HAMMOND®

World Atlas

HAMMOND®

Medallion

WORLD

ATLAS

HAMMOND® INCORPORATED

MAPLEWOOD, NEW JERSEY

Library of Congress Cataloging in Publication Data

Hammond Incorporated.
  Hammond medallion world atlas.

  Includes glossary and index.
  1. Atlases.   I. Title.   II. Title: Medallion
world atlas.
G1021.H273   1981   912   81-675340
ISBN 0-8437-1231-7   AACR2

Hammond Publications Advisory Board

Contents

Part IV—World History Map Collection

Part V—United States History Map Collection

Introduction to the World Atlas

As in previous editions, this Hammond World Atlas is organized to make the retrieval of information as simple and quick as possible. The guiding principle in organizing the atlas material has been to present separate subjects on *separate* maps. In this way, each individual map topic is shown with the greatest degree of clarity, unencumbered with extraneous information that is best revealed on separate maps. Of equal importance from the standpoint of good atlas design is the treatment of all current information on a given country or state as a single atlas unit. Thus, the basic reference map of an area is accompanied on adjacent pages by all supplementary information pertaining to that area. For example, the detailed index for a given map always appears on the same page as, or on the pages immediately following, the reference map. This same map index provides population data for the many cities, towns and villages shown on the map. Highlight information on the area, i.e., the total population and area, the capital, the highest point, is listed in the summary fact listings accompanying each unit. An adjacent locator map relates the subject area to the larger world beyond. A three-dimensional picture of the area is exhibited by means of the accompanying full-color topographic map. A separate economic map defines the vital agricultural, industrial and mineral resources of the area. In the case of the foreign maps, the flag of each independent nation appears on the appropriate page. Finally, certain country units contain special subject maps dealing with the history, climate, demography and vegetation of the area.

An outstanding new feature of the atlas is the addition of ZIP codes to the index entries for each of the legion of communities shown on the state maps. With the exception of the U.S. Postal Service directories of limited availability, the ZIP code listings herein are the most extensive published. In addition to listing ZIP codes for the communities possessing post offices, ZIP codes of the nearest post offices are listed for communities without postal facilities. It may be said with a fair degree of certainty that this new innovation in atlas content doubles the value of the work for home, office and school.

The back of the book contains a second type of index. This is a multi-paged "A to Z" index of all the world's places that appear on the maps. The use of this map index is essential when the name of a place is known but its country, state, or province is unknown. ZIP codes also are given here for each U.S. city, town, or community entry.

The numerous geographical changes of the decade are all recorded in the Hammond World Atlas. Over 5,000 changes, which occurred throughout the world since the last major revision, were entered on the maps. The state maps now reveal the many new towns and cities that have developed in the recent past. The majority of these are burgeoning suburbs on the fringes of our larger cities. On the other hand, large numbers of abandoned and defunct rural hamlets have been removed from the maps and map indexes. The trend toward metropolitan government is expressed in the new county-size city limits shown for Jacksonville, Florida, and Indianapolis, Indiana. Hundreds of other changes are also recorded on the state maps: new national parks and monuments, new dams, new reservoirs, name changes, etc.

Of course, the maps of foreign areas have been thoroughly updated. These revisions echo the new nations, shifting boundaries and the fluid internal divisions of many countries. New communities generated by the opening up of resources in the developing nations are also noted.

In closing it may be said that the atlas has truly been designed for contemporary use. Just as the information presented on the following pages is as current and up-to-date as the editors and cartographers could issue it, so the design and organization has been as well planned as possible to create a work useful to present generations.

President
HAMMOND INCORPORATED

Gazetteer-Index of the World

This alphabetical list of continents, countries, states, colonial possessions and other major geographical areas provides a quick reference to their area, population, capital or chief town, map page number and index key thereon. The last named indicates the square on the respective page in which the name may be found. An indication of the population sources used is also included, and refers both to the total figures given in this Gazetteer-Index and to the populations appearing in greater detail

with the maps throughout the atlas. The population figures used in each case are the latest reliable figures obtainable. A glance at the sources will show that the dates vary considerably throughout the world. In certain areas where no census has ever been taken, we must rely on official estimates. In other areas where censuses have been taken at infrequent intervals, we again rely on estimates. The key to the abbreviations used in the Gazetteer-Index follows:

adm = administrative	FC = final census	prov = provinces; provincial
cap = capital	int div = internal divisions	SSR = Soviet Socialist Republic
CE = census (undetermined)	isl, isls = island; islands	terr = territories; territory
cit = cities	MC = municipal census	TP = total population
co = counties	met = metropolitan	UK = United Kingdom
com = communes	mun = municipalities	UN = United Nations
dept = departments	OE = official estimate	USA = United States of America
dist = districts	oth = other populations	USSR = Union of Soviet
div = divisions	PC = preliminary census	Socialist Republics
est = estimate	pref = prefectures	ws = with suburbs

Country	Area (Square Miles)	Population	Capital or Chief Town	Page and Index Ref.	Sources of Population Data
★Afghanistan	250,775	19,280,000	Kabul	68/A 2	TP—75 OE; cap (& ws), cit over 100,000—73 OE; oth—70, 67, 59 OE
Africa	11,707,000	431,900,000	....	102/......	76 OE
Alabama, U.S.A.	51,609	3,890,061	Montgomery	194/......	80 FC & 70 FC & OE
Alaska, U.S.A.	586,412	400,481	Juneau	196/......	80 FC & 70 FC & OE
★Albania	11,100	2,482,000	Tiranë	45/E 5	TP—75 OE; cap—68 OE; oth—64 OE
Alberta, Canada	255,285	1,838,037	Edmonton	182/......	71 FC, T 76 FC
★Algeria	919,591	16,776,000	Algiers	106/D 3	TP—75 OE; met areas—67 OE; oth—66 PC
American Samoa	76	32,395	Pago Pago	87/J 7	TP—80 PC; oth—70 FC
Andorra	188	26,558	Andorra la Vella	33/G 1	75 OE
★Angola	481,351	6,761,000	Luanda	115/C 6	TP—76 OE; cap—68 OE; Malange & Huambo—64 OE; oth—60 FC
Anguilla	35	5,605	The Valley	156/F 3	60 FC
Antarctica	5,500,000	....		5/......	
Antigua	171	63,000	St. John's	156/G 3; 161/E11	TP—69 UN est; cap—66 OE; oth—60 FC
★Argentina	1,072,070	23,983,000	Buenos Aires	143/......	TP, cap—69 OE; oth—60 FC & PC
Arizona, U.S.A.	113,909	2,717,866	Phoenix	198/......	80 FC & 70 FC & OE
Arkansas, U.S.A.	53,104	2,285,513	Little Rock	202/......	80 FC & 70 FC & OE
Armenian S.S.R., U.S.S.R.	11,506	2,491,900	Erivan	52/F 6	70 FC & PC
Ascension Island, St. Helena	34	1,146	Georgetown	102/A 5	75 OE
Ashmore & Cartier Islands, Australia	1.9	....		88/C 2	....
Asia	17,128,500	2,535,333,000	....	54/......	76 OE
★Australia	2,967,909	13,684,900	Canberra	88/......	TP, states, cap (ws)—76 OE; Norfolk, Christmas & Cocos Is.—68 OE; oth—66 FC
Australian Capital Territory	939	204,200	Canberra	97/E 4	76 PC
★Austria	32,375	7,540,000	Vienna	41/......	TP—75 OE; cap, cit over 100,000—73 OE; oth—71 FC
Azerbaidzhan S.S.R., U.S.S.R.	33,436	5,117,100	Baku	52/G 6	70 FC & PC
Azores Islands, Portugal	902	275,900	Ponta Delgada, Angra do Heroísmo, Horta	32/......	TP, dist (& caps)—74 OE; oth—70 PC
★Bahamas	5,382	197,000	Nassau	156/C 1	TP—74 OE; cap (ws) & New Prov. I.—67 OE; oth—63 FC
★Bahrain	240	300,000	Manama	59/F 4	TP—76 OE; oth—65 FC
Balearic Islands, Spain	1,936	558,287	Palma	33/H 3	70 FC
★Bangladesh	55,126	82,900,000	Dacca	68/G 4	TP—76 OE; cit (ws)—69 OE; oth—61 FC
★Barbados	166	253,620	Bridgetown	161/B 8	TP, cap—70 PC; oth—60 FC
★Belgium	11,781	9,813,000	Brussels	27/......	TP—76 OE; oth (com)—70 FC
Belize	8,867	122,000	Belmopan	154/C 2	TP—70 OE; cap (& ws)—68 OE; oth—60 FC
★Benin	43,483	3,200,000	Porto-Novo	106/E 7	TP—76 OE; cap, Cotonou—69 OE; oth—61 OE
Bermuda	21	52,000	Hamilton	156/H 3	TP—69 OE; cap—66 OE; oth—60 FC
★Bhutan	18,147	1,200,000	Thimphu	68/G 3	TP—76 OE; oth—70 OE
Bismarck Archipelago, Papua New Guinea	18,976	209,051	Rabaul	87/E 6	TP—69 OE; oth—66 FC & PC
★Bolivia	424,163	4,804,000	La Paz, Sucre	136/......	TP, La Paz, Cochabamba, Sta. Cruz—69 OE; dept—67 OE; Sucre—65 OE; oth—62 OE & 50 FC
Bophuthatswana (aut. rep.), S. Africa	15,571	847,198	Mmabatho	118/D 5	70 FC
★Botswana	224,764	700,000	Gaborone	118/C 4	TP—75 OE; cap, Francistown—74 OE; oth—71 FC
★Brazil	3,284,426	90,840,000	Brasília	132/......	TP—69 OE; cit (ws)—70 OE; cit (com) over 100,000—68 OE; states—67 OE; oth—60 PC
British Columbia, Canada	366,255	2,466,608	Victoria	184/......	71 FC, T 76 FC
British Indian Ocean Terr.	29	600	(London, U.K.)	54/L10	75 OE
British Virgin Islands	59	10,484	Road Town	156/H 1	TP, cap, isls—70 PC; oth—60 FC
Brunei	2,226	155,000	Bandar Seri Begawan	85/E 4	TP—75 OE; cap—68 OE; oth—60 FC
★Bulgaria	42,823	8,800,000	Sofia	45/F 4	TP—76 OE; cap, cit over 100,000—68 OE; oth—65 FC
★Burma	261,789	31,240,000	Rangoon	72/B 2	TP—75 OE; cap (ws)—69 OE; cit over 100,000—70 OE; oth—53 CE
★Burundi	10,747	4,100,000	Bujumbura	115/E 4	TP—76 OE; cap—67 OE; oth—59 OE
★Byelorussian S.S.R. (White Russian S.S.R.), U.S.S.R.	80,154	9,522,000	Minsk	52/C 4	TP—77 OE; oth—70 FC & PC
California, U.S.A.	158,693	23,668,562	Sacramento	204/......	80 FC & 70 FC & OE
★Cambodia	69,898	8,110,000	Phnom Penh	72/E 4	TP—75 OE; cap—66 OE; oth—62 PC
★Cameroon	183,568	6,600,000	Yaoundé	115/B 2	TP—76 OE; cap, Douala—69 OE; oth—67, 63 & 61 OE
★Canada	3,851,809	22,992,604	Ottawa	162/......	TP, provs—71 & 76 FC, oth—71 FC
Canary Islands, Spain	2,808	1,170,224	Las Palmas, Santa Cruz	33/B 4	70 FC
Cape of Good Hope, South Africa	261,705	2,794,873	Cape Town	118/C 6	70 FC

★Member of the United Nations.

Gazetteer-Index of the World

Country	Area (Square Miles)	Population	Capital or Chief Town	Page and Index Ref.	Sources of Population Data
★Cape Verde	1,557	302,000	Praia	106/B 8	TP—75 OE; oth—60 PC
Caroline Islands, Terr. Pacific Is.	463	54,563	....	87/E 5	70 FC & 69 OE
Cayman Islands	100	10,652	Georgetown	156/B 3	TP, cap—70 PC; oth—70 PC & 60 FC
Celebes, Indonesia	72,986	7,665,000	Udjung Pandang	85/G 6	TP—70 OE; mun—61 PC; oth—60, 57 & 56 OE
★Central African Republic	236,293	1,800,000	Bangui	115/C 2	TP—76 OE; cap (ws)—67 OE; cap—64 MC; oth—67, 63 & 61 OE
Central America	197,575	19,800,000	....	154/......	76 OE
★Ceylon (Sri Lanka)	25,332	14,000,000	Colombo	68/E 7	TP—76 OE; cap, Jaffna—73 OE; oth—71 FC
★Chad	495,752	4,178,000	N'Djamena	111/C 4	TP—75 OE; cap, cit (part)—68 OE; oth—67, 63 & 61 OE
Channel Islands	74	128,000	Saint Helier, Saint Peter Port	13/E 7	TP—75 OE; oth—71 FC
★Chile	292,257	8,834,820	Santiago	138/......	TP, prov, cap (ws), cit (com)—70 PC; oth—60 FC
★China (People's Rep.)	3,691,000	853,000,000	Peking	77/......	TP—76 OE; cit over 100,000—70 OE; prov & cap—58 OE; oth—53 FC, 58 & 57 OE
China (Taiwan)	13,971	16,426,386	Taipei	77/K 7	TP—76 OE; cap, cit over 100,000—69 OE; oth—66 OE
Christmas Island, Australia	52	3,032	Flying Fish Cove	54/O11	75 OE
Cocos (Keeling Is.), Australia	5.4	604	West I.	54/N11	75 OE
★Colombia	439,513	21,117,000	Bogotá	126/......	TP, prov, cap (ws)—70 OE; cap, cit over 100,000—69 OE; oth—64 FC
Colorado, U.S.A.	104,247	2,888,834	Denver	208/......	80 FC & 70 FC & OE
★Comoros	719	266,000	Moroni	118/G 2	TP, cap—75 OE; oth—66 FC
★Congo	132,046	1,400,000	Brazzaville	115/B 4	TP—76 OE; cap (ws)—67 OE; oth—62 FC, 67 & 63 OE
Connecticut, U.S.A.	5,009	3,107,576	Hartford	210/......	80 FC & 70 FC & OE
Cook Islands	91	17,046	Avarua	87/K 7	TP—75 OE; oth—66 FC
Coral Sea Islands, Australia	8.5	....	(Norfolk Isl.)	88/J 3	....
Corsica, France	3,352	269,831	Ajaccio, Bastia	28/B 6	68 FC
★Costa Rica	19,575	1,800,000	San José	154/E 5	TP—70 OE; cap (ws)—69 OE; cap—66 OE; prov caps—65 OE; oth—63 FC
★Cuba	44,206	8,553,395	Havana	158/......	TP—70 PC; prov—70 OE; met areas—68 OE; cap (& ws), cit over 20,000—67 OE; cit over 5,000—65 OE; oth—53 FC
Curaçao, Neth. Antilles	182	196,170	Willemstad	161/G 8	TP—68 OE; oth—60 FC
★Cyprus	3,473	639,000	Nicosia	63/E 5	TP—75 OE; cit (ws)—68 OE; cap—64 OE; oth—65 OE & 60 FC
★Czechoslovakia	49,373	14,900,000	Prague	41/......	TP—76 OE; cap, cit over 100,000—75 OE; republics & regions—75 & 74 OE; oth—75 OE & 70 FC
Delaware, U.S.A.	2,057	595,225	Dover	245/......	80 FC & 70 FC & OE
★Denmark	16,629	5,065,313	Copenhagen	21/......	TP—75 OE; oth—75 & 73 OE & 70 FC
District of Columbia, U.S.A.	67	637,651	Washington	245/F 5	80 FC & 70 FC
★Djibouti	8,880	250,000	Djibouti	111/H 5	TP—75 OE; cap (ws)—69 OE; oth—61 OE
★Dominica	290	70,302	Roseau	161/E 7	70 PC
★Dominican Republic	18,704	4,011,589	Santo Domingo	158/......	70 PC
★East Germany (German Democratic Rep.)	41,768	16,850,000	Berlin (East)	22/......	75 OE
★Ecuador	109,483	6,144,000	Quito	128/......	TP—70 OE; cap & Guayaquil—69 OE; oth—62 FC
★Egypt	386,659	37,900,000	Cairo	111/E 2	TP—76 OE; cap, cit over 100,000—66 FC; Gaza Strip—76 OE & 67 CE; oth—60 FC
★El Salvador	8,260	3,418,455	San Salvador	154/C 4	69 OE
England, U.K.	50,516	46,417,600	London	13/......	TP, co, cap (boros & ws)—76 OE; cit—76 & 73 OE; oth—71 FC
★Equatorial Guinea	10,831	320,000	Malabo	115/A 3	TP—75 OE; terr—68 OE; oth—60 FC
Estonian S.S.R., U.S.S.R.	17,413	1,356,100	Tallinn	52/C 3; 53/......	70 FC & PC
★Ethiopia	471,776	27,946,000	Addis Ababa	111/G 5	TP—75 OE; cap, Asmara—68 OE; prov—67 OE; oth—65, 62 & 58 OE
Europe	4,057,000	666,116,000	....	7/......	76 OE
Faerøe Islands, Denmark	540	38,000	Tórshavn	21/B 2	69 OE
Falkland Islands & Dependencies	6,198	1,905	Stanley	120/E 8	TP—76 OE; cap—65 OE; oth—62 FC
★Fiji	7,055	569,468	Suva	87/H 8	TP—76 OE; oth—66 FC
★Finland	130,128	4,729,000	Helsinki	18/......	TP—76 OE; prov—75 OE; oth—75 OE & 70 FC
Florida, U.S.A.	58,560	9,739,992	Tallahassee	212/......	80 FC & 70 FC & OE
★France	210,038	53,300,000	Paris	28/......	TP—76 OE; cap (met area) & cit (ws)—69 OE; oth—68 FC
French Guiana	35,135	48,000	Cayenne	131/E 3	TP—69 UN est; oth—67 FC
French Polynesia	1,544	135,000	Papeete	87/L 8	TP—76 OE; oth—67 OE
★Gabon	103,346	526,000	Libreville	115/B 4	TP—75 OE; cap (ws)—67 OE; oth—67, 63 & 61 OE
★Gambia	4,127	524,000	Banjul	106/A 6	TP—75 OE; cap (& ws)—67 OE; oth—63 FC
Georgia, U.S.A.	58,876	5,464,265	Atlanta	216/......	80 FC & 70 FC & OE
Georgian S.S.R., U.S.S.R.	26,911	4,686,000	Tbilisi	52/F 6	70 FC & PC
★Germany, East (German Democratic Rep.)	41,768	16,850,000	Berlin (East)	22/......	75 OE
★Germany, West (Federal Republic)	95,985	61,644,600	Bonn	22/......	TP, states, cap—76 OE; oth—76 OE & 70 FC
★Ghana	92,099	9,900,000	Accra	106/D 7	TP—75 OE; cap (ws)—70 PC; cap, Kumasi (& ws), Sekondi-Takoradi (& ws)—68 OE; oth—60 FC
Gibraltar	2.28	30,000	Gibraltar	33/D 4	75 OE
Gilbert Islands (Kiribati)	264	56,000	Bairiki	87/J 6	TP—73 FC; isls (part)—68 FC; oth—68 PC
★Great Britain & Northern Ireland (United Kingdom)	94,399	56,076,000	London	10/......	TP—76 OE (see England, Wales, Scotland and Northern Ireland)
★Greece	50,944	9,046,000	Athens	45/F 6	TP—75 OE; cap (ws), Thessaloniki (ws)—68 OE; oth—61 FC
Greenland	840,000	54,000	Nûk (Godthåb)	4/B12	TP—75 OE; oth—66 CE
★Grenada	133	96,000	Saint George's	156/G 4; 161/D 9	TP—74 OE; cap—66 OE; oth—60 FC
Guadeloupe & Dependencies	687	324,000	Basse-Terre	156/F 4; 161/A 5	TP, cap, cit over 4,000—69 OE; oth—67 PC
Guam	212	105,816	Agaña	87/E 4	TP—80 PC; oth—70 FC
★Guatemala	42,042	5,200,000	Guatemala	154/B 3	TP, cap—70 OE; oth—64 PC
★Guinea	94,925	4,500,000	Conakry	106/B 6	TP—76 OE; cap (ws)—67 OE; Kankan, Kindia—64 OE; cap—60 MC; oth—61 OE
★Guinea-Bissau	13,948	517,000	Bissau	106/A 6	TP—75 OE; cap—64 OE; oth—60 PC
★Guyana	83,000	763,000	Georgetown	131/B 3	TP—70 OE; cap—69 OE; New Amsterdam—64 OE; oth—60 FC
★Haiti	10,694	4,867,190	Port-au-Prince	158/......	TP—70 OE; dept, cap (ws), cit (com)—69 OE; cap, Cap-Haitien—68 OE
Hawaii, U.S.A.	6,450	965,000	Honolulu	218/......	80 FC & 70 FC & OE
Heard & McDonald Islands, Australia	113	....	....	2/H 6	....
★Holland (Netherlands)	15,892	13,800,000	The Hague, Amsterdam	27/......	76 OE (com)
★Honduras	43,277	2,495,000	Tegucigalpa	154/D 3	TP, cap—69 OE; oth—68 OE
Hong Kong	403	4,400,000	Victoria	77/H 7	TP—76 OE; oth—66 CE
★Hungary	35,919	10,590,000	Budapest	41/......	TP—76 OE; cap, cit over 100,000—74 OE; oth—70 FC

Gazetteer-Index of the World

Country	Area (Square Miles)	Population	Capital or Chief Town	Page and Index Ref.	Sources of Population Data
★Iceland	39,768	220,000	Reykjavík	21/B 1	TP—76 OE; oth—70 FC
Idaho, U.S.A.	83,557	943,935	Boise	220/......	80 FC & 70 FC & OE
Illinois, U.S.A.	56,400	11,418,461	Springfield	222/......	80 FC & 70 FC & OE
★India	1,269,339	605,614,000	New Delhi	68/......	TP—76 OE; oth—71 FC
Indiana, U.S.A.	36,291	5,490,179	Indianapolis	227/......	80 FC & 70 FC & OE
★Indonesia	788,430	131,255,000	Djakarta	85/......	TP—75 OE; cap, cit & isls (part)—70 OE; mun—61 PC; oth—60, 57 & 56 OE
Iowa, U.S.A.	56,290	2,913,387	Des Moines	229/......	80 FC & 70 FC & OE
★Iran	636,293	32,900,000	Tehran	66/......	TP—76 PC; prov, cap, cit (exact pops)—66 FC; cit (rounded pops)—66 PC
★Iraq	172,476	11,400,000	Baghdad	66/......	TP—76 OE; oth—65 FC
★Ireland	27,136	3,109,000	Dublin	17/......	TP—75 OE; oth—71 FC
Ireland, Northern, U.K.	5,452	1,537,200	Belfast	17/......	TP, dist—76 OE; cap, Londonderry—73 OE; oth—71 FC
Isle of Man	227	59,000	Douglas	13/C 3	TP—75 OE; oth—71 FC
★Israel	7,847	3,459,000	Jerusalem	65/......	TP—76 OE; cap, cit over 100,000—75 OE; dist, cit over 5,000—72 OE; oth—61 FC
★Italy	116,303	56,110,000	Rome	34/......	TP—76 OE; oth—71 FC
★Ivory Coast	127,520	6,673,013	Abidjan	106/C 7	TP—75 PC; cap (ws)—67 OE; cap—61 OE; oth—64, 63 & 61 OE
★Jamaica	4,411	1,972,000	Kingston	158/......	TP—70 OE; oth—60 FC
★Japan	145,730	112,200,000	Tokyo	81/......	TP—76 OE; oth—75 PC
Java, Indonesia	48,842	69,323,000	Djakarta	85/J 2	TP—70 OE; mun—61 PC; oth—60, 57 & 56 OE
★Jordan	37,737	2,700,000	Amman	65/......	TP, cap—76 OE; cit over 100,000—74 OE; int div (E. Bank)—73 OE, (W. Bank)—68 OE; oth (W. Bank)—67 CE, (E. Bank)—61 FC
Kampuchea (Cambodia)	69,898	8,110,000	Phnom Penh	72/E 4	TP—75 OE; cap—66 OE; oth—62 PC
Kansas, U.S.A.	82,264	2,363,208	Topeka	232/......	80 FC & 70 FC & OE
Kazakh S.S.R., U.S.S.R.	1,048,300	14,185,000	Alma-Ata	48/G 5	TP—75 OE; oth—70 FC & PC
Kentucky, U.S.A.	40,395	3,661,433	Frankfort	237/......	80 FC & 70 FC & OE
★Kenya	224,960	13,300,000	Nairobi	115/G 3	TP—75 OE; prov, cap, cit over 9,000—69 PC; oth—62 FC
Kirgiz S.S.R., U.S.S.R.	76,641	2,932,800	Frunze	48/H 5	70 FC & PC
Kiribati	264	56,000	Bairiki	87/J 6	TP—73 FC; isls. (part)—68 FC; oth—68 PC
Korea, North	46,540	17,000,000	P'yongyang	81/......	TP, cap—76 OE; cit over 350,000—72 OE; oth—70 OE
Korea, South	38,175	34,688,079	Seoul	81/......	TP, cap, Pusan—75 PC; cit over 100,000—70 FC; oth—70 & 66 PC
★Kuwait	6,532	1,100,000	Al Kuwait	59/E 4	TP—76 OE; oth—70 PC
★Laos	91,428	3,500,000	Vientiane	72/D 3	TP—76 OE; cap—66 OE; oth—58 OE
Latvian S.S.R., U.S.S.R.	24,595	2,364,100	Riga	52/B 3; 53/......	70 FC & PC
★Lebanon	4,015	3,207,000	Beirut	63/F 6	TP—75 OE; cap (ws)—69 OE; cap, Tarabulus—64 OE; oth—61 OE
★Lesotho	11,720	1,100,000	Maseru	118/D 5	TP—76 OE; cap—72 OE; oth—66 FC
★Liberia	43,000	1,600,000	Monrovia	106/C 7	TP—76 OE; cap (ws)—68 OE; cap—66 OE; oth—62 PC
★Libya	679,358	2,500,000	Tripoli	111/......	TP—76 OE; Tripoli—68 OE; prov, Benghazi—64 FC; oth—64 PC
Liechtenstein	61	25,000	Vaduz	39/J 2	TP—75 OE; cap—61 OE; oth—60 FC
Lithuanian S.S.R., U.S.S.R.	25,174	3,128,000	Vilna	52/B 3; 53/......	70 FC & PC
Louisiana, U.S.A.	48,523	4,203,972	Baton Rouge	238/......	80 FC & 70 FC & OE
★Luxembourg	999	358,000	Luxembourg	27/J 9	TP—75 OE; cap—74 OE; oth—70 FC
Macao	6	300,000	Macao	77/H 7	TP—76 OE; oth—69 OE
★Madagascar	226,657	7,700,000	Antananarivo	118/H 3	TP—76 OE; oth—71 OE
Madeira Islands, Portugal	307	253,220	Funchal	33/A 2	70 PC
Maine, U.S.A.	33,215	1,124,660	Augusta	242/......	80 FC & 70 FC & OE
★Malawi	45,747	5,100,000	Lilongwe	115/F 6	TP—76 OE; oth—66 FC
Malaya, Malaysia	50,806	9,000,000	Kuala Lumpur	72/D 6	TP—69 UN est; states—66 OE; cap—64 OE; oth—57 FC
★Malaysia	128,308	12,368,000	Kuala Lumpur	72/D 6; 85/E 4	TP—75 OE; TP: Malaya, Sabah, Sarawak—69 UN est; states—66 OE; cap—64 OE; oth—60 FC (Sabah, Sarawak) & 57 FC (Malaya)
★Maldives	115	136,000	Male	54/L 9	TP—75 OE; cap—69 OE; oth—65 FC
★Mali	464,873	5,800,000	Bamako	106/C 6	TP—76 OE; cap (ws)—68 OE; oth—67, 63 & 61 OE
★Malta	122	319,000	Valletta	34/E 7	TP—76 OE; cap—74 OE; oth—73 OE
Man, Isle of	227	59,000	Douglas	13/C 3	TP—75 OE; oth—71 FC
Manitoba, Canada	251,000	1,021,506	Winnipeg	179/......	71 FC, T 76 FC
Mariana Islands, Terr. Pacific Is.	182	11,827	Chalan Kanoa (Saipan)	87/E 4	70 FC & 69 OE
Marquesas Islands, French Polynesia	492	5,174	Atuona	87/N 6	67 OE
Marshall Islands, Terr. Pacific Is.	69	19,328	Uliga (Majuro)	87/G 4	70 FC & 69 OE
Martinique	425	332,000	Fort-de-France	161/D 5	TP, cap—69 OE; oth—67 PC
Maryland, U.S.A.	10,577	4,216,446	Annapolis	245/......	80 FC & 70 FC & OE
Massachusetts, U.S.A.	8,257	5,737,037	Boston	249/......	80 FC & 70 FC & OE
★Mauritania	397,354	1,140,000	Nouakchott	106/B 5	TP—75 OE; cap—67 OE; oth—67, 65, 63 & 61 OE
★Mauritius	790	899,000	Port Louis	118/G 5	TP—75 UN est; cap, Curepipe, Quatre Bornes—74 OE; Mahebourg—72 PC; oth—62 FC
Mayotte	144	40,000	Mamoutzou	119/G 2	TP—75 OE; cap—66 FC
★Mexico	761,601	48,313,438	Mexico City	150/......	TP, states, cap, cit (mun)—70 PC
Michigan, U.S.A.	58,216	9,258,344	Lansing	250/......	80 FC & 70 FC & OE
Midway Islands	2	2,220		87/J 3	70 FC
Minnesota, U.S.A.	84,068	4,077,148	St. Paul	254/......	80 FC & 70 FC & OE
Mississippi, U.S.A.	47,716	2,520,638	Jackson	256/......	80 FC & 70 FC & OE
Missouri, U.S.A.	69,686	4,917,444	Jefferson City	261/......	80 FC & 70 FC & OE
Moldavian S.S.R., U.S.S.R.	13,012	3,823,000	Kishinev	52/C 5	TP—75 OE; oth—70 FC & PC
Monaco	368 acres	23,035	Monaco	28/G 6	68 FC
★Mongolia	606,163	1,500,000	Ulan Bator	77/......	TP—76 OE; cap—68 OE; Darkhan, Tsetserlig—66 OE; provs—62 CE; oth—65 OE
Montana, U.S.A.	147,138	786,690	Helena	262/......	80 FC & 70 FC & OE
Montserrat	40	12,300	Plymouth	156/F 3	TP—70 PC; cap—66 OE
★Morocco	172,413	16,800,000	Rabat	106/C 2	TP—76 OE; cap (ws), cit over 100,000—69 OE; oth—60 FC
★Mozambique	308,641	9,300,000	Maputo	118/E 5	TP—76 OE; oth—70 FC
Namibia (South-West Africa)	317,827	883,000	Windhoek	118/B 3	TP—75 UN est; oth—70 PC
Natal, South Africa	33,578	4,245,675	Pietermaritzburg	118/E 5	70 FC
Nauru	7.7	8,000	Yaren (dist.)	87/G 6	75 UN est
Nebraska, U.S.A.	77,227	1,570,006	Lincoln	264/......	80 FC & 70 FC & OE
★Nepal	54,663	12,900,000	Kathmandu	68/E 3	TP—76 OE; oth—71 FC
★Netherlands	15,892	13,800,000	The Hague, Amsterdam	27/......	76 OE (com)
Netherlands Antilles	390	220,000	Willemstad	156/E 4	TP—70 OE; isls—68 OE; oth—60 FC
Nevada, U.S.A.	110,540	799,184	Carson City	266/......	80 FC & 70 FC & OE
New Brunswick, Canada	28,354	677,250	Fredericton	170/......	71 FC, T 76 FC
New Caledonia & Dependencies	7,335	136,000	Nouméa	87/G 8	TP—76 OE; oth—69 PC
Newfoundland, Canada	156,185	557,725	St. John's	166/......	71 FC, T 76 FC
New Hampshire, U.S.A.	9,304	920,610	Concord	268/......	80 FC & 70 FC & OE

Country	Area (Square Miles)	Population	Capital or Chief Town	Page and Index Ref.	Sources of Population Data
New Hebrides (Vanuatu)	5,700	97,468	Vila	87/G 7	TP—76 OE; oth—69 OE
New Jersey, U.S.A.	7,836	7,364,158	Trenton	273/......	80 FC & 70 FC & OE
New Mexico, U.S.A.	121,666	1,299,968	Santa Fe	274/......	80 FC & 70 FC & OE
New South Wales, Australia	309,433	4,847,800	Sydney	97/......	TP—76 OE; oth—66 FC
New York, U.S.A.	49,576	17,557,288	Albany	276/......	80 FC & 70 FC & OE
★New Zealand	103,736	3,121,904	Wellington	100/......	TP—76 PC; cap (& ws), cit (ws)—69 OE; int div, cit over 2,500—68 OE; oth—66 FC
★Nicaragua	45,698	1,984,000	Managua	154/D 4	TP—70 OE; cap—65 OE; oth—63 FC
★Niger	489,189	4,700,000	Niamey	106/F 5	TP—76 OE; cap, int div caps—68 OE; cap (ws)—59 MC; oth—63 & 61 OE
★Nigeria	379,628	83,800,000	Lagos	106/F 6	TP—76 OE; cap, cit over 100,000—69 OE; oth—63 FC
Niue	100	2,992	Alofi	87/K 7	TP—74 OE; cap—66 FC
Norfolk Island, Australia	13.3	1,870	Kingston	88/L 5	75 OE
North America	9,363,000	314,000,000	....	146/......	69 UN est
North Carolina, U.S.A.	52,586	5,874,429	Raleigh	281/......	80 FC & 70 FC & OE
North Dakota, U.S.A.	70,665	652,695	Bismarck	282/......	80 FC & 70 FC & OE
Northern Ireland, U.K.	5,452	1,537,200	Belfast	17/......	TP, dist—76 OE; cap, Londonderry—73 OE; oth—71 FC
Northern Territory, Australia	520,280	98,400	Darwin	93/......	TP—76 OE; oth—66 FC
North Korea	46,540	17,000,000	P'yongyang	81/......	TP, cap—76 OE; cit over 350,000—72 OE; oth—70 OE
Northwest Territories, Canada	1,304,903	42,609	Yellowknife	187/......	71 FC, T 76 FC
★Norway	125,053	4,027,000	Oslo	18/......	TP—75 OE; co, Svalbard—76 OE; oth—76 OE & 70 FC
Nova Scotia, Canada	21,425	828,571	Halifax	168/......	71 FC, T 76 FC
Oceania	3,292,000	21,500,000	....	87/......	76 OE
Ohio, U.S.A.	41,222	10,797,419	Columbus	284/......	80 FC & 70 FC & OE
Oklahoma, U.S.A.	69,919	3,025,266	Oklahoma City	288/......	80 FC & 70 FC & OE
★Oman	120,000	800,000	Muscat	59/G 5	TP—76 OE; cap, Matrah—66 OE; Salala—68 OE; Kuria Muria Isls.—67 OE; Dhofar—65 OE
Ontario, Canada	412,582	8,264,465	Toronto	175, 177/......	71 FC, T 76 FC
Orange Free State, South Africa	49,866	1,674,139	Bloemfontein	118/D 4	70 FC
Oregon, U.S.A.	96,981	2,632,663	Salem	291/......	80 FC & 70 FC & OE
Orkney Islands, Scotland	376	17,675	Kirkwall	15/J 1	TP—75 OE; oth—73 OE & 71 FC
Pacific Islands, Territory of the	707	120,000	Kolonia	87/F 5	TP—75 OE; oth—70 FC & 69 OE
★Pakistan	310,403	72,370,000	Islamabad	68/......	TP—76 OE; prov, cit over 100,000—72 PC; cit (ws)—72 OE; oth—61 FC
Palau Islands, Terr. Pacific Is.	184	12,291	Koror	87/D 5	70 FC & 69 OE
★Panama	29,856	1,469,993	Panamá	154/G 6	70 PC
★Papua New Guinea	183,540	2,800,000	Port Moresby	85/B 7; 87/E 6	TP—76 OE; int div—69 OE; cap—70 MC; oth—66 FC & PC
★Paraguay	157,047	2,314,000	Asunción	144/......	TP—69 OE; cap (ws)—68 OE; cap—65 OE; dept—62 PC; oth—67 & 65 OE & 62 PC
Pennsylvania, U.S.A.	45,333	11,866,728	Harrisburg	294/......	80 FC & 70 FC & OE
★Persia (Iran)	636,293	32,900,000	Tehran	66/......	TP—76 OE; prov, cap, cit (exact pops)—66 FC; cit (rounded pops)—66 PC
★Peru	496,222	13,586,300	Lima	128/......	TP, dept, cap (ws), cit over 23,000—70 OE; oth—61 FC
★Philippines	115,707	43,751,000	Manila	82/......	TP—76 OE; cap, cit over 100,000—75 OE; met Manila—73 OE; prov, mun, isls—70 FC; oth—70 FC & PC
Pitcairn Islands	18	67	Adamstown	87/O 8	TP—75 OE; cap—69 OE
★Poland	120,725	34,364,000	Warsaw	47/......	TP—76 OE; oth—68 OE
★Portugal	35,549	8,825,000	Lisbon	33/......	TP—75 OE; cap (ws), Porto—76 OE; cap, Azores, Madeira—74 OE; oth—74 OE & 70 PC
Prince Edward Island, Canada	2,184	118,229	Charlottetown	168/E 2	71 FC, T 76 FC
Puerto Rico	3,435	3,187,570	San Juan	161/......	80 PC & 70 FC
★Qatar	4,247	150,000	Doha	59/F 4	TP—75 OE; cap—69 OE; oth—62 OE
Québec, Canada	594,860	6,234,445	Québec	172, 174/......	71 FC, T 76 FC
Queensland, Australia	666,991	2,015,300	Brisbane	95/......	TP—76 OE; oth—66 FC
Réunion	969	475,700	Saint–Denis	118/F 5	TP—75 OE; oth—67 FC
Rhode Island, U.S.A.	1,214	947,154	Providence	249/......	80 FC & 70 FC & OE
Rhodesia (Zimbabwe)	150,803	6,600,000	Salisbury	118/D 3	TP—76 OE; urban areas—74 OE; oth—69 FC
★Rumania	91,699	21,500,000	Bucharest	45/F 3	TP—76 OE; cap, cit (& ws) over 100,000—68 OE; cit (& ws) over 20,000—66 PC; oth—56 FC
Russian S.F.S.R., U.S.S.R.	6,592,812	133,913,000	Moscow	48/D 4	TP—75 OE; oth—70 FC & PC
★Rwanda	10,169	4,241,000	Kigali	115/E 4	TP—75 OE; cap—67 OE; oth—59 OE
Sabah, Malaysia	28,460	633,000	Kota Kinabalu	85/F 4	TP—69 UN est; oth—60 FC
Saint Christopher–Nevis–Anguilla	138	56,000	Basseterre	156/F 3; 161/D11	TP—69 OE; oth—60 FC
Saint Helena & Dependencies	162	6,438	Jamestown	102/B 6	75 OE
★Saint Lucia	238	110,000	Castries	161/G 6	TP—69 UN est; oth—60 FC
Saint Pierre & Miquelon	93.5	6,000	Saint–Pierre	166/C 4	TP—75 OE; oth—67 FC
Saint Vincent & the Grenadines	150	89,129	Kingstown	161/A 8	TP—69 UN est; oth—70 PC
Sakhalin, U.S.S.R.	29,500	600,000	Yuzhno–Sakhalinsk	48/P 4	70 FC & PC
★Salvador, El	8,260	3,418,455	San Salvador	154/C 4	69 OE
San Marino	23.4	20,000	San Marino	34/D 3	TP—75 OE; cap (& ws)—74 OE
★São Tomé e Príncipe	372	80,000	São Tomé	106/F 8	TP—75 OE; oth—60 FC
Sarawak, Malaysia	48,050	950,000	Kuching	85/E 5	TP—69 UN est; oth—60 FC
Sardinia, Italy	9,301	1,473,800	Cagliari	34/B 4	71 FC
Saskatchewan, Canada	251,700	921,323	Regina	181/......	71 FC, T 76 FC
★Saudi Arabia	829,995	7,200,000	Riyadh, Mecca	59/D 4	TP—75 OE; caps & Jidda—65 OE; prov—59 OE; oth—62 & 59 OE
Scotland, U.K.	30,414	5,261,000	Edinburgh	15/......	TP—76 OE; regions—75 OE; cit—75 & 73 OE & 71 FC; oth—71 FC
★Senegal	75,954	5,085,388	Dakar	106/A 5	TP—76 PC; cap (& ws)—69 OE; oth—65, 63 & 61 OE
★Seychelles	145	60,000	Victoria	118/H 5	TP—76 OE; cap (& ws), Anse Boileau, isls—71 FC; oth—60 FC
Shetland Islands, Scotland	552	18,494	Lerwick	15/M 3	TP—75 OE; oth—73 OE & 71 FC
★Siam (Thailand)	198,455	42,700,000	Bangkok	72/D 3	TP—76 OE; cap (ws)—68 OE; Thonburi (ws)—64 OE; oth—60 FC
Sicily, Italy	9,926	4,680,715	Palermo	34/E 6	71 FC
★Sierra Leone	27,925	3,100,000	Freetown	106/B 7	TP—76 OE; cap—69 OE; oth—63 FC
★Singapore	226	2,300,000	Singapore	72/F 6	TP—76 OE; cap—68 OE; oth—57 FC
Society Islands, French Polynesia	677	81,487	Papeete	87/L 7	67 OE
★Solomon Islands	11,500	196,708	Honiara	87/F 6	TP—76 PC; cap—69 PC; oth—69 PC, 64 & 63 OE
★Somalia	246,200	3,170,000	Mogadishu	115/H 3	TP—75 OE; cap—67 OE; prov—66 OE; oth—66 & 62 OE
★South Africa	472,359	24,400,000	Cape Town, Pretoria	118/C 5	TP—76 OE; oth—70 FC

Country	Area (Square Miles)	Population	Capital or Chief Town	Page and Index Ref.	Sources of Population Data
South America	6,875,000	186,000,000	....	120/......	69 UN est
South Australia, Australia	380,070	1,247,100	Adelaide	94/......	TP—76 OE; oth—66 FC
South Carolina, U.S.A.	31,055	3,119,208	Columbia	296/......	80 FC & 70 FC & OE
South Dakota, U.S.A.	77,047	690,178	Pierre	298/......	80 FC & 70 FC & OE
South Korea	38,175	34,688,079	Seoul	81/......	TP, cap, Pusan—75 PC; cit over 100,000—70 FC; oth—70 & 66 PC
South–West Africa (Namibia)	317,827	883,000	Windhoek	118/B 3	TP—75 UN est; oth—70 PC
★Spain	194,881	36,000,000	Madrid	33/......	TP, met areas—75 OE; oth—70 PC
★Sri Lanka	25,332	14,000,000	Colombo	68/E 7	TP—76 OE; cap, Jaffna—73 OE; oth—71 FC
★Sudan	967,494	18,347,000	Khartoum	111/E 4	TP—75 OE; cap, Omdurman—68 OE; cit over 25,000—65 OE; prov—64 OE; oth—56 FC
Sumatra, Indonesia	164,000	17,345,000	Medan	85/B 5	TP—70 OE; mun—61 PC; oth—60, 57 & 56 OE
★Suriname	55,144	389,000	Paramaribo	131/C 3	TP—69 UN est; dist—62 OE; oth—64 FC
Svalbard, Norway	23,957	2,828	Longyearbyen	18/D 2	76 OE
★Swaziland	6,705	500,000	Mbabane	118/E 5	TP—76 OE; Manzini—75 OE; cap—73 OE; Stegi—66 FC
★Sweden	173,665	8,236,461	Stockholm	18/......	TP, co—77 OE; oth—77 0E & 70 FC
Switzerland	15,943	6,327,000	Bern	39/......	TP, Cantons—78 OE; cap, cit over 100,000 (& ws)—74 OE; cit (com) over 30,000 (& ws)—73 OE; oth—70 FC
★Syria	71,498	7,585,000	Damascus	63/G 5	TP—76 OE; cap, cit over 100,000—68 OE; oth—62 OE
Tadzhik S.S.R., U.S.S.R.	55,251	2,900,000	Dushanbe	48/H 6	70 FC & PC
Tahiti, French Polynesia	402	61,519	Papeete	87/L 7	67 OE
★Tanzania	363,708	15,506,000	Dar es Salaam	115/F 5	TP—75 OE; oth—67 FC
Tasmania, Australia	26,383	410,800	Hobart	99/......	TP—76 OE; oth—66 FC
Tennessee, U.S.A.	42,244	4,590,750	Nashville	237/......	80 FC & 70 FC & OE
Texas, U.S.A.	267,339	14,228,383	Austin	302/......	80 FC & 70 FC & OE
★Thailand	198,455	42,700,000	Bangkok	72/D 3	TP—76 OE; cap (ws)—68 OE; Thonburi (ws)—64 OE; oth—60 FC
Tibet, China	471,660	1,270,000	Lhasa	77/C 5	TP—58 OE; cap—70 OE; oth—58 & 57 OE & 53 FC
★Togo	21,622	2,300,000	Lomé	106/E 7	TP—76 OE; cap (ws), cit (com) over 10,000—70 PC; cap—68 OE
Tokelau	3.9	1,603	Fakaofo	87/J 6	TP—75 OE; oth—67 OE
Tonga	270	102,000	Nuku'alofa	87/J 8	TP—75 OE; oth—66 FC
Transkei (aut. rep.), S. Afr.	14,180	1,967,289	Umtata	118/D 6	70 FC
Transvaal, South Africa	109,621	8,167,154	Pretoria	118/D 4	70 FC
★Trinidad and Tobago	1,980	1,040,000	Port-of-Spain	156/G 5; 161/A10	TP—69 UN est; cap (ws)—69 0E; cap, isls—67 OE; oth—60 FC
Tristan da Cunha, St. Helena	38	292	Edinburgh	2/G10	75 OE
Tuamotu Archipelago, French Polynesia	341	6,148	Apataki	87/M 7	67 CE
★Tunisia	63,170	5,776,000	Tunis	106/F 2	TP—75 OE; cap (ws)—69 OE; cap, Sousse, Sfax—68 OE; prov caps—66 PC; oth—61 OE
★Turkey	300,946	40,284,000	Ankara	63/......	TP—75 OE; oth—65 FC
Turkmen S.S.R., U.S.S.R.	188,455	2,158,880	Ashkhabad	48/F 6	70 FC & PC
Turks and Caicos Islands	166	6,000	Cockburn Town (Grand Turk)	156/D 2	TP—69 UN est; isl groups—69 OE; cap, Cockburn Hbr.—63 OE; oth—60 FC
Tuvalu	10	5,887	Fongafale (Funafuti)	87/H 6	TP—73 FC; oth—68 FC
★Uganda	91,076	11,400,000	Kampala	115/F 3	TP—75 OE; cap, Mbale—69 PC; oth—59 FC
★Ukrainian S.S.R., U.S.S.R.	233,089	49,438,000	Kiev	52/D 5	TP—77 OE; oth—70 FC & PC
★Union of Soviet Socialist Republics	8,649,490	258,402,000	Moscow	48/......	TP—77 OE; oth—70 FC & PC
★United Arab Emirates	32,278	240,000	Abu Dhabi	59/F 5	TP—75 OE; oth—68 FC
★United Kingdom	94,399	56,076,000	London	10/......	TP—76 OE (see England, Wales, Scotland & Northern Ireland)
★United States of America	3,615,123	226,504,825	Washington	188/......	80 FC & 70 FC & OE; States—80 FC & 70 FC
★Upper Volta	105,869	6,144,013	Ouagadougou	106/D 6	TP—75 PC; cap—66 OE; cap (ws)—63 OE; oth—63 & 61 OE
★Uruguay	72,172	2,900,000	Montevideo	145/......	TP, cap (ws)—70 OE; dept, cap, cit (part)—63 FC; oth—63 FC, 62 & 59 OE
Utah, U.S.A.	84,916	1,461,037	Salt Lake City	304/......	80 FC & 70 FC & OE
Uzbek S.S.R., U.S.S.R.	173,591	11,960,000	Tashkent	48/G 5	70 FC & PC
Vanuatu (New Hebrides)	5,700	97,468	Vila	87/G 7	TP—76 OE; oth—69 OE
Vatican City	116 acres	704	....	34/B 6	74 OE
Venda (aut. rep.), S. Afr.	2,510	449,000	Thohoyandou	119/E4	
★Venezuela	352,143	10,398,907	Caracas	124/......	TP, states, cap (& ws)—70 OE; cit (ws), cit over 100,000—69 OE; oth—61 FC
Vermont, U.S.A.	9,609	511,456	Montpelier	268/......	80 FC & 70 FC & OE
Victoria, Australia	87,884	3,713,200	Melbourne	97/......	TP—76 OE; oth—66 FC
★Vietnam	128,405	46,600,000	Hanoi	72/E 3	TP—76 OE; cap (ws)—70 OE; cit (North) over 100,000—70 OE; cit (South)—69 OE; oth—69 OE & 60 CE
Virginia, U.S.A.	40,817	5,346,279	Richmond	307/......	80 FC & 70 FC & OE
Virgin Islands, British	59	10,484	Road Town	156/H 1	TP, cap, isls—70 PC; oth—60 FC
Virgin Islands, U.S.A.	133	95,214	Charlotte Amalie	161/A–G4	TP—80 PC; cap, isls, cit over 1,000—70 PC; oth—60 FC
Wake Island	2.5	437	Wake Islet	87/G 4	74 OE
Wales, U.K.	8,017	2,778,000	Cardiff	13/......	TP—77 OE; co—76 OE; cit—76 & 73 OE; parishes—71 FC
Wallis and Futuna	106	9,000	Matautu	87/J 7	TP—75 UN est; cap—69 FC; isls—69 OE
Washington, U.S.A.	68,192	4,130,163	Olympia	310/......	80 FC & 70 FC & OE
Western Australia, Australia	975,920	1,148,100	Perth	92/......	TP—76 OE; oth—66 FC
Western Sahara	102,702	139,000	....	106/B 3	
★Western Samoa	1,133	159,000	Apia	87/J 7	TP—75 OE; cap—68 OE; oth—66 FC
★West Germany (Federal Republic)	95,985	61,644,600	Bonn	22/......	TP, states, cap—76 OE; oth—76 OE & 70 FC
West Virginia, U.S.A.	24,181	1,949,644	Charleston	312/......	80 FC & 70 FC & OE
★White Russian S.S.R. (Byelorussian S.S.R.), U.S.S.R.	80,154	9,522,000	Minsk	52/C 4	TP—77 OE; oth—70 FC & PC
Wisconsin, U.S.A.	56,154	4,705,335	Madison	317/......	80 FC & 70 FC & OE
World	57,970,000	4,240,700,000	....	1, 2/......	76 OE
Wyoming, U.S.A.	97,914	470,816	Cheyenne	319/......	80 FC & 70 FC & OE
★Yemen Arab Republic	77,220	5,600,000	San'a	59/D 7	TP—76 OE; caps—64 OE; oth—59 OE
★Yemen, Peoples Dem. Rep. of	111,101	1,700,000	Aden	59/E 7	TP—76 OE; Aden (& ws)—64 OE; Madinat ash Sha'b—60 OE; oth—65, 62, 61 & 60 OE
★Yugoslavia	98,766	21,520,000	Belgrade	45/C 3	TP—76 OE; cap (ws)—70 OE; cap—67 OE; int div—65 OE; cit over 100,000—68 OE; cit over 10,000—63 OE; oth—61 FC
Yukon Territory, Canada	207,076	21,836	Whitehorse	187/E 3	71 FC, T 76 FC
★Zaire	918,962	25,600,000	Kinshasa	115/D 4	TP—76 OE; prov, cap—70 FC; oth—70 FC & 57 OE
★Zambia	290,586	4,936,000	Lusaka	115/E 7	TP—75 OE; cap, cit over 4,000—69 PC; cap (ws), cit (ws)—68 OE; oth—63 FC & 61 OE
Zimbabwe	150,803	6,600,000	Salisbury	118/D 3	TP—76 OE; urban areas—74 OE; oth—69 FC

Introduction to the Maps and Indexes

The following notes have been added to aid the reader in making the best use of this atlas. Though he may be familiar with maps and map indexes, the publisher believes that a quick review of the material below will add to his enjoyment of this reference work.

Arrangement — The Plan of the Atlas. The atlas has been designed with maximum convenience for the user as its objective. All geographically related information pertaining to a country or region appears on adjacent pages, eliminating the task of searching throughout the entire volume for data on a given area. Thus, the reader will find, conveniently assembled, political, topographic, economic and special maps of a political area or region, accompanied by detailed map indexes, statistical data, and illustrations of the national flags of the area.

The sequence of country units in this American-designed atlas is international in arrangement. Units on the world as a whole are followed by a section on the polar regions which, in turn, is followed by pages devoted to Europe and its countries. Every continent map is accompanied by special population distribution, climatic and vegetation maps of that continent. Following the maps of the European continent and its countries, the geographic sequence plan proceeds as follows: Asia, the Pacific and Australia, Africa, South America, North America, and ends with detailed coverage on the United States.

Political Maps — The Primary Reference Tool. The most detailed maps in each country unit are the *political maps.* It is our feeling that the reader is likely to refer to these maps more often than to any other in the book when confronted by such questions as — Where? How big? What is it near? Answering these common queries is the function of the political maps. Each political map stresses *political* phenomena — countries, internal political divisions, boundaries, cities and towns. The major political unit or units, shown on the map, are banded in distinctive colors for easy identification and delineation. First-order political subdivisions (states, provinces, counties on the state maps) are shown, scale permitting.

The reader is advised to make use of the *legend* appearing under the title on each political map. Map *symbols,* the special "language" of maps, are explained in the legend. Each variety of dot, circle, star or interrupted line has a special meaning which should be clearly understood by the user so that he may interpret the map data correctly.

Each country has been portrayed at a *scale* commensurate with its political, areal, economic or tourist importance. In certain cases, a whole map unit may be devoted to a single nation if that nation is considered to be of prime interest to most atlas users. In other cases, several nations will be shown on a single map if, as separate entities, they are of lesser relative importance. Areas of dense settlement and important significance within a country have been enlarged and portrayed in inset maps inserted on the margins of the main map. The reader is advised to refer to the linear or "bar" scale appearing on each map or map inset in order to ascertain the basic scale of the map or to determine the distance between points.

The *projection* system used for each map is noted near the title of the map. Map projections are the special graphic systems used by cartographers to render the curved three-dimensional surface of the globe on a flat surface. Optimum map projections determined by the attributes of the area have been used by the publishers for each map in the atlas.

A word here as to the choice of place names on the maps. Throughout the atlas names appear, with a few exceptions, in their local official spellings. However, conventional Anglicized spellings are used for major geographical divisions and for towns and topographic features for which English forms exist; i.e., "Spain" instead of "España" or "Munich" instead of "München." Names of this type are normally followed by the local official spelling in parentheses. As an aid to the user the indexes are cross-referenced for all current and most former spellings of such names.

Names of cities and towns in the United States follow the forms listed in the *Directory of Post Offices* of the United States Postal Service. Domestic physical names follow the decisions of the Board on Geographic Names, U.S. Department of the Interior, and of various state geographic name boards.

It is the belief of the publishers that the boundaries shown in a general reference atlas should reflect current geographic and political realities. This policy has been followed consistently in the atlas. The presentation of *de facto* boundaries in cases of territorial dispute between various nations does not imply the political endorsement of such boundaries by the publisher, but simply the honest representation of boundaries as they exist at the time of the printing of the atlas maps.

Indexes — Pinpointing a Location. Each political map is accompanied by a comprehensive index of the place names appearing on the map. If you are unfamiliar with the location of a particular geographical place and wish to find its position within the confines of the subject area of the map, consult the map index as your first step. The name of the feature sought will be found in its proper alphabetical sequence with a key reference letter-number combination corresponding to its location on the map. After noting the key reference letter-number combination for the place name, turn to the map. The place name will be found within the square formed by the two lines of latitude and the two lines of longitude which enclose the co-ordinates — i.e., the marginal letters and numbers. The diagram below illustrates the system of indexing.

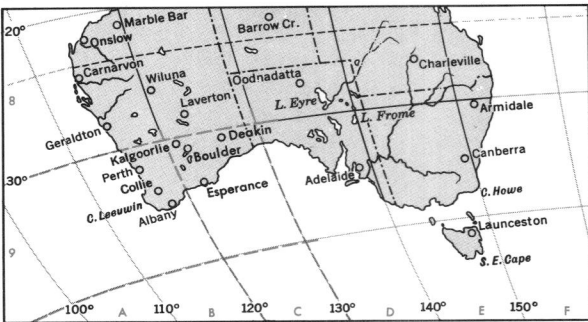

In the case of maps consisting entirely of insets, the place name is found near the intersection point of the imaginary lines connecting the co-ordinates at right angles. See below.

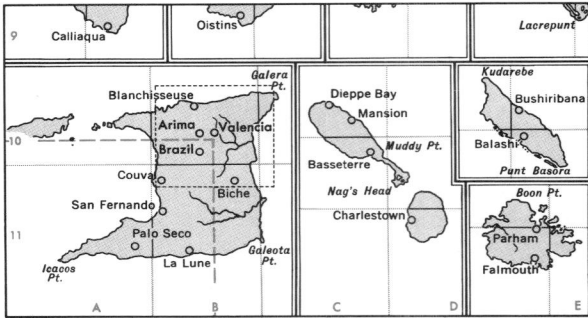

Where space on the map has not permitted giving the complete form of the place name, the complete form is shown in the index. Where a place is known by more than one name or by various spellings of the same name, the different forms have been included in the index. Physical features are listed under their proper names and not according to their generic terms; that is to say, Rio Negro will be found under Negro and not under Rio Negro. On the other hand, Rio Grande will be found under Rio Grande. Accompanying most index entries for cities and towns, and for other political units, are *population figures* for the particular entries. The large number of population figures in the atlas makes this work one of the most comprehensive statistical sources available to the public today. The population figures have been taken from the latest official censuses and estimates of the various nations. Dates and sources for the population figures are listed in the Gazetteer-Index of the World preceding this section.

Population and area figures for countries and major political units are listed in bold type *fact lists* on the margins of the indexes. In addition, the capital, largest city, highest point, monetary unit, principal languages and the prevailing religions of the country concerned are also listed. The Gazetteer-Index of the World on the preceding pages provides a quick reference index for countries and other important areas. Though population and area figures for each major unit area also found in the map section, the Gazetteer-Index provides a conveniently arranged statistical comparison contained in five pages. As mentioned, dates and sources of the population figures appearing in the country indexes are also listed in this section.

All index entries for cities and towns in the United States are preceded by a five-digit postal ZIP code number applying to the community. This useful feature permits the reader to address his mail so that it will be routed and delivered more efficiently and quickly by the U.S. Postal Service. A dagger (†) designates those places that do not possess a post office. The ZIP code number listed in such cases refers to that of the nearest post office. An asterisk (*) marks those larger cities which are divided into multiple ZIP code areas. Using the single ZIP code number listed in such cases will direct your letter to the proper city with dispatch. However, if the precise ZIP code number of the address within the city is needed, it is suggested that the reader refer to the latest National ZIP Code Directory at his local post office. This detailed guide lists every street in a multiple ZIP code city with the proper ZIP code for the street.

Relief Maps. Accompanying each political map is a relief map of the area. The purpose of the relief map is to illustrate the surface configuration (TOPOGRAPHY) of the region. A shading technique in color simulates the relative ruggedness of the terrain — plains, plateaus, valleys, hills and mountains. Graded colors, ranging from greens for lowlands, yellows for intermediate elevations to browns in the highlands, indicate the height above sea level of each part of the land. A vertical scale at the margin of the map shows the approximate height in meters and feet represented by each color.

Economic Maps — Agriculture, Industry and Resources. One of the most interesting features that will be found in each country unit is the economic map. From this map one can determine the basic activities of a nation as expressed through its economy. A perusal of the map yields a full understanding of the area's economic geography and natural resources.

The agricultural economy is manifested in two ways: color bands and commodity names. The color bands express broad categories of *dominant land use,* such as, cereal belts, forest lands, livestock range lands, nonagricultural wastes. The red commodity names, on the other hand, pinpoint the areas of production of *specific* crops; i.e., wheat, cotton, sugar beets, etc.

Major mineral occurrences are denoted by standard letter symbols appearing in blue. The relative size of the letter symbols signifies the relative importance of the deposit.

The manufacturing sector of the economy is presented by means of diagonal line patterns expressing the various *industrial areas* of consequence within a country. The products of each major industrial area are listed in boxes at the margin of the map.

The fishing industry is represented by names of commercial fish species appearing offshore in blue letters. Major waterpower sites are designated by blue symbols.

The publishers have tried to make this work the most comprehensive and useful atlas available, and it is hoped that it will prove a valuable reference work. Any constructive suggestions from the reader will be welcomed.

Glossary of Abbreviations

A

A. A. F. — Army Air Field
Acad. — Academy
A. C. T. — Australian Capital Territory
adm. — administration; administrative
adm. city-co. — administrative
city-county
A. F. B. — Air Force Base
Afgh., Afghan. — Afghanistan
Afr. — Africa
Ala. — Alabama
Alb. — Albania
Alg. — Algeria
Alta. — Alberta
Amer. — American
Amer. Samoa — American Samoa
And. — Andorra
Ant. — Antarctica
Ar. — Arabia
arch. — archipelago
Arg. — Argentina
Ariz. — Arizona
Ark. — Arkansas
A. S. S. R. — Autonomous Soviet
Socialist Republic
Austr., Austral. — Australian, Australia
aut. — autonomous
Aut. Obl. — Autonomous Oblast
aut. prov. — autonomous province

B

B. — bay
Bah. — Bahamas
Barb. — Barbados
Battlef. — Battlefield
Bch. — Beach
Belg. — Belgium
Berm. — Bermuda
Bol. — Bolivia
Bots. — Botswana
Br. — Branch
Br. — British
Braz. — Brazil
Br. Col. — British Columbia
Br. Ind. Oc. Terr. — British Indian
Ocean Territory
Bulg. — Bulgaria

C

C. — cape
Calif. — California
can. — canal
cap. — capital
Centr. Afr. Rep. — Central African
Republic
Cent. Amer. — Central America
C. G. Sta. — Coast Guard Station
C. H. — Court House
chan. — channel
Chan. Is. — Channel Islands
Chem. Ctr. — Chemical Center
co. — county
C. of G. H. — Cape of Good Hope
Col. — Colombia
Colo. — Colorado
comm. — commissary
Conn. — Connecticut
cont. — continent
cord. — cordillera (mountain range)
C. Rica — Costa Rica
C. S. — County Seat
C. Verde — Cape Verde
Cy. — City
Czech. — Czechoslovakia

D

D. C. — District of Columbia
Del. — Delaware
Dem. — Democratic
Den. — Denmark
depr. — depression
dept. — department
des. — desert
dist., dist's — district, districts
div. — division
Dom. Rep. — Dominican Republic
dry riv. — dry river

E

E. — East
Ec., Ecua. — Ecuador
E. Ger. — East Germany
elec. div. — electoral division

El Salv. — El Salvador
Eng. — England
Eq. Guin. — Equatorial Guinea
escarp. — escarpment
est. — estuary
Eth. — Ethiopia

F

Falk. Is. — Falkland Islands
Fin. — Finland
Fk., Fks. — Fork, Forks
Fla. — Florida
for. — forest
Fr. — France, French
Fr. Gui. — French Guiana
Fr. Poly. — French Polynesia
Ft. — Fort

G

G. — gulf
Ga. — Georgia
Game Res. — Game Reserve
Ger. — Germany
geys. — geyser
Gibr. — Gibraltar
glac. — glacier
gov. — governorate
Gr. — Group
Greenl. — Greenland
Gt. Brit. — Great Britain
Guad. — Guadeloupe
Guat. — Guatemala
Guy. — Guyana

H

har., harb., hbr. — harbor
hd. — head
highl. — highland, highlands
Hist. — Historic, Historical
Hond. — Honduras
Hts. — Heights
Hung. — Hungary

I

i., isl., — island, isle
Ice., Icel. — Iceland
Ida. — Idaho
Ill. — Illinois
Ind. — Indiana
ind. city — independent city
Indon. — Indonesia
Ind. Res. — Indian Reservation
int. div. — internal division
inten. — intendency
interm. str. — intermittent stream
Int'l — International
Ire. — Ireland
is., isls. — islands
Isr. — Israel
isth. — isthmus

J

Jam. — Jamaica
Jct. — Junction

K

Kans. — Kansas
Ky. — Kentucky

L

L. — Lake, Loch, Lough
La. — Louisiana
Lab. — Laboratory
lag. — lagoon
Ld. — Land
Leb. — Lebanon
Les. — Lesotho
Liecht. — Liechtenstein
Lux. — Luxembourg

M

Madag. — Madagascar
Man. — Manitoba
Mart. — Martinique
Mass. — Massachusetts
Maur. — Mauritania
Md. — Maryland
met. area — metropolitan area
Mex. — Mexico
Mich. — Michigan
Minn. — Minnesota
Miss. — Mississippi
Mo. — Missouri

Mon. — Monument
Mong. — Mongolia
Mont. — Montana
Mor. — Morocco
Moz., Mozamb. — Mozambique
mt. — mount
mtn. — mountain

N

N., No. — North, Northern
N. Amer. — North America
N. A. S. — Naval Air Station
Nat'l — National
Nat'l Cem. — National Cemetery
Nat'l Mem. Park — National Memorial
Park
Nat'l Mil. Park — National Military
Park
Nat'l Pkwy. — National Parkway
Nav. Base — Naval Base
Nav. Sta. — Naval Station
N. B., N. Br. — New Brunswick
N. C. — North Carolina
N. Dak. — North Dakota
Nebr. — Nebraska
Neth. — Netherlands
Neth. Ant. — Netherlands Antilles
Nev. — Nevada
New Cal. — New Caledonia
Newf. — Newfoundland
New Hebr. — New Hebrides
N. H. — New Hampshire
Nic. — Nicaragua
N. Ire. — Northern Ireland
N. J. — New Jersey
N. Mex. — New Mexico
Nor. — Norway, Norwegian
No. Terr. — Northern Territory
(Australia)
N. S. — Nova Scotia
N. S. W. — New South Wales
N. W. T. — Northwest Territories
(Canada)
N. Y. — New York
N. Z. — New Zealand

O

Obl. — Oblast
O. F. S. — Orange Free State
Okla. — Oklahoma
Okr. — Okrug
Ont. — Ontario
Ord. Depot — Ordnance Depot
Oreg. — Oregon

P

Pa. — Pennsylvania
Pac. — Pacific
Pac. Is. — Pacific Islands,
Territory of the
Pak. — Pakistan
Pan. — Panama
Par. — Paraguay
par. — parish
passg. — passage
P.D.R. Yemen — Peoples Democratic
Republic of Yemen
P. E. I. — Prince Edward Island
pen. — peninsula
Phil., Phil. Is. — Philippines
Pk. — Park
pk. — peak
plat. — plateau
P. N. G. — Papua New Guinea
Port. — Portugal, Portuguese
P. Rico — Puerto Rico
pref. — prefecture
prom. — promontory
prov. — province, provincial
prov. dist. — provincial district
pt. — point

Q

Que. — Québec
Queens. — Queensland

R

R. — River
ra. — range
Rec., Recr. — Recreation, Recreational
reg. — region
Rep. — Republic
res. — reservoir
Res. — Reservation, Reserve
Rho., Rhod. — Rhodesia

R. I. — Rhode Island
riv. — river
Rum. — Rumania

S

S. — South
Sa. — Sierra, Serra
S. Afr., S. Africa — South Africa
salt dep. — salt deposit
salt des. — salt desert
S. Amer. — South America
São T. & Pr. — São Tomé
and Príncipe
Sask. — Saskatchewan
Saudi Ar. — Saudi Arabia
S. Aust., S. Austral. — South Australia
S. C. — South Carolina
Scot. — Scotland
Sd. — Sound
S. Dak. — South Dakota
Sen. — Senegal
sen. dist. — senatorial district
Seych. — Seychelles
S. F. S. R. — Soviet Federated Social
Republic
Sing. — Singapore
S. Leone — Sierra Leone
S. Marino — San Marino
Sol. Is. — Solomon Islands
Sp. — Spanish
Spr., Sprs. — Spring, Springs
S. S. R. — Soviet Socialist Republic
St., Ste. — Saint, Sainte
Sta. — Station
St. Chr.-N.-A. — Saint Christopher-
Nevis-Anguilla
St. P. & M. — Saint Pierre and
Miquelon
St. Vinc. & Grens. — St. Vincent & The
Grenadines
str., strs. — strait, straits
Sur. — Suriname
S. W. Afr. — South-West Africa
Swaz. — Swaziland
Switz. — Switzerland

T

Tanz. — Tanzania
Tas. — Tasmania
Tenn. — Tennessee
terr., terrs. — territory, territories
Tex. — Texas
Thai. — Thailand
Trin. & Tob. — Trinidad and Tobago
Tun. — Tunisia
twp. — township

U

U.A.E. — United
Arab Emirates
U. K. — United Kingdom
Upp. Volta — Upper Volta
urb. area — urban area
Urug. — Uruguay
U. S. — United States
U. S. S. R. — Union of Soviet Socialist
Republics

V

Va. — Virginia
Vall. — Valley
Ven., Venez. — Venezuela
V. I. (Br.) — Virgin Islands (British)
V. I. (U. S.) — Virgin Islands (U. S.)
Vic. — Victoria
Vill. — Village
vol. — volcano
Vt. — Vermont

W

W. — West, Western
Wash. — Washington
W. Aust., W. Austral. — Western
Australia
W. Ger. — West Germany
Wis. — Wisconsin
W. Samoa — Western Samoa
W. Va. — West Virginia
Wyo. — Wyoming

Y

Yugo. — Yugoslavia
Yukon — Yukon Territory

Z

Zim. — Zimbabwe

Environment & life

The Sun: *Energy Source of the Solar System*

*For longer than the memory of man, a
glowing furnace of nuclear activity has held our solar
system within its gravitational orbit and,
deep within its interior, fused the nuclei of
hydrogen and helium, dispensing them as heat, light and the
other forms of radiation which nurture the very elements of
life on earth. The sun—with radiant energy so fierce that
it was deified by ancient man—still dominates the
lives of laymen and the minds of
scientists who seek to comprehend its nature
and utilize its mighty force.*

Structure of the Earth

The photographs (opposite) reveal views of the world seen only since the advent of satellites and space vehicles. Pictures such as these greatly increase man's understanding of the earth's structure and the visible forces which act upon it.

If man were big enough he could peel the earth somewhat like a complicated grape, finding at its heart what some scientists believe is the remains of its most primitive beginnings — a solid core of iron and nickel. Wrapped around this solid mass is a second, molten outer core which, set in motion by the earth's rotations, may be the source of its magnetic field. The solid rock mantle, extending to about 1,800 miles from the surface of the earth, is the next layer which in turn is covered by the crust and separated from it by a distinct boundary known as the Mohorovicic discontinuity. The crust, which is as deep as 40 miles under the continents, is only about 5 miles thick beneath the oceans.

To simplify the complex layerings of solids, liquids and gases which make up the structure of the earth, geologists have divided them into three zones: the lithosphere, containing all solids from the land surface to the earth's center; the hydrosphere, all surface water areas; and the atmosphere, the layered gaseous envelope extending about 600 miles above the earth's surface. From each of these three spheres the biologist has selected those parts which contain organic matter, plant as well as animal, and has grouped them together into a comprehensive zone known as the Biosphere. Here, in this world of life, man survives in relationship, however indirectly, with every other living organism.

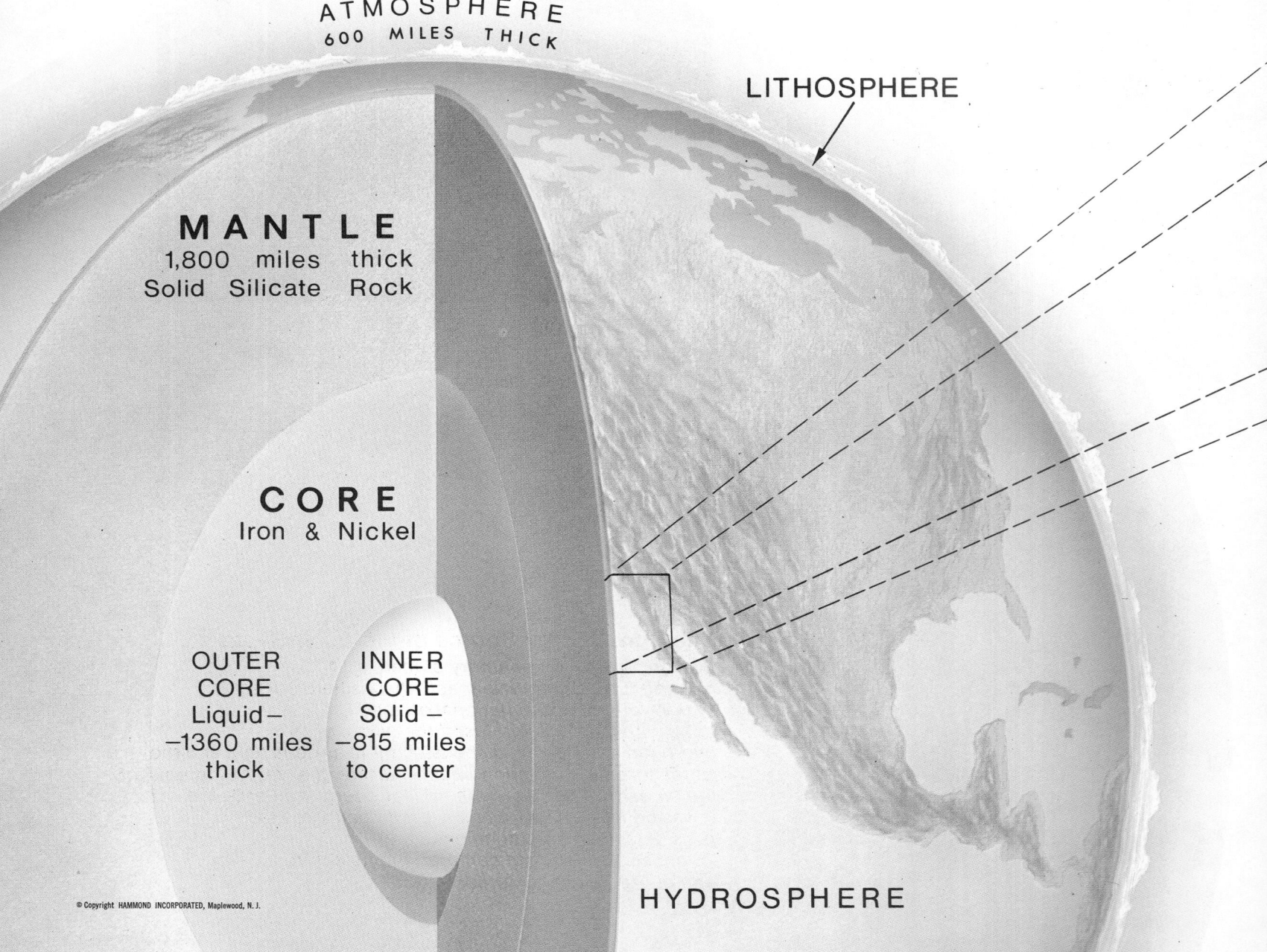

ATMOSPHERE
600 MILES THICK

LITHOSPHERE

MANTLE
1,800 miles thick
Solid Silicate Rock

CORE
Iron & Nickel

OUTER CORE
Liquid —
—1360 miles
thick

INNER CORE
Solid —
—815 miles
to center

HYDROSPHERE

Complex geologic structures, Northern Territory, Australia   NASA

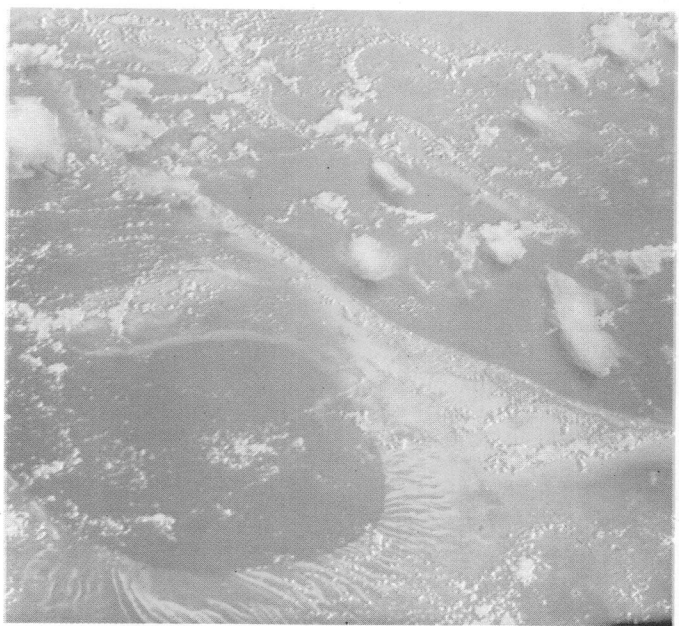

Ocean-bottom topography of the Great Bahama Bank   NASA

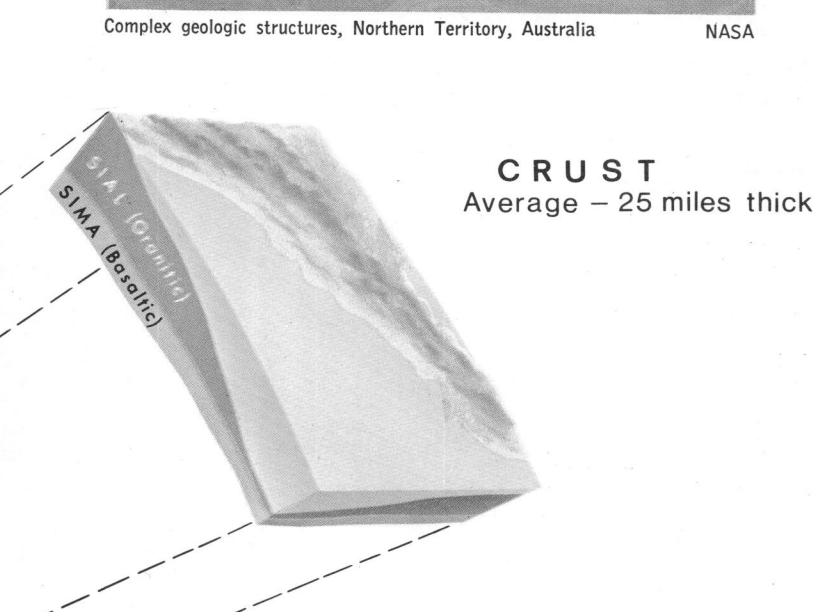

CRUST
Average — 25 miles thick

Classic dendritic drainage patterns, Saudi Arabia   NASA

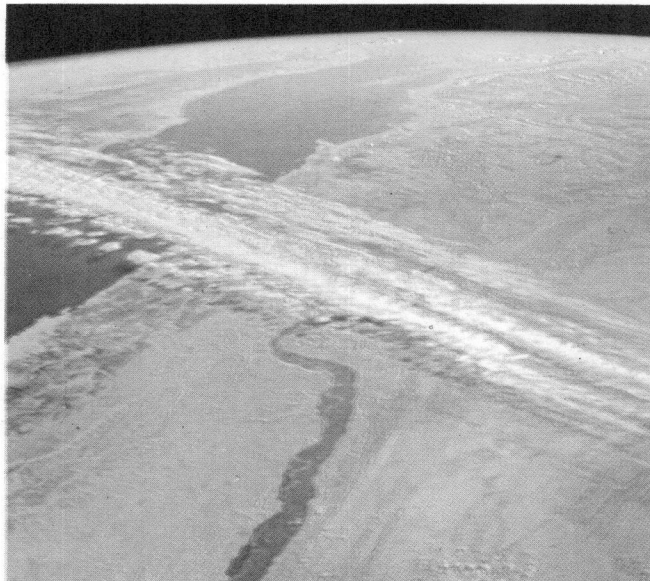

Jet stream over the Red Sea and Nile Valley   NASA

Cloud formations affecting the Indian Subcontinent   NASA

GEOLOGIC TIME

TIME DIVISION			YEARS AGO	MAJOR GEOLOGIC DEVELOPMENTS
CENOZOIC ERA	TERTIARY PERIOD / QUATERNARY PERIOD	RECENT	10,000	GREAT LAKES NORWEGIAN FJORDS ICE AGES BLACK SEA CASPIAN SEA
		PLEISTOCENE	1-2 million	
		PLIOCENE	11 million	
		MIOCENE	25 million	HIMALAYAS
		OLIGOCENE	40 million	ALPS
		EOCENE	60 million	
		PALEOCENE	70 million	ANDES MOUNTAINS ROCKY MOUNTAINS CHALK DEPOSITS
MESOZOIC ERA		CRETACEOUS PERIOD	135 million	COAST RANGES SIERRA NEVADA JURA MOUNTAINS
		JURASSIC PERIOD	180 million	NEW JERSEY PALISADES
		TRIASSIC PERIOD	225 million	CAUCASUS URAL MOUNTAINS APPALACHIAN MOUNTAINS
PALEOZOIC ERA		PERMIAN PERIOD	270 million	POTASH DEPOSITS
		PENNSYLVANIAN PERIOD	300 million	COAL DEPOSITS
		MISSISSIPPIAN PERIOD	350 million	ACADIAN MOUNTAINS
		DEVONIAN PERIOD	400 million	
		SILURIAN PERIOD	440 million	NIAGARA FALLS CAPROCK TACONIC MOUNTAINS
		ORDOVICIAN PERIOD	500 million	LIMESTONE DEPOSITS VERMONT MOUNTAINS
		CAMBRIAN PERIOD	600 million	ARIZONA MOUNTAINS
		PRE-CAMBRIAN		METALLIC ORE DEPOSITS LAURENTIAN MOUNTAINS ADIRONDACK MOUNTAINS

© Copyright HAMMOND INCORPORATED, Maplewood, N.J.

Like a giant Rosetta stone the secrets of the earth's creation lie spread in strata beneath our feet, revealing their hieroglyphic message to a few of the initiated.

For billions of years layers of rock — the sedimentary deposits of ages — have piled up on the earth's surface, entrapping the characteristics of time. Time when a lifeless nature prepared for the first microscopic living organisms; time when these organisms were destroyed or became extinct; time when, through endless subtle mutations, they evolved into new forms of life.

The Paleozoic, ancient era; Mesozoic, middle era; and Cenozoic, recent era, are the designations used for the broad periods of time during which life evolved. Locked within strata of rock, vestiges of life are found in the fossilized remains of creatures over a billion years old. In succeeding layers geologists and anthropologists find other clues to the mystery of time and life: the appearance of the lowest forms of animal life; the evolution of fish, amphibians, reptiles, birds and mammals. Late in the schedule of creation traces of a strange and wonderful animal appear, for it was only one million years ago that man left his first imprint on the geologic record.

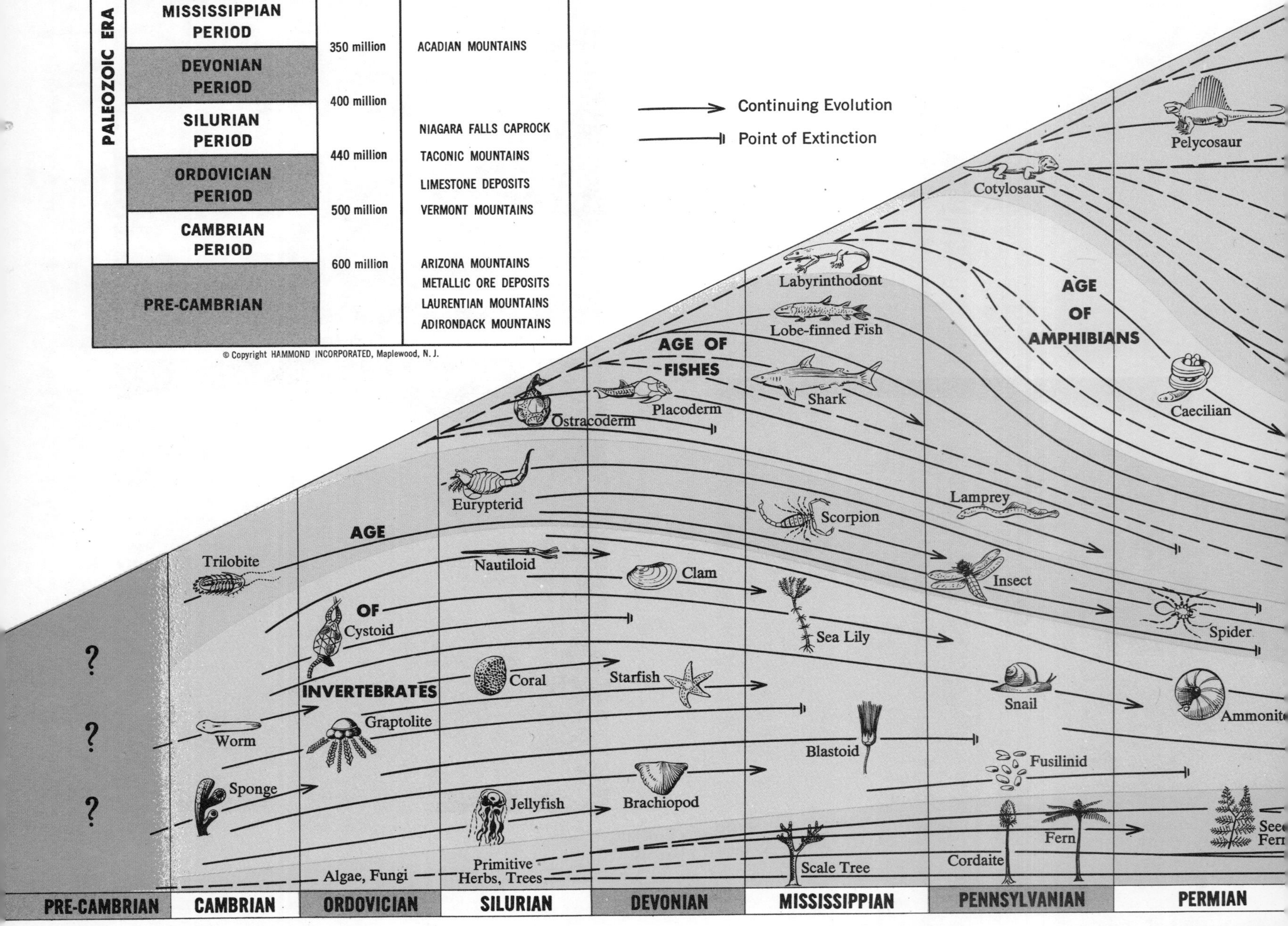

Continuing Evolution

Point of Extinction

AGE OF FISHES

AGE OF AMPHIBIANS

AGE OF INVERTEBRATES

Pelycosaur
Cotylosaur
Labyrinthodont
Lobe-finned Fish
Shark
Ostracoderm
Placoderm
Caecilian
Eurypterid
Scorpion
Lamprey
Nautiloid
Clam
Insect
Cystoid
Sea Lily
Spider
Coral
Starfish
Snail
Graptolite
Blastoid
Ammonite
Trilobite
Worm
Fusilinid
Sponge
Jellyfish
Brachiopod
Scale Tree
Cordaite
Fern
Seed Fern

Algae, Fungi
Primitive Herbs, Trees

PRE-CAMBRIAN	CAMBRIAN	ORDOVICIAN	SILURIAN	DEVONIAN	MISSISSIPPIAN	PENNSYLVANIAN	PERMIAN

The Geologic Record

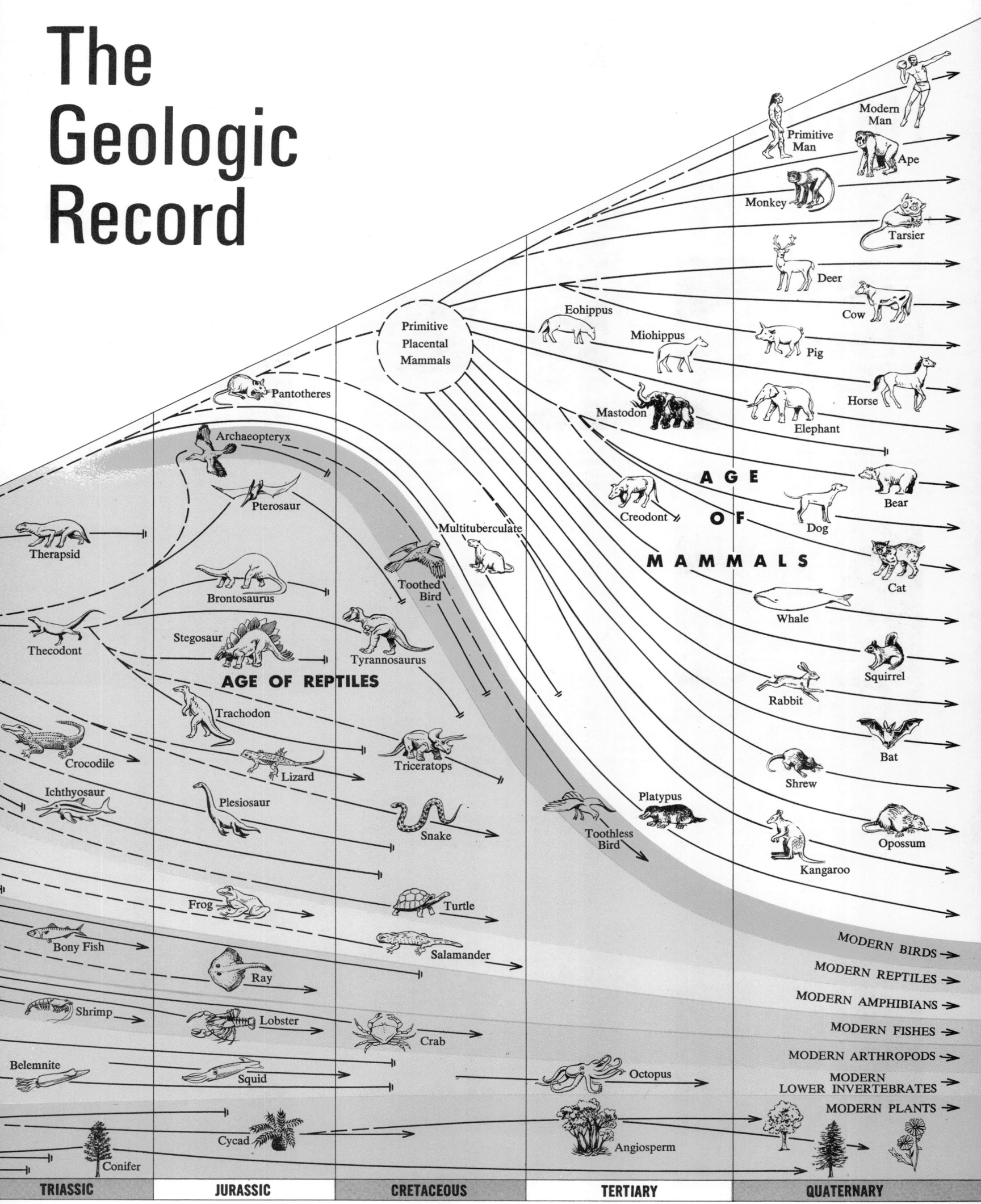

| TRIASSIC | JURASSIC | CRETACEOUS | TERTIARY | QUATERNARY |

The Biosphere: Realm of Living Things

Polar and mountainous regions of perpetual **ice and snow** cover one-tenth of the earth's land areas. Windswept, always below freezing, it can support life only peripherally, if at all.

A place of mosses, lichens and stunted flowering plants and trees, the **tundra** is an area so marginal that only specially adapted life-forms, such as reindeer, can live there.

As favorable climates produce and sustain an abundance of vegetation, the **mid-latitude forest** regions of the world continue to serve as home for a majority of the world's population.

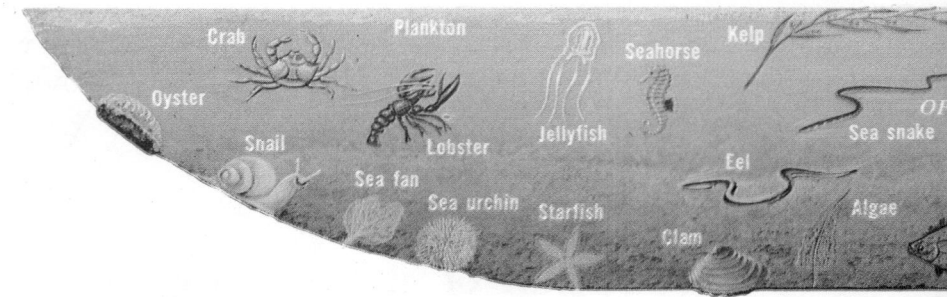

Ranging from the luxuriant vegetation of the rainforest to scrub-like woodlands in drier areas, the **tropical forest** is noted for containing a wide variety of insects, birds and small animals.

The **savanna** or tropical grassland is a land of tall grass interspersed with trees. A place of winter droughts and summer rainfall, it is the true jungle home of big-game animals.

On the **mid-latitude grasslands** are found many of the sheep and cattle ranches of the earth, and, where the land has been successfully cultivated, the great grain fields.

Except in scattered oases and irrigated lands, the **deserts** of the world are inhabited only by livestock-herding nomads and wildlife capable of surviving in moisture-deficient areas.

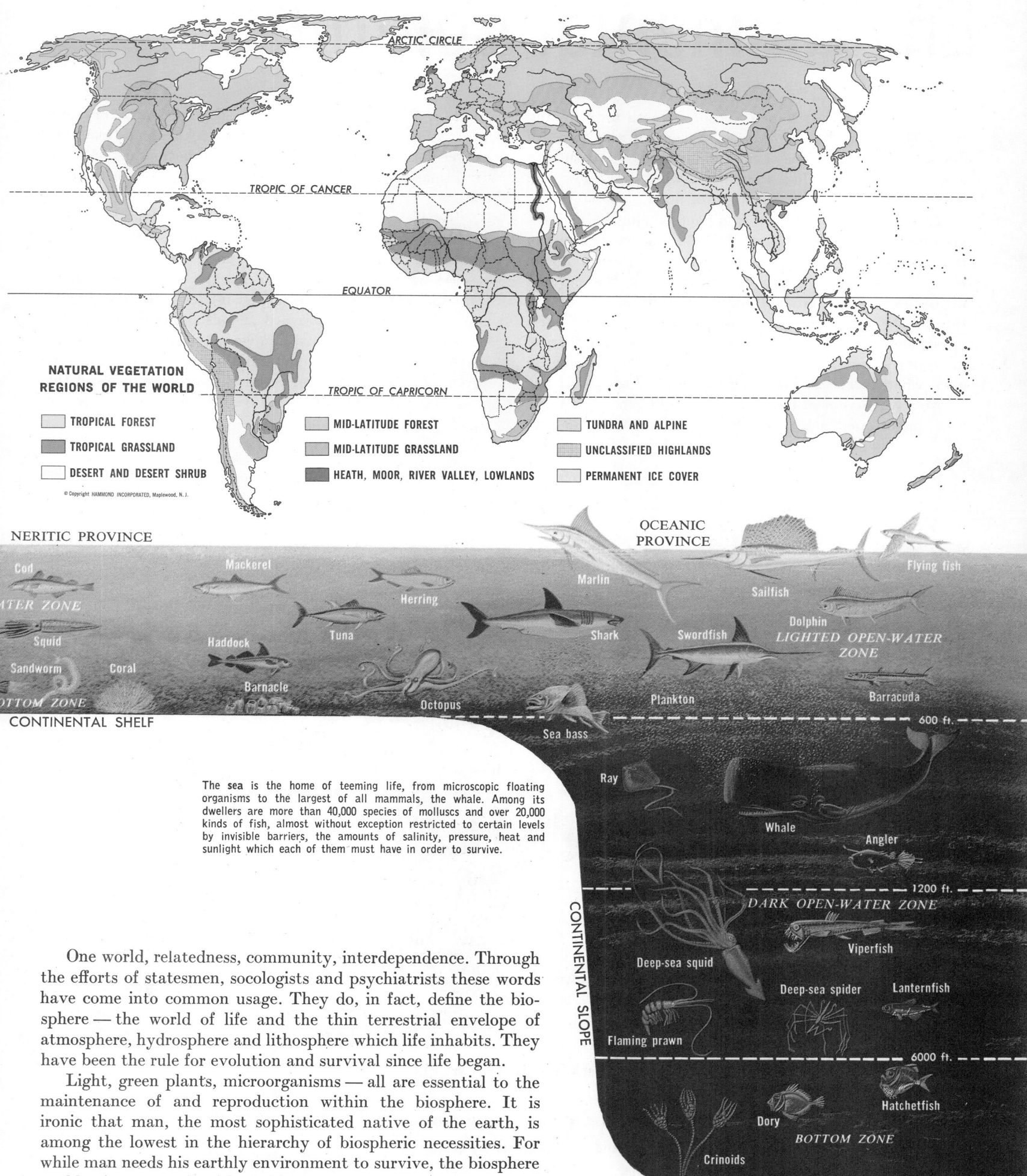

NATURAL VEGETATION
REGIONS OF THE WORLD

TROPICAL FOREST

TROPICAL GRASSLAND

DESERT AND DESERT SHRUB

MID-LATITUDE FOREST

MID-LATITUDE GRASSLAND

HEATH, MOOR, RIVER VALLEY, LOWLANDS

TUNDRA AND ALPINE

UNCLASSIFIED HIGHLANDS

PERMANENT ICE COVER

© Copyright HAMMOND INCORPORATED, Maplewood, N.J.

ARCTIC CIRCLE

TROPIC OF CANCER

EQUATOR

TROPIC OF CAPRICORN

NERITIC PROVINCE

OCEANIC PROVINCE

Cod

Mackerel

Marlin

Sailfish

Flying fish

WATER ZONE

Herring

Tuna

Shark

Swordfish

Dolphin

LIGHTED OPEN-WATER ZONE

Squid

Haddock

Sandworm

Coral

Barnacle

BOTTOM ZONE

Octopus

Plankton

Barracuda

CONTINENTAL SHELF

Sea bass

600 ft.

Ray

The **sea** is the home of teeming life, from microscopic floating organisms to the largest of all mammals, the whale. Among its dwellers are more than 40,000 species of molluscs and over 20,000 kinds of fish, almost without exception restricted to certain levels by invisible barriers, the amounts of salinity, pressure, heat and sunlight which each of them must have in order to survive.

Whale

Angler

1200 ft.

DARK OPEN-WATER ZONE

Deep-sea squid

Viperfish

Deep-sea spider

Lanternfish

Flaming prawn

6000 ft.

One world, relatedness, community, interdependence. Through the efforts of statesmen, socologists and psychiatrists these words have come into common usage. They do, in fact, define the biosphere — the world of life and the thin terrestrial envelope of atmosphere, hydrosphere and lithosphere which life inhabits. They have been the rule for evolution and survival since life began.

Light, green plants, microorganisms — all are essential to the maintenance of and reproduction within the biosphere. It is ironic that man, the most sophisticated native of the earth, is among the lowest in the hierarchy of biospheric necessities. For while man needs his earthly environment to survive, the biosphere could exist very well without him.

CONTINENTAL SLOPE

Hatchetfish

Dory

BOTTOM ZONE

Crinoids

OCEAN FLOOR

© Copyright HAMMOND INCORPORATED, Maplewood, N.J.

Environmental Controls

Primitive man worshiped the sun, danced for rain, and trembled when the angry gods unleashed the force of hurricane or hid the face of the sun in clouds. Modern man curses the drought, hides from the wind and snow and builds walls against the onslaught of flood.

Little has changed in the impact of climate and environment on the life of man. There are no vegetarians in the desert or in the ice-bound regions of the far north. Houses exposing vast expanses of glass to the burning fingers of the sun are not found in the Sahara, at the Equator or near the Poles. Man does not die of malaria in regions too dry or too cold to support the larvae of mosquitoes; swollen goiterous necks are never seen in areas where local water is naturally supplied with iodine.

Men who live near lakes or seas build boats while those near mountains climb or ski. The plainsman nurtures cattle or grain; the farmer in the valley cultivates tomatoes or legumes. In work, in play, in sickness and varying degrees of health — even in the formation of national traditions — the world of man is subject to the force of nature.

By a variety of adaptations man wrestles with the problems of his environment. He can air-condition or heat his home, refrigerate his food, quench parts of the thirsty deserts with irrigated water, drain the swamps and navigate the seas. He has developed intricate technologies to forecast earthquakes, blizzards, floods and hurricanes.

But the ancient sun still governs the movements of the earth within its orbit, determining heat and cold, the progress of the winds and ocean currents, the levels of the seas — the glacier's trail. Man continues to bow before the "god of day."

The interactions of sun, rain and wind are so closely related that they function as a single entity which is, perhaps, the most dominant force in creating man's environment.

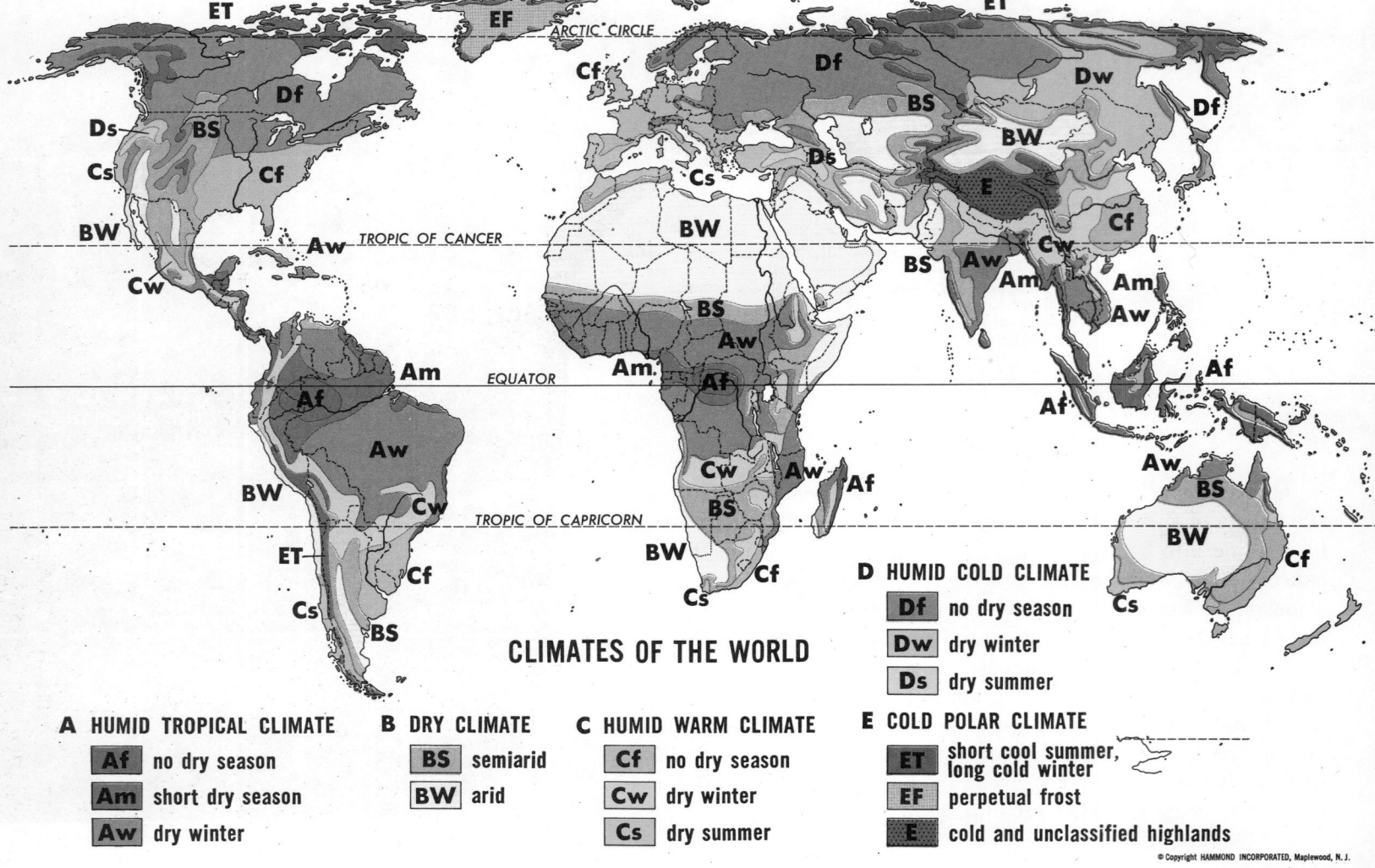

CLIMATES OF THE WORLD

A HUMID TROPICAL CLIMATE
- **Af** no dry season
- **Am** short dry season
- **Aw** dry winter

B DRY CLIMATE
- **BS** semiarid
- **BW** arid

C HUMID WARM CLIMATE
- **Cf** no dry season
- **Cw** dry winter
- **Cs** dry summer

D HUMID COLD CLIMATE
- **Df** no dry season
- **Dw** dry winter
- **Ds** dry summer

E COLD POLAR CLIMATE
- **ET** short cool summer, long cold winter
- **EF** perpetual frost
- **E** cold and unclassified highlands

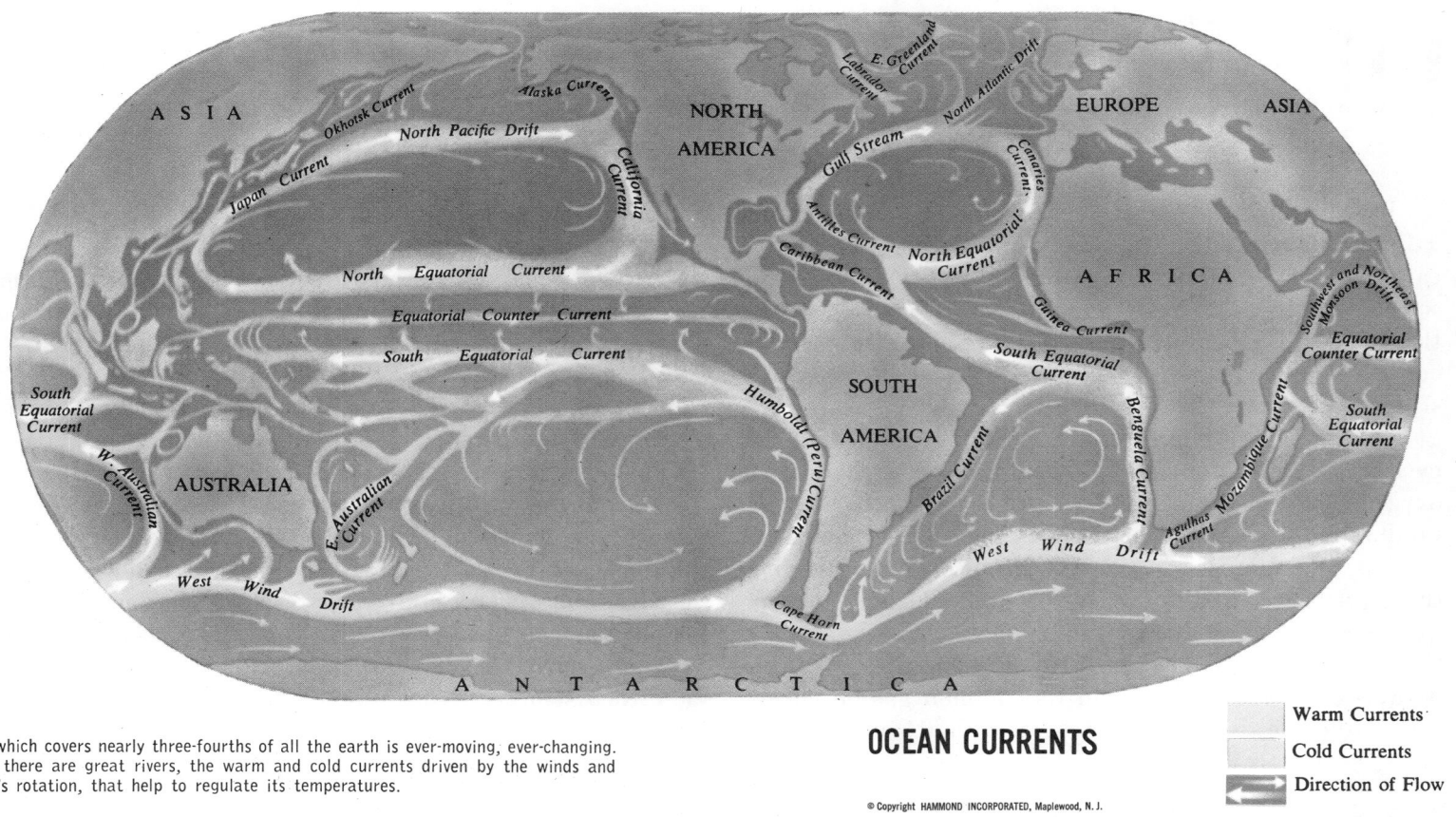

OCEAN CURRENTS

The sea, which covers nearly three-fourths of all the earth is ever-moving, ever-changing. Within it there are great rivers, the warm and cold currents driven by the winds and the earth's rotation, that help to regulate its temperatures.

Warm Currents
Cold Currents
Direction of Flow

© Copyright HAMMOND INCORPORATED, Maplewood, N.J.

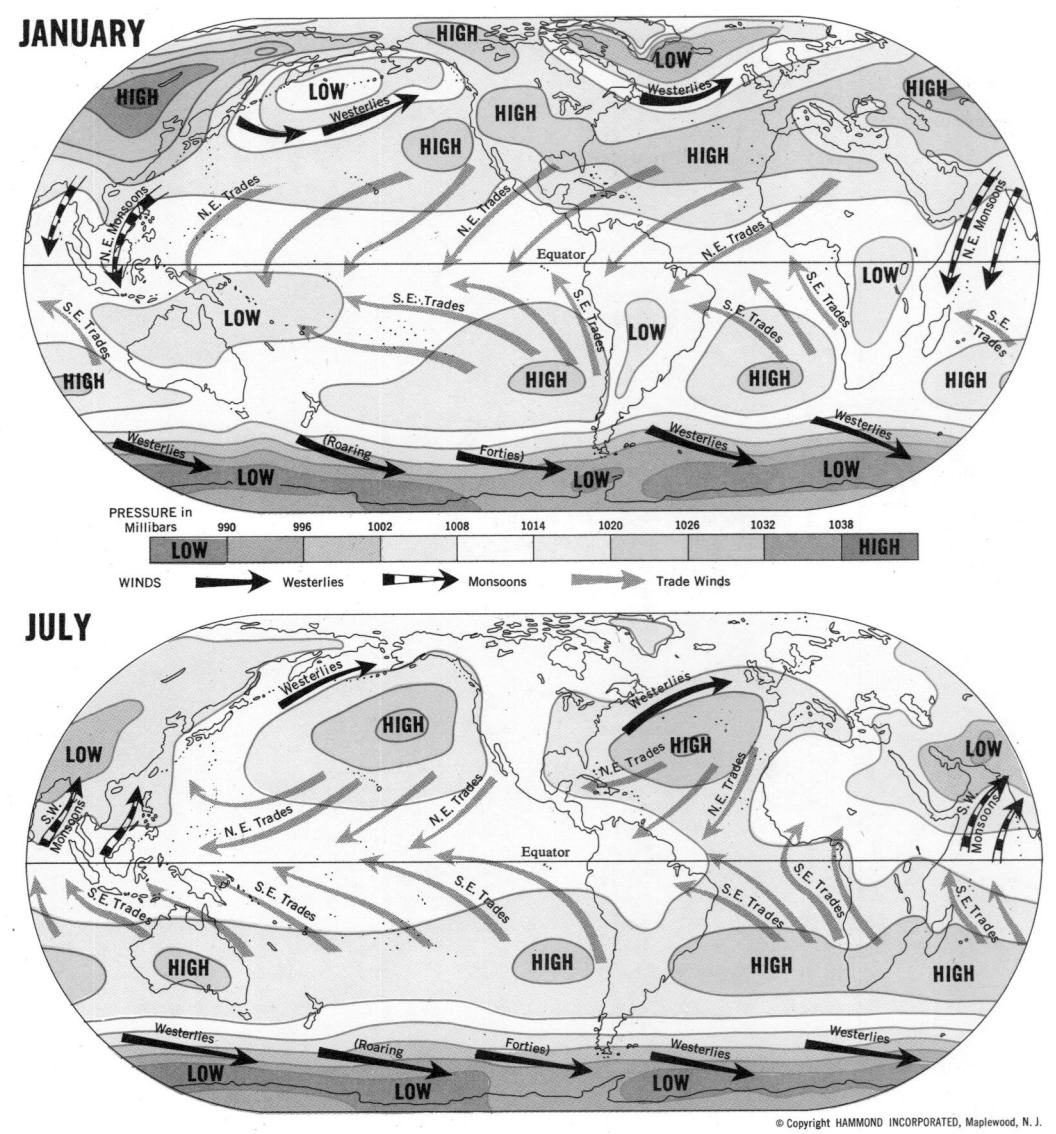

PRESSURE in Millibars	990	996	1002	1008	1014	1020	1026	1032	1038	
LOW										HIGH

WINDS → Westerlies → Monsoons → Trade Winds

AIR PRESSURE AND WINDS

Just as the atmosphere tends to equalize heat distribution, it tends to maintain equal pressure over the earth. Whenever this equilibrium, or balance, is disturbed, air flows from areas of higher pressure to areas of lower pressure. In the Northern Hemisphere winds flow clockwise around a high pressure area (high) and counterclockwise around the center of a low pressure area (low). These movements are reversed in the Southern Hemisphere.

© Copyright HAMMOND INCORPORATED, Maplewood, N.J.

Life Support Cycles

With an intuition clearly beyond their scientific knowledge, the ancients of India developed a theory of reincarnation which, in some philosophic ways, parallels what science has learned of the workings of the biosphere. In the remarkable thrift of nature nothing is lost — in tremendous complex cycles atoms from the first life on earth still move through the biosphere.

The miracle of energy is constantly performed in the cycles of the "life-giving" elements. Carbon, hydrogen, oxygen, nitrogen, sulfur and phosphorus act together to produce all living matter. While many other elements such as calcium, iodine and iron are also found in living things, they are not absolute essentials in all cases. Carbon, hydrogen and oxygen are vital for photosynthesis and are the components of the basic food substances — carbohydrates and fats. Carbon, in its common gaseous form, carbon dioxide, is absorbed by green plants and triggers

the production of carbohydrate compounds by reacting with molecules of water.

Some "energy" is stored within the plant in the form of new tissue; other "energy," in the form of oxygen is released into the air to be used by other organisms. The seemingly inexhaustible supply of carbon dioxide available for use is replenished in the atmosphere through the respiration of all living things, and in the soil as bacteria and fungi break down plant and animal cells,

Nitrogen, sulfur and phosphorus are essential to animals and plants for the production and maintenance of protein. Nitrogen, with carbon, hydrogen and oxygen, is used for the growth and repair of tissue. Sulfur acts as a "stiffening" agent in all protein. To perform their functions proteins must be folded and shaped in a particular way, and their structure is maintained by bonds between sulfur atoms. While phosphorus is not a constituent of protein,

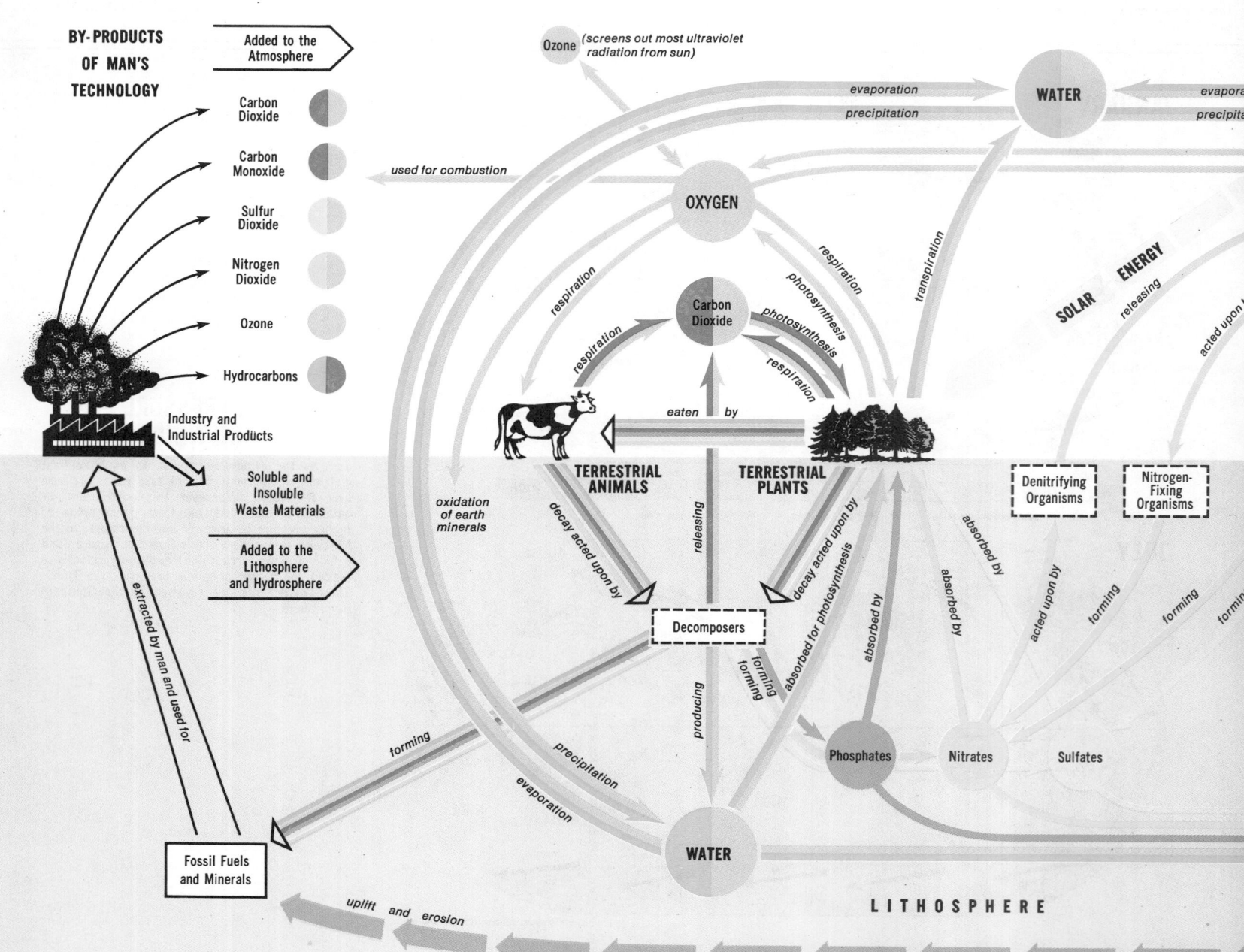

no protein can be made without it. Special phosphate compounds are the "fuel" for all biochemical work within the cell.

Although about four-fifths of the atmosphere is nitrogen, higher forms of life cannot make use of it in its "free" state and must absorb it at one or more points in its biospheric cycle. The decomposers — bacteria and fungi — act on waste matter, breaking down complex compounds into simpler usable forms including nitrogen. Some nitrogen-fixing bacteria are able to utilize atmospheric nitrogen in their own metabolism, while others convert it to those nitrogen-enriched substances necessary for all plant growth.

In nature, no part is greater than the whole and almost every element is dependent on another for some essential part of its cycle. Water, which is incorporated into every organism, is essential in the formation of free oxygen which in turn sustains the life of that organism. Water is also

the principal "carrier" in the cycling of all elements. When it evaporates, water returns certain elements to the atmosphere; when it seeps through the soil on its return to the sea, water distributes nutrients to plant roots.

Carbon monoxide, sulfur and nitrogen oxides, hydrocarbons — by-products of man's industry — are being injected into the biosphere in ever-increasing amounts. There, as the "new compounds," they must in some way co-exist with the life-support cycles established throughout millions of years of evolution. Their compatability with these cycles and the organisms they nurture will determine the future of life on our planet.

Already man has learned one thing. Although the question of reincarnation or any form of life after death remains unanswered for many, science has proved that there is no natural end to the raw materials of nature or to the "new compounds" man has made from them.

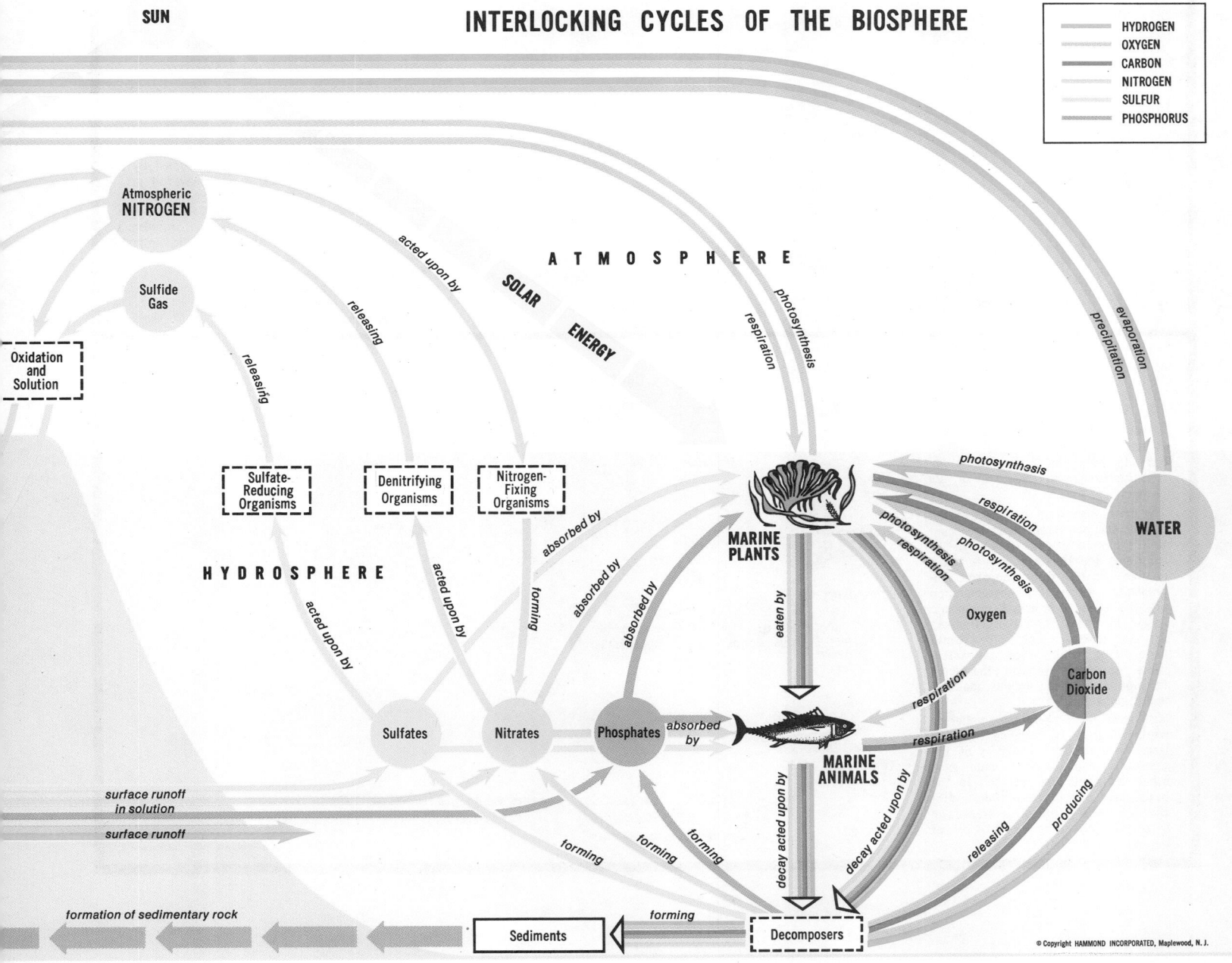

INTERLOCKING CYCLES OF THE BIOSPHERE

PHOTOSYNTHESIS: Converting the sun's energy

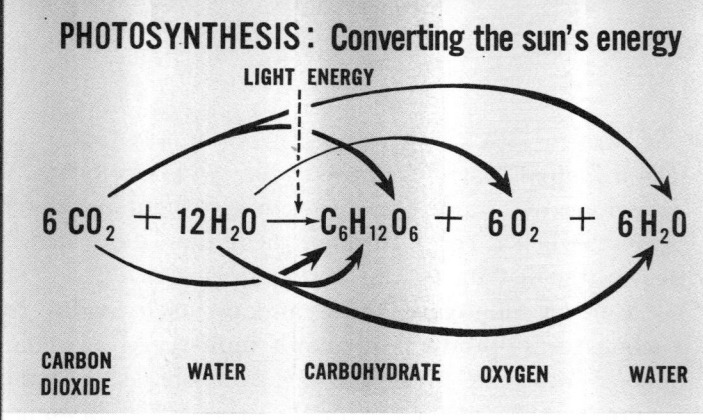

LIGHT ENERGY

$$6 CO_2 + 12 H_2O \longrightarrow C_6H_{12}O_6 + 6 O_2 + 6 H_2O$$

| CARBON DIOXIDE | WATER | CARBOHYDRATE | OXYGEN | WATER |

Using light energy, green plants build up organic foods such as carbohydrates — stored chemical energy to be used by the entire community — from the simple inorganic substances of carbon dioxide and water. The important by-product of this reaction is the release of oxygen, an element vital to the respiration of all living things.

THE LEAF: An organ of photosynthesis
CROSS SECTION

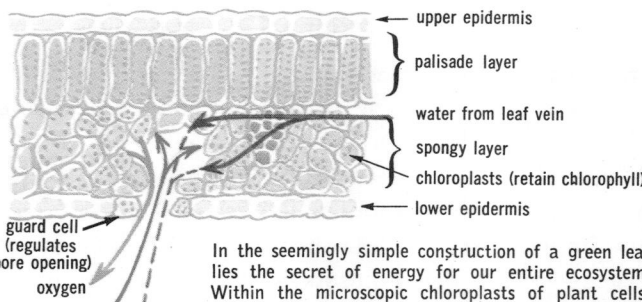

- upper epidermis
- palisade layer
- water from leaf vein
- spongy layer
- chloroplasts (retain chlorophyll)
- lower epidermis

guard cell (regulates pore opening)

oxygen

carbon dioxide

water vapor

In the seemingly simple construction of a green leaf lies the secret of energy for our entire ecosystem. Within the microscopic chloroplasts of plant cells, which contain the vital green pigment known as chlorophyll, carbon dioxide and water are absorbed, decomposed and converted into carbohydrate and oxygen molecules. Special "guard cells" control the surface pore openings to regulate the intake and output of materials.

PRODUCER - CONSUMER FOOD WEB

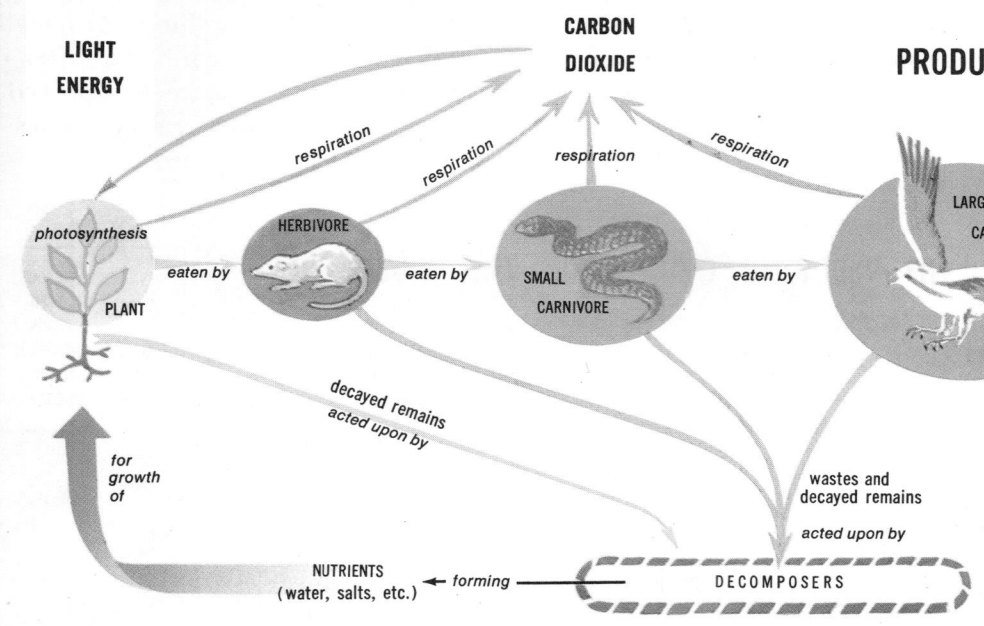

LIGHT ENERGY

CARBON DIOXIDE

respiration

photosynthesis

PLANT — eaten by — HERBIVORE — eaten by — SMALL CARNIVORE — eaten by — LARGE CARNIVORE

decayed remains acted upon by

for growth of

wastes and decayed remains

acted upon by

NUTRIENTS (water, salts, etc.) ← forming — DECOMPOSERS

Some of the complex relationships of life in an ecological system can be described by tracing the passage of energy through a simplified community in what is called a food chain or web.

The primary food source is the producer, that organism which uses light energy to manufacture its own food from inorganic substances (nutrients). This producer or plant is consumed by a plant-eating animal which in turn may fall prey to a flesh-eating animal or carnivore. A larger carnivore may extend the food chain further. During this process part of the consumed organism's energy is passed on to the consuming animal. Energy not passed on is released to the atmosphere during respiration or to the soil in the form of waste materials. Eventually, death and decay of all organisms lead to a recycling of nutrient compounds to be used by the producers.

CHAIN OF LIFE IN THE SEA

Although community members are constructed to adapt to their watery habitat, the chain of life in the sea is quite similar to the chain of life on land.

The most important members of the oceanic community are those that contain chlorophyll or a chlorophyll-like substance and thus are able to make organic matter from inorganic ingredients. Algae and phytoplankton are the ocean's principal producers. In the open seas the initial consumers are tiny crustacea only a few centimeters long, while in coastal waters these consumers include the more familiar starfish, sea urchins, molluscs and some worms.

Just as on land, where the smaller or weaker animal is consumed by the larger and stronger, members of the oceanic community feed upon each other. Nutrients are returned to the atmosphere through respiration and to the hydrosphere through a breakdown of complex organisms by the work of decomposing organisms.

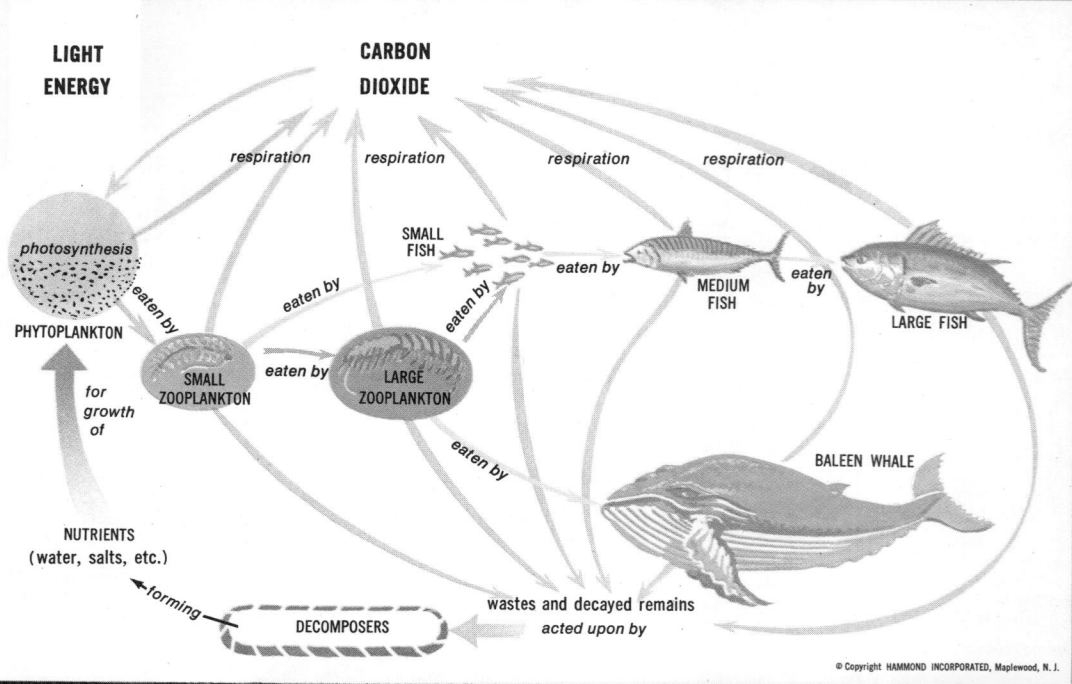

LIGHT ENERGY

CARBON DIOXIDE

respiration   respiration   respiration   respiration

photosynthesis

PHYTOPLANKTON — eaten by — SMALL ZOOPLANKTON — eaten by — LARGE ZOOPLANKTON — eaten by — SMALL FISH — eaten by — MEDIUM FISH — eaten by — LARGE FISH

eaten by — BALEEN WHALE

for growth of

NUTRIENTS (water, salts, etc.)

← forming — DECOMPOSERS ← acted upon by — wastes and decayed remains

Ecology:
INTERRELATION OF LIVING THINGS AND THEIR SURROUNDINGS

Freedom and independence do not exist in the universe except in the creative reaches of man's intellect which distinguishes him from the other living organisms with which he shares a portion of the biosphere.

Dependent on the sun for its creation, the earth is dependent on it still for solar energy to sustain and move all living things. The amount and types of earthly life are determined by the amounts and patterns of flow of this energy which is fixed by green plants and converted into the organic compounds to maintain the plants themselves and every other organism.

In a seemingly tangled web of forces — in competition, cooperation, neutrality — in a constantly changing and more or less suitable climate, and in the processes of evolution continually in flux throughout the thin layers of atmosphere, earth and sea, strands of mutual dependence have been woven. Each form of life, from the simple one-celled organism to the complexity of man, is subject to the same laws of nature, depending one upon the other for energy and food — creating it as they destroy it and are destroyed themselves.

The word "ecology" comes from two Greek words meaning "the study of the home," and in modern times has signified the study of all living things in relation to their environments — or homes — and to each other. Western man, particularly, has romanticised his notion of a home and often chose to think of it as a solitary fortress snug against intrusion by other men and the forces of nature. But the making and maintaining of a home for man as for other forms of life is a subtle combination and balance of light, heat, moisture and food any one of which may be disturbed or destroyed by natural calamity or inadvertent act.

Through a closer study of ecology and ecological systems man is learning, hopefully not too late, that even the "lilies of the field," which neither sow nor reap, are as essential to him as are the insects clinging to their leaves, the rodents burrowing at their feet, and the soil and air that they enrich.

A TYPICAL FOOD CHAIN

1. Through the process of photosynthesis a green plant or primary producer begins the food chain.

2. A cricket, feeding upon the plant, becomes a primary consumer.

3. A secondary consumer is the frog who devours the cricket.

4. It is the fate of the frog to turn into a meal for the snake, the third or tertiary consumer.

5. The food chain ends with a snake-eating hawk, the fourth consumer, who has no predator other than man.

Photos: Ernst G. Hofmann

Man's Impact Upon Nature

Since he could think man has been at war with death. He has fought his battles against destruction with science and technology as his weapons, virtually eliminating his own annihilation by predatory animals and from diseases such as leprosy, tuberculosis and diphtheria. He has walked into many valleys of death to fight malaria and yellow fever, and he has resolved that each year more of his own kind will live to finish out their threescore years and ten.

However, the victory over nature, which had balanced population with food supply and space, is bitter, for the population has "exploded" leaving man with the seemingly insolvable problem of providing more food and space for himself or reducing his numbers by starvation or by war.

Man outsmarted himself in many ways as he worked toward creating a more perfect world for himself without understanding that natural laws go beyond human manipulation. He has destroyed forests and meadows, polluted the water and air, eliminated organisms that tried to share his bread. However, he has yet to learn to recreate the wood and brush or the interdependent communities of bacteria, insects and animals that he learned — too late — enrich the air, the soil and the water and without which he cannot function.

Modern man knows how to manufacture "miraculous" materials to work for his pleasure or his seemingly insatiable needs, but the sophistications of technology have yet to control effectively the by-products. These new materials, still subject to the order of nature's cycles, penetrate the biosphere and eventually come to roost in his own vulnerable body.

New battles are being fought throughout the world and new standards bearing the slogans of ecology float in the "unsafe" air. It is somehow ironic to find that many people now believe that man has been fighting the wrong fight in his gigantic struggle with nature. That, after all, nature never was his enemy.

Man cannot turn back to his beginnings when he lived with, and not against, the natural world. But a compromise between technology and nature must take place for our "plundered planet" cries out for the day of reckoning.

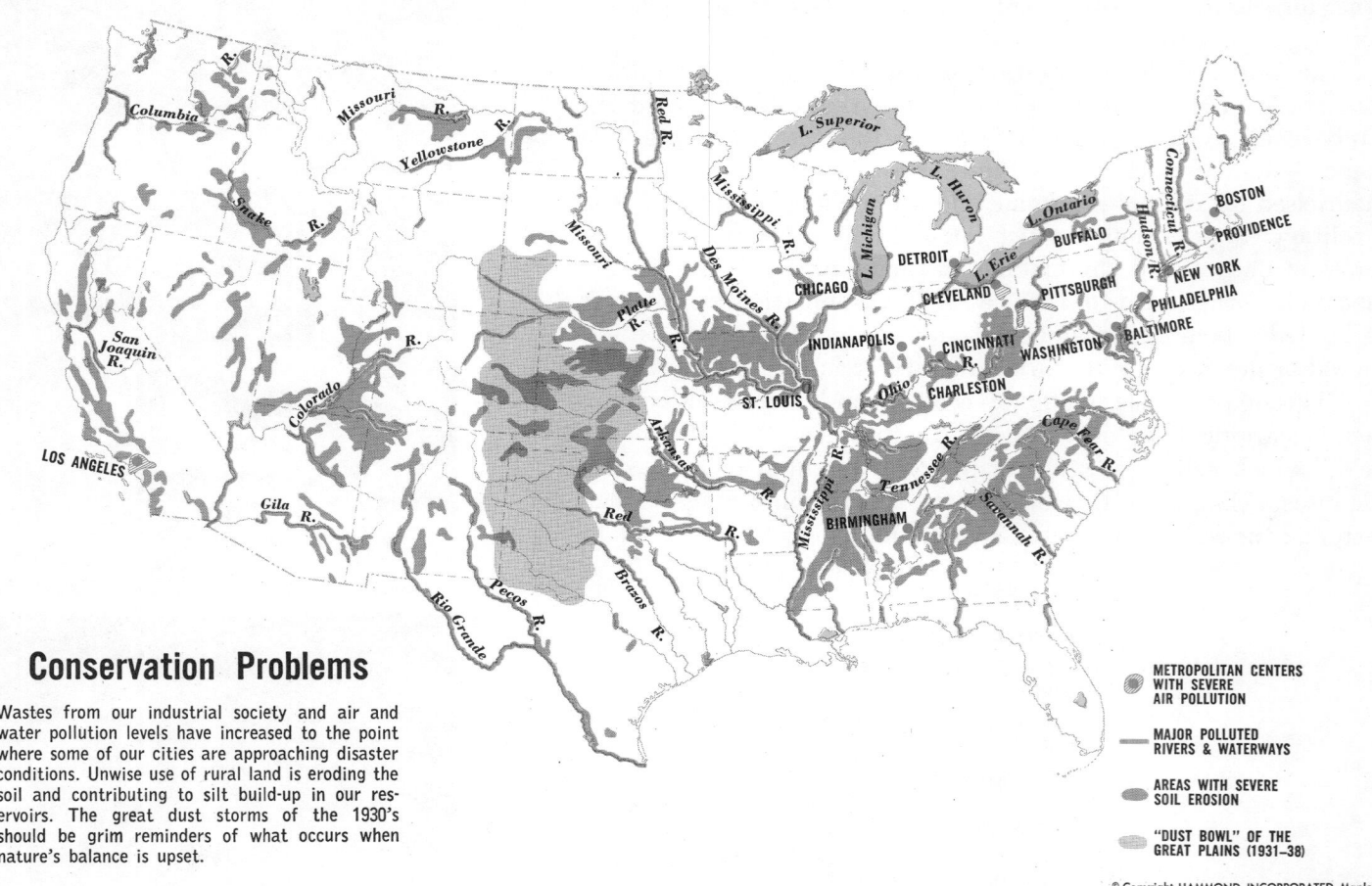

Conservation Problems

Wastes from our industrial society and air and water pollution levels have increased to the point where some of our cities are approaching disaster conditions. Unwise use of rural land is eroding the soil and contributing to silt build-up in our reservoirs. The great dust storms of the 1930's should be grim reminders of what occurs when nature's balance is upset.

● METROPOLITAN CENTERS WITH SEVERE AIR POLLUTION

— MAJOR POLLUTED RIVERS & WATERWAYS

● AREAS WITH SEVERE SOIL EROSION

● "DUST BOWL" OF THE GREAT PLAINS (1931–38)

© Copyright HAMMOND INCORPORATED, Maplewood, N. J.

A sloping barnyard provides a convenient runoff for chemical and organic fertilizers, causing overenrichment (eutrophication) of the pond.

Trash burning billows clouds of air pollution over the nation's capital.

A forest stripped of trees reduces the supply of oxygen-producing greenery and inhibits good soil development and maintenance.

Poor drainage procedures near a housing development produce unstable soil, resulting in earth slides.

Unauthorized dumping affects the beauty of the countryside and later will pollute the nearby river.

Photos: U.S. Department of Agriculture

This stream is rapidly becoming polluted because of the direct discharge of soap and detergent suds into it.

POLLUTION CIRCLE
TYPES OF POLLUTION AND THEIR EFFECT ON THE TOTAL ENVIRONMENT

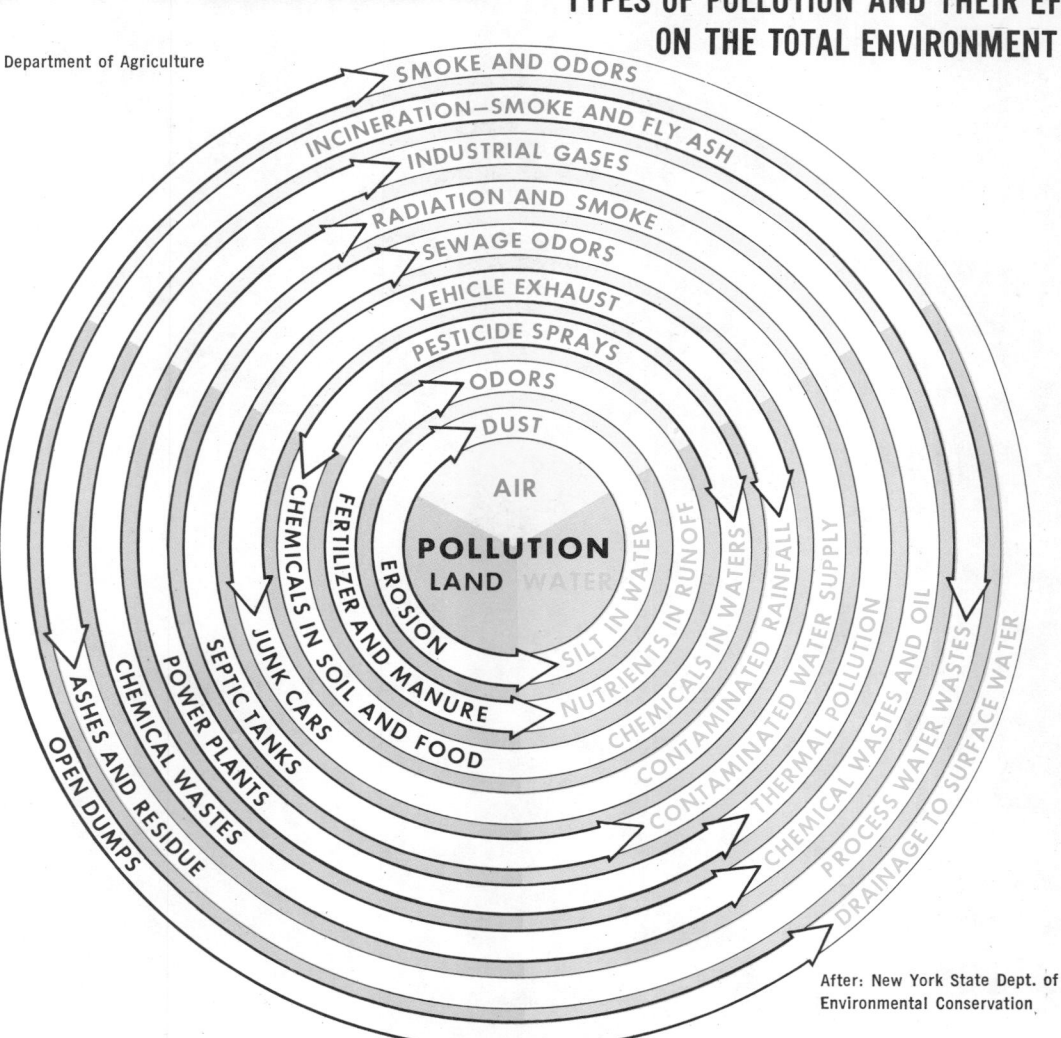

POLLUTION

AIR
LAND WATER

SMOKE AND ODORS
INCINERATION—SMOKE AND FLY ASH
INDUSTRIAL GASES
RADIATION AND SMOKE
SEWAGE ODORS
VEHICLE EXHAUST
PESTICIDE SPRAYS
ODORS
DUST

CHEMICALS IN SOIL AND FOOD
FERTILIZER AND MANURE
EROSION
JUNK CARS
SEPTIC TANKS
POWER PLANTS
CHEMICAL WASTES
ASHES AND RESIDUE
OPEN DUMPS

SILT IN WATER
NUTRIENTS IN RUNOFF
CHEMICALS IN WATERS
CONTAMINATED RAINFALL
CONTAMINATED WATER SUPPLY
THERMAL POLLUTION
CHEMICAL WASTES AND OIL
PROCESS WATER WASTES
DRAINAGE TO SURFACE WATER

After: New York State Dept. of Environmental Conservation

In. soaring cities, in golden plains of wheat, in the meanderings of highways, in the warmth of firesides — in homes, factories, forests, farms and seasides — we see the tracings of man's intellect and imagination. Unlike other creatures man's energies are not directed merely toward survival but to the challenge of creating his own environment.

For too many years man has played games with his environment without knowing nature's ground rules and it has become apparent, even to children, that the tools that mold the stuffs of nature to man's liking are double-edged.

It is unlikely that man will turn his wits and his technology toward a return to a simple and primitive way of life. It is also unlikely that man can stand still and survive.

Now man must begin to grapple with causes that have more than one effect. It is time for man to meditate on his heritage and to act, remembering that "knowledge is a fountain of life to him who possesses it."

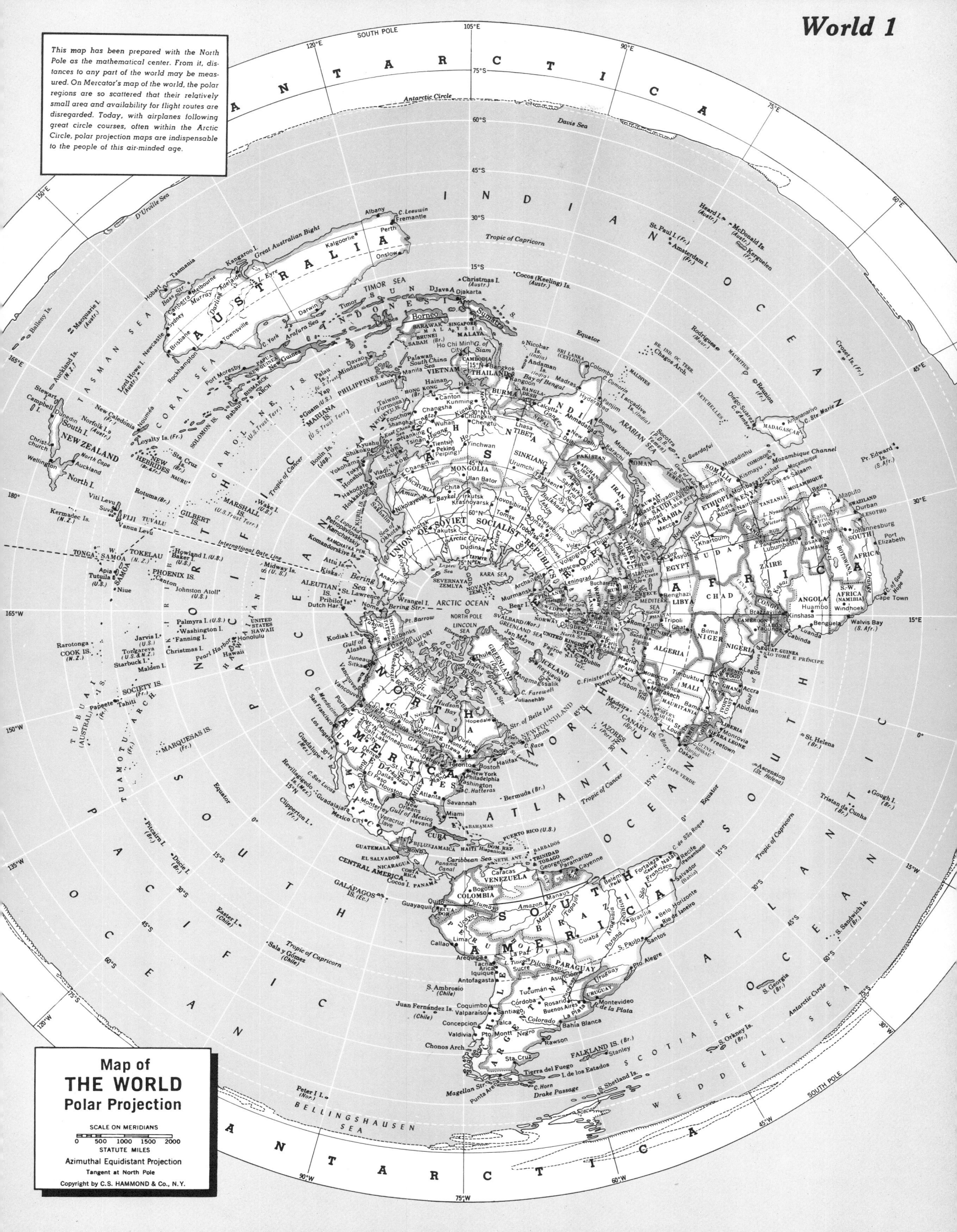

This map has been prepared with the North Pole as the mathematical center. From it, distances to any part of the world may be measured. On Mercator's map of the world, the polar regions are so scattered that their relatively small area and availability for flight routes are disregarded. Today, with airplanes following great circle courses, often within the Arctic Circle, polar projection maps are indispensable to the people of this air-minded age.

**Map of
THE WORLD
Polar Projection**

SCALE ON MERIDIANS

0   500   1000   1500   2000
STATUTE MILES

Azimuthal Equidistant Projection
Tangent at North Pole
Copyright by C.S. HAMMOND & CO., N.Y.

THE WORLD

BRIESEMEISTER ELLIPTICAL
EQUAL-AREA PROJECTION

Capitals of Countries .... ⊛
International Boundaries ....___

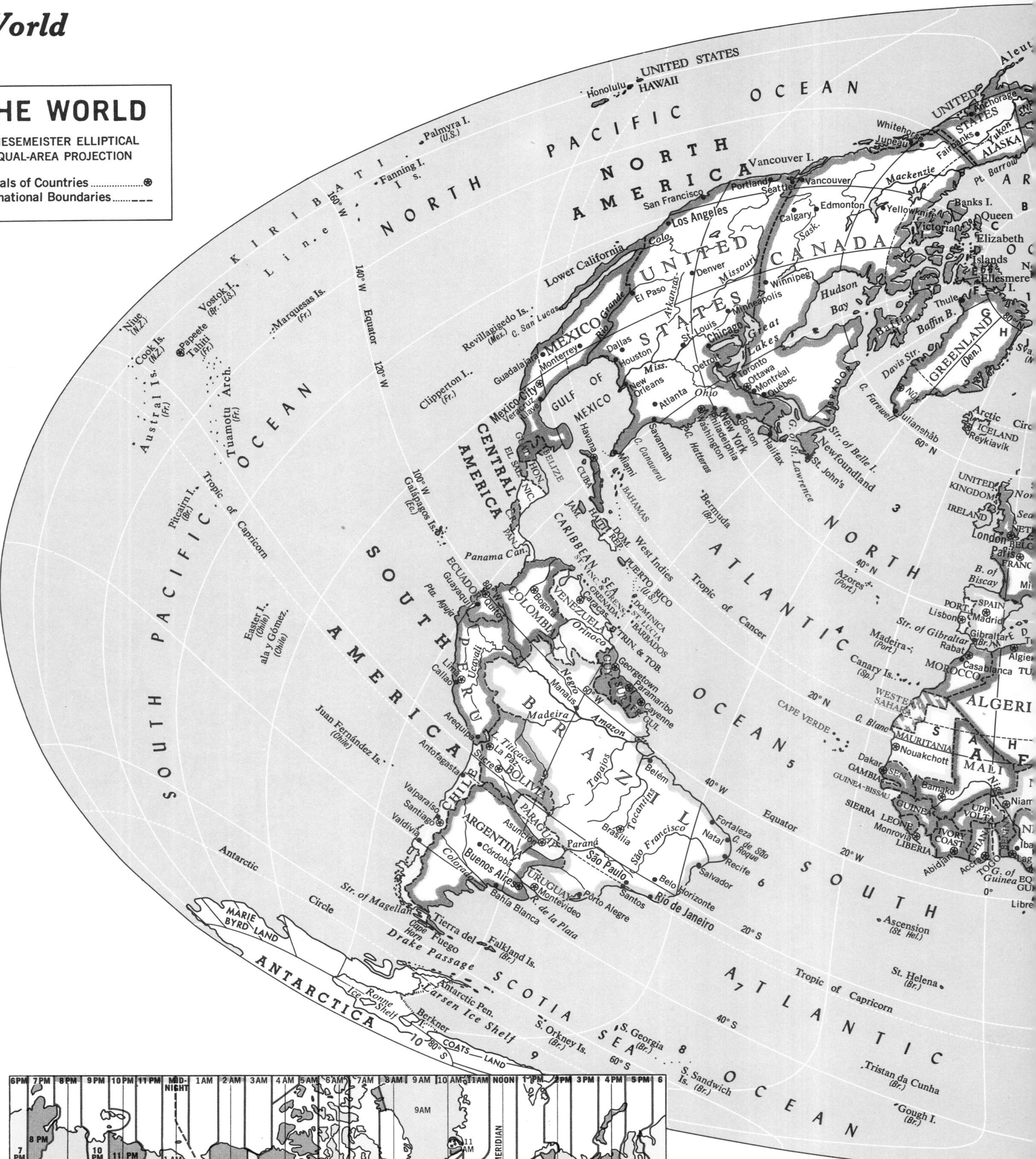

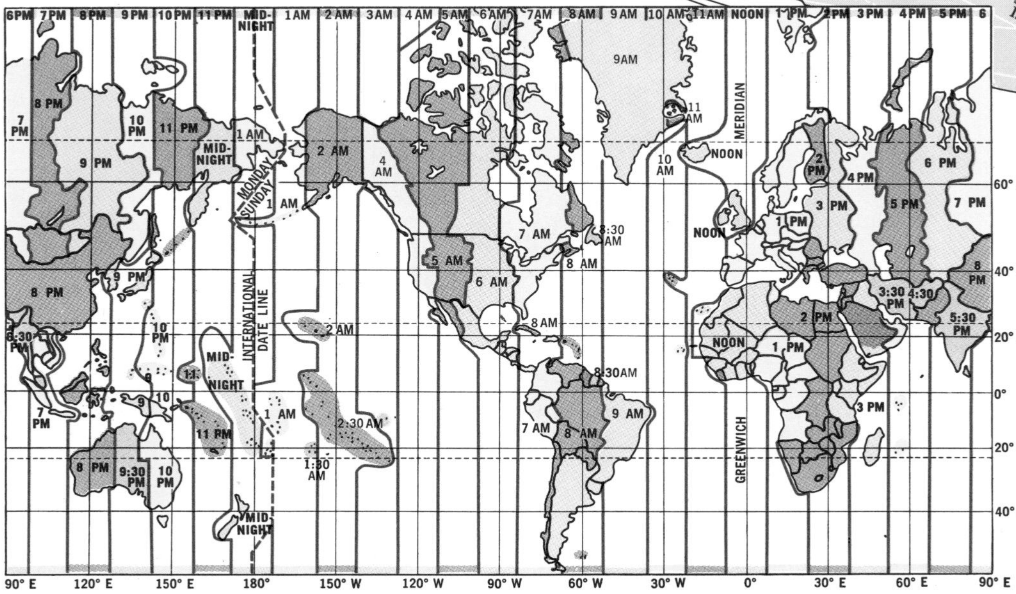

TIME ZONES

STANDARD
TIME
ZONES

Areas using half
hour deviations.

Areas not using
zone system.

NOTE: Standard time zones in the U.S.S.R. are
always advanced one hour.

NORTH PACIFIC OCEAN

SOUTH PACIFIC OCEAN

NORTH AMERICA

SOUTH AMERICA

NORTH ATLANTIC OCEAN

SOUTH ATLANTIC OCEAN

CENTRAL AMERICA

ANTARCTICA

UNITED STATES

CANADA

GREENLAND (Den.)

MEXICO

BRAZIL

ARGENTINA

CHILE

PERU

BOLIVIA

COLOMBIA

VENEZUELA

ECUADOR

URUGUAY

PARAGUAY

Honolulu — HAWAII

Vancouver I.

San Francisco
Los Angeles
Lower California
Denver
El Paso
Dallas
Houston
New Orleans
Atlanta
St. Louis
Chicago
Minneapolis
Detroit
Toronto
Ottawa
Montréal
Québec
New York
Boston
Philadelphia
Washington
Savannah
Miami
Havana

Winnipeg
Calgary
Edmonton
Yellowknife

Seattle
Portland
Vancouver

Whitehorse
Juneau
Fairbanks
Anchorage
ALASKA
Pt. Barrow

Hudson Bay
Great Lakes

Baffin B.
Thule
Julianehåb
Reykjavik
ICELAND

IRELAND
UNITED KINGDOM
London
Paris
SPAIN
Madrid
Lisbon
PORTUGAL
Gibraltar (Br.)
Rabat
Casablanca
MOROCCO
Algiers
ALGERIA
WESTERN SAHARA
MAURITANIA
Nouakchott
Dakar
SENEGAL
GAMBIA
GUINEA-BISSAU
SIERRA LEONE
Monrovia
LIBERIA
IVORY COAST
Abidjan
MALI
Bamako

Bogotá
Quito
Guayaquil
Lima
Callao
Arequipa
La Paz
Sucre
Antofagasta
Valparaíso
Santiago
Valdivia
Córdoba
Buenos Aires
Montevideo
Bahía Blanca
Asunción
Brasília
São Paulo
Rio de Janeiro
Santos
Pôrto Alegre
Belo Horizonte
Salvador
Recife
Natal
Fortaleza
Belém
Manaus

Amazon
Orinoco
Negro
Madeira
Tapajós
Tocantins
São Francisco
Paraná

Tropic of Cancer
Tropic of Capricorn
Equator
Antarctic Circle

Str. of Magellan
Cape Horn
Tierra del Fuego
Drake Passage
Falkland Is. (Br.)
SCOTIA SEA
S. Georgia (Br.)
S. Orkney Is.
S. Sandwich Is. (Br.)

Bermuda (Br.)
Azores (Port.)
Madeira (Port.)
Canary Is. (Sp.)
CAPE VERDE
C. Blanc
Ascension (St. Hel.)
St. Helena (Br.)
Tristan da Cunha (Br.)
Gough I. (Br.)

MARIE BYRD LAND
Ronne Shelf
Larsen Ice Shelf
Berkner I.
COATS LAND
Antarctic Pen.

6PM 7PM 8PM 9PM 10PM 11PM MIDNIGHT 1AM 2AM 3AM 4AM 5AM 6AM 7AM 8AM 9AM 10AM 11AM NOON 1PM 2PM 3PM 4PM 5PM 6

INTERNATIONAL DATE LINE
MERIDIAN
GREENWICH

90°E 120°E 150°E 180° 150°W 120°W 90°W 60°W 30°W 0° 30°E 60°E 90°E

WORLD
LAND AREA 57,970,000 sq. mi.
WATER AREA 139,781,000 sq. mi.
TOTAL SURFACE AREA 197,751,000 sq. mi.
POPULATION 4,240,700,000

ANTARCTICA

AZIMUTHAL EQUIDISTANT PROJECTION

Arctic Ocean

ARCTIC ICE
Bering Sea
Nome
UNITED STATES
ALASKA
Ambarchik
CANADA
Barrow
East Siberian Sea
U.S.S.R.
Beaufort Sea
Approximate Limit of Pack Ice in September
Laptev Sea
Nordvik
ARCTIC
NORTH POLE
OCEAN
CANADA
Kara Sea
Thule
Baffin Bay
Barents Sea
Godhavn
GREENLAND
Approximate Limit of Pack Ice in March
Murmansk
Archangel
Norwegian Sea
ATLANTIC OCEAN
ICELAND
FINLAND
U.S.S.R.
NORWAY
SWEDEN
© C.S. Hammond & Co.

ARCTIC OCEAN
AZIMUTHAL EQUIDISTANT PROJECTION
SCALE OF MILES
0 100 200 400 600
SCALE OF KILOMETRES
0 200 400 600 800 1000
Copyright by C. S. Hammond & Co., N.Y.
Longitude 17 West of 160° Greenwich 18
180° 1 Longitude 160° East of 2 Greenwich
Longitude 11 West of 20° Greenwich 10
0° 9 Longitude 20° East of 8 Greenwich
BERING SEA
SEA OF OKHOTSK
GULF OF ALASKA
ARCTIC OCEAN
BEAUFORT SEA
EAST SIBERIAN SEA
LAPTEV SEA
KARA SEA
BARENTS SEA
GREENLAND SEA
NORWEGIAN SEA
NORTH SEA
ATLANTIC OCEAN
GREENLAND
(KALÂTDLIT-NUNÂT)
(Denmark)
NORTH POLE
Peary Apr. 6, 1909
Byrd May 9, 1926 (airplane)
Amundsen-Ellsworth-Nobile May 12, 1926 (dirigible)
Anderson in U.S.S. Nautilus Aug. 3, 1958
EXPLORERS' ROUTES
Peary 1909
Byrd 1926
Amundsen, Ellsworth & Nobile 1926
Anderson in U. S. S. Nautilus 1958
By ship
By sledge
By airplane
By dirigible
By nuclear submarine

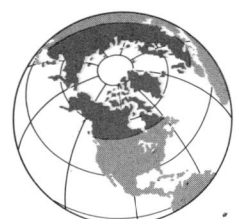

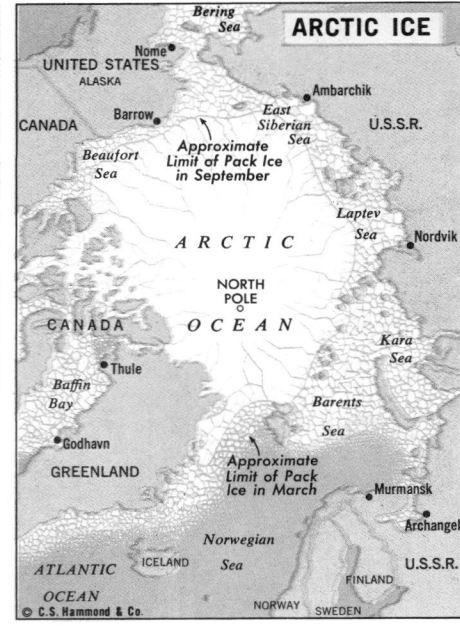

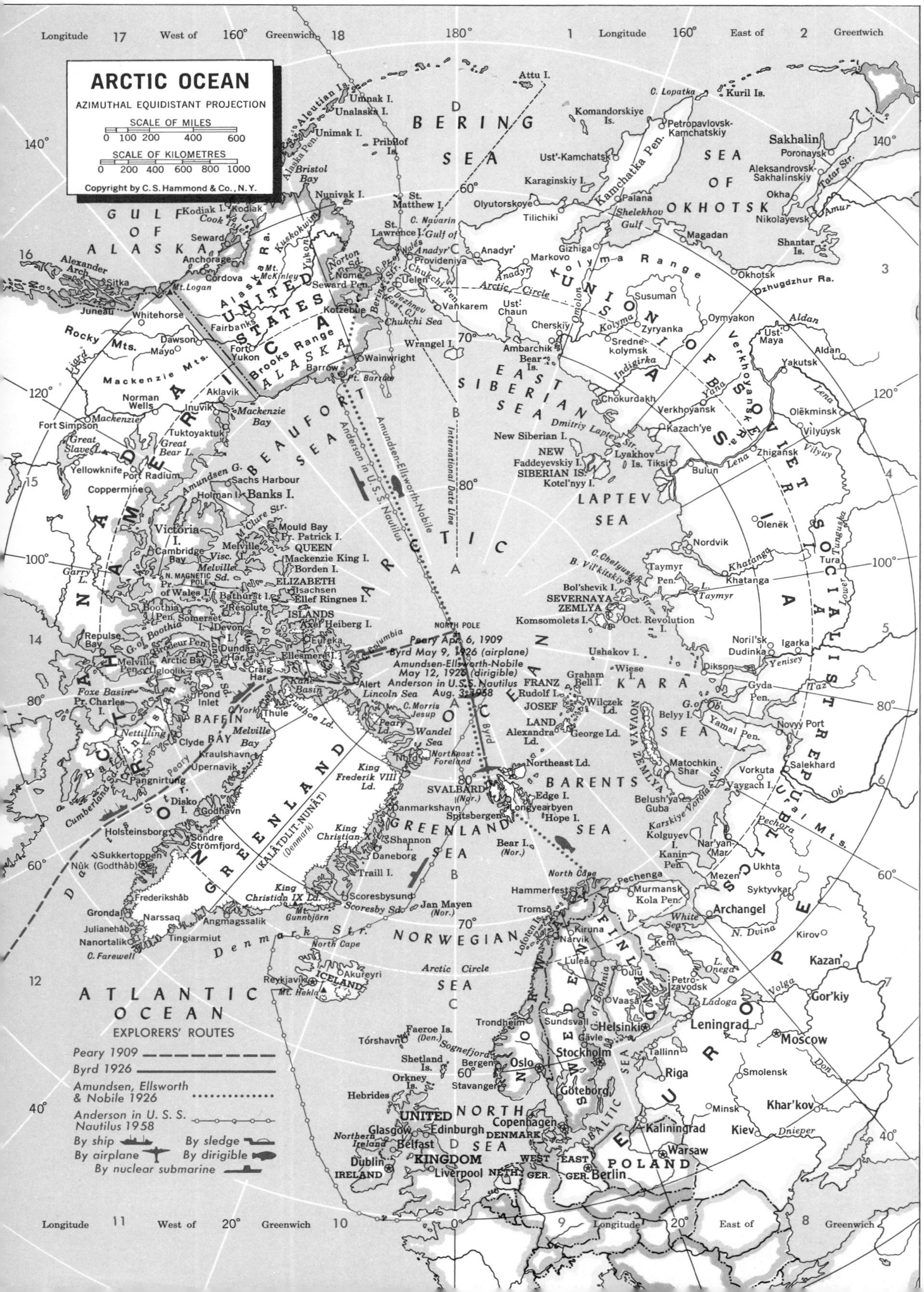

ANTARCTICA
AZIMUTHAL EQUIDISTANT PROJECTION

SCALE OF MILES
0 200 400 600 800

SCALE OF KILOMETRES
0 200 400 600 800 1000

© C. S. HAMMOND & Co., N.Y.

Adare (cape)	B 9		Luitpold Coast (region)	B17
Adelaide (isl.)	C15		Lützow-Holm (bay)	C 3
Adélie Coast (region)	C 7		Mackenzie (bay)	C 4
Alexander (isl.)	B15		Mac-Robertson Land	
American Highland	B 4		(region)	C 4
Amery Ice Shelf	C 4		Marguerite (bay)	C15
Amundsen (bay)	C 3		Marie Byrd Land	
Amundsen (sea)	B13		(region)	B12
Antarctic (pen.)	C15		Markham (mt.)	A 8
Balleny (isls.)	C 9		Mawson	C 4
Banzare Coast (region)	C 7		McMurdo (sound)	B 9
Barr Smith (mt.)	C 3		Mertz (glacier)	C 8
Batterbee (cape)	C 3		Mirnyy	C 5
Beardmore (glacier)	A 8		New Schwabenland	
Bellingshausen (sea)	C14		(region)	B 1
Berkner (isl.)	B16		Ninnis (glacier)	C 8
Biscoe (isls.)	B18		Norvegia (cape)	B18
Bouvet (isl.)	D 1		Oates Coast (region)	B 8
Bransfield (strait)	C16		Palmer (arch.)	C15
Budd Coast (region)	C 6		Palmer Land	
Byrd Station	A12		(region)	B15
Caird Coast (region)	B17		Palmer Station	C15
Charcot (isl.)	C15		Peter I (isl.)	C14
Clarie Coast (region)	C 7		Prince Edward (isls.)	E 2
Coats Land (region)	B18		Prince Olav Coast	
Colbeck (cape)	B10		(region)	C 3
Coronation (isl.)	C16		Princess Astrid Coast	
Daly (cape)	C 4		(region)	B 1
Darnley (cape)	C 4		Princess Martha Coast	B18
Dart (cape)	B12		Princess Ragnhild Coast	
Davis (sea)	C 5		(region)	B 2
Davis (sta.)	C 4		Prydz (bay)	C 4
Drake (passage)	C15		Queen Mary Coast	
Dumont d'Urville			(region)	C 5
(sta.)	C 7		Queen Maud Land	
Edith Ronne Ice Shelf	B16		(region)	B 1
Edward VII (pen.)	B11		Riiser–Larsen (pen.)	C 2
Eights Coast (region)	B14		Ronne Entrance (bay)	B15
Elephant (isl.)	C16		Roosevelt (isl.)	A10
Ellsworth Land (reg.)	A14		Ross (isl.)	B 9
Enderby Land (region)	B14		Ross (sea)	B10
English Coast (reg.)	B15		Ross Ice Shelf	A10
Executive Committee			Sabine (mt.)	B 9
(range)	B12		Sabrina Coast (region)	C 6
Farr (bay)	C 5		Sanae (sta.)	B18
Filchner Ice Shelf	B16		Scotia (sea)	D16
Ford (ranges)	B11		Scott (isl.)	C10
Gaussberg (mt.)	C 5		Shackleton Ice Shelf	C 5
George V Coast (region)	C 8		Sidley (mt.)	B12
Getz Ice Shelf	B12		Siple (mt.)	B12
Goodenough (cape)	C 7		South Georgia (isl.)	D17
Graham Land (region)	C15		South Magnetic	
Grytviken	D17		Polar Area	C 8
Hilton Inlet (bay)	B16		South Orkney (isls.)	C16
Hobbs Coast (region)	B12		South Polar (plateau)	A 1
Hollick-Kenyon			South Pole	A 4
(plateau)	B13		South Sandwich (isls.)	D17
Hope (bay)	C15		South Shetland (isls.)	C15
Joinville (isl.)	C16		Sulzberger (bay)	B11
Kainan (bay)	B10		Thurston (isl.)	C14
Keltie (cape)	C 7		Transantarctic (mts.)	A11
Kemp Coast (region)	C 3		Victoria Land (region)	B 8
King George (isl.)	C16		Vincennes (bay)	C 6
Kirkpatrick (mt.)	A 8		Vinson Massif (mt.)	B14
Knox Coast (region)	C 6		Walgreen Coast (region)	B13
Larsen Ice Shelf	C16		Weddell (sea)	C17
Lazarev (sta.)	C 1		West Ice Shelf	C 5
Levick (mt.)	B 8		Wilhelm II Coast (region)	C 5
Lister (mt.)	B 8		Wilkes Land (region)	C 7
Little America	B10			

EXPLORERS' ROUTES

Palmer 1820
Amundsen 1910-12
Scott 1910-13
Byrd 1928-30
Fuchs 1957-58
By ship   By sledge   By airplane
By snow tractor

Amundsen Dec. 14, 1911
Scott Jan. 17, 1912
Byrd Nov. 29, 1929 (airplane)
Fuchs Jan. 20, 1958

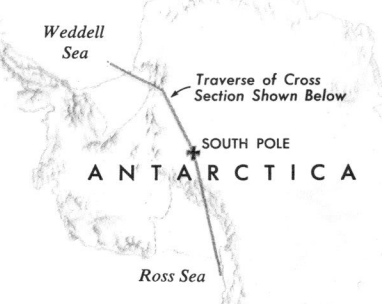

Weddell Sea

Traverse of Cross Section Shown Below

+ SOUTH POLE

ANTARCTICA

Ross Sea

ANTARCTIC CROSS SECTION: WEDDELL SEA TO ROSS SEA

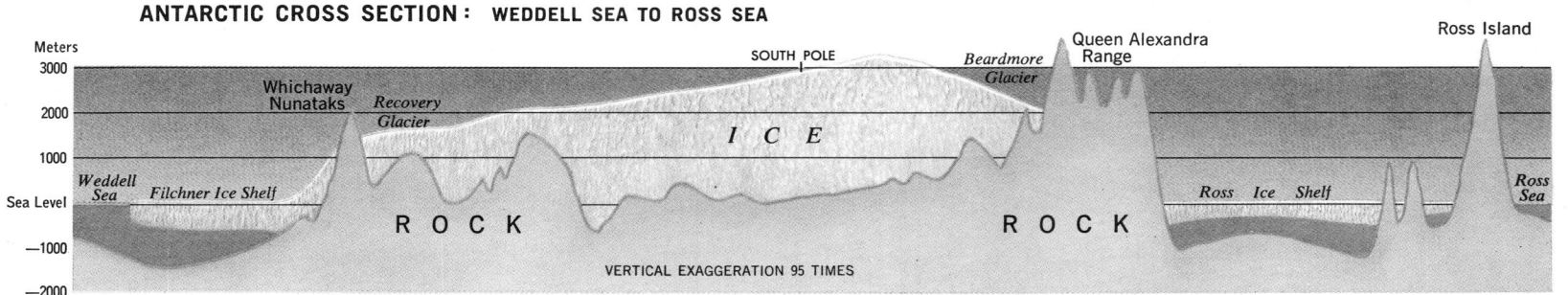

VERTICAL EXAGGERATION 95 TIMES

Information Based on American Geographical Society's "Antarctic Map Folio Series"

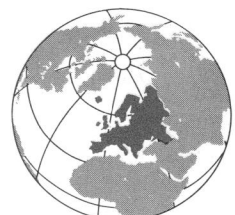

AREA 4,057,000 sq. mi.
POPULATION 666,116,000
LARGEST CITY London
HIGHEST POINT El'brus 18,481 ft.
LOWEST POINT Caspian Sea -92 ft.

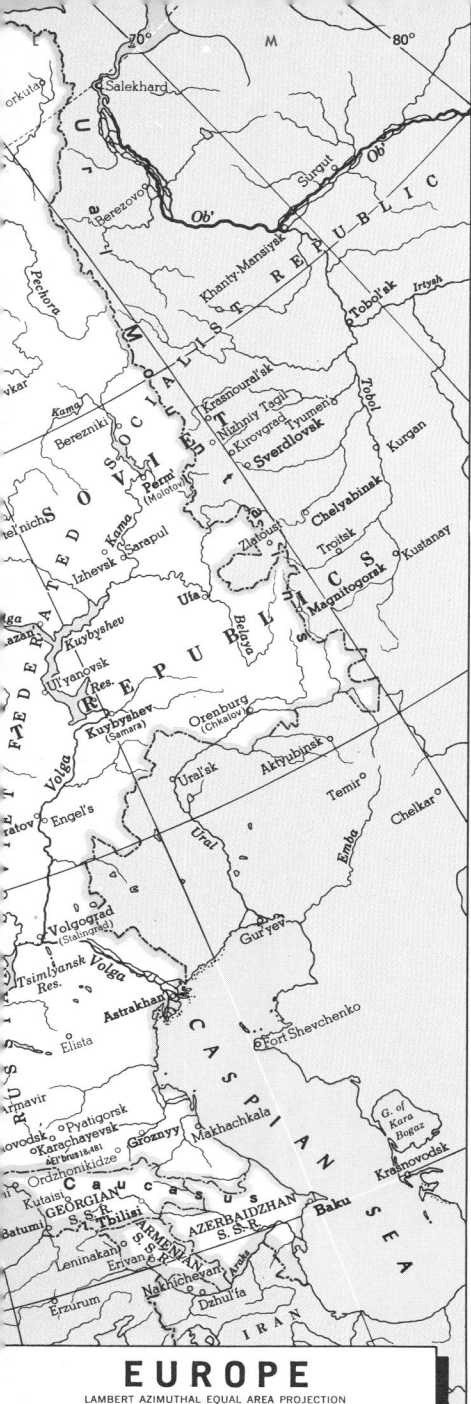

EUROPE

LAMBERT AZIMUTHAL EQUAL AREA PROJECTION

SCALE OF MILES

0   100   200   300   400   500

SCALE OF KILOMETRES

0   100   200   300   400   500

Capitals of Countries .... ☆
International Boundaries ...... ___·___·___
Canals ....

Copyright by C. S. Hammond & Co., N. Y.

POPULATION DISTRIBUTION

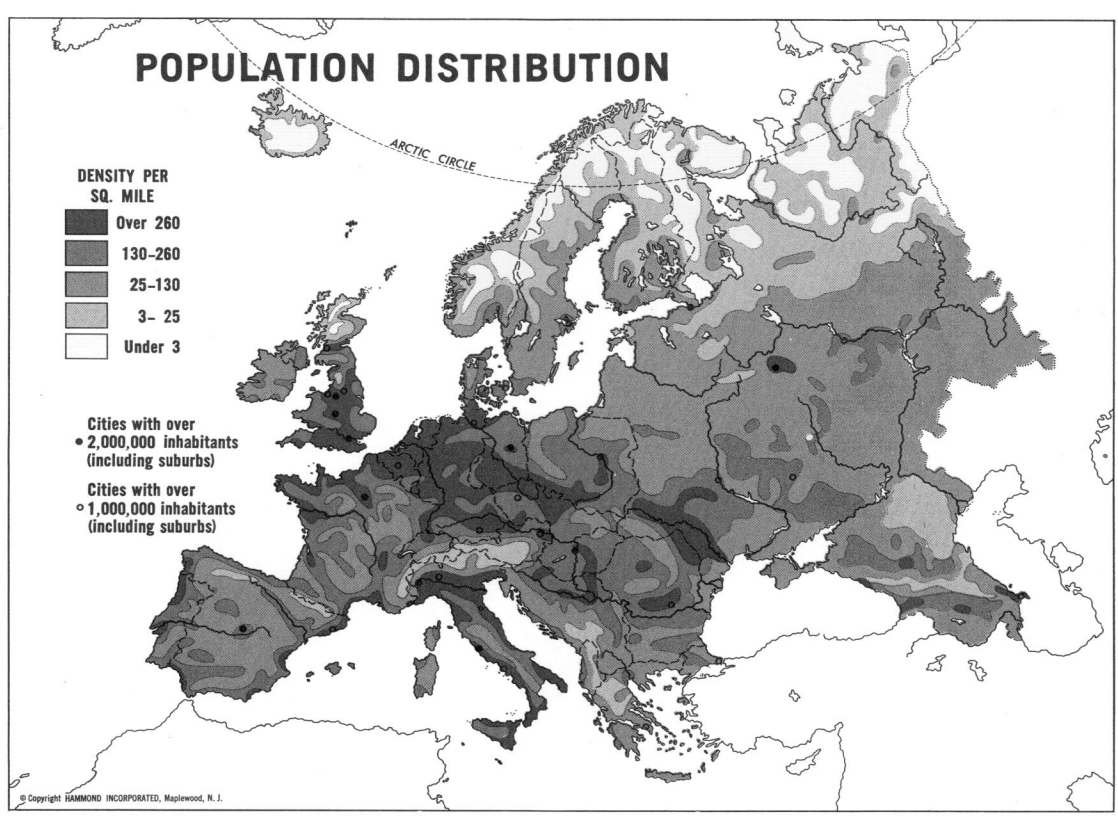

DENSITY PER
SQ. MILE

Over 260

130–260

25–130

3– 25

Under 3

● Cities with over
2,000,000 inhabitants
(including suburbs)

○ Cities with over
1,000,000 inhabitants
(including suburbs)

© Copyright HAMMOND INCORPORATED, Maplewood, N. J.

VEGETATION

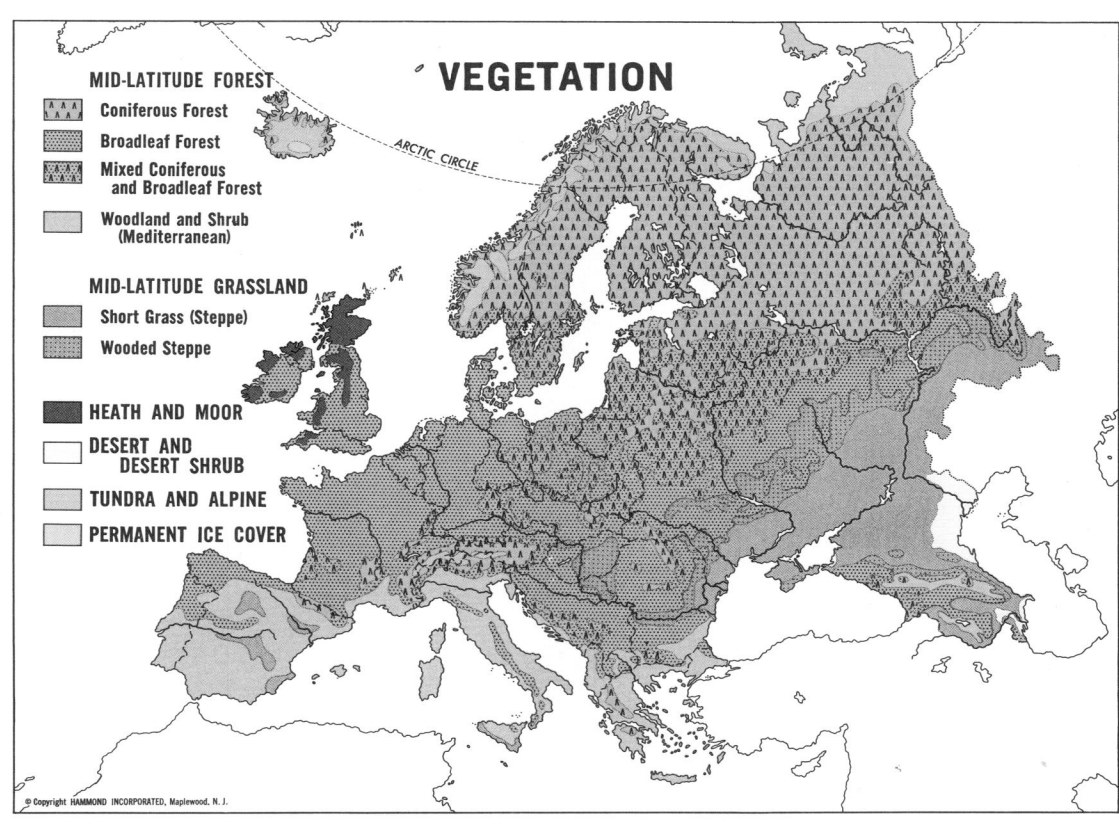

MID-LATITUDE FOREST

Coniferous Forest

Broadleaf Forest

Mixed Coniferous
and Broadleaf Forest

Woodland and Shrub
(Mediterranean)

MID-LATITUDE GRASSLAND

Short Grass (Steppe)

Wooded Steppe

HEATH AND MOOR

DESERT AND
DESERT SHRUB

TUNDRA AND ALPINE

PERMANENT ICE COVER

© Copyright HAMMOND INCORPORATED, Maplewood, N. J.

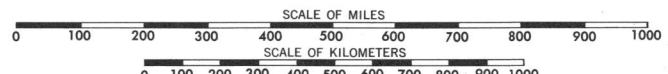

VEGETATION/RELIEF

SCALE OF MILES

0 100 200 300 400 500 600 700 800 900 1000

SCALE OF KILOMETERS

0 100 200 300 400 500 600 700 800 900 1000

Capitals of Countries .... ⊛
International Boundaries .... — ·· —
Canals ....
Elevations in Feet   Depths in Fathoms

Longitude West of Greenwich   0°   Longitude East of Greenwich

ICELAND

Reykjavik

Horn   Fontur

NORWEGIAN SEA

Faeroe Is.
(Den.)

Shetland Is.

Hebrides

Orkney Is.

Moray Firth

Aberdeen

UNITED

Glasgow

U.K.
Belfast

IRELAND

Dublin

IRISH SEA

Liverpool

St. George's Chan.

KINGDOM

Birmingham

London

Land's End

Channel Is.
(U.K.)

NORTH SEA

DENMARK

Copenhagen

Bornholm

Rügen

NETHERLANDS

Frisian Is.

Amsterdam

Hamburg

Elbe

EAST

Berlin

POLAND

Gdansk

Vistula

Warsaw

BELGIUM

Brussels

Cologne

WEST

GERMANY

Leipzig

Oder

Łódź

LUX

GERMANY

Prague

CZECHOSLOVAKIA

Cracow

L'vov

ATLANTIC OCEAN

English Channel

Le Havre

Seine

Paris

FRANCE

Nantes

Loire

Bordeaux

Dordogne

Garonne

Bilbao

Oporto

Douro

SPAIN

Madrid

Tagus

Guadiana

Pyrenees

Lyon

SWITZ

Munich

Stuttgart

AUSTRIA

Vienna

Graz

HUNGARY

Budapest

ROMANIA

Bucharest

YUGOSLAVIA

Belgrade

Zagreb

Genoa

MONACO

SAN MARINO

Corsica

VATICAN CITY

Rome

Naples

ITALY

Venice

ADRIATIC SEA

PORTUGAL

Lisbon

C. de São Vicente

C. Finisterre

Bay of Biscay

Gulf of Lions

Barcelona

Valencia

Balearic Is.

Minorca

Majorca

Ibiza

Málaga

Cádiz

Strait of Gibraltar

GIBRALTAR
(U.K.)

Tangier

Rabat

Casablanca

MOROCCO

Oran

Algiers

ALGERIA

Constantine

Sardinia

C. Teulada

TYRRHENIAN SEA

Palermo

Sicily

Etna
1,053

C. Bon

Tunis

TUNISIA

C. Passero

MALTA   Valletta

MEDITERRANEAN SEA

BULGARIA

Sofia

Skoplje

Balkan Mts.

Tirana

Thessaloniki

IONIAN SEA

Athens

Euboea

Lésvos

C. Tainaron

Crete

Rhodes

CYPRUS   Nicosia

LEBANON

Beirut

Istanbul

Bosporus

Dardanelles

BLACK SEA

SEA OF AZOV

Crimea

Krasnodar

Odessa

Kiev

Khar'kov

Dnieper

Don

Minsk

Bug

Western Dvina

Riga

Moscow

Volga

Gor'kiy

Leningrad

UNION OF

SOCIALIST

Lake Ladoga

Lake Onega

WHITE SEA

Archangel

Northern Dvina

FINLAND

Oulu

Tampere

Helsinki

Saaremaa

Hiiumaa

Gulf of Finland

Gulf of Bothnia

Åland Is.

Gotland

Stockholm

Västerås

Vänern

Göteborg

Kattegat

Skagerrak

Lindesnes

Hardangerfjord

Vestfjord

Lofoten Is.

Vesterålen

Kiruna

Narvik

NORWAY

SWEDEN

Sundsvall

Trondheim

BALTIC SEA

BARENTS SEA

Nordkapp

Hammerfest

Sørøy

Kola Pen.

Kolguyev I.

Kanin Pen.

Cheshkaya Bay

Arctic Circle

60°

50°

40°

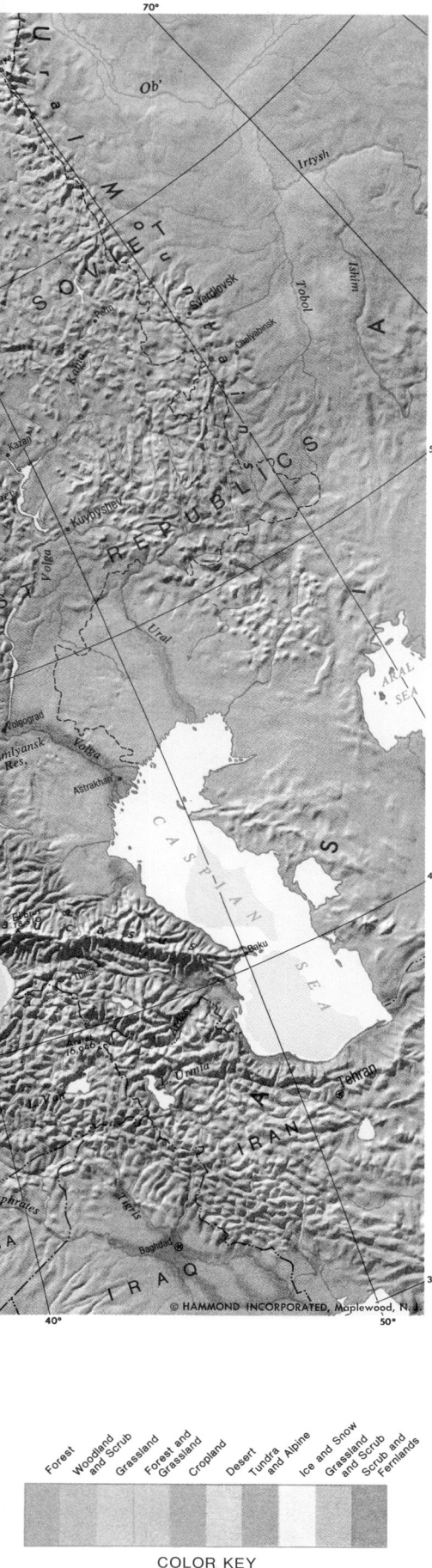

COLOR KEY

Forest | Woodland and Scrub | Grassland | Forest and Grassland | Cropland | Desert | Tundra and Alpine | Ice and Snow | Grassland and Scrub | Scrub and Fernlands

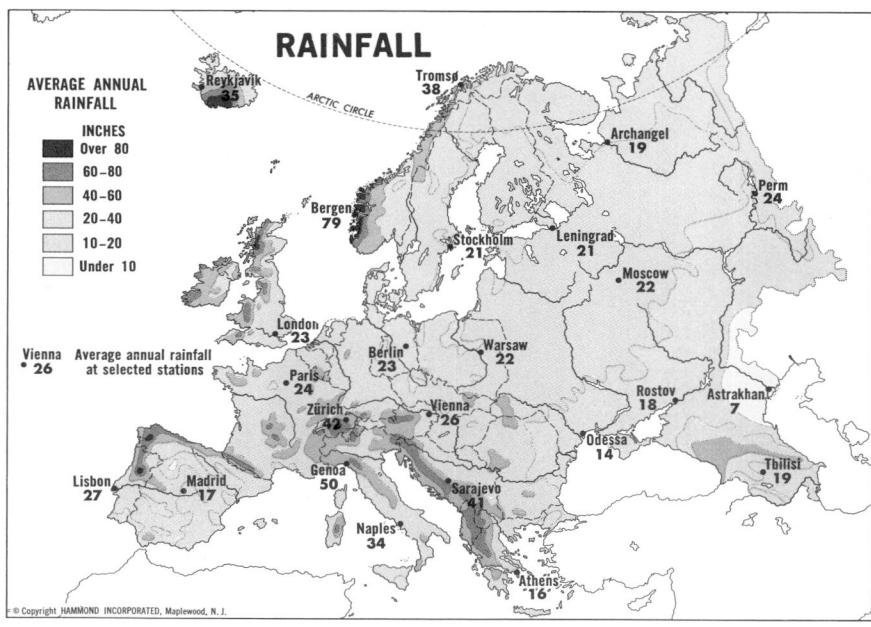

RAINFALL

AVERAGE ANNUAL RAINFALL

INCHES
- Over 80
- 60–80
- 40–60
- 20–40
- 10–20
- Under 10

Vienna
•26 Average annual rainfall at selected stations

Reykjavík 35
Tromsø 38
Archangel 19
Perm 24
Bergen 79
Stockholm 21
Leningrad 21
Moscow 22
London 23
Berlin 23
Warsaw 22
Paris 24
Vienna 26
Rostov 18
Astrakhan 7
Zürich 42
Odessa 14
Tbilisi 19
Lisbon 27
Madrid 17
Genoa 50
Sarajevo 41
Naples 34
Athens 16

© Copyright HAMMOND INCORPORATED, Maplewood, N. J.

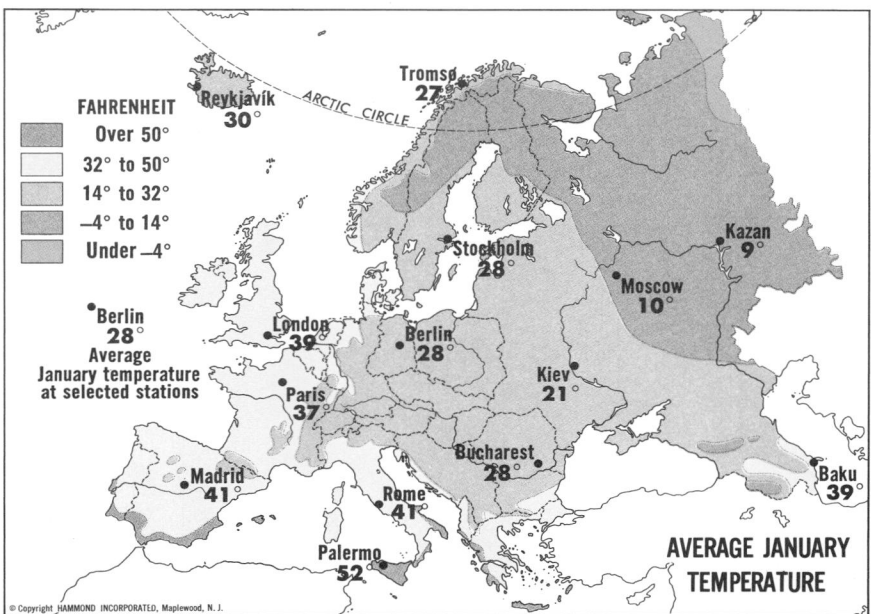

FAHRENHEIT
- Over 50°
- 32° to 50°
- 14° to 32°
- –4° to 14°
- Under –4°

Berlin 28° Average January temperature at selected stations

Reykjavík 30°
Tromsø 27°
Stockholm 28°
Moscow 10°
Kazan 9°
London 39°
Berlin 28°
Kiev 21°
Paris 37°
Bucharest 28°
Madrid 41°
Rome 41°
Baku 39°
Palermo 52°

AVERAGE JANUARY TEMPERATURE

© Copyright HAMMOND INCORPORATED, Maplewood, N. J.

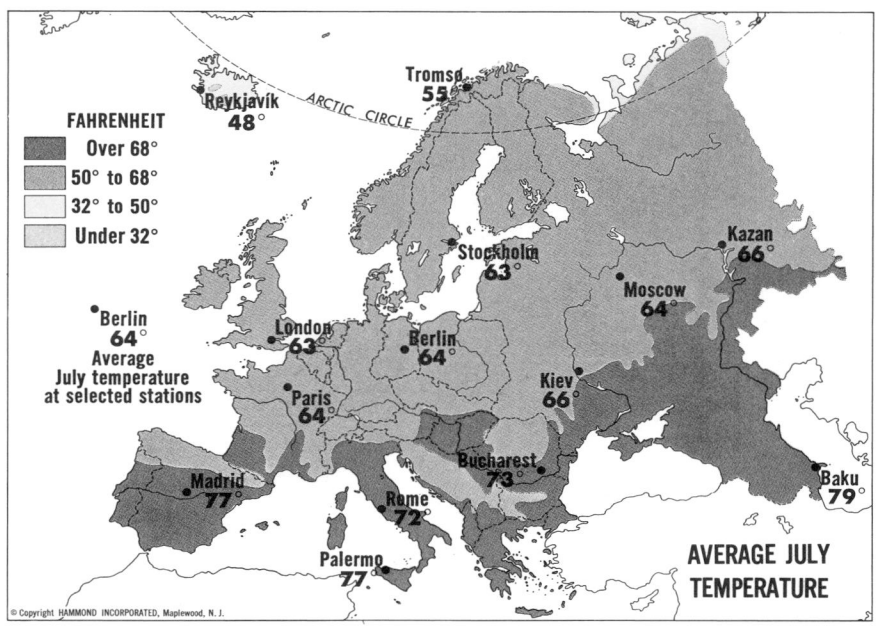

FAHRENHEIT
- Over 68°
- 50° to 68°
- 32° to 50°
- Under 32°

Berlin 64° Average July temperature at selected stations

Reykjavík 48°
Tromsø 55°
Stockholm 63°
Moscow 64°
Kazan 66°
London 63°
Berlin 64°
Kiev 66°
Paris 64°
Bucharest 73°
Madrid 77°
Rome 72°
Baku 79°
Palermo 77°

AVERAGE JULY TEMPERATURE

© Copyright HAMMOND INCORPORATED, Maplewood, N. J.

UNITED KINGDOM

AREA 94,399 sq. mi.
POPULATION 56,076,000
CAPITAL London
LARGEST CITY London
HIGHEST POINT Ben Nevis 4,406 ft.
MONETARY UNIT pound sterling
MAJOR LANGUAGES English, Gaelic, Welsh
MAJOR RELIGIONS Protestantism, Roman Catholicism

IRELAND

AREA 27,136 sq. mi.
POPULATION 3,109,000
CAPITAL Dublin
LARGEST CITY Dublin
HIGHEST POINT Carrantuohill 3,415 ft.
MONETARY UNIT Irish pound
MAJOR LANGUAGES English, Gaelic (Irish)
MAJOR RELIGION Roman Catholicism

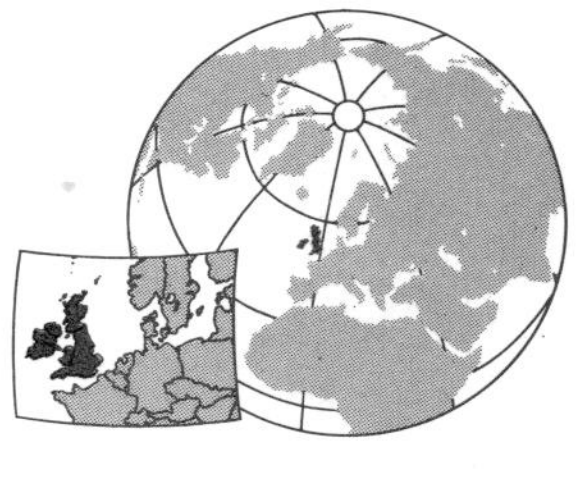

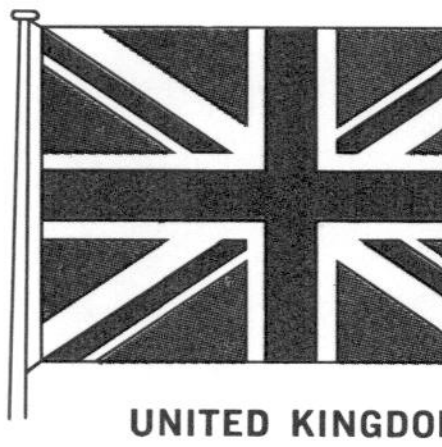

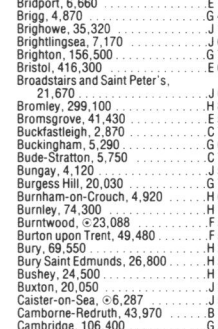

UNITED KINGDOM

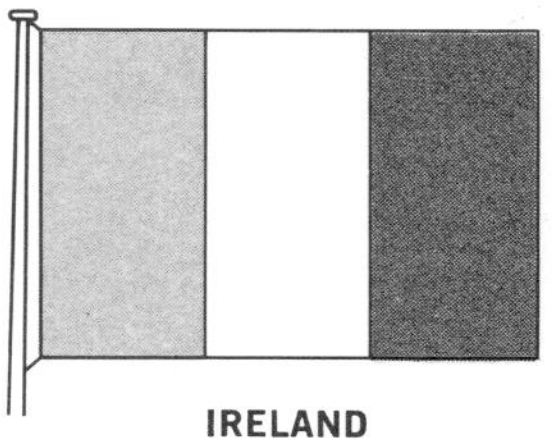

IRELAND

ENGLAND

AREA 50,516 sq.mi.
POPULATION 46,417,600
CAPITAL London
LARGEST CITY London
HIGHEST POINT Scafell Pike 3,210 ft.

WALES

AREA 8,017 sq. mi.
POPULATION 2,778,000
LARGEST CITY Cardiff
HIGHEST POINT Snowdon 3,560 ft.

SCOTLAND

AREA 30,414 sq. mi.
POPULATION 5,261,000
CAPITAL Edinburgh
LARGEST CITY Glasgow
HIGHEST POINT Ben Nevis 4,406 ft.

NORTHERN IRELAND

AREA 5,452 sq. mi.
POPULATION 1,537,200
CAPITAL Belfast
LARGEST CITY Belfast
HIGHEST POINT Slieve Donard 2,796 ft.

ENGLAND

COUNTIES

Avon, 920,200 ... E 6
Bedfordshire, 491,700 ... G 5
Berkshire, 659,000 ... F 6
Buckinghamshire, 512,000 ... G 6
Cambridgeshire, 563,000 ... G 5
Cheshire, 916,400 ... E 4
Cleveland, 567,900 ... F 3
Cornwall, 405,200 ... C 7
Cumbria, 473,600 ... D 3
Derbyshire, 887,600 ... F 5
Devon, 942,100 ... D 7
Dorset, 575,800 ... E 7
Durham, 610,400 ... F 3
East Sussex, 655,600 ... H 7
Essex, 1,426,200 ... H 6
Gloucestershire, 491,500 ... E 6
Greater London, 7,028,200 ... H 8
Greater Manchester, 2,684,100 ... H 2
Hampshire, 1,456,100 ... F 6
Hereford and Worcester, 594,200 ... E 5
Hertfordshire, 937,300 ... G 6
Humberside, 848,600 ... G 4
Isle of Wight, 111,300 ... F 7
Isles of Scilly, 1,900 ... A 7
Kent, 1,448,100 ... H 6
Lancashire, 1,375,500 ... E 4
Leicestershire, 837,900 ... F 5
Lincolnshire, 524,500 ... G 4
London, Greater, 7,028,200 ... H 8
Manchester, Greater, 2,684,100 ... H 2
Merseyside, 1,578,000 ... G 2
Norfolk, 662,500 ... H 5
Northamptonshire, 505,900 ... G 5
Northumberland, 287,300 ... E 2
North Yorkshire, 653,000 ... F 3
Nottinghamshire, 977,500 ... F 4
Oxfordshire, 541,800 ... F 6
Salop, 359,000 ... E 5
Somerset, 404,400 ... E 6
South Yorkshire, 1,318,300 ... F 4
Staffordshire, 997,600 ... E 5
Suffolk, 577,600 ... H 5
Surrey, 1,002,900 ... G 6
Sussex, East, 655,600 ... H 7
Sussex, West, 623,400 ... G 7
Tyne and Wear, 1,182,900 ... H 3
Warwickshire, 471,000 ... F 5
West Midlands, 2,743,300 ... F 5
West Sussex, 623,400 ... G 7
West Yorkshire, 2,072,500 ... J 1
Wiltshire, 512,800 ... E 6
Yorkshire, North, 653,000 ... F 3
Yorkshire, South, 1,318,300 ... F 4
Yorkshire, West, 2,072,500 ... J 1

CITIES and TOWNS

Abingdon, 20,130 ... F 6
Accrington, 36,470 ... H 1
Adwick le Street, 17,650 ... K 2
Aldeburgh, 2,750 ... J 5
Aldershot, 33,750 ... G 8
Aldridge Brownhills, 89,370 ... E 5
Alfreton, 21,560 ... F 4
Alnwick, 7,300 ... F 2
Altrincham, 40,800 ... H 2
Amersham, ⊙17,254 ... G 7
Andover, 27,620 ... F 6
Appleby, 2,240 ... E 3
Arnold, 35,090 ... F 4
Arundel, 2,390 ... G 7
Ashford, 36,380 ... H 6
Ashington, 24,720 ... F 2
Ashton-under-Lyne, 48,500 ... H 2
Axminster, ⊙4,515 ... D 7
Aycliffe, ⊙20,203 ... F 3
Aylesbury, 41,420 ... G 7
Bacup, 14,990 ... H 1
Bakewell, 4,100 ... J 2
Banbury, 31,060 ... F 5
Banstead, 44,100 ... H 8
Barking, 153,800 ... H 8
Barnet, 305,200 ... H 7
Barnsley, 74,730 ... J 2
Barnstaple, 17,820 ... D 6
Barrow-in-Furness, 73,400 ... D 3
Barton-upon-Humber, 7,750 ... G 4
Basildon, 135,720 ... J 8
Basingstoke, 60,910 ... F 6
Bath, 83,100 ... E 6
Batley, 41,630 ... J 1
Battle, ⊙4,987 ... H 7
Bebington, 62,500 ... G 2
Bedford, 74,390 ... G 5
Bedlington, 27,200 ... F 2
Bedworth, 41,600 ... F 5
Beeston and Stapleford, 65,360 ... F 5
Benfleet, 49,180 ... J 8
Bentley with Arksey, 22,320 ... F 4
Berkhamsted, 15,920 ... G 7
Beverley, 16,920 ... G 4
Bexhill, 34,680 ... H 7
Bexley, 213,500 ... H 8
Biddulph, 18,720 ... H 2
Birkenhead, 135,750 ... G 2
Birmingham, 1,058,800 ... F 5
Bishop Auckland, 32,940 ... E 3
Bishop's Stortford, 21,720 ... H 6
Blackburn, 101,670 ... H 1
Blackpool, 149,000 ... G 1
Blaydon, 31,940 ... H 3
Blyth, 35,390 ... F 2
Bodmin, 10,430 ... C 7
Bognor Regis, 34,620 ... G 7
Boldon, 24,430 ... J 3
Bolton, 154,480 ... H 2
Bootle, 71,160 ... G 2
Boston, 26,700 ... G 5
Bournemouth, 144,100 ... F 7
Bracknell, ⊙34,067 ... G 8
Bradford, 458,900 ... J 1
Braintree and Bocking, 26,300 ... H 6
Brent, 256,500 ... H 8
Brentwood, 58,690 ... J 8
Bridgwater, 26,700 ... E 6
Bridlington, 26,920 ... G 3
Bridport, 6,660 ... E 7
Brigg, 4,870 ... G 4
Brighowe, 35,320 ... J 1
Brightlingsea, 7,170 ... J 6
Brighton, 156,500 ... G 7
Bristol, 416,300 ... E 6
Broadstairs and Saint Peter's, 21,670 ... J 6
Bromley, 299,100 ... H 8
Bromsgrove, 41,430 ... E 5
Buckfastleigh, 2,870 ... C 7
Buckingham, 5,290 ... G 6
Bude-Stratton, 5,750 ... C 7
Bungay, 4,120 ... J 5
Burgess Hill, 20,030 ... G 7
Burnham-on-Crouch, 4,920 ... H 6
Burnley, 74,300 ... H 1
Burntwood, ⊙23,088 ... F 5
Burton upon Trent, 49,480 ... F 5
Bury, 69,550 ... H 2
Bury Saint Edmunds, 26,800 ... H 5
Bushey, 24,500 ... H 7
Buxton, 20,050 ... J 2
Caister-on-Sea, ⊙6,287 ... J 5
Camborne-Redruth, 43,970 ... B 7
Cambridge, 106,400 ... G 5
Camden, 185,800 ... H 8
Cannock, 56,440 ... E 5
Canterbury, 115,600 ... H 6
Canvey Island, 29,550 ... J 8
Carlisle, 99,600 ... D 3
Carlton, 46,690 ... F 5
Caterham and Warlingham, 35,840 ... H 8
Chatham, 59,550 ... J 8
Cheadle and Gatley, 62,460 ... H 2
Chelmsford, 58,320 ... J 7
Cheltenham, 75,910 ... E 6
Chertsey, 45,070 ... G 8
Chesham, 20,830 ... G 7
Cheshunt, 45,750 ... H 7
Chester, 117,200 ... G 2
Chesterfield, 69,480 ... J 2
Chester-le-Street, 20,720 ... J 3
Chichester, 20,940 ... G 7
Chigwell, 54,220 ... H 8
Chippenham, 18,550 ... E 6
Chorley, 31,800 ... G 2
Christchurch, 31,610 ... F 7
Cirencester, 14,500 ... E 6
Clacton, 39,380 ... J 6
Clay Cross, 9,630 ... J 2
Cleator Moor, ⊙7,686 ... D 3
Cleethorpes, 37,200 ... H 4
Clevedon, 15,140 ... D 6
Clun, ⊙1,261 ... D 6
Coalville, 28,740 ... F 5
Cockermouth, 6,480 ... D 3
Colchester, 79,600 ... H 6
Colne, 19,030 ... H 1
Colne Valley, 21,190 ... J 2
Congleton, 21,500 ... H 2
Consett, 35,080 ... H 3
Corby, 48,850 ... G 5
Coventry, 336,800 ... F 5
Cowes, 19,190 ... F 7
Crawley, 72,600 ... G 6
Crewe and Nantwich, 98,100 ... E 4
Cromer, 5,720 ... J 5
Crook and Willington, 21,120 ... E 3
Crosby, 56,750 ... G 2
Croydon, 330,600 ... H 8
Cuckfield, 26,500 ... G 6
Darlington, 85,120 ... F 3
Dartford, 44,130 ... J 8
Darton, 15,710 ... J 2
Darwen, 29,290 ... H 1
Deal, 26,840 ... J 6
Dearne, 24,780 ... K 2
Denton, 38,110 ... H 2
Derby, 213,700 ... F 5
Dewsbury, 50,560 ... J 1
Didcot, ⊙14,277 ... F 6
Doncaster, 81,530 ... F 4
Dorking, 22,410 ... G 8
Dover, 34,160 ... J 6
Downham Market, 4,120 ... H 5
Droitwich, 13,950 ... E 5
Dronfield, 20,000 ... J 2
Dudley, 187,110 ... E 5
Dunstable, 32,090 ... G 6
Durham, 88,800 ... J 3
Ealing, 293,800 ... H 8
Eastbourne, 73,200 ... H 7
East Grinstead, 19,420 ... G 6
Eastleigh, 46,340 ... F 7
East Retford, 18,260 ... G 4
Egham, 30,320 ... G 8
Egremont, ⊙7,253 ... D 3
Eling, ⊙20,006 ... F 7
Ellesmere, ⊙2,630 ... E 5
Ellesmere Port, 63,870 ... G 2
Enfield, 260,900 ... H 7
Epsom and Ewell, 70,700 ... G 8
Esher, 63,970 ... H 8
Eston, ⊙46,219 ... F 3
Eton, 4,950 ... G 8
Evesham, 14,090 ... F 5
Exeter, 93,300 ... D 7
Exminster, ⊙3,181 ... D 7
Exmouth, 26,840 ... D 7
Falmouth, 17,530 ... B 7
Fareham, 86,300 ... F 7
Farnborough, 43,520 ... G 8
Farnham, 33,140 ... G 8
Farnworth, 26,110 ... H 2
Faversham, 15,010 ... H 6
Felixstowe, 19,460 ... J 6
Felling, 38,990 ... J 3
Filey, 5,660 ... G 3
Fleet, 22,930 ... G 8
Fleetwood, 30,070 ... D 4
Folkestone, 45,610 ... J 6
Formby, 24,850 ... G 2
Framlingham, ⊙2,258 ... J 5
Frimley and Camberley, 47,390 ... G 8
Fulwood, 22,910 ... G 1
Gainsborough, 17,440 ... G 4
Gateshead, 91,230 ... J 3
Gillingham, Dorset, ⊙4,050 ... E 6
Gillingham, Kent, 93,900 ... J 8
Glastonbury, 6,580 ... E 6
Glossop, 24,820 ... J 2
Gloucester, 91,600 ... E 6
Godalming, 18,840 ... G 8
Golborne, 28,720 ... G 2
Goole, 17,920 ... G 4
Gosport, 82,300 ... F 7
Grange, 3,520 ... E 3
Grantham, 27,830 ... G 5
Gravesend, 53,500 ... J 8
Great Baddow, ⊙18,755 ... J 7
Great Torrington, 3,430 ... C 7
Great Yarmouth, 49,410 ... J 5
Greenwich, 207,200 ... H 8
Grimsby, 93,800 ... G 4
Guildford, 58,470 ... G 8
Guisborough, 14,860 ... F 3
Hackney, 192,500 ... H 8
Hale, 17,080 ... H 2
Halesowen, 54,120 ... E 5
Halifax, 88,580 ... J 1
Haltemprice, 54,850 ... G 4
Haltwhistle, ⊙3,511 ... E 2
Hammersmith, 170,000 ... H 8
Haringey, 228,200 ... H 8
Harlow, 79,160 ... H 7
Harrogate, 64,620 ... J 1
Harrow, 200,200 ... G 8
Hartlepool, 97,100 ... F 3
Harwich, 15,280 ... J 6
Haslingden, 15,140 ... H 1
Hastings, 74,600 ... H 7
Hatfield, ⊙25,359 ... H 7
Havant and Waterloo, 112,430 ... G 7
Haverhill, 14,550 ... H 5
Havering, 239,200 ... J 8
Hayle, ⊙5,378 ... B 7
Hazel Grove and Bramhall, 40,400 ... H 2
Heanor, 24,590 ... F 4
Hebburn, 23,150 ... J 3
Hedon, 3,010 ... G 4
Hemel Hempstead, 71,150 ... G 7
Hereford, 47,800 ... E 5
Hertford, 20,760 ... H 7
Hetton, 16,810 ... J 3
Hexham, 9,820 ... E 3
Heywood, 31,720 ... H 2
High Wycombe, 61,190 ... G 8
Hillingdon, 230,800 ... G 8
Hinckley, 49,310 ... F 5
Hinderwell, ⊙2,551 ... G 3
Hitchin, 29,190 ... G 6
Hoddesdon, 27,510 ... H 7
Holmfirth, 19,790 ... J 2
Horley, ⊙18,593 ... H 8
Hornsea, 7,280 ... G 4
Horsham, 26,770 ... G 6
Horwich, 16,670 ... G 2
Houghton-le-Spring, 33,150 ... J 3
Hounslow, 199,100 ... G 8
Hove, 72,000 ... G 7
Hoylake, 32,000 ... G 2
Hoyland Nether, 15,500 ... J 2
Hucknall, 27,110 ... F 4
Huddersfield, 130,060 ... J 2
Hugh Town, ⊙1,958 ... A 8
Hull, 276,600 ... G 4
Hunstanton, 4,140 ... H 5
Huntingdon and Godmanchester, 17,200 ... G 5
Huyton-with-Roby, 65,950 ... G 2
Hyde, 37,040 ... H 2
Ilfracombe, 9,350 ... C 6
Ilkeston, 33,690 ... F 5
Immingham, ⊙10,259 ... G 4
Ipswich, 121,500 ... J 5
Islington, 171,600 ... H 8
Jarrow, 28,510 ... J 3
Kendal, 22,440 ... E 3
Kenilworth, 19,730 ... F 5
Kensington and Chelsea, 161,400 ... G 8
Keswick, 4,790 ... D 3
Kettering, 44,480 ... G 5
Keynsham, 18,970 ... E 6
Kidderminster, 49,960 ... E 5
Kidsgrove, 22,690 ... E 4
King's Lynn, 29,990 ... H 5
Kingston upon Thames, 135,600 ... H 8
Kingswood, 30,450 ... E 6
Kirkburton, 20,320 ... J 2
Kirkby, 59,100 ... G 2
Kirkby Lonsdale, ⊙1,506 ... E 3
Kirkby Stephen, ⊙1,539 ... E 3
Knutsford, 14,840 ... H 2
Lambeth, 290,300 ... H 8
Lancaster, 126,300 ... E 3
Leatherhead, 40,830 ... G 8
Leeds, 744,500 ... J 1
Leek, 19,460 ... H 2
Leicester, 289,400 ... F 5
Leigh, 46,390 ... H 2
Leighton-Linslade, 22,590 ... F 7
Letchworth, 31,520 ... G 6
Lewes, 14,170 ... H 7
Lewisham, 237,300 ... H 8
Leyland, 23,690 ... G 1
Lichfield, 23,690 ... F 5
Lincoln, 73,700 ... G 4
Liskeard, 5,360 ... C 7
Litherland, 23,530 ... G 2
Littlehampton, 20,320 ... G 7

(continued on following page)

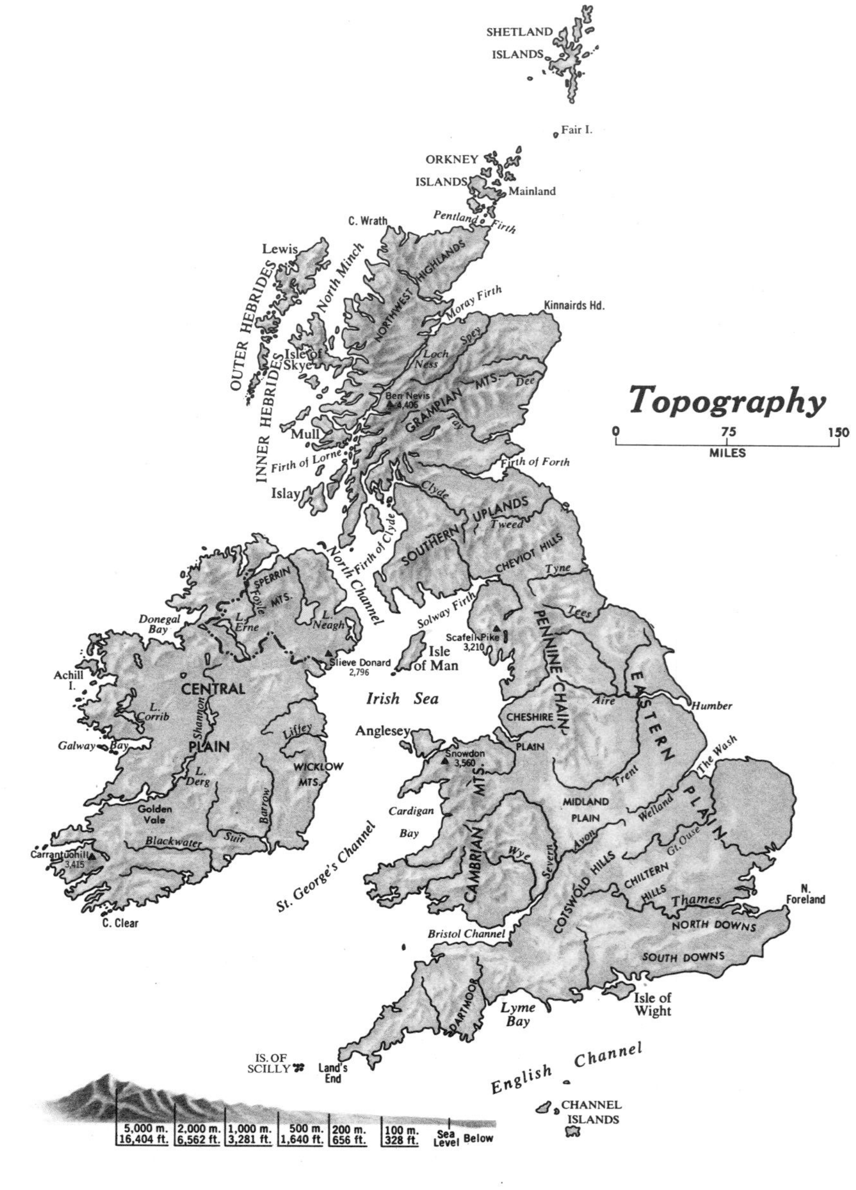

Topography
0 75 150
MILES
SHETLAND ISLANDS
Fair I.
ORKNEY ISLANDS
Mainland
C. Wrath
Pentland Firth
Lewis
OUTER HEBRIDES
North Minch
NORTHWEST HIGHLANDS
Moray Firth
Kinnairds Hd.
Loch Ness
Spey
Isle of Skye
INNER HEBRIDES
Ben Nevis 4,406
GRAMPIAN MTS.
Dee
Tay
Mull
Firth of Lorne
Firth of Forth
Islay
Clyde
Firth of Clyde
SOUTHERN UPLANDS
Tweed
CHEVIOT HILLS
Tyne
North Channel
SPERRIN MTS.
L. Neagh
L. Erne
Donegal Bay
Solway Firth
Scafell Pike 3,210
PENNINE CHAIN
Tees
Slieve Donard 2,796
Isle of Man
Achill I.
CENTRAL PLAIN
Shannon
L. Corrib
Irish Sea
Liffey
Aire
Humber
CHESHIRE PLAIN
EASTERN PLAIN
Galway Bay
L. Derg
Anglesey
Snowdon 3,560
The Wash
WICKLOW MTS.
Trent
Barrow
Golden Vale
Cardigan Bay
MIDLAND PLAIN
Welland
Suir
Blackwater
CAMBRIAN MTS.
Wye
Severn
Avon
Gt. Ouse
Carrantuohill 3,415
St. George's Channel
COTSWOLD HILLS
CHILTERN HILLS
Thames
N. Foreland
C. Clear
Bristol Channel
NORTH DOWNS
SOUTH DOWNS
DARTMOOR
Lyme Bay
Isle of Wight
IS. OF SCILLY
Land's End
English Channel
CHANNEL ISLANDS
5,000 m. 16,404 ft.
2,000 m. 6,562 ft.
1,000 m. 3,281 ft.
500 m. 1,640 ft.
200 m. 656 ft.
100 m. 328 ft.
Sea Level
Below

12 United Kingdom and Ireland

(continued)

Liverpool, 539,700 G 2
Loftus, 7,850 G 3
London (cap.), 7,028,200 H 8
London, ★12,332,900 H 8
Long Eaton, 33,560 F 5
Longbenton, 50,120 J 3
Looe, 4,060 C 7
Loughborough, 49,010 F 5
Lowestoft, 53,260 J 5
Ludlow, ⊙7,466 E 5
Luton, 164,500 G 6
Lydd, 4,670 H 7
Lyme Regis, 3,460 E 7
Lymington, 36,780 F 7
Lynton, 1,770 D 6
Lytham Saint Anne's, 42,120 G 1
Mablethorpe and Sutton, 6,750 H 4
Macclesfield, 45,420 H 2
Maidenhead, 48,210 G 8
Maidstone, 72,110 J 8
Maldon, 14,350 H 6
Malmesbury, 2,550 E 6
Malton, 4,010 G 3
Malvern, 30,420 E 5
Manchester, 490,000 H 2
Mangotsfield, 23,000 E 6
Mansfield, 58,450 K 2
Mansfield Woodhouse, 25,400 F 4
March, 14,560 H 5
Margate, 50,290 J 6
Market Harborough, 15,230 G 5
Marlborough, 6,370 F 6
Matlock, 20,300 J 2
Melton Mowbray, 20,680 G 5
Merton, 169,400 H 8
Middlesbrough, 153,900 F 3
Middleton, 53,340 H 2
Middlewich, 7,600 H 2
Mildenhall, ⊙9,269 H 5
Millom, ⊙7,101 D 3
Milton Keynes, 89,900 F 5
Minehead, 8,230 D 6
Moretonhampstead, ⊙1,440 C 7
Morpeth, 14,450 F 2
Mundesley, ⊙1,536 J 5
Nelson, 31,220 H 1
Neston, 18,210 G 2
Newark, 24,760 G 4
Newbury, 24,850 F 6
Newcastle upon Tyne, 295,800 H 3
Newcastle-under-Lyme, 75,940 E 4
Newham, 228,900 H 8
Newhaven, 9,970 H 7
Newport, 22,430 F 7
New Romney, 3,830 J 7
Newton Abbot, 19,940 D 7
Newton-le-Willows, 21,780 H 2
New Windsor, 29,660 G 8
Northallerton F 3
Northam, 8,310 C 6
Northampton, 128,290 F 5
Northfleet, 27,150 J 8
North Sunderland, ⊙1,725 F 2
Northwich, 17,710 H 2
Norton, 5,580 G 3
Norton-Radstock, 15,900 E 6
Norwich, 119,200 J 5
Nottingham, 280,300 F 5
Nuneaton, 69,210 F 5
Oadby, 20,700 F 5
Oakham, 7,280 G 5
Okehampton, 4,000 D 7
Oldham, 103,690 H 2
Ormskirk, 28,860 G 2
Oswaldtwistle, 14,270 H 1
Oxford, 117,400 F 6
Padstow, ⊙2,802 B 7
Penryn, 5,660 B 7
Penzance, 19,360 B 7
Peterborough, 118,900 G 5
Peterlee, ⊙21,846 J 3
Plymouth, 259,100 C 7
Polperro, ⊙1,491 C 7
Poole, 110,600 E 7
Porlock, ⊙1,290 D 6
Portishead, 9,680 E 6
Portland, 14,860 E 7
Portslade-by-Sea, 18,040 G 7
Portsmouth, 198,500 F 7
Potters Bar, 24,670 H 7
Poulton-le-Fylde, 16,340 G 1
Preston, 94,760 G 1
Prestwich, 32,850 H 2
Queenborough, 31,550 H 6
Radcliffe, 29,630 H 2
Ramsbottom, 16,710 H 2
Ramsgate, 40,090 J 6
Rawtenstall, 20,950 H 1
Rayleigh, 26,740 J 8
Reading, 131,200 G 8
Redbridge, 231,600 H 8
Redcar, ⊙46,325 F 3
Redditch, 44,750 E 5
Reigate, 55,600 H 8
Richmond upon Thames, 166,800 H 8
Rickmansworth, 29,030 G 8
Ripley, 18,060 F 4
Rochdale, 93,780 H 2
Rochester, 56,030 J 8
Rothbury, ⊙1,818 E 2
Rotherham, 84,770 K 2
Royal Leamington Spa, 44,950 F 5
Royal Tunbridge Wells, 44,800 H 6
Rugby, 60,380 F 5
Rugeley, 24,440 E 5
Runcorn, 42,730 G 2
Rushden, 21,840 G 5
Ryde, 23,170 F 7
Rye, 4,530 H 7
Ryton, 15,170 H 3
Saddleworth, 21,340 J 2
Saint Agnes, ⊙4,747 B 7
Saint Albans, 123,800 H 7
Saint Austell-with-Fowey, 32,710 C 7
Saint Columb Major, ⊙3,953 B 7
Saint Helens, 104,890 G 2
Saint Ives, Cornwall, 9,760 B 7
Saint Neots, 17,940 G 5
Salcombe, 2,370 D 7
Sale, 59,060 H 2
Salford, 261,100 H 2
Salisbury, 35,460 F 6
Saltburn and Marske-by-the-Sea, 21,170 G 3
Sandbach, 14,280 H 2
Sandown-Shanklin, 14,800 F 7
Sandwich, 4,420 J 6
Saxmundham, 1,820 J 5
Scarborough, 43,300 G 3
Scunthorpe, 68,100 G 4
Seaford, 18,020 H 7
Seaham, 22,470 J 3
Seascale, ⊙2,106 D 3
Seaton, 4,500 D 7
Seaton Valley, 35,880 J 3
Sedbergh, ⊙2,741 E 3
Selsey, ⊙6,491 G 7
Sevenoaks, 18,160 J 8
Shaftesbury, 4,180 E 7
Sheffield, 558,000 J 2
Sherborne, 9,230 E 7
Sheringham, 4,940 J 5
Shildon, 15,360 F 3
Shoreham-by-Sea, 19,620 G 7
Shrewsbury, 56,120 E 5
Silloth, ⊙2,662 D 3
Sittingbourne and Milton, 32,830 H 6
Skelmersdale, 35,850 G 2
Skelton and Brotton, 15,930 G 3
Sleaford, 8,050 G 5
Slough, 89,060 G 8
Solihull, 108,230 F 5
Southampton, 213,700 F 7
Southend-on-Sea, 159,300 H 6
Southport, 86,030 G 1
South Shields, 96,900 J 3
Southwark, 224,900 H 8
Southwold, 1,960 J 5
Sowerby Bridge, 15,700 H 1
Spalding, 17,040 G 5
Spenborough, 41,460 J 1
Spennymoor, 19,050 F 3
Stafford, 54,860 E 5
Staines, 56,380 G 8
Stamford, 14,980 G 5
Stanley, 42,280 H 3
Staveley, 17,620 K 2
Stevenage, 72,600 G 6
Stockport, 138,350 H 2
Stockton-on-Tees, 165,400 F 3
Stoke-on-Trent, 256,200 E 4
Stourbridge, 56,530 E 5
Stourport-on-Severn, 19,430 E 5
Stowmarket, 9,020 J 5
Stratford-upon-Avon, 20,080 F 5
Stretford, 52,450 H 2
Stroud, 19,600 E 6
Sudbury, 8,860 H 5
Sunbury-on-Thames, 40,070 G 8
Sunderland, 214,820 J 3
Sutton, 166,700 H 8
Sutton Bridge, ⊙3,113 H 5
Sutton in Ashfield, 40,330 K 2
Swadlincote, 21,060 F 5
Swanage, 8,000 E 7
Swindon, 90,680 F 6
Tamworth, 46,960 F 5
Taunton, 37,570 D 6
Tavistock, ⊙7,620 C 7
Telford, ⊙79,451 E 5
Tenbury, ⊙2,151 E 5
Tewkesbury, 9,210 E 6
Thetford, 15,690 H 5
Thirsk, ⊙2,884 F 3
Thornaby-on-Tees, ⊙42,385 F 3
Thorne, ⊙16,694 F 4
Thornton Cleveleys, 27,090 G 1
Thurrock, 127,700 J 8
Tiverton, 16,190 D 7
Todmorden, 14,540 H 1
Tonbridge, 31,410 H 8
Torbay, 109,900 D 7
Torpoint, 6,840 C 7
Tower Hamlets, 146,100 H 8
Tow Law, 2,460 H 4
Trowbridge, 20,120 E 6
Truro, 15,690 B 7
Turton, 22,800 H 2
Tynemouth, 67,090 J 3
Upton upon Severn, ⊙2,048 E 5
Urmston, 44,130 H 2
Uttoxeter, 9,100 E 5
Ventnor, 6,980 F 7
Wainfleet All Saints, ⊙1,116 H 4
Wakefield, 306,500 J 2
Wallasey, 94,520 G 2
Wallsend, 45,490 J 3
Walsall, 182,430 E 5
Waltham Forest, 223,700 H 8
Waltham Holy Cross, 14,810 H 7
Walton and Weybridge, 51,270 G 8
Walton-le-Dale, 27,660 G 1
Wandsworth, 284,600 H 8
Wantage, 8,490 F 6
Ware, 14,900 H 7
Wareham, 4,630 E 7
Warley, 161,260 E 5
Warminster, 14,440 E 6
Warrington, 65,320 G 2
Warwick, 17,870 F 5
Washington, 27,720 J 3
Watchet, 2,980 D 6
Watford, 77,000 H 7
Wellingborough, 39,570 G 5
Wells, 8,960 E 6
Wells-next-the-Sea, 2,450 H 5
Welwyn, 39,900 H 7
Wem, ⊙3,411 E 5
West Bridgford, 28,340 F 5
West Bromwich, 162,740 F 5
West Mersea, 4,730 H 6
Westminster, 216,100 H 8
Weston-super-Mare, 51,960 D 6
Weymouth and Melcombe Regis, 41,080 E 7
Whickham, 29,710 J 3
Whitchurch, ⊙7,142 E 5
Whitehaven, 26,260 D 3
Whitley Bay, 37,010 J 3
Widnes, 58,330 G 2
Wigan, 80,920 G 2
Wigston, 31,650 F 5
Wilmslow, 31,250 H 2
Wilton, 4,090 F 6
Winchester, 88,900 F 6
Windermere, 7,860 E 3
Winsford, 26,920 G 2
Wirral, 27,510 G 2
Wisbech, 16,990 H 5
Witham, 19,730 H 6
Withernsea, 6,300 H 4
Wivenhoe, 5,630 J 6
Woking, 79,300 G 8
Wokingham, 22,390 G 8
Wolverhampton, 266,400 E 5
Wombwell, 17,850 K 2
Woodhall Spa, 2,420 G 4
Woodley and Sandford, ⊙24,581 G 8
Woodstock, 2,070 F 6
Wooler, ⊙1,833 F 2
Worcester, 73,900 E 5
Workington, 28,260 D 3
Worksop, 36,590 F 4
Worsbrough, 15,180 J 2
Worsley, 49,530 H 2
Worthing, 89,100 G 7
Wymondham, 9,390 J 5
Yateley, ⊙16,505 G 8
Yeovil, 26,180 E 7
York, 101,900 F 4

OTHER FEATURES

Aire (riv.) F 4
Atlantic Ocean A 7
Avon (riv.) F 5
Avon (riv.) F 7
Axe Edge (mt.) H 2
Barnstaple (bay) C 6
Beachy (head) H 7
Bigbury (bay) C 7
Blackwater (riv.) H 6
Bristol (chan.) C 6
Brown Willy (mt.) C 7
Cheviot (hills) E 2
Cheviot, The (mt.) E 2
Chiltern (hills) G 6
Cleveland (hills) F 3
Colne (riv.) G 8
Cornwall (cape) B 7
Cotswold (hills) E 6
Cross Fell (mt.) E 3
Cumbrian (mts.) D 3
Dart (riv.) D 7
Dartmoor National Park C 7
Dee (riv.) D 4
Derwent (riv.) G 3
Derwent (riv.) H 3
Don (riv.) F 4
Dorset Heights (hills) E 7
Dove (riv.) J 2
Dover (str.) J 7
Dungeness (prom.) J 7
Dunkery (hill) D 6
Eddystone (rocks) C 7
Eden (riv.) E 3
English (chan.) D 8
Esk (riv.) D 2
Exe (riv.) D 7
Exmoor National Park D 6
Fens, The (reg.) G 5
Flamborough (head) G 3
Formby (head) G 2
Foulness Island (pen.) J 6
Gibraltar (pt.) H 4
Great Ouse (riv.) H 5
Hartland (pt.) C 6
High Willhays (mt.) C 7
Hodder (riv.) H 1
Holderness (pen.), 43,900 G 4
Holy (isl.), 189 F 2
Humber (riv.) G 4
Irish (sea) B 4
Kennet (riv.) F 6
Lake District National Park D 3
Land's End (prom.) B 7
Lea (riv.) G 6
Lincoln Wolds (hills) G 4
Lindisfarne (Holy) (isl.), 189 F 2
Liverpool (bay) D 4
Lizard, The (pen.), 7,371 B 8
Lundy (isl.), 49 C 6
Lune (riv.) E 3
Lyme (bay) D 7
Manacle (pt.) C 7
Medway (riv.) H 6
Mendip (hills) E 6
Mersea (isl.), 4,423 J 6
Mersey (riv.) G 2
Morecambe (bay) D 3
Mounts (bay) B 7
Naze, The (prom.) J 6
Nene (riv.) H 5
New (for.) F 6
North (sea) J 4
North Downs (hills) G 6
North Foreland (prom.) J 6
Northumberland National Park E 2
North York Moors National Park G 3
Orford Ness (prom.) J 5
Ouse (riv.) G 4
Ouse (riv.) G 6
Parrett (riv.) E 6
Peak District National Park F 4
Peak, The (mt.) J 2
Peel Fell (mt.) E 2
Pennine Chain (range) E 3
Plymouth (sound) C 7
Portland, Bill of (pt.) E 7
Prawle (pt.) D 7
Purbeck, Isle of (pen.), 39,500 F 7
Ribble (riv.) E 4
Saint Alban's (head) F 7
Saint Bees (head) D 3
Saint Martin's (isl.), 106 A 8
Saint Mary's (isl.), 1,958 A 8
Scafell Pike (mt.) D 3
Scilly (isls.), 1,900 A 7
Selsey Bill (prom.) G 7
Severn (riv.) E 6
Sheppey (isl.), 31,550 J 6
Sherwood (for.) F 4
Skiddaw (mt.) D 3
Solent (chan.) F 7
Solway (firth) D 3
South Downs (hills) G 7
Spithead (chan.) F 7
Spurn (head) H 4
Stonehenge (ruins) F 6
Stour (riv.) E 7
Stour (riv.) H 6
Stour (riv.) J 6
Swale (riv.) F 3
Tamar (riv.) C 7
Taw (riv.) D 7
Tees (riv.) F 3
Test (riv.) F 6
Thames (riv.) H 6
Tintagel (head) C 7
Torridge (riv.) C 7
Trent (riv.) G 4
Tresco (isl.), 246 A 8
Tweed (riv.) E 2
Tyne (riv.) F 3
Ure (riv.) F 3
Ver (riv.) H 7
Walney, Isle of (isl.), 11,241 D 3
Wash, The (bay) H 5
Weald, The (reg.) H 6
Wear (riv.) F 3
Weaver (riv.) G 2
Welland (riv.) G 5
Wey (riv.) G 6
Wharfe (riv.) E 3
Wirral (pen.), 432,900 G 2
Witham (riv.) G 4
Wolds, The (hills) G 4
Wye (riv.) D 5
Wyre (riv.) G 1
Yare (riv.) J 5
Yorkshire Dales National Park E 3

CHANNEL ISLANDS

CITIES and TOWNS

Saint Anne E 8
Saint Helier (cap.), Jersey, ⊙28,135 E 8
Saint Peter Port (cap.), Guernsey, ⊙16,303 E 8
Saint Sampson's, ⊙6,534 E 8

OTHER FEATURES

Alderney (isl.), 1,686 E 8
Guernsey (isl.), 51,351 E 8
Herm (isl.), 96 E 8
Jersey (isl.), 72,629 E 8
Sark (isl.), 590 E 8

ISLE of MAN

CITIES and TOWNS

Castletown, 2,820 C 3
Douglas (cap.), 20,389 C 3
Laxey, 1,170 C 3
Michael, 408 C 3
Onchan, 4,807 C 3
Peel, 3,081 C 3
Port Erin, 1,714 C 3
Port Saint Mary, 1,508 C 3
Ramsey, 5,048 C 3

OTHER FEATURES

Ayre (pt.) C 3
Calf of Man (isl.) C 3
Langness (prom.) C 3
Snaefell (mt.) C 3
Spanish (head) C 3

WALES

COUNTIES

Clwyd, 376,000 D 4
Dyfed, 323,100 C 6
Gwent, 439,600 D 6
Gwynedd, 225,100 C 4
Mid Glamorgan, 540,400 D 6
Powys, 101,500 D 5
South Glamorgan, 389,200 A 7
West Glamorgan, 371,900 D 6

CITIES and TOWNS

Aberaeron, 1,340 C 5
Abercarn, 18,370 B 6
Aberdare, 38,030 A 6
Abertillery, 20,550 B 6
Amlwch, 3,630 C 4
Bala, 1,650 D 5
Bangor, 16,030 C 4
Barmouth, 2,070 C 5
Barry, 42,780 B 7
Beaumaris, 2,090 C 4
Bedwellty, 25,460 B 6
Bethesda, 4,180 D 4
Betws-y-Coed, 720 D 4
Brecknock (Brecon), 6,460 D 6
Brecon, 6,460 D 6
Bridgend, 14,690 A 7
Brynmawr, 5,970 B 6
Builth Wells, 1,480 D 5
Burry Port, 5,990 C 6
Caernarfon, 8,840 C 4
Caerphilly, 42,190 B 6
Cardiff, 281,500 B 7
Cardigan, 3,830 C 5
Chepstow, 8,260 E 6
Chirk, ⊙3,564 D 5
Colwyn Bay, 25,370 D 4
Criccieth, 1,590 C 5
Cwmamman, 3,950 D 6
Cwmbran, 32,980 B 6
Denbigh, 8,420 D 4
Dolgellau, 2,430 D 5
Ebbw Vale, 25,670 B 6
Ffestiniog, 5,510 D 5
Fishguard and Goodwick, 5,020 B 5
Flint, 15,070 G 2
Gelligaer, 33,820 A 6
Harlech, ⊙332 C 5
Haverfordwest, 8,930 B 6
Hawarden, ⊙20,389 G 2
Hay, 1,200 D 5
Holywell, 8,570 G 2
Kidwelly, 3,090 C 6
Knighton, 2,190 D 5
Llandeilo, 1,780 C 6
Llandovery, 2,040 D 5
Llandrindod Wells, 3,460 D 5
Llandudno, 17,700 D 4
Llanelli, 25,870 C 6
Llanfairfechan, 3,800 D 4
Llangefni, 4,070 C 4
Llangollen, 3,050 D 5
Llanguicke, ⊙15,029 D 6
Llanidloes, 2,390 D 5
Llantrisant, ⊙27,490 A 7
Llanwrtyd Wells, 460 D 5
Llwchwr, 27,530 D 6
Machynlleth, 1,830 D 5
Maesteg, 21,100 D 6
Menai Bridge, 2,730 C 4
Merthyr Tydfil, 61,500 A 6
Milford Haven, 13,960 B 6
Mold, 8,700 G 2
Montgomery, 1,000 D 5
Mountain Ash, 27,710 A 6
Mynyddislwyn, 15,590 B 6
Narberth, 970 C 6
Neath, 27,280 D 6
Nefyn, ⊙2,086 C 5
Newcastle Emlyn, 690 C 5
Newport, Dyfed, ⊙1,062 C 5
Newport, Gwent, 110,090 B 6
New Quay, 760 C 5
Newtown, 6,400 D 5
Neyland, 2,690 B 6
Ogmore and Garw, 19,680 A 6
Pembroke, 14,570 C 6
Penarth, 24,180 B 7
Penmaenmawr, 4,050 C 4
Pontypool, 36,710 B 6
Pontypridd, 34,180 A 6
Porthcawl, 14,980 D 6
Porthmadog, 3,900 C 5
Port Talbot, 58,200 D 6
Prestatyn, 15,480 D 4
Presteigne, 1,330 D 5
Pwllheli, 4,020 C 5
Rhondda, 85,400 A 6
Rhyl, 22,150 D 4
Risca, 15,780 B 6
Ruthin, 4,780 D 4
Saint David's, ⊙1,638 B 6
Swansea, 190,800 C 6
Tenby, 4,930 C 6
Tredegar, 17,450 B 6
Tywyn, 3,850 C 5
Welshpool, 7,370 D 5
Wrexham, 39,530 E 4

OTHER FEATURES

Anglesey (isl.), 64,500 C 4
Aran Fawddwy (mt.) C 5
Bardsey (isl.), 9 C 5
Berwyn (mts.) D 5
Black (mts.) D 6
Braich-y-Pwll (prom.) C 5
Brecon Beacons (mt.) D 6
Brecon Beacons National Park D 6
Caldy (isl.), 70 C 6
Cambrian (mts.) D 5
Cardigan (bay) C 5
Carmarthen (bay) C 6
Cemmaes (head) C 5
Dee (riv.) D 4
Dovey (riv.) D 5
Ely (riv.) B 7
Gower (pen.), 17,220 C 6
Great Ormes (head) C 4
Holy (isl.), 13,715 C 4
Lleyn (pen.), 25,800 C 5
Menai (str.) C 4
Milford Haven (inlet) B 6
Pembrokeshire Coast National Park C 6
Plynlimon (mt.) D 5
Preseli (mts.) C 6
Radnor (for.) D 5
Rhymney (riv.) B 6
Saint Brides (bay) B 6
Saint David's (head) B 6
Saint George's (chan.) B 5
Saint Gowans (head) C 6
Severn (riv.) E 5
Snowdon (mt.) D 4
Snowdonia National Park D 4
Taff (riv.) B 7
Teifi (riv.) C 5
Towy (riv.) D 6
Tremadoc (bay) C 5
Usk (riv.) B 6
Wye (riv.) D 5
Ynys Môn (Anglesey) (isl.), 64,500 C 4

★Population of met. area.
⊙Population of parish.

SCOTLAND

(map on page 15)

REGIONS

Borders, 99,409 E 5
Central, 269,281 D 4
Dumfries and Galloway, 143,667 E 5
Fife, 336,339 E 4
Grampian, 448,772 F 3
Highland, 182,044 D 3
Lothian, 754,008 E 5
Orkney (islands area), 17,675 E 1
Shetland (islands area), 18,494 F 2
Strathclyde, 2,504,909 C 4
Tayside, 401,987 E 4
Western Isles (islands area), 29,615 A 3

CITIES and TOWNS

Aberchirder, 877 F 3
Aberdeen, 210,362 F 3
Aberdour, 1,576 D 1
Aberfeldy, 1,552 E 4
Aberfoyle, 793 D 4
Aberlady, 737 F 4
Aberlour, 842 E 3
Abernethy, 776 E 4
Aboyne, 1,040 F 3
Acharacle, ⊙764 C 4
Achiltibuie, ⊙1,564 C 3
Achnasheen, ⊙1,078 C 3
Ae, 239 E 5
Airdrie, 38,491 C 2
Alexandria, 9,758 A 1
Alford, 764 F 3
Alloa, 13,558 C 1
Alness, 2,560 D 3
Altnaharra, ⊙1,227 D 2
Alva, 4,593 C 1
Alyth, 1,738 E 4
Ancrum, 266 F 5
Annan, 6,250 E 6
Annat, ⊙550 C 3
Annbank Station, 2,530 D 5
Applecross, ⊙550 C 3
Arbroath, 22,706 F 4
Ardavasar, ⊙449 B 3
Ardersier, 942 E 3
Ardgay, 193 D 3
Ardrishaig, 946 C 4
Ardrossan, 11,072 D 5
Armadale, 7,200 C 2
Arrochar, 543 D 4
Ascog, 230 A 2
Auchenblae, 339 F 4
Auchencairn, 215 E 6
Auchinleck, 4,883 D 5
Auchterarder, 1,738 E 4
Auchtermuchty, 1,426 E 4
Auldearn, 405 E 3
Aviemore, 1,224 E 3
Avoch, 776 D 3
Ayr, 47,990 D 5
Ayton, 410 F 5
Bailivanish, 347 A 3
Baillieston, 7,671 B 2
Balallan, 283 B 2
Balerno, 3,576 D 2
Balfron, 1,149 B 1
Ballantrae, 262 C 5
Ballater, 981 F 3
Ballingry, 4,332 D 1
Ballinluig, 188 E 4
Balloch, Highland, 572 D 3
Balloch, Strathclyde, 1,484 B 1
Baltasound, 246 G 2
Banchory, 2,435 F 3
Banff, 3,832 F 3
Bankfoot, 868 E 4
Bankhead, 1,492 F 3
Bannockburn, 5,889 C 1
Barrhead, 18,736 B 2
Barrhill, 236 D 5
Barvas, 279 B 2
Bathgate, 14,038 C 2
Bayble, 543 B 2
Bearsden, 25,128 B 2
Beattock, 309 E 5
Beauly, 1,141 D 3
Beith, 5,859 D 5
Bellsbank, 3,066 D 5
Bellshill, 18,166 C 2
Berriedale, ⊙1,927 E 2
Bieldside, 1,137 F 3
Biggar, 1,718 E 5
Birnam, 659 E 4
Bishopbriggs, 21,570 B 2
Bishopton, 2,931 B 2
Blackburn, 7,636 C 2
Blackford, 529 E 4
Blair Atholl, 437 E 4
Blairgowrie and Rattray, 5,681 E 4
Blanefield, 835 B 1
Blantyre, 13,992 B 2
Blyth Bridge, ⊙441 E 5
Bo'ness, 12,959 C 1
Boat of Garten, 406 E 3
Boddam, 1,429 G 3
Bonar Bridge, 519 D 3
Bonhill, 4,385 B 1
Bonnybridge, 5,701 C 1
Bonnyrigg and Lasswade, 7,429 D 2
Bowmore, 947 B 5
Braemar, 394 E 3
Breasclete, 234 B 2
Brechin, 6,759 F 4
Bridge of Allan, 4,638 C 1
Bridge of Don, 4,086 F 3
Bridge of Weir, 4,724 A 2
Brightons, 3,106 C 1
Broadford, 310 B 3
Brodick, 630 C 5
Brora, 1,436 E 2
Broxburn, 7,776 D 1
Buchlyvie, 412 B 1
Buckhaven and Methil, 17,930 F 4
Buckie, 8,145 E 3
Bucksburn, 6,567 F 3
Bunessan, ⊙585 B 4
Burghead, 1,321 E 3
Burnmouth, 300 F 5
Burntisland, 5,626 D 1
Cairndow, ⊙874 D 4
Cairnryan, 199 D 6
Callander, 1,805 D 4
Cambuslang, 14,607 B 2
Campbeltown, 6,428 C 5
Cannich, 203 D 3
Canonbie, 234 F 5
Caol, 3,719 C 4
Carbost, ⊙772 B 3
Cardenden, 6,802 D 1
Carloway, 178 B 2
Carluke, 8,864 E 5
Carnoustie, 6,838 F 4
Carnwath, 1,246 E 5
Carradale, 262 C 5
Carrbridge, 416 E 3
Carron, 2,626 C 1
Carsphairn, 186 D 5
Castlebay, 284 A 4
Castle Douglas, 3,384 E 6
Castle Kennedy, 307 D 6
Castletown, 902 E 2
Catrine, 2,681 D 5
Cawdor, 111 E 3
Chirnside, 888 F 5
Chryston, 8,322 C 2
Clackmannan, 3,248 C 1
Clarkston, 8,404 B 2
Closeburn, 225 E 5
Clovulin, ⊙315 C 4
Clydebank, 47,538 B 2
Coalburn, 1,460 E 5
Coatbridge, 50,806 C 2
Cockburnspath, 233 F 5
Cockenzie and Port Seton, 3,539 D 1
Coldingham, 423 F 5
Coldstream, 1,393 F 5
Coll, 305 B 2
Colmonell, 218 D 5
Comrie, 1,119 E 4
Connel, 300 C 4
Cononbridge, 914 D 3
Corpach, 1,296 C 4
Coupar Angus, 2,010 E 4
Cove and Kilcreggan, 1,402 A 1
Cove Bay, 765 F 3
Cowdenbeath, 10,215 D 1
Cowie, 2,751 C 1
Craigellachie, 382 E 3
Craignure, ⊙544 C 4
Crail, 1,033 F 4
Crawford, 384 E 5
Creetown, 769 D 6
Crieff, 5,718 E 4
Crimond, 313 G 3
Crinan, ⊙462 C 4
Cromarty, 492 E 3
Crosshill, 535 D 5
Crossmichael, 317 D 6
Cruden Bay, 528 G 3
Cullen, 1,199 F 3
Culross, 504 C 1
Cults, 3,336 F 3
Cumbernauld, 41,200 C 1
Cumnock and Holmhead, 6,298 D 5
Cupar, 6,607 E 4
Currie, 6,764 D 2
Dailly, 1,258 D 5
Dalbeattie, 3,659 E 6
Daliburgh, 261 A 3
Dalkeith, 9,713 D 2
Dalmally, 283 D 4
Dalmellington, 1,949 D 5
Dalry, 5,833 D 5
Dalrymple, 1,336 D 5
Darvel, 3,177 D 5
Daviot, ⊙513 D 3
Denholm, 581 F 5
Denny and Dunipace, 10,424 C 1
Dervaig, ⊙1,081 B 4
Dingwall, 4,275 D 3
Dollar, 2,573 E 4
Dornoch, 880 D 3
Douglas, 1,843 E 5
Doune, 859 D 4
Drongan, 3,609 D 5
Drumbeg, ⊙833 C 2
Drummore, 336 D 6
Drumnadrochit, 359 D 3
Drymen, 659 B 1
Dufftown, 1,481 E 3
Dumbarton, 25,469 B 1
Dumfries, 29,259 E 5
Dunbar, 4,609 F 4
Dunbeath, 161 E 2
Dunbeg, 939 C 4
Dunblane, 5,222 E 4
Dundee, 194,732 F 4
Dundonald, 2,256 D 5
Dunfermline, 52,098 D 1
Dunkeld, 273 E 4
Dunning, 564 E 4
Dunoon, 8,759 A 2
Dunragit, 323 D 6
Duns, 1,812 F 5
Duntochter, 3,532 B 2
Dunure, 452 D 5
Dunvegan, 301 B 3
Dyce, 2,733 F 3
Eaglesfield, 581 E 5
Eaglesham, 2,788 D 5
Earlston, 1,415 F 5
East Calder, 2,690 D 2
East Kilbride, 71,200 B 2
East Linton, 882 F 5
Eastriggs, 1,455 E 5
Ecclefechan, 844 E 5
Edinburgh (cap.), 470,085 D 1
Edzell, 658 F 4
Elderslie, 5,204 B 2
Elgin, 17,042 E 3
Elie and Earlsferry, 807 F 4
Ellon, 2,855 F 3
Embo, 260 E 3
Errol, 762 E 4
Evanton, 562 D 3
Eyemouth, 2,704 F 5
Fairlie, 1,029 D 5
Falkirk, 36,901 C 1
Falkland, 998 E 4
Fallin, 3,159 C 1
Fauldhouse, 5,247 C 2
Ferness, ⊙287 E 3
Ferryden, 740 F 4
Findhorn, 664 E 3
Findochty, 1,229 E 3
Fintry, 296 B 1
Fochabers, 1,238 E 3
Forfar, 11,179 F 4
Forres, 5,317 E 3
Fort Augustus, 670 D 3
Forth, 2,929 C 2
Fortrose, 1,150 D 3
Fort William, 4,370 C 4
Foyers, 276 D 3
Fraserburgh, 10,930 G 3
Friockheim, 807 F 4
Furnace, 220 C 4
Fyvie, 405 F 3
Gairloch, 125 C 3
Galashiels, 12,808 F 5
Galston, 4,256 D 5
Gardenstown, 892 F 3
Garelochhead, 1,552 A 1
Gargunnock, 457 B 1
Garlieston, 385 D 6
Garmouth, 352 E 3
Garrabost, 307 B 2
Gartmore, 253 B 1
Gatehouse-of-Fleet, 835 D 6
Giffnock, 10,987 B 2
Gifford, 575 F 5
Girvan, 7,597 D 5
Glamis, 190 F 4
Glasgow, 880,617 B 2
Glasgow, ★1,674,789 B 2
Glenbarr, ⊙691 C 5
Glencaple, 275 E 5
Glencoe, 195 C 4
Glenelg, ⊙1,468 C 3
Glenluce, 725 D 6
Glenrothes, 31,400 E 4
Golspie, 1,374 E 3
Gordon, 320 F 5
Gorebridge, 3,426 D 2
Gourock, 11,192 A 1
Grangemouth, 24,430 C 1
Grantown-on-Spey, 1,578 E 3
Greenlaw, 574 F 5
Greenock, 67,275 A 2
Gretna, 1,907 E 5
Gullane, 1,701 F 4
Haddington, 6,767 F 5
Halkirk, 679 E 2
Hamilton, 45,495 C 2
Hamnavoe, 307 G 2
Harthill, 4,712 C 2
Hatton, 315 G 3
Hawick, 16,484 F 5
Heathhall, 1,365 E 5
Helensburgh, 13,327 A 1
Helmsdale, 727 E 2
Hill of Fearn, 233 D 3
Hillside, 692 F 4
Hillswick, ⊙696 G 2
Hopeman, 1,248 E 3
Huntly, 4,078 F 3
Hurlford, 4,294 D 5
Inchnadamph, ⊙833 D 2
Innellan, 922 A 2
Innerleithen, 2,293 E 5
Insch, 881 F 3
Inveraray, 473 C 4
Inverbervie, 853 F 4
Invercassley, ⊙1,067 D 3
Invergordon, 2,385 D 3
Invergowrie, 1,389 E 4
Inverie, ⊙1,468 C 3
Inverkeithing, 6,102 D 1
Inverness, 35,801 D 3
Inverurie, 5,534 F 3
Irvine, 48,500 D 5
Isle of Whithorn, 222 D 6
Jedburgh, 3,953 F 5
John O'Groats, 195 E 2
Johnshaven, 544 F 4
Johnstone, 23,251 B 2
Kames, 230 C 5
Keiss, 344 E 2
Keith, 4,192 F 3
Kelso, 4,934 F 5
Kelty, 6,573 D 1
Kemnay, 1,042 F 3
Kenmore, 211 E 4
Kilbarchan, 2,669 A 2
Kilbirnie, 8,259 A 2
Kilchoan, ⊙764 B 4
Kildonan, ⊙1,105 E 2
Killearn, 1,086 B 1
Killin, 600 D 4
Kilmacolm, 3,348 A 2
Kilmarnock, 50,175 D 5
Kilmaurs, 2,518 D 5
Kilninver, ⊙247 C 4
Kilrenny and Anstruther, 2,951 F 4
Kilsyth, 10,210 B 1
Kilwinning, 8,460 D 5
Kinbrace, ⊙1,105 E 2
Kincardine, 3,278 C 1
Kinghorn, 2,163 D 1
Kingussie, 1,036 D 3
Kinlochewe, ⊙1,794 C 3
Kinlochleven, 1,243 D 4
Kinloch Rannoch, 241 D 4
Kinloss, 2,378 E 3
Kinross, 2,829 E 4
Kintore, 970 F 3
Kippen, 529 B 1
Kirkcaldy, 50,207 D 1
Kirkcolm, 346 C 6
Kirkconnel, 3,318 E 5
Kirkcowan, 354 D 6
Kirkcudbright, 2,690 E 6
Kirkhill, 210 D 3
Kirkintilloch, 26,664 B 2
Kirkmuirhill, 2,575 E 5
Kirkton of Glenisla, ⊙331 E 4
Kirkwall, 4,777 E 2
Kirriemuir, 4,295 E 4
Kyleakin, 268 C 3
Kyle of Lochalsh, 687 C 3
Kylestrome, ⊙745 D 2
Ladybank, 1,216 E 4
Laggan, 393 D 3
Lairg, 572 D 2
Lamlash, 613 C 5
Lanark, 8,842 E 5
Langholm, 2,509 E 5
Larbert, 4,922 C 1
Largs, 9,461 A 2
Larkhall, 15,926 E 5
Lauder, 639 F 5
Laurencekirk, 1,416 F 4

(continued)

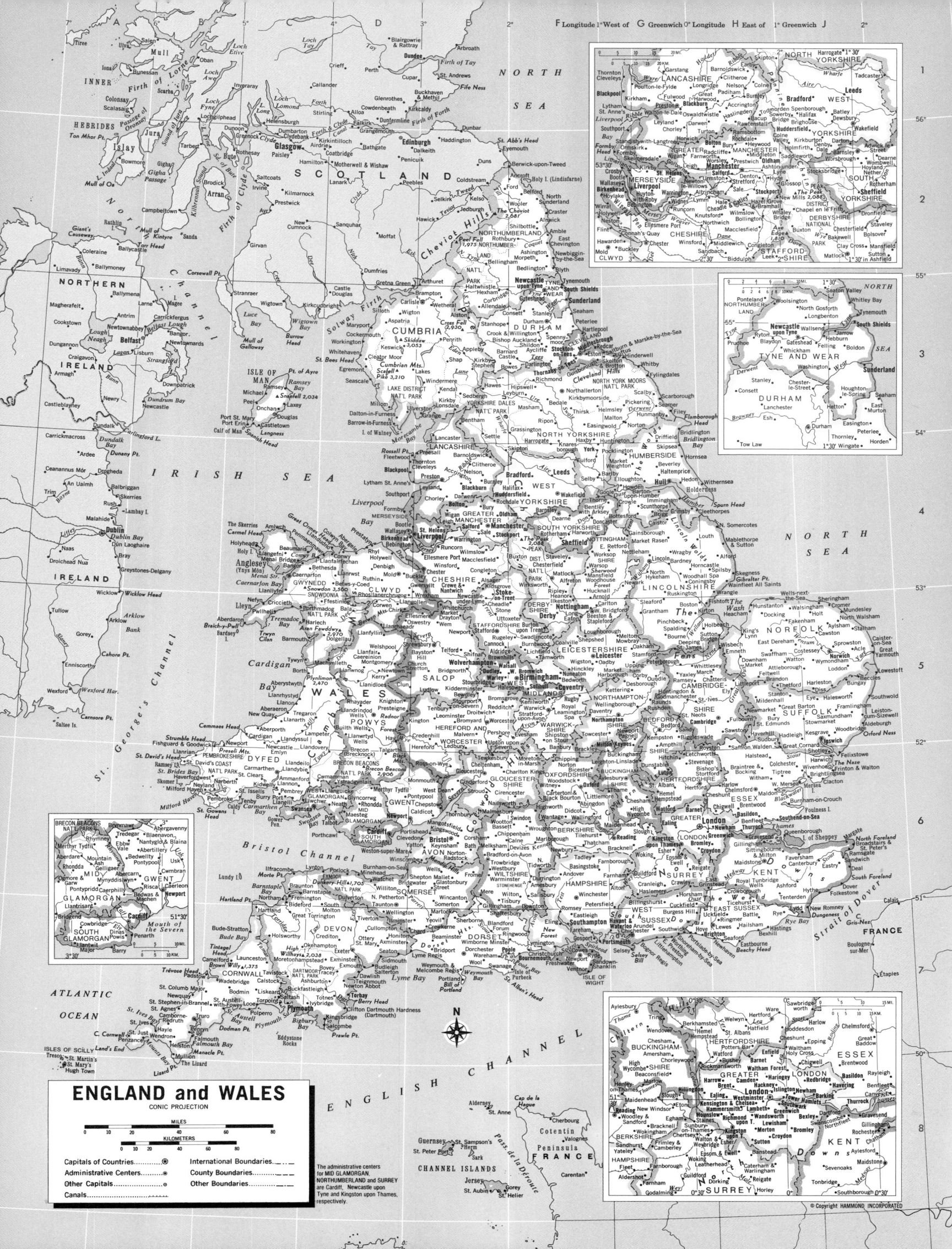

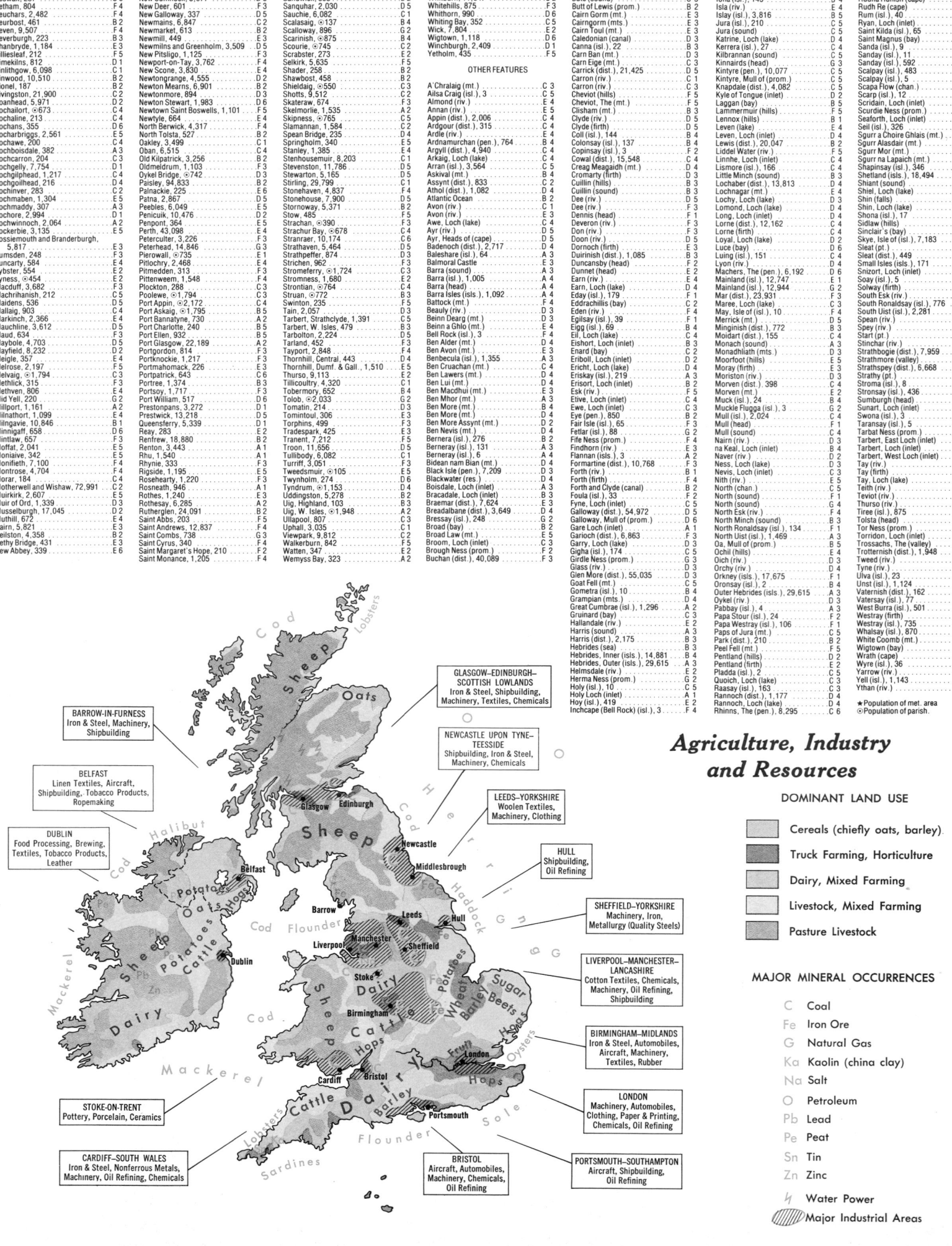

Agriculture, Industry and Resources

BARROW-IN-FURNESS
Iron & Steel, Machinery, Shipbuilding

BELFAST
Linen Textiles, Aircraft, Shipbuilding, Tobacco Products, Ropemaking

DUBLIN
Food Processing, Brewing, Textiles, Tobacco Products, Leather

GLASGOW–EDINBURGH–SCOTTISH LOWLANDS
Iron & Steel, Shipbuilding, Machinery, Textiles, Chemicals

NEWCASTLE UPON TYNE–TEESSIDE
Shipbuilding, Iron & Steel, Machinery, Chemicals

LEEDS–YORKSHIRE
Woolen Textiles, Machinery, Clothing

HULL
Shipbuilding, Oil Refining

SHEFFIELD–YORKSHIRE
Machinery, Iron, Metallurgy (Quality Steels)

LIVERPOOL–MANCHESTER–LANCASHIRE
Cotton Textiles, Chemicals, Machinery, Oil Refining, Shipbuilding

BIRMINGHAM–MIDLANDS
Iron & Steel, Automobiles, Aircraft, Machinery, Textiles, Rubber

LONDON
Machinery, Automobiles, Clothing, Paper & Printing, Chemicals, Oil Refining

STOKE-ON-TRENT
Pottery, Porcelain, Ceramics

CARDIFF–SOUTH WALES
Iron & Steel, Nonferrous Metals, Machinery, Oil Refining, Chemicals

BRISTOL
Aircraft, Automobiles, Machinery, Chemicals, Oil Refining

PORTSMOUTH–SOUTHAMPTON
Aircraft, Shipbuilding, Oil Refining

DOMINANT LAND USE

Cereals (chiefly oats, barley)
Truck Farming, Horticulture
Dairy, Mixed Farming
Livestock, Mixed Farming
Pasture Livestock

MAJOR MINERAL OCCURRENCES

C   Coal
Fe Iron Ore
G   Natural Gas
Ka Kaolin (china clay)
Na Salt
O   Petroleum
Pb Lead
Pe Peat
Sn Tin
Zn Zinc

Water Power
Major Industrial Areas

SCOTLAND

CONIC PROJECTION

MILES

KILOMETERS

Capital .... ⊛
Regional Centers .... ⊙
Canals ....

International Boundaries ....
Regional Boundaries ....
Other Boundaries ....

© Copyright HAMMOND INCORPORATED, Maplewood, N.J.

IRELAND

COUNTIES

Carlow, 34,237 . . . H 6
Cavan, 52,618 . . . G 4
Clare, 75,008 . . . D 6
Cork, 352,883 . . . D 7
Donegal, 108,344 . . . K 2
Dublin, 852,219 . . . J 5
Galway, 149,223 . . . D 5
Kerry, 112,772 . . . B 7
Kildare, 71,977 . . . H 5
Kilkenny, 61,473 . . . G 6
Laoighis, 45,259 . . . G 6
Leitrim, 28,360 . . . E 3
Leix (Laoighis), 45,259 . . . G 6
Limerick, 140,459 . . . D 7
Longford, 28,250 . . . F 4
Louth, 74,951 . . . J 4
Mayo, 109,525 . . . C 4
Meath, 71,729 . . . H 4
Monaghan, 46,242 . . . H 3
Offaly, 51,829 . . . F 5
Roscommon, 53,519 . . . E 4
Sligo, 50,275 . . . D 3
Tipperary, 123,565 . . . F 6
Waterford, 77,315 . . . F 7
Westmeath, 53,570 . . . G 5
Wexford, 86,351 . . . H 7
Wicklow, 66,295 . . . J 5

CITIES and TOWNS

Abbeydorney, 188 . . . B 7
Abbeyfeale, 1,337 . . . C 7
Abbeylara, ‡290 . . . F 4
Abbeyleix, 1,033 . . . G 6
Achill Sound, ‡1,163 . . . B 4
Aclare, ‡336 . . . D 3
Adare, 545 . . . D 6
Aghada-Farsid-Rostellan, 461 . . . E 8
Aghadoe, ‡497 . . . B 7
Aghagower, ‡693 . . . C 4
Ahascragh, 221 . . . E 5
Annagry, 201 . . . E 1
Annascaul, 236 . . . B 7
An Uaimh, 4,605 . . . H 4
An Uaimh, *6,665 . . . H 4
Ardagh, Limerick, 213 . . . C 7
Ardagh, Longford, ‡974 . . . F 4
Ardara, 683 . . . E 2
Ardee, *3,183 . . . H 4
Ardee, 3,096 . . . H 4
Ardfert, 286 . . . B 7
Ardfinnan, 510 . . . F 7
Ardmore, 233 . . . F 8
Ardrahan, ‡239 . . . D 5
Arklow, 6,948 . . . J 6
Arthurstown, 1,188 . . . H 7
Arva, 370 . . . F 4
Ashford, 341 . . . J 5
Askeaton, 844 . . . D 6
Athboy, 705 . . . H 4
Athea, 328 . . . C 7
Athenry, 1,240 . . . D 5
Athleague, ‡955 . . . E 4
Athlone, 9,825 . . . F 5
Athlone, *11,611 . . . F 5
Athy, 4,270 . . . H 6
Athy, *4,654 . . . H 6
Aughrim, 451 . . . J 6
Avoca, ‡620 . . . J 6
Bagenalstown (Muinebeag), 2,321 . . . H 6
Baile Átha Cliath (Dublin) (cap.), 567,866 . . . K 5
Bailieborough, 1,293 . . . G 4
Balbriggan, 3,741 . . . J 4
Balla, 293 . . . C 4
Ballaghaderreen, 1,121 . . . E 4
Ballina, Mayo, 6,063 . . . C 3
Ballina, *6,369 . . . C 3
Ballina, Tipperary, 336 . . . E 6
Ballinagh, 459 . . . G 4
Ballinakill, 300 . . . G 6
Ballineen . . . D 8
Ballinamore, 808 . . . F 3
Ballinasloe, 5,969 . . . E 5
Ballincollig-Carrigrohane, 2,110 . . . D 8
Ballindine, 232 . . . C 4
Ballingarry, Limerick, 422 . . . D 7
Ballingarry, Tipperary, ‡574 . . . F 6
Ballinlough, 242 . . . D 4
Ballinrobe, 1,272 . . . C 4
Ballintober, ‡867 . . . E 4
Ballintra, 197 . . . E 2
Ballisodare, 486 . . . E 3
Ballivor, 287 . . . H 4
Ballybay, 754 . . . G 3
Ballybay, *1,159 . . . G 3
Ballybofey-Stranorlar, 2,214 . . . F 2
Ballybunion, 1,287 . . . B 7
Ballycanew, ‡460 . . . J 6
Ballycarney, ‡294 . . . J 6
Ballycastle, ‡724 . . . C 3
Ballyconnell, 421 . . . F 3
Ballycotton, 389 . . . F 8
Ballydehob, 253 . . . C 8
Ballyduff, 406 . . . B 7
Ballygar, 359 . . . E 4
Ballygeary, 725 . . . J 7
Ballyhaise, 274 . . . G 3
Ballyhaunis, 1,093 . . . D 4
Ballyheigue, 450 . . . B 7
Ballyjamesduff, 673 . . . G 4
Ballylanders, 266 . . . E 7
Ballylongford, 504 . . . B 6
Ballymahon, 707 . . . F 4
Ballymakeery, 272 . . . C 8
Ballymore, ‡447 . . . F 5
Ballymore Eustace, 433 . . . J 5
Ballymote, 952 . . . D 3
Ballyporeen, ‡810 . . . E 7
Ballyragget, 519 . . . G 6
Ballyroan, ‡478 . . . G 6
Ballyshannon, 2,325 . . . E 3
Ballytore, ‡580 . . . H 5
Baltimore, 200 . . . C 9
Baltinglass, 909 . . . H 6
Baltray, 236 . . . J 4
Banagher, 1,052 . . . F 5
Bandon, 2,257 . . . D 8
Bandon, *4,071 . . . D 8
Bannow, ‡798 . . . H 7
Bansha, 184 . . . E 7
Bantry, 2,579 . . . C 8
Barna, ‡1,734 . . . C 5
Belmullet, 744 . . . B 3
Belturbet, 1,092 . . . G 3
Bennettsbridge, 367 . . . G 6
Birr, 3,319 . . . F 5
Birr, *3,881 . . . F 5
Blanchardstown, 3,279 . . . H 5
Blarney, 1,128 . . . D 8
Blessington, 637 . . . J 5
Boherbue, 372 . . . C 7
Borris, 430 . . . H 6
Borris-in-Ossory, 276 . . . F 6
Borrisokane, 769 . . . E 6
Borrisoleigh, 471 . . . E 6
Boyle, 1,727 . . . E 4
Boyle, *1,939 . . . E 4
Bray, 14,467 . . . K 5
Bray, *15,841 . . . K 5
Bri Chualann (Bray), 14,467 . . . K 5
Broadford, 226 . . . D 6
Brosna, 250 . . . C 7
Bruff, 547 . . . D 7
Bruree, 243 . . . D 7
Bunbeg-Derrybeg, 878 . . . E 1
Bunclody-Carrickduff, 929 . . . H 6
Buncrana, 2,955 . . . G 1
Buncrana, *3,334 . . . G 1
Bundoran, 1,337 . . . E 3
Burtonport, ‡1,288 . . . E 2
Buttevant, 1,045 . . . D 7
Cahir, 1,747 . . . F 7
Cahirciveen, 1,547 . . . A 8
Callan, 1,283 . . . G 7
Camolin, 306 . . . J 6
Campile, 231 . . . H 7
Cappamore, 567 . . . E 6
Cappawhite, 305 . . . E 6
Cappoquin, 872 . . . F 7
Carbury, ‡894 . . . H 5
Carlingford, 559 . . . J 3
Carlow, 9,588 . . . H 6
Carlow, *10,399 . . . H 6
Carndonagh, 1,146 . . . G 1
Carnew, 570 . . . H 6
Carrickmacross, 2,100 . . . H 4
Carrickmacross, *2,475 . . . H 4
Carrick-on-Shannon, 1,854 . . . F 4
Carrick-on-Suir, 5,006 . . . F 7
Carrigaholt, ‡493 . . . B 6
Carrigaline, 951 . . . E 8
Carrigallen, 230 . . . F 4
Carrigart, ‡753 . . . F 1
Carrigtwohill, 622 . . . E 8
Carrowkeel, ‡326 . . . G 1
Cashel, 2,692 . . . F 7
Castlebar, 5,979 . . . C 4
Castlebar, *6,476 . . . C 4
Castlebellingham, 407 . . . J 4
Castleblayney, 2,118 . . . H 3
Castleblayney, *2,395 . . . H 3
Castlecomer-Donaguile, 1,244 . . . G 6
Castledermot, 583 . . . H 6
Castlefin, 610 . . . F 2
Castlegregory, 216 . . . A 7
Castleisland, 1,929 . . . B 7
Castlemartyr, 491 . . . E 8
Castlepollard, 693 . . . G 4
Castlerea, 1,752 . . . D 4
Castletown, ‡504 . . . F 6
Castletownbere, 812 . . . B 8
Castletownroche, 399 . . . D 7
Castletownshend, 170 . . . C 9
Causeway, 215 . . . B 7
Cavan, 3,273 . . . G 3
Cavan, *4,312 . . . G 3
Ceanannus Mór, 2,391 . . . G 4
Ceanannus Mór, *2,653 . . . G 4
Celbridge, 1,568 . . . H 5
Charlestown-Bellahy, 677 . . . D 4
Charleville (Rathluirc), 2,232 . . . D 7
Clara, 2,156 . . . F 5
Claregalway, ‡594 . . . D 5
Claremorris, 1,718 . . . C 4
Clashmore, ‡379 . . . F 8
Clifden, 790 . . . B 5
Cloghan, 404 . . . F 5
Clogh-Chatsworth, 324 . . . G 6
Clogheen, 530 . . . F 7
Clogherhead, 649 . . . J 4
Clonakilty, 2,430 . . . D 8
Clonaslee, 285 . . . F 5
Clondalkin, 7,009 . . . J 5
Clonegal, 202 . . . H 6
Clones, 2,164 . . . G 3
Clonfert, ‡430 . . . E 5
Clonmany, ‡936 . . . G 1
Clonmel, 11,622 . . . F 7
Clonmel, *12,291 . . . F 7
Clonmellon, 328 . . . H 4
Clonroche, 222 . . . H 7
Clontuskert, 351 . . . E 4
Cloone, ‡460 . . . F 4
Cloughjordan, 480 . . . E 6
Cloyne, 654 . . . E 8
Coachford, 290 . . . D 8
Cóbh, 6,076 . . . E 8
Cóbh, *7,141 . . . E 8
Coill Dubh, 920 . . . H 5
Collon, 262 . . . J 4
Collooney, 546 . . . E 3
Cong, 233 . . . C 4
Convoy, 654 . . . F 2
Coolaney, ‡352 . . . D 3
Coolgreany, ‡603 . . . J 6
Cootehill, 1,415 . . . G 3
Cootehill, *1,542 . . . G 3
Cork, 128,645 . . . E 8
Cork, *134,430 . . . E 8
Corofin, 342 . . . C 6
Courtmacsherry, 210 . . . D 8
Courtown Harbour, 291 . . . J 6
Creeslough, 269 . . . F 1
Crookhaven, ‡400 . . . B 9
Croom, 756 . . . D 6
Crosshaven, 1,222 . . . E 8
Crossmolina, 1,077 . . . C 3
Crusheen, ‡405 . . . D 6
Culdaff, ‡621 . . . G 1
Daingean, 492 . . . G 5
Delvin, 223 . . . G 4
Dingle, 1,401 . . . A 7
Doaghbeg, ‡701 . . . F 1
Donabate, 426 . . . J 5
Donegal, 1,725 . . . E 2
Doneraile, 799 . . . D 7
Dooagh-Keel, 649 . . . A 4
Doon, 387 . . . E 6
Douglas, ‡4,448 . . . D 8
Drimoleague, 415 . . . C 8
Drishane, ‡1,548 . . . C 7
Drogheda, 19,762 . . . J 4
Drogheda, *20,095 . . . J 4
Droichead Nua, 5,053 . . . H 5
Droichead Nua, *6,444 . . . H 5
Dromahair, 177 . . . E 3
Drumcar, ‡1,215 . . . J 4
Drumconrath, ‡1,044 . . . H 4
Drumkeerin, ‡467 . . . E 3
Drumlish, 205 . . . F 4
Drumshanbo, 576 . . . E 3
Dublin (cap.), 567,866 . . . K 5
Dublin, *679,748 . . . K 5
Duleek, 658 . . . J 4
Duncannon, 228 . . . H 7
Dundalk, 21,672 . . . H 3
Dundalk, *23,816 . . . H 3
Dunfanaghy, 303 . . . F 1
Dungarvan, 5,583 . . . F 7
Dungloe, 940 . . . E 2
Dunkineely, 288 . . . E 2
Dún Laoghaire, 53,171 . . . K 5
Dún Laoghaire, *98,379 . . . K 5
Dunlavin, 423 . . . H 5
Dunleer, 855 . . . J 4
Dunmanway, 1,392 . . . C 8
Dunmore, 522 . . . D 4
Dunmore East, 656 . . . G 7
Dunshaughlin, ‡283 . . . H 5
Durrow, Laoighis, 596 . . . G 6
Durrow, Offaly, ‡441 . . . F 5
Easky, 184 . . . D 3
Edenderry, 2,953 . . . G 5
Edenderry, *3,116 . . . G 5
Elphin, 489 . . . E 4
Emyvale, 281 . . . G 3
Ennis, 5,972 . . . D 6
Ennis, *10,840 . . . D 6
Enniscorthy, 5,704 . . . J 7
Enniscorthy, *6,642 . . . J 7
Enniskerry, 772 . . . J 5
Ennistymon, 1,013 . . . C 6
Eyrecourt, 314 . . . E 5
Fahan, ‡1,023 . . . G 1
Falcarragh, 506 . . . E 1
Feakle, ‡398 . . . D 6
Fenit, 360 . . . B 7
Ferbane, 1,064 . . . F 5
Fermoy, 3,237 . . . E 7
Fermoy, *4,033 . . . E 7
Ferns, 712 . . . J 6
Fethard, Tipperary, 1,064 . . . F 7
Fethard, Wexford, ‡637 . . . H 7
Foxford, 868 . . . C 4
Foynes, 624 . . . C 6
Frankford (Kilcormac), 1,089 . . . F 5
Frenchpark, ‡693 . . . E 4
Freshford, 585 . . . G 6
Galbally, 258 . . . E 7
Galway, 27,726 . . . C 5
Galway, *29,375 . . . C 5
Geashill, ‡751 . . . G 5
Glandore, ‡695 . . . C 8
Glanmire-Riverstown, 1,113 . . . E 8
Glanworth, 335 . . . E 7
Glenamaddy, 315 . . . D 4
Glenbeigh, 266 . . . B 7
Glencolumbkille, ‡787 . . . D 2
Glengarriff, 244 . . . C 8
Glenties, 734 . . . E 2
Glenville, ‡264 . . . D 7
Glin, 623 . . . C 6
Golden, ‡640 . . . F 7
Gorey, 2,946 . . . J 6
Gorey, *3,024 . . . J 6
Gormanston, ‡1,384 . . . J 4
Gort, 975 . . . D 5
Gowran, 402 . . . G 6
Graiguenamanagh-Tinnahinch, 1,303 . . . H 6
Granard, 1,054 . . . F 4
Greencastle, 322 . . . H 1
Greenore, 882 . . . J 4
Greystones-Delgany, 4,517 . . . K 5
Gurteen, 165 . . . D 3
Hackettstown, 574 . . . H 6
Headford, 673 . . . C 5
Holycross, ‡902 . . . F 6
Hospital, 525 . . . E 7
Inchigeelagh, ‡516 . . . C 8
Inishannon, 190 . . . D 8
Inistioge, 179 . . . G 7
Inniscrone, 582 . . . C 3
Johnstown, 303 . . . G 6
Kanturk, 2,063 . . . D 7
Keel-Dooagh, 649 . . . A 4
Kells, ‡423 . . . G 6
Kells (Ceanannus Mór), 2,391 . . . G 4
Kenmare, 903 . . . B 8
Kilbaha, ‡471 . . . B 6
Kilbeggan, 635 . . . G 5
Kilcar, 273 . . . D 2
Kilcock, 827 . . . H 5
Kilconnell, ‡629 . . . E 5
Kilcoole, 679 . . . K 5
Kilcormac, 1,089 . . . F 5
Kilcullen, 880 . . . H 5
Kildare, 3,137 . . . H 5
Kildysart, 239 . . . C 6
Kilfenora, ‡441 . . . C 6
Kilfinane, 561 . . . D 7
Kilgarvan, 228 . . . B 8
Kilkee, 1,287 . . . B 6
Kilkelly, 225 . . . D 4
Kilkenny, 9,838 . . . G 6
Kilkenny, *13,306 . . . G 6
Killala, 368 . . . C 3
Killaloe, 871 . . . D 6
Killarney, 7,184 . . . C 7
Killarney, *7,541 . . . C 7
Killavullen, 221 . . . D 7
Killenaule, 592 . . . F 6
Killeshandra, 432 . . . F 3
Killimor, 221 . . . E 5
Killinaboy, ‡297 . . . C 6
Killorglin, 1,150 . . . B 7
Killucan-Rathwire, 290 . . . G 4
Killybegs, 1,094 . . . E 2
Kilmacrennan, 274 . . . F 1
Kilmacthomas, 396 . . . G 7
Kilmallock, 1,170 . . . D 7
Kilmeadan, ‡262 . . . G 7
Kilmihill, 284 . . . C 6
Kilmoganny, 181 . . . G 7
Kilmore Quay, 273 . . . H 7
Kilmurry, ‡387 . . . C 6
Kilnaleck, 273 . . . G 4
Kilronan, 243 . . . B 5
Kilrush, 2,671 . . . C 6
Kilsheelan, ‡665 . . . F 7
Kiltimagh, 978 . . . C 4
Kilworth, 360 . . . E 7
Kingscourt, 1,016 . . . H 4
Kingstown (Dún Laoghaire), 53,171 . . . K 5
Kinlough, 160 . . . E 3
Kinnegad, 362 . . . G 5
Kinnitty, ‡420 . . . F 5
Kinsale, 1,622 . . . D 8
Kinsale, *1,989 . . . D 8
Kinvara, 293 . . . D 5
Knightstown, 236 . . . A 8
Knock, ‡1,202 . . . D 4
Knocklong, 248 . . . D 7
Knocknagashel, 168 . . . C 7
Labasheeda, ‡468 . . . C 6
Laghey, ‡625 . . . E 2
Lahinch, 455 . . . C 6
Lanesborough-Ballyleague, 906 . . . E 4
Laracor, ‡404 . . . H 4
Laytown-Bettystown-Mornington, 1,882 . . . J 4
Leenane, ‡271 . . . B 4
Leighlinbridge, 379 . . . H 6
Leitrim, ‡544 . . . F 3
Leixlip, 2,402 . . . H 5
Letterkenny, 4,930 . . . F 2
Letterkenny, *5,207 . . . F 2
Lifford, 1,121 . . . F 2
Limerick, 57,161 . . . D 6
Limerick, *63,002 . . . D 6
Liscarroll, 231 . . . D 7
Lisdoonvarna, 459 . . . C 5
Lismore, 884 . . . F 7
Lismore, *1,041 . . . F 7
Listowel, 3,021 . . . C 7
Littleton, 322 . . . F 6
Longford, 3,876 . . . F 4
Longford, *4,791 . . . F 4
Lorrha, ‡685 . . . E 5
Loughrea, 3,075 . . . E 5
Louisburgh, 310 . . . B 4
Louth, 208 . . . J 4
Lucan-Doddsborough, 4,245 . . . J 5
Luimneach (Limerick), 57,161 . . . D 6
Lusk, 553 . . . J 4
Macroom, 2,256 . . . C 8
Malahide, 3,834 . . . J 5
Malin, ‡552 . . . G 1
Mallow, 5,901 . . . D 7
Mallow, *6,506 . . . D 7
Manorhamilton, 858 . . . E 3
Manulla, ‡660 . . . C 4
Maryborough (Portlaoighise), 3,902 . . . G 5
Maynooth, 1,296 . . . H 5
Meathas Truim, 546 . . . G 4
Midleton, 3,075 . . . E 8
Midleton, *4,666 . . . E 8
Milford, 763 . . . F 1
Millstreet, 1,319 . . . D 7
Milltown, 260 . . . A 7
Miltown-Malbay, 677 . . . C 6
Minard, ‡397 . . . A 7
Mitchelstown, 2,783 . . . E 7
Moate, 1,378 . . . F 5
Mohill, 868 . . . F 4
Monaghan, 5,256 . . . G 3
Monasterevan, 1,619 . . . H 5
Moneygall, 282 . . . F 6
Monivea, ‡405 . . . D 5
Mooncoin, 413 . . . G 7
Mount Bellew, 275 . . . D 5
Mountcharles, 445 . . . E 2
Mountmellick, 2,595 . . . G 5
Mountmellick, *2,864 . . . G 5
Mountrath, 1,098 . . . F 5
Moville, 1,089 . . . G 1
Moycullen, ‡498 . . . C 5
Moynalty, ‡583 . . . H 4
Muff, 240 . . . G 1
Muinebeag, 2,321 . . . H 6
Mullagh, 293 . . . H 4
Mullaghmore, ‡629 . . . E 3
Mullinahone, 262 . . . F 7
Mullinavat, 343 . . . G 7
Mullingar, 6,790 . . . G 4
Mullingar, *9,245 . . . G 4
Naas, 5,078 . . . H 5
Navan (An Uaimh), 4,605 . . . H 4
Nenagh, 5,085 . . . E 6
Nenagh, *5,174 . . . E 6
Newbliss, ‡547 . . . G 3
Newbridge (Droichead Nua), 5,053 . . . H 5
Newcastle, 2,549 . . . D 7
Newcastle, *2,680 . . . D 7
Newmarket, 886 . . . C 7
Newmarket-on-Fergus, 1,052 . . . D 6
New Pallas, ‡1,271 . . . E 6
Newport, Mayo, 420 . . . C 4
Newport, Tipperary, 582 . . . E 6
New Ross, 4,775 . . . H 7
New Ross, *5,153 . . . H 7
Newtownforbes, ‡495 . . . F 4
Newtownmountkennedy, 882 . . . J 5
Newtownsandes, 268 . . . C 6
O'Briensbridge-Montpelier, 237 . . . D 6
Oldcastle, 759 . . . G 4
Old Leighlin, ‡309 . . . G 6
Oola, 348 . . . E 6
Oranmore, 440 . . . D 5
Oughterard, 628 . . . C 5
Passage East, 408 . . . G 7
Passage West, 2,709 . . . E 8
Patrickswell, 415 . . . D 6
Pettigo, 332 . . . F 2
Piltown, 456 . . . G 7
Portarlington, 3,117 . . . G 5
Portlaoighise, 3,902 . . . G 5
Portlaoighise, *6,470 . . . G 5
Portlaw, 1,166 . . . G 7
Portmarnock, 1,726 . . . J 5
Portumna, 913 . . . E 5
Queenstown (Cobh), 6,076 . . . E 8
Rahan, ‡531 . . . F 5
Ramelton, 807 . . . F 1
Raphoe, 945 . . . F 2
Rathangan, 868 . . . G 5
Rathcoole, 1,740 . . . J 5
Rathcormac, 191 . . . E 7
Rathdowney, 892 . . . F 6
Rathdrum, 1,141 . . . J 6
Rathgormuck, ‡231 . . . F 7
Rathkeale, 1,543 . . . D 7
Rathluirc, 2,232 . . . D 7
Rathmore, 437 . . . J 5
Rathmullen, 486 . . . F 1
Rathnew-Merrymeeting, 954 . . . J 6
Rathowen, ‡294 . . . F 4
Rathvilly, 230 . . . H 6
Ratoath, 300 . . . J 5
Riverstown, 236 . . . E 3
Rockcorry, 233 . . . H 3
Rosapenna, ‡822 . . . F 1
Roscommon, 1,556 . . . E 4
Roscommon, *2,821 . . . E 4
Roscrea, 3,855 . . . F 6
Rosscarbery, 309 . . . C 8
Rosses Point, 464 . . . D 3
Rosslare, 588 . . . J 7
Rosslare Harbour (Ballygeary), 725 . . . J 7
Roundstone, 204 . . . A 5
Roundwood, 260 . . . J 5
Rush, 2,633 . . . J 4
Saint Johnston, 463 . . . F 2
Scarriff, 619 . . . E 6
Schull, 457 . . . B 8
Scotstown, 264 . . . H 3
Shanagolden, 231 . . . C 6
Shannon Airport, 3,657 . . . D 6
Shannon Bridge, 188 . . . F 5
Shercock, 313 . . . G 4
Shillelagh, 246 . . . J 6
Shinrone, 365 . . . F 5
Shrule, 288 . . . C 4
Sixmilebridge, 567 . . . D 6
Skerries, 3,044 . . . J 4
Skibbereen, 2,104 . . . C 8
Slane, 483 . . . H 4
Sligo, 14,080 . . . E 3
Sligo, *14,456 . . . E 3
Sneem, 285 . . . B 8
Spiddal, ‡819 . . . C 5
Stepaside, 748 . . . J 5
Stradbally, Laoighis, 891 . . . G 5
Stradbally, Waterford, 158 . . . F 7
Strokestown, 563 . . . E 4
Swanlinbar, 257 . . . F 3
Swinford, 1,105 . . . C 4
Swords, 4,133 . . . J 5
Taghmon, 369 . . . H 7
Tallaght, 6,174 . . . J 5
Tallow, 883 . . . F 7
Tarbert, 485 . . . C 6
Teltown, ‡739 . . . H 4
Templemore, 2,174 . . . F 6
Templetuohy, 197 . . . F 6
Termonfeckin, 328 . . . J 4
Thomastown, 1,270 . . . G 7
Thurles, 6,840 . . . F 6
Thurles, *7,087 . . . F 6
Timoleague, 257 . . . D 8
Tinahely, 450 . . . H 6
Tipperary, 4,631 . . . E 7
Tipperary, *4,717 . . . E 7
Toomevara, 272 . . . E 6
Tralee, 12,287 . . . B 7
Tralee, *13,263 . . . B 7
Tramore, 3,792 . . . G 7
Trim, 1,700 . . . H 4
Trim, *2,255 . . . H 4
Tuam, 3,808 . . . D 4
Tuam, *4,952 . . . D 4
Tubbercurry, 959 . . . D 3
Tulla, 415 . . . D 6
Tullamore, 6,809 . . . G 5
Tullamore, *7,474 . . . G 5
Tullaroan, ‡301 . . . G 6
Tullow, 1,838 . . . H 6
Tullow, *1,945 . . . H 6
Tynagh, ‡452 . . . E 5
Tyrrellspass, 289 . . . G 5
Urlingford, 652 . . . F 6
Virginia, 583 . . . G 4
Waterford, 31,968 . . . G 7
Waterford, *33,676 . . . G 7
Waterville, 547 . . . A 8
Westport, 3,023 . . . C 4
Wexford, 11,849 . . . H 7
Wexford, *13,293 . . . H 7
Whitegate, 370 . . . E 8
Wicklow, 3,786 . . . K 6
Wicklow, *3,915 . . . K 6
Woodenbridge, ‡620 . . . J 6
Woodford, 198 . . . E 5
Youghal, 5,445 . . . F 8
Youghal, *5,626 . . . F 8

OTHER FEATURES

Achill (isl.), 3,129 . . . A 4
Allen (lake) . . . E 3
Allen, Bog of (marsh) . . . H 5
Aran (isl.), 773 . . . D 2
Aran (isls.), 1,499 . . . B 5
Arklow (bank) . . . K 6
Arrow (lake) . . . E 3
Awbeg (riv.) . . . D 7
Ballinskelligs (bay) . . . A 8
Ballycotton (bay) . . . F 8
Ballyheige (bay) . . . B 7
Ballyhoura (hills) . . . E 7
Ballyteige (bay) . . . H 7
Bandon (riv.) . . . D 8
Bann (riv.) . . . J 6
Bantry (bay) . . . B 8
Barrow (riv.) . . . H 7
Baurtregaum (mt.) . . . B 7
Bear (isl.), 288 . . . B 8
Blacksod (bay) . . . A 3
Blackstairs (mt.) . . . H 6
Blackwater (riv.) . . . D 7
Blackwater (riv.) . . . H 4
Blasket (isls.) . . . A 7
Bloody Foreland (prom.) . . . E 1
Blue Stack (mts.) . . . E 2
Boderg (lake) . . . E 4
Boggeragh (mts.) . . . D 7
Boyne (riv.) . . . J 4
Brandon (head) . . . A 7
Bride (riv.) . . . E 7
Broad Haven (harb.) . . . B 3
Brosna (riv.) . . . F 5
Bull, The (isl.), 5 . . . A 8
Caha (mts.) . . . B 8
Carlingford (inlet) . . . J 3
Carnsore (pt.) . . . J 7
Carrantuohill (mt.) . . . B 7
Clare (riv.) . . . D 5
Clare (isls.), 168 . . . A 4
Clear (cape) . . . B 9
Clear (isl.), 192 . . . C 9
Clew (bay) . . . B 4
Comeragh (mts.) . . . F 7
Conn (lake) . . . C 3
Connacht (prov.), 390,902 . . . C 4
Connemara (dist.), 7,599 . . . B 5
Cork (harb.) . . . E 8
Corrib (lake) . . . C 5
Courtmacsherry (bay) . . . D 8
Curragh, The . . . H 5
Dee (riv.) . . . H 4
Deel (riv.) . . . D 7
Deele (riv.) . . . F 2
Derg (lake) . . . E 6
Derravaragh (lake) . . . G 4
Derryveagh (mts.) . . . E 2
Dingle (bay) . . . A 7
Donegal (bay) . . . D 3
Drum (hills) . . . F 7
Dublin (bay) . . . J 5
Dundalk (bay) . . . J 4
Dunmanus (bay) . . . B 8
Dursey (isl.), 38 . . . A 8
Ennell (lake) . . . G 5
Erne (riv.) . . . E 3
Errigal (mt.) . . . E 1
Erris (head) . . . A 3
Fanad (head) . . . F 1
Fastnet Rock (isl.), 3 . . . B 9
Feale (riv.) . . . C 7
Fergus (riv.) . . . D 6
Finn (riv.) . . . F 2
Finn (riv.) . . . G 3
Flesk (riv.) . . . C 7
Foyle (inlet) . . . G 1
Foyle (riv.) . . . G 2
Galley (head) . . . D 9
Galtee (mts.) . . . E 7
Galtymore (mt.) . . . E 7
Galway (bay) . . . C 5
Gara (lake) . . . D 4
Garadice (lake) . . . F 3
Gill (lake) . . . E 3
Glyde (riv.) . . . H 4
Golden Vale (plain) . . . E 7
Gorumna (isl.), 1,108 . . . B 5
Gowna (lake) . . . G 4
Grand (canal) . . . G 5
Greenore (pt.) . . . J 7
Gweebarra (bay) . . . D 2
Hags (head) . . . B 6
Helvick (head) . . . G 7
Hook (head) . . . H 7
Horn (head) . . . E 1
Iar Connacht (dist.), 10,774 . . . C 5
Inishbofin (isl.), 236 . . . A 4
Inishbofin (isl.), 103 . . . E 1
Inisheer (isl.), 313 . . . B 5
Inishmaan (isl.), 319 . . . C 5
Inishmore (isl.), 864 . . . B 5
Inishowen (head) . . . H 1
Inishowen (pen.), 24,109 . . . G 1
Inishtrahull (isl.), 3 . . . G 1
Inishturk (isls.), 83 . . . A 4
Inny (riv.) . . . A 8
Inny (riv.) . . . F 4
Inver (bay) . . . E 2
Ireland's Eye (isl.) . . . K 5
Irish (sea) . . . K 4
Joyce's Country (dist.), 2,021 . . . B 4
Kenmare (riv.) . . . A 8
Kerry (head) . . . A 7
Key (lake) . . . E 3
Kilkieran (bay) . . . B 5
Killala (bay) . . . C 3
Killary (harb.) . . . A 4
Kinsale (harb.) . . . E 8
Kippure (mt.) . . . J 5
Knockboy (mt.) . . . B 8
Knockmealdown (mts.) . . . E 7
Lady's Island Lake (inlet) . . . J 7
Lambay (isl.), 24 . . . K 4
Laune (riv.) . . . B 7
Leane (lake) . . . B 7
Leane (lake) . . . G 4
Lee (riv.) . . . D 8
Leinster (mt.) . . . H 6
Leinster (prov.), 1,498,140 . . . G 5
Lettermullan (isl.), 221 . . . B 5
Liffey (riv.) . . . H 5
Liscannor (bay) . . . B 6
Long Island (bay) . . . B 9
Loop (head) . . . A 6
Lugnaquillia (mt.) . . . J 5
Macgillicuddy's Reeks (mts.) . . . B 7
Macnean (lake) . . . F 3
Maigue (riv.) . . . D 6
Maine (riv.) . . . C 7
Malin (head) . . . F 1
Mask (lake) . . . C 4
Maumturk (mts.) . . . B 5
Melvin (lake) . . . E 3
Mizen (head) . . . B 9
Moher (cliffs) . . . B 6
Monavullagh (mts.) . . . F 7
Moy (riv.) . . . C 3
Mulkear (riv.) . . . E 6
Mullaghareirk (mts.) . . . C 7
Mulroy (bay) . . . F 1
Munster (prov.), 882,002 . . . D 7
Mweelrea (mt.) . . . B 4
Mweenish (isl.), 198 . . . B 5
Nagles (mts.) . . . E 7
Nenagh (riv.) . . . E 6
Nephin (mt.) . . . C 3
Nore (riv.) . . . G 7
North (sound) . . . B 5
Omey (isl.), 34 . . . A 5
Oughter (lake) . . . G 3
Ovoca (riv.) . . . J 6
Owenmore (riv.) . . . D 3
Owey (isl.), 51 . . . D 1
Paps, The (mt.) . . . C 7
Partry (mts.) . . . C 4
Pollaphuca (res.) . . . J 5
Punchestown . . . H 5
Rathlin O'Birne (isl.), 3 . . . C 2
Ree (lake) . . . F 4
Roaringwater (bay) . . . B 9
Rosses (bay) . . . D 1
Rosskeeragh (pt.) . . . D 3
Royal (canal) . . . G 4
Saint Finan's (bay) . . . A 8
Saint George's (chan.) . . . K 7
Saint John's (pt.) . . . D 2
Saltee (isls.) . . . H 7
Seven (heads) . . . D 8
Seven Hogs, The (isls.) . . . A 7
Shannon (riv.) . . . C 6
Sheeffry (hills) . . . B 4
Sheelin (lake) . . . G 4
Sheep Haven (harb.) . . . F 1
Sheeps (head) . . . B 8
Sherkin (isl.), 82 . . . C 9
Silvermine (mts.) . . . E 6
Slaney (riv.) . . . H 7
Slieve Aughty (mts.) . . . D 5
Slieve Bloom (mts.) . . . F 5
Slieve Gamph (mts.) . . . D 3
Slievenaman (mt.) . . . F 7
Sligo (bay) . . . D 3
Slyne (head) . . . A 5
South (sound) . . . B 5
Stacks (mts.) . . . B 7
Suck (riv.) . . . E 5
Suir (riv.) . . . G 7
Swilly (inlet) . . . F 1
Tara (hill) . . . H 4
Tory (isl.), 273 . . . E 1
Tory (sound) . . . E 1
Tralee (bay) . . . B 7
Trawbreaga (bay) . . . F 1
Ulster (part) (prov.), 207,204 . . . G 2
Valencia (Valentia) (isl.), 770 . . . A 8
Valentia (isl.), 770 . . . A 8
Waterford (harb.) . . . G 7
Wexford (bay) . . . J 7
Wicklow (head) . . . K 6
Wicklow (mts.) . . . J 5
Youghal (bay) . . . F 8

NORTHERN IRELAND

COUNTIES

Antrim, 37,600 . . . J 2
Ards, 52,100 . . . K 2
Armagh, 47,500 . . . H 3
Ballymena, 52,200 . . . J 2
Ballymoney, 22,700 . . . J 1
Banbridge, 28,800 . . . J 3
Belfast, 368,200 . . . J 2
Carrickfergus, 27,500 . . . K 2
Castlereagh, 63,600 . . . K 2
Coleraine, 44,900 . . . H 1
Cookstown, 27,500 . . . H 2
Craigavon, 71,200 . . . J 3
Down, 48,800 . . . K 3
Dungannon, 43,000 . . . H 3
Fermanagh, 50,900 . . . F 3
Larne, 29,000 . . . K 2
Limavady, 25,000 . . . H 1
Lisburn, 80,800 . . . J 2
Londonderry, 86,600 . . . G 2
Magherafelt, 32,200 . . . H 2
Mourne (Newry and Mourne), 75,300 . . . J 3
Moyle, 13,400 . . . J 1
Newtownabbey, 71,500 . . . J 2
North Down, 59,600 . . . K 2
Omagh, 41,800 . . . G 2
Strabane, 35,500 . . . G 2

CITIES and TOWNS

Ahoghill, ‡1,929 . . . J 2
Annalong, 1,001 . . . K 3
Antrim, 8,351 . . . J 2
Ardglass, 1,052 . . . K 3
Armagh, 13,606 . . . H 3
Armoy, ‡1,051 . . . J 1
Augher, ‡1,986 . . . G 3
Aughnacloy, ‡1,885 . . . H 3
Ballycastle, 2,899 . . . J 1
Ballyclare, 5,155 . . . J 2
Ballygawley, ‡2,165 . . . G 3
Ballykelly, 1,116 . . . G 1
Ballymena, 23,386 . . . J 2
Ballymoney, 5,697 . . . J 1
Ballynahinch, 3,485 . . . J 3
Banbridge, 7,968 . . . J 3
Bangor, 35,260 . . . K 2
Belfast (cap.), 353,700 . . . J 2
Belfast, *551,940 . . . J 2
Bellaghy, ‡2,265 . . . H 2
Belleek, ‡2,487 . . . E 3
Beragh, ‡2,137 . . . G 2
Bessbrook, 2,619 . . . J 3
Brookeborough, ‡2,534 . . . G 3
Broughshane, 1,288 . . . J 2
Bushmills, 1,288 . . . J 1
Caledon, ‡1,828 . . . H 3
Carnlough, 1,416 . . . J 2
Carrickfergus, 16,603 . . . K 2
Carrowdore, 2,548 . . . K 2
Castledawson, 1,162 . . . H 2
Castlederg, 1,766 . . . F 2
Castlewellan, 1,488 . . . K 3
Claudy, ‡2,507 . . . G 2
Clogher, ‡1,888 . . . G 3
Coalisland, 3,614 . . . H 2
Coleraine, 16,354 . . . H 1
Comber, 5,575 . . . K 2
Cookstown, 6,965 . . . H 2
Craigavon, 12,740 . . . J 3
Crossgar, 1,098 . . . K 3
Crossmaglen, 1,085 . . . H 3
Crumlin, 1,450 . . . J 2
Cullybackey, 1,649 . . . J 2
Derrygonnelly, ‡2,539 . . . F 3
Dervock, ‡1,191 . . . J 1
Donaghadee, 4,008 . . . K 2
Downpatrick, 7,918 . . . K 3
Draperstown, ‡2,247 . . . H 2
Dromore, Banbridge, 2,848 . . . J 3
Dromore, Omagh, ‡2,224 . . . G 3
Drumquin, ‡1,982 . . . F 2
Dundrum, ‡2,249 . . . K 3
Dungannon, 8,190 . . . H 3
Dungiven, 1,536 . . . H 2
Dunnamanagh, ‡2,242 . . . G 2
Ederny and Kesh, ‡2,497 . . . F 2
Enniskillen, 9,679 . . . F 3
Feeny, ‡1,459 . . . H 2
Fintona, 1,190 . . . G 3
Fivemiletown, ‡1,649 . . . G 3
Garvagh, ‡2,363 . . . H 2
Gilford, 1,592 . . . J 3
Glenarm, ‡1,728 . . . J 2
Glenavy, ‡2,360 . . . J 2
Glynn, ‡1,872 . . . K 2
Gortin, ‡2,033 . . . G 2
Greyabbey, ‡2,646 . . . K 2
Hillsborough, 1,021 . . . J 3
Holywood, 9,892 . . . K 2
Irvinestown, 1,457 . . . F 3
Keady, 2,145 . . . H 3
Kells, ‡2,560 . . . J 2
Kesh, ‡2,497 . . . F 3
Kilkeel, 4,090 . . . K 3
Killough, ‡3,295 . . . K 3
Killyleagh, 2,359 . . . K 3
Kilrea, 1,196 . . . H 2
Kircubbin, 1,075 . . . K 3
Larne, 18,482 . . . K 2
Limavady, 6,004 . . . H 1
Lisburn, 31,836 . . . J 2
Lisnaskea, 1,443 . . . G 3
Londonderry, 51,200 . . . G 2
Loughbrickland, ‡2,056 . . . J 3
Maghera, 2,085 . . . H 2
Magherafelt, 4,704 . . . H 2
Markethill, ‡2,352 . . . H 3
Millisle, 1,172 . . . K 2
Moneymore, 1,178 . . . H 2
Moy, ‡2,349 . . . H 3
Moygashel, 1,086 . . . H 3
Newcastle, 4,647 . . . J 3
Newry, 20,279 . . . J 3
Newtownabbey, 58,114 . . . K 2
Newtownards, 15,484 . . . K 2
Newtownbutler, ‡2,663 . . . G 3
Newtownhamilton, ‡1,936 . . . H 3
Newtownstewart, 1,433 . . . G 2
Omagh, 14,594 . . . G 2
Pomeroy, ‡1,786 . . . H 2
Portaferry, 1,730 . . . K 3
Portavogie, 1,310 . . . K 3
Portglenone, ‡2,061 . . . H 2
Portrush, 5,376 . . . H 1
Portstewart, 5,085 . . . H 1
Randalstown, 2,799 . . . J 2
Rathfriland, 1,886 . . . J 3
Rostrevor, 1,617 . . . J 3
Saintfield, ‡2,198 . . . K 3
Sion Mills, 1,588 . . . G 2
Sixmilecross, ‡1,980 . . . G 2
Stewartstown, ‡1,759 . . . H 2
Strabane, 9,413 . . . G 2
Strangford, ‡1,987 . . . K 3
Tandragee, 1,725 . . . J 3
Tempo, ‡2,282 . . . G 3
Trillick, ‡2,167 . . . G 3
Warrenpoint, 4,291 . . . J 3
Whitehead, 2,642 . . . K 2

OTHER FEATURES

Bann (riv.) . . . H 2
Belfast (inlet) . . . K 2
Blackwater (riv.) . . . H 3
Bush (riv.) . . . H 1
Derg (riv.) . . . F 2
Divis (mt.) . . . J 2
Dundrum (bay) . . . K 3
Erne (lake) . . . F 3
Foyle (inlet) . . . G 1
Foyle (riv.) . . . G 2
Giant's Causeway . . . H 1
Lagan (riv.) . . . K 2
Larne (inlet) . . . K 2
Magee, Island (pen.), 1,581 . . . K 2
Magilligan (pt.) . . . H 1
Main (riv.) . . . J 2
Mourne (mts.) . . . J 3
Mourne (riv.) . . . G 2
Neagh (lake) . . . J 2
North (chan.) . . . K 1
Rathlin (isl.), 109 . . . J 1
Red (bay) . . . K 1
Roe (riv.) . . . H 1
Saint John's (pt.) . . . K 3
Slieve Donard (mt.) . . . K 3
Sperrin (mts.) . . . G 2
Strangford (inlet) . . . K 3
Torr (head) . . . K 1
Ulster (part) (prov.), 1,537,200 . . . G 2
Upper Lough Erne (lake) . . . F 3

*City and suburbs.
‡Population of district.

IRELAND

CONIC PROJECTION

SCALE OF MILES

0 5 10   20   30   40

SCALE OF KILOMETERS

0 5 10   20   30   40

Capitals.....................☆   Country Boundaries.–·–·–·–

County Towns &   County & District
District Capitals..........△   Boundaries.............

Canals.......................

TRADITIONAL
DIVISIONS

NORTHERN IRELAND is divided internally into
26 districts bearing the same names as their
respective capitals, except:

DISTRICTS	CAPITALS
ARDS	Newtownards
CASTLEREAGH ①*	Belfast†
DOWN	Downpatrick
FERMANAGH	Enniskillen
MOURNE	Newry
MOYLE	Ballycastle
NEWTOWNABBEY ②*	Belfast†
NORTH DOWN	Bangor

* Indicated by number on map
† Belfast also serves as capital of Belfast District

© Copyright HAMMOND INCORPORATED, Maplewood, N.J.

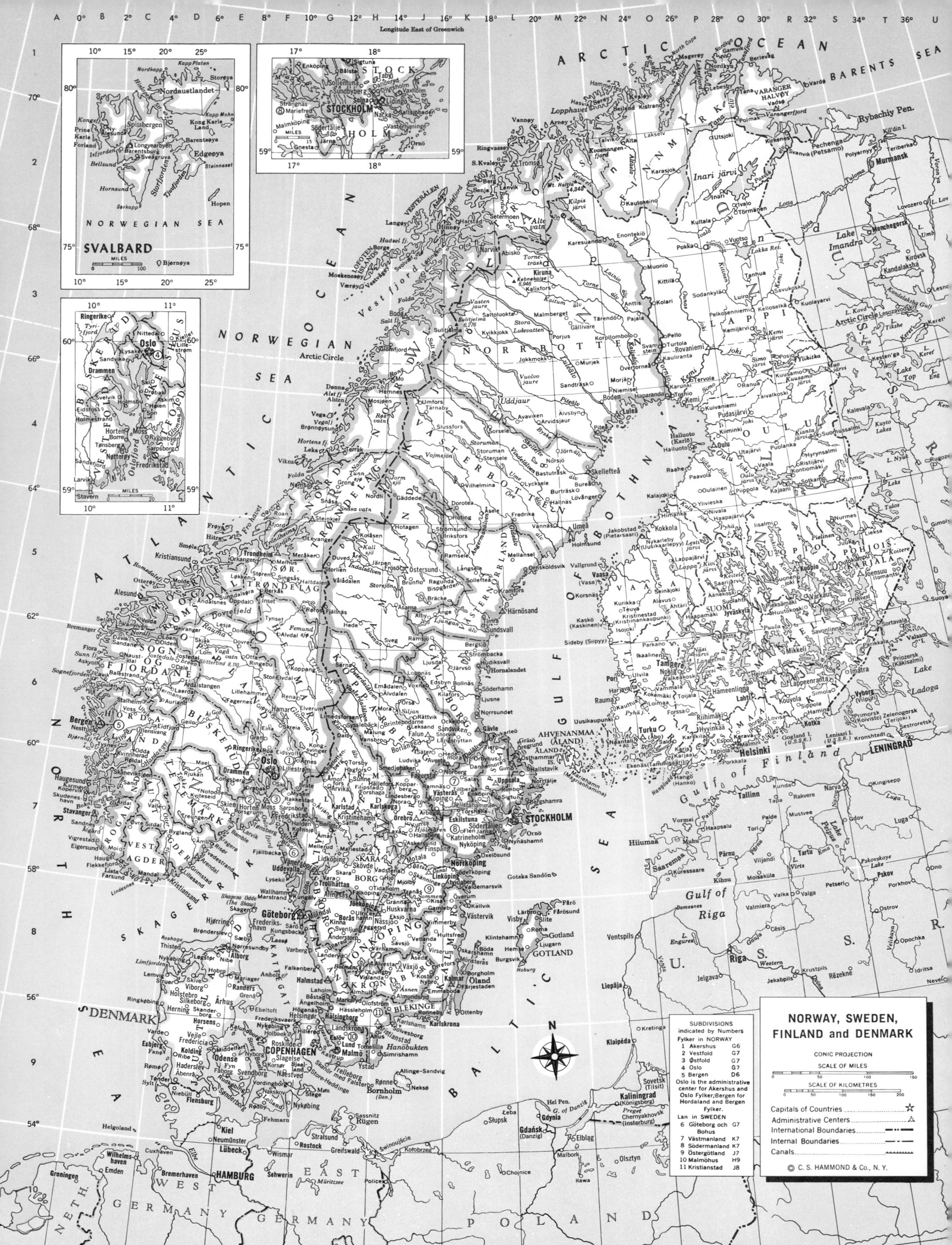

NORWAY, SWEDEN, FINLAND and DENMARK

CONIC PROJECTION

SCALE OF MILES

SCALE OF KILOMETRES

Capitals of Countries .... ☆
Administrative Centers .... △
International Boundaries .... —·—·—
Internal Boundaries .... —··—··—
Canals ....

© C. S. HAMMOND & Co., N. Y.

SUBDIVISIONS
indicated by Numbers
Fylker in NORWAY
1 Akershus G6
2 Vestfold G7
3 Østfold G7
4 Oslo G7
5 Bergen D6
Oslo is the administrative
center for Akershus and
Oslo Fylke; Bergen for
Hordaland and Bergen
Fylker.
Län in SWEDEN
6 Göteborg och G7
  Bohus
7 Västmanland K7
8 Södermanland K7
9 Östergötland J7
10 Malmöhus H9
11 Kristianstad J8

SVALBARD

Longitude East of Greenwich

NORWAY

AREA 125,053 sq. mi.
POPULATION 4,027,000
CAPITAL Oslo
LARGEST CITY Oslo
HIGHEST POINT Glittertind 8,110 ft.
MONETARY UNIT krone
MAJOR LANGUAGE Norwegian
MAJOR RELIGION Protestantism

SWEDEN

AREA 173,665 sq. mi.
POPULATION 8,236,461
CAPITAL Stockholm
LARGEST CITY Stockholm
HIGHEST POINT Kebnekaise 6,946 ft.
MONETARY UNIT krona
MAJOR LANGUAGE Swedish
MAJOR RELIGION Protestantism

FINLAND

AREA 130,128 sq. mi.
POPULATION 4,729,000
CAPITAL Helsinki
LARGEST CITY Helsinki
HIGHEST POINT Mt. Haltia 4,343 ft.
MONETARY UNIT markka
MAJOR LANGUAGES Finnish, Swedish
MAJOR RELIGION Protestantism

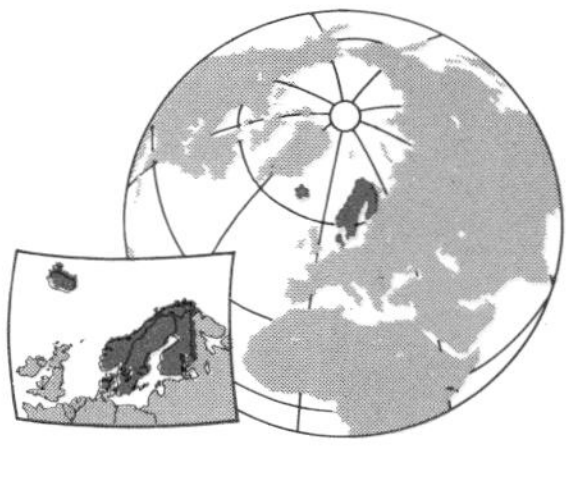

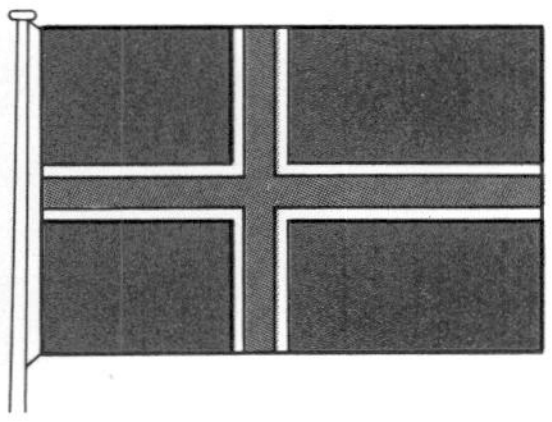

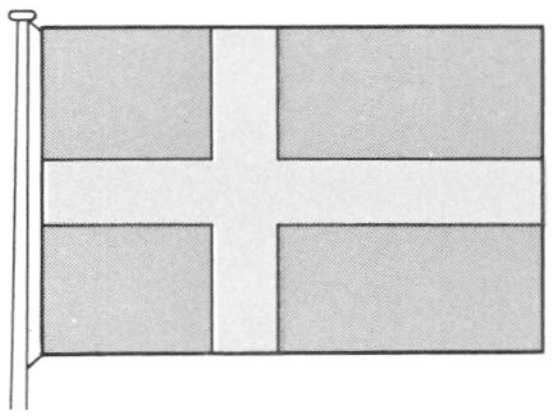

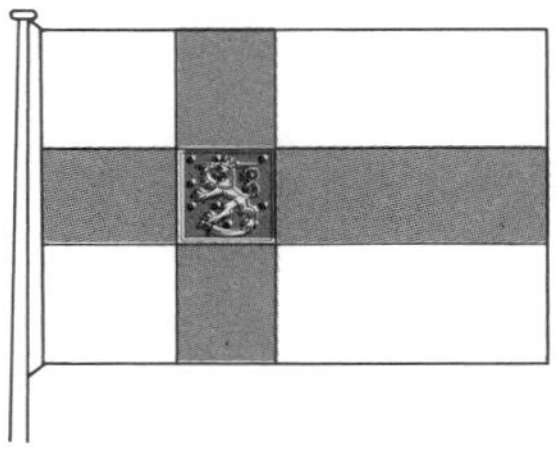

FINLAND

PROVINCES

Ahvenanmaa, 22,380	L 6
Åland (Ahvenanmaa), 22,380	L 6
Häme, 662,500	O 6
Keski-Suomi, 241,770	O 5
Kuopio, 252,023	P 5
Kymi, 346,478	Q 6
Lappi, 196,792	P 3
Mikkeli, 211,453	P 6
Oulu, 406,309	P 4
Pohjois-Karjala, 179,065	Q 5
Turku-Pori, 697,988	N 6
Uusimaa, 1,085,625	O 6
Vaasa, 425,283	N 5

CITIES and TOWNS

Äänekoski, 10,725	O 5
Åbo (Turku), 164,857	N 6
Alavus, 10,285	N 5
Borgå, 18,740	O 6
Ekenäs, 7,391	N 6
Espoo, 117,090	O 6
Forssa, 18,442	N 6
Haapajärvi, 7,791	O 5
Hämeenlinna, 40,761	O 6
Hamina, 11,055	P 6
Hangö, 10,374	N 7
Hanko (Hangö), 10,374	N 7
Harjavalta, 8,445	M 6
Heinola, 15,350	P 6
Helsinki (cap.), 502,961	O 6
Helsinki, *794,746	O 6
Huutokoski, ☆6,458	P 5
Hyvinkää, 35,865	O 6
Iisalmi, 21,159	P 5
Ikaalinen, 8,364	N 6
Ilomantsi, 2,211	R 5
Imatra, 35,590	Q 6
Ivalo, 2,661	P 2
Jakobstad, 20,397	N 5
Joensuu, 41,429	R 5
Jyväskylä, 61,209	O 5
Jyväskylä, *84,185	O 5
Kajaani, 20,583	P 4
Kalajoki, 3,624	N 4
Karis, 8,152	N 6
Karjaa (Karis), 8,152	N 6
Karkkila, 8,678	N 6
Kauttua, 3,297	M 6
Kelloselkä, ☆8,200	Q 3
Kemi, 27,893	O 4
Kemijärvi, 12,951	P 3
Kerava, 19,966	O 6
Kokemäki, 10,188	N 6
Kokkola, 22,096	N 5
Kotka, 34,026	P 6
Kotka, *60,235	P 6
Kouvola, 29,383	P 6
Kouvola, *59,507	P 6
Kristiinankaupunki (Kristinestad), 9,331	N 5
Kristinestad, 9,331	N 5
Kuhmo, 4,150	Q 4
Kuopio, 71,684	Q 5
Kuopio, *74,600	Q 5
Kurikka, 11,177	M 5
Kuusamo, 4,449	Q 4
Lahti, 94,864	O 6
Lahti, *112,129	O 6
Lappeenranta, 52,682	P 6
Lieksa, 20,274	R 5
Loimaa, 6,575	N 6
Lovisa, 8,674	P 6
Maarianhamina (Mariehamn), 9,574	M 7
Mänttä, 7,910	O 6
Mariehamn, 9,574	M 7
Mikkeli, 27,112	P 6
Naantali, 7,814	M 6
Nokia, 22,308	N 6
Nurmes, 11,721	Q 5
Nykarleby, 7,408	N 5
Oulainen, 7,322	O 4
Oulu, 93,707	O 4
Oulu, *103,044	O 4
Outokumpu, 10,736	Q 5
Parkano, 8,518	N 6
Pello, 1,960	O 3
Pieksämäki, 12,923	P 5
Pietarsaari (Jakobstad), 20,397	N 5
Pori, 80,343	M 6
Pori, *86,635	M 6
Porkkala, ☆15,558	O 7
Porvoo (Borgå), 18,740	O 6
Posio, ☆6,205	Q 3
Pudasjärvi, ☆12,594	P 4
Raahe, 15,379	O 4
Rauma, 29,081	M 6
Riihimäki, 24,106	O 6
Rovaniemi, 28,411	O 3
Saarijärvi, 2,714	O 5
Salo, 19,176	N 6
Savonlinna, 28,336	Q 6
Seinäjoki, 22,123	N 5
Sodankylä, 3,304	P 3
Sotkamo, 2,316	Q 4
Suolahti, 5,936	O 5
Suonenjoki, 9,286	P 5
Tammisaari (Ekenäs), 7,391	N 6
Tampere, 168,118	N 6
Tampere, *220,920	N 6
Toijala, 8,080	N 6
Tornio, 19,971	O 4
Turku, 164,857	N 6
Turku, *217,423	N 6
Turtola, ☆5,852	O 3
Ulvila, ☆8,040	N 6
Uusikaarlepyy (Nykarleby), 7,408	N 5
Uusikaupunki, 11,915	M 6
Vaasa, 54,402	M 5
Vaasa, *58,224	M 5
Valkeakoski, 22,588	N 6
Vammala, 16,363	N 6
Varkaus, 24,450	Q 5
Vasa (Vaasa), 54,402	M 5
Vuotso, ☆10,186	P 2
Ylivieska, 10,827	O 4

OTHER FEATURES

Åland (isls.), 22,380	L 6
Baltic (sea)	K 9
Bothnia (gulf)	M 5
Finland (gulf)	P 7
Hailuoto (isl.), 926	O 4
Haltia (mt.)	M 2
Hangöudd (prom.)	N 7
Haukivesi (lake)	Q 5
Iijoki (riv.)	O 4
Inarijärvi (lake)	P 2
Ivalojoki (riv.)	P 2
Juojärvi (lake)	Q 5
Kalajoki (riv.)	O 4
Kallavesi (lake)	P 5
Karlö (Hailuoto) (isl.), 926	O 4
Keitele (lake)	O 5
Kemijärvi (lake)	Q 3
Kemijoki (riv.)	O 3
Kiantajärvi (lake)	Q 4
Kilpisjärvi (lake)	M 2
Kitinen (riv.)	P 3
Kivijärvi (lake)	O 5
Koitere (lake)	R 5
Kuusamojärvi (lake)	Q 4
Längelmävesi (lake)	O 6
Lapland (reg.), 196,792	O 2
Lappajärvi (lake)	O 5
Lapuanjoki (riv.)	N 5
Lestijärvi (lake)	O 5
Lokka (res.)	Q 3
Muojärvi (lake)	R 4
Muonio (riv.)	M 2
Näsijärvi (lake)	O 6
Onkivesi (lake)	P 5
Orihvesi (lake)	Q 5
Oulujärvi (lake)	P 4
Oulujoki (riv.)	O 4
Ounasjoki (riv.)	O 3
Päijänne (lake)	O 6
Pielinen (lake)	Q 5
Puruvesi (lake)	Q 6
Puulavesi (lake)	P 5
Pyhäjärvi (lake)	O 5
Pyhäjärvi (lake)	M 6
Saimaa (lake)	Q 6
Siikajoki (riv.)	O 4
Simojärvi (lake)	P 3
Simojoki (riv.)	O 4
Tana (riv.)	P 2
Tornio (riv.)	O 3
Vallgrund (isl.), 1,480	M 5
Ylikitka (lake)	Q 3

NORWAY

COUNTIES

Akershus, 355,196	G 6
Aust-Agder, 86,216	E 7
Buskerud, 209,684	F 6
Finnmark, 79,373	O 2
Hedmark, 183,465	G 6
Hordaland, 386,492	E 6
Møre og Romsdal, 231,944	E 5
Nordland, 243,233	J 3
Nord-Trøndelag, 122,886	H 4
Oppland, 178,259	F 6
Oslo (city), 462,732	D 3
Østfold, 228,546	G 7
Rogaland, 287,653	E 7
Sogn og Fjordane, 103,135	E 6
Sør-Trøndelag, 241,361	G 5
Telemark, 158,853	F 7
Troms, 144,111	L 2
Vest-Agder, 131,659	E 7
Vestfold, 182,433	G 7

CITIES and TOWNS

Ålesund, 40,868	D 5
Ålgård, 2,322	D 7
Alta, 5,582	N 2
Åndalsnes, 2,574	F 5
Årdalstangen, 2,360	F 6
Arendal, 11,701	F 7
Arendal, *21,228	F 7
Årnes, 2,267	G 6
Askim, 8,413	E 4
Bamble, ⊙7,031	F 7
Barentsburg	C 2
Bergen, 213,434	D 6
Bodø, 31,077	J 3
Borge, ⊙3,294	H 2
Brate, ⊙2,107	G 7
Brønnøysund, 3,130	G 4
Dombås, 1,114	F 5
Drammen, 50,777	C 4
Drammen, *56,521	C 4
Drøbak, 4,538	D 4
Eidsvoll, 2,906	G 6
Eigersund, 11,379	D 7
Elverum, 7,391	G 6
Farsund, 8,908	E 7
Flekkefjord, 8,750	E 7
Flora, 8,822	D 6
Fredrikstad, 29,024	D 4
Fredrikstad, *51,141	D 4
Gjøvik, 25,963	G 6
Grimstad, 13,091	F 7
Halden, 27,087	G 7
Hamar, 16,418	G 6
Hamar, *25,138	G 6
Hammerfest, 7,610	N 1
Hammerfest, *8,005	N 1
Harstad, 21,125	K 2
Hauge, 2,079	E 7
Haugesund, 27,386	D 7
Haugesund, *29,277	D 7
Hermansverk, 706	E 6
Holmestrand, 8,246	C 4
Holmsbu, 273	D 4
Honningsvag, 3,780	O 1
Horten, 13,746	D 4
Horten, *17,246	D 4
Kirkenes, 4,466	Q 2
Kongsberg, 19,854	F 7
Kongsvinger, 16,146	H 6
Kopervik, 4,221	D 7
Kornsjø, ⊙6,079	G 7
Kragerø, 5,249	F 7
Kristiansand, 59,488	F 8
Kristiansund, 18,847	E 5
Kvinnherad, ⊙2,898	E 6
Larvik, 9,097	C 4
Larvik, *19,202	C 4
Lenvik, ☆11,098	L 2
Levanger, 5,066	G 5
Lillehammer, 21,248	F 6
Lillesand, 3,028	F 7
Lillestrøm, ⊙11,550	E 3
Løkken, 1,942	F 5
Longyearbyen	D 2
Lysaker, ☆81,612	D 3
Mandal, 11,579	E 7
Meråker, ⊙2,907	G 5
Mo, 21,033	J 3
Molde, 20,334	E 5
Mosjøen, 9,341	H 4
Moss, 25,786	D 4
Moss, *27,430	D 4
Mysen, 3,760	G 7
Namsos, 11,452	G 4
Narvik, 19,582	K 2
Nesttun, ⊙11,519	D 6
Nittedal, ⊙8,889	D 3
Notodden, 12,970	F 7
Nøtterøy, 11,944	D 4
Ny-Ålesund	C 2
Odda, 7,401	E 6
Oppdal, 2,173	F 5
Orkanger, 3,685	F 5
Oslo (cap.), 462,732	D 3
Oslo, *645,413	D 3
Otta, 1,916	F 6
Porsgrunn, 31,709	G 7
Rakkestad, 2,392	G 7
Ringerike, 30,156	C 3
Risør, 6,560	F 7
Rjukan, 5,334	F 7
Røros, 3,041	G 5
Ryggebyen, 1,954	D 4
Sandefjord, 33,350	C 4
Sandnes, 33,934	D 7
Sandvika, ☆34,337	C 3
Sarpsborg, 12,889	D 4
Sarpsborg, *36,449	D 4
Selje, ⊙3,386	D 5
Setermoen, 2,114	L 2
Ski, 9,081	D 4
Skien, 47,105	F 7
Skudeneshavn, 2,206	D 7
Stavanger, 86,639	D 7
Stavern, 2,604	D 4
Steinkjer, 20,553	G 4
Stor-Elvdal, ⊙2,993	G 6
Sunndalsøra, 5,114	F 5
Sveagruva	D 2
Svelvik, 2,256	D 4
Svolvaer, 3,942	J 2
Tana, ⊙1,893	Q 1
Tønsberg, 9,964	D 4
Tønsberg, *36,374	D 4
Tromsø, 43,830	L 2
Trondheim, 134,910	F 5
Ullensvang, ⊙2,326	E 6
Vadsø, 6,019	Q 1
Vanylven, ⊙1,966	E 5
Vardø, 3,875	R 1
Vik, 1,019	E 6
Volda, 3,511	E 5
Voss, 5,944	E 6

OTHER FEATURES

Alsten (isl.), 5,154	H 4
Andøy (isl.), 7,537	J 2
Arnøy (isl.), 887	M 1
Barduelv (riv.)	L 2
Bellsund	C 2
Bjørnafjorden (fjord)	D 6
Bjornøya (isl.)	D 3
Boknafjord (fjord)	D 7
Bremanger (isl.), 1,862	D 6
Dønna (isl.), 1,671	H 3
Dovrefjeld (hills)	F 5
Edgeøya (isl.)	E 2
Femundsjø (lake)	G 5
Folda (fjord)	G 4
Folda (fjord)	J 3
Frohavet (bay)	F 5
Frøya (isl.), 3,417	F 5
Glittertind (mt.)	F 6
Glomma (riv.)	G 6
Haltia (mt.)	M 2
Hardanger (plat.)	E 6
Hardangerfjord (fjord)	D 7
Hinlopen (str.)	C 1
Hinnøy (isl.), 29,944	K 2
Hitra (isl.), 2,929	F 5
Hopen (isl.)	E 2
Isfjorden (fjord)	C 2
Jostedalsbreen (glac.)	E 6
Karmøy (isl.), 23,136	D 7
Kjölen (mts.)	K 3
Kongsfjorden (fjord)	B 2
Kvaløy (isl.), 8,457	O 1
Lågen (riv.)	G 6
Laksefjorden (fjord)	P 1
Langøy (isl.), 15,685	J 2
Lapland (reg.), 466,717	K 2
Leka (isl.), 724	G 4
Lindesnes (cape)	E 8
Lista (pen.), 8,304	E 7
Lofoten (isls.), 26,587	H 2
Lopphavet (bay)	M 1
Magerøy (isl.), 5,043	P 1
Moskenesøy (isl.), 2,003	H 3
Namsen (riv.)	H 4
Nordaustlandet (isl.)	D 1
Nordfjord (fjord)	E 6
Nordkapp (pt.)	C 1
Nordkyn (headland)	Q 1
Nordkyn (pen.), 1,669	P 1
North (pt.)	P 1
Norwegian (sea)	F 3
Ofotfjorden (fjord)	K 2
Oslofjord (fjord)	D 4
Otterelv (riv.)	E 7
Otterøy (isl.), 1,702	E 5
Pasvikelv (riv.)	Q 2
Platen, Kapp (pt.)	D 1
Porsangerfjord (fjord)	O 1
Ran (fjord)	H 3
Rauma (riv.)	F 5
Ringvassøy (isl.), 1,301	L 2
Romsdalsfjorden (fjord)	E 5
Saltfjorden (fjord)	J 3
Seiland (isl.), 559	N 1
Senja (isl.), 9,858	K 2
Skagerrak (str.)	F 8
Smøla (isl.), 2,486	F 5
Sognefjorden (fjord)	D 6
Sørkapp (pt.)	C 2
Sør Kvaløy (isl.), 3,542	K 2
Sorøy (isl.), 1,808	N 1
Spitsbergen (isl.)	C 2
Storfjorden (fjord)	D 2
Sulitjelma (mt.)	K 3
Svalbard (isls.), 3,431	C 3
Tana (riv.)	P 1
Tanafjord (fjord)	Q 1
Tokke (riv.)	F 7
Trondheimsfjorden (fjord)	G 5
Tyrifjord (lake)	C 3
Vaerøy (isl.), 1,088	H 3
Vagåvatn (lake)	F 6
Vannøy (isl.), 1,219	L 1
Varanger Halvøy (pen.), 19,320	Q 1
Varangerfjord (fjord)	Q 2
Vega (isl.), 1,426	G 4
Vesterålen (isls.), 61,564	J 2
Vestfjord (fjord)	H 3
Vestvågoy (isl.), 10,798	H 3
Vikna (isls.), 3,410	G 4

(continued on following page)

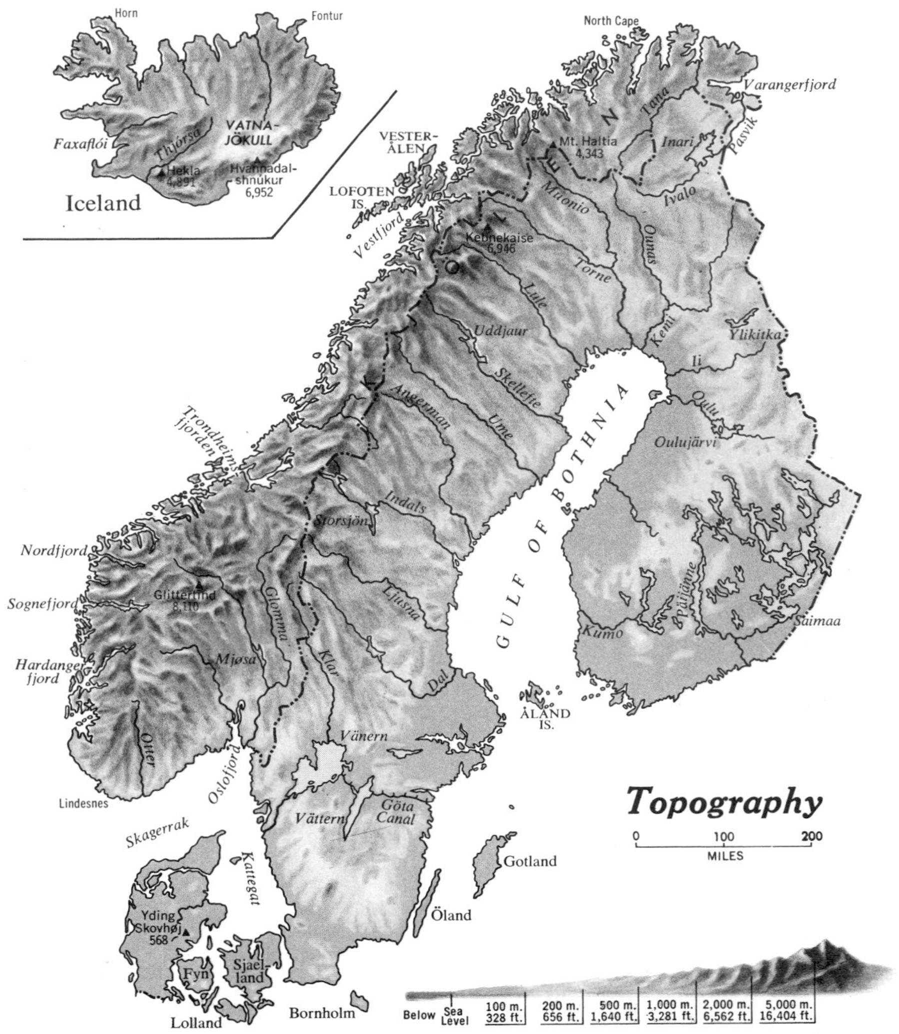
Horn
Fontur
Faxaflói
VATNA-JÖKULL
Hekla 4,891
Hvannadal-shnúkur 6,952
Iceland
North Cape
Varangerfjord
VESTER-ÅLEN
LOFOTEN IS.
Vestfjord
Mt. Haltia 4,343
Kebnekaise 6,946
Inari
Tana
Pasvik
Ivalo
Muonio
Ounas
Torne
Lule
Kemi
Uddjaur
Ylikitka
Skellefte
Ume
Ångerman
Oulujärvi
Trondheimsfjorden
GULF OF BOTHNIA
Indals
Storsjön
Nordfjord
Sognefjord
Glittertind 8,110
Glomma
Ljusna
Hardanger fjord
Mjøsa
Klar
Dal
Saimaa
Kumo
Päijänne
ÅLAND IS.
Otter
Vänern
Oslofjord
Lindesnes
Skagerrak
Vättern
Göta Canal
Kattegat
Gotland
Öland
Yding Skovhøj 568
Fyn
Sjælland
Lolland
Bornholm
Topography
0 100 200 MILES
Below Sea Level
100 m. 328 ft.
200 m. 656 ft.
500 m. 1,640 ft.
1,000 m. 3,281 ft.
2,000 m. 6,562 ft.
5,000 m. 16,404 ft.

20 Norway, Sweden, Finland, Denmark and Iceland
(continued)

SWEDEN

COUNTIES

Älvsborg, 420,199 ... H 7
Blekinge, 154,968 ... J 8
Gävleborg, 294,696 ... K 6
Göteborg och Bohus, 714,478 ... G 7
Gotland, 54,624 ... L 8
Halland, 222,967 ... H 8
Jämtland, 133,755 ... J 5
Jönköping, 302,161 ... H 8
Kalmar, 241,005 ... K 8
Kopparberg, 283,353 ... J 6
Kristianstad, 273,924 ... J 8
Kronoberg, 170,307 ... J 8
Malmöhus, 739,729 ... H 9
Norrbotten, 266,033 ... L 3
Örebro, 273,897 ... J 7
Östergötland, 389,416 ... J 7
Skaraborg, 264,316 ... H 7
Södermanland, 252,017 ... K 7
Stockholm, 1,500,736 ... L 7
Uppsala, 233,131 ... K 7
Värmland, 284,620 ... H 7
Västerbotten, 237,679 ... K 4
Västernorrland, 268,268 ... K 5
Västmanland, 260,182 ... K 7

CITIES and TOWNS

Åhus, 4,083 ... J 9
Alingsås, 18,761 ... H 7
Älmhult, 7,001 ... H 8
Alvesta, 7,544 ... J 8
Älvsbyn, 3,902 ... M 4
Åmål, 9,331 ... H 7
Ånge, 3,874 ... J 5
Ängelholm, 14,853 ... H 8
Arboga, 11,932 ... J 7
Årjäng, ⊙2,171 ... H 7
Arvidsjaur, 3,541 ... L 4
Arvika, 12,975 ... H 7
Åseda, 2,491 ... J 8
Åsele, 2,249 ... K 4
Askersund, 2,788 ... J 7
Åtvidaberg, 8,385 ... K 7
Avesta, 19,915 ... J 6
Bålsta, 4,972 ... G 1
Båstad, 2,395 ... H 8
Bengtsfors, 3,389 ... H 7
Boden, 18,642 ... M 4
Bollnäs, 13,003 ... K 6
Borås, 73,344 ... H 8
Borås, *104,451 ... H 8
Borgholm, 2,424 ... K 8
Borlänge, 35,436 ... J 6
Bräcke, 2,104 ... J 5
Brunflo, 2,380 ... J 5
Bureå, 2,031 ... M 4
Charlottenberg, 1,942 ... H 6
Danderyd, ☆27,103 ... H 1
Dannemora, 464 ... K 6
Edsbyn, 4,068 ... J 6
Eksjö, 9,214 ... J 8
Emmaboda, 3,860 ... J 8
Enköping, 19,066 ... G 1
Eskilstuna, 68,596 ... K 7
Eslöv, 13,186 ... H 9
Fagersta, ☆15,730 ... J 6
Falkenberg, 13,476 ... H 8
Falköping, 15,681 ... H 7
Falun, 28,788 ... J 6
Filipstad, 7,420 ... H 7
Finspång, 16,181 ... J 7
Flen, 6,768 ... K 7
Forshaga, 4,297 ... H 7
Frösö, 8,936 ... J 5
Frövi, 2,586 ... J 7
Gällivare, 7,773 ... M 3
Gamleby, 3,521 ... J 8
Gävle, 65,326 ... K 6
Gimo, 2,905 ... K 6
Gnesta, 2,908 ... G 2
Göteborg, 442,507 ... G 8
Göteborg, *692,210 ... G 8
Gränna, 2,052 ... J 8
Hagfors, 8,315 ... H 6
Hällefors, 7,953 ... J 7
Hallsberg, 7,559 ... J 7
Hallstahammar, 13,818 ... K 7
Hallstavik, 5,069 ... L 6
Halmstad, 49,725 ... H 8
Hälsingborg, 82,008 ... H 8
Hälsingborg, *101,352 ... H 8
Haparanda, 4,246 ... N 4
Härnösand, 18,683 ... L 5
Hässleholm, 16,984 ... H 8
Hedemora, 6,628 ... K 6
Hjo, 4,078 ... J 7
Höganäs, 10,554 ... H 8
Holmsund, 4,717 ... M 5
Hudiksvall, 14,351 ... K 6
Hultsfred, 5,417 ... K 8
Järna, 5,715 ... G 2
Jokkmokk, 2,966 ... L 3
Jönköping, 80,693 ... H 8
Jönköping, *108,182 ... H 8
Kalmar, 34,918 ... K 8
Karlshamn, 17,193 ... J 8
Karlskoga, ☆37,733 ... J 7
Karlskrona, 33,873 ... J 8
Karlstad, 52,044 ... H 7
Katrineholm, 22,616 ... K 7
Kinna, 12,467 ... H 8
Kiruna, 23,279 ... L 3
Kisa, 3,951 ... J 8
Köping, 21,740 ... J 7
Kopparberg, 4,014 ... J 7
Kramfors, 7,267 ... L 5
Kristianstad, 29,013 ... J 9
Kristinehamn, 21,043 ... H 7
Kumla, 10,734 ... J 7
Kungälv, ☆28,322 ... G 8
Kungsbacka, ☆39,778 ... G 8
Laholm, 3,695 ... H 8
Landskrona, 30,110 ... H 9
Långsele, 2,320 ... K 5
Långshyttan, 2,793 ... K 6
Laxå, 5,847 ... J 7
Leksand, 4,200 ... J 6
Lidingö, 29,799 ... H 1
Lidköping, 21,300 ... H 7
Lindesberg, 7,171 ... J 7
Linköping, 77,063 ... K 7
Linköping, *110,060 ... K 7
Ljungby, 12,596 ... J 8
Ljusdal, 6,489 ... J 6
Ljusne, 3,748 ... K 6
Ludvika, 18,266 ... J 6
Luleå, 36,743 ... N 4
Lund, 76,516 ... H 9
Lycksele, 7,879 ... L 4
Lysekil, 6,783 ... G 7
Malmberget, 10,315 ... M 3
Malmköping, 2,189 ... F 1
Malmö, 240,283 ... H 9
Malmö, *453,339 ... H 9
Malung, 6,028 ... H 6
Mariefred, 2,013 ... F 1
Mariestad, 16,637 ... H 7
Markaryd, 4,121 ... H 8
Marstrand, 1,072 ... G 8
Mellerud, 3,368 ... H 7
Mjölby, 12,245 ... J 7
Mölndal, ☆46,925 ... H 8
Mönsterås, 5,430 ... K 8
Mora, 7,891 ... J 6
Motala, 28,942 ... J 7
Nacka, 22,569 ... H 1
Nässjö, 19,434 ... J 8
Nora, 4,681 ... J 7
Norberg, 5,392 ... K 6
Norrköping, 91,034 ... K 7
Norrköping, *119,984 ... K 7
Norrtälje, 12,735 ... L 7
Nybro, 12,875 ... J 8
Nyköping, 30,943 ... K 7
Nynäshamn, 10,955 ... L 7
Ockelbo, 2,669 ... K 6
Olofström, 10,482 ... J 8
Örebro, 87,125 ... J 7
Örebro, *117,399 ... J 7
Örnsköldsvik, 28,428 ... L 5
Orrefors, 921 ... J 8
Orsa, 4,799 ... J 6
Oskarshamn, 17,143 ... K 8
Östersund, 27,320 ... J 5
Östhammar, 2,668 ... L 6
Överum, 2,483 ... K 7
Oxelösund, 15,085 ... K 7
Piteå, 15,067 ... M 4
Ramnäs, 1,920 ... J 7
Rättvik, 3,918 ... J 6
Rimbo, 3,237 ... L 7
Ronneby, 11,801 ... J 8
Säffle, 11,609 ... H 7
Sala, 10,476 ... K 7
Saltsjöbaden, 7,055 ... J 1
Sandviken, 28,410 ... K 6
Säter, 3,973 ... J 6
Sävsjö, 4,846 ... J 8
Sigtuna, 4,214 ... H 1
Simrishamn, 5,502 ... J 9
Skanör med Falsterbo, 3,127 ... H 9
Skara, 10,284 ... H 7
Skellefteå, 27,456 ... M 4
Skövde, 29,040 ... H 7
Smedjebacken, 8,395 ... J 6
Söderhamn, 13,721 ... K 6
Söderköping, 4,688 ... K 7
Södertälje, 57,494 ... G 1
Sollefteå, 8,414 ... K 5
Sollentuna, ☆44,582 ... H 1
Solna, ☆52,854 ... H 1
Sölvesborg, 6,797 ... J 9
Stockholm (cap.), 661,536 ... G 1
Stockholm, *1,364,056 ... G 1
Storuman, 2,456 ... K 4
Storvik, 2,615 ... K 6
Strängnäs, 9,509 ... F 1
Strömstad, 4,447 ... G 7
Strömsund, 3,578 ... K 5
Sundbyberg, ☆26,456 ... G 1
Sundsvall, 53,599 ... K 5
Sunne, 3,686 ... H 7
Sveg, 2,298 ... J 5
Svenljunga, 2,786 ... H 8
Täby, ☆42,493 ... H 1
Tidaholm, 7,663 ... J 7
Tierp, 4,497 ... K 6
Timrå, 11,055 ... K 5
Tomelilla, 4,923 ... J 9
Torsby, 3,094 ... H 6
Torshälla, 8,363 ... K 7
Tranås, 15,150 ... J 7
Trelleborg, 34,504 ... H 9
Trollhättan, 41,016 ... H 7
Trosa, 2,173 ... K 7
Uddevalla, 35,459 ... G 7
Ulricehamn, 7,699 ... H 8
Umeå, 47,692 ... M 5
Uppsala, 92,624 ... K 7
Uppsala, *139,883 ... L 7
Vaggeryd, 3,820 ... J 8
Valdemarsvik, 3,545 ... K 7
Vänersborg, 19,465 ... G 7
Vännäs, 4,066 ... L 5
Vansbro, 2,701 ... H 6
Vara, 2,827 ... H 7
Varberg, 17,768 ... G 8
Värnamo, 14,962 ... J 8
Västerås, 99,343 ... K 7
Västerås, *118,073 ... K 7
Västerhaninge, 12,966 ... H 1
Västervik, 20,168 ... K 8
Vaxholm, ☆28,678 ... J 1
Växjö, 39,019 ... J 8
Vetlanda, 12,024 ... J 8
Vilhelmina, 3,632 ... K 4
Vimmerby, 7,201 ... J 8
Virserum, 2,591 ... J 8
Visby, 19,245 ... L 8
Ystad, 14,164 ... H 9

OTHER FEATURES

Ångermanälven (riv.) ... K 5
Åsnen (lake) ... J 8
Baltic (sea) ... K 9
Bolmen (lake) ... H 8
Bothnia (gulf) ... N 4
Dalälven (riv.) ... K 6
Fårö (isl.), 727 ... L 8
Göta (canal) ... J 7
Göta (riv.) ... H 7
Gotland (isl.), 53,053 ... L 8
Gräsö (isl.), 618 ... L 6
Hanöbukten (bay) ... J 9
Hjälmaren (lake) ... J 7
Hoburg (cliff) ... L 8
Hornslandet (pen.) ... K 6
Indalsälven (riv.) ... H 5
Kalixälv (riv.) ... N 3
Kalmarsund (sound) ... K 8
Kattegat (str.) ... G 8
Kebnekaise (mt.) ... L 3
Kjölen (mts.) ... K 3
Klarälv (riv.) ... H 6
Lapland (reg.), 503,712 ... M 2
Ljusnan (riv.) ... H 5
Luleälv (riv.) ... M 3
Mälaren (lake) ... G 1
Muonioälv (riv.) ... M 2
Öland (isl.), 22,561 ... K 8
Öresund (sound) ... H 9
Ornö (isl.), 175 ... J 2
Österdalälven (riv.) ... H 6
Piteälv (riv.) ... M 4
Siljan (lake) ... J 6
Skagerrak (str.) ... F 8
Sommen (lake) ... J 7
Stora Lulevatten (lake) ... L 3
Storsjön (lake) ... J 5
Sulitjelma (mt.) ... K 3
Torneälv (riv.) ... M 3
Uddjaur (lake) ... L 4
Umeälv (riv.) ... L 4
Vänern (lake) ... H 7
Västerdalälven (riv.) ... H 6
Vättern (lake) ... J 7

*City and suburbs.
☆Population of commune.
⊙Population of parish.

DENMARK

INTERNAL DIVISIONS

Århus (county), 525,167 ... D 5
Bornholm (county), 47,405 ... F 9
Copenhagen (commune), 634,500 ... F 6
Færøe Islands, 38,000 ... B 2
Frederiksberg (commune), 102,751 ... F 6
Frederiksborg (county), 252,557 ... F 5
Fyn (county), 430,958 ... D 7
København (Copenhagen) (commune), 634,500 ... F 6
København (county), 609,469 ... F 6
Nordjylland (county), 455,062 ... D 4
Ribe (county), 196,894 ... B 6
Ringkøbing (county), 240,014 ... B 5
Roskilde (county), 147,434 ... E 6
Sønderjylland (county), 237,270 ... C 7
Storstrøm (county), 251,815 ... E 7
Vejle (county), 304,358 ... C 6
Vestsjælland (county), 256,997 ... E 6
Viborg (county), 220,214 ... B 4

CITIES and TOWNS

Åbenrå, 15,156 ... C 7
Åbybro, 6,309 ... C 3
Ærøskøbing, 1,228 ... D 8
Agerbæk, 804, ... B 6
Åkirkeby, 1,549 ... F 9
Ålborg, 82,346 ... D 4
Ålborg, *153,307 ... D 4
Ålestrup, 5,228 ... C 4
Allingåbro, 1,352 ... D 5
Allinge-Sandvig, 2,023 ... F 8
Ansager, 1,123 ... B 6
Arden, 1,353 ... C 4
Århus, 109,498 ... D 5
Århus, *232,173 ... D 5
Års, 5,075 ... C 4
Årup, †5,033 ... D 7
Aså, 1,348 ... D 3
Askov, 725 ... C 7
Asnæs, 2,493 ... E 6
Assens, Århus, 1,266 ... D 4
Assens, Fyn, †10,777 ... D 7
Augustenborg, 3,537 ... D 8
Auning, 1,367 ... D 5
Avlum, 3,694 ... B 5
Bælum, 1,922 ... D 4
Bagenkop, 774 ... D 8
Ballerup, †50,128 ... F 6
Bandholm, 1,248 ... E 8
Bested, 1,886 ... B 4
Birkerød, †20,835 ... F 6
Bjerringbro, 6,469 ... C 5
Bogense, †6,450 ... D 6
Bolderslev, 729 ... C 8
Børkop, †9,053 ... C 6
Borup, 2,344 ... E 7
Brabrand, 12,514 ... C 5
Brædstrup, 3,925 ... C 6
Bramminge, 5,937 ... B 7
Brande, 6,814 ... B 6
Bredebro, †3,747 ... B 7
Broager, †5,387 ... C 8
Brønderslev, 10,274 ... C 3
Brøns, 867 ... B 7
Brørup, 4,066 ... C 7
Brovst, †8,086 ... C 3
Christiansfeld, 958 ... C 7
Copenhagen (cap.), 634,500 ... F 6
Copenhagen, *1,346,720 ... F 6
Dronninglund, 9,179 ... D 3
Dybvad, 793 ... D 3
Ebeltoft, 3,168 ... D 5
Egernsund, 1,360 ... C 8
Egtved, 2,857 ... C 6
Ejby, 3,265 ... D 7
Esbjerg, 62,483 ... B 7
Fåborg, 5,630 ... D 7
Fakse, 7,268 ... F 7
Fakse Ladeplads, 1,639 ... F 7
Farsø, 4,126 ... C 4
Farum, †9,583 ... F 6
Fjerritslev, 2,686 ... C 3
Fredensborg, 3,977 ... F 6
Fredericia, 34,464 ... C 6
Frederiksberg, 102,751 ... F 6
Frederikshavn, 24,640 ... D 3
Frederikssund, 7,835 ... E 6
Frederiksværk, 4,385 ... E 6
Fuglebjerg, 5,082 ... E 7
Gedser, 1,195 ... F 8
Gedsted, 1,924 ... C 4
Gelsted, 2,461 ... C 7
Gentofte, †78,641 ... F 6
Gilleleje, 4,300 ... F 5
Give, 8,573 ... C 6
Gjerlev, 1,209 ... D 4
Glamsbjerg, †5,677 ... D 7
Glostrup, †28,169 ... F 6
Glumsø, 819 ... E 7
Glyngøre, 1,047 ... C 4
Gørding, 2,422 ... B 7
Gørlev, 2,437 ... E 6
Græsted, 2,899 ... F 5
Gram, 3,935 ... C 7
Gråsten, †6,336 ... C 8
Grenå, 13,277 ... D 5
Grindsted, 9,345 ... B 6
Gylling, 990 ... D 6
Haderslev, 20,291 ... C 7
Hadsten, 6,919 ... C 5
Hadsund, 6,862 ... D 4
Hals, 3,016 ... D 3
Hammel, 7,456 ... C 5
Hammerum, 2,415 ... C 5
Hanstholm, 3,358 ... B 3
Harboør, 2,224 ... A 4
Hårby, †4,671 ... D 7
Hårlev, 980 ... F 7
Hasle, 1,542 ... F 8
Haslev, 10,173 ... E 7
Havdrup, 5,163 ... F 6
Hedensted, 4,791 ... C 6
Hellebæk, 2,240 ... F 5
Helsinge, 4,707 ... F 6
Helsingør, 30,211 ... F 6
Herning, 32,512 ... B 5
Hillerød, 23,500 ... F 6
Hinnerup, †5,614 ... D 5
Hirtshals, 8,598 ... C 2
Hjallerup, 1,385 ... C 3
Hjerm, 1,421 ... B 5
Hjørring, 15,699 ... C 3
Hobro, 8,845 ... C 4
Højer, 1,407 ... B 8
Højslev, 2,863 ... C 4
Holbæk, 17,892 ... E 6
Holeby, 4,359 ... E 8
Holstebro, 24,009 ... B 5
Holsted, 2,773 ... B 6
Høng, †7,355 ... E 7
Hornslet, 3,371 ... D 5
Horsens, 35,621 ... C 6
Hørsholm, 18,060 ... F 6
Hørve, 2,829 ... E 6
Hov, 607 ... D 6
Humlum, 2,357 ... B 4
Hundested, †6,301 ... E 6
Hurup, 2,560 ... B 4
Hvidbjerg, 2,361 ... B 4
Hvide Sande, 1,775 ... A 6
Hviding, 750 ... B 7
Ikast, 11,110 ... C 5
Jelling, 4,780 ... C 6
Jerslev, 2,672 ... D 3
Juelsminde, 7,245 ... D 6
Jyderup, 3,246 ... E 6
Kalundborg, 11,762 ... D 6
Karby, 2,302 ... B 4
Karise, 1,733 ... F 7
Karup, 1,891 ... C 5
Kastrup ... F 6
Kerteminde, †10,296 ... D 7
Kibæk, 1,179 ... B 5
Kjellerup, 3,506 ... C 5
Klaksvík, Færøe Is., 3,894 ... B 2
København (Copenhagen), (cap.), 634,500 ... F 6
Køge, 17,360 ... F 7
Kolding, 39,609 ... C 7
Kolind, 2,590 ... D 5
Kørsør, 15,550 ... E 7
Kværndrup, 1,963 ... D 7
Langå, 2,801 ... C 5
Lem, 1,060 ... B 5
Lemvig, 6,766 ... B 4
Løgstør, 3,666 ... C 4
Løgumkloster, 2,089 ... B 7
Lohals, 634 ... D 7
Løjt Kirkeby, 2,724 ... C 7
Løkken, 1,388 ... C 3
Løsning, 2,418 ... C 6
Lundby, 2,392 ... E 7
Lunderskov, †4,402 ... C 7
Lyngby, †61,245 ... F 6
Malling, 4,332 ... D 5
Mariager, 3,733 ... D 4
Maribo, 5,235 ... E 8
Marstal, 4,095 ... D 8
Middelfart, 9,015 ... C 7
Møgeltønder, 1,181 ... B 8
Næstved, 24,831 ... E 7
Nakskov, 15,994 ... E 8
Neksø, 3,499 ... F 9
Nibe, 2,786 ... C 4
Nordborg, 3,016 ... C 7
Nordby, 2,353 ... B 7
Nørre Åby, †5,195 ... C 7
Nørre Alslev, 1,939 ... E 8
Nørre Broby, 858 ... D 7
Nørre Nebel, 867 ... B 6
Nørre Snede, 3,019 ... C 6
Nørresundby, 23,848 ... D 3
Nørre Vorupør, 632 ... B 4
Nyborg, 11,698 ... D 7
Nykøbing, Storstrøm, 17,364 ... E 8
Nykøbing, Vestsjælland, 4,905 ... E 6
Nykøbing, Viborg, 8,710 ... B 4
Nysted, 1,211 ... E 8
Odder, 8,144 ... D 6
Odense, 102,698 ... D 7
Odense, *163,593 ... D 7
Ølgod, 7,091 ... B 6
Ørsted, 1,925 ... D 5
Øster Vrå, 931 ... D 3
Otterup, †10,462 ... D 7
Ovtrup, 549 ... B 6
Pandrup, 1,383 ... C 3
Pedersborg, 1,560 ... E 7

Agriculture, Industry and Resources

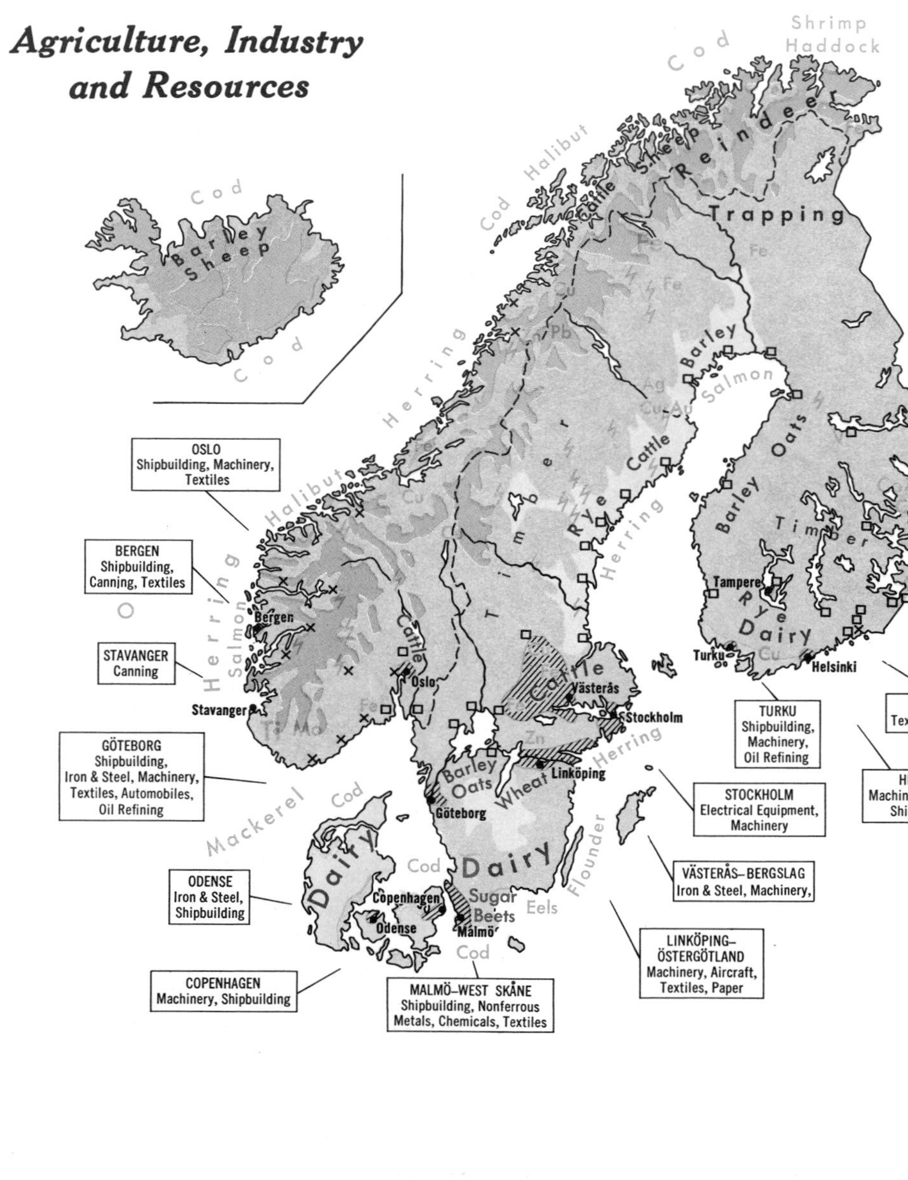

Cod
Barley
Sheep
Shrimp
Haddock
Halibut
Cattle
Sheep
Reindeer
Trapping
Fe
Pb
Barley
Ag
Cu
Salmon
Herring
Oats
Rye
Cattle
Timber
Barley
Tampere
Rye
Dairy
Turku
Helsinki
Cu
Bergen
Oslo
Västerås
Stockholm
Stavanger
Linköping
Göteborg
Mackerel
Dairy
Wheat
Oats
Flounder
Copenhagen
Odense
Sugar
Beets
Eels
Malmö
OSLO
Shipbuilding, Machinery, Textiles
BERGEN
Shipbuilding, Canning, Textiles
STAVANGER
Canning
GÖTEBORG
Shipbuilding, Iron & Steel, Machinery, Textiles, Automobiles, Oil Refining
ODENSE
Iron & Steel, Shipbuilding
COPENHAGEN
Machinery, Shipbuilding
MALMÖ–WEST SKÅNE
Shipbuilding, Nonferrous Metals, Chemicals, Textiles
LINKÖPING–ÖSTERGÖTLAND
Machinery, Aircraft, Textiles, Paper
VÄSTERÅS–BERGSLAG
Iron & Steel, Machinery,
STOCKHOLM
Electrical Equipment, Machinery
TURKU
Shipbuilding, Machinery, Oil Refining
TAMPERE
Textiles, Leather
HELSINKI
Machinery, Textiles, Shipbuilding

DOMINANT LAND USE

- Cash Cereals, Dairy
- Dairy, Cattle, Hogs
- Dairy, General Farming
- General Farming (chiefly cereals)
- Nomadic Sheep Herding
- Forests, Limited Mixed Farming
- Nonagricultural Land

MAJOR MINERAL OCCURRENCES

Ag Silver
Au Gold
Co Cobalt
Cu Copper
Fe Iron Ore
Mo Molybdenum
O Petroleum
Pb Lead
Ti Titanium
V Vanadium
Zn Zinc

Water Power
Major Industrial Areas
× Electrochemical & Electrometallurgical Centers
□ Paper, Pulp & Sawmilling Centers

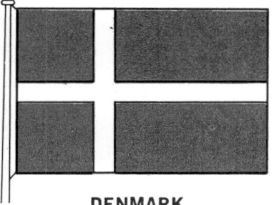

DENMARK

ICELAND

DENMARK

AREA 16,629 sq. mi
POPULATION 5,065,313
CAPITAL Copenhagen
LARGEST CITY Copenhagen
HIGHEST POINT Yding Skovhøj 568 ft.
MONETARY UNIT krone
MAJOR LANGUAGE Danish
MAJOR RELIGION Protestantism

ICELAND

AREA 39,768 sq. mi.
POPULATION 220,000
CAPITAL Reykjavík
LARGEST CITY Reykjavík
HIGHEST POINT Hvannadalshnúkur 6,952 ft.
MONETARY UNIT króna
MAJOR LANGUAGE Icelandic
MAJOR RELIGION Protestantism

DENMARK and ICELAND

CONIC PROJECTION

SCALE OF MILES

SCALE OF KILOMETERS

Capitals of Countries .... ☆
Capitals of Counties (amter) .... △
International Boundaries .... —·—·—
Internal Boundaries .... ———

Denmark is divided into fourteen counties plus Copenhagen and Frederiksberg communes.

© Copyright HAMMOND INCORPORATED, Maplewood, N.J.

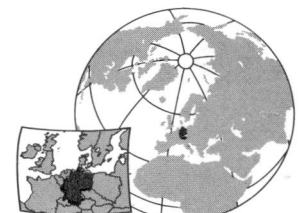

WEST GERMANY

AREA 95,985 sq. mi
POPULATION 61,644,600
CAPITAL Bonn
LARGEST CITY Berlin (West)
HIGHEST POINT Zugspitze 9,718 ft.
MONETARY UNIT Deutsche mark
MAJOR LANGUAGE German
MAJOR RELIGIONS Protestantism, Roman Catholicism

EAST GERMANY

AREA 41,768 sq. mi.
POPULATION 16,850,000
CAPITAL Berlin (East)
LARGEST CITY Berlin (East)
HIGHEST POINT Fichtelberg 3,983 ft.
MONETARY UNIT East German mark
MAJOR LANGUAGE German
MAJOR RELIGIONS Protestantism, Roman Catholicism

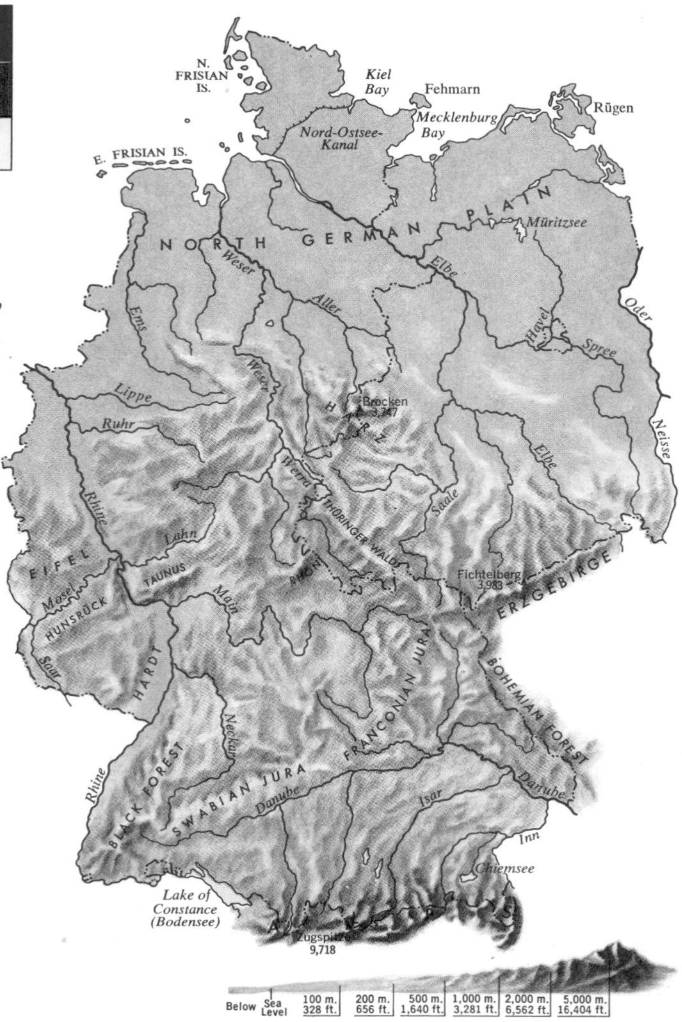

EAST GERMANY

DISTRICTS

Berlin, 1,094,147	F 4
Cottbus, 872,242	F 3
Dresden, 1,845,459	E 3
Erfurt, 1,247,213	D 3
Frankfurt, 688,637	F 2
Gera, 738,847	D 3
Halle, 1,890,187	D 3
Karl-Marx-Stadt, 1,994,115	E 3
Leipzig, 1,457,817	E 3
Magdeburg, 1,297,881	D 2
Neubrandenburg, 628,686	E 2
Potsdam, 1,124,892	E 2
Rostock, 867,806	E 1
Schwerin, 592,334	D 2
Suhl, 550,497	D 3

CITIES and TOWNS

Aken, 11,742	D 3
Altenburg, 51,193	E 3
Angermünde, 11,786	E 2
Anklam, 19,099	E 2
Annaberg-Buchholz, 26,561	E 3
Apolda, 28,649	D 3
Arnstadt, 29,462	D 3
Aue, 32,622	E 3
Auerbach, 18,168	E 3
Bad Doberan, 12,541	D 1
Bad Dürrenberg, 15,192	D 3
Bad Freienwalde, 11,497	F 2
Bad Langensalza, 166,282	D 3
Bad Salzungen, 17,277	C 3
Barth, 12,069	E 1
Bautzen, 45,851	F 3
Bergen, 13,244	E 1
Berlin (East) (cap.), 1,094,147	F 4
Bernau bei Berlin, 15,749	E 2
Bernburg, 44,428	D 3
Bischofswerda, 11,540	F 3
Bitterfeld, 27,062	E 3
Blankenburg am Harz, 18,784	D 3
Boizenburg an der Elbe, 12,428	D 2
Borna, 21,807	E 3
Brandenburg, 94,071	E 2
Burg bei Magdeburg, 29,027	D 2
Calbe, 15,976	D 3
Chemnitz (Karl-Marx-Stadt), 303,811	E 3
Coswig, Dresden, 22,149	E 3
Coswig, Halle, 12,473	E 3
Crimmitschau, 28,845	E 3
Delitzsch, 24,076	E 3
Demmin, 17,270	E 2
Dessau, 100,820	E 3
Döbeln, 27,624	E 3
Dresden, 507,692	E 3
Eberswalde-Finow, 47,141	F 2
Eilenburg, 22,245	E 3
Eisenach, 49,954	D 3
Eisenberg, 13,450	E 3
Eisenhüttenstadt, 46,455	F 2
Eisleben, 29,297	D 3
Erfurt, 202,979	D 3
Falkensee, 25,295	E 3
Falkenstein, 14,367	E 3
Finsterwalde, 22,466	E 3
Forst, 28,084	F 3
Frankfurt an der Oder, 70,817	F 2
Freiberg, 50,815	E 3
Freital, 46,061	E 3
Friedland	F 2
Fürstenwalde, 31,065	F 2
Gardelegen, 12,987	D 2
Genthin, 15,916	E 2
Gera, 113,108	E 3
Glauchau, 30,927	E 3
Görlitz, 84,658	F 3
Gotha, 59,243	D 3
Greifswald, 53,940	E 1
Greiz, 37,612	E 3
Grevesmühlen, 12,005	D 2
Grimma, 17,100	E 3
Grimmen, 14,571	E 3
Grossenhain, 18,712	E 3
Grossräschen, 12,889	E 3
Guben (Wilhelm-Pieck-Stadt), 32,731	F 3
Güstrow, 36,824	D 2
Hagenow, 11,254	D 2
Halberstadt, 46,669	D 3
Haldensleben, 19,194	D 3
Halle, 241,425	D 3
Havelberg	D 2
Heidenau, 21,315	E 3
Heiligenstadt, 13,931	D 3
Hennigsdorf bei Berlin, 24,853	E 2
Hettstedt, 20,291	D 3
Hildburghausen, 11,372	D 3
Hoyerswerda, 64,904	F 3
Ilmenau, 22,021	D 3
Jena, 99,431	E 3
Johanngeorgenstadt, 10,328	E 3
Jüterbog, 13,221	E 3
Kamenz, 18,221	F 3
Karl-Marx-Stadt, 303,811	E 3
Kleinmachnow, 14,059	E 4
Klingenthal, 13,614	E 3
Königs Wusterhausen, 11,825	E 2
Köpenick, 130,987	F 4
Köthen, 35,451	E 3
Kühlungsborn	D 1
Lauchhammer, 26,939	E 3
Leipzig, 570,972	E 3
Lichtenberg, 192,063	F 4
Limbach-Oberfrohna, 25,706	E 3
Löbau, 18,077	F 3
Lübben, 14,224	F 3
Lübbenau, 22,350	F 3
Luckenwalde, 28,544	E 2
Ludwigslust, 13,280	D 2
Magdeburg, 276,089	D 2
Markkleeberg, 22,380	E 3
Meerane, 25,037	E 3
Meiningen, 26,134	D 3
Meissen, 43,561	E 3
Merseburg, 54,269	D 3
Meuselwitz, 13,585	E 3
Mittweida, 19,259	E 3
Mühlhausen (Thomas-Müntzer-Stadt), 44,106	D 3
Nauen, 11,940	E 2
Naumburg, 36,358	D 3
Neubrandenburg, 59,971	E 2
Neuenhagen bei Berlin, 12,603	F 4
Neuruppin, 24,888	E 2
Neustrelitz, 27,074	E 2
Nordhausen, 44,442	D 3
Oelsnitz, 15,084	E 3
Oelsnitz im Erzgebirge, 16,063	E 3
Olbernhau, 13,479	E 3
Oranienburg, 24,452	E 2
Oschatz, 18,974	E 3
Oscherleben, 17,377	D 2
Pankow, 136,527	F 3
Parchim, 22,927	D 2
Pasewalk, 15,099	E 2
Peenemünde	E 1
Perleberg, 15,029	D 2
Pirna, 49,771	E 3
Plauen, 80,353	E 3
Pössneck, 18,648	D 3
Potsdam, 117,236	E 2
Prenzlau, 22,738	E 2
Pritzwalk, 11,887	D 2
Quedlinburg, 29,796	D 3
Radeberg, 18,528	E 3
Radebeul, 38,383	E 3
Rathenow, 32,011	E 2
Reichenbach, 27,440	E 3
Ribnitz-Damgarten, 17,254	E 1
Riesa, 49,999	E 3
Rosslau, 16,520	E 3
Rostock, 210,167	E 1
Rüdersdorf bei Berlin, 11,068	E 2
Rudolstadt, 31,698	D 3
Saalfeld, 33,648	D 3
Salzwedel, 21,741	D 2
Sangerhausen, 32,721	D 3
Sassnitz, 13,857	E 1
Schkeuditz, 15,585	E 3
Schmalkalden, 15,017	D 3
Schmölln, 13,406	E 3
Schneeberg, 20,376	E 3
Schönebeck, 45,197	D 2
Schwedt, 45,729	F 2
Schwerin, 104,984	D 2
Sebnitz, 13,470	F 3
Senftenberg, 29,953	F 3
Sömmerda, 20,712	D 3
Sondershausen, 23,383	D 3
Sonneberg, 29,193	D 3
Spremberg, 22,862	F 3
Stassfurt, 26,225	D 3
Stendal, 39,647	D 2
Stralsund, 72,167	E 1
Strausberg, 21,334	F 2
Suhl, 36,642	D 3
Tangermünde, 12,898	D 2
Teltow, 16,171	E 4
Templin, 11,718	E 2
Teterow, 11,156	E 2
Thale, 17,248	D 3
Torgau, 21,613	E 3
Treptow, 14,320	F 2
Treptow, 127,448	F 4
Ueckermünde, 11,423	F 2
Waldheim, 11,925	E 3
Waltershausen, 13,893	D 3
Waren, 22,921	E 2
Weida, 11,816	E 3
Weimar, 63,144	D 3
Weissenfels, 43,191	D 3
Weissensee, 78,451	F 4
Weisswasser, 25,910	F 3
Werdau, 22,921	E 3
Wernigerode, 34,658	D 3
Wilhelm-Pieck-Stadt, 32,731	F 3
Wismar, 56,765	D 2
Wittenberg, 51,364	E 3
Wittenberge, 32,907	D 2
Wittstock, 10,799	E 2
Wolgast, 16,384	E 1
Wurzen, 20,501	E 3
Zehdenick, 12,651	E 2
Zeitz, 44,582	E 3
Zella-Mehlis, 16,301	D 3
Zerbst, 19,356	E 3
Zeulenroda, 13,452	E 3
Zittau, 42,298	F 3
Zwickau, 123,069	E 3

OTHER FEATURES

Altmark (reg.), 267,229	D 2
Arkona (cape)	E 1
Baltic (sea)	E 1
Black Elster (riv.)	E 3
Brandenburg (reg.), 7,130,055	E 2
Elbe (riv.)	D 2
Elde (riv.)	D 2
Elster, Black (riv.)	E 3
Elster, White (riv.)	E 3
Erzgebirge (mts.)	E 3
Fichtelberg (mt.)	E 3
Harz (mts.)	D 3
Havel (riv.)	E 2
Lusatia (reg.), 594,784	F 3
Mecklenburg (bay)	D 1
Mecklenburg (reg.), 1,925,669	E 2
Mulde (riv.)	E 3
Neisse (riv.)	F 3
Oder (riv.)	F 2
Peene (riv.)	E 2
Pomerania (reg.), 630,524	E 1
Pomeranian (bay)	F 1
Rhön (mts.)	D 3
Rügen (isl.), 85,651	E 1
Saale (riv.)	D 3
Saxony (reg.), 5,148,714	E 3
Spree (riv.)	F 3
Spreewald (for.)	F 3
Thüringer Wald (for.)	D 3
Thuringia (reg.), 2,686,322	D 3
Ücker (riv.)	E 2
Unstrut (riv.)	D 3
Usedom (isl.)	F 1
Warnow (riv.)	D 2
Werra (riv.)	D 3
White Elster (riv.)	E 3

WEST GERMANY

STATES

Baden-Württemberg, 9,152,700	C 4
Bavaria, 10,810,400	D 4
Berlin (West) (free city), 1,984,800	E 4
Bremen, 716,800	C 2
Hamburg, 1,717,400	C 2
Hesse, 5,549,800	C 3
Lower Saxony, 7,238,500	C 2
North Rhine-Westphalia, 17,129,600	B 3
Rhineland-Palatinate, 3,665,800	B 4
Saarland, 1,096,300	B 4
Schleswig-Holstein, 2,582,400	C 1

CITIES and TOWNS

Aachen, 242,453	B 3
Aalen, 64,273	D 4
Ahaus, 27,126	B 2
Ahlen, 54,214	B 3
Ahrensburg, 24,964	D 1
Alfeld, 24,273	C 2
Alsdorf, 47,473	B 3
Alsfeld, 18,091	C 3
Altena, 26,753	B 3
Altona	C 2
Altötting, 11,010	E 4
Alzey, 15,190	C 4
Amberg, 46,954	D 4
Andernach, 27,132	B 3
Ansbach, 39,117	D 4
Arnsberg, 80,287	C 3
Arolsen, 15,619	C 3
Aschaffenburg, 55,398	C 4
Augsburg, 249,943	D 4
Aurich, 34,194	B 2
Backnang, 29,614	C 4
Bad Driburg, 17,478	C 3
Bad Ems, 10,487	B 3
Baden-Baden, 49,718	C 4
Bad Gandersheim, 11,614	D 3
Bad Harzburg, 25,786	D 3
Bad Hersfeld, 29,248	C 3
Bad Homburg vor der Höhe, 51,196	C 3
Bad Oldesloe, 19,640	D 2
Bad Pyrmont, 21,896	C 3
Bad Reichenhall, 13,048	E 5
Bad Salzuflen, 50,924	C 2
Bad Schwartau, 38,696	D 2
Bad Segeberg, 13,320	D 2
Bad Tölz, 12,458	D 5
Bad Vilbel, 25,012	C 3
Bad Waldsee, 14,296	C 5
Bad Wildungen, 15,418	C 3
Bad Wimpfen, 5,536	C 4
Baiersbronn, 14,845	C 4
Balingen, 29,310	C 4
Bamberg, 74,236	D 4

OTHER FEATURES

Bassum, 14,113	C 2
Bayreuth, 67,035	D 4
Bayrischzell, 1,639	E 5
Bebra, 14,591	C 3
Bendorf, 15,943	B 3
Bensheim, 32,653	C 4
Benshem, 13,681	B 2
Berchtesgaden, 8,558	E 5
Bergisch Gladbach, 99,517	B 3
Berleburg (Bad Berleburg), 20,415	C 3
Berlin (West), 1,984,837	E 4
Biberach an der Riss, 28,891	C 4
Bielefeld, 316,058	C 2
Bietigheim-Bissingen, 34,042	C 4
Bingen, 24,541	B 4
Birkenfeld, 5,883	B 4
Blaubeuren, 11,652	C 4
Böblingen, 40,547	C 4
Bocholt, 65,460	B 3
Bochum, 414,842	B 3
Bonn (cap.), 283,711	B 3
Boppard, 15,887	B 3
Borghorst, 17,238	B 2
Borken, 30,212	B 3
Bottrop, 101,495	B 3
Brake, 18,089	C 2
Bramsche, 24,119	B 2
Braunschweig (Brunswick), 268,519	D 2
Breisach am Rhein, 9,230	B 4
Bremen, 572,969	C 2
Bremerhaven, 143,836	C 2
Bremervörde, 17,565	C 2
Bretten, 22,140	C 4
Brilon, 24,595	C 3
Bruchsal, 38,929	C 4
Brühl, 44,675	B 3
Brunsbüttel, 11,451	C 2
Brunswick, 268,519	D 2
Buchholz in der Nordheide, 25,713	C 2
Bückeburg, 21,393	C 2
Büdingen, 16,845	C 3
Bühl, 21,596	C 4
Büren, 17,352	C 3
Burg auf Fehmarn, 5,874	D 1
Burghausen, 16,892	E 4
Burgsteinfurt, 31,367	B 2
Butzbach, 20,900	C 3
Buxtehude, 30,249	C 2
Celle, 74,347	D 2
Cham, 12,423	E 4
Charlottenburg, 201,732	E 4
Clausthal-Zellerfeld, 16,690	D 3
Cloppenburg, 19,757	B 2
Coburg, 46,244	D 3
Coesfeld, 30,617	B 3
Cologne, 1,013,771	B 3
Crailsheim, 24,506	D 4
Cuxhaven, 60,353	C 2
Dachau, 33,207	D 4
Dahlem	E 4
Darmstadt, 137,018	C 4
Deggendorf, 25,188	E 4
Delmenhorst, 71,488	C 2
Detmold, 65,629	C 3
Diepholz, 14,201	C 2
Dillenburg, 14,068	C 3
Dillingen an der Donau, 11,601	D 4
Dingolfing, 13,325	E 4
Dinkelsbühl, 10,034	D 4
Donaueschingen, 17,578	C 5
Donauwörth, 17,077	D 4
Dorsten, 65,718	B 3
Dortmund, 630,609	B 3
Duderstadt, 23,255	D 3
Dudweiler, 27,877	B 4
Duisburg, 591,635	B 3
Dülmen, 37,013	B 3
Düren, 87,774	B 3
Düsseldorf, 664,336	B 3
Ebenhausen, 15,834	C 4
Ebingen, 22,594	C 4
Eckernförde, 22,938	C 1
Eichstätt, 13,080	D 4
Einbeck, 29,821	C 3
Eiserfeld, 22,346	C 3

Ellwangen, 21,994	D 4
Elmshorn, 41,355	C 2
Emden, 53,509	B 2
Emmendingen, 24,722	B 4
Emmerich, 29,113	B 3
Erlangen, 100,671	D 4
Eschwege, 24,882	C 3
Eschweiler, 53,603	B 3
Espelkamp, 22,670	C 2
Essen, 677,568	B 3
Esslingen am Neckar, 95,298	C 4
Ettlingen, 35,159	C 4
Euskirchen, 43,558	B 3
Eutin, 17,701	D 1
Fellbach, 42,501	C 4
Flensburg, 93,213	C 1
Forchheim, 23,430	D 4
Frankenberg-Eder, 15,337	C 3
Frankenthal, 43,684	C 4
Frankfurt am Main, 636,157	C 3
Frechen, 41,453	B 3
Freiburg im Breisgau, 175,371	B 5
Freising, 31,524	D 4
Freudenstadt, 19,454	C 4
Friedberg, 24,762	C 3
Friedrichshafen, 51,544	C 5
Fritzlar, 15,079	C 3
Fürstenfeldbruck, 27,194	D 4
Fürth, 101,639	D 4
Füssen, 10,506	D 5
Gaggenau, 28,846	C 4
Garmisch-Partenkirchen, 26,831	D 5
Gatow	E 4
Geesthacht, 24,745	D 2
Geislingen an der Steige, 28,693	C 4
Gelnhausen, 17,889	C 3
Gelsenkirchen, 322,584	B 3
Geretsried, 17,330	D 5
Germersheim, 12,041	C 4
Gerolstein, 6,857	B 3
Giessen, 75,481	C 3
Gifhorn, 31,635	D 2
Glückstadt, 12,159	C 2
Goch, 28,213	B 3
Göppingen, 54,365	C 4

Goslar, 53,957	D 3
Göttingen, 123,797	D 3
Grevenbroich, 56,392	B 3
Griesheim, 18,548	C 4
Gronau, 40,527	B 2
Gummersbach, 49,316	B 3
Günzburg, 13,528	D 4
Gunzenhausen, 13,565	D 4
Gütersloh, 77,128	C 2
Haar, 18,624	D 4
Hagen, 229,224	B 3
Haltern, 29,750	B 3
Hamburg, 1,717,383	D 2
Hameln, 61,066	C 2
Hamm, 172,210	B 3
Hammelburg, 12,350	C 3
Hanau, 86,676	C 3
Hannover, 552,955	C 2
Harburg-Wilhelmsburg	C 2
Hasloch, 17,752	C 4
Haunstetten, 21,810	D 4
Hechingen, 15,926	C 4
Heide, 21,918	C 1
Heidelberg, 129,368	C 4
Heidenheim an der Brenz, 49,943	D 4
Heilbronn, 113,177	C 4
Helmstedt, 28,095	D 2
Hemer, 27,815	B 3
Herford, 64,385	C 2
Herne, 190,561	B 3
Hildesheim, 105,290	D 2
Hockenheim, 16,890	C 4
Hof, 54,357	D 3
Hofgeismar, 13,300	C 3
Holzminden, 23,650	C 3
Homburg, 41,861	B 4
Horn-Bad Meinberg, 16,927	C 3
Höxter, 32,759	C 3
Hünfeld, 13,873	C 3
Hürth, 51,692	B 3
Husum, 24,984	C 1
Hüttenfeld, 39,561	C 4
Idar-Oberstein, 37,179	B 4
Immenstadt im Allgäu, 13,720	C 5
Ingolstadt, 88,500	D 4
Iserlohn, 96,174	B 3
Isny im Allgäu, 12,367	D 5
Itzehoe, 35,077	C 2

Jever, 12,096	B 2
Jülich, 31,564	B 3
Kaiserslautern, 100,886	B 4
Karlsruhe, 280,448	C 4
Kassel, 205,534	C 3
Kaufbeuren, 42,224	D 5
Kehl, 29,861	B 4
Kelheim, 11,996	D 4
Kempten, 56,944	D 5
Kevelaer, 20,971	B 3
Kiel, 262,164	D 1
Kirchheim unter Teck, 31,666	C 4
Kitzingen, 19,116	C 4
Kleve, 44,043	B 3
Koblenz, 118,394	B 3
Köln (Cologne), 1,013,771	B 3
Königswinter, 34,586	B 3
Konstanz, 70,152	C 5
Korbach, 22,998	C 3
Kornwestheim, 27,771	C 4
Krefeld, 228,463	B 3
Kronach, 11,538	D 3
Kulmbach, 25,711	D 3
Lage, 31,724	C 3
Lahnstein (Oberlahnstein), 19,725	B 3
Lahr, 35,570	B 4
Langelsheim, 31,993	C 4
Landau in der Pfalz, 37,661	C 4
Landsberg am Lech, 15,862	D 4
Landshut, 55,858	E 4
Langen, 30,227	C 4
Langenhagen, 47,092	C 2
Lauenburg an der Elbe, 11,077	D 2
Lauf an der Pegnitz, 19,443	D 4
Lauingen, 8,778	D 4
Lauterbach, 15,077	C 3
Leer, 32,785	B 2
Lehrte, 38,272	D 2
Lemgo, 39,664	C 2
Lengerich, 20,803	B 2
Leverkusen, 165,947	B 3
Lichtenfels, 13,719	D 3
Limburg an der Lahn, 28,606	C 3
Lindau, 23,930	C 5
Lingen, 43,785	B 2
Lippstadt, 63,040	C 3
Lohr am Main, 16,435	C 4
Lörrach, 44,179	B 5

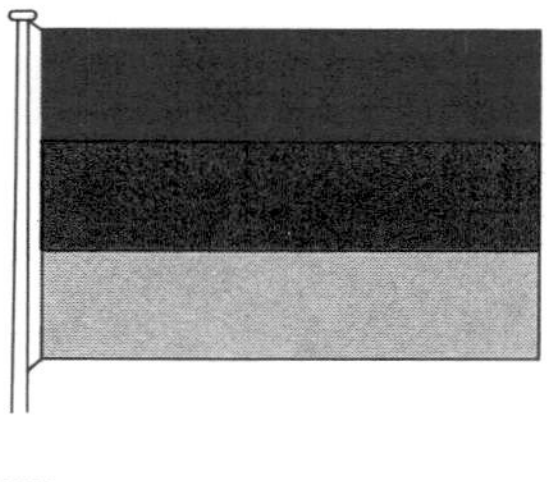

Topography

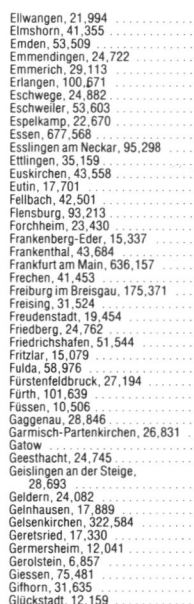

0   50   100
MILES

Below Sea Level | 100 m. 328 ft. | 200 m. 656 ft. | 500 m. 1,640 ft. | 1,000 m. 3,281 ft. | 2,000 m. 6,562 ft. | 5,000 m. 16,404 ft.

(continued on following page)

GERMANY Before World War I 1871-1914

GERMANY Between Wars 1919-1937

Occupied GERMANY 1945-1949

Agriculture, Industry and Resources

DOMINANT LAND USE

- Wheat, Sugar Beets
- Cereals (chiefly rye, oats, barley)
- Potatoes, Rye
- Dairy, Livestock
- Mixed Cereals, Dairy
- Truck Farming
- Grapes, Fruit
- Forests

MAJOR MINERAL OCCURRENCES

Ag Silver
Ba Barite
C Coal
Cu Copper
Fe Iron Ore
G Natural Gas
Gr Graphite
K Potash

Lg Lignite
Mg Magnesium
Na Salt
O Petroleum
Pb Lead
U Uranium
Zn Zinc

 Water Power

Major Industrial Areas

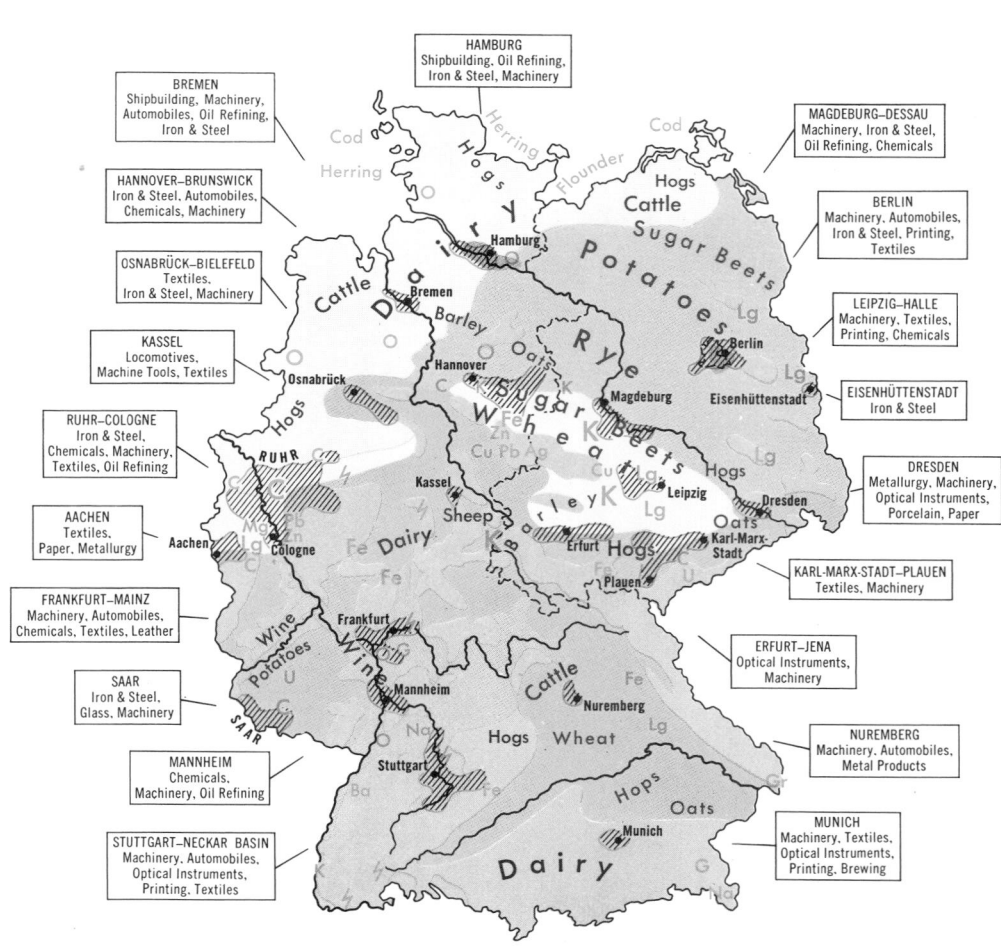

HAMBURG
Shipbuilding, Oil Refining, Iron & Steel, Machinery

BREMEN
Shipbuilding, Machinery, Automobiles, Oil Refining, Iron & Steel

MAGDEBURG–DESSAU
Machinery, Iron & Steel, Oil Refining, Chemicals

HANNOVER–BRUNSWICK
Iron & Steel, Automobiles, Chemicals, Machinery

BERLIN
Machinery, Automobiles, Iron & Steel, Printing, Textiles

OSNABRÜCK–BIELEFELD
Textiles, Iron & Steel, Machinery

LEIPZIG–HALLE
Machinery, Textiles, Printing, Chemicals

KASSEL
Locomotives, Machine Tools, Textiles

EISENHÜTTENSTADT
Iron & Steel

RUHR–COLOGNE
Iron & Steel, Chemicals, Machinery, Textiles, Oil Refining

DRESDEN
Metallurgy, Machinery, Optical Instruments, Porcelain, Paper

AACHEN
Textiles, Paper, Metallurgy

KARL-MARX-STADT–PLAUEN
Textiles, Machinery

FRANKFURT–MAINZ
Machinery, Automobiles, Chemicals, Textiles, Leather

ERFURT–JENA
Optical Instruments, Machinery

SAAR
Iron & Steel, Glass, Machinery

NUREMBERG
Machinery, Automobiles, Metal Products

MANNHEIM
Chemicals, Machinery, Oil Refining

MUNICH
Machinery, Textiles, Optical Instruments, Printing, Brewing

STUTTGART–NECKAR BASIN
Machinery, Automobiles, Optical Instruments, Printing, Textiles

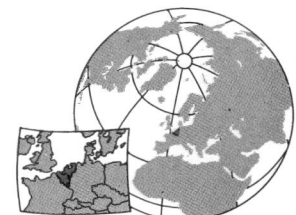

NETHERLANDS
AREA 15,892 sq. mi.
POPULATION 13,800,000
CAPITALS The Hague, Amsterdam
LARGEST CITY Amsterdam
HIGHEST POINT Vaalserberg 1,056 ft.
MONETARY UNIT guilder (florin)
MAJOR LANGUAGE Dutch
MAJOR RELIGIONS Protestantism, Roman Catholicism

BELGIUM
AREA 11,781 sq. mi.
POPULATION 9,813,000
CAPITAL Brussels
LARGEST CITY Brussels (greater)
HIGHEST POINT Botrange 2,277 ft.
MONETARY UNIT Belgian franc
MAJOR LANGUAGES French (Walloon), Flemish
MAJOR RELIGION Roman Catholicism

LUXEMBOURG
AREA 999 sq. mi.
POPULATION 358,000
CAPITAL Luxembourg
LARGEST CITY Luxembourg
HIGHEST POINT Ardennes Plateau 1,825 ft.
MONETARY UNIT Luxembourg franc
MAJOR LANGUAGES Luxembourgeois (Letze-burgisch), French, German
MAJOR RELIGION Roman Catholicism

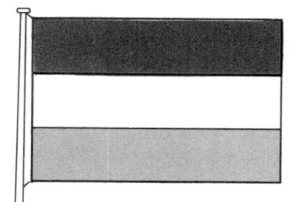

BELGIUM

PROVINCES

Antwerp, 1,533,249 .... F 6
Brabant, 2,176,373 .... F 7
East Flanders, 1,310,117 .... D 7
Hainault, 1,317,453 .... D 7
Liège, 1,008,905 .... H 7
Limburg, 652,547 .... G 7
Luxembourg, 217,310 .... G 9
Namur, 380,561 .... F 8
West Flanders, 1,054,429 .... B 7

☆CITIES and TOWNS

Aalst, 46,659 .... D 7
Aalter, 9,173 .... C 6
Aarlen (Arlon), 13,745 .... H 9
Aarschot, 12,474 .... F 7
Aat (Ath), 11,842 .... D 7
Adinkerke, 2,577 .... A 6
Aiken, 8,677 .... G 7
Alost (Aalst), 46,659 .... D 7
Amay, 7,617 .... G 8
Andenne, 8,091 .... G 8

Anderlecht, 103,796 .... B 9
Anderlues, 12,176 .... E 8
Antoing, 3,426 .... C 7
Antwerp, 224,543 .... E 6
Antwerp, *928,000 .... E 6
Antzerpen (Antwerp), 224,543 .... C 7
Ardooie, 7,081 .... C 7
Arendonk, 9,919 .... G 6
Arlon, 13,745 .... H 9
As, 5,496 .... H 7
Asse, 6,583 .... E 7
Assesse, 1,147 .... G 8
Ath, 11,842 .... D 7
Athus, 7,445 .... H 9
Audenarde (Oudenaarde), 26,615 .... D 7
Auderghem, 34,546 .... C 9
Autelbas, 1,501 .... H 9
Auvelais, 8,287 .... F 8
Aywaille, 3,850 .... H 8

Baerle-Duc, 2,121 .... F 6
Balen, 15,110 .... G 6
Barvaux, 1,934 .... H 8
Basècles, 4,164 .... D 7
Bastenaken (Bastogne), 6,816 .... H 9
Bastogne, 6,816 .... H 9
Beaumont, 1,790 .... E 8

Beauraing, 2,755 .... F 8
Berchem, 50,241 .... F 6
Berchem-Sainte-Agathe, 19,087 .... B 9
Bergen (Mons), 59,362 .... E 8
Bertrix, 4,562 .... G 9
Beveren, 15,913 .... E 6
Bilzen, 7,178 .... G 7
Binche, 10,098 .... E 8
Blankenberge, 13,969 .... C 6
Bocholt, 6,497 .... H 6
Boom, 16,584 .... E 6
Borgerhout, 49,002 .... E 6
Borgloon, 3,412 .... G 7
Borgworm (Waremme), 10,956 .... G 7
Bouillon, 2,944 .... G 9
Bourg-Léopold (Leopoldsburg), 9,593 .... G 6
Boussu, 11,474 .... D 8
Bovigny, 972 .... H 8
Braine-l'Alleud, 18,531 .... E 7
Braine-le-Comte, 11,957 .... D 7
Bredene, 9,244 .... B 6
Bree, 10,389 .... H 6
Bruges, 117,220 .... C 6
Brugge (Bruges), 117,220 .... C 6
Brussels (cap.), *1,054,970 .... C 9

Bruxelles (Brussels) (cap.), *1,054,970 .... C 9
Charleroi, 23,689 .... E 8
Charleroi, *458,000 .... E 8
Châtelet, 14,752 .... F 8
Châtelineau, 19,004 .... F 8
Chièvres, 3,283 .... D 7
Chimay, 3,288 .... E 8
Ciney, 7,536 .... G 8
Comblain-au-Pont, 3,582 .... G 8
Comines, 8,192 .... B 7
Couillet, 14,284 .... E 8
Courcelles, 17,015 .... E 8
Courtrai, 44,961 .... C 7
Couvin, 4,234 .... F 8
Cul-des-Sarts, 910 .... E 9
Deinze, 16,711 .... D 7
Denderleeuw, 9,925 .... E 7
Dendermonde, 22,119 .... E 6
De Panne, 6,985 .... B 6
Dessel, 7,505 .... G 6
Deurne, 80,766 .... E 6
Diegem, 4,906 .... C 9
Diest, 10,799 .... F 7
Diksmuide, 6,669 .... B 6
Dilbeek, 15,108 .... B 9

Dinant, 9,747 .... G 8
Dison, 8,466 .... H 7
Dixmude (Diksmuide), 6,669 .... B 6
Doel, 1,332 .... E 6
Doornik (Tournai), 32,794 .... C 7
Dour, 10,059 .... D 8
Drogenbos, 4,840 .... B 10
Drongen, 9,120 .... D 6
Duffel, 13,802 .... F 6
Ecaussinnes-d'Enghien, 6,630 .... E 7
Edingen (Enghien), 4,115 .... D 7
Eeklo, 19,144 .... D 6
Eernegem, 5,778 .... B 6
Eigenbrakel (Braine-l'Alleud), 18,531 .... E 7
Ekeren, 27,648 .... E 6
Ellezelles, 3,556 .... D 7
Enghien, 4,115 .... D 7
Ensival, 5,266 .... H 7
Erquelinnes, 4,471 .... E 8
Esneux, 6,183 .... H 7
Essen, 10,795 .... F 6
Etalle, 1,185 .... H 9
Etterbeek, 51,030 .... B 9
Eupen, 14,879 .... J 7
Evere, 26,957 .... C 9

Evergem, 12,886 .... D 6
Flémalle-Haute, 8,135 .... G 7
Fleurus, 8,523 .... F 8
Florennes, 4,107 .... F 8
Florenville, 2,529 .... G 9
Forest, 55,135 .... B 9
Fosses-la-Ville, 3,972 .... F 8
Frameries, 11,224 .... D 8
Frasnes-lez-Buissenal, 2,694 .... D 7
Furnes (Veurne), 9,496 .... B 6
Ganshoren, 21,147 .... B 9
Gaurain-Ramecroix, 3,507 .... D 7
Gedinne, 1,073 .... F 9
Geel, 29,346 .... F 6
Geldenaken (Jodoigne), 4,132 .... F 7
Gembloux, 11,249 .... F 7
Gemmenich, 2,501 .... H 7
Genk, 57,913 .... H 7
Gent (Ghent), 148,860 .... D 6
Gentbrugge, 22,214 .... D 6
Geraardsbergen, 17,533 .... D 7
Ghent, 148,860 .... D 6
Ghent, *477,000 .... D 6
Gilly, 23,241 .... E 8
Gosselies, 10,724 .... E 8
Grammont (Geraardsbergen), 17,533 .... D 7
Haacht, 4,436 .... F 7
Hal (Halle), 20,017 .... E 7
Halen, 5,322 .... G 7
Halle, 20,017 .... E 7
Hamme, 17,559 .... E 6
Hamont, 6,893 .... H 6
Hannut (Hannut), 7,232 .... G 7
Hannut, 7,232 .... G 7
Harelbeke, 18,498 .... C 7
Hasselt, 39,663 .... G 7
Havelange, 1,632 .... G 8
Heer, 569 .... F 8
Heist-Knokke, 27,582 .... C 6
Heist-op-den-Berg, 13,472 .... F 6
Herbeumont, 573 .... G 9
Herentals, 18,639 .... F 6
Herselt, 7,412 .... F 6
Herstal, 29,600 .... H 7
Herve, 4,118 .... H 7
Hoboken, 33,693 .... E 6
Hoei (Huy), 12,736 .... G 8
Hoeselt, 6,884 .... G 7
Hoogstraten, 4,381 .... F 6
Hornu, 10,712 .... D 8
Houffalize, 1,315 .... H 8
Huy, 12,736 .... G 8
Ieper, 20,825 .... B 7
Ingelmunster, 10,245 .... C 7
Ixelles, 86,450 .... C 9
Izegem, 22,928 .... C 7
Jambes, 15,840 .... F 8
Jemappes, 18,632 .... D 8
Jemeppe, 12,243 .... G 7
Jette, 40,013 .... B 9
Jodoigne, 4,132 .... F 7
Jumet, 28,029 .... E 8
Kain, 5,032 .... C 7
Kalmthout, 12,724 .... F 6
Kapellen, 13,352 .... E 6
Kessel-Lo, 23,104 .... F 7
Knokke-Heist, 27,582 .... C 6
Koekelare, 7,807 .... B 6
Koekelberg, 17,570 .... B 9
Koersel, 11,173 .... G 6
Kontich, 14,432 .... E 6
Kortemark, 5,904 .... C 6
Kortrijk (Courtrai), 44,961 .... C 7
Kraainem, 11,390 .... C 9
La Louvière, 23,310 .... E 8
La Louvière, *113,259 .... E 8
Lanaken, 8,659 .... H 7
Landen, 5,740 .... G 7
Langemark, 5,457 .... B 7
La Roche-en-Ardenne, 1,908 .... G 8
Lede, 10,316 .... D 7
Ledeberg, 10,338 .... D 7
Lens, 1,758 .... D 7
Leopoldsburg, 9,593 .... G 6
Lessen (Lessines), 8,906 .... D 7
Lessines, 8,906 .... D 7
Leuven (Louvain), 30,623 .... F 7
Leuze, 7,185 .... D 7
Libramont, 2,975 .... G 9
Lichtervelde, 7,459 .... C 6
Liedekerke, 10,482 .... D 7
Liège, 145,573 .... H 7
Liège, *622,000 .... H 7
Lier, 28,416 .... F 6
Lierneux, 2,740 .... H 8
Lierre (Lier), 28,416 .... F 6
Limbourg, 3,762 .... J 7
Limburg (Limbourg), 3,762 .... J 7
Linkebeek, 4,265 .... B 10
Lokeren, 26,740 .... D 6
Lommel, 21,984 .... G 6
Looz (Borgloon), 3,412 .... G 7
Louvain, 30,623 .... F 7
Luik (Liège), 145,573 .... H 7
Maaseik, 8,622 .... H 6

Mechelen, 7,057 .... C 9
Maldegem, 14,474 .... C 6
Malines (Mechelen), 65,466 .... F 6
Malmédy, 6,464 .... J 8
Marche-en-Famenne, 4,567 .... G 8
Marchin, 4,206 .... G 8
Marcinelle, 27,228 .... E 8
Mariembourg, 1,783 .... E 8
Martelange, 1,526 .... H 9
Mechelen, 65,466 .... F 6
Meerhout, 8,567 .... G 6
Meerle, 2,911 .... F 6
Melsbroek, 2,027 .... D 9
Menen, 22,037 .... C 7
Menin (Menen), 22,037 .... C 7
Merchtem, 8,998 .... E 7
Merelbeke, 13,837 .... D 7
Merksem, 39,768 .... E 6
Merksplas, 5,065 .... F 6
Messancy, 3,150 .... H 9
Mettet, 3,372 .... F 8
Meulebeke, 10,458 .... C 7
Moeskroen (Mouscron), 37,311 .... C 7
Mol, 28,823 .... G 6
Molenbeek-Saint-Jean, 68,411 .... B 9
Mons, 59,362 .... E 8
Montegnée, 11,823 .... G 7
Montignies-sur-Sambre, 23,572 .... F 8
Mortsel, 28,012 .... E 6
Mouscron, 37,311 .... C 7
Namen (Namur), 32,269 .... F 8
Namur, 32,269 .... F 8
Neerlinter, 2,912 .... G 7
Neerpelt, 8,771 .... G 6
Neufchâteau, 2,670 .... G 9
Nieuport (Nieuwpoort), 8,273 .... B 6
Nieuwpoort, 8,273 .... B 6
Nijvel (Nivelles), 16,126 .... E 7
Ninove, 12,428 .... D 7
Nivelles, 16,126 .... E 7
Oostende (Ostend), 71,227 .... B 6
Oostkamp, 8,999 .... C 6
Ophoven, 2,577 .... H 6
Opwijk, 9,699 .... E 7
Ostend, 71,227 .... B 6
Oudenaarde, 26,615 .... D 7
Oud-Turnhout, 9,245 .... F 6
Ougrée, 20,574 .... G 7
Overijse, 16,181 .... F 7
Overpelt, 10,470 .... G 6
Peer, 7,201 .... G 6
Péruwelz, 7,878 .... D 8
Perwez, 2,905 .... F 7
Philippeville, 2,076 .... F 8
Poperinge, 12,671 .... B 7
Poppel, 2,272 .... G 6
Putte, 6,953 .... F 6
Quaregnon, 17,688 .... D 8
Quiévrain, 5,510 .... D 8
Raeren, 3,655 .... J 7
Rance, 1,464 .... E 8
Rebecq-Rognon, 3,744 .... E 7
Renaix (Ronse), 25,056 .... D 7
Retie, 6,619 .... G 6
Rièzes, 276 .... E 9
Rochefort, 4,357 .... G 8
Roeselare, 40,428 .... C 7
Roeulx, 2,628 .... E 8
Ronse, 25,056 .... D 7
Roulers (Roeselare), 40,428 .... C 7
Ruisbroek, 5,824 .... B 9
Saint-Georges-sur-Meuse, 6,003 .... G 7
Saint-Gérard, 1,627 .... F 8
Saint-Gilles, 55,055 .... B 9
Saint-Hubert, 3,091 .... G 9
Saint-Josse-ten-Noode, 23,633 .... C 9
Saint-Léger, 1,586 .... H 9
Saint-Trond (Sint-Truiden), 21,473 .... G 7
Saint-Vith (Sankt Vith), 3,001 .... J 8
Sankt Vith, 3,001 .... J 8
Schaerbeek, 118,950 .... C 9
Schoten, 29,914 .... E 6
Seraing, 40,545 .... G 7
's-Gravenbrakel (Braine-le-Comte), 11,957 .... D 7
Sint-Amandsberg, 25,071 .... D 6
Sint-Lenaarts, 4,606 .... F 6
Sint-Niklaas, 49,214 .... E 6
Sint-Pieters-Leeuw, 16,856 .... B 9
Sint-Truiden, 21,473 .... G 7
Sivry, 1,373 .... E 8
Soignies, 12,006 .... D 7
Spa, 9,504 .... H 8
Staden, 5,740 .... B 7
Stavelot, 4,723 .... H 8
Steenokkerzeel, 4,037 .... C 9
Strombeek-Bever, 11,233 .... C 9
Tamines, 7,885 .... F 8
Tamise (Temse), 14,950 .... E 6
Schelen, 29,914 .... C 7
Templeuve, 3,902 .... C 7
Temse, 14,950 .... E 6
Termonde (Dendermonde), 22,119 .... E 6
Tessenderlo, 11,778 .... G 6
Theux, 5,316 .... H 8
Thuin, 5,777 .... E 8

(continued on following page)

Agriculture, Industry and Resources

DOMINANT LAND USE

- Dairy, Truck Farming
- Cash Crops, Livestock
- Mixed Cereals, Dairy
- Specialized Horticulture
- Grapes, Wine
- Forests
- Sand Dunes

MAJOR MINERAL OCCURRENCES

C Coal   Na Salt
Fe Iron Ore   O Petroleum
G Natural Gas

Major Industrial Areas

AMSTERDAM–HAARLEM
Shipbuilding, Machinery, Iron & Steel

ROTTERDAM
Shipbuilding, Machinery, Oil Refining

ENSCHEDE
Textiles, Cotton Industry

EINDHOVEN
Electrical Machinery, Automobiles

ANTWERP
Shipbuilding, Heavy Machinery, Oil Refining

LIÈGE
Iron & Steel, Machinery, Nonferrous Metals, Armaments

GHENT–FLANDERS
Textiles, Chemicals, Iron & Steel

BRUSSELS
Metallurgy, Textiles, Chemicals

VERVIERS
Textiles

LUXEMBOURG
Iron & Steel, Machinery, Chemicals

MONS–CHARLEROI
Iron & Steel, Metallurgy, Machinery, Chemicals

Topography

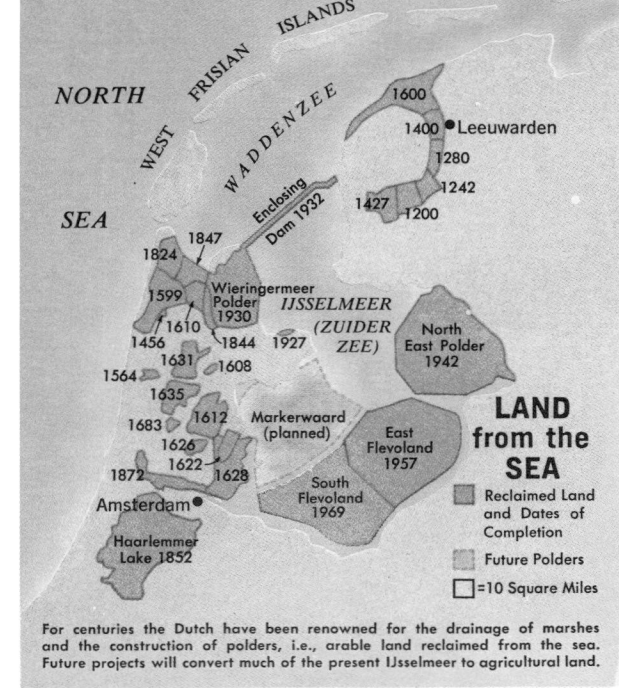

LAND from the SEA

■ Reclaimed Land and Dates of Completion

▨ Future Polders

□ =10 Square Miles

For centuries the Dutch have been renowned for the drainage of marshes and the construction of polders, i.e., arable land reclaimed from the sea. Future projects will convert much of the present IJsselmeer to agricultural land.

NETHERLANDS, BELGIUM and LUXEMBOURG

CONIC PROJECTION

SCALE OF MILES

0 5 10 20 30 40

SCALE OF KILOMETRES

0 5 10 20 30 40 50

Capitals of Countries ⭐

Provincial Capitals △

International Boundaries ▬ ▬

Provincial Boundaries ▬▬

Canals ┈┈┈┈

Copyright by C.S. Hammond & Co., N.Y.

FRANCE

CONIC PROJECTION

SCALE OF MILES

SCALE OF KILOMETRES

Capitals of Countries .... ★
Capitals of Departments .... △
International Boundaries .... —·—·—
Department Boundaries .... —··—··—
Canals .... ====

© C.S. HAMMOND & Co., N.Y.

PARIS and ENVIRONS

CORSICA

Same Scale as Main Map

DEPARTMENTS

Ain, 339,262 ... F 4
Aisne, 526,346 ... E 3
Allier, 386,533 ... E 4
Alpes-de-Haute-Provence, 104,813 ... G 5
Alpes-Maritimes, 722,070 ... G 6
Ardèche, 256,927 ... F 5
Ardennes, 309,380 ... F 3
Ariège, 138,478 ... D 6
Aube, 270,325 ... E 3
Aude, 278,323 ... E 6
Aveyron, 281,568 ... E 5
Bas-Rhin, 827,367 ... G 3
Belfort (terr.), 118,450 ... G 4
Bouches-du-Rhône, 1,470,271 ... F 6
Calvados, 519,695 ... C 3
Cantal, 169,330 ... E 5
Charente, 331,016 ... D 5
Charente-Maritime, 483,622 ... C 5
Cher, 304,601 ... E 4
Corrèze, 237,858 ... D 5
Corse-du-Sud, 121,771 ... B 7
Côte-d'Or, 421,192 ... F 4
Côtes-du-Nord, 506,102 ... B 3
Creuse, 156,876 ... D 4
Deux-Sèvres, 326,462 ... C 4
Dordogne, 374,073 ... D 5
Doubs, 426,363 ... G 4
Drôme, 342,891 ... F 5
Essonne, 674,157 ... E 3
Eure, 383,385 ... D 3
Eure-et-Loir, 302,207 ... D 3
Finistère, 768,929 ... A 3
Gard, 478,544 ... F 6
Gers, 181,577 ... D 6
Gironde, 1,009,390 ... C 5
Haut-Rhin, 585,018 ... G 4
Haute-Corse, 148,060 ... B 6
Haute-Garonne, 690,712 ... D 6
Haute-Loire, 208,337 ... E 5
Haute-Marne, 214,336 ... F 3
Haute-Saône, 214,176 ... G 4
Haute-Savoie, 378,550 ... G 5
Haute-Vienne, 341,589 ... D 5
Hautes-Alpes, 91,790 ... G 5
Hautes-Pyrénées, 225,730 ... D 6
Hauts-de-Seine, 1,461,619 ... A 2
Hérault, 591,397 ... E 6
Ille-et-Vilaine, 652,722 ... C 3
Indre, 247,178 ... D 4
Indre-et-Loire, 437,870 ... D 4
Isère, 768,450 ... F 5
Jura, 233,547 ... F 4
Landes, 277,381 ... C 5
Loir-et-Cher, 267,896 ... D 4
Loire, 722,383 ... F 5
Loire-Atlantique, 861,452 ... C 4
Loiret, 430,629 ... E 4
Lot, 151,198 ... D 5
Lot-et-Garonne, 290,592 ... D 5
Lozère, 77,258 ... E 5
Maine-et-Loire, 584,709 ... C 4
Manche, 451,939 ... C 3
Marne, 485,388 ... F 3
Mayenne, 252,762 ... C 3
Meurthe-et-Moselle, 705,413 ... G 3
Meuse, 209,513 ... F 3
Morbihan, 540,474 ... B 4
Moselle, 971,314 ... G 3
Nièvre, 247,702 ... E 4
Nord, 2,417,899 ... E 2
Oise, 540,988 ... E 3
Orne, 288,524 ... C 3
Paris, 2,590,771 ... B 2
Pas-de-Calais, 1,397,159 ... E 2
Puy-de-Dôme, 547,743 ... E 5
Pyrénées-Atlantiques, 508,734 ... C 6
Pyrénées-Orientales, 281,976 ... E 6
Rhône, 1,325,611 ... F 5
Saône-et-Loire, 550,362 ... F 4
Sarthe, 461,839 ... D 3
Savoie, 288,921 ... G 5
Seine-et-Marne, 604,340 ... E 3
Seine-Maritime, 1,113,977 ... D 3
Seine-Saint-Denis, 1,251,792 ... B 1
Somme, 512,113 ... E 3
Tarn, 332,011 ... E 6
Tarn-et-Garonne, 183,572 ... D 5
Val-de-Marne, 1,121,340 ... B 2
Val-d'Oise, 693,269 ... E 3
Var, 555,926 ... G 6
Vaucluse, 353,966 ... F 6
Vendée, 421,250 ... C 4
Vienne, 340,256 ... D 4
Vosges, 388,201 ... G 3
Yonne, 283,376 ... E 4
Yvelines, 853,386 ... D 3

CITIES and TOWNS

Abbeville, 23,770 ... D 2
Agde, 8,812 ... E 6
Agen, 34,592 ... D 5
Aix-en-Provence, 74,948 ... F 6
Aix-les-Bains, 20,594 ... G 5
Ajaccio, 38,776 ... B 7
Albert, 10,937 ... E 2
Albertville, 15,422 ... G 5
Albi, 38,867 ... E 6
Alençon, 30,368 ... D 3
Aléria, 1,000 ... B 6
Alès, 31,948 ... E 5
Ambérieu-en-Bugey, 8,570 ... F 5
Amboise, 8,408 ... D 4
Amiens, 116,107 ... D 3
Angers, 127,415 ... C 4
Angoulême, 46,584 ... D 5
Annecy, 53,361 ... G 5
Annonay, 19,591 ... F 5
Antibes, 47,393 ... G 6
Antony, 56,556 ... B 2
Apt, 8,502 ... F 6
Arcachon, 14,852 ... C 5
Argentan, 14,418 ... D 3
Argenteuil, 87,106 ... A 1
Arles, 33,575 ... F 6
Armentières, 24,460 ... E 2
Arras, 48,494 ... E 2
Asnières, 79,942 ... A 1
Aubagne, 17,055 ... F 6
Aubenas, 10,480 ... F 5
Aubervilliers, 73,559 ... B 1
Aubusson, 5,641 ... E 4
Auch, 18,072 ... D 6
Audincourt, 13,487 ... G 4
Aulnay-sous-Bois, 61,384 ... B 1
Auray, 8,180 ... B 4
Aurignac, 783 ... D 6
Aurillac, 26,776 ... E 5
Autun, 17,194 ... F 4
Auxerre, 33,700 ... E 4
Avallon, 6,615 ... E 4
Avesnes-sur-Helpe, 6,253 ... F 2
Avignon, 78,871 ... F 6
Avion, 22,390 ... E 2
Avranches, 9,751 ... C 3
Bagnères-de-Bigorre, 9,139 ... D 6
Bagnères-de-Luchon, 4,079 ... D 6
Bagnolet, 33,607 ... B 2
Bagnols-sur-Cèze, 15,336 ... F 5
Bar-le-Duc, 18,874 ... F 3
Bar-sur-Seine, 2,642 ... F 3
Barfleur, 825 ... C 3
Bastia, 48,800 ... B 6
Bayeux, 11,190 ... C 3
Bayonne, 39,761 ... C 6
Beaucaire, 8,820 ... F 6
Beaune, 16,441 ... F 4
Beauvais, 46,284 ... E 3
Bédarieux, 6,929 ... E 6
Belfort, 53,001 ... G 4
Belley, 5,958 ... F 5
Berck, 13,658 ... D 2
Bergerac, 24,184 ... D 5
Berney, 9,298 ... D 3
Besançon, 107,939 ... G 4
Bessèges, 5,421 ... F 5
Béthune, 26,144 ... E 2
Béziers, 74,517 ... E 6
Biarritz, 26,628 ... C 6
Blois, 39,279 ... D 4
Bobigny, 39,321 ... B 1
Bolbec, 12,517 ... D 3
Bondy, 51,555 ... B 1
Bordeaux, 263,808 ... C 5
Bordeaux, †648,000 ... C 5
Boulogne-Billancourt, 108,846 ... A 2
Boulogne-sur-Mer, 49,064 ... D 2
Bourg-en-Bresse, 35,064 ... F 4
Bourges, 67,137 ... E 4
Bressuire, 8,010 ... C 4
Brest, 150,696 ... A 3
Briançon, 7,551 ... G 5
Briare, 4,725 ... E 4
Brignoles, 8,010 ... G 6
Brive-la-Gaillarde, 45,314 ... D 5
Bruay-en-Artois, 38,608 ... E 2
Caen, 106,790 ... C 3
Cahors, 17,775 ... D 5
Calais, 70,153 ... D 2
Caluire-et-Cuire, 37,541 ... F 5
Calvi, 2,523 ... B 6
Cambrai, 37,290 ... E 2
Cannes, 66,590 ... G 6
Carcassonne, 40,580 ... D 6
Carentan, 5,207 ... C 3
Carmaux, 13,423 ... E 5
Carpentras, 18,092 ... F 5
Castelnaudary, 8,550 ... E 6
Castelsarrasin, 7,912 ... D 6
Castres, 35,975 ... E 6
Cavaillon, 14,815 ... F 6
Cayeux-sur-Mer, 2,489 ... D 2
Chalon-sur-Saône, 47,004 ... F 4
Châlons-sur-Marne, 48,558 ... F 3
Chambéry, 49,858 ... F 5
Chambord, 200 ... D 4
Chamonix-Mont Blanc, 5,907 ... G 5
Champigny-sur-Marne, 70,353 ... C 2
Chantilly, 10,156 ... E 3
Charenton-le-Pont, 22,220 ... B 2
Charleville-Mézières, 55,230 ... F 3
Chartres, 34,128 ... D 3
Château-du-Loir, 5,239 ... D 4
Château-Gontier, 7,881 ... C 4
Château-Renault, 5,082 ... D 4
Château-Thierry, 10,858 ... E 3
Châteaubriant, 11,196 ... C 4
Châteaudun, 13,715 ... D 3
Châteauneuf-sur-Loire, 4,603 ... E 4
Châteauroux, 48,867 ... D 4
Châtellerault, 33,491 ... D 4
Châtillon, 24,468 ... B 2
Châtillon-sur-Seine, 6,128 ... F 4
Chatou, 22,495 ... A 1
Chaumont, 25,602 ... F 3
Chauny, 13,714 ... E 3
Chelles, 22,111 ... C 1
Cherbourg, 37,933 ... C 3
Chinon, 5,435 ... D 4
Choisy-le-Roi, 41,080 ... B 2
Cholet, 40,224 ... C 4
Clamart, 54,866 ... A 2
Clermont, 7,119 ... E 3
Clermont-Ferrand, 145,856 ... E 5
Clichy, 52,398 ... B 1
Cluny, 3,552 ... F 4
Cluses, 12,391 ... G 4
Cognac, 21,137 ... C 5
Colmar, 58,623 ... G 3
Colombes, 80,224 ... A 1
Commentry, 8,129 ... E 4
Commercy, 7,043 ... F 3
Compiègne, 28,881 ... E 3
Concarneau, 16,458 ... A 4
Cosne-sur-Loire, 8,931 ... E 4
Coudekerque-Branche, 22,972 ... E 2
Coulommiers, 11,182 ... E 3
Courbevoie, 57,998 ... A 1
Coutances, 8,599 ... C 3
Coutras, 4,251 ... C 5
Creil, 31,792 ... E 3
Crépy-en-Valois, 8,506 ... E 3
Créteil, 48,757 ... B 2
Cusset, 12,286 ... E 4
Dax, 18,185 ... C 6
Deauville, 5,103 ... C 3
Decazeville, 9,581 ... E 5
Denain, 27,840 ... E 2
Dieppe, 29,829 ... D 3
Digne, 11,973 ... G 5
Digoin, 9,585 ... F 4
Dijon, 143,120 ... F 4
Dinan, 12,999 ... B 3
Dinard, 9,042 ... B 3
Dôle, 25,620 ... F 4
Domrémy-la-Pucelle, 184 ... F 3
Douai, 47,347 ... E 2
Douarnenez, 18,442 ... A 3
Draguignan, 16,139 ... G 6
Drancy, 69,226 ... B 1
Dreux, 28,156 ... D 3
Dunkirk (Dunkerque), 26,038 ... E 2
Elbeuf, 19,110 ... D 3
Embrun, 3,986 ... G 5
Épernay, 26,094 ... E 3
Épinal, 36,219 ... G 3
Épinay-sur-Seine, 41,538 ... B 1
Étampes, 15,542 ... E 3
Étaples, 9,092 ... D 2
Eu, 7,866 ... D 3
Évreux, 41,004 ... D 3
Évry, 7,047 ... E 3
Falaise, 6,977 ... C 3
Fécamp, 21,098 ... D 3
Figeac, 8,462 ... D 5
Firminy, 24,545 ... F 5
Flers, 16,677 ... C 3
Foix, 9,061 ... D 6
Fontainebleau, 17,565 ... E 3
Fontenay-le-Comte, 10,884 ... C 4
Fontenay-sous-Bois, 38,737 ... C 2
Forbach, 23,062 ... G 3
Fougères, 25,745 ... C 3
Fourmies, 14,895 ... F 2
Fréjus, 22,567 ... G 6
Gagny, 35,745 ... C 1
Gap, 22,027 ... G 5
Gardanne, 12,601 ... F 6
Gennevilliers, 45,925 ... B 1
Gentilly, 18,638 ... B 2
Gex, 3,078 ... G 4
Gien, 11,655 ... E 4
Gisors, 7,024 ... D 3
Givet, 7,697 ... F 2
Givors, 17,545 ... F 5
Granville, 12,315 ... C 3
Grasse, 24,398 ... G 6
Graulhet, 10,318 ... E 6
Gray, 7,782 ... F 4
Grenoble, 161,230 ... F 5
Guebwiller, 10,684 ... G 4
Guéret, 12,441 ... D 4
Guingamp, 9,091 ... B 3
Guise, 6,732 ... E 3
Haguenau, 22,335 ... G 3
Ham, 5,565 ... E 3
Harfleur, 15,503 ... D 3
Hautmont, 17,818 ... F 2
Hayange, 10,218 ... F 3
Hazebrouck, 16,768 ... E 2
Hendaye, 7,536 ... C 6
Hénin-Liétard, 25,067 ... E 2
Hennebont, 7,605 ... B 4
Héricourt, 7,376 ... G 4
Hirson, 11,764 ... F 3
Honfleur, 9,017 ... D 3
Hyères, 27,600 ... G 6
Issoire, 11,745 ... E 5
Issoudun, 14,559 ... D 4
Issy-les-Moulineaux, 50,260 ... A 2
Istres, 8,713 ... F 6
Ivry-sur-Seine, 60,342 ... B 2
Joigny, 9,609 ... E 3
La Baule-Escoublac, 11,962 ... B 4
La Ciotat, 19,485 ... F 6
La Courneuve, 42,812 ... B 1
La Flèche, 9,536 ... C 4
La Grand-Combe, 8,608 ... E 5
La Roche-sur-Yon, 32,279 ... C 4
La Rochelle, 72,075 ... C 4
La Seyne-sur-Mer, 42,958 ... F 6
La Tour-du-Pin, 5,649 ... F 5
L'Aigle, 7,478 ... D 3
Landerneau, 12,356 ... B 3
Langeac, 4,584 ... E 5
Langres, 8,945 ... F 4
Lannion, 10,066 ... B 3
Laon, 25,623 ... E 3
Laval, 45,051 ... C 3
Lavelanet, 8,512 ... E 6
Le Blanc-Mesnil, 48,212 ... B 1
Le Bourget, 9,625 ... B 1
Le Cateau, 8,922 ... E 2
Le Chesnay, 13,586 ... A 2
Le Creusot, 33,581 ... F 4
Le Croisic, 4,092 ... B 4
Le Havre, 198,021 ... C 3
Le Mans, 140,520 ... C 3
Le Puy, 24,816 ... F 5
Le Teil, 7,872 ... F 5
Le Tourquet-Paris-Plage, 4,403 ... D 2
Le Tréport, 6,194 ... D 2
Lens, 41,800 ... E 2
Les Andelys, 6,292 ... D 3
Les Sables-d'Olonne, 17,856 ... B 4
Levallois-Perret, 58,890 ... B 1
Lézignan-Corbières, 7,101 ... E 6
Libourne, 19,981 ... C 5
Liévin, 35,733 ... E 2
Lille, 189,697 ... E 2
Lille, †1,042,000 ... E 2
Limoges, 127,605 ... D 5
Limoux, 9,150 ... E 6
Lisieux, 23,337 ... D 3
Livry-Gargan, 32,015 ... C 1
Lodève, 6,899 ... E 6
Longwy, 21,052 ... F 3
Lons-le-Saunier, 18,649 ... F 4
Lorient, 66,023 ... B 4
Loudun, 6,118 ... D 4
Lourdes, 17,627 ... C 6
Louviers, 15,159 ... D 3
Lunel, 10,178 ... E 6
Lunéville, 22,961 ... G 3
Luxeuil-les-Bains, 9,203 ... G 4
Lyon, 524,500 ... F 5
Lyon, †1,305,000 ... F 5
Mâcon, 33,266 ... F 4
Maisons-Alfort, 53,118 ... B 2
Maisons-Laffitte, 24,041 ... A 1
Malakoff, 36,198 ... B 2
Manosque, 13,352 ... G 6
Mantes-la-Jolie, 25,842 ... D 3
Marmande, 12,145 ... C 5
Marseille, 880,527 ... F 6
Marseille, †1,015,000 ... F 6
Martigues, 17,771 ... F 6
Maubeuge, 31,992 ... F 2
Mayenne, 10,010 ... C 3
Mazamet, 14,650 ... E 6
Meaux, 29,966 ... E 3
Melun, 33,345 ... E 3
Mende, 9,424 ... E 5
Menton, 23,401 ... G 6
Metz, 105,533 ... G 3
Meudon, 30,735 ... A 2
Millau, 21,420 ... E 5
Moissac, 7,694 ... D 5
Mont-de-Marsan, 22,771 ... C 6
Mont-Dore, 2,045 ... E 5
Mont-Saint-Michel, 72 ... C 3
Montargis, 18,087 ... E 3
Montauban, 33,945 ... D 5
Montbéliard, 23,402 ... G 4
Montbrison, 8,733 ... E 5
Montceau-les-Mines, 18,621 ... F 4
Montdidier, 5,785 ... E 3
Montélimar, 23,831 ... F 5
Montfort, 2,563 ... C 3
Montigny-les-Metz, 24,417 ... G 3
Montluçon, 57,638 ... E 4
Montpellier, 152,105 ... E 6
Montreuil, 95,420 ... B 2
Montrouge, 44,788 ... B 2
Morlaix, 16,750 ... B 3
Moulins, 25,778 ... E 4
Moûtiers, 4,066 ... G 5
Moyeuvre-Grande, 14,559 ... G 3
Mulhouse, 115,632 ... G 4
Muret, 10,515 ... D 6
Nancy, 121,910 ... G 3
Nanterre, 90,124 ... A 1
Nantes, 253,105 ... C 4
Narbonne, 35,236 ... E 6
Nemours, 8,081 ... E 3
Neufchâteau, 7,656 ... F 3
Neufchâtel-en-Bray, 5,734 ... D 3
Neuilly-sur-Seine, 70,787 ... B 1
Nevers, 42,092 ... E 4
Nice, 301,400 ... G 6
Nîmes, 115,561 ... F 6
Niort, 46,749 ... C 4
Nogent-le-Rotrou, 11,040 ... D 3
Nogent-sur-Seine, 4,271 ... E 3
Noisy-le-Sec, 34,058 ... B 1
Noyon, 11,567 ... E 3
Nyons, 4,311 ... F 5
Oloron-Sainte-Marie, 12,597 ... C 6
Orange, 17,582 ... F 5
Orléans, 94,382 ... D 3
Orly, 30,151 ... B 2
Orthez, 8,778 ... C 6
Oullins, 26,520 ... F 5
Oyonnax, 19,571 ... F 4
Pamiers, 13,183 ... D 6
Pantin, 47,580 ... B 1
Paray-le-Monial, 10,324 ... F 4
Paris (cap.), 2,580,010 ... B 2
Paris, *7,953,065 ... B 2
Paris, †9,283,000 ... B 2
Parthenay, 11,177 ... C 4
Pau, 71,865 ... C 6
Périgueux, 36,991 ... D 5
Perpignan, 100,086 ... E 6
Pessac, 35,343 ... C 5
Ploërmel, 3,720 ... B 4
Poitiers, 68,082 ... D 4
Pont-à-Mousson, 13,283 ... G 3
Pont-l'Abbé, 6,227 ... A 4
Pont-l'Évêque, 2,823 ... D 3
Pontarlier, 16,250 ... G 4
Pontivy, 9,674 ... B 3
Pontoise, 16,633 ... E 3
Port-de-Bouc, 13,447 ... F 6
Port-Louis, 3,921 ... B 4

(continued on following page)

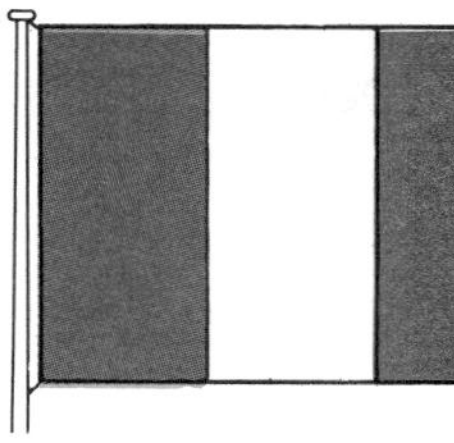

AREA 210,038 sq. mi.
POPULATION 53,300,000
CAPITAL Paris
LARGEST CITY Paris
HIGHEST POINT Mont Blanc 15,771 ft.
MONETARY UNIT franc
MAJOR LANGUAGE French
MAJOR RELIGION Roman Catholicism

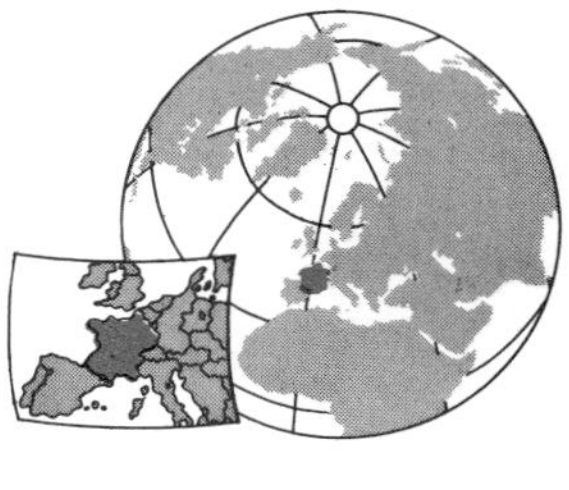

Topography

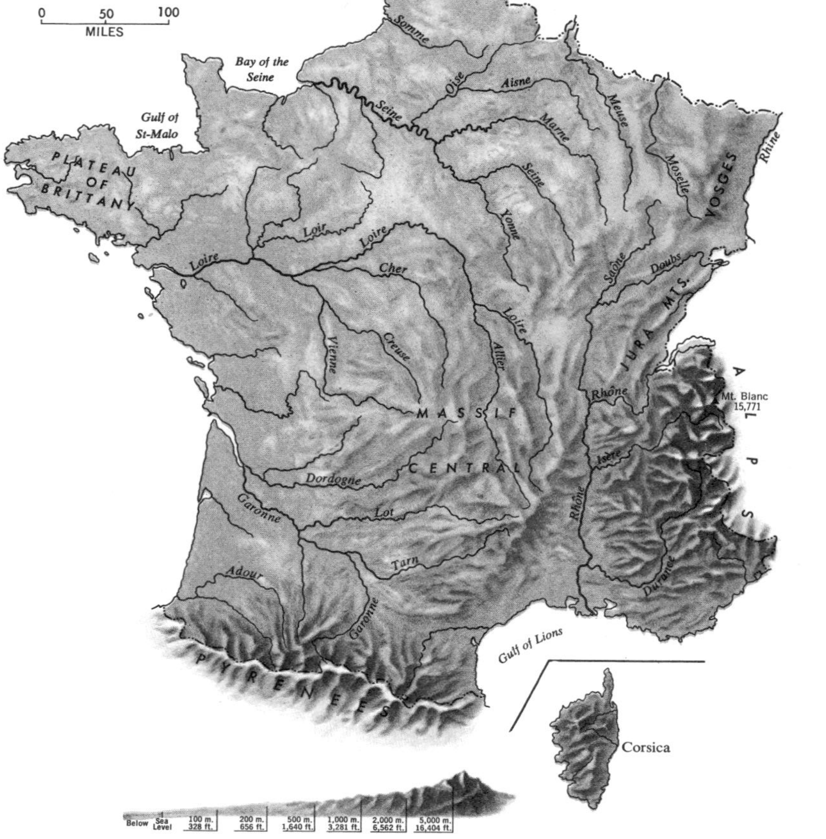

HISTORIC PROVINCES

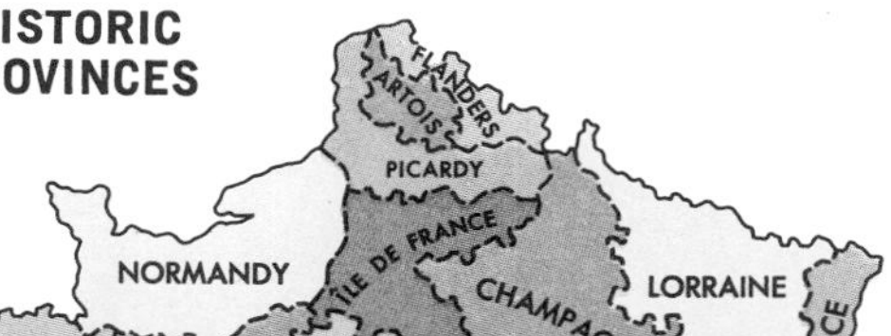

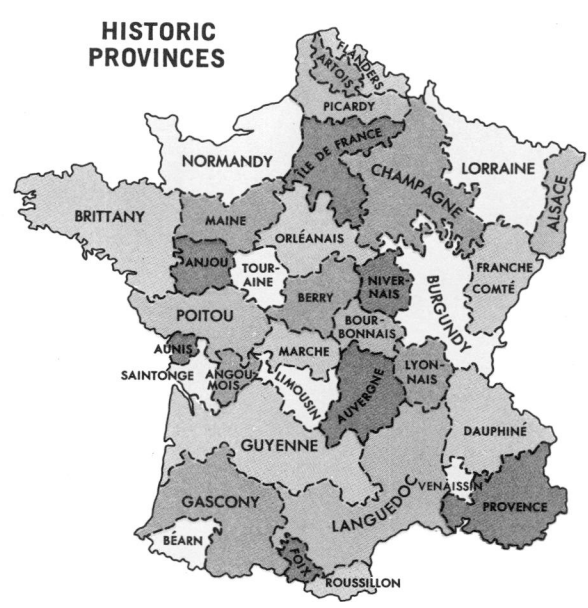

A resident of the city of Caen thinks of himself as a Norman rather than as a citizen of the modern department of Calvados. In spite of the passing of nearly two centuries, the historic provinces which existed before 1790 command the local patriotism of most Frenchmen.

Port-St-Louis-du-Rhône, 7,194 ....F 6
Port-Vendres, 5,358 ....E 6
Porto-Vecchio, 3,324 ....B 7
Privas, 8,113 ....F 5
Provins, 11,205 ....E 3
Puteaux, 37,801 ....A 2
Quiberon, 4,305 ....B 4
Quimper, 47,811 ....A 4
Quimperlé, 9,701 ....B 4
Rambouillet, 14,043 ....D 3
Redon, 8,767 ....C 4
Reims, 151,988 ....E 3
Remiremont, 9,018 ....G 4
Rennes, 176,024 ....C 3
Rethel, 7,737 ....F 3
Révin, 11,978 ....F 3
Rezé, 31,113 ....C 4
Rive-de-Gier, 15,483 ....F 5
Roanne, 53,178 ....E 4
Rochefort, 28,223 ....C 5
Rodez, 23,041 ....E 5
Romans-sur-Isère, 29,430 ....F 5
Romilly-sur-Seine, 16,867 ....E 3
Romorantin-Lanthenay, 13,516 .....D 4
Roubaix, 114,239 ....E 2
Rouen, 118,323 ....D 3
Royan, 17,187 ....C 5
Rueil-Malmaison, 60,130 ....A 2
Sablé-sur-Sarthe, 8,194 ....D 4
Saint-Affrique, 6,443 ....E 6
Saint-Amand-Mont-Rond, 11,035 ...E 4
Saint-Brieuc, 49,305 ....B 3
Saint-Céré, 3,682 ....D 5
Saint-Chamond, 35,362 ....F 5
Saint-Claude, 12,344 ....F 4
Saint-Cloud, 28,016 ....A 2
Saint-Denis, 99,027 ....B 1
Saint-Dié, 24,652 ....G 3
Saint-Dizier, 35,742 ....F 3
Saint-Étienne, 212,843 ....F 5
Saint-Florent-sur-Cher, 6,261 ....E 4
Saint-Flour, 5,582 ....E 5
Saint-Gaudens, 9,776 ....D 6
Saint-Germain-en-Laye, 36,251 ....D 3
Saint-Girons, 7,462 ....D 6
Saint-Jean-d'Angély, 8,883 ....C 4
Saint-Jean-de-Luz, 10,206 ....C 6
Saint-Jean-de-Maurienne, 8,407 ...G 5
Saint-Jean-Pied-de-Port, 1,677 ...C 6
Saint-Junien, 8,624 ....D 5
Saint-Lô, 17,347 ....C 3
Saint-Malo, 40,252 ....B 3
Saint-Mandé, 22,998 ....B 2
Saint-Maur-des-Fossés, 77,122 ....B 2
Saint-Mihiel, 5,262 ....F 3
Saint-Nazaire, 60,696 ....B 4
Saint-Omer, 17,647 ....E 2
Saint-Ouen, 48,304 ....B 1
Saint-Quentin, 63,932 ....E 3
Saint-Raphaël, 16,117 ....G 6
Saint-Tropez, 5,138 ....G 6
Saint-Vallier, 4,863 ....F 5
Saint-Yrieix-la-Perche, 4,655 ....D 5
Sainte-Mère-Église, 889 ....C 3
Sainte-Savine, 11,616 ....E 3

Saintes, 24,594 ....C 4
Salins-les-Bains, 4,084 ....F 4
Salon-de-Provence, 24,803 ....F 6
Sarrebourg, 11,104 ....G 3
Sarreguemines, 23,074 ....G 3
Sartène, 4,117 ....B 7
Sartrouville, 39,722 ....A 1
Saumur, 21,354 ....D 4
Saverne, 9,432 ....G 3
Sceaux, 19,837 ....A 2
Sedan, 22,998 ....F 3
Sélestat, 14,558 ....G 3
Senlis, 10,111 ....E 3
Sens, 22,658 ....E 3
Sèvres, 20,025 ....A 2
Sète, 40,220 ....E 6
Soissons, 25,409 ....E 3
Sotteville-lès-Rouen, 33,503 .....D 3
Stiring-Wendel, 13,757 ....G 3
Strasbourg, 247,526 ....H 3
Suresnes, 40,393 ....A 2
Tarare, 12,116 ....F 5
Tarascon, 8,848 ....F 6
Tarbes, 55,200 ....D 6
Thann, 8,108 ....G 4
Thiers, 14,430 ....E 5
Thionville, 35,747 ....G 3
Thonon-les-Bains, 20,095 ....G 4
Thouars, 11,526 ....C 4
Tonnerre, 5,562 ....E 4
Toulon, 169,593 ....F 6
Toulouse, 331,751 ....D 6
Tourcoing, 93,675 ....E 2
Tours, 126,414 ....D 4
Trouville-sur-Mer, 5,718 ....D 3
Troyes, 74,409 ....F 3
Tulle, 17,640 ....D 5
Uckange, 10,326 ....G 3
Uzès, 6,201 ....F 5
Valence, 60,662 ....F 5
Valenciennes, 46,237 ....E 2
Valognes, 5,182 ....C 3
Vannes, 36,380 ....B 4
Vence, 6,450 ....G 6
Vendôme, 15,854 ....D 4
Vénissieux, 47,460 ....F 5
Verdun-sur-Meuse, 21,306 ....F 3
Vernon, 16,983 ....D 3
Versailles, 89,035 ....A 2
Vesoul, 16,079 ....F 4
Vichy, 33,458 ....E 4
Vienne, 26,512 ....F 5
Vierzon, 32,429 ....E 4
Villefranche, 6,619 ....G 6
Villefranche-de-Rouergue, 9,382 ..E 5
Villefranche-sur-Saône, 25,995 ...F 4
Villejuif, 48,737 ....B 2
Villemomble, 28,731 ....C 1
Villeneuve-St-Georges, 30,229 ....E 3
Villeneuve-sur-Lot, 18,612 ....D 5
Villeurbanne, 119,420 ....F 5
Vincennes, 49,116 ....B 2
Vire, 10,819 ....C 3
Vitré, 10,125 ....C 3
Vitry-le-François, 16,409 ....F 3

Vitry-sur-Seine, 77,616 ....B 2
Vittel, 6,343 ....F 3
Voiron, 15,693 ....F 5
Wissembourg, 5,341 ....G 3
Yvetot, 9,208 ....D 3

OTHER FEATURES

Adour (river) ....C 6
Ain (river) ....F 4
Aisne (river) ....E 3
Ajaccio (gulf) ....B 7
Allier (river) ....E 5
Aube (river) ....E 5
Aubrac (mts.) ....E 5
Auvergne (mts.) ....E 5
Belle-Île (isl.), 4,442 ....B 4
Biscay (bay) ....B 5
Blanc (mt.) ....G 5
Bonifacio (strait) ....B 7
Calais (strait) ....D 2
Causses (region) ....E 5
Cévennes (mts.) ....E 5
Charente (river) ....C 5
Cher (river) ....D 4
Corse (cape) ....B 6
Corsica (isl.), 269,831 ....B 6
Côte-d'Or (mts.) ....F 4
Cotentin (pen.) ....C 3
Cottian Alps (range) ....G 5
Creuse (river) ....D 4
Dordogne (river) ....D 5
Dore (river) ....E 5
Doubs (river) ....G 4
Drôme (river) ....F 5
Dronne (river) ....D 5
Durance (river) ....F 6
English (channel) ....B 3
Eure (river) ....D 3
Forez (mts.) ....E 5
Fréjus (pass) ....G 5
Gard (river) ....F 5
Gave de Pau (river) ....C 6
Garonne (river) ....C 5
Geneva (lake) ....G 4
Gers (river) ....D 6
Gironde (river) ....C 5
Graian Alps (range) ....G 5
Gris-Nez (cape) ....D 2
Groix (isl.), 3,161 ....B 4
Hague (cape) ....C 3
Hérault (river) ....E 6
Hyères (isls.) ....F 6
Indre (river) ....D 4
Isère (river) ....F 5
Isle (river) ....C 5
Jura (mts.) ....F 4
Langres (plateau) ....F 4
Limousin (region) ....D 5
Lions (gulf) ....E 6
Little Saint Bernard (pass) ......G 5
Loir (river) ....D 4
Loire (river) ....E 4
Lot (river) ....D 5
Manche, La (English) (chan.) .....B 3
Maritime Alps (range) ....G 5

Marne (river) ....C 2
Mayenne (river) ....C 4
Mediterranean (sea) ....E 7
Médoc (reg.) ....C 5
Meuse (river) ....F 3
Mont Cenis (tunnel) ....G 5
Morvan (plateau) ....E 4
Moselle (river) ....G 3
Noirmoutier (isl.), 8,091 ....B 4
North (sea) ....E 1
Oise (river) ....E 3
Oléron, d' (isl.), 16,355 ....C 5
Omaha (beach) ....C 3
Orb (river) ....E 6
Orne (river) ....C 3
Ouessant (isl.), 1,817 ....A 3
Penmarch (point) ....A 4
Perche (reg.) ....D 3
Puy-de-Dôme (mt.) ....E 5
Pyrenees (range) ....C 6
Ré (isl.), 9,967 ....C 4
Rhine (river) ....H 3
Rhône (river) ....F 5
Risle (river) ....D 3
Riviera (region) ....G 6
Saint-Florent (gulf) ....B 6
Saint-Malo (gulf) ....B 3
Saône (river) ....F 4
Sarthe (river) ....D 4
Sein (isl.), 835 ....A 3
Seine (river) ....C 3
Seine (bay) ....D 3
Sologne (reg.) ....D 4
Somme (river) ....E 2
Tarn (river) ....E 6
Ushant (Ouessant) (isl.), 1,817 ..A 3
Utah (beach) ....C 3
Vaccarès (lagoon) ....F 6
Vienne (river) ....D 4
Vilaine (river) ....C 4
Vosges (mts.) ....G 3
Yeu, d' (isl.), 4,786 ....B 4
Yonne (river) ....E 4

*City and suburbs.
†Population of metropolitan area.

MONACO

CITIES and TOWNS

Monte Carlo, 9,948 ....G 6

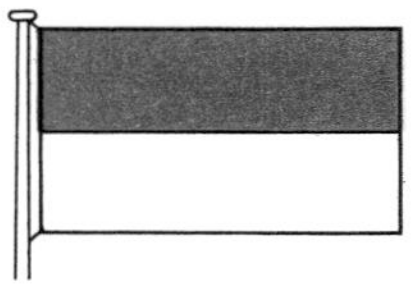

MONACO
AREA 368 acres
POPULATION 23,035

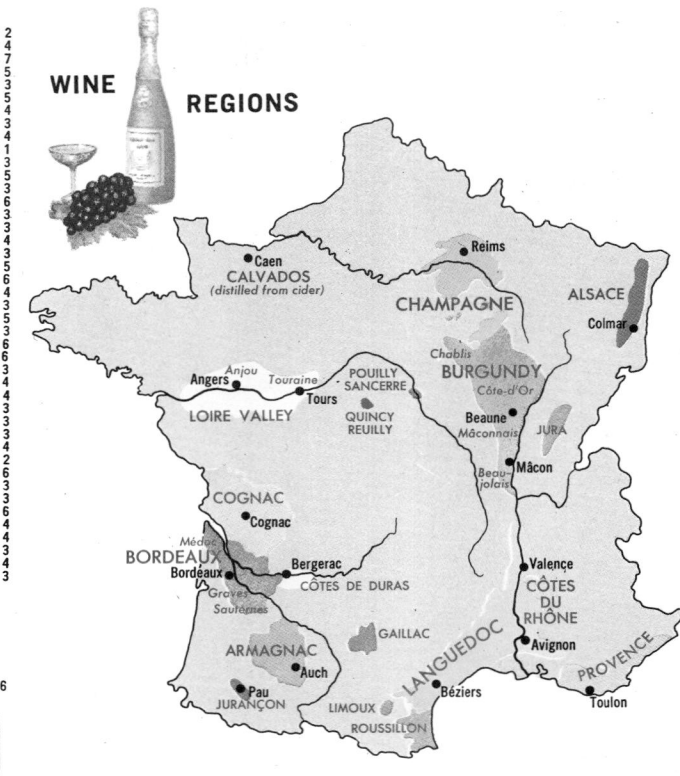

WINE REGIONS

Climate, soil and variety of grape planted determine the quality of wine. Long, hot and fairly dry summers with cool, humid nights constitute an ideal climate. The nature of the soil is such a determining influence that identical grapes planted in Bordeaux, Burgundy and Champagne, will yield wines of widely different types.

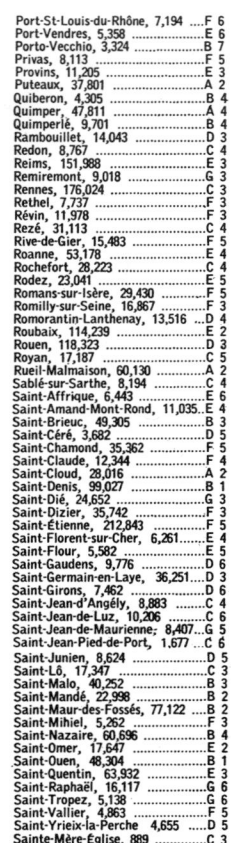

Agriculture, Industry and Resources

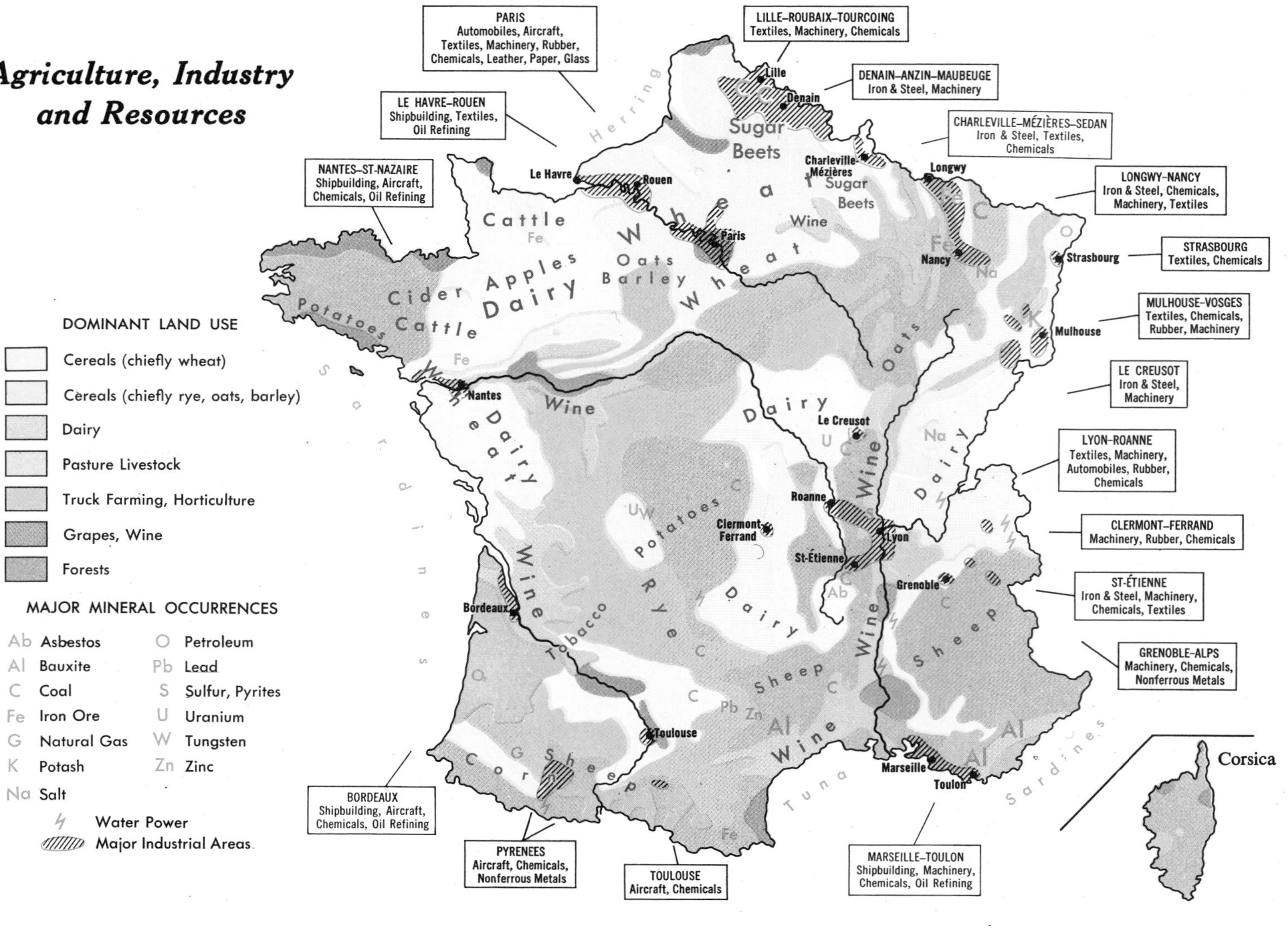

PARIS
Automobiles, Aircraft, Textiles, Machinery, Rubber, Chemicals, Leather, Paper, Glass

LILLE–ROUBAIX–TOURCOING
Textiles, Machinery, Chemicals

DENAIN–ANZIN–MAUBEUGE
Iron & Steel, Machinery

CHARLEVILLE–MÉZIÈRES–SEDAN
Iron & Steel, Textiles, Chemicals

LONGWY–NANCY
Iron & Steel, Chemicals, Machinery, Textiles

LE HAVRE–ROUEN
Shipbuilding, Textiles, Oil Refining

NANTES–ST-NAZAIRE
Shipbuilding, Aircraft, Chemicals, Oil Refining

STRASBOURG
Textiles, Chemicals

MULHOUSE–VOSGES
Textiles, Chemicals, Rubber, Machinery

LE CREUSOT
Iron & Steel, Machinery

LYON–ROANNE
Textiles, Machinery, Automobiles, Rubber, Chemicals

CLERMONT–FERRAND
Machinery, Rubber, Chemicals

ST-ÉTIENNE
Iron & Steel, Machinery, Chemicals, Textiles

GRENOBLE–ALPS
Machinery, Chemicals, Nonferrous Metals

BORDEAUX
Shipbuilding, Aircraft, Chemicals, Oil Refining

PYRENEES
Aircraft, Chemicals, Nonferrous Metals

TOULOUSE
Aircraft, Chemicals

MARSEILLE–TOULON
Shipbuilding, Machinery, Chemicals, Oil Refining

DOMINANT LAND USE

- Cereals (chiefly wheat)
- Cereals (chiefly rye, oats, barley)
- Dairy
- Pasture Livestock
- Truck Farming, Horticulture
- Grapes, Wine
- Forests

MAJOR MINERAL OCCURRENCES

Ab Asbestos
Al Bauxite
C Coal
Fe Iron Ore
G Natural Gas
K Potash
Na Salt

O Petroleum
Pb Lead
S Sulfur, Pyrites
U Uranium
W Tungsten
Zn Zinc

⚡ Water Power
▨ Major Industrial Areas

Corsica

SPAIN

PROVINCES

Álava, 204,323 E 1
Albacete, 335,026 E 3
Alicante, 920,105 F 3
Almería, 375,004 E 4
Ávila, 203,798 D 2
Badajoz, 687,599 C 3
Baleares, 558,287 H 3
Barcelona, 3,929,194 G 2
Burgos, 358,075 E 1
Cáceres, 457,777 C 3
Cádiz, 885,433 D 4
Castellón, 385,823 G 2
Ciudad Real, 507,650 D 3
Córdoba, 724,116 D 3
Cuenca, 247,158 E 2
Gerona, 414,397 H 1
Granada, 733,375 E 4
Guadalajara, 147,732 E 2
Guipúzcoa, 631,003 E 1
Huelva, 397,683 C 4
Huesca, 222,238 F 1
Jaén, 661,146 E 4
La Coruña, 1,004,188 B 1
Las Palmas, 579,710 C 4
León, 548,721 C 1
Lérida, 347,015 G 2
Logroño, 235,713 E 1
Lugo, 415,052 C 1
Madrid, 3,792,561 E 2
Málaga, 867,330 D 4
Murcia, 832,313 F 4
Navarra, 464,867 F 1
Orense, 413,733 C 1
Oviedo, 1,045,635 C 1
Palencia, 198,763 D 1
Pontevedra, 750,701 B 1
Salamanca, 371,607 C 2
Santa Cruz de Tenerife, 590,514 B 5
Santander, 467,138 D 1
Saragossa, 760,186 F 2
Segovia, 162,770 D 2
Seville, 1,327,190 D 4
Soria, 114,956 E 2
Tarragona, 431,961 G 2
Teruel, 170,284 F 2
Toledo, 468,925 D 3
Valencia, 1,767,327 F 3
Valladolid, 412,572 D 2
Vizcaya, 1,043,310 E 1
Zamora, 251,934 D 2

CITIES and TOWNS

Adra, 10,851 E 4
Aguilar, 12,893 D 4
Aguilas, 15,525 F 4
Alagón, 5,114 F 2
Alayor, 5,124 J 3
Albacete, 82,607 F 3
Albox, 5,072 E 4
Alburquerque, 7,530 C 3
Alcalá de Guadaira, 28,781 D 4
Alcalá de Henares, 59,783 G 4
Alcalá de los Gazules, 5,262 D 4
Alcalá la Real, 9,849 E 4
Alcanar, 5,961 G 2
Alcañiz, 10,229 F 2
Alcantarilla, 19,895 F 4
Alcaudete, 8,557 E 4
Alcázar de San Juan, 24,620 E 3
Alcira, 30,493 F 3
Alcora, 6,711 F 2
Alcoy, 61,371 F 3
Alfaro, 8,766 F 1
Algeciras, 74,754 D 4
Algemesí, 21,158 F 3
Alhama de Granada, 6,148 E 4
Alhama de Murcia, 9,274 F 4
Alicante, 177,918 F 3
Almadén, 10,713 D 3
Almagro, 9,066 E 3
Almansa, 16,965 F 3
Almendralejo, 21,929 C 3
Almería, 104,008 E 4
Almodóvar del Campo, 7,310 D 3
Almonte, 9,960 C 4
Almuñécar, 7,812 E 4
Álora, 8,209 D 4
Altea, 7,262 G 3
Amposta, 11,767 G 2
Andorra, 6,485 F 2
Andújar, 25,962 D 3
Antequera, 28,039 D 4
Aracena, 5,390 C 4
Aranda de Duero, 18,183 E 2
Aranjuez, 28,559 E 2
Aravaca F 4
Archena, 7,118 F 3
Archidona, 6,084 D 4
Arcos de la Frontera, 16,217 D 4
Arenas de San Pedro, 5,225 D 2
Arenys de Mar, 8,325 H 2
Arévalo, 5,807 D 2
Argamasilla de Alba, 6,192 E 3
Arganda, 11,876 G 4
Arnedo, 9,809 E 1
Arrecife, 21,310 C 4
Arroyo de la Luz, 8,130 C 3
Artá, 5,284 H 3
Arucas, 9,095 B 5
Aspe, 13,229 F 3
Astorga, 11,794 C 1
Ávila de los Caballeros, 30,958 D 2
Avilés, 67,186 C 1
Ayamonte, 9,897 C 4
Ayora, 5,249 F 3
Azpeitia, 7,835 E 1
Azuaga, 10,719 D 3
Badajoz, 80,793 C 3
Badalona, 162,888 H 2
Baena, 16,496 D 4
Baeza, 12,607 E 4
Bailén, 13,207 E 3
Balaguer, 11,676 G 2
Bañolas, 9,807 H 1
Barajas F 4
Barbastro, 13,243 F 1
Barcarrota, 5,012 C 3
Barcelona, 1,741,144 H 2
Barcelona, ★2,000,000 H 2
Baza, 14,290 E 4
Beas de Segura, 6,592 E 3
Béjar, 16,804 D 2
Bélmez, 5,161 D 3
Benavente, 11,779 D 1
Benicarló, 12,831 G 2
Berga, 11,163 G 1
Berja, 7,081 E 4
Bermeo, 16,714 E 1
Betanzos, 7,283 B 1
Bilbao, 393,179 E 1
Bilbao, ★450,000 E 1
Binéfar, 6,821 G 2
Blanes, 15,810 H 2
Borjas Blancas, 4,991 G 2
Bujalance, 8,236 D 4
Bullas, 8,131 F 4

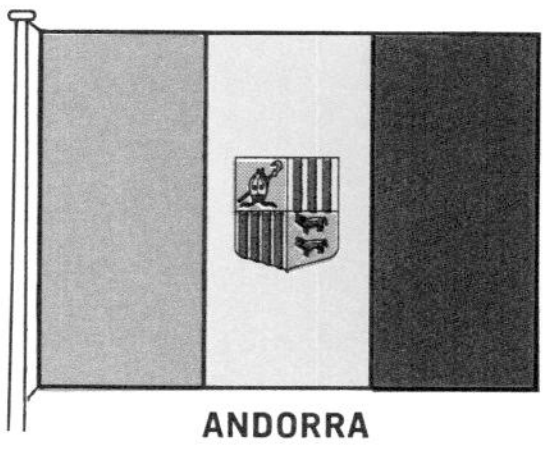

ANDORRA

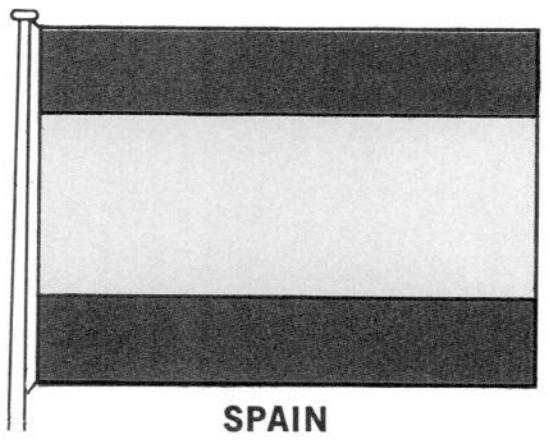

SPAIN

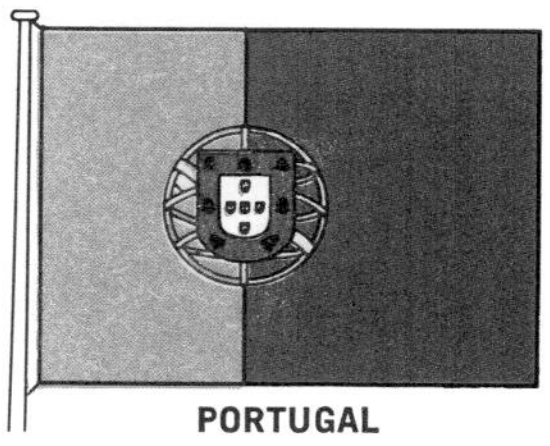

PORTUGAL

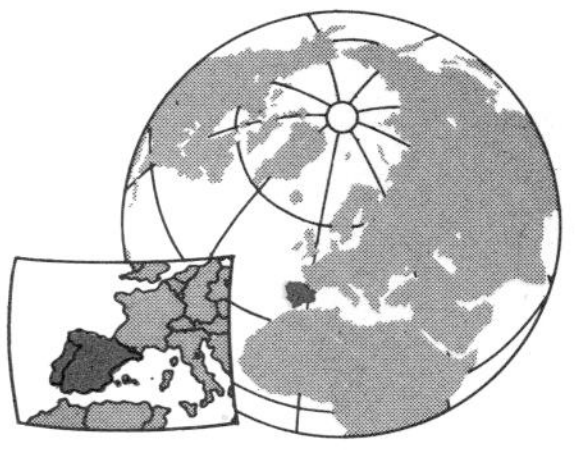

SPAIN

AREA 194,881 sq. mi.
POPULATION 36,000,000
CAPITAL Madrid
LARGEST CITY Madrid
HIGHEST POINT Pico de Teide 12,172 ft. (Canary Is.); Mulhacén 11,411 ft. (mainland)
MONETARY UNIT peseta
MAJOR LANGUAGES Spanish, Catalan, Basque, Galician, Valencian
MAJOR RELIGION Roman Catholicism

ANDORRA

AREA 188 sq. mi.
POPULATION 26,558
CAPITAL Andorra la Vella
MONETARY UNIT French franc, Spanish peseta
MAJOR LANGUAGE Catalan
MAJOR RELIGION Roman Catholicism

PORTUGAL

AREA 35,549 sq. mi.
POPULATION 8,825,000
CAPITAL Lisbon
LARGEST CITY Lisbon
HIGHEST POINT Malhão da Estrêla 6,532 ft.
MONETARY UNIT escudo
MAJOR LANGUAGE Portuguese
MAJOR RELIGION Roman Catholicism

GIBRALTAR

AREA 2.28 sq. mi.
POPULATION 30,000
CAPITAL Gibraltar
MONETARY UNIT pound sterling
MAJOR LANGUAGES English, Spanish
MAJOR RELIGION Roman Catholicism

Burgos, 118,366 E 1
Burriana, 21,298 G 3
Cabeza del Buey, 8,704 D 3
Cabra, 16,177 D 4
Cáceres, 53,108 C 3
Cádiz, 135,743 C 4
Calahorra, 16,315 E 1
Calasparra, 7,238 F 3
Calatayud, 16,524 F 2
Calella, 9,696 H 2
Callosa de Ensarriá, 5,701 G 3
Calzada de Calatrava, 5,751 E 3
Campanario, 7,722 D 3
Campillos, 7,014 D 4
Campo de Criptana, 12,604 E 3
Candás, 5,517 D 1
Candeleda, 5,153 D 2
Caniles, 5,099 E 4
Caravaca de le Cruz, 10,411 E 3
Carballo, 5,542 B 1
Carcagente, 18,223 F 3
Carmona, 22,832 D 4
Cartagena, 52,312 F 4
Caspe, 8,766 G 2
Cassa de la Selva, 5,248 H 2
Castellón de la Plana, 79,773 G 2
Castro del Río, 10,087 D 4
Castro-Urdiales, 8,369 E 1
Castuera, 8,060 D 3
Caudete, 7,332 F 3
Cazalla de la Sierra, 5,382 D 4
Cazorla, 6,938 E 4
Cehegín, 9,661 F 3
Cervera, 5,693 G 2
Ceuta, 60,639 D 5
Chiclana de la Frontera, 22,986 C 4
Chiva, 5,394 F 3
Ciempozuelos, 9,185 F 5
Cieza, 22,929 F 3
Ciudadela, 13,701 H 2
Ciudad Real, 39,931 D 3
Ciudad-Rodrigo, 11,694 C 2
Cocentaina, 8,375 F 3
Coín, 14,190 D 4
Colmenar de Oreja, 4,930 G 5
Colmenar Viejo, 12,886 F 4
Condado de Treviño, 245 E 1
Constantina, 10,227 D 4
Consuegra, 10,026 E 3
Córdoba, 216,049 D 4
Corella, 5,850 F 1
Coria, 8,083 C 3
Coria del Río, 18,085 C 4
Corral de Almaguer, 8,006 E 3
Crevillente, 15,749 F 3
Cuéllar, 6,118 D 2
Cuenca, 33,980 E 2
Cullera, 15,128 F 3
Daimiel, 17,710 E 3
Denia, 14,514 G 3
Dolores, 5,420 F 3
Don Benito, 21,351 C 3
Dos Hermanas, 36,921 D 4
Durango, 20,403 E 1
Écija, 27,295 D 4
Eibar, 36,729 E 1
Ejea de los Caballeros, 9,766 F 1
El Arahal, 14,703 D 4
Elche, 101,271 F 3
Elda, 41,404 F 3
El Ferrol del Caudillo, 75,464 B 1
Elizondo, 2,516 F 1
El Pardo F 4
El Puerto de Santa María, 36,451 C 4
Espejo, 5,925 D 4
Estella, 10,371 E 1
Estepa, 9,376 D 4
Estepona, 18,560 D 4
Felanitx, 9,100 H 3
Figueras, 22,087 H 1
Fraga, 9,665 G 2
Fregenal de la Sierra, 6,826 C 3
Fuengirola, 20,597 D 4
Fuente de Cantos, 5,967 C 3
Fuenterrabiá, 2,350 E 1
Fuentes de Andalucía, 8,257 D 4
Gandía, 30,702 F 3
Gerona, 37,095 H 2
Getafe, 68,680 F 4
Gijón, 159,806 D 1
Granada, 185,799 E 4
Granollers, 30,066 H 2
Guadalajara, 30,924 E 2
Guadix, 15,311 E 4
Guareña, 7,706 C 3
Guerníca y Luno, 12,046 E 1
Haro, 8,393 E 1
Hellín, 15,934 F 3
Herencia, 8,212 E 3
Hinojosa del Duque, 9,873 D 3
Hortaleza G 4
Hospitalet, 241,978 H 2
Huelma, 5,260 E 4
Huelva, 96,689 C 4
Huercal-Overa, 5,158 F 4
Huesca, 33,076 F 1
Huéscar, 6,384 E 4
Ibiza, 16,943 G 3
Igualada, 27,941 G 2
Inca, 16,930 H 3
Irún, 38,014 F 1
Iscar, 5,192 D 2
Isla Cristina, 11,402 C 4
Jaca, 9,936 F 1
Jaén, 71,145 E 4
Jaraíz de la Vera, 6,379 D 2
Játiva, 20,934 F 3
Jávea, 6,228 G 3
Jerez de la Frontera, 112,411 C 4
Jerez de los Caballeros, 8,607 C 3
Jijona, 8,117 F 3
Jódar, 11,973 E 4
Jumilla, 16,407 F 3
La Bañeza, 8,480 C 1
La Bisbal, 6,374 H 1
La Carolina, 13,138 E 3
La Coruña, 184,372 B 1
La Granja (San Ildefonso), 3,198 E 2
La Guardia, 4,967 B 2
La Línea de la Concepción, 51,021 D 4
La Orotava, 8,246 B 4
La Palma del Condado, 9,256 C 4
Laplaza, 15,587 E 1
La Puebla, 9,923 H 3
La Puebla de Montalbán, 6,629 D 3
La Rambla, 6,525 D 4
Laredo, 9,114 E 1
La Roda, 11,460 E 3
La Solana, 13,894 E 3
Las Palmas de Gran Canaria, 260,368 B 4
Las Pedroñeras, 5,846 E 3
La Unión, 9,998 F 4
Lebrija, 15,081 D 4
Leganés, 57,537 F 4
Lena, 5,760 D 1
León, 99,702 D 1
Lérida, 73,148 G 2
Linares, 45,330 E 3
Liria, 11,323 F 3
Llerena, 5,728 C 3
Llivia, 801 G 1
Lluchmayor, 9,630 H 3
Logroño, 83,117 E 1
Loja, 11,549 D 4
Lora del Río, 15,741 D 4
Lorca, 25,208 F 4
Los Santos de Maimona, 7,899 C 3
Los Yébenes, 5,477 E 3
Lucena, 21,527 D 4
Lugo, 53,504 C 1
Madrid (cap.), 3,146,071 F 4
Madrid, ★3,500,000 F 4
Madridejos, 9,948 E 3
Madroñera, 5,397 D 3
Mahón, 17,802 J 3
Málaga, 334,988 D 4
Málaga, ★400,000 D 4
Malagón, 7,732 E 3
Malpartida de Cáceres, 5,054 C 3
Manacor, 20,266 H 3
Mancha Real, 7,547 E 4
Manlleu, 13,169 H 1
Manresa, 52,526 G 2
Manzanares, 15,024 E 3
Marbella, 19,648 D 4
Marchena, 16,227 D 4
Marín, 10,948 B 1
Martos, 16,395 E 4
Mataró, 73,129 H 2
Medina del Campo, 16,345 D 2
Medina de Rioseco, 4,874 D 2
Medina-Sidonia, 7,523 D 4
Mérida, 36,916 C 3
Miajadas, 8,042 D 3
Mieres, 22,790 D 1
Minas de Ríotinto, 3,939 C 4
Miranda de Ebro, 29,355 E 1
Moguer, 7,629 C 4
Mollerusa, 6,685 G 2
Monasterio, 5,923 C 3
Monforte, 14,002 C 1
Monóvar, 9,071 F 3
Montehermoso, 5,952 C 2
Montellano, 6,658 D 4
Montijo, 11,931 C 3
Montilla, 18,670 D 4
Montoro, 9,295 D 3
Monzón, 14,089 G 2
Mora, 10,523 E 3
Moratalla, 5,101 E 3
Morón de la Frontera, 25,662 D 4
Mota del Cuervo, 5,130 E 3
Motril, 25,121 E 4
Mula, 9,168 F 3
Munera, 5,003 E 3
Murcia, 102,242 F 4
Navalcarnero, 6,212 F 4
Navalmoral de la Mata, 9,650 D 3
Nerja, 7,413 E 4
Nerva, 10,830 C 4
Novelda, 16,867 F 3
Nules, 9,027 F 3
Ocaña, 5,603 E 3
Oliva, 16,717 F 3
Oliva de la Frontera, 8,560 C 3
Olivenza, 7,616 C 3
Olot, 18,062 H 1
Olvera, 9,825 D 4
Onda, 13,012 F 3
Onteniente, 23,685 F 3
Orense, 63,542 C 1
Orihuela, 17,610 F 3
Osuna, 17,384 D 4
Oviedo, 130,021 C 1
Padul, 6,377 E 4
Palafrugell, 10,421 H 2
Palamós, 7,679 H 2
Palencia, 58,327 D 2
Palma, 191,416 H 3
Palma del Río, 15,075 D 4
Pamplona, 142,686 F 1
Pego, 8,861 F 3
Peñaranda de Bracamonte, 6,094 D 2
Peñarroya-Pueblonuevo, 15,649 D 3
Pinos-Puente, 7,634 E 4
Plasencia, 26,897 C 2
Pollensa, 7,625 H 3
Ponferrada, 22,838 C 1
Pontevedra, 27,118 B 1
Porcuna, 8,169 D 4
Port-Bou, 2,230 H 1
Portugalete, 45,589 E 1
Posadas, 7,245 D 4
Pozoblanco, 13,280 D 3
Pozuelo de Alarcón, 14,041 D 2
Priego de Córdoba, 12,676 D 4
Puente-Genil, 22,888 D 4
Puertollano, 50,609 D 3
Puerto Real, 13,993 D 4
Puigcerdá, 4,418 G 1
Quesada, 6,965 E 4
Quintana de la Serena, 5,171 D 3
Quintanar de la Orden, 7,764 E 3
Reinosa, 10,863 D 1
Requena, 9,836 F 3
Reus, 47,240 G 2
Ripoll, 9,283 H 1
Ronda, 22,094 D 4
Roquetas, 5,617 G 2
Rosas, 5,448 H 1
Rota, 20,021 C 4
Rute, 8,294 D 4
Sabadell, 148,223 H 2
Sagunto, 17,052 F 3
Salamanca, 125,132 D 2
Sallent, 7,118 H 2
Salobreña, 5,961 E 4

Agriculture, Industry and Resources

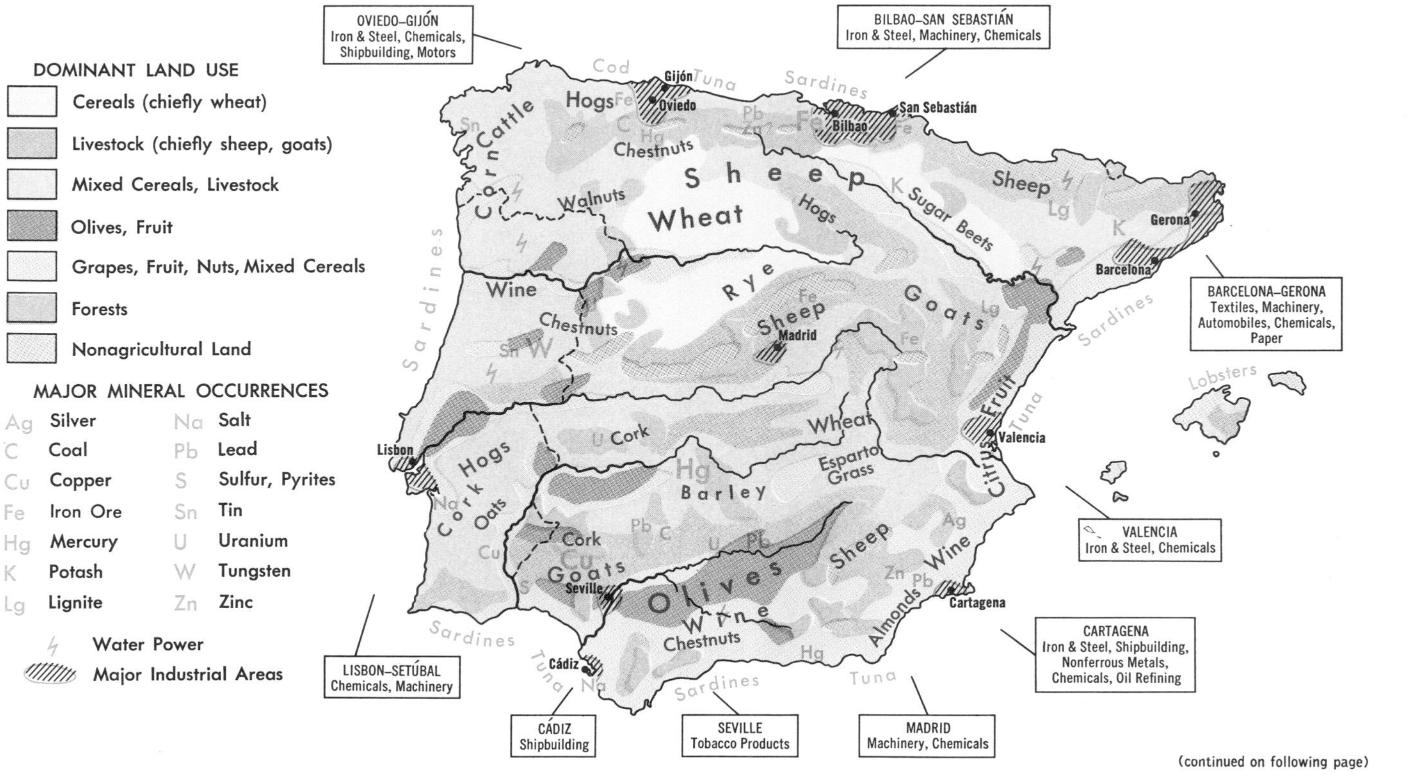
DOMINANT LAND USE
Cereals (chiefly wheat)
Livestock (chiefly sheep, goats)
Mixed Cereals, Livestock
Olives, Fruit
Grapes, Fruit, Nuts, Mixed Cereals
Forests
Nonagricultural Land
MAJOR MINERAL OCCURRENCES
Ag Silver
C Coal
Cu Copper
Fe Iron Ore
Hg Mercury
K Potash
Lg Lignite
Na Salt
Pb Lead
S Sulfur, Pyrites
Sn Tin
U Uranium
W Tungsten
Zn Zinc
Water Power
Major Industrial Areas
OVIEDO–GIJÓN
Iron & Steel, Chemicals, Shipbuilding, Motors
BILBAO–SAN SEBASTIÁN
Iron & Steel, Machinery, Chemicals
BARCELONA–GERONA
Textiles, Machinery, Automobiles, Chemicals, Paper
VALENCIA
Iron & Steel, Chemicals
CARTAGENA
Iron & Steel, Shipbuilding, Nonferrous Metals, Chemicals, Oil Refining
LISBON–SETÚBAL
Chemicals, Machinery
CÁDIZ
Shipbuilding
SEVILLE
Tobacco Products
MADRID
Machinery, Chemicals
Cod
Tuna
Sardines
Lobsters
Gijón
Oviedo
San Sebastián
Bilbao
Gerona
Barcelona
Madrid
Valencia
Lisbon
Seville
Cádiz
Cartagena
Hogs
Cattle
Corn
Chestnuts
Walnuts
Sheep
Wheat
Sugar Beets
Rye
Goats
Wine
Fruit
Citrus
Cork
Esparto Grass
Barley
Oats
Olives
Almonds

(continued on following page)

SPAIN (continued)

Salt, 5,572 .... H 1
Sama, 9,863 .... D 1
San Carlos de la Rápita, 8,946 .... G 2
San Clemente, 6,016 .... E 3
San Feliú de Guixols, 12,006 .... H 2
San Fernando, 59,309 .... C 4
San Ildefonso, 3,198 .... E 2
San Lorenzo de El Escorial, 8,098 .... E 2
Sanlúcar de Barrameda, 29,483 .... C 4
Sanlúcar la Mayor, 6,121 .... C 4
San Roque, 8,224 .... D 4
San Sebastián, 159,557 .... E 1
Santa Cruz de Mudela, 6,354 .... E 3
Santa Cruz de Tenerife, 74,910 .... B 4
Santa Eugenia, 5,946 .... B 1
Santafé, 8,990 .... E 4
Santander, 130,019 .... D 1
Santiago, 51,620 .... B 1
Santo Domingo de la Calzada, 5,638 .... E 1
Santoña, 9,546 .... E 1
San Vicente de Alcántara, 7,006 .... C 3
Saragossa, 449,319 .... F 2
Saragossa, ★500,000 .... F 2
Segorbe, 6,962 .... F 3
Segovia, 41,880 .... D 2
Seo de Urgel, 6,604 .... G 1
Sestao, 37,312 .... E 1
Seville, 511,447 .... D 4
Seville, ★560,000 .... D 4
Sitges, 8,906 .... G 2
Socuéllamos, 12,610 .... E 3
Sóller, 6,470 .... H 3
Solsona, 5,346 .... G 2
Sonseca, 6,594 .... D 3
Soria, 24,744 .... E 2
Sotrondio, 5,914 .... D 1
Sueca, 20,019 .... F 3
Tabernes de Valldigna, 13,962 .... G 3

Tafalla, 8,858 .... F 1
Talavera de la Reina, 39,889 .... D 2
Tarancón, 8,238 .... E 3
Tarazona, 11,067 .... E 2
Tarazona de la Mancha, 5,952 .... F 3
Tarifa, 9,201 .... D 4
Tarragona, 53,548 .... G 2
Tarrasa, 134,481 .... H 2
Tárrega, 9,036 .... G 2
Tauste, 6,832 .... F 2
Telde, 13,257 .... B 5
Teruel, 20,614 .... F 2
Toledo, 43,905 .... D 3
Tolosa, 15,164 .... E 1
Tomelloso, 26,041 .... E 3
Tordesillas, 5,815 .... D 2
Toro, 8,455 .... D 2
Torredonjimeno, 12,507 .... D 4
Torrejón de Ardoz, 21,081 .... G 4
Torrelavega, 19,933 .... D 1
Torremolinos, 20,484 .... D 4
Torrente, 38,397 .... F 3
Torrevieja, 9,431 .... F 4
Torrijos, 6,362 .... D 2
Torrox, 5,583 .... E 4
Tortosa, 20,030 .... G 2
Totana, 12,714 .... F 4
Trigueros, 6,887 .... C 4
Trujillo, 9,024 .... D 3
Tudela, 20,942 .... F 1
Úbeda, 28,306 .... E 3
Ubrique, 13,166 .... D 4
Utiel, 9,168 .... F 3
Utrera, 28,287 .... D 4
Valdemoro, 6,263 .... F 4
Valdepeñas, 24,018 .... E 3
Valencia, ★700,000 .... F 3
Valencia de Alcántara, 5,963 .... C 3
Valladolid, 227,511 .... D 2
Vall de Uxó, 23,976 .... F 3
Vallecas .... G 4
Valls, 14,189 .... G 2
Valverde del Camino, 10,566 .... C 4
Vejer de la Frontera, 6,184 .... C 4

Vélez-Málaga, 20,794 .... E 4
Vendrell, 7,951 .... G 2
Vera, 4,903 .... F 4
Vergara, 11,541 .... E 1
Vicálvaro .... G 4
Vich, 23,449 .... H 2
Vigo, 114,526 .... B 1
Villacañas, 9,883 .... E 3
Villacarrillo, 9,452 .... E 3
Villafranca de los Barros, 12,610 .... C 3
Villafranca del Penedés, 16,875 .... G 2
Villagarcía, 6,601 .... B 1
Villajoyosa, 12,573 .... F 3
Villanueva de Córdoba, 11,270 .... D 3
Villanueva del Arzobispo, 8,076 .... E 3
Villanueva de la Serena, 16,687 .... D 3
Villanueva de los Infantes, 8,154 .... E 3
Villanueva y Geltrú, 35,714 .... G 2
Villarejo de los Infantes, 29,482 .... G 3
Villarrobledo, 19,698 .... E 3
Villarrubia de los Ojos, 9,144 .... E 3
Villaverde .... G 4
Villena, 23,483 .... F 3
Vinaroz, 13,727 .... G 2
Vitoria, 124,791 .... E 1
Yecla, 19,352 .... F 3
Zafra, 11,583 .... C 3
Zalamea de la Serena, 6,017 .... D 3
Zamora, 48,791 .... D 2
Zaragoza (Saragossa), 449,319 .... F 2

OTHER FEATURES

Alborán (isl.) .... E 5
Alcaraz, Sierra de (range) .... E 3
Alcudia (bay) .... H 3
Almanzor (mt.) .... D 2
Almansa (riv.) .... F 4
Andalusia (reg.), 5,971,277 .... C 4
Aneto (peak) .... G 1
Aragon (reg.), 1,152,710 .... F 2
Arosa, Ría de (est.) .... B 1

Asturias (reg.), 1,045,635 .... C 1
Autza (mt.) .... F 1
Balaitous (mt.) .... F 1
Balearic (Baleares) (isls.), 558,287 .... H 3
Barbate (riv.) .... D 4
Biscay (bay) .... D 1
Cabrera (isl.) .... H 3
Cadiz (gulf) .... C 4
Cala Burras (pt.) .... H 3
Canary (isls.), 1,170,224 .... B 4
Cantabrian (range) .... C 1
Catalonia (reg.), 5,122,567 .... G 2
Cinca (riv.) .... G 2
Columbretes (isls.) .... G 3
Costa Brava (reg.) .... H 2
Costa de Sola (Costa del Sol) (reg.) .... D 4
Creus (cape) .... H 1
Cuenca, Sierra de (range) .... F 2
Demanda, Sierra de la (range) .... E 1
Douro (riv.) .... C 2
Ebro (riv.) .... G 2
Eresma (riv.) .... D 2
Esla (riv.) .... C 1
Estats (peak) .... G 1
Estremadura (reg.), 1,145,376 .... C 3
Finisterre (cape) .... B 1
Formentera (isl.), 2,965 .... G 3
Formentor (cape) .... H 2
Fuerteventura (isl.), 18,192 .... C 4
Gata (cape) .... F 4
Galicia (reg.), 2,583,674 .... B 1
Gata (cape) .... F 4
Genil (riv.) .... D 4
Gibraltar (str.) .... D 5
Gomera (isl.), 19,339 .... B 5
Gran Canaria (isl.), 519,606 .... B 5
Gredos, Sierra de (range) .... D 2
Guadalimar (riv.) .... E 3
Guadalquivir (riv.) .... C 4
Guadarrama, Sierra de (range) .... E 2
Guadarrama (riv.) .... F 4
Guadiana (riv.) .... D 3
Gudar, Sierra de (range) .... F 2

Henares (riv.) .... G 4
Hierro (isl.), 5,503 .... A 5
Ibiza (isl.), 45,075 .... G 3
Jalón (riv.) .... E 2
Jarama (riv.) .... G 2
Júcar (riv.) .... F 3
Lanzarote (isl.), 41,912 .... C 4
La Palma (isl.), 65,291 .... B 4
León (reg.), 1,172,262 .... C 1
Llobregat (riv.) .... H 2
Majorca (isl.), 462,995 .... H 3
Mallorca (Majorca) (isl.), 462,995 .... H 3
Mancha, La (reg.) .... E 3
Manzanares (riv.) .... F 4
Marismas, Las (marsh) .... C 4
Mar Menor (lag.) .... F 4
Mayor (cape) .... D 1
Menorca (Minorca) (isl.), 50,217 .... J 2
Minorca (isl.), 50,217 .... J 2
Miño (riv.) .... B 1
Moncayo, Sierra de (range) .... F 2
Mont Rouge (peak) .... G 1
Montserrat (mt.) .... G 2
Morena, Sierra (range) .... D 3
Mulhacén (mt.) .... E 4
Murcia (reg.), 1,167,339 .... F 3

Nao (cape) .... G 3
Navia (riv.) .... C 1
Nevada, Sierra (mts.) .... E 4
New Castile (reg.), 5,164,026 .... E 3
Odiel (riv.) .... C 4
Old Castile (reg.), 2,153,785 .... D 2
Órbigo (riv.) .... D 1
Peñalara (mt.) .... E 2
Peñas (cape) .... C 1
Peña Vieja (mt.) .... D 1
Peñíscola (cape) .... D 1
Penibética, Sistema (range) .... E 4
Perdido (mt.) .... F 1
Pyrenees (range) .... H 1
Rosas (gulf) .... H 1
San Jorge (gulf) .... G 2
Segura (riv.) .... F 3
Sil (riv.) .... C 1
Tagus (riv.) .... D 3
Tajo (Tagus) (riv.) .... D 3
Teide, Pico de (peak) .... B 5
Tenerife (isl.), 500,381 .... B 5
Ter (riv.) .... H 1
Tinto (riv.) .... C 4
Toledo (isls.) .... D 3
Tortosa (cape) .... G 2

Trafalgar (cape) .... C 4
Turia (riv.) .... F 3
Ulla (riv.) .... B 1
Urgel, Llanos de (plain) .... G 2
Valencia (gulf) .... G 3
Valencia (reg.), 3,073,255 .... F 3
Valencia, Albufera de (lag.) .... F 3
Vascongadas (reg.), 1,878,636 .... E 1

PORTUGAL

PROVINCES

Algarve, 266,621 .... B 4
Alto Alentejo, 304,542 .... C 3
Baixo Alentejo, 267,733 .... B 3
Beira Alta, 545,904 .... C 2
Beira Baixa, 275,379 .... C 2
Beira Litoral, 976,826 .... B 2
Douro Litoral, 1,518,804 .... B 2
Estremadura, 2,121,562 .... B 3
Madeira, 253,220 .... A 2
Minho, 867,296 .... B 2
Ribatejo, 467,730 .... B 3
Trás-os-Montes e Alto Douro, 511,722 .... C 2

Topography

Below Sea Level | 100 m. 328 ft. | 200 m. 656 ft. | 500 m. 1,640 ft. | 1,000 m. 3,281 ft. | 2,000 m. 6,562 ft. | 5,000 m. 16,404 ft.

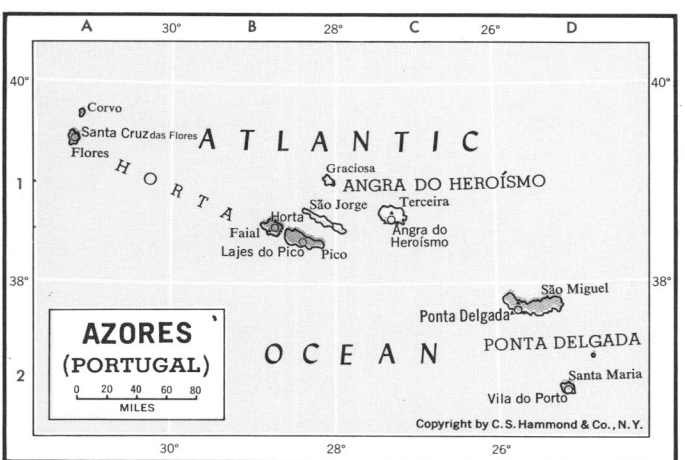

AZORES

INTERNAL DIVISIONS

Angra do Heroísmo (dist.), 83,500 .... C 1
Horta (dist.), 38,700 .... A 1
Ponta Delgada (dist.), 153,700 .... D 2

CITIES and TOWNS

Angra do Heroísmo, 13,795 .... C 1
Horta, 6,145 .... B 1
Lajes do Pico, 2,147 .... B 1
Ponta Delgada, 20,195 .... C 2
Santa Cruz das Flores, 1,880 .... A 1
Vila do Porto, 4,149 .... D 2

OTHER FEATURES

Azores (isls.), 275,900 .... A 2
Corvo (isl.), 469 .... A 1
Faial (isl.), 17,474 .... B 1
Flores (isl.), 5,302 .... A 1
Graciosa (isl.), 7,188 .... C 1
Pico (isl.), 18,014 .... B 1
Santa Maria (isl.), 9,487 .... D 2
São Jorge (isl.), 12,853 .... B 1
São Miguel (isl.), 149,873 .... C 1
Terceira (isl.), 70,368 .... C 1

Copyright by C. S. Hammond & Co., N. Y.

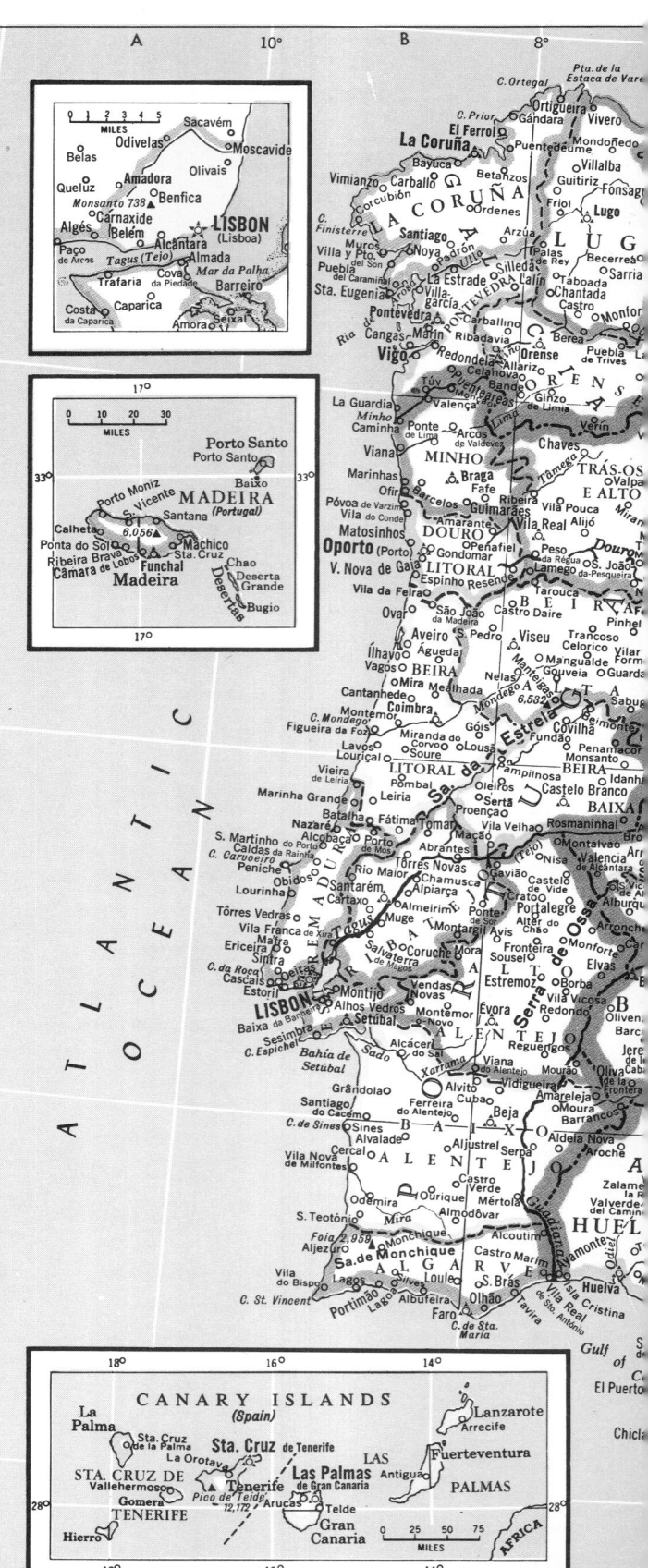

SPAIN and PORTUGAL

CONIC PROJECTION

SCALE OF MILES
0 20 40 60 80 100

SCALE OF KILOMETRES
0 20 40 60 80 100

Capitals of Countries _____ ★
Provincial Capitals _____ △
International Boundaries _____
Provincial Boundaries _____

© Copyright by C.S. HAMMOND & Co., Maplewood, N.J.

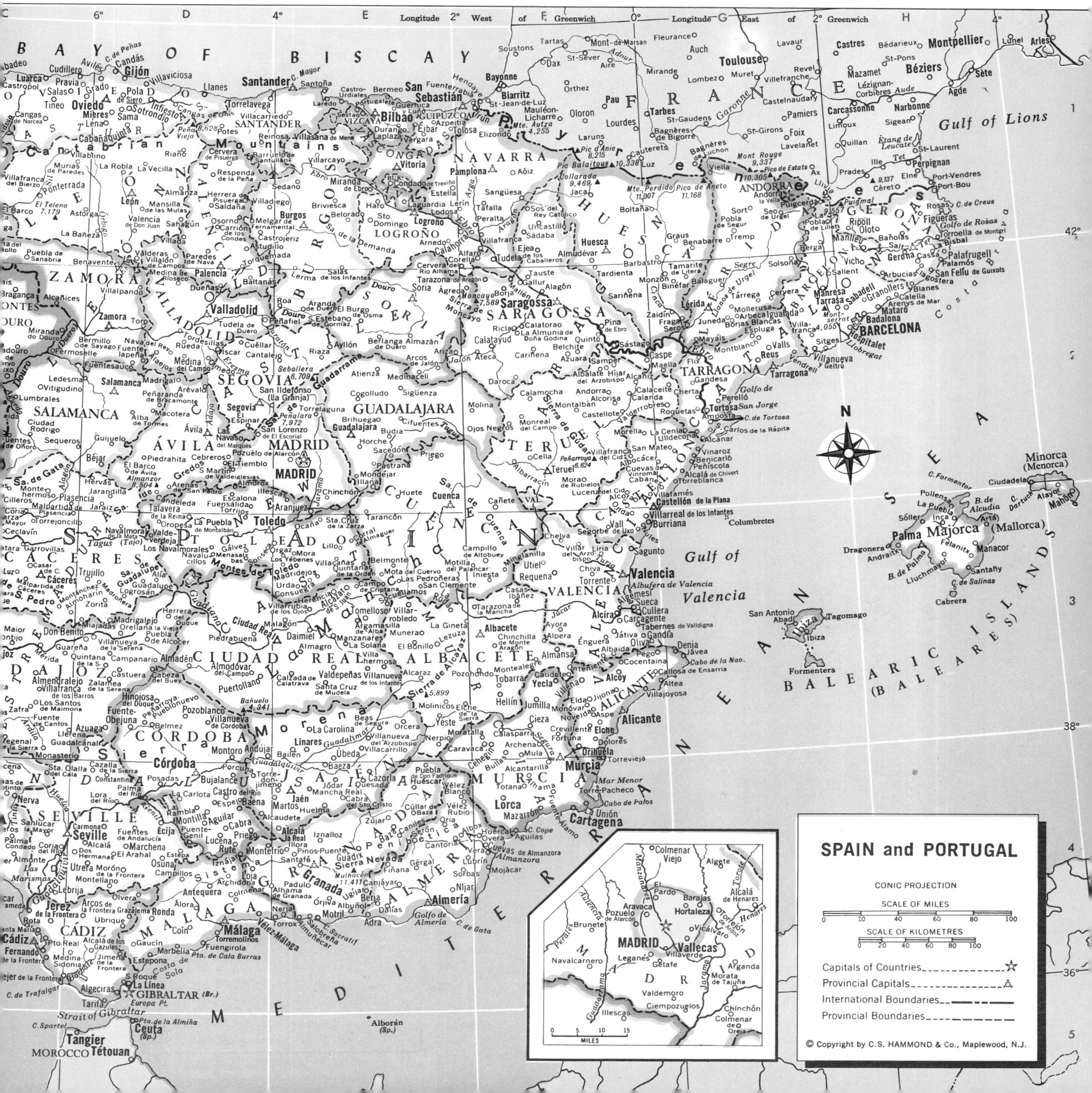

ITALY
CONIC PROJECTION

SCALE OF MILES

0   20   40   60   80   100

SCALE OF KILOMETERS

0 20 40 60 80 100

Capitals of Countries _____ ☆
Regional Capitals _____ ⌘
Provincial Capitals _____ △
International Boundaries _·_·_·_
Regional Boundaries _··_··_··_

ITALY is divided for administrative purposes into
20 regions, shown on the map in separate colors.
The regions are subdivided into provinces bearing
the same names as their respective capitals, except:

PROVINCE	CAPITAL
MASSA-CARRARA	Massa
PESARO-URBINO	Pesaro

Copyright by C.S. HAMMOND & Co., N.Y.

VATICAN CITY

SCALE

ROME and ENVIRONS

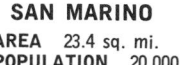

VATICAN CITY
AREA 116 acres
POPULATION 704

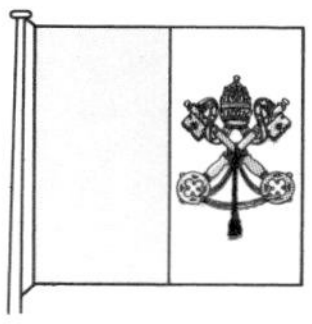

SAN MARINO
AREA 23.4 sq. mi.
POPULATION 20,000

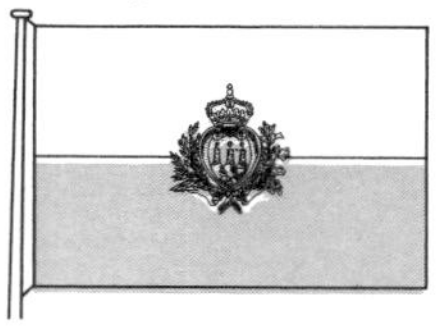

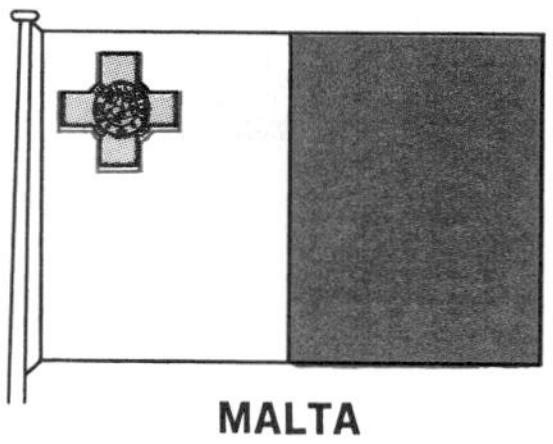

MALTA

AREA 122 sq. mi.
POPULATION 319,000
CAPITAL Valletta
LARGEST CITY Sliema
HIGHEST POINT 787 ft.
MONETARY UNIT Maltese pound
MAJOR LANGUAGES Maltese, English
MAJOR RELIGION Roman Catholicism

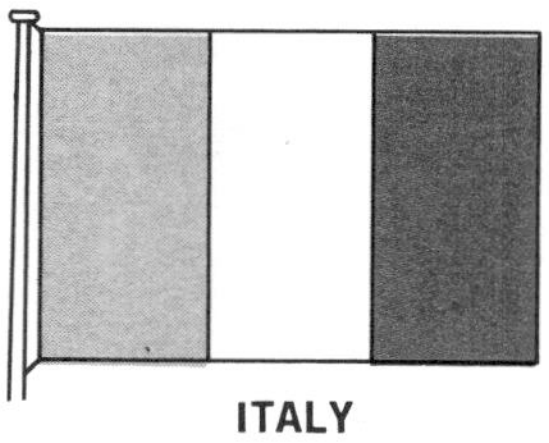

ITALY

AREA 116,303 sq. mi.
POPULATION 56,110,000
CAPITAL Rome
LARGEST CITY Rome
HIGHEST POINT Dufourspitze (Mte. Rosa) 15,203 ft.
MONETARY UNIT lira
MAJOR LANGUAGE Italian
MAJOR RELIGION Roman Catholicism

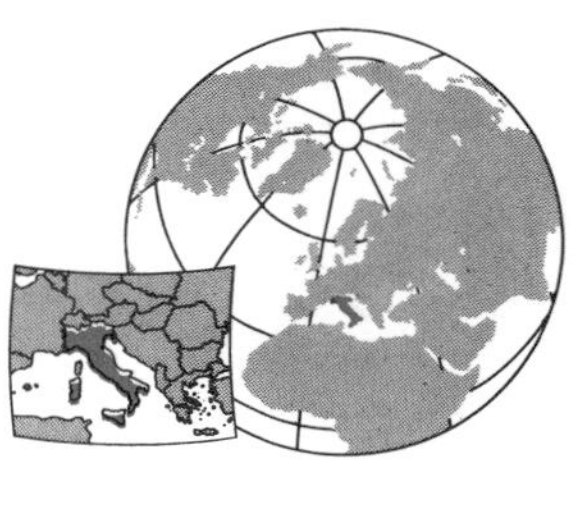

ITALY

REGIONS

Abruzzi, 1,166,664 D 3
Aosta, 109,150 A 2
Apulia (Puglia), 3,582,787 F 4
Basilicata, 603,064 F 4
Calabria, 1,988,051 F 5
Campania, 5,059,348 E 4
Emilia-Romagna, 3,846,755 C 2
Friuli-Venezia Giulia, 1,213,532 D 1
Latium (Lazio), 4,689,482 D 3
Liguria, 1,853,578 B 2
Lombardy, 8,543,657 B 2
Marche, 1,359,907 D 3
Molise, 319,807 E 4
Piedmont, 4,432,313 A 2
Sardinia, 1,473,800 B 4
Sicily, 4,680,715 D 6
Trentino-Alto Adige, 841,886 C 1
Tuscany, 3,473,097 C 3
Umbria, 775,783 D 3
Venetia (Veneto), 2,109,502 C 2

PROVINCES

Agrigento, 454,045 D 6
Alessandria, 483,183 B 2
Ancona, 416,611 D 3
Aosta, 109,150 A 2
Arezzo, 306,340 C 3
Ascoli Piceno, 340,758 D 3
Asti, 218,547 B 2
Avellino, 427,509 E 4
Bari, 1,351,288 F 4
Belluno, 221,155 D 1
Benevento, 286,499 E 4
Bergamo, 829,019 B 2
Bologna, 918,844 C 2
Bolzano-Bozen, 414,041 C 1
Brescia, 957,686 C 2
Brindisi, 366,027 G 4
Cagliari, 802,888 B 5
Caltanissetta, 282,069 D 6
Campobasso, 227,641 E 4
Caserta, 677,959 E 4
Catania, 938,273 E 6
Catanzaro, 718,069 F 5
Chieti, 351,567 E 3
Como, 720,463 B 2
Cosenza, 691,659 F 5
Cremona, 334,281 B 2
Cuneo, 540,504 A 2
Enna, 202,131 E 6
Ferrara, 383,639 C 2
Florence, 1,146,367 C 3
Foggia, 657,292 E 4
Forlì, 565,470 D 2
Frosinone, 422,630 D 4
Genoa, 1,087,973 B 2
Gorizia, D 2
Grosseto, 216,315 C 3
Imperia, 225,127 B 3
Isernia, 92,166 E 4
L'Aquila, 293,066 D 3
La Spezia, 244,435 B 2
Latina, 376,238 D 4
Lecce, 696,503 G 4
Leghorn, 335,265 C 3
Lucca, 380,356 C 3
Macerata, 286,155 D 3
Mantua, 376,892 C 2
Massa-Carrara, 200,955 C 2
Matera, 194,629 F 4
Messina, 654,703 E 5
Milan, 3,903,685 B 2
Modena, 553,852 C 2
Naples, 2,709,929 E 4
Novara, 496,811 B 2
Nuoro, 273,021 B 4
Padua, 762,998 C 2
Palermo, 1,124,015 D 5
Parma, 395,497 C 2
Pavia, 526,389 B 2
Perugia, 552,936 D 3
Pesaro e Urbino, 316,383 D 3
Pescara, 264,981 E 3
Piacenza, 284,881 B 2
Pisa, 375,933 C 3
Pistoia, 254,335 C 2
Pordenone, 253,906 D 2
Potenza, 408,435 E 4
Ragusa, 255,047 E 6
Ravenna, 351,876 D 2
Reggio di Calabria, 578,323 E 5
Reggio nell'Emilia, 392,696 C 2
Rieti, 143,162 D 3
Rome, 3,490,377 F 6
Rovigo, 251,908 C 2
Salerno, 957,452 E 4
Sassari, 397,891 B 4
Savona, 296,043 B 2
Siena, 257,221 C 3
Sondrio, 169,149 B 1
Syracuse, 365,039 E 6
Taranto, 511,677 F 4
Teramo, 257,080 D 3
Terni, 222,847 D 3
Trapani, 405,393 D 5
Trento, 427,845 C 1
Treviso, 668,620 D 2
Trieste, 300,304 E 2
Turin, 2,287,016 A 2
Udine, 516,910 D 1
Varese, 725,823 B 2
Venice, 807,251 D 2
Vercelli, 406,252 B 2
Verona, 733,595 C 2
Vicenza, 677,884 C 2
Viterbo, 257,075 C 3

CITIES and TOWNS

Acireale, 34,081 E 6
Acqui Terme, 20,099 B 2
Acri, 8,150 F 5
Adrano, 31,988 E 6
Adria, 11,951 D 2
Agira, 11,262 E 6
Agrigento, 40,513 D 6
Agropoli, 9,413 E 4
Alassio, 13,512 A 2
Alba, 23,522 B 2
Albano Laziale, 15,561 F 7
Albenga, 13,397 B 3
Albino, 8,837 B 2
Alcamo, 41,448 D 6
Alessandria, 78,644 B 2
Alghero, 28,454 B 4
Altamura, 44,879 F 4
Amalfi, 4,205 E 4
Amantea, 6,132 E 5
Ancona, 88,427 D 3
Andria, 76,405 F 4
Anzio, 14,966 D 4
Aosta, 35,053 A 2
Aprilia, 18,412 D 4
Aragona, 11,213 D 6
Arezzo, 56,693 C 3
Argenta, 6,682 D 2
Ariano Irpino, 9,796 E 4
Ariccia, 7,287 F 7
Ascoli Piceno, 43,041 D 3
Assisi, 4,630 D 3
Asti, 62,277 B 2
Augusta, 32,501 E 6
Avellino, 44,750 E 4
Aversa, 46,536 E 4
Avezzano, 26,456 D 3
Avola, 29,089 E 6
Bagheria, 32,465 D 5
Barcellona Pozzo di Gotto, 25,280 E 5
Bari, 339,110 F 4
Barletta, 75,116 F 4
Bassano del Grappa, 33,002 C 2
Bellagio, 3,258 B 2
Belluno, 22,180 D 1
Benevento, 48,523 E 4
Bergamo, 127,553 B 2
Biancavilla, 18,743 E 6
Biella, 46,453 B 2
Bisceglie, 45,014 F 4
Bitonto, 39,714 F 4
Bologna, 493,282 C 2
Bolzano, 102,806 C 1
Bondeno, 7,451 C 2
Bordighera, 8,994 A 3
Borgomanero, 16,655 B 2
Borgo San Lorenzo, 7,699 C 2
Bosa, 8,045 B 4
Bra, 18,399 A 2
Bracciano, 7,681 C 3
Brescia, 189,092 C 2
Bressanone, 12,261 C 1
Brindisi, 76,612 G 4
Bronte, 17,823 E 6
Busto Arsizio, 72,400 B 2
Cagliari, 211,015 B 5
Caltagirone, 34,444 E 6
Caltanissetta, 52,838 D 6
Camaiore, 8,578 C 3
Campobasso, 35,551 E 4
Campo Tures, 1,325 C 1
Canicatti, 28,761 E 6
Canosa di Puglia, 30,263 E 4
Cantù, 28,617 B 2
Capua, 13,938 E 4
Caravaggio, 11,298 B 2
Carbonia, 23,031 B 5
Carini, 14,255 D 5
Carloforte, 6,671 B 5
Carmagnola, 16,469 A 2
Carpi, 41,789 C 2
Carrara, 56,236 C 2
Casale Monferrato, 35,156 B 2
Casalmaggiore, 6,374 C 2
Cascina-Navacchio, 28,263 C 3
Caserta, 51,621 E 4
Cassano allo Ionio, 9,661 F 5
Cassino, 14,747 D 4
Castelfranco Veneto, 16,042 D 2
Castel Gandolfo, 2,965 F 7
Castellammare del Golfo, 13,144 D 5
Castellammare di Stabia, 64,341 E 4
Castel San Pietro Terme, 6,985 C 2
Castelvetrano, 29,167 D 6
Castrovillari, 15,207 F 5
Catania, 403,390 E 6
Catanzaro, 52,054 F 5
Cava de'Tirreni, 33,868 E 4
Cavarzere, 7,917 D 2
Cecina, 19,415 C 3
Cefalù, 11,043 E 5
Ceglie Messapico, 17,512 F 4
Celano, 9,531 D 3
Cerignola, 44,648 E 4
Cernobbio, 8,026 B 2
Cesena, 49,915 D 2
Cesenatico, 12,805 D 2
Chiari, 12,017 C 2
Chiavari, 29,950 B 2
Chieri, 27,548 A 2
Chieti, 31,895 E 3
Chioggia, 24,044 D 2
Chivasso, 21,369 A 2
Ciampino, 36,728 F 7
Cittadella, 9,321 C 2
Città di Castello, 18,880 C 3
Cittanova, 11,045 F 5
Cividale del Friuli, 8,345 D 1
Civitavecchia, 41,305 C 3
Clusone-Fiorine, 6,428 C 2
Codroipo, 6,117 D 2
Colle di Val d'Elsa, 8,657 C 3
Comacchio, 10,437 D 2
Comiso, 24,508 E 6
Como, 73,257 B 2
Conegliano, 28,635 D 2
Conversano, 16,805 F 4
Corato, 38,163 F 4
Cori, 6,829 F 7
Corigliano Calabro, 14,518 F 5
Corleone, 11,057 D 6
Correggio, 11,415 C 2
Cortina d'Ampezzo, 7,285 D 1
Cosenza, 94,565 F 5
Courmayeur, 1,401 A 2
Crema, 26,061 B 2
Cremona, 75,988 B 2
Crotone, 44,081 F 5
Cuneo, 41,633 A 2
Cuorgnè, 6,752 A 2
Desenzano del Garda, 14,624 C 2
Diano Marina, 6,001 B 3
Domodossola, 18,562 A 1
Dorgali, 6,714 B 4
Eboli, 19,787 E 4
Empoli, 30,526 C 3
Enna, 27,351 E 6
Este, 12,992 C 2
Fabriano, 18,355 D 3
Faenza, 36,241 D 2
Fano, 31,238 D 3
Fasano, 21,247 F 4
Favara, 27,940 D 6
Feltre, 11,806 C 1
Fermo, 17,521 D 3
Ferrandina, 8,372 F 4
Ferrara, 97,507 C 2
Fidenza, 18,064 B 2
Fiesole, 3,772 C 3
Finale Emilia, 7,474 C 2
Finale Ligure, 11,461 B 2
Firenze (Florence), 441,654 C 3
Fiumicino, 13,180 F 7
Florence, 441,654 C 3
Floridia, 16,562 E 6
Foggia, 136,436 E 4
Foligno, 26,887 D 3
Fondi, 16,472 D 4
Forlì, 83,303 D 2
Formia, 18,978 D 4
Fossano, 15,857 A 2
Fossombrone, 5,882 D 3
Francavilla Fontana, 30,347 F 4
Frascati, 14,217 F 7
Frosinone, 34,066 D 4
Gaeta, 21,973 D 4
Galatina, 22,137 G 4
Galatone, 13,880 F 4
Gallarate, 43,773 B 2
Gallipoli, 16,878 F 4
Gela, 66,845 E 6
Gemona, 6,863 D 1
Genoa, 787,011 B 2
Genova (Genoa), 787,011 B 2
Genzano di Roma, 14,147 F 7
Giarre, 18,233 E 6
Gioia del Colle, 23,299 F 4
Giovinazzo, 17,768 F 4
Giulianova, 17,926 E 3
Gorizia, 35,912 D 2
Gravina in Puglia, 32,006 F 4
Grosseto, 48,309 C 3
Grottaferrata, 10,639 F 7
Grottaglie, 23,556 F 4
Guastalla, 7,639 C 2
Gubbio, 12,371 D 3
Guidonia, 8,413 F 6
Iesi, 33,011 D 3
Iglesias, 24,472 B 5
Imola, 42,111 C 2
Imperia, 37,585 B 3
Isernia, 12,290 E 4
Ivrea, 26,530 B 2
Ladispoli, 6,625 E 6
La Maddalena, 10,405 B 4
Lanciano, 19,652 E 3
L'Aquila, 36,233 D 3
La Spezia, 121,254 B 2
Latina, 53,003 D 4
Lavello, 11,486 E 4
Lecce, 80,114 G 4
Lecco, 53,165 B 2
Leghorn, 170,369 C 3
Legnago, 15,534 C 2
Lendinara, 7,079 C 2
Lentini, 31,429 E 6
Leonforte, 16,317 E 6
Licata, 40,997 D 6
Lido di Ostia, 61,492 F 7
Lido di Venezia, 18,794 D 2
Livigno, 2,135 C 1
Livorno (Leghorn), 170,369 C 3
Lodi, 42,489 B 2
Lonigo, 6,368 C 2
Lucca, 54,280 C 3
Lucera, 29,355 E 4
Lugo, 19,497 D 2
Macerata, 33,470 D 3
Macomer, 9,433 B 4
Maglie, 13,326 G 4
Manduria, 25,194 F 4
Manfredonia, 44,463 F 4
Mantua, 59,529 C 2
Marino, 12,135 F 7
Marsala, 34,150 D 6
Martina Franca, 31,811 F 4
Massa, 56,591 C 2
Massafra, 22,610 F 4
Massa Marittima, 6,438 C 3
Matera, 43,026 F 4
Mazara del Vallo, 37,441 D 6
Mazzarino, 14,981 E 6
Melfi, 13,355 E 4
Menfi, 12,386 D 6
Merano, 30,951 C 1
Mesagne, 26,955 G 4
Messina, 203,937 E 5
Mestre, 184,818 D 2
Milan, 1,724,557 B 2
Milazzo, 18,576 E 5
Minturno, 2,428 D 4
Mirandola, 11,551 C 2
Mira Taglio, 10,194 D 2
Mistretta, 6,631 E 6
Modena, 149,029 C 2
Modica, 31,074 E 6
Mola di Bari, 23,778 F 4
Molfetta, 63,250 F 4
Moncalieri, 49,953 A 2
Mondovi Breo, 12,524 A 2
Monfalcone, 29,589 D 2
Monopoli, 29,776 F 4
Monreale, 19,348 D 5
Monselice, 9,047 C 2
Montebelluna, 9,573 D 2
Montefiascone, 6,885 D 3
Monterotondo, 15,869 F 6
Monte Sant'Angelo, 17,756 F 4
Montevarchi, 16,849 C 3
Monza, 110,735 B 2
Mortara, 13,929 B 2
Naples, 1,214,775 E 4
Nardò, 24,142 F 4
Narni, 6,213 D 3
Naro, 13,171 D 6
Nettuno, 20,927 D 4
Nicastro, 27,206 F 5
Nicosia, 13,982 E 6
Niscemi, 23,925 E 6
Nizza Monferrato, 7,532 B 2
Nocera Inferiore, 44,415 E 4
Noto, 21,606 E 6
Novara, 92,634 B 2
Novi Ligure, 29,944 B 2
Nuoro, 30,551 B 4
Olbia, 20,998 B 4
Oliena, 7,030 B 4
Orbetello, 6,884 C 3
Oristano, 20,966 B 5
Ortona, 11,966 E 3
Orvieto, 8,813 D 3
Osimo, 12,034 D 3
Ostia Antica, 2,583 F 7
Ostuni, 27,241 F 4
Otranto, 3,707 G 4
Ozieri, 9,149 B 4
Pachino, 20,427 E 6
Padua, 210,950 C 2
Palazzolo Acreide, 8,981 E 6
Palermo, 556,374 D 5
Palestrina, 9,239 F 7
Palma di Montechiaro, 22,381 D 6
Palmi, 14,405 E 5
Paola, 11,330 E 5
Parma, 151,967 C 2
Partanna, 10,303 D 6
Partinico, 25,447 D 6
Paterno, 41,504 E 6
Patti, 7,500 E 5
Pavia, 80,639 B 2
Penne, 5,889 D 3
Pergine Valsugana, 6,248 C 1
Perugia, 65,975 D 3
Pesaro, 72,104 D 3
Pescara, 125,391 E 3
Pescia, 9,918 C 3
Piacenza, 100,001 B 2
Piazza Armerina, 21,754 E 6
Pietrasanta, 6,620 B 3
Pinerolo, 33,935 A 2
Piombino, 35,641 C 3
Piove di Sacco, 7,035 C 2
Pisa, 91,156 C 3
Pisticci, 11,239 F 4
Pistoia, 55,403 C 2
Poggibonsi, 21,271 C 3
Pomezia, 11,915 F 7
Pontecorvo, 5,986 D 4
Pordenone, 43,230 D 2
Porto Civitanova, 25,773 D 3
Porto Empedocle, 15,986 D 6
Portoferraio, 7,579 C 3
Portofino, 720 B 2
Portogruaro, 12,258 D 2
Portomaggiore, 6,343 C 2
Porto Torres, 15,422 B 4
Potenza, 46,869 E 4
Pozzallo, 12,199 E 6
Pozzuoli, 53,546 D 4
Prato, 108,385 C 3
Prima Porta, 11,393 F 6
Priverno, 9,950 D 4
Putignano, 19,290 F 4
Quartu Sant'Elena, 29,715 B 5
Ragusa, 55,751 E 6
Rapallo, 22,272 B 2
Ravenna, 75,153 D 2
Recanati, 10,176 D 3
Reggio di Calabria, 110,291 E 5
Reggio nell'Emilia, 102,337 C 2
Rho, 39,206 B 2
Riesi, 15,855 E 6
Rieti, 26,775 D 3
Rimini, 101,579 D 2
Rionero in Vulture, 11,230 E 4
Riva del Garda, 8,513 C 2
Rome (cap.), 2,535,018 F 6
Ronciglione, 5,900 C 3
Rossano, 12,119 F 5
Rovereto, 26,827 C 2
Rovigo, 31,124 C 2
Ruvo di Puglia, 23,133 F 4
Sala Consilina, 8,177 E 4
Salemi, 10,180 D 6
Salerno, 146,534 E 4
Salsomaggiore Terme, 13,677 B 2
Saluzzo, 13,929 A 2
Sambiase, 10,567 F 5
San Bartolomeo in Galdo, 6,943 E 4
San Benedetto del Tronto, 40,108 E 3
San Cataldo, 19,609 D 6
San Giovanni in Fiore, 16,116 F 5

(continued on following page)

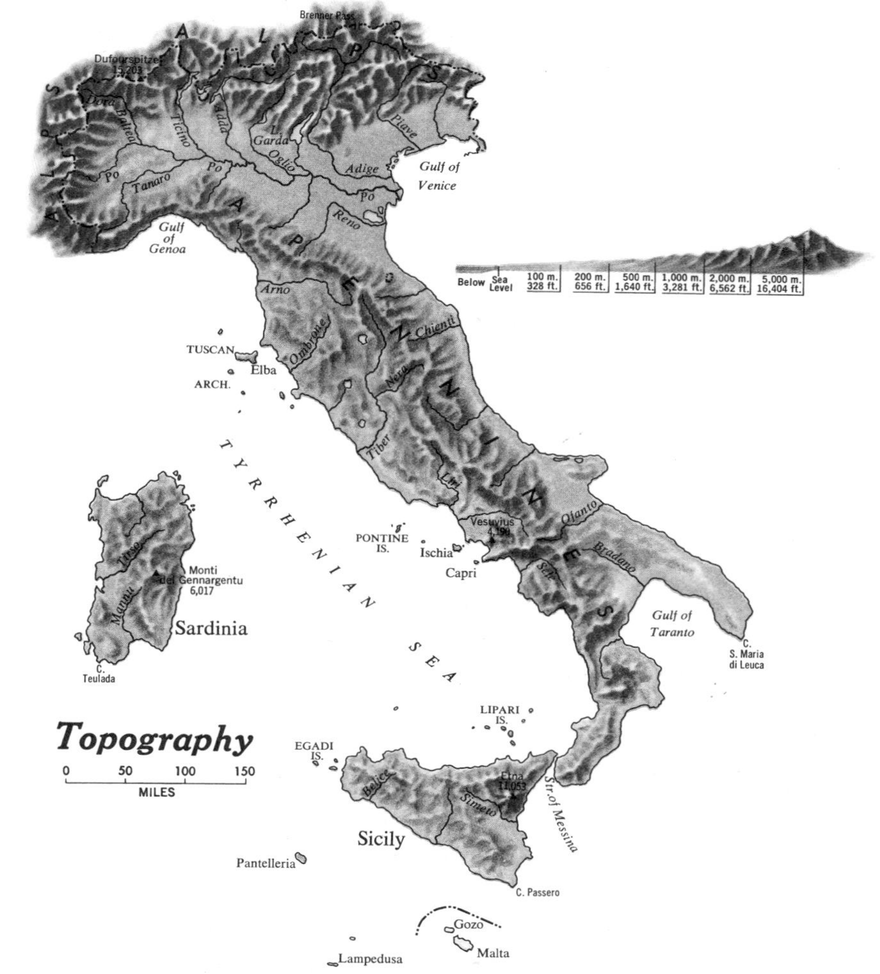
Brenner Pass
A L P S
Dufourspitze 15,203
Ticino
Adda
Garda
Oglio
Adige
Piave
Po
Tanaro
Gulf of Venice
Gulf of Genoa
Reno
A P E N N I N E S
Arno
Ombrone
Chienti
Tiber
Nera
Liri
Ofanto
Bradano
Sele
Vesuvius 4,190
TUSCAN ARCH.
Elba
T Y R R H E N I A N S E A
PONTINE IS.
Ischia
Capri
Monti del Gennargentu 6,017
Tirso
Mannu
Sardinia
C. Teulada
Gulf of Taranto
C. S. Maria di Leuca
LIPARI IS.
EGADI IS.
Etna 11,053
Belice
Simeto
Str. of Messina
Sicily
Pantelleria
C. Passero
Gozo
Malta
Lampedusa
Below Sea Level
100 m. 328 ft.
200 m. 656 ft.
500 m. 1,640 ft.
1,000 m. 3,281 ft.
2,000 m. 6,562 ft.
5,000 m. 16,404 ft.
Topography
0 50 100 150
MILES

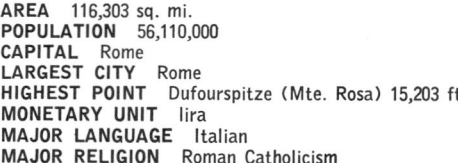

Agriculture, Industry and Resources

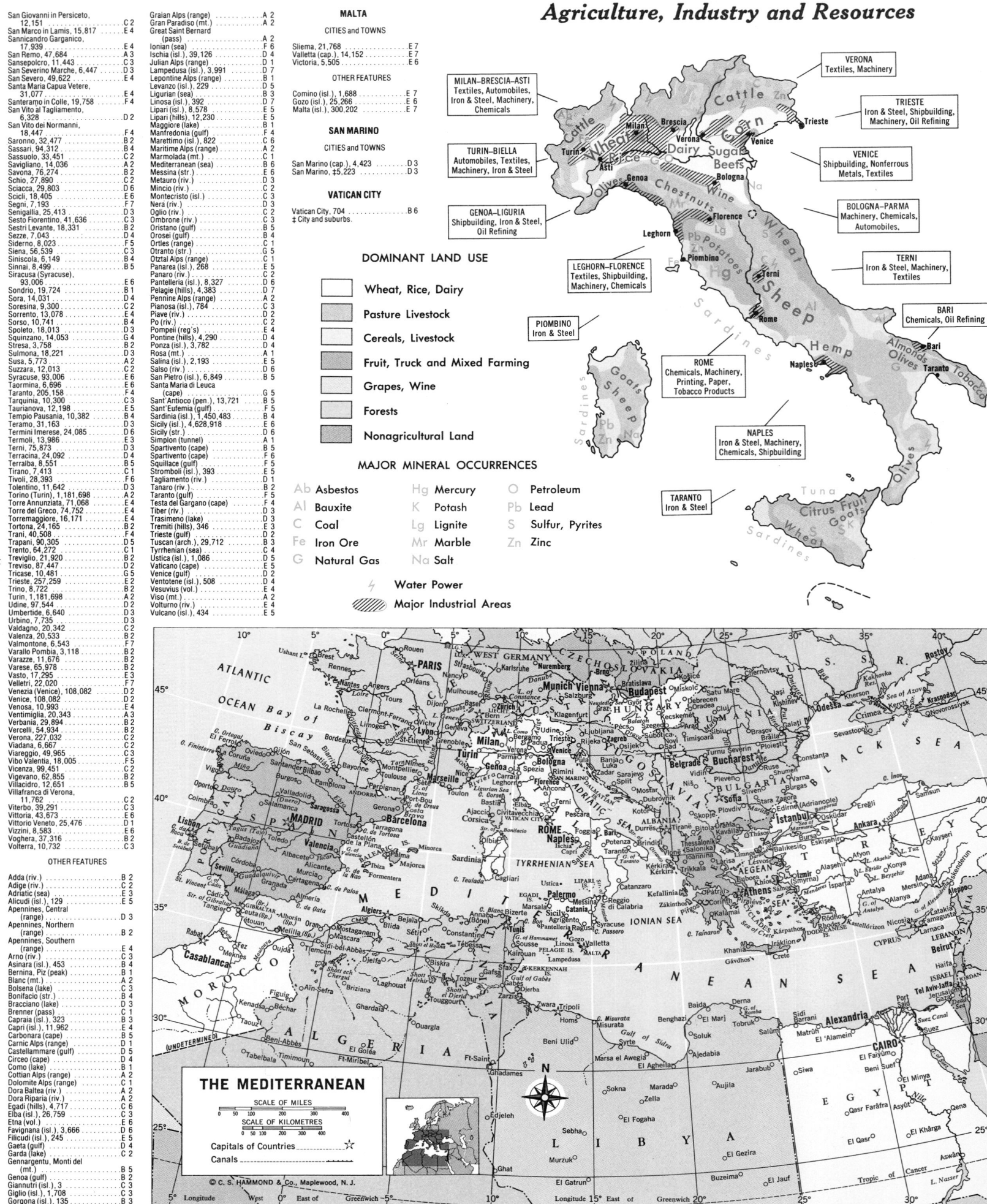

VERONA
Textiles, Machinery

MILAN–BRESCIA–ASTI
Textiles, Automobiles,
Iron & Steel, Machinery,
Chemicals

TRIESTE
Iron & Steel, Shipbuilding,
Machinery, Oil Refining

TURIN–BIELLA
Automobiles, Textiles,
Machinery, Iron & Steel

VENICE
Shipbuilding, Nonferrous
Metals, Textiles

GENOA–LIGURIA
Shipbuilding, Iron & Steel,
Oil Refining

BOLOGNA–PARMA
Machinery, Chemicals,
Automobiles.

LEGHORN–FLORENCE
Textiles, Shipbuilding,
Machinery, Chemicals

TERNI
Iron & Steel, Machinery,
Textiles

PIOMBINO
Iron & Steel

BARI
Chemicals, Oil Refining

ROME
Chemicals, Machinery,
Printing, Paper,
Tobacco Products

NAPLES
Iron & Steel, Machinery,
Chemicals, Shipbuilding

TARANTO
Iron & Steel

DOMINANT LAND USE

Wheat, Rice, Dairy
Pasture Livestock
Cereals, Livestock
Fruit, Truck and Mixed Farming
Grapes, Wine
Forests
Nonagricultural Land

MAJOR MINERAL OCCURRENCES

Ab Asbestos
Al Bauxite
C Coal
Fe Iron Ore
G Natural Gas
Hg Mercury
K Potash
Lg Lignite
Mr Marble
Na Salt
O Petroleum
Pb Lead
S Sulfur, Pyrites
Zn Zinc

Water Power
Major Industrial Areas

THE MEDITERRANEAN

SCALE OF MILES
0 50 100 200 300 400
SCALE OF KILOMETRES
0 50 100 200 300 400

Capitals of Countries ... ☆
Canals

© C. S. HAMMOND & Co., Maplewood, N.J.

SWITZERLAND

AREA 15,943 sq. mi.
POPULATION 6,327,000
CAPITAL Bern
LARGEST CITY Zürich
HIGHEST POINT Dufourspitze (Mte. Rosa) 15,203 ft.
MONETARY UNIT Swiss franc
MAJOR LANGUAGES German, French, Italian, Romansch
MAJOR RELIGIONS Protestantism, Roman Catholicism

LIECHTENSTEIN

AREA 61 sq. mi.
POPULATION 25,000
CAPITAL Vaduz
LARGEST CITY Vaduz
HIGHEST POINT Naafkopf 8,445 ft.
MONETARY UNIT Swiss franc
MAJOR LANGUAGE German
MAJOR RELIGION Roman Catholicism

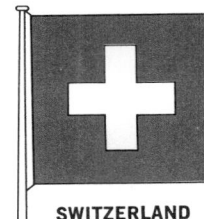

SWITZERLAND

LIECHTENSTEIN

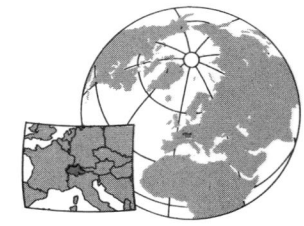

LANGUAGES

- German
- French
- Italian
- Romansch

Switzerland is a multilingual nation with four official languages. 70% of the people speak German, 19% French, 10% Italian and 1% Romansch.

SWITZERLAND

CANTONS

Aargau, 442,400	F 2
Appenzell, Ausser-Rhoden, 46,700	H 2
Appenzell, Inner-Rhoden, 13,500	H 2
Baselland, 219,500	E 2
Baselstadt, 209,700	E 2
Bern, 920,900	D 2
Fribourg, 181,600	C 4
Geneva, 338,600	B 4
Glarus, 35,700	H 3
Graubünden (Grisons), 164,300	J 3
Jura, 67,000	D 2
Luzern (Lucerne), 292,900	F 2
Neuchâtel, 162,200	C 3
Nidwalden, 26,900	F 3
Obwalden, 25,400	F 3
Sankt Gallen, 385,000	H 2
Schaffhausen, 69,300	G 1
Schwyz, 93,100	G 2
Solothurn (Soleure), 221,800	E 2
Thurgau, 183,500	H 1
Ticino, 264,400	G 4
Uri, 34,000	G 3
Valais, 214,000	E 4
Vaud, 523,500	C 3
Zug, 73,600	G 2
Zürich, 1,117,300	G 2

CITIES and TOWNS

Aadorf, 3,022	G 2
Aarau, 16,881	F 2
Aarau, ‡51,800	F 2
Aarberg, 3,122	D 2
Aarburg, 5,943	E 2
Adelboden, 3,326	E 3
Aeschi bei Spiez, 1,402	E 3
Affoltern am Albis, 7,363	F 2
Affoltern im Emmental, 1,223	E 2
Aigle, 6,532	C 4
Airolo, 2,140	G 3
Alle, 1,615	D 2
Allschwil, 17,638	D 1
Alpnach, 3,277	F 3
Altdorf, 8,647	G 3
Altstätten, 9,084	J 2
Amriswil, 7,601	H 1
Andeer, 714	H 3
Andermatt, 1,589	G 3
Appenzell, 5,217	H 2
Apples, 652	B 3
Arbedo-Castione, 2,456	G 4
Arbon, 12,227	H 1
Arbon, ‡15,400	H 1
Ardon, 1,498	D 4
Arosa, 2,717	J 3
Arth, 7,580	F 2
Ascona, 4,086	G 4
Attalens, 1,116	C 3
Aubonne, 1,983	B 4
Avenches, 2,235	D 3
Baar, 14,074	F 2
Baden, 14,115	F 2
Baden, ‡66,800	F 2
Bad Ragaz, 3,713	H 2
Balerna, 3,885	G 5
Ballaigues, 868	B 3
Balsthal, 5,607	E 2
Bäretswil, 2,733	G 2
Basel, 199,600	E 1

Basel, ‡379,700	E 1
Bassecourt, 2,985	D 2
Bätterkinden, 1,757	E 2
Baulmes, 811	C 3
Bauma, 3,159	G 2
Beatenberg, 1,263	E 3
Begnins, 981	B 4
Beinwil am See, 2,520	F 2
Belfaux, 1,075	D 3
Bellinzona, 16,979	H 4
Bellinzona, ‡31,000	H 4
Belp, 6,981	D 3
Bern (cap.), 154,700	D 3
Bern, ‡285,300	D 3
Beromünster, 1,552	F 2
Bex, 5,069	D 4
Biasca, 4,696	H 4
Biberist, 7,769	D 2
Biel, 63,400	D 2
Biel, ‡89,900	D 2
Biere, 1,252	B 3
Binningen, 15,344	D 1
Bischofszell, 4,233	H 1
Blumenstein, 1,049	E 3
Bodio, 1,425	G 4
Bolligen, 26,121	E 3
Boltigen, 1,519	D 3
Boncourt, 1,528	C 2
Bonfol, 888	D 2
Bönigen, 1,738	E 3
Boswil, 1,904	F 2
Boudry, 4,372	C 3
Bourg Saint-Pierre, 236	D 5
Breil-Brigels, 1,215	H 3
Breitenbach, 2,455	E 2
Bremgarten, 4,873	F 2
Brienz, 2,796	F 3
Brig, 5,191	F 4
Brissago, 2,120	G 4
Brittnau, 2,888	E 2
Brugg, 8,635	F 2
Brusio, 1,344	K 4
Bubendorf, 2,070	E 2
Bubikon, 3,244	G 2
Buchs, 8,454	H 2
Bülach, 11,043	G 1
Bulle, 7,556	D 3
Buochs, 3,232	F 3
Büren an der Aare, 3,085	D 2
Burgdorf, 15,888	E 2
Burgdorf, ‡18,400	E 2
Bürglen, Thurgau, 1,920	H 1
Bürglen, Uri, 3,401	G 3
Bussigny-près-Lausanne, 4,509	B 3
Bütschwil, 3,270	H 2
Buttes, 801	C 3
Carouge, 14,055	B 4
Castagnola, 4,430	G 4
Cazis, 1,687	H 3
Cernier, 1,717	C 2
Chalais, 1,651	E 4
Cham, 8,209	F 2
Chamoson, 2,049	D 4
Champéry, 926	C 4
Charmey, 1,155	D 3
Château-d'Oex, 3,203	D 4
Châtel-Saint-Denis, 2,842	C 3
Chavornay, 1,521	C 3
Chexbres, 16,072	C 3
Chiasso, 8,868	G 5
Chur, 32,400	J 3
Churwalden, 1,052	J 3
Claro, 1,143	G 4
Concise, 650	C 3
Conthey, 4,259	D 4
Coppet, 1,097	B 4
Corcelles-près-Payerne, 1,256	C 3
Corgémont, 1,645	D 2
Cossonay, 1,529	B 3
Courgenay, 1,954	D 2
Courroux, 1,788	D 2
Courtelary, 1,462	C 2
Courtételle, 1,864	D 2
Couvet, 3,481	C 3
Cully, 1,535	C 4
Davos, 10,238	J 3
Degersheim, 3,400	H 2
Delémont, 11,797	D 2
Derendingen, 4,917	E 2
Diemtigen, 1,913	D 3
Diessenhofen, 2,532	G 1
Dietikon, 22,705	F 2
Disentis-Mustér, 2,319	G 3
Dombresson, 1,109	C 2
Dornach, 5,258	E 2
Dübendorf, 19,639	G 2
Düdingen, 4,932	D 3
Dürnten, 4,820	G 2
Dürrenroth, 1,084	E 2
Ebnat-Kappel, 5,131	H 2
Echallens, 1,643	C 3
Egg, 5,250	G 2
Eggiwil, 2,391	E 3
Eglisau, 2,160	G 1
Egnach, 3,466	H 1
Einsiedeln, 10,020	G 2
Elgg, 2,970	G 2

(continued on following page)

Agriculture, Industry and Resources

DOMINANT LAND USE

- Cereals, Dairy
- Pasture Livestock
- General Farming, Livestock
- Fruit, Truck, Mixed Farming
- Forests
- Nonagricultural Land

⚡ Water Power
▨ Major Industrial Areas

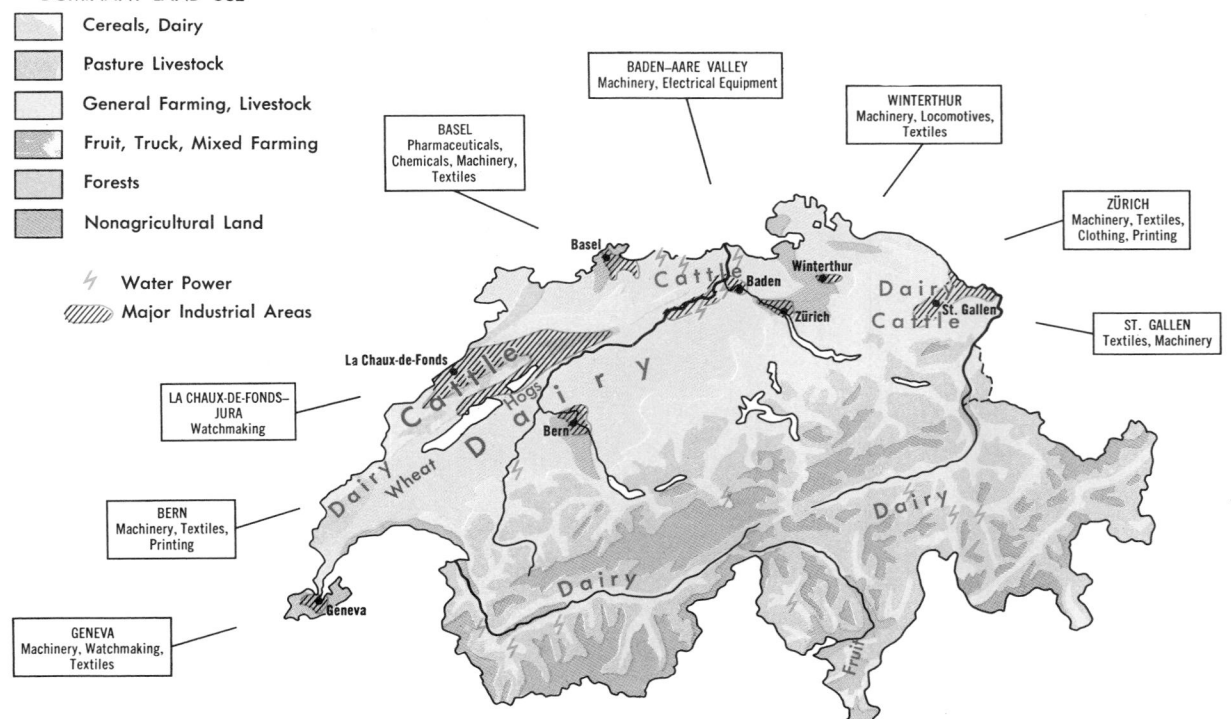

BADEN–AARE VALLEY
Machinery, Electrical Equipment

BASEL
Pharmaceuticals, Chemicals, Machinery, Textiles

WINTERTHUR
Machinery, Locomotives, Textiles

ZÜRICH
Machinery, Textiles, Clothing, Printing

ST. GALLEN
Textiles, Machinery

LA CHAUX-DE-FONDS–JURA
Watchmaking

BERN
Machinery, Textiles, Printing

GENEVA
Machinery, Watchmaking, Textiles

(continued)

Topography

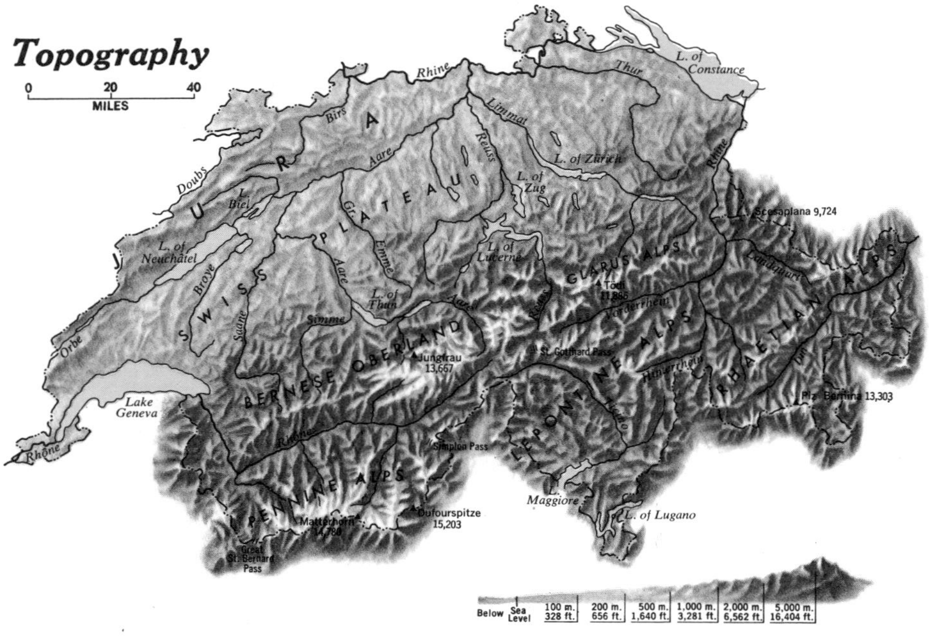

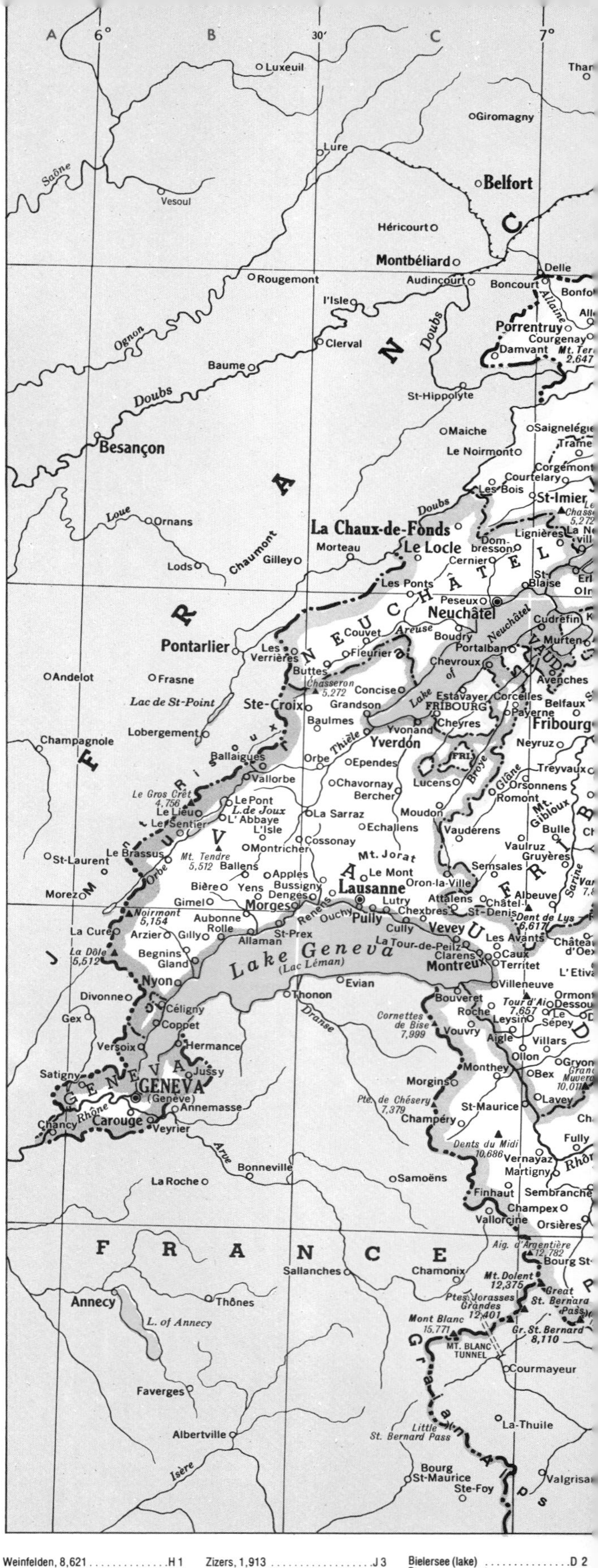

SWITZERLAND (continued)

Elm, 795 . . . . . H 3
Emmen, 22,040 . . . . . F 2
Engelberg, 2,841 . . . . . F 3
Engi, 837 . . . . . H 3
Ennenda, 2,762 . . . . . H 2
Entlebuch, 3,310 . . . . . F 3
Erlach, 1,052 . . . . . D 2
Erlenbach im Simmental, 1,436 . . . . . E 3
Ermatingen, 1,787 . . . . . H 1
Erstfeld, 4,516 . . . . . G 3
Eschenbach, 3,387 . . . . . G 2
Escholzmatt, 3,161 . . . . . E 3
Estavayer-le-Lac, 3,439 . . . . . C 3
Evolène, 1,403 . . . . . D 4
Faido, 1,866 . . . . . G 4
Finhaut, 681 . . . . . C 4
Flawil, 8,474 . . . . . H 2
Fleurier, 4,124 . . . . . C 3
Flims, 1,936 . . . . . H 3
Flüelen, 1,731 . . . . . G 3
Flums, 4,474 . . . . . H 2
Frauenfeld, 17,576 . . . . . G 1
Fribourg, 41,600 . . . . . D 3
Fribourg, ‡53,500 . . . . . D 3
Frick, 3,112 . . . . . E 1
Frutigen, 5,796 . . . . . E 3
Fully, 3,643 . . . . . D 4
Gais, 2,344 . . . . . H 2
Gampel, 1,021 . . . . . E 4
Gelterkinden, 5,157 . . . . . E 2
Geneva (Genève), 163,100 . . . . . B 4
Geneva (Genève), ‡320,200 . . . . . B 4
Gersau, 1,753 . . . . . G 2
Gimel, 1,205 . . . . . B 3
Giornico, 1,389 . . . . . G 4
Giswil, 2,760 . . . . . F 3
Giubiasco, 5,796 . . . . . H 4
Gland, 2,404 . . . . . B 4
Glarus, 6,189 . . . . . H 2
Glattfelden, 2,857 . . . . . F 1
Gordola, 2,586 . . . . . G 4
Göschenen, 888 . . . . . G 3
Gossau, 12,793 . . . . . H 2
Grabs, 4,245 . . . . . H 2
Grandson, 2,135 . . . . . C 3
Grenchen, 20,051 . . . . . D 2
Grenchen, ‡28,300 . . . . . D 2
Grindelwald, 3,511 . . . . . E 3
Grono, 845 . . . . . H 4
Grosswangen, 2,213 . . . . . F 2
Gruyères, 1,234 . . . . . D 3
Gryon, 752 . . . . . D 4
Gstaad, ... D 4
Gsteig, 865 . . . . . D 4
Guggisberg, 1,739 . . . . . D 3
Gurtnellen, 1,048 . . . . . G 3
Hallau, 1,836 . . . . . F 1
Heiden, 3,716 . . . . . H 2
Heimberg, 3,046 . . . . . E 3
Hérémence, 1,484 . . . . . D 4
Herisau, 14,597 . . . . . H 2
Herzogenbuchsee, 5,140 . . . . . E 2
Hinwil, 6,547 . . . . . G 2
Hochdorf, 5,222 . . . . . F 2
Horgen, 15,691 . . . . . G 2
Huttwil, 4,800 . . . . . E 2
Igis, 5,283 . . . . . J 3
Ilanz, 1,783 . . . . . H 3
Illnau, 13,693 . . . . . G 2
Ingenbohl, 5,111 . . . . . G 2
Innertkirchen, 1,064 . . . . . F 3
Ins, 2,435 . . . . . D 2
Interlaken, 4,735 . . . . . E 3
Intragna, 830 . . . . . G 4
Jaun, 689 . . . . . D 3
Jegenstorf, 2,858 . . . . . D 2
Jenaz, 1,124 . . . . . J 3
Jona, 9,286 . . . . . G 2
Jungfraujoch, ... E 3
Jussy, 692 . . . . . B 4
Kaltbrunn, 2,751 . . . . . H 2
Kandersteg, 957 . . . . . E 4
Kerns, 3,807 . . . . . F 3
Kerzers, 2,688 . . . . . D 3
Kirchberg, Bern, 3,595 . . . . . E 2
Kirchberg, St. Gallen, 6,309 . . . . . G 2
Kleinlützel, 1,271 . . . . . D 2
Klingnau, 2,545 . . . . . F 1
Klosters, 3,534 . . . . . J 3
Kloten, 16,388 . . . . . G 2
Koblenz, 1,439 . . . . . F 1
Kölliken, 3,219 . . . . . F 2
Köniz, 33,800 . . . . . D 3
Kreuzlingen, 15,760 . . . . . H 1
Kriens, 20,409 . . . . . F 2
Küblis, 796 . . . . . J 3
Küsnacht, 12,193 . . . . . G 2
Küssnacht am Rigi, 7,956 . . . . . F 2
Küttigen, 4,181 . . . . . F 2
L'Abbaye, 1,319 . . . . . B 3
La Chaux-de-Fonds, 42,500 . . . . . C 2
Lachen, 4,914 . . . . . G 2
La Neuveville, 3,917 . . . . . D 2
Langenthal, 13,077 . . . . . E 2
Langenthal, ‡22,100 . . . . . E 2
Langnau am Albis, 4,879 . . . . . G 2
Langnau in Emmental, 8,950 . . . . . E 3
La Roche, 1,069 . . . . . D 3
La Sarraz, 1,190 . . . . . C 3
La Tour-de-Peilz, 8,864 . . . . . C 4
Läufelfingen, 1,243 . . . . . E 2
Laufen, 4,723 . . . . . D 2
Laufenburg, 2,128 . . . . . F 1
Laupen, 2,139 . . . . . D 3
Lauperswil, 2,542 . . . . . E 3
Lausanne, 136,100 . . . . . C 3
Lausanne, ‡228,700 . . . . . C 3
Lauterbrunnen, 3,431 . . . . . E 3
Lavey-Morcles, 734 . . . . . D 4
Le Brassus, 5,465 . . . . . B 3
Le Châble, 4,541 . . . . . D 4
Le Lieu, 924 . . . . . B 3
Le Locle, 14,452 . . . . . C 2
Le Mont-sur-Lausanne, 2,692 . . . . . C 3
Lengnau, 4,736 . . . . . D 2
Lenk, 1,876 . . . . . D 4
Le Noirmont, 1,516 . . . . . C 2
Lens, 2,052 . . . . . D 4
Lenzburg, 7,594 . . . . . F 2
Les Bois, 1,110 . . . . . C 2
Les Ponts-de-Martel, 1,327 . . . . . C 2
Les Verrières, 898 . . . . . B 3
Leuk, 2,796 . . . . . E 4
Leukerbad, 1,056 . . . . . E 4
Leysin, 2,752 . . . . . C 4
Liestal, 12,500 . . . . . E 2
Liestal-Sissach, ‡40,800 . . . . . E 2
Linthal, 1,458 . . . . . H 3
Littau, 13,495 . . . . . F 2
Locarno, 14,143 . . . . . G 4
Locarno, ‡39,200 . . . . . G 4
Lodrino, 1,075 . . . . . G 4
Lucens, 2,144 . . . . . C 3
Lucerne, 70,200 . . . . . F 2
Lucerne, ‡158,600 . . . . . F 2
Lugano, 22,280 . . . . . G 4
Lugano, ‡64,200 . . . . . G 4
Lungern, 1,813 . . . . . F 3
Luthern, 1,706 . . . . . E 2
Lutry, 4,994 . . . . . C 3
Lützelflüh, 3,842 . . . . . E 3
Luzein, 1,032 . . . . . J 3
Luzern (Lucerne), 70,200 . . . . . F 2
Lyss, 8,131 . . . . . D 2
Maienfeld, 1,542 . . . . . J 2
Malans, 1,294 . . . . . J 3
Malters, 5,100 . . . . . F 2
Malvaglia, 1,099 . . . . . H 4
Männedorf, 7,419 . . . . . G 2
Marbach, 1,265 . . . . . E 3
Martigny, 10,478 . . . . . C 4
Meilen, 9,881 . . . . . G 2
Meiringen, 3,759 . . . . . F 3
Melide, 1,315 . . . . . G 5
Mellingen, 3,211 . . . . . F 2
Mels, 5,969 . . . . . H 2
Mendrisio, 6,223 . . . . . G 5
Menzingen, 3,483 . . . . . G 2
Menznau, 2,185 . . . . . E 2
Mesocco, 1,376 . . . . . H 4
Minusio, 5,027 . . . . . G 4
Möhlin, 6,003 . . . . . E 1
Mollis, 2,628 . . . . . H 2
Montana, 1,725 . . . . . D 4
Monthey, 10,114 . . . . . C 4
Montreux, 20,421 . . . . . C 4
Morges, 11,931 . . . . . B 3
Morges, ‡17,200 . . . . . B 3
Moudon, 3,773 . . . . . C 3
Moutier, 8,794 . . . . . D 2
Müllheim, 1,620 . . . . . G 1
Mümliswil-Ramiswil, 2,702 . . . . . E 2
Münchenbuchsee, 6,459 . . . . . E 2
Münsingen, 8,350 . . . . . E 3
Muotathal, 2,763 . . . . . G 3
Muri, 4,853 . . . . . F 2
Muri bei Bern, 3,057 . . . . . E 3
Mürren, ... E 3
Murten, 4,256 . . . . . D 3
Müstair, 645 . . . . . K 3
Muttenz, 15,518 . . . . . E 1
Näfels, 3,739 . . . . . H 2
Naters, 5,517 . . . . . E 4
Nebikon, 1,378 . . . . . F 2
Nesslau, 1,934 . . . . . H 2
Netstal, 2,771 . . . . . H 2
Neuchâtel, 38,400 . . . . . C 3
Neuchâtel, ‡61,700 . . . . . C 3
Neuenegg, 3,452 . . . . . D 3
Neuhausen am Rheinfall, 12,103 . . . . . G 1
Neunkirch, 1,239 . . . . . F 1
Niederbipp, 3,293 . . . . . E 2
Niederurnen, 3,354 . . . . . G 2
Nunningen, 1,450 . . . . . E 2
Nyon, 11,424 . . . . . B 4
Oberägeri, 2,992 . . . . . G 2
Oberburg, 3,015 . . . . . E 2
Oberdiessbach, 2,145 . . . . . E 3
Oberdorf, 1,210 . . . . . E 2
Oberriet, 6,123 . . . . . J 2
Oberuzwil, 4,659 . . . . . H 2
Oensingen, 3,387 . . . . . E 2
Olivone, 839 . . . . . G 3
Ollon, 4,470 . . . . . D 4
Olten, 21,209 . . . . . E 2
Olten, ‡49,000 . . . . . E 2
Orbe, 4,522 . . . . . C 3
Ormont-Dessous, 884 . . . . . D 4
Oron-la-Ville, 764 . . . . . C 3
Orsières, 2,470 . . . . . D 4
Osogna, 750 . . . . . H 4
Ouchy, ... C 4
Payerne, 6,899 . . . . . C 3
Peseux, 5,578 . . . . . C 3
Pfäffikon, 7,586 . . . . . G 2
Pfaffnau, 2,584 . . . . . E 2
Pieterlen, 3,485 . . . . . D 2
Pontresina, 1,646 . . . . . J 3
Porrentruy, 7,827 . . . . . C 2
Poschiavo, 3,563 . . . . . J 4
Pratteln, 15,127 . . . . . E 1
Pully, 15,917 . . . . . C 4
Quinto, 1,490 . . . . . G 3
Rafz, 2,215 . . . . . G 1
Ramsen, 1,217 . . . . . G 1
Rapperswil, 8,713 . . . . . G 2
Raron, 1,257 . . . . . E 4
Rechthalten, 878 . . . . . D 3
Regensdorf, 8,566 . . . . . F 2
Reichenbach im Kandertal, 2,900 . . . . . E 3
Reiden, 3,275 . . . . . F 2
Reinach, 5,862 . . . . . F 2
Renens, 17,391 . . . . . C 3
Rheinau, 2,075 . . . . . G 1
Rheineck, 3,275 . . . . . J 2
Rheinfelden, 6,866 . . . . . E 1
Richterswil, 7,380 . . . . . G 2
Riehen, 21,026 . . . . . E 1
Riggisberg, 2,193 . . . . . E 3
Riva San Vitale, 1,607 . . . . . G 5
Rivera, 1,146 . . . . . G 4
Roche, 848 . . . . . C 4
Roggwil, 3,403 . . . . . E 2
Rolle, 3,658 . . . . . B 4
Romanshorn, 8,329 . . . . . H 1
Romont, 3,276 . . . . . C 3
Rorschach, 11,963 . . . . . H 2
Rorschach, ‡24,200 . . . . . H 2
Rosenlaui, ... F 3
Rothrist, 5,883 . . . . . E 2
Rougemont, 824 . . . . . D 4
Roveredo, 2,037 . . . . . H 4
Rüeggisberg, 1,857 . . . . . E 3
Rüschegg, 1,346 . . . . . D 3
Ruswil, 4,756 . . . . . F 2
Rüthi, 1,493 . . . . . J 2
Rüti, Zürich, 9,546 . . . . . G 2
Saanen, 5,840 . . . . . D 4
Saas Fee, 895 . . . . . E 4
Sachseln, 3,059 . . . . . F 3
Saignelégier, 1,745 . . . . . D 2
Saint-Blaise, 2,586 . . . . . D 2
Sainte-Croix, 6,240 . . . . . B 3
Saint-Imier, 6,740 . . . . . D 2
Saint-Martin, 1,120 . . . . . E 4
Saint-Maurice, 3,808 . . . . . C 4
Saint Moritz, 5,699 . . . . . J 3
Saint Niklaus, 2,043 . . . . . E 4
Saint-Prex, 2,306 . . . . . B 4
Saint Stephan, 1,213 . . . . . D 3
Saint-Ursanne, 1,073 . . . . . D 2
Samedan, 2,574 . . . . . J 3
Sankt Gallen, 81,900 . . . . . H 2
Sankt Gallen, ‡90,400 . . . . . H 2
Sargans, 4,058 . . . . . H 2
Sarnen, 6,952 . . . . . F 3
Satigny, 1,877 . . . . . A 4
Savièse, 3,585 . . . . . D 4
Savognin, 820 . . . . . J 3
Saxon, 2,409 . . . . . D 4
Schaffhausen, 36,800 . . . . . G 1
Schaffhausen, ‡55,800 . . . . . G 1
Schangnau, 985 . . . . . E 3
Schänis, 2,355 . . . . . H 2
Schiers, 2,342 . . . . . J 3
Schinznach-Dorf, 1,154 . . . . . F 2
Schlarigna-Celerina, 983 . . . . . J 3
Schleitheim, 1,544 . . . . . G 1
Schlieren, 11,869 . . . . . F 2
Schönenwerd, 4,793 . . . . . E 2
Schüpfheim, 3,773 . . . . . F 3
Schwanden, 2,823 . . . . . H 2
Schwyz, 12,194 . . . . . G 2
Scuol, 1,686 . . . . . K 3
Sedrun, 1,273 . . . . . G 3
Seewis im Prättigau, 923 . . . . . J 2
Sembrancher, 712 . . . . . D 4
Sempach, 1,619 . . . . . F 2
Semsales, 829 . . . . . C 3
Sent, 704 . . . . . K 3
Seon, 3,628 . . . . . F 2
Sevelen, 2,742 . . . . . H 2
Sierre, 11,017 . . . . . D 4
Signau, 2,642 . . . . . E 3
Sigriswil, 3,540 . . . . . E 3
Silenen, 2,338 . . . . . G 3
Sils im Domleschg, 762 . . . . . H 3
Silvaplana, 714 . . . . . J 4
Sins, 2,435 . . . . . F 2
Sion, 21,925 . . . . . D 4
Sirnach, 3,706 . . . . . G 2
Sissach, 4,938 . . . . . E 2
Solothurn (Soleure), 17,708 . . . . . E 2
Solothurn, ‡35,600 . . . . . E 2
Somvix, 1,555 . . . . . G 3
Sonvico, 1,129 . . . . . G 4
Spiez, 9,911 . . . . . E 3
Stäfa, 9,937 . . . . . G 2
Stalden, 1,121 . . . . . E 4
Stans, 5,180 . . . . . F 3
Steckborn, 3,752 . . . . . G 1
Steffisburg, 12,621 . . . . . E 3
Stein, 1,763 . . . . . E 1
Stein am Rhein, 2,751 . . . . . G 1
Sulgen, 1,834 . . . . . H 1
Sulz, 1,021 . . . . . F 1
Sumiswald, 5,334 . . . . . E 2
Sursee, 7,052 . . . . . F 2
Tafers, 2,021 . . . . . D 3
Tamins, 828 . . . . . H 3
Täuffelen, 1,761 . . . . . D 2
Tavannes, 3,869 . . . . . D 2
Tavetsch (Sedrun), 1,273 . . . . . G 3
Thalwil, 13,591 . . . . . G 2
Thayngen, 3,640 . . . . . G 1
Therwil, 5,412 . . . . . E 1
Thun, 37,000 . . . . . E 3
Thun, ‡63,600 . . . . . E 3
Thusis, 2,381 . . . . . H 3
Trachselwald, 1,199 . . . . . E 2
Tramelan, 5,549 . . . . . D 2
Treyvaux, 946 . . . . . D 3
Trimmis, 1,109 . . . . . J 3
Trin, 714 . . . . . H 3
Trub, 1,833 . . . . . E 3
Trun, 1,607 . . . . . G 3
Turbenthal, 2,939 . . . . . G 2
Uetendorf, 3,132 . . . . . E 3
Unterägeri, 4,671 . . . . . G 2
Unterkulm, 2,596 . . . . . F 2
Unterseen, 4,192 . . . . . E 3
Untervaz, 1,230 . . . . . H 3
Urnäsch, 2,313 . . . . . H 2
Uster, 21,819 . . . . . G 2
Utzenstorf, 3,193 . . . . . E 2
Uznach, 3,984 . . . . . H 2
Uzwil, 9,133 . . . . . H 2
Vallorbe, 4,028 . . . . . B 3
Vals, 1,037 . . . . . H 3
Vaz-Obervaz, 2,003 . . . . . J 3
Vechigen, 3,595 . . . . . E 3
Vernayaz, 1,356 . . . . . D 4
Versoix, 5,627 . . . . . B 4
Vevey, 17,957 . . . . . C 4
Vevey-Montreux, ‡62,300 . . . . . C 4
Villeneuve, 3,705 . . . . . C 4
Visp, 5,252 . . . . . E 4
Vouvry, 1,851 . . . . . C 4
Wädenswil, 15,695 . . . . . G 2
Wahlern, 4,832 . . . . . D 3
Wald, 8,185 . . . . . G 2
Waldenburg, 1,449 . . . . . E 2
Waldkirch, 2,669 . . . . . H 2
Wallenstadt, 3,446 . . . . . H 2
Walzenhausen, 2,082 . . . . . J 2
Wangen an der Aare, 2,013 . . . . . E 2
Wängi, 2,730 . . . . . H 1
Wartau, 3,604 . . . . . H 2
Wassen, 764 . . . . . G 3
Wattwil, 8,566 . . . . . H 2
Weesen, 1,308 . . . . . H 2
Weggis, 2,517 . . . . . F 2
Weinfelden, 8,621 . . . . . H 1
Wettingen, 19,900 . . . . . F 2
Wetzikon, 13,469 . . . . . G 2
Wil, 14,646 . . . . . H 2
Wil, ‡20,500 . . . . . H 2
Wilchingen, 1,066 . . . . . F 1
Wilderswil, 1,666 . . . . . E 3
Wildhaus, 1,104 . . . . . H 2
Willisau, 2,728 . . . . . F 2
Wimmis, 1,833 . . . . . E 3
Windisch, 7,444 . . . . . F 1
Winterthur, 93,500 . . . . . G 1
Winterthur, ‡110,100 . . . . . G 1
Wohlen, 12,024 . . . . . F 2
Wohlen, ‡16,000 . . . . . F 2
Wohlen bei Bern, 4,190 . . . . . D 3
Wolfenschiessen, 1,470 . . . . . F 3
Wolhusen, 3,556 . . . . . F 2
Worb, 9,526 . . . . . E 3
Wynigen, 1,986 . . . . . E 2
Yverdon, 20,538 . . . . . C 3
Yvonand, 1,321 . . . . . C 3
Zell, Luzern, 1,590 . . . . . E 2
Zell, Zürich, 4,008 . . . . . G 2
Zermatt, 3,101 . . . . . E 4
Zernez, 906 . . . . . K 3
Zizers, 1,913 . . . . . J 3
Zofingen, 9,292 . . . . . F 2
Zollikofen, 9,069 . . . . . E 3
Zollikon, 12,117 . . . . . G 2
Zug, 22,972 . . . . . G 2
Zug, ‡51,300 . . . . . G 2
Zuoz, 1,165 . . . . . J 3
Zürich, 401,600 . . . . . F 2
Zürich, ‡718,100 . . . . . F 2
Zurzach, 3,098 . . . . . F 1
Zweisimmen, 2,738 . . . . . D 3

OTHER FEATURES

Aa (riv.) . . . . . F 3
Aare (riv.) . . . . . E 3
Agerisee (lake) . . . . . G 2
Aiguille d'Argentière (mt.) . . . . . C 5
Aletschhorn (mt.) . . . . . F 4
Aroser Rothorn (mt.) . . . . . J 3
Ault (peak) . . . . . H 3
Balmhorn (mt.) . . . . . E 4
Bernese Oberland (reg.) . . . . . E 3
Bernina (peak) . . . . . J 4
Bernina (pass) . . . . . K 4
Bielersee (lake) . . . . . D 2
Bietschhorn (mt.) . . . . . E 4
Birs (riv.) . . . . . D 2
Blinnenhorn (mt.) . . . . . F 4
Blümlisalp (mt.) . . . . . E 3
Bodensee (Constance) (lake) . . . . . H 1
Borgne (riv.) . . . . . D 4
Breithorn (mt.) . . . . . E 5
Breithorn (mt.) . . . . . E 4
Brienzer Rothorn (mt.) . . . . . F 3
Brienzersee (lake) . . . . . F 3
Broye (riv.) . . . . . C 3
Buchegg (mts.) . . . . . D 2
Buin (peak) . . . . . K 3
Campo Tencia (peak) . . . . . G 4
Chasseron (mt.) . . . . . C 3
Churfirsten (mt.) . . . . . H 2
Clariden (mt.) . . . . . G 3
Constance (lake) . . . . . H 1
Cornettes de Bise (mts.) . . . . . C 4
Dammastock (mt.) . . . . . F 3
Davos (valley) . . . . . J 3
Dent Blanche (mt.) . . . . . E 4
Dent de Lys (mt.) . . . . . D 4
Dent de Ruth (mt.) . . . . . D 3

SWITZERLAND and LIECHTENSTEIN

CONIC PROJECTION

SCALE OF MILES

0 5 10 20 30

SCALE OF KILOMETRES

0 5 10 20 30 40 50

Capitals of Countries	☆
Capitals of Cantons	◉
International Boundaries	▬ ▬
Canals	

Copyright by C.S. HAMMOND & Co., N.Y.

AUSTRIA

PROVINCES

Burgenland, 272,119 .... D 3
Carinthia, 525,728 .... B 3
Lower Austria, 1,414,161 .... C 2
Salzburg, 401,766 .... B 3
Styria, 1,192,442 .... C 3
Tirol, 540,771 .... A 3
Upper Austria, 1,223,444 .... B 2
Vienna (city), 1,614,841 .... D 2
Vorarlberg, 271,473 .... A 3

CITIES and TOWNS

Achenkirch, 1,763 .... A 3
Admont, 3,126 .... C 3
Aigen im Mühlkreis, 1,822 .... B 2
Allentsteig, 2,783 .... C 2
Alt Aussee, 1,951 .... B 3
Altheim, 4,766 .... B 2
Althofen, 3,886 .... C 3
Amstetten, 13,330 .... C 2
Andau, 3,058 .... D 3
Arnoldstein, 6,740 .... B 3
Aspang Markt, 2,316 .... D 3
Attnang-Puchheim, 7,837 .... B 2
Bad Aussee, 5,039 .... B 3
Baden, 22,631 .... D 2
Badgastein, 5,228 .... B 3
Bad Goisern, 6,360 .... B 3
Bad Hofgastein, 5,525 .... B 3
Bad Ischl, 12,740 .... B 3
Bad Sankt Leonhard im Lavanttal, 4,882 .... C 3
Berndorf, 8,371 .... C 3
Bischofshofen, 9,417 .... B 3
Bludenz, 12,050 .... A 3
Bramberg am Wildkogel, 3,129 .... B 3
Braunau am Inn, 16,432 .... B 2
Bregenz, 22,839 .... A 3
Bruck an der Leitha, 7,506 .... D 2
Bruck an der Mur, 16,359 .... C 3
Deutsch Feistritz, 3,820 .... C 3
Deutschkreutz, 3,673 .... D 3
Deutsch Landsberg, 6,614 .... C 3
Deutsch Wagram, 4,481 .... D 2
Dölsach, 1,752 .... B 3
Dornbirn, 33,810 .... A 3
Ebenfurth, 2,272 .... D 3
Ebensee, 9,413 .... B 3

Heiligenblut, 1,324 .... B 3
Hermagor-Presegersee, 7,531 .... B 3
Herzogenburg, 7,299 .... C 2
Hieflau, 1,699 .... C 3
Hohenau an der March, 3,591 .... D 2
Hohenberg, 2,016 .... C 2
Hohenems, 11,487 .... A 3
Hollabrunn, 6,563 .... C 2
Hopfgarten in Nordtirol, 4,784 .... B 3
Horn, 6,264 .... C 2
Hüttenberg, 3,251 .... C 3
Imst, 5,855 .... A 3
Innsbruck, 115,800 .... A 3
Innsbruck, *167,200 .... A 3
Jenbach, 5,868 .... A 3
Jennersdorf, 4,210 .... C 3
Judenburg, 11,346 .... C 3
Kapfenberg, 26,001 .... C 3
Kappl, 2,156 .... A 3
Kaprun, 2,604 .... B 3
Kindberg, 6,128 .... C 3
Kirchdorf an der Krems, 3,471 .... C 2
Kitzbühel, 7,995 .... B 3
Klagenfurt, 74,326 .... C 3
Klagenfurt, *112,600 .... C 3
Klosterneuburg, 21,912 .... D 2
Knittelfeld, 14,517 .... C 3
Königswiesen, 2,921 .... C 2
Korneuburg, 8,892 .... D 2
Kössen, 2,764 .... B 3
Kötschach-Mauthen, 3,740 .... B 3
Krems an der Donau, 21,733 .... C 2
Krimml, 794 .... B 3
Kufstein, 12,766 .... A 3
Kundl, 3,020 .... A 3
Laa an der Thaya, 5,455 .... D 2
Laakirchen, 7,664 .... B 3
Lambach, 2,301 .... C 2
Landeck, 7,388 .... A 3
Längenfeld, 2,838 .... A 3
Langenlois, 4,957 .... C 2
Langenwang, 4,071 .... C 3
Lavamünd, 4,120 .... C 3
Leibnitz, 6,646 .... C 3
Lenzing, 5,385 .... B 3
Leoben, 35,153 .... C 3
Leonfelden, 2,782 .... C 2
Lienz, 11,696 .... B 3
Liezen, 6,244 .... C 3
Lilienfeld, 3,126 .... C 3
Linz, 205,700 .... C 2

Ratten, 1,368 .... C 3
Rechnitz, 3,412 .... D 3
Reichenau an der Rax, 4,053 .... C 3
Retz, 4,780 .... C 2
Reutte, 5,006 .... A 3
Ried im Innkreis, 10,534 .... B 2
Rohrbach in Oberösterreich, 1,755 .... B 2
Rottenmann, 4,781 .... C 3
Saalfelden am Steinernen Meer, 10,172 .... B 3
Salzburg, 122,100 .... B 3
Salzburg, *213,430 .... B 3
Sankt Aegyd am Neuwalde, 3,165 .... C 3
Sankt Anton am Arlberg, 2,086 .... A 3
Sankt Johann in Tirol, 5,942 .... A 3
Sankt Michael im Lungau, 2,839 .... B 3
Sankt Michael in Obersteiermark, 3,717 .... C 3
Sankt Paul im Lavanttal, 6,721 .... C 3
Sankt Pölten, 43,300 .... C 2
Sankt Valentin, 8,715 .... C 2
Sankt Veit an der Glan, 11,047 .... C 3
Sankt Wolfgang im Salzkammergut, 2,476 .... B 3
Schärding, 5,874 .... B 2
Scheibbs, 4,419 .... C 2
Schladming, 3,460 .... B 3
Schrems, 3,393 .... C 2
Schruns, 3,607 .... A 3
Schwarzach im Pongau, 3,616 .... B 3
Schwaz, 10,253 .... A 3
Schwertberg, 3,881 .... C 2
Sierning, 8,162 .... C 2
Sigmundsherberg, 945 .... C 2
Sillian, 1,988 .... B 3
Solbad Hall in Tirol, 12,335 .... A 3
Spital am Pyhrn, 2,315 .... C 3
Spittal an der Drau, 13,690 .... B 3
Spitz, 1,504 .... C 2
Steinach, 2,698 .... A 3
Steyr, 40,578 .... C 2
Stockerau, 12,634 .... D 2
Strassburg, 2,850 .... C 3
Tamsweg, 5,060 .... B 3
Telfs, 6,589 .... A 3
Ternitz, 10,287 .... C 3
Traiskirchen, 8,878 .... C 2
Traun, 20,843 .... C 2
Trieben, 4,639 .... C 3
Trofaiach, 8,731 .... C 3

Tulln, 7,705 .... D 2
Velden am Wörthersee, 7,306 .... C 3
Vienna (cap.), 1,700,000 .... D 2
Vienna, 1,858,700 .... D 2
Villach, 50,979 .... B 3
Vils, 1,325 .... A 3
Vöcklabruck, 10,627 .... B 2
Voitsberg, 11,094 .... C 3
Völkermarkt, 10,772 .... C 3
Vorderberg, 2,508 .... C 3
Waidhofen an der Thaya, 4,200 .... C 2
Waidhofen an der Ybbs, 5,218 .... C 3
Weitensfeld-Flattnitz, 5,206 .... B 3
Weitra, 3,250 .... C 2
Weiz, 8,431 .... C 3
Wels, 47,277 .... C 2
Weyer Markt, 2,518 .... C 3
Wiener Neustadt, 34,774 .... C 3
Wildon, 2,002 .... C 3
Wilhelmsburg, 6,307 .... C 2
Windischgarsten, 1,805 .... C 3
Wolfsberg, 31,176 .... C 3
Wörgl, 7,811 .... A 3
Ybbs an der Donau, 6,422 .... C 2
Zams, 3,120 .... A 3
Zell am See, 7,456 .... B 3
Zell am Ziller, 1,882 .... A 3
Zirl, 4,157 .... A 3
Zistersdorf, 3,412 .... D 2
Zwettl-Niederösterreich, 11,624 .... C 2

OTHER FEATURES

Allgäu Alps (mts.) .... A 3
Bavarian Alps (mts.) .... A 3
Bodensee (Constance) (lake) .... A 3
Brenner (pass) .... A 3
Carnic Alps (mts.) .... B 3
Constance (lake) .... A 3
Danube (riv.) .... C 2
Donau (Danube) (riv.) .... D 2
Drau (riv.) .... C 3
Enns (riv.) .... C 3
Grossglockner (mt.) .... B 3
Hohe Tauern (range) .... B 3
Inn (riv.) .... A 3
Karawanken (range) .... C 3
March (riv.) .... D 2
Mühlviertel (reg.), 214,012 .... C 2
Mur (riv.) .... C 3

Neusiedler See (lake) .... D 3
Niedere Tauern (range) .... B 3
Ötztal Alps (mts.) .... A 3
Raab (riv.) .... C 3
Rhine (riv.) .... A 3
Salzach (riv.) .... B 2
Salzkammergut (reg.), 112,566 .... B 3
Semmering (pass) .... C 3
Thaya (riv.) .... C 2
Traun (riv.) .... C 2
Wildspitze (mt.) .... A 3
Zugspitze (mt.) .... A 3

CZECHOSLOVAKIA

REPUBLICS

Czech Socialist Rep., 9,964,338 .... B 1
Slovak Socialist Rep., 4,670,409 .... E 2

REGIONS

Bratislava (city), 333,000 .... D 2
Jihocesky, 662,002 .... C 2
Jihomoravsky, 1,966,850 .... D 2
Praha (city), 1,161,200 .... C 1
Severocesky, 1,122,035 .... C 1
Severomoravsky, 1,849,286 .... D 1
Stredocesky, 1,193,041 .... C 2
Stredoslovensky, 1,436,351 .... E 2
Vychodocesky, 1,214,581 .... C 1
Vychodoslovensky, 1,298,481 .... F 2
Zapadocesky, 865,094 .... B 2
Zapadoslovensky, 1,610,542 .... D 2

CITIES and TOWNS

As, 12,000 .... B 1
Austerlitz (Slavkov) .... D 2
Bánovce nad Bebravou, 11,400 .... E 2
Banská Bystrica, 53,000 .... E 2
Banská Stiavnica, 7,486 .... E 2
Bardejov, 17,400 .... F 2
Benesov, 11,100 .... C 2
Beroun, 17,600 .... C 2
Bilina, 17,800 .... B 1
Blansko, 13,800 .... D 2
Boskovice, 8,531 .... D 2
Brandys nad Labem-Stara Boleslav, 15,500 .... C 1
Bratislava, 333,000 .... D 2
Breclav, 21,100 .... D 2
Brezno, 14,800 .... E 2
Brno, 335,700 .... D 2
Broumov, 7,782 .... D 1
Bruntál, 12,300 .... D 1
Bystrice nad Pernstejnem, 6,471 .... D 2
Bystrice pod Hostynem, 6,681 .... D 2
Bytca, 6,922 .... E 2
Cadca, 16,800 .... E 2
Calovo, 6,591 .... D 2
Caslav, 10,200 .... C 2
Ceská Lipa, 18,600 .... C 1
Ceska Trebova, 14,700 .... D 2
Ceske Budejovice, 80,800 .... C 2
Cesky Brod, 6,640 .... C 1
Cesky Krumlov, 12,000 .... C 2
Cesky Tesin, 17,200 .... E 2

Cheb, 27,000 .... B 1
Chocen, 8,198 .... C 1 [partial]
Chodov, 14,400 .... B 1
Chomutov, 44,200 .... B 1
Chotebor, 6,692 .... C 2
Chrudim, 18,800 .... C 2
Cierny Balog, 6,435 .... E 2
Decin, 46,500 .... B 1
Detva, 13,100 .... E 2
Dobris, 6,378 .... C 2
Dobruska, 5,779 .... C 1
Dolny Kubin, 9,900 .... E 2
Domazlice, 9,100 .... B 2
Dubnica nad Vahom, 11,300 .... E 2
Duchcov, 9,712 .... B 1
Dunajska Streda, 13,000 .... D 2
Dvory nad Zitavou, 5,847 .... D 2
Dvůr Králové nad Labem, 16,800 .... C 1
Falknov (Sokolov), 23,900 .... B 1
Fil'akovo, 7,822 .... E 2
Frenstat pod Radhostem, 8,516 .... E 2
Frýdek-Mistek, 43,800 .... E 2
Frýdlant v Cechách, 5,948 .... C 1
Frýdlant nad Ostravici, 6,250 .... E 2
Galanta, 12,300 .... D 2
Gottwaldov, 84,300 .... E 2
Handlova, 16,200 .... E 2
Havirov, 85,000 .... E 2
Havlickuv Brod, 19,200 .... C 2
Hlinsko, 8,890 .... C 2
Hlohovec, 15,200 .... D 2
Hlucin, 15,300 .... E 2

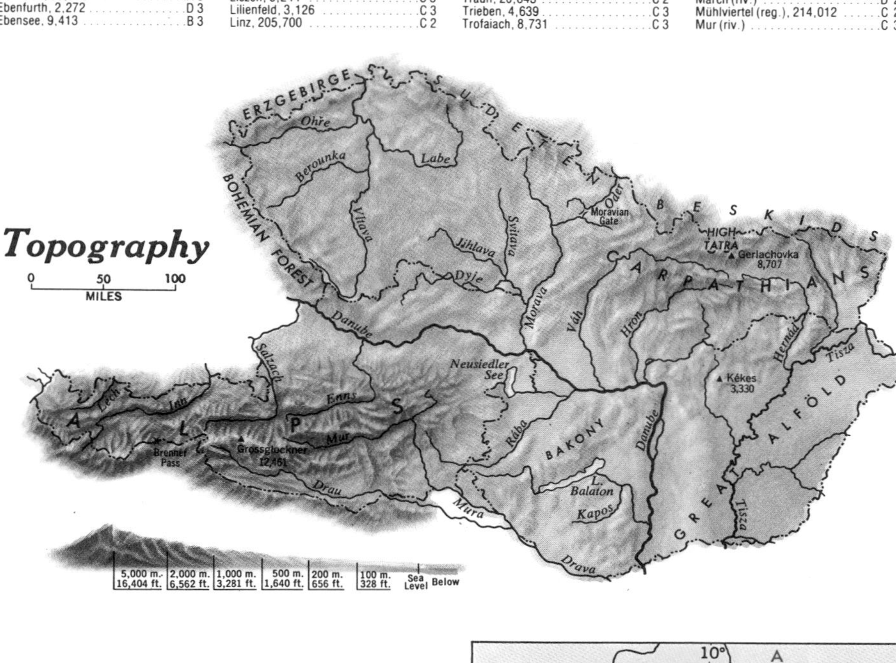

Topography

0 50 100
MILES

5,000 m. 2,000 m. 1,000 m. 500 m. 200 m. 100 m. Sea Below
16,404 ft. 6,562 ft. 3,281 ft. 1,640 ft. 656 ft. 328 ft. Level

Eferding, 3,014 .... B 2
Eggenburg, 3,730 .... C 2
Ehrwald, 2,198 .... A 3
Eisenerz, 11,563 .... C 3
Eisenkappel-Vellach, 3,761 .... C 3
Eisenstadt, 10,059 .... D 3
Eisenstadt, *43,582 .... D 3
Engelhartszell, 1,238 .... B 2
Enns, 9,622 .... C 2
Feldbach, 3,887 .... C 3
Feldkirch, 21,214 .... A 3
Feldkirchen in Kärnten, 11,188 .... B 3
Fels am Wagram, 1,896 .... C 2
Ferlach, 7,621 .... C 3
Fieberbrunn, 3,651 .... B 3
Fohnsdorf, 11,169 .... C 3
Frankenmarkt, 2,960 .... B 3
Frauenkirchen, 2,749 .... D 3
Freistadt, 5,956 .... C 2
Friedberg, 2,504 .... C 3
Friesach, 7,257 .... C 3
Frohnleiten, 5,081 .... C 3
Fulpmes, 2,553 .... A 3
Fürstenfeld, 6,054 .... C 3
Gaming, 4,181 .... C 3
Gänserndorf, 4,211 .... D 2
Gleisdorf, 4,921 .... C 3
Gloggnitz, 7,078 .... D 3
Gmünd, Carinthia, 2,267 .... B 3
Gmünd, Lower Austria, 6,323 .... C 2
Gmunden, 12,270 .... B 3
Golling an der Salzach, 3,089 .... B 3
Götzis, 2,931 .... A 3
Gratwein, 2,747 .... C 3
Graz, 251,900 .... C 3
Graz, *314,200 .... C 3
Grein, 2,767 .... C 2
Gries am Brenner, 1,396 .... A 3
Grieskirchen, 4,519 .... B 2
Gross Siegharts, 3,288 .... C 2
Grünburg, 3,775 .... C 3
Gurk, 1,689 .... C 3
Güssing, 3,675 .... D 3
Haag, 5,060 .... C 2
Hainburg an der Donau, 6,009 .... D 2
Hainfeld, 3,897 .... C 2
Hallein, 14,371 .... B 3
Hallstatt, 1,303 .... B 3
Hartberg, 5,702 .... C 3
Haslach an der Mühl, 2,636 .... C 2
Heidenreichstein, 4,340 .... C 2

Linz, *356,600 .... C 2
Lofer, 1,687 .... B 3
Lustenau, 15,239 .... A 3
Mallnitz, 1,008 .... B 3
Mannersdorf am Leithagebirge, 4,012 .... D 3
Marchegg, 2,678 .... D 2
Mariazell, 2,298 .... C 3
Matrei in Osttirol, 4,003 .... B 3
Mattersburg, 5,417 .... D 3
Mattighofen, 4,344 .... B 2
Mauerkirchen, 2,237 .... B 2
Mautern in Steiermark, 2,536 .... C 3
Mauterndorf, 4,419 .... C 2
Mauthen-Kötschach, 3,740 .... B 3
Mayrhofen, 3,174 .... A 3
Melk, 5,108 .... C 2
Mistelbach an der Zaya, 6,306 .... D 2
Mittersill, 4,361 .... B 3
Mödling, 18,712 .... D 2
Mondsee, 2,141 .... B 3
Murau, 2,710 .... C 3
Mürzzuschlag, 11,564 .... C 3
Nassereith, 1,888 .... A 3
Nauders, 1,302 .... A 3
Neuberg an der Mürz, 2,183 .... C 3
Neumarkt am Wallersee, 3,267 .... B 3
Neumarkt in Steiermark, 1,835 .... C 3
Neunkirchen, 10,922 .... C 3
Neusiedl am See, 3,999 .... D 3
Neustadtl, 5,808 [unclear]
Neustift im Stubaital, 2,789 .... A 3
Ober Grafendorf, 4,109 .... C 2
Oberndorf bei Salzburg, 3,293 .... B 3
Obervellach, 2,420 .... B 3
Oberwart, 5,661 .... C 3
Oberwölz, 870 .... C 3
Paternion, 5,805 .... C 3
Perg, 4,872 .... C 2
Peuerbach, 2,161 .... B 2
Pfunds, 2,043 .... A 3
Pinkafeld, 4,610 .... C 3
Pöchlarn, 3,199 .... C 2
Pöllau, 1,811 .... C 3
Pörtschach am Wörthersee, 2,511 .... C 3
Poysdorf, 5,774 .... D 2
Pregarten, 3,249 .... C 2
Raabs an der Thaya, 4,194 .... C 2
Radenthein, 6,847 .... B 3
Radkersburg, 2,000 .... C 3
Radstadt, 3,585 .... B 3
Rankweil, 8,440 .... A 3

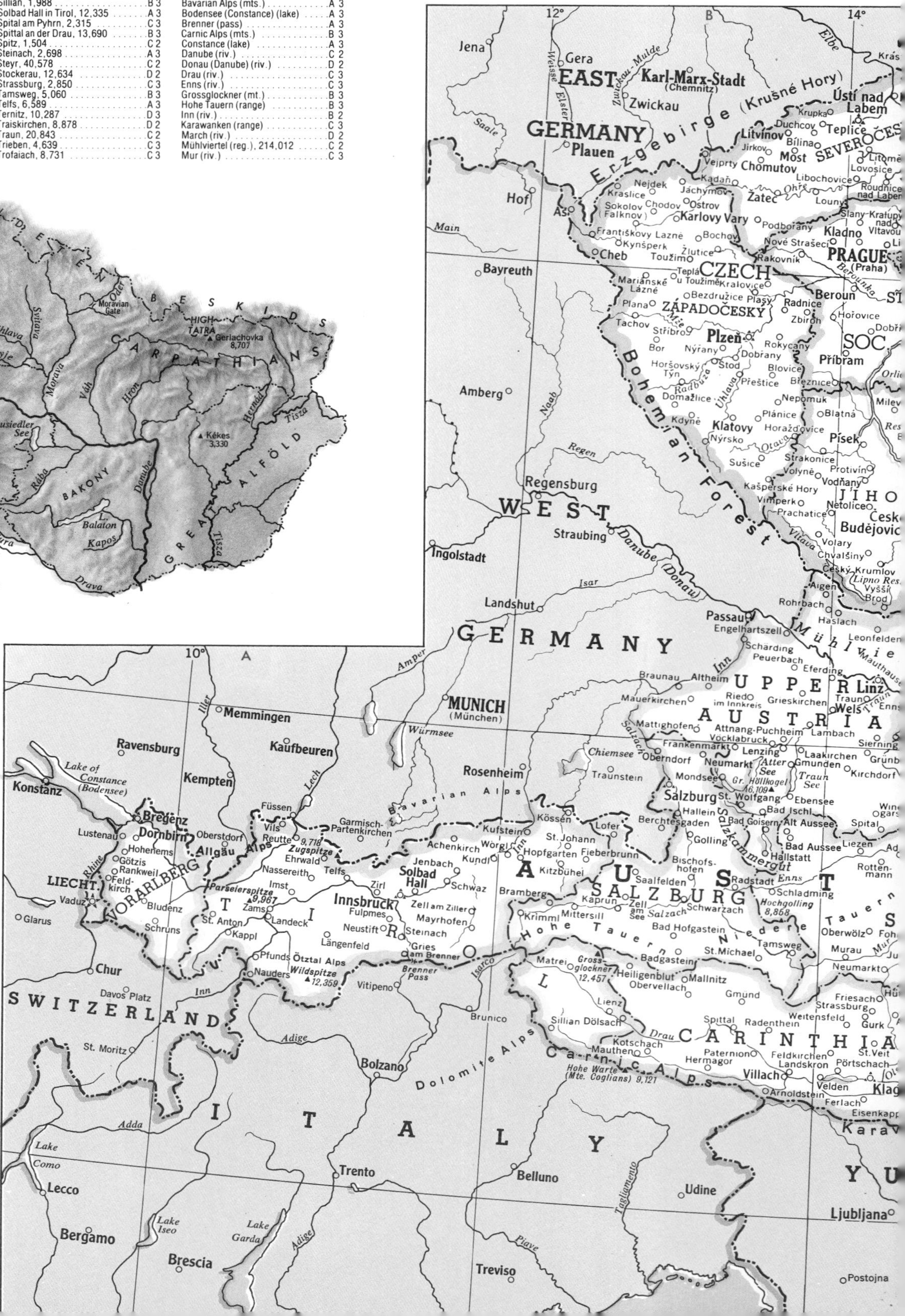

AUSTRIA
AREA 32,375 sq. mi.
POPULATION 7,540,000
CAPITAL Vienna
LARGEST CITY Vienna
HIGHEST POINT Grossglockner 12,457 ft.
MONETARY UNIT schilling
MAJOR LANGUAGE German
MAJOR RELIGION Roman Catholicism

CZECHOSLOVAKIA
AREA 49,373 sq. mi.
POPULATION 14,900,000
CAPITAL Prague
LARGEST CITY Prague
HIGHEST POINT Gerlachovka 8,707 ft.
MONETARY UNIT koruna
MAJOR LANGUAGES Czech, Slovak
MAJOR RELIGIONS Roman Catholicism, Protestantism

HUNGARY
AREA 35,919 sq. mi.
POPULATION 10,590,000
CAPITAL Budapest
LARGEST CITY Budapest
HIGHEST POINT Kékes 3,330 ft.
MONETARY UNIT forint
MAJOR LANGUAGE Hungarian
MAJOR RELIGIONS Roman Catholicism, Protestantism

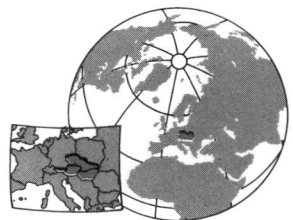

AUSTRIA

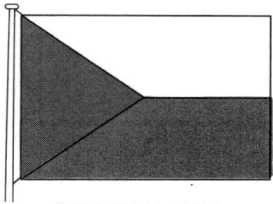

CZECHOSLOVAKIA

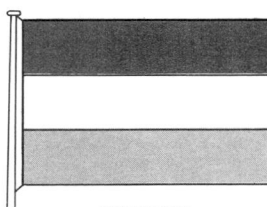

HUNGARY

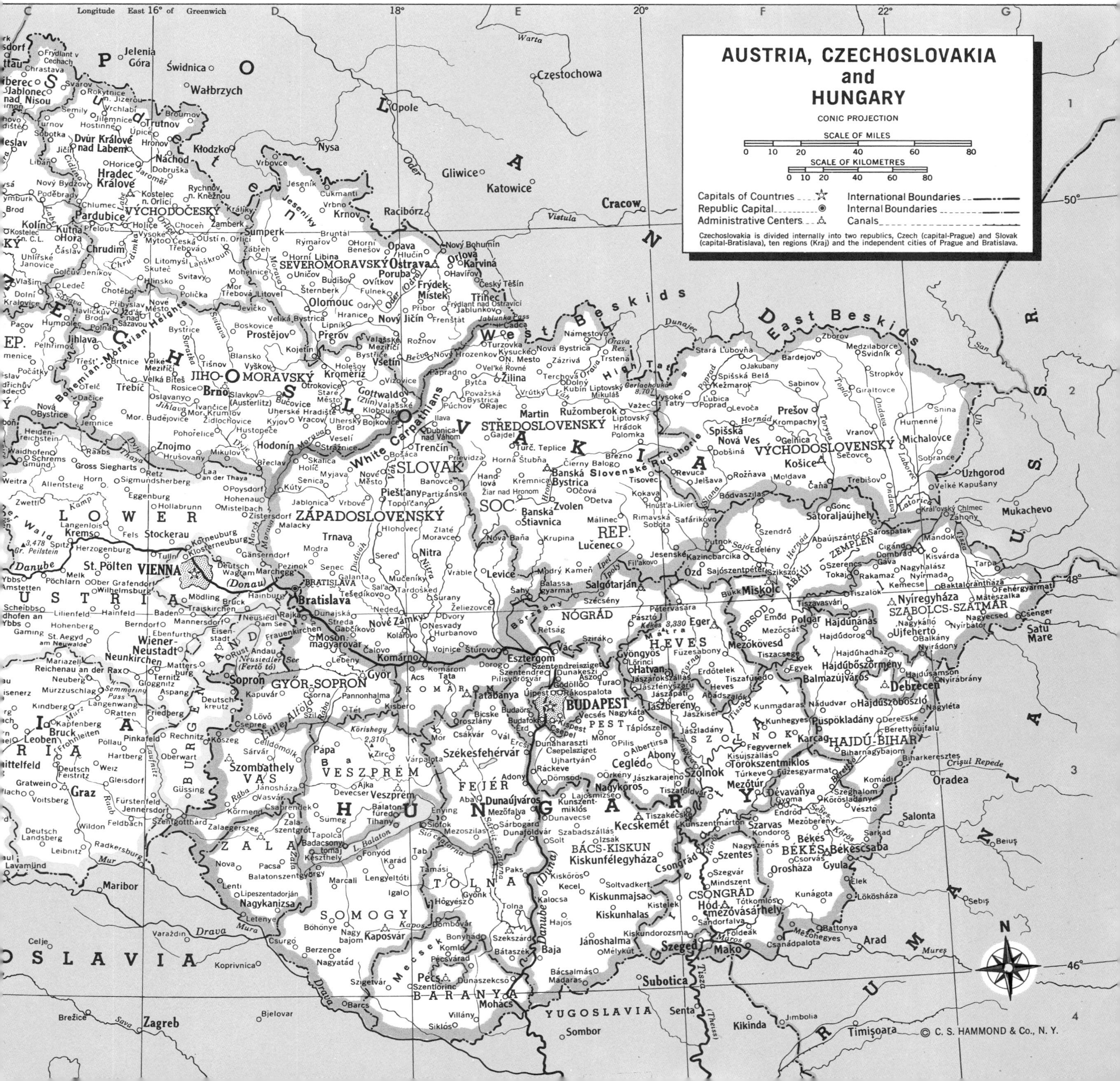

AUSTRIA, CZECHOSLOVAKIA and HUNGARY
CONIC PROJECTION

SCALE OF MILES
0 10 20   40   60   80

SCALE OF KILOMETRES
0 10 20 40 60 80

Capitals of Countries ... ☆   International Boundaries _____
Republic Capital .... ◉   Internal Boundaries _ _ _ _ _
Administrative Centers ... △   Canals _____

Czechoslovakia is divided internally into two republics, Czech (capital-Prague) and Slovak (capital-Bratislava), ten regions (Kraj) and the independent cities of Prague and Bratislava.

© C. S. HAMMOND & Co., N. Y.

Hnušt'a-Likier E 2
Hodonín, 22,600 D 2
Holešov, 9,091 D 2
Holíč, 7,602 D 2
Holice, 6,151 C 1
Horažd'ovice B 2
Hořice v Podkrkonoší, 7,715 C 1
Horná Štubňa E 2
Horní Benešov D 2
Horní Libina D 2
Hořovice, 5,665 C 2
Horšovský Týn B 2
Hostinné C 1
Hradec Králové, 85,600 C 1
Hranice, 13,300 D 2
Hronov, 9,767 D 1
Hrušovany D 2
Humenné, 22,200 G 2
Humpolec, 7,810 C 2
Hurbanovo E 3
Hustopeče D 2
Ilava E 2
Ivančice, 7,314 D 2
Jablonec nad Nisou, 36,300 C 1
Jablonica D 2
Jablunkov, 9,405 E 2
Jáchymov B 1
Jakubany F 2
Jaroměř, 11,600 C 1
Jelšava F 2
Jemnice C 2
Jeseník, 10,900 D 1
Jesenské F 2
Jevíčko D 2
Jičín, 13,200 C 1
Jihlava, 44,500 C 2
Jilemnice C 1
Jindřichův Hradec, 15,700 C 2
Jirkov, 11,400 B 1
Kadaň, 18,100 B 1
Kamenice C 2
Kaplice C 2
Karlovy Vary, 43,300 B 1
Karviná, 79,100 E 2
Kdyně B 2
Kežmarok, 11,000 F 2
Kladno, 61,200 B 1
Klatovy, 18,500 B 2
Kojetín, 5,852 D 2
Kokava nad Rimavicou, 5,391 E 2
Kolárovo, 10,500 D 3
Kolín, 29,100 C 1
Komárno, 28,200 D 3
Košice, 169,100 F 2
Kostelec nad Orlicí, 5,575 D 1
Kráľovský Chlmec, 5,329 G 2
Kralupy nad Vltavou, 16,900 C 1
Kraslice, 6,733 B 1
Kremnica, 5,941 E 2
Krnov, 25,000 D 1
Kroměříž, 23,200 D 2
Krompachy, 6,332 F 2
Krupina, 6,627 E 2
Krupka, 8,301 B 1
Kutná Hora, 19,200 C 2
Kyjov, 10,700 D 2
Kynšperk, 5,524 B 1
Kysucké Nové Mesto, 11,700 E 2
Lanškroun, 8,683 D 2
Levice, 19,000 E 2
Levoča, 10,100 F 2
Libáň C 1
Liberec, 75,600 C 1
Libochovice B 1
Lidice C 1
Lipník nad Bečvou, 7,358 D 2
Liptovský Hrádok E 2
Liptovský Mikuláš, 19,400 E 2
Lišov C 2
Litoměřice, 19,700 C 1
Litomyšl, 8,112 D 2
Litovel, 5,805 D 2
Litvínov, 23,300 B 1
Lomnice C 2
Louny, 15,200 B 1
Lovosice, 9,323 C 1
L'ubica F 2
Lučenec, 23,300 E 2
Lysá nad Labem, 9,920 C 1
Malacky, 13,200 D 2
Mariánské Lázně, 14,600 B 2
Martin, 47,800 E 2
Medzilaborce F 2
Mělník, 17,800 C 1
Michalovce, 23,600 G 2
Mikulov, 6,267 D 2
Milevsko, 7,091 C 2
Mimoň, 6,773 C 1
Mladá Boleslav, 36,900 C 1
Mladá Vožice C 2
Mnichovo Hradiště, 5,239 C 1
Modra, 7,219 D 2
Modrý Kameň, 6,200 E 2
Mohelnice, 6,050 D 2
Moldava nad Bodvou, 5,397 F 2
Moravská Třebová, 9,052 D 2
Moravské Budějovice, 5,576 D 2
Most, 59,400 B 1
Mučeníky D 2
Myjava, 6,657 D 2
Náchod, 19,300 D 1
Námestovo E 2
Neded D 2
Nejdek, 8,187 B 1
Nepomuk B 2
Nesvady, 5,453 E 3
Netolice C 2
Nitra, 50,000 E 2
Nová Baňa, 6,218 E 2
Nová Bystrica E 2
Nová Bystřice C 2
Nové Hrady C 2
Nové Město na Moravě, 6,581 D 2
Nové Mesto nad Váhom, 15,900 D 2
Nové Strašecí B 1
Nové Zámky, 27,300 D 3
Nový Bohumín, 16,700 E 2
Nový Bor, 7,621 C 1
Nový Bydžov, 6,824 C 1
Nový Hrozenkov E 2
Nový Jičín, 21,400 E 2
Nymburk, 13,600 C 1
Nýřany, 6,204 B 2
Nýrsko B 2
Odry D 2
Olomouc, 82,800 D 2
Opava, 53,800 E 2
Orlová, 25,500 E 2
Ostrava, 293,500 E 2
Ostrov, 18,200 B 1
Pardubice, 78,500 C 1
Partizánske, 15,100 E 2
Pelhřimov, 11,900 C 2
Pezinok, 13,100 D 2
Piešt'any, 25,400 D 2
Písek, 25,100 C 2
Plzeň, 155,000 B 2
Počátky C 2
Podbořany B 1
Poděbrady, 13,400 C 1
Pohořelice D 2
Polička, 6,529 D 2
Polná C 2
Polomka E 2
Poprad, 25,800 F 2
Považská Bystrica, 19,300 E 2
Prachatice, 7,900 B 2
Prague (Praha) (cap.), 1,161,200 C 1
Přelouč, 6,251 C 1
Přerov, 43,500 D 2
Prešov, 61,000 F 2
Přeštice B 2
Příbor, 7,726 E 2
Příbram, 31,300 B 2
Prievidza, 30,900 E 2
Prostějov, 44,200 D 2
Protivín C 2
Púchov, 9,306 E 2
Radnice B 2
Rajec E 2
Rakovník, 14,200 B 1
Revúca, 5,901 F 2
Říčany u Prahy, 8,407 C 2
Rimavská Sobota, 5,800 E 2
Rokycany, 12,800 B 2
Rokytnice nad Jizerou C 1
Rosice D 2
Roudnice nad Labem, 11,800 C 1
Rožňava, 12,400 F 2
Rožnov pod Radhoštěm, 11,600 E 2
Rumburk C 1
Ružomberok, 22,600 E 2
Rychnov nad Kněžnou, 7,500 D 1
Rýmařov, 7,522 D 2
Sabinov, 5,473 F 2
Šafárikovo F 2
Šahy, 5,049 E 2
Šal'a, 15,200 D 2
Sečovce, 5,744 F 2
Sedlčany C 2
Semily, 8,200 C 1
Senec, 8,544 D 2
Senica, 12,300 D 2
Sered', 12,500 D 2
Skalica, 11,100 D 2
Skuteč D 2
Slaný, 13,200 C 1
Slavkov D 2
Snina, 10,900 G 2
Soběslav, 6,140 C 2
Sobotka C 1
Sobrance G 2
Sokolov, 23,900 B 1
Spišská Belá F 2
Spišská Nová Ves, 26,100 F 2
Stará L'ubovňa, 5,800 F 2
Staré Město, 6,293 D 2
Šternberk, 13,700 D 2
Stod B 2
Strakonice, 19,000 B 2
Strážnice, 5,482 D 2
Stříbro B 2
Stropkov, 5,645 F 2
Štúrovo, 8,287 E 3
Šumperk, 25,900 D 1
Šurany, 6,693 E 2
Sušice, 10,300 B 2
Svárov C 1
Svidník, 4,600 F 2
Svitavy, 15,000 D 2
Tábor, 28,100 C 2
Tachov, 11,400 B 2
Telč, 5,285 C 2
Teplice, 52,300 B 1
Tišnov, 8,263 D 2
Topol'čany, 17,500 D 2
Třebíč, 23,900 C 2
Trebišov, 13,700 F 2
Třeboň, 6,068 C 2
Trenčín, 38,800 E 2
Třešť, 5,053 C 2
Třinec, 32,000 E 2
Trnava, 48,600 D 2
Trutnov, 24,500 D 1
Turnov, 13,600 C 1
Turzovka, 6,107 E 2
Uherské Hradiště, 32,100 D 2
Uherský Brod, 12,800 D 2
Uničov, 10,800 D 2
Úpice, 6,323 C 1
Ústí nad Labem, 74,900 C 1
Ústí nad Orlicí, 13,700 D 2
Valašské Meziříčí, 19,400 D 2
Varnsdorf, 14,700 C 1
Važec E 2
Vejprty B 1
Velká Bíteš D 2
Velká Bystřice D 2
Vel'ké Kapušany G 2
Velké Meziříčí, 7,590 D 2
Vel'ké Rovné E 2
Veselí nad Lužnicí C 2
Veselí nad Moravou, 11,500 D 2
Vimperk, 5,749 B 2
Vítkov, 5,138 D 2
Vizovice D 2
Vlašim, 8,873 C 2
Vodňany, 5,620 C 2
Vojnice E 3
Volary B 2
Volyně B 2
Votice C 2
Vráble E 2
Vracov D 2
Vranov nad Teplou, 14,700 F 2
Vrbno pod Pradědem, 5,594 D 1
Vrbovce D 1
Vrbové D 2
Vrchlabí, 11,700 C 1
Vrútky, 5,756 E 2
Vsetín, 24,100 D 2
Vyškov, 15,100 D 2
Vysoké Mýto, 8,830 D 2
Vysoké Tatry F 2
Vyšší Brod C 2
Zábřeh, 11,300 D 2
Žamberk, 5,040 D 1
Žatec, 17,400 B 1
Zázrivá E 2
Zbiroh B 2
Zborov F 2
Žd'ár nad Sázavou, 17,800 C 2
Želiezovce, 5,478 E 2
Žiar nad Hronom, 14,800 E 2
Židlochovice D 2
Žilina, 56,000 E 2
Zlaté Moravce, 10,300 E 2
Zlín (Gottwaldov), 84,300 D 2
Žlutice B 1
Znojmo, 28,500 D 2
Zvolen, 29,000 E 2

OTHER FEATURES

Berounka (riv.) C 2
Beskids, East (mts.) F 1
Beskids, West (mts.) E 2
Bohemian (for.) B 2
Bohemian-Moravian Heights (hills) C 2
Danube (riv.) C 2
Dunajec (riv.) F 2
Dyje (riv.) D 2
Erzgebirge (mts.) B 1
Gerlachovka (mt.) E 2
Hornád (riv.) F 2
Hron (riv.) E 2
Ipel' (riv.) E 2
Jablunka (pass) E 2
Jeseníky (mts.) D 1
Jihlava (riv.) D 2
Krušné Hory (Erzgebirge) (mts.) B 1
Labe (riv.) C 1
Lipno (res.) C 2
Lužnice (riv.) C 2
Moldau (Vltava) (riv.) C 2
Morava (riv.) D 2
Nitra (riv.) E 2
Oder (Odra) (riv.) D 2
Ohře (riv.) B 1
Ondava (riv.) F 2
Orava (riv.) E 2
Orlická (res.) C 2
Sázava (riv.) C 2
Slovenské Rudohorie (mts.) E 2
Sudeten (mts.) C 1
Svitava (riv.) D 2
Svratka (riv.) D 2
Tatra, High (mts.) E 2
Torysa (riv.) F 2
Úhlava (riv.) B 2
Váh (riv.) D 2
Vltava (riv.) C 2
White Carpathians (mts.) E 2

HUNGARY

COUNTIES

Bács-Kiskun, 574,009 E 3
Baranya, 424,857 E 4
Békés, 446,405 F 3
Borsod-Abaúj-Zemplén, 779,424 F 2
Budapest (city), 2,051,354 E 3
Csongrád, 441,399 F 3
Fejér, 390,655 E 3
Gy"or-Sopron, 403,860 D 3
Hajdú-Bihar, 531,508 F 3
Heves, 347,270 F 3
Komárom, 301,760 E 3
Nógrád, 240,129 E 3
Pest, 875,462 E 3
Somogy, 363,075 D 3
Szabolcs-Szatmár, 590,211 G 3
Szolnok, 449,001 F 3
Tolna, 258,789 E 3
Vas, 280,125 D 3
Veszprém, 412,298 D 3
Zala, 266,779 D 3

CITIES and TOWNS

Aba, 4,271 E 3
Abádszalók, 6,386 F 3
Abaújszántó, 4,209 F 2
Abony, 15,624 E 3
Ács, 8,423 E 3
Ajka, 20,263 D 3
Albertirsa, 11,252 E 3
Aszód, 6,218 E 3
Bácsalmás, 9,025 E 3
Badacsonytomaj, 2,933 D 3
Baja, 34,650 E 3
Baktalórántháza, 3,736 G 2
Balassagyarmat, 15,147 E 2
Balatonfüred, 9,736 D 3
Balatonszentgyörgy, 1,416 D 3
Balkány, 7,667 G 3
Balmazújváros, 17,371 F 3
Barcs, 7,703 D 4
Bátaszék, 7,274 E 3
Battonya, 9,324 F 3
Békés, 21,032 F 3
Békéscsaba, 57,060 F 3
Berettyóújfalu, 13,999 F 3
Berzence, 3,406 D 3
Bicske, 10,720 E 3
Biharkeresztes, 4,788 F 3
Biharnagybajom, 4,093 F 3
Bódvaszilas, 1,280 F 2
Böhönye, 3,215 D 3
Bonyhád, 12,377 E 3
Budafok, 40,623 E 3
Budaörs, 13,958 E 3
Budapest (cap.), 2,051,354 E 3
Cegléd, 38,040 E 3
Celldömölk, 10,493 D 3
Cigánd, 4,767 F 2
Csabrendek, 3,045 D 3
Csákvár, 5,238 E 3
Csanádpalota, 4,642 F 3
Csenger, 4,792 G 3
Csepel, 71,693 E 3
Csepreg, 4,079 D 3
Csongrád, 20,264 E 3
Csorna, 9,508 D 3
Csorvás, 6,826 F 3
Csurgó, 5,463 D 3
Debrecen, 179,755 F 3
Derecske, 9,579 F 3
Dévaványa, 11,208 F 3
Devecser, 5,482 D 3
Dombóvár, 16,670 E 3
Dombrád, 6,328 F 2
Dömsöd, 6,545 E 3
Dorog, 10,754 E 3
Dunaföldvár, 10,318 E 3
Dunaharaszti, 15,788 E 3
Dunakeszi, 19,280 E 3
Dunaszekcs"o, 2,999 E 3
Dunaújváros, 44,721 E 3
Dunavecse, 4,521 E 3
Edelény, 9,559 F 2
Eger, 45,236 F 3
Egyek, 7,956 F 3
Elek, 6,032 F 3
Endr"od, 8,136 F 3
Enying, 7,518 E 3
Érd, 31,188 E 3
Erd"otelek, 4,250 F 3
Esztergom, 26,965 E 3
Fegyvernek, 7,331 F 3
Fehérgyarmat, 6,688 G 3
Földeák, 3,855 F 3
Fonyód, 3,957 D 3
Füzesabony, 6,965 F 3
Füzesgyarmat, 7,097 F 3
Gödöll"o, 21,418 E 3
Gönc, 2,875 F 2
Gyoma, 10,392 F 3
Gyöngyös, 33,117 E 3
Gy"onk, 2,507 E 3
Gy"or, 114,709 D 3
Gyula, 26,438 F 3
Hajdúböszörmény, 30,464 F 3
Hajdúdorog, 10,118 F 3
Hajdúhadház, 13,626 F 3
Hajdúnánás, 17,906 F 3
Hajdúsámson, 7,492 F 3
Hajdúszoboszló, 22,003 F 3
Hajós, 5,113 E 3
Hatvan, 21,984 E 3
Heves, 10,943 F 3
Hódmez"ovásárhely, 52,777 F 3
H"ogyész, 3,534 E 3
Igal, 1,813 D 3
Izsák, 7,686 E 3
Jánoshalma, 12,534 E 3
Jánosháza, 3,274 D 3
Jászapáti, 10,424 E 3
Jászárokszállás, 10,139 E 3
Jászberény, 29,793 E 3
Jászfényszaru, 6,869 E 3
Jászkarajen"o, 4,101 E 3
Jászkisér, 6,816 F 3
Jászladány, 7,823 F 3
Kalocsa, 16,084 E 3
Kaposvár, 58,524 D 3
Kapuvár, 10,570 D 3
Karád, 2,754 D 3
Karcag, 24,638 F 3
Kazincbarcika, 25,948 F 2
Kecel, 10,493 E 3
Kecskemét, 77,963 E 3
Kemecse, 4,583 F 2
Keszthely, 17,082 D 3
Kisbér, 4,562 D 3
Kisk"orös, 14,150 E 3
Kiskunfélegyháza, 34,073 E 3
Kiskunhalas, 26,668 E 3
Kiskunmajsa, 14,439 E 3
Kispest, 65,106 E 3
Kistelek, 8,544 E 3
Kisújszállás, 13,470 F 3
Kisvárda, 13,725 G 2
Komádi, 8,765 F 3
Komárom, 11,300 E 3
Komló, 28,191 E 3
Kondoros, 7,319 F 3
Körmend, 9,942 D 3
Körösladány, 6,565 F 3
K"oszeg, 10,238 D 3
Kunágota, 4,622 F 3
Kunhegyes, 10,116 F 3
Kunmadaras, 7,343 F 3
Kunszentmárton, 11,103 F 3
Kunszentmiklós, 7,952 E 3
Lajosmizse, 12,872 E 3
Lébény, 6,190 D 3
Lengyeltóti, 3,389 D 3
Lenti, 4,476 D 3
Letenye, 4,395 D 3
Lispeszentadorján, 722 D 3
Lökösháza, 2,514 F 3
L"orinci, 10,679 E 3
Löv"o, 1,671 D 3
Madaras, 4,519 E 3
Makó, 30,073 F 3
Mándok, 5,093 G 2
Marcali, 8,282 D 3
Mátészalka, 12,413 G 3
Mélykút, 7,640 E 3
Mez"oberény, 12,702 F 3
Mez"ocsát, 6,729 F 3
Mez"ofalva, 5,008 E 3
Mez"ohegyes, 8,631 F 3
Mez"okövesd, 17,899 F 3
Mez"oszilas, 2,792 E 3
Mez"otúr, 21,851 F 3
Mindszent, 8,730 F 3
Miskolc, 194,648 F 2
Mohacs, 19,717 E 4
Monor, 16,838 E 3
Mór, 12,066 E 3
Mosonmagyaróvár, 24,440 D 3
Nádudvar, 9,447 F 3
Nagyatád, 10,358 D 3
Nagybajom, 4,402 D 3
Nagyecsed, 8,225 G 3
Nagyhalász, 6,437 F 2
Nagykálló, 11,282 F 3
Nagykanizsa, 39,559 D 3
Nagykáta, 11,922 E 3
Nagyk"orös, 25,927 E 3
Nagyszénás, 7,124 F 3
Nova, 1,329 D 3
Nyírábrány, 4,509 G 3
Nyíradony, 7,146 G 3
Nyírbátor, 11,022 G 3
Nyíregyháza, 73,013 F 3
Nyírmada, 4,744 F 2
Örkény, 5,013 E 3
Orosháza, 33,471 F 3
Oroszlány, 18,249 E 3
Ózd, 38,620 F 2
Pacsa, 1,984 D 3
Paks, 12,385 E 3
Pannonhalma, 3,731 D 3
Pápa, 28,640 D 3
Pásztó, 7,962 E 3
Pécs, 160,488 E 3
Pécsvárad, 3,672 E 3
Pétervására, 2,753 F 3
Pilis, 9,055 E 3
Pilisvörösvár, 10,217 E 3
Polgár, 9,429 F 3
Püspökladány, 15,730 F 3
Putnok, 7,103 F 2
Ráckeve, 7,534 E 3
Rajka, 2,448 D 3
Rakamaz, 5,407 F 2
Rákospalota, 60,983 E 3
Rétság, 1,591 E 3
Sajószentpéter, 13,992 F 2
Salgótarján, 40,095 E 2
Sándorfalva, 5,949 F 3
Sárbogárd, 11,178 E 3
Sarkad, 11,937 F 3
Sárospatak, 14,061 F 2
Sárvár, 12,754 D 3
Sátoraljaújhely, 16,982 F 2
Siklós, 7,083 E 4
Siófok, 17,315 E 3
Solt, 6,911 E 3
Soltvadkert, 7,934 E 3
Sopron, 44,956 D 3
Sümeg, 6,229 D 3
Szabadszállás, 8,223 E 3
Szarvas, 19,521 F 3
Szécsény, 5,690 E 2
Szeged, 166,040 E 3
Szeghalom, 9,736 F 3
Szegvár, 6,395 F 3
Székesfehérvár, 73,949 E 3
Szekszárd, 24,364 E 3
Szendr"o, 4,098 F 2
Szentendre, 12,859 E 3
Szentes, 33,436 F 3
Szentgotthárd, 5,837 D 3
Szentl"orinc, 3,926 E 3
Szerencs, 8,612 F 2
Szigetvár, 10,412 D 3
Szikszó, 6,419 F 2
Szil, 2,073 D 3
Szirák, 1,435 E 3
Szolnok, 61,559 F 3
Szombathely, 64,485 D 3
Tab, 3,922 E 3
Tamási, 7,602 E 3
Tápiószele, 5,575 E 3
Tapolca, 11,223 D 3
Tarpa, 3,436 G 2
Tata, 20,565 E 3
Tatabánya, 65,274 E 3
Tét, 4,441 D 3
Tihany, 1,390 D 3
Tiszacsege, 6,263 F 3
Tiszaföldvár, 12,560 F 3
Tiszafüred, 12,259 F 3
Tiszakécske, 12,378 E 3
Tiszalök, 6,230 F 2
Tiszavasvári, 13,292 F 3
Tokaj, 4,845 F 2
Tolna, 8,997 E 3
Törökszentmiklós, 24,301 F 3
Tótkomlós, 8,803 F 3
Tura, 8,235 E 3
Türkeve, 11,640 F 3
Újfehértó, 14,412 F 3
Újpest, 80,384 E 3
Vác, 28,847 E 3
Vál, 2,488 E 3
Várpalota, 25,312 E 3
Vasvár, 4,275 D 3
Vecsés, 19,193 E 3
Veszprém, 36,938 D 3
Vészt"o, 9,815 F 3
Villány, 2,764 E 4
Záhony, 3,049 G 2
Zalaegerszeg, 39,252 D 3
Zalaszentgrót, 5,346 D 3
Zirc, 5,980 D 3

OTHER FEATURES

Bakony (mts.) D 3
Balaton (lake) D 3
Berettyó (riv.) F 3
Bükk (mts.) F 2
Csepelsziget (isl.) E 3
Danube (riv.) E 3
Dráva (riv.) D 3
Duna (Danube) (riv.) E 3
Fert"o tó (Neusiedler See) (lake) D 3
Great Alfold (plain) F 3
Hernád (riv.) F 2
Kapos (riv.) D 3
Kékes (mt.) E 3
Körös (riv.) F 3
Maros (riv.) F 3
Mátra (mts.) E 3
Mecsek (mts.) D 3
Mura (riv.) D 3
Rába (riv.) D 3
Sajó (riv.) F 2
Sárviz csatorna (canal) E 3
Sió csatorna (canal) E 3
Szentendreisziget (isl.) E 3
Tisza (riv.) F 3
Zala (riv.) D 3

*City and suburbs.
☆Population of Austrian cities are communes.

Agriculture, Industry and Resources

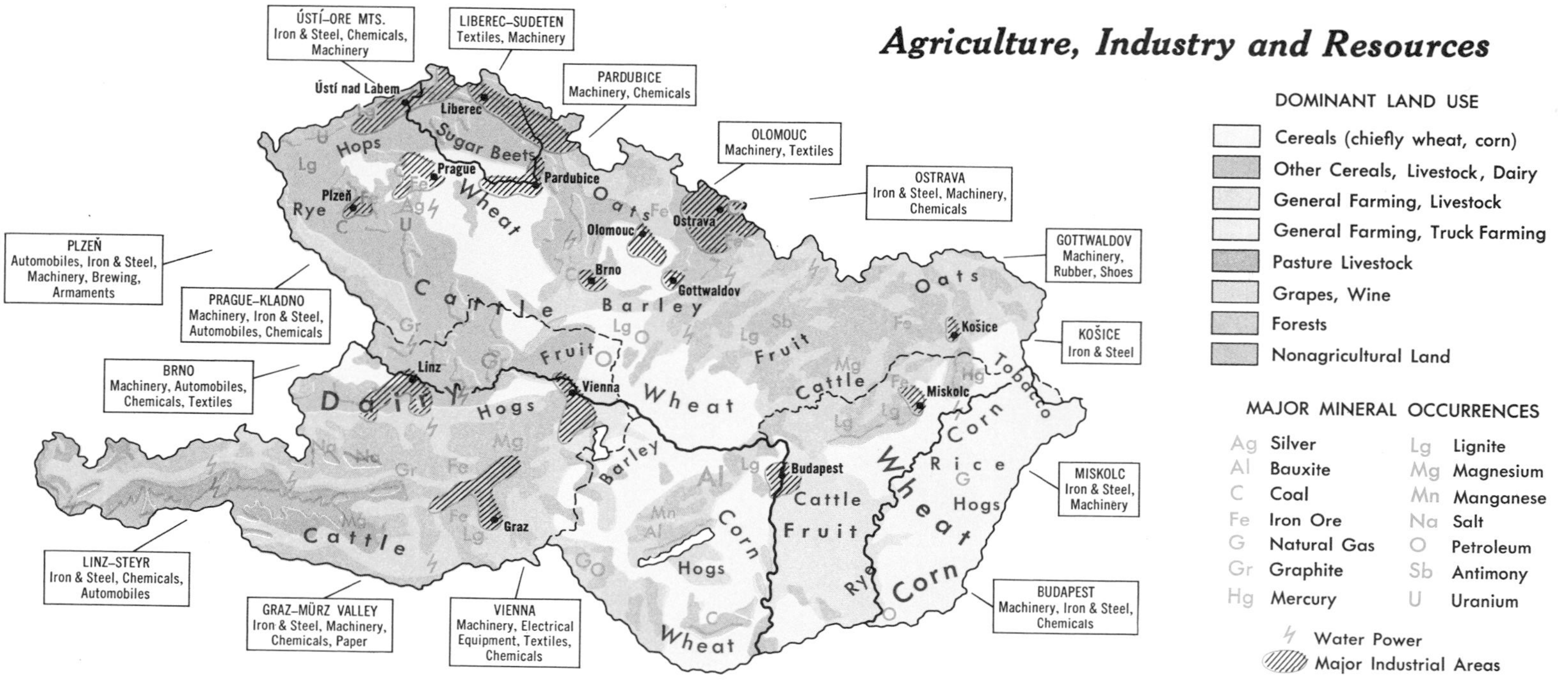
ÚSTÍ–ORE MTS.
Iron & Steel, Chemicals, Machinery
LIBEREC–SUDETEN
Textiles, Machinery
PARDUBICE
Machinery, Chemicals
OLOMOUC
Machinery, Textiles
OSTRAVA
Iron & Steel, Machinery, Chemicals
GOTTWALDOV
Machinery, Rubber, Shoes
KOŠICE
Iron & Steel
MISKOLC
Iron & Steel, Machinery
BUDAPEST
Machinery, Iron & Steel, Chemicals
VIENNA
Machinery, Electrical Equipment, Textiles, Chemicals
GRAZ–MÜRZ VALLEY
Iron & Steel, Machinery, Chemicals, Paper
LINZ–STEYR
Iron & Steel, Chemicals, Automobiles
BRNO
Machinery, Automobiles, Chemicals, Textiles
PRAGUE–KLADNO
Machinery, Iron & Steel, Automobiles, Chemicals
PLZEŇ
Automobiles, Iron & Steel, Machinery, Brewing, Armaments
Ústí nad Labem
Liberec
Prague
Pardubice
Plzeň
Olomouc
Ostrava
Brno
Gottwaldov
Košice
Linz
Vienna
Miskolc
Budapest
Graz
Hops
Sugar Beets
Wheat
Rye
Oats
Cattle
Barley
Fruit
Dairy
Hogs
Corn
Rice
Tobacco
DOMINANT LAND USE
Cereals (chiefly wheat, corn)
Other Cereals, Livestock, Dairy
General Farming, Livestock
General Farming, Truck Farming
Pasture Livestock
Grapes, Wine
Forests
Nonagricultural Land
MAJOR MINERAL OCCURRENCES
Ag Silver
Al Bauxite
C Coal
Fe Iron Ore
G Natural Gas
Gr Graphite
Hg Mercury
Lg Lignite
Mg Magnesium
Mn Manganese
Na Salt
O Petroleum
Sb Antimony
U Uranium
Water Power
Major Industrial Areas

YUGOSLAVIA

AREA 98,766 sq. mi.
POPULATION 21,520,000
CAPITAL Belgrade
LARGEST CITY Belgrade
HIGHEST POINT Triglav 9,393 ft.
MONETARY UNIT Yugoslav dinar
MAJOR LANGUAGES Serbo-Croatian, Slovenian, Macedonian, Montenegrin, Albanian
MAJOR RELIGIONS Eastern Orthodoxy, Roman Catholicism, Islam

ALBANIA

AREA 11,100 sq. mi.
POPULATION 2,482,000
CAPITAL Tiranë
LARGEST CITY Tiranë
HIGHEST POINT Korab 9,026 ft.
MONETARY UNIT lek
MAJOR LANGUAGE Albanian
MAJOR RELIGIONS Islam, Eastern Orthodoxy, Roman Catholicism

RUMANIA

AREA 91,699 sq. mi.
POPULATION 21,500,000
CAPITAL Bucharest
LARGEST CITY Bucharest
HIGHEST POINT Moldoveanul 8,343 ft.
MONETARY UNIT leu
MAJOR LANGUAGES Rumanian, Hungarian
MAJOR RELIGION Eastern Orthodoxy

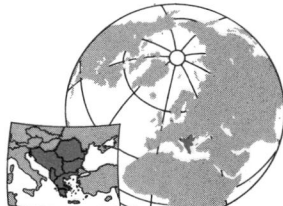

BULGARIA

AREA 42,823 sq. mi.
POPULATION 8,800,000
CAPITAL Sofia
LARGEST CITY Sofia
HIGHEST POINT Musala 9,597 ft.
MONETARY UNIT lev
MAJOR LANGUAGE Bulgarian
MAJOR RELIGION Eastern Orthodoxy

GREECE

AREA 50,944 sq. mi.
POPULATION 9,046,000
CAPITAL Athens
LARGEST CITY Athens
HIGHEST POINT Olympus 9,570 ft.
MONETARY UNIT drachma
MAJOR LANGUAGE Greek
MAJOR RELIGION Eastern (Greek) Orthodoxy

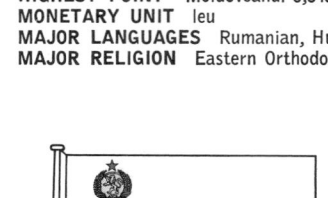
BULGARIA

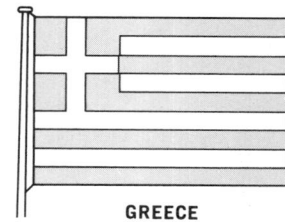
GREECE

YUGOSLAVIA

ALBANIA

RUMANIA

DOMINANT LAND USE

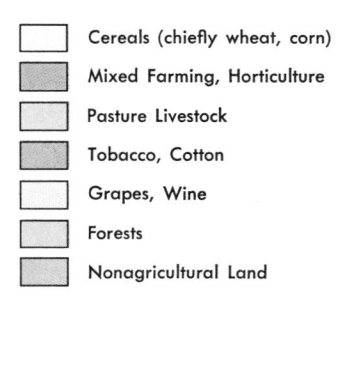

- Cereals (chiefly wheat, corn)
- Mixed Farming, Horticulture
- Pasture Livestock
- Tobacco, Cotton
- Grapes, Wine
- Forests
- Nonagricultural Land

Agriculture, Industry and Resources

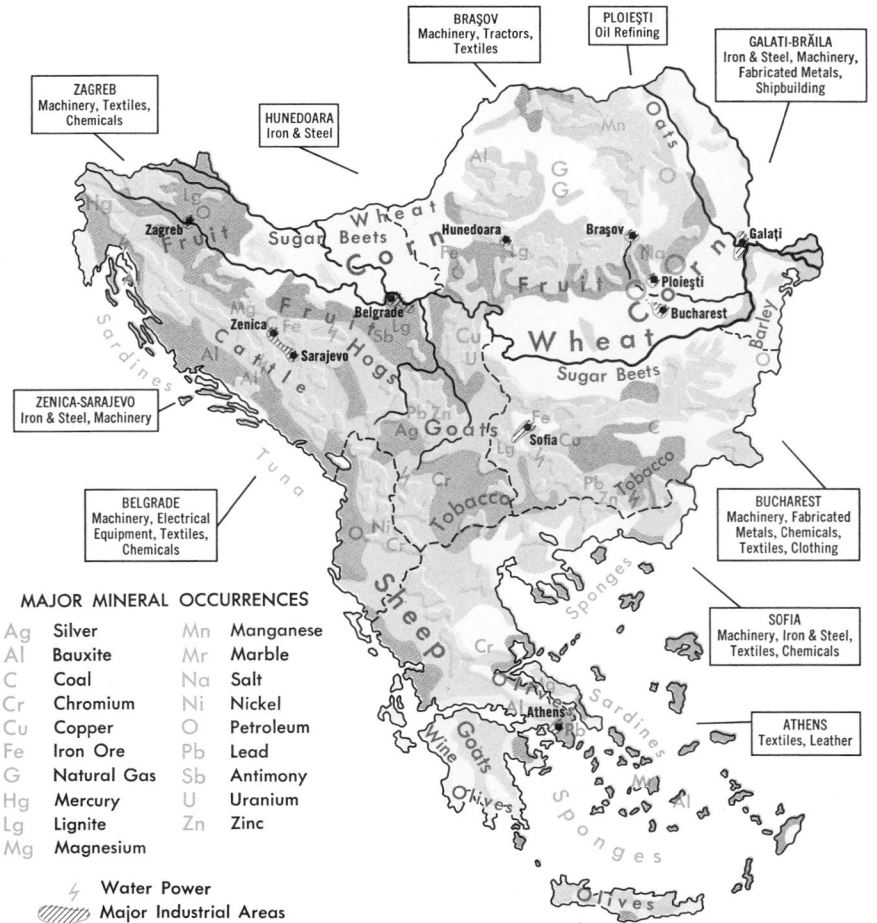

ZAGREB Machinery, Textiles, Chemicals

HUNEDOARA Iron & Steel

BRAŞOV Machinery, Tractors, Textiles

PLOIEŞTI Oil Refining

GALATI-BRĂILA Iron & Steel, Machinery, Fabricated Metals, Shipbuilding

ZENICA-SARAJEVO Iron & Steel, Machinery

BELGRADE Machinery, Electrical Equipment, Textiles, Chemicals

BUCHAREST Machinery, Fabricated Metals, Chemicals, Textiles, Clothing

SOFIA Machinery, Iron & Steel, Textiles, Chemicals

ATHENS Textiles, Leather

MAJOR MINERAL OCCURRENCES

Ag	Silver	Mn	Manganese
Al	Bauxite	Mr	Marble
C	Coal	Na	Salt
Cr	Chromium	Ni	Nickel
Cu	Copper	O	Petroleum
Fe	Iron Ore	Pb	Lead
G	Natural Gas	Sb	Antimony
Hg	Mercury	U	Uranium
Lg	Lignite	Zn	Zinc
Mg	Magnesium		

⚡ Water Power
▨ Major Industrial Areas

ALBANIA

CITIES and TOWNS

Berat, 22,000	D 5
Bajram Curi, 1,795	D 4
Burrel, 3,150	D 5
Çorovodë, 1,790	D 5
Delvinë, 5,700	D 6
Durrës, 47,900	D 5
Elbasan, 35,300	E 5
Ersekë, 2,150	E 5
Fier, 17,900	D 5
Gjirokastër, 15,000	D 5
Kavajë, 17,700	D 5
Korçë, 43,700	E 5
Krujë, 6,700	D 5
Kuçovë (Stalin), 12,300	D 5
Kukës, 3,900	E 4
Leskovik, 1,625	E 5
Lezh, 3,000	D 5
Lushnje, 16,000	D 5
Peqin, 3,800	D 5
Përmet, 4,000	E 5
Peshkopi, 5,500	E 5
Pogradec, 8,900	E 5
Pukë, 1,700	E 4
Sarandë, 7,700	D 6
Shijak, 5,100	D 5
Shkodër, 47,000	D 5
Stalin, 12,300	D 5
Tepelenë, 2,500	D 5
Tiranë (Tirana) (cap.), 170,000	E 5
Vlorë, 46,900	D 5

OTHER FEATURES

Adriatic (sea)	B 4
Drin (riv.)	E 4
Korab (mt.)	E 5
Ohrid (lake)	E 5
Otranto (str.)	D 5
Prespa (lake)	E 5
Sazan (isl.)	C 5
Scutari (lake)	D 4
Tomor (mt.)	E 5
Vijosë (riv.)	D 5

BULGARIA

CITIES and TOWNS

Alfatar, 3,650	H 4
Akhtopol, 1,058	H 4
Alfatar, 4,042	H 4
Ardino, 2,558	G 5
Asenovgrad, 37,411	G 5
Aytos, 15,769	H 4
Balchik, 8,714	H 4
Bansko, 7,851	F 5
Belogradchik, 5,174	F 4
Berkovitsa, 11,553	F 4
Blagoevgrad, 32,744	F 5
Botevgrad, 17,051	F 4
Bregovo, 4,725	F 3
Breznik, 4,093	F 4
Burgas, 122,212	H 4
Byala, 9,347	G 4
Byala Slatina, 14,942	F 4
Chirpan, 17,857	G 4
Devin, 4,475	F 5
Dimitrovgrad, 41,787	G 4
Dobrich (Tolbukhin), 55,111	H 4
Dryanovo, 8,187	G 4
Elena, 4,071	G 4
Elin Pelin, 8,074	F 4
Elkhovo, 11,315	H 4
Gabrovo, 57,758	G 4
General Toshevo, 8,251	H 4
Godech, 4,074	F 4
Gorna Oryakhovitsa (Blagoevgrad), 32,744	F 5
Gorna Oryakhovitsa, 26,290	G 4
Gotse Delchev, 14,457	F 5
Grudovo, 9,177	H 4
Ikhtiman, 10,325	F 4
Isperikh, 8,445	H 4
Ivaylovgrad, 2,907	H 5
Karapelit, 2,033	H 4
Karlovo (Levskigrad), 20,287	G 4
Karnobat (Polyanovgrad), 18,727	H 4
Kavarna, 8,291	H 4
Kazanlŭk, 44,418	G 4
Kharmanlii, 15,478	H 5
Khaskovo, 57,682	G 5
Kolarovgrad (Shumen), 59,362	H 4

Kotel, 7,209	H 4
Krumovgrad, 2,230	G 5
Kubrat, 7,531	H 4
Kula, 6,474	F 4
Kŭrdzhali, 33,319	G 5
Kyustendil, 38,199	F 4
Levskigrad, 20,287	G 4
Lom, 28,189	F 4
Lovech, 30,843	G 4
Lukovit, 9,716	G 4
Malko Tŭrnovo, 3,744	H 4
Maritsa, 8,532	H 4
Michurin, 2,783	H 4
Mikhaylovgrad, 27,240	F 4
Momchilgrad, 6,084	G 5
Nesebŭr, 2,333	H 4
Nikopol, 5,763	G 4
Nova Zagora, 19,257	H 4
Novi Pazar, 12,476	H 4
Omurtag, 8,148	H 4
Oryakhovo, 7,498	F 4
Panagyurishte, 18,298	G 4
Pazardzhik, 55,410	G 4
Pernik, 75,844	F 4
Peshtera, 14,606	G 4
Petrich, 20,653	F 5
Pirdop, 8,252	G 4
Pleven, 79,234	G 4
Plovdiv, 234,547	G 4
Polyanovgrad, 18,727	H 4
Pomorie, 9,567	H 4
Popina, 2,699	H 3
Popovo, 15,609	H 4
Provadiya, 13,837	H 4
Radomir, 8,458	F 4
Razgrad, 26,297	H 4
Razlog, 10,425	F 5
Rositsa, 1,505	H 4
Ruse, 142,894	H 4
Samokov, 21,585	F 4
Sandanski, 14,590	F 5
Sevlievo, 20,396	G 4
Shabla, 3,788	J 4
Shumen, 59,362	H 4
Silistra, 32,996	H 3
Simeonovgrad (Maritsa), 8,532	G 4
Sliven, 68,331	H 4
Smolyan, 17,479	G 5
Smyadovo, 5,349	H 4
Sofia (cap.), 840,113	F 4
Sofia, *923,400	F 4
Sozopol, 3,257	H 4
Stanke Dimitrov, 35,813	F 4
Stara Zagora, 100,565	G 4
Sveti Vrach (Sandanski), 14,590	F 5
Svilengrad, 12,438	G 5
Svishtov, 21,522	G 4
Teteven, 9,807	G 4
Tolbukhin, 55,111	H 4
Topolovgrad, 6,633	H 4
Troyan, 18,982	G 4
Trŭn, 2,922	F 4
Tŭrgovishte, 25,528	H 4
Tutrakan, 9,909	H 4
Varna, 200,827	J 4
Veliko Tŭrnovo, 37,269	G 4
Vidin, 36,820	F 4
Vratsa, 39,052	F 4
Yambol, 58,405	H 4
Zlatograd, 6,508	G 5

OTHER FEATURES

Balkan (mts.)	G 4
Black (sea)	J 4
Danube (Dunav) (riv.)	G 4
Emine (cape)	J 4
Iskŭr (riv.)	G 4
Kaliakra (cape)	J 4
Lom (riv.)	F 4
Maritsa (riv.)	G 5
Mesta (riv.)	F 5
Musala (mt.)	F 4
Osŭm (riv.)	G 4
Rhodope (mts.)	G 5
Ruen (mt.)	F 5
Struma (riv.)	F 5
Timok (riv.)	F 3
Tundzha (riv.)	H 4
Vit (riv.)	G 4

GREECE

REGIONS

Aegean Islands, 477,476	G 6
Áyion Óros (aut. dist.), 2,687	G 5
Central Greece and Euboea, 2,823,658	F 6
Crete, 483,258	G 8
Epirus, 352,604	E 6
Greater Athens, 1,852,709	F 7
Ionian Islands, 212,573	D 6
Macedonia, 1,890,654	F 5
Pelopónnisos, 1,096,390	F 7
Thessalía, 695,385	F 6
Thrace, 356,555	G 5

CITIES and TOWNS

Agrínion, 24,763	E 6
Aíyina, 4,989	F 7
Aíyion, 17,762	F 6
Alexandroúpolis, 18,712	H 5
Alivérion, 3,523	G 6
Almirós, 6,010	F 6
Amaliás, 15,468	E 6
Amfilokhía, 5,408	E 6
Ámfissa, 6,076	F 6
Ándissa, 2,530	H 6
Andravída, 3,155	E 6
Ándros, 2,032	G 7
Áno Viánnos, 1,820	G 8
Anóyia, 2,461	G 8
Andréa, 3,222	F 5
Argalastí, 1,864	F 6
Árgos, 16,712	F 7
Argostólion, 7,322	E 6
Arkhángelos, 2,918	J 7
Arnaía, 2,612	F 5
Árta, 16,899	E 6
Astipálaia, 1,205	H 7
Atalándi, 4,552	F 6
Athens (cap.), 627,564	F 7
Athens, *2,347,000	F 7
Áyios Matthaíos, 1,892	D 6
Áyios Nikólaos, 3,709	G 8
Candia (Iráklion), 63,458	G 8
Canea (Khaniá), 38,467	G 8
Chalcis (Khalkís), 24,745	F 6
Corinth, 15,892	F 7
Delvinákion, 1,076	E 6
Dhidhimótikhon, 7,287	H 5
Dhíkaia, 1,181	H 5
Dhimitsána, 1,300	F 7
Dhomokós, 2,017	F 6
Dráma, 32,195	F 5
Édhessa, 15,534	F 5
Elassón, 6,501	F 6
Elevtheroúpolis, 5,448	G 5
Ermoúpolis, 14,402	G 7
Fársala, 6,356	F 6
Filiátes, 3,065	E 6
Filiatrá, 6,753	E 7
Flórina, 11,933	E 5
Grevená, 6,892	E 6
Idhra, 2,546	F 7
Ierápetra, 6,488	G 8
Igoumenítsa, 3,235	E 6
Ioánnina, 34,997	E 6
Iráklion, 63,458	G 8
Istiaía, 3,882	F 6
Itháki, 2,632	E 6
Kalámai, 38,211	F 7
Kalampáka, 4,640	E 6
Kalávrita, 2,039	F 6
Kálimnos, 10,211	H 7
Kardhítsa, 23,708	E 6
Kariaí, 1,739	F 5
Kariaí, 429	G 5
Káristos, 3,335	G 6
Karpenísion, 3,523	E 6
Kassándra, 2,071	F 8
Kastéllion, 1,351	G 8
Kastoría, 10,162	E 5
Kateríni, 28,046	F 5
Kaválla, 44,517	G 5
Kéa, 1,788	G 7
Kérkira, 26,991	D 6
Khalkís, 24,745	F 6
Khaniá, 38,467	G 8
Khíos, 24,053	G 6
Kiáton, 6,069	F 6
Kilkís, 10,963	F 5
Kími, 3,252	F 6
Kiparissía, 4,602	E 7
Kíthira, 349	F 7
Komotiní, 28,355	G 5
Kónitsa, 3,485	E 5
Koropí, 7,862	G 7
Kos, 8,138	H 7

(continued on following page)

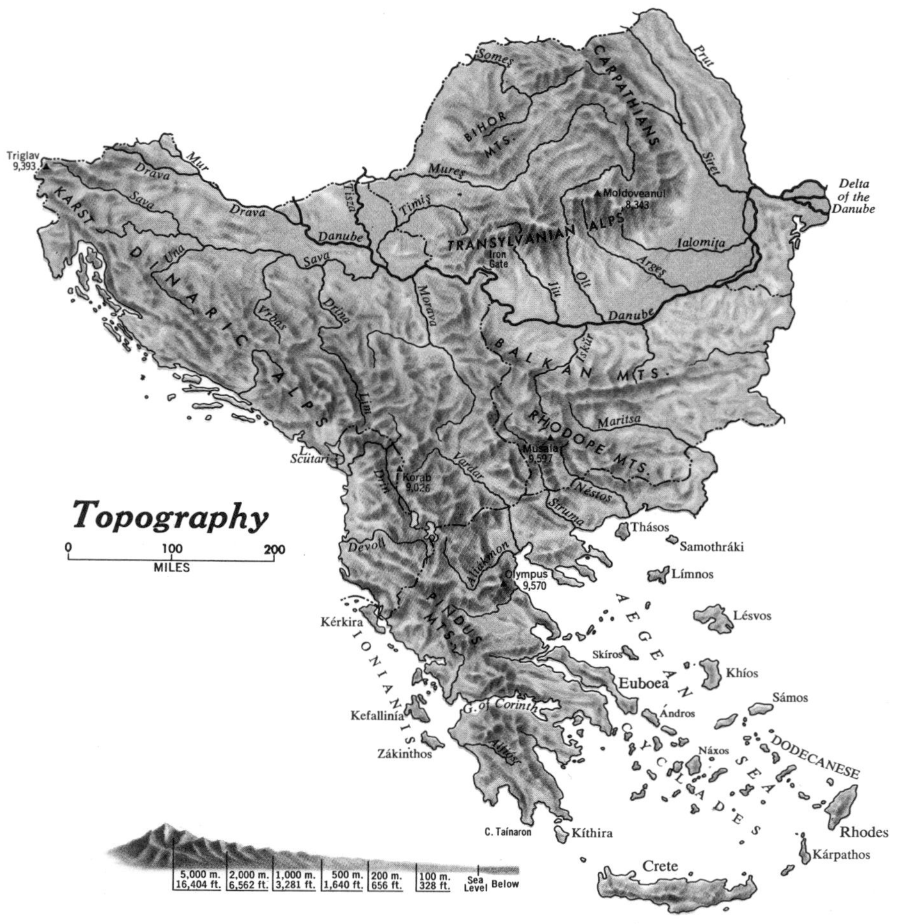
Topography
0 100 200
MILES
Triglav 9,393
Mur
Drava
Sava
Drava
KARST
DINARIC ALPS
Una
Vrbas
Danube
Sava
Drina
Tisza
Someș
Mureș
BIHOR MTS.
CARPATHIANS
Prut
Siret
Timiș
Moldoveanul 8,343
TRANSYLVANIAN ALPS
Iron Gate
Jiu
Olt
Argeș
Ialomița
Delta of the Danube
Danube
Morava
Iskar
BALKAN MTS.
Maritsa
RHODOPE MTS.
Lim
L. Scutari
Drin
Korab 9,026
Musala 9,597
Vardar
Nestos
Struma
Thásos
Samothráki
Límnos
Devoli
Aliákmon
Olympus 9,570
PINDUS MTS.
Kérkira
IONIAN SEA
AEGEAN SEA
Lésvos
Skíros
Euboea
Khíos
Sámos
Kefallinía
Zákinthos
G. of Corinth
Ándros
Náxos
CYCLADES
DODECANESE
Rhodes
Kárpathos
C. Taínaron
Kíthira
Crete
5,000 m. 16,404 ft.
2,000 m. 6,562 ft.
1,000 m. 3,281 ft.
500 m. 1,640 ft.
200 m. 656 ft.
100 m. 328 ft.
Sea Level
Below

GREECE (continued)

Kozáni, 21,537 ... F 5
Kranídhion, 3,942 ... F 7
Lamía, 21,509 ... F 6
Langadhás, 6,739 ... F 5
Lárisa, 55,391 ... F 6
Lávrion, 6,553 ... G 7
Leonídhion, 3,297 ... F 7
Levádhia, 12,609 ... F 6
Levkás, 6,552 ... E 6
Limenária, 1,999 ... G 5
Limín Vathéos, 5,469 ... H 7
Límni, 2,394 ... F 6
Litókhoron, 5,032 ... F 5
Lixoúrion, 3,977 ... E 6
Loutrá Aidhipsoú, 1,859 ... F 6
Marathón, 2,167 ... G 6
Megalópolis, 2,235 ... F 7
Mégara, 15,450 ... F 6
Meligalá, 1,960 ... F 7
Mesolóngion, 11,266 ... E 6
Messíni, 8,249 ... F 7
Métsovon, 2,976 ... E 6
Mikínai, 361 ... F 7
Mílos, 944 ... G 7
Mírina, 3,460 ... G 6
Missolonghi (Mesolóngion), 11,266 ... E 6
Míthimna, 1,828 ... G 6
Mitilíni, 25,758 ... H 6
Moláoi, 2,526 ... F 7
Monólithos, 496 ... H 7
Moúdhros, 1,236 ... G 6
Náousa, 15,492 ... F 5
Návpaktos, 7,080 ... F 6
Návplion, 8,918 ... F 7
Náxos, 2,458 ... G 7
Néa Filippiás, 3,001 ... E 6
Neápolis, 2,464 ... F 7
Neméa, 4,720 ... F 7
Néon Karlóvasi, 5,308 ... H 7
Nigríta, 9,979 ... F 5
Olimbía, 771 ... E 7
Orestiás, 10,281 ... H 5
Paramithiá, 2,827 ... E 6
Pátrai, 95,364 ... E 6
Péta, 2,522 ... E 6
Pigádhia, 1,281 ... H 8
Pílos, 2,434 ... E 7
Piraiévs (Piraeus), 183,877 ... F 7
Pírgos, 20,558 ... E 7
Pirgí, 1,914 ... G 6
Píthion, 1,535 ... H 5
Plomárion, 5,172 ... H 6
Políkastron, 3,821 ... F 5
Políkhnitos, 5,131 ... G 6
Políyiros, 3,541 ... F 5
Póros, 4,392 ... F 7
Préveza, 11,172 ... E 6
Psakhná, 4,433 ... F 6
Ptolemaís, 12,747 ... E 5
Réthimnon, 14,999 ... G 8
Ródhos (Rhodes), 27,393 ... J 7
Salamís, 11,161 ... F 6
Salonika (Thessaloníki), 448,000 ... F 5
Sámi, 1,065 ... E 6
Samothráki, 1,555 ... G 5
Sápai, 2,589 ... G 5
Sérrai, 40,063 ... F 5
Sérvia, 4,132 ... F 5
Siátista, 4,737 ... E 5
Sidhirókastron, 8,177 ... F 5
Sími, 2,982 ... H 7
Sitía, 5,327 ... H 8
Skíros, 2,411 ... G 6
Skópelos, 2,955 ... F 6
Souflíon, 6,693 ... H 5
Sparta, 10,412 ... F 7
Spétsai, 3,314 ... F 7
Stilís, 4,673 ... F 6
Thebes (Thívai), 15,779 ... F 6
Thessaloníki, 448,000 ... F 5
Thásos, 1,875 ... G 5
Thíra, 1,481 ... G 7
Thívai, 15,779 ... F 6
Timbákion, 2,816 ... G 8
Tínos, 2,888 ... G 7
Tríkkala, 27,876 ... E 6
Trípolis, 18,500 ... F 7
Vartholomión, 3,244 ... E 7
Vathí, 3,161 ... H 7
Velvendós, 4,158 ... F 5
Véroia, 25,765 ... F 5
Vólos, 49,221 ... F 6
Vólos, *67,424 ... F 6
Vónitsa, 2,996 ... E 6
Vrondádhes, 4,685 ... G 6
Xánthi, 26,377 ... G 5
Yiannitsá, 19,693 ... F 5
Yíthion, 4,992 ... F 7
Zákinthos, 9,506 ... E 7
Zante (Zákinthos), 9,506 ... E 7

OTHER FEATURES

Aegean (sea) ... G 6
Akrítas (cape) ... E 7
Aktí (pen.) ... G 5
Amorgós (isl.), 2,396 ... G 7
Anáfi (isl.), 471 ... G 7
Andikíthira (isl.), 178 ... F 8
Ándros (isl.), 12,928 ... G 7
Arda (riv.) ... G 5
Argolís (gulf) ... F 7
Astipálaia (isl.), 1,539 ... H 7
Áthos (mt.) ... G 5
Áyios Evstrátios (isl.), 1,061 ... G 6
Áyios Yeóryios (cape) ... G 5
Cephalonia (Kefallinía) (isl.), 39,793 ... E 6
Chios (Khíos) (isl.), 60,061 ... G 6
Corfu (Kérkira) (isl.), 99,092 ... D 6
Corinth (gulf) ... F 6
Crete (isl.), 483,075 ... G 8
Crete (sea) ... G 7
Cyclades (isls.), 99,959 ... G 7
Dhrépanon (cape) ... F 6
Dodecanese (isls.), 123,021 ... H 8
Euboea (isl.), 163,215 ... G 6
Évros (riv.) ... H 5
Gávdhos (isl.), 172 ... F 8
Ikaría (isl.), 9,577 ... G 7
Ionian (sea) ... D 7
Íos (isl.), 1,343 ... G 7
Itháki (Ithaca) (isl.), 5,210 ... E 6
Kálimnos (isl.), 10,211 ... H 7
Kafirévs (cape) ... G 6
6,689 ... H 8
Kárpathos (isl.), 6,689 ... H 8
Kásos (isl.), 1,422 ... H 8
Kassándra (pen.) ... F 6
Kéa (isl.), 2,361 ... G 7
Kefallinía (isl.), 39,793 ... E 6
Kérkira (isl.), 99,092 ... D 6
Khálki (isl.), 501 ... H 7
Khani, (gulf) ... G 8
Khíos (isl.), 60,061 ... G 6
Kiparissía (gulf) ... E 7
Kíthira (isl.), 5,340 ... F 7
Kíthnos (isl.), 2,064 ... G 7
Kos (isl.), 18,187 ... H 7
Kriós (cape) ... F 8
Lakonía (gulf) ... F 7
Léros (isl.), 6,611 ... H 7
Lésvos (isl.), 117,371 ... G 6
Levítha (isl.), 7 ... H 7
Levkás (isl.), 2,697 ... E 6
Límnos (isl.), 21,808 ... G 6
Maléa (cape) ... F 7
Matapan (Taínaron) (cape) ... F 7
Merabéllou (gulf) ... H 8
Mesará (gulf) ... G 8
Messíni (gulf) ... E 7
Míkonos (isl.), 3,633 ... G 7
Mílos (isl.), 4,910 ... G 7
Mirtóön (sea) ... F 7
Náxos (isl.), 16,703 ... G 7
Néstos (riv.) ... G 5
Nísiros (isl.), 1,788 ... H 7
Northern Sporades (isls.), 9,810 ... F 6
Olympus (mt.) ... F 5
Óssa (mt.) ... F 6
Parnassus (mt.) ... F 6
Páros (isl.), 7,830 ... G 7
Pátmos (isl.), 2,564 ... H 7
Paxoí (isl.), 2,678 ... D 6
Pindus (mts.) ... E 6
Piniós (riv.) ... E 6
Prespa (lake) ... E 5
Psará (isl.), 576 ... G 6
Rhodes (isl.), 63,951 ... H 7
Rhodope (mts.) ... G 5
Salonika (Thermaic) (gulf) ... F 6
Sámos (isl.), 41,124 ... H 7
Samothráki (isl.), 3,830 ... G 5
Saría (isl.), 18 ... H 8
Saronic (gulf) ... F 7
Sérifos (isl.), 1,878 ... G 7
Sídheros (cape) ... H 8
Sífnos (isl.), 2,258 ... G 7
Sími (isl.), 3,123 ... H 7
Síros (isl.), 19,570 ... G 7
Sithoniá (pen.) ... F 5
Skíros (isl.), 2,882 ... G 6
Spátha (cape) ... F 8
Strimón (gulf) ... G 5
Strofádhes (isls.), 10 ... E 7
Taínaron (cape) ... F 7
Thásos (isl.), 15,916 ... G 5
Thermaic (gulf) ... F 6
Thíra (isl.), 7,751 ... G 7
Tílos (isl.), 789 ... H 7
Tínos (isl.), 9,273 ... G 7
Toronaic (gulf) ... F 5
Vardar (riv.) ... F 5
Voïviïs (lake) ... F 6
Vólvi (lake) ... F 5
Voúxa (cape) ... F 8
Zákinthos (Zante) (isl.), 35,499 ... E 7

RUMANIA

CITIES and TOWNS

Aiud, 11,886 ... F 2
Alba Iulia, 22,225 ... F 2
Alexandria, 21,907 ... G 3
Anina, 11,837 ... E 3
Arad, 132,757 ... E 2
Arad, *137,444 ... E 2
Babadag, 5,549 ... J 3
Bacău, 73,481 ... H 2
Bacău, *87,465 ... H 2
Baia Mare, 62,769 ... F 2
Baia Mare, *108,709 ... F 2
Băileşti, 15,932 ... F 3
Balş, 6,956 ... G 3
Beiuş, 6,467 ... F 2
Bîrlad, 41,061 ... H 2
Bîrlad, *52,497 ... H 2
Bistriţa, 25,534 ... G 2
Blaj, 8,731 ... F 2
Botoşani, 35,185 ... H 2
Botoşani, *50,204 ... H 2
Brad, 9,963 ... F 2
Brăila, 147,495 ... H 3
Braşov, 175,264 ... G 3
Braşov, *264,537 ... G 3
Bucharest (Bucureşti) (cap.), 1,431,993 ... G 3
Bucharest, *1,518,725 ... G 3
Buhuş, 12,382 ... H 2
Buzău, 56,380 ... H 3
Buzău, *82,454 ... H 3
Buziaş, 5,140 ... E 3
Călafat, 8,069 ... F 3
Călăraşi, 35,698 ... H 3
Caracal, 22,715 ... G 3
Caransebeş, 15,195 ... F 3
Carei, 16,780 ... F 2
Cernavodă, 8,802 ... J 3
Cîmpia Turzii, 11,514 ... F 2
Cîmpina, 22,862 ... H 3
Cîmpulung, 24,891 ... G 3
Cîmpulung Moldovenesc, 13,627 ... G 2
Cisnădie, 12,246 ... F 3
Cluj, 193,375 ... F 2
Cluj, *223,519 ... F 2
Comaneşti, 12,392 ... H 2
Constanţa, 165,245 ... J 3
Constanţa, *202,024 ... J 3
Corabia, 11,502 ... G 4
Craiova, 166,249 ... F 3
Craiova, *174,669 ... F 3
Curtea de Argeş, 10,764 ... G 3
Dej, 26,968 ... F 2
Deva, 26,952 ... F 3
Deva, *45,836 ... F 3
Dorohoi, 14,771 ... H 2
Drăgăşani, 9,963 ... F 3
Făgăraş, 22,941 ... G 3
Fălticeni, 13,305 ... H 2
Feteşti, 21,425 ... H 3
Focşani, 35,075 ... H 3
Focşani, *40,701 ... H 3
Găeşti, 7,179 ... G 3
Galaţi, 160,097 ... H 3
Gheorgheni, 11,969 ... G 2
Gherla, 7,617 ... G 2
Giurgiu, 39,225 ... G 3
Giurgiu, *55,471 ... G 3
Haţeg, 3,853 ... F 3
Hîrşova, 4,761 ... J 3
Hunedoara, 68,303 ... F 3
Hunedoara, *100,953 ... F 3
Huşi, 20,703 ... J 2
Iaşi, 173,569 ... H 2
Iaşi, *196,167 ... H 2
Isaccea, 5,203 ... J 3
Jimbolia, 11,281 ... E 3
Lipova, 10,064 ... E 2
Lugoj, 35,388 ... F 3
Lupeni, 29,377 ... F 3
Mangalia, 4,792 ... J 4
Medgidia, 27,989 ... J 3
Mediaş, 46,396 ... G 2
Miercurea Ciuc, 11,996 ... G 2
Mizil, 7,460 ... H 3
Moineşti, 12,934 ... H 2
Moldova Nouă, 3,582 ... E 3
Moreni, 11,687 ... G 3
Năsăud, 5,725 ... G 2
Ocna Mureş, 10,701 ... G 2
Odobeşti, 4,977 ... H 3
Odorhei, 14,162 ... G 2
Olteniţa, 14,111 ... H 3
Oradea, 132,266 ... E 2
Oradea, *136,375 ... E 2
Orăştie, 10,488 ... F 3
Oraşul Gheorghe Gheorghiu-Dej, 35,689 ... H 2
Oraviţa, 8,175 ... E 3
Orşova, 6,527 ... F 3
Panciu, 7,679 ... H 3
Paşcani, 15,008 ... H 2
Petrila, 24,804 ... F 3
Petroşeni, 35,237 ... F 3
Petroşeni, *130,111 ... F 3
Piatra Neamţ, 45,925 ... G 2
Piatra Neamţ, *58,397 ... G 2
Piteşti, 60,094 ... G 3
Piteşti, *78,784 ... G 3
Ploieşti, 156,382 ... H 3
Ploieşti, *191,663 ... H 3
Pucioasa, 9,259 ... G 3
Rădăuţi, 15,949 ... G 2
Reghin, 23,317 ... G 2
Reşiţa, 58,683 ... E 3
Reşiţa, *121,458 ... E 3
Rîmnicu Sărat, 22,325 ... H 3
Rîmnicu Vîlcea, 23,880 ... F 3
Roman, 38,990 ... H 2
Roman, *49,496 ... H 2
Roşiori de Vede, 21,707 ... G 3
Săcele, 22,822 ... G 3
Salonta, 16,276 ... E 3
Satu Mare, 68,257 ... F 2
Sebeş, 11,628 ... F 3
Sfîntu Gheorge, 20,759 ... G 3
Sibiu, 117,020 ... G 3
Sighetul-Marmaţiei, 29,768 ... F 2
Sighişoara, 25,100 ... G 2
Şimleu Silvaniei, 8,560 ... F 2
Sinaia, 9,006 ... G 3
Sînnicolau Mare, 9,956 ... E 2
Siret, 5,664 ... G 1
Slănic, 6,842 ... G 3
Slatina, 13,381 ... G 3
Slobozia, 9,632 ... H 3
Solca, 2,384 ... G 2
Strehaia, 8,545 ... F 3
Suceava, 37,715 ... G 2
Suceava, *76,327 ... G 2
Sulina, 3,622 ... J 3
Techirghiol, 2,705 ... J 3
Tecuci, 28,458 ... H 3
Timişoara, 184,797 ... E 3
Timişoara, *194,159 ... E 3
Tîrgovişte, 29,754 ... G 3
Tîrgovişte, *48,005 ... G 3
Tîrgu Jiu, 30,837 ... F 3
Tîrgu Jiu, *33,019 ... F 3
Tîrgu Mureş, 86,458 ... G 2
Tîrgu Mureş, *104,922 ... G 2
Tîrgu Neamţ, 10,373 ... G 2
Tîrgu Ocna, 11,227 ... H 2
Tîrgu Secuiesc, 7,500 ... H 2
Tîrnăveni, 20,354 ... F 2
Topliţa, 8,944 ... G 2
Tulcea, 35,552 ... J 3
Turda, 42,318 ... G 2
Turda, *69,768 ... G 2
Turnu Măgurele, 26,409 ... G 4
Turnu Severin, 45,394 ... F 3
Turnu Severin, *52,497 ... F 3
Urlaţi, 8,658 ... H 3
Urziceni, 6,061 ... H 3
Vasile Roaită, 3,286 ... J 3
Vasluí, 14,850 ... H 2
Vatra Dornei, 10,822 ... G 2
Vişeu de Sus, 13,956 ... F 2
Zalău, 13,378 ... F 2
Zărneşti, 6,673 ... G 3
Zimnicea, 12,445 ... G 4

OTHER FEATURES

Argeş (riv.) ... G 3
Buzău (riv.) ... H 3
Carpathian (mts.) ... F 2
Crişul Alb (riv.) ... F 2
Crişul Repede (riv.) ... F 2
Danube (river) ... H 4
Ialomiţa (marshes) ... J 3
Jiu (riv.) ... F 3
Moldoveanul (mt.) ... G 3
Mureş (riv.) ... E 2
Negoiul (mt.) ... G 3
Olt (riv.) ... G 3
Pietrosul (mt.) ... G 2
Prut (riv.) ... J 2
Siret (riv.) ... H 2
Someş (riv.) ... F 2
Timiş (riv.) ... E 3
Transylvanian Alps (mts.) ... G 3

YUGOSLAVIA

INTERNAL DIVISIONS

Bosnia and Hercegovina (rep.), 3,594,000 ... C 3
Croatia (rep.), 4,281,000 ... C 3
Kosovo-Mitohiyan (aut. prov.), 1,089,000 ... E 4
Macedonia (rep.), 1,506,000 ... E 5
Montenegro (rep.), 471,894 ... D 4
Serbia (rep.), 7,637,800 ... E 3
Slovenia (rep.), 1,624,900 ... B 2
Voyvodina (aut. prov.), 1,880,000 ... D 3

CITIES and TOWNS

Aleksinac, 8,828 ... E 4
Apatin, 17,000 ... D 3
Bačka Topola, 14,000 ... D 3
Bakar ... B 3
Banja Luka, 55,000 ... C 3
Bar, 2,184 ... D 4
Bečej, 22,000 ... E 3
Bela Crkva, 11,000 ... E 3
Belgrade (Beograd) (cap.), 745,000 ... E 3
Belgrade, *1,050,000 ... E 3
Bihać, 17,000 ... B 3
Bijeljina, 19,000 ... D 3
Bijelo Polje, 5,856 ... D 4
Bileća, 2,491 ... D 4
Biograd, 2,418 ... B 4
Bitola (Bitolj), 52,000 ... E 5
Bjelovar, 16,000 ... C 3
Bled, 4,156 ... A 2
Bor, 19,000 ... E 3
Bosanska Dubica, 6,259 ... C 3
Bosanska Gradiška, 6,363 ... C 3
Bosanska Kostajnica, 2,034 ... B 3
Bosanska Krupa, 6,191 ... C 3
Bosanski Brod, 7,350 ... D 3
Bosanski Novi, 7,023 ... C 3
Bosanski Petrovac, 3,473 ... C 3
Bosanski Šamac, 3,654 ... D 3
Brčko, 20,000 ... D 3
Brežice, 2,641 ... B 3
Brod, 30,000 ... D 3
Bugojno, 5,453 ... C 3
Buje, 1,955 ... A 3
Čačak, 30,000 ... F 4
Čapljina, 3,275 ... C 4
Caribrod (Dimitrovgrad), 3,665 ... F 4
Celje, 28,000 ... B 2
Cetinje, 9,359 ... D 4
Ćuprija, 12,000 ... E 4
Debar, 6,323 ... E 5
Derventa, 9,843 ... C 3
Dimitrovgrad, 3,665 ... F 4
Djakovica, 22,000 ... E 4
Djakovo, 13,000 ... D 3
Donji Vakuf, 3,764 ... C 3
Drvar, 3,646 ... C 3
Dubrovnik, 24,000 ... C 4
Fiume (Rijeka), 108,000 ... B 3
Foča, 6,763 ... D 4
Fojnica, 1,549 ... C 4
Gacko, 1,368 ... D 4
Gevgelija, 7,332 ... F 5
Glamoč, 1,626 ... C 4
Gnjilane, 14,000 ... E 4
Gornji Vafuf, 1,860 ... C 4
Gospić, 6,767 ... B 3
Gostivar, 14,000 ... E 5
Gračac, 2,183 ... B 3
Gračanica, 7,656 ... D 3
Gradačac, 5,878 ... D 3
Grubišno Polje, 2,655 ... C 3
Gusinje, 2,756 ... D 4
Hercegnovi, 3,797 ... D 4
Ivangrad, 6,969 ... E 4
Jajce, 6,853 ... C 3
Jesenice, 16,000 ... A 2
Kamnik, 5,062 ... B 2
Kanjiža, 10,000 ... D 2
Kardeljevo, 3,267 ... C 4
Karlovac, 35,000 ... B 3
Kavadarci, 13,000 ... E 5
Kičevo, 11,000 ... E 5
Kikinda, 32,000 ... E 3
Kladanj, 2,825 ... D 3
Ključ, 2,320 ... C 3
Knin, 5,116 ... C 3
Knjaževac, 7,448 ... F 4
Kočevje, 5,819 ... B 3
Konjic, 5,927 ... D 4
Koper, 12,000 ... A 3
Koprivnica, 12,000 ... C 2
Korčula, 2,458 ... C 4
Kosovska Mitrovica, 29,000 ... E 4
Kostajnica, 2,080 ... C 3
Kotor, 4,764 ... D 4
Kragujevac, 56,000 ... E 3
Kraljevo (Rankovićevo), 26,000 ... E 4
Kranj, 23,000 ... B 2
Križevci, 6,642 ... C 2
Krk, 1,280 ... B 3
Krško, 3,518 ... B 3
Kruševac, 31,000 ... E 4
Kumanovo, 33,000 ... E 4
Leskovac, 37,000 ... E 4
Livno, 5,181 ... C 4
Ljubljana, 183,000 ... B 3
Ljubuški, 2,168 ... C 4
Loznica, 12,000 ... D 3
Maglaj, 4,556 ... D 3
Makarska, 3,634 ... C 4
Maribor, 89,000 ... B 2
Mladenovac, 12,000 ... E 3
Modriča, 5,053 ... D 3
Mostar, 53,000 ... D 4
Našice, 4,187 ... C 3
Negotin, 8,635 ... F 3
Nevesinje, 2,349 ... D 4
Nikšić, 25,000 ... D 4
Niš, 92,000 ... F 4
Nova Gradiška, 9,229 ... C 3
Novi, 2,075 ... B 3
Novi Pazar, 23,000 ... E 4
Novi Sad, 119,000 ... D 3
Novo Mesto, 6,885 ... B 3
Novska, 3,844 ... C 3
Ogulin, 3,522 ... B 3
Ohrid, 18,000 ... E 5
Omiš, 2,171 ... C 4
Opatija, 7,974 ... A 3
Osijek, 78,000 ... D 3
Pag, 2,431 ... B
Pančevo, 49,000 ... E
Paraćin, 17,000 ... E
Peć, 30,000 ... E
Petrinja, 7,366 ... B
Piran, 5,474 ... A
Pirot, 20,000 ... F
Plav, 2,535 ... D
Pljevlja, 12,000 ... D
Podgorica (Titograd), 37,000 ... D
Pola (Pula), 40,000 ... A
Poreč, 3,006 ... A
Postojna, 4,857 ... B
Požarevac, 23,000 ... E
Požega, 14,000 ... C
Preševo, 5,680 ... E
Priboj, 5,490 ... D
Prijedor, 13,000 ... C
Prijepolje, 4,566 ... D
Prilep, 40,000 ... E
Priština, 43,000 ... E
Prizren, 29,000 ... E
Prokuplje, 15,000 ... E
Prozor, 1,052 ... C
Ptuj, 7,392 ... C
Pula, 40,000 ... A
Rab, 1,548 ... B
Rača, 1,351 ... E
Radeče, 1,500 ... B
Radoviš, 6,246 ... F
Ragusa (Dubrovnik), 24,000 ... C
Rankovićevo, 26,000 ... E
Raška, 2,278 ... E
Rijeka, 108,000 ... B
Rogatica, 3,040 ... D
Rovinj, 7,155 ... A
Ruma, 21,000 ... D
Šabac, 30,000 ... D
Sanski Most, 5,096 ... C
Sarajevo, 223,000 ... D
Senj, 3,903 ... B
Senta, 22,000 ... D
Šibenik, 27,000 ... C
Sinj, 4,134 ... C
Sisak, 29,000 ... C
Škofja Loka, 3,429 ... A
Skopje, 230,000 ... E
Skradin, 1,118 ... C
Smederevo, 29,000 ... E
Sombor, 31,000 ... D
Split, 106,000 ... C
Srebrenica, 1,859 ... D
Sremska Mitrovica, 22,000 ... D
Sremski Karlovci, 6,390 ... D
Stari Majdan, 1,445 ... C
Štip, 22,000 ... F
Stolac, 2,970 ... D
Struga, 6,857 ... E
Strumica, 17,000 ... F
Subotica, 76,000 ... D
Surdulica, 5,007 ... F
Svetozarevo, 22,000 ... E
Svilajnac, 5,895 ... E
Tešanj, 3,148 ... C
Tetovo, 27,000 ... E
Titograd, 37,000 ... D
Titovo Užice, 26,000 ... D
Titov Veles, 29,000 ... E
Travnik, 12,000 ... C
Trbovlje, 16,000 ... B
Trebinje, 4,073 ... D
Trogir, 5,003 ... C
Tržič, 4,881 ... B
Tuzla, 55,000 ... D
Ulcinj, 5,705 ... D
Valjevo, 27,000 ... D
Varaždin, 28,000 ... C
Vareš, 7,647 ... D
Veliki Bečkerek (Zrenjanin), 56,000 ... E
Vinkovci, 24,000 ... D
Virovitica, 10,000 ... C
Višegrad, 3,309 ... D
Vranje, 18,000 ... F
Vrbas, 19,000 ... D
Vršac, 32,000 ... E
Vukovar, 25,000 ... D
Žabari, 1,984 ... E
Zadar, 28,000 ... B
Zagreb, 503,000 ... B
Zaječar, 18,000 ... F
Zara (Zadar), 28,000 ... B
Zenica, 50,000 ... C
Žepče, 2,709 ... C
Zrenjanin, 56,000 ... E
Zvornik, 5,444 ... D

OTHER FEATURES

Adriatic (sea) ... B
Bobotov Kuk (mt.) ... D
Bosna (riv.) ... D
Brač (isl.), 14,227 ... C
Čazma (riv.) ... C
Cres (isl.), 4,949 ... B
Danube (riv.) ... E
Dinaric Alps (mts.) ... B
Drava (riv.) ... C
Drina (riv.) ... D
Dugi Otok (isl.), 4,873 ... B
Hvar (isl.), 12,147 ... C
Ibar (riv.) ... E
Kamenjak (cape) ... A
Korab (mt.) ... E
Korčula (isl.), 10,245 ... C
Kornat (isl.), 6 ... B
Krk (isl.), 14,548 ... B
Kvarner (gulf) ... B
Lastovo (Lagosta) (isl.), 1,449 ... C
Lim (riv.) ... D
Lošinj (isl.), 5,068 ... B
Mljet (isl.), 1,963 ... C
Morava (riv.) ... E
Mur (riv.) ... B
Neretva (riv.) ... D
Ohrid (lake) ... E
Pag (isl.), 8,017 ... B
Pelagruž (Pelagosa) (isl.) ... C
Prespa (lake) ... E
Rab (isl.), 8,400 ... B
Ruen (mt.) ... F
Sava (riv.) ... D
Scutari (lake) ... D
Solta (isl.), 2,735 ... C
Tara (riv.) ... D
Timok (riv.) ... F
Tisza (riv.) ... E
Triglav (mt.) ... A
Una (riv.) ... C
Vardar (riv.) ... E
Vis (isl.), 7,004 ... C
Vrbas (riv.) ... C
Žirje (isl.), 506 ... B

*City and suburbs.

THE BALKAN STATES

CONIC PROJECTION

SCALE OF MILES

0 25 50 75 100 125 150 175

SCALE OF KILOMETRES

0 25 50 75 100 125 150 175

Capitals of Countries ----------- ☆
Administrative Centers ---------- △
International Boundaries ----------
Major Internal Boundaries -- -- --
Minor Internal Boundaries ········
Canals ----------

BULGARIA and GREECE are divided into counties and departments, respectively. Because of the scale no attempt has been made to delimit and name these subdivisions; their administrative centers have, however, been designated.

The larger divisions named in Greece are well-known geographical regions, without administrative function.

RUMANIA consists of thirty-nine counties and three cities of regional status, Bucharest, Constanța and Petroșeni. Scale does not permit delimiting these counties.

ALBANIA is divided into twenty-seven districts. Scale does not permit the delimitation of these divisions.

YUGOSLAVIA is a federation of six republics. The Serbian republic includes an autonomous province (Voyvodina), and an autonomous region (Kosovo-Mitohiyan).

© C. S. HAMMOND & Co., N.Y.

Topography

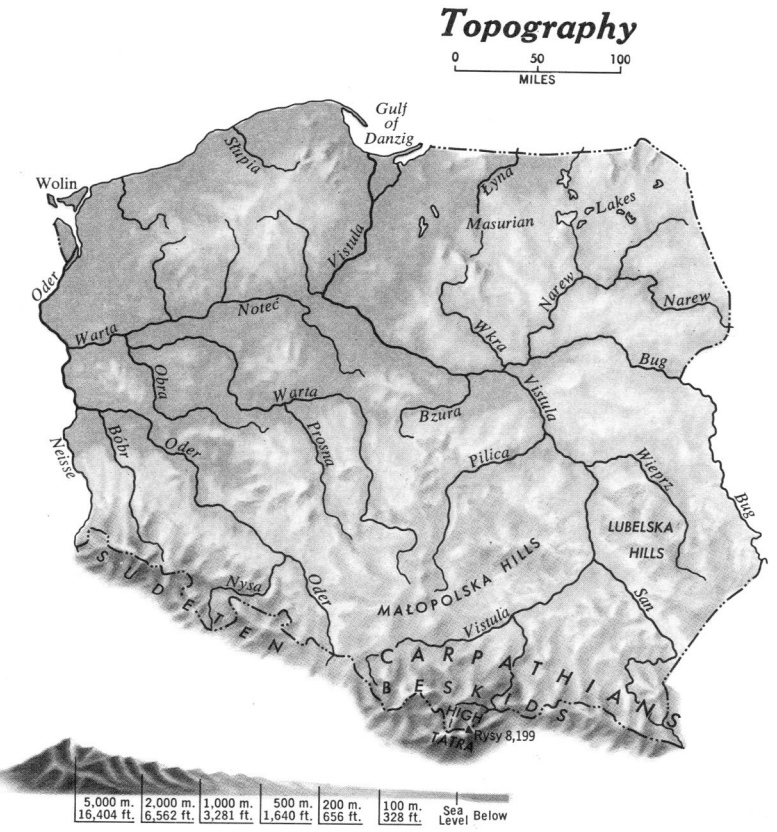

0   50   100
MILES

| 5,000 m. 16,404 ft. | 2,000 m. 6,562 ft. | 1,000 m. 3,281 ft. | 500 m. 1,640 ft. | 200 m. 656 ft. | 100 m. 328 ft. | Sea Level | Below |

POLAND 1938

0   50   100
MILES

PROVINCES

Biała Podlaska, 283,200 ...... F 3
Białystok, 613,800 .... F 2
Bielsko, 765,500 .... D 4
Bydgoszcz, 982,100 .... C 2
Chełm, 221,000 .... F 3
Ciechanów, 398,500 .... E 2
Cracow, 1,097,600 .... E 4
Cracow (city), 651,300 .... E 4
Częstochowa, 723,200 .... D 3
Elbląg, 419,800 .... D 1
Gdańsk, 1,220,500 .... D 1
Gorzów, 428,700 .... B 2
Jelenia Góra, 483,400 .... B 3
Kalisz, 640,300 .... D 3
Katowice, 3,439,700 .... D 3
Kielce, 1,030,400 .... E 3
Konin, 423,700 .... D 2
Koszalin, 428,500 .... C 1
Krosno, 418,000 .... E 4
Legnica, 405,600 .... C 3
Leszno, 340,600 .... C 3
Łódź, 1,063,700 .... D 3
Łódź (city), 777,800 .... D 3
Łomża, 320,600 .... F 2
Lublin, 875,300 .... F 3
Nowy Sącz, 600,300 .... E 4
Olsztyn, 654,400 .... E 2
Opole, 961,600 .... C 3
Ostrołęka, 360,700 .... E 2
Piła, 414,000 .... C 2
Piotrków, 581,900 .... D 3
Płock, 479,700 .... D 2
Poznań, 1,156,500 .... C 2
Przemyśl, 373,100 .... F 4
Radom, 674,400 .... E 3
Rzeszów, 602,200 .... F 4
Siedlce, 602,100 .... F 2
Sieradz, 388,000 .... D 3
Skierniewice, 388,300 .... E 3
Słupsk, 352,900 .... C 1
Suwałki, 412,700 .... F 1
Szczecin, 841,400 .... B 2
Tarnobrzeg, 532,200 .... E 3
Tarnów, 573,900 .... E 4
Toruń, 580,500 .... D 2
Wałbrzych, 709,600 .... C 3
Warsaw, 2,117,700 .... E 2
Warsaw (city), 1,377,100 ... E 2
Wrocław, 1,014,600 .... C 3
Zamość, 472,300 .... F 3
Zielona Góra, 575,000 .... B 3

CITIES and TOWNS

Aleksandrów Łódzki, 14,800 ...... D 3
Andrespol, 12,500 .... D 3
Andrychów, 14,300 .... D 4
Augustów, 20,200 .... F 2
Bartoszyce, 15,700 .... E 1
Będzin, 42,500 .... D 3
Bełchatów, 9,230 .... D 3
Bełżyce, 5,333 .... F 3
Biała Podlaska, 26,700 .... F 2
Białogard, 20,800 .... C 1
Białystok, 182,300 .... F 2
Bielawa, 31,300 .... C 3
Bielsk Podlaski, 14,600 .... F 2
Bielsko-Biała, 114,200 .... D 4
Biłgoraj, 13,600 .... F 3
Błonie, 12,500 .... E 2
Bochnia, 15,000 .... E 4
Bogatynia, 12,300 .... B 3
Boguszów-Gorce, 11,900 .... C 3
Bolesławiec, 31,400 .... B 3
Braniewo, 12,400 .... D 1
Brodnica, 17,700 .... D 2
Brzeg, 31,500 .... C 3
Brzeg Dolny, 10,900 .... C 3
Brzesko, 10,800 .... E 3

POLAND 1945

0   50   100
MILES

Agriculture, Industry and Resources

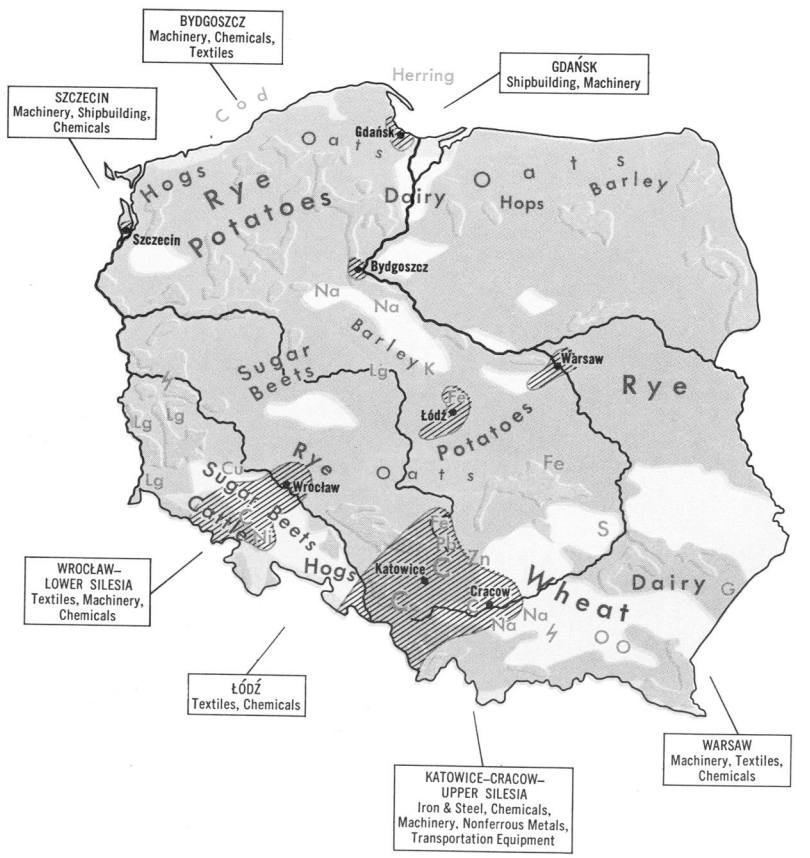

SZCZECIN
Machinery, Shipbuilding, Chemicals

BYDGOSZCZ
Machinery, Chemicals, Textiles

GDAŃSK
Shipbuilding, Machinery

WROCŁAW–
LOWER SILESIA
Textiles, Machinery, Chemicals

ŁÓDŹ
Textiles, Chemicals

KATOWICE–CRACOW–
UPPER SILESIA
Iron & Steel, Chemicals, Machinery, Nonferrous Metals, Transportation Equipment

WARSAW
Machinery, Textiles, Chemicals

DOMINANT LAND USE

- Cereals (chiefly wheat)
- Rye, Oats, Barley, Potatoes
- General Farming, Livestock
- Forests

MAJOR MINERAL OCCURRENCES

C   Coal
Cu Copper
Fe Iron Ore
G   Natural Gas
K   Potash
Lg Lignite

Na Salt
Ni Nickel
O   Petroleum
Pb Lead
S   Sulfur
Zn Zinc

⚡ Water Power
▨ Major Industrial Areas

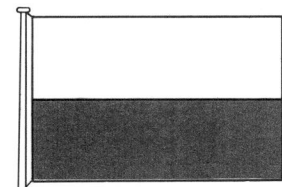

AREA 120,725 sq. mi.
POPULATION 34,364,000
CAPITAL Warsaw
LARGEST CITY Warsaw
HIGHEST POINT Rysy 8,199 ft.
MONETARY UNIT zloty
MAJOR LANGUAGE Polish
MAJOR RELIGION Roman Catholicism

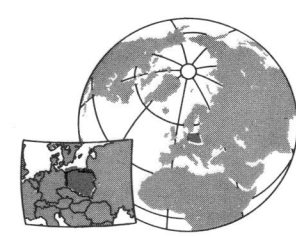

ozów, 8,591	F 4	Jaworzno, 64,500	B 4
sko-Zdrój, 11,400	E 3	Jędrzejów, 13,700	E 3
dgoszcz, 305,500	C 2	Jelenia Góra, 56,200	B 3
tom, 192,000	A 3	Kalisz, 82,400	D 3
tów, 10,900	C 1	Kamienna Góra, 21,200	B 3
elmo, 18,100		Kamień Pomorski, 8,725	B 1
elm, 40,000		Kartuzy,	C 1
elmza, 14,500	E 2	Katowice, 317,700	B 4
odzież, 14,300	C 2	Kazimierza Wielka, 8,571	E 3
ojnów, 11,100	B 3	Kędzierzyn, 34,200	C 3
orzów, 154,300	B 4	Kępno, 10,300	C 3
rzanów, 29,300		Kętrzyn, 19,600	E 1
echanów, 23,500		Kęty, 12,000	D 4
eplice Śląskie-Zdrój, 15,600	B 3	Kielce, 138,700	E 3
eszyn, 25,600		Kłobuck, 12,500	D 3
acow (Kraków), 651,300		Kłodzko, 26,300	C 3
echowice-Dziedzice, 25,700	B 4	Kluczbork, 18,200	D 3
eladź, 32,700		Knurów, 30,600	A 4
erwionka, 10,600		Kolno, 7,980	F 2
ęstochowa, 193,400	D 3	Kołobrzeg, 26,600	B 1
browa Górnicza, 62,400	B 4	Koło, 13,400	D 2
browa Tarnowska, 9,703	E 3	Konin, 42,800	D 2
bica, 23,600	C 1	Końskie, 15,500	E 3
blin, 11,500		Kościan, 19,000	C 2
no, 11,700		Kościerzyna, 15,500	C 1
błowo, 10,500	E 2	Kostrzyń, 11,700	B 2
ierzoniów, 33,400	D 1	Koszalin, 66,800	C 1
lag, 91,400	D 1	Kowary, 11,400	B 3
k, 27,900		Koźle, 13,300	C 3
ańsk, 394,000	D 1	Krapkowice, 14,200	D 3
ynia, 207,600	E 1	Kraśnik, 14,700	F 3
życe, 18,500		Kraśnik Fabryczny, 13,800	F 3
ogow, 22,700	C 3	Krasnystaw, 12,700	F 3
nowo, 13,200	D 2	Krosno, 27,200	E 4
ubczyce, 11,500	C 3	Krotoszyn, 22,200	C 3
ucholaży, 13,400	C 3	Krynica, 10,400	E 4
zew, 51,300		Kutno, 30,600	D 2
idap, 8,886	F 1	Kwidzyn, 23,400	D 2
elnie, 15,000		Łańcut, 12,300	F 3
ra, 9,905		Łaziska Górne, 10,900	A 4
flice, 16,000	E 4	Łęczyca, 13,900	D 2
rzów Wielkopolski, 76,200	C 2	Łędziny, 12,800	B 4
ostyń, 13,300		Legionowo, 21,000	E 2
ustyń, 12,200		Legnica, 76,800	A 4
ajewo, 11,400	F 2	Leszczyny, 12,100	A 4
odziec, 10,200	B 3	Leszno, 34,600	C 3
ozdzisk Mazowiecki, 21,000		Leżajsk, 9,647	F 3
ójec, 10,400	D 2	Libiąż, 10,700	D 4
udziądz, 76,600	D 2	Lidzbark Warmiński, 13,200	E 1
ryfino, 7,446	B 2	Lipno, 11,100	D 2
ryfice, 13,600	B 2	Łódź, 777,800	D 3
ajnówka, 14,600		Łomża, 26,400	F 2
rubieszów, 15,500	D 2	Łosice, 4,197	F 2
niewa, 17,100	D 2	Łowicz, 21,100	D 3
nezno, 4,419		Lubaczów, 8,298	F 3
anów Lubelski, 5,944	F 3	Lubań, 17,500	B 3
arcin, 18,300	C 3	Lubartów, 10,300	F 3
arosiau, 29,500	F 3	Lubin, 31,900	C 3
asło, 17,800		Lublin, 254,700	F 3
astrzębie-Zdrój, 34,400	D 3	Lubliniec, 20,100	D 3
awon, 15,700	C 3	Luboń, 17,000	C 2
		Lubsko, 13,000	B 3
		Łuków, 16,300	F 2
		Malbork, 31,500	D 1
		Maków Mazowiecki, 7,694	E 2

Międzyrzec Podlaski, 13,800	F 3	Piekary Śląskie, 36,600	B 3
Międzyrzec, 15,200	B 2	Piła, 44,500	C 2
Mielec, 27,700	E 3	Pińczów, 7,080	E 3
Mików, 21,800	A 4	Pionki, 14,000	E 3
Mińsk Mazowiecki, 24,900	E 2	Piotrków Trybunalski, 60,800	D 3
Mława, 20,600	E 2	Pisz, 11,400	F 1
Mońki, 9,560	F 2	Pleszew, 13,700	C 3
Morąg, 9,681	E 1	Płock, 74,100	D 2
Mrągowo, 13,700	E 1	Płońsk, 11,900	E 2
Myślenice, 12,400	E 4	Police, 13,200	B 2
Mysłowice, 45,100	A 4	Polkowice, 10,600	C 3
Myszków, 18,300	D 3	Poznań, 495,200	C 2
Nakło nad Notecią, 17,000	C 2	Prudnik, 20,400	C 3
Namysłów, 11,200	C 3	Pruszcz Gdański, 13,100	D 1
Nidzica, 10,000	E 1	Pruszków, 43,500	E 2
Nisko, 10,200	F 3	Przasnysz, 11,400	E 2
Nowa Ruda, 18,300	C 3	Przemyśl, 53,800	F 4
Nowa Sól, 34,000	B 3	Puławy, 34,600	F 3
Nowy Dwór Gdański, 7,146	D 1	Pułtusk, 12,800	E 2
Nowy Dwór Mazowiecki, 17,200	E 2	Pyskowice, 23,300	A 3
Nowy Sącz, 42,100	E 4	Rabka, 10,800	D 4
Nowy Targ, 22,600	E 4	Racibórz, 40,600	C 3
Nysa, 33,100	C 3	Radlin, 23,100	B 4
Oborniki, 10,300	C 2	Radom, 166,000	E 3
Oława, 18,500	C 3	Radomsko, 31,600	D 3
Olecko, 9,120	F 1	Radziejów, 4,165	D 2
Oleśnica, 28,100	C 3	Radzionków, 28,200	A 3
Olkusz, 16,500	E 3	Rawicz, 14,600	C 3
Olsztyn, 104,300	E 2	Ruda Śląska, 146,200	A 4
Opatów, 9,784	E 3	Rumia, 23,800	D 1
Opoczno, 12,400	E 3	Rybnik, 44,000	B 4
Opole, 87,800	C 3	Rydułtowy, 19,500	D 3
Ostróda, 21,600	E 2	Rypin, 10,200	D 2
Ostrołęka, 23,000	F 2	Rzeszów, 83,900	F 4
Ostrów Mazowiecka, 15,200	F 2	Sandomierz, 17,300	F 4
Ostrów Wielkopolski, 50,300	C 3	Sanok, 22,100	F 4
Ostrowiec Świętokrzyski, 51,400	E 3	Siedlce, 39,600	F 2
Oświęcim, 40,200	D 3	Siemianowice Śląskie, 67,800	A 4
Otwock, 40,200	E 2	Sieradz, 19,000	D 3
Ozorków, 18,400	D 3	Sierpc, 12,900	D 2
Pabianice, 63,500	D 3	Skarżysko-Kamienna, 39,700	E 3
Parczew, 6,952	F 2	Skawina, 16,300	D 4
Pasłęk, 8,030	D 1	Skierniewice, 25,800	E 3
Piaseczno, 20,500	E 2	Sławno, 10,900	C 1
		Słubice, 12,200	B 2

Słupca, 8,634	D 2	Tuchola, 9,439	D 2
Słupsk, 69,900	C 1	Turek, 18,700	D 2
Sochaczew, 21,000	D 2	Tychy, 72,800	B 4
Sokółka, 10,300	F 2	Ursus, 30,900	D 2
Sokołów Podlaski, 9,569	F 2	Wąbrzeźno, 11,900	D 2
Solec Kujawski, 10,800	C 2	Wadowice, 12,000	D 4
Sopot, 48,500	D 1	Wągrowiec, 16,500	C 2
Sosnowiec, 148,300	B 4	Wałbrzych, 127,400	C 3
Śrem, 16,400	C 2	Wałcz, 20,900	C 2
Środa Wielkopolska, 15,000	C 2	Warszawa (Warszawa) (cap.), 1,377,100	E 2
Stalowa Wola, 31,100	F 3	Wejherowo, 34,600	C 1
Starachowice, 43,700	E 3	Wieliczka, 14,000	E 3
Stargard Szczeciński, 45,600	B 2	Wieluń, 14,900	D 3
Starogard Gdański, 34,200	D 1	Wieruszów, 3,650	D 3
Staszów, 8,449	E 3	Włocławek, 79,900	D 2
Strzegom, 14,400	C 3	Włodawa, 7,354	F 3
Strzelce Opolskie, 15,000	D 3	Wodzisław Śląski, 27,500	B 4
Strzemieszyce Wielkie, 11,500	B 4	Wołomin, 24,100	E 2
Sulechów, 10,500	B 2	Wołów, 10,600	C 3
Suwałki, 26,500	F 1	Wrocław, 557,200	C 3
Swarzędz, 12,200	C 2	Września, 18,400	C 2
Świdnica, 48,200	C 3	Wschowa, 10,100	C 3
Świdnik, 23,100	F 3	Wysokie Mazowieckie, 5,296	F 2
Świdwin, 10,100	B 1	Wyszków, 12,200	E 2
Świebodzice, 18,900	C 3	Ząbki, 16,200	E 2
Świebodzin, 15,200	B 2	Ząbkowice Śląskie, 14,400	C 3
Świecie, 18,300	D 2	Zabrze, 200,700	A 4
Świętochłowice, 57,200	A 4	Żagań, 21,700	B 3
Świnoujście, 28,800	A 2	Zagórze, 13,000	B 4
Szamotuły, 14,800	C 2	Zakopane, 27,200	E 4
Szczecin, 355,600	B 2	Zambrów, 14,500	F 2
Szczecinek, 29,500	C 2	Zamość, 35,600	F 3
Szczytno, 17,900	E 2	Zawiercie, 39,800	D 3
Szprotawa, 11,500	B 3	Zduńska Wola, 29,500	D 3
Szydłowiec, 6,240	E 3	Zgierz, 44,100	D 3
Tarnobrzeg, 21,300	E 3	Zgorzelec, 28,800	B 3
Tarnów, 87,200	E 4	Zielona Góra, 75,000	B 3
Tarnowskie Góry, 35,000	A 3	Złocieniec, 10,400	C 2
Tczew, 42,100	D 1	Złotoryja, 12,400	C 3
Tomaszów Lubelski, 12,800	F 3	Złotów, 12,100	C 2
Tomaszów Mazowiecki, 55,600	E 3	Zwoleń, 5,216	E 3
Toruń, 139,000	D 2	
Trzcianka, 11,200	C 2	
Trzebinia-Siersza, 19,600	C 4	

Żyrardów, 33,300	E 2
Żywiec, 22,900	D 4

OTHER FEATURES

Baltic (sea)	B 1
Beskids (mts.)	D 4
Brda (river)	C 2
Brynica (river)	B 3
Bug (river)	F 2
Danzig (gulf)	D 1
Dukla (pass)	E 4
Dunajec (river)	E 4
Hel (pen.)	D 1
High Tatra (mts.)	D 4
Kłodnica (river)	A 4
Łyna (river)	E 1
Mamry (lake)	F 1
Masurian (lakes)	E 2
Narew (river)	E 2
Neisse (river)	B 3
Noteć (river)	C 2
Nysa Kłodzka (river)	C 3
Nysa Łużycka (Neisse) (riv.)	B 3
Oder (Odra) (river)	B 2
Orava (res.)	D 3
Pilica (river)	D 3
Pomeranian (bay)	B 1
Prosna (river)	C 3
Przemsza (river)	B 4
Rysy (mt.)	D 4
San (river)	F 3
Słupia (river)	C 1
Śniardwy (lake)	E 2
Sudeten (mts.)	B 3
Uznam (Usedom) (isl.)	B 1
Vistula (river)	D 2
Warmia (reg.)	D 1
Warta (river)	B 2
Wieprz (river)	E 3
Wisła (Vistula) (river)	D 2
Wkra (river)	E 2
Wolin (isl.)	B 2

POLAND
CONIC PROJECTION

SCALE OF MILES
0 10 20 40 60 80

SCALE OF KILOMETERS
0 10 20 40 60 80

Capitals of Countries .... ★
Other Capitals .... ◉
International Boundaries ____
Internal Boundaries ....
Canals ....

Poland is divided into 49 provinces (bearing the same name as their capitals) and the autonomous cities of Warsaw, Łódź and Cracow.

© Copyright HAMMOND INCORPORATED, Maplewood, N.J.

UNION REPUBLICS

Armenian S.S.R., 2,491,900 ....E 6
Azerbaidzhan S.S.R.,
  5,117,100 ....E 5
Estonian S.S.R., 1,356,100 ......C 4
Georgian S.S.R., 4,686,000 .....D 5
Kazakh S.S.R., 14,185,000 ......F 5
Kirgiz S.S.R., 2,932,800 ....H 5
Latvian S.S.R., 2,364,100 ....C 4
Lithuanian S.S.R.,
  3,128,000 ....C 4
Moldavian S.S.R., 3,823,000 ...C 5
Russian S.F.S.R.,
  133,913,000 ....D 4
Tadzhik S.S.R., 2,900,000 ....H 6
Turkmen S.S.R., 2,158,880 .....F 6
Ukrainian S.S.R.,
  49,438,000 ....C 5
Uzbek S.S.R., 11,960,000 ....G 5
White Russian S.S.R.,
  9,522,000 ....C 4

INTERNAL DIVISIONS

Abkhaz A.S.S.R., 487,000 ....E 5
Adygey Aut. Oblast,
  385,000 ....D 5
Adzhar A.S.S.R., 310,000 ....D 5
Aginsk-Buryat Nat'l Okrug,
  66,000 ....M 4
Bashkir A.S.S.R., 3,818,000 ....F 4
Buryat A.S.S.R., 812,000 ....M 4
Chechen-Ingush A.S.S.R.,
  1,065,000 ....E 5

Chukchi Nat'l Okrug,
  101,000 ....R 3
Chuvash A.S.S.R.,
  1,224,000 ....E 4
Dagestan A.S.S.R.,
  1,429,000 ....E 5
Evenki Nat'l Okrug,
  13,000 ....K 3
Gorno-Altay Aut. Oblast,
  168,000 ....J 4
Gorno-Badakhshan Aut. Oblast,
  98,000 ....H 6
Jewish Aut. Oblast,
  172,000 ....O 5
Kabardin-Balkar A.S.S.R.,
  588,000 ....E 5
Kalmuck A.S.S.R.,
  268,000 ....E 5
Karachay-Cherkess Aut. Oblast,
  345,000 ....E 5
Karakalpak A.S.S.R.,
  702,000 ....G 5
Karelian A.S.S.R.,
  713,000 ....D 3
Khakass Aut. Oblast,
  446,000 ....J 4
Khanty-Mansi Nat'l Okrug,
  271,000 ....H 3
Komi A.S.S.R., 965,000 ....F 3
Komi-Permyak Nat'l Okrug,
  212,000 ....F 4
Koryak Nat'l Okrug,
  31,000 ....R 3
Mari A.S.S.R., 685,000 ....E 4
Mordvinian A.S.S.R.,
  1,029,000 ....E 4

Nagorno-Karabakh Aut. Oblast,
  150,000 ....E 5
Nakhichevan' A.S.S.R.,
  202,000 ....E 6
Nenets Nat'l Okrug, 39,000 ....F 3
North Ossetian A.S.S.R.,
  552,000 ....E 5
South Ossetian Aut. Oblast,
  99,000 ....E 5
Tatar A.S.S.R., 3,131,000 ....F 4
Taymyr Nat'l Okrug, 38,000 ....K 2
Tuvinian A.S.S.R., 231,000 ......K 4
Udmurt A.S.S.R., 1,418,000 .....F 4
Ust'-Ordynsk-Buryat Nat'l Okrug,
  146,000 ....L 4
Yakut A.S.S.R., 664,000 ....N 3
Yamal-Nenets Nat'l Okrug,
  80,000 ....H 3

CITIES and TOWNS

Abakan, 90,000 ....J 4
Achinsk, 97,000 ....K 4
Adimi ....O 5
Aginskoye, 9,000 ....M 4
Akmolinsk (Tselinograd),
  180,000 ....H 4
Aktyubinsk, 150,000 ....F 4
Aldan, 19,000 ....N 4
Aleksandrovsk-Sakhalinskiy,
  168,000 ....P 5
Aleysk, 32,000 ....J 4
Allah, 17,000 ....F 5
Allakh-Yun' ....O 3
Alma-Ata, 730,000 ....H 5

Ambarchik ....R 3
Amderma ....F 3
Anadyr, 15,000 ....S 3
Anadyr' 8,000 ....S 3
Andizhan, 188,000 ....H 5
Angarsk, 203,000 ....L 4
Anzhero-Sudzhensk,
  ....J 4
Aral'sk, 26,000 ....G 5
Archangel, 343,000 ....E 3
Arkalyk, 15,000 ....G 4
Armavir, 145,000 ....E 5
Artem, 61,000 ....O 5
Artemovskiy ....M 4
Arzamas, 67,000 ....E 4
Ashkhabad, 253,000 ....F 6
Ashkhabad, *256,000 ....F 6
Asino, 30,000 ....J 4
Astrakhan', 410,000 ....E 5
Atbasar, 41,000 ....G 4
Atka ....Q 3
Ayaguz, 40,000 ....J 5
Aykhal ....M 3
Aykhal ....M 4
Baku, 852,000 ....F 5
Baku, *1,266,000 ....F 5
Balashov, 83,000 ....E 4
Balkhash, 76,000 ....H 5
Balturino, 30,000 ....K 4
Barabinsk, 40,000 ....J 4
Baranovichi, 101,000 ....C 4
Barnaul, 439,000 ....J 4
Batumi, 101,000 ....E 5
Baykit ....K 3
Baykonur ....G 5

Bayram-Ali, 33,000 ....G 6
Belgorod, 151,000 ....D 4
Belomorsk, 57,000 ....D 3
Beloretsk, 67,000 ....F 4
Belovo, 108,000 ....J 4
Berdichev, 71,000 ....C 5
Berdsk, 53,000 ....J 4
Berezniki, 146,000 ....F 4
Berezovo, 6,000 ....G 4
Beringovskiy ....T 3
Bilibino, 13,000 ....R 3
Birobidzhan, 56,000 ....O 5
Biysk, 186,000 ....J 4
Blagoveshchensk,
  128,000 ....N 4
Bobruysk, 138,000 ....C 4
Bodaybo, 19,000 ....M 4
Borisoglebsk, 64,000 ....E 4
Borzya, 28,000 ....M 4
Boschakul' ....H 4
Bratsk, 155,000 ....L 4
Brest, 122,000 ....C 4
Bryansk, 318,000 ....D 4
Bugul'ma, 72,000 ....F 4
Bukhara, 112,000 ....G 5
Bulun ....N 2
Buzuluk, 67,000 ....F 4
Chagda ....O 4
Chapayevo ....O 3
Chapayevsk, 86,000 ....F 4
Chardzhou, 96,000 ....G 6
Cheboksary, 216,000 ....E 4
Chelkar, 25,000 ....F 5
Chelyabinsk,
  875,000 ....G 4

Cheremkhovo, 99,000 ....L 4
Cherepovets, 188,000 ....D 4
Cherkessk, 67,000 ....E 5
Chernigov, 159,000 ....D 4
Chernovtsy, 187,000 ....C 5
Chernyshevsk, 10,000 ....M 4
Chernyshevskiy,
  10,000 ....M 3
Cherskiy ....Q 3
Chimbay, 20,000 ....G 5
Chimkent, 247,000 ....G 5
Chirchik, 107,000 ....H 5
Chita, 241,000 ....M 4
Chokurdakh ....P 2
Chul'man ....N 4
Chumikan ....O 4
Dalnegorsk, 33,500 ....O 5
Dalnerechensk, 30,000 ....O 5
Daugavpils, 100,400 ....C 4
Dikson ....J 2
Dimitrovgrad, 81,000 ....F 4
Dneropetrovsk,
  862,000 ....D 5
Dolinsk, 18,000 ....P 5
Donetsk, 879,000 ....D 5
Drogobych, 56,000 ....C 5
Druzhina ....P 3
Dudinka, 22,000 ....J 3
Dushanbe, 376,000 ....G 6
Dzerzhinsk, 221,000 ....E 4
Dzhalal-Abad, 44,000 ....H 5
Dzhalinda ....N 4
Dzhambul, 187,000 ....H 5
Dzhetygara, 39,000 ....G 4
Dzhezkazgan, 62,000 ....G 5
Ekibastuz, 46,000 ....H 4

Ekimchan ....O ...
El'dikan ....O ...
Eliista, 50,000 ....E ...
Engel's, 130,000 ....E ...
Erivan, 767,000 ....E ...
Evensk ....Q ...
Fergana, 111,000 ....H ...
Fort-Shevchenko,
  12,000 ....F ...
Frolovo, 30,000 ....E ...
Frunze, 430,600 ....H ...
Gasan-Kuli ....F ...
Gizhiga ....Q ...
Gol'chikha ....J ...
Gomel', 272,000 ....D ...
Gor'kiy, 1,170,000 ....E ...
Gorno-Altaysk,
  34,000 ....J ...
Grodno, 132,000 ....C ...
Groznyy, 341,000 ....E ...
Gubakha, 40,000 ....F ...
Gulistan, 31,000 ....G ...
Gur'yev, 114,000 ....F ...
Gusinoözersk, 10,000 ....L ...
Gydy ....H ...
Igarka, 22,000 ....J ...
Ilanskiy, 24,000 ....K ...
Iliysk, 17,000 ....H ...
Indiga ....F ...
Inta, 50,000 ....F ...
Iolotan', 10,000 ....G ...
Irkutsk, 451,000 ....L ...
Ishim, 56,000 ....G ...
Ishimbay, 54,000 ....F ...
Isil'-Kul', 26,000 ....H ...
Ivano-Frankovsk, 105,000 ......C ...

ADMINISTRATIVE DIVISIONS NOT NAMED ON MAP

Division	Ref.	Division	Ref.
1. Abkhaz A.S.S.R.	E5	13. Khakass Aut. Oblast	J4
2. Adygey Aut. Oblast	D5	14. Komi-Permyak Nat'l Okrug	F4
3. Adzhar A.S.S.R.	D5	15. Mari A.S.S.R.	E4
4. Aginsk-Buryat Nat'l Okrug	M4	16. Mordvinian A.S.S.R.	E4
5. Chechen-Ingush A.S.S.R.	E5	17. Nagorno-Karabakh Aut. Oblast	E5
6. Chuvash A.S.S.R.	E4	18. Nakhichevan' A.S.S.R.	E5
7. Gorno-Altay Aut. Oblast	J4	19. North Ossetian A.S.S.R.	E5
8. Gorno-Badakhshan Aut. Oblast	H6	20. South Ossetian Aut. Oblast	E5
9. Jewish Aut. Oblast	O5	21. Tatar A.S.S.R.	F4
10. Kabardin-Balkar A.S.S.R.	E5	22. Tuvinian A.S.S.R.	K4
11. Karachay-Cherkess Aut. Oblast	E5	23. Udmurt A.S.S.R.	F4
12. Karakalpak A.S.S.R.	G5	24. Ust'-Ordynsk-Buryat Nat'l Okrug	L4

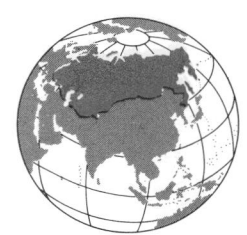

AREA 8,649,490 sq. mi.
POPULATION 258,402,000
CAPITAL Moscow
LARGEST CITY Moscow
HIGHEST POINT Communism Peak 24,590 ft.
MONETARY UNIT ruble
MAJOR LANGUAGES Russian, Ukrainian, White Russian, Uzbek, Azerbaidzhani, Tatar, Georgian, Lithuanian, Armenian, Yiddish, Latvian, Mordvinian, Kirgiz, Tadzhik, Estonian, Kazakh, Moldavian, German, Chuvash, Turkmenian, Bashkir
MAJOR RELIGIONS Eastern (Russian) Orthodoxy, Islam, Judaism, Protestantism (Baltic States)

UNION REPUBLICS

	AREA (sq. mi.)	POPULATION	CAPITAL and LARGEST CITY
RUSSIAN S.F.S.R.	6,592,812	133,913,000	Moscow 7,632,000
KAZAKH S.S.R.	1,048,300	14,185,000	Alma-Ata 836,000
UKRAINIAN S.S.R.	233,089	49,438,000	Kiev 1,947,000
TURKMEN S.S.R.	188,455	2,158,880	Ashkhabad 280,000
UZBEK S.S.R.	173,591	11,960,000	Tashkent 1,595,000
WHITE RUSSIAN S.S.R.	80,154	9,522,000	Minsk 1,147,000
KIRGIZ S.S.R.	76,641	2,932,800	Frunze 474,000
TADZHIK S.S.R.	55,251	2,900,000	Dushanbe 422,000
AZERBAIDZHAN S.S.R.	33,436	5,117,100	Baku 1,383,000
GEORGIAN S.S.R.	26,911	4,686,000	Tbilisi 1,006,000
LITHUANIAN S.S.R.	25,174	3,128,000	Vilna 420,000
LATVIAN S.S.R.	24,595	2,364,100	Riga 796,000
ESTONIAN S.S.R.	17,413	1,356,100	Tallinn 392,000
MOLDAVIAN S.S.R.	13,012	3,823,000	Kishinev 432,000
ARMENIAN S.S.R	11,506	2,491,900	Erivan 899,000

Topography

(continued on following page)

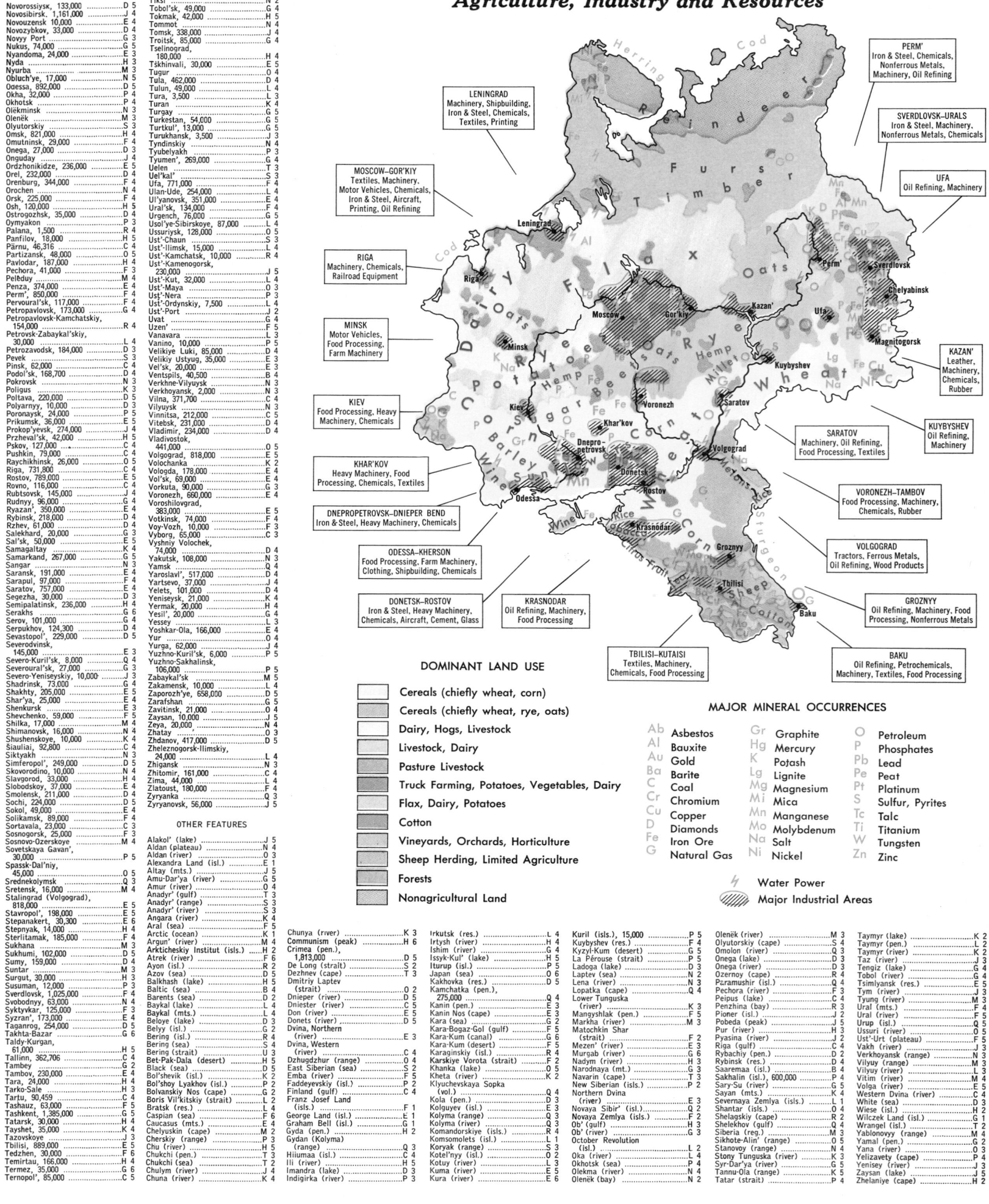

Agriculture, Industry and Resources

Map labels

PERM'
Iron & Steel, Chemicals, Nonferrous Metals, Machinery, Oil Refining

SVERDLOVSK–URALS
Iron & Steel, Machinery, Nonferrous Metals, Chemicals

UFA
Oil Refining, Machinery

LENINGRAD
Machinery, Shipbuilding, Iron & Steel, Chemicals, Textiles, Printing

MOSCOW–GOR'KIY
Textiles, Machinery, Motor Vehicles, Iron & Steel, Aircraft, Printing, Oil Refining

KAZAN'
Leather, Machinery, Chemicals, Rubber

RIGA
Machinery, Chemicals, Railroad Equipment

MINSK
Motor Vehicles, Food Processing, Farm Machinery

KIEV
Food Processing, Heavy Machinery, Chemicals

KUYBYSHEV
Oil Refining, Machinery

SARATOV
Machinery, Oil Refining, Food Processing, Textiles

KHAR'KOV
Heavy Machinery, Food Processing, Chemicals, Textiles

VORONEZH–TAMBOV
Food Processing, Machinery, Chemicals, Rubber

DNEPROPETROVSK–DNIEPER BEND
Iron & Steel, Heavy Machinery, Chemicals

VOLGOGRAD
Tractors, Ferrous Metals, Oil Refining, Wood Products

ODESSA–KHERSON
Food Processing, Farm Machinery, Clothing, Shipbuilding, Chemicals

GROZNYY
Oil Refining, Machinery, Food Processing, Nonferrous Metals

DONETSK–ROSTOV
Iron & Steel, Heavy Machinery, Chemicals, Aircraft, Cement, Glass

KRASNODAR
Oil Refining, Machinery, Food Processing

TBILISI–KUTAISI
Textiles, Machinery, Chemicals, Food Processing

BAKU
Oil Refining, Petrochemicals, Machinery, Textiles, Food Processing

DOMINANT LAND USE

- Cereals (chiefly wheat, corn)
- Cereals (chiefly wheat, rye, oats)
- Dairy, Hogs, Livestock
- Livestock, Dairy
- Pasture Livestock
- Truck Farming, Potatoes, Vegetables, Dairy
- Flax, Dairy, Potatoes
- Cotton
- Vineyards, Orchards, Horticulture
- Sheep Herding, Limited Agriculture
- Forests
- Nonagricultural Land

MAJOR MINERAL OCCURRENCES

Ab	Asbestos	Gr	Graphite	O	Petroleum
Al	Bauxite	Hg	Mercury	P	Phosphates
Au	Gold	K	Potash	Pb	Lead
Ba	Barite	Lg	Lignite	Pe	Peat
C	Coal	Mg	Magnesium	Pt	Platinum
Cr	Chromium	Mi	Mica	S	Sulfur, Pyrites
Cu	Copper	Mn	Manganese	Tc	Talc
D	Diamonds	Mo	Molybdenum	Ti	Titanium
Fe	Iron Ore	Na	Salt	W	Tungsten
G	Natural Gas	Ni	Nickel	Zn	Zinc

⚡ Water Power

▨ Major Industrial Areas

Agriculture, Industry and Resources

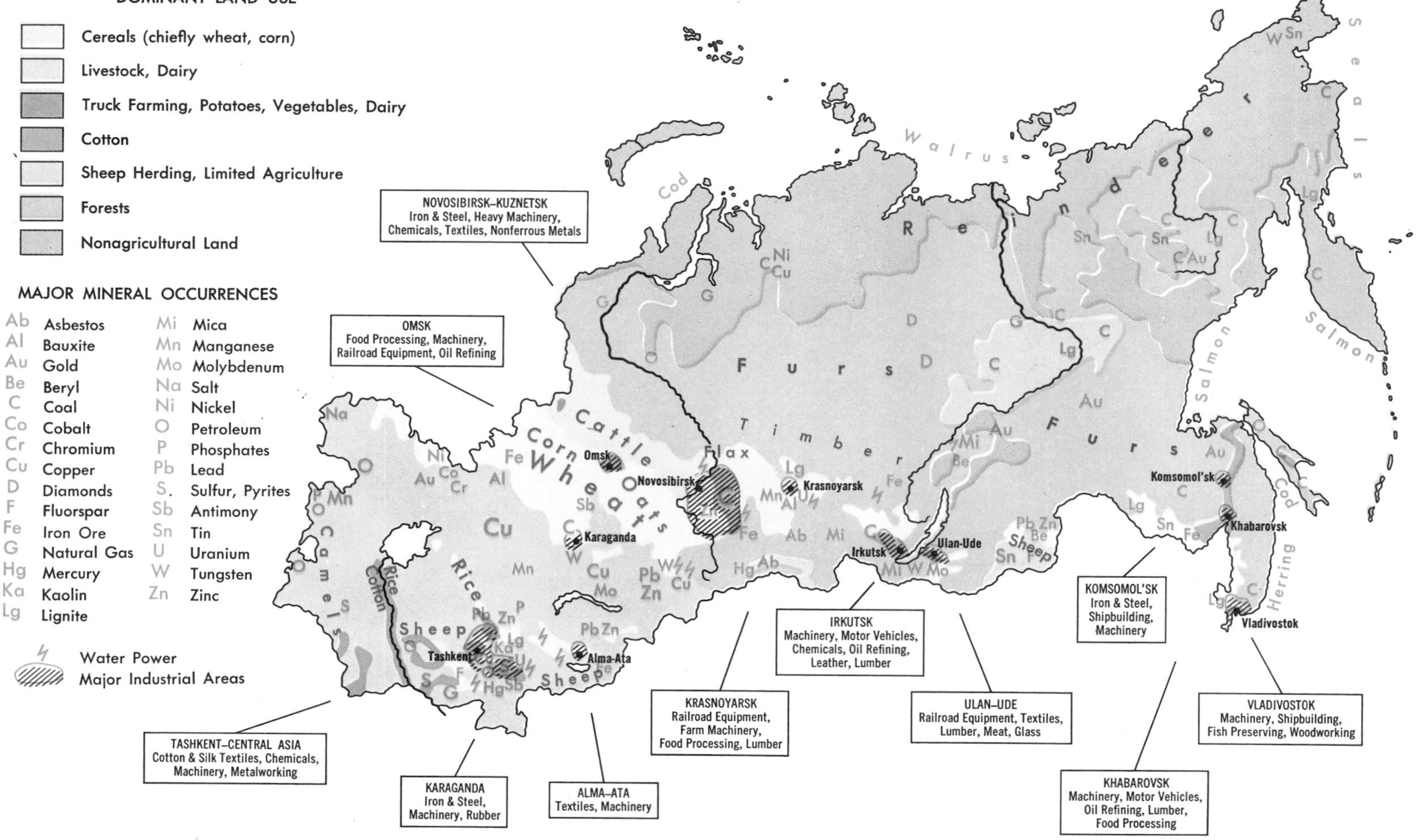
DOMINANT LAND USE
Cereals (chiefly wheat, corn)
Livestock, Dairy
Truck Farming, Potatoes, Vegetables, Dairy
Cotton
Sheep Herding, Limited Agriculture
Forests
Nonagricultural Land
MAJOR MINERAL OCCURRENCES
Ab Asbestos
Al Bauxite
Au Gold
Be Beryl
C Coal
Co Cobalt
Cr Chromium
Cu Copper
D Diamonds
F Fluorspar
Fe Iron Ore
G Natural Gas
Hg Mercury
Ka Kaolin
Lg Lignite
Mi Mica
Mn Manganese
Mo Molybdenum
Na Salt
Ni Nickel
O Petroleum
P Phosphates
Pb Lead
S. Sulfur, Pyrites
Sb Antimony
Sn Tin
U Uranium
W Tungsten
Zn Zinc
Water Power
Major Industrial Areas
NOVOSIBIRSK-KUZNETSK
Iron & Steel, Heavy Machinery, Chemicals, Textiles, Nonferrous Metals
OMSK
Food Processing, Machinery, Railroad Equipment, Oil Refining
TASHKENT-CENTRAL ASIA
Cotton & Silk Textiles, Chemicals, Machinery, Metalworking
KARAGANDA
Iron & Steel, Machinery, Rubber
ALMA-ATA
Textiles, Machinery
KRASNOYARSK
Railroad Equipment, Farm Machinery, Food Processing, Lumber
IRKUTSK
Machinery, Motor Vehicles, Chemicals, Oil Refining, Leather, Lumber
ULAN-UDE
Railroad Equipment, Textiles, Lumber, Meat, Glass
KOMSOMOL'SK
Iron & Steel, Shipbuilding, Machinery
KHABAROVSK
Machinery, Motor Vehicles, Oil Refining, Lumber, Food Processing
VLADIVOSTOK
Machinery, Shipbuilding, Fish Preserving, Woodworking
Walrus
Reindeer
Seals
Salmon
Cod
Herring
Furs
Timber
Flax
Cattle
Corn
Wheat
Oats
Rice
Cotton
Camels
Sheep
Omsk
Novosibirsk
Krasnoyarsk
Karaganda
Irkutsk
Ulan-Ude
Komsomol'sk
Khabarovsk
Vladivostok
Tashkent
Alma-Ata

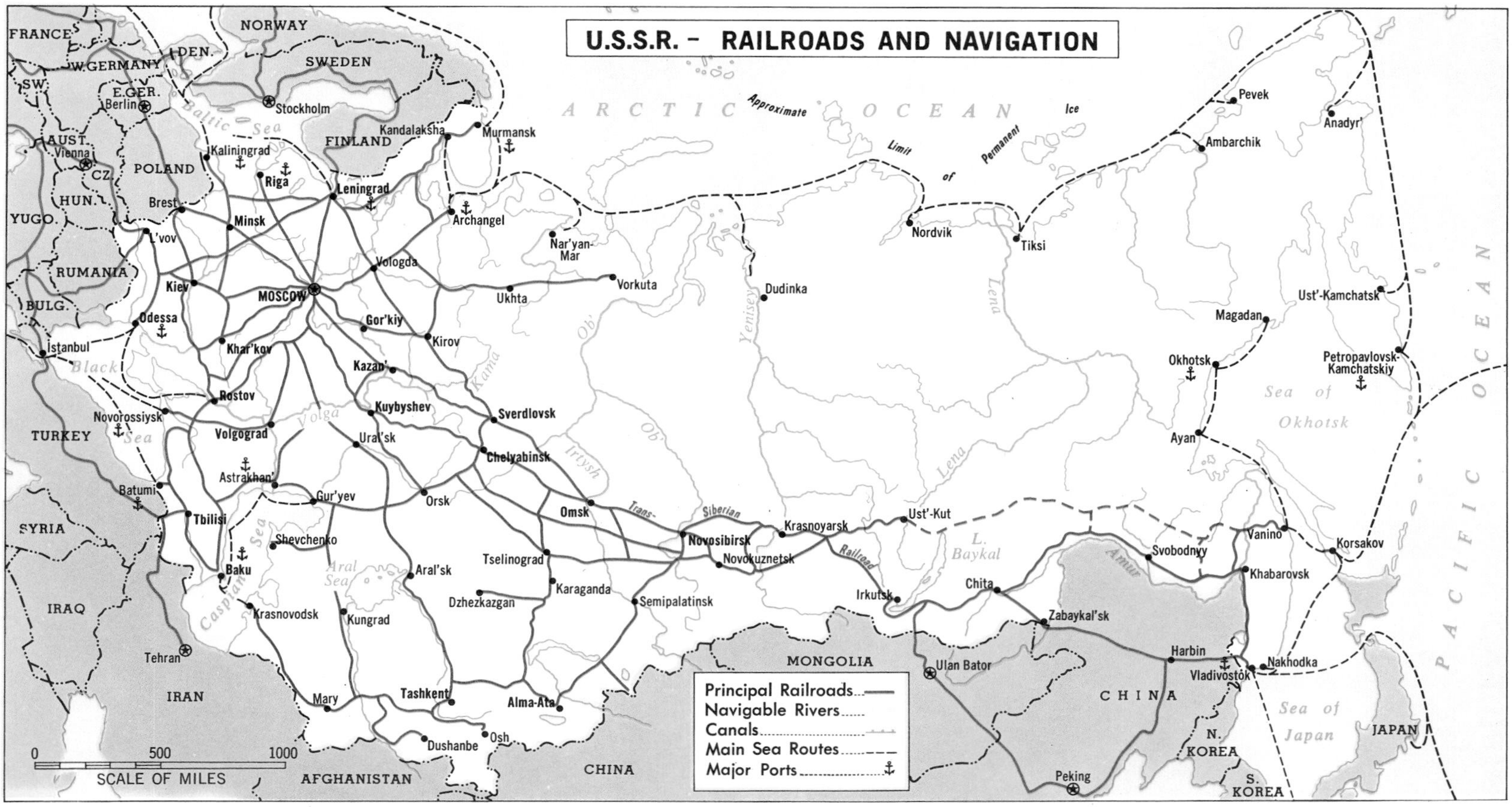
U.S.S.R. - RAILROADS AND NAVIGATION
ARCTIC OCEAN
Approximate Limit of Permanent Ice
PACIFIC OCEAN
Sea of Okhotsk
Sea of Japan
Baltic Sea
Black Sea
Caspian Sea
Aral Sea
L. Baykal
FRANCE
W.GERMANY
E.GER.
DEN.
NORWAY
SWEDEN
FINLAND
POLAND
AUST.
CZ.
SW.
HUN.
YUGO.
RUMANIA
BULG.
TURKEY
SYRIA
IRAQ
IRAN
AFGHANISTAN
CHINA
MONGOLIA
N. KOREA
S. KOREA
JAPAN
Berlin
Stockholm
Vienna
Kaliningrad
Riga
Leningrad
Murmansk
Kandalaksha
Archangel
Minsk
Brest
L'vov
Kiev
Odessa
Istanbul
Khar'kov
MOSCOW
Vologda
Gor'kiy
Kirov
Kazan'
Rostov
Novorossiysk
Volgograd
Kuybyshev
Astrakhan'
Batumi
Tbilisi
Baku
Ural'sk
Gur'yev
Shevchenko
Krasnovodsk
Kungrad
Tehran
Mary
Dushanbe
Tashkent
Osh
Alma-Ata
Aral'sk
Orsk
Sverdlovsk
Chelyabinsk
Omsk
Tselinograd
Karaganda
Dzhezkazgan
Semipalatinsk
Novosibirsk
Novokuznetsk
Krasnoyarsk
Irkutsk
Ust'-Kut
Chita
Ulan Bator
Zabaykal'sk
Harbin
Peking
Svobodnyy
Khabarovsk
Vanino
Korsakov
Vladivostok
Nakhodka
Ayan
Okhotsk
Magadan
Petropavlovsk-Kamchatskiy
Ust'-Kamchatsk
Anadyr'
Pevek
Ambarchik
Tiksi
Nordvik
Dudinka
Nar'yan-Mar
Ukhta
Vorkuta
Ob'
Yenisey
Lena
Irtysh
Kama
Volga
Amur
Trans-Siberian Railroad
Principal Railroads
Navigable Rivers
Canals
Main Sea Routes
Major Ports
0 500 1000
SCALE OF MILES

(continued on following page)

UNION OF SOVIET SOCIALIST REPUBLICS
European Part

CONIC PROJECTION

SCALE OF MILES

SCALE OF KILOMETRES

National Capitals	☆
Capitals of Union Republics	⌂
Administrative Centers	△
International boundaries	
Union Republic boundaries	
A.S.S.R., Oblast, Kray boundaries	
Autonomous Oblast boundaries	
National Okrug boundaries	
Canals	

The government of the United States has not recognized the incorporation of Estonia, Latvia and Lithuania into the Soviet Union, nor does it recognize as final the de facto western limit of Polish administration in Germany (the Oder-Neisse line).

Administrative Divisions bear same names as their respective Capitals or Centers, except:

Abkhaz A.S.S.R.	Sukhumi	F6
Adygey Aut. Oblast	Maykop	F6
Adzhar A.S.S.R.	Batumi	F6
Bashkir A.S.S.R.	Ufa	J4
Chechen-Ingush A.S.S.R.	Groznyy	G6
Chuvash A.S.S.R.	Cheboksary	G3
Crimean Oblast	Simferopol'	D6
Dagestan A.S.S.R.	Makhachkala	G6
Kabardin-Balkar A.S.S.R.	Nal'chik	F6
Kalmuck A.S.S.R.	Elista	F5
Karachay-Cherkess Aut. Obl.	Cherkessk	F6
Karelian A.S.S.R.	Petrozavodsk	D2
Komi A.S.S.R.	Syktyvkar	H2
Komi-Permyak Nat'l Okrug	Kudymkar	H3
Mari A.S.S.R.	Yoshkar-Ola	G3
Mordvinian A.S.S.R.	Saransk	G4
Nagorno-Karabakh Aut. Obl.	Stepanakert	G7
Nenets Nat'l Okrug	Nar'yan-Mar	H1
North Ossetian A.S.S.R.	Ordzhonikidze	F6
South Ossetian Aut. Obl.	Tskhinvali	F6
Tatar A.S.S.R.	Kazan'	G3
Trans-Carpathian Oblast	Uzhgorod	B5
Udmurt A.S.S.R.	Izhevsk	H3
Volyn Oblast	Lutsk	C4

U.S.S.R. - EUROPEAN

UNION REPUBLICS

Armenian S.S.R., 2,491,900 ... F 6
Azerbaidzhan S.S.R., 5,117,100 ... G 6
Estonian S.S.R., 1,356,100 ... C 3
Georgian S.S.R., 4,686,000 ... F 6
Latvian S.S.R., 2,364,100 ... B 3
Lithuanian S.S.R., 3,128,000 ... B 3
Moldavian S.S.R., 3,823,000 ... C 5
Russian S.F.S.R., 133,913,000 ... F 3
Ukrainian S.S.R., 49,438,000 ... D 5
White Russian S.S.R., 9,522,000 ... C 4

INTERNAL DIVISIONS

Abkhaz A.S.S.R., 487,000 ... F 6
Adygey Aut. Oblast, 385,000 ... F 6
Adzhar A.S.S.R., 310,000 ... F 6
Bashkir A.S.S.R., 3,818,000 ... J 4
Chechen-Ingush A.S.S.R., 1,065,000 ... G 6
Chuvash A.S.S.R., 1,224,000 ... G 3
Crimean Oblast, 1,813,000 ... D 6
Dagestan A.S.S.R., 1,429,000 ... G 6
Kabardin-Balkar A.S.S.R., 588,000 ... F 6
Kalmuck A.S.S.R., 268,000 ... F 5
Karachay-Cherkess Aut. Oblast, 345,000 ... F 6
Karelian A.S.S.R., 713,000 ... D 2
Komi A.S.S.R., 965,000 ... H 2
Komi-Permyak Nat'l Okrug, 212,000 ... H 3
Mari A.S.S.R., 685,000 ... G 3
Mordvinian A.S.S.R., 1,029,000 ... G 4
Nagorno-Karabakh Aut. Oblast, 150,000 ... G 7
Nakhichevan' A.S.S.R., 202,000 ... F 7
Nenets Nat'l Okrug, 39,000 ... H 1
North Ossetian A.S.S.R., 552,000 ... F 6
South Ossetian Aut. Oblast, 99,000 ... F 6
Tatar A.S.S.R., 3,131,000 ... G 3
Trans-Carpathian Oblast, 1,057,000 ... B 5
Udmurt A.S.S.R., 1,418,000 ... H 3
Volyn Oblast, 974,000 ... C 4

CITIES and TOWNS

Abdulino, 27,000 ... H 4
Agdam, 21,300 ... G 6
Agryz, 21,000 ... H 3
Akhaltsikhe, 20,000 ... F 6
Akhtubinsk, 33,000 ... G 5
Akhtyrka, 42,000 ... E 4
Alagir, 18,000 ... F 6
Alatyr', 47,000 ... G 4
Aleksandriya, 69,000 ... D 5
Alekseyevka, 24,000 ... E 4
Aleksin, 61,000 ... E 4
Ali-Bayramly, 33,900 ... G 7
Al'met'yevsk, 87,000 ... H 3
Alushta, 21,000 ... D 6
Anapa, 25,000 ... E 6
Apatity, 40,000 ... D 1
Apsheronsk, 36,000 ... F 6
Archangel (Arkhangel'sk), 343,000 ... F 2
Armavir, 145,000 ... F 5
Arzamas, 67,000 ... F 3
Astrakhan', 410,000 ... G 5
Atkarsk, 30,000 ... G 4
Azov, 59,000 ... E 5
Bakhchisaray, 12,000 ... D 6
Bakhmach, 14,000 ... D 4
Baku, 852,000 ... H 6
Baku, *1,266,000 ... H 6
Balakhna, 36,000 ... F 3
Balaklava, 5,000 ... D 6
Balakovo, 103,000 ... G 4
Balashoy, 83,000 ... F 4
Baltiysk, 18,000 ... A 4
Baranovichi, 101,000 ... C 4
Barysh, 21,000 ... G 4
Bataysk, 85,000 ... E 5
Batumi, 101,000 ... F 6
Belaya Tserkov', 109,000 ... C 5
Belebey, 35,000 ... H 4
Belev, 18,000 ... E 4
Belgorod, 151,000 ... E 4
Belgorod-Dnestrovskiy, 30,000 ... D 5
Belomorsk, 18,000 ... D 2
Beloretsk, 67,000 ... J 4
Bel'tsy, 101,800 ... C 5
Bendery, 72,300 ... C 5
Berdichev, 71,000 ... C 5
Berdyansk, 100,000 ... E 5
Beregovo, 30,000 ... B 5
Berezniki, 146,000 ... J 3
Beslan, 28,000 ... F 6
Bezhetsk, 31,000 ... E 3
Birsk, 36,000 ... J 3
Blagoveshchensk, 15,000 ... J 4
Bobruysk, 138,000 ... C 4
Bologoye, 32,000 ... D 3
Bor, 55,000 ... F 3
Borislav, 36,000 ... B 5
Borisoglebsk, 64,000 ... F 4
Borisov, 84,000 ... C 4
Borovichi, 55,000 ... D 3
Borzhomi, 17,000 ... F 6
Brest, 122,000 ... B 4
Bryansk, 318,000 ... D 4
Bugul'ma, 72,000 ... H 4
Buguruslan, 49,000 ... H 4
Buy, 25,000 ... F 3
Buynaksk, 41,000 ... G 6
Buzuluk, 67,000 ... H 4
Bykhov, 16,000 ... C 4
Cēsis, 17,700 ... C 3
Chadyr-Lunga, 20,200 ... C 5
Chapayevsk, 86,000 ... G 4
Chaykovskiy, 48,000 ... H 3
Cheboksary, 216,000 ... G 3
Cherepovets, 188,000 ... E 3
Cherkassy, 158,000 ... D 5
Cherkessk, 67,000 ... F 6
Chernigov, 159,000 ... D 4
Chernovtsy, 187,000 ... C 5
Chervonograd, 41,000 ... B 4
Chiatura, 30,000 ... F 6
Chistopol', 60,000 ... H 3
Chkalov (Orenburg), 344,000 ... J 4
Chortkov, 21,000 ... B 5
Chusovoy, 58,000 ... J 3
Danilov, 17,000 ... E 3
Daugavpils, 100,400 ... C 3
Davlekanovo, 22,000 ... H 4
Derbent, 57,000 ... G 6
Dimitrovgrad, 81,000 ... G 4
Dneprodzerzhinsk, 227,000 ... D 5
Dnepropetrovsk, 862,000 ... D 5
Dobrush, 17,000 ... D 4
Donetsk, 879,000 ... E 5
Drogobych, 56,000 ... B 5
Dubna, 43,700 ... E 3
Dubna, 8,000 ... E 4
Dvinsk (Daugavpils), 100,400 ... C 3
Dzerzhinsk, 221,000 ... F 3
Dzhankoy, 42,000 ... D 5
Elektrostal', 123,100 ... E 3
Elista, 50,000 ... F 5
Engel's, 130,000 ... G 4
Erivan, 767,000 ... F 6
Ertil', 20,000 ... F 4
Fastov, 42,000 ... C 4
Feodosiya, 65,000 ... D 5
Frolovo, 30,000 ... F 5
Furmanov, 44,000 ... F 3
Gagarin, 15,000 ... D 3
Gagra, 23,000 ... E 6
Galich, 20,000 ... F 3
Gandzha (Kirovabad), 189,800 ... G 6
Gatchina, 63,000 ... D 3
Gay, 35,000 ... J 4
Gaysin, 23,000 ... C 5
Gelendzhik, 24,000 ... E 6
Genichesk, 19,000 ... E 5
Georgiu-Dezh, 48,000 ... E 4
Glazov, 68,000 ... H 3
Glukhov, 30,000 ... D 4
Gomel', 272,000 ... D 4
Gori, 45,000 ... F 6
Gorki, 24,000 ... D 4
Gor'kiy, 1,170,000 ... F 3
Gorlovka, 335,000 ... E 5
Gornyatskiy, 30,000 ... K 1
Gorodets, 34,000 ... F 3
Gremyachinsk, 34,000 ... J 3
Grodno, 132,000 ... B 4
Groznyy, 341,000 ... G 6
Gryazi, 40,000 ... F 4
Gubakha, 40,000 ... J 3
Gubkin, 54,000 ... E 4
Gudauta, 14,000 ... F 6
Gukovo, 65,000 ... F 5
Gus'-Khrustal'nyy, 65,000 ... F 3
Ichnya, 14,000 ... D 4
Inta, 50,000 ... K 1
Inza, 20,000 ... G 4
Ishimbay, 54,000 ... J 4
Ivano-Frankovsk, 105,000 ... B 5
Ivanovo, 420,000 ... E 3
Izhevsk, 422,000 ... H 3
Izmail, 70,000 ... C 5
Izyum, 52,000 ... E 5
Jelgava, 55,300 ... B 3
Kadiyevka, 137,000 ... E 5
Kagul, 26,000 ... C 5
Kakhovka, 25,000 ... D 5
Kalach, 23,000 ... F 5
Kalinin, 345,000 ... E 3
Kaliningrad, 297,000 ... B 4
Kaliningrad, 105,900 ... E 3
Kalinkovichi, 22,000 ... C 4
Kaluga, 211,000 ... E 4
Kamenets-Podol'skiy, 57,000 ... C 5
Kamenka, 30,000 ... F 4
Kamensk-Shakhtinskiy, 68,000 ... F 5
Kamyshin, 97,000 ... F 4
Kanash, 45,000 ... G 3
Kandalaksha, 42,000 ... D 1
Kapsukas, 28,700 ... B 4
Kashin, 19,000 ... E 3
Kasimov, 37,000 ... F 4
Kaspiysk, 39,000 ... G 6
Kaunas, 306,200 ... B 4
Kazan', 869,000 ... G 3
Kazatin, 28,000 ... C 5
Kem', 21,000 ... D 2
Kerch', 128,000 ... E 5
Khachmas, 22,300 ... G 6
Khar'kov, 1,223,000 ... E 5
Khasavyurt, 54,000 ... G 6
Kherson, 261,000 ... D 5
Khmel'nitskiy, 113,000 ... C 5
Khorol, 13,000 ... D 5
Khvalynsk, 19,000 ... G 4
Kiev, 1,632,000 ... D 4
Kiliya, 26,000 ... C 5
Kimovsk, 44,000 ... E 4
Kimry, 53,000 ... E 3
Kinel', 38,000 ... H 4
Kineshma, 96,000 ... F 3
Kirov, 30,000 ... D 4
Kirov, 333,000 ... G 3
Kirovabad, 189,800 ... G 6
Kirovakan, 107,000 ... G 6
Kirovo-Chepetsk, 51,000 ... H 3
Kirovograd, 189,000 ... D 5
Kirovsk, 48,000 ... D 1
Kirsanov, 24,000 ... F 4
Kishinev, 356,900 ... C 5
Kislovodsk, 90,000 ... F 6
Kizel, 49,000 ... J 3
Kizlyar, 30,000 ... G 6
Klaipėda, 139,900 ... B 3
Klimovichi, 13,000 ... D 4
Klintsy, 58,000 ... D 4
Kobrin, 25,000 ... B 4
Kobuleti, 18,000 ... F 6
Kohtla-Järve, 68,318 ... C 3
Kolomna, 135,900 ... E 4
Kolpino, 70,000 ... D 3
Kommunarsk, 123,000 ... E 5
Komrat, 21,400 ... C 5
Kondopoga, 25,000 ... D 2
Königsberg (Kaliningrad), 297,000 ... B 4
Konotop, 68,000 ... D 4
Konstantinovka, 105,000 ... E 5
Korosten', 56,000 ... C 4
Kostroma, 223,000 ... F 3
Kotel'nich, 30,000 ... G 3
Kotel'nikovo, 21,000 ... F 5
Kotlas, 56,000 ... G 2
Kotovo, 20,000 ... G 4
Kotovsk, 38,000 ... C 5
Kotovsk, 32,000 ... F 4
Kovel', 35,000 ... C 4
Kovrov, 123,000 ... F 3
Kramatorsk, 150,000 ... E 5
Krasnoarmeysk, 21,000 ... G 4
Krasnodar, 464,000 ... E 6
Krasnograd, 18,000 ... E 5
Krasnokamsk, 55,000 ... H 3
Krasnovishersk, 16,000 ... J 2
Krasnyy Kut, 17,000 ... G 4
Krasnyy Luch, 103,000 ... E 5
Kremenchug, 148,000 ... D 5
Krichev, 26,000 ... D 4
Krivoy Rog, 573,000 ... D 5
Krolevets, 18,000 ... D 4
Kropotkin, 68,000 ... F 5
Krymsk, 44,000 ... E 6
Kuba, 18,900 ... G 6
Kudymkar, 20,000 ... H 3
Kulebaki, 48,000 ... F 3
Kumertau, 42,000 ... J 4
Kungur, 74,000 ... J 3
Kupyansk, 28,000 ... E 5
Kursk, 284,000 ... E 4
Kutaisi, 161,000 ... F 6

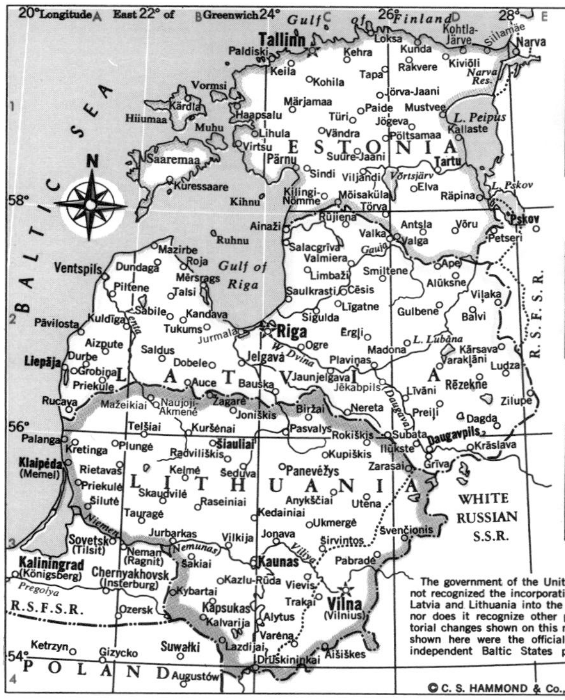

The government of the United States has not recognized the incorporation of Estonia, Latvia and Lithuania into the Soviet Union, nor does it recognize other post-war territorial changes shown on this map. The flags shown here were the official flags of the independent Baltic States prior to 1939.

© C. S. HAMMOND & Co., Maplewood, N. J.

ESTONIA

LATVIA

LITHUANIA

THE BALTIC STATES

SCALE OF MILES
0 25 50 75 100
SCALE OF KILOMETRES
0 30 60 90 120 150 180

Capitals ... ☆
International Boundaries ... —·—
Union Republic Boundaries ... —·—
Prewar boundaries of the Baltic States where divergent from present boundaries ... .

THE BALTIC STATES

Alytus, 27,900 ... C 3
Biržai, 11,400 ... C 2
Cēsis, 17,700 ... C 2
Daugava (Western Dvina) (riv.) ... C 2
Daugavpils, 100,400 ... D 3
Dobele, 10,100 ... B 2
Druskininkai, 11,200 ... C 3
Dvina, Western (river) ... C 2
Finland (gulf) ... D 1
Gauja (riv.) ... C 2
Haapsalu, 11,483 ... B 1
Hiiumaa (isl.) ... B 1
Jēkabpils, 22,400 ... C 2
Jelgava, 55,300 ... B 2
Jonava, 14,400 ... C 3
Jurmala, 53,800 ... B 2
Kapsukas, 28,700 ... B 3
Kaunas (cap.), Lithuania, 306,200 ... C 3
Kedainiai, 19,700 ... C 3
Kihnu (isl.) ... B 1
Kingisepp (Kuressaare), 12,140 ... B 1
Kivioli, 11,153 ... D 1
Klaipėda, 139,900 ... A 3
Kohtla-Järve, 68,318 ... D 1
Kretinga, 13,000 ... A 3
Kuldīga, 12,300 ... A 2
Kuressaare, 12,140 ... B 1
Kuršėnai, 11,500 ... B 2
Liepāja, 92,800 ... A 2
Lubāna (lake) ... D 2
Mažeikiai, 13,400 ... A 2
Memel (Klaipėda), 139,900 ... A 3
Muhu (isl.) ... B 1
Narva, 57,863 ... E 1
Naujoji-Akmene, 10,200 ... B 2
Niemen (Nemunas) (riv.) ... A 3
Ogre, 15,700 ... C 2
Panevėžys, 73,500 ... C 3
Pärnu, 46,316 ... C 1
Peipus (lake) ... D 1
Plungė, 13,600 ... B 3
Radviliškis, 16,900 ... B 3
Rakvere, 17,891 ... D 1
Rēzekne, 30,800 ... D 2
Riga (cap.), Latvia, 731,800 ... C 2
Riga (gulf) ... B 2
Saaremaa (isl.) ... B 1
Saldus, 10,000 ... B 2
Šiauliai, 92,800 ... B 3
Sillamäe, 13,505 ... D 1
Silutė, 12,400 ... A 3
Tallinn (cap.), Estonia, 362,706 ... C 1
Tapa, 10,037 ... C 1
Tartu, 90,459 ... D 1
Tauragė, 19,500 ... B 3
Telšiai, 20,200 ... B 2
Tukums, 14,800 ... B 2
Ukmergė, 21,600 ... C 3
Utena, 13,300 ... C 3
Valga, 16,795 ... D 2
Valmiera, 20,300 ... C 2
Venta (riv.) ... B 2
Ventspils, 40,500 ... A 2
Viliya (riv.) ... C 3
Viljandi, 20,814 ... C 1
Vilna (Vilnius), 371,700 ... C 3
Vormsi (isl.) ... B 1
Võrtsjärv (lake) ... D 1
Voru, 15,398 ... D 2
Western Dvina (riv.) ... C 2

Kuvandyk, 24,000 ... J 4
Kuybyshev, 1,045,000 ... H 4
Kuznetsk, 84,000 ... G 4
Labinsk, 50,000 ... F 6
Lebedin, 29,000 ... D 4
Leninakan, 165,000 ... F 6
Leningrad, 3,513,000 ... C 3
Leningrad, *3,950,000 ... C 3
Leninogorsk, 45,000 ... H 4
Lenkoran', 35,500 ... G 7
L'gov, 28,000 ... E 4
Lida, 48,000 ... C 4
Liepāja, 92,800 ... B 3
Lipetsk, 289,000 ... E 4
Lisichansk, 118,000 ... E 5
Livny, 37,000 ... E 4
Lodeynoye Pole, 20,000 ... D 2
Lozovaya, 34,000 ... E 5
Lubny, 39,000 ... D 4
Luga, 30,000 ... C 3
Lutsk, 94,000 ... B 4
L'vov (Lwów), 553,000 ... B 5
Lys'va, 73,000 ... J 3
Lyubertsy, 139,400 ... E 3
Lyubotin, 38,000 ... E 4
Lyudinovo, 33,000 ... D 4
Makeyevka, 392,000 ... E 5
Makhachkala, 186,000 ... G 6
Makharadze, 24,000 ... F 6
Manturovo, 21,000 ... F 3
Marganets, 47,000 ... E 5
Mariupol' (Zhdanov), 417,000 ... E 5
Marks, 18,000 ... G 4
Maykop, 110,000 ... F 6
Mednogorsk, 41,000 ... J 4
Medvezh'yegorsk, 18,000 ... D 2
Melenki, 19,000 ... F 3
Meleuz, 28,000 ... J 4
Melitopol', 137,000 ... D 5
Memel (Klaipėda), 139,900 ... B 3
Merefa, 32,000 ... E 5
Michurinsk, 94,000 ... F 4
Mikhaylovka, 50,000 ... F 4
Millerovo, 38,000 ... F 5
Mineralnye Vody, 55,000 ... F 6
Mingechaur, 43,100 ... G 6
Minsk, 907,000 ... C 4
Minsk, *917,000 ... C 4
Mirgorod, 28,000 ... D 5
Mogilev, 202,000 ... C 4
Mogilev-Podol'skiy, 27,000 ... C 5
Molodechno, 50,000 ... C 4
Molotov (Perm'), 850,000 ... J 3
Monchegorsk, 49,000 ... D 1
Morshansk, 45,000 ... F 4
Moscow (Moskva) (cap.), 6,942,000 ... E 3
Moscow, *7,061,000 ... E 3
Mozhaysk, 20,300 ... E 3
Mozhga, 34,000 ... H 3
Mozyr', 49,000 ... C 4
Mtsensk, 24,000 ... E 4
Mukachevo, 57,000 ... B 5
Murmansk, 309,000 ... D 1
Murom, 99,000 ... F 3
Mytishchi, 118,700 ... E 3
Naberezhnye Chelny, 38,000 ... H 3
Nakhichevan', 33,200 ... F 7
Nal'chik, 146,000 ... F 6
Narva, 57,863 ... C 3
Nar'yan-Mar, 15,000 ... H 1
Neftekamsk, 35,000 ... J 3
Nelidovo, 30,000 ... D 3
Nerekhta, 28,000 ... F 3
Nevinnomyssk, 85,000 ... F 6
Nezhin, 56,000 ... D 4
Nikel', 17,000 ... C 1
Nikolayev, 331,000 ... D 5
Nikopol', 125,000 ... D 5
Nizhnekamsk, 49,000 ... H 3
Nizhniy Lomov, 19,000 ... F 4
Nosovka, 23,000 ... D 4
Novaya Kakhovka, 40,000 ... D 5
Novgorod, 128,000 ... D 3
Novoanninskiy, 21,000 ... F 4
Novocherkassk, 162,000 ... F 5
Novograd-Volynskiy, 36,000 ... C 4
Novogrudok, 20,000 ... C 4
Novokuybyshevsk, 104,000 ... G 4
Novomoskovsk, 134,000 ... E 4
Novopolotsk, 40,000 ... C 3
Novorossiysk, 133,000 ... E 6
Novoshakhtinsk, 102,000 ... E 5
Novotroitsk, 83,000 ... J 4
Novoukrainka, 22,000 ... D 5
Novovolynsk, 40,000 ... B 4
Novozybkov, 33,000 ... D 4
Nyandoma, 24,000 ... F 2
Obninsk, 49,000 ... E 3
Ochamchire, 20,000 ... F 6
Odessa, 892,000 ... D 5
Oktyabr'sk, 36,000 ... G 4
Oktyabr'skiy, 77,000 ... H 4
Olenegorsk, 21,000 ... D 1
Omutninsk, 29,000 ... H 3
Onega, 27,000 ... E 2
Ordzhonikidze, 236,000 ... F 6
Orel, 232,000 ... E 4
Orenburg, 344,000 ... J 4
Orgeyev, 25,800 ... C 5
Orsha, 101,000 ... C 4
Orsk, 225,000 ... J 4
Osipenko (Berdyansk), 100,000 ... E 5
Osipovichi, 19,000 ... C 4
Ostashkov, 22,000 ... D 3
Ostrogozhsk, 35,000 ... E 4
Ostrov, 19,000 ... C 3
Otradnyy, 46,000 ... H 4
Panevėžys, 73,500 ... B 3
Pärnu, 46,316 ... C 3
Pavlovo, 63,000 ... F 3
Pechora, 41,000 ... J 1
Penza, 374,000 ... F 4
Perm', 850,000 ... J 3
Pervomaysk, 59,000 ... D 5
Pervomayskiy, 18,000 ... F 2
Petrovsk, 32,000 ... G 4
Petrozavodsk, 184,000 ... D 2
Pinsk, 62,000 ... C 4
Piryatin, 18,000 ... D 4
Pochep, 16,000 ... D 4
Podol'sk, 168,700 ... E 3
Polonnoye, 23,000 ... C 4
Polotsk, 64,000 ... C 3
Poltava, 220,000 ... D 5
Postavy, 13,000 ... C 3
Poti, 48,000 ... F 6
Povorino, 22,000 ... F 4
Prikumsk, 36,000 ... F 6
Priluki, 57,000 ... D 4
Primorsko-Akhtarsk, 30,000 ... E 5
Priyutovo, 20,000 ... H 4
Promyshlennyy, 22,000 ... K 1
Pskov, 127,000 ... C 3
Pugachev, 38,000 ... G 4
Pushkin, 79,000 ... C 3
Pyatigorsk, 93,000 ... F 6
Pyatikhatki, 20,000 ... D 5
Radomyshl', 12,000 ... C 4
Rakhov, 11,000 ... B 5
Rakvere, 17,891 ... C 3
Rasskazovo, 40,000 ... F 4
Rechitsa, 48,000 ... C 4
Revel (Tallinn), 362,706 ... B 3
Rēzekne, 30,800 ... C 3
Riga, 731,800 ... B 3
Rogachev, 12,000 ... D 4
Romny, 48,000 ... D 4
Roslavl', 48,000 ... D 4
Rossosh', 36,000 ... E 4
Rostov, 32,000 ... E 3
Rostov, 789,000 ... F 5
Rovno, 116,000 ... C 4
Rtishchevo, 40,000 ... F 4
Rubezhnoye, 58,000 ... E 5
Rustavi, 98,000 ... G 6
Ruzayevka, 38,000 ... F 4
Ryazan', 350,000 ... E 4
Rybinsk, 218,000 ... E 3
Rybnitsa, 32,400 ... C 5
Rzhev, 61,000 ... D 3
Safonovo, 44,000 ... D 3
Saki, 23,000 ... D 5
Salavat, 114,000 ... H 4
Sal'sk, 50,000 ... F 5
Sal'yany, 24,200 ... G 7
Samara (Kuybyshev), 1,045,000 ... H 4
Saransk, 191,000 ... G 4
Sarapul, 97,000 ... H 3
Saratov, 757,000 ... G 4
Sarny, 10,000 ... C 4
Sasovo, 28,000 ... F 4
Segezha, 30,000 ... D 2
Semenov, 25,000 ... F 3
Serdobel (Sortavala), 23,000 ... D 2
Serdobsk, 33,000 ... F 4
Serpukhov, 124,300 ... E 4
Sevastopol', 229,000 ... D 6
Severodonetsk, 90,000 ... E 5
Severodvinsk, 145,000 ... E 2
Severomorsk, 45,000 ... D 1
Shakhty, 205,000 ... F 5
Shakhun'ya, 22,000 ... G 3
Shar'ya, 25,000 ... G 3
Shchekino, 61,000 ... E 4
Shcherbakov (Rybinsk), 218,000 ... E 3
Sheki, 43,200 ... G 6
Shemakha, 17,900 ... G 6
Shepetovka, 39,000 ... C 4
Shostka, 64,000 ... D 4
Shumerlya, 33,000 ... G 3
Shuya, 69,000 ... F 3
Šiauliai, 92,800 ... B 3
Sibay, 42,000 ... J 4
Simferopol', 249,000 ... D 6
Skopin, 23,000 ... F 4
Slantsy, 40,000 ... C 3
Slavuta, 24,000 ... C 4
Slavyansk, 124,000 ... E 5
Slavyansk-na-Kubani, 52,000 ... E 5
Slobodskoy, 37,000 ... H 3
Slonim, 30,000 ... B 4
Slutsk, 36,000 ... C 4
Smela, 55,000 ... D 5
Smolensk, 211,000 ... D 4
Sochi, 224,000 ... E 6
Sokol, 49,000 ... F 3
Solikamsk, 89,000 ... J 3
Sol'-Iletsk, 25,000 ... J 4
Sorochinsk, 25,000 ... H 4
Soroki, 21,700 ... C 5
Sortavala, 23,000 ... D 2
Sosnogorsk, 25,000 ... H 2
Sovetsk, 38,000 ... B 4
Sovetsk, 19,000 ... G 3
Stalingrad (Volgograd), 818,000 ... F 5
Staraya Russa, 34,000 ... D 3
Staryy Oskol, 52,000 ... E 4
Stavropol', 198,000 ... F 5
Stepanakert, 30,300 ... G 7
Stepnoy (Elista), 50,000 ... G 5
Sterlitamak, 185,000 ... J 4
Stupino, 59,300 ... E 4
Sukhumi, 102,000 ... F 6
Sumgait, 124,400 ... G 6
Sumy, 159,000 ... E 4
Svetlogorsk, 40,000 ... C 4
Svetlograd, 30,000 ... F 5
Syktyvkar, 125,000 ... H 2
Syzran', 173,000 ... G 4
Taganrog, 254,000 ... E 5
Tallinn, 362,706 ... B 3
Tambov, 230,000 ... F 4
Tartu, 90,459 ... C 3
Tauragė, 19,500 ... B 3
Tbilisi, 889,000 ... F 6
Telavi, 23,000 ... G 6
Telšiai, 20,200 ... B 3
Temryuk, 28,000 ... E 5
Ternopol', 85,000 ... C 5
Teykovo, 34,000 ... E 3
Tiflis (Tbilisi), 889,000 ... F 6
Tighina (Bendery), 72,300 ... C 5
Tikhoretsk, 60,000 ... F 5
Tikhvin, 29,000 ... D 3
Timashevsk, 35,000 ... E 5
Tiraspol', 105,700 ... D 5
Togliatti, 251,000 ... G 4
Tokmak, 39,000 ... E 5
Torzhok, 47,000 ... D 3
Tskhinvali, 30,000 ... F 6
Tuapse, 51,000 ... E 6
Tula, 462,000 ... E 4
Tul'chin, 14,000 ... C 5
Tuymazy, 35,000 ... H 4
Tyrnyauz, 19,000 ... F 6
Uchaly, 18,000 ... J 4
Ufa, 771,000 ... J 4
Uglich, 36,000 ... E 3
Ukhta, 63,000 ... H 2
Ukmergė, 21,600 ... C 3
Ul'yanovsk, 351,000 ... G 4
Uman', 63,000 ... D 5
Uryupinsk, 37,000 ... F 4
Usman', 19,000 ... E 4
Uzhgorod, 65,000 ... B 5
Uzlovaya, 62,000 ... E 4
Valga, 16,795 ... C 3
Valmiera, 20,300 ... C 3
Valuyki, 29,000 ... E 4
Vasil'kov, 27,000 ... D 4
Velikiye Luki, 85,000 ... D 3
Velikiy Ustyug, 35,000 ... F 2
Vel'sk, 20,000 ... F 2
Ventspils, 40,500 ... B 3
Vichuga, 53,000 ... F 3
Viipuri (Vyborg), 65,000 ... C 2
Vilna (Vilnius), 371,700 ... C 4
Vinnitsa, 212,000 ... C 5
Vitebsk, 231,000 ... C 3
Vladimir, 234,000 ... F 3
Volgodonsk, 25,000 ... F 5
Volgograd, 818,000 ... F 5
Volkhov, 46,000 ... D 3
Volkovysk, 22,000 ... B 4
Vologda, 178,000 ... F 3
Vol'sk, 69,000 ... G 4
Volzhsk, 44,000 ... G 3
Volzhskiy, 142,000 ... G 5
Vorkuta, 90,000 ... K 1
Voronezh, 660,000 ... E 4
Voroshilovgrad, 383,000 ... F 5
Voskresensk, 66,900 ... E 3
Votkinsk, 74,000 ... H 3
Voznesensk, 36,000 ... D 5
Vyatskiye Polyany, 33,000 ... H 3
Vyaz'ma, 42,000 ... D 3
Vyborg, 65,000 ... C 2
Vyksa, 46,000 ... F 3
Vyshniy Volochek, 74,000 ... D 3
Yalta, 62,000 ... D 6
Yanaul, 18,000 ... J 3
Yaroslavl', 517,000 ... E 3
Yartsevo, 37,000 ... D 3
Yefremov, 47,000 ... E 4
Yelabuga, 36,000 ... H 3
Yelets, 101,000 ... E 4
Yenakiyevo, 92,000 ... E 5
Yershov, 20,000 ... G 4
Yessentuki, 65,000 ... F 6
Yevpatoria, 79,000 ... D 5
Yeysk, 64,000 ... E 5
Yoshkar-Ola, 166,000 ... G 3
Yur'yevets, 23,000 ... F 3
Zagorsk, 92,400 ... E 3
Zaporozh'ye, 658,000 ... E 5
Zelenodol'sk, 77,000 ... G 3
Zhdanov, 417,000 ... E 5
Zherdevka, 20,000 ... F 4
Zhigulevsk, 52,000 ... G 4
Zhitomir, 161,000 ... C 4
Zhlobin, 25,000 ... D 4
Zhmerinka, 34,000 ... C 5
Zhodino, 17,000 ... C 4
Znamenka, 30,000 ... D 5
Zolotonosha, 27,000 ... D 5
Zugdidi, 39,000 ... F 6
Zvenigorodka, 21,000 ... D 5

OTHER FEATURES

Apsheron (pen.) ... H 6
Araks (river) ... G 7
Azov (sea) ... E 5
Baltic (sea) ... B 3
Barents (sea) ... E 1
Belaya (river) ... H 3
Beloye (lake) ... E 2
Berezina (river) ... C 4
Black (sea) ... D 6
Bug (river) ... B 4
Bug (river) ... D 5
Caspian (sea) ... G 6
Caucasus (mts.) ... F 6
Central Ural (mts.) ... J 2
Chir (river) ... F 5
Crimea (pen.), 1,813,000 ... D 5
Dagö (Hiiumaa) (isl.) ... B 3
Denezhkin Kamen' (mt.) ... K 2
Desna (river) ... D 4
Dnieper (river) ... D 5
Dniester (river) ... C 5
Don (river) ... F 5
Donets (river) ... E 5
Dvina (bay) ... E 2
Dvina, Northern (river) ... F 2
Dvina, Western (river) ... C 3
Dykh-Tau (mt.) ... F 6
El'brus (mt.) ... F 6
Finland (gulf) ... C 3
Goryn' (river) ... C 4
Hiiumaa (isl.) ... B 3
Ilek (river) ... J 4
Il'men (lake) ... D 3
Izhma (river) ... H 2
Kakhovka (res.) ... D 5
Kama (river) ... H 3
Kandalaksha (gulf) ... D 1
Kanin (pen.) ... G 1
Kapydzhik (mt.) ... G 7
Kara (sea) ... K 1
Kazbek (mt.) ... F 6
Khoper (river) ... F 4
Kil'din (isl.) ... D 1
Kinel' (river) ... H 4
Kola (pen.) ... E 1
Kolguyev (isl.) ... G 1
Kolva (river) ... J 1
Kuban' (river) ... E 5
Kubeno (lake) ... E 3
Kura (river) ... G 6
Kuyto (lake) ... D 2
Ladoga (lake) ... D 2
Lapland (reg.) ... C 1
Lovat' (river) ... D 3
Mansel'ka (mts.) ... C 1
Manych-Gudilo (lake) ... F 5
Matveyev (isl.) ... J 1
Medveditsa (river) ... F 4
Mezen' (river) ... G 1
Mezhdusharskiy (isl.) ... G 1
Moksha (river) ... F 4
Moskva (river) ... E 3
Msta (river) ... D 3
Niemen (river) ... B 4
North Ural (mts.) ... K 1
Northern Dvina (river) ... F 2
Novaya Zemlya (isls.) ... H 1
Oka (river) ... F 4
Onega (bay) ... E 2
Onega (lake) ... E 2
Ösel (Saaremaa) (isl.) ... B 3
Pay-Yer (mt.) ... K 1
Pechora (river) ... H 1
Pechora (sea) ... H 1
Peipus (lake) ... C 3
Pinega (river) ... G 2
Ponoy (river) ... E 1
Pripet (marsh) ... C 4
Pripyat' (river) ... C 4
Prut (river) ... C 5
Psel (river) ... D 4
Riga (gulf) ... B 3
Russkiy Zavorot (cape) ... H 1
Rybachiy (pen.) ... D 1
Saaremaa (isl.) ... B 3
Samara (river) ... H 4
Seg (lake) ... D 2
Sevan (lake) ... G 6
Seym (river) ... D 4
Solovetskiye (isls.) ... E 1
South Ural (mts.) ... J 4
Suda (river) ... E 3
Sukhona (river) ... F 2
Sura (river) ... G 4
Svir' (river) ... D 2
Sysola (river) ... H 2
Tel'pos-Iz (mt.) ... K 2
Timan Ridge (mts.) ... H 1
Top (lake) ... D 1
Tuloma (river) ... D 1
Ufa (river) ... J 3
Undzha (river) ... F 3
Ural (mts.) ... J 2
Ural (river) ... J 4
Usa (river) ... K 1
Vaga (river) ... F 2
Valday (hills) ... D 3
Vaygach (isl.) ... K 1
Velikaya (river) ... C 3
Vetluga (river) ... G 3
Vodl (lake) ... E 2
Volga (river) ... G 5
Volga-Don (canal) ... F 5
Volkhov (river) ... D 3
Vorona (river) ... F 4
Vorskla (river) ... E 4
Vozhe (lake) ... F 2
Vyatka (river) ... H 3
Vychegda (river) ... G 2
Vyg (lake) ... E 2
Vym' (river) ... H 2
Western Dvina (river) ... C 3
White (sea) ... E 1
Yamantau (mt.) ... J 4
Yug (river) ... G 2
Yugorskiy (pen.) ... K 1

*City and suburbs.

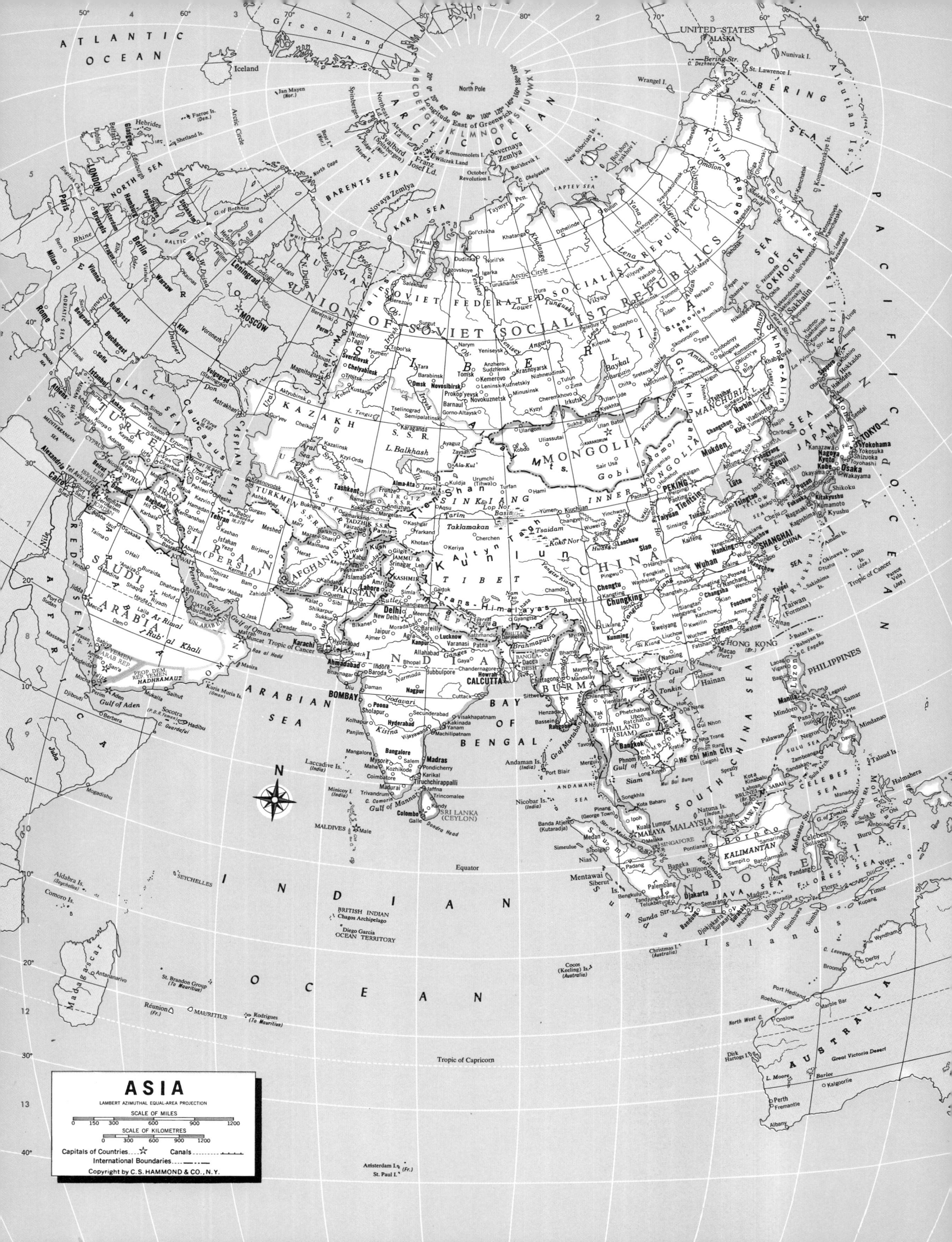

POPULATION DISTRIBUTION

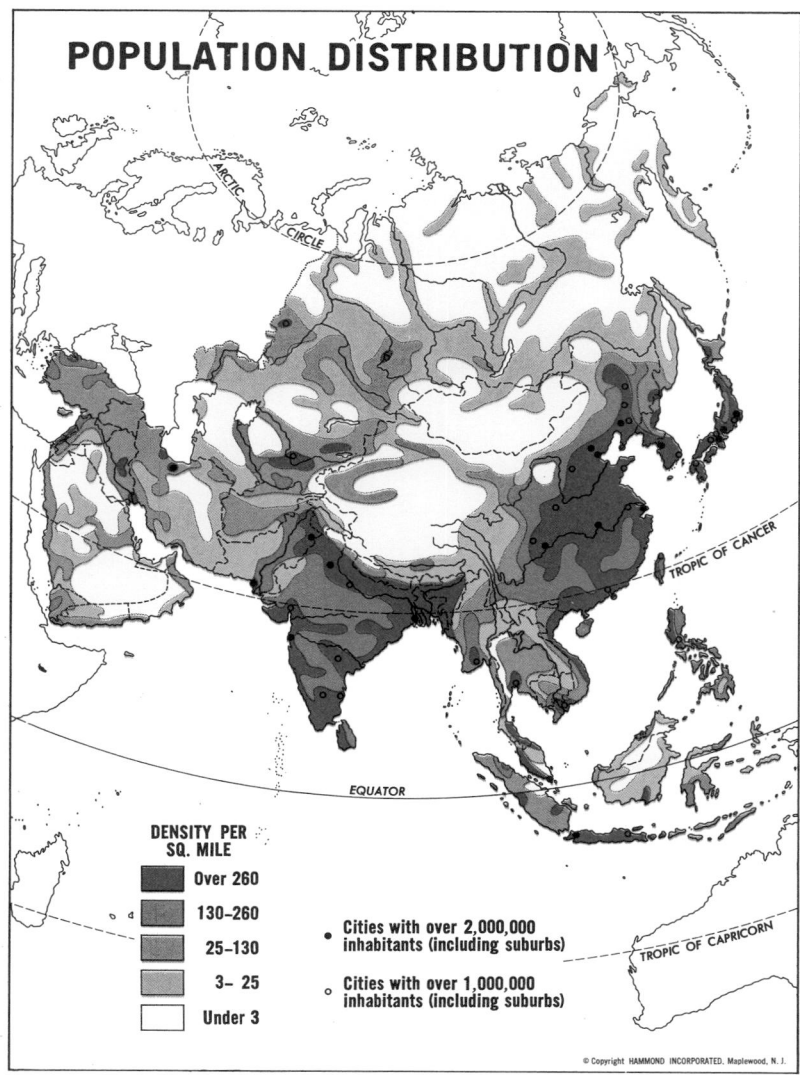

DENSITY PER SQ. MILE

- Over 260
- 130–260
- 25–130
- 3–25
- Under 3

- Cities with over 2,000,000 inhabitants (including suburbs)
- Cities with over 1,000,000 inhabitants (including suburbs)

© Copyright HAMMOND INCORPORATED, Maplewood, N. J.

AREA 17,128,500 sq. mi.
POPULATION 2,535,333,000
LARGEST CITY Tokyo
HIGHEST POINT Mt. Everest 29,028 ft.
LOWEST POINT Dead Sea –1,296 ft.

VEGETATION

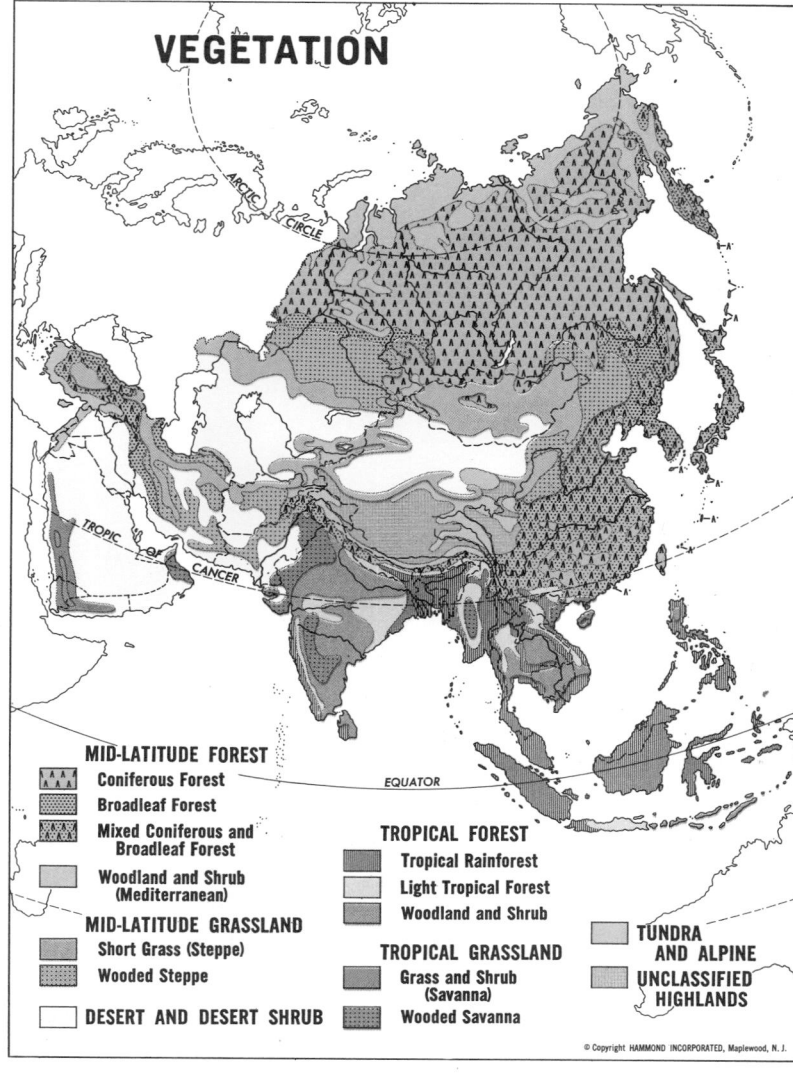

MID-LATITUDE FOREST
- Coniferous Forest
- Broadleaf Forest
- Mixed Coniferous and Broadleaf Forest
- Woodland and Shrub (Mediterranean)

MID-LATITUDE GRASSLAND
- Short Grass (Steppe)
- Wooded Steppe

DESERT AND DESERT SHRUB

TROPICAL FOREST
- Tropical Rainforest
- Light Tropical Forest
- Woodland and Shrub

TROPICAL GRASSLAND
- Grass and Shrub (Savanna)
- Wooded Savanna

TUNDRA AND ALPINE

UNCLASSIFIED HIGHLANDS

© Copyright HAMMOND INCORPORATED, Maplewood, N. J.

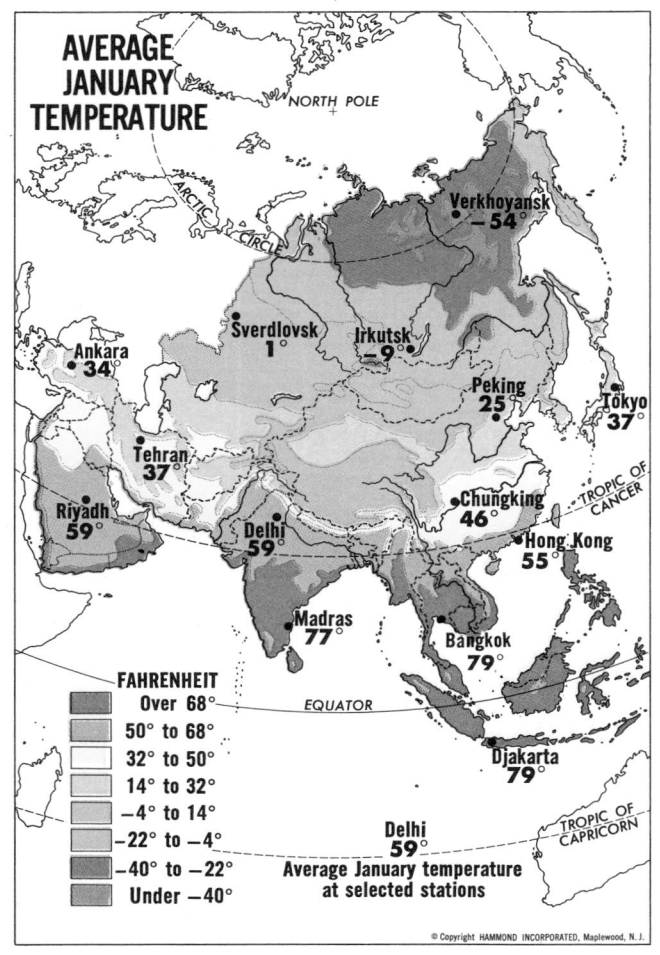

AVERAGE JANUARY TEMPERATURE

Verkhoyansk −54°
Sverdlovsk 1°
Irkutsk −9°
Ankara 34°
Peking 25°
Tokyo 37°
Tehran 37°
Chungking 46°
Riyadh 59°
Delhi 59°
Hong Kong 55°
Madras 77°
Bangkok 79°
Djakarta 79°

FAHRENHEIT
- Over 68°
- 50° to 68°
- 32° to 50°
- 14° to 32°
- −4° to 14°
- −22° to −4°
- −40° to −22°
- Under −40°

Delhi 59°
Average January temperature at selected stations

© Copyright HAMMOND INCORPORATED, Maplewood, N.J.

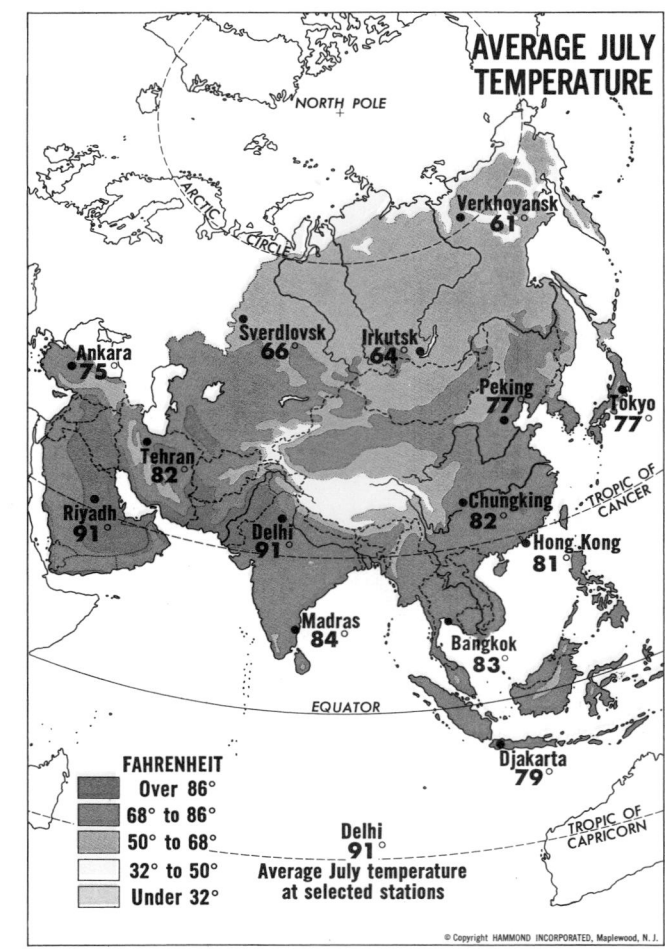

AVERAGE JULY TEMPERATURE

Verkhoyansk 61°
Sverdlovsk 66°
Irkutsk 64°
Ankara 75°
Peking 77°
Tokyo 77°
Tehran 82°
Chungking 82°
Riyadh 91°
Delhi 91°
Hong Kong 81°
Madras 84°
Bangkok 83°
Djakarta 79°

FAHRENHEIT
- Over 86°
- 68° to 86°
- 50° to 68°
- 32° to 50°
- Under 32°

Delhi 91°
Average July temperature at selected stations

© Copyright HAMMOND INCORPORATED, Maplewood, N.J.

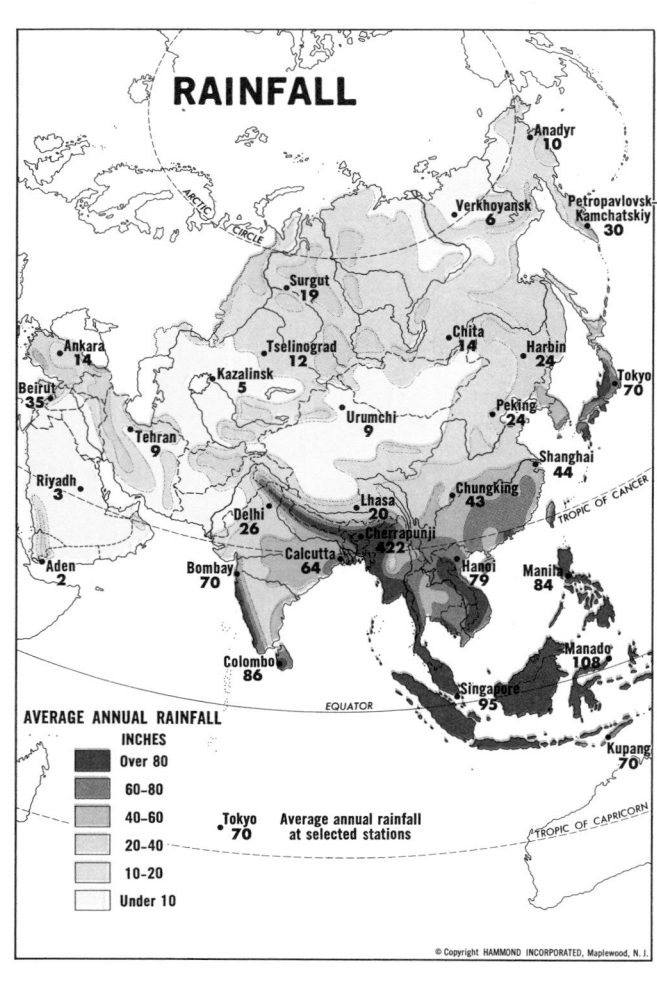

RAINFALL

Anadyr 10
Verkhoyansk 6
Petropavlovsk-Kamchatskiy 30
Surgut 19
Chita 14
Tselinograd 12
Harbin 24
Ankara 14
Kazalinsk 5
Beirut 35
Tokyo 70
Urumchi 9
Peking 24
Tehran 9
Shanghai 44
Riyadh 3
Lhasa 20
Chungking 43
Delhi 26
Cherrapunji 422
Aden 2
Calcutta 64
Bombay 70
Hanoi 79
Manila 84
Colombo 86
Manado 108
Singapore 95
Kupang 70

AVERAGE ANNUAL RAINFALL
INCHES
- Over 80
- 60–80
- 40–60
- 20–40
- 10–20
- Under 10

Tokyo 70
Average annual rainfall at selected stations

© Copyright HAMMOND INCORPORATED, Maplewood, N.J.

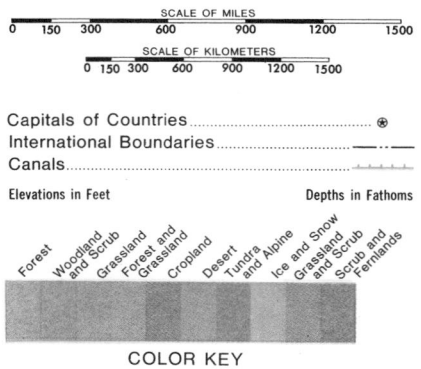

VEGETATION/RELIEF

SCALE OF MILES
0 150 300 600 900 1200 1500

SCALE OF KILOMETERS
0 150 300 600 900 1200 1500

Capitals of Countries .... ⊛
International Boundaries ....
Canals ....

Elevations in Feet   Depths in Fathoms

Forest
Woodland and Scrub
Grassland
Forest and Grassland
Cropland
Desert
Tundra and Alpine
Ice and Snow
Grassland and Scrub
Scrub and Fernlands

COLOR KEY

SAUDI ARABIA | KUWAIT | YEMEN ARAB REPUBLIC | BAHRAIN | QATAR | OMAN | PEOPLES DEM. REP. OF YEMEN

AFGHANISTAN

CITIES and TOWNS

Andkhui, 30,000 ....J 2	Charikar, 83,700 ....J 2	Haibak, 35,200 ....J 2	Kandahar, 127,036 ....J 3
Baghlan, 92,000 ....J 2	Daulatabad, 15,000 ....H 3	Herat, 71,563 ....H 3	Kandahar, *142,000 ....J 3
Bala Murghab, 10,000 ....H 2	Daulat Yar, 2,000 ....J 2	Jalalabad, 48,919 ....K 3	Khanabad, 30,000 ....J 2
Balkh, 15,000 ....H 2	Doshi, 5,000 ....J 2	Jurm, 10,000 ....K 2	Kushk, 10,000 ....H 2
Bamian, 25,000 ....J 3	Faizabad, 57,000 ....K 2	Juwain, 2,000 ....H 3	Landi Muhammad Amin Khan,
Chahar Burjak, 500 ....H 3	Farah, 26,400 ....H 3	Kabul (capital),	1,000 ....H 2
	Gardez, 33,000 ....J 3	472,313 ....J 3	Maimana, 48,750 ....H 2
	Ghazni, 39,900 ....J 3	Kabul, *600,000 ....J 3	Matun, 15,000 ....J 3
	Ghurian, 10,000 ....H 3	Kala Bist, 26,100 ....H 3	Mazar-i-Sharif, 43,197 ....J 2
	Girishk, 10,000 ....H 3	Kalat-i-Ghilzai, 40,500 ....J 3	Mukur, 10,000 ....J 3

Obeh, 5,000 ....H 3	Shindand (Sabzawar),	Gaud-i-Zirreh (marsh) ....H 4
Panjao, 3,000 ....J 3	5,000 ....H 3	Hari Rud (river) ....H 3
Qala Panja, 1,000 ....K 2	Taiwara, 5,000 ....H 3	Helmand (river) ....H 3
Qaleh-i-Kang, 15,600 ....H 3	Tashkurghan, 30,000 ....J 2	Hindu Kush (mts.) ....J 2
Rudbar, 1,000 ....H 3	Zebak, 5,000 ....K 2	Jam (mt.) ....J 3
Rustak, 10,000 ....J 2		Kabul (river) ....K 3
Sabzawar, 5,000 ....H 3	**OTHER FEATURES**	Kunar (river) ....K 2
Sar-i-Pul, 5,000 ....J 2		Kunduz (river) ....J 2
Shahjui, 5,000 ....J 3	Chagai (hills) ....H 4	Lora (river) ....J 3
Shibarghan, 50,440 ....H 2	Farah Rud (river) ....H 3	Margo, Dasht-i (desert) ....H 3

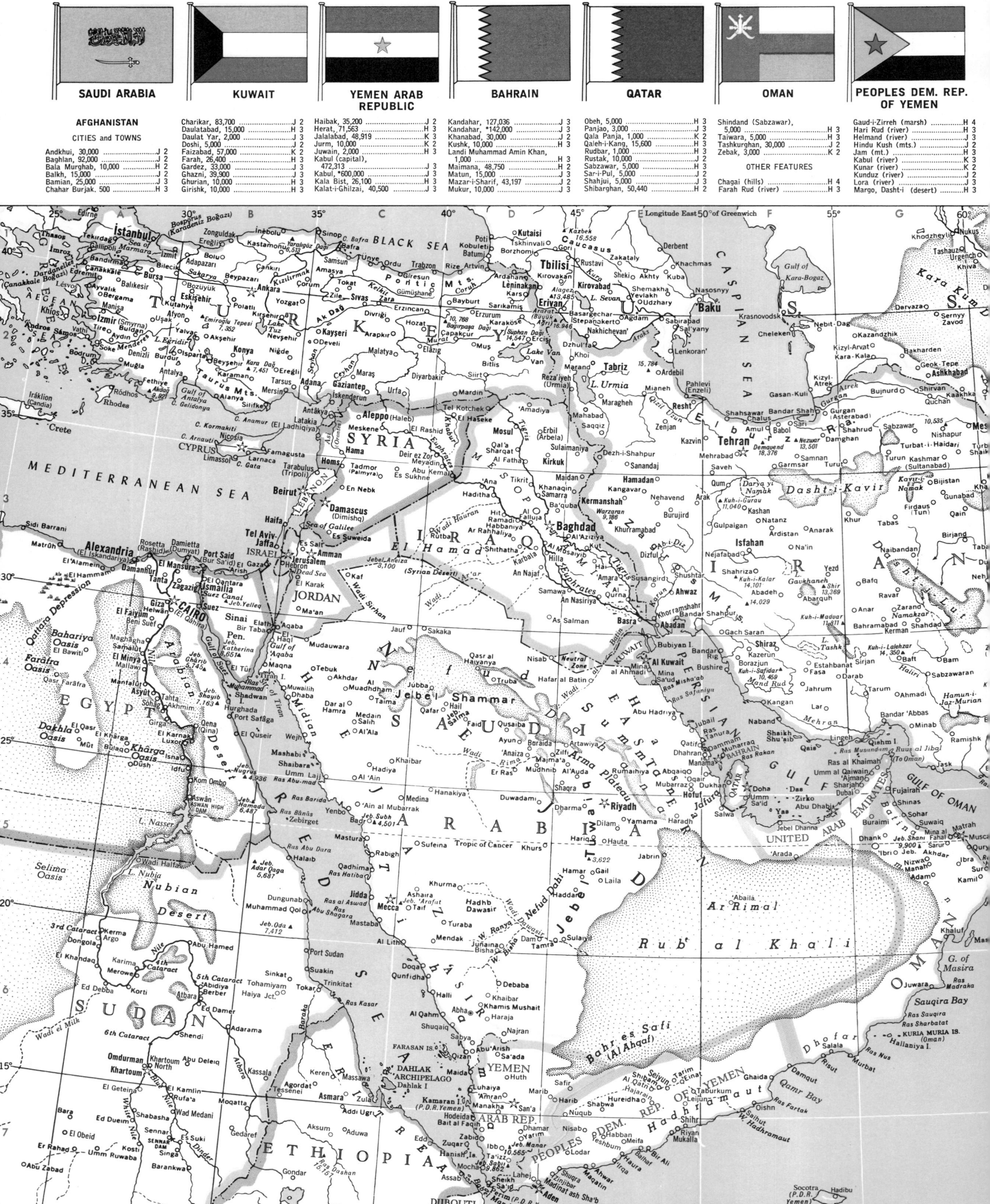

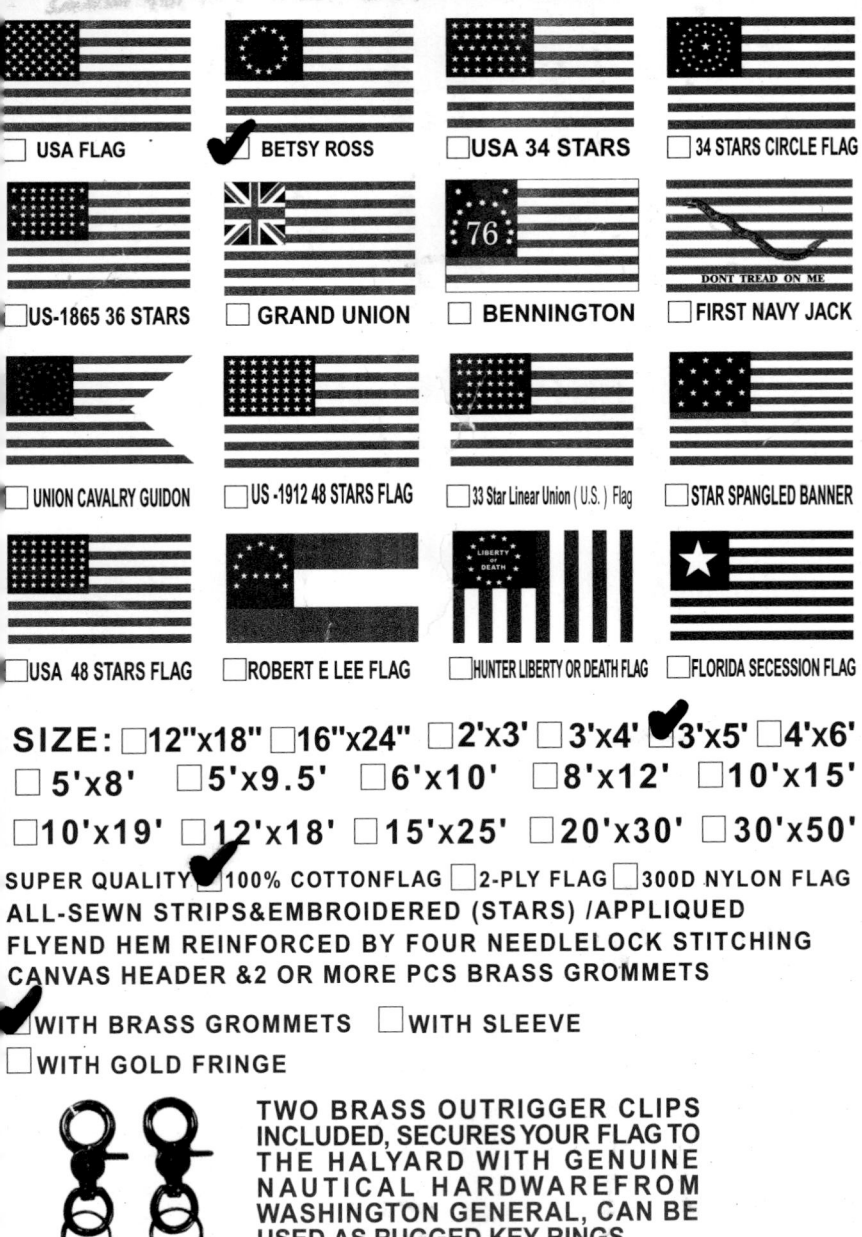

- ☐ USA FLAG
- ✔ BETSY ROSS
- ☐ USA 34 STARS
- ☐ 34 STARS CIRCLE FLAG
- ☐ US-1865 36 STARS
- ☐ GRAND UNION
- ☐ BENNINGTON
- ☐ FIRST NAVY JACK
- ☐ UNION CAVALRY GUIDON
- ☐ US -1912 48 STARS FLAG
- ☐ 33 Star Linear Union (U.S.) Flag
- ☐ STAR SPANGLED BANNER
- ☐ USA 48 STARS FLAG
- ☐ ROBERT E LEE FLAG
- ☐ HUNTER LIBERTY OR DEATH FLAG
- ☐ FLORIDA SECESSION FLAG

SIZE: ☐12"x18" ☐16"x24" ☐ 2'x3' ☐ 3'x4' ✔3'x5' ☐4'x6'
☐ 5'x8' ☐5'x9.5' ☐6'x10' ☐8'x12' ☐10'x15'
☐10'x19' ☐12'x18' ☐15'x25' ☐20'x30' ☐30'x50'

SUPER QUALITY ✔100% COTTONFLAG ☐2-PLY FLAG ☐300D NYLON FLAG
ALL-SEWN STRIPS&EMBROIDERED (STARS) /APPLIQUED
FLYEND HEM REINFORCED BY FOUR NEEDLELOCK STITCHING
CANVAS HEADER &2 OR MORE PCS BRASS GROMMETS

✔WITH BRASS GROMMETS ☐WITH SLEEVE
☐WITH GOLD FRINGE

TWO BRASS OUTRIGGER CLIPS INCLUDED, SECURES YOUR FLAG TO THE HALYARD WITH GENUINE NAUTICAL HARDWAREFROM WASHINGTON GENERAL, CAN BE USED AS RUGGED KEY RINGS

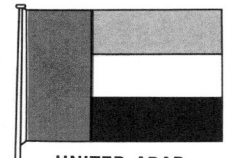

UNITED ARAB EMIRATES

Murghab (river) ....H 2
Namaksar (salt lake) ....H 3
Paropamisus (range) ....H 3
Pyandzh (river) ....K 2
Registan (desert) ....H 3

BAHRAIN

CITIES and TOWNS

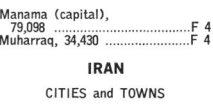

IRAN
CITIES and TOWNS

Abadan, 272,962 ....E 3
Abadeh, 16,000 ....F 3

Manama (capital),
79,098 ....F 4
Muharraq, 34,430 ....F 4

Abarquh, 8,000 ....F 3
Ahwaz, 206,375 ....E 3
Amol, 40,076 ....F 2
Anarak, 2,038 ....F 3
Arak, 71,925 ....E 3
Ardabil, 83,596 ....E 2
Ardistan, 6,645 ....F 3
Asterabad (Gurgan),
51,181 ....F 2
Babol, 49,973 ....F 2

Bafq, 5,000 ....G 3
Baft, 6,000 ....G 4
Bahramabad, 21,000 ....G 3
Bam, 22,000 ....G 4
Bandar 'Abbas, 34,627 ......G 4
Bandar Shah, 13,000 ....F 2
Bandar Shahpur, 6,000 ......E 3
Barfrush (Babol),
49,973 ....F 2
Birjand, 25,854 ....G 3

Borazjun, 20,000 ....F 4
Bujnurd, 31,248 ....G 2
Burujird, 71,476 ....E 3
Bushire, 26,032 ....F 4
Chalus, 15,000 ....F 2
Damghan, 13,000 ....F 2
Darab, 13,000 ....G 4
Dizful, 84,499 ....E 3
Duzdab (Zahidan),
40,000 ....H 4

(continued on following page)

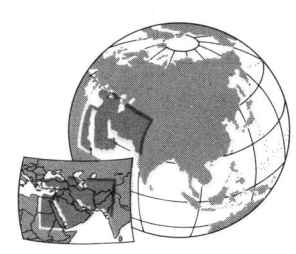

SAUDI ARABIA
AREA 829,995 sq. mi.
POPULATION 7,200,000
CAPITALS Riyadh, Mecca
MONETARY UNIT Saudi riyal
MAJOR LANGUAGE Arabic
MAJOR RELIGION Islam

YEMEN ARAB REPUBLIC
AREA 77,220 sq. mi.
POPULATION 5,600,000
CAPITAL San'a
MONETARY UNIT Yemeni rial
MAJOR LANGUAGE Arabic
MAJOR RELIGION Islam

BAHRAIN
AREA 240 sq. mi.
POPULATION 300,000
CAPITAL Manama
MONETARY UNIT Bahraini dinar
MAJOR LANGUAGE Arabic
MAJOR RELIGION Islam

UNITED ARAB EMIRATES
AREA 32,278 sq. mi.
POPULATION 240,000
CAPITAL Abu Dhabi
MONETARY UNIT dirham
MAJOR LANGUAGE Arabic
MAJOR RELIGION Islam

KUWAIT
AREA 6,532 sq. mi.
POPULATION 1,100,000
CAPITAL Al Kuwait
MONETARY UNIT Kuwaiti dinar
MAJOR LANGUAGE Arabic
MAJOR RELIGION Islam

PEOPLES DEMOCRATIC REPUBLIC OF YEMEN
AREA 111,101 sq. mi.
POPULATION 1,700,000
CAPITAL Aden
MONETARY UNIT Yemeni dinar
MAJOR LANGUAGE Arabic
MAJOR RELIGION Islam

QATAR
AREA 4,247 sq. mi.
POPULATION 150,000
CAPITAL Doha
MONETARY UNIT Qatari riyal
MAJOR LANGUAGE Arabic
MAJOR RELIGION Islam

OMAN
AREA 120,000 sq. mi.
POPULATION 800,000
CAPITAL Muscat
MONETARY UNIT Omani rial
MAJOR LANGUAGE Arabic
MAJOR RELIGION Islam

NEAR and MIDDLE EAST
CONIC PROJECTION
SCALE OF MILES
SCALE OF KILOMETRES

Capitals of Countries .... ☆
Other Capitals .... ◉
International Boundaries ....

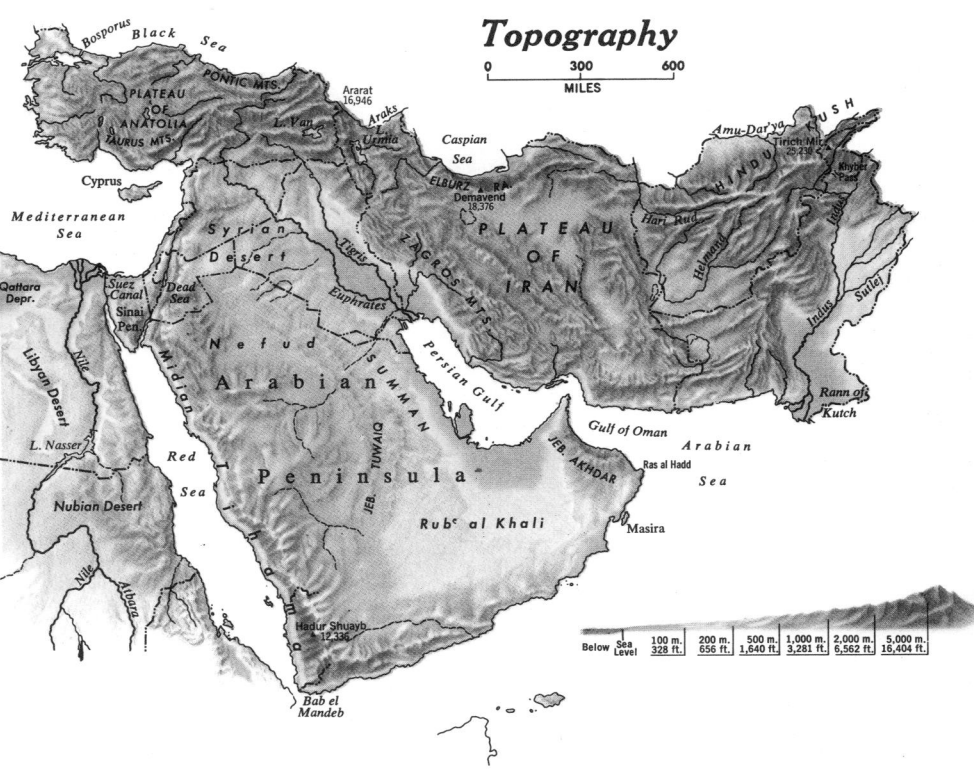

Topography

IRAN (continued)

Enzeli (Pahlevi), 41,785 .....E 2
Estahbanat, 18,187 .....F 4
Fahrej (Iranshahr),
5,000 .....H 4
Fasa, 19,000 .....F 4
Firdaus, 11,000 .....G 3
Gach Saran .....F 3
Garmsar, 4,723 .....F 2
Gulpaigan, 20,515 .....F 3
Gunabad, 8,000 .....G 3
Gurgan, 51,181 .....F 2
Hamadan, 124,167 .....E 3
Iranshahr, 5,000 .....H 4
Isfahan, 424,045 .....F 3
Jahrum, 38,236 .....F 4
Juimand (Gunabad),
6,000 .....G 3
Kangavar, 9,414 .....E 3
Kashan, 58,468 .....F 3
Kashmar, 17,000 .....G 2
Kazerun, 39,758 .....F 4
Kazvin, 88,106 .....E 2
Kerman, 85,404 .....G 3
Kermanshah, 187,930 .....E 3
Khaf, 5,000 .....H 3
Khoi, 47,648 .....E 2
Khorramshahr, 88,536 .....E 3
Khur, 2,912 .....G 3
Khurramabad, 59,578 .....E 3
Lar, 22,000 .....F 4
Mahabad, 28,610 .....E 2
Maragheh, 54,106 .....E 2
Marand, 24,000 .....E 2
Meshed, 409,616 .....H 2
Mianeh, 28,447 .....E 2
Mirjawa, 11,000 .....H 4
Na'in, 5,925 .....F 3
Naishapur (Nishapur),
33,482 .....G 2
Nasratabad (Zabul), 20,000 .....H 3
Natanz, 4,370 .....F 3
Nehavend, 24,000 .....E 3
Nejafabad, 43,384 .....F 3
Nishapur, 33,482 .....G 2
Pahlevi, 41,785 .....E 2
Qain, 6,000 .....G 3
Quchan, 29,133 .....G 2
Qum, 134,292 .....F 3
Ravar, 7,000 .....G 3
Resht, 143,557 .....E 2
Reza'iyeh, 110,749 .....D 2
Sabzawar, 42,415 .....G 2
Sabzawaran, 7,000 .....G 4
Samnan, 31,058 .....F 2
Sanandaj, 54,578 .....E 2
Saqiz, 17,000 .....E 2
Sari, 44,547 .....F 2
Saveh, 17,565 .....F 3
Shahr-i-Tajan (Sari),
44,547 .....F 2
Shahriza, 34,220 .....F 3
Shahrud, 30,767 .....F 2
Shahsawar, 12,000 .....F 2
Shiraz, 269,865 .....F 4
Shirvan, 11,000 .....G 2
Shushtar, 21,000 .....E 3
Sirjan, 12,160 .....G 4
Sultanabad (Arak), 71,925 .....F 3
Sultanabad (Kashmar),
17,000 .....G 2
Susangird, 21,000 .....E 3
Tabas (Tabas-Masina),
10,000 .....H 3
Tabriz, 403,413 .....E 2
Tehran (capital), 2,719,730 .....F 2
Tun (Firdaus), 11,000 .....G 3
Turbat-i-Haidari,
30,106 .....G 2
Turbat-i-Shaikh Jam,
13,000 .....H 2
Turshiz (Kashmar),
17,000 .....G 2
Turun .....G 2
Urmia (Reza'iyeh),
110,749 .....D 2
Yezd, 93,241 .....F 3
Zabul, 20,000 .....H 3
Zahidan, 39,732 .....H 4
Zarand, 5,000 .....G 3
Zenjan, 58,714 .....E 2

OTHER FEATURES

Araks (river) .....E 2
Atrek (river) .....G 2
Bazman, Kuh-i-(mt.) .....H 4
Demavend (mt.) .....F 2
Diz, Ab-i-(river) .....E 3
Elburz (mts.) .....F 2
Galvkhaneh (lake) .....E 2
Gurgan (river) .....G 2
Haliri (river) .....G 4
Jaz Murian, Hamun-i-
(marsh) .....G 4
Karun (river) .....E 3
Kavir, Dasht-i-
(salt desert) .....G 3
Kavir-i-Namak
(salt desert) .....G 3
Lut, Dasht-i-
(desert) .....G 3
Maidani, Ras (cape) .....F 4
Mand Rud (river) .....F 4
Mashkel (river) .....H 4
Mehran (river) .....F 4
Namak, Darya-i-
(salt lake) .....F 3
Namaksar (salt lake) .....H 3
Namakzar (marsh) .....H 3
Nezwar (mt.) .....E 2
Oman (gulf) .....G 5
Persian (gulf) .....F 4
Qais (isl.) .....F 4
Qishm (isl.) .....G 4
Qizil Uzun (river) .....E 2
Safidar, Kuh-i- (mt.) .....F 4
Shaikh Shu'aib (isl.) .....F 4
Shir (mt.) .....H 3
Taftan (mt.) .....H 4
Talab (river) .....H 4
Tashk (lake) .....F 4
Urmia (lake) .....E 2
Zagros (mts.) .....E 3

IRAQ

CITIES and TOWNS

Al 'Aziziya, 7,450 .....E 3
Al Falluja, 38,072 .....D 3
Al Musaiyib, 15,955 .....D 3
Al Qurna, 5,638 .....E 3
'Amadiya, 2,578 .....D 2
Amara, 64,847 .....E 3
An Najaf, 128,096 .....D 3
An Nasiriya, 60,405 .....D 3
'Ana, 6,884 .....D 3
Ar Rahhaliya .....D 3
Arbela (Erbil),
90,320 .....D 2
As Salman, 1,789 .....E 3
Baghdad (capital),
502,503 .....E 3
Baghdad, *1,745,328 .....E 3
Ba'quba, 34,575 .....D 3
Basra, 313,327 .....E 3
Erbil, 90,320 .....D 2
Habbaniya, 14,405 .....D 3
Haditha, 6,870 .....D 3
Hai, 16,988 .....E 3
Hilla, 84,717 .....D 3
Hit, 9,131 .....D 3
Karbala', 83,301 .....D 3
Khanaqin, 23,522 .....E 3
Kirkuk, 167,413 .....D 2
Kut, 42,116 .....E 3
Maidan, 354 .....D 2
Mosul, 315,157 .....D 2
Qal'a Sharqat, 2,434 .....D 2
Ramadi, 28,723 .....D 3
Rutba, 5,091 .....D 3
Samarra, 24,746 .....D 3
Samawa, 33,473 .....D 3
Shithatha, 2,326 .....D 3
Sulaimaniya, 86,822 .....E 2
Tikrit, 9,921 .....D 3

OTHER FEATURES

Al Batin, Wadi (river) .....E 4
'Aneiza, Jebel (mt.) .....D 3
El Hamad (desert) .....D 3
Euphrates (river) .....D 3
Hauran, Wadi
(dry river) .....D 3
Mesopotamia (reg.) .....E 3
Tigris (river) .....E 3

KUWAIT

CITIES and TOWNS

Al Kuwait (capital),
80,008 .....E 4
Al Kuwait, *217,364 .....E 4
Mina al-Ahmadi .....E 4

OTHER FEATURES

Bubiyan (isl.) .....E 4
Persian (gulf) .....F 4

OMAN

CITIES and TOWNS

Adam .....G 5
Buraimi .....G 5
Dhank .....G 5
Ibra .....G 5
'Ibri .....G 5
Juwara .....G 5
Kamil .....G 5
Khaluf .....G 5
Khasab .....G 4
Manah .....G 5
Matrah, 15,000 .....G 5
Mina al Fahal .....G 5
Murbat .....G 6
Muscat (capital),
7,500 .....G 5
Nizwa .....G 5
Quryat .....G 5
Risut .....F 6
Salala, 4,000 .....F 6
Sarur .....G 5
Shinas .....G 5
Sohar .....G 5
Sur .....G 5
Suwaiq .....G 5

OTHER FEATURES

Akhdar, Jebel (range) .....G 5

QATAR

CITIES and TOWNS

Doha (capital), 45,000 .....F 4
Dukhan, 2,500 .....F 4
Umm Sa'id, 3,500 .....F 5

OTHER FEATURES

Persian (gulf) .....F 4
Rakan, Ras (cape) .....F 4

SAUDI ARABIA

PROVINCES

'Asir, 900,000 .....D 6
Eastern, 2,250,000 .....E 4
Hejaz, 1,250,000 .....C 4
Nejd, 1,500,000 .....D 4

CITIES and TOWNS

Abha .....D 6
Abqaiq .....E 4
Abu 'Arish .....D 6
Abu Hadriya .....E 4
'Ain al Mubarrak .....C 4
Al 'Ain .....C 4
Al 'Ala .....C 4
Al 'Auda .....D 6
Al Lith .....C 5
Al Muaddham .....D 4
Al Qahm .....D 6
'Anaiza .....D 4
Artawiya .....E 4
Badr .....C 5
Buraida .....D 4
Buraimi .....G 5
Dam .....D 5
Dammam, 3,000 .....F 4
Dar al Hamra .....C 4
Dhaba .....C 4
Dharma .....E 5
Dilam .....E 5
Doqa .....D 5
Duwadami .....D 4
Er Ras .....D 4
Faid .....D 4
Haddar .....E 5
Hafar al Batin .....E 4
Halli .....D 6
Hamar .....E 5
Hanakiya .....D 5
Haql .....C 4
Haradh .....E 5
Haraja .....D 6
Hariq .....E 5
Hauta .....E 5
Hadd, Ras al (cape) .....G 5
Hallaniya (isl.), 78 .....G 6
Hofuf, 83,000 .....E 4
Jabrin .....E 5
Jauf, 5,000 .....C 4
Jidda, 194,000 .....C 5
Jibsh, Ras (cape) .....G 5
Jubba .....D 4
Jubba .....D 5
Junaina .....D 5
Kaf .....C 4
Khaibar .....D 4
Khamis Mushait .....D 6
Khurma .....D 5
Khurs .....E 5
Laila .....E 5
Majma'a .....D 4
Mastaba .....C 5
Mastura .....C 5
Mecca (capital), 185,000 .....C 5
Medain Salih .....C 4
Medina, 72,000 .....D 5
Mendak .....D 6
Mina Sa'ud .....E 4
Mubarraz .....E 4
Mudhnib .....D 4
Muwailih .....C 4
Najran .....D 6
Nisab .....E 4
Oqair .....E 4
Qadhima .....C 5
Qafar .....D 4
Qasr al Haiyana .....D 4
Qatif .....E 4
Qizan .....D 6
Qunfida .....D 6
Qusaiba .....D 4
Rabigh .....C 5
Ras Tanura .....F 4
Riyadh (capital),
225,000 .....E 5
Rumaihiya .....D 6
Sabya .....D 6
Sakaka .....D 4
Salwa .....F 5
Shaqra .....D 6
Shuqaiq .....D 6
Sufeina .....D 5
Sulaiyil .....E 5
Taif, 54,000 .....C 4
Taima .....C 4
Tamra .....D 4
Tebuk .....C 4
Truba .....D 5
Turaba .....D 5
Umm Lajj .....C 5
Wejh .....C 4
Yamama .....E 5
Yenbo .....C 5
Zilfi .....E 4

OTHER FEATURES

Abu-mad (cape) .....C 5
'Ar'ar, Wadi
(dry river) .....D 3
Al Ahqaf (Bahr es Safi)
(desert) .....E 6
'Aneiza, Jebel (mt.) .....C 3
'Aqaba (gulf) .....C 4
Arafat, Jebel (mt.) .....C 5
Ar'ar, Wadi (dry river) .....D 3
Arma (plateau) .....E 4
Aswad, Ras al (cape) .....C 5
Bahr es Safi (desert) .....E 6
Barida, Ras (cape) .....C 5
Bisha, Wadi
(dry river) .....D 5
Dahana (desert) .....E 4
Dawasir, Wadi
(dry river) .....E 5
Dawasir, Hadb
(range) .....D 5
Farasan (isls.) .....C 6
Hasa (reg.) .....E 4
Hatiba, Ras (cape) .....C 5
Jafura (desert) .....F 5
Mashabi (isl.) .....C 4
Midian (district) .....C 4
Misha'ab, Ras
(cape) .....E 4
Nefud (desert) .....D 4
Nefud Dahi (desert) .....D 5
Persian (gulf) .....E 4
Ranya, Wadi
(dry river) .....D 5
Red (Nefud) (desert) .....D 4
Red (sea) .....C 5
Rima, Wadi (river) .....D 4
Rimal, Ar (desert) .....F 5
Rub' al Khali
(desert) .....F 5
Safaniya, Ras
(cape) .....E 4
Salma, Jebel (mts.) .....D 4
Shaibara (isl.) .....C 4
Shammar, Jebel
(plateau) .....D 4
Sirhan, Wadi
(dry river) .....C 3
Subh, Jebel (mt.) .....C 5
Summan (plateau) .....E 4
Tihama (reg.) .....C 5
Tiran (isl.) .....B 4
Tiran (str.) .....B 4
Tuwaiq, Jebel
(range) .....E 5

UNITED ARAB EMIRATES

CITIES and TOWNS

Abu Dhabi (capital),
22,000 .....F 5
Abu Dhabi, *35,000 .....F 5
Ajman, 3,725 .....G 4
'Arada .....F 5
Buraimi .....G 5
Dubai, 13,092 .....F 4
Dubai, *57,400 .....F 4
Fujairah, 761 .....G 4
Jebel Dhauna .....F 5
Ras al Khaimah, 5,244 .....F 4
Sharjah, 19,198 .....F 4
Sharjah, *20,621 .....F 4
Umm al Qaiwain,
2,928 .....F 4

OTHER FEATURES

Das (isl.) .....F 4
Persian (gulf) .....F 4
Yas (isl.) .....F 5
Zirko (isl.) .....F 5

YEMEN ARAB REP.

CITIES and TOWNS

'Amran .....D 6
Bait al Faqih .....D 7
Dhamar .....D 7
Harib .....E 6
Hodeida, 40,000 .....D 7
Huth .....D 6
Ibb .....D 7

Luhaiya (Loheia) .....D 6
Maida, 2,500 .....D 6
Manakha .....D 7
Marib .....E 6
Mocha .....D 7
Sa'ada .....E 6
Safir .....E 6
San'a (capital),
100,000 .....D 7
Sheikh Sa'id .....D 7
Ta'izz, 80,000 .....D 7
Yarim, 5,000 .....D 7
Zabid, 8,000 .....D 7

OTHER FEATURES

Hanish (isls.) .....D 7
Manar, Jebel (mt.) .....D 7
Red (sea) .....C 6
Sabir, Jebel (mt.) .....D 7
Tihama (reg.) .....D 7
Zuqar (isl.) .....D 7

YEMEN, PEOPLES DEM. REPUBLIC OF

CITIES and TOWNS

Aden (capital), 150,000 .....E 7
Aden, *225,000 .....E 7
Ahwar .....E 7
Al Qatn .....E 7
Balhaf .....E 7
Bir 'Ali .....E 7
Damqut .....F 6
'Einat .....F 7
Ghaida .....F 7
Hadibu .....F 7
Hajarain .....E 7
Haura .....E 7
Hureidha .....E 7
'Irqa .....E 6
Lahej .....E 7
Leijun .....E 7
Lodar .....E 7
Madinat ash Sha'b,
29,897 .....E 7
Maqatin .....E 7
Meifa .....E 7
Mukalla, 30,000 .....F 7
Nisab .....E 7
Nuqub .....E 7
Qishn .....F 7
Riyan .....F 7
Saihut, 10,000 .....F 7
Seiyun .....E 7
Shabwa .....E 7
Shibam, 6,000 .....E 7
Shihr .....F 7
Shuqra .....E 7
Taburkum .....E 7
Tarim .....E 7
Yeshbum .....E 7
Zinjibar .....E 7

OTHER FEATURES

Fartak, Ras (cape) .....F 6
Hadhramaut (dist.),
350,000 .....E 7
Hadhramaut, Wadi
(dry river) .....E 7
Kamaran (island),
2,200 .....D 6
Mandeb, Bab el
(strait) .....D 7
Perim (isl.), 381 .....D 7
Socotra (island),
14,000 .....F 7

*City and suburbs.

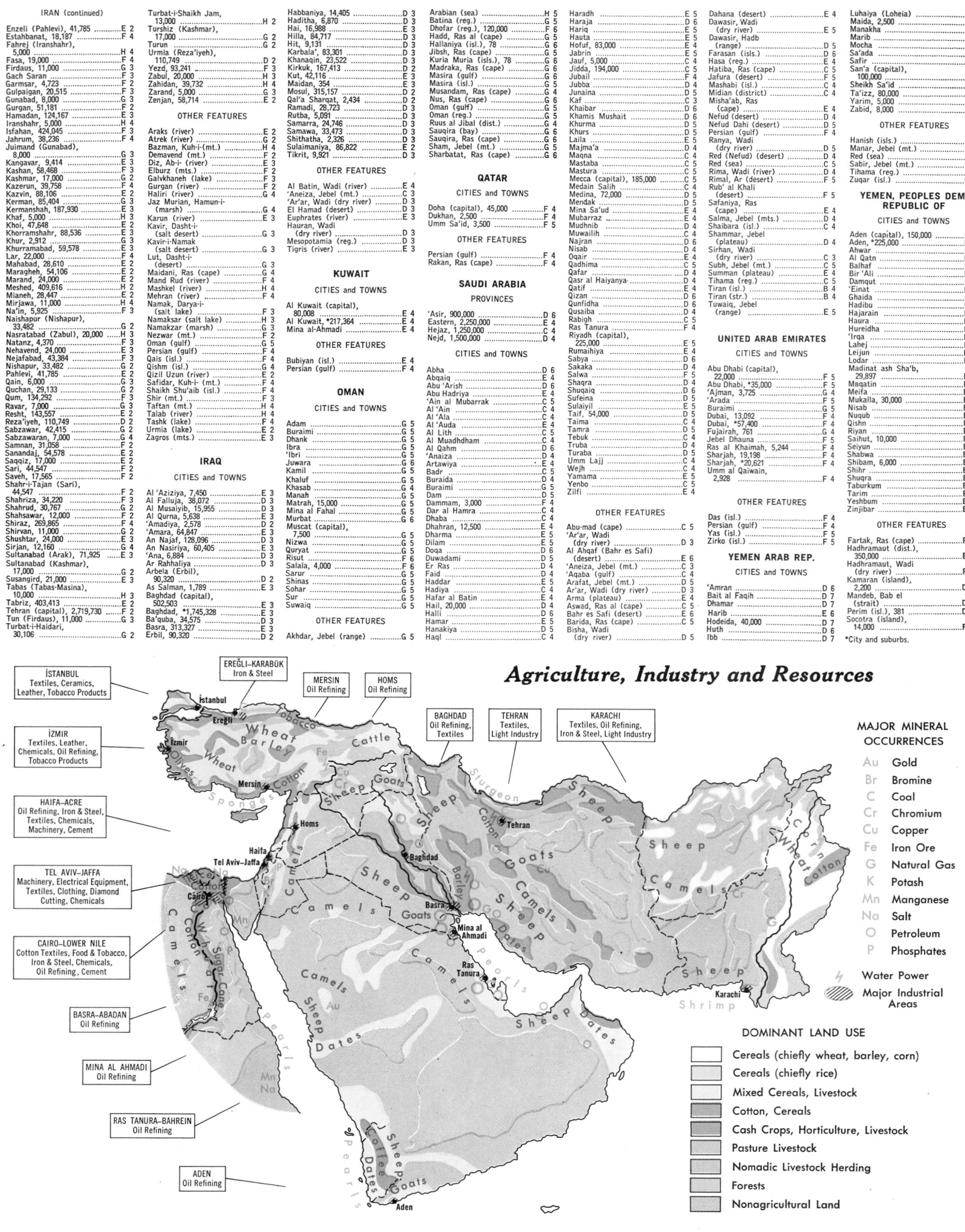

Agriculture, Industry and Resources

İSTANBUL — Textiles, Ceramics, Leather, Tobacco Products

EREĞLİ–KARABÜK — Iron & Steel

MERSIN — Oil Refining

HOMS — Oil Refining

BAGHDAD — Oil Refining, Textiles

TEHRAN — Textiles, Light Industry

KARACHI — Textiles, Oil Refining, Iron & Steel, Light Industry

İZMIR — Textiles, Leather, Chemicals, Oil Refining, Tobacco Products

HAIFA–ACRE — Oil Refining, Iron & Steel, Textiles, Chemicals, Machinery, Cement

TEL AVIV–JAFFA — Machinery, Electrical Equipment, Textiles, Clothing, Diamond Cutting, Chemicals

CAIRO–LOWER NILE — Cotton Textiles, Food & Tobacco, Iron & Steel, Chemicals, Oil Refining, Cement

BASRA–ABADAN — Oil Refining

MINA AL AHMADI — Oil Refining

RAS TANURA–BAHREIN — Oil Refining

ADEN — Oil Refining

MAJOR MINERAL OCCURRENCES

Au — Gold
Br — Bromine
C — Coal
Cr — Chromium
Cu — Copper
Fe — Iron Ore
G — Natural Gas
K — Potash
Mn — Manganese
Na — Salt
O — Petroleum
P — Phosphates

Water Power

Major Industrial Areas

DOMINANT LAND USE

Cereals (chiefly wheat, barley, corn)
Cereals (chiefly rice)
Mixed Cereals, Livestock
Cotton, Cereals
Cash Crops, Horticulture, Livestock
Pasture Livestock
Nomadic Livestock Herding
Forests
Nonagricultural Land

TURKEY

SYRIA

LEBANON

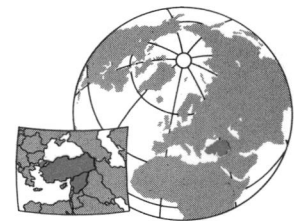
CYPRUS

TURKEY
AREA 300,946 sq. mi.
POPULATION 40,284,000
CAPITAL Ankara
LARGEST CITY Istanbul
HIGHEST POINT Ararat 16,946 ft.
MONETARY UNIT Turkish lira
MAJOR LANGUAGE Turkish
MAJOR RELIGION Islam

SYRIA
AREA 71,498 sq. mi.
POPULATION 7,585,000
CAPITAL Damascus
LARGEST CITY Damascus
HIGHEST POINT Hermon 9,232 ft.
MONETARY UNIT Syrian pound
MAJOR LANGUAGES Arabic, French, Kurdish, Armenian
MAJOR RELIGIONS Islam, Christianity

LEBANON
AREA 4,015 sq. mi.
POPULATION 3,207,000
CAPITAL Beirut
LARGEST CITY Beirut
HIGHEST POINT Qurnet es Sauda 10,131 ft.
MONETARY UNIT Lebanese pound
MAJOR LANGUAGE Arabic, French
MAJOR RELIGIONS Christianity, Islam

CYPRUS
AREA 3,473 sq. mi.
POPULATION 639,000
CAPITAL Nicosia
LARGEST CITY Nicosia
HIGHEST POINT Troodos 6,406 ft.
MONETARY UNIT Cypriot pound
MAJOR LANGUAGES Greek, Turkish, English
MAJOR RELIGIONS Eastern (Greek) Orthodoxy, Islam

CYPRUS
CITIES and TOWNS

Famagusta, 38,000 .....F 5
Famagusta, *41,000 .....F 5
Kyrenia, 3,500 .....E 5
Kyrenia, *4,500 .....E 5
Larnaca, 20,000 .....E 5
Larnaca, *21,000 .....E 5
Lefka, 3,673 .....E 5
Lefkara, 2,075 .....E 5
Limassol, 46,500 .....E 5
Limassol, *50,000 .....E 5
Morphou, 6,642 .....E 5
Nicosia (capital), 47,000 .....E 5
Nicosia, *112,000 .....E 5
Paphos, 10,000 .....E 5
Paphos, *11,500 .....E 5
Yialousa, 2,541 .....F 5

OTHER FEATURES

Andreas (cape) .....F 5
Arnauti (cape) .....E 5
Famagusta (bay) .....F 5
Gata (cape) .....E 5
Greco (cape) .....F 5
Klides (isls.) .....F 5
Kormakiti (cape) .....E 5
Larnaca (bay) .....F 5
Morphou (bay) .....E 5
Sovereign Base Area, 3,602 .....E 5
Troodos (mt.) .....E 5

LEBANON
CITIES and TOWNS

'Aleih, 18,630 .....F 6
Amyun, 7,926 .....F 5
Ba'albek, 15,560 .....G 5
Batrun, 5,976 .....F 5
Beirut (capital), 700,000 .....F 6
Beirut, *940,000 .....F 6
En Naqura, 967 .....F 6
Hermil, 2,652 .....G 5

Merj 'Uyun, 9,318 .....F 6
Rasheiya, 6,731 .....F 6
Rayak, 1,480 .....G 6
Saida, 32,200 .....F 6
Sidon (Saida), 32,200 .....F 6
Sur, 16,483 .....F 6
Tarabulus (Tripoli), 127,611 .....F 5
Tyre (Sur), 16,483 .....F 6
Zahle, 53,121 .....F 6
Zegharta, 18,210 .....G 5

OTHER FEATURES

Hermon (mt.) .....F 6
Lebanon (range) .....F 6
Litani (Leontes) (river) .....F 6
Sauda, Qurnet es (mt.) .....G 5

SYRIA
GOVERNORATES

Aleppo, 1,131,854 .....G 4
Damascus, 1,060,484 .....G 6
Damascus (municipality), 630,063 .....G 6
Deir ez Zor, 286,010 .....H 5
Der'a, 221,275 .....G 6
El Quneitra, 6,396 .....F 6
Es Suweida, 151,500 .....G 6
Hama, 390,084 .....G 5
Haseke, 309,279 .....J 4
Homs, 504,098 .....G 5
Idlib, 374,751 .....G 5
Latakia, 625,473 .....F 5
Rashid, 124,876 .....H 5

CITIES and TOWNS

Abu Kemal, 6,907 .....J 5
Aleppo, 566,770 .....G 4
A'zaz, 13,923 .....G 4
Baniyas, 8,537 .....F 5
Damascus (cap.), 789,840 .....G 6
Deir ez Zor, 60,335 .....H 5
Der'a, 20,465 .....G 6

Dimishq (Damascus) (capital), 789,840 .....G 6
Duma, 30,050 .....G 6
El Bab, 27,366 .....G 4
El Haseke, 23,074 .....J 4
El Ladhiqiya (Latakia), 72,378 .....F 5
El Quneitra, 206 .....F 6
El Rashid, 11,998 .....H 5
En Nebk, 16,334 .....G 5
Es Suweida, 17,592 .....G 6
Haleb (Aleppo), 566,770 .....G 4
Hama, 196,224 .....G 5
Harim, 6,837 .....G 4
Homs, 231,877 .....G 5
Idlib, 37,501 .....G 5
Jeble, 15,715 .....F 5
Jerablus, 8,610 .....H 4
Jisr esh Shughur, 13,131 .....G 5
Latakia, 72,378 .....F 5
Masyaf, 7,058 .....G 5
Membij, 13,796 .....G 4
Meyadin, 12,515 .....J 5
Palmyra (Tadmor), 10,670 .....H 5
Qamishliye, 31,448 .....J 4
Quteife, 4,993 .....G 6
Raqqa (El Rashid), 11,998 .....H 5
Safita, 9,650 .....G 5
Selemiya, 25,728 .....G 5
Tadmor, 10,670 .....H 5
Tartus, 19,137 .....F 5
Zebdani, 10,010 .....G 6

OTHER FEATURES

'Abdul 'Aziz, Jebel (mts.) .....J 4
Abu Rujmein, Jebel (mts.) .....H 5
'Asi (river) .....G 5
Druz, Jebel ed (mts.) .....G 6
Euphrates (El Furat) (river) .....J 5
Furat, El (river) .....H 4
Hermon (mt.) .....F 6
Khabur (river) .....J 5
Orontes ('Asi) (river) .....G 5
Ruad (island) .....F 5
Sharqi, Jebel esh (range) .....G 5
Tigris (river) .....K 4

TURKEY
PROVINCES

Adana, 902,712 .....F 4
Adıyaman, 267,288 .....H 4
Afyon-Karahisar, 502,248 .....D 3
Ağrı, 246,961 .....K 3
Amasya, 285,729 .....F 2
Ankara, 1,644,302 .....E 3
Antalya, 486,910 .....D 4
Artvin, 210,065 .....J 2
Aydın, 524,918 .....B 4
Balıkesir, 708,342 .....B 3
Bilecik, 139,041 .....D 2
Bingöl, 150,521 .....J 3
Bitlis, 154,069 .....J 3
Bolu, 383,939 .....D 2
Burdur, 194,950 .....D 4
Bursa, 755,504 .....C 2
Çanakkale, 350,317 .....B 2
Çankırı, 250,706 .....E 2
Çorum, 485,567 .....F 2
Denizli, 483,369 .....C 4
Diyarbakır, 475,916 .....H 4
Edirne, 303,234 .....B 2
Elâzığ, 322,727 .....H 3
Erzincan, 258,586 .....H 3
Erzurum, 628,001 .....J 3
Eskişehir, 415,101 .....D 3
Gaziantep, 511,026 .....G 4
Giresun, 428,015 .....H 2
Gümüşhane, 262,731 .....H 2
Hakkâri, 83,937 .....K 4
Hatay, 506,154 .....G 4
İçel, 511,273 .....F 4
Isparta, 266,240 .....D 4
Istanbul, 2,293,823 .....C 2
İzmir, 1,234,667 .....B 3
Kars, 606,313 .....K 2
Kastamonu, 441,638 .....E 2
Kayseri, 536,206 .....F 3
Kırklareli, 258,386 .....B 2
Kırşehir, 196,836 .....F 3
Kocaeli, 335,518 .....D 2
Konya, 1,122,622 .....E 4
Kütahya, 398,081 .....C 3

Malatya, 452,624 .....H 3
Manisa, 748,545 .....B 3
Maraş, 438,423 .....G 4
Mardin, 397,880 .....J 4
Muğla, 334,973 .....C 4
Muş, 198,716 .....J 3
Nevşehir, 203,316 .....F 3
Niğde, 362,044 .....F 4
Ordu, 543,863 .....G 2
Rize, 281,099 .....J 2
Sakarya, 404,078 .....D 2
Samsun, 755,946 .....F 2
Siirt, 264,832 .....J 4
Sinop, 266,069 .....F 2
Sivas, 705,186 .....G 3
Tekirdağ, 287,381 .....B 2
Tokat, 495,352 .....G 3
Trabzon, 595,782 .....H 2
Tunceli, 164,175 .....H 3
Urfa, 450,798 .....H 4
Uşak, 190,536 .....C 3
Van, 266,840 .....K 3
Yozgat, 437,883 .....F 3
Zonguldak, 650,191 .....D 2

CITIES and TOWNS

Abana, 2,455 .....F 1
Acıgöl, 3,265 .....F 3
Acıpayam, 4,514 .....C 4
Adalia (Antalya), 71,833 .....D 4
Adana, 289,919 .....F 4
Adapazarı, 86,124 .....D 2
Adilcevaz, 6,148 .....K 3
Adıyaman, 22,153 .....H 4
Afşin, 8,069 .....G 3
Afyon, 44,026 .....D 3
Ağlasun, 3,730 .....D 4
Ağrı, 3,425 .....K 3
Ağrı (Karaköse), 24,168 .....K 3
Ahlat, 5,065 .....K 3
Akçaabat, 7,600 .....H 2
Akçadağ, 5,995 .....G 3
Akçakale, 4,526 .....H 4
Akçakoca, 7,179 .....D 2
Akdağmadeni, 4,321 .....F 3
Akhisar, 46,167 .....B 3
Aksaray, 24,414 .....F 3

Akşehir, 25,269 .....D 3
Akseki, 2,505 .....D 4
Akviran, 3,786 .....E 4
Akyazı, 9,090 .....D 2
Alaca, 8,288 .....F 2
Alaçam, 7,833 .....F 2
Alanya, 12,436 .....D 4
Alaşehir, 16,012 .....C 3
Alexandretta (Iskenderun), 69,382 .....G 4
Aliağa, 3,087 .....B 3
Alibeyköyü, 15,199 .....D 6
Almus, 4,110 .....G 2
Alpu, 2,709 .....D 3
Altındağ, 89,838 .....E 2
Altınova, 6,368 .....B 3
Altıntaş, 2,361 .....C 3
Amasya, 34,168 .....F 2
Anadoluhisari, 13,959 .....D 6
Anamur, 11,246 .....E 4
Andırın, 3,695 .....G 4
Ankara (capital), 905,660 .....E 3
Antâkya, 57,855 .....G 4
Antalya, 71,833 .....D 4
Araç, 2,820 .....E 2
Aralık, 2,879 .....L 3
Arapkir, 7,056 .....H 3
Ardahan, 9,117 .....K 2
Ardeşen, 5,488 .....J 2
Arhavi, 4,510 .....J 2
Arnavutköy, 22,468 .....D 6
Arsin, 4,028 .....H 2
Artova, 2,863 .....G 2
Artvin, 9,847 .....J 2
Aşkale, 6,943 .....J 3
Aslanköy, 3,656 .....F 2
Avanos, 5,675 .....F 3
Ayancık, 5,320 .....F 2
Ayas, 3,873 .....E 2
Aybastı, 7,450 .....G 2
Aydın, 43,483 .....B 3
Ayvacık, 2,277 .....B 3
Ayvalık, 16,283 .....B 3
Babadağ, 5,511 .....C 4
Babaeski, 13,879 .....B 2
Bafra, 26,239 .....F 2
Bahçe, 2,264 .....G 4
Bakırköy, 65,285 .....D 6

Baklan, 2,680 .....C 4
Balâ, 3,646 .....E 3
Balıkesir, 69,341 .....B 3
Banaz, 3,495 .....C 3
Bandırma, 33,116 .....B 2
Barak, 3,117 .....G 4
Bartın, 14,259 .....E 1
Başkale, 4,007 .....K 3
Başmakçı, 5,093 .....D 4
Batman, 24,990 .....J 2
Bayburt, 15,184 .....H 2
Bayındır, 11,273 .....B 3
Bayramiç, 4,607 .....B 3
Bergama, 24,121 .....B 3
Beşiktaş, 58,814 .....D 6
Besni, 11,625 .....G 4
Beykoz, 37,730 .....D 6
Beylerbeyi, 21,741 .....D 6
Beyoğlu, 39,984 .....D 6
Beypazarı, 9,860 .....D 3
Beyşehir, 7,456 .....D 4
Biga, 12,063 .....B 2
Bigadiç, 4,820 .....C 3
Bilecik, 9,722 .....C 2
Bingöl (Çapakçur), 11,727 .....J 3
Birecik, 15,317 .....H 4
Bismil, 4,444 .....J 4
Bitlis, 18,725 .....J 3
Bodrum, 5,136 .....B 4
Boğazlıyan, 7,925 .....F 3
Bolu, 21,700 .....D 2
Bolvadin, 20,139 .....D 3
Bor, 14,309 .....F 4
Borçka, 3,763 .....J 2
Bornova, 30,445 .....B 3
Boyabat, 9,418 .....F 2
Bozdoğan, 6,739 .....C 4
Bozkır, 3,112 .....E 4
Bozkurt, 2,954 .....F 2
Bozova, 3,425 .....H 4
Bozüyük, 10,842 .....D 3
Bucak, 10,094 .....D 4
Bulancak, 9,343 .....G 2
Bulanık, 6,186 .....K 3
Buldan, 9,813 .....C 3
Bünyan, 8,467 .....F 3
Burdur, 29,268 .....D 4
Burhaniye, 12,597 .....B 3

(continued on following page)

Agriculture, Industry and Resources

DOMINANT LAND USE

- Cereals (chiefly wheat, barley), Livestock
- Cash Crops, Horticulture, Livestock
- Pasture Livestock
- Nomadic Livestock Herding
- Forests
- Nonagricultural Land

MAJOR MINERAL OCCURRENCES

- Ab Asbestos
- C Coal
- Cr Chromium
- Cu Copper
- Fe Iron Ore
- Hg Mercury
- Na Salt
- O Petroleum
- Pb Lead
- Sb Antimony
- Zn Zinc

- ⚡ Water Power
- ▨ Major Industrial Areas

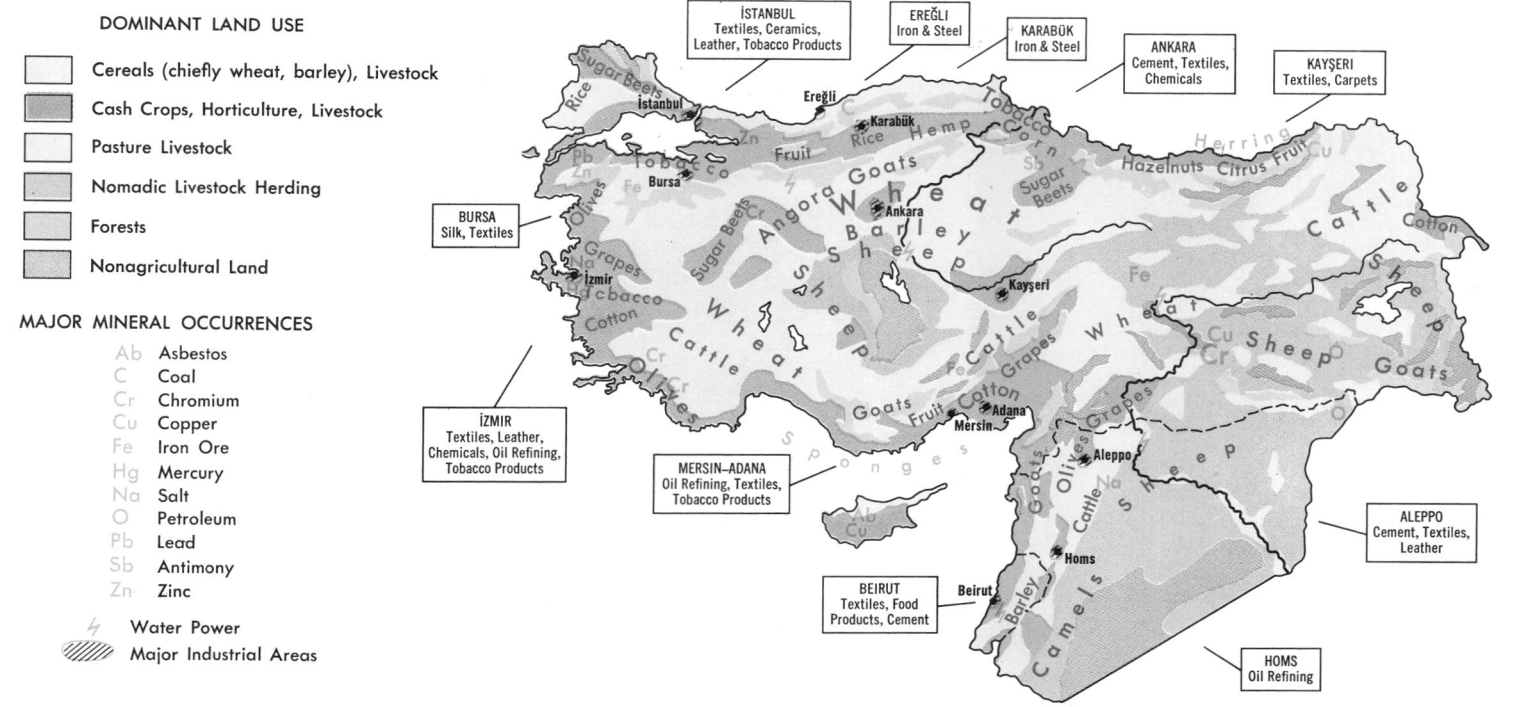

İSTANBUL — Textiles, Ceramics, Leather, Tobacco Products

EREĞLİ — Iron & Steel

KARABÜK — Iron & Steel

ANKARA — Cement, Textiles, Chemicals

KAYSERİ — Textiles, Carpets

BURSA — Silk, Textiles

İZMIR — Textiles, Leather, Chemicals, Oil Refining, Tobacco Products

MERSIN–ADANA — Oil Refining, Textiles, Tobacco Products

ALEPPO — Cement, Textiles, Leather

BEIRUT — Textiles, Food Products, Cement

HOMS — Oil Refining

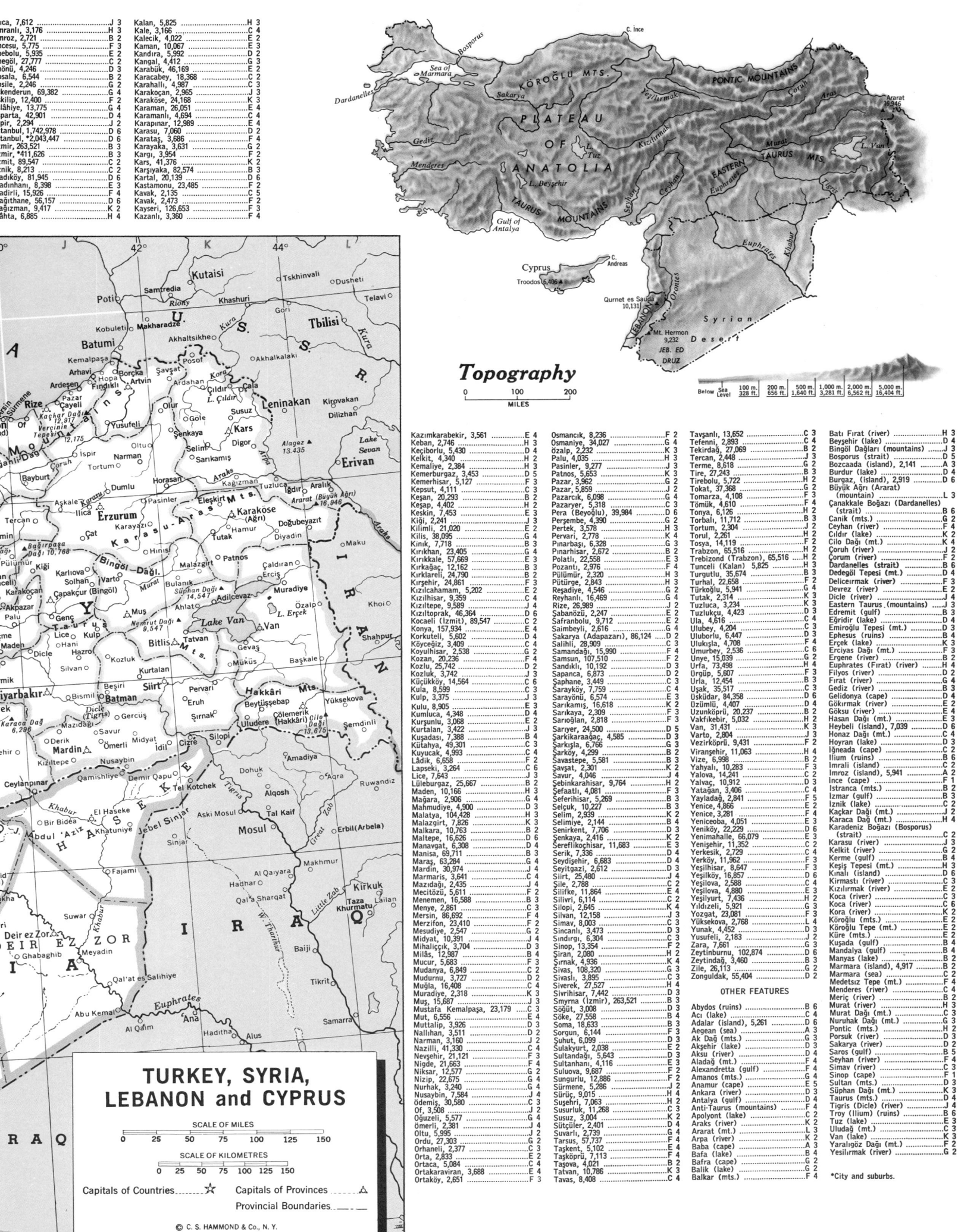

Ilıca, 7,612	J 3	Kalan, 5,825	H 3		
İmranlı, 3,176	H 3	Kale, 3,166	C 4		
İmroz, 2,721	A 2	Kalecik, 4,022	E 2		
İncesu, 5,775	F 3	Kaman, 10,067	E 3		
İnebolu, 5,935	E 2	Kandıra, 5,912	D 2		
İnegöl, 27,777	C 2	Kangal, 4,412	G 3		
İnönü, 4,246	D 3	Karabük, 46,169	E 2		
İpsala, 2,246	A 2	Karacabey, 18,368	C 2		
İpsile, 6,544	G 4	Karacahalı, 4,987	C 3		
İskenderun, 69,382	G 4	Karaçoban, 2,965	J 3		
İskilip, 12,400	F 2	Karaköse, 24,168	K 3		
İslâhiye, 13,775	G 4	Karaman, 26,051	E 4		
İsparta, 42,901	D 4	Karamanlı, 4,694	C 4		
İspir, 2,294	J 2	Karapınar, 12,989	E 4		
İstanbul, 1,742,978	D 6	Karasu, 7,060	D 2		
İstanbul, *2,043,447	D 6	Karataş, 3,686	F 4		
İzmir, 263,521	B 3	Karayaka, 3,631	G 2		
İzmir, *411,626	B 3	Kargı, 3,954	F 2		
İzmit, 89,547	C 2	Kars, 41,376	K 2		
İznik, 8,213	C 2	Karşıyaka, 82,574	B 3		
Kadıköy, 81,945	D 6	Kartal, 20,139	D 6		
Kadınhanı, 8,398	E 3	Kastamonu, 23,485	E 2		
Kadirli, 15,926	F 4	Kavak, 2,135	C 5		
Kağıthane, 56,157	D 6	Kavak, 2,473	F 2		
Kağızman, 9,417	K 2	Kayseri, 126,653	F 3		
Kâhta, 6,885	H 4	Kazanlı, 3,360	F 4		

Topography

MILES 0 100 200

Below Sea Level	100 m. 328 ft.	200 m. 656 ft.	500 m. 1,640 ft.	1,000 m. 3,281 ft.	2,000 m. 6,562 ft.	5,000 m. 16,404 ft.

Kazımkarabekir, 3,561	E 4	Osmancık, 8,236	F 2	Tavşanlı, 13,652	C 3	Batı Fırat (river)	H 3
Keban, 2,746	H 3	Osmaniye, 34,027	G 4	Tefenni, 2,893	C 4	Beyşehir (lake)	D 4
Keçiborlu, 5,430	D 4	özalp, 2,232	K 3	Tekirdağ, 27,069	B 2	Bingöl Dağları (mountains)	J 3
Kelkit, 4,340	H 2	Palu, 4,035	H 3	Tercan, 2,448	J 3	Bosporus (strait)	D 5
Kemaliye, 2,384	H 3	Pasinler, 9,277	J 3	Terme, 8,618	G 2	Bozcaada (island), 2,141	A 3
Kemerburgaz, 3,453	D 5	Patnos, 5,653	K 3	Tire, 27,243	B 3	Burdur (lake)	C 4
Kemerhisar, 5,127	F 3	Pazar, 3,962	H 2	Tirebolu, 5,722	H 2	Burgaz, (island), 2,919	D 6
Kepsut, 4,111	C 3	Pazar, 5,859	G 2	Tokat, 37,368	F 3	Büyük Ağrı (Ararat)	
Kepan, 20,293	B 2	Pazarcık, 6,098	G 4	Tomarza, 4,108	F 3	(mountain)	L 3
Keşap, 4,402	H 2	Pazaryer, 5,318	C 3	Tömük, 4,610	F 4	Çanakkale Boğazı (Dardanelles)	
Keskin, 7,453	E 3	Pera (Beyoğlu), 39,984	D 6	Tonya, 6,126	H 2	(strait)	B 6
Kiği, 2,241	J 3	Perşembe, 4,390	G 2	Torbalı, 11,712	B 3	Canik (mts.)	G 2
Kilimli, 21,020	E 2	Pertek, 3,578	H 3	Tortum, 2,304	J 2	Ceyhan (river)	F 4
Kilis, 38,095	G 4	Pervari, 2,778	K 4	Torul, 2,261	H 2	Cilo (lake)	K 2
Kınık, 7,718	B 3	Pınarbaşı, 6,328	G 3	Tosya, 14,119	F 2	Çoruh (river)	J 2
Kırıkhan, 23,405	G 4	Pınarhisar, 2,672	B 2	Trabzon, 65,516	H 2	Çorum (river)	F 2
Kırıkkale, 57,669	E 3	Polatlı, 22,558	E 3	Trebizond (Trabzon), 65,516	H 2	Dardanelles (strait)	B 6
Kırkağaç, 12,162	B 3	Pozantı, 2,976	F 4	Tunceli (Kalan), 5,825	H 3	Dedegöl Tepesi (mt.)	D 4
Kırklareli, 24,790	B 2	Pülümür, 2,320	H 3	Turgutlu, 35,674	B 3	Delice (river)	F 3
Kırşehir, 24,861	F 3	Pütürge, 2,843	H 3	Turhal, 22,658	F 2	Devrez (river)	E 2
Kızılcahamam, 5,202	E 2	Reşadiye, 4,546	G 2	Türkoğlu, 5,941	G 4	Dicle (river)	J 4
Kızılhisar, 9,359	C 4	Reyhanlı, 16,469	G 4	Tutak, 2,314	K 3	Eastern Taurus (mountains)	H 4
Kızıltepe, 9,589	J 4	Rize, 26,989	J 2	Tuzluca, 3,234	K 3	Edremit (gulf)	B 3
Kızıltoprak, 46,364	D 6	Şabanözü, 2,247	E 2	Tuzlukçu, 4,423	D 3	Eğridir (lake)	D 4
Kocaeli (İzmit), 89,547	C 2	Safranbolu, 9,712	E 2	Ula, 4,616	C 4	Emiroğlu Tepesi (mt.)	D 3
Konya, 157,934	E 4	Saimbeyli, 2,616	G 3	Uluborlu, 5,602	D 4	Ephesus (ruins)	B 4
Korkuteli, 5,602	D 4	Sakarya (Adapazarı), 86,124	D 2	Ulubey, 6,447	C 3	Erçek (lake)	K 3
Köyceğiz, 3,409	C 4	Salihli, 28,909	C 3	Ulukışla, 4,708	F 3	Erciyas Dağı (mt.)	F 3
Koyulhisar, 2,538	G 2	Samandağı, 15,990	F 4	Umurbey, 2,536	C 6	Ergene (river)	B 2
Kozan, 20,236	F 4	Samsun, 107,510	F 2	Unye, 15,039	G 2	Euphrates (Fırat) (river)	H 4
Kozlu, 25,742	D 2	Sandıklı, 10,192	D 3	Urfa, 73,498	H 4	Filyos (river)	E 2
Kozluk, 3,422	J 3	Sapanca, 6,873	D 2	Ürgüp, 5,607	F 3	Fırat (river)	G 4
Küçükköy, 14,564	C 6	Şaphane, 3,449	C 3	Urla, 12,454	B 3	Gediz (river)	C 3
Kula, 8,599	C 3	Sarayköy, 7,759	C 4	Üsküdar, 84,358	D 6	Gelidonya (cape)	D 4
Kulp, 3,375	J 3	Sarayönü, 6,574	E 3	Üzümlü, 4,407	D 4	Gökırmak (river)	E 2
Kulu, 8,905	E 3	Sarıkamış, 16,618	K 2	Uzunköprü, 20,237	A 2	Göksu (river)	E 4
Kumluca, 4,348	D 4	Sarıkaya, 2,309	F 3	Vakfıkebir, 5,032	H 2	Hasan Dağı (mt.)	E 3
Kurşunlu, 3,088	E 2	Sarıoğlan, 2,818	F 3	Van, 31,431	K 3	Heybeli (island), 7,039	D 6
Kurtalan, 3,422	J 3	Sarıyer, 24,500	D 5	Varto, 2,804	J 3	Honaz Dağı (mt.)	C 4
Kuşadası, 7,388	B 4	Şarkikaraağaç, 4,585	D 4	Vezirköprü, 9,431	F 2	Hoyran (lake)	D 4
Kütahya, 49,301	C 3	Şarkışla, 6,766	G 3	Viranşehir, 11,063	H 4	İğneada (cape)	C 2
Kuyucak, 4,993	C 4	Şarköy, 4,299	B 2	Vize, 6,998	B 2	Ilium (ruins)	B 3
Lâdik, 6,658	F 2	Savastepe, 5,581	B 3	Yahyalı, 10,283	F 3	İmralı (island)	C 2
Lapseki, 3,264	C 6	Şavşat, 2,301	J 2	Yalova, 14,241	C 2	İmroz (island), 5,941	A 2
Lice, 7,643	J 3	Savur, 4,046	J 4	Yalvaç, 10,912	D 4	İnce (cape)	F 1
Lüleburgaz, 25,667	B 2	Şebinkarahisar, 9,764	G 3	Yatağan, 3,406	C 4	İstranca (mts.)	B 2
Maden, 10,166	H 3	Şefaatli, 4,081	F 3	Yayladağ, 2,841	F 5	İzmar (gulf)	B 3
Mağara, 2,906	G 3	Seferihisar, 5,269	B 3	Yenice, 4,866	C 4	İznik (lake)	C 2
Mahmudiye, 4,900	D 3	Selçuk, 10,227	B 3	Yenice, 3,381	E 3	Kaçkar Dağı (mt.)	J 2
Malatya, 104,428	H 3	Selim, 2,939	K 2	Yeniceoba, 4,051	E 3	Karaca Dağ (mt.)	H 4
Malkara, 10,763	B 2	Selimiye, 2,144	B 4	Yeniköy, 22,229	D 6	Karadeniz Boğazı (Bosporus)	
Maltepe, 16,626	D 6	Şenirkent, 7,706	D 3	Yenişehir, 11,352	C 2	(strait)	C 2
Manavgat, 6,308	D 4	Şenkaya, 2,416	K 2	Yerkesik, 2,200	C 4	Karasu (river)	J 3
Manisa, 69,711	B 3	Şereflikoçhisar, 11,683	E 3	Yerköy, 11,962	F 3	Kelkit (river)	G 2
Maraş, 63,284	G 4	Serik, 7,336	D 4	Yeşilhisar, 8,647	F 3	Kerme (gulf)	B 4
Mardin, 30,974	J 4	Seydişehir, 6,883	D 3	Yeşilköy, 16,857	D 6	Keşiş Tepesi (mt.)	C 2
Marmaris, 3,641	C 4	Seyitgazi, 2,612	D 3	Yeşilova, 2,588	C 4	Kınalı (island)	D 6
Mazıdağı, 2,435	J 4	Siirt, 25,480	J 4	Yeşilova, 4,880	E 3	Kırmastı (river)	C 2
Mecitözü, 5,611	F 2	Şile, 2,187	D 6	Yeşilyurt, 7,436	H 2	Kızılırmak (river)	E 2
Menemen, 16,588	B 3	Silifke, 11,864	E 4	Yıldızeli, 5,921	G 3	Koca (river)	D 3
Menye, 2,861	C 3	Silivri, 6,114	C 2	Yozgat, 23,081	F 3	Koca (river)	K 2
Mersin, 86,692	F 4	Silopi, 2,645	K 4	Yüksekova, 2,768	L 4	Köroğlu (mts.)	D 2
Merzifon, 23,410	F 2	Silvan, 12,158	J 4	Yunak, 4,452	D 3	Köroğlu Tepe (mt.)	E 2
Mesudiye, 2,547	G 2	Simav, 8,003	C 3	Yusufeli, 2,183	J 2	Küre (mts.)	E 2
Midyat, 10,391	J 4	Sincanlı, 3,473	D 3	Zara, 7,661	G 3	Kuşada (gulf)	B 4
Mihalıçcık, 3,704	D 3	Sındırgı, 6,304	C 3	Zeytinburnu, 102,874	D 6	Mandalya (gulf)	B 4
Milâs, 12,987	B 4	Sinop, 13,354	F 2	Zeytindağ, 3,460	B 3	Manyas (lake)	C 2
Mucur, 5,683	F 3	Şiran, 2,980	H 2	Zile, 26,113	F 2	Marmara (island), 4,917	C 2
Mudanya, 6,849	C 2	Şırnak, 4,936	K 4	Zonguldak, 55,404	D 2	Marmara (sea)	C 2
Mudurnu, 3,727	D 2	Sivas, 108,320	G 3			Meandres (river)	C 4
Muğla, 16,408	C 4	Sivaslı, 3,895	C 3			Meriç (river)	A 2
Muradiye, 2,318	K 3	Siverek, 27,527	H 4			Murat (river)	H 3
Muş, 15,687	J 3	Sivrihisar, 7,442	D 3	**OTHER FEATURES**		Murat Dağı (mt.)	C 3
Mustafa Kemalpaşa, 23,179	C 3	Smyrna (İzmir), 263,521	B 3			Nuruhak Dağı (mt.)	H 2
Mut, 6,556	E 4	Söğüt, 3,008	D 3	Abydos (ruins)	B 6	Pontic (mts.)	G 2
Muttalip, 3,926	D 3	Söke, 27,558	B 3	Acı (lake)	D 4	Porsuk (river)	D 3
Nallıhan, 3,151	D 2	Soma, 18,633	B 3	Adalar (island), 5,261	D 6	Sakarya (river)	D 2
Narman, 3,160	J 2	Sorgun, 6,144	F 3	Aegean (sea)	A 3	Saros (gulf)	B 5
Nazilli, 41,330	C 4	Şuhut, 6,099	D 3	Ak Dağ (mts.)	F 3	Seyhan (river)	F 4
Nevşehir, 21,121	F 3	Sulakyurt, 2,038	E 2	Akşehir (lake)	D 3	Simav (river)	C 3
Niğde, 21,663	F 4	Sultandağı, 5,643	D 3	Aksu (river)	D 4	Sinop (cape)	F 1
Nizip, 22,675	G 4	Sultanhanı, 4,116	E 3	Aladağ (mt.)	F 4	Sultan (mts.)	D 3
Nurhak, 3,240	G 4	Suluova, 9,687	F 2	Alexandretta (gulf)	F 4	Süphan Dağı (mt.)	J 3
Nusaybin, 7,584	J 4	Sungurlu, 12,886	F 2	Amanos (mts.)	G 4	Taurus (mts.)	E 4
ödemiş, 30,580	C 3	Süfürü, 9,015	H 2	Anamur (cape)	E 4	Tigris (Dicle) (river)	J 4
Of, 3,508	J 2	Suşehri, 7,063	H 2	Ankara (river)	D 2	Troy (Ilium) (ruins)	B 6
Oğuzeli, 5,577	G 4	Susurluk, 11,268	C 3	Antalya (gulf)	D 4	Tuz (lake)	E 3
Ömerli, 2,381	J 4	Susuz, 3,004	K 2	Anti-Taurus (mountains)	G 3	Uludağ (mt.)	C 2
Oltu, 5,995	J 2	Sütçüler, 2,401	D 4	Apolyont (lake)	C 2	Van (lake)	K 3
Ordu, 27,303	G 2	Suvarlı, 2,739	G 4	Araks (river)	L 3	Yaralıgöz Dağı (mt.)	F 2
Orhaneli, 2,377	C 3	Tarsus, 57,737	F 4	Ararat (river)	K 3	Yeşilırmak (river)	G 2
Orta, 2,833	E 2	Taşkent, 5,102	E 4	Arpa (river)	K 3		
Ortaca, 5,084	C 4	Taşköprü, 7,113	F 2	Baba (cape)	A 3		
Ortakaraviran, 3,688	E 3	Taşova, 4,021	G 2	Bafa (lake)	B 4		
Ortaköy, 2,651	F 3	Tatvan, 10,786	K 3	Balık (lake)	F 2		
		Tavas, 8,408	C 4	Balkar (mts.)	F 4	*City and suburbs.	

TURKEY, SYRIA, LEBANON and CYPRUS

SCALE OF MILES
0 25 50 75 100 125 150

SCALE OF KILOMETRES
0 25 50 75 100 125 150

Capitals of Countries ⭐   Capitals of Provinces △

Provincial Boundaries ―――

© C. S. HAMMOND & Co., N.Y.

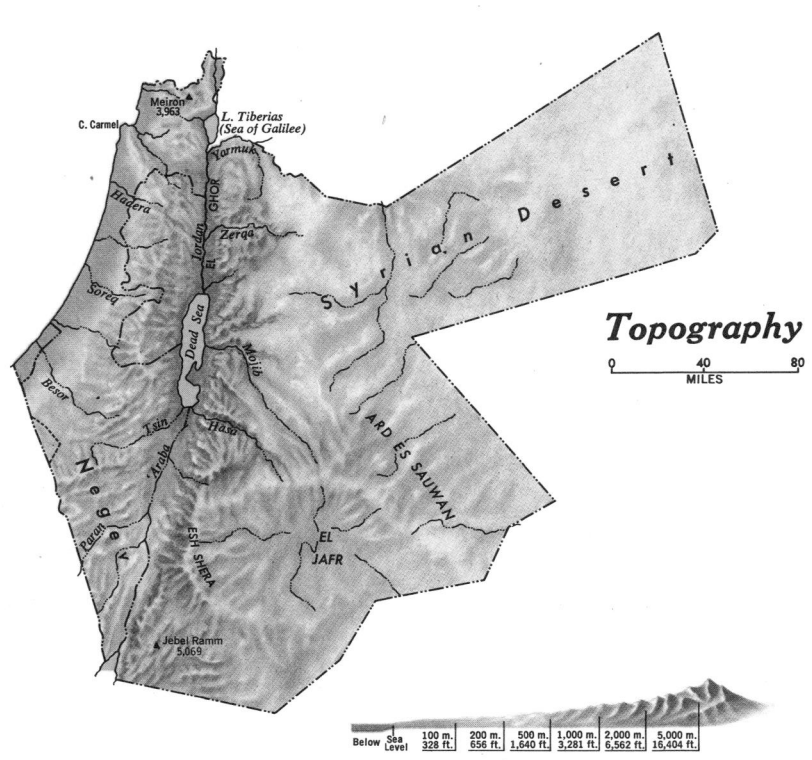

Topography

```
0        40        80
        MILES
```

| Below Sea Level | 100 m. 328 ft. | 200 m. 656 ft. | 500 m. 1,640 ft. | 1,000 m. 3,281 ft. | 2,000 m. 6,562 ft. | 5,000 m. 16,404 ft. |

ISRAEL

DISTRICTS

Central, 572,300 .... B 3
Haifa, 480,800 .... C 2
Jerusalem, 338,600 .... B 4
Northern, 473,700 .... C 2
Southern, 351,300 .... B 5
Tel Aviv, 905,100 .... B 3

CITIES and TOWNS

Acre, 34,400 .... C 2
Afiqim, 1,243 .... D 2
'Afula, 17,400 .... C 2
Ahuzzam, 407 .... B 4
Akko (Acre), 34,400 .... C 2
Arad, 5,400 .... C 5
'Arrabe, 6,000 .... C 2
Ashdod, 40,500 .... B 4
Ashdot Ya'aqov, 1,197 .... D 2
Ashqelon, 43,100 .... A 4
Atlit, 1,516 .... B 2
Avihayil, 579 .... B 3
Bat Shelomo, 218 .... B 2
Bat Yam, 114,000 .... B 3
Be'eri, 390 .... A 5
Beersheba, 104,000 .... B 5
Be'er Tuveya, 602 .... B 4
Beit Guvrin .... B 4
Bene Beraq, 74,100 .... B 3
Bet Dagan, 2,932 .... B 4
Bet Hagaddi, 566 .... B 5
Bet Qama, 228 .... B 5
Bet She'an, 11,300 .... D 3
Bet Shemesh, 10,100 .... B 4
Binyamina, 2,701 .... B 2
Carmiel .... C 2
Dafna, 577 .... D 1
Dalyat el-Karmel, 6,200 .... B 2
Dan, 498 .... D 1
Dimona, 23,700 .... D 4
Dor, 195 .... B 2
'Ein Harod, 1,372 .... C 2
Elath (Eilat), 12,800 .... D 5
El 'Auja .... D 5
Elyakim, 568 .... B 2
Elyashiv, 435 .... B 3
Even Yehuda, 3,464 .... B 3
Gal'on, 356 .... B 4
Gan Yavne, 2,668 .... B 4
Gat, 430 .... B 4
Gedera, 9,100 .... B 4
Gesher, 360 .... C 2
Gesher Haziv, 238 .... C 1
Gevar'am, 283 .... B 4
Gilat, 561 .... B 5
Ginnosar, 473 .... D 2
Giv'atayim, 48,500 .... B 3
Giv'at Brenner, 1,505 .... B 4
Giv'at Hayyim, 1,360 .... B 3
Gosh Halav (Jish), 1,498 .... C 1
Habonim, 189 .... B 2
Hadera, 31,900 .... B 3
Haifa, 225,000 .... B 2
Haifa, *353,700 .... B 2
Hatseva .... D 5
Hazerim, 127 .... B 5
Helez, 466 .... B 4
Herzeliyya, 41,200 .... B 3
Hod Hasharon, 13,500 .... B 3
Hodiyya, 400 .... B 4
Holon, 110,300 .... B 3
Iksal, 2,156 .... C 2
Jerusalem (cap.), 344,200 .... C 4
Jish, 1,498 .... C 1
Kafar Kanna, 5,200 .... C 2
Kafar Yasif, 2,975 .... C 2
Karkur-Pardes Hanna, 13,600 .... C 3
Kefar Atta, 27,000 .... C 2
Kefar Blum, 565 .... D 1
Kefar Gil'adi, 701 .... C 1
Kefar Ruppin, 306 .... D 3
Kefar Sava, 26,500 .... B 3
Kefar Vitkin, 808 .... B 3
Kefar Yona, 2,372 .... B 3
Kefar Zekhariya, 420 .... B 4
Kinneret, 909 .... D 2
Kurnub .... C 5
Lod (Lydda), 30,500 .... B 4
Lydda, 30,500 .... B 4
Magen, 149 .... A 5
Malkiya .... D 1
Mash 'Abbe Sade, 238 .... B 6
Mavqi'im, 177 .... B 4
Megiddo .... C 2
Me'ona, 317 .... C 1
Metula, 261 .... D 1
Migdal, 688 .... D 2
Mikhmoret, 608 .... B 3
Mishmar Hanegev, 336 .... B 5
Mishmar Hayarden .... D 1
Mivtahim, 398 .... A 5
Mizpe Ramon, 331 .... D 5
Moza Illit, 219 .... C 4
Mughar, 4,010 .... C 2
Muqeible, 459 .... C 2
Nahariyya, 24,000 .... C 1
Nazareth, 33,300 .... C 2
Negba, 453 .... B 4
Nesher, 9,400 .... C 2
Nes Ziyyona, 11,700 .... B 4
Nevatim, 436 .... B 5
Newe Yam, 211 .... B 2
Nir Am, 331 .... B 4
Nir Yitzhaq, 209 .... A 5
Nizzanim, 479 .... B 4
Oron .... C 6
Pardes Hanna-Karkur, 13,600 .... B 2
Peduyim, 361 .... B 5
Petah Tiqwa, 103,000 .... B 3
Qadima, 2,937 .... B 3
Qedma, 157 .... B 4
Qiryat Bialik, 18,000 .... C 2
Qiryat Gat, 19,200 .... B 4
Qiryat Haayin, 25,600 .... C 2
Qiryat Motzkin, 17,600 .... C 2
Qiryat Shemona, 15,200 .... C 1
Qiryat Tiv'on, 9,800 .... C 2
Qiryat Yam, 19,800 .... C 2
Ra'anana, 14,900 .... B 3
Ramat Gan, 120,200 .... B 3
Ramat Hasharon, 20,100 .... B 3
Rame, 2,986 .... C 2
Ramla, 34,100 .... B 4
Rehovot, 39,200 .... B 4
Re'im, 155 .... A 5
Revadim, 175 .... B 4
Revivim, 258 .... D 5
Rishon Le Ziyyon, 51,900 .... B 4
Rosh Pinna, 700 .... D 2
Ruhama, 497 .... B 4
Sa'ad, 418 .... B 5
Safad (Zefat), 13,600 .... C 2
Sakhnin, 8,400 .... C 2
Sede Boqer .... C 5
Sedom .... D 5
Sedot Yam, 511 .... B 2
Shave Ziyyon, 269 .... C 1
Shefar'am, 11,800 .... C 2
Shefayim, 614 .... B 3
Shoval, 393 .... B 4
Tayibe, 11,700 .... C 3
Tel Aviv-Jaffa, 357,600 .... B 3
Tel Aviv-Jaffa, *1,156,800 .... B 3
Tiberias, 23,800 .... D 2
Tirat Hakarmel, 14,400 .... B 2
Tirat Zevi, 353 .... D 3
Tur'an, 2,304 .... C 2
Umm el Fahm, 13,300 .... C 2
Urim, 203 .... A 5
Uzza, 487 .... B 4
Yad Mordekhai, 416 .... A 4
Yagur, 1,266 .... C 2
Yahav .... D 5
Yavne, 10,100 .... B 4
Yavne'el, 1,580 .... D 2
Yehud, 8,900 .... B 3
Yeroham, 5,800 .... B 6
Yesodot, 293 .... B 4
Yesud Hama'ala, 428 .... D 1
Yiftah .... D 1
Yirka, 2,715 .... C 2
Yoqne'am, 2,884 .... C 2
Yotvata .... D 5
Zavdi'el, 396 .... B 4
Ze'elim, 148 .... B 5
Zefat, 13,600 .... C 2
Zikhron Ya'aqov, 6,500 .... B 2
Zippori, 241 .... C 2

OTHER FEATURES

'Araba, Wadi (dry riv.) .... D 5
Beer Sheva' (dry riv.) .... B 5
Besor (riv.) .... B 5
Carmel (cape) .... C 2
Carmel (mt.) .... C 2
Dead (sea) .... C 4
'Ein Gedi (well) .... C 5
Galilee, Sea of (Tiberias) (lake) .... D 2
Galilee (reg.) .... C 2
Gerar (dry riv.) .... B 5
Hadera (dry riv.) .... B 3
Haniqra, Rosh (cape) .... C 1
Jordan (riv.) .... D 3
Judaea (reg.) .... B 4
Lakhish (dry riv.) .... B 4
Meiron (mt.) .... C 2
Negev (reg.) .... C 5
Qishon (riv.) .... C 2
Ramon (mt.) .... D 5
Rubin (dry riv.) .... B 4
Tabor (mt.) .... C 2
Tiberias (lake) .... D 2
Yarmuk (riv.) .... D 2
Yarqon (riv.) .... B 3

ARCHAEOLOGICAL SITES IN PALESTINE

■ Major Excavations

```
Miles
0    10    20    30
```

Mediterranean Sea

Sur / Tyre
Meirun / Merom
Acre
Tell el-Qedah / Hazor
Haifa / Tell Abu Hawam
Tell Hum / Capernaum
'Athlit
Sheikh Abreiq
Khirbet Kerak
Sea of Galilee
Shoikh Sa'd / Karnaim
Nazareth
el-Burj
Wadi el-Murgharah
Tell el-Mutesellim / Megiddo
el-Hammeh
Caesarea
Tell Ta'annek / Taanach
Tell el-Husn / Beth-shan
Tell el-Far'ah / Tirzah
Sabastiya / Samaria
Jarash / Gerasa
Tell Deir 'allah / Succoth
Balatah / Shechem
Tell el-Qasileh
Ras el-'Ain / Aphek
Tel Aviv-Jaffa
Seilun / Shiloh
Beitin / Bethel
et-Tell / Ai
Tell es-Sultan / Jericho
Amman / Philadelphia
Tell Jezer / Gezer
Tell en-Nasbeh / Mizpah
Tell el-Ful / Gibeah
Jerusalem
Teleilat el-Ghassul
Tell er-Rumeileh / Beth-shemesh
Bethlehem
Khirbet Qumran
Ma'daba
Ascalon
Tell Sandahannah
Tell el-Hesi / Eglon
Kh. et-Tubeiqah / Beth-zur
Gaza
Tell ed-Duweir / Lachish
Dhiban / Dibon
Tell el-'Ajjul
Tell Beit Mirsim / Debir
Dead Sea
Tell Jemmeh
Tell el-Far'ah / Sharuhen
Tell Abu Matar
Masada
Bab edh Dra'
Ader
Kurnub
Khirbet et-Tannur
Isbeita / Subaita

SYRIA
LEBANON
JORDAN
EGYPT

© C. S. Hammond & Co.

Agriculture, Industry and Resources

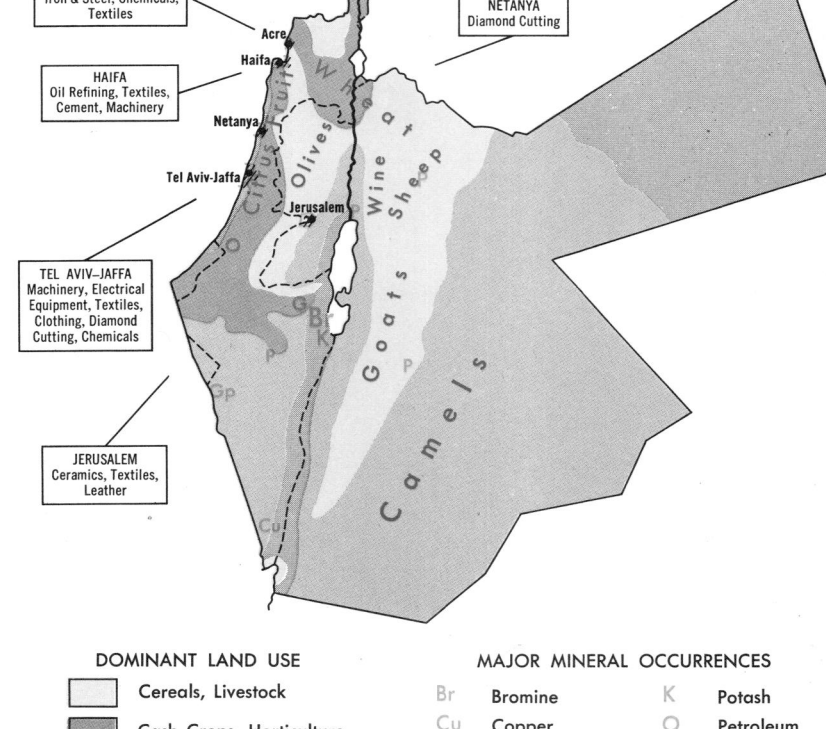

ACRE — Iron & Steel, Chemicals, Textiles

NETANYA — Diamond Cutting

HAIFA — Oil Refining, Textiles, Cement, Machinery

TEL AVIV-JAFFA — Machinery, Electrical Equipment, Textiles, Clothing, Diamond Cutting, Chemicals

JERUSALEM — Ceramics, Textiles, Leather

DOMINANT LAND USE

- ▢ Cereals, Livestock
- ▢ Cash Crops, Horticulture
- ▢ Nomadic Livestock Herding
- ▢ Nonagricultural Land

MAJOR MINERAL OCCURRENCES

Br	Bromine	K	Potash
Cu	Copper	O	Petroleum
G	Natural Gas	P	Phosphates
Gp	Gypsum		

▨ Major Industrial Areas

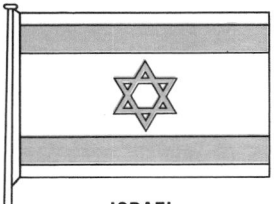

ISRAEL

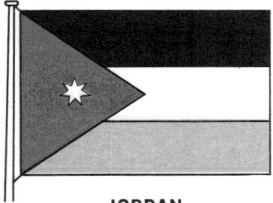

JORDAN

ISRAEL
AREA 7,847 sq. mi.
POPULATION 3,459,000
CAPITAL Jerusalem
LARGEST CITY Tel Aviv-Jaffa
HIGHEST POINT Meiron 3,963 ft.
MONETARY UNIT shekel
MAJOR LANGUAGES Hebrew, Arabic
MAJOR RELIGIONS Judaism, Islam,
Christianity

JORDAN
AREA 37,737 sq. mi.
POPULATION 2,700,000
CAPITAL Amman
LARGEST CITY Amman
HIGHEST POINT Jeb. Ramm 5,755 ft.
MONETARY UNIT Jordanian dinar
MAJOR LANGUAGE Arabic
MAJOR RELIGION Islam

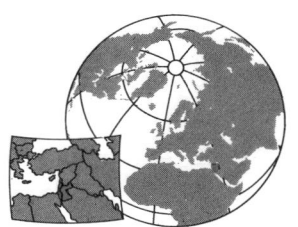

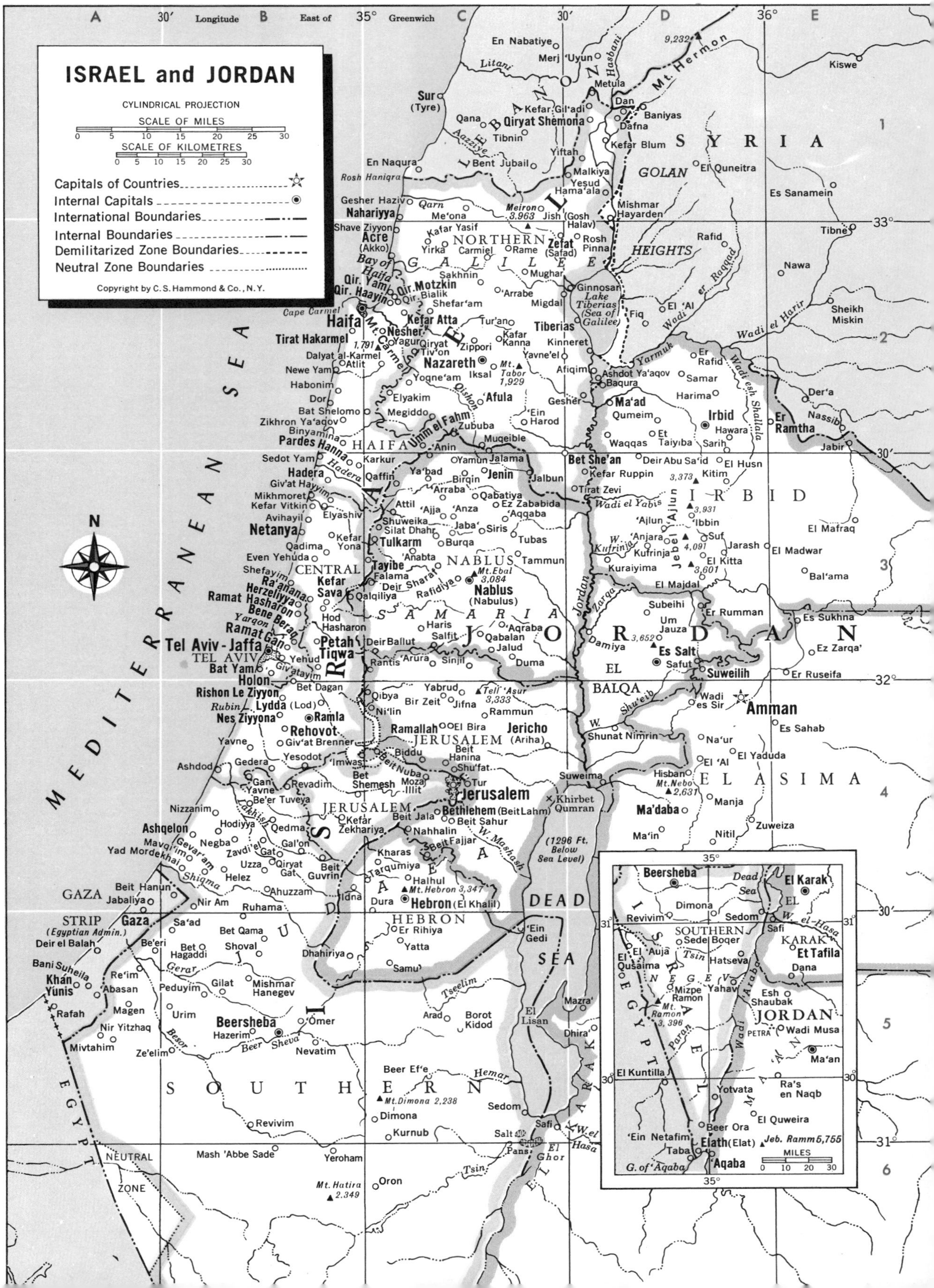

ISRAEL and JORDAN
CYLINDRICAL PROJECTION

SCALE OF MILES
0 5 10 15 20 25 30

SCALE OF KILOMETRES
0 5 10 15 20 25 30

Capitals of Countries .... ★
Internal Capitals _____ ◉
International Boundaries _____
Internal Boundaries _____
Demilitarized Zone Boundaries ___ ___
Neutral Zone Boundaries _____

Copyright by C.S. Hammond & Co., N.Y.

JORDAN
GOVERNORATES

El Asima, 526,000 ....D 4
El Balqa, 95,000 ....D 4
El Karak, 81,000 ....E 5
Hebron, 145,000 ....C 5
Irbid, 334,000 ....D 3
Jerusalem, 418,000 ....C 4
Ma'an, 58,000 ....D 5
Nablus, 414,000 ....C 3

CITIES and TOWNS

'Ajja, 1,322 ....C 3
'Ajlun, ‡42,000 ....D 4
Amman (cap.), 615,000 ....D 4
'Anabta, 3,426 ....C 3
'Anin, 914 ....C 3
'Anjara, 3,163 ....D 3
'Anza, 807 ....C 3
'Aqaba, 15,000 ....D 6
'Aqqaba, 1,127 ....C 4
'Aqraba, 2,501 ....C 4
Ariha (Jericho), 5,312 ....C 4
'Arraba, 4,231 ....C 3
'Arura, 849 ....C 4
'Attil, 3,808 ....C 3
Bal'ama, 769 ....E 3
Baqura, 3,042 ....D 2
Beit Fajjar, 2,474 ....C 4
Beit Hanun, 6,041 ....C 4
Beit Hanina, 1,177 ....C 4
Beit Jala, 9,974 ....C 4
Beit Nuba, 1,350 ....C 4
Beit Sahur, 5,380 ....C 4
Bethlehem, 14,439 ....C 4
Bethlehem, *16,313 ....C 4
Biddu, 1,259 ....C 4
Birgin, 2,036 ....C 3
Bir Zeit, 2,311 ....C 4
Burqa, 2,477 ....C 3
Damiya, 483 ....D 3
Dana, 844 ....E 5
Deir Abu Sa'id, 1,927 ....C 3
Deir Ballut, 1,058 ....C 3
Deir Sharaf, 973 ....C 3
Dhahiriya, 4,875 ....B 5
Dhira ....D 5
Duma, 524 ....C 3
Dura, 4,954 ....C 4
El 'Al, 492 ....D 4
El Bira, 9,674 ....C 4
El Bira, *13,037 ....C 4
El Husn, 3,728 ....C 3
El Karak, 10,000 ....E 4
El Khalil (Hebron), 38,309 ....C 4
El Kitta, 987 ....D 3
El Madwar, 164 ....E 3
El Mafraq, 15,500 ....E 3
El Majdal, 259 ....C 4
El Quweira, 268 ....E 5
El Yaduda, 251 ....E 4
Er Rafid, 787 ....D 2
Er Ramtha, 19,000 ....E 3
Er Rihiya, 679 ....C 5
Er Rumman, 293 ....E 3
Er Ruseifa, 6,200 ....E 3
Esh Shaubak, *4,634 ....E 5
Es Sahab, 2,580 ....E 4
Es Salt, 24,000 ....D 3
Es Sukhna, 649 ....E 3
Et Tafila, ‡17,000 ....E 5
Et Taiyiba, 2,606 ....C 3
Ez Zababida, 1,474 ....C 3
Ez Zarqa', 226,000 ....E 3
Falama, 162 ....C 3
Halhul, 6,041 ....C 4
Harima, 635 ....D 2
Haris, 941 ....C 4
Hawara, 2,342 ....D 2
Hisban, 718 ....D 4
'Ibbin, 1,364 ....D 3
Idna, 3,713 ....B 4
Irbid, 125,000 ....D 2
Jaba, 2,817 ....C 3
Jabir, 132 ....E 2
Jalama, 784 ....C 3
Jalbun, 914 ....C 3
Jalud, 221 ....C 3
Jarash, ‡29,000 ....D 3
Jenin, 8,346 ....C 3
Jenin, *13,365 ....C 3
Jericho, 5,312 ....C 4
Jericho, *6,931 ....C 4
Jifna, 655 ....C 4

Kharas, 1,364 ....C 4
Kitim, 1,026 ....D 3
Kufrinja, 3,922 ....D 3
Kuraiyima ....D 3
Ma'ad, 125 ....D 2
Ma'an, 9,500 ....D 5
Ma'daba, 22,600 ....D 4
Ma'in, 1,271 ....D 4
Manja, 353 ....C 4
Mazra' ....D 4
Nablus (Nabulus), 41,799 ....C 3
Nablus, *44,223 ....C 3
Nahhalin, 1,109 ....C 4
Na'ur, 2,382 ....D 4
Ni'lin, 1,227 ....C 4
Nitil, 348 ....D 4
Qabalan, 1,970 ....C 3
Qabatiya, 6,005 ....C 3
Qaffin, 2,480 ....C 3
Qalqiliya, 8,926 ....C 3
Qibya, 926 ....C 4
Qumeim, 955 ....D 2
Rafidiya, 1,123 ....C 3
Ramallah, 12,134 ....C 4
Rammun, 1,198 ....C 4
Rantis, 897 ....C 4
Ra's en Naqb, 225 ....E 5
Safi ....E 5
Safut, 4,210 ....D 3
Salfit, 3,201 ....C 3
Salt, 716 ....C 4
Samu', 3,784 ....C 5
Sarih, 3,390 ....D 2
Shu'fat, 14,000 ....D 4
Shunat Nimrin, 109 ....D 4
Shuweika, 2,332 ....C 3
Silat Dhahr, 2,104 ....C 3
Sinjil, 1,823 ....C 3
Siris, 1,285 ....C 3
Subeihi, 514 ....D 3
Suf ....D 3
Suweilih, 3,457 ....D 3
Suweima, 315 ....D 4
Tammun, 2,952 ....C 3
Tarqumiya, 2,412 ....C 4
Tubas, 5,262 ....C 3
Tulkarm, 10,255 ....C 3
Tulkarm, *15,275 ....C 3
Tur, 12,200 ....C 4
Um Jauza, 582 ....C 4
Wadi es Sir, 4,455 ....D 4
Wadi Musa, 654 ....E 5
Waqqas, 2,321 ....D 2
Ya'bad, 4,857 ....C 3
Yabrud, 277 ....C 4
Yamun, 4,384 ....C 3
Yatta, 7,281 ....C 5
Zububa, 633 ....C 2
Zuweiza, 126 ....D 4

OTHER FEATURES

'Ajlun (range) ....D 3
'Aqaba (gulf) ....D 5
'Araba, Wadi (dry riv.) ....D 5
Dead (sea) ....C 4
Ebal (mt.) ....C 3
El Ghor (reg.) ....C 6
El Lisan (pen.) ....C 5
Hebron (mt.) ....C 4
Jordan (riv.) ....D 3
Judaea (reg.) ....C 4
Khirbet Qumran (site) ....D 4
Nebo (mt.) ....D 4
Ramm, Jebel (mt.) ....D 5
Samaria (reg.) ....C 3
Tell 'Asur (mt.) ....C 3
Zarqa' (riv.) ....D 3

GAZA STRIP
CITIES and TOWNS

'Abasan, 1,481 ....A 5
Bani Suheila, 7,561 ....A 5
Beit Hanun, 4,756 ....A 5
Deir el Balah, 10,854 ....A 5
Deir el Balah, *18,118 ....A 5
Gaza, 87,793 ....A 5
Gaza, *118,272 ....A 5
Jabaliya, 10,508 ....A 4
Jabaliya, *43,604 ....A 4
Khan Yunis, 29,522 ....A 5
Khan Yunis, *52,997 ....A 5
Rafah, 10,812 ....A 5
Rafah, *49,812 ....A 5

*City and suburbs.
‡Population of subdivision.

IRAN

INTERNAL DIVISIONS

Bakhtiari (governorate),
298,448 ....F 4
Boyer Ahmedi and Kahkiluye
(governorate) ....G 5
Central (province), 4,979,081 ....G 3
East Azerbaijan (province),
2,596,439 ....E 1
Fars (province), 1,429,804 ....H 6
Gilan (province), 1,752,504 ....F 2
Hamadan (governorate),
889,888 ....F 3
Ilam (governorate) ....E 4
Isfahan (province),
1,703,701 ....H 4
Kerman (province), 761,851 ....K 6
Kermanshah (prov.), 924,717 ....E 3
Khurasan (prov.), 2,497,381 ......K 3
Khuzistan (prov.), 1,578,079 .....F 5
Kurdistan (province), 619,573 ....E 3
Luristan (governorate),
686,307 ....F 4
Mazanderan (province),
1,841,637 ....H 2
Ports and Islands
(province), 346,410 ....H 7
Samnan (governorate),
207,786 ....J 3
Seistan and Baluchistan (prov.),
454,996 ....M 6
Southern Coast (province),
251,921 ....G 6
West Azerbaijan (province),
1,087,182 ....D 1
Yezd (governorate) ....J 5
Zenjan (governorate) ....F 2

CITIES and TOWNS

Abadan, 272,962 ....F 5
Abadeh, 16,000 ....H 5
Abarquh, 8,000 ....H 5
Abhar, 11,000 ....F 2
Ahar, 24,000 ....E 1
Ahwaz, 206,375 ....F 5
Amul, 40,076 ....H 2
Anarak, 2,038 ....H 4
Andimeshk, 16,000 ....F 4
Aradan, 18,978 ....H 3
Arak, 71,925 ....F 3
Ardebil, 83,596 ....F 1
Ardistan, 6,645 ....H 4
Asadabad, 7,000 ....F 3
Asterabad (Gurgan),
51,181 ....J 2
Azarshahr, 6,000 ....D 2
Azna, 9,000 ....F 3
Babol, 49,973 ....H 2
Babulsar, 12,000 ....H 2
Bafq, 5,000 ....J 5
Baft, 6,000 ....K 6
Bahramabad, 21,000 ....K 5
Bam, 22,000 ....L 6
Bandar 'Abbas, 34,627 ....J 7
Bandar Ma'shur,
17,000 ....F 5
Bandar Shah, 13,000 ....J 2
Bandar Shahpur, 6,000 ....F 5
Behbehan, 39,874 ....G 5
Behshahr, 26,032 ....H 2
Bijar, 12,000 ....E 3
Birjand, 25,854 ....L 4
Borazjun, 20,000 ....G 6
Bujnurd, 31,248 ....K 2
Bukan, 9,000 ....E 2
Burujird, 71,476 ....F 4
Bushire, 26,032 ....G 6
Chalus, 15,000 ....G 2
Dalijan, 6,000 ....G 3
Damghan, 13,000 ....J 2
Darab, 15,000 ....H 6
Daran, 4,609 ....G 4
Dareh Gaz, 11,000 ....L 2
Daulatabad (Malayer), 28,434 ..F 3
Deh Haqq, 4,115 ....G 4
Demavend, 5,391 ....H 3
Dizful, 84,499 ....F 4
Duzdab (Zahidan), 40,000 ....M 6
Enzeli (Pahlevi), 41,785 ....F 2
Estahbanat, 18,187 ....H 6
Fahrej (Iranshahr), 5,000 ....M 7
Fariman, 8,000 ....L 3
Farrashband, 3,532 ....G 6
Fasa, 19,000 ....H 6
Firdaus, 11,000 ....K 3
Firuzabad, 8,718 ....H 6
Firuzkuh, 4,684 ....H 3
Fumen, 9,000 ....F 2
Gach Saran, 9,000 ....G 5
Ganaveh, 9,000 ....G 6
Garmsar, 4,723 ....H 3
Golshan (Tabas), 10,000 ....K 4
Gulpaigan, 20,515 ....G 4
Gumishan, 6,000 ....J 2
Gunabad, 8,000 ....L 3
Gunbad-i-Qabus, 40,667 ....K 2
Gurgan, 51,181 ....J 2
Haft Kel, 10,000 ....F 5
Hamadan, 124,167 ....F 3
Hashtpar, 5,000 ....F 2
Homayunshahr, 46,836 ....G 4
Ilam, 15,000 ....E 4
Iranshahr, 5,000 ....M 7
Isfahan, 424,045 ....G 4
Jahrum, 38,236 ....H 6

Kangavar, 9,414 ....F 3
Karaj, 44,243 ....G 3
Kashan, 58,468 ....G 3
Kashmar, 17,000 ....L 3
Kazerun, 39,758 ....G 6
Kazvin, 88,106 ....G 2
Kerman, 85,404 ....K 5
Kermanshah, 187,930 ....E 3
Khaf, 5,000 ....L 3
Khoi, 47,648 ....D 1
Khorramshahr, 88,536 ....F 5
Khunsar, 10,947 ....G 4
Khur, 2,912 ....J 4
Khurramabad, 59,578 ....F 4
Lahijan, 25,725 ....F 2
Lar, 22,000 ....H 7
Mahabad, 28,610 ....D 2
Mahallat, 12,000 ....G 4
Mahan, 8,000 ....K 5
Maibud, 15,000 ....H 4
Maku, 7,000 ....D 1
Malayer, 28,434 ....F 3
Maragheh, 54,106 ....D 1
Marand, 24,000 ....D 1
Marvdasht, 25,498 ....H 6
Masjid-i-Sulaiman, 64,488 ......F 5
Meshed, 409,616 ....L 2
Meshed-i-Sar (Babulsar) ....H 2
Meshkinshahr, 9,000 ....F 1
Mianeh, 28,447 ....E 2
Mirjawa, 11,000 ....M 6
Miyanduab, 19,000 ....D 1
Naft-i-Shah, 3,043 ....E 4
Na'in, 5,925 ....H 4
Nasratabad (Zabul), 20,000 .....M 5
Natanz, 4,370 ....H 4
Naushahr, 8,000 ....G 2
Nehavend, 24,000 ....F 3

Nejafabad, 43,384 ....G 4
Niriz, 16,114 ....J 6
Nishapur, 33,482 ....L 2
Pahlevi (Enzeli), 41,785 ....F 2
Qain, 6,000 ....L 3
Qasr-i-Shirin, 15,904 ....E 3
Quchan, 29,133 ....L 2
Qum, 134,292 ....G 3
Rafsenjan (Bahramabad),
21,000 ....K 5
Rai, 102,825 ....G 3
Ram Hormuz, 9,000 ....F 5
Ramsar, 12,000 ....G 2
Ravar, 7,000 ....K 5
Resht, 143,557 ....F 2
Reza'iyeh, 110,749 ....D 2
Sabzawar, 42,415 ....K 2
Sabzawaran, 7,000 ....K 6
Saidabad (Sirjan), 20,000 ....J 6
Samnan, 31,058 ....J 3
Sanandaj, 54,578 ....E 3
Sang-i-Sar, 9,000 ....H 3
Saqqiz, 17,000 ....E 2
Sarab, 16,000 ....E 2
Sardasht, 6,000 ....D 2
Sari, 44,547 ....H 2
Savanat (Estahbanat),
18,187 ....H 6
Saveh, 17,565 ....G 3
Shahabad, 12,000 ....E 3
Shahdegan, 6,000 ....F 5
Shahi, 38,898 ....H 2
Shahpur, 22,000 ....D 1
Shahr-i-Kurd, 24,000 ....G 4
Shahriza, 34,220 ....H 4
Shahrud, 30,767 ....J 2
Shahsawar, 12,000 ....G 2
Shiraz, 269,865 ....H 6
Shirvan, 11,000 ....K 2

Shushtar, 24,000 ....F 4
Sinneh (Sanandaj), 54,578 ......E 3
Sirjan, 20,000 ....J 6
Sultanabad (Kashmar),
17,000 ....L 3
Sunqur, 10,433 ....F 3
Susangird, 21,000 ....F 5
Tabas, 10,000 ....K 4
Tabriz, 403,413 ....D 1
Taft, 7,000 ....J 5
Tajrish, 157,486 ....G 3
Takistan, 13,485 ....G 2
Tehran (capital), 2,719,730 ......G 3
Tuiserkan, 12,000 ....F 3
Tun (Firdaus), 11,000 ....K 3
Turbat-i-Haidari, 20,000 ....L 3
Turbat-i-Shaikh Jam, 13,000 ...M 3
Urmia (Reza'iyeh), 110,749 ......D 2
Ushnuiyeh, 5,000 ....D 2
Veramin, 11,183 ....G 3
Yezd, 93,241 ....J 5
Zabul, 20,000 ....M 5
Zahidan, 39,732 ....M 6
Zarand, 5,000 ....K 5
Zarghan, 7,000 ....H 6
Zenjan, 58,714 ....F 2

OTHER FEATURES

Ab-i-Diz (river) ....F 4
Aji Chai (river) ....E 1
Arabi (isl.) ....G 7
Aras (Araks) (river) ....E 1
Atrek (river) ....K 2
Bakhtegan (lake) ....J 6
Baluchistan (region) ....M 7
Bampur (river) ....M 7
Behistun (ruins) ....E 3
Caspian (sea) ....F 1
Darya-yi-Namak (salt lake) ....H 3
Dasht-i-Kavir (salt desert) ....K 4
Dasht-i-Lut (desert) ....L 5
Demavend (mt.) ....H 3
Dez (Ab-i-Diz) (river) ....F 4
Elburz (range) ....G 2
Farsi (isl.) ....G 6
Gurgan (river) ....J 2
Hamun-i-Helmand (marsh) ......M 6
Hamun-i-Jaz-Murian
(marsh) ....L 6
Hamun-i-Sabari (lake) ....M 5
Hanjam (isl.) ....H 7
Hari Rud (river) ....M 3
Hashtadan (reg.) ....L 3
Hormuz (strait) ....J 7
Kalar, Kuh-i- (mt.) ....H 5
Karkheh (river) ....F 4
Karun (river) ....F 4
Kashaf Rud (river) ....L 2
Kharg (isl.), 647 ....G 6
Kuh, Ras el (cape) ....K 7
Kuh-i-Aladagh (mts.) ....K 2
Kuh-i-Bagraband (mts.) ....G 2
Kuh-i-Bazqush (mts.) ....E 2
Kuh-i-Dinar (mts.) ....G 5
Kuh-i-Jagatai (mts.) ....K 2
Kuh-i-Shah Jehan (mts.) ....K 2
Kur Rud (river) ....H 6
Kurang (river) ....G 4
Laristan (region) ....H 7
Maidani (cape) ....G 7
Makran (region) ....L 7
Mand Rud (river) ....G 6
Mashkel (river) ....M 7
Mehran (river) ....G 7
Mura, Qal'eh-i- (ruins) ....E 3
Namaksar (lake) ....M 3

IRAN

IRAQ

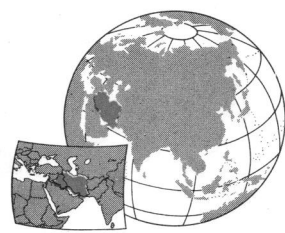

Index (Iraq)

kzar (dry lake)	L 4
ar (mt.)	H 3
g (river)	N 7
gadae (gulf)	M 8
gadae (ruins)	H 5
polis (ruins)	H 6
an (ruins)	F 6
i-Kuh (mts.)	E 4
(isl.)	J 7
eh Dagh (mts.)	E 1
Su (river)	E 2
Su (river)	G 2
aqu (river)	F 2
n (isl.)	H 8
Uzun (river)	F 2
h Shu'aib (island)	H 7
gh (river)	M 5
an (river)	E 3
Kuh (mts.)	L 3
(river)	M 8
(ruins)	N 6
k (lake)	D 2
(lake)	J 5
(region)	J 7
(mts.)	E 4
eh Rud (river)	H 4
eh (river)	E 2
Chai (river)	D 1
eh Rud (river)	F 5

IRAQ PROVINCES

	B 4
Najaf	C 5

Babil	D 4
Baghdad	D 4
Basra	E 5
Dhi Qar	E 5
Diyala	D 4
Dohuk	C 2
Erbil	C 3
Karbala'	D 4
Maysan	E 5
Muthanna	D 5
Ninawa	C 3
Qadisiya	D 4
Salahuddin	D 3
Sulaimaniya	C 3
Tamim	C 3
Wasit	D 4

CITIES and TOWNS

Ad Diwaniya, 60,553	D 5
'Afaq, 5,390	D 4
Al 'Azair, 2,255	E 5
Al 'Aziziya, 7,450	D 4
Al Falluja, 38,072	C 4
Al Kufa, 30,862	D 4
Al Kumait, 2,225	E 4
Al Musaiyib, 15,955	D 4
Al Qa'im, 3,372	B 3
Al Qaiyara, 3,060	C 3
Al Qosh, 3,863	C 2
Al Qurna, 5,638	E 5
'Ali Gharbi, 5,735	E 4
'Ali Sharqi, 1,980	E 4
'Amadiya, 2,578	C 2
'Amara, 64,847	E 5
An Najaf, 128,096	D 5
An Nasiriya, 60,405	D 5
'Ana, 6,884	B 3
'Aqra, 8,659	D 2
Ar Rahhaliya	C 4
Arbela (Erbil), 90,320	D 2
As Busaiya, 295	E 5
As Salman, 1,789	D 5
Ash Shabicha, 249	C 5
Az Zubair, 41,408	E 5
Badra, 3,564	D 4
Baghdad (capital), 502,503	D 4
Baghdad, *1,745,328	D 4
Baiji, 6,785	C 3
Ba'quba, 34,575	D 4
Basra, 313,327	E 5
Dohuk, 16,998	D 2
Erbil, 90,320	C 2
Fao, 15,399	F 6
Habbaniya, 14,405	C 4
Hadhar, 1,019	C 3
Hadith, 6,870	E 4
Hai, 16,988	E 4
Halabja, 11,206	D 3
Hilla, 84,717	D 4
Hindiya, 16,436	D 4
Hit, 9,131	C 4
Karbala', 83,301	D 4
Khanaqin, 23,522	D 3
Kifri, 8,500	D 3
Kirkuk, 167,413	D 3
Kut, 42,116	D 4
Lailan, 1,526	D 3
Maidan, 354	D 3
Makhmur, 2,556	C 3
Mandali, 11,262	D 4
Mosul, 315,157	C 2
Muqdadiyah, 12,181	D 4
Na'maniya, 11,943	D 4
Qal'at Sharqat, 2,434	C 3
Qal'at Diza, 6,250	D 2
Ramadi, 28,723	C 4
Rania, 4,090	D 2
Refa'i, 7,681	E 5
Rumaitha, 10,222	D 5
Rutba, 5,091	B 4
Ruwandiz, 5,807	D 2
Sa'diya, 5,285	D 3
Samarra, 24,746	C 3
Samawa, 33,473	D 5
Shaikh Sa'ad, 2,958	E 4
Shaqlawa, 6,814	D 2
Shatra, 18,822	E 5
Shithatha, 2,326	C 4
Sinjar, 7,942	B 2
Sulaimaniya, 86,822	D 3
Tal Kaif, 7,482	C 2
Tauq, 845	D 3
Taza Khurmatu, 2,681	D 3
Tikrit, 9,921	C 3
Tuz Khurmatu, 13,860	D 3
Zakho, 14,790	C 2
Zorbatiya, 1,602	D 4

OTHER FEATURES

Adhaim (river)	D 3
Al Hajara (plain)	D 5
'Aneiza, Jebel (mt.)	A 4
'Arab, Shatt-al- (river)	F 5
'Ar'ar, Wadi (dry river)	B 5
Babylon (ruins)	D 4
Bahr al Milh (lake)	D 4
Batin, Wadi al (dry river)	E 6
Ctesiphon (ruins)	D 4
Darbandikhan (dam)	D 3
Euphrates (river)	D 4
Great Zab (river)	C 2
Hajara, Al (plain)	D 5
Haji Ibrahim (mt.)	D 2
Hammar, Hor al (lake)	E 5
Hauran, Wadi (dry river)	B 4
Ibrahim, Haji (mt.)	D 2
Little Zab (river)	C 3
Mesopotamia (region)	B 3
Nineveh (ruins)	C 3
Sa'diya, Hor (lake)	E 4
Saniya, Hor (lake)	E 5
Sha'ib Hisb, Wadi (dry river)	C 5
Shatt-al-'Arab (river)	F 5
Sinjar, Jebel (mts.)	B 2
Siyah Kuh (mt.)	B 2
Syrian (desert)	B 4
Tigris (river)	C 2
Ubaiyidh, Wadi (dry river)	B 5
Ur (ruins)	D 5

*City and suburbs.
†Population of sub-district.

IRAN

AREA 636,293 sq. mi.
POPULATION 32,900,000
CAPITAL Tehran
LARGEST CITY Tehran
HIGHEST POINT Demavend 18,376 ft.
MONETARY UNIT Iranian rial
MAJOR LANGUAGES Persian, Azerbaijani, Kurdish
MAJOR RELIGIONS Islam, Zoroastrianism

IRAQ

AREA 172,476 sq. mi.
POPULATION 11,400,000
CAPITAL Baghdad
LARGEST CITY Baghdad
HIGHEST POINT Haji Ibrahim 11,811 ft.
MONETARY UNIT Iraqi dinar
MAJOR LANGUAGES Arabic, Kurdish
MAJOR RELIGION Islam

Topography

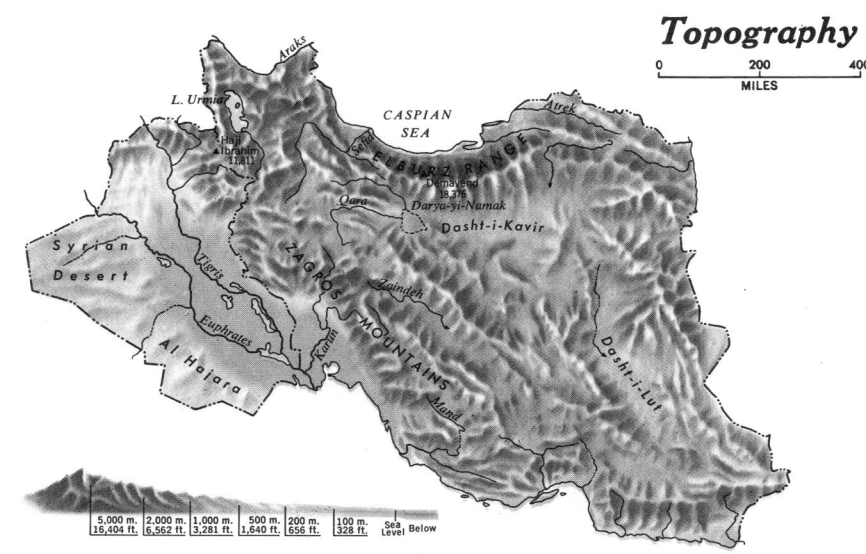

0   200   400
MILES

5,000 m. 2,000 m. 1,000 m. 500 m. 200 m. 100 m. Sea Below
16,404 ft. 6,562 ft. 3,281 ft. 1,640 ft. 656 ft. 328 ft. Level

Agriculture, Industry and Resources

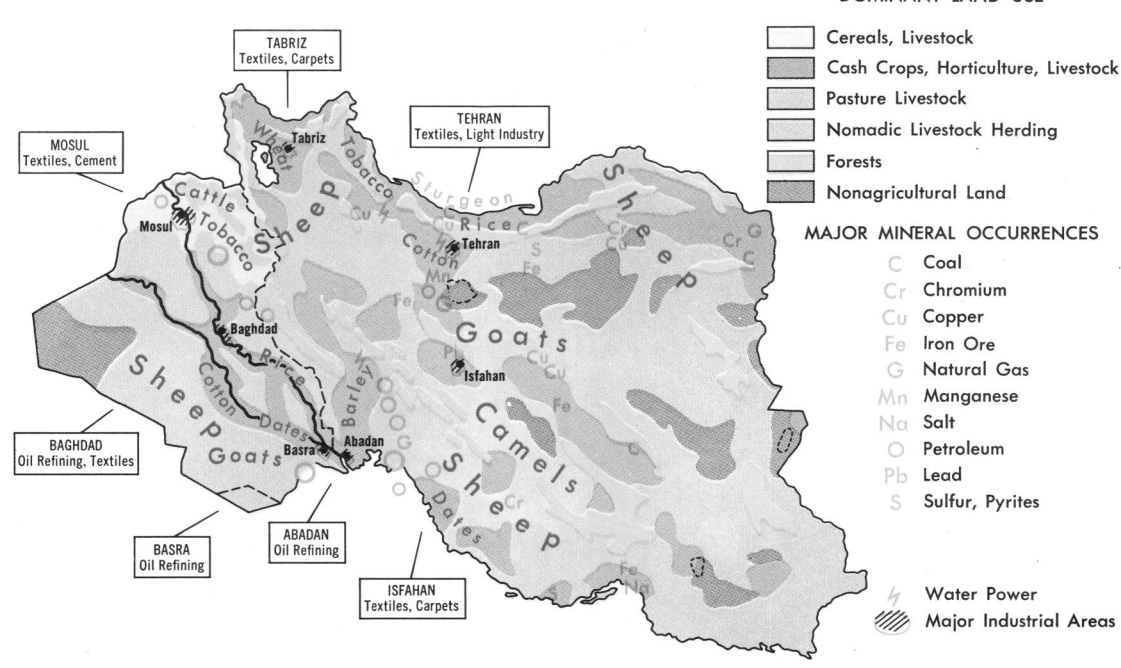

TABRIZ
Textiles, Carpets

TEHRAN
Textiles, Light Industry

MOSUL
Textiles, Cement

BAGHDAD
Oil Refining, Textiles

BASRA
Oil Refining

ABADAN
Oil Refining

ISFAHAN
Textiles, Carpets

DOMINANT LAND USE

- Cereals, Livestock
- Cash Crops, Horticulture, Livestock
- Pasture Livestock
- Nomadic Livestock Herding
- Forests
- Nonagricultural Land

MAJOR MINERAL OCCURRENCES

C	Coal
Cr	Chromium
Cu	Copper
Fe	Iron Ore
G	Natural Gas
Mn	Manganese
Na	Salt
O	Petroleum
Pb	Lead
S	Sulfur, Pyrites

⚡ Water Power
▨ Major Industrial Areas

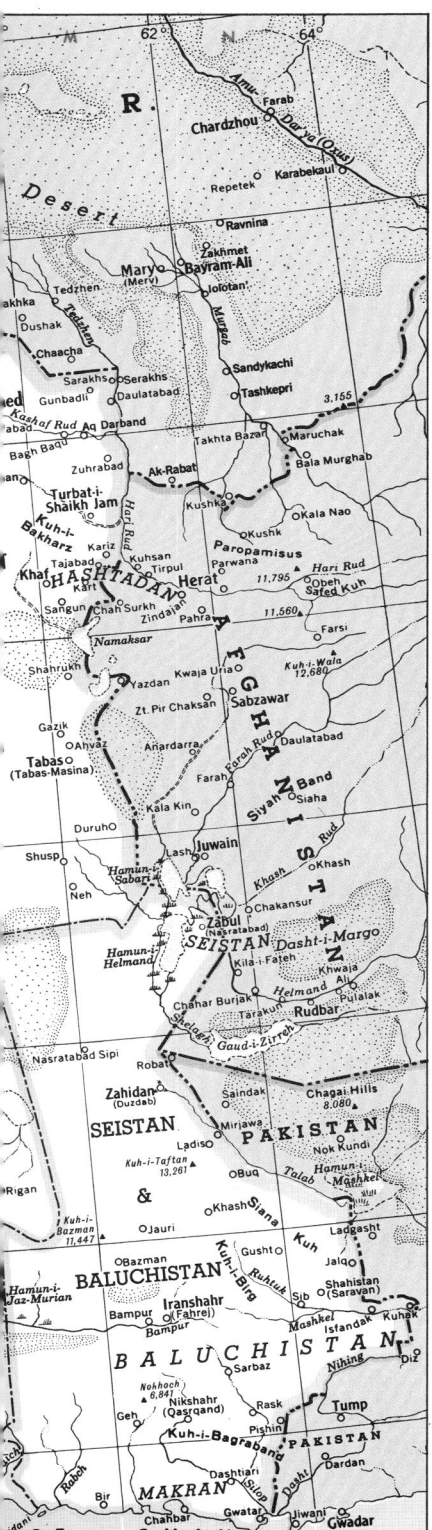

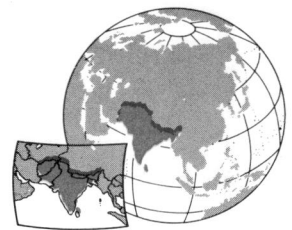

INDIA

AREA 1,269,339 sq. mi.
POPULATION 605,614,000
CAPITAL New Delhi
LARGEST CITY Calcutta (greater)
HIGHEST POINT K2 (Godwin Austen) 28,250 ft.
MONETARY UNIT Indian rupee
MAJOR LANGUAGES Hindi, English, Bihari, Telugu, Marathi, Bengali, Tamil, Gujarati, Rajasthani, Kanarese, Malayalam, Oriya, Punjabi, Assamese, Kashmiri, Urdu
MAJOR RELIGIONS Hinduism, Islam, Christianity, Sikhism, Buddhism, Jainism, Zoroastrianism, Animism

PAKISTAN

AREA 310,403 sq. mi.
POPULATION 72,370,000
CAPITAL Islamabad
LARGEST CITY Karachi
HIGHEST POINT Tirich Mir 25,230 ft.
MONETARY UNIT Pakistani rupee
MAJOR LANGUAGES Urdu, English, Punjabi, Pushtu, Sindhi, Baluchi, Brahui
MAJOR RELIGIONS Islam, Hinduism, Sikhism, Christianity, Buddhism

SRI LANKA (CEYLON)

AREA 25,332 sq. mi.
POPULATION 14,000,000
CAPITAL Colombo
LARGEST CITY Colombo
HIGHEST POINT Pidurutalagala 8,281 ft.
MONETARY UNIT Sri Lanka rupee
MAJOR UNIT Sinhala, Tamil, English
MAJOR RELIGIONS Buddhism, Hinduism, Christianity, Islam

AFGHANISTAN

AREA 250,775 sq. mi.
POPULATION 19,280,000
CAPITAL Kabul
LARGEST CITY Kabul
HIGHEST POINT Noshaq 24,581 ft.
MONETARY UNIT afghani
MAJOR LANGUAGES Pushtu, Dari, Uzbek
MAJOR RELIGION Islam

NEPAL

AREA 54,663 sq. mi.
POPULATION 12,900,000
CAPITAL Kathmandu
LARGEST CITY Kathmandu
HIGHEST POINT Mt. Everest 29,028 ft.
MONETARY UNIT Nepalese rupee
MAJOR LANGUAGES Nepali, Maithili, Tamang, Newari, Tharu
MAJOR RELIGIONS Hinduism, Buddhism

MALDIVES

AREA 115 sq. mi.
POPULATION 136,000
CAPITAL Male
LARGEST CITY Male
HIGHEST POINT 20 ft.
MONETARY UNIT Maldivian rupee
MAJOR LANGUAGE Divehi
MAJOR RELIGION Islam

BHUTAN

AREA 18,147 sq. mi.
POPULATION 1,200,000
CAPITAL Thimphu
LARGEST CITY Thimphu
HIGHEST POINT Kula Kangri 24,784 ft.
MONETARY UNIT tikchung
MAJOR LANGUAGES Dzongka, Nep
MAJOR RELIGIONS Buddhism, Hinduism

BANGLADESH

AREA 55,126 sq. mi.
POPULATION 82,900,000
CAPITAL Dacca
LARGEST CITY Dacca
HIGHEST POINT Mowdok Mual 3,292 ft.
MONETARY UNIT taka
MAJOR LANGUAGES Bengali, English
MAJOR RELIGIONS Islam, Hinduism, Christianity

INDIA

PAKISTAN

SRI LANKA (CEYLON)

BHUTAN

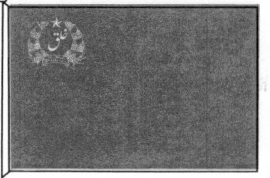
AFGHANISTAN

MALDIVES

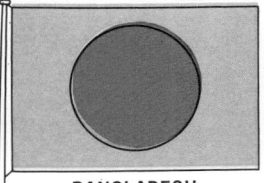
BANGLADESH

NEPAL

AFGHANISTAN

CITIES and TOWNS

Andkhui, 30,000	B 1
Baghlan, 110,874	B 1
Bala Murghab, 10,000	A 1
Balkh, 15,000	B 1
Bamian, 49,000	B 2
Chahardeh	B 2
Charikar, 100,443	B 1
Daulatabad, 15,000	A 2
Faizabad, 64,400	A 2
Farah, 29,400	A 2
Gardez, 40,100	B 2
Ghazni, 44,500	B 2
Girishk, 10,000	A 2
Haibak, 39,300	B 1
Herat, 108,750	A 2
Jalalabad, 50,100	B 2
Kabul (cap.), 318,094	B 2
Kabul, *534,350	B 2
Kala Bist, 26,100	A 2
Kalat-i-Ghilzai, 51,000	B 2
Kandahar, 140,024	B 2
Khanabad, 80,000	B 1
Kuhsan	A 2
Kushk, 10,000	A 1
Landi Muhammad Amin Khan, 1,000	A 2
Maimana, 56,900	A 1
Matun, 15,000	B 2
Mazar-i-Sharif, 44,300	B 1
Panjao, 3,000	A 2
Qaleh-i-Kang, 17,400	A 2
Sabzawar, 5,000	A 2
Shibarghan, 56,200	B 1
Shindand (Sabzawar), 5,000	A 2
Taiwara, 5,000	A 2
Tashkurghan, 30,000	B 1

OTHER FEATURES

Farah Rud (riv.)	A 2
Hari Rud (riv.)	A 1
Helmand (riv.)	B 2
Hindu Kush (mts.)	B 1
Jam (mt.)	A 2
Kabul (riv.)	C 2
Kunar (riv.)	C 1
Kunduz (riv.)	B 1
Lora (riv.)	B 2
Margo, Dasht-i- (des.)	A 2
Namaksar (salt lake)	A 2
Paropamisus (range)	A 2
Registan (reg.)	B 2
Tarnak (riv.)	B 2

BANGLADESH

CITIES and TOWNS

Barisal, 69,936	G 4
Bogra, 33,784	F 4
Mungla Anchorage	G 4
Chittagong, 416,733	G 4
Comilla, 54,504	G 4
Cox's Bazar (Maheshkhali)	G 4
Dacca (cap.), 1,310,976	G 4
Dacca, □2,539,991	G 4
Dinajpur, 37,711	F 3
Faridpur, 28,333	F 4
Habiganj	G 4
Jamalpur	F 4
Jessore, 46,366	F 4
Khulna, 436,000	F 4
Kishorganj	G 4
Madaripur	G 4

Maheshkhali	G 4
Mymensingh, 53,256	G 4
Narayanganj, 176,879	G 4
Nawabganj	F 4
Noakhali, 19,874	F 4
Pabna, 40,792	F 4
Rajshahi, 56,885	F 4
Rangamati, 6,416	G 4
Rangpur, 40,634	F 3
Siraiganj, 47,152	F 4
Sylhet, 37,740	G 4

OTHER FEATURES

Bengal, Bay of (sea)	F 5
Brahmaputra (riv.)	G 3
Ganges (riv.)	F 3
Sundarbans (reg.)	F 4

BHUTAN

CITIES and TOWNS

Bumthang, 10,000	G 3
Paro Dzong, 35,000	F 3
Punakha, 12,000	G 3
Taga Dzong, 18,000	G 3
Thimphu (cap.), 50,000	G 3
Tongsa Dzong, 2,500	G 3

OTHER FEATURES

Chomo Lhari (mt.)	F 3
Himalaya (mts.)	E 2
Kula Kangri (mt.)	G 3

INDIA

INTERNAL DIVISIONS

Andaman and Nicobar Isls. (terr.), 115,133	G 6
Andhra Pradesh (state), 43,502,708	D 5
Arunachal Pradesh (terr.), 467,511	G 3
Assam (state), 14,625,152	G 3
Bihar (state), 56,353,369	F 4
Chandigarh (terr.), 257,251	D 2
Dadra and Nagar Haveli (terr.), 74,170	C 4
Delhi (terr.), 4,065,698	D 3
Goa, Daman and Diu (terr.), 857,771	C 4
Gujarat (state), 26,697,475	C 4
Haryana (state), 10,036,808	D 3
Himachal Pradesh (state), 3,460,434	D 2
Jammu and Kashmir (state), 4,616,632	D 2
Karnataka (state), 29,299,014	D 6
Kerala (state), 21,347,375	D 6
Lakshadweep (terr.), 31,810	C 6
Madhya Pradesh (state), 41,654,119	D 4
Maharashtra (state), 50,412,235	C 5
Manipur (state), 1,072,753	G 4
Meghalaya (state), 1,011,699	G 3
Mizoram (state), 332,390	G 4
Nagaland (state), 516,449	G 3
Orissa (state), 21,944,615	E 5
Pondicherry (terr.), 471,707	E 6
Punjab (state), 13,551,060	D 2
Rajasthan (state), 25,765,806	C 3
Sikkim (state), 209,843	F 3
Tamil Nadu (state), 41,199,168	D 6
Tripura (state), 1,556,342	G 4

(continued on following page)

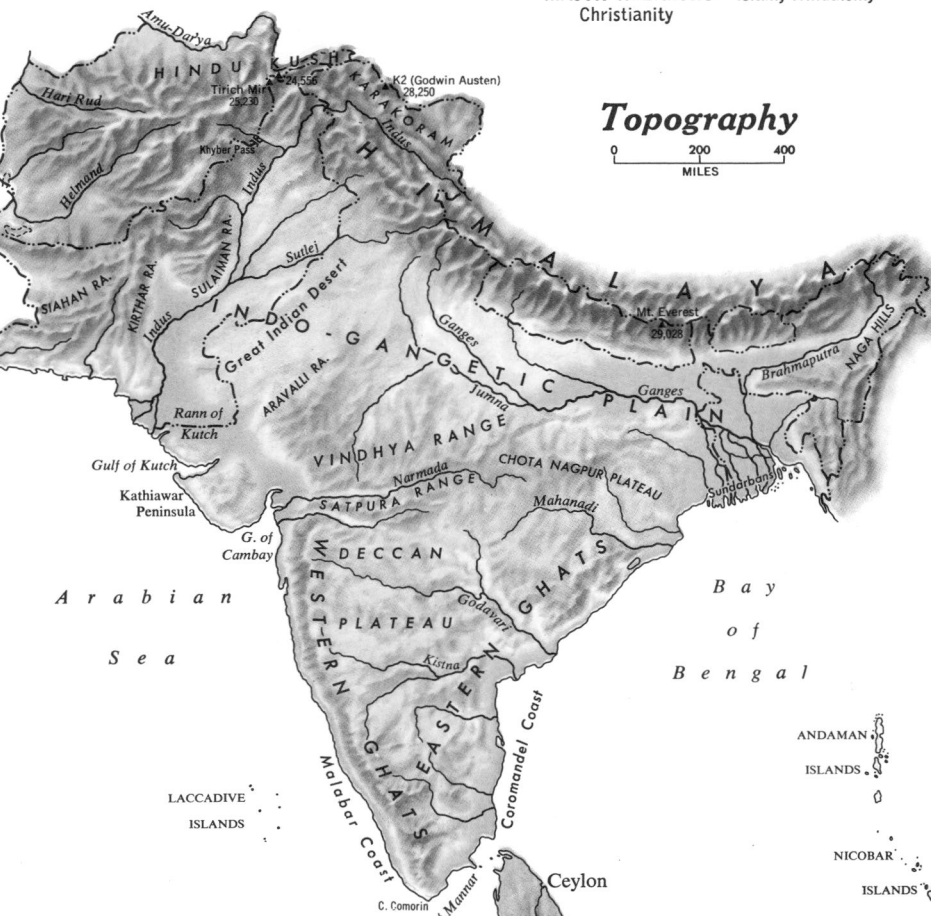

Topography

0 · 200 · 400
MILES

5,000 m. / 16,404 ft. · 2,000 m. / 6,562 ft. · 1,000 m. / 3,281 ft. · 500 m. / 1,640 ft. · 200 m. / 656 ft. · 100 m. / 328 ft. · Sea Level · Below

BRITISH INDIA

U.S.S.R.

GILGIT AGENCY

AFGHANISTAN

N.W. FRONTIER PROV.

KASHMIR & JAMMU

PUNJAB

IRAN

BALUCHISTAN

PUNJAB STATES

BAHAWALPUR (PUNJ. ST.)

DELHI

RAMPUR

TIBET

CHINA

PUNJ. ST.

RAJPUTANA

AJMER-MERWARA

UNITED

NEPAL

Gwadar (Oman)

SIND

GWALIOR

PROVINCES

SIKKIM

BHUTAN

E. ST.

ASSAM

KHASI HILLS

MANIPUR

BENARES

CENTRAL INDIA

BIHAR

EASTERN

BENGAL

TRIPURA (E. ST.)

WESTERN INDIA

CENTRAL

STATES

Chandernagore (Fr.)

Arabian Sea

Diu (Port.) Damão (Port.)

GUJARAT ST.

BERAR

CENTRAL PROVINCES

EASTERN

STATES

ORISSA

Bay of Bengal

BURMA

DECCAN STATES

HYDERABAD

Yanaon (Fr.)

Gôa (Port.)

MYSORE

Bangalore (Br.)

Mahé (Fr.)

COORG

Pondichéry (Fr.)

Karikal (Fr.)

Andaman Islands (Br.)

Cochin (Br.)

Laccadive Islands (Madras)

MADRAS STATES

MADRAS

Nicobar Islands (Br.)

CEYLON

British India. The provinces of British India were directly administered by Britain. A few areas were leased from the Indian princes.

Indian States. The Indian States, sometimes referred to as the "Native" or "Princely States," were under the nominal control of maharajas or other hereditary princes.

Possessions of Other Countries in India

State or Provincial Boundaries

Other Internal Boundaries

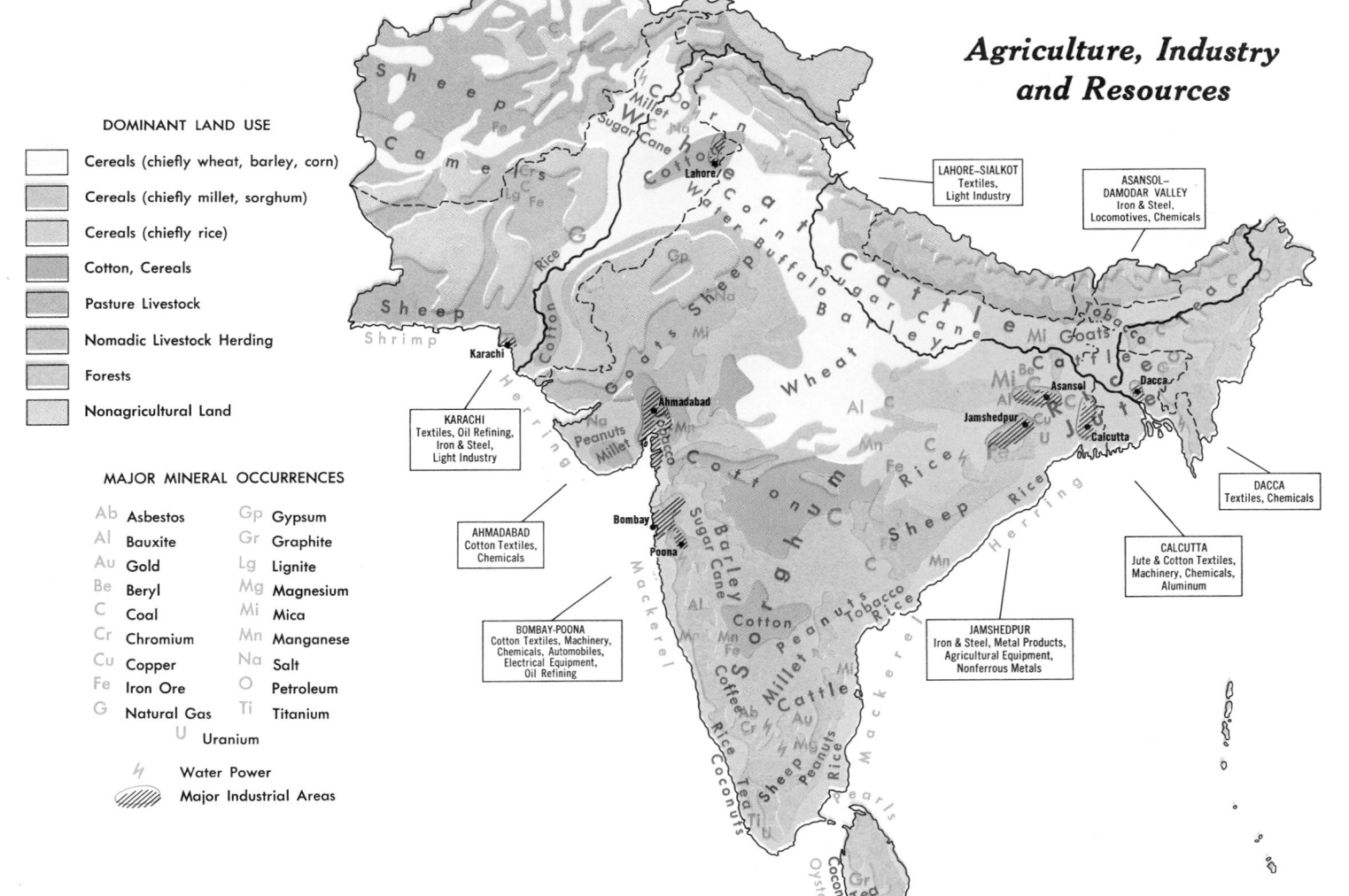

Agriculture, Industry and Resources

DOMINANT LAND USE

- Cereals (chiefly wheat, barley, corn)
- Cereals (chiefly millet, sorghum)
- Cereals (chiefly rice)
- Cotton, Cereals
- Pasture Livestock
- Nomadic Livestock Herding
- Forests
- Nonagricultural Land

MAJOR MINERAL OCCURRENCES

Ab Asbestos
Al Bauxite
Au Gold
Be Beryl
C Coal
Cr Chromium
Cu Copper
Fe Iron Ore
G Natural Gas
Gp Gypsum
Gr Graphite
Lg Lignite
Mg Magnesium
Mi Mica
Mn Manganese
Na Salt
O Petroleum
Ti Titanium
U Uranium

Water Power
Major Industrial Areas

LAHORE–SIALKOT
Textiles, Light Industry

ASANSOL–DAMODAR VALLEY
Iron & Steel, Locomotives, Chemicals

KARACHI
Textiles, Oil Refining, Iron & Steel, Light Industry

AHMADABAD
Cotton Textiles, Chemicals

DACCA
Textiles, Chemicals

CALCUTTA
Jute & Cotton Textiles, Machinery, Chemicals, Aluminum

BOMBAY–POONA
Cotton Textiles, Machinery, Chemicals, Automobiles, Electrical Equipment, Oil Refining

JAMSHEDPUR
Iron & Steel, Metal Products, Agricultural Equipment, Nonferrous Metals

BURMA, THAILAND,
INDOCHINA
and MALAYA

CONIC PROJECTION

SCALE OF MILES

SCALE OF KILOMETRES

International Boundaries
Division and State Boundaries
Capitals of Countries
Division and State Capitals

Copyright by C.S. HAMMOND & Co., N.Y.

BURMA

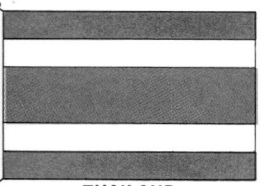

THAILAND

LAOS

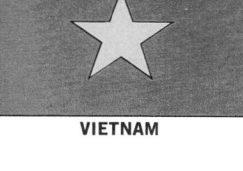

CAMBODIA

VIETNAM

MALAYSIA

SINGAPORE

BURMA

AREA 261,789 sq. mi.
POPULATION 31,240,000
CAPITAL Rangoon
LARGEST CITY Rangoon
HIGHEST POINT Hkakabo Razi 19,296 ft.
MONETARY UNIT kyat
MAJOR LANGUAGES Burmese, Karen, Shan,
Kachin, Chin, Kayah, English
MAJOR RELIGIONS Buddhism, Tribal religions

THAILAND

AREA 198,455 sq. mi.
POPULATION 42,700,000
CAPITAL Bangkok
LARGEST CITY Bangkok
HIGHEST POINT Doi Inthanon 8,452 ft.
MONETARY UNIT baht
MAJOR LANGUAGES Thai, Lao, Chinese,
Khmer, Malay
MAJOR RELIGIONS Buddhism, Tribal religions

LAOS

AREA 91,428 sq. mi.
POPULATION 3,500,000
CAPITAL Vientiane
LARGEST CITY Vientiane
HIGHEST POINT Phu Bia 9,252 ft.
MONETARY UNIT kip
MAJOR LANGUAGES Lao, French
MAJOR RELIGIONS Buddhism, Tribal religions

CAMBODIA

AREA 69,898 sq. mi.
POPULATION 8,110,000
CAPITAL Phnom Penh
LARGEST CITY Phnom Penh
HIGHEST POINT 5,948 ft.
MONETARY UNIT riel
MAJOR LANGUAGES Khmer (Cambodian),
French
MAJOR RELIGION Buddhism

VIETNAM

AREA 128,405 sq. mi.
POPULATION 46,600,000
CAPITAL Hanoi
LARGEST CITY Ho Chi Minh City (Saigon)
HIGHEST POINT Fan Si Pan 10,308 ft.
MONETARY UNIT dong
MAJOR LANGUAGES Vietnamese, Thai, Muong,
Meo, Yao, Khmer, French, Chinese, Cham
MAJOR RELIGIONS Buddhism, Taoism,
Confucianism, Roman Catholicsm, Cao-Dai

MALAYSIA

AREA 128,308 sq. mi.
POPULATION 12,368,000
CAPITAL Kuala Lumpur
LARGEST CITY Kuala Lumpur
HIGHEST POINT Mt. Kinabalu 13,455 ft.
MONETARY UNIT Malaysian dollar
MAJOR LANGUAGES Malay, Chinese,
English, Tamil, Dayak, Kadazan
MAJOR RELIGIONS Islam, Confucianism,
Buddhism, Tribal religions, Hinduism,
Taoism, Christianity, Sikhism

SINGAPORE

AREA 226 sq. mi.
POPULATION 2,300,000
CAPITAL Singapore
LARGEST CITY Singapore
HIGHEST POINT Bukit Timah 581 ft.
MONETARY UNIT Singapore dollar
MAJOR LANGUAGES Chinese, Malay,
Tamil, English, Hindi
MAJOR RELIGIONS Confucianism, Buddhism,
Taoism, Hinduism, Islam, Christianity

Topography

0   200   400
MILES

5,000 m. | 2,000 m. | 1,000 m. | 500 m. | 200 m. | 100 m. | Sea
16,404 ft. | 6,562 ft. | 3,281 ft. | 1,640 ft. | 656 ft. | 328 ft. | Level | Below

(continued on following page)

(continued)

CAMBODIA

CITIES and TOWNS

Banam, †87,048 E 5
Battambang, 38,846 D 4
Cheom Ksan E 4
Chhlong, †46,108 E 4
Chong Kal, †16,918 D 4
Kampot, 12,558 E 5
Kep, 7,565 E 5
Khemarak Phouinville D 5
Kohnieh E 4
Kompong Cham, 28,534 E 4
Kompong Chhnang, 12,847 D 4
Kompong Kleang E 4
Kompong Som, 6,578 D 5
Kompong Speu, 7,453 E 5
Kompong Thom, 9,682 E 4
Kompong Trabek, †108,227 E 5
Koulen E 4
Kratie, 11,908 E 4
Krauchmar, †63,262 E 4
Moung, †88,321 D 4
Pailin, †15,536 D 4
Phnom Penh (capital), *500,000 E 5
Phsar Babau D 4
Phsar Oudong, †50,456 E 5
Phum Rovieng, †21,151 E 4
Phum Troun E 4
Poipet D 4
Prek Po E 5
Prey Veng, 8,792 E 5
Pursat, 14,329 D 4
Ream D 5
Sambor, †11,213 E 4
Siem Pang, †8,959 E 4
Siem Reap, 10,230 D 4
Sisophon, †29,581 D 4
Sre Khtum E 4
Stung Treng, 3,369 E 4
Suong E 5
Svay Rieng, 11,184 E 5
Takeo, 11,312 E 5
Virachei, †16,912 E 4

OTHER FEATURES

Angkor Wat (ruins) E 4
Dang Raek, Phanom (mts.) D 4
Joncs (plain) E 5
Kas Kong (isl.) D 5
Kas Tang (isl.) D 5
Kong, Kas (isl.) D 5
Mekong (river) E 4
Phanom Dang Raek (mts.) D 4
Preapatang (rapids) E 4
Rong, Koh (isl.) D 5
Samit (point) D 5
Se Khong (river) E 4
Se San (river) E 4
Siam (gulf) D 5
Srepok (river) E 4
Stung Sen (river) E 4
Tang, Kas (isl.) D 5
Tonle Sap (lake) D 4

LAOS

CITIES and TOWNS

Attopeu, 2,750 E 4
Ban Bung Sai E 4
Borikhane D 3
Botene D 3
Boun Neua, 2,500 D 2
Boun Tai, †1,681 D 2
Champassak, 3,500 E 4
Houei Sai, 1,500 D 2
Hua Muong D 2
Keng Kok, 2,000 E 3
Kham Keut, †31,206 E 3
Khone E 4
Khong, 1,750 E 4
Khong Sédone, 2,000 E 4
Luang Prabang, 7,596 D 3
Mahaxay, 2,000 E 3
Muong Beng, †2,305 D 2
Muong Bo D 3
Muong Hai, †476 D 2
Muong Hôm D 3
Muong Lan, †836 D 3
Muong May E 4
Muong Phalane E 3
Muong Phine E 3
Muong Phong D 3
Muong Sai, 2,000 D 2
Muong Sing, 1,091 D 2
Muong Son D 2
Muong Song Khone, 2,000 E 3
Muong Wapi E 4
Muong Yo D 2
Nam Tha, 1,459 D 2
Napé E 3
Nong Het D 3
Ou Neua, †4,300 D 2
Pak Beng, †2,964 D 2
Pak Hin Boun, 1,750 E 3
Pak Sane, 2,500 D 3
Paklay, 2,000 D 3
Pakse, 8,000 E 4
Phiafay, †17,216 E 4
Phon Tiou E 3
Phong Saly, 2,500 D 2
Sam Neua, 3,000 D 2
Saravane, 2,350 E 4
Savannakhet, 8,500 E 3
Sayaboury, 2,500 D 3
Tchepone, 1,250 E 3
Tha-deua D 3
Thakhek, 5,500 E 3
Tourakom D 3
Vang Vieng, 1,250 D 3
Vien Phou Kha D 2
Vientiane (capital), 132,253 D 3
Vientiane, *162,297 D 3
Xieng Khouang, 3,500 D 3

OTHER FEATURES

Bolovens (plateau) E 4
Hou, Nam (river) D 2
Jars (plain) D 3
Mekong (river) D 3
Nam Hou (river) D 2
Nam Tha (river) D 2
Phu Bia (mt.) D 3
Phu Co Pi (mt.) E 3
Phu Loi (mt.) D 2
Rao Co (mt.) E 3
Se Khong (river) E 3
Tha, Nam (river) D 2
Tran Ninh (plateau) D 3

MALAYSIA

STATES

Federal Territory D 7
Johor, 1,236,412 D 7
Kedah, 885,775 D 6
Kelantan, 645,200 D 6
Melaka, 391,003 D 7
Negeri Sembilan, 488,318 D 7
Pahang, 405,156 D 7
Perak, 1,568,024 D 6
Perlis, 113,350 D 6
Pinang, 724,169 D 6
Selangor, 1,339,142 D 7
Terengganu, 360,388 D 6

CITIES and TOWNS

Alor Gajah, 2,135 D 7
Alor Setar, 52,915 D 6
Baling, 4,121 D 6
Bandar Maharani, 39,046 D 7
Bandar Penggaram, 39,294 D 7
Batu Gajah, 10,143 D 6
Bentong, 18,845 D 7
Butterworth, 42,504 D 6
Cameron Highlands D 6
Chukai, 10,803 D 6
Gemas, 4,873 D 7
George Town (Pinang), 234,903 C 6
Ipoh, 125,770 D 6
Johor Baharu, 74,909 F 5
Kampar, 24,602 D 6
Kangar, 6,064 D 6
Kelang, 75,649 D 7
Keluang, 31,181 D 7
Kota Baharu, 38,103 D 6
Kota Tinggi, 7,475 F 5
Kuala Dungun, 12,515 D 6
Kuala Lipis, 8,753 D 6
Kuala Lumpur (cap.), 325,000 D 7
Kuala Pilah, 12,024 D 7
Kuala Selangor, 2,285 D 7
Kuala Terengganu, 29,446 D 6
Kuantan, 23,034 D 7
Kulai, 7,759 F 5
Lumut, 2,947 D 6
Melaka (Malacca), 69,848 D 7
Mersing, 7,228 E 7
Pekan, 2,070 D 7
Pekan Nanas, 7,129 E 5
Pinang, 234,903 C 6
Pontian Kechil, 8,459 E 5
Port Dickson, 4,416 D 7
Port Swettenham, 16,925 D 7
Port Weld, 2,260 D 6
Raub, 15,363 D 7
Segamat, 18,445 D 7
Seremban, 52,091 D 7
Shah Alam D 7
Sungei Petani, 22,916 C 6
Taiping, 48,206 D 6
Tanah Merah, 775 D 6
Telok Anson, 37,042 D 6
Tumpat, 8,946 D 6

OTHER FEATURES

Aur, Pulau (isl.), 415 E 7
Belumut, Gunong (mt.) D 7
Gelang, Tanjong (point) D 6
Johor (river) F 5
Johore (str.) E 6
Kelantan (river) D 6
Langkawi, Palau (isl.), 16,535 C 6
Ledang, Gunong (mt.) D 7
Lima, Pulau (isl.) F 6
Malacca (str.) D 7
Malaya (region), 9,000,000 E 6
Pahang (river) D 7
Pangkor, Pulau (isl.), 2,580 D 6
Perak, Gunong (mt.) D 6
Perhentian (isls.), 447 D 6
Pulai (river) E 5
Pinang, Pulau (isl.), 338,898 C 6
Ramunia, Tanjong (point) F 6
Redang, Pulau (isl.), 470 D 6
Sedili Kechil, Tanjong (point) F 5
Tahan, Gunong (mt.) D 6
Temiang, Bukit (mt.) D 6
Tenggol, Pulau (isl.), 2,386 D 6
Tinggi, Pulau (isl.), 440 E 7

SINGAPORE

CITIES and TOWNS

Jurong E 6
Nee Soon, 6,043 F 6
Paya Lebar, 45,440 F 6
Serangoon, 3,798 F 6
Singapore (cap.), *1,987,900 F 6
Woodlands, 737 F 6

OTHER FEATURES

Johore (str.) E 6
Keppel (harb.) F 6
Main (str.) F 6
Singapore (str.) F 6
Tekong Besar, Pulau (isl.), 4,074 F 6

THAILAND (SIAM)

CITIES and TOWNS

Amnat, 11,335 E 4
Ang Thong, 6,458 C 4
Ayutthaya, 24,597 D 4
Ban Aranyaprathet, 11,112 D 4
Ban Kantang, 5,076 C 6
Ban Khlong Yai, 3,815 D 5
Ban Pak Phanang, 11,963 C 5
Ban Pua, 12,317 D 3
Ban Sattahip, 22,942 D 4
Ban Tha Uthen, 7,297 D 3
Bang Lamung, 9,087 D 4
Bang Saphan, 6,959 C 5
Bangkok (capital), 1,299,528 D 4
Bangkok, *2,000,000 D 4
Banphot Phisai, 6,036 C 3
Buriram, 12,579 D 4
Chachoengsao, 19,809 G 4
Chai Badan, 6,158 D 4
Chai Buri, †31,135 D 3
Chainat, 4,652 D 4
Chaiya, 3,607 C 5
Chaiyaphum, 9,633 D 4
Chang Khoeng, 6,037 C 3
Chanthaburi, 10,780 D 4
Chiang Dao, 8,017 C 3
Chiang Khan, 5,810 D 3
Chiang Rai, 11,663 C 3
Chiang Saen, 5,443 C 2
Chiengmai, 65,600 C 3
Chon Buri, 32,496 D 4
Chumphon, 9,342 C 5
Dan Sai, 6,710 D 3
Den Chai, 12,732 C 3
Hat Yai, 35,504 C 6
Hua Hin, 17,078 D 4
Kabin Buri, 3,703 D 4
Kalasin, 11,043 D 3
Kamphaeng Phet, 7,171 C 3
Kanchanaburi, 12,957 C 4
Khemmarat, 5,426 E 4
Khon Kaen, 19,591 D 3
Khorat (Nakhon Ratchasima), 41,037 D 4
Khu Khan, †122,206 E 4
Kra Buri, 3,717 C 5
Krung Thep (Bangkok) (cap.), 1,299,528 D 4
Kumphawapi, 20,759 D 3
Lae, 5,743 D 3
Lampang, 36,488 C 3
Lamphun, 10,602 C 3
Lang Suan, 4,108 C 5
Loei, 7,301 D 3
Lom Sak, 8,386 D 3
Lop Buri, 21,244 D 4
Maha Sarakham, 15,680 D 3
Mukdahan, 17,738 E 3
Nakhon Nayok, 8,048 D 4
Nakhon Pathom, 28,426 C 4
Nakhon Phanom, 14,799 D 3
Nakhon Ratchasima, 41,037 D 4
Nakhon Sawan, 34,947 D 4
Nakhon Si Thammarat, 25,919 D 5
Nan, 13,843 D 3
Nang Rong, 15,623 D 4
Narathiwat, 17,508 D 6
Ngao, †32,643 D 3
Nong Khai, 21,120 D 3
Pattani, 16,804 D 6
Phanat Nikhom, 9,307 D 4
Phangnga, 4,782 C 5
Phatthalung, 10,420 D 6
Phayao, 17,959 C 3
Phet Buri, 24,654 C 4
Phetchabun, 5,947 D 3
Phichai, 5,258 D 3
Phichit, 9,258 D 3
Phitsanulok, 30,364 D 3
Phon Phisai, 6,745 D 3
Phrae, 16,005 D 3
Phuket, 28,163 C 6
Phutthaisong, 9,315 D 4
Prachin Buri, 13,420 D 4
Prachuap Khiri Khan, 6,303 D 5
Pran Buri, 7,795 D 4
Rahaeng (Tak), 13,274 C 3
Ranong, 5,993 C 5
Rat Buri, 20,383 C 4
Rayong, 9,680 D 4
Roi Et, 12,930 D 4
Rong Kwang, †39,375 D 3
Sakon Nakhon, 16,457 E 3
Samut Prakan, 21,769 D 4
Samut Sakhon, 27,802 D 4
Samut Songkhram, 12,801 C 4
Sara Buri, 17,572 D 4
Satun, 4,369 C 6
Sawankhalok, 7,880 C 3
Selaphum, 10,395 E 3
Sing Buri, 8,384 D 4
Singora (Songkhla), 31,014 D 6
Sisaket, 9,519 E 4
Songkhla, 31,014 D 6
Sukhothai, 8,627 C 3
Suphan Buri, 13,859 C 4
Surat Thani, 19,738 C 5
Surin, 13,860 D 4
Suwannaphum, 15,731 D 4
Tak, 13,274 C 3
Takua Pa, 6,308 C 5
Thoen, 17,283 C 3
Thonburi, 403,818 D 4
Thonburi, *460,000 D 4
Trang, 17,158 C 6
Trat, 3,813 D 4
Ubon, 27,092 E 4
Udon Thani, 29,965 D 3
Uthai Thani, 10,729 C 4
Uttaradit, 9,120 D 3
Warin Chamrap, 7,067 E 4
Yala, 18,083 D 6
Yasothon, 9,717 D 4

OTHER FEATURES

Amya (pass) C 4
Bilauktaung (range) C 4
Chao Phraya, Mae Nam (river) D 4
Chi, Mae Nam (river) D 3
Chong Pak Phra (cape) C 5
Dang Raek, Phanom (mts.) D 4
Doi Inthanon (mt.) C 3
Doi Pha Hom Pok (mt.) C 2
Doi Pia Fai (mt.) D 4
Kao Prawa (mt.) C 3
Khao Luang (mt.) C 5
Khwae Noi, Mae Nam (river) C 4
Ko Chang (isl.) D 4
Ko Kut (isl.) D 5
Ko Lanta (isl.), 9,486 C 6
Ko Phangan (isl.) D 5
Ko Phuket (isl.), 75,652 C 5
Ko Samui (isl.), 30,818 C 5
Ko Tao (isl.) C 5
Ko Terutao (isl.) C 6
Ko Thalu (isls.) C 5
Kra (isthmus) C 5
Laem Pho (cape) D 6
Laem Talumphuk (cape) D 5
Luang (mt.) C 5
Mae Klong, Mae Nam (river) C 4
Mekong (river) D 3
Mulayit Taung (mt.) C 3
Mun, Mae Nam (river) D 4
Nan, Mae Nam (river) D 3
Nong Lahan (lake) D 3
Pa Sak, Mae Nam (river) D 4
Pakchan (river) C 5
Phanom Dang Raek (mts.) D 4
Ping, Mae Nam (river) C 3
Samui (str.) D 5
Siam (gulf) D 5
Tapi, Mae Nam (river) C 5
Tha Chin, Mae Nam (river) C 4
Thale Luang (lagoon) D 6
Three Pagodas (pass) C 4
Wang, Mae Nam (river) C 3

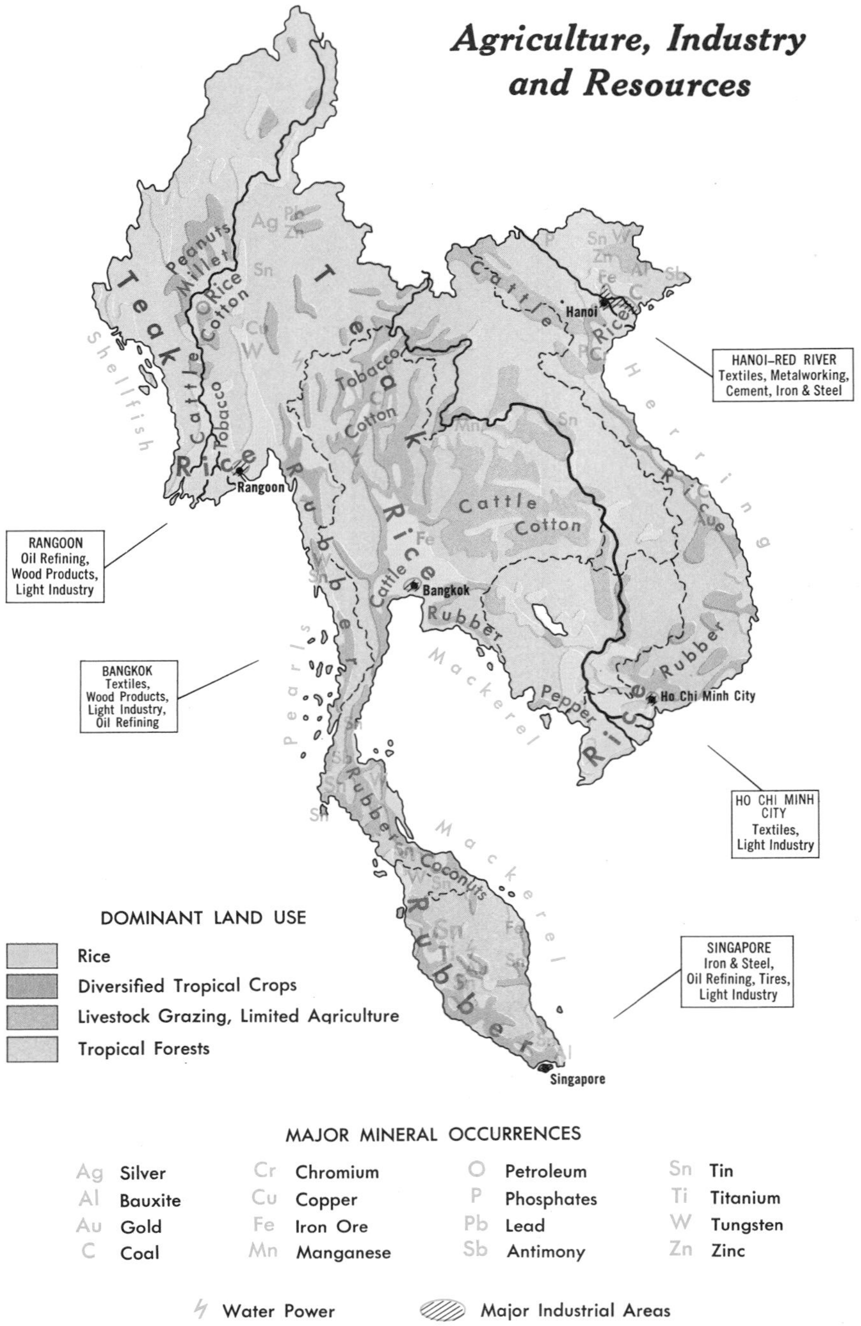

Agriculture, Industry and Resources
Teak
Peanuts
Millet
Rice
Cotton
Cattle
Tobacco
Shellfish
Rubber
Rangoon
Bangkok
Hanoi
Ho Chi Minh City
Singapore
Pearls
Mackerel
Herring
Pepper
Coconuts
Tea
RANGOON
Oil Refining, Wood Products, Light Industry
BANGKOK
Textiles, Wood Products, Light Industry, Oil Refining
HANOI–RED RIVER
Textiles, Metalworking, Cement, Iron & Steel
HO CHI MINH CITY
Textiles, Light Industry
SINGAPORE
Iron & Steel, Oil Refining, Tires, Light Industry
DOMINANT LAND USE
Rice
Diversified Tropical Crops
Livestock Grazing, Limited Agriculture
Tropical Forests
MAJOR MINERAL OCCURRENCES
Ag Silver
Al Bauxite
Au Gold
C Coal
Cr Chromium
Cu Copper
Fe Iron Ore
Mn Manganese
O Petroleum
P Phosphates
Pb Lead
Sb Antimony
Sn Tin
Ti Titanium
W Tungsten
Zn Zinc
Water Power
Major Industrial Areas

VIETNAM

CITIES and TOWNS

An Khe F 4
An Loc, 15,276 E 5
Bac Can E 2
Bac Lieu (Vinh Loi), 53,841 E 5
Bac Ninh, 22,560 E 2
Ba Don E 3
Bai Thuong E 3
Ban Me Thuot, 68,771 F 4
Bao Ha D 2
Bao Lac E 2
Bien Hoa, 87,135 E 5
Binh Dinh F 4
Binh Son F 4
Bong Son F 4
Bu Dop E 4
Cam Ranh, 84,281 F 5
Can Tho, 92,132 E 5
Cao Bang E 2
Cao Lanh, 16,482 E 5
Cap Saint-Jacques (Vung Tau), 79,270 E 5
Chau Phu, 37,175 E 5
Cheo Reo E 4
Chu Lai F 4
Co Lieu E 3
Con Cuong E 3
Cua Rao E 3
Dak Bla E 4
Da Lat, 83,992 F 5
Dam Doi E 5
Da Nang, 363,343 E 3
Dien Bien Phu D 2
Di Linh F 5
Dong Hoi E 3
Duong Dong D 5
Go Cong, 33,191 E 5
Go Quao E 5
Ha Giang E 2
Haiphong, 182,496 E 2
Haiphong, ‡*600,000 E 2
Ham Tan, 19,323 E 5
Hanoi (capital), 414,620 E 2
Hanoi, ‡*1,400,000 E 2
Ha Tien E 5
Ha Tinh E 3
Hoa Binh E 2
Hoa Da F 5
Ho Chi Minh City, 1,706,869 E 5
Hoi An, 45,059 F 4
Hoi Xuan E 2
Hon Chong E 5
Hon Gay, †100,000 E 2
Hue, 170,884 E 3
Huong Khe E 3
Ke Bao E 2
Khanh Hoa F 4
Khanh Hung, 59,015 E 5
Kontum, 33,554 E 4
Lai Chau D 2
Lang Mo E 3
Lang Son, 15,071 E 2
Lao Cai E 2
Loc Chou E 3
Loc Ninh E 5
Long Xuyen, 72,658 E 5
Luc An Chau E 2
Moc Hoa, 3,191 E 5
Mo Duc F 4
Mon Cay E 2
Muong Khuong E 2
My Tho, 109,967 E 5
Nam Dinh, ‡125,000 E 2
Nghia Lo D 2
Nha Trang, 103,184 F 4
Ninh Binh E 2
Phan Rang, 33,377 F 5
Phan Ri F 5
Phan Thiet, 80,122 F 5
Phoc Tuy, 16,419 E 5
Phuc Loi E 3
Phu Cuong, 28,267 E 5
Phu Dien E 3
Phu Lang Thuong E 2
Phu Loc E 3
Phuly E 2
Phu My F 4
Phu Qui E 3
Phu Rieng E 5
Phu Tho, 10,888 E 2
Phu Vinh (Tra Vinh), 48,485 E 5
Pleiku, 23,720 E 4
Pleime E 4
Quang Nam E 4
Quang Khe E 3
Quang Ngai, 14,119 F 4
Quang Tri, 15,874 E 3
Quang Yen E 2
Quan Long, 59,331 E 5
Qui Nhon, 116,821 F 4
Rach Gia, 66,745 E 5
Ron E 3
Sa Dec, 51,867 E 5
Saigon (Ho Chi Minh City), 1,706,869 E 5
Song Cau F 4
Son Ha F 4
Son La D 2
Son Tay, 19,213 E 2
Tam Ky, 38,532 F 4
Tam Quan F 4
Tan An, 38,082 E 5
Tay Ninh, 22,957 E 5
Thai Binh, 14,739 E 2
Thai Nguyen, ‡110,000 E 2
Thanh Hoa, 31,211 E 3
That Khe E 2
Tien Yen E 2
Tra Vinh, 48,485 E 5
Truc Giang, 68,629 E 5
Trung Khanh Phu E 2
Tuyen Quang E 2
Tuy Hoa, 63,552 F 4
Van Gia F 4
Van Hoa E 2
Van Yen E 2
Vinh, 43,954 E 3
Vinh Loi, 53,841 E 5
Vinh Long, 30,667 E 5
Vinh Yen E 2
Vo Dat E 5
Vu Liet E 3
Vung Tau, 79,270 E 5
Yen Bai E 2
Yen Minh E 2

OTHER FEATURES

Bach Long Vi, Dao (isl.) F 2
Batangan (cape) F 4
Bên Gôi (bay) F 4
Black (river) D 2
Ca Mau (Mui Bai Bung) (pt.) E 5
Cam Ranh (bay) F 5
Cat Ba, Dao (isl.) E 2
Chon May (bay) F 3
Chu Yang Sin (mt.) F 4
Con Son (isls.), 3,147 E 5
Cu Lao Hon (isls.) F 5
Dama, Poulo (isls.) D 5
Dao Bach Long Vi (isl.) F 2
Dao Phu Quoc (isl.) D 5
Darlac (plateau) F 4
Dent du Tigre (mt.) E 3
Deux Frères, Les (isls.) E 5
Fan Si Pan (mt.) D 2
Hon Khoai (isl.) E 5
Hon Panjang (isl.) D 5
Ia Drang (riv.) E 4
Joncs (plain) E 5
Ke Ga (point) F 5
Kontum (plateau) F 4
Lang Bian (mts.) F 4
Lay (cape) E 3
Mekong, Mouths of the (delta) E 5
Mui Bai Bung (pt.) E 5
Mui Dinh (cape) F 5
Mui Duong (cape) E 3
Nam Tram (cape) F 4
Nightingale (Bach Long Vi) (isl.) F 2
Nui Ba Den (mt.) E 5
Phu Quoc, Dao (isl.) D 5
Poulo Dama (isls.) D 5
Poulo Way (isls.) D 5
Rao Co (mt.) E 3
Red (river) E 2
Se San (river) E 4
Siam (gulf) D 5
Sip Song Chau Thai (mts.) D 2
Song Ba (river) F 4
Song Bo (Black) (river) D 2
Song Ca (river) E 3
Song Cai (river) F 4
Song Coi (Red) (river) E 2
South China (sea) F 4
Tigre (isl.) E 3
Tonkin (gulf) E 3
Varella (cape) F 4
Way, Poulo (isls.) D 5

★See page 84 for other Malaysian entries.
*City and suburbs.
†Population of district.

‡City populations courtesy of Kingsley Davis, Office of Int'l Pop. & Urban Research, Inst. of Int'l Studies, Univ. of California.

CHINA (MAINLAND)

AREA 3,691,000 sq. mi.
POPULATION 853,000,000
CAPITAL Peking
LARGEST CITY Shanghai
HIGHEST POINT Mt. Everest 29,028 ft.
MONETARY UNIT yüan
MAJOR LANGUAGES Chinese, Chuang, Uigur, Yi,
Tibetan, Miao, Mongol, Kazakh
MAJOR RELIGIONS Confucianism, Buddhism,
Taoism, Islam

CHINA (TAIWAN)

AREA 13,971 sq. mi.
POPULATION 16,426,386
CAPITAL Taipei
LARGEST CITY Taipei
HIGHEST POINT Hsinkao Shan 12,959 ft.
MONETARY UNIT new Taiwan yüan (dollar)
MAJOR LANGUAGES Chinese, Formosan
MAJOR RELIGIONS Confucianism, Buddhism,
Taoism, Christianity, Tribal religions

MONGOLIA

AREA 606,163 sq. mi.
POPULAIOTN 1,500,000
CAPITAL Ulan Bator
LARGEST CITY Ulan Bator
HIGHEST POINT Tabun Bogdo 14,288 ft.
MONETARY UNIT tugrik
MAJOR LANGUAGES Khalkha Mongolian,
Kazakh (Turkic)
MAJOR RELIGION Buddhism

HONG KONG

AREA 403 sq. mi.
POPULATION 4,400,000
CAPITAL Victoria
MONETARY UNIT Hong Kong dollar
MAJOR LANGUAGES Chinese, English
MAJOR RELIGIONS Confucianism, Buddhism,
Christianity

MACAO

AREA 6 sq. mi.
POPULATION 300,000
CAPITAL Macao
MONETARY UNIT pataca
MAJOR LANGUAGES Chinese, Portuguese
MAJOR RELIGIONS Confucianism, Buddhism,
Taoism, Christianity

CHINA (MAINLAND)

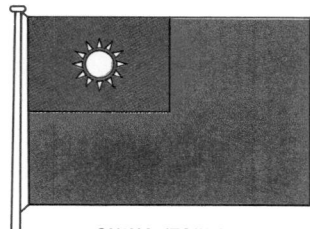

CHINA (TAIWAN)

MONGOLIA

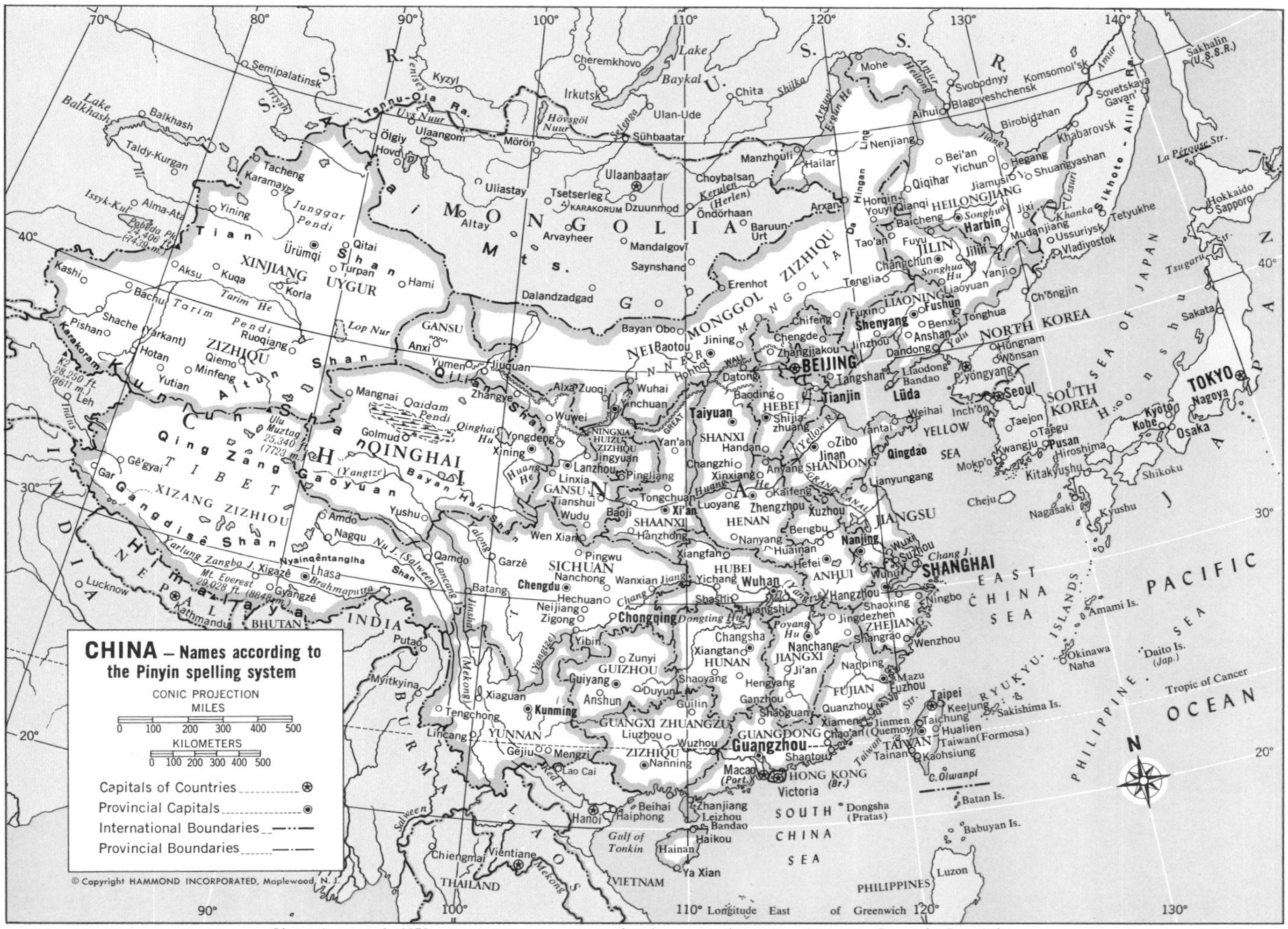

CHINA

PROVINCES

Anhwei, 33,560,000	J 5
Chekiang, 25,280,000	J 6
Fukien, 14,650,000	J 6
Heilungkiang, 14,860,000	L 2
Honan, 48,670,000	H 5
Hopei, 44,720,000	J 4
Hunan, 36,220,000	H 6
Hupei, 30,790,000	H 5
Inner Mongolian Autonomous	
Region, 9,200,000	G 3
Kansu, 12,800,000	F 4
Kiangsi, 18,610,000	J 6
Kiangsu, 45,230,000	K 5
Kirin, 12,550,000	L 3
Kwangsi Chuang Autonomous	
Region, 19,390,000	G 7
Kwangtung, 37,960,000	H 7
Kweichow, 16,890,000	G 6
Liaoning, 24,090,000	K 3
Ningsia Hui Autonomous Region,	
1,810,000	G 4
Shansi, 15,960,000	H 4
Shantung, 54,030,000	J 4
Shensi, 18,130,000	G 5
Sinkiang-Uigur Autonomous	
Region, 5,640,000	B 3
Szechwan, 72,160,000	F 5
Taiwan, 14,577,000	K 7
Tibet Aut. Reg., 1,270,000	C 5
Tsinghai, 2,050,000	E 4
Yünnan, 19,100,000	F 7

CITIES and TOWNS†

Ahpa	F 5
Aicheng	G 8
Aigun	L 1
Aihui (Aigun)	L 1
Alihu	K 2
Altai	C 2
Amoy, 400,000	J 7

Ankang	G 5
Anking, 160,000	J 5
Anshan, 1,500,000	K 3
Anshun, 40,000	G 6
Ansi	E 3
Anta, 110,000	L 2
Antung (Tantung), 450,000	K 3
Anyang, 225,000	H 4
Aqsu	A 4
Atushi, 5,000	A 4
Awati	B 3
Baba Hatim	B 3
Bai	B 3
Barkha	B 4
Barkhatu	B 3
Barkol	B 2
Bayinhot	E 4
Canton, 2,300,000	H 7
Chalainor	J 2
Chamdo	E 5
Changchih, 300,000	H 4
Changchow, 400,000	J 3
Changchow, 81,200	J 6
Changchun, 1,500,000	K 3
Changki	C 3
Changpeh	H 3
Changsha, 850,000	H 6
Changteh, 225,000	H 6
Changyeh, 45,000	E 4
Chankiang, 220,000	H 7
Chaoan (Chaochow), 101,000	J 7
Chaochow, 101,000	J 7
Chaotung, 50,000	F 6
Chaoyang, 30,000	J 3
Charkhliq	C 4
Chefoo, 180,000	K 4
Chengan	G 6
Chengchow, 1,500,000	H 5
Chengteh, 200,000	J 3
Chengtu, 2,000,000	F 5
Chenhsien, 50,000	H 6
Chenpa	G 5
Chenyüan	F 7
Chenyüeh	F 6
Cherchen	C 4
Chiai, 221,817	K 7
Chiehmo (Cherchen)	C 4
Chifeng, 49,000	J 3
Chihshui	G 6
Chihtan	G 4
Chimunai	C 2
Chinchow	G 7
Chinchow, 750,000	J 3
Chinkiang, 250,000	K 5
Chinsi, 45,000	K 3
Chinwangtao, 400,000	K 4
Chira	B 4
Chomo Dzong	J 7
Chüanchow, 130,000	J 7
Chucheng	J 4
Chuchow, 350,000	H 6
Chuguchak	B 2
Chühsien	J 5
Chumatien, 45,000	H 5
Chunghsin	K 7
Chungking, 3,500,000	G 6
Chungning	G 4
Chungshan, 135,000	H 7
Chungtien	F 6
Chushul	D 6
Dairen (in Lüta)	K 4
Denchin	E 5
Draya	E 5
Drepung	D 6
Durbuljin	B 2
Ed Dzong	D 5
Enshih	G 5
Erhlien	H 3
Fatshan, 120,000	H 7
Fengfeng, 45,000	H 4
Fenghsien	G 5
Fengkieh	G 5
Fengning	J 3
Fenyang, 25,000	H 4
Foochow, 900,000	J 6
Fowyang, 75,000	J 5
Fuchin	M 2
Fuhai	C 2
Fushun, 1,700,000	K 3
Fusin, 350,000	K 3
Fusingchen, 20,000	F 7
Fuyü, 62,969	J 2
Fuyüan	M 2
Gartok	D 5
Giamda Dzong (Taichao)	D 5
Golmo, 40,000	D 4
Gulo Gomba	B 5
Guma	A 4
Gyangtse	C 6
Gyatsa Dzong	D 6
Haikow (Hoihow), 500,000	H 7
Hailar, 60,000	J 2
Hailun	J 2
Hailung, 20,000	L 3
Hami	D 3
Hanchung, 120,000	G 5
Hangchow, 1,100,000	J 5
Hankow (in Wuhan)	H 5
Hantan, 500,000	H 4
Hanyang (in Wuhan)	H 5
Harbin, 2,750,000	L 2
Hengshui	H 4
Hengyang, 310,000	H 6
Hingi	G 7
Hochih	G 7
Hochwan, 75,000	G 6
Hofei, 400,000	J 5
Hofeng	H 5
Hoihow, 500,000	H 7
Hokang, 350,000	M 2
Hoppo, 80,000	G 7
Hotien (Khotan)	A 4
Hotso	F 5
Hsüchang, 58,000	H 5

(continued on following page)

CHINA — Names according to the Pinyin spelling system

CONIC PROJECTION

MILES
0 100 200 300 400 500

KILOMETERS
0 100 200 300 400 500

Capitals of Countries	⊛
Provincial Capitals	◉
International Boundaries	—·—·—
Provincial Boundaries	————

© Copyright HAMMOND INCORPORATED, Maplewood, N.J.

Since January 1, 1979, all proper names appearing in press dispatches from the People's Republic of China have been spelled according to the Pinyin system of transcribing Chinese speech sounds.

CHINA (continued)

Hsünkow	L 2
Huhehot, 700,000	H 3
Huma	L 1
Hunchun, 13,246	M 3
Hunkiang	L 3
Huocheng	B 3
Hwainan, 350,000	J 5
Hwaiteh, 60,000	K 3
Hwangchow	F 4
Hwangling	G 4
Hwangshih, 200,000	J 5
Hwangyüan	F 4
Hweili	H 6
Hwohsien	H 4
Ichang, 150,000	H 5
Ichun, 200,000	L 2
Ierhsieh	J 2
Iliang	F 7
Ining (Kuldja), 160,000	B 3
Ipin, 275,000	F 6
Ishan	G 7
Jechiang (Charkhliq)	C 4
Jyekundo	E 5
Kaifeng, 330,000	J 4
Kailu	K 3
Kalgan, 1,000,000	J 3
Kanchow, 135,000	H 6
Kangting	F 5
Kantse	F 5
Kaohsiung, 719,899	J 7
Karamai, 43,000	B 2
Kashgar, 175,000	A 4
Kashing, 132,000	K 5
Keelung, 304,740	K 6
Kelpin (Koping)	A 3
Kenho	K 1
Keriya	B 4
Khabakhe	C 2
Khana Abasa	D 2
Khetinsiring	C 2
Khobuk-Saur (Hofeng)	B 2
Khotan, 275,000	A 4
Kian, 100,000	J 6
Kiangling	H 5
Kiaoho	J 3
Kiaohsien	K 4
Kiayükwan	E 3
Kienko	G 5
Kienow	J 6
Kienshui	F 7
Kienyang, 50,000	K 2
Kinghung	F 7
Kingku	F 7
Kingpeng	J 3
Kingtehchen, 300,000	J 6
Kingyang	G 4
Kinhwa, 46,200	J 6
Kinta	E 3
Kirin, 1,200,000	L 3
Kishow	G 6
Kisi, 350,000	M 2
Kitai	C 3
Kiuchüan, 50,000	E 4
Kiukiang, 120,000	J 6
Kiungshan	H 8
Kokiu, 250,000	F 7
Kongmoon, 150,000	H 7
Koping	A 3
Kucha	C 3
Kueitun	C 3
Kulang	F 4
Kuldja, 160,000	B 3
Kungliu	C 3
Kunming, 1,700,000	F 6
Kurla	C 3
Kuyang	G 4
Kuyüan	G 4
Kwanghwa	H 5
Kweilin, 225,000	G 6
Kweiping	H 7
Kweisui (Huhehot)	H 3
Kweiyang, 1,500,000	G 6
Kweiyang	H 6
Laiyang, 250,000	K 4
Lanchow, 1,500,000	F 4
Lantang	E 7
Leiyang	J 6
Lhakang Dzong	D 6
Lhasa, 175,000	C 6
Lhatse Dzong	C 6
Lhuntse Dzong	D 6
Liangtang	G 5
Liaoyang, 250,000	K 3
Liaoyüan, 300,000	L 3
Lienyünkang, 300,000	J 4
Lihsien	F 4
Likiang	F 6
Linchwan, 45,000	J 6
Linfen	H 4
Lingling	J 6
Linhai	K 6
Linho	G 3
Linhsien	H 4
Linkow	M 2
Linping	H 7
Linsi	J 3
Linsia, 75,000	F 4
Lintsang	E 7
Lintsing, 45,000	J 4
Liping	G 6
Lishui	J 6
Litang	H 6
Liuchow, 250,000	G 7
Loho, 55,000	H 5
Loshan, 250,000	F 6
Loyang, 750,000	H 4
Luchow, 225,000	F 6
Luhsi	E 7
Lukchun	D 3
Lungchen, 14,000	L 2
Lungyen	J 6
Lupeh	H 5
Lüta, ‡4,000,000	K 4
Maerhkang	F 5
Mahai	D 4
Manass	C 3
Manchouli, 30,000	J 1
Mangyai	D 4
Mani	D 4
Manning (Wanning)	H 8
Maralbashi	A 4
Markham Dzong	E 6
Mato	E 4
Meihsien	J 7
Mendong Gomba	C 5
Menyüan	F 4
Merket	A 4
Miehning	F 6
Mienyang	G 5
Minhsien	F 5
Mintsin	F 4
Mishan	M 2
Moho	K 1
Mowming, 15,000	H 7
Moyü (Qara Qash)	B 4
Mukden, 3,750,000	K 3
Muli	F 6
Mutankiang, 400,000	M 3
Nachii	D 5
Nanchang, 900,000	J 6
Nancheng, 50,000	H 6
Nanchung, 275,000	G 5
Nangtsien	E 5
Nanhsiung	H 6
Nanking, 2,000,000	J 5
Nanning, 375,000	G 7
Nanping, 53,445	J 6
Neikiang, 240,000	F 6
Nenkiang	L 2
Ningan	L 3
Ningpo, 350,000	K 6
Ningsia (Yinchwan), 175,000	G 4
Ningsiang	H 6
Ningteh	J 6
Ningtu	J 6
Ningwu	H 4
Noh	B 5
Noho	K 2
Omin (Durbuljin)	B 2
Owpu	L 1
Pachen	D 5
Pachu (Maralbashi)	A 4
Pachung	F 5
Paicheng (Bai)	B 3
Paicheng, 75,000	K 2
Pailingmiao	H 3
Paiyin, 50,000	F 4
Paiyü	E 5
Pakhoi, 175,000	G 7
Pangkiang	H 3
Paochang	H 3
Paoki, 275,000	G 5
Paoshan	E 7
Paoting, 350,000	J 4
Paotow, 800,000	G 3
Pehan, 130,000	L 2
Peihai (Pakhoi), 175,000	G 7
Peiping (Peking) (cap.), ‡8,000,000	J 3
Peking (cap.), ‡8,000,000	J 3
Penglai	K 4
Pengpu, 400,000	J 5
Penki, 750,000	K 3
Phongdo Dzong	D 5
Pichieh	G 6
Piklang	E 6
Pingchüan	J 3
Pingliang, 60,000	G 4
Pinglo	G 7
Pingsiang, 7,000	J 6
Pingsiang, 210,000	G 7
Pingtung, 153,953	K 7
Pingwu	H 4
Pingyang	G 7
Pinyang	G 7
Pishan (Guma)	A 4
Pohsien, 75,000	J 5
Pokotu	K 2
Poli	M 2
Port Arthur (in Lüta)	K 4
Poseh	G 7
Pucheng	F 7
Puerh	F 7
Putien	J 6
Qara Qash	B 4
Qara Shahr	C 3
Qaraqum	A 4
Qarghaliq	A 4
Rima	E 6
Rudok	B 5
Rungmar Thok	B 5
Saka	E 6
Sanga Cho Dzong	E 6
Sanho	J 3
Sanming	J 6
Santai	F 5
Shahyar	B 3
Shangchih	H 2
Shanghai, ‡8,500,000	K 5
Shanghang	J 7
Shanghsien	H 4
Shangjao, 100,000	J 6
Shangkiu, 250,000	J 4
Shangnan	H 4
Shangshui, 100,000	J 5
Shanhaikwan	K 3
Shanshan	D 3
Shantan	F 4
Shaohing, 225,000	K 6
Shaoyang, 275,000	H 6
Sharasume (Altai)	C 2
Shasi, 125,000	H 5
Shentsa Dzong	D 5
Shenyang (Mukden), 3,750,000	K 3
Shigatse, 26,000	D 6
Shihchü	E 5
Shihchüan	G 5
Shihhotzu, 70,000	C 3
Shihkiachwang, 1,500,000	J 4
Shihtsuishan, 60,000	G 4
Shiukwan, 125,000	H 7
Shobando	J 7
Shwangcheng	L 3
Shwangliao	K 3
Shwangyashan, 150,000	M 2
Siaho	F 4
Siakwan, 26,200	E 7
Sian, 1,900,000	G 5
Siangfan, 150,000	H 5
Siangtan, 300,000	H 6
Siangyin	H 6
Sichang	G 6
Sienyang, 120,000	G 5
Silin	G 7
Silinhot, 20,000	H 3
Sinchu, 188,062	K 7
Singi Obo	C 5
Singsingsia	D 4
Singtai, 75,000	H 4
Sinhailien (Lienyünkang), 300,000	J 5
Sining, 250,000	F 4
Sinsiang, 300,000	H 4
Sinyang, 125,000	H 5
Siushui	J 6
Soche (Yarkand), 80,000	A 4
Solun	K 2
Soochow, 1,300,000	K 5
Süchow, 1,500,000	J 4
Suhsien	J 5
Suihsien	H 5
Suihwa, 36,000	L 2
Suining, 75,000	F 5
Suiteh	G 4
Sungpan	F 5
Sutsien	J 4
Süyung	F 6
Swatow, 400,000	J 7
Szeping, 100,000	K 3
Tahcheng (Chuguchak)	B 2
Tahsien	H 5
Taian, 20,000	J 4
Taichao	D 6
Taichung, 407,054	J 7
Tainan, 441,556	J 7
Taipei (cap.), 1,604,543	K 7
Taitung, 69,984	K 7
Taiyüan, 2,725,000	H 4
Taklakhar	B 5
Talai, 20,000	J 2
Tali	E 6
Tangshan, 1,200,000	J 4
Tanhsien	H 8
Tantung, 450,000	K 3
Taom, 75,000	K 2
Taocheng	F 6
Taofu	F 5
Tapanshang	A 4
Tardin	D 4
Tash Qurghan	A 4
Tashigong	B 5
Tatsaitan	D 4
Tatung, 300,000	H 3
Tayü	J 6
Tehchow, 45,000	J 4
Tehko	H 5
Tehtsin	F 6
Telingha	E 4
Tengchung	E 7
Tengkow	G 3
Tepao	G 7
Thok Daurakpa	B 5
Thok Jalung	B 5
Tiehling, 52,945	K 3
Tienshui, 100,000	G 5
Tientsin, ‡4,500,000	J 4
Tinghai	K 6
Tinghai	K 6
Tinghai	K 5
Tingri Dzong	C 6

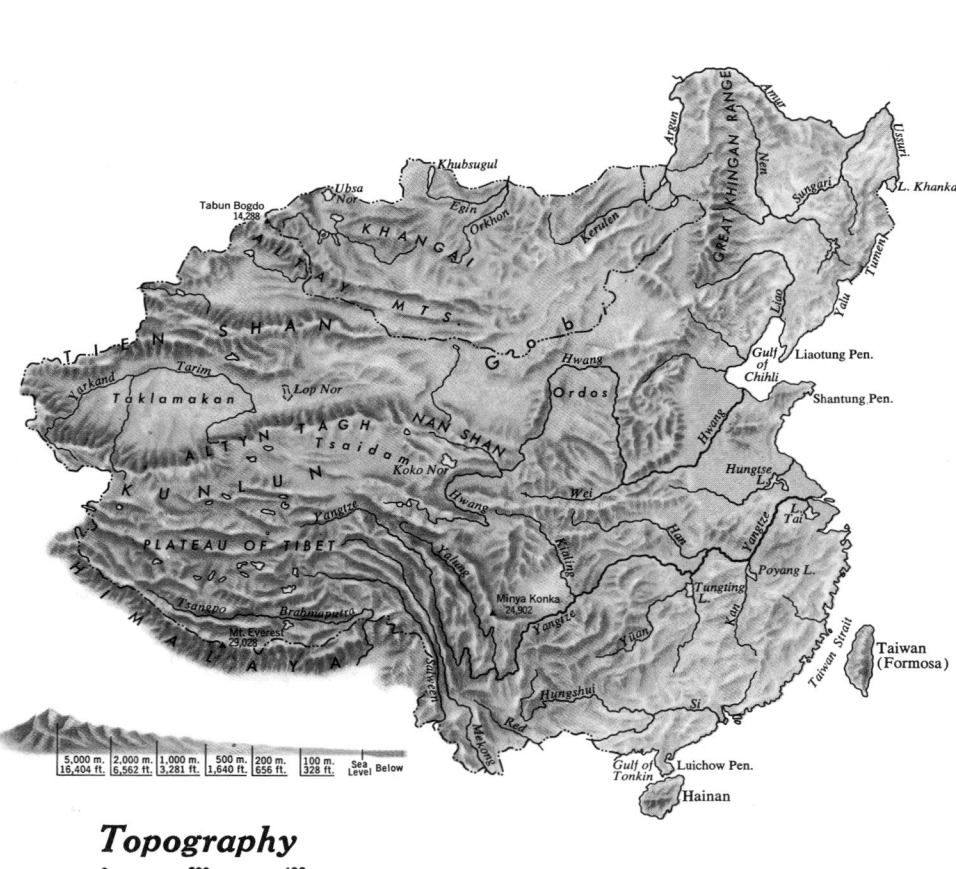

Topography

5,000 m. / 16,404 ft. — 2,000 m. / 6,562 ft. — 1,000 m. / 3,281 ft. — 500 m. / 1,640 ft. — 200 m. / 656 ft. — 100 m. / 328 ft. — Sea Level — Below

0 — 300 — 600
MILES

CHINA and MONGOLIA

CONIC PROJECTION

SCALE OF MILES

0 — 100 — 200 — 300 — 400 — 500

SCALE OF KILOMETRES

0 — 100 — 200 — 300 — 400 — 500

Capitals of Countries.... ☆   International Boundaries ———

Provincial Capitals....... ◉   Provincial Boundaries ———

Canals ....   Walls ww

© Copyright by C. S. HAMMOND & CO., N.Y.

*Wuhan municipality consists of
Hankow, Hanyang and Wuchang

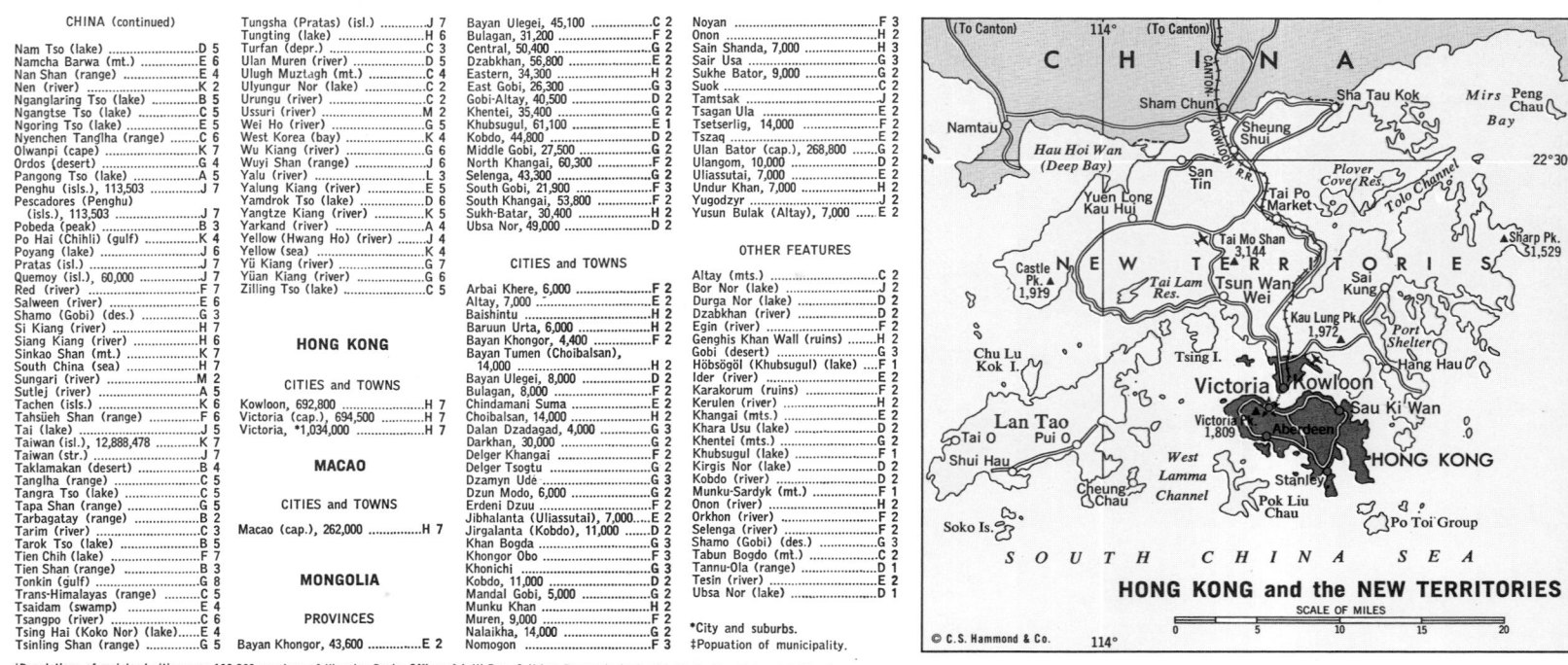

HONG KONG and the NEW TERRITORIES

© C.S. Hammond & Co.

Agriculture, Industry and Resources

DOMINANT LAND USE

- Cereals (chiefly wheat, millet)
- Cereals (chiefly wheat, rice, barley)
- Cereals (chiefly rice, barley)
- Livestock Herding, Limited Agriculture
- Forests
- Nonagricultural Land

MAJOR MINERAL OCCURRENCES

Ab	Asbestos
Ag	Silver
Al	Bauxite
Au	Gold
C	Coal
Cu	Copper
F	Fluorspar
Fe	Iron Ore
G	Natural Gas
Gp	Gypsum
Hg	Mercury
J	Jade
Mg	Magnesium
Mn	Manganese
Mo	Molybdenum
Na	Salt
O	Petroleum
Pb	Lead
Sb	Antimony
Sn	Tin
Tc	Talc
U	Uranium
W	Tungsten
Zn	Zinc

Water Power

Major Industrial Areas

JAPAN

AREA 145,730 sq. mi.
POPULATION 112,200,000
CAPITAL Tokyo
LARGEST CITY Tokyo
HIGHEST POINT Fuji 12,389 ft.
MONETARY UNIT yen
MAJOR LANGUAGE Japanese
MAJOR RELIGIONS Buddhism, Shintoism

NORTH KOREA

AREA 46,540 sq. mi.
POPULATION 17,000,000
CAPITAL P'yŏngyang
LARGEST CITY P'yŏngyang
HIGHEST POINT Paektu 9,003 ft.
MONETARY UNIT wŏn
MAJOR LANGUAGE Korean
MAJOR RELIGIONS Confucianism, Buddhism, Christianity, Ch'ŏndogyo

SOUTH KOREA

AREA 38,175 sq.mi.
POPULATION 34,688,079
CAPITAL Seoul
LARGEST CITY Seoul
HIGHEST POINT Halla 6,398 ft.
MONETARY UNIT wŏn
MAJOR LANGUAGE Korean
MAJOR RELIGIONS Confucianism, Buddhism, Ch'ŏndogyo, Christianity

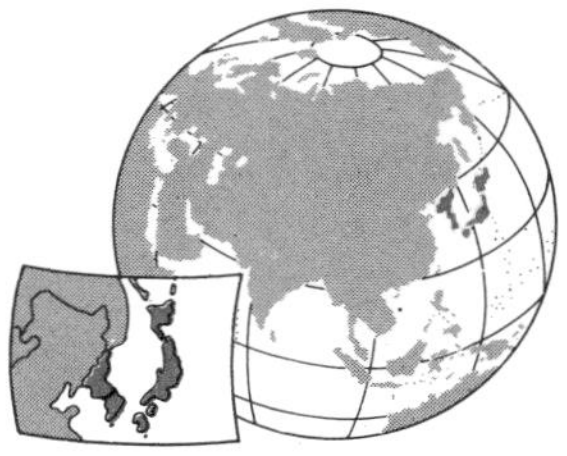

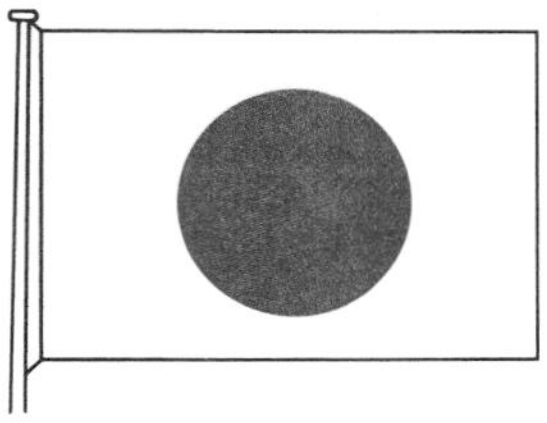

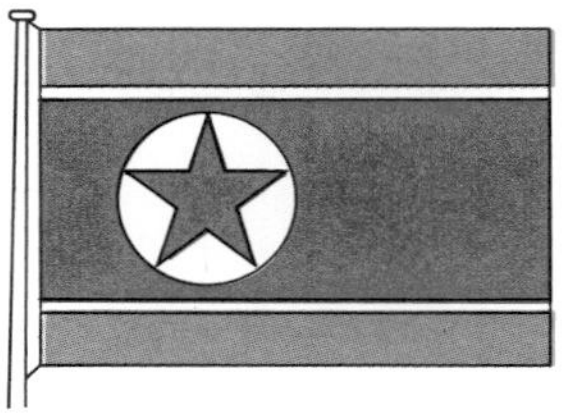

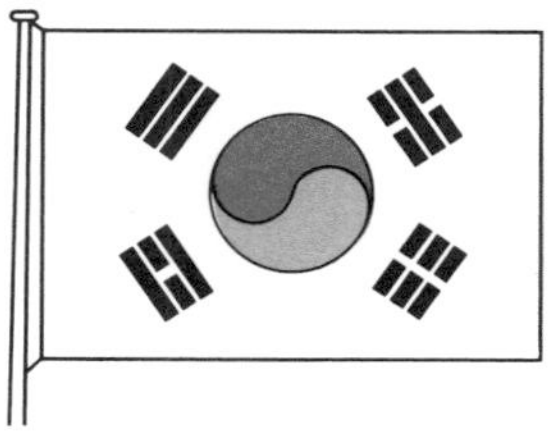

JAPAN

PREFECTURES

Aichi, 5,923,499	H 6
Akita, 1,232,493	J 4
Aomori, 1,468,571	K 3
Chiba, 4,149,132	P 2
Ehime, 1,465,205	F 7
Fukui, 773,597	G 5
Fukuoka, 4,292,997	D 7
Fukushima, 1,970,675	K 5
Gifu, 1,867,970	H 6
Gumma, 1,756,489	J 5
Hiroshima, 2,646,353	E 6
Hokkaido, 5,338,043	K 2
Hyogo, 4,991,910	H 7
Ibaraki, 2,342,173	K 5
Ishikawa, 1,069,871	H 5
Iwate, 1,385,566	K 4
Kagawa, 961,285	G 6
Kagoshima, 1,723,900	E 8
Kanagawa, 3,697,619	O 2
Kochi, 808,367	F 7
Kumamoto, 1,715,011	E 7
Kyoto, 2,424,830	J 7
Mie, 1,625,992	H 6
Miyagi, 1,955,274	K 4
Miyazaki, 1,085,057	E 8
Nagano, 2,017,544	J 5
Nagasaki, 1,571,919	D 7
Nara, 1,077,301	J 8
Niigata, 2,391,963	J 5
Oita, 1,190,307	E 7
Okayama, 1,814,300	F 6
Okinawa, 1,042,502	N 6
Osaka, 8,278,844	J 8
Saga, 837,680	E 7
Saitama, 4,821,349	O 2
Shiga, 985,515	J 7
Shimane, 768,876	F 6
Shizuoka, 3,308,796	H 6
Tochigi, 1,698,002	K 5
Tokushima, 805,090	G 7
Tokyo, 11,669,167	O 2
Tottori, 581,318	G 6
Toyama, 1,070,793	H 5
Wakayama, 1,072,078	G 6
Yamagata, 1,220,308	K 4
Yamaguchi, 1,555,233	E 6
Yamanashi, 783,054	J 6

CITIES and TOWNS

Abashiri, 43,821	M 1
Ageo, 146,359	O 2
Aikawa, 13,546	H 4
Aizuwakamatsu, 108,676	J 5
Ajigasawa, 18,094	J 3
Akabira, 26,363	K 2
Akashi, 234,905	H 8
Aki, 24,483	F 7
Akita, 261,242	J 4
Akkeshi, 16,778	M 2
Akune, 30,296	E 7
Amagasaki, 545,762	H 8
Amagi, 42,725	E 7
Anan, 60,369	G 7
Aomori, 264,187	K 3
Asahi, 34,028	K 6
Asahikawa, 320,526	L 2
Ashibetsu, 36,517	L 2
Ashikaga, 162,361	J 5
Ashiya, 76,211	H 8
Atami, 51,437	J 6
Atsugi, 108,952	O 2
Awaji, 9,622	H 8
Ayabe, 43,490	G 6
Beppu, 133,893	E 7
Bibai, 38,418	L 2
Chiba, 659,344	P 2
Chichibu, 61,797	J 5
Chigasaki, 152,024	O 3
Chitose, 61,031	K 2
Chofu, 175,858	O 2
Choshi, 90,375	K 6
Daito, 110,829	J 8
Ebetsu, 77,623	K 2
Esashi, Hokkaido, 10,172	L 1
Esashi, Hokkaido, 14,410	J 3
Esashi, Iwate, 36,338	K 4
Fuchu, Hiroshima, 50,217	F 6
Fuchu, Tokyo, 182,379	O 2
Fuji, 199,195	J 6
Fujieda, 90,356	J 6
Fujisawa, 265,938	O 3
Fukuchiyama, 60,004	G 6
Fukue, 32,016	D 7
Fukui, 231,365	G 5
Fukuoka, 1,002,214	D 7
Fukushima, 246,531	K 5
Fukuyama, 329,779	F 6
Funabashi, 423,106	P 2
Furukawa, 54,358	K 4
Gifu, 408,699	H 6
Gobo, 30,273	G 7
Gose, 37,555	J 8
Gosen, 39,378	J 5
Goshogawara, 49,048	K 3
Gotsu, 27,990	F 6
Habikino, 94,160	J 8
Haboro, 13,624	K 1
Hachinohe, 224,213	K 3
Hachioji, 322,558	O 2
Hagi, 52,724	E 6
Hakodate, 307,447	K 3
Hakui, 28,726	H 5
Hamada, 50,315	E 6
Hamamatsu, 468,886	H 6
Hanamaki, 65,829	K 4
Hanno, 55,925	O 2
Haramachi, 43,482	K 5
Hayama, 24,025	O 3
Higashiosaka, 524,731	J 8
Hikone, 85,068	H 6
Himeji, 436,099	G 6
Himi, 61,789	H 5
Hirakata, 297,618	J 7
Hirara, 29,292	L 7
Hirata, 30,943	F 6
Hiratsuka, 195,635	O 3
Hiroo, 11,399	L 2
Hirosaki, 164,924	K 3
Hiroshima, 852,607	E 6
Hitachi, 202,387	K 5
Hitachiota, 35,322	K 5
Hitoyoshi, 41,119	E 7
Hofu, 105,538	E 6
Hondo, 40,432	E 7
Honjo, 40,488	J 4
Hyuga, 53,449	E 7
Ibaraki, 210,286	J 7
Ibusuki, 32,338	E 8
Ichihara, 194,069	P 3
Ichikawa, 319,272	P 2
Ichinohe, 21,437	K 3
Ichinomiya, 238,457	H 6
Ichinoseki, 59,143	K 4
Ide, 9,112	J 7
Iida, 77,114	H 6
Iizuka, 75,417	E 7
Ikeda, Hokkaido, 12,306	L 2
Ikeda, Osaka, 100,263	H 7
Ikuno, 6,659	G 6
Imabari, 119,725	F 6
Imari, 60,914	D 7
Imazu, 11,520	G 6
Ina, 54,467	H 6
Isahaya, 73,339	D 7
Ise, 104,955	H 6
Ishigaki, 34,625	L 7
Ishige, 19,220	P 2
Ishinomaki, 115,084	K 4
Ishioka, 43,678	K 5
Itami, 171,979	H 7
Ito, 68,073	J 6
Itoigawa, 36,646	H 5
Itoman, 39,359	N 6
Iwaizumi, 20,218	K 4
Iwaki, 330,210	K 5
Iwakuni, 111,071	E 6
Iwami, 16,062	G 6
Iwamizawa, 72,303	L 2
Iwanai, 25,823	K 2
Iwasaki, 4,439	J 3
Iwata, 67,665	H 6
Iwatsuki, 83,825	O 2
Iyo, 27,808	F 7
Izuhara, 18,460	D 6
Izumi, 118,234	J 8
Izumiotsu, 66,243	J 8
Izumisano, 86,139	G 6
Izumo, 71,568	F 6
Joyo, 58,916	J 7
Kadoma, 143,235	J 7
Kaga, 61,598	H 5
Kagoshima, 456,818	E 8
Kaizuka, 79,506	H 8
Kakogawa, 169,297	G 6
Kamaishi, 68,982	L 4
Kamakura, 165,548	O 3
Kameoka, 58,184	J 7
Kaminoyama, 37,860	J 4
Kamiyaku, 8,666	E 8
Kamo, 8,954	J 7
Kanazawa, 395,262	H 5
Kanonji, 44,134	F 6
Kanoya, 67,949	E 8
Kanuma, 81,800	J 5
Karatsu, 75,224	D 7
Kaseda, 24,969	D 8
Kashihara, Nara, 95,697	J 8
Kashihara, Osaka, 63,585	J 8
Kashiwa, 203,063	P 2
Kashiwazaki, 80,353	J 5
Kasugai, 213,856	H 6
Kasukabe, 121,639	O 2
Katsuta, 79,997	K 5
Katsuura, 26,755	K 6
Kawachinagano, 66,945	J 8
Kawagoe, 225,467	O 2
Kawaguchi, 345,547	J 6
Kawanishi, 115,771	H 7
Kawasaki, 1,015,022	O 2
Kesennuma, 66,618	K 4
Kikonai, 10,034	K 3
Kiryu, 134,240	J 5
Kisarazu, 96,839	P 3
Kishiwada, 174,947	J 8
Kitaibaraki, 44,332	K 5
Kitakata, 37,472	J 5
Kitakyushu, 1,058,067	E 6
Kitami, 91,514	L 2
Kizu, 11,891	J 7
Kobayashi, 38,325	E 8
Kobe, 1,360,530	H 7
Kochi, 280,960	F 7
Kodaira, 156,182	O 2
Kofu, 193,887	J 6
Kokubu, 31,658	E 8
Komagane, 30,318	H 6
Komatsu, 100,276	H 5
Koriyama, 264,610	K 5
Koshigaya, 195,915	P 2
Kuji, 38,126	K 3
Kuki, 45,799	O 2
Kumagaya, 131,486	J 5
Kumamoto, 488,053	E 7
Kumano, 27,025	G 7
Kumiyama, 11,539	J 7
Kurashiki, 392,770	F 6
Kurayoshi, 50,786	F 6
Kure, 242,652	F 6
Kurume, 204,474	E 7
Kushikino, 30,457	E 8
Kushima, 30,036	E 8
Kushimoto, 18,998	G 7
Kushiro, 206,689	M 2
Kutchan, 18,668	K 2
Kyonan, 13,066	O 3
Kyoto, 1,461,050	J 7
Machida, 255,303	O 2
Maebashi, 250,241	J 5
Maibara, 12,834	G 6
Maizuru, 97,775	G 6
Makurazaki, 29,689	O 3
Mashike, 9,312	K 2
Masuda, 50,732	E 6
Matsubara, 132,662	H 8
Matsudo, 344,552	P 2
Matsue, 127,446	F 6
Matsumae, 18,307	J 3
Matsumoto, 185,577	H 5
Matsusaka, 108,891	H 6
Matsuto, 36,170	H 5
Matsuyama, 367,313	F 7
Mihara, 83,680	F 6
Miki, 55,730	H 7
Mikuni, 21,603	G 5
Minamata, 36,782	E 7
Minobu, 10,346	J 6
Minoo, 79,620	J 7
Misawa, 37,434	K 3
Mishima, 22,404	J 7
Mitaka, 164,852	O 2
Mito, 197,950	K 5
Mitsukaido, 38,820	P 2
Miura, 47,890	O 3
Miyako, 61,912	L 4
Miyakonojo, 118,284	E 8
Miyazaki, 234,348	E 8
Miyazu, 30,194	G 6
Miyoshi, 37,195	F 6
Mizusawa, 52,271	K 4
Mobara, 64,942	K 6
Mombetsu, 32,821	L 1
Mooka, 47,347	K 5
Mori, 17,030	K 2
Moriguchi, 178,379	J 7
Morioka, 216,211	K 4
Motobu, 17,809	N 6
Muko, 45,886	J 7
Murakami, 32,939	J 4
Muroran, 158,714	K 2
Muroto, 26,660	G 7
Musashino, 139,493	O 2
Mutsu, 44,651	K 3
Nachikatsuura, 23,597	H 7
Nagahama, Ehime, 13,144	F 7
Nagahama, Shiga, 53,966	H 6
Nagano, 306,643	J 5
Nagaoka, Kyoto, 65,557	J 7
Nagaoka, Niigata, 171,742	J 5
Nagasaki, 450,195	D 7
Nagato, 27,327	E 6
Nago, 45,207	N 6
Nagoya, 2,079,694	H 6
Naha, 295,091	N 6
Nakaminato, 33,144	K 5
Nakamura, 34,426	F 7
Nakasato, 14,247	K 3
Nakatsu, 59,111	E 7
Nanao, 49,491	H 5
Nankoku, 42,828	F 7
Naoetsu, 123,416	H 5
Nara, 257,482	J 8
Narashino, 117,851	P 2
Nayoro, 35,145	L 1
Naze, 46,337	O 5
Nemuro, 45,817	M 2
Neyagawa, 254,316	J 7
Nichinan, 52,171	E 8
Niigata, 423,204	J 5
Niihama, 131,707	F 6
Niimi, 30,014	F 6
Niitsu, 58,970	J 5
Nikko, 26,279	J 5
Nishinomiya, 400,590	H 8
Nishinoomote, 24,266	E 8
Nobeoka, 134,530	E 7
Noboribetsu, 50,890	K 2
Noda, 78,194	P 2
Nogata, 58,551	E 7
Nose, 9,751	J 7
Noshiro, 59,218	J 3
Noto, 15,815	H 5
Numata, 45,254	J 5
Numazu, 199,325	J 6
Obama, 33,891	G 6
Obihiro, 141,776	L 2
Oda, 37,450	F 6

(continued on following page)

Agriculture, Industry and Resources

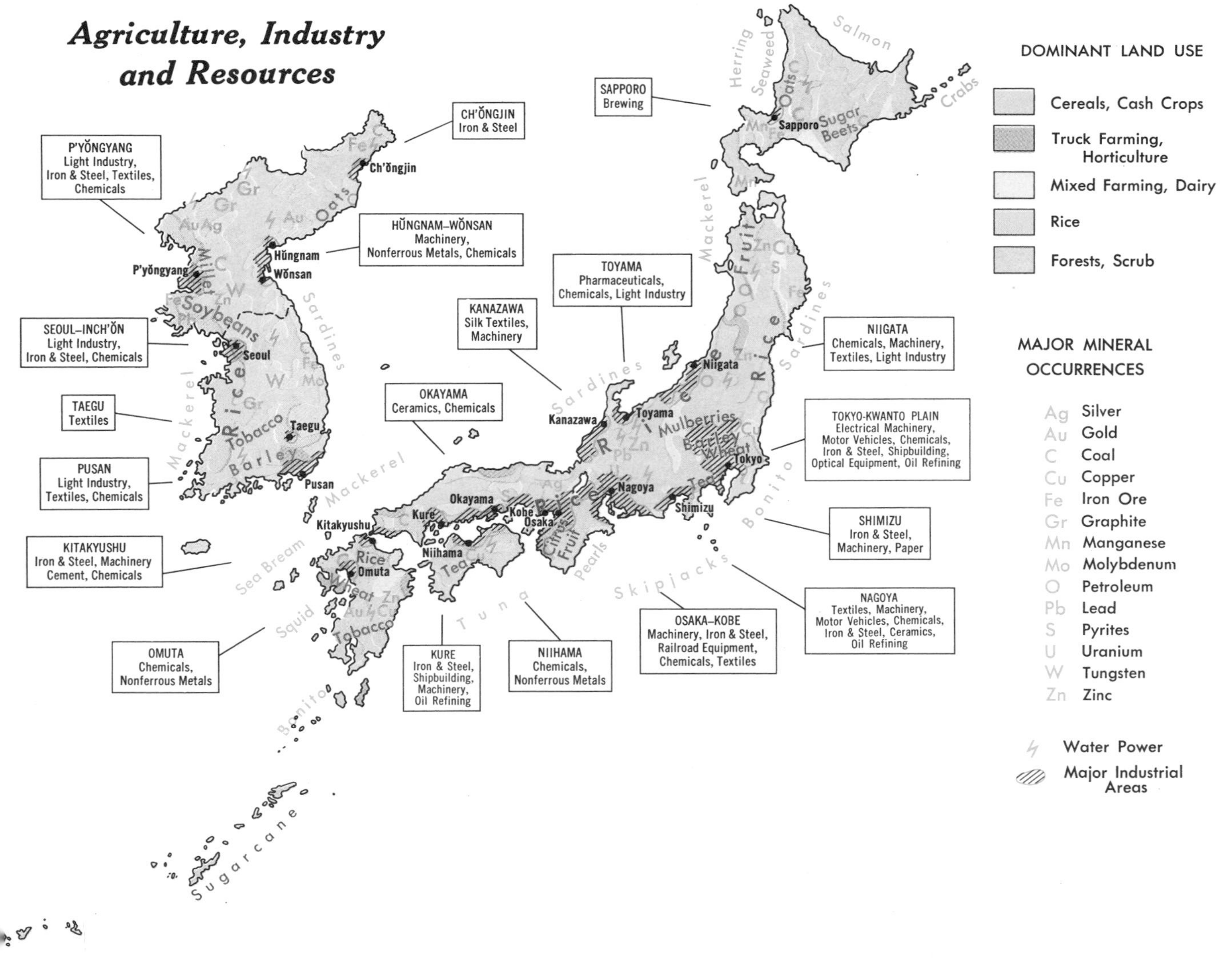
SAPPORO
Brewing
CH'ŎNGJIN
Iron & Steel
P'YŎNGYANG
Light Industry,
Iron & Steel, Textiles,
Chemicals
HŬNGNAM–WŎNSAN
Machinery,
Nonferrous Metals, Chemicals
TOYAMA
Pharmaceuticals,
Chemicals, Light Industry
KANAZAWA
Silk Textiles,
Machinery
SEOUL–INCH'ŎN
Light Industry,
Iron & Steel, Chemicals
NIIGATA
Chemicals, Machinery,
Textiles, Light Industry
OKAYAMA
Ceramics, Chemicals
TAEGU
Textiles
TOKYO-KWANTO PLAIN
Electrical Machinery,
Motor Vehicles, Chemicals,
Iron & Steel, Shipbuilding,
Optical Equipment, Oil Refining
PUSAN
Light Industry,
Textiles, Chemicals
SHIMIZU
Iron & Steel,
Machinery, Paper
KITAKYUSHU
Iron & Steel, Machinery
Cement, Chemicals
NAGOYA
Textiles, Machinery,
Motor Vehicles, Chemicals,
Iron & Steel, Ceramics,
Oil Refining
OSAKA–KOBE
Machinery, Iron & Steel,
Railroad Equipment,
Chemicals, Textiles
OMUTA
Chemicals,
Nonferrous Metals
KURE
Iron & Steel,
Shipbuilding,
Machinery,
Oil Refining
NIIHAMA
Chemicals,
Nonferrous Metals
Sapporo
Ch'ŏngjin
Hŭngnam
Wŏnsan
P'yŏngyang
Seoul
Taegu
Pusan
Niigata
Toyama
Kanazawa
Tokyo
Nagoya
Shimizu
Okayama
Kure
Kobe
Osaka
Niihama
Kitakyushu
Omuta
Salmon
Herring
Seaweed
Oats
Sugar Beets
Crabs
Mackerel
Fruit
Rice
Sardines
Soybeans
Millet
Tobacco
Barley
Mulberries
Wheat
Tea
Citrus Fruit
Pearls
Bonito
Skipjacks
Tuna
Sea Bream
Squid
Sugarcane
DOMINANT LAND USE
Cereals, Cash Crops
Truck Farming, Horticulture
Mixed Farming, Dairy
Rice
Forests, Scrub
MAJOR MINERAL OCCURRENCES
Ag Silver
Au Gold
C Coal
Cu Copper
Fe Iron Ore
Gr Graphite
Mn Manganese
Mo Molybdenum
O Petroleum
Pb Lead
S Pyrites
U Uranium
W Tungsten
Zn Zinc
Water Power
Major Industrial Areas

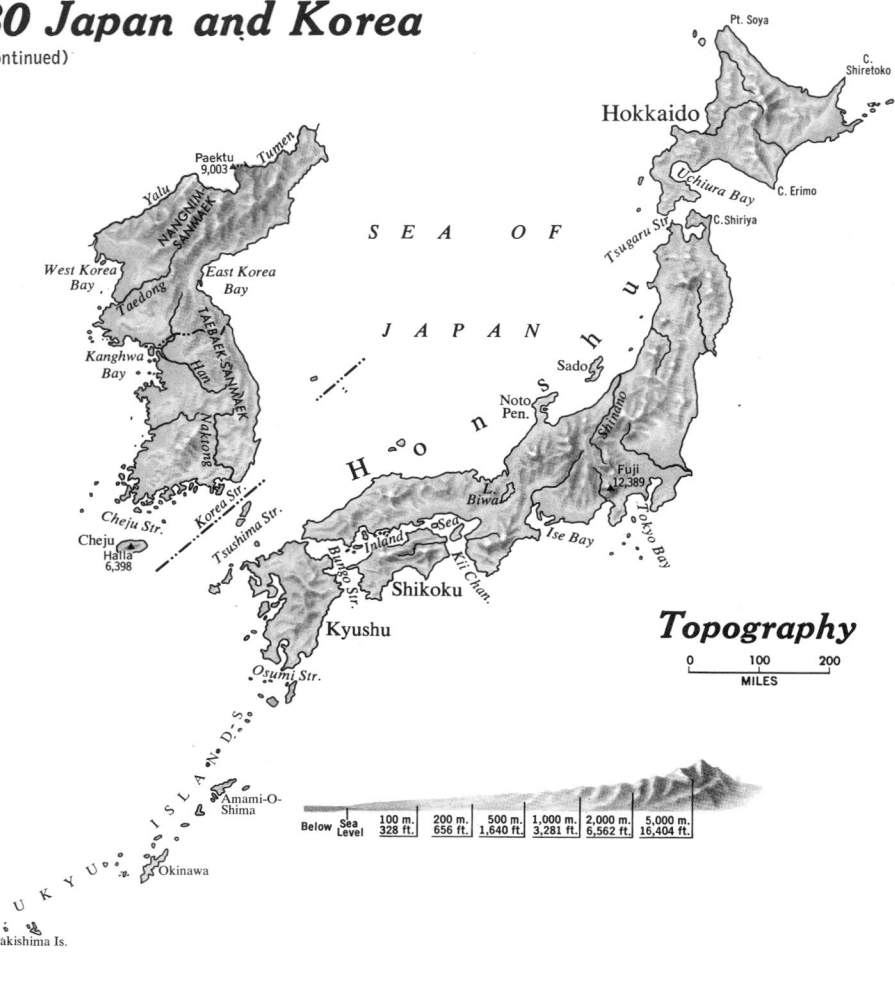

Topography

0   100   200
MILES

Below Sea Level | 100 m. 328 ft. | 200 m. 656 ft. | 500 m. 1,640 ft. | 1,000 m. 3,281 ft. | 2,000 m. 6,562 ft. | 5,000 m. 16,404 ft.

Sagami (bay)	O 3	Suzu (pt.)	H 5	Tsushima (str.)	D 7
Sagami (riv.)	O 2	Takeshima (isls.)	F 5	Uchiura (bay)	K 2
Sagami (sea)	J 6	Tama (riv.)	O 2	Unzen (mt.)	D 7
Saikai National Park	D 7	Tanega (isl.), 46,345	E 8	Unzen-Amakusa National Park	D 7
Sakishima (isls.), 63,361	K 7	Tappi (cape)	K 3	Volcano (isls.)	M 4
San in Kaigan National Park	G 6	Tarama (isl.), 1,805	L 7	Wakasa (bay)	G 6
Sata (cape)	E 8	Tazawa (lake)	K 3	Yaeyama (isls.), 5,622	K 7
Setonaikai National Park	H 7	Teshio (mt.)	L 1	Yaku (isl.), 16,108	E 8
Shikoku (isl.), 3,928,607	F 7	Teshio (riv.)	L 1	Yodo (riv.)	J 7
Shikotan (isl.)	N 2	Tobi (isl.)	J 4	Yonaguni (isl.), 2,153	K 7
Shikotsu (lake)	K 2	Tokachi (mt.)	L 2	Yoron (isl.), 6,973	N 6
Shikotsu-Toya National Park	K 2	Tokachi (riv.)	L 2	Yoshino (riv.)	H 7
Shimane (pen.), 199,148	F 6	Tokara (isls.)	O 5	Yoshino-Kumano National Park	H 7
Shimokita (pen.), 95,574	J 5	Tokuno (isl.), 35,396	O 5	Zao (isl.)	K 5
Shinano (riv.)	J 5	Tokyo (bay)	O 2		
Shiono (cape)	H 7	Tone (riv.)	K 6	**KOREA (NORTH)**	
Shiragami (cape)	J 3	Tosa (bay)	F 7		
Shirane (mt.)	H 5	Towada (lake)	K 3	CITIES and TOWNS	
Shirane (mt.)	H 6	Towada-Hachimantai National			
Shiretoko (cape)	M 1	Park	K 3	Ch'ongjin, 306,000	E 3
Shiriya (cape)	K 3	Toya (lake)	K 2	Chongju	B 4
Soya (isl.)	L 1	Toyama (bay)	H 5	Haeju, 140,000	B 4
Suo (sea)	E 7	Tsu (isls.), 52,478	D 6	Hamhung, 484,000	C 4
Suruga (bay)	J 6	Tsugaru (str.)	J 3	Heijo (P'yongyang) (cap.),	
Suwanose (isl.)	O 4	Tsurugi (mt.)	G 7	1,250,000	C 4

Odate, 71,828	K 3	Sunagawa, 26,023	K 2	Yokkaichi, 247,000	H 6	Ishikari (riv.)	L 2
Odawara, 173,521	J 6	Susaki, 31,016	F 7	Yokohama, 2,621,648	O 3	Ishikari (mt.)	L 2
Ofunato, 39,629	K 4	Suttsu, 6,511	J 2	Yokosuka, 389,559	O 3	Iwaki (mt.)	K 3
Oga, 39,621	J 4	Suwa, 49,595	H 6	Yokote, 43,030	K 4	Iwate (mt.)	K 4
Ogaki, 140,424	H 6	Suzu, 28,238	H 5	Yonago, 118,332	F 6	Iwo (isl.)	M 4
Ogi, 4,717	J 5	Suzuka, 141,829	H 6	Yonezawa, 91,975	K 5	Iyo (sea)	E 7
Ohata, 12,632	K 3	Tachikawa, 138,097	O 2	Yono, 71,045	O 2	Izu (isl.), 32,459	J 6
Oita, 320,236	E 7	Tajimi, 68,901	H 6	Yubari, 50,131	L 2	Izu (pen.), 274,136	J 6
Ojiya, 44,375	J 5	Takaishi, 66,824	H 8	Yubetsu, 6,693	L 1	Japan (sea)	G 4
Okawa, 50,397	E 7	Takamatsu, 298,997	G 6	Yukuhashi, 53,751	E 7	Joshinetsu-Kogen National	
Okaya, 61,776	H 5	Takaoka, 169,618	H 5	Yuzawa, 38,005	K 4	Park	J 5
Okayama, 513,452	F 6	Takarazuka, 162,622	H 7	Zushi, 56,298	O 3	Kagoshima (bay)	E 8
Okazaki, 234,506	H 6	Takasaki, 211,348	J 5			Kamui (cape)	K 2
Omagari, 40,581	K 4	Takatsuki, 330,571	J 7	OTHER FEATURES		Kariba (mt.)	K 2
Omiya, 327,696	O 2	Takawa, 61,465	E 7			Kasumiga (lag.)	K 5
Omu, 7,407	L 1	Takayama, 60,506	H 5	Abashiri (riv.)	M 1	Kazan-retto (Volcano) (isls.)	M 4
Omura, Bonin Is., 1,507	M 3	Takefu, 65,013	H 6	Abukuma (riv.)	K 4	Kerama (isls.), 1,687	M 6
Omura, Nagasaki, 60,919	E 7	Tanabe, Kyoto, 30,025	J 7	Agano (riv.)	J 4	Kii (chan.)	G 7
Omuta, 165,971	E 7	Tanabe, Wakayama, 67,001	G 7	Akan National Park	M 2	Kikai (isl.), 11,464	O 5
Onagawa, 16,945	K 4	Tateyama, 56,139	K 6	Amakusa (isls.), 175,495	D 7	Kino (riv.)	G 7
Ono, 41,918	H 6	Tendo, 48,077	K 4	Amami (isls.), 155,884	N 5	Kirishima-Yaku National Park	E 7
Onoda, 43,804	E 6	Tenri, 62,908	J 7	Amami-O-Shima (isl.), 85,168	N 5	Kita Iwo (isl.)	M 4
Onomichi, 102,954	F 6	Teshio, 17,351	K 1	Ara (riv.)	O 2	Kitakami (riv.)	K 4
Osaka, 2,778,975	J 8	Toba, 29,346	H 6	Asahi (mt.)	J 5	Komaga (mt.)	K 2
Ota, 110,724	J 5	Tobetsu, 17,351	K 1	Asama (mt.)	J 5	Korea (str.)	D 7
Otaru, 184,403	K 2	Togane, 33,404	K 6	Ashizuri (cape)	F 7	Koshiki (isls.), 8,979	D 8
Otawara, 42,331	K 5	Toi, 6,982	J 6	Aso (mt.)	E 7	Kuchino (isl.)	O 5
Otsu, 191,474	J 7	Tojo, 13,795	F 6	Aso National Park	E 7	Kuju (mt.)	E 7
Owase, 31,798	H 6	Tokushima, 239,285	G 7	Atsumi (bay)	H 6	Kume (isl.), 4,740	M 6
Oyabe, 35,791	H 5	Tokuyama, 106,963	F 6	Awa (isl.), 674	J 4	Kutcharo (lake)	M 2
Oyama, 120,259	J 5	Tokyo (cap.), 8,642,800	O 2	Awaji (isl.), 172,118	H 8	Kyushu (isl.), 11,775,985	E 7
Ozu, 37,296	E 7	Tomakomai, 132,480	K 2	Bandai (mt.)	K 4	Meakan (mt.)	L 2
Rausu, 8,249	M 1	Tomiyama, 7,390	J 6	Bandai-Asahi National Park	J 4	Minami Iwo (isl.)	M 5
Rikuzentakata, 29,440	K 4	Tondabayashi, 91,393	J 8	Biwa (lake)	H 6	Miura (pen.), 517,772	O 3
Rumoi, 36,878	K 2	Tosa, 30,679	F 7	Bonin (isls.), 1,507	M 3	Miyako (isl.), 40,160	L 7
Ryotsu, 22,109	J 4	Tosashimizu, 24,858	F 7	Boso (pen.), 976,493	K 6	Miyako (isls.), 57,739	L 7
Ryugasaki, 40,569	P 2	Tosu, 50,732	E 7	Bungo (str.)	F 7	Mogami (riv.)	K 4
Sabae, 57,252	H 5	Tottori, 122,312	G 6	Chichi (isl.), 1,507	M 3	Motsuta (cape)	J 2
Saga, 150,260	E 7	Towada, 54,369	K 3	Chichibu-Tama National Park	J 6	Muko (isl.)	M 3
Sagamihara, 377,341	O 2	Toyama, 290,145	H 5	Chokai (mt.)	K 4	Muko (mt.)	H 7
Saigo, 14,408	F 5	Toyohashi, 284,597	H 6	Chubu-Sangaku National Park	H 5	Muroto (pt.)	G 7
Saiki, 52,863	E 7	Toyonaka, 398,363	J 7	Dai (mt.)	F 6	Mutsu (bay)	K 3
Saito, 37,054	E 7	Toyooka, 46,211	G 6	Daimanji (mt.)	F 5	Naka (riv.)	K 4
Sakado, 51,230	O 2	Toyota, 248,774	H 6	Daio (cape)	H 6	Nampo-Shoto (isls.), 1,507	M 3
Sakai, Ibaraki, 24,347	P 1	Tsu, 139,537	H 6	Daisen-Oki National Park	F 6	Nansei Shoto (Ryukyu)	
Sakai, Osaka, 750,671	J 8	Tsubame, 43,265	J 5	Daisetsu (mt.)	L 2	(isls.), 1,198,386	M 6
Sakaide, 67,624	G 6	Tsuchiura, 104,031	J 5	Daisetsu-Zan National Park	L 2	Nantai (mt.)	J 5
Sakaiminato, 35,819	F 6	Tsuruga, 60,210	G 6	Dogo (isl.), 23,605	F 5	Nasu (mt.)	K 4
Sakata, 97,723	J 4	Tsurugi, 15,253	H 5	Dozen (isls.), 6,160	F 5	Nemuro (str.)	M 1
Saku, 56,145	J 5	Tsuruoka, 95,933	J 4	East China (sea)	C 8	Nii (isl.), 3,666	J 6
Sakurai, 54,315	J 8	Tsuyama, 79,907	F 6	Edo (riv.)	P 2	Nikko National Park	J 5
Sanda, 35,261	H 7	Ube, 161,971	E 6	Erimo (cape)	L 3	Nishino (isl.)	M 3
Sanjo, 81,806	J 5	Ueda, 105,147	J 5	Esan (pt.)	K 3	Nojima (cape)	K 6
Sapporo, 1,240,617	K 2	Ugo, 21,956	K 4	Fuji (mt.)	J 6	Nosappu (pt.)	M 1
Sarufutsu, 3,552	L 1	Uji, 133,396	J 7	Fuji (riv.)	J 6	Noto (pen.), 290,628	H 5
Sasebo, 250,723	D 7	Uozu, 48,419	H 5	Fuji-Hakone-Izu National		Nyudo (cape)	K 3
Satte, 43,083	O 1	Urakawa, 20,213	L 2	Park	H 6	Oani (riv.)	K 3
Sawara, 48,669	K 6	Urawa, 331,145	O 2	Gassan (mt.)	J 4	Obitsu (riv.)	K 6
Sayama, 98,548	O 2	Ushibuka, 24,252	D 7	Goto (isls.), 126,261	D 7	Oga (pen.), 39,621	J 4
Sendai, Kagoshima, 61,790	E 8	Usuki, 85,147	E 7	Habomai (isls.)	N 2	Ogasawara-gunto (Bonin)	
Sendai, Miyagi, 615,473	K 4	Utsunomiya, 344,417	K 5	Hachiro (lag.)	J 3	(isls.), 1,507	M 3
Shari, 15,996	M 2	Uwajima, 70,433	E 7	Haha (isl.)	M 3	Okhotsk (sea)	M 1
Shibata, 74,025	J 4	Wajima, 33,232	H 5	Hakken (mt.)	H 7	Oki (isls.), 29,765	F 5
Shibetsu, 30,028	M 2	Wakasa, 6,989	H 6	Haku (mt.)	H 5	Okinawa (isl.), 924,540	N 6
Shimabara, 45,178	E 7	Wakayama, 389,677	G 6	Hakusan National Park	H 5	Okinawa (isls.), 936,895	N 6
Shimizu, 243,045	J 6	Wakkanai, 55,464	K 1	Harima (sea)	H 6	Okinoerabu (isl.), 16,883	N 5
Shimoda, 31,700	J 6	Warabi, 76,312	O 2	Hida (riv.)	H 6	Okushiri (isl.), 5,746	J 2
Shimonoseki, 266,596	E 6	Yaizu, 94,102	J 6	Hodaka (mt.)	H 5	Oma (cape)	K 3
Shingu, 39,023	H 7	Yakumo, 19,260	K 2	Hokkaido (isl.), 5,312,404	L 2	Omono (riv.)	K 4
Shinjo, 42,229	K 4	Yamagata, 219,773	K 4	Honshu (isl.), 88,578,094	H 5	Ono (riv.)	E 7
Shiogama, 59,236	K 4	Yamaguchi, 106,099	E 6	Ie (isl.), 5,262	N 6	Ontake (mt.)	H 6
Shiroishi, 40,862	K 4	Yamato, 145,877	O 2	Iheya (isl.), 1,640	N 6	Osaka (bay)	H 7
Shizunai, 24,832	L 2	Yamatokoriyama, 71,000	J 8	Iki (isl.), 41,873	D 7	O-Shima (isl.), 11,096	J 6
Shizuoka, 446,952	H 6	Yamatotakada, 58,638	J 7	Ina (riv.)	H 7	Osumi (isls.), 62,453	E 8
Shobara, 23,867	F 6	Yao, 261,642	J 7	Inawashiro (lake)	J 4	Osumi (isls.), 33,575	E 8
Soka, 167,176	O 2	Yatabe, 22,225	J 7	Inubo (cape)	K 5	Osumi (str.)	E 8
Soma, 37,692	K 4	Yatsushiro, 103,693	E 7	Iriomote (isl.), 3,469	K 7	Otakine (mt.)	K 4
Sonobe, 14,827	J 7	Yawata, 50,131	J 7	Iro (cape)	J 6	Rebun (isl.), 6,525	K 1
Suita, 300,949	J 7	Yawatahama, 45,260	E 7	Ise (bay)	H 6	Rikuchu-Kaigan National Park	K 4
Sukagawa, 54,925	K 5	Yoichi, 25,816	K 2	Ise-Shima National Park	H 6	Rishiri (isl.), 13,368	K 1
Sukumo, 25,338	E 7	Yokawa, 8,012	H 7	Ishigaki (isl.), 34,625	K 7	Ryukyu (isls.), 1,198,386	J 4
Sumoto, 44,135	G 6			Ishikari (bay)	K 2	Sado (isl.), 87,504	J 4

Kaesŏng, 175,000	C 4	
Kilchu	D 3	
Kimch'aek, 100,000	D 3	
Koksan	C 4	
Kosong	C 4	
Kusong	B 4	
Manp'o	C 3	
Mupy'ong-ni	D 3	
Musan	D 2	
Myongch'on	D 3	
Najin	E 2	
Namp'o, 140,000	B 5	
Ongjin	B 5	
Onsong	D 2	
Paekam	D 3	
Pakch'on	B 4	
P'anmunjom	C 5	
Pukch'ong	D 3	
P'ungsan	D 3	
P'yonggang	C 4	
P'yongsan	C 4	
P'yongyang (cap.) 1,250,000	C 4	

Sariwon	C 4	
Sinch'on	B 4	
Sinp'o	D 4	

OTHER FEATURES

Baktu (Paektu) (mt.)	C 3	
Chang Pai Shan (range)	D 2	
Changjin (res.)	C 3	
East Korea (bay)	D 4	
Japan (sea)	G 4	
Kanghwa (bay)	B 5	
Komdok (mt.)	D 3	
Kŭmgang (mt.)	D 4	

Sinŭiju, 300,000	B 3	
Sŏhung	C 4	
Sŏnch'on	B 4	
Songnim	B 4	
Sunch'on	C 4	
Tanch'on	D 3	
T'ongch'on	D 4	
Ŭiju	B 3	
Unggi	E 2	
Unsan	C 4	
Wŏnsan, 275,000	C 4	
Yangdok	C 4	
Yangamp'o	B 4	
Yonghung	C 4	

OTHER FEATURES

KOREA (SOUTH)

CITIES and TOWNS

Andong, 76,434	D 5	
Ansong, 23,698	C 5	
Changhung, 30,166	C 6	
Changsong, 26,916	C 6	
Chech'on, 49,883	D 5	
Cheju, 104,493	C 7	
Chinhae, 80,804	D 6	

Kwanmo (mt.)	D 3	
Myohyang (mt.)	D 3	
Nangnim-sanmaek (range)	C 3	
Paektu (mt.)	C 3	
Puksubaek (mt.)	C 3	
Sasu (mt.)	C 4	
Supung (res.)	B 3	
Taedong (riv.)	C 4	
Tumen (riv.)	D 2	
Tuun (riv.)	C 4	
West Korea (bay)	B 4	
Yalu (riv.)	C 3	
Yellow (sea)	B 6	

Chinju, 119,371	D 6	
Choch'iwon, 25,423	C 5	
Ch'onan, 78,316	C 5	
Ch'ongju, 141,074	C 5	
Chongup, 47,036	C 6	
Chonju, 257,530	C 6	
Ch'orwon, 7,324	C 4	
Ch'unch'on, 120,517	C 5	
Ch'ungju, 87,727	C 5	
Hongch'on, 23,473	C 5	
Hongsong, 21,912	C 5	
Inch'on, 634,046	C 5	
Iri, 86,770	C 6	
Kanggyong, 26,430	C 5	
Kangnung, 74,489	D 5	
Kimch'on, 62,157	D 5	
Koch'ang, 24,177	C 6	
Kongju, 30,320	C 5	
Kunsan, 110,140	C 6	
Kwangju, 493,634	C 6	
Kyongju, 92,093	D 6	
Masan, 186,890	D 6	
Miryang, 40,288	D 6	
Mokp'o, 174,006	C 6	
Muju, 18,174	C 6	

Namwon, 44,193	C 6	
P'anmunjom	C 5	
P'ohang, 79,451	D 5	
Posong, 22,247	C 6	
Pusan, 2,451,000	D 6	
Samch'ok, 35,117	D 5	
Samnangjin, 21,936	D 6	
Sangju, 47,558	D 5	
Seoul (cap.) 6,884,000	C 5	
Sosan, 30,416	C 5	
Sunch'on, 90,910	C 6	
Suwon, 167,201	C 5	
Taegu, 1,063,553	D 6	
Taejon, 406,910	C 5	
Tamyang, 14,856	C 6	
Uisong, 24,306	D 5	
Ulchin, 27,579	D 5	
Ulsan, 157,088	D 6	
Wonju, 110,188	C 5	
Yangyang, 10,832	D 4	
Yongch'on, 44,305	D 5	
Yongdok, 19,220	D 5	
Yongju, 46,338	D 5	
Yosu, 111,455	C 6	

OTHER FEATURES

Cheju (isl.), 365,522	C 7	
Cheju (str.)	C 6	
Chiri (mt.)	C 6	
Dagelet (Ullung) (isl.), 23,248	E 5	
East China (sea)	C 8	
Halla (mt.)	C 7	
Han (riv.)	C 5	
Japan (sea)	G 4	
Kanghwa (bay)	B 5	
Kebang (mt.)	D 5	
Kŏje (isl.), 112,241	D 6	
Korea (str.)	D 6	
Kum (riv.)	C 5	
Naktong (riv.)	D 6	
Port Hamilton (So) (isl.)	C 7	
Quelpart (Cheju) (isl.), 365,522	C 7	
Taebaek (mt.)	D 5	
Ullung (isl.), 23,248	E 5	
Yellow (sea)	B 6	

OTHER FEATURES

JAPAN is divided into prefectures bearing the same names as their capitals except:

Prefecture	Capital	Ref.
AICHI	NAGOYA	H 6
EHIME	MATSUYAMA	F 7
GUMMA	MAEBASHI	J 5
HOKKAIDO	SAPPORO	K 2
HYOGO	KOBE	H 7
IBARAKI	MITO	K 5
ISHIKAWA	KANAZAWA	H 5
IWATE	MORIOKA	K 3
KAGAWA	TAKAMATSU	G 6
KANAGAWA	YOKOHAMA	O 3
MIE	TSU	H 6
MIYAGI	SENDAI	K 4
OKINAWA	NAHA	N 6
SAITAMA	URAWA	O 2
SHIGA	OTSU	J 7
SHIMANE	MATSUE	F 6
TOCHIGI	UTSUNOMIYA	K 5
YAMANASHI	KOFU	J 6

†Populations courtesy of Kingsley Davis, Office of Int'l Pop. & Urban Research, Inst. of Int'l Studies, Univ. of California.

*City and suburbs.

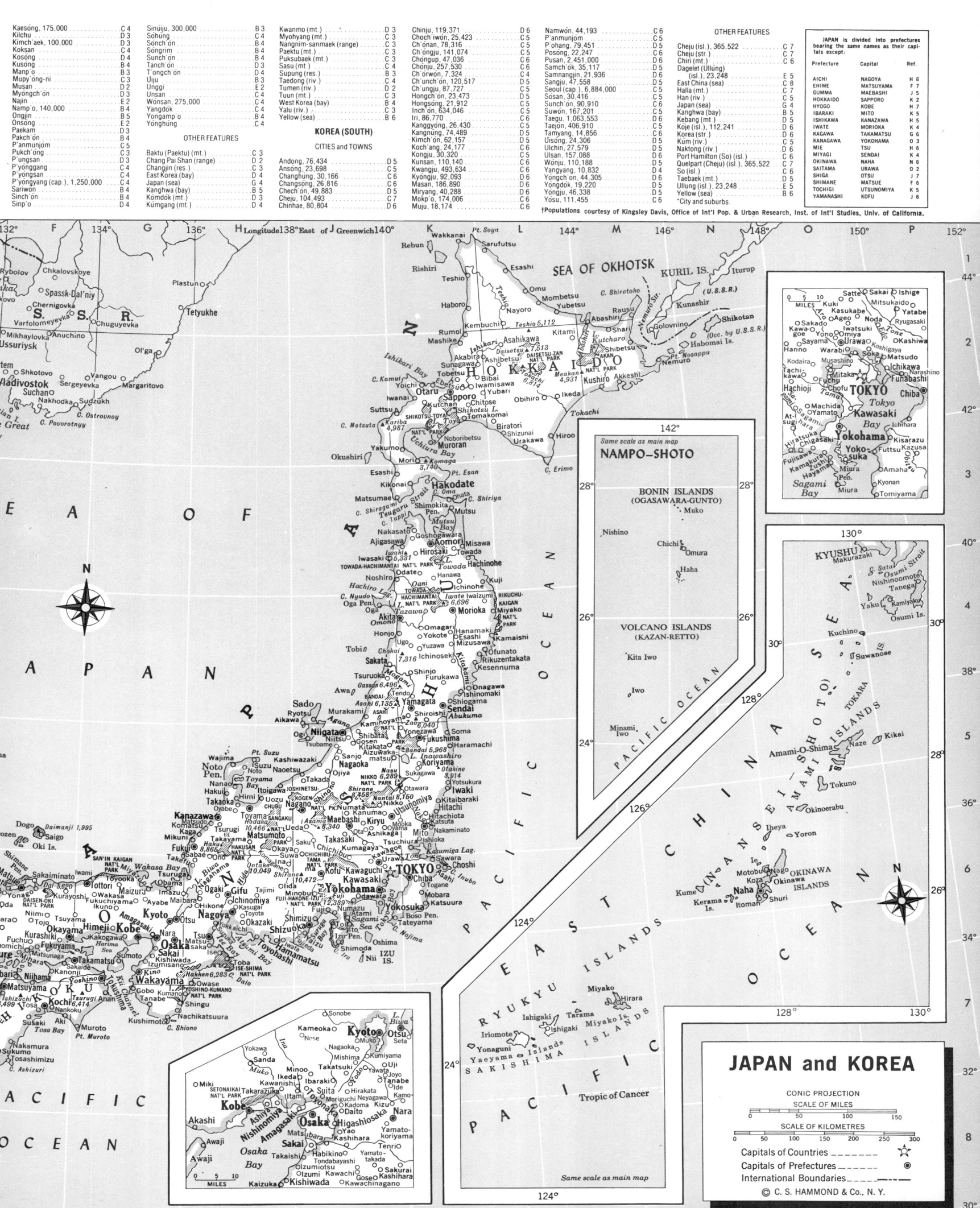

JAPAN and KOREA

CONIC PROJECTION

SCALE OF MILES

0   50   100   150

SCALE OF KILOMETRES

0   50   100   150   200   250   300

Capitals of Countries ⋯⋯⋯ ☆

Capitals of Prefectures ⋯⋯⋯ ◉

International Boundaries ⋯⋯⋯

© C. S. HAMMOND & Co., N.Y.

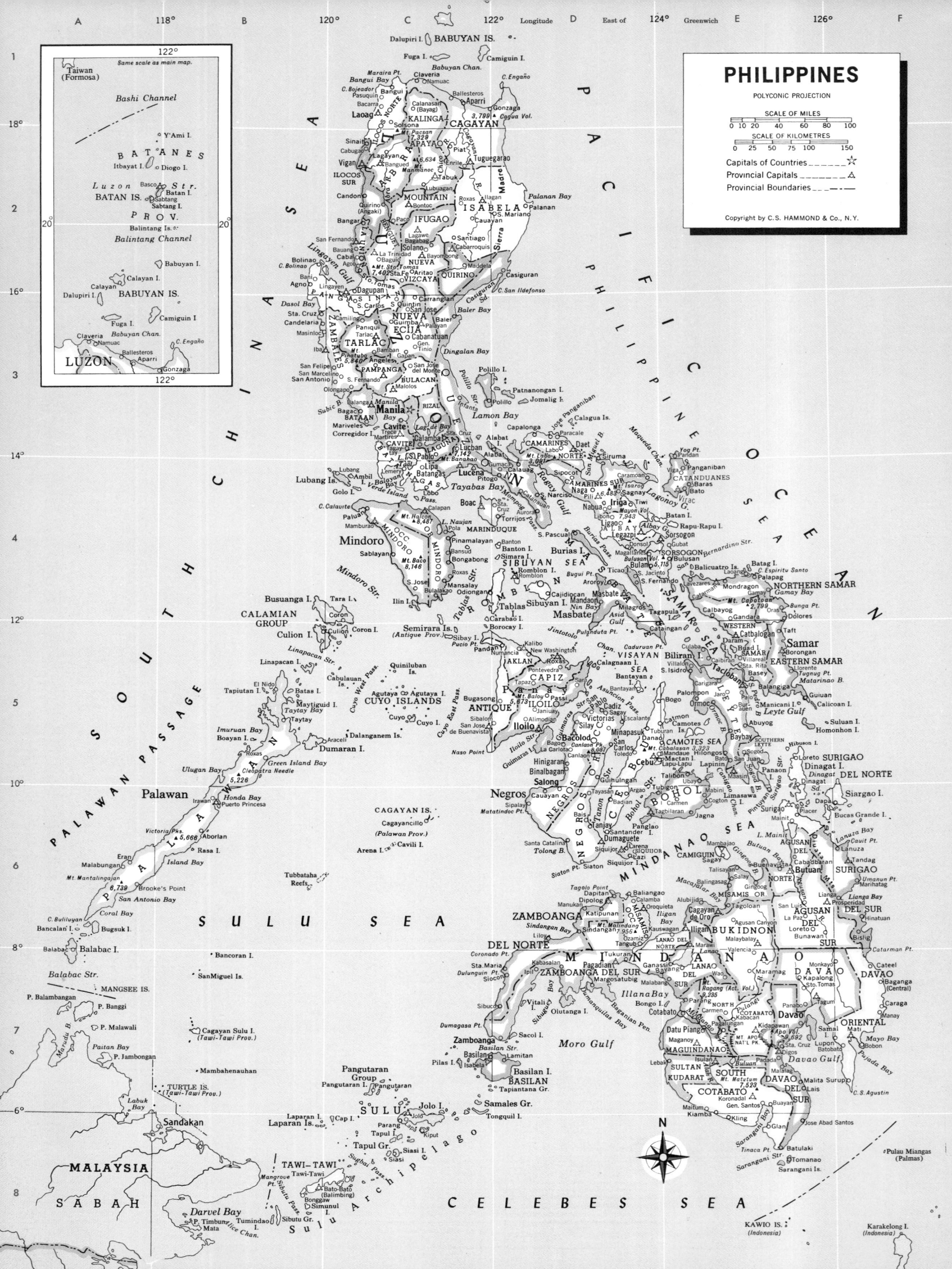

PHILIPPINES

POLYCONIC PROJECTION

SCALE OF MILES

0 10 20 40 60 80 100

SCALE OF KILOMETRES

0 25 50 75 100 150

Capitals of Countries _____ ☆

Provincial Capitals _____ △

Provincial Boundaries __ _ __ _ __

Copyright by C.S. Hammond & Co., N.Y.

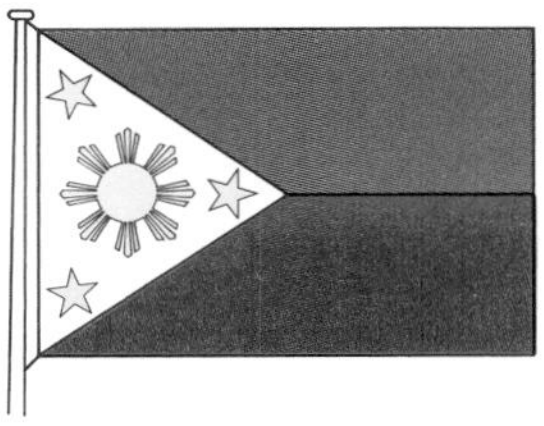

AREA 115,707 sq. mi.
POPULATION 43,751,000
CAPITAL Manila
LARGEST CITY Manila
HIGHEST POINT Apo 9,692 ft.
MONETARY UNIT piso
MAJOR LANGUAGES Pilipino (Tagalog), English, Spanish, Bisayan, Ilocano, Bikol
MAJOR RELIGIONS Roman Catholicism, Islam, Protestantism, Tribal religions

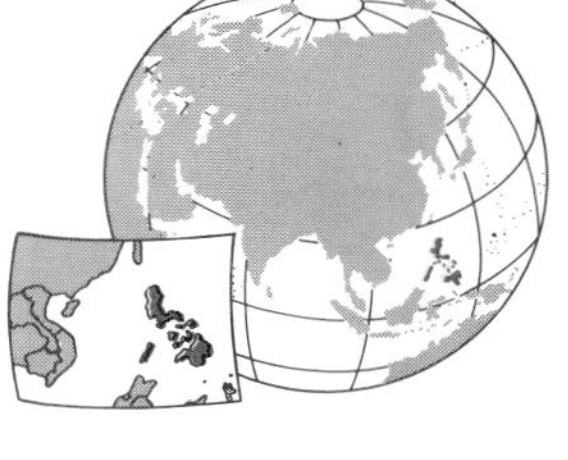

PROVINCES

Abra, 145,508	C 2
Agusan del Norte, 278,053	E 6
Agusan del Sur, 174,682	E 6
Aklan, 263,358	D 5
Albay, 673,981	D 4
Antique, 289,172	D 5
Basilan, 143,829	D 7
Bataan, 216,210	C 3
Batanes, 11,398	A 2
Batangas, 926,308	C 4
Benguet, 263,550	C 2
Bohol, 683,297	E 6
Bukidnon, 414,762	E 6
Bulacan, 836,431	C 3
Cagayan, 581,237	C 1
Camarines Norte, 262,207	D 3
Camarines Sur, 948,436	D 4
Camiguin, 53,913	E 6
Capiz, 394,041	D 5
Catanduanes, 162,302	E 4
Cavite, 520,180	C 3
Cebu, 1,634,182	D 5
Davao, 442,543	E 7
Davao del Sur, 785,398	E 7
Davao Oriental, 247,995	F 7
Eastern Samar, 271,000	E 5
Ifugao, 92,487	C 2
Ilocos Norte, 343,427	C 1
Ilocos Sur, 385,139	C 2
Iloilo, 1,167,973	D 5
Isabela, 648,123	C 2
Kalinga-Apayao, 136,249	C 1
Laguna, 699,736	C 3
Lanao del Norte, 349,942	E 6
Lanao del Sur, 455,508	E 7
La Union, 373,682	C 2
Leyte, 1,110,626	E 5
Maguindanao, 476,338	E 7
Manila, 3,868,239	C 3
Marinduque, 144,109	C 4
Masbate, 492,908	D 4
Misamis Occidental, 319,855	D 6
Misamis Oriental, 472,756	E 6
Mountain, 93,112	C 2
Negros Occidental, 1,503,782	D 6
Negros Oriental, 652,264	D 6
North Cotabato	E 7
Northern Samar, 306,114	E 4
Nueva Ecija, 851,294	C 3
Nueva Vizcaya, 169,198	C 2
Occidental Mindoro, 144,032	C 4
Oriental Mindoro, 328,364	C 4
Palawan, 236,635	B 6
Pampanga, 907,275	C 3
Pangasinan, 1,386,143	C 3
Quezon, 983,324	C 3
Quirino, 52,767	C 2
Rizal, 307,238	C 3
Romblon, 167,082	D 4
Siquijor, 62,976	D 6
Sorsogon, 427,047	E 4
South Cotabato, 466,110	E 7
Southern Leyte, 251,425	E 5
Sultan Kudarat, 191,315	E 7
Sulu, 315,421	C 7
Surigao del Norte, 238,714	F 5
Surigao del Sur, 258,680	F 6
Tarlac, 559,708	C 3
Tawi-Tawi, 110,196	B 8
Western Samar, 442,244	E 5
Zambales, 343,034	C 3
Zamboanga del Norte, 409,379	D 6
Zamboanga del Sur, 890,189	D 7

CITIES and TOWNS

Angeles, 175,694	C 3
Aparri, 14,597	C 1
Bacolod, 196,492	D 5
Bago, 71,653	D 5
Baguio, 100,209	C 2
Bais, 40,095	D 6
Balanga, 1,298	C 3
Baler, ◆14,632	C 3
Balimbing (Bato-Bato), 3,880	C 8
Bangued, 10,482	C 2
Bantayan, 11,771	D 5
Basco, ◆3,757	A 2
Basilan, 171,266	C 7
Batangas, 125,304	C 4
Bato-Bato, 3,880	C 8
Baybay, 11,989	E 5
Bayombong, 11,697	C 2
Binalbagan, 17,456	D 5
Bislig, 26,625	F 6
Boac, 3,497	C 4
Bogo, 11,069	E 5
Bontoc, 3,336	C 2
Buenavista, 9,211	E 6
Bulan, 19,716	D 4
Burauen, 12,172	E 5
Butuan, 173,429	E 6
Cabanatuan, 117,995	C 3
Cabarroquis	C 2
Cadiz, 130,199	D 5
Cagayan de Oro, 163,163	E 6
Calamba, Laguna, 22,750	C 3
Calapan, 11,376	C 4
Calbayog, 101,748	E 4
Camiling, 12,996	C 3
Canlaon, 23,598	D 5
Carigara, 11,824	E 5
Catarman, 13,018	E 4
Catbalogan, 18,413	E 5
Catmon, ◆14,837	E 5
Cavite, 75,739	C 3
Cebu, 418,517	D 5
Cotabato, 61,184	D 7
Daet, 23,739	D 3
Dagupan, 83,582	C 2
Danao, 47,662	D 5
Dapitan, 37,781	D 6
Davao, 515,520	E 7
Digos, 17,334	E 7
Dipolog, 46,368	D 6
Dumaguete, 52,000	D 6
Escalante, 16,324	D 5
Ganassi, ◆13,227	D 7
Gapan, 11,958	C 3
General Santos, 108,285	E 7
Gingoog, 65,522	E 6
Gubat, 11,369	E 4
Guimba, 10,077	C 3
Gumaca, 9,459	D 4
Hinigaran, 10,864	D 5
Iba, 4,486	B 3
Ilagan, 11,494	C 2
Iligan, 129,454	E 6
Iloilo, 247,956	D 5
Iriga, 77,382	D 4
Isabela, 12,879	C 7
Isulan, 10,075	E 7
Jolo, 46,586	C 8
Jose Panganiban, 9,970	D 3
Kalibo, 10,564	D 5
Kauswagan, ◆12,316	E 6
Kidapawan, 11,344	E 7
Koronadal, 14,003	E 7
La Carlota, 38,321	D 5
Lagawe, 3,038	C 2
Lais, 15,209	E 7
Laoag, 61,727	C 1
Lapu-Lapu, 69,268	E 5
La Trinidad, ◆18,551	C 2
Lazi, ◆14,875	D 6
Legazpi, 84,090	D 4
Lianga, 12,689	E 6
Lingayen, 15,333	C 2
Lipa, 112,006	C 4
Loreto, Agusan del Sur, ◆13,057	E 6
Lucban, 18,466	C 3
Lucena, 77,006	C 4
Maasin, 12,661	E 5
Maganoy, 1,648	E 7
Mainit, 3,559	E 6
Malabang, 9,244	D 7
Malaybalay, 10,193	E 6
Malita, 9,705	E 7
Malolos, 73,996	C 3
Mandaue, 58,579	E 5
Manila (cap.), 1,438,252	C 3
Manila (Metro.), *4,337,140	C 3
Marawi, 55,708	E 6
Mariveles, 4,502	C 3
Masbate, 17,749	D 4
Mati, 16,186	F 7
Mondragon, ◆14,974	E 4
Naga, 79,846	D 4
Olongapo, 134,453	C 3
Ormoc, 84,563	E 5
Oroquieta, 38,575	D 6
Ozamiz, 64,643	D 6
Padada, ◆14,402	E 7
Pagadian, 57,615	D 7
Paniqui, 11,789	C 3
Parang, Sulu, ◆21,115	C 8
Prosperidad, 3,043	F 6
Puerto Princesa, 12,278	B 6
Romblon, 4,241	D 4
Roxas, Capiz, 67,648	D 5
Roxas, Isabela, 9,849	C 2
Sablayan, ◆18,256	C 4
Sagay, Negros Occ., 36,855	D 5
Sagnay, ◆16,968	D 4
Salong, 35,137	D 5
San Antonio, 13,270	B 3
San Carlos, Negros Occ., 90,058	D 5
San Carlos, Pangasinan, 84,333	C 3
San Fernando, La Union, 11,084	C 2
San Fernando, Pampanga, 84,362	C 3
San Isidro, ◆23,569	E 5
San Jose, Nueva Ecija, 70,314	C 3
San Jose, Occ. Mindoro, 10,388	C 4
San Mariano, ◆20,227	D 2
San Pablo, Laguna, 125,720	C 3
Santa Cruz, Davao del Sur, 9,787	E 7
Santa Cruz, Laguna, 47,114	C 3
Santa Rita, ◆20,713	E 5
Santiago, ◆49,688	C 2
Siasi, 9,930	C 8
Silay, 69,200	D 5
Sindangan, 10,965	D 6
Sipalay, ◆34,771	D 6
Sipocot, ◆38,153	D 4
Siquijor, 766	D 6
Solano, 14,274	C 2
Solsona, ◆12,803	C 1
Sorsogon, 19,008	E 4
Surigao, 26,099	E 6
Tacloban, 76,531	E 5
Tagaytay, 10,907	C 3
Tagbilaran, 33,005	E 6
Tagum, 17,161	E 7
Tangub, 30,918	D 6
Tanjay, 12,676	D 6
Tarlac, 23,547	C 3
Toledo, 67,727	D 5
Tuguegarao, 14,116	C 2
Tukuran, ◆19,274	D 7
Victorias, 13,416	D 5
Vigan, 30,252	C 2
Virac, 10,314	E 4
Zamboanga, 240,066	C 7

OTHER FEATURES

Abra (riv.)	C 2
Agusan (riv.)	E 6
Agutaya (isl.), 2,464	C 5
Alabat (isl.), 22,666	D 3
Ambil (isl.), 323	C 4
Apo (vol.)	E 7
Asid (gulf)	D 4
Babuyan (isls.), 7,749	A 2
Baganian (pen.), 22,755	D 7
Balabac (isl.), 4,946	A 7
Balayan (bay)	C 4
Balicuatro (isls.), 6,349	E 4
Balintang (chan.)	A 2
Baloy (mt.)	D 5
Bancalan (isl.), 398	A 6
Bantayan (isl.), 57,311	D 5
Banton (isl.), 6,447	D 4
Bashi (chan.)	A 1
Basilan (isl.), 147,871	D 7
Batag (isl.), 4,142	E 4
Batan, Albay (isl.), 11,779	E 4
Batan, Batanes (isl.), 6,831	B 2
Batan (isls.), 11,398	A 2
Batas (isl.), 204	B 5
Bay, Laguna de (lake)	C 3
Biliran (isl.), 82,033	E 5
Bohol (isl.), 613,532	E 6
Bojeador (cape)	C 1
Bongo (isl.), 2,077	D 7
Borocay (isl.), 2,660	D 5
Buad (isl.), 12,064	E 5
Bucas Grande (isl.), 6,213	F 6
Bugsuk (isl.), 831	A 6
Buliluyan (cape)	A 6
Bunga (pt.)	E 4
Burias (isl.), 53,299	D 4
Busuanga (isl.), 16,136	B 4
Cabalasan (mt.)	E 5
Cabulauan (isls.), 570	C 5
Cagayan (isls.), 3,598	C 6
Cagayan (riv.)	C 2
Cagayan Sulu (isl.), 12,577	B 7
Cagua (vol.)	D 1
Calagnaan (isl.), 2,690	D 5
Calagua (isls.), 1,890	D 3
Calamian Group (isls.), 26,864	B 4
Calayan (isl.), 5,075	A 2
Calicoan (isl.), 2,966	E 5
Camiguin, Cagayan (isl.), 1,741	B 3
Camiguin, Camiguin (isl.), 53,913	E 6
Camotes (isls.), 55,479	E 5
Camotes (sea)	E 5
Canigao (chan.)	E 5
Canlaon (peak)	D 5
Capotoan (mt.)	E 4
Carabao (isl.), 4,562	D 4
Catanduanes (isl.), 160,614	E 4
Cebu (isl.), 1,426,804	D 5
Celebes (sea)	D 8
Cleopatra Needle (mt.)	B 5
Coron (isl.), 477	C 5
Corregidor (isl.), 91	C 3
Culion (isl.), 5,580	B 5
Cuyo (isl.), 9,489	C 5
Cuyo (isls.), 16,737	C 5
Dalanganem (isls.), 512	C 5
Daram (isl.), 26,087	E 5
Davao (gulf)	E 7
Dinagat (isl.), 23,337	E 5
Diuata (mts.)	E 6
Dumanquilas (bay)	D 7
Dumaran (isl.), 3,996	C 5
Engaño (cape)	D 1
Espiritu Santo (cape)	E 4
Fuga (isl.), 967	A 3
Golo (isl.), 1,300	C 4
Guimaras (isl.), 71,067	D 5
Halcon (mt.)	C 4
Hibuson (isl.), 531	E 5
Homonhon (isl.), 2,316	E 5
Honda (bay)	B 6
Iligan (bay)	E 6
Ilin (isl.), 6,647	C 4
Illana (bay)	D 7
Imuruan (bay)	B 5
Island (bay)	B 6
Itbayat (isl.), 2,760	A 2
Jintotolo (chan.)	D 5
Jolo (isl.), 208,110	C 7
Jomalig (isl.), 1,792	D 3
Lagonoy (gulf)	E 4
Lamon (bay)	C 3
Lanao (lake)	E 7
Laparan (isls.)	B 8
Lapinin (isl.), 9,229	E 5
Leyte (gulf)	E 5
Leyte (isl.), 1,223,667	E 5
Limasawa (isl.), 2,116	E 6
Linapacan (isl.), 1,121	B 5
Lingayen (gulf)	C 2
Lubang (isls.), 19,904	B 4
Luzon (isl.), 17,862,660	C 3
Luzon (str.)	A 2
Macajalar (bay)	E 6
Mactan (isl.), 70,729	E 5
Malindang (mt.)	D 6
Mangsee (isls.), 246	A 7
Manicani (isl.), 1,555	E 5
Manila (bay)	C 3
Mantalingajan (mt.)	A 6
Maqueda (chan.)	D 3
Maraira (pt.)	C 1
Marinduque (isl.), 140,924	C 4
Masbate (isl.), 387,721	D 4
Mayon (vol.)	D 4
Maytiguid (isl.), 632	B 5
Mindanao (isl.), 6,871,696	D 7
Mindanao (riv.)	E 7
Mindanao (sea)	D 6
Mindoro (isl.), 437,817	C 4
Mindoro (str.)	C 4
Mompog (passage)	D 4
Moro (gulf)	D 7
Mount Apo National Park	E 7
Naso (pt.)	C 5
Negros (isl.), 2,080,153	D 6
Olutanga (isl.), 16,680	D 7
Pacsan (mt.)	C 2
Palawan (isl.), 146,430	B 6
Palawan (passage)	A 6
Panaon (isl.), 31,149	E 5
Panay (isl.), 2,010,297	D 5
Panglao (isl.), 29,121	D 6
Pangutaran (isl.), 12,883	C 7
Pangutaran Group (isls.), 16,172	C 7
Patnanongan (isl.), 3,680	D 3
Philippine (sea)	D 3
Pilas (isl.), 8,666	C 7
Pinatubo (mt.)	C 3
Polillo (isl.), 27,716	C 3
Pujada (bay)	F 7
Pulangi (riv.)	E 7
Quiniluban (isls.), 653	C 5
Ragang (vol.)	E 7
Ragay (gulf)	D 4
Rapu-Rapu (isl.), 8,007	E 4
Romblon (isl.), 19,728	D 4
Sabtang (isl.), 1,359	B 2
Sacol (isl.), 7,994	D 7
Samal (isl.), 30,897	E 7
Samales Group (isls.), 9,095	D 7
Samar (isl.), 861,765	E 5
Samar (sea)	E 4
San Agustin (cape)	F 7
San Bernardino (str.)	E 4
San Miguel (bay)	D 3
San Pedro (bay)	E 5
Santo Tomas (mt.)	C 2
Sarangani (isls.), 6,791	E 8
Semirara (isls.), 7,932	C 5
Siargao (isl.), 40,632	F 6
Siasi (isl.), 24,026	C 8
Sibay (isl.), 1,544	C 5
Sibuguey (bay)	D 7
Sibutu Group (isls.), 13,738	B 8
Sibuyan (isl.), 32,079	D 4
Sibuyan (sea)	D 4
Sierra Madre (mts.)	D 2
Simara (isl.), 7,805	D 4
Simunul (isl.), 8,401	B 8
Siquijor (isl.), 62,976	D 6
South China (sea)	B 3
Subic (bay)	C 3
Sulu (arch.), 413,040	B 8
Sulu (sea)	B 6
Suluan (isl.), 966	F 5
Taal (lake)	C 4
Tablas (isl.), 89,642	D 4
Tablas (str.)	C 4
Tagapula (isl.), 5,691	E 4
Tagolo (pt.)	D 6
Tanon (str.)	D 6
Tapiantana Group (isls.), 6,697	D 7
Tapul (isl.), 8,830	C 8
Tapul Group (isls.), 72,119	C 8
Tara (isl.), 449	C 4
Tawi-Tawi (isl.), 13,216	B 8
Tayabas (bay)	C 4
Ticao (isl.), 62,270	D 4
Tinaca (pt.)	E 8
Tongquil (isl.), 2,599	D 8
Tumindao (isl.), 2,389	B 8
Turtle (isls.), 389	B 7
Verde Island (passage)	C 4
Victoria (peaks)	B 6
Visayan (sea)	D 5
Vitali (isl.), 6,026	D 7

*City and suburbs.
◆Population of municipality.

Topography

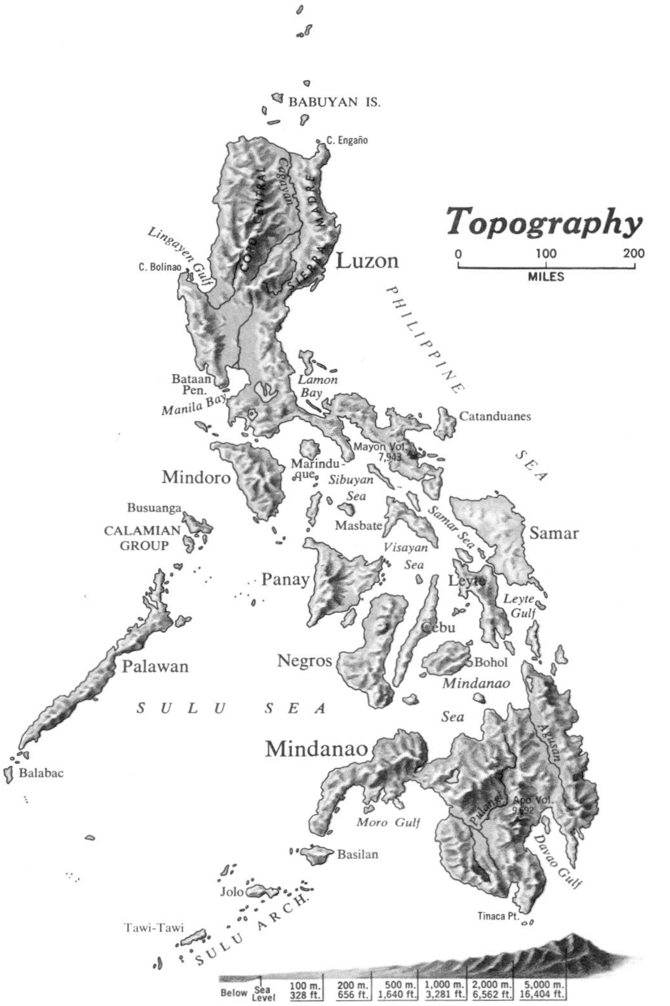
BABUYAN IS.
C. Engaño
Lingayen Gulf
C. Bolinao
Luzon
PHILIPPINE
SEA
Bataan Pen.
Manila Bay
Lamon Bay
Catanduanes
Mindoro
Mayon Vol.
Marindu-que
Sibuyan Sea
Busuanga
CALAMIAN GROUP
Masbate
Samar Sea
Samar
Visayan Sea
Panay
Leyte
Leyte Gulf
Cebu
Palawan
Negros
Bohol
Mindanao Sea
S U L U S E A
Mindanao
Balabac
Moro Gulf
Davao Gulf
Basilan
Jolo
Tawi-Tawi
SULU ARCH.
Tinaca Pt.
0 100 200 MILES
Below Sea Level
100 m. 328 ft.
200 m. 656 ft.
500 m. 1,640 ft.
1,000 m. 3,281 ft.
2,000 m. 6,562 ft.
5,000 m. 16,404 ft.

Agriculture, Industry and Resources

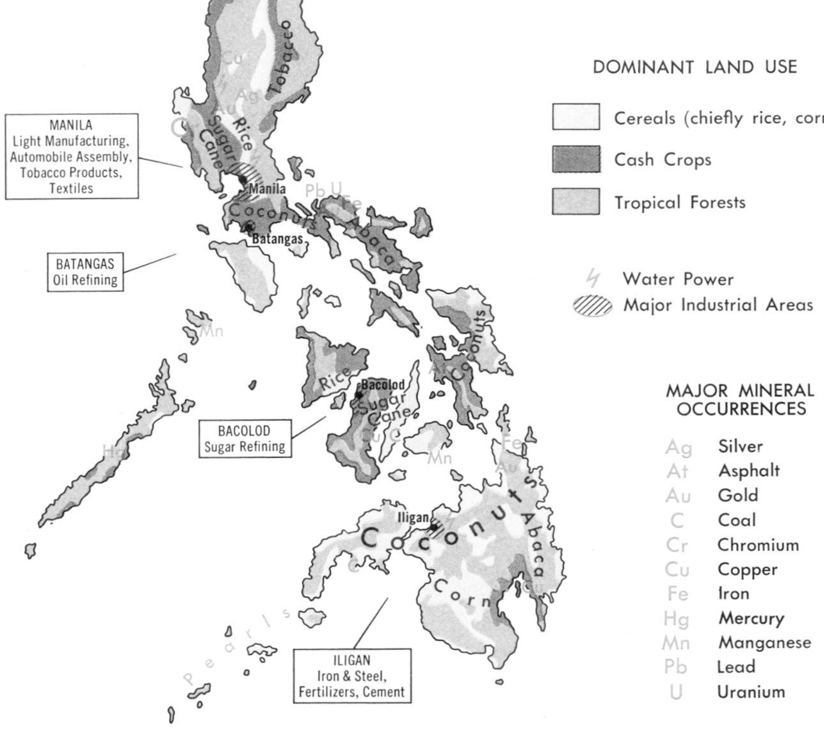
MANILA
Light Manufacturing, Automobile Assembly, Tobacco Products, Textiles
BATANGAS
Oil Refining
BACOLOD
Sugar Refining
ILIGAN
Iron & Steel, Fertilizers, Cement
Tobacco
Rice
Sugar Cane
Manila
Batangas
Coconuts
Bacolod
Iligan
Abaca
Corn
Pearls
DOMINANT LAND USE
Cereals (chiefly rice, corn)
Cash Crops
Tropical Forests
Water Power
Major Industrial Areas
MAJOR MINERAL OCCURRENCES
Ag Silver
At Asphalt
Au Gold
C Coal
Cr Chromium
Cu Copper
Fe Iron
Hg Mercury
Mn Manganese
Pb Lead
U Uranium

BRUNEI
CITIES and TOWNS

Bandar Seri Begawan (cap.), 37,000...E 4

INDONESIA
CITIES and TOWNS

Agats, 300...K 7
Amahai, 18,017...H 6
Amboina, 70,000...H 6
Ambon (Amboina), 70,000...H 6
Balikpapan, 113,000...F 6
Banda Atjeh, 49,000...A 4
Bandanaira, 13,686...H 6
Bandjarmasin, 264,000...E 6
Bandung, 1,006,000...H 2
Bangil, 34,132...K 2
Bangkalan, 129,536...K 2
Banjuwangi, 53,576...L 2
Bantul, 30,572...J 2
Barabai, 9,366...F 6
Barus, †35,716...B 5
Batang, 57,561...J 2
Batavia (Djakarta) (cap.), 3,429,000...H 1
Baturadja, 126,706...C 6
Batusangkar, 10,437...C 6
Bekasi, 32,012...H 1
Bengkajang, †17,029...E 5
Bengkalis, †36,433...C 5
Bengkulu, 31,000...C 6
Benteng, 7,035...F 7
Bindjai, 56,000...B 5
Bitung, 15,249...H 5
Blitar, 78,000...K 2
Blora, 49,296...J 2
Bodjonegoro, †61,749...J 2
Bogor, 172,000...H 2
Bondowoso, 144,215...L 2
Bonthain, †40,289...F 7
Brebes, †72,971...J 2
Bukittinggi, 62,000...B 6
Bula, 3,116...J 6
Bulukumba, 14,137...H 2
Bumiaju, †52,790...H 2
Demak, †42,915...J 2
Denpasar, †52,000...E 7
Dili, 78,000...H 7
Djailolo, †10,170...H 5
Djajapura, 14,462...K 6
Djakarta (cap.), 3,429,000...H 1
Djakarta, *5,692,000...H 1
Djambi (Telanaipura) 139,000...C 6
Djeneponto, 10,350...F 7
Djepara, †54,025...J 2
Djombang, †57,370...K 2
Djokjakarta, 385,000...J 2
Dompu, 8,886...F 7
Fakfak, 2,430...J 6
Galela, 17,384...H 5
Garut, †67,542...H 2
Gorontalo, 88,000...G 5
Gresik, 36,790...K 2
Hollandia (Djajapura), 14,462...K 6
Indramaju, 156,117...H 2

Isimu, 4,304...G 5
Kaimana, 1,128...J 6
Kajuagung, 15,000...D 6
Kalianda, †31,073...D 7
Kampung Baru (Tolitoli), 8,333...G 5
Karangasem, 16,022...F 7
Kau, 17,497...H 5
Kebumen, 164,874...J 2
Kediri, 196,000...K 2
Kendal, 23,129...J 2
Kendari, †91,065...G 6
Kendawangan, 6,845...D 6
Klaten, 33,400...J 2
Kolaka, 118,671...G 6
Kotaagung, 125,314...C 7
Kragan, 23,786...K 2
Krawang, 49,867...H 2
Kualakurun, †11,489...E 6
Kudus, 62,130...J 2
Kumai, 8,835...E 6
Kuningan, †77,181...H 2
Kupang, 17,171...G 8
Kutaradja (Banda Atjeh), 49,000...A 4
Kutoardjo, 44,962...J 2
Labuan, †22,259...G 2
Lahat, †25,781...C 6
Lamongan, 134,825...K 2
Langsa, †47,044...B 5
Lawang, 140,239...K 2
Longiram, 7,776...F 6
Longnawan, 116,234...F 5
Lubuklinggau, 14,890...C 6
Lubuksikaping, 11,778...B 5
Lumadjang, 55,700...K 2
Madiun, 152,000...J 2
Madjalengka, 147,055...H 2
Madjene, †37,727...F 6
Magelang, 119,000...J 2
Magetan, 154,159...K 2
Makassar (Udjung Pandang), 473,000...F 7
Malang, 419,000...K 2
Malili, 5,735...G 6
Malinau, 9,677...F 5
Manado, 160,000...G 5
Manokwari, 10,461...J 6
Marabahan, 8,893...E 6
Martapura, †53,216...F 6
Masamba, †15,152...G 6
Medan, 590,000...B 5
Menggala, 20,343...D 6
Meulaboh, 6,544...A 5
Merak, 136,293...H 2
Merauke, 5,989...K 7
Mindiptana, 1,577...K 7
Modjokerto, 64,000...K 2
Muarabungo, 10,706...C 6
Muaratewah, 6,135...F 6
Muntok, 15,883...D 6
Namlea, 16,018...H 6
Nangapinoh, †24,836...E 6
Nangatajap, 18,285...E 6
Negara, 10,161...F 6
Ngabang, †24,516...D 5
Ngawi, 29,220...K 2
Padang, 178,000...B 6
Padangpandjang, 32,000...B 6
Padangsidimpuan, †71,704...B 5
Painan, 12,060...B 6

Pajakumbuh, †74,393...C 6
Pakanbaru, 87,000...C 5
Palangkaraja, 9,000...E 6
Palélèh, 5,466...G 5
Palembang, 585,000...D 6
Pamangkat, †51,871...D 5
Pamekasan, †42,650...L 2
Pameungpeuk, †24,662...H 2
Panarukan, 6,846...K 2
Pandeglang, 124,823...G 2
Pangkalanberandan, †23,806...B 5
Pangkalpinang, 74,000...D 6
Pare, 185,528...K 2
Parepare, 84,000...F 6
Pariaman, †45,812...B 6
Pasuruan, 78,000...K 2
Pati, 156,749...J 2
Patjitan, 44,383...J 2
Pekalongan, 125,000...J 2
Pemalang, 193,608...J 2
Pematangsiantar, 142,000...B 5
Perahbumulih, 41,951...C 6
Pinrang, 23,818...F 6
Piru, †23,633...H 6
Ponorogo, 49,993...J 2
Pontianak, 185,000...D 6
Poso, 141,292...G 6
Praja, 26,729...F 7
Prapat, 5,552...B 5
Probolinggo, 85,000...K 2
Purbolinggo, 31,719...J 2
Purwakarta, †88,680...H 2
Purwodadi, 154,648...J 2
Purwokerto, 22,623...J 2
Purworedjo, 23,209...J 2
Putussibau, 18,357...E 5
Rangkasbitung, †51,176...G 2
Rantauprapat, 25,707...C 5
Rembang, 39,939...K 2
Rengat, †22,982...C 6
Ruteng, 15,814...G 7
Sabang, 6,747...B 4
Salatiga, 72,000...J 2
Samarinda, 87,000...F 6
Sambas, †53,290...D 5
Sampang, 47,596...K 2
Sanana, 23,388...H 6
Sanggau, †28,039...E 6
Sangkulirang, 6,108...F 6
Saparua, 53,390...H 6
Saumlaki, †22,732...J 7
Sawahlunto, 15,000...C 6
Semarang, 619,000...J 2
Semitau, 19,255...E 5
Senikang, †17,948...G 6
Serang, †43,661...G 1
Serui, 2,743...K 6
Sibolga, 48,000...B 5
Sidoardjo, †40,591...K 2
Sigli, 4,050...B 4
Sindjai, 18,390...G 7
Singaradja, †61,107...F 7
Singkawang, †24,836...D 5
Sintang, 125,067...E 5
Situbondo, 30,000...L 2
Sorong, 9,151...J 6
Sragen, 32,310...J 2
Subang, †22,825...H 2
Sukabumi, 90,000...H 2
Sukadana, 6,899...D 6
Sumbawa Besar, †22,308...F 7

Sumedang, †74,062...H 2
Sumenep, 33,628...L 2
Surabaja, 1,241,000...K 2
Surakarta, 453,000...J 2
Tandjungbalai, 36,000...C 5
Tandjungkarang-Telukbetung, 164,000...D 7
Tandjungpandan, †39,253...D 6
Tandjungpriok, †140,573...H 1
Tandjungpura, †20,726...B 5
Tangerang, †81,042...G 1
Tapaktuan, 9,650...A 5
Tarakan, 24,807...F 5
Tarutung, 141,041...B 5
Tasikmalaja, †101,466...H 2
Tebingtinggi, 37,762...B 5
Tegal, 110,000...J 2
Telanaipura, 139,000...C 6
Temanggung, 8,107...J 2
Tenggarong, †15,516...F 6
Ternate, 23,500...H 5
Tjiamis, 180,018...H 2
Tjiandjur, †77,927...H 2
Tjidulang, †32,475...H 2
Tjilatjap, 78,619...J 2
Tjimahi, †90,718...H 2
Tjirebon, 176,000...H 2
Tjurup, 14,480...C 6
Tobelo, †14,430...H 5
Tolitoli, 8,333...G 5
Tondano, †29,584...H 5
Trenggalek, †37,762...K 2
Tuban, 48,123...K 2
Tulungagung, 43,115...K 2
Turen, 157,711...K 2
Udjung Pandang, 473,000...F 7
Wahai, 18,781...H 6
Wonogiri, †45,704...J 2
Wonosobo, 33,917...J 2

OTHER FEATURES

Alas (str.)...F 7
Anambas (isls.), 15,700...D 5
Arafura (sea)...J 8
Aru (isls.), 27,006...J 7
Asahan (river)...B 5
Babar (isls.), 14,133...H 7
Bali (isls.), 2,196,000...F 7
Bali (sea)...F 7
Banda (sea)...H 7
Banggai (arch.), 144,747...G 6
Bangka (isl.), 384,000...D 6
Banjak (isls.), 1,696...B 5
Barisan (mts.)...B 6
Barito (river)...E 6
Batjan (isl.), 21,861...H 6
Bawean (isl.), 47,589...K 1
Belitung (Billiton) (isl.)...D 6
Bengalen (passage)...K 6
Berau (bay)...J 6
Biak (isl.), 31,139...K 6
Billiton (isl.), 126,000...D 6
Binongko (isl.), 10,580...G 7
Bintan (isl.), 65,301...C 5
Bone (gulf)...G 6
Borneo (isl.)...E 5
Borneo (Kalimantan) (reg.), 4,243,000...E 5

Bosch, van den (cape)...J 6
Bunguran (Natuna) (isls.), 15,261...D 5
Buru (isl.), 16,018...H 6
Butung (isl.), 311,000...G 7
Celebes (isl.), 7,665,000...G 6
Celebes (sea)...G 5
Ceram (isl.), 73,453...H 6
Damar (isl.)...H 7
Dampier (str.)...J 6
Diamond (point)...B 4
Digul (river)...K 7
Djaja (mt.)...K 6
Djajawidjaja (range)...K 6
Djemadja (isl.), 3,874...D 5
Doberai (pen.)...J 6
Dolak (isl.)...K 7
Enggano (isl.), 686...C 7
Ewab (isls.), 76,606...J 7
Flores (isls.), 1,108,000...G 7
Flores (sea)...F 7
Frederik Hendrik (Dolak) (isl.)...K 7
Gebe (isl.), 5,410...H 6
Geelvink (Sarera) (bay)...K 6
Good Hope (cape)...K 7
Gorong (isls.), 33,241...J 6
Halmahera (isl.), 97,133...H 5
Idenburg (river)...K 6
Japen (isl.), 23,701...K 6
Java (head)...H 2
Java (isl.), 69,323,000...J 2
Java (sea)...E 6
Kabaena (isl.), 14,380...G 7
Kabia (Salajar) (isl.), 107,000...G 7
Kai (Ewab) (isls.), 76,606...J 7
Kalao (isl.), 670...G 7
Kalaotoa (isl.), 2,031...G 7
Kalimantan (reg.), 4,243,000...E 5
Kangean (isls.), 52,893...F 7
Kapuas (river)...D 6
Karakelong (isl.), 15,276...H 5
Karimata (arch.), 1,623...D 6
Karimundjawa (isls.), 1,611...J 1
Kerintji (mt.)...C 6
Kisar (isl.), 16,569...H 7
Komodo (isl.)...F 7
Krakatau (Rakata) (isl.)...C 7
Laut (isl.), 42,099...F 6
Leuser (mt.)...B 5
Lingga (arch.), 39,307...D 5
Lingga (isl.), 14,309...D 6
Lombok (isl.), 1,602,000...F 7
Madura (isl.), 2,650,000...K 2
Mahakam (river)...F 6
Makassar (str.)...F 6
Malacca (str.)...C 5
Mamberamo (river)...K 6
Maoke (mts.)...K 6
Mapia (isls.)...J 5
Mentawai (isls.), 23,649...B 6
Misool (isl.), 3,022...J 6
Molucca (sea)...H 6
Moluccas (isls.), 973,000...H 6
Morotai (isl.), 19,523...H 5
Muli (str.)...K 7
Müller (mts.)...E 6
Muna (isl.), 139,000...G 7
Musi (river)...C 6
Natuna (isls.), 15,261...D 5
Ngundju (cape)...B 8

Obi (isls.), 6,358...H 6
Ombai (str.)...H 7
Perkam (cape)...K 6
Puting (cape), Borneo...E 6
Puting (cape), Sumatra...B 6
Radja Ampat Group (isls.), 17,158...H 6
Raja (mt.)...E 6
Rakata (isl.)...C 7
Rantekombola (mt.)...F 6
Riau (arch.), 342,000...C 5
Rokan (river)...B 5
Roti (isl.), 68,330...G 8
Rouffaer (river)...K 6
Salajar (isl.), 107,000...G 7
Salawati (isl.), 5,125...J 6
Sandalwood (Sumba) (isl.), 311,000...F 7
Sangihe (isls.), 83,585...H 5
Sangihe (isls.), 126,931...H 5
Sarera (bay)...K 6
Sawu (isls.), 78,785...G 8
Sawu (sea)...G 7
Schouten (isls.), 41,647...K 6
Schwaner (mts.)...E 6
Seaflower (channel)...F 5
Sebuko (bay)...F 6
Selatan (cape)...E 6
Semeru (mt.)...K 2
Siau (isl.), 29,762...H 5
Siberut (isl.)...B 6
Simeulue (isl.), 25,951...A 5
Singkep (isl.), 17,712...D 6
Sipora (isl.), 5,671...B 6
Slamet (mt.)...J 2
Sorik Merapi (mt.)...B 5
South Natuna (isls.), 3,318...D 5
Sudirman (range)...K 6

Sula (isls.), 30,779...H 6
Sulawesi (Celebes) (isl.)...G 6
Sumatra (isl.), 17,345,000...C 6
Sumba (isl.), 311,000...F 7
Sumba (str.)...F 7
Sumbawa (isl.), 625,000...F 7
Sunda (str.)...C 7
Tahulandang (isl.), 13,584...H 5
Talaud (isls.), 28,738...H 5
Taliabu (isl.), 7,391...G 6
Tambelan (isls.), 3,551...D 5
Tanimbar (isls.), 41,233...J 7
Tidore (isl.), 24,064...H 5
Timor (isl.)...G 7
Timor (reg.), 1,466,000...H 7
Toba (lake)...B 5
Tolo (gulf)...G 6
Tomini (gulf)...G 6
Tukangbesi (isls.), 59,775...G 7
Vals (cape)...K 7
Vogelkop (Deberai) (pen.)...J 6
Waigeo (isl.), 9,011...J 5
Wangiwangi (isl.), 19,719...G 7
Weh (isl.)...B 4
West Irian (reg.), 933,000...K 6
Wetar (isl.), 11,383...H 7

MALAYSIA★
STATES

Sabah, 633,000...F 4
Sarawak, 950,000...E 5

CITIES and TOWNS

Beaufort, †25,408...F 4

Topography

MILES
0   300   600

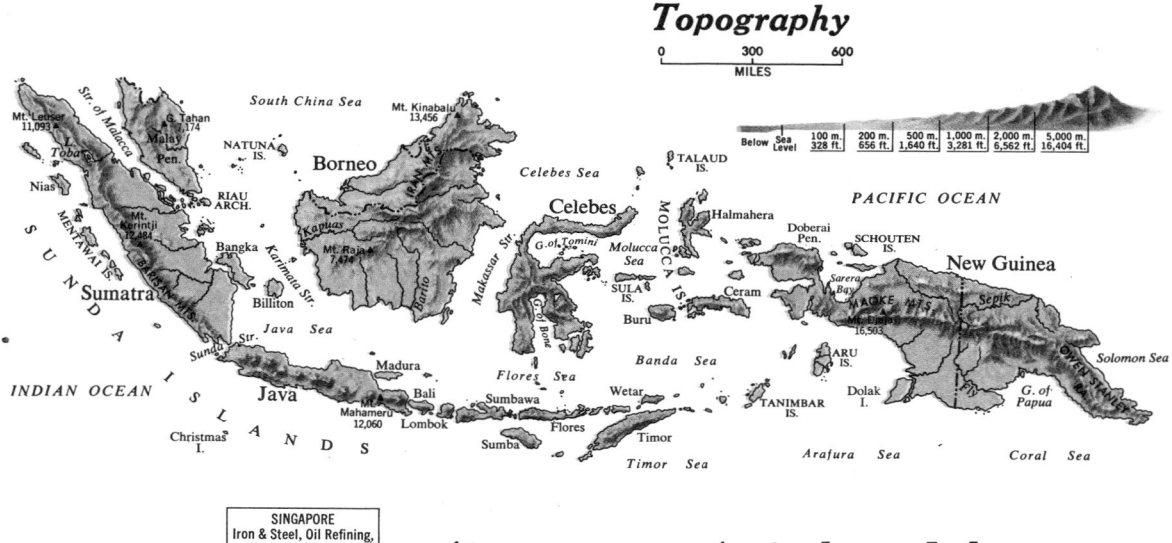

Below Sea Level | 100 m. 328 ft. | 200 m. 656 ft. | 500 m. 1,640 ft. | 1,000 m. 3,281 ft. | 2,000 m. 6,562 ft. | 5,000 m. 16,404 ft.

Agriculture, Industry and Resources

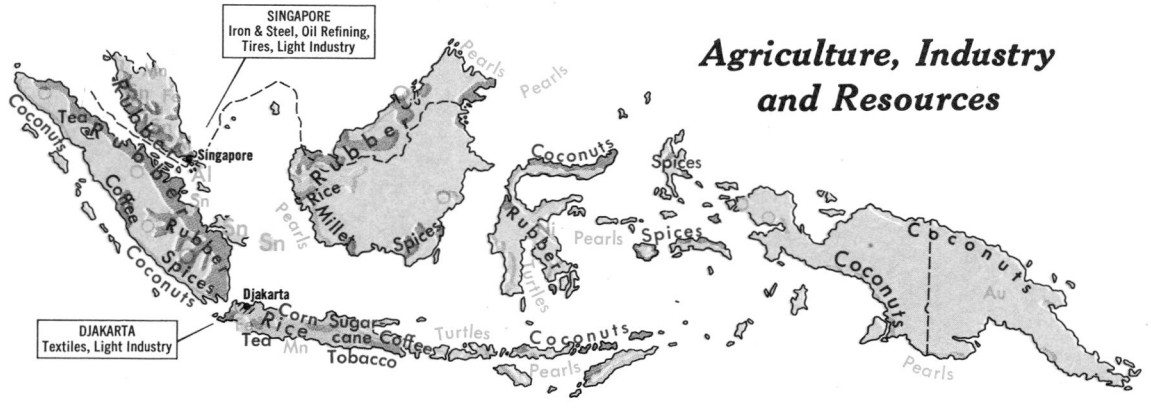

SINGAPORE
Iron & Steel, Oil Refining, Tires, Light Industry

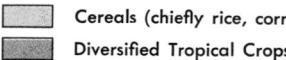
DJAKARTA
Textiles, Light Industry

DOMINANT LAND USE

Cereals (chiefly rice, corn)
Diversified Tropical Crops
Forests

MAJOR MINERAL OCCURRENCES

Al Bauxite
Au Gold
C Coal
Fe Iron Ore
Mn Manganese
Ni Nickel
○ Petroleum
Sn Tin

Major Industrial Areas

EASTERN NEW GUINEA
MILES
0 50 100 200

145°   150°

Bintulu, 5,307 .... E 5	Bogia, 639 .... B 6	New Britain (isl.), 138,689 ...... C 7
Keningau, 114,645 .... F 4	Bulolo, 2,724 .... B 7	Papua (gulf) .... B 7
Kota Kinabalu, 21,704 ...... F 4	Buna, 307 .... C 7	Ramu (river) .... B 7
Kuching, 56,000 .... E 5	Daru, 3,663 .... C 7	Rossel (isl.), 1,933 ...... D 8
Kudat, 3,660 .... F 4	Finschhafen, 436 .... C 7	Schouten (isls.), 6,633 ...... B 6
Lahad Datu, 119,534 ...... F 5	Goroka, 4,826 .... B 7	Sepik (river) .... B 6
Marudi, 2,663 .... E 5	Ioma, ‡3,552 .... B 7	Solomon (sea) .... C 7
Miri, 20,000 .... E 5	Kairuku, ‡4,582 .... B 7	Tagula (isl.), 1,654 ...... D 8
Papar, ‡28,210 .... F 4	Kerema, 820 .... B 7	Torres (str.) .... A 7
Ranau, 117,033 .... F 4	Kiunga, ‡918 .... C 7	Trobriand (isls.), 10,199 ...... C 7
Sandakan, 28,805 .... F 4	Kokoda, ‡1,615 .... C 7	Woodlark (isl.), 1,848 ...... C 7
Sematan .... D 5	Lae, 12,392 .... B 7	
Semporna, 116,895 .... F 5	Madang, 6,601 .... B 7	*City and suburbs.
Sibu, 29,630 .... E 5	Mendi, 1,687 .... C 7	†Population of district.
Simanggang, 5,648 .... E 5	Morobe, 12,132 .... C 7	‡Population of sub-district.
Tawau, 10,276 .... F 5	Popondetta, 2,139 .... C 7	
Victoria, 3,213 .... E 4	Rigo, ‡1,184 .... C 7	★See page 74 for other
	Saidor .... B 7	Malaysian entries.
OTHER FEATURES	Samarai, 2,201 .... C 8	
	Telefomin, ‡395 .... C 7	
Balambangan (isl.) .... F 4	Tufi, ‡462 .... C 7	
Banggi (isl.) .... F 4	Vanimo, 512 .... B 6	
Iran (mts.) .... E 5	Wau, 1,072 .... B 7	
Kinabalu (mt.) .... F 4	Wewak, 5,090 .... B 6	
Labuan (isl.), 14,904 .... F 4		
Labuk (bay) .... F 4	**OTHER FEATURES**	
Rajang (river) .... E 5		
Sirik (cape) .... E 5	Dampier (str.) .... C 7	
	D'Entrecasteaux (isls.), 32,288 .. C 7	
PAPUA NEW GUINEA	Fly (river) .... A 7	
	Huon (gulf) .... C 7	
CITIES and TOWNS	Karkar (isl.), 14,966 .... B 6	
	Kiriwina (isl.), 8,990 .... C 7	
Abau, ‡3,024 .... C 7	Long (isl.), 7,044 .... B 7	
Aitape, 540 .... B 6	Louisiade (arch.), 11,451 ...... D 8	
Ambunti, ‡697 .... B 6	Milne (bay) .... C 8	
Angoram, 1,822 .... B 6	Misima (isl.), 5,247 .... C 8	
Baniara, ‡1,110 .... C 7		

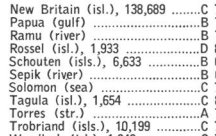

INDONESIA

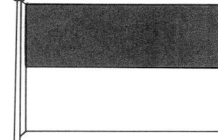

PAPUA NEW GUINEA

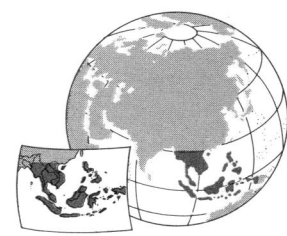

INDONESIA

AREA 788,430 sq. mi.
POPULATION 131,255,000
CAPITAL Djakarta
LARGEST CITY Djakarta
HIGHEST POINT Mt. Djaja 16,503 ft.
MONETARY UNIT rupiah
MAJOR LANGUAGES Bahasa Indonesia, Indonesian and Papuan languages, English
MAJOR RELIGIONS Islam, Tribal religions, Christianity, Hinduism

PAPUA NEW GUINEA

AREA 183,540 sq. mi.
POPULATION 2,800,000
CAPITAL Port Moresby
LARGEST CITY Port Moresby
HIGHEST POINT Mt. Wilhelm 15,400 ft.
MONETARY UNIT kina
MAJOR LANGUAGES Pidgin English, Hiri Motu, English
MAJOR RELIGIONS Tribal religions, Christianity

BRUNEI

AREA 2,226 sq. mi.
POPULATION 155,000
CAPITAL Bandar Seri Begawan

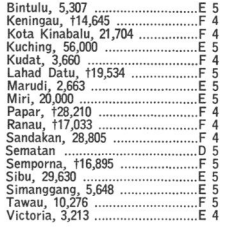

SOUTHEAST ASIA

LAMBERT AZIMUTHAL EQUAL-AREA PROJECTION

SCALE OF MILES

SCALE OF KILOMETRES

Capitals of Countries _____ ☆
Administrative Center _____ ◉
International Boundaries _____
Other Boundaries _____

Copyright by C.S. HAMMOND & CO., N.Y.

JAVA

MILES
0   25   50

86 Pacific Ocean

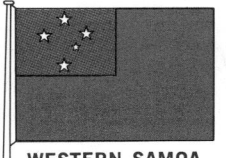
WESTERN SAMOA

SOLOMON ISLANDS

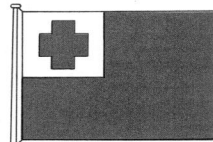
TONGA

FIJI

WESTERN SAMOA
AREA 1,133 sq. mi.
POPULATION 159,000
CAPITAL Apia
LARGEST CITY Apia
HIGHEST POINT Mt. Silisili 6,094 ft.
MONETARY UNIT tala
MAJOR LANGUAGES Samoan, English
MAJOR RELIGIONS Protestantism,
Roman Catholicism

TONGA
AREA 270 sq. mi.
POPULATION 102,000
CAPITAL Nuku'alofa
LARGEST CITY Nuku'alofa
HIGHEST POINT 3,389 ft.
MONETARY UNIT pa'anga
MAJOR LANGUAGES Tongan, English
MAJOR RELIGION Protestantism

NAURU
AREA 7.7 sq. mi.
POPULATION 8,000
CAPITAL Yaren (district)
MONETARY UNIT Australian dollar
MAJOR LANGUAGES Nauruan, English
MAJOR RELIGION Protestantism

SOLOMON ISLANDS
AREA 11,500 sq. mi.
POPULATION 196,708
CAPITAL Honiara
HIGHEST POINT Mount Popomanatseu 7,647
MONETARY UNIT Solomon Islands dollar
MAJOR LANGUAGES English, Pidgin English,
Melanesian dialects
MAJOR RELIGIONS Tribal religions, Protestantism,
Roman Catholicism

FIJI
AREA 7,055 sq. mi.
POPULATION 569,468
CAPITAL Suva
LARGEST CITY Suva
HIGHEST POINT Tomanivi 4,341 ft.
MONETARY UNIT Fijian dollar
MAJOR LANGUAGES Fijian, Hindi, English
MAJOR RELIGIONS Protestantism, Hinduism

TUVALU
AREA 9.78 sq. mi.
POPULATION 5,887
CAPITAL Fongafale
MONETARY UNIT Australian dollar
MAJOR LANGUAGES English, Tuvaluan
MAJOR RELIGION Protestantism

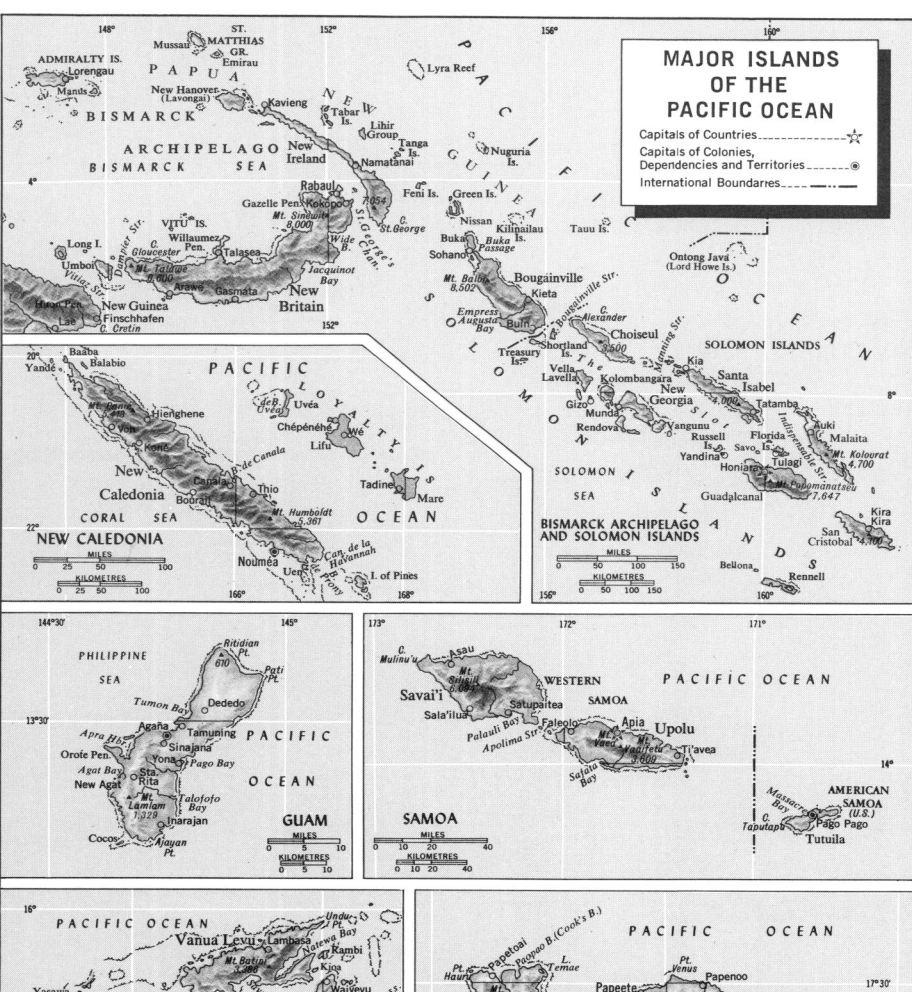

MAJOR ISLANDS
OF THE
PACIFIC OCEAN

Capitals of Countries .... ☆
Capitals of Colonies,
Dependencies and Territories .... ◉
International Boundaries .... ____

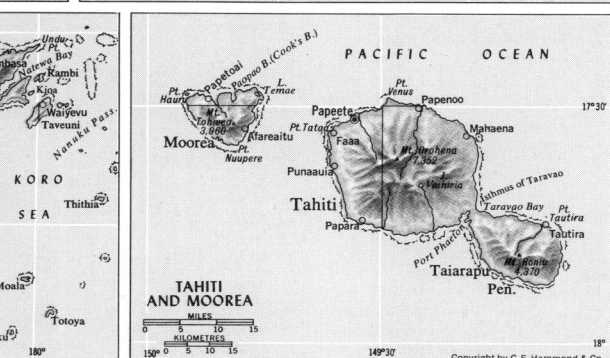

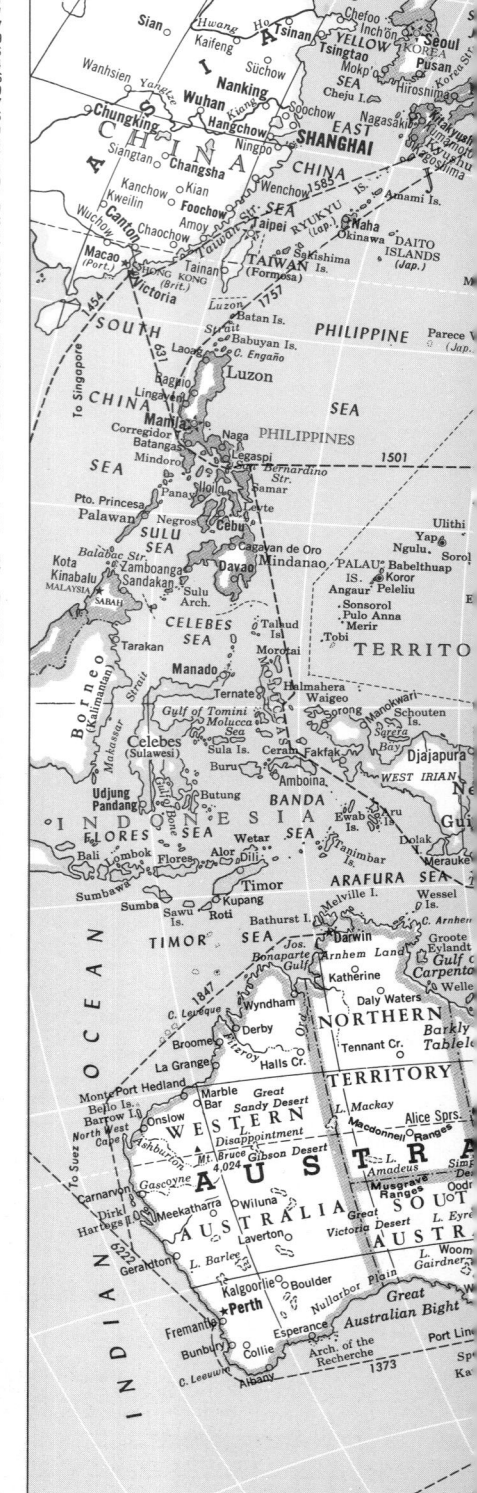

Copyright by C. S. Hammond & Co., N.Y.

KIRIBATI

AREA 264 sq. mi.
POPULATION 56,000
CAPITAL Bairiki
HIGHEST POINT 12 ft.
MONETARY UNIT Australian dollar
MAJOR LANGUAGES Gilbertese, English
MAJOR RELIGIONS Protestantism, Roman
Catholicism

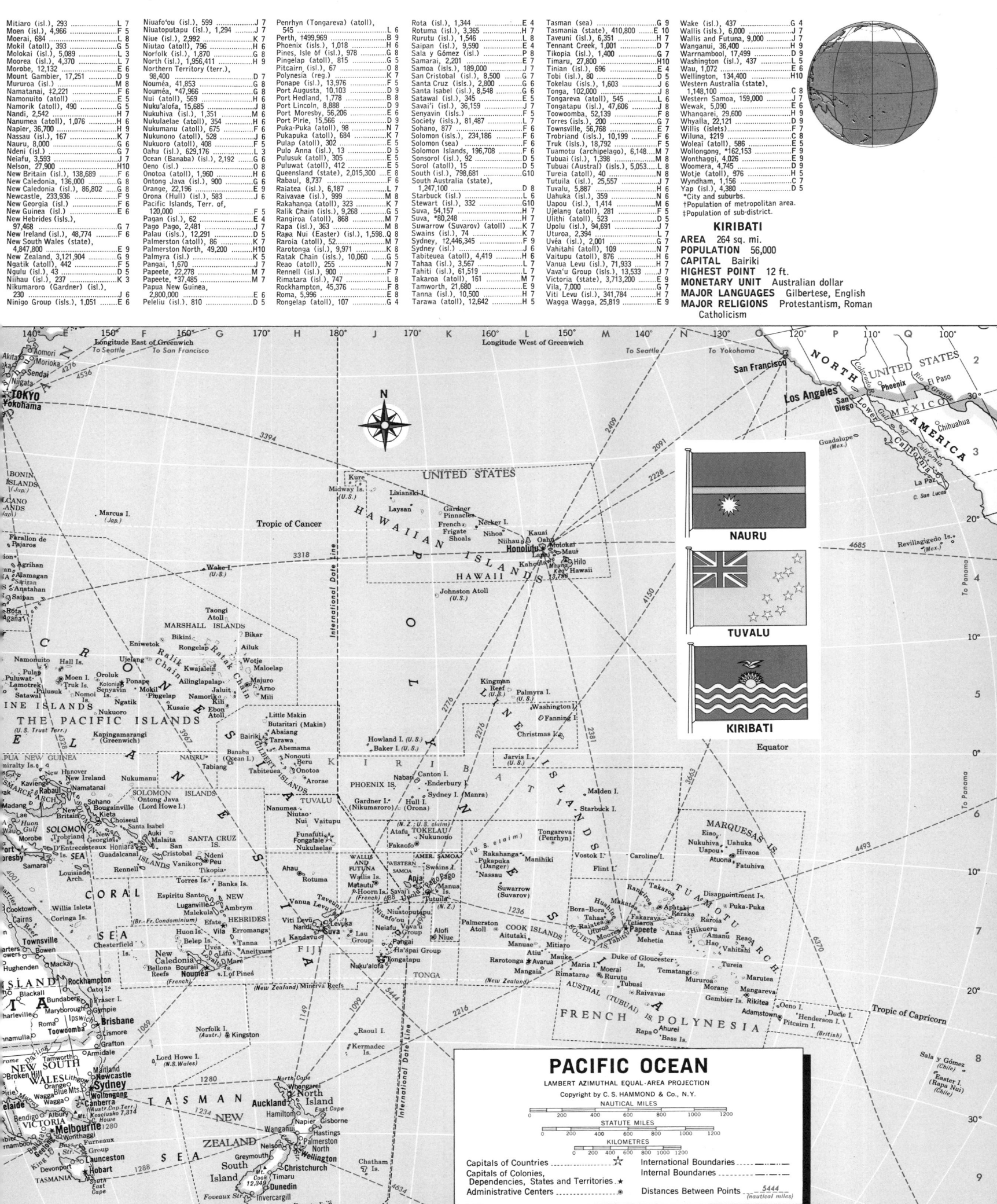

PACIFIC OCEAN
LAMBERT AZIMUTHAL EQUAL-AREA PROJECTION
Copyright by C. S. HAMMOND & Co., N.Y.

NAUTICAL MILES
STATUTE MILES
KILOMETRES

Capitals of Countries ☆
Capitals of Colonies, Dependencies, States and Territories ★
Administrative Centers ⊛
International Boundaries
Internal Boundaries
Distances Between Points 5444 (nautical miles)

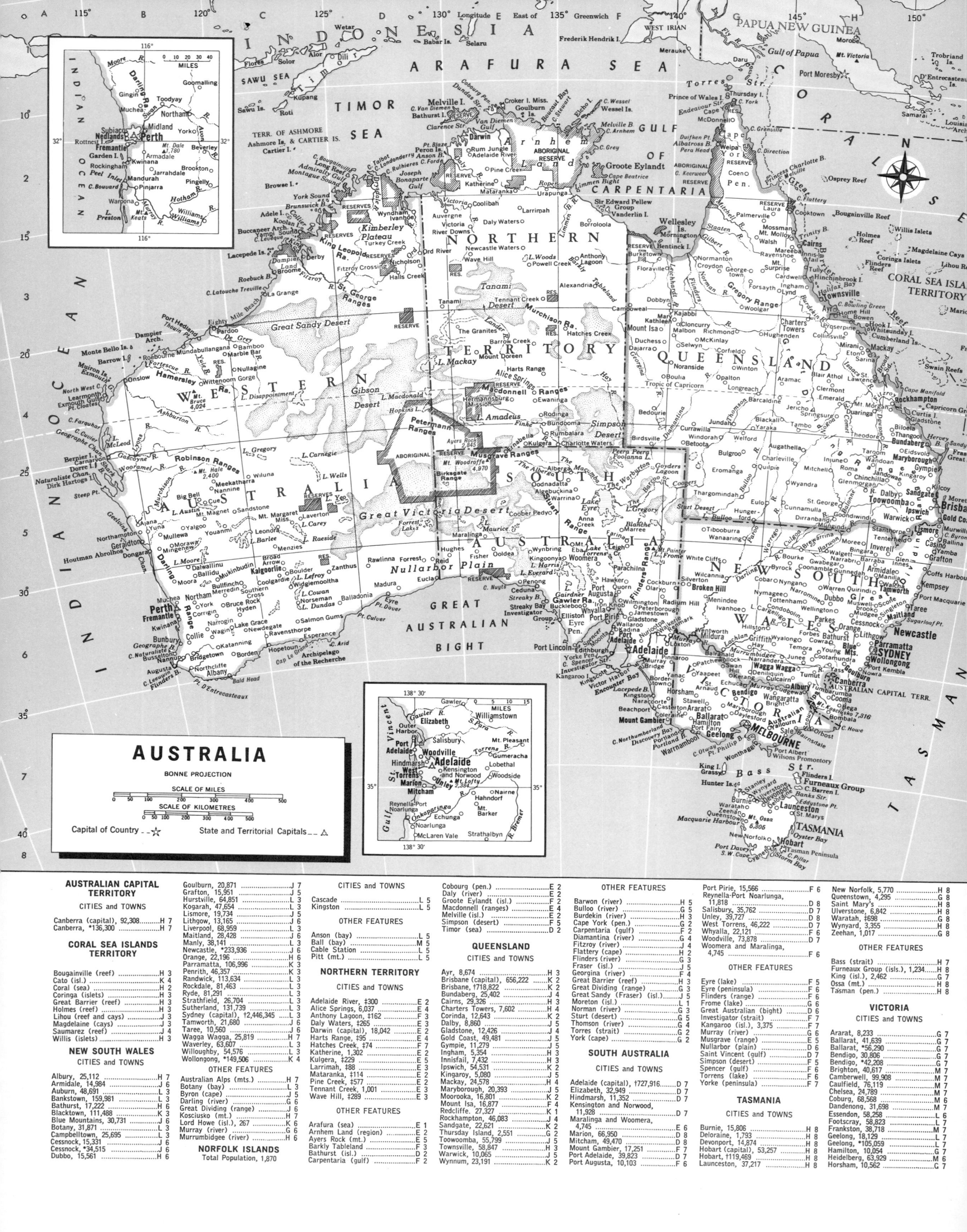

AUSTRALIA

BONNE PROJECTION

SCALE OF MILES

SCALE OF KILOMETRES

Capital of Country ⭐   State and Territorial Capitals △

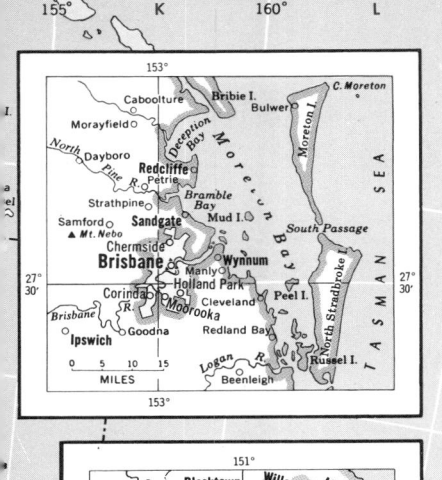

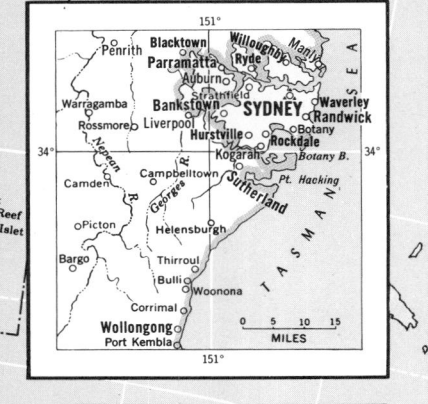

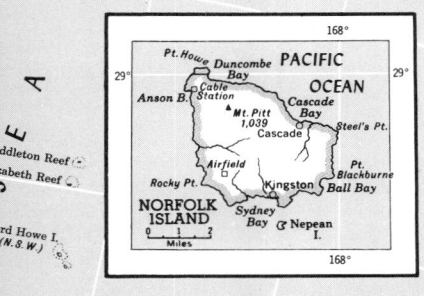

Copyright by C. S. HAMMOND & Co., N. Y.

AREA 2,967,909 sq. mi.
POPULATION 13,684,900
CAPITAL Canberra
LARGEST CITY Sydney
HIGHEST POINT Mt. Kosciusko 7,316 ft.
LOWEST POINT Lake Eyre -39 ft.
MONETARY UNIT Australian dollar
MAJOR LANGUAGE English
MAJOR RELIGIONS Protestantism, Roman Catholicism

Melbourne (capital),		
†2,110,168	......	H 7
Mildura, 12,931	......	G 6
Mordialloc, 28,076	......	M 7
Port Melbourne, 12,591	......	L 7
Preston, 89,767	......	M 6
Richmond, 32,530	......	M 7
Ringwood, 29,141	......	M 6
Saint Kilda, 58,129	......	H 7
Sale, 8,640	......	H 7
Sandringham, 36,671	......	M 7
Wangaratta, 15,175	......	H 7
Warrnambool, 17,499	......	G 7
Werribee, 8,228	......	L 7
Williamstown, 30,449	......	L 7

OTHER FEATURES

Australian Alps (mts.)	......	H 7
Bass (strait)	......	H 7
Murray (river)	......	G 6
Port Phillip (bay)	......	M 7
Tasman (sea)	......	J 7
Wilsons (promontory)	......	H 7

WESTERN AUSTRALIA

CITIES and TOWNS

Albany, 11,419	......	B 6
Armadale, 3,463	......	B 2
Boulder, 5,234	......	C 6
Bunbury, 15,459	......	A 6
Collie, 7,628	......	B 6
Fremantle, 25,284	......	B 2
Geraldton, 12,125	......	A 5
Kalgoorlie, 9,174	......	C 6
Kalgoorlie, *19,908	......	C 6
Midland, 9,335	......	B 2

Narrogin, 4,861	......	B 6
Nedlands, 23,320	......	B 2
Northam, 7,400	......	B 6
Perth (capital), 1⁄2499,969	......	B 2
Rockingham, 3,767	......	B 2
Subiaco, 16,621	......	B 2
Wittenoom Gorge	......	B 4

OTHER FEATURES

Ashburton (river)	......	B 4
Avon (river)	......	B 2
Bruce (mt.)	......	B 4
Dampier Land (region)	......	C 3
Exmouth (gulf)	......	A 4
Fitzroy (river)	......	C 3
Gascoyne (river)	......	B 5
Geographe (bay)	......	A 6
Gibson (desert)	......	C 4
Great Australian (bight)	......	D 6
Great Sandy (desert)	......	C 4
Great Victoria (desert)	......	D 5
Hamersley (range)	......	B 4
Joseph Bonaparte (gulf)	......	D 2
Kimberley (plateau)	......	D 3
Leeuwin (cape)	......	A 6
Lévêque (cape)	......	C 3
Nullarbor (plain)	......	D 6
Ord (river)	......	D 3
Shark (bay)	......	A 5
Swan (river)	......	B 2
Timor (sea)	......	D 2
Yule (river)	......	B 4

*City and suburbs.
†Population of metropolitan area.
‡Population of district.

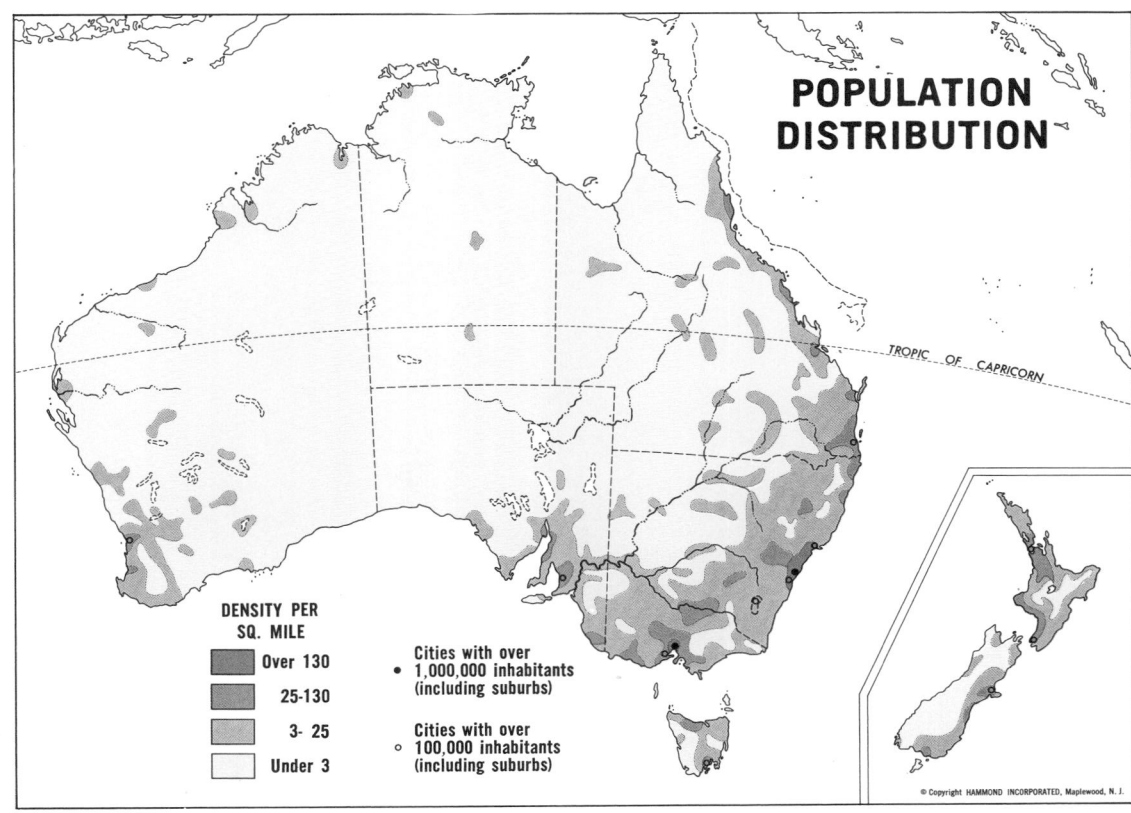

POPULATION DISTRIBUTION

DENSITY PER SQ. MILE

- Over 130
- 25-130
- 3- 25
- Under 3

- Cities with over 1,000,000 inhabitants (including suburbs)
- Cities with over 100,000 inhabitants (including suburbs)

© Copyright HAMMOND INCORPORATED, Maplewood, N. J.

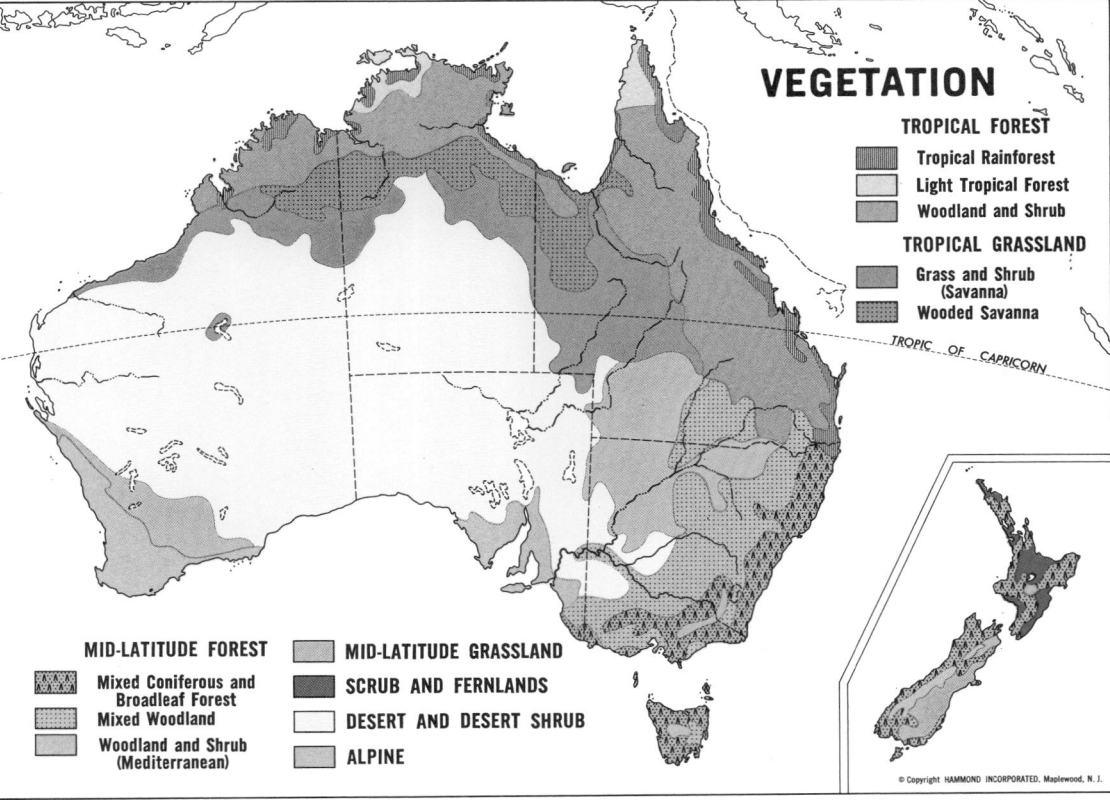

VEGETATION

TROPICAL FOREST
- Tropical Rainforest
- Light Tropical Forest
- Woodland and Shrub

TROPICAL GRASSLAND
- Grass and Shrub (Savanna)
- Wooded Savanna

MID-LATITUDE FOREST
- Mixed Coniferous and Broadleaf Forest
- Mixed Woodland
- Woodland and Shrub (Mediterranean)

MID-LATITUDE GRASSLAND

SCRUB AND FERNLANDS

DESERT AND DESERT SHRUB

ALPINE

© Copyright HAMMOND INCORPORATED, Maplewood, N. J.

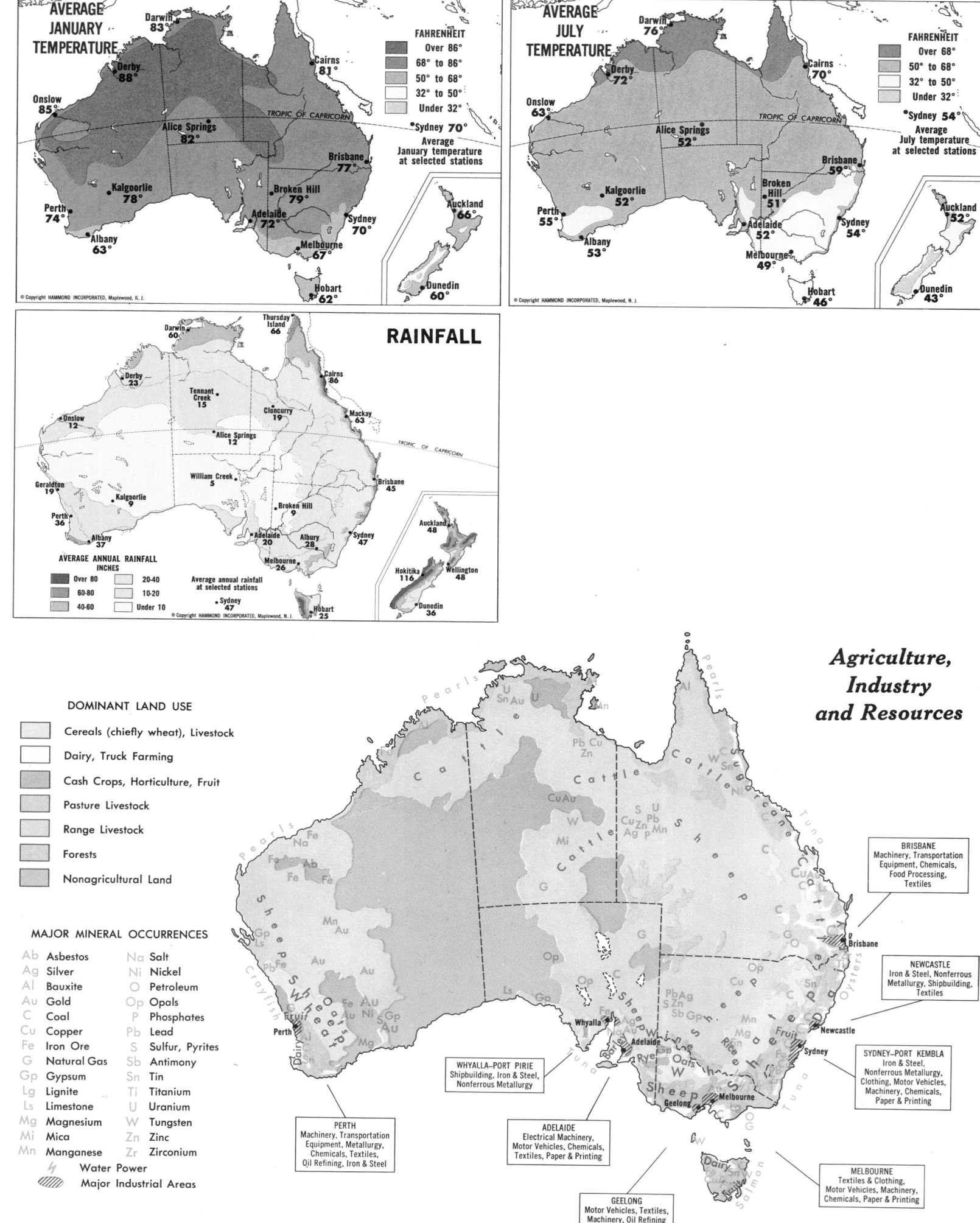

AVERAGE JANUARY TEMPERATURE

FAHRENHEIT
- Over 86°
- 68° to 86°
- 50° to 68°
- 32° to 50°
- Under 32°

•Sydney 70° Average January temperature at selected stations

Darwin 83°, Derby 88°, Onslow 85°, Cairns 81°, Alice Springs 82°, Kalgoorlie 78°, Perth 74°, Broken Hill 79°, Adelaide 72°, Albany 63°, Melbourne 67°, Sydney 70°, Brisbane 77°, Hobart 62°, Auckland 66°, Dunedin 60°

© Copyright HAMMOND INCORPORATED, Maplewood, N.J.

AVERAGE JULY TEMPERATURE

FAHRENHEIT
- Over 68°
- 50° to 68°
- 32° to 50°
- Under 32°

•Sydney 54° Average July temperature at selected stations

Darwin 76°, Derby 72°, Onslow 63°, Cairns 70°, Alice Springs 52°, Kalgoorlie 52°, Perth 55°, Broken Hill 51°, Adelaide 52°, Albany 53°, Melbourne 49°, Sydney 54°, Brisbane 59°, Hobart 46°, Auckland 52°, Dunedin 43°

© Copyright HAMMOND INCORPORATED, Maplewood, N.J.

RAINFALL

Darwin 60, Thursday Island 66, Derby 23, Tennant Creek 15, Cloncurry 19, Cairns 86, Mackay 63, Onslow 12, Alice Springs 12, Geraldton 19, William Creek 5, Brisbane 45, Kalgoorlie 9, Broken Hill 9, Perth 36, Albany 37, Adelaide 20, Albury 28, Sydney 47, Melbourne 26, Auckland 48, Hokitika 116, Wellington 48, Sydney 47, Hobart 25, Dunedin 36

AVERAGE ANNUAL RAINFALL
INCHES
- Over 80
- 60-80
- 40-60
- 20-40
- 10-20
- Under 10

Average annual rainfall at selected stations

© Copyright HAMMOND INCORPORATED, Maplewood, N.J.

Agriculture, Industry and Resources

DOMINANT LAND USE
- Cereals (chiefly wheat), Livestock
- Dairy, Truck Farming
- Cash Crops, Horticulture, Fruit
- Pasture Livestock
- Range Livestock
- Forests
- Nonagricultural Land

MAJOR MINERAL OCCURRENCES
- Ab Asbestos
- Ag Silver
- Al Bauxite
- Au Gold
- C Coal
- Cu Copper
- Fe Iron Ore
- G Natural Gas
- Gp Gypsum
- Lg Lignite
- Ls Limestone
- Mg Magnesium
- Mi Mica
- Mn Manganese
- Na Salt
- Ni Nickel
- O Petroleum
- Op Opals
- P Phosphates
- Pb Lead
- S Sulfur, Pyrites
- Sb Antimony
- Sn Tin
- Ti Titanium
- U Uranium
- W Tungsten
- Zn Zinc
- Zr Zirconium

↯ Water Power
▨ Major Industrial Areas

BRISBANE
Machinery, Transportation Equipment, Chemicals, Food Processing, Textiles

NEWCASTLE
Iron & Steel, Nonferrous Metallurgy, Shipbuilding, Textiles

SYDNEY–PORT KEMBLA
Iron & Steel, Nonferrous Metallurgy, Clothing, Motor Vehicles, Machinery, Chemicals, Paper & Printing

MELBOURNE
Textiles & Clothing, Motor Vehicles, Machinery, Chemicals, Paper & Printing

GEELONG
Motor Vehicles, Textiles, Machinery, Oil Refining

ADELAIDE
Electrical Machinery, Motor Vehicles, Chemicals, Textiles, Paper & Printing

WHYALLA–PORT PIRIE
Shipbuilding, Iron & Steel, Nonferrous Metallurgy

PERTH
Machinery, Transportation Equipment, Metallurgy, Chemicals, Textiles, Oil Refining, Iron & Steel

INDONESIA

Sumba   Timor

ARAFURA   SEA

New Guinea   PAPUA
                NEW
Port Moresby   GUINEA

TIMOR   SEA
Ashmore Is. TERR. OF ASHMORE
Cartier I.   & CARTIER IS.

Melville I.   Cobourg
              Pen.
Darwin   C. Wessel   Torres Strait
              Arnhem
              Land   Cape   C. York

INDIAN   Daly   Groote
                                Eylandt   York
                                              Peninsula   Great

              Kimberley   Gulf of   Mitchell
              Plateau   Carpentaria   Barrier
     Derby   Fitzroy   Ord   Cairns
                        Victoria   Reef
OCEAN   Barkly Tableland   Mt. Battle Frere
                        NORTHERN   5,287
                        Tanami   Townsville
                        Desert   Great
Port Hedland   TERRITORY   Mt. Isa
          Great Sandy Desert   QUEENSLAND
     WESTERN   Lake
North West Fortescue   Mackay   Georgina   Dividing
  C.   Hamersley Ra. Lake   Mackay
            Mt. Bruce   Disappointment Tropic of Capricorn Macdonnell Ranges
              8,024   Alice Springs   Simpson   Diamantina
            Gibson Desert   Finke   Rockhampton
                                                    Desert   Barcoo   Range
     Lake   Bundaberg
     Carnegie   AUSTRALIA   SOUTH   Ayers Rock   Grey Range
                                            2,845
Geraldton   Musgrave Ranges   Brisbane
                                                                             Gold Coast
     Lake   Great Victoria Desert   AUSTRALIA Lake
     Barlee   Eyre   Barcoo
                          Lake   Sturt   NEW SOUTH
     Kalgoorlie-   Torrens   Lake   Desert   Darling
     Boulder   Nullarbor Plain   Gairdner   Frome   Tamworth
Perth   Broken Hill   WALES
Fremantle Darling Ra.   Flinders Range   Newcastle
Bunbury   Great   Whyalla   Sydney
          C. Leeuwin   Australian Bight   Eyre   Lachlan Wollongong
     Albany   Pen.   Mt. Lofty Ra. Wagga Wagga
                                              Adelaide Murray   Canberra
                                                                 AUSTRALIAN CAPITAL
                          INDIAN   Kangaroo I.   Mt. Kosciusko TERRITORY
                                                        Bendigo 7,310
                                          Mt. Gambier Ballarat VICTORIA
     OCEAN   Geelong Melbourne C. Howe
                                                       King I.
                                                              Bass Strait   TASMAN
                                              Furneaux
                                              Group   SEA
                                          Launceston
                                                      TASMANIA
                                              Hobart
                                          South Cape

© HAMMOND INCORPORATED, Maplewood, N.J.

Longitude 140° East of Greenwich 145°

VEGETATION/RELIEF

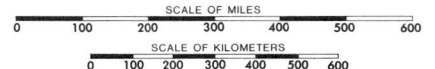

SCALE OF MILES
0   100   200   300   400   500   600
SCALE OF KILOMETERS
0   100   200   300   400   500   600

Capital of Country.................................⊛
State and Territorial Capitals..................⊛
International Boundaries.........................———
State and Territorial Boundaries...............———
Elevations in Feet   Depths in Fathoms

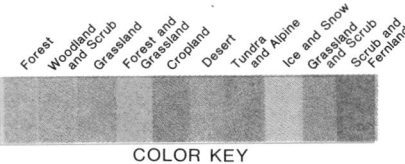

Forest
Woodland and Scrub
Grassland
Forest and Grassland
Cropland
Desert
Tundra and Alpine
Ice and Snow
Grassland and Scrub
Scrub and Fernlands

COLOR KEY

92 Western Australia

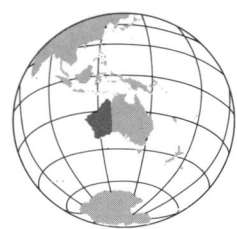

AREA 975,920 sq. mi.
POPULATION 1,148,100
CAPITAL Perth
LARGEST CITY Perth
HIGHEST POINT Mt. Bruce 4,024 ft.

Topography

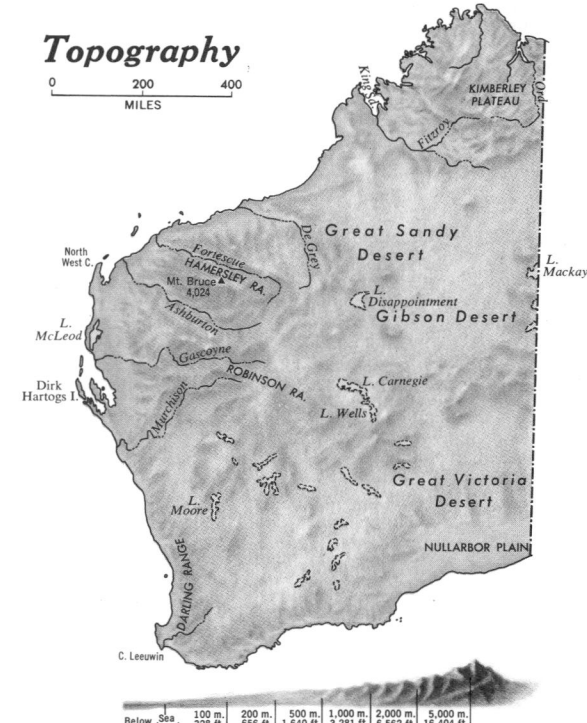

	MILES
0	200 400

Kimberley Plateau, Great Sandy Desert, Gibson Desert, Great Victoria Desert, Nullarbor Plain, Mt. Bruce 4,024, Hamersley Ra., Fortescue, De Grey, Fitzroy, Ashburton, Gascoyne, Robinson Ra., Murchison, L. Mackay, L. Disappointment, L. Carnegie, L. Wells, L. Moore, L. McLeod, Darling Range, North West C., Dirk Hartogs I., C. Leeuwin

CITIES and TOWNS

Albany, 11,419 .... B 6
Armadale, 3,463 .... A 1
Augusta, ⊙3,238 .... A 6
Beverley, ⊙1,773 .... B 1
Boddington, ⊙761 .... B 2
Boulder, 5,234 .... C 5
Bridgetown, 1,569 .... B 6
Brookton, ⊙1,341 .... B 2
Broome, 1,570 .... C 2
Bruce Rock, ⊙2,142 .... B 5
Bunbury, 15,459 .... A 2
Busselton, 4,278 .... A 6
Capel, ⊙2,132 .... A 2
Carnamah, ⊙996 .... A 5
Carnarvon, 2,956 .... A 4
Collie, 7,628 .... A 2
Coolgardie, ⊙762 .... C 5
Coorow, ⊙808 .... B 5

Corrigin, ⊙2,099 .... B 6
Cranbrook, ⊙1,419 .... B 6
Cuballing, ⊙732 .... B 2
Cue, ⊙430 .... B 4
Cunderdin, ⊙2,114 .... B 5
Dalwallinu, ⊙2,425 .... B 5
Dampier, 1,080 .... A 3
Dandaragan, ⊙619 .... A 5
Denmark, ⊙1,775 .... B 6
Derby, 1,424 .... C 2
Donnybrook, 981 .... A 2
Esperance, 2,677 .... C 6
Exmouth Gulf, ⊙2,248 .... A 3
Fremantle, 25,284 .... A 1
Geraldton, 12,125 .... A 5
Gingin, ⊙1,021 .... A 1
Gnowangerup, 981 .... B 6
Goomalling, ⊙1,567 .... B 1
Gosnells, 7,135 .... A 1
Halls Creek, ⊙577 .... D 2
Harvey, 2,066 .... A 2
Jarrahdale, ⊙1,728 .... B 2

Kalamunda-Gooseberry
Hill, 3,068 .... B 1
Kalgoorlie, 9,174 .... C 5
Kalgoorlie, ⊙19,908 .... C 5
Katanning, 3,506 .... B 6
Kellerberrin, 1,343 .... B 5
Kojonup, ⊙2,711 .... B 6
Kwinana, 1,272 .... A 1
Lake Grace, ⊙1,986 .... B 6
Learmonth .... A 3
Leonora, ⊙623 .... C 5
Mandurah, 2,730 .... A 2
Manjimup, 3,186 .... B 6
Marble Bar, ⊙567 .... C 3
Meekatharra, ⊙1,011 .... B 4
Menzies, ⊙404 .... C 5
Merredin, 3,599 .... B 5
Midland, 9,335 .... A 1
Mingenew, ⊙978 .... A 5
Moora, 1,185 .... B 5
Morawa, ⊙1,718 .... B 5
Mount Barker, 1,594 .... B 6

Mount Magnet, ⊙1,016 .... B 5
Mukinbudin, ⊙869 .... B 5
Mullewa, ⊙1,825 .... A 5
Nannup, ⊙1,272 .... B 6
Narrogin, 4,861 .... B 2
Nedlands, 23,320 .... A 1
Norseman, 1,863 .... C 6
Northam, 7,400 .... B 1
Northampton, ⊙2,021 .... A 5
Nullagine, ⊙211 .... C 3
Nungarin, ⊙539 .... B 5
Onslow, ... A 3
Pardoo, ... B 3
Pemberton, 930 .... A 6
Perenjori, ⊙1,311 .... B 5
Perth (cap.), ‡499,969 .... A 1
Pingelly, ⊙1,453 .... B 2
Port Hedland, 1,778 .... B 3
Quairading, ⊙1,687 .... B 5
Ravensthorpe, ⊙782 .... B 6
Rockingham, 3,767 .... A 2
Roebourne, ⊙702 .... B 3
South Perth, 32,042 .... A 1
Subiaco, 16,621 .... A 1
Tableland, ⊙1,815 .... D 2
Three Springs, ⊙1,038 .... A 5
Toodyay, ⊙1,388 .... B 1
Wagin, 1,750 .... B 2
Wandering, ⊙611 .... B 2
Wanneroo, 612 .... A 1
Waroona, 1,013 .... A 2
Wickepin, ⊙1,380 .... B 2
Williams, ⊙1,193 .... B 2
Wiluna, ⊙219 .... C 4
Wundowie, 1,040 .... B 1
Wyalkatchem, ⊙1,252 .... B 5
Wyndham, 1,156 .... E 1
Yalgoo, ⊙392 .... B 5
Yampi Sound, ... C 2
York, 1,421 .... B 1

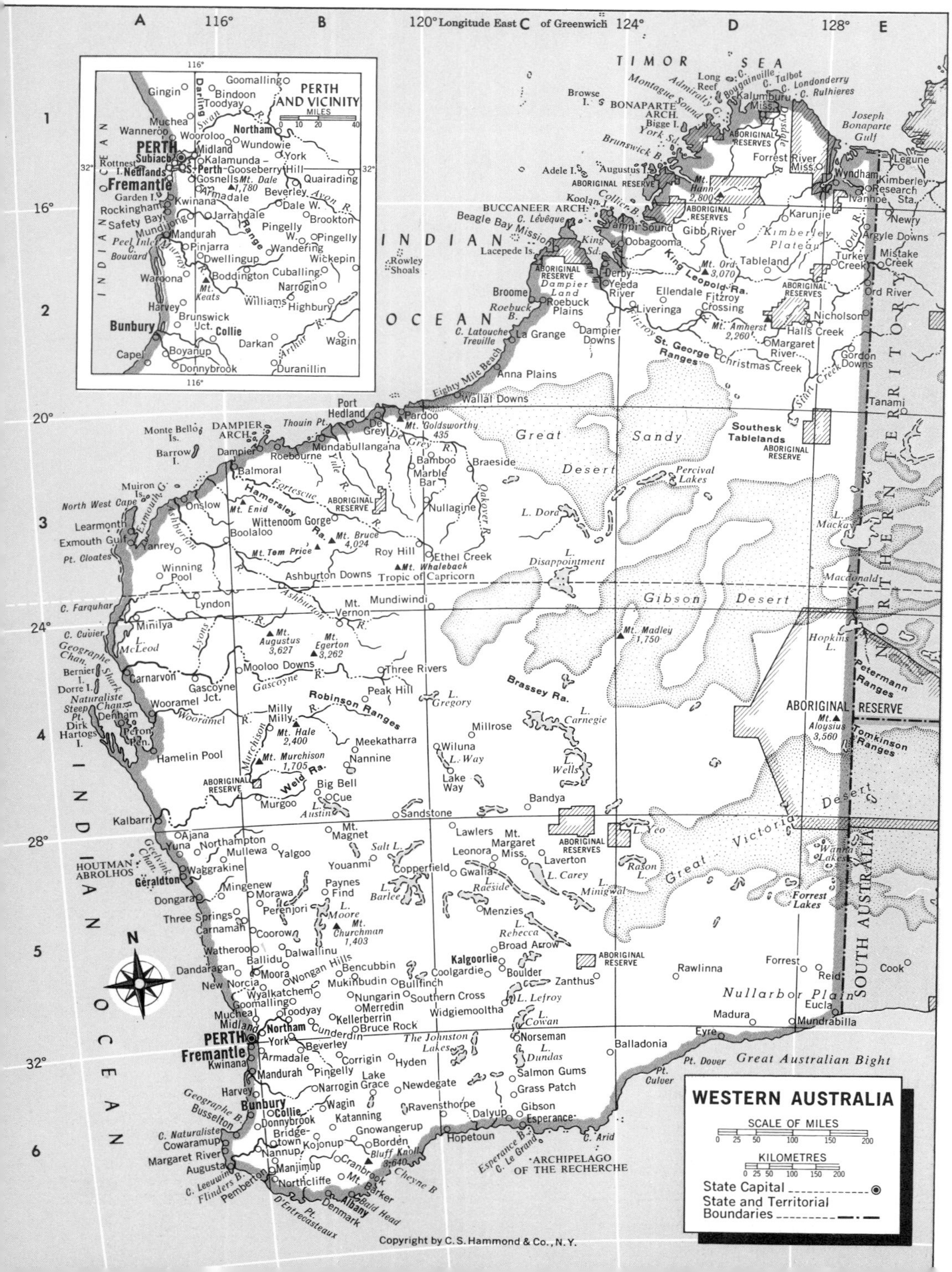

OTHER FEATURES

Adele (isl.) .... C 1
Admiralty (gulf) .... D 1
Aloysius (mt.) .... E 4
Amherst (mt.) .... D 2
Arid (cape) .... C 6
Arthur (riv.) .... A 3
Ashburton (riv.) .... A 3
Augustus (isl.) .... D 1
Augustus (mt.) .... B 4
Austin (lake) .... B 4
Avon (riv.) .... A 1
Bald (head) .... B 6
Barlee (lake) .... B 5
Barrow (isl.) .... A 3
Bernier (isl.) .... A 4
Bigge (isl.) .... D 1
Bluff Knoll (mt.) .... B 6
Bonaparte (arch.) .... D 1
Bougainville (cape) .... D 1
Bouvard (cape) .... A 2
Brassey (range) .... C 4
Browse (isl.) .... C 1
Bruce (mt.) .... B 3
Brunswick (bay) .... D 1
Buccaneer (arch.) .... C 2
Carey (lake) .... C 5
Carnegie (lake) .... C 4
Cheyne (bay) .... B 6
Churchman (mt.) .... B 5
Cloates (pt.) .... A 3
Collier (bay) .... C 1
Cowan (lake) .... C 5
Culver (pt.) .... D 6
Cuvier (cape) .... A 4
Dale (mt.) .... B 1
Dampier (arch.) .... B 3
Dampier Land (reg.) .... C 2
Darling (range) .... A 1
De Grey (riv.) .... B 3
D'Entrecasteaux (pt.) .... B 6
Dirk Hartogs (isl.) .... A 4
Disappointment (lake) .... C 3
Dora (lake) .... C 3
Dorre (isl.) .... A 4
Dover (pt.) .... D 6
Drysdale (riv.) .... D 1
Dundas (lake) .... C 6
Egerton (mt.) .... B 4
Eighty Mile (beach) .... C 2
Enid (mt.) .... B 3
Esperance (bay) .... C 6
Exmouth (gulf) .... A 3
Farquhar (cape) .... A 4
Fitzroy (riv.) .... D 2
Flinders (bay) .... A 6
Fortescue (riv.) .... B 3
Garden (isl.) .... A 1
Gascoyne (riv.) .... B 4
Geelvink (chan.) .... A 5
Geographe (bay) .... A 6
Geographe (chan.) .... A 4
Gibson (des.) .... C 4
Goldsworthy (mt.) .... B 3
Great Australian (bight) .... E 6
Great Sandy (des.) .... C 3
Great Victoria (des.) .... D 5
Gregory (lake) .... C 4
Hale (mt.) .... B 4
Hamersley (range) .... B 3
Hann (mt.) .... D 1
Hopkins (lake) .... E 4
Houtman Abrolhos (isls.) .... A 5

Indian Ocean .... A 5
Johnston, The (lakes) .... C 6
Joseph Bonaparte (gulf) .... E 1
Keats (mt.) .... A 2
Kimberley (plat.) .... D 2
King (sound) .... C 2
King Leopold (range) .... D 2
Koolan (isl.) .... C 1
Lacepede (isls.) .... C 2
Latouche Treville (cape) .... C 2
Leeuwin (cape) .... A 6
Lefroy (lake) .... C 5
Le Grand (cape) .... C 6
Lévêque (cape) .... C 2
Londonderry (cape) .... D 1
Long (reef) .... D 1
Lyons (riv.) .... A 4
Macdonald (lake) .... E 3
Mackay (lake) .... E 3
Madley (mt.) .... D 4
McLeod (lake) .... A 4
Minigwal (lake) .... C 5
Montague (sound) .... D 1
Monte Bello (isls.) .... A 3
Moore (lake) .... B 5
Muiron (isls.) .... A 3
Murchison (riv.) .... B 4
Murchison (riv.) .... A 4
Murray (riv.) .... A 2
Naturaliste (cape) .... A 6
Naturaliste (chan.) .... A 4
North West (cape) .... A 3
Nullarbor (plain) .... D 5
Oakover (riv.) .... C 3
Ord (lake) .... D 2
Ord (riv.) .... D 1
Peel (inlet) .... A 2
Percival (lakes) .... D 3
Peron (pen.) .... A 4
Petermann (ranges) .... E 4
Raeside (lake) .... C 5
Rason (lake) .... C 5
Rebecca (lake) .... C 5
Recherche (arch.) .... C 6
Robinson (ranges) .... B 4
Roebuck (bay) .... C 2
Rottnest (isl.) .... A 1
Rowley (shoals) .... B 2
Rulhieres (cape) .... D 1
Saint George (ranges) .... D 2
Salt (lake) .... B 5
Shark (bay) .... A 4
Southesk Tablelands .... D 3
Steep (pt.) .... A 4
Sturt (creek) .... D 2
Swan (riv.) .... A 1
Talbot (cape) .... D 1
Thouin (pt.) .... B 3
Timor (sea) .... D 1
Tomkinson (ranges) .... E 4
Tom Price (mt.) .... B 3
Wanna (lakes) .... E 5
Way (lake) .... C 4
Weld (lake) .... C 4
Weld (range) .... B 4
Wells (lake) .... C 4
Whaleback (mt.) .... B 3
Wooramel (riv.) .... A 4
Yeo (lake) .... D 5
York (sound) .... D 1
Yule (riv.) .... B 3

⊙ Population of district.
‡ Population of met. area.
□ Population of urban area.

WESTERN AUSTRALIA

SCALE OF MILES
0 25 50 100 150 200

KILOMETRES
0 25 50 100 150 200

State Capital .... ◉
State and Territorial
Boundaries .... —·—·—

Copyright by C. S. Hammond & Co., N.Y.

PERTH AND VICINITY

Gingin, Goomalling, Bindoon, Toodyay, Muchea, Woolooo, Wanneroo, Woorooloo, Northam, Wundowie, York, Rottnest I., PERTH, Subiaco, Midland, Kalamunda-Gooseberry Hill, Nedlands, Fremantle, Garden I., Gosnells, Mt. Dale, Quairading, Kwinana, Jarrahdale, Dale W., Brookton, Rockingham, Safety Bay, Mundijong, Pingelly, Pingelly, Peel Inlet, Mandurah, Pinjarra, Dwellingup, Wandering, Wickepin, Bouvard, Waroona, Boddington, Narrogin, Highbury, Harvey, Brunswick Jct., Williams, Collie, Bunbury, Boyanup, Darkan, Wagin, Capel, Donnybrook, Duranillin

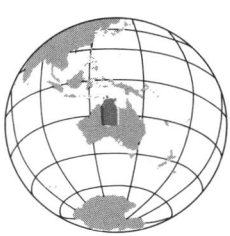

CITIES and TOWNS

Adelaide River, ⊙300....B 2
Aileron,....C 7
Alexandria,....E 5
Alice Springs, 6,037....D 7
Alroy Downs,....E 5
Andado,....D 8
Angas Downs,....C 8
Anthony Lagoon ⊙162....D 4
Areyonga,....C 8
Argadargada,....E 6
Arltunga,....D 7
Auvergne,....B 3
Avon Downs, ⊙231....E 5
Banka Banka,....C 5
Barrow Creek,....D 6
Batchelor, ⊙551....B 2
Bathurst Island Mission,....B 1
Birdum,....C 3
Birrimbah,....C 3
Birrindudu,....A 5
Bundooma,....D 8
Burramurra,....E 6
Calvert Hills,....E 4
Charlotte Waters,....D 8
Claravale,....B 3
Coniston,....C 7
Coolibah,....B 3
Creswell Downs,....E 4
Daly River, ⊙237....B 2
Daly Waters, ⊙265....C 3
Darwin (cap.), 18,042....B 2
Douglas,....B 2
Elliott, ⊙234....C 4
Epenarra,....D 6
Erldunda,....C 8
Eva Downs,....D 5

Ewaninga,....D 8
Fitzroy,....B 4
Frewena,....E 5
Harts Range, ⊙95....D 7
Hatches Creek, ⊙74....D 6
Helen Springs,....C 5
Henbury,....C 8
Humpty Doo,....B 2
Inverway,....A 4
Katherine, 1,302....B 3
Kildurk,....A 4
Killarney,....B 4
Koolpinyah,....C 2
Kulgera, ⊙229....C 8
Kurundi,....D 6
Lake Nash, ⊙113....E 6
Larrimah, ⊙88....C 3
Legune,....A 3
Limbunya,....B 4
Litchfield,....B 2
Lucy Creek,....E 7
Mainoru,....C 3
Mataranka, ⊙114....C 3
Mistake Creek,....A 4
Montejinni,....C 4
Mount Cavanagh,....C 8
Mount Doreen,....B 7
Murray Downs,....D 6
Napperby,....C 7
Newcastle Waters,....C 4
Newry,....A 3
Nutwood Downs,....D 3
O.T. Downs,....D 4
Pine Creek, ⊙577....C 2
Plenty River Mine,....D 7
Powell Creek,....C 5
Rankine Store,....E 5
Ringwood,....D 7

Robinson River,....E 4
Rockhampton Downs,....D 5
Rodinga,....D 8
Roper River Mission,
  ⊙357....D 3
Roper Valley,....D 3
Rosewood,....A 4
Rum Jungle,....B 2
Soudan,....E 6
Stirling,....C 6
Tanami,....B 6
Tarlton Downs,....E 7
Tea Tree Well Store,....C 7
Tempe Downs,....C 8
Tennant Creek, 1,001....C 5
The Granites,....B 6
Top Springs,....C 4
Ucharonidge,....D 4
Umbeara,....C 8
Urapunga,....D 3
Utopia,....D 7
Victoria River Downs,....A 4
Waterloo,....A 4
Wave Hill, ⊙289....B 4
White Quartz Hill,....D 7
Willeroo,....B 3
Willowra,....C 6
Wollogorang, ⊙87....F 4
Yambah,....C 7

OTHER FEATURES

Amadeus (lake)....B 8
Arafura (sea)....D 1
Arnhem (cape)....E 2
Arnhem Land (reg.)....D 2

Arnold (riv.)....D 3
Barkly Tableland....D 4
Bathurst (isl.)....A 1
Beagle (gulf)....A 2
Beatrice (cape)....B 3
Bennett (lake)....B 7
Bickerton (isl.)....E 2
Blaze (pt.)....A 2
Boucaut (bay)....D 1
Carpentaria (gulf)....E 3
Central Wedge (mt.)....C 7
Clarence (str.)....B 1
Cobourg (pen.)....C 1
Conner (pt.)....B 8
Croker (cape)....C 1
Daly (riv.)....B 2
Davenport (mt.)....B 7
Dobbie (mt.)....E 7
Drummond (mt.)....E 5
Dry (riv.)....B 3
Dundas (str.)....B 1
East Alligator (riv.)....C 2
Ehrenberg (range)....B 7
Elcho (isl.)....D 1
Ewing (mt.)....E 7
Finke (riv.)....C 8
Fitzmaurice (riv.)....B 3
Flora (riv.)....B 3
Ford (cape)....A 2
Georgina (riv.)....E 5
Goulburn (isls.)....C 1
Goyder (riv.)....D 2
Grey (cape)....E 2
Groote Eylandt (isl.)....E 2
Hale (riv.)....C 8
Hanson (riv.)....C 6
Hay (cape)....A 3
Hay (dry riv.)....E 7

Hogarth (mt.)....E 6
Hopkins (lake)....A 8
Joseph Bonaparte (gulf)....A 3
Katherine (riv.)....C 3
Lander (riv.)....C 6
Leisler (mt.)....A 7
Limmen (bight)....D 3
Limmen Bight (riv.)....D 4
Macdonald (lake)....A 8
Macdonnell (ranges)....C 7
MacKay (lake)....A 7
Mann (riv.)....D 2
Marshall (riv.)....D 7
Melville (bay)....E 2
Melville (isl.)....B 1
Murchison (range)....D 6
Napier (mt.)....A 4
Neale (lake)....A 8
Newcastle (creek)....C 4

Nicholson (riv.)....E 5
Old Marsh Bed....B 6
Olga (mt.)....B 8
Peron (isls.)....A 2
Petermann (ranges)....A 8
Port Darwin (inlet)....B 2
Ranken (riv.)....E 6
Robinson (riv.)....E 4
Roper (riv.)....C 3
Rose (riv.)....D 2
Sandover (riv.)....D 6
Simpson (des.)....E 8
Singleton (mt.)....B 6
Sir Edward Pellew Group
  (isls.)....E 3
South Alligator (riv.)....C 2
Stanley (mt.)....B 7
Stewart (cape)....D 1
Stirling (creek)....A 4

Sturt (plain)....C 4
Sylvester (lake)....D 5
Tanami (des.)....B 6
Timor (sea)....A 2
Todd (riv.)....D 8
Vanderlin (isl.)....E 3
Van Diemen (cape)....A 1
Van Diemen (gulf)....B 1
Victoria (riv.)....B 3
Warwick (chan.)....E 3
Wessel (cape)....E 1
Wessel (isls.)....E 1
West Baines (riv.)....A 4
White (lake)....A 6
Winnecke (creek)....B 5
Woods (lake)....C 4
Young (mt.)....D 3
Ziel (mt.)....C 7

⊙ Population of district.

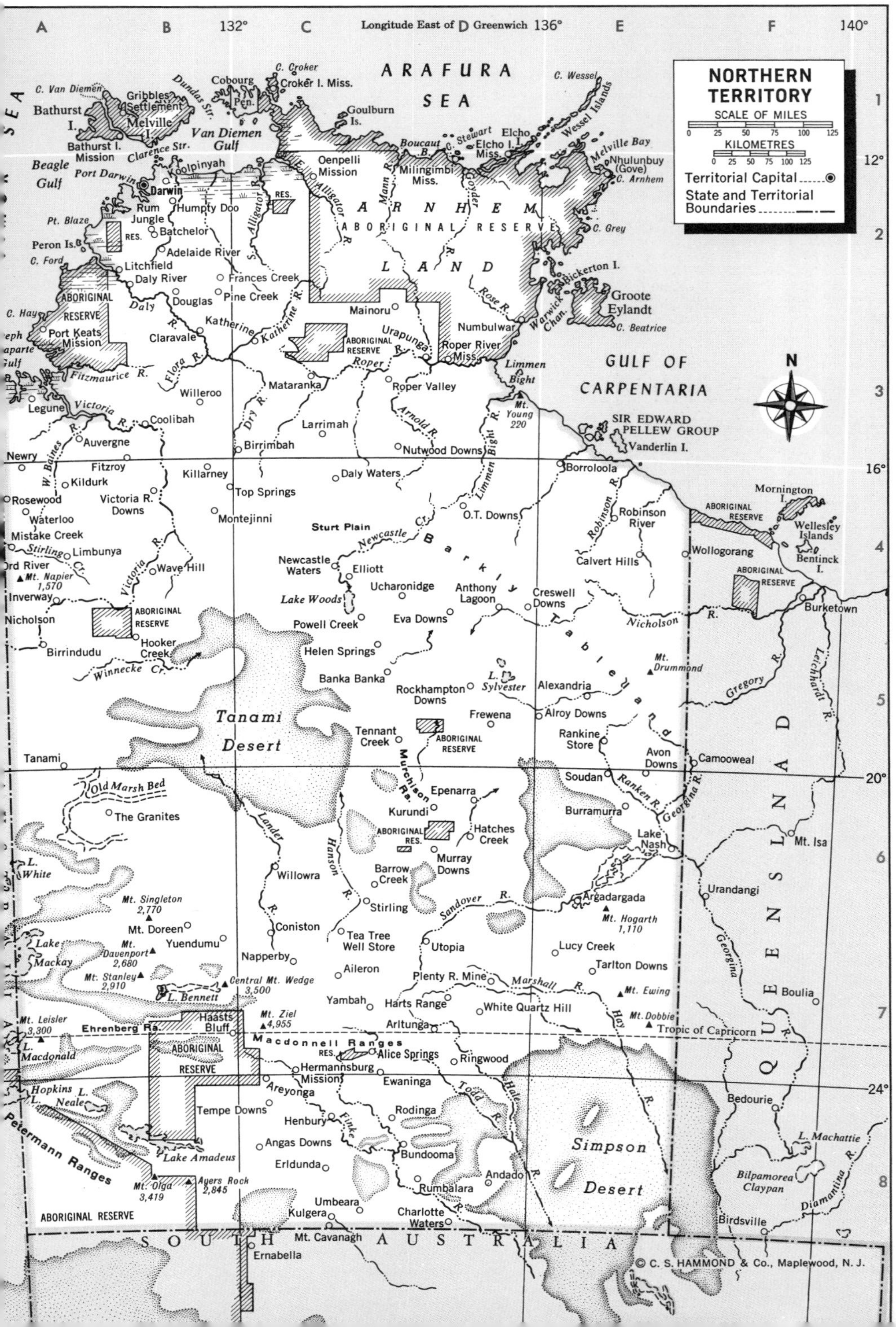

AREA 520,280 sq. mi.
POPULATION 98,400
CAPITAL Darwin
LARGEST CITY Darwin
HIGHEST POINT Mt. Ziel 4,955 ft.

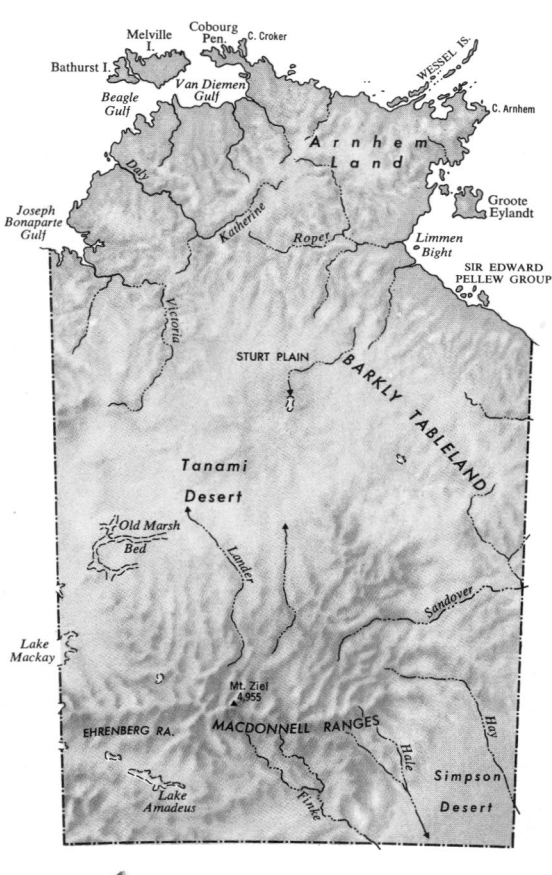

Topography

© C. S. HAMMOND & Co., Maplewood, N.J.

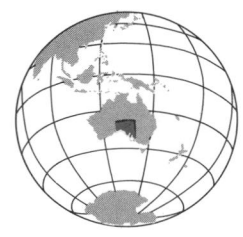

AREA 380,070 sq. mi.
POPULATION 1,247,100
CAPITAL Adelaide
LARGEST CITY Adelaide
HIGHEST POINT Mt. Woodroffe 4,970 ft.

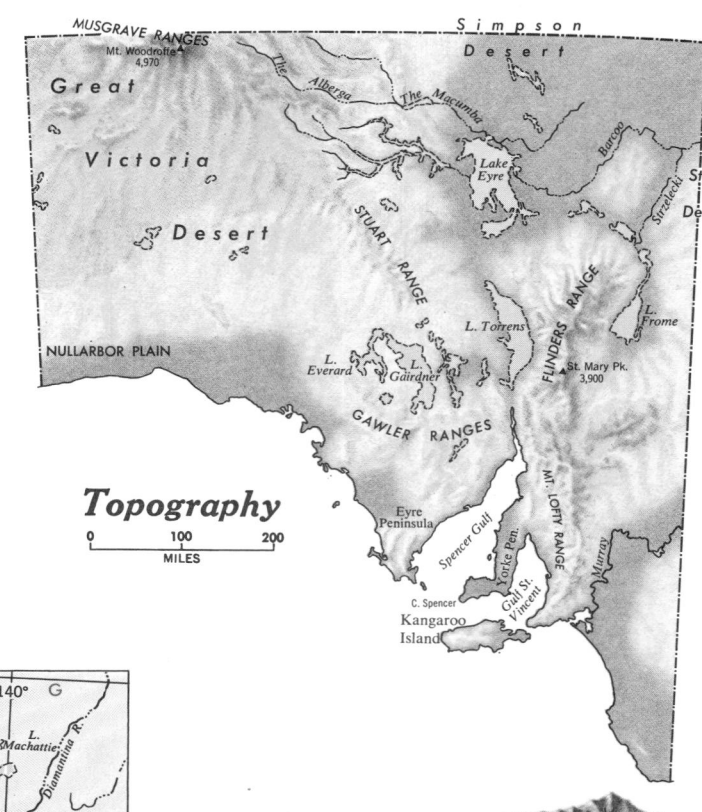

Topography

0   100   200
MILES

| Below Sea Level | 100 m. 328 ft. | 200 m. 656 ft. | 500 m. 1,640 ft. | 1,000 m. 3,281 ft. | 2,000 m. 6,562 ft. | 5,000 m. 16,404 ft. |

CITIES and TOWNS

Adelaide (cap.). ‡727,916 ..B 6
Angaston, 1,887 ....F 6
Balaklava, 1,199 ....F 6
Barmera, 1,484 ....G 6
Beachport,⊙1,903 ....F 7
Berri, 2,232 ....G 6
Bordertown, 1,758 ....G 7
Brighton, 22,620 ....A 8
Burnside, 38,758 ....B 8
Burra, 1,342 ....F 5
Campbelltown, 32,083.....B 7
Ceduna, 1,406 ....D 5
Clare, 1,579 ....F 5
Cleve, ⊙2,817 ....E 5
Colonel Light Gardens,
   3,404 ....A 8
Coober Pedy, ...D 3
Crystal Brook, 1,235 .....E 5
Elizabeth, 32,949 ....B 7
Elliston,⊙1,424 ....D 5

Enfield, 80,261 ....B 7
Gawler, 6,645 ....B 6
Gladstone, 1,035 ....F 5
Glenelg, 14,762 ....A 8
Gumeracha, ⊙2,654 .....C 7
Hindmarsh, 11,352 ......A 7
Hope Valley-Tea Tree
   Gully, ⊙21,314 ....B 7
Jamestown, 1,282 ....F 5
Kadina, 3,022 ....F 5
Kapunda, 1,119 ....F 6
Keith, 1,097 ....G 7
Kensington and Norwood,
   11,928 ....B 8
Kimba, ⊙1,703 ....E 5
Kingscote, 1,071 ....E 6
Kingston, 1,065 ....G 7
Lameroo, ⊙1,947 ....G 6
Leigh Creek, 1,014 ......F 4
Lobethal, 1,098 ....C 7
Loxton, 2,418 ....G 6
Maitland, 1,017 ....E 6

Mannum, 2,034...........F 6
Maralinga and Woomera,
   4,745 ....B 3
Marion, 66,950 ....A 8
Meadows, ⊙2,824 ....B 8
Meningie, ⊙4,104 ....F 6
Millicent, 4,533 ....F 7
Minlaton, ⊙2,504 ....E 6
Mitcham, 49,470 ....B 3
Moonta, 1,122 ....E 6
Mount Barker, 1,934 .....C 8
Mount Gambier, 17,251...G 7
Murray Bridge, 5,957 ....F 6
Nangwarry, 977 ....G 7
Naracoorte, 4,378 ....G 7
Nuriootpa, 2,041 ....F 6
Orroroo,⊙1,228 ....F 5
Payneham, 16,844 ......B 7
Penola, 1,383 ....G 7
Peterborough, 3,117 .....F 5
Pinnaroo,⊙1,717 ....G 6
Port Adelaide, 39,823 ...A 7

Port Augusta, 10,103.....E 5
Port Lincoln, 8,888 ......E 6
Port Pirie, 15,566 ....E 5
Prospect, 21,411 ....B 7
Radium Hill, ...G 5
Renmark, 6,275 ....G 6
Reynella-Port Noarlunga,
   11,818 ....A 8
Robe, ⊙941 ....F 7
Salisbury, 35,762 ....B 7
Snowtown, ⊙1,694 ......E 5
Stirling-Bridgewater,
   4,487 ....B 8
Strathalbyn, 1,449 ......F 6
Streaky Bay, ⊙2,134 ....D 5
Tailem Bend, 1,947 .....F 6
Tanunda, 1,986 ....C 6
Thebarton, 12,296 ......A 7
Tumby Bay, ⊙2,793 .....E 6
Unley, 39,727 ....B 8
Victor Harbor, 3,128 ....F 6
Waikerie, ⊙3,818 ....F 6
Wallaroo, 2,094 ....E 6
West Torrens, 46,222 ...A 8
Whyalla, 22,121 ....E 5
Willunga,⊙828 ....F 6
Wilmington, 1,449 ....F 5
Woodville, 73,878 ....A 7
Woomera and Maralinga,
   4,745 ....E 4
Yorketown,⊙2,734 ......E 6

Hack (mt.) ....F 6
Hamilton, The, (riv.) ....D 2
Harris (lake) ....D 4
Head of Bight (bay) .....B 4
Indian Ocean ....E 7
Investigator (str.) ......E 5
Investigator Group (isls.) D 5
Island (lag.) ....E 4
Jaffa (cape) ....F 7
Kangaroo (isl.), 3,375...F 7
Lacepede (bay) ....F 7
Little Para (riv.) ....B 7
Lofty (mt.) ....B 8
Macfarlane (lake) ....E 2
Macumba, The (riv.) ....D 2
Maurice (lake) ....B 3
Meramangye (lake) .....B 2
Morris (mt.) ....B 2
Mount Bold (res.) ....B 8
Murray (riv.) ....F 6
Musgrave (ranges) .....B 2
Neales, The (riv.) ......E 3
Neptune (isls.) ....E 6
Northumberland (cape) .F 7
Nukey Bluff (mt.) ....D 5
Nullarbor (plain) ....A 4
Nurrari (lakes) ....B 3
Nuyts (arch.) ....C 5
Nuyts (cape) ....C 5
Onkaparinga (riv.) ......B 8
Peera Peera Poolanna
   (lake) ....F 2
Saint Mary (peak) ......F 4
Saint Vincent (gulf) ....F 6
Serpentine (lakes) ......A 3
Simpson (des.) ....E 1
Sir Joseph Banks Group
   (isls.) ....E 6
South Para (riv.) ....C 7
Spencer (cape) ....E 6
Spencer (gulf) ....E 6
Stevenson, The (riv.) ...D 2
Streaky (bay) ....C 5
Strzelecki (creek) ......G 3
Stuart (range) ....D 3
Sturt (des.) ....G 3
Sturt (riv.) ....B 8
The Alberga (riv.) ......D 2
The Coorong (lag.) .....F 6
The Hamilton (riv.) .....D 2
The Macumba (riv.) ....D 2
The Neales (riv.) ....E 3
The Stevenson (riv.) ...D 2
The Warburton (riv.) ...F 2
Thistle (isl.) ....E 6
Torrens (lake) ....E 4
Torrens (riv.) ....B 7
Warburton, The (riv.) ..F 2
Warren (res.) ....C 7
Whidbey (isls.) ....D 6
Wilkinson (lakes) ......C 3
Wilson Bluff (prom.) ...A 4
Woodroffe (mt.) ....A 2
Wright (lake) ....A 2
Yarle (lakes) ....A 3
Yorke (pen.) ....E 6

OTHER FEATURES

Acraman (lake) ....D 5
Alberga, The (riv.) .....D 2
Alexandrina (lake) .....F 6
Anxious (bay) ....D 5
Arcakaringa (creek) ....D 2
Barcoo (creek) ....F 3
Barossa (res.) ....C 6
Birksgate (range) ......A 2
Blanche (lake) ....F 3
Brady (lake) ....D 3
Cadibarrawirracanna
   (lake) ....D 3
Callabonna (lake) ......F 3
Catastrophe (cape) ....D 6
Coffin (bay) ....D 6
Coffin Bay (pen.) ......D 6
Coopers (Barcoo) (creek) F 3
Coorong, The (lag.) ....F 6
Dey Dey (lake) ....B 3
Encounter (bay) ....F 6
Everard (lake) ....D 4
Everard (ranges) ....C 2
Eyre (pen.) ....D 5
Eyre North (lake) ......E 3
Eyre South (lake) ......E 3
Finke (riv.) ....C 1
Flinders (range) ....F 4
Frome (lake) ....G 4
Gairdner (lake) ....E 4
Gawler (ranges) ....E 5
Gawler (riv.) ....B 6
Gilles (lake) ....E 5
Goyders (lag.) ....F 2
Great Australian (bight) A 5
Great Victoria (des.) ...B 3
Gregory (lake) ....F 3

⊙ Population of district.
‡ Population of met. area.

A   **B**   132° Long.   **C**   East of Greenwich   **D**   136°   **E**   **F**   140°   **G**

NORTHERN TERRITORY

WESTERN AUSTRALIA

QUEENSLAND

NEW SOUTH WALES

VICTORIA

Simpson Desert

ABORIGINAL RESERVE

Great Victoria Desert

Nullarbor Plain

Great Australian Bight

INDIAN OCEAN

Flinders Range

Eyre Peninsula

Yorke Pen.

Kangaroo I.

ADELAIDE

Spencer G.

Gulf St. Vincent

ADELAIDE AND VICINITY

Roseworthy
Gawler
Lyndoch
Tanunda
Virginia
Elizabeth
Williamstown
Salisbury
Birdwood
Gumeracha
Hope Valley-Tea Tree Gully
Port Adelaide
Enfield
Woodville
Prospect
Campbelltown
Hindmarsh
Thebarton
Payneham
Kensington and Norwood
Lenswood
West Torrens
Lobethal
ADELAIDE
Glenelg
Unley
Burnside
Uraidla
Woodside
Marion
Mitcham
Mt. Lofty 2,384
Brighton
Colonel Light Gardens
Stirling-Bridgewater
Hahndorf
Nairne
Reynella-Port Noarlunga
Mt. Bold Res.
Mt. Barker
Noarlunga
Kangarilla
Meadows

SOUTH AUSTRALIA

SCALE OF MILES
0 25 50 100 150

KILOMETRES
0 25 50 100 150

State Capital .... ⊙
State and Territorial
Boundaries .... _ _ _ _

Copyright by C. S. Hammond & Co., N.Y.

AREA 666,991 sq. mi.
POPULATION 2,015,300
CAPITAL Brisbane
LARGEST CITY Brisbane
HIGHEST POINT Mt. Bartle Frere 5,287 ft.

CORAL SEA ISLANDS TERR.
Total Population 3

PHYSICAL FEATURES

Bougainville (reef)	C	2
Flinders (reefs)	D	3
Great Barrier (reef)	D	3
Heralds (cays)	D	3
Holmes (reef)	E	3
Marion (reef)	E	4
Osprey (reef)	C	2
Saumarez (reef)	E	4

QUEENSLAND
CITIES and TOWNS

Ascot, 16,450	E	2
Ayr, 8,674	C	3
Balmoral, 15,758	E	2
Biloela, 3,537	D	5
Bowen, 5,144	C	3
Brisbane (cap.), 656,222	D	2
Brisbane, ‡718,822	D	2
Bundaberg, 25,402	D	5
Cairns, 29,326	C	3
Caloundra, 3,657	E	5
Camp Hill, 12,392	E	3
Cardwell, ⊙5,640	C	3
Charleville, 4,871	C	5
Charters Towers, 7,602	C	4
Chermside, 26,189	D	2
Camp Hill, 12,392	E	3
Coopers Plains, 16,817	D	3
Corinda, 12,643	D	3
Dalby, 8,860	D	5
East Brisbane, 10,780	E	3
Ekibin, 13,224	D	3
Esk, ⊙6,120	E	5
Geebung, 17,850	E	2
Gladstone, 12,426	D	4
Gold Coast, 49,481	E	6
Goondiwindi, 3,529	D	6
Greenslopes, 13,351	E	3
Gympie, 11,279	E	5
Holland Park, 22,645	E	3
Home Hill, 3,507	C	3
Inala, 18,705	D	3
Indooroopilly, 15,321	D	3
Ingham, 5,354	C	3
Innisfail, 7,432	C	3
Ipswich, 54,531	E	5
Kingaroy, 5,080	D	5
Longreach, 3,871	B	4
Mackay, 24,578	D	4
Mareeba, 4,799	C	3
Maryborough, 20,393	E	5
Mary Kathleen,	A	4
Mirani, ⊙5,379	D	4
Mitchelton, 13,998	D	2
Moorooka, 16,801	D	3
Mount Isa, 16,877	A	4
Mount Morgan, 4,055	D	4
Nambour, 6,219	E	5
Newmarket, 12,212	D	2
Nundah, 15,609	E	2
Redcliffe, 27,327	E	5
Rockhampton, 46,083	D	4
Roma, 5,996	D	5
Sandgate, 22,621	D	2
Stafford, 17,692	D	2
Stanthorpe, 3,641	D	6
Taroom, ⊙3,367	D	5
Toowoomba, 52,139	D	5
Townsville, 58,847	C	3
Warwick, 10,065	D	6
Weipa,	B	2
Windsor, 14,023	D	2
Wynnum, 23,191	E	5
Yeppoon, 3,418	D	4
Yeronga, 11,769	D	3

OTHER FEATURES

Albatross (bay)	B	2
Alice (riv.)	C	4
Archer (riv.)	B	2
Balonne (riv.)	D	6
Banks (isl.)	B	1
Barcoo (creek)	B	5
Barkly Tableland	A	4
Bartle Frere (mt.)	C	3
Beal (range)	B	5
Belyando (riv.)	C	4
Bentinck (isl.)	A	3
Bigge (range)	D	5
Bowling Green (cape)	C	3
Bramble (bay)	E	2
Brisbane (riv.)	D	2
Brisbane Airport	E	2
Broad (sound)	D	4
Bulimba (creek)	E	3
Bulloo (lake)	B	6
Bulloo (riv.)	B	6
Bunker Group (isls.)	E	4
Burdekin (riv.)	C	3
Cabbage Tree (creek)	D	2
Cape York (pen.)	B	2
Capricorn (chan.)	D	4
Capricorn Group (isls.)	E	4
Carnarvon (range)	D	5
Carpentaria (gulf)	A	2

Caryapundy (swamp)	B	6
Clarke (range)	C	4
Cloncurry (riv.)	B	4
Coleman (riv.)	B	2
Comet (riv.)	D	5
Condamine (riv.)	D	5
Coopers (Barcoo) (creek)	B	5
Coral (sea)	C	1
Culgoa (riv.)	C	6
Cumberland (isls.)	D	4
Curtis (isl.)	D	4
Darling Downs	D	5
Dawson (riv.)	D	5

Diamantina (riv.)	B	4
Direction (cape)	B	2
Downfall (creek)	D	2
Drummond (range)	C	5
Duifken (pt.)	B	2
Endeavour (str.)	B	1
Enoggera (creek)	D	2
Fitzroy (riv.)	D	4
Flattery (cape)	C	2
Flinders (riv.)	B	3
Fraser (isl.)	E	5
Galilee (lake)	C	4
Georgina (riv.)	A	4

Longitude East 144° of Greenwich
PAPUA NEW GUINEA
CORAL SEA
GREAT BARRIER REEF
GULF OF CARPENTARIA
NORTHERN TERRITORY
SOUTH AUSTRALIA
NEW SOUTH WALES
Tropic of Capricorn
Copyright by C. S. Hammond & Co., N.Y.

QUEENSLAND
SCALE OF MILES
0 50 100 150 200
KILOMETRES
0 50 100 150 200
Territorial Capital ⊚
State and Territorial Boundaries

BRISBANE AND VICINITY
MILES

Topography

MILES
0 100 200

Torres Strait
Thursday I.
C. York
Cape York
Peninsula
Princess Charlotte Bay
C. Melville
Osprey Reef
Mornington I.
WELLESLEY IS.
Great Barrier Reef
Mt. Bartle Frere 5,287
GREAT DIVIDING RANGE
GREY RANGE
BEAL RANGE
BARKLY TABLELAND
Simpson Desert
Sturt Desert
Lake Yamma Yamma
Lake Eyre
Hervey Bay
Sandy C.
Fraser or Gt. Sandy I.
Broad Sd.
Capricorn Channel
Fitzroy
DARLING DOWNS
AUSTRALIA

	5,000 m.	2,000 m.	1,000 m.	500 m.	200 m.	100 m.	Sea
	16,404 ft.	6,562 ft.	3,281 ft.	1,640 ft.	656 ft.	328 ft.	Level	Below

Gilbert (riv.)	B	3
Great Dividing (range)	C	4
Great Sandy (Fraser) (isl.)	E	5
Gregory (range)	B	3
Gregory (riv.)	A	3
Grenville (cape)	B	1
Grey (range)	B	5
Halifax (bay)	C	3
Hamilton (riv.)	A	4
Hervey (bay)	E	5
Hinchinbrook (isl.)	C	3
Holroyd (riv.)	B	2
Hook (isl.)	D	4
Isaacs (riv.)	D	4
Kedron (brook)	D	2
Keerweer (cape)	B	2
Leichhardt (range)	C	4
Leichhardt (riv.)	A	3
Machattie (lake)	B	5
Macintyre (riv.)	D	6
Manifold (cape)	D	4
Maranoa (riv.)	C	5

Mary (riv.)	E	5
McIlwraith (range)	B	2
Melville (cape)	C	2
Mitchell (riv.)	B	2
Moonah (creek)	A	4
Moreton (bay)	E	5
Moreton (isl.)	E	5
Mornington (isl.)	A	3
Nicholson (riv.)	A	3
Nogoa (riv.)	C	5
Norman (creek)	D	3
Norman (riv.)	B	3
Normandy (riv.)	C	2
Northumberland (isls.)	D	4
Oxley (creek)	D	3
Palmer (riv.)	B	2
Paroo (riv.)	C	6
Peak (range)	D	4
Pera (head)	B	2
Prince of Wales (isl.)	B	1
Princess Charlotte (bay)	C	2
Sandy (cape)	E	5

Selwyn (range)	B	4
Sidmouth (cape)	C	2
Simpson (des.)	A	5
Staaten (riv.)	B	3
Sturt (des.)	B	5
Suttor (riv.)	C	4
Swain (reefs)	E	4
Thompson (riv.)	B	5
Torres (str.)	B	1
Trinity (bay)	C	3
Tully (falls)	C	3
Warrego (range)	C	5
Warrego (riv.)	C	5
Wellesley (isls.)	A	3
Whitsunday (isl.)	D	4
Wide (bay)	E	5
Willies (range)	C	5
Wilson (riv.)	B	5
Yamma Yamma (lake)	B	5
York (cape)	B	1

⊙ Population of district.
‡ Population of met. area.

NEW SOUTH WALES
AREA 309,433 sq. mi.
POPULATION 4,847,800
CAPITAL Sydney
LARGEST CITY Sydney
HIGHEST POINT Mt. Kosciusko
7,316 ft.

VICTORIA
AREA 87,884 sq. mi.
POPULATION 3,713,200
CAPITAL Melbourne
LARGEST CITY Melbourne
HIGHEST POINT Mt. Bogong
6,508 ft.

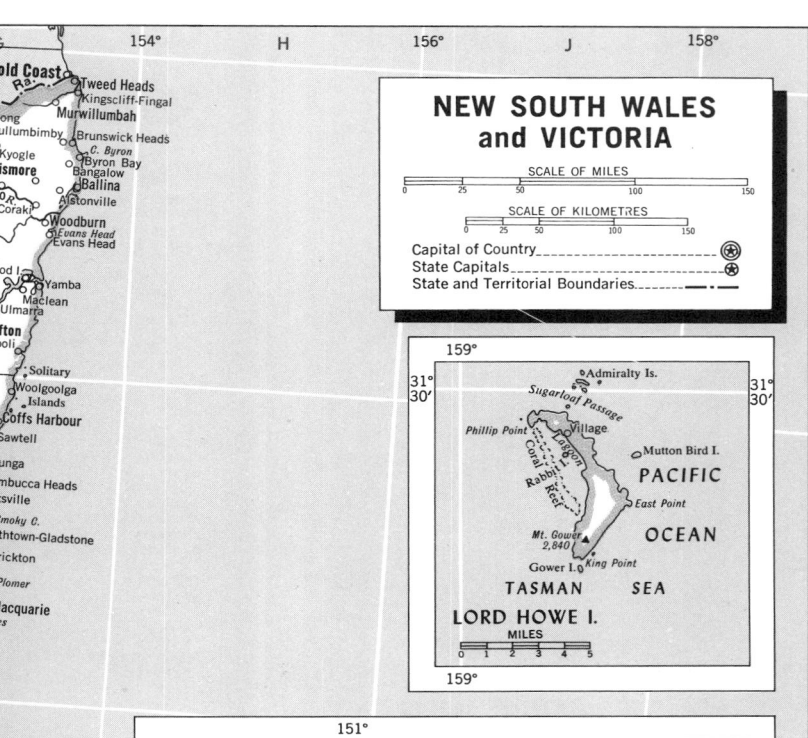

Topography

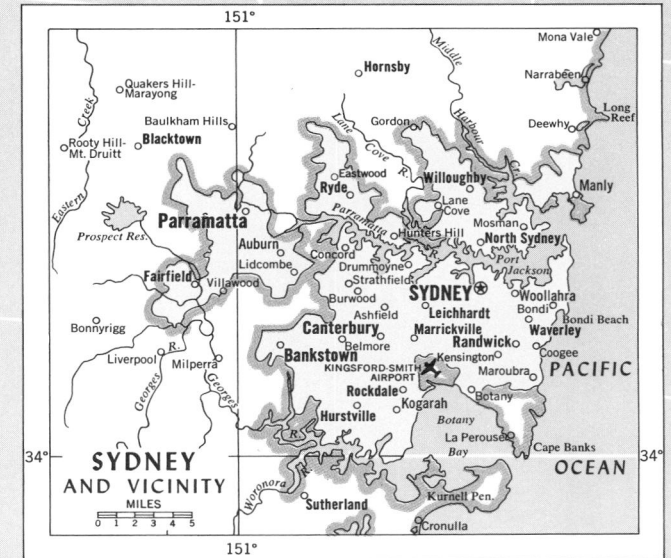

		Below Sea Level	100 m. 328 ft.	-200 m. 656 ft.	500 m. 1,640 ft.	1,000 m. 3,281 ft.	2,000 m. 6,562 ft.	5,000 m. 16,404 ft.

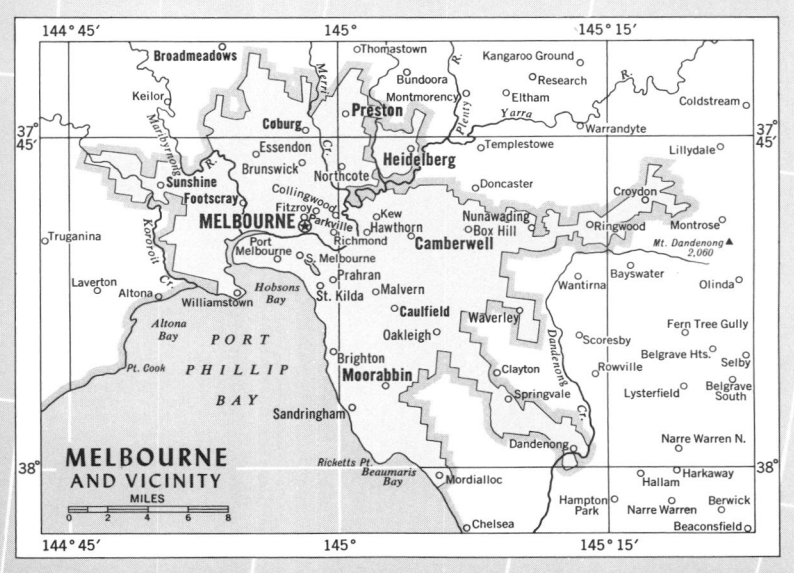

(continued on following page)

IRRIGATION AREAS AND ARTESIAN BASINS IN AUSTRALIA

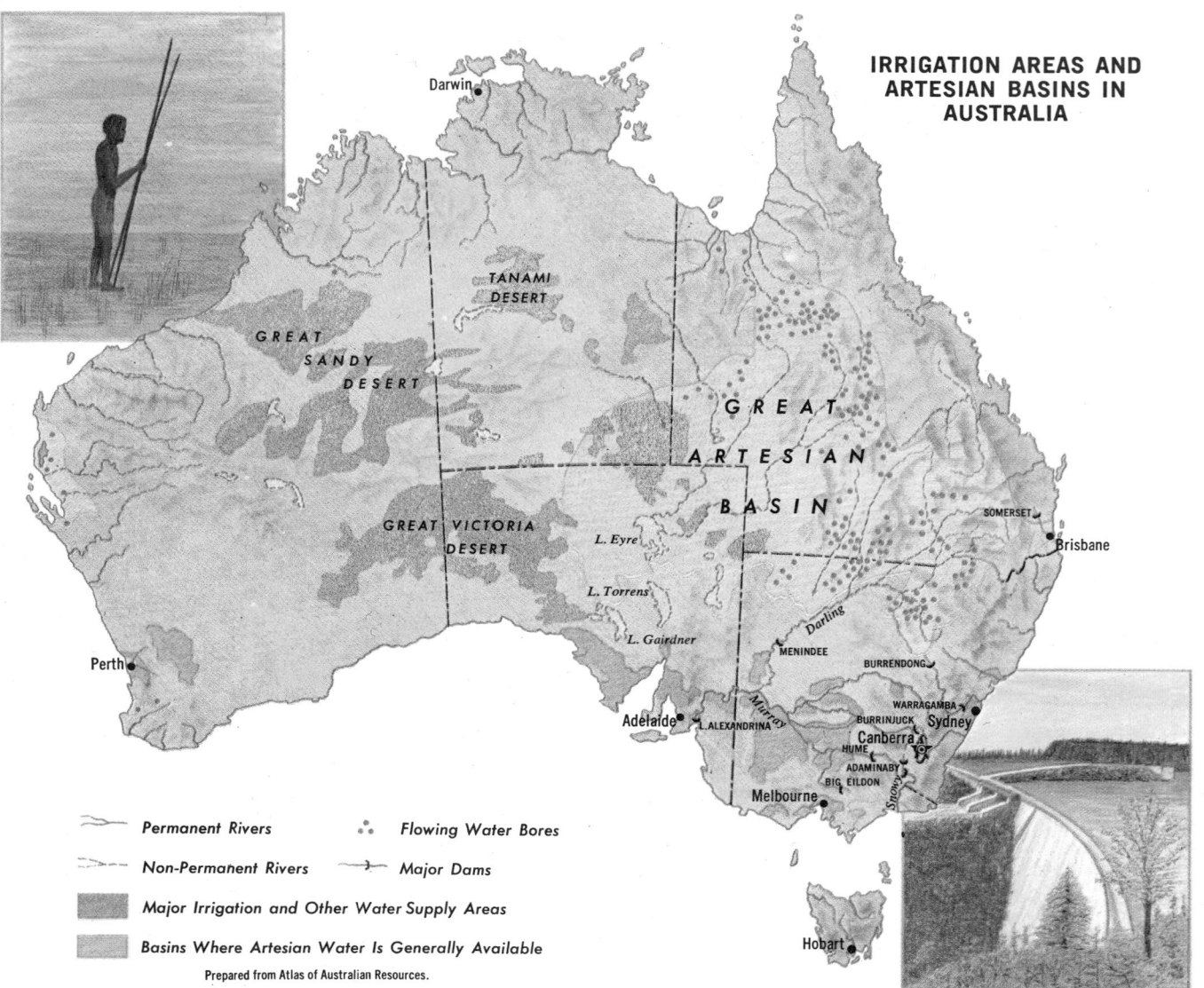

Darwin

TANAMI DESERT

GREAT SANDY DESERT

GREAT ARTESIAN BASIN

GREAT VICTORIA DESERT

L. Eyre
L. Torrens
L. Gairdner

SOMERSET

Brisbane

Perth

Darling

MENINDEE

BURRENDONG

Adelaide
L. ALEXANDRINA
Murray
WARRAGAMBA
BURRINJUCK
Sydney
Canberra
HUME
ADAMINABY
Snowy
BIG EILDON

Melbourne

Indian Ocean

Hobart

Permanent Rivers
Non-Permanent Rivers
Flowing Water Bores
Major Dams
Major Irrigation and Other Water Supply Areas
Basins Where Artesian Water Is Generally Available

Prepared from Atlas of Australian Resources.

AREA 26,383 sq. mi.
POPULATION 410,800
CAPITAL Hobart
LARGEST CITY Hobart
HIGHEST POINT Mt. Ossa 5,305 ft.

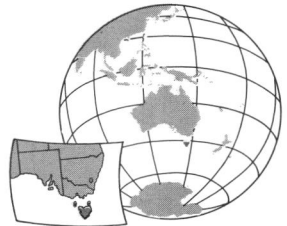

Gordon (riv.)	B 4	Long (pt.)	E 3	Pieman (riv.)	B 3	Stanley (mt.)	A 1

Gordon (riv.) ....B 4
Great (lake) ....C 3
Great Western Tiers (mts.) .C 3
Grim (cape) ....A 2
Hartz (mt.) ....C 5
Hibbs (pt.) ....B 4
High Rocky (pt.) ....B 4
Hogan Group (isls.) ....D 1
Hummock (isl.) ....D 2
Hunter (isl.) ....A 2
Hunter (isls.) ....B 2
Huon (riv.) ....C 5
Indian Ocean ....A 4
Kent Group (isls.) ....D 1
King (isl.), 2,462 ....A 1
King (riv.) ....B 4
King William (lake) ....C 4
Lake (riv.) ....D 3
Legges Tor (mt.) ....D 3
Leven (riv.) ....C 3
Lodi (cape) ....E 3
Lofty (range) ....B 3

Long (pt.) ....E 3
Low Rocky (pt.) ....B 4
Lyell (mt.) ....B 4
Maatsuyker (isls.) ....C 5
Macquarie (harb.) ....B 4
Macquarie (riv.) ....D 3
Maria (isl.) ....E 4
Marion (bay) ....E 4
Mersey (riv.) ....C 3
Munro (mt.) ....E 2
Naturaliste (cape) ....E 2
Nive (riv.) ....C 4
Norfolk (bay) ....D 4
North (pt.) ....E 1
North Bruny (isl.) ....D 5
North Esk (riv.) ....D 3
Ossa (mt.) ....C 3
Ouse (riv.) ....C 4
Oyster (bay) ....E 4
Peron (cape) ....E 4
Phoques (bay) ....A 1
Picton (mt.) ....C 5

Pieman (riv.) ....B 3
Pillar (cape) ....E 5
Port Davey (inlet) ....B 5
Portland (cape) ....D 2
Ramsey (mt.) ....B 3
Raoul (cape) ....D 5
Reid (rocks) ....B 1
Ringarooma (bay) ....D 2
Robbins (isl.) ....B 2
Rocky (cape) ....B 2
Saint Clair (lake) ....C 4
Saint Helens (pt.) ....E 2
Saint Vincent (cape) ....B 5
Sandy (cape) ....A 3
Schouten (isl.) ....E 4
Sorell (cape) ....B 4
Sorell (lake) ....D 4
South (cape) ....C 5
South Bruny (isl.) ....D 5
South East (cape) ....C 5
South Esk (riv.) ....D 3
South West (cape) ....B 5

Stanley (mt.) ....A 1
Stokes (pt.) ....A 1
Stony (head) ....C 2
Storm (bay) ....D 5
Strzelecki (mt.) ....D 2
Swan (isl.) ....E 2
Tamar (riv.) ....D 3
Tasman (head) ....D 5
Tasman (pen.) ....E 4
Tasman (sea) ....E 4
Three Hummock (isl.) ....B 2
Tooms (lake) ....D 4
Vansittart (isl.) ....E 2
Walker (isl.) ....B 2
Waterhouse (isl.) ....D 2
West (pt.) ....A 2
West Sister (isl.) ....D 1
Wickham (cape) ....A 1

⊙ Population of district.
‡ Population of met. area.

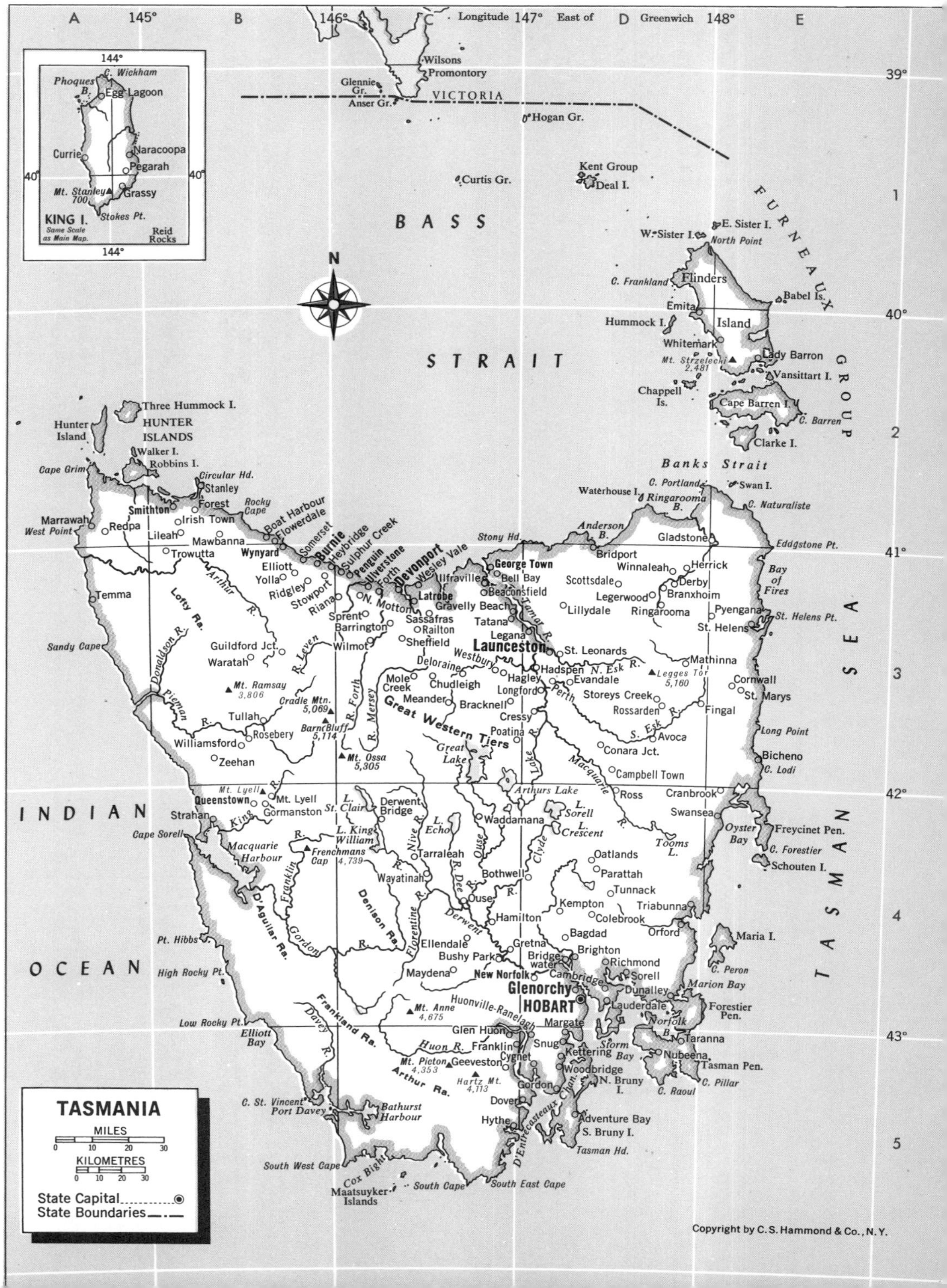

Topography

0   30   60
MILES

CITIES and TOWNS

Adventure Bay, ...D 5
Avoca, ...D 3
Bagdad, ...D 4
Barrington, ...C 3
Beaconsfield, 1,028 ....C 3
Bell Bay, ...D 3
Bicheno, ...E 3
Boat Harbour, ...B 2
Bothwell, ⊙1,008 ....C 4
Bracknell, ...D 3
Branxholm, ...D 3
Bridgewater, ...D 4
Bridport, ...D 3
Brighton, 1,150 ....D 4
Burnie, 15,806 ....B 3
Bushy Park, ...C 4
Cambridge, ...D 4
Campbell Town, ⊙1,753 ....D 3
Chudleigh, ...C 3
Colebrook, ...D 4
Conara Junction, ...D 3
Cornwall, ...E 3
Cranbrook, ...D 3
Cressy, ...C 3
Currie, ...A 1
Cygnet, ...C 5
Deloraine, 1,793 ....C 3
Derby, ...D 3
Derwent Bridge, ...C 4
Devonport, 14,874 ....C 3
Dover, ...C 5
Dunalley, ...D 4
Egg Lagoon, ...A 1
Ellendale, ...C 4
Elliott, ...B 3
Emita, ...D 2
Evandale, ⊙1,554 ....D 3
Fingal, ⊙3,791 ....E 3
Flowerdale, ...B 2
Forest, ...B 2
Forth, ...C 3
Franklin, ...C 5
George Town, 4,086 ....C 3
Glenorchy, 37,770 ....D 4
Gormanston, ⊙540 ....B 4
Hamilton, ⊙4,329 ....C 4
Hobart (cap.), 53,257 ....D 4
Hobart, ‡119,469 ....D 4
Latrobe, 2,241 ....C 3
Lauderdale, 916 ....D 4
Launceston, 37,217 ....D 3
Launceston, ‡60,456 ....D 3
Lillydale, ⊙7,841 ....D 3
Longford, 1,688 ....C 3
New Norfolk, 5,770 ....C 4
Oatlands, ⊙2,501 ....D 4
Penguin, 2,149 ....C 3
Perth, 1,002 ....D 3
Queenstown, 4,295 ....B 4
Richmond, ⊙1,658 ....D 4
Ringarooma, ⊙2,866 ....D 3

Rosebery, 1,774 ....B 3
Ross, ⊙617 ....D 4
Saint Leonards, ⊙13,660 ....D 3
Scottsdale, 1,698 ....D 3
Smithton, 2,698 ....A 2
Somerset, 2,236 ....B 3
Sorell, 1,652 ....D 4
Strahan, ⊙470 ....B 4
Temma, ...A 3
Ulverstone, 6,842 ....C 3
Waratah, ⊙698 ....B 3
Westbury, ⊙4,964 ....C 3
Wynyard, 3,355 ....B 3
Zeehan, 1,017 ....B 3

OTHER FEATURES

Anderson (bay) ....D 2
Anne (mt.) ....C 4
Anser Group (isls.) ....C 1
Arthur (lake) ....D 4
Arthur (range) ....C 5
Arthur (riv.) ....B 3
Babel (isls.) ....E 1
Banks (str.) ....D 2
Barn Bluff (mt.) ....C 4
Barren (cape) ....E 2
Bass (str.) ....C 1
Bathurst (harb.) ....B 5
Cape Barren (isl.) ....E 2
Chappell (isls.) ....D 2
Circular (head) ....B 2
Clarke (isl.) ....E 2
Clyde (riv.) ....C 4
Cox (bight) ....B 5
Cradle (mt.) ....C 3
Crescent (lake) ....C 4
Curtis Group (isls.) ....C 1
D'Aguilar (range) ....B 4
Davey (riv.) ....B 4
Deal (isl.) ....D 1
Dee (riv.) ....C 4
Denison (range) ....B 4
D'Entrecasteaux (chan.) ....D 5
Derwent (riv.) ....C 4
Donaldson (riv.) ....B 3
East Sister (isl.) ....E 1
Echo (lake) ....C 4
Eddystone (pt.) ....E 2
Elliott (bay) ....B 5
Fires (bay) ....E 3
Florence (riv.) ....B 4
Forestier (cape) ....E 4
Forestier (pen.) ....E 4
Forth (riv.) ....C 3
Frankland (cape) ....D 1
Frankland (range) ....B 4
Franklin (riv.) ....B 4
Frenchmans Cap (mt.) ....B 4
Freycinet (pen.) ....E 4
Furneaux Group (isls.),
..............1,234 ....E 1

Copyright by C.S. Hammond & Co., N.Y.

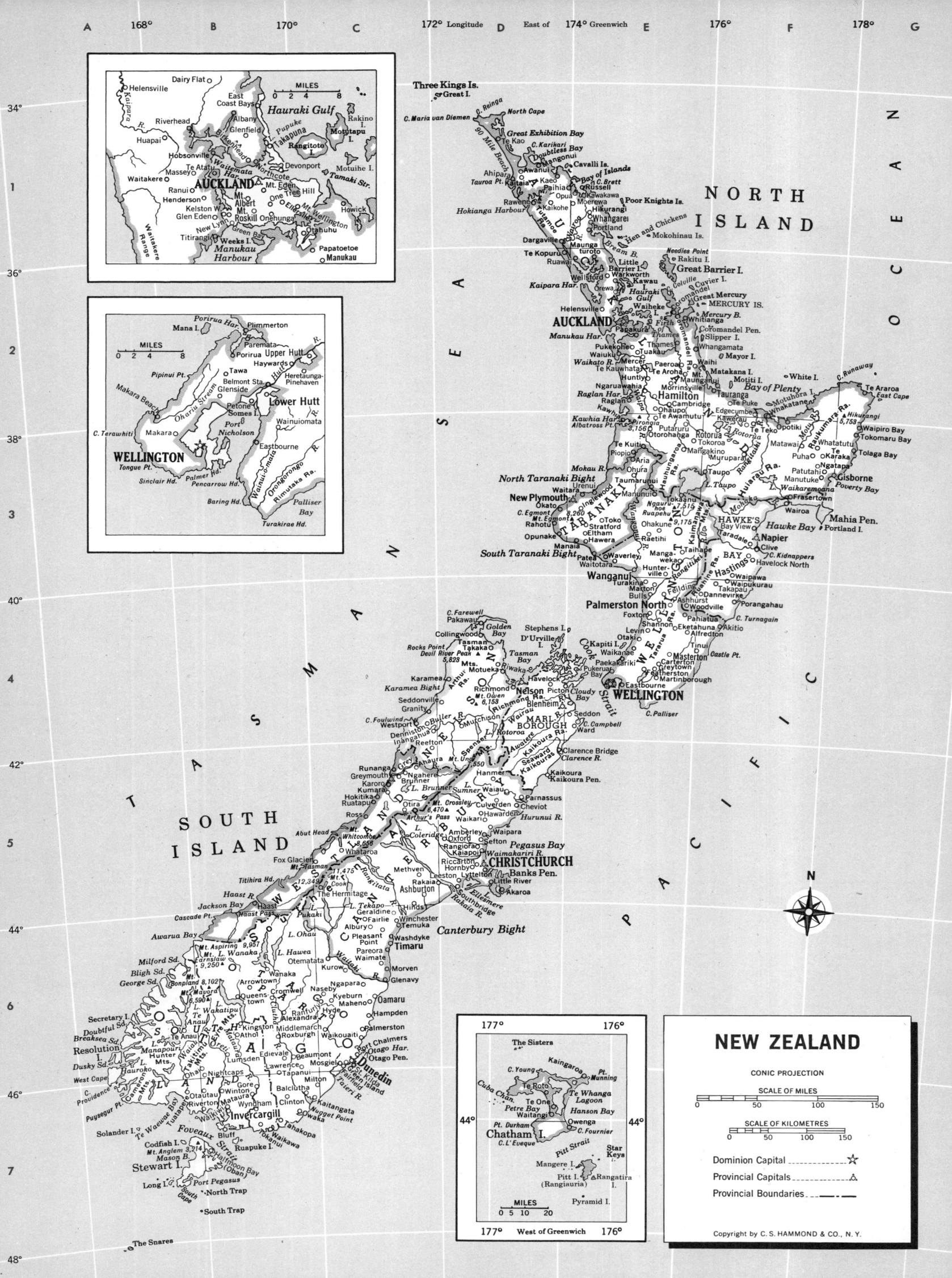

NEW ZEALAND

CONIC PROJECTION

SCALE OF MILES

SCALE OF KILOMETRES

Dominion Capital .... ☆

Provincial Capitals .... △

Provincial Boundaries .... ─ ─ ─

Copyright by C. S. HAMMOND & CO., N.Y.

Topography

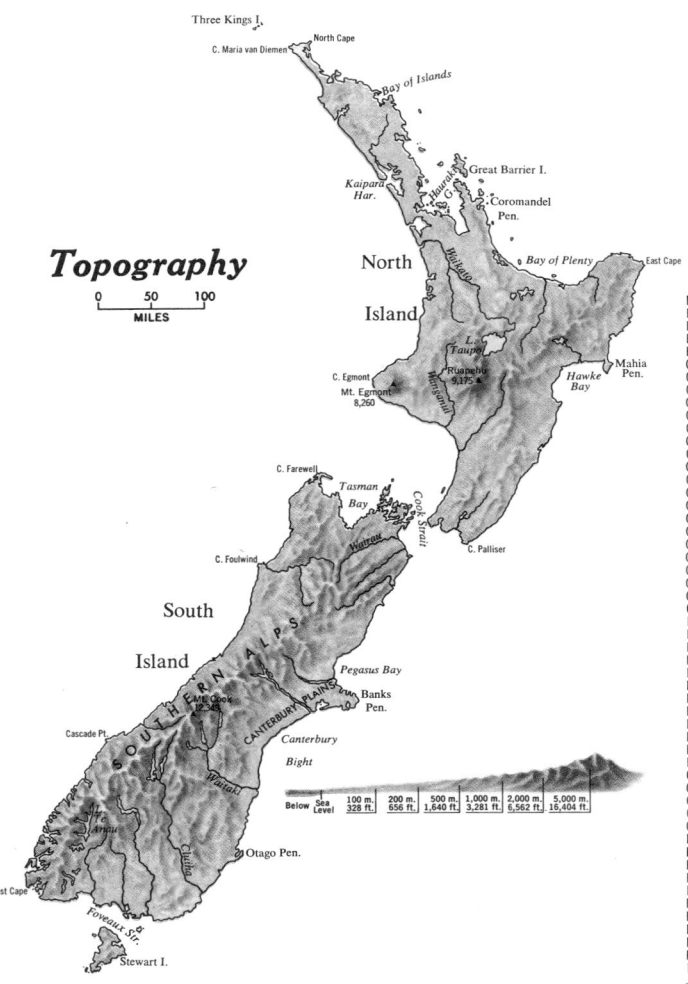

Three Kings I.
North Cape
C. Maria van Diemen
Bay of Islands
North Island
Kaipara Har.
Great Barrier I.
Coromandel Pen.
Bay of Plenty
East Cape
L. Taupo
Ruapehu 9,175
C. Egmont
Mt. Egmont 8,260
Hawke Bay
Mahia Pen.
C. Farewell
Tasman Bay
Cook Strait
C. Palliser
C. Foulwind
South Island
SOUTHERN ALPS
Pegasus Bay
Banks Pen.
Canterbury Bight
CANTERBURY PLAINS
Cascade Pt.
West Cape
Otago Pen.
Foveaux Str.
Stewart I.

0 50 100
MILES

Below Sea Level | 100 m. 328 ft. | 200 m. 656 ft. | 500 m. 1,640 ft. | 1,000 m. 3,281 ft. | 2,000 m. 6,562 ft. | 5,000 m. 16,404 ft.

AREA 103,736 sq. mi.
POPULATION 3,121,904
CAPITAL Wellington
LARGEST CITY Auckland
HIGHEST POINT Mt. Cook 12,349 ft.
MONETARY UNIT New Zealand dollar
MAJOR LANGUAGES English, Maori
MAJOR RELIGION Protestantism

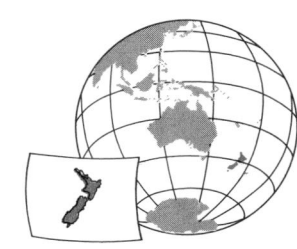

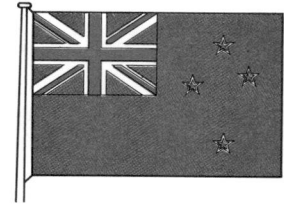

DISTRICTS

Auckland (prov. dist.), 1,189,811 .... E 2
Canterbury (prov. dist.), 385,981 .... C 5
Hawke's Bay (prov. dist.), 128,300 .... F 3
Marlborough (prov. dist.), 30,200 .... D 4
Nelson (prov. dist.), 68,300 .... D 4
Otago (prov. dist.), 290,100 .... A 6
Otago (land dist.), 183,200 .... B 6
Southland (land dist.), 106,900 .... A 6
Taranaki (prov. dist.), 101,200 .... E 3
Wellington (prov. dist.), 537,100 .... E 4
Westland (prov. dist.), 24,100 .... C 5

CITIES and TOWNS

Alexandra, 3,160 .... B 6
Ashburton, 12,950 .... C 5
Ashhurst, 922 .... E 4
Massey .... B 1
Auckland, 152,200 .... B 1
Auckland, 1588,400 .... B 1
Balclutha, 4,570 .... B 7
Bay View, 945 .... F 3
Belmont Hill, 1,119 .... B 2
Birkenhead, 12,800 .... B 1
Blenheim, 13,950 .... D 4
Bluff, 3,300 .... B 7
Bulls, 1,803 .... E 4
Cambridge, 6,060 .... E 2
Carterton, 3,640 .... E 4
Christchurch, 165,000 .... D 5
Christchurch, †256,300 .... D 5
Clive, 1,017 .... F 3
Cromwell, 1,062 .... B 6
Dannevirke, 5,780 .... E 4
Dargaville, 3,910 .... D 1
Devonport, 11,100 .... C 1
Dunedin, 77,800 .... C 6
Dunedin, †109,800 .... C 6
Eastbourne, 4,610 .... B 3
East Coast Bays, 13,150 .... C 1
Edgecumbe, 1,277 .... F 2
Ellerslie, 4,260 .... B 1
Eltham, 2,319 .... E 3
Fairfield, 1,106 .... C 6
Featherston, 1,857 .... E 4
Feilding, 9,360 .... E 4
Foxton, 2,830 .... E 4
Geraldine, 1,876 .... C 6
Gisborne, 25,600 .... G 3
Gisborne, †28,500 .... G 3
Glen Eden, 6,230 .... B 1
Glenfield, 16,450 .... B 1
Gore, 8,380 .... B 7
Green Bay, 2,022 .... B 1
Green Island, 5,990 .... C 7
Greymouth, 8,590 .... C 5
Greytown, 1,715 .... E 4
Hamilton, 67,700 .... E 2
Hamilton, 168,000 .... E 2
Hastings, 28,100 .... F 3
Hastings, †39,200 .... F 3
Havelock North, 5,950 .... F 3
Hawera, 8,210 .... E 3
Helensville, 1,305 .... E 2
Henderson, 5,780 .... C 1
Heretaunga-Pinehaven, 4,990 .... C 2
Hikurangi, 1,091 .... E 1
Hobsonville, 1,612 .... B 1
Hokitika, 3,310 .... C 5
Hornby, 6,780 .... D 5
Howick, 9,890 .... C 1
Huntly, 5,420 .... E 2
Hutt, †118,400 .... B, C 2
Inglewood, 2,003 .... E 3
Invercargill, 45,300 .... B 7
Invercargill, †47,800 .... B 7
Kaiapoi, 3,610 .... D 5
Kaikohe, 3,120 .... D 1
Kaikoura, 1,571 .... D 4
Kaitaia, 3,110 .... D 1
Kaitangata, 1,208 .... B 7
Kawakawa, 1,032 .... E 1
Kawerau, 6,010 .... F 3
Kelston West, 5,490 .... B 1
Levin, 11,950 .... E 4
Lower Hutt, 58,700 .... C 2
Lyttelton, 3,510 .... D 5
Mangakino, 1,466 .... E 3
Manukau, 84,700 .... C 1
Martinborough, 1,462 .... E 4
Marton, 4,780 .... E 4
Massey .... B 1
Masterton, 17,950 .... E 4
Mataura, 2,720 .... B 7
Milton, 1,861 .... C 7
Moerewa, 1,090 .... E 1
Morrinsville, 4,530 .... E 2
Mosgiel, 8,100 .... C 6
Motueka, 3,840 .... D 4
Mount Albert, 25,700 .... B 1
Mount Eden, 18,400 .... B 1
Mount Maunganui, 7,210 .... F 2
Mount Roskill, 34,400 .... B 1
Mount Wellington, 19,650 .... C 1
Murupara, 2,670 .... F 3
Napier, 36,700 .... F 3
Napier, 139,900 .... F 3
Nelson, 27,900 .... D 4
Nelson, †28,400 .... D 4
New Lynn, 10,150 .... B 1
New Plymouth, 32,300 .... D 3
New Plymouth, †35,800 .... D 3
Ngaruawahia, 3,790 .... E 2
Northcote, 8,640 .... B 1
Oamaru, 13,350 .... C 6
Ohai, 939 .... A 6
Ohakune, 1,458 .... E 3
One Tree Hill, 12,900 .... B 1
Onehunga, 16,050 .... B 1
Opotiki, 2,560 .... F 3
Opua, 151 .... D 1
Orewa, 1,357 .... E 2
Otahuhu, 10,000 .... C 1
Otaki, 3,660 .... E 4
Otematata, 3,890 .... B 6
Otorohanga, 1,951 .... E 3
Paekakariki, 1,934 .... C 2
Pahiatua, 2,590 .... E 4
Palmerston North, 49,200 .... E 4
Palmerston North, 150,900 .... E 4
Papakura, 12,950 .... C 2
Papatoetoe, 21,400 .... C 1
Patea, 2,013 .... E 3
Petone, 10,200 .... C 2
Picton, 2,610 .... D 4
Pinehaven (Heretaunga-Pinehaven), 4,990 .... C 2
Plimmerton-Paremata, 3,910 .... B 2
Porirua, 24,900 .... B 2
Port Chalmers, 3,040 .... C 6
Pukekohe, 6,800 .... E 2
Pukerua Bay, 1,220 .... E 4
Putaruru, 4,500 .... E 3
Queenstown, 1,634 .... B 6
Raetihi, 1,376 .... E 3
Raglan, 1,019 .... E 2
Ranfurly, 946 .... B 6
Rangiora, 4,270 .... D 5
Ranui, 1,897 .... B 1
Reefton, 1,730 .... C 5
Riccarton, 7,220 .... D 5
Richmond, 4,870 .... D 4
Riverton, 1,258 .... A 7
Riwaka, 993 .... D 4
Rotorua, 27,600 .... F 3
Rotorua, †35,300 .... F 3
Runanga, 1,683 .... C 5
Saint Kilda, 6,720 .... C 7
Shannon, 1,544 .... E 4
Stratford, 5,470 .... E 3
Taihape, 2,880 .... E 3
Takapuna, 23,800 .... C 1
Taradale .... F 3
Taumarunui, 6,080 .... E 3
Taupo, 8,530 .... E 3
Tauranga, 25,500 .... F 2
Tauranga, †33,500 .... F 2
Tawa, 10,200 .... B 2
Te Anau, 951 .... A 6
Te Aroha, 3,220 .... E 2
Te Atatu .... B 1
Te Awamutu, 6,780 .... E 2
Te Karaka, 637 .... F 3
Te Kuiti, 4,830 .... E 3
Temuka, 3,190 .... C 6
Te Puke, 3,090 .... F 2
Thames, 5,680 .... E 2
The Hermitage, 306 .... C 6
Timaru, 27,800 .... C 6
Timaru, †28,400 .... C 6
Titirangi, 5,740 .... B 1
Tokoroa, 12,450 .... E 2
Tuakau, 1,677 .... E 2
Tuatapere, 954 .... A 7
Upper Hutt, 19,750 .... C 2
Waihi, 3,500 .... E 2
Waikanae, 1,570 .... E 4
Waimate, 3,300 .... C 6
Wainuiomata, 15,000 .... B 3
Waipawa, 1,848 .... F 3
Waipukurau, 3,670 .... F 4
Wairoa, 5,700 .... F 3
Waitangi, 179 .... D 7
Waitara, 4,870 .... E 3
Waiuku, 1,759 .... E 2
Wanganui, 36,400 .... E 3
Wanganui, †38,500 .... E 3
Warkworth, 1,200 .... E 2
Waverley, 1,062 .... E 3
Wellington (capital), 134,400 .... A 3
Wellington, †175,500 .... A 3
Wellsford, 1,431 .... E 2
Westport, 5,230 .... C 4
Whakatane, 9,080 .... F 2
Whangarei, 29,600 .... E 1
Whangarei, †31,600 .... E 1
Winton, 1,740 .... B 7
Woodville, 1,529 .... F 4

OTHER FEATURES

Abut (head) .... B 5
Arthur (range) .... D 4
Arthur's (pass) .... C 5
Aspiring (mt.) .... A 6
Awarua (bay) .... A 6
Banks (pen.) .... D 5
Bligh (sound) .... A 6
Breaksea (sound) .... A 6
Bream (bay) .... E 1
Brett (cape) .... E 1
Brunner (lake) .... C 5
Buller (river) .... D 4
Cameron (mts.) .... A 7
Campbell (cape) .... E 4
Canterbury (bight) .... D 6
Cascade (point) .... A 6
Castle (point) .... F 4
Chatham, 467 .... D 7
Chatham (isls.), 520 .... D 7
Christina (mt.) .... B 6
Clarence (river) .... E 5
Cloudy (bay) .... E 4
Clutha (river) .... B 6
Codfish (isl.) .... A 7
Coleridge (lake) .... C 5
Colville (cape) .... E 2
Cook (mt.) .... C 5
Cook (strait) .... E 4
Coromandel (pen.) .... E 2
Coromandel (range) .... E 2
Crossley (mt.) .... C 5
Cuvier (isl.), 12 .... E 2
D'Urville (isl.), 91 .... D 4
Devil River (peak) .... D 4
Durham (pt.) .... D 7
Dusky (sound) .... A 6
Earnslaw (mt.) .... B 6
East (cape) .... G 2
Egmont (mt.) .... D 3
Ellesmere (lake) .... D 6
Eyre (mts.) .... B 6
Farewell (cape) .... D 4
Foulwind (cape) .... C 4
Foveaux (strait) .... A 7
George (sound) .... A 6
Golden (bay) .... D 4
Great Barrier (isl.), 272 .... F 2
Great Mercury (isl.), 7 .... E 2
Grey (river) .... C 5
Hauhangaroa (range) .... E 3
Hauraki (gulf) .... E 2
Hawea (lake) .... B 6
Hawke's (bay) .... F 3
Hen and Chickens (isls.) .... E 1
Hikurangi (mt.) .... G 2
Hokianga (harb.) .... D 1
Hunter (mts.) .... A 6
Hurunui (river) .... D 5
Hutt (river) .... C 2
Islands, Bay of (bay) .... E 1
Jackson (bay) .... A 6
Kaikoura (range) .... D 4
Kaikoura (pen.) .... D 5
Kaimanawa (mts.) .... E 3
Kaipara (harb.) .... D 2
Kapiti (isl.), 2 .... E 4
Karamea (bight) .... C 4
Karikari (cape) .... D 1
Kawau (isl.), 103 .... E 2
Kawhia (harb.) .... E 3
Kidnappers (cape) .... F 3
Little Barrier (isl.), 4 .... E 2
Mahia (pen.) .... G 3
Mana (isl.), 5 .... B 2
Manapouri (lake) .... A 6
Manukau (harb.) .... D 2
Maria van Diemen (cape) .... D 1
Mason (bay) .... A 7
Matakana (isl.), 396 .... F 2
Mataura (river) .... B 6
Mayor (isl.), 47 .... F 2
Mercury (bay) .... F 2
Mercury (isls.), 7 .... F 2
Milford (sound) .... A 6
Mokau (river) .... E 3
Mokohinau (isls.), 7 .... E 1
Motiti (isl.) .... F 2
Mothurora (isl.) .... E 1
Motuihe (isl.), 6 .... C 1
Motutapu (isl.), 27 .... C 1
Munning (point) .... E 7
Needles (point) .... E 4
Ninety-Mile (beach) .... D 1
North (isl.), 1,956,411 .... F 1
North Taranaki (bight) .... D 3
Nugget (point) .... C 7
Ohariu (stream) .... B 2
Otago (pen.), ... C 6
Owen (mt.) .... D 4
Palliser (bay) .... C 3
Palliser (cape) .... E 4
Pegasus (bay) .... D 5
Pitt (isl.), 53 .... E 7
Plenty (bay) .... F 2
Poor Knights (isls.) .... E 1
Port Nicholson (inlet) .... B 3
Port Pegasus (inlet) .... B 7
Portland (isl.), 14 .... G 3
Poverty (bay) .... G 3
Pukaki (lake) .... B 6
Pupuke (lake) .... B 1
Puysegur (point) .... A 7
Pyramid (isl.) .... E 7
Rakino (isl.), 5 .... C 1
Rakitu (isl.), 2 .... E 2
Rangatira (isl.) .... E 7
Rangiauria (Pitt) (isl.), 53 .... E 7
Rangitoto (isl.), 48 .... C 1
Raukumara (range) .... F 3
Reinga (cape) .... D 1
Resolution (isl.) .... A 6
Richmond (range) .... D 4
Rimutaka (range) .... B 3
Rocks (point) .... C 4
Rotorua (lake) .... F 2
Ruahine (range) .... E 4
Ruapehu (mt.) .... E 3
Ruapuke (isl.) .... B 7
Runaway (cape) .... G 2
Secretary (isl.) .... A 6
Slipper (isl.), 4 .... F 2
Somes (isl.), 2 .... B 2
South (isl.), 798,681 .... B 5
South Taranaki (bight) .... D 3
Southern Alps (range) .... C 5
Spenser (mts.) .... D 5
Stephens (isl.), 9 .... D 4
Stewart (isl.), 332 .... A 7
Sumner (lake) .... D 5
Taieri (river) .... C 7
Tasman (bay) .... D 4
Tasman (mt.) .... C 5
Tasman (sea) .... E 3
Taupo (lake) .... E 3
Tauroa (point) .... D 1
Te Anau (lake) .... A 6
Tekapo (lake) .... C 5
Three Kings (isls.) .... C 1
Titihiri (head) .... B 5
Tongue (point) .... A 3
Turnagain (cape) .... F 4
Tutumoe (range) .... D 1
Una (mt.) .... D 5
Waiau (river) .... A 6
Waiheke (isl.), 2,013 .... E 2
Waikato (river) .... E 2
Waimakariri (river) .... D 5
Wairau (river) .... D 4
Wairoa (river) .... E 1
Waitaki (river) .... B 6
Wakatipu (lake) .... B 6
Wanaka (lake) .... B 6
Wanganui (river) .... E 3
West (cape) .... A 6
Whitcombe (mt.) .... C 5
White (isl.) .... F 2

†Population of urban area.

Agriculture, Industry and Resources

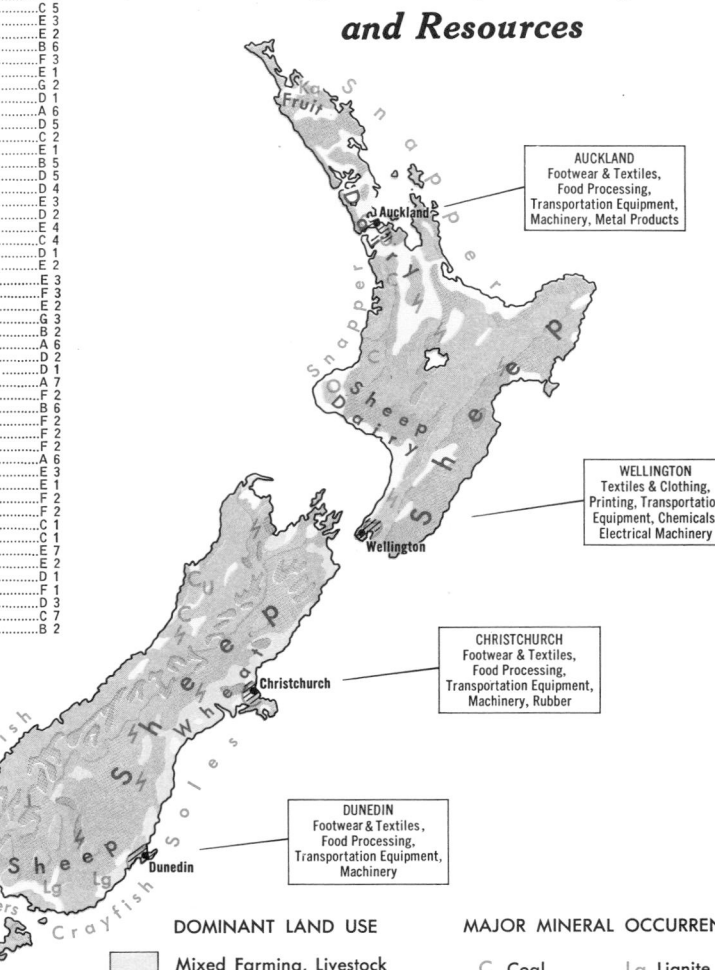

AUCKLAND
Footwear & Textiles, Food Processing, Transportation Equipment, Machinery, Metal Products

WELLINGTON
Textiles & Clothing, Printing, Transportation Equipment, Chemicals, Electrical Machinery

CHRISTCHURCH
Footwear & Textiles, Food Processing, Transportation Equipment, Machinery, Rubber

DUNEDIN
Footwear & Textiles, Food Processing, Transportation Equipment, Machinery

DOMINANT LAND USE

Mixed Farming, Livestock
Dairy
Truck Farming, Horticulture
Pasture Livestock (chiefly sheep)
Livestock Herding
Forests
Nonagricultural Land

MAJOR MINERAL OCCURRENCES

C Coal
J Jade
Ka Kaolin
Lg Lignite
O Petroleum
U Uranium

⚡ Water Power
▨ Major Industrial Areas

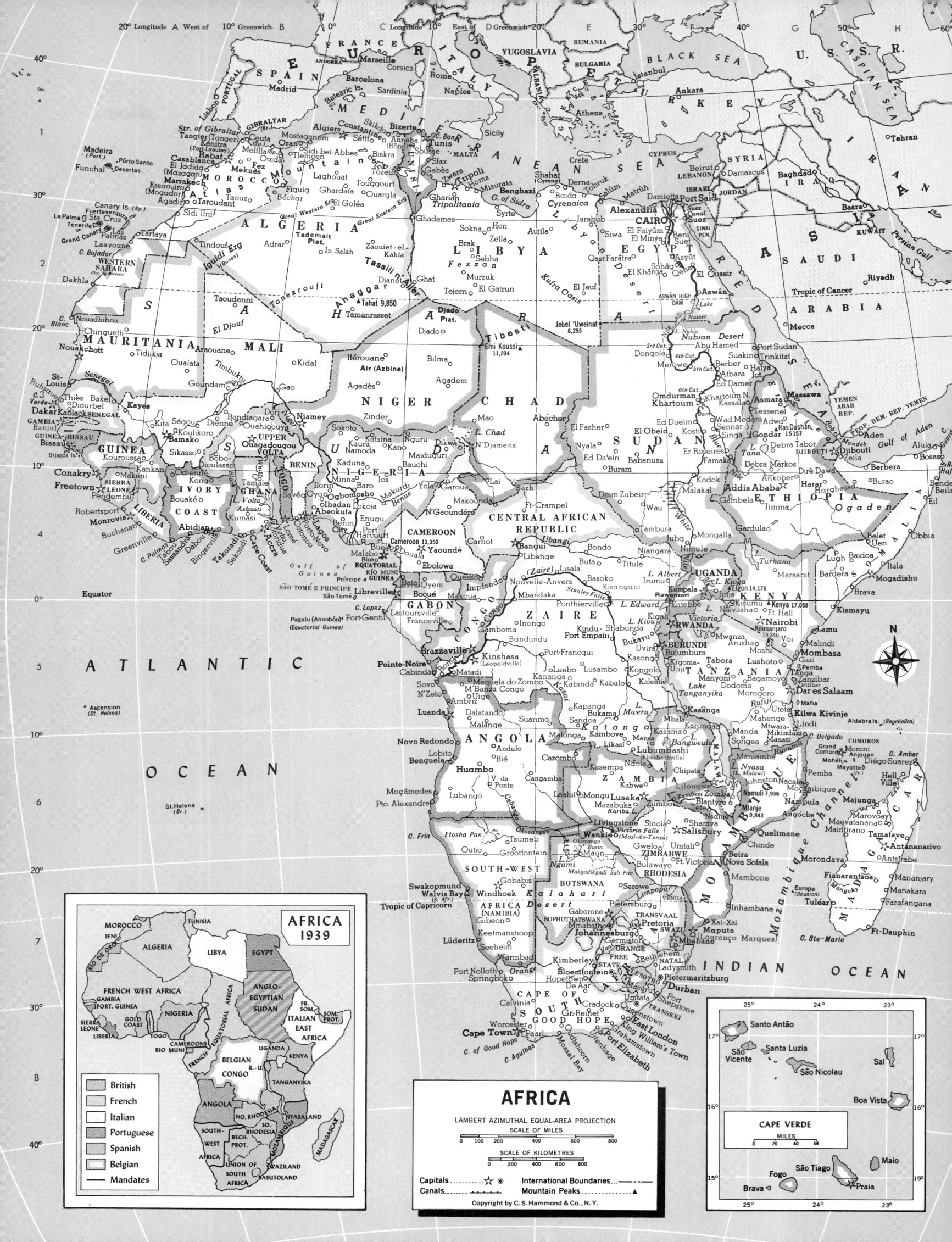

AFRICA

LAMBERT AZIMUTHAL EQUAL-AREA PROJECTION

SCALE OF MILES

0   100   200   400   600   800

SCALE OF KILOMETRES

0   200   400   600   800

Capitals............ ☆ ◉   International Boundaries........ — — —

Canals............ ⊢⊣   Mountain Peaks............. ▲

Copyright by C. S. Hammond & Co., N.Y.

AFRICA 1939

British
French
Italian
Portuguese
Spanish
Belgian
— Mandates

CAPE VERDE

MILES

0   20   40   60

POPULATION DISTRIBUTION

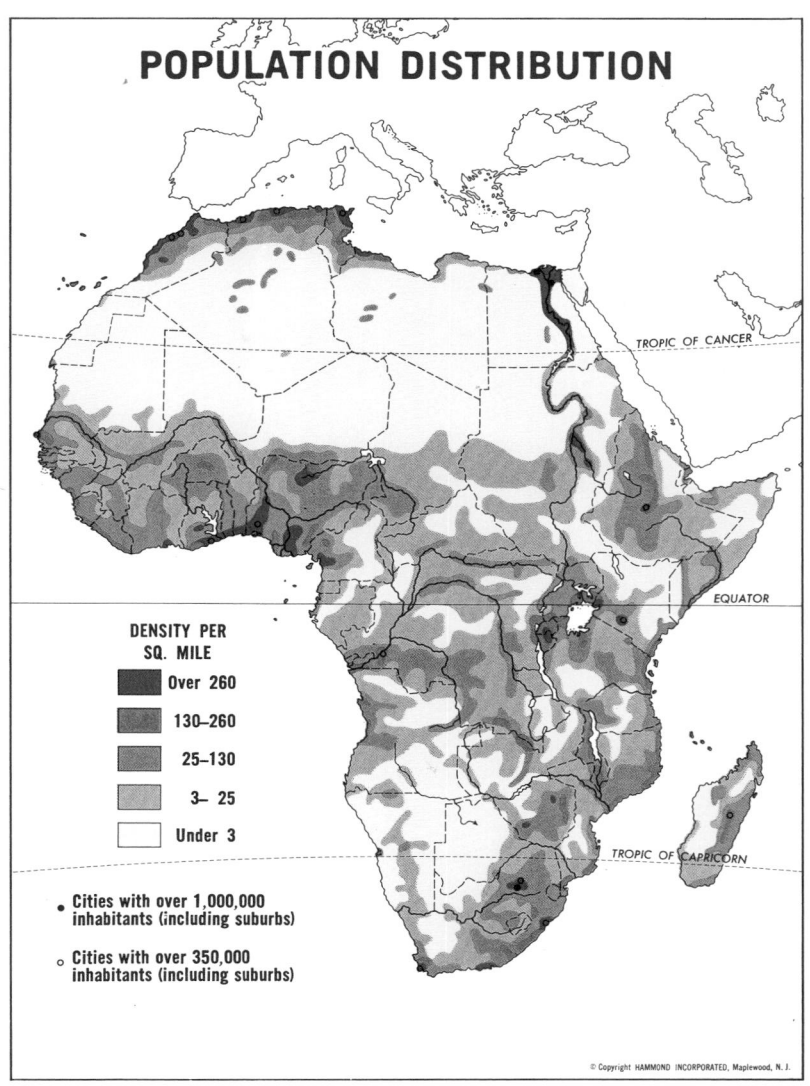

DENSITY PER SQ. MILE

- Over 260
- 130–260
- 25–130
- 3– 25
- Under 3

● Cities with over 1,000,000 inhabitants (including suburbs)

○ Cities with over 350,000 inhabitants (including suburbs)

© Copyright HAMMOND INCORPORATED, Maplewood, N. J.

AREA 11,707,000 sq. mi.
POPULATION 431,900,000
LARGEST CITY Cairo
HIGHEST POINT Kilimanjaro 19,340 ft.
LOWEST POINT Qattara Depression -436 ft.

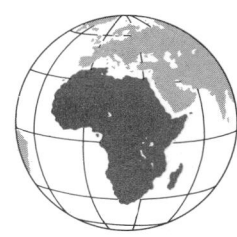

VEGETATION

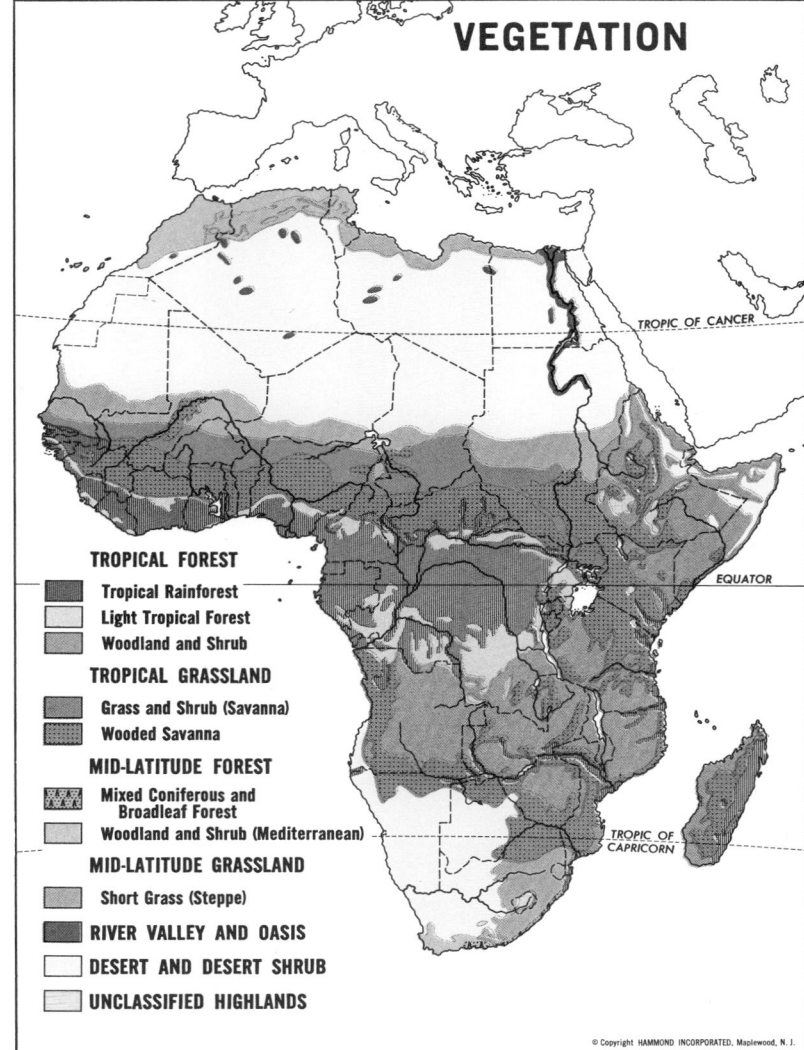

TROPICAL FOREST

- Tropical Rainforest
- Light Tropical Forest
- Woodland and Shrub

TROPICAL GRASSLAND

- Grass and Shrub (Savanna)
- Wooded Savanna

MID-LATITUDE FOREST

- Mixed Coniferous and Broadleaf Forest
- Woodland and Shrub (Mediterranean)

MID-LATITUDE GRASSLAND

- Short Grass (Steppe)

RIVER VALLEY AND OASIS

DESERT AND DESERT SHRUB

UNCLASSIFIED HIGHLANDS

© Copyright HAMMOND INCORPORATED, Maplewood, N. J.

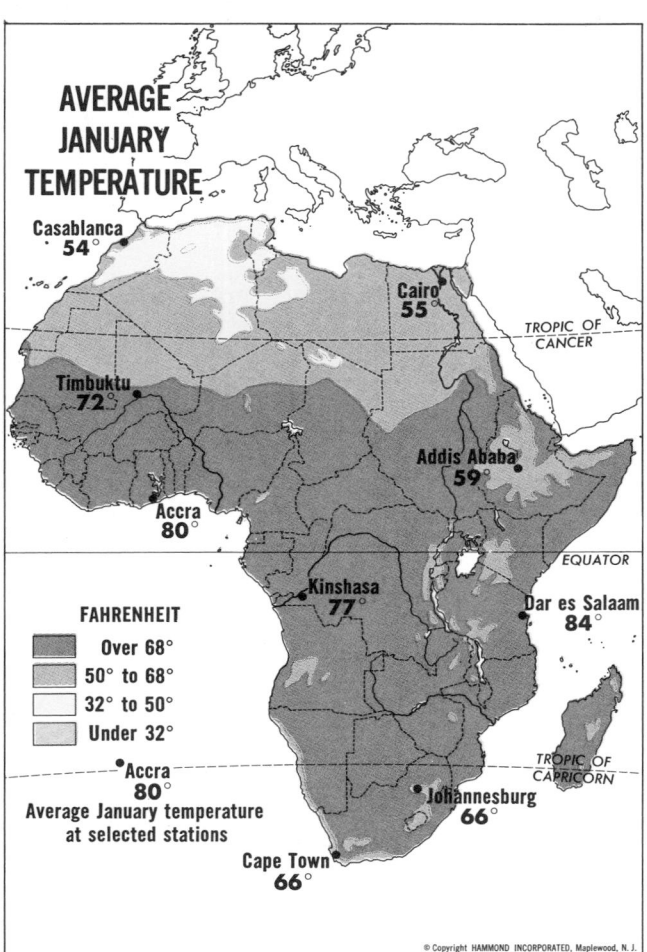

AVERAGE JANUARY TEMPERATURE

Casablanca 54°
Cairo 55°
Timbuktu 72°
Accra 80°
Addis Ababa 59°
Kinshasa 77°
Dar es Salaam 84°
Johannesburg 66°
Cape Town 66°

TROPIC OF CANCER
EQUATOR
TROPIC OF CAPRICORN

FAHRENHEIT
Over 68°
50° to 68°
32° to 50°
Under 32°

Accra 80°
Average January temperature at selected stations

© Copyright HAMMOND INCORPORATED, Maplewood, N.J.

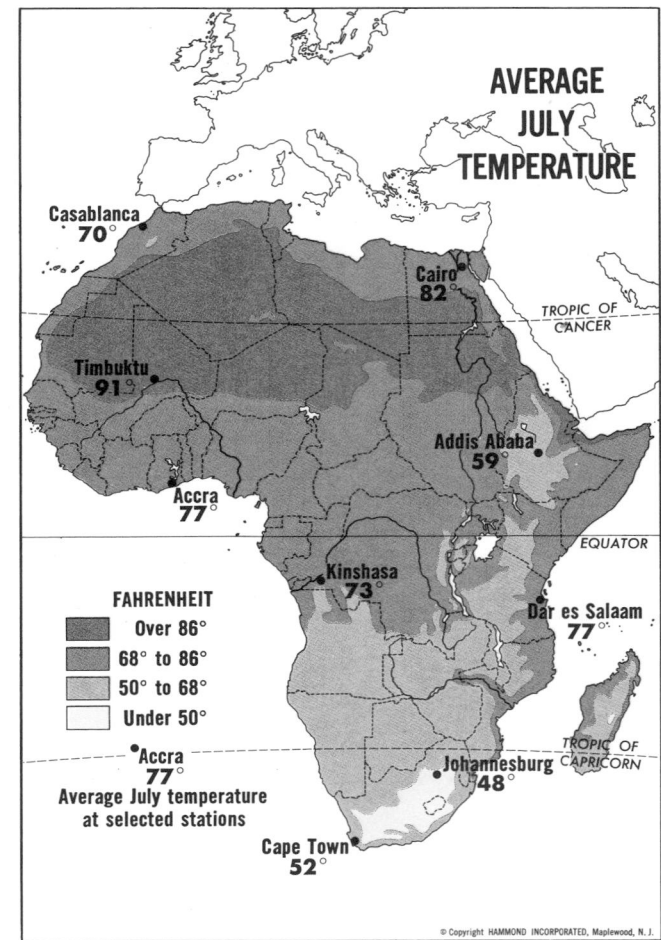

AVERAGE JULY TEMPERATURE

Casablanca 70°
Cairo 82°
Timbuktu 91°
Accra 77°
Addis Ababa 59°
Kinshasa 73°
Dar es Salaam 77°
Johannesburg 48°
Cape Town 52°

TROPIC OF CANCER
EQUATOR
TROPIC OF CAPRICORN

FAHRENHEIT
Over 86°
68° to 86°
50° to 68°
Under 50°

Accra 77°
Average July temperature at selected stations

© Copyright HAMMOND INCORPORATED, Maplewood, N.J.

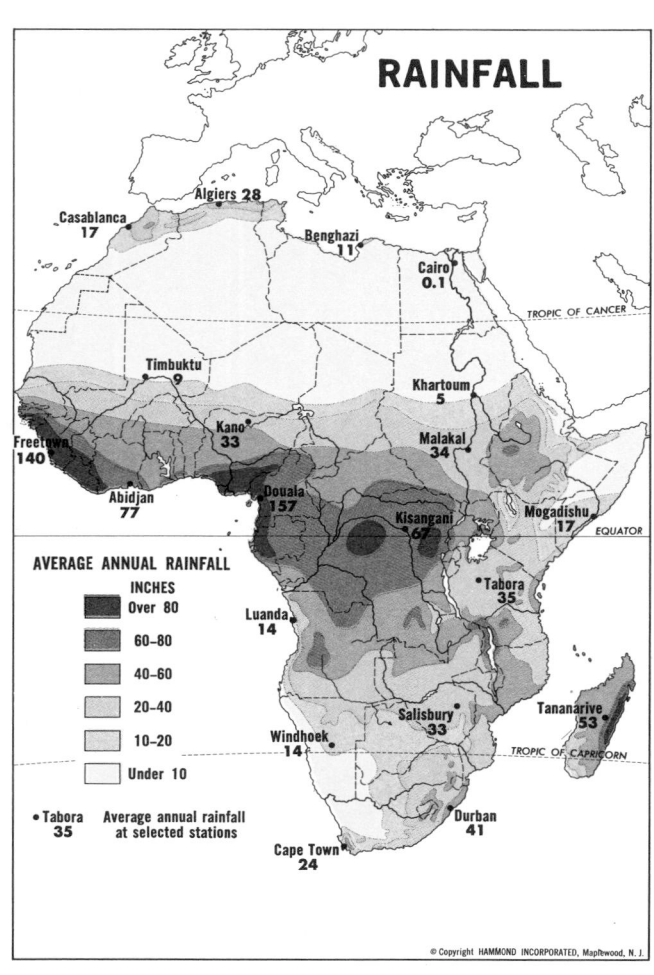

RAINFALL

Algiers 28
Casablanca 17
Benghazi 11
Cairo 0.1
Timbuktu 9
Khartoum 5
Kano 33
Malakal 34
Freetown 140
Abidjan 77
Douala 157
Kisangani 67
Mogadishu 17
Luanda 14
Tabora 35
Salisbury 33
Tananarive 53
Windhoek 14
Durban 41
Cape Town 24

TROPIC OF CANCER
EQUATOR
TROPIC OF CAPRICORN

AVERAGE ANNUAL RAINFALL
INCHES
Over 80
60–80
40–60
20–40
10–20
Under 10

• Tabora 35   Average annual rainfall at selected stations

© Copyright HAMMOND INCORPORATED, Maplewood, N.J.

VEGETATION/RELIEF

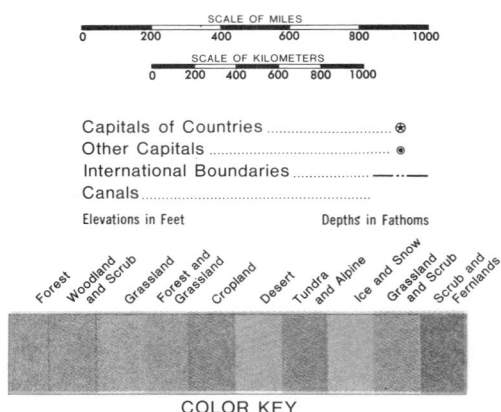

SCALE OF MILES
0   200   400   600   800   1000

SCALE OF KILOMETERS
0   200   400   600   800   1000

Capitals of Countries .... ⊛
Other Capitals .... ⊛
International Boundaries .... — ·· —
Canals ....

Elevations in Feet   Depths in Fathoms

Forest
Woodland and Scrub
Grassland
Forest and Grassland
Cropland
Desert
Tundra and Alpine
Ice and Snow
Grassland and Scrub
Scrub and Fernlands

COLOR KEY

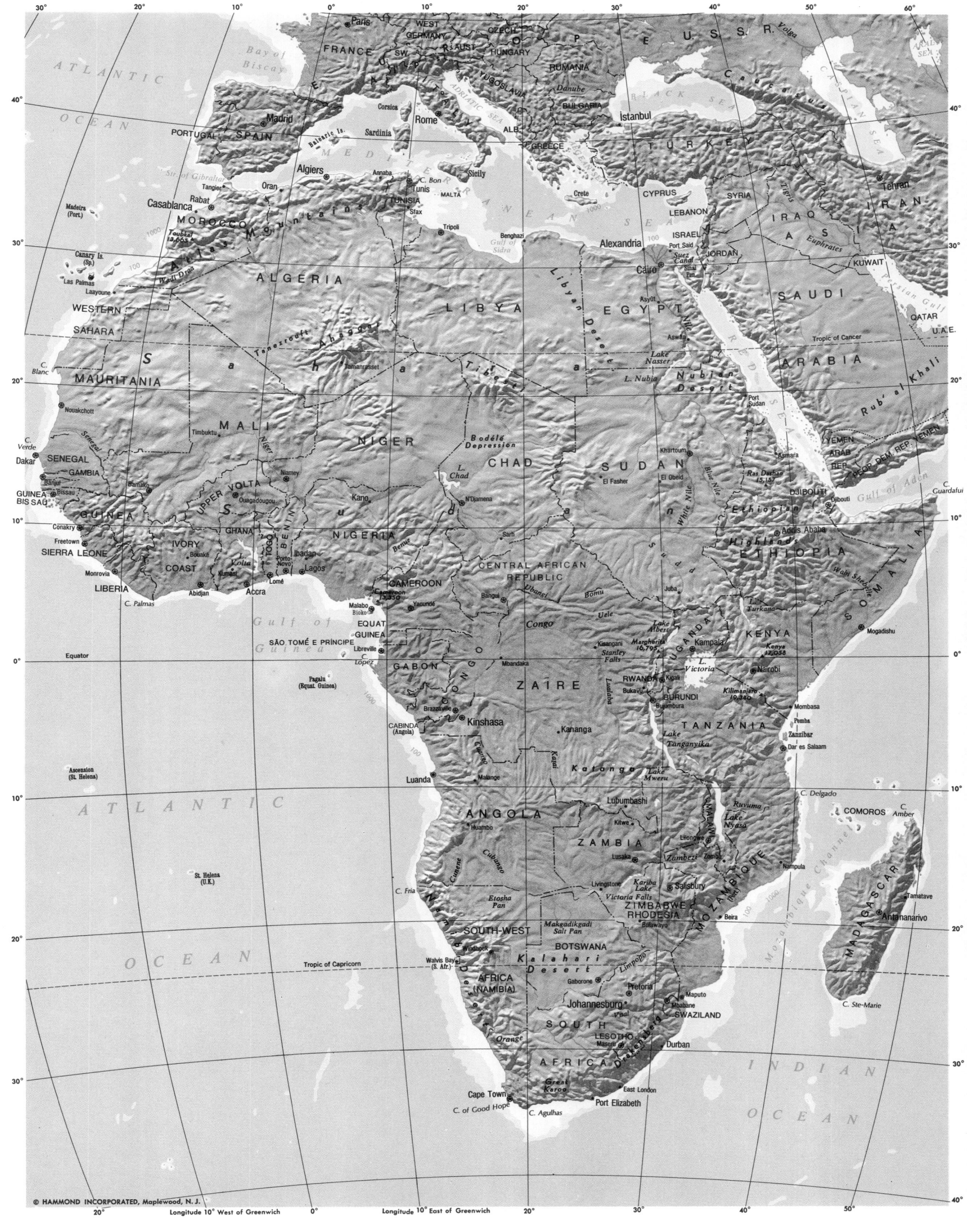

WESTERN AFRICA

CONIC EQUAL AREA PROJECTION

SCALE OF MILES

0 100 200 400

SCALE OF KILOMETERS

0 100 200 400

Capitals of Countries _ _ _ ☆   International Boundaries _____
Other Capitals _ _ _ _ ◉   Internal Boundaries _ _ _ _

© C. S. HAMMOND & Co., Maplewood, N. J.

CAPE VERDE

Santo Antão
São Vicente
Mindelo
Santa Luzia
São Nicolau

NORTH

ATLANTIC

OCEAN

São Tiago
Praia
Brava
Fogo

Sal
Sta. Maria
Sal Rei
Boa Vista
Maio

MILES

0 25 50 75 100

ALGERIA
AREA 919,591 sq. mi.
POPULATION 16,776,000
CAPITAL Algiers
LARGEST CITY Algiers
HIGHEST POINT Tahat 9,850 ft.
MONETARY UNIT Algerian dinar
MAJOR LANGUAGES Arabic, Berber, French
MAJOR RELIGION Islam

BENIN
AREA 43,483 sq. mi.
POPULATION 3,200,000
CAPITAL Porto-Novo
LARGEST CITY Cotonou
HIGHEST POINT Atakora Mts. 2,083 ft.
MONETARY UNIT CFA franc
MAJOR LANGUAGES Fon, Somba, Yoruba, Bariba, French, Mina, Dendi
MAJOR RELIGIONS Tribal religions, Islam, Roman Catholicism

CAPE VERDE
AREA 1,557 sq. mi.
POPULATION 302,000
CAPITAL Praia
LARGEST CITY Praia
HIGHEST POINT 9,281 ft.
MONETARY UNIT Cape Verde escudo
MAJOR LANGUAGE Portuguese
MAJOR RELIGION Roman Catholicism

GAMBIA
AREA 4,127 sq. mi.
POPULATION 524,000
CAPITAL Bathurst
LARGEST CITY Bathurst
HIGHEST POINT 100 ft.
MONETARY UNIT dalasi
MAJOR LANGUAGES Mandingo, Fulani, Wolof, English, Malinke
MAJOR RELIGIONS Islam, Tribal religions, Christianity

GHANA
AREA 92,099 sq. mi.
POPULATION 9,900,000
CAPITAL Accra
LARGEST CITY Accra
HIGHEST POINT Togo Hills 2,900 ft.
MONETARY UNIT new cedi
MAJOR LANGUAGES Twi, Fante, Dagbani, Ewe, Ga, English, Hausa, Akan
MAJOR RELIGIONS Tribal religions, Christianity, Islam

GUINEA
AREA 94,925 sq. mi.
POPULATION 4,500,000
CAPITAL Conakry
LARGEST CITY Conakry
HIGHEST POINT Nimba Mts. 6,070 ft.
MONETARY UNIT syli
MAJOR LANGUAGES Fulani, Mandingo, Susu, French
MAJOR RELIGIONS Islam, Tribal religions

GUINEA-BISSAU
AREA 13,948 sq. mi.
POPULATION 517,000
CAPITAL Bissau
LARGEST CITY Bissau
HIGHEST POINT 689 ft.
MONETARY UNIT Guinea-Bissau peso
MAJOR LANGUAGES Balante, Fulani, Crioulo, Mandingo, Portuguese
MAJOR RELIGIONS Islam, Tribal religions, Roman Catholicism

IVORY COAST
AREA 127,520 sq. mi.
POPULATION 6,673,013
CAPITAL Abidjan
LARGEST CITY Abidjan
HIGHEST POINT Nimba Mts. 5,745 ft.
MONETARY UNIT CFA franc
MAJOR LANGUAGES Bale, Bete, Senufu, French, Dioula
MAJOR RELIGIONS Tribal religions, Islam

LIBERIA
AREA 43,000 sq. mi.
POPULATION 1,600,000
CAPITAL Monrovia
LARGEST CITY Monrovia
HIGHEST POINT Wutivi 5,584 ft.
MONETARY UNIT Liberian dollar
MAJOR LANGUAGES Kru, Kpelle, Bassa, Vai, English
MAJOR RELIGIONS Christianity, Tribal religions, Islam

MALI
AREA 464,873 sq. mi.
POPULATION 5,800,000
CAPITAL Bamako
LARGEST CITY Bamako
HIGHEST POINT Hombori Mts. 3,789 ft.
MONETARY UNIT Mali franc
MAJOR LANGUAGES Bambara, Senufu, Fulani, Soninke, French
MAJOR RELIGIONS Islam, Tribal religions

MAURITANIA
AREA 397,354 sq. mi.
POPULATION 1,140,000
CAPITAL Nouakchott
LARGEST CITY Nouakchott
HIGHEST POINT 2,972 ft.
MONETARY UNIT ouguiya
MAJOR LANGUAGES Arabic, French, Wolof, Tukolor
MAJOR RELIGION Islam

MOROCCO
AREA 172,413 sq. mi.
POPULATION 16,800,000
CAPITAL Rabat
LARGEST CITY Casablanca
HIGHEST POINT Jeb. Toubkal 13,665 ft.
MONETARY UNIT dirham
MAJOR LANGUAGES Arabic, Berber, French
MAJOR RELIGIONS Islam, Judaism, Christianity

NIGER
AREA 489,189 sq. mi.
POPULATION 4,700,000
CAPITAL Niamey
LARGEST CITY Niamey
HIGHEST POINT Banguezane 6,234 ft.
MONETARY UNIT CFA franc
MAJOR LANGUAGES Hausa, Songhai, Fulani, French, Tamashek, Djerma
MAJOR RELIGIONS Islam, Tribal religions

NIGERIA
AREA 379,628 sq. mi.
POPULATION 83,800,000
CAPITAL Lagos
LARGEST CITY Lagos
HIGHEST POINT Vogel 6,700 ft.
MONETARY UNIT naira
MAJOR LANGUAGES Hausa, Yoruba, Ibo, Ijaw, Fulani, Tiv, Kanuri, Ibibio, English, Edo
MAJOR RELIGIONS Islam, Christianity, Tribal religions

SÃO TOMÉ E PRÍNCIPE
AREA 372 sq. mi.
POPULATION 80,000
CAPITAL São Tomé
LARGEST CITY São Tomé
HIGHEST POINT Pico 6,640 ft.
MONETARY UNIT São Tomean escudo
MAJOR LANGUAGES Bantu languages, Portuguese
MAJOR RELIGIONS Tribal religions, Roman Catholicism

SENEGAL
AREA 75,954 sq. mi.
POPULATION 5,085,388
CAPITAL Dakar
LARGEST CITY Dakar
HIGHEST POINT Futa Jallon 1,640 ft.
MONETARY UNIT CFA franc
MAJOR LANGUAGES Wolof, Peul (Fulani), French, Mende, Mandingo, Dida
MAJOR RELIGIONS Islam, Tribal religions, Roman Catholicism

SIERRA LEONE
AREA 27,925 sq. mi.
POPULATION 3,100,000
CAPITAL Freetown
LARGEST CITY Freetown
HIGHEST POINT Loma Mts. 6,390 ft.
MONETARY UNIT leone
MAJOR LANGUAGES Mende, Temne, Vai, English, Krio (pidgin)
MAJOR RELIGIONS Tribal religions, Islam, Christianity

TOGO
AREA 21,622 sq. mi.
POPULATION 2,300,000
CAPITAL Lomé
LARGEST CITY Lomé
HIGHEST POINT Agou 3,445 ft.
MONETARY UNIT CFA franc
MAJOR LANGUAGES Ewe, French, Twi, Hausa
MAJOR RELIGIONS Tribal religions, Roman Catholicism, Islam

TUNISIA
AREA 63,170 sq. mi.
POPULATION 5,776,000
CAPITAL Tunis
LARGEST CITY Tunis
HIGHEST POINT Jeb. Chambi 5,066 ft.
MONETARY UNIT Tunisian dinar
MAJOR LANGUAGES Arabic, French
MAJOR RELIGION Islam

UPPER VOLTA
AREA 105,869 sq. mi.
POPULATION 6,144,013
CAPITAL Ouagadougou
LARGEST CITY Ouagadougou
HIGHEST POINT 2,352 ft.
MONETARY UNIT CFA franc
MAJOR LANGUAGES Mossi, Lobi, French, Samo, Gourounsi
MAJOR RELIGIONS Islam, Tribal religions, Roman Catholicism

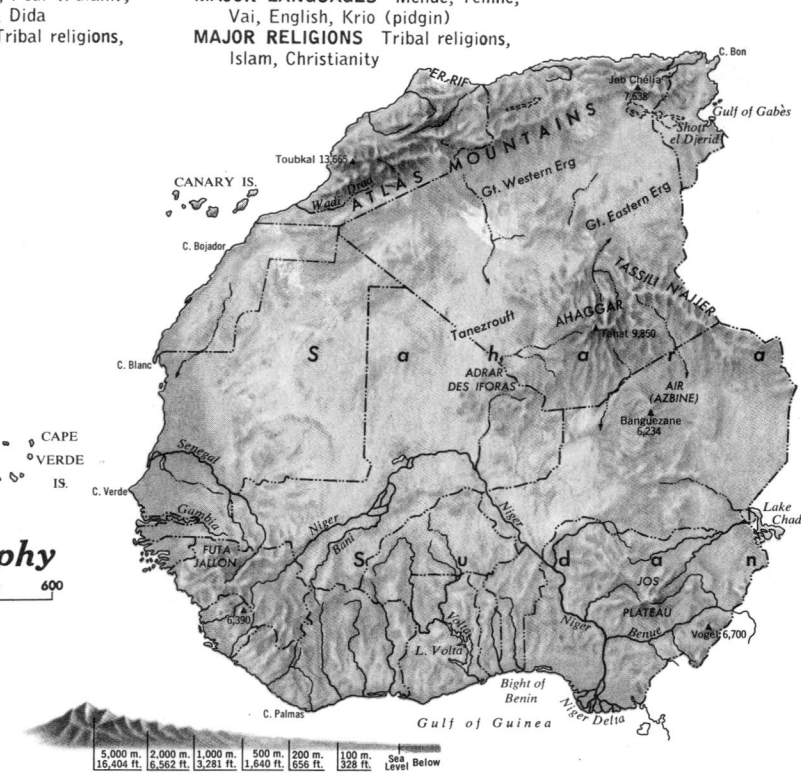

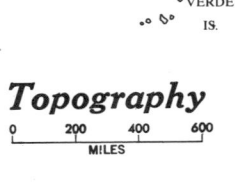

Topography

0   200   400   600
MILES

5,000 m. 2,000 m. 1,000 m. 500 m. 200 m. 100 m. Sea
16,404 ft. 6,562 ft. 3,281 ft. 1,640 ft. 656 ft. 328 ft. Level Below

(continued on following page)

(continued)

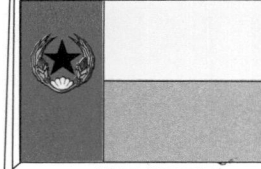

ALGERIA · BENIN · CAPE VERDE · GAMBIA · GHANA · GUINEA · GUINEA-BISSAU · IVORY COAST · LIBERIA · MALI · MAURITANIA · MOROCCO · NIGER · NIGERIA · SÃO TOMÉ E PRÍNCIPE · SENEGAL · SIERRA LEONE · TOGO · TUNISIA · UPPER VOLTA

ALGERIA

CITIES and TOWNS

Abadla, 7,288 .... D 2
Adrar, 13,332 .... D 3
Aïn-Béïda, 30,757 .... F 1
Aïn-Sefra, 16,818 .... D 2
Aïn-Témouchent, 33,481 .... D 1
Algiers (cap.), 943,142 .... E 1
Algiers, *1,800,000 .... E 1
Amguid .... F 3
Annaba, 152,006 .... F 1
Annaba, *223,000 .... F 1
Aoulef, 11,285 .... E 3
Arak .... E 3
Batna, 69,090 .... F 1
Béchar, 46,505 .... D 2
Béjaïa, 64,876 .... F 1
Beni-Abbès, 3,943 .... D 2
Beni-Ounif, 5,271 .... D 2
Beni-Saf, 23,368 .... D 1
Berga .... E 3
Bidon 5 (Poste Maurice Cordier) .... E 4
Biskra, 59,275 .... F 2
Blida, 99,238 .... E 1
Bordj-Bou-Arréridj, 43,494 .... E 1
Bordj Fly Sainte-Marie .... D 3
Boufarik, 33,881 .... E 1
Bougie (Béjaïa), 64,876 .... F 1
Bou-Saâda, 26,262 .... E 1
Briziana, 7,498 .... E 2
Charouïn .... D 3
Cherchell, 27,464 .... E 1
Constantine, 243,558 .... F 1
Deldoul .... F 3
Dellys, 23,718 .... E 1
Djamaâ, 25,925 .... F 2
Djanet .... F 4
Djelfa, 30,304 .... E 2
Djidjelli, 35,371 .... F 1
Edjeleh .... F 3
El Abiod-Sidi-Cheikh, 10,512 .... E 2
El Asnam, 69,745 .... E 1
El Bayadh, 24,770 .... E 2
El Djezair (Algiers) (cap.), 943,142 .... E 1
El Goléa, 16,679 .... E 2
El Oued, 43,547 .... F 2
Fort-Lallemand .... F 2
Fort-Mac-Mahon .... E 3
Fort-Miribel .... E 3
Ghardaïa, 46,609 .... E 2
Ghazaouet, 20,785 .... D 2
Guelma, 39,817 .... F 1
Guémar, 20,394 .... F 2
Guerara, 14,173 .... E 2
Guerzim .... D 3
Hassi-Messaoud .... F 2
Hassi-R'Mel .... E 2
Idelès .... F 4
Ighil-Izane, 43,547 .... E 1
Igli, 2,912 .... D 2
Illizi, 4,000 .... F 3
In-Amenas .... F 3
In-Amguel .... E 4
In-Eker .... F 4
In-Rhar .... E 3
In Salah, 12,645 .... E 3
Kenadsa, 7,258 .... D 2
Kerzaz, 2,492 .... D 3
Khémis-Miliana, 36,530 .... E 1
Ksar-el-Boukhari, 30,338 .... E 1
Laghouat, 38,166 .... E 2
Mascara, 43,108 .... D 1
Méchéria, 12,151 .... D 2
Médéa, 53,567 .... E 1
Metlili Chaamba, 17,999 .... E 2
Miliana, 28,410 .... E 1
Mohammadia, 38,441 .... D 1
Mostaganem, 75,332 .... D 1
M'Sila, 36,930 .... E 1
Oran, 327,493 .... D 1
Oran, *393,000 .... D 1
Ouallene .... E 4
Ouargla, 48,323 .... F 2
Ouled-Djellal, 14,597 .... F 2
Philippeville (Skikda), 72,742 .... F 1
Poste Maurice Cordier .... E 4
Poste Weygand .... D 4
Reggan, 11,075 .... D 3
Saïda, 38,348 .... E 2
Sba .... D 3
Sétif, 98,337 .... F 1
Sidi-bel-Abbès, 91,527 .... D 1
Silet .... E 4
Skikda, 72,742 .... F 1
Souk-Ahras, 42,680 .... F 1
Tabelbala, 1,972 .... D 3
Tamanrasset, 16,298 .... F 4
Tamentit .... D 3
Taourirt .... E 3
Tarat .... F 3
Tarhit .... D 2
Tébessa, 46,148 .... F 1
Temacine .... F 2
Ténès, 22,881 .... E 1
Tiaret, 40,934 .... E 1
Tiguentourine .... F 3
Timimoun, 15,349 .... E 3
Tindouf, 3,414 .... C 3
Tizi-Ouzou, 53,546 .... E 1
Tlemcen, 87,210 .... D 2
Touggourt, 50,159 .... F 2
Zaouiet-el-Kahla, 1,080 .... F 3
Zaouïet-Kounta, 11,455 .... D 3

OTHER FEATURES

Adrar des Iforas (plat.) .... E 4
Ahaggar (range) .... F 4
Aouïnet Legraa (well) .... C 3
Atlas (mts.) .... E 2
Aurés (mts.) .... F 1
Azzel Mati, Sebkra (lake) .... E 3
Bougaroun (cape) .... F 1
Chech Erg (des.) .... D 3
Chélia (mt.) .... F 1
Chéliff (riv.) .... E 1
Chenachane (well) .... D 3
Chergui, Shott Ech (salt lake) .... E 2
Gourara (oasis), 28,893 .... E 3
Great Eastern Erg (des.) .... F 2
Great Western Erg (des.) .... E 2
High Plateaus (ranges) .... D 2
Iguidi Erg (des.) .... C 3
In-Ezzane (well) .... G 4
In-Guezzam (well) .... F 5
Irharhar, Wadi (dry riv.) .... F 3
Issaouane Erg (des.) .... F 3
Kabylia (reg.) .... E 1
Medjerda (riv.) .... F 1
Mekerhane, Sebkra (salt lake) .... E 3
Melrhir, Shott (salt lake) .... F 2
Mouydir (mts.) .... E 3
Mya, Wadi (dry riv.) .... E 2
Mzab (oasis), 52,500 .... E 2
Raoui Erg (des.) .... D 3
Rhir, Wadi (dry riv.) .... F 2
Sahara (des.) .... E 4
Saharan Atlas (mts.) .... E 2
Saoura, Wadi (dry riv.) .... D 3
Souf (oasis), 92,014 .... F 2
Tademait (plat.) .... E 3
Tahat (mt.) .... F 4
Tamanrasset, Wadi (dry river) .... E 4
Tanezrouft (des.) .... E 4
Tassili n'Ahaggar (plat.) .... E 4
Tassili n'Ajjer (plat.) .... F 3
Tidikelt (oasis), 17,280 .... E 3
Timgad (ruins) .... F 1
Timmissao (well) .... E 4
Tindouf, Sebkra de (salt lake) .... C 3
Tinrhert Hamada (des.) .... F 3
Tni Haïa (well) .... D 4
Touat (oasis), 35,537 .... E 3
Touila (well) .... C 3

BENIN

CITIES and TOWNS

Abomey, 19,000 .... E 7
Athiémé, 1,782 .... E 7
Cotonou, 120,000 .... E 7
Djougou, 7,000 .... E 7
Grand-Popo, 2,545 .... E 7
Kandi, 5,100 .... E 6
Malanville, 1,900 .... E 6
Natitingou, 2,260 .... E 6
Nikki .... E 7
Ouidah, 18,915 .... E 7
Parakou, 10,600 .... E 7
Porto-Novo (cap.), 80,000 .... E 7
Savalou, 5,000 .... E 7
Savé, 6,262 .... E 7

OTHER FEATURES

Atakora (mts.) .... E 6
Benin (bight) .... E 8
Guinea (gulf) .... E 8
Ouémé (riv.) .... E 7
Slave Coast (reg.) .... E 7

CAPE VERDE

CITIES and TOWNS

Mindelo, 7,312 .... A 7
Praia (cap.), 3,628 .... B 8
Ribeira Grande, †17,573 .... B 7
Sal Rei, †3,309 .... B 8
Santa Maria, †2,626 .... B 8

OTHER FEATURES

Boa Vista (isl.), 3,309 .... B 8
Brava (isl.), 8,646 .... B 8
Fogo (isl.), 25,457 .... B 8
Maio (isl.), 2,718 .... B 8
Sal (isl.), 2,626 .... B 7
Santa Luzia (isl.) .... B 8
Santo Antão (island), 36,703 .... A 7
São Nicolau (island), 13,894 .... B 8
São Tiago (island), 86,835 .... B 8
São Vicente (island), 21,361 .... B 7

GAMBIA

CITIES and TOWNS

Banjul (cap.), 31,800 .... A 6
Banjul, *48,333 .... A 6
Basse, 1,639 .... B 6
Brikama, 4,195 .... A 6
Georgetown, 1,592 .... A 6

GHANA

CITIES and TOWNS

Accra (cap.), 337,828 .... D 7
Accra, *848,825 .... D 7
Ada Foah, 3,332 .... E 7
Akim Oda, 19,666 .... D 7
Amedika Akuse, 3,638 .... E 7
Attebubu, 4,216 .... D 7
Axim, 5,619 .... D 8
Bawku, 12,719 .... D 6
Bekwai, 9,093 .... D 7
Berekum, 11,148 .... D 7
Bole, 3,118 .... D 7
Bolgatanga, 5,515 .... D 6
Cape Coast, 41,230 .... D 7
Daboya, 1,579 .... D 7
Damongo, 6,575 .... D 7
Dunkwa, 12,689 .... D 7
Elmina, 8,534 .... D 8
Enkyi, 4,007 .... D 7
Gambaga, 2,936 .... D 6
Gyasikan, 4,989 .... D 7
Half Assini, 4,575 .... D 8
Ho, 14,519 .... E 7
Keta, 16,719 .... E 7
Kete Krakye, 3,928 .... E 7
Kintampo, 4,678 .... D 7
Koforidua, 34,856 .... D 7
Kpandu, 8,070 .... D 7
Kumasi, 281,600 .... D 7
Kumasi, *340,200 .... D 7
Lawra, 3,237 .... D 6
Mampong, 7,943 .... D 7
Mpraeso, 5,193 .... D 7
Navrongo, 5,274 .... D 6
Obuasi, 22,818 .... D 7
Prestea, 13,246 .... D 7
Salaga, 4,199 .... D 7
Sehwi Wiawso, 4,430 .... D 7
Sekondi, 34,513 .... D 8
Sekondi-Takoradi, 128,200 .... D 8
Sekondi-Takoradi, *209,400 .... D 8
Sunyani, 12,160 .... D 7
Takoradi, 40,937 .... D 8
Tamale, 40,443 .... D 7
Tarkwa, 13,545 .... D 7
Tema, 14,937 .... E 7
Tumu, 2,773 .... D 6
Wa, 14,342 .... D 6
Wenchi, 10,672 .... D 7
Winneba, 25,376 .... D 7
Yapei, 515 .... D 7
Yendi, 16,096 .... D 7
Zuarungu, 1,278 .... D 6

OTHER FEATURES

Ashanti (region), 1,109,133 .... D 7
Black Volta (riv.) .... D 6
Gold Coast (reg.) .... D 8
Guinea (gulf) .... E 8
Oti (riv.) .... E 7
Saint Paul (cape) .... E 7
Three Points (cape) .... D 8
Volta (lake) .... D 7
Volta (riv.) .... E 7
White Volta (riv.) .... D 6

GUINEA

CITIES and TOWNS

Beyla, 6,035 .... C 7
Boffa, 1,014 .... B 6
Boké, 6,000 .... B 6
Conakry (capital), 43,000 .... B 7
Conakry, *197,267 .... B 7
Dabola, 5,600 .... B 6
Dalaba, 5,450 .... B 6
Dinguiraye, 2,600 .... B 6
Dubréka, 740 .... B 7
Faranah, 4,000 .... B 6
Forécariah, 5,250 .... B 7
Gaoual, 3,208 .... B 6
Guéckédou, 1,421 .... B 7
Kankan, 50,000 .... C 6
Kérouané .... C 7
Kindia, 25,000 .... B 6
Kissidougou, 12,000 .... B 7
Kouroussa, 6,100 .... C 6
Labé, 11,609 .... B 6
Macenta, 22,500 .... C 7
Mamou, 9,000 .... B 6
N'Zérékoré, 11,000 .... C 7
Siguiri, 12,000 .... C 6
Tougué, 9,810 .... B 6
Victoria, 1,913 .... B 6

OTHER FEATURES

Bafing (riv.) .... B 6
Futa Jallon (mts.) .... B 6
Los (isls.) .... B 7
Milo (riv.) .... C 7
Niger (riv.) .... C 6
Nimba (mts.) .... C 7
Verga (cape) .... B 6

GUINEA-BISSAU

CITIES and TOWNS

Bissau (capital), 20,000 .... A 6
Bolama, †4,642 .... A 6
Buba .... B 6
Bubaque .... A 6
Cacheu, †70,233 .... A 6

OTHER FEATURES

Bijagós (isls.), 9,332 .... A 6

IVORY COAST

CITIES and TOWNS

Abengourou, 18,000 .... D 7
Abidjan (capital), 180,000 .... D 7
Abidjan, *425,000 .... D 7
Aboisso, 3,310 .... D 7
Agboville, 15,475 .... D 7
Bingerville, 2,500 .... D 7
Bondoukou, 5,216 .... D 7
Bouaflé, 5,000 .... C 7
Bouaké, 100,000 .... D 7
Bouna, 3,410 .... D 7
Boundiali, 3,608 .... C 7
Dabakala, 1,500 .... D 7
Dabou, 4,500 .... D 7
Daloa, 20,000 .... C 7
Danané, 5,200 .... C 7
Dimbokro, 10,260 .... D 7
Ferkessédougou, 9,110 .... D 7
Fresco, 719 .... C 7
Gagnoa, 18,000 .... C 7
Grand-Bassam, 12,330 .... D 7
Grand-Lahou, 4,040 .... C 8
Guiglo, 3,867 .... C 7
Katiola, 7,778 .... C 7
Kong, 4,073 .... D 7
Korhogo, 25,000 .... C 7
Man, 24,000 .... C 7
Odienné, 6,000 .... C 7
Port-Bouet .... D 7
San Pedro, 21 .... C 8
Sassandra, 5,300 .... D 7
Séguéla, 7,598 .... C 7
Sinfra, 5,965 .... C 7
Tabou, 3,030 .... C 8
Touba, 1,217 .... C 7
Toumodi, 3,000 .... D 7

OTHER FEATURES

Aby (lag.) .... D 8
Bandama (riv.) .... C 7
Cavally (riv.) .... C 7
Comoé (riv.) .... D 7
Ebrié (lag.) .... D 8
Ivory Coast (reg.) .... C 8
Sassandra (riv.) .... C 7

LIBERIA

CITIES and TOWNS

Bomi Hills, 2,441 .... B 7
Buchanan, 11,909 .... B 7
Gbarnga, 2,810 .... C 7
Grand Bassa (Buchanan), 11,909 .... B 7
Grand Cess .... C 8
Greenville, 3,962 .... C 8
Harper, 6,095 .... C 8
Kolahun .... C 7
Marshall .... B 7
Monrovia (capital), 85,000 .... B 7
Monrovia, *100,000 .... B 7
River Cess .... C 7
Robertsport, 2,417 .... B 7
Salala .... B 7
Sass Town .... C 8
Sinoe (Greenville), 3,962 .... C 8
Tappita .... C 7
Tchien, 945 .... C 7
Zwedru (Tchien), 945 .... C 7

OTHER FEATURES

Bong (mts.) .... B 7
Cavally (riv.) .... C 7
Grain Coast (reg.) .... B 8
Kru Coast (reg.), 21,280 .... C 8
Mano (riv.) .... B 7
Mount (cape) .... B 7
Nimba (mts.) .... C 7
Palmas (cape) .... C 8
Roberts International Airport .... B 7

MALI

CITIES and TOWNS

Anéfis .... E 5
Ansongo, 1,200 .... E 5
Araouane .... D 5
Badougou .... C 6
Bafoulabé, 1,300 .... B 6
Bamako (cap.), 88,500 .... C 6
Bamako, *182,000 .... C 6
Bamba .... D 5
Bandiagara, 6,700 .... D 6
Bou Djebeha .... D 5
Bougouni, 5,500 .... C 6
Bourem, 2,700 .... E 5
Dioila, 1,900 .... C 6
Dire, 3,300 .... D 5
Djenné, 8,200 .... D 6
Douentza, 7,100 .... D 6
Gao, 15,400 .... E 5
Goumbou, 5,000 .... C 6
Goundam, 10,000 .... D 5
Gourma-Rharous, 2,700 .... D 5
Hombori, 3,600 .... D 5
Kangaba, 6,200 .... C 6
Kati, 5,900 .... C 6
Kayes, 23,600 .... B 6
Ké-Macina, 3,100 .... C 6
Kéniéba, 800 .... B 6
Kerchoual .... E 5
Kidal, 1,200 .... E 5
Kita, 8,600 .... C 6
Kolokani, 7,300 .... C 6
Koulikoro, 10,000 .... C 6
Kourouba, 807 .... B 6
Koutiala, 11,300 .... C 6
Mabrouk .... D 5
Ménaka, 1,400 .... E 5
Mopti, 32,000 .... D 6
Nampala .... C 5
Nara, 2,500 .... C 5
Niafunké, 5,100 .... D 5
Niono, 4,000 .... C 6
Nioro, 11,000 .... C 5
San, 14,900 .... D 6
Satadougou, 180 .... B 6
Ségou, 27,200 .... C 6
Sikasso, 21,800 .... C 6
Sokolo, 3,457 .... C 6
Taoudenni .... D 4
Tessalit .... E 4
Timbuktu, 14,900 .... D 5
Tin-Zaouatene .... E 5
Yelimané, 1,700 .... B 5

OTHER FEATURES

Achourat (well) .... D 4
Adrar des Iforas (plat.) .... E 4
Asselar (well) .... D 5
Azaouad (reg.) .... D 5
Azaouak (dry riv.) .... E 5
Bafing (riv.) .... B 6
Bagoé (riv.) .... C 6
Bakoy (riv.) .... B 6
Bani (riv.) .... C 6
Baoulé (riv.) .... C 6
Bir Ounane (well) .... D 4
Chech Erg (des.) .... D 3
Debo (lake) .... D 5
El-Mraiti (well) .... D 5
Faguibine (lake) .... D 5
Falémé (riv.) .... B 6
Haricha Hamada (des.) .... D 4
Hombori (mts.) .... D 5
In Dagouber (well) .... D 4
Macina (depr.) .... D 6
Mina (mt.) .... C 6
Niger (riv.) .... D 5
Oum el Asel (well) .... D 4
Sahara (des.) .... D 4
Sekkane (des.) .... D 4
Tadjnout Hagguerete (well) .... D 4
Terhazza (ruins) .... C 4
Tilemsi (valley) .... E 5
Toufourine (well) .... C 4

MAURITANIA

CITIES and TOWNS

Aïoun el Atrous, 3,054 .... C 5
Akjoujt, 2,500 .... B 5
Akreïjit .... C 5
Aleg, 1,000 .... B 5
Atar, 7,120 .... B 4
Bassikounou .... C 5
Bir Mogrein, 1,052 .... B 4
Boghé, 2,316 .... B 5
Boutilimit, 3,000 .... B 5
Chinguetti, 600 .... B 4
Cité de Cansado .... A 4
Dakhla, 4,000 .... A 4
F'Dérick, †900 .... B 4
Kaédi, 11,000 .... B 5
Kankossa, †13,000 .... B 5
Kiffa, 2,600 .... B 5
Maghama, 3,157 .... B 5
Mal .... B 5
M'Bout, 1,400 .... B 5
Méderdra, 1,473 .... A 5
Moudjéria, 753 .... B 5
Néma, 2,946 .... C 5
Nouadhibou, 11,250 .... A 4
Nouakchott (capital), 14,500 .... A 5
Ouadane .... B 4
Oualata, 1,285 .... C 5
Oujaf .... C 5
Oujeft .... B 4
Rosso, 3,923 .... A 5
Sélibaby, 2,600 .... B 5
Tamchakett, 641 .... B 5
Tamsagout .... C 4
Tazadit .... A 4
Tichitt, 1,000 .... C 5
Tidjikja, 5,900 .... B 5
Timbédra, 1,200 .... C 5

OTHER FEATURES

Adafer (reg.) .... B 5
Adrar (reg.), 50,920 .... B 4
Affolé (reg.) .... B 5
Agmar (well) .... B 3
Agueraktem (well) .... C 4
Aïn ben Tili (well) .... C 3
Arguin (bay) .... A 4
Assaba (reg.), 100,000 .... B 5
Atoui, Wadi (dry riv.) .... B 4
Ausert (well) .... B 4
Barbas (cape) .... A 4
Ben Guerdane (well) .... B 3
Bir el Khzaim (well) .... C 4
Bir Ganduz (well) .... A 4
Bir Nzaran (well) .... B 4
Blanc (cape) .... A 4
Brakna (reg.), 82,020 .... B 5
Chegga (well) .... C 3
Djouf, El (des.) .... C 4
Durnford (pt.) .... A 4
El Mrayer (well) .... C 4
El Mreïti (well) .... C 4
Gorgol (reg.), 54,037 .... B 5
Hodh (reg.), 183,945 .... C 5
Iguidi Erg (des.) .... C 3
Inchiri (reg.), 15,443 .... A 5
Kumbi Saleh (ruins) .... C 5
Lévrier (bay) .... A 4
Makteïr (des.) .... B 4
Meraia (reg.) .... C 5
Mirik (Timiris) (cape) .... A 5
Ouarane (reg.) .... B 4
Sahara (des.) .... C 4
Senegal (riv.) .... B 5
Tagant (reg.), 52,703 .... B 5
Tichlá (well) .... B 4
Tidra (isl.) .... A 5
Timiris (cape) .... A 5
Touila (well) .... C 3
Trarza (reg.), 105,737 .... A 5

MOROCCO

CITIES and TOWNS

Agadir, 16,695 .... C 2
Al Hoceima, 11,262 .... D 1
Asilah, 10,839 .... C 1
Azemmour, 12,449 .... C 2
Azrou, 14,143 .... C 2
Beni-Mellal, 28,933 .... C 2
Berguent, 2,607 .... D 2
Bouârfa, 8,775 .... D 2
Bou-Izakarn, 661 .... C 3

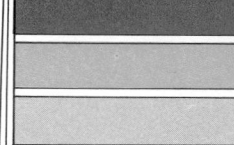

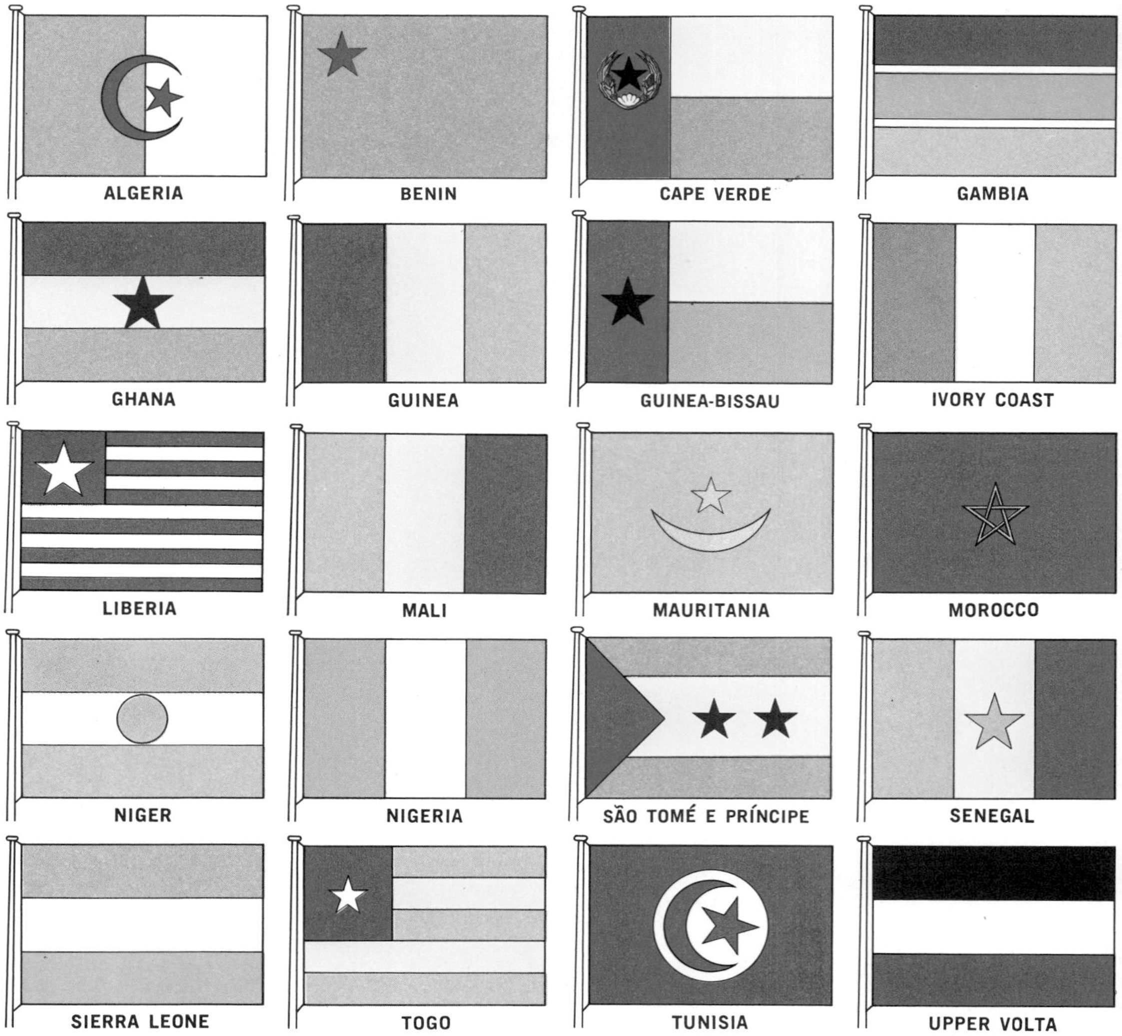

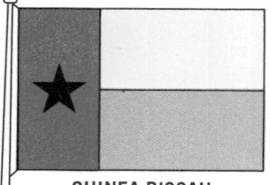

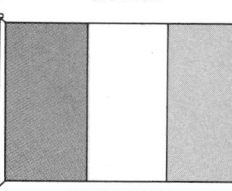

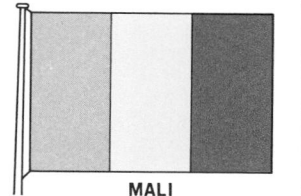

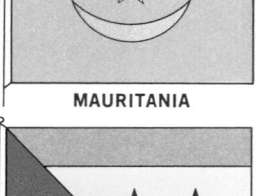

Boujad, 14,728 C 2
Casablanca, 1,320,000 C 2
Chechaouen, 13,712 D 1
Dar-el-Beida (Casablanca), 1,320,000 C 2
El Jadida, 40,302 C 2
El Kelâa des Srarhna, 10,187 C 2
Erfoud, 4,491 D 2
Essaouira, 26,392 B 2
Fédala (Mohammedia), 35,010 C 2
Fez, 280,000 D 2
Figuig, 12,108 D 2
Goulmima, 1,804 C 2
Inezgane, 6,917 C 2
Jerada, 18,872 D 2
Kénitra, 125,000 C 2
Khenifra, 18,503 C 2
Khouribga, 40,838 C 2
Ksar-el-Kebir, 34,035 C 2
Ksar-es-Souk, 6,554 D 2
Laayoune, 10,000 B 3
Larache, 30,763 C 1
Marrakech, 295,000 C 2
Mazagan (El Jadida), 40,302 C 2
Meknès, 235,000 C 2
Mogador (Essaouira), 26,392 B 2
Mohammedia, 35,010 C 2
Nador, 17,583 D 1
Ouarzazate, 4,200 C 2
Oued-Zem, 18,640 C 2
Ouezzane, 26,203 C 2
Oujda, 150,000 D 2
Petitjean (Sidi-Kacem), 19,478 C 2
Port-Lyautey (Kénitra), 125,000 C 2
Rabat (capital), 227,445 C 2
Rabat, *435,000 C 2
Safi, 125,000 C 2
Saïdia, 1,102 D 2
Salé, 75,799 C 2
Sefrou, 21,478 D 2
Semara, 1,000 B 3
Settat, 29,617 C 2
Sidi Ifni, 12,751 B 3
Sidi-Kacem, 19,478 C 2
Tagounite, 354 C 3
Tangier (Tanger), 160,000 C 1
Tantan, 2,153 B 3
Taourirt, 7,343 D 2
Taouz, 641 D 2
Tarfaya, 1,521 B 3
Taroudant, 17,141 C 2
Taza, 31,667 D 2
Tendrara, 1,563 D 2
Tétouan (Tetuán), 120,000 C 1
Tinjoub C 3
Tiznit, 7,694 B 3
Youssoufia, 8,302 C 2
Zagora, 2,200 C 2

OTHER FEATURES

Anti-Atlas (ranges) C 3
Atlas (mts.) C 2
Bani, Jebel (mts.) C 3
Bojador (cape) B 3
Cantin (cape) C 2
Dra Hamada (des.) C 3
Dra, Wadi (dry riv.) C 3
Er Rif (range) D 2
Gibraltar (str.) C 1
Guelta de Zemmur (well) B 3
High Atlas (ranges) C 2
Juby (cape) B 3
Middle Atlas (ranges) C 2
Moulouya (riv.) D 2
Rhéris, Wadi (dry riv.) D 2
Rhir (cape) B 2
Rif, Er (range) D 2
Saguia el Hamra (dry riv.) B 3
Saguia el Hamra (region) B 3
Sarro, Jebel (mts.) C 2
Sebou (riv.) C 2
Sim (cape) B 2
Toubkal, Jebel (mt.) C 2
Ziz, Wadi (dry riv.) D 2

NIGER

CITIES and TOWNS

Agadès, 7,100 F 5
Bilma, 1,500 G 5
Birni-N'Konni, 7,900 E 6
Bosso, 509 G 6
Chirfa G 4
Dakoro, 2,400 F 6
Dessa E 6
Diffa, 477 G 6
Djado G 4
Dogondoutchi, 7,700 E 6
Dosso, 3,500 E 6
Fachi, 1,060 G 5
Filingué, 6,000 E 6
Gangara F 6
Gaya, 4,200 E 6
Gouré, 2,100 G 6
Iférouane F 5
In-Gall, 1,555 F 5
Madama G 4
Madaoua, 2,800 F 6
Magaria, 4,000 F 6
Mainé-Soroa, 1,500 G 6
Maradi, 22,400 F 6
N'Guigmi, 4,000 G 6
Niamey (cap.), 42,000 E 6
Niamey, *122,672 E 6
Say, 2,700 E 6
Tahoua, 18,100 F 6
Tanout, 1,600 F 6
Téra, 6,600 E 6
Tessaoua, 6,700 F 6
Tillabéry, 1,600 E 6
Zinder, 24,000 F 6

OTHER FEATURES

Achégour (well) G 5
Agadem (well) G 5
Air (mts.) F 5
Anaye (well) G 5
Assakarai (dry riv.) F 5
Azaoua (reg.) E 5
Azbine (Air) (mts.) F 5
Bagam (well) F 5
Banguezane (mt.) F 5
Bedouaram (well) G 5
Chad (lake) G 6
Dallol Bosso (dry riv.) E 6
Dillia (dry riv.) G 5
Djado (plat.) G 4
El War (well) G 4
In-Azaoua (well) F 4
Mantas (well) E 5
Niger (riv.) E 6
Sudan (reg.) E 6
Talak (reg.) E 5
Ténéré (des.) G 5
Timboulaga (well) F 5
Tummo (El War) (well) G 4
Zoo Baba (well) G 5

NIGERIA

STATES

Benue-Plateau, 4,009,408 F 7
East-Central, 6,223,831 F 7
Kano, 5,774,842 F 6
Kwara, 2,406,265 E 7
Lagos, 1,443,567 E 7
Mid-Western, 2,535,839 F 7
North-Central, 4,098,305 F 6
North-Eastern, 7,815,443 G 6
North-Western, 5,733,296 E 6
Rivers, 1,544,314 F 8
South-Eastern, 4,626,317 F 7
Western, 9,487,576 E 7

CITIES and TOWNS

Aba, 151,923 F 7
Abeokuta, 217,201 E 7
Abuja F 7
Ado, 182,673 E 7
Afikpo F 7
Aku, 20,809 F 7
Akure, 38,853 F 7
Argungu E 6
Asaba, 17,387 F 7
Azare G 6
Baga G 6
Bama G 6
Baro F 7
Bauchi F 6
Benin City, 116,774 F 7
Bida F 7
Birnin Kebbi E 6
Biu G 6
Bonny F 8
Brass F 8
Burutu, 6,784 F 7
Calabar, 46,705 F 8
Deba Habe G 6
Degema F 8
Dikwa G 6
Donga F 7
Ede, 156,036 E 7
Eha Amufu, 29,434 F 7
Enugu, 160,567 F 7
Forcados F 7
Funtua F 6
Gashaka G 7
Gbogo F 7
Geidam G 6
Gombe G 6
Gumel F 6
Gummi F 6
Gusau, 40,202 F 6
Gwadabawa F 6
Hadejia G 6
Ibadan, 727,565 E 7
Ibi F 7
Ife, 150,818 E 7
Ijebu-Ode, 27,558 E 7
Ikom F 7
Ilesha, 192,302 E 7
Ilorin, 241,849 E 7
Isa F 6
Iseyin, 49,680 E 7
Iwo, 183,907 E 7
Jalingo G 7
Jebba E 7
Jega E 6
Jos, 38,527 F 7
Kabba, 7,305 F 7
Kaduna, 173,849 F 6
Kaiama E 7
Kalmalo F 6
Kano, 342,610 F 6
Katsina, 52,672 F 6
Katsina Ala F 7
Kaura Namoda F 6
Keffi F 7
Koko E 6
Kontagora F 6
Kukawa G 6
Kumo G 7
Kuta F 7
Lafia F 7
Lafiagi F 7
Lagos (cap.), 841,749 E 7
Lere F 7
Lokoja, 13,103 F 7
Maiduguri, 162,316 G 6
Maigatari F 6
Makurdi F 7
Minna F 7
Mubi G 6
Mushin, 169,287 E 7
Nasarawa F 7
New Bussa, 10,000 E 6
Nguru, 23,084 G 6
Nnewi, 28,777 F 7
Nsukka F 7
Numan G 7
Offa, 20,668 E 7
Ogbomosho, 370,963 E 7
Ogoja F 7
Okene, 32,602 F 7
Ondo, 36,233 E 7
Onitsha, 189,067 F 7
Oron F 8
Oshogbo, 242,336 E 7
Owo, 30,662 F 7
Oyo, 130,290 E 7
Pankshin F 7
Panyam F 7
Port Harcourt, 208,237 F 8
Ringim F 6
Sapele, 33,638 F 7
Shaki, 22,983 E 7
Shendam F 7
Sokoto, 47,643 F 6
Toungo G 7
Uromi, 22,339 F 7
Vom F 7
Wamba F 7
Warri, 19,526 F 7
Wukari F 7
Yan G 7
Yelwa F 6
Yola G 7
Zaria, 192,706 F 6
Zungeru F 7

OTHER FEATURES

Adamawa (reg.) G 7
Benin (bight) E 8
Benue (riv.) F 7
Biafra (bight) F 8
Bornu (reg.) G 6
Chad (lake) G 6
Cross (riv.) F 7
Donga (riv.) G 7
Foge (isl.) E 6
Gongola (riv.) G 6
Guinea (gulf) E 8
Hadejia (riv.) F 6
Kaduna (riv.) F 7
Kainji (res.) E 6
Kebbi (riv.) E 6
Komadugu Yobe (riv.) G 6
Niger (delta) F 8
Niger (riv.) F 7
Osse (riv.) F 7
Slave Coast (reg.) E 7
Sokoto (riv.) F 6
Sudan (reg.) F 6
Vogel (peak) G 7

PORTUGAL—Madeira

CITIES and TOWNS

Funchal, 43,301 A 2

OTHER FEATURES

Desertas (isls.) A 2
Madeira (island), 265,432 A 2
Madeira (islands), 268,700 A 2
Pôrto Santo (island), 3,505 A 2
Salvage (isls.) A 2

SÃO TOMÉ E PRÍNCIPE

CITIES and TOWNS

Santo António, †4,605 F 8
São Tomé (capital), 7,364 F 8

OTHER FEATURES

Príncipe (isl.), 4,605 F 8
São Tomé (isl.), 58,880 F 8

SENEGAL

CITIES and TOWNS

Bakel, 2,500 B 6
Bignona, 5,432 A 6
Dagana, 4,000 A 5
Dakar (cap.), 550,000 A 6
Dakar, *661,000 A 6
Diourbel, 30,000 A 6
Kaolack, 70,000 A 6
Kédougou, 1,938 B 6
Louga, 15,000 A 5
Matam, 5,000 B 5
M'Bour, 15,000 A 6
Nioro-du-Rip, 2,788 A 6
Podor, 5,000 B 5
Richard Toll, 894 A 5
Rufisque, 50,000 A 6
Saint-Louis, 50,000 A 5
Sedhiou, 2,419 A 6
Tambacounda, 10,027 B 6
Thiès, 70,000 A 5
Tivaouane, 8,000 A 5
Touba, 2,575 A 6
Yarboutenda B 6
Ziguinchor, 30,000 A 6

OTHER FEATURES

Casamance (riv.) A 6
Falémé (riv.) B 6
Ferlo (reg.) B 6
Gambia (riv.) B 6
Senegal (riv.) B 5
Verde (cape) A 6

SIERRA LEONE

CITIES and TOWNS

Bo, 26,613 B 7
Bonthe, 6,230 B 7
Freetown (capital), 170,600 B 7
Kabala, 4,610 B 7
Kambia, 3,700 B 7
Kenema, 13,246 B 7
Lungi, 2,170 B 7
Makeni, 12,304 B 7
Moyamba, 4,564 B 7
Pendembu, 2,696 B 7
Pepel B 7
Port Loko, 5,809 B 7
Pujehun, 2,034 B 7

OTHER FEATURES

Loma (mts.) B 7
Moa (riv.) B 7
Sherbro (isl.), 6,894 B 7
Yawri (bay) B 7

SPAIN—Canary Islands, Ceuta and Melilla

CITIES and TOWNS

Arrecife, 12,748 B 3
Ceuta, 88,000 C 1
La Laguna, 15,899 A 3
Las Palmas de Gran Canaria, 166,236 B 3
Melilla, 77,000 D 1
Santa Cruz de la Palma, 9,928 A 3
Santa Cruz de Tenerife, 82,620 A 3

OTHER FEATURES

Canary (isls.), 944,448 A 3
Fuerteventura (island), 18,138 B 3
Gomera (isl.), 27,790 A 3
Grand Canary (island), 400,837 A 3
Hierro (isl.), 7,957 A 3
Lanzarote (isl.), 34,805 B 3
La Palma (isl.), 67,141 A 3
Tenerife (isl.), 387,767 A 3

TOGO

CITIES and TOWNS

Anécho, ‡11,040 E 7
Atakpamé, ‡18,008 E 7
Kpémé, 2,229 E 7
Lama-Kara E 7
Lomé (cap.), 90,600 E 7
Lomé, *149,879 E 7
Palimé, ‡20,331 E 7
Sansanné-Mango E 6
Sokodé, ‡30,271 E 7

OTHER FEATURES

Guinea (gulf) E 8
Mono (riv.) E 7
Oti (riv.) E 7
Slave Coast (reg.) E 7

TUNISIA

CITIES and TOWNS

Beja, 28,100 F 1
Ben Gardane, 2,138 G 2
Bizerte, 51,700 F 1
El Djem, 6,800 G 1
El Kef, 23,200 F 1
Fort-Saint F 2
Gabès, 32,300 F 2
Gafsa, 32,400 F 2
Halq el Oued, 27,500 G 1
Jendouba, 14,800 F 1
Kairouan, 46,200 F 1
Kalaa-Kebira, 16,800 F 1
Kasserine, 9,800 F 1
La Skhirra, 1,500 G 2
Mahdia, 10,900 G 1
Mareth, 153 F 2
Mateur, 15,600 F 1
Médenine, 8,000 F 2
Menzel Bourguiba, 36,700 F 1
Menzel-Temime, 12,500 G 1
Moknine, 18,500 G 1
Monastir, 16,500 G 1
Msaken, 27,500 G 1
Nabeul, 34,100 G 1
Nefta, 15,000 F 2
Remada, 1,866 F 2
Sbeitla, 4,000 F 1
Sfax, 65,000 G 2
Sousse, 48,200 G 1
Tabarka, 356 F 1
Tatahouine, 3,100 G 2
Tozeur, 11,820 F 2
Tunis (cap.), 662,000 G 1
Tunis, *800,000 G 1
Zarzis, 30,080 G 2

OTHER FEATURES

Abiad, Ras el (Blanc) (cape) G 1
Blanc (cape) G 1
Bon (cape) G 1
Chambi, Jebel (mt.) F 2
Djerba (isl.), 62,445 G 2
Djerid, Shott el (salt lake) F 2
Gabès (gulf) G 2
Hammamet (gulf) G 1
Jefara (reg.) G 2
Kerkennah (isls.), 13,704 G 2
Merjerda (riv.) F 1
Tib, Ras el (Bon) (cape) G 1
Tunis (gulf) G 1

UPPER VOLTA

CITIES and TOWNS

Aribinda, 3,150 D 6
Banfora, 4,511 D 6
Batié, 1,335 D 6
Bobo-Dioulasso, 56,100 D 6
Bogandé, 3,125 E 6
Dédougou, 3,680 D 6
Diapaga, 3,050 E 6
Djibo D 6
Dori, 3,500 D 6
Fada-N'Gourma, 4,867 E 6
Gaoua, 5,907 D 6
Houndé, 1,153 D 6
Kaya, 10,304 D 6
Koudougou, 7,940 D 6
Koupela, 3,800 D 6
Léo, 2,139 D 6
Ouagadougou (capital), 77,500 D 6
Ouagadougou, *100,000 D 6
Ouahigouya, 12,960 D 6
Pama, 1,411 E 6
Po, 4,000 D 6
Tenkodogo, 6,561 E 6
Tougan, 5,000 D 6
Yako, 5,110 D 6

OTHER FEATURES

Black Volta (riv.) D 6
Red Volta (riv.) D 6
Sudan (reg.) E 6
White Volta (riv.) D 6

*City and suburbs.
†Population of sub-district or division.
‡Population of commune.

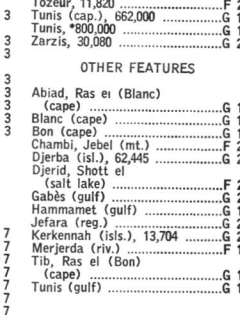

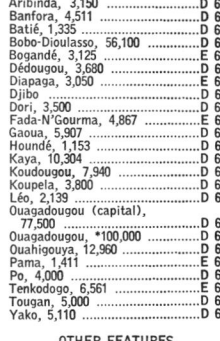

Agriculture, Industry and Resources

DOMINANT LAND USE

Cereals, Horticulture, Livestock
Market Gardening, Diversified Tropical Crops
Plantation Agriculture
Oases
Pasture Livestock
Nomadic Livestock Herding
Forests
Nonagricultural Land

MAJOR MINERAL OCCURRENCES

Al Bauxite
Au Gold
C Coal
Co Cobalt
Cr Chromium
Cu Copper
D Diamonds
Fe Iron Ore
G Natural Gas
Gn Granite
Gp Gypsum
Mn Manganese
Na Salt
O Petroleum
P Phosphates
Pb Lead
Sb Antimony
Sn Tin
Ti Titanium
Zn Zinc
Water Power
Major Industrial Areas

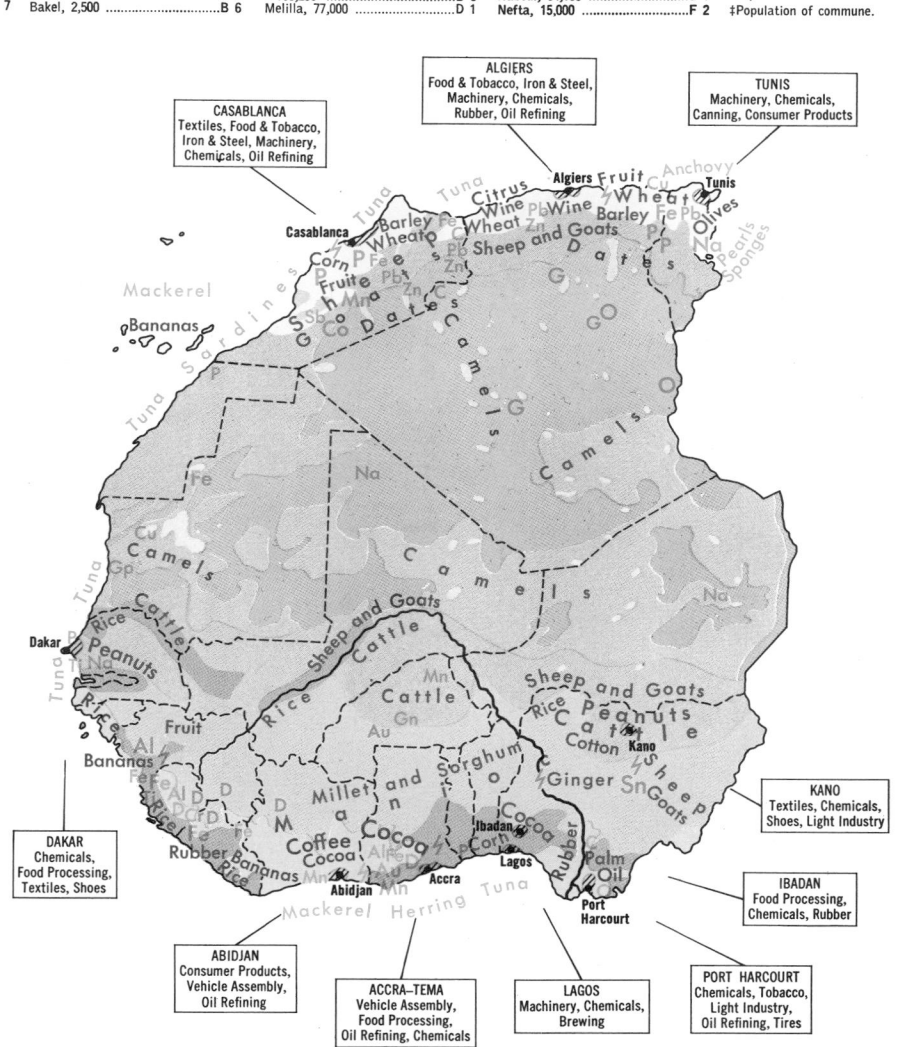

ALGIERS
Food & Tobacco, Iron & Steel, Machinery, Chemicals, Rubber, Oil Refining
TUNIS
Machinery, Chemicals, Canning, Consumer Products
CASABLANCA
Textiles, Food & Tobacco, Iron & Steel, Machinery, Chemicals, Oil Refining
Casablanca
Algiers
Tunis
Mackerel
Bananas
Sardines
Tuna
Citrus
Wine
Wheat
Barley
Olives
Pearls
Sponges
Sheep and Goats
Dates
Camels
Dakar
Rice
Peanuts
Cattle
Sheep and Goats
Fruit
Bananas
Millet and Sorghum
Cocoa
Coffee
Rubber
Ginger
Cotton
Kano
Palm Oil
Ibadan
Lagos
Abidjan
Accra
Port Harcourt
Herring
KANO
Textiles, Chemicals, Shoes, Light Industry
DAKAR
Chemicals, Food Processing, Textiles, Shoes
IBADAN
Food Processing, Chemicals, Rubber
ABIDJAN
Consumer Products, Vehicle Assembly, Oil Refining
ACCRA–TEMA
Vehicle Assembly, Food Processing, Oil Refining, Chemicals
LAGOS
Machinery, Chemicals, Brewing
PORT HARCOURT
Chemicals, Tobacco, Light Industry, Oil Refining, Tires

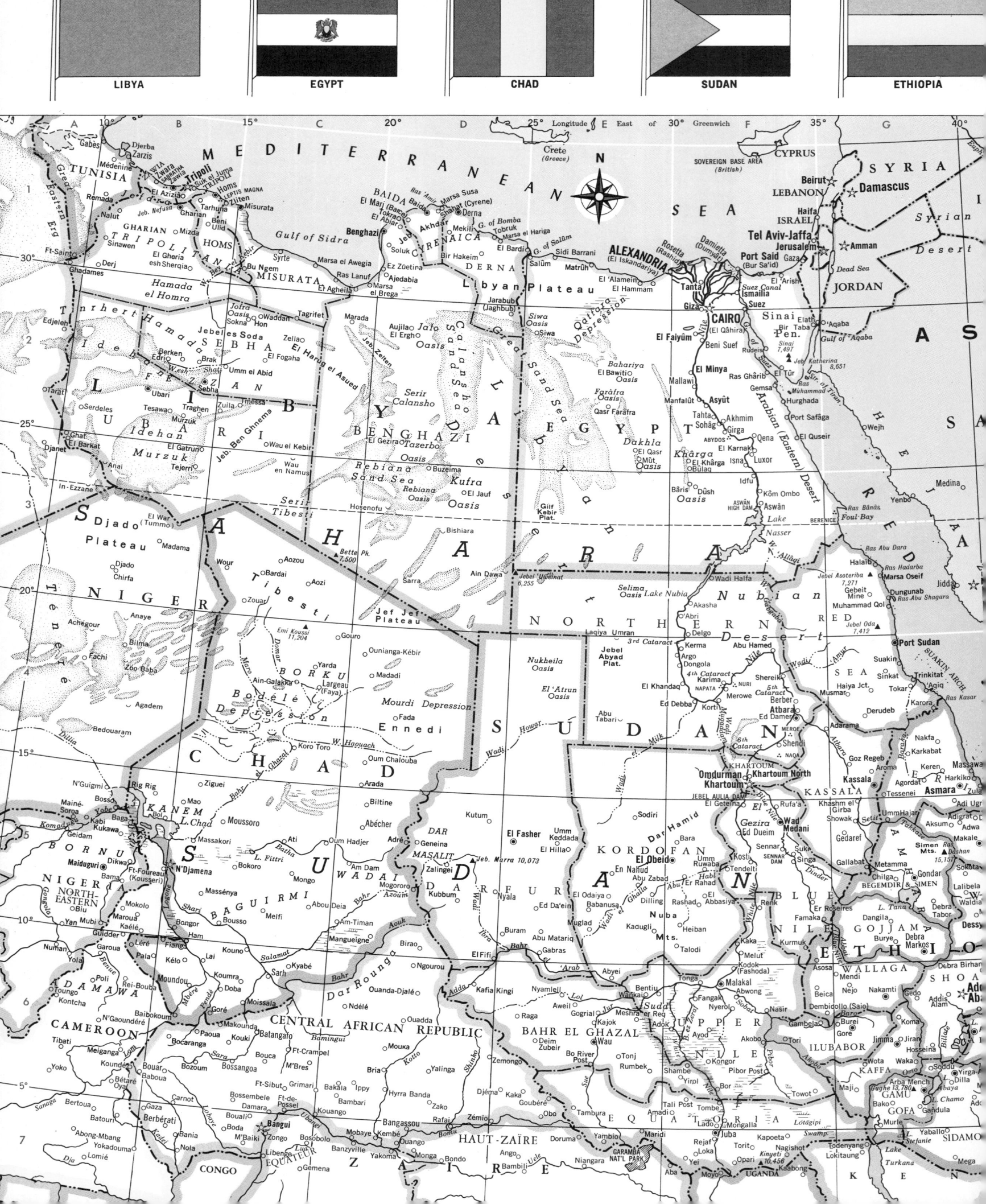

LIBYA | EGYPT | CHAD | SUDAN | ETHIOPIA

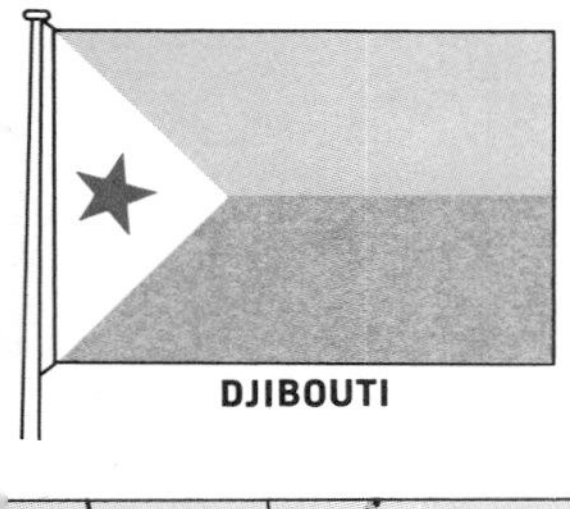

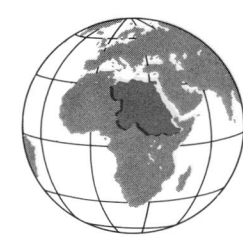

DJIBOUTI

LIBYA
AREA 679,358 sq. mi.
POPULATION 2,500,000
CAPITAL Tripoli
LARGEST CITY Tripoli
HIGHEST POINT Bette Pk. 7,500 ft.
MONETARY UNIT Libyan dinar
MAJOR LANGUAGES Arabic, Berber, Italian
MAJOR RELIGION Islam

DJIBOUTI
AREA 8,880 sq. mi.
POPULATION 250,000
CAPITAL Djibouti
LARGEST CITY Djibouti
HIGHEST POINT Moussa Ali 6,768 ft.
MONETARY UNIT Djibouti franc
MAJOR LANGUAGES Arabic, Somali, Afar, French
MAJOR RELIGIONS Islam, Roman Catholicism

EGYPT
AREA 386,659 sq. mi.
POPULATION 37,900,000
CAPITAL Cairo
LARGEST CITY Cairo
HIGHEST POINT Jeb. Katherina 8,651 ft.
MONETARY UNIT Egyptian pound
MAJOR LANGUAGE Arabic
MAJOR RELIGIONS Islam, Coptic Christianity

CHAD
AREA 495,752 sq. mi.
POPULATION 4,178,000
CAPITAL N'Djamena
LARGEST CITY N'Djamena
HIGHEST POINT Emi Koussi 11,204 ft.
MONETARY UNIT CFA franc
MAJOR LANGUAGES Arabic, Bagirmi, French, Sara, Massa, Moudang
MAJOR RELIGIONS Islam, Tribal religions

SUDAN
AREA 967,494 sq. mi.
POPULATION 18,347,000
CAPITAL Khartoum
LARGEST CITY Khartoum
HIGHEST POINT Jeb. Marra 10,073 ft.
MONETARY UNIT Sudanese pound
MAJOR LANGUAGES Arabic, Dinka, Nubian, Beja, Nuer, English
MAJOR RELIGIONS Islam, Tribal religions

ETHIOPIA
AREA 471,776 sq. mi.
POPULATION 27,946,000
CAPITAL Addis Ababa
LARGEST CITY Addis Ababa
HIGHEST POINT Ras Dashan 15,157 ft.
MONETARY UNIT Ethiopian dollar
MAJOR LANGUAGES Amharic, Gallinya, Tigrinya, Somali, Sidamo, Arabic, Ge'ez, Italian
MAJOR RELIGIONS Coptic Christianity, Islam

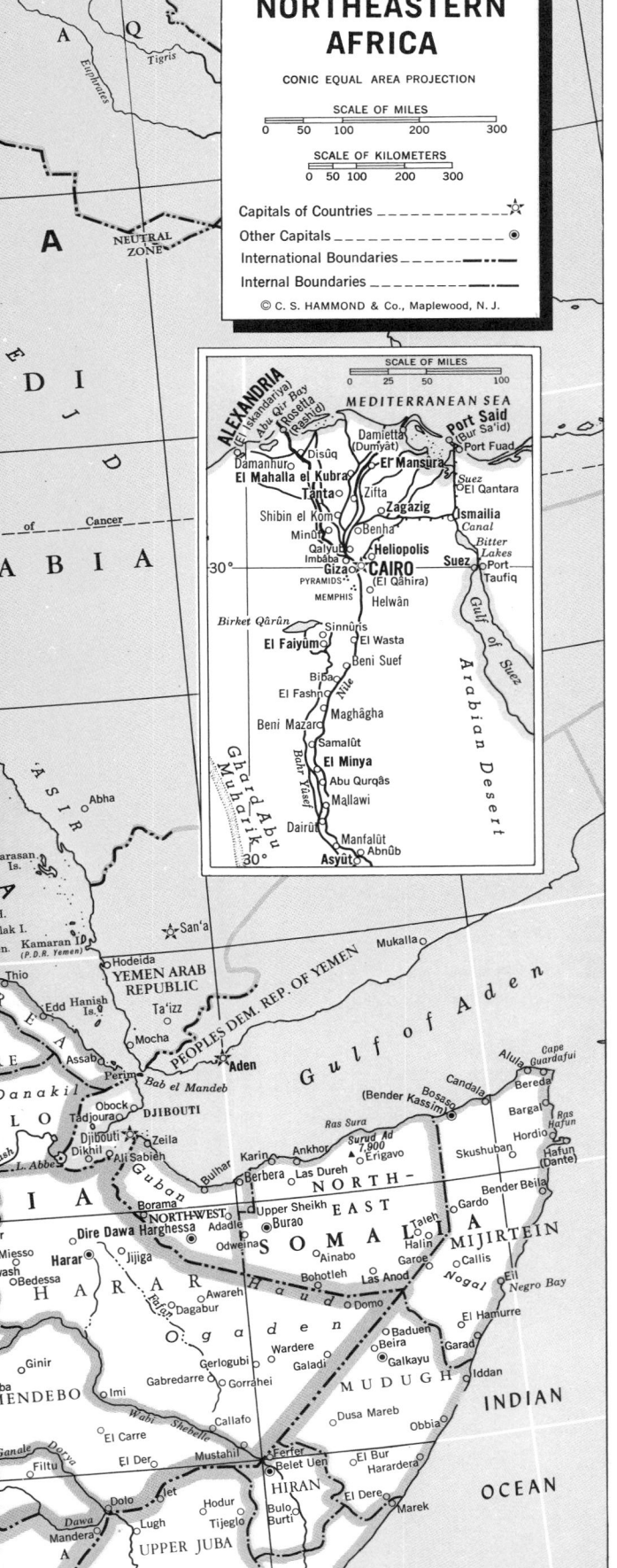

NORTHEASTERN AFRICA
CONIC EQUAL AREA PROJECTION

SCALE OF MILES
0 50 100 200 300

SCALE OF KILOMETERS
0 50 100 200 300

Capitals of Countries _____ ☆
Other Capitals _____ ⊙
International Boundaries _____
Internal Boundaries _____

© C. S. HAMMOND & Co., Maplewood, N.J.

CHAD
CITIES and TOWNS

Abécher, 19,650 ....D 5
Abou Deia, 1,100 ....C 5
Adré ....D 5
Ain-Galakka ....C 4
Am-Dam, 1,002 ....D 5
Am-Timan, 1,500 ....D 5
Aozi ....C 3
Aozou ....C 3
Arada ....D 4
Ati, 6,000 ....C 5
Baibokoum, 3,138 ....C 6
Bardai, 800 ....C 3
Biltine, 4,000 ....D 5
Bokoro, 4,700 ....C 5
Bol, 1,500 ....B 5
Bongor, 11,000 ....C 6
Bousso, 1,800 ....C 5
Doba, 7,375 ....C 6
Fada, 1,500 ....D 4
Faya (Largeau), 5,200 ....C 4
Fianga, 923 ....C 6
Goré ....C 6
Ham ....C 5
Kélo, 6,067 ....C 6
Koro Toro ....C 4
Koumra, 6,351 ....C 6
Kouno ....C 5
Kyabé, 3,000 ....C 6
Lai, 8,000 ....C 6
Largeau, 5,200 ....C 4
Léré, 3,500 ....B 6
Madadi ....D 4
Manqueigne, 1,700 ....D 5
Mao ....C 5
Massakori, 2,000 ....C 5
Massénya, 1,700 ....C 5
Melfi, 3,000 ....C 5
Mogororo ....D 5
Moissala, 3,000 ....C 6
Mongo, 7,000 ....C 5
Moundou, 34,100 ....C 6
Moussoro ....C 5
N'Djamena (capital), 132,500 ....C 5
Oum Chalouba ....D 4
Oum Hadjer, 4,500 ....C 5
Ounianga-Kébir ....D 4
Pala, 4,200 ....B 6
Rig Rig, 286 ....B 5
Sarh, 35,000 ....C 6
Yarda ....C 4
Ziguei ....C 5
Zouar ....C 3

OTHER FEATURES

Baguirmi (region), 81,666 ....C 5
Bahr el Ghazal (dry riv.) ....C 5
Batha (riv.) ....C 5
Bodélé (depr.) ....C 4
Borku (region), 21,962 ....C 4
Chad (lake) ....C 5
Domar (dry riv.) ....C 4
Emi Koussi (mt.) ....C 4
Ennedi (plat.) ....D 4
Fittri (lake) ....C 5
Haouach, Wadi (dry riv.) ....C 4
Jef Jef (plat.) ....D 3
Kanem (region), 261,108 ....C 5
Logone (riv.) ....C 6
Maro (dry riv.) ....C 4
Mbéré (riv.) ....C 6
Mourdi (depr.) ....D 4
Pendé (riv.) ....C 6
Sahara (des.) ....C 3
Salamat (riv.) ....C 6
Sara (riv.) ....C 6
Shari (riv.) ....C 5
Sudan (reg.) ....C 5
Tibesti (mts.) ....C 3
Wadai (region) 314,775 ....D 5

DJIBOUTI
CITIES and TOWNS

Ali Sabieh, 2,000 ....H 5
Dikhil, 1,000 ....H 5
Djibouti (capital), 130,000 ....H 5
Obock, 582 ....H 5
Tadjoura, 2,000 ....H 5

OTHER FEATURES

Abbe (lake) ....H 5

Aden (gulf) ....J 5
Bab el Mandeb (str.) ....H 5

EGYPT
CITIES and TOWNS

Abnûb, 27,751 ....J 4
Abu Qurqâs, 19,318 ....J 4
Akhmin, 41,580 ....F 2
Alexandria, 1,803,900 ....J 2
Aswân, 127,700 ....F 3
Asyût, 154,100 ....J 4
Bâris, 1,347 ....F 3
Benha, 52,686 ....J 3
Beni Mazar, 30,583 ....J 4
Beni Suef, 78,829 ....J 3
Biba, 20,773 ....J 4
Bûlaq, 928 ....F 2
Bur Sa'id (Port Said), 283,400 ....K 3
Cairo (cap.), 4,219,853 ....J 3
Dairût, 24,364 ....J 4
Damanhur, 146,300 ....J 3
Damietta, 71,780 ....J 3
Dumyât (Damietta), 71,780 ....J 3
Dûsh, 794 ....F 3
El 'Alamein, 593 ....E 1
El 'Arish, 29,973 ....F 1
El Bawiti, 2,478 ....E 2
El Fashn, 25,961 ....J 4
El Faiyûm, 133,800 ....J 3

[Egypt inset map labels]

ALEXANDRIA (El Iskandarîya)
Abu Qir Bay
Rosetta (Rashid)
MEDITERRANEAN SEA
Damietta (Dumyât)
Port Said (Bur Sa'id)
Port Fuad
Damanhur
Disûq
El Mansura
El Mahalla el Kubra
Tântâ
Zifta
Zagazig
El Qantara
Ismailia
Shibin el Kom
Minûf
Benha
Qalyub
Imbâba
Heliopolis
Gizao
CAIRO (El Qâhira)
Suez
Port Taufiq
Gulf of Suez
PYRAMIDS
MEMPHIS
Helwân
Bitter Lakes
Suez Canal
Birket Qârûn
Sinnûris
El Faiyûm
El Wasta
Beni Suef
BiBao
El Fashn
Maghâgha
Beni Mazar
Samalût
El Minya
Abu Qurqâs
Mallawi
Dairût
Manfalût
Abnûb
Asyût
Nile
Bahr Yûsef
Arabian Desert
Ghardaña
Abu Muharik
Tropic of Cancer

Topography

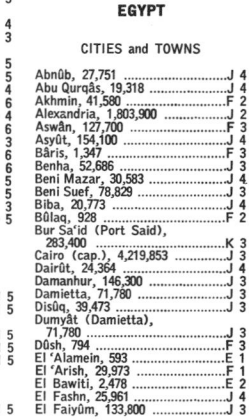

Gulf of Sidra
Nile Delta
Suez Canal
Sinai Pen.
Qattara Depr.
Jeb. Katherina 8,651
EL HARUG EL ASUED
Idehan
Libyan Desert
Kufra Oasis
Arabian Desert
L. Nasser
L. Nubia
Nubian Desert
TIBESTI
Emi Koussi 11,204
Bette Pk. 7,500
Sahara
Bodélé Depression
Lake Chad
Shari
Bahr el Ghazal
Logone
MARRA MTS.
Jeb. Marra 10,073
Sudan
Blue Nile
White Nile
Atbara
Sudd
ETHIOPIAN HIGHLANDS
Ras Dashan 15,157
OGADEN
Shebeli
Kinyeti 10,456

0 200 400 600
MILES

5,000 m. / 16,404 ft. | 2,000 m. / 6,562 ft. | 1,000 m. / 3,281 ft. | 500 m. / 1,640 ft. | 200 m. / 656 ft. | 100 m. / 328 ft. | Sea Level | Below

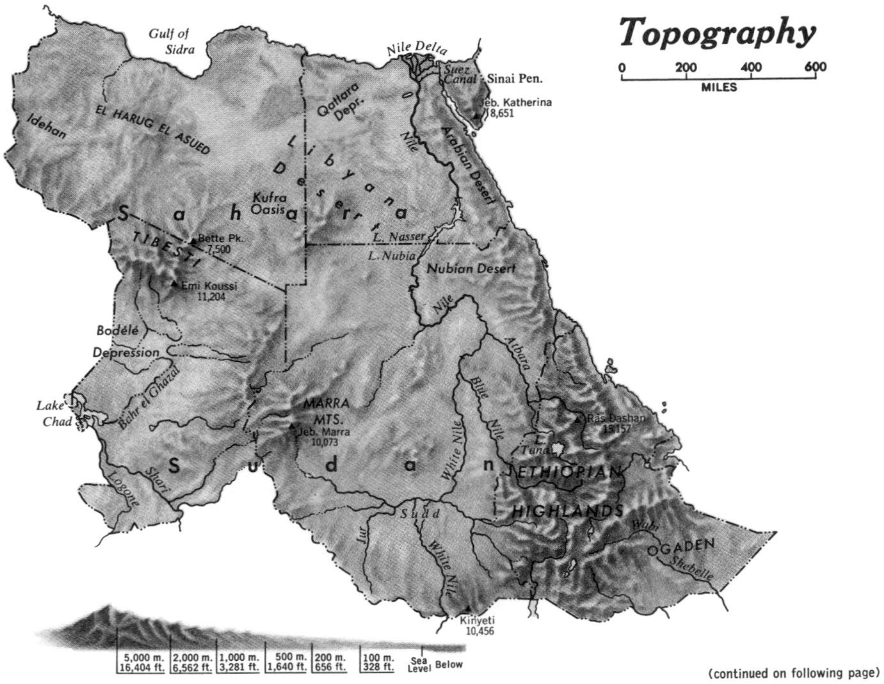

(continued on following page)

[Main map labels - left side]

IRAN
IRAQ
Tigris
Euphrates
NEUTRAL ZONE
ARABIA
'ASIR
Abha
Birket Qârûn
San'a
Kamaran I. (P.D.R. Yemen)
Hodeida
YEMEN ARAB REPUBLIC
Ta'izz
Mocha
Thio
Edd
Hanish Is.
Assab
Danakil
Perim
Bab el Mandeb
Mukalla
PEOPLES DEM. REP. OF YEMEN
Aden
Gulf of Aden
Cape Guardafui
Alula
Candala
Bereda
Bargal
Ras Hafun
Hafun (Dante)
Bosaso (Bender Kassim)
Ras Sura
Ankhor
Surud Ad 7,900
Erigavo
Skushuban
Hordio
DJIBOUTI
Obock
Tadjoura
Zeila
Djibouti
Ali Sabieh
Dikhil
L. Abbe
Karin
Bulhar
Berbera
Las Dureh
NORTH-EAST
Bender Beila
Guban
Upper Sheikh
Burao
Gardo
MIJIRTEIN
Borama
NORTHWEST
Adadle
Hargheisa
Dire Dawa
Odweina
Ainabo
Garoe
Callis
Harar
Jijiga
Taleh
Halin
Las Anod
Bohotleh
HARAR
Awareh
Negro Bay
Dagabur
Nogal
Gabredarre
Wardere
El Hamurre
Gerlogubi
Baduen
Galadi
Beira
Garad
Ogaden
Galkayu
Iddan
MUDUGH
Ginir
Imi
Dusa Mareb
Obbia
ENDEBO
Callafo
INDIAN OCEAN
El Carre
Mustahil
Ferfer
El Bur
El Der
Ganale Dorya
Dolo
Jet
Hodur
Tijeglo
Bulo Burti
HIRAN
El Dere
Marek
Filtu
Lugh
Mandera
UPPER JUBA
Dawa

Agriculture, Industry and Resources

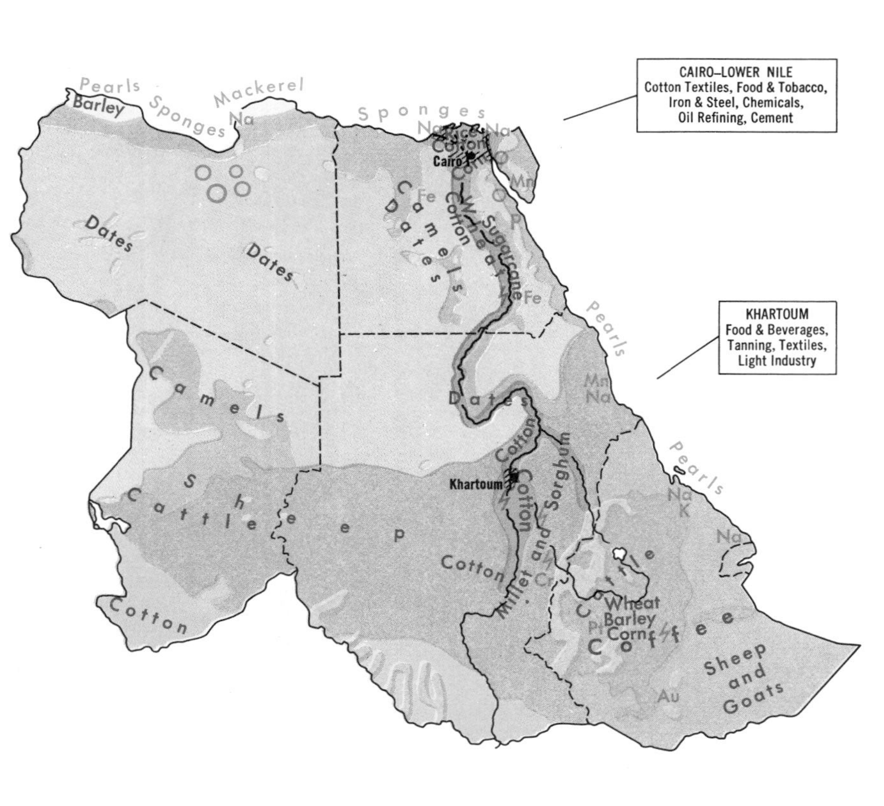

CAIRO–LOWER NILE
Cotton Textiles, Food & Tobacco,
Iron & Steel, Chemicals,
Oil Refining, Cement

KHARTOUM
Food & Beverages,
Tanning, Textiles,
Light Industry

DOMINANT LAND USE

Cereals, Horticulture, Livestock
Cash Crops, Mixed Cereals
Cotton, Cereals
Market Gardening, Diversified Tropical Crops
Plantation Agriculture
Oases
Pasture Livestock
Nomadic Livestock Herding
Forests
Nonagricultural Land

MAJOR MINERAL OCCURRENCES

Au Gold
Cr Chromium
Fe Iron Ore
K   Potash
Mn Manganese
Na Salt
O   Petroleum
P   Phosphates
Pt Platinum

⚡ Water Power
▨ Major Industrial Areas

ANGOLA
- **AREA** 481,351 sq. mi.
- **POPULATION** 6,761,000
- **CAPITAL** Luanda
- **LARGEST CITY** Luanda
- **HIGHEST POINT** Mt. Moco 8,593 ft.
- **MONETARY UNIT** Angolan escudo
- **MAJOR LANGUAGES** Mbundu, Kongo, Lunda, Portuguese
- **MAJOR RELIGIONS** Tribal religions, Roman Catholicism

BURUNDI
- **AREA** 10,747 sq. mi.
- **POPULATION** 6,400,000
- **CAPITAL** Bujumbura
- **LARGEST CITY** Bujumbura
- **HIGHEST POINT** 8,858 ft.
- **MONETARY UNIT** Burundi franc
- **MAJOR LANGUAGES** Kirundi, French, Swahili
- **MAJOR RELIGIONS** Tribal religions, Roman Catholicism, Islam

CAMEROON
- **AREA** 183,568 sq.mi.
- **POPULATION** 6,600,000
- **CAPITAL** Yaoundé
- **LARGEST CITY** Douala
- **HIGHEST POINT** Cameroon 13,350 ft.
- **MONETARY UNIT** CFA franc
- **MAJOR LANGUAGES** Fang, Bamileke, Fulani, Duala, French, English
- **MAJOR RELIGIONS** Tribal religions, Christianity, Islam

CENTRAL AFRICAN REPUBLIC
- **AREA** 236,293 sq. mi.
- **POPULATION** 1,800,000
- **CAPITAL** Bangui
- **LARGEST CITY** Bangui
- **HIGHEST POINT** Gao 4,659 ft.
- **MONETARY UNIT** CFA franc
- **MAJOR LANGUAGES** Banda, Gbaya, Sangho, French
- **MAJOR RELIGIONS** Tribal religions, Christianity, Islam

CONGO
- **AREA** 132,046 sq. mi.
- **POPULATION** 1,400,000
- **CAPITAL** Brazzaville
- **LARGEST CITY** Brazzaville
- **HIGHEST POINT** Leketi Mts. 3,412 ft.
- **MONETARY UNIT** CFA franc
- **MAJOR LANGUAGES** Kikongo, Bateke, Lingala, French
- **MAJOR RELIGIONS** Christianity, Tribal religions, Islam

EQUATORIAL GUINEA
- **AREA** 10,831 sq. mi.
- **POPULATION** 320,000
- **CAPITAL** Malabo
- **LARGEST CITY** Malabo
- **HIGHEST POINT** 9,868 ft.
- **MONETARY UNIT** ekuele
- **MAJOR LANGUAGES** Fang, Bubi, Spanish, English, Ibo
- **MAJOR RELIGIONS** Tribal religions, Christianity

GABON
- **AREA** 103,346 sq. mi.
- **POPULATION** 526,000
- **CAPITAL** Libreville
- **LARGEST CITY** Libreville
- **HIGHEST POINT** Ibounzi 5,165 ft.
- **MONETARY UNIT** CFA franc
- **MAJOR LANGUAGES** Fang and other Bantu languages, French
- **MAJOR RELIGIONS** Tribal religions, Christianity, Islam

KENYA
- **AREA** 224,960 sq. mi.
- **POPULATION** 13,300,000
- **CAPITAL** Nairobi
- **LARGEST CITY** Nairobi
- **HIGHEST POINT** Kenya 17,058 ft.
- **MONETARY UNIT** Kenya shilling
- **MAJOR LANGUAGES** Kikuyu, Luo, Kavirondo, Kamba, Swahili, English
- **MAJOR RELIGIONS** Tribal religions, Christianity, Hinduism, Islam

MALAWI
- **AREA** 45,747 sq. mi.
- **POPULATION** 5,100,000
- **CAPITAL** Lilongwe
- **LARGEST CITY** Blantyre
- **HIGHEST POINT** Mlanje 9,843 ft.
- **MONETARY UNIT** Malawi kwacha
- **MAJOR LANGUAGES** Chichewa, Yao, English, Nyanja, Tumbuka, Tonga, Ngoni
- **MAJOR RELIGIONS** Tribal religions, Islam, Christianity

RWANDA
- **AREA** 10,169 sq. mi.
- **POPULATION** 4,241,000
- **CAPITAL** Kigali
- **LARGEST CITY** Kigali
- **HIGHEST POINT** Karisimbi 14,780 ft.
- **MONETARY UNIT** Rwanda franc
- **MAJOR LANGUAGES** Kinyarwanda, French, Swahili
- **MAJOR RELIGIONS** Tribal religions, Roman Catholicism, Islam

SOMALIA
- **AREA** 246,200 sq. mi.
- **POPULATION** 3,170,000
- **CAPITAL** Mogadishu
- **LARGEST CITY** Mogadishu
- **HIGHEST POINT** Surud Ad 7,900 ft.
- **MONETARY UNIT** Somali shilling
- **MAJOR LANGUAGES** Somali, Arabic, Italian, English
- **MAJOR RELIGIONS** Islam

TANZANIA
- **AREA** 363,708 sq. mi.
- **POPULATION** 15,506,000
- **CAPITAL** Dar es Salaam
- **LARGEST CITY** Dar es Salaam
- **HIGHEST POINT** Kilimanjaro 19,340 ft.
- **MONETARY UNIT** Tanzanian shilling
- **MAJOR LANGUAGES** Nyamwezi-Sukuma, Swahili, English
- **MAJOR RELIGIONS** Tribal religions, Christianity, Islam

UGANDA
- **AREA** 91,076 sq. mi.
- **POPULATION** 11,400,000
- **CAPITAL** Kampala
- **LARGEST CITY** Kampala
- **HIGHEST POINT** Margherita 16,795 ft.
- **MONETARY UNIT** Ugandan shilling
- **MAJOR LANGUAGES** Luganda, Acholi, Teso, Nyoro, Soga, Nkole, English, Swahili
- **MAJOR RELIGIONS** Tribal religions, Christianity, Islam

ZAIRE
- **AREA** 918,962 sq. mi.
- **POPULATION** 25,600,000
- **CAPITAL** Kinshasa
- **LARGEST CITY** Kinshasa
- **HIGHEST POINT** Margherita 16,795 ft.
- **MONETARY UNIT** zaire
- **MAJOR LANGUAGES** Tshiluba, Mongo, Kikongo, Kingwana, Zande, Lingala, Swahili, French
- **MAJOR RELIGIONS** Tribal religions, Christianity

ZAMBIA
- **AREA** 290,586 sq. mi.
- **POPULATION** 4,936,000
- **CAPITAL** Lusaka
- **LARGEST CITY** Lusaka
- **HIGHEST POINT** Sunzu 6,782 ft.
- **MONETARY UNIT** Zambian kwacha
- **MAJOR LANGUAGES** Bemba, Tonga, Lozi, Luvale, Nyanja, English, Afrikaans
- **MAJOR RELIGIONS** Tribal religions

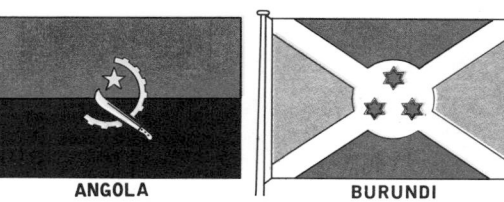

ANGOLA

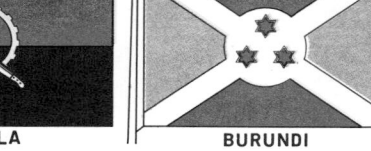

BURUNDI

CAMEROON

CENTRAL AFRICAN REP.

CONGO

EQUATORIAL GUINEA

GABON

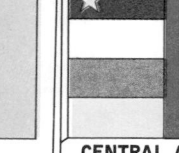

KENYA

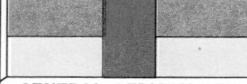

MALAWI

RWANDA

SOMALIA

TANZANIA

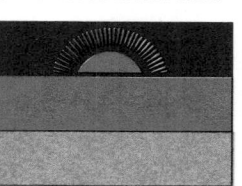

UGANDA

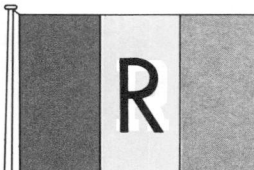

ZAIRE

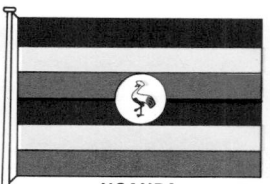

ZAMBIA

(continued on following page)

Zémio, 1,500 ..... D 2
Zemongo ..... E 2

OTHER FEATURES

Bamingui (riv.) ..... D 2
Dar Rounga (region), 25,000 ..... D 2
Gao (mt.) ..... C 2
Kadei (riv.) ..... C 3
Kotto (riv.) ..... D 2
Lobaye (riv.) ..... C 3
Pendé (riv.) ..... C 2
Sara (riv.) ..... C 2
Shari (riv.) ..... C 2

Shinko (riv.) ..... D 2
Ubangi (riv.) ..... C 3

CONGO

CITIES and TOWNS

Boko, 800 ..... B 4
Brazzaville (capital), 94,000 ..... C 4
Brazzaville, *200,000 ..... C 4
Djambala, 2,000 ..... C 4
Dolisie, 20,000 ..... B 4
Madingo, 2,500 ..... B 4

Dongou, 2,190 ..... C 3
Epéna, 8,446 ..... C 3
Ewo, 700 ..... B 4
Fort-Rousset, 5,082 ..... C 4
Gamboma, 1,700 ..... C 4
Ikelemba, 400 ..... C 3
Impfondo, 2,000 ..... C 3
Kayes, 1,500 ..... B 4
Kellé, 1,282 ..... B 4
Kibangou, 1,000 ..... B 4
Kinkala, 1,000 ..... B 4
Komono, 750 ..... B 4
Loudima, 400 ..... B 4
Madingo, 2,500 ..... B 4

Makoua, 2,000 ..... C 3
Mindouli, 1,600 ..... B 4
Mossaka, 2,128 ..... C 4
Mossendjo, 3,000 ..... B 4
M'Pouya ..... C 4
M'Vouti ..... B 4
Okoyo ..... C 4
Ouesso, 4,464 ..... C 3
Pangala ..... B 4
Pointe-Noire, 100,000 ..... B 4
Sembé ..... B 4
Sibiti, 1,000 ..... B 4
Souanké, 280 ..... B 4
Zanaga, 800 ..... B 4

OTHER FEATURES

Alima (riv.) ..... B 4
Congo (riv.) ..... C 4
Crystal (mts.) ..... B 4
Kouilou (riv.) ..... B 4
Niari (riv.) ..... B 4
Sanga (riv.) ..... C 3
Ubangi (riv.) ..... C 3

EQUATORIAL GUINEA

TERRITORIES

Macías Nguema Biyogo, 78,000 ..... A 3
Río Muni, 203,000 ..... A 3

CITIES and TOWNS

Bata, 27,024 ..... B 3
Luba, 19,933 ..... A 3
Malabo (capital), 37,237 ..... A 3
Mbini, 14,503 ..... A 3

OTHER FEATURES

Corisco (isl.) ..... A 3
Elobey (isls.) ..... A 3
Macías Nguema Biyogo (island), 78,000 ..... A 3

GABON

CITIES and TOWNS

Bitam, 2,080 ..... B 3
Booué, 114 ..... B 3
Cocobeach, 100 ..... B 3
Franceville, 2,000 ..... B 4
Kango, 300 ..... B 4
Koula-Moutou, 3,170 ..... B 4
Lalara, 1,333 ..... B 3
Lambaréné, 7,000 ..... B 4
Lastoursville, 2,000 ..... B 4
Lekoni, 3,020 ..... B 4
Libreville (cap.), *57,000 ..... A 3
Makokou, 1,150 ..... B 3
Mayumba, 1,000 ..... A 4
M'Bigou, 1,500 ..... B 4
Mekambo, 800 ..... B 3
Mimongo, 350 ..... B 4
Minvoul, 200 ..... B 3
Mitzic, 1,180 ..... B 3
Moanda, 2,700 ..... B 4
Mouila, 1,800 ..... B 4
N'Dendé, 1,560 ..... B 4
N'Djolé, 1,600 ..... B 4
Okondja, 1,600 ..... B 4
Oyem, 3,050 ..... B 3
Port-Gentil, 30,000 ..... A 4
Setté-Cama, 1,609 ..... A 4
Tchibanga, 2,080 ..... B 4

OTHER FEATURES

Crystal (mts.) ..... B 4
Ibounzi (mt.) ..... B 3
Ivindo (riv.) ..... B 3
Lopez (cape) ..... A 4
N'Dogo (lag.) ..... A 4
N'Gounié (riv.) ..... B 4
N'Komi (lag.) ..... A 4
Ogooué (riv.) ..... A 4
Onangué (lake) ..... A 4
Pongara (pt.) ..... A 3

KENYA

PROVINCES

Central, 1,664,000 ..... G 4
Coast, 924,800 ..... G 4
Eastern, 1,899,200 ..... G 4
Nairobi (city district), 477,600 ..... G 4
North Eastern, 244,200 ..... G 3
Nyanza, 2,115,908 ..... F 4
Rift Valley, 2,219,400 ..... G 3
Western, 1,335,100 ..... G 3

CITIES and TOWNS

Baragoi ..... G 3
Eldoret, 16,900 ..... G 3
El Wak ..... H 3

Embu, 5,213 ..... G 4
Fort Hall, 5,389 ..... G 4
Garissa ..... G 4
Garsen ..... G 4
Gazi, 6,452 ..... G 4
Gilgil ..... G 3
Hadu ..... G 4
Isiolo, 5,445 ..... G 3
Kajiado ..... G 4
Kakamega ..... F 4
Karungu ..... F 4
Kericho, 10,900 ..... F 4
Kiambu ..... G 4
Kibwezi ..... H 4
Kipini ..... H 4
Kisii ..... F 4
Kisumu, 30,700 ..... F 4
Kitale, 11,500 ..... G 3
Kitui ..... G 4
Konza ..... G 4
Kwale ..... G 4
Laisamis ..... G 3
Lamu, 5,828 ..... H 4
Lodwar ..... F 3
Lokitaung ..... G 3
Lolgorien ..... F 4
Machakos ..... G 4
Magadi ..... G 4
Malindi, 5,818 ..... H 4
Marsabit ..... G 3
Meru ..... G 4
Mombasa, 234,400 ..... G 4
Moyale ..... G 3
Nairobi (capital), 477,600 ..... G 4
Naivasha ..... G 4
Nakuru, 47,800 ..... G 4
Namanga ..... G 4
Nanyuki, 11,200 ..... G 3
Ngong ..... G 4
North Horr ..... G 3
Nyeri, 9,900 ..... G 4
Port Victoria ..... F 3
Rumuruti ..... G 3
South Horr ..... G 3
Thika, 18,100 ..... G 4
Thomson's Falls, 5,316 ..... G 3
Todenyang ..... G 3
Tsavo ..... G 4
Vanga ..... G 4
Voi ..... G 4
Wajir ..... H 3
Witu ..... G 4

OTHER FEATURES

Dawa (riv.) ..... H 3
Elgon (mt.) ..... F 3
Formosa (bay) ..... H 4
Galana (riv.) ..... G 4
Gedi (ruins) ..... H 4
Kavirondo (gulf) ..... F 4
Kenya (mt.) ..... G 4
Lorian (swamp) ..... G 3
Lotagipi (swamp) ..... F 2
Nyira (mt.) ..... G 3
Patta (isl.) ..... H 4
Royal Tsavo Nat'l Park ..... G 4
Tana (riv.) ..... G 4
Turkana (Rudolf) (lake) ..... G 3
Victoria (lake) ..... F 4

MALAWI

CITIES and TOWNS

Bandawe ..... F 6
Blantyre, 109,461 ..... F 7
Chilumbe ..... F 6
Chipoka ..... F 6
Chiromo ..... F 7
Chitipa, 1,429 ..... F 5
Cholo, 1,394 ..... F 7
Dedza, 2,318 ..... F 6
Dowa, 750 ..... F 6
Fort Johnston, 1,467 ..... F 6
Karonga, 1,128 ..... F 5
Kasungu, 1,628 ..... F 6
Lilongwe (cap.), 19,425 ..... F 6
Livingstonia ..... F 6
Mchinji, 831 ..... F 6
Mzimba, 4,156 ..... F 6
Ncheu, 1,118 ..... F 6
Nkhata Bay, 1,188 ..... F 6
Nkhota Kota, 1,117 ..... F 6
Nsanje, 1,373 ..... G 7

Salima, 2,307 ..... F 6
Zomba, 19,666 ..... G 7

OTHER FEATURES

Chilwa (lake) ..... G 7
Malawi (Nyasa) (lake) ..... F 6
Mlanje (mt.) ..... G 7
Nyasa (lake) ..... F 6
Shire (riv.) ..... G 7

RWANDA

CITIES and TOWNS

Butare, 3,714 ..... E 4
Cyangugu, 284 ..... E 4
Gisenyi, 3,956 ..... E 4
Kigali (cap.), 24,000 ..... E 4
Nyabisindu, 1,010 ..... F 4

OTHER FEATURES

Kagera Nat'l Park ..... F 4
Karisimbi (mt.) ..... E 4
Kivu (lake) ..... E 4
Ruzizi (riv.) ..... E 4

SOMALIA

PROVINCES

Benadir, 392,189 ..... H 3
Hiran, 176,603 ..... J 3
Lower Juba, 113,774 ..... H 3
Mijirtein, 82,710 ..... J 2
Mudugh, 141,197 ..... J 2
North-East ..... J 1
North-West ..... H 2
Upper Juba, 362,397 ..... H 3

CITIES and TOWNS

Adadle ..... H 2
Afgoi, ⊙16,575 ..... H 3
Afmadu, 2,580 ..... H 3
Alula, ⊙6,063 ..... K 1
Ankhor ..... J 1
Audegle, ⊙8,865 ..... H 3
Baduen ..... J 2
Baidoa, ⊙14,962 ..... H 3
Balad, ⊙1,936 ..... H 3
Barawa (Brava), ⊙6,168 ..... H 3
Bardera, 7,874 ..... H 3
Bargal, ⊙2,222 ..... K 1
Belet Uen, ⊙11,426 ..... J 3
Bender Beila, 6,084 ..... K 2
Bender Kasim (Bosaso), ⊙7,560 ..... J 1
Berbera, ⊙12,219 ..... J 2
Bereda, 8,323 ..... K 1
Birikao (Bur Gavo) ..... H 4
Bohotleh ..... J 2
Borama, ⊙3,244 ..... H 2
Bosaso, ⊙7,560 ..... J 1
Brava, ⊙6,168 ..... H 3
Bulhar ..... J 2
Bulo Burti, ⊙5,247 ..... J 3
Bur Acaba, ⊙10,924 ..... H 3
Burao, ⊙12,617 ..... J 2
Bur Gavo ..... H 4
Candala, ⊙3,213 ..... K 1
Coriolei, ⊙4,341 ..... H 3
Dante (Hafun) ..... H 2
Dif ..... H 3
Dinsor, ⊙4,301 ..... H 3
Dusa Mareb, ⊙3,125 ..... J 2
Eil, ⊙2,234 ..... J 2
El Athale (Itala), ⊙900 ..... J 3
El Bur, ⊙3,224 ..... J 2
El Dere, ⊙10,924 ..... J 3
El Hamurre ..... J 2
Erigavo, ⊙4,279 ..... J 1
Ferfer ..... J 2
Galkayu, ⊙9,477 ..... J 2
Garad ..... J 2
Gardo, ⊙4,076 ..... J 2
Garoe, ⊙5,672 ..... J 2
Gobwen ..... H 4
Hafun ..... K 1
Harardera, ⊙824 ..... J 3
Harghessa, 40,254 ..... H 2
Hodur, ⊙3,137 ..... J 2
Hordio ..... K 1
Iddan ..... J 2

(continued on following page)

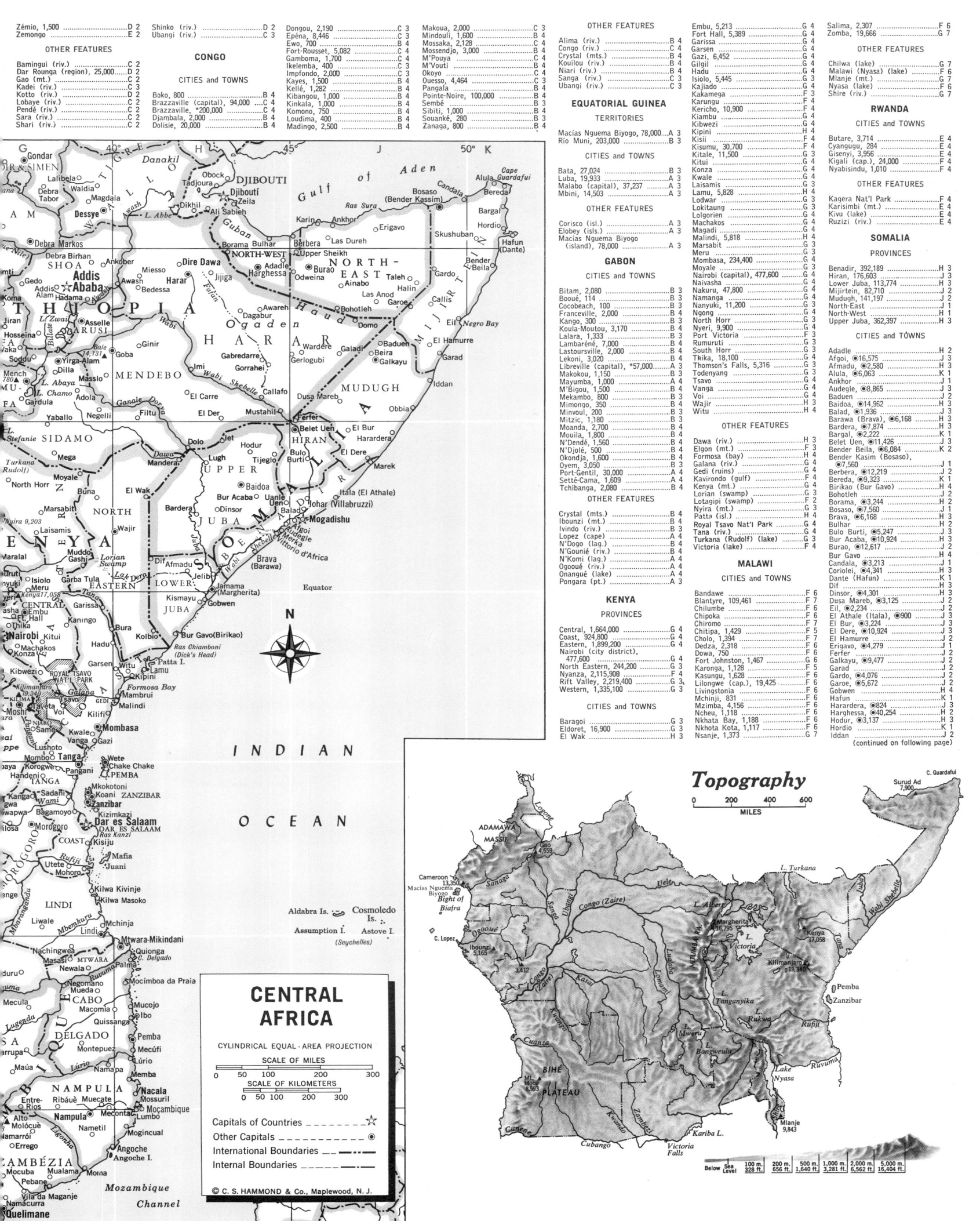

CENTRAL AFRICA

CYLINDRICAL EQUAL-AREA PROJECTION

SCALE OF MILES
0 50 100 200 300

SCALE OF KILOMETERS
0 50 100 200 300

Capitals of Countries ——————— ★
Other Capitals ——————— ⊙
International Boundaries ——————
Internal Boundaries ——————

© C. S. HAMMOND & Co., Maplewood, N.J.

Topography

MILES
0 200 400 600

Below sea Level | 100 m. 328 ft. | 200 m. 656 ft. | 500 m. 1,640 ft. | 1,000 m. 3,281 ft. | 2,000 m. 6,562 ft. | 5,000 m. 16,404 ft.

(continued)

SOMALIA (cantinued)

Iet, ◉1,370 .... H 3
Itala, ◉900 .... J 3
Jamama, ◉22,030 .... H 3
Jelib, ◉3,232 .... H 3
Johar, ◉13,156 .... H 3
Kismayu, ◉17,872 .... H 4
Las Anod, ◉2,441 .... J 2
Las Dureh .... J 1
Las Khoreh, ◉2.245 .... J 1
Lugh, ◉3,768 .... H 3
Marek .... J 3
Margherita (Jamama), ◉22,030 .... H 3
Merka, ◉56,385 .... H 3
Mogadishu, 172,677 .... J 3
Obbia, ◉2,106 .... J 2
Odweina, ◉1,422 .... J 2
Skushuban, ◉1,384 .... J 1
Taleh .... J 2
Tijeglo, ◉5,459 .... H 3
Uanle Uen, ◉9,650 .... H 3
Upper Sheikh .... J 2
Villabruzzi (Johar), ◉13,156 .... J 3
Vittorio d'Africa .... H 3
Zeila, ◉1,226 .... H 1

OTHER FEATURES

Aden (gulf) .... J 1
Chiamboni, Ras (cape) .... H 4
Guardafui (cape) .... K 1
Guban (reg.) .... H 1
Hafun, Ras (cape) .... K 1
Haud (plat.) .... J 2
Juba (riv.) .... H 3
Negro (bay) .... J 2
Nogal (reg.) .... J 2
Surud Ad (mt.) .... J 1
Wabi Shebelle (riv.) .... H 3

TANZANIA

REGIONS

Arusha .... G 4
Coast .... G 5
Dar es Salaam .... G 5
Dodoma .... G 5
Iringa .... G 5
Kigoma .... F 4
Kilimanjaro .... G 4
Lindi .... G 5
Mara .... F 4
Mbeya .... F 5
Morogoro .... G 5
Mtwara .... G 6
Mwanza .... F 4
Pemba .... H 5
Rukwa .... F 5
Ruvuma .... G 6
Shinyanga .... F 4
Singida .... F 5
Tabora .... F 5
Tanga .... G 5
West Lake .... F 4
Zanzibar Mjini .... H 5
Zanzibar Shambani North .... G 5
Zanzibar Shambani South .... G 5

CITIES and TOWNS

Arusha, 32,452 .... G 4
Bagamoyo, 5,112 .... G 5
Biharamulo, 1,011 .... F 4
Bukene, 2,288 .... F 4
Bukoba, 8,141 .... F 4
Chake Chake, 4,862 .... G 5
Chunya, 2,398 .... F 5
Dar es Salaam (capital), 272,821 .... G 5
Dodoma, 23,559 .... G 5
Geita, 3,066 .... F 4
Ifakara, †21,101 .... G 5
Iringa, 21,746 .... G 5
Itigi, †6,633 .... F 5
Kahama, 3,211 .... F 4
Kaliua, †13,071 .... F 5
Karema, †3,171 .... F 5
Kasanga, †10,462 .... F 5
Kibara, †18,827 .... F 4
Kibaya, †4,422 .... G 5
Kibondo .... F 4
Kigoma-Ujiji, 21,369 .... E 4
Kilosa, 4,458 .... G 5
Kilwa Kivinje, 2,790 .... G 5
Kilwa Masoko .... G 5
Kinyangiri, †14,111 .... G 4
Kipili, †2,964 .... F 5
Kisiju, †26,298 .... G 5
Kitunda, †2,491 .... F 5
Kizimkazi, 992 .... G 5
Koani, 1,102 .... G 5
Kondoa, 4,514 .... G 4
Kongwa, †27,411 .... G 5
Korogwe, 6,675 .... G 5
Lindi, 13,352 .... G 5
Liwale, †22,205 .... G 5
Longido, †1,998 .... G 4
Lushoto, 1,803 .... G 4
Mahenge, †32,047 .... G 5
Makumbako .... G 5
Manyoni, †4,362 .... G 5
Mbamba Bay, †10,936 .... G 6
Mbeya, 12,479 .... F 5
Mbulu, †7,004 .... G 4
Mchinga, †5,778 .... H 5
Mkokotoni, 2,200 .... G 5
Mohoro-Kikobo, †6,112 .... G 5
Mombo, †29,782 .... G 4
Morogoro, 25,262 .... G 5
Moshi, 26,864 .... G 4
Mpanda, †4,220 .... F 5
Mpwapwa, 2,429 .... G 5
Mtwara-Mikindani, 20,413 .... H 6
Murongo, †20,118 .... F 4
Musoma, 15,412 .... F 4
Muwale .... F 5
Mwadui, 7,383 .... F 4
Mwanza, 34,861 .... F 4
Mwaya, †15,940 .... F 5
Mwesi, †803 .... F 5
Nachingwea, 3,751 .... G 6
Newala, †7,458 .... G 6
Ngara .... F 4
Njombe .... F 5
Nzega, 2,386 .... F 4
Pangani, 2,955 .... G 5
Rungwa, †903 .... F 5
Sadani, †760 .... G 5
Same, †8,105 .... G 4
Sekenke .... F 4
Shinyanga, 5,135 .... F 4
Singida, 9,478 .... F 4
Songea, 5,430 .... G 6
Sumbawanga, †34,106 .... F 5
Tabora, 21,012 .... F 5
Tanga, 61,058 .... G 4
Tukuyu, 4,089 .... F 5
Tunduru .... G 6
Urambo, †16,625 .... F 4
Utete, †5,642 .... G 5
Uvinza, †12,812 .... F 5
Wete, 8,469 .... G 4
Zanzibar, 68,490 .... G 5
Zanzibar, *95,047 .... G 5

OTHER FEATURES

Eyasi (lake) .... F 4
Gombe (riv.) .... F 4
Great Ruaha (riv.) .... G 5
Juani (isl.), 696 .... G 5
Kalambo (falls) .... F 5
Kanzi (cape) .... G 5
Kilimanjaro (mt.) .... G 4
Kilombero (riv.) .... G 5
Kungwe (mt.) .... F 5
Mafia (isl.), 15,459 .... H 5
Manyara (lake) .... G 4
Masai (steppe) .... G 4
Mbarangandu (riv.) .... G 5
Mbemkuru (riv.) .... G 5
Meru (mt.) .... G 4
Natron (lake) .... G 4
Ngorongoro (crater) .... F 4
Njombe (riv.) .... F 5
Nyasa (lake) .... F 6
Olduvai Gorge (canyon) .... G 4
Pangani (riv.) .... G 4
Pemba (isl.), 164,321 .... H 5
Rufiji (riv.) .... G 5
Rukwa (lake) .... F 5
Rungwa (riv.) .... F 5
Rungwe (mt.) .... F 5
Ruvuma (riv.) .... G 4
Serengeti Nat'l Park .... F 4
Tanganyika (lake) .... E 5
Victoria (lake) .... F 4
Wami (riv.) .... G 5
Wembere (riv.) .... F 4
Zanzibar (isl.), 190,494 .... G 5

UGANDA

CITIES and TOWNS

Arua, 4,645 .... F 3
Atura, 119 .... F 3
Butiaba, 1,216 .... F 3
Entebbe, 10,941 .... F 4
Fort Portal, 8,317 .... F 3
Gulu, 4,770 .... F 3
Hoima, 1,056 .... F 3
Jinja, 29,741 .... F 3
Kaabong .... F 3
Kabale, 10,919 .... E 4
Kampala (capital), 330,000 .... F 3
Kasese, 1,564 .... F 3
Katwe, 2,057 .... F 4
Kilembe .... F 3
Kitgum, 3,454 .... F 3
Lira, 2,929 .... F 3
Masaka, 4,785 .... F 4
Masindi, 1,571 .... F 3
Mbale, 23,539 .... F 3
Mbarara, 3.844 .... F 4
Moroto, 2.082 .... F 3
Moyo, 2,009 .... F 3
Mubende, 1,878 .... F 3
Namasagali .... F 3
Pakwach, 1,467 .... F 3
Rhino Camp, 3,478 .... F 3
Soroti, 6,645 .... F 3
Tororo, 6,365 .... F 3
Yumbe, 949 .... F 3

OTHER FEATURES

Albert (lake) .... F 3
Edward (lake) .... E 4
Elgon (mt.) .... F 3
George (lake) .... F 4
Kioga (lake) .... F 3
Margherita (mt.) .... E 3
Murchison (falls) .... F 3
Owen Falls (dam) .... F 3
Queen Elizabeth Nat'l Park .... F 4
Ruwenzori (range) .... E 3
Sese (isls.) .... F 4
Victoria (lake) .... F 4

ZAIRE

PROVINCES

Bandundu, 2,600,556 .... C 4
Bas-Zaïre, 1,504,361 .... B 4
Equateur, 2,431,812 .... D 3
Haut-Zaïre, 3,356,419 .... E 3
Kasai-Occidental, 2,433,861 .... D 4
Kasai-Oriental, 1,872,231 .... D 5
Katanga, 2,753,714 .... E 5
Kinshasa (city), 1,323,039 .... C 4
Kivu, 3,361,883 .... E 4

CITIES and TOWNS

Aba .... F 3
Abumombazi, †5,773 .... D 3
Aketi, 15,339 .... D 3
Ango .... E 3
Avakubi .... E 3
Bagata .... C 4
Balangala .... D 3
Bambesa .... E 3
Bambili .... E 3
Banana .... B 5
Bandundu, 74,467 .... C 4
Banzyville, 6,608 .... D 3
Baraka .... E 4
Basankusu, 5,613 .... C 3
Basoko .... D 3
Basongo .... D 4
Batama .... E 3
Baudouinville .... E 5
Befale, 3,407 .... D 3
Bena-Dibele .... D 4
Beni .... E 3
Bikoro, 6,491 .... C 4
Boende, 391 .... D 4
Bokungu, 4,952 .... D 4
Bolobo .... C 4
Bolomba, 5,636 .... C 3
Boma, 33,143 .... B 5
Bomboma, 1,319 .... C 3
Bomongo, 4,827 .... C 3
Bondo, 453 .... D 3
Bongandanga, 4,476 .... D 3
Bosobolo, 2,809 .... D 3
Budjala, 415 .... C 3
Bukama .... E 5
Bukavu, 134,861 .... E 4
Bumba, 5,182 .... D 3
Bunia, 12,410 .... E 3
Bunkeya .... E 6
Busanga, †2,792 .... D 6
Businga, 2,827 .... D 3
Busu-Djanoa, †5,520 .... D 3
Buta, 10,845 .... D 3
Butembo, 9,980 .... E 3
Dekese .... D 4
Demba .... D 5
Dibaya .... D 5
Dibaya-Lubue .... C 4
Dilolo .... D 6
Dimbelenge .... D 5
Djolu, 2,516 .... D 3
Djugu .... F 3
Djuma .... C 4
Dongo, 559 .... C 3
Doruma .... E 3
Dungu .... E 3
Elila .... E 4
Equateur .... C 3
Etoile .... E 6
Faradje .... E 3
Feshi .... C 5
Fizi .... E 4
Gandajika .... D 5
Gemena, 8,135 .... D 3
Goma, 14,115 .... E 4
Gombari .... E 3
Gumba-Mobeka, †7,023 .... C 3
Idiofa .... C 4
Ikela, 3,166 .... D 4
Imese, 115 .... C 3
Ingende, 6,730 .... C 4
Inongo .... C 4
Irumu .... E 3
Isangi .... D 3
Isangila .... B 5
Isiro, 17,430 .... E 3
Kabalo .... E 5
Kabare .... E 4
Kabinda .... D 5
Kabongo .... E 5
Kabunda .... E 6
Kahemba .... C 5
Kalehe .... E 4
Kalemie, 29,934 .... E 5
Kalima .... E 4
Kaloko .... E 5
Kama .... E 4
Kambove (with Shinkolobwe), 14,517 .... E 6
Kamina, 20,915 .... D 5
Kananga, 428,960 .... D 5
Kanda Kànda .... D 5
Kaniama .... D 5
Kapanga .... D 5
Kasaji .... D 6
Kasangulu .... C 4
Kasenyi .... E 3
Kasese .... E 4
Kasongo .... E 4
Kasongo-Lunda .... C 5
Katako-Kombe .... D 4
Katana .... E 4
Katenga .... E 5
Kazumba .... D 5
Kenge .... C 4
Kibombo .... E 4
Kikwit, 111,960 .... C 5
Kilo .... E 3
Kilwa .... E 5
Kindu-Port Empain, 19,385 .... E 4
Kiniama .... E 6
Kinshasa (capital), 1,323,039 .... C 4
Kipushi, 22,602 .... E 6
Kirundu .... E 4
Kisangani, 229,596 .... E 3
Kolwezi, 45,192 .... E 6
Komba .... D 3
Kongolo, 10,434 .... E 5
Kungu, 7,912 .... C 3
Kutu, †2,072 .... C 4
Kwamouth .... C 4
Libenge, 2,632 .... C 3
Lienartville .... E 3
Likasi, 146,394 .... E 6
Likati .... D 3
Lisala, 574 .... D 3
Lodja, 7,227 .... D 4
Lokolama .... D 4
Lomela, †7,757 .... D 4
Loto .... D 4
Lotumbe .... C 4
Luashi .... D 6
Lubefu .... D 4
Lubudi, 5,915 .... E 5
Lubumbashi, 318,000 .... E 6
Lubutu .... E 4
Luebo .... D 5
Luena .... E 5
Luishia .... E 6
Lukula .... B 4
Lunyama .... E 5
Luofu .... E 4
Luozi .... B 5
Luputa .... D 5
Lusambo, 9,395 .... D 4
Lusangi .... E 4
Madimba .... C 5
Malonga .... D 6
Mambasa .... E 3
Manono, 12,234 .... E 5
Masi-Manimba .... C 4
Masisi .... E 4
Matadi, 110,436 .... B 5
Mbandaka, 107,910 .... C 3
Mbuji-Mayi, 256,154 .... D 5
Moanda .... B 5
Moba .... E 5
Moliro .... E 5
Monga .... D 3
Monkoto, 5,209 .... D 4
Monveda .... D 3
Mungbere .... E 3
Mushie, 12,118 .... C 4
Mutshatsha .... D 6
Muyumba .... E 5
Mwadingusha .... E 6
Mwanza .... E 5
Mwene Ditu .... D 5
Mwenga .... E 4
Niangara .... E 3
Niemba .... E 5
Nouvelle-Anvers, †4,330 .... C 3
Nyunzu .... E 5
Oshwe .... C 4
Panda .... E 6
Pangi .... E 4
Penge .... D 5
Piana-Mwanga .... E 5
Poie .... D 4
Poko .... E 3
Ponthierville .... D 4
Port-Francqui .... D 4
Punia .... E 4
Pweto .... E 5
Rutshuru .... E 4
Sakania .... E 6
Sampwe .... E 5
Sandoa .... D 5
Shabunda .... E 4
Shinkolobwe (with Kambove), 14,517 .... E 6
Songololo .... B 5
Thysville, 16,369 .... C 5
Titule .... E 3
Tolo .... C 4
Tondo .... C 4
Tshela .... B 4
Tshikapa .... D 5
Tshofa .... D 5
Uvira .... E 4
Vanga .... C 4
Wafania, 584 .... D 4
Waka, 264 .... D 3
Wamba .... E 3
Watsa, 6,077 .... E 3
Yakoma, †5,685 .... D 3
Yangambi, 18,849 .... D 3
Zongo, †4,128 .... C 3

OTHER FEATURES

Albert (lake) .... F 3
Albert Nat'l Park .... E 4
Aruwimi (riv.) .... E 3
Bomu (riv.) .... D 3
Congo (riv.) .... C 4
Edward (lake) .... E 4
Elila (riv.) .... E 4
Fimi (riv.) .... C 4
Garamba Nat'l Park .... E 3
Giri (riv.) .... C 3
Itimbiri (riv.) .... D 3
Ituri (for.) .... E 3
Karisimbi (mt.) .... E 4
Kasai (riv.) .... C 4
Kivu (lake) .... E 4
Kwa (riv.) .... C 4
Kwango (riv.) .... C 5
Kwilu (riv.) .... C 5
Léopold II (lake) .... C 4
Lindi (riv.) .... E 3
Livingstone (falls) .... B 5
Loange (riv.) .... C 5
Lokoro (riv.) .... C 4
Lomami (riv.) .... D 4
Lomela (riv.) .... D 4
Lowa (riv.) .... E 4
Lua (riv.) .... C 3
Lualaba (riv.) .... E 4
Luapula (riv.) .... E 6
Lubilash (riv.) .... D 5
Lufira (riv.) .... E 5
Luilaka (riv.) .... D 4
Lukenie (riv.) .... D 4
Lukuga (riv.) .... E 5
Lulua (riv.) .... D 5
Luvua (riv.) .... E 5
Margherita (mt.) .... E 3
Mweru (lake) .... E 5
Marungu (mts.) .... E 5
Ruwenzori (range) .... E 3
Ruzizi (riv.) .... E 4
Sankuru (riv.) .... D 4
Stanley (falls) .... E 3
Stanley Pool (lake) .... C 4
Tanganyika (lake) .... E 5
Tshuapa (riv.) .... D 4
Tumba (lake) .... C 4
Ubangi (riv.) .... C 3
Uele (riv.) .... E 3
Ulindi (riv.) .... E 4
Upemba (lake) .... E 5
Upemba Nat'l Park .... E 5
Virunga (range) .... E 4
Zaire (Congo) (riv.) .... C 4

ZAMBIA

CITIES and TOWNS

Abercorn (Mbala), ‡5,200 .... F 5
Balovale, 2,260 .... D 6
Bancroft (Chililabombwe), ‡39,900 .... E 6
Broken Hill (Kabwe), ‡67,200 .... E 6
Chilanga, 2,510 .... E 7
Chililabombwe, ‡39,900 .... E 6
Chingola, ‡92,800 .... E 6
Chinsali, 1,110 .... F 6
Chipata, ‡13,300 .... F 6
Chisamba, 790 .... E 6
Choma, ‡11,300 .... E 7
Feira, 310 .... E 7
Fort Rosebery (Mansa), ‡5,700 .... E 6
Isoka, 1,370 .... F 6
Kabompo, 990 .... D 6
Kabwe, ‡67,200 .... E 6
Kafue, 2,490 .... E 7
Kalabo, 2,420 .... D 6
Kalomo, 2,560 .... E 7
Kapiri Mposhi, 440 .... E 6
Kasama, ‡8,900 .... F 6
Kasempa, 670 .... E 6
Kawambwa, 1,430 .... E 5
Kitwe, ‡179,300 .... E 6
Lealui .... D 6
Livingstone, ‡43,000 .... E 7
Luanshya, ‡90,400 .... E 6
Lukulu .... D 6
Lundazi, 1,750 .... F 6
Lusaka (capital), ‡238,200 .... E 7
Luwingu, 850 .... E 6
Mankoya, 1,600 .... D 6
Mansa, ‡5,700 .... E 6
Mazabuka, ‡9,400 .... E 7
Mbala, ‡5,200 .... F 5
Mongu, ‡10,700 .... D 7
Monze, ‡4,300 .... E 7
Mpika, 660 .... F 6
Mporokoso, 790 .... F 5
Mpulungu, 1,830 .... F 5
Mufulira, ‡101,200 .... E 6
Mumbwa, 1,400 .... E 6
Mwinilunga, 700 .... D 6
Nakonde .... F 5
Namwala, 880 .... E 7
Nchanga, 35,030 .... E 6
Ndola, ‡150,800 .... E 6
Nkana, 54,500 .... E 6
Petauke, 1,640 .... F 6
Roan Antelope, 36,300 .... E 6
Senanga, 1,500 .... D 7
Serenje, 1,650 .... F 6
Sesheke, 910 .... D 7
Solwezi, 1,930 .... E 6

OTHER FEATURES

Bangweulu (lake) .... F 6
Barotseland (reg.), 417,000 .... D 7
Chambeshi (riv.) .... F 6
Dongwe (riv.) .... D 6
Kabampo (riv.) .... D 6
Kafue (riv.) .... E 7
Kariba (dam) .... E 7
Kariba (lake) .... E 7
Kwando (riv.) .... D 7
Luangwa (riv.) .... F 6
Mosi-Ao-Tunya (Victoria) (falls) .... E 7
Mulungushi (dam) .... E 6
Mweru (lake) .... E 5
Sunzu (mt.) .... F 5
Tanganyika (lake) .... E 5
Victoria (falls) .... E 7
Zambezi (riv.) .... D 7

*City and suburbs.
†Population of sub-district or division.
‡Population of urban area.
◉Population of municipality.

Agriculture, Industry and Resources

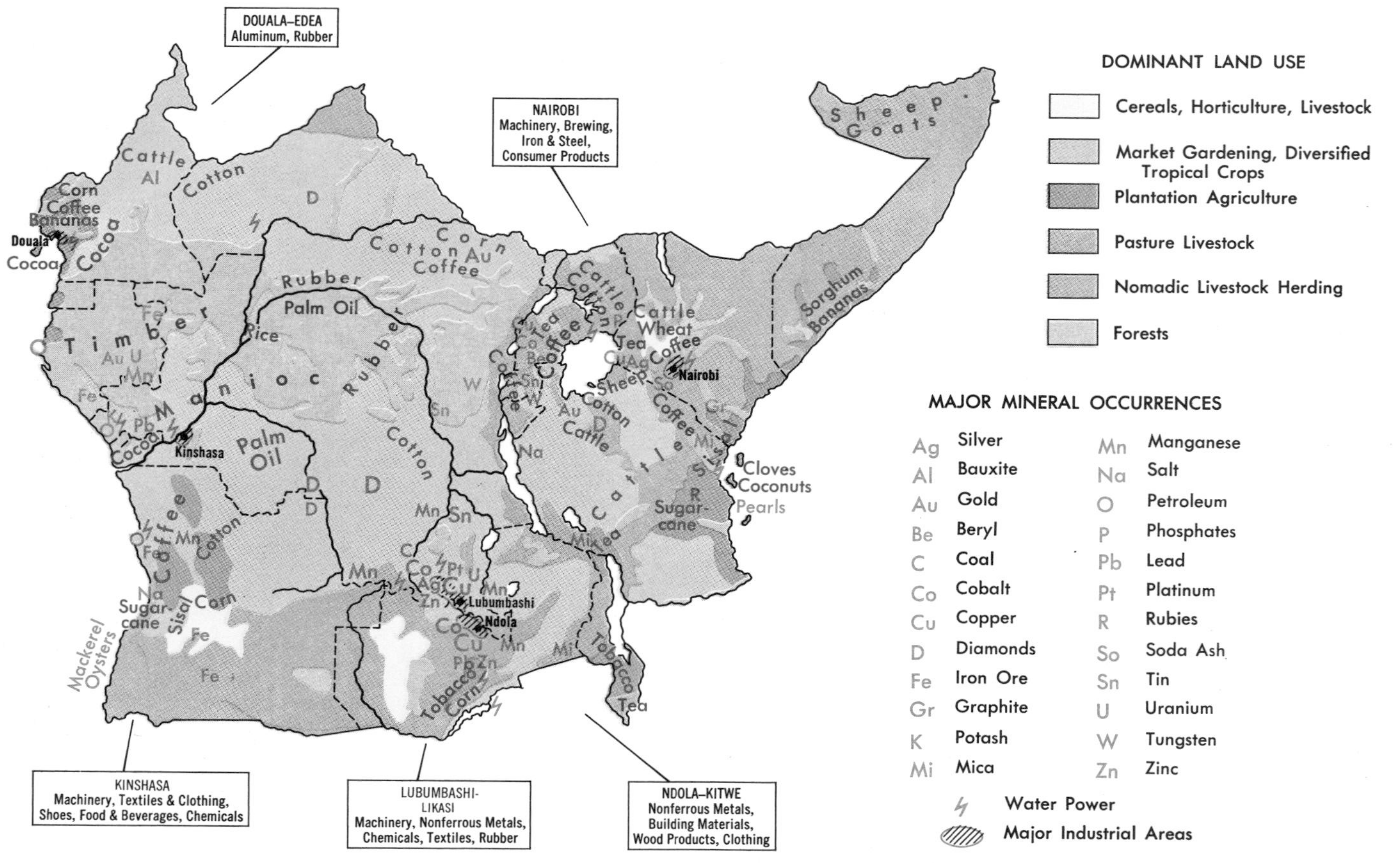

DOUALA–EDEA
Aluminum, Rubber
NAIROBI
Machinery, Brewing, Iron & Steel, Consumer Products
KINSHASA
Machinery, Textiles & Clothing, Shoes, Food & Beverages, Chemicals
LUBUMBASHI-LIKASI
Machinery, Nonferrous Metals, Chemicals, Textiles, Rubber
NDOLA–KITWE
Nonferrous Metals, Building Materials, Wood Products, Clothing
Douala
Kinshasa
Nairobi
Lubumbashi
Ndola
Cattle
Cotton
Corn
Coffee
Bananas
Cocoa
Timber
Rubber
Palm Oil
Rice
Manioc
Sheep
Goats
Wheat
Tea
Sorghum
Sisal
Cloves
Coconuts
Pearls
Sugar-cane
Tobacco
Mackerel
Oysters
DOMINANT LAND USE
Cereals, Horticulture, Livestock
Market Gardening, Diversified Tropical Crops
Plantation Agriculture
Pasture Livestock
Nomadic Livestock Herding
Forests
MAJOR MINERAL OCCURRENCES
Ag Silver
Al Bauxite
Au Gold
Be Beryl
C Coal
Co Cobalt
Cu Copper
D Diamonds
Fe Iron Ore
Gr Graphite
K Potash
Mi Mica
Mn Manganese
Na Salt
O Petroleum
P Phosphates
Pb Lead
Pt Platinum
R Rubies
So Soda Ash
Sn Tin
U Uranium
W Tungsten
Zn Zinc
Water Power
Major Industrial Areas

SOUTH-WEST AFRICA (NAMIBIA)
AREA 317,827 sq. mi.
POPULATION 883,000
CAPITAL Windhoek
LARGEST CITY Windhoek
HIGHEST POINT Brandberg 8,550 ft.
MONETARY UNIT rand
MAJOR LANGUAGES Ovambo, Hottentot, Herero, Afrikaans, English
MAJOR RELIGIONS Tribal religions, Protestantism

SOUTH AFRICA
AREA 458,179 sq. mi.
POPULATION 24,400,000
CAPITALS Cape Town, Pretoria
LARGEST CITY Johannesburg
HIGHEST POINT Injasuti 11,182 ft.
MONETARY UNIT rand
MAJOR LANGUAGES Afrikaans, English, Xhosa, Zulu, Sesotho
MAJOR RELIGIONS Protestantism, Roman Catholicism, Islam, Hinduism

LESOTHO
AREA 11,720 sq. mi.
POPULATION 1,100,000
CAPITAL Maseru
LARGEST CITY Maseru
HIGHEST POINT 11,425 ft.
MONETARY UNIT South African rand
MAJOR LANGUAGES Sesotho, English
MAJOR RELIGIONS Tribal religions, Christianity

BOTSWANA
AREA 224,764 sq. mi.
POPULATION 700,000
CAPITAL Gaborone
LARGEST CITIES Selebi-Pikwe
HIGHEST POINT Tsodilo Hill 5,922 ft.
MONETARY UNIT pula
MAJOR LANGUAGES Setswana, Shona, Bushman, English, Afrikaans
MAJOR RELIGIONS Tribal religions, Protestantism

MOZAMBIQUE
AREA 308,641 sq. mi.
POPULATION 9,300,000
CAPITAL Maputo
LARGEST CITY Maputo
HIGHEST POINT Mt. Binga 7,992 ft.
MONETARY UNIT Mozambique escudo
MAJOR LANGUAGES Makua, Thonga, Shona, Portuguese
MAJOR RELIGIONS Tribal religions, Roman Catholicism, Islam

SWAZILAND
AREA 6,705 sq. mi.
POPULATION 500,000
CAPITAL Mbabane
LARGEST CITY Mbabane
HIGHEST POINT Emlembe 6,109 ft.
MONETARY UNIT lilangeni
MAJOR LANGUAGES siSwati, English
MAJOR RELIGIONS Tribal religions, Christianity

ZIMBABWE RHODESIA
AREA 150,803 sq. mi.
POPULATION 6,600,000
CAPITAL Salisbury
LARGEST CITY Salisbury
HIGHEST POINT Mt. Inyangani 8,517 ft.
MONETARY UNIT Rhodesian dollar
MAJOR LANGUAGES English, Shona, Ndebele
MAJOR RELIGIONS Tribal religions, Protestantism

MADAGASCAR
AREA 226,657 sq. mi.
POPULATION 7,700,000
CAPITAL Antananarivo
LARGEST CITY Antananarivo
HIGHEST POINT Maromokotro 9,436 ft.
MONETARY UNIT Madagascar franc
MAJOR LANGUAGES Malagasy, French
MAJOR RELIGIONS Tribal religions, Roman Catholicism, Prostestantism

COMOROS
AREA 719 sq. mi.
POPULATION 266,000
CAPITAL Moroni
LARGEST CITY Moroni
HIGHEST POINT Karthala 8,399 ft.
MONETARY UNIT CFA franc
MAJOR LANGUAGES Arabic, French, Swahili
MAJOR RELIGION Islam

MAURITIUS
AREA 790 sq. mi.
POPULATION 899,000
CAPITAL Port Louis
LARGEST CITY Port Louis
HIGHEST POINT 2,711 ft.
MONETARY UNIT Mauritian rupee
MAJOR LANGUAGES English, French, French Creole, Hindi, Urdu
MAJOR RELIGIONS Hinduism, Christianity, Islam

SEYCHELLES
AREA 145 sq. mi.
POPULATION 60,000
CAPITAL Victoria
LARGEST CITY Victoria
HIGHEST POINT Morne Seychellois 2,970 ft.
MONETARY UNIT Seychellois rupee
MAJOR LANGUAGES English, French, Creole
MAJOR RELIGION Roman Catholicism

RÉUNION
AREA 969 sq. mi.
POPULATION 475,700
CAPITAL St-Denis

MAYOTTE
AREA 144 sq. mi.
POPULATION 40,000
CAPITAL Mamoutzou

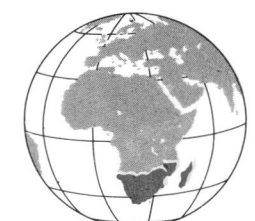

ZIMBABWE RHODESIA

BOTSWANA

SOUTH AFRICA

LESOTHO

SWAZILAND

MOZAMBIQUE

COMOROS

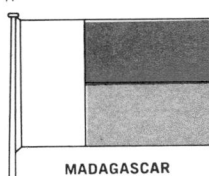
MADAGASCAR

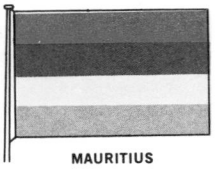
MAURITIUS

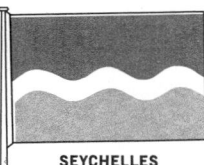
SEYCHELLES

Agriculture, Industry and Resources

MAJOR MINERAL OCCURRENCES

Ab Asbestos
Ag Silver
Au Gold
Be Beryl
C Coal
Cr Chromium
Cu Copper
D Diamonds
Fe Iron Ore
Gr Graphite
Lt Lithium
Mg Magnesium
Mi Mica
Mn Manganese
Na Salt
Ni Nickel
P Phosphates
Pb Lead
Pt Platinum
Sb Antimony
Sn Tin
U Uranium
V Vanadium
W Tungsten
Zn Zinc

⚡ Water Power
▨ Major Industrial Areas

DOMINANT LAND USE

Cereals, Horticulture, Livestock
Market Gardening, Diversified Tropical Crops
Plantation Agriculture
Pasture Livestock
Nomadic Livestock Herding
Forests
Nonagricultural Land

SALISBURY–GWELO
Metal Products, Machinery, Transportation Equipment, Building Materials, Wood Products, Chemicals, Clothing, Iron & Steel

BULAWAYO
Metal Products, Machinery, Clothing, Wood Products, Chemicals, Building Materials

CAPE TOWN
Food & Tobacco, Textiles, Clothing, Machinery, Chemicals, Leather

JOHANNESBURG–WITWATERSRAND
Iron & Steel, Machinery, Electrical Goods, Chemicals, Building Materials, Textiles, Food Processing, Printing

DURBAN–PIETERMARITZBURG
Oil Refining, Machinery, Sugar Refining, Rubber, Chemicals

PORT ELIZABETH
Automobile Assembly, Textiles, Rubber, Leather

(continued on following page)

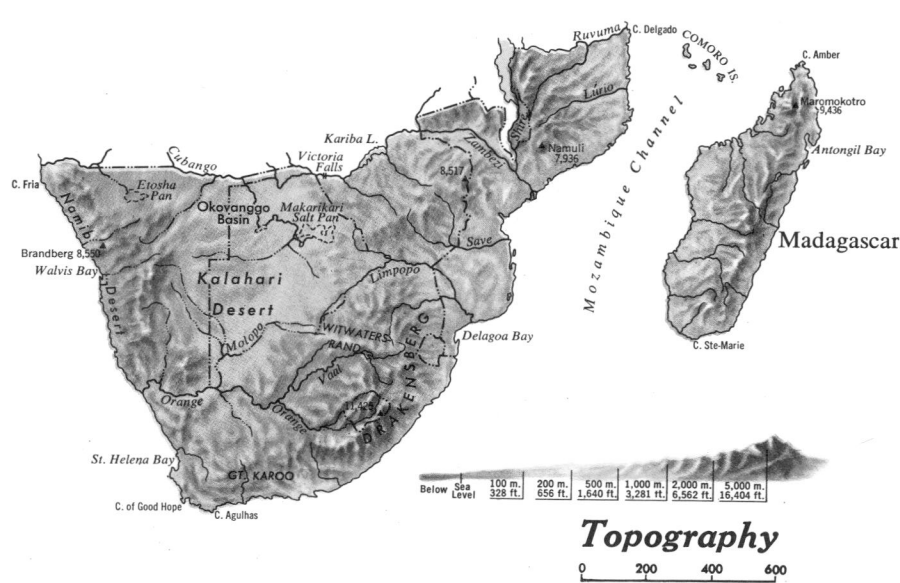

Topography

Below Sea Level | 100 m. 328 ft. | 200 m. 656 ft. | 500 m. 1,640 ft. | 1,000 m. 3,281 ft. | 2,000 m. 6,562 ft. | 5,000 m. 16,404 ft.

0   200   400   600
MILES

SOUTHERN AFRICA

CONIC PROJECTION

SCALE OF MILES
0   50   100   200   300

SCALE OF KILOMETERS
0   50   100   200   300

★ Capitals of Countries
◉ Other Capitals
International Boundaries
Internal Boundaries

Copyright by C.S. HAMMOND & CO., N.Y.

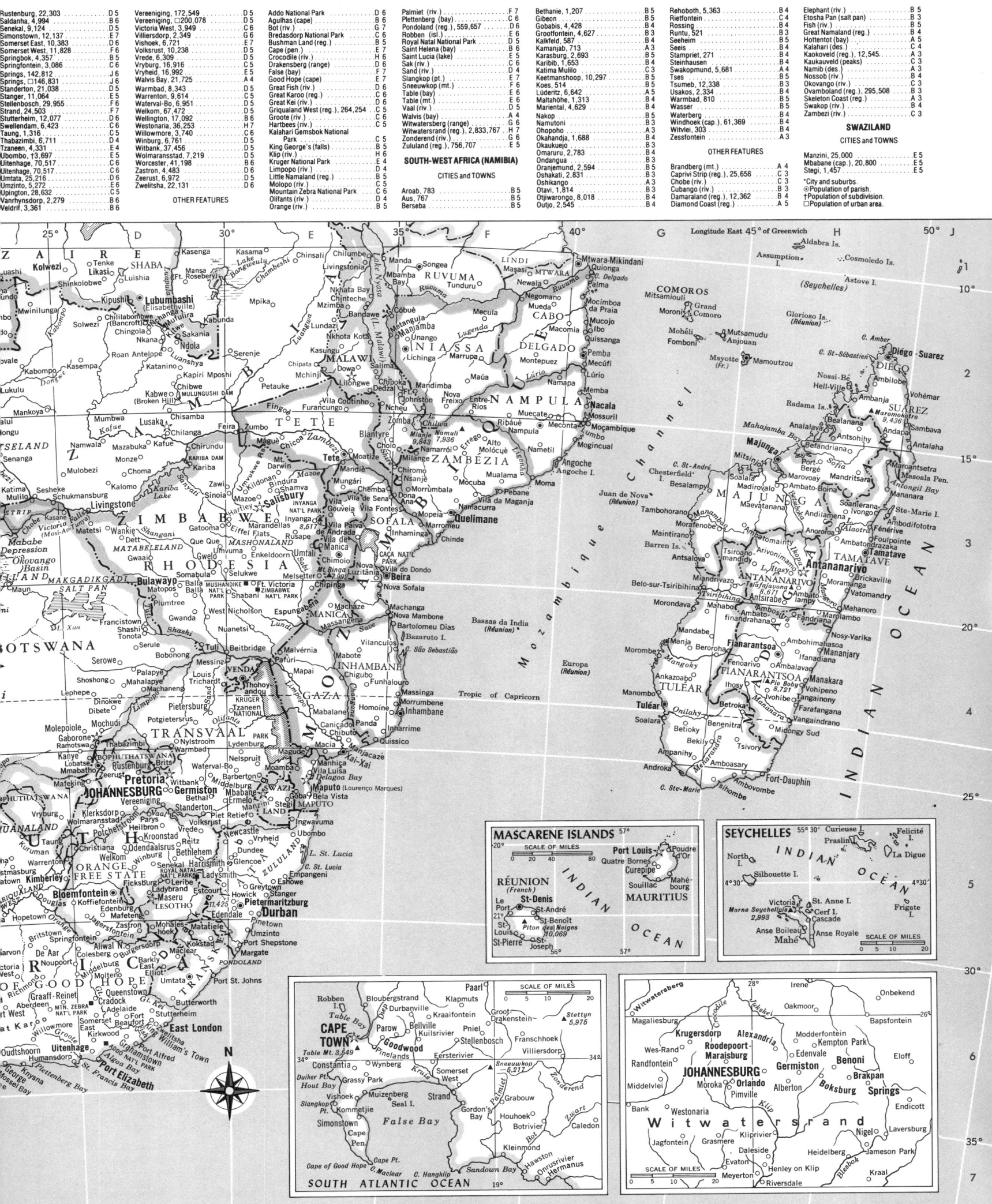

SOUTH AMERICA

LAMBERT AZIMUTHAL EQUAL-AREA PROJECTION

SCALE OF MILES

0 100 200 400 600

SCALE OF KILOMETRES

0 100 200 400 600

Capitals of Countries _____ ☆
International Boundaries _____ - - - -
Canals _____ _____

© C.S. HAMMOND & Co., N.Y.

GALAPAGOS ISLANDS
(ARCHIPIELAGO DE COLON)
(ECUADOR)

SCALE OF MILES

0 50 100 150

PACIFIC OCEAN

Equator

I. Pinta
I. Marchena
I. Santiago
I. Chaves
I. San Cristóbal
Fernandina
Isla Isabéla
I. Floreana
Española

POPULATION DISTRIBUTION

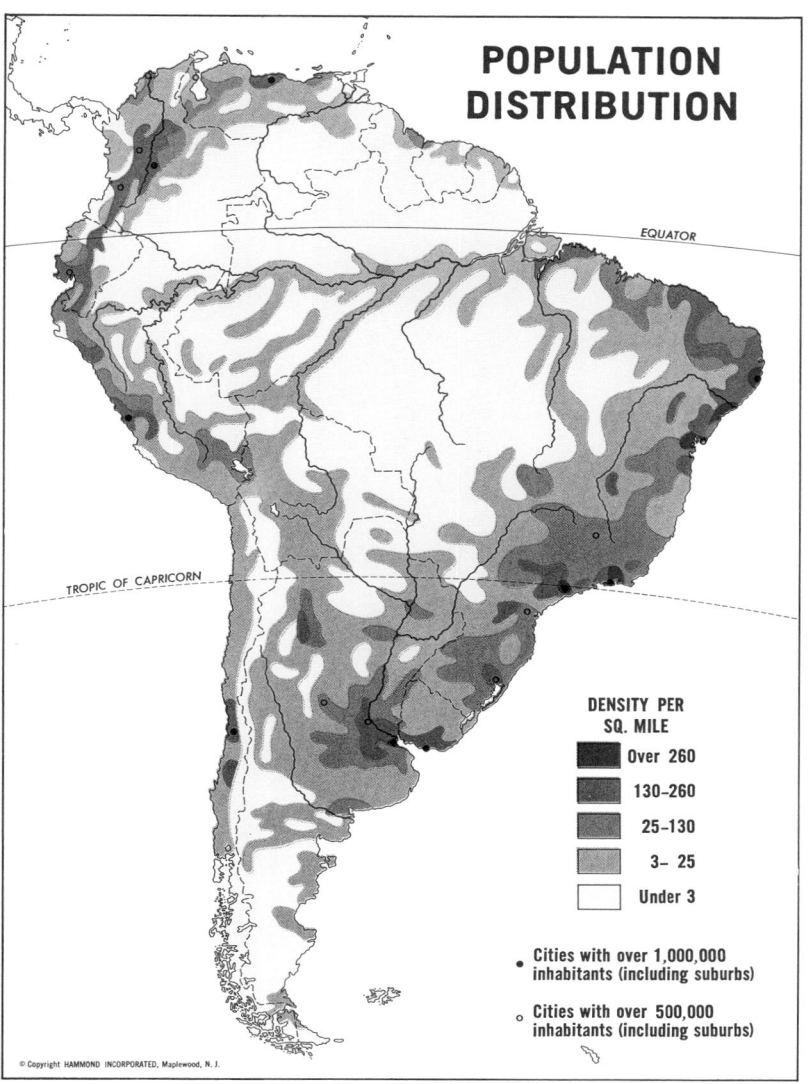

AREA 6,875,000 sq. mi.
POPULATION 186,000,000
LARGEST CITY Buenos Aires (greater)
HIGHEST POINT Cerro Aconcagua 22,831 ft.
LOWEST POINT Salina Grande -131 ft.

DENSITY PER SQ. MILE

- Over 260
- 130–260
- 25–130
- 3–25
- Under 3

● Cities with over 1,000,000 inhabitants (including suburbs)

○ Cities with over 500,000 inhabitants (including suburbs)

© Copyright HAMMOND INCORPORATED, Maplewood, N.J.

VEGETATION

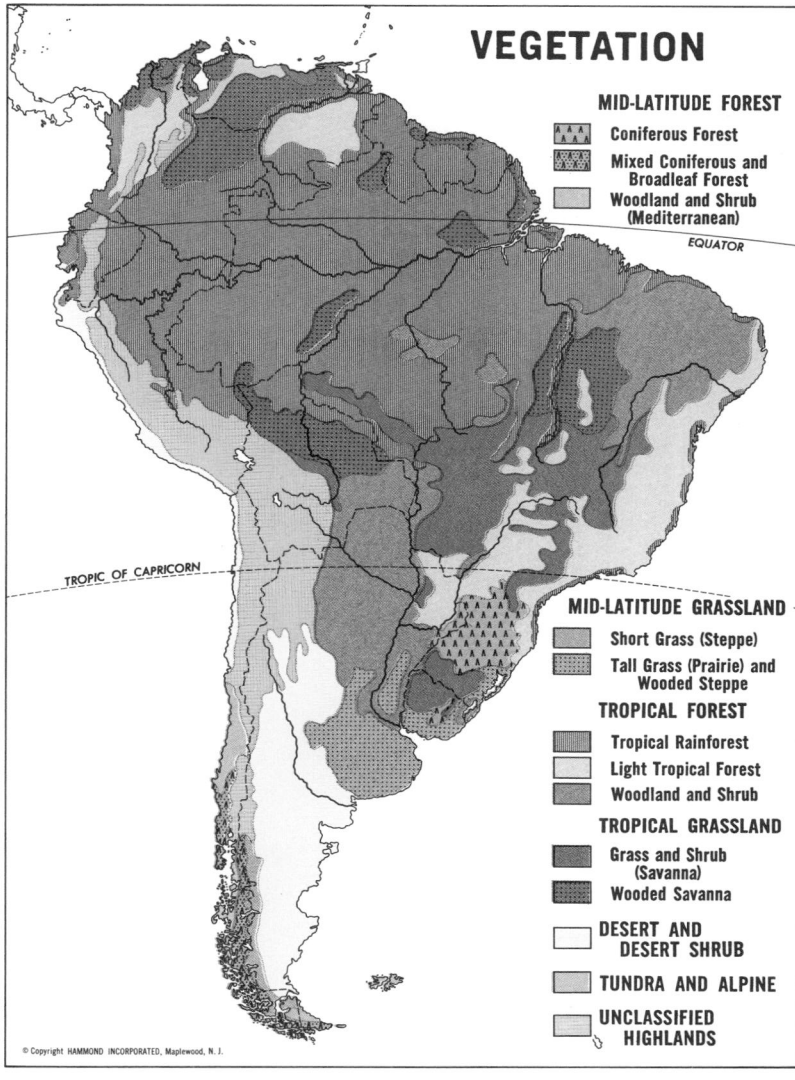

MID-LATITUDE FOREST
- Coniferous Forest
- Mixed Coniferous and Broadleaf Forest
- Woodland and Shrub (Mediterranean)

MID-LATITUDE GRASSLAND
- Short Grass (Steppe)
- Tall Grass (Prairie) and Wooded Steppe

TROPICAL FOREST
- Tropical Rainforest
- Light Tropical Forest
- Woodland and Shrub

TROPICAL GRASSLAND
- Grass and Shrub (Savanna)
- Wooded Savanna

DESERT AND DESERT SHRUB

TUNDRA AND ALPINE

UNCLASSIFIED HIGHLANDS

© Copyright HAMMOND INCORPORATED, Maplewood, N.J.

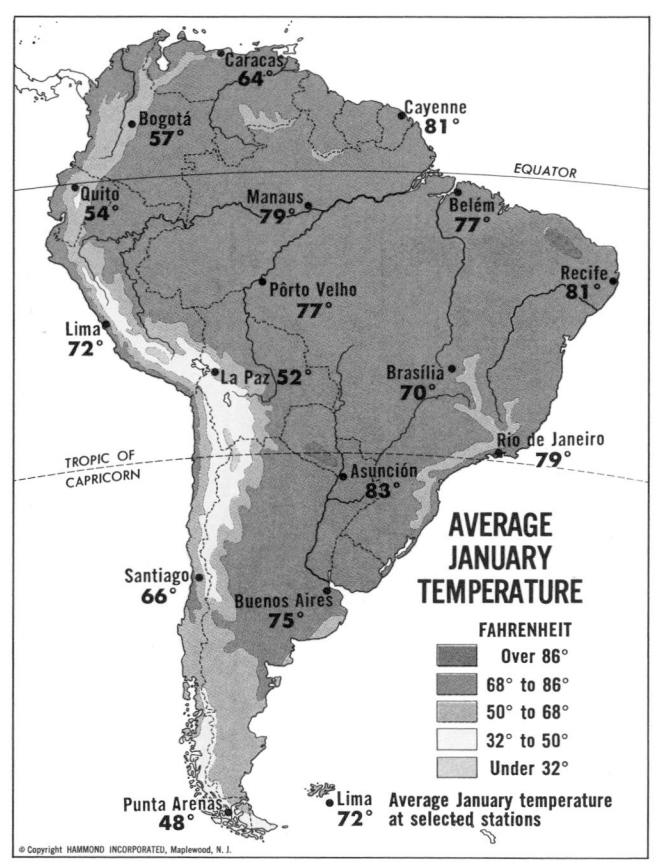

AVERAGE JANUARY TEMPERATURE

Caracas 64°
Bogotá 57°
Cayenne 81°
Quito 54°
Manaus 79°
Belém 77°
Pôrto Velho 77°
Recife 81°
Lima 72°
La Paz 52°
Brasília 70°
Rio de Janeiro 79°
Asunción 83°
Santiago 66°
Buenos Aires 75°
Punta Arenas 48°

EQUATOR
TROPIC OF CAPRICORN

FAHRENHEIT
Over 86°
68° to 86°
50° to 68°
32° to 50°
Under 32°

● Lima 72° Average January temperature at selected stations

© Copyright HAMMOND INCORPORATED, Maplewood, N. J.

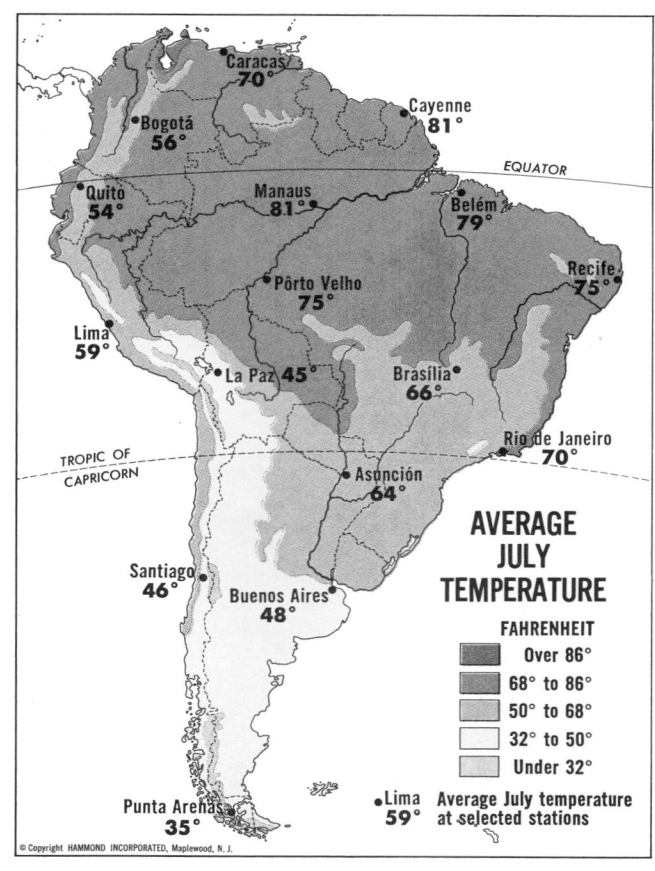

AVERAGE JULY TEMPERATURE

Caracas 70°
Bogotá 56°
Cayenne 81°
Quito 54°
Manaus 81°
Belém 79°
Pôrto Velho 75°
Recife 75°
Lima 59°
La Paz 45°
Brasília 66°
Rio de Janeiro 70°
Asunción 64°
Santiago 46°
Buenos Aires 48°
Punta Arenas 35°

EQUATOR
TROPIC OF CAPRICORN

FAHRENHEIT
Over 86°
68° to 86°
50° to 68°
32° to 50°
Under 32°

● Lima 59° Average July temperature at selected stations

© Copyright HAMMOND INCORPORATED, Maplewood, N. J.

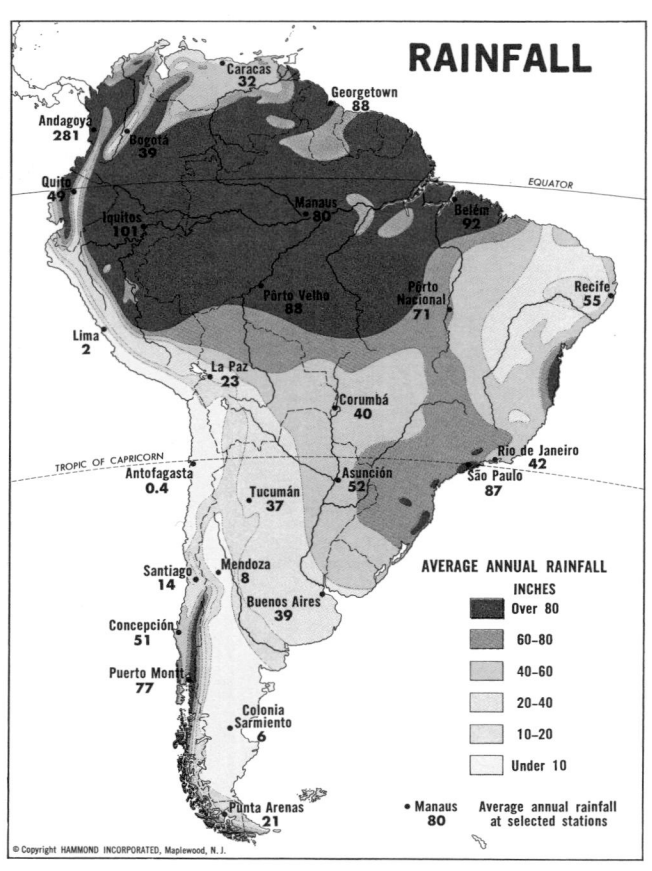

RAINFALL

Caracas 32
Georgetown 88
Andagoyá 281
Bogotá 39
Quito 49
Iquitos 101
Manaus 80
Belém 92
Pôrto Velho 88
Pôrto Nacional 71
Recife 55
Lima 2
La Paz 23
Corumbá 40
Rio de Janeiro 42
Antofagasta 0.4
Asunción 52
São Paulo 87
Tucumán 37
Santiago 14
Mendoza 8
Buenos Aires 39
Concepción 51
Puerto Montt 77
Colonia Sarmiento 6
Punta Arenas 21

EQUATOR
TROPIC OF CAPRICORN

AVERAGE ANNUAL RAINFALL
INCHES
Over 80
60–80
40–60
20–40
10–20
Under 10

● Manaus 80 Average annual rainfall at selected stations

© Copyright HAMMOND INCORPORATED, Maplewood, N. J.

VEGETATION/RELIEF

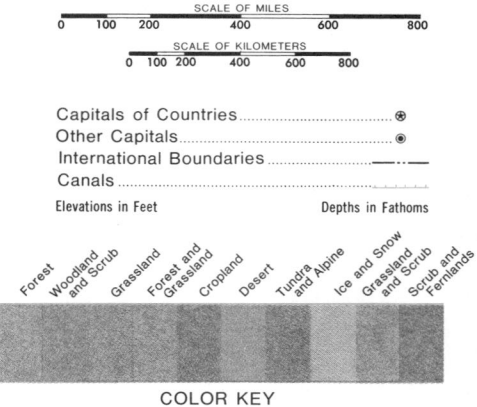

SCALE OF MILES
0   100   200   400   600   800

SCALE OF KILOMETERS
0   100 200   400   600   800

Capitals of Countries .... ⊛
Other Capitals .... ⊛
International Boundaries ....
Canals ....

Elevations in Feet   Depths in Fathoms

Forest
Woodland and Scrub
Grassland
Forest and Grassland
Cropland
Desert
Tundra and Alpine
Ice and Snow
Grassland and Scrub
Scrub and Fernlands

COLOR KEY

80°   70°   60°   50°   40°

CARIBBEAN   SEA

G. of Venezuela
Pta. Gallinas
NETH. ANTILLES
Aruba
Curaçao
Bonaire
Willemstad
West Indies
GRENADA
Tobago
TRINIDAD & TOBAGO
Port of Spain
Trinidad
BARBADOS

Barranquilla
Maracaibo
Caracas
L. Maracaibo
Pico Bolívar 16,427

PANAMA
Panamá Canal
G. of Panama

10°

Medellín
Bogotá
Cali
COLOMBIA

VENEZUELA
Bucaramanga
Arauca
Meta
Orinoco
Ciudad Guayana
Guri Res.
Angel Fall
Caroní
Roraima

GUYANA
Georgetown
Paramaribo
SURINAME
FRENCH GUIANA
Cayenne

Quito
Chimborazo 20,561
ECUADOR
Guayaquil
Gulf of Guayaquil
Pta. Aguja

Pico da Neblina 9,889
Vaupés
Negro
Japurá
Içá
Iquitos
Amazon
Yavarí
Juruá

Amazon
Manaus
Selvas
Madeira
Purus
Tapajós
Xingu
Tocantins

Amazon
I. de Marajó
Belém
São Luís

Equator 0°

Fortaleza
Cabo de São Roque
Natal
Recife

Trujillo
Huascarán 22,205

PERU
Callao
Lima
Cuzco

BOLIVIA
Lake Titicaca
Ancohuma 21,490
La Paz
Cochabamba
Lake Poopó
Sucre

Planalto de
Mato Grosso
Brazilian
Highlands

Teresina
Parnaíba
Caatingas

10°

BRAZIL
Paraguaçu
Salvador
São Francisco
Jequitinhonha
Belo Horizonte
Pico da Bandeira 9,482

Arica
Antofagasta
Tropic of Capricorn

Volcán Llullaillaco 22,057

CHILE
I. de San Félix (Chile)
I. San Ambrosio (Chile)

Ojos del Salado 22,572

Gran
Chaco
PARAGUAY
Asunción
Paraguay
Pilcomayo
Bermejo
Campo Grande
Paraná
Iguassú Falls
Iguaçu

Goiânia
Brasília
Tietê
Grande
Paraná

São Paulo
Santos
Curitiba
I. de Santa Catarina
C. de São Tomé
C. Frio
Rio de Janeiro
Paraíba

20°

Tucumán
I. Alejandro Selkirk
I. Robinson Crusoe
Juan Fernandez Is. (Chile)

Córdoba
Santa Fé
Rosario
ARGENTINA
Salado
Mendoza
Aconcagua 22,831
Valparaíso
Santiago

PAMPAS
Negro
Buenos Aires
La Plata
URUGUAY
Montevideo
Río de la Plata
C. San Antonio

Porto Alegre
Lagoa dos Patos
Lagoa Mirim
Salado do Sul

30°

Concepción
Bahía Blanca
Colorado
Limay
Negro

PATAGONIA
Golfo San Matías
Pen. Valdés

ATLANTIC OCEAN

Puerto Montt
Isla de Chiloé
Archipiélago de los Chonos
Pen. Taitao
G. de Penas
Chubut
Golfo San Jorge
C. Tres Puntas
Deseado

40°

PACIFIC OCEAN

Archipiélago
Reina Adelaida
Str. of Magellan
Tierra del Fuego
Cape Horn
Bahía Grande
Str. of Magellan
Punta Arenas

Falkland Islands (U.K.)
Stanley

50°

© HAMMOND INCORPORATED, Maplewood, N.J.

90°   80°   70°   60°   50°   40°   30° Longitude West of Greenwich 20°

124 Venezuela

INTERNAL DIVISIONS

Amazonas (terr.), 12,831 ....E 5
Anzoátegui (state),
 501,384 ....F 3
Apure (state), 158,487 ....D 4
Aragua (state), 429,344 ....E 3
Barinas (state), 193,914 ....C 3
Bolívar (state), 383,315 ....F 4
Carabobo (state), 512,173 ......D 2
Cojedes (state), 95,177 ....D 3
Delta Amacuro (terr.), 34,278 ..H 3
Dependencias Federales (terr.),
 1,000 ....E 2
Distrito Federal, 2,009,561 .....E 2
Falcón (state), 408,051 ....D 2
Guárico (state), 330,147 ....E 3
Lara (state), 611,192 ....C 2
Mérida (state), 335,428 ....C 3
Miranda (state), 702,603 ....E 3
Monagas (state), 316,732 ....G 3
Nueva Esparta (state),
 112,611 ....G 2
Portuguesa (state),
 284,523 ....D 3
Sucre (state), 493,840 ....G 2
Táchira (state), 525,840 ....B 3
Trujillo (state), 382,441 ....C 3
Yaracuy (state), 222,041 ....D 2
Zulia (state), 1,342,994 ....B 2

CITIES and TOWNS

Acarigua, 30,683 ....D 3
Achaguas, 1,934 ....D 4
Adícora, 563 ....D 2
Aguada Grande, 1,601 ....D 2
Agua Fría, 539 ....D 3
Aguasay, 1,458 ....G 3
Agua Linda, 255 ....G 5
Altagracia, 7,362 ....C 2
Altagracia de Orituco, 13,013 ..E 3
Amuay, 998 ....D 2
Anaco, 23,105 ....F 3
Aparurén, 739 ....G 4
Apurito, 739 ....D 4
Arabopó ....G 4
Aragua de Barcelona,
 8,241 ....F 3
Aragua de Maturín,
 2,643 ....G 3
Araure, 12,316 ....D 3
Aricagua, 230 ....C 3
Arichuna, 983 ....E 4
Aripao, 400 ....F 4
Arismendi, 1,243 ....D 4
Aroa, 6,356 ....D 2
Atapirire, 203 ....F 3
Bachaquero, 14,490 ....C 2
Baragua, 831 ....D 2
Barbacoas, 1,379 ....E 3
Barcelona, 42,379 ....F 2
Barinas, 25,748 ....C 3
Barinitas, 7,208 ....C 3
Barquisimeto, 280,086 ....D 2
Barrancas, Barinas, 3,154 ......C 3
Barrancas, Monagas,
 4,189 ....G 3

Betijoque, 3,915 ....C 3
Biruaca, 631 ....E 4
Biscucuy, 3,900 ....D 3
Bobare, 970 ....D 3
Bobures, 2,159 ....C 3
Boca de Aroa, 1,674 ....D 2
Boca del Mangle, 1,075 ....C 2
Boca del Pao, 283 ....F 3
Boconó, 10,430 ....C 3
Borbón, 373 ....F 4
Borojó, 367 ....D 2
Bruzual, 556 ....D 4
Buena Vista, Anzoátegui, 2,335 ..F 3
Buena Vista, Apure, 64 ....D 4
Buena Vista, Falcón, 786 ....C 2
Cabimas, 141,314 ....C 2
Cabruta, 813 ....E 3
Cabudare, 4,480 ....D 2
Cabure, 1,440 ....D 2
Cachipo, 1,091 ....G 3
Cacuri, 45 ....F 5
Cagua, 16,233 ....E 3
Caicara, 4,781 ....G 2
Caicara de Orinoco, 3,281 ......E 4
Calabozo, 15,739 ....E 3
Calderas, 857 ....C 3
Camaguán, 1,917 ....E 3
Camatagua, 1,419 ....E 3
Campo Claro, 1,620 ....D 2
Candelaria, 158 ....F 4
Cantaura, 14,068 ....F 3
Capatárida, 1,278 ....C 2
Capure, 459 ....G 2
Carabobo, Bolívar ....H 4

Carabobo, Carabobo,
 2,319 ....D 3
Caracas (cap.), 786,710 ....E 2
Caracas, *2,064,033 ....E 2
Carache, 2,635 ....C 3
Carapa, 115 ....C 3
Cariaco, 4,281 ....G 2
Caribén, 25 ....F 4
Caripe, 3,583 ....G 2
Caripito, 21,598 ....G 3
Carirubana, 3,421 ....D 2
Carmelo, 1,944 ....C 2
Carora, 23,227 ....C 2
Carrasquero, 1,353 ....C 2
Carúpano, 38,197 ....G 2
Casanay, 3,561 ....G 2
Casigua, Falcón, 406 ....C 2
Casigua, Zulia, 5,320 ....B 3
Caucagua, 4,705 ....E 2
Cazorla, 657 ....E 3
Chaguaramas, 1,363 ....E 3
Chichiriviche, 2,512 ....D 2
Chivacoa, 12,871 ....D 2
Choroní, 352 ....E 2
Churuguara, 4,538 ....D 2
Ciudad Bolívar, 63,266 ....G 3
Ciudad Bolivia, 2,080 ....C 3
Ciudad de Nutrias, 541 ....D 3
Ciudad Guayana, 127,681 ......G 3
Ciudad Ojeda, 53,745 ....C 2
Ciudad Piar, 4,598 ....G 4
Clarines, 2,018 ....F 3
Cojoro, 156 ....B 1
Colón, 169 ....E 6

Comunidad, 44 ....E 6
Coporito, 659 ....H 3
Coro, 45,506 ....D 2
Corozo Pando, 286 ....E 3
Cúa, 5,567 ....E 2
Cubiro, 1,742 ....D 3
Cuchivero, 122 ....F 4
Cumaná, 69,937 ....G 2
Cumanacoa, 7,354 ....G 2
Cunaviche, 596 ....E 4
Curiapo, 375 ....H 3
Dabajuro, 3,927 ....C 2
Delicias, 1,398 ....B 4
Democracia, 12 ....E 6
Dolores, 1,122 ....D 3
Duaca, 5,457 ....C 3
Ejido, 5,457 ....C 3
El Almacén, 31 ....G 4
El Amparo de Apure, 1,087 ....C 4
El Baúl, 1,550 ....D 3
El Callao, 5,039 ....G 4
El Calvario, 567 ....E 3
El Carmen ....E 3
El Chaparro, 1,703 ....F 3
El Cristo, 328 ....G 4
El Dorado, 2,094 ....H 4
El Empedrado, 1,739 ....C 3
El Guapo, 842 ....E 2
El Manteco, 999 ....G 4
El Miamo, 269 ....H 4
El Pao, Anzoátegui, 586 ....F 3
El Pao, Bolívar, 2,115 ....G 3

El Pao, Cojedes, 1,081 ....D 3
El Perú, 1,487 ....G 4
El Pilar, 3,326 ....G 2
El Rastro, 748 ....E 3
El Roque, 348 ....D 3
El Samán de Apure, 1,099 ......D 4
El Socorro, 3,153 ....E 3
El Sombrero, 5,712 ....E 3
El Tigre, 41,961 ....F 3
El Tocuyo, 14,560 ....C 3
El Toro, 199 ....G 4
El Vigía, 8,874 ....C 3
El Vínculo, 1,224 ....D 1
El Yagual, 435 ....D 4
Encontrados, 2,991 ....B 3
Esperanza, 15 ....E 6
Espino, 470 ....E 3
Garcitas, 1,224 ....C 3
Guacara, 11,353 ....D 2
Guacara, 462 ....D 3
Guadarrama, 461 ....D 3
Guaina, 87 ....G 5
Guana, 87 ....G 5
Guanare, 18,452 ....D 3
Guanarito, 1,048 ....D 3
Guanoco, 437 ....G 2
Guanta, 8,048 ....F 2
Guardatinajas, 704 ....E 3
Guarenas, 646 ....E 2
Guárico, 3,653 ....D 2
Guariquén, 633 ....G 2
Guasdualito, 4,586 ....C 4
Guasimal, 303 ....D 4
Guasipati, 3,446 ....H 4

Guayabal, 40 ....E 6
Guayabal, 841 ....E 3
Güiria, 11,061 ....G 2
Guri, 158 ....G 4
Guzmán Blanco, 151 ....E 6
Higuerote, 3,852 ....E 2
Icabarú, 475 ....H 5
Independencia, 3,658 ....B 3
Irapa, 4,532 ....G 2
Juangriego, 4,505 ....G 2
Judibana, 4,375 ....C 2
Jusepín, 2,471 ....G 3
Kavanayen, 401 ....G 4
La Aduana, 106 ....G 2
La Asunción, 5,517 ....G 2
La Canoa, 256 ....F 3
La Ceiba, Apure, 13 ....D 4
La Ceiba, Trujillo, 199 ....C 2
La Concepción, 18,015 ....B 2
La Concepción, 9,488 ....C 3
La Esmeralda, 30 ....F 6
La Esperanza ....H 3
La Fría, 4,771 ....B 3
La Grita, 7,866 ....C 3
La Guaira, 20,497 ....E 2
Lagunetas, 522 ....C 3
La Horqueta, 330 ....G 3
La Inglesa, 100 ....G 3
La Leona, 327 ....G 3
La Luz, 414 ....G 3
La Margarita ....C 3
La Pàragua, 833 ....G 4
Las Bonitas, 306 ....E 4
Las Lajitas ....F 4

Las Mercedes, 5,410 E 3
Las Piedras, Falcón, 2,068 C 2
Las Piedras, Zulia, 2,069 B 2
Las Trincheras, 157 F 4
Las Vegas, 1,190 D 3
La Tigra, 234 H 4
La Trinidad, 141 C 3
La Trinidad de Arauca, 68 D 3
La Trinidad de Orichuna, 820 D 4
La Unión, 1,068 E 3
La Urbana, 444 E 4
La Vela de Coro, 4,963 D 2
La Victoria, Apure, 109 D 4
La Victoria, Aragua, 22,293 E 2
Libertad, Barinas, 1,218 D 3
Libertad, Cojedes, 1,000 D 3
Los Castillos, 92 G 3
Los Taques, 2,097 C 2
Los Teques, 36,073 E 2
Macareo Santo Niño, 376 H 3
Machiques, 11,115 B 3
Macuro, 899 H 2
Macuto, 7,041 E 2
Maiquetía, 75,687 E 2
Mantecal, Apure, 987 D 4
Mantecal, Bolívar, 21 F 4
Maparari, 1,330 D 2
Mapire, 658 F 4
Maporal, 224 C 4
Maracaibo, 625,101 C 2
Maracaibo, *655,000 C 2
Maracay, 185,655 E 2

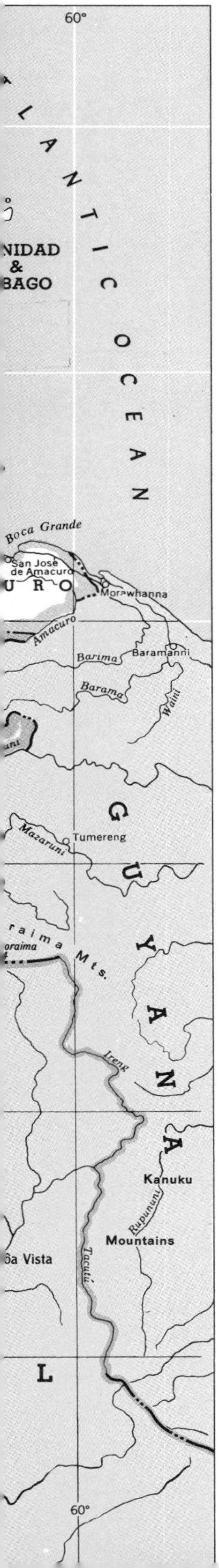

60°
NIDAD
&
BAGO
Boca Grande
San José de Amacuro
Morawhanna
Amacuro
Barima
Baramanni
Barama
Waini
Mazaruni
Tumereng
Roraima
Mts.
Ireng
Kanuku
Rupununi
Mountains
Takutu
Boa Vista
60°

Marigüitar, 3,075 G 2
Maripa, 802 F 4
Maroa, 417 E 6
Matu, 87 F 4
Maturín, 54,362 G 3
Mene de Mauroa, 3,597 C 2
Mene Grande, 11,673 C 3
Mérida, 46,339 C 3
Mesa Bolívar, 1,227 C 3
Mirimire, 1,473 D 2
Moitaco, 364 F 4
Morganito, 103 E 5
Morón, 7,079 D 2
Mucuchachí, 391 C 3
Mucuchíes, 1,034 C 3
Naricual, 656 F 2
Nirgua, 7,371 D 2
Nuevo Mamo, 284 G 3
Obispos, 651 D 3
Ocumare de la Costa, 1,332 E 2
Ocumare del Tuy, 15,006 E 2
Onoto, 1,090 F 3
Ortiz, 1,309 E 3
Ospino, 1,590 D 3
Palmarejo, 943 C 2
Palmarito, Apure, 1,176 D 4
Palmarito, Guárico, 74 F 3
Palmarito, Mérida, 903 C 3
Papelón, 414 D 3
Paraguaipoa, 1,443 C 2
Paraíso de Chabasquén, 2,324 D 3
Pariaguán, 6,236 F 3
Parmana, 322 F 4
Pedernales, 788 G 3
Pedregal, 1,483 C 2
Peraitepuí, 81 H 5
Piacoa, 377 H 3
Pimichín, 19 E 6
Píritu, Anzoátegui, 1,438 F 2
Píritu, Falcón, 1,859 D 2
Píritu, Portuguesa, 4,879 D 3
Platanal, 8 F 6
Porlamar, 21,787 G 2
Pozuelos, 6,488 F 2
Pregonero, 2,894 C 3
Pueblo Nuevo, 2,680 D 1
Puerto Ayacucho, 5,465 E 5
Puerto Cabello, 52,493 E 2
Puerto Cumarebo, 8,029 D 2
Puerto de Nutrias, 565 D 3
Puerto Hierro, 1,096 H 2
Puerto La Cruz, 59,033 F 2
Puerto Miranda, 374 E 4
Puerto Páez, 767 E 4
Puerto Píritu, 2,407 F 2
Punta Cardón, 7,461 C 2
Punta de Mata, 6,525 G 3
Punta de Piedras, 2,342 F 2
Punto Fijo, 34,457 D 2
Puruey, 343 F 4
Puruname, 8 E 6
Quíbor, 7,046 D 3
Quiriquire, 7,393 G 3
Quisiro, 816 C 2
Río Caribe, 7,774 G 2
Río Chico, 2,612 F 2
Río Claro, 1,374 D 3
Río Tocuyo, 1,650 C 2
Rosario, 10,442 B 2
Rubio, 11,774 B 4
Sabaneta, Barinas, 1,997 D 3
Sabaneta, Falcón, 414 D 2
Samariapo, 19 E 5
San Antonio, Monagas, 3,337 G 2
San Antonio, Zulia, 510 C 3
San Antonio de Caparo, 1,412 C 4
San Antonio del Táchira, 14,247 B 4
San Antonio de Orinoco, 48 E 6
San Antonio de Tabasca, 434 G 3
Sanare, 3,599 D 3
San Carlos, Cojedes, 11,934 D 3
San Carlos, Zulia, 686 C 2
San Carlos del Zulia, 14,880 C 3
San Carlos de Río Negro, 474 E 7
San Casimiro, 3,485 E 3

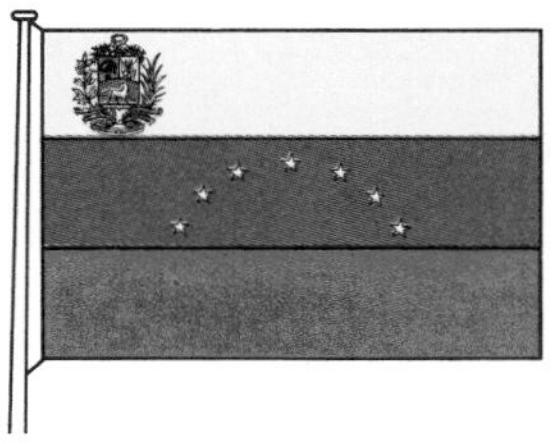

AREA 352,143 sq. mi.
POPULATION 10,398,907
CAPITAL Caracas
LARGEST CITY Caracas
HIGHEST POINT Pico Bolívar 16,427 ft.
MONETARY UNIT bolívar
MAJOR LANGUAGE Spanish
MAJOR RELIGION Roman Catholicism

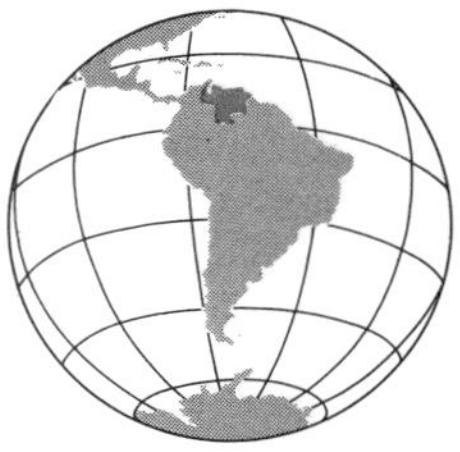

San Cristóbal, 149,063 B 4
San Diego de Cabrutica, 455 F 3
San Felipe, Yaracuy, 28,744 D 2
San Felipe, Zulia, 570 B 3
San Félix, 424 C 2
San Fernando, 24,470 E 4
San Fernando de Atabapo, 898 E 5
San Francisco, 967 C 2
San Ignacio, 697 B 2
San José, Amazonas E 5
San José, Zulia, 2,991 B 3
San José de Amacuro, 22 H 3
San José de Areocuar, 1,000 G 2
San José de Guanipa, 20,746 G 3
San José de la Costa, 505 D 2
San José de Río Chico, 3,368 F 2
San José de Tiznados, 504 E 3
San Juan de Colón, 8,944 B 3
San Juan de las Galdonas, 1,104 G 2
San Juan de los Cayos, 1,191 D 2
San Juan de los Morros, 28,556 E 3
San Juan de Manapiare, 46 E 5
San Juan de Payara, 945 E 4
San Lorenzo, Falcón, 527 D 2
San Lorenzo, Zulia, 1,552 C 3
San Luis, 1,266 D 2
San Mateo, 1,849 F 3
San Mauricio, 43 E 3
San Pedro de las Bocas, 288 G 4
San Rafael, 6,390 C 2
San Rafael de Atamaica, 597 E 4
San Rafael de Orituco, 991 E 3
San Sebastián, 4,090 E 2
Santa Ana, Anzoátegui, 3,609 F 3
Santa Ana, Táchira, 3,677 B 4
Santa Bárbara, Amazonas E 6
Santa Bárbara, Barinas, 2,029 C 4
Santa Bárbara, Monagas, 1,720 G 3
Santa Bárbara, Zulia, 105 C 3
Santa Catalina, Barinas, 425 D 4
Santa Catalina, Delta Amacuro, 440 H 3
Santa Cruz, 3,224 C 3
Santa Cruz de Bucaral, 1,829 D 2
Santa Cruz del Zulia, 2,041 B 3
Santa Cruz de Mara, 1,919 C 2
Santa Cruz de Orinoco, 419 F 3
Santa Elena, 752 H 5
Santa Inés, Anzoátegui, 917 F 3
Santa Inés, Barinas, 257 C 3
Santa Isabel F 7
Santa Lucía, 563 E 3
Santa María, Bolívar, 468 G 3
Santa María de Erebató, 468 F 5
Santa María de Ipire, 3,167 F 3
Santa María del Orinoco, 57 E 4
Santa Rita, Guárico, 306 E 3
Santa Rita, Zulia, 5,342 C 2

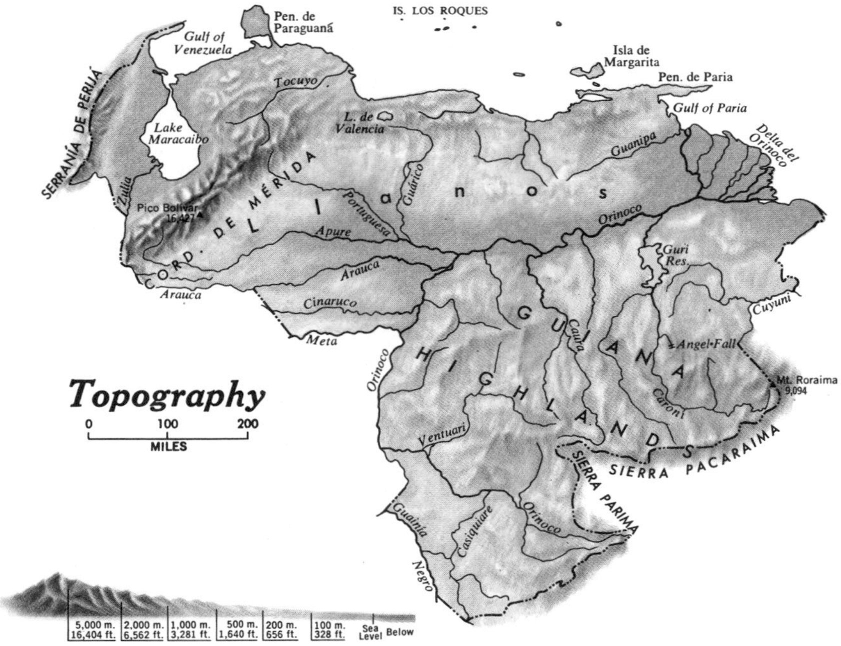

Topography
0 100 200
MILES
Pen. de Paraguaná
IS. LOS ROQUES
Isla de Margarita
Pen. de Paria
Gulf of Paria
Delta del Orinoco
Gulf of Venezuela
Tocuyo
L. de Valencia
Guanipa
Lake Maracaibo
SERRANÍA DE PERIJÁ
Zulia
Pico Bolívar 16,427
CORD. DE MÉRIDA
Llanos
Portuguesa
Guárico
Apure
Orinoco
Arauca
Cinaruco
Meta
Guri Res.
Cuyuní
GUIANA HIGHLANDS
Caura
Caroní
Angel Fall
Mt. Roraima 9,094
SIERRA PACARAIMA
Ventuari
SIERRA PARIMA
Orinoco
Casiquiare
Guainía
Negro
5,000 m. 16,404 ft.
2,000 m. 6,562 ft.
1,000 m. 3,281 ft.
500 m. 1,640 ft.
200 m. 656 ft.
100 m. 328 ft.
Sea Level
Below

Santa Rosa, Anzoátegui, 1,036 F 3
Santa Rosa, Apure, 27 D 4
Santa Rosa, Barinas, 957 D 3
Santa Rosa de Amanadona, 163 E 7
Santa Rosalía, 239 F 4
Santa Teresa del Tuy, 6,958 E 2
San Timoteo, 2,823 C 3
San Tomé, 5,625 F 3
San Vicente, Amazonas, 14 E 5
San Vicente, Apure, 252 D 4
Sarare, 2,664 D 3
Seboruco, 2,440 B 3
Simaraña G 5
Sinamaica, 1,345 B 2
Siquisique, 2,579 D 2
Solano E 6
Soledad, 5,653 G 3
Sucre, 65 D 3

Suripa, 128 D 4
Tamatama, 35 F 6
Táriba, 9,835 B 4
Temblador, 2,041 G 3
Tia Juana, 5,846 C 2
Timotes, 2,548 C 3
Tinaco, 4,485 D 3
Tinaquillo, 8,142 D 3
Tocópero, 721 D 2
Tocuyo de la Costa, 3,351 D 2
Torunos, 676 C 3
Tovar, 9,614 C 3
Trujillo, 18,957 C 3
Tucacas, 3,853 D 2
Tucupido, 7,016 F 3
Tucupita, 9,922 H 3
Tumeremo, 3,926 H 4
Tupí, 91 D 2
Turén, 341 D 3
Turiamo, 31 E 2

Turmero, 7,639 E 2
Upata, 12,717 G 3
Urachiche, 3,630 D 2
Uracoa, 858 H 3
Urica, 1,577 F 3
Urimán, 237 G 5
Urumaco, 941 C 2
Uruyén G 5
Uverito, 336 F 3
Valencia, 177,199 E 2
Valencia, *224,552 E 2
Valera, 46,643 C 3
Valle de Guanape, 3,254 F 3
Valle de la Pascua, 24,308 F 3
Villa Bruzual, 10,278 D 3
Villa de Cura, 19,945 E 2
Villa Frontado, 1,597 G 2
Yaguaraparo, 2,673 G 2
Yaritagua, 14,740 D 2
Yavita, 49 E 6
Yericaña F 5
Yoco, 2,181 G 2
Zanja de Lira, 58 E 3
Zaraza, 10,084 F 3
Zuata, 783 F 3

OTHER FEATURES

Amacuro (river) H 4
Angel (Salto Angel) (fall) G 5
Apongua (river) H 5
Apure (river) E 4
Arauca (river) E 4
Arichuna (river) D 4
Aro (river) F 4
Atabapo (river) E 6
Auyantepui (mt.) G 5
Baria (river) E 7
Blanquilla, La (isl.), 46 F 2
Bolívar (mt.) C 3
Bolívar (mt.) G 4
Canagua (river) C 3
Caño Capure (river) H 3
Caño Macareo (river) H 3
Caño Mánamo (river) G 3
Capanaparo (river) E 4
Caparo (river) C 4
Caroní (river) G 4
Carrao (river) G 5
Caruai (river) H 5
Casiquiare, Brazo (river) E 6
Catatumbo (river) B 3
Caura (river) F 5
Cerbatana, La (mts.) E 4
Chicanán (river) H 4
Chimantá–tepuí (mt.) G 5
Chivapure (river) E 4
Cinaruco (river) D 4
Coche (isl.) F 2
Codera (cape) E 2
Cojedes (river) D 3
Cuao (river) E 5
Cubagua (isl.) F 2
Cuchivero (river) F 4
Cuquenán (river) H 5
Curutú (river) G 5
Cuyuní (river) H 4
Delgado Chalbaud (mt.) G 6
Dragons Mouth (strait) H 2
Duida (mt.) F 6
Erebato (river) F 5
Gran Sabana, La (plain) G 5
Guainía (river) E 6
Guampí (mts.) F 4
Guanare (river) D 3
Guanare Viejo (river) D 3
Guanipa (river) G 3
Guárico (res.) E 3
Guárico (river) E 3
Guayapo (mts.) E 5
Güere (river) F 3

Guri (dam) G 4
Guri (res.) G 4
Hermanos, Los (isls.) F 2
Icabaru (river) G 5
Imataca (mts.) H 4
Imeri (mts.) E 7
La Blanquilla (isl.), 46 F 2
La Grand Sabana (plain) G 5
La Orchila (isl.), 35 E 2
Las Aves (isl.), 6 E 2
La Tortuga (isl.), 25 F 2
Los Hermanos (isls.) F 2
Los Monjes (isls.) C 1
Los Roques (isls.), 537 E 2
Los Testigos (isls.), 59 G 2
Macanao (pen.) F 2
Maigualida (mts.) F 4
Manapire (river) E 3
Maracaibo (lake) C 3
Margarita (isl.), 85,296 F 2
Mavaca (river) F 6
Médanos (isthmus) D 2
Merevari (river) E 4
Mérida (mts.) C 3
Meta (river) E 4
Monjes, Los (isls.) C 1
Morichal Largo (river) G 3
Neblina (Phelps) (pk.) E 7
Negro (river) E 7
Nuria (mts.) H 4
Ocamo (river) F 6
Orchila, La (isl.), 35 E 2
Orinoco (delta) H 3
Orinoco (river) G 3
Orituco (river) E 3
Pacaraima (mts.) G 5
Pao (river) D 3
Pao (river) F 3
Paragua (river) G 4
Paraguaná (peninsula), 104,535 C 1
Paria (gulf) H 2
Paria (pen.) G 2
Parida, La (Bolívar) (mt.) G 4
Parima (mts.) F 6
Perijá (mts.) B 2
Phelps (pk.) E 7
Portuguesa (river) D 3
Roques, Los (isls.), 537 E 2
Roraima (mt.) H 5
Salto Angel (fall) G 5
Sarare (river) C 4
Serpents Mouth (strait) H 3
Siapa (river) E 7
Sipapo (river) E 5
Suapure (river) E 4
Suripá (river) C 4
Tapirapecó (mts.) F 7
Testigos, Los (isls.), 59 G 2
Tigre (river) G 3
Tocuco (river) B 3
Tocuyo (river) D 2
Tortuga, La (isl.), 25 F 2
Tramán–tepuí (mt.) G 5
Triste (gulf) D 2
Turagua (mts.) F 4
Tuy (river) E 2
Unare (river) F 3
Valencia (lake) E 2
Venamo (mt.) H 4
Venamo (river) H 4
Venezuela (gulf) C 2
Ventuari (river) E 5
Votamo (river) F 6
Yatua (river) E 7
Yuruari (river) H 4
Zuata (river) F 3
Zulia (river) B 3

*City and suburbs.

Agriculture, Industry and Resources

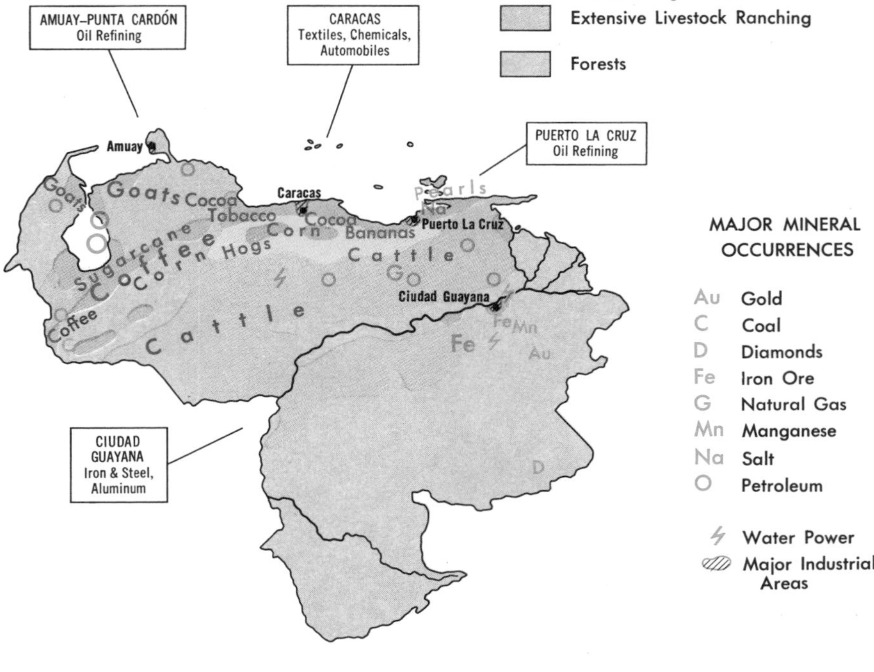

AMUAY–PUNTA CARDÓN
Oil Refining
CARACAS
Textiles, Chemicals, Automobiles
PUERTO LA CRUZ
Oil Refining
CIUDAD GUAYANA
Iron & Steel, Aluminum
Amuay
Caracas
Puerto La Cruz
Ciudad Guayana
Goats
Cocoa
Tobacco
Pearls
Na
Corn
Bananas
Sugarcane
Coffee
Hogs
Cattle
Fe
Mn
Au
D
DOMINANT LAND USE
Diversified Tropical Crops (chiefly plantation agriculture)
Upland Cultivated Areas
Upland Livestock Grazing, Limited Agriculture
Extensive Livestock Ranching
Forests
MAJOR MINERAL OCCURRENCES
Au Gold
C Coal
D Diamonds
Fe Iron Ore
G Natural Gas
Mn Manganese
Na Salt
O Petroleum
Water Power
Major Industrial Areas

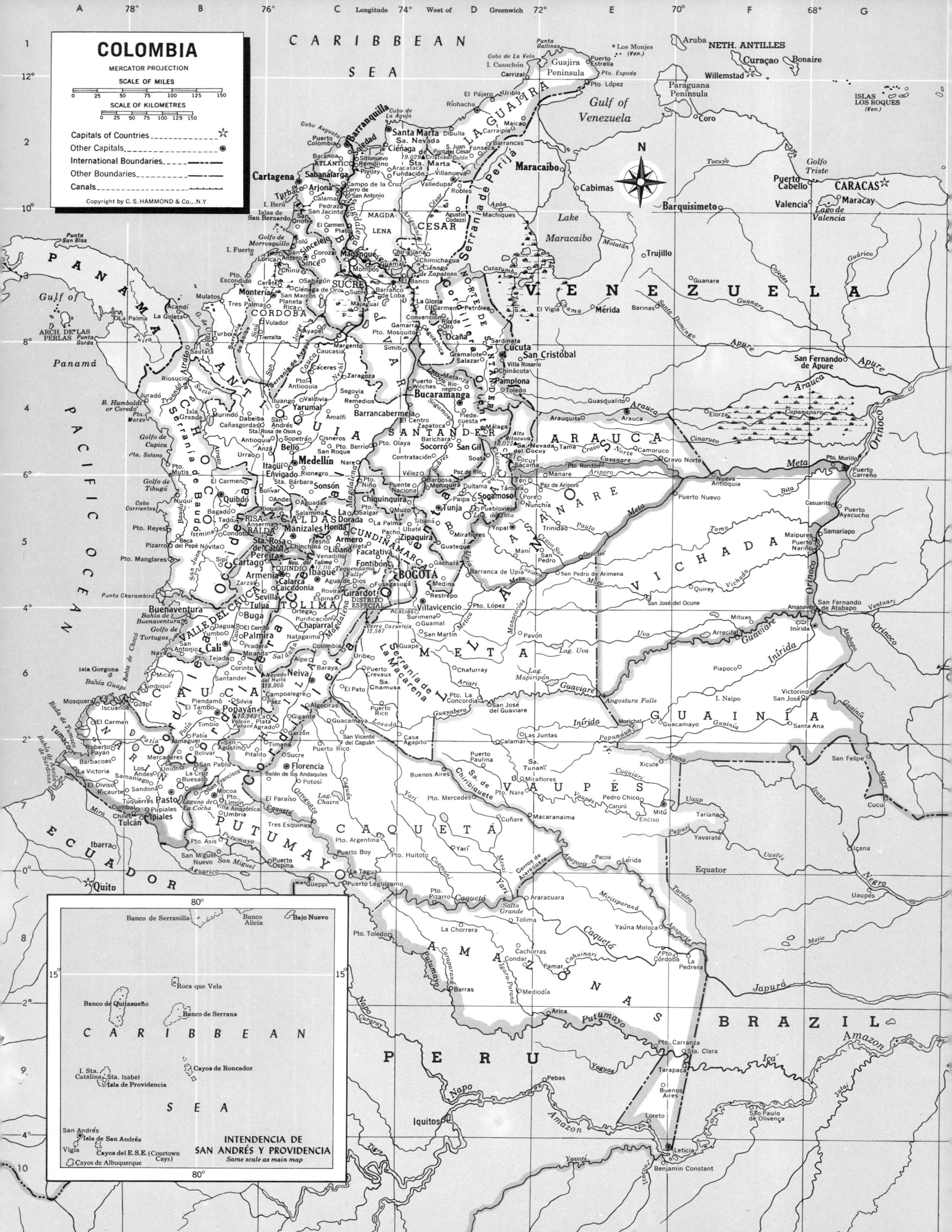

INTERNAL DIVISIONS

Amazonas (intendency), 16,000...D 8
Antioquia (dept.), 3,031,000........C 4
Arauca (commissary), 32,000......E 4
Atlántico (dept.), 903,000 ....C 2
Bolívar (dept.), 849,000 ....C 3
Boyacá (dept.), 1,104,000 ....D 5
Caldas (dept.), 810,000 ....C 5
Caquetá (intendency), 157,000....C 7
Casanare (intendency), 90,000 ....E 5
Cauca (dept.), 696,000 ....B 6
Cesar (dept.), 357,000 ....D 3
Chocó (dept.), 210,000 ....B 4
Córdoba (dept.), 760,000 ....C 3
Cundinamarca (dept.), 1,187,000 ....C 5
Distrito Especial, 2,416,000 ....C 5
Guainía (comm.), 5,000 ....F 6
Guajira, La (dept.), 173,000 ......D 2
Huila (dept.), 485,000 ....C 6
La Guajira (dept.), 173,000 ......D 2
Magdalena (dept.), 683,000 ....D 3
Meta (dept.), 248,000 ....D 6
Nariño (dept.), 787,000 ....B 7
Norte de Santander (dept.), 615,000 ....D 4
Putumayo (comm.), 77,000 ....C 7
Quindío (dept.), 346,000 ....C 5
Risaralda (dept.), 512,000...........C 5
San Andrés y Providencia (intendency), 27,000 ....B10
Santander (dept.), 1,137,000 ....D 4
Sucre (dept.), 361,000 ....C 3
Tolima (dept.), 902,000 ....C 5
Valle del Cauca (dept.), 2,114,000 ....B 6
Vaupés (commissary), 18,000 ....E 7
Vichada (commissary), 9,000 .....F 5

CITIES and TOWNS

Acacías, 6,508 ....D 6
Acandí, 1,686 ....B 3
Agrado, 2,751 ....C 6
Agua de Dios, 7,401 ....C 5
Aguachica, 8,556 ....D 3
Aguadas, 10,822 ....C 5
Agustín Codazzi, 11,673 ....D 3
Aipe, 3,404 ....C 6
Algeciras, 3,778 ....C 6
Almaguer, 1,251 ....B 7
Amalfi, 4,667 ....C 4
Amanavén, †1,164 ....G 6
Andes, 11,135 ....C 5
Anserma, 14,129 ....B 5
Antioquia, 6,002 ....B 4
Anza, 680 ....C 4
Aracataca, 5,304 ....D 2
Araracuara ....E 8
Arauca, 4,280 ....E 4
Arauquita, 413 ....E 4
Arjona, 16,510 ....C 2
Armenia, 162,837 ....B 5
Armero, 17,495 ....C 5
Ayapel, 5,610 ....C 3
Bagado, 865 ....B 5
Baranoa, 14,064 ....C 2
Baraya, 2,696 ....C 6
Barbacoas, 4,011 ....A 7
Barbosa, 6,018 ....D 5
Barichara, 2,798 ....D 4
Barrancabermeja, 59,625 ....C 4
Barrancas, 2,010 ....D 2
Barranco de Loba, 1,648 ....C 3
Barranquilla, 816,706 ....C 2
Belén de los Andaquíes, 1,420.....C 7
Bello, 127,377 ....C 4
Boca del Pepé, 566 ....B 5
Bogotá (cap.), 2,037,904 ....D 5
Bogotá, *2,416,000 ....D 5
Bolívar, Antioquia, 9,532 ....C 5
Bolívar, Cauca, 3,641 ....B 7
Bucaramanga, 279,703 ....D 4
Buenaventura, 113,301 ....B 6
Buesaco, 2,278 ....B 7
Buga, 65,535 ....B 6
Caicedonia, 16,327 ....C 5
Calamar, Bolívar, 6,055 ....C 2
Calamar, Vaupés ....D 7
Calarcá, 30,342 ....C 5
Cali, 820,809 ....B 6
Camoruco ....E 4
Campo de la Cruz, 10,044 ....C 2
Campoalegre, 9,768 ....C 6
Cañasgordas, 4,464 ....B 4
Cartagena, 229,040 ....C 2
Cartago, 55,682 ....B 5
Carurú, 277 ....E 7
Casuarito, †75 ....G 4
Caucasia, 5,616 ....C 4
Cereté, 11,849 ....C 3
Cerro de San Antonio, 3,397 ....C 2
Chaparral, 13,261 ....C 6
Chimichagua, 5,093 ....D 3
Chinácota, 4,081 ....D 4
Chinchiná, 15,944 ....C 5
Chinú, 7,552 ....C 3
Chiquinquirá, 16,926 ....C 5
Chiriguaná, 6,516 ....D 3
Ciénaga, 142,893 ....C 2
Ciénaga de Oro, 8,047 ....C 3
Cisneros, 7,554 ....C 4
Colombia, 1,599 ....C 6
Colón, 1,133 ....B 7
Condoto, 4,094 ....B 5
Contratación, 3,117 ....D 4
Convención, 7,371 ....D 3
Corinto, 5,008 ....B 6
Corozal, 14,000 ....C 3
Cravo Norte, 566 ....F 4
Cúcuta, 207,091 ....D 4
Cumbal, 2,549 ....B 7
Cuñare ....D 7
Dabeiba, 4,218 ....B 4
Dagua, 4,635 ....B 6
Dibulla ....D 2
Duitama, 31,865 ....D 5
El Banco, 14,889 ....D 3
El Carmen, Chocó, 1,689 ....B 5
El Carmen, Norte de Santander, 2,737 ....D 3
El Carmen de Bolívar, 19,196.....C 3
El Cerrito, 12,200 ....B 6
El Cocuy, 2,869 ....D 4
El Tambo, 4,003 ....B 6
Envigado, 40,686 ....C 4
Espinal, 22,791 ....C 5
Facatativá, 20,742 ....C 5
Florencia, 17,709 ....C 7
Fonseca, 5,190 ....D 2
Fontibón ....C 5
Fresno, 7,058 ....C 5
Fundación, 14,128 ....D 2
Fusagasugá, 18,755 ....C 5
Gachalá, 1,253 ....D 5
Gamarra, 4,664 ....D 3
Garzón, 11,999 ....C 6
Gigante, 4,594 ....C 6
Girardot, 66,584 ....C 5
Gramalote, 3,098 ....D 4
Guacamaya ....C 6
Guamal, Magdalena, 4,695 ....C 3
Guamal, Meta, 2,113 ....D 6
Guape ....D 6
Guapí, 3,066 ....B 6
Guateque, 4,646 ....D 5
Honda, 19,945 ....C 5
Ibagué, 178,821 ....C 5
Inírida ....G 6
Ipiales, 23,320 ....B 7
Iscuandé, 1,777 ....A 6
Istmina, 3,996 ....B 5
Itagüí, 101,066 ....C 4
Ituango, 3,466 ....C 4
Jurado, 708 ....B 4
La Cruz, 4,014 ....B 7
La Dorada, 26,168 ....C 5
La Gloria, 2,915 ....D 3
La Palma, 4,594 ....C 5
La Plata, 5,863 ....C 6
La Unión, 3,875 ....B 7
Leticia, 4,013 ....F10
Líbano, 18,640 ....C 5
Lorica, 12,880 ....C 3
Los Andes, 1,392 ....B 7
Macaranaima ....E 7
Magangué, 27,354 ....C 3
Maicao, 9,347 ....D 2
Maipures ....F 5
Majagual, 2,197 ....C 3
Málaga, 9,674 ....D 4
Manare ....E 4
Maní, 586 ....D 5
Manizales, 267,543 ....C 5
Matanza, 1,264 ....D 4
Medellín, 967,825 ....C 4
Medina, 893 ....D 5
Mercaderes, 2,376 ....B 7
Micay ....B 6
Miraflores, Boyacá, 3,257 ....D 5
Miraflores, Vaupés, 245 ....E 7
Miranda, 5,527 ....B 6
Mitú, 1,623 ....E 7
Mituas ....F 6
Mocoa, 2,571 ....B 7
Mompós, 10,965 ....C 3
Moniquirá, 4,882 ....D 5
Montería, 167,446 ....B 3
Morichal, †2,512 ....E 6
Mosquera, 766 ....A 6
Murindó, 319 ....B 4
Muzo, 792 ....D 5
Natagaima, 8,372 ....C 6
Naya ....B 6
Neiva, 111,727 ....C 6
Nóvita, 883 ....B 5
Nueva Antioquia, †236 ....F 5
Nunchía, 461 ....D 5
Nuquí, 1,500 ....B 5
Ocaña, 28,028 ....D 3
Orocué, 1,600 ....E 5
Ortega, 4,450 ....C 6
Pacho, 7,192 ....C 5
Pacoa, 1960 ....G 6
Páez, 1,570 ....C 6
Paipa, 3,105 ....D 5
Palmira, 164,394 ....B 6
Pamplona, 25,502 ....D 4
Pasto, 123,153 ....B 7
Patía, 3,045 ....B 6
Paz de Ariporo, 1,216 ....E 5
Paz de Río, 2,748 ....D 4
Pedraza, 1,757 ....C 2
Pereira, 224,421 ....C 5
Piedecuesta, 12,278 ....D 4
Pitalito, 10,818 ....B 7
Pivijay, 8,200 ....C 2
Planeta Rica, 5,959 ....C 3
Plato, 13,364 ....C 3
Popayán, 58,500 ....B 6
Pore, 193 ....D 5
Potosí, 1,149 ....C 7
Pradera, 11,223 ....B 6
Puente Nacional, 2,913 ....D 5
Puerto Asís, 2,902 ....B 7
Puerto Berrío, 15,812 ....C 4
Puerto Carreño, 1,115 ....G 4
Puerto Colombia, 7,143 ....C 2
Puerto Escondido, 1,543 ....B 3
Puerto Leguízamo, 3,014 ....C 8
Puerto López, La Guajira ....E 2
Puerto López, Meta, 3,586 ....D 5
Puerto Murillo, †1,014 ....G 4
Puerto Nariño, †926 ....F 5
Puerto Rico, Caquetá, †10,328 ....C 7
Puerto Rico, Meta ....C 6
Puerto Rondón, 951 ....E 4
Puerto Salgar, 6,398 ....C 5
Puerto Tejada, 14,863 ....B 6
Puerto Wilches, 4,635 ....D 4
Pupiales, 2,432 ....B 7
Purificación, 7,044 ....C 6
Quibdó, 19,989 ....B 5
Remedios, 2,090 ....C 4
Remolino, 3,373 ....C 2
Restrepo, 2,603 ....D 5
Ricaurte, 866 ....A 7
Río de Oro, 2,482 ....D 3
Riohacha, 11,708 ....D 2
Rionegro, Antioquia, 2,708 ....D 4
Rionegro, Santander, 12,541 ....C 4
Riosucio, Caldas, 11,274 ....C 5
Riosucio, Chocó, 1,817 ....B 4
Roberto Payán, 402 ....A 7
Robles, 4,278 ....D 2
Rovira, 4,582 ....C 5
Sabanalarga, 20,254 ....C 2
Sácama, 54 ....D 4
Sahagún, 11,560 ....C 3
Salamina, 14,263 ....C 5
Salazar, 3,020 ....D 4
Samaniego, 3,181 ....B 7
San Agustín, 3,250 ....B 7
San Andrés, Antioquia, 1,773 ....C 4
San Andrés, San Andrés y Providencia, 9,040 ....A10
San Antero, 6,596 ....C 3
San Felipe, 187 ....G 7
San Francisco, 1,248 ....B 7
San Gil, 18,518 ....D 4
San Jacinto, 10,210 ....C 3
San José del Guaviare, 215 ....D 6
San José del Ocuné, 105 ....E 5
San Juan del César, 9,347 ....D 2
San Marcos, 7,083 ....C 3
San Martín, 6,739 ....D 6
San Onofre, 10,737 ....C 3
San Pablo, 4,103 ....B 7
San Roque, 3,272 ....C 4
San Vicente del Caguán, 1,764....C 6
Sandoná, 6,776 ....B 7
Santa Bárbara, 7,779 ....C 5
Santa Isabel, 468 ....B 9
Santa Marta, 137,474 ....D 2
Santa Rosa de Cabal, 31,646 ....C 5
Santa Rosa de Osos, 6,860 ....C 4
Santander, 11,426 ....B 6
Santiago, 929 ....B 7
Sardinata, 2,964 ....D 3
Segovia, 9,234 ....C 4
Sevilla, 26,757 ....C 5
Sibundoy-Las Casas, 1,999 ....B 7
Silvia, 3,180 ....B 6
Simití, 2,825 ....C 4
Sincé, 10,631 ....C 3
Sincelejo, 44,001 ....C 3
Sipí, 155 ....B 5
Sitionuevo, 5,969 ....C 2
Soatá, 4,361 ....D 4
Socorro, 13,716 ....D 4
Sogamoso, 32,274 ....D 5
Soledad, 37,617 ....C 2
Sonsón, 16,955 ....C 5
Sopetrán, 3,646 ....C 4
Sucre, Bolívar, 3,035 ....C 3
Sucre, Caquetá ....C 7
Tadó, 1,947 ....B 5
Támara, 1,034 ....D 5
Tame, 3,063 ....E 4
Tibaná, 924 ....D 5
Tierralta, 4,415 ....C 3
Timaná, 2,999 ....C 7
Timbío, 4,145 ....B 6
Timbiquí, 1,406 ....B 6
Toledo, 2,314 ....D 4
Tolú, 7,954 ....C 3
Trinidad, 572 ....E 5
Tuluá, 56,539 ....B 6
Tumaco, 25,145 ....A 7
Tunja, 40,451 ....D 5
Túquerres, 10,698 ....B 7
Turbaco, 14,255 ....C 2
Turbo, 7,375 ....B 3
Ubaté, 6,261 ....D 5
Uribia, 1,763 ....D 2
Urrao, 7,712 ....B 4
Valdivia, 2,264 ....C 4
Valledupar, 120,009 ....D 2
Vélez, 7,033 ....D 4
Venadillo, 6,931 ....C 5
Villanueva, 8,288 ....D 2
Villa Amazónica, 1,344 ....B 7
Villa Rosario, 5,184 ....D 4
Villavicencio, 45,277 ....D 5
Villeta, 5,280 ....C 5
Yarumal, 16,823 ....C 4
Yavaraté, †1,963 ....F 7
Yopal, 2,878 ....D 5
Zapatoca, 7,305 ....D 4
Zaragoza, 2,134 ....C 4
Zarzal, 17,768 ....B 5
Zipaquirá, 22,648 ....D 5

OTHER FEATURES

Abibe (mts.) ....B 4
Aguja (cape) ....C 2
Albuquerque (cays) A10
Alicia (bank) ....B 8
Alto Ritacuva (mt.) ....D 4
Amazon (Amazonas) (river) ....E 9
Ancón de Sardinas (bay) ....A 7
Angostura (falls) ....E 6
Apaporis (river) ....F 8
Araracuara (mts.) ....E 7
Arauca (river) ....E 4
Ariari (river) ....D 6
Ariguaní (river) ....D 3
Ariporo (river) ....E 4
Atabapo (river) ....G 6
Atrato (river) ....B 4
Augusta (cape) ....C 2
Ayapel (mts.) ....C 4
Bajo Nuevo (shoal) ....C 8
Baudó (mts.) ....B 5
Baudó (river) ....B 5
Bita (river) ....F 5
Caguán (river) ....C 7
Cahuinari (river) ....E 8
Caquetá (river) ....E 8
Caraparaná (river) ....D 8
Casanare (river) ....E 4
Cauca (river) ....C 4
Cazueleja (mt.) ....C 6
Central (mts.) ....C 5
César (river) ....D 2
Chaira (lagoon) ....C 7
Chamusa (mts.) ....C 6
Charambirá (point) ....B 5
Chiribiquete (mts.) ....D 7
Chocó (bay) ....B 6
Cocha (lake) ....B 7
Cocuy (mts.) ....D 4
Coredó (Humboldt) (bay) ....B 4
Corrientes (cape) ....B 5
Courtown (Este Sudeste) (cays) A10
Cravo Norte (river) ....E 4
Cravo Sur (river) ....E 5
Cristóbal Colón (mt.) ....D 2
Cuemaní (river) ....D 7
Cupica (gulf) ....B 4
Cuquiari (river) ....E 7
Cusiana (river) ....D 5
Este Sudeste (cays) A10
Gallinas (point) ....E 1
Grande (isl.) ....B 4
Guainía (river) ....F 6
Guajira (pen.) ....E 1
Guapí (bay) ....A 6
Guaviare (river) ....F 6
Guayabero (river) ....D 6
Huila (mt.) ....C 6
Humboldt (Coredó) (bay) ....B 4
Igara-Paraná (river) ....D 8
Inírida (river) ....F 6
Isana (river) ....F 7
Lebrija (river) ....D 4
Llanos (plains) ....D 5
Losada (river) ....C 6
Macarena (mts.) ....D 6
Magdalena (river) ....C 3
Manacacías (river) ....D 6
Mapiripán (lake) ....E 6
Marzo (cape) ....B 4
Mesai (river) ....D 7
Meta (river) ....E 5
Metica (river) ....D 6
Miritiparaná (river) ....E 8
Morrosquillo (gulf) ....C 3
Muco (river) ....E 5
Naipo (isl.) ....F 6
Nechí (river) ....C 4
Occidental, Cordillera (mts.) ....B 5
Oriental, Cordillera (mts.) ....D 5
Orinoco (river) ....G 5
Orteguaza (river) ....C 7
Papunáua (river) ....E 6
Patía (river) ....B 6
Pauto (river) ....E 5
Perijá (mts.) ....D 2
Providencia (isl.), 2,318 ....B 9
Pupurí (river) ....F 7
Puracé (volcano) ....B 6
Putumayo (river) ....E 9
Quitasueño (bank) ....A 8
Riosucio (river) ....C 5
Roncador (cays) ....B 9
Saldaña (river) ....C 6
Salto Grande (falls) ....D 8
San Andrés (isl.), 14,413 ....A10
San Jorge (river) ....C 3
San Juan (river) ....B 5
Santa Marta, Nev. de (range)...D 2
Serrana (bank) ....B 9
Serranilla (bank) ....B 8
Sinú (river) ....B 3
Sogamoso (river) ....D 4
Solano (point) ....B 4
Suárez (river) ....D 4
Taraíra (river) ....F 8
Tequendama (falls) ....C 5
Tibugá (gulf) ....B 5
Tolima (mt.) ....C 5
Tomo (river) ....F 5
Tortugas (gulf) ....B 6
Truandó (river) ....B 4
Tumaco (inlet) ....A 6
Tunahí (mts.) ....E 7
Upía (river) ....D 5
Urabá (gulf) ....B 3
Uva (lake) ....E 6
Uva (river) ....E 6
Vaupés (river) ....E 7
Vela (cape) ....D 1
Vela, Roca que (cay) ....B 8
Vichada (river) ....F 5
Yarí (river) ....D 8
Zapatosa (swamp) ....D 3

*City and suburbs.

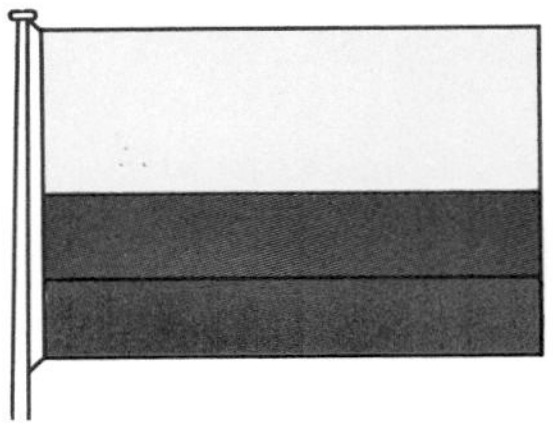

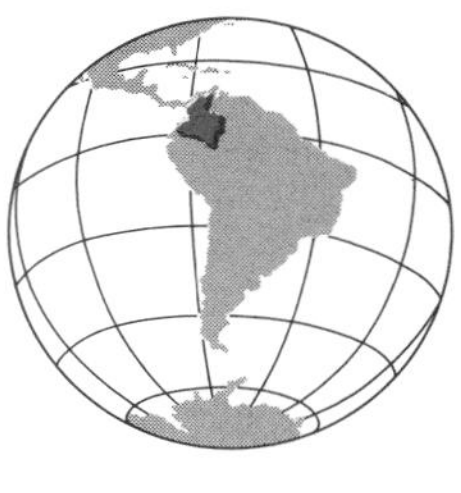

AREA 439,513 sq. mi.
POPULATION 21,117,000
CAPITAL Bogotá
LARGEST CITY Bogotá
HIGHEST POINT Pico Cristóbal Colón 19,029 ft.
MONETARY UNIT Colombian peso
MAJOR LANGUAGE Spanish
MAJOR RELIGION Roman Catholicism

Agriculture, Industry and Resources

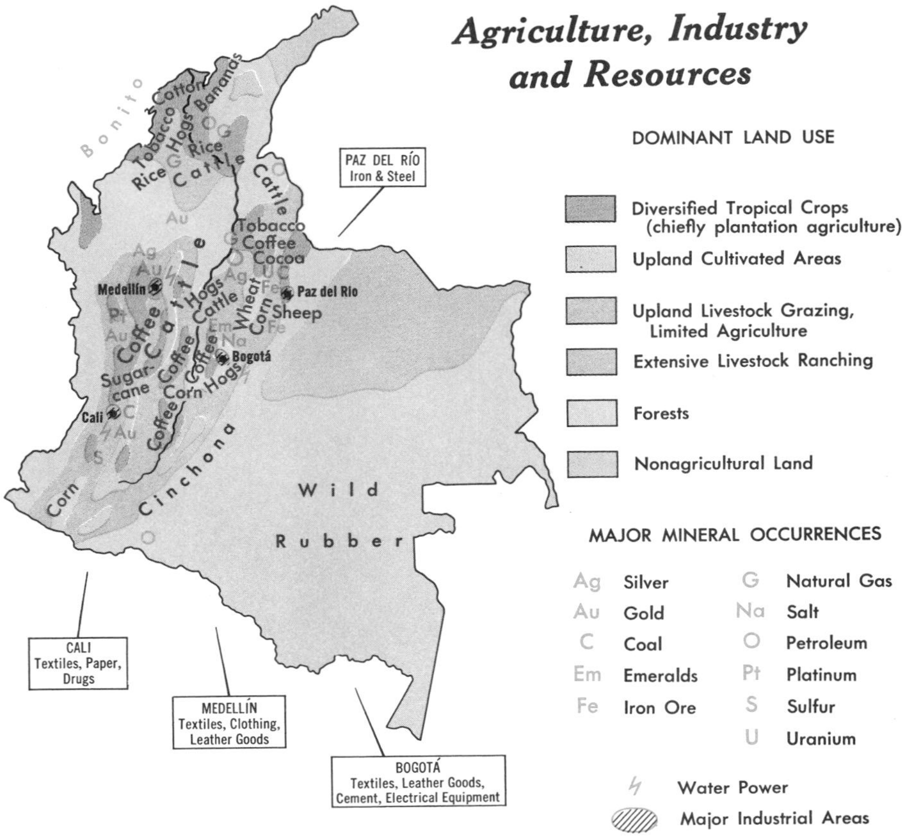

PAZ DEL RÍO Iron & Steel
CALI Textiles, Paper, Drugs
MEDELLÍN Textiles, Clothing, Leather Goods
BOGOTÁ Textiles, Leather Goods, Cement, Electrical Equipment
Medellín
Paz del Río
Bogotá
Cali
Bonito
Wild Rubber
Cinchona
DOMINANT LAND USE
Diversified Tropical Crops (chiefly plantation agriculture)
Upland Cultivated Areas
Upland Livestock Grazing, Limited Agriculture
Extensive Livestock Ranching
Forests
Nonagricultural Land
MAJOR MINERAL OCCURRENCES
Ag Silver
Au Gold
C Coal
Em Emeralds
Fe Iron Ore
G Natural Gas
Na Salt
O Petroleum
Pt Platinum
S Sulfur
U Uranium
Water Power
Major Industrial Areas

Topography

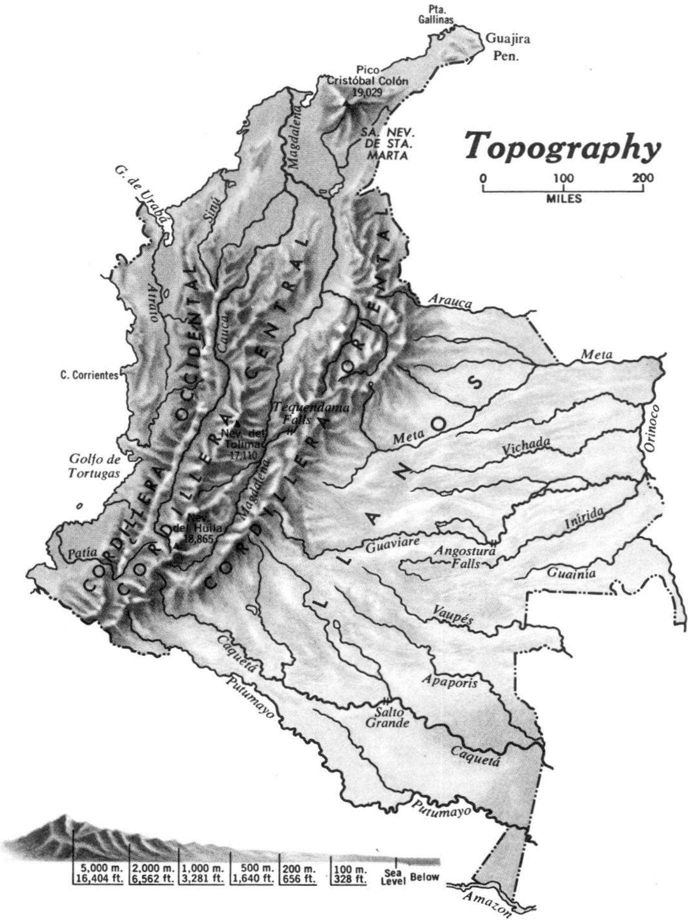

0 100 200 MILES
Pta. Gallinas
Guajira Pen.
Pico Cristóbal Colón 19,029
SA. NEV. DE STA. MARTA
G. de Urabá
C. Corrientes
Golfo de Tortugas
CORDILLERA OCCIDENTAL
CORDILLERA CENTRAL
CORDILLERA ORIENTAL
LLANOS
Tequendama Falls
Nev. del Huila 18,865
Arauca
Meta
Vichada
Inírida
Guaviare
Angostura Falls
Guainía
Vaupés
Apaporis
Caquetá
Putumayo
Salto Grande
Amazon
Orinoco
Patía
Cauca
Magdalena
Sinú
Atrato
5,000 m. 16,404 ft.
2,000 m. 6,562 ft.
1,000 m. 3,281 ft.
500 m. 1,640 ft.
200 m. 656 ft.
100 m. 328 ft.
Sea Level
Below

PERU and ECUADOR

BIPOLAR OBLIQUE CONIC CONFORMAL PROJECTION

SCALE OF MILES
0   50   100   150   200

SCALE OF KILOMETRES
0   50   100   150   200

Capitals of Countries ⋯⋯⋯☆
Other Capitals ⋯⋯⋯◉
International Boundaries ▬ ▪ ▬ ▪ ▬
Other Boundaries ⋯⋯⋯⋯

Copyright by C. S. Hammond & Co., N.Y.

GALÁPAGOS ISLANDS
(ARCHIPIÉLAGO DE COLÓN)
(Ecuador)
Same scale as main map

PROVINCES OF ECUADOR
INDICATED BY NUMBERS

1 Imbabura	C-2	5 Bolívar	C-3
2 Cotopaxi	C-3	6 Chimborazo	C-3
3 Tungurahua	C-3	7 Cañar	C-4
4 Los Ríos	C-3	8 El Oro	C-4

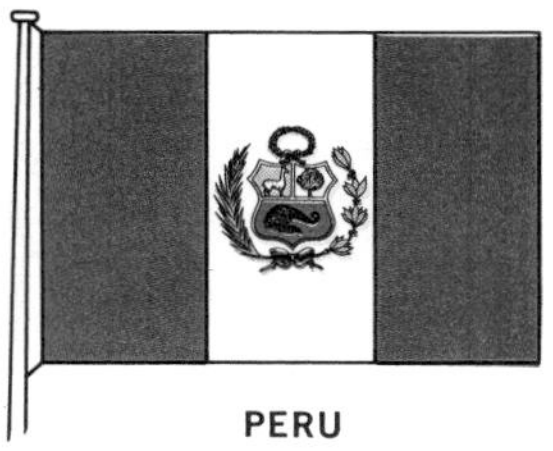

PERU

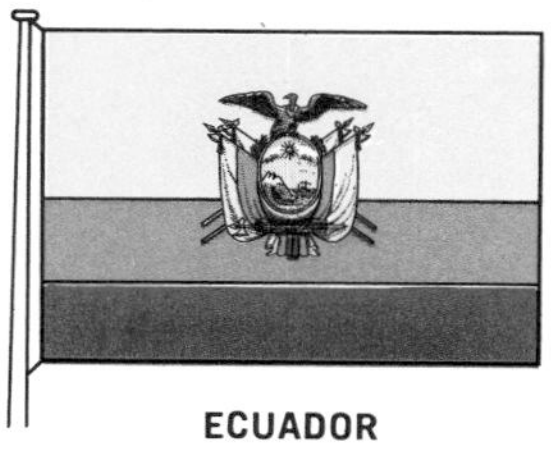

ECUADOR

PERU

AREA 496,222 sq. mi.
POPULATION 13,586,300
CAPITAL Lima
LARGEST CITY Lima
HIGHEST POINT Huascarán 22,205 ft.
MONETARY UNIT sol
MAJOR LANGUAGES Spanish, Quechua, Aymara
MAJOR RELIGION Roman Catholicism

ECUADOR

AREA 109,483 sq. mi.
POPULATION 6,144,000
CAPITAL Quito
LARGEST CITY Guayaquil
HIGHEST POINT Chimborazo 20,561 ft.
MONETARY UNIT sucre
MAJOR LANGUAGES Spanish, Quechua
MAJOR RELIGION Roman Catholicism

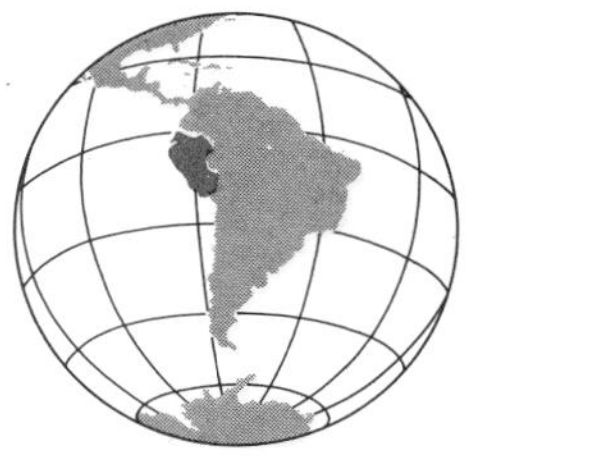

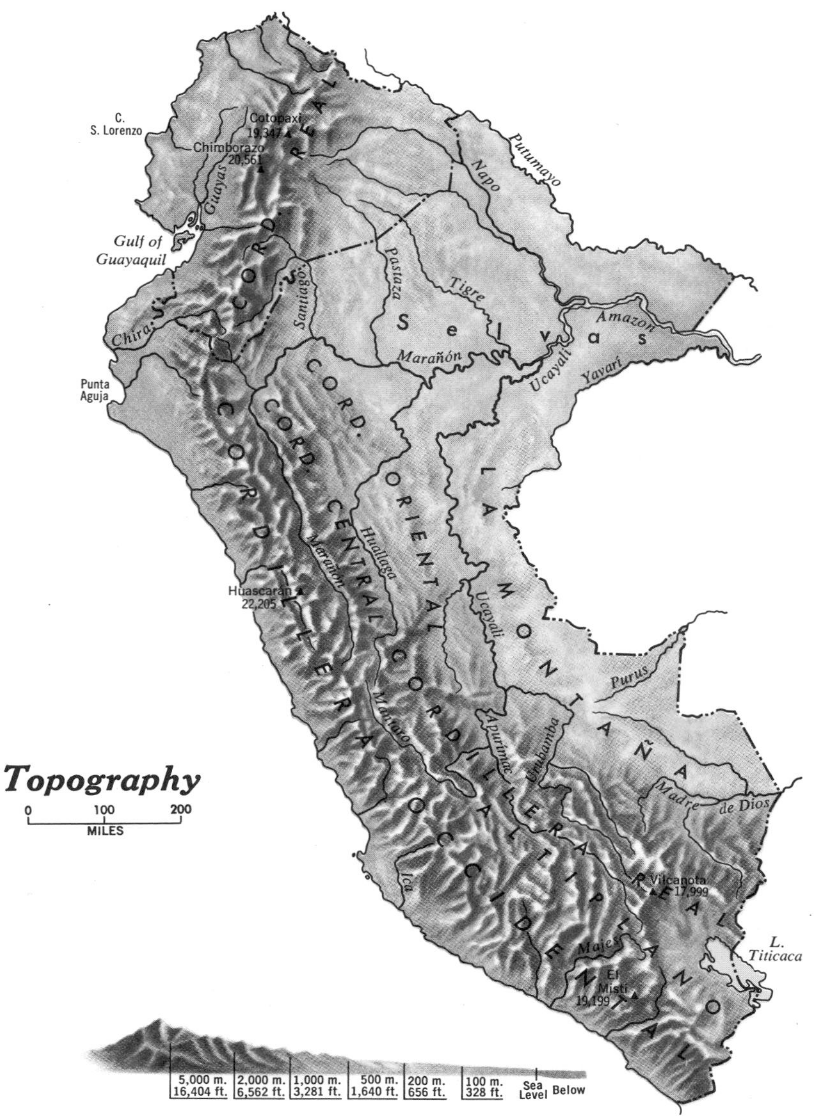

PERU

DEPARTMENTS

Amazonas, 171,100 .... C 5
Ancash, 744,700 .... D 7
Apurímac, 330,400 .... F10
Arequipa, 518,300 .... F10
Ayacucho, 474,100 .... E 9
Cajamarca, 1,007,600 .... C 6
Callao (province), 335,400 .... D 9
Cuzco, 756,100 .... F 9
Huancavelica, 367,100 .... E 9
Huánuco, 430,100 .... D 7
Ica, 362.700 .... E10
Junín, 699,100 .... E 8
La Libertad, 784,900 .... C 6
Lambayeque, 485,500 .... B 6
Lima, 3,155,800 .... D 8
Loreto, 504,600 .... E 5
Madre de Dios, 24,200 .... G 8
Moquegua, 68,800 .... G11
Pasco, 188,000 .... E 8
Piura, 922,300 .... B 5
Puno, 848,200 .... G10
San Martín, 229,400 .... D 6
Tacna, 93,900 .... G11
Tumbes, 84,000 .... B 4

CITIES and TOWNS

Abancay, 9,053 .... F 9
Acarí, 1,428 .... E10
Acobamba, 2,167 .... E 9
Acolla, 4,415 .... E 8
Acomayo, Cuzco, 1,874 .... G 9
Acomayo, Huánuco, 1,198 .... E 7
Acora, 941 .... H11
Acuracay, 96 .... F 5
Aija, 1,710 .... D 7
Alca, 539 .... F10
Ambo, 1,606 .... D 8
Ancón, 3,760 .... D 8
Andahuaylas, 4,674 .... F 9
Andamarca, 339 .... E 8
Anta, 2,574 .... F 9
Antabamba, 2,294 .... F10
Aplao, 1,316 .... F11
Aquia, 897 .... D 8
Arequipa, 194,700 .... G11
Ascope, 3,845 .... C 6
Astillero .... H 9
Atalaya, 816 .... E 8
Atico, 297 .... F11
Ayabaca, 3,415 .... C 5
Ayacucho, 28,500 .... F 9
Ayavirí, 7,553 .... G10
Azángaro, 4,771 .... H10
Bagua, 2,343 .... C 5
Balsapuerto, 203 .... D 5
Bambamarca, 4,281 .... C 6
Barranca, Lima, 11,320 .... C 8
Barranca, Loreto, 184 .... D 5
Bartra Antiguo .... E 4
Bartra Nuevo .... E 4
Bayóvar .... B 5
Bellavista, 2,129 .... C 5
Bolívar, 1,057 .... D 6
Bolognesi .... F 6
Bolognesi, 516 .... F 8
Borja, 300 .... D 5
Bretaña, 766 .... E 5
Buldibuyo, 616 .... D 7
Caballococha, 1,197 .... G 4
Cabana, 1,910 .... C 7
Cabo Blanco .... B 5
Cahuapanas, 125 .... D 5
Cailloma, 607 .... G10
Cajabamba, 5,253 .... C 6
Cajacay, 809 .... D 8
Cajamarca, 28,200 .... C 6
Cajatambo, 2,257 .... D 8
Calca, 3,489 .... G 9
Callalli, 133 .... G10
Callao, 335,400 .... D 9
Camaná, 5,120 .... F11
Candarave, 859 .... G11
Cangallo, 1,578 .... E 9
Canta, 2,491 .... D 8
Capachica, 193 .... H10
Carás, 4,033 .... D 7
Caravelí, 1,954 .... F10
Carhuás, 2,175 .... D 7
Carumás, 727 .... G11
Cascas, 2,403 .... C 6
Casma, 4,975 .... C 7
Castilla, 29,541 .... B 5
Castrovirreyna, 784 .... E 9
Catacaos, 12,135 .... B 5
Celendín, 5,646 .... D 6
Cerro Azul, 1,571 .... D 9
Cerro de Pasco, 23,400 .... D 8
Chachapoyas, 6,860 .... D 6
Chala, 1,054 .... E10
Chalhuanca, 2,840 .... F10
Chancay, 6,145 .... D 8
Chao .... C 7
Chepén, 16,119 .... C 6
Chicama, 1,362 .... C 6
Chiclayo, 140,800 .... C 6
Chilca (Pucusana), 1,331 .... D 9
Chilete, 1,105 .... C 6
Chimbote, 102,800 .... C 7
Chincha Alta, 26,500 .... D 9
Chiquián, 3,354 .... D 8
Chirinos, 490 .... C 5
Chivay, 2,320 .... G10
Chorrillós, 31,703 .... D 9
Chosica .... D 8
Chota, 4,961 .... C 6
Chulucanas, 19,714 .... B 5
Chupaca, 2,180 .... E 9
Chuquibamba, 2,983 .... F10
Chuquibambilla, 1,423 .... F 9
Churín, 610 .... D 8
Cocachacra, 2,869 .... G11
Cocama .... G 8
Cojata, 763 .... H10
Colasay, 466 .... C 5
Colcamar, 1,370 .... D 6
Conaica, 1,408 .... E 9
Concepción, 4,184 .... E 8
Concordia, 66 .... E 5
Contamana, 4,708 .... E 6
Contumazá, 2,532 .... C 6
Coracora, 4,116 .... F10
Córdova, 620 .... E10
Corongo, 2,241 .... D 7
Cotahuasi, 1,618 .... F10
Culebras .... C 7
Cumaría .... F 7
Cutervo, 4,702 .... C 6
Cuyocuyo, 708 .... H10
Cuzco, 108,900 .... F 9
Desaguadero, 948 .... H11
Deustua, 416 .... G10
Dos de Mayo, 970 .... E 6
Echarate, 374 .... F 9
El Portugués .... C 7
Esperanza, 261 .... G 7
Ferreñafe, 12,112 .... C 6
Fitzcarrald .... G 8
Francisco de Orellana, 306 .... F 4
Guadalupe, 2,896 .... E 9
Güeppi .... E 3
Huacho, 29,400 .... D 8
Huacrachuco, 757 .... D 7
Hualgayoc, 1,223 .... C 6
Hualla, 2,586 .... F 9
Huallanca, Ancash, 491 .... D 7
Huallanca, Huánuco, 1,202 .... D 7
Huamachuco, 5,730 .... D 6
Huancabamba, 3,215 .... C 5
Huancané, 4,053 .... H10
Huancapi, 2,415 .... E 9
Huancavelica, 11,039 .... E 9
Huancayo, 95,000 .... E 9
Huanchaco, 1,006 .... C 7
Huanta, 5,728 .... E 9
Huánuco, 34,500 .... E 7
Huaral, 11,481 .... D 8
Huaráz, 20,345 .... D 7
Huari, 2,467 .... D 7
Huariaca, 1,534 .... E 8
Huarmey, 5,232 .... C 8
Huarochirí, 2,125 .... D 9
Huarocondo, 2,921 .... F 9
Huaura, 1,442 .... D 8
Huaylas, 1,258 .... C 7
Iberia, 526 .... F 5
Ica, 72,300 .... E10
Ichuña, 183 .... G11
Ilave, 4,278 .... H11
Ilo, 9,986 .... G11
Imperial, 6,345 .... D 9
Inambari, 9 .... H 9
Iñapari, 159 .... H 8
Intutu, 344 .... E 4
Iparia, 171 .... E 7
Iquitos, 76,100 .... F 4
Jaén, 4,420 .... C 5
Jauja, 12,751 .... E 8
Jayanca, 4,240 .... B 6
Jeberos, 1,842 .... D 5
Juanjuí, 5,105 .... D 6
Juli, 3,874 .... H11
Juliaca, 35,000 .... G10
Jumbilla, 876 .... C 5
Junín, 5,004 .... E 8
Lagunas, 3,637 .... E 5
La Huaca, 1,863 .... B 5
La Jalca, 1,401 .... D 6
La Joya, 1,305 .... G11
Lamas, 7,139 .... D 6
Lambayeque, 10,629 .... B 6
Lampa, 3,123 .... G10
Lamud, 2,609 .... C 6
Lanlacuni Bajo, 229 .... G 9
La Oroya, 32,600 .... D 8
Las Piedras, 13 .... H 9
Las Yaras, 367 .... G11
La Tina .... B 5
La Unión, 2,013 .... D 7
Leimebamba, 1,026 .... D 6
Lima (capital), *2,541,300 .... D 8
Limbani, 903 .... H10
Lircay, 2,077 .... E 9
Llata, 2,255 .... D 7
Lobitos, 3,071 .... B 5
Locumba, 349 .... G11
Lomas, 111 .... E10
Lucerna .... H 9
Lurín, 2,741 .... D 9
Machupicchu, 1,026 .... F 9
Macusani, 1,601 .... G10
Madre de Dios, †802 .... G 9
Máncora, 7,943 .... B 5
Manú, †686 .... G 9
Marcapata, 334 .... G 9
Marcona, 6,744 .... E10
Margos, 1,195 .... D 8
Masisea, 1,520 .... E 7
Matarani F11
Matucana, 2,883 .... D 8
Mavila .... H 8
Mazán, 411 .... F 4
Mazocruz, 156 .... H11
Mendoza, 1,002 .... D 6
Miraflores, 52,142 .... G11
Mishagua .... F 8
Moho, 1,377 .... H10
Mollendo, 12,483 .... F11
Monsefú, 11,141 .... C 6
Moquegua, 7,795 .... G11
Morales, 2,430 .... D 6
Morococha, 6,519 .... D 8
Morropón, 4,730 .... C 5
Motupe, 1,286 .... C 6
Moyobamba, 8,373 .... D 6
Nauta, 1,905 .... F 5
Nazca, 13,587 .... E10
Negritos, 14,810 .... B 5
Nueva Alejandría, †264 .... F 5
Nuñoa, 2,137 .... G10
Ocoña, 1,207 .... F11
Ocros, 1,204 .... D 8
Ollachea, 903 .... G 9
Ollantaytambo, 1,632 .... F 9
Olmos, 3,628 .... C 5
Omaguas .... F 4
Omas, 217 .... D 9
Omate, 856 .... G11
Orcotuna, 2,716 .... E 8
Orellana, 1,596 .... E 6
Otuzco, 4,311 .... C 6
Oxapampa, 2,535 .... E 8
Oyón, 2,171 .... D 8
Pacasmayo, 11,956 .... C 6
Pachiza, 1,307 .... D 6
Paijan, 5,815 .... C 6
Paita, 9,615 .... B 5
Palpa, 2,615 .... E10
Pampachiri, 448 .... F10
Pampacolca, 1,876 .... F10
Pampas, 2,495 .... E 9
Panao, 1,262 .... E 7
Pantoja, 528 .... E 3
Parinari, 126 .... E 5
Paruro, 1,905 .... F 9
Pataz, 324 .... D 6
Pativilca, 15,325 .... D 8
Paucarbamba, 715 .... E 9
Paucartambo, Cuzco, 1,928 .... E 8
Paucartambo, Pasco, 1,717 .... G 9
Pevas, 696 .... G 4
Picota, 2,014 .... D 6
Pimentel, 6,252 .... B 6
Pinquén .... G 9
Pisac, 1,230 .... G 9
Pisco, 27,300 .... D 9
Piura, 111,400 .... B 5
Pizacoma, 86 .... H11
Pomabamba, 2,522 .... D 7
Porvenir .... E 5
Poto, 161 .... H10
Pozuzo, 121 .... E 8
Puca Barranca .... F 4
Pucallpa, 45,600 .... E 7
Pucará, 1,119 .... G10
Pucaurco, 12 .... G 4
Pucusana, 1,331 .... D 9
Puerto Alianza .... D 5
Puerto América, 150 .... D 5
Puerto Arturo .... F 3
Puerto Bermúdez, 230 .... E 8
Puerto Caballas E10
Puerto Chicama, 3,002 .... C 6
Puerto Eten, 2,192 .... B 6
Puerto José Pardo .... D 4
Puerto Leguía, Loreto .... D 4
Puerto Leguía, Puno .... G 9
Puerto Maldonado, 3,518 .... H 9
Puerto Morín .... C 7
Puerto Ocopa, 1,304 .... E 8
Puerto Pardo .... F 7
Puerto Pizarro .... B 4
Puerto Portillo, 49 .... F 7
Puerto Prado, 419 .... E 8
Puerto Samanco, 1,733 .... C 7
Puerto Tahuantinsuyo .... G 9
Puerto Victoria .... E 7
Puno, 32,100 .... G10
Punta de Bombón, 3,943 .... F11
Punta Moreno .... C 6
Puquina, 1,030 .... G11
Puquio, 8,144 .... F10
Putina, 3,512 .... H10
Querecotillo, 6,205 .... B 5
Quicacha, 299 .... F10
Quilca, 171 .... F11
Quillabamba, 8,644 .... F 9
Quince Mil .... G 9
Ramón Castilla, †8,106 .... G 5
Recuay, 1,755 .... D 7
Requena, 3,931 .... F 5
Reventazón .... B 6
Rioja, 4,361 .... D 6
Salaverry, 4,605 .... C 7
San José, 2,612 .... B 6
San José de Sisa, 4,190 .... D 6
San Juan, 717 .... E10
San Lorenzo, 84 .... H 8
San Martín .... E 3
San Miguel, Ayacucho, 1,271 .... F 9
San Miguel, Cajamarca, 1,871 .... C 6
San Pedro de Lloc, 7,497 .... C 6
San Ramón, 3,016 .... E 8
San Vicente de Cañete, 7,184 .... D 9
Saña, 18,421 .... C 6
Sandia, 3,026 .... H10
Santa, 2,966 .... C 7
Santa Clotilde, 824 .... E 4
Santa Cruz, Cajamarca, 1,729 .... C 6
Santa Cruz, Loreto, 739 .... E 5
Santa Elena, 271 .... F 5
Santa Isabel de Sihuas, 118 .... F11
Santa María de Nanay, 123 .... F 4
Santiago, 1,613 .... E10
Santiago de Cao, 1,033 .... C 6
Santiago de-Chocorvos, 344 .... E 9
Santiago de Chuco, 4,649 .... C 7
Santo Tomás, Amazonas, 1,097 .... C 6
Santo Tomás, Cuzco, 1,659 .... G10
Santo Tomás de Andoas, 65 .... D 4
Saposoa, 4,456 .... D 6
Saquena, 688 .... F 5
Satipo, 2,499 .... E 8
Sauce, 1,761 .... D 6
Sayán, 1,764 .... D 8
Sechura, 5,157 .... B 5
Sicuani, 10,664 .... G10
Sihuas, 1,404 .... D 7
Sullana, 43,500 .... B 5
Sumbay G10
Sumbilca, 1,365 .... D 8
Supe, 2,499 .... D 8
Tacna, 41,200 .... G11
Tahuamanu, †4,011 .... H 8
Talara, 39,600 .... B 5
Tambo de Mora, 1,128 .... D 9
Tambo Grande, 4,404 .... B 5
Tamshiyacu, 1,623 .... F 5
Tarapoto, 13,907 .... D 6
Tarata, 2,673 .... H11
Tarma, 15,452 .... E 8
Tarqui .... E 3
Tayabamba, 1,519 .... D 7
Ticaco, 1,206 .... H11
Tingo María, 5,208 .... D 7
Tiruntán, 847 .... E 6
Tocache, 1,607 .... D 7
Tonegrama .... D 4
Topara, 1,437 .... D 9
Toquepala G11
Torata, 669 .... G11
Tournavista .... E 7
Trujillo, 156,200 .... C 7
Tumbes, 30,000 .... B 4
Ubinas, 348 .... G11
Uchiza, 1,006 .... D 7
Unini .... F 8
Urcos, 2,733 .... G 9
Urubamba, 3,325 .... F 9
Vinchos, 473 .... E 9
Virú, 2,647 .... C 7
Vitor, 117 .... G11
Yambrasbamba, 306 .... D 5
Yanahuanca, 962 .... D 8
Yanaoca, 1,146 .... G10
Yauca, 2,364 .... E10
Yauli, 1,696 .... D 8
Yauri, 2,834 .... G10
Yauyos, 1,456 .... E 9
Yunguyo, 2,506 .... H11
Yurimaguas, 11,655 .... E 5
Zarumilla, 3,499 .... B 4
Zorritos, 2,862 .... B 4

OTHER FEATURES

Acarí (river) E10
Aguaytía (river) .... E 7
Aguja (point) .... B 5
Amazon (river) .... F 4
Andes, Cordillera de los (mts.) F10
Apurímac (river) .... F 9
Azángaro (river) G10
Azul, Cordillera (mts.) .... E 7
Blanca, Cordillera (mts.) .... D 7
Blanco (cape) .... B 5
Blanco (river) .... F 6
Boquerón, El (pass) .... E 7
Cañete (river) .... D 9
Casma (river) .... C 7
Chimbote (bay) .... C 7
Chincha (isls.) .... D 9
Chira (river) .... B 5
Coles (point) G11
Cóndor, Cordillera del (mts.) .... C 5
Coropuna, Nudo (mt.) F10
Corrientes (river) .... E 4
El Boquerón (pass) .... E 7
El Misti (mt.) G11
Ene (river) .... E 8
Ferrol (pen.) .... C 7
Grande (river) E10
Guañape (isls.) .... C 7
Heath (river) .... H 9
Huallaga (river) .... D 5
Huasaga (river) .... D 4
Huascarán (mt.) .... D 7
Huayabamba (river) .... D 6
Ica (river) E10
Inambari (river) .... H 9
Independencia (bay) D10
Junín (lake) .... E 8
La Montaña (reg.) .... F 8
Lachay (Salinas) (point) .... D 8
Las Piedras (river) .... G 8
Las Viejas (isl.) D10
Lobos de Afuera (isls.) .... B 6
Lobos de Tierra (isl.) .... B 6
Locumba (river) G11
Madre de Dios (river) .... G 9
Majes (river) F11
Mantaro (river) .... E 8
Manú (river) .... G 8
Marañón (river) .... E 5
Mayo (river) .... D 6
Misti, El (mt.) G11
Montaña, La (reg.) .... F 8
Morona (river) .... D 5
Nanay (river) .... E 4
Napo (river) .... F 4
Negra, Cordillera (mts.) .... D 7
Negra (point) .... B 6
Ñermete (point) .... B 5
Nudo Coropuna (mt.) F10
Occidental, Cordillera (mts.) F10
Ocoña (river) F11
Oriental, Cordillera (mts.) H10
Pachitea (river) .... E 7
Paita (bay) .... B 5
Pampas (river) .... E 9
Paracas (pen.), †727 .... D 9
Parinacochas (lake) F10
Pariñas (point) .... B 5
Pastaza (river) .... D 5
Pativilca (river) .... D 8
Perené (river) .... E 8
Pichis (river) .... E 8
Piedras, Las (river) .... G 8
Pisco (bay) .... D 9
Pisco (river) .... D 9
Pirua (river) .... B 5
Puinagua, Canal de (river) .... E 5
Purus (river) .... G 8
Putumayo (river) .... G 4
Rímac (river) .... D 9
Salinas (Lachay) (point) .... D 8
Sama (river) G11

(continued on following page)

Agriculture, Industry and Resources

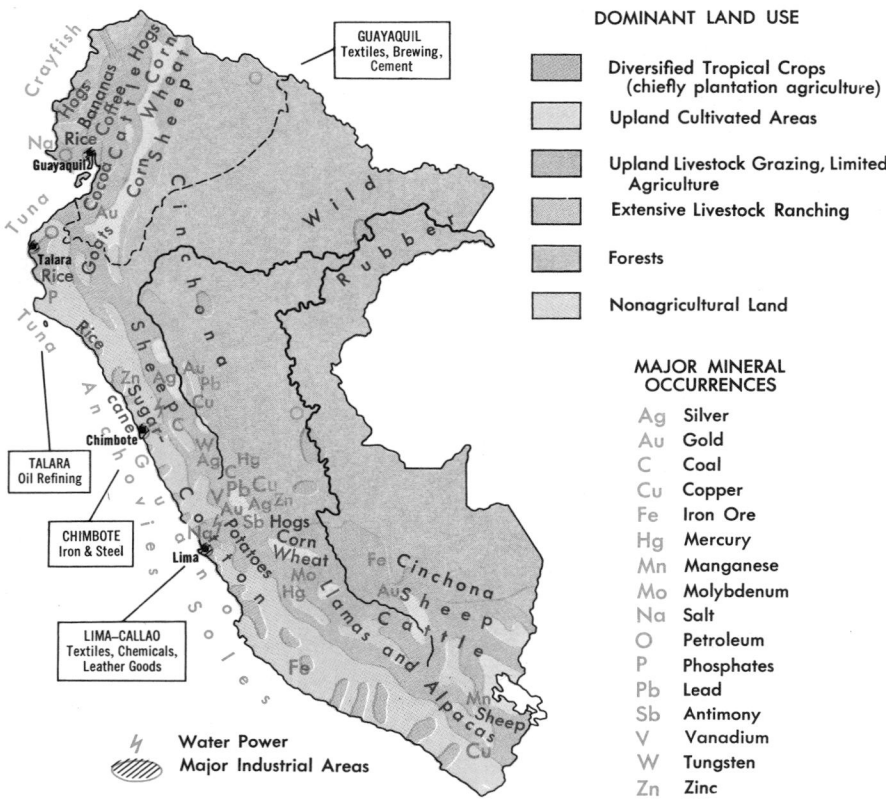

GUAYAQUIL
Textiles, Brewing, Cement

TALARA
Oil Refining

CHIMBOTE
Iron & Steel

LIMA–CALLAO
Textiles, Chemicals, Leather Goods

DOMINANT LAND USE

- Diversified Tropical Crops (chiefly plantation agriculture)
- Upland Cultivated Areas
- Upland Livestock Grazing, Limited Agriculture
- Extensive Livestock Ranching
- Forests
- Nonagricultural Land

⚡ Water Power
Major Industrial Areas

MAJOR MINERAL OCCURRENCES

Ag	Silver
Au	Gold
C	Coal
Cu	Copper
Fe	Iron Ore
Hg	Mercury
Mn	Manganese
Mo	Molybdenum
Na	Salt
O	Petroleum
P	Phosphates
Pb	Lead
Sb	Antimony
V	Vanadium
W	Tungsten
Zn	Zinc

Agriculture, Industry and Resources

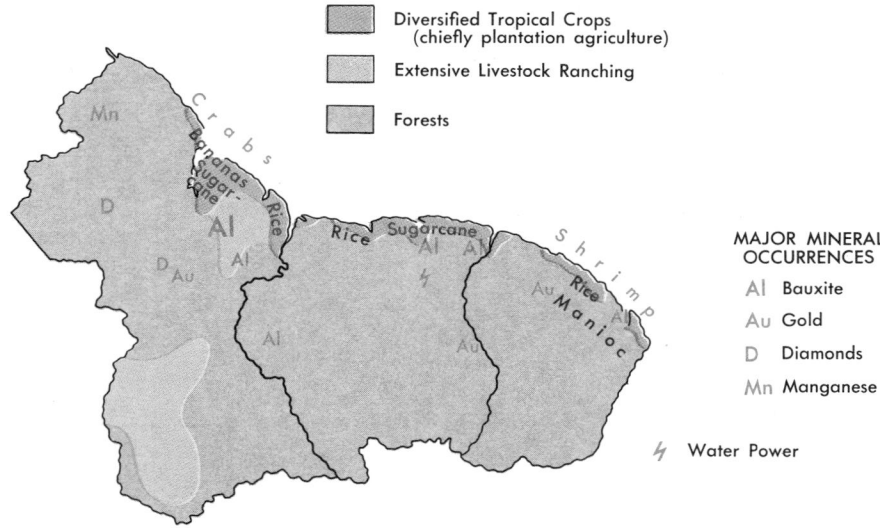

DOMINANT LAND USE

- Diversified Tropical Crops (chiefly plantation agriculture)
- Extensive Livestock Ranching
- Forests

MAJOR MINERAL OCCURRENCES

Al	Bauxite
Au	Gold
D	Diamonds
Mn	Manganese

⚡ Water Power

GUYANA
AREA 83,000 sq. mi.
POPULATION 763,000
CAPITAL Georgetown
LARGEST CITY Georgetown
HIGHEST POINT Mt. Roraima 9,094 ft.
MONETARY UNIT Guyana dollar
MAJOR LANGUAGES English, Hindi
MAJOR RELIGIONS Christianity, Hinduism, Islam

SURINAME
AREA 55,144 sq. mi.
POPULATION 389,000
CAPITAL Paramaribo
LARGEST CITY Paramaribo
HIGHEST POINT Julianatop 4,200 ft.
MONETARY UNIT Surinam guilder
MAJOR LANGUAGES Dutch, Hindi, Indonesian
MAJOR RELIGIONS Christianity, Islam, Hinduism

FRENCH GUIANA
AREA 35,135 sq. mi.
POPULATION 48,000
CAPITAL Cayenne
LARGEST CITY Cayenne
HIGHEST POINT 2,723 ft.
MONETARY UNIT French franc
MAJOR LANGUAGE French
MAJOR RELIGIONS Roman Catholicism, Protestantism

GUYANA

Kuyuwini (river)	B 4
Kwitaro (river)	B 4
Leguan (isl.), 6,567	B 2
Marudi (mts.)	B 5
Mazaruni (river)	A 2
Moruka (river)	B 2
New (river)	C 4
Pakaraima (mts.)	A 3
Playa (point)	B 1
Pomeroon (river)	B 2
Potaro (river)	B 3
Puruni (river)	B 2
Roraima (mt.)	A 4
Rupununi (river)	B 4
Sororieng (river)	A 3
Surwakwima (fall)	A 2
Takutu (river)	B 4
Venamo (mt.)	A 3
Waini (river)	B 1
Wenamu (river)	A 2

SURINAME

DISTRICTS

Brokopondo, 1,376	D 4
Commewijne, 18,796	D 3
Coronie, 4,069	C 3
Marowijne, 10,074	D 3
Nickerie, 24,730	C 3
Para	D 3
Paramaribo, 122,634	D 3
Saramacca, 10,979	C 3
Suriname, 80,870	D 3

CITIES and TOWNS

Ajoewa	C 4
Alalapadu	C 4
Albina, 1,000	D 3
Asidonhoppo	D 4
Berg-en-Dal	D 3
Bitagron	D 3
Brokopondo	D 3
Burnside	C 2
Calcutta, 1,100	D 3

Cottica	D 4
Domburg, 1,200	D 3
Groningen, 600	D 3
Huwelijkszorg	D 3
Kwakoegron	D 3
Kwatta	D 3
Lelydorp, 300	D 3
Magalie	D 4
Marienburg, 3,500	D 3
Moengo, 2,100	D 3
Nieuw-Amsterdam, 1,400	D 2
Nieuw-Nickerie, 7,400	C 2
Paramaribo (cap.), 110,867	D 2
Paramaribo, *182,100	D 2
Paranam	D 3
Saramaccapolder	D 2
Totness, 1,300	C 3
Wageningen, 800	C 3
Zanderij	D 3

OTHER FEATURES

Bakhuys (mts.)	C 3
Coeroeni (river)	C 4
Commewijne (river)	D 3
Coppename (river)	C 3
Corantijn (river)	C 3
Cottica (river)	D 3
Eilerts-de-Haan (mts.)	C 4
Frederik Willem IV (falls)	C 4
Julianatop (mt.)	C 4
Kayser (mts.)	C 4
Lely (mts.)	D 3
Litani (river)	D 4
Marowijne (river)	D 3
Nickerie (river)	C 3
Orange (mts.)	D 4
Saramacca (river)	D 3
Sipaliwini (river)	C 4
Suriname (river)	D 3
Tapanahoni (river)	D 3
Toekomstig (res.)	C 4
Van Blommestein (lake)	D 3
Wilhelmina (mts.)	C 4

*City and suburbs.
†Population of municipality.

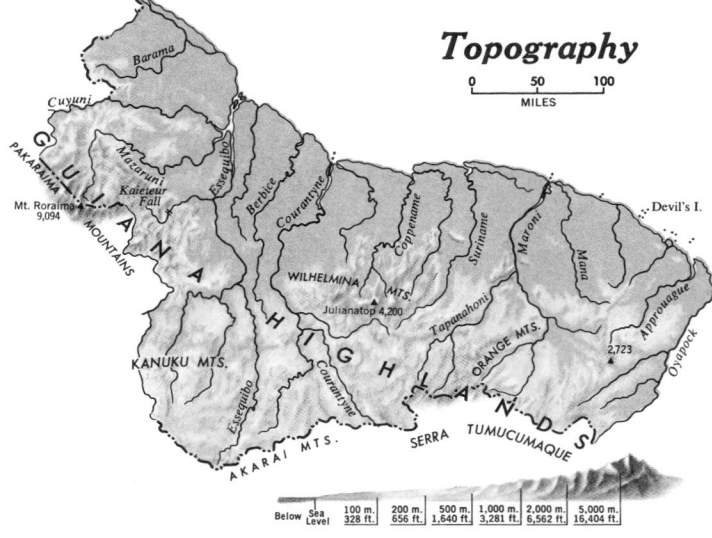

Topography

0 50 100
MILES

Mt. Roraima 9,094

Barama

Cuyuni

PAKARAIMA MOUNTAINS

Mazaruni

Kaieteur Fall

Essequibo

Berbice

Courantyne

Coppename

Suriname

Maroni

Mana

Approuague

Devil's I.

GUIANA HIGHLANDS

WILHELMINA MTS.

Julianatop 4,200

KANUKU MTS.

Courantyne

Essequibo

Tapanahoni

ORANGE MTS.

2,723

Oyapock

AKARAI MTS.

SERRA TUMUCUMAQUE

Below Sea Level | 100 m. 328 ft. | 200 m. 656 ft. | 500 m. 1,640 ft. | 1,000 m. 3,281 ft. | 2,000 m. 6,562 ft. | 5,000 m. 16,404 ft.

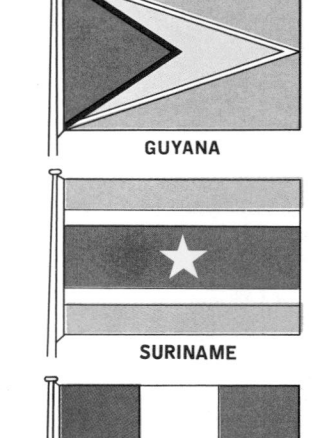

GUYANA

SURINAME

FRENCH GUIANA

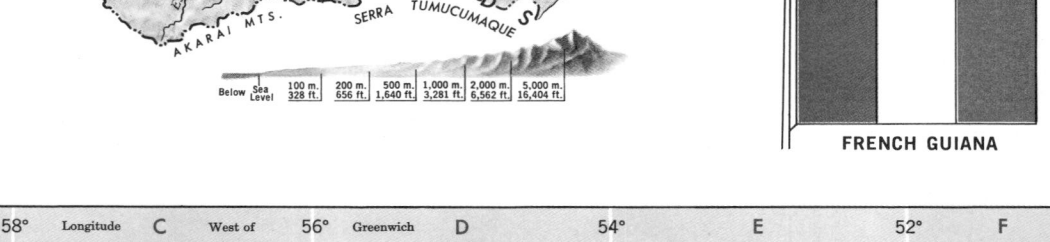

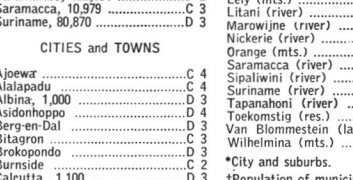

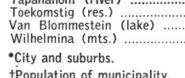

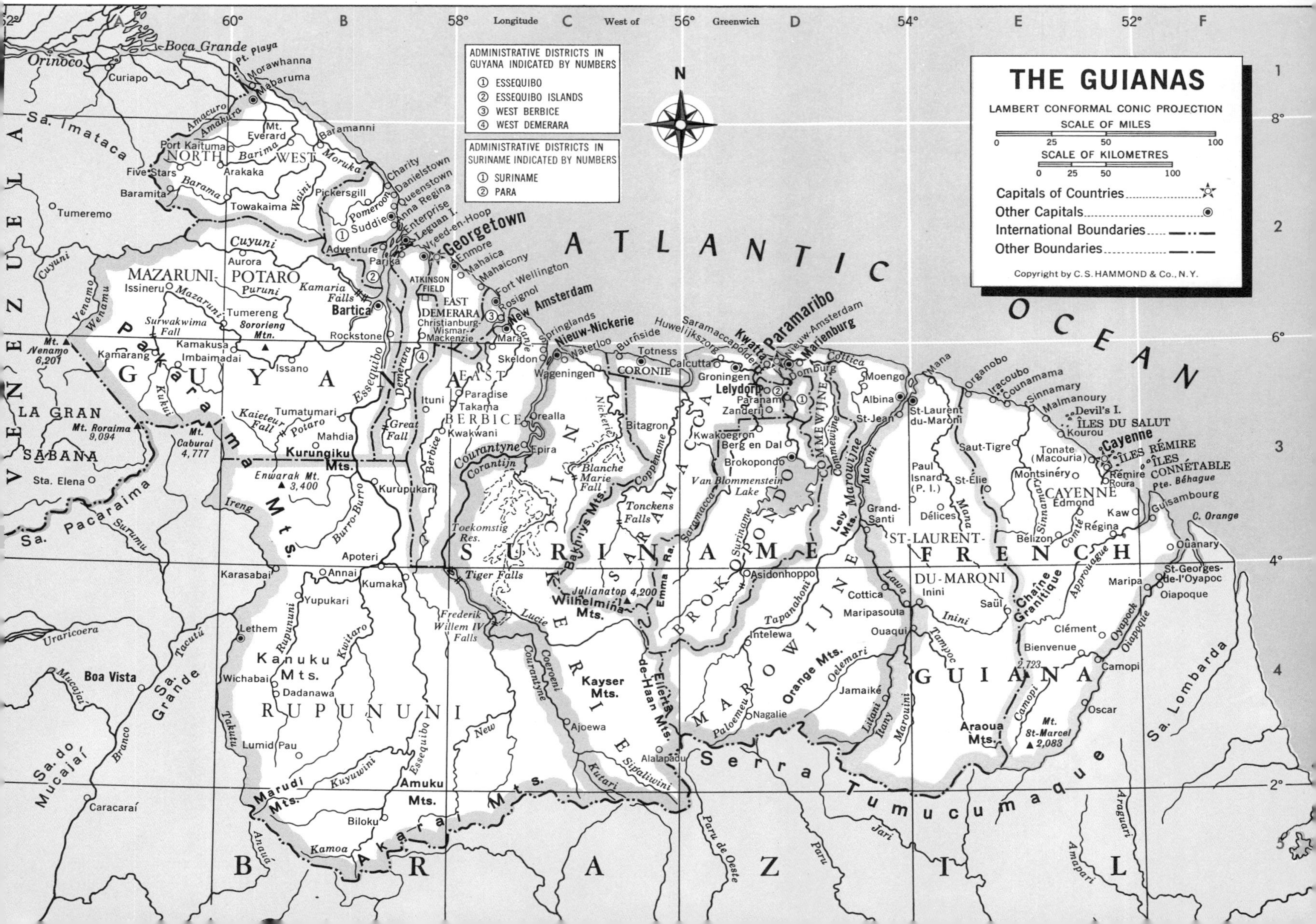

THE GUIANAS
LAMBERT CONFORMAL CONIC PROJECTION

SCALE OF MILES
0 25 50 100

SCALE OF KILOMETRES
0 25 50 100

Capitals of Countries .... ☆
Other Capitals .... ◉
International Boundaries .... —·—·—
Other Boundaries .... ———

Copyright by C.S. HAMMOND & Co., N.Y.

ADMINISTRATIVE DISTRICTS IN GUYANA INDICATED BY NUMBERS
① ESSEQUIBO
② ESSEQUIBO ISLANDS
③ WEST BERBICE
④ WEST DEMERARA

ADMINISTRATIVE DISTRICTS IN SURINAME INDICATED BY NUMBERS
① SURINAME
② PARA

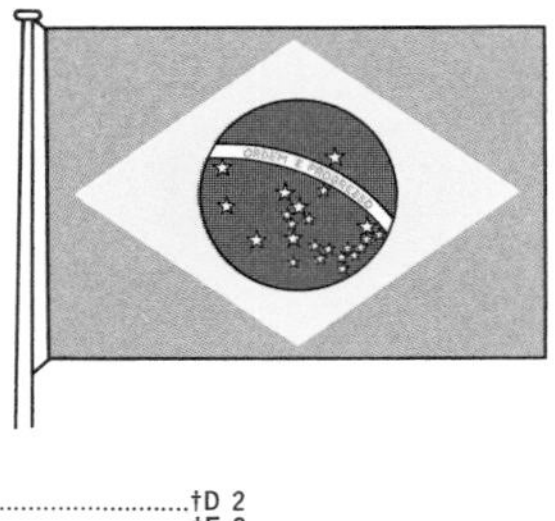

AREA 3,284,426 sq. mi.
POPULATION 90,840,000
CAPITAL Brasília
LARGEST CITY São Paulo (greater)
HIGHEST POINT Pico da Neblina 9,889 ft.
MONETARY UNIT cruzeiro
MAJOR LANGUAGE Portuguese
MAJOR RELIGION Roman Catholicism

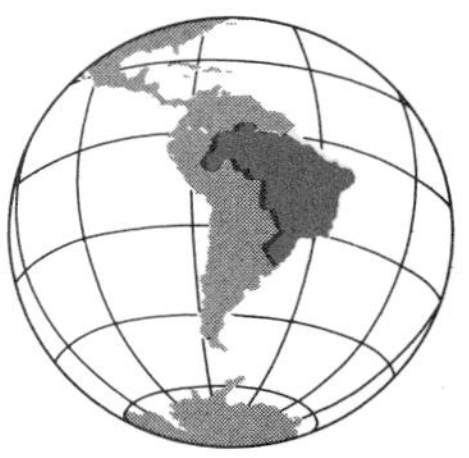

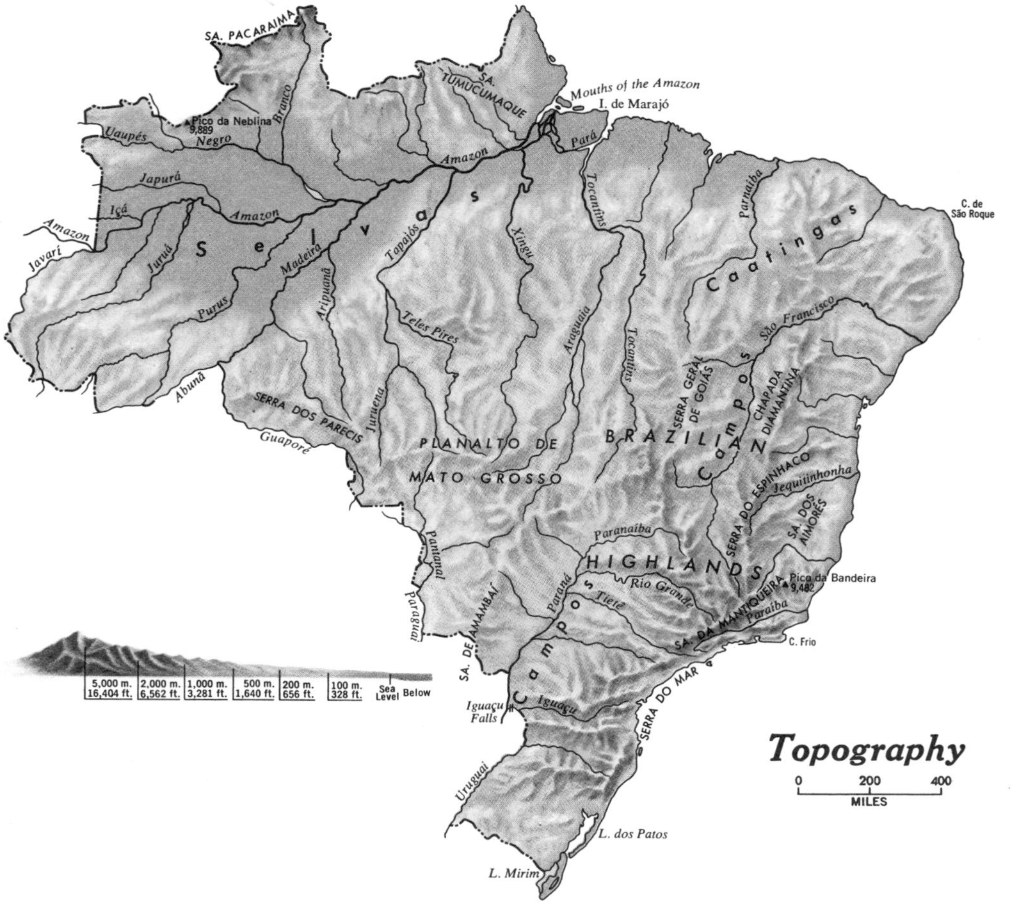
SA. PACARAIMA
Pico da Neblina 9,889
Uaupés
Negro
Branco
SA. TUMUCUMAQUE
Mouths of the Amazon
I. de Marajó
Pará
Amazon
Japurá
Içá
Amazon
Javari
Juruá
Purus
Madeira
Aripuanã
Tapajós
Xingu
Tocantins
Parnaíba
C. de São Roque
Selvas
Caatingas
São Francisco
Teles Pires
Araguaia
Abunã
SERRA DOS PARECIS
Juruena
Guaporé
PLANALTO DE MATO GROSSO
SERRA GERAL DE GOIÁS
CHAPADA DIAMANTINA
Campos
BRAZILIAN HIGHLANDS
SERRA DO ESPINHAÇO
Jequitinhonha
SA. DOS AIMORÉS
Paranaíba
Pico da Bandeira 9,482
Rio Grande
Tietê
Paraíba
SA. DA MANTIQUEIRA
C. Frio
Pantanal
Paraguai
Paraná
SA. DE AMAMBAÍ
Iguaçu Falls
Iguaçu
SERRA DO MAR
Uruguai
L. dos Patos
L. Mirim
5,000 m. 16,404 ft.
2,000 m. 6,562 ft.
1,000 m. 3,281 ft.
500 m. 1,640 ft.
200 m. 656 ft.
100 m. 328 ft.
Sea Level
Below
Topography
0 200 400
MILES

STATES and TERRITORIES

Acre, 196,000 ... G10
Alagoas, 1,381,000 ... G 5
Amapá (terr.), 100,000 ... D 2
Amazonas, 875,000 ... G 9
Bahia, 6,778,000 ... F 6
Ceará, 3,764,000 ... G 4
Espírito Santo, 1,446,000 ... F 7
Federal District, 348,000 ... E 6
Goiás, 2,950,000 ... D 6
Guaporé (Rondônia) (terr.), 97,000 ... H10
Maranhão, 3,314,000 ... E 4
Mato Grosso ... B 6
Mato Grosso do Sul ... C 7
Minas Gerais, 11,230,000 ... E 7, †D 2
Pará, 1,872,000 ... C 4
Paraíba, 2,219,000 ... G 4
Paraná, 6,743,000 ... D 9, †B 4
Pernambuco, 4,645,000 ... G 5
Piauí, 1,391,000 ... F 4
Rio de Janeiro, 8,347,000 ... F 8, †E 3
Rio Grande do Norte, 1,271,000 ... G 4
Rio Grande do Sul, 6,397,000 ... C10
Rondônia (terr.), 107,000 ... H10
Roraima (terr.), 40,000 ... H 8
Santa Catarina, 2,624,000 ... D 9
São Paulo, 16,081,000 ... D 8, †B 2
Sergipe, 838,000 ... G 5

CITIES and TOWNS

Abaeté, 7,988 ... E 7
Abaetetuba, 11,196 ... D 3
Acaraú, 3,042 ... F 3
Acopiara, 3,953 ... G 4
Acorizal, 892 ... C 6
Açu, 8,158 ... G 4
Afuá, 600 ... D 3
Agudos, 6,564 ... †B 3
Alagoa Grande, 12,115 ... H 4
Alagoinhas, 38,246 ... G 6
Alcobaça, 1,812 ... G 7
Alegre, 7,487 ... †F 2
Alegrete, 33,735 ... B10
Além Paraíba, 18,399 ... †E 2
Alenquer, 7,027 ... C 3
Alfenas, 16,051 ... †C 2
Alfredo Chaves, 1,209 ... F 8
Altamira, 2,939 ... C 3
Alto Araguaia, 2,077 ... C 7
Alto Longa, 784 ... F 4
Alto Parnaiba, 1,300 ... E 5
Altos, 5,056 ... F 4
Amambaí, 2,601 ... C 8
Amarante, 3,199 ... F 4
Amargosa, 6,059 ... F 6
Americana, 32,000 ... †C 3
Amparo, 14,348 ... †C 3
Anápolis, 48,847 ... D 7
Andaraí, 2,510 ... F 6
Angra dos Reis, 10,634 ... †D 3
Anicuns, 3,642 ... D 7
Andrelândia, 4,617 ... †D 2
Antonina, 8,520 ... †B 4
Aparecida, 15,290 ... †D 3
Apiaí, 2,728 ... †B 4
Aquidauana, 11,997 ... C 8
Aracaju, *156,243 ... G 5
Aracati, 11,016 ... G 4
Araçatuba, 53,563 ... †A 2
Araçuaí, 6,763 ... F 7
Araguacema, 1,745 ... D 5
Araguaiana, 568 ... C 6
Araguari, 35,520 ... D 7
Araioses, 1,487 ... F 3
Araranguá, 7,775 ... D10
Araraquara, 58,076 ... †B 2
Araras, 23,898 ... †C 3
Arari, 4,004 ... E 3
Araxá, 24,041 ... E 7
Arcoverde, 18,008 ... G 5
Areia Branca, 8.904 ... G 4
Aripuanã, 178 ... B 5
Arraias, 1,446 ... E 6
Assis, 30,207 ... †A 3
Aurora, 3,622 ... G 4
Avaré, 20,334 ... †B 3
Bacabal, *19,753 ... E 4
Bagé, 47,930 ... C10
Bahia (Salvador), *892,392 ... G 6
Baião, 2,265 ... D 3
Baixo Guandu, 6,975 ... F 7
Balsas, 1,946 ... E 4
Bambuí, 8,148 ... †C 2
Barão de Cocais, 7,223 ... †E 1
Barbacena, 41,931 ... †E 2
Barcelos, 1,904 ... H 9
Bariri, 8,403 ... †B 3
Barra, 7,237 ... F 5
Barra-do-Bugres, 658 ... B 6
Barra-do-Corda, 3,723 ... E 4
Barra do Piraí, 29,398 ... †E 3
Barra Mansa, 47,398 ... †D 3
Barras, 3,388 ... F 4
Barreiras, 7,175 ... E 6
Barreirinha, 701 ... B 3
Barreirinhas, 2,184 ... F 3
Barreiros, 10,402 ... H 5
Barretos, 39,950 ... †B 2
Batalha, 15,559 ... F 3
Batatais, 15,266 ... †C 2
Baturité, 7,198 ... G 4
Bauru, *110,961 ... †B 3
Bebedouro, 18,249 ... †B 2
Bela Vista, 8,878 ... C 8
Bela Vista de Goiás, 2,687 ... D 7
Belém, *563,996 ... E 3
Belmonte, 7,897 ... G 6
Belo Horizonte, *1,167,026 ... †D 1
Belo Horizonte, ‡1,300,000 ... †D 1
Beneditinos, 828 ... F 4
Benjamin Constant, 3,224 ... G 9
Bento Gonçalves, 13,662 ... C10
Bertolínia, 714 ... F 4
Betim, 8,963 ... †D 2
Bicas, 7,469 ... †E 2
Birigui, 18,721 ... †A 2
Blumenau, 46,591 ... D 9
Boa Esperança, 9,263 ... †D 2
Boa Vista, 10,180 ... H 8
Bôca do Acre, 2,994 ... G10
Bocaiúva, 5,952 ... E 7
Boiaçu, 180 ... H 8
Bom Conselho, 6,840 ... G 5
Bom Despacho, 13,568 ... †D 1
Bom Jesus, 1,431 ... E 5
Bom Jesus da Lapa, 6,107 ... F 6
Bom Retiro, 1,601 ... D10
Bom Sucesso, 6,173 ... †D 2
Borba, 1,304 ... H 9
Botucatu, 33,878 ... †B 3
Bragança, 12,848 ... E 3
Bragança Paulista, 27,328 ... †C 3
Brasiléia, 1,902 ... G10
Brasília (capital), 130,968 ... D 6
Brasília, ‡379,699 ... D 6
Brasília, 3,182 ... F 7
Brumado, 7,054 ... F 6
Brusque, 16,127 ... D 9
Buri, 2,666 ... †B 3
Buriti, 1,951 ... F 3
Buriti Alegre, 5,042 ... D 7
Buriti dos Lopes, 1,812 ... F 3
Cabedelo, 10,738 ... H 4
Cabo Frio, 13,117 ... †F 3
Caçador, 10,480 ... D 9
Caçapava, 7,987 ... †D 3
Caçapava do Sul, 6,712 ... C10
Cáceres, 8,246 ... B 7
Cachoeira, 11,415 ... G 6
Cachoeira do Arari, 2,532 ... D 3
Cachoeira do Sul, 38,661 ... C10
Cachoeiro de Itapemirim, *110,301 ... G 8
Caeté, 10,840 ... †E 1
Caetite, 4,823 ... F 6
Cafelândia, 6,573 ... †B 2
Caiapônia, 2,476 ... C 7
Caicó, 15,826 ... G 4
Cajàzeiras, 15,884 ... G 4
Cajuru, 4,971 ... †C 2
Camaquã, 9,732 ... C10
Cambará, 6,028 ... †A 3
Cametá, 5,695 ... D 3
Camocim, 10,788 ... F 3
Campanha, 6,178 ... †D 2
Campina Grande, *157,149 ... G 4
Campinas, *252,145 ... †C 3
Campina Verde, 4,464 ... D 7
Campo Belo, 15,742 ... †D 2
Campo Florido, 1,307 ... †B 1
Campo Formoso, 3,925 ... F 5
Campo Grande, *111,205 ... C 8
Campo Largo, 7,915 ... †B 4
Campo Maior, 13,939 ... F 4
Campos, *389,045 ... †F 2
Campos Altos, 5,243 ... †C 1
Cananéia, 1,948 ... †C 4
Canavieiras, 10,264 ... G 6
Cândido Mendes, 819 ... E 3
Canguaretama, 4,261 ... H 4
Canindé, 5,854 ... G 4
Canoas, *122,040 ... D10
Canoinhas, 9,252 ... D 9
Cantagalo, 3,479 ... †E 3
Canto do Buriti, 1,636 ... F 5
Canutama, 977 ... G 9
Capanema, 9,678 ... E 3
Capão Bonito, 6,829 ... †B 4
Capela, 5,172 ... G 5
Caraguatatuba, 4,655 ... †D 3
Carandaí, 2,792 ... †E 2
Carangola, 11,896 ... †E 2
Caratinga, *123,344 ... †E 1
Caraúbas, 3,066 ... G 4
Caravelas, 3,096 ... G 7
Carinhanha, 2,163 ... E 6
Carolina, 8,137 ... E 4
Caruaru, *115,414 ... G 5
Carutapera, 2,477 ... E 3
Casa Branca, 8,980 ... †C 2
Casa Nova, 1,525 ... F 5
Cascatinha, 19,497 ... †E 3
Cascavel, 3,336 ... G 4
Cássia, 7,034 ... †C 2
Castanhal, 9,528 ... E 3
Castelo, 5,729 ... F 8
Castelo do Piauí, 1,185 ... F 4
Castro, 9,249 ... †B 4
Castro Alves, 7,388 ... G 6
Cataguases, 21,476 ... †E 2
Catalão, 11,471 ... D 7
Catanduva, 37,307 ... †B 2
Catolé do Rocha, 5,217 ... G 4
Cavalcante, 660 ... D 6
Caxambu, 10,491 ... †D 2
Caxias, *124,403 ... F 4
Caxias do Sul, *110,241 ... D10
Ceará (Fortaleza), *846,069 ... G 3
Ceará-Mirim, 8,290 ... H 4
Ceres, 6,895 ... D 7
Cêrro Azul, 1,460 ... †B 4
Chaves, 428 ... D 3
Cicero Dantas, 2,972 ... G 5
Coari, 5,908 ... H 9
Codajás, 1,505 ... H 9
Codó, *100,933 ... E 4
Colatina, *140,729 ... F 7
Colinas, 2,972 ... F 4
Conceição da Barra, 2,229 ... G 7
Conceição do Araguaia, 2,332 ... D 5
Concórdia, 5,864 ... D 9
Conde, 4,190 ... G 5
Conselheiro Lafaiete, 29,208 ... †E 2
Corinto, 12,247 ... E 7
Cornélio Procópio, 17,524 ... D 8
Coroatá, 7,720 ... F 3
Coromandel, 5,148 ... E 7
Corrente, 2,214 ... E 5
Correntina, 2,636 ... E 6
Corumbá, 36,744 ... B 7
Coxim, 1,371 ... C 7
Crateús, 14,572 ... F 4
Crato, 27,649 ... G 4
Criciúma, 25,331 ... D10
Cristalina, 3,810 ... E 7
Cruz Alta, 33,190 ... C10
Cruzeiro, 27,005 ... †D 3
Cruzeiro do Sul, 2,826 ... G10
Cubatão, 18,885 ... †C 3
Cuiabá, 43,112 ... C 6
Curaça, 1,264 ... G 5
Curitiba, *616,548 ... †B 4
Currais Novos, 7,782 ... G 4
Curuçá, 3,871 ... E 3
Cururupu, 4,822 ... E 3
Curvelo, 21,772 ... E 7
Diamantina, 14,252 ... F 7
Diamantino, 645 ... B 6
Dianópolis, 2,145 ... E 5
Divinópolis, 41,544 ... †D 2
Dois Córregos, 7,272 ... †B 3
Dom Pedrito, 15,429 ... C10
Dores do Indaiá, 10,354 ... E 7
Dourados, 10,757 ... C 8
Duque de Caxias, *324,261 ... †E 3
Eirunepé, 3,023 ... G10
Eldorado, 1,524 ... †B 4
Erechim, 24,941 ... C 9
Erval, 1,404 ... C11
Escada, 13,761 ... H 5
Esperança, 9,105 ... G 4
Esplanada, 3,792 ... G 5
Estância, 16,106 ... G 5
Exu, 2,549 ... G 4
Faro, 1,434 ... B 3
Feira de Santana, *136,000 ... G 5
Fernandópolis, 14,375 ... †A 2
Ferreira Gomes, 439 ... D 2
Ferros, 2,456 ... F 7
Flores, 2,102 ... G 4
Floriano, 16,063 ... F 4
Florianópolis, *130,012 ... E 9
Formiga, 18,763 ... †D 2
Formosa, 9,449 ... E 6
Fortaleza, *846,069 ... G 3
Foz do Iguaçu, 7,407 ... C 9
Franca, 47,244 ... †C 2
Fronteiras, 1,320 ... F 4
Frutal, 8,252 ... †B 2
Garanhuns, 34,050 ... G 5
Garça, 18,155 ... †B 3
Gilbués, 588 ... E 5
Goiana, 19,026 ... H 4
Goiandira, 3,169 ... E 7
Goiânia, *345,085 ... D 7
Goiás, 7,121 ... D 6
Governador Valadares, *124,606 ... F 7
Grajaú, 2,539 ... E 4
Granja, 5,074 ... F 3
Guacuí, 7,724 ... †F 2
Guajará-Mirim, 7,115 ... H10
Guamá, 2,470 ... E 3
Guarabira, 15,848 ... H 4
Guarapuava, *126,080 ... C 9
Guaratinguetá, 38,293 ... †D 3
Guarujá, 6,506 ... †C 4
Guarulhos, *119,572 ... †C 3
Guarus, 21,492 ... †F 2
Guaxupé, 14,168 ... †C 2
Guimarães, 1,512 ... E 3
Guiratinga, 4,203 ... C 7
Gurupá, 912 ... D 3
Gurupi, 4,148 ... D 5
Humaitá, 1,192 ... H10
Ibaiti, 3,628 ... †A 3
Ibiá, 6,999 ... E 7
Ibipetuba, 2,298 ... F 5
Ibitinga, 8,881 ... †B 2
Icó, 5,586 ... G 4
Icoraci, 11,512 ... D 3
Igarapava, 9,083 ... †C 2
Igarapé-Miri, 2,591 ... D 3
Iguape, 5,465 ... †C 4
Iguatu, 16,540 ... G 4
Ijuí, 19,671 ... C10
Ilhéus, *100,687 ... G 6
Imbituba, 6,638 ... D10
Imbituva, 3,290 ... †A 4
Imperatriz, 9,004 ... E 4
Inhumas, 8,298 ... D 7
Ipameri, 8,987 ... E 7
Ipiaú, 13,164 ... G 6
Ipu, 7,724 ... F 4
Irati, 12,764 ... †A 4
Itabaiana, Paraíba, 11,847 ... H 4
Itabaiana, Sergipe, 11,050 ... G 5
Itaberaba, 8,555 ... F 6
Itabira, 15,539 ... F 7
Itabirito, 10,511 ... †E 2
Itabuna, 54,268 ... G 6
Itacoatiara, 8,818 ... B 3
Itaguatins, 1,596 ... D 4
Itaí, 1,601 ... †B 3
Itajaí, 38,889 ... D 9
Itajubá, 31,262 ... †D 3
Itamarandiba, 2,404 ... F 7
Itanhaém, 5,376 ... †C 4
Itapecerica, 7,696 ... †D 2
Itapecuru-Mirim, 3,385 ... F 3
Itapemirim, 4,095 ... F 8
Itaperuna, 18,095 ... †F 2
Itapetininga, 29,468 ... †B 3
Itapeva, 13,510 ... †B 3
Itapicuru, 900 ... G 5
Itapipoca, 7,186 ... G 3
Itapira, 16,859 ... †C 3
Itapiranga, 477 ... B 3
Itápolis, 7,430 ... †B 2
Itaporanga, 5,328 ... G 4
Itaqui, 13,223 ... B10
Itararé, 12,812 ... †B 4
Itariri, 1,318 ... †C 4
Itatiba, 12,336 ... †C 3
Itaúna, 22,319 ... †D 2
Itu, 23,435 ... †C 3
Ituaçu, 1,431 ... F 6
Ituberá, 4,097 ... G 6
Ituiutaba, 29,724 ... D 7
Itumbiara, 12,575 ... D 7
Iturama, 1,518 ... †A 1
Ituverava, 11,890 ... †C 2
Jaboticabal, 20,231 ... †B 2
Jacareí, 28,131 ... †D 3
Jacarèzinho, 14,813 ... †A 3
Jacobina, 12,373 ... F 5
Jacupiranga, 2,144 ... †B 4
Jaguaquara, 5,363 ... F 6
Jaguarão, 12,336 ... C11
Jaguariaíva, 6,465 ... †B 4
Jaicós, 1,308 ... F 4
Januária, 9,741 ... E 6
Jaraguá, 3,813 ... D 6
Jardim, 3,104 ... G 4
Jataí, 14,022 ... D 7
Jaú, 31,229 ... †B 3
Jequié, 40,158 ... F 6
Jequitinhonha, 5,410 ... F 7
Jeremoabo, 3,177 ... G 5
Joaçaba, 7,921 ... D 9
João Pessoa, *189,096 ... H 4
João Pinheiro, 3,433 ... E 7
Joaquim Tavora, 3,574 ... †B 3
Joinville, 44,255 ... D 9
Juàzeiro, 21,196 ... G 5
Juàzeiro do Norte, 53,421 ... F 4
Juiz de Fora, *194,135 ... †E 2
Jundiaí, *124,368 ... †C 3
Lábrea, 2,080 ... G10
Laguna, 17,451 ... D10
Lajes, 35,112 ... D 9
Lambari, 6,825 ... †D 2
Lapa, 7,167 ... D 9
Laranjeiras, 4,296 ... G 5
Laranjeiras do Sul, 3,802 ... C 9
Lavras, 23,793 ... †D 2
Leme, 11,785 ... †C 3
Lençóis, 2,483 ... F 6
Leopoldina, 17,726 ... †E 2
Lima Duarte, 3,554 ... †E 2
Limeira, 45,256 ... †C 3
Limoeiro, 21,252 ... H 4
Limoeiro do Norte, 5,705 ... G 4
Linhares, 5,751 ... F 7
Lins, 32,204 ... †B 2
Londrina, *226,332 ... D 8
Lorena, 26,068 ... †D 3
Luís Correia, 1,523 ... F 3
Luz, 5,633 ... †D 1
Luziânia, 4,849 ... E 7
Luzilândia, 3,434 ... F 3
Macaé, 19,830 ... †F 3
Macapá, 27,585 ... D 2
Macau, 11,876 ... G 4
Macaúbas, 2,504 ... F 6
Maceió, *221,250 ... H 5
Machado, 8,373 ... †C 2
Mafra, 12,981 ... D 9
Magé, 10,712 ... †E 3
Mallet, 1,816 ... D 9
Manacapuru, 2,584 ... H 9
Manaus, *249,797 ... H 9
Manga, 2,000 ... E 6
Manhuaçu, 10,546 ... †E 2
Manhumirim, 9,477 ... †E 2
Manicoré, 2,268 ... H 9
Marabá, 8,533 ... D 4
Maragogipe, 12,575 ... G 6
Maranguape, 8,715 ... G 3
Marapanim, 3,542 ... E 3
Marechal-Deodoro, 5,269 ... H 5
Mariana, 6,378 ... †E 2
Marília, *107,305 ... †A 3
Marques de Valença, 18,935 ... †D 3
Massapê, 4,760 ... G 3
Mata de São João, 8,117 ... G 6
Mato Grosso, 520 ... B 6
Maués, 4,161 ... B 3
Mazagão, 919 ... B 3
Miguel Alves, 4,537 ... F 4
Mimoso do Sul, 5,278 ... †F 2
Minas Novas, 1,708 ... F 7
Mineiros, 5,105 ... C 7
Miracema, 9,810 ... †E 2
Mirador, 818 ... B 4
Miranda, 2,075 ... C 8
Mirassol, 13,674 ... †B 2
Mocajuba, 1,352 ... D 3
Mococa, 14,306 ... †C 2
Mogi das Cruzes, *111,554 ... †C 3
Mogi-Mirim, 18,345 ... †C 3
Monte Alegre, 3,911 ... C 3
Monte Alegre de Minas, 4,464 ... D 7
Monte Aprazível, 7,235 ... †A 2
Monte Azul, 4,860 ... F 6
Monteiro, 6,028 ... G 4
Montenegro, 14,491 ... D10
Monte Santo, 1,607 ... G 5
Montes Claros, *121,428 ... E 7
Morrinhos, 9,879 ... D 7
Morro do Chapéu, 2,039 ... F 5
Mossoró, 38,833 ... G 4
Mucugê, 723 ... F 6
Mucuri, 603 ... G 7
Mundo Novo, 3,237 ... F 5
Muqui, 4,262 ... F 8
Muriaé, 22,571 ... †E 2
Muzambinho, 18,073 ... †C 2
Natal, *239,590 ... H 4

(continued on following page)

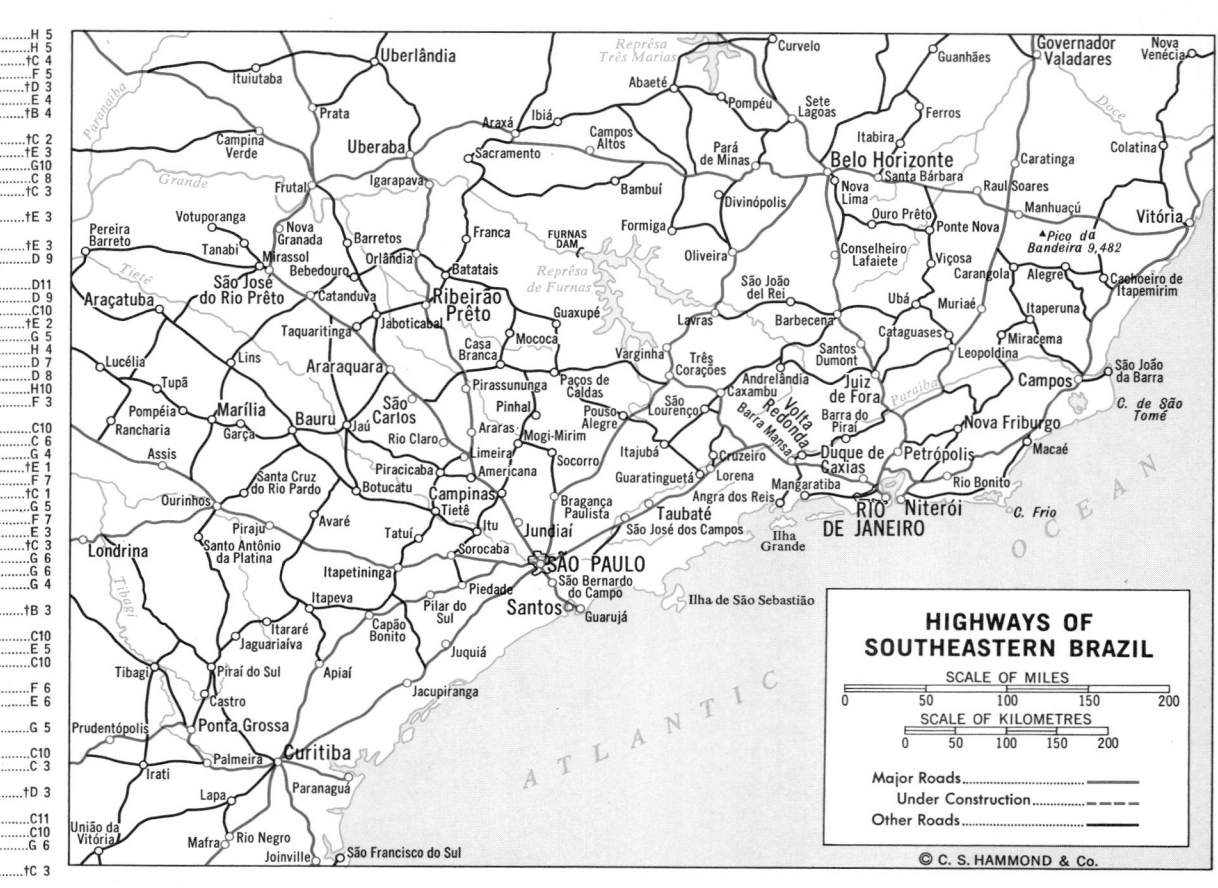

HIGHWAYS OF SOUTHEASTERN BRAZIL

SCALE OF MILES
0   50   100   150   200

SCALE OF KILOMETRES
0   50   100   150   200

Major Roads ....
Under Construction ....
Other Roads ....

© C. S. HAMMOND & Co.

Agriculture, Industry and Resources

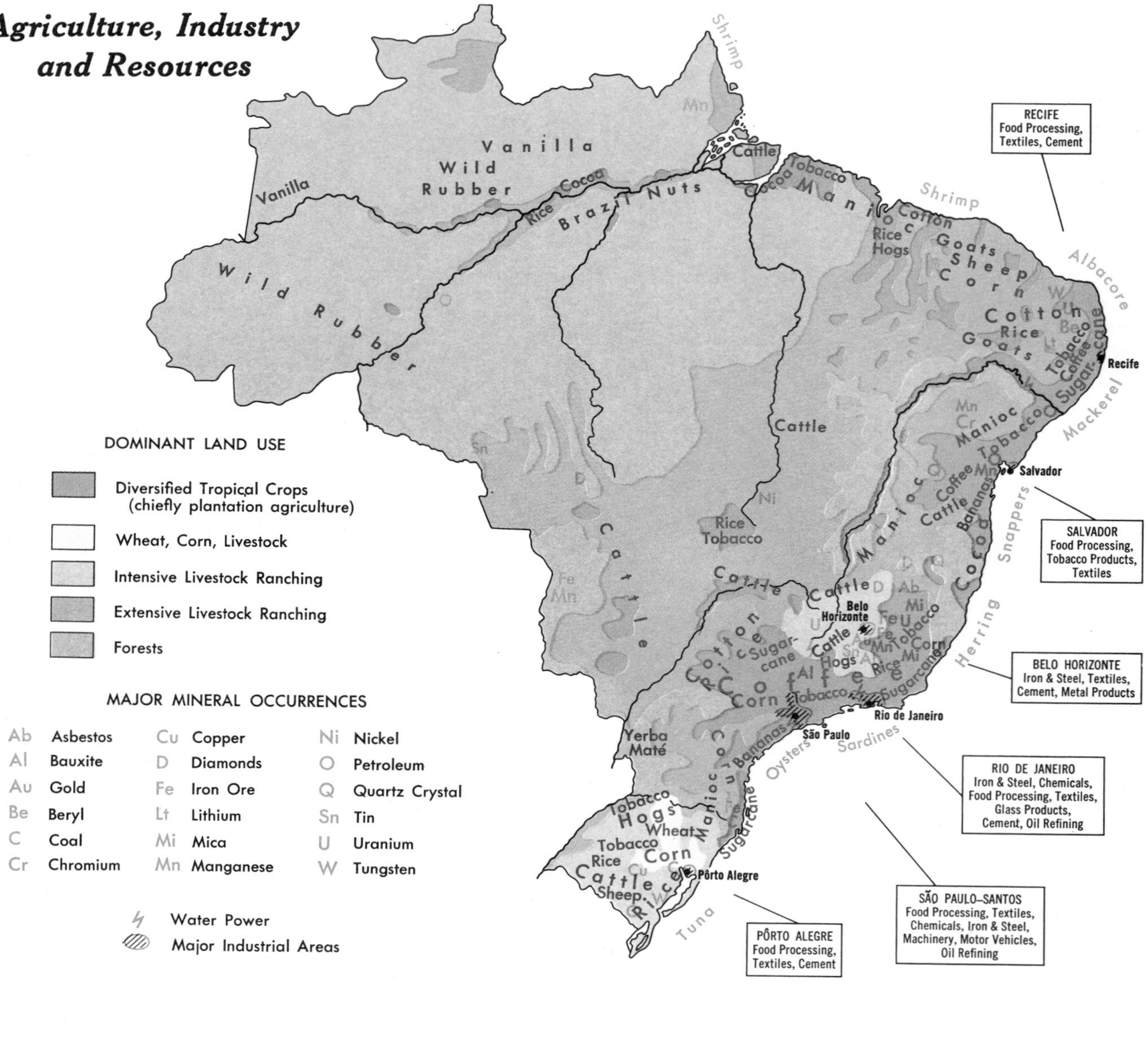

RECIFE
Food Processing,
Textiles, Cement

SALVADOR
Food Processing,
Tobacco Products,
Textiles

BELO HORIZONTE
Iron & Steel, Textiles,
Cement, Metal Products

RIO DE JANEIRO
Iron & Steel, Chemicals,
Food Processing, Textiles,
Glass Products,
Cement, Oil Refining

SÃO PAULO–SANTOS
Food Processing, Textiles,
Chemicals, Iron & Steel,
Machinery, Motor Vehicles,
Oil Refining

PÔRTO ALEGRE
Food Processing,
Textiles, Cement

DOMINANT LAND USE

Diversified Tropical Crops
(chiefly plantation agriculture)

Wheat, Corn, Livestock

Intensive Livestock Ranching

Extensive Livestock Ranching

Forests

MAJOR MINERAL OCCURRENCES

Ab Asbestos
Al Bauxite
Au Gold
Be Beryl
C   Coal
Cr Chromium

Cu Copper
D   Diamonds
Fe Iron Ore
Lt Lithium
Mi Mica
Mn Manganese

Ni Nickel
O   Petroleum
Q   Quartz Crystal
Sn Tin
U   Uranium
W   Tungsten

Water Power

Major Industrial Areas

Santo Ângelo, 25,415 ....C10
Santo Antônio da Platina, 9,378 ....†A 3
Santo Antonio do Leverger, 2,028 ....C 6
Santos, *313,771 ....†C 3
Santos Dumont, 20,414 ....†E 3
São Bento, 7,094 ....E 3
São Bernardo do Campo, 61,645 ....†C 3
São Borja, 20,339 ....C10
São Caetano do Sul, *135,095 ....†C 3
São Carlos, 50,010 ....†C 3
São Cristóvão, 7,624 ....G 5
São Domingos, 907 ....E 6
São Félix, 5,993 ....G 6
São Fidélis, 6,145 ....†E 2
São Francisco, 4,074 ....E 6
São Francisco do Sul, 11,593 ....E 9
São Gabriel, 22,967 ....C10
São João da Boa Vista, 25,226 ....†C 2
São João del Rei, 34,654 ....†D 2
São João do Piauí, 2,688 ....F 5
São João dos Patos, 2,590 ....F 4
São João Nepomuceno, 9,436 ....†E 2
São Joaquim da Barra, 13,853 ....†C 2
São José, 3,295 ....D 9
São José da Laje, 5,822 ....H 5
São José de Mipibu, 5,179 ....H 4
São José do Rio Pardo, 14,186 ....†C 2
São José do Rio Prêto, 66,476 ....†B 2
São José dos Campos, 55,349 ....†D 3
São José dos Pinhais, 7,574 ....D10
São Leopoldo, 41,023 ....D10
São Lourenço, 14,680 ....†D 3
São Lourenço do Sul, 6,877 ....C10
São Luís, *218,783 ....F 3
São Luís Gonzaga, 12,926 ....C10
São Manuel, 10,009 ....†B 3
São Mateus, 6,075 ....G 7
São Miguel Arcanjo, 3,633 ....†C 3
São Miguel dos Campos, 6,511 ....G 5
São Miguel Paulista, 39,644 ....†C 3
São Paulo, *5,684,706 ....†C 3
São Paulo, ‡6,300,000 ....†C 3
São Pedro, 4,474 ....†C 3
São Pedro do Piauí, 2,139 ....F 4

São Raimundo Nonato, 3,751 ....F 5
São Roque, 12,409 ....†C 3
São Sebastião, 3,490 ....†D 3
São Sebastião do Paraíso, 14,451 ....†C 2
São Simão, 5,742 ....†C 2
São Vicente, 73,578 ....†C 4
Senador Pompeu, 8,210 ....G 4
Sena Madureira, 1,962 ....G10
Senhor do Bonfim, 13,958 ....F 5
Serra do Navio, 9 ....C 2
Serra Talhada, 12,164 ....G 4
Serrinha, 10,284 ....G 5
Sertânia, 7,556 ....G 5
Sertanópolis, 6,469 ....D 8
Sete Lagoas, 36,302 ....E 7
Sítio da Abadia, 482 ....D 7
Silvânia, 2,920 ....D 7
Sobral, 32,281 ....F 3
Socorro, 6,402 ....†C 3
Sorocaba, *142,835 ....†C 3
Soure, 6,666 ....D 3
Taquaritinga, 11,624 ....†B 2
Tarauacá, 2,292 ....G10
Tatuí, 22,550 ....†C 3
Taubaté, 64,863 ....E 8
Tefé, 2,781 ....G 9
Teófilo-Otoni, *134,476 ....F 7
Teresina, *184,836 ....F 4
Teresópolis, 29,540 ....†E 3
Tibagi, 1,746 ....†A 4
Tietê, 8,729 ....†C 3
Tijucas, 4,420 ....D 9
Tocantínia, 1,414 ....D 5
Tocantinópolis, 4,927 ....D 4
Três Corações, 17,498 ....†D 2
Três Lagoas, 14,520 ....C 8
Três Pontas, 11,534 ....†D 2
Três Rios, 22,246 ....†E 3
Tubarão, 20,615 ....D10
Tucano, 4,007 ....G 5
Tupã, 28,723 ....†A 2
Tupaciretã, 8,659 ....C10
Tutóia, 3,337 ....F 3
Uaupés, 571 ....G 9
Ubá, 21,767 ....†E 2
Ubaíra, 2,352 ....G 5
Ubaitaba, 3,581 ....G 6
Ubatuba, 3,748 ....†D 3
Uberaba, *100,634 ....†C 2
Uberlândia, *101,149 ....E 7
Unaí, 4,214 ....E 7
União, 4,296 ....F 4
União da Vitória, 15,822 ....D 9
União dos Palmares, 10,406 ....H 5
Uruaçu, 4,392 ....D 5
Uruçuí, 2,233 ....E 5
Urucurituba, 520 ....B 3
Uruguaiana, 48,358 ....B10
Valença, 17,137 ....G 6

Valença do Piauí, 3,046 ....F 4
Valparaíso, 7,974 ....D 8
Varginha, 24,944 ....†D 2
Vera Cruz, 5,535 ....†B 3
Viçosa, Alagoas, 7,285 ....G 5
Viçosa, Minas Gerais, 9,342 ....†E 2
Vigia, 7,246 ....E 3
Visconde do Rio Branco, 12,363 ....†E 2
Viseu, 1,606 ....E 3
Vitória, *121,843 ....G 8
Vitória da Conquista, 46,778 ....F 6
Vitória de Santo Antão, 27,053 ....H 5
Volta Redonda, *118,114 ....†D 3
Votuporanga, 18,722 ....†B 2
Xapecó, 8,465 ....C 9
Xapuri, 2,000 ....G10
Xique-Xique, 5,467 ....F 5

OTHER FEATURES

Abacaxis (river) ....B 4
Abunã (river) A10
Acaraí (range) ....C 7
Acre (river) G10
Amambaí (range) ....C 7
Amaparí (river) ....C 2
Amazon (river) ....C 3
Anauá (river) ....B 3
Aporé (river) ....C 7
Araguaia (river) ....D 6
Araguarí (river) ....D 7
Araruama (lagoon) ....†E 3
Arinos (river) ....B 5
Aripuanã (river) ....A 4
Balsas (river) ....E 4
Bananal (isl.) ....D 5
Bandeira, Pico da (mt.) ....E 7
Branco (river) ....H 8
Buzios (cape) ....†F 3
Canumã (river) ....B 4
Capim (river) ....D 3
Carajás (range) ....D 4
Cardoso (isl.) ....†C 4
Cassiporé (cape) ....C 1
Caviana (isl.) ....D 2
Chavantes (range) ....D 5
Claro (river) ....C 6
Coluene (river) ....C 6
Comprida (isl.) ....†C 4
Cuiabá (river) ....B 7
Doce (river) ....E 7
Dois Irmãos (range) ....F 5
Erepecuru (river) ....B 3
Espigão Mestre (Geral) (range) ....E 6
Espinhaço (range) ....F 7
Estrondo (range) ....D 5
Feia (lake) ....†F 3
Feio (river) ....†B 2

Formosa (range) ....C 5
Frio (cape) ....†F 3
Furnas (dam) ....†C 2
Furnas (res.) ....†C 2
Geral (range) ....D 9
Geral de Goiás (range) ....E 6
Gi-Paraná (river) H10
Gradaús (range) ....D 4
Grajaú (river) ....E 4
Grande (isl.) ....†D 3
Grande (river) ....†B 1, D 8
Guanabara (bay) ....†E 3
Guaporé (river) H10
Guariba (river) ....B 4
Gurguéia (river) ....E 5
Gurupi (range) ....E 3
Gurupi (river) ....E 3
Ibicuí (river) C10
Içá (river) ....B 9
Iguaçu (river) ....C 9
Iguaçú (falls) ....B 9
Ilha Grande (bay) ....†D 3
Iriri (river) ....C 3
Itapecuru (river) ....F 4
Itararé (river) ....C 8
Ivaí (river) ....C 8
Jacuípe (river) ....G 5
Jaguaribe (river) ....G 4
Japurá (river) ....B 9
Jarí (river) ....C 2
Javarí (river) ....F 9
Jequitinhonha (river) ....F 7
Juruá (river) G10
Juruena (river) ....B 5
Madeira (river) ....A 4
Manso (river) ....C 6
Mantiqueira (range) ....†D 3
Mar (range) ....†C 4, E 9
Maracá (isl.) ....C 2
Marajó (isl.) ....D 3
Mato Grosso (plateau) ....B 6
Mirim (lagoon) C11
Moji Guaçu (river) ....†C 2
Mortes (Manso) (river) ....D 6
Neblina, Pico da (mt.) ....G 8
Negro (river) ....H 9
Nhamundá (river) ....B 3
Norte (range) ....†B 4
Orange (cape) ....D 1
Orgãos (range) ....†E 3
Oyapock (river) ....C 2
Pacajá Grande (river) ....D 4
Pacaraima (range) ....H 8
Papagaio (river) ....B 6
Pará (river) ....D 3
Paracatu (river) D10
Paraguaçu (river) ....F 6
Paraguai (river) ....B 7
Paraíba (river) ....†E 2
Paraná (river) ....E 6
Paraná (river) ....C 8

Paranapanema (river) ....†B 3, C 8
Paranapiacaba (range) ....†B 4
Paranatinga (river) ....C 6
Pardo (river) ....†B 2, D 8
Pardo (river) ....B 6
Parecis (range) ....B 6
Parnaíba (river) ....E 5
Paru (river) ....C 3
Patos (lagoon) D10
Peixoto (dam) ....†C 2
Penitente (range) ....E 5
Piauí (river) ....F 5
Piauí (river) ....E 2
Piracambu (range) ....E 3
Purus (river) ....H 9
Ribeira (river) ....†B 4

Roncador (range) ....D 5
Roosevelt (river) ....A 5
Santa Catarina (isl.), 98,520 ....E 9
São Francisco (river) ....F 5
São Lourenço (river) ....B 7
São Marcos (bay) ....F 3
São Roque (cape) ....H 4
São Sebastião (isl.), 1,823 ....†D 3
São Tomé (cape) ....G 8
Sapucaí (river) ....†D 2
Sepetiba (bay) ....†D 3
Sete Quedas (falls) ....B 8
Tacutú (river) ....H 8
Tapajós (river) ....B 4
Taquarí (river) ....C 7
Teles Pires (river) ....B 5

Tibagi (river) ....†A 4
Tietê (river) ....†B 2, D 8
Tocantins (river) ....D 4
Tombador (range) ....B 6
Trombetas (river) ....B 3
Tumucumaque (range) ....B 2
Turvo (river) ....†B 2
Uaupés (river) ....G 9
Uraricuera (river) ....H 8
Urucún, Morro do (mt.) ....B 7
Uruguai (river) ....C 9
Verde (river) ....C 8
Xingu (river) ....C 3

‡Population of metropolitan area.
*Population of municipality.
†Keys refer to map on page 135.

BRASÍLIA
MILES
0   5
© C. S. Hammond & Co., Maplewood, N.J.

SOUTHEASTERN BRAZIL
POLYCONIC PROJECTION
SCALE OF MILES
0   25   50   100   150
SCALE OF KILOMETRES
0   25   50   100   150
State Capitals ....◉
State Boundaries ....
© Copyright by C. S. HAMMOND & Co., Maplewood, N.J.

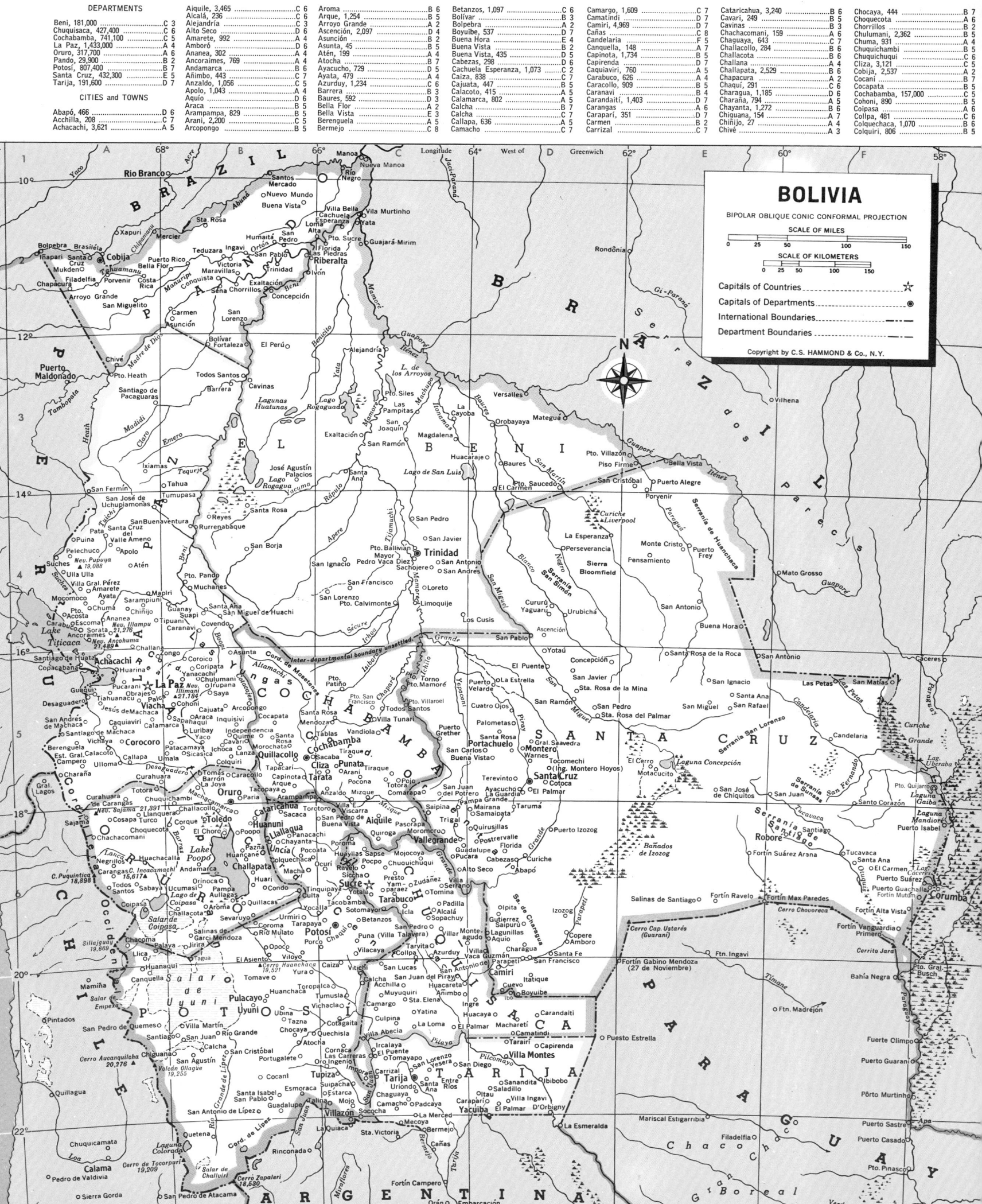

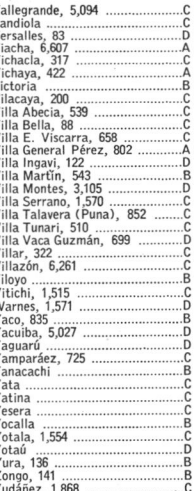

Comarapa, 1,096 .... C 5
Concepción .... B 2
Concepción, 1,056 .... D 5
Condo .... B 6
Conquista .... B 2
Copacabana, 1,981 .... A 5
Copere .... D 6
Coripata, 1,647 .... B 5
Cornaca, 264 .... C 7
Corocoro, 4,431 .... A 5
Coroico, 2,235 .... B 5
Coroma .... B 6
Corque, 423 .... B 6
Cosapa, 297 .... A 6
Costa Rica .... A 2
Cotagaita, 1,353 .... C 7
Cotoca, 915 .... D 5
Covendo, 71 .... B 4
Cuatro Ojos .... D 5
Cuevo, 902 .... D 7
Culpina, 981 .... C 7
Culta .... B 6
Curahuara, 510 .... A 5
Curahuara de Carangas, 235 .... A 5
Curiche, 257 .... D 6
Cururú .... D 4
Desaguadero, 201 .... A 5
D'Orbigny .... D 7
El Asiento .... B 6
El Carmen, 232 .... D 3
El Carmen .... F 6
El Cerro, 117 .... E 5
El Choro, 224 .... B 6
El Palmer .... D 7
El Palmar, 437 .... D 5
El Palmar, 832 .... D 7
El Perú .... B 3
El Puente .... C 7
El Puente .... D 5
Entre Ríos, 1,011 .... C 7
Escoma, 220 .... A 4
Esmoraca .... B 7
Estación General Campero .... A 5
Estarca .... C 7
Exaltación .... B 2
Exaltación, 405 .... C 3
Filadelfia .... A 2
Florida .... C 2
Florida, 128 .... D 6
Fortaleza .... B 3
Fortín Alta Vista .... F 6
Fortín Campero .... C 8
Fortín Max Paredes .... F 6
Fortín Mutum .... F 6
Fortín Ravelo .... E 6
Fortín Suárez Arana .... F 6
Fortín Vanguardia Primero .... F 6
General Saavedra, 1,006 .... D 5
Guadalupe, 71 .... B 7
Guadalupe, 2,355 .... C 6
Guanay, 574 .... B 4
Guaqui, 2,266 .... A 5
Gutiérrez, 770 .... D 6
Huacaraje, 673 .... D 3
Huacareta, 239 .... C 7
Huacaya, 229 .... D 7
Huachacalla, 801 .... A 6
Huanaqui, 359 .... A 7
Huancané, 148 .... B 6
Huanchaca .... B 7
Huanuni, 5,696 .... B 6
Huari, 1,070 .... B 6
Huarina, 1,151 .... A 5
Huayllas, 206 .... C 6
Humaitá .... B 2
Ibibobo .... D 7
Ibo, 425 .... D 7
Ichoca, 591 .... B 5
Icla, 196 .... C 6
Impora, 274 .... C 7
Independencia, 1,742 .... B 5
Ingavi .... B 2
Ingeniero Montero Hoyos (Tocomechi), 575 .... D 5
Ingre, 162 .... D 7
Inquisivi, 520 .... B 5
Ipitá, 441 .... D 6
Ircalaya .... C 7
Irupana, 1,937 .... B 5
Itatique .... D 7
Itaú, 102 .... D 7
Ivón .... C 2
Ixiamas, 292 .... A 3
Izozog .... D 6
Jesús de Machaca, 529 .... A 5
Jirira .... B 6
José Agustín Palacios .... B 3
La Cayoba .... C 3
La Esmeralda .... D 8
La Esperanza .... D 4
La Estrella .... D 5
La Guardia, 470 .... D 5

La Joya, 401 .... B 5
La Loma .... C 7
La Merced .... C 8
La Paz (cap.), 525,000 .... B 5
Lagunillas, 840 .... D 6
Lanza, 526 .... B 5
Las Carreras, 155 .... C 7
Las Pampitas .... C 3
Las Petas .... F 5
Las Piedras .... C 2
Limoquije .... C 4
Llallagua, 6,719 .... B 6
Llanquera, 613 .... A 6
Llica, 560 .... A 6
Loma Alta .... B 2
Loreto, 589 .... C 4
Los Cusis .... D 4
Luribay, 392 .... B 5
Macha, 1,050 .... B 6
Machacamarca, 1,746 .... B 5
Machareti .... D 7
Magdalena, 1,724 .... C 3
Mairana, 508 .... D 6
Manoa .... C 1
Mapiri, 289 .... B 4
Maravillas .... B 2
Mategua, 38 .... D 3
Mayor Pedro Vaca Diez, 358 .... C 4
Mecoya .... C 8
Mendoza .... C 5
Mercier .... B 2
Mizque, 870 .... C 5
Mocomoco, 977 .... A 4
Mojo, 469 .... C 7
Mojocoya, 498 .... C 6
Monte Cristo .... E 4
Monteagudo, 971 .... D 6
Montero, 2,713 .... D 5
Morochata, 461 .... B 5
Moromoro, 556 .... C 6
Motacucito .... E 5
Muchanes .... B 4
Mukden .... A 2
Muyuquiri .... C 7
Negrillos, 85 .... A 6
Nueva Manoa .... C 1
Nuevo Mundo .... B 2
Obrajes .... A 5
Ocurí, 1,531 .... C 6
Opoco .... B 6
Orinoca .... B 6
Oro Ingenio .... C 7
Orobayaya .... D 3
Oruro, 86,985 .... B 5
Padcaya, 324 .... C 7
Padilla, 2,462 .... C 6
Palaya, 300 .... A 6
Palca, 887 .... A 5
Palometas .... D 5
Pampa Aullagas .... B 6
Pampa Grande, 727 .... D 5
Panacachi, 952 .... B 6
Paria, 335 .... B 5
Pasorapa, 1,016 .... C 6
Pata, 122 .... A 4
Patacamaya, 1,278 .... B 5
Pazña, 671 .... B 6
Pelechuco, 873 .... A 4
Pensamiento .... E 4
Perseverancia .... D 4
Piso Firme .... D 3
Pocoata, 859 .... B 6
Pocona, 518 .... C 5
Pocpo .... C 6
Pojo, 1,047 .... C 5
Poopó, 736 .... B 6
Porco, 817 .... B 6
Poroma, 171 .... C 6
Portachuelo, 2,456 .... D 5
Portugalete .... B 7
Porvenir .... A 2
Porvenir .... E 4
Postrervalle, 750 .... D 6
Potosí, 55,233 .... C 6
Presto, 725 .... C 6
Pucara, 762 .... C 6
Pucarani, 1,041 .... A 5
Puerto Acosta, 1,302 .... A 4
Puerto Alegre .... E 3
Puerto Ballivián .... C 4
Puerto Calvimonte .... C 4
Puerto Frey .... E 4
Puerto General Busch .... G 7
Puerto Grether .... C 5
Puerto Guachalla .... F 6
Puerto Heath .... A 3
Puerto Isabel .... G 6
Puerto Izozog .... D 6
Puerto Mamoré .... C 5
Puerto Pando .... B 4
Puerto Patiño .... C 5
Puerto Quiiarro, 1,006 .... G 5

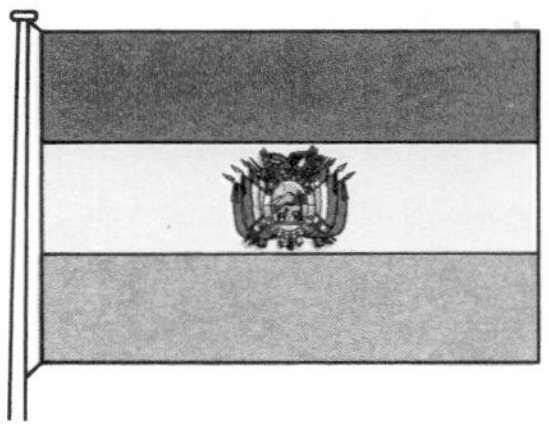

AREA 424, 163 sq. mi.
POPULATION 4,804,000
CAPITALS La Paz, Sucre
LARGEST CITY La Paz
HIGHEST POINT Nevada Ancohuma 21,489 ft.
MONETARY UNIT Bolivian peso
MAJOR LANGUAGES Spanish, Quechua, Aymara
MAJOR RELIGION Roman Catholicism

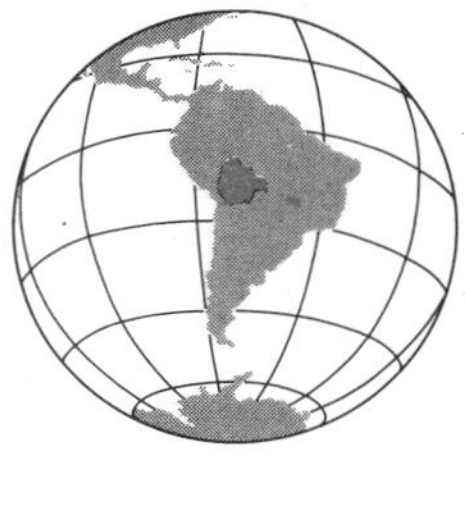

Puerto Rico .... B 2
Puerto San Francisco .... C 5
Puerto Saucedo .... D 3
Puerto Siles, 357 .... C 3
Puerto Suárez, 1,159 .... F 6
Puerto Sucre, 1,470 .... C 2
Puerto Torno .... C 5
Puerto Velarde .... D 5
Puerto Villaroel .... C 5
Puerto Villazón .... D 3
Puina .... A 4
Pulacayo, 7,984 .... B 7
Puna, 852 .... C 6
Punata, 5,014 .... C 5
Quechisla, 171 .... C 7
Quetena, 183 .... B 8
Quillacas, 1,170 .... B 6
Quillacollo, 9,123 .... B 5
Quime, 1,256 .... B 5
Quiroga .... C 6
Quirusillas, 433 .... D 6
Ravelo, 907 .... C 6
Reyes, 1,404 .... B 4
Riberalta, 6,549 .... C 2
Río Grande, 281 .... B 7
Río Mulato, 381 .... B 6
Río Negro .... C 1
Roboré, 3,715 .... F 6
Rurrenabaque, 1,225 .... B 4
Sabaya, 649 .... A 6
Sacaba, 2,752 .... C 5
Sacaca, 1,778 .... B 6
Sachojere, 401 .... C 4
Saipina, 573 .... C 6
Saipurú .... D 6
Sajama, 231 .... A 6
Saladillo .... D 7
Salinas de Garci Mendoza, 335 .... B 6
Salinas de Santiago .... E 6
Samaipata, 1,656 .... D 6
San Agustín .... B 7
San Andrés, 399 .... C 4
San Andrés de Machaca, 101 .... A 5
San Antonio, 436 .... C 4
San Antonio .... E 4
San Antonio de Lípez .... B 7
San Antonio del Parapetí, 497 .... D 7
San Borja, 708 .... B 4
San Buenaventura, 307 .... A 4
San Carlos, 570 .... D 5
San Cristóbal .... B 7
San Cristóbal .... E 3
San Diego .... D 7
San Fermín .... A 3
San Francisco, 185 .... C 4
San Francisco .... D 7
San Ignacio, 1,757 .... C 4
San Ignacio, 1,819 .... E 5
San Javier, 233 .... C 4
San Javier, 564 .... D 5
San Joaquín, 1,959 .... C 3
San José de Chiquitos, 1,933 .... E 5
San José de Uchupiamonas, 277 .... A 4
San Juan, 131 .... B 7
San Juan .... F 5
San Juan del Piray, 541 .... C 7
San Juan del Potrero, 263 .... C 5
San Lorenzo .... B 2
San Lorenzo, 496 .... C 4
San Lorenzo, 785 .... C 7
San Lucas, 925 .... C 7
San Matías, 887 .... F 5
San Miguel, 502 .... E 5
San Miguel de Huachi, 25 .... B 4
San Miguelito .... A 2
San Pablo .... B 2
San Pablo, 11 .... B 7
San Pablo .... D 4
San Pedro .... B 2
San Pedro, 262 .... C 4
San Pedro, 182 .... C 6

San Pedro, 80 .... D 5
San Pedro de Buena Vista, 1,094 .... C 6
San Pedro de Quemes .... A 7
San Rafael .... E 5
San Ramón, 1,161 .... C 3
San Ramón, 379 .... D 5
Sanandita, 379 .... D 7
Santa Ana, 171 .... B 4
Santa Ana, 2,225 .... C 3
Santa Ana .... C 7
Santa Ana, 275 .... E 5
Santa Ana, 663 .... F 6
Santa Cruz .... A 2
Santa Cruz, 108,720 .... D 5
Santa Cruz del Valle Ameno, 442 .... A 4
Santa Elena .... C 7
Santa Fe .... D 6
Santa Isabel .... B 7
Santa Rosa .... B 2
Santa Rosa, 765 .... B 4
Santa Rosa, 491 .... B 5
Santa Rosa .... C 5
Santa Rosa, 995 .... D 5
Santa Rosa de la Mina, 99 .... D 5
Santa Rosa de la Roca, 101 .... E 5
Santa Roso del Palmar, 441 .... E 5
Santiago, 172 .... A 7
Santiago, 765 .... F 6
Santiago de Huata, 948 .... A 5
Santiago de Machaca, 218 .... A 5
Santiago de Pacaguaras .... A 3
Santo Corazón .... F 5
Santos Mercado .... B 2
Sapahaqui, 55 .... B 5
Sapse .... C 6
Sarampiuni, 138 .... A 4
Saya, 339 .... B 5
Sena .... B 2
Sevaruyo, 475 .... B 6
Sicasica, 1,486 .... B 5
Siccha .... C 6
Sococha .... C 7
Sopachuy, 713 .... C 6
Sorata, 2,087 .... A 4
Sotomayor, 510 .... C 6
Suapi .... B 4
Suches .... A 4
Sucre (capital), 58,359 .... C 6
Suipacha .... C 7
Tablas .... C 5
Tacobamba .... C 6
Tacopaya, 795 .... B 5
Tagua .... B 6
Tahua, 114 .... B 3
Talina, 122 .... B 7
Tapacarí, 980 .... B 5
Tarabuco, 2,833 .... C 6
Tarairí .... D 7
Tarapaya, 357 .... B 6
Tarata, 3,016 .... C 5
Tarija, 20,851 .... C 7
Tarumá .... D 6
Tarvita, 404 .... C 6
Tazna .... B 7
Teduzara .... B 2
Terevinto .... D 5
Tiahuanacu, 1,227 .... A 5
Tinquipaya, 766 .... C 6
Tipuani .... B 4
Tiraque, 1,390 .... C 5
Tiraque, 234 .... C 5
Tocomechi (Ingeniero Montero Hoyos), 575 .... D 5
Todos Santos, 68 .... A 6
Todos Santos .... B 3
Todos Santos, 408 .... C 5
Toledo, 3,273 .... B 6
Tomás Barrón, 1,852 .... B 5
Tomave, 201 .... B 7
Tomayapo .... C 7

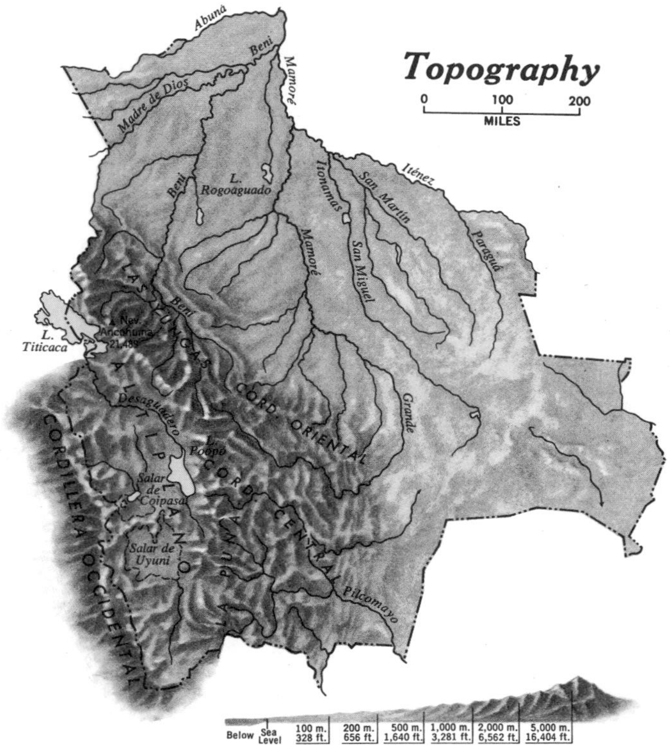
Topography
0 100 200
MILES
Abuná
Beni
Mamoré
Madre de Dios
Iténez
San Martín
L. Rogoaguado
Itonamas
Paraguá
San Miguel
Grande
L. Titicaca
Nev. Ancohuma
Desaguadero
Poopó
Salar de Coipasa
Salar de Uyuni
CORD. ORIENTAL
CORDILLERA OCCIDENTAL
Pilcomayo
Below Sea Level
100 m. 328 ft.
200 m. 656 ft.
500 m. 1,640 ft.
1,000 m. 3,281 ft.
2,000 m. 6,562 ft.
5,000 m. 16,404 ft.

Tomina, 708 .... C 6
Toropalca .... B 7
Torotoro, 1,233 .... C 6
Totora, 210 .... A 5
Totora, 2,290 .... C 5
Trigal, 749 .... C 6
Trinidad .... B 2
Trinidad, 14,505 .... C 4
Tucavaca .... F 6
Tumupasa, 349 .... B 4
Tumusla .... C 7
Tupiza, 8,248 .... C 7
Turco, 131 .... A 6
Ubina .... B 7
Ucumasi .... B 6
Ulla Ulla, 52 .... A 4
Ulloma, 116 .... A 5
Umala, 481 .... B 5
Uncía, 4,507 .... B 6
Uriondo, 860 .... C 7
Urmiri .... B 6
Urubichá, 1,369 .... D 4
Uyuni, 6,968 .... B 7

Vallegrande, 5,094 .... C 6
Vandiola .... C 5
Versalles, 83 .... D 3
Viacha, 6,607 .... A 5
Vichacla, 317 .... C 7
Vichaya, 422 .... A 5
Victoria .... B 2
Vilacaya, 200 .... C 6
Villa Abecia, 539 .... C 7
Villa Bella, 88 .... C 2
Villa E. Viscarra, 658 .... C 6
Villa General Pérez, 802 .... A 4
Villa Ingavi, 122 .... D 7
Villa Martín, 543 .... B 7
Villa Montes, 3,105 .... D 7
Villa Serrano, 1,570 .... C 6
Villa Talavera (Puna), 852 .... C 6
Villa Tunari, 510 .... C 5
Villa Vaca Guzmán, 699 .... D 6
Villar, 322 .... C 6
Villazón, 6,261 .... C 7
Viloyo .... B 6
Vitichi, 1,515 .... C 7
Warnes, 1,571 .... D 5
Yaco, 835 .... B 5
Yacuiba, 5,027 .... D 7
Yaguarú .... D 4
Yamparáez, 725 .... C 6
Yanacachi .... B 5
Yata .... C 2
Yatina .... C 7
Yesera .... C 7
Yocalla .... B 6
Yotala, 1,554 .... C 6
Yotaú .... D 5
Yura, 136 .... B 7
Zongo, 141 .... B 5
Zudáñez, 1,868 .... C 6

OTHER FEATURES

Altamachi (river) .... B 5
Ancohuma, Nevada (mt.) .... A 4
Andes (mts.) .... A 3
Apere (river) .... C 4
Arroyas, Los (lake) .... C 3
Barras (river) .... B 6
Baures (river) .... D 3
Beni (river) .... B 2
Bermejo (river) .... C 8
Blanco (river) .... D 4
Bloomfield, Sierra (mts.) .... D 4
Boopi (river) .... B 4
Cáceres (lagoon) .... F 6
Candelaria (river) .... F 5
Capitán Ustarés, Cerro (mt.) .... E 6
Central, Cordillera (mts.) .... C 6
Challviri (salt depr.) .... B 8
Chaparé (river) .... C 5
Charagua (mts.) .... D 6
Chipamanu (river) .... A 2
Coipasa (lake) .... B 6
Coipasa (salt depr.) .... A 6
Colorada (lagoon) .... A 8
Concepción (lagoon) .... E 5
Cotacajes (river) .... B 5
Desaguadero (river) .... B 5
Empexa (salt depr.) .... A 7
Gaiba (lagoon) .... G 5
Grande (marsh) .... F 5
Grande (river) .... C 4
Grande (river) .... C 6
Grande de Lípez (river) .... B 7
Guaporé (river) .... C 3
Guaraní (Capitán Ustarés) (mt.) .... E 6
Heath (river) .... A 3
Huanchaca, Cerro (mt.) .... B 7
Huanchaca, Serranía de (mts.) .... E 4
Ichilo (river) .... C 5
Illampu, Nevada (mt.) .... A 4
Illimani, Nevada (mt.) .... B 5
Incacamachi, Cerro (mt.) .... A 6
Isiboro (river) .... C 5
Iténez (Guaporé) (river) .... C 3
Itonamas (river) .... C 3
Izozog (swamp) .... E 6
Las Petas (river) .... F 5
Las Yungas (region) .... B 5
Lauca (river) .... A 6
Lípez, Cordillera de (mts.) .... B 8
Liverpool (swamp) .... D 4
Machupo (river) .... C 3
Madidi (river) .... A 3
Madre de Dios (river) .... A 3
Mamoré (river) .... C 2
Mandioré (lagoon) .... G 6
Manuripi (river) .... B 2
Mizque (river) .... C 6
Mosetenes, Cordillera de (mts.) .... B 5
Negro (river) .... D 4
Occidental, Cordillera (mts.) .... A 6
Ollagüe (volcano) .... A 7
Oriental, Cordillera (mts.) .... C 5
Ortón (river) .... B 2
Otuquis (river) .... F 6
Paraguá (river) .... E 4
Paraguay (river) .... F 7
Parapetí (river) .... D 6
Petas, Las (river) .... F 5
Pilaya (river) .... C 7
Pilcomayo (river) .... D 7
Piray (river) .... D 5
Poopó (lake) .... B 6
Pupuya, Nevada (mt.) .... A 4
Puquintica, Cerro (mt.) .... A 6
Rápulo (river) .... C 4
Real, Cordillera (mts.) .... A 5
Rogagua (lake) .... B 3
Rogaguado (lake) .... C 3
Sajama, Nevada (mt.) .... A 6
San Fernando (river) .... F 5
San Juan (river) .... C 7
San Luis (lake) .... C 3
San Martín (river) .... D 3
San Miguel (river) .... D 4
San Simón, Serranía (mts.) .... D 4
Santiago, Serranía de (mts.) .... F 6
Sillajguay (mt.) .... A 6
Suches (river) .... A 4
Tahuamanu (river) .... A 2
Tarija (river) .... C 8
Titicaca (lake) .... A 4
Tocorpuri, Cerros de (mt.) .... A 8
Tucavaca (river) .... F 6
Tuichi (river) .... A 4
Uberaba (lagoon) .... F 5
Uyuni (salt depr.) .... B 7
Yacuma (river) .... B 3
Yapacani (river) .... C 5
Yata (river) .... C 3
Yungas, Las (region) .... B 5
Zapaleri, Cerro (mt.) .... B 8

Agriculture, Industry and Resources

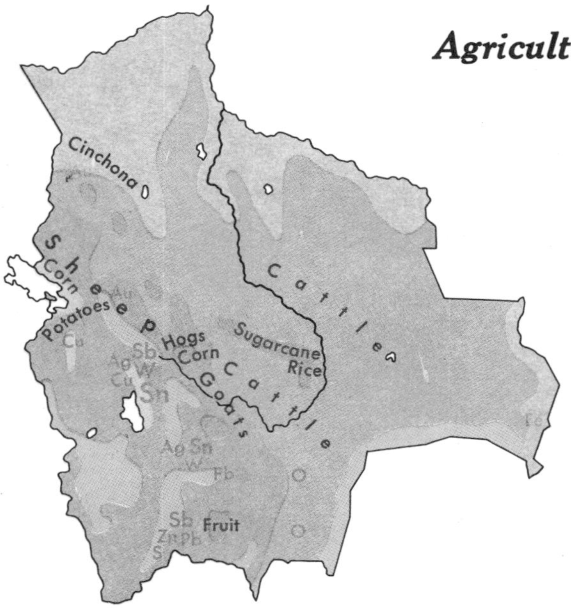
Cinchona
Sheep
Corn
Potatoes
Hogs
Corn
Sugarcane
Rice
Cattle
Goats
Cattle
Fruit
Ag Sn
Sb
Cu
Fb
Zn Pb

DOMINANT LAND USE

- Diversified Tropical Crops (chiefly plantation agriculture)
- Upland Cultivated Areas
- Upland Livestock Grazing, Limited Agriculture
- Extensive Livestock Ranching
- Forests
- Nonagricultural Land

MAJOR MINERAL OCCURRENCES

Ag	Silver	O	Petroleum	Sn	Tin
Au	Gold	Pb	Lead	W	Tungsten
Cu	Copper	S	Sulfur	Zn	Zinc
Fe	Iron Ore	Sb	Antimony		

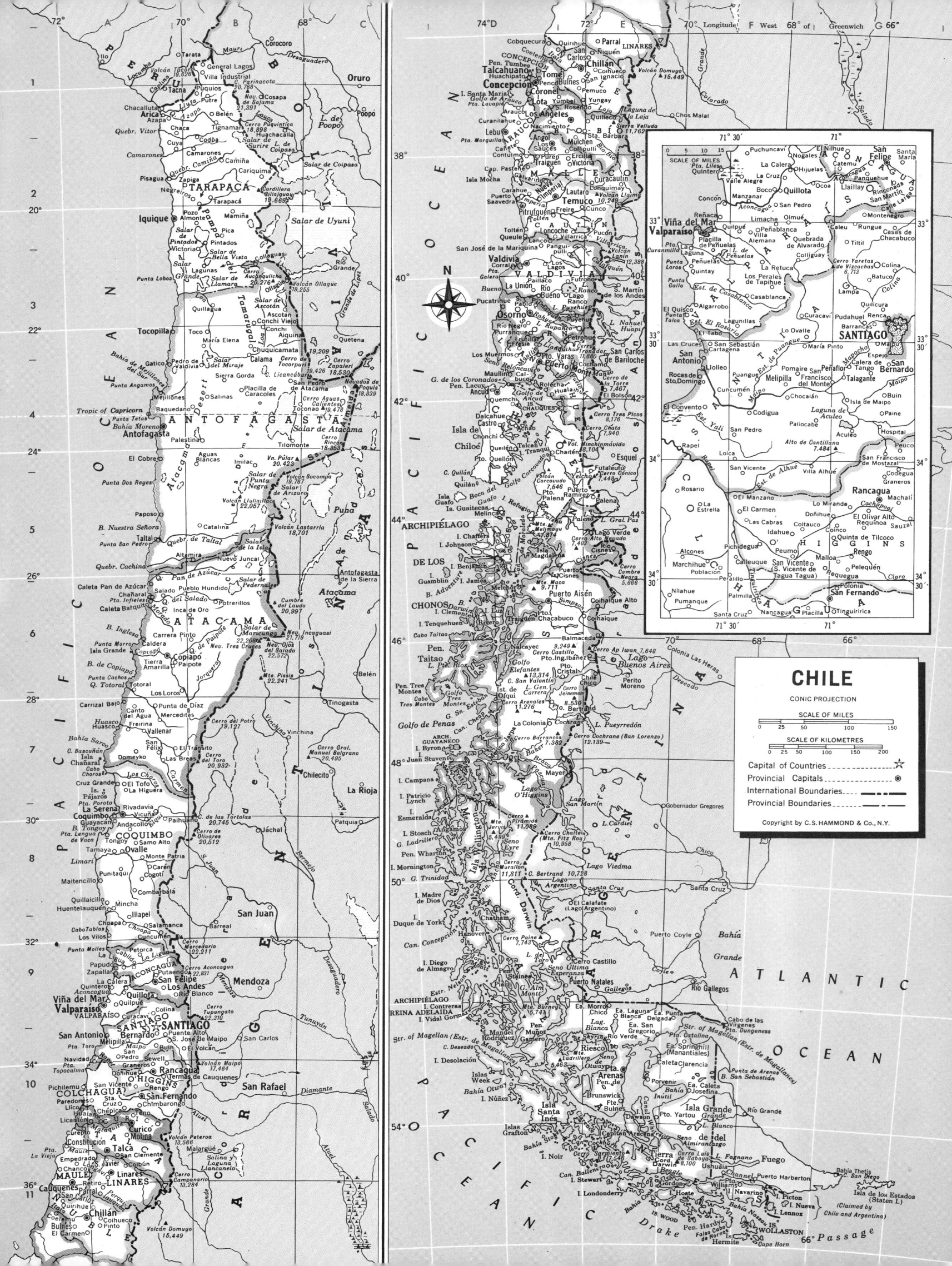

CHILE

CONIC PROJECTION

SCALE OF MILES
0 25 50 100 150

SCALE OF KILOMETRES
0 25 50 100 150 200

Capital of Countries .... ☆
Provincial Capitals .... ◉
International Boundaries ....
Provincial Boundaries ....

Copyright by C.S. Hammond & Co., N.Y.

Topography

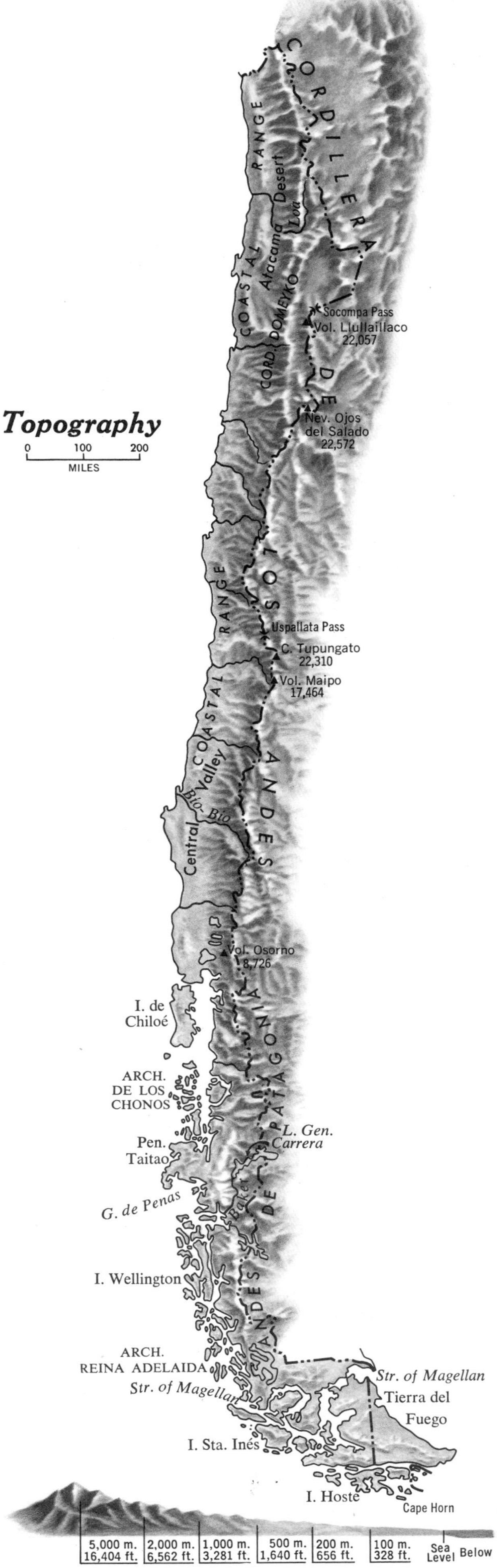
0 100 200
MILES
CORDILLERA DE LOS ANDES
COASTAL RANGE
Atacama Desert
Loa
CORD. DOMEYKO
Socompa Pass
Vol. Llullaillaco
22,057
Nev. Ojos del Salado
22,572
Uspallata Pass
C. Tupungato
22,310
Vol. Maipo
17,464
Central Valley
Bío Bío
Vol. Osorno
8,726
I. de Chiloé
ARCH. DE LOS CHONOS
Pen. Taitao
L. Gen. Carrera
G. de Penas
Baker
ANDES DE PATAGONIA
I. Wellington
ARCH. REINA ADELAIDA
Str. of Magellan
Str. of Magellan
Tierra del Fuego
I. Sta. Inés
I. Hoste
Cape Horn
5,000 m. 16,404 ft.
2,000 m. 6,562 ft.
1,000 m. 3,281 ft.
500 m. 1,640 ft.
200 m. 656 ft.
100 m. 328 ft.
Sea Level
Below

AREA 292,257 sq. mi.
POPULATION 8,834,820
CAPITAL Santiago
LARGEST CITY Santiago
HIGHEST POINT Ojos del Salado 22,572 ft.
MONETARY UNIT Chilean escudo
MAJOR LANGUAGE Spanish
MAJOR RELIGION Roman Catholicism

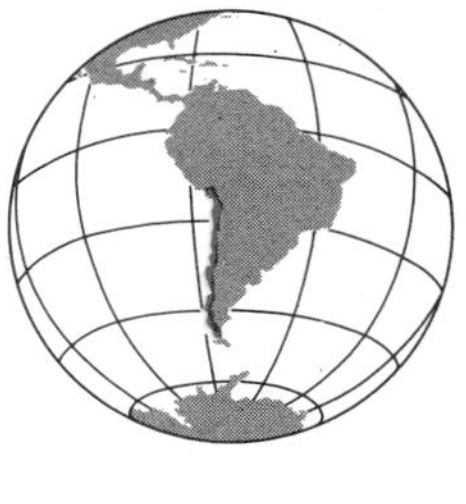

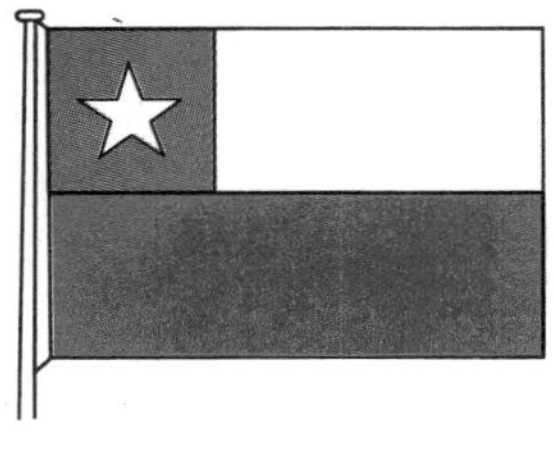

PROVINCES

Aconcagua, 160,821 ... A 9
Aisén, 51,022 ... D 6
Antofagasta, 250,665 ... B 4
Arauco, 98,810 ... D 1
Atacama, 152,326 ... B 6
Bío-Bío, 193,002 ... D 1
Cautín, 420,682 ... E 2
Chiloé, 110,728 ... D 4
Colchagua, 167,899 ... A10
Concepción, 638,118 ... D 1
Coquimbo, 336,821 ... A 8
Curicó, 113,710 ... A10
Linares, 189,010 ... A11
Llanquihue, 197,986 ... D 3
Magallanes, 88,706 ... E10
Malleco, 176,060 ... E 2
Maule, 82,339 ... A11
Ñuble, 314,738 ... E 1
O'Higgins, 306,739 ... A10
Osorno, 158,673 ... D 3
Santiago, 3,217,870 ... A 9
Talca, 231,088 ... A11
Tarapacá, 174,730 ... B 2
Valdivia, 275,404 ... D 3
Valparaíso, 726,953 ... A 9

CITIES and TOWNS

Achao, †11,501 ... D 4
Aculeo, 20 ... G 4
Aguas Blancas, †203 ... B 4
Aiquina, 105 ... B 3
Alcones, 682 ... F 5
Algarrobo, †3,941 ... F 3
Altamira, 93 ... B 5
Ancud, †22,127 ... D 4
Andacollo, †9,987 ... A 8
Angol, †35,995 ... D 1
Antofagasta, †126,252 ... A 4
Arauco, †20,018 ... D 1
Arica, †92,394 ... A 1
Ascotán, 23 ... B 3
Azapa, 225 ... A 1
Balmaceda, 735 ... E 6
Baquedano, 1,412 ... A 4
Barrancas, †184,241 ... G 3
Batuco, 1,125 ... G 3
Belén, †925 ... B 1
Boco, 1,655 ... F 2
Buin, †31,233 ... G 4
Bulnes, †16,107 ... E 1
Cabildo, †13,018 ... A 9
Calama, †71,983 ... B 3
Calbuco, †21,673 ... D 4
Caldera, †3,268 ... A 6
Calera de Tango, †6,198 ... G 4
Caleta Barquito, 932 ... A 6
Caleta Clarencia, 60 ... E10
Caleta Pan de Azúcar, 8 ... A 6
Caleu, 187 ... G 2
Calle Larga, †7,172 ... G 2
Calleuque ... F 5
Camarones, 259 ... B 2
Camiña, 234 ... B 2
Cañete, †15,179 ... D 2
Canto del Agua, 269 ... A 7
Capitán Pastene, 1,669 ... D 2
Carahue, †12,733 ... D 2
Carén, 225 ... A 8
Cariquima, 20 ... B 2
Carrera Pinto, 68 ... B 6
Carrizal Bajo, 207 ... A 7
Cartagena, †7,124 ... F 3
Casablanca, †12,292 ... F 3
Castro, †22,682 ... D 4
Catalina, †1,637 ... B 5
Catemu, †8,728 ... G 2
Cauquenes, †38,476 ... A11
Cerro Castillo, †537 ... E 9
Chaca, 37 ... B 1
Chacalluta, 75 ... A 1
Chaitén, †4,067 ... E 4
Chañaral, †36,949 ... A 6
Chanco, †12,433 ... A11
Chépica, †11,199 ... A10
Chile Chico, 1,926 ... E 6
Chillán, †102,361 ... A11
Chimbarongo, †17,592 ... A10
Choapa, 258 ... A 9
Chocalán, 187 ... F 4
Chonchi, †8,911 ... D 4
Chuquicamata, 24,798 ... B 3
Cobquecura, †6,298 ... D 1
Cochamó, †5,042 ... E 3
Codegua, †6,757 ... G 4
Codigua, 530 ... F 4
Codpa, †950 ... B 1
Coelemu, †11,967 ... D 1
Cogotí, 212 ... A 8
Coihaique, †24,032 ... E 6
Coihaique Alto, 24 ... E 6
Coihueco, †17,276 ... A11
Coinco, †4,942 ... G 5
Colbún, †12,924 ... A11
Colina, †18,058 ... G 3
Collaguasi, 8 ... B 3
Colliguay, 102 ... F 3
Collipulli, †15,058 ... E 2
Coltauco, †11,857 ... F 5
Combarbalá, †17,332 ... A 8
Concepción, †189,929 ... D 1
Conchi, 9 ... B 3
Conchi Viejo, 17 ... B 3
Concón, 5,381 ... F 2
Constitución, †23,543 ... A11
Contulmo, †13,987 ... D 2
Copiapó, †51,809 ... B 6
Coquimbo, †55,360 ... A 8
Coronel, †73,568 ... D 1
Corral, †5,533 ... D 3
Cruz Grande, 478 ... A 7
Cunco, †18,836 ... E 2
Cuncumén, Coquimbo, 1,052 ... A 9
Cuncumén, Santiago ... F 4
Curacautín, †15,862 ... E 2
Curacaví, †11,481 ... G 3
Curanilahue, †21,207 ... D 1
Curepto, †13,020 ... A10
Curicó, †59,621 ... A10
Cuya, 86 ... B 2
Dalcahue, †7,084 ... D 4
Domeyko, 1,814 ... A 7
Doñihue, †8,837 ... G 5
El Carmen, Ñuble, †13,226 ... A11
El Carmen, O'Higgins, 625 ... F 5
El Cobre, 7 ... A 4
El Convento, 733 ... F 4
El Manzano, 1,073 ... F 5
El Ñilhue, 341 ... G 1
El Olivar Alto, †5,414 ... G 5
El Quisco, †2,152 ... E 3
El Tabo, †2,180 ... F 3
El Tofo, 1,175 ... A 7
El Tránsito, 235 ... B 7
El Volcán, 250 ... B10
Empedrado, †7,887 ... A11
Ercilla, †8,061 ... E 2
Espejo, 3,481 ... G 3
Estancia Caleta Josefina, †1,042 ... F10
Estancia Laguna Blanca, 119 ... E 9
Estancia Morro Chico, †785 ... E 9
Estancia Punta Delgada, 233 ... E 9
Estancia San Gregorio, †1,156 ... E 9
Estancia Springhill (Manantiales), 291 ... F10
Freire, †23,313 ... E 2
Freirina, †5,523 ... A 7
Fresia, †15,359 ... D 3
Frutillar, †12,721 ... D 3
Fuerte Bulnes, 18 ... E10
Futaleufú, †2,366 ... E 4
Futrono, †7,109 ... E 3
Galvarino, †9,495 ... D 2
Gatico, 16 ... A 4
General Lagos, †810 ... B 1
Graneros, †13,523 ... G 5
Guayacán, 1,514 ... A 8
Hijuelas, †7,128 ... F 2
Hospital, 460 ... G 4
Huachipato, †16,336 ... D 1
Hualaihué, 391 ... E 4
Hualañé, †6,912 ... A10
Huara, †1,934 ... B 2
Huasco, †4,971 ... A 7
Huentelauquén, 355 ... A 8
Idahue, 1,832 ... F 5
Illapel, †20,660 ... A 8
Imalac, 27 ... B 4
Inca de Oro, 1,406 ... B 6
Iquique, †64,900 ... A 2
Isla de Maipo, †12,903 ... G 4
La Calera, †28,728 ... F 2
La Colonia, 41 ... D 7
La Cruz, †8,907 ... F 2
La Estrella, †3,707 ... F 5
La Higuera, †6,991 ... A 7
La Laguna, 316 ... F 2
La Ligua, †15,719 ... A 9
La Retuca, 173 ... F 3
La Serena, †71,898 ... A 8
La Unión, †32,010 ... D 3
Lago Ranco, †12,767 ... D 3
Lago Verde, 193 ... E 5
Lagunas, †5,653 ... B 3
Lagunillas, 468 ... F 3
Lampa, †10,220 ... G 3
Lanco, †14,479 ... D 2
Las Breas, 14 ... B 7
Las Cabras †12,119 ... F 5
Las Cruces, 612 ... F 3
Lautaro, †26,011 ... E 2
Lebu, †16,946 ... D 1
Licantén, †6,354 ... A10
Limache, †22,472 ... F 2
Linares, †61,011 ... A11
Llaillay, †14,074 ... G 2
Llico, 330 ... A10
Llolleo, 9,846 ... F 4
Lo Miranda, 2,270 ... G 5
Lo Ovalle, 129 ... F 3
Loica, 446 ... F 4
Loncoche, †17,539 ... D 2
Longaví, †15,909 ... A11
Lonquimay, †9,524 ... E 2
Los Andes, †30,408 ... B 9
Los Ángeles, †89,810 ... D 1
Los Lagos, †14,934 ... D 3
Los Loros, 269 ... A 6
Los Muermos, †9,296 ... D 3
Los Perales de Tapihue, 176 ... F 3
Los Sauces, †7,613 ... D 2
Los Vilos, †10,453 ... A 9
Lota, †51,548 ... D 1
Machalí, †28,415 ... G 5
Maipú, †117,872 ... G 3
Maitencillo, 31 ... A 8
Malloa, †9,742 ... G 5
Mamiña, 341 ... B 2
Manantiales, 291 ... F10
Manzanar, 248 ... F 2
Marchihue, †4,451 ... F 5
María Elena, 9,572 ... B 3
María Pinto, †5,980 ... G 3
Maullín, †14,544 ... D 4
Mayer, 29 ... E 7
Mejillones, †3,333 ... A 4
Melinca, 166 ... D 5
Melipilla, †49,306 ... F 4
Merceditas, 33 ... B 7
Mincha, †11,329 ... A 8
Molina, †30,398 ... A10
Montenegro, 327 ... G 2
Monte Patria, †18,927 ... A 8
Mulchén, †23,379 ... E 1
Nacimiento, †17,651 ... D 1
Nancagua, †11,076 ... F 6
Navidad, †6,618 ... A10
Negreiros, †1,144 ... B 2
Nilahue, 428 ... E 6
Ñiquén, †13,640 ... E 1
Nogales, †18,529 ... F 2
Nueva Imperial, †30,286 ... D 2
Nuevo Juncal, 2 ... B 5
Ocoa, 871 ... G 2
Ollagüe, 333 ... B 3
Olmué, †8,804 ... F 2
Osorno, †105,793 ... D 3
Ovalle, †53,433 ... A 8
Paihuano, †6,048 ... B 8
Paillaco, †13,612 ... D 3
Paine, †21,876 ... G 4
Paipote, 2,278 ... B 6
Palena, †2,508 ... E 5
Palestina, 7 ... B 4
Paliocabe, 77 ... F 4
Palmilla, †12,429 ... F 6
Panguipulli, †32,834 ... E 2
Panquehue, †4,230 ... G 2
Paposo, 87 ... A 5
Papudo, †2,594 ... A 9
Paredones, †7,404 ... A10
Parral, †30,427 ... A11
Pedro de Valdivia, 11,028 ... B 4
Pelequen, 1,068 ... G 5
Pemuco, †7,577 ... E 1
Peñablanca, 5,586 ... F 2
Peñaflor, †37,788 ... G 4
Penco, †33,962 ... D 1
Peñuelas, 359 ... F 3
Peralillo, †7,965 ... F 5
Petorca, †8,343 ... A 9
Petrohué, 40 ... E 3
Peuco, 211 ... G 4
Peumo, †11,308 ... F 5
Pica, †1,487 ... B 2
Pichidegua, †13,550 ... F 5
Pichilemu, †8,042 ... A10
Pintados, 144 ... B 2
Pinto, †8,687 ... A11
Pisagua, †1,880 ... A 2
Pitrufquén, †16,797 ... D 2
Placilla, †6,411 ... F 6
Placilla de Caracoles, 2 ... B 4
Placilla de Peñuelas, 1,495 ... F 2
Población, 1,026 ... F 5
Polonia ... G 6
Pomaire, 1,366 ... F 4
Porvenir, †3,600 ... E10
Potrerillos, 6,168 ... B 6
Pozo Almonte, †1,798 ... B 2
Puangue ... F 4
Pucatrihue, 60 ... D 3
Puchuncaví, †7,542 ... F 2
Pucón, †16,872 ... E 2
Pudahuel, 172 ... G 3
Pueblo Hundido, 2,123 ... B 6
Puente Alto, †81,031 ... B10
Puerto Aisén, †15,000 ... E 6
Puerto Bertrand, 52 ... E 7
Puerto Chacabuco, 130 ... D 6
Puerto Cisnes, †2,800 ... E 5
Puerto Cristal, 698 ... E 6
Puerto Ingeniero Ibáñez, †1,900 ... E 6
Puerto Montt, †86,750 ... E 4
Puerto Natales, †13,577 ... E 9
Puerto Palena, 105 ... D 5
Puerto Quellón, †7,734 ... D 4
Puerto Ramírez, 82 ... E 5
Puerto Saavedra, 805 ... D 2
Puerto Varas, †21,003 ... E 3
Puerto Williams, †949 ... F11
Puerto Yartou, 14 ... E10
Pumanque, †3,137 ... F 6
Punitaqui, †16,167 ... A 8
Punta Arenas, †64,958 ... E10
Punta de Díaz, 11 ... B 7
Puquios, 105 ... B 1
Purén, †11,604 ... D 2
Purranque, †18,201 ... D 3
Putaendo, †12,806 ... A 9
Putre, †855 ... B 1
Puyehue, 39 ... E 3
Quebrada de Alvarado, 429 ... F 2
Queilén, †6,055 ... D 4
Quemchi, †6,707 ... D 4
Queule, 235 ... D 2
Quilicura, †22,644 ... G 3
Quillagua, 288 ... B 3
Quillaicillo, 195 ... A 8
Quilleco, †16,043 ... E 1
Quillota, †49,202 ... F 2
Quilpué, †56,399 ... F 2
Quinta de Tilcoco, †6,513 ... G 5
Quintay, 166 ... F 3
Quintero, †11,847 ... F 2
Quirihue, †11,178 ... E 1
Rancagua, †95,030 ... G 5
Rapel, 699 ... F 4
Reñaca, 1,267 ... F 2
Renca, †67,168 ... G 3
Rengo, †28,230 ... G 5
Requegua, 1,699 ... G 5
Requíhoa, †10,730 ... G 5
Retiro, †15,146 ... A11
Rinconada San Martín, †4,118 ... G 2
Río Blanco, 456 ... B 9
Río Bueno, †28,469 ... D 3
Río Cisnes, 244 ... E 5
Río Negro, †15,582 ... D 3
Río Verde, †554 ... E10
Rivadavia, 443 ... A 7
Rocas de Santo Domingo, †4,114 ... F 4
Rolecha, 573 ... D 4
Rosario, †3,383 ... F 5
Rungue, 312 ... G 2
Salado, 1,375 ... A 6
Salamanca, †18,741 ... A 9
Salinas, 7 ... B 4
Samo Alto, †5,689 ... A 8
San Antonio, †53,100 ... F 3
San Bernardo, †117,766 ... G 4
San Carlos, †30,651 ... E 1
San Clemente, †23,273 ... A11
San Felipe, †34,292 ... G 2
San Félix, 495 ... A 7
Sán Fernando, †44,160 ... G 6
San Francisco de Mostazal, †11,439 ... G 4
San Francisco del Monte, †14,897 ... G 4
San Ignacio, †13,523 ... E 1
San Javier, †27,592 ... A11
San José de la Mariquina, 2,878 ... D 2
San José de Maipo, †9,601 ... B10
San Pablo, †7,978 ... D 3
San Pedro, Santiago, †8,255 ... F 4
San Pedro, Valparaíso, 1,420 ... F 2
San Pedro de Atacama, 515 ... C 4
San Rosendo, †14,337 ... E 1
San Sebastián, 494 ... F 3
San Vicente, 230 ... F 4
San Vicente (San Vicente de Tagua Tagua), †28,333 ... F 5
Santa Bárbara, †14,345 ... E 1
Santa Cruz, †19,338 ... F 6
Santa María, †8,162 ... G 2
Santiago (capital), 2,596,929 ... G 3
Sewell, 10,866 ... A10
Sierra Gorda, †8,805 ... B 4
Talagante, †23,619 ... G 4
Talca, †102,522 ... A11
Talcahuano, †150,011 ... D 1
Taltal, †7,417 ... A 5
Tamaya, 248 ... A 8
Tarapacá, 130 ... B 2
Temuco, †146,039 ... E 2
Teno, †17,675 ... A10
Termas de Cauquenes, 210 ... B10
Tierra Amarilla, †6,842 ... A 6
Tignamar, 226 ... B 1
Tilomonte, 3 ... B 4
Tiltil, †9,198 ... G 2
Tinguiririca, 1,012 ... G 6
Toco, †8,734 ... B 3
Toconao, 452 ... C 4
Tocopilla, †22,301 ... A 3
Toltén, †16,265 ... D 2
Tomé, †44,480 ... D 1
Tongoy, 935 ... A 8
Totoral, 109 ... A 6
Traiguén, †21,084 ... D 2
Valdivia, †90,942 ... D 3
Valle Alegre, 241 ... F 2
Vallenar, †41,907 ... A 7
Valparaíso, †251,459 ... E 2
Victoria, Malleco, †28,382 ... E 2
Victoria, Tarapacá, 4,943 ... B 3
Vicuña, †13,806 ... A 8
Villa Alemana, †37,547 ... F 2
Villa Alhué, †5,078 ... G 4
Villa Industrial, 28 ... B 1
Villarrica, †23,924 ... E 2
Viña del Mar, †184,332 ... F 2
Yumbel, †21,858 ... E 1
Yungay, †10,725 ... E 1
Zapallar, †2,894 ... A 9

OTHER FEATURES

Aconcagua (river) ... F 2
Aculeo (lagoon) ... G 4
Adventure (bay) ... D 5
Aguas Calientes (mt.) ... C 4
Alhué (river) ... F 4
Almirantazgo (bay) ... F11
Almeida (mts.) ... C 4
Almirante Montt (gulf) ... D 9
Alto Nevado (mt.) ... E 5
Ancho (channel) ... D 8
Ancud (gulf) ... D 4
Angamos (isl.) ... D 8
Angamos (point) ... A 4
Ap Iwan (mt.) ... E 6
Arauco (gulf) ... D 1
Arenales (mt.) ... D 7
Ascotán (salt deposit) ... B 3
Atacama (desert) ... B 4
Atacama (salt deposit) ... C 4
Aucanquilcha (mt.) ... B 3
Azapa (river) ... B 1
Baker (river) ... D 7
Ballenero (channel) ... E11
Barrancos (mt.) ... D 7
Bascuñán (cape) ... A 7
Beagle (channel) ... E11
Bella Vista (salt deposit) ... B 3
Benjamín (isl.), 16 ... D 5
Bertrand (mt.) ... D 8
Bío-Bío (river) ... E 2
Blanca (lagoon) ... E10
Blanco (lake) ... F10
Bravo (river) ... D 7
Brunswick (pen.) ... E10

(continued on following page)

Agriculture, Industry and Resources

DOMINANT LAND USE

- Cereals, Livestock
- Mediterranean Agriculture (cereals, fruit, livestock)
- Pasture Livestock
- Extensive Livestock Ranching
- Limited Seasonal Grazing
- Forests
- Nonagricultural Land

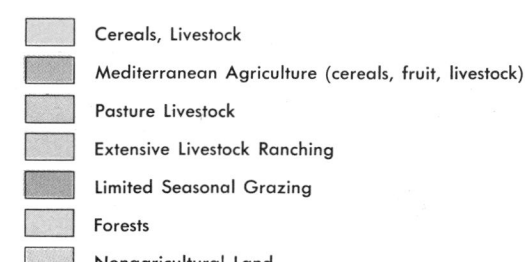

MAJOR MINERAL OCCURRENCES

Ag	Silver	Hg	Mercury
Au	Gold	Id	Iodine
C	Coal	Mn	Manganese
Cu	Copper	Mo	Molybdenum
Fe	Iron Ore	N	Nitrates
G	Natural Gas	Na	Salt
Gp	Gypsum	O	Petroleum
		S	Sulfur

⚡ Water Power   ▧ Major Industrial Areas

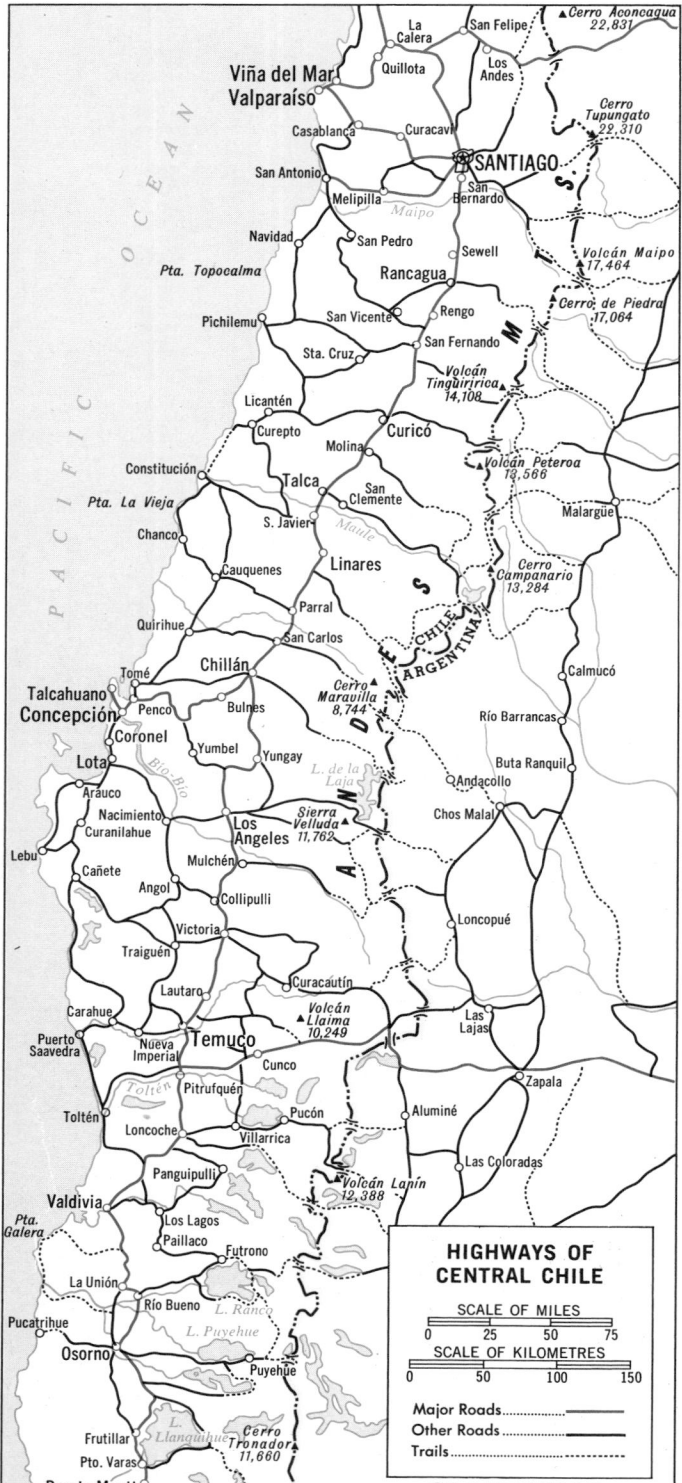

HIGHWAYS OF CENTRAL CHILE

SCALE OF MILES
0   25   50   75

SCALE OF KILOMETRES
0   50   100   150

Major Roads ————
Other Roads ---------
Trails ··········

© C. S. HAMMOND & Co.

VALPARAÍSO
Textiles, Chemicals, Metal Products, Oil Refining

SANTIAGO
Food Processing, Textiles & Clothing, Leather Goods, Chemicals

CONCEPCIÓN
Iron & Steel, Food Processing, Textiles, Oil Refining

PROVINCES

Buenos Aires, 6,734,548 ....D 4
Catamarca, 172,407 ....C 2
Chaco, 535,443 ....D 2
Chubut, 142,195 ....C 5
Córdoba, 1,759,997 ....D 3
Corrientes, 543,226 ....E 2
Distrito Federal (fed. dist.), 2,966,816 ....H 7
Entre Ríos, 803,505 ....E 3
Formosa, 178,458 ....D 1
Jujuy, 239,783 ....C 1
La Pampa, 158,489 ....C 4
La Rioja, 128,270 ....C 2
Mendoza, 825,535 ....C 4
Misiones, 391,094 ....F 2
Neuquén, 111,008 ....C 4
Río Negro, 192,595 ....C 5
Salta, 412,652 ....D 1
San Juan, 352,461 ....C 3
San Luis, 174,251 ....C 3
Santa Cruz, 52,853 ....C 6
Santa Fe, 1,865,537 ....D 3
Santiago del Estero, 477,156 ....D 2
Tierra del Fuego, Antártida e Islas del Atlántico Sur (terr.), 13,452 ....C 7
Tucumán, 780,348 ....C 2

CITIES and TOWNS

Abra Pampa, 1,391 ....C 1
Acebal, 2,026 ....F 6
Acevedo. 1.057 ....F 6
Acuña, 805 ....G 5
Adolfo Alsina, 5,836 ....D 4
Aguilares, 9,816 ....C 2
Aimogasta, 2,721 ....C 2
Alberti, 4,447 ....G 7
Alcaraz, 376 ....G 5
Alcorta, 3,781 ....F 6
Alejandra, 881 ....F 5
Allen, 11,389 ....C 4
Alpachiri, 733 ....D 4
Alta Gracia, 11,570 ....D 3
Aluminé, 744 ....B 4
Alvear, 4,252 ....E 2
Ameghino, 2,770 ....D 3
Aminga, 480 ....C 2
Añatuya, 11,753 ....D 2
Anchorena, 862 ....C 4
Andacollo, 587 ....B 4
Andalgalá, 3,260 ....C 2
Angélica, 434 ....E 5
Anguil, 734 ....D 4
Antofagasta de la Sierra, 462 ....C 2
Apóstoles, 6,507 ....E 2
Arrecifes, 7,635 ....F 6
Arribeños, 1,739 ....F 7
Arroyo Seco, 5,193 ....F 6
Ascensión, 1,775 ....F 7
Astra, 1,019 ....C 6
Avellaneda, †329,626 ....G 7
Ayacucho, 9,220 ....E 4
Azul, 28,609 ....E 4
Bahía Blanca, †150,354 ....D 4
Bahía Thetis, †438 ....C 7
Baibiene, 380 ....G 4
Baigorrita, 1,206 ....F 7
Balcarce, 15,210 ....E 4
Balnearia, 4,306 ....D 3
Bañado de Ovanta, 198 ....C 2
Bandera, 2,035 ....D 2
Baradero, 10,194 ....G 6
Barrancas, 1,953 ....F 6
Barranqueras, 19,779 ....E 2
Barreal, 1,790 ....C 3
Basavilbaso, 6,614 ....G 6
Batavia, 457 ....C 3
Beazley, 1,070 ....C 3
Belén, 5,469 ....C 2
Bella Vista, Corrientes, 8,334 ....E 2
Bella Vista, Tucumán, 6,816 ......D 2
Bell Ville, 15,796 ....D 3
Bernardo de Irigoyen, 1,400........F 2
Bolívar, 14,010 ....D 4
Bovril, 1,955 ....G 5
Bragado, 16,104 ....F 7
Buenos Aires (capital), 3,549,000 ....H 7
Buenos Aires, *9,070,000 ....H 7
Bustinza, 918 ....F 6
Cachi, 491 ....C 2
Cafayate, 2,407 ....C 2
Calchaqui, 2,782 ....F 5
Caleta Olivia, 3,639 ....C 6
Caleufú, 1,197 ....D 4
Camarones, 501 ....D 5
Campana, 14,452 ....G 6
Campo Gallo, 2,336 ....D 2
Cañada de Gómez, 12,354 ....F 6
Cañada Honda, 345 ....C 3
Canals, 5,359 ....D 3
Cañuelas, 5,614 ....G 7
Carabelas, 3,476 ....F 6
Carcaraña, 4,516 ....F 6
Carlos Casares, 7,558 ....F 7
Carlos Tejedor, 2,897 ....D 4
Carmen de Areco, 4,411 ....F 7
Carmen de Patagones, 5,423 ....D 5
Caseros, 4,975 ....D 4
Casilda, 11,023 ....F 6
Castelli, Buenos Aires, 3,263 .....H 7
Castelli, Chaco, 4,131 ....D 2
Catamarca, 45,929 ....C 2
Catriló, 1,794 ....D 4
Cayasta, 592 ....F 5
Cayastacito, 483 ....F 5
Cereales, 367 ....D 4
Ceres, 6,525 ....D 2
Chabas, 2,937 ....F 6
Chacabuco, 12,530 ....F 7
Chajarí, 9,075 ....G 5
Chamical, 3,756 ....C 3
Charadai, 1,872 ....D 2
Charata, 8,953 ....D 2
Chascomús, 9,105 ....H 7
Chepes, 2,941 ....C 3
Chicoana, 1,093 ....C 2
Chilecito, 9,809 ....C 2
Chivilcoy, 23,386 ....F 7
Choele-Choel, 3,079 ....C 4
Chos Malal, 2,874 ....C 4
Chumbicha, 2,188 ....C 2
Cinco Saltos, 10,196 ....C 4
Cipolletti, 19,862 ....C 4
Clarke, 506 ....F 6
Clodomira, 4,685 ....D 2
Clorinda, 10,043 ....E 2
Colón, Buenos Aires, 5,628 ....F 6

AREA 1,072,070
POPULATION 23,983,000
CAPITAL Buenos Aires
LARGEST CITY Buenos Aires
HIGHEST POINT Cerro Aconcagua 22,831 ft.
MONETARY UNIT Argentine peso
MAJOR LANGUAGE Spanish
MAJOR RELIGION Roman Catholicism

Agriculture, Industry and Resources

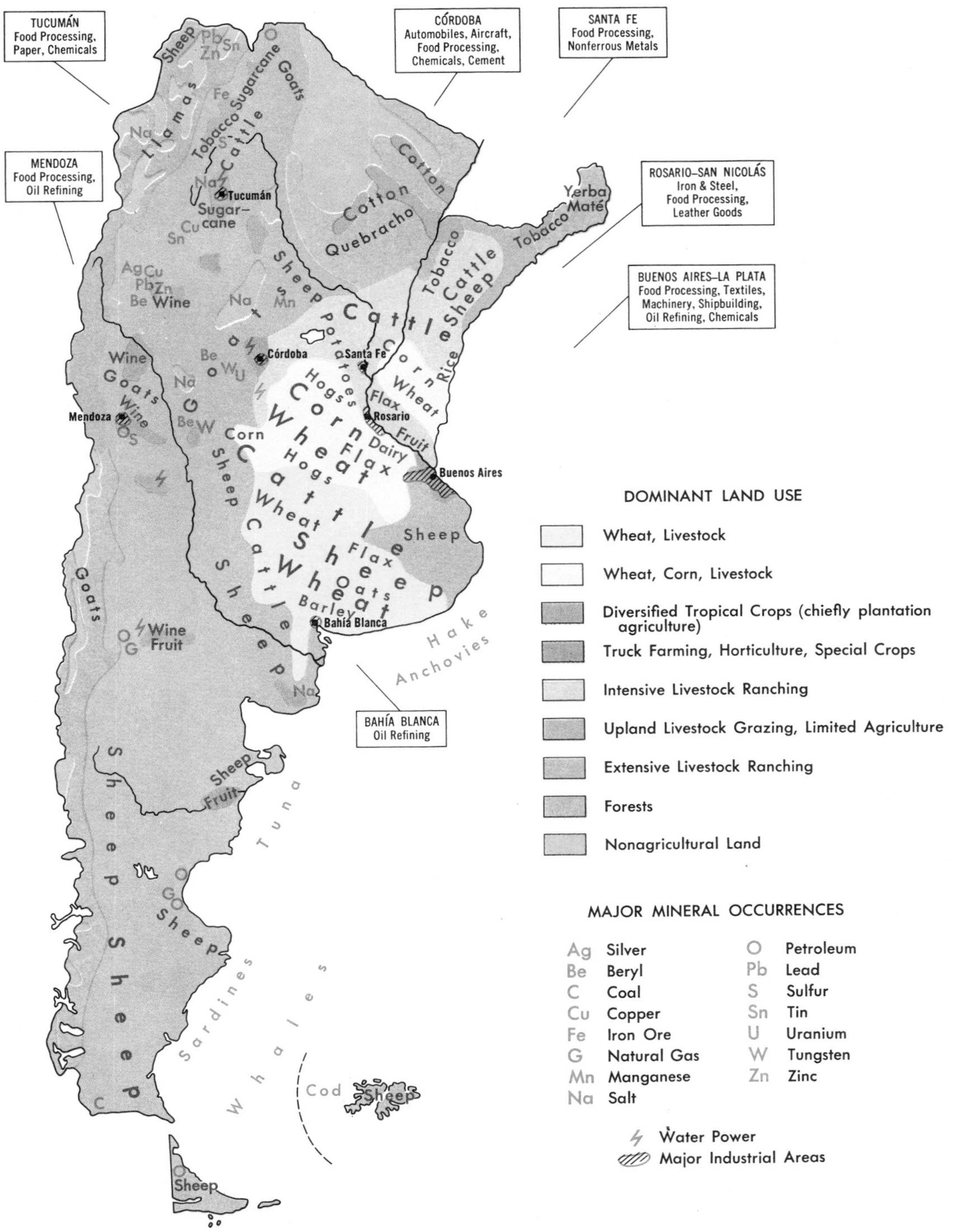
TUCUMÁN
Food Processing, Paper, Chemicals
CÓRDOBA
Automobiles, Aircraft, Food Processing, Chemicals, Cement
SANTA FE
Food Processing, Nonferrous Metals
MENDOZA
Food Processing, Oil Refining
ROSARIO–SAN NICOLÁS
Iron & Steel, Food Processing, Leather Goods
BUENOS AIRES–LA PLATA
Food Processing, Textiles, Machinery, Shipbuilding, Oil Refining, Chemicals
BAHÍA BLANCA
Oil Refining
Tucumán
Córdoba
Santa Fe
Rosario
Mendoza
Buenos Aires
Bahía Blanca
Llamas
Tobacco
Sugarcane
Sugar-cane
Cattle
Goats
Cotton
Quebracho
Yerba Maté
Tobacco
Sheep
Wine
Potatoes
Hogs
Corn
Wheat
Flax
Dairy
Fruit
Rice
Oats
Barley
Hake
Anchovies
Tuna
Sardines
Whales
Cod
DOMINANT LAND USE
Wheat, Livestock
Wheat, Corn, Livestock
Diversified Tropical Crops (chiefly plantation agriculture)
Truck Farming, Horticulture, Special Crops
Intensive Livestock Ranching
Upland Livestock Grazing, Limited Agriculture
Extensive Livestock Ranching
Forests
Nonagricultural Land
MAJOR MINERAL OCCURRENCES
Ag Silver
Be Beryl
C Coal
Cu Copper
Fe Iron Ore
G Natural Gas
Mn Manganese
Na Salt
O Petroleum
Pb Lead
S Sulfur
Sn Tin
U Uranium
W Tungsten
Zn Zinc
Water Power
Major Industrial Areas

Colón, Entre Ríos, 6,813 ....G 6
Colonia Elisa, 1,338 ....E 2
Colonia Las Heras, 1,880 ....C 6
Comandante Fontana, 1,686 ....D 2
Comandante Luis Piedrabuena, 1,441 ....C 6
Comodoro Rivadavia, 35,966 ......C 6
Concepción, Corrientes, 2,593 ....E 2
Concepción, Tucumán, 15,832 .....C 2
Concepción del Uruguay, 36,486 ....G 6
Concordia, 56,654 ....G 5
Copacabana, 957 ....C 2
Córdoba, †589,153 ....D 3
Coronda, 4,656 ....F 6
Coronel Bogado, 1,264 ....F 6
Coronel Brandsen, 3,803 ....H 7
Coronel Dorrego, 7,245 ....D 4
Coronel Moldes, 1,695 ....C 2
Coronel Pringles, 12,844 ....D 4
Coronel Suárez, 11,133 ....D 4
Corral de Bustos, 3,900 ....D 3
Corrientes, 97,507 ....E 2
Cosquín, 7,746 ....D 3
Crespo, 5,706 ....F 6
Cruz del Eje, 15,563 ....C 3
Cuadro Nacional, 1,879 ....C 3
Curuzú Cuatiá, 16,567 ....G 5
Cutral-Có, 11,292 ....C 4
Deán Funes, 13,840 ....D 3
Del Carril, 475 ....G 7
Diamante, 10,948 ....F 6
Díaz, 1,288 ....F 6
Doblas, 902 ....D 4
Dolavón, 1,277 ....C 5
Dolores, 14,438 ....E 4
Dudignac, 1,503 ....F 7
Eduardo Castex, 4,020 ....D 4
El Bolsón, 2,607 ....B 5
El Calafate, 567 ....B 7
El Chorro, 377 ....D 1
Eldorado, 2,778 ....F 2
El Huecu, 298 ....B 4
Elisa, 579 ....F 5
El Maitén, 2,382 ....B 5
Elortondo, 3,514 ....F 6
El Pintado, 388 ....D 1
El Quebrachal, 1,212 ....D 2
Embárcación, 6,371 ....D 1
Emilio Ayarza, 1,357 ....F 7
Empedrado, 3,735 ....E 2
Enrique Carbó, 956 ....G 6
Ensenada, †35,030 ....H 7
Escobar, 3,693 ....G 7
Esperanza, 10,035 ....F 5
Esquel, 9,900 ....B 5
Esquina, 7,619 ....G 5
Famatina, 1,330 ....C 2
Federación, 4,247 ....G 5
Fernández, 3,115 ....D 2
Fiambalá, 1,450 ....C 2
Firmat, 4,051 ....F 6
Fives Lille, 667 ....F 5
Formosa, 36,499 ....E 2
French, 4,007 ....F 7
Frías, 11,862 ....D 2
Gaiman, 1,286 ....C 5
Gálvez, 2,475 ....F 6
Gálvez, 7,891 ....F 6
Gan Gan, 281 ....C 5
General Acha, 4,709 ....C 4
General Alvarado, 3,537 ....E 4
General Alvear, Buenos Aires, 2,548 ....F 7
General Alvear, Mendoza, 12,325 ....C 3
General Arenales, 2,182 ....F 7
General Belgrano, 3,789 ....G 7
General Campos, 1,400 ....G 5
General Conesa, 716 ....C 5
General Galarza, 2,435 ....G 6
General Juan Madariaga, 7,073 ....E 4
General José de San Martín, 5,390 ....E 2
General La Madrid, 3,572 ....D 4
General Las Heras, 3,820 ....G 7
General Lavalle, 1,663 ....E 4
Gral. M. M. de Güemes, 8,748....D 1
General O'Brien, 2,988 ....F 7
General Paz, 1,689 ....E 2
General Pico, 11,121 ....D 4
General Roca, 21,969 ....C 4
General San-Martín, 2,501 ....D 4
General Villegas, 4,738 ....D 4
Gobernador Crespo, 6,000 ....F 5
Gobernador Gregores, 772 ....C 6
Gobernador Mansilla, 947 ....G 6
Godoy Cruz, 80,024 ....C 3
Goya, 30,011 ....G 4
Gualeguay, 16,542 ....G 6
Gualeguaychú, 29,863 ....G 6
Guandacol, 1,255 ....C 2
Guardia Mitre, 746 ....D 5
Guatrache, 1,259 ....D 4
Guaymallén, 85,718 ....C 3
Hasenkamp, 1,789 ....F 5
Helvecia, 3,390 ....F 5
Hernández, 283 ....F 6
Hernando, 4,869 ....D 3
Herradura, 1,679 ....E 2
Herrera, 1,685 ....D 2
Huinca Renancó, 4,391 ....D 3
Humahuaca, 2,530 ....C 1
Humberto, 3,434 ....F 5
Ibarreta, 4,366 ....D 2
Ibicuy, 3,356 ....G 6
Icaño, Catamarca, 1,114 ....C 2
Icaño, Santiago del Estero, 1,926 ....D 2
Iglesia, 575 ....C 3
Ingeniero Huergo, 3,083 ....C 4
Ingeniero Jacobacci, 2,656 ....C 5
Ingeniero Luiggi, 1,665 ....D 4
Intendente Alvear, 2,760 ....D 4
Irigoyen, 3,500 ....F 6
Itacaruaré, 422 ....F 2
Jáchal, 6,886 ....C 3
Jaramillo, 437 ....C 6
Jesús María, 6,284 ....D 3
Joaquín V. González, 3,274 ....D 2
Jobson, 7,667 ....F 5
José de San Martín, 1,143 ....B 5
José M. Micheo, 1,165 ....G 7
Juan B. Arruabarrena, 1,997 ....G 5
Juan B. Molino, 1,483 ....F 6
Juan Ortíz, 6,240 ....F 6
Juan Pujol, 625 ....G 5
Juárez, 7,602 ....D 4
Jujuy, 44,188 ....C 1
Juncal, 943 ....F 6
Junín, 36,149 ....F 7
Junín de los Andes, 1,183 ....B 4
La Banda, 23,772 ....D 2
Labougle, 503 ....G 5
Laboulaye, 9,032 ....D 3
La Clarita, 389 ....G 5
La Cumbre, 3,961 ....C 3
La Esmeralda, 348 ....G 5
La Falda, 2,847 ....D 3
La Gallareta, 3,736 ....F 5
Lago Argentino (El Calafate), 567 ....B 7
Laguna Paiva, 7,196 ....F 5
Lanús, 381,561 ....H 7
La Paz, Entre Ríos, 11,028 ....G 5
La Paz, Mendoza, 2,502 ....C 3
La Plata, †330,310 ....H 7
La Quiaca, 6,290 ....C 1
La Rioja, 35,431 ....C 2
Las Flores, 9,287 ....E 4
Las Lajas, 1,805 ....B 4
Las Lomitas, 1,650 ....D 1
Las Palmas, 3,590 ....E 2
Las Parejas, 1,973 ....F 6
Las Plumas, 182 ....C 5
Las Rosas, 6,153 ....F 6
Las Varillas, 5,950 ....D 3
La Toma, 2,352 ....C 3
Lavalle, 1,571 ....G 4
Leleque, 401 ....B 5
Lezama, 1,962 ....H 7
Libertador General San Martín, Jujuy, 5,051 ....D 1
Libertador General San Martín, Misiones, 2,267 ....E 2
Lincoln, 12,695 ....F 7
Lobería, 7,916 ....E 4
Lobos, 8,372 ....G 7
Lomas de Zamora, †275,219 ....G 7
Loncopué, 856 ....B 4
Los Antiguos, 709 ....B 6
Los Menucos, 1,749 ....C 5
Los Toldos, 5,342 ....F 7
Lucas González, 1,145 ....G 6
Luján, 19,176 ....G 7
Lules, 4,828 ....C 2
Macachín, 1,793 ....D 4
Maciel, 1,832 ....F 6
Magdalena, 4,114 ....H 7
Maipú, 5,469 ....E 4
Makallé, 1,462 ....E 2
Malabrigo, 1,532 ....F 4
Malargüe, 4,523 ....C 4
Manucho, 2,800 ....F 5
Maquinchao, 1,851 ....C 5
Mar del Plata, 141,886 ....E 4
Marcos Juárez, 9,556 ....D 3
Marcos Paz, 4,115 ....G 7
Margarita, 1,461 ....F 5
María Grande, 2,819 ....F 5
Mburucuyá, 2,555 ....E 2
Médanos, Buenos Aires, 2,229 ....D 4
Médanos, Entre Ríos, 647 ....G 6
Mencué, 208 ....C 5
Mendoza, 109,122 ....C 3
Mercedes, Buenos Aires, 16,932 ....G 7

(continued on following page)

(continued)

Mercedes, Corrientes, 13,368 .....G 4
Mercedes, San Luis, 35,449 ....C 3
Merlo, 8,385 .....G 7
Metán, 12,849 .....D 2
Milagro, 1,967 .....C 3
Miñones, 204 .....G 5
Miramar (General Alvarado), 3,537 .....E 4
Moisés Ville, 3,166 .....E 5
Molinos, 174 .....C 2
Monte, 2,491 .....G 7
Monte Caseros, 12,930 .....G 5
Monte Comán, 4,278 .....C 3
Monte Quemado, 4,083 .....D 2
Monteros, 11,938 .....C 2
Morteros, 5,993 .....D 3
Mosconi, 333 .....F 7
Naré, 346 .....F 5
Navarro, 2,547 .....G 7
Necochea, 17,808 .....E 4
Nelson, 866 .....F 5
Neuquén, 16,738 .....C 4
Niquivil, 1,301 .....C 3
Nogoyá, 10,911 .....F 6
Norberto de la Riestra, 2,809 .....G 7
Ñorquincó, 602 .....B 5
Nueve (9) de Julio, 13,678 .....F 7
Obera, 12,322 .....F 2
Olavarría, 24,204 .....D 4
Oliva, 8,701 .....D 3
Olta, 1,226 .....C 3
Orán, 14,286 .....D 1
Ordoqui, 402 .....F 7
Palo Santo, 1,123 .....E 2
Pampa del Chañar, 1,521 .....C 2
Pampa del Infierno, 1,261 .....D 2
Paraná, 107,551 .....F 5
Paso de Indios, 1,067 .....C 5
Paso de los Libres, 15,054 .....E 2
Patquía, 839 .....C 3
Paz, 2,495 .....F 6
Pedernal, 250 .....G 5
Pehuajó, 13,537 .....D 4
Pellegrini, 2,310 .....D 4
Pérez, 3,433 .....F 6
Pergamino, 32,382 .....F 6
Perito Moreno, 1,587 .....B 6
Perugorria 1,110 .....G 4
Pico Truncado, 1,527 .....C 6
Pigüé, 5,869 .....D 4
Pila, 1,009 .....H 7
Pilar, 2,508 .....F 5
Pipinas, 658 .....H 7
Pirané, 5,285 .....E 2
Plaza Huincul, 4,906 .....B 4
Pomán, 1,100 .....C 2
Posadas, 70,691 .....E 2
Pozo Hondo, 872 .....D 2
Presidencia de la Plaza, 4,568 .....D 2
Presidencia Roque Sáenz Peña, 14,381 .....D 2
Puán, 3,191 .....D 4
Puerto Coyle, 251 .....C 7
Puerto Deseado, 3,120 .....D 6
Puerto Madryn, 5,586 .....C 5
Puerto Pirámides, 425 .....D 5
Punta Alta, 19,852 .....D 4
Quebracho Coto. 271 .....D 2
Quemú-Quemú, 2,735 .....D 4
Quequén, 4,760 .....E 4
Quimilí, 2,902 .....D 2
Quines, 3,319 .....C 3
Quiroga, 1,827 .....F 7
Quitilipi, 5,217 .....D 2
Rafaela, 23,665 .....F 5
Raíces, 452 .....G 6
Ramallo, 4,824 .....F 6
Ranchos, 2,475 .....H 7
Rauch, 5,274 .....E 4
Rawson, Buenos Aires, 2,425.....F 7
Rawson, Chubut, 4,109 .....D 5
Reconquista, 12,729 .....D 2
Recreo, 2,834 .....C 2
Resistencia, 84,036 .....E 2
Rigby, 737 .....F 6
Rinconada, 782 .....C 1
Río Colorado, Río Negro, 5,892 .....D 4
Río Cuarto, 48,706 .....D 3
Río Gallegos, 14,439 .....C 7
Río Grande, 5,103 .....C 7
Río Segundo, 5,873 .....D 3
Río Tercero, 10,683 .....D 3
Rivadavia, Mendoza, 14,358 .....C 3
Rivadavia, Salta, 215 .....D 1
Rivas, 429 .....G 7
Rojas, 6,608 .....F 7
Roldán, 3,402 .....F 6
Romang, 1,906 .....F 4
Roque Pérez, 2,841 .....G 7
Rosario, †671,852 .....F 6
Rosario de la Frontera, 7,134 .....D 2
Rosario de Lerma, 4,241 .....C 1
Rosario del Tala, 7,350 .....G 6
Rufino, 10,987 .....D 3
Saforcada, 146 .....F 7
Saladas, 3,883 .....E 2
Saladillo, 7,586 .....G 7
Salta, 117,400 .....C 1
San Andrés de Giles, 5,392 .....G 7
San Antonio de Areco, 7,436 .....G 7
San Antonio de los Cobres, 1,439 .....C 1
San Antonio Oeste, 5,278 .....C 5
San Carlos, Corrientes, 1,858 .....E 2
San Carlos, Mendoza, 809 .....C 3
San Carlos, Santa Fe, 3,126 .....F 5
San Carlos de Bariloche, 15,995 .....B 5
San Cristóbal, 9,071 .....F 5
San Fernando, †91,644 .....G 7
San Francisco, Córdoba, 24,354 .....D 3
San Francisco, San Luis, 1,864.....C 3
San Francisco del Chañar, 817.....C 2
San Genaro, 1,522 .....F 6
San Ignacio, 2,106 .....E 2
San Isidro, 2,271 .....C 2
San Javier, Río Negro, 370.....D 5
San Javier, Santa Fe, 2,961 .....F 5
San José, 2,188 .....G 6
San José de Feliciano, 3,721 .....G 5
San Juan, 106,564 .....C 3
San Julián, 3,649 .....C 6
San Justo, 6,571 .....F 5
San Lorenzo, 11,109 .....F 6
San Luis, 40,420 .....C 3
San Martín, 20,466 .....C 3
San Martín de los Andes, 4,567 .....C 5
San Martín Norte, 485 .....F 5
San Miguel, 1,300 .....E 2
San Nicolás. 25,029 .....G 6
San Pedro, Buenos Aires, 12,778 .....F 6
San Pedro, Jujuy, 15,354 .....D 1
San Rafael, 46,599 .....C 3
San Salvador, 2,108 .....G 5
San Sebastián, †3,154 .....C 7
Santa Catalina, 331 .....C 1
Santa Clara, 3,700 .....F 6
Santa Cruz, 1,178 .....C 7
Santa Elena, 8,174 .....F 5
Santa Fe, †259,560 .....F 5
Santa Lucia, Buenos Aires, 1,831 .....F 6
Santa Lucia, Corrientes, 2,930 ...E 2
Santa María, 2,826 .....C 2
Santa Rosa, Córdoba, 2,999 .....D 3
Santa Rosa, La Pampa, 14,623.....C 4
Santa Rosa, San Luis, 2,880 .....C 3
Santa Victoria, 165 .....D 1
Santiago del Estero, 80,395.....D 2
Santo Tomé, Corrientes, 10,121 .....E 2
Santo Tomé Santa Fe, 4,446 .....F 5
San Urbano, 1,721 .....F 6
Sarmiento, 4,922 .....B 6
Sauce, 3,448 .....G 5
Sauce Luna, 501 .....G 5
Seguí, 2,161 .....G 6
Selva, 1,070 .....D 2
Sierra Colorada, 541 .....C 5
Sierra Grande, 512 .....C 5
Solari, 1,636 .....G 4
Soledad, 794 .....F 5
Suipacha, 3,006 .....G 7
Sunchales, 5,048 .....F 5
Suncho Corral, 2,693 .....D 2
Susana, 484 .....F 5
Susques, 537 .....C 1
Tafí Viejo, 21.197 .....C 2
Tamberías, 1,129 .....C 3
Tandil, 32,309 .....E 4
Tapalquén, 3,018 .....E 4
Tartagal, 16,740 .....D 1
Telsen, 490 .....C 5
Tigre, †91,824 .....G 7
Tilcara, 1,675 .....C 1
Tinogasta, 3,557 .....C 2
Tintina, 1,500 .....D 2
Toay, 2,457 .....D 4
Tornquist, 2,782 .....D 4
Tostado, 5,234 .....D 2
Trelew, 11,852 .....C 5
Trenel, 1,206 .....D 4
Trenque Lauquen, 10,887 .....D 4
Tres Arroyos, 29,996 .....D 4
Tres Lomas, 3,425 .....D 4
Trevelín, 1,642 .....B 5
Tricao Malal, 370 .....C 4
Tucumán, 271,546 .....D 2
Tunuyán, 9,781 .....C 3
Ulapes, 438 .....C 3
Unión, 630 .....C 3
Urdinarrain, 3,484 .....G 6
Ushuaia, 4,950 .....C 7
Valcheta, 1,697 .....C 5
Valle Fértil, 1,293 .....C 3
Vedia, 3,676 .....F 7
Veinticinco (25) de Mayo, 9,063 ..F 7
Venado Tuerto, 15,947 .....D 3
Vergara, 1,077 .....H 7
Verónica, 2,405 .....H 7
Victoria, 15,108 .....F 6
Victorica, 2,475 .....C 4
Vicuña Mackenna, 3,032 .....D 3
Viedma, 7,253 .....D 5
Villa Ana, 5,413 .....E 2
Villa Ángela, 18,518 .....D 2
Villa Atamisqui, 1,122 .....D 2
Villa Atuel, 6,072 .....C 3
Villa Bustos, 1,314 .....C 2
Villa Cañas, 7,099 .....F 6
Villa Clara, 1,557 .....G 5
Villa Constitución, 9,183 .....F 6
Villa del Rosario, 4,461 .....D 3
Villa Dolores, 13,835 .....C 2
Villa Domínguez, 984 .....G 6
Villa Elisa, 2,715 .....G 6
Villa Federal, 5,256 .....G 5
Villa General Ramírez, 3,203 .....F 6
Villa General Roca, 325 .....C 3
Villaguay, 12,463 .....G 5
Villa Guillermina, 7,471 .....D 2
Villa Hernandarias, 2,788 .....F 5
Villalonga, 392 .....D 5
Villa Larroque, 1,993 .....G 6
Villa Mantero, 989 .....G 6
Villa María, 30,362 .....D 3
Villa Ocampo, 4,897 .....D 2
Villa Ojo de Agua, 1,505 .....D 2
Villa Regina, 11,360 .....C 4
Villa San Martín, 3,354 .....D 2
Villa Unión, 1,696 .....C 2
Vinchina, 395 .....C 2
Winifreda, 1,063 .....D 4
Yacimiento Río Turbio, 3,506 .....B 7
Yofré, 826 .....G 4
Zapala, 7,497 .....B 4
Zárate, 35,197 .....G 6
Zavalla, 1,799 .....F 6

OTHER FEATURES

Aconcagua (mt.) .....C 3
Alerces, Los (park) .....C 5
Andes (mts.) .....C 2
Argentino (lake) .....B 7
Arizaro (salt dep.) .....C 2
Arrecifes (river) .....G 6
Atacama, Puna de (reg.) .....C 2
Atuel (river) .....C 4
Barrancas (river) .....G 5
Bermejo (river) .....E 2
Blanca (bay) .....D 4
Brazo Sur (river) .....E 1
Buenos Aires (lake) .....B 6
Campanario (mt.) .....C 4
Chaco Austral (reg.) .....D 2
Chaco Central (reg.) .....D 1
Chato (mt.) .....B 5
Chico (river) .....C 5
Chico (river) .....C 6

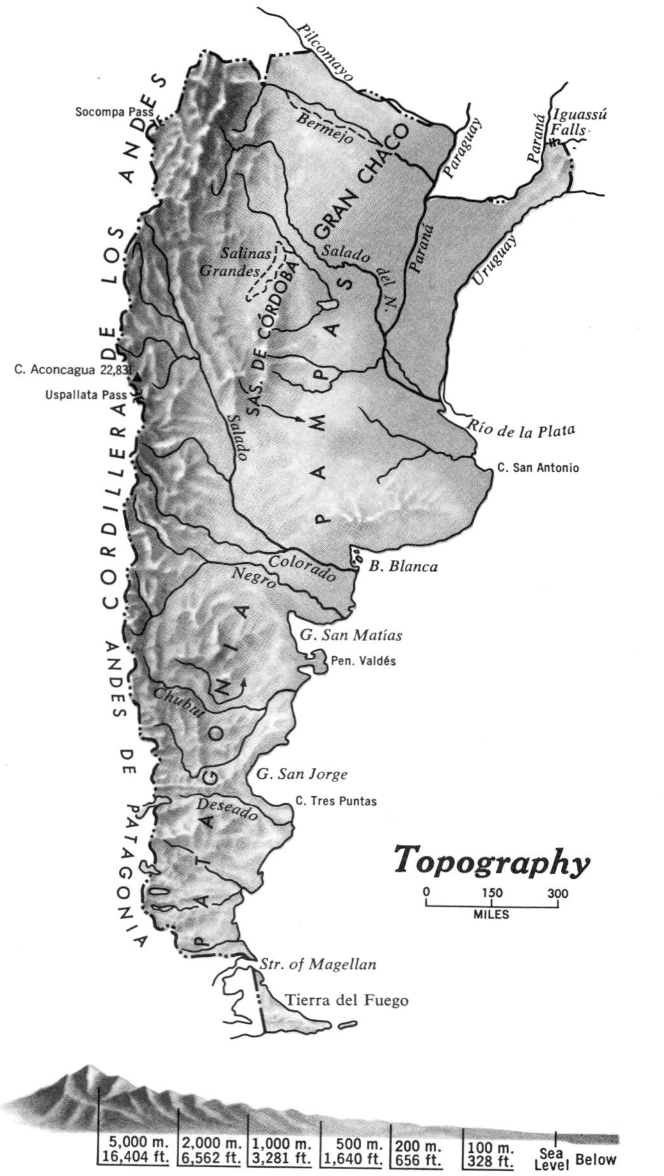

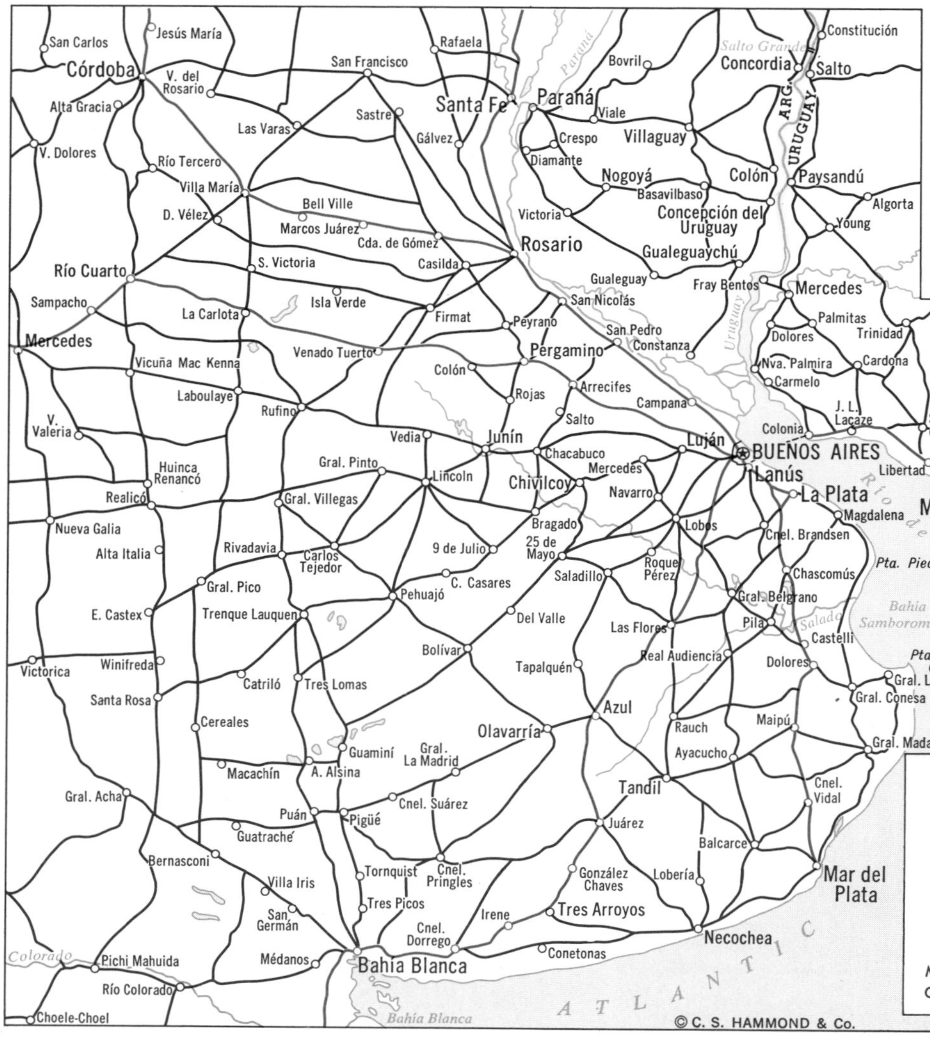

Chubut (river) .....C 5
Colhué Huapí (lake) .....C 6
Colorado (river) .....D 4
Cónico (mt.) .....B 5
Corrientes (river) .....E 2
Coyle (river) .....B 7
Cuarto (river) .....D 3
Delgada (point) .....D 5
Desaguadero (river) .....C 3
Deseado (river) .....C 6
Diamante (river) .....C 3
Domuyo (vol.) .....B 4
Dos Bahías (cape) .....D 5
Dulce (river) .....D 2
Dungeness (point) .....C 7
El Chocón (res.) .....C 4
Estados (isl.) .....D 7
Fagnano (lake) .....C 7
Famatina (mts.) .....C 2
Feliciano (river) .....G 5
Flores, Las (river) .....G 7
Gallegos (river) .....B 7
General Manuel Belgrano (mt.) ..C 2
Glaciares, Los (park) .....B 6
Gran Chaco (reg.) .....D 1
Grande (bay) .....C 7
Grande (falls) .....G 5
Grande (river) .....C 4
Gualeguay (river) .....G 5
Guayaquilaró (river) .....G 5
Iguazú (falls) .....F 2
Iguazú (park) .....E 2
Incahuasi (mt.) .....C 2
Lanín (park) .....B 4
Lanín (vol.) .....B 4
Laudo (mt.) .....C 2
Lechiguanas (isls.) .....G 6
Lennox (isl.) .....C 8
Limay (river) .....C 4
Llancanelo (lag.) .....C 4
Llullaillaco (vol.) .....C 1
Magallanes (Magellan) (str.) ....C 7
Maipo (vol.) .....C 3
Mar Chiquita (lake) .....D 3
Martín García (isl.), 1,575.....H 7
Mendoza (river) .....C 3
Mercedario (mt.) .....B 3
Mogotes (point) .....E 4
Montemayor (plateau) .....C 5
Murallón (mt.) .....B 6
Nahuel Huapi (lake) .....B 5
Nahuel Huapi (park) .....B 5
Negro (river) .....D 4
Neuquén (river) .....C 4
Ninfas (point) .....D 5
Norte (point) .....D 5
Norte del Cabo San Antonio (point) .....E 4
Nuevo (gulf) .....D 5
Ojos del Salado (mt.) .....C 2
Olivares (mt.) .....B 3
Pampa de las Tres Hermanas (plain) .....C 6
Pampas (plain) .....D 3
Paraná (river) .....E 2
Patagonia (reg.) .....C 5
Peteroa (vol.) .....B 4
Pilcomayo (river) .....E 1
Pissis (mt.) .....C 2
Plata, Río de la (est.) .....E 4
Pueyrredón (lake) .....B 6
Puna de Atacama (reg.) .....C 2
Quinto (river) .....D 3
Rincón (mt.) .....C 1
Saladillo (river) .....D 2
Salado (river) .....H 7
Salado (river) .....C 4
Salado del Norte (river) .....D 2
Sali (river) .....C 2
Salto (river) .....F 7
Samborombón (bay) .....E 4
San Antonio (cape) .....E 4
San Diego (cape) .....D 7
San Jorge (gulf) .....C 6
San Juan (river) .....C 3
San Lorenzo (mt.) .....B 6
San Martín (lake) .....B 6
San Matías (gulf) .....D 5
Santa Cruz (river) .....B 7
Senguerr (river) .....B 6
Staten (Estados) (isl.) .....D 7
Sur del Cabo San Antonio (point) .....E 4
Tarija (river) .....D 1
Tercero (river) .....D 3
Teuco (river) .....D 1
Tierra del Fuego, Isla Grande de (isl.), 10,620 .....C 7
Toro (mt.) .....B 2
Tres Picos (mt.) .....B 5
Tres Puntas (cape) .....D 6
Trinidad (isl.) .....D 4
Tronador (mt.) .....B 5
Tunuyán (river) .....C 3
Tupungato (mt.) .....B 3
Uruguay (river) .....E 3
Valdés (pen.) .....D 5
Vallimanca (river) .....F 7
Viedma (lake) .....B 6
Zapaleri (mt.) .....C 1

*City and suburbs.
†Population of department.

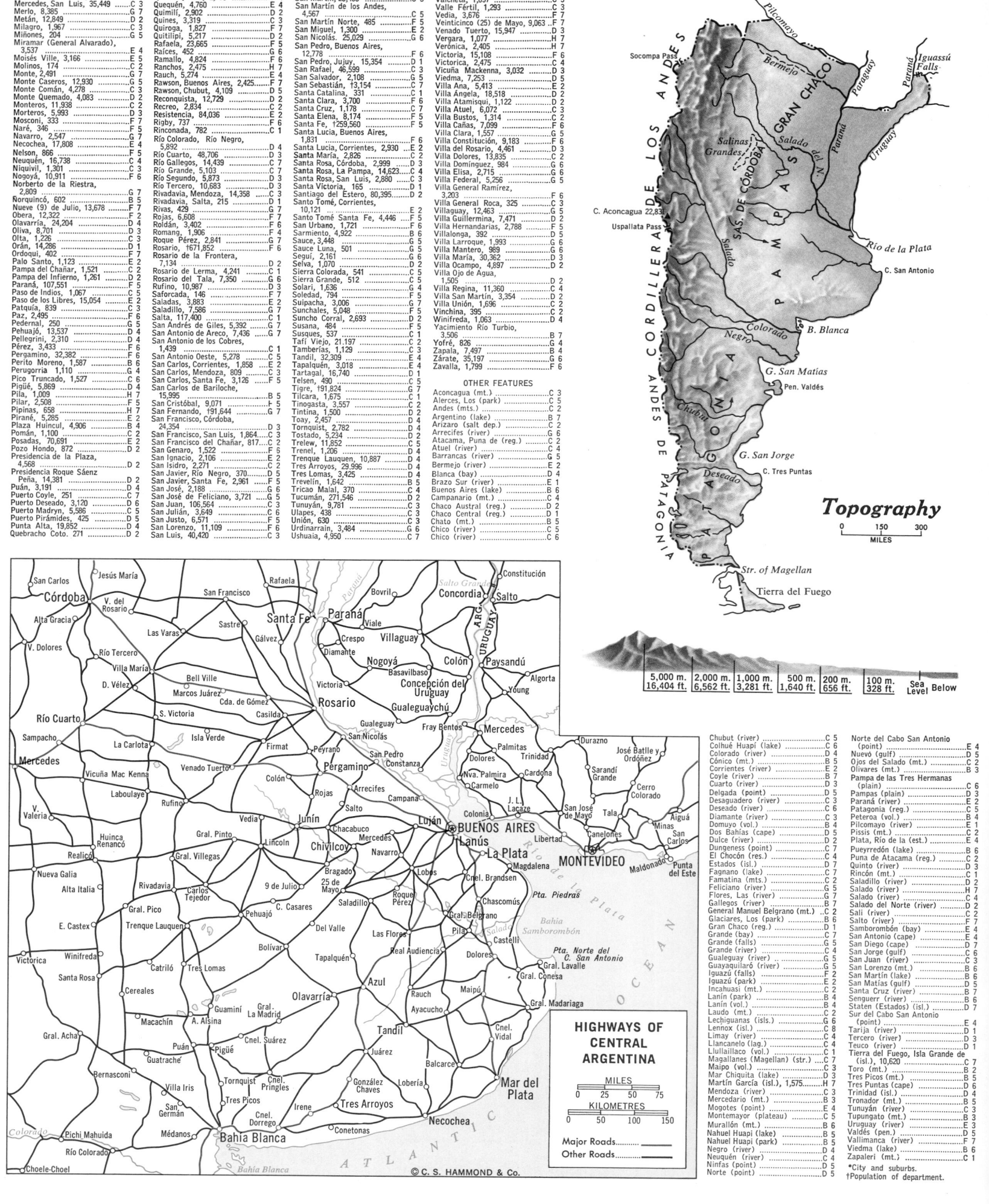

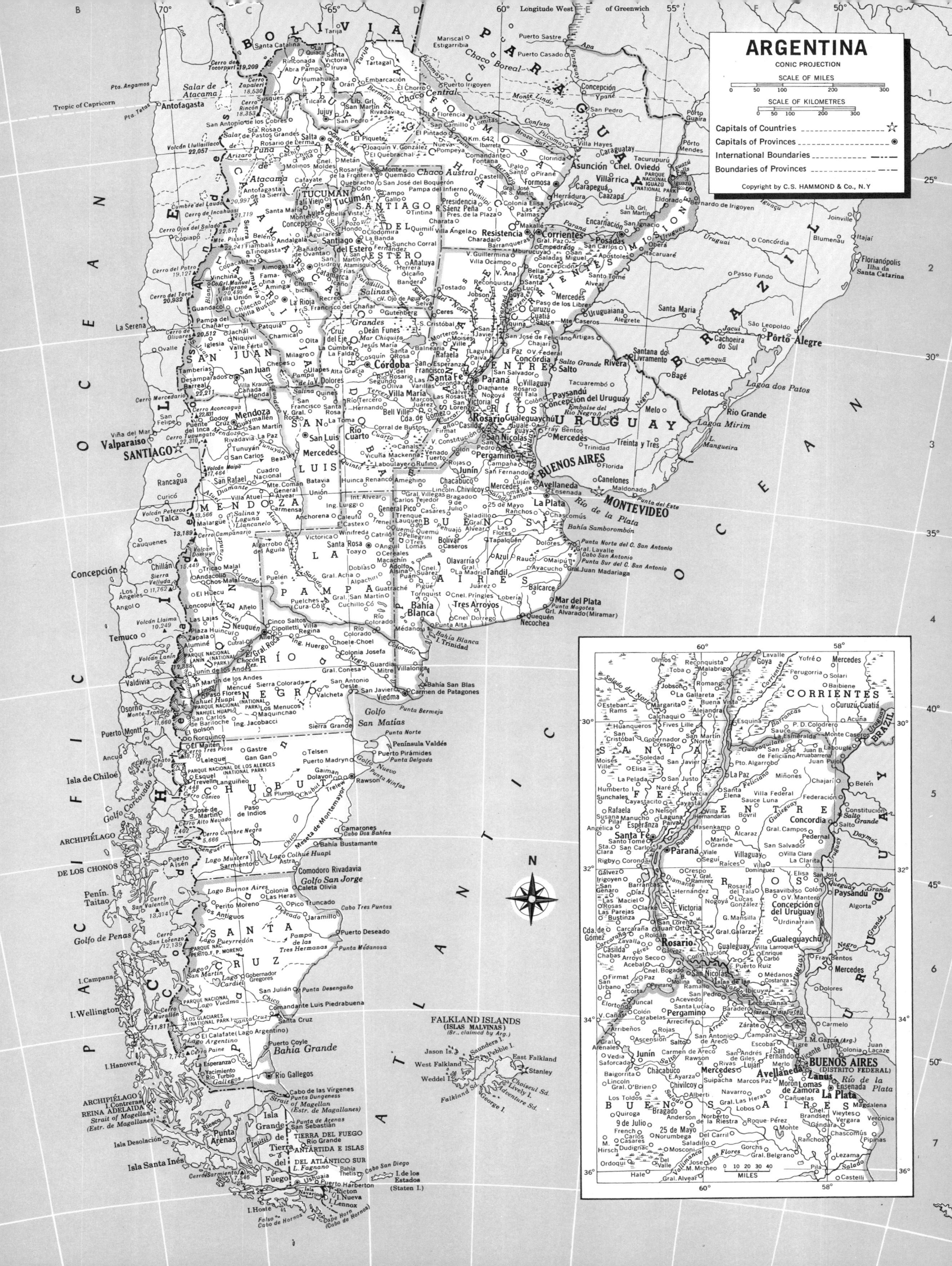

Map

BOLIVIA

BRAZIL

ARGENTINA

CHACO

NUEVA ASUNCIÓN

ALTO PARAGUAY

BOQUERÓN

PRESIDENTE HAYES

CONCEPCIÓN

AMAMBAY

SAN PEDRO

CANENDIYÚ

CORDILLERA

CAAGUAZÚ

ALTO PARANÁ

PARAGUARÍ

GUAIRÁ

CAAZAPÁ

ITAPÚA

MISIONES

ÑEEMBUCÚ

CENTRAL

Tropic of Capricorn

Inset map
PRESIDENTE HAYES, **SAN PEDRO**, **CORDILLERA**, **CENTRAL**, **CAAGUAZÚ**, **PARAGUARÍ**, **GUAIRÁ**, **CAAZAPÁ**, **ÑEEMBUCÚ**

Map legend
PARAGUAY
CONIC PROJECTION

SCALE OF MILES
0 20 40 60 80 100 120 140

SCALE OF KILOMETERS
0 20 40 60 80 100 120 140

★ Capitals of Countries
◉ Capitals of Departments
—— International Boundaries
— — Department Boundaries
© Copyright HAMMOND INCORPORATED, Maplewood, N.J.

PARAGUAY

DEPARTMENTS

Alto Paraguay .... C 3
Alto Paraná .... E 5
Amambay .... E 4
Asunción (capital) .... A 6
Boquerón .... B 4
Caaguazú .... E 5
Caazapá .... D 6
Canendiyu .... E 5
Central .... D 5
Chaco .... B 4
Concepción .... D 4
Cordillera .... D 5
Guairá .... D 5
Itapúa .... D 6
Misiones .... D 6
Ñeembucú .... C 6
Nueva Asunción .... B 3
Paraguarí .... D 6
Presidente Hayes .... C 4
San Pedro .... D 5

CITIES and TOWNS

Abaí, 1,507 .... E 6
Acahay, 2,622 .... B 7
Alberdi, 1,787 .... D 6
Altos, 1,348 .... B 6
Antequera, 1,123 .... D 5
Aregúa, 3,699 .... B 6
Arroyos y Esteros, 1,447 .... B 6
Asunción (cap.), 350,000 .... A 6
Asunción, *411,500 ....
Atyrá, 1,246 .... B 6
Belén, 2,523 .... D 4
Bella Vista, 2,331 .... D 4
Bella Vista, 1,421 .... A 5
Benjamín Aceval, 3,463 .... D 5
Buena Vista, 1,954 .... E 5
Caacupé, 6,329 .... B 6
Caaguazú, 2,291 .... E 5
Caapucú, 1,513 .... C 6
Caazapá, 3,079 .... D 6
Caballero, 1,553 .... D 6
Capiatá, 2,062 .... A 6
Caraguatay, 1,935 .... B 6
Carapeguá, 2,628 .... D 6
Carayaó, 1,376 .... D 6
Carmen del Paraná, 1,813 .... D 6
Cerrito, 801 .... D 6
Concepción, 33,500 .... D 4
Coronel Bogado, 3,885 .... D 6
Coronel Martínez, 1,270 .... C 6
Coronel Oviedo, 9,468 .... C 6
Desmochados, 681 .... C 6
Doctor Cecilio Báez, 1,300 .... D 5
Doctor Juan L. Mallorquín, 1,913 .... E 5
Doctor Juan Manuel Frutos, 1,494 .... E 5
Emboscada, 1,040 .... B 6
Encarnación, 35,000 .... D 6
Eusebio Ayala, 2,532 .... B 6
Fernando de la Mora, 10,194 .... A 6
Filadelfia, 12,639 .... C 4
Fortín General Díaz, 1508 .... B 4
Fram, 1,090 .... D 6
Fuerte Olimpo, 2,588 .... C 3
General Artigas, 3,450 .... E 6
General Elizardo Aquino, 1,162 .... D 5
General Eugenio A. Garay, ... B 3
Guarambaré, 3,167 .... A 6
Hernandarias, 1,646 .... E 5
Hohenau, 1,877 .... D 6
Horqueta, 5,095 .... D 4
Hugo Stroessner, 536 .... C 6
Humaitá, 781 .... C 6
Isla Pucu, 1,938 .... B 6
Itá, 6,265 .... B 6
Itacurubí de la Cordillera, 2,137 .... C 6
Itacurubí del Rosario, 1,776 .... D 5
Itapé, 1,235 .... C 6
Itaquyry, 788 .... E 5
Itauguá, 3,064 .... B 6
Iturbe, 3,274 .... C 7
Jesús, 1,814 .... B 6
Juan de Mena, 1,450 .... D 6
La Colmena, 1,804 .... B 7
Lambaré, 8,300 .... A 6
Lima, 751 .... D 4
Limpio, 1,438 .... B 6
Loreto, 1,866 .... D 4
Luque, 11,008 .... A 6
Mariano Roque Alonso, 1,492 .... A 6

Mariscal Estigarribia, 1,824 .... B 4
Mayor Pablo Lagerenza .... B 2
Mbocayaty, 701 .... C 6
Mbuyapey, 1,310 .... D 6
Ñacunday, 1,119 .... E 6
Natalicio Talavera, 1,020 .... D 5
Nueva Germania, 511 .... D 4
Nueva Italia, 1,517 .... B 6
Paraguarí, 4,880 .... D 6
Paso de Patria, 608 .... C 6
Pedro Juan Caballero, 10,355 .... E 4
Pilar, 10,500 .... C 6
Pirayú, 2,753 .... B 6
Piribebuy, 4,038 .... D 5
Primero de Marzo, 672 .... B 6
Puerto Antequera, 1,123 .... D 5
Puerto Casado, 1,891 .... C 4
Puerto Guaraní, 1,055 .... C 3
Puerto Pinasco, 3,872 .... C 4
Puerto Presidente Franco, 4,152 .... E 5
Puerto Presidente Stroessner, 1764 .... E 5
Puerto Sastre, 1,408 .... D 4
Quiindy, 2,851 .... B 7
Quyquyó, 1,168 .... B 7
Roque Gonzáles de Santa Cruz, 1,436 .... B 7
Rosario, 3,313 .... D 5
Salto del Guairá .... E 5
San Antonio, 4,247 .... A 6
San Bernardino, 570 .... A 6
San Carlos, 870 .... D 4
San Cosme y Damián, 554 .... D 6
San Estanislao, 3,569 .... D 5
San Ignacio, 5,141 .... C 6
San José, 2,802 .... B 6
San Juan Bautista de las Misiones, 5,972 .... D 6
San Juan Bautista de Ñeembucú, 454 .... C 6
San Juan Nepomuceno, 3,118 .... E 6
San Lázaro, 807 .... D 4
San Lorenzo, 8,593 .... B 6
San Miguel, 1,034 .... D 6
San Patricio, 1,130 .... D 6
San Pedro del Paraná, 2,263 .... E 6
San Pedro de Ycuámanddyú, 3,306 .... D 5
San Salvador, 1,393 .... C 7
Santa Elena, 1,364 .... C 6
Santa María, 754 .... D 6
Santa Rosa, 2,641 .... D 6
Santiago, 1,689 .... D 6
Sapucaí, 1,708 .... B 6
Tacuatí, 615 .... D 4
Tavai, 528 .... E 6
Tobatí, 2,520 .... B 6
Trinidad, 518 .... E 6
Unión, 806 .... D 5
Valenzuela, 994 .... C 6
Valle Mí, 1,141 .... C 4
Villa Florida, 1,141 .... C 6
Villa Hayes, 4,712 .... A 6
Villa Oliva, 813 .... C 5
Villarrica, 30,500 .... C 6
Villeta, 3,020 .... A 6
Yaguarón, 2,763 .... B 6
Yataity, 1,050 .... C 6
Ybycuí, 3,056 .... B 6
Ybytimí, 1,410 .... B 6
Yegros, 1,158 .... C 6
Yhú, 1,240 .... D 6
Ypacaraí, 5,281 .... B 6
Ypané, 1,469 .... A 6
Yuty, 2,573 .... D 6

OTHER FEATURES

Acaray (river) .... E 5
Aguaray-Guazú (river) .... C 5
Alto Paraná (river) .... D 6
Amambay, Cord. de (mts.) .... E 4
Apa (river) .... D 4
Aquidabán (river) .... D 4
Chaco Boreal (reg.) .... B 3
Chovoreca (hill) .... C 2
Confuso (river) .... B 4
Coronel F. Cabrera (hill) .... B 2
Gonzáles, Riacho (river) .... C 4
Gran Chaco (reg.) .... A 4
Guairá (falls) .... E 5
Mbaracayú, Cord. de (mts.) .... E 4
Monday (river) .... E 5
Montelindo (river) .... C 4
Mosquito, Riacho (river) .... C 4
Negro (river) .... D 5
Paraguay (river) .... D 5
Patiño, Estero (swamp) .... B 5
Pilcomayo (river) .... A 4
Tebicuary (river) .... C 6
Tímane (river) .... C 3

Agriculture, Industry and Resources

Quebracho

Yerba Maté

Cattle

Corn

Tobacco, Cotton, Manioc

Yerba Maté

Cattle, Sheep, Fruit, Wheat, Flax, Sheep, Dairy, Corn, Wine, Fruit, Cattle, Rice, Sunflowers

Montevideo

DOMINANT LAND USE

Diversified Tropical Crops (chiefly plantation agriculture)

Extensive Livestock Ranching

Forests

Nonagricultural Land

Wheat, Corn, Livestock

Truck Farming, Horticulture, Fruit

Intensive Livestock Ranching

MAJOR MINERAL OCCURRENCES

Mr Marble

MONTEVIDEO
Textiles, Food Processing, Leather Goods

⚡ Water Power

Major Industrial Areas

Topography

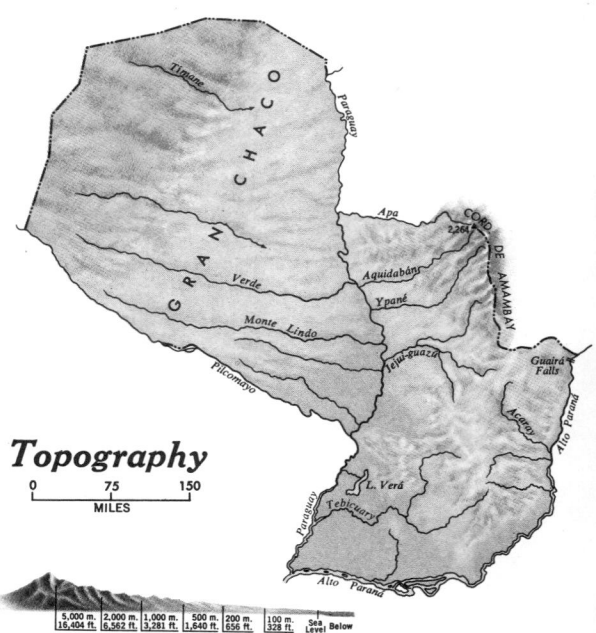

GRAN CHACO

CORD. DE AMAMBAY

Guairá Falls

0   75   150
MILES

5,000 m.   2,000 m.   1,000 m.   500 m.   200 m.   100 m.   Sea   Below
16,404 ft.   6,562 ft.   3,281 ft.   1,640 ft.   656 ft.   328 ft.   Level

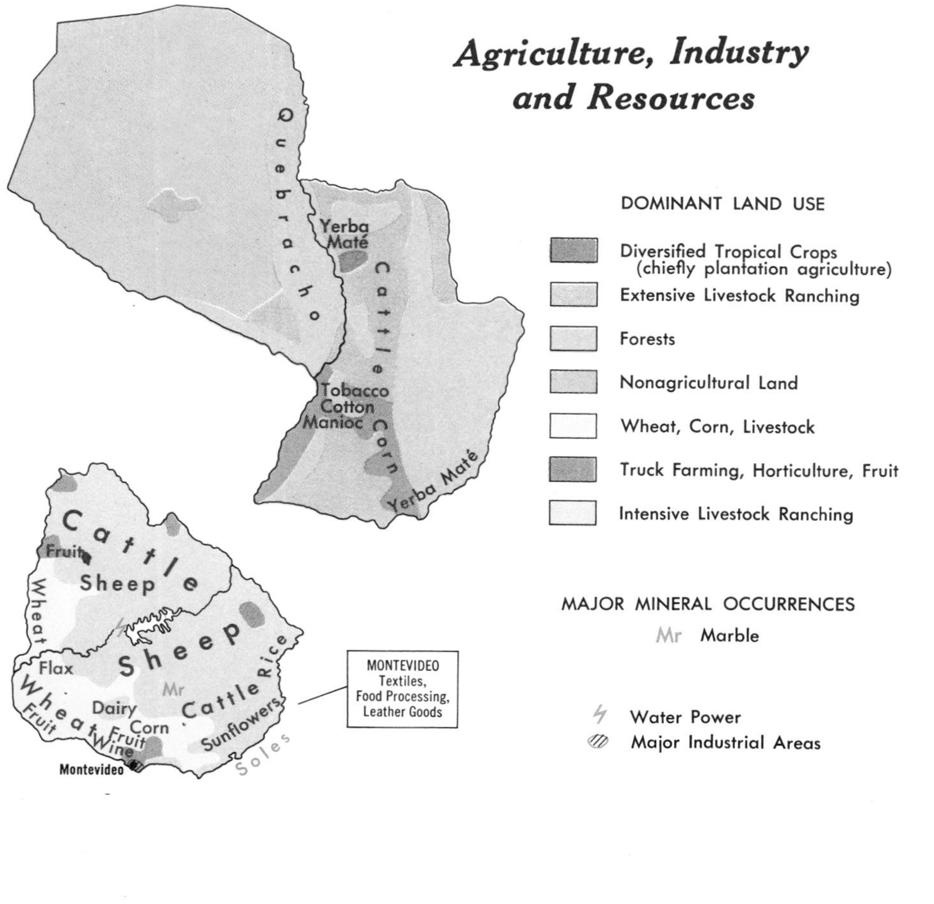

Verá (lagoon) ....B 7
Verde (river) ....C 4
Yacaré (river) ....C 4
Ypané (river) ....D 4
Ypoá (lake) ....B 6

URUGUAY

DEPARTMENTS

Artigas, 52,261 ....B 1
Canelones, 211,644 ....D 5
Cerro Largo, 118,880 ....E 3
Colonia, 135,185 ....B 5
Durazno, 113,797 ....C 3
Flores, 35,457 ....C 4
Florida, 104,739 ....D 4
Lavalleja, 114,090 ....D 5
Maldonado, 62,344 ....E 5
Montevideo, 1,173,114 ....B 7
Paysandú, 89,908 ....B 3
Río Negro, 49,258 ....B 3
Rivera, 86,430 ....D 2
Rocha, 84,210 ....E 4
Salto, 105,698 ....B 2
San José, 94,541 ....C 5
Soriano, 78,234 ....B 4
Tacuarembó, 119,690 ....D 3
Treinta y Tres, 81,887 ....E 4

CITIES and TOWNS

Achar, 460 ....C 3
Aiguá, 2,715 ....E 5
Algorta, 650 ....B 3
Arroyo Grande, 1,000 ....B 4
Artigas, 23,429 ....C 1
Balneario El Tesoro, 84 ....E 5
Balneario La Barra, 124 ....E 5
Balneario Solís, 225 ....D 5
Baltasar Brum, 1,764 ....B 1
Belén, 2,933 ....B 1
Bella Unión, 4,955 ....B 1
Bernabé Rivera, 683 ....B 1
Bizcocho, 117 ....B 4
Campamento, 187 ....C 1
Cañada Nieto, 407 ....B 4
Canelones, 27,000 ....B 6
Cardona, 4,110 ....B 4
Carlos Reyles, 940 ....C 4
Carmelo, 11,923 ....A 4
Carmen, 1,687 ....D 4
Castillos, 5,345 ....F 5
Casupá, 1,652 ....D 5
Cerro Chato, Treinta y Tres, 2,045 ....D 4
Clara, 1,000 ....D 3
Colonia, 9,825 ....B 5
Colonia Agraciada, 409 ....A 4
Colonia Arrué ....B 5
Colonia Artigas, 234 ....B 1
Colonia Concordia, 755 ....A 4
Colonia Itacumbú, 738 ....B 1
Colonia Lavalleja ....C 2
Colonia Palma, 94 ....B 1
Colonia Rossel y Rius ....D 4
Colonia Valdense, 1,126 ....B 5
Conchillas, 590 ....B 5
Constancia, 150 ....B 3
Constitución, 1,600 ....A 2
Corrales (J. P. Varela), 2,700 ..E 4
Cuaró ....D 2
Cufré ....B 5
Curtina ....C 3
Diego Lamas, 94 ....B 1
Dolores, 12,480 ....A 4
Durazno, 19,486 ....C 4
Egaña, 675 ....B 4
Estación Atlántida, 1,007 ....B 6
Estación Cuaró, 203 ....C 1
Estación José Ignacio, 131 ....E 5
Estación Rincón ....F 3
Estación Sosa Díaz ....C 6
Estación Villasboas ....C 4
Estanzuela ....B 5
Florida, 17,243 ....C 5
Fortaleza de Santa Teresa ....F 5
Fraile Muerto, 1,876 ....E 3
Fray Bentos, 14,625 ....A 4
Fray Marcos, 1,095 ....D 5
Garzón, 345 ....E 5
Guichón, 4,625 ....B 3
Itapeby ....B 2
Javier de Viana, 317 ....C 1
Joaquín Suárez, Canelones, 1,752 ....B 6
Joaquín Suárez, Colonia ....B 5
José Batlle y Ordóñez, 1,781 ....D 4
José Enrique Rodo, 1,319 ....B 4
José Pedro Varela (Corrales), 2,955 ....E 4
Juan D. Jackson, 163 ....C 4
Juan L. Lacaze, 9,916 ....B 5
La Bolsa, 274 ....C 1
La Cruz, 2,000 ....C 4
La Paz, Canelones, 5,214 ....B 6
La Paz, Colonia ....B 5
La Sierra, 241 ....D 5
Las Flores, 404 ....D 5
Las Piedras, 15,724 ....B 6
Lascano, 4,204 ....E 4
Libertad, 4,622 ....C 5
Mal Abrigo, 630 ....C 5
Maldonado, 15,005 ....D 6
Manga ....B 7
Mariscala, 1,305 ....E 5
Martín Chico ....A 5
Mazangano ....E 3
Melo, 28,673 ....E 3
Mercedes, 31,325 ....B 4
Merinos, 1,200 ....C 3
Migues, 1,017 ....C 6
Minas, 21,133 ....D 5
Minas de Corrales, 2,320 ....D 2
Molles (Carlos Reyles), 940 ......C 4
Montevideo (cap.), 1,154,465......B 7
Montevideo, *1,400,000 ....B 7
Nico Pérez ....D 4
Nueva Helvecia ....B 5
Nueva Palmira, 4,611 ....A 4
Nuevo Berlín, 1,531 ....B 3
Olimar, 2,499 ....E 3
Ombúes de Lavalle, 1,067 ....B 4
Palmitas, 1,288 ....B 4
Pan de Azúcar, 4,190 ....D 5
Pando, 11,623 ....B 6
Parada Esperanza, 250 ....B 3
Paso de Andrés Pérez ....B 3
Paso de León, 184 ....B 1
Paso de los Toros, 10,624 ....C 3
Paso de Ramos, 23 ....C 1
Paso del Borracho ....D 2
Paso del Parque ....B 2
Paysandú, 47,875 ....A 3
Piedras Coloradas, 200 ....B 3
Piñera, 1,000 ....C 3
Pintado, 160 ....C 1
Pirarajá, 1,000 ....E 4
Piriápolis, 4,546 ....D 5
Polanco del Yí, 300 ....D 4
Porvenir, 1,000 ....B 3
Progreso ....B 6
Puerto Amaro ....F 3
Puerto Arazatí ....C 5
Punta del Este, 5,272 ....E 6
Quebracho, 1,002 ....B 2
Río Branco, 3,345 ....F 3
Rivera, 42,623 ....D 1
Rocha, 19,895 ....E 5
Rodríguez, 1,097 ....C 5
Rosario, 6,398 ....B 5
Salto, 55,425 ....B 2
San Bautista, 1,500 ....B 6
San Carlos, 13,695 ....E 5
San Gregorio, San José ....C 4
San Gregorio, Tacuarembó 1,606 ....D 3
San José de Mayo, 21,048 ....C 5
San Ramón, 3,983 ....D 5
Sánchez ....B 3
Santa Catalina, 824 ....B 4
Santa Clara de Olimar ....D 3
Santa Lucía, 9,126 ....B 6
Santa Rosa, 1,596 ....B 6
Sarandí del Yí, 5,900 ....D 4
Sarandí de Navarro, 630 ....C 3
Sarandí Grande, 5,620 ....C 4
Sauce, Canelones, 1,570 ....B 6
Sauce, Rocha ....E 5
Sequeira, 880 ....C 1
Soca, 1,200 ....C 6
Solís, 1,531 ....D 5
Soriano, 1,036 ....A 4
Tacuarembó, 17,854 ....D 2
Tala, 1,957 ....D 5
Tambores, 1,273 ....C 2
Toledo, 1,200 ....B 6
Tomás Gomensoro, 2,144 ....B 1
Topador, 183 ....C 1
Tranqueras, 3,340 ....D 2
Treinta y Tres, 18,856 ....E 4
Tres Árboles, 400 ....C 3
Trinidad, 17,233 ....B 4
Tupambaé, 1,359 ....E 3
Veinticinco de Agosto, 1,139 ....A 6
Velázquez, 1,199 ....D 5
Vergara, 2,480 ....E 3
Villa Darwin, 445 ....B 4
Young, 6,485 ....B 3
Zapicán, 1,500 ....E 4

OTHER FEATURES

Aiguá (river) ....E 4
Alférez (river) ....E 5
Arapey Chico (river) ....B 1
Arapey Grande (river) ....B 2
Arroyo Negro (river) ....B 3
Belén (range) ....C 1
Bonete (dam) ....C 3
Brava (point) ....B 7
Cañas (range) ....C 2
Caraguatá (river) ....D 3
Castillos (lagoon) ....F 5
Cebollatí (river) ....F 4
Cordobés (river) ....D 3
Cuareim (river) ....B 1
Cuñapirú (river) ....D 2
Daymán (range) ....B 2
Daymán (river) ....B 2
Durazno (range) ....D 4
Espinillo (point) ....A 7
Este (point) ....D 6
Flores (isl.) ....D 5
Garzón (lagoon) ....E 5
Grande (range) ....D 4
Grande (river) ....B 4
Grande Inferior (range) ....C 4
Haedo (range) ....C 2
India Muerta (river) ....E 4
José Ignacio (lagoon) ....E 5
La Plata (river) ....B 5
Lobos (isl.), 11 ....E 6
Maciel (river) ....C 4
Mirador Nacional (mt.) ....D 5
Mirim (lagoon) ....F 4
Negra (lagoon) ....F 5
Negra (range) ....D 2
Negro (river) ....B 4
Negro (river) ....B 3
Olimar Grande (river) ....E 4
Pando (river) ....B 6
Parao (river) ....E 3
Plata, La (river) ....B 5
Polonio (cape) ....F 5
Queguay Chico (river) ....B 3
Queguay Grande (river) ....B 3
Río Negro (res.) ....D 3
Rocha (lagoon) ....E 5
Salto Grande (falls) ....A 2
San José (river) ....C 4
San Miguel (swamp) ....F 4
San Salvador (river) ....B 4
Santa Ana (range) ....D 2
Santa Lucía (river) ....D 5
Santa Lucía Chico (river) ....D 4
Santa María (cape) ....F 5
Sauce (lagoon) ....D 5
Sopas (river) ....C 2
Tacuarembó (river) ....D 2
Tacuarí (river) ....E 3
Tigre (isl.) ....A 7
Uruguay (river) ....A 3
Yaguarón (river) ....F 3
Yí (river) ....B 4

*City and suburbs.
†Population of district.

PARAGUAY

AREA 157,047 sq. mi.
POPULATION 2,314,000
CAPITAL Asunción
LARGEST CITY Asunción
HIGHEST POINT Amambay Range 2,264 ft.
MONETARY UNIT guaraní
MAJOR LANGUAGES Spanish, Guaraní
MAJOR RELIGION Roman Catholicism

URUGUAY

AREA 72,172 sq. mi.
POPULATION 2,900,000
CAPITAL Montevideo
LARGEST CITY Montevideo
HIGHEST POINT Mirador Nacional 1,644 ft.
MONETARY UNIT Uruguayan peso
MAJOR LANGUAGE Spanish
MAJOR RELIGION Roman Catholicism

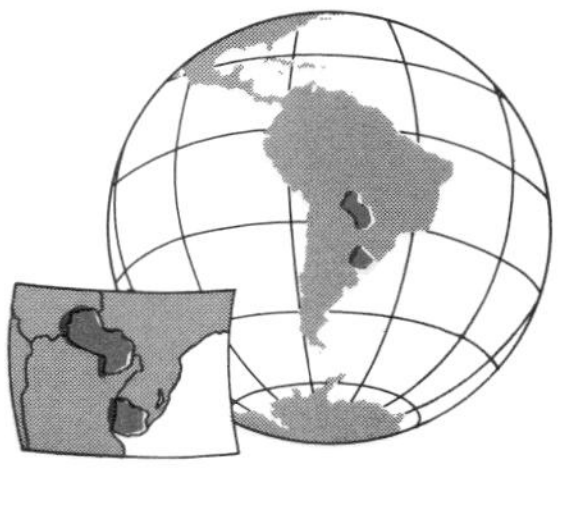

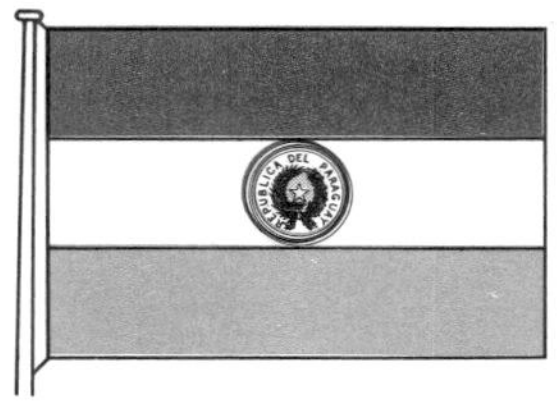

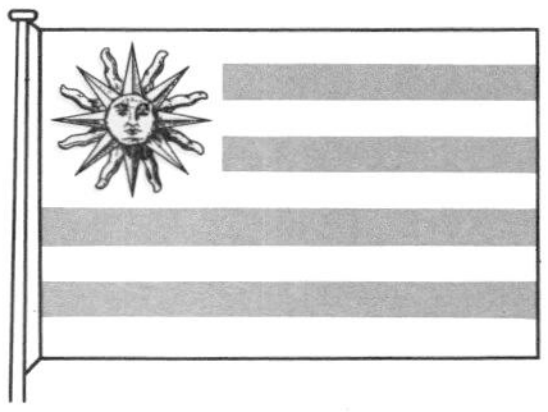

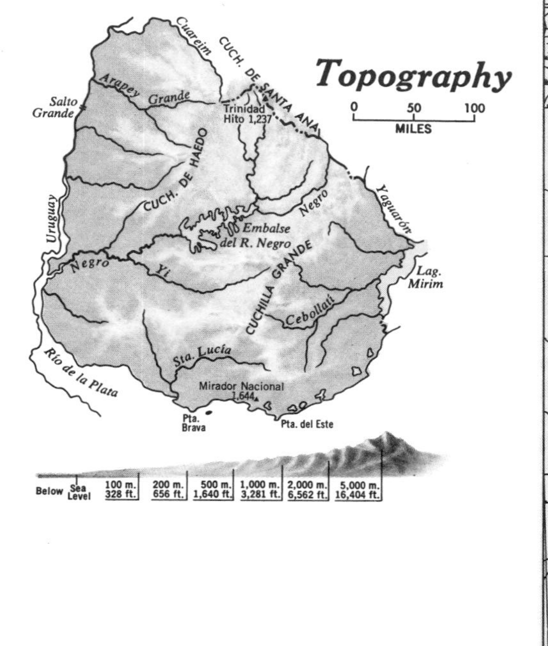
Topography
0 50 100
MILES
Cuareim
CUCH. DE SANTA ANA
Arapey Grande
Salto Grande
Trinidad Hito 1,237
CUCH. DE HAEDO
Uruguay
Negro
Yaguarón
Embalse del R. Negro
Yí
CUCHILLA GRANDE
Lag. Mirim
Cebollatí
Sta. Lucía
Río de la Plata
Mirador Nacional 1,644
Pta. Brava
Pta. del Este
Below Sea Level
100 m. 328 ft.
200 m. 656 ft.
500 m. 1,640 ft.
1,000 m. 3,281 ft.
2,000 m. 6,562 ft.
5,000 m. 16,404 ft.

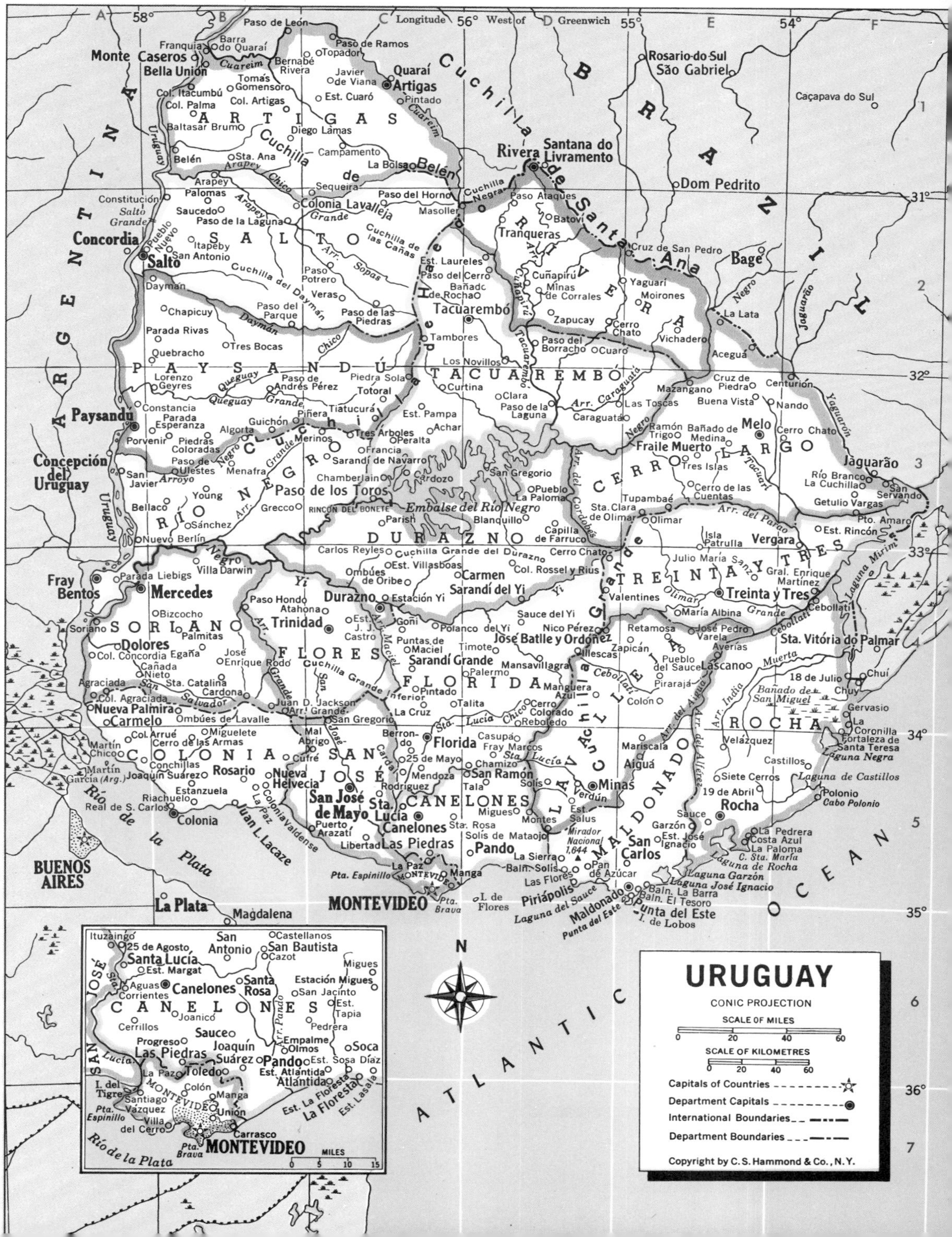
Longitude 56° West of Greenwich
ARGENTINA
BRAZIL
ATLANTIC OCEAN
MONTEVIDEO
BUENOS AIRES
La Plata
Río de la Plata
ARTIGAS
SALTO
PAYSANDÚ
RÍO NEGRO
SORIANO
COLONIA
SAN JOSÉ
FLORES
FLORIDA
DURAZNO
TACUAREMBÓ
RIVERA
CERRO LARGO
TREINTA Y TRES
LAVALLEJA
MALDONADO
ROCHA
CANELONES
Embalse del Río Negro
Cuchilla Grande
Cuchilla de Haedo
Cuchilla de Santa Ana
Laguna Merín
URUGUAY
CONIC PROJECTION
SCALE OF MILES
0 20 40 60
SCALE OF KILOMETRES
0 20 40 60
Capitals of Countries
Department Capitals
International Boundaries
Department Boundaries
Copyright by C. S. Hammond & Co., N. Y.

POPULATION DISTRIBUTION

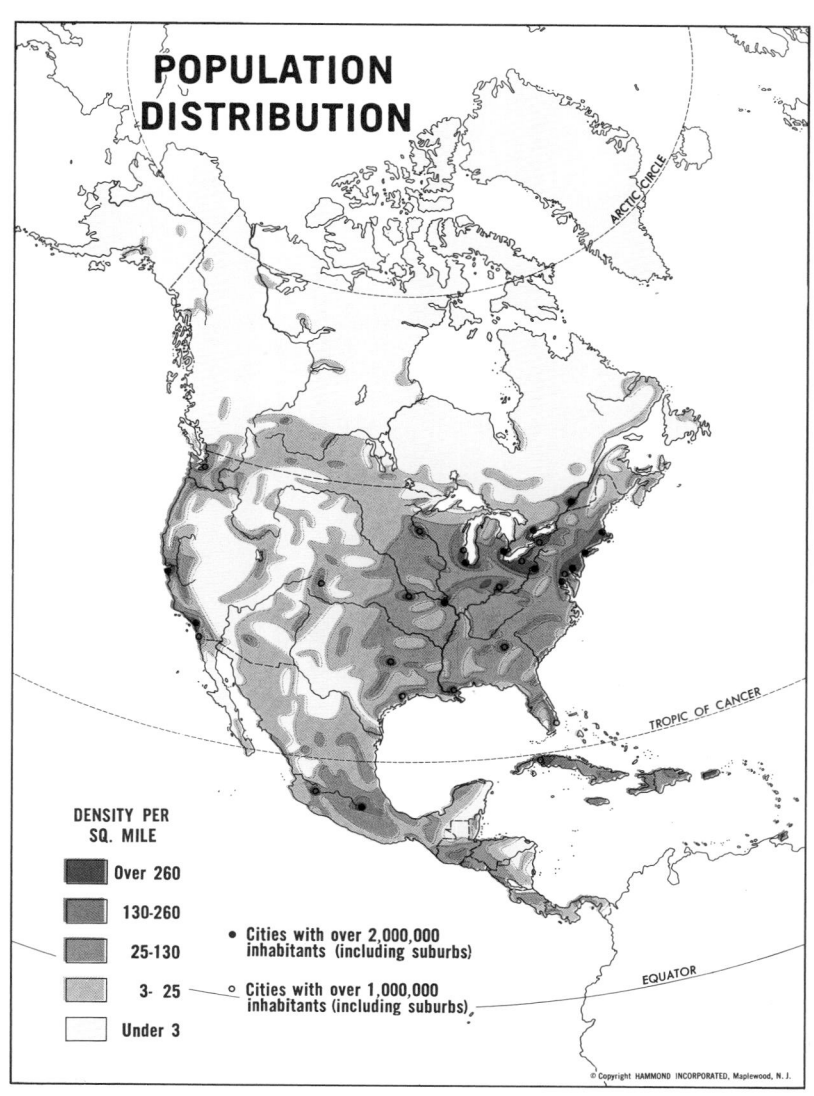

AREA 9,363,000 sq. mi.
POPULATION 314,000,000
LARGEST CITY New York
HIGHEST POINT Mt. McKinley 20,320 ft.
LOWEST POINT Death Valley -282 ft.

DENSITY PER SQ. MILE

- Over 260
- 130-260
- 25-130
- 3-25
- Under 3

• Cities with over 2,000,000 inhabitants (including suburbs)
○ Cities with over 1,000,000 inhabitants (including suburbs)

© Copyright HAMMOND INCORPORATED, Maplewood, N.J.

VEGETATION

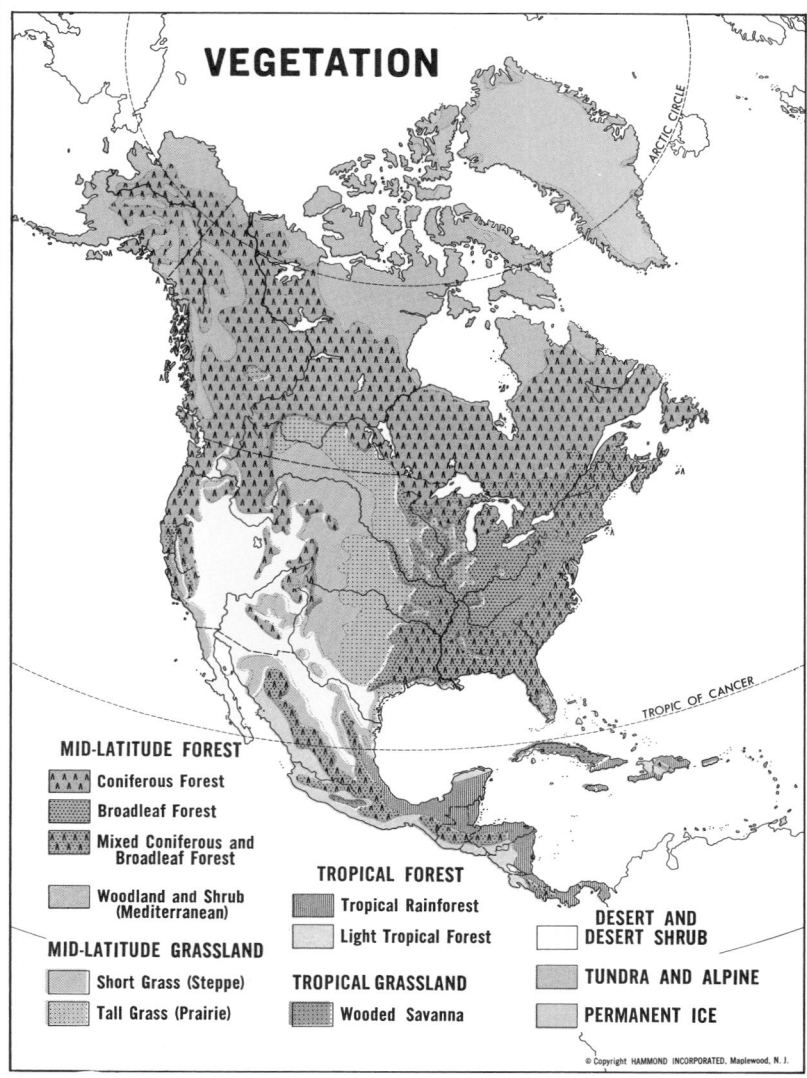

MID-LATITUDE FOREST
- ▲ Coniferous Forest
- Broadleaf Forest
- Mixed Coniferous and Broadleaf Forest
- Woodland and Shrub (Mediterranean)

MID-LATITUDE GRASSLAND
- Short Grass (Steppe)
- Tall Grass (Prairie)

TROPICAL FOREST
- Tropical Rainforest
- Light Tropical Forest

TROPICAL GRASSLAND
- Wooded Savanna

DESERT AND DESERT SHRUB

TUNDRA AND ALPINE

PERMANENT ICE

© Copyright HAMMOND INCORPORATED, Maplewood, N.J.

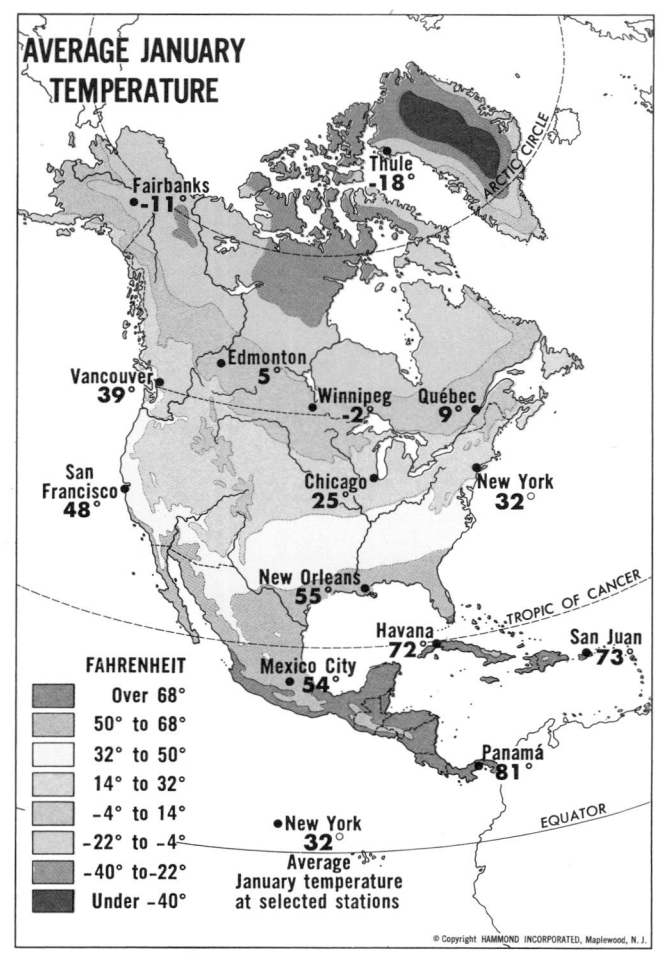

AVERAGE JANUARY TEMPERATURE

Thule -18°
Fairbanks -11°
Edmonton 5°
Vancouver 39°
Winnipeg -2°
Québec 9°
San Francisco 48°
Chicago 25°
New York 32°
New Orleans 55°
Havana 72°
San Juan 73°
Mexico City 54°
Panamá 81°

FAHRENHEIT
- Over 68°
- 50° to 68°
- 32° to 50°
- 14° to 32°
- -4° to 14°
- -22° to -4°
- -40° to -22°
- Under -40°

• New York 32°
Average January temperature at selected stations

© Copyright HAMMOND INCORPORATED, Maplewood, N.J.

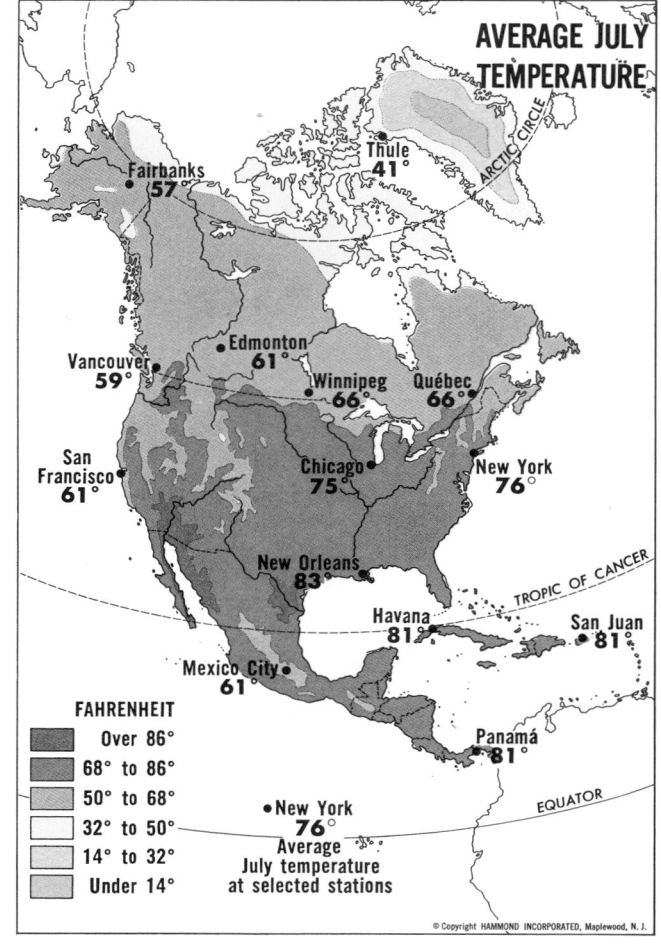

AVERAGE JULY TEMPERATURE

Thule 41°
Fairbanks 57°
Edmonton 61°
Vancouver 59°
Winnipeg 66°
Québec 66°
San Francisco 61°
Chicago 75°
New York 76°
New Orleans 83°
Havana 81°
San Juan 81°
Mexico City 61°
Panamá 81°

FAHRENHEIT
- Over 86°
- 68° to 86°
- 50° to 68°
- 32° to 50°
- 14° to 32°
- Under 14°

• New York 76°
Average July temperature at selected stations

© Copyright HAMMOND INCORPORATED, Maplewood, N.J.

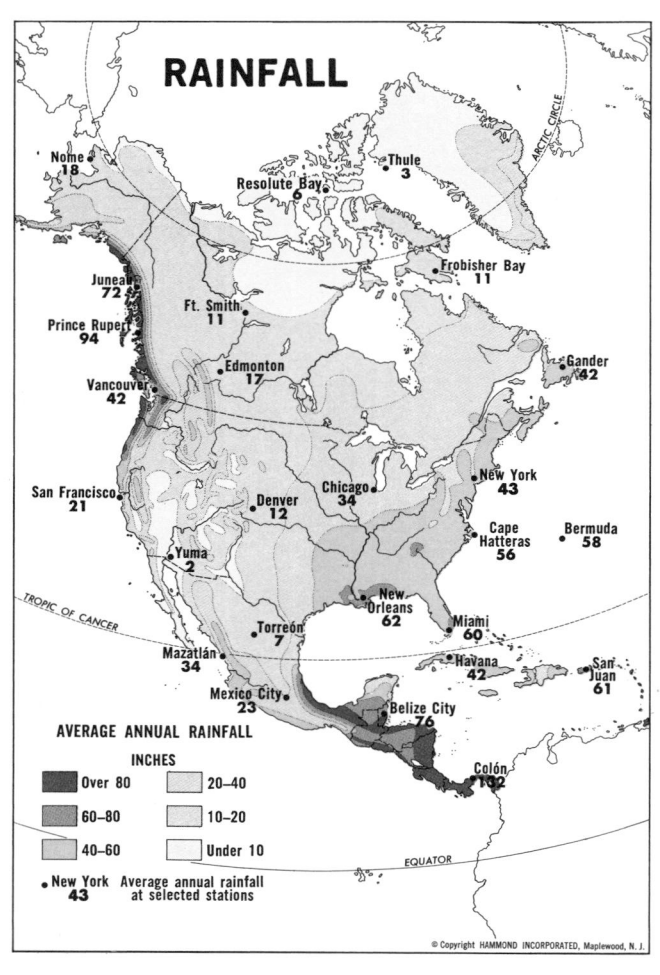

RAINFALL

Nome 18
Thule 3
Resolute Bay 6
Frobisher Bay 11
Juneau 72
Ft. Smith 11
Prince Rupert 94
Edmonton 17
Gander 42
Vancouver 42
San Francisco 21
Denver 12
Chicago 34
New York 43
Cape Hatteras 56
Bermuda 58
Yuma 2
New Orleans 62
Miami 60
Torreón 7
Mazatlán 34
Havana 42
San Juan 61
Mexico City 23
Belize City 76
Colón 102

AVERAGE ANNUAL RAINFALL
INCHES
- Over 80
- 60–80
- 40–60
- 20–40
- 10–20
- Under 10

• New York 43
Average annual rainfall at selected stations

© Copyright HAMMOND INCORPORATED, Maplewood, N.J.

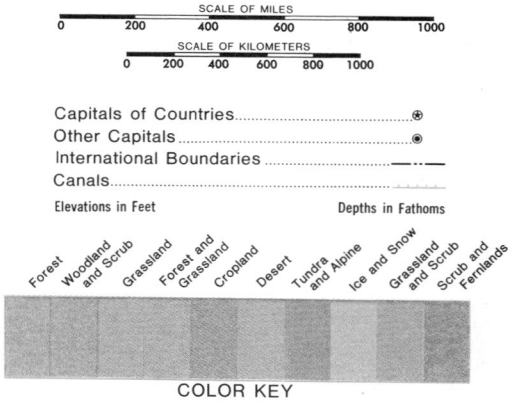

VEGETATION/RELIEF

SCALE OF MILES
0 200 400 600 800 1000

SCALE OF KILOMETERS
0 200 400 600 800 1000

Capitals of Countries .... ⊛
Other Capitals .... ⊛
International Boundaries ....
Canals ....

Elevations in Feet   Depths in Fathoms

Forest · Woodland and Scrub · Grassland · Forest and Grassland · Cropland · Desert · Tundra and Alpine · Ice and Snow · Grassland and Scrub · Scrub and Fernlands

COLOR KEY

Longitude 90° West of Greenwich

Topography

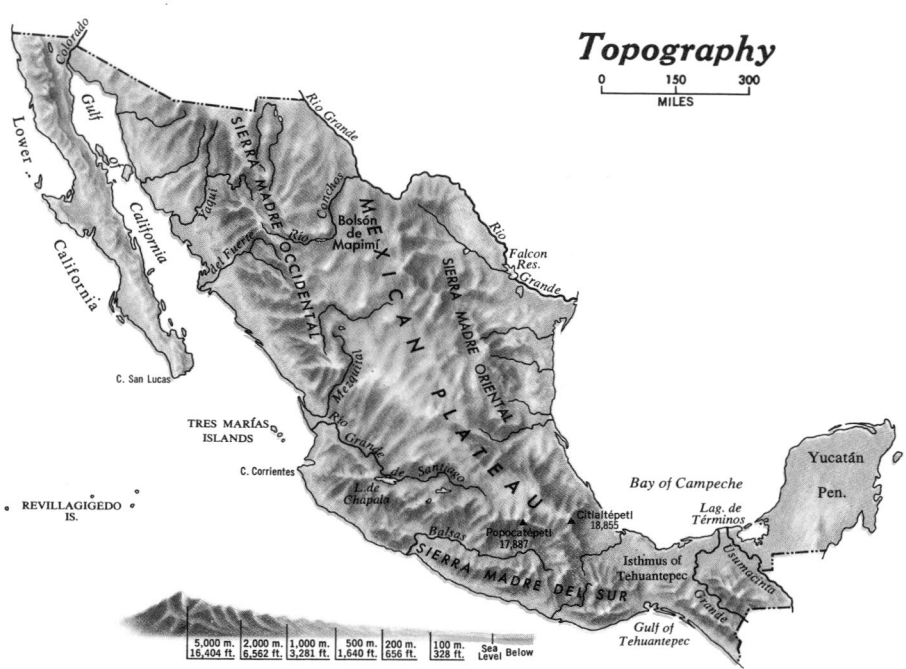

0   150   300
MILES

5,000 m. 2,000 m. 1,000 m. 500 m. 200 m. 100 m. Sea
16,404 ft. 6,562 ft. 3,281 ft. 1,640 ft. 656 ft. 328 ft. Level Below

MEXICO

CONIC PROJECTION

SCALE OF MILES

0 .... 100 200

SCALE OF KILOMETRES

0 ... 100 ... 200 ... 300

National Capitals .... ☆   State Capitals .... ◉
International Boundaries ----   State Boundaries ....

Copyright by C.S. HAMMOND & Co., N.Y.

AREA 761,601 sq. mi.
POPULATION 48,313,438
CAPITAL Mexico City
LARGEST CITY Mexico City
HIGHEST POINT Citlaltépetl 18,855 ft.
MONETARY UNIT Mexican peso
MAJOR LANGUAGE Spanish
MAJOR RELIGION Roman Catholicism

States Indicated by Numbers

1 Tlaxcala
2 Morelos
3 Distrito Federal
4 México
5 Hidalgo
6 Querétaro
7 Guanajuato
8 Aguascalientes
9 Nayarit
10 Colima

HIGHWAYS OF MIDDLE AMERICA

Limited Access Highways
Major Highways
Other Important Roads
U.S. Interstate Numbers
U.S. Route Numbers
Other Route Numbers

© C. S. HAMMOND & Co., Maplewood, N.J.

Agriculture, Industry and Resources

CHIHUAHUA — Nonferrous Metals

PIEDRAS NEGRAS — Iron & Steel

MONCLOVA — Iron & Steel, Chemicals

MONTERREY–SALTILLO — Iron & Steel, Nonferrous Metals, Metalworking, Chemicals, Food Processing

TORREÓN — Nonferrous Metals, Chemicals, Textiles

SAN LUIS POTOSÍ — Nonferrous Metals, Textiles

TAMPICO — Oil Refining, Chemicals, Food Processing

SALAMANCA — Chemicals, Textiles, Food Processing

VERACRUZ LLAVE — Iron & Steel, Textiles, Metalworking

GUADALAJARA — Metalworking, Textiles, Food Processing, Leather Products

ORIZABA — Textiles, Cement

MEXICO CITY–PUEBLA — Metalworking, Textiles, Leather Products, Food Processing, Chemicals, Automobile Assembly

DOMINANT LAND USE

- Wheat, Livestock
- Cereals (chiefly corn), Livestock
- Diversified Tropical Cash Crops
- Cotton, Mixed Cereals
- Livestock, Limited Agriculture
- Range Livestock
- Forests
- Nonagricultural Land

MAJOR MINERAL OCCURRENCES

Ag	Silver	G	Natural Gas	O	Petroleum
Au	Gold	Gr	Graphite	Pb	Lead
C	Coal	Hg	Mercury	S	Sulfur
Cu	Copper	Mn	Manganese	Sb	Antimony
F	Fluorspar	Mo	Molybdenum	Sn	Tin
Fe	Iron Ore	Na	Salt	W	Tungsten
				Zn	Zinc

⚡ Water Power

Major Industrial Areas

GUATEMALA

AREA 42,042 sq. mi.
POPULATION 5,200,000
CAPITAL Guatemala
LARGEST CITY Guatemala
HIGHEST POINT Tajumulco 13,845 ft.
MONETARY UNIT quetzal
MAJOR LANGUAGES Spanish, Quiché
MAJOR RELIGION Roman Catholicism

BELIZE

AREA 8,867 sq. mi.
POPULATION 122,000
CAPITAL Belmopan
LARGEST CITY Belize City
HIGHEST POINT Victoria Peak, 3,681 ft.
MONETARY UNIT Belize dollar
MAJOR LANGUAGES English, Spanish, Mayan
MAJOR RELIGIONS Protestantism, Roman Catholicism

EL SALVADOR

AREA 8,260 sq. mi.
POPULATION 3,418,455
CAPITAL San Salvador
LARGEST CITY San Salvador
HIGHEST POINT Santa Ana 7,825 ft.
MONETARY UNIT colón
MAJOR LANGUAGE Spanish
MAJOR RELIGION Roman Catholicism

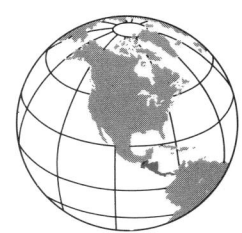

HONDURAS

AREA 43,277 sq. mi.
POPULATION 2,495,000
CAPITAL Tegucigalpa
LARGEST CITY Tegucigalpa
HIGHEST POINT Las Minas 9,347 ft.
MONETARY UNIT lempira
MAJOR LANGUAGE Spanish
MAJOR RELIGION Roman Catholicism

NICARAGUA

AREA 45,698 sq. mi.
POPULATION 1,984,000
CAPITAL Managua
LARGEST CITY Managua
HIGHEST POINT Cerro Mocotón 6,913 ft.
MONETARY UNIT córdoba
MAJOR LANGUAGE Spanish
MAJOR RELIGION Roman Catholicism

COSTA RICA

AREA 19,575 sq. mi.
POPULATION 1,800,000
CAPITAL San José
LARGEST CITY San José
HIGHEST POINT Chirripó Grande 12,530 ft.
MONETARY UNIT colón
MAJOR LANGUAGE Spanish
MAJOR RELIGION Roman Catholicism

PANAMA

AREA 29,856 sq. mi.
POPULATION 1,469,993
CAPITAL Panamá
LARGEST CITY Panamá
HIGHEST POINT Vol. Chiriquí 11,401 ft.
MONETARY UNIT balboa
MAJOR LANGUAGE Spanish
MAJOR RELIGION Roman Catholicism

Agriculture, Industry and Resources

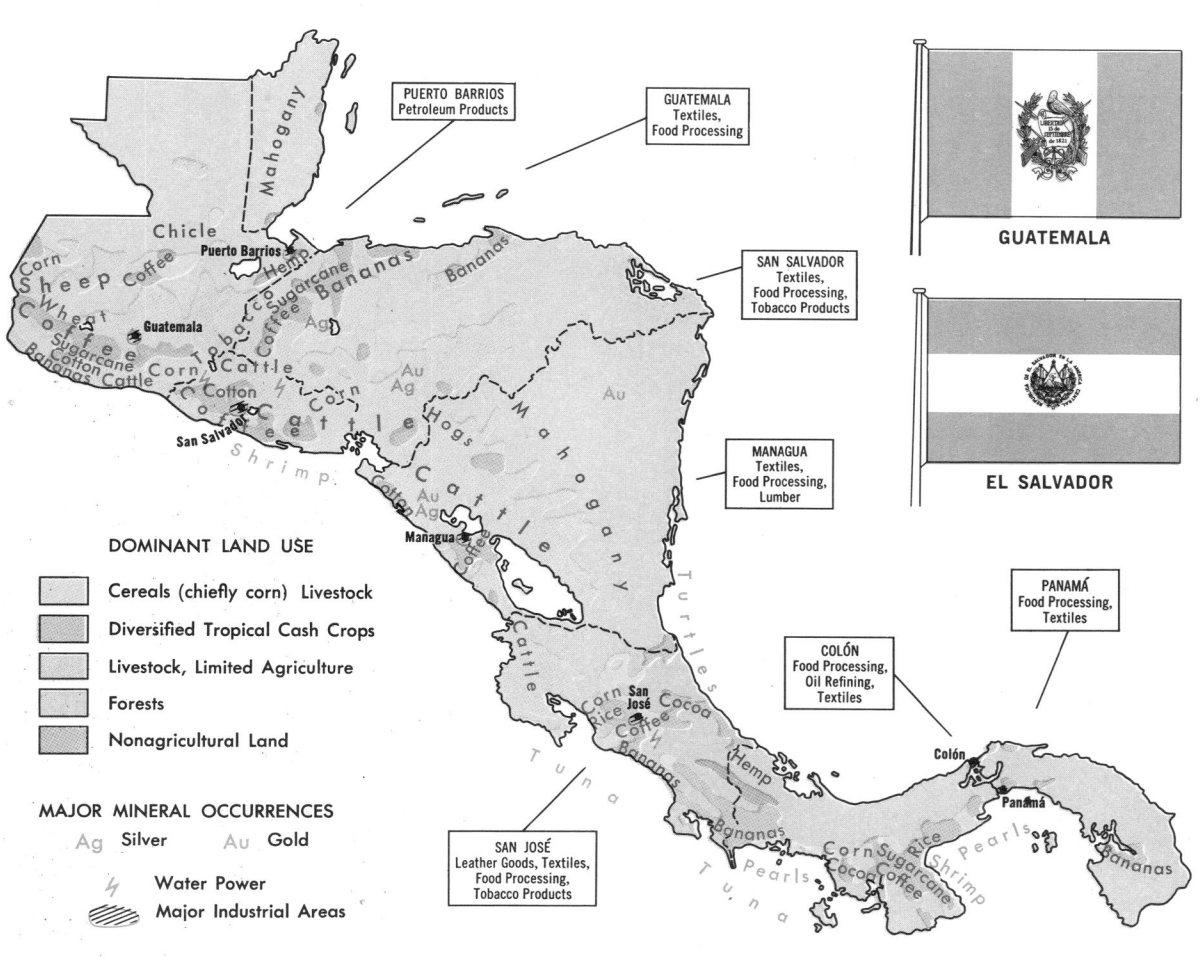

DOMINANT LAND USE

- Cereals (chiefly corn) Livestock
- Diversified Tropical Cash Crops
- Livestock, Limited Agriculture
- Forests
- Nonagricultural Land

MAJOR MINERAL OCCURRENCES

Ag Silver   Au Gold

⚡ Water Power
Major Industrial Areas

BELIZE

GUATEMALA
Textiles,
Food Processing

PUERTO BARRIOS
Petroleum Products

SAN SALVADOR
Textiles,
Food Processing,
Tobacco Products

MANAGUA
Textiles,
Food Processing,
Lumber

PANAMÁ
Food Processing,
Textiles

COLÓN
Food Processing,
Oil Refining,
Textiles

SAN JOSÉ
Leather Goods, Textiles,
Food Processing,
Tobacco Products

GUATEMALA

EL SALVADOR

HONDURAS

NICARAGUA

COSTA RICA

PANAMA

El Paraíso, Copán, 1,787 ...C 3
El Paraíso, El Paraíso, 5,758 ...D 4
El Porvenir, 529 ...D 3
El Progreso, 8,718 ...D 3
El Triunfo, 2,136 ...D 4
Goascorán, 1,184 ...D 3
Gracias, 2,484 ...C 3
Guaimaca, 2,620 ...D 3
Gualpatanta ...E 3
Guanaja, 1,253 ...E 2
Guarita, 599 ...C 3
Guayape, 610 ...D 3
Iriona, 119 ...E 2
Jacaleapa, 992 ...D 3
Jesús de Otoro, 2,775 ...D 3
Jutiapa, 1,711 ...D 3
Juticalpa, 7,912 ...D 3
La Ceiba, 33,934 ...D 3
La Concepción ...C 3
La Esperanza, 2,000 ...D 3
La Guata, 281 ...E 3
La Paz, 5,542 ...D 3
La Protección ...C 3
Lauterique, 272 ...D 3
Limón, 1,934 ...E 3
Manto, 943 ...D 3
Marcala, 1,968 ...C 3
Melcher ...D 3

Morazán, 3,924 ...D 3
Morocelí, 1,472 ...D 3
Nacaome, 4,376 ...D 4
Namasigüe, 1,024 ...D 4
Naranjito, 3,291 ...C 3
Nueva Armenia, 866 ...D 4
Nueva Ocotepeque, 4,608 ...C 3
Olanchito, 5,008 ...D 3
Omoa, 1,384 ...C 3
Paso Real ...E 3
Patuca ...D 3
Pespire, 1,758 ...D 3
Puerto Castilla ...D 2
Puerto Cortés, 21,600 ...C 3
Roatán, 1,883 ...D 2
Sabanagrande, 1,657 ...D 3
Salado ...D 3
San Esteban, 763 ...D 3
San Francisco, 1,122 ...D 3
San Francisco de la Paz, 1,971 ...D 3
San Juan de Flores, 1,174 ...D 3
San Luis, 2,631 ...C 3
San Marcos, 1,576 ...C 3
San Pedro Sula, 90,538 ...C 3
San Pedro Zacapa, 765 ...C 3
Santa Bárbara, 6,129 ...C 3
Santa Cruz de Yojoa, 1,833 ...D 3

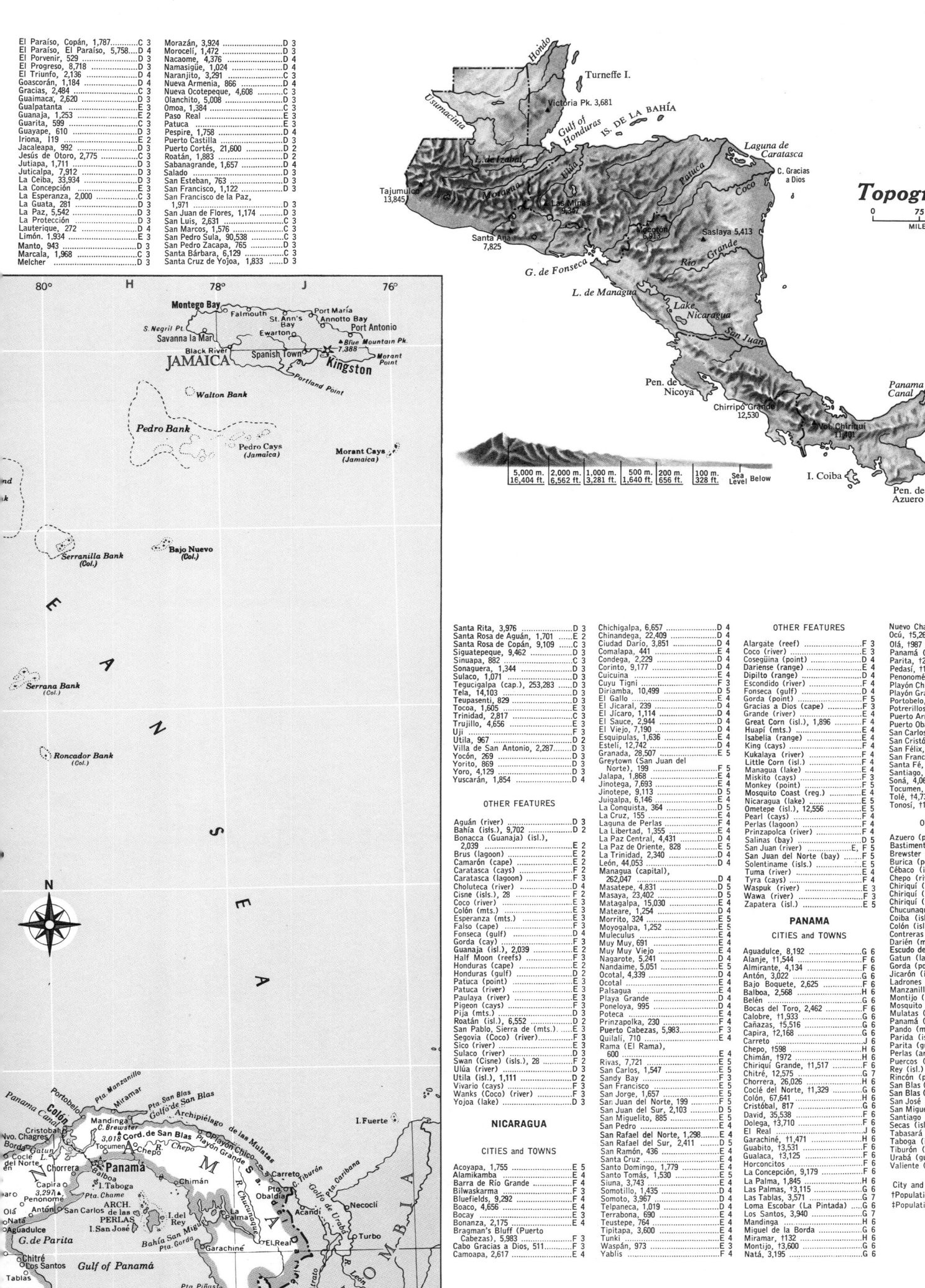

Santa Rita, 3,976 ...D 3
Santa Rosa de Aguán, 1,701 ...E 2
Santa Rosa de Copán, 9,109 ...C 3
Siguatepeque, 9,462 ...D 3
Sinuapa, 882 ...C 3
Sonaguera, 1,344 ...D 3
Sulaco, 1,071 ...D 3
Tegucigalpa (cap.), 253,283 ...D 3
Tela, 14,103 ...D 3
Teupasenti, 829 ...D 3
Tocoa, 1,605 ...E 3
Trinidad, 2,817 ...D 3
Trujillo, 4,656 ...E 3
Uji ...F 3
Utila, 967 ...D 2
Villa de San Antonio, 2,287 ...D 3
Yocón, 269 ...D 3
Yorito, 869 ...D 3
Yoro, 4,129 ...D 3
Yuscarán, 1,854 ...D 4

OTHER FEATURES

Aguán (river) ...D 3
Bahía (isls.), 9,702 ...D 2
Bonacca (Guanaja) (isl.), 2,039 ...E 2
Brus (lagoon) ...E 2
Camarón (cape) ...E 2
Caratasca (cays) ...F 2
Caratasca (lagoon) ...F 3
Choluteca (river) ...D 3
Cisne (isls.), 28 ...E 2
Coco (river) ...E 3
Colón (mts.) ...E 3
Esperanza (mts.) ...E 3
Falso (cape) ...F 3
Fonseca (gulf) ...D 3
Gorda (cay) ...F 2
Guanaja (isl.), 2,039 ...E 2
Half Moon (reefs) ...F 3
Honduras (cape) ...D 2
Honduras (gulf) ...D 2
Patuca (point) ...E 3
Patuca (river) ...E 3
Paulaya (river) ...E 3
Pigeon (cays) ...F 3
Pija (mts.) ...D 3
Roatán (isl.), 6,552 ...D 2
San Pablo, Sierra de (mts.) ...E 3
Segovia (Coco) (river) ...F 3
Sico (river) ...E 3
Sulaco (river) ...D 3
Swan (Cisne) (isls.), 28 ...E 2
Ulúa (river) ...D 3
Utila (isl.), 1,111 ...D 2
Vivario (cays) ...F 3
Wanks (Coco) (river) ...D 3
Yojoa (lake) ...D 3

Chichigalpa, 6,657 ...D 4
Chinandega, 22,409 ...D 4
Ciudad Darío, 3,851 ...D 4
Comalapa, 441 ...E 4
Condega, 2,229 ...D 4
Corinto, 9,177 ...D 4
Cuicuina ...E 4
Cuyu Tigni ...F 3
Diriamba, 10,499 ...D 5
El Gallo ...E 4
El Jicaral, 239 ...D 4
El Jícaro, 1,114 ...D 4
El Sauce, 2,944 ...D 4
El Viejo, 7,190 ...D 4
Esquipulas, 1,636 ...E 4
Estelí, 12,742 ...D 4
Granada, 28,507 ...E 5
Greytown (San Juan del Norte), 199 ...F 5
Jalapa, 1,868 ...E 4
Jinotega, 7,693 ...E 4
Jinotepe, 9,113 ...D 5
Juigalpa, 6,146 ...E 4
La Conquista, 364 ...D 5
La Cruz, 155 ...E 5
La Libertad, 1,355 ...E 4
La Paz Central, 4,431 ...D 4
La Paz de Oriente, 828 ...E 5
La Trinidad, 2,340 ...E 4
León, 44,053 ...D 4
Managua (capital), 262,047 ...D 4
Masatepe, 4,831 ...D 5
Masaya, 23,402 ...D 5
Matagalpa, 15,030 ...E 4
Mateare, 1,254 ...D 4
Morrito, 324 ...E 5
Moyogalpa, 1,252 ...E 5
Muluculus ...E 4
Muy Muy, 691 ...E 4
Muy Muy Viejo ...E 4
Nagarote, 5,241 ...D 4
Nandaime, 5,051 ...E 5
Ocotal, 4,339 ...E 4
Ocotal ...E 4
Palsagua ...E 4
Playa Grande ...D 4
Poneloya, 995 ...D 4
Poteca ...E 4
Prinzapolka, 230 ...F 4
Puerto Cabezas, 5,983 ...F 3
Quilalí, 710 ...E 4
Rama (El Rama), 600 ...E 4

NICARAGUA

CITIES and TOWNS

Acoyapa, 1,755 ...E 5
Alamikamba ...F 4
Barra de Río Grande ...F 4
Bilwaskarma ...F 3
Bluefields, 9,292 ...F 4
Boaco, 4,656 ...E 4
Bocay ...E 4
Bonanza, 2,175 ...E 4
Bragman's Bluff (Puerto Cabezas), 5,983 ...F 3
Cabo Gracias a Dios, 511 ...F 3
Camoapa, 2,617 ...E 4

Rivas, 7,721 ...E 5
San Carlos, 1,547 ...E 5
Sandy Bay ...F 3
San Francisco ...E 5
San Jorge, 1,657 ...E 5
San Juan del Norte, 199 ...F 5
San Juan del Sur, 2,103 ...D 5
San Miguelito, 885 ...E 5
San Pedro ...E 4
San Rafael del Norte, 1,298 ...E 4
San Rafael del Sur, 2,411 ...D 5
San Ramón, 436 ...E 4
Santa Cruz ...E 4
Santo Domingo, 1,779 ...E 4
Santo Tomás, 1,530 ...E 4
Siuna, 3,743 ...E 4
Somotillo, 1,435 ...D 4
Somoto, 3,967 ...D 4
Telpaneca, 1,019 ...D 4
Terrabona, 690 ...E 4
Teustepe, 764 ...E 4
Tipitapa, 3,600 ...E 4
Tunki ...E 4
Waspán, 973 ...F 3
Yablis ...F 4

OTHER FEATURES

Alargate (reef) ...F 3
Coco (river) ...E 3
Coseguina (point) ...D 4
Dariense (range) ...E 4
Dipilto (range) ...D 4
Escondido (river) ...F 4
Fonseca (gulf) ...D 4
Gorda (point) ...F 4
Gracias a Dios (cape) ...F 3
Grande (river) ...F 4
Great Corn (isl.), 1,896 ...F 4
Huapí (mts.) ...E 4
Isabelia (range) ...E 4
King (cays) ...F 4
Kukalaya (river) ...F 4
Little Corn (isl.) ...F 4
Managua (lake) ...E 4
Miskito (cays) ...F 3
Monkey (point) ...F 4
Mosquito Coast (reg.) ...E 4
Nicaragua (lake) ...E 5
Ometepe (isl.), 12,556 ...E 5
Pearl (cays) ...F 4
Perlas (lagoon) ...F 4
Prinzapolca (river) ...F 4
Salinas (bay) ...D 5
San Juan (river) ...E, F 5
San Juan del Norte (bay) ...F 5
Solentiname (isls.) ...E 5
Tuma (river) ...E 4
Tyra (cays) ...F 4
Waspuk (river) ...E 3
Wawa (river) ...F 3
Zapatera (isl.) ...E 5

PANAMA

CITIES and TOWNS

Aguadulce, 8,192 ...G 6
Alanje, †1,544 ...F 6
Almirante, 4,134 ...F 6
Antón, 3,022 ...G 6
Bajo Boquete, 2,625 ...F 6
Balboa, 2,568 ...H 6
Belén ...G 6
Bocas del Toro, 2,462 ...F 6
Calobre, †1,933 ...G 6
Cañazas, †5,516 ...G 6
Capira, †2,168 ...G 6
Carreto ...J 6
Chepo, †598 ...H 6
Chimán, 1972 ...H 6
Chiriquí Grande, †1,517 ...F 6
Chitré, 12,575 ...G 7
Chorrera, 26,026 ...H 6
Coclé del Norte, †1,329 ...G 6
Colón, 67,641 ...H 6
Cristóbal, 817 ...H 6
David, 35,538 ...F 6
Dolega, †3,710 ...F 6
El Real ...J 6
Garachiné, †1,471 ...H 6
Guabito, †3,531 ...F 6
Gualaca, †3,125 ...F 6
Horconcitos ...F 6
La Concepción, 9,179 ...F 6
La Palma, 1,845 ...H 6
Las Palmas, †3,115 ...G 6
Las Tablas, 3,571 ...G 7
Loma Escobar (La Pintada) ...G 6
Los Santos, 3,940 ...G 7
Mandinga ...H 6
Miguel de la Borda ...G 6
Miramar, †132 ...F 6
Montijo, †3,600 ...G 6
Natá, 3,195 ...G 6

Nuevo Chagres ...G 6
Ocú, †5,267 ...G 7
Olá, †987 ...G 6
Panamá (cap.), 418,013 ...H 6
Parita, 12,320 ...G 7
Pedasí, †1,302 ...G 7
Penonomé, 5,067 ...G 6
Playón Chico ...H 6
Playón Grande ...H 6
Portobelo, 1626 ...H 6
Potrerillos ...F 6
Puerto Armuelles, 12,022 ...F 6
Puerto Obaldía ...J 6
San Carlos, †1,421 ...H 6
San Cristóbal ...G 6
San Félix, †1,314 ...F 6
San Francisco, †1,576 ...G 6
Santa Fé, †1,768 ...G 6
Santiago, 14,391 ...G 6
Soná, 4,066 ...G 6
Tocumen, †5,905 ...H 6
Tolé, †4,734 ...F 6
Tonosí, †1,301 ...G 7

OTHER FEATURES

Azuero (pen.) ...G 7
Bastimentos (isl.), 574 ...G 6
Brewster (mt.) ...H 6
Burica (point) ...F 6
Cébaco (isl.) ...G 7
Chepo (river) ...H 6
Chiriquí (gulf) ...F 7
Chiriquí (lagoon) ...F 6
Chiriquí (volcano) ...F 6
Chucunaque (river) ...J 7
Coiba (isl.) ...F 7
Colón (isl.) ...F 6
Contreras (isls.) ...F 7
Darién (mts.) ...J 6
Escudo de Veraguas (isl.) ...G 6
Gatún (lake) ...H 6
Gorda (point) ...H 6
Jicarón (isl.) ...G 7
Ladrones (isls.) ...F 6
Manzanillo (point) ...H 6
Montijo (gulf) ...G 7
Mosquito (gulf) ...G 6
Mulatas (arch.) ...J 6
Panamá (gulf) ...H 7
Pando (mt.) ...F 6
Parida (isl.) ...F 6
Parita (gulf) ...G 6
Perlas (arch.) ...H 7
Puercos (prom.) ...G 7
Rey (isl.) ...H 6
Rincón (point) ...H 6
San Blas (gulf) ...H 6
San Blas (range) ...H 6
San José (isl.) ...H 6
San Miguel (bay) ...H 6
Santiago (mt.) ...G 7
Secas (isls.) ...F 6
Tabasará (mts.) ...F 6
Taboga (isl.), 1,747 ...H 6
Tiburón (cape) ...J 6
Urabá (gulf) ...J 6
Valiente (pen.) ...G 6

City and suburbs.
†Population of sub-district.
‡Population of district.

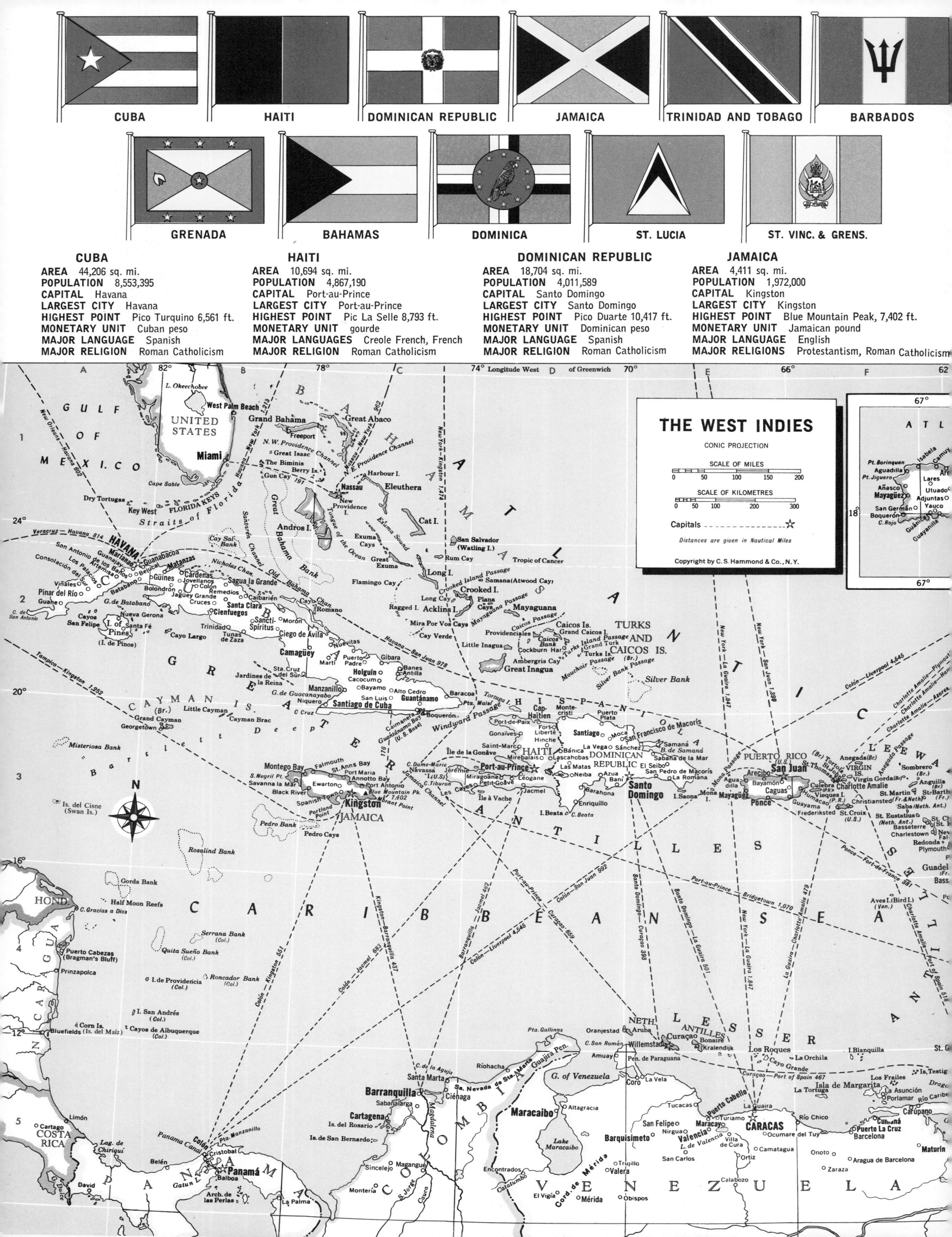

CUBA

HAITI

DOMINICAN REPUBLIC

JAMAICA

TRINIDAD AND TOBAGO

BARBADOS

GRENADA

BAHAMAS

DOMINICA

ST. LUCIA

ST. VINC. & GRENS.

CUBA
AREA 44,206 sq. mi.
POPULATION 8,553,395
CAPITAL Havana
LARGEST CITY Havana
HIGHEST POINT Pico Turquino 6,561 ft.
MONETARY UNIT Cuban peso
MAJOR LANGUAGE Spanish
MAJOR RELIGION Roman Catholicism

HAITI
AREA 10,694 sq. mi.
POPULATION 4,867,190
CAPITAL Port-au-Prince
LARGEST CITY Port-au-Prince
HIGHEST POINT Pic La Selle 8,793 ft.
MONETARY UNIT gourde
MAJOR LANGUAGES Creole French, French
MAJOR RELIGION Roman Catholicism

DOMINICAN REPUBLIC
AREA 18,704 sq. mi.
POPULATION 4,011,589
CAPITAL Santo Domingo
LARGEST CITY Santo Domingo
HIGHEST POINT Pico Duarte 10,417 ft.
MONETARY UNIT Dominican peso
MAJOR LANGUAGE Spanish
MAJOR RELIGION Roman Catholicism

JAMAICA
AREA 4,411 sq. mi.
POPULATION 1,972,000
CAPITAL Kingston
LARGEST CITY Kingston
HIGHEST POINT Blue Mountain Peak, 7,402 ft.
MONETARY UNIT Jamaican pound
MAJOR LANGUAGE English
MAJOR RELIGIONS Protestantism, Roman Catholicism

THE WEST INDIES

CONIC PROJECTION

SCALE OF MILES

SCALE OF KILOMETRES

Capitals ------------ ☆

Distances are given in Nautical Miles

Copyright by C. S. Hammond & Co., N.Y.

SAINT LUCIA
AREA 238 sq. mi.
POPULATION 111,800
CAPITAL Castries
HIGHEST POINT Mt. Gimie 3,117 ft.
MONETARY UNIT East Caribbean dollar
MAJOR LANGUAGES English, French patois
MAJOR RELIGIONS Roman Catholicism, Protestantism

GRENADA
AREA 133 sq. mi.
POPULATION 96,000
CAPITAL St. George's
LARGEST CITY St. George's
HIGHEST POINT Mt. St. Catherine 2,757 ft.
MONETARY UNIT East Caribbean dollar
MAJOR LANGUAGES English, French patois
MAJOR RELIGIONS Roman Catholicism, Protestantism

SAINT VINCENT & THE GRENADINES
AREA 150 sq. mi.
POPULATION 104,000
CAPITAL Kingstown
HIGHEST POINT Soufrière 4,000 ft.
MONETARY UNIT East Caribbean dollar
MAJOR LANGUAGES English
MAJOR RELIGIONS Protestantism, Roman Catholicism

TRINIDAD AND TOBAGO
AREA 1,980 sq. mi.
POPULATION 1,040,000
CAPITAL Port of Spain
LARGEST CITY Port of Spain
HIGHEST POINT Mt. Aripo 3,084 ft.
MONETARY UNIT Trinidad and Tobago dollar
MAJOR LANGUAGES English, Hindi
MAJOR RELIGIONS Roman Catholicism, Protestantism, Hinduism, Islam

DOMINICA
AREA 290 sq. mi.
POPULATION 70,302
CAPITAL Roseau
HIGHEST POINT Morne Diablotin 4,747
MONETARY UNIT East Caribbean dollar
MAJOR LANGUAGES English, French patois
MAJOR RELIGIONS Roman Catholicism, Protestantism

BAHAMAS
AREA 5,382 sq. mi.
POPULATION 197,000
CAPITAL Nassau
LARGEST CITY Nassau
HIGHEST POINT Mt. Alvernia 206 ft.
MONETARY UNIT Bahamian dollar
MAJOR LANGUAGE English
MAJOR RELIGIONS Roman Catholicism, Protestantism

BARBADOS
AREA 166 sq. mi.
POPULATION 253,620
CAPITAL Bridgetown
LARGEST CITY Bridgetown
HIGHEST POINT Mt. Hillaby 1,104 ft.
MONETARY UNIT East Caribbean dollar
MAJOR LANGUAGE English
MAJOR RELIGION Protestantism

NETHERLANDS ANTILLES
AREA 390 sq. mi.
POPULATION 220,000
CAPITAL Willemstad
MONETARY UNIT Antilles guilder
MAJOR LANGUAGES Dutch, Papiamento, English
MAJOR RELIGIONS Roman Catholicism, Protestantism

PUERTO RICO
AREA 3,435 sq. mi.
POPULATION 2,712,033
CAPITAL San Juan
MONETARY UNIT U.S. dollar
MAJOR LANGUAGES Spanish, English
MAJOR RELIGION Roman Catholicism

VIRGIN ISLANDS (BR.)
AREA 59 sq. mi.
POPULATION 10,484
CAPITAL Road Town
MONETARY UNIT British West Indian dollar
MAJOR LANGUAGES English, Creole
MAJOR RELIGION Protestantism

VIRGIN ISLANDS (U.S.)
AREA 133 sq. mi.
POPULATION 62,468
CAPITAL Charlotte Amalie
MONETARY UNIT U.S. dollar
MAJOR LANGUAGES English, Creole
MAJOR RELIGIONS Roman Catholicism, Protestantism

BERMUDA
AREA 21 sq. mi.
POPULATION 52,000
CAPITAL Hamilton
MONETARY UNIT Bermuda dollar
MAJOR LANGUAGE English
MAJOR RELIGION Protestantism

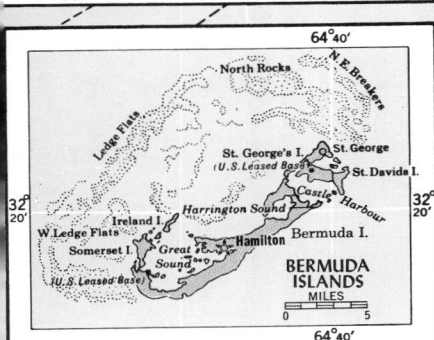

ANTIGUA
Barbuda (isl.), 1,145 ....G 3
Redonda (isl.) ....F 3
Saint John's (cap.), 24,367 ......G 3

BAHAMAS
Acklins (isl.), 1,160 ....C 2
Andros (isl.), 7,460 ....B 1
Atwood (Samana) (cay), 32.....D 2
Berry (isls.), 266 ....B 1
Biminis, The (isl.), 1,576.........B 1
Cat (isl.), 3,131 ....C 1
Crooked (isl.), 764 ....D 2
Eleuthera (isl.), 7,247 ....C 1
Exuma (isls.), 220 ....C 1
Exuma (Great Exuma) (isl.),
  2,854 ....C 2
Grand Bahama (isl.), 7,847......B 1
Great Abaco (isl.), 4,746 ....C 1
Great Exuma (isl.), 2,854 ....C 2
Great Inagua (isl.), 1,240 ....D 2
Great Issac (cay), 5 ....B 1
Gun (cay), 3 ....B 1
Harbour (isl.), 997 ....C 1
Long (cay), 22 ....C 2
Long (isl.), 4,176 ....C 2
Mayaguana (isl.), 707 ....D 2
Nassau (cap.), *100,000...........C 1
New Providence (isl.), 100,000...C 1
Plana (cays), 3 ....D 2
Ragged (isl.), 371 ....C 2
Rum (cay), 77 ....C 2
Samana (cay), 32 ....D 2
San Salvador (isl.), 968 ....C 1
Tongue of the Ocean (chan.)....C 1
Watling (San Salvador) (isl.),
  968 ....C 1

BARBADOS
Bridgetown (cap.), 12,430.........G 4

BERMUDA
Bermuda (isl.) ....H 3
Castle (harb.) ....H 2
Great (sound) ....G 3
Hamilton (cap.), 3,000 ....H 3
Hamilton, *14,156 ....H 3
Harrington (sound) ....G 3
Ireland (isl.) ....G 3
Saint David's (isl.) ....H 2
Saint George, 1,335 ....H 2
Saint George's (isl.) ....H 2
Somerset (isl.) ....G 3

CAYMAN ISLANDS
Total Population, 10,652
Cayman Brac (isl.), 1,240 ....B 3
Georgetown (cap.), 4,106 ....B 3
Grand Cayman (isl.), 9,309 ......B 3
Little Cayman (isl.), 23 ....B 3

CUBA
Bayamo, 45,400 ....C 2
Camagüey, 178,600 ....B 2
Cárdenas, 67,400 ....B 2
Ciego de Ávila, 54,700 ....B 2
Cienfuegos, 91,800 ....B 2
Florida (straits) ....B 1
Guanabacoa, 41,000 ....B 2
Guantánamo, 135,100 ....C 2
Güines, 45,000 ....B 2
Havana (cap.), *1,577,200 ....A 2
Holguín, 100,500 ....C 2
Manzanillo, 91,200 ....C 2
Marianao, 454,700 ....A 2
Matanzas, 84,100 ....B 2
Pinar del Río, 67,600 ....A 2
Pines (Pinos) (isl.), 20,630.......A 2
Sagua la Grande, 35,200 ....B 2
Sancti-Spíritus, 62,500 ....B 2
San Felipe (cay), 391 ....A 2

DOMINICA
Roseau (cap.), *16,677 ....G 4

DOMINICAN REPUBLIC
Barahona, 37,889 ....D 3
La Romana, 36,722 ....E 3
La Vega, 31,085 ....D 3
Puerto Plata, 32,181 ....D 3
San Francisco de Macorís,
  43,941 ....E 3
San Pedro de Macorís, 42,473...E 3
Santiago, 155,151 ....D 3
Santo Domingo (cap.), 671,402...E 3

GRENADA
Carriacou (isl.), 6,958 ....G 4
Gouyave, 2,356 ....F 4
Grenadines (isls.), 5,612...........G 4
Saint George's (cap.), *26,843...F 5

GUADELOUPE
Basse-Terre (cap.), 16,000 ....F 4
Saint-Barthélemy (isl.), 2,351....F 3
Saint-Martin (isl.), 5,062 ....F 3

HAITI
Cap-Haïtien, 30,000 ....D 3
Gonâve (isl.), 45,411 ....D 3
Jacmel, †199,598 ....D 3
Léogane, †140,607 ....D 3
Les Cayes, †95,446 ....C 3
Port-au-Prince (cap.), *352,681..D 3
Tortuga (Tortue) (isl.), 13,723..D 2

SANTA CLARA / CUBA (cont.)
Santa Clara, 137,700 ....B 2
Santiago de Cuba, 259,000 ......B 2
Viñales, 1,602 ....A 2
Windward (passage) ....C 3

JAMAICA
Blue Mountain (peak) ....C 3
Jamaica (channel) ....C 3
Kingston (cap.), *376,520 ....C 3
Montego Bay, 23,610 ....B 3
Pedro (cays) ....C 3
Port Antonio, 7,830 ....C 3
Savanna la Mar, 9,789 ....B 3
Spanish Town, 14,706 ....C 3

MARTINIQUE
Forte-de-France (cap.), 100,000..G 4
Pelée (isl.) ....G 4

MONTSERRAT
Total Population, 12,300
Plymouth (cap.), 3,000 ....F 3

NETHERLANDS ANTILLES
Aruba (isl.), 58,868 ....E 4
Bonaire (isl.), 5,755 ....E 4
Curaçao (isl.), 196,170 ....E 4
Saba (isl.), 1,094 ....F 3
Saint Eustatius (isl.), 1,020......F 3
Sint Maarten (Saint Martin)
  (isl.), 4,970 ....F 3
Willemstad (cap.), *94,133........E 4

PUERTO RICO
Aguadilla, 21,031 ....F 1
Arecibo, 35,484 ....G 1
Bayamón, 147,552 ....G 1
Caguas, ‡95,661 ....G 1
Cataño, 26,459 ....G 1
Cayey, 21,562 ....G 1
Culebra (isl.), 732 ....G 1
Guayama, 20,318 ....G 1
Humacao, 12,411 ....G 1
Mayagüez, ‡85,857 ....F 1
Mona (isl.), 6 ....F 1
Ponce, ‡158,981 ....F 1
San Juan (cap.), ‡851,247 ....G 1
Vieques (isl.), 7,767 ....G 1

SAINT CHRISTOPHER-NEVIS-ANGUILLA
Anguilla (isl.), 5,605 ....F 3
Basseterre (cap.), 15,726 ....F 3
Sombrero (isl.), 5 ....F 3

SAINT LUCIA
Castries (cap.), *15,291 ....G 4

SAINT VINCENT & THE GRENADINES
Bequia (isl.) ....G 4
Canouan (isl.) ....G 4
Grenadines (isls.), 6,428 ....G 4
Kingstown (cap.), *23,482 ....G 4
Union (isl.) ....G 4

TRINIDAD AND TOBAGO
Port of Spain (cap.), *250,000...G 5
Scarborough, 1,931 ....G 5
Tobago (isl.), 36,850 ....G 5
Trinidad (isl.), 973,250 ....G 5

TURKS AND CAICOS IS.
Total Population, 6,000
Caicos (isls.), 2,200 ....D 2
Cockburn Harbour, 866 ....D 2
Grand Turk (isl.), 2,339 ....D 2
Providenciales (isl.), 510 ....D 2
Turks (isls.), 3,800 ....D 2

VIRGIN ISLANDS (BRITISH)
Anegada (isl.), 290 ....H 1
Road Town (cap.), 2,183 ....H 1

VIRGIN ISLANDS (U.S.)
Charlotte Amalie (cap.), 12,220..H 1
Saint Croix (isl.), 31,779 ....H 1
Saint John (isl.), 1,729 ....H 1
Saint Thomas (isl.), 28,960 ......H 1

WEST INDIES
Antilles Gtr. (isls.), 22,094,100...D 3
Antilles, Lesser, 2,749,000 ....F 4
Hispaniola (isl.), 8,878,800 ......D 2
Leeward (isls.), 599,300 ....F 3
Navassa (isl.) ....C 3
Windward (isls.), 2,149,750......G 4

*City and suburbs.
†Population of commune.
‡Population of met. area.

Topography
0   100   200
MILES

Below Sea Level | 100 m. 328 ft. | 200 m. 656 ft. | 500 m. 1,640 ft. | 1,000 m. 3,281 ft. | 2,000 m. 6,562 ft. | 5,000 m. 16,404 ft.

CUBA

PROVINCES

Camagüey, 889,600 ....G 2
Havana (La Habana), 2,150,300...C 1
Las Villas, 1,320,900 ....E 2
Matanzas, 483,300 ....D 1
Oriente, 2,857,200 ....H 4
Pinar del Río, 648,100 ....A 1

CITIES and TOWNS

Abreus, 1,682 ....D 2
Agramonte, 2,948 ....D 2
Aguada de Pasajeros, 9,000........D 2
Alacranes, 3,165 ....D 1
Alquízar, 9,600 ....C 1
Alto Cedro, 679 ....J 4
Alto Songo, 2,197 ....J 4
Amarillas, 1,935 ....D 2
Antilla, 7,500 ....J 3
Arcos de Canasí, 1,103 ....C 1
Artemisa, 27,300 ....C 1
Báez, 2,223 ....E 2
Bahía Honda, 5,200 ....B 1
Baire, 5,300 ....H 4
Banagüises, 1,245 ....D 2
Banes, 27,900 ....J 3
Baracoa, 13,000 ....K 4
Bartle, 1,052 ....G 3
Bauta, 16,800 ....C 1
Bayamo, 45,400 ....H 4
Bejucal, 12,900 ....C 1
Bolondrón, 3,444 ....D 1
Boquerón, ...K 4
Bueycito, 1,109 ....H 4
Cabaiguán, 20,800 ....E 2
Cabañas, 2,226 ....B 1
Cacocum, 2,724 ....J 3
Caibarién, 26,400 ....H 2

Caimanera, 8,600 ....K 4
Calabazar de Sagua, 3,286 ....E 1
Calimete, 2,260 ....D 1
Camagüey, 178,600 ....G 3
Camajuaní, 14,200 ....E 1
Campechuela, 7,600 ....G 4
Cañas, 1,789 ....B 1
Candelaria, 3,548 ....B 1
Caney, 2,009 ....J 4
Caonao, 3,403 ....E 2
Cárdenas, 67,400 ....D 1
Cartagena, 1,239 ....D 2
Cascajal, 1,493 ....E 1
Cascorro, 2,442 ....H 3
Casilda, 2,445 ....E 2
Cauto, 3,137 ....H 4
Cayo Mambí, 1,553 ....K 3
Central Amancia Rodríguez,
    3,800 ....G 3
Central Amazonas, 1,405 ....F 2
Central América ....H 4
Central Antonio Guiteras, 8,300..H 3
Central Baraguá, 2,267 ....F 3
Central Colombia, 9,800 ....G 3
Central Jesús Menéndez, 7,400...H 3
Central Máximo Gómez, 5,100 ....J 2
Central Merceditas, 1,146 ....B 1
Central Niágara ....B 1
Central Santa Marta, 1,326 ....G 3
Central Tacajó, 1,298 ....J 3
Céspedes, 7,300 ....G 2
Chambas, 3,046 ....F 2
Cidra, 1,463 ....D 1
Ciego de Ávila, 54,700 ....F 2
Cienfuegos, 91,800 ....D 2
Cobre, 2,586 ....J 4
Cojímar, 7,400 ....C 1
Colón, 22,900 ....D 1
Consolación del Norte, 2,254 ....B 1
Consolación del Sur, 7,300 ....B 2
Contramaestre, 13.000 ....G 3

Corralillo, 1,123 ....D 1
Cristo, 6,200 ....J 4
Cruces, 15,100 ....E 2
Cueto, 8,700 ....J 4
Cumanayagua, 5,300 ....E 2
Cunagua, 1,879 ....F 2
Daiquirí ....J 4
Dos Caminos, 2,004 ....J 4
Encrucijada, 6,500 ....E 1
Esmeralda, 5,400 ....F 2
Esperanza, 7,300 ....E 2
Falla, 1,876 ....F 2
Flamenco de San Pedro ....F 3
Florida, 33,800 ....G 2
Fomento, 8,800 ....E 2
Fray Benito, 1,456 ....J 3
Garden City ....G 2
Gaspar, 1,740 ....F 2
Gibara, 8,400 ....J 3
Guadalupe, 1,098 ....F 2
Guáimaro, 4,800 ....G 3
Guamo, 2,507 ....H 3
Guanabacoa, 41,000 ....C 1
Guanajay, 13,700 ....B 1
Guane, 4,400 ....A 2
Guantánamo, 135,100 ....K 4
Guaro, 1,362 ....J 4
Guasimal, 1,752 ....E 2
Guayabal, Camagüey, 9,000 ....G 3
Guayabal, Oriente ....K 4
Guayos, 5,600 ....E 2
Güines, 45,000 ....C 1
Güira de Melena, 18,900 ....C 1
Guisa, 7,700 ....H 4
Hatuey, 1,737 ....G 3
Havana (cap.), 1,008,500 ....C 1
Havana, †1,577,200 ....C 1
Havana, ‡1,760,000 ....C 1
Holguín, 100,500 ....J 3
Imías ....K 4
Isabela de Sagua, 3,701 ....E 1
Martí, Camagüey ....G 2

Isabel María ....A 2
Isabel Rubio, 1,394 ....A 2
Itabo ....D 1
Jagüey Grande, 6,600 ....D 2
Jamaica ....K 4
Jaruco, 6,700 ....C 1
Jatibonico, 5,700 ....F 2
Jíbaro ....F 2
Jiguaní, 9,000 ....H 4
Jiquí, 1,135 ....E 2
Jobabo, 3,246 ....H 3
Jovellanos, 12,400 ....D 1
Júcaro, 1,411 ....F 2
La Coloma, 1,907 ....A 2
La Fé ....A 2
La Maya, 6,500 ....J 4
La Negros ....K 4
Las Martinas ....A 2
Laguna Larga ....G 2
Limonar, 3,301 ....D 1
Los Arabos, 1,690 ....E 1
Los Caños ....K 4
Los Indios, 1,103 ....B 2
Los Negros ....K 4
Los Palacios, 7,000 ....B 1
Lugareño, 3,135 ....G 2
Maceo, 1,433 ....H 3
Magarabomba ....G 2
Maisí ....K 4
Majagua ....F 2
Manacas, 2,515 ....E 1
Manatí, 2,318 ....H 3
Manguito, 2,569 ....D 1
Manicaragua, 3,993 ....E 2
Mantua ....A 2
Manzanillo, 91,200 ....H 4
Marianao, 454,700 ....C 1
Mariel, 6,700 ....B 1
Martí, Camagüey ....G 2

Martí, Matanzas, 2,605 ....D 1
Matanzas, 84,100 ....C 1
Matún ....D 2
Máximo Gómez ....D 1
Mayajigua, 2,950 ....F 2
Mayarí, 7,400 ....J 3
Mayarí Arriba, 900 ....J 4
McKinley ....B 2
Media Luna, ...G 4
Meneses, 1,650 ....F 2
Minas, 3,827 ....G 2
Minas de Matahambre, 5,400 ...A 1
Minas de Santa Lucía ....A 1
Miranda, 2,186 ....J 4
Morón, 26,600 ....F 2
Nicaro, 3,074 ....J 3
Niquero, 8,600 ....G 4
Nueva Gerona, 9,000 ....B 2
Nuevitas, 16,300 ....G 2
Omaja ....H 3
Orozco ....B 1
Palma Soriano, 33,700 ....J 4
Palmarito, 1,985 ....J 4
Palmira, 8,700 ....E 2
Palo Alto ....F 2
Paso Real de San Diego, 1,436...B 1
Pedro Betancourt, 8,000 ....D 1
Perico, 7,380 ....D 1
Piedrecitas, 1,619 ....F 2
Pilotos ....B 1
Pinar del Río, 67,600 ....B 2
Placetas, 38,800 ....E 2
Presidio Modelo ....C 2
Preston, 3,827 ....J 3
Puerta de Golpe, 1,512 ....B 2
Puerto Esperanza, 1,867 ....A 1
Puerto Padre, 15,900 ....H 3
Puerto Samá ....J 3
Puerto Tarafa ....H 3
Puerto Vita ....J 4

Quemado de Güines, 6,500 ....E 1
Quiebra Hacha, 1,584 ....B 1
Ramón de las Yaguas ....J 4
Rancho Veloz, 2,789 ....D 1
Ranchuelo, 12,500 ....E 2
Remates ....A 2
Remedios, 12,400 ....E 1
Río Seco, 1,615 ....A 2
Rodas, 5,900 ....D 2
Sábalo ....A 2
Sabana ....K 4
Sagua de Tánamo, 10,700 ....K 3
Sagua la Grande, 35,200 ....E 1
Salado ....H 3
San Agustín ....E 2
San Andrés, 1,655 ....H 3
San Antonio, 1,300 ....E 1
San Antonio de los Baños, 23,700 C 1
San Cristóbal, 5,600 ....B 1
San Germán, 9,700 ....J 3
San José de la Plata ....E 1
San José de las Lajas, 18,000 ....C 1
San José de los Ramos, 1,269 ......D 1
San Juan y Martínez, 6,700 ....A 2
San Luis, Oriente, 15,700 ....J 4
San Luis, Pinar del Río, 2,735 ......B 2
San Manuel, 2,105 ....J 3
San Miguel ....H 4
San Nicolás, 7,000 ....C 1
San Pedro ....H 4
San Ramón, 1,037 ....H 4
Sancti-Spíritus, 62,500 ....E 2
Santa Bárbara ....E 2
Santa Clara, 137,700 ....E 2
Santa Cruz del Norte, 3,537 ....C 1
Santa Cruz del Sur, 4,200 ....G 3
Santa Fé, 11,900 ....B 2
Santa Isabel de las Lajas, 6,200...E 2
Santa Lucía, Oriente ....J 3
Santa Lucía, Oriente ....H 2
Santa Rita, 1,655 ....H 4

Santiago de Cuba, 259,000 ....J 4
Santiago de las Vegas, 10,300.....C 1
Santo, 2,210 ....E 1
Santo Domingo, 9,600 ....E 1
Senado, 1,314 ....G 2
Sibanicú, 3,378 ....G 3
Siboney ....J 4
Stewart, 1,943 ....F 2
Surgidero de Batabanó, 5,075 .....C 1
Taco-Taco ....B 1
Tánamo, 2,032 ....K 3
Tiguabos, 1,286 ....K 4
Torriente ....D 2
Trinidad, 28,000 ....E 2
Tunas de Zaza, 1,380 ....F 2
Unión de Reyes, 5,500 ....C 1
Uvero Quemado ....A 2
Varadero, 2,640 ....D 1
Veguitas, 2,014 ....H 4
Velasco, 1,444 ....J 3
Vertientes, 10,200 ....G 3
Victoria de las Tunas, 29,700 ......H 3
Viñales, 1,602 ....A 1
Vista Hermosa ....H 4
Yaguajay, 5,900 ....F 2
Yara, 3,246 ....H 4
Yuraguanal ....J 4
Zarzal, 1,421 ....H 4
Zaza del Medio, 4,252 ....F 2
Zulueta, 4,254 ....E 1

OTHER FEATURES

Abalos (point) ....A 2
Ana María (gulf) ....F 3
Anclitas (key) ....G 3
Batabanó (gulf) ....C 1
Birama (point) ....G 3
Broa (inlet) ....C 1
Buena Vista (bay) ....F 2
Caballones (chan.) ....F 3

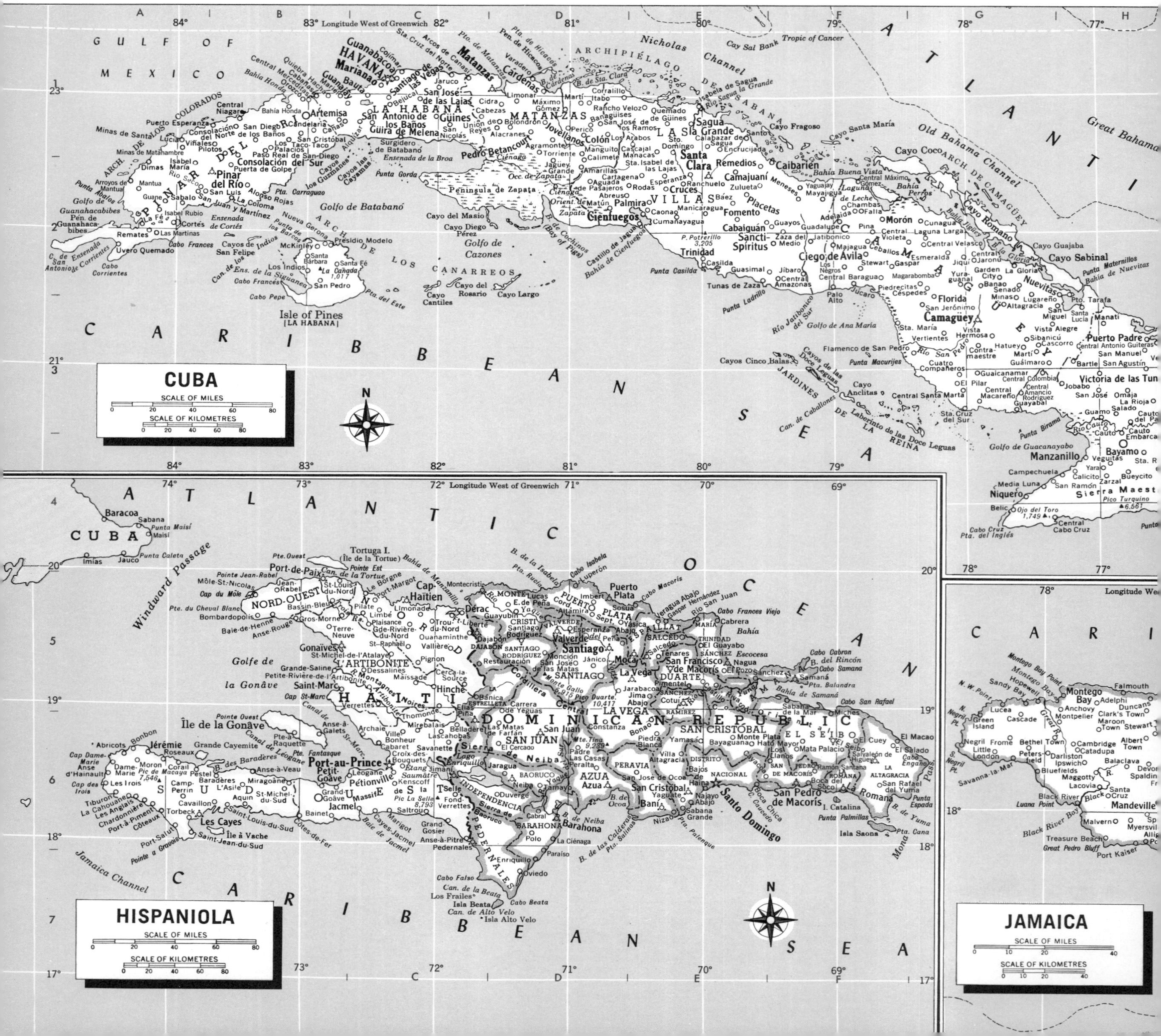

CUBA
SCALE OF MILES
0 20 40 60 80
SCALE OF KILOMETRES
0 20 40 60 80

HISPANIOLA
SCALE OF MILES
0 20 40 60 80
SCALE OF KILOMETRES
0 10 20 40 60 80

JAMAICA
SCALE OF MILES
0 20 40
SCALE OF KILOMETRES
0 10 20 40

Camagüey (arch.) .... G 2
Cantiles (cay) .... C 3
Cárdenas (bay) .... D 1
Carraguao (point) .... B 2
Casilda (point) .... E 2
Cauto (river) .... H 3
Cayamas (cays) .... C 2
Cazones (gulf) .... C 2
Cienfuegos (bay) .... D 2
Cinco Balas (cays) .... E 3
Cochinos (bay) .... D 2
Coco (cay) .... G 1
Corrientes (cape) .... A 2
Corrientes (inlet) .... A 2
Cortés (inlet) .... B 2
Cristal, Sierra del (mts.) .... J 4
Cruz (cape) .... G 4
Diego Pérez (cay) .... C 2
Doce Leguas (cays) .... F 3
Este (point) .... C 3
Fragoso (cay) .... F 1
Francés (cape) .... A 2
Gorda (point) .... C 2
Gran Piedra (mt.) .... J 4
Guacanayabo (gulf) .... G 4
Guajaba (cay) .... H 2
Guanahacabibes (gulf) .... A 2
Guanahacabibes (pen.) .... A 2
Guantánamo (bay) .... J 4
Guantánamo Bay U.S. Naval Reserve .... J 4
Guarico (point) .... K 3
Guzmanes (cays) .... B 2
Hicacos (pen.) .... D 1
Hicacos (point) .... D 1
Honda (bay) .... B 1
Indios (chan.) .... B 2
Inglés (point) .... G 4
Jardines de la Reina (arch.) .... F 3
Jatibonico del Sur (river) .... F 3
Jigüey (bay) .... G 2
Laberinto de las Doce Leguas (cays) .... F 3
La Cañada (mt.) .... B 2
La Gloria (bay) .... G 2
Ladrillo (point) .... E 2
Largo (cay) .... D 2
Leche (lagoon) .... F 2
Los Barcos (point) .... B 2
Los Canarreos (arch.) .... C 2
Los Colorados (arch.) .... A 1
Lucrecia (cape) .... J 3
Macurijes (point) .... F 3
Maestra, Sierra (mts.) .... H 4
Maisí (point) .... K 4
Mangle (point) .... J 3
Masio (cay) .... C 2
Matanzas (bay) .... D 1
Matanzas (point) .... H 2
Mayarí (river) .... J 4
Nicholas (chan.) .... E 1
Nipe (bay) .... J 3
Nuevitas (bay) .... H 2
Ojo del Toro (mt.) .... G 4
Old Bahama (chan.) .... G 1
Pepe (cape) .... B 1
Perros (bay) .... G 2
Pigs (Cochinos) (bay) .... D 2
Pines (isl.), 20,630 .... G 3
Potrerillo (peak) .... E 2
Quemado (point) .... A 4
Romano (cay) .... G 2
Rosario (cay) .... C 2
Sabana (arch.) .... E 1
Sabinal (cay) .... H 2
Sagua la Grande (river) .... E 1
San Antonio (cape) .... A 2
San Felipe (cays) .... B 2
San Pedro (river) .... G 3
Santa Clara (bay) .... D 1
Santa María (cay) .... F 1
Siguanea (bay) .... B 2
Tabacal (point) .... H 4
Toa, Cuchillas de (mts.) .... K 4
Tortuguilla (point) .... K 4
Turquino (peak) .... H 4
Zapata (pen.) .... C 2
Zapata Occidental (swamp) .... D 2
Zapata Oriental (swamp) .... D 2

DOMINICAN REPUBLIC

PROVINCES

Azua, 91,511 .... D 6
Baoruco, 66,572 .... D 6
Barahona, 112,914 .... D 6
Dajabón, 50,780 .... D 5
Distrito Nacional, 817,467 .... E 6
Duarte, 200,813 .... E 5
El Seibo, 132,795 .... F 6
Espaillat, 139,579 .... E 5
Independencia, 32,580 .... D 6
La Altagracia, 87,180 .... F 6
La Estrelleta, 53,228 .... C 5
La Romana, 56,955 .... F 6
La Vega, 293,694 .... D 6
María Trinidad Sánchez, 97,043 .... E 5
Montecristi, 69,276 .... D 5
Pedernales, 12,547 .... D 7
Peravia, 127,587 .... E 6
Puerto Plata, 185,800 .... D 5
Salcedo, 89,773 .... E 5
Samaná, 53,893 .... E 5
San Cristóbal, 324,395 .... E 6
San Juan, 191,065 .... D 6
San Pedro de Macorís, 105,490 .... F 6
Sánchez Ramírez, 106,177 .... E 5
Santiago, 386,269 .... D 5
Santiago Rodríguez, 49,598 .... D 5
Valverde, 76,608 .... D 5

CITIES and TOWNS

Altamira, 1,573 .... D 5
Azua, 18,584 .... D 6
Bajos de Haina, 10,396 .... E 6
Baní, 23,716 .... E 6
Bánica, 1,303 .... D 5
Barahona, 37,889 .... D 6
Bayaguana, 2,947 .... E 6
Bonao .... E 6
Cabral, 5,575 .... D 6
Cabrera, 1,899 .... E 5
Castillo, 3,191 .... E 5
Cayacoa .... E 6
Ciudad Trujillo (Santo Domingo) (cap.), 671,402 .... E 6
Constanza, 4,316 .... D 6
Cotuí, 7,574 .... E 5
Dajabón, 6,027 .... D 5
Duvergé, 7,979 .... D 6
El Cercado, 3,369 .... D 6
El Cuey .... F 6
El Guayabo .... E 5
El Pozo .... E 5
El Salado .... F 6
El Seibo, 8,958 .... F 6
Elías Piña, 5,099 .... C 6
Enriquillo, 4,103 .... D 7
Esperanza, 10,684 .... D 5
Gaspar Hernández, 2,222 .... E 5
Guayubín, 1,369 .... D 5
Hato Mayor, 9,985 .... F 6
Imbert, 4,321 .... D 5
Jánico, 1,117 .... D 5
Jarabacoa, 6,329 .... E 5
Jaragua, 4,853 .... D 6
Jimaní, 2,248 .... C 6
La Romana, 36,722 .... F 6
La Vega, 31,085 .... D 5
Las Matas de Farfán, 7,138 .... D 6
Los Llanos, 1,849 .... F 6
Lucas E. de Peña .... D 5
Luperón, 1,991 .... D 5
Mata Palacio .... F 6
Miches, 4,410 .... F 6
Moca, 18,965 .... D 5
Monción, 2,007 .... D 5
Montecristi, 8,252 .... C 5
Monte Plata, 3,636 .... E 6
Nagua, 13,937 .... E 5
Najayo Abajo .... E 6
Neiba, 10,194 .... D 6
Nizao, 3,178 .... E 6
Oviedo, 2,117 .... D 7
Padre Las Casas, 2,953 .... D 6
Paraíso, 3,496 .... D 7
Pedernales, 5,919 .... C 7
Peña .... D 5
Peralta .... D 6
Pimentel, 5,954 .... E 5
Polo .... D 6
Puerto Plata, 32,181 .... D 5
Ramón Santana, 4,139 .... F 6
Restauración, 1,784 .... D 5
Río San Juan, 2,764 .... E 5
Sabana de la Mar, 6,841 .... F 5
Sabana Grande de Palenque, 1,950 .... E 6
Salcedo, 11,459 .... E 5
Salvaleón de Higüey, 21,741 .... F 6
Samaná, 4,435 .... F 5
Sánchez, 6,583 .... E 5
San Cristóbal, 25,829 .... E 6
San Francisco de Macorís, 43,941 .... E 5
San José de las Matas, 3,228 .... D 5
San José de Ocoa, 9,382 .... E 6
San Juan, 32,248 .... D 6
San Pedro de Macorís, 42,473 .... E 6
San Rafael del Yuma, 1,944 .... F 6
Santiago, 155,151 .... D 5
Santiago Rodríguez, 9,637 .... D 5
Santo Domingo (cap.), 671,402 .... E 6
Sosúa, 4,204 .... E 5
Tamayo, 4,177 .... D 6
Tenares, 2,663 .... E 5
Valverde, 27,111 .... D 5
Villa Altagracia, 10,300 .... E 6
Villa Riva 2,165 .... E 5
Yaguate, 1,854 .... E 6
Yamasá, 2,642 .... E 6
Yásica Abajo .... E 5

OTHER FEATURES

Alto Velo (chan.) .... C 7
Alto Velo (isl.) .... D 7
Balandra (point) .... F 5
Baoruco, Sierra de (mts.) .... D 6
Beata (cape) .... D 7
Beata (chan.) .... C 7
Beata (isl.) .... C 7
Cabrón (cape) .... F 5
Calderas (bay) .... D 6
Cana (point) .... F 6
Catalina (isl.) .... F 6
Caucedo (cape) .... E 6
Central, Cordillera (range) .... D 5
Duarte (peak) .... D 5
Engaño (cape) .... F 5
Enriquillo (lake) .... C 6
Escocesa (bay) .... E 5
Espada (point) .... F 6
Falso (cape) .... C 7
Francés Viejo (cape) .... E 5
Gallo (mt.) .... D 5
Isabela (bay) .... D 5
Isabela (cape) .... D 5
Los Frailes (isl.) .... C 7
Macorís (cape) .... E 5
Manzanillo (bay) .... C 5
Mona (passage) .... F 6
Neiba (bay) .... D 6
Neiba (mt.) .... D 6
Ocoa (bay) .... D 6
Oriental, Cordillera (range) .... F 6
Palenque (point) .... E 6
Palmillas (point) .... F 6
Rincón (bay) .... F 5
Rucia (point) .... D 5
Salinas (point) .... E 6
Samaná (bay) .... F 5
Samaná (cape) .... F 5
San Rafael (cape) .... F 5
Saona (isl.) .... F 6
Septentrional, Cord. (range) .... D 5
Tina (mt.) .... D 6
Yaque del Norte (river) .... D 5
Yaque del Sur (river) .... D 6
Yuma (bay) .... F 6
Yuna (river) .... E 5

HAITI

DEPARTMENTS

Artibonite, 748,357 .... C 5
Nord, 747,360 .... C 5
Nord-Ouest, 247,326 .... B 5
Ouest, 1,983,826 .... C 6
Sud, 1,041,232 .... A 6

CITIES and TOWNS

Abricots, †26,612 .... B 6
Anse-à-Pitre, †16,195 .... C 6
Anse-à-Veau, †41,690 .... B 6
Anse-d'Hainault, †18,416 .... A 6
Anse-Rouge, †14,657 .... B 5
Aquin, †95,283 .... B 6
Archaie, †52,221 .... C 6
Baie-de-Henne, †6,927 .... B 5
Baradères, †33,575 .... B 6
Bassin-Bleu, †23,623 .... B 5
Belladère, †35,706 .... C 6
Bombardopolis, †13,556 .... B 5
Bonbon, †8,711 .... A 6
Camp-Perrin, †25,398 .... A 6
Cap-Haïtien, 30,000 .... C 5
Cavaillon, †50,479 .... A 6
Cayes-Jacmel, †39,726 .... C 6
Cerca-la-Source, †20,671 .... C 5
Chardonnière, †15,270 .... A 6
Corail, †47,936 .... A 6
Côteaux, †28,327 .... A 6
Côtes-de-Fer, †122,568 .... B 6
Croix-des-Bouquets; †83,250 .... C 6
Dame-Marie, †27,430 .... A 2
Dessalines, †86,348 .... C 5
Fort-Liberté, †26,942 .... C 5
Gonaïves, †99,140 .... B 5
Grand-Goâve, †60,589 .... B 6
Grand-Gosier, †29,102 .... C 6
Grande-Rivière-du-Nord, †29,904 .... C 5
Grande-Saline, †30,628 .... B 5
Gros-Morne, †90,116 .... B 4
Hinche, †63,796 .... C 5
Jacmel, †199,598 .... C 6
Jean-Rabel, †55,834 .... B 5
Jérémie, †92,500 .... A 6
Kenscoff, †24,219 .... C 6
La Cahouane .... A 6
Lascahobas, †29,760 .... C 6
Le Borgne, †51,325 .... C 5
Léogane, †140,607 .... C 6
Les Anglais, †15,321 .... A 6
Les Cayes, †95,446 .... B 6
Limbé, †52,315 .... C 5
Limonade, †21,395 .... C 5
Maissade, †26,568 .... C 5
Marigot, †65,402 .... C 6
Miragoâne, †50,059 .... B 6
Mirebalais, †78,060 .... C 6
Môle-Saint-Nicolas, †14,352 .... B 5
Moron, †17,020 .... A 6
Ouanaminthe, †55,717 .... C 5
Pestel, †33,007 .... A 6
Pétionville, †52,221 .... C 6
Petit-Goâve, †123,157 .... B 6
Petite-Rivière-de-l'Artibonite, †65,772 .... B 5
Pignon, †15,512 .... C 5
Pilate, †40,293 .... C 5
Plaisance, †47,896 .... C 5
Pointe-à-Raquette .... B 6
Port-à-Piment, †14,072 .... A 6
Port-au-Prince (cap.), 265,000 .... C 6
Port-au-Prince, *352,681 .... C 6
Port-de-Paix, †54,016 .... B 5
Port-Margot, †33,043 .... C 5
Port-Salut, †41,055 .... A 6
Roseaux, †25,984 .... A 6
Saint-Jean-du-Sud, †18,923 .... B 6
Saint-Louis-du-Nord, †44,898 .... B 5
Saint-Louis-du-Sud, †42,807 .... B 6
Saint-Marc, †61,359 .... B 5
Saint-Michel-de-l'Atalaye, †68,813 .... C 5
Saint-Raphaël, †25,708 .... C 5
Saltrou, †57,067 .... C 6
Savanette, †55,505 .... C 6
Terre-Neuve, †15,953 .... B 5
Thomonde, †15,660 .... C 6
Tiburon, †9,860 .... A 6
Torbeck, †66,480 .... A 6
Trou-du-Nord, †29,324 .... C 5
Vallière, †16,089 .... C 5
Verrettes, †39,327 .... C 5

OTHER FEATURES

Artibonite (river) .... C 5
Baradères (bay) .... B 6
Cheval Blanc (point) .... B 5
Dame-Marie (cape) .... A 6
Est (point) .... C 4
Fantasque (point) .... B 6
Gonâve (gulf) .... B 5
Gonâve (isl.), 45,411 .... B 6
Grande Cayemite (isl.) .... B 6
Gravois (point) .... A 6
Irois (cape) .... A 6
Jean-Rabel (point) .... B 5
La Selle (mts.) .... C 6
La Selle (peak) .... C 6
Macaya (peak) .... A 6
Manzanillo (bay) .... C 5
Môle (cape) .... B 5
Noires (mts.) .... C 5
Ouest (point) .... B 4
Ouest (point) .... B 6
Saint-Marc (cape) .... B 5
Saint-Marc (chan.) .... B 6
Saumâtre (lake) .... C 6
Tortue (chan.) .... C 5
Tortue (isl.), 13,723 .... C 4
Tortuga (Tortue) (isl.), 13,723 .... C 4
Trois-Rivières (river) .... B 5
Vache (isl.) .... B 6
Windward (passage) .... A 5

JAMAICA

CITIES and TOWNS

Adelphi .... H 5
Albany, 1,590 .... J 6
Albert Town, 1,650 .... H 6
Alley .... J 7
Alligator Pond .... H 6
Anchovy .... H 5
Annotto Bay, 3,559 .... K 6
Balaclava, 1,153 .... H 6
Bath, 1,979 .... K 6
Bethel Town .... G 6
Black River, 3,077 .... H 6
Bluefields .... H 6
Bog Walk, 2,808 .... J 6
Brown's Town, 3,899 .... H 6
Buff Bay, 2,821 .... K 6
Cambridge .... H 6
Castleton .... J 6
Catadupa .... H 6
Chapelton, 4,417 .... J 6
Christiana, 4,404 .... H 6
Claremont, 1,417 .... J 6
Clark's Town, 1,543 .... H 6
Darliston .... H 6
Devon .... H 6
Discovery Bay .... J 5
Ewarton .... J 6
Falmouth, 3,727 .... H 5
Four Paths .... J 6
Frankfield, 2,123 .... H 6
Golden Grove .... K 6
Green Island .... G 6
Hayes .... J 6
Highgate, 3,313 .... J 6
Hope Bay .... K 6
Hopewell .... G 5
Kingston (cap.), 123,403 .... K 6
Kingston, *376,520 .... K 6
Lacovia .... H 6
Linstead, 3,781 .... J 6
Lionel Town, 2,664 .... J 7
Little London .... G 6
Lluidas Vale .... J 6
Lucea, 2,803 .... G 5
Maggotty .... H 6
Malvern .... H 6
Manchioneal .... K 6
Mandeville, 8,416 .... H 6
Maroon Town .... H 6
May Pen, 14,085 .... J 6
Moneague .... J 6
Montego Bay, 23,610 .... H 5
Moore Town .... K 6
Morant Bay, 5,054 .... K 7
Myersville .... H 6
Negril .... G 6
Ocho Rios, 4,570 .... J 6
Old England .... H 6
Old Harbour, 4,192 .... J 6
Oracabessa, 1,313 .... J 5
Petersfield .... G 6
Port Antonio, 7,830 .... K 6
Port Kaiser .... H 7
Port Maria, 3,998 .... J 6
Port Morant, 2,284 .... K 6
Port Rhoades .... J 6
Port Royal, 37,673 .... J 6
Porus, 2,723 .... H 6
Richmond .... J 6
Runaway Bay .... J 5
Saint Ann's Bay, 5,087 .... J 5
Saint Margaret's Bay .... K 6
Sandy Bay .... G 5
Santa Cruz, 1,426 .... H 6
Savanna la Mar, 9,789 .... G 6
Spaldings, 2,003 .... H 6
Spanish Town, 14,706 .... J 6
Stewart Town .... H 6
Tobolski .... J 6
Treasure Beach .... H 6
Trinityville .... K 6
Trout Hall .... J 6
Ulster Spring .... H 6
Williamsfield .... H 6
Yallahs .... K 6

OTHER FEATURES

Black (river) .... H 6
Black River (bay) .... G 6
Blue (mts.) .... K 6
Blue Mountain (peak) .... K 6
Galina (point) .... J 6
Grande (river) .... K 6
Great (river) .... H 6
Great Pedro Bluff (prom.) .... H 6
Long (bay) .... H 7
Luana (point) .... G 6
Minho (river) .... J 6
Montego (bay) .... G 5
Montego Bay (point) .... G 5
North East (point) .... K 6
North Negril (point) .... G 6
North West (point) .... G 5
Old Harbour (bay) .... J 6
Portland (point) .... J 7
Sir John's (peak) .... K 6
South East (point) .... K 6
South Negril (point) .... G 6

*City and suburbs.
†Population of commune.
‡Population of met. area.

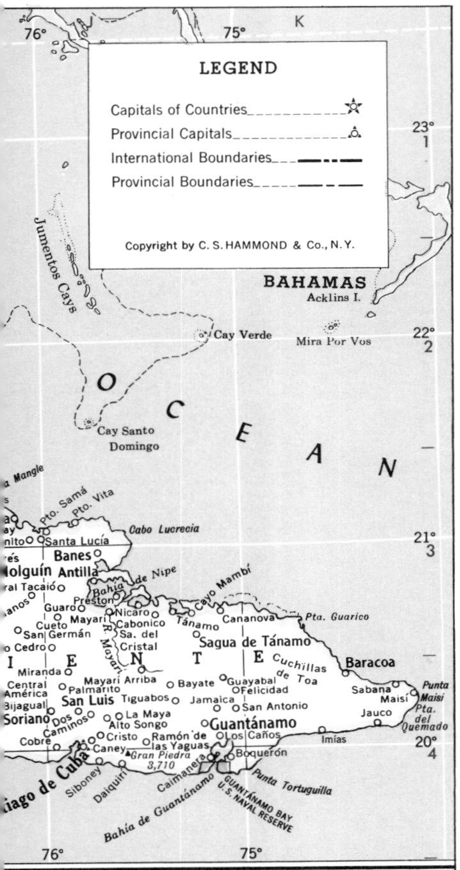

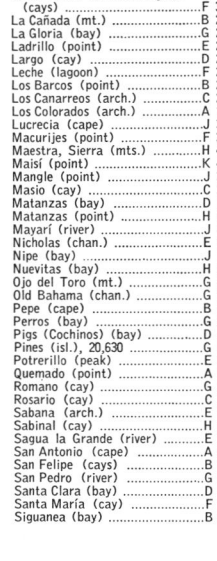

LEGEND
Capitals of Countries
Provincial Capitals
International Boundaries
Provincial Boundaries
Copyright by C. S. HAMMOND & Co., N.Y.
BAHAMAS
Acklins I.
Cay Verde
Mira Por Vos
Cay Santo Domingo
O C E A N
Cabo Lucrecia
Banes
Holguín
Antilla
Sagua de Tánamo
Baracoa
Guantánamo
Pta. Guarico
Punta Maisí
Imías
Punta Tortuguilla
Bahía de Guantánamo
GUANTANAMO BAY U.S. NAVAL RESERVE

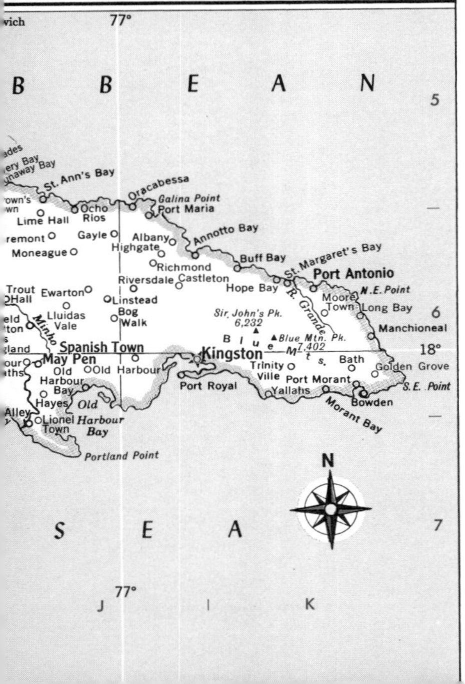

B B E A N
St. Ann's Bay
Oracabessa
Galina Point
Port Maria
Annotto Bay
Buff Bay
St. Margaret's Bay
Port Antonio
N.E. Point
Long Bay
Manchioneal
Spanish Town
Kingston
May Pen
Old Harbour
Port Royal
Morant Bay
S.E. Point
Portland Point
S E A

Agriculture, Industry and Resources

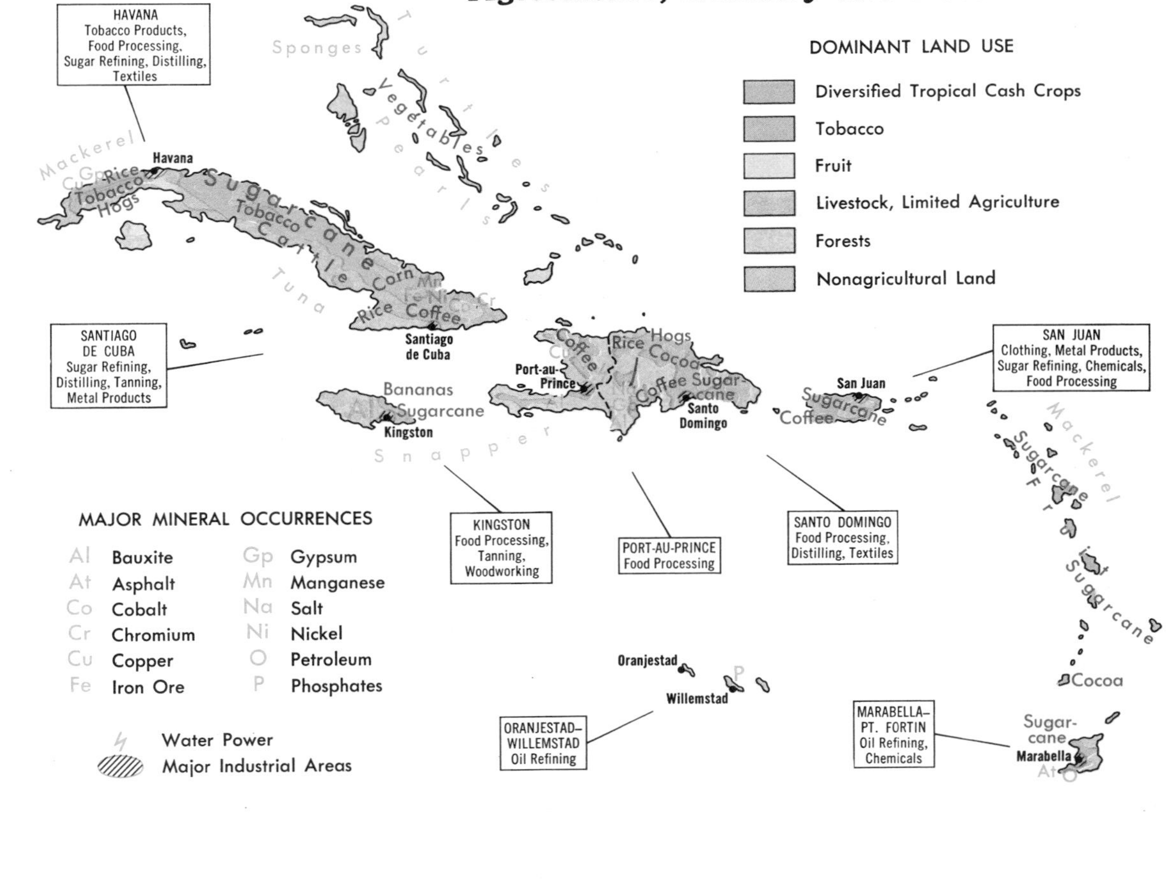

HAVANA
Tobacco Products, Food Processing, Sugar Refining, Distilling, Textiles
SANTIAGO DE CUBA
Sugar Refining, Distilling, Tanning, Metal Products
SAN JUAN
Clothing, Metal Products, Sugar Refining, Chemicals, Food Processing
KINGSTON
Food Processing, Tanning, Woodworking
PORT-AU-PRINCE
Food Processing
SANTO DOMINGO
Food Processing, Distilling, Textiles
ORANJESTAD-WILLEMSTAD
Oil Refining
MARABELLA-PT. FORTIN
Oil Refining, Chemicals
Havana
Santiago de Cuba
Port-au-Prince
Kingston
Santo Domingo
San Juan
Oranjestad
Willemstad
Marabella
Cocoa
Sponges
Vegetables
Sugarcane
Tobacco
Coffee
Bananas
DOMINANT LAND USE
Diversified Tropical Cash Crops
Tobacco
Fruit
Livestock, Limited Agriculture
Forests
Nonagricultural Land
MAJOR MINERAL OCCURRENCES
Al Bauxite
At Asphalt
Co Cobalt
Cr Chromium
Cu Copper
Fe Iron Ore
Gp Gypsum
Mn Manganese
Na Salt
Ni Nickel
Petroleum
P Phosphates
Water Power
Major Industrial Areas

PUERTO RICO

DISTRICTS

Aguadilla, 284,983 A 1
Arecibo, 270,492 C 1
Bayamón, 359,499 D 1
Guayama, 335,305 D 2
Humacao, 283,481 F 2
Mayagüez, 267,731 B 2
Ponce, 308,968 C 2
San Juan, 601,554 E 1

CITIES and TOWNS

Adjuntas, 5,319 B 2
Aguada, 4,590 A 1
Aguadilla, 21,031 A 1
Aguas Buenas, 3,426 E 2
Aibonito, 7,582 D 2
Añasco, 4,416 A 1
Ángeles, †2,817 B 2
Arecibo, 35,484 B 1
Arroyo, 5,429 E 3
Arus C 3
Bahomamey, †146 A 1
Bajadero C 1
Barceloneta, 4,515 C 1
Barranquitas, 4,508 D 2
Bayamón, 147,552 D 1
Boquerón, †2,790 A 3
Cabo Rojo, 7,181 A 2
Caguas, 63,215 E 2
Caguas, ‡95,661 E 2
Camuy, 3,892 B 1
Carolina, 94,271 E 1
Cataño, 26,459 D 1
Cayey, 21,562 D 2
Ceiba, 2,147 F 2
Central Aguirre, 1,237 D 3
Ciales, 4,046 C 1
Cidra, 6,306 D 2
Coamo, 12,077 D 2
Comerío, 6,297 D 2
Coquí, 2,643 D 3
Corozal, 5,211 D 1
Corral Viejo C 2
Coto Laurel, 1,761 C 2
Culebra, 611 G 1
Dewey (Culebra), 611 G 1
Dorado, 4,388 D 1
Ensenada, 1,268 B 3
Esperanza, †1,312 G 2
Fajardo, 18,249 F 1
Florida, 1,716 C 1
Guánica, 8,979 B 3
Guayama, 20,318 E 3
Guayanilla, 5,189 B 3
Guaynabo, 55,310 D 1
Gurabo, 6,290 E 2
Hatillo, 2,760 B 1
Hato Rey, †60,539 E 1
Hormigüeros, 6,531 A 2
Humacao, 12,411 E 2
Isabela, 9,515 A 1
Isabel Segunda, 2,378 G 2
Jayuya, 3,826 C 2
Jobos, 2,720 D 3
Juana Díaz, 8,765 C 2
Juncos, 7,985 E 2
Lajas, 3,391 A 3
Lares, 4,545 B 2
Las Marías, 474 B 2
Las Piedras, 4,636 E 2
Levittown, 17,079 D 1
Loíza, 2,707 E 1
Loíza Aldea, 3,350 E 1
Luquillo, 2,459 F 1
Manatí, 13,483 C 1
Maricao, 1,492 B 2
Maunabo, 1,829 E 3
Mayagüez, 68,872 A 2
Mayagüez, ‡85,857 A 2
Moca, 2,378 A 1
Morovis, 2,892 D 1
Naguabo, 4,169 F 2
Naranjito, 3,283 D 1
Orocovis, 3,684 C 2
Palmer, 1,456 F 1
Palo Seco, †489 D 1
Parquera, 1,028 A 3
Patillas, 2,543 E 3
Peñuelas, 3,169 B 2
Playa de Fajardo F 1
Playa de Humacao, 1,912 F 2
Playa de Ponce, †15,574 C 3
Ponce, 128,233 C 3
Ponce, ‡158,981 C 3
Puerto Nuevo, †37,644 D 1
Puerto Real, 1,502 A 2
Puerto Real (Playa de Fajardo) F 1
Punta Santiago (Playa de Humacao), 1,912 F 2
Quebradillas, 2,840 B 1
Rincón, 1,538 A 1
Río Blanco, †2,659 F 2
Río Grande, 4,164 E 1
Río Piedras, †3,761 E 1
Rosario, 640 A 2
Sabana Grande, 5,561 B 2
Sabana Seca, 5,023 D 1
Salinas, 4,461 D 3
San Antonio, 2,484 A 1
San Germán, 11,613 A 2
San Juan (capital), 452,749 E 1
San Juan, ‡851,247 E 1
San Lorenzo, 7,702 E 2
San Sebastián, 7,169 B 1
Santa Isabel, 4,495 C 3
Santurce, †128,232 E 1
Tallaboa, 1,155 B 3
Toa Alta, 3,199 D 1
Toa Baja, 2,026 D 1
Trujillo Alto, 18,477 E 1
Utuado, 11,573 B 2
Vega Alta, 8,688 D 1
Vega Baja, 17,089 C 1
Vieques (Isabel Segunda), 2,378 G 2
Villalba, 4,134 C 2
Yabucoa, 5,119 E 2
Yauco, 12,922 B 2

OTHER FEATURES

Aguadillo (bay) A 1
Algarrobo (pt.) A 2
Añasco (bay) A 1
Arenas (pt.) F 2
Bauta (river) C 2
Bayamón (river) D 1
Boquerón (bay) A 3
Borinquen (pt.) A 1
Cabullón (pt.) C 3
Caja de Muertos (isl.) C 3
Camuy (river) B 1
Candelero (pt.) F 2
Canovanas (river) E 1
Caonillas (lake) C 2
Carite (lake) E 2
Carraízo (lake) E 1
Cayey, Sierra de (mts.) D 2
Central, Cordillera (range) C 2
Cerro Gordo (pt.) D 1
Coamo (res.) D 3
Coamo (river) D 3
Culebra (isl.), 732 G 1
Culebrinas (river) A 1
Culebrita (isl.) G 2
El Toro (mt.) F 2
El Yunque (mt.) F 1
Este (pt.) G 2
Fajardo (river) F 1
Figuras (pt.) E 3
Fosforescente (bay) A 3
Grande de Añasco (river) B 2
Grande de Arecibo (river) C 1
Grande de Loíza (river) E 1
Grande de Manatí (river) C 1
Guajataca (lake) B 1
Guanajibo (pt.) A 2
Guanajibo (river) A 2
Guánica (lake) B 3
Guaniquilla (pt.) A 2
Guayabal (lake) C 2
Guayanés (pt.) F 2
Guayanés (river) E 2
Guayanilla (bay) B 3
Guayo (lake) B 2
Guilarte (mt.) B 2
Honda (bay) F 2
Humacao (river) E 2
Jacaguas (river) C 2
Jaicoa (mts.) B 1
Jiguero (pt.) A 1
Jobos (bay) D 3
La Bandera (pt.) F 1
Lima (pt.) F 2
Lobo (cay) G 1
Luquillo, Sierra de (mts.) E 2
Manglillo (pt.) B 3
Mayagüez (bay) A 2
Miquillo (pt.) F 1
Molinos (pt.) G 1
Mona (passage) A 2
Negra (pt.) G 2
Nigua (river) D 2
Ola Grande (pt.) D 3
Palmas Altas (pt.) C 1
Patillas (lake) E 2
Peñón (pt.) B 1
Petrona (pt.) D 3
Pirata (mt.) F 2
Plata (river) D 2
Puerca (pt.) F 2
Puerto Medio Mundo (bay) F 2
Puerto Nuevo (pt.) C 1
Punta, Cerro de (mt.) C 2
Ramey A.F.B., 7,507 A 1
Rincón (bay) D 3
Rojo (cape) A 3
Salinas (pt.) D 1
San José (lake) E 1
San Juan, Cabezas de (prom.) F 1
San Juan National Hist. Site D 1
Sardina (pt.) A 1
Soldado (pt.) G 2
Sucia (bay) A 3
Tanamá (river) B 1
Torrecilla (lagoon) E 1
Tortuguero (lake) D 1
Tuna (pt.) E 3
Vacía Talega (pt.) E 1
Viento (pt.) E 3
Vieques (isl.), 7,767 G 2
Vieques (passage) F 2
Vieques (sound) G 2
Yagüez (river) A 2
Yauco (lake) B 2
Yeguas (pt.) F 3

ANTIGUA

Total Population, 63,000

CITIES and TOWNS

All Saints, 2,077 D11
Cedar Grove, 899 E11
Falmouth, 239 E11
Freetown, 1,026 E11
Jennings, 850 D11
Johnsons Point, 339 D11
Liberta, 1,988 E11
Old Road, 1,178 D11
Parham, 1,123 E11
Saint John's (capital) 24,367 E11
Willikies, 1,330 E11

OTHER FEATURES

Antigua (isl.), 54,304 E11
Boggy (peak) D11
Boon (pt.) E11
Green (isl.) E11
Guiana (isl.) E11
Long (isl.) E11
Saint John's (harb.) D11
Standfast (pt.) E11
Willoughby (bay) E11

BARBADOS

CITIES and TOWNS

Bathsheba B 8
Belleplaine B 8
Bridgetown (capital), 12,430 B 9
Carlton B 8
Cave Hill B 9
Checker Hall B 8
Codrington B 8
Crab Hill B 8
Crane C 9
Drax Hall B 8
Ellerton B 9
Greenland B 8
Holetown B 8
Kendal B 8
Lodge Hill B 8
Marchfield B 9
Maxwell B 9
Maxwell Hill B 9
Mount Standfast B 8
Portland B 8
Rose Hill B 8
Rouen B 9
Saint Lawrence B 9
Saint Martins B 9
Scarboro B 9
Seawell B 9
Six Mens B 8
Speightstown, 2,415 B 8
Spring Hall B 8
Welchman Hall B 8

OTHER FEATURES

Carlisle (bay) B 9
Hillaby (mt.) B 8
Long (bay) B 9
North (pt.) B 8
Oistins (bay) B 9
Pelican (isl.) B 9
Ragged (pt.) C 8
Sam Lord's Castle C 9
South (pt.) B 9

DOMINICA

Total Population, 70,302

CITIES and TOWNS

Barroui E 6
Castle Bruce, 1,474 F 6
Coulihaut, 972 E 6
Delice, 377 F 7
Grand Bay, 2,385 F 7
Hampstead, 559 E 5
La Plaine, 746 F 6
Laudat, 364 E 6
Mahaut, 1,688 E 6
Marigot, 3,200 E 6
Petit Soufrière, 799 F 6
Portsmouth, 4,146 E 5
Rosalie, 781 F 6
Roseau (capital), 10,157 E 7
Roseau, *16,677 E 7
Saint Joseph, 2,646 E 6
Salybia, 297 F 6
Soufrière, 934 E 7
Vieille Case, 1,372 E 5
Wesley, 2,063 F 5

OTHER FEATURES

Capuchin (cape) E 5
Carib Reserve, 1,974 F 6
Clyde (river) F 6
Crampton (pt.) F 5
Diablotin, Morne (mt.) E 6
Dominica (passage) E 5
Douglas (bay) E 5
Grand (bay) F 7
Jaquet (pt.) E 5
Layou (river) E 6
Martinique (passage) E 7
Micotrin (mt.) F 6
Pagoua (bay) F 6
Prince Rupert (bay) E 5
Roseau (river) E 7
Scotts (head) E 7
Soufrière (bay) E 7
Trois Pitons, Morne (mt.) E 6

GRENADA

Total Population, 105,000

CITIES and TOWNS

Crochu D 8
Gouyave, 2,356 C 8
Grand Anse C 9
Grand Roy C 8
Grenville, 1,747 D 8
Hermitage D 8
La Taste D 8
Marquis D 8
Mount Tivoli D 8
Providence D 9
Saint George's, (capital), 9,000 C 9
Saint George's, *26,843 C 9
Sauteurs, 925 D 8
Union D 8
Victoria, 1,692 D 8
Woburn C 9
Woodford C 8

OTHER FEATURES

Bedford (pt.) D 8
David (pt.) D 8
Great Bacolet (pt.) D 8
Green (isl.) D 8
Grenville (bay) D 8
Gros (pt.) C 8
Halifax (harb.) C 8
Irvins (bay) D 8
Les Tantes (isls.) D 7
Molinière (pt.) C 8
Prickly (pt.) C 9
Ronde (isl.) D 7
Saint Catherine (mt.) D 8
Saline (pt.) C 9
Sinai (mt.) D 8
Telescope (pt.) D 8

GUADELOUPE

Total Population, 324,000

CITIES and TOWNS

Anse-Bertrand, 2,597 B 5
Baie-Mahault, 2,518 A 6
Baillif, 3,056 A 7
Baninier A 7
Basse-Terre (capital), 16,000 A 7
Bouillante, 1,993 A 6
Bourg-des-Saintes, 1,174 A 7
Capesterre, 7,000 A 7
Capesterre, 861 B 7
Deshaies, 754 A 6
Ferry A 6
Gosier, 5,000 B 6
Gourbeyre, 3,024 A 7
Goyave, 1,191 A 6
Grand-Bourg, 3,299 B 7
Grippon B 6
Lamentin, 1,457 A 6
Le Moule, 8,000 B 6
Les Abymes, 6,600 B 6
Morne-à-l'Eau, 10,000 A 6
Petit-Bourg, 3,896 A 6
Petit-Canal, 1,725 A 6
Pigeon A 6
Pointe-à-Pitre, 50,000 B 6
Pointe-Noire, 2,473 A 6
Port-Louis, 5,000 B 5
Saint-Claude, 4,800 A 7
Saint-François, 3,200 B 6
Saint-Louis, 1,500 B 7
Sainte-Anne, 3,573 B 6
Sainte-Marguerite B 6
Sainte-Marie A 6
Sainte-Rose, 3,043 A 6
Trois-Rivières, 1,743 A 7
Vieux-Fort, 1,213 B 7
Vieux-Habitants, 1,621 A 7

OTHER FEATURES

Allègre (pt.) A 6
Antigues (pt.) A 5
Basse-Terre (isl.), 134,601 A 6
Châteaux (pt.) B 6
Constant, Morne (hill) B 7
Désirade (isl.), 1,559 B 6
Fajou (isl.) A 6
Grand Cul-de-Sac Marin (bay) A 6
Grand Îlet (isl.) A 7
Grande-Terre (isl.), 150,576 B 5
Grande Vigie (pt.) B 5
Guadeloupe (isl.), 285,177 B 6
Guadeloupe (passage) A 5
Kahouanne (isl.) A 6
Marie-Galante (isl.), 15,870 B 7
Nord (pt.) B 7
Nord-Est (bay) B 6
Petit Cul-de-Sac Marin (bay) A 6
Petite-Terre (isls.) B 6
Saintes (isls.), 3,272 A 7
Saintes, Canal des (chan.) A 7
Salée (river) A 6
Sans Toucher (mt.) A 6
Soufrière (mt.) A 7
Terre-de-Bas (isl.), 1,795 A 7
Terre-de-Haut (isl.), 1,477 A 7
Vieux-Fort (pt.) A 7

MARTINIQUE

Total Population, 332,000

CITIES and TOWNS

Ajoupa-Bouillon, 1,397 C 5
Anses-d'Arlet, 1,102 C 7
Basse-Pointe, 2,324 C 5
Belle-Fontaine, 1,082 C 6
Carbet, 2,593 C 6
Case-Pilote, 1,625 C 6
Diamant, 629 D 7
Ducos, 1,976 D 6
Fond-Lahaye C 6
Fonds-Saint-Denis, 780 C 6
Fort-de-France (capital), 100,000 C 6
Fort-Desaix D 6
François, 3,195 D 6
Grande-Rivière, 1,493 C 5
Gros-Morne, 979 D 6
Lamentin, 6,721 D 6
Lorrain, 1,848 D 5
Macouba, 1,329 C 5
Marigot, 1,449 D 5
Marin, 1,789 D 7
Morne-Rouge, 2,655 C 5
Morne-Vert, 493 C 6
Prêcheur, 2,312 C 5
Rivière-Pilote, 2,039 D 7
Rivière-Salée, 1,725 D 7
Robert, 2,077 D 6
Saint-Esprit, 3,214 D 6
Saint-Joseph, 1,995 C 6
Saint-Pierre, 5,556 C 6
Sainte-Anne, 960 D 7
Sainte-Luce, 1,243 D 7
Sainte-Marie, 2,933 D 5
Schoelcher, 10,817 C 6
Trinité, 3,566 D 6
Trois-Îlets, 1,400 C 6
Vauclin, 2,908 D 6
Vert-Pré D 6

OTHER FEATURES

Cabet, Pitons du (mt.) C 6
Cabri (isl.) D 7
Caravelle (pen.) D 6
Cul-de-Sac du Marin (bay) D 7
Diable (pt.) D 5
Ferré (cape) E 7
Fort-de-France (bay) C 6
Galion (bay) D 6
Lézarde (river) D 6
Long, Îlet (isl.) D 6
Lorrain (river) D 5
Martinique (passage) C 5
Pelée (vol.) C 5
Pilote (river) D 7
Ramiers, Îlet-à- (isl.) C 6
Ramville, Îlet (isl.) D 6
Robert (harb.) D 6
Rocher du Diamant (isl.) C 7
Rose (pt.) D 6
Saint-Martin (cape) C 5
Saint-Pierre (bay) C 6
Salines (pt.) D 7
Salomon (pt.) C 7
Vauclin (mt.) D 6

NETHERLANDS ANTILLES

CITIES and TOWNS

Aresji D 9
Ascension F 8
Bacuna E 8
Balashi E10
Boven Bolivia E 8
Bubali D10
Bushiribana E10
Dokterstuin D 8
Druif D10
Emmastad G 9
Entrejo E 8
Fontein E 8
Fuik G 9
Groot Sint Joris G 9
Hato G 8
Kralendijk (capital), Bonaire, 839 E 8
Lago E10
Lagoen F 8
Montanja di Reij G 9
New Port G 9
Noord di Salinja E 8
Onima E 8
Oranjestad (capital), Aruba, 15,398 D10
Otrabanda F 9
Patrick F 8
Rincon E 8
Rooi E 8
Sabana Westpunt F 8
Santa Barbara G 9
Santa Catharina G 9
Savaneta E10
Savonet F 8
Sint Anna D10
Sint Jan D 8
Sint Kruis F 8
Sint Martha F 8
Sint Michiel F 9
Sint Nicolaas E10
Sint Willebrordus F 8
Terra Corra E 8
Westpunt D10
Willemstad (capital), 43,547 F 9
Willemstad, *94,133 F 9

OTHER FEATURES

Aruba (isl.), 58,868 E 9
Basora (pt.) E10
Bonaire (isl.), 5,755 E 9
Bullen (bay) F 8
Caracas (bay) G 9
Curaçao (isl.), 196,170 G 7
Goto (lake) D 8
Jamanota (mt.) E10
Kanon (pt.) G 9
Klein Bonaire (isl.) E 8
Kudarebe (pt.) D 9
Lac (bay) D 9
Lacre (pt.) E 9
Malmok (mt.) D 8
Noord (pt.) D 8
Noord (pt.) F 8
Paarden (bay) D10
Palm (beach) D10
Pekelmeer (lake) E 9
Piscadera (bay) F 9
Schottegat (bay) G 9
Sint Anna (bay) F 9
Sint Christoffel Berg (mt.) F 8
Sint Joris (bay) G 9
Slag (bay) D 8
Vierkant (pt.) E 8

SAINT CHRISTOPHER-NEVIS-ANGUILLA

Total Population, 56,000

CITIES and TOWNS

Basseterre (capital), 15,726 C10
Cayon, 1,524 C10
Charlestown, 2,852 C11
Cotton Ground, 747 C11
Dieppe Bay, 949 C10
Gingerland D11
Golden Rock C10
Newcastle, 361 D11
Old Road, 1,206 C10
Sadlers Village, 1,091 C10
Sandy Point, 3,608 C10
Tabernacle, 1,250 C10
Zion Hill D11

OTHER FEATURES

Brimstone (hill) C10
Dogwood (pt.) D11
Fort (pt.) C11
Great Salt (pond) D10
Heldens (pt.) C10
Horse Shoe (pt.) C11
Misery (mt.) C10
Monkey (hill) C10
Muddy (pt.) C10
Narrows, The (str.) D11
Nevis (isl.), 12,762 D11
Nevis (peak) D11
North Friars (bay) D10
Palmetto (pt.) C10
Saint Christopher (isl.), 38,291 D10
Saint Kitts (Saint Christopher) (isl.), 38,291 D10
South Friars (bay) C10

SAINT LUCIA

Total Population, 110,000

CITIES and TOWNS

Anse la Raye, 2,053 F 6
Canaries, 1,676 G 6
Castries (capital), 4,353 G 6
Castries, *15,291 G 6
Choc G 5
Choiseul, 513 F 7
Dauphin G 5
Dennery, 2,252 G 6
Gros Islet, 1,016 G 5
Laborie, 1,591 G 7
Marigot G 6
Marquis G 6
Micoud, 2,040 G 6
Praslin G 6
Soufrière, 2,692 F 6
Vieux Fort, 3,228 G 7

OTHER FEATURES

Beaumont (pt.) F 6
Canaries, Piton (mt.) G 6
Cannelles (pt.) G 7
Cannelles (river) G 6
Cap (pt.) G 5
Choc (bay) G 5
Fond d'Or (bay) G 6
Gimie (mt.) G 6
Grand Caille (pt.) F 6
Grand Cul de Sac (river) G 6
Gros Islet (bay) G 5
Gros Piton (mt.) G 6
Maria (isl.) G 7
Ministre (pt.) G 7
Moule à Chique (cape) G 7
Petit Piton (mt.) G 6
Pigeon (isl.) G 5
Port Castries (harb.) G 6
Port Praslin (bay) G 6
Roseau (river) G 6
Saint Lucia (chan.) G 5
Saint Vincent (passage) G 7
Savannes (bay) G 7
Sorcière, La (mt.) G 6
Soufrière (bay) F 6
Vierge (pt.) G 6
Vieux Fort (river) G 6

SAINT VINCENT & THE GRENADINES

Total Population, 89,129

CITIES and TOWNS

Barrouallie, †2,459 A 9
Calliaqua, †3,589 A 9
Camden Park A 9
Chateaubelair, †2,173 A 8
Colonarie, †1,550 A 9
Georgetown, †2,645 A 8
Kingstown (capital), 17,258 A 9
Kingstown, *23,482 A 9
Layou, †3,060 A 9
Turema A 8
Wallibu A 8

OTHER FEATURES

Colonarie (pt.) A 9
Cumberland (bay) A 8
Dark (head) A 8
De Volet (pt.) A 8
Espagnol (pt.) A 8
Greathead (bay) A 9
Kingstown (bay) A 9
Owia (bay) A 8
Porter (pt.) A 8
Richmond (peak) A 8
Saint Andrew (mt.) A 9
Saint Vincent (passage) A 8
Soufrière (mt.) A 8
Yambu (head) A 9

TRINIDAD and TOBAGO

CITIES and TOWNS

Arima, 10,982 B10
Arouca, 4,781 B10
Basse Terre B11
Biche, 1,986 B10
Blanchisseuse, 205 B10
California A11
Carapichaima B10
Caroni, 678 B10
Cedros, 1,388 A11
Chaguanas, 3,509 A10
Chaguaramas A10
Couva, 3,567 B10
Cunapo B10
Débé, 2,189 B11
Ecclesville B11
Flanagin Town B10
Fullarton A11
Fyzabad, 1,869 A11
Gran Couva B10
Grande Rivière, 301 B10
Guaico B10
Guayaguayare, 287 B11
La Brea, 4,828 A11
La Lune, 252 B11
Marabella, 8,937 A11
Matelot, 289 B10
Matura B10
Mayaro, 1,828 B11
Moruga, 656 B11
Mucurapo, 2,851 A10
Nestor B10
Palo Seco A11
Peñal, 3,594 B11
Piarco B10
Point Fortin, 8,753 A11
Port-of-Spain (capital), 86,150 A10
Port-of-Spain, *250,000 A10
Princes Town, 6,681 B11
Redhead, 302 B10
Rio Claro, 2,174 B11
Sadhoowa B11
Saint Joseph, 4,079 B10
Saint Joseph B11
San Fernando, 39,830 A11
San Francique A11
San Juan, 19,064 A10
Sangre Grande, 5,087 B10
Sans Souci, 295 B10
Siparia, 4,174 B11
Tabaquite B11
Tableland B11
Tacarigua, 6,704 B10
Talparo B10
Toco, 979 B10
Tunapuna, 11,287 B10
Upper Manzanilla B11
Valencia, 370 B10
Waterloo A10

OTHER FEATURES

Aripo, El Cerro del (mt.) B10
Boca Grande (passage) A10
Casa Cruz (cape) B11
Chacachacare (isl.) A10
Chupara (pt.) B10
Cocos (bay) B11
Dragons Mouth (passage) A10
Erin (bay) A11
Erin (pt.) A11
Galeota (pt.) B11
Galera (pt.) C10
Guapo (bay) A11
Guatuaro (pt.) B11
Icacos (pt.) A11
Matura (bay) B10
Mayaro (bay) B11
Monos (isl.) A10
Nariva (swamp) B10
Oropuche (river) B10
Ortoire (river) B11
Paria (gulf) A10
Pitch (lake) A11
Serpents Mouth (passage) A11
Tamana (mt.) B10
Trinidad (isl.), 973,250 A 9
Tucuche, El (mt.) B10
U.S. Naval Base A10

VIRGIN ISLANDS (BRITISH)

CITIES and TOWNS

Road Town (capital), 2,183 D 3
West End, 105 C 4

OTHER FEATURES

Flanagan (passage) D 4
Frenchman (cay) C 4
Great Thatch (isl.) C 4
Great Tobago (isl.) B 3
Jost Van Dyke (isl.), 124 C 3
Little Tobago (isl.) B 3
Narrow, The (str.) C 4
Norman (isl.) D 4
Peter (isl.) D 4
Road (bay) D 3
Sage (mt.) D 4
Sir Francis Drake (chan.) D 4
Tortola (isl.), 8,939 D 3

VIRGIN ISLANDS (U. S.)

CITIES and TOWNS

Bethlehem E 4
Canebay E 3
Charlotte Amalie (capital), 12,220 B 4
Christiansted, 3,020 F 4
Cruz Bay, †1,497 C 4
Diamond F 4
East End, †26 D 4
Emmaus C 4
Fredensdal F 4
Frederiksted, 1,531 E 4
Grove Place E 4
Kingshill F 4
Longford F 4
Negro Bay E 4

OTHER FEATURES

Altona (lagoon) F 4
Annaly (bay) E 3
Baron Bluff (prom.) E 3
Bordeaux (mt.) C 4
Brass (isls.) A 4
Buck (isl.) G 3
Buck Island (chan.) F 3
Buck Island Reef National Mon. G 3
Butler (bay) E 4
Caneel (bay) B 4
Capella (isls.) B 5
Christiansted National Hist. Site F 4
Coral (bay) C 4
Crown (mt.) A 4
Dutchcap (cay) A 4
Eagle (mt.) E 4
East (pt.) G 4
Flanagan (passage) D 4
Flat (cays) A 4
Grass (pt.) G 4
Great (pond) F 4
Great Pond (bay) F 4
Green (cay) F 4
Hams Bluff (prom.) E 3
Hans Lollik (isls.) B 4
Hassel (isl.) B 4
Jersey (bay) B 4
Krause (lagoon) F 4
Leeward (passage) B 4
Long (pt.) B 4
Long (pt.) E 4
Lovango (cay) C 4
Magens (bay) B 4
Maho (bay) C 4
Narrows, The (str.) C 4
Nulliberg (mt.) B 4
Perseverance (bay) A 4
Picara (pt.) B 4
Pillsbury (sound) B 4
Privateer (pt.) D 4
Pull (pt.) F 3
Ram (head) C 4
Red (pt.) D 4
Reef (bay) C 4
Saba (isl.) A 4
Saint Croix (isl.), 31,779 G 4
Saint James (isls.) B 4
Saint John (isl.), 1,729 C 4
Saint Thomas (harb.) B 4
Saint Thomas (isl.), 28,960 A 4
Salt (cay) A 4
Salt (river) F 4
Salt River (bay) F 3
Sandy (pt.) D 4
Savana (isl.) A 4
Southwest (cape) E 4
Tague (bay) G 4
Thatch (cay) B 4
Turner Hole (bay) G 4
U.S. Naval Air Sta. A 4
Vagthus (pt.) F 4
Virgin (passage) A 4
Virgin Islands National Park C 4
Water (isl.) A 4
Westend Saltpond (lagoon) E 4

*City and suburbs.
†Population of municipality or sub-division.

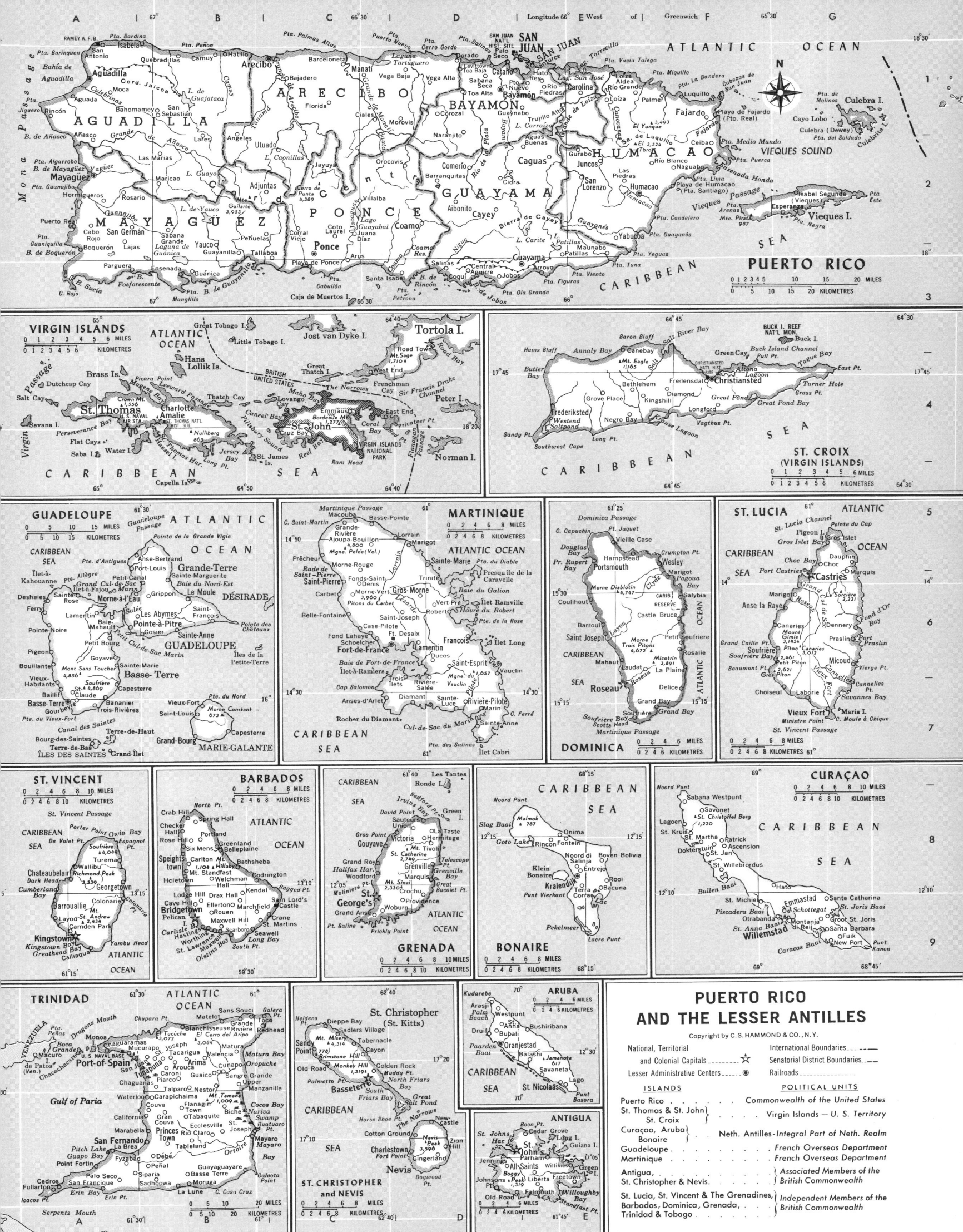

PUERTO RICO AND THE LESSER ANTILLES

Copyright by C.S. HAMMOND & CO., N.Y.

National, Territorial and Colonial Capitals ☆
Lesser Administrative Centers ⊙
International Boundaries ▬ ▬ ▬
Senatorial District Boundaries ▬ ▬ ▬
Railroads ▬▬▬

ISLANDS   POLITICAL UNITS

Puerto Rico . . . . Commonwealth of the United States

St. Thomas & St. John
St. Croix . . . . Virgin Islands — U. S. Territory

Curaçao, Aruba
Bonaire . . . . Neth. Antilles–Integral Part of Neth. Realm

Guadeloupe . . . . French Overseas Department
Martinique . . . . French Overseas Department

Antigua,
St. Christopher & Nevis . . . Associated Members of the British Commonwealth

St. Lucia, St. Vincent & The Grenadines,
Barbados, Dominica, Grenada,
Trinidad & Tobago . . . . Independent Members of the British Commonwealth

CANADA

SCALE

0 50 100   200   300   400   500 MI.

0 50 100 200   300   400   500 KM.

Capitals of Countries .... ☆
Provincial & Territorial Capitals .... △
International Boundaries .... ▬ ▬ ▬
Provincial Boundaries .... ▬ ∙ ▬ ∙
Canals .... ▬

© C.S. HAMMOND & Co., N.Y.

QUEEN ELIZABETH ISLANDS

0 50 100 200 MI.
0 50 100 200 KM.

AREA 3,851,809 sq. mi.
POPULATION 21,568,311 ('71); 22,992,604 ('76)
CAPITAL Ottawa
LARGEST CITY Montréal
HIGHEST POINT Mt. Logan 19,850 ft.
MONETARY UNIT Canadian dollar
MAJOR LANGUAGES English, French
MAJOR RELIGIONS Protestantism, Roman Catholicism

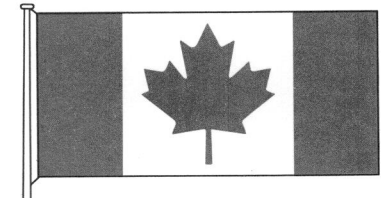

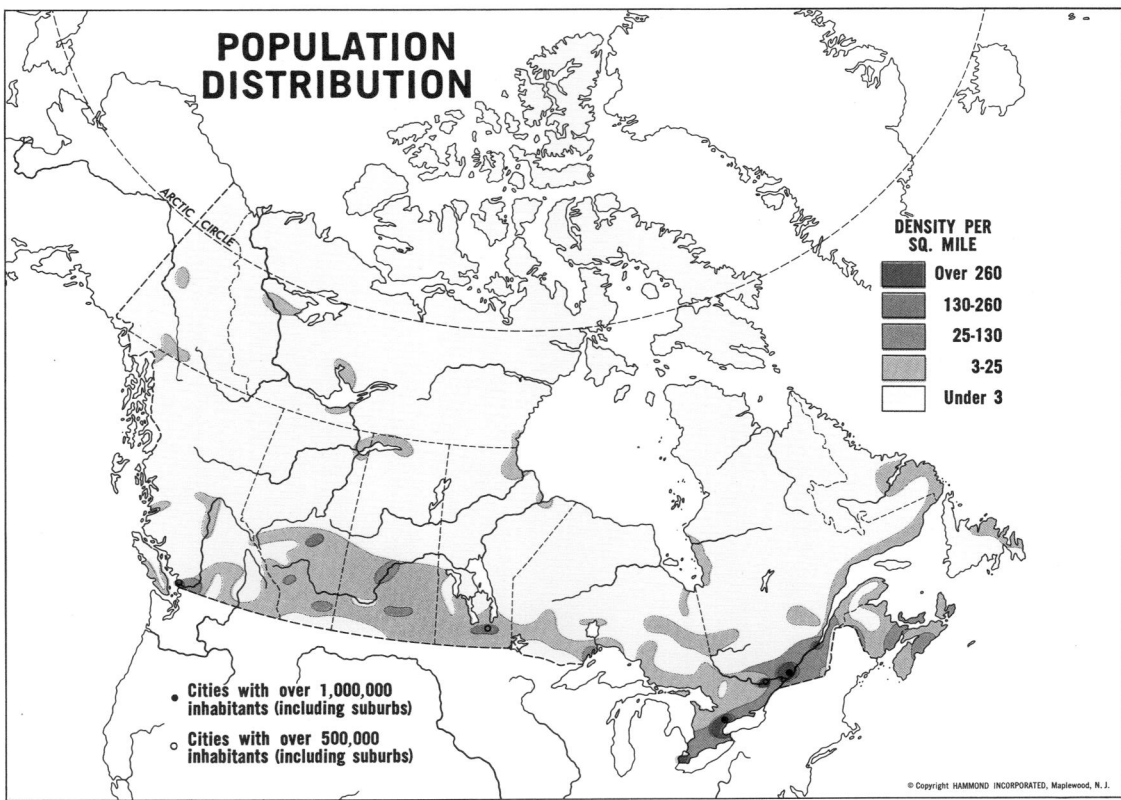

POPULATION DISTRIBUTION

DENSITY PER SQ. MILE

Over 260
130-260
25-130
3-25
Under 3

● Cities with over 1,000,000 inhabitants (including suburbs)
○ Cities with over 500,000 inhabitants (including suburbs)

© Copyright HAMMOND INCORPORATED, Maplewood, N.J.

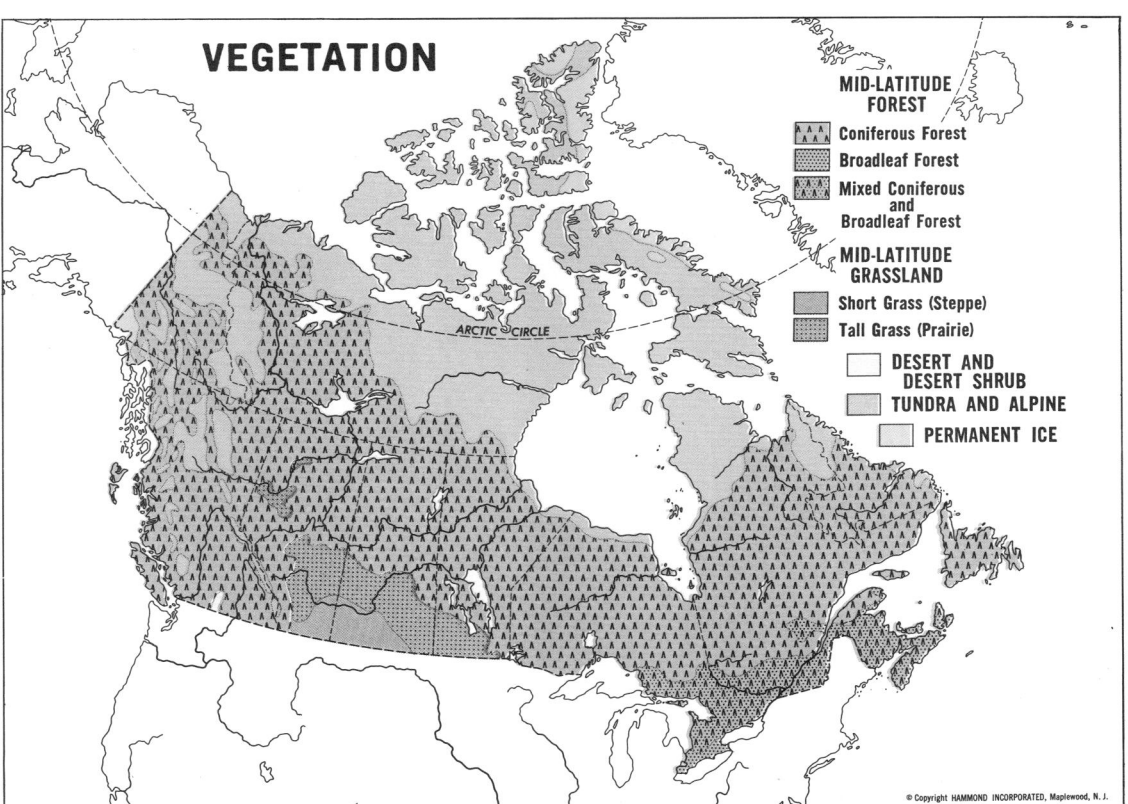

VEGETATION

MID-LATITUDE FOREST

Coniferous Forest
Broadleaf Forest
Mixed Coniferous and Broadleaf Forest

MID-LATITUDE GRASSLAND

Short Grass (Steppe)
Tall Grass (Prairie)

DESERT AND DESERT SHRUB
TUNDRA AND ALPINE
PERMANENT ICE

© Copyright HAMMOND INCORPORATED, Maplewood, N.J.

(continued)

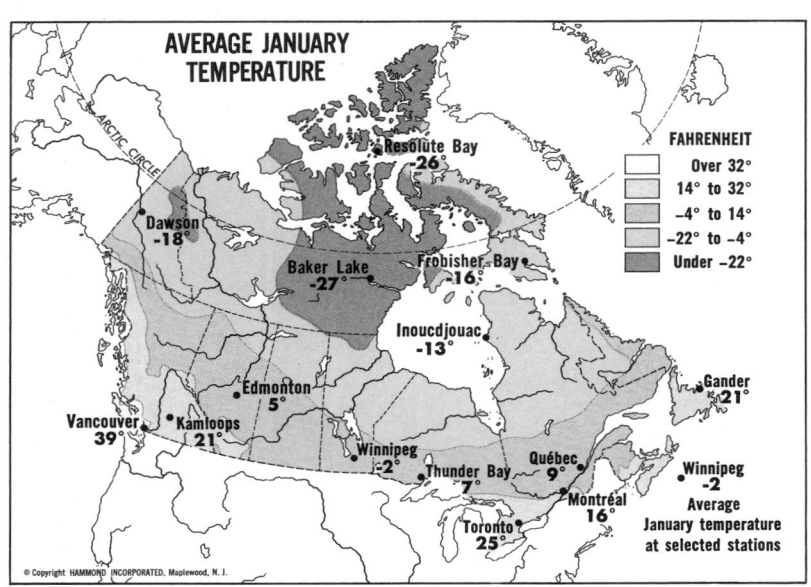

AVERAGE JANUARY TEMPERATURE
FAHRENHEIT
Over 32°
14° to 32°
-4° to 14°
-22° to -4°
Under -22°
ARCTIC CIRCLE
Resolute Bay -26°
Dawson -18°
Baker Lake -27°
Frobisher Bay -16°
Inoucdjouac -13°
Edmonton 5°
Gander 21°
Vancouver 39°
Kamloops 21°
Winnipeg -2°
Thunder Bay 7°
Québec 9°
Montréal 16°
Toronto 25°
Winnipeg -2
Average January temperature at selected stations
© Copyright HAMMOND INCORPORATED, Maplewood, N. J.

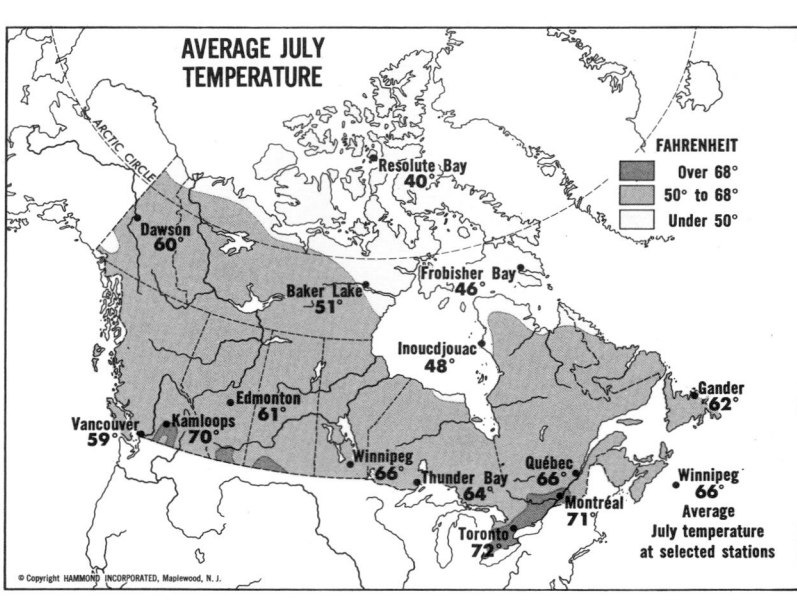

AVERAGE JULY TEMPERATURE
FAHRENHEIT
Over 68°
50° to 68°
Under 50°
ARCTIC CIRCLE
Resolute Bay 40°
Dawson 60°
Baker Lake 51°
Frobisher Bay 46°
Inoucdjouac 48°
Edmonton 61°
Gander 62°
Vancouver 59°
Kamloops 70°
Winnipeg 66°
Thunder Bay 64°
Québec 66°
Montréal 71°
Toronto 72°
Winnipeg 66°
Average July temperature at selected stations
© Copyright HAMMOND INCORPORATED, Maplewood, N. J.

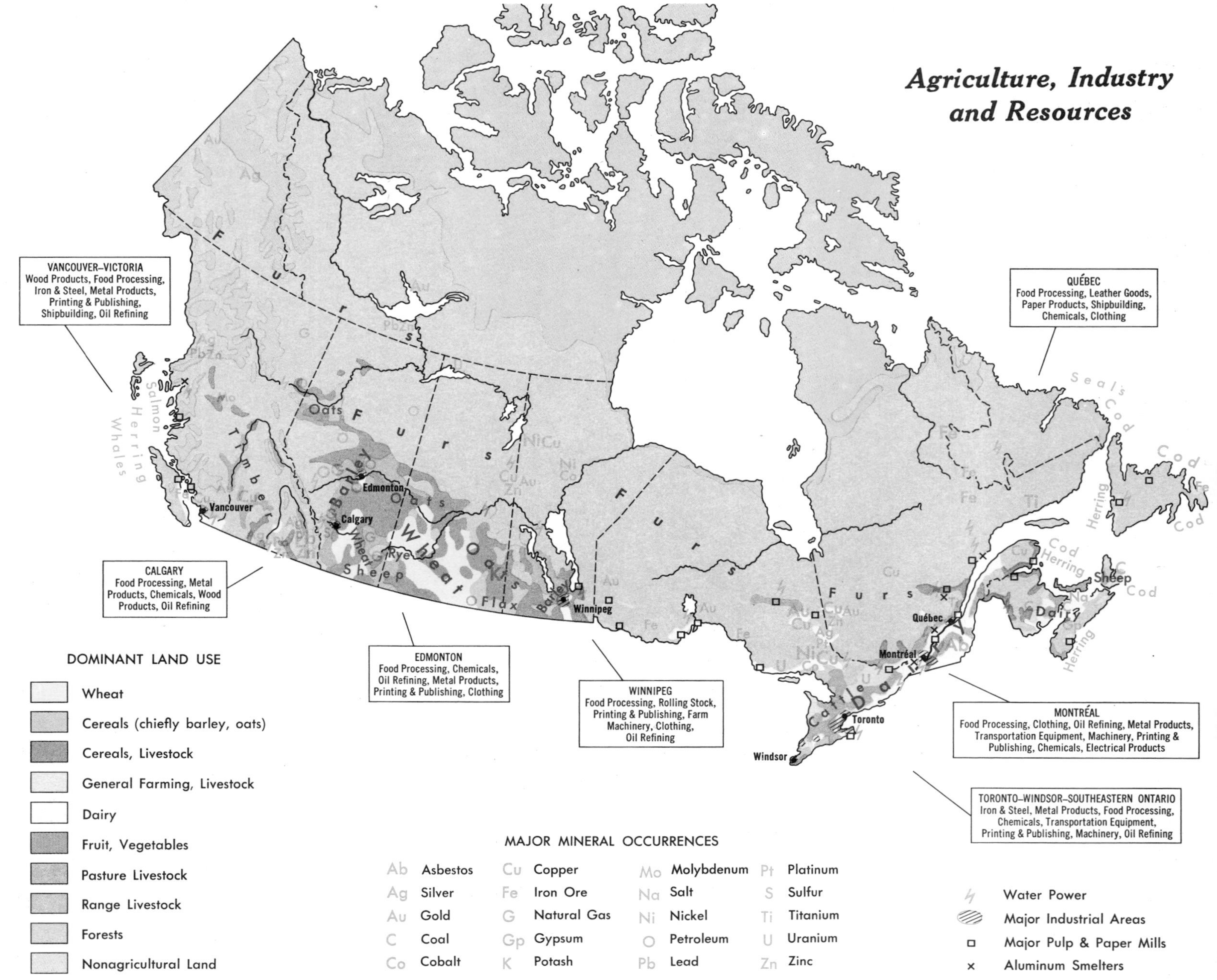

Agriculture, Industry and Resources
VANCOUVER–VICTORIA
Wood Products, Food Processing, Iron & Steel, Metal Products, Printing & Publishing, Shipbuilding, Oil Refining
CALGARY
Food Processing, Metal Products, Chemicals, Wood Products, Oil Refining
EDMONTON
Food Processing, Chemicals, Oil Refining, Metal Products, Printing & Publishing, Clothing
WINNIPEG
Food Processing, Rolling Stock, Printing & Publishing, Farm Machinery, Clothing, Oil Refining
QUÉBEC
Food Processing, Leather Goods, Paper Products, Shipbuilding, Chemicals, Clothing
MONTRÉAL
Food Processing, Clothing, Oil Refining, Metal Products, Transportation Equipment, Machinery, Printing & Publishing, Chemicals, Electrical Products
TORONTO–WINDSOR–SOUTHEASTERN ONTARIO
Iron & Steel, Metal Products, Food Processing, Chemicals, Transportation Equipment, Printing & Publishing, Machinery, Oil Refining
Vancouver
Calgary
Edmonton
Winnipeg
Québec
Montréal
Toronto
Windsor
Furs
Timber
Oats
Barley
Wheat
Rye
Sheep
Flax
Dairy
Cattle
Salmon
Herring
Whales
Seals
Cod
DOMINANT LAND USE
Wheat
Cereals (chiefly barley, oats)
Cereals, Livestock
General Farming, Livestock
Dairy
Fruit, Vegetables
Pasture Livestock
Range Livestock
Forests
Nonagricultural Land
MAJOR MINERAL OCCURRENCES
Ab Asbestos
Ag Silver
Au Gold
C Coal
Co Cobalt
Cu Copper
Fe Iron Ore
G Natural Gas
Gp Gypsum
K Potash
Mo Molybdenum
Na Salt
Ni Nickel
O Petroleum
Pb Lead
Pt Platinum
S Sulfur
Ti Titanium
U Uranium
Zn Zinc
Water Power
Major Industrial Areas
Major Pulp & Paper Mills
Aluminum Smelters

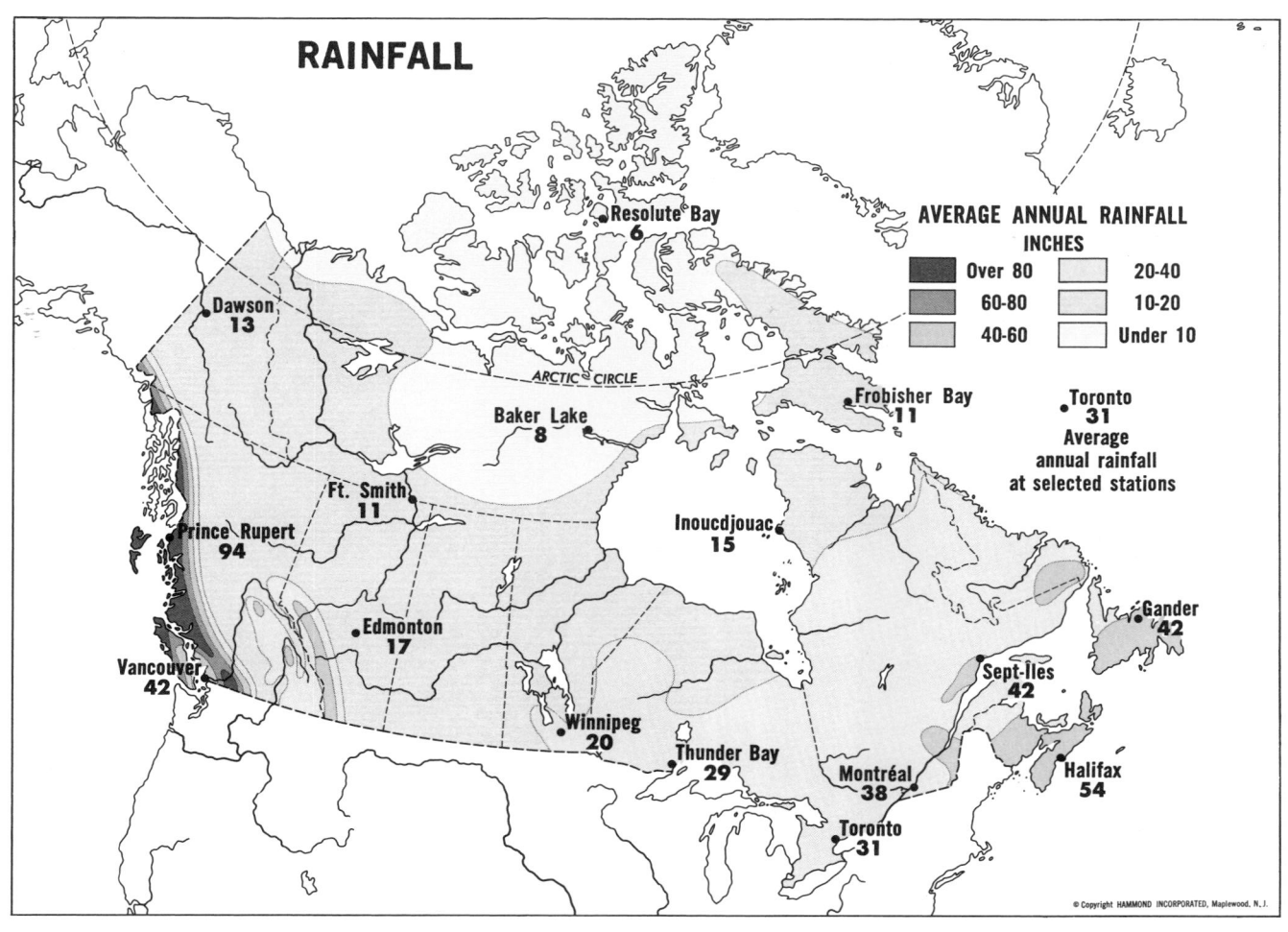

RAINFALL

AVERAGE ANNUAL RAINFALL
INCHES

Over 80	20-40
60-80	10-20
40-60	Under 10

Resolute Bay 6

Dawson 13

ARCTIC CIRCLE

Baker Lake 8

Frobisher Bay 11

Toronto 31
Average annual rainfall at selected stations

Ft. Smith 11

Prince Rupert 94

Inoucdjouac 15

Edmonton 17

Gander 42

Vancouver 42

Sept-Îles 42

Winnipeg 20

Thunder Bay 29

Montréal 38

Halifax 54

Toronto 31

© Copyright HAMMOND INCORPORATED, Maplewood, N.J.

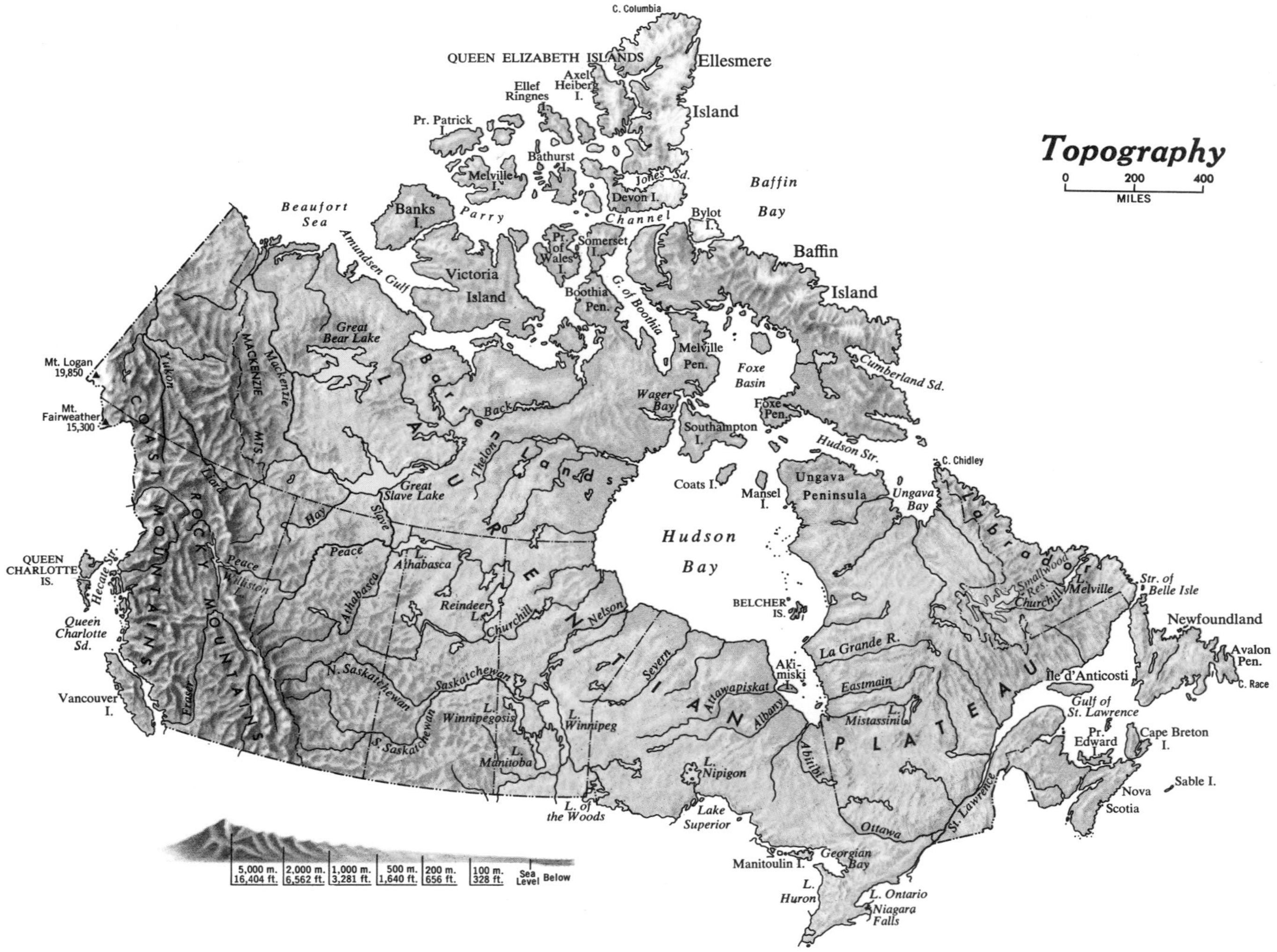

Topography

0   200   400
MILES

C. Columbia

QUEEN ELIZABETH ISLANDS

Ellesmere

Axel Heiberg I.
Ellef Ringnes

Island

Pr. Patrick I.

Bathurst

Baffin Bay

Melville I.

Jones Sd.
Devon I.

Banks I.

Parry Channel

Bylot I.

Beaufort Sea

Amundsen Gulf

Pr. of Wales I.
Somerset

Baffin Island

Victoria Island

Boothia Pen.

Gf. of Boothia

Great Bear Lake

Melville Pen.

Cumberland Sd.

Mt. Logan 19,850

Wager Bay

Foxe Basin

Foxe Pen.

Mt. Fairweather 15,300

Back

Southampton I.

Hudson Str.

C. Chidley

Great Slave Lake

Coats I.

Mansel I.

Ungava Peninsula

Ungava Bay

QUEEN CHARLOTTE IS.

Peace

Athabasca

Reindeer L.

Churchill

Hudson Bay

BELCHER IS.

Melville

Str. of Belle Isle

Queen Charlotte Sd.

Nelson

La Grande R.

Newfoundland

Vancouver I.

N. Saskatchewan

Saskatchewan

Winnipegosis

L. Winnipeg

Severn

Attawapiskat

Albany

Akimiski I.

Eastmain

Mistassini

Île d'Anticosti

Avalon Pen.

C. Race

Gulf of St. Lawrence

Pr. Edward

Cape Breton I.

L. Manitoba

S. Saskatchewan

L. of the Woods

Lake Superior

L. Nipigon

Abitibi

PLATEAU

Nova Scotia

Sable I.

Manitoulin I.

Georgian Bay

St. Lawrence

Ottawa

L. Huron

Lake Erie

L. Ontario
Niagara Falls

5,000 m.
16,404 ft.

2,000 m.
6,562 ft.

1,000 m.
3,281 ft.

500 m.
1,640 ft.

200 m.
656 ft.

100 m.
328 ft.

Sea Level

Below

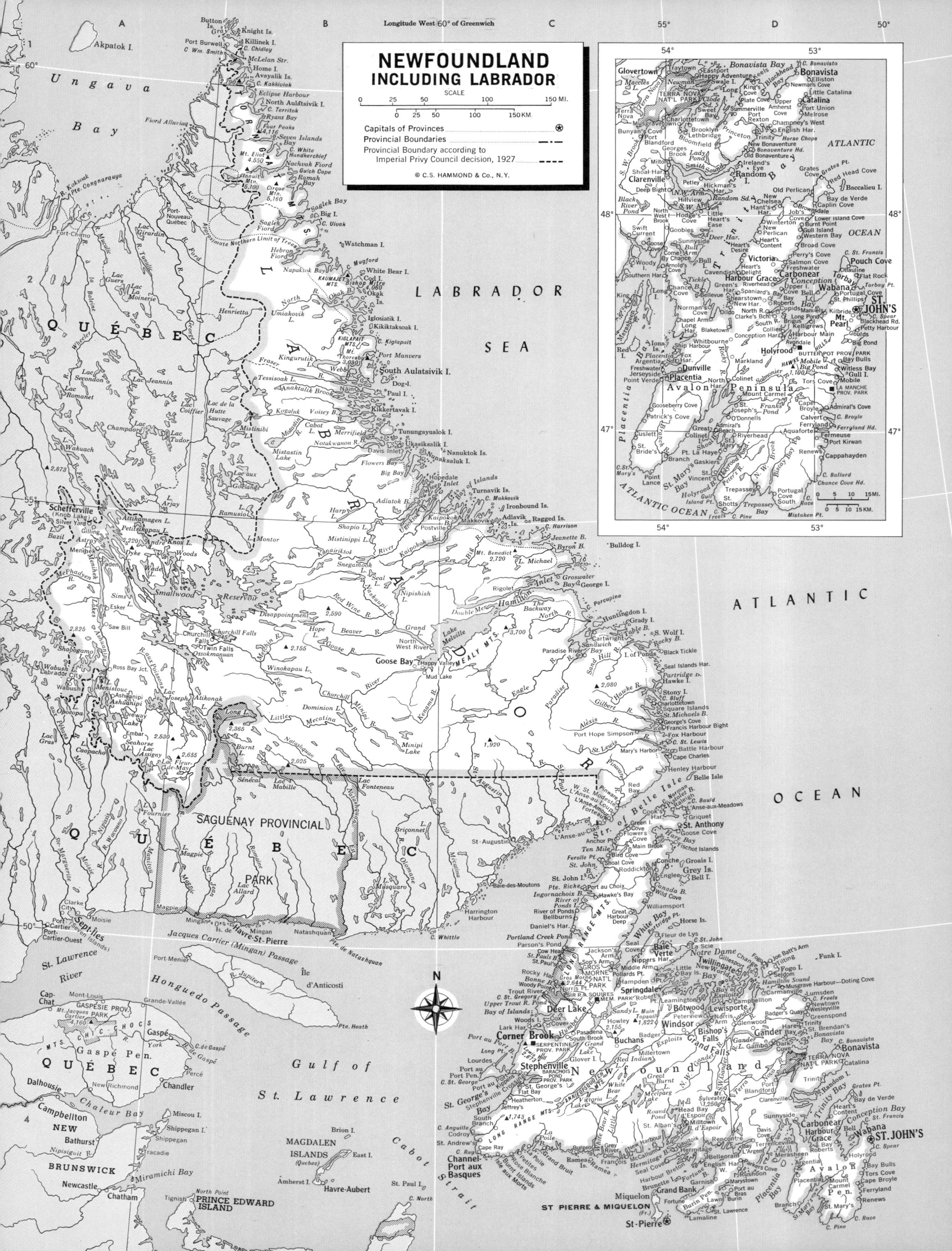

NEWFOUNDLAND
INCLUDING LABRADOR

SCALE

0 25 50 100 150 MI.

0 25 50 100 150 KM.

Capitals of Provinces .... ✪

Provincial Boundaries .... —·—·—

Provincial Boundary according to
Imperial Privy Council decision, 1927 .... ——

© C.S. HAMMOND & Co., N.Y.

AREA 156,185 sq. mi.
POPULATION 522,104 ('71); 557,725 ('76)
CAPITAL St. John's
LARGEST CITY St. John's
HIGHEST POINT Cirque Mtn. 5,160 ft.
SETTLED IN 1610
ADMITTED TO CONFEDERATION 1949
PROVINCIAL FLOWER Pitcher Plant

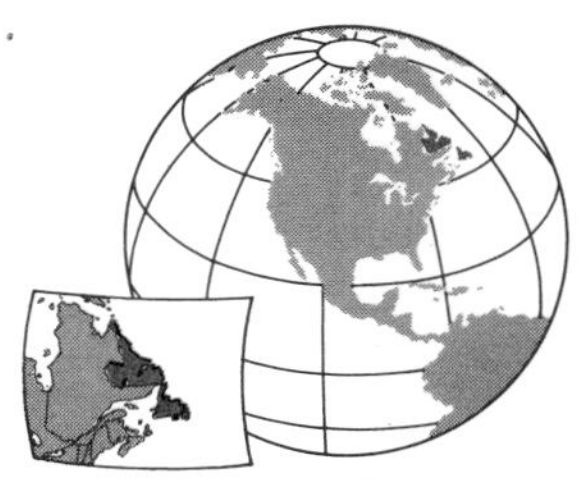

CITIES and TOWNS

Admiral's Beach, 402 ....D 2
Admiral's Cove, 121 ....D 2
Anchor Point, 275 ....C 3
Aquaforte, 186 ....D 2
Argentia, 13 ....C 2
Arnold's Cove, 919 ....C 2
Avondale, 944 ....D 2
Badger, 1,187 ....C 4
Badger's Quay, 904 ....D 4
Baie Verte, 2,397 ....C 4
Battle Harbour, 75 ....C 3
Bauline, 297 ....D 2
Bay Bulls, 1,011 ....D 2
Bay de Verde, 826 ....D 2
Bay L'Argent, 453 ....D 4
Bay Roberts, 3,702 ....D 2
Bellburns, 165 ....C 3
Belleoram, 530 ....C 4
Bellevue, 293 ....D 2
Bird Cove, 339 ....C 3
Bishop's Falls, 4,133 ....C 4
Blackhead Road, 1,672 ....D 2
Black Tickle, 164 ....C 3
Blaketown, 399 ....D 2
Bloomfield, 597 ....D 2
Bonavista, 4,215 ....D 2
Botwood, 4,115 ....C 4
Branch, 516 ....D 2
Brigus, 746 ....D 2
Broad Cove, 198 ....D 2
Brooklyn, 167 ....D 2
Brownsdale, 189 ....D 2
Buchans, 1,907 ....C 4
Bunyan's Cove, 494 ....C 2
Burgeo, 2,226 ....C 4
Burin, 2,586 ....C 4
Burnt Islands, 799 ....C 4
Burnt Point, 257 ....D 2
Calvert, 470 ....D 2
Campbellton, 730 ....D 4
Cape Broyle, 677 ....D 2
Cape Ray, 302 ....C 4
Caplin Cove, 164 ....D 2
Carbonear, 4,732 ....D 2
Carmanville, 839 ....D 4
Cartwright, 752 ....C 3
Catalina, 1,131 ....D 2
Cavendish, 286 ....D 2
Champney's West, 195 ....D 2
Chance Cove, 446 ....D 2
Change Islands, 609 ....D 4
Channel-Port aux Basques, 5,942 ....C 4
Chapel Arm, 659 ....D 2
Charlottetown, 309 ....D 2
Churchill Falls, 2,357 ....B 3
Clarenville, 2,193 ....C 2
Clarke's Beach, 877 ....D 2
Codroy, 321 ....C 4
Colinet, 264 ....D 2
Colliers, 650 ....D 2
Come By Chance, 364 ....C 2
Conception Harbour, 783 ....D 2
Conche, 505 ....C 3
Cook's Harbour, 325 ....C 3
Corner Brook, 26,309 ....C 4
Cow Head, 501 ....C 4
Cox's Cove, 797 ....C 4
Cupids, 691 ....D 2
Cuslett, 124 ....C 2
Daniel's Harbour, 415 ....C 3
Dark Cove, 1,198 ....D 4
Davis Inlet, 193 ....B 2
Deep Bight, 169 ....C 2
Deer Lake, 4,421 ....C 4
Dildo, 878 ....D 2
Dunville, 1,742 ....D 2
Eastport, 438 ....D 1
Elliston, 551 ....D 2
Englee, 1,050 ....C 3
English Harbour West, 393 ....C 4
Fermeuse, 404 ....D 2
Ferryland, 716 ....D 2
Flat Bay, 357 ....C 4
Flat Rock, 680 ....D 2
Fleur de Lys, 672 ....C 3
Flowers Cove, 372 ....C 3
Fogo, 1,155 ....D 4
Forteau, 312 ....C 3
Fortune, 2,164 ....C 4
Fox Harbour, 214 ....C 3
Fox Harbour, 685 ....D 2
François, 220 ....C 4
Freshwater, 1,562 ....C 2
Freshwater, 222 ....D 2
Gambo, 491 ....D 4
Gander, 7,748 ....D 4
Garnish, 618 ....C 4
Gaskiers, 300 ....D 2
Gaultois, 509 ....C 4
Georges Brook, 209 ....D 2
Gillesport, 314 ....D 4
Glenwood, 979 ....D 4
Glovertown, 1,915 ....C 1
Goobies, 137 ....D 2
Goose Bay, 496 ....B 3
Gooseberry Cove, 145 ....C 2
Goose Cove, 239 ....C 2
Goose Cove, 349 ....C 3
Goulds, 4,695 ....D 2
Grand Bank, 3,476 ....C 4
Grand Falls, 7,677 ....C 4
Grates Cove, 328 ....D 2
Great Harbour Deep, 329 ....C 3
Green Island Cove, 224 ....C 3
Green's Harbour, 710 ....D 2
Greenspond, 449 ....D 4
Grey River, 204 ....C 4
Griquet, 825 ....C 3
Gull Island, 361 ....D 2
Hampden, 739 ....C 4
Hant's Harbour, 522 ....D 2
Happy Adventure, 364 ....D 2
Happy Valley, 4,937 ....B 3
Harbour Breton, 2,196 ....C 4
Harbour Grace, 2,771 ....D 2
Harbour Main, 652 ....D 2
Hare Bay, 1,485 ....D 4
Hawke's Bay, 462 ....C 3
Head of Bay d'Espoir, 514 ....C 4
Heart's Content, 599 ....D 2
Heart's Delight, 543 ....D 2
Heart's Desire, 347 ....D 2
Heatherton, 329 ....C 4
Hermitage, 520 ....C 4
Hickman's Harbour, 414 ....D 2
Hillview, 281 ....D 2
Hodge's Cove, 391 ....D 2
Holyrood, 1,282 ....D 2
Hopedale, 375 ....B 2
Howley, 409 ....C 4
Isle aux Morts, 1,158 ....C 4
Jackson's Arm, 491 ....C 4
Jeffrey's, 280 ....C 4
Jerseyside, 1,061 ....B 3
Job's Cove, 182 ....D 2
Joe Batt's Arm, 886 ....D 4
Keels, 146 ....D 1
Kelligrews, 2,046 ....D 2
Kilbride, 2,148 ....D 2
King's Cove, 271 ....D 1
King's Point, 651 ....C 4
Kippens, 1,383 ....C 4
Labrador City, 7,622 ....A 3
Lamaline, 553 ....C 4
L'Anse-au-Clair, 233 ....C 3
L'Anse-au-Loup, 448 ....C 3
La Poile, 173 ....C 4
Lark Harbour, 590 ....C 4
La Scie, 1,255 ....C 4
Lawn, 1,000 ....C 4
Lethbridge, 657 ....D 2
Lewisporte, 3,175 ....C 4
Little Bay Islands, 394 ....C 4
Little Catalina, 722 ....D 2
Little Heart's Ease, 395 ....D 2
Long Harbour, 376 ....D 2
Long Pond, 1,758 ....D 2
Lourdes, 903 ....C 4
Lower Island Cove, 406 ....D 2
Lumsden, 630 ....D 4
Main Brook, 590 ....C 3
Makkovik, 292 ....C 2
Manuels, 1,006 ....D 2
Markland, 311 ....D 2
Mary's Harbour, 134 ....C 3
Marystown, 4,960 ....D 4
McCallum, 216 ....C 4
Melrose, 378 ....D 2
Middle Arm, 474 ....C 4
Millertown, 316 ....C 4
Milltown, 712 ....C 4
Milton, 290 ....C 2
Mount Carmel, 435 ....D 2
Mount Pearl, 7,211 ....D 2
Musgrave Harbour-Doting Cove, 1,238 ....D 4
Musgravetown, 586 ....C 2
Nain, 708 ....B 2
New Chelsea, 215 ....D 2
New Harbour, 704 ....D 2
Newmans Cove, 235 ....D 2
New Perlican, 308 ....D 2
Newtown, 513 ....D 4
Nippers Harbour, 275 ....C 4
Norman's Cove, 997 ....D 2
Norris Arm, 1,191 ....C 4
Norris Point, 986 ....C 4
North Harbour, 146 ....D 2
North River, 256 ....D 2
North West Brook, 302 ....C 2
North West River, 931 ....B 3
O'Donnells, 268 ....D 2
Old Perlican, 597 ....D 2
Paradise River, 146 ....C 3
Parkers Cove, 405 ....D 4
Parson's Pond, 491 ....C 3
Pasadena, 964 ....C 4
Patrick's Cove, 170 ....C 2
Perry's Cove, 165 ....D 2
Peterview, 953 ....C 4
Petley, 177 ....D 2
Petty Harbour, 940 ....D 2
Pinware, 186 ....C 3
Placentia, 2,211 ....C 2
Plate Cove, 517 ....D 2
Point La Haye, 320 ....D 2
Point Lance, 133 ....C 2
Point Leamington, 940 ....C 4
Point Verde, 309 ....C 2
Pollards Point, 439 ....C 4
Port au Bras, 393 ....D 4
Port au Choix, 861 ....C 3
Port au Port, 605 ....C 4
Port Blandford, 779 ....C 2
Port Hope Simpson, 232 ....C 3
Port Kirwan, 159 ....D 2
Port Rexton, 384 ....D 2
Portugal Cove, 1,411 ....D 2
Portugal Cove South, 371 ....D 2
Port Union, 578 ....D 2
Pouch Cove, 1,483 ....D 2
Princeton, 180 ....D 2
Raleigh, 292 ....C 3
Ramea, 1,208 ....C 4
Red Bay, 296 ....C 3
Red Head Cove, 234 ....D 2
Rencontre East, 235 ....C 4
Renews, 497 ....D 2
Rigolet, 182 ....C 3
Riverhead, 329 ....D 2
River of Ponds, 258 ....C 3
Robert's Arm, 1,044 ....C 4
Rocky Harbour, 982 ....C 4
Roddickton, 1,239 ....C 3
Rose Blanche, 703 ....C 4
Rushoon, 506 ....D 4
Saint Alban's, 1,941 ....C 4
Saint Andrew's, 257 ....C 4
Saint Anthony, 2,593 ....C 3
Saint Brendan's, 276 ....D 4
Saint Bride's, 598 ....C 2
Saint George's, 2,082 ....C 4
Saint John's (cap.), 88,102 ....D 2
Saint John's, ‡131,814 ....D 2
Saint Joseph's, 305 ....D 2
Saint Lawrence, 2,173 ....C 4
Saint Mary's, 375 ....D 2
Saint Paul's, 347 ....C 4
Saint Phillips, 573 ....D 2
Saint Shotts, 226 ....D 2
Saint Vincent's, 593 ....D 2
Salmon Cove, 653 ....D 2
Seal Cove, 698 ....C 3
Seal Cove, 457 ....C 4
Seldom, 442 ....D 4
Ship Harbour, 255 ....D 2
Shoal Cove, 236 ....C 3
Shoal Harbour, 715 ....C 2
Sop's Arm, 382 ....C 4
South Branch, 339 ....C 4
South Brook, 802 ....C 4
Southern Harbour, 679 ....C 2
South River, 554 ....D 2
Spaniard's Bay, 1,764 ....D 2
Springdale, 3,224 ....C 4
Stephenville, 7,770 ....C 4
Stephenville Crossing, 2,129 ....C 4
Summerville, 374 ....D 2
Sunnyside, 716 ....D 2
Sweet Bay, 192 ....D 2
Swift Current, 426 ....C 2
Terrenceville, 700 ....D 4
Tilting, 406 ....D 4
Torbay, 2,090 ....D 2
Tors Cove, 325 ....D 2
Traytown, 344 ....D 1
Trepassey, 1,443 ....D 2
Trinity, 577 ....D 2
Trinity, 288 ....D 4
Trout River, 689 ....C 4
Twillingate, 1,437 ....C 4
Upper Island Cove, 1,819 ....D 2
Victoria, 1,601 ....D 2
Wabana, 5,421 ....D 2
Wabush, 3,387 ....A 3
Wesleyville, 1,142 ....D 4
Western Bay, 430 ....D 2
West Saint Modeste, 294 ....C 3
Whitbourne, 1,235 ....D 2
Wild Cove, 172 ....C 3
Windsor, 6,644 ....C 4
Winterton, 794 ....D 2
Witless Bay, 754 ....D 2
Woody Point, 300 ....C 4

OTHER FEATURES

Alexis (riv.) ....C 3
Anguille (cape) ....C 4
Annieopscotch (mts.) ....C 4
Ashuanipi (lake) ....A 3
Ashuanipi (riv.) ....A 3
Atikonak (lake) ....B 3
Attikamagen (lake) ....A 3
Avalon (pen.) ....D 2
Barachois Pond Prov. Park ....C 4
Bauld (cape) ....C 3
Bell (isl.) ....C 3
Bell (isl.), 6,079 ....D 2
Belle Isle (isl.), 25 ....C 3
Belle Isle (str.) ....C 3
Blackhead (bay) ....D 2
Bonavista (bay) ....D 1
Bonavista (cape) ....D 1
Bonne (bay) ....C 4
Broyle (cape) ....D 2
Bull Arm (inlet) ....D 2
Burin (pen.) ....C 4
Butter Pot Prov. Park ....D 2
Cabot (str.) ....B 4
Canada (bay) ....C 3
Chidley (cape) ....B 1
Churchill (falls) ....B 3
Churchill (riv.) ....B 3
Cirque (mt.) ....B 2
Clode (sound) ....D 2
Conception (bay) ....D 2
Deep (inlet) ....B 2
Double Mer (lake) ....C 3
Dyke (lake) ....A 3
Eagle (riv.) ....C 3
Espoir (bay) ....C 4
Exploits (bay) ....C 4
Exploits (riv.) ....C 4
Fogo (isl.), 4,094 ....D 4
Fortune (bay) ....C 4
Freels (cape) ....D 3
Gander (lake) ....D 4
Gander (riv.) ....D 4
Glover (isl.) ....C 4
Goose (riv.) ....B 3
Grand (lake) ....B 3
Grand (lake) ....C 4
Grates (pt.) ....D 2
Great Colinet (isl.) ....D 2
Grey (isls.) ....C 3
Groais (isl.) ....C 3
Gros Morne (mt.) ....C 4
Gros Morne Nat'l Park ....C 4
Groswater (bay) ....C 3
Hamilton (inlet) ....C 3
Hamilton (sound) ....D 4
Hare (bay) ....C 3
Hawke (hills) ....D 2
Hebron (fjord) ....B 2
Hermitage (bay) ....C 4
Holyrood (bay) ....D 2
Horse (isls.) ....C 3
Horse Chops (head) ....D 2
Humber (riv.) ....C 4
Ingornachoix (bay) ....C 3
Innuit (mt.) ....B 2
Ireland's Eye (isl.) ....D 2
Islands (bay) ....C 4
Kaipokok (bay) ....B 2
Kanairiktok (riv.) ....B 3
Kaumajet (mts.) ....B 2
Kingurutuk (lake) ....B 2
Labrador (reg.), 28,166 ....B 2
Labrador (sea) ....C 2
La Manche Prov. Park ....D 2
La Poile (bay) ....C 4
Little Mecatina (riv.) ....B 3
Long (isl.) ....C 2
Long (lake) ....A 3
Long (pt.) ....C 4
Long Range (mts.) ....C 4
Main Topsail (mt.) ....C 4
Makkovik (cape) ....C 2
McLelan (str.) ....B 1
Mealy (mts.) ....C 3
Meelpaeg (lake) ....C 4
Melville (lake) ....C 3
Menihek (lakes) ....A 3
Merasheen (isl.) ....C 2
Mistaken (pt.) ....D 2
Mistastin (lake) ....B 2
Nachvak (fjord) ....B 2
Naskaupi (riv.) ....B 3
Newfoundland (isl.), 493,938 ....C 4
Newman (sound) ....D 2
New World (isl.), 4,563 ....C 4
Norman (cape) ....C 3
North Aulatsivik (isl.) ....B 2
Notre Dame (bay) ....C 4
Okak (bay) ....B 2
Ossokmanuan (res.) ....B 3
Petitsikapau (lake) ....A 3
Pine (cape) ....D 2
Pinware (riv.) ....C 3
Pistolet (bay) ....C 3
Placentia (bay) ....C 2
Ponds (isl.), 164 ....C 3
Port au Port (bay) ....C 4
Port au Port (pen.) ....C 4
Port Manvers (harb.) ....B 2
Race (cape) ....D 2
Ramah (bay) ....B 2
Ramea (isls.), 1,208 ....C 4
Random (isl.), 1,353 ....D 2
Random (sound) ....D 2
Ray (cape) ....C 4
Red (isl.) ....C 2
Red Indian (lake) ....C 4
Red Wine (riv.) ....B 3
Rocky (riv.) ....D 2
Round (pond) ....C 4
Saglek (bay) ....B 2
Saint Francis (cape) ....D 2
Saint George (cape) ....C 4
Saint George's (bay) ....C 4
Saint John (bay) ....C 3
Saint John (cape) ....C 3
Saint Lawrence (gulf) ....B 4
Saint Lewis (cape) ....C 3
Saint Mary's (bay) ....C 2
Saint Mary's (cape) ....C 2
Saint Michaels (bay) ....C 3
Salmonier (riv.) ....D 2
Sandwich (bay) ....C 3
Serpentine Prov. Park ....C 4
Shabogamo (lake) ....A 3
Shoal (bay) ....D 2
Sir R.A. Squires Mem. Park ....C 4
Smallwood (res.) ....B 3
Smith (sound) ....D 2
South Aulatsivik (isl.) ....B 2
Spear (cape) ....D 2
Swale (isl.) ....D 1
Sylvester (mt.) ....C 4
Terra Nova (riv.) ....C 2
Terra Nova Nat'l Park ....D 2
Territok (cape) ....B 2
Thoresby (mt.) ....B 2
Tickle (bay) ....D 2
Torbay (pt.) ....D 2
Torngat (mts.) ....B 2
Trespassey (bay) ....D 2
Trinity (bay) ....D 2
Tunungayualok (isl.) ....B 2
Ukasiksalik (isl.), 193 ....B 2
Victoria (lake) ....C 4
Wabush (lake) ....A 3
White (bay) ....C 3
White Bear (lake) ....C 4
White Handkerchief (cape) ....B 2

SAINT PIERRE & MIQUELON

CITIES and TOWNS

Saint-Pierre (cap.), 4,565 ....C 4

OTHER FEATURES

Miquelon (isl.), 621 ....C 4
Saint Pierre (isl.), 4,565 ....C 4

‡ Population of metropolitan area.

Agriculture, Industry and Resources

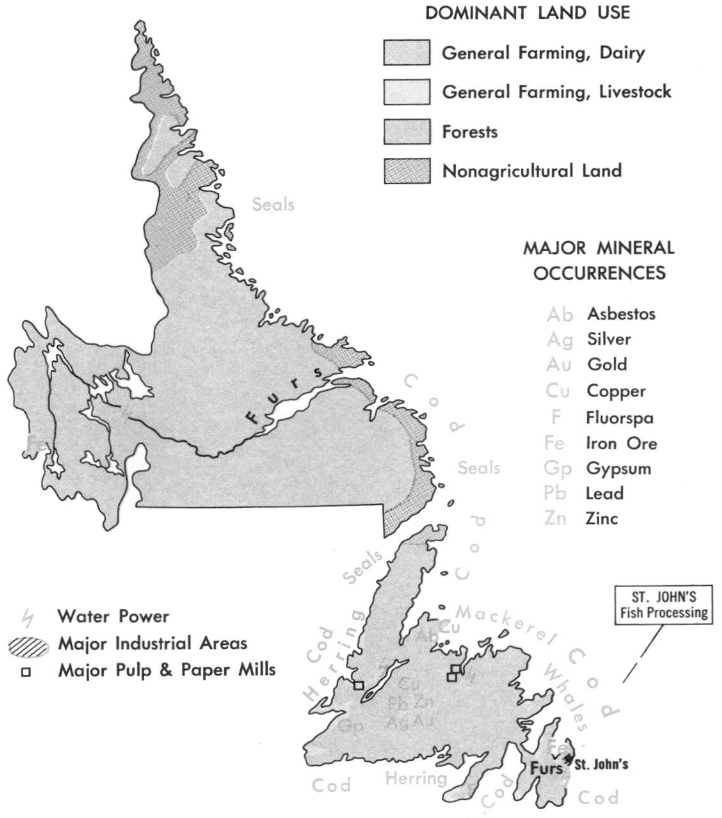

DOMINANT LAND USE
General Farming, Dairy
General Farming, Livestock
Forests
Nonagricultural Land
MAJOR MINERAL OCCURRENCES
Ab Asbestos
Ag Silver
Au Gold
Cu Copper
F Fluorspa
Fe Iron Ore
Gp Gypsum
Pb Lead
Zn Zinc
Water Power
Major Industrial Areas
Major Pulp & Paper Mills
Seals
Furs
Cod
Herring
Mackerel
Whales
ST. JOHN'S Fish Processing
St. John's

Topography

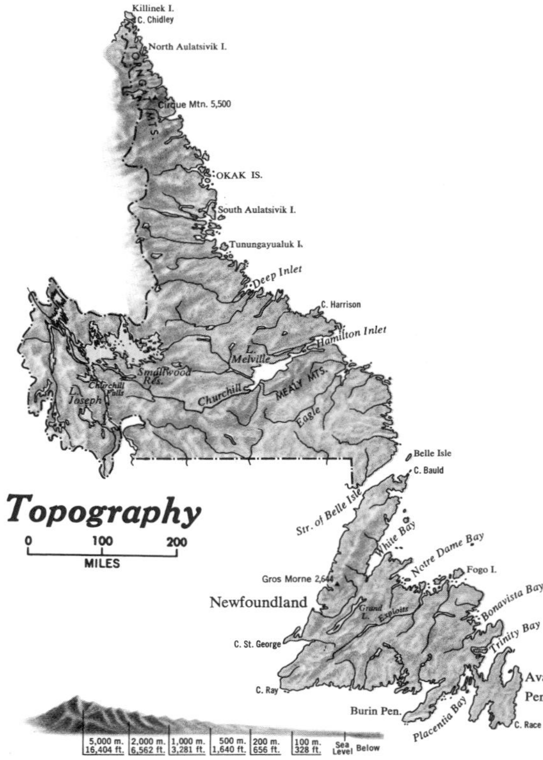

Killinek I.
C. Chidley
North Aulatsivik I.
Cirque Mtn. 5,500
OKAK IS.
South Aulatsivik I.
Tunungayualuk I.
Deep Inlet
C. Harrison
Hamilton Inlet
Melville
Smallwood Res.
Churchill
MEALY MTS.
Eagle
Belle Isle
C. Bauld
Str. of Belle Isle
White Bay
Notre Dame Bay
Fogo I.
Gros Morne 2,644
Newfoundland
Bonavista Bay
Trinity Bay
C. St. George
C. Ray
Burin Pen.
Placentia Bay
Avalon Pen.
C. Race
0 100 200
MILES
5,000 m. 16,404 ft.
2,000 m. 6,562 ft.
1,000 m. 3,281 ft.
500 m. 1,640 ft.
200 m. 656 ft.
100 m. 328 ft.
Sea Level
Below

NOVA SCOTIA

COUNTIES

Annapolis, 21,841 .... C 4
Antigonish, 16,814 .... F 3
Cape Breton, 129,075 .... H 2
Colchester, 37,735 .... E 3
Cumberland, 35,160 .... D 3
Digby, 20,349 .... C 4
Guysborough, 12,864 .... F 3
Halifax, 261,461 .... E 4
Hants, 28,935 .... D 4
Inverness, 20,375 .... G 2
Kings, 44,975 .... C 3
Lunenburg, 38,422 .... D 4
Pictou, 46,104 .... F 3
Queens, 12,950 .... C 4
Richmond, 12,734 .... H 3
Shelburne, 16,661 .... C 5
Victoria, 7,823 .... H 2

CITIES and TOWNS

Yarmouth, 24,682 .... C 5

Abercrombie, 532 .... F 3
Alder Point, 844 .... H 2
Aldershot, 1,729 .... D 3
Amherst⊙, 9,966 .... D 3
Annapolis Royal⊙, 758 .... C 4
Antigonish⊙, 5,489 .... F 3
Arcadia, 425 .... B 5
Arichat⊙, 829 .... H 3
Auburn, 519 .... D 3
Aylesford, 680 .... C 3
Baddeck⊙, 831 .... H 2
Barrington Passage, 551 .... C 5
Bear River, 733 .... C 4
Beaverbank, 958 .... E 4
Belliveau Cove, 486 .... B 4
Belmont, 663 .... E 3
Berwick, 1,412 .... D 4

Bible Hill, 3,505 .... E 3
Block House, 418 .... D 4
Blue Rock, 394 .... D 4
Bras d'Or, 655 .... H 2
Bridgetown, 1,039 .... C 4
Bridgewater, 5,231 .... D 4
Brookfield, 658 .... E 3
Brooklyn, 1,253 .... D 4
Caledonia, 459 .... C 4
Cambridge Station, 699 .... D 3
Canning, 809 .... D 3
Canso, 1,209 .... H 3
Cape North, 118 .... H 2
Centreville, 552 .... D 3
Chester, 1,031 .... D 4
Chester Basin, 588 .... D 4
Chéticamp, 1,016 .... G 2
Church Point, 258 .... B 4
Clark's Harbour, 1,082 .... C 5
Clementsport, 479 .... C 4
Comeauville, 365 .... B 4
Concession, 404 .... B 4
Conquerall Bank, 480 .... D 4

Conway, 363 .... C 4
Dartmouth, 64,770 .... E 4
Debert, 703 .... E 3
Deep Brook, 494 .... C 4
Digby⊙, 2,363 .... C 4
Dominion, 2,879 .... J 2
Donkin, 910 .... J 2
East Chester, 485 .... D 4
East Chezzetcook, 617 .... E 4
Ellershouse, 424 .... D 4
Elmsdale, 758 .... E 4
Enfield, 1,056 .... E 4
Fall River, 969 .... E 4
Falmouth, 759 .... D 3
Florence, 1,958 .... H 2
Freeport, 475 .... B 4
Glace Bay, 22,440 .... J 2
Gold River, 448 .... D 4
Granville Ferry, 445 .... C 4
Great Village, 494 .... E 3
Grosses Coques, 360 .... B 4
Guysborough⊙, 494 .... G 3
Halifax (cap.)⊙, 122,035 .... E 4

Halifax, ‡222,637 .... E 4
Hantsport, 1,447 .... D 3
Havre Boucher, 385 .... G 3
Head of Jeddore, 445 .... E 4
Head of Saint Margarets Bay, 644 .... E 4
Heatherton, 368 .... G 3
Hebron, 463 .... B 5
Herring Cove, 1,487 .... E 4
Hilden, 803 .... E 3
Hopewell, 439 .... F 3
Hubbards, 427 .... D 4
Ingonish, 338 .... H 2
Ingonish Beach, 640 .... H 2
Inverness, 1,846 .... G 2
Joggins, 777 .... D 3
Judique, 409 .... G 3
Kentville⊙, 5,198 .... D 3
Kingston, 1,429 .... D 3
Lakeside, 1,687 .... E 4
Lantz, 661 .... E 4
L'Ardoise West, 432 .... H 3
Lawrencetown, 512 .... C 4

Lequille, 526 .... C 4
Little Dover, 585 .... G 3
Liverpool⊙, 3,654 .... C 5
Lockeport, 1,208 .... C 5
Louisbourg, 1,582 .... J 3
Louisdale, 1,036 .... H 3
Lower Wedgeport, 561 .... C 5
Lower West Pubnico, 743 .... C 5
Lower Woods Harbour, 589 .... C 5
Lunenburg⊙, 3,215 .... D 4
Lyons Brook, 441 .... F 3
Mabou, 421 .... G 2
Maccan, 492 .... D 3
Mahone Bay, 1,333 .... D 4
Main-à-Dieu, 394 .... J 2
Meaghers Grant, 388 .... E 4
Melvern Square, 427 .... C 3
Meteghan, 909 .... B 4
Meteghan Centre, 368 .... B 4
Meteghan River, 414 .... B 4
Middle Musquodoboit, 638 .... E 3

Middleton, 1,870 .... C 4
Middlewood, 395 .... D 4
Milford Station, 650 .... E 3
Milton, 1,854 .... C 5
Mira Road, 1,503 .... H 2
Monastery, 418 .... G 3
Mount Uniacke, 813 .... E 4
Mulgrave, 1,196 .... G 3
Musquodoboit Harbour, 768 .... E 4
New Germany, 584 .... D 4
New Glasgow, 10,849 .... F 3
New Minas, 1,503 .... D 3
Newport, 471 .... D 3
New Road, 1,333 .... C 4
New Victoria, 1,377 .... J 2
New Waterford, 9,579 .... J 2
Nictaux, 578 .... C 4
North Sydney, 8,604 .... H 2
Oxford, 1,473 .... D 3
Parkers Cove, 395 .... C 4
Parrsboro, 1,807 .... D 3
Petit-de-Grat, 1,032 .... H 3

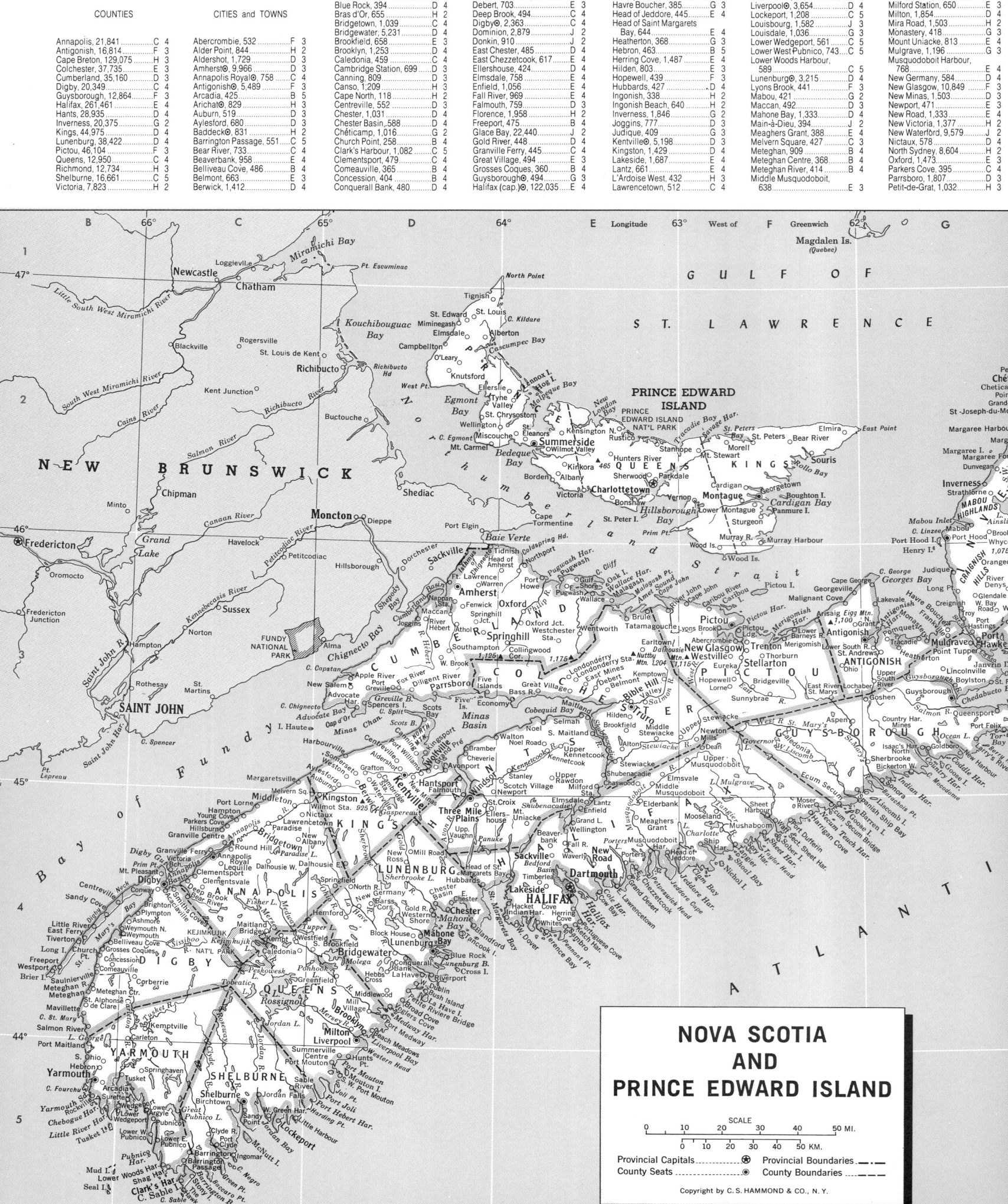

NOVA SCOTIA
AND
PRINCE EDWARD ISLAND

SCALE

0   10   20   30   40   50 MI.

0   10   20   30   40   50 KM.

Provincial Capitals .... ⊛   Provincial Boundaries ___ . ___

County Seats .... ⊙   County Boundaries ____ ____

Copyright by C. S. HAMMOND & CO., N.Y.

PRINCE EDWARD ISLAND
AREA 2,184 sq. mi.
POPULATION 111,641 ('71); 118,229 ('76)
CAPITAL Charlottetown
LARGEST CITY Charlottetown
HIGHEST POINT 465 ft.
SETTLED IN 1720
ADMITTED TO CONFEDERATION 1873
PROVINCIAL FLOWER Lady's Slipper

NOVA SCOTIA
AREA 21,425 sq. mi.
POPULATION 788,960 ('71); 828,571 ('76)
CAPITAL Halifax
LARGEST CITY Halifax
HIGHEST POINT Cape Breton Highlands 1,747 ft.
SETTLED IN 1605
ADMITTED TO CONFEDERATION 1867
PROVINCIAL FLOWER Trailing Arbutus or Mayflower

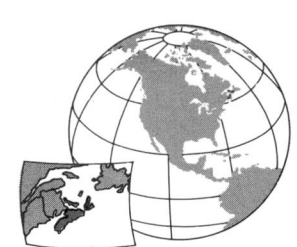

Topography

0 30 60
MILES

PRINCE EDWARD ISLAND

Agriculture, Industry and Resources

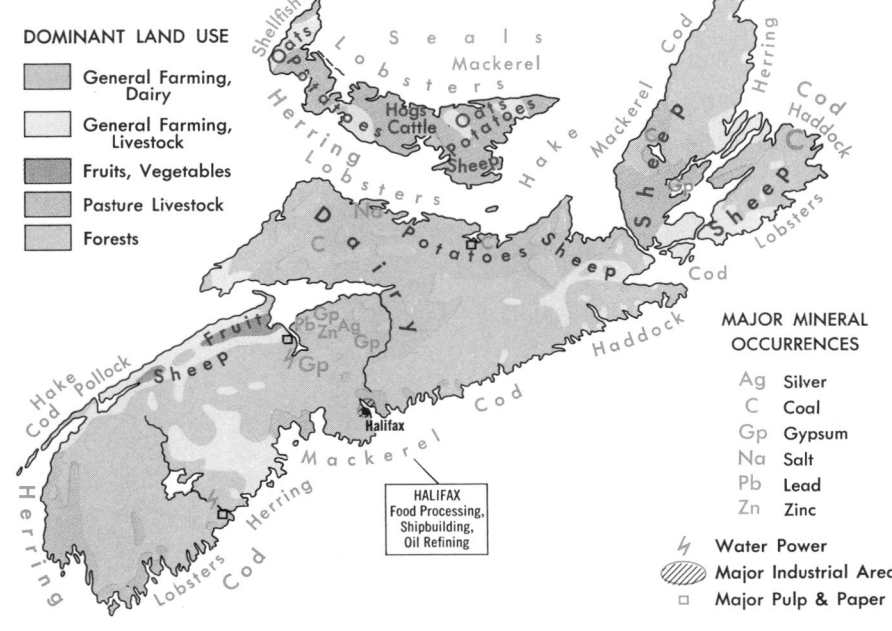

DOMINANT LAND USE

- General Farming, Dairy
- General Farming, Livestock
- Fruits, Vegetables
- Pasture Livestock
- Forests

HALIFAX
Food Processing, Shipbuilding, Oil Refining

MAJOR MINERAL OCCURRENCES

Ag Silver
C Coal
Gp Gypsum
Na Salt
Pb Lead
Zn Zinc

↯ Water Power
Major Industrial Areas
□ Major Pulp & Paper Mills

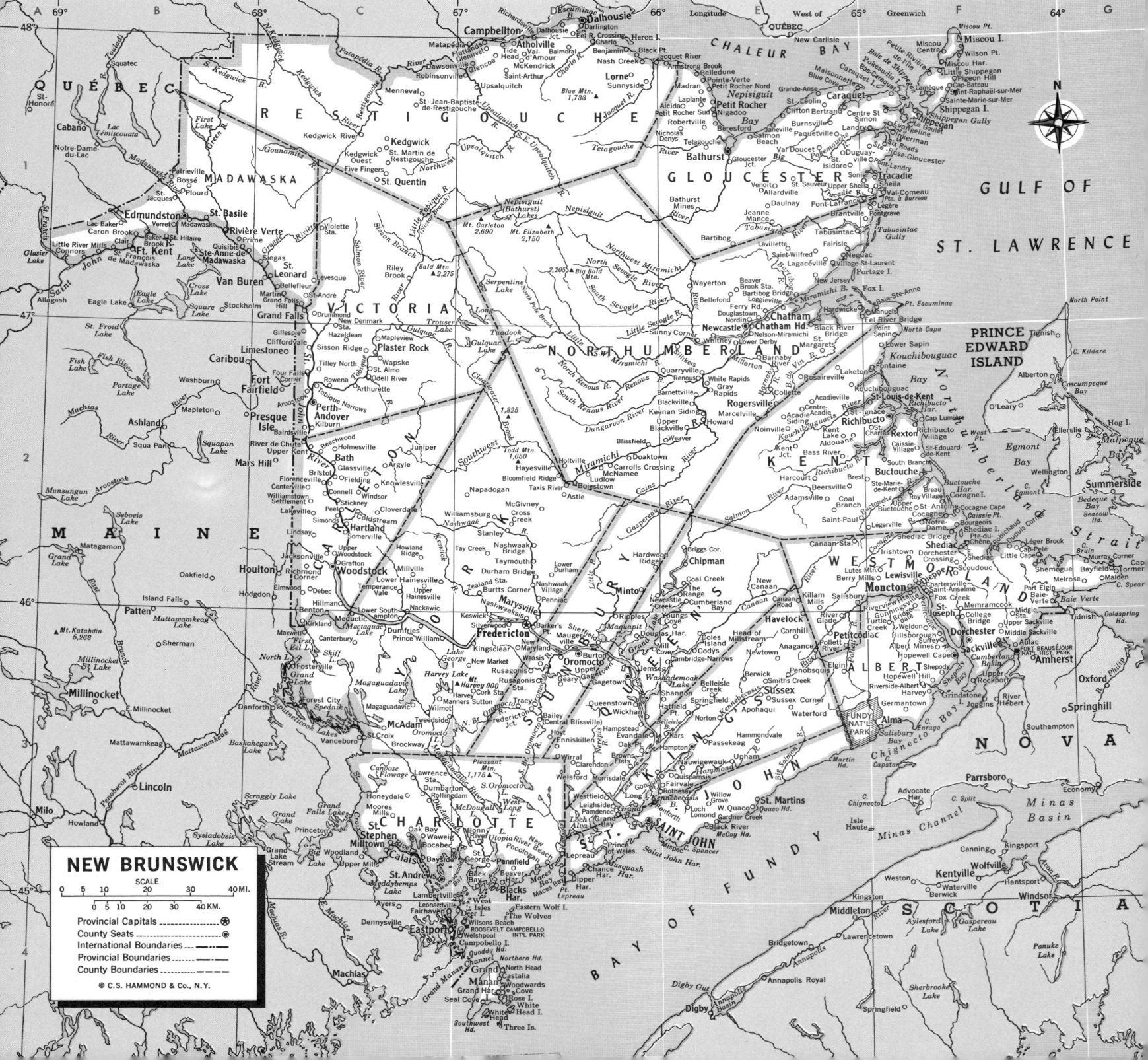

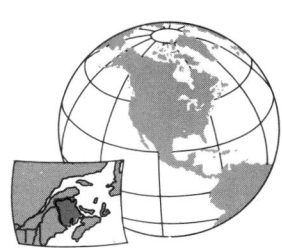

AREA 28,354 sq. mi.
POPULATION 634,557 ('71); 677,250 ('76)
CAPITAL Fredericton
LARGEST CITY Saint John
HIGHEST POINT Mt. Carleton 2,690 ft.
SETTLED IN 1611
ADMITTED TO CONFEDERATION 1867
PROVINCIAL FLOWER Purple Violet

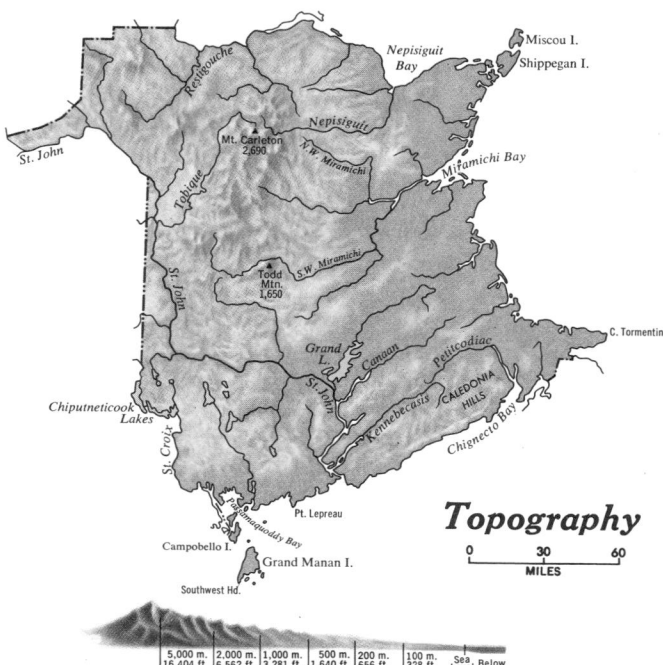

Topography

0   30   60
MILES

5,000 m. / 16,404 ft. | 2,000 m. / 6,562 ft. | 1,000 m. / 3,281 ft. | 500 m. / 1,640 ft. | 200 m. / 656 ft. | 100 m. / 328 ft. | Sea Level | Below

Agriculture, Industry and Resources

SAINT JOHN
Food Processing, Shipbuilding,
Pulp & Paper, Wood Products,
Metal Products

DOMINANT LAND USE

- Cereals, Livestock
- Dairy
- Potatoes
- General Farming, Livestock
- Pasture Livestock
- Forests

MAJOR MINERAL OCCURRENCES

Ag Silver   Pb Lead
C Coal   Zn Zinc
Cu Copper

⚡ Water Power
▨ Major Industrial Areas
▫ Major Pulp & Paper Mills

Topography

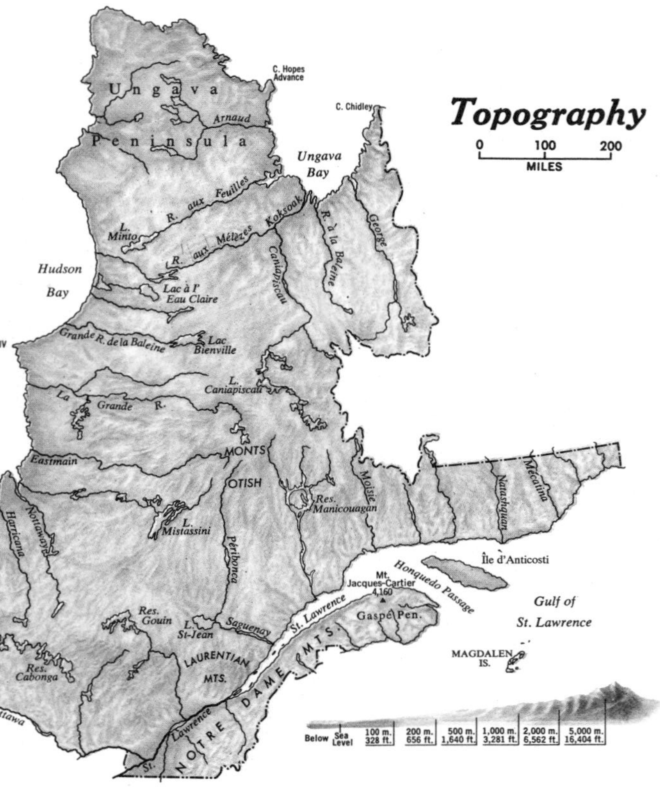
Topography
0 100 200
MILES
Ungava
Peninsula
C. Hopes Advance
C. Chidley
Arnaud
Ungava Bay
Hudson Bay
R. aux Feuilles
L. Minto
R. aux Mélèzes
Koksoak
Caniapiscau
R. à la Baleine
George
Lac à l'Eau Claire
Pte. Louis-XIV
Grande R. de la Baleine
Lac Bienville
L. Caniapiscau
La Grande R.
Eastmain
MONTS
OTISH
Res. Manicouagan
Moisie
Natashquan
Mécatina
L. Mistassini
Nottaway
Harricana
Péribonca
Île d'Anticosti
Mt. Jacques-Cartier 4,160
Honguedo Passage
Gulf of St. Lawrence
Res. Gouin
L. St-Jean
Saguenay
St. Lawrence
Gaspé Pen.
LAURENTIAN MTS.
NOTRE DAME MTS.
MAGDALEN IS.
Res. Cabonga
Ottawa
Below Sea Level 100 m. 328 ft. 200 m. 656 ft. 500 m. 1,640 ft. 1,000 m. 3,281 ft. 2,000 m. 6,562 ft. 5,000 m. 16,404 ft.

QUÉBEC

COUNTIES

Argenteuil, 31,319 C 4
Arthabaska, 51,524 E 4
Bagot, 23,591 E 4
Beauce, 63,960 G 3
Beauharnois, 52,137 C 4
Bellechasse, 23,517 G 3
Berthier, 27,288 C 3
Bonaventure, 41,701 C 2
Brome, 15,311 E 4
Chambly, 231,590 J 4
Champlain, 113,150 E 2
Charlevoix-Est, 16,780 G 2
Charlevoix-Ouest, 13,650 G 2
Châteauguay, 53,737 D 4
Chicoutimi, 163,348 G 1
Compton, 21,367 F 4
Deux-Montagnes, 52,369 C 4
Dorchester, 32,473 C 3
Drummond, 64,144 E 4
Frontenac, 27,293 G 4
Gaspé-Est, 41,727 D 1
Gaspé-Ouest, 18,754 C 1
Gatineau, 55,729 B 3
Hull, 109,946 B 4
Huntingdon, 15,358 C 4
Iberville, 20,400 D 4
île-de-Montréal, 1,959,143 H 4
île-Jésus, 228,010 H 4
Joliette, 52,088 C 3
Kamouraska, 26,264 H 2
Labelle, 30,582 B 3
Lac-Saint-Jean-Est, 45,220 F 1
Lac-Saint-Jean-Ouest, 57,074 E 1
Laprairie, 61,691 H 4
L'Assomption, 62,198 D 4
Lévis, 62,776 J 3
L'Islet, 23,187 G 2
Lotbinière, 27,373 F 3
Maskinongé, 21,257 D 3
Matane, 30,261 B 1
Matapédia, 26,856 B 2
Mégantic, 58,020 F 3
Missisquoi, 33,953 D 4
Montcalm, 21,546 C 3
Montmagny, 26,307 G 3
Montmorency No. 1, 20,401 F 2
Montmorency No. 2, 5,435 G 3
Napierville, 12,067 D 4
Nicolet, 30,004 E 3
Papineau, 31,793 B 4
Pontiac, 19,570 A 3
Portneuf, 51,540 E 3
Québec, 423,162 F 3
Richelieu, 47,093 D 4
Richmond, 41,044 E 4
Rimouski, 64,263 J 1
Rivière-du-Loup, 39,488 H 2
Rouville, 31,759 D 4
Saguenay, 111,272 H 1
Saint-Hyacinthe, 50,494 D 4
Saint-Jean, 45,892 D 4
Saint-Maurice, 108,366 D 3
Shefford, 62,361 E 4
Sherbrooke, 101,470 E 4
Soulanges, 11,449 C 4
Stanstead, 36,266 F 4
Témiscouata, 23,189 J 2
Terrebonne, 139,945 H 4
Vaudreuil, 36,593 C 4
Verchères, 35,273 J 4
Wolfe, 16,197 F 4
Yamaska, 15,206 E 3

CITIES and TOWNS

Acton Vale, 4,564 E 4
Albanel, 788 E 1
Alma⊙, 22,622 F 1
Amqui⊙, 3,797 B 2
Ancienne-Lorette, 8,304 H 3
Angers, 881 B 4
Anjou, 33,886 H 4
Armagh, 987 G 3
Arthabaska⊙, 4,479 F 3
Arvida, 18,448 F 1
Asbestos, 9,749 F 4
Ayer's Cliff⊙, 873 E 4
Aylmer, 7,198 B 4
Bagotville, 6,041 G 1
Baie-Comeau, 12,109 A 1
Baie-de-Shawinigan, 847 E 3
Baie-des-Sables, 638 A 1
Baie-d'Urfé, 3,881 G 4
Baie-Saint-Paul⊙, 4,163 G 2
Baie-Trinité, 734 B 1
Beaconsfield, 19,389 H 4
Beauceville, 2,098 G 3
Beauceville-Est⊙, 2,192 G 3
Beauharnois⊙, 8,121 D 4
Beaulieu, 659 J 3
Beaumont, 630 F 3
Beauport, 14,681 J 3
Beaupré, 2,862 G 2
Bécancour⊙, 8,182 E 3
Bedford⊙, 2,786 E 4
Beebe Plain, 1,236 E 4
Bélair, 4,505 H 3
Beloeil, 12,274 D 4
Bernierville, 2,415 F 3
Berthierville⊙, 4,080 D 3
Bic, 1,157 J 1
Black Lake, 4,123 F 3
Blainville, 9,630 H 4
Bois-des-Filion, 4,061 H 4
Bolduc, 1,496 G 4
Bonaventure, 1,079 C 2
Boucherville, 19,997 J 4
Breakeyville, 800 J 3
Bromont, 1,089 E 4
Bromptonville, 2,771 F 4
Brossard, 23,452 H 4
Brownsburg, 3,481 C 4
Buckingham, 7,304 B 4
Cabano, 3,063 J 2
Calumet, 764 C 4
Candiac, 5,185 J 4
Cap-à-l'Aigle, 679 G 2
Cap-Chat, 3,868 B 1
Cap-de-la-Madeleine, 31,463 E 3
Caplan, 693 C 2
Cap-Rouge, 1,750 H 3
Cap-Saint-Ignace, 1,338 G 2
Cap-Santé⊙, 610 F 3
Carignan, 3,340 J 4
Carleton, 899 C 2
Caughnawaga, 3,982 H 4
Causapscal, 2,965 B 2
Chambly, 11,469 J 4
Chambord, 1,106 E 1
Champlain, 632 E 3
Chandler, 3,843 D 2
Charlemagne, 4,111 H 4
Charlesbourg, 33,443 J 3
Charny, 5,175 J 3
Châteauguay, 15,797 H 4
Châteauguay-Centre, 17,942 H 4
Château-Richer⊙, 3,111 F 3
Chénéville, 718 B 4
Chicoutimi⊙, 33,893 G 1
Chicoutimi-Jonquière, ‡133,703 G 1
Chicoutimi-Nord, 14,086 G 1
Chute-aux-Outardes, 1,930 A 1
Clermont, 3,386 G 2
Coaticook, 6,569 F 4
Coleraine, 1,474 F 4
Contrecoeur, 2,694 D 4
Cookshire⊙, 1,484 F 4
Coteau-du-Lac, 838 C 4
Coteau-Landing⊙, 846 C 4
Côte-Saint-Luc, 24,375 H 4
Courcelles, 679 G 4
Courville, 6,222 J 3
Cowansville, 11,920 E 4
Crabtree, 1,706 D 4
Danville, 2,566 E 4
Daveluyville, 998 E 3
Deauville, 761 E 4
Dégelis, 3,046 J 2
Delson, 2,941 H 4
Desbiens, 1,813 E 1
Deschaillons-sur-Saint-Laurent, 1,176 E 3
Deschambault, 995 E 3
Deschênes, 1,806 B 4
Deux-Montagnes, 8,631 H 4
Didyme, 720 E 1
Disraëli, 3,384 F 4
Dolbeau, 7,633 E 1
Dollard-des-Ormeaux, 25,217 H 4
Donnacona, 5,940 F 3
Dorion, 6,209 C 4
Dorval, 20,469 H 4
Douville, 3,267 D 4
Drummondville⊙, 31,813 E 4
Drummondville-Sud, 8,989 E 4
East Angus, 4,715 F 4
East Broughton, 1,380 F 3
East Broughton Station, 1,127 F 3
Escoumins, 1,968 H 1
Farnham, 6,496 E 4
Ferme-Neuve, 1,990 B 3
Forestville, 1,606 H 1
Frampton, 711 G 3
Francoeur, 1,186 F 3
Gaspé, 17,211 D 1
Gatineau, 22,321 B 4
Giffard, 13,135 J 3
Girardville, 933 E 1
Glenwood Domaine, 3,997 B 4
Godbout, 653 B 1
Gracefield, 1,049 A 3
Granb, 34,385 E 4
Grande-Rivière, 1,330 D 2
Grandes-Bergeronnes, 802 H 1
Grande-Vallée, 779 D 1
Grand'Mère, 17,137 E 3
Greenfield Park, 15,348 J 4
Grenville, 1,495 C 4
Hampstead, 7,033 H 4
Ham-Sud⊙, 64 F 4
Hauterive, 13,181 A 1
Hébertville-Station, 1,163 F 1
Hemmingford, 810 D 4
Henryville, 666 D 4
Hudson, 4,345 C 4
Hull⊙, 63,580 B 4
Huntingdon⊙, 3,087 C 4
Iberville⊙, 9,331 D 4
île-Bizard, 2,950 H 4
île-Perrot, 4,021 G 4
Inverness⊙, 362 F 3
Joliette⊙, 20,127 D 3
Jonquière, 28,430 F 1
Kénogami, 10,970 F 1
Kirkland, 2,917 H 4
Labelle, 1,492 C 3
Lac-au-Saumon, 1,3i4 B 2
Lac-aux-Sables, 844 E 3
Lac-Beauport, 42 F 3
Lac-Bouchette, 954 E 1
Lac-Brome⊙, 4,063 E 4
Lac-Carré, 660 C 3
Lac-Etchemin, 2,789 G 3
Lachine, 44,423 H 4
Lachute⊙, 11,813 C 4
Lac-Mégantic⊙, 6,770 G 4
Lacolle, 1,254 D 4
Lac-Saint-Charles, 1,693 H 3
Lafontaine, 2,980 C 4
La Guadeloupe, 1,934 F 4
La Malbaie⊙, 4,036 C 2
Lambton, 767 F 4
L'Ange-Gardien, 1,605 F 3
L'Annonciation, 2,162 C 3
Lanoraie, 1,151 D 4
La Pérade, 1,123 E 3
La Pocatière, 4,256 H 2
La Prairie⊙, 8,309 J 4
La Providence, 4,709 E 4
La Salle, 72,912 H 4
L'Ascension, 1,034 F 1
L'Assomption⊙, 4,915 D 4
La Station-du-Coteau, 885 C 4
La Tuque, 13,099 E 2
Laurentides, 1,746 D 4
Laurier-Station, 946 F 3
Laurierville, 922 F 3
Lauzon, 12,809 J 3
Laval, 228,010 H 4
Lavaltrie, 1,261 D 4
Le Moyne, 8,194 J 4
Lennoxville, 3,859 F 4
L'Épiphanie, 2,752 D 4
Léry, 2,247 H 4
Les Méchins, 792 B 1
Lévis, 16,597 J 3
Linière, 1,220 G 3
L'Islet, 1,195 G 2
L'Islet-sur-Mer, 772 G 2
L'Isle-Verte, 1,360 G 1
Longueuil⊙, 97,590 J 4
Loretteville⊙, 11,644 H 3
Lorraine, 3,145 H 4
Louiseville⊙, 4,042 E 3
Luceville, 1,411 J 1
Lyster, 879 F 3
Magog, 13,281 E 4
Maniwaki⊙, 6,689 B 3
Manouane, 751 C 2
Manseau, 756 E 3
Maple Grove, 1,708 H 4
Maria, 1,157 C 2
Marieville⊙, 4,563 D 4
Mascouche, 8,812 H 4
Maskinongé, 996 E 3
Masson, 2,336 B 4
Massueville, 632 E 4
Matane⊙, 11,841 B 1
Melocheville, 1,601 C 4
Mercier, 4,011 H 4
Mistassini, 3,601 E 1
Mont-Carmel, 800 H 2
Montebello, 1,285 B 4
Mont-Joli, 6,698 J 1
Mont-Laurier⊙, 8,240 B 3
Mont-Louis, 815 C 1
Montmagny⊙, 12,432 G 3
Montmorency, 4,949 J 3
Montréal⊙, 1,214,352 H 4
Montréal, ‡2,743,208 H 4
Montréal-Est, 5,076 J 4
Montréal-Nord, 89,139 H 4
Mont-Rolland, 1,503 C 4
Mont-Royal, 21,561 H 4
Mont-Saint-Hilaire, 5,758 D 4
Morin Heights, 710 C 4
Murdochville, 2,891 C 1
Napierville⊙, 1,987 D 4
Neuville, 798 F 3
New Carlisle⊙, 1,384 D 2
New Richmond, 3,957 C 2
Nicolet, 4,714 E 3
Nitro, 1,827 D 4
Nominingue, 699 B 3
Normandin, 1,823 E 1
North Hatley, 728 F 4
Notre-Dame-de-la-Doré, 1,127 E 1
Notre-Dame-des-Anges, 790 E 3

Agriculture, Industry and Resources

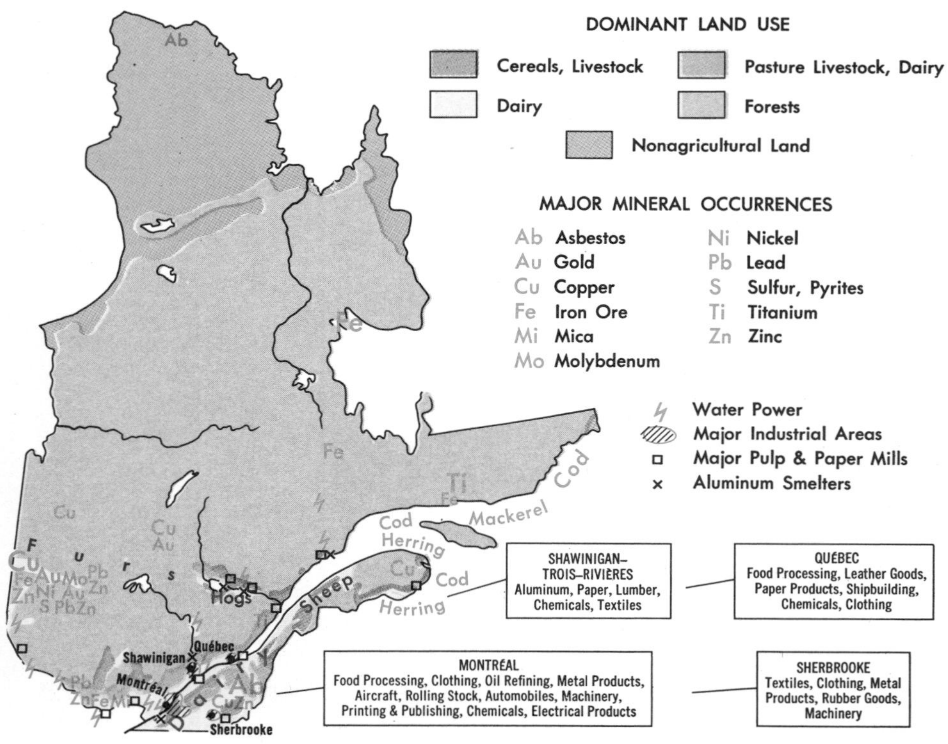
DOMINANT LAND USE
Cereals, Livestock
Pasture Livestock, Dairy
Dairy
Forests
Nonagricultural Land
MAJOR MINERAL OCCURRENCES
Ab Asbestos
Au Gold
Cu Copper
Fe Iron Ore
Mi Mica
Mo Molybdenum
Ni Nickel
Pb Lead
S Sulfur, Pyrites
Ti Titanium
Zn Zinc
Water Power
Major Industrial Areas
Major Pulp & Paper Mills
Aluminum Smelters
Cod
Mackerel
Herring
Hogs
Sheep
Québec
Shawinigan
Montréal
Sherbrooke
SHAWINIGAN–TROIS-RIVIÈRES
Aluminum, Paper, Lumber, Chemicals, Textiles
QUÉBEC
Food Processing, Leather Goods, Paper Products, Shipbuilding, Chemicals, Clothing
MONTRÉAL
Food Processing, Clothing, Oil Refining, Metal Products, Aircraft, Rolling Stock, Automobiles, Machinery, Printing & Publishing, Chemicals, Electrical Products
SHERBROOKE
Textiles, Clothing, Metal Products, Rubber Goods, Machinery

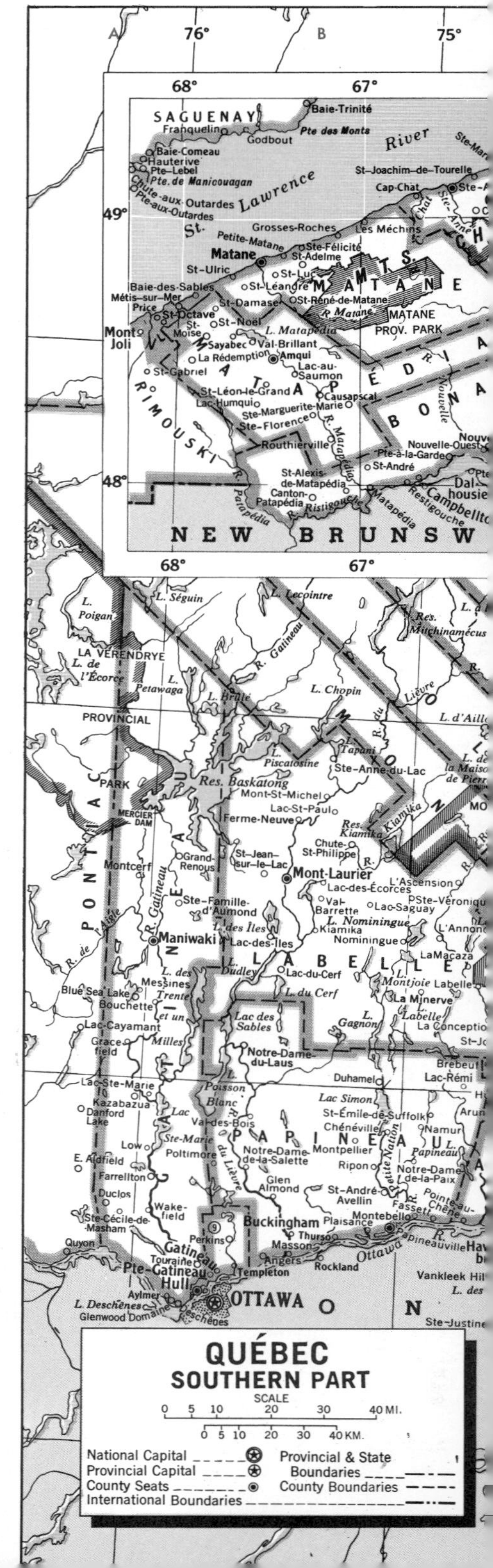
QUÉBEC
SOUTHERN PART
SCALE
0 5 10 20 30 40 MI.
0 5 10 20 30 40 KM.
National Capital
Provincial Capital
County Seats
International Boundaries
Provincial & State Boundaries
County Boundaries
76°
75°
68°
67°
49°
48°
SAGUENAY
Baie-Trinité
Franquelin
Godbout
Pte des Monts
Baie-Comeau
Hauterive
Pte-Lebel
Pte. de Manicouagan
St. Lawrence River
Matane
MATANE PROV. PARK
Mont Joli
Amqui
Causapscal
RIMOUSKI
NEW BRUNSWICK
OTTAWA
Hull
Gatineau
Buckingham
Maniwaki
Mont-Laurier
Aylmer
Glenwood Domaine

Notre-Dame-des-Laurentides, 5,080........H 3
Notre-Dame-des-Prairies, 3,541........D 3
Notre-Dame-d'Hébertville, 1,506........F 1
Notre-Dame-du-Bon-Conseil, 1,048........E 4
Notre-Dame-du-Lac⊙, 2,107........J 2
Nouvelle, 722........C 2
Omerville, 1,102........E 4
Ormstown, 1,517........D 4
Orsainville, 12,520........H 3
Otterburn Park, 3,512........D 4
Ouiatchouan, 1,217........E 1
Outremont, 28,552........H 4
Pabos-Mills, 668........D 2
Papineauville⊙, 1,384........C 4
Paspébiac, 1,317........D 2
Percé, 5,617........D 1
Petite-Matane, 668........B 1
Petit-Saguenay (Saint-François-d'Assise), 691........G 1
Pierrefonds, 33,010........H 4
Pierreville, 1,455........E 3
Pincourt, 5,899........D 4
Pintendre, 796........J 3
Plaisance, 651........B 4
Plessisville, 7,204........F 3
Pointe-à-la-Croix, 753........C 2
Pointe-au-Pic, 1,231........G 2
Pointe-aux-Outardes, 836........A 1

Pointe-aux-Trembles, 35,567........J 4
Pointe-Calumet, 2,214........G 4
Pointe-Claire, 27,303........H 4
Pointe-du-Lac, 1,314........E 3
Pointe-Gatineau, 15,640........B 4
Pointe-Lebel, 756........A 1
Pont-Rouge, 3,272........F 3
Port-Alfred, 9,228........G 1
Portneuf, 1,347........F 3
Price, 2,740........A 1
Princeville, 3,829........F 3
Québec (cap.), 186,088........H 3
Québec, ‡480,502........H 3
Quyon, 879........A 4
Rawdon, 2,740........D 3
Repentigny, 19,520........J 4
Restigouche, 1,155........C 2
Richelieu, 1,777........D 4
Richmond⊙, 4,317........E 4
Rigaud, 2,138........C 4
Rimouski⊙, 26,887........J 1
Rimouski-Est, 2,069........J 1
Rivière-à-Pierre, 691........E 3
Rivière-du-Loup⊙, 12,760........H 2
Rivière-du-Moulin, 4,393........G 1
Rivière-Portneuf, 987........H 1
Robertsonville, 1,294........F 3
Roberval⊙, 8,330........E 1
Rock Forest, 793........F 4
Rock Island, 1,341........E 4
Rosemère, 6,710........H 4
Rougemont, 853........D 4
Roxboro, 7,633........H 4

Roxton Falls, 1,139........E 4
Sacré-Coeur-de-Jésus, 1,252........H 1
Saint-Adelphe, 708........E 3
Saint-Agapitville, 1,493........F 3
Saint-Alban, 770........E 3
Saint-Alexandre-de-Kamouraska, 927........H 2
Saint-Alexis-des-Monts, 1,905........D 3
Saint-Amable, 1,051........J 4
Saint-Ambroise, 1,629........F 1
Saint-Anaclet, 955........J 1
Saint-André-Avellin, 1,088........B 4
Saint-André-Est, 1,201........C 4
Saint-Anselme, 1,400........J 3
Saint-Antoine, 5,831........H 4
Saint-Antonin, 748........H 2
Saint-Aubert, 952........G 2
Saint-Augustin-de-Québec, 688........H 3
Saint-Basile-le-Grand, 4,402........J 4
Saint-Basile-Sud, 1,731........F 3
Saint-Bernard-sur-Mer, 667........G 2
Saint-Boniface-de-Shawinigan, 2,581........D 3
Saint-Bruno, 1,276........F 1
Saint-Bruno-de-Montarville, 15,780........J 4
Saint-Camille-de-Bellechasse, 774........G 3
Saint-Casimir, 1,239........E 3

Saint-Césaire, 2,279........D 4
Saint-Charles, 969........G 3
Saint-Charles-de-Drummond, 2,266........E 4
Saint-Charles-de-Mandeville, 900........D 3
Saint-Chrysostome, 1,077........D 4
Saint-Coeur-de-Marie, 1,218........F 1
Saint-Côme, 914........D 3
Saint-Constant, 4,139........H 4
Saint-Cyprien 743........J 2
Saint-Cyrille, 1,125........E 4
Saint-Damien-de-Buckland, 1,799........G 3
Saint-David-de-Falardeau, 770........F 1
Saint-David-de-l'Auberivière, 3,818........J 3
Saint-Denis, 899........D 4
Saint-Dominique, 1,722........E 4
Saint-Donat-de-Montcalm, 1,536........C 3
Sainte-Adélaïde-de-Pabos, 627........D 2
Sainte-Adèle, 2,581........C 4
Sainte-Agathe, 646........F 3
Sainte-Agathe-des-Monts, 5,532........C 3
Sainte-Angèle-de-Mérici, 688........J 1
Sainte-Anne-de-Beaupré, 1,797........F 2

Sainte-Anne-de-Bellevue, 4,976........H 4
Sainte-Anne-des-Monts⊙, 5,546........C 1
Sainte-Anne-des-Plaines, 2,093........H 4
Sainte-Blandine, 941........J 1
Sainte-Catherine, 913........F 1
Sainte-Claire-de-Joliette, 1,490........G 3
Sainte-Croix⊙, 1,545........F 3
Sainte-Famille-d'Orléans, 295........J 3
Sainte-Félicité, 816........B 1
Sainte-Foy, 68,385........H 3
Sainte-Geneviève, 2,847........H 4
Sainte-Geneviève-de-Batiscan⊙, 556........E 3

Sainte-Hedwidge-de-Roberval, 641........E 1
Sainte-Hélène-de-Kamouraska, 656........H 2
Sainte-Hénédine⊙, 533........F 3
Sainte-Jeanne-d'Arc, 936........E 1
Sainte-Julie-de-Verchères, 1,214........J 4
Sainte-Julienne⊙, 839........D 4
Sainte-Justine, 980........G 3
Sainte-Éleuthère, 1,083........H 2
Sainte-Marie, 4,307........H 3
Sainte-Martine⊙, 1,931........D 4
Saint-émile, 2,645........H 3
Sainte-Monique, 697........F 1
Sainte-Perpétue-de-L'Islet, 1,048........H 2

Saint-éphrem-de-Tring, 954........G 3
Sainte-Pudentienne, 799........E 4
Sainte-Scholastique, 14,787........C 4
Saint-Esprit, 937........D 3
Sainte-Thècle, 1,725........E 3
Sainte-Thérèse, 17,175........H 4
Sainte-Thérèse-Ouest, 7,278........H 4
Saint-Étienne-des-Grès, 870........E 3
Saint-Eugène, 656........G 2
Saint-Eustache, 9,479........H 4
Saint-Eustache-Est, 4,993........H 4
Saint-Fabien, 1,537........J 1
Saint-Félicien, 4,952........E 1
Saint-Félix-de-Valois, 1,455........D 3

AREA 594,860 sq. mi.
POPULATION 6,027,764 ('71); 6,234,445 ('76)
CAPITAL Québec
LARGEST CITY Montréal
HIGHEST POINT Mt. Jacques Cartier 4,160 ft.
SETTLED IN 1608
ADMITTED TO CONFEDERATION 1867
PROVINCIAL FLOWER White Garden Lily

Saint-Féréol-les-Neiges, 692 ....G 2
Saint-Flavien, 645 ....F 3
Saint-François-d'Assise, 691 ....G 1
Saint-François-du-Lac◎, 1,001 ....E 3
Saint-Fulgence, 999 ....G 1
Saint-Gabriel, 3,383 ....D 3
Saint-Gédéon, Frontenac, 1,174 ....G 4
Saint-Gédéon, Lac-St-Jean-E., 885 ....F 1
Saint-Georges, Beauce, 7,554 ....G 3
Saint-Georges, Champlain, 2,061 ....E 3
Saint-Georges-de-Cacouna, 1,001 ....H 2
Saint-Georges-Ouest, 6,000 ....G 3
Saint-Germain-de-Grantham, 1,104 ....E 4
Saint-Gilles, 694 ....F 3
Saint-Grégoire, 655 ....D 4
Saint-Grégoire-de-Greenlay, 694 ....E 4
Saint-Henri, 1,160 ....J 3
Saint-Honoré, Beauce, 1,045 ....G 4
Saint-Honoré, Chicoutimi, 1,055 ....F 1
Saint-Hubert, 36,854 ....J 4
Saint-Hubert-de-Témiscouata, 832 .....J 2
Saint-Hyacinthe◎, 24,562 .D 4
Saint-Isidore, 736 ....F 3
Saint-Isidore-de-Laprairie, 749 ....D 4
Saint-Jacques, 1,975 ....D 4
Saint-Jean◎, 32,863 ....D 4
Saint-Jean-Chrysostome, 1,905 ....J 3
Saint-Jean-de-Boischatel, 1,685 ....J 3
Saint-Jean-de-Dieu, 1,148 .J 2
Saint-Jean-de-Matha, 943 .D 3
Saint-Jean-Port-Joli◎, 1,795 ....G 2
Saint-Jérôme, Lac-St-Jean-E., 1,910 ....F 1
Saint-Jérôme, Terrebonne◎, 26,524...H 4
Saint-Joachim, 920 ....G 2
Saint-Joachim-de-Tourelle, 1,021......C 1

Saint-Joseph, 4,945 ....E 4
Saint-Joseph-de-Beauce, 2,893 ....G 3
Saint-Joseph-de-la-Rivière-Bleue, 1,429 ..J 2
Saint-Joseph-de-Sorel, 3,290 ....D 3
Saint-Jovite, 3,132.........C 3
Saint-Lambert, 18,616....J 4
Saint-Laurent, 62,955.....H 4
Saint-Léonard, 52,040....H 4
Saint-Léonard-d'Aston, 995 ....E 3
Saint-Léon-de-Standon, 830 ....G 3
Saint-Léon-le-Grand, 695..B 2
Saint-Liboire◎, 667 ....E 4
Saint-Louis-de-Terrebonne, 1,113 ....H 4
Saint-Louis-du-Ha! Ha!, 733 H 2
Saint-Luc, 4,850 ....D 4
Saint-Marc-des-Carrières, 2,650 ....E 3
Saint-Méthode-de-Frontenac, 793 ....F 3
Saint-Michel-de-Bellechasse, 967 ....G 3
Saint-Michel-des-Saints, 1,647 ....D 3
Saint-Nazaire-de-Chicoutimi, 884 ....F 1
Saint-Nicolas, 1,975 ....H 3
Saint-Noël, 910 ....B 1
Saint-Odilon, 704 ....G 3
Saint-Ours, 838 ....D 4
Saint-Pacôme, 1,180 ....G 2
Saint-Pamphile, 3,542 .....H 2
Saint-Pascal, 2,513 ....H 2
Saint-Paul-de-Montminy, 746 ....G 3
Saint-Paul◎, 809 ....D 4
Saint-Paul-l'Ermite, 3,165..J 4
Saint-Philippe-de-Néri, 701 ....H 2
Saint-Pie, 1,709 ....E 4
Saint-Pierre, 6,801 ....H 4
Saint-Prime, 2,350 ....E 1
Saint-Prosper-de-Dorchester, 1,696 .....G 3
Saint-Raphaël◎, 1,216.....G 3
Saint-Raymond, 4,036.....F 3
Saint-Rédempteur, 1,652 ..J 3
Saint-Régis, 727 ....C 4
Saint-Rémi, 2,282 ....D 4
Saint-Roch-de-l'Achigan, 962 ....D 4

Saint-Roch-de-Richelieu, 721 ....D 4
Saint-Romuald-d'Etchemin◎, 8,394 .J 3
Saint-Sauveur-des-Monts, 1,846 ....C 4
Saint-Siméon, 1,186 ....G 2
Saint-Thomas-de-Joliette, 728 ....D 4
Saint-Timothée, 1,613 .....C 4
Saint-Tite, 3,130 ....E 3
Saint-Ubald, 809 ....E 3
Saint-Ulric, 936 ....B 1
Saint-Urbain-de-Charlevoix, 1,172.......G 2
Saint-Victor, 1,017.........G 3
Saint-Zacharie, 1,390......G 3
Saint-Zotique, 1,243.......C 4
Sault-au-Mouton, 951 .....H 1
Sawyerville, 864 ....F 4
Sayabec, 1,789 ....B 2
Scotstown, 917 ....F 4
Senneville, 1,412 ....G 4
Shawbridge, 969 ....C 4
Shawinigan, 27,792 ....E 3
Shawinigan-Sud, 11,470...E 4
Sherbrooke◎, 80,711 .....E 4
Sillery, 13,932 ....J 3
Sorel◎, 19,347 ....D 4
Squatec, 950 ....J 2
Stanstead Plain, 1,192 .....F 4
Sully, 776 ....H 2
Sutton, 1,884 ....E 4
Tadoussac◎, 1,010.........H 1
Templeton, 3,648 ....B 4
Terrebonne, 9,212.........H 4
Thetford Mines, 22,003....F 3
Thurso, 3,219 ....B 4
Touraine, 6,978 ....B 4
Tourville, 811 ....H 2
Tracy, 11,842 ....D 4
Tring-Jonction, 1,283 .....F 3
Trois-Pistoles, 4,678.......H 1
Trois-Rivières, 55,869.....E 3
Trois-Rivières-Ouest, 8,057 ....E 3
Upton, 818 ....E 4
Val-Brillant, 690 ....B 1
Valcourt, 2,411 ....E 4
Val-David, 1,627 ....C 3
Vallée-Jonction, 1,295 .....G 3
Valleyfield, 30,173 ....C 4
Val-Saint-Michel, 2,050....H 3
Vanier, 9,717 ....J 3
Varennes, 2,382 ....J 4
Vaudreuil◎, 3,843 ....C 4

Verchères◎, 1,840 ....J 3
Verdun, 74,718 ....H 4
Victoriaville, 22,047 ....F 3
Villeneuve, 4,062 ....J 3
Warwick, 2,847 ....F 3
Waterloo, 4,936 ....E 4
Waterville, 1,476 ....F 4
Weedon-Centre, 1,429 .....F 4
Westmount, 23,606 ....H 4
Windsor, 6,023 ....F 4
Wottonville, 683 ....F 4
Yamachiche◎, 1,147 ....E 3

OTHER FEATURES

Alma (isl.) ....F 1
Aylmer (lake) ....F 4
Baskatong (res.) ....B 3
Batiscan (riv.) ....E 2
Bécancour (riv.) ....F 3
Bonaventure (isl.) ....D 1
Bonaventure (riv.) ....C 1
Brome (lake) ....E 4
Brompton (lake) ....E 4
Cascapédia (riv.) ....C 1
Chaleur (bay) ....C 2
Champlain (lake) ....D 4
Chaudière (riv.) ....F 3
Chic-Chocs (mts.) ....C 1
Chicoutimi (riv.) ....F 1
Coudres (isl.), 1,522 ....G 2
Deschênes (lake) ....A 4
Deux Montagnes (lake) ....C 4
Ditton (riv.) ....F 4
Forillon Nat'l Park ....D 1
Fort Chambly Nat'l Hist. Park ....J 4
Gaspé (bay) ....D 1
Gaspé (cape) ....D 1
Gaspé (pen.) ....C 1
Gaspésie Prov. Park ....C 1
Gatineau (riv.) ....B 3
Îles (lake) ....B 3
Jacques-Cartier (mt.) .....C 1
Jacques-Cartier (riv.) .....F 2
Kénogami (lake) ....F 1
Kiamika (lake) ....C 3
La Maurice Nat'l Park .....D 3
Laurentides Prov. Park ....F 2
La Vérendrye Prov. Park ...A 2
Lièvre (riv.) ....B 4
Lièvres (isl.) ....H 2
Maskinongé (riv.) ....D 3
Matane (riv.) ....B 1
Matane Prov. Park ....B 1
Matapédia (riv.) ....B 1
Matawin (res.) ....D 3

Mégantic (lake) ....G 4
Memphremagog (lake) .....E 4
Mercier (dam) ....A 3
Métabetchouane (riv.) .....F 1
Mille Îles (riv.) ....H 4
Montmorency (riv.) ....F 2
Mont-Tremblant Prov. Park .C 3
Nicolet (riv.) ....E 3
Nominingue (lake) ....C 3
Nord (riv.) ....C 4
Orléans (isl.), 5,435.......J 3
Ottawa (riv.) ....B 4
Ouareau (riv.) ....D 3
Patapédia (riv.) ....B 2
Péribonca (riv.) ....F 1
Petite Nation (riv.) ....B 3
Prairies (riv.) ....H 4
Rimouski (riv.) ....J 1
Ristigouche (riv.) ....B 2
Saguenay (riv.) ....G 1
Sainte-Anne (riv.) ....F 3
Sainte-Anne (riv.) ....B 1
Saint-François (lake) ....F 4
Saint-François (riv.) ....E 4
Saint-Jean (lake) ....E 1
Saint Lawrence (gulf) .....D 2
Saint Lawrence (riv.) .....H 3
Saint-Louis (lake) ....H 4
Saint-Maurice (riv.) ....D 3
Saint-Pierre (lake) ....E 3
Shawinigan (riv.) ....E 3
Shipshaw (riv.) ....F 1
Sœurs (isl.) ....H 4
Témiscouata (lake) ....H 2
Tremblant (lake) ....C 3
Trente et un Milles (lake) ..B 3
Verte (isl.), 175 ....H 1
Yamaska (riv.) ....E 4
York (riv.) ....D 1

◎ County seat.
‡ Population of metropolitan area.

QUÉBEC, NORTHERN

INTERNAL DIVISIONS

Abitibi (co.), 112,244....B 2
Abitibi (terr.), 21,308 .B 3
Chicoutimi (county), 163,348 ....C 2
Lac-Saint-Jean-Ouest (county), 57,074 .....C 2
Mistassini (terr.), 2,702 B 2
Nouveau-Québec (terr.), 10,002 ....E 2

Pontiac (co.), 19,570....B 3
Saguenay (co.), 111,272 D 2
Témiscamingue (county), 54,656 ....B 3

CITIES and TOWNS

Aguanish, 442 ....E 2
Amos◎, 6,984 ....B 3
Angliers, 404 ....B 3
Baie-du-Poste, 1,598 .....C 2
Barraute, 1,288 ....B 3
Belleterre, 614 ....B 3
Betsiamites, 1,574 ....D 2
Cadillac, 1,102 ....B 3
Chapais, 2,914 ....B 3
Chibougamau, 9,701 .....C 3
Clarke City, 750 ....D 2
Dolbeau, 7,633 ....C 2
Duparquet, 786 ....B 3
Dupuy, 439 ....B 3
Évain, 605 ....B 3
Forestville, 1,606 ....D 3
Fort-Chimo, 693 ....F 2
Fort-George, 1,280 ....B 2
Gagnon, 3,787 ....D 2
Godbout, 653 ....D 3
Hauterive, 13,181 ....D 3
Havre-St-Pierre, 2,999....E 2
Inoucdjouac, 525 ....E 1
La Reine, 450 ....B 3
La Sarre, 5,185 ....B 3
La Tabatière, 475 ....F 2
Lebel-sur-Quevillon, 2,936 ....B 3
Lorrainville, 906 ....B 3
Macamic, 1,705 ....B 3
Malartic, 5,347 ....B 3
Manicouagan, 500 ....D 2
Matagami, 2,411 ....B 3
Micoua, 851 ....D 3
Moisie, 570 ....D 2
Noranda, 10,741 ....B 3
Normétal, 1,851 ....B 3
Nouveau-Comptoir, 514...B 2
Obedjiwan, 712 ....B 3
Parent, 452 ....C 3
Port-Cartier, 3,730 ....D 2
Port-Cartier-Ouest, 500..D 2
Port-Menier, 394 ....E 2
Poste-de-la-Baleine, 987 B 1
Povungnituk, 676 ....E 1
Rivière-au-Tonnerre, 520 D 2
Rouyn, 17,821 ....B 3
Rupert House, 757 ....B 2

Saglouc, 402 ....E 1
Saint-Augustin, 916 ....F 2
Scheferville, 3,271 ....D 2
Senneterre, 4,303 ....B 3
Sept-Îles, 24,320 ....D 2
Témiscaming, 2,428 ....B 3
Val-d'Or, 17,421 ....B 3
Ville-Marie◎, 1,995 ....B 3

OTHER FEATURES

Anticosti (isl.), 419 ....E 2
Baleine, Grande Rivière de la (riv.) ....B 2
Betsiamites (riv.) ....D 2
Bienville (lake) ....B 2
Cabonga (res.) ....B 3
Caniapiscau (riv.) ....D 1
Daniel-Johnson (dam)....D 2
Dozois (res.) ....B 3
Eastmain (riv.) ....B 2
George (riv.) ....F 2
Gouin (res.) ....C 3
Grande Rivière, La (riv.) ....B 2
Guillaume-Delisle (lake) ..B 2
Harricana (riv.) ....B 3
Honguedo (passg.) ....E 2
Hudson (bay) ....A 1
Hudson (str.) ....E 1
Jacques-Cartier (passg.)..E 2
James (bay) ....B 2
Koksoak (riv.) ....D 1
La Vérendrye Prov. Park ....B 3
Louis-XIV (pt.) ....B 2
Manicouagan (res.) ....D 2
Mistassibi (riv.) ....C 3
Mistassini (lake) ....C 3
Mistassini (riv.) ....C 3
Moisie (riv.) ....D 2
Natashquan (riv.) ....E 2
Nottaway (riv.) ....B 2
Nouveau-Québec (crater) ....F 1
Otish (mts.) ....C 2
Ottawa (riv.) ....B 3
Reed (mt.) ....D 2
Romaine (riv.) ....E 2
Saguenay (riv.) ....E 2
Saguenay Prov. Park .....E 2
Saint Lawrence (gulf) ....E 2
Saint Lawrence (riv.) .....D 3
Ungava (bay) ....F 1
Ungava (pen.) ....E 1
Wolstenholme (cape) .....E 1
Wright (mt.) ....D 2

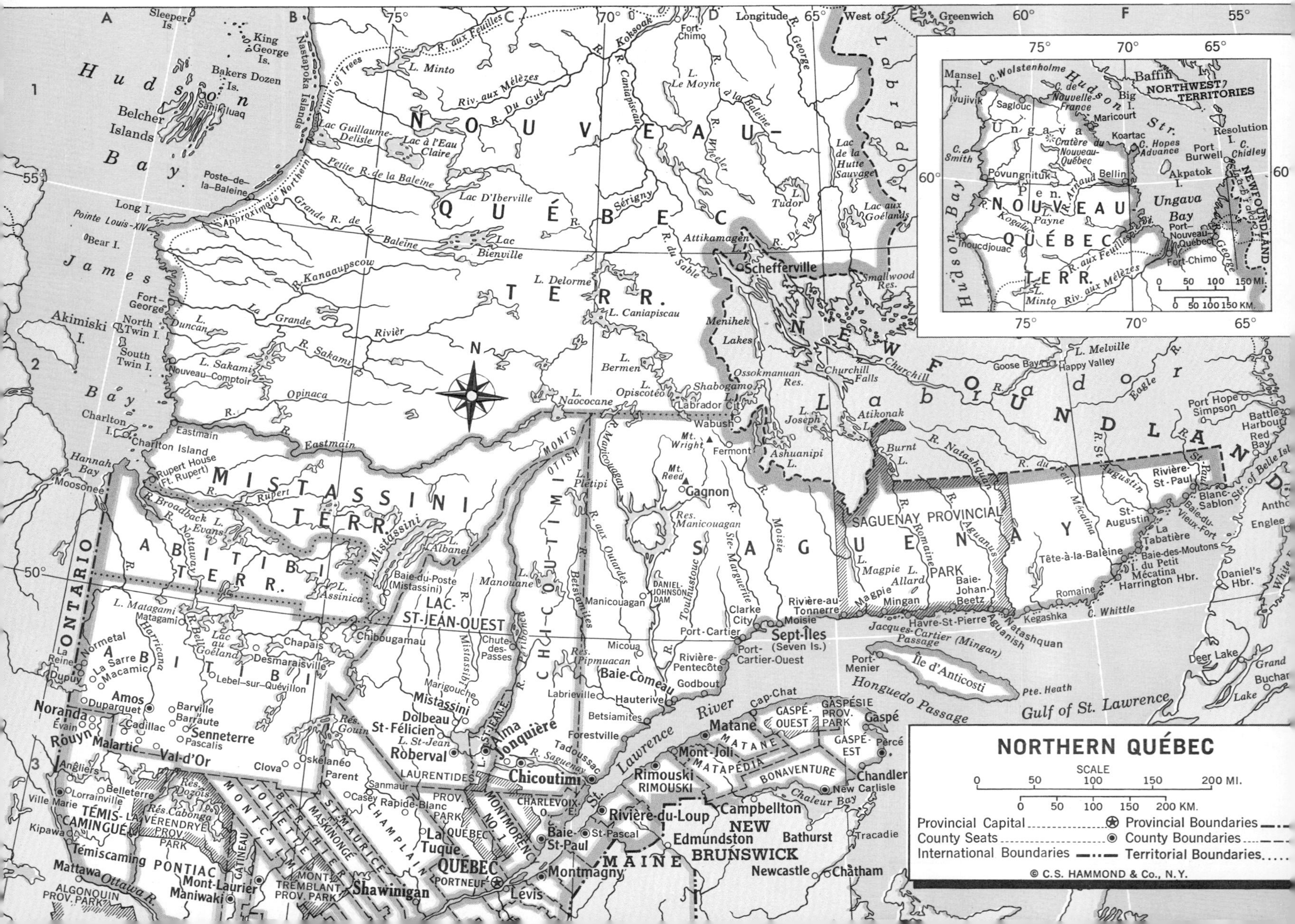

© C.S. HAMMOND & Co., N.Y.

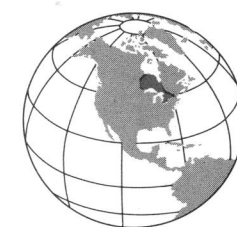

ONTARIO, NORTHERN

INTERNAL DIVISIONS

Algoma (terr. dist.),
121,937 ....D 3
Cochrane (terr. dist.),
95,836 ....D 2
Kenora (terr. dist.), 53,230 C 2
Manitoulin (terr. dist.),
10,931 ....D 3
Nipissing (terr. dist.),
78,867 ....E 3
Parry Sound (terr. dist.),
30,244 ....E 3
Rainy River (terr. dist.),
25,750 ....B 3
Renfrew (county), 90,875 .E 3
Sudbury (reg. munic.),
168,224 ....D 3
Sudbury (terr. dist.),
198,079 ....D 3
Thunder Bay (terr. dist.),
145,390 ....C 3
Timiskaming (terr. dist.),
46,485 ....D 3

CITIES and TOWNS

Atikokan, 6,007 ....B 3
Blind River, 3,450 ....D 3
Capreol, 3,994 ....D 3
Chalk River, 1,094 .....E 3
Chapleau, 3,365 ....C 3
Cochrane ⊙, 4,965 ......D 3
Deep River, 5,671 ....E 3
Dryden, 6,939 ....B 3
Elliot Lake, 8,727 ......D 3
Espanola, 6,045 ....D 3
Fort Albany, 25 ....D 2
Fort Frances ⊙, 9,947 ..B 3
Geraldton, 3,178 ....C 3
Haileybury ⊙, 5,280 ....D 3
Hearst, 5,354 ....D 3
Huntsville, 9,784 ......E 3
Iroquois Falls, 7,055 ...D 3
Kapuskasing, 12,834 ....D 3
Kenora ⊙, 10,952 ....B 3
Kirkland Lake, 13,599 ..D 3
Manitouwadge, 3,258 ...C 3
Mattawa, 2,881 ....E 3
Moose Factory, 849 ....D 2
Moosonee, 1,793 ....D 2

New Liskeard, 5,488 .....E 3
Nickel Centre, 13,037 ...D 3
North Bay ⊙, 49,187 ....E 3
Onaping Falls, 7,511 ...D 3
Parry Sound ⊙, 5,842 ..D 3
Pembroke ⊙, 16,544 ...E 3
Renfrew, 9,173 ....E 3
Sault Sainte Marie ⊙,
80,332 ....D 3
Sturgeon Falls, 6,662 ...E 3
Sudbury, 99,512 ....D 3
Sudbury, ‡155,424 .....D 3
Thunder Bay ⊙, 108,411 .C 3
Thunder Bay, ‡112,093 ..C 3
Timmins, 43,182 ....D 3
Valley East, 17,937 .....D 3
Walden, 10,788 ....D 3
Wawa, 4,375 ....C 3

OTHER FEATURES

Abitibi (lake) ....E 3
Abitibi (riv.) ....D 2
Albany (riv.) ....C 2
Algonquin Prov. Park 337E 3
Attawapiskat (riv.) ....C 2
Big Trout (lake) ......B 2
Caribou (isl.), 3 ......C 3
Eabamet (lake) ....C 2
Ekwan (riv.) ....C 2
English (riv.) ....B 2
Groundhog (riv.) ......D 3
Hannah (bay) ....D 2
Henrietta Maria (cape) .D 1
Hudson (bay) ....D 1
James (bay) ....D 2
Kapuskasing (riv.) .....D 3
Kenogami (riv.) ....C 2
Lake of the Woods (lake) B 3
Lake Superior Prov. Park C 3
Manitoulin (isl.), 10,064 D 3
Mattagami (riv.) ....D 3
Michipicoten (isl.), 4 ..C 3
Mille Lacs (lake) ......B 3
Missinaibi (riv.) ......D 2
Nipigon (lake) ....C 3
North Caribou (lake) ...B 2
Ogidaki (mt.) ....D 3
Ogoki (riv.) ....C 2
Ottawa (riv.) ....E 3
Pipestone (riv.) ....B 2
Polar Bear Prov. Park ..D 2
Quetico Prov. Park ....B 3
Rainy (lake) ....B 3

Red (lake) ....B 2
Sachigo (riv.) ....B 2
Saint Joseph (lake) ....B 2
Sandy (lake) ....B 2
Seine (riv.) ....B 3
Seul (lake) ....B 2
Severn (riv.) ....B 2
Sibley Prov. Park , 2 ..C 3
Slate (isls.), 4 ....C 3
Superior (lake) ....C 3
Sutton (riv.) ....D 2
Thunder (bay) ....C 3
Timagami (lake) ....D 3
Timiskaming (lake) ....E 3
Winisk (riv.) ....C 2
Winnipeg (riv.) ....A 2
Woods (lake) ....B 2

ONTARIO

INTERNAL DIVISIONS

Algoma (terr. dist.),
121,937 ....J 5
Brant (county), 96,767 ..D 4
Bruce (county), 47,385 ..C 3
Cochrane (terr. dist.),
95,836 ....J 4
Dufferin (county), 21,200 .D 3
Dundas (county), 17,457 .J 2
Durham (reg. munic.),
221,503 ....F 4
Elgin (county), 66,608 ..C 5
Essex (county), 306,399 .B 5
Frontenac (county),
101,692 ....H 3
Glengarry (county), 18,480 K 2
Grenville (county), 24,316 .J 3
Grey (county), 66,403 ...D 3
Haldimand-Norfolk (reg.
munic.), 86,772 ....D 5
Haliburton (county), 9,081 F 2
Hamilton-Wentworth (reg.
munic.), 401,883 ...D 4
Halton (reg. munic.),
190,469 ....E 4
Hastings (county), 99,393 G 3
Huron (county), 52,951 ..C 4
Kenora (terr. dist.), 53,230 G 5
Kent (county), 101,118 ..B 5
Lambton (county),
114,314 ....B 5
Lanark (county), 42,259 .H 3

Leeds (county), 50,093 ...H 3
Lennox and Addington
(county), 28,359 ...G 3
Manitoulin (terr. dist.),
10,931 ....B 2
Middlesex (county),
282,014 ....C 4
Muskoka (dist. munic.)
31,938 ....E 3
Niagara (reg. munic.)
347,328 ....E 4
Nipissing (terr. dist.),
78,867 ....F 2
Northumberland (county),
60,102 ....G 3
Ottawa-Carleton (reg. munic.)
471,931 ....J 2
Oxford (county), 80,349 .D 4
Parry Sound (terr. dist.),
30,244 ....D 2
Peel (reg. munic.),
259,402 ....E 4
Perth (county), 62,973 ..C 4
Peterborough (county),
92,417 ....F 3
Prescott (county),
27,832 ....K 2
Prince Edward (county),
20,640 ....G 3
Rainy River (terr. dist.),
25,750 ....G 5
Renfrew (county),
90,875 ....G 2
Russell (county), 16,287 .J 2
Simcoe (county),
175,604 ....E 3
Stormont (county),
61,302 ....K 2
Sudbury (reg. munic.),
168,224 ....K 6
Sudbury (terr. dist.),
198,079 ....J 5
Thunder Bay (terr. dist.),
145,390 ....H 5
Timiskaming (terr. dist.),
46,485 ....K 5
Toronto (metro. munic.),
2,086,017 ....K 4
Victoria (county),
36,641 ....F 3
Waterloo (reg. munic.),
254,037 ....D 4
Wellington (county),
108,581 ....D 4
York (reg. munic.),
166,060 ....E 4

AREA 412,582 sq. mi.
POPULATION 7,703,106 ('71); 8,264,465 ('76)
CAPITAL Toronto
LARGEST CITY Toronto
HIGHEST POINT Tip Top Hill 2,120 ft.
SETTLED IN 1749
ADMITTED TO CONFEDERATION 1867
PROVINCIAL FLOWER White Trillium

CITIES and TOWNS

Ailsa Craig, 608 ....C 4
Ajax, 15,052 ....E 4
Alban, 420 ....D 1
Alcona Beach, 659 .....E 3
Alexandria, 3,240 .....K 2
Alfred, 1,230 ....K 2
Alliston, 3,176 ....E 3
Almonte, 3,696 ....H 2
Alvinston, 702 ....B 5
Amherstburg, 5,169 ...A 5
Amherst View, 3,121 ..H 3
Ancaster, 15,326 .....D 4
Angus, 3,174 ....E 3
Apple Hill, 318 ....K 2
Arkona, 469 ....C 4
Armstrong, 574 ....H 4
Arnprior, 6,016 ....H 2
Arthur, 1,414 ....D 4
Athens, 1,071 ....J 3
Atherley, 392 ....E 3
Atikokan, 6,007 ......G 5
Atwood, 692 ....D 4
Aurora, 13,614 ....J 3
Avonmore, 287 ....K 2
Aylmer, 4,755 ....C 5
Ayr, 1,272 ....D 4
Ayton, 423 ....D 4
Baden, 959 ....D 4
Bala, 462 ....E 2
Bancroft, 2,276 ......G 2
Barrie ⊙, 27,676 .....E 3
Barry's Bay, 1,432 ...G 2
Batawa, 667 ....G 3
Batchawana Bay, 586 ..J 5
Bath, 810 ....H 3
Bayfield, 503 ....C 4

Bayside, 1,732 ....G 3
Baysville, 283 ....E 2
Beachburg, 549 ....H 2
Beachville, 995 ......D 4
Beardmore, 754 ......H 5
Beaverton, 1,485 .....E 3
Beeton, 1,061 ....E 3
Belle River, 2,877 ...B 5
Belleville ⊙, 35,128 .G 3
Belmont, 798 ....C 5
Bethany, 325 ....F 3
Bewdley, 446 ....F 3
Bicroft, 576 ....F 2
Blackburn, 3,841 .....J 2
Blenheim, 3,490 ......C 5
Blind River, 3,450 ...J 5
Bloomfield, 730 ......G 4
Blyth, 814 ....C 4
Bobcaygeon, 1,518 ....F 3
Bonfield, 694 ....E 1
Bothwell, 810 ....C 5
Bourget, 855 ....J 2
Bracebridge ⊙, 6,903 .E 2
Bradford, 3,401 ......E 3
Braeside, 522 ....H 2
Brampton ⊙, 73,570 ..J 4
Brantford ⊙, 64,421 ..D 4
Bridgenorth, 1,380 ...F 3
Brigden, 582 ....B 5
Brighton, 2,956 ......G 3
Brights Grove, 730 ...B 4
Britt, 500 ....D 2
Brockville ⊙, 19,765 .J 3
Bruce Mines, 505 ....J 5
Brussels, 908 ....C 4
Burford, 1,291 ....D 4
Burgessville, 329 ....D 4

Burlington, 87,023 ...E 4
Cache Bay, 727 ......D 1
Caesarea, 352 ....F 3
Calabogie, 299 ......H 2
Caledon, 13,480 .....E 4
Callander, 1,190 .....E 1
Cambridge, 64,114 ...D 4
Campbellford, 3,522 ..G 3
Cannington, 1,083 ...E 3
Cape Croker, 681 ....D 3
Capreol, 3,994 ......K 5
Caramat, 520 ....H 5
Cardinal, 1,865 ......J 3
Carleton Place, 5,020 .H 2
Carlisle, 488 ....D 4
Carp, 516 ....J 2
Cartier, 740 ....J 5
Casselman, 1,337 ....J 2
Castleton, 289 ......F 3
Cedar Springs, 302 ..B 5
Chalk River, 1,094 ..G 1
Chapleau, 3,365 .....J 5
Charing Cross, 436 ..B 5
Chatham ⊙, 35,317 ..B 5
Chatsworth, 399 .....D 3
Chesley, 1,693 ......C 3
Chesterville, 1,252 ..J 2
Chute-à-Blondeau, 420 .K 2
City View, 4,500 ....J 2
Clarence Creek, 411 ..J 2
Clarksburg, 389 .....D 3
Clifford, 555 ....D 4
Clinton, 3,154 ......C 4
Cobalt, 2,197 ....K 5
Cobden, 926 ....H 2
Coboconk, 477 ....F 3
Cobourg ⊙, 11,282 ..F 4
Cochrane ⊙, 4,965 ..K 5
Colchester, 1,588 ...G 4

Colchester, 752 ......B 6
Coldwater, 759 ......E 3
Collingwood, 9,775 ..D 3
Collins Bay, 2,089 ...H 3
Comber, 642 ....B 5
Consecon, 332 ....G 3
Cookstown, 847 .....E 3
Cornwall ⊙, 47,116 ..K 2
Corunna, 3,052 ......B 5
Cottam, 530 ....B 5
Courtland, 574 ......D 5
Courtright, 590 .....B 5
Coverdale, 670 ......F 4
Crediton, 409 ....C 4
Creemore, 978 ......D 3
Crysler, 481 ....J 2
Cumberland, 759 ....J 2
Cumberland Beach, 477 .E 3
Dashwood, 434 ......C 4
Deep River, 5,671 ...G 1
Delaware, 627 ....C 5
Delhi, 3,894 ....D 5
Delta, 465 ....H 3
Deseronto, 1,863 ....G 3
Dorchester, 1,796 ...C 5
Douglas, 307 ....H 2
Drayton, 752 ....D 4
Dresden, 2,369 ......B 5
Drumbo, 460 ....D 4
Dryden, 6,939 ....G 4
Dublin, 314 ....C 4
Dubreuilville, 654 ...J 5
Dundalk, 1,022 ......D 3
Dundas, 17,208 .....D 4
Dunnville, 11,422 ...E 5
Durham, 2,448 ......D 3
Dutton, 878 ....C 5
East York, 104,784 ..J 4
Echo Bay, 493 ......J 5
Eganville, 1,395 .....G 2
Egmondville, 492 ....C 4
Elgin, 322 ....H 3
Elk Lake, 627 ....K 5
Elliot Lake, 8,727 ...B 1
Elmira, 4,730 ....D 4
Elmvale, 1,103 ......E 3
Elmwood, 345 ....C 3
Elora, 1,904 ....D 4
Embro, 703 ....D 4
Embrun, 1,452 ......J 2
Emeryville, 1,719 ...B 5
Emo, 768 ....F 5
Englehart, 1,721 ....K 5
Erieau, 509 ....C 5
Erin, 1,446 ....D 4
Espanola, 6,045 .....J 5
Essex, 4,002 ....B 5
Etobicoke, 282,686 ..J 4
Everett, 405 ....D 3
Exeter, 3,354 ....C 4
Fauquier, 643 ....J 5
Fenelon Falls, 1,616 .F 3
Fergus, 5,433 ....D 4
Field, 655 ....E 1
Finch, 397 ....J 2
Fingal, 322 ....C 5
Fitzroy Harbour, 317 .H 2
Flesherton, 524 .....D 3
Foleyet, 637 ....J 5
Fordwich, 325 ....C 4

(continued on following page)

NORTHERN ONTARIO

SCALE

0   25   50   100   150   200 MI.

0 25 50   100   150   200 KM.

Provincial Capital .... ⍟ Provincial and
County Seats .... ⊙ State Boundaries —·—·—
International Boundaries — —   County Boundaries — — —

© C.S. HAMMOND & Co., N.Y.

Forest, 2,355	C 4
Formosa, 370	C 3
Fort Erie, 23,113	E 5
Fort Frances ⊙, 9,947	F 5
Foxboro, 590	G 3
Frankford, 1,862	G 3
Fraserdale, 337	J 4
Gananoque, 5,212	H 3
Geraldton, 3,178	H 5
Glencoe, 1,387	C 5
Glen Miller, 736	G 3
Glen Robertson, 345	K 2
Glen Walter, 656	K 2
Goderich ⊙, 6,813	C 4
Gogama, 578	J 5
Goodwood, 356	E 3
Gore Bay ⊙, 770	B 2
Gorrie, 380	C 4
Grafton, 395	G 4
Grand Bend, 696	C 4
Grand Valley, 904	D 4
Granton, 350	C 4
Gravenhurst, 7,133	E 3
Green Valley, 1,423	K 2
Grimsby, 15,770	E 4
Guelph ⊙, 60,087	D 4
Hagar, 290	D 1
Haileybury ⊙, 5,280	K 5
Haldimand, 15,839	E 5
Haliburton, 899	F 2
Halton Hills, 31,500	E 4
Hamilton ⊙, 309,173	E 4
Hamilton, ‡498,523	E 4
Hanover, 5,063	C 3
Harriston, 1,785	D 4
Harrow, 1,971	B 5

Harrowsmith, 550	H 3
Hastings, 938	G 3
Havelock, 1,225	G 3
Hawkesbury, 9,276	K 2
Hawkestone, 283	E 3
Hawk Junction, 396	J 5
Hearst, 5,354	J 5
Hensall, 970	C 4
Hepworth, 372	C 3
Highgate, 424	C 5
Hillsburgh, 674	D 4
Hillsdale, 308	E 3
Holland Landing, 896	E 3
Hornepayne, 1,826	J 5
Hudson, 543	G 4
Huntsville, 9,784	E 2
Huron Park, 1,217	C 4
Ignace, 334	G 5
Ilderton, 297	C 4
Ingersoll, 7,783	C 4
Ingleside, 899	J 2
Innerkip, 584	C 4
Iron Bridge, 874	A 1
Iroquois, 1,224	J 3
Iroquois Falls, 7,055	J 4
Johnstown, 414	J 3
Kakabeka Falls, 325	G 5
Kaladar, 289	H 3
Kanata, 4,635	J 2
Kapuskasing, 12,834	J 5
Kearney, 308	E 2
Keene, 334	F 3
Keewatin, 2,112	F 5
Kemptville, 2,413	J 2
Kenora ⊙, 10,952	F 4
Keswick, 1,031	E 3

Killaloe Station, 810	G 2
Killarney, 475	G 2
Kincardine, 3,239	C 3
King City, 2,091	J 3
Kingston ⊙, 59,047	H 3
Kingsville, 4,076	B 6
Kinmount, 371	F 3
Kiosk, 332	F 1
Kirkfield, 288	E 3
Kirkland Lake, 15,205	K 5
Kitchener ⊙, 116,096	D 4
Kitchener, ‡226,846	D 4
Komoka, 698	C 5
Lakefield, 2,245	F 3
Lambeth, 3,023	C 5
Lanark, 861	H 2
Lancaster, 617	K 2
Langton, 478	D 5
Lansdowne, 520	J 3
Latchford, 535	K 5
Leamington, 10,435	B 5
Lefroy, 629	E 3
Limoges, 355	J 2
Lincoln, 14,247	E 4
Lindsay ⊙, 12,746	F 3
Linwood, 482	D 4
Lion's Head, 467	C 2
Listowel, 4,677	D 4
Little Britain, 337	F 3
Little Current, 1,565	B 2
London ⊙, 223,222	C 5
London, ‡286,011	C 5
Longlac, 1,400	H 5
Long Sault, 965	K 2
L'Orignal ⊙, 1,405	K 2
Lucan, 1,178	C 4

Lucknow, 1,047	C 4
Lyn, 556	J 3
MacGregor's Bay, 312	G 2
MacTier, 794	E 2
Madawaska, 371	F 2
Madoc, 1,353	G 3
Maitland, 670	J 3
Mallorytown, 347	J 3
Manitouwadge, 3,258	H 5
Manitowaning, 437	C 2
Manotick, 476	J 2
Marathon, 2,409	H 5
Markdale, 1,236	D 3
Markham, 36,684	K 4
Markstay, 491	D 1
Marmora, 1,350	G 3
Martintown, 394	K 2
Massey, 1,278	C 1
Matachewan, 549	J 5
Matheson, 535	K 5
Mattawa, 2,881	F 1
Mattice, 860	J 5
Maxville, 846	K 2
Maynooth, 328	G 2
McGregor, 665	B 5
Meaford, 4,045	D 3
Melbourne, 305	C 5
Merlin, 757	B 5
Merrickville, 930	J 3
Metcalfe, 473	J 2
Midhurst, 342	E 3
Midland, 10,992	D 3
Mildmay, 963	C 3
Millbrook, 908	F 3
Milton ⊙, 10,463	E 4
Milverton, 1,193	D 4

Minaki, 299	F 4
Mindemoya, 458	B 2
Minden ⊙, 697	F 3
Mississauga, 172,352	J 4
Mitchell, 2,545	C 4
Monkton, 550	C 4
Moonbeam, 920	J 5
Moorefield, 311	D 4
Moose Creek, 391	K 2
Morrisburg, 2,055	J 3
Mount Albert, 705	E 3
Mount Brydges, 1,484	C 5
Mount Forest, 3,037	D 4
Mount Hope, 565	E 4
Mount Pleasant, 574	D 4
Nairn, 461	C 1
Nakina, 673	H 4
Napanee ⊙, 4,638	G 3
Nanticoke, 20,453	D 5
Neustadt, 579	D 3
Newboro, 296	H 3
Newburgh, 620	H 3
Newbury, 338	C 5
Newcastle, 27,198	F 4
New Hamburg, 3,008	D 4
New Liskeard, 5,488	K 5
Newmarket ⊙, 18,941	E 3
Niagara Falls, 67,163	E 4
Niagara-on-the-Lake, 12,552	E 4
Nickel Centre, 13,037	D 1
Nipigon, 2,141	H 5
Nobel, 484	D 2
Nobleton, 1,356	J 3
Noelville, 856	D 1
North Bay ⊙, 49,187	E 1

North Gower, 363	J 2
North York, 504,150	J 4
Norwich, 1,806	D 5
Norwood, 1,183	F 3
Nottawa, 401	D 3
Novar, 294	E 2
Oakville, 61,483	E 4
Oakwood, 310	F 3
Odessa, 1,020	H 3
Oil Springs, 570	B 5
Omemee, 777	F 3
Onaping Falls, 7,511	J 5
Orangeville ⊙, 8,074	D 4
Orillia, 24,040	E 3
Orleans, 2,810	J 2
Osgoode, 823	J 2
Oshawa, 94,994	F 4
Ottawa (cap.), Canada ⊙, 302,341	J 2
Ottawa-Hull, ‡602,510	J 2
Otterville, 754	D 5
Owen Sound ⊙, 18,469	D 3
Paincourt, 324	B 5
Painswick, 727	E 3
Paisley, 793	C 3
Pakenham, 371	H 2
Palmerston, 1,855	D 4
Paris, 6,483	D 4
Parkhill, 1,167	C 4
Parry Sound ⊙, 5,842	E 2
Pefferlaw, 432	E 3
Pelham, 9,997	E 4
Pembroke ⊙, 16,544	G 2
Penetanguishene, 5,497	D 3
Perkinsfield, 368	E 3
Perth ⊙, 5,537	H 3

Petawawa, 5,784	G 2
Peterborough ⊙, 58,111	F 3
Petrolia, 4,044	B 5
Pickering, 31,734	K 4
Picton ⊙, 4,875	G 3
Plantagenet, 909	J 2
Plattsville, 526	D 4
Point Anne, 373	G 3
Point Edward, 2,773	B 4
Pontypool, 288	F 3
Port Burwell, 700	D 5
Port Carling, 617	E 2
Port Colborne, 21,420	E 5
Port Elgin, 2,855	C 3
Port Hope, 8,872	F 4
Port Lambton, 714	B 5
Port Loring, 331	E 2
Port McNicoll, 1,450	E 3
Port Perry, 2,977	F 3
Port Rowan, 856	D 5
Port Stanley, 1,725	C 5
Pottageville, 381	J 3
Powassan, 1,163	E 1
Prescott ⊙, 5,165	J 3
Princeton, 456	D 4
Rainy River, 1,196	F 5
Rayside-Balfour, 15,445	K 5
Red Rock, 1,407	H 5
Renfrew, 9,173	H 2
Richards Landing, 318	J 5
Richmond, 2,122	J 2
Richmond Hill, 32,384	J 4
Ridgetown, 2,836	C 5
Ripley, 448	C 3
Rockcliffe Park, 2,138	J 2
Rockland, 3,649	J 2

Rockwood, 996 . . . . D 4
Rodney, 1,016 . . . . C 5
Rolphton, 418 . . . . G 1
Russell, 583 . . . . J 2
Ruthven, 461 . . . . B 6
Saint Catharines ⊙,
  109,722 . . . . E 4
Saint Catharines-Niagara,
  ‡303,429 . . . . E 4
Saint Charles, 468 . . . . . . D 1
Saint Clair Beach, 1,987 . . B 5
Saint-Eugène, 512 . . . . . . K 2
Saint George, 949 . . . . . . D 4
Saint Isidore de Prescott,
  615 . . . . K 2
Saint Jacobs, 787 . . . . . . D 4
Saint Mary's, 4,650 . . . . . C 4
Saint Thomas ⊙, 25,545 . . C 5
Saint Williams, 437 . . . . . D 5
Salem, 348 . . . . D 4
Sarnia ⊙, 57,644 . . . . . . B 5
Sauble Beach, 338 . . . . . . C 3
Sault Sainte Marie ⊙,
  80,332 . . . . J 5
Scarborough, 334,310 . . . . K 4
Schomberg, 677 . . . . J 3
Schreiber, 2,072 . . . . H 5
Scotland, 542 . . . . D 4
Seaforth, 2,134 . . . . C 4
Searchmont, 375 . . . . J 5
Sebringville, 571 . . . . . . C 4
Seeleys Bay, 406 . . . . . . H 3
Shallow Lake, 385 . . . . . . C 3
Shanty Bay, 316 . . . . E 3
Sharbot Lake, 461 . . . . . . H 3
Shedden, 277 . . . . C 5

Shelburne, 1,790 . . . . . . D 3
Simcoe ⊙, 10,793 . . . . . . D 5
Sioux Lookout, 2,530 . . . . G 4
Smithfield, 319 . . . . G 3
Smiths Falls, 9,585 . . . . . H 3
Smithville, 1,418 . . . . . . E 4
Smooth Rock Falls, 1,239 . . J 5
Sombra, 685 . . . . B 5
Southampton, 2,036 . . . . . C 3
South River, 1,052 . . . . . E 2
Spanish, 1,257 . . . . J 5
Spencerville, 386 . . . . . . J 3
Springfield, 522 . . . . C 5
Springford, 296 . . . . D 5
Stayner, 1,937 . . . . E 3
Stirling, 1,500 . . . . G 3
Stittsville, 1,994 . . . . . . J 2
Stoney Creek, 27,373 . . . . E 4
Stoney Point, 749 . . . . . . B 5
Straffordville, 717 . . . . . D 5
Stratford ⊙, 24,508 . . . . . C 4
Strathroy, 6,592 . . . . . . C 5
Stroud, 548 . . . . E 3
Sturgeon Falls, 6,662 . . . . E 1
Sudbury ⊙, 99,512 . . . . . K 5
Sudbury, ‡155,424 . . . . . K 5
Sultan, 343 . . . . J 5
Sunderland, 807 . . . . E 3
Sundridge, 723 . . . . E 2
Sutton, 2,500 . . . . E 3
Sydenham, 556 . . . . H 3
Tamworth, 375 . . . . H 3
Tara, 643 . . . . C 3
Tavistock, 1,490 . . . . . . D 4
Tecumseh, 5,165 . . . . . . B 5
Teeswater, 983 . . . . C 3

Terrace Bay, 1,819 . . . . . H 5
Thamesford, 1,185 . . . . . . C 4
Thamesville, 1,028 . . . . . C 5
Thedford, 719 . . . . C 4
Thessalon, 1,879 . . . . . . J 5
Thornbury, 1,220 . . . . . . D 3
Thorndale, 463 . . . . C 4
Thornton, 313 . . . . E 3
Thorold, 15,065 . . . . E 4
Thunder Bay ⊙, 108,411 . . H 5
Thunder Bay, ‡112,093 . . . H 5
Tilbury, 3,580 . . . . B 5
Tillsonburg, 6,608 . . . . . D 5
Timagami, 693 . . . . K 5
Timmins, 43,182 . . . . . . J 5
Tiverton, 567 . . . . C 3
Tobermory, 315 . . . . C 2
Toronto (cap.) ⊙, 712,786 . K 4
Toronto (Metro.),
  2,086,017 . . . . K 4
Toronto, ‡2,628,043 . . . . . K 4
Tottenham, 1,616 . . . . . . E 3
Trenton, 14,589 . . . . G 3
Trout Creek, 586 . . . . . . E 2
Turkey Point, 373 . . . . . . D 5
Tweed, 1,738 . . . . G 3
Uxbridge, 3,077 . . . . E 3
Vanier, 22,477 . . . . J 2
Vankleek Hill, 1,691 . . . . K 2
Vars, 395 . . . . J 2
Vaughan, 15,873 . . . . . . J 4
Vermilion Bay, 637 . . . . . G 4
Verner, 1,011 . . . . D 1
Verona, 689 . . . . H 3
Victoria Harbour, 1,243 . . . D 3
Vienna, 390 . . . . D 5
Vittoria, 455 . . . . D 5
Wabigoon, 312 . . . . G 4
Walden, 10,788 . . . . J 5
Walkerton ⊙, 4,479 . . . . . C 3
Wallaceburg, 10,550 . . . . B 5
Wardsville, 388 . . . . C 5
Warkworth, 562 . . . . G 3
Warren, 613 . . . . D 1
Wasaga Beach, 1,923 . . . . D 3
Washago, 423 . . . . E 3
Waterdown, 2,146 . . . . . . D 4
Waterloo, 37,893 . . . . . . D 4
Watford, 1,400 . . . . C 5
Waubaushene, 718 . . . . . D 3
Wawa, 4,375 . . . . J 5
Webbwood, 585 . . . . C 1
Welland, 44,397 . . . . E 5
Wellesley, 816 . . . . D 4
Wellington, 988 . . . . G 4
Wendover, 313 . . . . J 2
West Lorne, 1,094 . . . . . C 5
Westport, 601 . . . . H 3
Wheatley, 1,657 . . . . B 5
Yarker, 335 . . . . H 3
Whitby ⊙, 25,324 . . . . . . F 4
Whitchurch-Stouffville,
  11,262 . . . . J 3
White River, 945 . . . . . . J 5
Whitney, 826 . . . . F 2
Wiarton, 2,222 . . . . C 3
Wikwemikong, 895 . . . . . C 2
Williamsburg, 398 . . . . . . J 3
Williamstown, 312 . . . . . . K 2
Winchester, 1,575 . . . . . . J 2
Windsor ⊙, 203,300 . . . . . B 5
Windsor, ‡258,643 . . . . . . B 5

Wingham, 2,913 . . . . C 4
Wolfe Island, 335 . . . . . . H 3
Woodstock ⊙, 26,173 . . . . D 4
Woodville, 473 . . . . F 3
Wroxeter, 291 . . . . C 4
Wyoming, 1,279 . . . . B 5
Zephyr, 337 . . . . E 3
Zurich, 767 . . . . C 4

OTHER FEATURES

Abitibi (riv.) . . . . J 5
Algonquin Prov. Park, 337 F 2
Amherst (isl.), 367 . . . . . H 3
Balsam (lake) . . . . F 3
Barrie (isl.), 109 . . . . . . B 1
Bays (lake) . . . . F 2

Big Rideau (lake) . . . . . . H 3
Black (riv.) . . . . E 3
Bruce (pen.) . . . . C 2
Buckhorn (lake) . . . . . . F 3
Cabot (head) . . . . C 2
Charleston (lake) . . . . . . J 3
Christian (isl.), 506 . . . . D 3
Clear (lake) . . . . F 3
Cockburn (isl.) . . . . A 2
Couchiching (lake) . . . . . E 3
Croker (cape) . . . . D 3
Don (riv.) . . . . J 4
Doré (lake) . . . . G 2
Douglas (pt.) . . . . C 3
Erie (lake) . . . . E 5
Flowerpot (isl.) . . . . . . C 2
French (riv.) . . . . D 1
Georgian (bay) . . . . D 2
Georgian Bay Is. Nat'l Park D 3

Georgina (isl.), 181 . . . . . E 3
Grand (riv.) . . . . D 4
Humber (riv.) . . . . J 3
Hurd (cape) . . . . C 2
Huron (lake) . . . . B 3
Ipperwash Prov. Park, 32 C 4
Joseph (lake) . . . . D 2
Killbear Point Prov. Park . D 2
Lake of the Woods (lake) F 5
Lake Superior Prov. Park . J 5
Lonely (isl.), 3 . . . . C 2
Long (pt.) . . . . D 5
Long Point (bay) . . . . . . D 5
Madawaska (riv.) . . . . . . G 2
Magnetawan (riv.) . . . . . D 2
Main (chan.) . . . . C 2
Manitou (lake) . . . . C 2
Manitoulin (isl.), 10,064 . . B 2
Mattagami (riv.) . . . . . . J 5
Michipicoten (isl.), 4 . . . . H 5
Missinaibi (riv.) . . . . . . J 5
Mississagi (riv.) . . . . . . A 1
Mississippi (lake) . . . . . H 3
Muskoka (lake) . . . . E 2
Niagara (riv.) . . . . E 4
Nipigon (lake) . . . . H 5
Nipissing (lake) . . . . . . E 1
North (chan.) . . . . C 2
Nottawasaga (bay) . . . . . D 3
Ogidaki (mt.) . . . . J 5
Ontario (lake) . . . . G 4
Opeongo (lake) . . . . F 2
Ottawa (riv.) . . . . H 2
Owen (sound) . . . . D 3
Panache (lake) . . . . C 1
Parry (isl.), 318 . . . . . . D 2
Parry (sound) . . . . D 2
Pelee (pt.) . . . . B 6

Petre (pt.) . . . . G 4
Point Pelee Nat'l Park, 202 B 6
Presqu'île Prov. Park, 67 G 4
Quetico Prov. Park . . . . . G 5
Rainy (lake) . . . . F 3
Rice (lake) . . . . F 3
Rideau (lake) . . . . H 3
Rondeau Prov. Park, 103 . C 5
Rosseau (lake) . . . . E 2
Saint Clair (riv.) . . . . . . B 5
Saint Lawrence (lake) . . . K 3
Saint Lawrence (riv.) . . . J 3
Saint Lawrence Is. Nat'l
  Park . . . . J 3
Saugeen (riv.) . . . . C 3
Scugog (lake) . . . . F 3
Seul (lake) . . . . G 4
Severn (riv.) . . . . E 3
Sibley Prov. Park, 2 . . . . H 5
Simcoe (lake) . . . . E 3
South (bay) . . . . C 2
Spanish (riv.) . . . . C 1
Stony (lake) . . . . G 3
Superior (lake) . . . . H 5
Sydenham (riv.) . . . . . . B 5
Thames (riv.) . . . . B 5
Theano (pt.) . . . . J 5
Thousand (isls.), 1,447 . . H 3
Timagami (lake) . . . . . . K 5
Trout (lake) . . . . E 1
Vernon (lake) . . . . E 2
Walpole (isl.), 1,420 . . . . B 5
Welland (canal) . . . . . . E 5
Woods (lake) . . . . F 5

⊙ County seat.
‡ Population of metropolitan area.

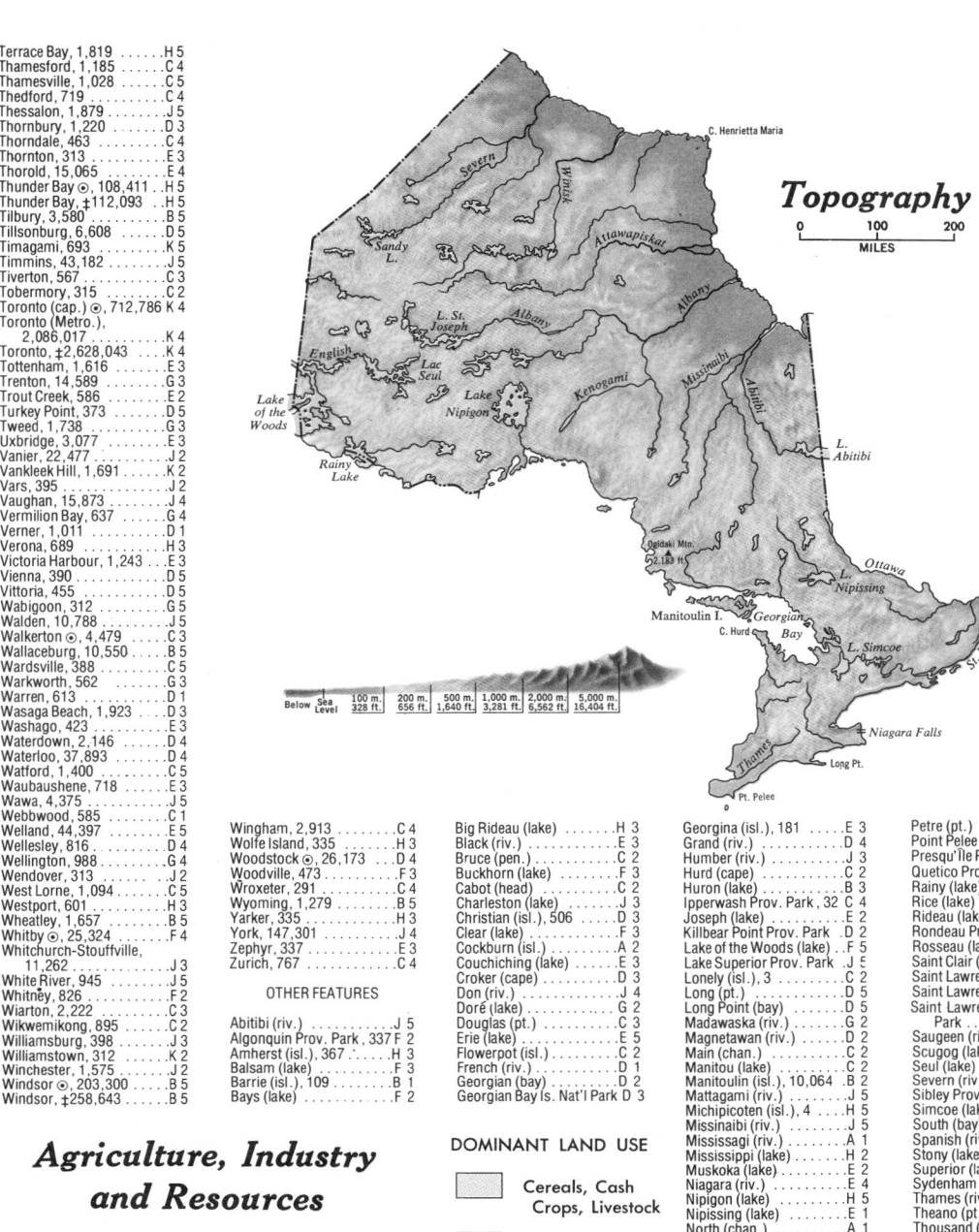

Topography

0   100   200
MILES

Below Sea Level | 100 m. 328 ft. | 200 m. 656 ft. | 500 m. 1,640 ft. | 1,000 m. 3,281 ft. | 2,000 m. 6,562 ft. | 5,000 m. 16,404 ft.

Agriculture, Industry and Resources

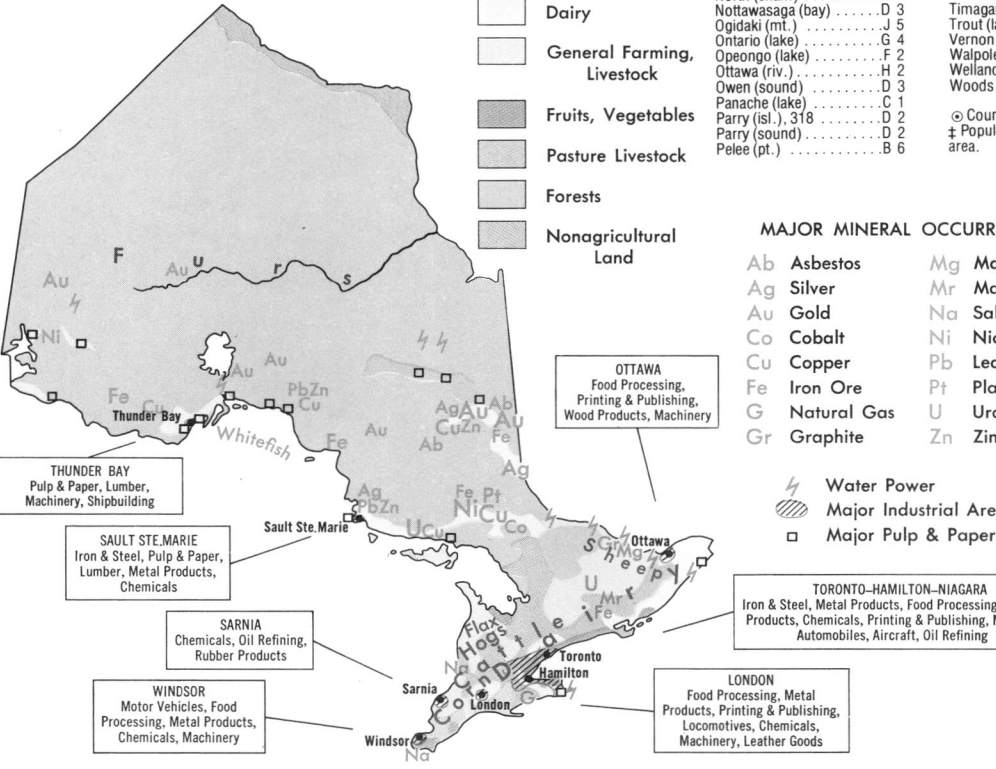

DOMINANT LAND USE

Cereals, Cash Crops, Livestock

Dairy

General Farming, Livestock

Fruits, Vegetables

Pasture Livestock

Forests

Nonagricultural Land

MAJOR MINERAL OCCURRENCES

Ab Asbestos
Ag Silver
Au Gold
Co Cobalt
Cu Copper
Fe Iron Ore
G   Natural Gas
Gr Graphite

Mg Magnesium
Mr Marble
Na Salt
Ni Nickel
Pb Lead
Pt Platinum
U   Uranium
Zn Zinc

⚡ Water Power
▨ Major Industrial Areas
□ Major Pulp & Paper Mills

OTTAWA
Food Processing, Printing & Publishing, Wood Products, Machinery

THUNDER BAY
Pulp & Paper, Lumber, Machinery, Shipbuilding

SAULT STE.MARIE
Iron & Steel, Pulp & Paper, Lumber, Metal Products, Chemicals

SARNIA
Chemicals, Oil Refining, Rubber Products

WINDSOR
Motor Vehicles, Food Processing, Metal Products, Chemicals, Machinery

TORONTO-HAMILTON-NIAGARA
Iron & Steel, Metal Products, Food Processing, Electrical Products, Chemicals, Printing & Publishing, Machinery, Automobiles, Aircraft, Oil Refining

LONDON
Food Processing, Metal Products, Printing & Publishing, Locomotives, Chemicals, Machinery, Leather Goods

ONTARIO
SOUTHERN PART

SCALE
0   10   20   30   40   50 MI.
0 10 20 30 40 50 KM.

National Capital . . . . . . ⊛
Provincial Capital . . . . . ⊛
County Seats . . . . ⊙
International Boundaries ____
Provincial & State Boundaries ____
County Boundaries ---
Canals +++

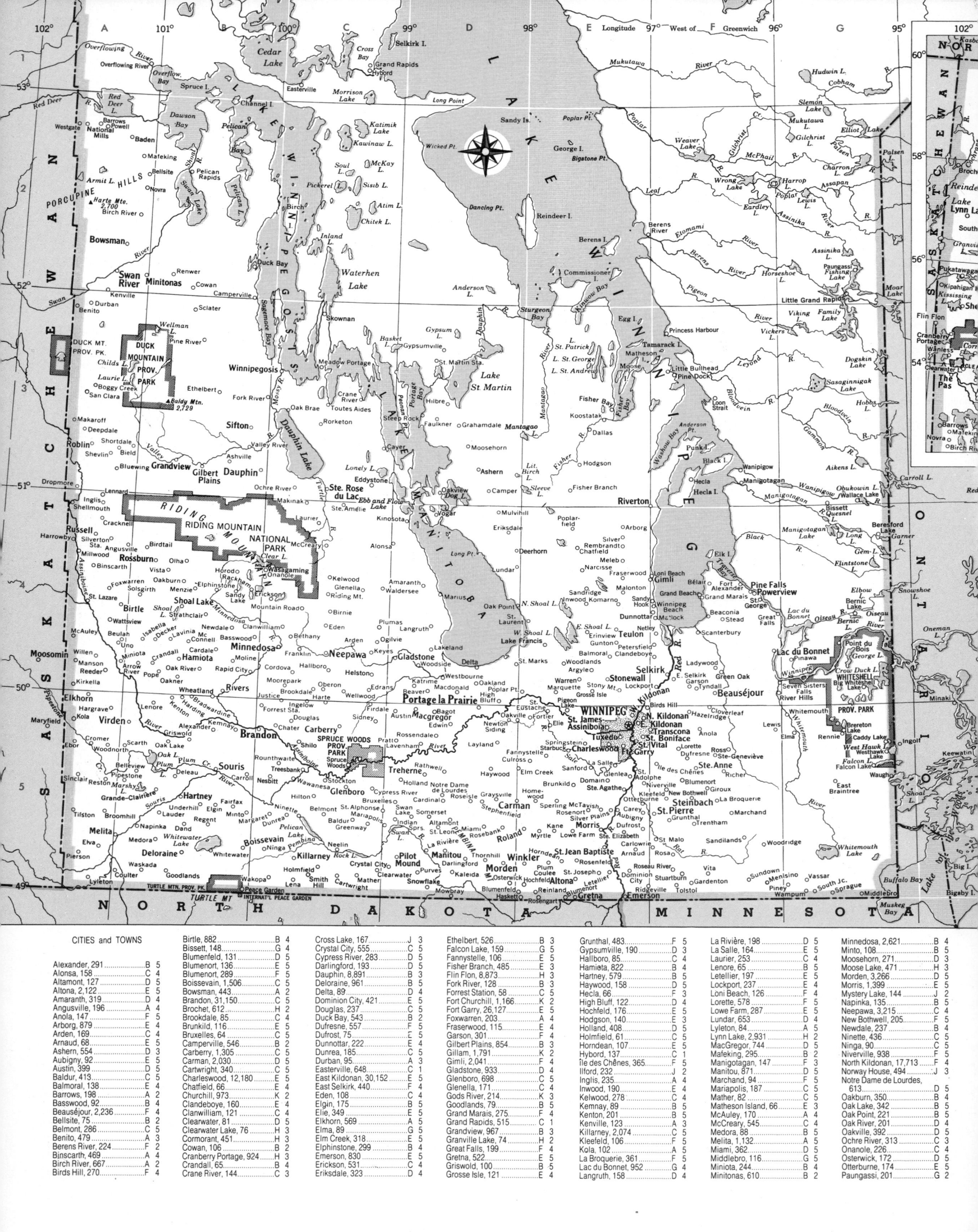

CITIES and TOWNS

Alexander, 291	B 5	
Alonsa, 158	C 4	
Altamont, 127	D 5	
Altona, 2,122	E 5	
Amaranth, 319	C 4	
Angusville, 196	A 4	
Anola, 147	F 5	
Arborg, 879	E 4	
Arden, 169	C 4	
Arnaud, 68	E 5	
Ashern, 554	D 3	
Aubigny, 92	E 5	
Austin, 399	D 5	
Baldur, 413	C 5	
Balmoral, 138	E 4	
Barrows, 198	A 2	
Basswood, 92	B 4	
Beauséjour, 2,236	F 4	
Bellsite, 75	B 2	
Belmont, 286	C 5	
Benito, 479	A 3	
Berens River, 224	F 2	
Binscarth, 469	A 4	
Birch River, 667	A 2	
Birds Hill, 270	F 4	

Birtle, 882 ... B 4
Bissett, 148 ... G 4
Blumenfeld, 131 ... D 5
Blumenort, 136 ... E 5
Blumenort, 289 ... F 5
Boissevain, 1,506 ... C 5
Bowsman, 443 ... A 2
Brandon, 31,150 ... C 5
Brookdale, 85 ... C 4
Brunkild, 116 ... E 5
Bruxelles, 64 ... C 5
Camperville, 546 ... B 2
Carberry, 1,305 ... C 5
Carman, 2,030 ... D 5
Cartwright, 340 ... C 5
Charleswood, 12,180 ... E 4
Chatfield, 66 ... E 4
Churchill, 973 ... K 2
Clandeboye, 160 ... E 4
Clanwilliam, 121 ... C 4
Clearwater, 81 ... D 5
Clearwater Lake, 76 ... H 3
Cormorant, 451 ... H 3
Cowan, 106 ... B 2
Cranberry Portage, 924 ... H 3
Crandall, 65 ... B 4
Crane River, 144 ... C 3

Cross Lake, 167 ... J 3
Crystal City, 555 ... C 5
Cypress River, 283 ... D 5
Darlingford, 193 ... D 5
Dauphin, 8,891 ... B 3
Delta, 89 ... D 4
Deloraine, 961 ... B 5
Dominion City, 421 ... E 5
Douglas, 237 ... C 5
Duck Bay, 543 ... B 2
Dufresne, 557 ... F 5
Dufrost, 75 ... E 5
Dunnottar, 222 ... E 4
Dunrea, 185 ... C 5
Durban, 95 ... A 3
Easterville, 648 ... C 1
East Kildonan, 30,152 ... F 4
East Selkirk, 440 ... F 4
Eden, 108 ... C 4
Elgin, 175 ... B 5
Elie, 349 ... E 5
Elkhorn, 569 ... A 4
Elma, 89 ... G 5
Elm Creek, 318 ... D 4
Elphinstone, 299 ... B 4
Emerson, 830 ... E 5
Erickson, 531 ... C 4
Eriksdale, 323 ... D 4

Ethelbert, 526 ... B 3
Falcon Lake, 159 ... G 5
Fannystelle, 106 ... E 5
Fisher Branch, 485 ... E 3
Flin Flon, 8,873 ... H 3
Fork River, 128 ... B 3
Forrest Station, 58 ... C 5
Fort Churchill, 1,166 ... K 2
Fort Garry, 26,127 ... F 4
Foxwarren, 203 ... A 4
Fraserwood, 115 ... E 4
Garson, 301 ... F 4
Gilbert Plains, 854 ... B 3
Gillam, 1,791 ... K 2
Gimli, 2,041 ... F 4
Gladstone, 933 ... D 4
Glenboro, 698 ... C 5
Glenella, 171 ... C 4
Gods River, 214 ... K 3
Goodlands, 79 ... B 5
Grand Marais, 275 ... F 4
Grand Rapids, 515 ... C 1
Grandview, 967 ... B 3
Granville Lake, 74 ... H 2
Great Falls, 199 ... F 4
Gretna, 522 ... E 5
Griswold, 100 ... B 5
Grosse Isle, 121 ... E 4

Grunthal, 483 ... F 5
Gypsumville, 190 ... D 3
Hallboro, 85 ... C 4
Hamiota, 822 ... B 4
Hartney, 579 ... B 5
Haywood, 158 ... D 5
Hecla, 66 ... E 3
High Bluff, 122 ... D 4
Hochfeld, 176 ... E 5
Hodgson, 140 ... E 3
Holland, 408 ... D 5
Holmfield, 61 ... C 5
Horndean, 107 ... E 5
Hybord, 137 ... C 1
Île des Chênes, 365 ... F 5
Ilford, 232 ... J 2
Inglis, 235 ... A 3
Inwood, 190 ... E 4
Kelwood, 278 ... C 4
Kemnay, 89 ... B 5
Kenton, 201 ... B 4
Kenville, 123 ... A 3
Killarney, 2,074 ... C 5
Kleefeld, 106 ... F 5
Kola, 102 ... A 5
La Broquerie, 361 ... F 5
Lac du Bonnet, 952 ... G 4
Langruth, 158 ... D 4

La Rivière, 198 ... D 5
La Salle, 164 ... E 5
Laurier, 253 ... C 4
Lenore, 65 ... B 5
Letellier, 197 ... E 5
Lockport, 237 ... E 4
Loni Beach, 126 ... F 4
Lorette, 578 ... F 5
Lowe Farm, 287 ... D 5
Lundar, 653 ... D 4
Lyleton, 84 ... A 5
Lynn Lake, 2,931 ... H 2
MacGregor, 744 ... D 5
Mafeking, 295 ... B 2
Manigotagan, 147 ... F 3
Manitou, 871 ... D 5
Marchand, 94 ... F 5
Mariapolis, 187 ... C 5
Mather, 82 ... C 5
Matheson Island, 66 ... E 3
McAuley, 170 ... A 4
McCreary, 545 ... C 4
Medora, 84 ... B 5
Melita, 1,132 ... A 5
Miami, 362 ... D 5
Middlebro, 116 ... G 5
Miniota, 244 ... A 4
Minitonas, 610 ... B 2

Minnedosa, 2,621 ... B 4
Minto, 108 ... B 5
Moosehorn, 271 ... D 3
Moose Lake, 471 ... H 3
Morden, 3,266 ... D 5
Morris, 1,399 ... E 5
Mystery Lake, 144 ... J 2
Napinka, 135 ... B 5
Neepawa, 3,215 ... C 4
New Bothwell, 205 ... F 5
Newdale, 237 ... B 4
Ninette, 436 ... C 5
Ninga, 90 ... C 5
Niverville, 938 ... F 5
North Kildonan, 17,713 ... F 4
Norway House, 494 ... J 3
Notre Dame de Lourdes, 613 ... D 5
Oakbank, 350 ... B 4
Oak Lake, 342 ... B 5
Oak Point, 201 ... D 4
Oak River, 201 ... B 4
Oakville, 392 ... D 5
Ochre River, 313 ... C 3
Onanole, 226 ... C 4
Osterwick, 172 ... D 5
Otterburne, 174 ... E 5
Paungassi, 201 ... G 2

MANITOBA
NORTHERN PART

0 40 80 120 MI.
0 40 80 120 KM.

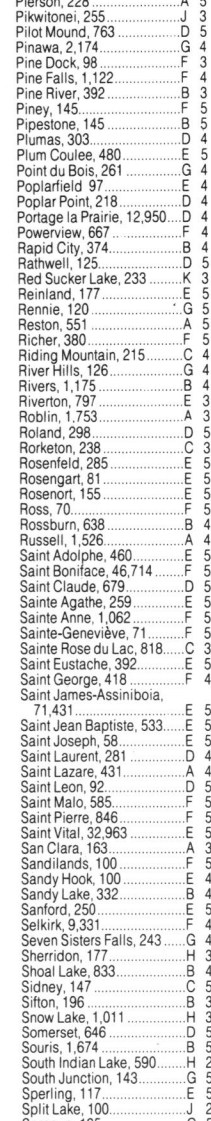

MANITOBA
SOUTHERN PART
SCALE

0 5 10 20   40   60 MI.
0 5 10 20   40   60 KM.

Provincial Capital _____ ⊛
International Boundaries _ _ _ _ _
Provincial Boundaries _ _ _ _ _

© C.S. HAMMOND & Co., N.Y.

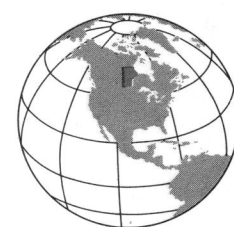

AREA 251,000 sq. mi.
POPULATION 988,247 ('71); 1,021,506 ('76)
CAPITAL Winnipeg
LARGEST CITY Winnipeg
HIGHEST POINT Baldy Mtn. 2,727 ft.
SETTLED IN 1812
ADMITTED TO CONFEDERATION 1870
PROVINCIAL FLOWER Prairie Crocus

Pelican Rapids, 217 ....B 2
Petersfield, 146 ....E 4
Pierson, 228 ....A 5
Pikwitonei, 255 ....J 3
Pilot Mound, 763 ....D 5
Pinawa, 2,174 ....G 4
Pine Dock, 98 ....F 3
Pine Falls, 1,122 ....F 4
Pine River, 392 ....B 3
Piney, 145 ....F 5
Pipestone, 145 ....A 5
Plumas, 303 ....D 4
Plum Coulee, 480 ....E 5
Point du Bois, 261 ....G 4
Poplarfield 97 ....E 4
Poplar Point, 218 ....D 4
Portage la Prairie, 12,950..D 4
Powerview, 667 ....F 4
Rapid City, 374 ....B 4
Rathwell, 125 ....D 5
Red Sucker Lake, 233 .....K 3
Reinland, 177 ....E 5
Rennie, 120 ....G 5
Reston, 551 ....A 5
Richer, 380 ....F 5
Riding Mountain, 215 ....C 4
River Hills, 126 ....G 4
Rivers, 1,175 ....B 4
Riverton, 797 ....E 3
Roblin, 1,753 ....A 3
Roland, 298 ....D 5
Rorketon, 238 ....C 3
Rosenfeld, 285 ....E 5
Rosengart, 81 ....E 5
Rosenort, 155 ....F 5
Ross, 70. ....F 5
Rossburn, 638 ....B 4
Russell, 1,526 ....A 4
Saint Adolphe, 460 ....E 5
Saint Boniface, 46,714 ....E 5
Saint Claude, 679 ....D 5
Sainte Agathe, 259 ....E 5
Sainte Anne, 1,062 ....F 5
Sainte-Geneviève, 71 ......F 5
Sainte Rose du Lac, 818...C 3
Saint Eustache, 392 ....E 4
Saint George, 418 ....F 4
Saint James-Assiniboia,
71,431 ....E 5
Saint Jean Baptiste, 533...E 5
Saint Joseph, 58 ....E 5
Saint Laurent, 281 ....D 4
Saint Lazare, 431 ....A 4
Saint Leon, 92 ....D 5
Saint Malo, 585 ....F 5
Saint Pierre, 846 ....E 5
Saint Vital, 32,963 ....E 5
San Clara, 163 ....A 3
Sandilands, 100 ....F 5
Sandy Hook, 100 ....E 4
Sandy Lake, 332 ....B 4
Sanford, 250 ....E 5
Selkirk, 9,331 ....E 4
Seven Sisters Falls, 243 ..G 4
Sherridon, 177 ....H 3
Shoal Lake, 833 ....B 4
Sidney, 147 ....C 5
Sifton, 196 ....B 3
Snow Lake, 1,011 ....H 3
Somerset, 646 ....D 5
Souris, 1,674 ....C 5
South Indian Lake, 590 ...H 2
South Junction, 143 ....G 5
Sperling, 117 ....E 5
Split Lake, 100 ....J 2
Sprague, 195. ....G 5
Springstein, 117 ....E 5
Spruce Woods, 183 ....C 5

Starbuck, 263 ....E 5
Steep Rock, 146 ....D 3
Steinbach, 5,197 ....F 5
Stockton, 58. ....C 5
Stonewall, 1,583 ....E 4
Stony Mountain, 1,268 ....E 4
Strathclair, 404 ....B 4
Sundown, 296 ....F 5
Swan Lake, 300 ....D 5
Swan River, 3,522 ....A 2
Teulon, 828. ....E 4
The Pas, 19,001 ....H 3
Thicket Portage, 318 ....J 3
Thompson, 6,062 ....J 3
Tilston, 72 ....A 5
Tolstoi, 88. ....F 5
Transcona, 22,490 ....F 5
Treherne, 628 ....D 5
Tuxedo, 3,258 ....E 5
Tyndall, 400. ....F 4
Vassar, 240. ....G 5
Virden, 2,823 ....A 5
Vista, 71. ....C 5
Vita, 349. ....F 5
Vogar, 126. ....D 4
Wabowden, 809 ....J 3
Wanless, 123. ....H 3
Warren, 267 ....E 4
Wasagaming, 122 ....C 4
Waskada, 247. ....B 5
Wawanesa, 478. ....C 5
Wellwood, 79. ....C 4
Westbourne, 113. ....D 4
West Kildonan, 23,959 ....E 4
Wheatland, 67 ....B 4
Whitemouth, 366 ....G 5
Winkler, 2,983 ....E 5
Winnipeg (cap.), 246,246..E 5
Winnipeg, †540,262 ....E 5
Winnipeg Beach, 687 ......F 4
Winnipegosis, 887 ....B 3
Woodlands, 123 ....E 4
Woodridge, 228. ....G 5

OTHER FEATURES

Assiniboine (riv.) ....C 5
Assinika (riv.) ....G 2
Baldy (mt.) ....B 3
Berens (riv.) ....F 2
Bernic (lake) ....G 5
Birch (isl.) ....C 2
Black (isl.) ....F 3
Bloodvein (riv.) ....F 3
Bonnet (lake) ....G 4
Burntwood (riv.) ....J 2
Cedar (lake) ....B 1
Charron (lake) ....G 2

Childs (lake) ....A 3
Chitek (lake) ....C 2
Churchill (cape) ....K 2
Churchill (riv.) ....J 2
Clear (lake) ....C 4
Clearwater Prov. Park .....H 3
Cormorant (lake) ....H 3
Cross (lake) ....J 3
Crow Duck (lake) ....G 4
Dauphin (lake) ....C 3
Dauphin (riv.) ....D 3
Dawson (bay) ....B 2
Dog (lake) ....D 3
Duck Mountain Prov. Park ..B 3
East Shoal (lake) ....E 4
Ebb and Flow (lake) ....C 3
Elk (isl.) ....F 4
Falcon (lake) ....G 5
Family (lake) ....G 3
Fisher (bay) ....E 3
Fishing (lake) ....G 2
Fox (riv.) ....K 2
Garner (lake) ....G 4
George (lake) ....G 4
Gods (lake) ....K 3
Gods (riv.) ....K 3
Granville (lake) ....H 2
Grass (riv.) ....J 3
Grass River Prov. Park ....H 3
Harte (mt.) ....A 2
Hayes (riv.) ....K 3
Hecla (isl.) ....F 3
Hudson (bay) ....K 2
International Peace
Garden ....B 5
Island (lake) ....K 3
Kawinaw (lake) ....C 2
Kississing (lake) ....H 3
Lake of the Woods (lake)..H 5
Lonely (lake) ....C 3
Long (pt.) ....D 1
Manigotagan (riv.) ....G 4
Manitoba (lake) ....D 3
Mantagao (riv.) ....E 3
Minnedosa (riv.) ....B 4
Moose (isl.) ....E 3
Mossy (riv.) ....C 3
Mukutawa (riv.) ....E 1
Nejanilini (lake) ....J 1
Nelson (riv.) ....J 2
Northern Indian (lake) .....J 2
North Shoal (lake) ....E 4
Nueltin (lake) ....H 1
Oak (lake) ....B 5
Oiseau (riv.) ....G 4
Overflowing (riv.) ....A 1
Oxford (lake) ....J 3
Paint (lake) ....J 2
Pelican (bay) ....B 2
Pelican (lake) ....B 2

Pelican (lake) ....C 5
Pembina (mt.) ....D 5
Pembina (riv.) ....C 5
Peonan (pt.) ....D 3
Pigeon (riv.) ....F 2
Pipestone (creek) ....A 5
Plum (creek) ....B 5
Poplar (riv.) ....D 2
Porcupine (hills) ....A 2
Portage (bay) ....D 3
Rat (riv.) ....D 3
Red (riv.) ....F 4
Red Deer (lake) ....A 2
Reindeer (isl.) ....E 2
Reindeer (lake) ....J 1
Riding (mt.) ....B 4
Riding Mountain Nat'l
Park, 158 ....B 4
Rock (lake) ....C 5
Ross (isl.) ....J 3
Sagemace (bay) ....B 3
Saint George (lake) ....E 3
Saint Martin (lake) ....D 3
Sale (riv.) ....E 5
Sasaginnigak (lake) ....G 3
Seal (riv.) ....J 2
Setting (lake) ....H 3
Shoal (riv.) ....B 3
Sipiwesk (lake) ....J 3
Souris (riv.) ....B 5
Southern Indian (lake) ....H 2
South Knife (riv.) ....J 2
Split (lake) ....J 2
Spruce Woods Prov. Park ..C 5
Sturgeon (bay) ....E 3
Swan (lake) ....B 2
Swan (lake) ....D 5
Swan (riv.) ....A 3
Tadoule (lake) ....J 2
Tatnam (cape) ....K 2
Traverse (bay) ....F 4
Turtle (riv.) ....J 3
Turtle Mountain Prov. Park..B 5
Valley (riv.) ....B 3
Wanipigow (riv.) ....G 3
Washow (bay) ....F 3
Waterhen (lake) ....C 3
Weaver (lake) ....F 2
West Hawk (lake) ....G 5
West Shoal (lake) ....E 4
Whitemouth (lake) ....G 5
Whitemouth (riv.) ....G 5
Whiteshell Prov. Park ......G 4
Whitewater (lake) ....B 5
Winnipeg (lake) ....E 2
Winnipeg (riv.) ....G 4
Winnipegosis (lake) ....C 3
Woods (lake) ....H 5

‡ Population of metropolitan
area.

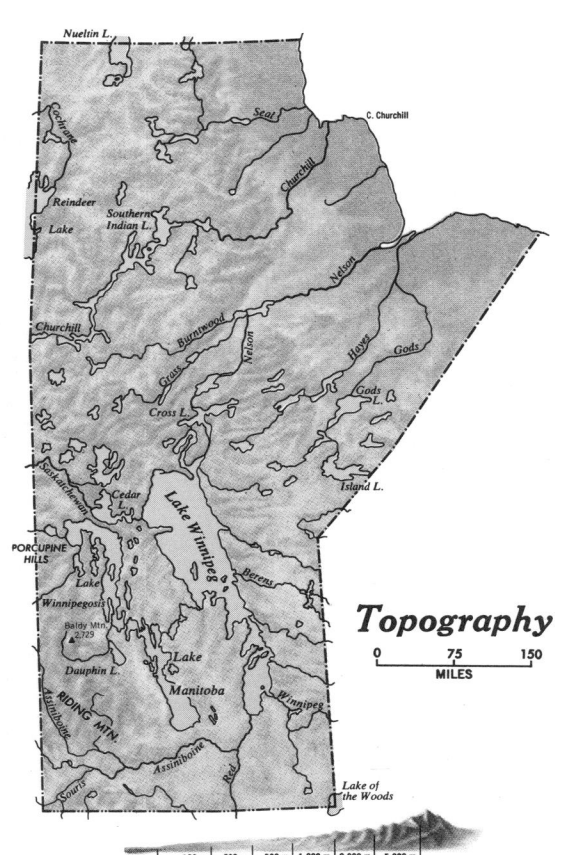

Topography

0   75   150
MILES

Below 100 m. 200 m. 500 m. 1,000 m. 2,000 m. 5,000 m.
Sea Level 328 ft. 656 ft. 1,640 ft. 3,281 ft. 6,562 ft. 16,404 ft.

Agriculture, Industry and Resources

DOMINANT LAND USE

Cereals (chiefly barley, oats)
Cereals, Livestock
Dairy
Livestock
Forests
Nonagricultural Land

MAJOR MINERAL OCCURRENCES

Au Gold   Ni Nickel
Co Cobalt   O   Petroleum
Cu Copper   Pb Lead
Na Salt   Pt Platinum
                  Zn Zinc

⚡ Water Power
▨ Major Industrial Areas
▫ Major Pulp & Paper Mills

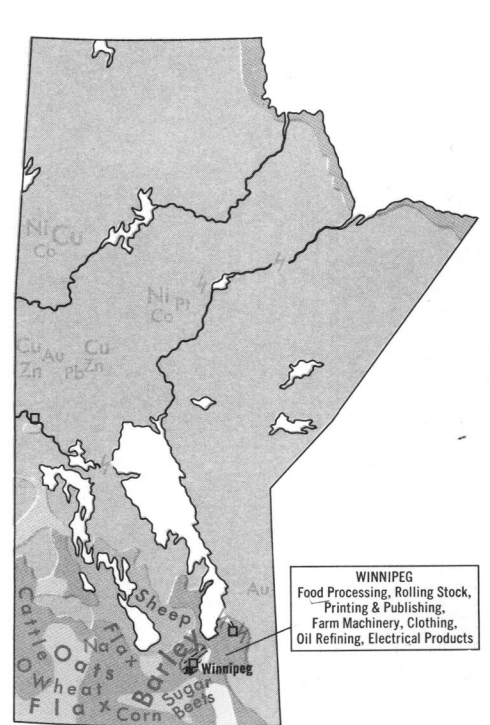

WINNIPEG
Food Processing, Rolling Stock,
Printing & Publishing,
Farm Machinery, Clothing,
Oil Refining, Electrical Products

Topography

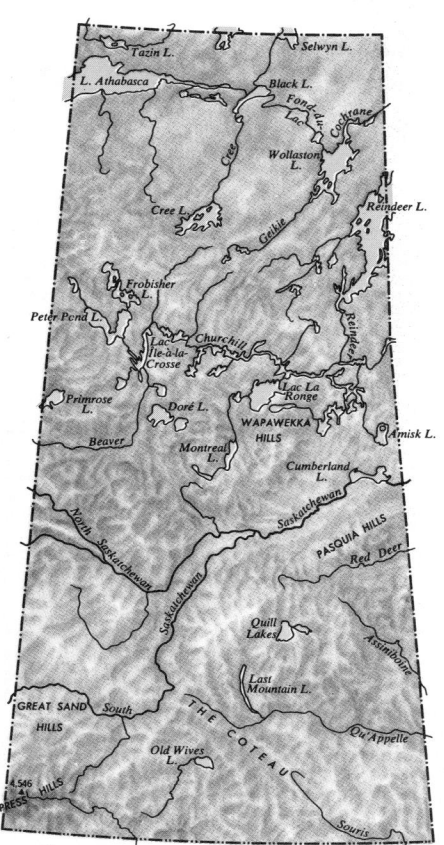

```
0      60    120
       MILES
```

5,000 m. / 2,000 m. / 1,000 m. / 500 m. / 200 m. / 100 m. / Sea Level
16,404 ft. / 6,562 ft. / 3,281 ft. / 1,640 ft. / 656 ft. / 328 ft. / Below

Duval, 133 .... G 4
Dysart, 243 .... H 5
Earl Grey, 243 .... G 5
Eastend, 784 .... C 6
Eatonia, 610 .... B 4
Ebenezer, 140 .... J 4
Edam, 334 .... C 2
Edenwold, 129 .... G 5
Elbow, 361 .... E 4
Eldorado, 289 .... L 2
Elfros, 253 .... H 4
Elrose, 573 .... D 4
Elstow, 150 .... E 4
Endeavour, 193 .... J 3
Englefeld, 218 .... H 3
Ernfold, 100 .... D 5
Erwood, 94 .... J 3
Esterhazy, 2,896 .... K 5
Estevan, 9,150 .... J 6
Eston, 1,418 .... C 4
Eyebrow, 181 .... E 5
Fairlight, 127 .... K 6
Fenwood, 112 .... H 4
Ferland, 109 .... D 6
Fillmore, 396 .... H 5
Findlater, 96 .... F 5
Fiske, 85 .... C 4
Flaxcombe, 99 .... B 4
Fleming, 183 .... K 5
Flin Flon, 471 .... N 4
Foam Lake, 1,331 .... H 4
Fond du Lac, 328 .... L 2
Forget, 100 .... J 6
Fort Qu'Appelle, 1,606 ... H 5
Fosston, 119 .... H 3
Fox Valley, 489 .... B 5
Francis, 159 .... H 5
Frenchman Butte, 86 ..... B 2
Frobisher, 245 .... J 6
Frontier, 249 .... C 6
Gainsborough, 375 .... K 6
Garrick, 120 .... G 2
Gerald, 174 .... K 5
Girvin, 86 .... F 4
Gladmar, 131 .... G 6
Glaslyn, 357 .... C 2
Glenavon, 340 .... J 5
Glen Ewen, 223 .... K 6
Glenside, 94 .... E 4
Glentworth, 126 .... E 6
Golden Prairie, 144 .... B 5
Goodeve, 169 .... H 4
Goodsoil, 219 .... L 1
Gorlitz, 97 .... J 4
Govan, 354 .... G 4
Grand Coulee, 131 .... G 5
Gravelbourg, 1,428 .... E 5
Grayson, 260 .... J 5
Green Lake, 450 .... L 4
Grenfell, 1,350 .... J 5
Griffin, 90 .... H 6
Gronlid, 138 .... G 2
Guernsey, 142 .... F 4
Gull Lake, 1,156 .... C 5
Hafford, 580 .... D 3
Hague, 431 .... E 3
Halbrite, 166 .... H 6
Hanley, 390 .... E 4
Harris, 254 .... D 4
Hawarden, 190 .... E 4
Hazel Dell, 105 .... H 4
Hazenmore, 127 .... D 6
Hazlet, 198 .... C 5
Hepburn, 305 .... E 3
Herbert, 1,024 .... D 5
Herschel, 89 .... C 4
Hitchcock, 91 .... J 6
Hodgeville, 399 .... E 5
Hoey, 95 .... F 3

Holdfast, 399 .... F 5
Hubbard, 119 .... H 4
Hudson Bay, 1,971 .... J 3
Humboldt, 3,881 .... G 3
Hyas, 215 .... J 4
Île-à-la-Crosse, 908 ...... L 3
Imperial, 486 .... F 4
Indian Head, 1,810 ...... H 5
Invermay, 412 .... H 4
Ituna, 960 .... H 4
Jansen, 241 .... G 4
Kamsack, 2,783 .... K 4
Kayville, 84 .... F 6
Kelliher, 460 .... H 4
Kelvington, 1,053 .... H 3
Kenaston, 402 .... E 4
Kendal, 90 .... H 5
Kennedy, 264 .... J 5
Kenosee Park, 103 .... J 5
Kerrobert, 1,180 .... C 4
Khedive, 91 .... G 5
Killaly, 139 .... J 5
Kincaid, 306 .... D 6
Kindersley, 3,451 .... B 4
Kinistino, 767 .... G 3
Kinoosao, 95 .... N 3
Kipling, 927 .... J 5
Kisbey, 260 .... J 6
Krydor, 106 .... D 3
Kuroki, 167 .... H 4
Kyle, 509 .... C 5
Lacadena, 84 .... C 5
Lac Vert, 111 .... G 3
Laflèche, 715 .... E 6
Laird, 218 .... E 3
Lake Alma, 173 .... G 6
Lake Lenore, 392 .... G 3
La Loche, 1,136 .... L 3
Lampman, 830 .... J 6
Lancer, 199 .... C 5
Landis, 297 .... C 3
Lang, 183 .... G 5
Langenburg, 1,236 ...... K 5
Langham, 535 .... E 3
Lanigan, 1,430 .... F 4
La Ronge, 906 .... L 1
Lashburn, 494 .... B 2
Leader, 1,105 .... B 5
Leask, 439 .... E 2
Lebret, 278 .... H 5
Leipzig, 87 .... C 3
Lemberg, 409 .... H 5
Leoville, 399 .... D 2
Leross, 91 .... H 4
Leroy, 435 .... G 4
Leslie, 87 .... H 4
Lestock, 452 .... G 4
Liberty, 141 .... F 4
Limerick, 178 .... E 6
Lintlaw, 212 .... H 3
Lipton, 401 .... H 5
Livelong, 126 .... C 2
Lloydminster, 3,953 .... A 2
Lone Rock, 120 .... A 2
Loon Lake, 348 .... B 1
Loreburn, 252 .... E 4
Love, 133 .... G 2
Lucky Lake, 378 .... D 5
Lumsden, 900 .... G 5
Luseland, 728 .... B 3
Macdowall, 173 .... E 2
Macklin, 829 .... A 3
MacNutt, 184 .... K 4
Macoun, 172 .... H 6
Macrorie, 120 .... E 4
Maidstone, 691 .... B 2
Major, 164 .... B 4
Makwa, 126 .... C 2
Manitou Beach, 118 .. F 4

Mankota, 424 .... D 6
Manor, 409 .... K 6
Maple Creek, 2,268 .. B 6
Marcelin, 306 .... E 3
Marchwell, 129 ...... K 5
Marengo, 133 .... B 4
Margo, 225 .... H 4
Marquis, 131 .... F 5
Marsden, 241 .... B 3
Marshall, 195 .... B 2
Martensville, 870 .... E 3
Maryfield, 408 .... K 6
Mayfair, 134 .... D 2
Maymont, 167 .... D 3
McKague, 91 .... H 3
McLean, 178 .... G 5
Meacham, 186 ...... F 4
Meadow Lake, 3,435 . C 1
Meath Park, 251 ..... F 2
Medstead, 172 ...... C 2
Melfort, 4,725 .... G 3
Melville, 5,375 ...... J 5
Mendham, 163 ..... B 5
Meota, 233 .... C 2
Mervin, 198 .... C 2
Meyronne, 142 ..... E 6
Midale, 647 .... H 6
Middle Lake, 292 .. F 3
Mikado, 90 .... J 4
Milden, 239 .... D 4
Milestone, 483 .... G 5
Minton, 215 .... G 6
Mistatim, 165 ..... H 3
Molanosa, 213 .... M 4
Montmartre, 510 .. H 5
Moose Jaw, 31,854 . F 5
Moosomin, 2,407 .. K 5
Morse, 455 .... D 5
Mortlach, 310 ..... E 5
Mossbank, 460 .... F 5
Mozart, 93 .... G 4
Muenster, 280 .... F 3
Naicam, 711 ...... G 3
Neilburg, 298 ..... B 3
Neuanlage, 107 ... E 3
Neudorf, 469 ..... J 5
Neville, 154 ...... D 6
Nipawin, 4,057 ... H 2
Nokomis, 533 .... F 4
Norquay, 513 .... J 4
North Battleford, 12,698 . C 3
North Portal, 189 . J 6
Odessa, 224 ..... H 5
Ogema, 457 ..... G 6
Ormiston, 173 ... F 5
Osler, 182 ...... E 3
Outlook, 1,767 .. E 4
Oxbow, 1,380 ... J 6
Paddockwood, 230 . F 2
Pambrun, 91 .... D 6
Pangman, 242 .. G 6
Paradise Hill, 344 . B 2
Parkside, 112 ... E 2
Payton, 204 .... B 2
Pelican Narrows, 265 . N 3
Pelly, 426 ...... K 4
Pennant, 215 ... C 5
Pense, 270 ..... G 5
Perdue, 411 .... D 3
Piapot, 160 .... B 6
Pierceland, 271 . K 1
Pilger, 109 ..... F 3
Pilot Butte, 403 . G 5
Pine House, 427 . M 3
Pleasantdale, 153 . G 3
Plenty, 208 .... C 4
Plunkett, 152 .. F 4
Ponteix, 786 ... D 6
Porcupine Plain, 830 . H 3

Preeceville, 1,118 ...... J 4
Prelate, 407 .... B 5
Prince Albert, 28,464 .. F 2
Prud'homme, 260 ..... F 3
Punnichy, 451 .... G 4
Qu'Appelle, 451 ...... H 5
Quill Lake, 566 .... G 3
Quinton, 195 .... G 4
Rabbit Lake, 206 ..... D 2
Radisson, 416 .... D 3
Radville, 1,024 .... G 6
Rama, 188 .... H 4
Raymore, 523 .... G 4
Redvers, 846 .... K 6
Regina (cap.), 139,469 . G 5
Regina †140,734 ..... G 5
Regina Beach, 334 ... G 5
Regway, 19 .... G 6
Reserve, 153 .... J 3
Rhein, 295 .... J 4
Rhineland, 84 .... D 5
Riceton, 112 .... G 5
Richmound, 208 .... B 5
Ridgedale, 169 ..... H 2
Riverhurst, 264 ..... E 5
Rocanville, 891 ..... K 5
Roche Percée, 167 ... J 6
Rockglen, 550 ...... F 6
Rosetown, 2,614 .... D 4
Rose Valley, 591 .... H 3
Rosthern, 1,431 ..... E 3
Rouleau, 395 .... G 5

Rush Lake, 162 .... D 5
Saint Benedict, 193 ... F 3
Saint Brieux, 367 ..... G 3
Saint Front, 92 .... G 3
Saint Gregor, 125 .... G 3
Saint Louis, 387 ..... F 3
Saint Victor, 85 ..... F 6
Saint Walburg, 656 .. B 2
Saltcoats, 509 ...... J 4
Sandy Bay, 494 ..... N 3
Saskatoon, 126,449 . E 3
Saskatoon, ‡126,449 . E 3
Sceptre, 234 .... B 5
Scott, 254 .... C 3
Sedley, 268 .... H 5
Semans, 331 ...... G 4
Senlac, 94 .... B 3
Shamrock, 105 .... E 5
Shaunavon, 2,244 . C 6
Sheho, 320 .... H 4
Shellbrook, 1,048 . E 2
Shell Lake, 255 ... D 2
Simmie, 100 ...... C 6
Simpson, 239 ..... F 4
Sintaluta, 272 .... H 5
Smeaton, 315 .... G 2
Smiley, 124 ...... B 4
Snowden, 87 .... G 2
Sonningdale, 106 . D 3
Southey, 548 .... G 5
Sovereign, 91 ... D 4
Spalding, 329 ... G 3

CITIES and TOWNS

Abbey, 246 .... C 5
Aberdeen, 288 .... E 3
Abernethy, 253 .... H 5
Air Ronge, 239 .... M 3
Alameda, 370 .... J 6
Alida, 230 .... K 6
Allan, 712 .... E 4
Alsask, 819 .... B 4
Alvena, 143 .... E 3
Aneroid, 163 .... D 6
Annaheim, 182 .... G 3
Antler, 115 .... K 6
Arborfield, 418 .... H 2
Archerwill, 302 .... H 3
Arcola, 539 .... J 6
Arran, 120 .... K 4
Asquith, 355 .... D 3
Assiniboia, 2,675 .... E 6
Avonlea, 391 .... G 5
Aylesbury, 88 .... F 5
Aylsham, 170 .... H 2
Balcarres, 678 ...... H 5
Balgonie, 518 ...... G 5
Batoche, 27 .... E 3
Battleford, 1,803 ... C 3
Beatty, 97 .... G 3
Beauval, 436 ...... L 3
Beechy, 342 ...... D 5
Bellevue, 122 ..... F 3
Bengough, 650 ... F 6
Bethune, 291 .... F 5
Bienfait, 823 .... J 6
Biggar, 2,607 ... C 3
Big River, 836 .. D 2
Birch Hills, 696 . F 3
Birsay, 123 ..... D 4
Bjorkdale, 223 .. H 3
Black Lake, 471 . M 2
Bladworth, 125 . E 4
Blaine Lake, 671 . D 3
Borden, 187 .... D 3
Bradwell, 100 ... E 4
Bredenbury, 472 . K 5
Briercrest, 130 .. F 5
Broadview, 959 .. J 5
Brock, 205 ...... C 4
Broderick, 115 ... E 4
Brownlee, 121 ... F 5
Bruno, 728 ...... F 3
Buchanan, 442 ... J 4
Buffalo Narrows, 794 . L 3
Bulyea, 109 ..... G 5
Burstall, 507 .... B 5
Cabri, 737 ...... C 5
Cadillac, 217 ... D 6
Calder, 186 .... K 4
Camsell Portage, 87 . L 2

Cando, 193 .... C 3
Canoe Lake, 138 .... L 3
Canora, 2,603 .... J 4
Canwood, 325 .... E 2
Carievale, 229 .... K 6
Carlyle, 1,101 .... J 6
Carmel, 90 .... F 3
Carnduff, 1,075 ...... K 6
Caron, 96 .... F 5
Carragana, 137 ..... J 3
Carrot River, 953 ... H 2
Central Butte, 522 .. E 5
Ceylon, 279 .... G 6
Chamberlain, 161 .. F 5
Chaplin, 368 ...... E 5
Chelan, 101 ...... H 3
Chitek Lake, 131 . D 2
Choiceland, 456 .. G 2
Christopher Lake, 143 . F 2
Churchbridge, 973 . J 5
Clair, 86 .... G 3
Clavet, 482 ...... E 4
Climax, 341 ..... C 6
Cochin, 163 ..... C 2
Coderre, 161 .... E 5
Codette, 175 .... H 2
Coleville, 482 ... B 4
Colonsay, 526 ... F 4
Conquest, 261 .. E 4
Consul, 205 .... B 6
Coronach, 379 .. F 6
Craik, 503 ..... F 5
Crane Valley, 84 . F 6
Craven, 126 .... G 5
Creelman, 197 .. H 6
Creighton, 1,857 . N 4
Crooked River, 106 . H 3
Cudworth, 799 .. F 3
Cupar, 573 ..... H 5
Cutbank, 217 ... E 4
Cut Knife, 560 . B 3
Dalmeny, 417 .. E 3
Davidson, 1,043 . F 4
Debden, 340 ... E 2
Delisle, 653 .... D 4
Delmas, 161 ... C 3
Denare Beach, 235 . M 4
Denzil, 287 .... B 3
Deschambault Lake, 127 . M 3
Dilke, 130 ..... F 5
Dinsmore, 421 . D 4
Dodsland, 404 . C 4
Dollard, 92 .... C 6
Domremy, 253 . F 3
Dorintosh, 87 . L 1
Drake, 238 .... F 4
Drinkwater, 118 . F 5
Dubuc, 153 ... J 5
Duck Lake, 584 . E 3
Duff, 90 ..... H 5
Dundurn, 354 . E 4

Agriculture, Industry and Resources

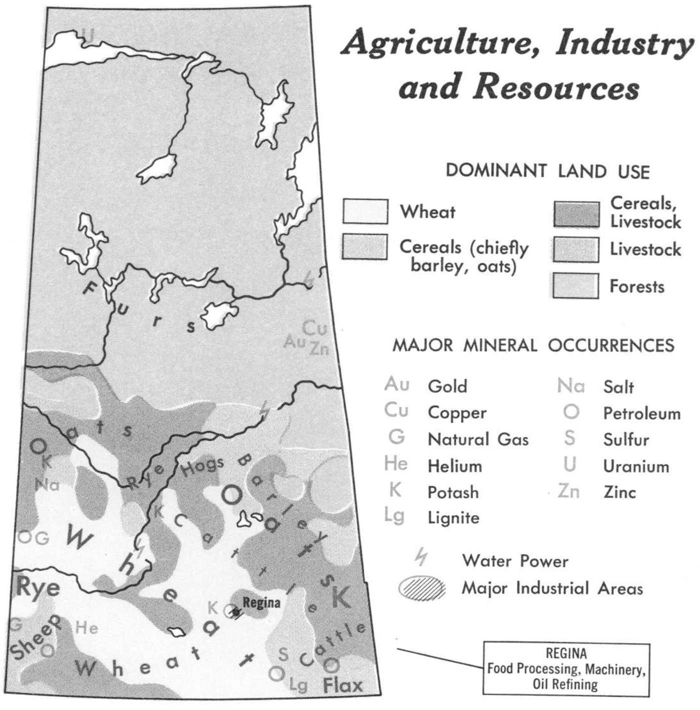

DOMINANT LAND USE

- Wheat
- Cereals (chiefly barley, oats)
- Cereals, Livestock
- Livestock
- Forests

MAJOR MINERAL OCCURRENCES

Au	Gold	Na	Salt
Cu	Copper	O	Petroleum
G	Natural Gas	S	Sulfur
He	Helium	U	Uranium
K	Potash	Zn	Zinc
Lg	Lignite		

⚡ Water Power

▨ Major Industrial Areas

REGINA
Food Processing, Machinery, Oil Refining

AREA 251,700 sq. mi.
POPULATION 926,242 ('71); 921,323 ('76)
CAPITAL Regina
LARGEST CITY Regina
HIGHEST POINT Cypress Hills 4,546 ft.
SETTLED IN 1774
ADMITTED TO CONFEDERATION 1905
PROVINCIAL FLOWER Prairie Lily

SASKATCHEWAN
NORTHERN PART

SASKATCHEWAN
SOUTHERN PART

SCALE
0 5 10 20 40 60 MI.
0 5 10 20 40 60 KM.

Provincial Capital ⊛
International Boundaries
Provincial Boundaries

© C.S. Hammond & Co., N.Y.

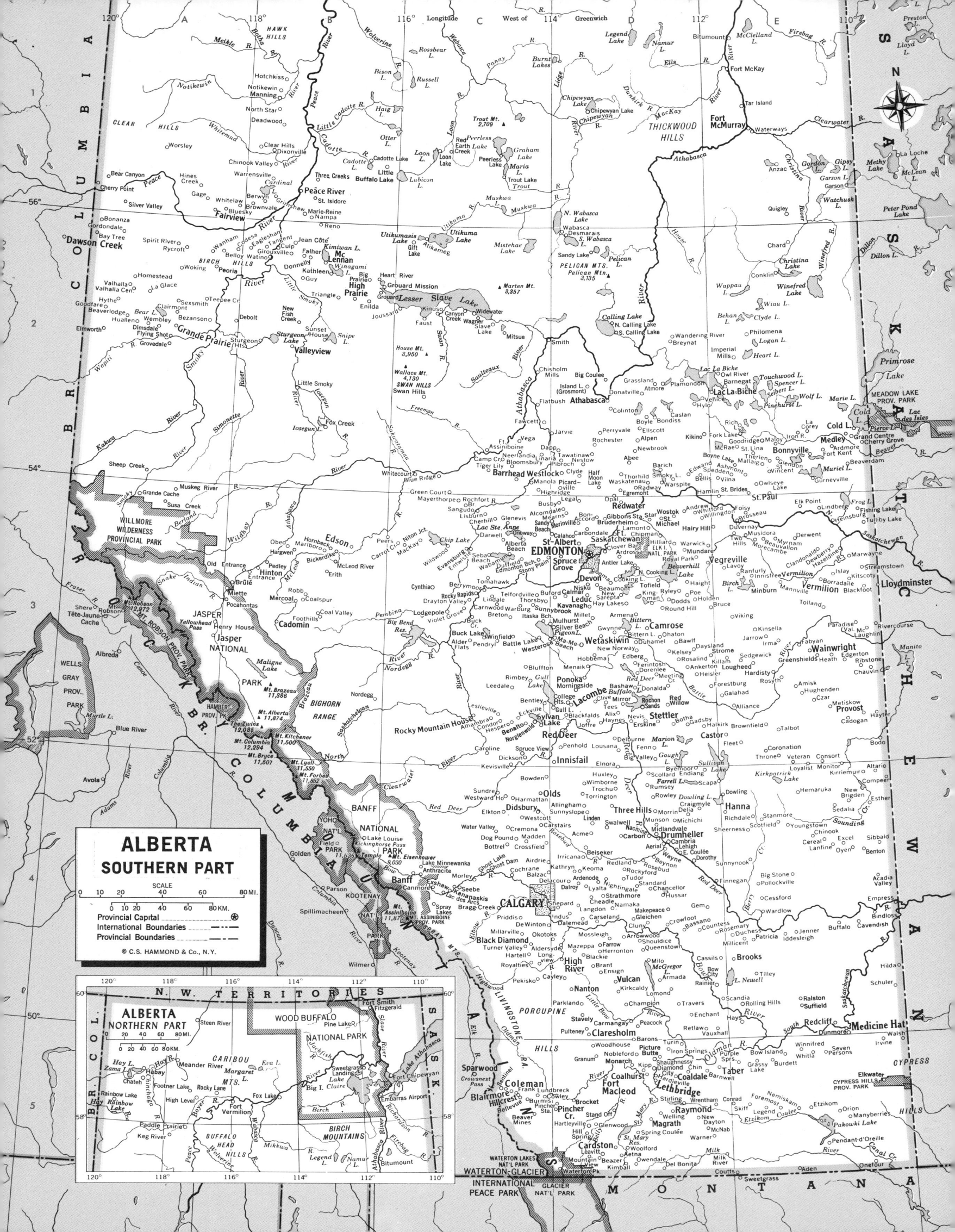

ALBERTA
SOUTHERN PART

SCALE
0 10 20   40   60   80 MI.
0 10 20   40   60   80 KM.

Provincial Capital .... ⊗
International Boundaries ....
Provincial Boundaries ....

© C.S. HAMMOND & Co., N.Y.

ALBERTA
NORTHERN PART
20 40 60 80 MI.
20 40 60 80 KM.

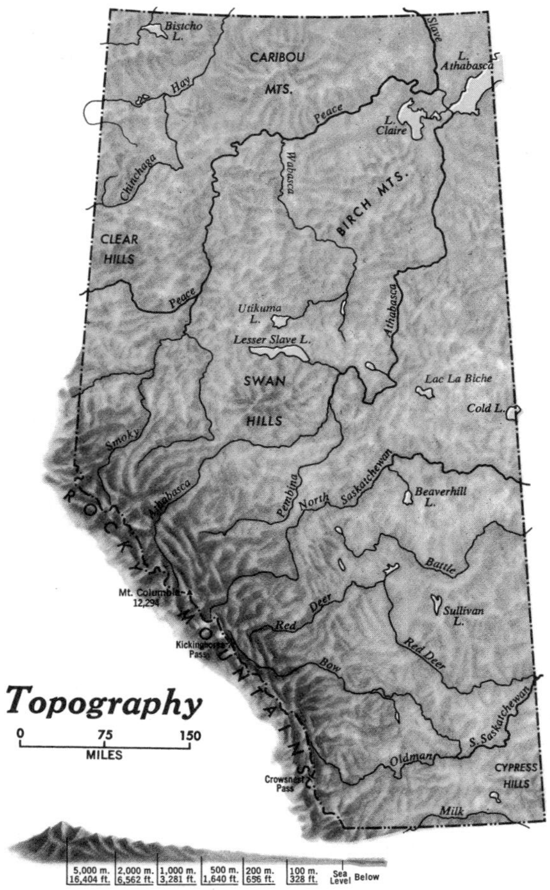
Bistcho L.
CARIBOU MTS.
Slave
L. Athabasca
Hay
Peace
L. Claire
Chinchaga
Wabasca
BIRCH MTS.
CLEAR HILLS
Peace
Utikuma L.
Lesser Slave L.
Athabasca
SWAN HILLS
Lac La Biche
Cold L.
Smoky
Athabasca
Pembina
North Saskatchewan
Beaverhill L.
Battle
Mt. Columbia 12,294
Red Deer
Sullivan L.
Kickinghorse Pass
Bow
Red Deer
S. Saskatchewan
Oldman
Crowsnest Pass
CYPRESS HILLS
Milk
ROCKY MOUNTAINS
0 75 150
MILES
5,000 m. 16,404 ft.
2,000 m. 6,562 ft.
1,000 m. 3,281 ft.
500 m. 1,640 ft.
200 m. 656 ft.
100 m. 328 ft.
Sea Level Below

Topography

AREA 255,285 sq. mi.
POPULATION 1,627,874 ('71); 1,838,037 ('76)
CAPITAL Edmonton
LARGEST CITY Edmonton
HIGHEST POINT Mt. Columbia 12,294 ft.
SETTLED IN 1861
ADMITTED TO CONFEDERATION 1905
PROVINCIAL FLOWER Wild Rose

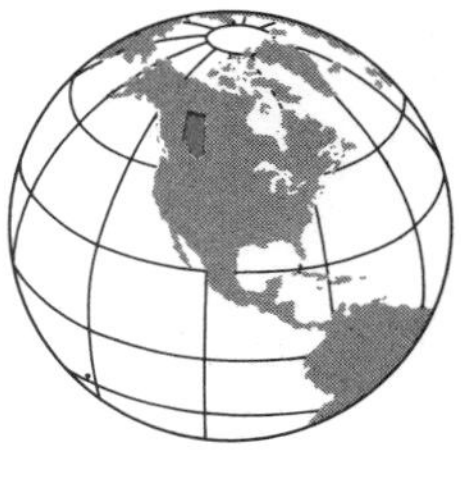

CITIES and TOWNS

Acadia Valley, 166	E 4
Acme, 300	D 4
Aerial, 151	D 4
Airdrie, 1,089	C 4
Alberta Beach, 320	C 3
Alder Flats, 133	C 3
Alix, 565	D 3
Alliance, 230	E 3
Amisk, 134	E 3
Andrew, 466	D 3
Anzac, 114	E 1
Ardmore, 230	E 2
Ardrossan, 137	D 3
Arrowwood, 166	D 4
Ashmont, 150	E 2
Athabasca, 1,765	D 2
Atikameg, 117	C 2
Banff, 3,219	C 4
Barnwell, 341	D 5
Barons, 237	D 4
Barrhead, 2,803	C 2
Bashaw, 757	D 3
Bassano, 861	D 4
Bawlf, 182	D 3
Beaumont, 337	D 3
Beaverlodge, 1,157	A 2
Beiseker, 414	D 4
Bellevue, 1,242	C 5
Bentley, 621	C 3
Berwyn, 474	B 1
Big Valley, 306	D 3
Black Diamond, 945	C 4
Blackfalds, 904	D 3
Blackfoot, 175	E 3
Blackie, 168	D 4
Blairmore, 2,037	C 5
Blue Ridge, 239	C 2
Bluesky, 124	A 1
Bon Accord, 332	D 3
Bonnyville, 2,587	E 2
Bowden, 560	C 4
Bow Island, 1,159	E 5
Boyle, 460	D 2
Bragg Creek, 203	C 4
Breton, 352	C 3
Brooks, 3,986	E 4
Brownvale, 161	B 1
Bruce, 110	E 3
Bruderheim, 350	D 3
Brûlé, 104	B 3
Buck Lake, 159	C 3
Burdett, 206	E 5
Cadomin, 109	B 3
Cadotte Lake, 192	B 1
Calgary, 403,319	C 4
Calgary, ‡403,319	C 4
Calmar, 799	D 3
Camrose, 8,673	D 3
Canmore, 1,538	C 4
Canyon Creek, 205	C 2
Carbon, 343	D 4
Carbondale, 115	D 3
Cardston, 2,685	D 5
Carmangay, 230	D 4
Caroline, 339	C 3
Carseland, 105	D 4
Carstairs, 884	D 4
Caslan, 117	D 2
Castor, 1,166	D 3
Cayley, 122	D 4
Cereal, 220	E 4
Champion, 335	D 4
Chateh, 400	A 5
Chauvin, 349	E 3
Chipewyan Lake, 118	D 1
Chipman, 181	D 3
Clairmont, 309	A 2
Clandonald, 119	E 3
Claresholm, 2,935	D 4
Clive, 247	D 3
Clyde, 233	D 2
Coaldale, 2,798	D 5
Coalhurst, 426	D 5
Cochrane, 1,046	C 4
Cold Lake, 1,309	E 2
Coleman, 1,534	C 5
Colinton, 125	D 2
College Heights, 331	D 3
Conklin, 119	E 2
Consort, 659	E 3
Cooking Lake, 196	D 3
Coronation, 877	E 3
Coutts, 407	D 5
Cowley, 201	D 5
Cremona, 186	C 4
Crossfield, 638	C 4
Czar, 196	E 3
Daysland, 593	D 3
Delburne, 383	D 3
Delia, 241	D 4
Derwent, 203	E 3
Desmarais, 258	D 2
Devon, 1,468	D 3
Dewberry, 160	E 3
Didsbury, 1,821	C 4
Dixonville, 113	B 1
Donalda, 232	D 3
Donnelly, 274	B 2
Drayton Valley, 3,900	C 3
Drumheller, 5,446	D 4
Duchess, 228	E 4
Eaglesham, 218	B 2
East Coulée, 312	D 4
Eckville, 660	C 3
Edberg, 145	D 3
Edgerton, 296	E 3
Edmonton (cap.), 438,152	D 3
Edmonton, ‡495,702	D 3
Edmonton Beach, 148	C 3
Edson, 3,818	B 3
Elk Point, 729	E 3
Elnora, 213	D 3
Empress, 266	E 4
Enilda, 201	B 2
Entwistle, 353	C 3
Erskine, 233	D 3
Evansburg, 528	C 3
Exshaw, 548	C 4
Fairview, 2,109	A 1
Falher, 918	B 2
Faust, 353	C 2
Fawcett, 141	C 2
Ferintosh, 127	D 3
Foremost, 568	E 5
Forestburg, 669	E 3
Fort Assiniboine, 173	C 2
Fort Chipewyan, 1,122	C 5
Fort Kent, 113	E 2
Fort Macleod, 2,715	D 5
Fort McKay, 200	E 1
Fort McMurray, 6,847	E 1
Fort Saskatchewan, 5,726	D 3
Fort Vermilion, 740	B 5
Fox Creek, 1,281	B 2
Frank, 224	C 5
Galahad, 179	E 3
Garden River, 134	B 5
Gibbons, 551	D 3
Gift Lake, 379	C 2
Girouxville, 347	B 2
Gleichen, 367	D 4
Glendon, 354	E 2
Glenwood, 200	D 5
Grand Centre, 2,088	E 2
Grande Cache, 2,525	A 3
Grande Prairie, 13,079	A 2
Granum, 324	D 5
Grassy Lake, 196	E 5
Grimshaw, 1,714	B 1
Grouard Mission, 277	C 2
Halkirk, 136	D 3
Hanna, 2,545	E 4
Hardieville, 473	D 5
Hardisty, 594	E 3
Hay Lakes, 211	D 3
Heisler, 199	D 3
High Level, 1,614	A 5
High Prairie, 2,354	B 2
High River, 2,676	D 4
Hillcrest, 613	C 5
Hill Spring, 213	D 5
Hines Creek, 438	A 1
Hinton, 4,911	B 3
Holden, 448	D 3
Hughenden, 267	E 3
Hussar, 170	D 4
Hythe, 487	A 2
Imperial Mills, 118	E 2
Innisfail, 2,474	D 3
Innisfree, 252	E 3
Irma, 423	E 3
Irricana, 139	D 4
Irvine, 194	E 5
Jarvie, 104	D 2
Jasper, 2,932	B 3
Joussard, 269	B 2
Kikino, 202	D 2
Killam, 851	E 3
Kinuso, 267	C 2
Kitscoty, 320	E 3
Lac La Biche, 1,791	E 2
Lacombe, 3,436	D 3
Lake Louise, 165	B 4
Lamont, 899	D 3
Langdon, 109	D 4
Lavoy, 114	E 3
Leduc, 4,000	D 3
Legal, 563	D 3
Leslieville, 159	C 3
Lethbridge, 41,217	D 5
Linden, 226	D 4
Little Buffalo Lake, 165	B 1
Lloydminster, 4,738	E 3
Lodgepole, 144	C 3
Lomond, 165	D 4
Longview, 189	C 4
Loon Lake, 135	C 1
Lougheed, 217	E 3
Lundbreck, 113	C 5
Magrath, 1,215	D 5
Mallaig, 190	E 2
Manning, 1,071	B 1
Mannville, 646	E 3
Marlboro, 156	B 3
Marwayne, 351	E 3
Mayerthorpe, 1,036	C 3
McLennan, 1,090	B 2
Meander River, 233	A 5
Medicine Hat, 26,518	E 4
Midlandvale, 392	D 4
Milk River, 775	D 5
Millet, 456	D 3
Milo, 117	D 4
Minburn, 106	E 3
Mirror, 365	D 3
Monarch, 102	D 5
Morinville, 1,475	D 3
Morrin, 197	D 4
Mulhurst, 139	D 3
Mundare, 511	D 3
Myrnam, 403	E 3
Nacmine, 350	D 4
Nampa, 283	B 1
Nanton, 991	D 4
Newbrook, 154	D 2
New Norway, 200	D 3
New Sarepta, 202	D 3
Nobleford, 401	D 5
North Calling Lake, 103	D 2
Okotoks, 1,247	C 4
Olds, 3,376	D 4
Onoway, 496	C 3
Oyen, 929	E 4
Paradise Valley, 144	E 3
Peace River, 5,039	B 1
Peerless Lake, 134	C 1
Peers, 129	B 3
Penhold, 452	D 3
Pibroch, 112	D 2
Picardville, 130	D 2
Picture Butte, 1,008	D 5
Pincher Creek, 3,227	D 5
Plamondon, 189	D 2
Pollockville, 29	E 4
Ponoka, 4,414	D 3
Provost, 1,489	E 3
Radway, 170	D 2
Rainbow Lake, 355	A 5
Ralston, 475	E 4
Ranfurly, 110	E 3
Raymond, 2,156	D 5
Redcliff, 2,255	E 4
Red Deer, 27,674	D 3
Redwater, 1,287	D 3
Rimbey, 1,450	C 3
Robb, 256	B 3
Rochester, 111	D 2
Rockyford, 286	D 4
Rocky Mountain House, 2,968	C 3
Rolling Hills, 127	E 4
Rosalind, 203	D 3
Rosemary, 208	E 4
Rycroft, 461	A 2
Ryley, 428	D 3
Saint Albert, 11,800	D 3
Saint Paul, 4,161	E 3
Sangudo, 360	C 3
Seba Beach, 165	C 3
Sedgewick, 730	E 3
Seebe, 108	C 4
Sexsmith, 559	A 2
Shaughnessy, 323	D 5
Sherwood Park, 14,282	D 3
Slave Lake, 2,052	C 2
Smith, 445	D 2
Smoky Lake, 881	D 2
Spirit River, 1,091	A 2
Spruce Grove, 3,029	D 3
Spruce View, 104	C 3
Standard, 267	D 4
Stavely, 351	D 4
Stettler, 4,168	D 3
Stirling, 436	D 5
Stony Plain, 1,770	C 3
Strathmore, 1,148	D 4
Strome, 226	E 3
Sundre, 933	C 4
Swan Hills, 1,376	C 2
Sylvan Lake, 1,597	C 3
Taber, 4,765	E 5
Thorhild, 509	D 2
Thorsby, 595	C 3
Three Hills, 1,354	D 4
Tilley, 270	E 4
Tofield, 924	D 3
Torrington, 118	D 4
Trochu, 739	D 4
Trout Lake, 162	C 1
Turin, 102	D 5
Turner Valley, 766	C 4
Two Hills, 979	E 3
Valleyview, 1,708	B 2
Vauxhall, 1,016	D 4
Vegreville, 3,691	E 3
Vermilion, 2,915	E 3
Veteran, 267	E 3
Viking, 1,178	E 3
Vilna, 303	E 2
Vulcan, 1,384	D 4
Wabamun, 336	C 3
Wabasca, 172	D 2
Wainwright, 3,872	E 3
Wanham, 268	A 2
Warburg, 464	C 3
Warner, 408	D 5
Warspite, 110	D 2
Waskatenau, 233	D 2
Waterton Park, 236	D 5
Wembley, 348	A 2
Westlock, 3,246	C 2
Westward Ho, 104	C 4
Wetaskiwin, 6,267	D 3
Whitecourt, 3,202	C 2
Whitelaw, 192	A 1
Widewater, 126	C 2
Wildwood, 386	C 3
Willingdon, 325	E 3
Winfield, 209	C 3
Youngstown, 305	E 4

OTHER FEATURES

Alberta (mt.)	B 3
Assiniboine (mt.)	C 4
Athabasca (lake)	C 5
Athabasca (riv.)	D 1
Banff Nat'l Park, 3,532	B 4
Battle (riv.)	D 3
Beaverhill (lake)	D 3
Belly (riv.)	D 5
Berry (creek)	E 4
Biche (lake)	E 2
Big Bend (res.)	C 3
Bighorn (range)	B 3
Birch (hills)	A 2
Birch (lake)	E 3
Birch (mts.)	B 5
Bow (riv.)	D 4
Boyer (riv.)	A 5
Brazeau (mt.)	B 3
Brazeau (riv.)	B 3
Buffalo (lake)	D 3
Buffalo Head (hills)	B 5
Cadotte (riv.)	B 1
Calling (lake)	D 2
Caribou (mts.)	B 5
Chinchaga (riv.)	A 5
Chip (lake)	C 3
Chipewyan (riv.)	D 1
Christina (riv.)	E 1
Claire (lake)	B 5
Clear (hills)	A 1
Clearwater (riv.)	C 4
Clearwater (riv.)	E 1
Cold (lake)	E 2
Columbia (mt.)	B 3
Crowsnest (pass)	C 5
Cypress (hills)	E 5
Cypress Hills Prov. Park	E 5
Eisenhower (mt.)	C 4
Elbow (riv.)	C 4
Elk Island Nat'l Park, 46	D 3
Etzikom Coulee (riv.)	E 5
Firebag (riv.)	E 1
Forbes (mt.)	B 4
Frog (lake)	E 3
Gordon (lake)	E 1
Gough (lake)	D 3
Graham (lake)	C 1
Gull (lake)	C 3
Hawk (hills)	B 1
Hay (riv.)	A 5
Highwood (riv.)	C 4
Iosegun (lake)	B 2
Jasper Nat'l Park, 3,064	A 3
Kickinghorse (pass)	B 4
Kimiwan (lake)	B 2
Kitchener (mt.)	B 3
Lesser Slave (lake)	C 2
Little Bow (riv.)	D 4
Little Smoky (riv.)	B 2
Livingstone (range)	C 4
Lyell (mt.)	B 4
Maligne (lake)	B 3
McGregor (lake)	D 4
McLeod (riv.)	B 3
Milk (riv.)	D 5
Muriel (lake)	E 2
Muskwa (riv.)	C 1
North Saskatchewan (riv.)	E 3
North Wabasca (lake)	D 1
Notikewin (riv.)	A 1
Oldman (riv.)	D 5
Pakowki (lake)	E 5
Peace (riv.)	B 1
Peerless (lake)	C 1
Pelican (mts.)	D 2
Pembina (riv.)	C 3
Pigeon (lake)	D 3
Porcupine (hills)	C 4
Red Deer (riv.)	D 4
Rocky (mts.)	C 4
Rosebud (riv.)	D 4
Sainte Anne (lake)	C 3
Saint Mary (riv.)	D 5
Saulteaux (riv.)	C 2
Slave (riv.)	C 5
Smoky (riv.)	A 2
Sounding (creek)	E 4
South Saskatchewan (riv.)	E 4
South Wabasca (lake)	D 2
Spray (mts.)	C 4
Sullivan (lake)	D 3
Swan (hills)	C 2
Temple (mt.)	B 4
The Twins (mt.)	B 3
Thickwood (hills)	D 1
Utikuma (lake)	C 2
Vermilion (riv.)	E 3
Wabasca (riv.)	C 1
Waterton-Glacier Int'l Peace Park, 259	C 5
Waterton Lakes Nat'l Park, 259	C 5
Whitemud (riv.)	A 1
Willmore Wilderness Prov. Park	A 3
Winagami (lake)	B 2
Winefred (lake)	E 2
Wood Buffalo Nat'l Park, 186	B 5
Yellowhead (pass)	A 3

‡ Population of metropolitan area.

Agriculture, Industry and Resources

DOMINANT LAND USE

- Wheat
- Cereals (chiefly barley, oats)
- Cereals, Livestock
- Dairy
- Pasture Livestock
- Range Livestock
- Forests
- Nonagricultural Land

MAJOR MINERAL OCCURRENCES

- C Coal
- G Natural Gas
- Na Salt
- O Petroleum
- S Sulfur
- Water Power
- Major Industrial Areas

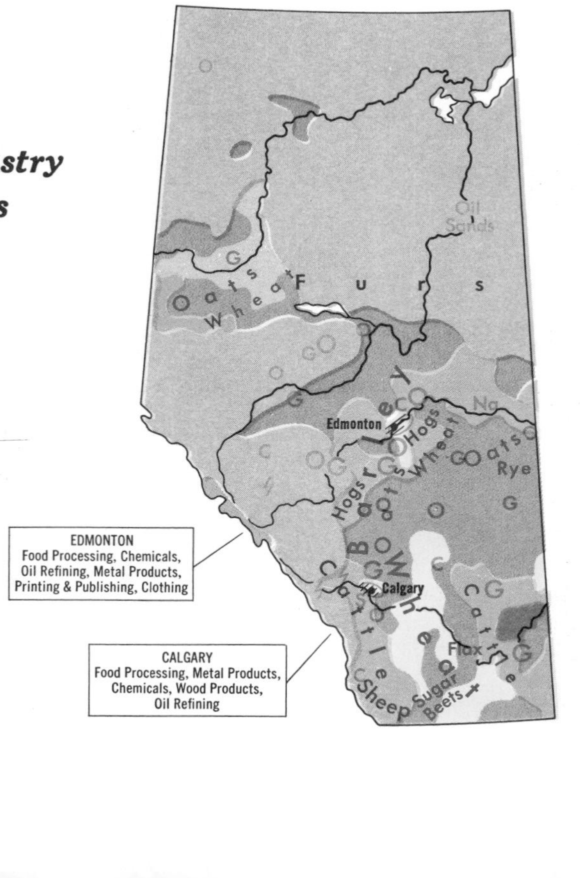
Oil Sands
Furs
Oats
Wheat
Edmonton
Hogs
Barley
Oats
Wheat
Rye
Calgary
Cattle
Flax
Sheep
Sugar Beets
EDMONTON
Food Processing, Chemicals, Oil Refining, Metal Products, Printing & Publishing, Clothing
CALGARY
Food Processing, Metal Products, Chemicals, Wood Products, Oil Refining

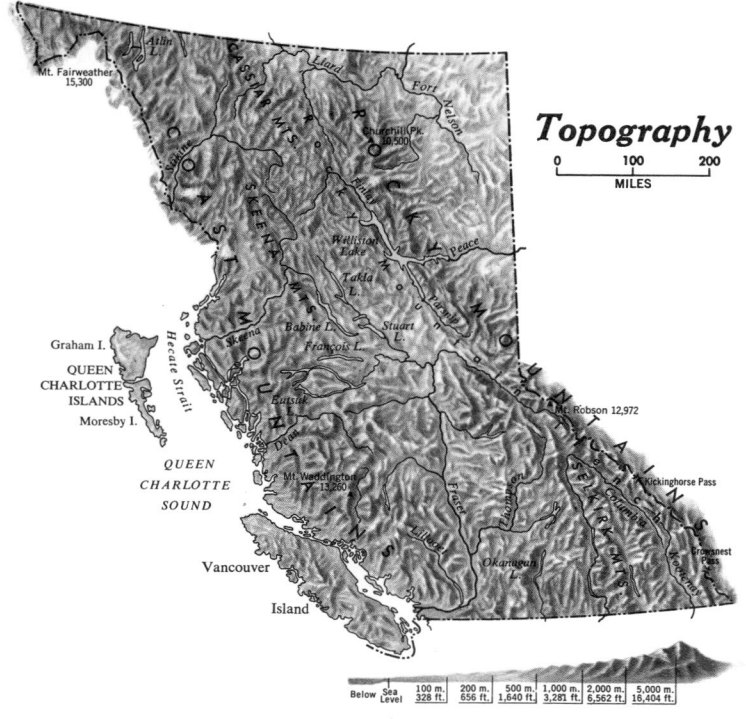

Topography

0   100   200
MILES

Below Sea Level | 100 m. 328 ft. | 200 m. 656 ft. | 500 m. 1,640 ft. | 1,000 m. 3,281 ft. | 2,000 m. 6,562 ft. | 5,000 m. 16,404 ft.

Agriculture, Industry and Resources

KITIMAT Aluminum

VANCOUVER–VICTORIA
Wood Products, Food Processing, Iron & Steel, Metal Products, Printing & Publishing, Shipbuilding, Oil Refining

DOMINANT LAND USE

- Cereals, Livestock
- Dairy
- Fruits, Vegetables
- Pasture Livestock
- Forests
- Nonagricultural Land

MAJOR MINERAL OCCURRENCES

Ab	Asbestos	Gp	Gypsum
Ag	Silver	Mo	Molybdenum
Au	Gold	Ni	Nickel
C	Coal	O	Petroleum
Cu	Copper	Pb	Lead
Fe	Iron Ore	S	Sulfur
G	Natural Gas	Sn	Tin
		Zn	Zinc

⚡ Water Power
▨ Major Industrial Areas
□ Major Pulp & Paper Mills

CITIES and TOWNS

Abbotsford, 706 .... L 3
Albert Head, 330 .... J 4
Alert Bay, 760 .... D 5
Alexandria, 168 .... F 4
Armstrong, 1,648 .... H 5
Ashcroft, 1,916 .... G 5
Ashton Creek, 318 .... H 5
Athalmer, 255 .... K 5
Atlin, 258 .... J 1
Avola, 265 .... H 4
Balfour, 195 .... J 5
Barrière, 829 .... H 4
Bear Lake, 302 .... F 3
Beaverdell, 241 .... H 5
Bella Coola, 273 .... D 4
Big Eddy, 654 .... H 4
Birch Island, 219 .... H 4
Blue River, 475 .... H 4
Boston Bar, 548 .... G 5
Bowen Island, 351 .... K 3
Bowser, 169 .... H 2
Brackendale, 692 .... F 5
Bralorne, 379 .... F 5
Britannia Beach, 738 .... K 2
Brouse, 446 .... J 5
Burnaby, ●125,660 .... K 3
Burns Lake, 1,259 .... D 3
Cache Creek, 1,013 ...... G 5
Campbell River, ●10,000 .. E 5
Campbell River, 9,770 .... E 5
Canal Flats, 902 .... K 5
Cassiar, 1,073 .... K 2
Castlegar, 3,072 .... J 5
Cawston, 642 .... H 5
Caycuse, 297 .... J 3
Cedarside, 218 .... H 4
Celista, 178 .... H 4
Central Saanich, ●5,136 .. K 3
Charlie Lake, 214 .... G 2
Chase, 1,212 .... H 5
Chase River, 728 .... J 3
Chemainus, 2,129 .... J 3
Cherry Creek, 449 .... G 5
Cherryville, 284 .... H 5
Chetwynd, 1,260 .... G 2
Chilliwack, 9,135 .... M 3
Chilliwack, ●23,739 ...... M 3
Clearbrook, 3,653 .... L 3
Clearwater, 513 .... G 4
Clinton, 905 .... G 4
Coal Harbour, 334 .... D 5
Cobble Hill, 280 .... K 3
Coldstream, ●3,602 ...... H 5
Comox, 3,980 .... H 2
Coquitlam, ●53,073 ...... K 3
Courtenay, 7,152 .... E 5
Cranbrook, 12,000 ...... K 5
Crawford Bay, 244 ...... J 5
Creston, 3,204 .... K 5
Crofton, 972 .... J 3
Cultus Lake, 554 .... M 3
Cumberland, 1,718 ...... E 5
Dawson Creek, 11,885 .. G 2
Delta, ●45,860 .... K 3
Departure Bay, 3,744 .... J 3
Donald, 235 .... J 4
Duncan, 4,388 .... J 3
East Kelowna, 826 ...... H 5
Eddontenajon, 180 ...... K 2

Edgewater, 346 .... J 5
Elko, 196 .... K 5
Endako, 242 .... E 3
Enderby, 1,158 .... H 5
Errington, 464 .... J 3
Esquimalt, ●12,922 ...... K 4
Extension, 181 .... J 3
Falkland, 375 .... H 5
Fernie, 4,422 .... K 5
Field, 358 .... J 4
Flood, 295 .... M 3
Forest Grove, 238 .... G 4
Fort Fraser, 385 .... E 3
Fort Langley, 1,342 ...... L 3
Fort Nelson, 2,289 ...... M 2
Fort Saint James, 1,483 .. E 3
Fort Saint John, 8,264 .... G 2
Franklin River, 187 ...... H 3
Fraser Lake, 1,292 ...... E 3
Fraser Mills, ●157 ...... K 3
Fruitvale, 1,379 .... J 5
Gabriola Island, 655 .... J 3
Galiano Island, 412 ...... K 3
Ganges, 333 .... K 3
Gibsons, 1,934 .... K 3
Gillies Bay, 543 .... H 2
Giscome, 416 .... F 3
Gold River, 1,896 .... D 5
Golden, 3,012 .... J 4
Grand Forks, 3,173 ...... H 6
Granisle, 451 .... D 3
Granthams Landing, 404 .. J 3
Greenwood, 868 .... H 5
Grindrod, 283 .... H 5
Hagensborg, 315 .... D 4
Haney, 3,221 .... L 3
Harrison Hot Springs, 598 .. M 3
Hatzic, 547 .... L 3
Hazelton, 351 .... D 2
Hedley, 385 .... G 5
Heffley Creek, 503 ...... G 5
Hendrix Lake, 341 ...... G 4
Heriot Bay, 187 .... E 5
Hixon, 385 .... F 3
Holberg, 333 .... C 5
Honeymoon Bay, 546 .... J 3
Hope, 3,153 .... M 3
Houston, ●2,232 .... D 3
Houston, 905 .... D 3
Hudson Hope, 1,116 .... F 2
Hudson's Hope, ●1,741 .. F 2
Huntingdon, 202 .... L 3
Invermere, 1,065 ...... J 5
Ioco, 308 .... K 3
Jaffray, 193 .... K 5
Kaleden, 640 .... H 5
Kamloops, 26,168 ...... G 5
Kaslo, 755 .... J 5
Kelly Lake, 231 .... G 4
Kelowna, 19,412 .... H 5
Kemano, 346 .... D 3
Kent, ●2,966 .... M 3
Keremeos, 605 .... G 5
Kimberley, 7,641 ...... K 5
Kinnaird, 2,846 .... J 5
Kitimat, 11,824 .... C 3
Kitsault, 343 .... C 2
Kitwanga, 217 .... D 2
Kokish, 222 .... D 5
Lac La Hache, 417 .... G 4
Ladysmith, 3,664 ...... J 3
Lake Cowichan, 2,364 .. J 3

Lang Bay, 285 .... E 5
Langley, ●21,936 .... L 3
Langley, 4,684 .... L 3
Lantzville, 565 .... G 5
Lillooet, 1,514 .... G 5
Lion's Bay, 396 .... K 3
Lone Butte, 206 .... G 4
Louis Creek, 289 ...... H 4
Lower Nicola, 361 ...... G 5
Lower Post, 206 .... K 1
Lumby, 940 .... H 5
Lytton, 494 .... G 5
Mackenzie, ●2,332 .... F 3
Mackenzie, 1,976 ...... F 2
Madeira Park, 351 .... J 3
Maple Bay, 509 .... K 3
Maple Ridge, ●24,476 .. L 3
Masset, 975 .... B 3
Matsqui, ●23,554 ...... L 3
Mayne Island, 293 .... J 3
McBride, 658 .... G 4
McConnell Creek, 233 .. D 2
McLure, 193 .... H 4
Merritt, 5,289 .... G 5
Merville, 227 .... E 5
Mesachie Lake, 266 .. J 3
Metchosin, 540 ...... K 3
Mica Creek, 772 ...... H 4
Midway, 502 .... H 6
Mill Bay, 347 .... J 2
Milnes Landing, 254 .. J 3
Mission, ●10,220 ...... L 3
Mission City, 3,649 .... L 3
Moberly, 175 .... J 4
Monte Lake, 176 ...... G 5
Montrose, 1,137 ...... J 5
Nakusp, 1,163 .... J 5
Nanaimo, 14,948 ...... J 3
Naramata, 461 .... H 5
Nelson, 9,400 .... J 5
New Denver, 644 ...... J 5
New Hazelton, 475 .... D 2
New Westminster, 42,835 .. K 3
Nicholson, 619 ...... J 4
Nicomen Island, 527 .. L 3
Nootka, 2 .... D 5
North Bend, 291 ...... G 5
North Cowichan, ●12,170 .. J 3
North Pender Island, 407 .. K 3
North Saanich, ●3,601 .. K 3
North Vancouver, ●57,861 .. K 3
North Vancouver, 31,847 .. K 3
Nukko Lake, 182 ...... F 3
Oak Bay, ●18,426 ...... K 4
Ocean Falls, 1,085 .... D 4
Okanagan Centre, 266 .. H 5
Okanagan Falls, 621 .... H 5
Okanagan Landing, 656 .. H 5
Okanagan Mission, 857 .. H 5
Old Barkerville, 3 ...... G 3
Oliver, 1,615 .... H 5
One Hundred Mile House, 1,120 .... G 4
Osoyoos, 1,285 ...... H 5
Oyama, 326 .... H 5
Parksville, 2,169 .... J 3
Parson, 306 .... J 4
Peachland, ●1,446 .... G 5
Penticton, 18,146 .... H 5
Pine Valley, 264 .... F 2
Pitt Meadows, ●2,771 .. L 3
Popkum, 286 .... M 3
Port Alberni, 20,063 .. H 3
Port Alice, 1,507 .... D 5
Port Clements, 406 .. B 3
Port Coquitlam, 19,560 .. L 3
Port Edward, 1,019 .. B 3
Port Hammond, 1,556 .. L 3
Port Hardy, ●1,761 .... D 5
Port McNeill, 934 .... D 5
Port Moody, 10,778 .. L 3
Port Renfrew, 362 .... J 3
Pouce-Coupé, 595 .... G 2
Powell River, ●13,726 .. E 5
Prince George, 33,101 .. F 3
Prince Rupert, 15,747 .. B 3
Princeton, 2,601 .... G 5
Procter, 183 .... J 5
Qualicum Beach, 1,245 .. J 3
Queen Charlotte, 665 .. A 3
Quesnel, 6,252 ...... F 4
Radium Hot Springs, 393 .. J 5
Rayleigh, 652 .... G 5
Revelstoke, 4,867 .... J 5
Richmond, ●62,121 .... K 3
Riondel, 572 .... J 5
Robson, 1,046 .... J 5
Rossland, 3,896 ...... H 6
Royston, 532 .... H 2
Rutland, 3,279 ...... H 5
Saanich, ●65,040 .... K 3
Salmo, 872 .... J 5
Salmon Arm, ●7,793 .. H 5
Salmon Arm, 1,981 .. H 5
Saltair, 1,008 ...... J 3
Sandspit, 459 .... B 3
Sardis, 1,194 .... M 3
Saseenos, 574 ...... J 3
Saturna Island, 174 .. K 3
Savona, 670 .... G 5
Sayward, 465 .... D 5
Sechelt, 590 .... J 2
Seventy Mile House, 225 .. G 4
Shawnigan Lake, 213 .. J 3
Shoreacres, 345 .... J 5
Sicamous, 814 ...... H 5
Sidney, 4,868 .... K 3
Silverton, 246 ...... J 5
Slocan, 346 .... J 5
Slocan Park, 360 .... J 5
Smithers, 3,864 .... D 3
Sointula, 575 .... D 5
Sooke, 836 .... J 4
Sorrento, 269 .... H 5
South Fort George, 1,282 .. F 3
South Hazelton, 483 .. D 2
South Slocan, 278 .... J 5

South Wellington, 460 .. J 3
Sparwood, 2,990 .... K 5
Sparwood, 2,154 .... K 5
Spences Bridge, 199 .... G 5
Sproat Lake, 321 .... H 3
Squamish, ●6,121 ...... F 5
Squamish, 1,597 .... F 5
Stewart, 1,357 .... C 2
Stoner, 182 .... F 3
Summerland, ●5,551 .... G 5
Surrey, ●98,601 .... K 3
Tahsis, 1,351 .... D 5
Tasu, 331 .... A 4
Taylor, 605 .... G 2
Telkwa, 712 .... D 3
Terrace, ●9,991 .... C 3
Terrace, 7,820 .... C 3
Thrums, 365 .... J 5
Tofino, 461 .... E 5
Trail, 11,149 .... J 6
Ucluelet, 1,018 .... E 5
Union Bay, 407 .... H 2
Upper Fraser, 339 ...... G 3
Valemount, 693 .... H 4
Valleyview, 3,787 ...... G 3
Vananda, 497 .... E 5
Vancouver, 426,256 .... K 3
Vancouver, ‡1,082,352 .. K 3
Vancouver (Greater), ●1,028,334 ...... K 3
Vanderhoof, 1,653 .... E 3
Vavenby, 331 .... H 4
Vernon, 13,283 .... H 5

Victoria (cap.), 61,761 .. K 4
Victoria, ‡195,800 ...... K 4
Warfield, 2,132 .... J 5
Wasa, 355 .... K 5
Wells, 409 .... G 3
Westbank, 747 .... H 5
West Vancouver, ●36,440 .. K 3
Westwold, 434 .... G 5
White Rock, 10,349 .... K 3
Williams Lake, 4,072 .. F 4
Willow River, 422 ...... F 3
Wilmer, 200 .... J 5
Wilson Creek, 408 .... J 2
Windermere, 421 ...... J 5
Winfield, 875 .... H 5
Winlaw, 383 .... J 5
Woodfibre, 408 .... K 2
Woss Lake, 394 ...... D 5
Wynndel, 579 .... J 5
Yahk, 192 .... J 5
Yale, 224 .... M 2
Yarrow, 1,039 .... M 3
Ymir, 292 .... J 5
Youbou, 1,109 .... J 3
Zeballos, 186 .... D 5

OTHER FEATURES

Adams (riv.) .... H 4
Alberni (inlet) .... H 3
Alsek (riv.) .... H 1

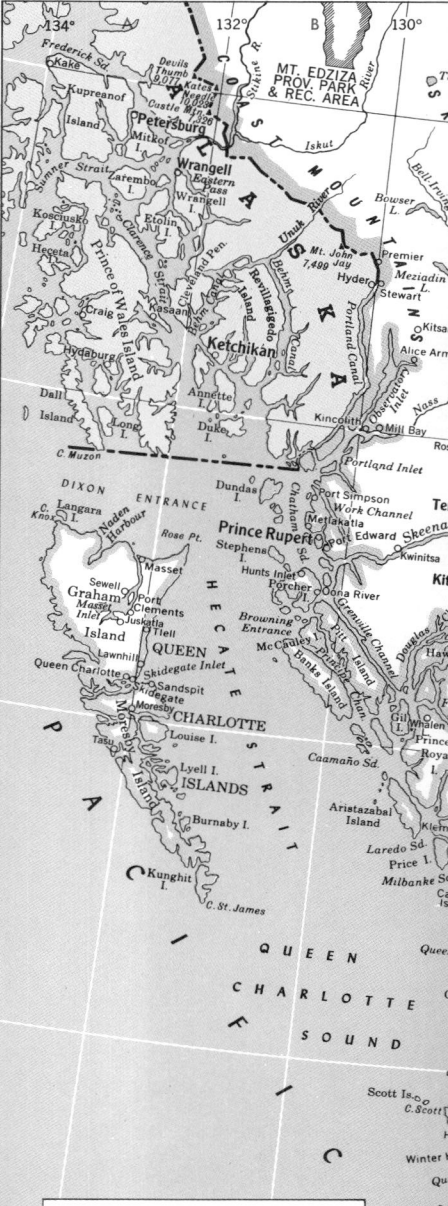

BRITISH COLUMBIA

SCALE
0 15 30 60 90 120 MI.
0 15 30 60 90 120 KM.

Provincial Capital .... ⊛
State Capital .... ◉
International Boundaries .... — ·· — ··
Provincial Boundaries ...... — · — ·

© C.S. HAMMOND & Co., N.Y.

AREA 366,255 sq. mi.
POPULATION 2,184,621 ('71); 2,466,608 ('76)
CAPITAL Victoria
LARGEST CITY Vancouver
HIGHEST POINT Mt. Fairweather 15,300 ft.
SETTLED IN 1806
ADMITTED TO CONFEDERATION 1871
PROVINCIAL FLOWER Dogwood

‡ Population of metropolitan area.
• Population of municipality.

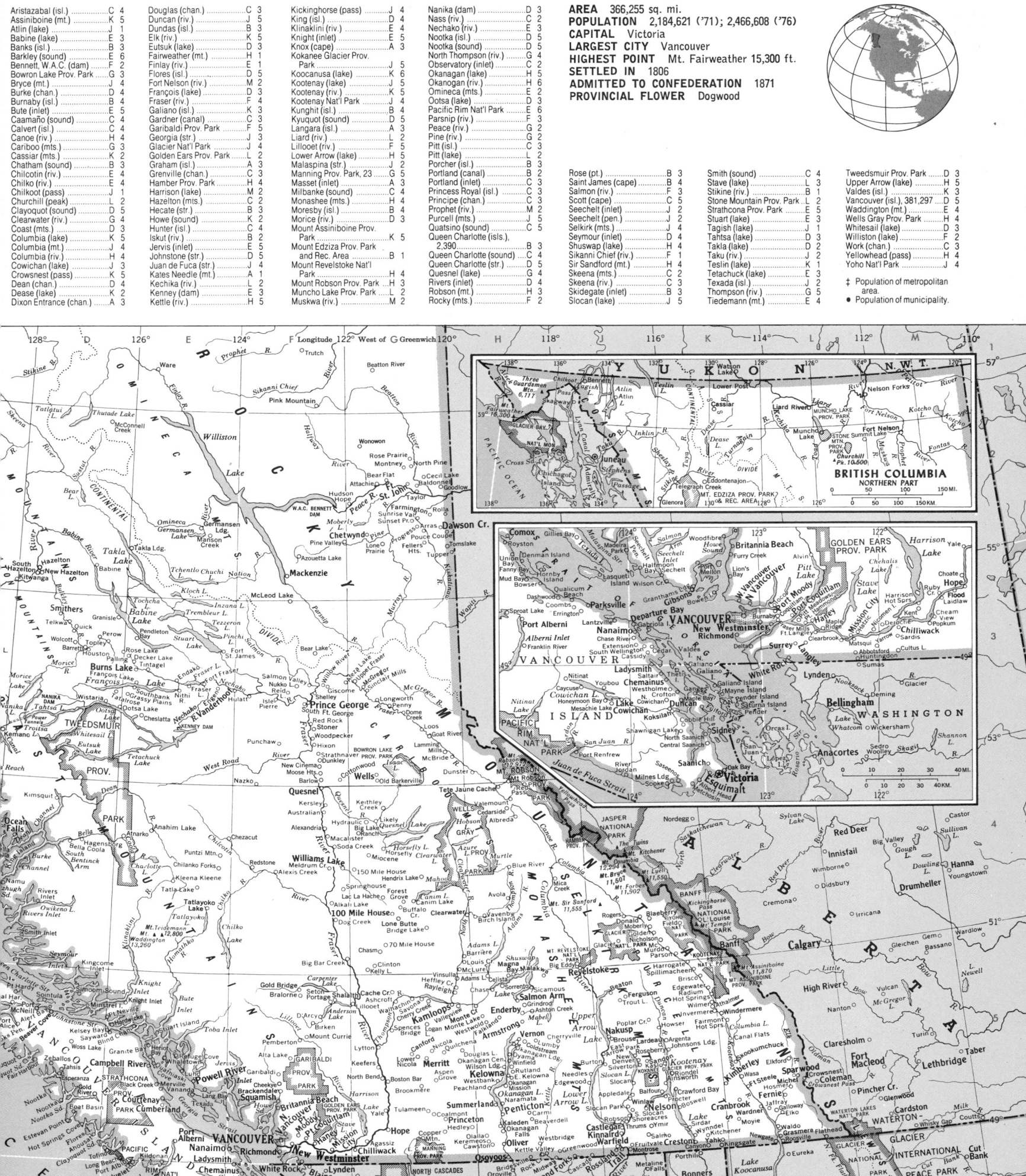

Topography

0 200 400
MILES

QUEEN ELIZABETH
ISLANDS

5,000 m. / 16,404 ft. — 2,000 m. / 6,562 ft. — 1,000 m. / 3,281 ft. — 500 m. / 1,640 ft. — 200 m. / 656 ft. — 100 m. / 328 ft. — Sea Level — Below

DOMINANT LAND USE

 Forests

Nonagricultural Land

MAJOR MINERAL OCCURRENCES

Ab	Asbestos	Cu	Copper
Ag	Silver	Fe	Iron Ore
Au	Gold	O	Petroleum
C	Coal	Pb	Lead
		Zn	Zinc

Agriculture, Industry and Resources

Prince Albert (pen.) .... G 2	Smith (bay) .... L 2
Prince Albert (sound) .... G 2	Smith (cape) .... L 3
Prince Charles (isl.) .... L 3	Smith (sound) .... L 2
Prince Gustav Adolf (sea) .... H 2	Snare (riv.) .... G 3
Prince of Wales (isl.) .... J 2	Snowbird (lake) .... H 3
Prince of Wales (str.) .... G 2	Somerset (isl.) .... J 2
Prince Patrick (isl.) .... F 2	South (bay) .... L 3
Prince Regent (inlet) .... J 2	Southampton (isl.) .... K 3
Queen Elizabeth (isls.) .... H 1	South Nahanni (riv.) .... F 3
Queen Maud (gulf) .... H 3	Stallworthy (cape) .... J 1
Queens (chan.) .... J 2	Steensby (inlet) .... K 2
Raanes (pen.) .... K 2	Stefansson (isl.) .... H 2
Rae (isth.) .... K 3	Sverdrup (chan.) .... J 1
Rae (riv.) .... G 3	Sverdrup (isls.) .... J 2
Rae (str.) .... J 3	Talbot (inlet) .... L 2
Ramparts (riv.) .... E 3	Taltson (riv.) .... G 3
Resolution (isl.) .... M 3	Tathlina (lake) .... G 3
Richard Collinson (inlet) .... G 2	Tha-anne (riv.) .... J 3
Richards (mts.) .... E 3	Thelon (riv.) .... H 3
Richardson (mts.) .... E 3	Thlewiaza (riv.) .... J 3
Robeson (chan.) .... M 1	Trout (lake) .... F 3
Roes Welcome (sound) .... K 3	Ungava (bay) .... M 4
Royal Geographical	Vansittart (isl.) .... K 3
Society (isls.) .... J 3	Victoria (isl.) .... G 2
Russell (isl.) .... J 2	Victoria (str.) .... H 3
Sabine (pen.) .... H 2	Viscount Melville (sound) .... G 2
Salisbury (isl.) .... L 3	Wager (bay) .... K 3
Seahorse (pt.) .... L 3	Wales (isl.) .... K 3
Selwyn (lake) .... H 4	Walsingham (cape) .... M 3
Sherman (inlet) .... J 3	Wellington (chan.) .... J 2
Simpson (pen.) .... K 3	Wholdaia (lake) .... H 3
Sir James MacBrien (mt.) .... F 3	Winter (harb.) .... H 2
Slave (riv.) .... G 3	Wollaston (pen.) .... G 3

YUKON TERRITORY

AREA 207,076 sq. mi.
POPULATION 18,388 ('71); 21,836 ('76)
CAPITAL Whitehorse
LARGEST CITY Whitehorse
HIGHEST POINT Mt. Logan 19,850 ft.
SETTLED IN 1897
ADMITTED TO CONFEDERATION 1898
PROVINCIAL FLOWER Fireweed

NORTHWEST TERRITORIES

AREA 1,304,903 sq. mi.
POPULATION 34,807 ('71); 42,609 ('76)
CAPITAL Yellowknife
LARGEST CITY Yellowknife
HIGHEST POINT United States Range 9,600 ft.
SETTLED IN 1800
ADMITTED TO CONFEDERATION 1870
PROVINCIAL FLOWER Mountain Avens

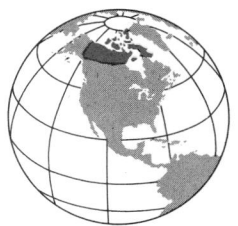

Wood Buffalo Nat'l Park ..... G 3	Beaver Creek, 120 .... D 3	Keno Hill, 79 .... E 3
Wynniatt (bay) .... G 2	Burwash Landing, 67 .... D 3	Mayo, 462 .... E 3
Yathkyed (lake) .... J 3	Carcross, 188 .... E 3	McCabe Creek, 12 .... E 3
Yellowknife (riv.) .... G 3	Carmacks, 348 .... E 3	Old Crow, 206 .... E 3
	Clinton Creek, 381 .... D 3	Pelly Crossing, 141 .... E 3
	Cowley, 11 .... E 3	Ross River, 317 .... E 3
YUKON	Dawson, 762 .... D 3	Stewart Crossing, 43 .... E 3
	Destruction Bay, 82 .... E 3	Stewart River, 4 .... D 3
	Dominion, 12 .... E 3	Swift River, 33 .... E 3
CITIES and TOWNS	Donjek, 11 .... D 3	Tagish, 4 .... E 3
	Eagle River, 12 .... E 3	Teslin, 340 .... E 3
	Elsa, 298 .... E 3	Toobally Lake, 1 .... F 3
Bear Creek, 4 .... E 3	Faro, 863 .... E 3	Tuchitua Lake, 17 .... E 3
	Fort Selkirk, 3 .... E 3	Upper Liard, 219 .... F 3
	Haines Junction, 179 .... E 3	Watson Lake, 553 .... F 3
	Herschel, 5 .... E 3	Whitehorse (cap.), 11,217 .... E 3

OTHER FEATURES		
Alsek (riv.) .... E 3	Macmillan (riv.) .... E 3
British (mts.) .... D 3	Mayo (lake) .... E 3
Cassiar (mts.) .... E 3	Ogilvie (mts.) .... E 3
Frances (lake) .... E 3	Peel (riv.) .... E 3
Herschel (isl.) .... E 3	Pelly (mts.) .... E 3
Hess (riv.) .... E 3	Pelly (riv.) .... E 3
Hyland (riv.) .... F 3	Porcupine (riv.) .... E 3
Keele (peak) .... E 3	Richardson (mts.) .... E 3
Klondike (riv.) .... E 3	Rocky (mts.) .... F 4
Kluane (lake) .... E 3	Saint Elias (mt.) .... D 3
Kluane Nat'l Park .... E 3	Saint Elias (mts.) .... D 3
Logan (mt.) .... D 3	Selwyn (mts.) .... E 3
Mackenzie (bay) .... E 3	Stewart (riv.) .... E 3
Mackenzie (mts.) .... E 3	Teslin (riv.) .... E 3
	White (riv.) .... D 3
	Yukon (riv.) .... E 3

(Map: Yukon and Northwest Territories)

YUKON AND NORTHWEST TERRITORIES

SCALE

0 50 100   200   300 MI.

0 50 100   200   300 KM.

Territorial Capitals ⊛
International Boundaries
Provincial & Territorial Boundaries
District Boundaries

All islands in Hudson and James Bays
lie within the District of Keewatin.

UNITED STATES

POLYCONIC PROJECTION

SCALE

0 50 100 200 300 400 MI.

0 50 100 200 300 400 KM.

Capitals of Countries .... ☆
State Capitals .... △
International Boundaries .... — · — · —
State Boundaries .... — — —

© C.S. HAMMOND & Co., N.Y.

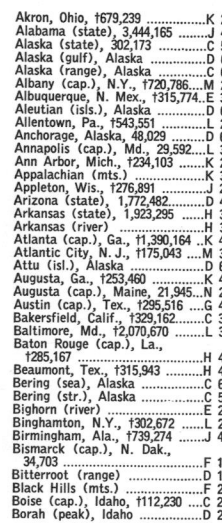

Akron, Ohio, †679,239 ......K 2	Boston (cap.), Mass., †2,753,700 M 2	Connecticut (state), 3,032,217 ..M 2	Golden Gate (chan.), Calif. ...B 3	Kentucky (state), 3,219,311 ..J 3	Minneapolis, Minn., †1,813,647..H 2

Akron, Ohio, †679,239 ......K 2
Alabama (state), 3,444,165 ..J 4
Alaska (state), 302,173 ......C 5
Alaska (gulf), Alaska ....D 6
Alaska (range), Alaska ....C 5
Albany (cap.), N.Y., †720,786..M 2
Albuquerque, N. Mex., †315,774..E 3
Aleutian (isls.), Alaska ......D 6
Allentown, Pa., †543,551 .....L 2
Anchorage, Alaska, 48,029 ...D 6
Annapolis (cap.), Md., 29,592..L 3
Ann Arbor, Mich., †234,103 ..K 2
Appalachian (mts.) ....K 3
Appleton, Wis., †276,891 .....J 2
Arizona (state), 1,772,482 ...D 4
Arkansas (state), 1,923,295 ..H 3
Arkansas (river) ....H 3
Atlanta (cap.), Ga., †1,390,164 ..K 4
Atlantic City, N.J., †175,043 ..M 3
Attu (isl.), Alaska ....D 6
Augusta, Ga., †253,460 ......K 4
Augusta (cap.), Maine, 21,945..N 2
Austin (cap.), Tex., †295,516 ..G 4
Bakersfield, Calif., †329,162 ..C 3
Baltimore, Md., †2,070,670 ...L 3
Baton Rouge (cap.), La.,
  †285,167 ....H 4
Beaumont, Tex., †315,943 ....H 4
Bering (sea), Alaska ....C 6
Bering (str.), Alaska ....B 5
Bighorn (river) ....E 2
Binghamton, N.Y., †302,672 ..L 2
Birmingham, Ala., †739,274 ..J 4
Bismarck (cap.), N. Dak.,
  34,703 ....F 1
Bitterroot (range) ....D 1
Black Hills (mts.) ....F 2
Boise (cap.), Idaho, †112,230..D 2
Borah (peak), Idaho ....D 2

Boston (cap.), Mass., †2,753,700 M 2
Brazos (river), Tex. ....G 4
Bridgeport, Conn., †388,953 ..M 2
Brooks (range), Alaska ....C 5
Buffalo, N.Y., †1,349,211 .....L 2
California (state), 19,953,134..C 3
Canadian (river) ....F 3
Canaveral (cape), Fla. ....L 5
Canton, Ohio, †372,210 ......K 2
Cape Fear (river), N.C. ....L 4
Carson City (cap.), Nev.,
  15,468 ....C 3
Cascade (range) ....B 1
Cedar Rapids, Iowa, †163,213..H 2
Champlain (lake) ....M 2
Charleston, S.C., †303,849 ...L 4
Charleston (cap.), W. Va.,
  †229,515 ....K 3
Charlotte, N.C., †409,370 ....K 3
Chattahoochee (river) ....J 4
Chattanooga, Tenn., †304,927..J 3
Chesapeake (bay) ....L 3
Cheyenne (cap.), Wyo., 40,914..F 2
Cheyenne (river) ....F 2
Chicago, Ill., †6,978,947 .....J 2
Cimarron (river) ....G 3
Cincinnati, Ohio, †1,384,911 ..K 3
Cleveland, Ohio, †2,064,194 ..K 2
Coast (range) ....B 2
Cod (cape), Mass. ....N 2
Colorado (state), 2,207,259 ..E 3
Colorado (river) ....D 4
Colorado (river), Tex. ....G 4
Columbia (cap.), S.C., †322,880..K 4
Columbia (river) ....B 1
Columbus, Ga., †238,584 .....K 4
Columbus (cap.), Ohio, †916,228..K 3
Concord (cap.), N.H., 30,022..M 2

Connecticut (state), 3,032,217 ..M 2
Connecticut (river) ....M 2
Corpus Christi, Tex., †284,832..G 5
Cumberland (river) ....J 3
Dallas, Tex., †1,555,950 ......G 4
Davenport, Iowa, †362,638 ...H 2
Dayton, Ohio, †850,266 ......K 3
Death Valley (depr.), Calif. ...C 3
Delaware (state), 548,104 .....L 3
Delaware (bay) ....M 3
Denver (cap.), Colo., †1,227,529..F 3
Des Moines (cap.), Iowa,
  †286,101 ....H 2
Detroit, Mich., †4,199,931 ....K 2
District of Columbia, 756,510..L 3
Dover (cap.), Del., 17,488 ....L 3
Duluth, Minn., †265,350 .....H 1
Durham, N.C., †190,388 .....L 3
Elbert (mt.), Colo. ....E 3
El Paso, Tex., †359,291 ......E 4
Erie, Pa., †263,654 ....K 2
Erie (lake) ....K 2
Eugene, Oreg., †213,358 .....B 2
Evansville, Ind., †232,775 ....J 3
Everglades (swamp), Fla. .....K 5
Fayetteville, N.C., †212,042 ..L 3
Flint, Mich., †496,658 ....K 2
Florida (state), 6,789,443 ....K 5
Florida (keys), Fla. ....K 6
Ft. Smith, Ark., †160,421 ....H 3
Ft. Wayne, Ind., †280,455 ...J 2
Ft. Worth, Tex., †762,086 ...G 4
Frankfort (cap.), Ky., 21,356..K 3
Fresno, Calif., †413,053 .....C 3
Galveston, Tex., †169,812 ....H 5
Gary, Ind., †633,367 ....J 2
Georgia (state), 4,589,575 ....K 4
Gila (river) ....D 4
Glacier Nat'l Park, Mont. .....D 1

Golden Gate (chan.), Calif. ...B 3
Grand Canyon Nat'l Park, Ariz..D 3
Grand Rapids, Mich., †539,225..J 2
Great Salt (lake), Utah ....D 2
Greensboro, N.C., †603,895 ...K 3
Greenville, S.C., †299,502 ....K 4
Hamilton, Ohio, †226,207 ....K 3
Harrisburg (cap.), Pa., †410,626..L 2
Hartford (cap.), Conn.,
  †663,891 ....M 2
Hatteras (cape), N.C. ....M 3
Havasu (lake) ....D 3
Hawaii (state), 769,913 ......F 6
Hawaii (isl.), Hawaii ....G 6
Helena (cap.), Mont., 22,730..D 1
Honolulu (cap.), Hawaii,
  †629,176 ....F 5
Houston, Tex., †1,985,031 ....G 5
Huntington, W. Va., †253,743..K 3
Huntsville, Ala., †228,239 ....J 4
Huron (lake), Mich. ....K 2
Idaho (state), 713,008 ....D 2
Illinois (state), 11,113,976 ...J 3
Indiana (state), 5,193,669 ....J 3
Indianapolis (cap.), Ind.,
  †1,109,882 ....J 3
Iowa (state), 2,825,041 ......H 2
Jackson (cap.), Miss., †258,906..H 4
Jacksonville, Fla., †528,865 ..K 4
Jefferson City (cap.), Mo.,
  32,407 ....H 3
Jersey City, N.J., †609,266 ...M 2
Johnstown, Pa., †262,822 ....L 2
Juneau (cap.), Alaska, 13,556..E 6
Kalamazoo, Mich., †201,550 ..J 2
Kansas (state), 2,249,071 ....G 3
Kansas City, Kans.-Mo.,
  †1,256,649 ....H 3
Kauai (isl.), Hawaii ....E 5

Kentucky (state), 3,219,311 ..J 3
Kentucky (lake) ....J 3
Knoxville, Tenn., †400,337 ...K 3
Lancaster, Pa., †319,693 .....L 2
Lansing (cap.), Mich.,
  †378,423 ....K 2
Las Vegas, Nev., †273,288 ...C 3
Lawrence, Mass., †232,395 ...M 2
Lexington, Ky., †174,323 .....K 3
Lima, Ohio, †171,472 ....K 2
Lincoln (cap.), Nebr., †167,972..G 2
Little Rock (cap.), Ark.,
  †323,296 ....H 4
Long (isl.), N.Y. ....M 2
Long Beach, Calif., 358,633 ..C 4
Los Angeles, Calif., †7,032,075..C 4
Louisiana (state), 3,643,180 ..H 4
Louisville, Ky., †826,553 .....J 3
Lowell, Mass., †212,860 .....M 2
Lubbock, Tex., †179,295 .....F 4
Macon, Ga., †206,342 ....K 4
Madison (cap.), Wis., †290,272..H 2
Maine (state), 993,663 ....N 1
Maryland (state), 3,922,399 ..L 3
Massachusetts (state),
  5,689,170 ....M 2
Mauna Kea (mt.), Hawaii .....G 6
Mauna Loa (mt.), Hawaii .....G 6
May (cape), N.J. ....M 3
McKinley (mt.), Alaska ....D 5
Mead (lake) ....D 3
Memphis, Tenn., †770,120 ...J 3
Mendocino (cape), Calif. .....B 2
Mexico (gulf) ....J 5
Miami, Fla., †1,267,792 ......K 6
Michigan (state), 8,875,083 ..J 1
Michigan (lake) ....J 2
Milwaukee, Wis., †1,403,887..J 2

Minneapolis, Minn., †1,813,647..H 2
Minnesota (state), 3,805,069 ..H 1
Mississippi (state), 2,216,912 ..J 4
Mississippi (river) ....H 4
Missouri (state), 4,677,399 ...H 3
Missouri (river) ....H 3
Mitchell (mt.), N.C. ....K 3
Mobile, Ala., †376,690 ....J 4
Montana (state), 694,409 .....E 1
Montgomery (cap.), Ala.,
  †201,325 ....J 4
Montpelier (cap.), Vt., 8,609..M 2
Nantucket (isl.), Mass. ....N 2
Nashville (cap.), Tenn., †540,982..J 3
Nebraska (state), 1,483,791 ..F 2
Nevada (state), 488,738 ......C 3
Newark, N.J., †1,856,556 .....M 2
New Hampshire (state), 737,681..M 2
New Haven, Conn., †355,538..M 2
New Jersey (state), 7,168,164..M 3
New Mexico (state), 1,016,000..E 4
New Orleans, La., †1,045,809..H 5
New York (state), 18,190,740..L 2
New York, N.Y., †11,528,649 ..M 2
Newport News, Va., †292,159..L 3
Norfolk, Va., †680,600 ....L 3
North Carolina (state), 5,082,059..L 3
North Dakota (state), 617,761..F 1
Oahu (isl.), Hawaii ....F 5
Oakland, Calif., 361,561 .....B 3
Ohio (state), 10,652,017 .....K 2
Ohio (river) ....J 3
Oklahoma (state), 2,559,253 ..G 3
Oklahoma City (cap.), Okla.,
  †640,889 ....G 3
Olympia (cap.), Wash., 23,111..B 1
Olympic Nat'l Park, Wash. ....A 1
Omaha, Nebr., †541,453 ......G 2
Ontario (lake), N.Y. ....L 2

Oregon (state), 2,091,385 ....B 2
Orlando, Fla., †428,003 ......K 5
Ozark (mts.) ....H 3
Paterson, N.J., †1,358,794 ...M 2
Pennsylvania (state), 11,793,909..L 2
Pensacola, Fla., †243,075 ....J 4
Peoria, Ill., †341,979 ....J 2
Philadelphia, Pa., †4,817,914..M 3
Phoenix (cap.), Ariz., †968,487..D 4
Pierre (cap.), S. Dak., 9,699..F 2
Pikes (peak), Colo. ....F 3
Pittsburgh, Pa., †2,401,245 ..L 2
Platte (river), Nebr. ....G 2
Pontchartrain (lake), La. .....H 4
Portland, Maine, †141,625 ...N 2
Portland, Oreg., †1,009,129 ..B 1
Potomac (river) ....L 3
Providence (cap.), R.I., †914,110..M 2
Racine, Wis., †70,838 ....J 2
Rainier (mt.), Wash. ....B 1
Raleigh (cap.), N.C., †228,453..L 3
Reading, Pa., †296,382 ......L 2
Red (river) ....G 4
Red River of the North (river)..G 1
Rhode Island (state), 949,723..M 2
Richmond (cap.), Va., †518,319..L 3
Rio Grande (river) ....F 5
Roanoke, Va., †181,436 ......K 3
Rochester, N.Y., †882,667 ...L 2
Rockford, Ill., †272,063 ......J 2
Rocky (mts.) ....F 2
Sacramento (cap.), Calif.,
  †800,592 ....B 3
Saginaw, Mich., †219,743 ....K 2
Saint Clair (lake), Mich. ......K 2
Saint Lawrence (river), N.Y. ..N 1
Saint Louis, Mo., †2,363,017 ..H 3
Saint Paul (cap.), Minn.,
  309,980 ....H 1

UNITED STATES
POPULATION 203,235,298 ('70); 226,504,825 ('80)
AREA 3,615,123 sq. mi.
CAPITAL Washington
LARGEST CITY New York
HIGHEST POINT Mt. McKinley 20,320 ft.
MONETARY VALUE U.S. dollar
MAJOR LANGUAGE English
MAJOR RELIGIONS Protestantism, Roman Catholicism, Judaism

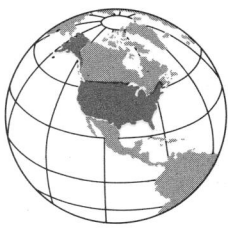

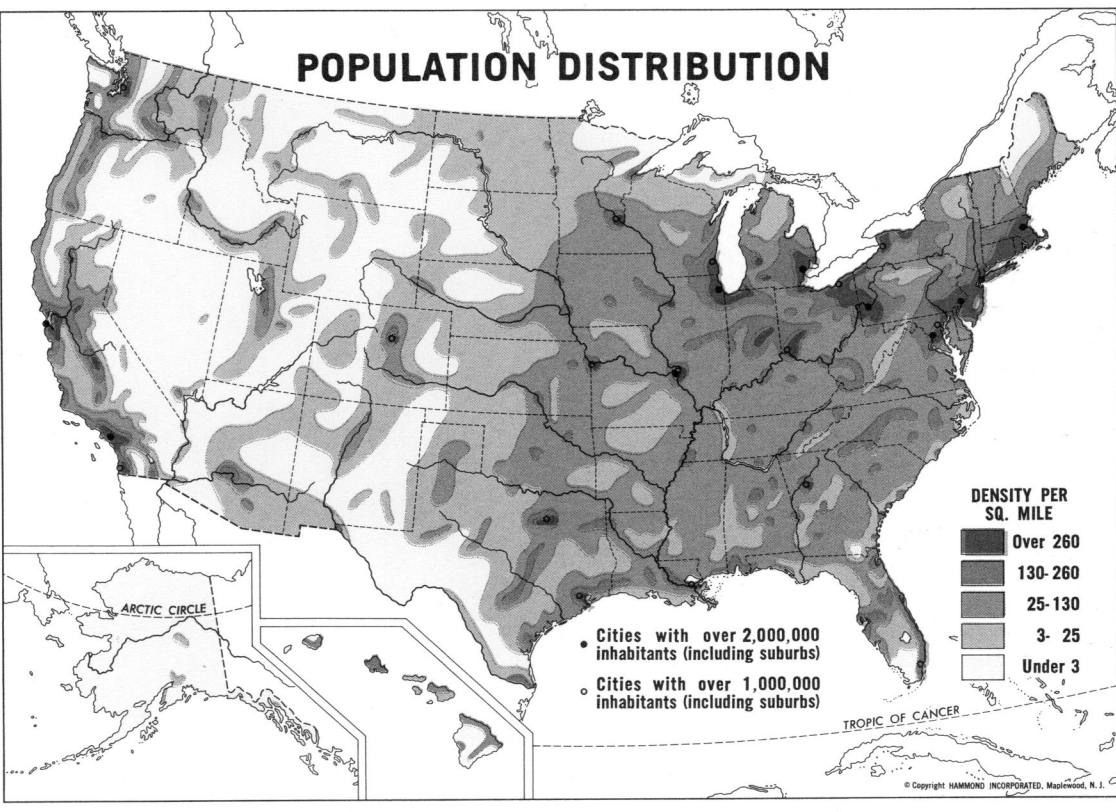

POPULATION DISTRIBUTION

ARCTIC CIRCLE

DENSITY PER SQ. MILE
Over 260
130- 260
25- 130
3- 25
Under 3

• Cities with over 2,000,000 inhabitants (including suburbs)
○ Cities with over 1,000,000 inhabitants (including suburbs)

TROPIC OF CANCER

© Copyright HAMMOND INCORPORATED, Maplewood, N. J.

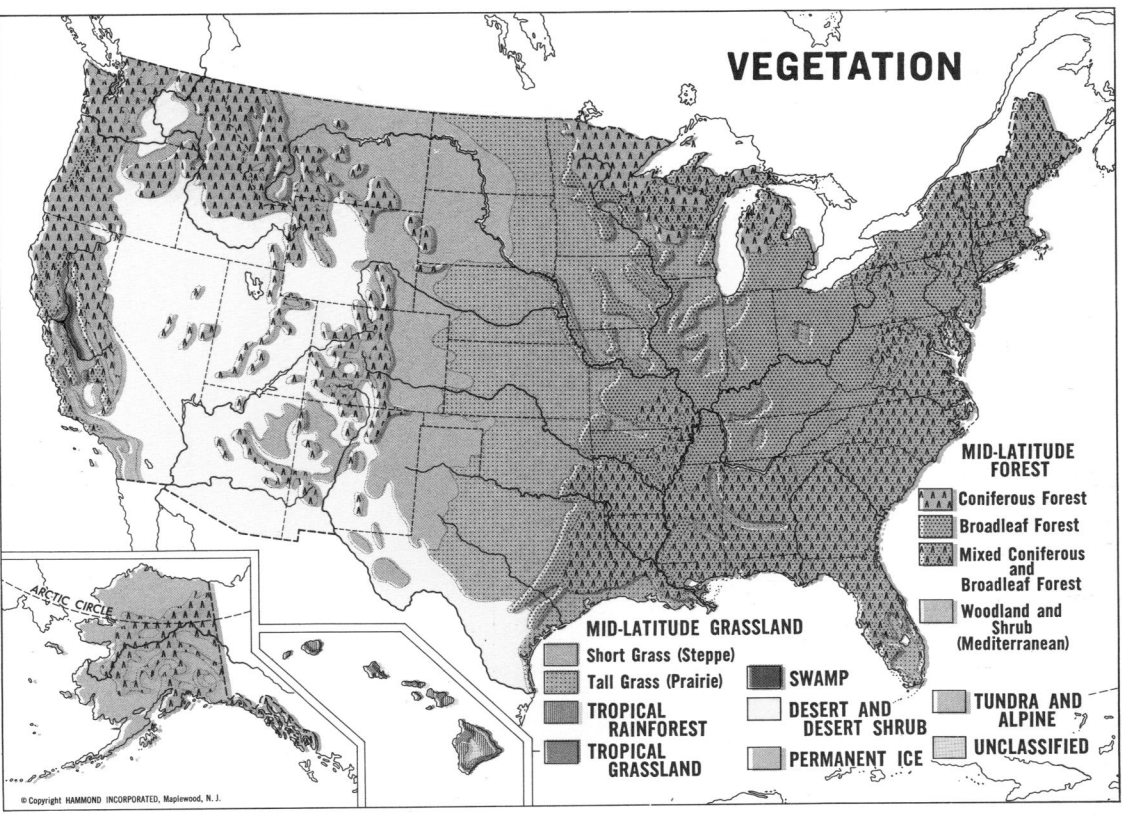

VEGETATION

ARCTIC CIRCLE

MID-LATITUDE FOREST
▲ Coniferous Forest
Broadleaf Forest
Mixed Coniferous and Broadleaf Forest
Woodland and Shrub (Mediterranean)

MID-LATITUDE GRASSLAND
Short Grass (Steppe)
Tall Grass (Prairie)

SWAMP
DESERT AND DESERT SHRUB
PERMANENT ICE

TROPICAL RAINFOREST
TROPICAL GRASSLAND

TUNDRA AND ALPINE
UNCLASSIFIED

© Copyright HAMMOND INCORPORATED, Maplewood, N. J.

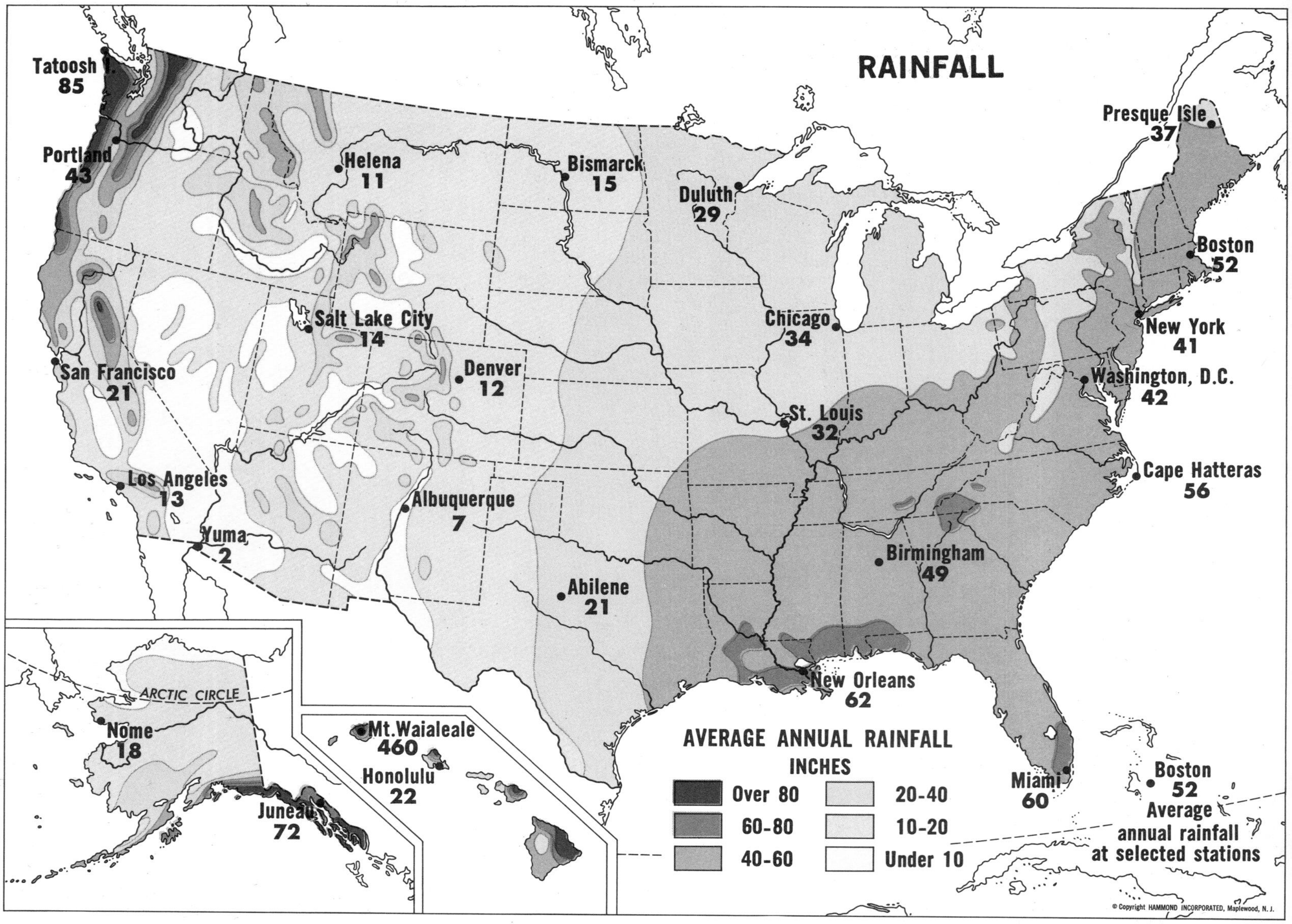

RAINFALL

Tatoosh I.
85

Portland
43

Helena
11

Bismarck
15

Duluth
29

Presque Isle
37

Boston
52

Salt Lake City
14

Chicago
34

New York
41

San Francisco
21

Denver
12

St. Louis
32

Washington, D.C.
42

Los Angeles
13

Albuquerque
7

Cape Hatteras
56

Yuma
2

Abilene
21

Birmingham
49

New Orleans
62

Miami
60

ARCTIC CIRCLE

Nome
18

Mt.Waialeale
460

Honolulu
22

Juneau
72

AVERAGE ANNUAL RAINFALL
INCHES

Over 80	20–40
60–80	10–20
40–60	Under 10

Boston
52
Average annual rainfall at selected stations

© Copyright HAMMOND INCORPORATED, Maplewood, N.J.

AVERAGE JANUARY TEMPERATURE

Seattle
39°

Bismarck
9°

Minneapolis
12°

Chicago
25°

New York
30°

San Francisco
48°

Denver
30°

St. Louis
31°

Washington
34°

Los Angeles
55°

Phoenix
52°

Dallas
46°

Atlanta
43°

Chicago
25°
Average January temperature at selected stations

New Orleans
55°

Miami
69°

ARCTIC CIRCLE

Fairbanks
-11°

Honolulu
73°

TROPIC OF CANCER

FAHRENHEIT

Over 68°	14° to 32°
50° to 68°	-4° to 14°
32° to 50°	Under -4°

© Copyright HAMMOND INCORPORATED, Maplewood, N.J.

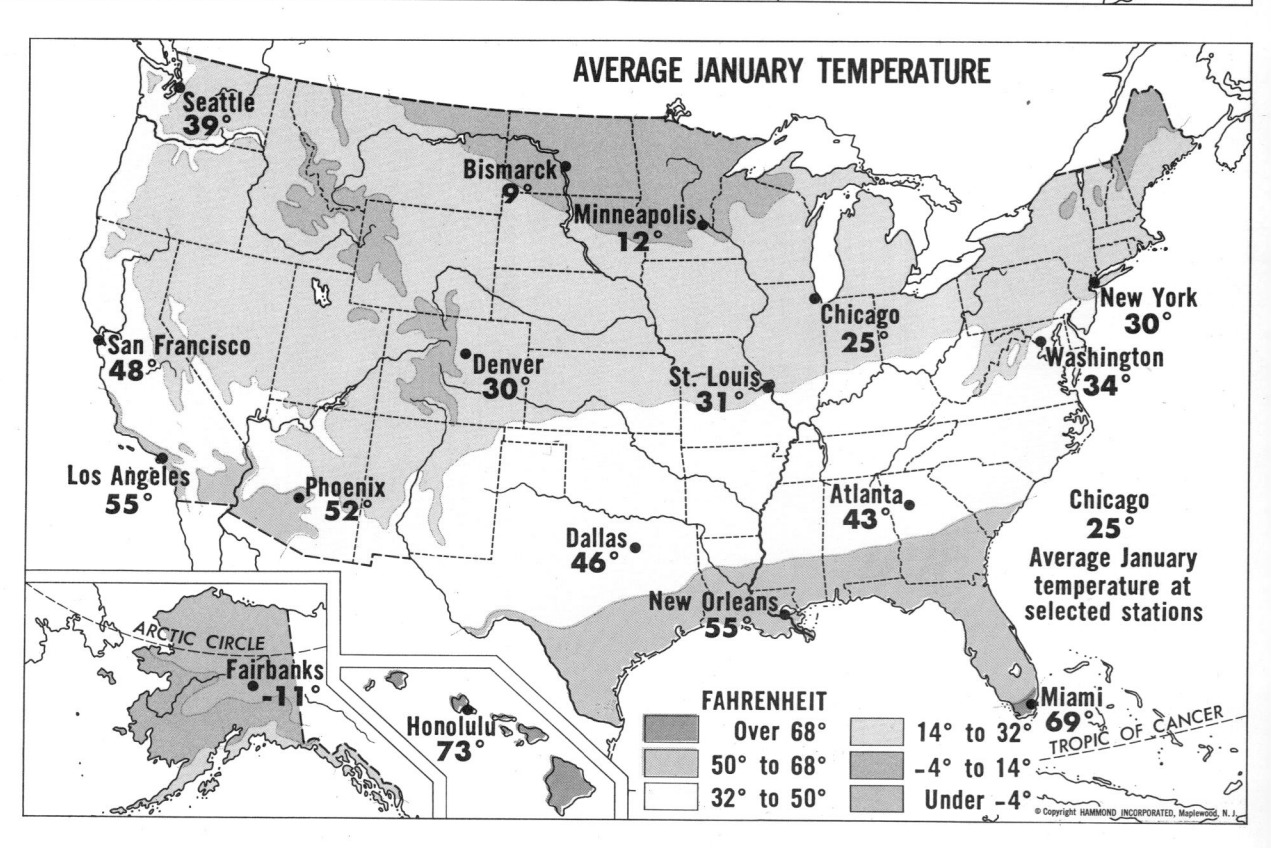

Topography

MILES
0   200   400

PACIFIC OCEAN

C. Flattery
Mt. Rainier 14,410
COAST RANGE
CASCADE
COLUMBIA
PLATEAU
BITTERROOT RANGE
Columbia
Snake
Snake
SIERRA NEVADA
Sacramento
Central Valley
Mt. Whitney 14,494
Great Basin
Great Salt Lake
ROCKY
Missouri
Yellowstone
Fort Peck Lake
GREAT
Lake Sakakawea
Missouri
James
Red
Rainy
Lake Superior
Keweenaw Pen.
St. Lawrence
L. Champlain
C. Cod

Pt. Conception
SANTA BARBARA IS.
Mojave Desert
Grand Canyon
L. Mead
Lake Powell
Colorado
COLORADO
Mt. Elbert 14,431
PLATEAU
MOUNTAINS
Colorado
N. Platte
Platte
PLAINS
Des Moines
Illinois
Missouri
Wisconsin
Lake Michigan
Lake Huron
Lake Ontario
Niagara Falls
Lake Erie
Ohio
Potomac
ALLEGHENY MTS.
APPALACHIAN MOUNTAINS
ATLANTIC COASTAL PLAIN
Long Island
Chesapeake Bay
C. Hatteras
ATLANTIC
OCEAN

Rio Grande
Gila
Colorado
LLANO ESTACADO
Arkansas
Canadian
Red
Arkansas
OZARK PLATEAU
Tennessee
Wabash
Mt. Mitchell 6,684
Wheeler L.
Chattahoochee
Savannah
C. Fear

Pecos
EDWARDS PLATEAU
Colorado
Brazos
Red
Mississippi
GULF COASTAL PLAIN
Mississippi Delta
C. Canaveral
L. Okeechobee
The Everglades
FLORIDA KEYS

Rio Grande
Gulf of Mexico

ARCTIC OCEAN
MILES
0   200   400
BROOKS RA.
St. Lawrence I.
Bering Str.
Yukon
Tanana
Alaska Ra.
Mt. McKinley 20,320
BERING SEA
Gulf of Alaska
Aleutian Islands
Alaska Pen.
Kodiak I.
ALEXANDER ARCHIPELAGO

HAWAIIAN ISLANDS
PACIFIC OCEAN
Kauai
Oahu
Molokai
Maui
Mauna Kea 13,796
Hawaii
MILES
0   50   100

| 5,000 m. 16,404 ft. | 2,000 m. 6,562 ft. | 1,000 m. 3,281 ft. | 500 m. 1,640 ft. | 200 m. 656 ft. | 100 m. 328 ft. | Sea Level | Below |

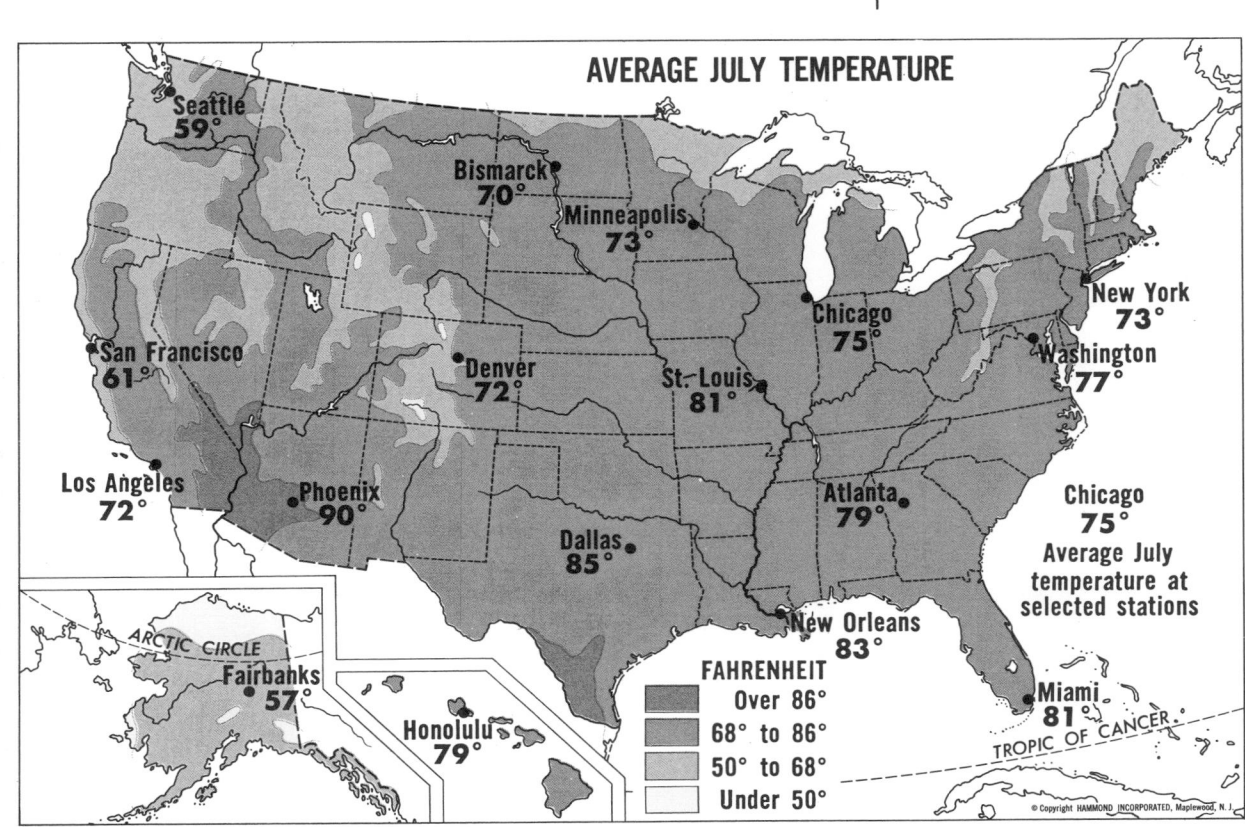

AVERAGE JULY TEMPERATURE

Seattle 59°
Bismarck 70°
Minneapolis 73°
Chicago 75°
New York 73°
Washington 77°
San Francisco 61°
Denver 72°
St. Louis 81°
Los Angeles 72°
Phoenix 90°
Dallas 85°
Atlanta 79°
New Orleans 83°
Miami 81°

Chicago 75°
Average July temperature at selected stations

Fairbanks 57°
ARCTIC CIRCLE
Honolulu 79°
TROPIC OF CANCER

FAHRENHEIT
Over 86°
68° to 86°
50° to 68°
Under 50°

© Copyright HAMMOND INCORPORATED, Maplewood, N.J.

LAND USE

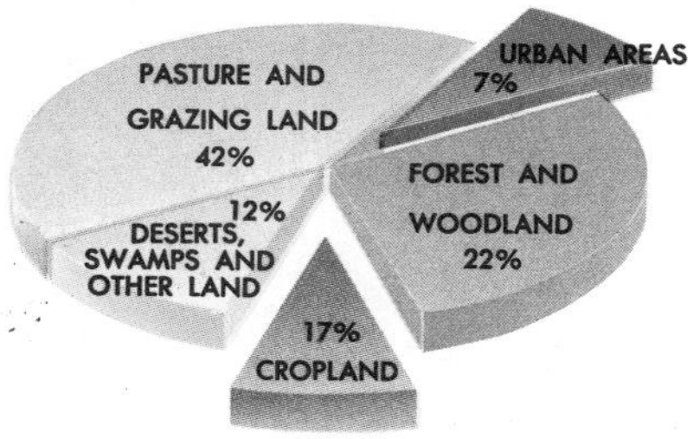
PASTURE AND GRAZING LAND 42%
URBAN AREAS 7%
FOREST AND WOODLAND 22%
12% DESERTS, SWAMPS AND OTHER LAND
17% CROPLAND

EMPLOYMENT

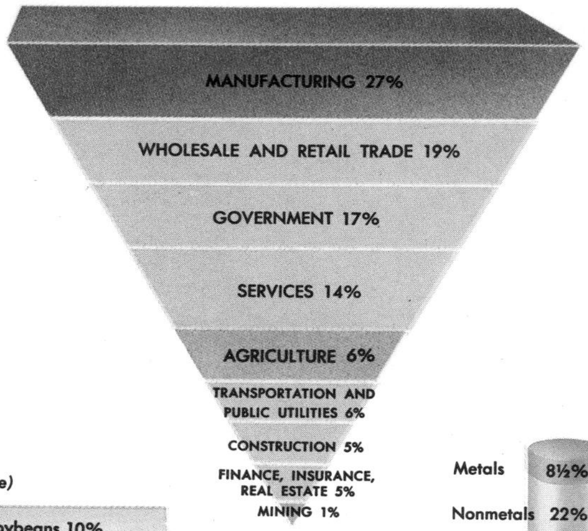
MANUFACTURING 27%
WHOLESALE AND RETAIL TRADE 19%
GOVERNMENT 17%
SERVICES 14%
AGRICULTURE 6%
TRANSPORTATION AND PUBLIC UTILITIES 6%
CONSTRUCTION 5%
FINANCE, INSURANCE, REAL ESTATE 5%
MINING 1%

TOTAL VALUE ADDED BY MANUFACTURING

(percent by industry group)

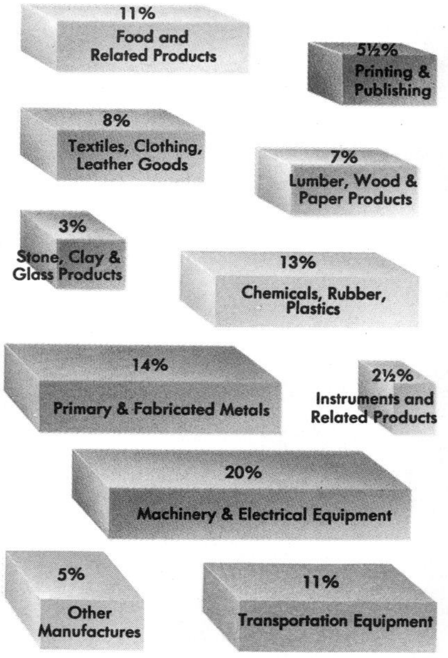
11% Food and Related Products
5½% Printing & Publishing
8% Textiles, Clothing, Leather Goods
7% Lumber, Wood & Paper Products
3% Stone, Clay & Glass Products
13% Chemicals, Rubber, Plastics
14% Primary & Fabricated Metals
2½% Instruments and Related Products
20% Machinery & Electrical Equipment
5% Other Manufactures
11% Transportation Equipment

CROPLAND *(percent of total acreage)*

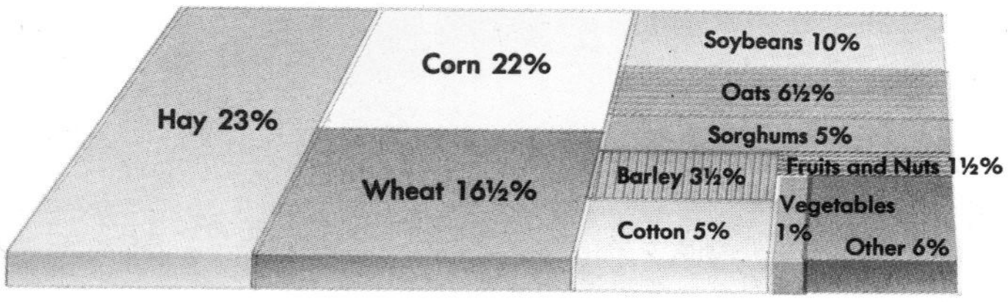
Hay 23%
Corn 22%
Soybeans 10%
Oats 6½%
Sorghums 5%
Wheat 16½%
Barley 3½%
Fruits and Nuts 1½%
Cotton 5%
Vegetables 1%
Other 6%

VALUE OF MINERAL PRODUCTION

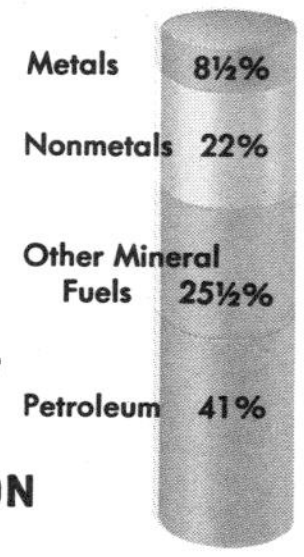
Metals 8½%
Nonmetals 22%
Other Mineral Fuels 25½%
Petroleum 41%

Agriculture, Industry and Resources

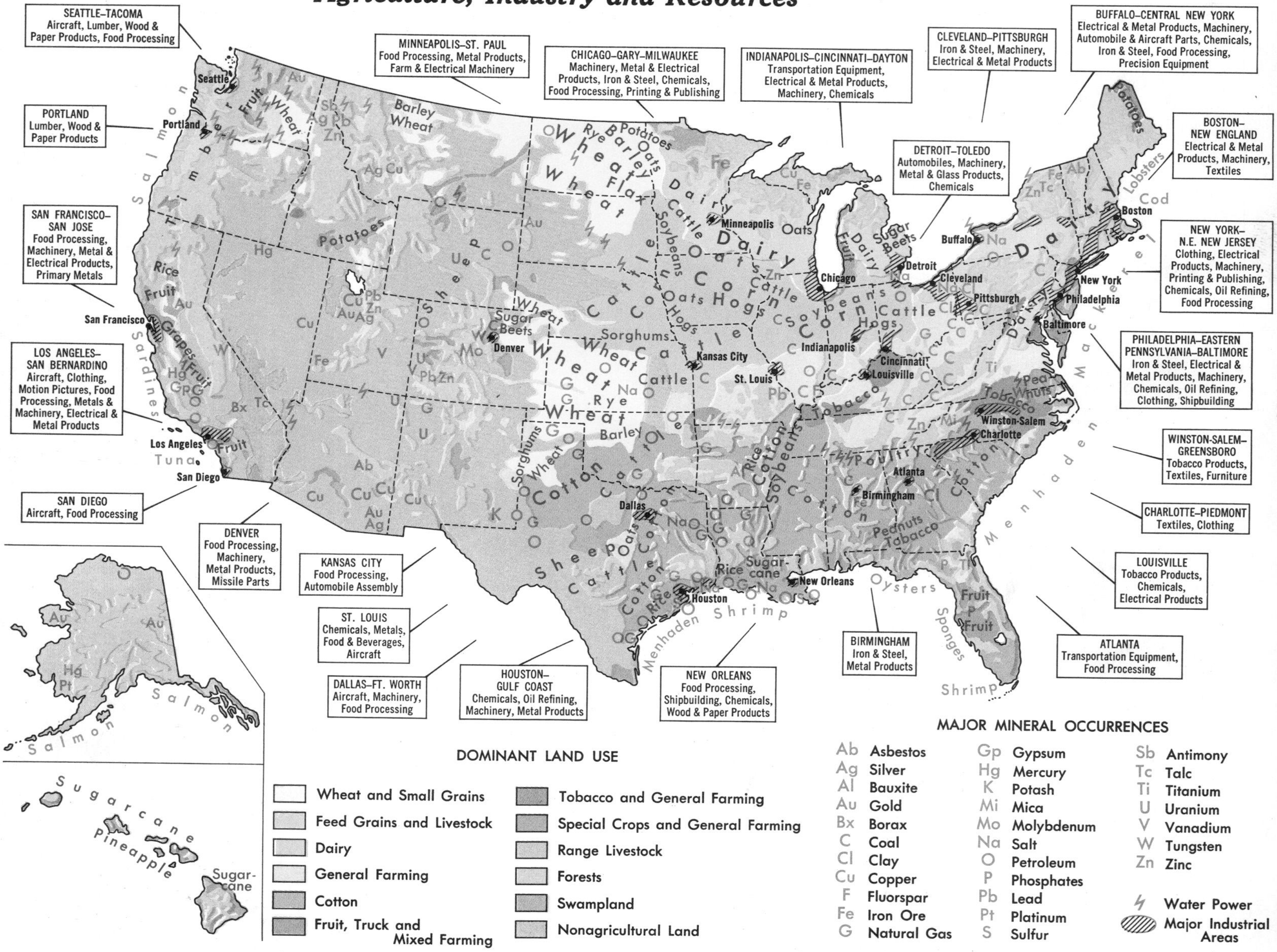
SEATTLE–TACOMA
Aircraft, Lumber, Wood & Paper Products, Food Processing
PORTLAND
Lumber, Wood & Paper Products
SAN FRANCISCO–SAN JOSE
Food Processing, Machinery, Metal & Electrical Products, Primary Metals
LOS ANGELES–SAN BERNARDINO
Aircraft, Clothing, Motion Pictures, Food Processing, Metals & Machinery, Electrical & Metal Products
SAN DIEGO
Aircraft, Food Processing
DENVER
Food Processing, Machinery, Metal Products, Missile Parts
KANSAS CITY
Food Processing, Automobile Assembly
ST. LOUIS
Chemicals, Metals, Food & Beverages, Aircraft
DALLAS–FT. WORTH
Aircraft, Machinery, Food Processing
HOUSTON–GULF COAST
Chemicals, Oil Refining, Machinery, Metal Products
NEW ORLEANS
Food Processing, Shipbuilding, Chemicals, Wood & Paper Products
BIRMINGHAM
Iron & Steel, Metal Products
MINNEAPOLIS–ST. PAUL
Food Processing, Metal Products, Farm & Electrical Machinery
CHICAGO–GARY–MILWAUKEE
Machinery, Metal & Electrical Products, Iron & Steel, Chemicals, Food Processing, Printing & Publishing
INDIANAPOLIS–CINCINNATI–DAYTON
Transportation Equipment, Electrical & Metal Products, Machinery, Chemicals
CLEVELAND–PITTSBURGH
Iron & Steel, Machinery, Electrical & Metal Products
DETROIT–TOLEDO
Automobiles, Machinery, Metal & Glass Products, Chemicals
BUFFALO–CENTRAL NEW YORK
Electrical & Metal Products, Machinery, Automobile & Aircraft Parts, Chemicals, Iron & Steel, Food Processing, Precision Equipment
BOSTON–NEW ENGLAND
Electrical & Metal Products, Machinery, Textiles
NEW YORK–N.E. NEW JERSEY
Clothing, Electrical Products, Machinery, Printing & Publishing, Chemicals, Oil Refining, Food Processing
PHILADELPHIA–EASTERN PENNSYLVANIA–BALTIMORE
Iron & Steel, Electrical & Metal Products, Machinery, Chemicals, Oil Refining, Clothing, Shipbuilding
WINSTON-SALEM–GREENSBORO
Tobacco Products, Textiles, Furniture
CHARLOTTE–PIEDMONT
Textiles, Clothing
LOUISVILLE
Tobacco Products, Chemicals, Electrical Products
ATLANTA
Transportation Equipment, Food Processing
Seattle
Portland
San Francisco
Los Angeles
San Diego
Denver
Kansas City
St. Louis
Dallas
Houston
New Orleans
Birmingham
Atlanta
Minneapolis
Chicago
Indianapolis
Cincinnati
Louisville
Detroit
Cleveland
Pittsburgh
Buffalo
Boston
New York
Philadelphia
Baltimore
Winston-Salem
Charlotte
Salmon
Sardines
Tuna
Oysters
Shrimp
Menhaden
Sponges
Mackerel
Cod
Lobsters
Pineapple
Sugarcane
DOMINANT LAND USE
Wheat and Small Grains
Feed Grains and Livestock
Dairy
General Farming
Cotton
Fruit, Truck and Mixed Farming
Tobacco and General Farming
Special Crops and General Farming
Range Livestock
Forests
Swampland
Nonagricultural Land
MAJOR MINERAL OCCURRENCES
Ab Asbestos
Ag Silver
Al Bauxite
Au Gold
Bx Borax
C Coal
Cl Clay
Cu Copper
F Fluorspar
Fe Iron Ore
G Natural Gas
Gp Gypsum
Hg Mercury
K Potash
Mi Mica
Mo Molybdenum
Na Salt
O Petroleum
P Phosphates
Pb Lead
Pt Platinum
S Sulfur
Sb Antimony
Tc Talc
Ti Titanium
U Uranium
V Vanadium
W Tungsten
Zn Zinc
Water Power
Major Industrial Areas

COUNTIES

Autauga, 24,460 .... E 5
Baldwin, 59,382 .... C 9
Barbour, 22,543 .... H 7
Bibb, 13,812 .... D 5
Blount, 26,853 .... E 2
Bullock, 11,824 .... G 6
Butler, 22,007 .... E 7
Calhoun, 103,092 .... G 3
Chambers, 36,356 .... H 5
Cherokee, 15,606 .... G 2
Chilton, 25,180 .... E 5
Choctaw, 16,589 .... B 6
Clarke, 26,724 .... C 7
Clay, 12,636 .... G 4
Cleburne, 10,996 .... G 3
Coffee, 34,872 .... G 8
Colbert, 49,632 .... C 1
Conecuh, 15,645 .... E 8
Coosa, 10,662 .... F 5
Covington, 34,079 .... F 8
Crenshaw, 13,188 .... F 7
Cullman, 52,445 .... E 2
Dale, 52,938 .... G 8
Dallas, 55,296 .... D 6
De Kalb, 41,981 .... G 2
Elmore, 33,535 .... F 5
Escambia, 34,906 .... D 8
Etowah, 94,144 .... F 2
Fayette, 16,252 .... C 3
Franklin, 23,933 .... C 2
Geneva, 21,924 .... G 8
Greene, 10,650 .... C 5
Hale, 15,888 .... C 5
Henry, 13,254 .... H 7
Houston, 56,574 .... H 8
Jackson, 39,202 .... F 1
Jefferson, 644,991 .... E 3
Lamar, 14,335 .... B 3
Lauderdale, 68,111 .... C 1
Lawrence, 27,281 .... D 1
Lee, 61,268 .... H 5
Limestone, 41,699 .... E 1
Lowndes, 12,897 .... E 6
Macon, 24,841 .... G 6
Madison, 186,540 .... E 1
Marengo, 23,819 .... C 6
Marion, 23,788 .... C 2
Marshall, 54,211 .... F 2
Mobile, 317,308 .... B 9
Monroe, 20,883 .... D 7
Montgomery, 167,790 .... F 6
Morgan, 77,306 .... E 2
Perry, 15,388 .... D 5
Pickens, 20,326 .... B 4
Pike, 25,038 .... G 7
Randolph, 18,331 .... H 4
Russell, 45,394 .... H 6
Saint Clair, 27,956 .... F 3
Shelby, 38,037 .... E 4
Sumter, 16,974 .... B 5
Talladega, 65,280 .... F 4
Tallapoosa, 33,840 .... G 5
Tuscaloosa, 116,029 .... C 4
Walker, 56,246 .... D 3
Washington, 16,241 .... B 8
Wilcox, 16,303 .... D 7
Winston, 16,654 .... D 2

CITIES and TOWNS

Zip *Name/Pop.* *Key*

36310 Abbeville⊙, 2,996 .... H 7
35440 Abernant, 602 .... D 4
35005 Adamsville, 2,412 .... D 3
35540 Addison, 692 .... D 2
35006 Adger, 1,550 .... D 4
35441 Akron, 535 .... C 5
35007 Alabaster, 2,642 .... E 4
35950 Albertville, 9,963 .... F 2
† 35115 Aldrich, 476 .... E 4
35010 Alexander City, 12,358 .... G 5
36250 Alexandria, 600 .... G 3
35442 Aliceville, 2,807 .... B 4
35013 Allgood, 272 .... F 3
† 35616 Allsboro, 300 .... B 1
35015 Alton, 500 .... E 3
35952 Altoona, 781 .... F 2
36420 Andalusia⊙, 10,092 .... E 8
35610 Anderson, 400 .... D 1
36201 Anniston⊙, 31,533 .... G 3
35016 Arab, 4,399 .... E 2
35805 Ardmore, 761 .... E 1
36311 Ariton, 643 .... G 7
35033 Arkadelphia, 325 .... E 3
† 35035 Ashby, 500 .... E 4
36312 Ashford, 1,980 .... H 8
36251 Ashland⊙, 1,921 .... G 4
35953 Ashville, 986 .... F 3
35611 Athens⊙, 14,360 .... E 1
36502 Atmore, 8,293 .... C 8
35954 Attalla, 7,510 .... F 2
36830 Auburn, 22,767 .... H 5
36003 Autaugaville, 870 .... E 6
† 36312 Avon, 374 .... H 8
36505 Axis, 600 .... B 9
35019 Baileyton, 500 .... E 2
36004 Baker Hill, 350 .... H 7
36506 Barlow Bend, 300 .... C 8
† 36532 Barnwell, 700 .... C 10
36533 Battles Wharf, 300 .... C 10
36507 Bay Minette⊙, 6,727 .... C 9
36509 Bayou La Batre, 2,664 .... B 10
35543 Bear Creek, 336 .... C 2
36425 Beatrice, 455 .... D 7
35544 Beaverton, 265 .... B 3
† 35653 Belgreen, 500 .... C 2
36901 Bellamy, 700 .... B 6
35546 Berry, 679 .... C 3
35020 Bessemer, 33,428 .... D 4
* 35201 Birmingham⊙, 300,910 .... D 3
Birmingham, ‡739,274 .... D 3
36902 Bladon Springs, 300 .... B 7
† 36874 Bleecker, 250 .... H 5
35031 Blountsville, 1,254 .... E 2
36201 Blue Mountain, 446 .... G 3
35226 Bluff Park, 12,372 .... E 4
35957 Boaz, 5,621 .... F 2
36903 Bolinger, 250 .... B 7
36007 Bolling, 250 .... E 7
36511 Bon Secour, 850 .... C 10
36110 Boylston, 2,943 .... F 6
36009 Brantley, 1,066 .... F 7
35034 Brent, 2,093 .... D 5
36426 Brewton⊙, 6,747 .... D 8
35740 Bridgeport, 2,908 .... G 1
35035 Brierfield, 950 .... E 4
35020 Brighton, 2,277 .... D 4
35548 Brilliant, 726 .... C 2
36429 Brooklyn, 350 .... E 8
35036 Brookside, 990 .... E 3
35444 Brookwood, 450 .... D 4
35445 Brownville, 300 .... C 4
36010 Brundidge, 2,709 .... G 7
35446 Buhl, 500 .... C 4
36725 Burkville, 250 .... E 6
36431 Burnt Corn, 250 .... D 7
36904 Butler⊙, 2,064 .... B 6
† 36767 Cahaba, 50 .... D 6
35040 Calera, 1,655 .... E 4
36012 Calhoun, 950 .... F 6
36513 Calvert, 500 .... B 8
36726 Camden⊙, 1,742 .... D 7
36850 Camp Hill, 1,554 .... G 5
36514 Canoe, 560 .... D 8
† 36726 Canton Bend, 250 .... D 6
35549 Carbon Hill, 1,929 .... D 3
36515 Carlton, 275 .... C 8
35447 Carrollton⊙, 923 .... B 4
† 36023 Carrville, 895 .... G 5
† 36548 Carson, 250 .... C 8
36432 Castleberry, 666 .... D 8
36013 Cecil, 250 .... F 6
35959 Cedar Bluff, 956 .... G 2
36014 Central, 300 .... F 5
35960 Centre⊙, 2,418 .... G 2
35042 Centreville⊙, 2,233 .... D 5
36729 Chance, 350 .... C 7
36015 Chapman, 400 .... E 7
36518 Chatom⊙, 1,059 .... B 8
35043 Chelsea, 615 .... E 4
35616 Cherokee, 1,484 .... C 1
36611 Chickasaw, 8,447 .... B 9
35044 Childersburg, 4,831 .... F 4
36254 Choccolocco, 300 .... G 3
36905 Choctaw, 600 .... B 6
36520 Chrysler, 300 .... C 8
36521 Chunchula, 400 .... B 9
36522 Citronelle, 1,935 .... B 8
35045 Clanton⊙, 5,868 .... E 5
36015 Clayton⊙, 1,626 .... G 7
35049 Cleveland, 413 .... E 3
36017 Clio, 1,065 .... G 7
35617 Cloverdale, 650 .... C 1
35449 Coaling, 300 .... D 4
36523 Coden, 500 .... B 10
36318 Coffee Springs, 329 .... G 8
36524 Coffeeville, 441 .... B 7
35452 Coker, 800 .... C 4
35961 Collinsville, 1,300 .... G 2
36319 Columbia, 891 .... H 8
35051 Columbiana⊙, 2,248 .... E 4

AREA 51,609 sq. mi.
POPULATION 3,444,165 ('70); 3,890,061 ('80)
CAPITAL Montgomery
LARGEST CITY Birmingham
HIGHEST POINT Cheaha Mtn. 2,407 ft.
SETTLED IN 1702
ADMITTED TO UNION December 14, 1819
POPULAR NAME Heart of Dixie; Cotton State
STATE FLOWER Camellia
STATE BIRD Yellowhammer

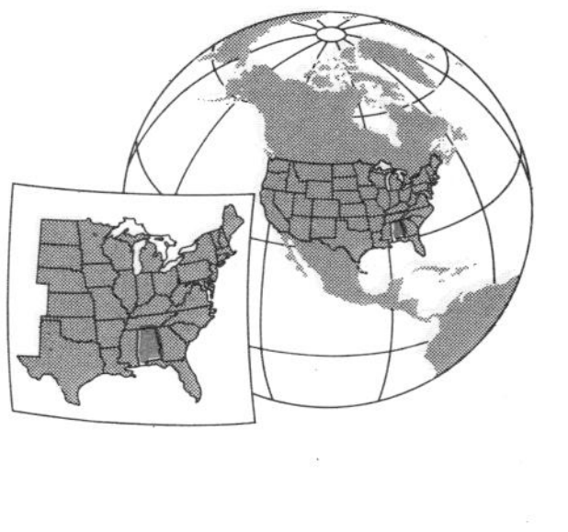

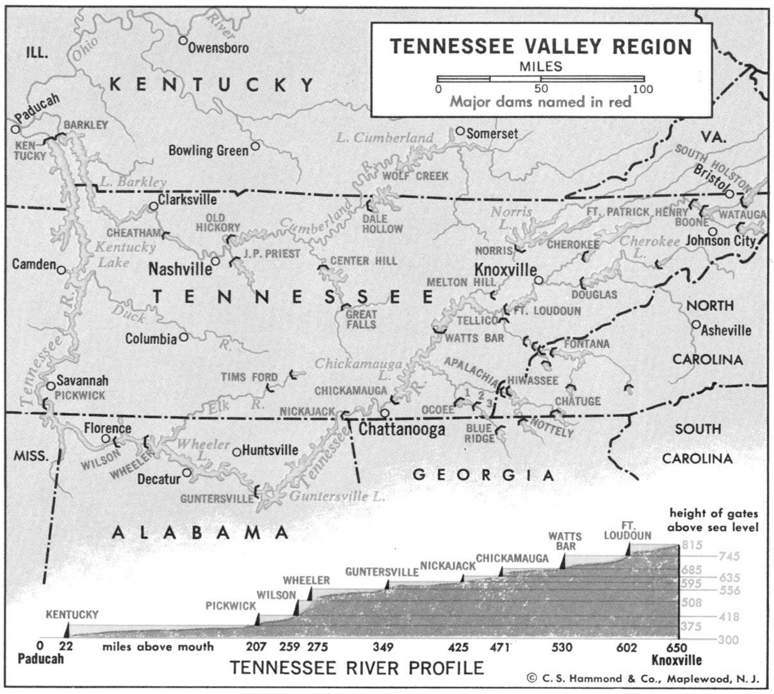
TENNESSEE VALLEY REGION
MILES
0 50 100
Major dams named in red
ILL.
KENTUCKY
TENNESSEE
ALABAMA
GEORGIA
MISS.
VA.
NORTH CAROLINA
SOUTH CAROLINA
Owensboro
Paducah
Bowling Green
Somerset
Clarksville
Nashville
Knoxville
Johnson City
Bristol
Asheville
Camden
Columbia
Savannah
Florence
Huntsville
Decatur
Chattanooga
KENTUCKY
BARKLEY
CHEATHAM
OLD HICKORY
J. P. PRIEST
CENTER HILL
DALE HOLLOW
WOLF CREEK
NORRIS
FT. PATRICK HENRY
BOONE
WATAUGA
CHEROKEE
DOUGLAS
MELTON HILL
FT. LOUDOUN
TELLICO
WATTS BAR
FONTANA
GREAT FALLS
TIMS FORD
CHICKAMAUGA
NICKAJACK
OCOEE
BLUE RIDGE
NOTTELY
HIWASSEE
CHATUGE
APALACHIA
PICKWICK
WILSON
WHEELER
GUNTERSVILLE
L. Cumberland
L. Barkley
Kentucky Lake
Norris L.
Cherokee L.
Chickamauga L.
Wheeler L.
Guntersville L.
TENNESSEE RIVER PROFILE
height of gates above sea level
KENTUCKY
PICKWICK
WILSON
WHEELER
GUNTERSVILLE
NICKAJACK
CHICKAMAUGA
WATTS BAR
FT. LOUDOUN
0 22 miles above mouth 207 259 275 349 425 471 530 602 650
Paducah
Knoxville
815
745
685
635
595
556
508
418
375
300
© C. S. Hammond & Co., Maplewood, N. J.

36019 Cooper, 250 .... E 5
36020 Coosada, 600 .... F 5
35550 Cordova, 2,750 .... D 3
† 35546 Corona, 300 .... C 3
35088 Cottage Grove, 300 .... F 5
35453 Cottondale, 600 .... D 4
36851 Cottonton, 415 .... H 6
36320 Cottonwood, 1,149 .... H 8
35618 Courtland, 547 .... D 1
36321 Cowarts, 350 .... H 8
36435 Coy, 950 .... D 7
36525 Creola, 950 .... B 9
36906 Cromwell, 700 .... B 6
35962 Crossville, 1,035 .... G 2
36907 Cuba, 386 .... B 6
35055 Cullman⊙, 12,601 .... E 2
36920 Cullomburg, 325 .... B 7
36852 Cusseta, 250 .... H 5
36853 Dadeville⊙, 2,847 .... G 5
36322 Daleville, 5,182 .... G 8
35619 Danville, 400 .... D 2
36526 Daphne, 2,382 .... C 9
36528 Dauphin Island, 950 .... B 10
36256 Daviston, 247 .... G 4
36257 De Armanville, 500 .... G 3
36022 Deatsville, 350 .... F 5
35601 Decatur⊙, 38,044 .... D 1
36529 Deer Park, 300 .... B 8
36732 Demopolis, 7,651 .... C 6
36436 Dickinson, 350 .... C 7
36736 Dixons Mills, 285 .... C 6
35061 Dolomite, 1,237 .... D 4
35062 Dora, 1,862 .... D 3
36301 Dothan⊙, 36,733 .... H 8
35553 Double Springs⊙, 957 .... D 2
35964 Douglas, 527 .... F 2
36028 Dozier, 304 .... F 7
36259 Duke, 250 .... G 3
35744 Dutton, 423 .... G 1
† 36507 Dyas, 250 .... C 9
36260 Eastaboga, 500 .... F 3
36426 East Brewton, 2,336 .... E 8
35457 Echola, 300 .... C 4
36024 Eclectic, 1,184 .... F 5
† 36317 Edwin, 296 .... H 7
36323 Elba⊙, 4,634 .... F 8
36530 Elberta, 395 .... C 10
35554 Eldridge, 350 .... C 3
35620 Elkmont, 394 .... E 1
36025 Elmore, 656 .... F 5
35458 Elrod, 600 .... C 4
35459 Emelle, 300 .... B 5
35063 Empire, 400 .... D 3
36330 Enterprise, 15,591 .... G 8
35460 Epes, 293 .... B 5
36027 Eufaula, 9,102 .... H 7
35462 Eutaw⊙, 2,805 .... C 5
36401 Evergreen⊙ 3,924 .... E 8
36439 Excel, 422 .... D 8
35746 Fackler, 250 .... G 1
36854 Fairfax, 2,772 .... H 5
35064 Fairfield, 14,369 .... E 3
36532 Fairhope, 5,720 .... C 10
35208 Fairview, 313 .... E 2
35622 Falkville, 946 .... E 2
35555 Fayette⊙, 4,568 .... C 3
36440 Finchburg, 300 .... D 7
36855 Five Points, 247 .... H 4
† 35129 Flat Creek-Wegra, 1,066 .... D 3
35966 Flat Rock, 750 .... G 1
36739 Flatwood, 300 .... C 6
† 35601 Flint City, 404 .... D 1
36441 Flomaton, 1,584 .... D 8
36442 Florala, 2,701 .... F 8
35630 Florence⊙, 34,031 .... C 1
36535 Foley, 3,368 .... C 10
35214 Forestdale, 6,091 .... E 3
36030 Forest Home, 450 .... E 7
36740 Forkland, 400 .... C 5
36031 Fort Davis, 500 .... G 6
36032 Fort Deposit, 1,438 .... E 7
36856 Fort Mitchell, 2,400 .... H 6
35967 Fort Payne⊙, 8,435 .... G 2
35463 Fosters, 400 .... C 4
36444 Franklin, 500 .... D 7
36538 Frankville, 550 .... B 7
† 31833 Fredonia, 300 .... H 5
36445 Frisco City, 1,286 .... D 8
36539 Fruitdale, 275 .... B 8
36446 Fulton, 628 .... C 7
35068 Fultondale, 5,163 .... E 3
36741 Furman, 300 .... E 6
35971 Fyffe, 311 .... G 2
* 35901 Gadsden⊙, 53,928 .... G 2
Gadsden, ‡94,144 .... G 2
36540 Gainestown, 300 .... C 8
35464 Gainesville, 255 .... B 5
35972 Gallant, 475 .... F 2
36038 Gantt, 380 .... E 8
35070 Garden City, 745 .... E 2
35071 Gardendale, 6,502 .... E 3
36340 Geneva⊙, 4,398 .... G 8
36033 Georgiana, 2,148 .... E 7
35974 Geraldine, 610 .... G 2
35559 Glen Allen, 276 .... C 3
35905 Glencoe, 2,901 .... G 3
36034 Glenwood, 378 .... F 7
† 36024 Good Hope, 840 .... E 2
35072 Goodwater, 2,172 .... F 4
35466 Gordo, 1,991 .... C 4
36343 Gordon, 312 .... H 8
35561 Gorgas, 500 .... D 3
36035 Goshen, 279 .... F 7
36450 Gosport, 400 .... C 7
36036 Grady, 298 .... F 7
36541 Grand Bay, 950 .... B 10
35747 Grant, 382 .... F 1
35073 Graysville, 3,182 .... D 3
35074 Green Pond, 500 .... D 4
36744 Greensboro⊙, 3,371 .... C 5

(continued on following page)

Agriculture, Industry and Resources

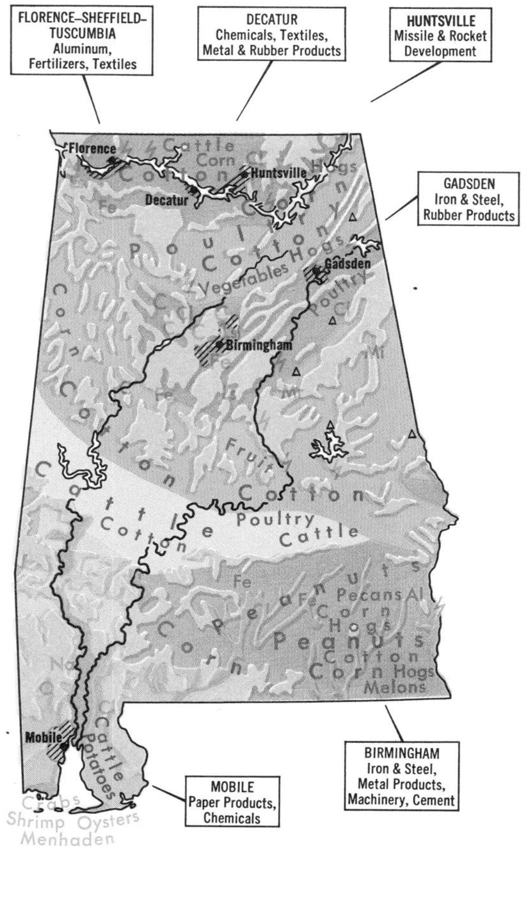
FLORENCE–SHEFFIELD–TUSCUMBIA
Aluminum, Fertilizers, Textiles
DECATUR
Chemicals, Textiles, Metal & Rubber Products
HUNTSVILLE
Missile & Rocket Development
GADSDEN
Iron & Steel, Rubber Products
BIRMINGHAM
Iron & Steel, Metal Products, Machinery, Cement
MOBILE
Paper Products, Chemicals
Florence
Huntsville
Decatur
Gadsden
Birmingham
Mobile
Cattle
Corn
Cotton
Hogs
Poultry
Vegetables
Fruit
Peanuts
Pecans
Melons
Potatoes
Crabs
Shrimp
Oysters
Menhaden

DOMINANT LAND USE

- Specialized Cotton
- Cotton, Livestock
- Cotton, General Farming
- Cotton, Hogs, Peanuts
- Cotton, Forest Products
- Peanuts, General Farming
- Truck and Mixed Farming
- Forests
- Swampland, Limited Agriculture

MAJOR MINERAL OCCURRENCES

Al	Bauxite	Ls	Limestone
At	Asphalt	Mi	Mica
C	Coal	Mr	Marble
Cl	Clay	Na	Salt
Fe	Iron Ore	O	Petroleum

Water Power
Major Industrial Areas
△ Major Textile Manufacturing Centers

ALABAMA

SCALE

0 5 10   20   30   40 MI.

0 5 10   20   30   40 KM.

State Capitals ⊛

County Seats ⊙

© C.S. HAMMOND & Co., N.Y.

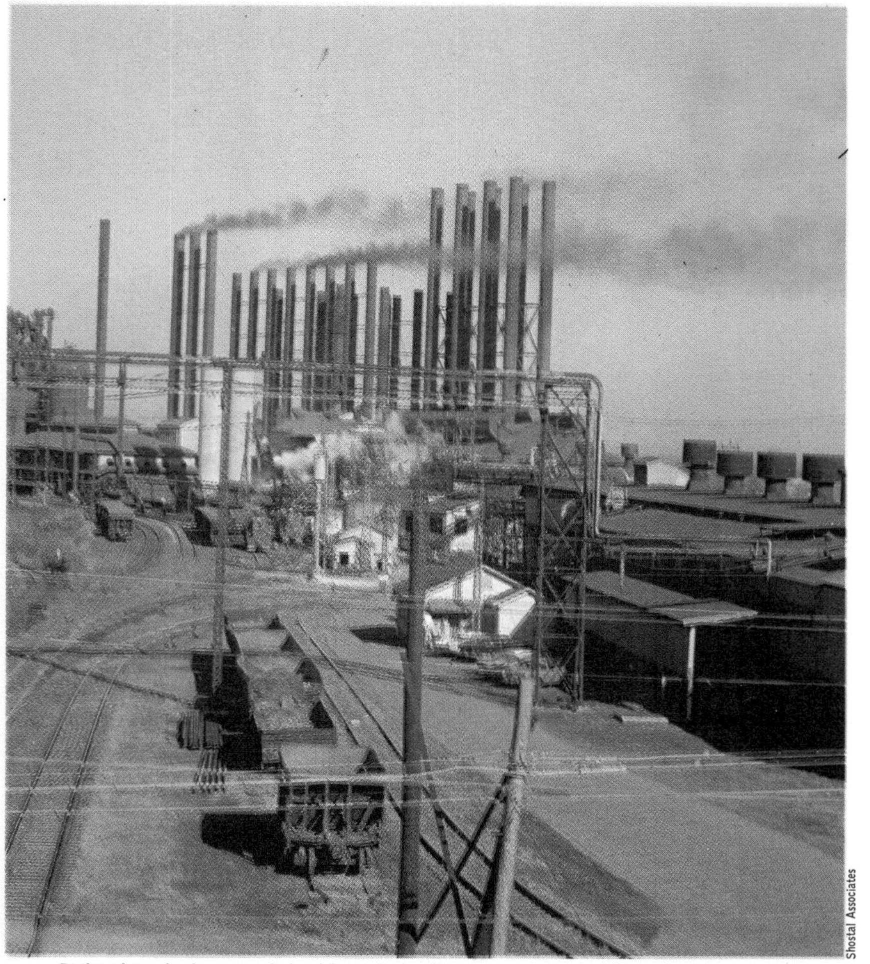

Shostal Associates

Railroad tracks form tangled spider webs leading to voracious steel furnaces. Native coal, iron ore and limestone are delivered to Ensley (Birmingham), Alabama plant.

Topography

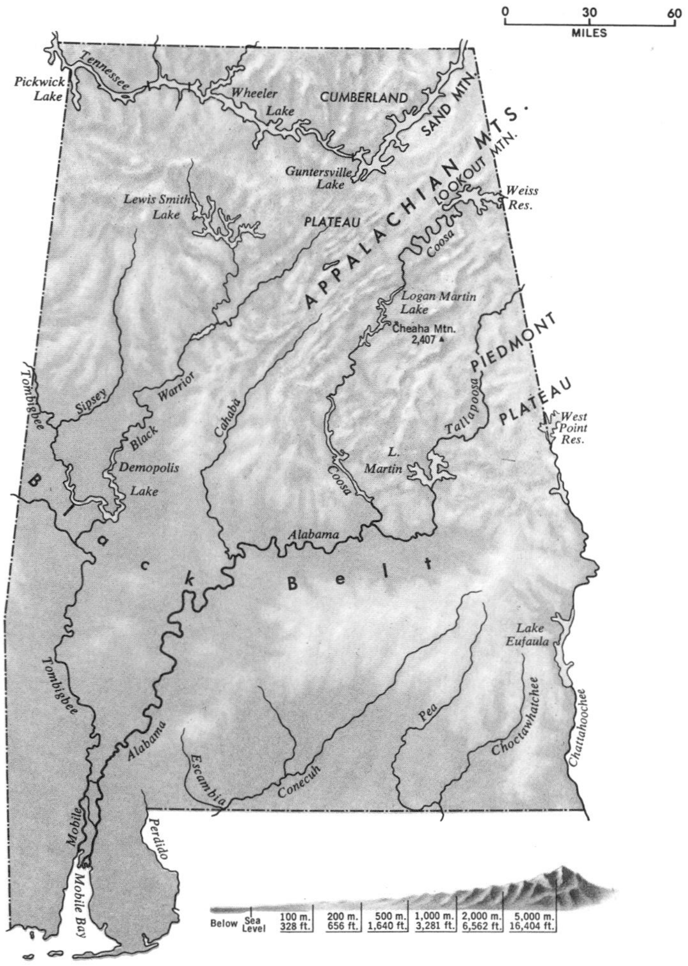

0
30
60
MILES
Pickwick Lake
Tennessee
Wheeler Lake
CUMBERLAND
SAND MTN.
Guntersville Lake
APPALACHIAN MTS.
LOOKOUT MTN.
Weiss Res.
Lewis Smith Lake
PLATEAU
Coosa
Logan Martin Lake
Cheaha Mtn. 2,407
PIEDMONT
PLATEAU
Tallapoosa
West Point Res.
Sipsey
Black Warrior
Cahaba
Tombigbee
Demopolis Lake
L. Martin
Coosa
Alabama
Black Belt
Lake Eufaula
Tombigbee
Alabama
Escambia
Conecuh
Pea
Choctawhatchee
Chattahoochee
Mobile
Perdido
Mobile Bay
Below Sea Level
100 m. 328 ft.
200 m. 656 ft.
500 m. 1,640 ft.
1,000 m. 3,281 ft.
2,000 m. 6,562 ft.
5,000 m. 16,404 ft.

36037 Greenville⊙, 8,033 E 7
36451 Grove Hill⊙, 1,825 C 7
35975 Groveoak, 275 F 2
35563 Guin, 2,220 C 3
36542 Gulf Shores, 909 C 10
35976 Guntersville⊙, 6,491 F 2
35748 Gurley, 647 F 1
35564 Hackleburg, 726 C 2
35565 Haleyville, 4,134 C 2
36909 Halsell, 250 B 6
35570 Hamilton⊙, 3,088 C 2
35077 Hanceville, 2,027 E 2
36039 Hardaway, 300 G 6
35078 Harpersville, 639 F 4
36344 Hartford, 2,648 G 8
35640 Hartselle, 7,355 E 2
35749 Harvest, 500 E 1
36858 Hatchechubbee, 250 H 6
† 35672 Hatton, 950 D 1
36040 Hayneville⊙, 473 E 6
36345 Headland, 2,545 H 8
36264 Heflin⊙, 2,872 G 3
35080 Helena, 1,110 E 4
35978 Henagar, 812 G 1
35979 Higdon, 450 G 1
35081 Hissop, 250 F 5
† 36201 Hobson City, 1,124 G 3
35903 Hokes Bluff, 2,133 G 3
35082 Hollins, 600 F 4
35083 Holly Pond, 325 E 2
35751 Hollytree, 245 F 1
35752 Hollywood, 301 G 1
35401 Holt, 2,000 D 4
36859 Holy Trinity, 400 H 6
35209 Homewood, 21,245 E 4
† 35226 Hoover, 1,393 E 4
36043 Hope Hull, 975 F 6
35980 Horton, 271 F 2
35020 Hueytown, 7,095 D 4
* 35801 Huntsville⊙, 137,802 E 1
Huntsville, ‡228,339 E 1
† 36507 Hurricane, 300 C 9
36860 Hurtsboro, 937 H 6
36452 Hybart, 250 D 7
35981 Ider, 500 G 1
35210 Irondale, 3,166 E 3
36910 Jachin, 250 B 6
36545 Jackson, 5,957 C 8
36861 Jacksons Gap, 450 G 5
36265 Jacksonville, 7,715 G 3
35501 Jasper⊙, 10,798 D 3
36745 Jefferson, 500 C 6
35085 Jemison, 1,423 E 5
† 36268 Jenifer, 300 G 3
35086 Johns, 241 D 4
35087 Joppa, 350 E 2
35089 Kellyton, 500 F 5
35574 Kennedy, 415 B 3
36045 Kent, 500 G 5
35645 Killen, 683 D 1

35091 Kimberly, 847 E 3
36746 Kimbrough, 250 C 6
36453 Kinston, 540 F 8
35469 Knoxville, 500 C 4
35754 Laceys Spring, 500 E 1
36862 Lafayette⊙, 3,530 H 5
36747 Lamison, 275 C 6
36863 Lanett, 6,908 H 5
36864 Langdale, 2,235 H 5
35755 Langston, 250 G 1
36046 Lapine, 300 F 7
35768 Larkinsville, 425 F 1
36911 Lavaca, 550 B 6
35094 Leeds, 6,991 E 3
35646 Leighton, 1,231 D 1
36548 Leroy, 350 B 8
36047 Letohatchee, 250 E 6
35648 Lexington, 278 D 1
36549 Lillian, 600 D 10
35096 Lincoln, 1,127 F 3
36748 Linden⊙, 2,697 C 6
36266 Lineville, 1,984 G 4
35020 Lipscomb, 3,225 E 4
36912 Lisman, 628 B 6
36550 Little River, 400 C 8
† 36876 Little Shawmut, 2,682 H 5
35654 Littleville, 858 C 1
35470 Livingston⊙, 2,358 B 5
36865 Loachapoka, 400 G 5
36455 Lockhart, 698 F 8
† 35045 Lomax, 300 E 5
36048 Louisville, 785 G 7
36751 Lower Peach Tree, 950 C 7
36551 Loxley, 859 C 9
36049 Luverne⊙, 2,440 F 7
35575 Lynn, 286 C 2
35758 Madison, 3,086 E 1
36754 Magnolia, 350 C 6
36555 Magnolia Springs, 726 C 10
36556 Malcolm, 300 B 8
† 35501 Manchester, 400 D 3
† 36586 Manila, 300 C 7
36750 Maplesville, 596 E 5
35112 Margaret, 685 F 3
† 35616 Margerum, 250 B 1
36756 Marion⊙, 4,289 D 5
36759 Marion Junction, 300 D 6
† 36801 Marvyn, 300 H 6
35111 McCalla, 450 E 4
36552 McCullough, 500 D 8
36553 McIntosh, 600 B 8
36456 McKenzie, 491 E 7
36753 McWilliams, 525 D 7
36913 Melvin, 300 B 7
35984 Mentone, 407 G 1
35759 Meridianville, 950 F 1
36458 Mexia, 250 D 8
35228 Midfield, 6,399 E 4
36350 Midland City, 1,172 H 8
36053 Midway, 558 H 6

† 35150 Mignon, 1,726 F 4
36054 Millbrook, 800 F 6
36760 Millers Ferry, 300 D 6
35576 Millport, 1,070 B 3
36558 Millry, 911 B 7
36761 Minter, 450 D 6
* 36601 Mobile⊙, 190,026 B 9
Mobile, ‡376,690 B 9
36460 Monroeville⊙, 4,846 D 7
† 35804 Monrovia, 500 E 1
35115 Montevallo, 3,719 E 4
* 36101 Montgomery (cap.)⊙, 133,386 F 6
Montgomery, ‡201,325 F 6
36559 Montrose, 900 C 9
† 35125 Moody, 504 F 3
35116 Morris, 519 E 3
36762 Morvin, 350 C 7
35650 Moulton⊙, 2,470 D 2
35474 Moundville, 996 C 5
† 35957 Mountainboro, 311 F 2
35223 Mountain Brook, 19,474 E 4
† 36047 Mount Carmel, 400 F 6
36057 Mount Meigs, 250 F 6
36560 Mount Vernon, 1,079 B 8
† 36012 Mount Willing, 364 E 6
36268 Munford, 950 F 3
35660 Muscle Shoals, 6,907 C 1
36763 Myrtlewood, 334 C 6
36764 Nanafalia, 250 B 6
35578 Nauvoo, 265 D 3
36765 Newbern, 286 C 5
36351 New Brockton, 1,374 G 8
35760 New Hope, 1,300 F 1
35761 New Market, 600 F 1
35010 New Site, 378 G 4
36352 Newton, 1,865 G 8
36353 Newville, 465 H 8
35476 Northport, 9,435 C 4
36866 Notasulga, 833 G 5
† 35014 Nottingham, 400 F 4
35579 Oakman, 853 D 3
35120 Odenville, 533 F 3
36271 Ohatchee, 445 G 3
35121 Oneonta⊙, 4,390 E 3
36801 Opelika⊙, 19,027 H 5
36467 Opp, 6,493 F 8
36561 Orange Beach, 300 C 10
36767 Orrville, 362 D 6
35763 Owens Cross Roads, 767 E 1
36201 Oxford, 4,361 G 3
36360 Ozark⊙, 13,555 G 8
35477 Panola, 300 B 5
36370 Pansey, 300 H 8
35580 Parrish, 1,742 D 3
35124 Pelham, 931 E 4
35125 Pell City⊙, 5,381 F 3
36916 Pennington, 276 B 6
36562 Perdido, 325 C 8
36530 Perdido Beach, 300 C 10

36471 Peterman, 750 D 7
35478 Peterson, 1,040 D 4
36867 Phenix City⊙, 25,281 H 6
35581 Phil Campbell, 1,230 C 2
36272 Piedmont, 5,063 G 3
36371 Pinckard, 609 G 8
36768 Pine Apple, 347 E 7
36769 Pine Hill, 697 C 7
36065 Pine Level, 300 F 6
35126 Pinson, 2,500 E 3
35765 Pisgah, 519 G 1
36871 Pittsview, 400 H 6
36758 Plantersville, 550 E 5
36564 Point Clear, 850 C 10
36067 Prattville⊙, 13,116 E 6
36610 Prichard, 41,578 B 9
35766 Princeton, 250 F 1
36772 Putnam, 305 B 6
† 36507 Rabun, 300 C 8
35131 Ragland, 1,239 F 3
35901 Rainbow City, 3,107 F 3
35986 Rainsville, 2,099 G 2
35480 Ralph, 500 C 4
36069 Ramer, 750 F 6
36273 Ranburne, 371 H 3
36473 Range, 275 D 8
35582 Red Bay, 2,464 B 2
36474 Red Level, 616 E 8
† 35954 Reece City, 496 G 2
35481 Reform, 1,893 C 4
† 36720 Rehoboth, 300 D 6
† 35160 Renfroe, 400 F 4
36475 Repton, 277 D 8
† 35203 Republic, 500 E 3
36918 Riderwood, 400 B 6
36476 River Falls, 580 E 8
35135 Riverside, 351 F 3
36872 River View, 1,109 H 5
36274 Roanoke, 5,251 H 4
36567 Robertsdale, 2,078 C 9
35136 Rockford⊙, 603 F 5
36274 Rock Mills, 800 H 4
35652 Rogersville, 950 D 1
† 35020 Roosevelt City, 3,663 E 4
35653 Russellville⊙, 7,814 C 2
36071 Rutledge, 353 F 7
35137 Saginaw, 300 E 4
35138 Saint Bernard, 896 E 2
† 35146 Saint Clair Springs, 300 F 3
36568 Saint Elmo, 650 B 10
36569 Saint Stephens, 400 B 7
36874 Salem, 475 H 5
36570 Salitpa, 500 C 7
36477 Samson, 2,257 F 8
36478 Sanford, 256 F 8
35583 Saragossa, 300 D 3
36571 Saraland, 7,840 B 9
36775 Sardis, 300 E 6
36775 Sardis, 368 F 2
36572 Satsuma, 2,035 B 9

35139 Sayre, 700 E 3
35768 Scottsboro⊙, 9,324 F 1
36875 Seale, 400 H 6
35771 Section, 702 G 1
36701 Selma⊙, 27,379 E 6
† 36701 Selmont, 2,270 E 6
36574 Seminole, 275 D 10
36575 Semmes, 800 B 9
36876 Shawmut, 2,181 H 5
35660 Sheffield, 13,115 C 1
35143 Shelby, 500 E 4
36075 Shorter, 500 G 6
36373 Shorterville, 330 H 7
36733 Shortleaf, 253 C 6
36919 Silas, 345 B 7
35144 Siluria, 678 E 4
36576 Silverhill, 552 C 9
† 36268 Silver Run, 250 G 3
35584 Sipsey, 608 D 3
36375 Slocomb, 1,883 G 8
36877 Smiths, 2,500 H 5
35952 Snead, 347 F 2
† 36104 Snowdoun, 250 F 6
36778 Snow Hill, 500 E 7
35901 Southside, 983 F 3
36527 Spanish Fort, 983 C 9
† 35674 Spring Valley, 600 C 1
35146 Springville, 1,153 E 3
35585 Spruce Pine, 600 C 2
36878 Standing Rock, 500 H 4
36578 Stapleton, 975 C 9
35987 Steele, 798 F 3
35147 Sterrett, 450 F 4
35772 Stevenson, 2,390 G 1
† 35150 Stewartville, 250 F 4
36579 Stockton, 1,400 C 9
35586 Sulligent, 1,762 B 3
35148 Sumiton, 2,374 D 3
36580 Summerdale, 550 C 10
36780 Sunny South, 250 C 7
36781 Suttle, 256 D 5
36782 Sweet Water, 265 C 6
35149 Sycamore, 800 F 4
35150 Sylacauga, 12,255 F 4
35988 Sylvania, 476 G 1
35160 Talladega⊙, 17,662 F 4
36078 Tallassee, 4,809 G 5
35671 Tanner, 600 E 1
35217 Tarrant, 6,835 E 3
36582 Theodore, 1,950 B 9
36783 Thomaston, 824 C 6
36784 Thomasville, 3,769 C 7
35171 Thorsby, 944 E 5
35672 Town Creek, 1,203 D 1
35587 Townley, 500 D 3
36921 Toxey, 304 B 7
35172 Trafford, 628 E 3
35673 Trinity, 881 D 1
36081 Troy⊙, 11,482 G 7
35173 Trussville, 2,985 E 3

36479 Tunnel Springs, 300 D 7
35401 Tuscaloosa⊙, 65,773 C 4
Tuscaloosa, ‡116,029 C 4
35674 Tuscumbia⊙, 8,828 C 1
36083 Tuskegee⊙, 11,028 G 6
36088 Tuskegee Institute, 5,800 G 6
36089 Union Springs⊙, 4,324 G 6
36786 Uniontown, 2,133 D 6
36480 Uriah, 1,200 D 8
35775 Valhermoso Springs, 500 E 2
35989 Valley Head, 470 G 1
35176 Vandiver, 700 F 4
36091 Verbena, 350 E 5
35592 Vernon⊙, 2,190 B 3
35216 Vestavia Hills, 8,311 E 4
35593 Vina, 366 B 2
35178 Vincent, 1,419 F 4
35179 Vinemont, 480 E 2
36481 Vredenburgh, 622 D 7
36276 Wadley, 626 G 4
36585 Wagarville, 350 B 8
36586 Walker Springs, 500 C 7
35180 Warrior, 2,621 E 3
35677 Waterloo, 262 B 1
35182 Wattsville, 500 F 3
36879 Waverly, 247 G 5
36277 Weaver, 2,091 G 3
36376 Webb, 354 H 8
36278 Wedowee⊙, 842 H 4
† 35129 Wegra-Flat Creek, 1,066 D 3
35183 Weogufka, 350 F 4
35184 West Blocton, 1,172 D 4
† 36201 West End-Cobb Town, 5,515 G 3
35185 Westover, 1,400 E 4
36092 Wetumpka⊙, 3,786 F 5
36482 Whatley, 500 C 7
† 35618 Wheeler, 300 D 1
† 36040 White Hall, 300 E 6
† 36862 White Plains, 350 G 3
† 35094 Whites Chapel, 334 F 3
36923 Whitfield, 500 B 6
† 36352 Wicksburg, 400 G 8
36587 Wilmer, 720 B 9
35186 Wilsonville, 659 E 4
35187 Wilton, 573 E 4
35594 Winfield, 3,292 C 3
35188 Woodstock, 320 D 4
35776 Woodville, 322 F 1
36924 Yantley, 500 B 6
36789 Yellow Bluff, 350 C 7
36925 York, 3,044 B 6

⊙ County seat.
‡ Population of metropolitan area.
† Zip of nearest p.o.
* Multiple zips

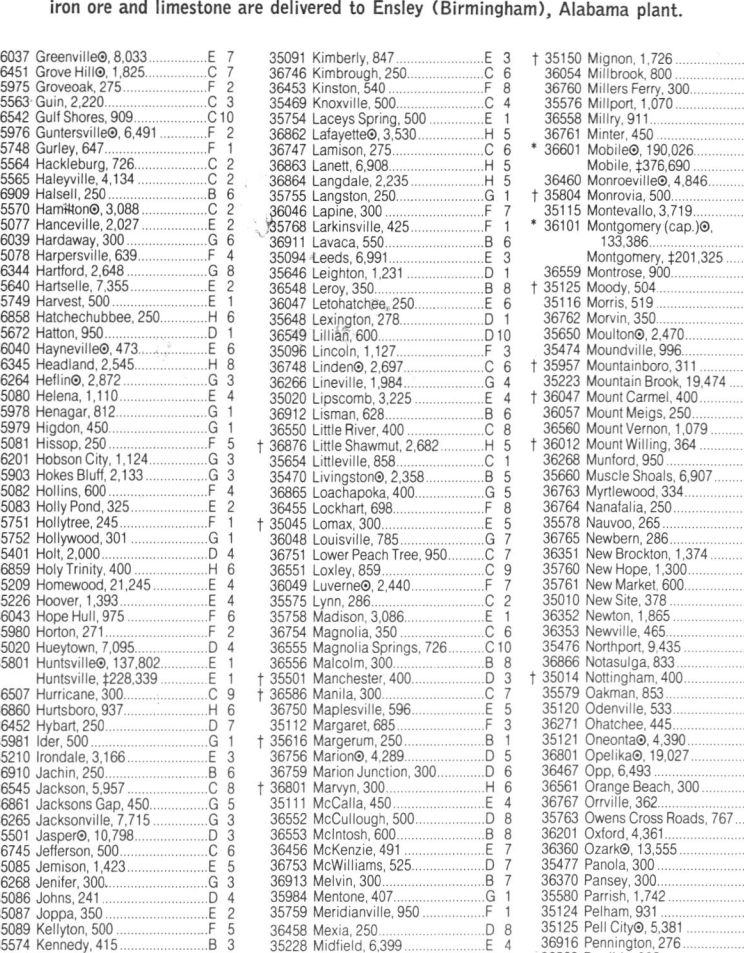

Agriculture, Industry and Resources

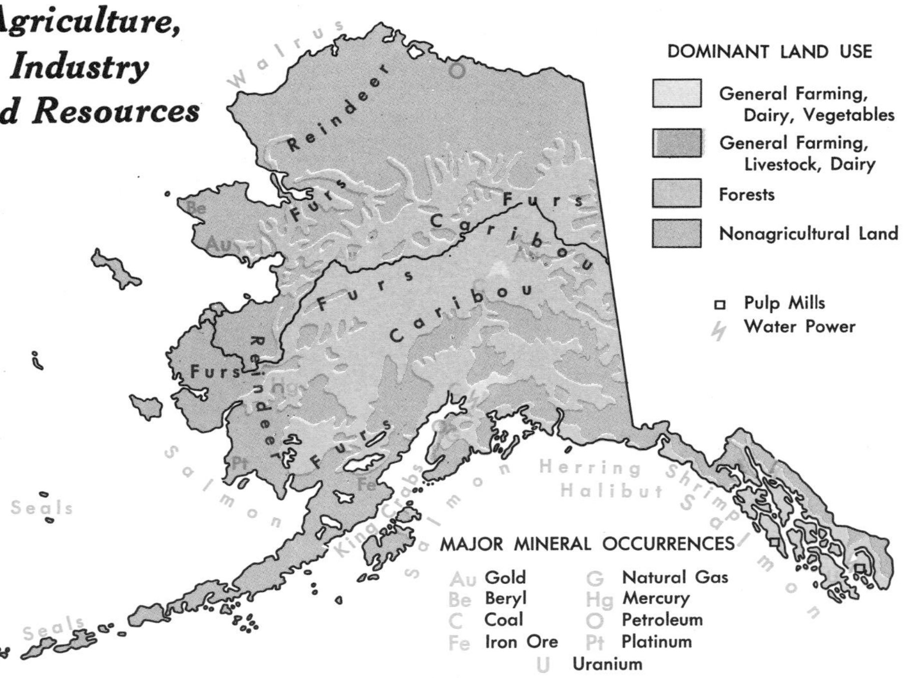

DOMINANT LAND USE

- General Farming, Dairy, Vegetables
- General Farming, Livestock, Dairy
- Forests
- Nonagricultural Land

□ Pulp Mills
⚡ Water Power

MAJOR MINERAL OCCURRENCES

Au	Gold	G	Natural Gas
Be	Beryl	Hg	Mercury
C	Coal	O	Petroleum
Fe	Iron Ore	Pt	Platinum
		U	Uranium	

Topography

200   400
0
MILES

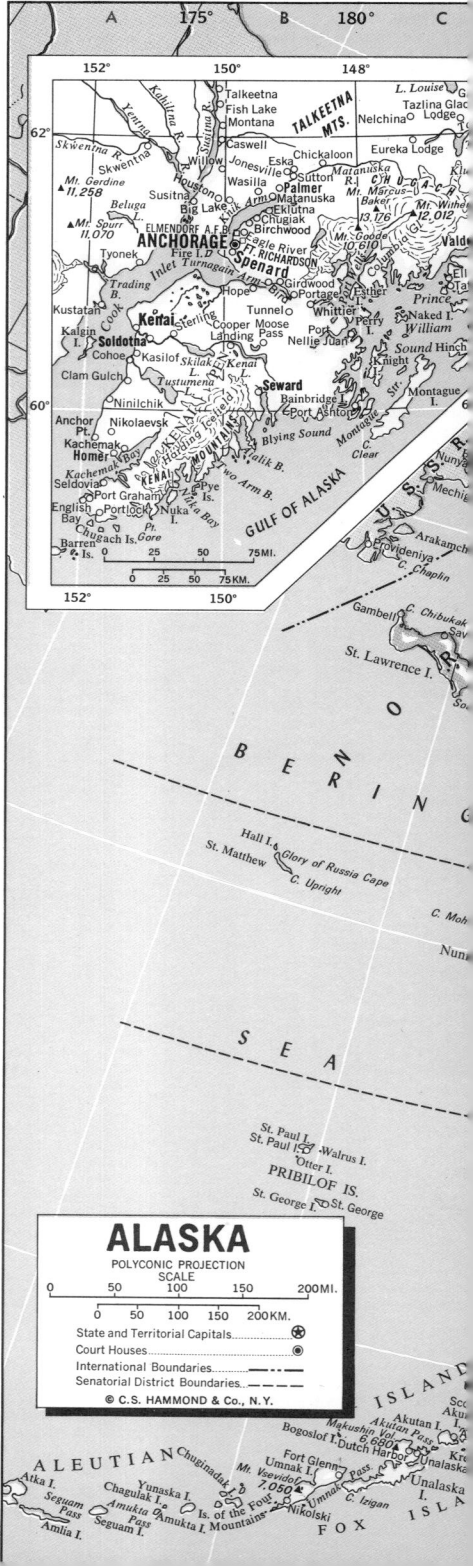

ALASKA

POLYCONIC PROJECTION

SCALE

0   50   100   150   200MI.

0   50   100   150   200KM.

State and Territorial Capitals .... ⊛
Court Houses .... ⊚
International Boundaries ------
Senatorial District Boundaries ------

© C.S. HAMMOND & Co., N.Y.

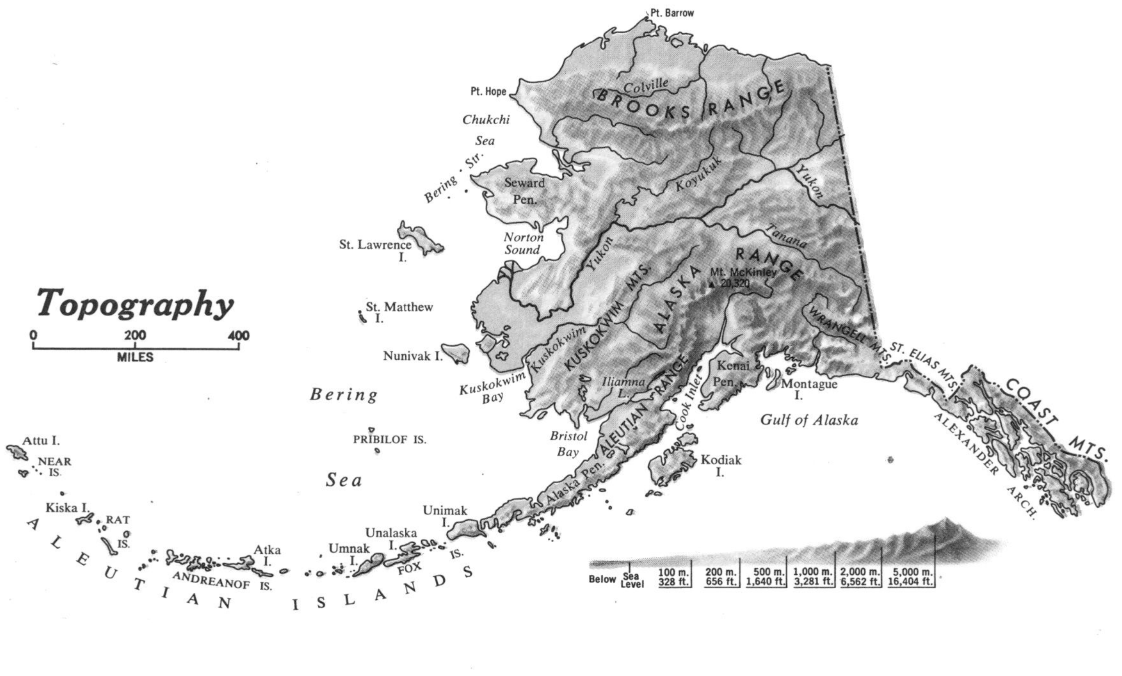

ZIP	Place	Ref
† 99723	Prudhoe Bay, 49	J 1
99655	Quinhagak, 340	F 3
99767	Rampart, 36	H 1
99656	Red Devil, 81	G 2
99768	Ruby, 145	G 2
99657	Russian Mission, 146	F 2
† 99660	Saint George, 163	E 3
99658	Saint Marys, 384	F 2
99659	Saint Michael, 207	F 2
99660	Saint Paul Island, 450	D 3
99661	Sand Point, 360	G 3
99769	Savoonga, 364	E 2
† 99901	Saxman, 135	N 2
99662	Scammon Bay, 166	E 2
99770	Selawik, 429	G 1
99663	Seldovia, 437	B 2
99664	Seward, 1,587	C 1
99665	Shageluk, 167	F 2
99771	Shaktoolik, 151	F 2
99666	Sheldon Point, 125	E 2
99772	Shishmaref, 267	E 1
99773	Shungnak, 165	G 1
99835	Sitka, 3,370	M 1
99840	Skagway, 675	M 1
99668	Sleetmute, 109	G 2
99669	Soldotna, 1,202	B 1
99670	South Naknek, 154	G 3
99503	Spenard, 18,089	C 1
99671	Stebbins, 231	F 2
99672	Sterling, 30	B 1
99774	Stevens Village, 74	J 1
99673	Stony River, 74	G 2
† 99729	Summit, 34	J 2
† 99743	Suntrana, 67	J 2
† 99501	Susitna, 50	B 1
99674	Sutton, 76	C 1
99676	Talkeetna, 182	C 1
99776	Tanacross, 84	K 2
99777	Tanana, 120	H 1
99677	Tatitlek, 111	D 1
99778	Teller, 220	E 1
99841	Tenakee Springs, 86	M 1
99779	Tetlin, 114	K 1
† 99801	Thane, 70	N 1
† 99678	Thorne Bay, 443	M 2
99679	Togiak, 383	F 3
99780	Tok, 214	K 2
99679	Tuluksak, 195	F 2
99680	Tuntutuliak, 158	F 2
99681	Tununak, 274	F 2
99682	Tyonek, 232	B 1
† 99701	Umiat, 45	H 1
99684	Unalakleet, 434	G 2
99685	Unalaska, 178	E 4
99686	Valdez, 1,005	D 1
99781	Venetie, 112	J 1
99782	Wainwright, 315	F 1
99783	Wales, 131	E 1
99928	Ward Cove, 105	N 2
99687	Wasilla, 300	C 1
99784	White Mountain, 87	F 2
99501	Whittier, 130	C 1
99688	Willow, 38	B 1
† 99615	Woody Island, 41	H 3
99929	Wrangell, 2,029	N 2
99689	Yakutat, 190	L 2

⊙ Court House
† Zip of nearest p.o.
* Multiple zips

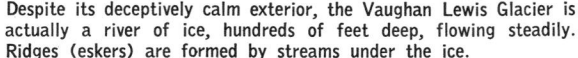

Despite its deceptively calm exterior, the Vaughan Lewis Glacier is actually a river of ice, hundreds of feet deep, flowing steadily. Ridges (eskers) are formed by streams under the ice.

Arthur A. Twomey — Shostal Associates

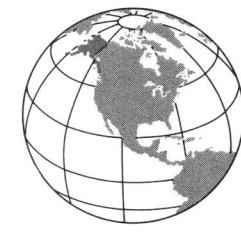

AREA 586,412 sq. mi.
POPULATION 302,173 ('70); 400,481 ('80)
CAPITAL Juneau
LARGEST CITY Anchorage
HIGHEST POINT Mt. McKinley 20,320 ft.
SETTLED IN 1801
ADMITTED TO UNION January 3, 1959
POPULAR NAME Great Land
STATE FLOWER Forget-me-not
STATE BIRD Willow Ptarmigan

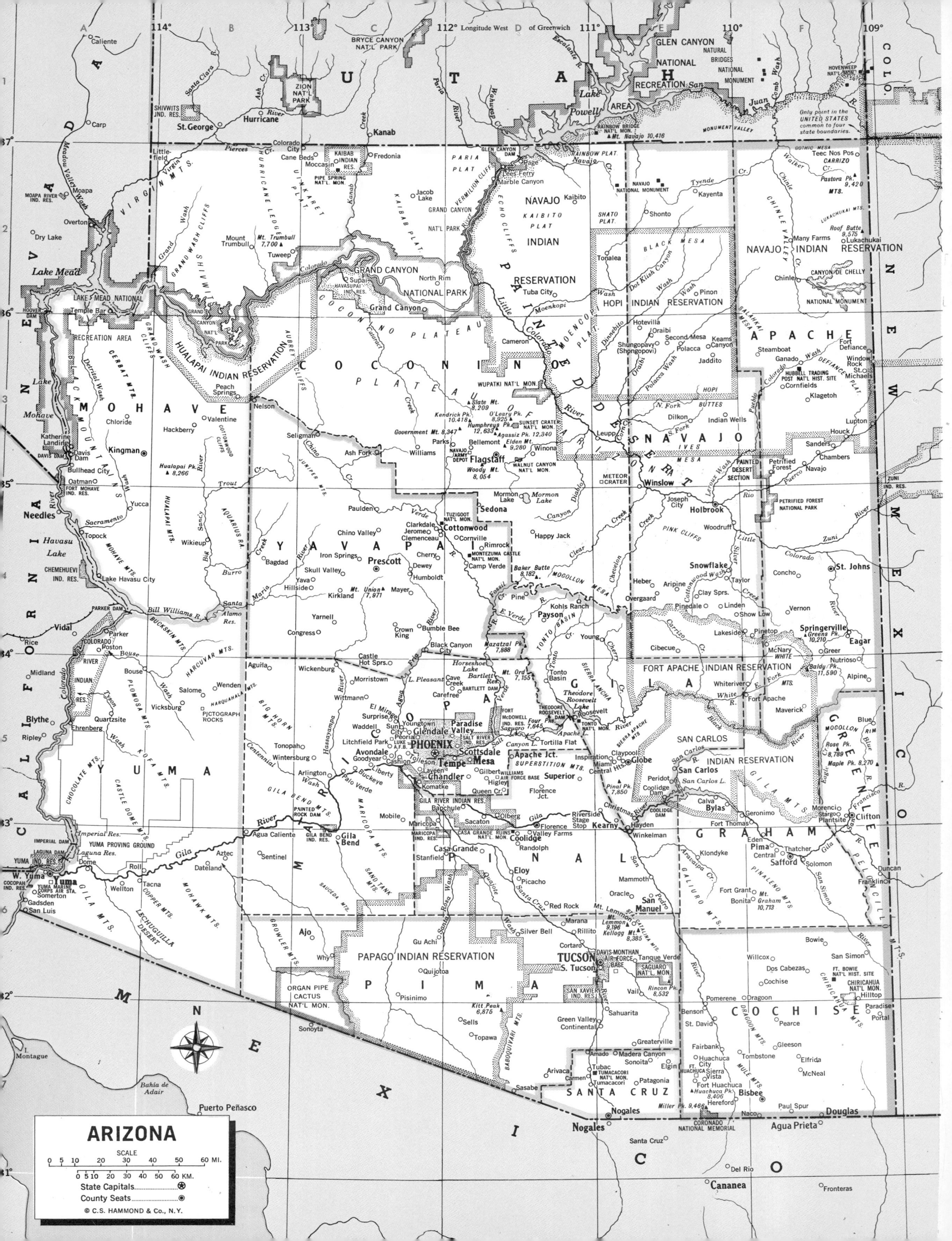

Topography

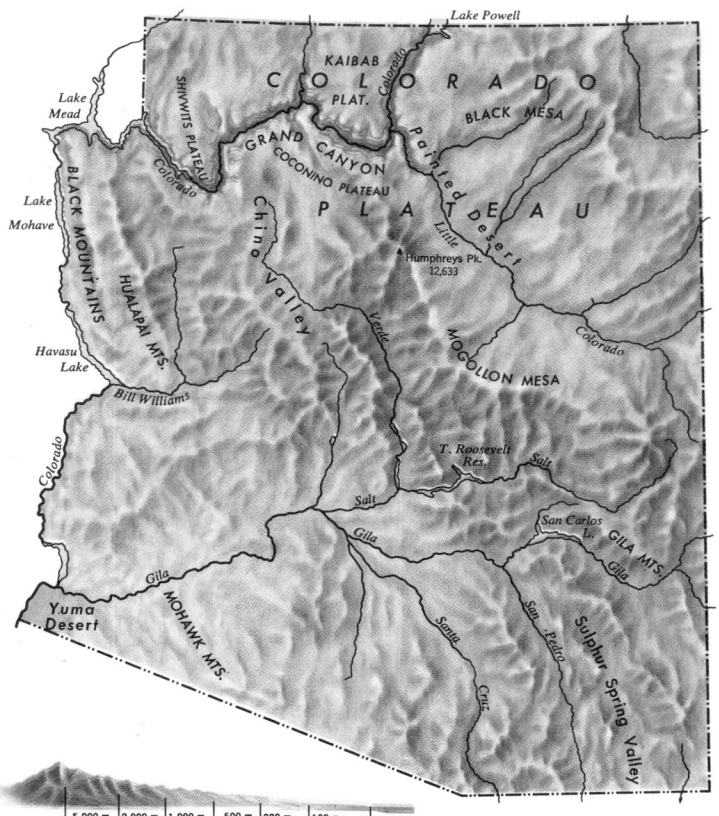

0   50   100
MILES

5,000 m. | 2,000 m. | 1,000 m. | 500 m. | 200 m. | 100 m. | Sea Level | Below
16,404 ft. | 6,562 ft. | 3,281 ft. | 1,640 ft. | 656 ft. | 328 ft. |

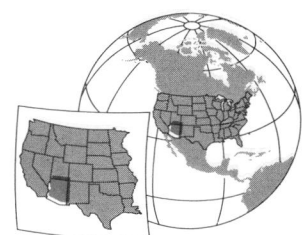

AREA 113,909 sq. mi.
POPULATION 1,772,482 ('70); 2,717,866 ('80)
CAPITAL Phoenix
LARGEST CITY Phoenix
HIGHEST POINT Humphreys Pk. 12,633 ft.
SETTLED IN 1580
ADMITTED TO UNION February 14, 1912
POPULAR NAME Grand Canyon State
STATE FLOWER Saguaro Cactus Blossom
STATE BIRD Cactus Wren

Agriculture, Industry and Resources

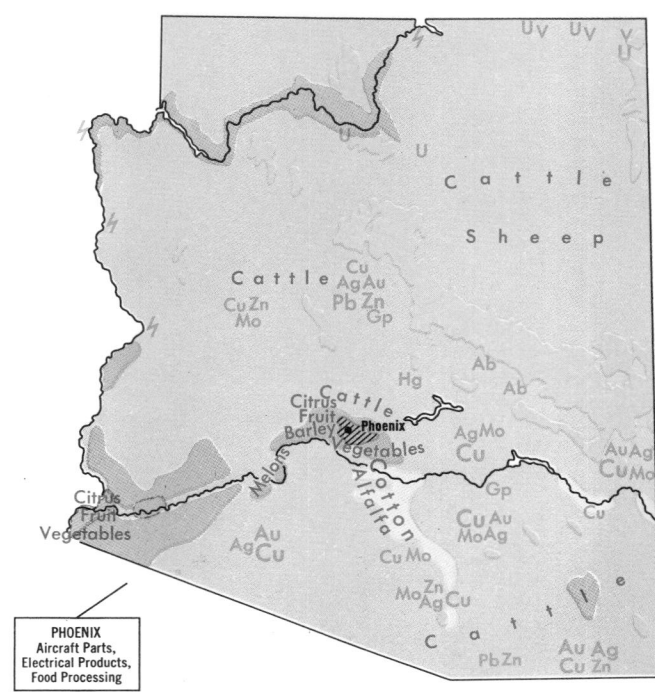

PHOENIX
Aircraft Parts,
Electrical Products,
Food Processing

MAJOR MINERAL OCCURRENCES

Ab	Asbestos	Gp	Gypsum	U	Uranium
Ag	Silver	Hg	Mercury	V	Vanadium
Au	Gold	Mo	Molybdenum	Zn	Zinc
Cu	Copper	Pb	Lead		

DOMINANT LAND USE

- Fruit, Truck and Mixed Farming
- Cotton and Alfalfa
- General Farming, Livestock, Special Crops
- Range Livestock
- Forests
- Nonagricultural Land

⚡ Water Power

▨ Major Industrial Areas

COUNTIES

Apache, 32,298 ....F 3
Cochise, 61,910 ....F 7
Coconino, 48,326 ....C 3
Gila, 29,255 ....E 5
Graham, 16,578 ....E 6
Greenlee, 10,330 ....F 5
Maricopa, 967,522 ....C 5
Mohave, 25,857 ....A 3
Navajo, 47,715 ....E 3
Pima, 351,667 ....D 6
Pinal, 67,916 ....D 6
Santa Cruz, 13,966 ....E 7
Yavapai, 36,733 ....C 4
Yuma, 60,827 ....A 5

CITIES and TOWNS

Zip   Name/Pop.   Key

† 85333 Agua Caliente, 30 ....B 6
85320 Aguila, 450 ....B 5
85321 Ajo, 5,881 ....C 6
85920 Amado, 450 ....F 5
85640 Amado, 75 ....D 7
85220 Apache Junction, 2,390 ....D 5
† 85901 Aripine, 25 ....E 4
85601 Arivaca, 165 ....D 7
85322 Arlington, 950 ....C 5
85320 Ash Fork, 800 ....C 3
85323 Avondale, 6,304 ....C 5
† 85333 Aztec, 20 ....B 6
86321 Bagdad, 2,079 ....B 4
85221 Bapchule, 300 ....C 5
86001 Bellemont, 6 ....D 3
85602 Benson, 2,839 ....E 7
85603 Bisbee⊙, 8,328 ....F 7
85324 Black Canyon City, 600 ....C 4
85922 Blue, 50 ....F 5
† 85643 Bonita, 20 ....E 6
85325 Bouse, 200 ....A 5
85605 Bowie, 600 ....F 6
85326 Buckeye, 2,599 ....C 5
86430 Bullhead City, 2,900 ....A 3
85327 Bumble Bee, 15 ....C 4
85530 Bylas, 1,125 ....E 5
85530 Calva, 10 ....E 5
86322 Camp Verde, 1,500 ....D 4
† 86022 Cane Beds, 30 ....B 2
85331 Carefree, 350 ....D 5
† 85640 Carmen, 200 ....D 7
85222 Casa Grande, 10,536 ....D 6
85329 Cashion, 2,705 ....C 5
† 85342 Castle Hot Springs, 50 ....C 5
85331 Cave Creek, 300 ....C 5
85531 Central, 300 ....F 6
† 85501 Central Heights, 2,289 .....E 5
86502 Chambers, 500 ....F 3

85224 Chandler, 13,763 ....D 5
† 86327 Cherry, 20 ....C 4
86503 Chinle, 500 ....F 2
86323 Chino Valley, 970 ....C 4
86431 Chloride, 225 ....A 3
† 85292 Christmas, 201 ....E 5
85901 Cibecue, 100 ....E 4
86324 Clarkdale, 892 ....C 4
85532 Claypool, 2,245 ....E 5
† 85934 Clay Springs, 225 ....E 4
† 86326 Clemenceau, 300 ....C 4
85533 Clifton⊙, 5,087 ....F 5
85606 Cochise, 150 ....F 6
86021 Colorado City, 350 ....B 2
85924 Concho, 100 ....F 4
85332 Congress, 350 ....C 4
85640 Continental, 250 ....D 7
85228 Coolidge, 4,651 ....D 6
† 85542 Coolidge Dam, 42 ....E 5
† 86505 Cornfields, 200 ....F 3
85325 Cornville, 425 ....D 4
85230 Cortaro, 75 ....D 6
86326 Cottonwood, 2,815 ....C 4
86333 Crown King, 100 ....C 4
85333 Dateland, 100 ....B 6
† 86430 Davis Dam, 125 ....A 3
86327 Dewey, 100 ....C 4
86047 Dilkon, 90 ....E 3
† 85364 Dome, 48 ....A 6
† 85643 Dos Cabezas, 30 ....F 6
85607 Douglas, 12,462 ....F 7
85609 Dragoon, 150 ....F 6
85534 Duncan, 773 ....F 6
85925 Eagar, 1,279 ....F 4
85535 Eden, 89 ....E 6
85334 Ehrenburg, 93 ....A 5
† 85617 Elfrida, 700 ....F 7
† 85637 Elgin, 247 ....E 7
85335 El Mirage, 3,258 ....C 5
85231 Eloy, 5,381 ....D 6
85612 Fairbank, 100 ....E 7
86001 Flagstaff⊙, 26,117 ....D 3
85232 Florence⊙, 2,173 ....D 5
85233 Florence Junction, 35 ......D 5
85926 Fort Apache, 500 ....F 5
86504 Fort Defiance, 900 ....F 3
85643 Fort Grant, 240 ....E 6
85613 Fort Huachuca, 159 ....E 7
85536 Fort Thomas, 450 ....E 5
85534 Franklin, 300 ....F 6
86022 Fredonia, 798 ....C 2
85336 Gadsden, 250 ....A 6
86505 Ganado, 300 ....F 3
† 85536 Geronimo, 25 ....E 5
85337 Gila Bend, 1,795 ....C 6
85234 Gilbert, 1,971 ....D 5
† 85617 Gleeson, 15 ....F 7
85301 Glendale, 36,228 ....C 5
85501 Globe⊙, 7,333 ....E 5

85338 Goodyear, 2,140 ....C 5
86023 Grand Canyon, 1,011 ......C 2
† 85637 Greaterville, 15 ....E 7
85614 Green Valley, 5,971 ....D 7
85927 Greer, 60 ....F 4
† 85634 Gu-Achi, 339 ....C 6
86401 Hackberry, 250 ....B 3
86024 Happy Jack, 50 ....D 4
85235 Hayden, 1,283 ....E 5
85928 Heber, 750 ....E 4
85615 Hereford, 10 ....E 7
85236 Higley, 500 ....D 5
85301 Hillside, 100 ....B 4
† 85632 Hilltop, 9 ....F 6
86025 Holbrook⊙, 4,759 ....E 3
86030 Hotevilla, 600 ....E 3
86506 Houck, 325 ....F 3
85616 Huachuca City, 1,233 ......E 7
86329 Humboldt, 424 ....C 4
86031 Indian Wells, 150 ....E 3
85537 Inspiration, 500 ....D 5
86330 Iron Springs, 175 ....C 4
86022 Jacob Lake, 16 ....C 2
† 86025 Jeddito, 20 ....E 3
86331 Jerome, 290 ....C 4
86032 Joseph City, 650 ....E 3
86044 Kaibito, 275 ....D 2
† 86401 Katherine Landing, 102 ...A 3
86033 Kayenta, 500 ....E 2
86034 Keams Canyon, 400 ....E 3
85237 Kearny, 2,829 ....E 5
86401 Kingman⊙, 7,312 ....A 3
86332 Kirkland, 100 ....C 4
† 86505 Klagetoh, 200 ....F 3
85643 Klondyke, 86 ....E 6
85538 Kohls Ranch, 100 ....D 4
† 85339 Komatke, 300 ....C 5
86403 Lake Havasu City, 5,700 ..A 4
85929 Lakeside, 700 ....E 4
85339 Laveen, 800 ....C 5
† 86036 Lees Ferry, 10 ....D 2
86035 Leupp, 150 ....E 3
† 85326 Liberty, 150 ....C 5
† 85901 Linden, 50 ....E 4
85340 Litchfield Park, 1,664 ......C 5
86432 Littlefield, 40 ....B 2
86507 Lukachukai, 350 ....F 2
85341 Lukeville, 50 ....C 7
86508 Lupton, 250 ....F 3
† 85637 Madera Canyon, 75 ....E 7
85618 Mammoth, 1,953 ....E 6
86503 Many Farms, 250 ....F 2
85238 Marana, 2,900 ....D 6
86036 Marble Canyon, 6 ....D 2
85239 Maricopa, 750 ....C 5
† 85920 Maverick, 50 ....F 5
86333 Mayer, 810 ....C 4
85930 McNary, 950 ....F 4
85617 McNeal, 100 ....F 7

(continued on following page)

Indigo-blue Lake Mead is surrounded by color-streaked cliffs and ranges, set off by the bright concrete of Arizona's Hoover Dam. One of the world's largest man-made lakes, Lake Mead provides water storage, dependable water supply and water sports.

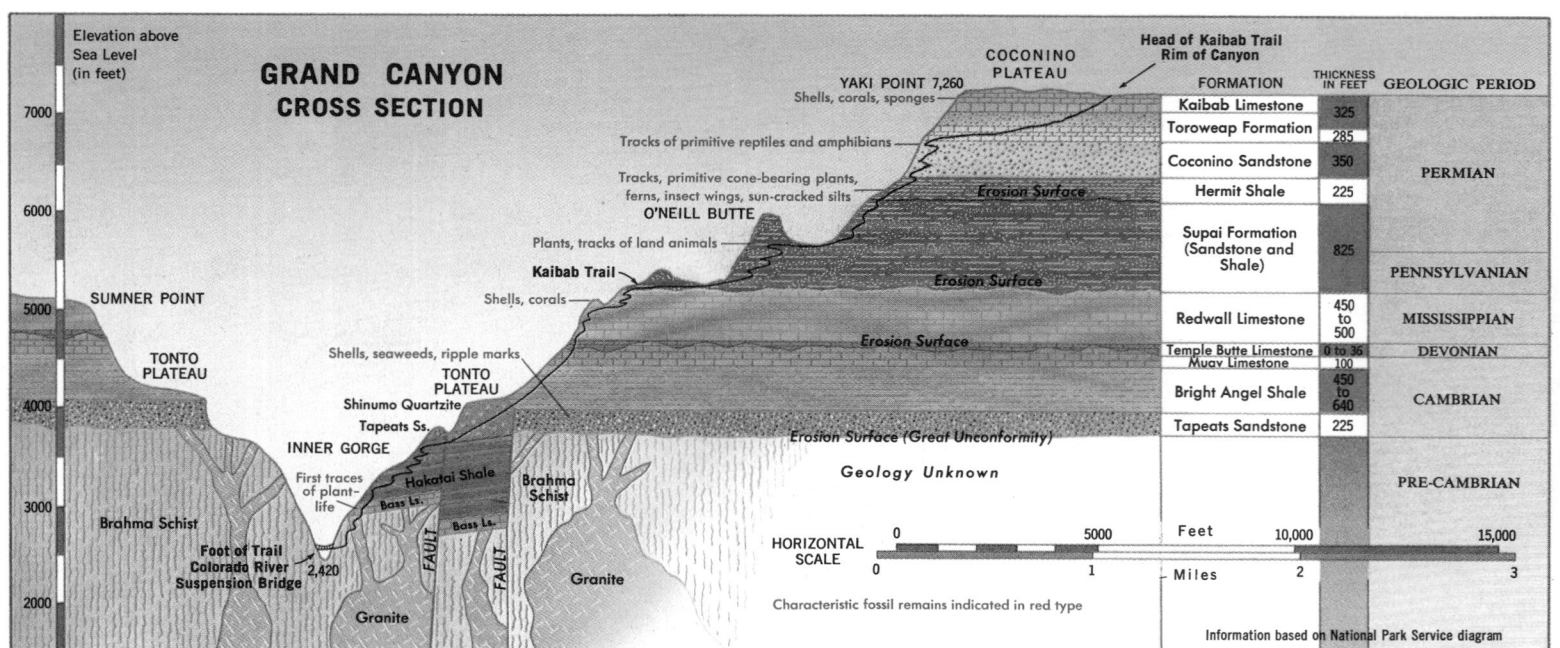

GRAND CANYON CROSS SECTION

Elevation above Sea Level (in feet)

FORMATION	THICKNESS IN FEET	GEOLOGIC PERIOD
Kaibab Limestone	325	
Toroweap Formation	285	PERMIAN
Coconino Sandstone	350	PERMIAN
Hermit Shale	225	PERMIAN
Supai Formation (Sandstone and Shale)	825	PENNSYLVANIAN
Redwall Limestone	450 to 500	MISSISSIPPIAN
Temple Butte Limestone	0 to 36	DEVONIAN
Muav Limestone	100	CAMBRIAN
Bright Angel Shale	450 to 640	CAMBRIAN
Tapeats Sandstone	225	CAMBRIAN
		PRE-CAMBRIAN

Head of Kaibab Trail — Rim of Canyon
COCONINO PLATEAU
YAKI POINT 7,260 — Shells, corals, sponges
Tracks of primitive reptiles and amphibians
Erosion Surface
Tracks, primitive cone-bearing plants, ferns, insect wings, sun-cracked silts
O'NEILL BUTTE
Plants, tracks of land animals
Kaibab Trail
Erosion Surface
Shells, corals
SUMNER POINT
Erosion Surface
TONTO PLATEAU
Shells, seaweeds, ripple marks
TONTO PLATEAU
Shinumo Quartzite
Tapeats Ss.
INNER GORGE
Erosion Surface (Great Unconformity)
Geology Unknown
First traces of plant life
Hakatai Shale
Bass Ls.
Brahma Schist
Brahma Schist
Bass Ls.
FAULT
FAULT
Foot of Trail — Colorado River Suspension Bridge 2,420
Granite
Granite

HORIZONTAL SCALE

Feet 0 ... 5000 ... 10,000 ... 15,000
Miles 0 ... 1 ... 2 ... 3

Characteristic fossil remains indicated in red type

Information based on National Park Service diagram

Ray Manley — Shostal Associates

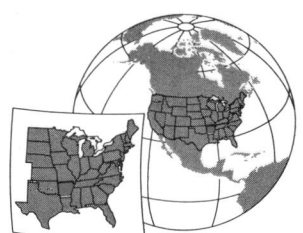

COUNTIES

Arkansas, 23,347 .... H 5
Ashley, 24,976 .... G 7
Baxter, 15,319 .... F 1
Benton, 50,476 .... B 1
Boone, 19,073 .... D 1
Bradley, 12,778 .... F 7
Calhoun, 5,573 .... E 6
Carroll, 12,301 .... C 1
Chicot, 18,164 .... H 7
Clark, 21,537 .... D 5
Clay, 18,771 .... K 1
Cleburne, 10,349 .... F 2
Cleveland, 6,605 .... F 6
Columbia, 25,952 .... D 7
Conway, 16,805 .... E 3
Craighead, 52,068 .... J 2
Crawford, 25,677 .... B 2
Crittenden, 48,106 ...... K 3
Cross, 19,783 .... J 3
Dallas, 10,022 .... E 6
Desha, 18,761 .... H 6
Drew, 15,157 .... G 6
Faulkner, 31,572 .... F 3

Franklin, 11,301 .... C 2
Fulton, 7,699 .... G 1
Garland, 54,131 .... D 4
Grant, 9,711 .... F 5
Greene, 24,765 .... J 1
Hempstead, 19,308 ...... C 6
Hot Spring, 21,963 ...... E 5
Howard, 11,412 .... C 5
Independence, 22,723 ... G 2
Izard, 7,381 .... G 1
Jackson, 20,452 .... H 2
Jefferson, 85,329 .... G 5
Johnson, 13,630 .... C 2
Lafayette, 10,018 ...... C 7
Lawrence, 16,320 .... H 1
Lee, 18,884 .... J 4
Lincoln, 12,913 .... G 6
Little River, 11,194 .... B 6
Logan, 16,789 .... C 3
Lonoke, 26,249 .... G 4
Madison, 9,453 .... C 1
Marion, 7,000 .... E 1
Miller, 33,385 .... C 7
Mississippi, 62,060 .... K 2
Monroe, 15,657 .... H 4
Montgomery, 5,821 .... C 4

Nevada, 10,111 .... D 6
Newton, 5,844 .... D 2
Ouachita, 30,896 .... E 6
Perry, 5,634 .... E 4
Phillips, 40,046 .... J 5
Pike, 8,711 .... C 5
Poinsett, 26,822 .... J 2
Polk, 13,297 .... B 5
Pope, 28,607 .... D 3
Prairie, 10,249 .... G 4
Pulaski, 287,189 .... F 4
Randolph, 12,645 ...... H 1
Saint Francis, 30,799 .. J 3
Saline, 36,107 .... E 4
Scott, 8,207 .... B 4
Searcy, 7,731 .... E 2
Sebastian, 79,237 ..... B 3
Sevier, 11,272 .... B 6
Sharp, 8,233 .... G 1
Stone, 6,838 .... F 2
Union, 45,428 .... E 7
Van Buren, 8,275 ..... E 2
Washington, 77,370 ... B 2
White, 39,253 .... G 3
Woodruff, 11,566 ..... H 3
Yell, 14,208 .... D 4

AREA 53,104 sq. mi.
POPULATION 1,923,295 ('70); 2,285,513 ('80)
CAPITAL Little Rock
LARGEST CITY Little Rock
HIGHEST POINT Magazine Mtn. 2,753 ft.
SETTLED IN 1685
ADMITTED TO UNION June 15, 1836
POPULAR NAME Land of Opportunity; Wonder State
STATE FLOWER Apple Blossom
STATE BIRD Mockingbird

Agriculture, Industry and Resources

DOMINANT LAND USE

Fruit and Mixed Farming
Specialized Cotton
Cotton, General Farming
Rice, General Farming
General Farming, Livestock, Truck Farming, Cotton
Forests
Swampland, Limited Agriculture

MAJOR MINERAL OCCURRENCES

Al Bauxite
Ba Barite
C Coal
Cl Clay
D Diamonds
Zn Zinc

G Natural Gas
Gp Gypsum
Mr Marble
O Petroleum
Sp Soapstone

⚡ Water Power   ///// Major Industrial Areas

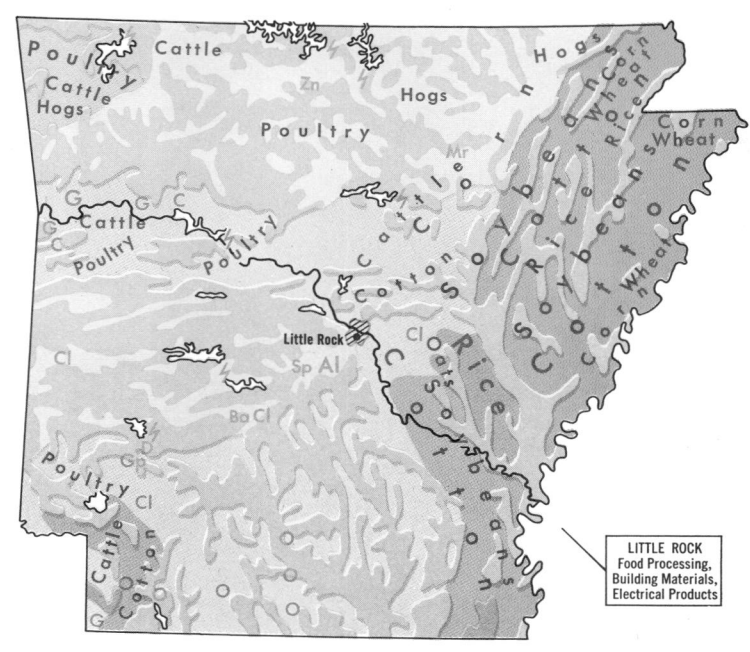

LITTLE ROCK
Food Processing,
Building Materials,
Electrical Products

Soybeans, Arkansas' leading cash crop, valued primarily as high protein food and feed, also has a wide range of uses, including plastics and agricultural sprays.

Eric Carle — Shostal Associates

CITIES and TOWNS

Zip	Name/Pop.	Key
72920	Abbott, 210	B 3
72001	Adona, 204	E 3
72510	Agnos, 130	G 1
72002	Alexander, 297	F 4
72410	Alicia, 246	H 2
72820	Alix, 250	C 3
† 72046	Allport, 307	G 4
72921	Alma, 1,613	B 3
72003	Almyra, 220	H 5
72611	Alpena, 309	D 1
72004	Altheimer, 1,037	G 5
72821	Altus, 418	C 3
72005	Amagon, 136	H 2
71921	Amity, 614	D 5
71922	Antoine, 182	D 5
72822	Appleton, 150	E 3
71923	Arkadelphia⊙, 9,841	D 5
71630	Arkansas City⊙, 615	H 6
† 72055	Arkansas Post, 15	H 5
72310	Armorel, 300	L 2
71822	Ashdown⊙, 3,522	B 6
72513	Ash Flat⊙, 211	G 1
72823	Atkins, 2,015	E 3
72311	Aubrey, 351	J 4
72006	Augusta⊙, 2,777	H 3
72007	Austin, 236	G 4
72008	Auvergne, 150	H 2
72711	Avoca, 173	B 1
72010	Bald Knob, 2,094	G 3
71631	Banks, 189	F 6
72923	Barling, 1,739	B 3
72312	Barton, 400	J 4
72313	Bassett, 265	K 2
72501	Batesville⊙, 7,209	G 2
72411	Bay, 751	J 2
71720	Bearden, 1,272	E 6
72012	Beebe, 2,805	G 3
72014	Beedeville, 144	H 3
71721	Beirne, 140	D 6
72712	Bella Vista, 500	B 1
† 72601	Bellefonte, 300	D 1
72824	Belleville, 379	D 3
71823	Ben Lomond, 155	B 6
72015	Benton⊙, 16,499	E 4
72712	Bentonville⊙, 5,508	B 1
72615	Bergman, 249	E 1
72616	Berryville⊙, 2,271	C 1
† 72764	Bethel Heights, 284	B 1
† 72501	Bethesda, 285	G 2
72016	Bigelow, 258	E 3
72617	Bigflat, 189	F 1
72413	Biggers, 372	J 1
† 72386	Birdsong, 150	K 3
72017	Biscoe, 340	H 4
71929	Bismarck, 200	D 5

Zip	Name/Pop.	Key
72414	Black Oak, 272	K 2
72415	Black Rock, 498	H 1
† 72069	Blackton, 175	H 4
71825	Blevins, 265	C 6
† 72933	Bloomer, 150	B 3
71722	Bluff City, 244	D 6
72827	Bluffton, 198	C 4
72315	Blytheville⊙, 24,752	L 2
† 71858	Bodcaw, 158	D 6
72926	Boles, 163	B 4
† 72901	Bonanza, 342	B 3
72416	Bono, 428	J 2
72927	Booneville⊙, 3,239	C 3
72020	Bradford, 826	G 3
71826	Bradley, 706	C 7
72928	Branch, 325	C 3
† 72017	Brasfield, 200	H 4
72828	Briggsville, 200	C 4
72021	Brinkley, 5,275	H 4
72417	Brookland, 465	J 2
72618	Bruno, 130	E 1
72022	Bryant, 1,199	F 4
71827	Buckner, 392	D 7
72619	Bull Shoals, 430	E 1
72321	Burdette, 173	L 2
72023	Cabot, 2,903	F 4
71935	Caddo Gap, 125	C 5
72322	Caldwell, 292	J 3
72519	Calico Rock, 723	F 1
71724	Calion, 535	E 7
71701	Camden⊙, 15,147	E 6
† 72201	Cammack Village, 1,165	E 4
† 72473	Campbell Station, 218	H 2
71829	Canfield, 365	C 7
72419	Caraway, 952	K 2
72024	Carlisle, 2,048	G 4
71725	Carthage, 566	E 5
72025	Casa, 208	D 3
72421	Cash, 265	J 2
72026	Casscoe, 200	H 4
† 72951	Caulksville, 208	C 3
72521	Cave City, 807	G 2
72718	Cave Springs, 469	B 1
72930	Cecil, 234	C 3
72450	Center Hill, 1,201	J 1
71830	Center Point, 144	C 5
72027	Center Ridge, 220	E 3
72719	Centerton, 312	B 1
71901	Central City, 150	B 3
† 71832	Chapel Hill, 154	B 5
72933	Charleston⊙, 1,497	B 3
72522	Charlotte, 158	H 2
72323	Chatfield, 155	K 3
72542	Cherokee Village, 1,300	G 1
† 71953	Cherry Hill, 250	B 4
72324	Cherry Valley, 556	J 3
71726	Chidester, 232	D 6
72029	Clarendon⊙, 2,563	H 4

Zip	Name/Pop.	Key
72325	Clarkedale, 250	K 3
72830	Clarksville⊙, 4,616	D 3
72031	Clinton⊙, 1,029	F 2
72832	Coal Hill, 733	C 3
72476	College City, 645	J 1
71655	College Heights, 2,050	G 6
72326	Colt, 301	J 3
71831	Columbus, 258	C 6
72523	Concord, 163	G 2
72032	Conway⊙, 15,510	F 3
72422	Corning⊙, 2,705	J 1
72626	Cotter, 858	E 1
72036	Cotton Plant, 1,657	H 3
71937	Cove, 334	B 5
72037	Coy, 240	G 4
72327	Crawfordsville, 831	K 3
71635	Crossett, 6,191	G 7
71728	Curtis, 500	D 6
72526	Cushman, 427	G 2
† 71923	Dalark, 132	E 5
72039	Damascus, 255	F 3
72833	Danville⊙, 1,362	D 3
72834	Dardanelle⊙, 3,297	D 3
72424	Datto, 142	J 1
72722	Decatur, 847	A 1
72723	Delaney, 150	C 2
72425	Delaplaine, 145	J 1
72835	Delaware, 200	D 3
71940	Delight, 439	C 5
72426	Dell, 358	K 2
72836	Denning, 203	C 3
71832	De Queen⊙, 3,863	B 5
71638	Dermott, 4,250	H 7
72040	Des Arc⊙, 1,714	H 4
72041	De Valls Bluff⊙, 622	H 4
72042	De Witt⊙, 3,728	H 5
72644	Diamond City, 282	E 1
72043	Diaz, 283	H 2
71833	Dierks, 1,101	B 5
71834	Doddridge, 125	C 7
71941	Donaldson, 500	E 5
72837	Dover, 662	D 3
72530	Drasco, 300	F 2
† 72943	Driggs, 125	C 3
71639	Dumas, 4,600	H 6
72935	Dyer, 486	B 3
71729	Eagle Mills, 149	E 6
72331	Earle, 3,146	K 3
71701	East Camden, 589	E 6
72044	Edgemont, 125	F 2
72332	Edmondson, 412	K 3
72333	Elaine, 1,210	J 5
71730	El Dorado⊙, 25,283	E 7
72727	Elkins, 418	C 1
72728	Elm Springs, 260	B 1
72045	El Paso, 131	F 3
71740	Emerson, 393	D 7
71835	Emmet, 433	D 6

(continued on following page)

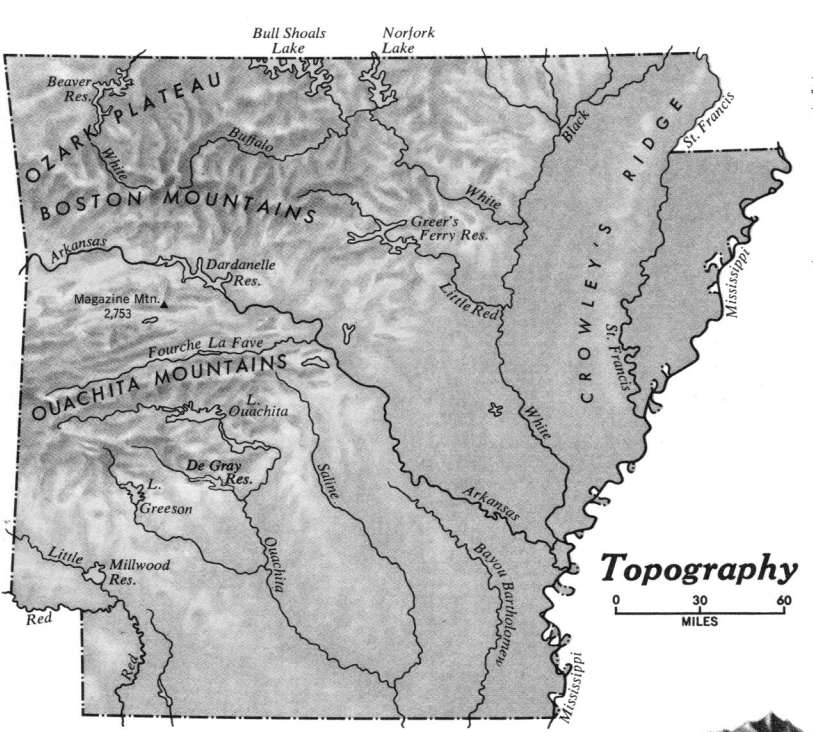

Bull Shoals Lake • Norfork Lake • Beaver Res. • OZARK PLATEAU • Buffalo • White • BOSTON MOUNTAINS • White • CROWLEY'S RIDGE • St. Francis • Arkansas • Greer's Ferry Res. • Dardanelle Res. • Little Red • Magazine Mtn. 2,753 • OUACHITA MOUNTAINS • Ouachita • L. • Saline • White • Arkansas • St. Francis • Mississippi • De Gray Res. • L. Greeson • Fourche La Fave • Bayou Bartholomew • Little • Millwood Res. • Red • Mississippi

Topography

0   30   60
MILES

Below Sea Level | 100 m. 328 ft. | 200 m. 656 ft. | 500 m. 1,640 ft. | 1,000 m. 3,281 ft. | 2,000 m. 6,562 ft. | 5,000 m. 16,404 ft.

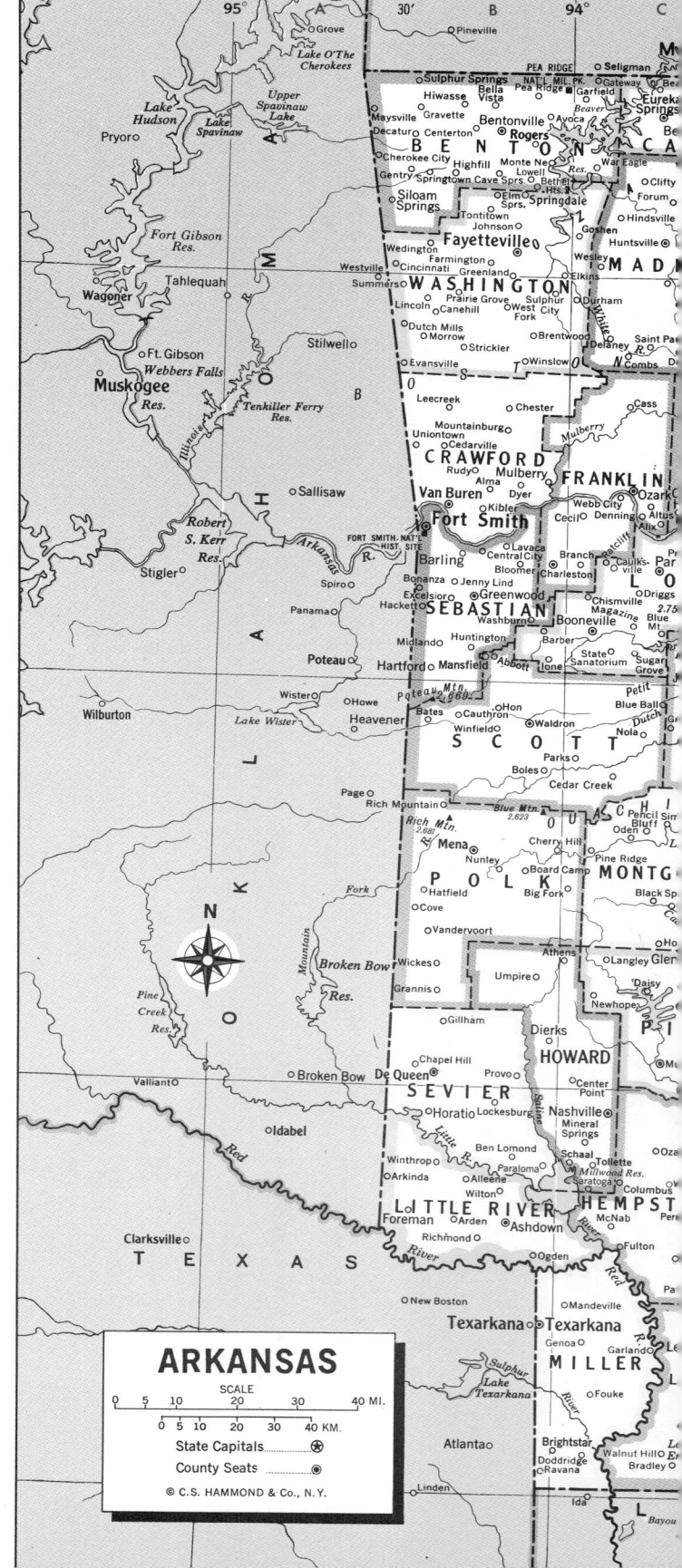

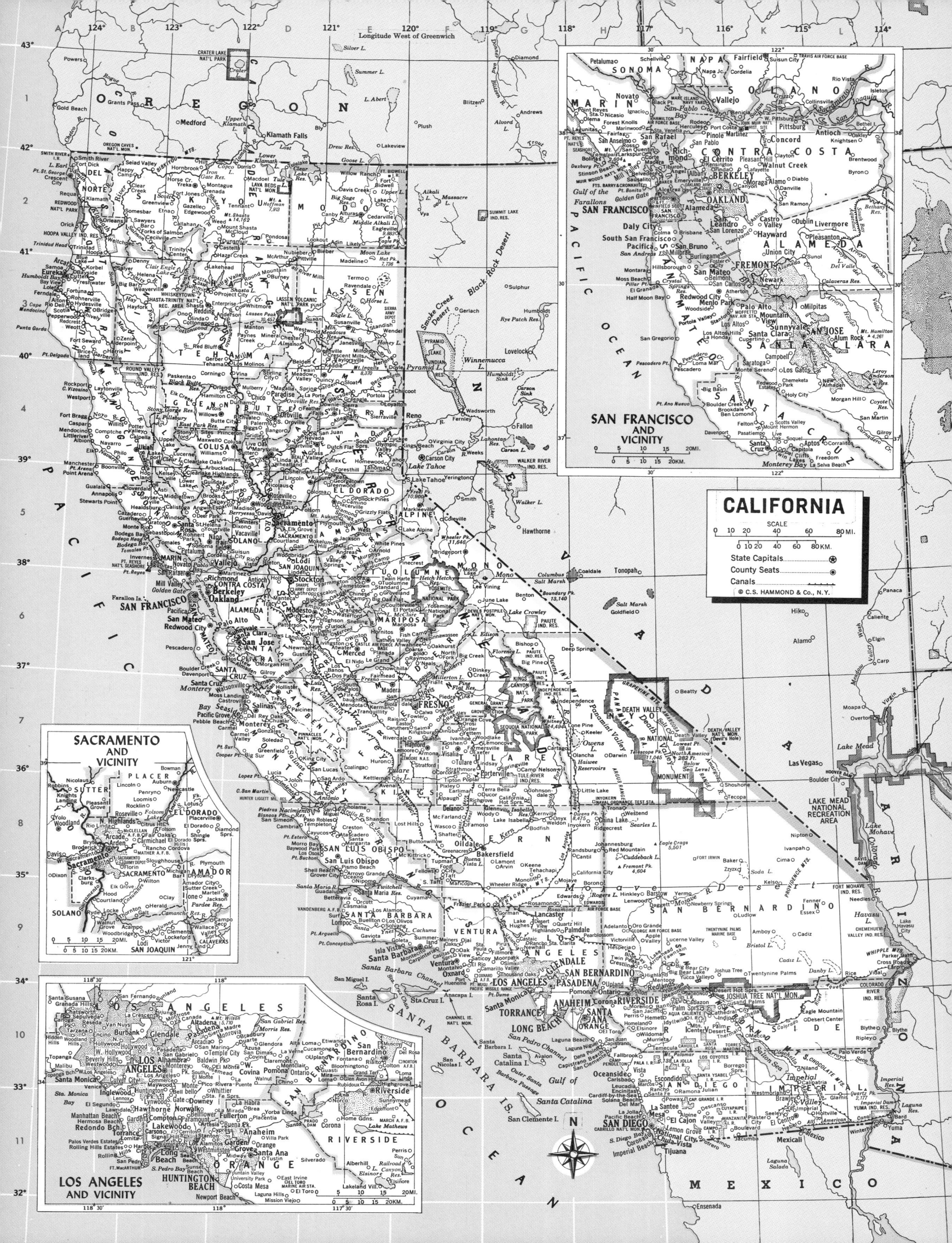

CALIFORNIA

SCALE

0 10 20   40   60   80 MI.

0 10 20 40 60 80 KM.

State Capitals ⊛
County Seats ◉
Canals

© C.S. HAMMOND & Co., N.Y.

SAN FRANCISCO AND VICINITY

SCALE
0   5   10   15   20MI.
0   5 10 15 20KM.

SACRAMENTO AND VICINITY

0 5 10 15 20MI.
0 5 10 15 20KM.

LOS ANGELES AND VICINITY

0   5   10   15   20MI.
0 5 10 15 20KM.

PACIFIC OCEAN

MEXICO

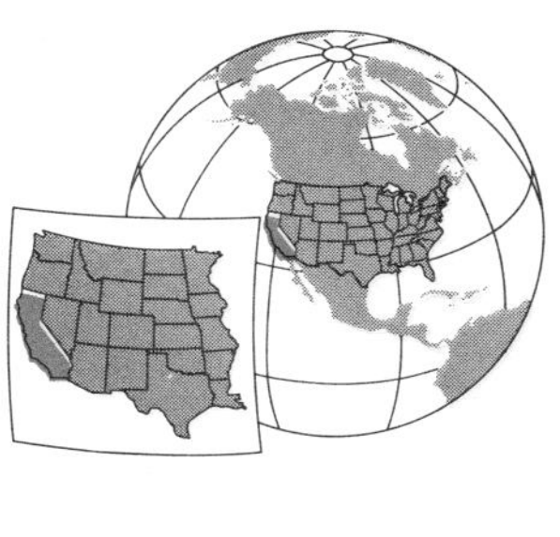

AREA 158,693 sq. mi.
POPULATION 19,953,134 ('70); 23,668,562 ('80)
CAPITAL Sacramento
LARGEST CITY Los Angeles
HIGHEST POINT Mt. Whitney 14,494 ft.
SETTLED IN 1769
ADMITTED TO UNION September 9, 1850
POPULAR NAME Golden State
STATE FLOWER Golden Poppy
STATE BIRD California Valley Quail

COUNTIES

Alameda, 1,073,184	D 6
Alpine, 484	F 5
Amador, 11,821	E 5
Butte, 101,969	D 4
Calaveras, 13,585	E 5
Colusa, 12,430	C 4
Contra Costa, 558,389	D 6
Del Norte, 14,580	B 2
El Dorado, 43,833	E 5
Fresno, 413,053	E 7
Glenn, 17,521	C 4
Humboldt, 99,692	B 3
Imperial, 74,492	K 10
Inyo, 15,571	H 7
Kern, 329,162	G 8
Kings, 64,610	F 8
Lake, 19,548	C 4
Lassen, 14,960	E 3
Los Angeles, 7,032,075	G 9
Madera, 41,519	F 6
Marin, 206,038	C 5
Mariposa, 6,015	E 6
Mendocino, 51,101	B 4
Merced, 104,629	E 6
Modoc, 7,469	E 2
Mono, 4,016	F 5
Monterey, 250,071	D 7
Napa, 79,140	C 5
Nevada, 26,346	E 4
Orange, 1,420,386	H 10
Placer, 77,306	E 4
Plumas, 11,707	E 4
Riverside, 459,074	J 10
Sacramento, 631,498	D 5
San Benito, 18,226	D 7
San Bernardino, 684,072	J 9
San Diego, 1,357,854	J 10
San Francisco (city county), 715,674	J 2
San Joaquin, 290,208	D 6
San Luis Obispo, 105,690	E 8
San Mateo, 556,234	C 6
Santa Barbara, 264,324	E 9
Santa Clara, 1,064,714	D 6
Santa Cruz, 123,790	C 6
Shasta, 77,640	C 3
Sierra, 2,365	E 4
Siskiyou, 33,225	C 2
Solano, 169,941	D 5
Sonoma, 204,885	C 5
Stanislaus, 194,506	D 6
Sutter, 41,935	D 4
Tehama, 29,517	C 3
Trinity, 7,615	B 3
Tulare, 188,322	G 7
Tuolumne, 22,169	F 5
Ventura, 376,430	F 9
Yolo, 91,788	D 5
Yuba, 44,736	D 4

CITIES and TOWNS

Zip	Name/Pop.	Key
92301	Adelanto, 2,115	H 9
96006	Adin, 550	E 2
93601	Ahwahnee, 503	F 6
94501	Alameda, 70,968	J 2
94507	Alamo-Danville, 14,059	K 2
94706	Albany, 14,674	J 2
* 91801	Alhambra, 62,125	C 10
93201	Alpaugh, 800	F 8
92001	Alpine, 1,570	J 11
91001	Altadena, 42,380	C 10
91701	Alta Loma, 6,100	E 10
96101	Alturas⊙, 2,799	E 2
† 95101	Alum Rock, 18,355	L 3
* 92801	Anaheim, 166,701	D 11
	Anaheim-Santa Ana-Garden Grove, ‡1,420,386	D 11
96007	Anderson, 5,492	C 3
95222	Angels Camp, 1,710	E 5
94508	Angwin, 2,690	C 5
94509	Antioch, 28,060	L 1
92307	Apple Valley, 6,702	H 9
95003	Aptos, 8,704	K 4
95912	Arbuckle, 1,037	C 4
95825	Arcade-Arden, 82,498	B 8
91006	Arcadia, 42,868	C 10
95521	Arcata, 8,985	A 3
93202	Armona, 1,392	F 7
93420	Arroyo Grande, 7,454	E 8
90701	Artesia, 14,757	C 11
93203	Arvin, 5,090	G 8
† 94578	Ashland, 14,810	K 2
95413	Asti, 50	C 5
93422	Atascadero, 10,290	E 8
94025	Atherton, 8,085	K 3
95301	Atwater, 11,640	E 6
93602	Auberry, 515	F 6
95603	Auburn⊙, 6,570	C 8
90704	Avalon, 1,520	G 10
93204	Avenal, 3,035	E 8
91702	Azusa, 25,217	D 10
92309	Baker, 600	J 8
* 93301	Bakersfield⊙ 69,515	G 8
	Bakersfield ‡, 329,271	G 8
91706	Baldwin Park, 47,285	D 10
92220	Banning, 12,034	J 10
92311	Barstow, 17,442	H 9
† 95501	Bayview, 2,340	A 3
† 93401	Baywood Park-Los Osos, 3,487	E 8
92223	Beaumont, 5,484	J 10
90201	Bell, 21,836	C 11
90706	Bellflower, 51,454	C 11
94002	Belmont, 23,667	J 3
94920	Belvedere, 2,599	H 2
94510	Benicia, 8,783	K 1
95005	Ben Lomond, 2,793	K 4
* 94701	Berkeley, 116,716	J 2
94511	Bethel Island, 1,398	L 1
* 90210	Beverly Hills, 33,416	B 10
92314	Big Bear City, 850	J 9
92315	Big Bear Lake, 5,268	J 9
95917	Biggs, 1,115	D 4
93513	Big Pine, 839	G 6
93920	Big Sur, 500	D 7
93606	Biola, 950	E 7
93514	Bishop, 3,498	G 6
† 94947	Black Point, 500	J 1
92316	Bloomington, 11,957	E 10
95525	Blue Lake, 1,112	A 3
92225	Blythe, 7,047	L 10
94923	Bodega Bay, 700	B 5
94924	Bolinas, 700	H 1
95415	Boonville, 715	B 5
93516	Boron, 1,999	H 8
92004	Borrego Springs, 860	J 10
95006	Boulder Creek, 1,806	J 4
95707	Bowman, 2,089	C 8
91010	Bradbury, 1,098	D 10
92227	Brawley, 13,746	K 11
92621	Brea, 18,447	D 11
94513	Brentwood, 2,649	L 2
93517	Bridgeport⊙, 525	F 5
94005	Brisbane, 3,003	J 2
95605	Broderick-Bryte, 12,782	B 8
95007	Brookdale, 630	J 4
95605	Bryte-Broderick, 12,782	B 8
93427	Buellton, 1,402	E 9
90620	Buena Park, 63,646	D 11
* 91501	Burbank, 88,871	C 10
94010	Burlingame, 27,320	J 2
96013	Burney, 2,190	D 3
93206	Buttonwillow, 1,193	F 8
94514	Byron, 800	L 2
92230	Cabazon, 598	J 10
92231	Calexico, 10,625	K 11
93501	California City, 1,309	H 8
92233	Calipatria, 1,824	K 10
94515	Calistoga, 1,882	C 5
95418	Calpella, 900	B 4
93745	Calwa, 5,191	F 7
93010	Camarillo, 19,219	F 9
93428	Cambria, 1,716	D 8
95709	Camino, 800	E 5
95008	Campbell, 24,770	K 3
92006	Campo, 850	J 11
95226	Campo Seco, 700	D 9
* 91303	Canoga Park, 109,127	B 10
92672	Capistrano Beach, 4,149	H 10
95010	Capitola, 5,080	K 4
92007	Cardiff-by-the-Sea, 5,724	H 10
92008	Carlsbad, 14,944	H 10
93921	Carmel, 4,525	D 7
93924	Carmel Valley, 3,026	D 7
95608	Carmichael, 37,625	C 8
93013	Carpinteria, 6,982	F 9
90744	Carson, 71,150	C 11
93609	Caruthers, 950	E 7
† 93001	Casitas Springs, 1,113	F 9
95420	Caspar, 578	B 4
91310	Castaic, 800	G 9
94546	Castro Valley, 44,760	K 2
95012	Castroville, 3,235	D 7
92234	Cathedral City, 3,640	J 10
93430	Cayucos, 1,772	E 8
96104	Cedarville, 825	E 2
96019	Central Valley, 2,361	C 3
95307	Ceres, 6,029	D 6
90701	Cerritos, 15,856	C 11
91311	Chatsworth, 24,000	B 10
95044	Chemeketa Park-Redwood Estates, 1,452	K 4
† 94521	Cherryland, 9,969	K 2
96020	Chester, 1,531	D 3
95926	Chico, 19,580	D 4
93555	China Lake, 11,105	H 8
95309	Chinese Camp, 150	E 6
91710	Chino, 20,411	D 10
93610	Chowchilla, 4,349	E 6
* 92010	Chula Vista, 67,901	J 11
95610	Citrus Heights, 21,760	C 8
91711	Claremont, 23,464	D 10
95612	Clarksburg, 554	B 9
94517	Clayton, 1,385	K 2
95422	Clearlake Highlands, 2,836	C 5
95423	Clearlake Oaks, 975	C 4
95425	Cloverdale, 3,251	B 5
93612	Clovis, 13,856	F 7
92236	Coachella, 8,353	J 10
93210	Coalinga, 6,161	E 7
95713	Colfax, 798	E 4
94014	Colma, 537	J 2
92324	Colton, 19,974	E 10
95932	Colusa⊙, 3,842	C 4
† 90001	Commerce, 10,536	C 10
* 90220	Compton, 78,611	C 11
* 94520	Concord, 85,164	K 1
93212	Corcoran, 5,249	F 7
96021	Corning, 3,573	C 4
91720	Corona, 27,519	E 11
92118	Coronado, 20,910	H 11
95076	Corralitos, 600	L 4
94925	Corte Madera, 8,464	J 2
* 92626	Costa Mesa, 72,660	D 11
96022	Cottonwood, 1,288	C 3
95428	Covelo, 900	B 4
91722	Covina, 30,380	D 10
95531	Crescent City⊙, 2,586	A 2
92325	Crestline, 3,509	H 9
94525	Crockett, 2,900	J 1
91730	Cucamonga, 5,796	E 10
90230	Culver City, 31,035	B 10
95014	Cupertino, 18,216	K 3
93615	Cutler, 2,503	F 7
95534	Cutten, 2,228	A 3
90630	Cypress, 31,026	D 11
92327	Daggett, 950	H 9
* 94014	Daly City, 66,922	H 2
92629	Dana Point, 4,745	H 10
94526	Danville-Alamo, 14,059	K 2
95616	Davis, 23,488	B 8
94576	Deer Park, 975	C 5
93215	Delano, 14,559	F 8
95315	Delhi, 2,063	E 6
92014	Del Mar, 3,956	H 11
93940	Del Rey Oaks, 1,823	D 7
92404	Del Rosa, 8,000	E 10
92240	Desert Hot Springs, 2,738	J 9
† 93550	Desert View Highlands, 2,172	G 9
94528	Diablo, 950	K 2
95619	Diamond Springs, 900	D 8
93618	Dinuba, 7,917	F 7
95620	Dixon, 4,432	B 9
96023	Dorris, 840	D 2
93620	Dos Palos, 2,496	E 6
* 90240	Downey, 88,445	C 11
95936	Downieville⊙, 375	E 4
91010	Duarte, 14,981	D 10
94566	Dublin, 13,641	K 2
95937	Dunnigan, 550	C 5
96025	Dunsmuir, 2,214	C 2
95938	Durham, 700	D 4
92241	Eagle Mountain, 2,453	K 10
93219	Earlimart, 3,080	F 8
† 92225	East Blythe, 1,252	L 10
90804	East Los Angeles, 105,033	C 10
93706	Easton, 1,065	F 7
93523	Edwards, 900	G 9
* 92020	El Cajon, 52,273	J 11
92243	El Centro⊙, 19,272	K 11
94530	El Cerrito, 25,190	J 2
95623	El Dorado, 900	C 8
95630	El Dorado Hills, 2,000	C 8
94018	El Granada, 1,473	H 3
95624	Elk Grove, 3,721	B 9
* 91731	El Monte, 69,837	D 10
95318	El Portal, 675	F 6
93030	El Rio, 6,173	F 9
90245	El Segundo, 15,620	B 11
92330	Elsinore, 3,530	F 11
92630	El Toro, 8,654	E 11
94608	Emeryville, 2,681	J 2
95319	Empire, 2,016	D 6
92024	Encinitas, 5,375	H 10
91316	Encino, 40,000	B 10
96001	Enterprise, 11,486	C 3
95320	Escalon, 2,366	E 6
92025	Escondido, 36,792	J 10
95627	Esparto, 1,088	C 5
91739	Etiwanda, 900	E 10
96027	Etna, 667	C 2
95501	Eureka⊙, 24,337	A 3
93221	Exeter, 4,475	F 7
94930	Fairfax, 7,661	H 1
94533	Fairfield⊙, 44,146	K 1
95628	Fair Oaks, 11,256	C 8
92028	Fallbrook, 6,945	H 10
96028	Fall River Mills, 600	D 3
93223	Farmersville, 3,456	F 7
93224	Fellows, 530	F 8
95018	Felton, 2,062	K 4
95536	Ferndale, 1,352	A 3
93015	Fillmore, 6,285	G 9
93622	Firebaugh, 2,517	E 7
95828	Florin, 9,646	B 8
95630	Folsom, 5,810	C 8
92335	Fontana, 20,673	E 10
† 93268	Ford City, 3,503	F 8
† 95703	Foresthill, 900	E 4
94933	Forest Knolls, 900	H 1
95437	Fort Bragg, 4,455	B 4
95538	Fort Dick, 850	A 2
96032	Fort Jones, 515	C 2
95540	Fortuna, 4,203	A 3
94404	Foster City, 9,327	J 2
92708	Fountain Valley, 31,826	D 11
93625	Fowler, 2,239	F 7
93225	Frazier Park, 1,167	F 9
95019	Freedom, 5,563	L 4
* 94536	Fremont, 100,869	K 3
* 93701	Fresno⊙, 165,972	F 7
	Fresno, ‡413,053	F 7
* 92631	Fullerton, 85,987	D 11
95632	Galt, 3,200	C 9
* 90247	Gardena, 41,021	C 11
* 92640	Garden Grove, 122,524	D 11
95634	Georgetown, 700	E 5
96035	Gerber, 800	C 3
95441	Geyserville, 887	B 5
95020	Gilroy, 12,665	D 6
† 92501	Glen Avon Heights, 5,759	E 10
* 91201	Glendale, 132,752	C 10
91740	Glendora, 31,349	D 10
93017	Goleta, 3,500	F 9
93926	Gonzales, 2,575	D 7
93227	Goshen, 1,324	F 7
91344	Granada Hills, 50,000	B 10
92324	Grand Terrace, 5,901	E 10
95945	Grass Valley, 5,149	D 4
95444	Graton, 975	C 5
93308	Greenacres, 2,116	F 8
93927	Greenfield, 2,608	D 7
95947	Greenville, 1,073	E 3
95948	Gridley, 3,534	D 4
93433	Grover City, 5,939	E 8
93434	Guadalupe, 3,145	E 9
95445	Gualala, 585	B 5
95446	Guerneville, 900	B 5
95322	Gustine, 2,793	D 6
94019	Half Moon Bay, 4,023	H 3
95951	Hamilton City, 961	C 4
93230	Hanford⊙, 15,179	F 7
96039	Happy Camp, 925	B 2
90710	Harbor City, 17,500	C 11
90250	Hawthorne, 53,304	C 11
96041	Hayfork, 900	B 3
* 94541	Hayward, 93,058	K 2
95448	Healdsburg, 5,438	B 5
92249	Heber, 875	K 11
92343	Hemet, 12,252	H 10
96113	Herlong, 900	E 3
90254	Hermosa Beach, 17,412	B 11
92345	Hesperia, 4,592	H 9
† 91302	Hidden Hills, 1,529	B 10
92507	Highgrove, 2,158	E 10
92346	Highland, 13,290	H 9
95324	Hilmar, 850	E 6
92347	Hinkley, 900	H 9
95023	Hollister⊙, 7,663	D 7
90028	Hollywood, 85,047	C 10
92250	Holtville, 3,496	K 11
† 91720	Home Gardens, 5,116	E 11
92348	Homeland, 1,187	H 10
95546	Hoopa, 850	B 2
95449	Hopland, 817	B 5
95326	Hughson, 2,144	E 6
* 92646	Huntington Beach, 115,960	C 11
90255	Huntington Park, 33,744	C 11
93234	Huron, 1,525	E 7
92349	Idyllwild, 950	J 10
94947	Ignacio, 4,500	H 1
92251	Imperial, 3,094	K 11
92032	Imperial Beach, 20,244	H 11
93526	Independence⊙, 748	H 7
92201	Indio, 14,459	J 10
* 90301	Inglewood, 89,985	B 11
94937	Inverness, 800	B 5
95640	Ione, 2,369	C 9
93017	Isla Vista, 13,441	E 9
95641	Isleton, 909	L 1
93235	Ivanhoe, 1,595	F 7
95642	Jackson⊙, 1,924	C 9
92034	Jacumba, 700	J 11
95327	Jamestown, 950	E 6
92252	Joshua Tree, 1,211	J 9
95451	Kelseyville, 950	C 5
† 94701	Kensington, 5,823	J 2
93600	Kerman, 2,667	E 7
93238	Kernville, 900	G 8
93239	Kettleman City, 600	E 7
95328	Keyes, 1,875	E 6
93930	King City, 3,717	D 7
95719	Kings Beach, 600	F 4
93631	Kingsburg, 3,843	F 7
95645	Knights Landing, 846	B 8
91011	La Canada, 20,652	C 10
91214	La Crescenta-Montrose, 19,594	C 10
94549	Lafayette, 20,484	K 2
* 92651	Laguna Beach, 14,550	G 10
92653	Laguna Hills, 13,676	D 11
92677	Laguna Niguel, 4,644	H 10
90631	La Habra, 41,350	D 11
94020	La Honda, 650	J 3
92037	La Jolla, 30,000	H 11
92352	Lake Arrowhead, 2,682	H 9
93532	Lake Hughes, 750	G 9
93240	Lake Isabella, 850	G 8
† 92330	Lakeland Village, 1,724	E 11
95453	Lakeport⊙, 3,005	C 4
* 90712	Lakewood, 82,973	C 11
92041	La Mesa, 39,178	H 11
90638	La Mirada, 30,808	D 11
93241	Lamont, 7,007	G 8
93534	Lancaster, 30,948	G 9
* 91744	La Puente, 31,092	D 10
94939	Larkspur, 10,487	H 1
95076	La Selva Beach, 1,171	K 4
95330	Lathrop, 2,137	D 6
93242	Laton, 1,071	F 7
91750	La Verne, 12,965	D 10

(continued on following page)

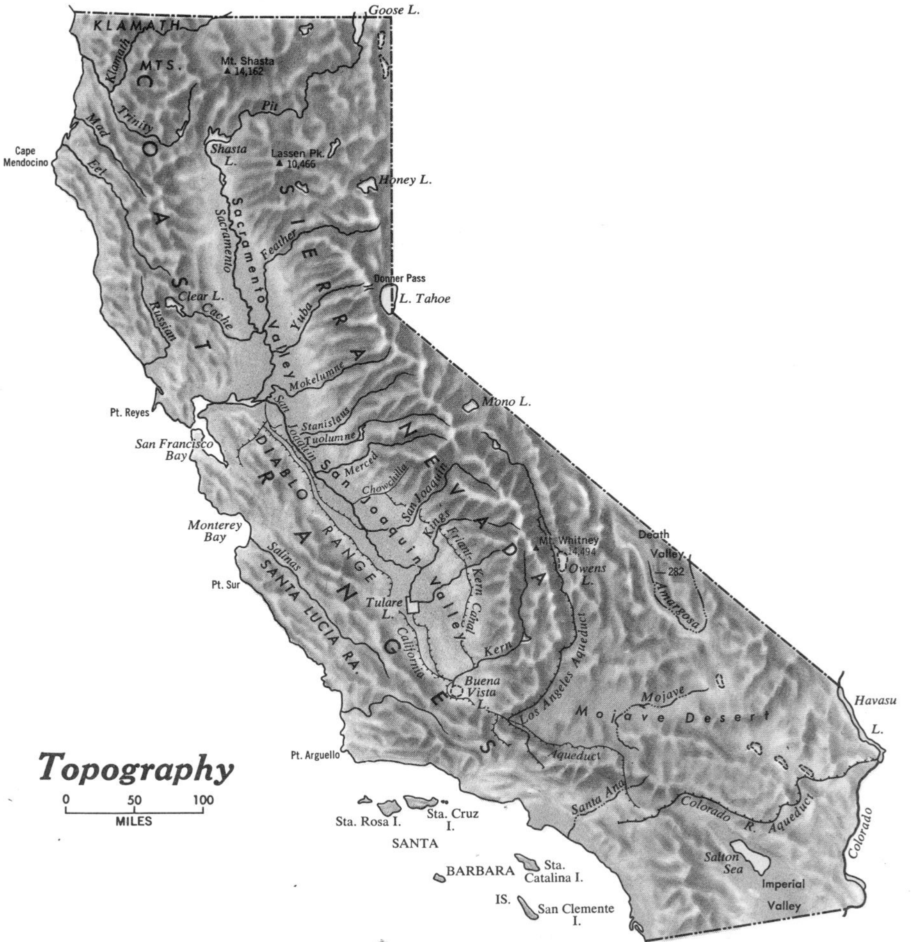

Agriculture, Industry and Resources

DOMINANT LAND USE

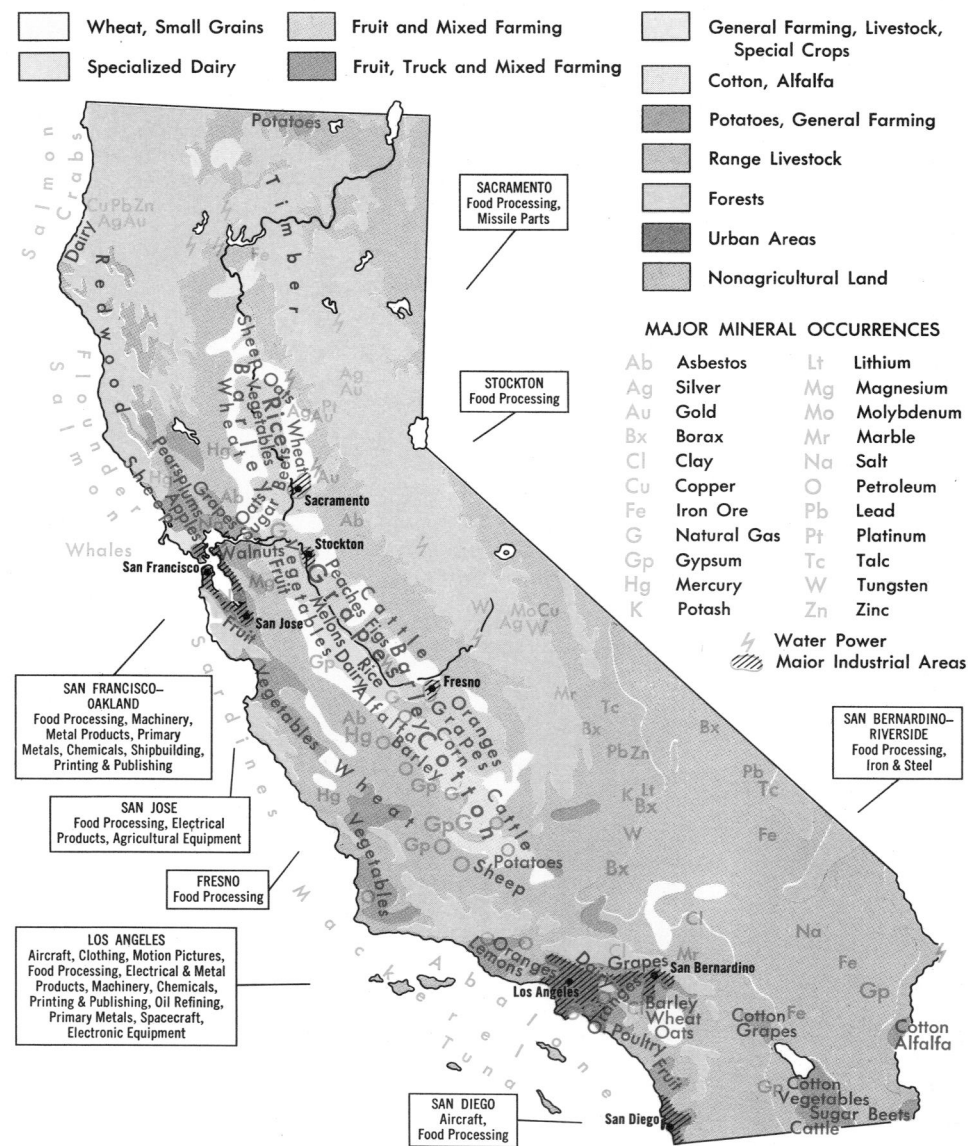

- Wheat, Small Grains
- Specialized Dairy
- Fruit and Mixed Farming
- Fruit, Truck and Mixed Farming
- General Farming, Livestock, Special Crops
- Cotton, Alfalfa
- Potatoes, General Farming
- Range Livestock
- Forests
- Urban Areas
- Nonagricultural Land

MAJOR MINERAL OCCURRENCES

Ab	Asbestos	Lt	Lithium
Ag	Silver	Mg	Magnesium
Au	Gold	Mo	Molybdenum
Bx	Borax	Mr	Marble
Cl	Clay	Na	Salt
Cu	Copper	O	Petroleum
Fe	Iron Ore	Pb	Lead
G	Natural Gas	Pt	Platinum
Gp	Gypsum	Tc	Talc
Hg	Mercury	W	Tungsten
K	Potash	Zn	Zinc

⚡ Water Power

/// Major Industrial Areas

SACRAMENTO
Food Processing, Missile Parts

STOCKTON
Food Processing

SAN BERNARDINO–RIVERSIDE
Food Processing, Iron & Steel

SAN FRANCISCO–OAKLAND
Food Processing, Machinery, Metal Products, Primary Metals, Chemicals, Shipbuilding, Printing & Publishing

SAN JOSE
Food Processing, Electrical Products, Agricultural Equipment

FRESNO
Food Processing

LOS ANGELES
Aircraft, Clothing, Motion Pictures, Food Processing, Electrical & Metal Products, Machinery, Printing & Publishing, Oil Refining, Primary Metals, Spacecraft, Electronic Equipment

SAN DIEGO
Aircraft, Food Processing

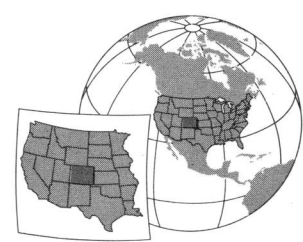

COUNTIES

Adams, 185,789 ....L 3
Alamosa, 11,422 ....H 7
Arapahoe, 162,142 ....L 3
Archuleta, 2,733 ....E 8
Baca, 5,674 ....O 8
Bent, 6,493 ....N 7
Boulder, 131,889 ....J 2
Chaffee, 10,162 ....G 5
Cheyenne, 2,396 ....O 5
Clear Creek, 4,819 ....H 3
Conejos, 7,846 ....H 8
Costilla, 3,091 ....J 8
Crowley, 3,086 ....M 6
Custer, 1,120 ....J 6
Delta, 15,286 ....D 5
Denver, 514,678 ....K 3
Dolores, 1,641 ....C 7
Douglas, 8,407 ....K 4
Eagle, 7,498 ....F 3
Elbert, 3,903 ....L 4
El Paso, 235,972 ....K 5
Fremont, 21,942 ....J 5
Garfield, 14,821 ....C 3
Gilpin, 1,272 ....H 3
Grand, 4,107 ....G 2
Gunnison, 7,578 ....E 5
Hinsdale, 202 ....E 7
Huerfano, 6,590 ....K 7
Jackson, 1,811 ....G 1
Jefferson, 233,031 ....J 3
Kiowa, 2,029 ....O 6
Kit Carson, 7,530 ....O 4
Lake, 8,282 ....G 4
La Plata, 19,199 ....D 8
Larimer, 89,900 ....H 1
Las Animas, 15,744 ....K 8
Lincoln, 4,836 ....M 5
Logan, 18,852 ....N 1
Mesa, 54,374 ....B 5
Mineral, 786 ....F 7
Moffat, 6,525 ....C 1
Montezuma, 12,952 ....B 8
Montrose, 18,366 ....D 6
Morgan, 20,105 ....M 2
Otero, 23,523 ....M 7
Ouray, 1,546 ....D 6
Park, 2,185 ....H 4
Phillips, 4,131 ....P 1
Pitkin, 3,653 ....F 4
Prowers, 13,258 ....P 7
Pueblo, 118,238 ....K 6
Rio Blanco, 4,842 ....C 3
Rio Grande, 10,494 ....G 7
Routt, 6,592 ....E 1
Saguache, 3,827 ....G 6
San Juan, 831 ....D 7
San Miguel, 1,949 ....C 6
Sedgwick, 3,405 ....P 1
Summit, 2,665 ....G 3
Teller, 3,316 ....J 5
Washington, 5,550 ....N 3
Weld, 89,297 ....L 1
Yuma, 8,544 ....P 2

CITIES and TOWNS

Zip Name/Pop. Key

80101 Agate, 120 ....M 4
80020 Aguilar, 699 ....K 8
80720 Akron⊙, 1,775 ....N 2
81101 Alamosa⊙, 6,985 ....H 8
80510 Allenspark, 100 ....J 2
80420 Alma, 73 ....G 4
81210 Almont, 15 ....F 5
80721 Amherst, 105 ....P 1
80801 Anton, 65 ....N 3
81120 Antonito, 1,113 ....H 8
80802 Arapahoe, 100 ....P 5
81021 Arlington, 10 ....N 6
80804 Arriba, 254 ....N 4
† 81323 Arriola, 50 ....B 8
80002 Arvada, 46,814 ....J 3
81611 Aspen⊙, 2,404 ....F 4
80722 Atwood, 75 ....N 1
80610 Ault, 841 ....K 1
80010 Aurora, 74,974 ....K 3
81410 Austin, 1,163 ....D 5
81620 Avon, 50 ....F 3
81022 Avondale, 750 ....L 6
80421 Bailey, 200 ....H 4
† 80624 Barnesville, 20 ....L 2
81621 Basalt, 419 ....E 4
81122 Bayfield, 320 ....D 8
81411 Bedrock, 20 ....B 6
80758 Beecher Island, 5 ....P 3
80512 Bellvue, 335 ....J 1
80102 Bennett, 613 ....L 3
80513 Berthoud, 1,446 ....J 2
80438 Berthoud Pass, 200 ....H 3
80805 Bethune, 99 ....P 4
81023 Beulah, 425 ....K 6
80908 Black Forest, 700 ....K 4
81001 Blende, 950 ....K 6
† 80424 Blue River, 8 ....G 4
81155 Bonanza, 10 ....G 6
81024 Boncarbo, 50 ....K 8
80423 Bond, 63 ....F 3
81025 Boone, 448 ....L 6
* 80301 Boulder⊙, 66,870 ....J 2
80806 Boyero, 25 ....N 5
81026 Brandon, 10 ....P 6
81027 Branson, 70 ....M 8
80424 Breckenridge⊙, 548 ....G 4
80611 Briggsdale, 440 ....L 1
80601 Brighton⊙, 8,309 ....K 3
81028 Bristol, 250 ....P 7
80901 Broadmoor, 3,871 ....K 5
† 81212 Brookside, 173 ....J 6
80020 Broomfield, 7,261 ....J 3
80723 Brush, 857 ....M 2
80742 Buckingham, 6 ....L 1
81211 Buena Vista, 1,962 ....G 5
80425 Buffalo Creek, 150 ....J 4
80807 Burlington⊙, 2,828 ....P 4
80426 Burns, 100 ....F 3
80103 Byers, 490 ....L 3

81320 Cahone, 125 ....B 7
80808 Calhan, 465 ....L 4
81029 Campo, 206 ....O 8
81212 Canon City⊙, 9,206 ....J 6
81324 Capulin, 600 ....G 8
81623 Carbondale, 726 ....E 4
80612 Carr, 47 ....K 1
80809 Cascade, 950 ....K 5
80104 Castle Rock⊙, 1,531 ....K 4
81413 Cedaredge, 581 ....D 5
81125 Center, 1,470 ....G 7
80427 Central City⊙, 228 ....J 3
81126 Chama, 400 ....J 8
81030 Cheraw, 129 ....N 6
80810 Cheyenne Wells⊙, 982 ....P 5
81127 Chimney Rock, 51 ....E 8
81031 Chivington, 15 ....O 6
81128 Chromo, 150 ....F 8
80428 Clark, 55 ....F 1
† 80731 Clarkville, 4 ....P 2
81323 Clifton, 950 ....C 4
80429 Climax, 975 ....G 4
81221 Coal Creek, 225 ....J 6
81222 Coaldale, 104 ....H 6
80430 Coalmont, 12 ....F 1
81032 Cokedale, 101 ....K 8
80611 Cornish, 2 ....L 2
81321 Cortez⊙, 6,032 ....B 8
81223 Cotopaxi, 150 ....H 6
80434 Cowdrey, 10 ....G 1
81625 Craig⊙, 4,205 ....D 2
81415 Crawford, 375 ....D 5
81130 Creede⊙, 653 ....E 7
81224 Crested Butte, 372 ....E 5
81131 Crestone, 34 ....H 7
80813 Cripple Creek⊙, 425 ....J 5
80726 Crook, 199 ....O 1
81033 Crowley, 216 ....M 6
81055 Cuchara, 43 ....J 8
80514 Dacono, 360 ....K 2
† 80728 Dailey, 20 ....O 1
81630 De Beque, 155 ....C 4
80135 Deckers, 4 ....J 4
80105 Deer Trail, 374 ....M 3
81034 Delhi, 10 ....M 7
81132 Del Norte⊙, 1,569 ....G 7
81416 Delta⊙, 3,694 ....D 5
* 80201 Denver (cap.)⊙, 514,678 ....K 3
 Denver, ‡1,227,529 ....K 3
81035 Deora, 25 ....O 7
80435 Dillon, 182 ....H 3
81610 Dinosaur, 247 ....B 2

80814 Divide, 50 ....J 5
81323 Dolores, 820 ....C 8
81324 Dove Creek⊙, 619 ....A 7
† 81239 Doyleville, 75 ....F 6
80515 Drake, 75 ....J 2
81301 Durango⊙, 10,333 ....D 8
81036 Eads⊙, 795 ....O 6
81631 Eagle⊙, 790 ....F 3
80615 Eaton, 1,389 ....K 1
81418 Eckert, 850 ....C 5
80727 Eckley, 193 ....P 2
80214 Edgewater, 4,866 ....J 3
81632 Edwards, 100 ....F 3
81325 Egnar, 84 ....B 7
80106 Elbert, 150 ....L 4
80437 Eldora, 100 ....H 3
80107 Elizabeth, 493 ....K 4
81633 Elk Springs, 56 ....C 2
80438 Empire, 249 ....H 3
80110 Englewood, 33,695 ....K 3
80516 Erie, 1,090 ....K 2
80517 Estes Park, 1,616 ....J 2
† 81433 Eureka, 25 ....D 7
80620 Evans, 2,570 ....K 2
80439 Evergreen, 2,321 ....J 3
80440 Fairplay⊙, 419 ....H 4
81037 Farisita, 45 ....J 7
† 80030 Federal Heights, 1,502 ....J 3
80520 Firestone, 570 ....K 2
† 80810 Firstview, 6 ....O 5
80815 Flagler, 615 ....N 4
80728 Fleming, 349 ....O 1
81226 Florence, 2,846 ....J 6
80816 Florissant, 75 ....J 5
80521 Fort Collins⊙, 43,337 ....J 1
81133 Fort Garland, 400 ....J 8
80621 Fort Lupton, 2,489 ....K 2
81038 Fort Lyon, 135 ....N 6
80701 Fort Morgan⊙, 7,594 ....M 2
80817 Fountain, 3,515 ....K 5
81039 Fowler, 1,241 ....L 6
80441 Foxton, 75 ....J 4
80116 Franktown, 157 ....K 4
80442 Fraser, 221 ....H 3

80530 Frederick, 696 ....K 2
80820 Freshwater (Guffey), 24 ....H 5
80443 Frisco, 471 ....G 3
81521 Fruita, 1,822 ....B 4
† 81501 Fruitvale, 950 ....C 4
80622 Galeton, 200 ....K 1
81134 Garcia, 90 ....J 8
81040 Gardner, 75 ....J 7
81227 Garfield, 11 ....G 5
81522 Gateway, 250 ....B 5
80818 Genoa, 161 ....N 4
80444 Georgetown⊙, 542 ....H 3
80623 Gilcrest, 382 ....K 2
80624 Gill, 250 ....L 2
81634 Gilman, 400 ....G 3
81523 Glade Park, 69 ....B 5
80485 Glendevey, 50 ....H 1
80532 Glen Haven, 50 ....J 2
81601 Glenwood Springs⊙, 4,106 ...E 4
80401 Golden⊙, 9,817 ....J 3
80625 Goodrich, 85 ....M 2
80445 Gould, 12 ....G 2
81041 Granada, 551 ....P 6
80446 Granby, 554 ....H 2
81501 Grand Junction⊙, 20,170 ....B 4
80439 Grand Lake, 189 ....H 2
81635 Grand Valley, 270 ....D 4
81228 Granite, 23 ....G 4
80448 Grant, 50 ....H 4
80631 Greeley⊙, 38,902 ....K 2
80118 Greenland, 47 ....K 4
80819 Green Mountain Falls, 359 .....K 5
81636 Greystone, 2 ....B 1
80729 Grover, 121 ....L 1
80820 Guffey, 24 ....H 5
81042 Gulnare, 100 ....K 8
81230 Gunnison⊙, 4,613 ....E 5
81637 Gypsum, 420 ....F 3
80730 Hale, 12 ....P 3
81638 Hamilton, 30 ....D 2
81043 Hartman, 129 ....P 6
80449 Hartsel, 75 ....H 4
81044 Hasty, 150 ....O 6
81045 Haswell, 135 ....N 6
80731 Haxtun, 899 ....O 1

80839 Hayden, 763 ....E 2
80732 Hereford, 50 ....L 1
81326 Hesperus, 78 ....C 8
80733 Hillrose, 121 ....N 2
81232 Hillside, 79 ....H 6
81046 Hoehne, 400 ....L 8
81047 Holly, 993 ....P 6
80734 Holyoke⊙, 1,640 ....P 1
81136 Hooper, 80 ....H 7
81419 Hotchkiss, 507 ....D 5
80451 Hot Sulphur Springs⊙, 220 ......H 2
81233 Howard, 175 ....H 6
80641 Hoyt, 175 ....L 2
80642 Hudson, 54 ....K 2
80821 Hugo⊙, 759 ....N 4
80533 Hygiene, 400 ....J 2
80452 Idaho Springs, 2,003 ....H 3
80735 Idalia, 100 ....P 3
81137 Ignacio, 613 ....D 8
80736 Iliff, 193 ....N 1
81427 Ironton, 5 ....D 7
† 80901 Ivywild, 12,000 ....K 5
80455 Jamestown, 185 ....J 2
81048 Jansen, 267 ....K 8
81138 Jaroso, 50 ....H 8
80456 Jefferson, 45 ....H 4
80822 Joes, 100 ....O 3
80534 Johnstown, 1,191 ....K 2
80737 Julesburg⊙, 1,578 ....P 1
80823 Karval, 70 ....N 5
80643 Keenesburg, 427 ....L 2
80738 Keota, 6 ....L 1
80644 Kersey, 474 ....L 2
81049 Kim, 200 ....N 8
80117 Kiowa⊙, 235 ....L 4
80824 Kirk, 100 ....P 3
81230 Kit Carson, 220 ....O 5
† 80435 Kokomo, 75 ....G 4
80459 Kremmling, 764 ....G 2
80826 Kutch, 2 ....M 5
80026 Lafayette, 3,498 ....J 2
81139 La Garita, 50 ....G 7
80739 Laird, 105 ....P 2
81140 La Jara, 768 ....H 8
81050 La Junta⊙, 7,938 ....M 7
81235 Lake City⊙, 91 ....E 6
80827 Lake George, 29 ....J 5
80215 Lakewood, 92,787 ....J 3
81052 Lamar⊙, 7,797 ....O 6
80535 Laporte, 950 ....J 1
80118 Larkspur, 350 ....K 4
80645 La Salle, 1,227 ....K 2
81054 Las Animas⊙, 3,148 ....N 6
† 81151 Lasauces, 120 ....H 8
† 81153 Lavalley, 237 ....J 8
81055 La Veta, 589 ....J 8
† 80452 Lawson, 108 ....H 3
81625 Lay, 8 ....C 2
81420 Lazear, 60 ....D 5
80461 Leadville⊙, 4,314 ....G 4
† 81323 Lebanon, 50 ....B 8
81327 Lewis, 350 ....B 8
80828 Limon, 1,814 ....M 4
† 81212 Lincoln Park, 2,984 ....J 6
80740 Lindon, 50 ....N 3
80120 Littleton⊙, 26,466 ....K 3
80536 Livermore, 20 ....J 1
† 80701 Log Lane Village, 329 ....M 2
81524 Loma, 100 ....B 4
80501 Longmont, 23,209 ....J 2
80135 Longview, 10 ....J 4
80027 Louisville, 2,409 ....J 3
80131 Louviers, 306 ....K 4
80537 Loveland, 16,220 ....J 2
80646 Lucerne, 150 ....K 2
81056 Lycan, 4 ....P 7
80540 Lyons, 958 ....J 2
81525 Mack, 175 ....B 4
81421 Maher, 80 ....D 5
† 80461 Malta, 200 ....G 4
81141 Manassa, 814 ....H 8
81328 Mancos, 709 ....C 8
80829 Manitou Springs, 4,278 ....J 5
81058 Manzanola, 451 ....M 6
† 81623 Marble, 1 ....E 4
81329 Marvel, 100 ....C 8
80541 Masonville, 200 ....J 2
† 80649 Masters, 50 ....L 2
80830 Matheson, 100 ....M 4
81640 Maybell, 82 ....C 2
81057 McClave, 165 ....O 6
80463 McCoy, 14 ....F 3
80542 Mead, 195 ....K 2
81641 Meeker⊙, 1,597 ....D 2
81642 Meredith, 48 ....F 4
80741 Merino, 260 ....N 2
81005 Mesa, 295 ....C 4
81330 Mesa Verde National Park,
 70 ....C 8
81142 Mesita, 50 ....H 8
80543 Milliken, 702 ....K 2
80477 Milner, 75 ....F 2
81059 Minturn, 706 ....G 3
81143 Moffat, 98 ....H 6
81646 Molina, 120 ....D 4
81144 Monte Vista, 3,909 ....G 7
80464 Montezuma, 6 ....H 3

(continued on following page)

AREA 104,247 sq. mi.
POPULATION 2,207,259 ('70); 2,888,834 ('80)
CAPITAL Denver
LARGEST CITY Denver
HIGHEST POINT Mt. Elbert 14,433 ft.
SETTLED IN 1858
ADMITTED TO UNION August 1, 1876
POPULAR NAME Centennial State
STATE FLOWER Mountain Columbine
STATE BIRD Lark Bunting

This view of Bear Lake and Longs Peak is typical of the beautiful mountain scenery found in Rocky Mountain National Park, an area which many call "the roof of America."

Colorado Department of Public Relations

Topography

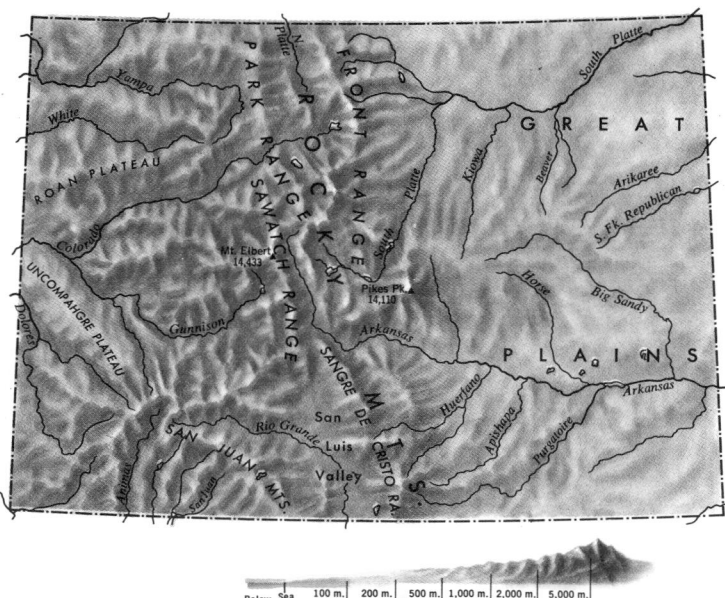

| Below Sea Level | 100 m. 328 ft. | 200 m. 656 ft. | 500 m. 1,640 ft. | 1,000 m. 3,281 ft. | 2,000 m. 6,562 ft. | 5,000 m. 16,404 ft. |

Agriculture, Industry and Resources

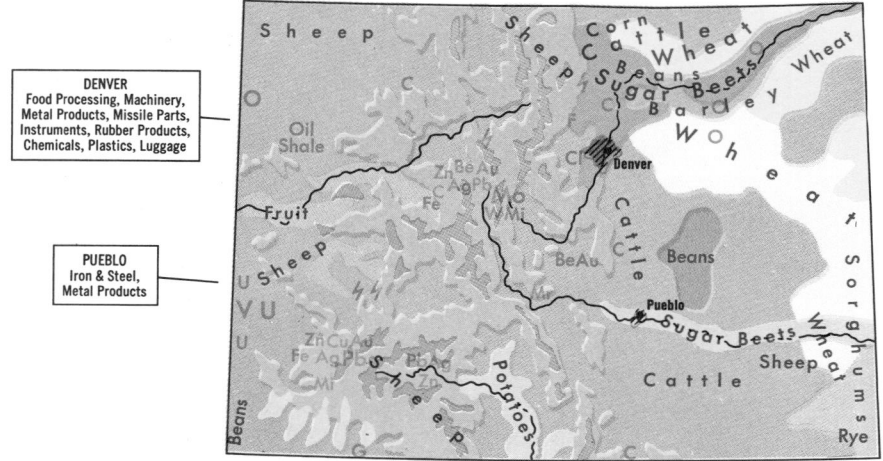

DENVER
Food Processing, Machinery, Metal Products, Missile Parts, Instruments, Rubber Products, Chemicals, Plastics, Luggage

PUEBLO
Iron & Steel, Metal Products

DOMINANT LAND USE

- Specialized Wheat
- Wheat, Range Livestock
- Wheat, Grain Sorghums, Range Livestock
- Dry Beans, General Farming
- Sugar Beets, Dry Beans, Livestock, General Farming
- Fruit, Mixed Farming
- General Farming, Livestock, Special Crops
- Range Livestock
- Forests
- Urban Areas
- Nonagricultural Land

MAJOR MINERAL OCCURRENCES

Ag	Silver	Mi	Mica
Au	Gold	Mo	Molybdenum
Be	Beryl	Mr	Marble
C	Coal	O	Petroleum
Cl	Clay	Pb	Lead
Cu	Copper	U	Uranium
F	Fluorspar	V	Vanadium
Fe	Iron Ore	W	Tungsten
G	Natural Gas	Zn	Zinc

⚡ Water Power

▨ Major Industrial Areas

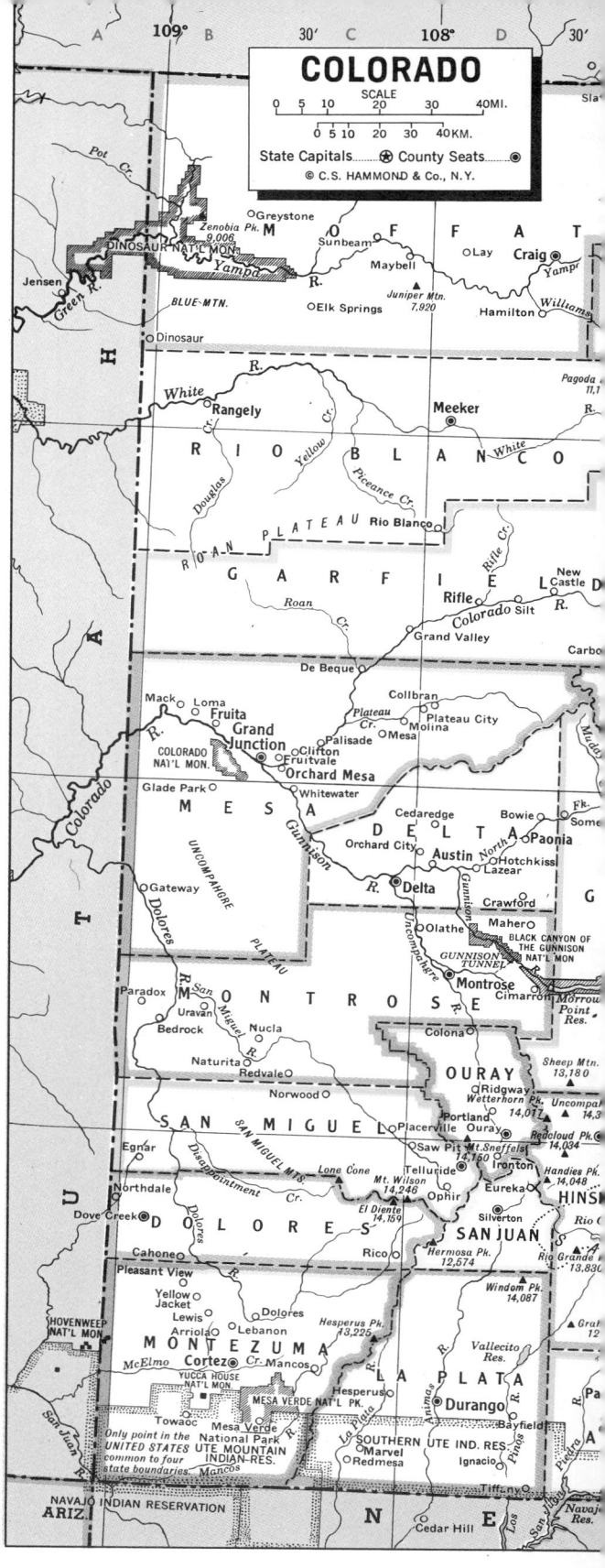

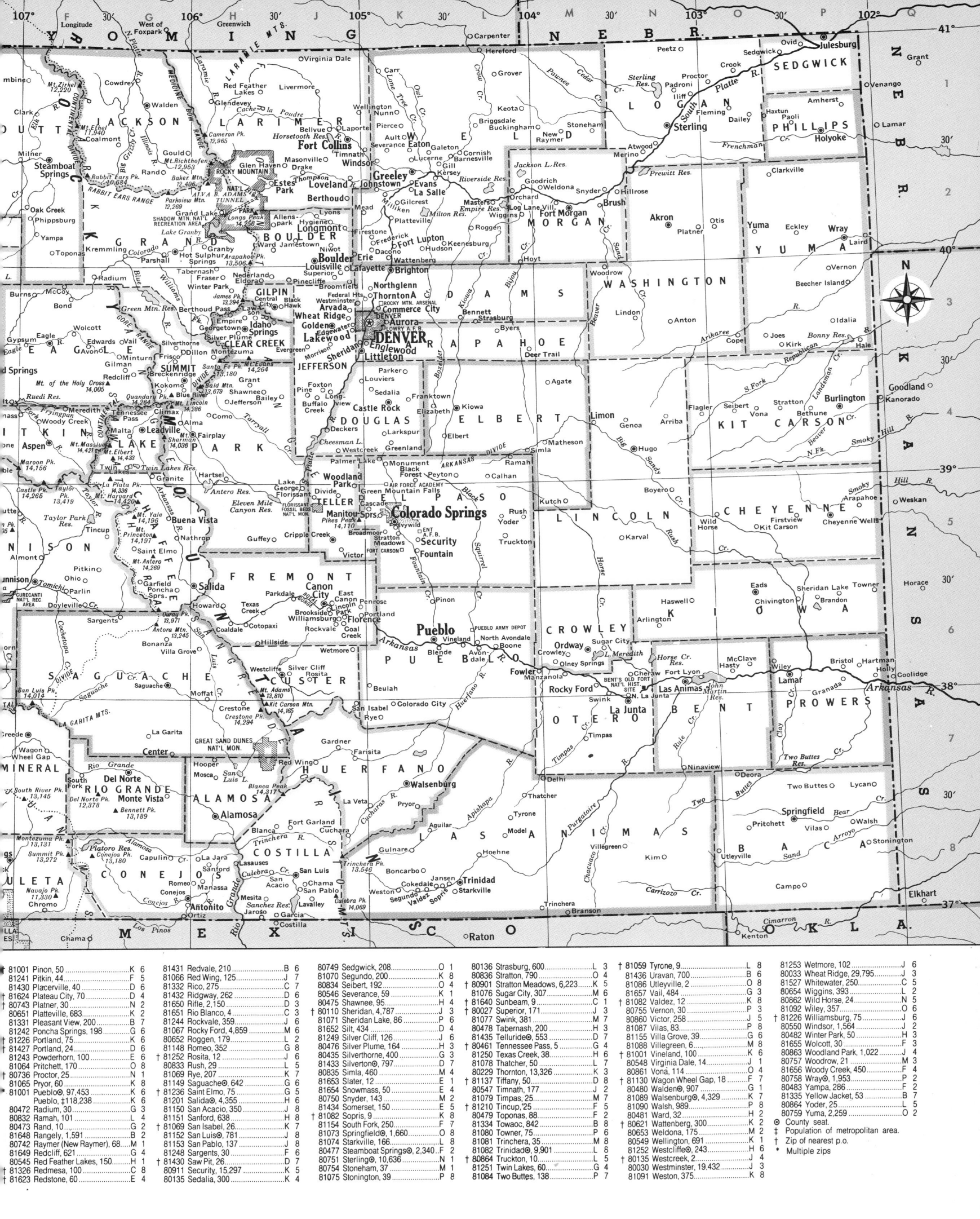

◉ County seat.
‡ Population of metropolitan area.
⊚ Zip of nearest p.o.
* Multiple zips

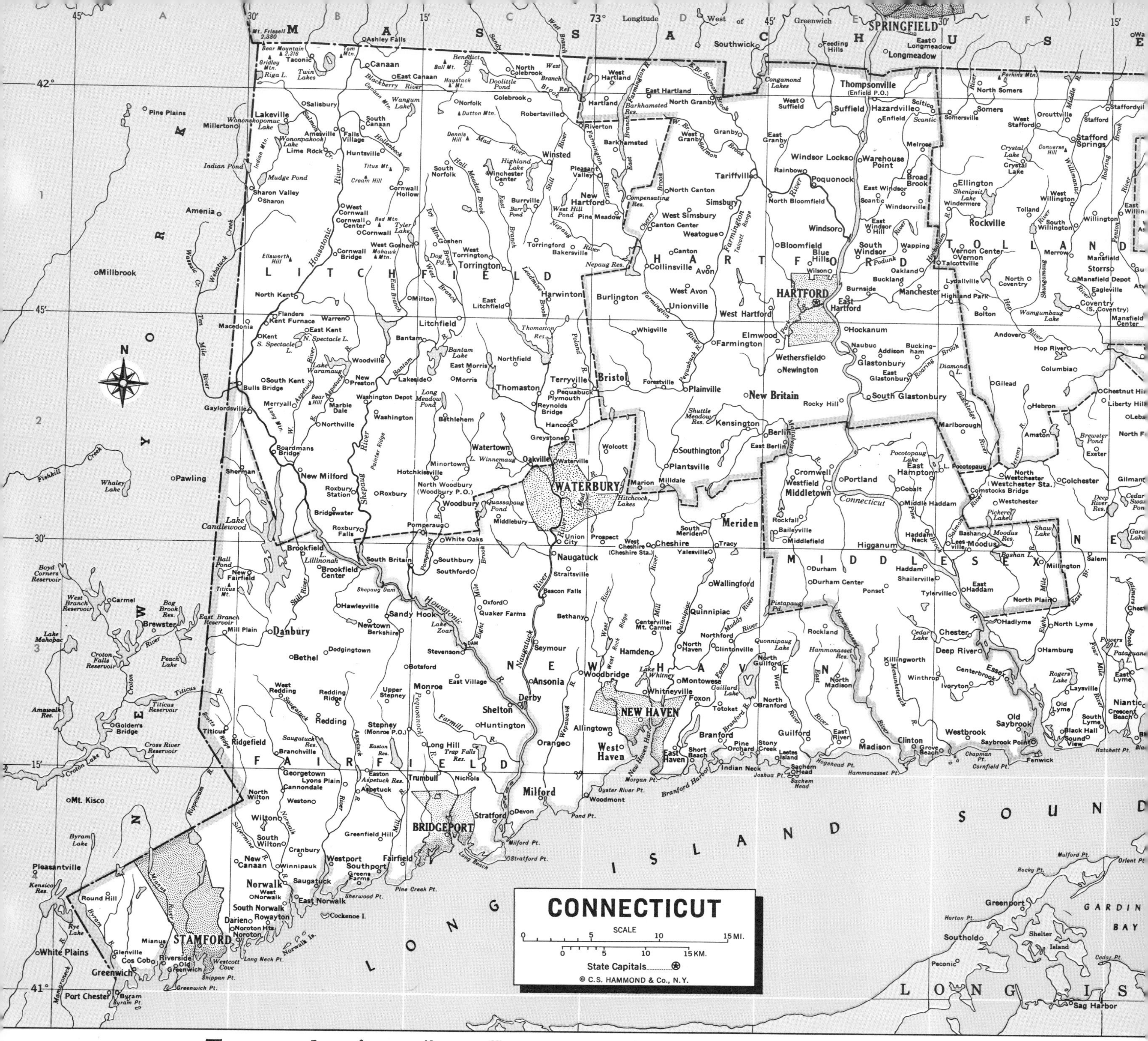

CONNECTICUT

SCALE

0   5   10   15 MI.

0   5   10   15 KM.

State Capitals .... ⊛

© C.S. HAMMOND & Co., N.Y.

Topography

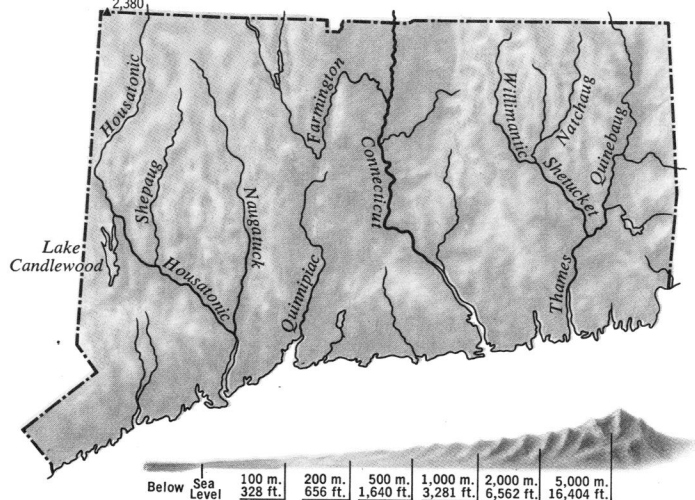

Mt. Frissell 2,380

Lake Candlewood

0   15   30
MILES

| Below Sea Level | 100 m. 328 ft. | 200 m. 656 ft. | 500 m. 1,640 ft. | 1,000 m. 3,281 ft. | 2,000 m. 6,562 ft. | 5,000 m. 16,404 ft. |

COUNTIES

Fairfield, 792,814 ....B 3
Hartford, 816,737 ....D 1
Litchfield, 144,091 ....B 1
Middlesex, 114,816 ....E 3
New Haven, 744,948 ....D 3
New London, 230,348 ....G 2
Tolland, 103,448 ....F 1
Windham, 84,515 ....H 1

CITIES and TOWNS

Zip	Name/Pop.	Key
† 06516	Allingtown, 7,000	D 3
06231	Amston, 1,963	F 2
06232	Andover, △2,099	F 2
06401	Ansonia, 21,160	C 3
† 06250	Ashford, △2,156	G 1
06001	Avon, △8,352	D 1
06330	Baltic, 1,500	G 2
† 06063	Barkhamsted, △2,066	D 1
06403	Beacon Falls, △3,546	C 3
06037	Berlin, △14,149	E 2
† 06801	Bethel, △10,945	B 3
06751	Bethlehem, △1,923	C 2
06002	Bloomfield, △18,301	E 1
06002	Bloomfield, 8,000	E 1
06112	Blue Hills, 5,000	E 1
06040	Bolton, △3,691	F 1
06405	Branford, △20,444	D 3
* 06405	Branford, 2,080	D 3
* 06601	Bridgeport, 156,542	C 4
	Bridgeport, ‡388,953	C 4
06752	Bridgewater, △1,277	B 2
06010	Bristol, 55,487	D 2
06016	Broad Brook, 1,548	E 1
06804	Brookfield, △9,688	B 3
06804	Brookfield, 6,000	B 3
06805	Brookfield Center, 3,000	B 3
06234	Brooklyn, △4,965	H 1
06085	Burlington, △4,070	D 1
06085	Burlington, 950	D 1
06018	Canaan, △931	B 1
06018	Canaan, 1,083	B 1
06331	Canterbury, △2,673	H 2
06019	Canton, △6,868	D 1
06332	Central Village, 1,200	H 2
06235	Chaplin, △1,621	G 1
06410	Cheshire, △19,051	D 2
06412	Chester, △2,982	F 3
06412	Chester, 1,569	F 3
06413	Clinton, △10,267	E 3
06413	Clinton, 5,957	E 3
† 06473	Clintonville, 1,300	D 3
06415	Colchester, △6,603	F 2
06415	Colchester, 3,529	F 2
06021	Colebrook, △1,020	C 1
06022	Collinsville, 2,897	D 1
06238	Coventry, △8,140	F 1
06238	Coventry, 3,735	F 1
06416	Cromwell, △7,400	E 2
06810	Danbury, 50,781	B 3
06239	Danielson, 4,580	H 1
06820	Darien, △20,411	A 4
06241	Dayville, △950	H 1
06417	Deep River, △3,690	F 3
06417	Deep River, 2,333	F 3
06418	Derby, 12,599	C 3
† 06460	Devon, 2,750	C 4
06422	Durham, △4,489	E 3
06023	East Berlin, 1,100	E 2
† 06239	East Brooklyn, 1,377	H 1
06242	Eastford, △922	G 1
06026	East Granby, △3,352	E 1
06423	East Haddam, △4,474	F 3
06424	East Hampton, △7,078	E 2
06424	East Hampton, 1,982	E 2
06108	East Hartford, △57,583	E 1
06512	East Haven, 25,120	D 3
06333	East Lyme, △11,399	G 3
† 06856	East Norwalk, 9,500	A 4
06425	Chester, △4,885	E 3
† 06088	East Windsor, △8,513	E 1
06029	Ellington, △7,707	F 1
06110	Elmwood, 18,500	D 2
06082	Enfield, △46,189	E 1
06082	Enfield P.O. (Thompsonville), 27,000	E 1
06426	Essex, △4,911	F 3
06426	Essex, 2,473	F 3
06430	Fairfield, △56,487	B 4
06032	Farmington, △14,390	D 2
† 06010	Forestville, 20,000	D 2

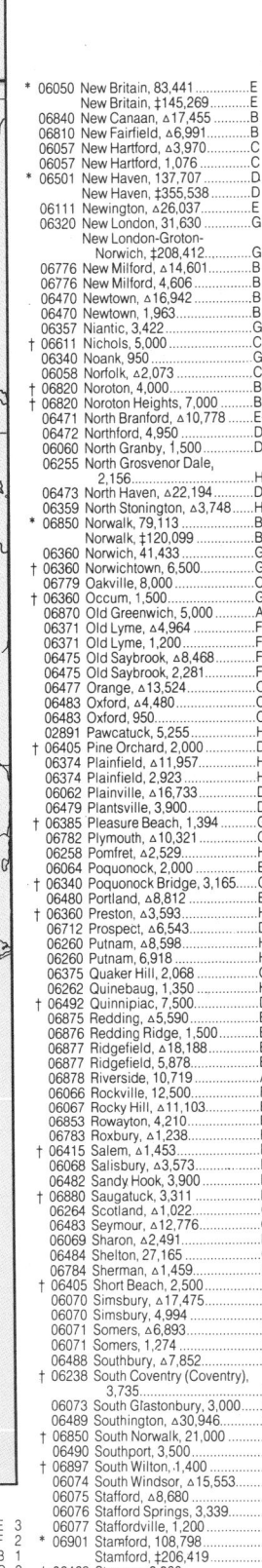

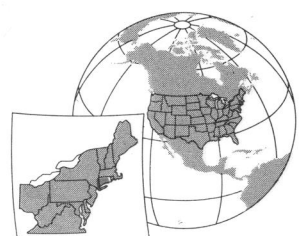

AREA 5,009 sq. mi.
POPULATION 3,032,217 ('70); 3,107,576 ('80)
CAPITAL Hartford
LARGEST CITY Hartford
HIGHEST POINT Mt. Frissell (S. Slope) 2,380 ft.
SETTLED IN 1635
ADMITTED TO UNION January 9, 1788
POPULAR NAME Constitution State; Nutmeg State
STATE FLOWER Mountain Laurel
STATE BIRD Robin

Agriculture, Industry and Resources

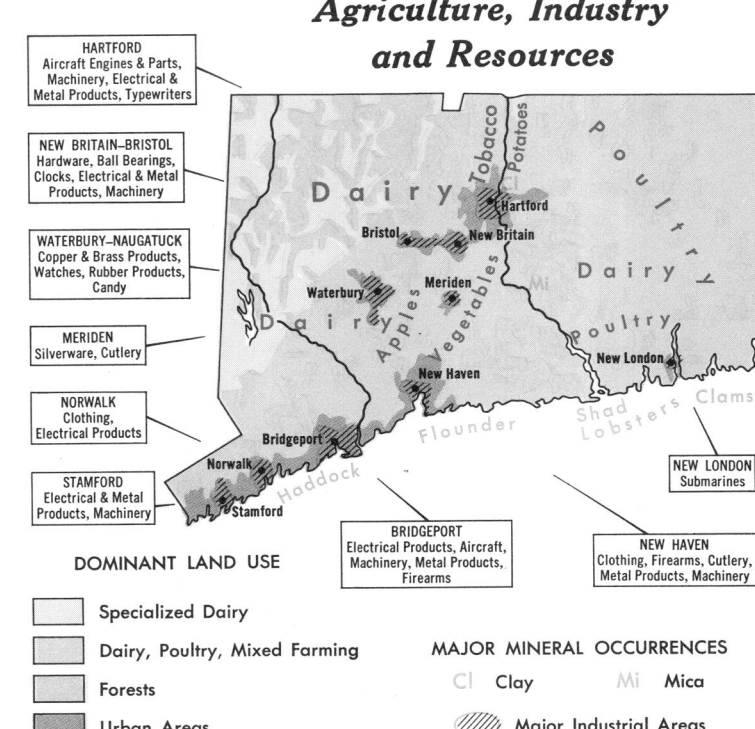

HARTFORD
Aircraft Engines & Parts, Machinery, Electrical & Metal Products, Typewriters

NEW BRITAIN–BRISTOL
Hardware, Ball Bearings, Clocks, Electrical & Metal Products, Machinery

WATERBURY–NAUGATUCK
Copper & Brass Products, Watches, Rubber Products, Candy

MERIDEN
Silverware, Cutlery

NORWALK
Clothing, Electrical Products

STAMFORD
Electrical & Metal Products, Machinery

BRIDGEPORT
Electrical Products, Aircraft, Machinery, Metal Products, Firearms

NEW LONDON
Submarines

NEW HAVEN
Clothing, Firearms, Cutlery, Metal Products, Machinery

DOMINANT LAND USE

Specialized Dairy
Dairy, Poultry, Mixed Farming
Forests
Urban Areas

MAJOR MINERAL OCCURRENCES
Cl Clay   Mi Mica
Major Industrial Areas

* 06050 New Britain, 83,441	E	2
New Britain, ‡145,269	E	2
06840 New Canaan, △17,455	B	4
06810 New Fairfield, △6,991	B	3
06057 New Hartford, △3,970	C	1
06057 New Hartford, 1,076	C	1
* 06501 New Haven, 137,707	D	3
New Haven, ‡355,538	D	3
06111 Newington, △26,037	E	2
06320 New London, 31,630	G	3
New London-Groton-Norwich, ‡208,412	G	3
06776 New Milford, △14,601	B	2
06776 New Milford, 4,606	B	2
06470 Newtown, △16,942	B	3
06470 Newtown, 1,963	B	3
06357 Niantic, 3,422	G	3
† 06611 Nichols, 5,000	C	4
06340 Noank, 950	G	3
06058 Norfolk, △2,073	C	1
† 06820 Noroton, 4,000	B	4
† 06820 Noroton Heights, 7,000	B	4
06471 North Branford, △10,778	E	3
06472 Northford, 4,950	D	3
06060 North Granby, 1,500	D	1
06255 North Grosvenor Dale, 2,156	H	1
06473 North Haven, △22,194	D	3
06359 North Stonington, △3,748	H	3
* 06850 Norwalk, 79,113	B	4
Norwalk, ‡120,099	B	4
06360 Norwich, 41,433	G	2
† 06360 Norwichtown, 6,500	G	2
06779 Oakville, 8,000	C	2
† 06360 Occum, 1,500	G	2
06870 Old Greenwich, 5,000	A	4
06371 Old Lyme, △4,964	F	3
06371 Old Lyme, 1,200	F	3
06475 Old Saybrook, △8,468	F	3
06475 Old Saybrook, 2,281	F	3
06477 Orange, △13,524	C	3
06483 Oxford, △4,480	C	3
06483 Oxford, 950	C	3
02891 Pawcatuck, 5,255	H	3
† 06405 Pine Orchard, 2,000	D	3
06374 Plainfield, △11,957	H	2
06374 Plainfield, 2,923	H	2
06062 Plainville, △16,733	D	2
06479 Plantsville, 3,900	D	2
06385 Pleasure Beach, 1,394	G	3
06782 Plymouth, △10,321	C	2
06258 Pomfret, △2,529	H	1
06064 Poquonock, 2,000	E	1
† 06340 Poquonock Bridge, 3,165	G	3
06480 Portland, △8,812	E	2
06360 Preston, △3,593	H	2
06712 Prospect, △6,543	D	2
06260 Putnam, △8,598	H	1
06260 Putnam, 6,918	H	1
06235 Quaker Hill, 2,068	G	3
06262 Quinebaug, 1,350	H	1
† 06492 Quinnipiac, 7,500	D	3
06875 Redding, 5,590	B	3
06876 Redding Ridge, 1,500	B	3
06877 Ridgefield, △18,188	B	3
06877 Ridgefield, 5,878	B	3
06878 Riverside, 10,719	A	4
06066 Rockville, 12,500	F	1
06067 Rocky Hill, △11,103	E	2
06853 Rowayton, 4,210	B	4
06783 Roxbury, △1,238	B	2
† 06415 Salem, △1,453	F	3
06068 Salisbury, △3,573	B	1
06482 Sandy Hook, 3,900	B	3
† 06880 Saugatuck, 3,311	B	4
06264 Scotland, △1,022	G	2
06483 Seymour, △12,776	C	3
06069 Sharon, △2,491	B	1
06484 Shelton, 27,165	C	3
06784 Sherman, △1,459	B	2
† 06405 Short Beach, 2,500	D	3
06070 Simsbury, △17,475	D	1
06070 Simsbury, 4,994	D	1
06071 Somers, △6,893	F	1
06071 Somers, 1,274	F	1
06488 Southbury, △7,852	C	3
† 06238 South Coventry (Coventry), 3,735	F	1
06073 South Glastonbury, 3,000	E	2
06489 Southington, △30,946	D	2
† 06850 South Norwalk, 21,000	B	4
06490 Southport, 3,500	B	4
† 06897 South Wilton, 1,400	B	4
06074 South Windsor, △15,553	E	1
06075 Stafford, △8,680	F	1
06076 Stafford Springs, 3,339	F	1
06077 Staffordville, 1,200	G	1

06492 Wallingford, △35,714	D	3
† 06074 Wapping, 1,600	E	1
06088 Warehouse Point, 2,400	E	1
06754 Warren, △827	B	2
06793 Washington, △3,121	B	2
* 06701 Waterbury, 108,033	C	2
Waterbury, ‡208,956	C	2
06385 Waterford, △17,227	G	3
06795 Watertown, △18,610	C	2
06795 Watertown, 9,000	C	2
06714 Waterville, 4,295	C	2
06387 Wauregan, 1,100	H	2
06089 Weatogue, 2,396	D	1
† 06001 West Avon, 4,500	D	1
06498 Westbrook, △3,820	F	3
06498 Westbrook, 1,507	F	3
† 06410 West Cheshire, 2,000	D	3
06457 Westfield, 9,000	E	2
06107 West Hartford, △68,031	D	1
06516 West Haven, 52,851	D	3
06388 West Mystic, 3,694	H	3
06856 West Norwalk, 950	B	4
06880 Weston, △7,417	B	4
06880 Weston, 3,000	B	4
06880 Westport, △27,414	B	4
06896 West Redding, 1,200	B	3
06092 West Simsbury, 1,419	D	1
06093 West Suffield, 2,400	E	1
06109 Wethersfield, 26,662	E	2
06517 Whitneyville, 18,438	D	3
06226 Willimantic, △14,402	G	2
† 06279 Willington, △3,755	F	1
06897 Wilton, △13,572	B	4
06897 Wilton, 4,500	B	4
06094 Winchester, △11,106	C	1
06094 Winchester Center, 350	C	1
06280 Windham, △19,626	G	2
06095 Windsor, △22,502	E	1
06096 Windsor Locks, △15,080	E	1
06098 Winsted, 8,954	C	1
06716 Wolcott, △12,495	D	2
† 06501 Woodbridge, △7,673	D	3
06798 Woodbury, △5,869	C	2
06798 Woodbury, 1,200	C	2
06798 Woodbury P.O. (North Woodbury), 1,342	C	2
‡ 06460 Woodmont, 2,400	D	4
06281 Woodstock, △4,311	H	1
‡ 06492 Yalesville, 1,500	D	3
‡ 06389 Yantic, 1,200	G	2

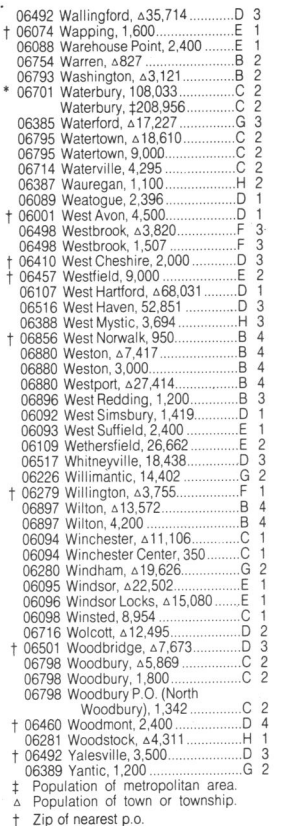

Bark whaler "Charles W. Morgan," on view at Mystic, Connecticut, covered more miles and caught more whales than any other ship of her kind.

† 06254 Franklin, △1,356	G	2
06335 Gales Ferry, 6,200	G	3
06829 Georgetown, 1,101	B	4
06033 Glastonbury, △20,651	E	2
06756 Goshen, △1,351	C	1
06035 Granby, △6,150	D	1
† 06430 Greenfield Hill, 2,500	B	4
06436 Greens Farms, 3,147	B	4
06830 Greenwich, △59,755	A	4
06340 Groton, △38,523	G	3
06340 Groton, 8,933	G	3
06437 Guilford, △12,033	E	3
06437 Guilford, 3,632	E	3
06438 Haddam, △4,934	E	3
06438 Haddam, 950	E	3
06514 Hamden, △49,357	D	3
06247 Hampton, △1,129	G	1
* 06101 Hartford (cap.), 158,017	E	1
Hartford, ‡663,891	E	1
† 06091 Hartland, △1,303	D	1
06790 Harwinton, △4,318	C	1
06082 Hazardville, 10,000	E	1
06248 Hebron, △3,815	F	2
06441 Higganum, 2,600	E	2
† 06108 Hockanum, 6,500	F	1
† 06484 Huntington, 1,559	C	3
† 06405 Indian Neck, 1,500	D	3
06442 Ivoryton, 1,500	F	3
06351 Jewett City, 3,372	H	2
06037 Kensington, 6,000	D	2
06757 Kent, △1,990	B	2
† 06241 Killingly, △13,573	H	1
† 06413 Killingworth, △2,435	E	3
† 06424 Lake Pocotopaug, 1,515	F	2
06039 Lakeville, 2,100	B	1
06249 Lebanon, △3,804	G	2
06339 Ledyard, △14,558	G	3
06759 Litchfield, △7,399	C	2
06759 Litchfield, 1,559	C	2
06443 Madison, △9,768	E	3
06443 Madison, 4,310	E	3
06040 Manchester, △47,994	E	1
† 06250 Mansfield, △19,994	F	1
06444 Marion, 1,800	D	2
† 06424 Marlborough, △2,991	F	2
06450 Meriden, 55,959	D	2
Meriden, ‡55,959	D	2
06762 Middlebury, △5,542	C	2
06455 Middlefield, △4,132	E	2
06457 Middletown, 36,924	E	2
06460 Milford, 50,858	C	4
06467 Milldale, 1,175	D	2
06468 Monroe, △12,047	C	3
06468 Monroe P.O. (Stepney), 3,000	B	3
† 06473 Montowese, 2,500	D	3
06353 Montville, 1,688	G	3
06353 Montville, 15,662	G	3
06469 Moodus, 1,352	F	2
06354 Moosup, 3,374	H	2
06385 Morningside Park, 3,458	G	3
06763 Morris, △1,609	C	2
06355 Mystic, 2,568	H	3
06770 Naugatuck, 23,034	C	3

06901 Stamford, 108,798	A	4
Stamford, ‡206,419	A	4
† 06468 Stepney, 2,300	B	3
06377 Sterling, △1,853	H	2
06491 Stevenson, 1,500	C	3
06378 Stonington, △15,940	H	3
06378 Stonington, 1,413	H	3
† 06405 Stony Creek, 2,800	E	3
06268 Storrs, 10,691	F	1
06497 Stratford, 49,775	C	4
06078 Suffield, △8,634	E	1
06380 Taftville, 2,000	G	2
06081 Tariffville, 1,337	D	1
06786 Terryville, 6,900	C	2
06360 Thamesville, 1,500	G	2
06787 Thomaston, △6,233	C	2
06277 Thompson, △7,580	H	1
06277 Thompson, 1,200	H	1
06082 Thompsonville, 27,000	E	1
06084 Tolland, △7,857	F	1
06790 Torrington, 3,500	C	1
06790 Torrington, 31,952	C	1
† 06405 Totoket, 950	D	3
06611 Trumbull, △31,394	C	4
06611 Trumbull, 10,000	C	4
06382 Uncasville, 1,750	G	3
† 06076 Union, △443	G	1
06770 Union City, 5,000	C	3
06085 Unionville, 3,000	D	1
06086 Vernon, △27,237	F	1
06384 Voluntown, △1,452	H	2

‡ Population of metropolitan area.
△ Population of town or township.
† Zip of nearest p.o.
* Multiple zips

Edmund V. Balliman

COUNTIES

Alachua, 104,764 ....D 2
Baker, 9,242 ....D 1
Bay, 75,283 ....C 6
Bradford, 14,625 ....D 2
Brevard, 230,006 ....F 3
Broward, 620,100 ....F 5
Calhoun, 7,624 ....D 6
Charlotte, 27,559 ....E 5
Citrus, 19,196 ....D 3
Clay, 32,059 ....E 2
Collier, 38,040 ....E 5
Columbia, 25,250 ....D 1
Dade, 1,287,792 ....F 6
De Soto, 13,060 ....E 4
Dixie, 5,480 ....C 2
Duval, 528,865 ....E 1
Escambia, 205,334 ....B 6
Flagler, 4,454 ....E 2
Franklin, 7,065 ....B 2
Gadsden, 39,184 ....B 1
Gilchrist, 3,551 ....D 2
Glades, 3,669 ....E 5
Gulf, 10,096 ....D 7
Hamilton, 7,787 ....D 1
Hardee, 14,889 ....E 4
Hendry, 11,859 ....E 5
Hernando, 17,004 ....D 3
Highlands, 29,507 ....E 4
Hillsborough, 490,265 ....D 4
Holmes, 10,720 ....C 5
Indian River, 35,992 ....F 4
Jackson, 34,434 ....D 5
Jefferson, 8,778 ....C 1
Lafayette, 2,892 ....C 2
Lake, 69,305 ....E 3
Lee, 105,216 ....E 5
Leon, 103,047 ....B 1
Levy, 12,756 ....D 2
Liberty, 3,379 ....B 1
Madison, 13,481 ....C 1
Manatee, 97,115 ....D 4
Marion, 69,030 ....D 2
Martin, 28,035 ....F 4
Monroe, 52,586 ....E 7
Nassau, 20,626 ....E 1
Okaloosa, 88,187 ....C 6
Okeechobee, 11,233 ....F 4
Orange, 344,311 ....E 3
Osceola, 25,267 ....E 3
Palm Beach, 348,753 ....F 5
Pasco, 75,955 ....D 3
Pinellas, 522,329 ....D 4
Polk, 227,222 ....E 4
Putnam, 36,290 ....E 2
Saint Johns, 30,727 ....E 2
Saint Lucie, 50,836 ....F 4
Santa Rosa, 37,741 ....B 6
Sarasota, 120,413 ....D 4
Seminole, 83,692 ....E 3
Sumter, 14,839 ....D 3
Suwannee, 15,559 ....C 1
Taylor, 13,641 ....C 1
Union, 8,112 ....D 1
Volusia, 169,487 ....E 2
Wakulla, 6,308 ....B 1
Walton, 16,087 ....C 6
Washington, 11,453 ....C 6

CITIES and TOWNS

Zip	Name/Pop.	Key
32615	Alachua, 2,252	D 2
32420	Alford, 402	D 6
32421	Altha, 423	A 1
32702	Altoona, 800	E 3
33820	Alturas, 468	E 4
33920	Alva, 900	E 4
33501	Anna Maria, 1,137	D 4
32617	Anthony, 500	D 2
32320	Apalachicola⊙, 3,102	A 2
33570	Apollo Beach, 1,042	C 3
32703	Apopka, 4,045	E 3
33821	Arcadia⊙, 5,658	E 4
32618	Archer, 898	D 2
32422	Argyle, 155	C 6
33502	Aripeka, 300	D 3
† 32327	Arran, 160	B 1
32705	Astatula, 388	E 3
32002	Astor, 300	E 2
33823	Auburndale, 5,386	E 4
† 32344	Aucilla, 150	C 1
33825	Avon Park, 6,712	E 4
33827	Babson Park, 950	E 4
32530	Bagdad, 850	B 6
32531	Baker, 500	C 5
32234	Baldwin, 1,272	E 1
† 33101	Bal Harbour, 2,038	C 4
32005	Barberville, 300	E 2
† 32533	Barrineau Park, 150	B 6
32532	Barth, 200	B 6
33830	Bartow⊙, 12,891	E 4
32423	Bascom, 200	A 1
33428	Basinger, 300	F 4
† 33101	Bay Harbour Islands, 4,619	B 4
33504	Bay Pines, 1,100	B 3
† 33902	Bayshore, 150	E 5
† 36502	Bay Springs, 125	B 6
33429	Bean City, 155	F 5
33578	Bee Ridge, 2,100	D 4
32619	Bell, 227	D 2
33540	Belleair, 2,962	B 3
† 33540	Belleair Beach, 952	B 3
33540	Belleair Bluffs, 1,910	B 3
33430	Belle Glade, 15,949	F 5
† 33430	Belle Glade Camp, 1,892	F 5
† 32801	Belle Isle, 2,705	E 3
32620	Belleview, 916	D 2
33152	Biscayne Park, 2,717	B 4
† 32801	Bithlo, 684	E 3
32424	Blountstown⊙, 2,384	A 1
† 32535	Bluffsprings, 160	B 6
33921	Boca Grande, 600	D 5
33432	Boca Raton, 28,506	F 5
33922	Bokeelia, 750	D 5
32425	Bonifay⊙, 2,068	C 5
33923	Bonita Springs, 1,932	E 5
32007	Bostwick, 500	E 2
33834	Bowling Green, 1,357	E 4
33435	Boynton Beach, 18,115	F 5
33505	Bradenton⊙, 21,040	D 4
33510	Bradenton Beach, 1,370	D 4
33835	Bradley, 1,276	D 4
33511	Brandon, 12,749	D 4
32008	Branford, 820	D 2
† 33435	Briny Breezes, 481	G 5
32321	Bristol⊙, 626	B 1
32621	Bronson⊙, 698	D 2
32622	Brooker, 340	D 2
33512	Brooksville⊙, 4,060	D 3

AREA 58,560 sq. mi.
POPULATION 6,789,443 ('70); 9,739,992 ('80)
CAPITAL Tallahassee
LARGEST CITY Jacksonville
HIGHEST POINT 345 ft. (Walton County)
SETTLED IN 1565
ADMITTED TO UNION March 3, 1845
POPULAR NAME Sunshine State; Peninsula State
STATE FLOWER Orange Blossom
STATE BIRD Mockingbird

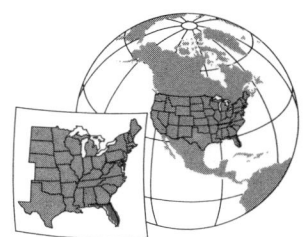

Topography

0   50   100
MILES

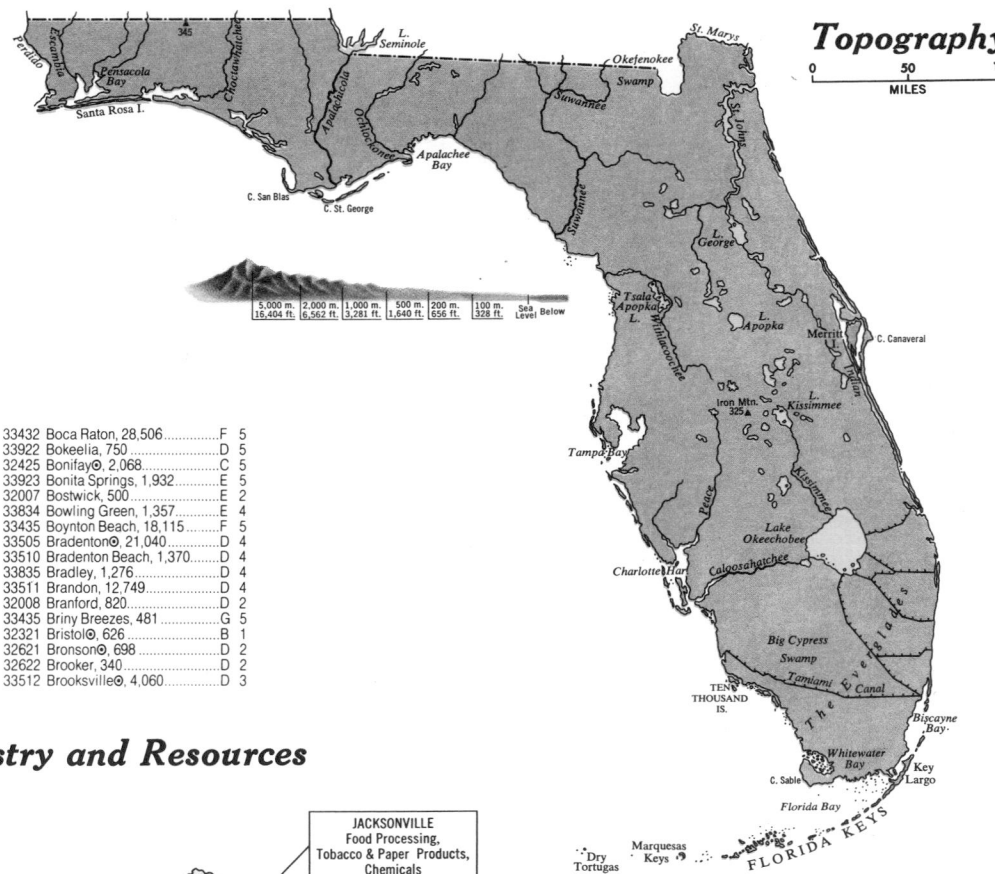

5,000 m. 16,404 ft.	2,000 m. 6,562 ft.	1,000 m. 3,281 ft.	500 m. 1,640 ft.	200 m. 656 ft.	100 m. 328 ft.	Sea Level Below

Agriculture, Industry and Resources

PENSACOLA
Lumber, Wood & Paper Products, Chemicals

TAMPA–ST. PETERSBURG
Food Processing, Chemicals, Cigars

JACKSONVILLE
Food Processing, Tobacco & Paper Products, Chemicals

MIAMI–WEST PALM BEACH
Aircraft, Metal & Electrical Products, Food Processing, Clothing, Furniture

DOMINANT LAND USE

- Fruit, Truck & Mixed Farming
- Truck & Mixed Farming
- Truck Farming
- Cotton, Tobacco, Hogs, Peanuts
- Peanuts, General Farming
- General Farming, Forest Products, Truck Farming, Cotton
- Livestock Grazing
- Forests
- Swampland, Limited Agriculture
- Urban Areas
- Nonagricultural Land

MAJOR MINERAL OCCURRENCES

Cl Clay
Ls Limestone
P Phosphates
⚡ Water Power
Pe Peat
Ti Titanium
Zr Zirconium
▨ Major Industrial Areas

† 33101	Browns Village, 23,442	B 4	32533	Cottagehill, 500	B 6
32455	Bruce, 221	C 6	32431	Cottondale, 765	D 6
33439	Bryant, 400	F 5	32327	Crawfordville⊙, 750	B 1
† 33054	Bunche Park, 5,773	B 4	32012	Crescent City, 1,734	E 2
32010	Bunnell⊙, 1,687	E 2	32536	Crestview⊙, 7,952	C 6
33513	Bushnell⊙, 700	D 3	32628	Cross City⊙, 2,268	C 2
32011	Callahan, 772	E 1	32463	Crystal Lake, 125	D 6
32401	Callaway, 3,240	D 6	32629	Crystal River, 1,696	D 3
32426	Campbellton, 304	D 6	33524	Crystal Springs, 300	D 3
33438	Canal Point, 900	F 5	33157	Cutler Ridge, 17,441	F 6
32624	Candler, 500	E 2	32432	Cypress, 266	A 1
32533	Cantonment, 3,241	B 6	33880	Cypress Gardens, 3,757	E 4
32920	Cape Canaveral, 4,258	F 3	† 33972	Cypress Quarters, 1,310	F 4
33904	Cape Coral, 10,193	E 5	33525	Dade City⊙, 4,241	D 3
33924	Captiva, 150	D 5	33004	Dania, 9,013	B 4
33054	Carol City, 27,361	B 4	† 32464	Darlington, 175	C 5
32322	Carrabelle, 1,044	B 2	33837	Davenport, 828	E 3
32427	Caryville, 724	C 6	33314	Davie, 2,856	B 4
32706	Cassadaga, 250	E 3	32013	Day, 200	C 1
32707	Casselberry, 9,438	E 3	* 32014	Daytona Beach, 45,327	F 2
† 32401	Cedar Grove, 689	D 6	32016	Daytona Beach Shores, 768	F 2
32625	Cedar Key, 714	C 2	32713	De Bary, 3,154	E 3
33514	Center Hill, 371	D 3	33441	Deerfield Beach, 17,130	F 5
32535	Century, 2,679	B 5	32433	De Funiak Springs⊙, 4,966	C 6
† 32302	Chaires, 150	B 1	32720	De Land⊙, 11,641	E 2
33950	Charlotte Harbor, 990	E 5	32028	De Leon Springs, 1,134	E 2
32324	Chattahoochee, 7,944	B 1	33444	Delray Beach, 19,366	F 5
† 32401	Cherry Lake Farms, 400	C 1	32763	Deltona, 4,868	E 2
32626	Chiefland, 1,965	D 2	† 33870	De Soto City, 250	E 4
32428	Chipley⊙, 3,347	C 6	32541	Destin, 1,536	C 6
33925	Chokoloskee, 230	E 6	32030	Doctors Inlet, 800	E 1
32709	Christmas, 800	E 3	33527	Dover, 2,094	D 4
† 32548	Cinco Bayou, 362	B 6	32060	Dowling Park, 200	C 1
32627	Citra, 500	D 2	33838	Dundee, 1,660	E 3
32922	City Point, 350	F 3	33528	Dunedin, 17,639	B 2
32430	Clarksville, 250	D 6	32630	Dunnellon, 1,146	D 2
* 33515	Clearwater⊙, 52,074	B 2	33899	Eagle Lake, 1,373	E 4
32711	Clermont, 3,661	E 3	32631	Earleton, 350	D 2
† 33950	Cleveland, 150	E 5	† 33601	East Lake-Orient Park, 5,697	C 2
33440	Clewiston, 3,896	E 5	† 33940	East Naples, 6,152	E 5
32922	Cocoa, 16,110	F 3	32031	East Palatka, 1,446	E 2
32931	Cocoa Beach, 9,952	F 3	32328	Eastpoint, 1,188	C 2
† 33060	Coconut Creek, 1,359	F 5	32437	Ebro, 125	C 6
33521	Coleman, 614	D 3	32032	Edgewater, 3,348	F 3
32448	Compass Lake, 200	D 6	* 32801	Edgewood, 392	E 3
† 32333	Concord, 300	B 1	† 33601	Egypt Lake, 7,556	C 2
33314	Cooper City, 2,535	F 5	33531	Elfers, 500	D 3
33926	Copeland, 500	E 6	32033	Elkton, 240	E 2
† 83559	Coral Cove, 1,520	D 4	† 33101	El Portal, 2,068	B 4
33134	Coral Gables, 42,494	B 5	33533	Englewood, 5,182	D 5
33836	Cornwell, 700	E 4	32504	Ensley, 2,400	B 6
33522	Cortez, 600	D 4			

(continued on following page)

(continued)

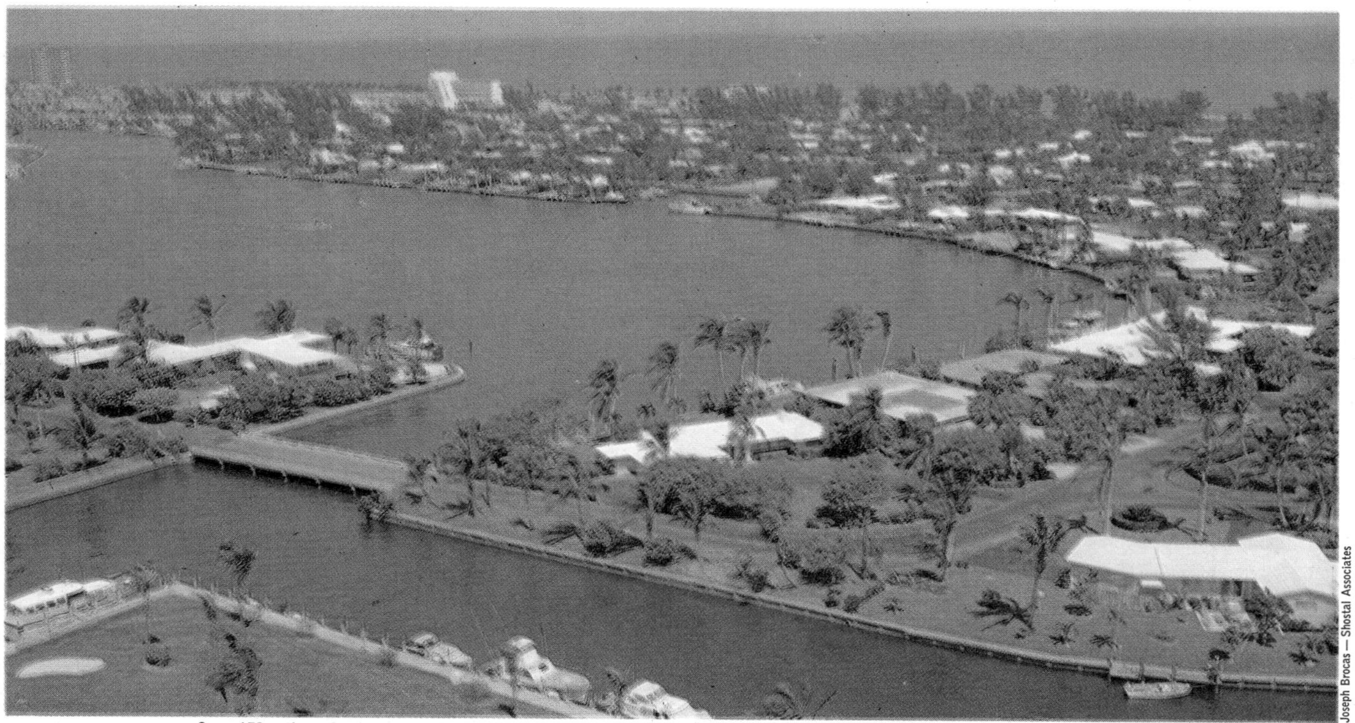
Joseph Brocas — Shostal Associates

Over 150 miles of inland waterways provide a Venetian atmosphere in the modern city of Fort Lauderdale, Florida.

† 32010 Espanola, 300 ... E 2
33928 Estero, 950 ... E 5
32425 Esto, 210 ... C 5
32726 Eustis, 6,722 ... E 3
33929 Everglades City, 462 ... E 6
† 32601 Fairbanks, 380 ... D 2
† 32804 Fairvilla, 950 ... E 3
33930 Felda, 125 ... E 5
32948 Fellsmere, 813 ... F 4
32034 Fernandina Beach⊙, 6,955 ... E 1
† 33301 Fern Crest Village, 1,009 ... B 4
32036 Flagler Beach, 1,042 ... E 2
32635 Florahome, 400 ... E 2
32636 Floral City, 975 ... D 3
33030 Florida City, 5,133 ... F 6
† 32570 Floridatown, 297 ... B 6
† 32569 Florosa, 200 ... B 6
† 32347 Foley, 500 ... C 1
† 33935 Fort Denaud, 300 ... E 5
† 33472 Fort Drum, 100 ... F 4
33834 Fort Green, 300 ... E 4
* 33301 Fort Lauderdale⊙, 139,590 ... C 4
Fort Lauderdale-Hollywood, ‡620,100 ... C 4
32637 Fort McCoy, 900 ... E 2
33841 Fort Meade, 4,374 ... E 4
* 33901 Fort Myers⊙, 27,351 ... E 5
33931 Fort Myers Beach, 4,305 ... E 5
33842 Fort Ogden, 700 ... E 4
33450 Fort Pierce⊙, 29,721 ... F 4
32548 Fort Walton Beach, 19,994 ... C 6
32038 Fort White, 365 ... D 2
32438 Fountain, 650 ... D 6
32439 Freeport, 950 ... C 6
† 32430 Frink, 275 ... D 6
33843 Frostproof, 2,814 ... E 4
32731 Fruitland Park, 1,359 ... D 3
33578 Fruitville, 1,531 ... D 4
32601 Gainesville⊙, 64,510 ... D 2
32732 Geneva, 950 ... E 3
32039 Georgetown, 687 ... E 2
33534 Gibsonton, 1,900 ... C 3
32960 Gifford, 5,772 ... F 4
32040 Glen Saint Mary, 357 ... D 1
32722 Glenwood, 400 ... E 2
33160 Golden Beach, 849 ... C 4
33940 Golden Gate, 1,410 ... E 5
† 33455 Gomez, 400 ... F 4
32560 Gonzalez, 750 ... B 6
33933 Goodland, 500 ... E 6
† 32502 Goulding, 500 ... B 6
33170 Goulds, 6,690 ... F 6
32440 Graceville, 2,560 ... D 5
32042 Graham, 150 ... D 2
32638 Grandin, 150 ... E 2
32442 Grand Ridge, 512 ... A 1
32949 Grant, 500 ... F 4
33460 Greenacres City, 1,731 ... F 5
32043 Green Cove Springs⊙, 3,857 ... E 2
32330 Greensboro, 716 ... B 1
32331 Greenville, 1,141 ... C 1
32443 Greenwood, 515 ... A 1
32332 Gretna, 883 ... B 1
33533 Grove City, 1,178 ... F 5
32736 Groveland, 1,928 ... E 3
32561 Gulf Breeze, 4,190 ... B 6
32639 Gulf Hammock, 300 ... D 2
† 33552 Gulf Harbors, 1,177 ... D 3
33737 Gulfport, 9,730 ... B 3
† 33444 Gulf Stream, 408 ... F 5
† 32601 Hague, 200 ... D 2
33844 Haines City, 8,956 ... E 3
33009 Hallandale, 23,849 ... B 4
32044 Hampton, 386 ... D 2
33440 Harlem, 2,006 ... F 5
32563 Harold, 150 ... B 6
32045 Hastings, 320 ... E 2
32333 Havana, 2,022 ... B 1
32640 Hawthorne, 1,126 ... D 2
32642 Hernando, 524 ... D 3
* 33010 Hialeah, 102,297 ... B 4
† 33010 Hialeah Gardens, 492 ... B 4
33846 Highland City, 900 ... E 4
† 33515 High Point, 800 ... B 3
32643 High Springs, 2,787 ... D 2
32401 Hiland Park, 3,691 ... C 6
† 33827 Hillcrest Heights, 154 ... E 4
32046 Hilliard, 1,205 ... E 1
† 32327 Hilliardville, 150 ... B 1
† 33060 Hillsboro Beach, 713 ... F 5
† 32333 Hinson, 250 ... B 1
33455 Hobe Sound, 2,029 ... F 4
32645 Holder, 134 ... D 3
32047 Hollister, 500 ... E 2
32017 Holly Hill, 8,191 ... E 2
* 33020 Hollywood, 106,873 ... B 4
† 33020 Hollywood Ridge Farms, 302 ... B 4
33509 Holmes Beach, 2,699 ... D 4
32564 Holt, 850 ... C 6
33030 Homestead, 13,674 ... F 6
† 32646 Homosassa, 850 ... D 3
32647 Homosassa Springs, 550 ... D 3
32634 Hosford, 975 ... B 1
32737 Howey In The Hills, 466 ... E 3
33568 Hudson, 2,278 ... D 3
† 33460 Hypoluxo, 336 ... F 5
33934 Immokalee, 3,764 ... E 5
32901 Indialantic, 2,685 ... F 3
32935 Indian Harbour Beach, 5,371 ... F 3
33535 Indian Rocks Beach, 2,666 ... B 3
† 33535 Indian Rocks Beach South Shore, 791 ... B 3
33456 Indiantown, 2,283 ... F 4
32649 Inglis, 449 ... D 2
33848 Intercession City, 600 ... E 3
32048 Interlachen, 478 ... E 2
32650 Inverness⊙, 2,299 ... D 3
33036 Islamorada, 1,251 ... F 7
32654 Island Grove, 200 ... D 2
* 32201 Jacksonville⊙, 528,865 ... E 1
Jacksonville, ‡528,865 ... E 1
32250 Jacksonville Beach, 12,049 ... E 1
32052 Jasper⊙, 2,221 ... D 1
32565 Jay, 646 ... B 5
32053 Jennings, 582 ... C 1
33457 Jensen Beach, 3,000 ... F 4
† 32901 June Park, 3,090 ... F 3
† 33404 Juno Beach, 747 ... F 5
33458 Jupiter, 3,136 ... F 5
† 33455 Jupiter Island, 295 ... F 4
† 33849 Kathleen, 900 ... D 3
32739 Kenansville, 450 ... F 4
33156 Kendall, 35,497 ... B 5
† 32670 Kendrick, 200 ... D 2
33709 Kenneth City, 3,862 ... B 3
33149 Key Biscayne, 4,563 ... B 5
33051 Key Colony Beach, 371 ... F 7
33037 Key Largo, 2,866 ... F 6
32656 Keystone Heights, 800 ... E 2
33040 Key West⊙, 27,563 ... E 7
32449 Kinard, 450 ... D 6
32741 Kissimmee⊙, 7,119 ... E 3
† 32010 Korona, 200 ... E 2
33935 La Belle⊙, 1,823 ... E 5
33537 Lacoochee, 1,380 ... D 3
32658 La Crosse, 365 ... D 2
32659 Lady Lake, 382 ... E 3
33850 Lake Alfred, 2,847 ... E 3
32054 Lake Butler⊙, 1,598 ... D 1
† 33601 Lake Carroll, 5,577 ... C 2
32055 Lake City⊙, 10,575 ... D 1
32057 Lake Como, 340 ... E 2
33459 Lake Harbor, 300 ... F 5
32744 Lake Helen, 1,303 ... E 3
32745 Lake Jem, 314 ... E 3
* 33801 Lakeland, 41,550 ... D 3
† 33601 Lake Magdalene, 9,266 ... D 3
32746 Lake Mary, 900 ... E 3
32747 Lake Monroe, 500 ... E 3
33403 Lake Park, 6,993 ... F 5
33852 Lake Placid, 656 ... E 4
† 33471 Lakeport, 375 ... E 5
33853 Lake Wales, 8,240 ... E 4
32566 Lakewood, 525 ... C 5
33460 Lake Worth, 23,714 ... G 5
32336 Lamont, 500 ... C 1
33539 Land O'Lakes, 900 ... D 3
33460 Lantana, 7,126 ... F 5
33540 Largo, 22,031 ... B 3
33308 Lauderdale-by-the-Sea, 2,879 ... C 3
† 33301 Lauderdale Lakes, 10,577 ... B 4
33313 Lauderhill, 8,465 ... B 4
32567 Laurel Hill, 418 ... C 5
33545 Laurel-Nokomis, 3,238 ... D 4
32058 Lawtey, 636 ... D 1
32661 Lecanto, 125 ... D 3
32059 Lee, 240 ... C 1
32748 Leesburg, 11,869 ... E 3
33936 Lehigh Acres, 4,394 ... E 5
33030 Leisure City, 2,900 ... F 6
† 33601 Leto, 8,458 ... C 2
33064 Lighthouse Point, 9,071 ... F 5
† 33865 Limestone, 200 ... E 4
32060 Live Oak⊙, 6,830 ... D 1
32337 Lloyd, 225 ... C 1
32662 Lochloosa, 175 ... E 2
33548 Longboat Key, 2,850 ... D 4
33001 Long Key, 150 ... F 7
32750 Longwood, 3,203 ... E 3
33857 Lorida, 950 ... E 4
33858 Loughman, 950 ... E 3
32663 Lowell, 350 ... D 2
33470 Loxahatchee, 950 ... F 5
33549 Lutz, 950 ... D 3
32444 Lynn Haven, 4,044 ... C 6
32063 Macclenny⊙, 2,733 ... D 1
33738 Madeira Beach, 4,158 ... B 3
32340 Madison⊙, 3,737 ... C 1
32751 Maitland, 7,157 ... E 3
32950 Malabar, 634 ... F 3
32445 Malone, 667 ... A 1
33550 Mango, 950 ... D 3
33050 Marathon, 4,397 ... E 7
33937 Marco, 900 ... E 6
33063 Margate, 8,867 ... F 5
32446 Marianna⊙, 6,741 ... A 1
† 32084 Marineland, 13 ... E 2
32569 Mary Esther, 3,192 ... B 6
33512 Masaryktown, 389 ... D 3
32753 Mascotte, 966 ... E 3
32066 Mayo⊙, 793 ... C 1
32568 McDavid, 500 ... B 5
32664 McIntosh, 287 ... D 2
† 33101 Medley, 351 ... B 4
32901 Melbourne, 40,236 ... F 3
32951 Melbourne Beach, 2,262 ... F 3
32666 Melrose, 950 ... D 2
† 33301 Melrose Park, 6,111 ... B 4
† 33561 Memphis, 3,207 ... D 4
32952 Merritt Island, 29,233 ... F 3
32410 Mexico Beach, 588 ... D 6
* 33101 Miami⊙, 334,859 ... B 5
Miami, ‡1,267,792 ... B 5
33139 Miami Beach, 87,072 ... C 5
† 33101 Miami Lakes, 3,500 ... B 4
33153 Miami Shores, 9,425 ... B 4
33166 Miami Springs, 13,279 ... B 5
32667 Micanopy, 759 ... D 2
† 32960 Micco, 400 ... F 4
32309 Miccosukee, 275 ... B 1
32068 Middleburg, 950 ... E 1
32343 Midway, 900 ... B 1
32537 Milligan, 950 ... C 6
32570 Milton⊙, 5,360 ... B 6
32754 Mims, 8,309 ... F 3
32755 Minneola, 878 ... E 3
33023 Miramar, 23,973 ... B 4
32577 Molino, 850 ... B 6
† 32696 Montbrook, 250 ... D 2
32344 Monticello⊙, 2,473 ... C 1
32756 Montverde, 308 ... E 3
33471 Moore Haven⊙, 974 ... E 5
32434 Mossy Head, 160 ... C 6
32757 Mount Dora, 4,543 ... E 3
32352 Mount Pleasant, 150 ... B 1
33860 Mulberry, 2,701 ... E 4
33551 Myakka City, 672 ... D 4
32506 Myrtle Grove, 16,186 ... B 6
33940 Naples⊙, 12,042 ... E 5
† 33940 Naples Park, 1,522 ... E 5
33030 Naranja, 2,900 ... F 6
32233 Neptune Beach, 2,868 ... E 1
32669 Newberry, 1,247 ... D 2
33552 New Port Richey, 6,098 ... D 3
32069 New Smyrna Beach, 10,580 ... F 2
32578 Niceville, 4,024 ... C 6
33863 Nichols, 300 ... E 4
33864 Nocatee, 950 ... E 4
33555 Nokomis-Laurel, 3,238 ... D 4
32452 Noma, 234 ... C 5
33141 North Bay Village, 4,831 ... B 4
33903 North Fort Myers, 8,798 ... E 5
33161 North Miami, 34,767 ... B 4
33161 North Miami Beach, 30,723 ... C 4
† 33940 North Naples, 3,201 ... E 5
33403 North Palm Beach, 9,035 ... F 5
33595 North Port Charlotte, 2,244 ... D 4
† 33708 North Redington Beach, 768 ... B 3
† 33054 Norwood, 14,973 ... B 4
32759 Oak Hill, 747 ... F 3
32760 Oakland, 672 ... E 3
33307 Oakland Park, 16,261 ... B 3
32071 O'Brien, 200 ... D 1
32670 Ocala⊙, 22,583 ... D 2
† 33457 Ocean Breeze, 714 ... F 4
33444 Ocean Ridge, 1,074 ... F 5
33943 Ochopee, 200 ... E 6
32761 Ocoee, 3,937 ... E 3
33556 Odessa, 500 ... D 3
33163 Ojus, 12,000 ... B 4
32762 Okahumpka, 470 ... D 3
33472 Okeechobee⊙, 3,715 ... F 4
32679 Oklawaha, 700 ... E 2
33557 Oldsmar, 1,538 ... B 2
32680 Old Town, 500 ... C 2
32072 Olustee, 400 ... D 1
33865 Ona, 236 ... E 4
33558 Oneco, 3,246 ... D 4
33054 Opa-locka, 11,902 ... B 4
32763 Orange City, 1,777 ... E 3
32681 Orange Lake, 900 ... D 2
32073 Orange Park, 7,619 ... E 1
32682 Orange Springs, 500 ... E 2
* 32801 Orlando⊙, 99,006 ... E 3
Orlando, ‡428,003 ... E 3
32074 Ormond Beach, 14,063 ... E 2
33559 Osprey, 1,115 ... D 4
32764 Osteen, 875 ... E 3
32683 Otter Creek, 400 ... D 2
32765 Oviedo, 1,870 ... E 3
32684 Oxford, 490 ... D 3
33560 Ozona, 900 ... B 3
32570 Pace, 1,776 ... B 6
33476 Pahokee, 5,663 ... F 5
32077 Palatka⊙, 9,310 ... E 2
32901 Palm Bay, 6,927 ... F 3
33480 Palm Beach, 9,086 ... G 4
† 33404 Palm Beach Shores, 1,214 ... G 5
33490 Palm City, 900 ... F 4
33561 Palmetto, 7,422 ... D 4
33563 Palm Harbor, 1,763 ... D 3
33619 Palm River-Clair Mel, 8,536 ... C 3
32935 Palm Shores, 202 ... F 3
33460 Palm Springs, 4,340 ... F 5
32346 Panacea, 950 ... B 1
32401 Panama City⊙, 32,096 ... C 6
32401 Parker, 4,212 ... C 6
33564 Parrish, 950 ... D 4
32538 Paxton, 243 ... C 5
† 33023 Pembroke Park, 2,949 ... B 4
33023 Pembroke Pines, 15,520 ... B 4
32079 Penney Farms, 561 ... E 2
* 32501 Pensacola⊙, 59,507 ... B 6
Pensacola, ‡243,075 ... B 6
33157 Perrine, 10,257 ... F 6
32347 Perry⊙, 7,701 ... C 1
33867 Pierce, 500 ... E 4
32080 Pierson, 654 ... E 2
33565 Pinellas Park, 22,287 ... B 3
32350 Pinetta, 300 ... C 1
† 33042 Pirates Cove, 150 ... E 7
33946 Placida, 250 ... D 5
33314 Plantation, 23,523 ... B 4
33566 Plant City, 15,451 ... D 3
32768 Plymouth, 950 ... E 3
33868 Polk City, 151 ... E 3
32081 Pomona Park, 578 ... E 2
* 33060 Pompano Beach, 37,724 ... F 5
32455 Ponce de Leon, 288 ... C 6
† 32019 Ponce Inlet, 328 ... F 2
32082 Ponte Vedra Beach, 2,100 ... E 1
33950 Port Charlotte, 10,769 ... D 5
† 32439 Portland, 228 ... C 6
† 33438 Port Mayaca, 400 ... F 5
32019 Port Orange, 3,781 ... F 2
33568 Port Richey, 1,259 ... D 3
32456 Port Saint Joe, 4,401 ... D 6
33450 Port Saint Lucie, 330 ... F 4
33492 Port Salerno, 1,161 ... F 4
33171 Princeton, 1,900 ... F 6
† 33619 Progress, 1,328 ... C 3
† 32061 Providence, 150 ... D 2
33950 Punta Gorda⊙, 3,879 ... E 5
32351 Quincy⊙, 8,334 ... B 1
32083 Raiford, 500 ... D 1
† 32696 Raleigh, 275 ... D 2
32455 Redbay, 500 ... C 6
32686 Reddick, 305 ... D 2
33708 Redington Beach, 1,583 ... B 3
† 33708 Redington Shores, 1,733 ... B 3
† 33599 Richland, 928 ... D 3
† 33158 Richmond Heights, 6,663 ... F 6
33569 Riverview, 2,225 ... D 4
33404 Riviera Beach, 21,401 ... G 5
32955 Rockledge, 10,523 ... F 3
32957 Roseland, 550 ... F 4
32447 Round Lake, 275 ... D 6
33570 Ruskin, 2,414 ... C 3
33572 Safety Harbor, 3,103 ... B 2
32084 Saint Augustine⊙, 12,352 ... E 2
32084 Saint Augustine Beach, 632 ... E 2
33573 Saint Catherine, 350 ... D 3
32769 Saint Cloud, 5,041 ... E 3
33956 Saint James City, 500 ... D 5
33574 Saint Leo, 1,145 ... D 3
† 33450 Saint Lucie, 428 ... F 4
32355 Saint Marks, 366 ... B 1
* 33701 Saint Petersburg, 216,232 ... B 3
33736 Saint Petersburg Beach, 8,024 ... B 3
32356 Salem, 150 ... C 2
33505 Samoset, 4,070 ... D 4
† 32069 Samsula, 270 ... E 2
33576 San Antonio, 473 ... D 3
32087 Sanderson, 150 ... D 1
32771 Sanford⊙, 17,393 ... E 3
33957 Sanibel, 750 ... D 5
32088 San Mateo, 975 ... E 2
† 32670 Santos, 150 ... D 2
* 33577 Sarasota⊙, 40,237 ... D 4
32935 Satellite Beach, 6,558 ... F 3
32089 Satsuma, 610 ... E 2
32775 Scottsmoor, 850 ... F 3
† 33301 Sea Ranch Lakes, 660 ... C 3
32958 Sebastian, 825 ... F 4
33870 Sebring⊙, 7,223 ... E 4
33584 Seffner, 2,000 ... D 4
33540 Seminole, 2,410 ... B 3
32090 Seville, 500 ... E 2
† 33457 Sewalls Point, 298 ... F 4
32579 Shalimar, 578 ... C 6
† 32628 Shamrock, 200 ... C 2
32959 Sharpes, 427 ... F 3
32688 Silver Springs, 500 ... D 2
32460 Sneads, 1,550 ... B 1
32358 Sopchoppy, 460 ... B 1
32776 Sorrento, 500 ... E 3
33493 South Bay, 2,958 ... F 5
32021 South Daytona, 4,979 ... F 2
† 36441 South Flomaton, 329 ... B 5
33143 South Miami, 19,571 ... B 5
33707 South Pasadena, 2,063 ... B 3
† 32401 Southport, 1,560 ... C 6
32690 Sparr, 450 ... D 2
32401 Springfield, 5,949 ... D 6
32091 Starke⊙, 4,848 ... D 2
32359 Steinhatchee, 800 ... C 2
33494 Stuart⊙, 4,820 ... F 4
32335 Sumatra, 150 ... B 1
32691 Summerfield, 450 ... D 2
33042 Summerland Key, 350 ... E 7
33586 Sun City, 2,143 ... D 4
† 33450 Sunland Gardens, 1,900 ... F 4
33160 Sunny Isles, 950 ... C 4
† 33577 Sunnyland, 4,900 ... D 4
32461 Sunnyside, 370 ... C 6
33313 Sunrise Golf Village, 7,403 ... B 4
33154 Surfside, 3,614 ... B 4
32692 Suwannee, 203 ... C 2
† 33144 Sweetwater, 3,307 ... B 5
† 33601 Sweetwater Creek, 19,453 ... B 2
† 32043 Switzerland, 500 ... E 1
32809 Taft, 1,183 ... E 3
* 32301 Tallahassee (cap.)⊙, 71,897 ... B 1
Tallahassee, ‡103,047 ... B 1
† 33301 Tamarac, 5,078 ... B 3
* 33601 Tampa⊙, 277,767 ... C 2
Tampa-Saint Petersburg, ‡1,012,594 ... C 2
33589 Tarpon Springs, 7,118 ... D 3
32778 Tavares⊙, 3,261 ... E 3
33070 Tavernier, 900 ... F 6
32360 Telogia, 300 ... B 1
33617 Temple Terrace, 7,347 ... C 2
33458 Tequesta, 2,642 ... F 5
33591 Terra Ceia, 450 ... D 4
33592 Thonotosassa, 900 ... D 3
33905 Tice, 7,254 ... E 5
32780 Titusville⊙, 30,515 ... F 3
33740 Treasure Island, 6,120 ... B 3
32693 Trenton⊙, 1,074 ... D 2
33593 Trilby, 930 ... D 3
32784 Umatilla, 1,600 ... E 3
32580 Valparaiso, 6,504 ... C 6
33595 Venice, 6,648 ... D 4
33960 Venus, 300 ... E 4
32462 Vernon, 691 ... C 6
32960 Vero Beach⊙, 11,908 ... F 4
† 32548 Villa Tasso, 200 ... C 6
† 33166 Virginia Gardens, 2,524 ... B 5
32970 Wabasso, 950 ... F 4
32361 Wacissa, 275 ... B 1
† 32327 Wakulla, 225 ... B 1
32694 Waldo, 800 ... D 2
32568 Walnut Hill, 500 ... B 6
32507 Warrington, 15,848 ... B 6
† 32055 Watertown, 3,624 ... D 1
33873 Wauchula⊙, 3,007 ... E 4
32463 Wausau, 288 ... D 6
33877 Waverly, 1,172 ... E 4
33597 Webster, 739 ... D 3
32695 Weirsdale, 995 ... D 3
32093 Welaka, 496 ... E 2
32094 Wellborn, 600 ... D 1
32401 Westbay, 350 ... C 6
† 32901 West Melbourne, 3,050 ... F 3
† 33101 West Miami, 5,494 ... B 5
* 33401 West Palm Beach⊙, 57,375 ... F 5
West Palm Beach, ‡348,753 ... F 5
32401 West Panama City Beach, 1,052 ... C 6
32505 West Pensacola, 20,924 ... B 6
32464 Westville, 475 ... C 6
† 33101 Westwood Lakes, 12,811 ... B 5
32465 Wewahitchka⊙, 1,733 ... D 6
† 32465 White City, 600 ... F 4
32096 White Springs, 767 ... D 1
32785 Wildwood, 2,082 ... D 3
32696 Williston, 1,939 ... D 2
33305 Wilton Manors, 10,948 ... B 3
33598 Wimauma, 650 ... D 4
32786 Windermere, 894 ... E 3
32971 Winter Beach, 350 ... F 4
32787 Winter Garden, 5,153 ... E 3
33880 Winter Haven, 16,136 ... E 3
32789 Winter Park, 21,895 ... E 3
32362 Woodville, 900 ... B 1
32697 Worthington Springs, 214 ... D 2
32797 Yalaha, 675 ... E 3
32698 Yankeetown, 490 ... D 2
32466 Youngstown, 400 ... D 6
32097 Yulee, 950 ... E 1
32798 Zellwood, 550 ... E 3
33599 Zephyrhills, 3,369 ... D 3
33890 Zolfo Springs, 1,117 ... E 4

⊙ County seat.
‡ Population of metropolitan area.
† Zip of nearest p.o.
* Multiple zips

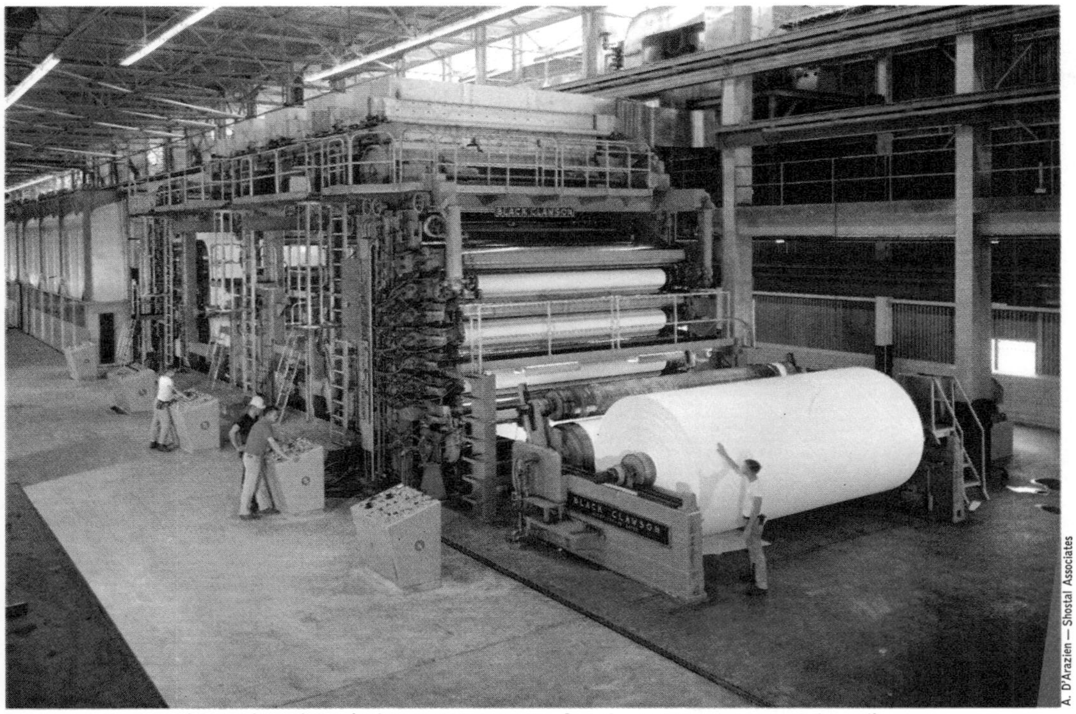

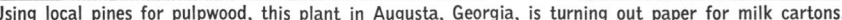

A. D'Arazien — Shostal Associates

Using local pines for pulpwood, this plant in Augusta, Georgia, is turning out paper for milk cartons.

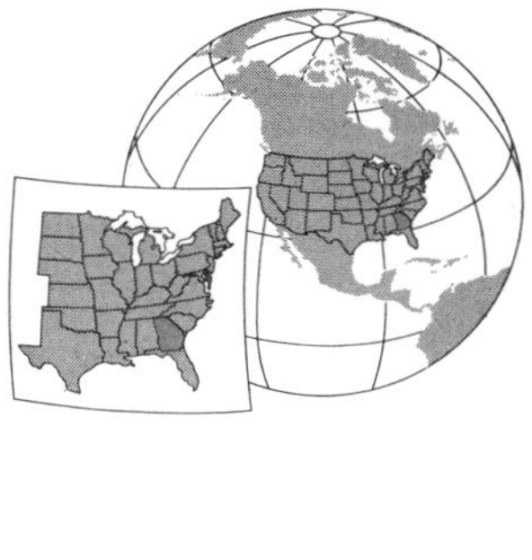

AREA 58,876 sq. mi.
POPULATION 4,589,575 ('70); 5,464,265 ('80)
CAPITAL Atlanta
LARGEST CITY Atlanta
HIGHEST POINT Brasstown Bald 4,784 ft.
SETTLED IN 1733
ADMITTED TO UNION January 2, 1788
POPULAR NAME Empire State of the South; Peach State
STATE FLOWER Cherokee Rose
STATE BIRD Brown Thrasher

COUNTIES

Name/Pop.	Key
Appling, 12,726	H 7
Atkinson, 5,879	G 8
Bacon, 8,233	G 7
Baker, 3,875	D 8
Baldwin, 34,240	F 4
Banks, 6,833	E 2
Barrow, 16,859	E 2
Bartow, 32,663	C 2
Ben Hill, 13,171	F 7
Berrien, 11,556	F 8
Bibb, 143,418	E 5
Bleckley, 10,291	F 6
Brantley, 5,940	J 8
Brooks, 13,739	E 9
Bryan, 6,539	K 6
Bulloch, 31,585	J 6
Burke, 18,255	J 4
Butts, 10,560	E 4
Calhoun, 6,606	C 7
Camden, 11,334	J 9
Candler, 6,412	H 6
Carroll, 45,404	B 3
Catoosa, 28,271	B 1
Charlton, 5,680	H 9
Chatham, 187,767	K 6
Chattahoochee, 25,813	C 6
Chattooga, 20,541	B 1
Cherokee, 31,059	D 2
Clarke, 65,177	F 3
Clay, 3,636	B 7
Clayton, 98,043	D 3
Clinch, 6,405	G 9
Cobb, 196,793	C 3
Coffee, 22,828	G 8
Colquitt, 32,200	E 8
Columbia, 22,327	H 3
Cook, 12,129	F 8
Coweta, 32,310	C 4
Crawford, 5,748	E 5
Crisp, 18,087	E 7
Dade, 9,910	A 1
Dawson, 3,639	D 2
Decatur, 22,310	C 9
De Kalb, 415,387	D 3
Dodge, 15,658	F 6
Dooly, 10,404	E 6
Dougherty, 89,639	D 7
Douglas, 28,659	C 3
Early, 12,682	C 8
Echols, 1,924	G 9
Effingham, 13,632	K 6
Elbert, 17,262	G 2
Emanuel, 18,189	H 5
Evans, 7,290	J 6
Fannin, 13,357	D 1
Fayette, 11,364	C 4
Floyd, 73,742	B 2
Forsyth, 16,928	D 2
Franklin, 12,784	F 2
Fulton, 607,592	D 3
Gilmer, 8,956	D 1
Glascock, 2,280	G 4
Glynn, 50,528	J 8
Gordon, 23,570	C 2
Grady, 17,826	D 9
Greene, 10,212	F 3
Gwinnett, 72,349	D 2
Habersham, 20,691	E 1
Hall, 59,405	E 2
Hancock, 9,019	G 4
Haralson, 15,927	B 3
Harris, 11,520	C 5
Hart, 15,814	G 2
Heard, 5,354	B 4
Henry, 23,724	D 4
Houston, 62,924	E 6
Irwin, 8,036	F 7
Jackson, 21,093	E 2
Jasper, 5,760	E 4
Jeff Davis, 9,425	G 7
Jefferson, 17,174	H 4
Jenkins, 8,332	J 5
Johnson, 7,727	G 5
Jones, 12,218	E 5
Lamar, 10,688	D 4
Lanier, 5,031	F 8
Laurens, 32,738	G 6
Lee, 7,044	D 7
Liberty, 17,569	J 7
Lincoln, 5,895	H 3
Long, 3,746	J 7
Lowndes, 55,112	F 9
Lumpkin, 8,728	D 1
Macon, 12,933	D 6
Madison, 13,517	F 2
Marion, 5,099	C 6
McDuffie, 15,276	H 4
McIntosh, 7,371	K 7
Meriwether, 19,461	C 4
Miller, 6,397	C 8
Mitchell, 18,956	D 8
Monroe, 10,991	E 4
Montgomery, 6,099	G 6
Morgan, 9,904	F 3
Murray, 12,986	C 1
Muscogee, 167,377	C 6
Newton, 26,282	E 3
Oconee, 7,915	F 3
Oglethorpe, 7,598	F 3
Paulding, 17,520	C 3
Peach, 15,990	E 5
Pickens, 9,620	D 2
Pierce, 9,281	H 8
Pike, 7,316	D 4
Polk, 29,656	B 3
Pulaski, 8,066	E 6
Putnam, 8,394	F 4
Quitman, 2,180	B 7
Rabun, 8,327	F 1
Randolph, 8,734	C 7
Richmond, 162,347	H 4
Rockdale, 18,152	D 3
Schley, 3,097	D 6
Screven, 12,591	J 5
Seminole, 7,059	C 9
Spalding, 39,514	D 4
Stephens, 20,331	F 1
Stewart, 6,511	C 6
Sumter, 26,931	D 6
Talbot, 6,625	C 5
Taliaferro, 2,423	G 3
Tattnall, 16,557	J 6
Taylor, 7,865	D 5
Telfair, 11,381	G 7
Terrell, 11,416	D 7
Thomas, 34,515	E 9
Tift, 27,288	E 7
Toombs, 19,151	H 6
Towns, 4,565	E 1
Treutlen, 5,647	G 6
Troup, 44,466	B 4
Turner, 8,790	E 7
Twiggs, 8,222	F 5
Union, 6,811	E 1
Upson, 23,505	D 5
Walker, 50,691	B 1
Walton, 23,404	E 3
Ware, 33,525	H 8
Warren, 6,669	G 4
Washington, 17,480	G 4
Wayne, 17,858	J 7
Webster, 2,362	C 6
Wheeler, 4,596	G 6
White, 7,742	E 1
Whitfield, 55,108	B 1
Wilcox, 6,998	F 7
Wilkes, 10,184	G 3
Wilkinson, 9,393	F 5
Worth, 14,770	E 8

CITIES and TOWNS

Zip	Name/Pop.	Key
31001	Abbeville⊙, 781	F 7
30101	Acworth, 3,929	C 2
30103	Adairsville, 1,676	C 2
31620	Adel⊙, 4,972	F 8
31002	Adrian, 705	G 5
30410	Ailey, 487	G 6
30411	Alamo⊙, 833	G 6
31622	Alapaha, 633	F 8
* 31701	Albany⊙, 72,623	D 7
	Albany, ‡89,639	D 7
† 30204	Aldora, 322	D 4
30801	Alexander, 200	J 4
31301	Allenhurst, 230	J 7
31003	Allentown, 295	F 5
31510	Alma⊙, 3,756	G 7
† 30209	Almon, 400	E 3
30201	Alpharetta, 2,455	D 2
30510	Alto, 372	E 2
† 30161	Alto Park, 2,963	B 2
31512	Ambrose, 253	G 7
31709	Americus⊙, 16,091	D 6
31711	Andersonville, 274	D 6
30802	Appling⊙, 212	H 3
31712	Arabi, 305	E 7
30104	Aragon, 850	B 2
† 30549	Arcade, 229	E 2
31520	Arco, 6,009	J 8
31623	Argyle, 206	G 8
31713	Arlington, 1,698	C 8
30105	Armuchee, 600	B 2
31714	Ashburn⊙, 4,209	E 7
† 30521	Ashland, 350	F 2
30601	Athens⊙, 44,342	F 3
* 30301	Atlanta (cap.)⊙, 496,973	D 3
	Atlanta, ‡1,390,164	D 3
31715	Attapulgus, 513	D 9
30203	Auburn, 361	E 2
* 30901	Augusta⊙, 59,864	J 4
	Augusta, ‡253,460	J 4
30001	Austell, 2,632	C 3
† 30557	Avalon, 204	F 1
30803	Avera, 217	G 4
30002	Avondale Estates, 1,735	D 3
31624	Axson, 250	G 8
31716	Baconton, 710	D 8
31717	Bainbridge⊙, 10,887	C 9
30511	Baldwin, 772	E 2
30107	Ball Ground, 617	D 2
30204	Barnesville⊙, 4,935	D 4
† 31601	Barretts, 275	F 8
30413	Bartow, 333	G 5
31720	Barwick, 381	E 9
31513	Baxley⊙, 3,503	H 7
† 31792	Beachton, 200	D 9
30414	Bellville, 234	H 6
† 31601	Bemiss, 325	F 9
31722	Berlin, 422	E 8
30748	Berryton, 200	B 2
30620	Bethlehem, 304	E 3
31904	Bibb City, 812	B 5
30621	Bishop, 235	F 3
31516	Blackshear⊙, 2,624	H 8
30512	Blairsville⊙, 491	E 1
31723	Blakely⊙, 5,267	C 8
† 31308	Blitchton, 256	J 6
31302	Bloomingdale, 1,588	K 6
30513	Blue Ridge⊙, 1,602	D 1
30805	Blythe, 333	H 4
30622	Bogart, 667	E 3
31626	Boston, 1,443	E 9
30623	Bostwick, 289	E 3
30108	Bowdon, 1,753	B 3
30109	Bowdon Junction, 200	B 3
30516	Bowersville, 301	G 2
30624	Bowman, 724	G 2
31801	Box Springs, 600	C 5
30517	Braselton, 386	E 2
30110	Bremen, 3,484	B 3
31701	Bridgeboro, 250	E 8
31725	Brinson, 231	C 9
31726	Bronwood, 500	D 7
31727	Brookfield, 860	F 8
30415	Brooklet, 683	J 6
31519	Broxton, 957	G 7
31520	Brunswick⊙, 19,585	K 8
30113	Buchanan⊙, 800	B 3
31803	Buena Vista⊙, 1,486	C 6
30518	Buford, 4,640	D 2
† 31020	Bullard, 230	F 5
31006	Butler⊙, 1,589	D 5
31007	Byromville, 419	E 6
31008	Byron, 1,368	E 5
31009	Cadwell, 354	G 6
31728	Cairo⊙, 8,061	D 9
30701	Calhoun⊙, 4,748	C 1
31729	Calvary, 500	D 9
30807	Camak, 224	G 4
31730	Camilla⊙, 4,987	D 8
30520	Canon, 709	F 2
30114	Canton⊙, 3,654	C 2
† 30720	Carbondale, 300	B 1
30203	Carl, 234	E 3
30627	Carlton, 294	F 2
30521	Carnesville⊙, 510	F 2
30117	Carrollton⊙, 13,520	C 3
† 30540	Cartecay, 250	D 1
30120	Cartersville⊙, 9,929	C 2
30123	Cassville, 350	C 2
31804	Cataula, 500	C 5
30124	Cave Spring, 1,305	B 2
31627	Cecil, 265	F 8
30125	Cedartown⊙, 9,253	B 2
† 30601	Center, 213	F 2
31093	Centerville, 1,725	E 5
† 31816	Chalybeate Springs, 266	C 5
30341	Chamblee, 9,127	D 3
30705	Chatsworth⊙, 2,706	C 1
31011	Chauncey, 308	F 6
31012	Chester, 409	F 6
30707	Chickamauga, 1,842	B 1
† 30512	Choestoe, 215	E 1
31733	Chula, 300	E 7
30523	Clarkesville⊙, 1,294	F 1
30021	Clarkston, 3,127	D 3
30417	Claxton⊙, 2,669	J 6
30525	Clayton⊙, 1,569	F 1
30128	Clem, 350	B 3
30527	Clermont, 290	E 2
30528	Cleveland⊙, 1,353	E 1
31734	Climax, 275	D 9
31604	Clyattville, 500	F 9
31303	Clyo, 300	K 6
30420	Cobbtown, 321	H 6
31014	Cochran⊙, 5,161	F 6
30710	Cohutta, 300	C 1
30628	Colbert, 532	F 2
30337	College Park, 18,203	C 3
30421	Collins, 574	H 6
31737	Colquitt⊙, 2,026	C 8
* 31901	Columbus⊙, 154,168	C 6
	Columbus, ‡238,584	C 6
30629	Comer, 828	F 2
30529	Commerce, 3,702	E 2
30206	Concord, 312	D 4
30207	Conyers⊙, 4,890	D 3
31738	Coolidge, 717	E 8
30129	Coosa, 600	B 2
31015	Cordele⊙, 10,733	E 7
30531	Cornelia, 3,014	E 1
30209	Covington⊙, 10,267	E 3
30630	Crawford, 624	F 3
30631	Crawfordville⊙, 735	G 3
† 30105	Crystal Springs, 500	B 2
31016	Culloden, 272	D 5
30130	Cumming⊙, 2,031	D 2
31805	Cusseta⊙, 1,251	C 6
31740	Cuthbert⊙, 3,972	C 7
30211	Dacula, 782	E 3
30533	Dahlonega⊙, 2,658	D 1
30132	Dallas⊙, 2,133	C 3
30720	Dalton⊙, 18,872	C 1
31741	Damascus, 272	C 8
30633	Danielsville⊙, 378	F 2
31017	Danville, 515	F 5
31305	Darien⊙, 1,826	K 8
31601	Dasher, 452	F 9
31018	Davisboro, 476	G 5
31742	Dawson⊙, 5,383	D 7
30534	Dawsonville⊙, 288	D 2
30808	Dearing, 555	H 4
* 30030	Decatur⊙, 21,943	D 3
† 31501	Deenwood, 3,015	H 8
30535	Demorest, 1,070	F 1
31532	Denton, 244	G 7
31743	De Soto, 321	D 7
31019	Dexter, 438	G 6
† 31520	Dock Junction (Arco), 6,009	J 8
31744	Doerun, 1,157	E 8
31745	Donalsonville⊙, 2,907	C 8
30340	Doraville, 9,039	D 3
31533	Douglas⊙, 10,195	G 7
30134	Douglasville⊙, 5,472	C 3
31020	Dry Branch, 700	F 5
31021	Dublin⊙, 15,143	G 5
31022	Dudley, 423	F 5
30136	Duluth, 1,810	D 2
31630	Du Pont, 252	G 9
30538	Eastanollee, 365	F 1
31021	East Dublin, 1,986	G 5
30539	East Ellijay, 488	C 1
31023	Eastman⊙, 5,416	F 6
† 30263	East Newnan, 1,634	C 4
30344	East Point, 39,315	C 3
31024	Eatonton⊙, 4,125	F 4
31307	Eden, 300	K 6
31746	Edison, 1,210	C 7
† 31093	Elberta, 500	E 5
30635	Elberton⊙, 6,438	G 2
30060	Elizabeth, 950	C 2
31025	Elko, 450	E 6
31308	Ellabell, 400	K 6
31806	Ellaville⊙, 1,391	D 6
31747	Ellenton, 337	E 8
31807	Ellerslie, 615	C 5
30540	Ellijay⊙, 1,326	C 1
30137	Emerson, 813	C 2
31026	Empire, 325	F 6
31749	Enigma, 505	F 8
† 30217	Ephesus, 212	B 4
30541	Epworth, 300	D 1
30724	Eton, 286	C 1
† 31331	Eulonia, 500	K 7
30809	Evans, 1,500	H 3
31536	Everett, 300	J 8
30212	Experiment, 2,256	D 4
30213	Fairburn, 3,143	C 3
30139	Fairmount, 623	C 2
31631	Fargo, 800	G 9
30214	Fayetteville⊙, 2,160	C 4
30140	Felton, 300	B 3
31750	Fitzgerald⊙, 8,015	F 7
† 31313	Flemington, 265	K 7
30215	Flippen, 600	D 3
30216	Flovilla, 289	E 4
30542	Flowery Branch, 779	E 2
31537	Folkston⊙, 2,112	H 9
30050	Forest Park, 19,994	D 3
31029	Forsyth⊙, 3,736	E 4
31751	Fort Gaines⊙, 1,255	C 7
30741	Fort Oglethorpe, 3,869	B 1
31030	Fort Valley⊙, 9,251	E 5
31752	Fowlstown, 400	D 9
30217	Franklin⊙, 749	B 4
30639	Franklin Springs, 501	F 2
37317	Fry, 300	D 1
31753	Funston, 293	E 8
30501	Gainesville⊙, 15,459	E 2
31408	Garden City, 5,741	K 6
30425	Garfield, 214	H 5
31810	Geneva, 250	C 5
31754	Georgetown⊙, 578	B 7
30810	Gibson⊙, 701	G 4
30426	Girard, 241	J 4
30427	Glennville, 2,965	J 7
30428	Glenwood, 670	G 6
30641	Good Hope, 202	E 3
31031	Gordon, 2,553	F 5
30811	Gough, 300	H 4
30812	Gracewood, 1,200	H 4
30220	Grantville, 1,128	C 4
31032	Gray⊙, 2,014	F 4
30221	Grayson, 366	E 3
30642	Greensboro⊙, 2,583	F 3
30222	Greenville⊙, 1,085	C 4
† 31620	Greggs, 250	F 8
30223	Griffin⊙, 22,734	D 4
† 31036	Grovania, 300	E 6
30813	Grovetown, 3,169	H 4
31312	Guyton, 742	K 6
30544	Habersham, 225	F 1
31033	Haddock, 600	F 4
30429	Hagan, 572	J 6
31632	Hahira, 1,326	F 9
31811	Hamilton⊙, 357	C 5
30228	Hampton, 1,551	D 4
30354	Hapeville, 9,567	D 3
31034	Hardwick, 14,047	F 4
30814	Harlem, 1,540	H 4
31035	Harrison, 329	G 5
30643	Hartwell⊙, 4,865	G 2
31036	Hawkinsville⊙, 4,077	E 6
31539	Hazlehurst⊙, 4,065	G 7
30545	Helen, 252	E 1
31037	Helena, 1,230	G 6
30815	Hephzibah, 987	H 4
30546	Hiawassee⊙, 415	E 1
31038	Hillsboro, 250	E 4
30467	Hilltonia, 294	J 5
31313	Hinesville⊙, 4,115	J 7
30141	Hiram, 441	C 3
31542	Hoboken, 424	H 8
30230	Hogansville, 3,075	C 4
30142	Holly Springs, 575	D 2
30523	Hollywood, 300	E 1
† 31537	Homeland, 595	H 9
30547	Homer⊙, 365	F 2
31634	Homerville⊙, 3,025	G 8
31543	Hortense, 400	J 8
30548	Hoschton, 509	E 2
30646	Hull, 222	F 2
30561	Hurst, 216	D 1
31041	Ideal, 543	D 6
30647	Ila, 202	F 2
30231	Indian Springs, 300	E 4
30232	Inman, 475	D 4
31759	Iron City, 351	C 8
31042	Irwinton⊙, 757	F 5
31760	Irwinville, 550	F 7
31406	Isle of Hope, 975	K 7
† 31031	Ivey, 245	F 5
30233	Jackson⊙, 3,778	E 4
31544	Jacksonville, 214	G 7
30143	Jasper⊙, 1,202	D 2

(continued on following page)

GEORGIA

SCALE

0 5 10 20 30 40 MI.

0 5 10 20 30 40 KM.

State Capitals.....................⊛

County Seats.....................◉

© C.S. Hammond & Co., N.Y.

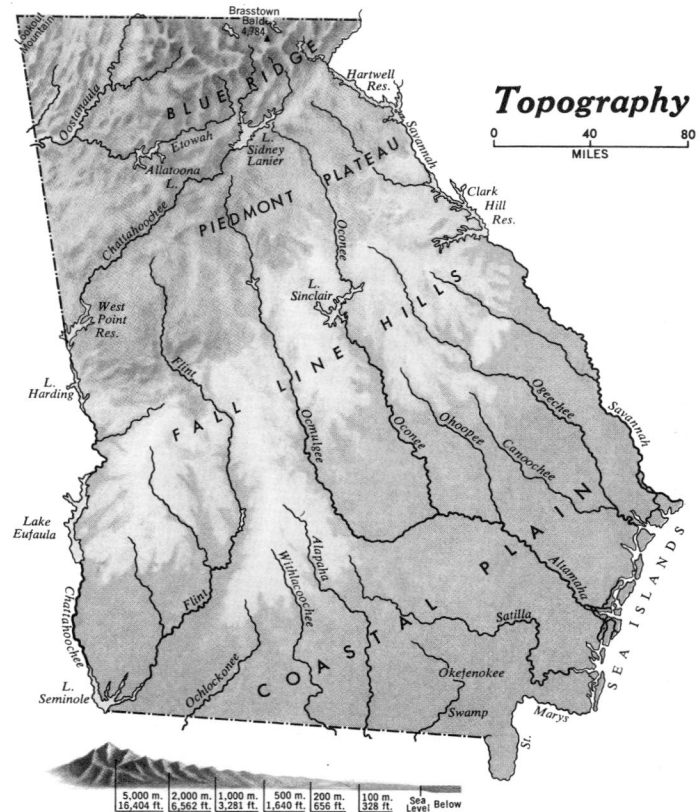

Topography

0 — 40 — 80
MILES

5,000 m. / 16,404 ft. — 2,000 m. / 6,562 ft. — 1,000 m. / 3,281 ft. — 500 m. / 1,640 ft. — 200 m. / 656 ft. — 100 m. / 328 ft. — Sea Level — Below

30549 Jefferson⊙, 1,647....F 2
31044 Jeffersonville⊙, 1,302....F 5
30234 Jenkinsburg, 382....E 4
31545 Jesup⊙, 9,091....J 7
30236 Jonesboro⊙, 4,105....D 4
31046 Juliette, 600....E 4
31812 Junction City, 269....C 5
31813 Juniper, 525....C 5
30551 Juno, 522....D 2
30144 Kennesaw, 3,548....C 2
† 30214 Kenwood, 500....D 3
30816 Keysville, 300....H 4
31548 Kingsland, 1,831....J 9
30145 Kingston, 714....C 2
31049 Kite, 336....G 5
31050 Knoxville⊙, 25....E 5
30728 La Fayette⊙, 6,044....B 1
30240 La Grange⊙, 23,301....B 4
† 30260 Lake, 2,306....D 3
31635 Lakeland⊙, 2,569....F 8
30552 Lakemont, 295....F 1
31636 Lake Park, 361....F 9
30553 Lavonia, 2,044....F 2
30245 Lawrenceville⊙, 5,115....D 3
† 31650 Lax, 350....F 8
† 30528 Leaf, 250....E 1
† 30802 Leah, 210....H 3
31762 Leary, 907....C 8
30146 Lebanon, 500....D 2
31763 Leesburg⊙, 996....D 7
31637 Lenox, 860....F 8
31764 Leslie, 562....D 7
30648 Lexington⊙, 322....F 3
30247 Lilburn, 1,668....D 3
† 30286 Lincoln Park, 1,852....D 5
30817 Lincolnton⊙, 1,442....G 3
30147 Lindale, 2,768....B 2
† 30728 Linwood, 588....B 1
30057 Lithia Springs, 950....C 3
30058 Lithonia, 2,270....D 3
31052 Lizella, 975....E 5
30248 Locust Grove, 642....D 4
30249 Loganville, 1,318....D 3
† 30741 Lookout Mountain, 1,538....B 1
30434 Louisville⊙, 2,691....H 4
31814 Louvale, 263....C 6
31316 Ludowici⊙, 1,419....J 7
† 30175 Ludville, 205....C 2
30554 Lula, 736....E 2
31549 Lumber City, 1,377....G 7
31815 Lumpkin⊙, 1,431....C 6
30251 Luthersville, 400....C 4
30730 Lyerly, 426....B 2
30436 Lyons⊙, 3,739....H 6
30059 Mableton, 9,500....C 3
* 31201 Macon⊙, 122,423....E 5
         Macon, ‡206,342....E 5
30650 Madison⊙, 2,890....F 3
31816 Manchester, 4,779....C 5
31550 Manor, 500....G 8
30255 Mansfield, 340....E 4
30148 Marblehill, 300....D 2
30060 Marietta, 27,216....D 3
† 31312 Marlow, 500....K 6
31057 Marshallville, 1,376....D 6

30557 Martin, 201....F 2
30907 Martinez, 950....H 3
30671 Maxeys, 229....F 3
30558 Maysville, 553....E 2
† 30908 McBean, 300....H 4
30555 McCaysville, 1,619....D 1
30253 McDonough⊙, 2,675....D 4
31054 McIntyre, 471....F 5
31055 McRae⊙, 3,151....G 6
30256 Meansville, 313....D 4
31765 Meigs, 1,226....D 8
31318 Meldrim, 500....K 6
30731 Menlo, 593....B 2
30819 Mesena, 400....G 4
† 31792 Metcalf, 213....E 9
30439 Metter⊙, 2,912....H 6
31820 Midland, 250....C 5
30441 Midville, 665....H 5
31060 Milan, 1,084....G 6
31061 Milledgeville⊙, 11,601....F 4
30442 Millen⊙, 3,713....J 5
30257 Milner, 270....D 4
30207 Milstead, 1,157....D 3
30258 Molena, 389....D 4
30655 Monroe⊙, 8,071....D 3
31063 Montezuma, 4,125....E 6
31064 Monticello⊙, 2,132....E 4
30259 Moreland, 363....C 4
31766 Morgan⊙, 280....C 7
30560 Morganton, 205....D 1
31638 Morven, 449....E 9
31768 Moultrie⊙, 14,302....E 8
30562 Mountain City, 594....F 1
† 30075 Mountain Park, 268....D 2
30563 Mount Airy, 463....F 1
30149 Mount Berry, 1,500....B 2
30445 Mount Vernon⊙, 1,579....G 6
30261 Mountville, 218....C 4
30150 Mount Zion, 264....B 3
30564 Murrayville, 550....D 2
31769 Mystic, 250....F 7
31553 Nahunta⊙, 974....H 8
† 31808 Nankipooh, 500....C 5
31639 Nashville⊙, 4,323....F 8
31641 Naylor, 244....F 9
30151 Nelson, 613....D 2
30262 Newborn, 294....E 3
† 30501 New Holland, 950....D 2
30446 Newington, 402....J 5
30263 Newnan⊙, 11,205....C 4
31770 Newton⊙, 624....D 8
31554 Nicholls, 1,150....G 7
30565 Nicholson, 397....F 2
† 30728 Noble, 250....B 1
30071 Norcross, 2,755....D 3
31771 Norman Park, 912....E 8
30114 North Canton, 950....C 2
† 30645 North High Shoals, 165....E 3
30821 Norwood, 272....G 4
31903 Oak Park, 226....H 6
30566 Oakwood, 250....D 2
31773 Ochlocknee, 611....E 9
31774 Ocilla⊙, 3,185....F 7
31067 Oconee, 262....G 5
31555 Odum, 379....H 7

31556 Offerman, 500....H 8
31406 Oglethorpe⊙, 1,286....D 6
30449 Oliver, 217....J 5
31775 Omega, 831....E 8
† 30701 Oostanaula, 300....B 1
30267 Oxford, 1,373....E 3
30268 Palmetto, 2,045....C 3
31777 Parrott, 222....D 7
31557 Patterson, 788....H 8
31778 Pavo, 775....E 9
† 31201 Payne, 225....E 5
30214 Peachtree City, 793....C 4
31642 Pearson⊙, 1,700....G 8
31779 Pelham, 4,539....D 8
31321 Pembroke⊙, 1,361....J 6
30567 Pendergrass, 267....E 2
30822 Perkins, 250....J 5
31069 Perry⊙, 7,771....E 6
† 31794 Phillipsburg, 2,335....E 8
† 31629 Pidcock, 210....E 9
31071 Pinehurst, 405....E 6
30152 Pine Log, 205....C 2
31822 Pine Mountain, 862....C 5
† 31312 Pineora, 266....K 6
31728 Pine Park, 330....D 9
31071 Pineview, 528....F 6
31072 Pitts, 345....E 7
31780 Plains, 683....D 6
31322 Pooler, 1,517....K 6
30450 Portal, 643....J 5
30270 Porterdale, 1,773....E 3
31407 Port Wentworth, 3,905....K 6
31781 Poulan, 766....E 8
30073 Powder Springs, 2,559....C 3
31824 Preston⊙, 226....C 6
30451 Pulaski, 230....J 5
31782 Putney, 750....D 8
31643 Quitman⊙, 4,818....E 9
30568 Rabun Gap, 250....F 1
31645 Ray City, 617....F 8
30660 Rayle, 300....G 3
31783 Rebecca, 266....E 7
30272 Red Oak, 3,500....C 3
30452 Register, 300....J 6
30453 Reidsville⊙, 1,806....H 6
31601 Remerton, 523....F 9
31075 Rentz, 392....G 5
31077 Rhine, 471....F 6
31076 Reynolds, 1,253....D 5
30735 Resaca, 500....C 1
31323 Riceboro, 252....K 7
31825 Richland, 1,823....C 6
31324 Richmond Hill, 826....K 6
31326 Rincon, 1,854....K 6
30736 Ringgold⊙, 1,381....B 1
30738 Rising Fawn, 400....A 1
30274 Riverdale, 2,521....D 3
31204 Riverside, 1,159....E 5
31078 Roberta, 746....D 5
† 30545 Robertstown, 290....E 1
31079 Rochelle, 1,380....F 7
30153 Rockmart, 3,857....B 2
30740 Rocky Face, 500....C 1
30455 Rocky Ford, 252....J 5
30161 Rome⊙, 30,759....B 2

30170 Roopville, 221....B 4
30741 Rossville, 3,869....B 1
30075 Roswell, 5,430....D 2
30662 Royston, 2,428....F 2
† 30680 Russell, 378....E 3
30663 Rutledge, 628....E 3
31646 Saint George, 600....H 9
31558 Saint Marys, 900....J 9
31522 Saint Simons Island, 5,346....K 8
31784 Sale City, 323....D 8
31082 Sandersville⊙, 5,546....G 5
31327 Sapelo Island, 250....K 7
30456 Sardis, 643....J 5
30275 Sargent, 800....C 4
31785 Sasser, 339....D 7
30571 Sautee-Nacoochee, 350....E 1
* 31401 Savannah⊙, 118,349....L 6
         Savannah, ‡187,767....L 6
31328 Savannah Beach, 1,786....L 6
31083 Scotland, 261....G 6
31095 Scott, 215....G 5
31560 Screven, 936....H 7
31561 Sea Island, 600....K 8
30276 Senoia, 910....C 4
30172 Shannon, 1,563....B 2
31786 Shellman, 1,166....C 7
31826 Shiloh, 298....C 5
† 31781 Shingler, 300....E 7
30665 Siloam, 319....F 3
30173 Silver Creek, 450....B 2
31086 Smarr, 350....E 5
31787 Smithville, 713....D 7
30080 Smyrna, 19,157....D 3
30278 Snellville, 1,990....D 3
30279 Social Circle, 1,961....E 3
30457 Soperton⊙, 2,596....G 6
31647 Sparks, 1,337....F 8
31087 Sparta⊙, 2,172....F 4
31329 Springfield⊙, 1,001....K 6
30705 Spring Place, 241....C 1
30823 Stapleton, 390....H 4
31648 Statenville⊙, 700....G 9
30458 Statesboro⊙, 14,616....J 6
30666 Statham, 817....E 3
31088 Stevens Pottery, 350....F 5
30464 Stillmore, 354....H 6
30281 Stockbridge, 1,561....D 3
31649 Stockton, 500....G 9
30083 Stone Mountain, 1,899....D 3
30282 Stonewall, 950....C 3
† 30747 Subligna, 300....B 1
30572 Suches, 400....E 1
30518 Sugar Hill, 1,745....D 2
† 30747 Summerville⊙, 5,043....B 2
31789 Sumner, 207....E 8
30284 Sunny Side, 209....D 4
31563 Surrency, 352....H 7
30174 Suwanee, 615....D 2
30401 Swainsboro⊙, 7,325....H 5
31790 Sycamore, 547....E 7
30467 Sylvania⊙, 3,199....J 5
31791 Sylvester⊙, 4,226....E 7
31827 Talbotton⊙, 1,045....C 5
30176 Tallapoosa, 2,896....B 3
30573 Tallulah Falls, 255....F 1
30177 Tate, 950....D 2
30178 Taylorsville, 253....C 2
30179 Temple, 864....B 3
30751 Tennga, 300....C 1
31089 Tennille, 1,753....G 5
† 30286 Thomaston⊙, 10,024....D 5
31792 Thomasville, 18,155....E 9

30824 Thomson⊙, 6,503....H 4
31404 Thunderbolt, 2,750....K 6
31794 Tifton⊙, 12,179....F 8
30576 Tiger, 312....F 1
30668 Tignall, 756....G 3
30577 Toccoa⊙, 6,971....F 1
31090 Toomsboro, 682....F 5
31331 Townsend, 300....J 7
30752 Trenton⊙, 1,523....A 1
30753 Trion, 1,965....B 1
30755 Tunnel Hill, 900....C 1
30289 Turin, 242....C 4
30471 Twin City, 1,119....H 5
31795 Ty Ty, 447....E 8
31091 Unadilla, 1,457....E 6
30291 Union City, 3,031....D 3
30669 Union Point, 1,624....F 3
31794 Unionville, 1,646....F 8
30473 Uvalda, 663....H 6
31601 Valdosta⊙, 32,303....F 9
30756 Varnell, 400....C 1
30474 Vidalia, 9,507....H 6
31092 Vienna⊙, 2,341....E 6
30180 Villa Rica, 3,922....C 3
30182 Waco, 431....B 3
30477 Wadley, 1,989....H 5
30183 Waleska, 487....D 2
31333 Walthourville, 300....J 7
31564 Waresboro, 350....H 8
31830 Warm Springs, 523....C 5
31093 Warner Robins, 33,491....E 5
30828 Warrenton⊙, 2,073....G 4
31796 Warwick, 466....E 7
30673 Washington⊙, 4,094....G 3
30677 Watkinsville⊙, 986....E 3
31565 Waverly, 250....J 8
31831 Waverly Hall, 671....C 5
31501 Waycross⊙, 18,996....H 8
30830 Waynesboro⊙, 5,530....J 4
31566 Waynesville, 500....J 8
31833 West Point, 4,232....B 5
31797 Whigham, 381....D 9
30184 White, 462....C 2
30603 White Hall, 400....F 2
30678 White Plains, 236....F 4
31566 Whitemarsh Island....J 8
31091 Whitesburg, 720....B 4
30186 Whitestone, 450....C 1
† 31833 Whitesville, 250....C 5
30581 Wiley, 300....F 1
31650 Willacoochee, 1,120....G 8
30292 Williamson, 284....D 4
31404 Wilmington Island, 3,284....L 7
† 30824 Winfield, 444....H 3
30187 Winston, 625....C 3
30683 Winterville, 551....F 3
31569 Woodbine⊙, 1,002....J 9
30293 Woodbury, 1,422....C 5
31836 Woodland, 689....D 5
30188 Woodstock, 870....D 2
30670 Woodville, 379....F 3
30833 Wrens, 2,204....H 4
31096 Wrightsville⊙, 2,106....G 5
31097 Yatesville, 423....D 5
30582 Young Harris, 544....E 1
30295 Zebulon⊙, 776....D 4

⊙ County seat.
‡ Population of metropolitan area.
† Zip of nearest p.o.
* Multiple zips

Agriculture, Industry and Resources

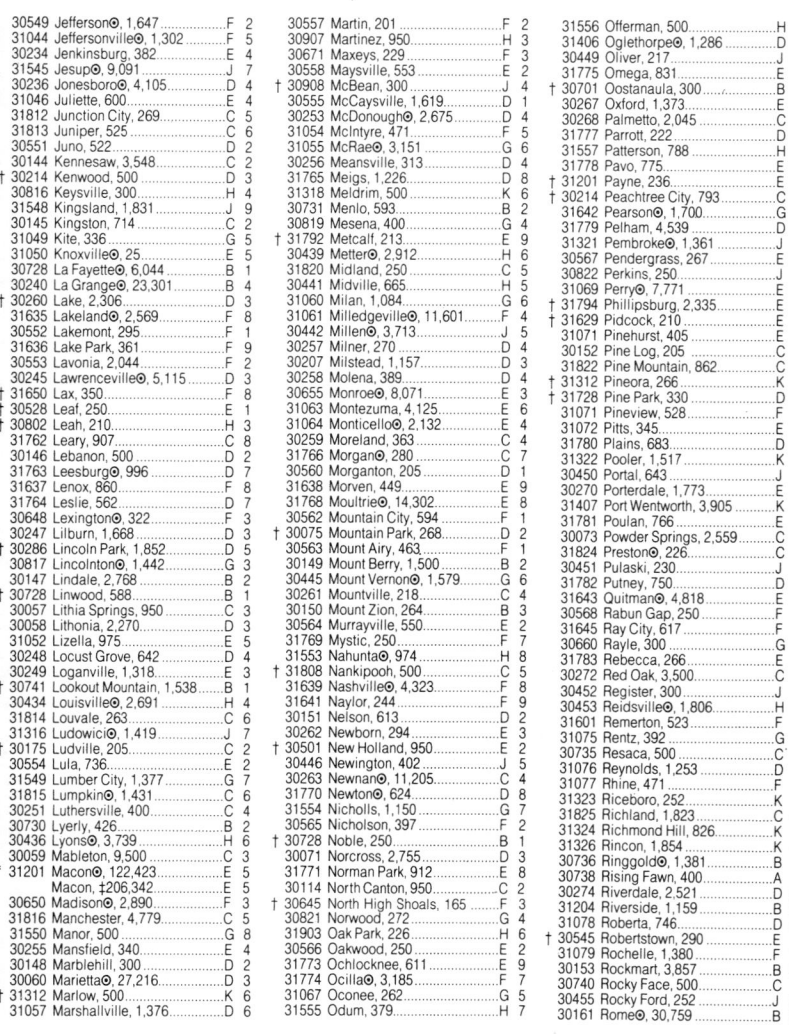

DOMINANT LAND USE

- Specialized Cotton
- Cotton, General Farming
- Cotton, Tobacco, Hogs, Peanuts
- Peanuts, General Farming
- General Farming, Livestock, Fruit, Tobacco
- General Farming, Forest Products, Cotton, Truck Farming
- Forests
- Swampland, Limited Agriculture
- Urban Areas

ATLANTA
Transportation Equipment,
Food Processing, Printing &
Publishing, Clothing

COLUMBUS
Food Processing,
Textiles

SAVANNAH
Food Processing,
Wood & Paper Products,
Chemicals

MAJOR MINERAL OCCURRENCES

- Al Bauxite
- Ba Barite
- Cl Clay
- Fe Iron Ore
- Gn Granite
- Mi Mica
- Mn Manganese
- Mr Marble
- Sl Slate
- Tc Talc
- Ti Titanium
- ⚡ Water Power
- ▨ Major Industrial Areas
- △ Major Textile Manufacturing Centers

Topography

0　40　80
MILES

5,000 m. | 2,000 m. | 1,000 m. | 500 m. | 200 m. | 100 m. | Sea
16,404 ft. | 6,562 ft. | 3,281 ft. | 1,640 ft. | 656 ft. | 328 ft. | Level
Below

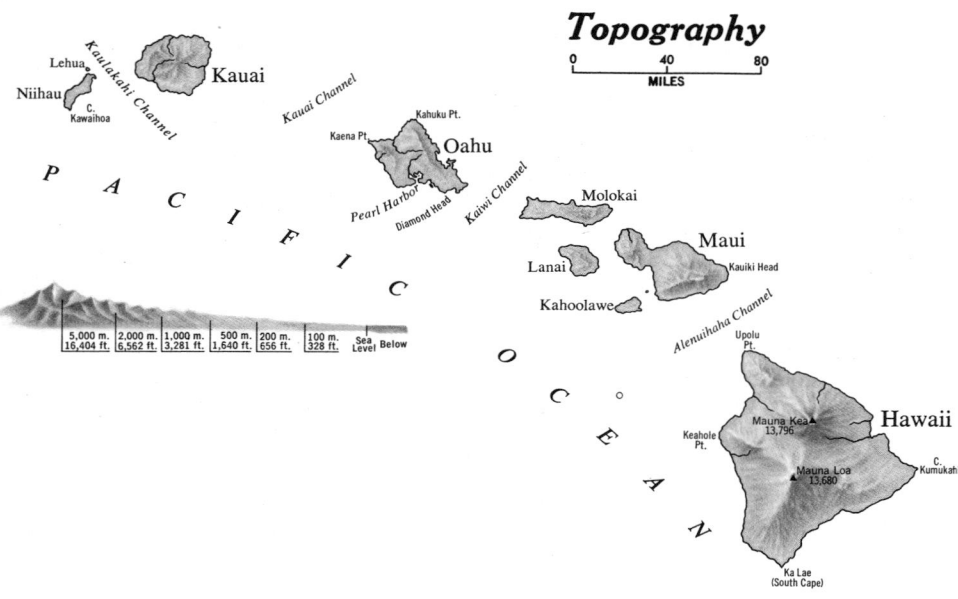

Niihau
Lehua
Kaulakahi Channel
Kawaihoa C.
Kauai
Kauai Channel
Kaena Pt.
Kahuku Pt.
Oahu
Pearl Harbor
Diamond Head
Kaiwi Channel
Molokai
Maui
Lanai
Kauiki Head
Kahoolawe
Alenuihaha Channel
Upolu Pt.
Keahole Pt.
Mauna Kea 13,796
Hawaii
C. Kumukahi
Mauna Loa 13,680
Ka Lae (South Cape)

PACIFIC OCEAN

Sharp spikes bristle protectively around their precious fruit crop on Pineapple Hill, west Maui. Second only to sugarcane, pineapples rank high in Hawaii's economy.

David Muench — Shostal Associates

Agriculture, Industry and Resources

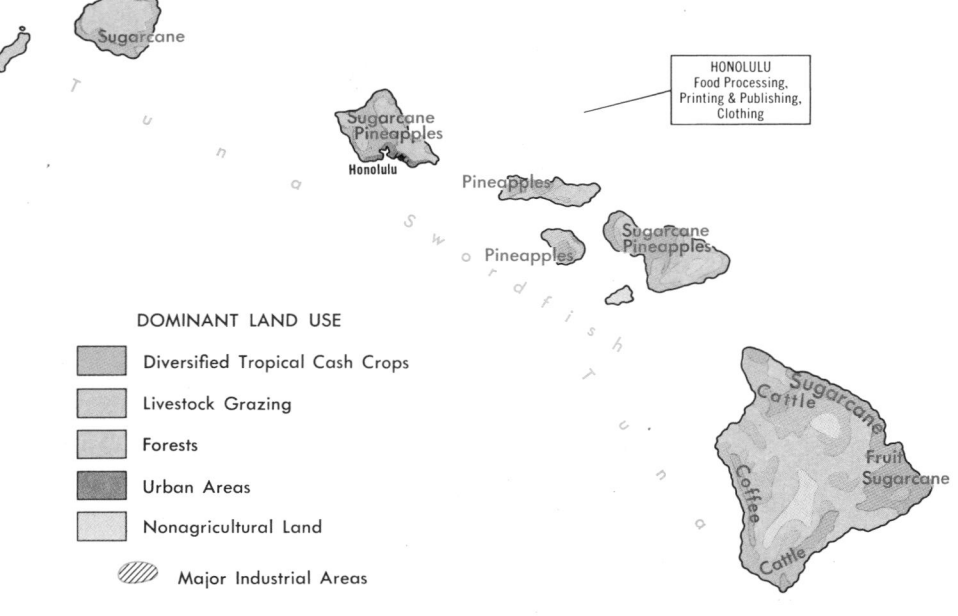

Sugarcane
Sugarcane Pineapples
Honolulu
Pineapples
Pineapples
Sugarcane Pineapples
Sugarcane Cattle
Coffee
Fruit Sugarcane
Cattle

HONOLULU
Food Processing, Printing & Publishing, Clothing

Tuna
Swordfish
Tuna

DOMINANT LAND USE

- Diversified Tropical Cash Crops
- Livestock Grazing
- Forests
- Urban Areas
- Nonagricultural Land
- Major Industrial Areas

COUNTIES

Hawaii, 63,468		K	7
Honolulu, 629,176		D	3
Kalawao, 172		G	1
Kauai, 29,761		A	1
Maui, 45,984		J	1

CITIES and TOWNS

Zip	Name/Pop.	Key
96701	Aiea, 12,560	B 3
96821	Aina Haina, 15,000	F 2
96703	Anahola, 638	C 1
† 96706	Barbers Point Housing, 1,947	E 2
96704	Captain Cook, 1,263	G 5
96705	Eleele, 758	C 2
96706	Ewa, 2,906	A 4
96706	Ewa Beach, 7,765	A 4
96701	Foster Village, 3,755	B 3
† 96714	Haena, 75	C 1
96708	Haiku, 464	J 2
96709	Haina, 333	H 3
96710	Hakalau, 742	J 4
† 96701	Halawa Heights, 5,809	B 3
96712	Haleiwa, 2,626	E 1
96787	Haliimaile, 638	J 2
96713	Hana, 459	K 2
96714	Hanalei, 153	C 1
96715	Hanamaulu, 2,461	C 1
96716	Hanapepe, 1,388	C 2
96717	Hauula, 2,048	E 1
96718	Hawaii National Park, 100	J 6
96719	Hawi, 797	H 3
96824	Hickam Housing, 7,352	B 4
96720	Hilo⊙, 26,353	J 5
96725	Holualoa, 850	G 5
96726	Honaunau, 950	G 6
† 96710	Honohina, 125	J 4
96727	Honokaa, 1,555	H 4
† 96761	Honokahua, 431	H 2
† 96740	Honokohau, 200	G 5
* 96801	Honolulu (cap)⊙, 324,871	C 4
	Honolulu, ‡630,528	C 4
96728	Honomu, 737	J 4
† 96706	Honouliuli, 600	A 3
96729	Hoolehua, 1,090	G 1
† 96740	Huehue, 100	G 5
† 96706	Iroquois Point, 4,572	A 4
† 96801	Iwilei, 1,835	C 4
96730	Kaaawa, 848	F 1
† 96761	Kaanapali, 250	H 2
† 96801	Kahala, 14,288	D 5
† 96744	Kahaluu, 1,657	E 2
96731	Kahuku, 917	E 1
96732	Kahului, 8,280	J 2
96734	Kailua, 33,783	F 2
† 96740	Kailua, 365	F 5
96740	Kailua Kona (Kailua), 365	F 5
96816	Kaimuki, 25,315	D 4

KAUAI COUNTY

SCALE
0　5　10　15 MI.
0　5　10　15 KM.

160° Longitude West of Greenwich 159°

Hanalei Bay
Haena Pt.
Haena
Wainiha
Wainiha R.
Makaha Pt.
Nohili Pt.
Kawaikini Pk. ▲ 5,170
Mana
K A U
Lehua
Paniau Pk. 1,281
Kaunuopou Pt.
Kokole Pt.
Kekaha
Waimea
Puuwai
Waimea Bay
Makaweli
Kaumakani
Puolo Pt.
Eleele
Hanapepe
Hanapepe Bay
Kamalino
NIIHAU
Halalii Lake
Pueo Pt.
Cape Kawaihoa
Kaulakahi Channel

A　B　C

HONOLULU & PEARL HARBOR

158°
Waipahu
Pearl City
Waimalu
Halawa Hts.
Aiea
Halawa Stream
Moanalua Stream
East Loch
Ford I.
West Loch
Middle Loch
FORD I. N.A.S.
Waipio Pen.
Southeast Loch
Honouliuli
Waipio Pt.
Foster Village
Salt Lake
FT. SHAFTER
PEARL HARBOR
Hickam Housing
HICKAM A.F.B.
HONOLULU INTERN'L AIRPORT
Keehi Lagoon
Kalihi
Puunui
Kalihl
Palama
Iwilei
Punchbowl ▲ 500
⊛ Honol
Ewa
Ewa Beach
Iroquois Point
Keahi Pt.
Ahua Pt.
Kalihi Entrance
MAMALA BAY
Honolulu Harbor
Anuenue

SCALE
0　1　2 MI.
0　1　2 KM.

HAWAII

180°　176°　172°　168°
Kure
Eastern I.
Sand I.
Midway Is. (U.S.)
Pearl and Hermes Reef
H A W A I I A N
Lisianski I.
Laysan I.
Maro Reef
Gardner Pinnac
French Frigate Shoals
International Date Line
P A C I F I C
O C E A N

State Capital .... ⊛
County Seats .... ⊙

Johnston Atoll (U.S.)

© C.S. HAMMOND & Co., N.Y.

AREA 6,450 sq. mi.
POPULATION 769,913 ('70); 965,000 ('80)
CAPITAL Honolulu
LARGEST CITY Honolulu
HIGHEST POINT Mauna Kea 13,796 ft.
SETTLED IN —
ADMITTED TO UNION August 21, 1959
POPULAR NAME Aloha State; Paradise of the Pacific
STATE FLOWER Red Hibiscus
STATE BIRD Nene (Hawaiian Goose)

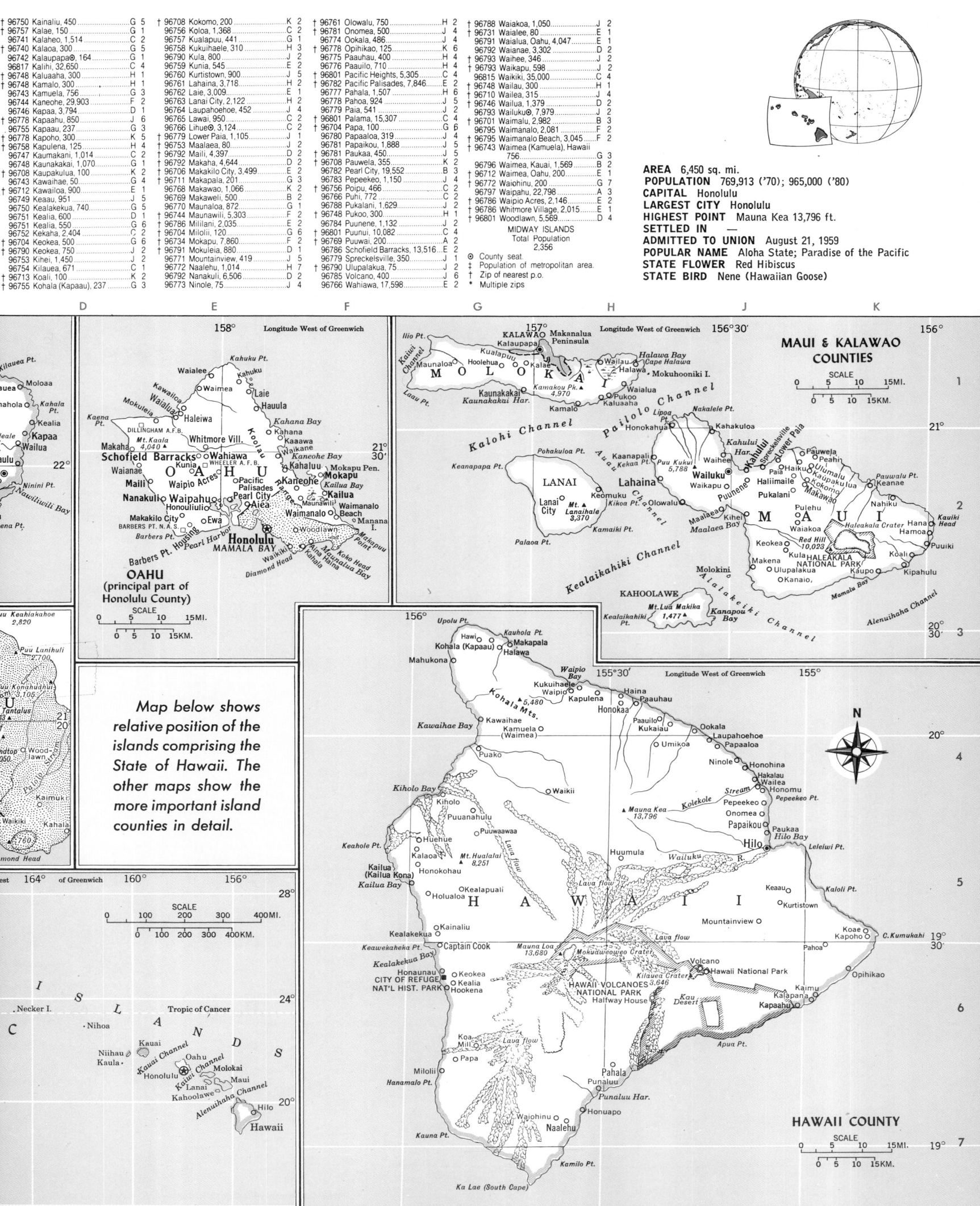

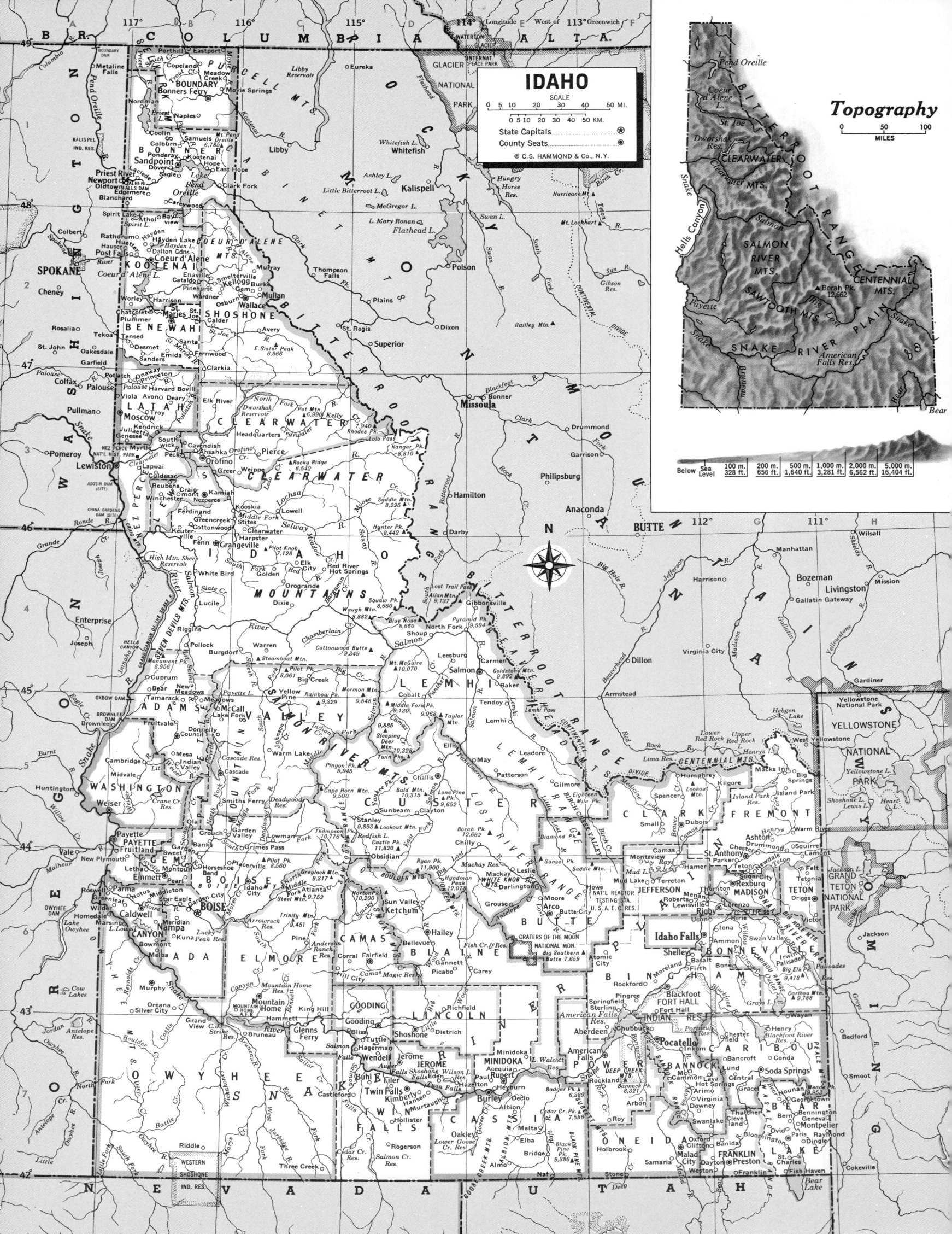

COUNTIES

Name/Pop.	Key
Ada, 112,230	B 6
Adams, 2,877	B 5
Bannock, 52,200	F 7
Bear Lake, 5,801	G 7
Benewah, 6,230	B 2
Bingham, 29,167	F 6
Blaine, 5,749	D 6
Boise, 1,763	C 6
Bonner, 15,560	B 1
Bonneville, 51,250	G 6
Boundary, 6,371	B 1
Butte, 2,925	E 6
Camas, 728	D 6
Canyon, 61,288	B 6
Caribou, 6,534	G 7
Cassia, 17,017	E 7
Clark, 741	F 5
Clearwater, 10,871	C 3
Custer, 2,967	D 5
Elmore, 17,479	C 6
Franklin, 7,373	G 7
Fremont, 8,710	G 5
Gem, 9,387	B 6
Gooding, 8,645	D 6
Idaho, 12,891	C 4
Jefferson, 11,619	F 6
Jerome, 10,253	D 7
Kootenai, 35,332	B 2
Latah, 24,891	B 3
Lemhi, 5,566	D 4
Lewis, 3,867	B 3
Lincoln, 3,057	D 6
Madison, 13,452	G 6
Minidoka, 15,731	E 7
Nez Perce, 30,376	B 3
Oneida, 2,864	F 7
Owyhee, 6,422	B 7
Payette, 12,401	B 5
Power, 4,864	F 7
Shoshone, 19,718	B 2
Teton, 2,351	G 6
Twin Falls, 41,807	D 7
Valley, 3,609	C 5
Washington, 7,633	B 5

CITIES and TOWNS

Zip	Name/Pop.	Key
83210	Aberdeen, 1,542	F 7
83310	Acequia, 107	E 7
83520	Ahsahka, 500	B 3
83311	Albion, 229	E 7
83312	Almo, 170	E 7
83211	American Falls⊙, 2,769	E 7
83401	Ammon, 1,338	G 6
83212	Arbon, 75	F 7
83213	Arco⊙, 1,244	E 6
83214	Arimo, 252	F 7
83420	Ashton, 1,187	G 5
83801	Athol, 190	B 2
83601	Atlanta, 50	C 6
83215	Atomic City, 24	F 6
83802	Avery, 250	C 2
83461	Baker, 98	E 4
83217	Bancroft, 366	G 7
83264	Banida, 76	G 7
83602	Banks, 49	B 5
83218	Basalt, 349	F 6
83803	Bayview, 300	B 2
83313	Bellevue, 537	D 6
83219	Bennington, 60	G 7
83220	Bern, 135	G 7
83221	Blackfoot⊙, 8,716	F 6
83804	Blanchard, 120	A 1
83314	Bliss, 114	D 7
83223	Bloomington, 186	G 7
* 83701	Boise (cap.)⊙, 74,990	B 6
	Boise, ‡112,230	B 6
83805	Bonners Ferry⊙, 2,796	B 1
83806	Bovill, 343	B 3
† 83651	Bowmont, 100	B 6
83315	Bridge, 140	E 7
83604	Bruneau, 150	C 7
83316	Buhl, 2,975	D 7
83807	Burke, 150	C 2
83318	Burley⊙, 8,279	E 7
† 83213	Butte City, 42	E 6
83808	Calder, 140	B 2
83605	Caldwell⊙, 14,219	B 6
83610	Cambridge, 383	B 5
83320	Carey, 750	E 6
83809	Careywood, 60	B 1
83462	Carmen, 40	E 4
83611	Cascade⊙, 833	C 5
83321	Castleford, 174	C 7
83810	Cataldo, 275	B 2
† 83241	Central, 60	G 7
83226	Challis⊙, 784	D 5
† 83851	Chatcolet, 95	B 2
83421	Chester, 206	G 5
† 83217	Chesterfield, 50	G 7
83201	Chubbuck, 2,924	F 7
83811	Clark Fork, 367	B 1
83812	Clarkia, 147	B 2
83227	Clayton, 36	D 5
83521	Clearwater, 110	C 3
† 83263	Cleveland, 60	G 7
83228	Clifton, 137	F 7
83229	Cobalt, 35	D 4
83814	Coeur d'Alene⊙, 16,228	B 2
83865	Colburn, 200	B 1
83230	Conda, 250	G 7
83821	Coolin, 110	B 1
83322	Corral, 21	D 6
83522	Cottonwood, 867	B 3
83612	Council⊙, 899	B 5
83523	Craigmont, 554	B 3
† 83622	Crouch, 71	B 5
83524	Culdesac, 211	B 3
† 83814	Dalton Gardens, 1,559	B 2
83232	Dayton, 198	F 7
83823	Deary, 411	B 3
83323	Declo, 251	E 7
83824	Desmet, 154	B 2
83324	Dietrich, 84	D 7
83233	Dingle, 300	G 7
83615	Donnelly, 114	B 5
83825	Dover, 300	B 1
83234	Downey, 586	F 7
83422	Driggs⊙, 727	G 6
83423	Dubois⊙, 400	F 5
83616	Eagle, 525	B 6
† 83836	East Hope, 175	B 1
83826	Eastport, 83	B 1
83325	Eden, 343	D 7
83326	Elba, 87	E 7
83525	Elk City, 500	C 4
83827	Elk River, 383	B 3
83235	Ellis, 75	D 5
83828	Emida, 135	B 2
83617	Emmett⊙, 3,945	B 6
83829	Enaville, 90	B 2
83327	Fairfield⊙, 157	D 6
83424	Felt, 90	G 6
83531	Fenn, 45	B 4
83526	Ferdinand, 157	B 3
83830	Fernwood, 360	B 2
83328	Filer, 1,173	D 7
83236	Firth, 362	F 6
83261	Fish Haven, 120	G 7
83203	Fort Hall, 750	F 6
83237	Franklin, 402	G 7
83619	Fruitland, 1,576	B 6
83620	Fruitvale, 90	B 5
83621	Gardena, 44	B 5
83704	Garden City, 2,368	B 6
83622	Garden Valley, 100	C 5
† 83873	Gem, 50	C 2
83832	Genesee, 619	B 3
83238	Geneva, 200	G 7
83239	Georgetown, 421	G 7
83463	Gibbonsville, 85	E 4
83623	Glenns Ferry, 1,386	C 7
83330	Gooding⊙, 2,599	D 7
83241	Grace, 826	G 7
83624	Grand View, 450	B 7
83530	Grangeville⊙, 3,636	B 4
83533	Greencreek, 72	B 3
83626	Greenleaf, 425	B 6
† 83544	Greer, 70	B 3
83332	Hagerman, 436	D 7
83333	Hailey⊙, 1,425	D 6
83425	Hamer, 81	F 6
83627	Hammett, 653	C 7
83334	Hansen, 415	D 7
† 83521	Harpster, 250	C 4
83833	Harrison, 249	B 2
83834	Harvard, 50	B 3
† 83854	Hauser, 349	A 2
† 83835	Hayden, 1,285	B 2
83835	Hayden Lake, 260	B 2
83335	Hazelton, 396	E 7
83534	Headquarters, 350	C 3
† 83443	Heise, 84	G 6
83336	Heyburn, 1,637	E 7
83337	Hill City, 30	D 6
83243	Holbrook, 100	F 7
† 83301	Hollister, 57	D 7
83628	Homedale, 1,411	A 6
83836	Hope, 63	B 1
83629	Horseshoe Bend, 511	B 6
83244	Howe, 428	F 6
† 83854	Huetter, 49	B 2
83631	Idaho City⊙, 164	C 6
83401	Idaho Falls⊙, 35,776	F 6
83632	Indian Valley, 72	B 5
83245	Inkom, 522	F 7
83427	Iona, 890	G 6
83428	Irwin, 228	G 6
83429	Island Park, 136	G 5
83338	Jerome⊙, 4,183	D 7
83535	Juliaetta, 423	B 3
83536	Kamiah, 1,307	B 3
83837	Kellogg, 3,811	B 2
83537	Kendrick, 426	B 3
83340	Ketchum, 1,454	D 6
83538	Keuterville, 26	B 3
† 83423	Kilgore, 50	G 5
83341	Kimberly, 1,557	D 7
83633	King Hill, 150	C 6
83539	Kooskia, 809	C 3
83840	Kootenai, 168	B 1
83634	Kuna, 593	B 6
83841	Laclede, 200	B 1
83635	Lake Fork, 141	B 5
83430	Lamont, 30	G 6
83540	Lapwai, 400	B 3
83246	Lava Hot Springs, 516	F 7
83464	Leadore, 111	E 5
83465	Lemhi, 36	E 5
83249	Leslie, 100	E 6
83636	Letha, 115	B 6
83501	Lewiston⊙, 26,068	A 3
83431	Lewisville, 468	F 6
83432	Lorenzo, 125	G 6
† 83242	Lost River, 58	E 6
83637	Lowman, 45	C 5
83542	Lucile, 105	B 4
† 83241	Lund, 100	G 7
83251	Mackay, 539	E 6
83433	Macks Inn, 150	G 5
83252	Malad City⊙, 1,848	F 7
83342	Malta, 196	E 7
83639	Marsing, 610	B 6
83253	May, 120	E 5
83638	McCall, 1,758	C 5
83250	McCammon, 623	F 7
83640	Meadows, 250	B 5
83641	Melba, 197	B 6
83434	Menan, 545	F 6
83642	Meridian, 2,616	B 6
83643	Mesa, 25	B 5
83644	Middleton, 739	B 6
83645	Midvale, 176	B 5
83343	Minidoka, 131	E 7
83435	Monteview, 110	F 6
83646	Montour, 138	B 6
83254	Montpelier, 2,604	G 7
83255	Moore, 156	E 6
83256	Moreland, 500	F 6
83843	Moscow⊙, 14,146	B 3
83647	Mountain Home⊙, 6,451	C 6
83845	Moyie Springs, 203	B 1
† 83450	Mud Lake, 194	F 6
83846	Mullan, 1,279	C 2
83650	Murphy⊙, 75	B 6
83874	Murray, 100	C 2
83344	Murtaugh, 124	D 7
83345	Naf, 42	E 7
83651	Nampa, 20,768	B 6
83847	Naples, 463	B 1
83436	Newdale, 267	G 6
83654	New Meadows, 605	B 4
83655	New Plymouth, 986	B 6
83543	Nezperce⊙, 555	B 3
83848	Nordman, 168	B 1
83466	North Fork, 150	D 4
83656	Notus, 304	B 6
† 83254	Nounan, 92	G 7
83346	Oakley, 656	D 7
83259	Obsidian, 22	D 6
83657	Ola, 78	B 5
† 99156	Oldtown, 161	A 1
† 83855	Onaway, 166	B 3
83659	Oreana, 115	B 6
83544	Orofino⊙, 3,883	B 3
† 83525	Orogrande, 34	C 4
83849	Osburn, 2,248	B 2
83260	Ovid, 150	G 7
† 83263	Oxford, 75	F 7
83437	Palisades, 95	G 6
83261	Paris⊙, 615	G 7
83438	Parker, 266	G 6
83660	Parma, 1,228	B 6
83347	Paul, 911	E 7
83661	Payette⊙, 4,521	B 5
83545	Peck, 238	B 3
83348	Picabo, 50	D 6
83546	Pierce, 1,218	C 3
83850	Pinehurst, 1,934	B 2
83262	Pingree, 115	F 6
83851	Plummer, 443	B 2
83201	Pocatello⊙, 40,036	F 7
83547	Pollock, 50	B 4
83852	Ponderay, 275	B 1
83853	Porthill, 39	B 1
83854	Post Falls, 2,371	A 2
83855	Potlatch, 871	A 3
83263	Preston⊙, 3,310	G 7
83856	Priest River, 1,493	A 1
83857	Princeton, 124	B 3
83858	Rathdrum, 741	A 2
† 83114	Raymond, 65	G 7
83548	Reubens, 81	B 3
83440	Rexburg⊙, 8,272	G 6
83349	Richfield, 290	D 6
† 89832	Riddle, 44	B 7
83442	Rigby⊙, 2,293	F 6
83549	Riggins, 533	B 4
83443	Ririe, 575	G 6
83444	Roberts, 393	F 6
† 83221	Rockford, 150	F 6
83271	Rockland, 209	F 7
83302	Rogerson, 45	D 7
† 83660	Roswell, 65	A 6
83350	Rupert⊙, 4,563	E 7
83860	Sagle, 100	B 1
83445	Saint Anthony⊙, 2,877	G 6
83272	Saint Charles, 200	G 7
† 83861	Saint Joe, 50	B 2
83861	Saint Maries⊙, 2,571	B 2
83467	Salmon⊙, 2,910	D 4
83252	Samaria, 137	F 7
83862	Samuels, 467	B 1
83863	Sanders, 27	B 2
83864	Sandpoint⊙, 4,144	B 1
83866	Santa, 100	B 2
83274	Shelley, 2,614	F 6
83352	Shoshone⊙, 1,233	D 7
† 83650	Silver City, 1	B 6
† 83423	Small, 35	F 5
83868	Smelterville, 967	B 2
83276	Soda Springs⊙, 2,977	G 7
83550	Southwick, 38	B 3
83446	Spencer, 45	F 5
83869	Spirit Lake, 622	A 2
83277	Springfield, 180	F 6
83447	Squirrel, 43	G 5
83278	Stanley, 47	D 5
83669	Star, 500	B 6
83279	Sterling, 73	F 6
83552	Stites, 263	C 3
83280	Stone, 114	F 7
83448	Sugar City, 617	G 6
83353	Sun Valley, 180	D 6
83281	Swanlake, 145	F 7
83449	Swan Valley, 235	G 6
83670	Sweet, 120	B 6
83468	Tendoy, 150	E 5
83870	Tensed, 151	B 2
83450	Terreton, 42	F 6
83451	Teton, 390	G 6
83452	Tetonia, 176	G 6
83283	Thatcher, 300	G 7
83453	Thornton, 177	G 6
83871	Troy, 541	B 3
83354	Tuttle, 53	D 7
83301	Twin Falls⊙, 21,914	D 7
83454	Ucon, 664	F 6
83455	Victor, 241	G 6
83872	Viola, 300	B 3
† 83234	Virginia, 100	F 7
83873	Wallace⊙, 2,206	C 2
83875	Wardner, 492	B 2
83611	Warm Lake, 200	C 5
83285	Wayan, 50	G 7
83553	Weippe, 713	C 3
83672	Weiser⊙, 4,108	B 5
83355	Wendell, 1,122	D 7
83286	Weston, 230	F 7
83554	White Bird, 185	B 4
83676	Wilder, 564	A 6
83555	Winchester, 274	B 3
83876	Worley, 235	B 2
83677	Yellow Pine, 45	C 4

⊙ County seat.
‡ Population of metropolitan area.
† Zip of nearest p.o.
* Multiple zips

AREA 83,557 sq. mi.
POPULATION 713,008 ('70); 943,935 ('80)
CAPITAL Boise
LARGEST CITY Boise
HIGHEST POINT Borah Pk. 12,662 ft.
SETTLED IN 1842
ADMITTED TO UNION July 3, 1890
POPULAR NAME Gem State
STATE FLOWER Syringa
STATE BIRD Mountain Bluebird

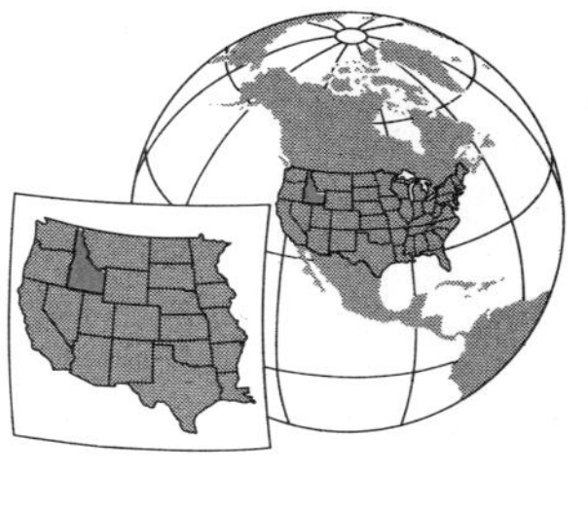

Agriculture, Industry and Resources

DOMINANT LAND USE

- Wheat, General Farming
- Wheat, Peas
- Specialized Dairy
- Potatoes, Beans, Sugar Beets, Livestock, General Farming
- General Farming, Dairy, Hay, Sugar Beets
- General Farming, Livestock, Special Crops
- General Farming, Dairy, Range Livestock
- Range Livestock
- Forests

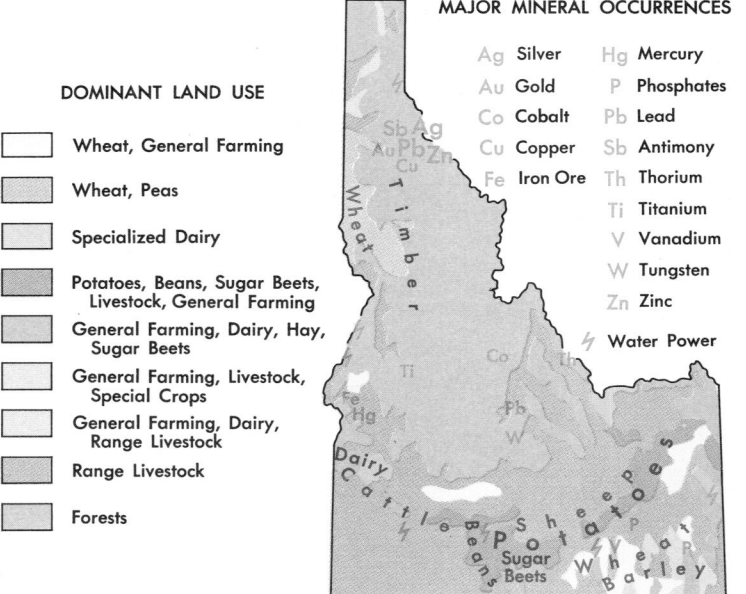

MAJOR MINERAL OCCURRENCES

Ag	Silver	Hg	Mercury
Au	Gold	P	Phosphates
Co	Cobalt	Pb	Lead
Cu	Copper	Sb	Antimony
Fe	Iron Ore	Th	Thorium
		Ti	Titanium
		V	Vanadium
		W	Tungsten
		Zn	Zinc

Water Power

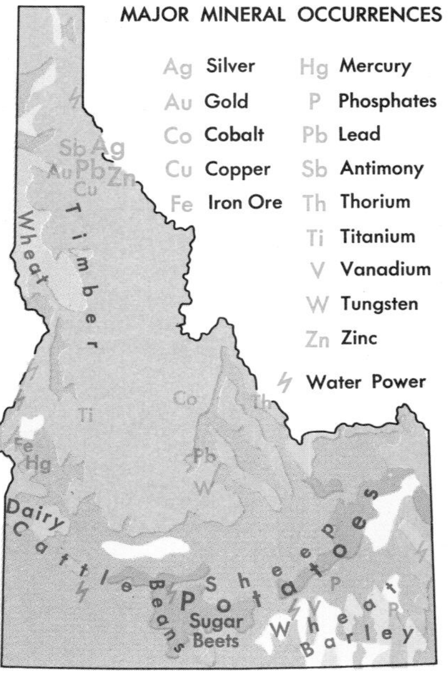

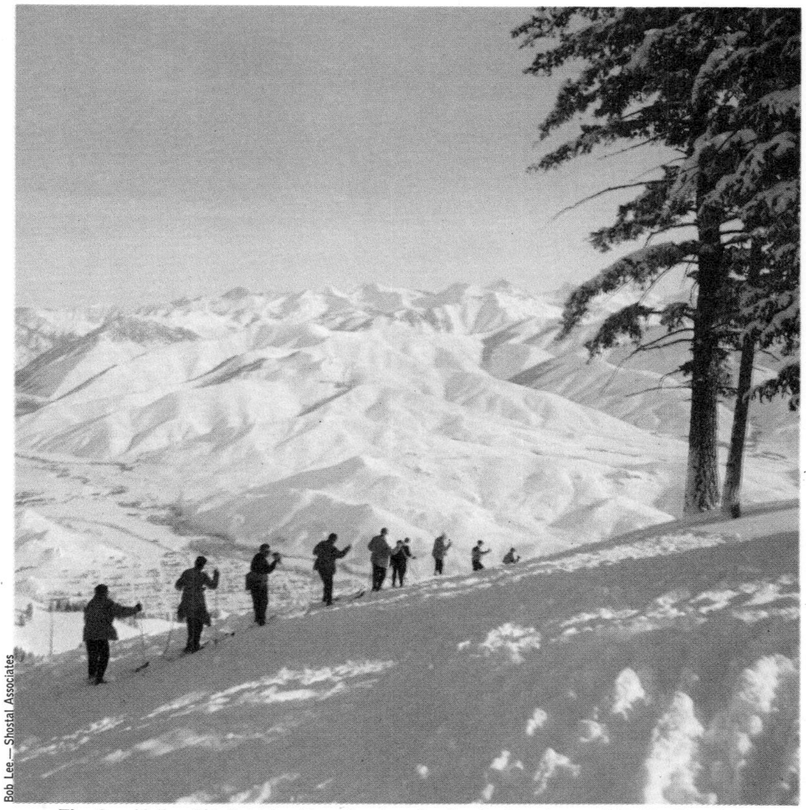

Bob Lee—Shostal Associates

The Sun Valley Ski Patrol adds a touch of color to the slopes of Baldy Mountain. Here, in one of the country's most popular resorts, visitors acquire tropical tans while swimming in heated pools, skiing, skijoring, dogsledding or just sunbathing in the glacial air.

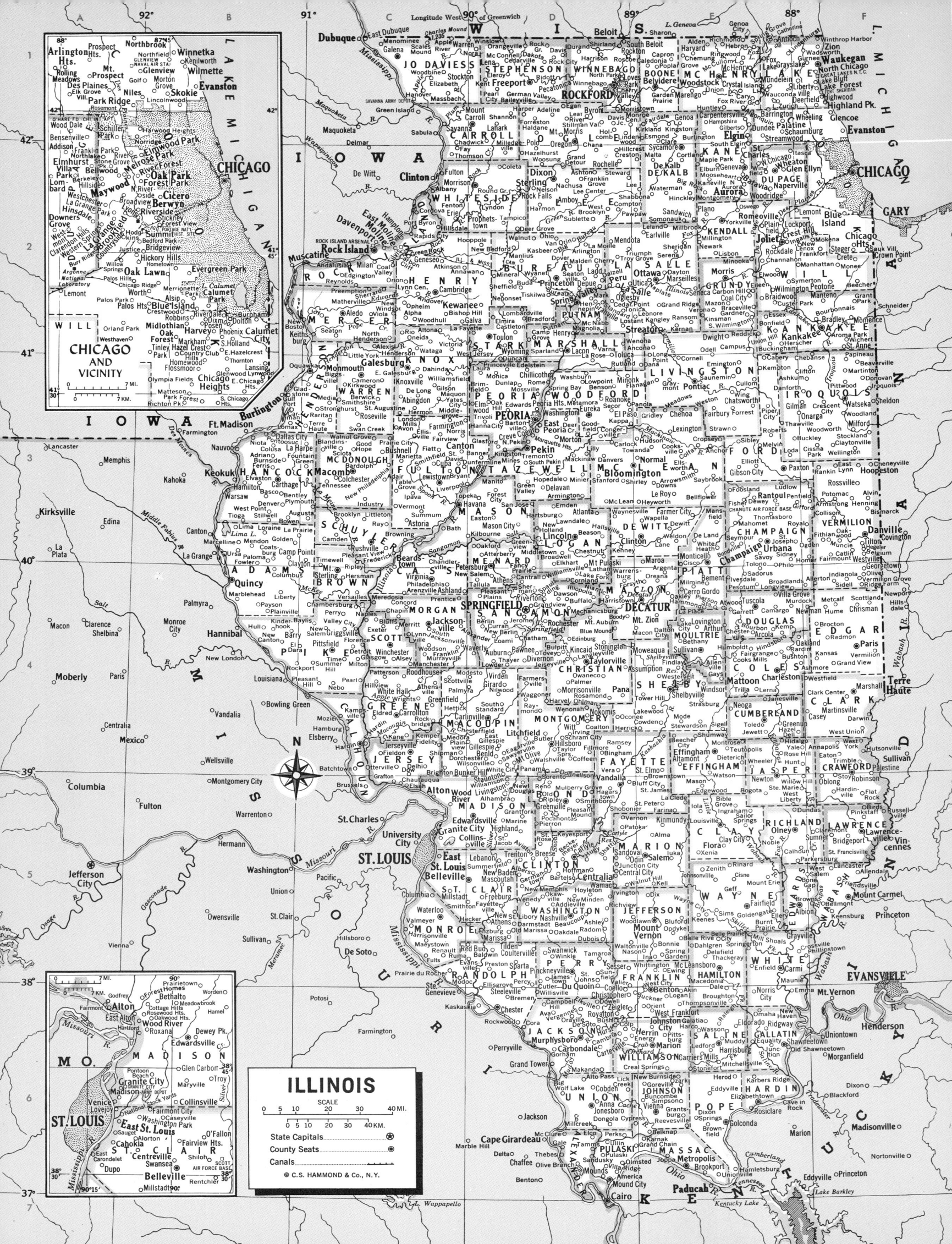

ILLINOIS

SCALE

State Capitals ⊛
County Seats ⊙
Canals

© C.S. HAMMOND & Co., N.Y.

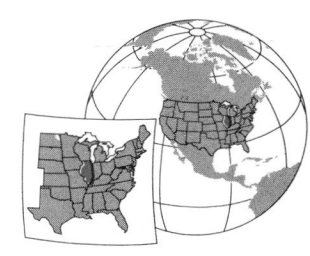

AREA 56,400 sq. mi.
POPULATION 11,113,976 ('70); 11,418,461 ('80)
CAPITAL Springfield
LARGEST CITY Chicago
HIGHEST POINT Charles Mound 1,235 ft.
SETTLED IN 1720
ADMITTED TO UNION December 3, 1818
POPULAR NAME Prairie State
STATE FLOWER Violet
STATE BIRD Cardinal

Agriculture, Industry and Resources

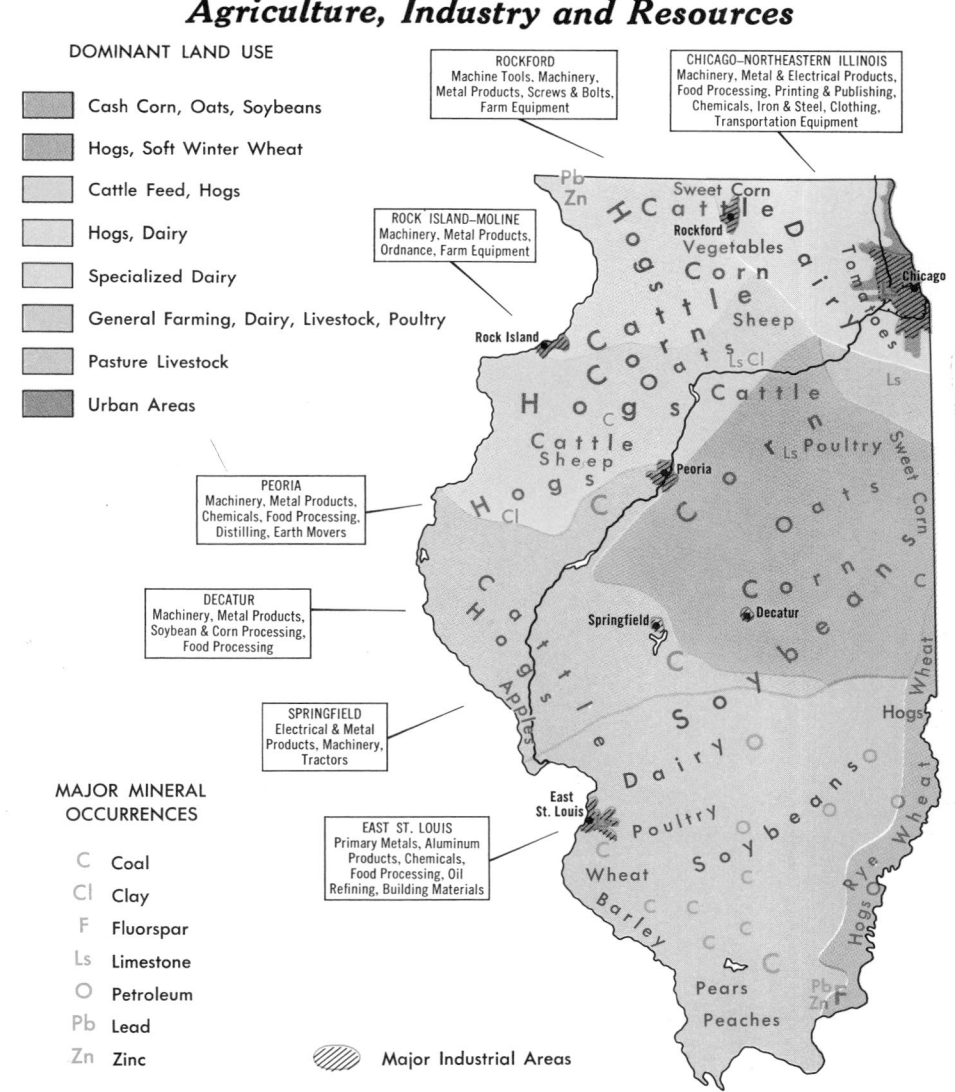

DOMINANT LAND USE

- Cash Corn, Oats, Soybeans
- Hogs, Soft Winter Wheat
- Cattle Feed, Hogs
- Hogs, Dairy
- Specialized Dairy
- General Farming, Dairy, Livestock, Poultry
- Pasture Livestock
- Urban Areas

ROCKFORD
Machine Tools, Machinery,
Metal Products, Screws & Bolts,
Farm Equipment

CHICAGO–NORTHEASTERN ILLINOIS
Machinery, Metal & Electrical Products,
Food Processing, Printing & Publishing,
Chemicals, Iron & Steel, Clothing,
Transportation Equipment

ROCK ISLAND–MOLINE
Machinery, Metal Products,
Ordnance, Farm Equipment

PEORIA
Machinery, Metal Products,
Chemicals, Food Processing,
Distilling, Earth Movers

DECATUR
Machinery, Metal Products,
Soybean & Corn Processing,
Food Processing

SPRINGFIELD
Electrical & Metal
Products, Machinery,
Tractors

EAST ST. LOUIS
Primary Metals, Aluminum
Products, Chemicals,
Food Processing, Oil
Refining, Building Materials

MAJOR MINERAL
OCCURRENCES

C   Coal
Cl Clay
F   Fluorspar
Ls Limestone
O   Petroleum
Pb Lead
Zn Zinc

▨ Major Industrial Areas

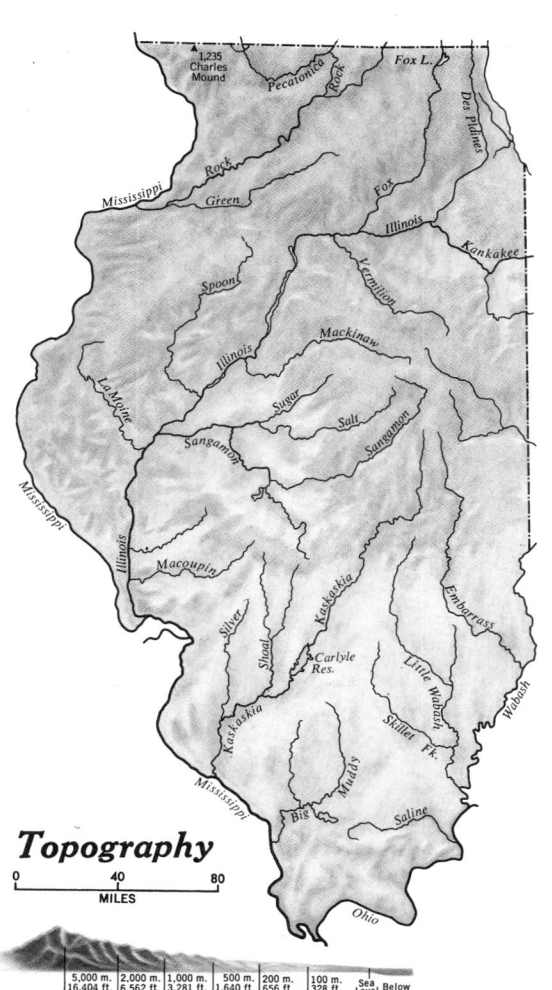

Topography

0   40   80
    MILES

5,000 m. | 2,000 m. | 1,000 m. | 500 m. | 200 m. | 100 m. | Sea
16,404 ft. | 6,562 ft. | 3,281 ft. | 1,640 ft. | 656 ft. | 328 ft. | Level
                                                              Below

(continued)

61733 Deer Creek, 647 D 3
60015 Deerfield, 18,949 F 1
60115 De Kalb, 32,949 E 2
61734 Delavan, 1,844 D 3
61322 Depue, 1,919 D 2
62924 De Soto, 966 D 6
* 60016 Des Plaines, 57,239 A 1
† 62025 Dewey Park, 2,029 B 6
62530 Divernon, 1,010 D 4
† 60469 Dixmoor, 4,735 B 2
61021 Dixon⊙, 18,147 D 2
60419 Dolton, 25,937 B 2
62926 Dongola, 825 D 6
60515 Downers Grove, 32,751 A 2
61736 Downs, 651 E 3
60118 Dundee (East and West Dundee), 6,215 E 1
61525 Dunlap, 656 D 3
62239 Dupo, 2,842 A 6
62832 Du Quoin, 6,691 D 5
61024 Durand, 972 D 1
60420 Dwight, 3,841 E 2
60518 Earlville, 1,410 E 2
62024 East Alton, 7,309 B 6
† 60411 East Chicago Heights, 5,000 B 3
61025 East Dubuque, 2,408 C 1
† 60118 East Dundee (Dundee), 2,920 E 1
61430 East Galesburg, 706 C 3
† 60429 East Hazelcrest, 1,885 B 2
61244 East Moline, 20,832 C 2
† 61611 East Peoria, 18,455 D 3
* 62201 East Saint Louis, 69,996 B 6
62531 Edinburg, 1,153 D 4
62025 Edwardsville⊙, 11,070 B 6
62401 Effingham⊙, 9,458 E 4
60119 Elburn, 1,122 E 2
62930 Eldorado, 3,876 E 6
60120 Elgin, 55,691 E 1
61028 Elizabeth, 707 C 1
62931 Elizabethtown⊙, 436 E 6
60007 Elk Grove Village, 24,516 A 1
62932 Elkville, 850 D 6
60126 Elmhurst, 50,547 A 2
61529 Elmwood, 2,014 D 3
60635 Elmwood Park, 26,160 B 2
61738 El Paso, 2,291 D 3
60421 Elwood, 794 E 2
62635 Emden, 552 D 3
62933 Energy, 812 E 6
62835 Enfield, 764 E 5
62934 Equality, 732 E 6
61250 Erie, 1,566 C 2
61530 Eureka⊙, 3,028 D 3
* 60201 Evanston, 79,808 B 1
62242 Evansville, 838 D 5
60642 Evergreen Park, 25,487 B 2
61739 Fairbury, 3,359 E 3
62837 Fairfield⊙, 5,897 E 5
† 62002 Fairmont, 1,521 A 6
† 62201 Fairmont City, 2,769 B 6
61841 Fairmount, 785 F 3
61432 Fairview 601 C 3
62232 Fairview Heights, 8,625 B 6
62838 Farina, 634 E 5
61842 Farmer City, 2,217 E 3
61531 Farmington, 2,959 C 3
62534 Findlay, 809 E 4
61843 Fisher, 1,525 E 3
61844 Fithian, 562 F 3
61740 Flanagan, 878 E 3
62839 Flora, 5,283 E 5
60422 Flossmoor, 7,846 B 3
† 62018 Forest Homes, 1,998 B 6
60130 Forest Park, 15,472 B 2
† 60402 Forest View, 927 B 2
61741 Forrest, 1,219 E 3
61030 Forreston, 1,227 D 1
60020 Fox Lake, 4,511 E 1
60021 Fox River Grove, 2,245 E 1
60423 Frankfort, 2,325 F 2
62638 Franklin, 565 C 4
61031 Franklin Grove, 968 D 2
60131 Franklin Park, 20,497 A 2
62243 Freeburg, 2,495 D 5
61032 Freeport⊙, 27,736 D 1
61252 Fulton, 3,630 C 2
62935 Galatia, 792 E 6
61036 Galena⊙, 3,930 C 1
61401 Galesburg⊙, 36,290 C 3
61434 Galva, 3,061 D 2
60424 Gardner, 1,212 E 2
61254 Geneseo, 5,840 C 2
60134 Geneva⊙, 9,115 E 2
60135 Genoa, 3,003 E 1
61846 Georgetown, 3,984 F 4
62245 Germantown, 1,108 D 5
60936 Gibson City, 3,454 E 3
61847 Gifford, 814 E 3
62033 Gillespie, 3,457 D 4
60938 Gilman, 1,786 E 3
62640 Girard, 1,881 D 4
61533 Glasford, 1,066 D 3
62034 Glen Carbon, 1,897 B 6
60022 Glencoe, 10,542 F 1
60137 Glen Ellyn, 21,909 F 2
60025 Glenview, 24,880 B 1
60425 Glenwood, 7,416 B 3
62035 Godfrey, 1,225 A 6
62938 Golconda⊙, 922 E 6
62339 Golden, 571 B 3
62939 Goreville, 1,109 E 6
62037 Grafton, 1,018 C 5
61325 Grand Ridge, 698 E 2
62942 Grand Tower, 664 D 6
† 62701 Grandview, 2,242 D 4
62040 Granite City, 40,440 B 6
60940 Grant Park, 801 F 2
61326 Granville, 1,232 D 2
60030 Grayslake, 4,907 E 1
62844 Grayville, 2,035 E 5
62044 Greenfield, 1,179 C 4
† 61241 Green Rock, 2,744 C 2
62428 Greenup, 1,618 E 4
61534 Green Valley, 617 D 3
62642 Greenview, 740 D 3
62246 Greenville⊙, 4,631 D 5
61744 Gridley, 1,007 E 3
62340 Griggsville, 1,245 C 4
60031 Gurnee, 2,738 F 1
62341 Hamilton, 2,764 B 3
60140 Hampshire, 1,611 E 1
61256 Hampton, 1,612 C 2
61536 Hanna City, 1,282 D 3
61041 Hanover, 1,243 C 1
62047 Hardin⊙, 1,035 C 4
62946 Harrisburg⊙, 9,535 E 6
62048 Hartford, 2,243 B 6
60033 Harvard, 5,177 E 1
60426 Harvey, 34,636 B 2
60656 Harwood Heights, 9,060 B 1
62644 Havana⊙, 4,376 D 3
60429 Hazel Crest, 10,329 B 2
60034 Hebron, 781 E 1
† 61832 Hegeler, 1,595 F 3
61327 Hennepin⊙, 535 D 2
61537 Henry, 2,610 D 2
62948 Herrin, 9,623 E 6
60941 Herscher, 988 E 2
61745 Heyworth, 1,441 E 3
60457 Hickory Hills, 13,176 B 2
62249 Highland, 5,981 D 5
60035 Highland Park, 32,263 F 1
60040 Highwood, 4,973 F 1
61244 Hillcrest, 630 D 2
62049 Hillsboro⊙, 4,267 D 4
60162 Hillside, 8,888 A 2
60520 Hinckley, 1,053 E 2
60521 Hinsdale, 15,918 A 2
60525 Hodgkins, 2,270 A 2
61849 Homer, 1,354 F 3
60456 Hometown, 6,729 B 2
60430 Homewood, 18,871 B 3
60942 Hoopeston, 6,461 F 3
61747 Hopedale, 923 D 3
61748 Hudson, 802 E 3
62343 Hull, 585 B 4
60142 Huntley, 1,432 E 1
62949 Hurst, 934 D 6
62539 Illiopolis, 1,122 D 4
61440 Industry, 558 C 3
† 60431 Ingalls Park, 5,615 F 2
61441 Ipava, 608 C 3
62051 Irving, 599 D 4
60042 Island Lake, 1,973 E 1
60143 Itasca, 4,638 F 2
62650 Jacksonville⊙, 20,553 C 4
† 62701 Jerome, 1,673 D 4
62052 Jerseyville⊙, 7,446 C 4
62951 Johnston City, 3,928 E 6
* 60431 Joliet⊙, 80,378 E 2
62952 Jonesboro⊙, 1,676 D 6
† 60453 Justice, 9,473 A 2
60901 Kankakee⊙, 30,944 F 2
61933 Kansas, 779 F 4
62956 Karnak, 641 E 6
† 63673 Kaskaskia, 79 C 6
61442 Keithsburg, 836 B 2
60043 Kenilworth, 2,980 B 1
61443 Kewanee, 15,762 C 2
62540 Kincaid, 1,424 D 4
62854 Kinmundy, 759 E 5
60146 Kirkland, 1,138 E 1
61447 Kirkwood, 817 C 3
61448 Knoxville, 2,930 C 3
61540 Lacon⊙, 2,147 D 2
61329 Ladd, 1,328 D 2
60525 La Grange, 16,773 A 2
60525 La Grange Park, 15,626 A 2
61450 La Harpe, 1,240 C 3
60044 Lake Bluff, 4,979 F 1
† 60002 Lake Catherine, 1,219 E 1
60045 Lake Forest, 15,642 F 1
60047 Lake Zurich, 4,082 E 1
61330 La Moille, 669 D 2
61046 Lanark, 1,495 D 1
60438 Lansing, 25,805 B 3
61301 La Salle, 10,736 D 2
62439 Lawrenceville⊙, 5,863 F 5
61047 Leaf River, 633 D 1
62254 Lebanon, 3,564 D 5
60531 Leland, 743 E 2
60439 Lemont, 5,080 A 2
61048 Lena, 1,691 D 1
61752 Le Roy, 2,435 E 3
61542 Lewistown⊙, 2,706 C 3
61753 Lexington, 1,615 E 3
60048 Libertyville, 11,684 F 1
62656 Lincoln⊙, 17,582 D 3
† 60601 Lincolnwood, 12,929 B 1
60046 Lindenhurst, 3,141 F 1
62056 Litchfield, 7,190 D 4
62058 Livingston, 916 D 5
60441 Lockport, 9,985 F 2
61454 Lomax, 565 B 3
60148 Lombard, 35,977 A 2
61544 London Mills, 600 C 3
62858 Louisville⊙, 1,020 E 5
62059 Lovejoy, 1,702 A 6
61111 Loves Park, 12,390 E 1
61937 Lovington, 1,303 E 4
61261 Lyndon, 673 D 2
† 60411 Lynwood, 1,042 B 3
60534 Lyons, 11,124 B 2
61755 Mackinaw, 1,293 D 3
61455 Macomb⊙, 19,643 C 3
62544 Macon, 1,249 E 4
62060 Madison, 7,042 B 6
81853 Mahomet, 1,296 E 3
60150 Malta, 961 E 2
60442 Manhattan, 1,530 F 2
61546 Manito, 1,334 D 3
61854 Mansfield, 870 E 3
60950 Manteno, 2,864 F 2
60151 Maple Park, 660 E 2
60152 Marengo, 4,235 E 1
62061 Marine, 882 D 5
62059 Marion⊙, 11,724 E 6
62257 Marissa, 2,004 D 5
60426 Markham, 15,987 B 2
61756 Maroa, 1,467 E 3
† 61554 Marquette Heights, 2,758 D 3
61341 Marseilles, 4,320 E 2
62441 Marshall⊙, 3,468 F 4
62442 Martinsville, 1,374 F 4
62062 Maryville, 809 B 6
62258 Mascoutah, 5,045 D 5
62664 Mason City, 2,611 D 3
61263 Matherville, 699 C 2
60443 Matteson, 4,741 B 3
61938 Mattoon, 19,681 E 4
60153 Maywood, 30,036 A 2
60444 Mazon, 727 E 2
62957 McClure, 800 D 6
† 60050 McCullom Lake, 873 E 1
60050 McHenry, 6,772 E 1
61754 McLean, 820 D 3
62859 McLeansboro⊙, 2,630 E 5
† 62010 Meadowbrook, 1,295 B 6
* 60160 Melrose Park, 22,706 A 2
62351 Mendon, 883 B 3
61342 Mendota, 6,902 D 2
62665 Meredosia, 1,178 C 4
† 60601 Merrionette Park, 2,303 B 2
61548 Metamora, 2,176 D 3
62960 Metropolis⊙, 6,940 E 6
62666 Middletown, 626 D 3
60445 Midlothian, 15,939 B 2
61264 Milan, 4,873 C 2
60953 Milford, 1,656 F 3
61051 Milledgeville, 1,130 D 1
62260 Millstadt, 2,168 B 6
61759 Minier, 986 D 3
61760 Minonk, 2,267 D 3
60447 Minooka, 768 E 2
60448 Mokena, 1,643 F 2
61265 Moline, 46,237 C 2
60954 Momence, 2,836 F 2
60449 Monee, 940 F 2
61462 Monmouth⊙, 11,022 C 3
60538 Montgomery, 3,278 E 2
61856 Monticello⊙, 4,130 E 3
60539 Mooseheart, 850 E 2
60450 Morris⊙, 8,194 E 2
61270 Morrison⊙, 4,387 C 2
62546 Morrisonville, 1,178 D 4
† 61101 Morristown, 669 D 1
61550 Morton, 10,419 D 3
60053 Morton Grove, 26,369 B 1
62963 Mound City⊙, 1,177 D 6
62964 Mounds, 1,718 D 6
62863 Mount Carmel⊙, 8,096 F 5
61053 Mount Carroll⊙, 2,143 D 1
61054 Mount Morris, 3,173 D 1
62069 Mount Olive, 2,288 D 4
60056 Mount Prospect, 34,995 A 1
62548 Mount Pulaski, 1,677 D 3
62353 Mount Sterling⊙, 2,182 C 4
62864 Mount Vernon⊙, 15,980 E 5
62549 Mount Zion, 2,343 E 4
62550 Moweaqua, 1,687 E 4
62262 Mulberry Grove, 697 D 5
60060 Mundelein, 16,128 E 1
62966 Murphysboro⊙, 10,013 D 6
62668 Murrayville, 595 C 4
60540 Naperville, 23,885 E 2
† 61350 Naplate, 686 E 2
62263 Nashville⊙, 3,027 D 5
62354 Nauvoo, 1,047 B 3
62447 Neoga, 1,270 E 4
60541 Newark, 590 E 2
62264 New Athens, 2,000 D 5
62265 New Baden, 1,953 D 5
62670 New Berlin, 754 D 4
61272 New Boston, 706 B 2
62867 New Haven, 606 E 6
60451 New Lenox, 2,855 F 2
61942 Newman, 1,018 F 4
62448 Newton⊙, 3,024 E 5
61465 New Windsor, 723 C 2
62551 Niantic, 705 D 4
60648 Niles, 31,432 A 1
62868 Noble, 719 E 5
62075 Nokomis, 2,532 D 4
61761 Normal, 26,396 E 3
† 60601 Norridge, 16,880 B 1
62869 Norris City, 1,319 E 6
60542 North Aurora, 4,833 E 2
60062 Northbrook, 27,297 A 1
60064 North Chicago, 47,275 F 1
60093 Northfield, 5,010 B 1
60164 Northlake, 14,212 A 2
† 61101 North Park, 15,679 D 1
† 61554 North Pekin, 1,886 D 3
60546 North Riverside, 8,097 B 2
† 61373 North Utica (Utica), 974 E 2
60452 Oak Forest, 17,870 B 2
61943 Oakland, 1,012 F 4
* 60453 Oak Lawn, 60,305 B 2
60303 Oak Park, 62,511 B 2
61858 Oakwood, 1,367 F 3
† 62095 Oakwood Heights, 3,229 B 6
62449 Oblong, 1,860 F 5
60460 Odell, 1,076 E 2
62870 Odin, 1,263 D 5
62269 O'Fallon, 7,268 B 6
61348 Oglesby, 4,175 D 2
62271 Okawville, 992 D 5
62969 Olive Branch, 600 D 6
62450 Olney⊙, 8,974 E 5
60461 Olympia Fields, 3,478 B 3
60955 Onarga, 1,436 F 3
61467 Oneida, 728 C 2
61469 Oquawka⊙, 1,352 C 3
62554 Oreana, 1,092 E 4
61061 Oregon⊙, 3,539 D 1
61273 Orion, 1,801 C 2
60462 Orland Park, 6,391 A 2
60543 Oswego, 1,862 E 2
61350 Ottawa⊙, 18,716 E 2
60067 Palatine, 25,904 E 1
62451 Palestine, 1,640 F 4
62674 Palmyra, 776 C 4
60463 Palos Heights, 9,915 A 2
60465 Palos Hills, 6,629 A 2
60464 Palos Park, 3,297 A 2
62557 Pana, 6,326 D 4
61944 Paris⊙, 9,971 F 4
60466 Park Forest, 30,638 B 3
60068 Park Ridge, 42,466 A 1
62875 Patoka, 562 D 5
62558 Pawnee, 1,936 D 4
61353 Pawpaw, 846 E 2
60957 Paxton⊙, 4,373 E 3
62360 Payson, 589 B 4
61063 Pecatonica, 1,781 D 1
61554 Pekin⊙, 31,375 D 3
* 61601 Peoria⊙, 126,963 D 3
Peoria, ‡341,979 D 3
61614 Peoria Heights, 7,943 D 3
60468 Peotone, 2,345 F 2
62272 Percy, 967 D 5
61354 Peru, 11,772 D 2
62675 Petersburg⊙, 2,632 D 4
61864 Philo, 1,022 E 3
† 60426 Phoenix, 3,596 B 2
62274 Pinckneyville⊙, 3,377 D 5
60959 Piper City, 817 E 3
62363 Pittsfield⊙, 4,244 C 4
60544 Plainfield, 2,928 E 2
60545 Plano, 4,664 E 2
62366 Pleasant Hill, 1,064 C 4
62677 Pleasant Plains, 644 D 4
62367 Plymouth, 740 C 3
62275 Pocahontas, 764 D 5
61074 Polo, 2,542 D 1
61764 Pontiac⊙, 9,031 E 3
61065 Poplar Grove, 607 E 1
61275 Port Byron, 1,222 C 2
60469 Posen, 5,498 B 2
61865 Potomac, 909 F 3
61470 Prairie City, 630 C 3
62277 Prairie du Rocher, 658 C 5
61356 Princeton⊙, 6,959 D 2
61559 Princeville, 1,455 D 3
61277 Prophetstown, 1,915 D 2
60070 Prospect Heights, 13,333 A 1
62301 Quincy⊙, 45,288 B 4
62080 Ramsey, 830 D 4
60960 Rankin, 727 F 3
61866 Rantoul, 25,562 E 3
61278 Rapids City, 656 C 2
62560 Raymond, 890 D 4
62278 Red Bud, 2,559 D 5
61279 Reynolds, 610 C 2
60071 Richmond, 1,153 E 1
60471 Richton Park, 2,558 B 3
61870 Ridge Farm, 1,015 F 4
62979 Ridgway, 1,160 E 6
60627 Riverdale, 15,806 B 2
60305 River Forest, 13,402 B 2
60171 River Grove, 11,465 A 2
60546 Riverside, 10,432 B 2
62561 Riverton, 2,090 D 4
61561 Roanoke, 2,040 D 3
60472 Robbins, 9,641 B 2
62454 Robinson⊙, 7,178 F 5
61068 Rochelle, 8,594 D 2
62563 Rochester, 1,667 D 4
60436 Rockdale, 2,085 E 2
61071 Rock Falls, 10,287 D 2
* 61101 Rockford⊙, 147,370 D 1
Rockford, ‡272,063 D 1
61201 Rock Island⊙, 50,166 C 2
Rock Island-Moline-Davenport, ‡362,638 C 2
61072 Rockton, 2,099 E 1
60008 Rolling Meadows, 19,178 A 1
61562 Rome, 1,919 D 3
† 60441 Romeoville, 12,674 E 2
62082 Roodhouse, 2,357 C 4
61073 Roscoe, 949 D 1
60018 Rosemont, 4,360 A 1
61473 Roseville, 1,111 C 3
† 62024 Rosewood Heights, 3,391 B 6
62982 Rosiclare, 1,421 E 6
60963 Rossville, 1,420 F 3
62084 Roxana, 1,882 B 6
62983 Royalton, 1,166 D 6
62681 Rushville⊙, 3,300 C 3
60964 Saint Anne, 1,271 F 2
60174 Saint Charles, 12,928 E 2
61563 Saint David, 773 C 3
62458 Saint Elmo, 1,676 E 4
62460 Saint Francisville, 997 F 5
62281 Saint Jacob, 659 D 5
61873 Saint Joseph, 1,554 E 3
62881 Salem⊙, 6,187 E 5
62882 Sandoval, 1,332 D 5
60548 Sandwich, 5,056 E 2
62682 San Jose, 681 D 3
60411 Sauk Village, 7,479 F 2
61074 Savanna, 4,942 C 1
61874 Savoy, 592 E 3
61770 Saybrook, 814 E 3
60172 Schaumburg, 18,730 E 1
60176 Schiller Park, 12,712 A 1
† 62049 Schram City, 657 D 4
61360 Seneca, 1,781 E 2
62884 Sesser, 2,125 D 5
61875 Seymour, 850 E 3
60550 Shabbona, 730 E 2
61078 Shannon, 848 D 1
62984 Shawneetown⊙, 1,742 E 6
61361 Sheffield, 1,038 D 2
62565 Shelbyville⊙, 4,597 E 4
60966 Sheldon, 1,455 F 3
60551 Sheridan, 724 E 2
61281 Sherrard, 808 C 2
† 62220 Shiloh, 945 B 6
61876 Sidell, 645 F 4
61877 Sidney, 915 E 3
61282 Silvis, 5,907 C 2
60076 Skokie, 68,627 B 1
62285 Smithton, 847 C 5
60552 Somonauk, 1,112 E 2
62086 Sorento, 625 D 5
61080 South Beloit, 3,804 E 1
60411 South Chicago Heights, 4,923 B 3
60177 South Elgin, 4,289 E 2
60473 South Holland, 23,931 B 2
62650 South Jacksonville, 2,950 C 4
61564 South Pekin, 955 D 3
60474 South Wilmington, 725 E 2
61565 Sparland, 585 D 2
62286 Sparta, 4,307 D 5
* 62701 Springfield (cap.)⊙, 91,753 D 4
Springfield, ‡161,335 D 4
61362 Spring Valley, 5,605 D 2
61774 Stanford, 657 D 3
62088 Staunton, 4,396 D 5
62288 Steeleville, 1,957 D 6
60475 Steger, 8,104 F 2
61081 Sterling, 16,113 D 2
62463 Stewardson, 729 E 4
60402 Stickney, 6,601 B 2
61084 Stillman Valley, 871 D 1
61085 Stockton, 1,930 C 1
60165 Stone Park, 4,451 A 2
62567 Stonington, 1,096 D 4
60103 Streamwood, 18,176 E 1
61364 Streator, 15,600 E 2
61480 Stronghurst, 836 C 3
61951 Sullivan⊙, 4,112 E 4
60501 Summit, 11,569 B 2
62466 Sumner, 1,201 F 5
62221 Swansea, 5,432 B 6
60178 Sycamore⊙, 7,843 E 2
62688 Tallula, 643 D 4
62888 Tamaroa, 799 D 5
62988 Tamms, 645 D 6
61283 Tampico, 838 D 2
62089 Taylor Springs, 620 D 4
62568 Taylorville⊙, 10,644 D 4
62467 Teutopolis, 1,249 E 4
62689 Thayer, 616 D 4
61878 Thomasboro, 806 E 3
61285 Thomson, 617 C 2
60476 Thornton, 3,714 B 3
62292 Tilden, 909 D 5
† 61832 Tilton, 2,544 F 3
60477 Tinley Park, 12,382 B 2
61368 Tiskilwa, 973 D 2
62468 Toledo⊙, 1,068 E 4
61880 Tolono, 2,027 E 3
61369 Toluca, 1,319 D 2
61370 Tonica, 821 E 2
61483 Toulon⊙, 1,207 D 2
61776 Towanda, 578 E 3
62571 Tower Hill, 683 E 4
61568 Tremont, 1,942 D 3
62293 Trenton, 2,328 D 5
62294 Troy, 2,144 B 6
61953 Tuscola⊙, 3,917 E 4
60180 Union, 579 E 1
61801 Urbana⊙, 32,800 E 3
61373 Utica, 974 E 2
62891 Valier, 628 D 5
62295 Valmeyer, 733 C 5
62471 Vandalia⊙, 5,160 D 5
62090 Venice, 4,680 A 6
61484 Vermont, 947 C 3
61485 Victoria, 782 C 2
62995 Vienna⊙, 1,325 E 6
61956 Villa Grove, 2,605 E 4
60181 Villa Park, 25,891 A 2
61486 Viola, 946 C 2
62690 Virden, 3,504 D 4
62691 Virginia⊙, 1,814 C 4
60083 Wadsworth, 756 F 1
61376 Walnut, 1,295 D 2
† 62801 Wamac, 1,347 D 5
61777 Wapella, 572 E 3
61087 Warren, 1,523 C 1
62573 Warrensburg, 738 D 4
62379 Warsaw, 1,758 B 3
61570 Washburn, 1,173 D 3
61571 Washington, 6,790 D 3
62204 Washington Park, 9,524 B 6
61488 Wataga, 570 C 2
62298 Waterloo⊙, 4,546 C 5
60556 Waterman, 990 E 2
60970 Watseka⊙, 5,294 F 3
60084 Wauconda, 5,460 E 1
60085 Waukegan⊙, 65,269 F 1
62692 Waverly, 1,442 D 4
62895 Wayne City, 985 E 5
61882 Weldon, 553 E 3
61377 Wenona, 1,080 E 2
60153 Westchester, 20,033 A 2
60185 West Chicago, 10,111 E 2
† 62812 West City, 637 E 5
† 60118 West Dundee (Dundee), 3,295 E 1
60558 Western Springs, 12,147 A 2
62474 Westfield, 678 F 4
62896 West Frankfort, 8,836 E 6
60559 Westmont, 8,482 A 2
62476 West Salem, 979 F 5
61883 Westville, 3,655 F 3
60187 Wheaton⊙, 31,138 E 2
60090 Wheeling, 14,746 F 1
62092 White Hall, 2,979 C 4
61489 Williamsfield, 552 C 3
62693 Williamsville, 923 D 4
62997 Willisville, 659 D 6
60480 Willow Springs, 3,318 A 2
60091 Wilmette, 32,134 B 1
60481 Wilmington, 4,335 E 2
62093 Wilsonville, 691 D 4
62694 Winchester⊙, 1,788 C 4
61957 Windsor, 1,126 E 4
† 61465 Windsor (New Windsor), 723 C 2
60190 Winfield, 4,285 E 2
61088 Winnebago, 1,285 D 1
60093 Winnetka, 14,131 B 1
60096 Winthrop Harbor, 4,794 F 1
62094 Witt, 1,040 D 4
60191 Wood Dale, 8,831 A 1
61490 Woodhull, 898 C 2
60515 Woodridge, 11,028 E 2
62095 Wood River, 13,186 B 6
60098 Woodstock⊙, 10,226 E 1
62097 Worden, 1,091 B 6
60482 Worth, 11,999 A 2
61379 Wyanet, 1,005 D 2
61491 Wyoming, 1,563 D 2
61572 Yates City, 840 C 3
60560 Yorkville⊙, 2,049 E 2
62999 Zeigler, 1,940 D 6
60099 Zion, 17,268 F 1

⊙ County seat.
‡ Population of metropolitan area.
† Zip of nearest p.o.
* Multiple zips

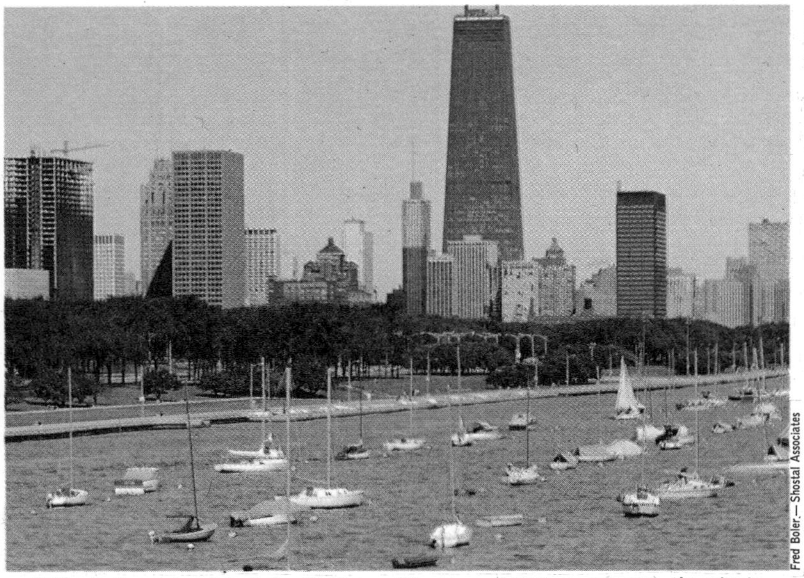

Fred Boler.—Shostal Associates

Sailboats lie anchored in Lake Michigan while many of their owners turn the wheels of industry behind Chicago's steel and glass facade.

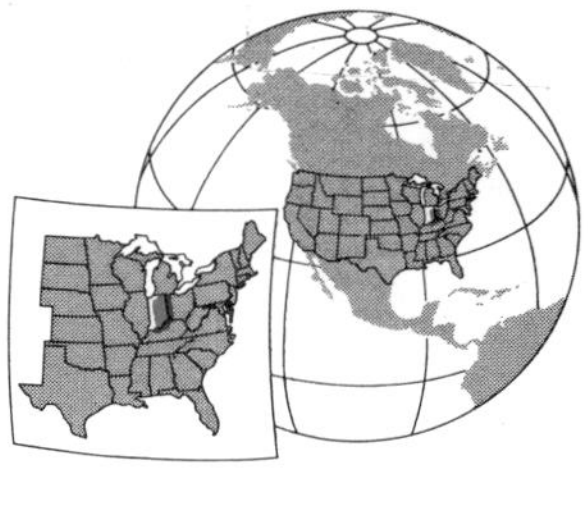

AREA 36,291 sq. mi.
POPULATION 5,193,669 ('70); 5,490,179 ('80)
CAPITAL Indianapolis
LARGEST CITY Indianapolis
HIGHEST POINT 1,257 ft. (Wayne County)
SETTLED IN 1730
ADMITTED TO UNION December 11, 1816
POPULAR NAME Hoosier State
STATE FLOWER Peony
STATE BIRD Cardinal

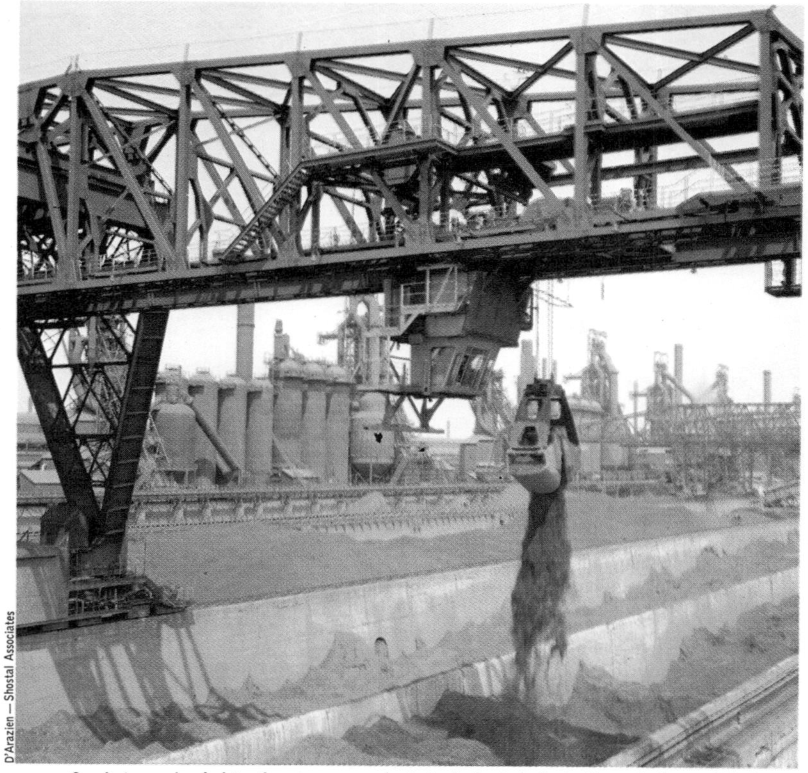

D'Arazien—Shostal Associates

Ore being unloaded in the storage yard at steel plant docks in Gary, Indiana. Aided by the state's outstanding natural supply of limestone, mills in the Lake Michigan area produce more than 15 million tons of steel yearly.

COUNTIES

Adams, 26,871 H 3
Allen, 280,455 G 2
Bartholomew, 57,022 F 6
Benton, 11,262 C 3
Blackford, 15,888 G 4
Boone, 30,870 E 4
Brown, 9,057 E 6
Carroll, 17,734 D 3
Cass, 40,456 E 3
Clark, 75,876 F 8
Clay, 23,933 C 6
Clinton, 30,547 E 4
Crawford, 8,033 E 8
Daviess, 26,602 C 7
Dearborn, 29,430 H 6
Decatur, 22,738 G 6
De Kalb, 30,837 H 2
Delaware, 129,219 G 4
Dubois, 30,934 D 8
Elkhart, 126,529 F 1
Fayette, 26,216 G 5
Floyd, 55,622 F 8
Fountain, 18,257 C 4
Franklin, 16,943 G 6
Fulton, 16,984 E 2
Gibson, 30,444 B 8
Grant, 83,955 F 3
Greene, 26,894 D 6
Hamilton, 54,532 E 4
Hancock, 35,096 F 5
Harrison, 20,423 E 8
Hendricks, 53,974 D 5
Henry, 52,603 G 5
Howard, 83,198 E 4
Huntington, 34,970 G 3
Jackson, 33,187 E 7
Jasper, 20,429 C 2
Jay, 23,575 G 4
Jefferson, 27,006 G 7
Jennings, 19,454 F 7
Johnson, 61,138 E 6
Knox, 41,546 C 7
Kosciusko, 48,127 F 2
Lagrange, 20,890 G 1
Lake, 546,253 C 2
LaPorte, 105,342 D 1
Lawrence, 38,038 E 7
Madison, 138,451 F 4
Marion, 792,299 E 5
Marshall, 34,986 E 2
Martin, 10,969 D 7
Miami, 39,246 E 3
Monroe, 84,849 D 6
Montgomery, 33,930 D 4
Morgan, 44,176 E 6
Newton, 11,606 C 3
Noble, 31,382 G 2
Ohio, 4,289 H 7
Orange, 16,968 E 7
Owen, 12,163 D 6
Parke, 14,600 C 5
Perry, 19,075 D 8
Pike, 12,281 C 8
Porter, 87,114 C 2
Posey, 21,740 B 8
Pulaski, 12,534 D 2
Putnam, 26,932 D 5
Randolph, 28,915 G 4
Ripley, 21,138 G 6
Rush, 20,352 G 5
Saint Joseph, 245,045 E 1
Scott, 17,144 F 7
Shelby, 37,797 F 5
Spencer, 17,134 C 9
Starke, 19,280 D 2
Steuben, 20,159 G 1
Sullivan, 19,889 C 6
Switzerland, 6,306 G 7
Tippecanoe, 109,378 D 4
Tipton, 16,650 E 4
Union, 6,582 H 5
Vanderburgh, 168,772 B 8
Vermillion, 16,793 C 5
Vigo, 114,528 C 6
Wabash, 35,553 F 3
Warren, 8,705 C 4
Warrick, 27,972 C 8
Washington, 19,278 E 7
Wayne, 79,109 G 5
Wells, 23,821 G 3
White, 20,995 D 3
Whitley, 23,395 F 2

CITIES and TOWNS

Zip Name/Pop. Key

47240 Adams, 300 F 6
† 46947 Adamsboro, 325 E 3
46102 Advance, 561 D 5
46910 Akron, 1,019 E 2
47320 Albany, 2,293 G 4
46701 Albion⊙, 1,498 G 2
† 47283 Alert, 210 F 6
46001 Alexandria, 5,097 F 4
† 46738 Altona, 209 G 2
47917 Ambia, 300 C 4
46911 Amboy, 473 F 3
† 46131 Amity, 400 E 6
46103 Amo, 422 D 5
* 46011 Anderson⊙, 70,787 F 4
Anderson, ‡138,451 F 4
† 47024 Andersonville, 250 G 5
46702 Andrews, 1,207 F 3
46703 Angola⊙, 5,117 G 1
46030 Arcadia, 1,338 E 4
46704 Arcola, 325 G 2
† 46624 Ardmore, 800 E 1
46501 Argos, 1,393 E 2
46104 Arlington, 550 F 5
46705 Ashley, 721 G 1
46031 Atlanta, 620 E 4
47918 Attica, 4,262 C 4
46502 Atwood, 300 F 2
46706 Auburn⊙, 7,337 G 2
47001 Aurora, 4,293 H 6
47102 Austin, 4,902 F 7
46710 Avilla, 881 G 2
47420 Avoca, 400 D 7
46105 Bainbridge, 703 D 5
46106 Bargersville, 873 E 5
47006 Batesville, 3,799 G 6
47920 Battle Ground, 818 D 3
47421 Bedford⊙, 13,087 E 7
46107 Beech Grove, 13,468 E 5
† 46526 Benton, 221 F 2
46711 Berne, 2,988 H 3
46301 Beverly Shores, 946 C 1
47512 Bicknell, 3,717 C 7
46713 Bippus, 220 F 3
47513 Birdseye, 404 D 8
† 46401 Blackoak, 9,624 C 1
47831 Blanford, 700 B 5
47170 Blocher, 350 F 7
47424 Bloomfield⊙, 2,565 D 6
47832 Bloomingdale, 391 C 5
47401 Bloomington⊙, 42,890 D 6
† 47360 Blountsville, 220 G 4
† 46176 Blue Ridge, 236 F 5
46714 Bluffton⊙, 8,297 G 3
46110 Boggstown, 200 F 5
46302 Boone Grove, 225 C 2
47601 Boonville⊙, 5,736 C 8
47106 Borden, 337 F 8
47324 Boston, 210 H 5
47921 Boswell, 998 C 3
46504 Bourbon, 1,606 E 2
47833 Bowling Green, 200 D 6
47107 Bradford, 400 E 8
47834 Brazil⊙, 8,163 C 5
46506 Bremen, 3,487 E 2
47836 Bridgeton, 350 C 5
† 45030 Bright, 450 H 6
46720 Brimfield, 258 G 2
46913 Bringhurst, 250 E 3
46507 Bristol, 1,100 F 1
† 47354 Bronson (Losantville), 212 G 4
47922 Brook, 919 C 3
46111 Brooklyn, 911 E 5
47923 Brookston, 1,232 D 3
47012 Brookville⊙, 2,864 G 6
46112 Brownsburg, 5,186 E 5
47220 Brownstown⊙, 2,376 F 7
47325 Brownsville, 285 H 5
47516 Bruceville, 627 C 7
47326 Bryant, 320 G 3
47924 Buck Creek, 260 D 4
47517 Buckskin, 275 C 8
47925 Buffalo, 350 D 3
46914 Bunker Hill, 956 E 3
46508 Burket, 210 F 2
46915 Burlington, 685 E 4
47926 Burnettsville, 510 D 3
47222 Burney, 344 F 6
† 46401 Burns Harbor, 1,284 C 1
46916 Burrows, 259 E 3
46721 Butler, 2,394 H 2
47223 Butlerville, 275 F 6
† 46371 Byron, 200 C 5
† 47362 Cadiz, 207 G 5
47327 Cambridge City, 2,481 G 5
46917 Camden, 577 D 3
47108 Campbellsburg, 678 E 7
47520 Cannelton⊙, 2,280 D 9
47837 Carbon, 344 C 5
47838 Carlisle, 714 C 7
46032 Carmel, 6,568 E 5
46114 Cartersburg, 400 E 5
46115 Carthage, 946 F 5
† 47460 Cataract, 200 D 6
47928 Cayuga, 1,090 C 5
47016 Cedar Grove, 248 H 6
46303 Cedar Lake, 7,589 C 2
47521 Celestine, 300 D 8
† 47842 Centenary, 225 B 5
46918 Center, 310 E 4
47840 Centerpoint, 275 C 6
46116 Centerton, 250 E 5
47330 Centerville, 2,380 H 5
47929 Chalmers, 544 D 3
47610 Chandler, 2,032 C 8
47111 Charlestown, 5,890 F 8
46117 Charlottesville, 500 F 5
† 47138 Chelsea, 200 F 7
46017 Chesterfield, 3,001 F 4
46304 Chesterton, 6,177 D 1
47611 Chrisney, 550 C 8
46723 Churubusco, 1,528 G 2
46034 Cicero, 1,378 E 4
47225 Clarksburg, 347 G 6
47930 Clarks Hill, 741 D 4
47130 Clarksville, 13,806 F 8
47841 Clay City, 900 C 6
46510 Claypool, 468 F 2
46118 Clayton, 736 D 5
47426 Clear Creek, 250 E 6
† 46737 Clear Lake, 271 H 1
47226 Clifford, 275 F 6
47842 Clinton, 5,340 C 5
46120 Cloverdale, 870 D 5
47427 Coal City, 300 D 6
47845 Coalmont, 400 C 6
46121 Coatesville, 453 D 5
47931 Colburn, 300 D 3
46035 Colfax, 633 D 4
47978 Collegeville, 1,700 C 3
46725 Columbia City⊙, 4,911 G 2
47201 Columbus⊙, 27,141 E 6
47331 Connersville⊙, 17,604 G 5
46919 Converse, 1,163 F 3
47228 Cortland, 200 F 7
46730 Corunna, 359 G 2
47112 Corydon⊙, 2,719 E 8
47932 Covington⊙, 2,641 C 4
† 47302 Cowan, 428 G 4
47522 Crane, 339 D 7
47933 Crawfordsville⊙, 13,842 D 4
46732 Cromwell, 475 F 2
47229 Crothersville, 1,663 F 7
46307 Crown Point⊙, 10,931 C 2
46511 Culver, 1,783 E 2
46229 Cumberland, 479 E 5
47612 Cynthiana, 793 B 8
47523 Dale, 1,113 D 8
47334 Daleville, 1,730 F 4
47847 Dana, 720 C 5
46122 Danville⊙, 3,771 D 5
47940 Darlington, 802 D 4
47941 Dayton, 840 D 4
46733 Decatur⊙, 8,445 H 3
47524 Decker, 268 B 7
† 46917 Deer Creek, 250 E 3
46923 Delphi⊙, 2,582 D 3
46310 Demotte, 1,697 C 2
46926 Denver, 566 E 3
47230 Deputy, 255 F 7
47302 Desoto, 385 G 4
47018 Dillsboro, 840 G 6
46513 Donaldson, 250 E 2
† 47118 Doolittle Mills, 200 D 8
47335 Dublin, 1,021 G 5
47525 Dubois, 500 D 8
47848 Dugger, 1,150 C 6
† 46304 Dune Acres, 301 C 1
47336 Dunkirk, 3,465 G 4
† 46514 Dunlap, 1,900 F 1
47337 Dunreith, 200 F 5
47231 Dupont, 357 G 7
46311 Dyer, 4,906 C 1
† 46074 Eagletown, 365 E 4
47942 Earl Park, 478 C 3
46312 East Chicago, 46,982 C 1
47019 East Enterprise, 250 H 7
46405 East Gary, 9,858 C 1
† 47370 East Germantown (Pershing), 447 G 5
47338 Eaton, 1,594 G 4
47116 Eckerty, 200 D 8
47339 Economy, 285 G 5
† 46011 Edgewood, 2,326 F 4
46124 Edinburg, 4,906 E 6
47528 Edwardsport, 482 C 7
† 47150 Edwardsville, 700 F 8
47613 Elberfeld, 834 C 8
47232 Elizabethtown, 519 F 6
46514 Elkhart, 43,152 F 1
47429 Ellettsville, 1,627 D 6
47529 Elnora, 873 C 7
† 47018 Elrod, 200 G 6
† 47901 Elston, 500 D 4
46036 Elwood, 11,196 F 4
46125 Eminence, 200 D 5
47118 English⊙, 664 E 8
46524 Etna Green, 516 E 2
† 47928 Eugene, 300 B 5
* 47701 Evansville⊙, 138,764 C 9
Evansville, ‡232,775 C 9
46126 Fairland, 950 F 5
46928 Fairmount, 3,427 F 4
† 47842 Fairview Park, 1,067 C 5
47850 Farmersburg, 962 C 6
47340 Farmland, 1,262 G 4
47532 Ferdinand, 1,432 D 8
46128 Fillmore, 600 D 5
46129 Finly, 350 F 5
46038 Fishers, 628 E 5
47234 Flat Rock, 289 F 6
46929 Flora, 1,877 E 3
47119 Floyds Knobs, 350 F 8
47851 Fontanet, 200 C 5
46039 Forest, 400 E 4
47533 Fort Branch, 2,535 B 8
46040 Fortville, 2,460 F 5
* 46801 Fort Wayne⊙, 177,671 G 2
Fort Wayne, ‡280,455 G 2
47341 Fountain City, 852 H 5
46130 Fountaintown, 225 F 5
47944 Fowler⊙, 2,643 C 3
46930 Fowlerton, 337 F 4
47946 Francesville, 1,015 D 3
47534 Francisco, 621 B 8
46041 Frankfort⊙, 14,956 E 4
46131 Franklin⊙, 11,477 E 6
46044 Frankton, 1,796 F 4
47120 Fredericksburg, 207 E 8
47431 Freedom, 262 D 6
47535 Freelandville, 710 C 7
47235 Freetown, 550 E 7
46737 Fremont, 1,043 H 1
47432 French Lick, 2,059 D 7
46931 Fulton, 372 E 3
† 47119 Galena, 250 F 8
46932 Galveston, 1,284 E 3
46738 Garrett, 4,715 G 2
* 46401 Gary, 175,415 C 1
Gary-Hammond-East Chicago, ‡633,367 C 1
46933 Gas City, 5,742 F 4
47342 Gaston, 928 G 4
46740 Geneva, 1,100 H 3
47537 Gentryville, 281 C 8
47122 Georgetown, 1,273 F 8
47343 Glenwood, 452 G 5
† 47567 Glezen, 300 C 8
46045 Goldsmith, 235 E 4
47948 Goodland, 1,176 C 3
46526 Goshen⊙, 17,171 F 1
47433 Gosport, 692 D 6
46741 Grabill, 570 H 2
47615 Grandview, 696 C 9
46530 Granger, 200 E 1
46135 Greencastle⊙, 8,852 D 5
† 47025 Greendale, 3,783 H 6
46140 Greenfield⊙, 9,986 F 5
47344 Greensboro, 225 G 5
47240 Greensburg⊙, 8,620 G 6
47345 Greens Fork, 444 H 5
46936 Greentown, 1,870 E 4
47124 Greenville, 611 F 8
46142 Greenwood, 11,408 E 5
46319 Griffith, 18,168 C 1
46144 Gwynneville, 240 F 5
47346 Hagerstown, 2,059 G 5
46742 Hamilton, 537 H 1
46532 Hamlet, 761 D 2
* 46320 Hammond, 107,790 B 1
46340 Hanna, 500 D 2
47243 Hanover, 3,018 F 7
47125 Hardinsburg, 263 E 8
46743 Harlan, 840 H 2
47853 Harmony, 750 C 5
47434 Harrodsburg, 400 D 6
47348 Hartford City⊙, 8,207 G 4
47244 Hartsville, 434 F 6
47617 Hatfield, 800 C 9
47539 Haubstadt, 1,171 B 8
† 47546 Haysville, 585 D 8
47540 Hazleton, 416 B 8
46341 Hebron, 1,624 C 2
47436 Heltonville, 400 E 7
46937 Hemlock, 200 F 4
47126 Henryville, 1,500 F 7
46322 Highland, 24,947 B 1
46046 Hillisburg, 225 E 4
47949 Hillsboro, 505 C 4
47854 Hillsdale, 500 C 5
46745 Hoagland, 530 H 3
46342 Hobart, 21,485 C 1
46047 Hobbs, 400 F 4
47541 Holland, 662 C 8
47023 Holton, 610 G 6
46146 Homer, 245 F 5
47246 Hope, 1,603 F 6
† 46069 Hortonville, 240 E 4
46746 Howe, 800 G 1
46747 Hudson, 464 G 1
46552 Hudson Lake, 1,134 D 1
46748 Huntertown, 775 G 2
47542 Huntingburg, 4,794 D 8
46750 Huntington⊙, 16,217 G 3
† 46064 Huntsville, 450 G 4
47437 Huron, 580 D 7
47855 Hymera, 907 C 6
47950 Idaville, 600 D 3
* 46201 Indianapolis (cap.)⊙ 744,624 E 5
Indianapolis, ‡1,109,882 E 5
46048 Ingalls, 888 F 5
47545 Ireland, 527 C 8
46147 Jamestown, 938 D 5
47438 Jasonville, 2,335 C 6
47546 Jasper⊙, 8,641 D 8
47130 Jeffersonville⊙, 20,008 F 8
† 47565 Johnson, 250 B 8
† 46074 Jolietville, 265 E 4
46938 Jonesboro, 2,466 F 4
47247 Jonesville, 202 F 6
46049 Kempton, 469 E 4
46755 Kendallville, 6,838 G 2
47351 Kennard, 518 G 5
47951 Kentland⊙, 1,864 C 3
46939 Kewanna, 614 E 2
46759 Keystone, 200 G 3
46760 Kimmell, 350 F 2
† 47952 Kingman, 530 C 5
46345 Kingsbury, 314 D 1
46346 Kingsford Heights, 1,200 D 2
46050 Kirklin, 736 E 4
46148 Knightstown, 2,456 F 5
47857 Knightsville, 788 C 5
46534 Knox⊙, 3,519 D 2
46901 Kokomo⊙, 44,042 E 4
† 46574 Koontz Lake, 900 D 2
46347 Kouts, 1,388 C 2
46348 La Crosse, 696 D 2
47954 Ladoga, 1,099 D 5
* 47901 Lafayette⊙, 44,955 D 4
Lafayette-West Lafayette, ‡109,378 D 4
46940 La Fontaine, 793 F 3
46761 Lagrange⊙, 2,053 F 1
46941 Lagro, 552 F 3
† 46703 Lake James, 400 H 1
46943 Laketon, 500 F 3
46349 Lake Village, 600 C 2
46536 Lakeville, 712 E 1
† 46567 Lake Wawasee, 600 F 2
47136 Lanesville, 586 E 8
46763 Laotto, 312 G 2
46537 Lapaz, 604 E 2
46051 Lapel, 1,725 F 4
46350 LaPorte⊙, 22,140 D 1
46764 Larwill, 324 F 2
47024 Laurel, 753 G 6
46226 Lawrence, 16,646 E 5
47025 Lawrenceburg⊙, 4,636 H 6
47137 Leavenworth, 330 E 8
46052 Lebanon⊙, 9,766 D 4
46538 Leesburg, 561 F 2
46945 Leiters Ford, 250 E 2
46765 Leo, 500 G 2
46355 Leroy, 350 C 2
† 47240 Letts, 247 F 6
47352 Lewisville, 530 G 5
47138 Lexington, 400 F 7
47353 Liberty⊙, 1,831 H 5
46766 Liberty Center, 300 G 3
46946 Liberty Mills, 200 F 2
46767 Ligonier, 3,034 F 2
47955 Linden, 713 D 4
46769 Linn Grove, 300 H 3
47441 Linton, 5,450 C 6
† 46755 Lisbon, 200 G 2
46149 Lizton, 397 D 5
46947 Logansport⊙, 19,255 E 3
† 46360 Long Beach, 2,740 D 1
47553 Loogootee, 2,953 D 7
47354 Losantville, 212 G 4
46356 Lowell, 3,839 C 2
† 46601 Lydick, 1,341 E 1
† 47874 Lyford, 400 C 5
47355 Lynn, 1,360 H 4
47619 Lynnville, 556 C 8
47443 Lyons, 702 C 7
46951 Macy, 273 E 3
47250 Madison⊙, 13,081 G 7
† 47001 Manchester, 250 H 6
46150 Manilla, 300 F 5
† 47872 Mansfield, 200 C 5
47140 Marengo, 767 E 8
47556 Mariah Hill, 275 D 8
† 46176 Marietta, 280 F 6
46952 Marion⊙, 39,607 F 3
46770 Markle, 963 G 3
46056 Markleville, 457 F 5
47859 Marshall, 365 C 5
46151 Martinsville⊙, 9,723 D 6
46957 Matthews, 728 F 4
46154 Maxwell, 245 F 5
46055 McCordsville, 500 F 5
47860 Mecca, 800 C 5
47957 Medaryville, 732 D 2
47260 Medora, 788 E 7
47958 Mellott, 325 C 4
47143 Memphis, 324 F 8
46539 Mentone, 830 E 2
47861 Merom, 305 B 6
46410 Merrillville, 15,918 C 2
47030 Metamora, 400 G 6
† 46703 Metz, 200 H 1
46958 Mexico, 850 E 3
46959 Miami, 420 E 3
46360 Michigan City, 39,369 C 1

(continued on following page)

Topography

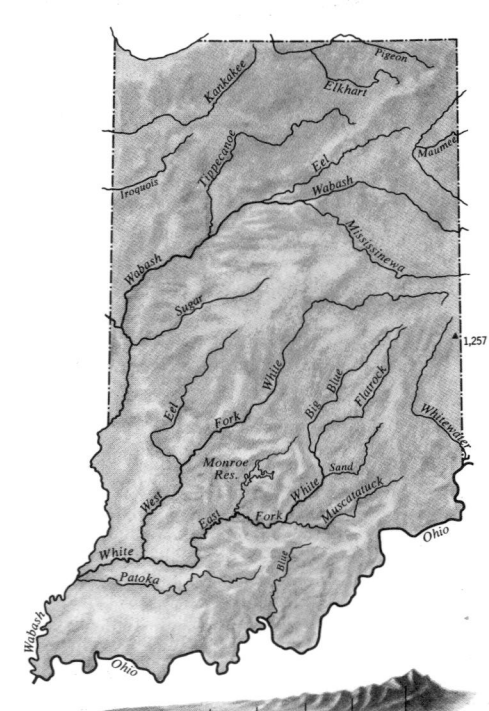

Agriculture, Industry and Resources

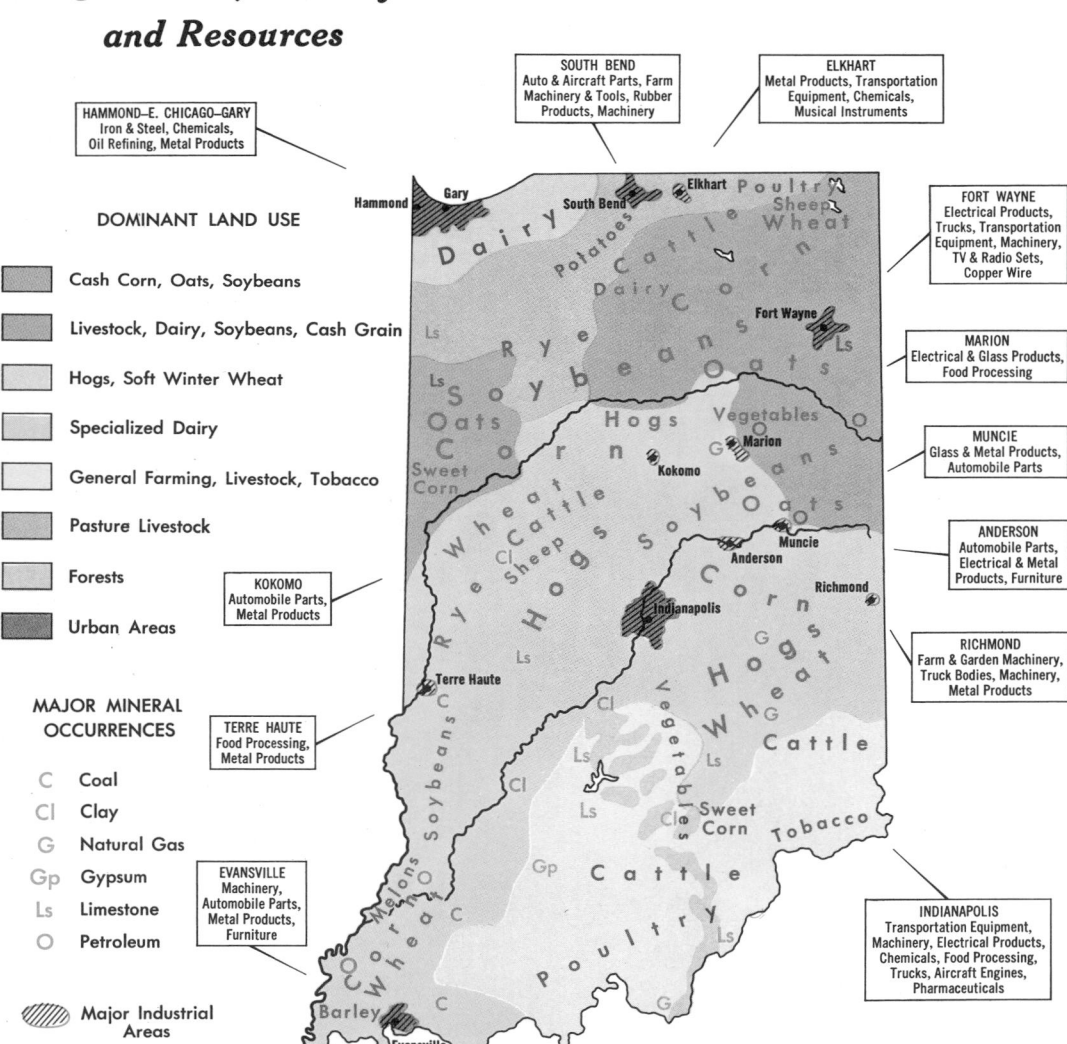

DOMINANT LAND USE
- Cash Corn, Oats, Soybeans
- Livestock, Dairy, Soybeans, Cash Grain
- Hogs, Soft Winter Wheat
- Specialized Dairy
- General Farming, Livestock, Tobacco
- Pasture Livestock
- Forests
- Urban Areas

MAJOR MINERAL OCCURRENCES
C Coal
Cl Clay
G Natural Gas
Gp Gypsum
Ls Limestone
O Petroleum
Major Industrial Areas

HAMMOND–E. CHICAGO–GARY: Iron & Steel, Chemicals, Oil Refining, Metal Products
SOUTH BEND: Auto & Aircraft Parts, Farm Machinery & Tools, Rubber Products, Machinery
ELKHART: Metal Products, Transportation Equipment, Chemicals, Musical Instruments
FORT WAYNE: Electrical Products, Trucks, Transportation Equipment, Machinery, TV & Radio Sets, Copper Wire
MARION: Electrical & Glass Products, Food Processing
MUNCIE: Glass & Metal Products, Automobile Parts
ANDERSON: Automobile Parts, Electrical & Metal Products, Furniture
RICHMOND: Farm & Garden Machinery, Truck Bodies, Machinery, Metal Products
KOKOMO: Automobile Parts, Metal Products
TERRE HAUTE: Food Processing, Metal Products
EVANSVILLE: Machinery, Automobile Parts, Metal Products, Furniture
INDIANAPOLIS: Transportation Equipment, Machinery, Electrical Products, Chemicals, Food Processing, Trucks, Aircraft Engines, Pharmaceuticals

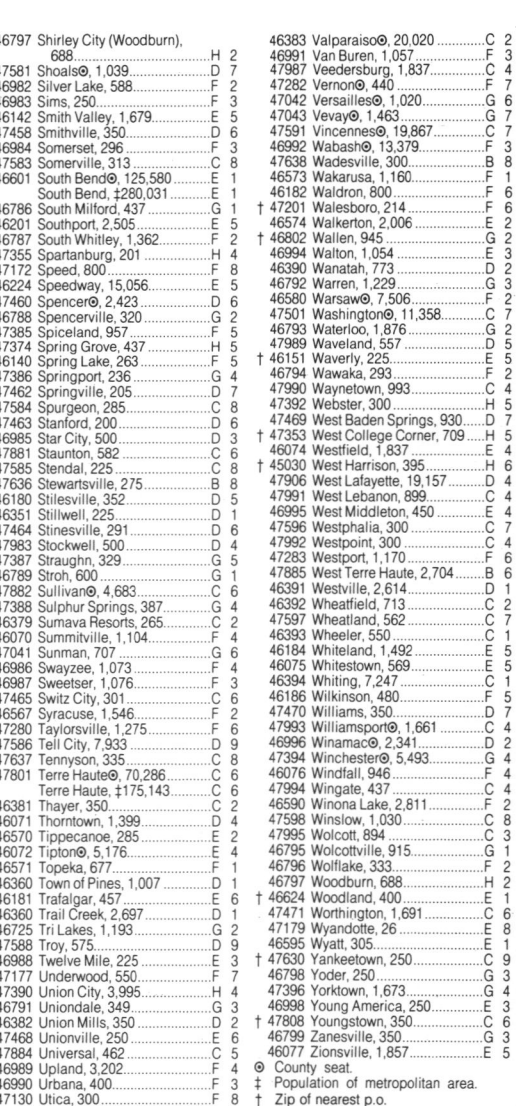

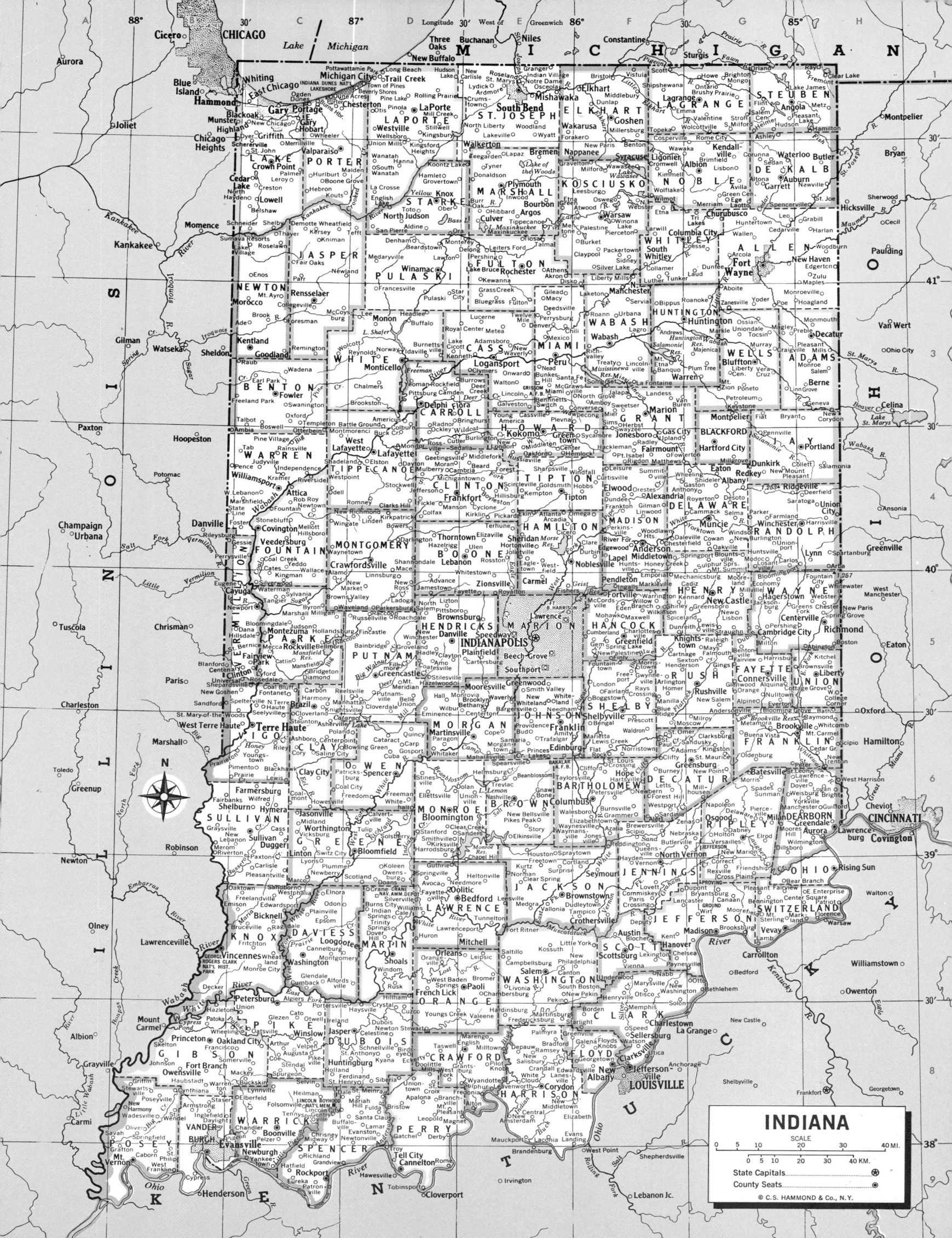

INDIANA

SCALE
0 5 10   20   30   40 MI.
0 5 10   20   30   40 KM.
State Capitals...............⊛
County Seats................⊙
© C.S. HAMMOND & Co., N.Y.

COUNTIES

Adair, 9,487	E 6	
Adams, 6,322	D 6	
Allamakee, 14,968	L 2	
Appanoose, 15,007	H 7	
Audubon, 9,595	D 5	
Benton, 22,885	J 4	
Black Hawk, 132,916	J 4	
Boone, 26,470	F 5	
Bremer, 22,737	J 3	
Buchanan, 21,746	K 4	
Buena Vista, 20,693	C 3	
Butler, 16,953	H 3	
Calhoun, 14,287	D 4	
Carroll, 22,912	D 4	
Cass, 17,007	D 6	
Cedar, 17,655	L 5	
Cerro Gordo, 49,335	G 2	
Cherokee, 17,269	B 3	
Chickasaw, 14,969	J 2	
Clarke, 7,581	F 6	
Clay, 18,464	C 2	
Clayton, 20,606	L 3	
Clinton, 56,749	M 5	
Crawford, 18,780	C 4	
Dallas, 26,085	E 5	
Davis, 8,207	J 7	
Decatur, 9,737	F 7	
Delaware, 18,770	L 4	
Des Moines, 46,982	L 7	
Dickinson, 12,565	C 2	
Dubuque, 90,609	M 4	
Emmet, 14,009	D 2	
Fayette, 26,898	K 3	
Floyd, 19,860	H 2	
Franklin, 13,255	G 3	
Fremont, 9,282	B 7	
Greene, 12,716	E 5	
Grundy, 14,119	H 4	
Guthrie, 12,243	D 5	
Hamilton, 18,383	F 4	
Hancock, 13,227	F 2	
Hardin, 22,248	H 4	
Harrison, 16,240	B 5	
Henry, 18,114	K 6	
Howard, 11,442	J 2	
Humboldt, 12,519	E 3	
Ida, 9,190	C 4	
Iowa, 15,419	J 5	
Jackson, 20,839	M 4	
Jasper, 35,425	G 5	
Jefferson, 15,774	K 6	
Johnson, 72,127	K 5	
Jones, 19,868	L 4	
Keokuk, 13,943	J 6	
Kossuth, 22,937	E 2	
Lee, 42,996	L 7	
Linn, 163,213	K 4	
Louisa, 10,682	L 6	
Lucas, 10,163	G 6	
Lyon, 13,340	A 2	
Madison, 11,558	E 6	
Mahaska, 22,177	H 6	
Marion, 26,352	G 6	
Marshall, 41,076	G 4	
Mills, 11,606	B 6	
Mitchell, 13,108	H 2	
Monona, 12,069	B 4	
Monroe, 9,357	H 7	
Montgomery, 12,781	C 6	
Muscatine, 37,181	L 5	
O'Brien, 17,522	B 2	
Osceola, 8,555	B 2	
Page, 18,507	C 7	
Palo Alto, 13,289	D 2	
Plymouth, 24,312	A 3	
Pocahontas, 12,729	D 3	
Polk, 286,101	F 5	
Pottawattamie, 86,991	B 6	
Poweshiek, 18,803	H 5	
Ringgold, 6,373	E 7	
Sac, 15,573	C 4	
Scott, 142,687	M 5	
Shelby, 15,528	C 5	
Sioux, 27,996	A 2	
Story, 62,783	F 4	
Tama, 20,147	H 4	
Taylor, 8,790	D 7	
Union, 13,557	E 7	
Van Buren, 8,643	K 7	
Wapello, 42,149	J 6	
Warren, 27,432	G 6	
Washington, 18,967	K 6	
Wayne, 8,405	G 7	
Webster, 48,391	E 4	
Winnebago, 12,990	F 2	
Winneshiek, 21,758	K 2	
Woodbury, 103,052	B 4	
Worth, 8,968	G 2	
Wright, 17,294	F 3	

CITIES and TOWNS

Zip	Name/Pop.	Key
50601	Ackley, 1,794	G 3
50002	Adair, 750	D 6
50003	Adel⊙, 2,419	E 5
50830	Afton, 823	E 6
52530	Agency, 610	J 7
52201	Ainsworth, 455	K 6
51001	Akron, 1,324	A 3
50510	Albert City, 683	C 3
52531	Albia, 4,151	H 6
52720	Atalissa, 244	L 5
50005	Albion, 772	H 4
52202	Alburnett, 418	K 4
50006	Alden, 876	G 4
50420	Alexander, 249	G 3
50511	Algona⊙, 6,032	E 2
50602	Allison⊙, 1,071	H 3
51002	Alta, 1,717	C 3
50603	Alta Vista, 283	J 2
51003	Alton, 1,018	A 3
50009	Altoona, 2,854	G 5
52203	Amana, 610	K 5
50010	Ames, 39,505	F 4
52205	Anamosa⊙, 4,389	L 4
50020	Andrew, 335	M 4
50021	Ankeny, 9,151	F 5
51004	Anthon, 711	B 4
50020	Anita, 1,101	D 6
50514	Armstrong, 1,061	D 2
51331	Arnolds Park, 970	C 2
51431	Arthur, 273	C 4
52001	Asbury, 410	M 4
51232	Ashton, 483	B 2
52720	Atalissa, 244	L 5
52206	Atkins, 581	K 4
50022	Atlantic⊙, 7,306	D 6
50025	Audubon⊙, 2,907	D 5
51433	Auburn, 329	C 4
51005	Aurelia, 1,065	B 3
50607	Aurora, 229	K 3
51521	Avoca, 1,535	C 6
50515	Ayrshire, 243	D 2
50516	Badger, 465	E 3
50026	Bagley, 365	E 5
50517	Bancroft, 1,103	E 2
52027	Barnes City, 238	H 6
52533	Batavia, 525	J 7
51006	Battle Creek, 837	B 4
50028	Baxter, 788	G 5
50029	Bayard, 628	D 5
52534	Beacon, 338	H 6
50609	Beaman, 222	H 4
50833	Bedford⊙, 1,733	D 7
52208	Belle Plaine, 2,810	J 5
52031	Bellevue, 2,336	M 4

Zip	City, Population	Ref
50421	Belmond, 2,358	F 3
52721	Bennett, 385	L 5
52722	Bettendorf, 22,126	N 5
52535	Birmingham, 452	K 7
50034	Blairsburg, 287	F 4
52209	Blairstown, 612	J 5
52536	Blakesburg, 403	H 7
51523	Blencoe, 255	A 5
50836	Blockton, 273	D 7
52537	Bloomfield, 2,718	J 7
52726	Blue Grass, 1,032	M 5
50519	Bode, 372	E 3
52620	Bonaparte, 517	K 7
50035	Bondurant, 462	G 5
50036	Boone◉, 12,468	F 4
50040	Boxholm, 242	E 4
51234	Boyden, 670	B 2
52210	Brandon, 432	K 4
51436	Breda, 518	C 4
52540	Brighton, 632	K 6
50611	Bristow, 230	H 3
50423	Britt, 2,069	F 2
52211	Brooklyn, 1,410	J 5
52728	Buffalo, 1,513	M 6
50424	Buffalo Center, 1,118	F 2
52601	Burlington◉, 32,366	L 7
50522	Burt, 608	E 2
50044	Bussey, 498	H 6
52729	Calamus, 396	M 5
50523	Callender, 421	E 4
52132	Calmar, 1,941	K 2
51009	Calumet, 219	B 3
52730	Camanche, 3,470	N 5
50046	Cambridge, 661	G 5
52542	Cantril, 258	J 7
50047	Carlisle, 2,246	G 6
51401	Carroll◉, 8,716	C 4
51525	Carson, 756	C 6
† 68101	Carter Lake, 3,268	K 3
52033	Cascade, 1,744	L 4
50048	Casey, 561	D 5
52133	Castalia, 210	K 2
51010	Castana, 211	B 4
50613	Cedar Falls, 29,597	H 3
* 52401	Cedar Rapids◉, 110,642	K 5
	Cedar Rapids, ‡163,213	K 5
52213	Center Point, 1,456	K 4
52544	Centerville◉, 6,531	H 7
52214	Central City, 1,116	K 4
50049	Chariton◉, 5,009	G 6
50616	Charles City◉, 9,268	H 3
52731	Charlotte, 444	M 5
51439	Charter Oak, 715	C 4
52215	Chelsea, 381	J 5
51012	Cherokee◉, 7,272	B 3
50050	Churdan, 598	D 4
50627	Cincinnati, 570	G 7
50524	Clare, 249	E 3
52216	Clarence, 915	M 5
51632	Clarinda◉, 5,420	C 7
50525	Clarion◉, 2,972	F 3
50619	Clarksville, 1,360	H 3
50840	Clearfield, 430	D 7
50428	Clear Lake, 6,430	G 2
51014	Cleghorn, 274	B 3
52135	Clermont, 582	K 2
52732	Clinton◉, 34,719	N 5
50053	Clive, 3,005	F 5
52217	Clutier, 275	J 4
† 50501	Coalville, 275	E 4
52218	Coggon, 656	L 4
51636	Coin, 294	C 7
52035	Colesburg, 379	L 3
50054	Colfax, 2,293	G 5
51637	College Springs, 295	C 7
50055	Collins, 404	G 5
50056	Colo, 606	G 4
52737	Columbus City, 312	L 6
52738	Columbus Junction, 1,205	L 6
52739	Conesville, 295	L 6
50631	Conrad, 932	H 4

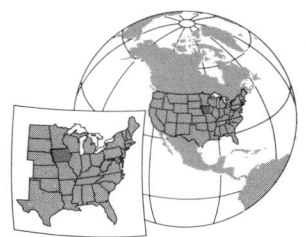

AREA 56,290 sq. mi.
POPULATION 2,825,041 ('70); 2,913,387 ('80)
CAPITAL Des Moines
LARGEST CITY Des Moines
HIGHEST POINT 1670 ft. (Osceola Co.)
SETTLED IN 1788
ADMITTED TO UNION December 28, 1846
POPULAR NAME Hawkeye State
STATE FLOWER Wild Rose
STATE BIRD Eastern Goldfinch

IOWA

SCALE
0 5 10 20 30 40 MI.
0 5 10 20 30 40 KM.

State Capitals .... ✪
County Seats .... ◉

© C. S. HAMMOND & Co., Maplewood, N.J.

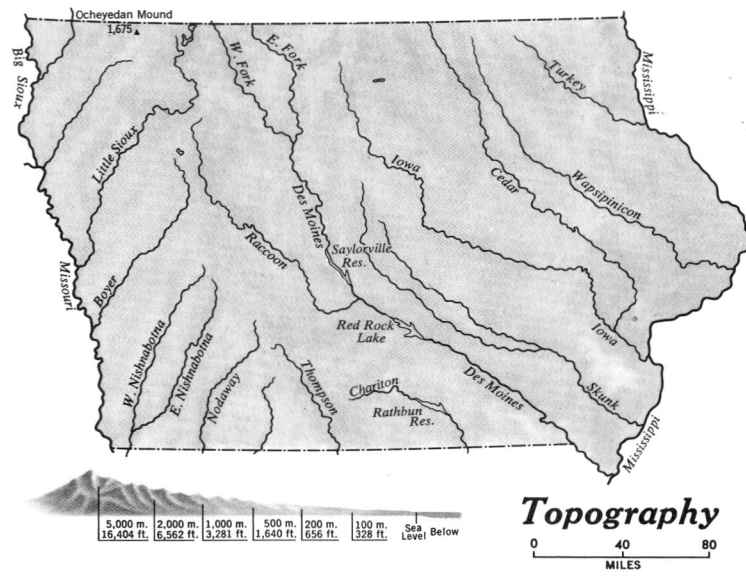

5,000 m. 2,000 m. 1,000 m. 500 m. 200 m. 100 m. Sea Below
16,404 ft. 6,562 ft. 3,281 ft. 1,640 ft. 656 ft. 328 ft. Level

Topography

0 40 80
MILES

Zip	City, Population	Ref
50058	Coon Rapids, 1,381	D 5
52240	Coralville, 6,130	K 5
50841	Corning◉, 2,095	D 7
51016	Correctionville, 870	B 4
50430	Corwith, 407	F 3
50060	Corydon◉, 1,745	G 7
50431	Coulter, 262	G 3
51501	Council Bluffs◉, 60,348	B 6
52621	Crawfordsville, 288	K 6
51526	Crescent, 284	B 6
52136	Cresco◉, 3,927	J 2
50801	Creston◉, 8,234	E 6
50432	Crystal Lake, 276	F 2
50843	Cumberland, 385	D 6
50529	Dakota City◉, 746	E 3
50062	Dallas, 438	G 6
50063	Dallas Center, 1,128	E 5
51019	Danbury, 527	B 4
52623	Danville, 948	L 7
50065	Davis City, 301	F 7
* 52801	Davenport◉, 98,469	M 5
	Davenport-Rock Island- Moline, ‡362,638	M 5
50066	Dawson, 232	E 5
50530	Dayton, 909	E 4
52101	Decorah◉, 7,458	K 2
51440	Dedham, 325	D 5
52222	Deep River, 323	J 5
51527	Defiance, 392	C 5
52223	Delhi, 527	L 4
52037	Delmar, 599	M 4
51441	Deloit, 279	C 4
52550	Delta, 475	J 6
51442	Denison◉, 5,882	C 4
52624	Denmark, 375	L 7
50622	Denver, 1,169	J 3
* 50301	Des Moines (cap.)◉, 200,587	G 5
	Des Moines, ‡286,101	G 5
50069	De Soto, 369	E 5
52742	De Witt, 3,647	N 5
50070	Dexter, 652	E 5
50845	Diagonal, 327	E 7
51333	Dickens, 240	C 2
50624	Dike, 794	H 4
52745	Dixon, 276	M 5
52746	Donahue, 216	M 5
52625	Donnellson, 798	K 7
51235	Doon, 437	A 2
52551	Douds, 247	J 7
51528	Dow City, 571	B 5
50071	Dows, 777	F 3
52001	Dubuque◉, 62,309	M 3
	Dubuque, ‡90,609	M 3
50625	Dumont, 724	H 3
50532	Duncombe, 418	E 4
50626	Dunkerton, 563	J 3
51529	Dunlap, 1,292	B 5
52747	Durant, 1,472	M 5
52040	Dyersville, 3,437	L 3
52224	Dysart, 1,251	J 4
50533	Eagle Grove, 4,489	F 3
50072	Earlham, 974	E 6
51530	Earling, 573	C 5
52041	Earlville, 751	L 4
50535	Early, 727	C 4
52553	Eddyville, 945	H 6
52042	Edgewood, 786	K 3
52554	Eldon, 1,319	J 7
50627	Eldora◉, 3,223	G 4
52748	Eldridge, 1,535	M 5
52141	Elgin, 613	K 3
52043	Elkader◉, 1,592	L 3
50073	Elkhart, 269	F 5
51531	Elk Horn, 667	C 5
† 50700	Elk Run Heights, 1,175	J 4
51532	Elliott, 423	C 6
50075	Ellsworth, 443	F 4
50628	Elma, 601	J 2
52227	Ely, 275	K 5
51533	Emerson, 484	C 6
50536	Emmetsburg◉, 4,150	D 2
52045	Epworth, 1,132	M 4
51638	Essex, 770	C 7
51334	Estherville◉, 8,108	D 2
50707	Evansdale, 5,038	J 4
51338	Everly, 699	C 2
50076	Exira, 966	D 5
52555	Exline, 224	H 7
50629	Fairbank, 810	K 3
52228	Fairfax, 635	K 5
52556	Fairfield◉, 8,715	J 6
52046	Farley, 1,096	L 4
52047	Farmersburg, 232	L 3
52626	Farmington, 800	K 7
50538	Farnhamville, 393	D 4
51639	Farragut, 521	C 7
52142	Fayette, 1,947	K 3
50539	Fenton, 403	E 2
50434	Fertile, 394	G 2
50435	Floyd, 380	H 2
50540	Fonda, 980	D 3
50846	Fontanelle, 752	E 6
50436	Forest City◉, 3,841	F 2
52144	Fort Atkinson, 339	J 2
50501	Fort Dodge◉, 31,263	E 4
52627	Fort Madison◉, 13,996	L 7
51340	Fostoria, 219	C 2
50630	Fredericksburg, 912	J 3
52561	Fremont, 480	H 6
51020	Galva, 319	C 3
50103	Garden Grove, 285	F 7
52049	Garnavillo, 634	L 3
50438	Garner◉, 2,217	F 2
52229	Garrison, 383	J 4
50632	Garwin, 563	H 4
51237	George, 1,194	B 2
50105	Gilbert, 521	F 4
50634	Gilbertville, 655	J 4
50106	Gilman, 513	H 5
50541	Gilmore City, 766	D 3
50635	Gladbrook, 961	H 4
51534	Glenwood◉, 4,195	B 6
51443	Glidden, 964	D 4
50542	Goldfield, 722	F 3
50439	Goodell, 218	F 3
52750	Gooselake, 218	N 5
50543	Gowrie, 1,225	E 4
51342	Graettinger, 907	D 2
50440	Grafton, 254	G 2
50107	Grand Junction, 967	E 4
52751	Grand Mound, 627	M 5
50108	Grand River, 211	F 7
52752	Grandview, 357	L 6
50109	Granger, 661	F 5
51022	Granville, 383	B 3
50848	Gravity, 286	D 7
52050	Greeley, 323	L 3
50636	Greene, 1,363	H 3
50849	Greenfield◉, 2,212	D 6
50111	Grimes, 834	F 5
50112	Grinnell, 8,402	H 5
51535	Griswold, 1,181	C 6
52638	Grundy Center◉, 2,712	H 4
50115	Guthrie Center◉, 1,834	D 5
52052	Guttenberg, 2,177	L 3
51444	Halbur, 235	D 4
51640	Hamburg, 1,649	B 7
50441	Hampton◉, 4,376	G 3
51536	Hancock, 228	C 6
50544	Harcourt, 305	E 4
51537	Harlan◉, 5,049	C 5
52146	Harpers Ferry, 227	L 2
50118	Hartford, 762	G 6
51346	Hartley, 1,694	C 2
50119	Harvey, 217	H 6
51540	Hastings, 229	C 6
50546	Havelock, 220	D 3
51023	Hawarden, 2,789	A 2
52147	Hawkeye, 529	J 3
50641	Hazleton, 626	K 3
52563	Hedrick, 790	J 6
51541	Henderson, 211	B 6
52233	Hiawatha, 2,416	K 4
52235	Hills, 507	K 5
52630	Hillsboro, 252	K 7
51024	Hinton, 488	A 3
50642	Holland, 258	H 4
51025	Holstein, 1,445	B 4
52053	Holy Cross, 290	L 3
52237	Hopkinton, 800	L 4
51026	Hornick, 250	A 4
51238	Hospers, 646	B 2
50122	Hubbard, 842	G 4
50643	Hudson, 1,535	H 4
51239	Hull, 1,523	A 2
50548	Humboldt, 4,665	E 3
50123	Humeston, 673	G 7
50124	Huxley, 937	F 5
51445	Ida Grove◉, 2,261	B 4
50644	Independence◉, 5,910	K 4
50125	Indianola◉, 8,852	F 6
51240	Inwood, 644	A 2
50645	Ionia, 270	J 2
52240	Iowa City◉, 46,850	L 5
50126	Iowa Falls, 6,454	G 3
51027	Ireton, 582	A 3
51446	Irwin, 446	C 5
50128	Jamaica, 271	E 5
50647	Janesville, 741	J 3
50129	Jefferson◉, 4,735	E 5
50648	Jesup, 1,662	J 4
50130	Jewell, 1,152	F 4
50131	Johnston, 222	F 5
52247	Kalona, 1,488	K 6
50132	Kamrar, 243	F 4
50447	Kanawha, 705	F 3
50133	Kellerton, 299	E 7

(continued on following page)

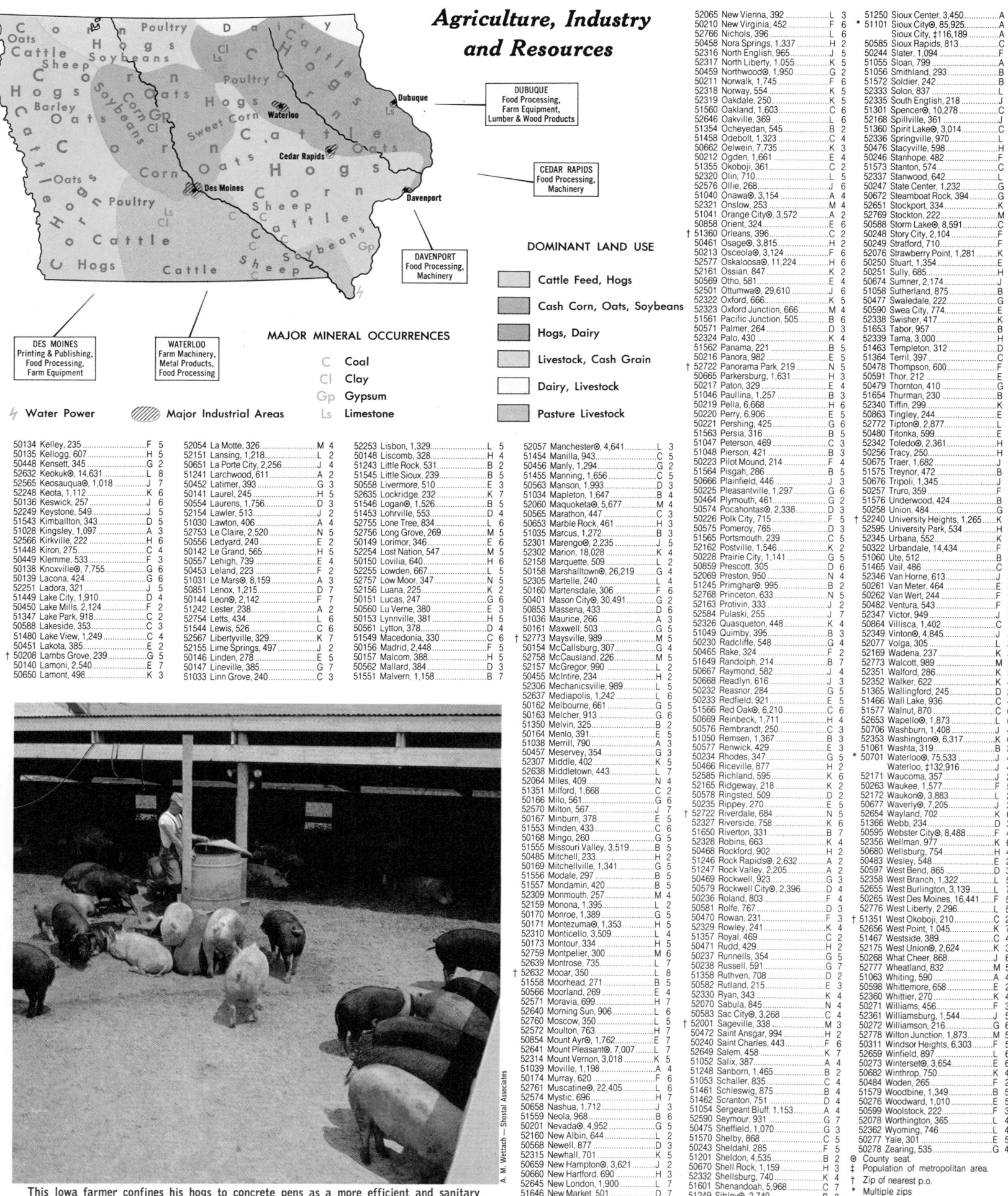

Agriculture, Industry and Resources

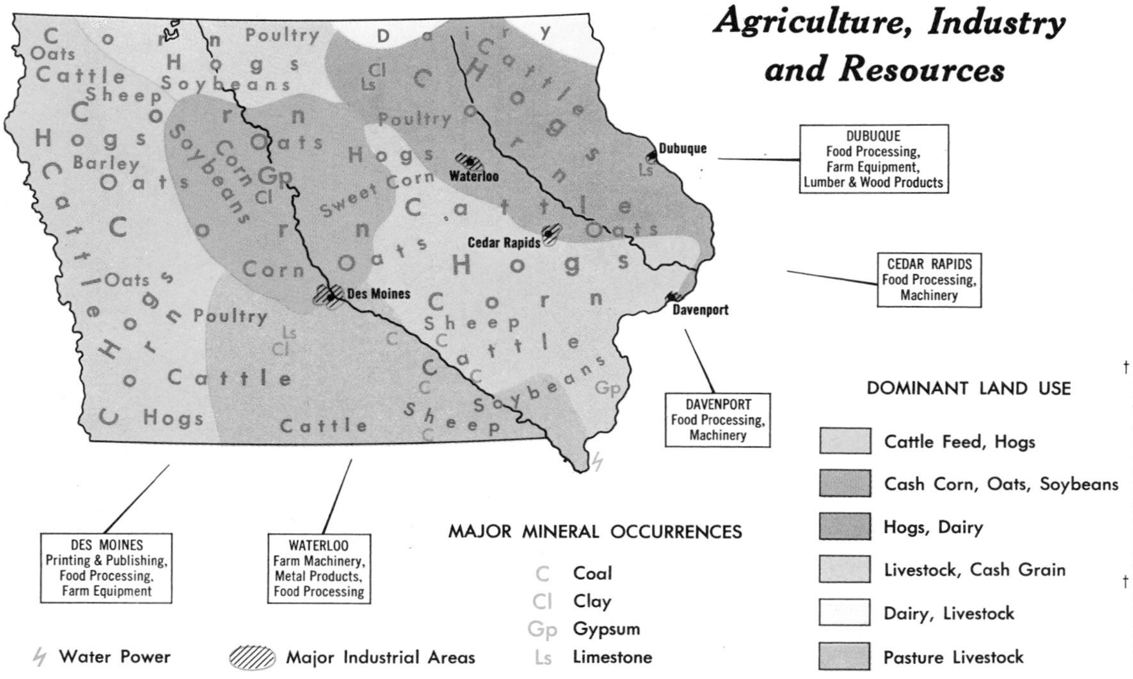
Poultry
Dairy
Cattle
Oats
Hogs
Soybeans
Sheep
Corn
Barley
Sweet Corn
Cl
Ls
C
Gp
Waterloo
Dubuque
Cedar Rapids
Des Moines
Davenport
DUBUQUE
Food Processing,
Farm Equipment,
Lumber & Wood Products
CEDAR RAPIDS
Food Processing,
Machinery
DAVENPORT
Food Processing,
Machinery
DES MOINES
Printing & Publishing,
Food Processing,
Farm Equipment
WATERLOO
Farm Machinery,
Metal Products,
Food Processing
DOMINANT LAND USE
Cattle Feed, Hogs
Cash Corn, Oats, Soybeans
Hogs, Dairy
Livestock, Cash Grain
Dairy, Livestock
Pasture Livestock
MAJOR MINERAL OCCURRENCES
C Coal
Cl Clay
Gp Gypsum
Ls Limestone
Water Power
Major Industrial Areas

	ZIP	Place, population	Key
	50134	Kelley, 235	F 5
	50135	Kellogg, 607	H 5
	50448	Kensett, 345	G 2
	52632	Keokuk⊙, 14,631	L 8
	52565	Keosauqua⊙, 1,018	J 7
	52248	Keota, 1,112	K 6
	50136	Keswick, 257	J 6
	52249	Keystone, 549	J 5
	51543	Kimballton, 343	D 5
	51028	Kingsley, 1,097	A 3
	52566	Kirkville, 222	H 6
	51448	Kiron, 275	C 4
	50449	Klemme, 533	F 3
	50138	Knoxville⊙, 7,755	G 6
	50139	Lacona, 424	G 6
	52251	Ladora, 321	J 5
	51449	Lake City, 1,910	D 4
	50450	Lake Mills, 2,124	F 2
	51347	Lake Park, 918	C 2
	50588	Lakeside, 353	C 3
	51480	Lake View, 1,249	C 4
	50451	Lakota, 385	E 2
†	50208	Lambs Grove, 239	G 5
	50140	Lamoni, 2,540	E 7
	50650	Lamont, 498	K 3
	52054	La Motte, 326	M 4
	52151	Lansing, 1,218	L 2
	50651	La Porte City, 2,256	J 4
	51241	Larchwood, 611	A 2
	50452	Latimer, 393	G 3
	50141	Laurel, 245	H 5
	50554	Laurens, 1,756	D 3
	52154	Lawler, 513	J 2
	51030	Lawton, 406	A 4
	52753	Le Claire, 2,520	N 5
	50556	Ledyard, 240	E 2
	50142	Le Grand, 565	H 5
	50557	Lehigh, 739	E 4
	50453	Leland, 223	F 2
	51031	Le Mars⊙, 8,159	A 3
	50851	Lenox, 1,215	D 7
	50144	Leon⊙, 2,142	F 7
	51242	Lester, 238	A 2
	52754	Letts, 434	L 6
	51544	Lewis, 526	C 6
	52567	Libertyville, 329	K 7
	52155	Lime Springs, 497	J 2
	50146	Linden, 278	E 5
	50147	Lineville, 385	G 7
	51033	Linn Grove, 240	C 3
	52253	Lisbon, 1,329	L 5
	50148	Liscomb, 328	H 4
	51243	Little Rock, 531	B 2
	51545	Little Sioux, 239	B 5
	50558	Livermore, 510	E 3
	52635	Lockridge, 232	K 7
	51546	Logan⊙, 1,526	B 5
	51453	Lohrville, 553	D 4
	52755	Lone Tree, 834	L 6
	52756	Long Grove, 269	M 5
	50149	Lorimor, 346	E 6
	52254	Lost Nation, 547	M 5
	50150	Lovilia, 640	H 6
	52255	Lowden, 667	L 5
	52757	Low Moor, 347	N 5
	52156	Luana, 225	K 2
	50151	Lucas, 247	G 6
	50560	Lu Verne, 380	E 3
	50153	Lynnville, 381	H 5
	50561	Lytton, 378	D 4
	51549	Macedonia, 330	C 6
	50156	Madrid, 2,448	F 5
	50157	Malcom, 388	H 5
	50562	Mallard, 384	D 3
	51551	Malvern, 1,158	B 7
	52057	Manchester⊙, 4,641	L 3
	51454	Manilla, 943	C 5
	50456	Manly, 1,294	G 2
	51455	Manning, 1,656	C 5
	50563	Manson, 1,993	D 3
	51034	Mapleton, 1,647	B 4
	52060	Maquoketa⊙, 5,677	M 4
	50565	Marathon, 447	C 3
	50653	Marble Rock, 461	H 3
	51035	Marcus, 1,272	B 3
	52301	Marengo⊙, 2,235	J 5
	52302	Marion, 18,028	K 4
	52158	Marquette, 509	L 2
	50158	Marshalltown⊙, 26,219	G 4
	52305	Martelle, 240	L 4
	50160	Martensdale, 306	F 6
	50401	Mason City⊙, 30,491	G 2
	50853	Massena, 433	D 6
	51036	Maurice, 266	A 3
	50161	Maxwell, 503	G 5
†	52773	Maysville, 989	M 5
	50154	McCallsburg, 307	G 4
	52758	McCausland, 226	M 5
	52157	McGregor, 990	L 2
	50455	McIntire, 234	H 2
	52306	Mechanicsville, 989	L 5
	52637	Mediapolis, 1,242	L 6
	50162	Melbourne, 661	G 5
	50163	Melcher, 913	G 6
	51350	Melvin, 325	B 2
	50164	Menlo, 391	E 5
	51038	Merrill, 790	A 3
	50457	Meservey, 354	G 3
	52307	Middle, 402	K 5
	52638	Middletown, 443	L 7
	52064	Miles, 409	N 4
	51351	Milford, 1,668	C 2
	50166	Milo, 561	G 6
	52570	Milton, 567	J 7
	50167	Minburn, 378	E 5
	51553	Minden, 433	C 6
	50168	Mingo, 260	G 5
	51555	Missouri Valley, 3,519	B 5
	50485	Mitchell, 233	H 2
	50169	Mitchellville, 1,341	G 5
	51556	Modale, 297	B 5
	51557	Mondamin, 420	B 5
	52309	Monmouth, 257	M 4
	52159	Monona, 1,395	L 2
	50170	Monroe, 1,389	G 5
	50171	Montezuma⊙, 1,353	H 5
	52310	Monticello, 3,509	L 4
	50173	Montour, 334	H 5
	52759	Montpelier, 300	M 6
	52639	Montrose, 735	L 7
†	52632	Mooar, 350	L 8
	51558	Moorhead, 271	B 5
	50566	Moorland, 269	E 4
	52571	Moravia, 699	H 7
	52640	Morning Sun, 906	L 6
	52760	Moscow, 350	L 5
	52572	Moulton, 763	H 7
	50854	Mount Ayr⊙, 1,762	E 7
	52641	Mount Pleasant⊙, 7,007	L 7
	52314	Mount Vernon, 3,018	K 5
	51039	Moville, 1,198	A 4
	50174	Murray, 620	F 6
	52761	Muscatine⊙, 22,405	L 6
	52574	Mystic, 696	H 7
	50658	Nashua, 1,712	J 3
	51559	Neola, 968	B 6
	50201	Nevada⊙, 4,952	G 5
	52160	New Albin, 644	L 2
	50568	Newell, 877	D 3
	52315	Newhall, 701	K 5
	50659	New Hampton⊙, 3,621	J 2
	50660	New Hartford, 690	H 3
	52645	New London, 1,900	L 7
	51646	New Market, 501	D 7
	50206	New Providence, 208	G 4
	50207	New Sharon, 944	H 6
	50208	Newton⊙, 15,619	H 5
	52065	New Vienna, 392	L 3
	50210	New Virginia, 452	F 6
	52766	Nichols, 396	L 6
	50458	Nora Springs, 1,337	H 2
	52316	North English, 965	J 5
	52317	North Liberty, 1,055	K 5
	50459	Northwood⊙, 1,950	G 2
	50211	Norwalk, 1,745	F 6
	52318	Norway, 554	K 5
	52319	Oakdale, 250	K 5
	51560	Oakland, 1,603	C 6
	52646	Oakville, 369	L 6
	51354	Ocheyedan, 545	B 2
	51458	Odebolt, 1,323	C 4
	50662	Oelwein, 7,735	K 3
	50212	Ogden, 1,661	E 4
	51355	Okoboji, 361	C 2
	52320	Olin, 710	L 5
	52576	Ollie, 268	J 6
	51040	Onawa⊙, 3,154	A 4
	52321	Onslow, 253	M 4
	51041	Orange City⊙, 3,572	A 2
	50858	Orient, 324	E 6
†	51360	Orleans, 396	C 2
	50461	Osage⊙, 3,815	H 2
	50213	Osceola⊙, 3,124	F 6
	52577	Oskaloosa⊙, 11,224	H 6
	52161	Ossian, 847	K 2
	50569	Otho, 581	E 4
	52501	Ottumwa⊙, 29,610	J 6
	52322	Oxford, 666	K 5
	52323	Oxford Junction, 666	M 4
	51561	Pacific Junction, 505	B 6
	50571	Palmer, 264	D 3
	52324	Palo, 430	K 4
	51562	Panama, 221	B 5
	50216	Panora, 982	E 5
†	52722	Panorama Park, 219	N 5
	50665	Parkersburg, 1,631	H 3
	50217	Paton, 329	E 4
	51046	Paullina, 1,257	B 3
	50219	Pella, 6,668	H 6
	50220	Perry, 6,906	E 5
	50221	Pershing, 425	G 6
	51563	Persia, 316	B 5
	51047	Peterson, 469	C 3
	51048	Pierson, 421	B 3
	50223	Pilot Mound, 214	F 4
	51564	Pisgah, 286	B 5
	50666	Plainfield, 446	J 3
	50225	Pleasantville, 1,297	G 6
	50464	Plymouth, 461	G 2
	50574	Pocahontas⊙, 2,338	D 3
	50226	Polk City, 715	F 5
	50575	Pomeroy, 765	D 3
	51565	Portsmouth, 239	C 5
	52162	Postville, 1,546	K 2
	50228	Prairie City, 1,141	G 5
	50859	Prescott, 305	D 6
	52069	Preston, 950	N 4
	51245	Primghar⊙, 995	B 2
	52768	Princeton, 633	N 5
	52163	Protivin, 333	J 2
	52584	Pulaski, 255	J 7
	52326	Quasqueton, 448	K 4
	51049	Quimby, 395	B 3
	50230	Radcliffe, 548	G 4
	50465	Rake, 324	F 2
	51649	Randolph, 214	B 7
	50667	Raymond, 582	J 4
	50668	Readlyn, 616	J 3
	50232	Reasnor, 284	G 5
	50233	Redfield, 921	E 5
	51566	Red Oak⊙, 6,210	C 6
	50669	Reinbeck, 1,711	H 4
	50576	Rembrandt, 250	C 3
	51050	Remsen, 1,367	B 3
	50577	Renwick, 429	E 3
	50234	Rhodes, 347	G 5
	50466	Riceville, 877	H 2
	52585	Richland, 595	K 6
	52165	Ridgeway, 218	K 2
	50578	Ringsted, 509	D 2
	50235	Rippey, 270	E 5
†	52722	Riverdale, 684	N 5
	52327	Riverside, 758	K 6
	51650	Riverton, 331	B 7
	52328	Robins, 663	K 4
	50468	Rockford, 902	H 2
	51246	Rock Rapids⊙, 2,632	A 2
	51247	Rock Valley, 2,205	A 2
	50469	Rockwell, 923	G 3
	50579	Rockwell City⊙, 2,396	D 4
	50236	Roland, 803	F 4
	50581	Rolfe, 767	D 3
	50470	Rowan, 231	F 3
	52329	Rowley, 241	K 4
	51357	Royal, 469	C 2
	50471	Rudd, 429	H 2
	50237	Runnells, 354	G 5
	50238	Russell, 591	G 7
	51358	Ruthven, 708	D 2
	50582	Rutland, 215	E 3
	52330	Ryan, 343	K 4
	52070	Sabula, 845	N 4
	50583	Sac City⊙, 3,268	C 4
†	52001	Sageville, 338	M 3
	50472	Saint Ansgar, 994	H 2
	50240	Saint Charles, 443	F 6
	52649	Salem, 458	K 7
	51052	Salix, 387	A 4
	51248	Sanborn, 1,465	B 2
	51053	Schaller, 835	C 4
	51461	Schleswig, 875	B 4
	51462	Scranton, 751	D 4
	51054	Sergeant Bluff, 1,153	A 4
	52590	Seymour, 931	G 7
	50475	Sheffield, 1,070	G 3
	51570	Shelby, 868	C 5
	50243	Sheldahl, 285	F 5
	51201	Sheldon, 4,535	B 2
	50670	Shell Rock, 1,159	H 3
	52332	Shellsburg, 740	K 4
	51601	Shenandoah, 5,968	C 7
	51249	Sibley⊙, 2,749	B 2
	51652	Sidney⊙, 1,061	B 7
	52591	Sigourney⊙, 2,319	J 6
	51571	Silver City, 272	B 6
	51250	Sioux Center, 3,450	A 2
*	51101	Sioux City⊙, 85,925	A 3
		Sioux City, ‡116,189	A 3
	50585	Sioux Rapids, 813	C 3
	50244	Slater, 1,094	F 5
	51055	Sloan, 799	A 4
	51056	Smithland, 293	B 4
	51572	Soldier, 242	B 5
	52333	Solon, 837	L 5
	52335	South English, 218	J 6
	51301	Spencer⊙, 10,278	C 2
	52168	Spillville, 361	J 2
	51360	Spirit Lake⊙, 3,014	C 2
	52336	Springville, 970	L 4
	50476	Stacyville, 598	H 2
	50246	Stanhope, 482	F 4
	51573	Stanton, 574	C 7
	52337	Stanwood, 642	L 5
	50247	State Center, 1,232	G 5
	50672	Steamboat Rock, 394	G 4
	52651	Stockport, 334	K 7
	52769	Stockton, 222	M 5
	50588	Storm Lake⊙, 8,591	C 3
	50248	Story City, 2,104	F 4
	50249	Stratford, 710	F 4
	52076	Strawberry Point, 1,281	K 3
	50250	Stuart, 1,354	E 6
	50251	Sully, 685	H 5
	50674	Sumner, 2,174	J 3
	51058	Sutherland, 875	B 3
	50477	Swaledale, 222	G 3
	50590	Swea City, 774	E 2
	52338	Swisher, 417	K 5
	51653	Tabor, 957	B 7
	52339	Tama, 3,000	H 5
	51463	Templeton, 312	D 5
	51364	Terril, 397	C 2
	50478	Thompson, 600	F 2
	50591	Thor, 212	E 3
	50479	Thornton, 410	G 3
	51654	Thurman, 230	B 7
	52340	Tiffin, 299	K 5
	50863	Tingley, 244	E 7
	52772	Tipton⊙, 2,877	L 5
	50480	Titonka, 599	E 2
	52342	Toledo⊙, 2,361	H 4
	50256	Tracy, 250	H 6
	50675	Traer, 1,682	J 4
	51575	Treynor, 472	B 6
	50676	Tripoli, 1,345	J 3
	50257	Truro, 359	F 6
	51576	Underwood, 424	B 6
	50258	Union, 484	G 4
†	52240	University Heights, 1,265	K 5
	52595	University Park, 534	H 6
	52345	Urbana, 552	K 4
	50322	Urbandale, 14,434	F 5
	51060	Ute, 512	B 4
	51465	Vail, 486	C 4
	52346	Van Horne, 613	J 4
	50261	Van Meter, 464	E 5
	50262	Van Wert, 244	F 7
	50482	Ventura, 543	F 2
	52347	Victor, 949	J 5
	50864	Villisca, 1,402	C 7
	52349	Vinton⊙, 4,845	J 4
	52077	Volga, 305	L 3
	52169	Wadena, 237	K 3
	52773	Walcott, 989	M 5
	52351	Walford, 286	K 5
	52352	Walker, 622	K 4
	51365	Wallingford, 245	D 2
	51466	Wall Lake, 936	C 4
	51577	Walnut, 870	C 6
	52653	Wapello⊙, 1,873	L 6
	50706	Washburn, 1,408	J 4
	52353	Washington⊙, 6,317	K 6
	51061	Washta, 319	B 3
*	50701	Waterloo⊙, 75,533	J 4
		Waterloo, ‡132,916	J 4
	52171	Waucoma, 357	J 2
	50263	Waukee, 1,577	F 5
	52172	Waukon⊙, 3,883	L 2
	50677	Waverly⊙, 7,205	J 3
	52654	Wayland, 702	K 6
	51366	Webb, 234	D 3
	50595	Webster City⊙, 8,488	F 4
	52356	Wellman, 977	K 6
	50680	Wellsburg, 754	H 4
	50483	Wesley, 548	E 2
	50597	West Bend, 865	D 3
	52358	West Branch, 1,322	L 5
	52655	West Burlington, 3,139	L 7
	50265	West Des Moines, 16,441	F 5
	52776	West Liberty, 2,296	L 5
†	51351	West Okoboji, 210	C 2
	52656	West Point, 1,045	K 7
	51467	Westside, 389	C 4
	52175	West Union⊙, 2,624	K 3
	50268	What Cheer, 868	J 6
	52777	Wheatland, 832	M 5
	51063	Whiting, 590	A 4
	50598	Whittemore, 658	E 2
	52360	Whittier, 270	K 4
	50271	Williams, 456	F 3
	52361	Williamsburg, 1,544	J 5
	50272	Williamson, 216	G 6
	52778	Wilton Junction, 1,873	M 5
	50311	Windsor Heights, 6,303	F 5
	52659	Winfield, 897	L 6
	50273	Winterset⊙, 3,654	E 6
	50682	Winthrop, 750	K 4
	50484	Woden, 265	F 2
	51579	Woodbine, 1,349	B 5
	50276	Woodward, 1,010	E 5
	50599	Woolstock, 222	F 3
	52078	Worthington, 365	L 4
	52362	Wyoming, 746	L 4
	50277	Yale, 301	E 5
	50278	Zearing, 535	G 4

⊙ County seat.
‡ Population of metropolitan area.
† Zip of nearest p.o.
* Multiple zips

A. M. Wettach — Shostal Associates

This Iowa farmer confines his hogs to concrete pens as a more efficient and sanitary method of raising healthy animals for market. Iowa's record-breaking hog production is due largely to the availability of corn for fodder.

Agriculture, Industry and Resources

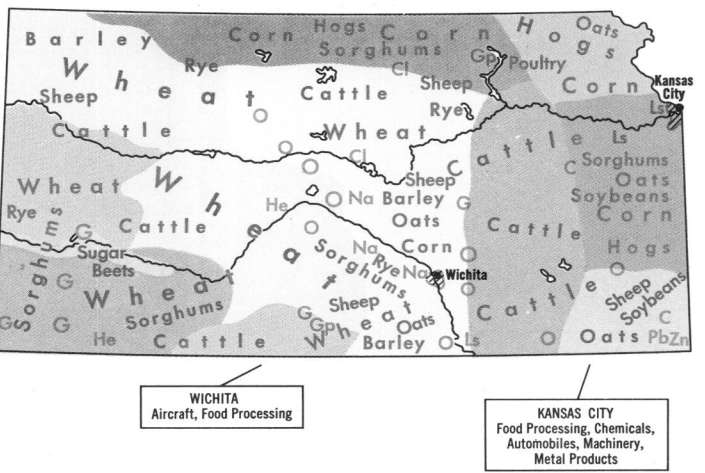

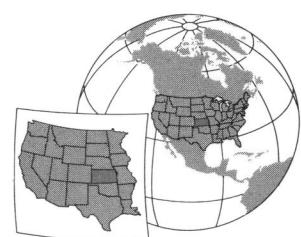

AREA 82,264 sq. mi.
POPULATION 2,249,071 ('70); 2,363,208 ('80)
CAPITAL Topeka
LARGEST CITY Wichita
HIGHEST POINT Mt. Sunflower 4,039 ft.
SETTLED IN 1831
ADMITTED TO UNION January 29, 1861
POPULAR NAME Sunflower State
STATE FLOWER Sunflower
STATE BIRD Western Meadowlark

WICHITA
Aircraft, Food Processing

KANSAS CITY
Food Processing, Chemicals, Automobiles, Machinery, Metal Products

DOMINANT LAND USE

- Specialized Wheat
- Wheat, General Farming
- Wheat, Range Livestock
- Wheat, Grain Sorghums, Range Livestock
- Cattle Feed, Hogs
- Livestock, Cash Grain
- Livestock, Cash Grain, Dairy
- General Farming, Livestock, Cash Grain
- General Farming, Livestock, Special Crops
- Range Livestock

MAJOR MINERAL OCCURRENCES

C	Coal	Ls	Limestone
Cl	Clay	Na	Salt
G	Natural Gas	O	Petroleum
Gp	Gypsum	Pb	Lead
He	Helium	Zn	Zinc

///// Major Industrial Areas

Loaded with wheat for storage, a truck pulls onto a weighing platform at the Salina grain elevators. Wheat is grown here on such a scale that Kansas is known as the Breadbasket of the World.

Robert Leahey — Shostal Associates

(continued on following page)

KANSAS

SCALE

0 5 10   20   30   40   50 MI.

0 5 10 20   30   40   50 KM.

⊛ State Capitals

⊙ County Seats

© C.S. HAMMOND & Co., N.Y.

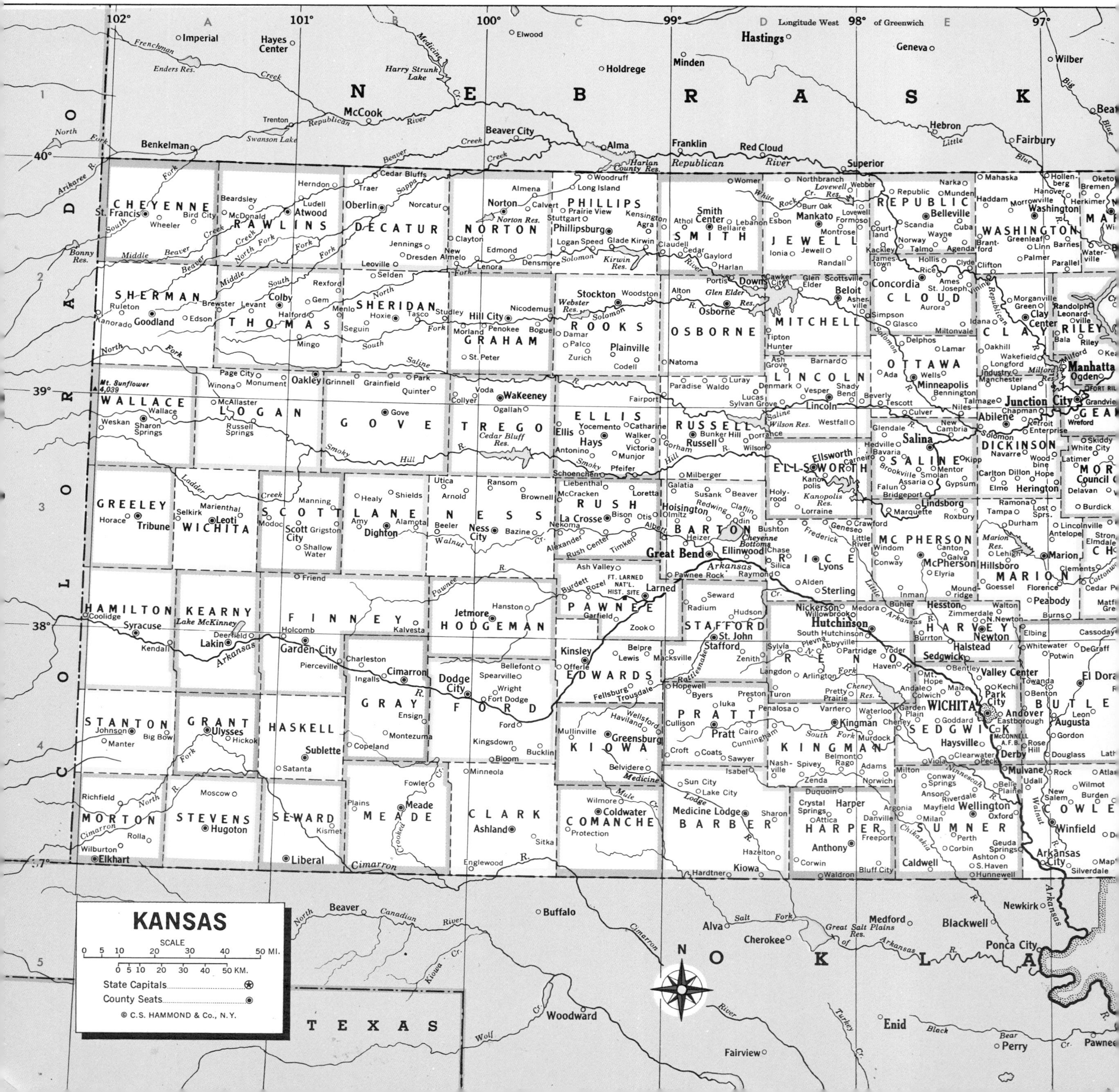

66449 Leonardville, 412......F 2
67861 Leoti◉, 1,916......A 3
66857 Le Roy, 551......G 3
67743 Levant, 425......A 2
67552 Lewis, 525......C 4
67901 Liberal◉, 13,471......B 4
67351 Liberty, 185......G 4
67553 Liebenthal, 169......C 3
66858 Lincoln◉, 1,582......D 2
66858 Lincolnville, 218......F 3
67456 Lindsborg, 2,764......E 3
66953 Linn, 388......F 2
66052 Linwood, 323......G 2
67457 Little River, 493......E 2
67646 Logan, 760......C 2
67647 Long Island, 195......C 2
67352 Longton, 304......F 4
67459 Lorraine, 153......D 3
66859 Lost Springs, 103......E 3
66053 Louisburg, 1,033......H 3
66450 Louisville, 204......F 2
67648 Lucas, 524......D 2
67649 Luray, 303......D 2
67451 Lyndon◉, 958......G 3
67554 Lyons◉, 4,355......D 3
67557 Macksville, 484......D 4

66860 Madison, 1,061......F 3
66955 Mahaska, 122......E 2
67101 Maize, 785......E 4
66502 Manhattan◉, 27,575......F 2
66956 Mankato◉, 1,287......D 2
67862 Manter, 219......A 4
66507 Maple Hill, 327......F 2
66754 Mapleton, 112......H 3
67863 Marienthal, 120......A 3
66861 Marion◉, 2,052......E 3
67464 Marquette, 578......E 3
66508 Marysville◉, 3,588......F 2
66509 Mayetta, 246......G 2
67103 Mayfield, 110......E 4
67556 McCracken, 333......C 3
66753 McCune, 487......G 4
67745 McDonald, 269......A 2
66501 McFarland, 209......F 2
66054 McLouth, 623......G 2
67460 McPherson◉, 10,851......E 3
67864 Meade◉, 1,899......B 4
67104 Medicine Lodge◉, 2,545......D 4
67558 Medora, 110......E 3
66510 Melvern, 455......G 3
66512 Meriden, 472......G 2
66203 Merriam, 10,851......H 3

Topography

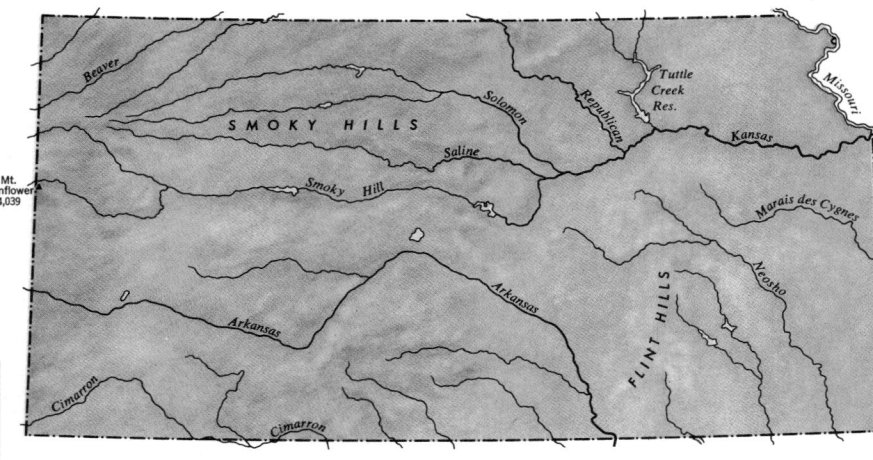

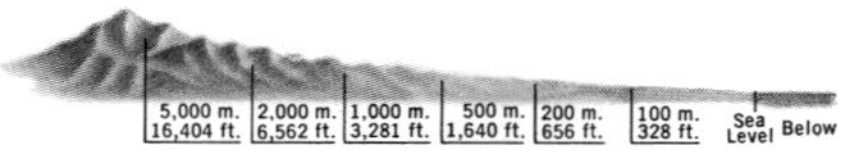

5,000 m. 16,404 ft.   2,000 m. 6,562 ft.   1,000 m. 3,281 ft.   500 m. 1,640 ft.   200 m. 656 ft.   100 m. 328 ft.   Sea Level   Below

67105 Milan, 162......E 4
66514 Milford, 296......F 2
67466 Miltonvale, 718......E 2
67467 Minneapolis◉, 1,971......E 2
67865 Minneola, 630......C 4
67222 Mission, 8,376......H 2
67353 Moline, 555......F 4
67867 Montezuma, 606......B 4
66755 Moran, 550......G 4
67468 Morganville, 257......E 2
67650 Morland, 300......B 2
66515 Morrill, 308......F 2
66958 Morrowville, 201......E 2
67952 Moscow, 228......A 4
66056 Mound City◉, 714......H 3
67107 Moundridge, 1,271......E 3
67354 Mound Valley, 467......G 4
67108 Mount Hope, 665......E 4
66758 Mulberry, 622......H 4
67109 Mullinville, 376......C 4
67110 Mulvane, 3,185......E 4
66959 Munden, 123......E 2
† 67601 Munjor, 200......C 3
66058 Muscotah, 206......G 2
66960 Narka, 130......E 2
67651 Natoma, 603......D 2
66757 Neodesha, 3,295......G 4
66758 Neosho Falls, 184......G 3
66864 Neosho Rapids, 234......F 3
67560 Ness City◉, 1,756......C 3
66516 Netawaka, 192......G 2
67470 New Cambria, 160......E 3
67117 North Newton, 963......E 3
67654 Norcatur, 284......B 2
67117 North Newton, 963......E 3
67654 Norton◉, 3,627......C 2
66060 Nortonville, 727......G 2
67118 Norwich, 414......E 4
67748 Oakley◉, 2,327......B 2
67749 Oberlin◉, 2,291......B 2
67562 Odin, 117......C 3
67563 Offerle, 212......C 4
66756 Ogallah, 110......C 3
66517 Ogden, 1,491......F 2
66518 Oketo, 133......F 2
67061 Olathe◉, 17,917......H 3
67564 Olmitz, 161......D 3
66865 Olpe, 453......F 3
66520 Olsburg, 151......F 2
66521 Onaga, 761......F 2
66522 Oneida, 112......G 2
66760 Opolis, 160......H 4
66523 Osage City, 2,600......G 3
66064 Osawatomie, 4,294......H 3
67473 Osborne◉, 1,980......D 2
66066 Oskaloosa◉, 955......G 2
67356 Oswego◉, 2,200......G 4
67565 Otis, 387......C 3
66067 Ottawa◉, 11,036......G 3
66524 Overbrook, 748......G 3
66204 Overland Park, 76,623......H 3
67070 Ozawkie, 137......G 2
67657 Palco, 398......C 2
66962 Palmer, 166......E 2
66071 Paola◉, 4,622......H 3
66758 Paradise, 145......D 2
67751 Park, 178......B 2
67219 Park City, 2,529......E 4
66072 Parker, 255......H 3
67357 Parsons, 13,015......G 4
67566 Partridge, 302......D 4
66619 Pauline, 800......G 3
67567 Pawnee Rock, 442......D 3
66526 Paxico, 216......F 2
66866 Peabody, 1,368......E 3
67120 Peck, 150......E 4
66073 Perry, 664......G 2
67360 Peru, 289......F 4
67660 Pfeifer, 175......C 3
67122 Piedmont, 116......F 4
67868 Pierceville, 175......B 4

66761 Piqua, 107......G 4
66762 Pittsburg, 20,171......H 4
67869 Plains, 857......B 4
67663 Plainville, 2,627......C 2
66075 Pleasanton, 1,216......H 3
67568 Plevna, 124......D 4
66076 Pomona, 541......G 3
67474 Portis, 178......D 2
67123 Potwin, 497......F 4
66527 Powhattan, 111......G 2
67664 Prairie View, 201......C 2
66208 Prairie Village, 28,138......H 2
67124 Pratt◉, 6,736......D 4
66767 Prescott, 222......H 3
67569 Preston, 239......D 4
67570 Pretty Prairie, 561......D 4
66078 Princeton, 159......G 3
67127 Protection, 673......C 4
66528 Quenemo, 429......G 3
67752 Quinter, 930......C 3
67475 Ramona, 121......E 3
66963 Randall, 195......D 2
66554 Randolph, 106......F 2
67572 Ransom, 416......C 3
66079 Rantoul, 163......G 3
67573 Raymond, 133......D 3
66868 Reading, 247......F 3
66769 Redfield, 138......H 4
66964 Republic, 243......E 2
66529 Reserve, 117......G 2
67753 Rexford, 231......B 2
66080 Richmond, 464......G 3
66531 Riley, 668......F 2
66770 Riverton, 500......H 4
67152 Robinson, 278......G 2
† 66205 Roeland Park, 9,974......H 2
67954 Rolla, 400......A 4
67132 Rosalia, 130......F 4
67133 Rose Hill, 387......E 4
66533 Rossville, 934......G 2
67476 Roxbury, 110......E 3
67574 Rozel, 236......C 3
67575 Rush Center, 237......C 3
67665 Russell◉, 5,371......D 3
66534 Sabetha, 2,376......G 2
66535 Saint Francis◉, 1,725......A 2
66535 Saint George, 241......F 2
67576 Saint John◉, 1,434......D 3
66536 Saint Marys, 1,434......F 2
66771 Saint Paul, 804......G 4
67401 Salina◉, 37,714......E 3
67870 Satanta, 1,161......B 4
66772 Savonburg, 109......G 4
67134 Sawyer, 164......D 4
66773 Scammon, 457......H 4
66966 Scandia, 567......E 2
67667 Schoenchen, 182......C 3
67871 Scott City◉, 4,001......B 3
66537 Scranton, 575......G 3
67361 Sedan◉, 1,555......F 4
67135 Sedgwick, 1,083......E 4
66538 Seneca◉, 2,182......F 2
66081 Severance, 128......G 2
67137 Severy, 384......F 4
67872 Shallow Water, 106......B 3
67138 Sharon, 265......D 4
66758 Sharon Springs◉, 1,012......A 3
66203 Shawnee, 20,482......H 2
67874 Shields, 110......B 3
66539 Silver Lake, 811......G 2
67478 Simpson, 131......E 2
66967 Smith Center◉, 2,389......D 2
67479 Smolan, 175......E 3
66540 Solomon, 173......E 3
67480 Solomon, 973......E 3
† 67501 South Hutchinson, 1,879......D 3
66083 Spearville, 738......C 3
67876 Spearville, 738......C 3
67578 Spring Hill, 1,186......H 3
67578 Stafford, 1,414......D 4
66084 Stanley, 450......H 3
66775 Stark, 124......G 4
67579 Sterling, 2,312......D 3
66085 Stilwell, 350......H 3

66669 Stockton◉, 1,818......C 2
66869 Strong City, 545......F 3
67877 Sublette◉, 1,208......B 4
66541 Summerfield, 254......F 2
67143 Sun City, 119......D 4
66019 Sunflower, 1,744......H 3
67363 Sycamore, 125......G 4
67581 Sylvia, 390......D 4
67878 Syracuse◉, 1,720......A 3
67482 Talmage, 125......E 2
67483 Tampa, 154......E 3
66542 Tecumseh, 270......G 2
67484 Tescott, 393......E 2
66776 Thayer, 430......G 4
67582 Timken, 123......C 3
67485 Tipton, 315......D 2
66086 Tonganoxie, 1,717......G 2
* 66601 Topeka (cap.)◉, 125,011......G 2
Topeka, ‡155,322......
66777 Toronto, 431......G 4
67144 Towanda, 1,190......E 4
66778 Treece, 225......H 4
67879 Tribune◉, 1,013......A 3
66087 Troy◉, 1,047......G 2
67583 Turon, 430......D 4
67364 Tyro, 206......G 4
67146 Udall, 668......E 4
67880 Ulysses◉, 3,779......A 4
66779 Uniontown, 286......G 4
67584 Utica, 297......B 3
67147 Valley Center, 2,551......E 4
66088 Valley Falls, 1,169......G 2
66544 Vermillion, 191......F 2
67671 Victoria, 1,246......C 3
67149 Viola, 193......E 4
66870 Virgil, 179......F 4
67672 WaKeeney◉, 2,334......C 2
67487 Wakefield, 583......E 2
67673 Waldo, 123......D 2
67761 Wallace, 112......A 3
66680 Walnut, 330......G 4
67151 Walton, 211......E 3
66547 Wamego, 2,507......F 2
66968 Washington◉, 1,584......E 2
66548 Waterville, 632......F 2
66090 Wathena, 1,150......H 2
66871 Waverly, 510......G 3
67481 Weir, 740......H 4
66091 Welda, 149......G 3
67152 Wellington◉, 8,072......E 4
66092 Wellsville, 1,183......G 3
66782 Weskan, 350......A 3
67762 West Mineral, 232......H 4
66549 Westmoreland◉, 485......F 2
66093 Westphalia, 185......G 3
67869 West Plains (Plains), 857......B 4
66550 Wetmore, 392......G 2
66551 Wheaton, 106......F 2
66872 White City, 458......F 3
66094 White Cloud, 210......G 2
67154 Whitewater, 520......E 4
66552 Whiting, 256......G 2
* 67201 Wichita◉, 276,554......E 4
Wichita, ‡389,352......E 4
† 66601 Willard, 124......G 2
66095 Williamsburg, 286......G 3
66873 Wilsey, 169......F 3
67490 Wilson, 870......D 2
66097 Winchester, 492......G 2
67491 Windom, 183......E 3
67156 Winfield◉, 11,405......E 4
67764 Winona, 293......A 2
67492 Woodbine, 170......E 3
67675 Woodston, 211......C 2
67882 Wright, 173......C 3
66783 Yates Center◉, 1,967......G 4
67585 Yoder, 155......D 3
67159 Zenda, 142......D 4
67876 Zurich, 189......C 2

◉ County seat.
‡ Population of metropolitan area.
† Zip of nearest p.o.
* Multiple zips

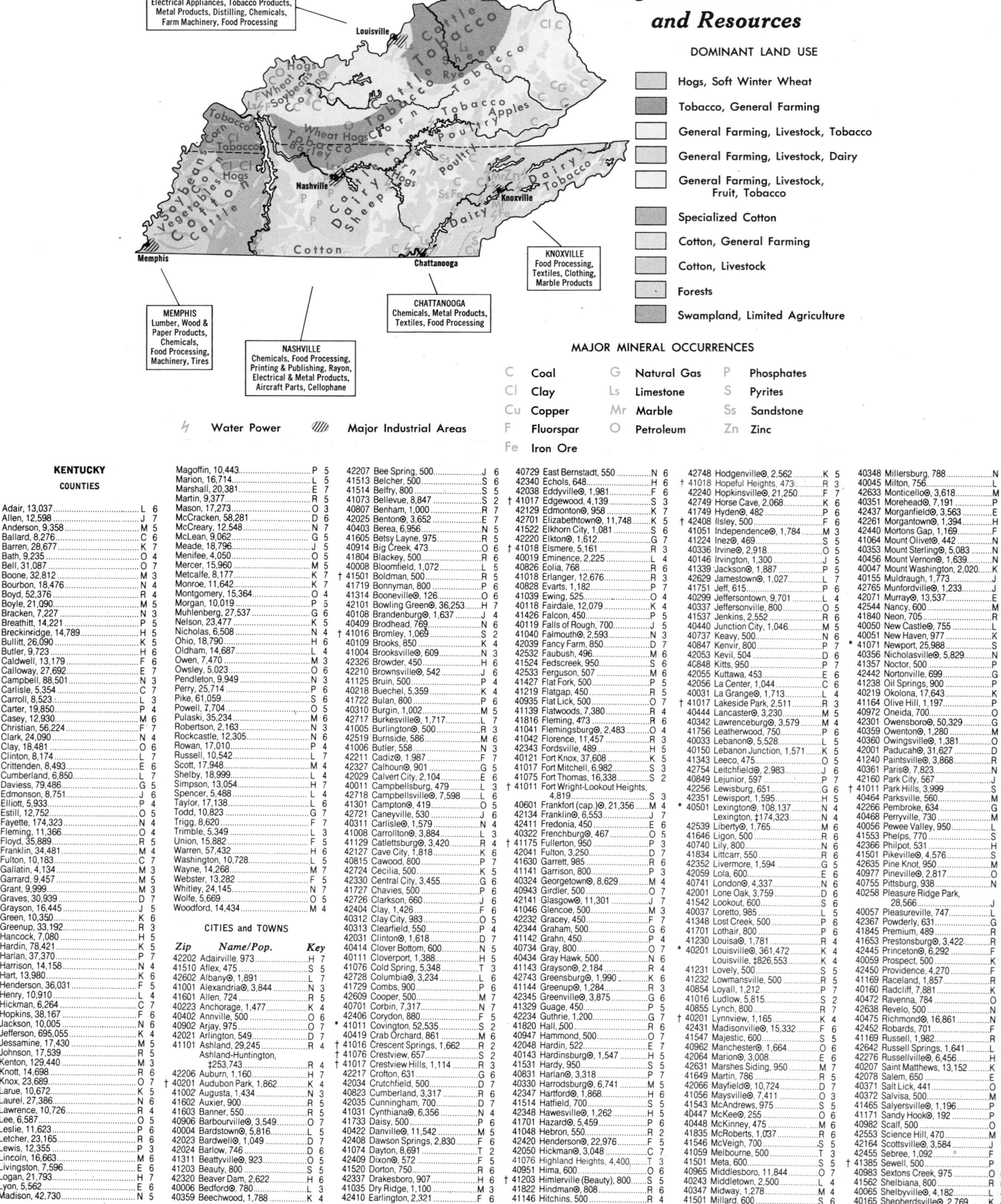

Agriculture, Industry and Resources

LOUISVILLE
Electrical Appliances, Tobacco Products, Metal Products, Distilling, Chemicals, Farm Machinery, Food Processing

KNOXVILLE
Food Processing, Textiles, Clothing, Marble Products

CHATTANOOGA
Chemicals, Metal Products, Textiles, Food Processing

NASHVILLE
Chemicals, Food Processing, Printing & Publishing, Rayon, Electrical & Metal Products, Aircraft Parts, Cellophane

MEMPHIS
Lumber, Wood & Paper Products, Chemicals, Food Processing, Machinery, Tires

DOMINANT LAND USE

- Hogs, Soft Winter Wheat
- Tobacco, General Farming
- General Farming, Livestock, Tobacco
- General Farming, Livestock, Dairy
- General Farming, Livestock, Fruit, Tobacco
- Specialized Cotton
- Cotton, General Farming
- Cotton, Livestock
- Forests
- Swampland, Limited Agriculture

MAJOR MINERAL OCCURRENCES

C	Coal	G	Natural Gas	P	Phosphates
Cl	Clay	Ls	Limestone	S	Pyrites
Cu	Copper	Mr	Marble	Ss	Sandstone
F	Fluorspar	O	Petroleum	Zn	Zinc
Fe	Iron Ore				

⚡ Water Power   ▨ Major Industrial Areas

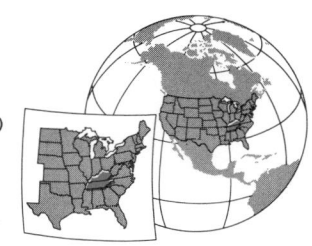

(continued on following page)

Sleek racehorses enjoy a patch of shade on a Calumet Farm pasture in Lexington, Kentucky. More than half the country's winning racehorses are from Inner Bluegrass area farms.

Jack Zehrt—Shostal Associates

Eugene Belt—Shostal Associates

Using field glasses to bridge the gap, a naturalist observes the wildlife in Cades Cove, Tennessee. Mist-shrouded Great Smoky Mountains are in the distance.

TENNESSEE (continued)

37352 Lynchburg⊙, 361 .... J 10
37115 Madison,■ .... H 8
37354 Madisonville⊙, 2,614 .... N 9
38354 Malesus, 600 .... D 9
37355 Manchester⊙, 6,208 .... J 10
† 37771 Martel, 500 .... N 9
38237 Martin, 7,781 .... D 8
† 38471 Martins Mills, 440 .... F 10
37801 Maryville⊙, 13,808 .... O 9
37806 Mascot, 1,050 .... O 8
38049 Mason, 443 .... B 10
38050 Maury City, 813 .... C 9
37807 Maynardville⊙, 702 .... O 8
37353 McDonald, 500 .... M 10
37101 McEwen, 1,237 .... F 8
38201 McKenzie, 4,873 .... E 8
37110 McMinnville⊙, 10,662 .... K 9
38355 Medina, 755 .... D 9
* 38101 Memphis⊙, 623,530 .... B 10
Memphis, ‡770,120 .... B 10
38052 Middleton, 654 .... D 10
38358 Milan, 7,313 .... D 9
37682 Milligan College, 1,170 .... S 8
38053 Millington, 21,106 .... B 10
37356 Monteagle, 934 .... K 10
38574 Monterey, 2,351 .... L 8
† 37660 Morrison City, 2,178 .... R 7
37814 Morristown⊙, 20,318 .... P 8
38057 Moscow, 448 .... C 10
37818 Mosheim, 450 .... R 8
37683 Mountain City⊙, 1,883 .... T 8
37122 Mount Juliet, 800 .... H 8
38474 Mount Pleasant, 3,530 .... G 9
38058 Munford, 1,281 .... B 10
37130 Murfreesboro⊙, 26,360 .... J 9
* 37201 Nashville (cap.)⊙, 447,877 .... H 8
Nashville, ‡540,982 .... H 8
† 37901 Neubert, 1,500 .... O 9
38059 Newbern, 2,124 .... C 8
37819 Newcomb, 550 .... N 7
37134 New Johnsonville, 970 .... E 8
37820 New Market, 950 .... O 8
37821 Newport⊙, 7,328 .... P 9
37825 New Tazewell, 1,192 .... O 8
37826 Niota, 629 .... M 9
37828 Norris, 1,359 .... N 8
† 37201 Oak Hill, ... H 8
37830 Oak Ridge, 28,319 .... N 8
38240 Obion, 1,010 .... C 8
37138 Old Hickory,■ .... H 8
37840 Oliver Springs, 3,405 .... N 8
37841 Oneida, 2,602 .... N 7
37363 Ooltewah, 1,200 .... M 10
† 37660 Orebank, 1,111 .... R 7
38577 Pall Mall, 500 .... M 7
37365 Palmer, 898 .... K 10
38242 Paris⊙, 9,892 .... E 8
38363 Parsons, 2,167 .... E 9
37143 Pegram, 850 .... H 8
37144 Petersburg, 463 .... H 10
37845 Petros, 800 .... M 8
37846 Philadelphia, 554 .... M 9
37862 Pigeon Forge, 1,361 .... O 9
37367 Pikeville⊙, 1,454 .... L 9
37148 Portland, 2,872 .... H 7
37849 Powell, 1,200 .... N 8
† 37201 Providence, ... H 8
38478 Pulaski⊙, 6,989 .... G 10
38251 Puryear, 458 .... E 8
38128 Raleigh, 2,500 .... B 10
37415 Red Bank, 12,715 .... L 10
37150 Red Boiling Springs, 726 .... K 7
37370 Riceville, 500 .... M 10
38580 Rickman, 500 .... L 8
38080 Ridgely, 1,657 .... B 8
† 37401 Ridgeside, 458 .... L 10
37152 Ridgetop, 810 .... H 8
38063 Ripley⊙, 4,794 .... B 9
38253 Rives, 5,259 .... C 8
37687 Roan Mountain, 950 .... S 8
37853 Rockford, 950 .... O 9
37854 Rockwood, 5,259 .... M 9
37857 Rogersville⊙, 4,045 .... P 8
38053 Rosemark, 950 .... B 10
37860 Russellville, 850 .... P 8
38369 Rutherford, 1,385 .... C 8
37861 Rutledge⊙, 863 .... P 8
38481 Saint Joseph, 637 .... G 10
37373 Sale Creek, 900 .... L 10
38254 Samburg, 463 .... C 8
38372 Savannah⊙, 5,576 .... E 10
38374 Scotts Hill, 476 .... E 10
38375 Selmer⊙, 3,495 .... D 10
37374 Sequatchie, 450 .... K 10
37862 Sevierville⊙, 2,661 .... P 9
37375 Sewanee, 1,886 .... K 10
37865 Seymour, 500 .... O 9
38255 Sharon, 1,188 .... D 8
37160 Shelbyville⊙, 12,262 .... H 10
37377 Signal Mountain, 4,839 .... L 10
37166 Smithville⊙, 2,997 .... K 9
37167 Smyrna, 5,698 .... H 9
37869 Sneedville⊙, 874 .... P 7
37379 Soddy-Daisy, 7,569 .... L 10
38068 Somerville⊙, 1,816 .... C 10
† 37030 South Carthage, 859 .... K 8
† 37311 South Cleveland, 5,070 .... M 10
† 37716 South Clinton, 1,484 .... N 8
42041 South Fulton, 3,122 .... D 8
37380 South Pittsburg, 3,613 .... K 10
37171 Southside, 800 .... G 8
38583 Sparta⊙, 4,930 .... K 9
38585 Spencer⊙, 1,179 .... L 9
37381 Spring City, 1,756 .... M 9
38378 Spring Creek, 500 .... D 9
37172 Springfield⊙, 9,720 .... H 8
37174 Spring Hill, 685 .... H 9
37871 Strawberry Plains, 680 .... O 8
† 37660 Sullivan Gardens, 950 .... R 7
38483 Summertown, 700 .... G 10
37382 Summitville, 500 .... K 9
37872 Sunbright, 500 .... M 8
37873 Surgoinsville, 1,285 .... R 8
37874 Sweetwater, 4,340 .... N 9
37877 Talbott, 975 .... P 8
37879 Tazewell⊙, 1,860 .... O 8
37385 Tellico Plains, 773 .... N 10
37880 Ten Mile, 700 .... M 9
37178 Tennessee Ridge, 664 .... F 8
† 37401 Tiftona, 1,750 .... L 11
38079 Tiptonville⊙, 2,229 .... B 8
37387 Tracy City, 1,388 .... K 10
37883 Treadway, 712 .... P 8
38382 Trenton⊙, 4,226 .... D 9
38258 Trezevant, 877 .... D 8
38259 Trimble, 675 .... C 8
38260 Troy, 826 .... C 8
37388 Tullahoma, 15,311 .... J 10
37743 Tusculum, 1,157 .... R 8
37692 Unicoi, 500 .... S 8
38261 Union City⊙, 11,925 .... C 8
37393 Victoria, 800 .... K 10
37885 Vonore, 524 .... N 9
37887 Wartburg⊙, 541 .... M 8
37183 Wartrace, 616 .... J 9
37184 Watertown, 1,061 .... J 8
37185 Waverly⊙, 3,794 .... F 8
38485 Waynesboro⊙, 1,983 .... F 10
38074 Western State Hospital, 2,900 .... C 10
37186 Westmoreland, 1,423 .... J 7
37187 White Bluff, 516 .... G 8
38116 Whitehaven, 19,000 .... A 10
37188 White House, 650 .... H 8
37890 White Pine, 1,532 .... P 8
37891 Whitesburg, 500 .... P 8
37396 Whiteside, 523 .... K 10
38075 Whiteville, 992 .... C 10
37397 Whitwell, 1,669 .... K 10
37398 Winchester⊙, 5,211 .... J 10
37892 Winfield, 950 .... M 7
37190 Woodbury⊙, 1,725 .... J 9
37191 Woodlawn, 500 .... G 7

⊙ County seat.
‡ Population of metropolitan area.
† Zip of nearest p.o.
* Multiple zips
■ Name not shown on map.

Topography

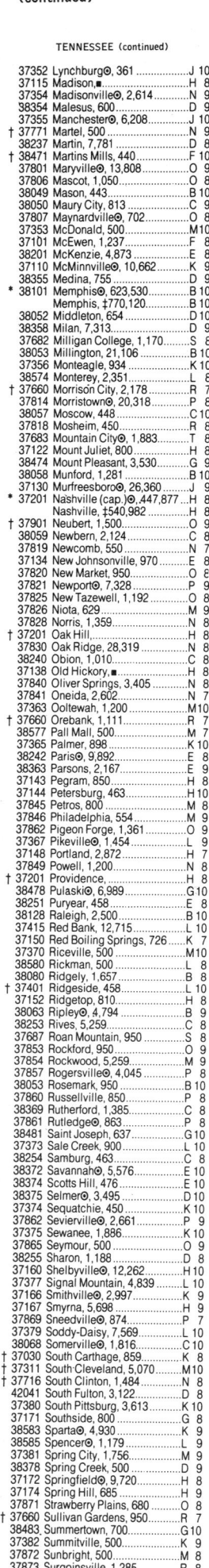

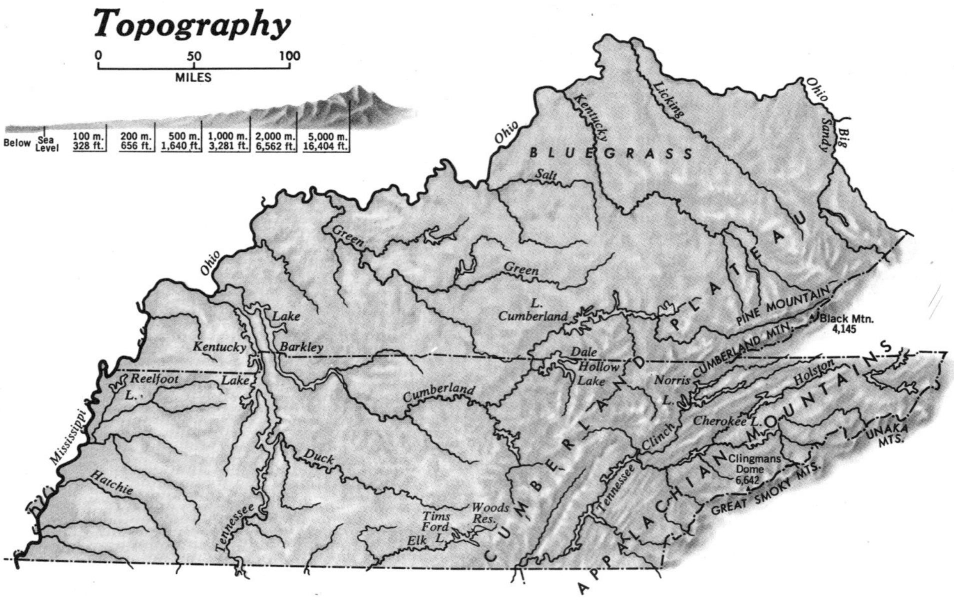

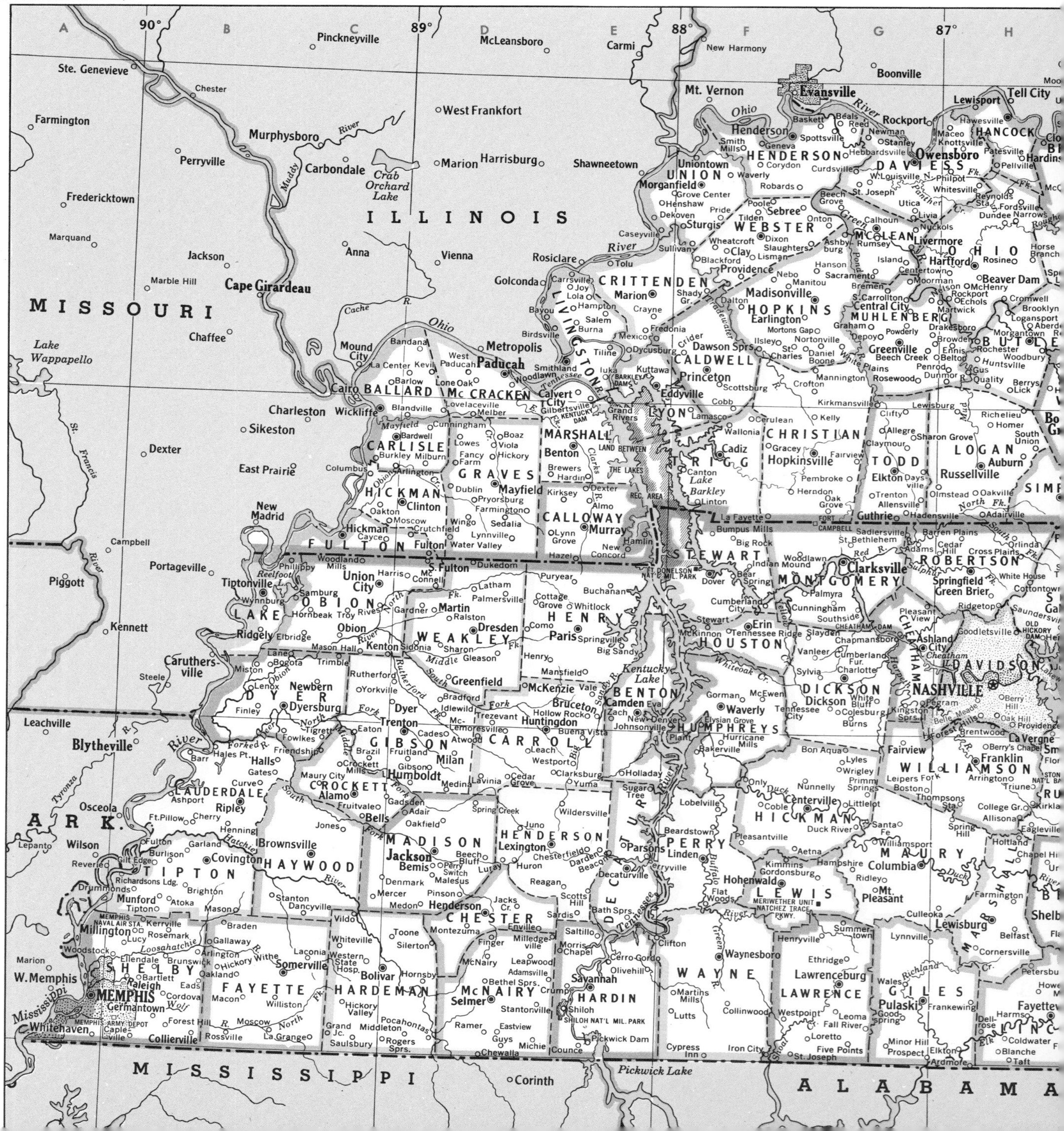

KENTUCKY
and
TENNESSEE

SCALE
0 5 10 20 30 40MI.
0 40KM.

State Capitals .... ⊛
County Seats .... ◉

© C.S. HAMMOND & Co., N.Y.

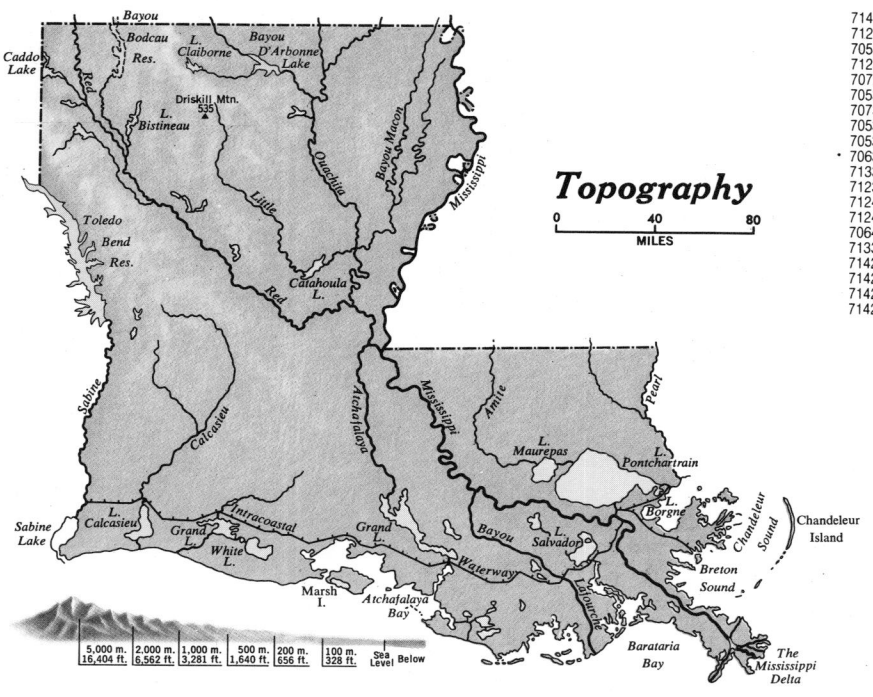

Topography

0   40   80
MILES

Driskill Mtn. 535

5,000 m. 2,000 m. 1,000 m. 500 m. 200 m. 100 m. Sea Level Below
16,404 ft. 6,562 ft. 3,281 ft. 1,640 ft. 656 ft. 328 ft. Level

The Mississippi Delta

LOUISIANA

SCALE
0   5   10   20   30   40 MI.
0   5   10   20   30   40 KM.

State Capitals .... ⊛
Parish Seats .... ⊙
Canals ....

© C.S. HAMMOND & Co., N.Y.

(continued on following page)

AREA 48,523 sq. mi.
POPULATION 3,643,180 ('70); 4,203,972 ('80)
CAPITAL Baton Rouge
LARGEST CITY New Orleans
HIGHEST POINT Driskill Mtn. 535 ft.
SETTLED IN 1699
ADMITTED TO UNION April 30, 1812
POPULAR NAME Pelican State
STATE FLOWER Magnolia
STATE BIRD Eastern Brown Pelican

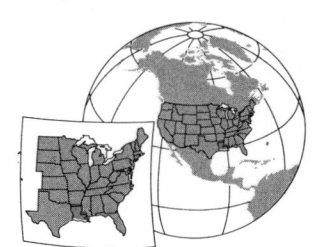

Agriculture, Industry and Resources

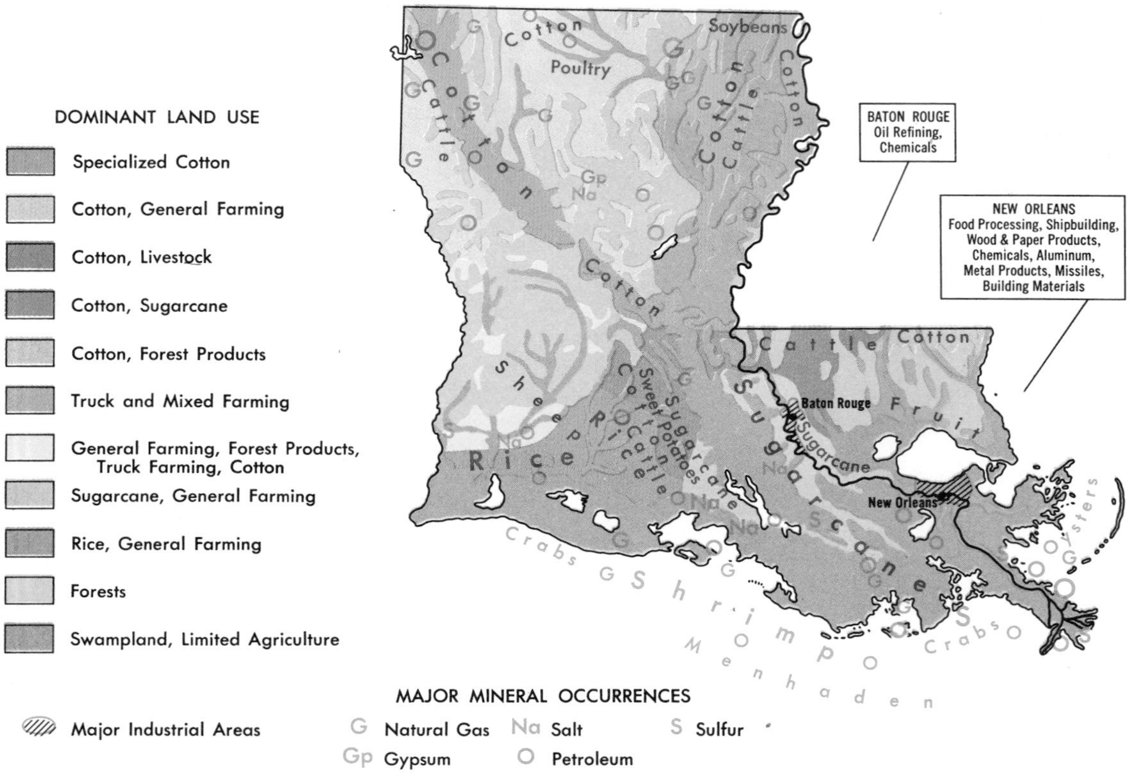

DOMINANT LAND USE
Specialized Cotton
Cotton, General Farming
Cotton, Livestock
Cotton, Sugarcane
Cotton, Forest Products
Truck and Mixed Farming
General Farming, Forest Products, Truck Farming, Cotton
Sugarcane, General Farming
Rice, General Farming
Forests
Swampland, Limited Agriculture
Major Industrial Areas
MAJOR MINERAL OCCURRENCES
G Natural Gas
Na Salt
S Sulfur
Gp Gypsum
O Petroleum
Cotton
Soybeans
Poultry
Cattle
Sheep
Rice
Sweet Potatoes
Sugarcane
Fruit
Oysters
Crabs
Shrimp
Menhaden
Baton Rouge
New Orleans
BATON ROUGE
Oil Refining,
Chemicals
NEW ORLEANS
Food Processing, Shipbuilding,
Wood & Paper Products,
Chemicals, Aluminum,
Metal Products, Missiles,
Building Materials

71047 Keithville, 500 C 2
71441 Kelly, 250 F 3
70062 Kenner, 29,858 N 4
70444 Kentwood, 2,736 J 5
71253 Kilbourne, 370 H 1
† 70462 Killian, 275 M 2
70066 Killona, 600 M 3
70648 Kinder, 2,307 E 6
70370 Klotzville, 248 K 3
70371 Kraemer, 510 M 4
70750 Krotz Springs, 1,435 G 5
70372 Labadieville, 700 K 4
70650 Lacassine, 494 E 6
70445 Lacombe, 750 L 6
70501 Lafayette⊙, 68,908 F 6
Lafayette, ‡109,716 F 6
70067 Lafitte, 1,223 K 7
† 70301 Lafourche, 200 J 7
70549 Lake Arthur, 3,551 E 6
70601 Lake Charles⊙, 77,998 D 6
Lake Charles, ‡145,415 D 6
70752 Lakeland, 400 H 5
71254 Lake Providence⊙, 6,183 H 1
70068 Laplace, 5,953 N 3
70373 Larose, 4,267 K 7
71344 Larto, 500 G 4
70550 Lawtell, 600 F 5
71345 Lebeau, 270 F 5
71346 Lecompte, 1,518 F 4
71446 Leesville⊙, 8,928 D 4
71447 Lena, 250 E 4
70551 Leonville, 512 G 6
70753 Lettsworth, 200 G 5
† 70525 Lewisburg, 265 F 6
71348 Libuse, 500 F 4
71256 Lillie, 160 E 1
71048 Lisbon, 151 E 1
† 71343 Lismore, 380 G 3
† 70062 Little Farms, 15,713 N 4
70754 Livingston⊙, 1,398 L 1
70755 Livonia, 611 G 5
70374 Lockport, 1,995 K 7
71049 Logansport, 1,330 C 3
† 71367 Lonepine, 850 F 5
71448 Longleaf, 250 E 4
71050 Longstreet, 182 B 2
70652 Longville, 250 D 5
70446 Loranger, 200 N 1
70552 Loreauville, 728 G 6
70756 Lottie, 350 G 5
70069 Lucy, 825 M 3
70070 Luling, 3,255 N 4
70071 Lutcher, 3,911 L 3
70447 Madisonville, 801 K 6
70554 Mamou, 3,275 F 5
70448 Mandeville, 2,282 L 6
71259 Mangham, 544 G 2
71052 Mansfield⊙, 6,432 C 2
71350 Mansura, 1,699 G 4
71449 Many⊙, 3,112 C 3
70663 Maplewood, 1,900 D 6
70757 Maringouin, 1,365 G 6
71260 Marion, 796 F 1
71351 Marksville⊙, 4,519 G 4
70072 Marrero, 29,015 O 4
70375 Mathews, 600 J 7
70449 Maurepas, 200 M 2
70555 Maurice, 476 F 6
† 71433 McNary, 220 E 5
71451 Melder, 200 E 4
71353 Melville, 2,076 G 5
70556 Mermentau, 756 E 6
71261 Mer Rouge, 819 G 1
70653 Merryville, 1,286 D 5
* 70001 Metairie, 135,816 O 4
70557 Midland, 500 F 6
70558 Milton, 500 F 6
71055 Minden⊙, 13,996 D 1
70376 Modeste, 230 K 3
71201 Monroe⊙, 56,374 F 1
Monroe, ‡115,387 F 1
70377 Montegut, 950 J 8
71354 Monterey, 800 G 4
71454 Montgomery, 923 E 3
70422 Montpelier, 211 M 1
† 70068 Montz, 200 M 3
71060 Mooringsport, 830 B 1
71455 Mora, 378 E 4
71355 Moreauville, 807 G 4
70380 Morgan City, 16,586 H 7
70759 Morganza, 836 G 5
71356 Morrow, 350 F 5
70559 Morse, 759 F 6
70076 Mount Airy, 700 M 3
70077 Nairn, 500 L 8
70390 Napoleonville⊙, 1,008 K 4
70451 Natalbany, 900 N 1
71456 Natchez, 600 D 3
71457 Natchitoches⊙, 15,974 D 3
† 71342 Nebo, 200 F 3
71460 Negreet, 200 C 4
71357 Newellton, 1,403 H 2
† 71354 New Era, 200 G 4
70560 New Iberia⊙, 30,147 G 6
71461 Newllano, 1,800 D 4
* 70101 New Orleans⊙, 593,471 O 4
New Orleans, ‡1,045,809 O 4
70760 New Roads⊙, 3,945 G 5
70078 New Sarpy, 1,643 N 4
71462 Noble, 209 C 3
70079 Norco, 4,773 N 3
† 71247 North Hodge, 640 E 2
70761 Norwood, 348 H 5
71463 Oakdale, 7,301 E 5
71263 Oak Grove⊙, 1,980 H 1
71264 Oak Ridge, 276 G 1
70655 Oberlin⊙, 1,857 E 5
† 71369 Odenburg, 175 G 5
71061 Oil City, 907 C 1
† 70560 Olivier, 300 G 7
71465 Olla, 1,387 F 3
70570 Opelousas⊙, 20,121 G 5
70762 Oscar, 700 H 5
71358 Palmetto, 312 G 5
70391 Paincourtville, 600 K 3
70080 Paradis, 750 M 4
70582 Parks, 491 G 6
† 70544 Patoutville, 230 G 7
70392 Patterson, 4,409 H 7
70763 Paulina, 500 L 3
70452 Pearl River, 1,361 L 6
† 70548 Pecan Island, 480 F 7
70575 Perry, 225 F 7
† 70042 Phoenix, 525 L 7
70453 Pine Grove, 500 J 5
70576 Pine Prairie, 515 E 5
71360 Pineville, 8,951 F 4
71266 Pioneer, 188 H 1
70656 Pitkin, 700 E 5
71064 Plain Dealing, 2,116 C 1
70764 Plaquemine⊙, 7,739 J 2
70393 Plattenville, 400 K 4
71362 Plaucheville, 224 G 5
71065 Pleasant Hill, 826 C 3
70082 Pointe a la Hache⊙, 750 L 7
71467 Pollock, 341 F 3
70454 Ponchatoula, 4,545 N 2
70767 Port Allen⊙, 5,728 J 2
70577 Port Barre, 2,133 G 5
† 70791 Port Hudson, 200 J 1
70083 Port Sulphur, 3,022 L 8
† 70726 Port Vincent, 387 L 2
71066 Powhatan, 277 D 3
70769 Prairieville, 500 K 2
71067 Princeton, 350 C 1
71468 Provencal, 530 D 3
71268 Quitman, 169 E 2
70394 Raceland, 4,880 J 7
70578 Rayne, 9,510 F 6
71269 Rayville⊙, 3,962 G 2
70580 Reddell, 800 F 5
70658 Reeves, 214 D 5
† 70085 Reggio, 400 L 7
† 70763 Remy, 850 L 3
70084 Reserve, 6,381 M 3
71334 Ridgecrest, 1,076 G 3
71068 Ringgold, 1,731 D 2
† 70427 Rio, 250 L 5
70581 Roanoke, 640 E 6
71469 Robeline, 274 D 3
70455 Robert, 600 N 1
71069 Rodessa, 273 B 1
70772 Rosedale, 621 G 6
70456 Roseland, 1,273 J 5
70659 Rosepine, 587 D 5
71365 Ruby, 350 F 4
71270 Ruston⊙, 17,365 E 1
70774 Saint Amant, 900 L 2
70457 Saint Benedict, 200 K 5
70085 Saint Bernard, 750 L 7
70775 Saint Francisville⊙ 1,603 H 5
70776 Saint Gabriel, 975 K 2
70086 Saint James, 600 L 3
71366 Saint Joseph⊙, 1,864 H 3
71367 Saint Landry, 950 F 5
70582 Saint Martinville⊙, 7,153 G 6
71471 Saint Maurice, 650 E 3
70087 Saint Rose, 2,106 N 4
71070 Saline, 307 E 2
71301 Samtown, 4,210 F 4
71071 Sarepta, 882 D 1
70395 Schriever, 700 J 7
70807 Scotlandville, 22,557 J 1
70583 Scott, 1,334 F 6
† 70560 Segura, 200 G 6
† 70764 Seymourville, 2,506 J 2
71072 Shongaloo, 173 D 1
* 71101 Shreveport⊙, 182,064 C 1
Shreveport, ‡294,703 C 1
71073 Sibley, 869 D 1
71368 Sicily Island, 630 G 3
71472 Sieper, 200 E 4
71473 Sikes, 237 F 2
71369 Simmesport, 2,027 G 5
71474 Simpson, 491 D 4
71275 Simsboro, 412 E 1
70660 Singer, 400 D 5
71475 Slagle, 200 D 4
70777 Slaughter, 580 H 5
70458 Slidell, 16,101 L 6
† 70346 Smoke Bend, 300 K 3
71276 Sondheimer, 325 H 1
70778 Sorrento, 1,182 L 3
† 71052 South Mansfield, 439 C 3
71277 Spearsville, 197 E 1
70462 Springfield, 423 M 2
71075 Springhill, 6,496 D 1
† 71465 Standard, 190 F 3
70661 Starks, 750 C 6
71279 Start, 200 G 2
71280 Sterlington, 1,118 F 1
71078 Stonewall, 500 C 2
70663 Sulphur, 13,551 D 6
71079 Summerfield, 170 E 1
70463 Sun, 288 L 5
70584 Sunset, 1,675 F 6
70780 Sunshine, 900 K 2
70396 Supreme, 617 K 4
71281 Swartz, 650 G 1
† 70601 Sweet Lake, 300 D 7
70464 Talisheek, 292 L 5
71282 Tallulah⊙, 9,643 H 2
70465 Tangipahoa, 469 J 5
71080 Taylor, 500 D 1
† 71290 Tendal, 200 H 2
† 70053 Terry Town, 13,832 O 4
70397 Theriot, 950 J 8
70301 Thibodaux⊙, 14,925 J 7
70466 Tickfaw, 370 M 1
71477 Tioga, 457 F 4
71286 Transylvania, 400 H 1
71081 Trees, 247 B 1
† 70041 Triumph-Buras, 4,113 L 8
71371 Trout, 500 F 3
71479 Tullos, 600 F 3
70782 Tunica, 475 G 5
70585 Turkey Creek, 280 F 5
70723 Union, 665 L 3
71480 Urania, 950 F 3
70090 Vacherie, 2,145 L 3
† 70757 Valverda, 200 G 5
70467 Varnado, 320 L 5
70091 Venice, 900 M 8
71372 Vick, 500 F 4
71373 Vidalia⊙, 5,538 G 3
71270 Vienna, 250 E 1
70586 Ville Platte⊙, 9,692 F 5
70668 Vinton, 3,454 C 6
70092 Violet, 975 P 4
71082 Vivian, 4,046 B 1
70784 Wakefield, 200 H 5
70785 Walker, 1,363 L 1
† 70049 Wallace, 200 M 3
71374 Walters, 500 G 3
71289 Warden, 350 H 1
† 71301 Wardville, 1,087 F 4
70589 Washington, 1,473 G 5
71375 Waterproof, 1,438 H 3
70786 Watson, 700 L 1
71290 Waverly, 350 H 2
† 70569 Weeks, 400 G 7
70093 Welcome, 450 L 3
70591 Welsh, 3,203 E 6
70669 Westlake, 4,082 D 6
71291 West Monroe, 14,868 F 1
† 70082 West Pointe a la Hache, 250 L 7
70094 Westwego, 11,402 O 4
70787 Weyanoke, 500 H 5
70788 White Castle, 2,206 J 3
† 70462 Whitehall, 380 M 2
71376 Whiteville, 450 F 5
71377 Wildsville, 650 G 3
70789 Wilson, 606 H 5
71483 Winnfield⊙, 7,142 E 3
71295 Winnsboro⊙, 5,349 G 2
71378 Wisner, 1,339 G 3
71485 Woodworth, 409 E 4
70592 Youngsville, 1,002 G 6
70791 Zachary, 4,964 K 1
71486 Zwolle, 2,169 C 3

⊙ Parish seat.
‡ Population of metropolitan area.
† Zip of nearest p.o.
* Multiple zips

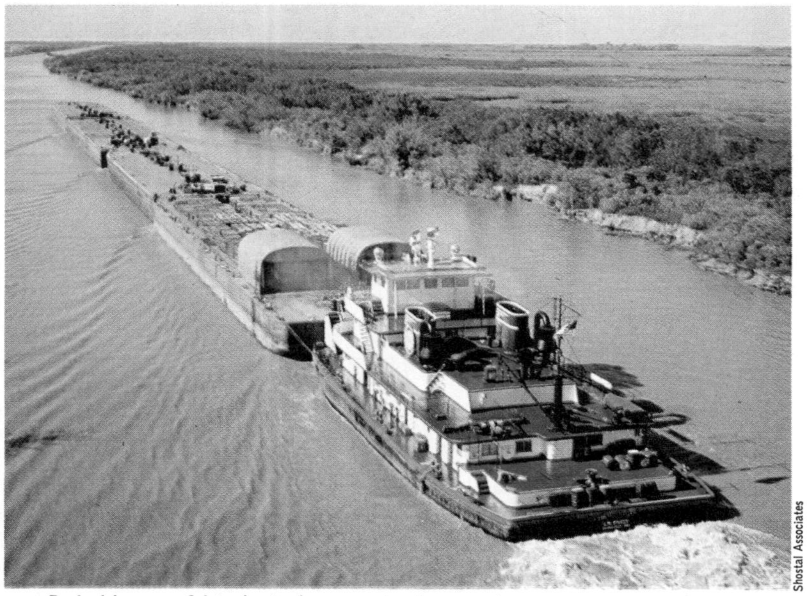
Shostal Associates

Pushed by powerful tugboats, barges make their way from the Mississippi down the shallow Gulf Intracoastal Waterway to deliver their cargoes to New Orleans, Morgan City and Lake Charles, Louisiana.

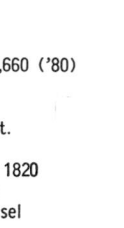

AREA 33,215 sq. mi.
POPULATION 993,663 ('70); 1,124,660 ('80)
CAPITAL Augusta
LARGEST CITY Portland
HIGHEST POINT Katahdin 5,268 ft.
SETTLED IN 1624
ADMITTED TO UNION March 15, 1820
POPULAR NAME Pine Tree State
STATE FLOWER Pine Cone & Tassel
STATE BIRD Chickadee

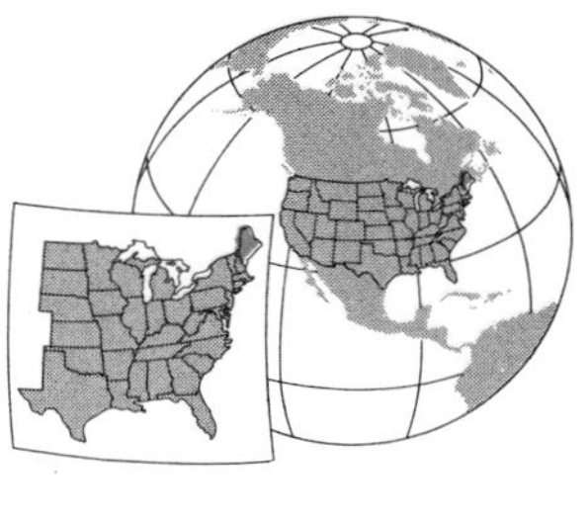

COUNTIES

Androscoggin, 91,279	C 7
Aroostook, 92,463	F 2
Cumberland, 192,528	C 8
Franklin, 22,444	B 5
Hancock, 34,590	G 6
Kennebec, 95,247	D 7
Knox, 29,013	E 7
Lincoln, 20,537	D 7
Oxford, 43,457	B 7
Penobscot, 125,393	F 5
Piscataquis, 16,285	E 4
Sagadahoc, 23,452	D 7
Somerset, 40,597	C 4
Waldo, 23,328	E 6
Washington, 29,859	H 6
York, 111,576	B 9

CITIES and TOWNS

Zip	Name/Pop.	Key
04406	Abbot Village, △453	D 5
04001	Acton, △697	B 8
04606	Addison, △773	H 6
04910	Albion, △1,056	E 6
† 04610	Alexander, △169	H 5
04002	Alfred⊙, △1,211	B 9
† 04774	Allagash, △456	F 1
† 04938	Allens Mills, 150	C 6
04535	Alna, △315	D 7
† 04468	Alton, △340	F 5
† 04408	Amherst, △148	G 6
04216	Andover, △791	B 6
04216	Andover, 350	B 6
04911	Anson, △2,168	D 6
04911	Anson, 950	D 6
† 04862	Appleton, △628	E 7
04732	Ashland, △1,761	G 2
04732	Ashland, 750	G 2
04912	Athens, △592	D 6
04912	Athens, 200	D 6
† 04426	Atkinson, △213	E 5
04210	Auburn⊙, 24,151	C 7
04330	Augusta (cap.)⊙, 21,945	D 7
04408	Aurora, △72	G 6
04003	Bailey Island, 400	D 8
04409	Bancroft, △53	H 4
04401	Bangor⊙, 33,168	F 6
04609	Bar Harbor, △3,716	G 7
04609	Bar Harbor, 2,392	G 7
04610	Baring, 150	J 5
04004	Bar Mills, 800	C 8
04653	Bass Harbor, 413	G 7
04530	Bath⊙, 9,679	D 8
04915	Bayside, 238	F 7
04611	Beals, △663	H 7
† 04622	Beddington, △32	H 6
04915	Belfast⊙, 5,957	F 7
04917	Belgrade, △1,302	D 7
04917	Belgrade, 300	D 7
04918	Belgrade Lakes, 700	D 6
† 04915	Belmont, △349	E 7
04733	Benedicta, △177	G 4
† 04919	Benton, △1,729	D 6
03901	Berwick, △3,136	B 9
03901	Berwick, 1,765	B 9
† 04285	Berry Mills, 245	C 6
04217	Bethel, △2,220	B 7
04217	Bethel, 750	B 7
04005	Biddeford, 19,983	B 9
04006	Biddeford Pool, 500	C 9
04920	Bingham, △1,254	D 5
04920	Bingham, 1,184	D 5
04613	Birch Harbor, 210	H 7
04734	Blaine, △903	H 2
04734	Blaine-Mars Hill, 1,854	H 2
† 04406	Blanchard, △56	D 5
04614	Blue Hill, △1,367	F 7
04615	Blue Hill Falls, 850	F 7
† 04040	Bolsters Mills, 150	B 7
04537	Boothbay, △1,814	D 8
04537	Boothbay, 700	D 8
04538	Boothbay Harbor, 2,320	D 8
04008	Bowdoinham, △1,294	D 7
04481	Bowerbank, △29	E 5
04410	Bradford, △569	F 5
04410	Bradford, 150	F 5
04411	Bradley, △1,010	F 6
04412	Brewer, 9,300	F 6
04735	Bridgewater, △895	H 3
04009	Bridgton, △2,967	B 7
04009	Bridgton, 1,779	B 7
† 04990	Brighton, △58	D 5
04539	Bristol, △1,721	D 8
04539	Bristol, 160	D 8
04616	Brooklin, △598	F 7
04921	Brooks, △751	E 6
04617	Brooksville, △673	F 7
04413	Brookton, 225	H 4
04010	Brownfield, △478	B 8
04010	Brownfield, 200	B 8
04414	Brownville, △1,490	E 5
04414	Brownville, 1,641	E 5
04415	Brownville Junction, 950	E 5
04011	Brunswick, △16,195	C 8
04011	Brunswick, 10,867	C 8
04219	Bryant Pond, 350	B 7
04220	Buckfield, △929	C 7
04618	Bucks Harbor, 161	J 6
04416	Bucksport, △3,756	F 6
04416	Bucksport, 2,456	F 6
04417	Burlington, △266	G 5
04922	Burnham, △802	E 6
† 04093	Buxton, △3,135	C 8
† 04275	Byron, △132	B 6
04619	Calais, 4,044	J 5
04923	Cambridge, △281	E 5
04843	Camden, △4,115	F 7
04843	Camden, 3,492	F 7
04924	Canaan, △904	D 6
04221	Canton, △742	C 7
03902	Cape Neddick, 850	B 9
04014	Cape Porpoise, 500	C 9
04925	Caratunk, △96	C 5
04418	Cardville, 223	F 5
04736	Caribou, 10,419	G 2
04419	Carmel, △1;301	E 6
04420	Carroll, △132	G 5
† 04224	Carthage, △354	C 6
† 04465	Cary, △184	H 4
04015	Casco, △1,256	B 7
04015	Casco, 250	B 7
04421	Castine, △1,080	F 7
† 04623	Centerville, △19	H 6
† 04757	Chapman, △328	G 2
04422	Charleston, △909	F 5
† 04666	Charlotte, △199	J 5
04017	Chebeague Island, 400	C 8
† 04345	Chelsea, △2,095	D 7
04622	Cherryfield, △771	H 6
† 04458	Chester, △255	F 5
† 04938	Chesterville, △643	C 6
04926	China, △1,850	E 7
04926	China, 336	E 7
04222	Chisholm, 1,530	C 7
† 04428	Clifton, △233	G 6
04927	Clinton, △1,971	D 6
04927	Clinton, 1,124	D 6
† 04623	Columbia, △162	H 6
04623	Columbia Falls, △367	H 6
† 04638	Cooper, △88	H 6
04341	Coopers Mills, 200	E 7
04624	Corea, 300	H 7
04928	Corinna, △1,700	E 6
04020	Cornish, △839	B 8
† 04976	Cornville, △623	D 6
04423	Costigan, 200	F 5
04625	Cranberry Isles, △186	G 7
† 04610	Crawford, △74	H 5
† 04015	Crescent Lake, 175	C 7
04738	Crouseville, 300	G 2
† 04747	Crystal, △281	G 4
04021	Cumberland Center, △4,096	C 8
04021	Cumberland Center, 950	C 8
04011	Cundys Harbor, 150	D 8
† 04563	Cushing, △522	E 7
04626	Cutler, △588	J 6
04626	Cutler, 153	J 6
04543	Damariscotta, △1,264	E 7
04543	Damariscotta-Newcastle, 1,188	E 7
04424	Danforth, △794	H 4
04424	Danforth, 650	H 4
† 04622	Deblois, △20	H 6
† 04429	Dedham, △522	F 6
04627	Deer Isle, △1,211	F 7
04627	Deer Isle, 600	F 7
04022	Denmark, △397	B 8
04628	Dennysville, △278	J 6
04425	Derby, 300	E 5
04929	Detroit, △663	E 6
04930	Dexter, △3,725	E 5
04936	Dexter, 2,732	E 5
04224	Dixfield, △2,188	C 6
04224	Dixfield, 1,535	C 6
04932	Dixmont, △559	E 6
04426	Dover-Foxcroft, △4,178	E 5
04426	Dover-Foxcroft⊙, 3,102	E 5
04342	Dresden, △787	D 7
04225	Dryden, 675	C 6
† 04039	Dry Mills, 700	C 8
† 04747	Dyer Brook, △165	G 3
04739	Eagle Lake, △908	F 1
04739	Eagle Lake, 675	F 1
04226	East Andover, 194	B 6
04024	East Baldwin, 175	B 8
04629	East Blue Hill, 150	G 7
04544	East Boothbay, 400	D 8
04427	East Corinth, 525	F 5
04227	East Dixfield, 288	C 6
04428	East Eddington, 200	F 6
04026	East Hiram, 198	B 8
04429	East Holden, 450	F 6
04027	East Lebanon, 950	B 9
† 04049	East Limington, 200	B 8
04228	East Livermore, 290	C 7
04630	East Machias, △1,057	J 6
04630	East Machias, 750	J 6
† 04950	East Madison, 400	D 6
04430	East Millinocket, △2,567	F 4
04430	East Millinocket, 2,564	F 4
04740	Easton, △1,305	H 2
† 04270	East Otisfield, 200	B 7
04229	East Peru, 350	C 7
04230	East Poland, 700	C 7
04631	Eastport, 1,989	K 6
04231	East Stoneham, 150	B 7
04632	East Sullivan, 300	G 6
† 04862	East Union, 220	E 7
04935	East Vassalboro, 300	D 7
04030	East Waterboro, 365	B 8
04234	East Wilton, 650	C 6
† 04428	Eddington, △1,358	F 6
† 04428	Eddington, 250	F 6
04545	Edgecomb, △549	D 8
† 04628	Edmunds, 229	J 6
03903	Eliot, △3,497	B 9
04605	Ellsworth⊙, 4,603	F 6
04433	Enfield, △1,148	F 5
04433	Enfield, 150	F 5
04434	Etna, △526	E 6
04936	Eustis, △595	B 5
04435	Exeter, △663	E 6
† 04938	Fairbanks, 300	C 6
04937	Fairfield, △5,684	D 6
04937	Fairfield, 3,694	D 6
† 04937	Fairfield Center, 975	D 6
04105	Falmouth, △6,291	C 8
04105	Falmouth, 1,621	C 8
† 04105	Falmouth Foreside (Falmouth), 1,621	C 8
† 04345	Farmingdale, △2,423	D 7
† 04345	Farmingdale, 1,832	D 7
04938	Farmington, △5,657	C 6
04938	Farmington⊙, 3,096	C 6
04940	Farmington Falls, 500	C 6
04344	Fayette, △447	C 7
04546	Five Islands, 161	D 8
04742	Fort Fairfield, △4,859	H 2
04742	Fort Fairfield, 2,322	H 2
04743	Fort Kent, △4,575	F 1
04743	Fort Kent, 2,876	F 1
04744	Fort Kent Mills, 300	F 1
04438	Frankfort, △620	F 6
04634	Franklin, △708	G 6
04634	Franklin, 350	G 6
04941	Freedom, △373	E 7
04032	Freeport, △4,781	C 8
04032	Freeport, 1,822	C 8
04745	Frenchville, △1,375	G 1
04745	Frenchville, 800	G 1
04547	Friendship, △834	E 7
04547	Friendship, 700	E 7
04037	Fryeburg, △2,208	A 7
04037	Fryeburg, 1,075	A 7
04345	Gardiner, 6,685	D 7
04939	Garland, △596	E 5
04939	Garland, 300	E 5
04548	Georgetown, △464	D 8
04548	Georgetown, 190	D 8
† 04217	Gilead, △153	B 7
† 04401	Glenburn, △1,196	F 6
04846	Glen Cove, 300	E 7
† 04005	Goodwins Mills, 340	B 8
† 04046	Goose Rocks Beach, 200	C 9
04038	Gorham, △7,839	C 8
04038	Gorham, 3,337	C 8
04636	Gouldsboro, △1,310	H 7
04636	Gouldsboro, 296	H 7
04746	Grand Isle, △797	G 1
04746	Grand Isle, 400	G 1
04637	Grand Lake Stream, △186	H 5
04039	Gray, △2,939	C 8
04039	Gray, 525	C 8
04236	Greene, △1,772	C 7
04441	Greenville, △1,894	D 5
04441	Greenville, 1,714	D 5
04442	Greenville Junction, 150	D 5
04443	Guilford, △1,694	E 5
04443	Guilford, 1,216	E 5
04347	Hallowell, 2,814	D 7
† 04785	Hamlin, △357	H 1
04444	Hampden, △4,693	F 6
04444	Hampden, 2,207	F 6
04445	Hampden Highlands, 950	F 6
04640	Hancock, △1,070	G 6
04237	Hanover, △275	B 7
04942	Harmony, △650	D 6
04942	Harmony, 350	D 6
† 04011	Harpswell, △2,552	D 8
04643	Harrington, △553	H 6
04040	Harrison, △1,045	B 7
† 04221	Hartford, △312	C 7
04943	Hartland, △1,414	D 6
04943	Hartland, 975	D 6
04446	Haynesville, △157	G 4
04238	Hebron, △532	C 7
† 04401	Hermon, △2,376	F 6
† 04082	Highland Lake, 600	C 8
04944	Hinckley, 317	D 6
04041	Hiram, △686	B 8
04041	Hiram, 175	B 8
04730	Hodgdon, △933	H 3
† 04429	Holden, △1,789	H 3
† 04429	Holden, 900	H 3
04042	Hollis Center, △1,560	B 8
04847	Hope, △500	E 7
04847	Hope, 175	E 7
04730	Houlton, △8,111	H 3
04730	Houlton⊙, 6,760	H 3
04448	Howland, △1,468	F 5
04448	Howland, 1,418	F 5
04449	Hudson, △482	F 5
04644	Hulls Cove, 200	G 7
04747	Island Falls, △913	G 3
04645	Isle au Haut, △45	F 7
04848	Islesboro, △421	F 7
04848	Islesboro, 200	F 7
04945	Jackman, △848	C 4
04945	Jackman, 700	C 4
04647	Jacksonville, 200	J 6
04239	Jay, △3,954	C 7
04239	Jay, 850	C 7
04348	Jefferson, △1,242	D 7
04648	Jonesboro, △448	J 6
04649	Jonesport, △1,326	H 6
04649	Jonesport, 1,073	H 6
04748	Keegan, 450	G 1
04450	Kenduskeag, △733	E 6
04043	Kennebunk, △5,646	B 9
04043	Kennebunk, 2,764	B 9
04046	Kennebunkport, △2,160	C 9
04046	Kennebunkport, 1,097	C 9
04349	Kents Hill, 250	D 7
04047	Kezar Falls, 680	B 8
04947	Kingfield, △877	C 6
04451	Kingman, 250	G 4
† 04990	Kingsbury, △7	D 5
03904	Kittery, △11,028	B 9
03904	Kittery, 7,363	B 9
03905	Kittery Point, 1,172	B 9
† 04986	Knox, △443	E 6
04453	La Grange, △393	F 5
04453	La Grange, 250	F 5
† 04463	Lake View, △16	F 5
† 04605	Lamoine, △615	G 7
04455	Lee, △599	G 5
† 04263	Leeds, △1,031	C 7
04456	Levant, △862	F 6
04240	Lewiston, 41,779	C 7
	Lewiston-Auburn, ‡72,474	C 7
04949	Liberty, △515	E 7
04949	Liberty, 200	E 7
04749	Lille, 300	G 1
04048	Limerick, △963	B 8
04750	Limestone, △8,745	H 2
04750	Limestone, 1,572	H 2
04049	Limington, △1,066	B 8
04049	Limington, 250	B 8
04457	Lincoln, △4,759	G 5
04457	Lincoln, 3,482	G 5
04458	Lincoln Center, 325	G 5
04849	Lincolnville, △955	E 7
04849	Lincolnville, 800	E 7
04755	Linneus, △608	H 3
04250	Lisbon, △6,544	C 7
* 04250	Lisbon-Lisbon Center, 1,475	C 7
04252	Lisbon Falls, 3,257	D 7
04350	Litchfield, △1,222	D 7
04650	Little Deer Isle, 275	F 7
† 04760	Littleton, △958	H 3
04253	Livermore, △1,610	C 7
04253	Livermore, 280	C 7
04254	Livermore Falls, △3,450	C 7
04254	Livermore Falls, 2,378	C 7
04255	Locke Mills, 300	B 7
04051	Lovell, △607	B 7
04051	Lovell, 180	B 7
† 04433	Lowell, △154	F 5
04652	Lubec, △1,949	K 6
04652	Lubec, 900	K 6
† 04730	Ludlow, △259	G 3
04654	Machias, △2,441	J 6
04654	Machias⊙, 1,368	J 6
04655	Machiasport, △887	H 6
04655	Machiasport, 374	H 6
† 04451	Macwahoc, △126	G 4
04756	Madawaska, △5,585	G 1
04756	Madawaska, 4,452	G 1
04950	Madison, △4,278	D 6
04950	Madison, 2,920	D 6
† 04966	Madrid, △107	B 6
04351	Manchester, △1,331	D 7
04757	Mapleton, △1,598	G 2
04758	Mars Hill, △1,875	H 2
04758	Mars Hill-Blaine, 1,854	H 2
04759	Masardis, △317	G 3
04459	Mattawamkeag, △988	G 5
04256	Mechanic Falls, △2,193	C 7
04256	Mechanic Falls, 1,872	C 7
04657	Meddybemps, △76	J 5
† 04453	Medford, △146	F 5
04460	Medway, △1,491	G 4
04957	Mercer, △313	D 6
04257	Mexico, △4,309	B 6
04257	Mexico, 3,325	B 6
04658	Milbridge, △1,154	H 6
04461	Milford, △1,828	F 6
04461	Milford, 1,519	F 6
04462	Millinocket, △7,742	F 4
04462	Millinocket, 7,558	F 4
04463	Milo, △2,572	F 5
04463	Milo, 1,514	F 5
04258	Minot, △919	C 7
04258	Minot, 250	C 7
04852	Monhegan, △44	E 8
04259	Monmouth. △2,062	D 7

(continued on following page)

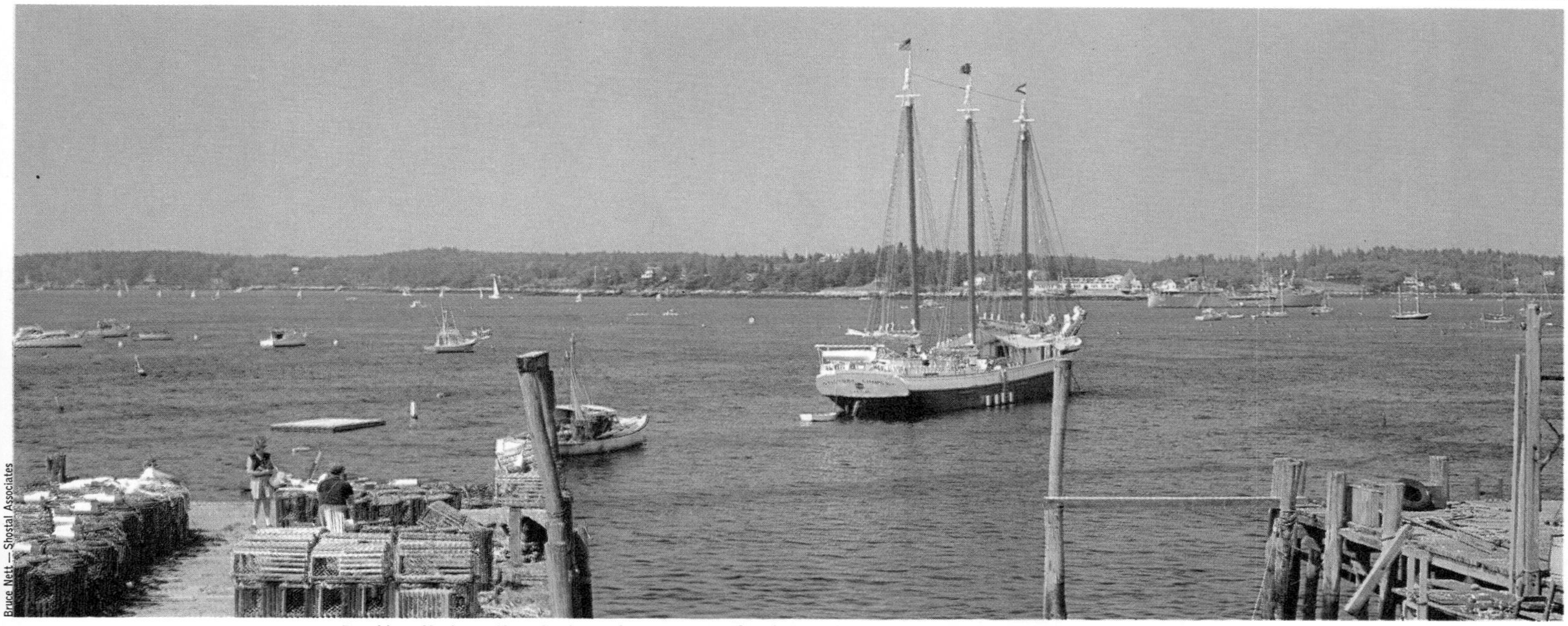

Bruce Nett—Shostal Associates

Boothbay Harbor offers facilities for a variety of sailing craft—yachts, rented party boats and commercial fishermen, all seen here at anchor. This active port rates high among Maine's popular coastal resort towns.

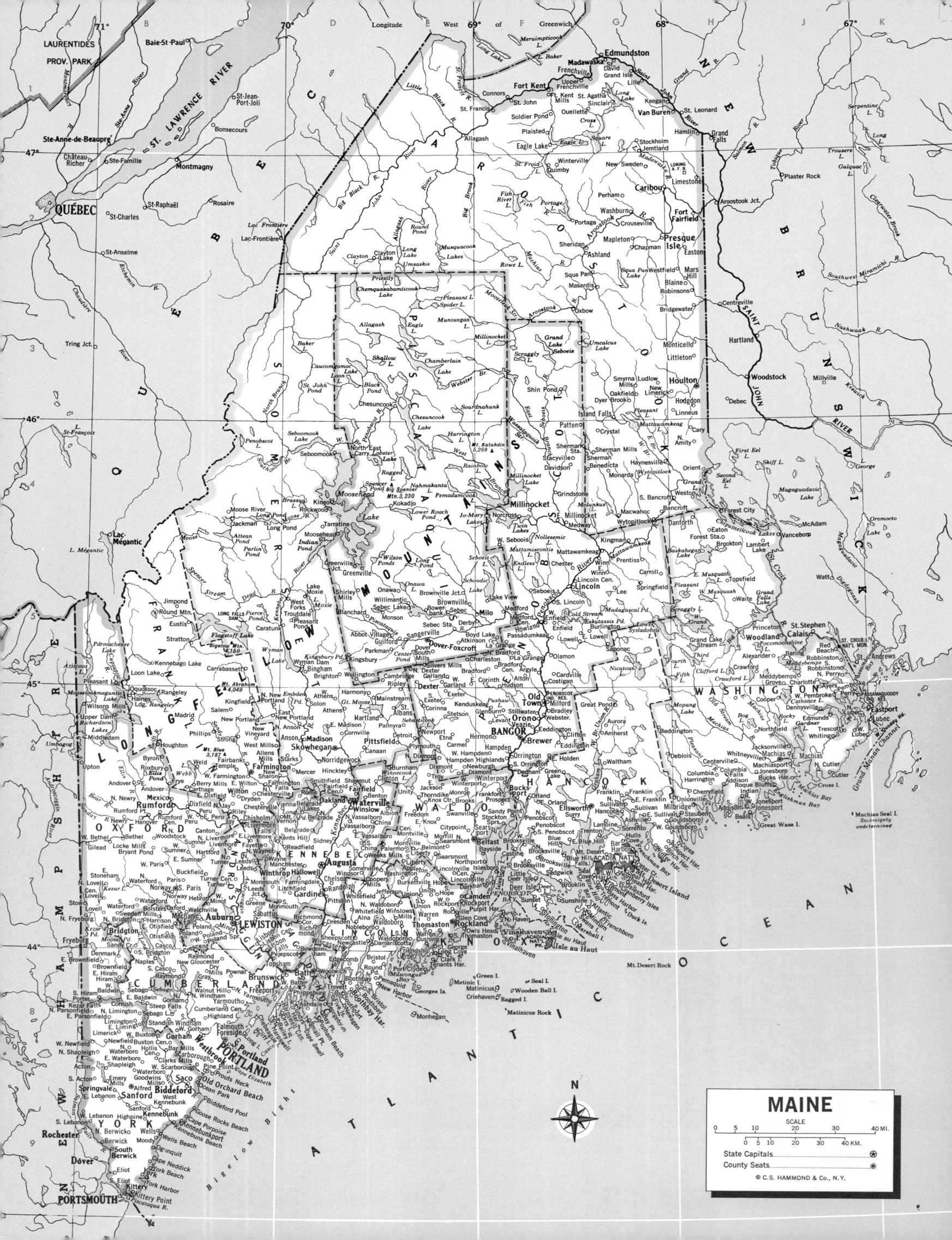

04259 Monmouth, 500 D 7
04951 Monroe, ▵478 E 6
04464 Monson, ▵669 E 5
04760 Monticello, ▵1,072 H 3
† 04941 Montville, ▵430 E 7
04054 Moody, 500 B 9
† 04945 Moose River, ▵255 C 4
04952 Morrill, ▵410 E 7
04660 Mount Desert, ▵1,659 G 7
04352 Mount Vernon, ▵680 D 7
04055 Naples, ▵956 B 8
† 04445 Newburgh, ▵835 F 6
04553 Newcastle, ▵1,076 D 7
04553 Newcastle-Damariscotta, 1,188 E 7
04056 Newfield, ▵458 B 8
04056 Newfield, 165 B 8
04260 New Gloucester, ▵2,811 C 8
04260 New Gloucester, 400 C 8
04554 New Harbor, 580 E 8
04761 New Limerick, ▵427 G 3
04953 Newport, ▵2,260 E 6
04953 Newport, 1,588 E 6
04954 New Portland, ▵559 C 6
04954 New Portland, 201 C 6
04261 Newry, ▵208 B 6
04955 New Sharon, ▵725 C 6
04762 New Sweden, ▵639 G 2
04762 New Sweden, 400 G 2
04956 New Vineyard, ▵444 C 6
04555 Nobleboro, ▵850 D 7
04957 Norridgewock, ▵1,964 D 6
04957 Norridgewock, 1,067 D 6
04958 North Anson 950 D 6
04959 North Belgrade, 300 D 7
03906 North Berwick, ▵2,224 B 9
03906 North Berwick, 1,449 B 9
04057 North Bridgton, 200 B 7
† 04626 North Cutler, 153 J 6
04662 Northeast Harbor, 700 G 7
† 04654 Northfield, ▵57 H 6
04058 North Fryeburg, 250 B 7
04853 North Haven, ▵399 F 7
04853 North Haven, 300 F 7
04262 North Jay, 800 C 6
† 04049 North Limington, 400 B 8
† 04254 North Livermore, 280 C 7
04663 North Lubec, 250 J 6
04961 North New Portland, 300 C 6
† 04849 Northport, ▵744 E 7
04664 North Sullivan, 280 G 6
04266 North Turner, 300 C 7
04962 North Vassalboro, 950 D 7
† 04572 North Waldoboro, 250 E 7
04061 North Waterboro, 200 B 8
04267 North Waterford, 217 B 7
† 04284 North Wayne, 175 C 7
04353 North Whitefield, 300 D 7
04062 North Windham, 600 C 8
† 04219 North Woodstock, 400 B 7
† 04096 North Yarmouth, ▵1,383 C 8
† 04096 North Yarmouth, 500 C 8
04268 Norway, ▵3,595 B 7
04268 Norway, 2,430 B 7
04763 Oakfield, ▵836 G 3
04963 Oakland, ▵5,273 D 6
04963 Oakland, 2,261 D 6
03907 Ogunquit, 800 B 9
04064 Old Orchard Beach, ▵5,404 C 9
04064 Old Orchard Beach, 5,273 C 9
04468 Old Town, 9,057 F 6
04964 Oquossoc, 210 B 6
04471 Orient, ▵83 H 4
04472 Orland, ▵1,307 F 6
04472 Orland, 500 F 6
04473 Orono, ▵9,989 F 6
04473 Orono, 9,146 F 6
04474 Orrington, ▵2,702 F 6
04474 Orrington, 250 F 6
04066 Orrs Island, 500 D 8
† 04270 Otisfield, ▵589 B 7
04665 Otter Creek, 350 G 7
04854 Owls Head, ▵1,281 F 7
04764 Oxbow, ▵92 G 3
04270 Oxford, ▵1,892 B 7
04270 Oxford, 550 B 7
04354 Palermo, ▵645 E 7
04965 Palmyra, ▵1,104 E 6
04271 Paris, ▵3,739 B 7
† 04443 Parkman, ▵457 D 5
04475 Passadumkeag, ▵326 F 5
04765 Patten, ▵1,266 F 4
04765 Patten, 1,068 F 4
04067 Pejepscot, 200 D 8
04558 Pemaquid, 160 E 8
04666 Pembroke, ▵700 J 6
04666 Pembroke, 300 J 6
04476 Penobscot, ▵786 F 7
04766 Perham, ▵436 G 2
04667 Perry, ▵878 J 6
04272 Peru, ▵1,345 C 6
04966 Phillips, ▵979 C 6
04562 Phippsburg, ▵1,229 D 8
04562 Phippsburg, 280 D 8
† 04064 Pine Point, 650 C 8
04967 Pittsfield, ▵4,274 E 6
04967 Pittsfield, 3,398 E 6
† 04345 Pittston, ▵1,617 D 7
04969 Plymouth, ▵542 E 6
04273 Poland, ▵2,015 C 7
04273 Poland, 300 C 7
04768 Portage, ▵477 G 2
04855 Port Clyde, 300 E 8
04068 Porter, ▵1,115 B 8
04068 Porter, 225 B 8
* 04101 Portland⊙, 65,116 C 8
Portland, ‡141,625 C 8
04069 Pownal, ▵800 C 8
04477 Prentiss, ▵159 G 5
04769 Presque Isle, 11,452 H 2
04668 Princeton, ▵956 H 5
† 04981 Prospect, ▵358 F 6
04669 Prospect Harbor, 350 H 7
† 04345 Randolph, ▵1,741 D 7
† 04345 Randolph, 1,548 D 7
04970 Rangeley, ▵941 B 6
04970 Rangeley, 600 B 6
04071 Raymond, ▵1,328 B 8
04071 Raymond, 550 B 8
04355 Readfield, ▵1,258 D 7
04355 Readfield, 300 D 7
04670 Red Beach, 210 J 5
04357 Richmond, ▵2,168 D 7
04357 Richmond, 1,449 D 7
† 04357 Richmond Corner, 200 D 7
† 04930 Ripley, ▵297 E 5
04671 Robbinston, ▵396 J 5
04671 Robbinston, 200 J 5
† 04734 Robinsons, 487 H 3
04841 Rockland⊙, 8,505 E 7
04856 Rockport, ▵2,067 F 7
04856 Rockport, 875 F 7
† 04841 Rockville, 250 E 7
04478 Rockwood, 250 D 4
† 04957 Rome, ▵362 D 6
† 04654 Roque Bluffs, ▵153 H 6
04564 Round Pond, 375 E 8
04275 Roxbury, ▵271 B 6
04276 Rumford, ▵9,363 B 6
04276 Rumford, 6,198 B 6
04278 Rumford Center, 325 B 7
04280 Sabattus, 950 C 7
04072 Saco, 11,678 C 8
04772 Saint Agatha, ▵868 G 1
04971 Saint Albans, ▵1,041 E 6
04773 Saint David, 915 G 1
04774 Saint Francis, ▵811 E 1
04857 Saint George, ▵1,639 E 7
04857 Saint George, 250 E 7
† 04743 Saint John, ▵377 F 1
† 04983 Salem, 300 C 6
04972 Sandy Point, 300 F 7
04073 Sanford, ▵10,457 B 9
04073 Sanford, 15,812 B 9
04479 Sangerville, ▵1,107 E 5
04074 Scarborough, ▵7,845 C 8
04074 Scarborough, 500 C 8
04675 Seal Harbor, 336 G 7
04973 Searsmont, ▵624 E 7
04973 Searsmont, 400 E 7
04974 Searsport, ▵1,951 E 7
04974 Searsport, 1,110 E 7
04075 Sebago Lake, 500 B 8
04481 Sebec, ▵325 E 5
04484 Seboeis, ▵63 F 5
04676 Sedgwick, ▵578 F 7
04076 Shapleigh, ▵559 B 8
04975 Shawmut, 250 D 6
04775 Sheridan, 250 F 2
† 04777 Sherman, ▵949 G 4
† 04777 Sherman, 165 G 4
04776 Sherman Mills, 600 G 4
04777 Sherman Station, 300 F 4
04485 Shirley Mills, ▵174 D 5
04485 Shirley Mills, 180 D 5
† 04330 Sidney, ▵1,319 D 7
04779 Sinclair, 260 G 1
04976 Skowhegan, ▵7,601 D 6
04976 Skowhegan⊙, 6,571 D 6
04978 Smithfield, ▵527 D 6
04780 Smyrna Mills, ▵318 G 3
04780 Smyrna Mills, 250 G 3
04781 Soldier Pond, 500 F 1
04979 Solon, ▵712 D 6
† 04341 Somerville, ▵215 D 7
04677 Sorrento, ▵199 G 7
03908 South Berwick, ▵3,488 B 9
03908 South Berwick, 1,863 B 9
04568 South Bristol, ▵664 D 8
04077 South Casco, 200 B 8
04358 South China, 225 D 7
† 03903 South Eliot, 1,635 B 9
04079 South Harpswell, 650 C 8
04080 South Hiram, 175 B 8
† 04862 South Hope, 200 E 7
† 03901 South Lebanon, 200 A 9
† 04259 South Monmouth, 168 D 7
† 04474 South Orrington, 400 F 6
04281 South Paris⊙, 2,315 C 7
† 04569 Southport, ▵473 D 8
04569 Southport, 175 D 8
04106 South Portland, 23,267 C 8
† 04073 South Sanford, 850 B 9
04858 South Thomaston, ▵831 E 7
† 04864 South Union, 180 E 7
† 04572 South Waldoboro, 300 E 7
04081 South Waterford, 320 B 7
04679 Southwest Harbor, ▵1,657 G 7
04082 South Windham, 1,453 C 8
04487 Springfield, ▵336 G 5
04083 Springvale, 2,914 B 9
04782 Stacyville, ▵547 F 4
04084 Standish, ▵3,122 B 8
04084 Standish, 700 B 8
04980 Starks, ▵323 D 6
04085 Steep Falls, 500 B 8
04488 Stetson, ▵395 E 6
04680 Steuben, ▵697 H 6
04680 Steuben, 200 H 6
04489 Stillwater, 600 F 6
04783 Stockholm, ▵388 G 1
04981 Stockton Springs, ▵1,142 F 7
04981 Stockton Springs, 500 F 7
04681 Stonington, ▵1,291 F 7
† 04058 Stow, ▵109 A 7
04982 Stratton, 450 B 5
04983 Strong, ▵1,132 C 6
04682 Sullivan, ▵824 G 6
† 04292 Sumner, ▵525 C 7
04683 Sunset, 170 F 7
† 04627 Sunshine, 175 G 7
04684 Surry, ▵623 F 7
04685 Swans Island, ▵323 G 7
† 04915 Swanville, ▵487 E 6
† 04040 Sweden, ▵110 B 7
04984 Temple, ▵367 C 6
04860 Tenants Harbor, 600 E 8
04861 Thomaston, ▵2,646 E 7
04861 Thomaston, 2,160 E 7
04986 Thorndike, ▵439 E 6
04490 Topsfield, 180 H 5
04086 Topsham, ▵5,022 D 8
04086 Topsham, 2,700 D 8
† 04653 Tremont, ▵1,003 G 7
† 04653 Tremont, 175 G 7
† 04605 Trenton, ▵392 G 7
† 04652 Trescott, 200 J 6
04571 Trevett, 275 D 8
04987 Troy, ▵543 E 6
04282 Turner, ▵2,246 C 7
04282 Turner, 400 C 7
04862 Union, ▵1,189 E 7
04862 Union, 300 E 7
04988 Unity, ▵1,280 E 6
04784 Upper Frenchville, 375 G 1
04261 Upton, ▵54 B 6
04785 Van Buren, ▵3,971 G 1
04785 Van Buren, 3,429 G 1
04491 Vanceboro, ▵263 J 4
04989 Vassalboro, ▵2,618 D 7
04401 Veazie, ▵1,556 F 6
04401 Veazie, 1,174 F 6
04360 Vienna, ▵205 D 6
04863 Vinalhaven, ▵1,135 F 7
04492 Waite, ▵70 H 5
† 04915 Waldo, ▵431 E 7
04572 Waldoboro, ▵3,146 E 7
04572 Waldoboro, 824 E 7
† 04021 Walnut Hill, 400 C 8
† 04605 Waltham, ▵167 G 6
04864 Warren, ▵1,864 E 7
04864 Warren, 770 E 7
04786 Washburn, ▵1,914 G 2
04786 Washburn, 1,098 G 2
04574 Washington, ▵723 E 7
04087 Waterboro, ▵1,208 B 8
04087 Waterboro, 400 B 8
04088 Waterford, ▵760 B 7
04901 Waterville, 18,192 D 6
04284 Wayne, ▵577 D 7
04284 Wayne, 175 D 7
04361 Weeks Mills, 235 E 7
04285 Weld, ▵360 C 6
04990 Wellington, ▵232 D 5
04090 Wells, ▵4,448 B 9
04090 Wells, 950 B 9
04090 Wells Beach, 600 B 9
04686 Wesley, ▵110 H 6
† 04530 West Bath, ▵836 D 8
04286 West Bethel, 155 B 7
04092 Westbrook, 14,444 C 8
† 04617 West Brooksville, 156 F 7
04093 West Buxton, 185 B 8
04493 West Enfield, 500 F 5
04992 West Farmington, 700 C 6
04787 Westfield, ▵517 G 2
† 04634 West Franklin, 350 G 6
† 04345 West Gardiner, ▵1,435 D 7
† 04445 West Hampden, 800 E 6
04649 West Jonesport, 400 H 6
† 04652 West Lubec, 275 J 6
04288 West Minot, 200 C 7
04095 West Newfield, 225 B 8
04494 Weston, ▵162 H 4
04289 West Paris, ▵1,171 B 7
04290 West Peru, 650 C 7
04291 West Poland, 300 C 7
04865 West Rockport, 350 E 7
04074 West Scarborough, 850 C 8
04690 West Tremont, 200 G 7
04362 Whitefield, ▵1,131 D 7
04362 Whitefield, 550 D 7
04691 Whiting, ▵269 J 6
04692 Whitneyville, ▵155 H 6
† 04443 Willimantic, ▵126 E 5
04294 Wilton, ▵3,802 C 6
04294 Wilton, 2,225 C 6
04363 Windsor, ▵1,097 D 7
04495 Winn, ▵516 G 5
04495 Winn, 250 G 5
04901 Winslow, ▵7,299 D 6
04901 Winslow, 5,389 D 6
04693 Winter Harbor, ▵1,028 G 7
04496 Winterport, ▵1,963 F 6
04496 Winterport, 900 F 6
04788 Winterville, ▵164 F 2
04364 Winthrop, ▵4,335 C 7
04364 Winthrop, 2,571 C 7
04578 Wiscasset⊙, ▵2,244 D 7
04694 Woodland, 1,534 H 5
04579 Woolwich, ▵1,710 D 8
† 04920 Wyman Dam, 300 D 5
04497 Wytopitlock, 200 G 4
04096 Yarmouth, ▵4,854 C 8
04096 Yarmouth, 2,421 C 8
03909 York, ▵5,690 B 9
03909 York, 2,912 B 9
03910 York Beach, 900 B 9
03911 York Harbor, 950 B 9

⊙ County seat.
‡ Population of metropolitan area.
▵ Population of town or township.
† Zip of nearest p.o.
* Multiple zips

Agriculture, Industry and Resources

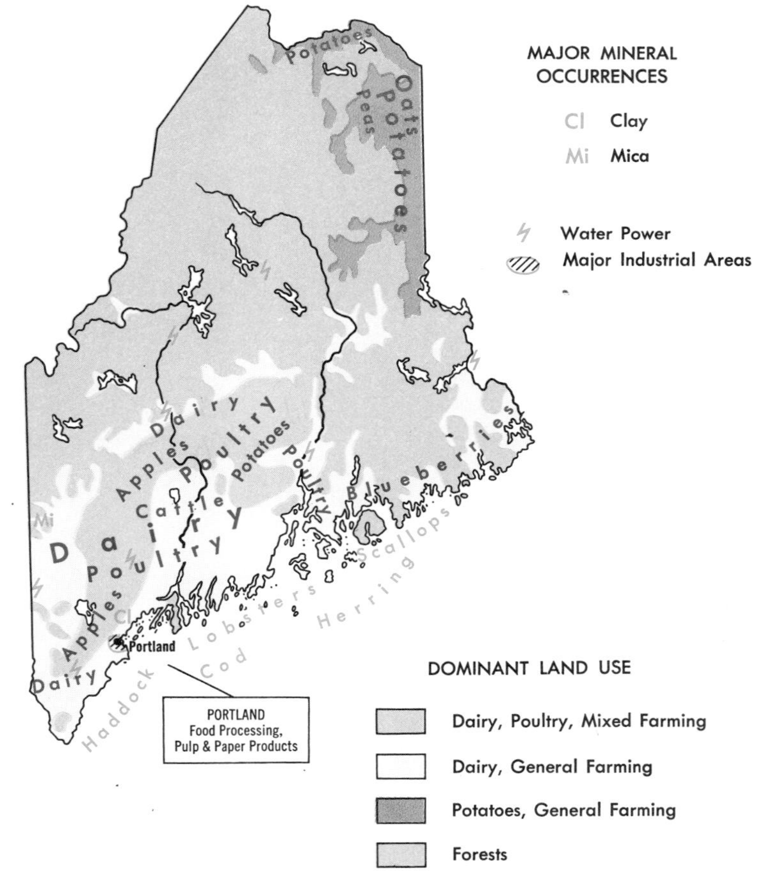
MAJOR MINERAL OCCURRENCES
Cl Clay
Mi Mica
Water Power
Major Industrial Areas
Potatoes
Oats
Peas
Potatoes
Potatoes
Dairy
Apples
Poultry
Cattle
Potatoes
Poultry
Blueberries
Dairy
Poultry
Apples
Scallops
Lobsters
Herring
Cod
Haddock
Portland
PORTLAND
Food Processing,
Pulp & Paper Products
DOMINANT LAND USE
Dairy, Poultry, Mixed Farming
Dairy, General Farming
Potatoes, General Farming
Forests

Topography

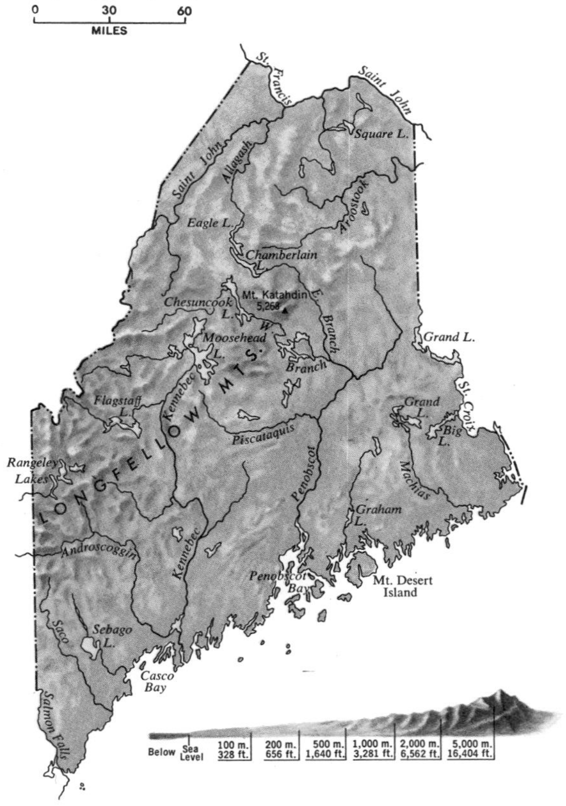
0 30 60
MILES
St. Francis
Saint John
Square L.
Saint John
Allagash
Aroostook
Eagle L.
Chamberlain
Mt. Katahdin
Chesuncook L.
Moosehead L.
Branch
Grand L.
Flagstaff L.
Kennebec
LONGFELLOW MTS.
Piscataquis
Grand
Big L.
St. Croix
Rangeley Lakes
Penobscot
Machias
Graham L.
Androscoggin
Kennebec
Penobscot Bay
Mt. Desert Island
Sebago L.
Saco
Casco Bay
Salmon Falls
Below Sea Level
100 m. 328 ft.
200 m. 656 ft.
500 m. 1,640 ft.
1,000 m. 3,281 ft.
2,000 m. 6,562 ft.
5,000 m. 16,404 ft.

MARYLAND

COUNTIES

Allegany, 84,044	C 2
Anne Arundel, 297,539	M 4
Baltimore, 621,077	M 3
Baltimore (city county), 905,759	M 3
Calvert, 20,682	M 6
Caroline, 19,781	P 5
Carroll, 69,006	K 2
Cecil, 53,291	P 2
Charles, 47,678	K 6
Dorchester, 29,405	O 7
Frederick, 84,927	J 3
Garrett, 21,476	A 2
Harford, 115,378	N 2
Howard, 61,911	L 4
Kent, 16,146	O 3
Montgomery, 522,809	J 4
Prince Georges, 660,567	L 5
Queen Annes, 18,422	P 4
Saint Marys, 47,388	M 7
Somerset, 18,924	R 8
Talbot, 23,692	O 5
Washington, 103,829	G 2
Wicomico, 54,236	R 7
Worcester, 24,442	S 8

CITIES and TOWNS

Zip	Name/Pop.	Key
21001	Aberdeen, 12,375	O 2
21009	Abingdon, 3,000	N 3
21520	Accident, 237	A 2
20607	Accokeek, 450	L 6
21710	Adamstown, 265	H 3
21810	Allen, 200	R 7
† 21043	Allview, 2,314	L 4
* 21401	Annapolis (cap.)⊙, 29,592	M 5
20701	Annapolis Junction, 775	M 4
† 21782	Antietam, 150	H 3
20608	Aquasco, 950	L 6
† 20785	Ardmore, 500	G 4
† 20015	Aspen Hill, 16,799	K 4
* 21201	Baltimore, 905,759	M 3
	Baltimore, ‡2,070,670	M 3
21607	Barclay, 187	P 4
20703	Barnesville, 162	J 4
20610	Barstow, 500	M 6
21521	Barton, 723	B 2
† 21901	Bayview, 250	P 2
21014	Bel Air⊙, 6,307	N 2
20611	Bel Alton, 675	L 7
† 21662	Bellevue, 300	O 6
20705	Beltsville, 8,912	G 3
20612	Benedict, 700	M 6
21811	Berlin, 1,942	T 7
† 20740	Berwyn Heights, 3,934	G 4
20014	Bethesda, 71,621	E 4
21609	Bethlehem, 200	P 6
21610	Betterton, 327	O 3
21611	Bishops Head, 250	O 7
21813	Bishopville, 300	T 7
21814	Bivalve, 450	P 7
20710	Bladensburg, 7,488	G 4
21523	Bloomington, 235	B 3
21713	Boonsboro, 1,410	H 2
† 21532	Borden Shaft, 208	B 2
21020	Boring, 283	L 2
† 20027	Boulevard Heights, 500	F 5
† 20678	Bowens, 250	M 6
20715	Bowie, 35,028	L 4
20720	Boyds, 300	J 4
21612	Bozman, 500	N 5
20613	Brandywine, 525	L 6
20722	Brentwood, 3,426	F 4
21715	Brownsville, 185	H 3
21716	Brunswick, 3,566	H 3
21717	Buckeystown, 400	J 3
21718	Burkittsville, 221	H 3
20730	Burtonsville, 3,000	L 4
20618	Bushwood, 675	L 7
21023	Butler, 150	M 2
20731	Cabin John, 2,500	E 4
20619	California, 350	M 7
† 20705	Calverton, 6,453	L 4
21613	Cambridge⊙, 11,595	O 6
20031	Camp Springs, 22,776	G 6
20027	Capitol Heights, 2,852	G 5
21024	Cardiff, 510	N 2
† 20780	Carrollton, 13,395	G 4
21025	Carrollton, 174	L 2
† 21034	Castleton, 675	N 2
† 21788	Catoctin Furnace, 516	J 2
21228	Catonsville, 54,812	M 3
21720	Cavetown, 325	H 2
21913	Cecilton, 581	P 3
† 20767	Cedar Grove, 300	K 4
† 20027	Cedar Heights, 6,049	G 5
21617	Centreville⊙, 1,853	O 4
21816	Chance, 500	P 8
20621	Chaptico, 300	M 7
21914	Charlestown, 721	P 2
20622	Charlotte Hall, 200	M 7
21027	Chase, 900	N 3
20623	Cheltenham, 950	L 6
† 21921	Cherry Hill, 214	P 2
20732	Chesapeake Beach, 934	N 6
21915	Chesapeake City, 1,031	P 2
21619	Chester, 950	N 5
21620	Chestertown⊙, 3,476	O 4
20785	Cheverly, 6,696	G 4
20015	Chevy Chase, 16,424	E 4
21721	Chewsville, 350	H 2
20783	Chillum, 35,656	F 4
21623	Church Hill, 247	O 4
21028	Churchville, 500	N 2
21624	Claiborne, 150	N 5
20734	Clarksburg, 400	J 4
21029	Clarksville, 500	L 4
21722	Clear Spring, 499	G 2
20624	Clements, 800	L 7
20735	Clinton, 1,900	G 6
21030	Cockeysville, 2,900	M 3
20740	College Park, 26,156	G 4
† 20722	Colmar Manor, 1,715	F 4
21917	Colora, 500	O 2
20626	Coltons Point, 310	M 8
21043	Columbia, 8,815	L 5
20627	Compton, 500	M 7
21918	Conowingo, 150	O 2
21723	Cooksville, 497	K 3
† 20027	Coral Hills, 7,105	G 5
21625	Cordova, 365	O 5
21524	Corriganville, 850	C 2
† 20722	Cottage City, 993	F 4
† 20611	Cox Station (Bel Alton), 675	L 7
† 21788	Creagerstown, 240	J 2
21525	Crellin, 500	A 3
21502	Cresaptown, 1,731	C 2
21817	Crisfield, 3,078	P 9
21627	Crocheron, 150	O 8
21113	Crofton, 4,478	M 4
21032	Crownsville, 1,900	M 4
21628	Crumpton, 375	P 4
21502	Cumberland⊙, 29,724	D 2
20750	Damascus, 2,638	K 3
20628	Dameron, 500	N 8
21820	Dames Quarter, 300	P 8
† 25425	Dargan, 245	H 3
21034	Darlington, 800	N 2
20760	Darnestown, 950	J 4
21035	Davidsonville, 250	M 5
20751	Deale, 1,059	M 5
21821	Deal Island, 800	P 8
21550	Deer Park, 310	A 3
† 19940	Delmar, 1,191	R 7
21629	Denton⊙, 1,561	P 5
20855	Derwood, 450	K 4
20753	Dickerson, 500	J 4
20028	District Heights, 8,424	G 5
† 21710	Doubs, 273	J 3
† 21795	Downsville, 255	G 2
20630	Drayden, 450	N 8
† 21154	Dublin, 366	N 2
21222	Dundalk, 85,377	N 3
† 20608	Eagle Harbor, 200	M 6
† 21146	Earleigh Heights, 1,500	M 4
21631	East New Market, 251	P 6
21601	Easton⊙, 6,809	O 5
21528	Eckhart Mines, 900	C 2
21040	Edgewood, 8,551	N 3
† 20781	Edmonston, 1,441	F 4
† 21784	Eldersburg, 1,739	L 3
21920	Elk Mills, 500	P 2
† 21901	Elk Neck, 700	P 2
21227	Elkridge, 4,900	M 4
21921	Elkton⊙, 5,362	P 2
21529	Ellerslie, 950	C 2
21043	Ellicott City⊙, 9,506	L 3
21727	Emmitsburg, 1,532	J 2
21221	Essex, 38,193	N 3
21824	Ewell, 350	O 9
† 21620	Fairlee, 300	O 4
† 20027	Fairmont Heights, 1,972	G 5
21047	Fallston, 617	N 2
21632	Federalsburg, 1,917	P 6
21061	Ferndale, 9,929	M 4
21048	Finksburg, 950	L 3
21634	Fishing Creek, 595	N 7
21530	Flintstone, 395	D 2
† 20907	Forest Glen, 1,900	F 4
† 20001	Forest Heights, 3,600	F 5
21050	Forest Hill, 450	N 2
† 20028	Forestville, 16,152	G 5
† 20013	Fort Foote, 700	F 6
† 20735	Fort Washington, 1,650	L 6
† 21740	Fountain Head, 2,029	H 2
† 21760	Foxville, 400	J 2
21701	Frederick⊙, 23,641	J 3
21053	Freeland, 500	M 2
21531	Friendsville, 566	A 2
† 21157	Frizzellburg, 300	K 2
21532	Frostburg, 7,327	C 2
21826	Fruitland, 2,315	R 7
21734	Funkstown, 1,051	H 2
20760	Gaithersburg, 8,344	K 4
21635	Galena, 361	P 3
21054	Gambrills, 460	M 4
20766	Garrett Park, 1,258	E 3
21055	Garrison, 950	L 3
20767	Germantown, 260	J 4
21829	Girdletree, 850	S 8
20801	Glenarden, 4,502	G 4
21057	Glen Arm, 350	N 3
21061	Glen Burnie, 38,608	M 4
20768	Glen Echo, 297	E 4
† 20013	Glen Echo Heights, 2,025	E 4
21737	Glenelg, 400	L 3
21071	Glyndon-Reisterstown, 14,037	L 3
21636	Goldsboro, 231	P 4
† 20715	Good Luck, 10,584	G 4
† 21788	Graceham, 300	J 2
† 21163	Granite, 950	L 3
21536	Grantsville, 517	B 2
21638	Grasonville, 1,182	O 5
20770	Greenbelt, 18,199	G 4
21122	Green Haven, 1,841	M 4
21072	Greenmount, 325	L 2
21639	Greensboro, 1,173	P 5
21740	Hagerstown⊙, 35,862	G 2
† 21740	Halfway, 6,106	G 2
† 20850	Halpine, 5,912	K 4
21074	Hampstead, 961	L 2
21750	Hancock, 1,832	F 2
21201	Hanover, 500	M 4
† 21787	Harney, 250	K 2
21078	Havre de Grace, 9,791	O 2
21830	Hebron, 705	R 7
21080	Henryton, 400	L 3
† 21111	Hereford, 680	M 2
21753	Highfield, 500	J 2
† 20901	Hillandale, 19,520	F 4
† 20001	Hillcrest Heights, 24,037	F 5
21641	Hillsboro, 177	P 5
20636	Hollywood, 500	M 7
21642	Hoopersville, 300	O 7
20637	Hughesville, 500	L 6
20639	Huntingtown, 450	M 6
21643	Hurlock, 1,056	P 6
† 21864	Hursley Station (Stockton), 500	S 8
20734	Hyattstown, 150	J 3
* 20780	Hyattsville, 14,998	F 4
20640	Indian Head, 1,350	K 6
21644	Ingleside, 180	P 4

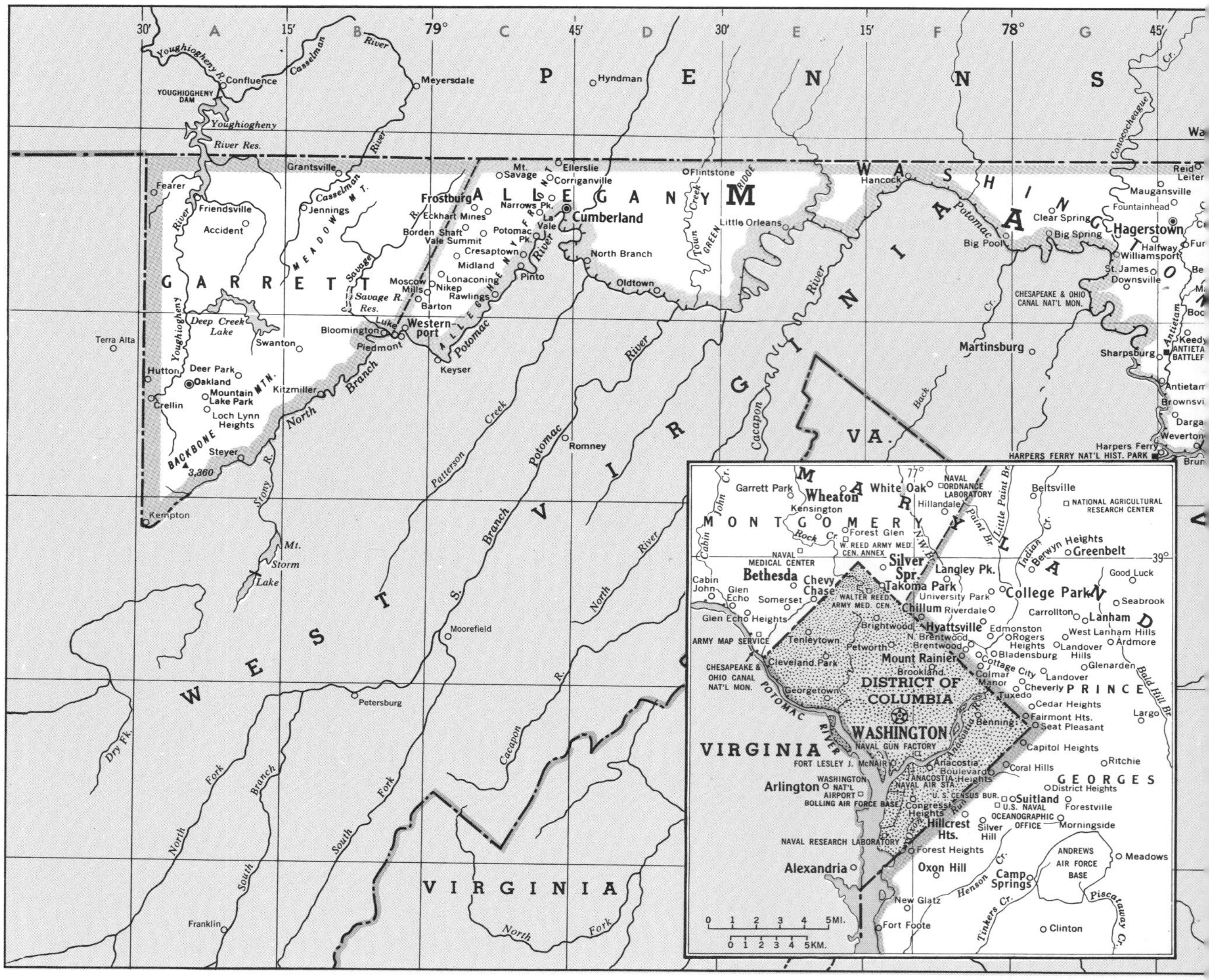

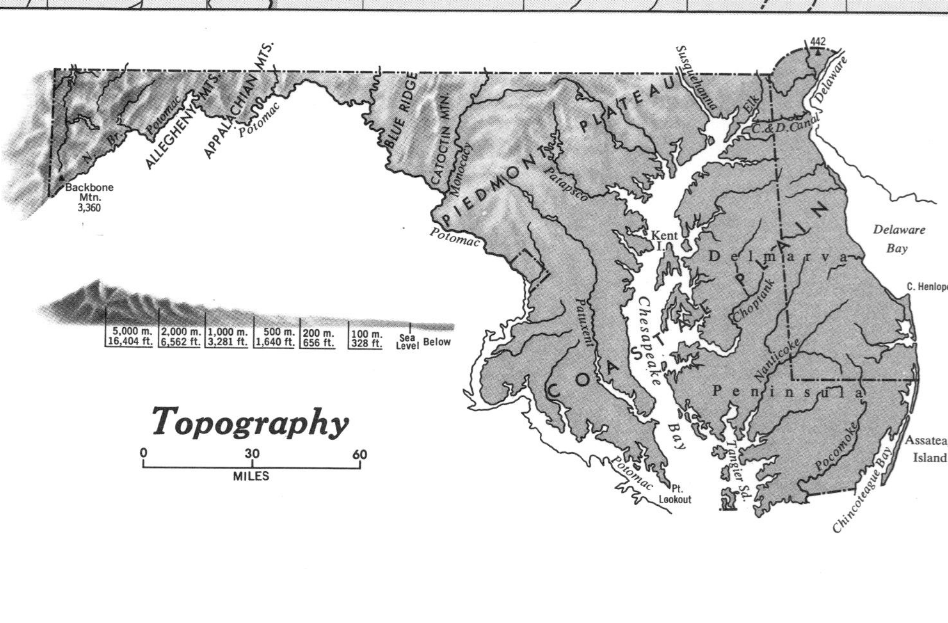

Topography

† 20685	Island Creek, 400	M	7
20645	Issue, 250	L	7
21084	Jarrettsville, 400	M	2
21755	Jefferson, 300	J	3
† 21101	Joppatowne, 9,092	N	3
21756	Keedysville, 431	H	3
21645	Kennedyville, 250	P	3
20795	Kensington, 2,322	E	4
21757	Keymar, 220	K	2
21087	Kingsville, 800	N	3
21538	Kitzmiller, 443	B	3
21758	Knoxville, 525	H	3
20785	Landover, 5,597	G	4
20784	Landover Hills, 2,691	G	4
20787	Langley Park, 11,564	F	4
20801	Lanham-Seabrook, 13,244	G	4
21227	Lansdowne, 16,976	M	3
20646	La Plata⊙, 1,561	L	6
20810	Laurel, 10,525	L	4
21502	La Vale-Narrows Park, 3,971	C	2
20760	Laytonsville, 293	K	4
21761	Le Gore, 500	J	2
† 21740	Leitersburg, 450	H	2
20650	Leonardtown⊙, 1,406	M	7
21701	Lewistown, 600	J	2
20653	Lexington Park, 9,136	M	7
21931	Liberty Grove, 150	O	2
21762	Libertytown, 500	J	3
21763	Lime Kiln, 230	J	3
21088	Lineboro, 300	L	2
21835	Linkwood, 250	P	6
21090	Linthicum Heights, 9,830	M	4
21764	Linwood, 191	K	2
21765	Lisbon, 150	K	3
21766	Little Orleans, 157	E	2
† 21550	Loch Lynn Heights, 507	A	3
21204	Loch Raven, 25,000	M	3
21539	Lonaconing, 1,572	C	2
† 21037	Londontowne, 3,864	M	4
21092	Long Green, 250	M	3
20656	Loveville, 600	M	7
21562	Luke, 424	B	3
20657	Lusby, 150	N	7
21093	Lutherville-Timonium, 24,055	M	3
21648	Madison, 300	O	6
21102	Manchester, 1,466	L	2
21836	Manokin, 400	P	8
20658	Marbury, 900	K	6
21837	Mardela Springs, 356	P	7
21838	Marion Station, 400	R	8

(continued on following page)

MARYLAND

AREA 10,577 sq. mi.
POPULATION 3,922,399 ('70); 4,216,446 ('80)
CAPITAL Annapolis
LARGEST CITY Baltimore
HIGHEST POINT Backbone Mtn. 3,360 ft.
SETTLED IN 1634
ADMITTED TO UNION April 28, 1788
POPULAR NAME Old Line State; Free State
STATE FLOWER Black-eyed Susan
STATE BIRD Baltimore Oriole

DELAWARE

AREA 2,057 sq. mi.
POPULATION 548,104 ('70); 595,225 ('80)
CAPITAL Dover
LARGEST CITY Wilmington
HIGHEST POINT Ebright Road 442 ft.
SETTLED IN 1627
ADMITTED TO UNION December 7, 1787
POPULAR NAME First State; Diamond State
STATE FLOWER Peach Blossom
STATE BIRD Blue Hen Chicken

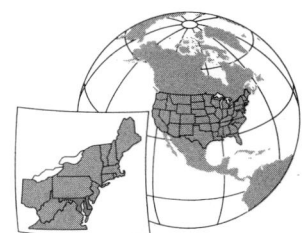

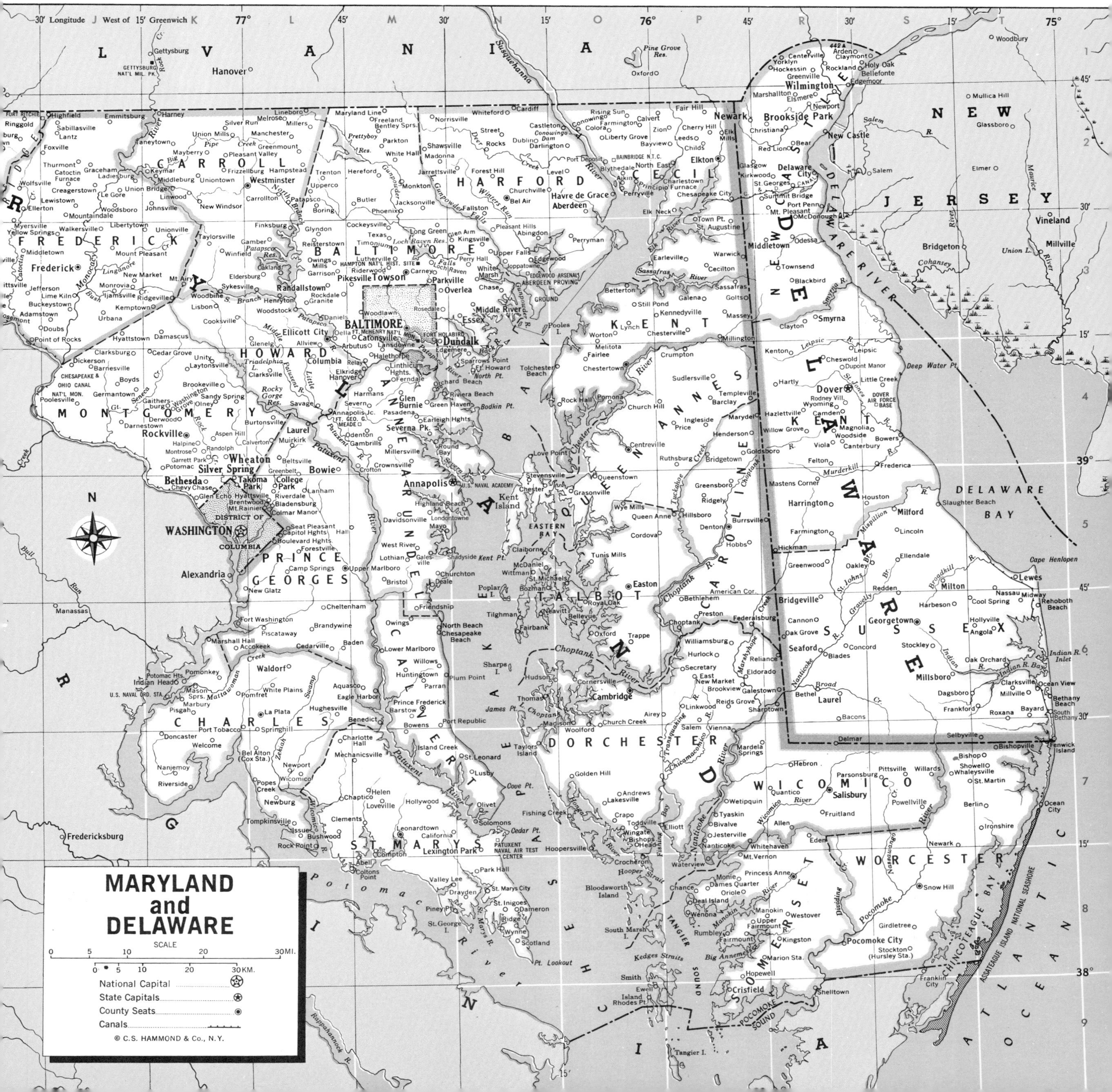

Antietam Battlefield, near Sharpsburg, Maryland, the scene of the country's bloodiest one-day battle on September 17, 1862. A national battlefield site today, it is surrounded by farms, some of whose cattle graze among the cannons and monuments.

J. C. Maycock—Shostal Associates

In Lewes, Delaware, settled by the Dutch in 1631, the Thompson Country Store sign establishes its origin as c.1800. The home of generations of Delaware River ship pilots, this seafaring town survives a history of shipwreck, bombardment and plundering.

Dorothy Bacheller

Agriculture, Industry and Resources

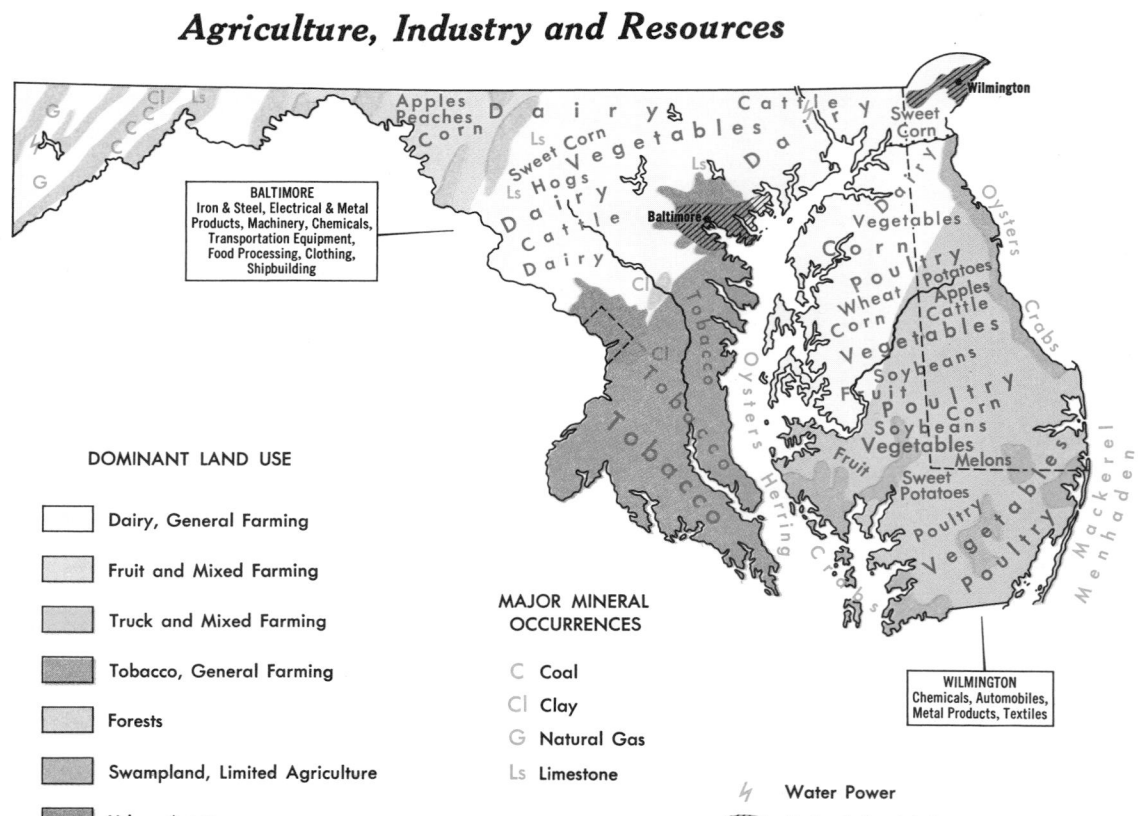

BALTIMORE
Iron & Steel, Electrical & Metal Products, Machinery, Chemicals, Transportation Equipment, Food Processing, Clothing, Shipbuilding

WILMINGTON
Chemicals, Automobiles, Metal Products, Textiles

DOMINANT LAND USE

Dairy, General Farming

Fruit and Mixed Farming

Truck and Mixed Farming

Tobacco, General Farming

Forests

Swampland, Limited Agriculture

Urban Areas

MAJOR MINERAL OCCURRENCES

C Coal
Cl Clay
G Natural Gas
Ls Limestone

↯ Water Power
▨ Major Industrial Areas

MASSACHUSETTS

AREA 8,257 sq. mi.
POPULATION 5,689,170 ('70); 5,737,037 ('80)
CAPITAL Boston
LARGEST CITY Boston
HIGHEST POINT Mt. Greylock 3,491 ft.
SETTLED IN 1620
ADMITTED TO UNION February 6, 1788
POPULAR NAME Bay State; Old Colony
STATE FLOWER Mayflower
STATE BIRD Chickadee

RHODE ISLAND

AREA 1,214 sq. mi.
POPULATION 949,723 ('70); 947,154 ('80)
CAPITAL Providence
LARGEST CITY Providence
HIGHEST POINT Jerimoth Hill 812 ft.
SETTLED IN 1636
ADMITTED TO UNION May 29, 1790
POPULAR NAME Little Rhody
STATE FLOWER Violet
STATE BIRD Rhode Island Red

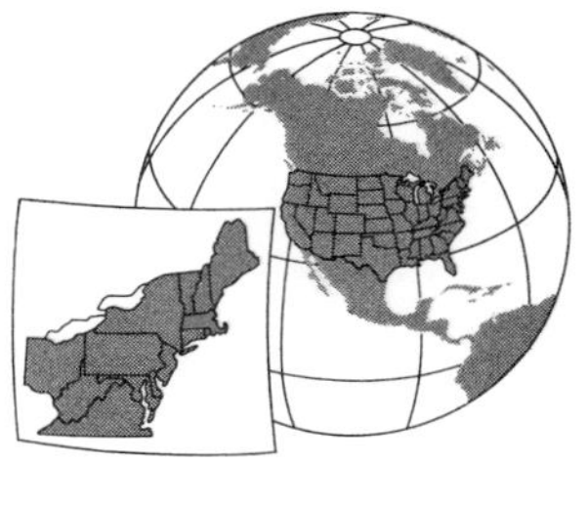

Agriculture, Industry and Resources

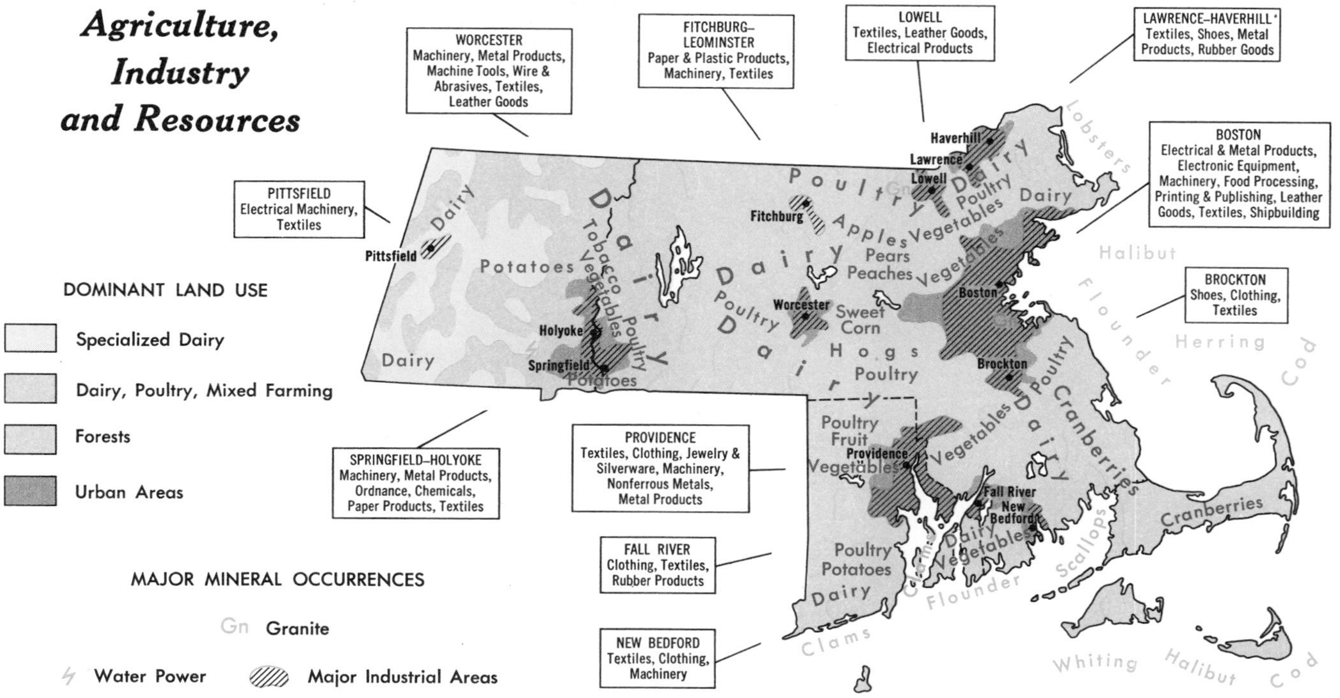

WORCESTER
Machinery, Metal Products, Machine Tools, Wire & Abrasives, Textiles, Leather Goods
FITCHBURG–LEOMINSTER
Paper & Plastic Products, Machinery, Textiles
LOWELL
Textiles, Leather Goods, Electrical Products
LAWRENCE–HAVERHILL
Textiles, Shoes, Metal Products, Rubber Goods
BOSTON
Electrical & Metal Products, Electronic Equipment, Machinery, Food Processing, Printing & Publishing, Leather Goods, Textiles, Shipbuilding
PITTSFIELD
Electrical Machinery, Textiles
BROCKTON
Shoes, Clothing, Textiles
SPRINGFIELD–HOLYOKE
Machinery, Metal Products, Ordnance, Chemicals, Paper Products, Textiles
PROVIDENCE
Textiles, Clothing, Jewelry & Silverware, Machinery, Nonferrous Metals, Metal Products
FALL RIVER
Clothing, Textiles, Rubber Products
NEW BEDFORD
Textiles, Clothing, Machinery
DOMINANT LAND USE
Specialized Dairy
Dairy, Poultry, Mixed Farming
Forests
Urban Areas
MAJOR MINERAL OCCURRENCES
Gn Granite
Water Power
Major Industrial Areas
Haverhill
Lawrence
Lowell
Fitchburg
Pittsfield
Worcester
Holyoke
Springfield
Boston
Brockton
Providence
Fall River
New Bedford
Dairy
Potatoes
Tobacco
Vegetables
Poultry
Apples
Pears
Peaches
Sweet Corn
Hogs
Fruit
Cranberries
Lobsters
Halibut
Flounder
Herring
Cod
Scallops
Clams
Whiting

MASSACHUSETTS

COUNTIES

Barnstable, 96,656 ... N 6
Berkshire, 149,402 ... B 3
Bristol, 444,301 ... K 5
Dukes, 6,117 ... M 7
Essex, 637,887 ... L 2
Franklin, 59,210 ... D 2
Hampden, 459,050 ... D 4
Hampshire, 123,981 ... D 3
Middlesex, 1,397,268 ... J 3
Nantucket, 3,774 ... O 7
Norfolk, 605,051 ... K 4
Plymouth, 333,314 ... L 5
Suffolk, 735,190 ... K 3
Worcester, 637,969 ... G 3

CITIES and TOWNS

Zip *Name/Pop.* *Key*

02351 Abington, △12,334 ... L 4
02351 Abington, 5,900 ... L 4
01720 Acton, △14,770 ... J 3
01220 Adams, △11,772 ... B 2
01220 Adams, 11,256 ... B 2
01001 Agawam, △21,717 ... D 4
† 01261 Alford, △302 ... A 4
01913 Amesbury, △11,388 ... L 1
01913 Amesbury, 10,088 ... L 1
01002 Amherst, △26,331 ... E 3
01002 Amherst, 17,926 ... E 3
01810 Andover, △23,695 ... K 2
02174 Arlington, △53,524 ... C 6
01430 Ashburnham, △3,484 ... G 2
01431 Ashby, △2,274 ... G 2
01330 Ashfield, △1,274 ... C 2
01721 Ashland, △8,882 ... J 3
01331 Athol, △11,185 ... F 2
01331 Athol, 9,723 ... F 2
02703 Attleboro, 32,907 ... J 5
02763 Attleboro Falls, 5,000 ... J 5
01501 Auburn, △15,347 ... G 4
† 02166 Auburndale, 7,235 ... B 7
02322 Avon, △5,295 ... K 4
* 01432 Ayer, △7,393 ... H 2
02630 Barnstable⊙, △19,842 ... N 6
01005 Barre, △3,825 ... F 3
01223 Becket, △929 ... B 3
01730 Bedford, △13,513 ... B 6
01007 Belchertown, △5,936 ... E 3
02019 Bellingham, △13,967 ... J 4
02019 Bellingham, 4,228 ... J 4
02178 Belmont, △28,285 ... C 6
† 02780 Berkley, △2,027 ... K 5
01503 Berlin, △2,099 ... H 3
01337 Bernardston, △1,659 ... D 2
01915 Beverly, 38,348 ... E 5
01821 Billerica, △31,648 ... J 2
01504 Blackstone, △6,566 ... H 4
01008 Blandford, △863 ... C 4
01740 Bolton, △1,905 ... H 3
* 02101 Boston (cap.)⊙, 641,071 ... D 7
Boston, ‡2,753,700 ... D 7
02532 Bourne, △12,636 ... M 6
† 01720 Boxborough, △1,451 ... H 3
01921 Boxford, △4,032 ... L 2
01505 Boylston, △2,774 ... H 3
02184 Braintree, △35,050 ... D 8
02631 Brewster, △1,790 ... O 5
02324 Bridgewater, △11,829 ... K 5
02324 Bridgewater, 4,032 ... K 5
01010 Brimfield, △1,907 ... F 4
* 02401 Brockton, 89,040 ... K 4
Brockton, ‡189,820 ... K 4
01506 Brookfield, △2,063 ... F 4
02147 Brookline, △58,886 ... C 7
01338 Buckland, △1,892 ... C 2
01803 Burlington, △21,980 ... C 5
† 02138 Cambridge⊙, 100,361 ... C 7
02021 Canton, △17,100 ... C 8
01741 Carlisle, △2,871 ... J 2
02330 Carver, △2,420 ... M 5
01339 Charlemont, △897 ... C 2
01507 Charlton, △4,654 ... F 4
02633 Chatham, △4,554 ... P 6
01824 Chelmsford, △31,432 ... J 2
02150 Chelsea, 30,625 ... D 6
01225 Cheshire, △3,006 ... B 2
01011 Chester, △1,025 ... C 3
01012 Chesterfield, △704 ... C 3
* 01013 Chicopee, 66,676 ... D 4
02535 Chilmark, △340 ... M 7
01510 Clinton, △13,383 ... H 3
01778 Cochituate, 6,000 ... A 7
02025 Cohasset, △6,954 ... F 7
02025 Cohasset, 3,900 ... F 7
† 01826 Collinsville, 4,000 ... J 2
01340 Colrain, △1,420 ... D 2
01742 Concord, △16,148 ... B 6
01742 Concord, 5,900 ... B 6
01341 Conway, △998 ... D 2
01026 Cummington, △562 ... C 3
01226 Dalton, △7,505 ... B 3
01923 Danvers, △26,151 ... D 5
02714 Dartmouth, △18,800 ... K 6
02026 Dedham⊙, △26,938 ... C 7
01342 Deerfield, △3,850 ... D 2
02638 Dennis, △6,454 ... O 5
02715 Dighton, △4,667 ... K 5
† 02122 Dorchester, 153,061 ... D 7
† 01516 Douglas, △2,947 ... H 4
02030 Dover, △4,529 ... B 7
01826 Dracut, △18,214 ... J 2
01570 Dudley, △8,087 ... G 4
01827 Dunstable, △1,292 ... J 2
02332 Duxbury, △7,636 ... M 4
02332 Duxbury, 2,477 ... M 4
† 02184 East Braintree, 12,000 ... D 8
02333 East Bridgewater, △8,347 ... L 4
01515 East Brookfield, △1,800 ... G 4
02642 Eastham, △2,043 ... O 5
01027 Easthampton, △13,012 ... D 3
01028 East Longmeadow, △13,029 ... E 4
† 02186 East Milton, 9,500 ... D 7
02334 Easton, △12,157 ... K 4
01437 East Pepperell, 4,200 ... H 2
† 01906 East Saugus, 4,200 ... D 6
02032 East Walpole, 4,500 ... C 8
† 02189 East Weymouth, 20,000 ... E 8
02539 Edgartown, △1,481 ... M 7
02539 Edgartown⊙, 1,006 ... M 7
01344 Erving, △1,260 ... E 2
02112 Essex, △2,670 ... L 2
02149 Everett, 42,485 ... D 6
02719 Fairhaven, △16,332 ... L 6
* 02720 Fall River, 96,898 ... K 6
Fall River, ‡149,976 ... K 6
* 02540 Falmouth, △15,942 ... M 6
* 02540 Falmouth, 5,806 ... M 6
01030 Feeding Hills, 9,500 ... D 4
01420 Fitchburg, 43,343 ... G 2
Fitchburg-Leominster, ‡97,164 ... G 2
† 01247 Florida, △672 ... B 2
02035 Foxboro, △14,218 ... J 4
02035 Foxboro, 4,090 ... J 4
01701 Framingham, 64,048 ... A 7
01701 Framingham Center, 16,000 ... J 3
02038 Franklin, △17,830 ... J 4
02038 Franklin, 8,863 ... J 4
01440 Gardner, 19,748 ... G 2
† 02535 Gay Head, △118 ... L 7
01830 Georgetown, △5,290 ... L 2
† 01376 Gill, △1,100 ... D 2
01930 Gloucester, 27,941 ... M 2
01032 Goshen, △483 ... C 3
01519 Grafton, △11,659 ... H 4
01033 Granby, △5,473 ... E 3
01034 Granville, △1,008 ... C 4
01230 Great Barrington, △7,537 ... A 4
01301 Greenfield, △18,116 ... D 2
01301 Greenfield⊙, 14,642 ... D 2
01880 Greenwood, 7,500 ... D 6
01450 Groton, △5,109 ... H 2
01830 Groveland, △5,382 ... L 1
01035 Hadley, △3,750 ... D 3
02338 Halifax, △3,537 ... L 5
01936 Hamilton, △6,373 ... L 2
01036 Hampden, △4,572 ... E 4
01237 Hancock, △675 ... A 2
02339 Hanover, △10,107 ... L 4
02341 Hanson, △7,148 ... L 4
01037 Hardwick, △2,379 ... F 3
01451 Harvard, △13,426 ... H 2
02645 Harwich, △5,892 ... O 6
02645 Harwich, 3,842 ... O 6
01038 Hatfield, △2,825 ... D 3
01830 Haverhill, 46,120 ... K 1
01346 Heath, △383 ... C 2
02043 Hingham, △18,845 ... E 8
01235 Hinsdale, △1,588 ... B 3
02343 Holbrook, △11,775 ... D 8
01520 Holden, △12,564 ... G 3
† 01550 Holland, △931 ... F 4
01746 Holliston, △12,069 ... A 8
01746 Holliston, 3,900 ... A 8
01040 Holyoke, 50,112 ... D 4
01747 Hopedale, △4,292 ... H 4
01748 Hopkinton, △5,981 ... J 4
01452 Hubbardston, △1,437 ... F 3
01749 Hudson, △16,084 ... H 3
01749 Hudson, 14,283 ... H 3
02045 Hull, △9,961 ... E 7
01050 Huntington, △1,593 ... C 4
02601 Hyannis, 6,847 ... N 6
02136 Hyde Park, 25,000 ... C 7
01938 Ipswich, △10,750 ... L 2
01938 Ipswich, 5,022 ... L 2
02090 Islington, 3,800 ... C 8
02130 Jamaica Plain, 50,000 ... C 7
02360 Kingston, △5,999 ... M 5
02360 Kingston, 3,772 ... M 5
02346 Lakeville, △4,376 ... L 5
01523 Lancaster, △6,095 ... H 3
01237 Lanesboro, △2,972 ... A 2
* 01840 Lawrence, 66,915 ... K 2
Lawrence-Haverhill, ‡232,395 ... K 2
01238 Lee, △6,426 ... B 3
01524 Leicester, △9,140 ... G 4
01240 Lenox, △5,804 ... A 3
01240 Lenox, 2,208 ... A 3
01453 Leominster, 32,939 ... G 2
01054 Leverett, △1,005 ... E 3
02173 Lexington, △31,886 ... B 6
† 01301 Leyden, △376 ... D 2
01773 Lincoln, △7,567 ... B 6
01460 Littleton, △6,380 ... H 2
01106 Longmeadow, △15,630 ... D 4
* 01850 Lowell, 94,239 ... J 2
Lowell, ‡212,860 ... J 2
01056 Ludlow, △17,580 ... E 4
02745 Lunds Corner, 7,020 ... L 6
01462 Lunenburg, △7,419 ... H 2
* 01901 Lynn, 90,294 ... D 6
01940 Lynnfield, △10,826 ... D 5
† 01940 Lynnfield Center (Lynnfield P.O.), 6,500 ... C 5
02148 Malden, 56,127 ... D 6
01944 Manchester, △5,151 ... F 5
02048 Mansfield, △9,939 ... J 4
02048 Mansfield, 4,778 ... J 4
01945 Marblehead, △21,295 ... E 7
02738 Marion, △3,466 ... L 6
01752 Marlborough, 27,936 ... H 3
02050 Marshfield, △15,223 ... M 4
02649 Mashpee, △1,288 ... M 6
02126 Mattapan, 18,500 ... C 7
02739 Mattapoisett, △4,500 ... L 6
01754 Maynard, △9,710 ... J 3
02052 Medfield, △9,821 ... B 8
02052 Medfield, 3,900 ... B 8
02155 Medford, 64,397 ... C 6
02053 Medway, △7,938 ... J 4
02053 Medway, 3,716 ... J 4
02176 Melrose, 33,180 ... D 6
01756 Mendon, △2,524 ... H 4
01860 Merrimac, △4,245 ... L 1
01844 Methuen, 35,456 ... K 2
02346 Middleboro, △13,607 ... L 5
02346 Middleboro, 6,259 ... L 5
01243 Middlefield, △288 ... B 3
01949 Middleton, △4,044 ... K 2
01757 Milford, △19,352 ... H 4
01757 Milford, 13,740 ... H 4
01527 Millbury, △11,987 ... H 4
02054 Millis, △5,686 ... A 8
01529 Millville, △1,764 ... H 4
02186 Milton, △27,190 ... D 7
01057 Monson, △7,355 ... E 4
01351 Montague, △8,451 ... E 2
01245 Monterey, △600 ... B 4
† 12517 Mount Washington, △52 ... A 4
01908 Nahant, △4,119 ... E 6
02554 Nantucket, △3,774 ... O 7
02554 Nantucket⊙, 2,461 ... O 7
01760 Natick, △31,057 ... A 7
02192 Needham, △29,748 ... B 7
02194 Needham Heights, 10,000 ... B 7
† 02122 Neponset, 25,000 ... D 7
* 02740 New Bedford, 101,777 ... K 6
New Bedford, ‡152,642 ... K 6
01531 New Braintree, △631 ... F 3
01950 Newbury, △3,804 ... L 1
01950 Newburyport, 15,807 ... L 1
† 01230 New Marlboro, △1,031 ... B 4
01355 New Salem, △474 ... E 2
† 02158 Newton, 91,066 ... C 7
† 02159 Newton Center, 20,790 ... C 7
† 02161 Newton Highlands, 6,900 ... C 7
† 02160 Newtonville, 14,000 ... C 7
02790 Noquochoke P.O. (Westport), △950 ... K 6
02056 Norfolk, △4,656 ... J 4
02351 North Abington, 6,200 ... L 4
01247 North Adams, 19,195 ... B 2
01060 Northampton⊙, 29,664 ... D 3
01845 North Andover, △16,284 ... K 2
* 02760 North Attleboro, △18,665 ... J 5
01862 North Billerica, 4,900 ... J 2
01532 Northboro, △9,218 ... H 3
01532 Northboro, 3,900 ... H 3
01536 Northbridge, △11,795 ... H 4
01535 North Brookfield, △3,967 ... F 3
01863 North Chelmsford, 3,700 ... J 2
02747 North Dartmouth, 6,000 ... K 6
02356 North Easton, 6,000 ... K 4
01360 Northfield, △2,631 ... E 2
01536 North Grafton, 5,500 ... H 4
01864 North Reading, △11,264 ... C 5
02060 North Scituate, 5,507 ... F 8
† 02191 North Weymouth, 13,000 ... D 8
01067 North Wilbraham, 5,700 ... E 4
02766 Norton, △9,487 ... K 5
02061 Norwell, △7,796 ... F 8
02062 Norwood, △30,815 ... B 8
02557 Oak Bluffs, △1,385 ... M 7
01068 Oakham, △730 ... F 3
† 01566 Old Sturbridge Village, 500 ... F 4
01364 Orange, △6,104 ... E 2
01364 Orange, 3,847 ... E 2
02653 Orleans, △3,055 ... O 5
01253 Otis, △820 ... B 4
01540 Oxford, △10,345 ... G 4
01540 Oxford, 6,109 ... G 4
01069 Palmer, △11,680 ... E 4
01069 Palmer, 3,649 ... E 4
01612 Paxton, △3,731 ... G 3
01960 Peabody, 48,080 ... E 5
† 01002 Pelham, △937 ... E 3
02359 Pembroke, △11,193 ... L 4
01463 Pepperell, △5,887 ... H 2
01366 Petersham, △1,014 ... F 3
† 01331 Phillipston, △872 ... F 2
01866 Pinehurst, 5,681 ... B 5
01201 Pittsfield⊙, 57,020 ... A 3
Pittsfield, ‡79,727 ... A 3
01070 Plainfield, △287 ... C 2
02762 Plainville, △4,953 ... J 4
* 02360 Plymouth, △18,606 ... M 5
* 02360 Plymouth⊙, 6,940 ... M 5
02367 Plympton, △1,224 ... L 5
† 02726 Pottersville, 3,722 ... K 6
01541 Princeton, △1,681 ... G 3
02657 Provincetown, △2,911 ... O 4
† 02169 Quincy, 87,966 ... D 7
02368 Randolph, △27,035 ... D 8
02767 Raynham, △6,705 ... K 5
01867 Reading, △22,539 ... C 5
02137 Readville, 10,000 ... C 8
02769 Rehoboth, △6,512 ... K 5
02151 Revere, 43,159 ... D 6
01254 Richmond, △1,461 ... A 3
02770 Rochester, △1,770 ... L 6
02370 Rockland, △15,674 ... L 4
01966 Rockport, △5,636 ... M 2
01966 Rockport, 4,166 ... M 2
01367 Rowe, △277 ... C 2
01969 Rowley, △3,040 ... L 2
† 02119 Roxbury, 200,000 ... C 7
01368 Royalston, △809 ... F 2
01071 Russell, △1,382 ... C 4
01543 Rutland, △3,198 ... G 3
01970 Salem⊙, 40,556 ... E 5
01950 Salisbury, △4,179 ... L 1
01255 Sandisfield, △547 ... B 4
02563 Sandwich, △5,239 ... N 5
01906 Saugus, △25,110 ... D 6
01256 Savoy, △322 ... B 2
01701 Saxonville, 15,000 ... A 7
02066 Scituate, △16,973 ... F 8
02066 Scituate, 3,738 ... F 8
02771 Seekonk, △11,116 ... J 5
02067 Sharon, △12,367 ... K 4
01810 Shawsheen Village, 5,200 ... K 2
01257 Sheffield, △2,374 ... A 4
01770 Sherborn, △3,309 ... A 8
01464 Shirley, △4,909 ... H 2
01545 Shrewsbury, △19,196 ... H 3
01072 Shutesbury, △489 ... E 3
02726 Somerset, △18,088 ... K 5
† 02143 Somerville, 88,779 ... C 6
01073 Southampton, △3,069 ... C 4
01772 Southborough, △5,798 ... H 3
† 02185 South Braintree, 6,000 ... D 8

(continued on following page)

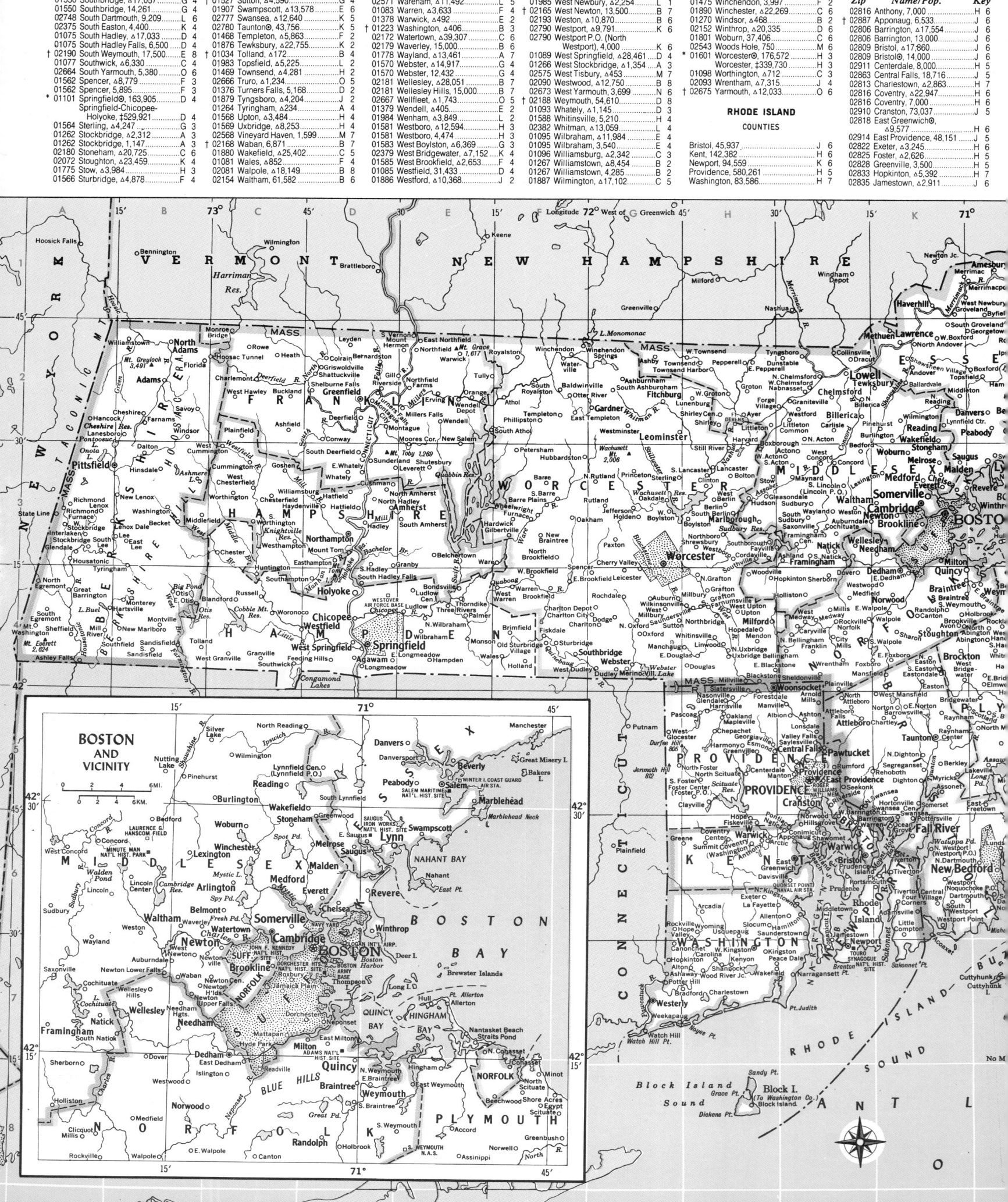

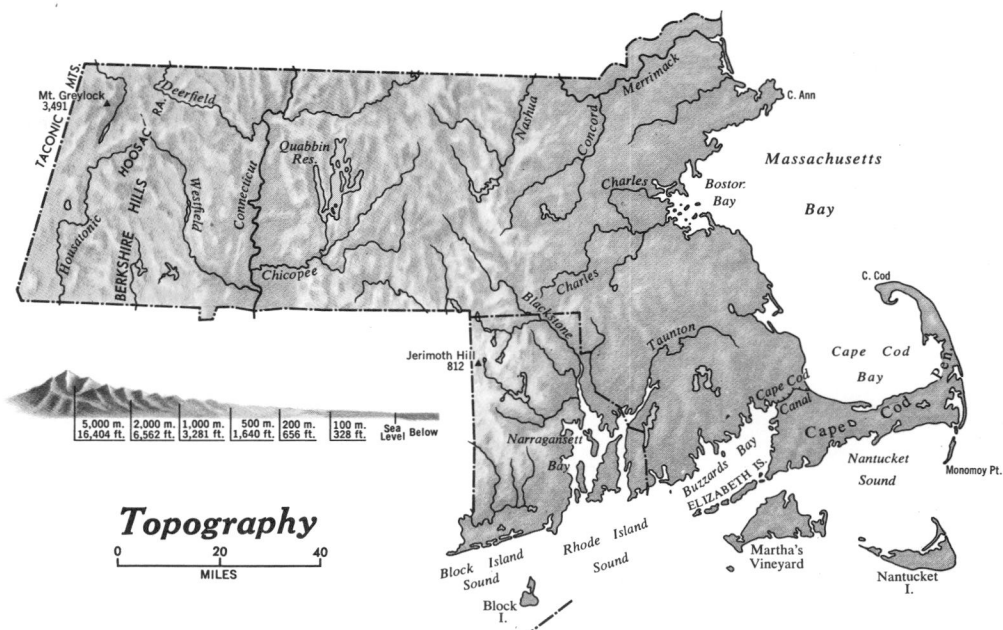

Topography

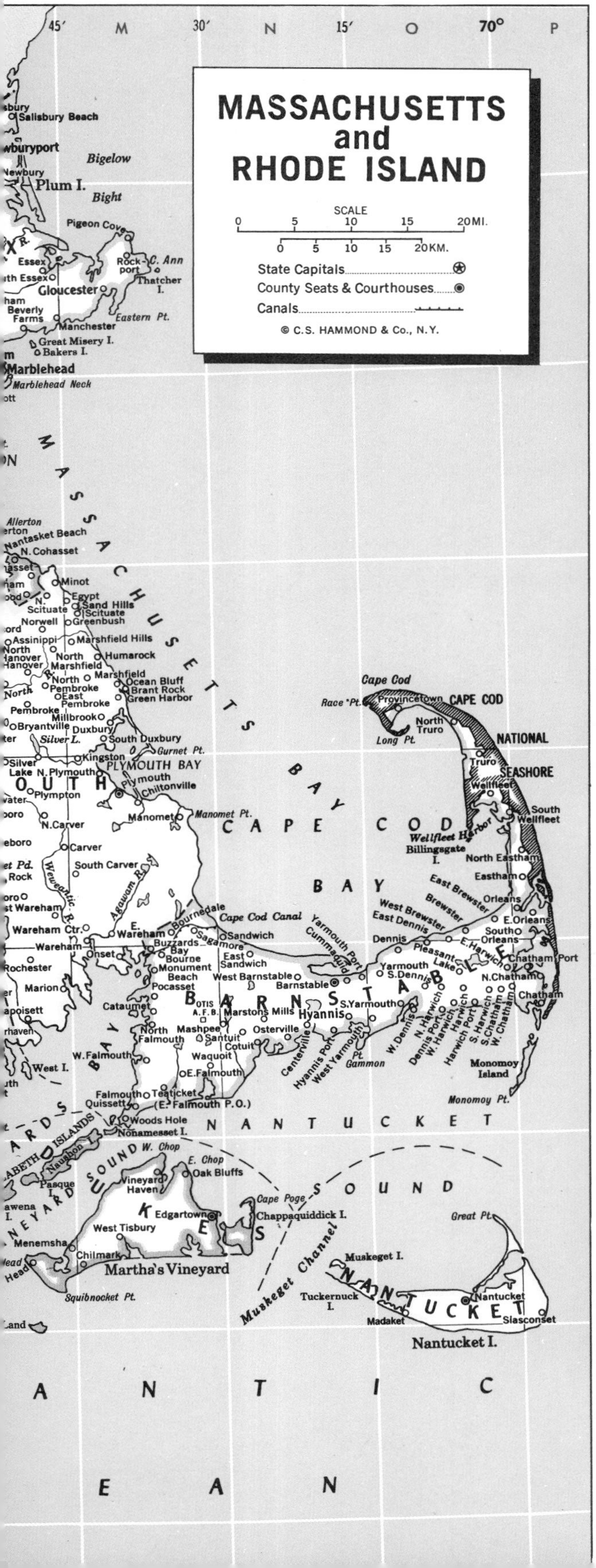

Marking the site of the first battle of the Revolutionary War on April 19, 1775, the Minuteman Statue faces the line of advancing Redcoats at Lexington, Massachusetts.

Jack Zehrt — Shostal Associates

Typical Newport turn-of-the-century grandeur in a French chalet-style mansion, with mansard roof and wrought iron gates.

Dorothy Bachellor

AREA 58,216 sq. mi.
POPULATION 8,875,083 ('70); 9,258,344 ('80)
CAPITAL Lansing
LARGEST CITY Detroit
HIGHEST POINT Mt. Curwood 1,980 ft.
SETTLED IN 1650
ADMITTED TO UNION January 26, 1837
POPULAR NAME Wolverine State
STATE FLOWER Apple Blossom
STATE BIRD Robin

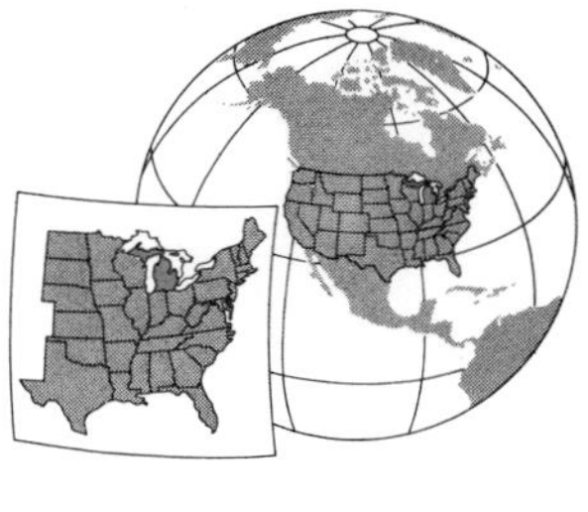

Topography

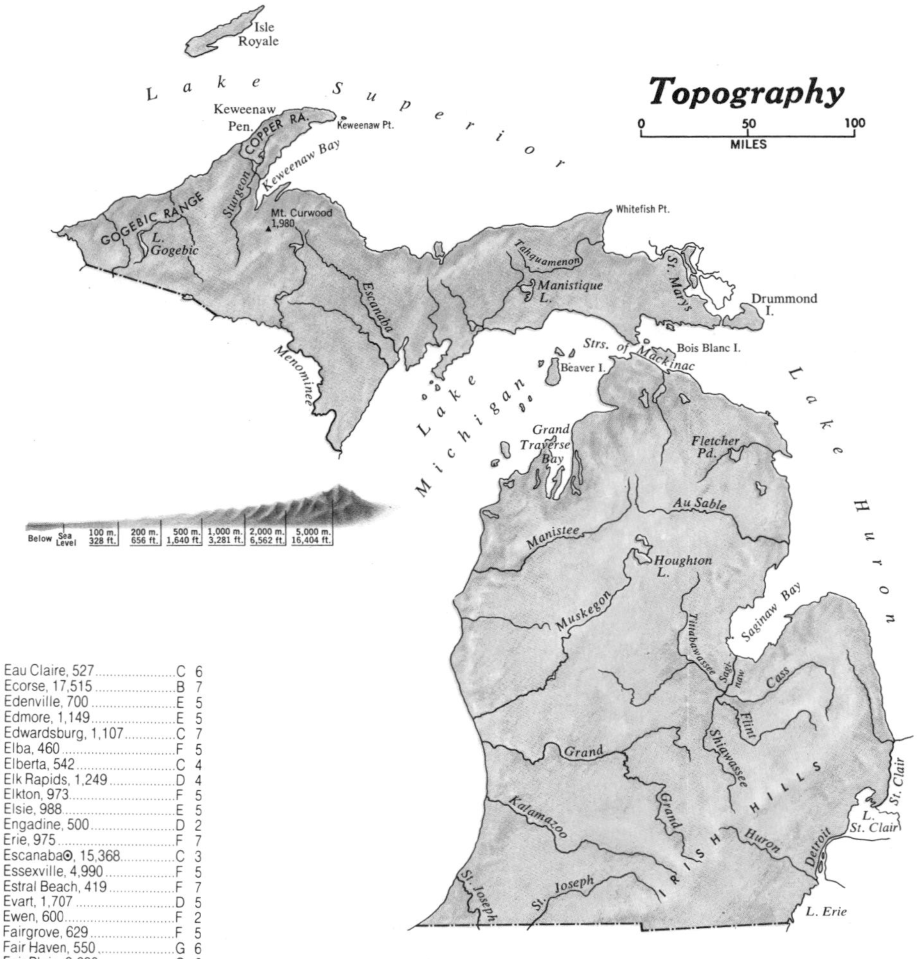
0 50 100
MILES
Isle Royale
Lake Superior
Keweenaw Pen.
COPPER RA.
Keweenaw Pt.
Keweenaw Bay
Sturgeon
GOGEBIC RANGE
L. Gogebic
Mt. Curwood 1,980
Whitefish Pt.
Tahquamenon
St. Marys
Manistique L.
Drummond I.
Escanaba
Menominee
Strs. of Mackinac
Bois Blanc I.
Beaver I.
Lake Michigan
Lake Huron
Grand Traverse Bay
Fletcher Pd.
Au Sable
Manistee
Houghton L.
Muskegon
Tittabawassee
Saginaw Bay
Saginaw
Cass
Flint
Shiawassee
Grand
Kalamazoo
IRISH HILLS
Huron
St. Clair
L. St. Clair
Detroit
St. Joseph
L. Erie
Below Sea Level
100 m. 328 ft.
200 m. 656 ft.
500 m. 1,640 ft.
1,000 m. 3,281 ft.
2,000 m. 6,562 ft.
5,000 m. 16,404 ft.

COUNTIES

Alcona, 7,113	F 4
Alger, 8,568	C 2
Allegan, 66,575	D 6
Alpena, 30,708	F 4
Antrim, 12,612	D 3
Arenac, 11,149	F 4
Baraga, 7,789	A 2
Barry, 38,166	D 6
Bay, 117,339	E 5
Benzie, 8,593	C 4
Berrien, 163,875	C 7
Branch, 37,906	D 7
Calhoun, 141,963	D 6
Cass, 43,312	C 7
Charlevoix, 16,541	D 3
Cheboygan, 16,573	E 3
Chippewa, 32,412	E 2
Clare, 16,695	E 5
Clinton, 48,492	E 6
Crawford, 6,482	E 4
Delta, 35,924	C 2
Dickinson, 23,753	B 2
Eaton, 68,892	E 6
Emmet, 18,331	E 3
Genesee, 444,341	F 5
Gladwin, 13,471	E 4
Gogebic, 20,676	F 2
Grand Traverse, 39,175	D 4
Gratiot, 39,246	E 5
Hillsdale, 37,171	E 7
Houghton, 34,652	G 1
Huron, 34,083	F 5
Ingham, 261,039	E 6
Ionia, 45,848	D 6
Iosco, 24,905	F 4
Iron, 13,813	G 2
Isabella, 44,594	E 5
Jackson, 143,274	E 6
Kalamazoo, 201,550	D 6
Kalkaska, 5,272	D 4
Kent, 411,044	D 5
Keweenaw, 2,264	A 1
Lake, 5,661	D 5
Lapeer, 52,317	F 5
Leelanau, 10,872	D 4
Lenawee, 81,609	E 7
Livingston, 58,967	F 6
Luce, 6,789	D 2
Mackinac, 9,660	D 2
Macomb, 625,309	G 6
Manistee, 20,094	C 4
Marquette, 64,686	B 2
Mason, 22,612	C 4
Mecosta, 27,992	D 5
Menominee, 24,587	B 3
Midland, 63,769	E 5
Missaukee, 7,126	D 4
Monroe, 118,479	F 7
Montcalm, 39,660	D 5
Montmorency, 5,247	E 3
Muskegon, 157,246	C 5
Newaygo, 27,992	D 5
Oakland, 907,871	F 6
Oceana, 17,984	C 5
Ogemaw, 11,903	E 4
Ontonagon, 10,548	F 1
Osceola, 14,838	D 5
Oscoda, 4,726	E 4
Otsego, 10,422	E 3
Ottawa, 128,181	C 6
Presque Isle, 12,836	F 3
Roscommon, 9,892	E 4
Saginaw, 219,743	E 5
Saint Clair, 120,175	G 6
Saint Joseph, 47,392	D 7
Sanilac, 34,889	G 5
Schoolcraft, 8,226	C 2
Shiawassee, 63,075	E 6
Tuscola, 48,603	F 5
Van Buren, 56,173	C 6
Washtenaw, 234,103	F 6
Wayne, 2,666,751	F 6
Wexford, 19,717	D 4

CITIES and TOWNS

Zip	Name/Pop.	Key
49220	Addison, 595	E 7
49221	Adrian⊙, 20,382	F 7
48701	Akron, 525	F 5
48764	Alabaster, 46	F 4
49224	Albion, 12,112	E 6
48001	Algonac, 3,684	G 6
49010	Allegan⊙, 4,516	D 6
48101	Allen Park, 40,747	B 7
48801	Alma, 9,790	E 5
48003	Almont, 1,634	F 6
49707	Alpena⊙, 13,805	F 3
49903	Amasa, 450	G 2
48004	Anchorville, 440	G 6
* 48103	Ann Arbor⊙, 99,797	F 6
	Ann Arbor, ‡234,103	F 6
† 49659	Antrim, 475	D 4
48410	Argyle, 800	G 5
48005	Armada, 1,352	G 6
48806	Ashley, 521	E 5
49011	Athens, 996	D 6
49709	Atlanta⊙, 475	E 3
49905	Atlantic Mine, 785	G 1
48611	Auburn, 1,919	F 5
48057	Auburn Heights, 7,500	F 6
48703	Au Gres, 564	F 4
49012	Augusta, 1,025	D 6
† 48750	Au Sable-Oscoda, 3,475	F 4
† 48640	Averill, 800	E 5
48413	Bad Axe⊙, 2,999	G 5
49304	Baldwin⊙, 612	D 5
48414	Bancroft, 724	E 6
49013	Bangor, 2,050	C 6
49908	Baraga, 1,116	G 1
49807	Bark River, 550	B 3
49101	Baroda, 439	C 7
48808	Bath, 600	E 6
* 49014	Battle Creek, 38,931	D 6
48706	Bay City⊙, 49,449	F 5
	Bay City, ‡117,339	F 5
48720	Bay Port, 600	F 5
49770	Bay View, 500	E 3
48612	Beaverton, 954	E 5
49020	Bedford, 450	D 6
† 49423	Beechwood, 2,714	C 6
48809	Belding, 5,121	D 5
49615	Bellaire⊙, 897	D 4
48111	Belleville, 2,406	F 6
49021	Bellevue, 1,297	E 6
49022	Benton Harbor, 16,481	C 6
† 49022	Benton Heights, 8,067	C 6
49910	Bergland, 635	F 1
48072	Berkley, 22,618	B 6
49103	Berrien Springs, 1,951	C 7
49911	Bessemer⊙, 2,805	F 2
49617	Beulah⊙, 461	C 4
49307	Big Rapids⊙, 11,995	D 5
48415	Birch Run, 932	F 5
* 48008	Birmingham, 26,170	B 6
49228	Blissfield, 2,753	F 7
48013	Bloomfield Hills, 3,672	B 6
49026	Bloomingdale, 496	C 6
49712	Boyne City, 2,969	E 3
48615	Breckenridge, 1,257	E 5
48722	Bridgeport, 1,900	F 5
49106	Bridgman, 1,621	C 7
48116	Brighton, 2,457	F 6
49715	Brimley, 490	E 2
49229	Britton, 697	F 6
49028	Bronson, 2,390	D 7
49230	Brooklyn, 1,112	E 6
48416	Brown City, 1,142	G 5
49716	Brutus, 431	E 3
49107	Buchanan, 4,645	C 7
49314	Burnips, 725	D 6
49030	Burr Oak, 873	D 7
48418	Byron, 655	E 6
49315	Byron Center, 900	D 6
49601	Cadillac⊙, 9,990	D 4
49316	Caledonia, 716	D 6
49913	Calumet, 1,007	A 1
48014	Capac, 1,279	G 5
48117	Carleton, 1,503	F 6
48723	Caro⊙, 3,701	F 5
48724	Carrollton, 7,300	E 5
48811	Carson City, 1,217	E 5
48419	Carsonville, 621	G 5
48725	Caseville, 607	F 5
49915	Caspian, 1,165	G 2
48726	Cass City, 1,974	F 5
49031	Cassopolis⊙, 2,108	C 7
49422	Castle Park, 500	C 6
49319	Cedar Springs, 1,807	D 5
49719	Cedarville, 800	E 2
49233	Cement City, 531	E 6
48015	Center Line, 10,379	B 6
49622	Central Lake, 741	D 3
49032	Centreville⊙, 1,044	D 7
49814	Champion, 550	B 2
49815	Channing, 550	B 2
49720	Charlevoix⊙, 3,519	D 3
48813	Charlotte⊙, 8,244	E 6
49623	Chase, 534	D 5
49721	Cheboygan⊙, 5,553	E 3
48118	Chelsea, 3,858	E 6
48616	Chesaning, 2,876	E 5
48617	Clare, 2,639	E 5
49234	Clarklake, 500	E 6
48016	Clarkston, 1,034	F 6
48017	Clawson, 17,617	B 6
49235	Clayton, 505	E 7
48727	Clifford, 472	F 5
49034	Climax, 594	D 6
49236	Clinton, 1,677	F 6
48420	Clio, 2,357	F 5
49036	Coldwater⊙, 9,099	D 7
48618	Coleman, 1,295	E 5
49038	Coloma, 1,814	C 6
49040	Colon, 1,172	D 7
48421	Columbiaville, 935	F 5
49041	Comstock, 5,003	D 6
49237	Concord, 983	E 6
49042	Constantine, 1,733	D 7
49722	Conway, 560	E 3
49404	Coopersville, 2,129	C 5
49818	Cornell, 640	B 3
48817	Corunna⊙, 2,829	E 6
49043	Covert, 650	C 6
48422	Croswell, 1,954	G 5
48818	Crystal, 649	E 5
49920	Crystal Falls⊙, 2,000	A 2
† 49501	Cutlerville, 6,267	D 6
48819	Dansville, 486	E 6
48423	Davison, 5,259	F 5
* 48120	Dearborn, 104,199	B 7
48127	Dearborn Heights, 80,069	B 7
49045	Decatur, 1,764	C 6
48427	Deckerville, 817	G 5
49238	Deerfield, 834	F 7
49725	De Tour Village, 494	E 3
* 48201	Detroit⊙, 1,511,482	B 7
	Detroit, ‡4,199,931	B 7
† 48161	Detroit Beach, 2,053	F 7
48820	De Witt, 1,829	E 6
48130	Dexter, 1,729	F 6
48821	Dimondale, 970	E 6
49922	Dollar Bay, 950	G 1
49323	Dorr, 550	D 6
49406	Douglas, 813	C 6
49047	Dowagiac, 6,583	C 6
48020	Drayton Plains, 16,462	F 6
49726	Drummond Island, 700	F 3
48428	Dryden, 654	F 6
48131	Dundee, 2,472	F 7
48429	Durand, 3,678	E 6
49924	Eagle River⊙, 36	A 1
48021	East Detroit, 45,920	B 6
† 49506	East Grand Rapids, 12,565	D 6
49727	East Jordan, 2,041	D 3
† 49801	East Kingsford, 1,155	A 3
49626	Eastlake, 512	C 4
48823	East Lansing, 47,540	E 6
48730	East Tawas, 2,372	F 4
† 49001	Eastwood, 9,682	D 6
48827	Eaton Rapids, 4,494	E 6
49111	Eau Claire, 527	C 6
48229	Ecorse, 17,515	B 7
48620	Edenville, 700	E 5
48829	Edmore, 1,149	E 5
49112	Edwardsburg, 1,107	C 7
† 48446	Elba, 460	F 5
49628	Elberta, 542	C 4
49629	Elk Rapids, 1,249	D 4
48731	Elkton, 973	F 5
48831	Elsie, 988	E 5
49827	Engadine, 500	D 2
48133	Erie, 975	F 7
49829	Escanaba⊙, 15,368	C 3
48732	Essexville, 4,990	F 5
† 48166	Estral Beach, 419	F 7
49631	Evart, 1,707	D 5
49925	Ewen, 600	F 2
48733	Fairgrove, 629	F 5
48023	Fair Haven, 550	G 6
49022	Fair Plain, 3,680	C 6
48621	Fairview, 600	F 4
48024	Farmington, 13,337	F 6
48622	Farwell, 777	E 5
49408	Fennville, 811	C 6
48430	Fenton, 8,284	F 6
48220	Ferndale, 30,850	B 6
49409	Ferrysburg, 2,196	C 5
48134	Flat Rock, 5,643	F 6
* 48501	Flint⊙, 193,317	F 6
	Flint, ‡496,658	F 6
48433	Flushing, 7,190	F 5
48835	Fowler, 1,020	E 5
48836	Fowlerville, 1,978	F 6
48734	Frankenmuth, 2,834	F 5
49635	Frankfort, 1,660	C 4
48025	Franklin, 3,344	B 6
48026	Fraser, 11,868	B 6
48623	Freeland, 1,303	E 5
49325	Freeport, 501	D 6
49412	Fremont, 3,465	D 5
49415	Fruitport, 1,409	C 5
49052	Fulton, 500	D 6
49927	Gaastra, 479	G 2
49053	Galesburg, 1,355	D 6
49113	Galien, 691	C 7
49735	Gaylord⊙, 3,012	E 3
48437	Genesee, 950	F 5
49836	Germfask, 750	C 2
48173	Gibraltar, 3,325	F 6
49837	Gladstone, 5,237	C 3
48624	Gladwin⊙, 2,071	E 5
49055	Gobles, 801	D 6
49737	Good Hart, 500	D 3
48438	Goodrich, 774	F 6
48439	Grand Blanc, 5,132	F 6
49417	Grand Haven⊙, 11,884	C 5
48837	Grand Ledge, 6,032	E 6
49839	Grand Marais, 650	D 2
* 49501	Grand Rapids⊙, 197,649	D 5
	Grand Rapids, ‡539,225	D 5
49418	Grandville, 10,764	D 6
49327	Grant, 772	D 5
49240	Grass Lake, 1,061	E 6
49738	Grayling⊙, 2,143	E 4
48738	Greenbush, 650	F 4
48838	Greenville, 7,493	D 5
48138	Grosse Ile, 7,799	B 7
48236	Grosse Pointe, 6,637	B 7
† 48236	Grosse Pointe Farms, 11,701	B 6
† 48236	Grosse Pointe Park, 15,585	B 7
† 48236	Grosse Pointe Shores, 3,042	B 6
† 48236	Grosse Pointe Woods, 21,878	B 6
49840	Gulliver, 962	D 2
49841	Gwinn, 1,054	B 2
48739	Hale, 500	F 4
48139	Hamburg, 500	F 6
49419	Hamilton, 950	C 6
48212	Hamtramck, 27,245	B 6
49930	Hancock, 4,820	G 1
49241	Hanover, 513	E 6
48441	Harbor Beach, 2,134	G 5
49740	Harbor Springs, 1,662	D 3
48236	Harper Woods, 20,186	B 6
48625	Harrison⊙, 1,460	E 4
48740	Harrisville⊙, 541	F 4
48028	Harsens Island, 750	G 6
49420	Hart⊙, 2,139	C 5
49057	Hartford, 2,508	C 6
48840	Haslett, 3,492	E 6
49058	Hastings⊙, 6,501	D 6
48030	Hazel Park, 23,784	B 6
48626	Hemlock, 900	E 5
48841	Henderson, 600	E 5
49847	Hermansville, 950	B 3
49744	Herron, 950	F 3
49421	Hesperia, 877	D 5
49745	Hessel, 500	E 2
48203	Highland Park, 35,444	B 6
49242	Hillsdale⊙, 7,728	E 7
49423	Holland, 26,337	C 6
48442	Holly, 4,355	F 6
48842	Holt, 6,980	E 6
49425	Holton, 500	C 5
49245	Homer, 1,617	E 6
49328	Hopkins, 566	D 6
49931	Houghton⊙, 6,067	G 1
48629	Houghton Lake, 500	E 4
48630	Houghton Lake Heights, 1,252	E 4
49329	Howard City, 1,060	D 5
48843	Howell⊙, 5,224	E 6
49934	Hubbell, 1,251	A 1
49247	Hudson, 2,618	E 7
49426	Hudsonville, 3,523	D 6
48140	Ida, 970	F 7
49642	Idlewild, 800	D 5
48444	Imlay City, 1,980	F 5
49749	Indian River, 950	E 3
48141	Inkster, 38,595	B 7
49643	Interlochen, 800	D 4
48846	Ionia⊙, 6,361	D 6
49801	Iron Mountain⊙, 8,702	B 3
49935	Iron River, 2,684	G 2
49938	Ironwood, 8,711	F 2
49849	Ishpeming, 8,245	B 2
48847	Ithaca⊙, 2,749	E 5
* 49201	Jackson⊙, 45,484	E 6
	Jackson, ‡143,274	E 6
49428	Jenison, 11,266	D 6
49061	Jones, 420	D 7
49250	Jonesville, 2,081	E 7
* 49001	Kalamazoo⊙, 85,555	D 6
	Kalamazoo, ‡201,550	D 6
49646	Kalkaska⊙, 1,475	D 4
48631	Kawkawlin, 450	F 5
48030	Keego Harbor, 3,092	F 6
49330	Kent City, 686	D 5
49508	Kentwood, 20,310	D 6
48445	Kinde, 618	G 5
49801	Kingsford, 5,276	A 3
49649	Kingsley, 632	D 4
48741	Kingston, 464	F 5
48848	Laingsburg, 1,159	E 6
48632	Lake, 600	E 5
49651	Lake City⊙, 704	D 4
48143	Lakeland, 720	F 6
49945	Lake Linden, 1,214	A 1
† 49039	Lake Michigan Beach, 1,201	C 6
48849	Lake Odessa, 1,924	D 6
48850	Lakeview, 1,198	D 5
† 49440	Lakewood Club, 590	C 5
48144	Lambertville, 5,721	F 7
49946	L'Anse⊙, 2,538	G 1
* 48901	Lansing (cap.), 131,546	E 6
	Lansing, ‡378,423	E 6
48446	Lapeer⊙, 6,270	F 5
49913	Laurium, 2,868	A 1
49064	Lawrence, 790	C 6
49065	Lawton, 1,358	D 6
49654	Leland⊙, 776	D 3
49251	Leslie, 1,894	E 6
49755	Levering, 967	E 3
49756	Lewiston, 750	E 4
48450	Lexington, 834	G 5
48146	Lincoln Park, 52,984	B 7
48451	Linden, 1,546	F 6
48634	Linwood, 950	F 5
49252	Litchfield, 1,167	E 6
49833	Little Lake, 950	B 2
* 48150	Livonia, 110,109	F 6
48743	Long Lake, 900	F 4
49331	Lowell, 3,068	D 6
49431	Ludington⊙, 9,021	C 5
48157	Luna Pier, 1,418	F 7
48851	Lyons, 758	E 6
49757	Mackinac Island, 517	E 3
49701	Mackinaw City, 810	E 3
48071	Madison Heights, 38,599	F 6
49659	Mancelona, 1,255	E 4
48158	Manchester, 1,650	E 6
49660	Manistee⊙, 7,723	C 4
49854	Manistique⊙, 4,324	C 3
49663	Manton, 1,107	D 4
48853	Maple Rapids, 683	E 5
49067	Marcellus, 1,139	D 6
49947	Marenisco, 865	F 2
48039	Marine City, 4,567	G 6
49665	Marion, 891	D 4
48453	Marlette, 1,706	G 5
49435	Marne, 950	D 5
49855	Marquette⊙, 21,967	B 2
49068	Marshall⊙, 7,253	E 6
49070	Martin, 502	D 6
48040	Marysville, 5,610	G 6
48854	Mason⊙, 5,468	E 6
49948	Mass, 850	G 1
49071	Mattawan, 1,569	D 6
48159	Maybee, 485	F 6
48744	Mayville, 872	F 5
49657	McBain, 520	D 4
48122	Melvindale, 13,862	B 7
48041	Memphis, 1,121	G 6
49072	Mendon, 949	D 7
49858	Menominee⊙, 10,748	B 3

(continued on following page)

Recognized as the country's leading automotive center, Detroit, with its fine harbor on the Detroit River, is also one of the busiest ports in the United States.

Michigan Travel Bureau

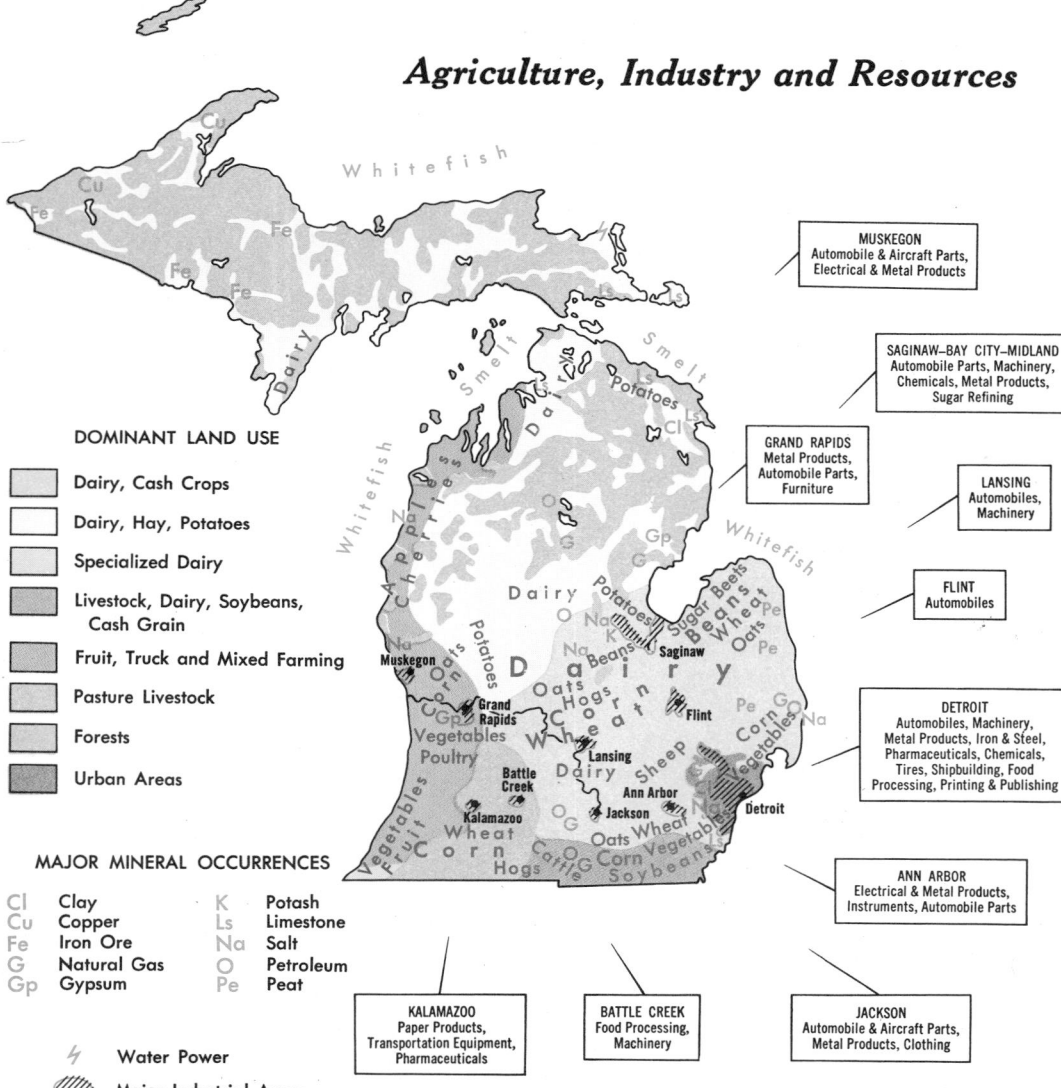

Agriculture, Industry and Resources

MUSKEGON
Automobile & Aircraft Parts, Electrical & Metal Products

SAGINAW–BAY CITY–MIDLAND
Automobile Parts, Machinery, Chemicals, Metal Products, Sugar Refining

GRAND RAPIDS
Metal Products, Automobile Parts, Furniture

LANSING
Automobiles, Machinery

FLINT
Automobiles

DETROIT
Automobiles, Machinery, Metal Products, Iron & Steel, Pharmaceuticals, Chemicals, Tires, Shipbuilding, Food Processing, Printing & Publishing

ANN ARBOR
Electrical & Metal Products, Instruments, Automobile Parts

KALAMAZOO
Paper Products, Transportation Equipment, Pharmaceuticals

BATTLE CREEK
Food Processing, Machinery

JACKSON
Automobile & Aircraft Parts, Metal Products, Clothing

DOMINANT LAND USE

- Dairy, Cash Crops
- Dairy, Hay, Potatoes
- Specialized Dairy
- Livestock, Dairy, Soybeans, Cash Grain
- Fruit, Truck and Mixed Farming
- Pasture Livestock
- Forests
- Urban Areas

MAJOR MINERAL OCCURRENCES

Cl	Clay	K	Potash
Cu	Copper	Ls	Limestone
Fe	Iron Ore	Na	Salt
G	Natural Gas	O	Petroleum
Gp	Gypsum	Pe	Peat

⚡ Water Power

▨ Major Industrial Areas

AREA 84,068 sq. mi.
POPULATION 3,805,069 ('70); 4,077,148 ('80)
CAPITAL St. Paul
LARGEST CITY Minneapolis
HIGHEST POINT Eagle Mtn. 2,301 ft.
SETTLED IN 1805
ADMITTED TO UNION May 11, 1858
POPULAR NAME North Star State; Gopher State
STATE FLOWER Lady-slipper
STATE BIRD Loon

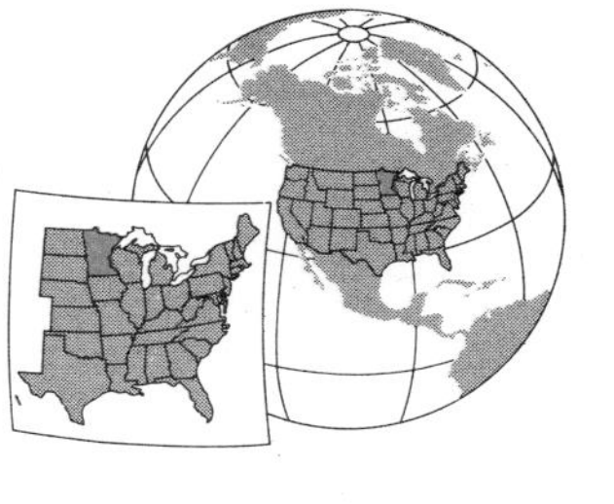

COUNTIES

Aitkin, 11,403 E 4
Anoka, 154,556 E 5
Becker, 24,372 C 4
Beltrami, 26,373 C 2
Benton, 20,841 D 5
Big Stone, 7,941 B 5
Blue Earth, 52,322 D 6
Brown, 28,887 D 6
Carlton, 28,072 F 4
Carver, 28,310 E 6
Cass, 17,323 D 4
Chippewa, 15,109 C 5
Chisago, 17,492 F 5
Clay, 46,585 B 4
Clearwater, 8,013 C 3
Cook, 3,423 H 3
Cottonwood, 14,887 C 6
Crow Wing, 34,826 D 4
Dakota, 139,808 E 6
Dodge, 13,037 F 7
Douglas, 22,892 C 5
Faribault, 20,896 D 7
Fillmore, 21,916 F 7
Freeborn, 38,064 E 7
Goodhue, 34,763 F 6
Grant, 7,462 B 5
Hennepin, 960,080 E 5
Houston, 17,556 G 7
Hubbard, 10,583 D 3
Isanti, 16,560 E 5
Itasca, 35,530 E 3
Jackson, 14,352 C 7
Kanabec, 9,775 E 5
Kandiyohi, 30,548 C 5
Kittson, 6,853 B 2
Koochiching, 17,731 E 2
Lac qui Parle, 11,164 B 6
Lake, 13,351 G 3
Lake of the Woods, 3,987 D 2
Le Sueur, 21,332 E 6
Lincoln, 8,143 B 6
Lyon, 24,273 C 6
Mahnomen, 5,638 C 3
Marshall, 13,060 B 2
Martin, 24,316 D 7
McLeod, 27,662 D 6
Meeker, 18,810 D 5
Mille Lacs, 15,703 E 5
Morrison, 26,949 D 4
Mower, 43,783 F 7
Murray, 12,508 C 6
Nicollet, 24,518 D 6
Nobles, 23,208 C 7
Norman, 10,008 B 3
Olmsted, 84,104 F 7
Otter Tail, 46,097 C 4
Pennington, 13,266 B 2
Pine, 16,821 F 4
Pipestone, 12,791 B 6
Polk, 34,435 B 3
Pope, 11,107 C 5
Ramsey, 476,255 E 5
Red Lake, 5,388 B 3
Redwood, 20,024 C 6
Renville, 21,139 C 6
Rice, 41,582 E 6
Rock, 11,346 B 7
Roseau, 11,569 C 2
Saint Louis, 220,693 F 3
Scott, 32,423 E 6
Sherburne, 18,344 E 5
Sibley, 15,845 D 6
Stearns, 95,400 D 5
Steele, 26,931 E 7
Stevens, 11,218 B 5
Swift, 13,177 C 5
Todd, 22,114 D 4
Traverse, 6,254 B 5
Wabasha, 17,224 F 6
Wadena, 12,412 D 4
Waseca, 16,663 E 6
Washington, 82,948 F 5
Watonwan, 13,298 D 7
Wilkin, 9,389 B 4
Winona, 44,409 G 6
Wright, 38,933 D 5
Yellow Medicine, 14,418 B 6

CITIES and TOWNS

Zip Name/Pop. Key

56510 Ada⊙, 2,076 B 3
55909 Adams, 771 F 7
56110 Adrian, 1,350 C 7
55001 Afton, 248 F 6
56430 Ah-Gwah-Ching, 500 D 3
56431 Aitkin⊙, 1,553 E 4
56433 Akeley, 468 D 3
56307 Albany, 1,599 D 5
56207 Alberta, 140 B 5
56007 Albert Lea⊙, 19,418 E 7
55301 Albertville, 451 E 5
56009 Alden, 713 E 7
56308 Alexandria⊙, 6,973 C 5
55002 Almelund, 150 F 5
56111 Alpha, 179 D 7
55910 Altura, 334 G 6
56710 Alvarado, 302 B 2
56010 Amboy, 571 D 7
55703 Angora, 287 F 3
55302 Annandale, 1,234 D 5
55303 Anoka⊙, 13,489 E 5
56208 Appleton, 1,789 C 5
† 55378 Apple Valley, 8,502 G 6
56113 Arco, 121 B 6
56713 Argyle, 739 B 2
55307 Arlington, 1,823 D 6
† 55801 Arnold, 750 F 4
56309 Ashby, 415 C 4
55704 Askov, 287 F 4
56209 Atwater, 956 D 5
56511 Audubon, 297 C 4
55705 Aurora, 2,531 F 3
55912 Austin⊙, 25,074 E 7
56114 Avoca, 203 C 7
56310 Avon, 725 D 5
55706 Babbitt, 3,076 G 3
56435 Backus, 257 D 4
56714 Badger, 327 B 2
56621 Bagley⊙, 1,314 C 3
56115 Balaton, 649 C 6
56622 Ball Club, 150 E 3
56514 Barnesville, 1,782 B 4
55707 Barnum, 382 F 4
56311 Barrett, 342 B 5
56515 Battle Lake, 772 C 4
56623 Baudette⊙, 1,547 D 2
† 56401 Baxter, 1,556 D 4
† 56444 Bay Lake, 250 E 4
55003 Bayport, 2,987 F 5
56211 Beardsley, 366 B 5
† 55723 Bear River, 250 E 3
55601 Beaver Bay, 362 G 3
56116 Beaver Creek, 235 B 7
55308 Becker, 365 E 5
56516 Bejou, 157 B 3
56312 Belgrade, 713 C 5
† 55027 Bellechester, 199 F 6
56011 Belle Plaine, 2,328 E 6
56212 Bellingham, 263 B 5
56517 Beltrami, 171 B 3
56214 Belview, 429 C 6
56601 Bemidji⊙, 11,490 D 3
56626 Bena, 169 D 3
56215 Benson⊙, 3,484 C 5
56437 Bertha, 512 C 4
56117 Bigelow, 262 C 7
56627 Big Falls, 534 E 2
56628 Bigfork, 399 E 3
55309 Big Lake, 1,015 E 5
56118 Bingham Lake, 214 C 7
55310 Bird Island, 1,309 D 6
55708 Biwabik, 1,483 F 3
56630 Blackduck, 595 D 3
† 55303 Blaine, 20,640 G 5
† 56011 Blakeley, 125 E 6
56216 Blomkest, 172 D 6
55917 Blooming Prairie, 1,804 E 7
55420 Bloomington, 81,970 G 6
56013 Blue Earth⊙, 3,965 D 7
56518 Bluffton, 195 C 4
56519 Borup, 128 B 3
55709 Bovey, 858 E 3
56314 Bowlus, 268 D 5
56218 Boyd, 311 C 6
55006 Braham, 744 E 5
56401 Brainerd⊙, 11,667 D 4
† 55056 Branch, 880 F 5
56315 Brandon, 414 C 5
56520 Breckenridge⊙, 4,200 B 4
† 56472 Breezy Point Village, 233 D 4
56119 Brewster, 563 C 7
56014 Bricelyn, 470 E 7
55710 Britt, 175 F 3
55429 Brooklyn Center, 35,173 G 5
† 55401 Brooklyn Park, 26,230 G 5
56715 Brooks, 163 B 3
55711 Brookston, 137 F 4
56316 Brooten, 615 C 5
56438 Browerville, 665 D 4
55918 Brownsdale, 625 F 7
56219 Browns Valley, 906 B 5
55919 Brownsville, 417 G 7
55312 Brownton, 688 D 6
55712 Bruno, 130 F 4
† 55051 Brunswick, 144 E 5
56317 Buckman, 158 D 5
55313 Buffalo⊙, 3,275 E 5
55314 Buffalo Lake, 758 D 6
55713 Buhl, 1,303 F 3
55378 Burnsville, 19,940 E 6
56318 Burtrum, 135 D 5
56120 Butterfield, 619 D 7
† 56723 Bygland, 475 B 3
55920 Byron, 1,419 F 6
55921 Caledonia⊙, 2,619 G 7
56521 Callaway, 233 C 3
55316 Calumet, 460 E 3
55008 Cambridge⊙, 3,467 E 5
56522 Campbell, 339 B 4
56220 Canby, 2,081 B 6
55009 Cannon Falls, 2,072 F 6
55922 Canton, 391 F 7
55717 Canyon, 125 F 3
56319 Carlos, 260 C 5
55718 Carlton⊙, 884 F 4
55315 Carver, 669 E 6
56633 Cass Lake, 1,317 D 3
55010 Castle Rock, 150 E 6
55012 Center City⊙, 324 F 5
† 55038 Centerville, 534 E 5
56121 Ceylon, 487 D 7
55316 Champlin, 2,275 G 5
56122 Chandler, 319 C 7
55317 Chanhassen, 4,879 F 6
55318 Chaska⊙, 4,352 F 6
55923 Chatfield, 1,885 F 7
55013 Chisago City, 1,068 E 5
55719 Chisholm, 5,913 E 3
56221 Chokio, 455 B 5
55014 Circle Pines, 3,918 G 5
56222 Clara City, 1,491 C 6
55924 Claremont, 520 E 6
56440 Clarissa, 599 C 4
56223 Clarkfield, 1,084 C 6
56016 Clarks Grove, 480 E 7
56634 Clearbrook, 599 C 3
55319 Clear Lake, 280 E 5
55320 Clearwater, 282 D 5
56224 Clements, 252 D 6
56017 Cleveland, 492 E 6
56523 Climax, 255 B 3
56225 Clinton, 608 B 5
56524 Clitherall, 131 C 4
56226 Clontarf, 147 C 5
55720 Cloquet, 8,699 F 4
55015 Cloverton, 150 F 4
55721 Cohasset, 536 E 3
55321 Cokato, 1,735 D 5
56320 Cold Spring, 2,006 D 5
55722 Coleraine, 1,086 E 3
56321 Collegeville, 1,600 D 5
55322 Cologne, 518 E 6
55421 Columbia Heights, 23,997 G 5
56019 Comfrey, 525 D 6
56525 Comstock, 135 B 4
56020 Conger, 167 E 7
55723 Cook, 687 F 3
55433 Coon Rapids, 30,505 G 5
† 55340 Corcoran, 1,656 F 5
56228 Cosmos, 570 D 6
55016 Cottage Grove, 13,419 F 6
55724 Cotton, 350 F 3
56229 Cottonwood, 794 C 6
56021 Courtland, 360 D 6
55725 Crane Lake, 350 F 2
55726 Cromwell, 181 F 4
56716 Crookston⊙, 8,312 B 3
56441 Crosby, 2,241 D 4
56442 Crosslake, 358 E 4
† 55005 Crown, 200 E 5
† 55401 Crystal, 30,925 G 5
55323 Crystal Bay, 6,787 F 5
56123 Currie, 368 C 6
56323 Cyrus, 289 C 5
55925 Dakota, 369 G 7
56324 Dalton, 221 C 4
56230 Danube, 497 C 6
56231 Danvers, 136 C 5
56022 Darfur, 179 D 6
55324 Darwin, 224 D 5
55325 Dassel, 1,058 D 5
56232 Dawson, 1,699 B 6
55327 Dayton, 517 E 5
55391 Deephaven, 3,853 G 5
56527 Deer Creek, 287 C 4
56636 Deer River, 815 E 3
56444 Deerwood, 448 E 4
56233 De Graff, 195 C 5
55328 Delano, 1,851 E 5
56023 Delavan, 281 D 7
56234 Delhi, 154 C 6
† 55110 Dellwood, 514 F 5
55018 Dennison, 162 E 6
56528 Dent, 156 C 4
56501 Detroit Lakes⊙, 5,797 C 4
55926 Dexter, 252 F 7
56529 Dilworth, 2,321 B 4
55927 Dodge Center, 1,603 F 6
56235 Donnelly, 252 B 5
55929 Dover, 321 F 7
55930 Dresbach, 250 G 7
* 55801 Duluth⊙, 100,578 F 4
Duluth-Superior, ‡265,350 F 4
56236 Dumont, 204 B 5
55019 Dundas, 460 E 6
56126 Dundee, 138 C 7
56127 Dunnell, 237 D 7
56446 Eagle Bend, 557 D 4
† 55005 East Bethel, 2,586 E 5
55024 Eagle Lake, 839 E 6
† 56031 East Chain, 171 D 7
56721 East Grand Forks, 7,607 B 3
† 56401 East Gull Lake, 440 D 4
56025 Easton, 352 E 7
56237 Echo, 356 C 6
55343 Eden Prairie, 6,938 G 6
55329 Eden Valley, 776 D 5
56128 Edgerton, 1,119 B 7
55424 Edina, 44,046 G 5
56639 Effie, 165 E 3
55931 Eitzen, 208 G 7
† 55910 Elba, 158 F 6
56531 Elbow Lake⊙, 1,484 B 5
55932 Elgin, 580 F 6
56533 Elizabeth, 188 B 4
55330 Elk River⊙, 2,252 E 5
55933 Elkton, 134 F 7
56026 Ellendale, 569 E 7
56129 Ellsworth, 588 C 7
56027 Elmore, 910 D 7
56325 Elrosa, 203 C 5
55731 Ely, 4,904 G 3
56028 Elysian, 445 E 6
55732 Embarrass, 195 F 3
56447 Emily, 386 E 4
56029 Emmons, 412 E 7
56534 Erhard, 748 B 4
56640 Ericsburg, 300 E 2
56535 Erskine, 571 B 3
55733 Esko, 500 F 4
56722 Euclid, 130 B 3
56238 Evan, 126 D 6
56326 Evansville, 553 C 4
55734 Eveleth, 4,721 F 3
55331 Excelsior, 2,563 F 6
55934 Eyota, 639 F 6
55332 Fairfax, 1,432 D 6
55383 Fairhaven, 129 D 5
56031 Fairmont⊙, 10,751 D 7
55113 Falcon Heights, 5,507 G 5
55021 Faribault⊙, 16,595 E 6
55024 Farmington, 3,104 E 6
56641 Federal Dam, 147 D 3
56536 Felton, 232 B 3
56537 Fergus Falls⊙, 12,443 B 4
56540 Fertile, 955 B 3
56448 Fifty Lakes, 143 D 4
55603 Finland, 300 G 3
55735 Finlayson, 192 F 4
56723 Fisher, 383 B 3
56328 Flensburg, 259 D 5
55736 Floodwood, 650 E 4
† 55792 Florenton, 635 F 3
56329 Foley⊙, 1,271 D 5
† 56308 Forada, 158 C 5
55738 Forbes, 225 F 3
55025 Forest Lake, 3,207 F 5
56330 Foreston, 273 E 5
56542 Fosston, 1,684 C 3
55935 Fountain, 347 F 7
56543 Foxhome, 185 B 4
55333 Franklin, 557 D 6
56544 Frazee, 1,015 C 4
56032 Freeborn, 296 E 7
56331 Freeport, 593 D 5
† 55801 French River, 200 G 4
55421 Fridley, 29,233 G 5
55026 Frontenac, 223 F 6
56033 Frost, 290 D 7
56131 Fulda, 1,226 C 7
56034 Garden City, 270 D 6
56332 Garfield, 198 C 5
56450 Garrison, 125 E 4
56132 Garvin, 201 C 6
56545 Gary, 265 B 3
55334 Gaylord⊙, 1,720 D 6
56035 Geneva, 358 E 7
56717 Gentilly, 163 B 3
56546 Georgetown, 141 B 3
55740 Gheen, 145 F 3
56239 Ghent, 301 C 6
55335 Gibbon, 877 D 6
55741 Gilbert, 2,287 F 3
† 56431 Glen, 125 E 4
55336 Glencoe⊙, 4,217 D 6
56036 Glenville, 740 E 7
56334 Glenwood⊙, 2,584 C 5
56547 Glyndon, 674 B 4
55427 Golden Valley, 24,246 G 5
56644 Gonvick, 344 C 3
55027 Goodhue, 539 F 6
55742 Goodland, 175 E 3
56725 Goodridge, 144 C 2
56037 Good Thunder, 489 D 6
55027 Goodview, 1,829 G 6
56240 Graceville, 735 B 5
56039 Granada, 381 D 7
55604 Grand Marais⊙, 1,301 G 2
55936 Grand Meadow, 869 F 7
55744 Grand Rapids⊙, 7,247 E 3
55029 Grandy, 155 E 5
56241 Granite Falls⊙, 3,225 C 6
55030 Grasston, 132 E 5
56726 Greenbush, 787 B 2
† 55373 Greenfield, 977 F 5
55338 Green Isle, 363 E 6
56242 Green Valley, 129 C 6
56335 Greenwald, 244 D 5
56336 Grey Eagle, 325 D 5
56243 Grove City, 502 D 5
56727 Grygla, 211 C 2
56452 Hackensack, 220 D 4
56133 Hadley, 119 C 7
56728 Hallock⊙, 1,477 A 2
56548 Halstad, 598 B 3
55339 Hamburg, 377 D 6
55340 Hamel, 2,396 F 5
55938 Hammond, 179 F 6
55031 Hampton, 369 E 6
56244 Hancock, 806 C 5
56245 Hanley Falls, 265 C 6
55341 Hanover, 365 E 5
56041 Hanska, 442 D 6
56364 Harding, 119 E 4
56134 Hardwick, 274 B 7
55939 Harmony, 1,130 F 7
55032 Harris, 559 F 5
56042 Hartland, 331 E 7
† 55374 Hassan, 778 E 5
55033 Hastings⊙, 12,195 F 6
56549 Hawley, 1,371 B 4
55940 Hayfield, 939 F 7
56043 Hayward, 261 E 7
55342 Hector, 1,178 D 6
56044 Henderson, 730 E 6
56136 Hendricks, 712 B 6
56550 Hendrum, 311 B 3
56551 Henning, 850 C 4
56248 Herman, 619 B 5
56137 Heron Lake, 777 C 7
56453 Hewitt, 198 C 4
55746 Hibbing, 16,104 F 3
55748 Hill City, 357 E 4
56138 Hills, 571 B 7
55037 Hinckley, 885 E 4
56552 Hitterdal, 178 B 4
56339 Hoffman, 627 C 5
55941 Hokah, 697 G 7
56340 Holdingford, 551 D 5
56139 Holland, 263 B 6
56045 Hollandale, 287 E 7
56249 Holloway, 146 C 5
55749 Holyoke, 190 F 4
55942 Homer, 150 G 6
56045 Hope, 125 E 7
55343 Hopkins, 13,428 G 5
55943 Houston, 1,090 G 7
55606 Hovland, 150 G 2
55349 Howard Lake, 1,162 D 5
55750 Hoyt Lakes, 3,634 F 3
55038 Hugo, 751 F 5
56047 Huntley, 139 D 7
55350 Hutchinson, 8,031 D 6
56140 Ihlen, 132 B 7
† 55359 Independence, 1,993 F 5
56649 International Falls⊙, 6,439 E 2
55075 Inver Grove Heights, 12,148 E 6
56141 Iona, 260 C 7
55751 Iron, 150 F 3
56455 Ironton, 562 D 4
55040 Isanti, 679 E 5
56342 Isle, 551 E 4
56142 Ivanhoe⊙, 738 B 6
56143 Jackson⊙, 3,550 C 7
55752 Jacobson, 225 E 4
56048 Janesville, 1,557 E 6
56144 Jasper, 754 B 7
56145 Jeffers, 436 C 6
56456 Jenkins, 148 D 4
55352 Jordan, 1,836 E 6
† 56669 Kabetogama, 150 F 2
56251 Kandiyohi, 295 D 5
56732 Karlstad, 727 B 2
56050 Kasota, 732 D 6
55944 Kasson, 1,883 F 6
55753 Keewatin, 1,382 E 3
56650 Kelliher, 289 D 3
55945 Kellogg, 403 G 6
55754 Kelly Lake, 950 F 3
55755 Kelsey, 151 F 3
56733 Kennedy, 424 B 2
56343 Kensington, 308 C 5
56553 Kent, 139 B 4
55946 Kenyon, 1,575 E 6
56252 Kerkhoven, 641 C 5
55757 Kettle River, 173 E 4
56051 Kiester, 681 E 7
56052 Kilkenny, 182 E 6
55353 Kimball, 567 D 5
55758 Kinney, 325 F 3
55609 Knife River, 350 G 4
55947 La Crescent, 3,142 G 7
56054 Lafayette, 498 D 6
56149 Lake Benton, 759 B 6
56734 Lake Bronson, 325 B 2
55041 Lake City, 3,594 F 6
56055 Lake Crystal, 1,807 D 6
55042 Lake Elmo, 4,032 F 6
56150 Lakefield, 1,820 C 7
† 55398 Lake Fremont (Zimmerman), 495 E 5
56458 Lake George, 200 D 3
55043 Lakeland, 962 F 6
56253 Lake Lillian, 316 C 6
56554 Lake Park, 658 B 4
† 55043 Lake Saint Croix Beach, 1,111 F 6
† 56401 Lake Shore, 410 D 4
55044 Lakeville, 7,556 E 6
56151 Lake Wilson, 378 B 7
56152 Lamberton, 962 C 6
56735 Lancaster, 382 B 2
55949 Lanesboro, 850 G 7
55950 Lansing, 300 F 7
56461 Laporte, 154 D 3
† 55744 La Prairie, 413 E 3
56056 La Salle, 132 D 6

(continued on following page)

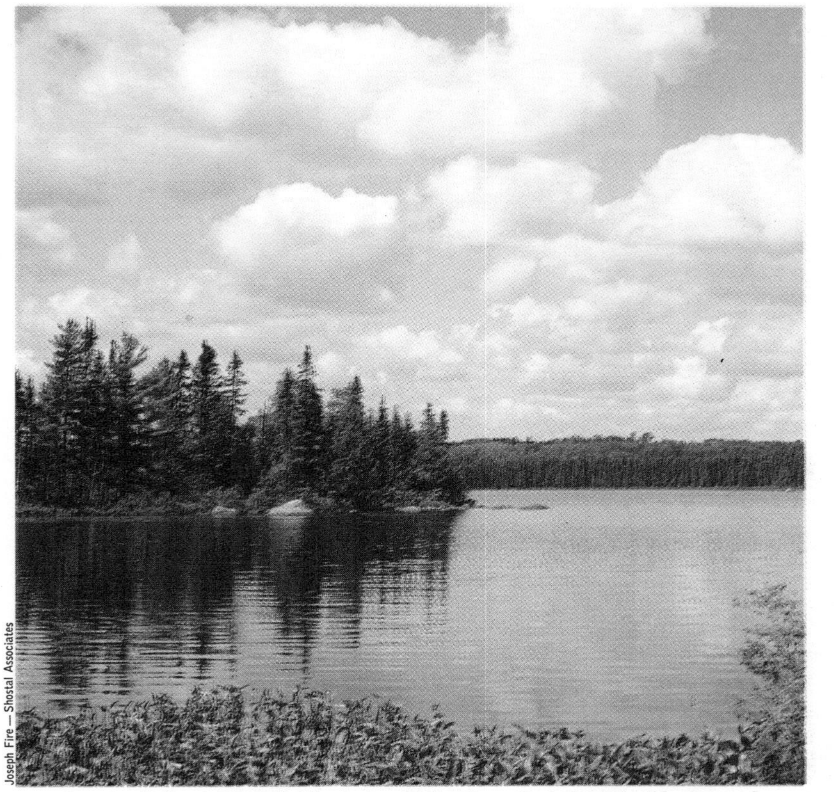

Joseph Fire—Shostal Associates

Superior National Forest in Minnesota contains the nation's largest wilderness park with primitive virgin timberlands, protected wildlife and 5,000 restocked lakes.

Minnesota 255
(continued)

56344 Lastrup, 161 .... D 4
† 55101 Lauderdale, 2,419 .... G 5
56057 Le Center⊙, 1,890 .... E 6
56651 Lengby, 140 .... C 3
† 55734 Leonidas, 157 .... F 3
56153 Leota, 285 .... C 7
55951 Le Roy, 870 .... F 7
55354 Lester Prairie, 1,162 .... D 6
56058 Le Sueur, 3,745 .... E 6
55952 Lewiston, 1,000 .... G 7
56060 Lewisville, 291 .... D 7
† 55014 Lexington, 1,926 .... G 5
† 55050 Lilydale, 664 .... G 5
55045 Lindstrom, 1,260 .... F 5
† 55038 Lino Lakes, 3,692 .... G 5
56155 Lismore, 323 .... B 7
55355 Litchfield⊙, 5,262 .... D 5
56345 Little Falls⊙, 7,467 .... D 5
56653 Littlefork, 824 .... E 2
55611 Little Marais, 175 .... G 3
† 56334 Long Beach, 219 .... C 5
55356 Long Lake, 1,506 .... F 5
56347 Long Prairie⊙, 2,416 .... D 5
56655 Longville, 171 .... D 4
55046 Lonsdale, 622 .... E 6
55357 Loretto, 340 .... F 5
56349 Lowry, 257 .... C 5
56255 Lucan, 254 .... C 6
55612 Lutsen, 620 .... F 2
56156 Luverne⊙, 4,703 .... B 7
55953 Lyle, 522 .... F 7
56157 Lynd, 267 .... C 6
55954 Mabel, 888 .... G 7
56062 Madelia, 2,316 .... D 6
56256 Madison⊙, 2,242 .... B 5
56063 Madison Lake, 587 .... E 6
56158 Magnolia, 233 .... B 7
56557 Mahnomen⊙, 1,313 .... C 3
55115 Mahtomedi, 2,640 .... F 5
55762 Mahtowa, 167 .... F 4
56001 Mankato⊙, 30,895 .... E 6
55955 Mantorville⊙, 479 .... F 6
† 55369 Maple Grove, 6,275 .... F 5
55358 Maple Lake, 1,124 .... D 5
55359 Maple Plain, 1,169 .... F 5
56065 Mapleton, 1,307 .... E 7
† 55912 Mapleview, 328 .... E 7
55109 Maplewood, 25,222 .... G 5
55764 Marble, 682 .... E 3
56657 Marcell, 350 .... E 3
56257 Marietta, 264 .... B 5
55047 Marine on Saint Croix, 513 .... F 5
56258 Marshall⊙, 9,886 .... C 6
55360 Mayer, 325 .... E 6
56260 Maynard, 455 .... C 6
55956 Mazeppa, 498 .... F 6
55760 McGregor, 331 .... E 4
56556 McIntosh, 753 .... C 3
55761 McKinley, 317 .... F 3
55765 Meadowlands, 128 .... F 3
55049 Medford, 690 .... E 6
55427 Medicine Lake, 930 .... G 5
† 55340 Medina (Hamel), 2,396 .... F 5
† 56352 Meire Grove, 171 .... C 5
56352 Melrose, 2,273 .... D 5
56464 Menahga, 835 .... C 4
55050 Mendota, 327 .... G 5
† 55050 Mendota Heights, 6,165 .... G 6
56736 Mentor, 236 .... B 3
56465 Merrifield, 300 .... D 4
56737 Middle River, 369 .... B 2
† 55033 Miesville, 192 .... F 6
56353 Milaca⊙, 1,940 .... E 5
56262 Milan, 427 .... C 5
55957 Millville, 139 .... F 6
56263 Milroy, 247 .... C 6
56354 Miltona, 172 .... C 4
* 55401 Minneapolis⊙, 434,400 .... G 5
Minneapolis-Saint Paul, ‡1,813,647 .... G 5
56264 Minneota, 1,320 .... C 6
55959 Minnesota City, 301 .... G 6
56068 Minnesota Lake, 738 .... E 7
55343 Minnetonka, 35,776 .... G 5
† 55364 Minnetrista, 2,878 .... F 5
56265 Montevideo⊙, 5,661 .... C 6
56069 Montgomery, 2,281 .... E 6
55362 Monticello, 1,636 .... E 5
55363 Montrose, 379 .... E 5
56560 Moorhead⊙, 29,687 .... B 4
Moorhead-Fargo, ‡120,238 .... B 4
55767 Moose Lake, 1,400 .... F 4
56266 Mora⊙, 2,582 .... E 5
56266 Morgan, 972 .... D 6
56267 Morris⊙, 5,366 .... C 5
55052 Morristown, 659 .... E 6
56270 Morton, 591 .... C 6
56466 Motley, 351 .... D 4
55364 Mound, 7,572 .... E 6
† 55112 Mounds View, 9,988 .... G 5
55768 Mountain Iron, 1,698 .... F 3
56159 Mountain Lake, 1,986 .... D 7
56271 Murdock, 358 .... C 5
55769 Nashwauk, 1,341 .... E 3
56272 Nassau, 126 .... B 5
56566 Naytahwaush, 350 .... C 3
56355 Nelson, 175 .... C 5
55053 Nerstrand, 231 .... E 6
55772 Nett Lake, 470 .... E 2
56467 Nevis, 308 .... D 4
55366 New Auburn, 274 .... D 6
55112 New Brighton, 19,507 .... G 5
56738 Newfolden, 390 .... B 2
55367 New Germany, 303 .... E 6
56273 New London, 736 .... C 5
55054 New Market, 215 .... E 6
56356 New Munich, 307 .... D 5
55055 Newport, 2,922 .... F 6
56071 New Prague, 2,680 .... E 6
56072 New Richland, 1,113 .... E 7
† 55031 New Trier, 153 .... F 6
56073 New Ulm⊙, 13,051 .... D 6
56567 New York Mills, 791 .... C 4
† 56431 Nichols, 125 .... E 4
56074 Nicollet, 618 .... D 6
56568 Nielsville, 156 .... B 3
56468 Nisswa, 1,011 .... D 4
55770 Nopeming, 268 .... F 4
56274 Norcross, 137 .... B 5
55056 North Branch, 1,106 .... F 5
† 56442 North Crosslake, 362 .... D 4
55057 Northfield, 10,235 .... E 6
56001 North Mankato, 7,347 .... D 6
56661 Northome, 351 .... D 3
56275 North Redwood, 155 .... D 6
56075 Northrop, 188 .... D 7
55109 North Saint Paul, 11,950 .... E 5
55368 Norwood, 1,058 .... E 6
56276 Odessa, 194 .... B 5
56160 Odin, 166 .... D 7
56569 Ogema, 236 .... C 3
56358 Ogilvie, 384 .... E 5
56161 Okabena, 237 .... C 7
56742 Oklee, 536 .... C 3
56277 Olivia⊙, 2,553 .... C 6
56359 Onamia, 670 .... E 4
† 55044 Orchard Lake, 200 .... E 6
56162 Ormsby, 199 .... D 7
† 55323 Orono (Crystal Bay), 6,787 .... F 5
55960 Oronoco, 564 .... F 6
55771 Orr, 315 .... F 2
56278 Ortonville⊙, 2,665 .... B 5
56570 Osage, 175 .... C 4
56360 Osakis, 1,306 .... C 5
56744 Oslo, 417 .... A 2
55369 Osseo, 2,908 .... G 5
55961 Ostrander, 216 .... F 7
† 56058 Ottawa, 125 .... E 6
56571 Ottertail, 180 .... C 4
56662 Outing, 425 .... E 4
55060 Owatonna⊙, 15,341 .... E 6
56469 Palisade, 149 .... E 4
† 55801 Palmers, 150 .... G 4
† 55705 Palo, 158 .... F 3
56361 Parkers Prairie, 882 .... C 4
56470 Park Rapids⊙, 2,772 .... D 4
56362 Paynesville, 1,920 .... D 5
56363 Pease, 187 .... E 5
† 56472 Pelican Lakes (Breezy Point Village), 233 .... D 4
56572 Pelican Rapids, 1,835 .... B 4
56078 Pemberton, 128 .... E 7
55775 Pengilly, 625 .... E 3
56279 Pennock, 255 .... C 5
56472 Pequot Lakes, 499 .... D 4
56573 Perham, 1,933 .... C 4
56574 Perley, 149 .... B 3
55962 Peterson, 269 .... G 7
† 55948 Pickwick, 150 .... G 7
56364 Pierz, 893 .... D 5
56473 Pillager, 374 .... D 4
55063 Pine City⊙, 2,143 .... F 5
55963 Pine Island, 1,640 .... F 6
56474 Pine River, 803 .... D 4
56164 Pipestone⊙, 5,328 .... B 7
55964 Plainview, 2,093 .... F 6
55370 Plato, 303 .... D 6
56748 Plummer, 285 .... B 3
† 55401 Plymouth, 17,593 .... G 5
56666 Ponemah, 531 .... D 2
56280 Porter, 207 .... B 6
55965 Preston⊙, 1,413 .... F 7
55371 Princeton, 2,531 .... E 5
56281 Prinsburg, 448 .... C 6
55372 Prior Lake, 1,114 .... E 6
55810 Proctor, 3,123 .... F 4
† 55752 Rabey, 125 .... E 4
55967 Racine, 197 .... F 7
56475 Randall, 536 .... D 4
55065 Randolph, 350 .... E 6
56668 Ranier, 255 .... E 2
56669 Ray, 200 .... E 2
56282 Raymond, 589 .... C 5
56165 Reading, 150 .... C 7
55968 Reads Landing, 150 .... F 6
56670 Redby, 475 .... D 3
56671 Redlake, 300 .... C 3
56750 Red Lake Falls⊙, 1,740 .... B 3
55066 Red Wing⊙, 10,441 .... F 6
56283 Redwood Falls⊙, 4,774 .... C 6
56672 Remer, 403 .... E 3
56284 Renville, 1,252 .... C 6
56166 Revere, 166 .... C 6
56367 Rice, 366 .... D 5
55423 Richfield, 47,231 .... G 6
56368 Richmond, 866 .... D 5
55422 Robbinsdale, 16,845 .... G 5
55901 Rochester⊙, 53,766 .... F 6
55067 Rock Creek, 805 .... F 5
55373 Rockford, 730 .... F 5
56369 Rockville, 302 .... D 5
55374 Rogers, 544 .... E 5
55969 Rollingstone, 450 .... G 6
56371 Roscoe, 195 .... D 5
56751 Roseau⊙, 2,552 .... C 2
55970 Rose Creek, 390 .... F 7
† 56216 Roseland, 123 .... C 6
55068 Rosemount, 1,337 .... E 6
55113 Roseville, 34,518 .... G 5
56579 Rothsay, 448 .... B 4
56167 Round Lake, 506 .... C 7
56373 Royalton, 534 .... D 5
55069 Rush City, 1,130 .... F 5
55971 Rushford, 1,318 .... G 7
56168 Rushmore, 394 .... C 7
56169 Russell, 398 .... C 6
56170 Ruthton, 405 .... B 6
55778 Rutledge, 123 .... F 4
56580 Sabin, 333 .... B 4
56285 Sacred Heart, 707 .... C 6
55779 Saginaw, 407 .... F 4
55414 Saint Anthony Falls, 9,239 .... G 5
55375 Saint Bonifacius, 685 .... F 5
55972 Saint Charles, 1,942 .... F 7
56080 Saint Clair, 488 .... E 6
56301 Saint Cloud⊙, 39,691 .... D 5
55070 Saint Francis, 897 .... E 5
56554 Saint Hilaire, 337 .... B 2
56081 Saint James⊙, 4,027 .... D 7
56374 Saint Joseph, 1,786 .... D 5
55426 Saint Louis Park, 48,883 .... G 5
56376 Saint Martin, 188 .... D 5
55376 Saint Michael, 1,021 .... E 5
* 55101 Saint Paul (cap.)⊙, 309,980 .... G 6
55071 Saint Paul Park, 5,587 .... G 6
56082 Saint Peter⊙, 8,339 .... E 6
56375 Saint Stephen, 331 .... D 5
56755 Saint Vincent, 177 .... A 2
56083 Sanborn, 505 .... C 6
55072 Sandstone, 1,641 .... F 4
56377 Sartell, 1,323 .... D 5
56378 Sauk Centre, 3,750 .... C 5
56379 Sauk Rapids, 5,051 .... D 5
55378 Savage, 3,611 .... G 6
55780 Sawyer, 200 .... F 4
55073 Scandia, 200 .... F 5
† 55720 Scanlon, 1,132 .... F 4
55613 Schroeder, 550 .... G 3
56287 Seaforth, 132 .... C 6
56084 Searles, 160 .... D 6
56477 Sebeka, 668 .... C 4
55074 Shafer, 149 .... F 5
55379 Shakopee⊙, 6,876 .... F 6
56581 Shelly, 260 .... B 3
56171 Sherburn, 1,190 .... D 7
56676 Shevlin, 185 .... C 3
† 55021 Shieldsville, 150 .... E 6
† 55331 Shorewood, 4,223 .... F 5
55614 Silver Bay, 3,504 .... G 3
55380 Silver Creek, 125 .... D 5
55381 Silver Lake, 694 .... D 6
† 56001 Skyline, 400 .... D 6
56172 Slayton⊙, 2,351 .... C 7
56085 Sleepy Eye, 3,461 .... D 6
† 56345 Sobieski, 189 .... D 5
55782 Soudan, 900 .... F 3
55382 South Haven, 238 .... D 5
56679 South International Falls, 2,116 .... E 2
55075 South Saint Paul, 25,016 .... G 6
56288 Spicer, 586 .... C 5
56087 Springfield, 2,530 .... C 6
55974 Spring Grove, 1,290 .... G 7
55432 Spring Lake Park, 6,417 .... E 5
55384 Spring Park, 1,087 .... F 5
55975 Spring Valley, 2,572 .... F 7
55079 Stacy, 278 .... E 5
55080 Stanchfield, 155 .... E 5
56479 Staples, 2,657 .... D 4
56381 Starbuck, 1,138 .... C 5
56173 Steen, 191 .... B 7
56757 Stephen, 904 .... A 2
55385 Stewart, 666 .... D 6
55976 Stewartville, 2,802 .... F 7
55082 Stillwater⊙, 10,191 .... F 5
55988 Stockton, 346 .... G 6
56174 Storden, 364 .... C 6
56758 Strandquist, 138 .... B 2
55783 Sturgeon Lake, 167 .... F 4
56289 Sunburg, 144 .... C 5
† 55075 Sunfish Lake, 269 .... E 6
56290 Svea, 125 .... C 6
56382 Swanville, 300 .... D 5
55785 Swatara, 250 .... E 4
55786 Taconite, 352 .... E 3
56291 Taunton, 195 .... B 6
55084 Taylors Falls, 587 .... F 5
56683 Tenstrike, 138 .... D 3
56701 Thief River Falls⊙, 8,618 .... B 2
† 56319 Thomson, 159 .... F 4
56583 Tintah, 167 .... B 5
55615 Tofte, 400 .... H 3
55789 Toivola, 185 .... F 3
† 55331 Tonka Bay, 1,397 .... F 5
55790 Tower, 699 .... F 3
56175 Tracy, 2,516 .... C 6
56176 Trimont, 835 .... D 7
56088 Truman, 1,137 .... D 7
55791 Twig, 165 .... F 4
56089 Twin Lakes, 230 .... E 7
56584 Twin Valley, 868 .... B 3
55616 Two Harbors⊙, 4,437 .... G 3
56178 Tyler, 1,069 .... B 6
56585 Ulen, 486 .... B 3
56586 Underwood, 278 .... C 4
56384 Upsala, 312 .... D 5
† 56361 Urbank, 125 .... C 4
55979 Utica, 240 .... G 7
† 55101 Vadnais Heights, 3,391 .... G 5
56587 Vergas, 281 .... C 4
55085 Vermillion, 359 .... F 6
56481 Verndale, 570 .... C 4
† 55752 Verndon, 135 .... E 4
56090 Vernon Center, 347 .... D 7
55086 Veseli, 150 .... E 6
56292 Vesta, 330 .... C 6
55386 Victoria, 850 .... F 6
56385 Villard, 221 .... C 5
56588 Vining, 121 .... C 4
55792 Virginia, 12,450 .... F 3
55981 Wabasha⊙, 2,371 .... G 6
56293 Wabasso, 738 .... C 6
55387 Waconia, 2,445 .... E 6
56482 Wadena⊙, 4,640 .... C 4
56386 Wahkon, 208 .... E 4
56387 Waite Park, 2,824 .... D 5
56091 Waldorf, 285 .... E 7
56484 Walker⊙, 2,073 .... D 3
56180 Walnut Grove, 756 .... C 6
56092 Walters, 152 .... E 7
55982 Waltham, 189 .... F 7
55983 Wanamingo, 574 .... F 6
56294 Wanda, 124 .... C 6
55743 Warba, 148 .... E 3
56762 Warren⊙, 1,999 .... B 2
56763 Warroad, 1,086 .... C 2
55087 Warsaw, 200 .... E 6
56093 Waseca⊙, 6,789 .... E 6
55388 Watertown, 1,390 .... E 6
56096 Waterville, 1,539 .... E 6
55389 Watkins, 785 .... D 5
56295 Watson, 228 .... C 5
56589 Waubun, 345 .... C 3
55390 Waverly, 546 .... E 5
55391 Wayzata, 3,700 .... G 5
55088 Webster, 175 .... E 6
56181 Welcome, 694 .... D 7
56097 Wells, 2,791 .... E 7
56590 Wendell, 247 .... B 4
56183 Westbrook, 990 .... C 6
55985 West Concord, 718 .... F 6
55118 West Saint Paul, 18,799 .... G 5
56296 Wheaton⊙, 2,029 .... B 5
56485 Whipholt, 142 .... D 3
55110 White Bear Lake, 23,313 .... G 5
56591 White Earth, 150 .... C 3
56184 Wilder, 132 .... C 7
55090 Willernie, 697 .... G 5
56686 Williams, 220 .... D 2
56201 Willmar⊙, 12,869 .... C 5
55795 Willow River, 331 .... F 4
56185 Wilmont, 390 .... C 7
56687 Wilton, 119 .... C 3
56101 Windom⊙, 3,952 .... C 7
56592 Winger, 228 .... B 3
56098 Winnebago, 1,791 .... D 7
55987 Winona⊙, 26,438 .... G 6
55395 Winsted, 1,266 .... D 6
55396 Winthrop, 1,391 .... D 6
55796 Winton, 193 .... G 3
56594 Wolverton, 171 .... B 4
† 55798 Woodbury, 6,184 .... F 6
56297 Wood Lake, 418 .... C 6
56186 Woodstock, 217 .... B 7
56187 Worthington⊙, 9,825 .... C 7
55797 Wrenshall, 147 .... F 4
55798 Wright, 132 .... E 4
55990 Wykoff, 450 .... F 7
55092 Wyoming, 695 .... F 5
55397 Young America, 611 .... E 6
55799 Zim, 608 .... F 3
55398 Zimmerman, 495 .... E 5
55991 Zumbro Falls, 203 .... F 6
55992 Zumbrota, 1,929 .... F 6

⊙ County seat.
‡ Population of metropolitan area.
† Zip of nearest p.o.
* Multiple zips

Agriculture, Industry and Resources

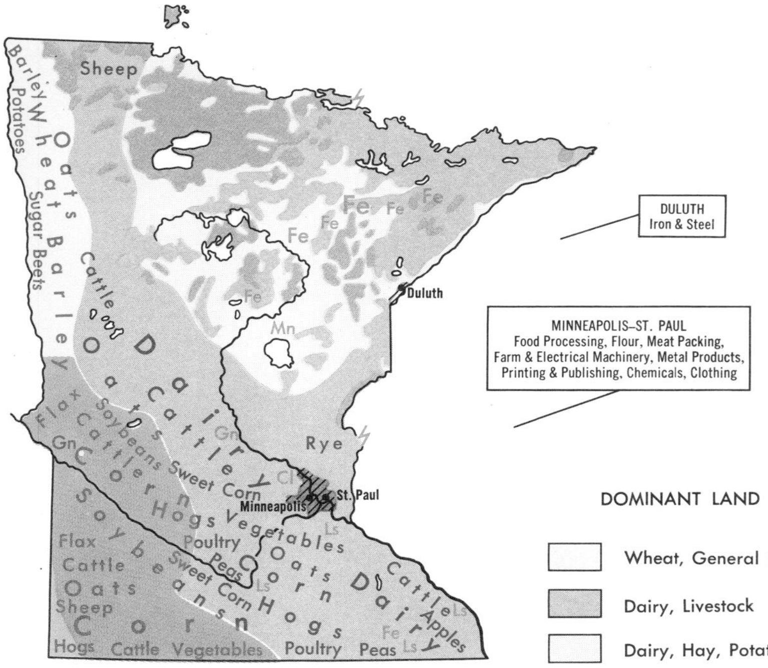

Sheep
Barley
Wheat
Potatoes
Oats
Sugar Beets
Cattle
Barley
Dairy
Fe
Mn
Duluth
DULUTH
Iron & Steel
MINNEAPOLIS–ST. PAUL
Food Processing, Flour, Meat Packing,
Farm & Electrical Machinery, Metal Products,
Printing & Publishing, Chemicals, Clothing
Rye
Cl
Minneapolis
St. Paul
Flax
Soybeans
Cattle
Sweet Corn
Corn
Hogs
Vegetables
Poultry
Peas
Gn
Ls
Apples
Hogs Cattle Vegetables Poultry Peas

MAJOR MINERAL OCCURRENCES

Cl Clay
Fe Iron Ore
Gn Granite
Ls Limestone
Mn Manganese

Water Power
Major Industrial Areas

DOMINANT LAND USE

Wheat, General Farming
Dairy, Livestock
Dairy, Hay, Potatoes
Cattle Feed, Hogs
Livestock, Cash Grain
Forests
Swampland, Limited Agriculture
Urban Areas

Topography

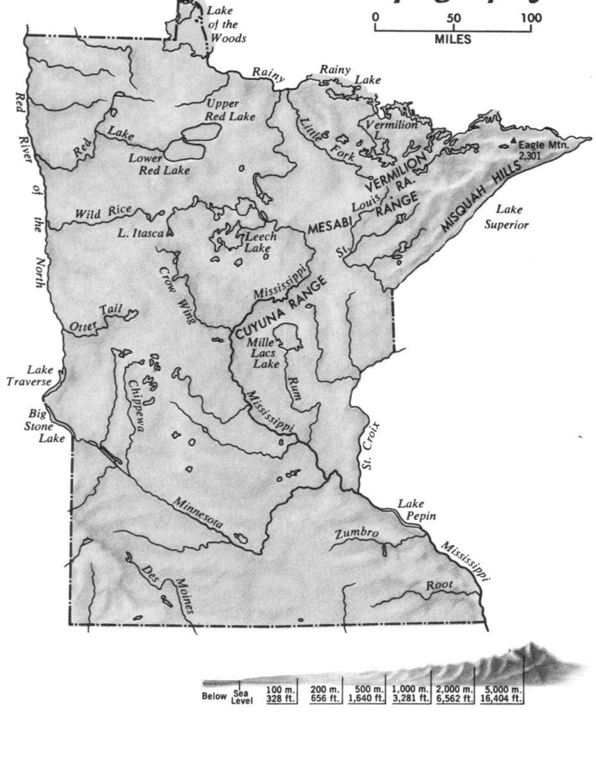

0 50 100
MILES
Lake of the Woods
Rainy
Rainy Lake
Upper Red Lake
Red Lake
Lower Red Lake
Red River of the North
Little Fork
Vermilion Lake
Eagle Mtn. 2,301
Vermilion Ra.
Louis
Mesabi Range
Misquah Hills
Lake Superior
St.
Wild Rice
L. Itasca
Leech Lake
Crow Wing
Mississippi
Cuyuna Range
Mille Lacs Lake
Otter Tail
Lake Traverse
Chippewa
Rum
Big Stone Lake
St. Croix
Minnesota
Lake Pepin
Zumbro
Mississippi
Root
Des Moines
Below Sea Level
100 m. 328 ft.
200 m. 656 ft.
500 m. 1,640 ft.
1,000 m. 3,281 ft.
2,000 m. 6,562 ft.
5,000 m. 16,404 ft.

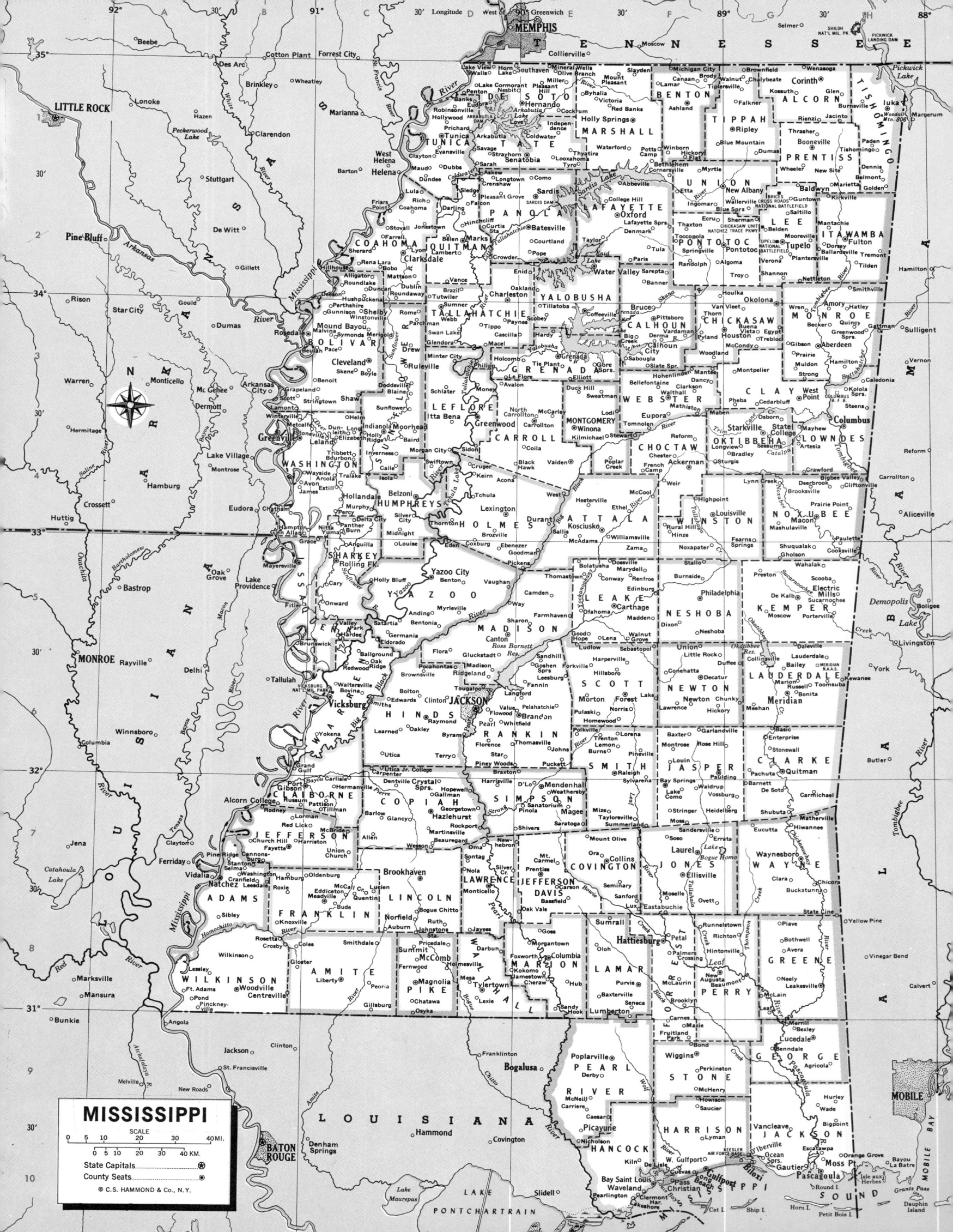

MISSISSIPPI

SCALE

0 5 10 20 30 40 MI.

0 5 10 20 30 40 KM.

State Capitals .... ✪
County Seats .... ◉

© C.S. Hammond & Co., N.Y.

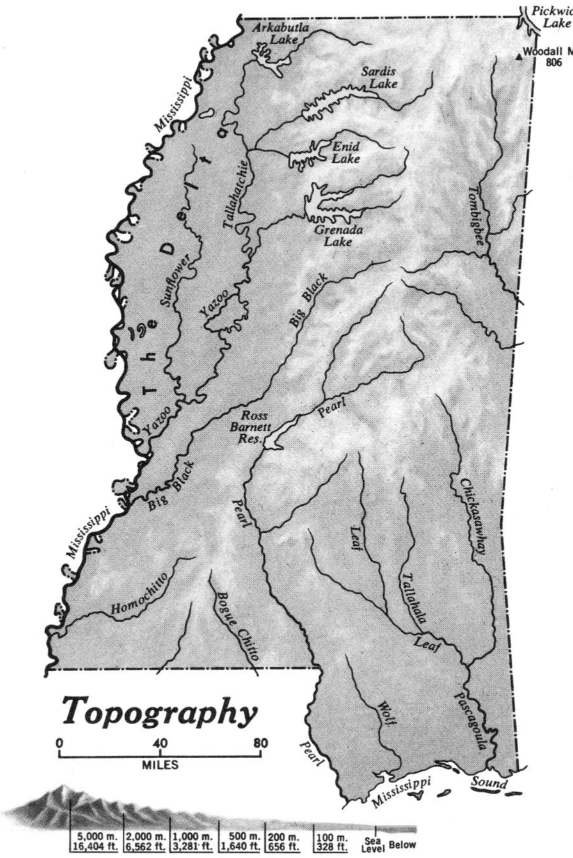
Pickwick Lake
Woodall Mtn. 806
Arkabutla Lake
Sardis Lake
Enid Lake
Grenada Lake
Mississippi
Tallahatchie
Tombigbee
Sunflower
Yazoo
Big Black
The Delta
Ross Barnett Res.
Pearl
Chickasawhay
Leaf
Tallahala
Homochitto
Bogue Chitto
Wolf
Pascagoula
Mississippi Sound
Topography
0 40 80
MILES
5,000 m. 16,404 ft.
2,000 m. 6,562 ft.
1,000 m. 3,281 ft.
500 m. 1,640 ft.
200 m. 656 ft.
100 m. 328 ft.
Sea Level
Below

AREA 47,716 sq. mi.
POPULATION 2,216,912 ('70); 2,520,638 ('80)
CAPITAL Jackson
LARGEST CITY Jackson
HIGHEST POINT Woodall Mtn. 806 ft.
SETTLED IN 1716
ADMITTED TO UNION December 10, 1817
POPULAR NAME Magnolia State
STATE FLOWER Magnolia
STATE BIRD Mockingbird

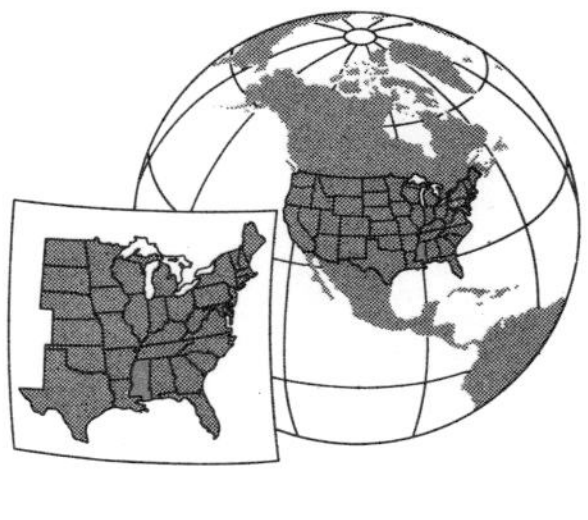

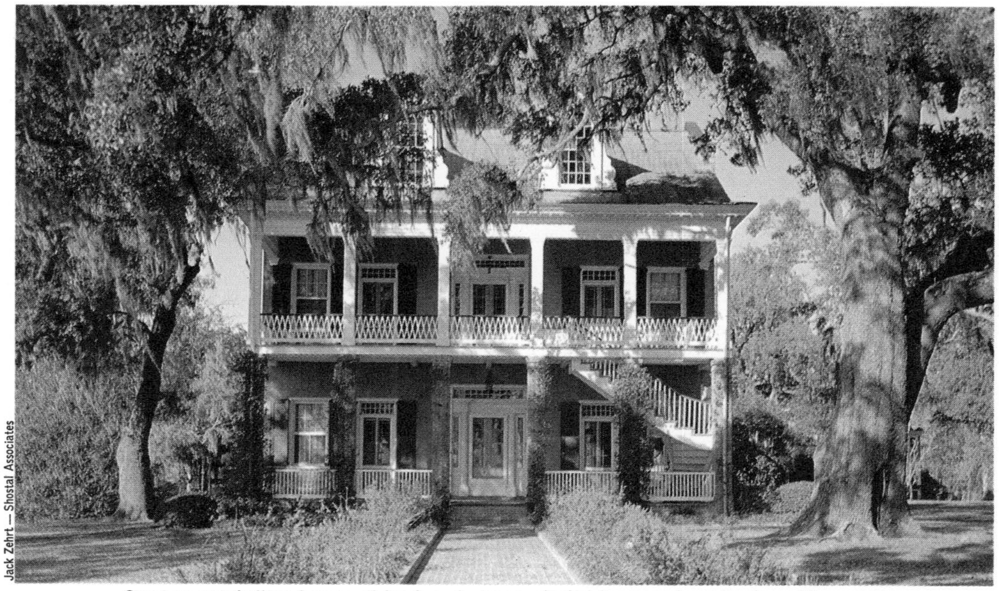
Jack Zehrt — Shostal Associates

Gracious antebellum houses of brick and stucco, shaded by moss-draped oaks, add a sense of permanence to the older section of Biloxi, Mississippi.

COUNTIES

Adams, 37,293 B 8
Alcorn, 27,179 G 1
Amite, 13,763 C 8
Attala, 19,570 E 4
Benton, 7,505 F 1
Bolivar, 49,409 C 3
Calhoun, 14,623 F 3
Carroll, 9,397 E 4
Chickasaw, 16,805 G 3
Choctaw, 8,440 F 4
Claiborne, 10,086 C 7
Clarke, 15,049 G 6
Clay, 18,840 G 3
Coahoma, 40,447 C 2
Copiah, 24,749 D 7
Covington, 14,002 E 7
De Soto, 35,885 E 1
Forrest, 57,849 F 8
Franklin, 8,011 C 8
George, 12,459 G 9
Greene, 8,545 G 8
Grenada, 19,854 E 3
Hancock, 17,387 E 10
Harrison, 134,582 F 10
Hinds, 214,973 D 6
Holmes, 23,120 D 4
Humphreys, 14,601 C 4
Issaquena, 2,737 B 5
Itawamba, 16,847 H 2
Jackson, 87,975 G 9
Jasper, 15,994 F 6
Jefferson, 9,295 B 7
Jefferson Davis, 12,936 E 7
Jones, 56,357 F 7
Kemper, 10,233 G 5
Lafayette, 24,181 E 2
Lamar, 15,209 E 8
Lauderdale, 67,087 G 6
Lawrence, 11,137 D 7
Leake, 17,085 E 5
Lee, 46,148 G 2
Leflore, 42,111 D 3
Lincoln, 26,198 D 8
Lowndes, 49,700 H 4
Madison, 29,737 D 5
Marion, 22,871 E 8
Marshall, 24,027 E 1
Monroe, 34,043 H 3
Montgomery, 12,918 E 4
Neshoba, 20,802 F 5
Newton, 18,983 F 6
Noxubee, 14,288 G 4
Oktibbeha, 28,752 G 4
Panola, 26,829 E 2
Pearl River, 27,802 E 9
Perry, 9,065 G 8
Pike, 31,756 D 8
Pontotoc, 17,363 F 2
Prentiss, 20,133 G 1
Quitman, 15,888 D 2
Rankin, 43,933 E 6
Scott, 21,369 E 6
Sharkey, 8,937 C 5
Simpson, 19,947 E 7
Smith, 13,561 E 6
Stone, 8,101 F 9
Sunflower, 37,047 C 3
Tallahatchie, 19,338 D 3
Tate, 18,544 E 1
Tippah, 15,852 G 1
Tishomingo, 14,940 H 1
Tunica, 11,854 D 1
Union, 19,096 F 2
Walthall, 12,500 D 8
Warren, 44,981 C 6
Washington, 70,581 C 4
Wayne, 16,650 G 7
Webster, 10,047 F 3
Wilkinson, 11,099 B 8
Winston, 18,406 F 4
Yalobusha, 11,915 E 2
Yazoo, 27,304 D 5

CITIES and TOWNS

Zip *Name/Pop.* *Key*
38601 Abbeville, 600 F 2
39730 Aberdeen⊙, 6,157 H 3
39735 Ackerman⊙, 1,502 F 4
† 39095 Acona, 200 D 4
† 39452 Agricola, 200 G 9
39096 Alcorn College, 2,380 B 7
38820 Algoma, 150 G 2
38720 Alligator, 280 C 2
38821 Amory, 7,236 H 3
38721 Anguilla, 612 C 5
38722 Arcola, 517 C 4
38602 Arkabutla, 195 D 1
39736 Artesia, 444 G 4
38603 Ashland⊙, 348 F 1
38604 Askew, 200 D 1
† 39664 Auburn, 500 C 8
38912 Avalon, 275 D 3
† 39456 Avera, 150 G 8
38723 Avon, 400 B 4
39320 Bailey, 320 G 6
38724 Baird, 212 C 4
38824 Baldwyn, 2,366 G 2
† 38801 Ballardsville, 105 H 2
† 38664 Banks, 100 D 1
38913 Banner, 200 F 2
39421 Bassfield, 354 E 8
38606 Batesville⊙, 3,796 E 2
† 39343 Baxter, 225 F 6
† 39455 Baxterville, 100 E 8
39520 Bay Saint Louis⊙, 6,752 F 10
39422 Bay Springs⊙, 1,801 F 7
39423 Beaumont, 1,061 G 8
† 39191 Beauregard, 199 D 7
38825 Becker, 450 G 3
38826 Belden, 241 G 2
38609 Belen, 500 D 2
39737 Bellefontaine, 360 F 3
38827 Belmont, 968 H 1
39038 Belzoni⊙, 3,146 C 4
† 39450 Benndale, 500 G 9
38725 Benoit, 473 C 3
39039 Benton, 500 D 5
39040 Bentonia, 544 D 5
† 38659 Bethlehem, 210 F 1
38726 Beulah, 443 B 3
39453 Bexley, 130 G 9
39738 Bigbee Valley, 370 H 4
38914 Big Creek, 148 F 3
† 39567 Bigpoint, 100 H 9
* 39530 Biloxi, 48,486 G 10
Biloxi-Gulfport, ‡134,582 G 10
38918 Black Hawk, 100 E 4
38610 Blue Mountain, 677 G 1
38828 Blue Springs, 125 G 2
38728 Bobo, 200 C 2
39629 Bogue Chitto, 658 D 8
39041 Bolton, 787 D 6
39550 Bond, 350 F 9
39321 Bonita, 300 G 6
38829 Booneville⊙, 5,895 G 1
† 39456 Bothwell, 100 G 8
38729 Bourbon, 350 C 4
38730 Boyle, 861 C 3
39042 Brandon⊙, 2,685 E 6
39044 Braxton, 180 D 6
38956 Brazil, 229 D 2
39601 Brookhaven⊙, 10,700 C 7
39425 Brooklyn, 750 F 8
39739 Brooksville, 978 G 4
† 38683 Brownfield, 300 G 1
† 39041 Brownsville, 200 D 6
† 39095 Brozville, 150 D 4
38915 Bruce, 2,033 F 3
† 39180 Brunswick, 90 C 5
39322 Buckatunna, 500 G 7
39630 Bude, 1,146 C 8
† 39153 Burns, 100 E 6
38833 Burnsville, 435 H 1
38611 Byhalia, 702 E 1
† 39205 Byram, 250 D 6
† 38754 Caile, 350 C 4
39740 Caledonia, 245 H 3
38916 Calhoun City, 1,847 F 3
39045 Camden, 248 E 5
38612 Canaan, 200 F 1
† 39120 Cannonsburg, 240 B 7
39046 Canton⊙, 10,503 D 5
39049 Carlisle, 350 C 7
† 39360 Carmichael, 150 G 7
39426 Carriere, 900 E 9
38917 Carrollton⊙, 295 E 4
39427 Carson, 285 E 7
39051 Carthage⊙, 3,031 E 5
39054 Cary, 517 C 5
38920 Cascilla, 150 D 3
39741 Cedarbluff, 180 G 3
39631 Centreville, 1,819 B 8
38684 Chalybeate, 350 G 1
38921 Charleston⊙, 2,821 D 2
39632 Chatawa, 300 D 8
† 39483 Cheraw, 100 E 8
39323 Chunky, 280 G 6
39324 Clara, 400 G 7
38614 Clarksdale⊙, 21,673 D 2
† 39752 Clarkson, 100 F 3
39551 Clermont Harbor, 200 F 10
38732 Cleveland⊙, 13,327 C 3
39742 Cliftonville, 280 H 4
39056 Clinton, 7,246 D 6
38617 Coahoma, 350 C 2
38922 Coffeeville⊙, 1,024 E 3
38618 Coldwater, 1,450 E 1
39639 Coles, 195 C 8
† 38655 College Hill, 175 E 2
39428 Collins⊙, 1,934 E 7
39325 Collinsville, 700 G 6
39429 Columbia⊙, 7,587 E 8
39701 Columbus⊙, 25,795 H 3
38619 Como, 1,003 E 1
† 39051 Conway, 125 E 5
38834 Corinth⊙, 11,581 G 1
† 38659 Cornersville, 235 F 1
38620 Courtland, 316 E 2
† 39095 Coxburg, 300 D 5
† 39120 Cranfield, 100 B 7
39743 Crawford, 391 G 4
38621 Crenshaw, 1,271 D 2
39633 Crosby, 491 B 8
38622 Crowder, 815 D 2
38924 Cruger, 415 D 4
39059 Crystal Springs, 4,180 D 7
† 39571 Cuevas, 200 F 10
† 38606 Curtis Station, 200 D 2
† 39751 Dancy, 116 F 3
† 39643 Darbun, 100 D 8
38623 Darling, 250 D 2
39327 Decatur⊙, 1,311 F 6
39328 De Kalb⊙, 1,072 G 5
† 39571 De Lisle, 450 F 10
39061 Delta City, 300 C 4
38838 Dennis, 175 H 1
† 39470 Derby, 189 E 9
38839 Derma, 660 F 3
39360 De Soto, 150 G 7
39532 D'Iberville, 7,288 G 10
† 39350 Dixon, 125 F 5
39062 D'Lo, 485 E 7
38736 Doddsville, 276 C 3
38840 Dorsey, 100 H 2
38737 Drew, 2,574 C 3
38739 Dublin, 385 C 2
38925 Duck Hill, 809 E 3
† 39337 Duffee, 100 G 6
38625 Dumas, 200 G 1
38740 Duncan, 599 C 2
† 38756 Dunleith, 140 C 4
39063 Durant, 2,752 E 4
39436 Eastabuchie, 200 F 8
39064 Ebenezer, 150 D 5
38841 Ecru, 417 F 2
39634 Eddiceton, 175 C 8
39065 Eden, 152 D 5
† 39051 Edinburg, 200 F 5
39066 Edwards, 1,236 C 6
38842 Egypt, 100 G 3
39329 Electric Mills, 200 G 5
38742 Elizabeth, 540 C 4
38926 Elliott, 200 E 3
39437 Ellisville⊙, 4,643 F 7
39330 Enterprise, 458 G 6
39552 Escatawpa, 1,579 G 10
† 38748 Estill, 100 C 4
39067 Ethel, 560 F 4
38627 Etta, 100 F 2
† 38632 Eudora, 200 D 1
39744 Eupora, 1,792 F 3
38628 Falcon, 230 D 2
38629 Falkner, 500 G 1
† 39042 Fannin, 250 E 6
38630 Farrell, 400 C 2
39069 Fayette⊙, 1,725 B 7
39635 Fernwood, 600 D 8
39070 Fitler, 800 B 5
39071 Flora, 987 D 5
39073 Florence, 404 D 6
† 39201 Flowood, 352 D 6
39074 Forest⊙, 4,085 F 6
39076 Forkville, 180 E 6
39636 Fort Adams, 129 B 8
39483 Foxworth, 950 E 8
39745 French Camp, 174 F 4
38631 Friars Point, 1,177 C 2
38843 Fulton⊙, 2,899 H 2
† 39345 Garlandville, 150 F 6
38844 Gattman, 175 H 3
39553 Gautier, 2,087 G 10
39078 Georgetown, 339 D 7
† 39083 Glancy, 120 C 7
38846 Glen, 250 H 1
38744 Glen Allan, 400 B 4
38928 Glendora, 201 D 3
39638 Gloster, 1,401 B 8
39110 Gluckstadt, 150 D 5
38847 Golden, 115 H 2
† 39094 Good Hope, 125 E 5
39079 Goodman, 1,194 E 5
38929 Gore Springs, 120 E 3
† 39042 Goshen Springs, 100 E 6
† 39429 Goss, 100 E 8
38745 Grace, 325 C 5
† 38725 Grapeland, 200 B 3
38701 Greenville⊙, 39,648 B 4
38930 Greenwood⊙, 22,400 D 4
38848 Greenwood Springs, 170 H 3
38901 Grenada⊙, 9,944 E 3
39501 Gulfport⊙, 40,791 F 10
38746 Gunnison, 545 C 3
38849 Guntown, 304 G 2
39746 Hamilton, 350 H 3
† 38744 Hampton, 200 B 4
† 39177 Hardee, 100 C 5
39080 Harperville, 260 E 6
39081 Harriston, 500 C 7
39082 Harrisville, 500 D 7
† 38821 Hatley, 500 H 3
39401 Hattiesburg⊙, 38,277 F 8
39083 Hazlehurst⊙, 4,577 D 7
39439 Heidelberg, 1,112 F 7
39086 Hermanville, 500 C 7
38632 Hernando⊙, 2,499 E 1
† 39192 Hesterville, 100 E 4
39332 Hickory, 570 F 6
38633 Hickory Flat, 354 F 1
39087 Hillsboro, 350 E 6
† 38646 Hinchcliff, 125 D 2
† 39462 Hintonville, 100 F 8
† 39108 Hinze, 140 F 4
39333 Hiwannee, 250 G 7
† 39751 Hohenlinden, 96 F 3
38748 Hollandale, 3,260 C 4
39068 Holly Bluff, 250 C 5
38749 Holly Ridge, 375 C 4
38635 Holly Springs⊙, 5,728 E 1
† 38676 Hollywood, 125 D 1
† 39648 Holmesville, 200 D 8
† 39059 Hopewell, 300 D 7
38637 Horn Lake, 850 D 1
38850 Houlka, 646 G 2
38851 Houston⊙, 2,720 G 3
39535 Hurley, 500 H 9
† 38774 Hushpuckena, 100 C 2
38638 Independence, 150 E 1
38751 Indianola⊙, 8,947 C 4
† 38652 Ingomar, 150 F 2
38753 Inverness, 1,119 C 4
38754 Isola, 458 C 4
38941 Itta Bena, 2,489 D 4
38852 Iuka⊙, 2,389 H 1
† 38865 Jacinto, 150 H 1
* 39201 Jackson (cap.)⊙, 153,968 D 6
Jackson, ‡258,906 D 6
† 38748 James, 100 B 4
39641 Jayess, 150 D 8
† 39042 Johns, 90 E 6
38639 Jonestown, 1,110 D 2
39334 Kewanee, 100 H 6
39747 Kilmichael, 543 E 4
39556 Kiln, 750 F 10
† 38856 Kirkville, 200 H 2
† 39661 Knoxville, 100 B 8
39643 Kokomo, 150 E 8
† 39740 Kolola Springs, 150 H 3
39090 Kosciusko⊙, 7,266 E 4
38834 Kossuth, 227 G 1
39092 Lake, 441 F 6
† 39422 Lake Como, 150 F 7
38641 Lake Cormorant, 300 D 1
39558 Lakeshore, 550 F 10
† 38680 Lake View, 125 D 1
38642 Lamar, 135 F 1
38643 Lambert, 1,511 D 2
38755 Lamont, 450 B 3
† 39042 Langford, 100 E 6
39335 Lauderdale, 600 G 5
39440 Laurel⊙, 24,145 F 7
39336 Lawrence, 200 F 6
39450 Leaf, 350 G 8
39451 Leakesville⊙, 1,090 G 8
39093 Learned, 116 C 6
38942 Le Flore, 99 D 3
38756 Leland, 6,000 C 4
† 39074 Lemon, 90 E 6
39094 Lena, 233 E 5
39644 Lessley, 100 B 8
† 39667 Lexie, 270 D 8
39095 Lexington⊙, 2,756 D 4
39645 Liberty⊙, 612 C 8
39337 Little Rock, 130 F 5
† 38828 Long, 110 G 2
39560 Long Beach, 6,170 F 10
† 38665 Longtown, 150 D 1
39749 Longview, 800 G 4
† 38668 Looxahoma, 200 E 1
† 39153 Lorena, 90 F 6
39096 Lorman, 500 B 7
39338 Louin, 382 F 6
39097 Louise, 444 C 5
39339 Louisville⊙, 6,626 G 4
39452 Lucedale⊙, 2,083 G 9
39098 Ludlow, 300 E 5
38644 Lula, 445 C 2
39455 Lumberton, 2,084 E 8
† 39501 Lyman, 500 F 10
38645 Lyon, 383 D 2
39750 Maben, 862 F 3
39341 Macon⊙, 2,612 G 4
39109 Madden, 450 F 5
39110 Madison, 853 D 6
39111 Magee, 2,973 E 7
39652 Magnolia⊙, 1,913 D 8

(continued on following page)

258 Mississippi

(continued)

† 38769 Malvina, 100 ... C 3
38855 Mantachie, 200 ... H 2
39751 Mantee, 142 ... F 3
38856 Marietta, 250 ... H 2
39342 Marion, 550 ... G 6
38646 Marks⊙, 2,609 ... D 2
† 39083 Martinsville, 250 ... D 7
† 39051 Marydell, 125 ... F 5
† 39341 Mashulaville, 227 ... G 4
† 39360 Matherville, 150 ... G 7
39752 Mathiston, 570 ... F 3
38758 Mattson, 200 ... C 2
† 39425 Maxie, 100 ... F 9
39113 Mayersville⊙, 500 ... B 5
39753 Mayhew, 200 ... G 4
39107 McAdams, 240 ... E 4
39647 McCall Creek, 250 ... C 7
38943 McCarley, 250 ... E 3
39648 McComb, 11,969 ... D 8
38854 McCondy, 150 ... G 3
39108 McCool, 225 ... F 4
39561 McHenry, 550 ... F 9
39456 McLain, 632 ... G 8
† 39401 McLaurin, 100 ... F 8
39457 McNeill, 800 ... E 9
39653 Meadville⊙, 594 ... C 8
† 39301 Meehan, 100 ... G 6
39114 Mendenhall⊙, 2,402 ... E 7
39301 Meridian⊙, 45,083 ... G 6
38759 Merigold, 772 ... C 3
† 39452 Merrill, 100 ... G 9
38760 Metcalfe, 600 ... B 4
38647 Michigan City, 350 ... F 1
39115 Midnight, 450 ... C 4
38648 Mineral Wells, 250 ... E 1
38944 Minter City, 300 ... D 3
39116 Mize, 372 ... E 7
38945 Money, 350 ... D 3
39654 Monticello⊙, 1,790 ... D 7
39754 Montpelier, 200 ... G 3
39343 Montrose, 160 ... F 6
38857 Mooreville, 200 ... G 2
38761 Moorhead, 2,284 ... C 4
38946 Morgan City, 300 ... D 4
39484 Morgantown, 305 ... E 8
39117 Morton, 2,672 ... E 6
39459 Moselle, 525 ... F 8
39460 Moss, 150 ... F 7
39563 Moss Point, 19,321 ... G 10
38762 Mound Bayou, 2,134 ... C 3
39119 Mount Olive, 923 ... E 7
38649 Mount Pleasant, 250 ... E 1
† 38748 Murphy, 100 ... C 4
38650 Myrtle, 308 ... F 1
39120 Natchez⊙, 19,704 ... B 7
39461 Neely, 200 ... G 8
38651 Nesbit, 300 ... D 1
39344 Neshoba, 250 ... F 5
38858 Nettleton, 1,591 ... G 2
38652 New Albany⊙, 6,426 ... G 2
39462 New Augusta⊙, 511 ... F 8
39140 Newhebron, 456 ... D 7
39345 Newton, 3,556 ... F 6
39463 Nicholson, 400 ... E 10
38763 Nitta Yuma, 150 ... C 4
† 39665 Nola, 120 ... D 7
† 39629 Norfield, 225 ... C 8
38947 North Carrollton, 611 ... E 3

39346 Noxapater, 554 ... F 5
38948 Oakland, 493 ... E 2
† 39154 Oakley, 420 ... D 6
† 39180 Oak Ridge, 350 ... C 6
39656 Oak Vale, 166 ... E 8
39564 Ocean Springs, 9,580 ... G 10
39141 Ofahoma, 850 ... E 5
38860 Okolona⊙, 3,002 ... G 2
38654 Olive Branch, 1,513 ... E 1
† 39482 Oloh, 100 ... E 8
39142 Oma, 100 ... D 7
† 39428 Ora, 140 ... E 7
† 39501 Orange Grove, 200 ... H 10
39657 Osyka, 628 ... D 8
39464 Ovett, 250 ... F 8
38655 Oxford⊙, 13,846 ... F 2
38764 Pace, 629 ... C 3
39347 Pachuta, 271 ... G 6
38861 Paden, 97 ... H 1
† 39401 Palmers Crossing, 250 ... F 8
38765 Panther Burn, 400 ... C 4
38738 Parchman, 200 ... D 3
38949 Paris, 253 ... F 2
39567 Pascagoula⊙, 27,264 ... G 10
39571 Pass Christian, 2,979 ... F 10
39144 Pattison, 540 ... C 7
39348 Paulding⊙, 769 ... F 6
39349 Paulette, 230 ... H 4
† 38920 Paynes, 100 ... D 3
39208 Pearl, 9,623 ... D 6
39572 Pearlington, 500 ... E 10
39145 Pelahatchie, 1,306 ... E 6
† 38664 Penton, 175 ... D 1
† 39645 Peoria, 100 ... C 8
39573 Perkinston, 950 ... F 9
39465 Petal, 6,986 ... F 8
39755 Pheba, 280 ... G 3
39350 Philadelphia⊙, 6,274 ... F 5
38950 Philipp, 975 ... D 3
† 39476 Piave, 250 ... G 8
39466 Picayune, 10,467 ... E 9
39146 Pickens, 1,012 ... E 5
† 39120 Pine Ridge, 175 ... B 7
39148 Piney Woods, 300 ... D 6
39149 Pinola, 102 ... E 7
38951 Pittsboro⊙, 188 ... F 3
38862 Plantersville, 910 ... G 2
38657 Pleasant Grove, 150 ... D 2
† 38651 Pleasant Hill, 400 ... E 1
39118 Polkville, 500 ... E 6
38863 Pontotoc⊙, 3,453 ... G 2
38568 Pope, 210 ... E 2
† 39747 Poplar Creek, 100 ... E 4
39470 Poplarville⊙, 2,312 ... E 9
39352 Porterville, 150 ... G 5
39150 Port Gibson⊙, 2,589 ... B 7
38659 Potts Camp, 459 ... F 1
39353 Prairie Point, 150 ... H 4
39474 Prentiss⊙, 1,789 ... E 7
39354 Preston, 120 ... G 5
† 39666 Pricedale, 400 ... D 8
38660 Prichard, 150 ... D 1
39151 Puckett, 333 ... E 6
39152 Pulaski, 108 ... E 6
39475 Purvis⊙, 1,860 ... F 8
† 38851 Pyland, 120 ... F 3
39660 Quentin, 150 ... C 8
39355 Quitman⊙, 2,702 ... G 6

Agriculture, Industry and Resources

DOMINANT LAND USE

- Specialized Cotton
- Cotton, Livestock
- Cotton, General Farming
- Cotton, Forest Products
- Truck and Mixed Farming
- Forests
- Swampland, Limited Agriculture

MAJOR MINERAL OCCURRENCES

- Cl Clay
- Fe Iron Ore
- G Natural Gas
- O Petroleum

Major Industrial Areas

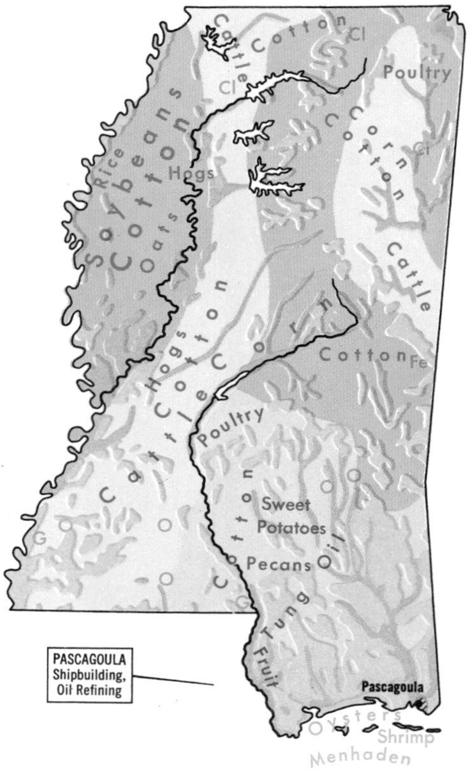
Cattle
Cotton
Cl
Poultry
Rice
Soybeans
Cotton
Oats
Hogs
Corn
Cattle
Cotton
Fe
Poultry
Sweet Potatoes
Pecans
Tung Oil
Fruit
PASCAGOULA
Shipbuilding,
Oil Refining
Pascagoula
Oysters
Shrimp
Menhaden

39153 Raleigh⊙, 1,018 ... F 6
38864 Randolph, 205 ... F 2
39154 Raymond⊙, 1,620 ... D 6
38661 Red Banks, 350 ... F 1
† 39096 Red Lick, 250 ... B 7
39156 Redwood, 400 ... C 6
39757 Reform, 150 ... F 4
38767 Rena Lara, 400 ... C 2
† 39051 Renfroe, 100 ... F 5
39476 Richton, 1,110 ... G 8
39157 Ridgeland, 1,650 ... D 6
38865 Rienzi, 363 ... G 1
38663 Ripley⊙, 3,482 ... G 1
38664 Robinsonville, 285 ... D 1

† 39083 Rockport, 100 ... D 7
† 39096 Rodney, 200 ... B 7
39159 Rolling Fork⊙, 2,034 ... C 5
38768 Rome, 171 ... C 3
38769 Rosedale⊙, 2,599 ... B 3
39356 Rose Hill, 300 ... F 6
† 38614 Roundaway, 175 ... C 2
† 38740 Roundlake, 105 ... C 2
39661 Roxie, 662 ... B 8
38771 Ruleville, 2,351 ... D 3
† 39401 Runnelstown, 200 ... F 8
† 39108 Rural Hill, 125 ... F 4
39357 Russell, 300 ... G 6
39662 Ruth, 150 ... D 8

† 38955 Sabougla, 100 ... F 3
39160 Sallis, 213 ... E 4
38866 Saltillo, 836 ... G 2
39112 Sanatorium, 400 ... E 7
39477 Sandersville, 694 ... F 7
39161 Sandhill, 392 ... E 5
39478 Sandy Hook, 108 ... E 8
39479 Sanford, 150 ... F 8
38665 Sarah, 300 ... D 1
38666 Sardis⊙, 2,391 ... E 2
38867 Sarepta, 650 ... F 2
39574 Saucier, 100 ... F 9
38667 Savage, 100 ... D 1
38952 Schlater, 398 ... D 3
38953 Scobey, 100 ... E 3
39358 Scooba, 626 ... G 5
38772 Scott, 500 ... B 3
39359 Sebastopol, 268 ... F 5
39479 Seminary, 269 ... E 7
38668 Senatobia⊙, 4,247 ... E 1
39758 Sessums, 100 ... G 4
38868 Shannon, 575 ... G 2
38773 Shaw, 2,513 ... C 3
38774 Shelby, 2,645 ... C 3
38669 Sherard, 160 ... C 2
38869 Sherman, 468 ... G 2
39164 Shivers, 100 ... E 7
39360 Shubuta, 602 ... G 7
39361 Shuqualak, 591 ... G 5
39165 Sibley, 250 ... B 8
38954 Sidon, 348 ... D 4
39166 Silver City, 370 ... C 4
39663 Silver Creek, 257 ... D 7
38775 Skene, 300 ... C 3
38955 Slate Spring, 105 ... F 3
† 38642 Slayden, 310 ... F 1
38670 Sledge, 516 ... D 2
39664 Smithdale, 200 ... C 8
38870 Smithville, 552 ... H 2
39665 Sontag, 200 ... D 7
39480 Soso, 230 ... F 7
38671 Southaven, 8,931 ... E 1
† 38863 Springville, 100 ... F 2
† 39350 Stallo, 100 ... F 5
39167 Star, 575 ... D 6
39759 Starkville⊙, 11,369 ... G 4
39762 State College, 4,595 ... G 4
39362 State Line, 598 ... G 8
39766 Steens, 125 ... H 3
39767 Stewart, 150 ... F 4
38776 Stoneville, 700 ... C 4
39363 Stonewall, 1,161 ... G 6
38672 Stovall, 260 ... C 2
† 38665 Strayhorn, 800 ... D 1
39481 Stringer, 340 ... F 7
38777 Stringtown, 300 ... C 3
39769 Sturgis, 321 ... G 4
† 39168 Summerland, 150 ... F 7
39666 Summit, 1,640 ... D 8
38957 Sumner⊙, 533 ... D 3
39482 Sumrall, 955 ... E 8
38778 Sunflower, 983 ... C 3
38958 Swan Lake, 250 ... D 3
38959 Swiftown, 400 ... D 4
39153 Sylvarena, 115 ... F 6
† 38769 Symonds, 200 ... C 3
38673 Taylor, 92 ... E 2
39168 Taylorsville, 1,299 ... F 7
39169 Tchula, 1,729 ... D 4
39170 Terry, 546 ... D 6
38871 Thaxton, 250 ... F 2
39171 Thomastown, 350 ... E 5
38872 Thorn, 125 ... F 3
39172 Thornton, 120 ... D 4

† 38829 Thrasher, 800 ... G 1
† 38668 Thyatira, 100 ... E 1
38960 Tie Plant, 950 ... E 3
† 38843 Tilden, 250 ... H 2
38961 Tillatoba, 102 ... E 3
38674 Tiplersville, 120 ... G 1
38962 Tippo, 200 ... D 3
38873 Tishomingo, 410 ... H 1
38874 Toccopola, 175 ... F 2
39770 Tomnolen, 225 ... F 4
39364 Toomsuba, 500 ... G 6
39174 Tougaloo, 1,720 ... D 6
38757 Tralake, 200 ... C 4
38875 Trebloc, 750 ... G 3
38876 Tremont, 250 ... H 2
38779 Tribbett, 200 ... C 4
† 38863 Troy, 150 ... G 2
38675 Tula, 100 ... F 2
38676 Tunica⊙, 1,685 ... D 1
38801 Tupelo⊙, 20,471 ... G 2
38963 Tutwiler, 1,103 ... D 2
39667 Tylertown⊙, 1,736 ... D 8
39365 Union, 1,856 ... F 5
39668 Union Church, 194 ... C 7
39175 Utica, 1,019 ... C 6
39175 Utica Junior College, 700 ... C 6
39176 Vaiden⊙, 716 ... E 4
39177 Valley Park, 350 ... C 5
39178 Value, 327 ... D 6
38964 Vance, 500 ... D 2
† 39564 Vancleave, 505 ... G 9
† 38851 Van Vleet, 300 ... G 3
38878 Vardaman, 777 ... F 3
38879 Verona, 1,877 ... G 2
39180 Vicksburg⊙, 25,478 ... C 6
38679 Victoria, 400 ... E 1
39366 Vossburg, 250 ... F 7
39575 Wade, 800 ... G 9
† 39422 Waldrup, 125 ... F 7
38680 Walls, 850 ... D 1
38683 Walnut, 458 ... G 1
39189 Walnut Grove, 398 ... F 5
† 39180 Waltersville, 150 ... C 6
39771 Walthall⊙, 161 ... F 3
39190 Washington, 250 ... B 7
38685 Waterford, 375 ... E 1
38965 Water Valley⊙, 3,285 ... E 2
39576 Waveland, 3,108 ... F 10
39367 Waynesboro⊙, 4,368 ... G 7
38780 Wayside, 250 ... C 4
38966 Webb, 751 ... D 3
39772 Weir, 573 ... F 4
38886 Wenasoga, 125 ... G 1
39191 Wesson, 1,253 ... D 7
39192 West, 305 ... E 4
† 39501 West-Gulfport, 6,996 ... F 10
39773 West Point⊙, 8,714 ... G 3
38880 Wheeler, 600 ... G 1
39193 Whitfield, 6,200 ... E 6
39577 Wiggins⊙, 2,995 ... F 9
† 39090 Williamsville, 250 ... F 4
† 38659 Winborn, 122 ... F 1
38967 Winona⊙, 5,521 ... E 4
38781 Winstonville, 536 ... C 3
38782 Winterville, 500 ... B 4
39776 Woodland, 130 ... F 3
39669 Woodville⊙, 1,734 ... B 8
† 39730 Wren, 150 ... G 3
39194 Yazoo City⊙, 10,796 ... D 5
† 39090 Zama, 125 ... F 5

⊙ County seat.
‡ Population of metropolitan area.
† Zip of nearest p.o.
* Multiple zips

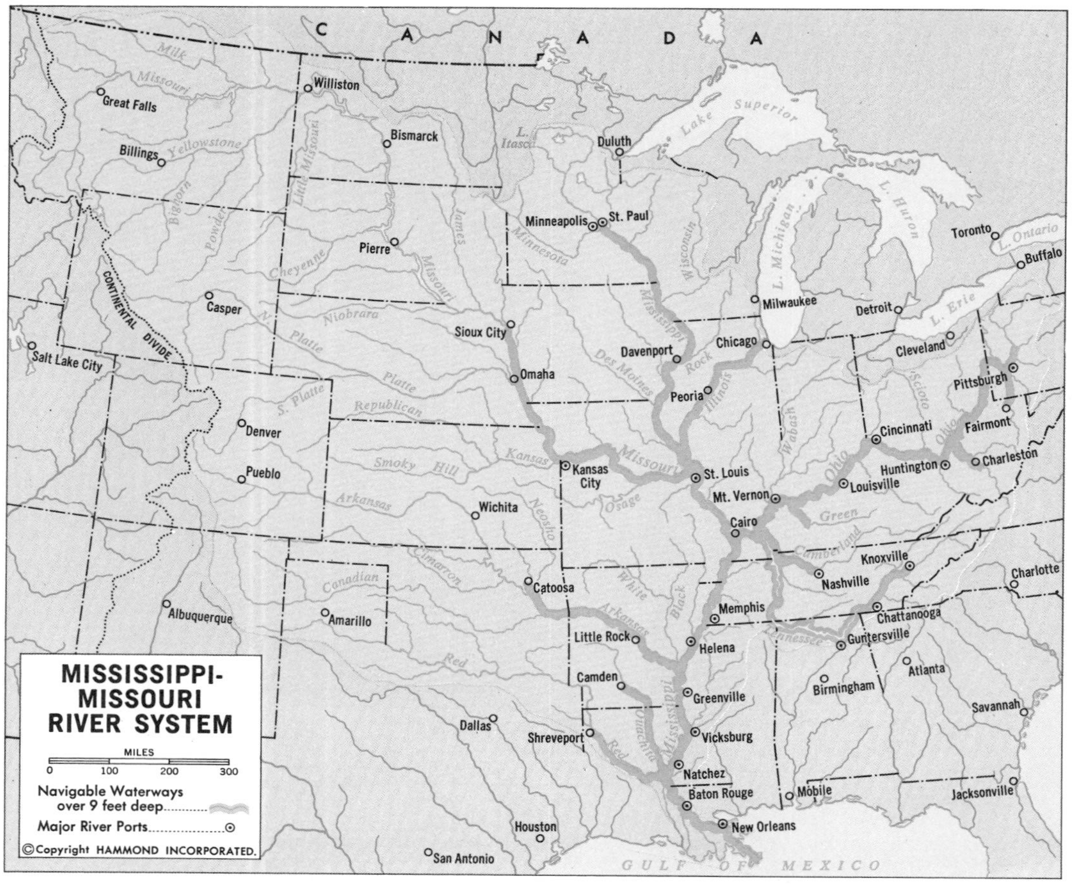
MISSISSIPPI-MISSOURI RIVER SYSTEM
MILES
0 100 200 300
Navigable Waterways over 9 feet deep
Major River Ports
©Copyright HAMMOND INCORPORATED.
CANADA
GULF OF MEXICO
Great Falls
Billings
Williston
Bismarck
Duluth
Minneapolis
St. Paul
Pierre
Casper
Salt Lake City
Sioux City
Omaha
Denver
Pueblo
Kansas City
Wichita
Albuquerque
Amarillo
Catoosa
Dallas
Shreveport
Houston
San Antonio
Little Rock
Camden
Memphis
Helena
Greenville
Vicksburg
Natchez
Baton Rouge
New Orleans
Mobile
St. Louis
Mt. Vernon
Cairo
Nashville
Knoxville
Chattanooga
Guntersville
Birmingham
Atlanta
Savannah
Jacksonville
Charlotte
Louisville
Cincinnati
Huntington
Charleston
Fairmont
Pittsburgh
Cleveland
Detroit
Toronto
Buffalo
Milwaukee
Chicago
Davenport
Peoria
CONTINENTAL DIVIDE
Lake Superior
L. Michigan
L. Huron
L. Erie
L. Ontario

AREA 69,686 sq. mi.
POPULATION 4,677,399 ('70); 4,917,444 ('80)
CAPITAL Jefferson City
LARGEST CITY St. Louis
HIGHEST POINT Taum Sauk Mtn. 1,772 ft.
SETTLED IN 1764
ADMITTED TO UNION August 10, 1821
POPULAR NAME Show Me State
STATE FLOWER Hawthorn
STATE BIRD Bluebird

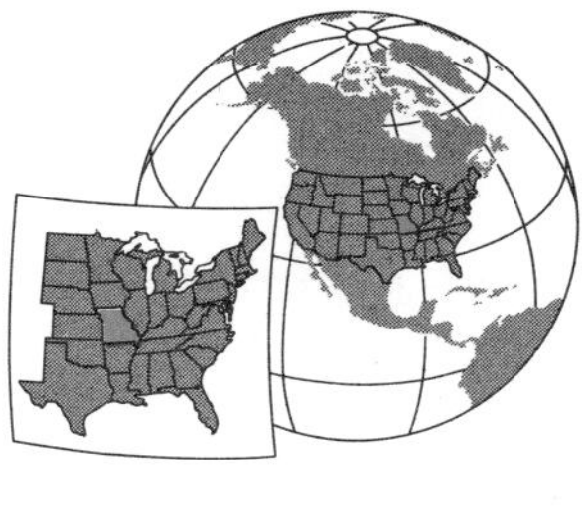

COUNTIES

Name/Pop.	Key
Adair, 22,472	G 2
Andrew, 11,913	C 3
Atchison, 9,240	B 2
Audrain, 25,362	J 4
Barry, 19,597	E 9
Barton, 10,431	D 7
Bates, 15,468	D 6
Benton, 9,695	F 6
Bollinger, 8,820	M 8
Boone, 80,911	H 4
Buchanan, 86,915	C 3
Butler, 33,529	M 9
Caldwell, 8,351	E 3
Callaway, 25,850	J 5
Camden, 13,315	G 6
Cape Girardeau, 49,350	N 8
Carroll, 12,565	F 4
Carter, 3,878	L 9
Cass, 39,448	D 5
Cedar, 9,424	E 7
Chariton, 11,084	F 3
Christian, 15,124	F 9
Clark, 8,260	J 2
Clay, 123,322	D 4
Clinton, 12,462	D 3
Cole, 46,228	H 6
Cooper, 14,732	G 5
Crawford, 14,828	K 7
Dade, 6,850	E 8
Dallas, 10,054	F 7
Daviess, 8,420	E 3
De Kalb, 7,305	D 3
Dent, 11,457	J 7
Douglas, 9,268	G 9
Dunklin, 33,742	M10
Franklin, 55,116	K 6
Gasconade, 11,878	J 6
Gentry, 8,060	D 2
Greene, 152,929	F 8
Grundy, 11,819	E 2
Harrison, 10,257	E 2
Henry, 18,451	E 6
Hickory, 4,481	F 7
Holt, 6,654	B 2
Howard, 10,561	G 4
Howell, 23,521	J 9
Iron, 9,529	L 7
Jackson, 654,558	D 5
Jasper, 79,852	D 8
Jefferson, 105,248	L 6
Johnson, 34,172	E 5
Knox, 5,692	H 2
Laclede, 19,944	G 7
Lafayette, 26,626	E 4
Lawrence, 24,585	E 8
Lewis, 10,993	J 2
Lincoln, 18,041	L 4
Linn, 15,125	F 3
Livingston, 15,368	E 3
Macon, 15,432	G 3
Madison, 8,641	M 8
Maries, 6,851	J 6
Marion, 28,121	J 3
McDonald, 12,357	D 9
Mercer, 4,910	E 2
Miller, 15,026	H 6
Mississippi, 16,647	O 9
Moniteau, 10,742	G 5
Monroe, 9,542	H 3
Montgomery, 11,000	K 5
Morgan, 10,068	G 6
New Madrid, 23,420	N 9
Newton, 32,901	D 9
Nodaway, 22,467	C 2
Oregon, 9,180	K 9
Osage, 10,994	J 6
Ozark, 6,226	H 9
Pemiscot, 26,373	N 10
Perry, 14,393	N 7
Pettis, 34,137	F 5
Phelps, 29,481	J 7
Pike, 16,928	K 4
Platte, 32,081	C 4
Polk, 15,415	F 7
Pulaski, 53,781	H 7
Putnam, 5,916	F 2
Ralls, 7,764	J 3
Randolph, 22,434	G 3
Ray, 17,599	E 4
Reynolds, 6,106	L 8
Ripley, 9,803	L 9
Saint Charles, 92,954	L 5
Saint Clair, 7,667	E 6
Sainte Genevieve, 12,867	M 7
Saint Francois, 36,818	M 7
Saint Louis, 951,353	M 5
Saint Louis (city county), 622,236	M 5
Saline, 24,633	F 4
Schuyler, 4,665	G 2
Scotland, 5,499	H 2
Scott, 33,250	N 8
Shannon, 7,196	K 8
Shelby, 7,906	H 3
Stoddard, 25,771	N 9
Stone, 9,921	F 9
Sullivan, 7,572	F 2
Taney, 13,023	F 9
Texas, 18,320	J 8
Vernon, 19,065	D 7
Warren, 9,699	K 5
Washington, 15,086	L 7
Wayne, 8,546	L 8
Webster, 15,562	G 8
Worth, 3,359	D 2
Wright, 13,667	H 8

CITIES and TOWNS

Zip	*Name/Pop.*	*Key*
64720	Adrian, 1,259	D 6
63730	Advance, 903	N 8
63123	Affton, 24,067	P 3
† 64836	Airport Drive, 300	C 8
64830	Alba, 365	D 8
64402	Albany⊙, 1,804	D 2
63430	Alexandria, 453	K 2
63001	Allenton, 800	N 3
64001	Alma, 380	E 4
64620	Altamont, 225	D 3
63732	Altenburg, 277	O 7
65606	Alton⊙, 715	K 9
64421	Amazonia, 326	C 3
64722	Amoret, 219	C 6
64831	Anderson, 1,065	D 9
63620	Annapolis, 330	L 8
63820	Anniston, 515	O 9
64724	Appleton City, 1,058	D 6
63821	Arbyrd, 575	M10
63621	Arcadia, 627	L 7
64725	Archie, 525	D 5
65001	Argyle, 262	J 6
65230	Armstrong, 354	G 4
63010	Arnold, 11,994	P 4
65604	Ash Grove, 934	E 8
65010	Ashland, 769	H 5
63530	Atlanta, 377	H 3
63332	Augusta, 259	M 3
65605	Aurora, 5,359	E 9
65231	Auxvasse, 808	J 4
65608	Ava⊙, 2,504	G 9
64010	Avondale, 748	P 5
63011	Ballwin, 10,656	O 3
63531	Baring, 206	H 2
64423	Barnard, 206	C 2
64011	Bates City, 229	E 5
† 65619	Battlefield, 291	F 8
63622	Belgrade, 349	L 7
63735	Bell City, 424	N 8
65013	Belle, 1,133	J 6
† 63101	Bellefontaine Neighbors, 13,987	R 2
63623	Belleview, 225	L 7
63333	Bellflower, 360	K 4
64012	Belton, 9,783	C 5
63736	Benton⊙, 640	O 8
63014	Berger, 226	K 5
63134	Berkeley, 19,743	P 2
63822	Bernie, 1,641	M 9
63823	Bertrand, 604	O 9
64424	Bethany⊙, 2,914	E 2
63532	Bevier, 806	G 3
65610	Billings, 760	F 8
65438	Birch Tree, 573	K 9
† 64068	Birmingham, 266	P 5
63624	Bismarck, 1,387	L 7
65321	Blackburn, 294	F 4
† 63031	Black Jack, 3,500	P 2
65322	Blackwater, 249	G 5
65014	Bland, 621	J 6
63824	Blodgett, 220	O 8
63825	Bloomfield⊙, 1,584	M 9
63627	Bloomsdale, 411	M 6
64015	Blue Springs, 6,779	R 6
† 64101	Blue Summit, 1,283	R 5
64426	Blythedale, 213	E 2
64622	Bogard, 294	E 4
65612	Bois D'Arc, 250	F 8
64427	Bolckow, 225	C 2
65613	Bolivar⊙, 4,769	F 7
63628	Bonne Terre, 3,622	L 7
65016	Bonnots Mill, 210	J 5
65233	Boonville⊙, 7,514	G 5
64723	Bosworth, 386	F 4
65441	Bourbon, 955	K 6
63334	Bowling Green⊙, 2,936	K 4
63826	Braggadocio, 285	N 10
63827	Bragg City, 210	N 10
65616	Branson, 2,175	F 9
63533	Brashear, 316	H 2
64624	Braymer, 919	E 3
64625	Breckenridge, 598	E 3
† 63101	Breckenridge Hills, 7,011	O 2
63144	Brentwood, 11,248	P 3
63044	Bridgeton, 19,992	O 2
64728	Bronaugh, 203	C 7
64628	Brookfield, 5,491	F 3
64630	Browning, 412	F 2
65236	Brunswick, 1,870	F 4
64631	Bucklin, 654	G 3
64016	Buckner, 1,695	R 5
65622	Buffalo⊙, 1,915	F 7
65237	Bunceton, 437	G 5
63629	Bunker, 447	K 8
64428	Burlington Junction, 634	B 2
64730	Butler⊙, 3,984	D 6
65689	Cabool, 1,848	H 8
63630	Cadet, 300	L 6
64632	Cainsville, 454	E 2
65239	Cairo, 248	H 4
65323	Calhoun, 360	E 6
65018	California⊙, 3,105	H 5
63534	Callao, 373	G 3
64017	Camden, 286	D 4
65020	Camdenton⊙, 1,636	G 6
64429	Cameron, 3,960	D 3
63933	Campbell, 1,979	M 9
63828	Canalou, 358	N 9
63435	Canton, 2,680	J 2
63701	Cape Girardeau, 31,282	O 8
63829	Cardwell, 859	M10
64834	Carl Junction, 1,661	C 8
64633	Carrollton⊙, 4,847	E 4
64835	Carterville, 1,716	D 8
64836	Carthage⊙, 11,035	D 8
63830	Caruthersville⊙, 7,350	N 10
65625	Cassville⊙, 1,910	E 9
63015	Catawissa, 250	N 4
65022	Cedar City, 454	H 5
63016	Cedar Hill, 500	L 6
63436	Center, 588	J 3
65023	Centertown, 277	H 5
64019	Centerview, 234	E 5
63633	Centerville⊙, 209	L 8
65240	Centralia, 3,618	H 4
63740	Chaffee, 2,793	N 8
65024	Chamois, 615	J 5
63834	Charleston⊙, 5,131	O 9
63017	Chesterfield, 13,000	O 3
64733	Chilhowee, 297	E 5
64601	Chillicothe⊙, 9,519	E 3
64635	Chula, 244	F 3
63437	Clarence, 1,050	H 3
65243	Clark, 271	H 4
65025	Clarksburg, 343	G 5
64430	Clarksdale, 248	D 3
63336	Clarksville, 668	K 4
63837	Clarkton, 1,177	M10
64119	Claycomo, 1,841	P 5
63105	Clayton⊙, 16,222	P 3
64431	Clearmont, 226	C 1
64734	Cleveland, 256	C 5
65631	Clever, 430	F 8
64735	Clinton⊙, 7,504	E 6
65325	Cole Camp, 1,038	F 6
65201	Columbia⊙, 58,804	H 5
63742	Commerce, 234	O 8
64434	Conception Junction, 237	C 2
64020	Concordia, 1,854	E 5
65632	Conway, 547	G 7
63839	Cooter, 414	N 10
64021	Corder, 476	E 4
63338	Cottleville, 275	N 2
† 64501	Country Club Village, 221	C 3
64637	Cowgill, 232	E 3
64437	Craig, 369	B 2
65633	Crane, 1,003	E 9
64739	Creighton, 294	D 6
63018	Crescent, 425	N 3
† 63101	Crestwood, 15,398	O 3
63141	Creve Coeur, 8,967	O 3
65452	Crocker, 814	H 7
65634	Cross Timbers, 204	F 6
63019	Crystal City, 3,898	M 6
65453	Cuba, 2,070	K 6
63339	Curryville, 337	K 4
64439	Dearborn, 543	C 3
64740	Deepwater, 565	E 6
64440	De Kalb, 287	C 3
63744	Delta, 462	N 8
63636	Des Arc, 222	L 8
63601	Desloge, 2,818	M 7
63020	De Soto, 5,984	M 6
63131	Des Peres, 5,333	O 3
63841	Dexter, 6,024	N 9
64840	Diamond, 554	D 9
65459	Dixon, 1,387	H 6
63637	Doe Run, 900	M 7
63935	Doniphan⊙, 1,850	L 9
† 65550	Doolittle, 509	J 7
63844	Dorena, 500	O 9
63536	Downing, 406	H 2
64742	Drexel, 723	C 6
63936	Dudley, 248	M 9
64841	Duenweg, 656	D 8
† 64801	Duquesne, 738	D 8
64442	Eagleville, 388	D 2
64743	East Lynne, 255	D 5
63845	East Prairie, 3,275	O 9
65462	Edgar Springs, 450	J 7
64444	Edgerton, 477	C 4
63537	Edina⊙, 1,574	H 2
65026	Eldon, 3,520	G 6
64744	El Dorado Springs, 3,300	E 7
63638	Ellington, 1,094	L 8
63011	Ellisville, 4,681	N 3
63937	Ellsinore, 342	L 9
63343	Elsberry, 1,398	L 4
63639	Elvins, 1,603	L 7
65466	Eminence⊙, 520	K 8
65327	Emma, 224	F 5
63344	Eolia, 321	L 4
63846	Essex, 493	N 9
† 63601	Esther, 1,040	M 7
63025	Eureka, 2,384	N 3
65646	Everton, 264	E 8
63440	Ewing, 330	J 2
64024	Excelsior Springs, 9,411	R 4
65647	Exeter, 434	D 9
64446	Fairfax, 835	B 2
65648	Fair Grove, 431	F 8
65649	Fair Play, 328	E 7
64842	Fairview, 263	D 9
63345	Farber, 470	J 4
63640	Farmington⊙, 6,590	M 7
65248	Fayette⊙, 3,520	G 4
63026	Fenton, 2,275	P 3
63135	Ferguson, 28,915	P 2
63028	Festus, 7,530	M 6
64449	Fillmore, 251	C 2
63940	Fisk, 503	M 9
63601	Flat River, 4,550	M 7
* 63031	Florissant, 65,908	P 2
63347	Foley, 224	L 4
65652	Fordland, 399	G 8
64451	Forest City, 365	B 3
63348	Foristell, 273	M 2
65653	Forsyth⊙, 803	F 9
63441	Frankford, 472	K 4
65250	Franklin, 252	G 4
63645	Fredericktown⊙, 3,799	M 7
65035	Freeburg, 577	J 6
64746	Freeman, 417	C 5
63748	Frohna, 225	N 7
† 63101	Frontenac, 3,920	O 3
65251	Fulton⊙, 12,148	J 5
65655	Gainesville⊙, 627	G 9
65656	Galena⊙, 391	F 9
64640	Gallatin⊙, 1,833	E 3
64641	Galt, 261	F 2
64747	Garden City, 633	D 5
65036	Gasconade, 235	J 5
63037	Gerald, 762	K 6
63848	Gideon, 1,112	N 10
65330	Gilliam, 248	F 4
64642	Gilman City, 376	D 2
64118	Gladstone, 23,128	P 5
65254	Glasgow, 1,336	G 4
† 64068	Glenaire, 505	R 5
63038	Glencoe, 2,500	N 3
63122	Glendale, 6,891	P 3
64748	Golden City, 810	D 8
63843	Goodman, 565	C 9
63543	Gorin, 220	H 2
64454	Gower, 758	C 3
64455	Graham, 213	C 2
64029	Grain Valley, 709	S 6
64844	Granby, 1,678	D 9
63943	Grandin, 243	L 9
64030	Grandview, 17,456	P 6
63650	Graniteville, 375	L 7
64456	Grant City⊙, 1,095	D 2
65037	Gravois Mills, 994	G 6
63850	Grayridge, 300	N 9
63039	Gray Summit, 950	M 3
63544	Green Castle, 235	G 2
63545	Green City, 629	F 2
65661	Greenfield⊙, 1,172	E 8
65332	Green Ridge, 403	F 5
63546	Greentop, 351	H 2
63944	Greenville⊙, 328	M 8
64034	Greenwood, 925	R 6
63040	Grover, 550	O 3
64643	Hale, 461	F 3
65255	Hallsville, 790	H 4
64644	Hamilton, 1,645	E 3
63401	Hannibal, 18,609	K 3
64035	Hardin, 683	E 4
64701	Harrisonville⊙, 4,928	D 5
65667	Hartville⊙, 524	G 8
63349	Hawk Point, 354	K 5
63851	Hayti, 3,841	N 10
* 63042	Hazelwood, 14,082	P 2
63047	Hematite, 300	L 6
64460	Hemple, 350	D 3
64036	Henrietta, 466	E 4
63048	Herculaneum, 1,885	M 6
65041	Hermann⊙, 2,658	K 5
65668	Hermitage⊙, 284	F 7
65257	Higbee, 641	H 4
64037	Higginsville, 4,318	E 4
63049	High Ridge, 350	O 4
63050	Hillsboro⊙, 432	L 6
63852	Holcomb, 593	N 10
64040	Holden, 2,089	E 5
63853	Holland, 329	N 10
65672	Hollister, 906	F 9
64048	Holt, 319	D 4
64461	Hopkins, 656	C 1
† 63070	Horine, 850	M 6
63855	Hornersville, 693	M10
63051	House Springs, 500	O 4
65483	Houston⊙, 2,178	J 8
65333	Houstonia, 312	F 5
65674	Humansville, 825	E 7
64752	Hume, 350	C 6
63443	Hunnewell, 304	J 3
65259	Huntsville⊙, 1,442	H 4
63547	Hurdland, 225	H 2
65486	Iberia, 741	H 6
63754	Illmo, 1.232	O 8
63052	Imperial, 900	P 4
* 64050	Independence⊙, 111,662	R 5
63648	Irondale, 319	L 7
63650	Ironton⊙, 1,452	L 7
63755	Jackson⊙, 5,896	N 8
64648	Jamesport, 614	E 3
65046	Jamestown, 243	G 5
64755	Jasper, 796	D 8
65101	Jefferson City (cap.)⊙, 32,407	H 5
63136	Jennings, 19,379	P 2
63351	Jonesburg, 479	K 5
64801	Joplin, 39,256	C 8
† 63385	Josephville, 250	N 2
63445	Kahoka⊙, 2,207	J 2
* 64101	Kansas City, 507,087	P 5
	Kansas City, ‡1,253,916	P 5
64060	Kearney, 984	D 4
63758	Kelso, 401	O 8
63857	Kennett⊙, 9,852	M10
65261	Keytesville⊙, 730	G 4
64649	Kidder, 231	D 3
63053	Kimmswick, 268	M 6
64463	King City, 1,023	D 2
64650	Kingston⊙, 291	E 3
64061	Kingsville, 284	D 5
63140	Kinloch, 5,629	P 2
63501	Kirksville⊙, 15,560	H 2
63122	Kirkwood, 31,890	O 3
65336	Knob Noster, 2,264	E 5
63446	Knox City, 284	H 2
63054	Koch, 600	P 4
65692	Koshkonong, 216	J 9
† 63090	Krakow, 300	K 6
63055	Labadie, 350	N 3
63447	La Belle, 848	J 2
64651	Laclede, 430	F 3
63352	Laddonia, 745	J 4
† 64758	Ladue, 10,491	P 3
63448	La Grange, 1,237	K 2
64063	Lake Lotawana, 1,786	R 6
65049	Lake Ozark, 507	G 6
† 64015	Lake Tapawingo, 867	R 6
† 64034	Lake Winnebago, 432	R 6
64759	Lamar⊙, 3,760	D 8
65337	La Monte, 814	F 5
64847	Lanagan, 374	C 9
63548	Lancaster⊙, 821	H 1
63549	La Plata, 1,377	H 2
64652	Laredo, 383	E 2
64465	Lathrop, 1,268	D 3
64062	Lawson, 1,034	D 4
† 63640	Leadington, 299	M 7
63653	Leadwood, 1,397	L 7
65535	Leasburg, 218	K 6
65536	Lebanon⊙, 8,616	G 7
64063	Lee's Summit, 16,230	R 6
64761	Leeton, 425	E 5
63125	Lemay, 40,115	P 3
63654	Lesterville, 275	L 8
64066	Levasy, 283	S 5
63452	Lewistown, 615	J 2
64067	Lexington⊙, 5,388	E 4
64762	Liberal, 644	D 7
64068	Liberty⊙, 13,679	R 5
65542	Licking, 1,002	J 8
63862	Lilbourn, 1,152	N 9
65338	Lincoln, 574	F 6
65051	Linn⊙, 1,289	J 5
65052	Linn Creek, 268	G 6
64653	Linneus⊙, 400	F 3
65682	Lockwood, 887	E 8
65054	Loose Creek, 370	J 5
63353	Louisiana, 4,533	K 4
64763	Lowry City, 520	E 6
63762	Lutesville, 626	M 8
63552	Macon⊙, 5,301	H 3
65263	Madison, 540	H 4
64466	Maitland, 319	B 2
63863	Malden, 5,374	M 9
65339	Malta Bend, 342	F 4
65704	Mansfield, 1,056	G 8
63143	Maplewood, 12,785	P 3
63764	Marble Hill⊙, 589	N 8
64658	Marceline, 2,622	F 3
65705	Marionville, 1,496	E 8
63655	Marquand, 400	M 8
65340	Marshall⊙, 11,847	F 4
65706	Marshfield⊙, 2,961	G 8
63866	Marston, 666	N 9
63357	Marthasville, 415	L 5
65264	Martinsburg, 318	J 4
64468	Maryville⊙, 9,970	C 2
63857	Matthews, 538	N 9
64469	Maysville⊙, 1,045	D 3
64071	Mayview, 330	E 4
64657	McFall, 203	D 2
64659	Meadville, 409	F 3
63555	Memphis⊙, 2,081	H 2
64660	Mendon, 289	F 3
64661	Mercer, 364	F 2
65058	Meta, 387	H 6
65265	Mexico⊙, 11,807	J 4
65344	Miami, 205	F 4
63359	Middletown, 235	J 4
63556	Milan⊙, 1,794	F 2
65707	Miller, 676	E 8
63952	Mill Spring, 207	L 8
64769	Mindenmines, 279	D 8
63659	Mine La Motte, 200	M 7
† 63801	Miner, 640	N 9
63660	Mineral Point, 369	L 7
64072	Missouri City, 375	R 5
65270	Moberly, 12,988	G 4

(continued on following page)

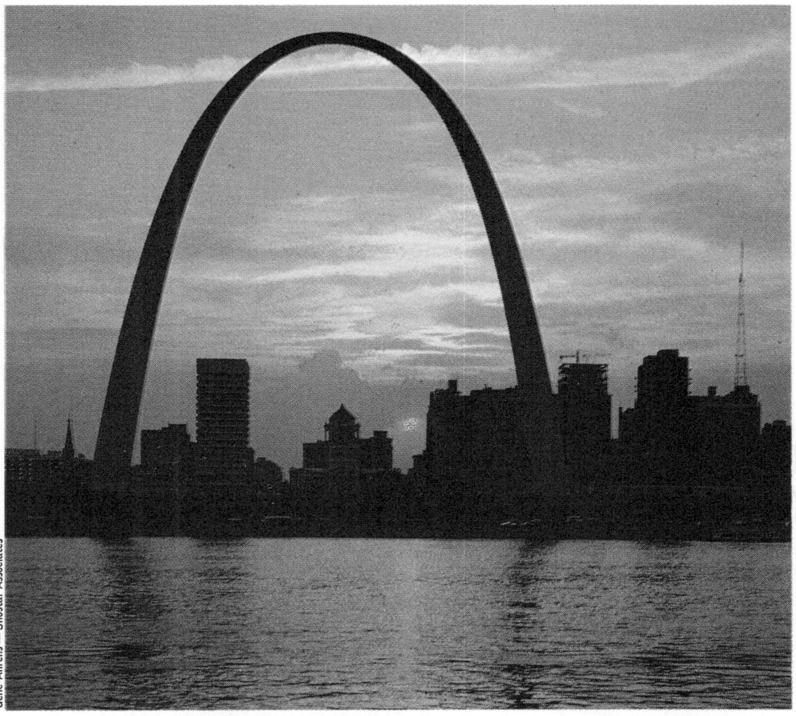

Gene Ahrens — Shostal Associates

The Gateway Arch soars in silhouette against the St. Louis skyline. A Saarinen design, the monument is the centerpiece of the Jefferson National Expansion Memorial. Internal passenger trains carry sightseers up either leg to the long observation room.

Agriculture, Industry and Resources

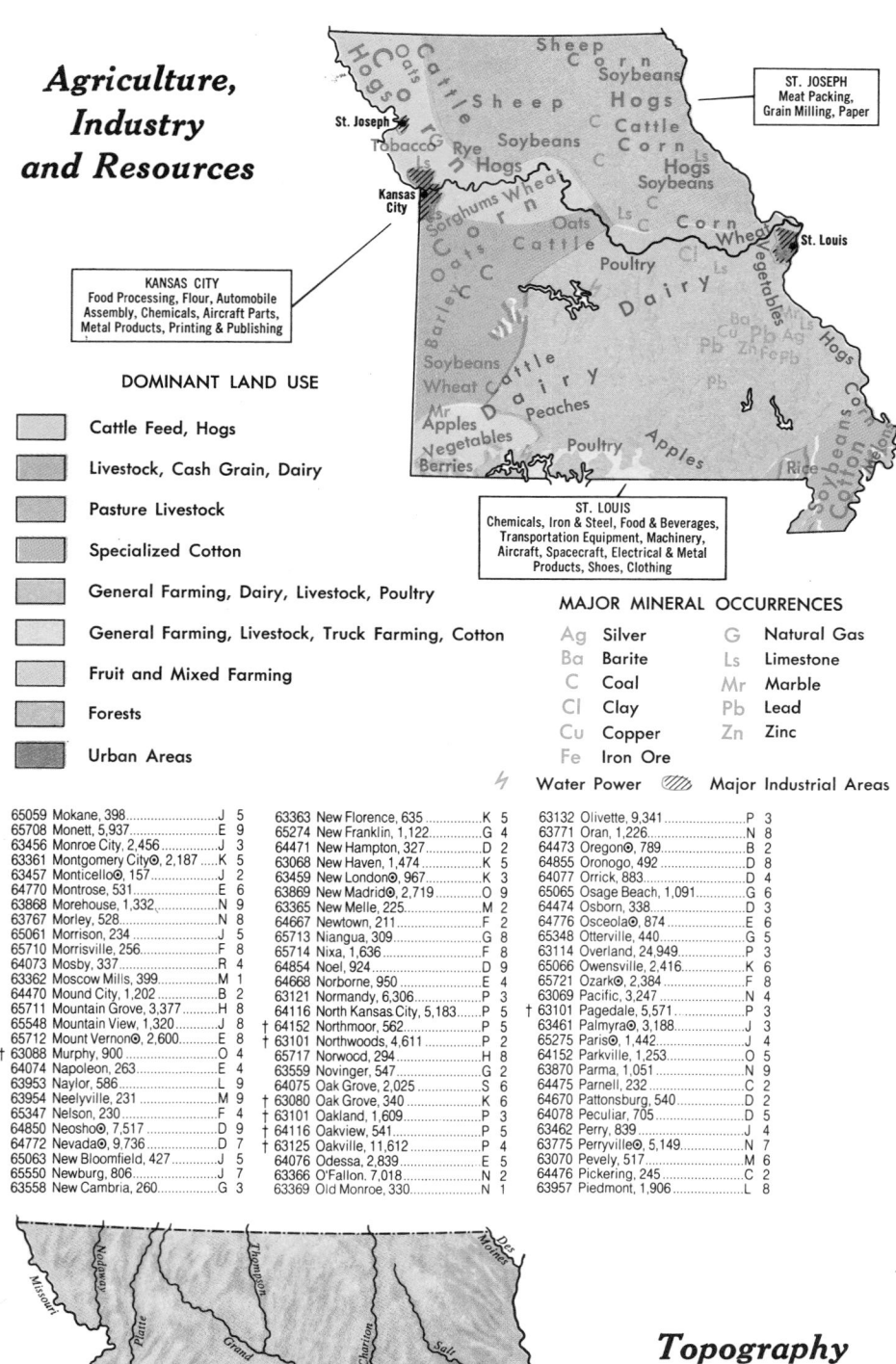

St. Joseph

Kansas City

ST. JOSEPH
Meat Packing, Grain Milling, Paper

KANSAS CITY
Food Processing, Flour, Automobile Assembly, Chemicals, Aircraft Parts, Metal Products, Printing & Publishing

St. Louis

DOMINANT LAND USE

- Cattle Feed, Hogs
- Livestock, Cash Grain, Dairy
- Pasture Livestock
- Specialized Cotton
- General Farming, Dairy, Livestock, Poultry
- General Farming, Livestock, Truck Farming, Cotton
- Fruit and Mixed Farming
- Forests
- Urban Areas

ST. LOUIS
Chemicals, Iron & Steel, Food & Beverages, Transportation Equipment, Machinery, Aircraft, Spacecraft, Electrical & Metal Products, Shoes, Clothing

MAJOR MINERAL OCCURRENCES

Ag	Silver	G	Natural Gas
Ba	Barite	Ls	Limestone
C	Coal	Mr	Marble
Cl	Clay	Pb	Lead
Cu	Copper	Zn	Zinc
Fe	Iron Ore		

⚡ Water Power   ▨ Major Industrial Areas

Topography

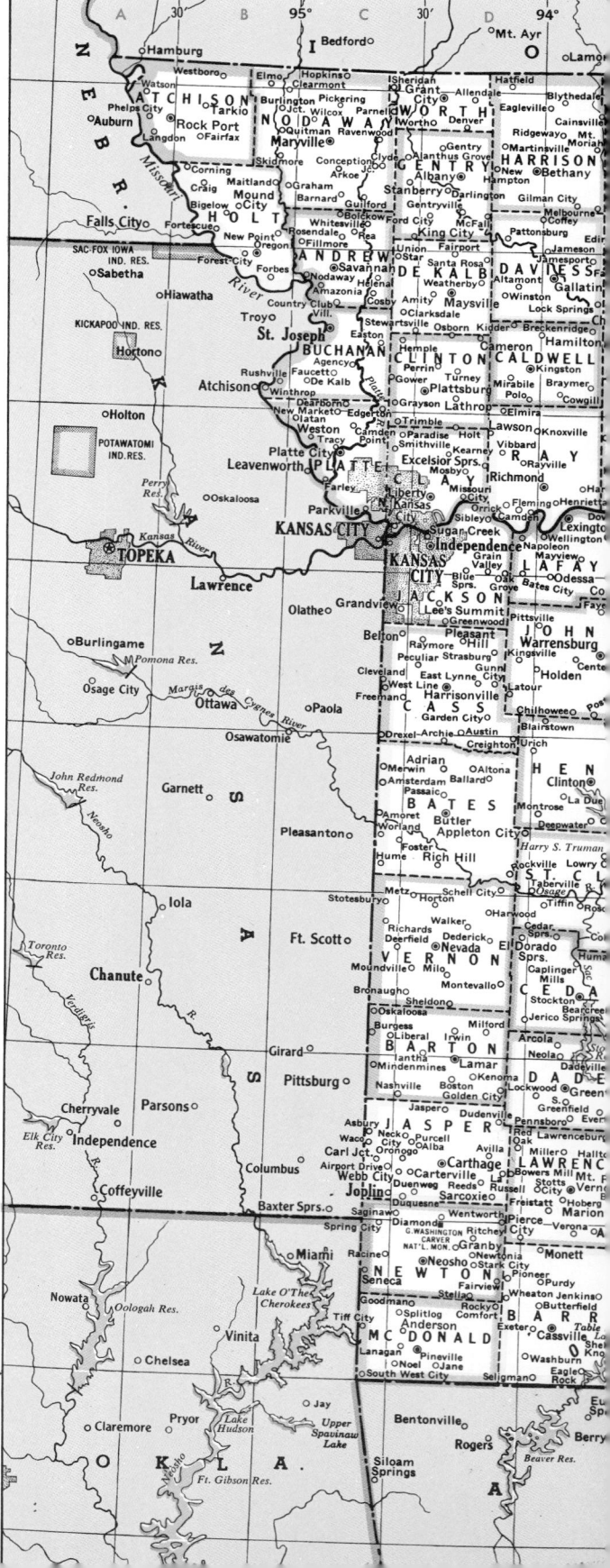

Topography scale: 0 — 40 — 80 MILES

5,000 m. / 16,404 ft. | 2,000 m. / 6,562 ft. | 1,000 m. / 3,281 ft. | 500 m. / 1,640 ft. | 200 m. / 656 ft. | 100 m. / 328 ft. | Sea Level | Below

COUNTIES

CITIES and TOWNS

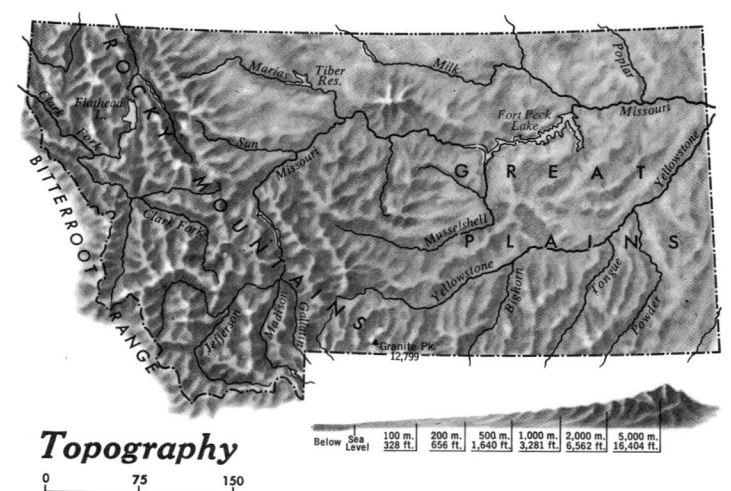

Topography

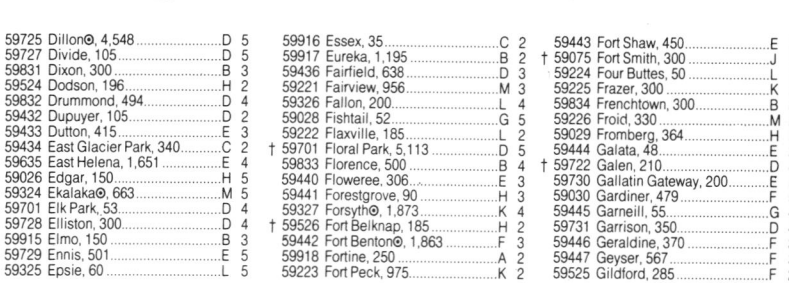

Below Sea Level	100 m. 328 ft.	200 m. 656 ft.	500 m. 1,640 ft.	1,000 m. 3,281 ft.	2,000 m. 6,562 ft.	5,000 m. 16,404 ft.

0 — 75 — 150
MILES

MONTANA

SCALE

0 5 10 20 40 60 MI.

0 5 10 20 40 60 KM.

State Capitals .... ⊛

County Seats .... ⊙

© C.S. HAMMOND & Co., N.Y.

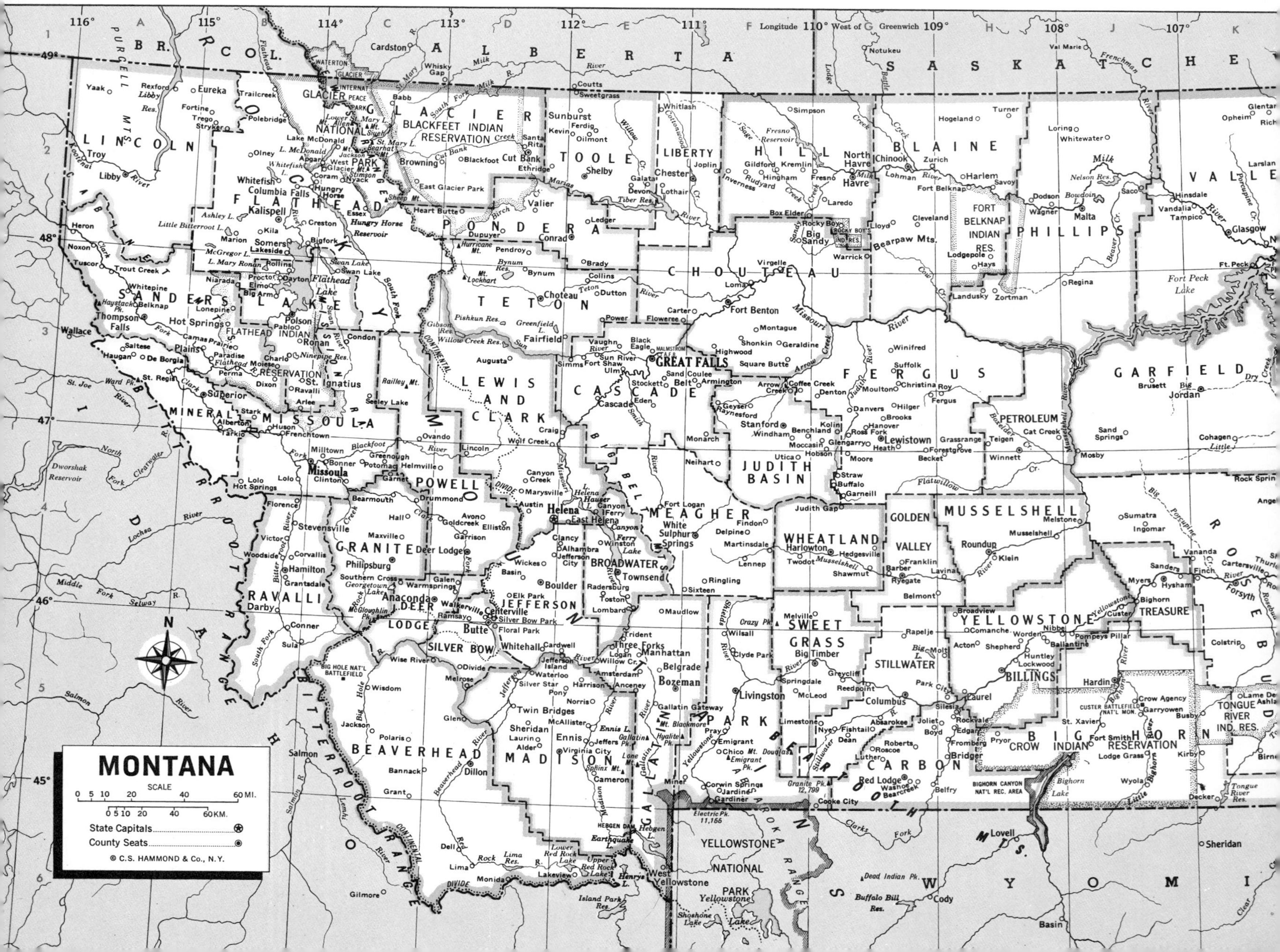

Surrounded by the wide open spaces, a Montana ranch basks in the reflected glory of the Rocky Mountains while it awaits cattle returning from the range. Ranches accommodate so many head of cattle that the state's residents are outnumbered six to one.

AREA 147,138 sq. mi.
POPULATION 694,409 ('70); 786,690 ('80)
CAPITAL Helena
LARGEST CITY Billings
HIGHEST POINT Granite Pk. 12,799 ft.
SETTLED IN 1809
ADMITTED TO UNION November 8, 1889
POPULAR NAME Treasure State
STATE FLOWER Bitterroot
STATE BIRD Western Meadowlark

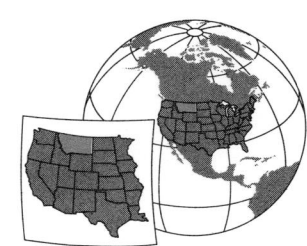

Agriculture, Industry and Resources

DOMINANT LAND USE

- Specialized Wheat
- Wheat, Range Livestock
- General Farming, Dairy, Range Livestock
- General Farming, Livestock, Special Crops
- Range Livestock
- Sugar Beets, Beans, Livestock, General Farming
- Forests

MAJOR MINERAL OCCURRENCES

Ag	Silver	O	Petroleum
Au	Gold	P	Phosphates
Cu	Copper	Pb	Lead
G	Natural Gas	Th	Thorium
Gp	Gypsum	Zn	Zinc
Mn	Manganese	⚡	Water Power

Zip	Place	Ref
59230	Glasgow⊙, 4,700	K 2
† 59725	Glen, 100	D 5
59330	Glendive⊙, 6,305	M 3
59240	Glentana, 40	K 2
59733	Goldcreek, 76	D 4
59835	Grantsdale, 250	B 4
59032	Grassrange, 181	H 3
59401	Great Falls⊙, 60,091	E 3
	Great Falls, ‡81,804	E 3
59836	Greenough, 100	C 4
59837	Hall, 95	C 4
59840	Hamilton⊙, 2,499	B 4
59034	Hardin⊙, 2,733	J 5
59526	Harlem, 1,094	H 2
59036	Harlowton⊙, 1,375	F 4
59735	Harrison, 275	E 5
59333	Hathaway, 45	K 4
59842	Haugan, 40	A 3
59501	Havre⊙, 10,558	G 2
59527	Hays, 950	H 2
59448	Heart Butte, 450	C 2
59601	Helena (cap.)⊙, 22,730	E 4
59843	Helmville, 76	C 4
59844	Heron, 185	A 2
59450	Highwood, 360	F 3
59451	Hilger, 40	G 3
59528	Hingham, 262	F 2
59241	Hinsdale, 500	K 2
59452	Hobson, 192	G 4
† 59353	Hodges, 50	M 4
59529	Hogeland, 68	H 2
59242	Homestead, 75	M 2
59845	Hot Springs, 664	B 3
59919	Hungry Horse, 700	C 2
59037	Huntley, 225	H 5
59846	Huson, 40	B 3
59038	Hysham⊙, 373	J 4
59039	Ingomar, 55	J 4
59335	Intake, 60	M 3
59530	Inverness, 150	F 2
59336	Ismay, 40	M 4
59736	Jackson, 196	C 5
59737	Jeffers, 70	E 5
59638	Jefferson City, 99	E 4
† 59721	Jefferson Island, 31	E 5
59041	Joliet, 412	G 5
59531	Joplin, 350	F 2
59337	Jordan⊙, 529	J 3
59453	Judith Gap, 160	G 4
59901	Kalispell⊙, 10,526	B 2
59454	Kevin, 250	D 2
59920	Kila, 44	B 2
† 59072	Klein, 200	H 4
59532	Kremlin, 347	F 2
59922	Lakeside, 663	B 2
59243	Lambert, 141	M 3
59043	Lame Deer, 460	K 5
59533	Landusky, 50	H 3
59244	Larslan, 140	K 2
59044	Laurel, 4,454	H 5

Zip	Place	Ref
59738	Laurin, 60	D 5
59046	Lavina, 169	H 4
59457	Lewistown⊙, 6,437	G 3
59923	Libby⊙, 3,286	A 2
59739	Lima, 351	D 6
59639	Lincoln, 473	D 4
59339	Lindsay, 40	L 3
59047	Livingston⊙, 6,883	F 5
59535	Lloyd, 70	G 2
59340	Locate, 49	L 4
† 59101	Lockwood, 950	H 5
59050	Lodge Grass, 806	J 5
† 59524	Lodgepole, 39	H 2
59763	Logan, 53	E 5
59847	Lolo, 300	B 4
59460	Loma, 172	F 3
59461	Lothair, 35	E 2
59538	Malta⊙, 2,195	J 2
59741	Manhattan, 816	E 5
59925	Marion, 120	B 2
59053	Martinsdale, 203	F 4
59640	Marysville, 42	D 4
59742	Maudlow, 75	E 4
53850	Maxville, 44	C 4
59740	McAllister, 62	E 5
59247	Medicine Lake, 393	M 2
59743	Melrose, 350	D 5
59054	Melstone, 227	H 4
59055	Melville, 150	F 4
59301	Miles City⊙, 9,023	L 4
59851	Milltown, 500	C 4
59801	Missoula⊙, 29,497	C 4
59462	Moccasin, 100	F 3
59463	Monarch, 80	F 3
59464	Moore, 219	G 3
59059	Musselshell, 32	H 4
59248	Nashua, 513	K 2
59465	Neihart, 109	F 4
59745	Norris, 35	E 5
† 59501	North Havre, 1,073	G 2
59853	Noxon, 250	A 3
† 59936	Nyack, 31	C 2
59061	Nye, 65	G 5
59466	Oilmont, 75	E 2
59927	Olney, 250	B 2
59250	Opheim, 306	K 2
59251	Oswego, 75	L 2
59252	Outlook, 153	M 2
59854	Ovando, 102	C 4
59855	Pablo, 350	B 3
59856	Paradise, 500	B 3
59063	Park City, 400	H 5
59253	Peerless, 100	L 2
59467	Pendroy, 35	D 2
59858	Philipsburg⊙, 1,128	C 4
59859	Plains, 1,046	B 3
59254	Plentywood⊙, 2,381	M 2
59344	Plevna, 189	M 4
59860	Polson⊙, 2,464	B 3
59064	Pompeys Pillar, 69	J 5

Zip	Place	Ref
59747	Pony, 111	E 5
59255	Poplar, 1,389	L 2
59862	Potomac, 58	C 4
59468	Power, 91	E 3
59929	Proctor, 108	B 3
59066	Pryor, 150	H 5
59641	Radersburg, 65	E 4
59748	Ramsay, 140	D 4
59067	Rapelje, 295	G 5
59863	Ravalli, 150	B 3
59256	Raymond, 34	M 2
59469	Raynesford, 100	F 3
59068	Red Lodge⊙, 1,844	H 5
59257	Redstone, 77	M 2
59069	Reedpoint, 125	G 5
59258	Reserve, 90	M 2
59930	Rexford, 243	A 2
59259	Richey, 389	L 3
59260	Richland, 37	K 2
59642	Ringling, 51	F 4
59070	Roberts, 291	G 5
† 59521	Rocky Boy, 150	G 2
59931	Rollins, 200	B 3
59864	Ronan, 1,347	C 3
59347	Rosebud, 120	K 4
59072	Roundup⊙, 2,116	H 4
59471	Roy, 175	H 3
59540	Rudyard, 550	F 2
59074	Ryegate⊙, 261	G 4
59261	Saco, 356	J 2
59865	Saint Ignatius, 925	C 3
59866	Saint Regis, 500	A 3
59075	Saint Xavier, 110	J 5
59867	Saltese, 95	A 3
59472	Sand Coulee, 500	E 3
59076	Sanders, 50	J 4
59473	Santa Rita, 125	D 2
59262	Savage, 300	M 3
59263	Scobey⊙, 1,486	L 2
59868	Seeley Lake, 400	C 4
59078	Shawmut, 60	G 4
† 59347	Sheffield, 40	K 4
59474	Shelby⊙, 3,111	E 2
59079	Shepherd, 100	H 5
59749	Sheridan, 636	D 5
59270	Sidney⊙, 4,543	M 3
59080	Silesia, 90	H 5
† 59701	Silver Bow Park, 5,524	D 4
59751	Silver Star, 100	D 5
59477	Simms, 299	E 3
59541	Simpson, 70	F 2
59932	Somers, 950	B 2
59348	Sonnette, 42	L 5
59442	Square Butte, 48	F 3
59479	Stanford⊙, 505	F 3
† 59846	Stark, 51	B 3
59870	Stevensville, 829	C 4
59480	Stockett, 500	E 3
59933	Stryker, 60	B 2
59481	Suffolk, 45	G 3

Zip	Place	Ref
59482	Sunburst, 604	E 2
59483	Sun River, 190	E 3
59872	Superior⊙, 993	B 3
59911	Swan Lake, 200	C 3
59484	Sweetgrass, 120	E 2
59349	Terry⊙, 870	L 4
59873	Thompson Falls⊙, 1,356	A 3
59752	Three Forks, 1,188	E 5
† 59347	Thurlow, 40	K 4
59643	Toston, 75	E 4
59644	Townsend⊙, 1,371	E 4
59934	Trego, 50	B 2
59753	Trident, 50	E 5
59874	Trout Creek, 200	A 3
59935	Troy, 1,046	A 2
59542	Turner, 175	H 2
59754	Twin Bridges, 613	D 5
59085	Twodot, 118	F 4
59485	Ulm, 450	E 3
59452	Utica, 40	F 4
59486	Valier, 651	D 2
† 59237	Vananda, 50	K 4
59487	Vaughn, 345	E 3
59875	Victor, 500	B 4
59274	Vida, 52	L 3
59755	Virginia City⊙, 149	E 5
59701	Walkerville, 1,097	D 4
59756	Warmsprings, 1,600	D 4
59757	Waterloo, 102	D 5
† 59314	Watkins, 40	K 3
59275	Westby, 287	M 2
59936	West Glacier, 348	C 2
59758	West Yellowstone, 756	E 6
59937	Whitefish, 3,349	B 2
59759	Whitehall, 1,035	D 5
† 59784	Whitepine, 50	A 3
59645	White Sulphur Springs⊙, 1,200	E 4
59276	Whitetail, 125	L 2
59544	Whitewater, 100	J 2
59353	Wibaux⊙, 644	M 3
59760	Willow Creek, 325	E 5
59086	Wilsall, 200	F 5
59488	Windham, 60	F 3
59489	Winifred, 190	G 3
59087	Winnett⊙, 271	H 4
59647	Winston, 115	E 4
59761	Wisdom, 155	C 5
59762	Wise River, 125	C 5
59648	Wolf Creek, 200	D 4
59201	Wolf Point⊙, 3,095	L 2
† 59875	Woodside, 80	B 4
59088	Worden, 350	H 5
59089	Wyola, 110	J 5
† 59935	Yaak, 75	A 2
59547	Zurich, 89	G 2

⊙ County seat.
‡ Population of metropolitan area.
† Zip of nearest p.o.
* Multiple zips

COUNTIES

Adams, 30,553	F	4
Antelope, 9,047	F	2
Arthur, 606	C	3
Banner, 1,034	A	3
Blaine, 847	E	3
Boone, 8,190	F	3
Box Butte, 10,094	A	2
Boyd, 3,752	F	2
Brown, 4,021	D	2
Buffalo, 31,222	E	4
Burt, 9,247	H	3
Butler, 9,461	G	3
Cass, 18,076	H	4
Cedar, 12,192	G	2
Chase, 4,129	C	4
Cherry, 6,846	C	2
Cheyenne, 10,778	A	3
Clay, 8,266	F	4
Colfax, 9,498	G	3
Cuming, 12,034	H	3
Custer, 14,092	E	3
Dakota, 13,137	H	2
Dawes, 9,693	A	2
Dawson, 19,467	E	4
Deuel, 2,717	B	3
Dixon, 7,453	H	2
Dodge, 34,782	H	3
Douglas, 389,455	H	3
Dundy, 2,926	C	4
Fillmore, 8,137	G	4
Franklin, 4,566	F	4
Frontier, 3,982	D	4
Furnas, 6,897	E	4
Gage, 25,719	H	4
Garden, 2,929	B	3
Garfield, 2,411	F	3
Gosper, 2,178	E	4
Grant, 1,019	C	3
Greeley, 4,000	F	3
Hall, 42,851	F	4
Hamilton, 8,867	F	4
Harlan, 4,357	E	4
Hayes, 1,530	C	4
Hitchcock, 4,051	C	4
Holt, 12,933	F	2
Hooker, 939	C	3
Howard, 6,807	F	3
Jefferson, 10,436	G	4
Johnson, 5,743	H	4
Kearney, 6,707	F	4
Keith, 8,487	C	3
Keya Paha, 1,340	E	2
Kimball, 6,009	A	3
Knox, 11,723	G	2
Lancaster, 167,972	H	4
Lincoln, 29,538	D	4
Logan, 991	D	3
Loup, 854	E	3
Madison, 27,402	G	3
McPherson, 623	C	3
Merrick, 8,751	F	3
Morrill, 5,813	A	3
Nance, 5,142	F	3
Nemaha, 8,976	J	4
Nuckolls, 7,404	F	4
Otoe, 15,576	H	4
Pawnee, 4,473	H	4
Perkins, 3,423	C	4
Phelps, 9,553	E	4
Pierce, 8,493	G	2
Platte, 26,508	G	3
Polk, 6,468	G	3
Red Willow, 12,191	D	4
Richardson, 12,277	J	4
Rock, 2,231	E	2
Saline, 12,809	G	4
Sarpy, 63,696	H	3
Saunders, 17,018	H	3
Scotts Bluff, 36,432	A	3
Seward, 14,460	G	4
Sheridan, 7,285	B	2
Sherman, 4,725	F	3
Sioux, 2,034	A	2
Stanton, 5,758	G	3
Thayer, 7,779	G	4
Thomas, 954	D	3
Thurston, 6,942	H	2
Valley, 5,783	E	3
Washington, 13,310	H	3
Wayne, 10,400	G	2
Webster, 6,477	F	4
Wheeler, 1,054	F	3
York, 13,685	G	4

CITIES and TOWNS

Zip	Name/Pop.	Key	
68301	Adams, 463	H	4
69210	Ainsworth⊙, 2,073	D	2
68620	Albion⊙, 2,074	F	3
68810	Alda, 456	F	4
68710	Allen, 309	H	2
69301	Alliance⊙, 6,862	A	2
68920	Alma⊙, 1,299	E	4
68814	Ansley, 631	E	3
68922	Arapahoe, 1,147	E	4
68815	Arcadia, 418	F	3
68002	Arlington, 910	H	3
69120	Arnold, 752	D	3
69121	Arthur⊙, 175	C	3
68003	Ashland, 2,176	H	3
68305	Auburn⊙, 3,650	J	4
68818	Aurora⊙, 3,180	F	4
68924	Axtell, 500	E	4
68004	Bancroft, 545	H	2
68622	Bartlett⊙, 193	F	3
69020	Bartley, 283	D	4
68714	Bassett⊙, 983	E	2
68715	Battle Creek, 1,158	G	3
69334	Bayard, 1,338	A	3
68310	Beatrice⊙, 12,389	H	4
68926	Beaver City⊙, 802	E	4
68313	Beaver Crossing, 400	G	4
68716	Beemer, 699	H	3
68005	Bellevue, 19,449	J	3
68624	Bellwood, 361	G	3
69021	Benkelman⊙, 1,349	C	4
68317	Bennet, 489	H	4
68007	Bennington, 683	H	3
68927	Bertrand, 662	E	4
69122	Big Springs, 472	B	3
68928	Bladen, 293	F	4
68008	Blair⊙, 6,106	H	3
68718	Bloomfield, 1,287	G	2
68930	Blue Hill, 1,201	F	4
68318	Blue Springs, 494	H	4
68010	Boys Town, 989	H	3
68319	Bradshaw, 347	G	4
69123	Brady, 311	D	3
68626	Brainard, 309	G	3
68821	Brewster⊙, 54	D	3
69336	Bridgeport⊙, 1,490	A	3
68822	Broken Bow⊙, 3,734	E	3
68321	Brownville, 174	J	4
69127	Brule, 423	C	3
68322	Bruning, 315	G	4
68823	Burwell⊙, 1,341	E	3
68722	Butte⊙, 575	F	2
68824	Cairo, 686	F	4
69022	Callaway, 523	D	3
69022	Cambridge, 1,145	D	4
68932	Campbell, 447	F	4
68015	Cedar Bluffs, 616	H	3
68627	Cedar Rapids, 449	F	3
68724	Center⊙, 111	G	2
68826	Central City⊙, 2,803	F	3
68017	Ceresco, 474	H	3
69337	Chadron⊙, 5,853	B	2
68725	Chambers, 321	F	2
68827	Chapman, 371	F	3
69129	Chappell⊙, 1,204	B	3
68327	Chester, 459	G	4
68628	Clarks, 480	G	3
68629	Clarkson, 805	G	3
68933	Clay Center⊙, 952	F	4
68726	Clearwater, 398	F	2
68727	Coleridge, 608	G	2
68601	Columbus⊙, 15,471	G	3
68329	Cook, 328	H	4
68331	Cortland, 326	H	4
69130	Cozad, 4,219	E	4
68019	Craig, 295	H	3
69339	Crawford, 1,291	A	2
68729	Creighton, 1,461	G	2
68333	Crete, 4,444	G	4
68730	Crofton, 677	G	2
69024	Culbertson, 801	C	4
69025	Curtis, 1,166	D	4
68731	Dakota City⊙, 1,057	H	2
69131	Dalton, 354	B	3
68831	Dannebrog, 384	F	3
68335	Davenport, 427	G	4
68632	David City⊙, 2,380	G	3
68020	Decatur, 679	H	3
68340	Deshler, 937	G	4
68341	De Witt, 651	H	4
68342	Diller, 287	H	4
69133	Dix, 342	A	3
68633	Dodge, 704	H	3
68832	Doniphan, 542	F	4
68343	Dorchester, 492	G	4
68634	Duncan, 298	G	3
68347	Eagle, 441	H	4
68935	Edgar, 707	F	4
68636	Elgin, 917	F	3
68022	Elkhorn, 1,184	H	3
68836	Elm Creek, 798	E	4
68349	Elmwood, 548	H	4
68937	Elwood⊙, 601	E	4
68733	Emerson, 850	H	2
69028	Eustis, 400	D	4
68735	Ewing, 552	F	2
68351	Exeter, 759	G	4
68352	Fairbury⊙, 5,265	G	4
68938	Fairfield, 487	G	4
68354	Fairmont, 761	G	4
68355	Falls City⊙, 5,444	J	4
68358	Firth, 328	H	4
68023	Fort Calhoun, 642	J	3
68939	Franklin⊙, 1,193	E	4
68025	Fremont⊙, 22,962	H	3
68359	Friend, 1,126	G	4
68638	Fullerton⊙, 1,444	F	3
68361	Geneva⊙, 2,275	G	4
68640	Genoa, 1,174	G	3
69341	Gering⊙, 5,639	A	3
68840	Gibbon, 1,388	F	4
68841	Giltner, 408	F	4
68941	Glenvil, 332	F	4
69343	Gordon, 2,106	B	2
69138	Gothenburg, 3,154	D	4
68801	Grand Island⊙, 31,269	F	4
69140	Grant⊙, 1,099	C	4
68842	Greeley⊙, 580	F	3
68366	Greenwood, 506	H	3
68028	Gretna, 1,557	H	3
68942	Guide Rock, 318	F	4
68843	Hampton, 387	G	4
69345	Harrisburg⊙, 80	A	3
69346	Harrison⊙, 377	A	2
68739	Hartington⊙, 1,581	G	2
68944	Harvard, 1,230	F	4
68901	Hastings⊙, 23,580	F	4
69032	Hayes Center⊙, 237	C	4
69347	Hay Springs, 682	B	2
68370	Hebron⊙, 1,667	G	4
69348	Hemingford, 734	A	2
68371	Henderson, 901	G	4
68739	Herman, 323	H	3
69143	Hershey, 526	D	3
68372	Hickman, 415	H	4
68947	Hildreth, 352	E	4
68948	Holbrook, 307	D	4
68949	Holdrege⊙, 5,635	E	4
68030	Homer, 457	H	2
68031	Hooper, 895	H	3
68641	Howells, 682	H	3
68376	Humboldt, 1,194	J	4

J. Gordon Miller—Shostal Associates

Miles of pens hold thousands of head of cattle in the Union Stockyards, Omaha. Next stop — the meat packers' plant.

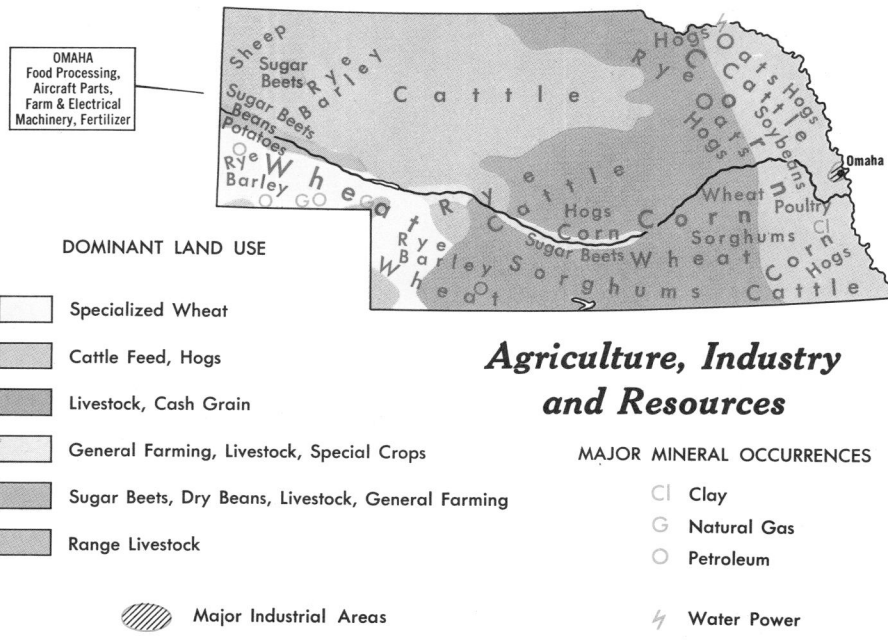

OMAHA
Food Processing, Aircraft Parts, Farm & Electrical Machinery, Fertilizer

DOMINANT LAND USE

- Specialized Wheat
- Cattle Feed, Hogs
- Livestock, Cash Grain
- General Farming, Livestock, Special Crops
- Sugar Beets, Dry Beans, Livestock, General Farming
- Range Livestock
- Major Industrial Areas

Agriculture, Industry and Resources

MAJOR MINERAL OCCURRENCES

Cl Clay
G Natural Gas
O Petroleum
⚡ Water Power

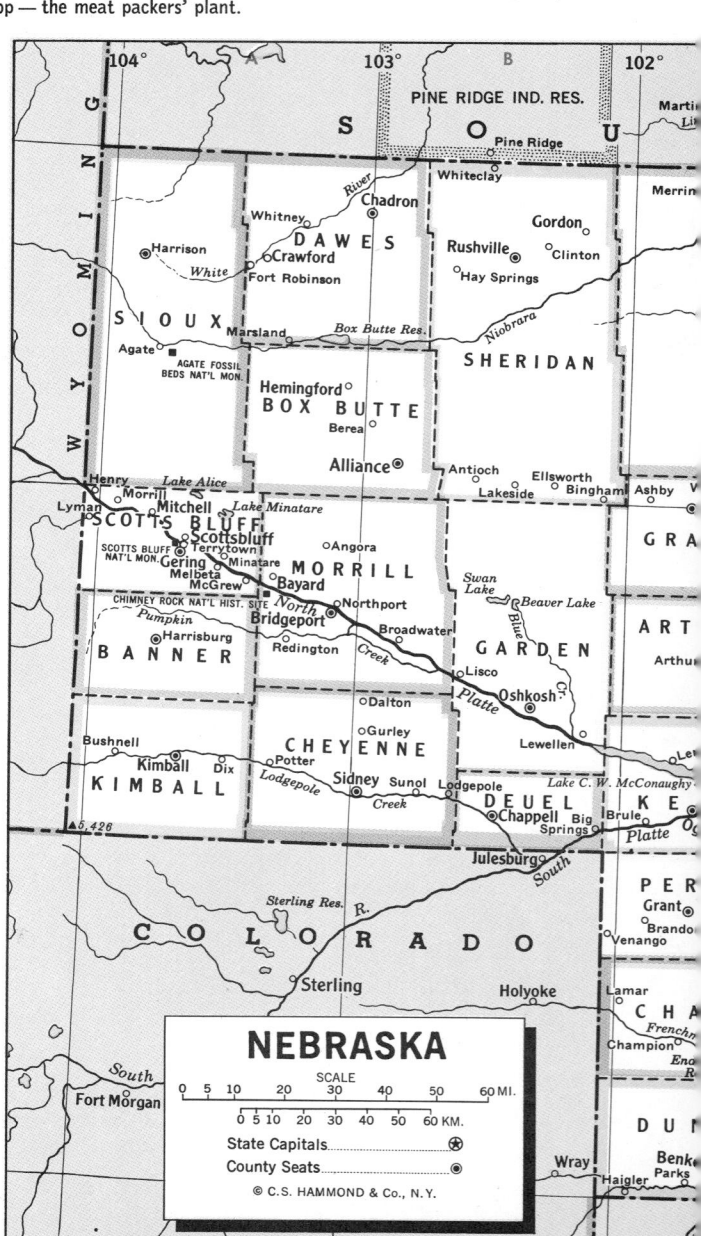

NEBRASKA

SCALE
0 5 10 20 30 40 50 60 MI.
0 5 10 20 30 40 50 60 KM.

State Capitals ⊛
County Seats ⊙

© C.S. HAMMOND & Co., N.Y.

AREA 77,227 sq. mi.
POPULATION 1,483,791 ('70); 1,570,006 ('80)
CAPITAL Lincoln
LARGEST CITY Omaha
HIGHEST POINT 5,426 ft. (Kimball Co.)
SETTLED IN 1847
ADMITTED TO UNION March 1, 1867
POPULAR NAME Cornhusker State
STATE FLOWER Goldenrod
STATE BIRD Western Meadowlark

Topography

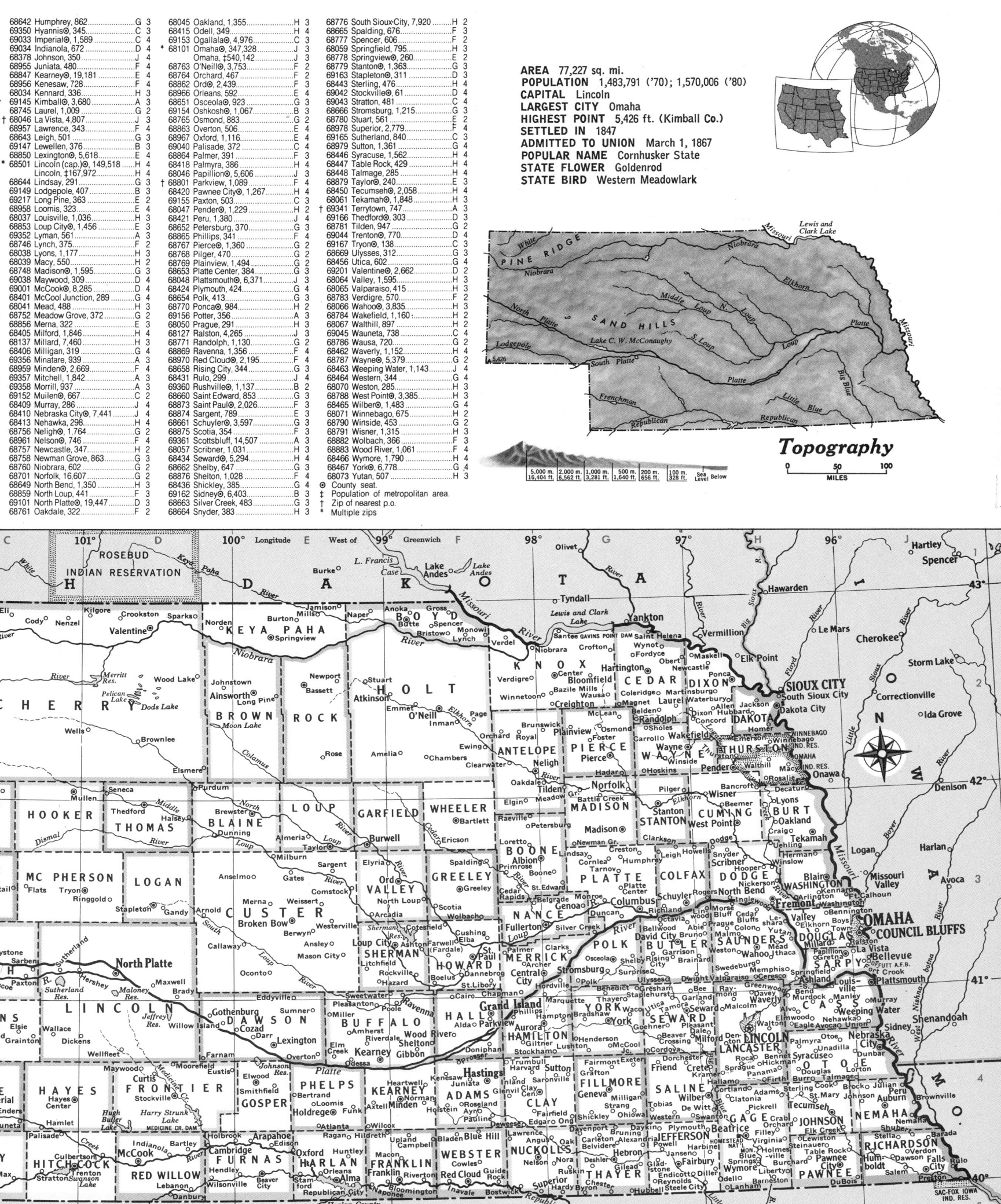

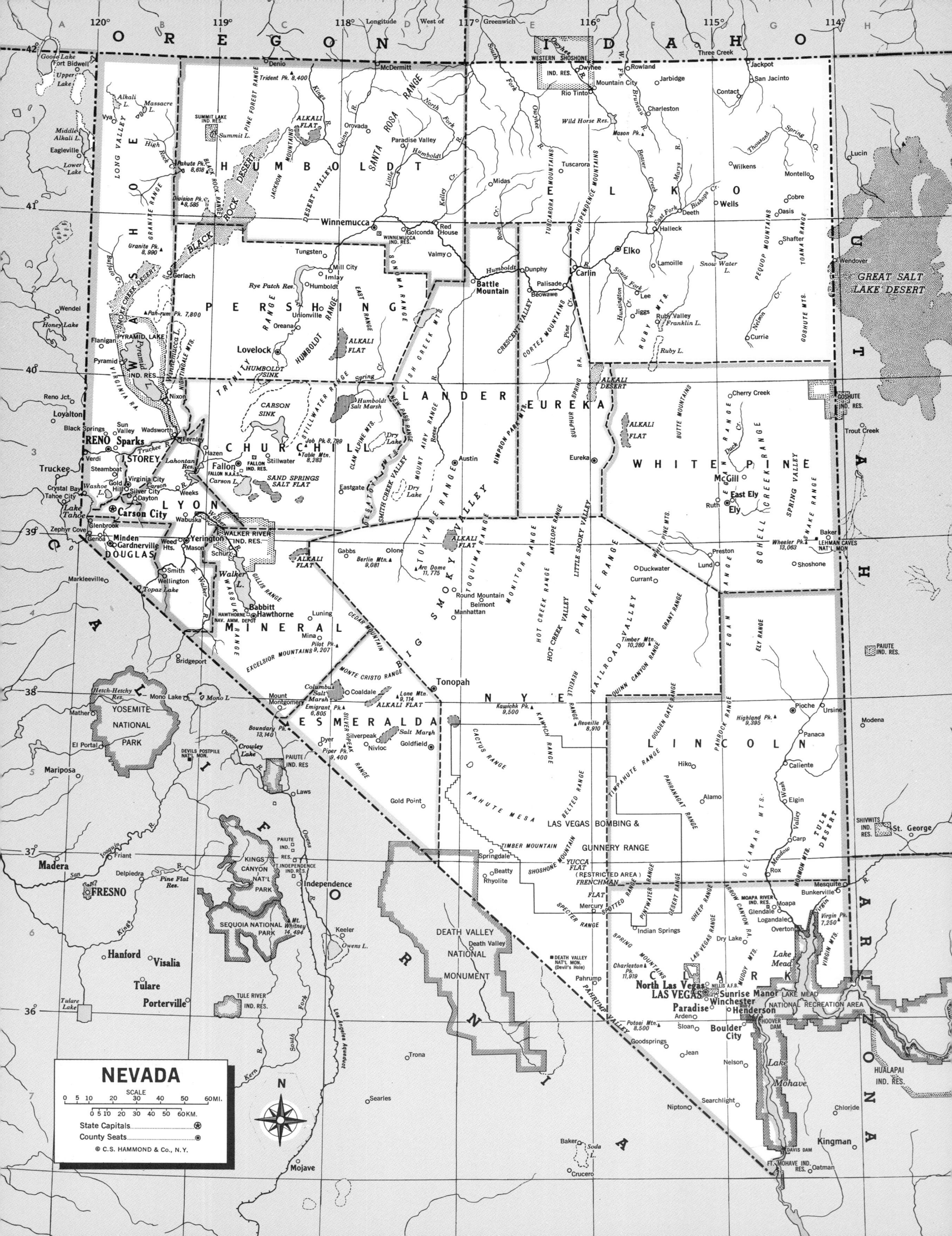

NEVADA

SCALE
0 5 10   20   30   40   50   60 MI.
0 5 10   20   30   40   50   60 KM.

State Capitals .... ⊛
County Seats .... ◉

© C.S. HAMMOND & Co., N.Y.

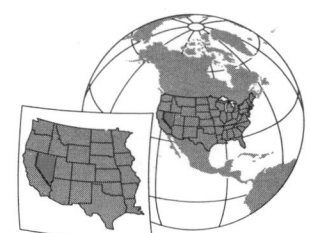

COUNTIES

Carson City (city), 15,468......B 3
Churchill, 10,513......C 3
Clark, 273,288......F 6
Douglas, 6,882......B 4
Elko, 13,958......F 1
Esmeralda, 629......D 5
Eureka, 948......E 3
Humboldt, 6,375......C 1
Lander, 2,666......D 3
Lincoln, 2,557......F 5
Lyon, 8,221......B 3
Mineral, 7,051......C 4
Nye, 5,599......E 4
Pershing, 2,670......C 2
Storey, 695......B 3
Washoe, 121,068......B 2
White Pine, 10,150......F 3

CITIES and TOWNS

Zip   Name/Pop.   Key
89001 Alamo, 300......F 5
89310 Austin⊙, 300......E 3
89416 Babbitt, 1,579......C 4
89311 Baker, 75......G 3
89820 Battle Mountain, 1,856......E 2
89003 Beatty, 570......E 6
† 89045 Belmont, 25......E 4
89821 Beowawe, 104......E 2
89508 Black Springs, 2,500......B 3
89005 Boulder City, 5,223......G 6
89007 Bunkerville, 150......G 6
89008 Caliente, 916......G 5
89822 Carlin, 1,313......E 2
89009 Carp, 32......G 5
89701 Carson City (cap.), 15,468......B 3
† 89801 Charleston, 14......F 1
89312 Cherry Creek, 75......F 2
† 89508 Coaldale, 31......D 4
† 89830 Cobre, 14......G 1
† 89825 Contact, 9......F 1
89402 Crystal Bay, 950......A 3
† 89314 Currant, 30......F 4
89313 Currie, 15......G 2
89403 Dayton, 350......B 3
89823 Deeth, 27......F 1
89404 Denio, 28......C 1
† 89040 Dry Lake, 5......G 6
89314 Duckwater, 85......F 4
† 89821 Dunphy, 25......E 2
89010 Dyer, 60......C 5
89315 East Ely, 1,992......F 3
† 89406 Eastgate, 17......D 3
89112 East Las Vegas, 6,501......F 6
† 89009 Elgin, 8......G 5
89801 Elko⊙, 7,621......F 2
89301 Ely⊙, 4,176......G 3
89316 Eureka⊙, 300......E 3
89406 Fallon⊙, 2,959......C 3
89408 Fernley, 750......B 3
89409 Gabbs, 874......D 4
89410 Gardnerville, 800......B 4
89411 Genoa, 170......B 4
89412 Gerlach, 150......B 2
89413 Glenbrook, 800......B 3
† 89025 Glendale, 20......G 6
89414 Golconda, 150......D 2
89013 Goldfield⊙, 213......D 5
† 89440 Gold Hill, 50......B 3
† 89013 Gold Point, 10......D 5
89019 Goodsprings, 120......F 7
89824 Halleck, 50......F 2
89415 Hawthorne⊙, 3,539......C 4
89417 Hazen, 60......C 3

89015 Henderson, 16,395......G 6
89017 Hiko, 150......F 5
† 89418 Humboldt, 12......C 2
89418 Imlay, 150......C 2
89018 Indian Springs, 500......F 6
† 89310 Ione, 15......D 4
89825 Jackpot, 400......G 1
89826 Jarbidge, 25......F 1
89019 Jean, 100......F 7
89827 Jiggs, 6......F 2
89828 Lamoille, 51......F 2
89829 Lee, 180......F 2
89021 Logandale, 410......G 6
89419 Lovelock⊙, 1,571......C 2
89317 Lund, 300......F 4
89420 Luning, 55......C 4
89022 Manhattan, 28......E 4
† 89447 Mason, 200......B 4
89318 McGill, 2,164......G 3
89421 McDermitt, 300......D 1
89023 Mercury, 2,200......E 6
89024 Mesquite, 500......G 6
89414 Midas, 6......E 1
† 89418 Mill City, 4......D 2
89422 Mina, 375......C 4
89423 Minden⊙, 520......B 4
89025 Moapa, 250......G 6
89830 Montello, 150......G 1
89831 Mountain City, 80......F 1
† 89422 Mount Montgomery, 10......C 5
89046 Nelson, 67......G 7
89424 Nixon, 300......B 3
89030 North Las Vegas, 36,216......F 6
† 89830 Oasis, 5......G 1
† 89419 Oreana, 18......C 2
89425 Orovada, 250......D 1
89040 Overton, 900......G 6
89832 Owyhee, 100......F 1
89041 Pahrump, 400......E 6
† 89822 Palisade, 5......E 2
89042 Panaca, 500......G 5
† 89101 Paradise, 24,477......F 6
89426 Paradise Valley, 110......D 1
89043 Pioche⊙, 525......G 5
† 89301 Preston, 44......G 4
89414 Red House, 4......D 2
* 89501 Reno⊙, 72,863......B 3
Reno, ‡121,068......B 3
† 89003 Rhyolite, 8......E 6
† 89831 Rio Tinto, 5......E 1
89045 Round Mountain, 100......E 4
† 89831 Rowland, 10......F 1
† 89009 Rox, 12......G 6
89833 Ruby Valley, 225......F 2
89319 Ruth, 750......F 3
† 89825 San Jacinto, 8......G 1
89427 Schurz, 350......C 4
89046 Searchlight, 279......F 7
† 89835 Shafter, 7......G 2
† 89301 Shoshone, 15......G 4
89428 Silver City, 100......B 3
89047 Silverpeak, 80......D 5
† 89114 Sloan, 25......F 7
89430 Smith, 300......B 4
89431 Sparks, 24,187......B 3
89436 Steamboat, 560......B 3
89406 Stillwater, 30......C 3
* 89101 Sunrise Manor, 10,886......F 6
89431 Sun Valley, 2,414......B 3
89049 Tonopah⊙, 1,716......D 4
89834 Tuscarora, 15......E 1
† 89418 Unionville, 18......C 2
† 89043 Ursine, 40......G 5
89438 Valmy, 50......D 2

89439 Verdi, 100......B 3
89440 Virginia City⊙, 300......B 3
† 96104 Vya, 12......B 1
† 89447 Wabuska, 50......B 3
89442 Wadsworth, 375......B 3
89443 Weed Heights, 750......B 4
† 89447 Weeks, 15......B 3
89835 Wells, 1,081......G 1
† 89835 Wilkins, 6......G 1
† 89101 Winchester, 13,981......F 6
89445 Winnemucca⊙, 3,587......D 2
89447 Yerington⊙, 2,010......B 4
89448 Zephyr Cove, 400......A 3

⊙ County seat.
‡ Population of metropolitan area.
○ Zip of nearest p.o.
* Multiple zips

AREA and FACTS

AREA 110,540 sq. mi.
POPULATION 488,738 ('70); 799,184 ('80)
CAPITAL Carson City
LARGEST CITY Las Vegas
HIGHEST POINT Boundary Pk. 13,140 ft.
SETTLED IN 1850
ADMITTED TO UNION October 31, 1864
POPULAR NAME Silver State
STATE FLOWER Sagebrush
STATE BIRD Mountain Bluebird

An incandescent oasis in the Nevada desert, Reno beckons travelers to its varied diversions — from games of chance and nightclub entertainment to annual rodeos and skiing in the Sierra Nevada.

Agriculture, Industry and Resources

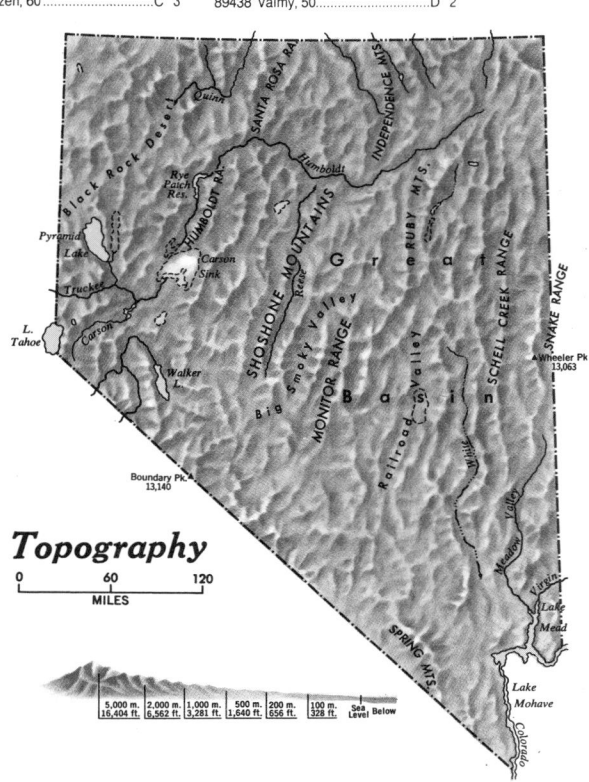

Topography

```
0    60    120
     MILES
```

5,000 m. 2,000 m. 1,000 m. 500 m. 200 m. 100 m. Sea Below
16,404 ft. 6,562 ft. 3,281 ft. 1,640 ft. 656 ft. 328 ft. Level

MAJOR MINERAL OCCURRENCES

Ag Silver
Au Gold
Ba Barite
Cu Copper
Gp Gypsum
Hg Mercury
Lt Lithium
Mg Magnesium
Mo Molybdenum
Na Salt
O Petroleum
Pb Lead
S Sulfur
W Tungsten
Zn Zinc

⚡ Water Power

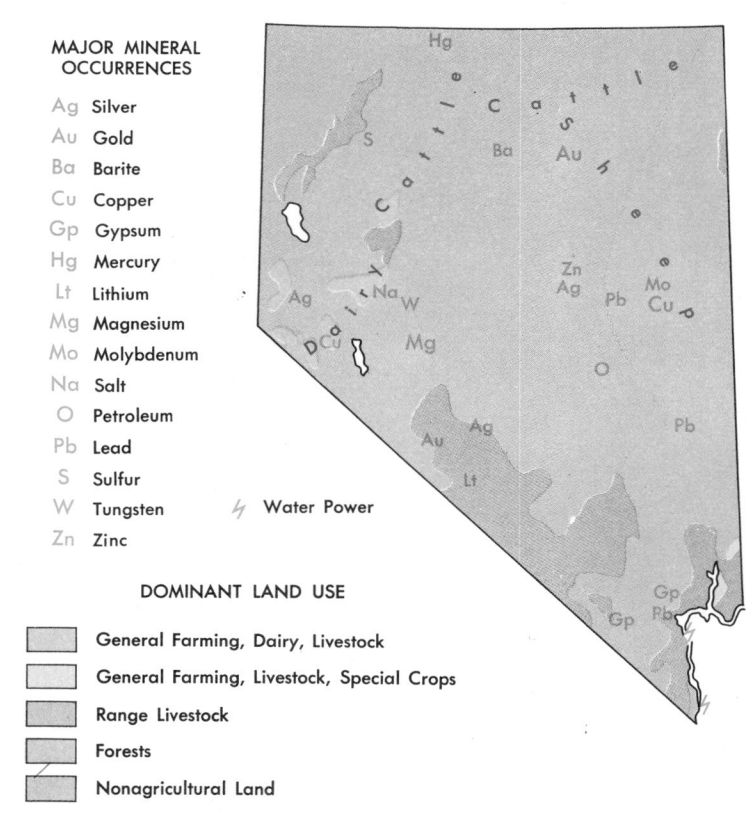

DOMINANT LAND USE

General Farming, Dairy, Livestock
General Farming, Livestock, Special Crops
Range Livestock
Forests
Nonagricultural Land

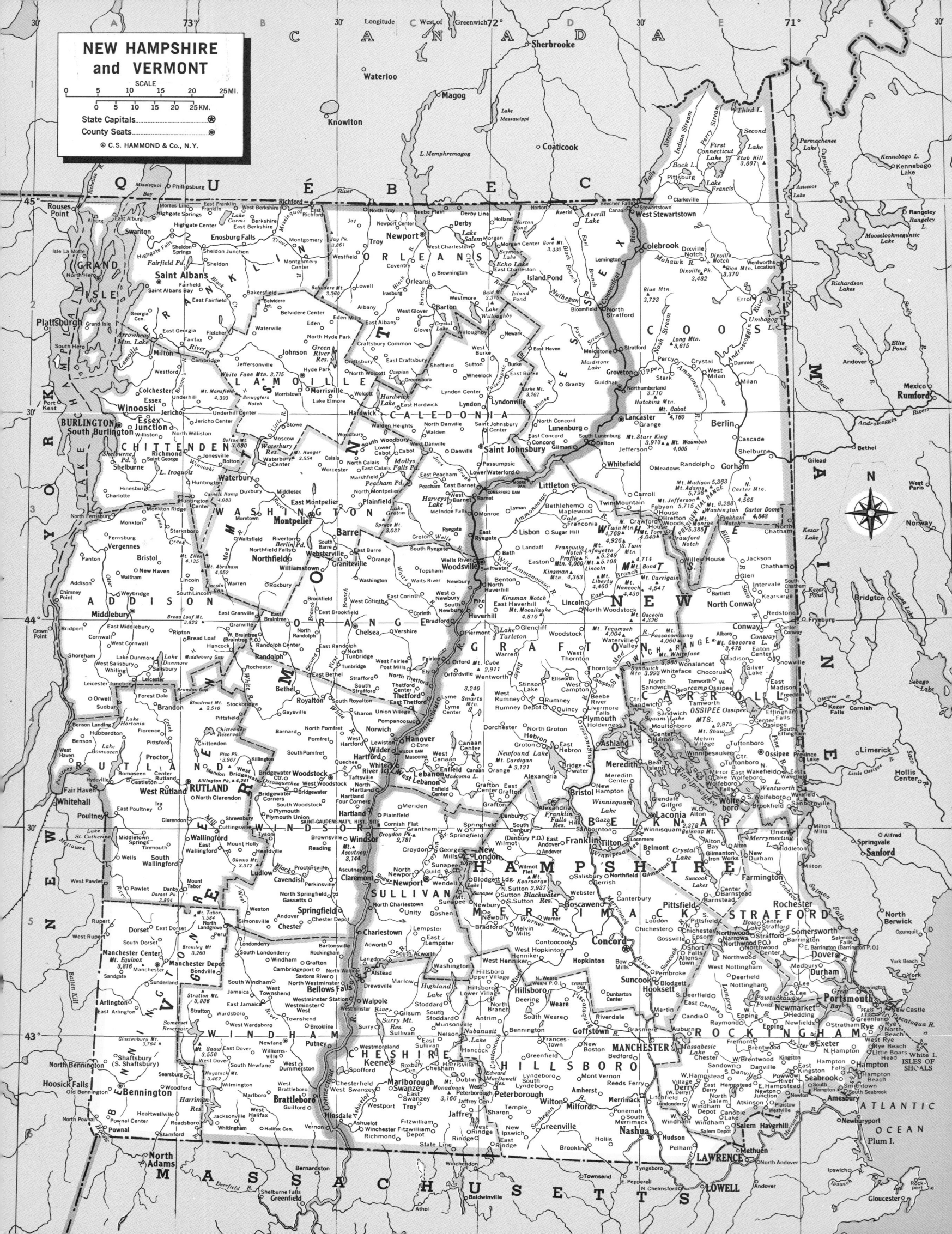

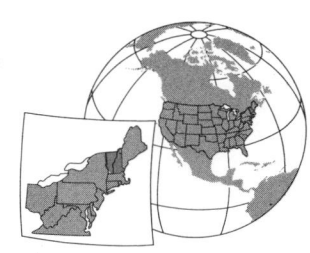

NEW HAMPSHIRE

COUNTIES

Belknap, 32,367	D	4
Carroll, 18,548	E	4
Cheshire, 52,364	C	6
Coos, 34,291	E	2
Grafton, 54,914	D	4
Hillsboro, 223,941	D	6
Merrimack, 80,925	D	5
Rockingham, 138,951	E	5
Strafford, 70,431	E	5
Sullivan, 30,949	C	5

CITIES and TOWNS

Zip	Name/Pop.	Key	
03601	Acworth, △459	C	5
† 03864	Albany, △259	E	4
† 03222	Alexandria, △466	D	4
† 03275	Allenstown, △2,732	E	5
03602	Alstead, △1,185	C	5
03602	Alstead, 450	C	5
03809	Alton, △1,647	E	5
03809	Alton, 450	E	5
03031	Amherst, △4,605	D	6
03810	Amherst, 600	D	6
03216	Andover, △1,138	D	5
03216	Andover, 500	D	5
03440	Antrim, △2,122	D	5
03440	Antrim, 750	D	5
03217	Ashland, △1,599	D	4
03217	Ashland, 1,391	D	4
03441	Ashuelot, 750	C	6
03811	Atkinson, △2,291	E	6
03032	Auburn, △2,035	E	5
03218	Barnstead, △1,119	E	5
03218	Barnstead, 400	E	5
† 03825	Barrington, △1,865	F	5
03812	Bartlett, 1,098	E	3
03812	Bartlett, 600	E	3
03740	Bath, △607	D	3
03102	Bedford, △5,859	D	6
03220	Belmont, △2,493	E	5
03220	Belmont, 900	E	5
03442	Bennington, △639	D	5

† 03785	Benton, △194	D	3
03570	Berlin, 15,256	E	3
03574	Bethlehem, △1,142	D	3
03574	Bethlehem, 500	D	3
03301	Boscawen, △3,162	D	5
03301	Bow Mills, 600	D	5
03221	Bradford, △679	D	5
03833	Brentwood, △1,468	E	6
03575	Bretton Woods, 6	E	3
03222	Bridgewater, △398	D	4
03222	Bristol, △1,670	D	4
03222	Bristol, 1,080	D	4
† 03872	Brookfield, △198	E	4
03033	Brookline, △1,167	D	6
03223	Campton, △1,171	D	4
03741	Canaan, △1,923	C	4
03741	Canaan, 500	C	4
03034	Candia, △1,997	E	5
† 03079	Canobie Lake, 500	E	6
03224	Canterbury, △895	D	5
† 03595	Carroll, △310	D	3
03813	Center Conway, 450	E	4
03226	Center Harbor, △540	D	4
03814	Center Ossipee, 550	E	4
03603	Charlestown, △3,274	C	5
03603	Charlestown, 1,285	C	5
04037	Chatham, △134	E	3
03036	Chester, △1,382	E	6
03443	Chesterfield, △1,817	C	6
03443	Chesterfield, 450	C	5
03258	Chichester, △1,083	C	5
03743	Claremont, 14,221	C	5
† 05902	Clarksville, △166	E	1
03576	Colebrook, △2,094	E	2
03576	Colebrook, 1,070	E	2
03301	Concord (cap.)⊙, 30,022	D	5
03229	Contoocook, 975	D	5
03818	Conway, △4,865	E	4
03818	Conway, 1,489	E	4
03753	Croydon, △396	C	5
† 03598	Dalton, △425	D	3
03230	Danbury, △489	D	4
03819	Danville, △924	E	6
03037	Deerfield, △1,178	D	5
† 03244	Deering, △578	D	5
03038	Derry, △11,712	E	6
03038	Derry, 6,090	E	6

† 03266	Dorchester, △141	D	4
03820	Dover⊙, 20,850	F	5
03444	Dublin, △837	C	6
03588	Dummer, △225	E	2
† 03301	Dunbarton, △825	D	5
03824	Durham, △8,869	F	5
03824	Durham, 7,221	F	5
03231	East Andover, 450	D	5
03041	East Derry, 600	E	6
03827	East Kingston, △838	F	6
† 03580	Easton, △92	D	3
03446	East Swanzey, 500	C	6
† 03894	East Wolfeboro, 400	E	4
03832	Eaton, △221	E	4
† 03264	Ellsworth, △13	D	4
03748	Enfield, △2,345	C	4
03748	Enfield, 1,408	C	4
03042	Epping, △2,356	E	5
03042	Epping, 1,097	E	5
03234	Epsom, △1,469	E	5
03579	Errol, △199	E	2
03750	Etna, 550	C	4
03833	Exeter, △8,892	F	6
03833	Exeter⊙, 6,439	F	6
03835	Farmington, △3,588	E	5
03835	Farmington, 2,884	E	5
03447	Fitzwilliam, △1,362	C	6
03447	Fitzwilliam, 750	C	6
03043	Francestown, △525	D	6
03580	Franconia, △655	D	3
03235	Franklin, 7,292	D	5
03836	Freedom, △387	E	4

NEW HAMPSHIRE

AREA 9,304 sq. mi.
POPULATION 737,681 ('70); 920,610 ('80)
CAPITAL Concord
LARGEST CITY Manchester
HIGHEST POINT Mt. Washington 6,288 ft.
SETTLED IN 1623
ADMITTED TO UNION June 21, 1788
POPULAR NAME Granite State
STATE FLOWER Purple Lilac
STATE BIRD Purple Finch

VERMONT

AREA 9,609 sq. mi.
POPULATION 444,732 ('70); 511,456 ('80)
CAPITAL Montpelier
LARGEST CITY Burlington
HIGHEST POINT Mt. Mansfield 4,393 ft.
SETTLED IN 1764
ADMITTED TO UNION March 4, 1791
POPULAR NAME Green Mountain State
STATE FLOWER Red Clover
STATE BIRD Hermit Thrush

Topography

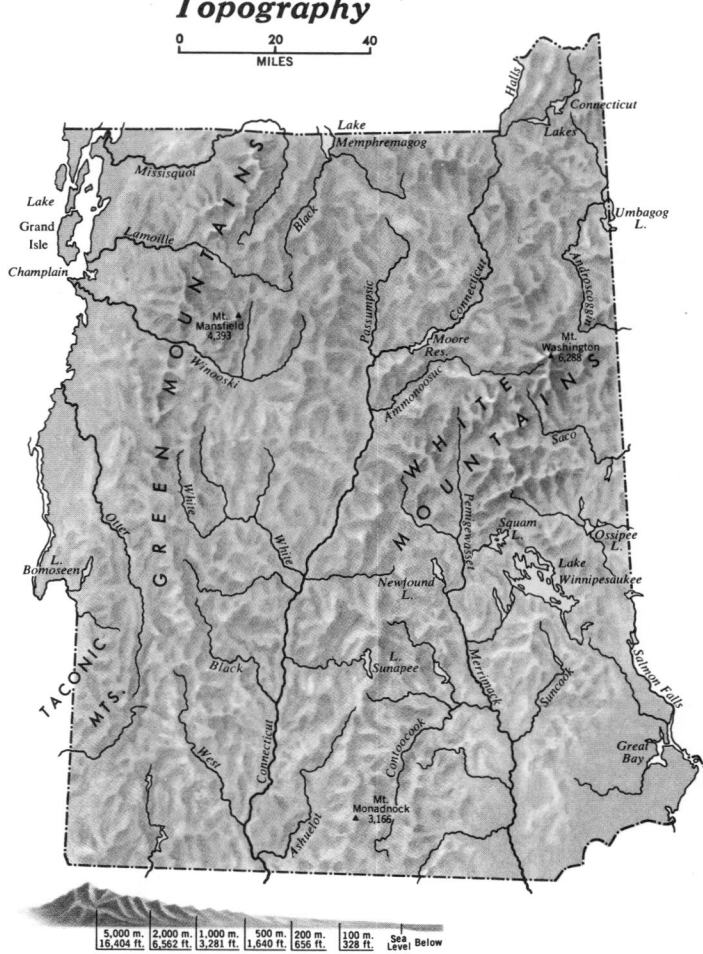

```
0        20        40
        MILES
```

5,000 m.	2,000 m.	1,000 m.	500 m.	200 m.	100 m.	Sea Level	Below
16,404 ft.	6,562 ft.	3,281 ft.	1,640 ft.	656 ft.	328 ft.		

Agriculture, Industry and Resources

DOMINANT LAND USE

- Specialized Dairy
- Dairy, General Farming
- Dairy, Poultry, Mixed Farming
- Forests

⚡ Water Power

▨ Major Industrial Areas

MANCHESTER •
Leather Goods, Textiles,
Electrical Products

MAJOR MINERAL OCCURRENCES

Ab	Asbestos		Mr	Marble
Be	Beryl		Sl	Slate
Gn	Granite		Tc	Talc
Mi	Mica		Th	Thorium

03044	Fremont, △993	E	6
† 03246	Gilford, △3,219	E	4
03237	Gilmanton, △1,010	E	5
03448	Gilsum, △570	C	5
03045	Goffstown, △9,284	D	5
03045	Goffstown, 2,272	D	5
03581	Gorham, △2,998	E	3
03581	Gorham, 2,020	E	3
03752	Goshen, △395	C	5
03239	Gossville, 800	E	5
03240	Grafton, △370	D	4
03753	Grantham, △366	D	5
03045	Grasmere, 513	D	5
03047	Greenfield, △1,058	D	6
03840	Greenland, △1,784	F	5
03048	Greenville, △1,587	D	6
03048	Greenville, 1,332	D	6
† 03241	Groton, △120	D	4
03582	Groveton, 1,597	D	2
03841	Hampstead, △2,401	E	6
03841	Hampstead, 500	E	6
03842	Hampton, △8,011	F	6
03842	Hampton, 5,407	F	6
03842	Hampton Beach, 975	F	6
03844	Hampton Falls, △1,254	F	6
03449	Hancock, △909	C	6
03755	Hanover, △8,494	C	4
03755	Hanover, 6,147	C	4
03450	Harrisville, △584	C	6
03765	Haverhill, △3,090	C	3
03765	Haverhill, 400	C	3
03241	Hebron, △234	D	4
03242	Henniker, △2,348	D	5
03242	Henniker, 950	D	5
03243	Hill, △450	D	4
03244	Hillsboro, △2,775	D	5
03244	Hillsboro, 1,784	D	5
03451	Hinsdale, △3,276	C	6
03451	Hinsdale, 1,059	C	6
03245	Holderness, △1,048	D	4
03049	Hollis, △2,616	D	6
03049	Hollis, 500	D	6
03106	Hooksett, △5,564	E	5
03106	Hooksett, 1,303	E	5

03301	Hopkinton, △3,007	D	5
03301	Hopkinton, 500	D	5
03051	Hudson, △10,638	E	6
03051	Hudson, 4,900	E	6
03845	Intervale, 500	E	3
03846	Jackson, △404	E	3
03452	Jaffrey, △3,353	C	6
03452	Jaffrey, 1,922	C	6
03583	Jefferson, △714	D	3
03431	Keene⊙, 20,467	C	6
03848	Kingston, △2,882	E	6
03246	Laconia⊙, 14,888	E	4
03584	Lancaster, △3,166	D	3
03584	Lancaster⊙, 2,120	D	3
† 03585	Landaff, △292	D	3
03602	Langdon, △337	C	5
03766	Lebanon, 9,725	C	4
† 03857	Lee, △1,481	F	5
03606	Lempster, △360	C	5
03251	Lincoln, △1,341	D	3
03251	Lincoln, 900	D	3
03585	Lisbon, △1,480	D	3
03585	Lisbon, 1,247	D	3
† 03051	Litchfield, △1,420	E	6
03561	Littleton, △5,290	D	3
03561	Littleton, 4,180	D	3
03252	Lochmere, 500	D	5
03053	Londonderry, △5,346	E	6
03301	Loudon, △1,707	E	5
† 03585	Lyman, △213	D	3
03768	Lyme, △1,112	C	4
03768	Lyme, 400	C	4
† 03082	Lyndeboro, △789	D	6
03820	Madbury, △704	F	5
03849	Madison, △572	E	4
* 03101	Manchester, 87,754	E	6
	Manchester, ‡108,461	E	6
03455	Marlborough, △1,671	C	6
03455	Marlborough, 1,231	C	6
03456	Marlow, △390	C	5
03253	Meredith, △2,904	D	4
03253	Meredith, 1,017	D	4
03770	Meriden, 495	C	4
03054	Merrimack, △8,595	D	6

03054	Merrimack, 850	D	6
† 03887	Middleton, △430	E	5
03588	Milan, △713	E	2
03055	Milford, △6,622	D	6
03055	Milford, 4,997	D	6
03851	Milton, △1,859	F	5
03851	Milton, 750	F	5
03771	Monroe, △385	C	3
03057	Mont Vernon, △906	D	6
03254	Moultonboro, △1,310	E	4
03060	Nashua⊙, 55,820	D	6
† 03457	Nelson, △304	C	5
03070	New Boston, △1,390	D	6
03070	New Boston, 450	D	6
03255	Newbury, △509	C	5
03854	New Castle, △975	F	5
03855	New Durham, △583	E	5
03856	Newfields, △843	F	5
03256	New Hampton, △946	D	4
† 03801	Newington, △798	F	5
03071	New Ipswich, △1,803	D	6
03257	New London, △2,236	D	5
03257	New London, 1,347	D	5
03857	Newmarket, △3,361	F	5
03857	Newmarket, 2,645	F	5
03773	Newport, △5,899	C	5
03773	Newport⊙, 3,296	C	5
03858	Newton, △1,920	E	6
03858	Newton, 483	E	6
03859	Newton Junction, 500	E	6
03258	North Chichester, 450	E	5
03860	North Conway, 1,723	E	3
† 03276	Northfield, △2,193	D	5
† 03276	Northfield-Tilton, 2,420	D	5
03862	North Hampton, △3,259	F	6
03862	North Hampton, 750	F	6
03774	North Haverhill, 750	D	3
03590	North Stratford, 650	D	2
03073	North Salem, 950	E	6
† 03773	North Newport, 500	C	5
† 03281	North Weare, 600	D	5
† 03582	Northumberland, △2,493	D	2
03608	North Walpole, 950	C	5
† 03281	North Weare, 600	D	5
03261	Northwood, △1,526	E	5

(continued on following page)

(continued)

NEW HAMPSHIRE (continued)

	Zip	Name/Pop.	Key
	03262	North Woodstock, 650	D 3
	03290	Nottingham, Δ952	E 5
†	03741	Orange, Δ103	D 4
	03777	Orford, Δ793	C 4
	03864	Ossipee⊙, Δ1,647	E 4
	03076	Pelham, Δ5,408	E 6
†	03275	Pembroke, Δ4,261	E 5
	03458	Peterborough, Δ3,807	D 6
	03458	Peterborough, 2,078	D 6
	03779	Piermont, Δ462	C 4
	03592	Pittsburg, Δ726	E 1
	03263	Pittsfield, Δ2,517	E 5
	03263	Pittsfield, 1,662	E 5
	03781	Plainfield, Δ1,323	C 4
	03865	Plaistow, Δ4,712	E 6
	03865	Plaistow, 950	E 6
	03264	Plymouth, Δ4,225	D 4
	03264	Plymouth, 3,109	D 4
	03801	Portsmouth, 25,717	F 5
	03593	Randolph, Δ169	E 3
	03077	Raymond, Δ3,003	E 5
†	03470	Richmond, Δ287	C 6
	03461	Rindge, Δ2,175	C 6
	03867	Rochester, 17,938	E 5
†	03431	Roxbury, Δ161	C 6
	03266	Rumney, Δ870	D 4
	03870	Rye, Δ4,083	F 5
	03870	Rye, 750	F 5
	03871	Rye Beach, 750	F 6
†	03870	Rye North Beach, 700	F 5
	03079	Salem, Δ20,142	E 6
	03079	Salem, 950	E 6
†	03079	Salem Depot, 975	E 6
	03268	Salisbury, Δ589	D 5
†	03820	Salmon Falls, 950	F 5
	03269	Sanbornton, Δ1,022	D 5
	03872	Sanbornville, 550	F 4
	03873	Sandown, Δ741	E 6
	03270	Sandwich, Δ666	E 4
	03874	Seabrook, Δ3,053	F 6
	03874	Seabrook, 950	F 6
†	03458	Sharon, Δ136	D 6
†	03581	Shelburne, Δ199	E 3
	03878	Somersworth, 9,026	F 5
†	03037	South Deerfield, 500	E 5
†	01913	South Hampton, Δ558	F 6
	03083	South Merrimack, 650	D 6
†	03874	South Seabrook, 500	F 6
	03462	Spofford, 631	C 6
†	03284	Springfield, Δ310	C 4
†	03582	Stark, Δ343	E 2
†	03576	Stewartstown, Δ1,008	E 2
	03464	Stoddard, Δ242	C 5
	03884	Strafford, Δ965	E 5
†	03590	Stratford, Δ980	D 2
	03885	Stratham, Δ1,512	F 5
	03585	Sugar Hill, Δ336	D 3
†	03445	Sullivan, Δ376	C 5
	03782	Sunapee, Δ1,384	C 5
	03782	Sunapee, 750	C 5
	03275	Suncook, 4,280	D 5
	03431	Surry, Δ507	C 5
†	03260	Sutton, Δ642	D 5
†	03431	Swanzey, Δ4,254	C 6
†	03431	Swanzey, 950	C 6
	03886	Tamworth, Δ1,054	E 4
	03084	Temple, Δ441	D 6
†	03285	Thornton, Δ594	D 4
	03276	Tilton, Δ2,579	D 5
	03276	Tilton-Northfield, 2,420	D 5
	03465	Troy, Δ1,713	C 6
†	03816	Tuftonboro, Δ910	E 4
†	03743	Unity, Δ709	C 5
	03888	Wakefield, Δ1,420	F 4
	03608	Walpole, Δ2,966	C 5
	03608	Walpole, 900	C 5
	03278	Warner, Δ1,441	D 5
	03278	Warner, 600	D 5
	03279	Warren, Δ539	D 4
	03280	Washington, Δ248	C 5
	03223	Waterville Valley, Δ109	D 4
	03281	Weare, Δ1,851	D 5
	03281	Weare P.O. (North Weare), 600	D 5
†	03301	Webster, Δ680	D 5
	03282	Wentworth, Δ376	D 4
†	03579	Wentworths Location, Δ37	E 2
†	03038	West Derry (Derry), 6,090	E 6
	03784	West Lebanon, 4,200	C 4
	03467	Westmoreland, Δ998	C 6
	03597	West Stewartstown, 600	E 2
	03469	West Swanzey, 950	C 6
	03892	Westville, 500	E 6
	03598	Whitefield, Δ1,538	D 3
	03598	Whitefield, 1,093	D 3
†	03287	Wilmot, Δ516	D 5
	03086	Wilton, Δ2,276	D 6
	03086	Wilton, 1,161	D 6
	03470	Winchester, Δ2,869	C 6
	03470	Winchester, 938	C 6
	03087	Windham, Δ3,008	E 6
	03289	Winnisquam, 500	E 5
	03894	Wolfeboro, Δ3,036	E 4
	03894	Wolfeboro, 1,718	E 4
	03896	Wolfeboro Falls, 650	E 4
	03293	Woodstock, Δ897	D 4
	03785	Woodsville⊙, 1,336	C 3

VERMONT

COUNTIES

County	Key
Addison, 24,266	A 3
Bennington, 29,282	A 6
Caledonia, 22,789	C 2
Chittenden, 99,131	A 3
Essex, 5,416	D 2
Franklin, 31,282	B 2
Grand Isle, 3,574	A 2
Lamoille, 13,309	B 2
Orange, 17,676	C 3
Orleans, 20,153	C 2
Rutland, 52,637	A 4
Washington, 47,659	B 3
Windham, 33,074	B 5
Windsor, 44,082	B 4

CITIES and TOWNS

	Zip	Name/Pop.	Key
†	05491	Addison, Δ717	A 3
	05820	Albany, Δ528	C 2
	05440	Alburg, Δ1,271	A 2
	05440	Alburg, 520	A 2
†	05143	Andover, Δ239	B 5
	05250	Arlington, Δ1,934	A 5
	05250	Arlington, 1,212	A 5
	05030	Ascutney, 500	C 5
	05901	Averill, Δ8	D 2
	05441	Bakersfield, Δ635	B 2
	05031	Barnard, Δ569	B 4
	05821	Barnet, Δ1,342	C 3
	05641	Barre, 10,209	C 3
	05641	Barre, Δ6,509	C 3
	05822	Barton, Δ2,874	C 2
	05822	Barton, 1,051	C 2
	05902	Beecher Falls, 640	D 2
	05101	Bellows Falls, 3,505	C 5
	05442	Belvidere, Δ189	B 2
	05201	Bennington, Δ14,586	A 6
	05201	Bennington⊙, 7,950	A 6
	05731	Benson, Δ583	A 4
†	05476	Berkshire, Δ931	B 2
	05032	Bethel, Δ1,347	B 4
†	03590	Bloomfield, Δ196	D 2
†	05466	Bolton, Δ427	B 3
	05732	Bomoseen, 500	A 4
	05033	Bradford, Δ1,627	C 3
	05033	Bradford, 709	C 3
	05646	Braintree, Δ751	B 4
	05733	Brandon, Δ3,697	A 4
	05733	Brandon, 1,720	A 4
	05301	Brattleboro, Δ12,239	B 6
	05301	Brattleboro, 9,055	B 6
	05034	Bridgewater, Δ783	B 4
	05734	Bridport, Δ809	A 4
	05443	Bristol, Δ2,744	A 3
	05443	Bristol, 1,737	A 3
	05036	Brookfield, Δ606	B 3
†	05345	Brookline, Δ180	B 5
†	05860	Brownington, Δ522	C 2
†	05871	Burke, Δ1,053	D 2
	05401	Burlington⊙, 38,633	A 3
	05647	Cabot, Δ663	C 3
	05648	Calais, Δ749	B 3
	05444	Cambridge, Δ1,528	B 2
	05903	Canaan, Δ949	D 2
	05735	Castleton, Δ2,837	A 4
	05735	Castleton, 450	A 4
	05142	Cavendish, Δ1,264	B 5
	05736	Center Rutland, 500	A 4
	05445	Charlotte, Δ1,802	A 3
	05038	Chelsea⊙, Δ983	C 4
	05038	Chelsea, 525	C 4
	05143	Chester, Δ2,371	B 5
	05143	Chester, 950	B 5
	05144	Chester Depot, 500	B 5
	05737	Chittenden, Δ646	B 4
	05737	Chittenden, 525	B 4
†	05759	Clarendon, Δ1,537	A 4
	05446	Colchester, Δ8,776	A 2
	05824	Concord, Δ896	D 3
	05039	Corinth, Δ683	C 3
†	05753	Cornwall, Δ900	A 4
	05825	Coventry, Δ492	C 2
	05826	Craftsbury, Δ632	C 2
	05739	Danby, Δ910	A 5
	05828	Danville, Δ1,405	C 3
	05828	Danville, 450	C 3
	05829	Derby, Δ3,252	C 2
	05829	Derby (Derby Center), 547	C 2
	05830	Derby Line, 834	C 2
	05251	Dorset, Δ1,293	A 5
	05251	Dorset, 450	A 5
†	05676	Duxbury, Δ621	B 3
	05252	East Arlington, 500	A 5
	05649	East Barre, 950	C 3
	05448	East Fairfield, 700	B 2
	05837	East Haven, Δ197	D 2
	05740	East Middlebury, 500	A 4
	05651	East Montpelier, Δ1,597	B 3
	05651	East Montpelier, 550	B 3
	05652	Eden, Δ513	B 2
	05450	Enosburg Falls, 1,266	B 2
	05451	Essex, Δ10,951	A 2
	05451	Essex, 850	A 2
	05452	Essex Junction, 6,511	A 3
	05454	Fairfax, Δ1,366	B 2
	05455	Fairfield, Δ1,285	B 2
	05743	Fair Haven, Δ2,777	A 4
	05743	Fair Haven, 2,287	A 4
	05045	Fairlee, Δ604	C 4
	05045	Fairlee, 425	C 4
	05456	Ferrisburg, Δ1,875	A 3
†	05444	Fletcher, Δ456	B 2
	05745	Forest Dale, 500	A 4
	05457	Franklin, Δ821	B 2
†	05478	Georgia, Δ1,711	A 2
	05904	Gilman, 700	D 3
	05839	Glover, Δ649	C 2
	05146	Grafton, Δ465	B 5
	05840	Granby, Δ52	D 2
	05458	Grand Isle, Δ809	A 2
	05654	Graniteville, 1,120	C 3
	05747	Granville, Δ255	B 4
	05841	Greensboro, Δ593	C 2
	05046	Groton, Δ666	C 3
	05046	Groton, 438	C 3
	05905	Guildhall⊙, Δ169	D 2
†	05301	Guilford, Δ1,108	B 6
†	05358	Halifax, Δ295	B 6
	05748	Hancock, Δ283	B 4
	05843	Hardwick, Δ2,466	C 2
	05843	Hardwick, 1,503	C 2
	05047	Hartford, Δ6,477	C 4
	05047	Hartford, 650	C 4
	05047	Hartland, Δ1,806	C 4
†	05459	Highgate, Δ1,936	B 2
	05459	Highgate Center, 927	B 2
	05461	Hinesburg, Δ1,775	A 3
†	05830	Holland, Δ383	D 2
	05749	Hubbardton, Δ228	A 4
	05462	Huntington, Δ748	B 3
	05655	Hyde Park, Δ1,347	B 2
	05655	Hyde Park⊙, 418	B 2
	05750	Hydeville, 450	A 4
†	05777	Ira, Δ284	A 4
	05845	Irasburg, Δ775	C 2
	05846	Island Pond, 1,123	D 2
	05463	Isle La Motte, Δ262	A 2
	05343	Jamaica, Δ590	B 5
†	05859	Jay, Δ182	C 2
	05465	Jericho, Δ2,343	B 3
	05465	Jericho, 450	A 2
	05656	Johnson, Δ1,927	B 2
	05656	Johnson, 1,296	B 2
†	05752	Leicester, Δ583	A 4
†	03576	Lemington, Δ120	D 2
†	05443	Lincoln, Δ599	B 3
	05148	Londonderry, Δ1,037	B 5
	05847	Lowell, Δ515	C 2
	05149	Ludlow, Δ2,463	B 5
	05149	Ludlow, 1,508	B 5
	05906	Lunenburg, Δ1,061	D 3
	05849	Lyndon, Δ3,705	C 2
	05851	Lyndonville, 1,415	D 2
†	05905	Maidstone, Δ94	D 2
	05254	Manchester, Δ2,919	A 5
	05254	Manchester⊙, 435	A 5
	05255	Manchester Center, 900	A 5
	05256	Manchester Depot, 1,560	B 5
	05344	Marlboro, Δ592	B 6
	05658	Marshfield, Δ1,033	C 3
†	05701	Mendon, Δ743	B 4
	05753	Middlebury, Δ6,532	A 3
	05753	Middlebury⊙, 4,500	A 3
†	05602	Middlesex, Δ857	B 3
	05757	Middletown Springs, Δ426	A 5
	05468	Milton, Δ4,495	A 2
	05468	Milton, 1,164	A 2
	05469	Monkton, Δ765	A 3
	05470	Montgomery, Δ651	B 2
	05602	Montpelier (cap.)⊙, 8,609	B 3
	05660	Moretown, Δ904	B 3
	05853	Morgan, Δ286	D 2
†	05661	Morristown, Δ4,052	B 2
	05661	Morrisville, 2,116	B 2
	05758	Mount Holly, Δ687	B 5
†	05739	Mount Tabor, Δ184	B 5
†	05871	Newark, Δ144	D 2
	05051	Newbury, Δ1,440	C 3
	05051	Newbury, 450	C 3
	05345	Newfane, Δ900	B 6
	05345	Newfane⊙, 183	B 6
	05472	New Haven, Δ1,039	A 3
	05855	Newport, Δ1,125	C 2
	05855	Newport⊙, 4,664	C 2
	05257	North Bennington, 984	A 6
	05759	North Clarendon, 750	B 4
	05663	Northfield, Δ4,870	B 3
	05663	Northfield, 2,139	B 3
	05664	Northfield Falls, 700	B 3
	05474	North Hero⊙, Δ364	A 2
	05260	North Pownal, 600	A 6
	05150	North Springfield, 1,100	B 5
	05859	North Troy, 774	C 2
	05907	Norton, Δ207	D 2
	05055	Norwich, Δ1,966	C 4
	05055	Norwich, 500	C 4
†	05649	Orange, Δ540	C 3
	05860	Orleans, 1,138	C 2
	05760	Orwell, Δ851	A 4
†	05491	Panton, Δ416	A 3
	05761	Pawlet, Δ1,184	A 5
	05862	Peacham, Δ446	C 3
	05152	Peru, Δ243	B 5
	05762	Pittsfield, Δ249	B 4
	05763	Pittsford, Δ2,306	A 4
	05763	Pittsford, 682	A 4
	05667	Plainfield, Δ1,399	C 3
	05667	Plainfield, 949	C 3
	05056	Plymouth, Δ283	B 4
†	05067	Pomfret, Δ620	B 4
	05764	Poultney, Δ3,217	A 4
	05764	Poultney, 1,914	A 4
	05261	Pownal, Δ2,441	A 6
	05261	Pownal, 700	A 6
	05765	Proctor, Δ2,095	A 4
	05765	Proctor, 1,950	A 4
	05153	Proctorsville, 512	B 5
	05346	Putney, Δ1,727	B 6
	05346	Putney, 1,115	B 6
	05059	Quechee, 420	C 4
	05060	Randolph, Δ3,882	B 4
	05060	Randolph, 2,115	B 4
	05062	Reading, Δ564	B 5
	05350	Readsboro, Δ638	B 6
	05350	Readsboro, 469	B 6
	05476	Richford, Δ2,116	B 2
	05476	Richford, 1,527	B 2
	05477	Richmond, Δ2,249	A 3
	05477	Richmond, 935	A 3
	05766	Ripton, Δ187	A 4
	05767	Rochester, Δ884	B 4
†	05101	Rockingham, Δ5,501	C 5
	05669	Roxbury, Δ354	B 3
	05063	Royalton, Δ1,399	B 4
	05768	Rupert, Δ582	A 5
	05701	Rutland, Δ2,248	B 4
	05701	Rutland⊙, 19,293	B 4
	05042	Ryegate, Δ830	C 3
	05478	Saint Albans, Δ3,270	A 2
	05478	Saint Albans⊙, 8,082	A 2
†	05401	Saint George, Δ477	A 2
	05819	Saint Johnsbury, Δ8,409	D 3
	05819	Saint Johnsbury⊙, 7,000	D 3
	05769	Salisbury, Δ649	A 4
†	05250	Sandgate, Δ127	A 5
	05154	Saxtons River, 581	B 5
†	05363	Searsburg, Δ84	A 6
	05262	Shaftsbury, Δ2,411	A 6
	05065	Sharon, Δ541	C 4
	05866	Sheffield, Δ307	C 2
	05482	Shelburne, Δ3,728	A 3
	05482	Shelburne, 2,591	A 3
	05483	Sheldon, Δ1,481	B 2
	05770	Shoreham, Δ790	A 4
†	05738	Shrewsbury, Δ570	B 4
	05670	South Barre, 865	B 3
	05401	South Burlington, Δ10,032	A 3
	05486	South Hero, Δ868	A 2
	05155	South Londonderry, 600	B 5
	05068	South Royalton, 625	C 4
	05156	Springfield, Δ10,063	B 5
	05156	Springfield, 5,632	B 5
†	01247	Stamford, Δ752	A 6
	05487	Starksboro, Δ668	A 3
	05772	Stockbridge, Δ389	B 4
	05672	Stowe, Δ2,388	B 3
	05672	Stowe, 435	B 3
	05072	Strafford, Δ536	C 4
†	05360	Stratton, Δ104	B 5
†	05733	Sudbury, Δ253	A 4
†	05250	Sunderland, Δ601	A 5
	05867	Sutton, Δ438	C 2
	05488	Swanton, Δ4,622	A 2
	05488	Swanton, 2,630	A 2
	05074	Thetford, Δ1,422	C 4
†	05773	Tinmouth, Δ268	A 5
	05076	Topsham, Δ686	C 3
	05353	Townshend, Δ668	B 5
	05868	Troy, Δ1,457	C 2
	05077	Tunbridge, Δ791	C 4
	05489	Underhill, Δ1,198	B 2
	05491	Vergennes, 2,242	A 3
	05354	Vernon, Δ1,024	B 6
	05079	Vershire, Δ299	C 4
	05673	Waitsfield, Δ837	B 3
†	05873	Walden, Δ442	C 3
	05773	Wallingford, Δ1,676	B 5
	05773	Wallingford, 815	B 5
†	05491	Waltham, Δ265	A 3
	05355	Wardsboro, Δ391	B 5
	05674	Warren, Δ588	B 3
	05675	Washington, Δ667	C 3
	05676	Waterbury, Δ4,614	B 3
	05676	Waterbury, 2,840	B 3
	05677	Waterbury Center, 900	B 3
	05492	Waterville, Δ397	B 2
	05678	Websterville, 700	B 3
	05774	Wells, Δ560	A 5
	05081	Wells River, 419	C 3
	05301	West Brattleboro, 2,200	B 6
	05083	West Fairlee, Δ337	C 4
	05874	Westfield, Δ375	C 2
	05494	Westford, Δ991	A 2
†	05743	West Haven, Δ240	A 4
	05158	Westminster, Δ1,875	C 5
†	05860	Westmore, Δ195	C 2
	05161	Weston, Δ507	B 5
	05161	Weston, 450	B 5
	05777	West Rutland, Δ2,381	A 4
	05777	West Rutland, 1,875	A 4
†	05753	Weybridge, Δ618	A 3
†	05851	Wheelock, Δ238	C 2
	05001	White River Junction, 2,379	C 4
	05778	Whiting, Δ359	A 4
	05361	Whitingham, Δ1,011	B 6
	05088	Wilder, 1,328	C 4
	05679	Williamstown, Δ1,822	B 3
	05679	Williamstown, 650	B 3
	05495	Williston, Δ3,187	A 3
	05363	Wilmington, Δ1,184	B 6
	05363	Wilmington, 544	B 6
†	05359	Windham, Δ174	B 5
	05089	Windsor, Δ4,158	C 5
	05089	Windsor, 3,400	C 5
	05404	Winooski, 7,309	A 3
	05680	Wolcott, Δ676	C 2
†	05681	Woodbury, Δ399	C 3
†	05201	Woodford, Δ286	A 6
	05091	Woodstock, Δ2,608	B 4
	05091	Woodstock⊙, 1,154	B 4
	05682	Worcester, Δ505	B 3

⊙ County seat.
Δ Population of town or township.
‡ Population of metropolitan area.
† Zip of nearest p.o.
* Multiple zips

Edmund V. Ballman

Designed to protect wooden structures from the ravages of weather, a few early covered bridges are still standing in New Hampshire. This barn-red relic is in Jackson.

Elizabeth L. Schultz

Located in the heart of Vermont, Barre rightfully boasts of its granite quarries which provide a sculptured panorama set off by surrounding green hills.

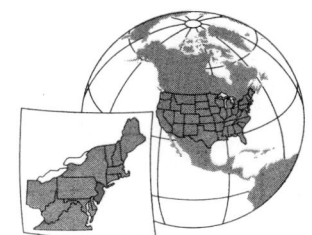

COUNTIES

CITIES and TOWNS

AREA, POPULATION

AREA 7,836 sq. mi.
POPULATION 7,168,164 ('70); 7,364,158 ('80)
CAPITAL Trenton
LARGEST CITY Newark
HIGHEST POINT High Point 1,803 ft.
SETTLED IN 1617
ADMITTED TO UNION December 18, 1787
POPULAR NAME Garden State
STATE FLOWER Violet
STATE BIRD Eastern Goldfinch

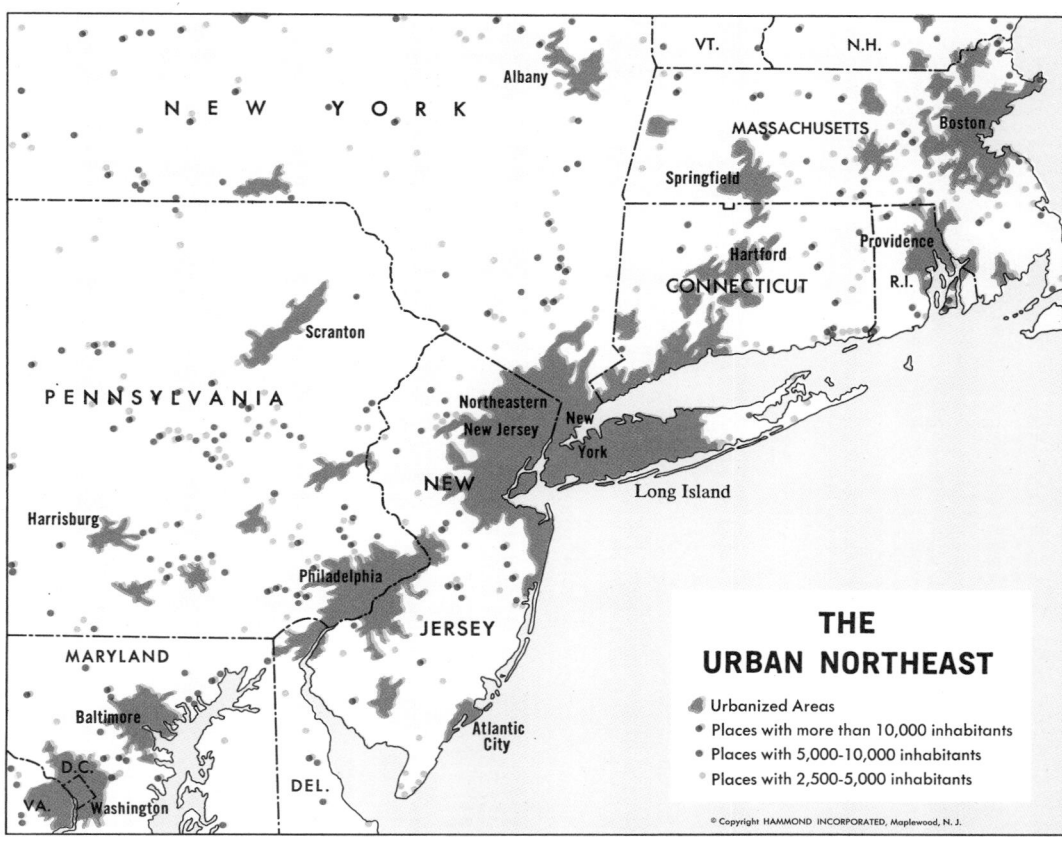

THE URBAN NORTHEAST

- Urbanized Areas
- Places with more than 10,000 inhabitants
- Places with 5,000-10,000 inhabitants
- Places with 2,500-5,000 inhabitants

© Copyright HAMMOND INCORPORATED, Maplewood, N. J.

Agriculture, Industry and Resources

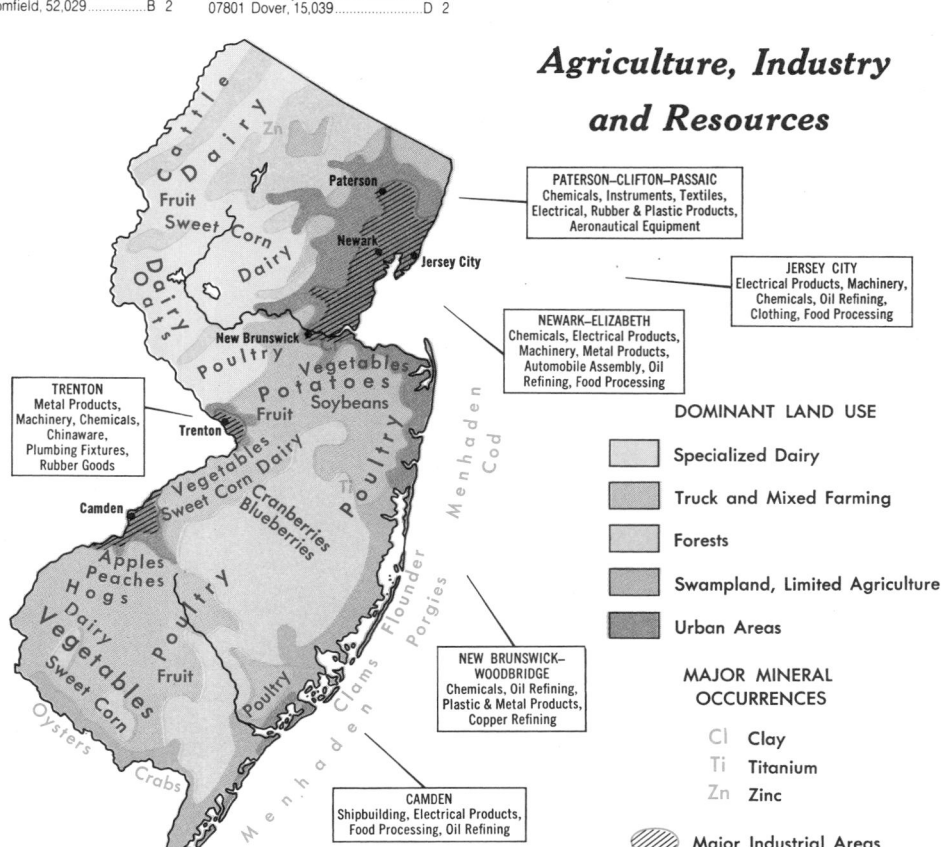

PATERSON–CLIFTON–PASSAIC
Chemicals, Instruments, Textiles, Electrical, Rubber & Plastic Products, Aeronautical Equipment

JERSEY CITY
Electrical Products, Machinery, Chemicals, Oil Refining, Clothing, Food Processing

NEWARK–ELIZABETH
Chemicals, Electrical Products, Machinery, Metal Products, Automobile Assembly, Oil Refining, Food Processing

TRENTON
Metal Products, Machinery, Chemicals, Chinaware, Plumbing Fixtures, Rubber Goods

NEW BRUNSWICK–WOODBRIDGE
Chemicals, Oil Refining, Plastic & Metal Products, Copper Refining

CAMDEN
Shipbuilding, Electrical Products, Food Processing, Oil Refining

DOMINANT LAND USE

- Specialized Dairy
- Truck and Mixed Farming
- Forests
- Swampland, Limited Agriculture
- Urban Areas

MAJOR MINERAL OCCURRENCES

- Cl Clay
- Ti Titanium
- Zn Zinc

- Major Industrial Areas

(continued on following page)

(continued)

08732 Island Heights, 1,397 .... E 4
08527 Jackson, ▵18,276 .... E 3
08831 Jamesburg, 4,584 .... E 3
* 07301 Jersey City⊙, 260,545 .... B 2
Jersey City, ‡609,266 .... B 2
07734 Keansburg, 9,720 .... E 3
07032 Kearny, 37,585 .... B 2
08832 Keasbey, 1,200 .... E 2
08824 Kendall Park, 7,412 .... D 3
07033 Kenilworth, 9,165 .... E 2
07735 Keyport, 7,205 .... E 3
08528 Kingston, 1,200 .... D 3
07405 Kinnelon, 7,600 .... E 2
08043 Kirkwood, 800 .... B 4
07848 Lafayette, 900 .... D 1
07034 Lake Hiawatha, 11,389 .... E 2
07849 Lake Hopatcong, 1,941 .... D 2
08733 Lakehurst, 2,641 .... E 3
† 07871 Lake Mohawk, 6,262 .... D 1
08701 Lakewood, 17,874 .... E 3
08530 Lambertville, 4,359 .... D 3
07850 Landing, 2,370 .... D 2
08734 Lanoka Harbor, 1,066 .... E 4
08021 Laurel Springs, 2,566 .... B 4
08879 Laurence Harbor, 6,715 .... E 3
08735 Lavallette, 1,509 .... E 4
08045 Lawnside, 2,757 .... B 3
08648 Lawrenceville, 1,464 .... D 3
08833 Lebanon, 885 .... D 2
07852 Ledgewood, 2,800 .... D 2
08327 Leesburg, 800 .... D 5
07737 Leonardo, 4,000 .... E 3
07605 Leonia, 8,847 .... C 2
07938 Liberty Corner, 1,900 .... D 2
07035 Lincoln Park, 9,034 .... A 1
07738 Lincroft, 4,900 .... E 3
07036 Linden, 41,409 .... A 3
08021 Lindenwold, 12,199 .... B 4
08221 Linwood, 6,159 .... D 5
07424 Little Falls, ▵11,727 .... B 2
07643 Little Ferry, 9,042 .... B 2
07739 Little Silver, 6,010 .... F 3
07039 Livingston, ▵30,127 .... E 2
07644 Lodi, 25,213 .... B 2
08008 Long Branch, 31,774 .... F 3
08403 Longport, 1,225 .... D 5
07853 Long Valley, 1,645 .... D 2
08048 Lumberton, 600 .... D 4
07071 Lyndhurst, ▵22,729 .... B 2
07939 Lyons, 3,900 .... D 2
07940 Madison, 16,710 .... E 2
08049 Magnolia, 5,893 .... B 3
07430 Mahwah, ▵10,539 .... E 1
08328 Malaga, 950 .... C 4
08050 Manahawkin, 1,278 .... E 4
08736 Manasquan, 4,971 .... E 3
08051 Mantua, 5,530 .... C 4
08835 Manville, 13,029 .... D 2
08052 Maple Shade, ▵16,464 .... B 3
07040 Maplewood, ▵24,932 .... E 2
† 07866 Marcella, 540 .... E 2
08402 Margate City, 10,576 .... E 5
07746 Marlboro, 2,380 .... E 3
08053 Marlton, 10,180 .... D 4
08223 Marmora, 650 .... D 5
08836 Martinsville, 3,500 .... D 2
08054 Masonville, 900 .... D 4
07747 Matawan, 9,136 .... E 3
08330 Mays Landing⊙, 1,272 .... D 5
07607 Maywood, 11,087 .... B 2
07428 McAfee, 800 .... D 1
† 08232 McKee City, 950 .... D 5
08055 Medford, 1,448 .... D 4
08055 Medford Lakes, 4,792 .... D 4
07945 Mendham, 3,729 .... D 2
08817 Menlo Park, 10,000 .... E 2
08619 Mercerville, 5,456 .... D 3
08109 Merchantville, 4,425 .... B 3
08840 Metuchen, 16,031 .... E 2
08056 Mickleton, 950 .... C 4
08846 Middlesex, 15,038 .... E 2
07748 Middletown, ▵54,623 .... E 3
07432 Midland Park, 8,159 .... B 1
08848 Milford, 1,230 .... C 2
07041 Millburn, ▵21,307 .... E 2
07946 Millington, 975 .... D 2
08849 Millstone, 630 .... D 2
08850 Milltown, 6,470 .... E 3
08332 Millville, 21,366 .... C 5
07438 Milton, 2,220 .... D 1
† 07801 Mine Hill, ▵3,557 .... D 2
08342 Mizpah, 900 .... D 5
07750 Monmouth Beach, 2,042 .... F 3
08852 Monmouth Junction, 1,900 .... D 3
07434 Monroe, ▵9,138 .... E 3
† 12771 Montague, 750 .... D 1
* 07042 Montclair, 44,043 .... B 2
07645 Montvale, 7,327 .... B 1
07045 Montville, 4,900 .... E 2
07074 Moonachie, 2,937 .... B 2
08057 Moorestown, 14,179 .... B 3
07950 Morris Plains, 5,540 .... D 2
07960 Morristown⊙, 17,662 .... D 2
07046 Mountain Lakes, 4,739 .... E 2
07092 Mountainside, 7,520 .... E 2
† 07470 Mountain View, 9,000 .... B 2
07856 Mount Arlington, 3,590 .... D 2
08059 Mount Ephraim, 5,625 .... B 3
07970 Mount Freedom, 1,621 .... D 2
08060 Mount Holly⊙, ▵12,713 .... D 4
† 07885 Mount Hope, 1,510 .... D 2
08061 Mount Royal, 850 .... C 4
08062 Mullica Hill, 800 .... C 4
† 08087 Mystic Islands, 900 .... E 4
08063 National Park, 3,730 .... B 3
07752 Navesink, 2,400 .... E 3
07753 Neptune, ▵27,863 .... E 3
07753 Neptune City, 5,502 .... E 3
† 08853 Neshanic, 752 .... D 3
07857 Netcong, 2,858 .... D 2
* 07101 Newark⊙, 382,417 .... B 2
Newark, ‡2,056,556 .... B 2
* 08901 New Brunswick⊙, 41,885 .... E 3
08533 New Egypt, 1,769 .... E 3
08344 Newfield, 1,487 .... D 4
07435 Newfoundland, 900 .... D 1
08224 New Gretna, 700 .... E 4
07646 New Milford, 20,201 .... B 1
08345 Newport, 700 .... C 5
07974 New Providence, 13,796 .... E 2
07724 New Shrewsbury, 5,925 .... E 3
07860 Newton⊙, 7,297 .... D 1
08346 Newtonville, 750 .... D 4
07976 New Vernon, 1,900 .... D 2
08817 Nixon, 12,000 .... E 2
08347 Norma, 1,200 .... C 4
07032 North Arlington, 18,096 .... B 2
07047 North Bergen, ▵47,751 .... B 2
08876 North Branch, 610 .... D 2
08902 North Brunswick, ▵16,691 .... E 3
† 07006 North Caldwell, 6,425 .... B 2
08204 North Cape May, 3,812 .... C 6
08225 Northfield, 8,875 .... D 5
07508 North Haledon, 7,614 .... B 1
07060 North Plainfield, 21,796 .... E 2
07647 Northvale, 5,177 .... F 1
08260 North Wildwood, 3,914 .... D 6
07648 Norwood, 4,398 .... C 1
07110 Nutley, 32,099 .... B 2
07755 Oakhurst, 5,558 .... E 3
07436 Oakland, 14,420 .... B 1
08107 Oaklyn, 4,626 .... B 3
07438 Oak Ridge, 750 .... E 1
08226 Ocean City, 10,575 .... D 5
08740 Ocean Gate, 1,081 .... E 4
07756 Ocean Grove, 7,000 .... F 3
07757 Oceanport, 7,503 .... F 3
08230 Ocean View, 950 .... D 5
08231 Oceanville, 600 .... D 5
07439 Ogdensburg, 2,222 .... D 1
08857 Old Bridge, 25,176 .... E 3
07675 Old Tappan, 3,917 .... C 1
08858 Oldwick, 600 .... D 2
07649 Oradell, 8,903 .... B 1
* 07050 Orange, 32,566 .... B 2
08723 Osbornsville, 3,900 .... E 3
07863 Oxford, 1,411 .... C 2
07470 Packanack Lake, 4,000 .... B 1
† 08226 Palermo, 600 .... D 5
07650 Palisades Park, 13,351 .... C 2
08065 Palmyra, 6,969 .... B 3
07652 Paramus, 29,495 .... B 1
† 08087 Parkertown, 600 .... E 4
07656 Park Ridge, 8,709 .... B 1
07054 Parsippany, ▵55,112 .... E 2
* 07055 Passaic, 55,124 .... E 2
* 07501 Paterson⊙, 144,824 .... B 2
Paterson-Clifton-Passaic, ‡1,358,794 .... B 2
08066 Paulsboro, 8,084 .... C 4
07977 Peapack-Gladstone, 1,924 .... D 2
08067 Pedricktown, 1,500 .... C 4
08068 Pemberton, 1,344 .... D 4
08534 Pennington, 2,151 .... D 3
08110 Pennsauken, ▵36,394 .... B 3
08069 Penns Grove, 5,727 .... C 4
08070 Pennsville, 11,014 .... C 4
07440 Pequannock, 4,900 .... B 1
* 08861 Perth Amboy, 38,798 .... E 2
08865 Phillipsburg, 17,849 .... C 2
08741 Pine Beach, 1,395 .... E 4
07058 Pine Brook, 3,500 .... E 2
08021 Pine Hill, 5,132 .... D 4
08854 Piscataway, ▵36,418 .... D 2
08071 Pitman, 10,257 .... C 4
* 07060 Plainfield, 46,862 .... E 2
08536 Plainsboro, 1,200 .... D 3
08232 Pleasantville, 13,778 .... D 5
08742 Point Pleasant, 15,968 .... E 3
08742 Point Pleasant Beach, 4,882 .... E 3
08240 Pomona, 900 .... D 5
07442 Pompton Lakes, 11,397 .... A 1
07444 Pompton Plains, 9,500 .... B 1
07758 Port Monmouth, 4,556 .... E 3
† 07850 Port Morris, 950 .... D 2
07865 Port Murray, 800 .... D 2
08349 Port Norris, 1,955 .... C 5
07064 Port Reading, 4,900 .... E 2
08241 Port Republic, 586 .... D 4
08540 Princeton, 12,311 .... D 3
08550 Princeton Junction, 950 .... D 3
† 07885 Prospect Park, 5,176 .... B 1
08072 Quinton, 575 .... C 4
* 07065 Rahway, 29,114 .... E 2
† 07945 Ralston, 650 .... D 2
† 08057 Ramblewood, 5,556 .... D 4
07446 Ramsey, 12,571 .... B 1
08869 Raritan, 6,691 .... D 2
07701 Red Bank, 12,847 .... E 3
08350 Richland, 950 .... D 5
07657 Ridgefield, 11,308 .... B 2
07660 Ridgefield Park, 14,453 .... B 2
* 07450 Ridgewood, 27,547 .... B 1
08551 Ringoes, 682 .... D 3
07456 Ringwood, 10,393 .... E 1
08242 Rio Grande, 1,203 .... D 5
07457 Riverdale, 2,729 .... A 1
07661 River Edge, 12,850 .... B 1
08075 Riverside, ▵8,616 .... B 3
08077 Riverton, 3,412 .... B 3
08691 Robbinsville, 650 .... D 3
07662 Rochelle Park, ▵6,380 .... B 2
07866 Rockaway, ▵18,955 .... D 2
07866 Rockaway, 6,383 .... D 2
08553 Rocky Hill, 917 .... D 3
08554 Roebling-Florence, 7,551 .... D 3
08555 Roosevelt, 814 .... E 3
07068 Roseland, 4,453 .... A 2
07203 Roselle, 22,585 .... B 2
07204 Roselle Park, 14,277 .... A 2
08352 Rosenhayn, 950 .... C 5
† 07876 Roxbury, ▵15,754 .... D 2
07760 Rumson, 7,421 .... F 3
08078 Runnemede, 10,475 .... B 3
* 07070 Rutherford, 20,802 .... B 2
07662 Saddle Brook, ▵15,098 .... B 1
07458 Saddle River, 2,437 .... B 1
08079 Salem⊙, 7,648 .... C 4
08872 Sayreville, 32,508 .... E 3
07076 Scotch Plains, ▵22,279 .... E 2
07760 Sea Bright, 1,339 .... F 3
08302 Seabrook, 1,569 .... C 5
08750 Sea Girt, 2,207 .... E 3
08243 Sea Isle City, 1,712 .... D 5
08751 Seaside Heights, 1,248 .... E 4
08752 Seaside Park, 1,432 .... E 4
07094 Secaucus, 13,228 .... B 2
07077 Sewaren, 3,200 .... E 2
08080 Sewell, 2,210 .... C 4
08353 Shiloh, 573 .... C 5
08008 Ship Bottom, 1,079 .... E 4
07078 Short Hills, 14,000 .... E 2
07701 Shrewsbury, 3,315 .... E 3
08081 Sicklerville, 1,700 .... D 4
† 07424 Singac, 3,942 .... B 2
08558 Skillman, 1,955 .... D 3
† 07728 Smithburg, 750 .... E 3
08083 Somerdale, 6,510 .... B 4
08244 Somers Point, 7,919 .... D 5
08876 Somerville⊙, 13,652 .... D 2
08879 South Amboy, 9,338 .... E 3
† 07719 South Belmar, 1,490 .... E 3
08880 South Bound Brook, 4,525 .... E 2
† 08852 South Brunswick, ▵14,058 .... E 3
07079 South Orange, 16,971 .... A 2
07080 South Plainfield, 21,142 .... E 2
08882 South River, 15,428 .... E 3
08246 South Seaville, 600 .... D 5
08753 South Toms River, 3,981 .... E 4
07871 Sparta, 3,000 .... D 1
08884 Spotswood, 7,891 .... E 3
07081 Springfield, ▵15,740 .... E 2
07762 Spring Lake, 3,896 .... F 3
07762 Spring Lake Heights, 4,602 .... E 3
07874 Stanhope, 3,040 .... D 2
08885 Stanton, 700 .... D 2
08886 Stewartsville, 950 .... C 2
07980 Stirling, 1,450 .... E 2
07460 Stockholm, 1,477 .... D 1
08559 Stockton, 619 .... D 3
08247 Stone Harbor, 1,089 .... D 5
08084 Stratford, 9,801 .... B 4
† 07747 Strathmore, 7,674 .... E 3
07876 Succasunna, 5,000 .... D 2
07901 Summit, 23,620 .... E 2
08008 Surf City, 1,129 .... E 4
07461 Sussex, 2,038 .... D 1
08085 Swedesboro, 2,287 .... C 4
07878 Tabor, 1,500 .... E 2
07666 Teaneck, ▵42,355 .... B 2
07670 Tenafly, 14,827 .... C 1
07608 Teterboro, 14 .... B 2
08086 Thorofare, 4,200 .... B 4
08887 Three Bridges, 750 .... D 2
08560 Titusville, 900 .... D 3
08753 Toms River⊙, 7,303 .... E 4
07511 Totowa, 11,580 .... B 1
07082 Towaco, 2,500 .... E 2
* 08601 Trenton (cap.)⊙, 104,638 .... D 3
Trenton, ‡303,968 .... D 3
08087 Tuckerton, 1,926 .... E 4
07083 Union, ▵53,077 .... A 2
07735 Union Beach, 6,472 .... E 3
07087 Union City, 58,537 .... C 2
† 07421 Upper Greenwood Lake 1,505 .... E 1
† 07458 Upper Saddle River, 7,949 .... B 1
† 07724 Vail Homes, 1,164 .... E 3
07088 Vauxhall, 9,245 .... A 2
08406 Ventnor City, 10,385 .... E 5
07462 Vernon, 800 .... E 1
07044 Verona, 15,067 .... B 2
08251 Villas, 3,155 .... D 5
08088 Vincentown, 900 .... D 4
08360 Vineland, 47,399 .... C 5
Vineland-Millville-Bridgeton, ‡121,374 .... C 5
07463 Waldwick, 12,313 .... B 1
07719 Wall, ▵16,498 .... E 3
07055 Wallington, 10,284 .... B 2
† 07712 Wanamassa, 4,600 .... E 3
07465 Wanaque, 8,636 .... B 1
08758 Waretown, 1,800 .... E 4
07882 Washington, 5,943 .... D 2
07060 Watchung, 4,750 .... E 2
08089 Waterford Works, 950 .... D 4
07470 Wayne, ▵49,141 .... A 1
07087 Weehawken, ▵13,383 .... C 2
08090 Wenonah, 2,364 .... C 4
07006 West Caldwell, 11,887 .... A 2
† 08204 West Cape May, 1,005 .... D 6
08092 West Creek, 630 .... E 4
* 07090 Westfield, 33,720 .... E 2
07764 West Long Branch, 6,845 .... F 3
07480 West Milford, 950 .... E 1
07093 West New York, 40,627 .... C 2
07052 West Orange, 43,715 .... A 2
07424 West Paterson, 11,692 .... B 2
08628 West Trenton, 5,900 .... D 3
08093 Westville, 5,170 .... B 3
07675 Westwood, 11,105 .... B 1
07885 Wharton, 5,535 .... D 2
07981 Whippany, 7,500 .... E 2
08888 Whitehouse, 800 .... D 2
08889 White House Station, 1,019 .... D 2
08252 Whitesboro, 700 .... D 5
† 08701 Whitesville, 600 .... E 3
08759 Whiting, 750 .... E 4
07765 Wickatunk, 950 .... E 3
08260 Wildwood, 4,110 .... D 6
08260 Wildwood Crest, 3,483 .... D 6
08094 Williamstown, 4,075 .... D 4
08046 Willingboro, ▵43,414 .... D 3
† 07036 Winfield, ▵2,184 .... B 2
08270 Woodbine, 2,625 .... D 5
07095 Woodbridge, ▵98,944 .... E 2
08096 Woodbury⊙, 12,408 .... B 4
08097 Woodbury Heights, 3,621 .... B 4
07675 Woodcliff Lake, 5,506 .... B 1
08107 Wood-Lynne, 3,101 .... B 3
† 07885 Woodport, 2,100 .... D 2
07075 Wood-Ridge, 8,311 .... B 2
08098 Woodstown, 3,137 .... C 4
08562 Wrightstown, 2,719 .... D 3
07481 Wyckoff, ▵16,039 .... B 1
08620 Yardville, 9,500 .... D 3

⊙ County seat.
‡ Population of metropolitan area.
▵ Population of town or township.
† Zip of nearest p.o
* Multiple zips

Topography

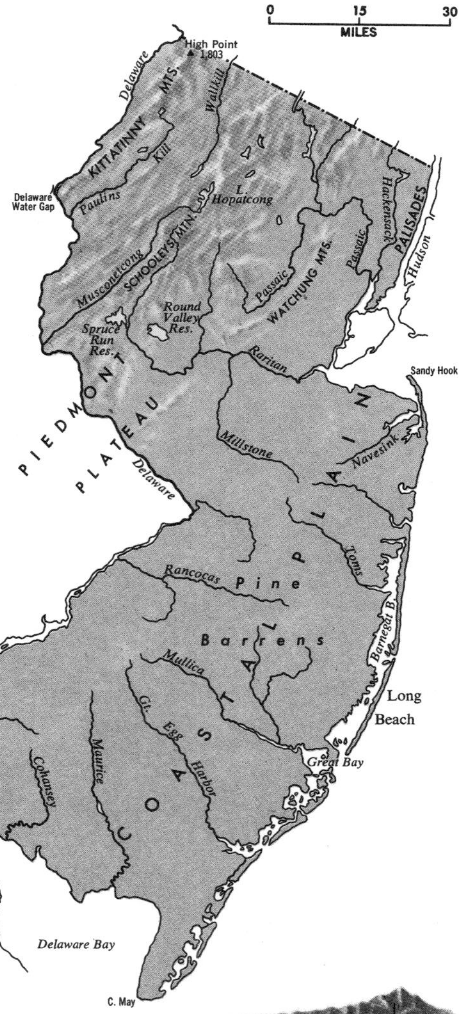

0 15 30
MILES
High Point 1,803
Delaware
KITTATINNY MTS.
Wallkill
Kill
Delaware Water Gap
Paulins
L. Hopatcong
SCHOOLEYS MTN.
Musconetcong
Hackensack
PALISADES
Hudson
Passaic
WATCHUNG MTS.
Round Valley Res.
Spruce Run Res.
Raritan
Sandy Hook
PIEDMONT
PLATEAU
Millstone
Navesink
Delaware
COASTAL PLAIN
Rancocas
Pine
Barrens
Toms
Barnegat B.
Mullica
Long Beach
Great Bay
Gt. Egg Harbor
Maurice
Cohansey
Delaware Bay
C. May
Below Sea Level
100 m. 328 ft.
200 m. 656 ft.
500 m. 1,640 ft.
1,000 m. 3,281 ft.
2,000 m. 6,562 ft.
5,000 m. 16,404 ft.

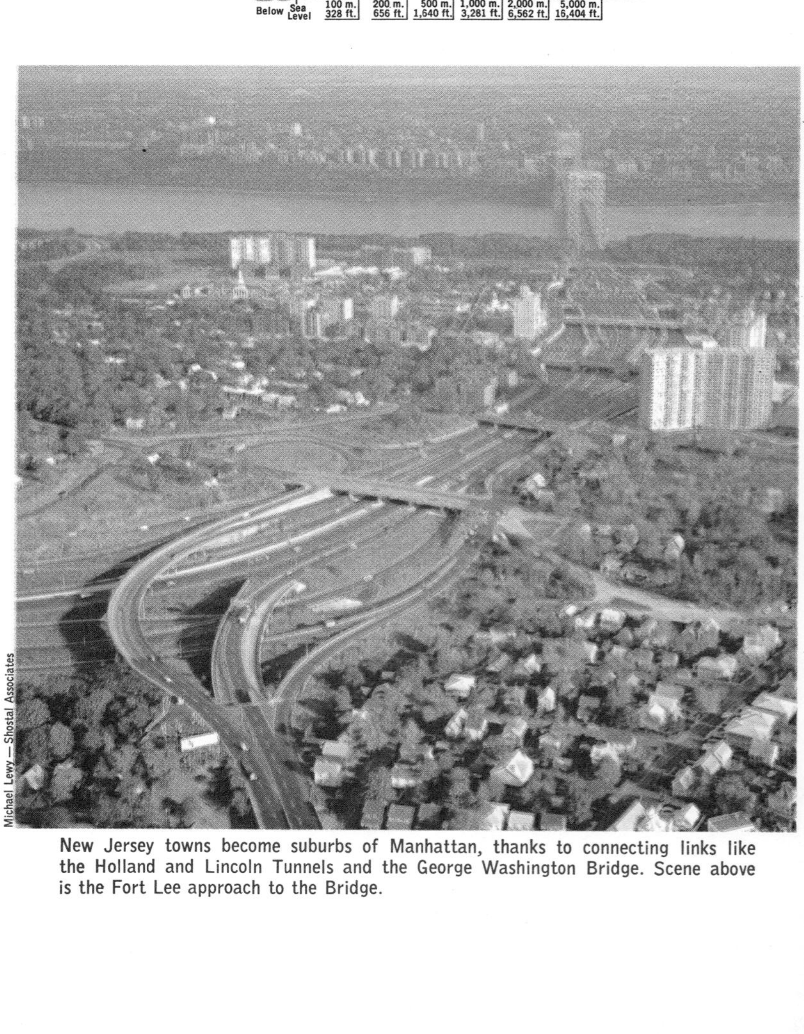

Michael Lewy — Shostal Associates

New Jersey towns become suburbs of Manhattan, thanks to connecting links like the Holland and Lincoln Tunnels and the George Washington Bridge. Scene above is the Fort Lee approach to the Bridge.

NEW JERSEY

SCALE

0   5   10   15   20 MI.

0   5   10   15   20 KM.

State Capitals .... ⊛
County Seats .... ⊙
Canals ....

© C.S. HAMMOND & Co., N.Y.

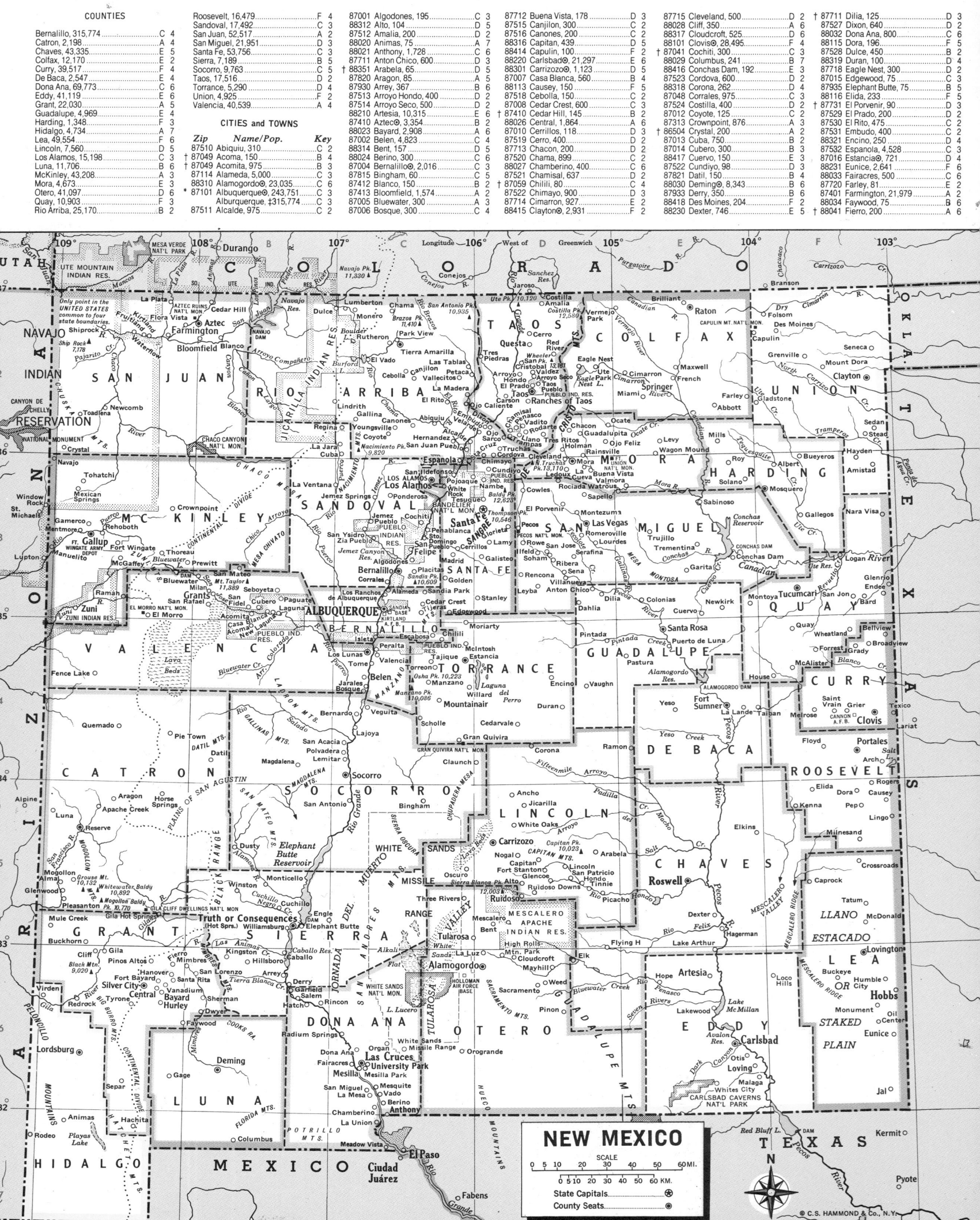

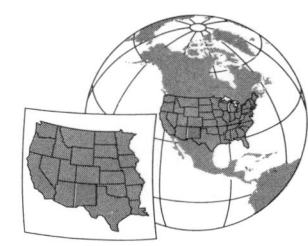

AREA 121,666 sq. mi.
POPULATION 1,016,000 ('70); 1,299,968 ('80)
CAPITAL Santa Fe
LARGEST CITY Albuquerque
HIGHEST POINT Wheeler Pk. 13,161 ft.
SETTLED IN 1605
ADMITTED TO UNION January 6, 1912
POPULAR NAME Land of Enchantment
STATE FLOWER Yucca
STATE BIRD Road Runner

Stephen Voynick — Shostal Associates

Golden adobe against the blue Sangre de Cristo Mountains. Clear, pure colors, magnificent surroundings and congenial atmosphere combine to draw artists and writers to Taos, New Mexico.

Topography

0   50   100
MILES

100 m. / 328 ft. — 200 m. / 656 ft. — 500 m. / 1,640 ft. — 1,000 m. / 3,281 ft. — 2,000 m. / 6,562 ft. — 5,000 m. / 16,404 ft.
Below Sea Level

Agriculture, Industry and Resources

DOMINANT LAND USE

Wheat, Grain Sorghums, Range Livestock

General Farming, Livestock, Special Crops

General Farming, Livestock, Cash Grain

Dry Beans, General Farming

Cotton, Forest Products

Range Livestock

Forests

Nonagricultural Land

MAJOR MINERAL OCCURRENCES

Ag Silver
Au Gold
C Coal
Cu Copper
G Natural Gas
Gp Gypsum
K Potash
Mo Molybdenum
Mr Marble
Na Salt
O Petroleum
Pb Lead
U Uranium
V Vanadium
Zn Zinc
⚡ Water Power

NEW YORK

SCALE

0 5 10 20 30 40 MI.

0 5 10 20 30 40 KM.

State Capitals .... ⊛
County Seats .... ⊙
Canals .... ———

© C.S. HAMMOND & Co., N.Y.

COUNTIES

	Key
Albany, 285,618	M 5
Allegany, 46,458	D 6
Bronx, 1,472,216	N 9
Broome, 221,815	J 6
Cattaraugus, 81,666	C 6
Cayuga, 77,439	G 4
Chautauqua, 147,305	B 6
Chemung, 101,537	G 6
Chenango, 46,368	J 6
Clinton, 72,934	N 1
Columbia, 51,519	N 6
Cortland, 45,894	H 5
Delaware, 44,718	K 6
Dutchess, 222,295	N 7
Erie, 1,113,491	C 5
Essex, 34,631	N 2
Franklin, 43,931	M 1
Fulton, 52,637	M 4
Genesee, 58,722	D 4
Greene, 33,136	M 6
Hamilton, 4,714	L 3
Herkimer, 67,440	L 4
Jefferson, 88,508	J 2
Kings, 2,601,852	N 9
Lewis, 23,644	K 3
Livingston, 54,041	E 5
Madison, 62,864	J 5
Monroe, 711,917	E 4
Montgomery, 55,883	M 5
Nassau, 1,422,905	N 9
New York, 1,524,541	N 9
Niagara, 235,720	C 4
Oneida, 273,037	J 4
Onondaga, 472,185	H 5
Ontario, 78,849	F 5
Orange, 220,558	M 8
Orleans, 37,305	D 4
Oswego, 100,897	H 4
Otsego, 56,181	K 5
Putnam, 56,696	N 8
Queens, 1,973,708	N 9
Rensselaer, 152,510	O 5
Richmond, 295,443	M 9
Rockland, 229,903	N 8
Saint Lawrence, 111,991	K 2
Saratoga, 121,679	N 4
Schenectady, 160,979	M 5
Schoharie, 24,750	M 5
Schuyler, 16,737	G 6
Seneca, 35,083	G 5
Steuben, 99,546	F 6
Suffolk, 1,116,672	O 9
Sullivan, 52,580	L 7
Tioga, 46,513	H 6
Tompkins, 76,879	H 6
Ulster, 141,241	M 7
Warren, 49,402	N 3
Washington, 52,725	O 4
Wayne, 79,404	F 4
Westchester, 891,409	N 8
Wyoming, 37,688	D 5
Yates, 19,831	F 5

CITIES and TOWNS

Zip	Name/Pop.	Key
13605	Adams, 1,951	J 3
13606	Adams Center, 900	H 3
14801	Addison, 2,104	F 6
13730	Afton, 1,064	J 6
14001	Akron, 2,863	C 4
* 12201	Albany (cap.)⊙, 114,873	N 5
	Albany-Schenectady-Troy, ‡720,786	N 5
14411	Albion⊙, 5,122	D 4
14004	Alden, 2,651	C 5
13607	Alexandria Bay, 1,440	J 2
14802	Alfred, 3,804	E 6
14706	Allegany, 2,050	C 6
12009	Altamont, 1,561	M 5
11930	Amagansett, 900	R 9
12501	Amenia, 1,157	N 7
11701	Amityville, 9,857	O 9
12010	Amsterdam, 25,524	M 5
14806	Andover, 1,214	E 6
14709	Angelica, 948	E 6
14006	Angola, 2,676	C 5
13732	Apalachin, 1,233	H 6
14009	Arcade, 1,972	D 5
10502	Ardsley, 4,470	E 7
14807	Arkport, 984	E 6
12603	Arlington, 11,203	N 7
12015	Athens, 1,718	N 6
14808	Atlanta, 900	F 5
11509	Atlantic Beach, 1,640	N 9
14011	Attica, 2,911	D 5
13021	Auburn⊙, 34,599	G 5
13026	Aurora, 1,072	G 5
12912	Au Sable Forks, 1,900	N 2
12018	Averill Park, 1,471	O 5
14809	Avoca, 1,153	F 6
14414	Avon, 3,260	E 5
* 11702	Babylon, 12,588	O 9
13733	Bainbridge, 1,674	J 6
11510	Baldwin, 34,525	R 7
13027	Baldwinsville, 6,298	H 4
† 12550	Ballston Spa⊙, 4,968	N 5
14020	Batavia⊙, 17,338	D 5
14810	Bath⊙, 6,053	F 6
11705	Bayport, 7,995	O 9
11706	Bay Shore, 11,119	O 9
11709	Bayville, 6,147	R 9
12508	Beacon, 13,255	N 7
10507	Bedford Hills, 3,900	N 8
11426	Bellerose, 1,654	R 7
11710	Bellmore, 18,431	R 7
11713	Bellport, 3,046	P 9
14813	Belmont⊙, 1,102	E 6
14416	Bergen, 1,018	E 4
12022	Berlin, 975	O 5
14814	Big Flats, 2,509	G 6
13901	Binghamton⊙, 64,123	J 6
	Binghamton, ‡302,672	J 6
13612	Black River, 1,307	J 3
14219	Blasdell, 3,910	C 5
14024	Bliss, 950	D 5
14715	Bolivar, 1,379	D 6
12814	Bolton Landing, 950	N 3
13309	Boonville, 2,488	K 4
14025	Boston, 950	C 5
12815	Brant Lake, 1,200	N 3
13613	Brasher Falls, 950	L 1
14816	Breesport, 950	G 6
11717	Brentwood, 27,868	O 9
13029	Brewerton, 1,985	H 4
10509	Brewster, 1,638	N 8
11932	Bridgehampton, 900	R 9
12025	Broadalbin, 1,452	M 4
14420	Brockport, 7,878	D 4
14716	Brocton, 1,370	B 6
* 10401	Bronx (borough)⊙, 1,472,216	N 9
10708	Bronxville, 6,674	O 7
* 11201	Brooklyn⊙, 2,601,852	N 9
13615	Brownville, 1,187	J 3
10511	Buchanan, 2,110	N 8
* 14201	Buffalo⊙, 462,768	B 5
	Buffalo, ‡1,349,211	B 5
12413	Cairo, 950	M 6
14423	Caledonia, 2,327	E 5
12723	Callicoon, 950	K 7
12816	Cambridge, 1,769	O 4
† 13316	Camden, 2,936	J 4
13031	Camillus, 1,534	H 4
13317	Canajoharie, 2,686	L 5
14424	Canandaigua⊙, 10,488	F 5
13032	Canastota, 5,033	J 4
13743	Candor, 939	H 6
14823	Canisteo, 2,772	E 6
13617	Canton⊙, 6,398	K 1
10512	Carmel⊙, 3,395	N 8
13619	Carthage, 3,889	J 3
14718	Cassadaga, 905	B 6
14427	Castile, 1,330	D 5
12033	Castleton-on-Hudson, 1,730	N 5
12414	Catskill⊙, 5,317	N 6
14719	Cattaraugus, 1,200	C 6
13035	Cazenovia, 3,031	J 5
11516	Cedarhurst, 6,941	R 7
14720	Celoron, 1,616	B 6
11720	Centereach, 9,427	O 9
11934	Center Moriches, 3,802	P 9
11722	Central Islip, 36,369	O 9
13036	Central Square, 1,298	H 4
10917	Central Valley, 975	M 8
13319	Chadwicks, 975	K 4
12919	Champlain, 1,426	N 1
12920	Chateaugay, 976	N 1
12037	Chatham, 2,239	N 5
14722	Chautauqua, 500	A 6
14225	Cheektowaga, △113,844	C 5
13745	Chenango Bridge, 5,059	J 6
10918	Chester, 1,622	M 8
12817	Chestertown, 950	N 3
13037	Chittenango, 3,605	J 4
14428	Churchville, 1,065	E 4
13040	Cincinnatus, 900	H 5
14031	Clarence, 2,014	C 5
14430	Clarkson, 1,300	E 4
13624	Clayton, 1,970	H 2
† 12118	Clifton Park, △14,867	N 5

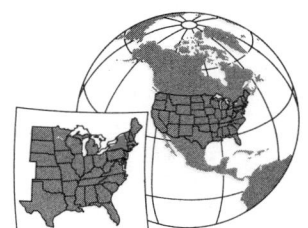

AREA 49,576 sq. mi.
POPULATION 18,241,266 ('70); 17,557,288 ('80)
CAPITAL Albany
LARGEST CITY New York
HIGHEST POINT Mt. Marcy 5,344 ft.
SETTLED IN 1614
ADMITTED TO UNION July 26, 1788
POPULAR NAME Empire State
STATE FLOWER Rose
STATE BIRD Bluebird

Topography

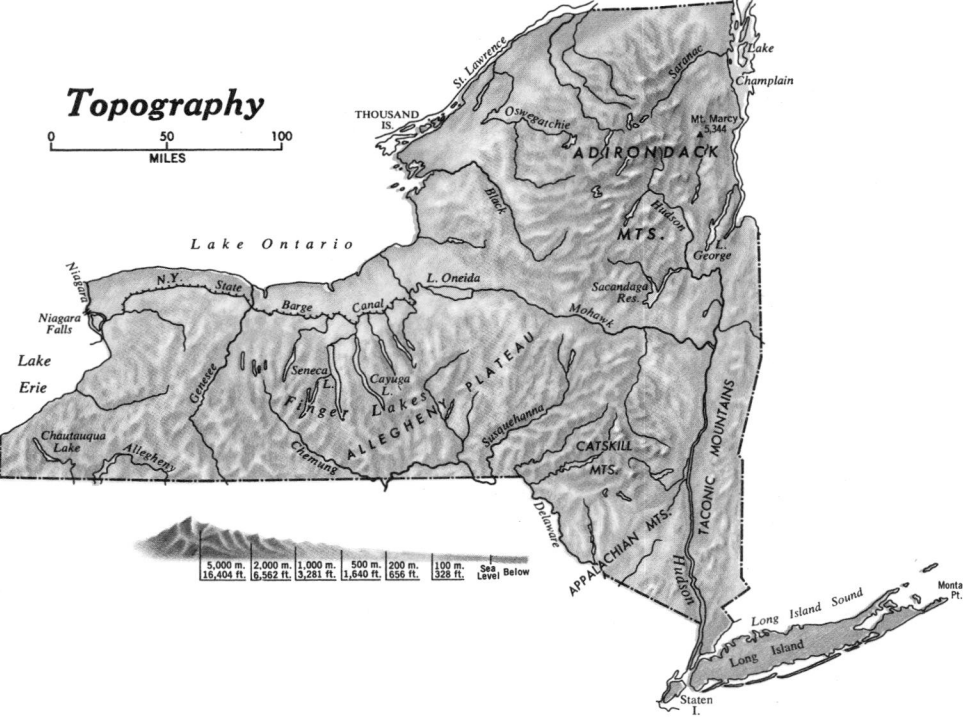

14432 Clifton Springs, 2,058	F 4	† 12601 Fairview, 8,517	N 7
13323 Clinton, 2,271	K 4	14733 Falconer, 2,983	B 6
14433 Clyde, 2,828	G 4	11735 Farmingdale, 9,297	N 9
12043 Cobleskill, 4,368	L 5	13066 Fayetteville, 4,996	J 4
12045 Coeymans, 975	N 6	12524 Fishkill, 913	N 7
12047 Cohoes, 18,613	N 5	* 11001 Floral Park, 18,422	R 7
14033 Colden, 950	C 5	10921 Florida, 1,674	M 8
10516 Cold Spring, 2,083	N 8	13337 Fly Creek, 910	K 5
† 12201 Colonie, 8,701	N 5	12068 Fonda⊙, 1,120	M 5
13326 Cooperstown⊙, 2,403	L 5	14062 Forestville, 908	B 6
12822 Corinth, 3,267	M 5	12937 Fort Covington, 983	M 1
14830 Corning, 15,792	F 6	12828 Fort Edward, 3,733	O 4
12518 Cornwall, 2,032	M 8	13339 Fort Plain, 2,809	L 5
13045 Cortland⊙, 19,621	H 5	13340 Frankfort, 3,305	K 4
12051 Coxsackie, 2,399	N 6	14737 Franklinville, 1,948	D 6
10519 Croton Falls, 950	N 8	14063 Fredonia, 10,326	B 6
10520 Croton-on-Hudson, 7,523	D 6	11520 Freeport, 40,374	R 7
14727 Cuba, 1,735	D 6	14738 Frewsburg, 1,772	B 6
12929 Dannemora, 3,735	N 1	14739 Friendship, 1,285	D 6
14437 Dansville, 5,436	E 5	13069 Fulton, 14,003	H 4
11729 Deer Park, 31,120	O 9	11542 Glen Cove, 25,770	R 6
14042 Delevan, 994	D 6	11545 Glen Head, 4,000	R 7
13753 Delhi⊙, 3,017	L 6	12801 Glens Falls, 17,222	N 4
12054 Delmar, 7,500	N 5	12078 Gloversville, 19,677	M 4
14043 Depew, 22,158	C 5	10526 Golden's Bridge, 1,101	N 8
13754 Deposit, 2,061	K 6	10924 Goshen⊙, 4,342	M 8
14047 Derby, 4,900	B 5	13642 Gouverneur, 4,574	K 2
13214 DeWitt, 10,032	H 4	14070 Gowanda, 3,110	B 6
13634 Dexter, 1,061	H 2	12434 Grand Gorge, 950	L 6
10522 Dobbs Ferry, 10,353	O 6	14072 Grand Island, 900	B 5
13329 Dolgeville, 2,872	L 4	12832 Granville, 2,784	O 4
12522 Dover Plains, 975	O 7	* 11020 Great Neck, 10,724	R 7
13053 Dryden, 1,490	H 6	14616 Greece, Δ75,136	E 4
14837 Dundee, 1,539	F 5	13778 Greene, 1,874	J 6
14048 Dunkirk, 16,855	B 5	12183 Green Island, 3,297	N 5
13054 Durhamville, 975	J 4	11944 Greenport, 2,481	P 8
13332 Earlville, 1,050	J 5	12834 Greenwich, 2,092	O 4
14052 East Aurora, 7,033	C 5	10925 Greenwood Lake, 2,262	M 8
12061 East Greenbush, 985	N 5	13073 Groton, 2,112	H 5
11937 East Hampton, 1,753	R 9	13780 Guilford, 995	J 6
11554 East Meadow, 46,252	R 7	12086 Hagaman, 1,410	M 5
11940 East Moriches, 1,702	P 9	14075 Hamburg, 10,215	C 5
11731 East Northport, 12,392	O 9	13346 Hamilton, 3,636	J 5
11941 Eastport, 1,308	P 9	14840 Hammondsport, 1,066	F 6
14445 East Rochester, 8,347	F 4	11946 Hampton Bays, 1,862	P 9
11518 East Rockaway, 10,323	R 7	13783 Hancock, 1,688	K 7
13057 East Syracuse, 4,333	H 4	10926 Harriman, 955	M 8
14057 Eden, 2,962	C 5	10528 Harrison, 9,250	P 7
* 14226 Eggertsville, 55,000	C 5	10706 Hastings on Hudson, 9,479	O 6
13060 Elbridge, 1,040	G 5	10927 Haverstraw, 8,198	M 8
12932 Elizabethtown⊙, 607	N 2	10532 Hawthorne, 5,000	O 6
14428 Ellenville, 4,482	M 7	11550 Hempstead, 39,411	R 7
14731 Ellicottville, 955	C 6	13650 Henderson, 900	H 3
14059 Elma, 2,784	C 5	13650 Herkimer⊙, 8,960	L 4
* 14901 Elmira⊙, 39,945	G 6	(continued on following page)	
14903 Elmira Heights, 4,906	G 6		
11003 Elmont, 29,363	R 7		
10523 Elmsford, 3,911	P 6		
13760 Endicott, 16,556	H 6		
13760 Endwell, 15,999	H 6		
14450 Fairport, 6,474	F 4		

(continued on following page)

Lower Manhattan's skyline in an unusual view from a pier at the Brooklyn Port Authority Marine Terminal.

Agriculture, Industry and Resources

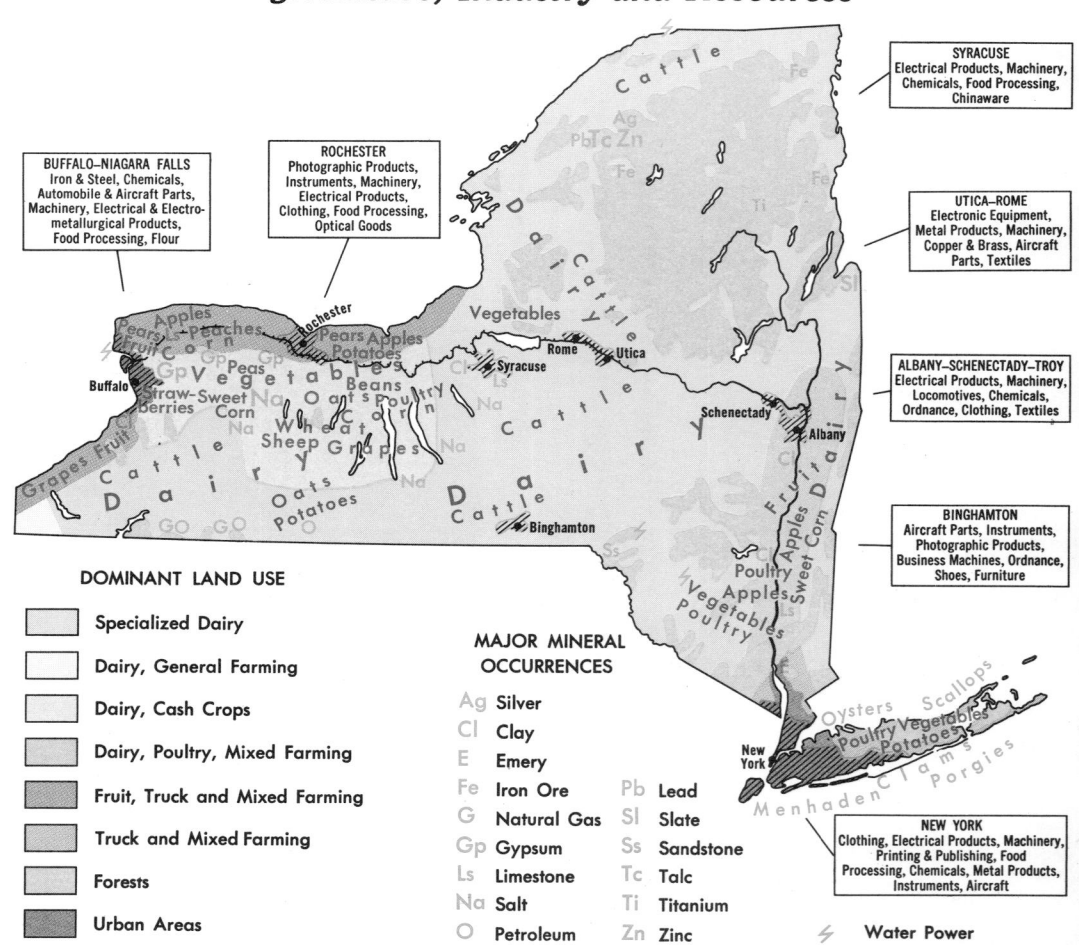

DOMINANT LAND USE

- Specialized Dairy
- Dairy, General Farming
- Dairy, Cash Crops
- Dairy, Poultry, Mixed Farming
- Fruit, Truck and Mixed Farming
- Truck and Mixed Farming
- Forests
- Urban Areas

MAJOR MINERAL OCCURRENCES

Ag	Silver		
Cl	Clay		
E	Emery		
Fe	Iron Ore	Pb	Lead
G	Natural Gas	Sl	Slate
Gp	Gypsum	Ss	Sandstone
Ls	Limestone	Tc	Talc
Na	Salt	Ti	Titanium
O	Petroleum	Zn	Zinc

⚡ Water Power

▨ Major Industrial Areas

SYRACUSE
Electrical Products, Machinery, Chemicals, Food Processing, Chinaware

UTICA–ROME
Electronic Equipment, Metal Products, Machinery, Copper & Brass, Aircraft Parts, Textiles

ALBANY–SCHENECTADY–TROY
Electrical Products, Machinery, Locomotives, Chemicals, Ordnance, Clothing, Textiles

BINGHAMTON
Aircraft Parts, Instruments, Photographic Products, Business Machines, Ordnance, Shoes, Furniture

NEW YORK
Clothing, Electrical Products, Machinery, Printing & Publishing, Food Processing, Chemicals, Metal Products, Instruments, Aircraft

ROCHESTER
Photographic Products, Instruments, Machinery, Electrical Products, Clothing, Food Processing, Optical Goods

BUFFALO–NIAGARA FALLS
Iron & Steel, Chemicals, Automobile & Aircraft Parts, Machinery, Electrical & Electro-metallurgical Products, Food Processing, Flour

COUNTIES

County	Key
Alamance, 96,362	L 3
Alexander, 19,466	G 3
Alleghany, 8,134	G 1
Anson, 23,488	J 4
Ashe, 19,571	F 2
Avery, 12,655	F 2
Beaufort, 35,980	R 4
Bertie, 20,528	P 2
Bladen, 26,477	M 5
Brunswick, 24,223	N 6
Buncombe, 145,056	D 3
Burke, 60,364	F 3
Cabarrus, 74,629	H 4
Caldwell, 56,699	F 3
Camden, 5,453	S 2
Carteret, 31,603	R 5
Caswell, 19,055	L 2
Catawba, 90,873	G 3
Chatham, 29,554	L 3
Cherokee, 16,330	A 4
Chowan, 10,764	R 2
Clay, 5,180	B 4
Cleveland, 72,556	F 4
Columbus, 46,937	M 6
Craven, 62,554	P 4
Cumberland, 212,042	M 4
Currituck, 6,976	S 2
Dare, 6,995	T 3
Davidson, 95,627	J 3
Davie, 18,855	H 3
Duplin, 38,015	O 5
Durham, 132,681	M 3
Edgecombe, 52,341	O 3
Forsyth, 214,348	J 2
Franklin, 26,820	N 2
Gaston, 148,415	G 4
Gates, 8,524	R 2
Graham, 6,562	B 4
Granville, 32,762	M 2
Greene, 14,967	O 3
Guilford, 288,590	K 3
Halifax, 53,884	O 2
Harnett, 49,667	M 4
Haywood, 41,710	C 3
Henderson, 42,804	D 4
Hertford, 23,529	P 2
Hoke, 16,436	L 4
Hyde, 5,571	S 3
Iredell, 72,197	H 3
Jackson, 21,593	C 4
Johnston, 61,737	N 4
Jones, 9,779	P 4
Lee 30,467	L 4
Lenoir, 55,204	O 4
Lincoln, 32,682	G 3
Macon, 15,788	B 4
Madison, 16,003	D 3
Martin, 24,730	P 3
McDowell, 30,648	E 3
Mecklenburg, 354,656	H 4
Mitchell, 13,447	E 2
Montgomery, 19,267	K 4
Moore, 39,048	L 4
Nash, 59,122	O 2
New Hanover, 82,996	O 6
Northampton, 24,009	P 2
Onslow, 103,126	P 5
Orange, 57,707	L 2
Pamlico, 9,467	R 4
Pasquotank, 26,824	S 2
Pender, 18,149	O 5
Perquimans, 8,351	S 2
Person, 25,914	M 2
Pitt, 73,900	P 3
Polk, 11,735	E 4
Randolph, 76,358	K 3
Richmond, 39,889	K 4
Robeson, 84,842	L 5
Rockingham, 72,402	K 2
Rowan, 90,035	H 3
Rutherford, 47,337	E 4
Sampson, 44,954	N 4
Scotland, 26,929	L 5
Stanly, 42,822	J 4
Stokes, 23,782	J 2
Surry, 51,415	H 2
Swain, 7,861	B 3
Transylvania, 19,713	D 4
Tyrrell, 3,806	S 3
Union, 54,714	H 4
Vance, 32,691	N 2
Wake, 228,453	M 3
Warren, 15,810	N 2
Washington, 14,038	R 3
Watauga, 23,404	F 2
Wayne, 85,408	N 4
Wilkes, 49,524	G 2
Wilson, 57,486	O 3
Yadkin, 24,599	H 2
Yancey, 12,629	E 3

AREA 52,586 sq. mi.
POPULATION 5,082,059 ('70); 5,874,429 ('80)
CAPITAL Raleigh
LARGEST CITY Charlotte
HIGHEST POINT Mt. Mitchell 6,684 ft.
SETTLED IN 1650
ADMITTED TO UNION November 21, 1789
POPULAR NAME Tarheel State
STATE FLOWER Flowering Dogwood
STATE BIRD Cardinal

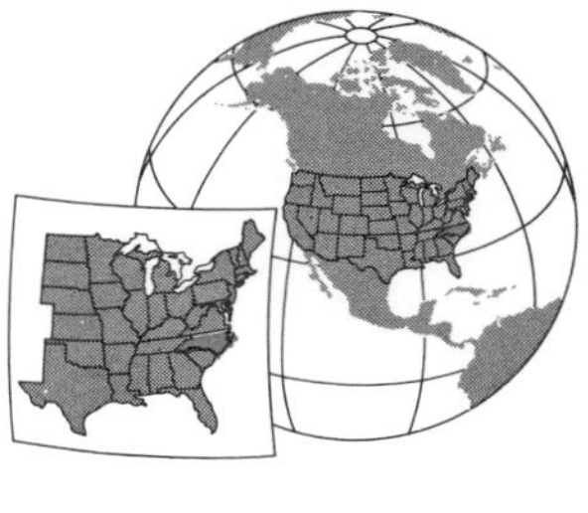

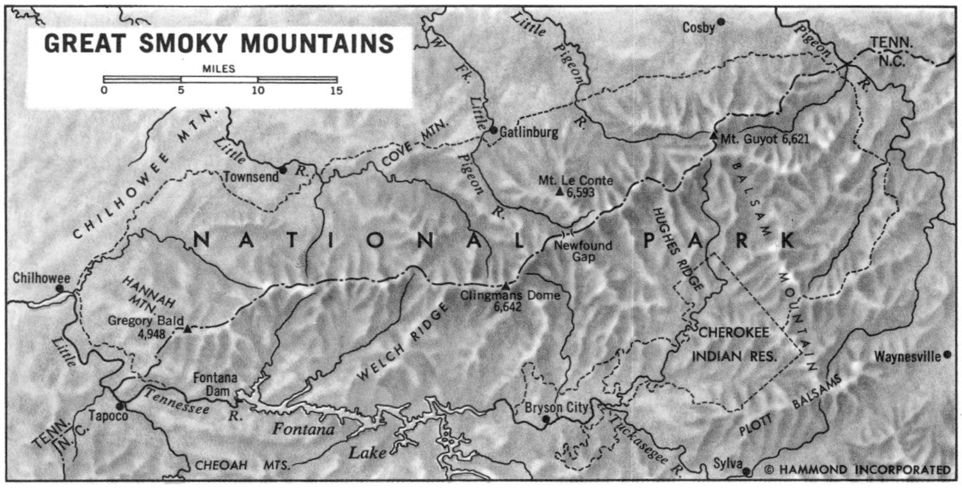
GREAT SMOKY MOUNTAINS
MILES
0 5 10 15
Cosby
TENN.
N.C.
Little Pigeon R.
Pigeon R.
W. Fk. Little Pigeon R.
Gatlinburg
Mt. Guyot 6,621
CHILHOWEE MTN.
Little R.
Townsend
COVE MTN.
Mt. Le Conte 6,593
BALSAM MOUNTAIN
HUGHES RIDGE
NATIONAL PARK
Newfound Gap
Chilhowee
HANNAH MTN.
Gregory Bald 4,948
Clingmans Dome 6,642
CHEROKEE INDIAN RES.
WELCH RIDGE
Waynesville
Little
Fontana Dam
Tennessee R.
Tapoco
Bryson City
PLOTT BALSAMS
Fontana Lake
Tuckasegee R.
CHEOAH MTS.
Sylva
© HAMMOND INCORPORATED

CITIES and TOWNS

	Zip	Name/Pop.	Key
	28321	Abbottsburg, 425	M 5
	28315	Aberdeen, 1,592	L 4
	27006	Advance, 206	J 3
	27910	Ahoskie, 5,105	P 2
	27201	Alamance, 450	K 2
†	28713	Alarka, 900	C 4
	28001	Albemarle⊙, 11,126	J 4
†	27589	Alert, 200	N 2
	28701	Alexander, 200	D 3
	28509	Alliance, 577	R 4
†	28364	Alma, 200	L 5
	28702	Almond, 200	B 4
	27202	Altamahaw, 900	L 2
	28901	Andrews, 1,384	B 4
	27501	Angier, 1,431	M 4
	28007	Ansonville, 694	J 4
	27502	Apex, 2,192	M 3
	28510	Arapahoe, 212	R 4
	27263	Archdale, 6,103	K 3
	27589	Arcola, 300	N 2
	28704	Arden, 850	D 4
†	28642	Arlington, 711	H 2
	28420	Ash, 250	N 6
	27203	Asheboro⊙, 10,797	K 3
*	28801	Asheville⊙, 57,681	D 3
		Asheville, ‡145,056	D 3
	28603	Ashford, 225	F 3
†	27983	Askewville, 247	R 2
	28421	Atkinson, 325	N 5
	28511	Atlantic, 950	S 5
	28512	Atlantic Beach, 300	R 5
	27805	Aulander, 947	P 2
	27806	Aurora, 620	R 4
	28318	Autryville, 213	M 4
	27915	Avon, 400	U 4
†	28076	Avondale-Henrietta, 1,307	F 4
	28513	Ayden, 3,450	P 4
	28009	Badin, 1,626	J 4
	27503	Bahama, 280	M 2
	27807	Bailey, 724	N 3
	28705	Bakersville⊙, 409	E 2
	28706	Balfour, 2,014	E 4
†	27203	Balfours, 4,836	K 3
	28707	Balsam, 300	C 4
†	27030	Bannertown, 1,138	H 1
	27917	Barco, 325	T 2
†	28739	Barker Heights, 2,933	D 4
	28710	Bat Cave, 400	E 4
	27808	Bath, 231	R 4
	27809	Battleboro, 688	O 2
	28515	Bayboro⊙, 665	R 4
	27207	Bear Creek, 500	L 3
	28516	Beaufort⊙, 3,368	R 5
	27810	Belhaven, 2,259	R 3
	28012	Belmont, 4,814	H 4
	27919	Belvidere, 275	S 2
†	28621	Benham, 400	G 2
	27208	Bennett, 200	K 3
	27504	Benson, 2,267	N 4
†	27565	Berea, 200	M 2
	28016	Bessemer City, 5,217	G 4
†	28779	Beta, 500	C 4
	27812	Bethel, 1,514	P 3
	28518	Beulaville, 1,156	O 5
†	28803	Biltmore Forest, 1,298	E 3
	27209	Biscoe, 1,244	K 4
	27813	Black Creek, 449	O 3
	28711	Black Mountain, 3,204	E 3
	28320	Bladenboro, 783	M 5
	27212	Blanch, 210	L 2
	28605	Blowing Rock, 801	F 2
†	28438	Boardman, 233	M 6
	28092	Boger City, 2,203	G 4
†	28570	Bogue, 600	R 5
	28461	Boiling Spring Lakes, 245	N 7
	28017	Boiling Springs, 2,284	F 4
	28423	Bolton, 534	N 6
	27213	Bonlee, 275	L 3
	28606	Boomer, 212	G 2
	28607	Boone⊙, 8,754	F 2
	27011	Boonville, 687	H 2
	28322	Bowdens, 250	N 4
	28712	Brevard⊙, 5,243	D 4
	28519	Bridgeton, 520	R 4
	27505	Broadway, 694	L 4
	28601	Brookford, 590	G 3
	27214	Browns Summit, 500	K 2
	28424	Brunswick, 206	M 6
	28713	Bryson City⊙, 1,290	C 4
†	28377	Buies, 275	L 5
	27506	Buies Creek, 2,024	M 4
	27507	Bullock, 550	M 2
	27508	Bunn, 284	N 3
	28323	Bunnlevel, 200	M 4
	28425	Burgaw⊙, 1,744	N 5
	27215	Burlington, 35,930	K 2
	28714	Burnsville⊙, 1,348	E 3
	27509	Butner, 3,538	M 2
	28324	Butters, 225	M 5
	27920	Buxton, 700	U 4
	27228	Bynum, 400	L 3
	28325	Calypso, 462	N 4
	27921	Camden⊙, 300	S 2
	28326	Cameron, 204	L 4
	28715	Candler, 950	D 3
	27229	Candor, 561	K 4
	28716	Canton, 5,158	D 3
	28019	Caroleen, 975	F 4
	28428	Carolina Beach, 1,663	O 6
	27510	Carrboro, 3,472	L 3
	28327	Carthage⊙, 1,034	K 4
	27511	Cary, 7,430	M 3
	28020	Casar, 350	F 3
	28717	Cashiers, 230	C 4
	27816	Castalia, 265	O 2
	28429	Castle Hayne, 900	O 6
	28609	Catawba, 565	G 3
†	28754	Catharine Lake, 500	O 5
	27230	Cedar Falls, 500	K 3
	28520	Cedar Island, 250	S 5
	28718	Cedar Mountain, 250	D 4
	28431	Chadbourn, 2,213	M 6
	27514	Chapel Hill, 25,537	M 3
*	28201	Charlotte⊙, 241,178	H 4
		Charlotte, ‡409,370	H 4
	28719	Cherokee, 975	C 4
	28021	Cherryville, 5,258	G 4
	28023	China Grove, 1,788	H 3
	28521	Chinquapin, 350	O 5
	27817	Chocowinity, 566	P 4
	28610	Claremont, 788	G 3
	28432	Clarendon, 300	M 6
	28433	Clarkton, 662	M 6
	27520	Clayton, 3,103	N 3
	27012	Clemmons, 4,900	J 2
	27013	Cleveland, 614	H 3
	28024	Cliffside, 950	F 4
	27233	Climax, 475	K 3
	28328	Clinton⊙, 7,157	N 5
	28721	Clyde, 900	D 3
	27521	Coats, 1,051	M 4
	27922	Cofield, 422	R 2
	27923	Coinjock, 650	S 2
	27924	Colerain, 373	R 2
	27234	Coleridge, 600	K 3
	28611	Collettsville, 275	F 3
	27925	Columbia⊙, 902	S 3
	28722	Columbus⊙, 731	E 4
	28522	Comfort, 340	O 5
	27818	Como, 211	P 1
	28025	Concord⊙, 18,464	H 4
	28612	Connellys Springs, 500	F 3
	28613	Conover, 3,355	G 3
	27820	Conway, 694	P 2
	27014	Cooleemee, 1,115	H 3
	28031	Cornelius, 1,296	H 4
	28523	Cove City, 485	P 4
	28032	Cramerton, 2,142	G 4
	27522	Creedmoor, 1,405	M 2
	27928	Creswell, 633	S 3
	28033	Crouse, 850	G 4
†	28716	Cruso, 800	D 4
	28723	Cullowhee, 6,300	C 4
	28331	Cumberland, 800	M 5
	28435	Currie, 294	N 6
	27929	Currituck⊙, 500	T 2
	27015	Cycle, 210	H 2
	28034	Dallas, 4,059	G 4
†	27043	Dalton, 400	J 2
	27016	Danbury⊙, 152	J 2
	28036	Davidson, 2,931	H 4
	28524	Davis, 600	R 5
	28436	Delco, 450	N 6
	27239	Denton, 1,017	J 3
	28725	Dillsboro, 215	C 4
	27017	Dobson⊙, 933	H 2
†	28685	Dockery, 300	G 2
	28526	Dover, 585	P 4
	28619	Drexel, 1,431	F 3
	28332	Dublin, 283	M 5
	28334	Dunn, 8,302	M 4
*	27701	Durham⊙, 95,438	M 2
		Durham, ‡190,388	M 2
†	28761	Dysartsville, 950	F 3
	27242	Eagle Springs, 500	K 4
	28038	Earl, 300	F 4
	27018	East Bend, 485	H 2
	28726	East Flat Rock, 2,627	E 4
	28352	East Laurinburg, 487	L 5
†	28752	East Marion, 3,015	F 3
	28039	East Spencer, 2,217	J 3
	27288	Eden, 15,871	K 1
	27932	Edenton⊙, 4,766	R 2
	27243	Efland, 600	L 2
	27909	Elizabeth City⊙, 14,069	S 2
	28337	Elizabethtown⊙, 1,418	M 5
	28621	Elkin, 2,899	H 2
	28622	Elk Park, 503	F 2
	28040	Ellenboro, 465	F 4
	28338	Ellerbe, 913	K 4
	27822	Elm City, 1,201	O 3
	27244	Elon College, 2,150	L 2
	27823	Enfield, 3,272	O 2
	27824	Engelhard, 500	T 3
	28728	Enka, 500	D 3
	28527	Ernul, 350	P 4
	28339	Erwin, 2,852	M 4
	27247	Ether, 375	K 4
	28729	Etowah, 700	D 4
	27830	Eureka, 263	O 3
	28438	Evergreen, 250	M 6
	28439	Fair Bluff, 1,039	M 6
	27826	Fairfield, 954	S 3
	28340	Fairmont, 2,827	L 6
	28730	Fairview, 800	D 3
	28341	Faison, 598	N 4
	28041	Faith, 506	J 3
	28342	Falcon, 357	M 4
†	27028	Farmington, 300	H 3
	27828	Farmville, 4,424	O 3
*	28301	Fayetteville⊙, 53,510	M 4
		Fayetteville, ‡212,042	M 4
	28731	Flat Rock, 650	E 4
	28732	Fletcher, 950	E 4
	28043	Forest City, 7,179	E 4
†	27028	Fork, 250	J 3
	27829	Fountain, 434	O 3
	27524	Four Oaks, 1,057	M 4
	28734	Franklin⊙, 2,336	C 4
	27525	Franklinton, 1,459	N 2
	27248	Franklinville, 794	K 3
	28440	Freeland, 500	N 6
	27830	Fremont, 1,596	N 3
	27936	Frisco, 325	T 4
	27526	Fuquay-Varina, 3,576	M 3
	28441	Garland, 656	N 5
	27529	Garner, 4,923	M 3
	27831	Garysburg, 231	O 2

(continued on following page)

Agriculture, Industry and Resources

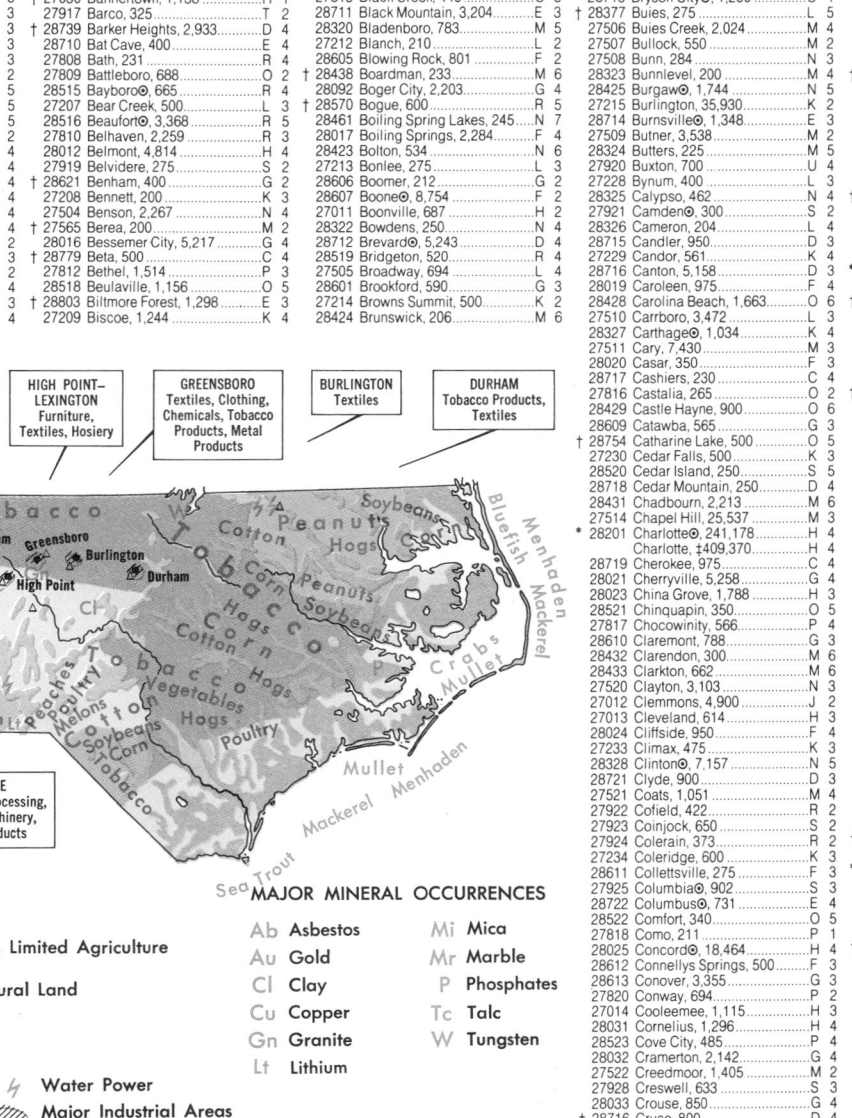

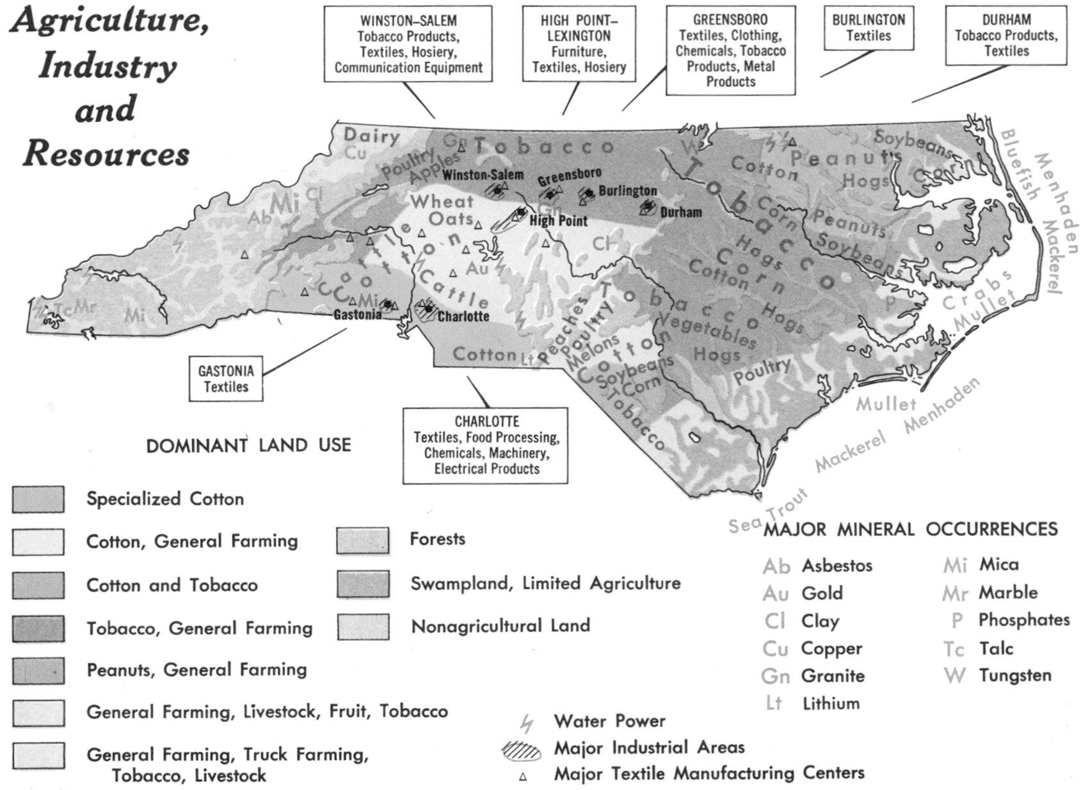
WINSTON-SALEM
Tobacco Products, Textiles, Hosiery, Communication Equipment
HIGH POINT-LEXINGTON
Furniture, Textiles, Hosiery
GREENSBORO
Textiles, Clothing, Chemicals, Tobacco Products, Metal Products
BURLINGTON
Textiles
DURHAM
Tobacco Products, Textiles
GASTONIA
Textiles
CHARLOTTE
Textiles, Food Processing, Chemicals, Machinery, Electrical Products
Dairy
Cu
Tobacco
Poultry
Apples
Winston-Salem
Greensboro
Burlington
Durham
High Point
Wheat
Oats
Cattle
Peanuts
Hogs
Cotton
Corn
Soybeans
Gastonia
Charlotte
Vegetables
Peaches
Melons
Sweet Potatoes
Bluefish
Menhaden
Mackerel
Crabs
Mullet
Sea Trout
DOMINANT LAND USE
Specialized Cotton
Cotton, General Farming
Cotton and Tobacco
Tobacco, General Farming
Peanuts, General Farming
General Farming, Livestock, Fruit, Tobacco
General Farming, Truck Farming, Tobacco, Livestock
Forests
Swampland, Limited Agriculture
Nonagricultural Land
Water Power
Major Industrial Areas
Major Textile Manufacturing Centers
MAJOR MINERAL OCCURRENCES
Ab Asbestos
Au Gold
Cl Clay
Cu Copper
Gn Granite
Lt Lithium
Mi Mica
Mr Marble
P Phosphates
Tc Talc
W Tungsten

27832 Gaston, 1,105....O 1
28052 Gastonia◉, 47,142....G 4
27937 Gates, 225....R 2
27938 Gatesville◉, 338....R 2
28343 Gibson, 502....K 5
27249 Gibsonville, 2,019....F 2
28628 Glen Alpine, 797....F 3
27251 Glendon, 250....L 3
27215 Glen Raven, 2,848....L 2
28736 Glenville, 400....C 3
28737 Glenwood, 400....F 3
28071 Gold Hill, 350....J 3
27530 Goldsboro◉, 26,810....O 4
27252 Goldston, 364....L 3
27253 Graham◉, 8,172....L 2
27939 Grandy, 425....T 2
28630 Granite Falls, 2,388....G 3
28072 Granite Quarry, 1,344....H 3
28529 Grantsboro, 900....R 4
28740 Greenmountain, 500....E 3
* 27401 Greensboro◉, 144,076....K 2
Greensboro-Winston-Salem-
High Point, ‡603,895....K 2
27834 Greenville◉, 29,063....P 3
28530 Grifton, 1,860....P 3
27837 Grimesland, 394....P 3
28073 Grover, 555....G 4
27256 Gulf, 300....L 3
27839 Halifax◉, 335....O 2
28442 Hallsboro, 300....M 6
27840 Hamilton, 579....P 3
28345 Hamlet, 4,627....K 5
28443 Hampstead, 400....O 6
27020 Hamptonville, 250....H 2
27941 Harbinger, 460....T 2
28531 Harkers Island, 1,633....R 5
28634 Harmony, 377....H 3
28444 Harrells, 249....N 5
28075 Harrisburg, 800....H 4
27943 Hatteras, 500....T 4
28532 Havelock, 5,283....P 5
27258 Haw River, 1,542....L 2
28904 Hayesville◉, 428....B 4
† 28318 Hayne, 300....M 5
28635 Hays, 750....L 2
† 27559 Haywood, 500....L 3
28738 Hazelwood, 2,057....C 4
27536 Henderson◉, 13,896....N 2
28739 Hendersonville◉, 6,443....D 4
28076 Henrietta-Avondale, 1,307....F 4
27944 Hertford◉, 2,023....S 2
28601 Hickory, 20,569....G 3
28636 Hiddenite, 800....G 3
28741 Highlands, 583....C 4
* 27260 High Point, 63,204....J 2
28077 High Shoals, 900....G 4
28637 Hildebran, 481....F 3
27278 Hillsborough◉, 1,444....L 2
27843 Hobgood, 530....P 2
28537 Hobucken, 500....S 4
28347 Hoffman, 434....K 4
27844 Hollister, 750....O 2
28445 Holly Ridge, 415....P 6
27540 Holly Springs, 697....M 3
28538 Hookerton, 441....O 4
28348 Hope Mills, 1,721....M 5
28743 Hot Springs, 653....D 3
28539 Hubert, 980....P 5
28638 Hudson, 2,820....G 3
28078 Huntersville, 1,538....H 4
28666 Icard, 1,100....G 3
28079 Indian Trail, 405....H 4
27589 Inez, 250....N 2
28080 Iron Station, 250....G 4
27845 Jackson◉, 762....P 2
27281 Jackson Springs, 225....K 4
28540 Jacksonville◉, 16,021....O 5
28550 James City, 2,577....R 4
27282 Jamestown, 1,297....J 2
27846 Jamesville, 533....R 3
27947 Jarvisburg, 350....T 2
28640 Jefferson◉, 943....G 2
† 28352 Johns, 250....K 5
28642 Jonesville, 1,659....H 2
27283 Julian, 500....J 3
28787 Jupiter, 208....D 3
28081 Kannapolis, 36,293....H 4
27847 Kelford, 295....P 2
28349 Kenansville◉, 762....O 5
27542 Kenly, 1,370....N 3
27284 Kernersville, 4,815....J 2
27948 Kill Devil Hills, 357....T 3
27021 King, 1,033....J 2
28086 Kings Mountain, 8,465....G 4
28501 Kinston◉, 22,309....O 4
27544 Kittrell, 427....N 2
27949 Kitty Hawk, 600....T 2

27545 Knightdale, 815....N 3
27950 Knotts Island, 450....T 2
28449 Kure Beach, 394....O 7
28551 La Grange, 2,558....O 4
28746 Lake Lure, 456....E 4
28747 Lake Toxaway, 750....D 4
28350 Lakeview, 449....L 4
28450 Lake Waccamaw, 924....M 6
28088 Landis, 2,297....H 3
28643 Lansing, 283....F 1
28089 Lattimore, 449....F 4
28351 Laurel Hill, 1,215....K 5
† 28739 Laurel Park, 581....D 4
28352 Laurinburg◉, 8,859....K 5
28090 Lawndale, 544....F 4
27291 Leasburg, 400....L 2
28748 Leicester, 265....D 3
28451 Leland, 500....N 6
28645 Lenoir◉, 14,705....G 3
27849 Lewiston, 327....P 2
27292 Lexington◉, 17,205....J 3
27298 Liberty, 2,167....K 3
28091 Lilesville, 641....K 5
27546 Lillington◉, 1,155....M 4
28092 Lincolnton◉, 5,293....G 4
28356 Linden, 205....M 4
28646 Linville, 400....F 2
27299 Linwood, 300....J 3
27850 Littleton, 903....O 2
28461 Long Beach, 493....N 7
27548 Longhurst, 1,485....L 2
28648 Longisland, 350....H 3
28601 Long View, 3,360....G 3
28852 Longwood, 650....N 6
† 28345 Longwood Park, 1,284....K 5
27549 Louisburg◉, 2,941....N 2
28098 Lowell, 3,307....G 4
27024 Lowgap, 660....H 1
28552 Lowland, 538....S 4
27851 Lucama, 610....N 3

28358 Lumberton◉, 16,961....L 5
28750 Lynn, 550....E 4
27852 Macclesfield, 536....O 3
27951 Mackeys, 250....R 3
27025 Madison, 2,018....J 2
28751 Maggie, 400....C 3
28453 Magnolia, 614....O 5
28650 Maiden, 2,416....G 3
27552 Mamers, 500....L 4
† 28387 Manly, 225....L 4
27953 Manns Harbor, 365....T 3
† 27855 Mapleton, 250....P 2
28905 Marble, 950....B 4
28752 Marion◉, 3,335....E 3
28753 Marshall◉, 982....D 3
28553 Marshallberg, 700....S 5
28754 Mars Hill, 1,623....D 3
28103 Marshville, 1,405....J 4
28105 Matthews, 783....H 4
28554 Maury, 421....O 4
28364 Maxton, 1,885....L 5
27027 Mayodan, 2,875....K 2
28555 Maysville, 952....P 5
28361 McCain, 950....L 4
27302 Mebane, 2,433....L 2
28516 Merrimon, 500....R 5
27555 Micro, 300....N 3
27557 Middlesex, 729....N 3
28107 Midland, 950....J 4
† 28377 Midstate Mill, 925....L 4
28544 Midway Park, 4,900....O 5
27305 Milton, 235....L 1
27854 Milwaukee, 376....P 2
28212 Mint Hill, 1,200....H 4
28109 Misenheimer, 1,450....J 4
27028 Mocksville◉, 2,529....H 3
27559 Moncure, 800....L 3
28110 Monroe◉, 11,282....J 5
28757 Montreat, 450....E 3

28114 Mooresboro, 275....F 4
28115 Mooresville, 8,808....H 3
28654 Moravian Falls, 375....G 2
28557 Morehead City, 5,233....R 5
28655 Morganton◉, 13,625....F 3
28119 Morven, 562....J 5
27730 Mount Airy, 7,325....H 1
27306 Mount Gilead, 1,286....K 4
28120 Mount Holly, 5,107....H 4
28123 Mount Mourne, 950....H 3
28365 Mount Olive, 4,914....O 4
28124 Mount Pleasant, 1,174....J 4
27345 Mount Vernon Springs, 225....L 3
27958 Moyock, 325....S 1
27855 Murfreesboro, 3,508....R 2
28906 Murphy◉, 2,082....B 4
27959 Nags Head, 414....T 3
27856 Nashville◉, 1,670....O 3
27561 Neuse, 500....M 3
28560 New Bern◉, 14,660....P 4
28657 Newland◉, 524....F 2
28127 New London, 285....J 4
28570 Newport, 1,735....R 5
28658 Newton◉, 7,624....G 3
28366 Newton Grove, 546....N 4
28123 Norlina, 969....N 2
† 28752 North Cove, 257....F 3
† 28532 North Harlowe, 975....R 5
28659 North Wilkesboro, 3,357....G 2
27564 Northside, 400....M 2
28128 Norwood, 1,896....J 4
28129 Oakboro, 568....J 4
27857 Oak City, 559....P 3
27310 Oak Ridge, 950....K 2
27960 Ocracoke, 500....T 4
28762 Old Fort, 676....E 3
27961 Old Trap, 400....T 2
28368 Olivia, 400....L 4
28571 Oriental, 445....R 4
28805 Oteen, 2,863....E 3

27565 Oxford◉, 7,178....M 2
28371 Pantego, 218....R 3
28371 Parkton, 550....M 5
27861 Parmele, 373....P 3
28661 Patterson, 344....F 2
28133 Peachland, 556....J 5
28091 Pee Dee, 210....K 5
27311 Pelham, 350....L 1
28372 Pembroke, 1,982....L 5
28766 Penrose, 600....D 4
27041 Pilot Mountain, 1,309....K 2
28373 Pinebluff, 577....K 4
27042 Pine Hall, 550....K 2
28374 Pinehurst, 1,056....K 4
27568 Pine Level, 983....N 4
28662 Pineola, 875....F 2
27864 Pinetops, 1,379....O 3
27865 Pinetown, 278....R 3
28134 Pineville, 1,948....H 4
28572 Pink Hill, 522....O 4
27043 Pinnacle, 725....J 2
28768 Pisgah Forest, 850....D 4
27312 Pittsboro◉, 1,447....L 3
27866 Pleasant Hill, 250....P 2
27962 Plymouth◉, 4,774....R 3
28135 Polkton, 845....J 4
28136 Polkville, 450....F 4
28573 Pollocksville, 456....P 5
27965 Poplar Branch, 400....T 2
27966 Powells Point, 375....T 2
27967 Powellsville, 247....R 2
27569 Princeton, 1,044....N 4
† 27886 Princeville, 654....P 3
28376 Raeford◉, 3,180....L 5
* 27601 Raleigh (cap.)◉, 121,577....M 3
Raleigh, ‡228,453....M 3
27316 Ramseur, 1,328....K 3
27317 Randleman, 2,312....K 3

† 28906 Ranger, 500....A 4
28052 Ranlo, 2,092....G 4
27868 Red Oak, 359....N 2
28377 Red Springs, 3,383....L 5
27320 Reidsville, 13,636....K 2
28378 Rex, 975....M 5
28133 Rhodhiss, 784....F 3
† 28092 Rhyne, 2,273....G 4
28137 Richfield, 306....J 4
28574 Richlands, 935....O 5
28456 Riegelwood, 459....N 6
27870 Roanoke Rapids, 13,508....O 2
28669 Roaring Gap, 450....G 2
28669 Roaring River, 500....G 2
27325 Robbins, 1,059....L 4
28771 Robbinsville◉, 777....B 4
† 28379 Roberdel, 350....K 5
27871 Robersonville, 1,910....P 3
28379 Rockingham◉, 5,852....K 5
28138 Rockwell, 999....J 3
27801 Rocky Mount, 34,284....O 3
28457 Rocky Point, 975....O 6
28571 Rolesville, 529....N 3
28670 Ronda, 465....H 2
27970 Roper, 649....R 3
28382 Roseboro, 1,235....N 5
28458 Rose Hill, 1,448....O 5
28772 Rosman, 407....D 4
27572 Rougemont, 400....L 2
28383 Rowland, 1,358....L 5
28573 Roxboro, 5,370....L 2
27872 Roxobel, 347....P 2
† 27587 Royal Cotton Mills, 600....M 2
27326 Ruffin, 600....L 1
27045 Rural Hall, 2,338....J 2
† 28139 Ruth, 500....F 4
28671 Rutherford College, 950....F 3
28139 Rutherfordton◉, 3,245....E 4

Topography

0   40   80
MILES

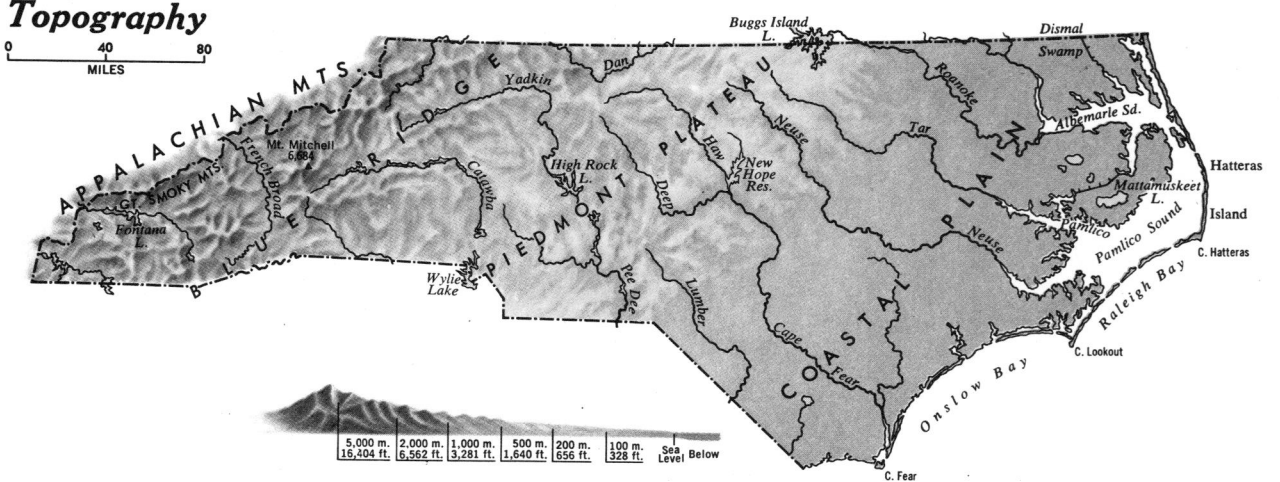

5,000 m. | 2,000 m. | 1,000 m. | 500 m. | 200 m. | 100 m. | Sea Level
16,404 ft. | 6,562 ft. | 3,281 ft. | 1,640 ft. | 656 ft. | 328 ft. | Below

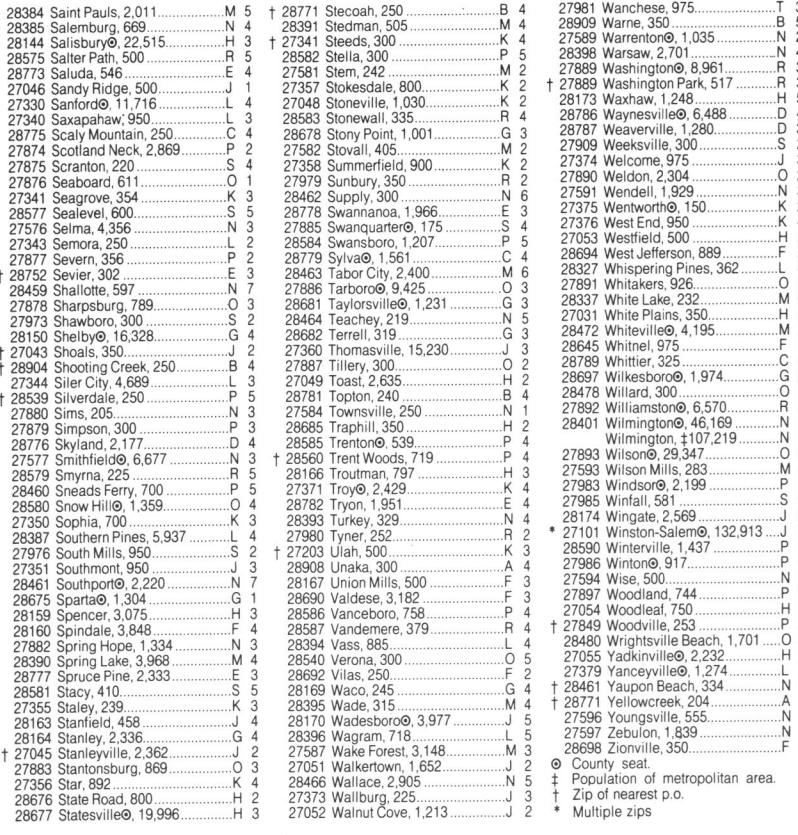

ZIP	Place	Grid
28384	Saint Pauls, 2,011	M 5
28385	Salemburg, 669	N 4
28144	Salisbury⊙, 22,515	H 3
28575	Salter Path, 500	R 5
28773	Saluda, 546	E 4
27046	Sandy Ridge, 500	J 1
27330	Sanford⊙, 11,716	L 4
27340	Saxapahaw, 950	L 3
28775	Scaly Mountain, 250	C 4
28774	Scotland Neck, 2,869	P 2
28785	Scranton, 220	S 4
28876	Seaboard, 611	O 2
27341	Seagrove, 354	K 3
28577	Sealevel, 600	S 5
27576	Selma, 4,356	M 3
27343	Semora, 250	L 2
27877	Severn, 356	O 2
† 28752	Sevier, 302	E 3
28459	Shallotte, 597	N 7
27878	Sharpsburg, 789	O 3
27973	Shawboro, 300	S 2
28150	Shelby⊙, 16,328	G 4
† 27043	Shoals, 350	J 2
† 28904	Shooting Creek, 250	B 4
27344	Siler City, 4,689	L 3
† 28539	Silverdale, 250	P 5
27880	Sims, 205	N 3
28776	Skyland, 2,177	D 4
27577	Smithfield⊙, 6,677	M 3
28579	Smyrna, 225	R 5
28460	Sneads Ferry, 700	P 5
28580	Snow Hill⊙, 1,359	O 4
27350	Sophia, 700	J 3
28387	Southern Pines, 5,937	L 4
27976	South Mills, 950	S 2
27351	Southmont, 950	J 3
28461	Southport⊙, 2,220	N 7
28675	Sparta⊙, 1,304	G 1
28159	Spencer, 3,075	H 3
28160	Spindale, 3,848	F 4
27882	Spring Hope, 1,334	N 3
28390	Spring Lake, 3,968	M 4
28777	Spruce Pine, 2,333	E 3
28581	Stacy, 410	S 5
27355	Staley, 239	K 3
28163	Stanfield, 458	H 4
28164	Stanley, 2,336	G 4
† 27045	Stanleyville, 2,362	J 2
27883	Stantonsburg, 869	O 3
27356	Star, 892	K 4
28676	State Road, 800	H 2
28677	Statesville⊙, 19,996	H 2
† 28771	Stecoah, 250	B 4
28391	Stedman, 505	M 4
† 27341	Steeds, 300	K 3
28582	Stella, 300	P 5
27581	Stem, 242	M 2
27357	Stokesdale, 800	K 2
27048	Stoneville, 1,030	J 2
28583	Stonewall, 335	R 4
28678	Stony Point, 1,001	G 3
27582	Stovall, 405	M 2
27358	Summerfield, 900	K 2
27979	Sunbury, 350	R 2
28462	Supply, 300	N 6
28778	Swannanoa, 1,966	E 3
27885	Swanquarter⊙, 175	S 4
28584	Swansboro, 1,207	P 5
28779	Sylva⊙, 1,561	C 4
28463	Tabor City, 2,400	M 6
27886	Tarboro⊙, 9,425	O 3
28681	Taylorsville⊙, 1,231	G 3
28464	Teachey, 219	N 5
28682	Terrell, 319	G 4
27360	Thomasville, 15,230	J 3
27887	Tillery, 300	O 2
27049	Toast, 2,635	J 2
28781	Topton, 240	B 4
27584	Townsville, 250	N 1
28685	Traphill, 350	H 2
28585	Trenton⊙, 539	P 4
† 28560	Trent Woods, 719	P 4
28166	Troutman, 797	H 3
27371	Troy⊙, 2,429	K 4
28782	Tryon, 1,951	E 4
28393	Turkey, 329	N 4
27980	Tyner, 252	R 2
† 27203	Ulah, 500	K 3
28908	Unaka, 300	A 4
28167	Union Mills, 500	F 3
28690	Valdese, 3,182	F 3
28586	Vanceboro, 758	P 4
28587	Vandemere, 379	R 4
28394	Vass, 885	L 4
28540	Verona, 300	O 5
28692	Vilas, 250	F 2
28169	Vaux, 245	G 4
28395	Wade, 315	M 4
28170	Wadesboro⊙, 3,977	G 4
28396	Wagram, 718	L 5
27587	Wake Forest, 3,148	M 3
27051	Walkertown, 1,652	J 2
28466	Wallace, 2,905	N 5
27373	Wallburg, 225	J 2
27052	Walnut Cove, 1,213	J 2
27981	Wanchese, 975	T 3
28909	Warne, 350	B 5
27589	Warrenton⊙, 1,035	N 2
28398	Warsaw, 2,701	N 4
27889	Washington⊙, 8,961	R 3
† 27889	Washington Park, 517	R 3
28173	Waxhaw, 1,248	H 5
28786	Waynesville⊙, 6,488	D 4
28787	Weaverville, 1,280	D 4
27909	Weeksville, 300	S 2
27374	Welcome, 975	J 3
27890	Weldon, 2,304	O 2
27591	Wendell, 1,929	N 3
27375	Wentworth⊙, 150	K 2
27376	West End, 950	K 4
27053	Westfield, 500	H 2
28694	West Jefferson, 889	F 2
28327	Whispering Pines, 362	L 4
27891	Whitakers, 926	O 2
28337	White Lake, 232	M 5
27031	White Plains, 350	H 2
28472	Whiteville⊙, 4,195	M 6
28645	Whitnel, 975	F 3
28789	Whittier, 325	C 4
28697	Wilkesboro⊙, 1,974	G 2
28478	Willard, 300	N 5
27892	Williamston⊙, 6,570	R 3
28401	Wilmington⊙, 46,169	N 6
	Wilmington, ‡107,219	N 6
27893	Wilson⊙, 29,347	O 3
27593	Wilson Mills, 283	M 3
27983	Windsor⊙, 2,199	R 2
27985	Winfall, 581	S 2
28174	Wingate, 2,569	H 5
* 27101	Winston-Salem⊙, 132,913	J 2
28590	Winterville, 1,437	P 3
27986	Winton⊙, 917	R 2
27594	Wise, 500	N 2
27897	Woodland, 744	O 2
27054	Woodleaf, 750	H 3
† 27849	Woodville, 253	P 2
28480	Wrightsville Beach, 1,701	O 6
27055	Yadkinville⊙, 2,232	H 2
27379	Yanceyville⊙, 1,274	L 2
28693	Yaupon Beach, 334	N 7
† 28771	Yellowcreek, 204	A 4
27596	Youngsville, 555	N 3
27597	Zebulon, 1,839	N 3
28698	Zionville, 350	F 2

⊙ County seat.
‡ Population of metropolitan area.
† Zip of nearest p.o.
* Multiple zips

Weeding "green gold" — tobacco is North Carolina's money crop.

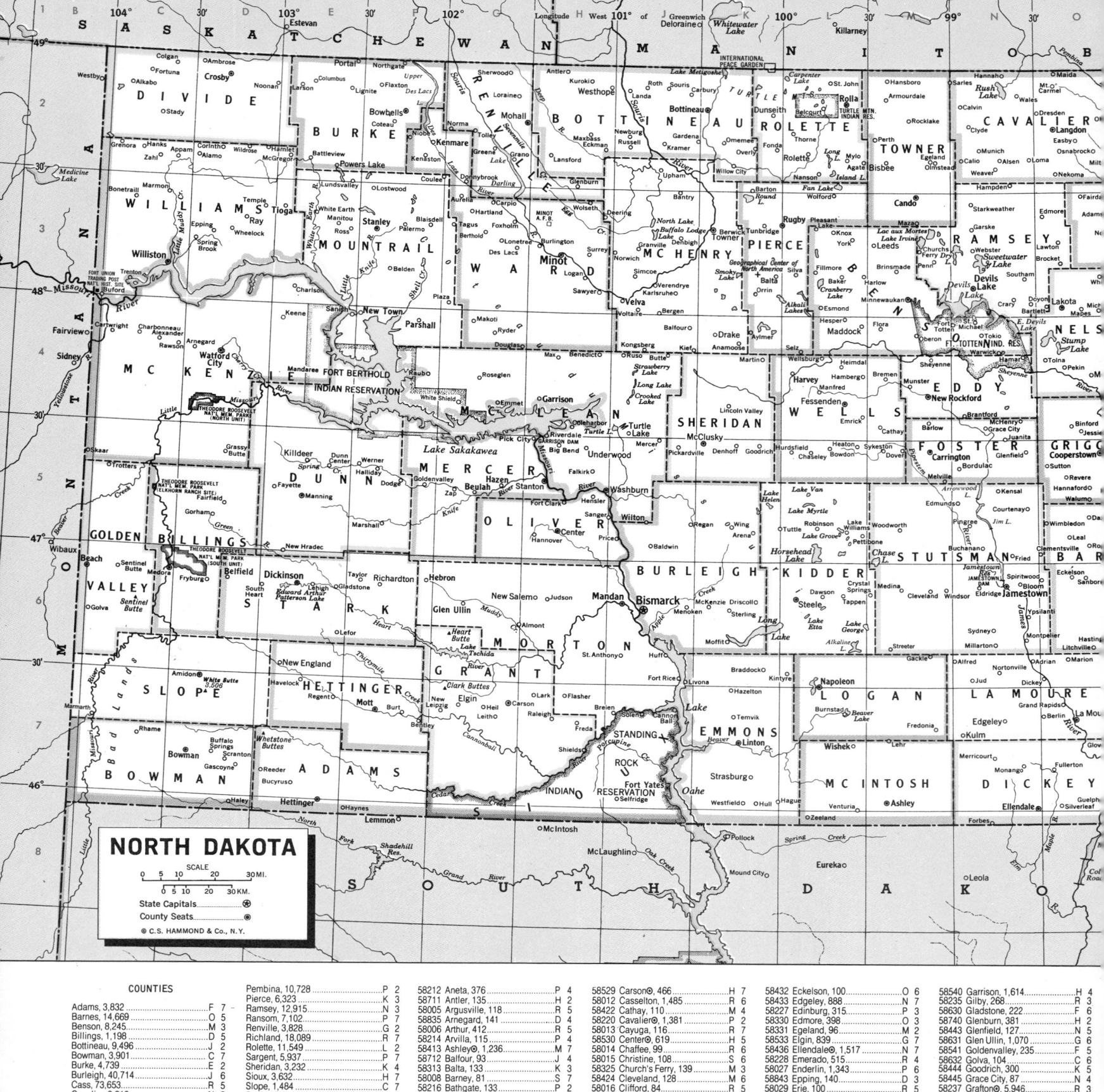

NORTH DAKOTA

SCALE
0 5 10   20   30 MI.
0 5 10   20   30 KM.

State Capitals.................⊛
County Seats..................◉

⊛ C.S. HAMMOND & Co., N.Y.

COUNTIES

Adams, 3,832 ....F 7
Barnes, 14,669 ....O 5
Benson, 8,245 ....M 3
Billings, 1,198 ....D 5
Bottineau, 9,496 ....J 2
Bowman, 3,901 ....C 7
Burke, 4,739 ....E 2
Burleigh, 40,714 ....J 6
Cass, 73,653 ....R 5
Cavalier, 8,213 ....N 2
Dickey, 6,976 ....N 7
Divide, 4,564 ....C 2
Dunn, 4,895 ....E 5
Eddy, 4,103 ....L 4
Emmons, 7,200 ....K 7
Foster, 4,832 ....N 5
Golden Valley, 2,611 ....C 5
Grand Forks, 61,102 ....P 3
Grant, 5,009 ....G 6
Griggs, 4,184 ....O 5
Hettinger, 5,075 ....E 7
Kidder, 4,362 ....L 6
La Moure, 7,117 ....N 7
Logan, 4,245 ....L 7
McHenry, 8,977 ....J 3
McIntosh, 5,545 ....L 7
McKenzie, 6,127 ....D 4
McLean, 11,251 ....G 5
Mercer, 6,175 ....G 5
Morton, 20,310 ....H 6
Mountrail, 8,437 ....E 3
Nelson, 5,776 ....O 4
Oliver, 2,322 ....H 5

Pembina, 10,728 ....P 2
Pierce, 6,323 ....K 3
Ramsey, 12,915 ....N 3
Ransom, 7,102 ....P 7
Renville, 3,828 ....G 2
Richland, 18,089 ....R 7
Rolette, 11,549 ....L 2
Sargent, 5,937 ....P 7
Sheridan, 3,232 ....K 4
Sioux, 3,632 ....H 7
Slope, 1,484 ....C 7
Stark, 19,613 ....E 6
Steele, 3,749 ....P 4
Stutsman, 23,550 ....M 5
Towner, 4,645 ....M 2
Traill, 9,571 ....R 5
Walsh, 16,251 ....P 3
Ward, 58,560 ....G 3
Wells, 7,847 ....L 4
Williams, 19,301 ....C 3

CITIES and TOWNS

Zip	Name/Pop.	Key
58001	Abercrombie, 262	S 7
58210	Adams, 284	O 3
58830	Alamo, 124	D 2
58831	Alexander, 208	C 4
58003	Alice, 83	P 6
58520	Almont, 109	H 6
58311	Alsen, 201	N 2
58833	Ambrose, 106	D 2
58620	Amidon⊙, 54	D 7
58710	Anamoose, 401	K 4
58212	Aneta, 376	P 4
58711	Antler, 135	H 2
58005	Argusville, 118	R 5
58835	Arnegard, 141	D 4
58006	Arthur, 412	R 5
58214	Arvilla, 115	P 4
58413	Ashley⊙, 1,236	M 7
58712	Balfour, 93	J 4
58313	Balta, 133	K 3
58008	Barney, 81	S 7
58216	Bathgate, 133	P 2
58621	Beach⊙, 1,408	C 6
58316	Belcourt, 950	L 2
58622	Belfield, 1,130	D 6
58718	Berthold, 398	G 3
58523	Beulah, 1,344	G 5
58416	Binford, 242	O 4
58317	Bisbee, 305	M 3
58501	Bismarck (cap.)⊛, 34,703	J 6
58318	Bottineau⊙, 2,760	J 2
58721	Bowbells⊙, 584	F 2
58418	Bowdon, 229	L 5
58623	Bowman⊙, 1,762	D 7
58524	Braddock, 106	K 6
58321	Brocket, 95	O 3
58420	Buchanan, 100	N 5
58011	Buffalo, 241	R 6
58722	Burlington, 247	G 3
58723	Butte, 193	H 4
58218	Buxton, 235	R 4
58324	Cando⊙, 1,512	M 3
58528	Cannon Ball, 550	J 7
† 58241	Canton (Hensel), 81	P 2
58725	Carpio, 215	G 3

58529	Carson⊙, 466	H 7
58012	Casselton, 1,485	R 6
58422	Cathay, 110	M 4
58220	Cavalier⊙, 1,381	P 2
58013	Cayuga, 116	P 7
58530	Center⊙, 619	H 5
58014	Chaffee, 99	R 6
58015	Christine, 108	S 6
58325	Church's Ferry, 139	M 3
58424	Cleveland, 128	M 6
58016	Clifford, 84	R 5
58017	Cogswell, 203	P 7
58425	Cooperstown⊙, 1,485	O 5
58426	Courtenay, 125	N 5
58327	Crary, 150	N 3
58730	Crosby⊙, 1,545	D 2
58222	Crystal, 272	P 2
58021	Davenport, 147	R 6
58428	Dawson, 131	L 6
58429	Dazey, 128	O 5
58430	Denhoff, 85	K 5
58733	Des Lacs, 197	G 3
58301	Devils Lake⊙, 7,078	N 3
58431	Dickey, 118	N 6
58601	Dickinson⊙, 12,405	E 6
58625	Dodge, 121	F 5
58734	Donnybrook, 163	G 2
58735	Dodge, 144	G 4
58736	Drake, 636	K 4
58225	Drayton, 1,095	P 2
58532	Driscoll, 128	K 6
58626	Dunn Center, 107	E 5
58329	Dunseith, 811	K 2
58024	Dwight, 93	S 7

58432	Eckelson, 100	O 6
58433	Edgeley, 888	N 7
58227	Edinburg, 315	P 3
58330	Edmore, 309	O 3
58331	Egeland, 96	M 2
58533	Elgin, 839	G 7
58436	Ellendale⊙, 1,517	N 7
58228	Emerado, 515	R 4
58027	Enderlin, 1,343	P 6
58843	Epping, 140	D 3
58029	Erie, 100	R 5
58332	Esmond, 416	L 3
58229	Fairdale, 102	O 3
58030	Fairmount, 412	S 7
58102	Fargo⊙, 53,365	S 6
	Fargo-Moorhead, ‡120,238	S 6
58438	Fessenden⊙, 815	L 4
58031	Finley, 166	P 6
58230	Finley, 809	P 4
58535	Flasher, 467	H 7
58737	Flaxton, 286	F 2
58439	Forbes, 88	N 8
58231	Fordville, 361	P 3
58233	Forest River, 169	P 3
58032	Forman⊙, 596	P 7
58033	Fort Ransom, 121	P 6
58835	Fort Totten, 550	M 4
58538	Fort Yates⊙, 1,153	J 7
58440	Fredonia, 100	M 7
58441	Fullerton, 107	O 7
58442	Gackle, 470	M 6
58035	Galesburg, 134	R 5
58739	Gardena, 84	J 2
58036	Gardner, 96	R 5

58540	Garrison⊙, 1,614	H 4
58235	Gilby, 268	R 3
58630	Gladstone, 222	F 6
58740	Glenburn, 381	H 2
58443	Glenfield, 127	N 5
58631	Glen Ullin, 1,070	G 6
58541	Goldenvalley, 235	F 5
58632	Golva, 104	C 6
58444	Goodrich, 300	K 5
58445	Grace City, 87	N 4
58237	Grafton⊙, 5,946	R 3
58201	Grand Forks⊙, 39,008	R 4
58038	Grandin, 187	R 5
58741	Granville, 282	J 3
58039	Great Bend, 86	S 7
58845	Grenora, 401	C 2
58040	Gwinner, 623	P 7
58542	Hague, 146	L 7
58636	Halliday, 413	F 5
58238	Hamilton, 110	R 2
58338	Hampden, 114	N 3
58041	Hankinson, 1,125	S 7
58448	Hannaford, 244	O 5
58239	Hannah, 145	N 2
58340	Harlow, 85	L 4
58341	Harvey, 2,361	L 4
58042	Harwood, 200	S 6
58240	Hatton, 808	R 4
58043	Havana, 156	P 7
58544	Hazelton, 374	K 7
58545	Hazen, 1,240	G 5
58638	Hebron, 1,103	G 6
58342	Heimdal, 101	L 4
58547	Hensler, 100	H 5
58639	Hettinger⊙, 1,655	E 7

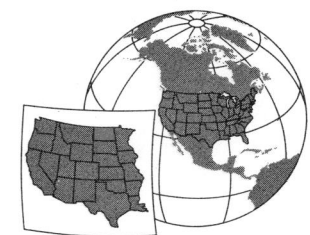

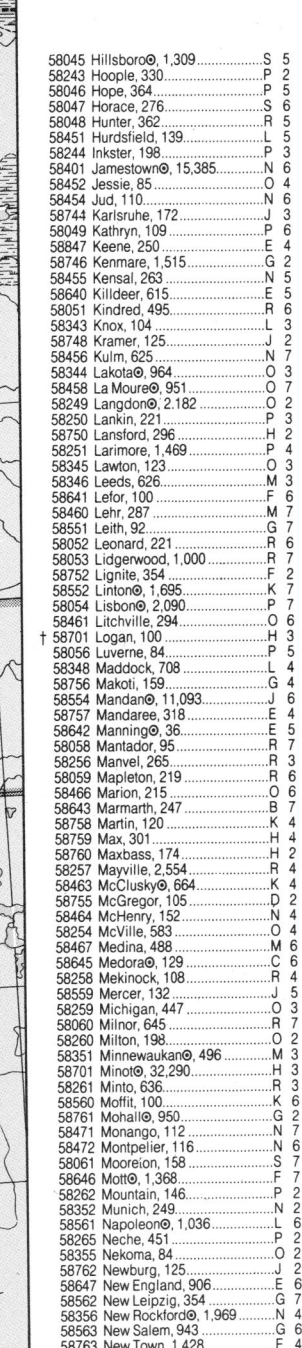

AREA 70,665 sq. mi.
POPULATION 617,761 ('70); 652,695 ('80)
CAPITAL Bismarck
LARGEST CITY Fargo
HIGHEST POINT White Butte 3,506 ft.
SETTLED IN 1780
ADMITTED TO UNION November 2, 1889
POPULAR NAME Flickertail State; Sioux State
STATE FLOWER Prairie Rose
STATE BIRD Meadowlark

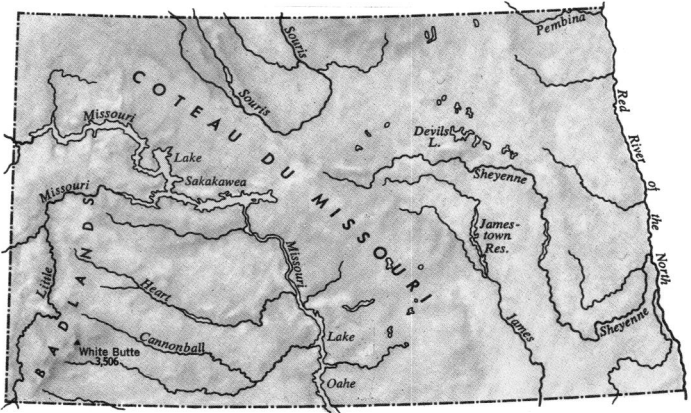

Topography

5,000 m. 16,404 ft.	2,000 m. 6,562 ft.	1,000 m. 3,281 ft.	500 m. 1,640 ft.	200 m. 656 ft.	100 m. 328 ft.	Sea Level	Below

0   50   100
MILES

58045 Hillsboro⊙, 1,309..............S 5
58243 Hoople, 330......................P 2
58046 Hope, 364.........................P 5
58047 Horace, 276......................S 6
58048 Hunter, 362......................R 5
58451 Hurdsfield, 139.................L 5
58244 Inkster, 198.....................P 3
58401 Jamestown⊙, 15,385.......N 6
58452 Jessie, 85..........................O 4
58454 Jud, 110............................N 6
58744 Karlsruhe, 172...................J 3
58049 Kathryn, 109.....................P 6
58847 Keene, 250........................E 4
58746 Kenmare, 1,515.................J 2
58455 Kensal, 263.......................N 5
58640 Killdeer, 615......................E 5
58051 Kindred, 495......................R 6
58343 Knox, 104.........................L 3
58748 Kramer, 125.......................J 2
58456 Kulm, 625..........................N 7
58344 Lakota⊙, 964.....................O 3
58458 La Moure⊙, 951................O 7
58249 Langdon⊙, 2,182..............O 2
58250 Lankin, 221........................P 3
58750 Lansford, 296....................H 2
58251 Larimore, 1,469.................P 4
58345 Lawton, 123.......................O 3
58346 Leeds, 626........................M 3
58641 Lefor, 100..........................F 6
58460 Lehr, 287...........................M 7
58551 Leith, 92............................G 7
58052 Leonard, 221......................R 6
58053 Lidgerwood, 1,000.............R 7
58752 Lignite, 354.......................F 2
58552 Linton⊙, 1,695...................K 7
58054 Lisbon⊙, 2,090..................P 7
58461 Litchville, 294....................O 6
† 58701 Logan, 100.......................H 3
58056 Luverne, 84........................P 5
58348 Maddock, 708....................L 4
58756 Makoti, 159.......................G 4
58554 Mandan⊙, 11,093............J 6
58757 Mandaree, 318....................E 4
58642 Manning, 36.......................E 5
58058 Mantador, 95......................R 7
58256 Manvel, 265.......................R 3
58059 Mapleton, 219....................R 6
58466 Marion, 215........................O 6
58643 Marmarth, 247....................B 7
58758 Martin, 120.........................K 4
58759 Max, 301............................H 4
58760 Maxbass, 174.....................H 2
58257 Mayville, 2,554..................R 4
58463 McClusky⊙, 664.................K 4
58755 McGregor, 105....................D 2
58464 McHenry, 152.....................N 4
58254 McVille, 583.......................O 4
58467 Medina, 488.......................M 6
58645 Medora⊙, 129....................C 6
58258 Mekinock, 108....................R 4
58559 Mercer, 132........................J 5
58259 Michigan, 447.....................O 3
58060 Milnor, 645.........................R 7
58260 Milton, 198.........................P 3
58351 Minnewaukan⊙, 496.........M 3
58701 Minot⊙, 32,290................H 3
58261 Minto, 636..........................R 3
58560 Moffit, 100..........................K 6
58761 Mohall⊙, 950.....................G 2
58471 Monango, 112....................N 7
58472 Montpelier, 116..................N 6
58061 Mooreton, 186....................S 7
58646 Mott⊙, 1,368.....................E 7
58262 Mountain, 146....................P 2
58352 Munich, 249.......................N 2
58561 Napoleon⊙, 1,036.............L 6
58265 Neche, 451.........................P 2
58355 Nekoma, 84........................O 2
58762 Newburg, 125.....................J 2
58647 New England, 906.............E 6
58562 New Leipzig, 354...............G 7
58356 New Rockford⊙, 1,969.......N 4
58563 New Salem, 943..................G 6
58763 New Town, 1,428...............F 4
58266 Niagara, 115.......................P 4
58062 Nome, 103..........................P 6

58765 Noonan, 403.......................D 2
58267 Northwood, 1,189...............P 4
58473 Nortonville, 90....................N 6
58474 Oakes, 1,742......................O 7
†58237 Oakwood, 91....................R 3
58357 Oberon, 151........................M 4
58063 Oriska, 128.........................P 6
58269 Osnabrock, 255...................O 2
58064 Page, 367...........................P 5
58769 Palermo, 146.......................F 3
58270 Park River, 1,680................P 3
58770 Parshall, 1,246....................F 4
58361 Pekin, 120...........................O 4
58271 Pembina, 741......................P 2
58272 Petersburg, 266...................P 3
58475 Pettibone, 173.....................L 5
†58545 Pick City, 119....................G 5
58273 Pisek, 154...........................P 3
58771 Plaza, 291...........................G 3
58772 Portal, 251...........................E 2
58274 Portland, 534.......................R 5
58773 Powers Lake, 523................E 2
58849 Ray, 776.............................D 3
58649 Reeder, 306.........................E 7
58650 Regent, 344.........................E 7
58275 Reynolds, 236......................R 4
58651 Rhame, 206.........................C 7
58652 Richardton, 799...................F 6
58565 Riverdale, 600......................H 4
58478 Robinson, 125......................L 5
58365 Rocklake, 270......................M 2
58479 Rogers, 96...........................O 5
58366 Rolette, 579.........................L 2
58367 Rolla⊙, 1,458......................L 2
58776 Ross, 125.............................E 3
58368 Rugby⊙, 2,889....................L 3
58067 Rutland, 225........................P 7

58779 Ryder, 211...........................G 4
58369 Saint John, 367....................L 2
58276 Saint Thomas, 508..............R 2
58480 Sanborn, 255.......................O 6
58580 Sanish, 25...........................E 4
58372 Sarles, 148..........................N 2
58781 Sawyer, 373........................H 3
58653 Scranton, 360......................D 7
58568 Selfridge, 346......................J 7
58373 Selz, 110.............................L 4
58654 Sentinel Butte, 125..............C 6
58277 Sharon, 201.........................P 4
58068 Sheldon, 192........................P 6
58782 Sherwood, 369....................G 2
58374 Sheyenne, 362.....................M 4
58569 Shields, 125.........................H 7
58570 Solen, 180...........................J 7
58783 Souris, 151..........................J 2
58655 South Heart, 132.................D 6
58481 Spiritwood, 100...................N 6
58784 Stanley⊙, 1,581..................F 3
58571 Stanton⊙, 517....................H 5
58377 Starkweather, 193...............N 3
58482 Steele⊙, 696.......................L 6
58573 Strasburg, 642.....................K 7
58483 Streeter, 324.......................M 6
58785 Surrey, 361..........................H 3
58484 Sutton, 87...........................O 5
58486 Sykeston, 232.....................M 5
58487 Tappen, 294.........................L 6
58656 Taylor, 162..........................F 6
58278 Thompson, 291....................R 4
58852 Tioga, 1,667........................E 3
58379 Tokio, 130...........................N 4
58787 Tolley, 163...........................G 2
58380 Tolna, 247...........................O 4
58071 Tower City, 289...................P 6

58788 Towner⊙, 870.....................K 3
58853 Trenton, 150........................C 3
58575 Turtle Lake, 712..................J 4
58488 Tuttle, 216...........................L 5
58576 Underwood, 781.................H 5
58789 Upham, 272.........................J 2
58072 Valley City⊙, 7,843............P 6
58790 Velva, 1,241........................J 3
58490 Verona, 140.........................O 7
58075 Wahpeton⊙, 7,076............S 7
58077 Walcott, 175........................R 6
58281 Wales, 116...........................N 2
58282 Walhalla, 1,471...................P 2
58577 Washburn⊙, 804................J 5
58854 Watford City⊙, 1,768.........D 4
58569 West Fargo, 5,161...............S 6
†58078 West Fargo Industrial Park,
    104...................................S 6
58793 Westhope, 705.....................H 2
58794 White Earth, 128..................E 3
58795 Wildrose, 235......................D 2
58801 Williston⊙, 11,280.............C 3
58384 Willow City, 403..................K 2
58579 Wilton, 695.........................J 5
58492 Wimbledon, 337...................O 5
58494 Wing, 223...........................K 5
58495 Wishek, 1,275.....................L 7
58496 Woodworth, 139..................M 5
58081 Wyndmere, 516...................R 7
58386 York, 102............................L 3
58497 Ypsilanti, 139......................N 6
58580 Zap, 271..............................G 5
58071 Zeeland, 313........................L 8

⊙ County seat.
● Population of metropolitan area.
† Zip of nearest p.o.
* Multiple zips

North Dakota's wealth springs from her soil. The state has the largest farms and leads in production of barley, wheat and flaxseed.

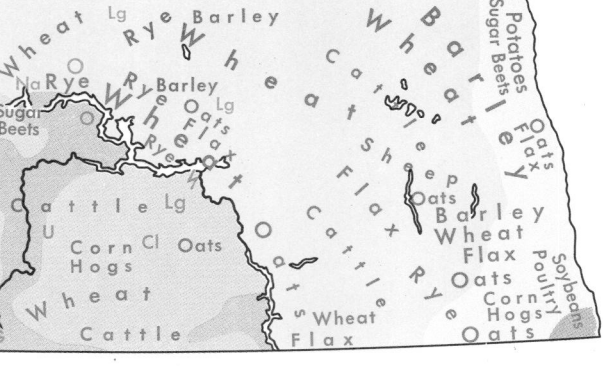

DOMINANT LAND USE

Agriculture, Industry and Resources

☐ Specialized Wheat
☐ Wheat, General Farming
☐ Wheat, Range Livestock
☐ Livestock, Cash Grain
☐ Sugar Beets, Dry Beans, Livestock, General Farming
☐ Range Livestock
⚡ Water Power

MAJOR MINERAL OCCURRENCES

Cl   Clay
G   Natural Gas
Lg   Lignite
Na   Salt
O   Petroleum
U   Uranium

OHIO

SCALE

0 5 10   20   30   40 MI.

0 5 10   20   30   40KM.

State Capitals............⭐

County Seats............◉

© C.S. HAMMOND & Co., N.Y.

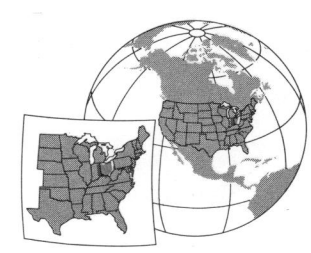

COUNTIES

Adams, 18,957 ....D 8
Allen, 111,144 ....B 4
Ashland, 43,303 ....F 4
Ashtabula, 98,237 ....J 2
Athens, 54,889 ....F 7
Auglaize, 38,602 ....B 4
Belmont, 80,917 ....J 5
Brown, 26,635 ....C 7
Butler, 258,207 ....A 7
Carroll, 21,579 ....H 4
Champaign, 30,491 ....C 5
Clark, 157,115 ....C 5
Clermont, 95,725 ....B 7
Clinton, 31,464 ....C 7
Columbiana, 108,310 ....J 4
Coshocton, 33,486 ....G 5
Crawford, 50,364 ....E 4
Cuyahoga, 1,721,300 ....G 3
Darke, 49,141 ....A 5
Defiance, 36,949 ....A 3
Delaware, 42,908 ....D 5
Erie, 75,909 ....E 3
Fairfield, 73,301 ....E 6
Fayette, 25,461 ....D 6
Franklin, 833,249 ....E 5
Fulton, 33,071 ....B 2
Gallia, 25,239 ....F 8
Geauga, 62,977 ....H 3
Greene, 125,057 ....C 6
Guernsey, 37,665 ....H 5
Hamilton, 924,018 ....A 7
Hancock, 61,217 ....C 3
Hardin, 30,813 ....C 4
Harrison, 17,013 ....H 5
Henry, 27,058 ....B 3
Highland, 28,996 ....C 7
Hocking, 20,322 ....F 6
Holmes, 23,024 ....G 4
Huron, 49,587 ....E 3
Jackson, 27,174 ....E 7
Jefferson, 96,193 ....J 5
Knox, 41,795 ....F 5
Lake, 197,200 ....H 2
Lawrence, 56,868 ....E 8
Licking, 107,799 ....F 5
Logan, 35,072 ....C 5
Lorain, 256,843 ....F 3
Lucas, 484,370 ....C 2
Madison, 28,318 ....D 5
Mahoning, 303,424 ....J 4
Marion, 64,724 ....D 4
Medina, 82,717 ....G 3
Meigs, 19,799 ....F 7
Mercer, 35,265 ....A 4
Miami, 84,342 ....B 5
Monroe, 15,739 ....H 6
Montgomery, 606,148 ....B 6
Morgan, 12,375 ....G 6
Morrow, 21,348 ....E 4
Muskingum, 77,826 ....G 5
Noble, 10,428 ....G 6
Ottawa, 37,099 ....D 2
Paulding, 19,329 ....A 3
Perry, 27,434 ....F 6
Pickaway, 40,071 ....D 6
Pike, 19,114 ....D 7
Portage, 125,868 ....H 3
Preble, 34,719 ....A 6
Putnam, 31,134 ....B 3
Richland, 129,997 ....E 4
Ross, 61,211 ....D 7
Sandusky, 60,983 ....D 3
Scioto, 76,951 ....D 8
Seneca, 60,696 ....D 3
Shelby, 37,748 ....B 5
Stark, 372,210 ....H 4
Summit, 553,371 ....G 3
Trumbull, 232,579 ....J 3
Tuscarawas, 77,211 ....H 5
Union, 23,786 ....D 5
Van Wert, 29,194 ....A 4
Vinton, 9,420 ....E 7
Warren, 84,925 ....B 7
Washington, 57,160 ....H 7
Wayne, 87,123 ....G 4
Williams, 33,669 ....A 2
Wood, 89,722 ....C 3
Wyandot, 21,826 ....D 4

CITIES and TOWNS

Zip	Name/Pop.	Key
45101	Aberdeen, 1,165	C 8
45810	Ada, 5,309	C 4
45001	Addyston, 1,336	B 9
43901	Adena, 1,134	J 5
* 44301	Akron◉, 275,425	G 3
	Akron, ‡679,239	G 3
45710	Albany, 899	F 7
43001	Alexandria, 588	E 5
45812	Alger, 1,071	C 4
44601	Alliance, 26,547	H 4
43102	Amanda, 788	E 6
† 45201	Amberley, 5,574	C 9
45102	Amelia, 820	D 10
44001	Amherst, 9,902	F 3
43903	Amsterdam, 882	J 5
44003	Andover, 1,179	J 2
45302	Anna, 792	B 5
45303	Ansonia, 1,044	A 5
45813	Antwerp, 1,735	A 3
44606	Apple Creek, 784	G 4
44804	Arcadia, 689	D 3
45304	Arcanum, 1,993	A 6
43502	Archbold, 3,047	B 2
45814	Arlington, 1,066	C 4
† 45201	Arlington Heights, 1,476	C 9
44805	Ashland◉, 19,872	F 4
43003	Ashley, 1,034	E 5
44004	Ashtabula, 24,313	J 2
43103	Ashville, 1,772	E 6
45701	Athens◉, 23,310	F 7
44807	Attica, 1,005	E 3
44201	Atwater, 975	H 3

Zip	Name/Pop.	Key
44202	Aurora, 6,549	H 3
44010	Austinburg, 900	J 2
44515	Austintown, 29,393	J 3
44011	Avon, 7,214	F 3
44012	Avon Lake, 12,261	F 2
† 43512	Ayersville, 950	B 3
45612	Bainbridge, 1,057	D 7
† 43420	Ballville, 1,652	D 3
43804	Baltic, 571	G 5
43105	Baltimore, 2,418	E 6
44203	Barberton, 33,052	G 4
43713	Barnesville, 4,292	H 6
43905	Barton, 975	J 5
45103	Batavia◉, 1,894	B 7
† 44870	Bay View, 798	E 3
44140	Bay Village, 18,163	G 4
44608	Beach City, 1,133	H 4
† 44101	Beachwood, 9,631	J 9
45808	Beaverdam, 525	C 4
44146	Bedford, 17,552	H 9
† 44146	Bedford Heights, 13,063	J 9
43906	Bellaire, 9,655	J 5
45305	Bellbrook, 1,268	C 6
43310	Belle Center, 985	C 4
43311	Bellefontaine◉, 11,255	C 5
44811	Bellevue, 8,604	E 3
44813	Bellville, 1,685	E 4
43718	Belmont, 666	J 5
44609	Beloit, 921	J 4
45714	Belpre, 7,189	G 7
44017	Berea, 22,396	G 10
43908	Bergholz, 914	J 4
44814	Berlin Heights, 828	F 3
45106	Bethel, 2,214	B 8
43719	Bethesda, 1,157	H 5
44815	Bettsville, 833	D 3
45715	Beverly, 1,396	G 6
43209	Bexley, 14,888	E 6
45107	Blanchester, 3,080	B 7
44817	Bloomdale, 727	D 3
43106	Bloomingburg, 895	D 6
44818	Bloomville, 884	D 3
† 45201	Blue Ash, 8,324	C 9
45817	Bluffton, 2,935	C 4
44512	Boardman, 30,852	J 4
44612	Bolivar, 1,084	H 4
† 44264	Boston Heights, 846	J 10
45306	Botkins, 1,057	B 5
43402	Bowling Green◉, 21,760	C 3
45308	Bradford, 2,163	B 5
43406	Bradner, 1,140	C 3
† 44101	Bratenahl, 1,613	J 9
44141	Brecksville, 9,137	H 10
43107	Bremen, 1,413	F 6
44613	Brewster, 2,020	H 4
† 44215	Briarwood Beach, 508	G 3
43912	Bridgeport, 3,001	J 5
† 45201	Bridgetown, 13,352	B 9
43913	Brilliant, 2,178	J 5
44240	Brimfield, 950	H 3
44402	Bristolville, 900	J 3
† 44141	Broadview Heights, 11,463	H 10
44403	Brookfield, 1,200	J 3
44144	Brooklyn, 13,142	H 9
† 44131	Brooklyn Heights, 1,527	H 9

Zip	Name/Pop.	Key
44142	Brook Park, 30,774	G 9
† 43912	Brookside, 939	J 5
45309	Brookville, 4,403	B 6
44212	Brunswick, 15,852	G 3
43506	Bryan◉, 7,008	A 3
45716	Buchtel, 592	F 7
43008	Buckeye Lake, 2,961	F 6
44820	Bucyrus◉, 13,111	E 4
43722	Buffalo, 710	G 6
45680	Burlington, 900	F 9
44021	Burton, 1,214	H 3
44822	Butler, 1,052	F 4
43723	Byesville, 2,097	G 6
43907	Cadiz◉, 3,060	J 5
45820	Cairo, 587	B 4
43920	Calcutta, 2,900	J 4
43724	Caldwell◉, 2,082	G 6
43314	Caledonia, 792	D 4
43725	Cambridge◉, 13,656	G 5
45311	Camden, 1,507	A 6
44405	Campbell, 12,577	J 3
45111	Camp Dennison, 550	D 9
44614	Canal Fulton, 2,367	H 4
43110	Canal Winchester, 2,412	E 6
44406	Canfield, 4,997	J 3
* 44701	Canton◉, 110,053	H 4
	Canton, ‡372,210	H 4
43315	Cardington, 1,730	E 5
43316	Carey, 3,523	D 4
45005	Carlisle, 3,821	B 6
43112	Carroll, 614	E 6
44615	Carrollton◉, 2,817	J 4
44824	Castalia, 1,045	E 3
45314	Cedarville, 2,342	C 6
45822	Celina◉, 7,779	A 4
43011	Centerburg, 1,038	E 5
45459	Centerville, 10,333	B 6
44022	Chagrin Falls, 4,848	J 9
44024	Chardon◉, 3,991	H 2
45719	Chauncey, 1,117	F 7
* 45202	Cherry Grove, 850	C 10
45619	Chesapeake, 1,364	E 9
44026	Chesterland, 11,500	H 2
45211	Cheviot, 11,135	B 9
45601	Chillicothe◉, 24,842	E 7
45389	Christiansburg, 724	C 5
* 45201	Cincinnati◉, 452,524	B 9
	Cincinnati, ‡1,384,851	B 9
43113	Circleville◉, 11,687	D 6
45113	Clarksville, 574	C 7
45315	Clayton, 773	B 6
* 44101	Cleveland◉, 750,903	H 9
	Cleveland, ‡2,074,194	H 9
44118	Cleveland Heights, 60,767	H 9
45002	Cleves, 2,044	B 9
44216	Clinton, 1,335	G 4
43410	Clyde, 5,503	E 3
† 45638	Coal Grove, 2,759	E 9
45621	Coalton, 550	E 7
45828	Coldwater, 3,533	A 5
† 44034	Colebrook, 700	J 2
44028	Columbia Station, 518	G 10
44408	Columbiana, 4,959	J 4
* 43201	Columbus (cap.)◉, 539,677	E 6
	Columbus, ‡916,228	E 6
45830	Columbus Grove, 2,290	B 4

(continued on following page)

AREA 41,222 sq. mi.
POPULATION 10,652,017 ('70); 10,797,419 ('80)
CAPITAL Columbus
LARGEST CITY Cleveland
HIGHEST POINT Campbell Hill 1,550 ft.
SETTLED IN 1788
ADMITTED TO UNION March 1, 1803
POPULAR NAME Buckeye State
STATE FLOWER Scarlet Carnation
STATE BIRD Cardinal

Topography

Agriculture, Industry and Resources

DOMINANT LAND USE

Hogs, Soft Winter Wheat

Livestock, Dairy, Soybeans, Cash Grain

Dairy, General Farming

General Farming, Livestock, Tobacco

Fruit, Truck and Mixed Farming

Forests

Urban Areas

MAJOR MINERAL OCCURRENCES

C Coal
Cl Clay
G Natural Gas
Gp Gypsum
Ls Limestone
Na Salt
O Petroleum
Ss Sandstone

▨ Major Industrial Areas

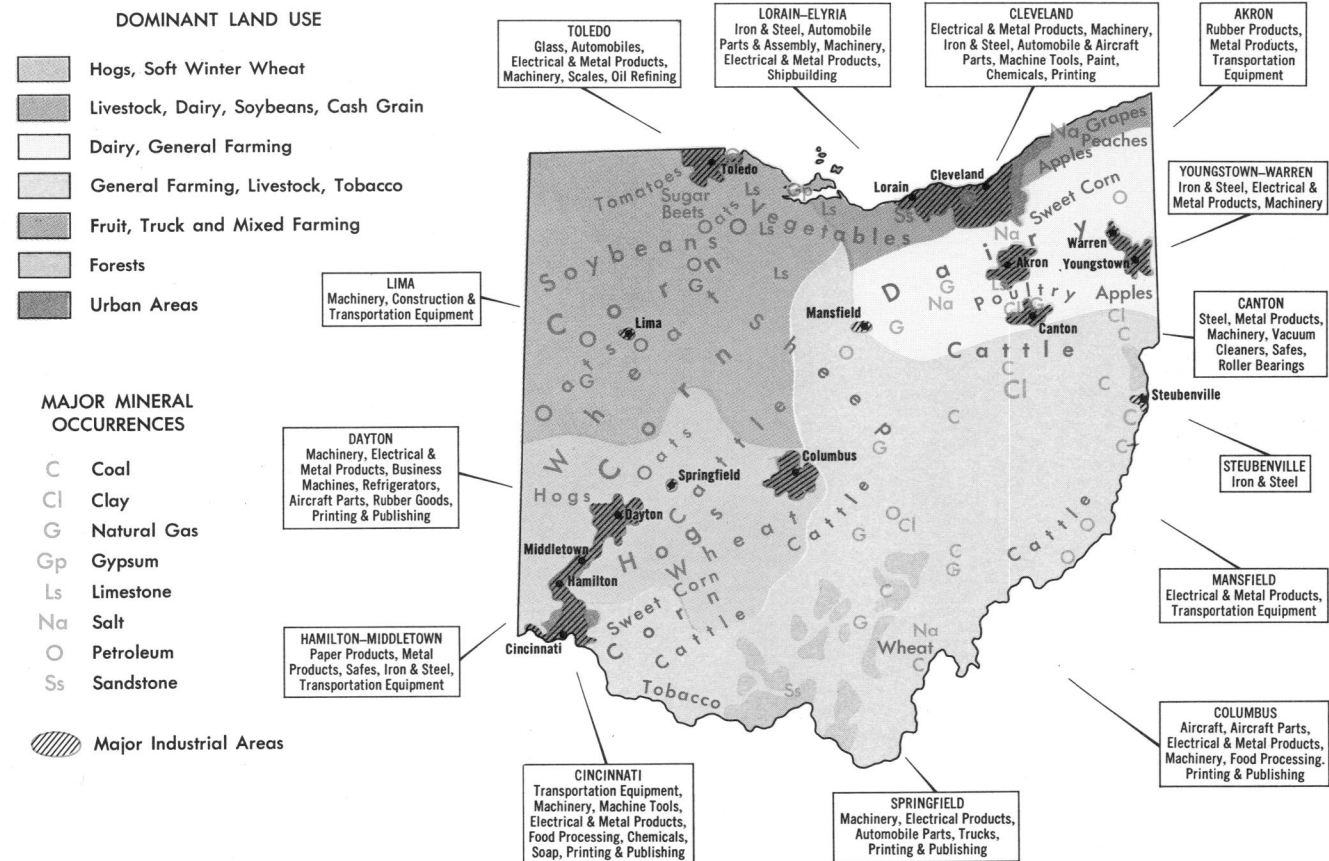

(continued)

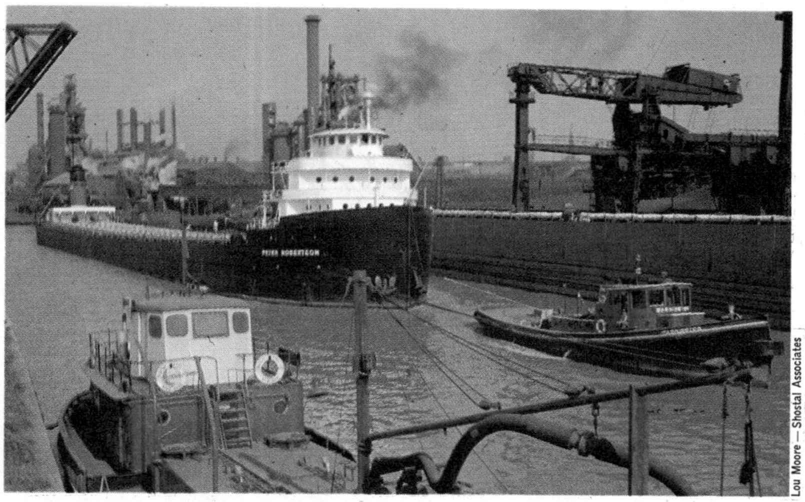
Lou Moore — Shostal Associates

Reminiscent of children's book illustrations, the tugboat "Washington" guides ore-carrier "Peter Robertson" through Cleveland's Industrial Flats, past a Milwaukee fuel tanker.

44030 Conneaut, 14,552 J 2
45831 Continental, 1,185 B 3
45832 Convoy, 991 A 4
45723 Coolville, 672 G 7
43730 Corning, 838 F 6
44410 Cortland, 2,525 J 3
43812 Coshocton⊙, 13,747 G 5
† 45201 Covedale, 6,639 B 10
45318 Covington, 2,575 B 5
† 44429 Craig Beach, 1,451 H 3
44827 Crestline, 5,947 E 4
44217 Creston, 1,632 G 3
45806 Cridersville, 1,103 B 4
43731 Crooksville, 2,828 F 6
† 45341 Crystal Lakes, 5,851 C 6
* 44221 Cuyahoga Falls, 49,678 G 3
† 44101 Cuyahoga Heights, 866 H 9
43413 Cygnet, 629 C 3
44618 Dalton, 1,177 G 4
43014 Danville, 1,025 F 5
43123 Darbydale, 743 D 6
* 45401 Dayton⊙, 243,601 B 6
Dayton, ‡850,266 B 6
44411 Deerfield, 800 H 3
45236 Deer Park, 7,415 C 9
43512 Defiance⊙, 16,281 B 3
43318 Degraff, 1,117 C 5
43015 Delaware⊙, 15,008 E 5
45833 Delphos, 7,608 B 4
43515 Delta, 2,544 B 2
44621 Dennison, 3,506 H 5
† 45202 Dent, 800 B 9
43516 Deshler, 1,938 C 3
45750 Devola, 1,989 H 7
43917 Dillonvale, 1,095 J 5
44622 Dover, 11,516 G 4
44230 Doylestown, 2,373 G 4
43821 Dresden, 1,516 G 5
43017 Dublin, 681 D 5
43734 Duncan Falls, 900 G 6
45836 Dunkirk, 1,036 C 4
44730 East Canton, 1,631 H 4
44112 East Cleveland, 39,600 H 9
44094 Eastlake, 19,690 J 8
43920 East Liverpool, 20,020 J 4
44413 East Palestine, 5,604 J 4
44626 East Sparta, 959 H 4
45320 Eaton⊙, 6,020 A 6
† 44035 Eaton Estates, 2,076 G 3
43517 Edgerton, 2,126 A 3
44004 Edgewood, 3,437 J 2
43320 Edison, 569 E 4
43518 Edon, 803 A 2
45807 Elida, 1,211 B 4
43416 Elmore, 1,316 D 3
45216 Elmwood Place, 3,525 B 9
* 44035 Elyria⊙, 53,427 F 3
45322 Englewood, 7,885 B 6
45323 Enon, 1,929 C 6
44117 Euclid, 71,552 J 9
† 45201 Evendale, 1,967 C 9
45042 Excello, 900 B 7
45324 Fairborn, 32,267 B 6
† 45201 Fairfax, 2,705 C 9
45014 Fairfield, 14,680 A 7
44313 Fairlawn, 6,102 G 3
44077 Fairport Harbor, 3,665 H 2
44126 Fairview Park, 21,681 G 9
45325 Farmersville, 865 A 6
43521 Fayette, 1,175 B 2
45120 Felicity, 786 B 8
45840 Findlay⊙, 35,800 C 3
45326 Fletcher, 539 B 5
43977 Flushing, 1,207 J 5
45843 Forest, 1,535 C 4
45405 Forest Park, 15,139 B 9
† 45202 Forestville, 950 C 10
45844 Fort Jennings, 533 B 4
45845 Fort Loramie, 744 B 5
† 45401 Fort McKinley, 11,536 B 6
45846 Fort Recovery, 1,348 A 5
† 45801 Fort Shawnee, 3,436 B 4
44830 Fostoria, 16,037 D 3
45628 Frankfort, 949 D 7
45005 Franklin, 10,075 B 6
45629 Franklin Furnace, 975 E 8
43822 Frazeysburg, 941 F 5
44627 Fredericksburg, 601 G 4
43019 Fredericktown, 1,935 F 5
43420 Fremont⊙, 18,490 D 3
45630 Friendship, 600 D 8
43230 Gahanna, 12,400 E 5
44833 Galion, 13,123 E 4
45631 Gallipolis⊙, 7,490 F 8
43022 Gambier, 1,571 F 5
44125 Garfield Heights, 41,417 J 9
44231 Garrettsville, 1,718 H 3
44040 Gates Mills, 2,378 J 9
44041 Geneva, 6,449 J 2
44043 Geneva-on-the-Lake, 877 H 2
43430 Genoa, 2,139 D 2
45121 Georgetown⊙, 2,949 C 8
45327 Germantown, 4,088 B 6
45328 Gettysburg, 526 A 5
43431 Gibsonburg, 2,585 D 3
44420 Girard, 14,119 J 3
45848 Glandorf, 732 B 3
45246 Glendale, 2,690 C 9
† 44139 Glenwillow, 526 J 10
45732 Glouster, 2,121 F 6
44629 Gnadenhutten, 1,466 G 5
† 45201 Golf Manor, 5,170 C 9
45122 Goshen, 1,174 B 7
44044 Grafton, 1,771 F 3
43522 Grand Rapids, 976 C 3
44045 Grand River, 613 H 2
† 43201 Grandview Heights, 8,460 D 6
43023 Granville, 3,963 E 5
45330 Gratis, 621 A 6
43322 Green Camp, 537 D 4
45123 Greenfield, 4,780 D 7
45218 Greenhills, 6,092 B 9
44232 Greensburg, 950 G 4
44836 Green Springs, 1,279 E 3
44630 Greentown, 1,150 H 4
45331 Greenville⊙, 12,380 A 5
44837 Greenwich, 1,473 E 3
45239 Groesbeck, 5,000 B 9
43123 Grove City, 13,911 D 6
43125 Groveport, 2,490 E 6
45849 Grover Hill, 536 B 3
45634 Hamden, 953 F 7
45130 Hamersville, 567 C 8
* 45011 Hamilton⊙, 67,865 A 7
Hamilton-Middletown, ‡226,207 A 7
43524 Hamler, 681 B 3
43931 Hannibal, 550 J 6
† 43055 Hanover, 626 F 5
43126 Harrisburg, 556 D 6
45030 Harrison, 4,408 A 9
45850 Harrod, 533 C 4
† 44085 Hartsgrove, 775 J 2
44632 Hartville, 1,752 H 4
43525 Haskins, 549 C 3
43127 Haydenville, 650 F 7
43055 Heath, 6,768 F 5
43025 Hebron, 1,699 E 6
43526 Hicksville, 3,461 A 3
† 44143 Highland Heights, 5,926 J 9
43026 Hilliard, 8,369 D 5
45133 Hillsboro⊙, 5,584 C 7
44234 Hiram, 1,484 H 3
43527 Holgate, 1,541 B 3
43528 Holland, 1,108 C 2
45033 Hooven, 550 A 9
43976 Hopedale, 916 J 5
44425 Hubbard, 8,583 J 3
45424 Huber Heights, 18,943 B 6
44236 Hudson, 3,933 H 3
† 44022 Hunting Valley, 797 J 9
44839 Huron, 6,896 E 3
44131 Independence, 7,034 H 9
† 45201 Indian Hill, 5,651 C 9
43932 Irondale, 602 J 4
45638 Ironton⊙, 15,030 E 8
45640 Jackson⊙, 6,843 E 7
45334 Jackson Center, 1,119 B 5
45740 Jacksonville, 545 F 7
45335 Jamestown, 1,790 C 6
44047 Jefferson⊙, 2,472 J 2
† 43162 Jefferson (West Jefferson), 3,664 D 6
43128 Jeffersonville, 1,031 C 6
44840 Jeromesville, 559 F 4
43986 Jewett, 901 H 5
43031 Johnstown, 3,208 E 5
43748 Junction City, 732 F 6
45853 Kalida, 900 B 4
44240 Kent, 28,183 H 3
43326 Kenton⊙, 8,315 C 4
45429 Kettering, 69,599 B 6
44637 Killbuck, 893 G 5
45034 Kings Mills, 800 B 7
45644 Kingston, 1,157 E 7
44048 Kingsville, 1,129 J 2
44428 Kinsman, 900 J 3
43033 Kirkersville, 578 E 6
44094 Kirtland, 5,530 H 2
43951 Lafferty, 900 H 5
44050 Lagrange, 1,074 F 3
44250 Lakemore, 2,708 H 3
43440 Lakeside, 850 E 2
43331 Lakeview, 1,026 C 4
44107 Lakewood, 70,173 G 9
43130 Lancaster⊙, 32,911 E 6
43934 Lansing, 950 J 5
43332 La Rue, 867 D 4
43135 Laurelville, 624 E 7
† 45501 Lawrenceville, 687 C 6
44430 Leavittsburg, 4,979 J 3
45036 Lebanon⊙, 7,934 B 7
45135 Leesburg, 984 D 7
44431 Leetonia, 2,342 J 4
45856 Leipsic, 2,072 C 3
44251 Leroy, 715 G 3
45338 Lewisburg, 1,553 A 6
44904 Lexington, 2,972 E 4
43532 Liberty Center, 1,007 B 3
* 45801 Lima⊙, 53,734 B 4
Lima, ‡171,472 B 4
† 45201 Lincoln Heights, 6,099 C 9
43442 Lindsey, 652 D 3
44432 Lisbon⊙, 3,521 J 4
44253 Litchfield, 650 F 3
43136 Lithopolis, 705 E 6
45742 Little Hocking, 520 G 7
45215 Lockland, 5,288 C 9
44254 Lodi, 2,399 F 3
43138 Logan⊙, 6,269 F 6
43140 London⊙, 6,481 C 6
* 44052 Lorain, 78,185 F 3
Lorain-Elyria, ‡256,843 F 3
44842 Loudonville, 2,865 F 4
44641 Louisville, 6,298 H 4
45140 Loveland, 7,144 D 9
45744 Lowell, 852 H 6
44436 Lowellville, 1,836 J 3
44843 Lucas, 771 F 4
45648 Lucasville, 900 E 8
43443 Luckey, 996 D 3
45142 Lynchburg, 1,186 C 7
44124 Lyndhurst, 19,749 J 9
43533 Lyons, 630 B 2
44056 Macedonia, 6,375 J 10
† 45202 Mack, 5,000 B 9
45243 Madeira, 6,713 C 9
44057 Madison, 1,678 H 2
44643 Magnolia, 1,064 H 4
43758 Malta, 1,017 G 6
44644 Malvern, 1,256 H 4
45144 Manchester, 2,195 C 8
* 44901 Mansfield⊙, 55,047 F 4
Mansfield, ‡129,997 F 4
44255 Mantua, 1,199 H 3
44137 Maple Heights, 34,093 H 9
† 43440 Marblehead, 726 E 2
45860 Maria Stein, 950 A 5
45227 Mariemont, 4,540 C 9
45750 Marietta⊙, 16,861 G 7
43302 Marion⊙, 38,646 D 4
44645 Marshallville, 693 G 4
43935 Martins Ferry, 10,757 J 5
43040 Marysville⊙, 5,744 D 5
45040 Mason, 5,677 B 7
44646 Massillon, 32,539 H 4
44438 Masury, 2,060 J 3
45069 Maud, 550 B 7
43537 Maumee, 15,937 C 2
† 44121 Mayfield, 3,548 J 9
† 44101 Mayfield Heights, 22,139 J 9
45651 McArthur⊙, 1,543 F 7
43534 McClure, 699 C 3
45858 McComb, 1,329 C 3
43756 McConnelsville⊙, 2,107 G 6
44437 McDonald, 3,177 J 3
45859 McGuffey, 704 C 4
43044 Mechanicsburg, 1,686 D 5
44256 Medina⊙, 10,913 G 3
45862 Mendon, 672 A 4
44060 Mentor, 36,912 H 2
44060 Mentor-on-the-Lake, 6,517 G 2
43540 Metamora, 594 C 2
45342 Miamisburg, 14,797 B 6
45041 Miamitown, 800 A 9
44652 Middlebranch, 600 H 4
† 44017 Middleburg Heights, 12,367 G 10
44062 Middlefield, 1,726 H 3
45863 Middle Point, 543 B 4
45760 Middleport, 2,784 F 7
45042 Middletown, 48,767 A 6
44653 Midvale, 636 H 5
44846 Milan, 1,405 E 3
45150 Milford, 4,828 D 9
43045 Milford Center, 753 D 5
43447 Millbury, 771 D 2
44654 Millersburg⊙, 2,979 F 4
43046 Millersport, 777 E 6
45013 Millville, 697 A 7
44656 Mineral City, 860 H 4
44440 Mineral Ridge, 1,500 J 3
44657 Minerva, 4,359 H 4
† 43201 Minerva Park, 1,402 E 5
43938 Mingo Junction, 5,278 J 5
45865 Minster, 2,405 B 5
44260 Mogadore, 3,858 H 3
45050 Monroe, 3,492 B 7
44847 Monroeville, 1,455 E 3
45242 Montgomery, 5,683 C 9
43543 Montpelier, 4,184 A 2
45439 Moraine, 4,898 B 6
† 44022 Moreland Hills, 3,000 J 9
45152 Morrow, 1,486 B 7
43338 Mount Gilead⊙, 2,971 E 4
45231 Mount Healthy, 7,446 B 9
45154 Mount Orab, 1,306 C 7
43939 Mount Pleasant, 635 J 5
43143 Mount Sterling, 1,536 D 6
43050 Mount Vernon⊙, 13,373 E 5
43340 Mount Victory, 633 D 4
44262 Munroe Falls, 3,794 H 3
43144 Murray City, 562 F 6
43545 Napoleon⊙, 7,791 B 3
44662 Navarre, 1,607 H 4
43940 Neffs, 900 J 5
44441 Negley, 600 J 4
45764 Nelsonville, 4,812 F 7
44849 Nevada, 917 D 4
43054 New Albany, 513 E 5
43055 Newark⊙, 41,836 F 5
45662 New Boston, 3,325 E 8
45869 New Bremen, 2,185 B 5
† 44101 Newburgh Heights, 3,396 H 9
† 45201 New Burlington, 900 B 9
45344 New Carlisle, 6,112 C 6
43832 Newcomerstown, 4,155 G 5
43762 New Concord, 2,318 G 6
43145 New Holland, 796 D 6
45871 New Knoxville, 852 B 5
45345 New Lebanon, 4,248 B 6
43764 New Lexington⊙, 4,921 F 6
44851 New London, 2,336 F 3
45346 New Madison, 959 A 6
45767 New Matamoras, 940 J 6
45011 New Miami, 3,273 A 7
44442 New Middletown, 1,664 J 4
45347 New Paris, 1,692 A 6
44663 New Philadelphia⊙, 15,184 G 5
45768 Newport, 975 H 7
45157 New Richmond, 2,650 B 8
43766 New Straitsville, 947 F 6
44444 Newton Falls, 5,378 J 3
45244 Newtown, 2,047 C 10
45159 New Vienna, 849 C 7
44854 New Washington, 1,251 E 4
44445 New Waterford, 735 J 4
44446 Niles, 21,581 J 3
45872 North Baltimore, 3,143 C 3
45052 North Bend, 638 B 9
44450 North Bloomfield, 650 J 3
44720 North Canton, 15,228 H 4
45239 North College Hill, 12,363 B 9
44855 North Fairfield, 540 E 3
44067 Northfield, 1,089 J 10
44707 North Industry, 2,000 H 4
44068 North Kingsville, 2,458 J 2
43060 North Lewisburg, 840 C 5
44452 North Lima, 800 J 4
44070 North Olmsted, 34,861 G 9
† 44081 North Perry, 851 H 2
† 44101 North Randall, 1,212 H 9
44035 North Ridgeville, 13,152 F 3
44133 North Royalton, 12,807 H 10
† 43601 Northwood, 4,222 D 2
† 43701 North Zanesville, 3,399 G 6
44203 Norton, 12,308 G 3
44857 Norwalk⊙, 13,386 E 3
45212 Norwood, 30,420 C 9
43449 Oak Harbor, 2,807 D 2
45656 Oak Hill, 1,642 E 8
45873 Oakwood, 10,095 B 6
45873 Oakwood, 3,127 H 9
45873 Oakwood, 804 B 3
44074 Oberlin, 8,761 F 3
43207 Obetz, 2,248 E 6
45874 Ohio City, 816 A 4
44138 Olmsted Falls, 2,504 G 9
44862 Ontario, 4,345 E 4
† 44101 Orange, 2,112 J 9
43616 Oregon, 16,563 D 2
44667 Orrville, 7,408 G 4
44076 Orwell, 965 J 2
45875 Ottawa⊙, 3,622 B 3
† 43601 Ottawa Hills, 4,270 C 2
45876 Ottoville, 914 B 4
45160 Owensville, 707 B 7
45056 Oxford, 15,868 A 6
44077 Painesville⊙, 16,536 H 2
45877 Pandora, 857 C 4
44080 Parkman, 750 H 3
44129 Parma, 100,216 H 9
† 44129 Parma Heights, 27,192 G 9
43062 Pataskala, 1,831 E 5
45879 Paulding⊙, 2,983 A 3
45880 Payne, 1,351 A 3
45660 Peebles, 1,629 D 8
43450 Pemberville, 1,301 C 3
44264 Peninsula, 692 G 3
44124 Pepper Pike, 5,933 J 9
44081 Perry, 917 H 2
43551 Perrysburg, 7,693 C 2
44864 Perrysville, 752 F 4
45354 Phillipsburg, 831 B 6
43771 Philo, 846 G 6
43147 Pickerington, 696 E 6
45661 Piketon, 1,347 E 7
43554 Pioneer, 968 A 2
45356 Piqua, 20,741 B 5
43064 Plain City, 2,254 D 5
45359 Pleasant Hill, 1,025 B 5
43148 Pleasantville, 754 F 6
44865 Plymouth, 1,993 E 4
† 45042 Poasttown, 650 B 6
44514 Poland, 3,097 J 3
45769 Pomeroy⊙, 2,672 G 7
43452 Port Clinton⊙, 7,202 E 2
45770 Portland, 550 G 7
45662 Portsmouth⊙, 27,633 D 8
43837 Port Washington, 550 G 5
43942 Powhatan Point, 2,167 J 6
45669 Proctorville, 881 F 9
43342 Prospect, 1,031 D 5
43456 Put-in-Bay, 135 E 2
43773 Quaker City, 510 H 6
43343 Quincy, 686 C 5
45771 Racine, 583 G 8
43066 Radnor, 950 D 5
44265 Randolph, 900 H 3
44266 Ravenna⊙, 11,780 H 3
43943 Rayland, 617 J 5
45215 Reading, 14,303 C 9
† 45202 Remington, 600 C 9
45773 Reno, 576 H 7
† 43412 Reno Beach, 1,049 D 2
44867 Republic, 705 D 3
43068 Reynoldsburg, 13,921 E 6
44286 Richfield, 3,228 G 3
43944 Richmond, 777 J 5
† 44045 Richmond (Grand River), 613 H 2
45673 Richmond Dale, 950 E 7
44143 Richmond Heights, 9,220 H 9
43344 Richwood, 2,072 D 5
45674 Rio Grande, 814 F 8
45167 Ripley, 2,745 C 8
43457 Risingsun, 730 C 3
44270 Rittman, 6,308 G 4
† 43085 Riverlea, 558 D 5
44670 Robertsville, 600 H 4
44084 Rock Creek, 731 J 2
45882 Rockford, 1,207 A 4
44116 Rocky River, 22,958 G 9
44085 Rome, 648 J 2
44272 Rootstown, 900 H 3
† 45662 Rosemount, 1,786 D 8
43777 Roseville, 1,767 F 6
45061 Ross (Venice), 1,661 B 9
43460 Rossford, 5,302 C 2
45236 Rossmoyne, 2,900 C 9
† 43943 Rush Run, 560 J 5
43347 Rushsylvania, 526 C 5
43348 Russells Point, 1,104 C 5
45775 Rutland, 663 F 7
45169 Sabina, 2,160 C 7
† 44067 Sagamore Hills, 4,100 J 10
45217 Saint Bernard, 6,080 B 9
43950 Saint Clairsville⊙, 4,754 J 5
45883 Saint Henry, 1,276 A 5
45885 Saint Marys, 7,699 B 4
43072 Saint Paris, 1,646 C 5
44460 Salem, 14,186 J 4
43945 Salineville, 1,686 J 4
44870 Sandusky⊙, 32,674 E 3
44671 Sandyville, 543 H 4
45171 Sardinia, 824 C 7
43946 Sardis, 700 J 6
43988 Scio, 1,002 H 5
† 45662 Sciotodale, 950 E 8
45679 Seaman, 866 C 8
44672 Sebring, 4,954 H 4
† 44101 Seven Hills, 12,700 H 9
45062 Seven Mile, 699 A 7
44273 Seville, 1,402 G 3
43947 Shadyside, 5,070 J 6
44120 Shaker Heights, 36,306 H 9
45241 Sharonville, 10,985 C 9
43782 Shawnee, 914 F 6
† 44052 Sheffield, 1,730 F 3
44054 Sheffield Lake, 8,734 F 3
44875 Shelby, 9,847 E 4
43556 Sherwood, 784 A 3
44878 Shiloh, 817 E 4
44676 Shreve, 1,635 F 4
45365 Sidney⊙, 16,332 B 5
† 44221 Silver Lake, 3,637 G 3
† 45201 Silverton, 6,588 C 9
43948 Smithfield, 1,245 J 5
44677 Smithville, 1,278 G 4
44139 Solon, 11,519 J 9
43783 Somerset, 1,417 F 6
† 44001 South Amherst, 2,913 F 3
† 43103 South Bloomfield, 610 D 6
45368 South Charleston, 1,500 C 6
44121 South Euclid, 29,579 H 9
45065 South Lebanon, 3,014 B 7
45680 South Point, 2,243 E 9
† 44022 South Russell, 2,673 H 3
45369 South Vienna, 545 C 6
45682 South Webster, 825 E 8
43701 South Zanesville, 1,436 F 6
44275 Spencer, 758 F 3
45887 Spencerville, 2,241 B 4
45066 Springboro, 2,799 B 6
45246 Springdale, 8,127 B 9
* 45501 Springfield⊙, 81,926 C 6
Springfield, ‡157,115 C 6
45370 Spring Valley, 667 C 6
44276 Sterling, 550 G 4
43952 Steubenville⊙, 30,771 J 5
Steubenville-Weirton, ‡165,627 J 5
43154 Stoutsville, 573 E 6
44224 Stow, 19,847 H 3
44680 Strasburg, 1,874 G 4
44240 Streetsboro, 7,966 H 3
44136 Strongsville, 15,182 G 10
44471 Struthers, 15,343 J 3
43557 Stryker, 1,296 B 3
† 44260 Suffield, 650 H 3
44681 Sugarcreek, 1,771 G 5
43074 Sunbury, 2,512 E 5
43558 Swanton, 2,927 C 2
44882 Sycamore, 1,096 D 4
43560 Sylvania, 12,031 C 2
45779 Syracuse, 684 G 7
44278 Tallmadge, 15,274 H 3
† 43771 Taylorsville (Philo), 846 G 6
45174 Terrace Park, 2,266 D 9
45780 The Plains, 1,568 F 7
43076 Thornville, 679 F 6
44883 Tiffin⊙, 21,596 D 3
43963 Tiltonsville, 2,123 J 5
† 44094 Timberlake, 964 J 8
45371 Tipp City, 5,090 B 6
† 45245 Tobasco, 950 C 10
* 43601 Toledo⊙, 383,818 D 2
Toledo, ‡692,571 D 2
43964 Toronto, 7,705 J 5
45067 Trenton, 5,278 B 7
45782 Trimble, 542 F 7
45373 Troy⊙, 17,186 B 5
44682 Tuscarawas, 830 H 5
44087 Twinsburg, 6,432 J 10
44683 Uhrichsville, 5,731 H 5
45322 Union, 3,654 B 6
† 47390 Union City, 1,808 A 5
44685 Uniontown, 875 H 4
44118 University Heights, 17,055 H 9
43221 Upper Arlington, 38,630 D 6
43351 Upper Sandusky⊙, 5,645 D 4
43078 Urbana⊙, 11,237 C 5
† 43123 Urbancrest, 754 D 6
43080 Utica, 1,977 F 5
† 43201 Valley View, 909 D 6
† 44101 Valley View, 1,422 H 9
45377 Vandalia, 10,796 B 6
45890 Vanlue, 539 C 4
45891 Van Wert⊙, 11,320 A 4
44870 Venice, 1,661 B 9
44089 Vermilion, 9,872 F 3
45378 Verona, 593 A 6
45380 Versailles, 2,441 A 5
44473 Vienna, 1,200 J 3
† 44473 Vienna (South Vienna), 545 C 6
44281 Wadsworth, 13,142 G 3
† 44094 Waite Hill, 514 H 2
44889 Wakeman, 514 F 3
43465 Walbridge, 3,208 C 2
44687 Walnut Creek, 550 G 4
† 44146 Walton Hills, 2,508 J 10
45895 Wapakoneta⊙, 7,324 B 4
* 44481 Warren⊙, 63,494 J 3
† 44100 Warrensville Heights, 18,925 H 9
43844 Warsaw, 725 G 5
43160 Washington Court House⊙, 12,495 D 6
44490 Washingtonville, 747 J 4
45786 Waterford, 600 G 6
43566 Waterville, 2,940 C 3
43567 Wauseon⊙, 4,932 B 2
45690 Waverly⊙, 4,858 D 7
43466 Wayne, 921 C 3
44688 Waynesburg, 1,337 H 4
45896 Waynesfield, 704 C 4
45068 Waynesville, 1,638 B 6
44090 Wellington, 4,137 F 3
45692 Wellston, 5,410 F 7
43968 Wellsville, 5,891 J 4
45381 West Alexandria, 1,553 A 6
45449 West Carrollton, 10,748 B 6
43081 Westerville, 12,530 D 5
44491 West Farmington, 650 J 3
43162 West Jefferson, 3,664 D 6
43845 West Lafayette, 1,719 G 5
44145 Westlake, 15,689 G 9
43357 West Liberty, 1,580 C 5
43358 West Mansfield, 753 C 5
45383 West Milton, 3,696 B 6
43569 Weston, 1,269 C 3
† 45662 West Portsmouth, 3,396 D 8
44287 West Salem, 1,058 F 4
45693 West Union⊙, 1,951 C 8
43570 West Unity, 1,589 B 2
† 44138 Westview, 2,523 G 10
45694 Wheelersburg, 3,709 E 8
43213 Whitehall, 25,263 E 6
43571 Whitehouse, 1,542 C 2
44092 Wickliffe, 21,354 J 9
44890 Willard, 5,510 E 3
45176 Williamsburg, 2,054 B 7
44093 Williamsfield, 950 J 2
43164 Williamsport, 857 D 6
44094 Willoughby, 18,634 J 8
† 44094 Willoughby Hills, 5,247 J 9
44094 Willowick, 21,237 J 8
45898 Willshire, 623 A 4
45177 Wilmington⊙, 10,051 C 7
45697 Winchester, 760 C 8
44288 Windham, 3,360 H 3
43952 Wintersville, 4,921 J 5
45245 Withamsville, 975 C 10
† 45201 Woodlawn, 3,251 C 9
† 44101 Woodmere, 976 J 9
43793 Woodsfield⊙, 3,239 H 6
43469 Woodville, 1,834 D 3
44691 Wooster⊙, 18,703 G 4
43085 Worthington, 15,326 E 5
45215 Wyoming, 9,089 C 9
45385 Xenia⊙, 25,373 C 6
45387 Yellow Springs, 4,624 C 6
43971 Yorkville, 1,656 J 5
* 44501 Youngstown⊙, 139,788 J 3
Youngstown-Warren, ‡536,003 J 3
43701 Zanesville⊙, 33,045 G 6

⊙ County seat.
‡ Population of metropolitan area.
† Zip of nearest p.o.
* Multiple zips

AREA 69,919 sq. mi.
POPULATION 2,559,253 ('70); 3,025,266 ('80)
CAPITAL Oklahoma City
LARGEST CITY Oklahoma City
HIGHEST POINT Black Mesa 4,973 ft.
SETTLED IN 1889
ADMITTED TO UNION November 16, 1907
POPULAR NAME Sooner State
STATE FLOWER Mistletoe
STATE BIRD Scissor-tailed Flycatcher

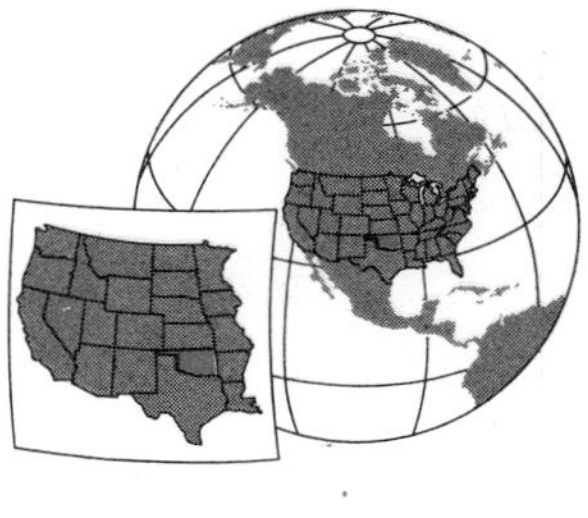

COUNTIES

Adair, 15,141	S	3
Alfalfa, 7,224	K	1
Atoka, 10,972	O	6
Beaver, 6,282	E	1
Beckham, 15,754	G	4
Blaine, 11,794	K	3
Bryan, 25,552	O	7
Caddo, 28,931	K	4
Canadian, 32,245	K	3
Carter, 37,349	M	6
Cherokee, 23,174	R	3
Choctaw, 15,141	P	6
Cimarron, 4,145	A	1
Cleveland, 81,839	M	4
Coal, 5,525	O	5
Comanche, 108,144	K	5
Cotton, 6,832	K	6
Craig, 14,722	R	1
Creek, 45,532	O	3
Custer, 22,665	H	3
Delaware, 17,767	S	2
Dewey, 5,656	H	2
Ellis, 5,129	G	2
Garfield, 55,365	L	2
Garvin, 24,874	M	5
Grady, 29,354	L	5
Grant, 7,117	L	1
Greer, 7,979	G	5
Harmon, 5,136	G	5
Harper, 5,151	G	1
Haskell, 9,578	R	4
Hughes, 13,228	O	4
Jackson, 30,902	H	5
Jefferson, 7,125	L	6
Johnston, 7,870	N	6
Kay, 48,791	M	1
Kingfisher, 12,857	L	3
Kiowa, 12,532	J	5
Latimer, 8,601	R	5
Le Flore, 32,137	S	5
Lincoln, 19,482	N	3
Logan, 19,645	M	3
Love, 5,637	M	7
Major, 7,529	K	2
Marshall, 7,682	N	6
Mayes, 23,302	R	2
McClain, 14,157	M	5
McCurtain, 28,642	S	6
McIntosh, 12,472	P	4
Murray, 10,669	M	6
Muskogee, 59,542	R	3
Noble, 10,043	M	2
Nowata, 9,773	P	1
Okfuskee, 10,683	O	3
Oklahoma, 526,805	M	3
Okmulgee, 35,358	P	3
Osage, 29,750	O	1
Ottawa, 29,800	S	1
Pawnee, 11,338	N	2
Payne, 50,654	N	2
Pittsburg, 37,521	P	5
Pontotoc, 27,867	N	5
Pottawatomie, 43,134	N	4
Pushmataha, 9,385	R	6
Roger Mills, 4,452	G	3
Rogers, 28,425	P	2
Seminole, 25,144	N	4
Sequoyah, 23,370	S	3
Stephens, 35,902	L	6
Texas, 16,352	C	1
Tillman, 12,901	J	6
Tulsa, 401,663	P	2
Wagoner, 22,163	P	3
Washington, 42,277	P	1
Washita, 12,141	J	4
Woods, 11,920	J	1
Woodward, 15,537	H	2

CITIES and TOWNS

	Zip	Name/Pop.	Key	
	74720	Achille, 382	O	7
	74820	Ada⊙, 14,859	N	5
	74330	Adair, 459	R	2
	73901	Adams, 175	D	1
	74520	Adamson, 150	P	5
	73520	Addington, 123	L	6
	74331	Afton, 1,022	S	1
	74824	Agra, 335	N	3
†	74955	Akins, 250	S	3
	74721	Albany, 100	O	7
	73001	Albert, 110	K	4
	74521	Albion, 186	R	5
	74522	Alderson, 215	P	5
	73002	Alex, 492	L	5
†	73015	Alfalfa, 70	J	4
	73716	Aline, 260	K	1
	74825	Allen, 974	O	5
	73521	Altus⊙, 23,302	H	5
	73717	Alva⊙, 7,440	J	1
	73004	Amber, 300	L	4
	73718	Ames, 227	K	2
†	73723	Amorita, 63	K	1
	73719	Anadarko⊙, 6,682	K	4
	74523	Antlers⊙, 2,685	P	6
	73006	Apache, 1,421	K	5
†	74633	Apperson, 40	N	1
	73620	Arapaho⊙, 531	H	3
	73007	Arcadia, 500	M	3
	73401	Ardmore⊙, 20,881	M	6
	74901	Arkoma, 2,098	T	4
	73832	Arnett⊙, 711	G	2
	74826	Asher, 437	N	5
	74524	Ashland, 73	O	5
	74525	Atoka⊙, 3,346	O	6
	74827	Atwood, 200	O	5
	74001	Avant, 439	O	2
	73833	Avard, 59	J	1
	74526	Bache, 100	P	5
	74420	Bacone, 786	R	3
	73930	Baker, 63	D	1
	73931	Balko, 100	E	1
	74002	Barnsdall, 1,579	O	1
†	74965	Baron, 100	S	3
	74003	Bartlesville⊙, 29,683	O	1
	74722	Battiest, 150	S	6
	74828	Bearden, 260	O	4
	73932	Beaver⊙, 1,853	F	1
	74421	Beggs, 1,107	P	3
†	74523	Belzoni, 50	R	6
	74929	Bengal, 75	R	5
	74723	Bennington, 288	P	7
	74527	Bentley, 125	O	6
†	73662	Berlin, 50	G	4
	74331	Bernice, 189	S	1
	73622	Bessie, 210	H	4
	73008	Bethany, 21,785	L	3
	74724	Bethel, 297	S	6
†	74801	Bethel Acres, 1,083	M	4
	74332	Big Cabin, 198	R	1
	74630	Billings, 618	M	1
	73009	Binger, 730	K	4
	73720	Bison, 80	L	2
	74008	Bixby, 3,973	P	3
	74058	Blackburn, 88	N	2
†	74962	Blackgum, 258	S	3
	74631	Blackwell, 8,645	M	1
	73526	Blair, 1,114	H	5
	73010	Blanchard, 1,580	L	4
	74528	Blanco, 200	P	5
	74529	Blocker, 151	P	4
	74725	Blue, 150	O	7
	74333	Bluejacket, 234	R	1
†	74525	Boggy Depot, 100	O	6
	73933	Boise City⊙, 1,993	B	1
	74726	Bokchito, 607	O	6
	74930	Bokoshe, 588	S	4
	74829	Boley, 514	O	4
	74727	Boswell, 755	P	6
	74830	Bowlegs, 540	N	4
	74009	Bowring, 100	O	1
	74422	Boynton, 522	P	3
	73011	Bradley, 247	L	5
	74423	Braggs, 325	R	3
	74632	Braman, 295	M	1
	73012	Bray, 90	L	5
	73721	Breckinridge, 70	L	2
	74424	Briartown, 100	R	4
	73013	Bridgeport, 142	K	3
	74010	Bristow, 4,653	O	3
	74012	Broken Arrow, 11,787	P	2
	74728	Broken Bow, 2,980	S	7
	74530	Bromide, 231	N	6
†	74873	Brooksville, 80	M	4
†	74437	Bryant, 86	P	4
	73834	Buffalo⊙, 1,579	G	1
	74931	Bunch, 90	S	3
	74633	Burbank, 188	N	1
	73722	Burlington, 165	K	1
	73430	Burneyville, 106	M	7
	73624	Burns Flat, 988	H	4
	73625	Butler, 315	H	3
	74831	Byars, 247	N	5
†	74820	Byng, 50	N	5
	73723	Byron, 72	K	1
	73527	Cache, 1,106	J	5
	74729	Caddo, 886	O	6
	74730	Calera, 1,063	O	7
	73014	Calumet, 386	K	3
	74531	Calvin, 359	O	5
	73835	Camargo, 236	H	2
	74932	Cameron, 311	T	4
	74425	Canadian, 304	P	4
	74533	Caney, 200	O	6
	73724	Canton, 844	J	2
	73626	Canute, 420	H	4
	73725	Capron, 80	J	1
	74335	Cardin, 950	S	1
	73726	Carmen, 519	J	1
	73015	Carnegie, 1,723	J	4
	74832	Carney, 396	N	3
	73727	Carrier, 125	K	2
	73627	Carter, 311	H	4
†	74633	Carter Nine, 50	N	1
	74934	Cartersville, 119	S	4
	73016	Cashion, 329	L	3
	74833	Castle, 212	O	4
	74015	Catoosa, 970	P	2
	73017	Cement, 892	K	5
†	74820	Center, 100	N	5
	74534	Centrahoma, 155	O	5
	74336	Centralia, 43	R	1
	74834	Chandler⊙, 2,529	N	3
	73528	Chattanooga, 302	J	6
	74426	Checotah, 3,074	R	4
	74016	Chelsea, 1,622	P	1
	73728	Cherokee⊙, 2,119	K	1
	73838	Chester, 135	J	2
	73628	Cheyenne⊙, 892	G	3
	73018	Chickasha⊙, 14,194	L	4
	74635	Chilocco, 712	M	1
	73020	Choctaw, 4,750	M	3
	74337	Chouteau, 1,046	R	2
†	74965	Christie, 70	S	3
	74017	Claremore⊙, 9,084	R	2
	74535	Clarita, 90	O	6
	74536	Clayton, 718	R	5
	74835	Clearview, 350	O	4
†	73437	Clemscot, 150	L	6
†	74331	Cleora, 87	S	1
	73729	Cleo Springs, 344	K	2
	74020	Cleveland, 2,573	O	2
	73601	Clinton, 8,513	H	3
	73632	Cloud Chief, 40	J	4
	74537	Cloudy, 175	R	6
	74538	Coalgate⊙, 1,859	O	5
†	73059	Cogar, 40	K	4
	74733	Colbert, 814	O	7
	74338	Colcord, 438	S	2
†	73010	Cole, 75	L	4
	73432	Coleman, 125	O	6
	74021	Collinsville, 3,009	P	2
	73021	Colony, 250	J	4
	73529	Comanche, 1,862	L	6
	74339	Commerce, 2,593	R	1
	73022	Concho, 500	L	3
	74836	Connerville, 150	N	6
	73023	Cooperton, 55	J	5
	74022	Copan, 558	P	1
	73632	Cordell⊙, 3,261	H	4
†	74751	Corinne, 100	R	6
	73024	Corn, 409	J	4
†	73456	Cornish, 90	L	6
	74428	Council Hill, 135	P	3
	73025	Countyline, 500	L	6
	73730	Covington, 605	L	2
	74429	Coweta, 2,457	P	3
†	74934	Cowlington, 751	S	4
	73082	Cox City, 285	L	5
	73027	Coyle, 303	M	3
	73028	Crescent, 1,568	L	3
	74837	Cromwell, 287	N	4
	74430	Crowder, 339	P	4
	73433	Cumberland, 150	N	6
	74023	Cushing, 7,529	N	3
	73639	Custer, 486	J	3
	73029	Cyril, 1,302	K	5
	73731	Dacoma, 226	J	1
	74540	Daisy, 250	P	5
	74838	Dale, 155	M	4
†	74523	Darwin, 50	P	6
	74026	Davenport, 831	N	3
	73530	Davidson, 515	J	6
	73030	Davis, 2,223	M	5
	74636	Deer Creek, 203	L	1
	74027	Delaware, 534	P	1
	73115	Del City, 27,133	L	4
	73640	Delhi, 41	G	4
	74028	Depew, 739	O	3
	73531	Devol, 129	J	6
	74431	Dewar, 933	P	4
	74029	Dewey, 3,958	P	1
†	74868	Dewright, 100	N	4
	73031	Dibble, 184	L	4
†	73401	Dickson, 798	M	6
	73641	Dill City, 578	H	4
	74340	Disney, 303	S	2
	73032	Dougherty, 211	M	6
	73733	Douglas, 79	L	2
	73734	Dover, 566	L	3
	74541	Dow, 300	P	5
	73735	Drummond, 326	L	2
	74030	Drumright, 2,931	O	3
	73532	Duke, 486	G	5
	73533	Duncan⊙, 19,718	L	5
	74701	Durant⊙, 11,118	O	6
	73642	Durham, 43	G	3
	74839	Dustin, 502	O	4
	73643	Eagle City, 56	J	3
	74734	Eagletown, 850	S	6
	73033	Eakly, 228	K	4
	74840	Earlsboro, 248	N	4
†	73532	East Duke, 250	H	5
	73034	Edmond, 16,633	M	3
	73537	Eldorado, 737	G	6
	73538	Elgin, 840	K	5
	73644	Elk City, 7,323	G	4
	73539	Elmer, 138	H	6
	73035	Elmore City, 653	M	5
	73036	El Reno⊙, 14,510	K	3
	73701	Enid⊙, 44,008	L	2
†	74561	Enterprise, 130	R	4
	73645	Erick, 1,285	G	4
	74342	Eucha, 66	S	2
	74432	Eufaula⊙, 2,355	P	4
	74637	Fairfax, 1,889	N	1
	74343	Fairland, 814	S	1
	73736	Fairmont, 154	L	2
	73737	Fairview⊙, 2,894	J	2
	74935	Fanshawe, 199	S	5
	73840	Fargo, 262	G	2
	74542	Farris, 100	P	6
	73540	Faxon, 121	J	6
	73646	Fay, 75	J	3
†	74561	Featherston, 75	P	4
	73937	Felt, 105	A	1
	73434	Fillmore, 250	N	6
	74543	Finley, 400	R	6
	74842	Fittstown, 325	N	5
	74843	Fitzhugh, 212	N	5
	73541	Fletcher, 950	K	5
	74638	Foraker, 52	O	1
†	73101	Forest Park, 835	M	3
	73938	Forgan, 496	E	1
	73038	Fort Cobb, 722	K	4
	74434	Fort Gibson, 1,418	R	3
	73841	Fort Supply, 550	G	1
	74735	Fort Towson, 430	R	7
	73647	Foss, 150	H	4
	73039	Foster, 50	M	5
	73435	Fox, 400	M	6
	74031	Foyil, 164	R	2
	74844	Francis, 283	N	5
	73542	Frederick⊙, 6,132	H	6
	73842	Freedom, 292	H	1
	73843	Gage, 536	G	2
	74936	Gans, 238	S	4
	73738	Garber, 1,011	M	2
	74736	Garvin, 117	S	7
	73844	Gate, 151	F	1
	73040	Geary, 1,380	K	3
	73436	Gene Autry, 120	N	6
	73543	Geronimo, 587	K	6
	74544	Gerty, 139	O	5
	74032	Glencoe, 421	M	2
	74033	Glenpool, 770	P	3
	74728	Glover, 244	S	6
	74737	Golden, 275	S	6
†	73093	Goldsby, 298	M	4
	73739	Goltry, 282	K	1
†	74740	Goodwater, 100	S	7
	73939	Goodwell, 1,467	C	1
	74435	Gore, 478	R	3
	73041	Gotebo, 376	J	4

(continued on following page)

Agriculture, Industry and Resources

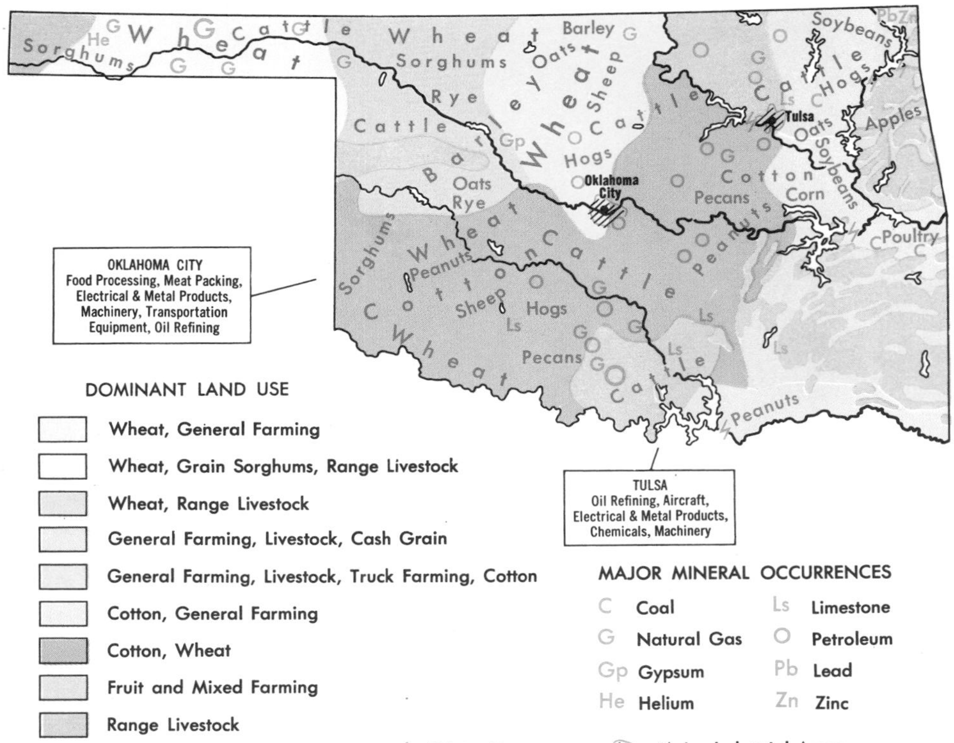

OKLAHOMA CITY
Food Processing, Meat Packing, Electrical & Metal Products, Machinery, Transportation Equipment, Oil Refining

TULSA
Oil Refining, Aircraft, Electrical & Metal Products, Chemicals, Machinery

DOMINANT LAND USE

- Wheat, General Farming
- Wheat, Grain Sorghums, Range Livestock
- Wheat, Range Livestock
- General Farming, Livestock, Cash Grain
- General Farming, Livestock, Truck Farming, Cotton
- Cotton, General Farming
- Cotton, Wheat
- Fruit and Mixed Farming
- Range Livestock
- Forests

MAJOR MINERAL OCCURRENCES

C	Coal	Ls	Limestone
G	Natural Gas	O	Petroleum
Gp	Gypsum	Pb	Lead
He	Helium	Zn	Zinc

Water Power — Major Industrial Areas

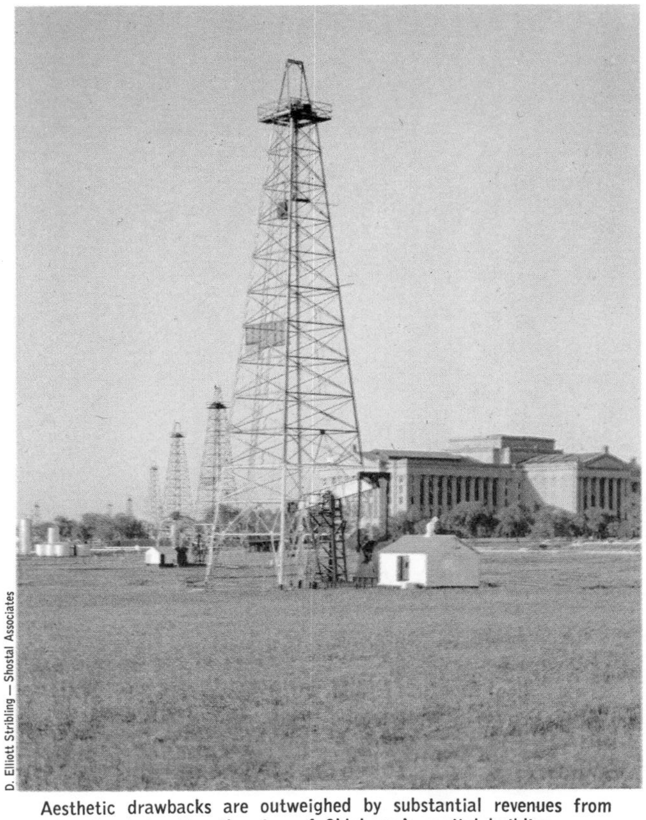
D. Elliott Stribling—Shostal Associates

Aesthetic drawbacks are outweighed by substantial revenues from oil wells obstructing the view of Oklahoma's capitol building.

(continued)

73544 Gould, 368 G 5
74545 Gowen, 350 R 5
73042 Gracemont, 424 K 4
73437 Graham, 250 M 6
74639 Grainola, 66 N 1
73546 Grandfield, 1,524 J 6
73547 Granite, 1,808 H 5
74738 Grant, 273 R 7
† 74437 Grayson (Wildcat), 142 P 3
73043 Greenfield, 143 K 3
74344 Grove, 2,000 S 1
73044 Guthrie⊙, 9,575 M 3
73942 Guymon⊙, 7,674 D 1
74546 Haileyville, 928 P 5
74034 Hallett, 125 N 2
73650 Hammon, 677 H 3
74845 Hanna, 181 P 4
† 74955 Hanson, 250 S 4
74846 Harden City, 150 N 5
73944 Hardesty, 223 D 1
73045 Harrah, 1,931 M 4
74739 Harris, 200 S 7
74547 Hartshorne, 2,121 R 5
74436 Haskell, 2,063 P 3
73548 Hastings, 184 K 6
74740 Haworth, 293 S 7
74548 Haywood, 175 P 5
73549 Headrick, 139 H 5
73438 Healdton, 2,324 M 6
74937 Heavener, 2,566 S 5
73741 Helena, 769 K 1
74741 Hendrix, 117 O 7
73046 Hennepin, 306 M 5
73742 Hennessey, 2,181 L 2
74437 Henryetta, 6,430 O 4
† 73539 Hess, 65 H 6
† 73086 Hickory, 62 N 5
73743 Hillsdale, 77 K 1
73047 Hinton, 889 K 4
73744 Hitchcock, 160 K 3
74438 Hitchita, 160 P 3
73651 Hobart⊙, 4,638 J 5
74345 Hockerville, 125 S 1
74939 Hodgen, 150 S 5
74439 Hoffman, 262 P 4
74848 Holdenville⊙, 5,181 O 4
73550 Hollis⊙, 3,150 G 5
73551 Hollister, 105 J 6
73745 Homestead, 75 K 2
74035 Hominy, 2,274 O 2
74549 Honobia, 250 R 5
73945 Hooker, 1,615 D 1
73746 Hopeton, 75 J 1
74940 Howe, 403 S 5
74440 Hoyt, 110 R 4
74743 Hugo⊙, 6,585 R 6
† 67333 Hulah, 50 O 1
74441 Hulbert, 505 R 3
† 73521 Humphreys, 44 H 5
74640 Hunter, 274 L 1
73048 Hydro, 805 J 3
74745 Idabel⊙, 5,946 S 7
73552 Indiahoma, 434 J 5
74442 Indianola, 205 P 4
74036 Inola, 948 P 2
73747 Isabella, 89 K 2
74346 Jay⊙, 1,594 S 2
73748 Jefferson, 128 L 1
74037 Jenks, 1,997 P 2
74038 Jennings, 338 N 2
73749 Jet, 317 K 1
73049 Jones, 1,666 M 3
74551 Jumbo, 40 P 6
74347 Kansas, 317 S 2
74641 Kaw, 283 N 1
† 74401 Keefeton, 70 R 3
74039 Kellyville, 685 O 3
74747 Kemp, 153 O 7
† 74741 Kemp City (Hendrix), 117 O 7
74040 Kendrick, 126 N 3
74748 Kenefic, 153 O 6
74348 Kenwood, 125 S 2
74941 Keota, 685 S 4
74349 Ketchum, 238 R 1
73947 Keyes, 569 B 1
† 74574 Kiamichi, 100 R 5
74041 Kiefer, 803 O 3
74642 Kildare, 79 M 1
73750 Kingfisher⊙, 4,042 L 3
73439 Kingston, 710 N 7
74552 Kinta, 247 R 4
74553 Kiowa, 754 P 5

73847 Knowles, 52 F 1
74849 Konawa, 1,719 N 5
† 74557 Kosoma, 50 P 6
74554 Krebs, 1,515 P 5
73753 Kremlin, 200 L 1
73754 Lahoma, 299 K 2
74850 Lamar, 153 O 4
74643 Lamont, 478 L 1
74555 Lane, 218 O 6
74350 Langley, 481 R 2
73050 Langston, 486 M 3
73848 Laverne, 1,373 G 1
73501 Lawton⊙, 74,470 K 5
Lawton, ‡108,144 K 5
74351 Leach, 75 S 2
73440 Lebanon, 240 N 7
73654 Leedey, 465 H 3
74942 Leflore, 175 S 5
74556 Lehigh, 296 O 6
74042 Lenapah, 325 P 1
73441 Leon, 112 M 7
74043 Leonard, 115 P 3
74943 Lequire, 100 R 4
73051 Lexington, 1,516 M 4
† 74858 Lima (New Lima), 238 D 4
73052 Lindsay, 3,705 L 5
† 74637 Little Chief, 40 N 1
† 73446 Little City, 80 N 6
73442 Loco, 193 L 6
74352 Locust Grove, 1,090 R 2
73443 Lone Grove, 1,240 M 6
73655 Lone Wolf, 584 H 5
73755 Longdale, 331 K 2
73053 Lookeba, 165 K 4
73756 Loyal, 107 K 3

73757 Lucien, 150 M 2
† 74825 Lula, 40 O 5
73054 Luther, 836 M 3
† 74578 Lutie, 250 R 5
74852 Macomb, 41 M 4
73446 Madill⊙, 2,875 N 6
73758 Manchester, 165 L 1
73554 Mangum⊙, 4,066 G 5
73555 Manitou, 308 J 5
74044 Mannford, 892 O 2
73447 Mannsville, 364 N 6
74045 Maramec, 128 N 2
74945 Marble City, 299 S 3
73448 Marietta⊙, 2,013 M 7
74644 Marland, 236 M 1
73055 Marlow, 3,995 K 5
73056 Marshall, 420 L 2
73556 Martha, 268 H 5
74853 Mason, 75 O 3
74854 Maud, 1,143 N 4
73851 May, 91 G 1
73057 Maysville, 1,380 M 5
74353 Mazie, 300 R 2
74501 McAlester⊙, 18,802 P 5
74944 McCurtain, 575 R 4
74851 McLoud, 2,159 M 4
73449 Mead, 210 O 7
73759 Medford⊙, 1,304 L 1
73557 Medicine Park, 562 J 5
74855 Meeker, 683 N 4
† 74074 Mehan, 60 M 2
73760 Meno, 119 K 2
73058 Meridian, 104 M 3
74354 Miami⊙, 13,880 S 1
† 74882 Micawber, 41 N 3

73110 Midwest City, 48,114 M 4
73450 Milburn, 275 O 6
74046 Milfay, 150 N 3
74856 Mill Creek, 234 N 6
74750 Millerton, 350 S 7
73451 Milo, 85 M 6
† 74944 Milton, 90 S 4
73059 Minco, 1,129 L 4
74946 Moffett, 312 S 4
74947 Monroe, 300 S 4
74444 Moodys, 200 S 2
† 71821 Moon, 50 S 7
73060 Moore, 18,761 M 4
73852 Mooreland, 1,196 H 2
74445 Morris, 1,119 P 3
73061 Morrison, 421 M 2
74047 Mounds, 766 O 3
73559 Mountain Park, 458 J 5
73062 Mountain View, 1,110 J 4
74557 Moyers, 125 P 6
74948 Muldrow, 1,680 S 4
73063 Mulhall, 250 M 2
74949 Muse, 75 S 5
74401 Muskogee⊙, 37,331 R 3
73064 Mustang, 2,637 L 4
73853 Mutual, 94 H 2
74646 Nardin, 135 M 1
73761 Nash, 294 K 1
74558 Nashoba, 100 R 6
† 74056 Nelagoney, 62 O 1
74857 Newalla, 350 M 4
74049 New Alluwe, 116 R 1
73065 Newcastle, 1,271 L 4
† 73632 New Cordell (Cordell)⊙, 3,261 H 4

74647 Newkirk⊙, 2,173 N 1
74858 New Lima, 238 O 4
† 74060 New Prue (Prue), 202 O 2
† 73466 New Woodville (Woodville), 118 N 7
† 73101 Nichols Hills, 4,478 L 3
73066 Nicoma Park, 2,560 M 4
73067 Ninnekah, 300 L 5
73068 Noble, 2,241 M 4
73069 Norman⊙, 52,117 M 4
† 73701 North Enid, 730 L 2
74358 North Miami, 503 R 1
74048 Nowata⊙, 3,679 P 1
74050 Oakhurst, 500 P 2
73452 Oakland, 317 N 6
74359 Oaks, 219 S 2
73658 Oakwood, 129 J 3
74051 Ochelata, 330 P 1
74958 Octavia, 40 S 5
74052 Oilton, 1,087 N 2
73762 Okarche, 826 L 3
74446 Okay, 419 R 3
73763 Okeene, 1,421 K 2
74859 Okemah⊙, 2,913 O 4
† 74003 Okesa, 165 O 1
* 73101 Oklahoma City (cap.)⊙, 366,481 L 4
Oklahoma City, ‡640,889 L 4
74447 Okmulgee⊙, 15,180 O 3
74450 Oktaha, 193 R 3
74751 Oleta, 50 R 6
† 74030 Olive, 100 O 2
† 74538 Olney, 42 O 6
73560 Olustee, 819 H 5
74053 Oologah, 458 P 2

73948 Optima, 103 D 1
73073 Orlando, 202 M 2
74054 Osage, 170 O 2
73561 Oscar, 61 L 7
73453 Overbrook, 120 M 6
74055 Owasso, 3,491 P 2
74860 Paden, 442 N 3
74951 Panama, 1,121 S 4
74559 Panola, 100 R 5
73074 Paoli, 480 M 5
74451 Park Hill, 125 R 3
† 74824 Parkland, 55 N 3
73075 Pauls Valley⊙, 5,769 M 5
74056 Pawhuska⊙, 4,238 O 1
74058 Pawnee⊙, 2,443 N 2
74861 Pearson, 60 N 4
74648 Peckham, 65 M 1
74452 Peggs, 82 R 2
† 74301 Pensacola, 56 R 2
† 66713 Peoria, 179 S 1
74059 Perkins, 1,029 M 3
73076 Pernell, 117 M 5
73077 Perry⊙, 5,341 M 2
74862 Pharoah, 100 O 4
† 74538 Phillips, 106 O 6
74360 Picher, 2,363 S 1
74752 Pickens, 350 S 6
73078 Piedmont, 269 L 3
74560 Pittsburg, 282 P 5
74753 Platter, 275 O 7
74952 Plunkettville, 125 S 6
73079 Pocasset, 200 L 4
74902 Pocola, 1,840 T 4
74601 Ponca City, 25,940 M 1
73766 Pondcreek, 903 L 1

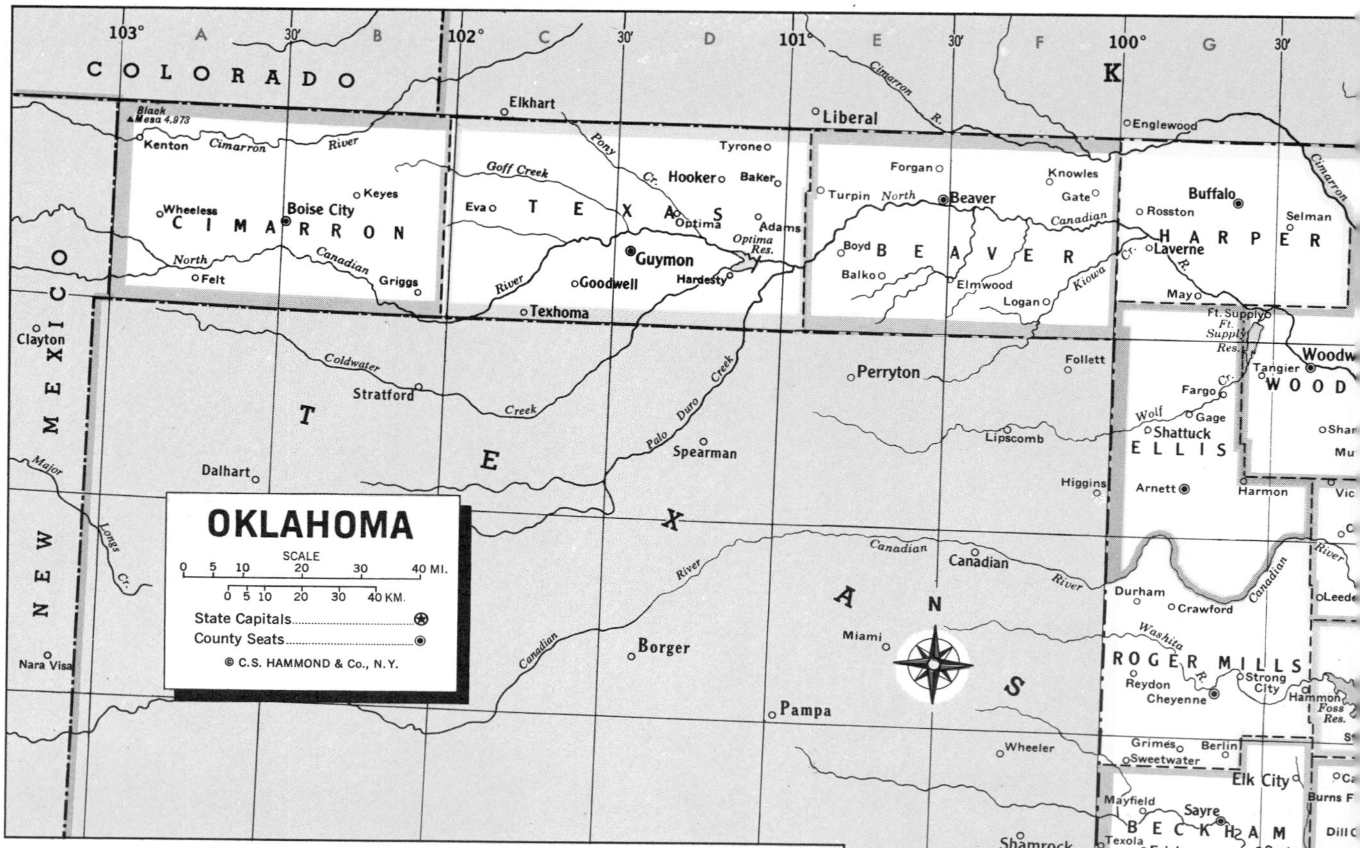

OKLAHOMA
SCALE
0 5 10 20 30 40 MI.
0 5 10 20 30 40 KM.
State Capitals
County Seats
© C.S. HAMMOND & Co., N.Y.
COLORADO
NEW MEXICO
TEXAS
CIMARRON
TEXAS
BEAVER
HARPER
ELLIS
ROGER MILLS
BECKHAM
GREER
HARMON
JACKSON
Black Mesa 4,973
Kenton
Boise City
Guymon
Hooker
Beaver
Buffalo
Liberal
Elkhart
Texhoma
Perryton
Stratford
Dalhart
Spearman
Borger
Pampa
Canadian
Shamrock
Wellington
Childress
Quanah
Paducah
Elk City
Sayre
Mangum
Hollis
Altus
Arnett
Cheyenne

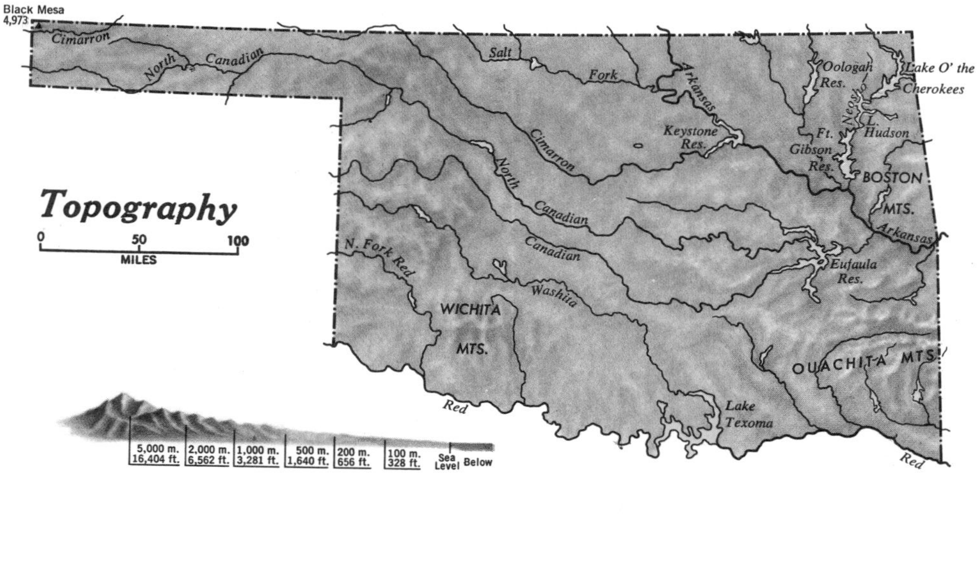

Topography
0 50 100
MILES
Black Mesa 4,973
Cimarron
North Canadian
Salt Fork
Arkansas
Keystone Res.
Oologah Res.
Lake O' the Cherokees
Ft. Gibson Res.
BOSTON MTS.
Eufaula Res.
WICHITA MTS.
OUACHITA MTS.
Lake Texoma
Red
Washita
5,000 m. 16,404 ft.
2,000 m. 6,562 ft.
1,000 m. 3,281 ft.
500 m. 1,640 ft.
200 m. 656 ft.
100 m. 328 ft.
Sea Level
Below

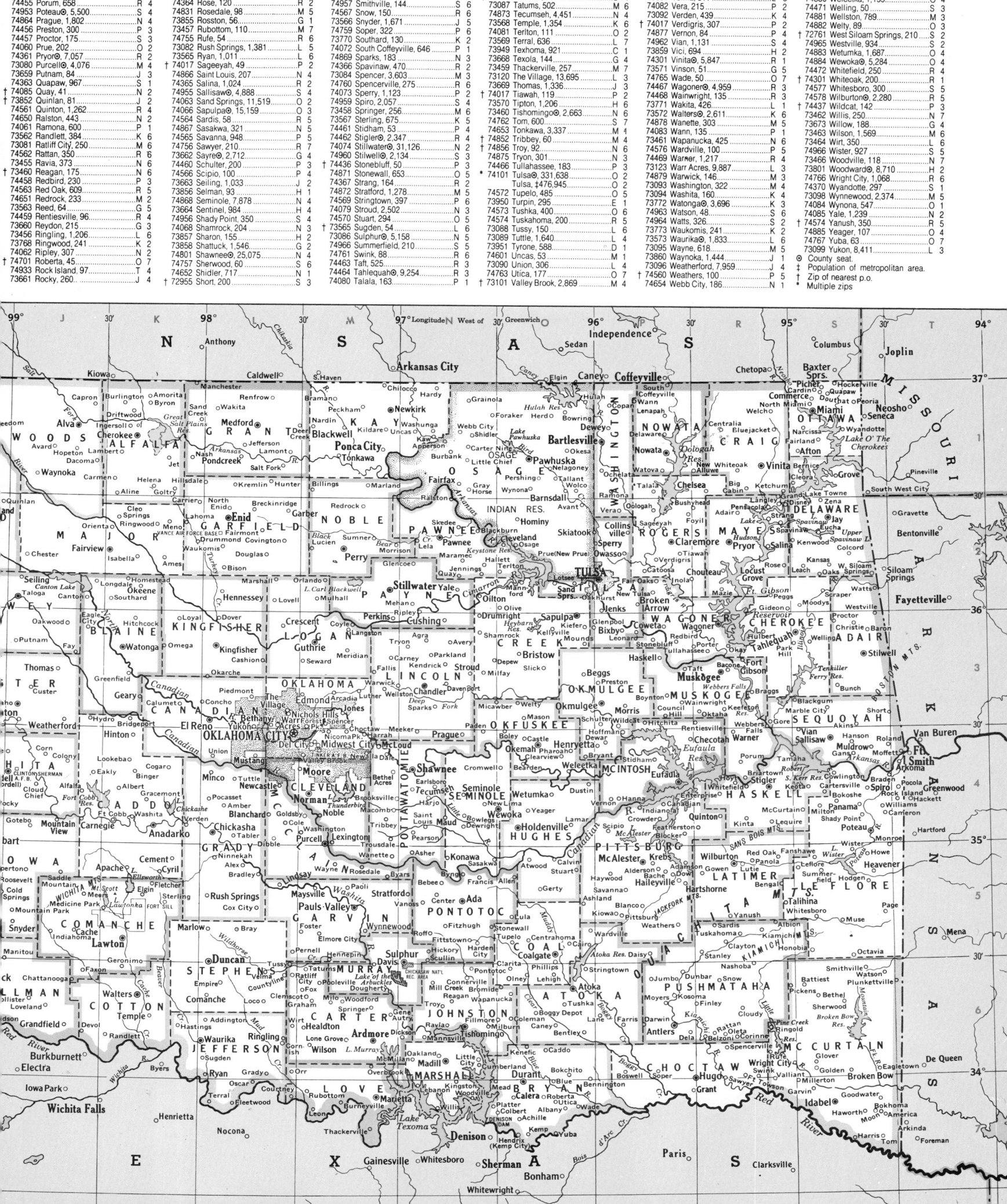

COUNTIES

Baker, 14,919		K 3
Benton, 53,776		D 3
Clackamas, 166,088		E 2
Clatsop, 28,473		D 1
Columbia, 28,790		D 2
Coos, 56,515		C 4
Crook, 9,985		G 3
Curry, 13,006		C 5
Deschutes, 30,442		F 3
Douglas, 71,743		D 4
Gilliam, 2,342		G 2
Grant, 6,996		J 3
Harney, 7,215		H 4
Hood River, 13,187		F 2
Jackson, 94,533		D 5
Jefferson, 8,548		F 3
Josephine, 35,746		D 5
Klamath, 50,021		E 5
Lake, 6,343		G 5
Lane, 213,358		D 4
Lincoln, 25,755		D 3
Linn, 71,914		E 3
Malheur, 23,169		K 4
Marion, 151,309		E 3
Morrow, 4,465		H 2
Multnomah, 556,667		E 2
Polk, 35,349		D 3
Sherman, 2,139		G 2
Tillamook, 17,930		D 2
Umatilla, 44,923		J 2
Union, 19,377		K 2
Wallowa, 6,247		K 2
Wasco, 20,133		F 2
Washington, 157,920		D 2
Wheeler, 1,849		G 3
Yamhill, 40,213		D 2

CITIES and TOWNS

Zip	Name/Pop.	Key
97810	Adams, 219	J 2
97620	Adel, 200	H 5
97901	Adrian, 140	K 4
97320	Agate Beach, 975	C 3
97406	Agness, 120	C 5
† 97361	Airlie, 45	D 3
97321	Albany◎, 18,181	D 3
† 97601	Algoma, 77	F 5
97811	Alicel, 30	J 2
97407	Allegany, 200	D 4
97006	Aloha, 6,000	A 2
97408	Alpine, 80	D 3
97324	Alsea, 600	D 3
† 97601	Altamont, 15,746	F 5
97409	Alvadore, 350	D 3
97101	Amity, 708	D 3
97001	Antelope, 51	G 3
97530	Applegate, 125	D 5
97458	Arago, 200	C 4
† 97812	Arlington, 375	G 2
97473	Ash, 80	D 4
97520	Ashland, 12,342	E 5
97103	Astoria◎, 10,244	D 1
97813	Athena, 872	J 2
97325	Aumsville, 590	E 3
97002	Aurora, 306	D 2
97817	Austin, 170	J 3
97410	Azalea, 40	D 4
97814	Baker◎, 9,354	K 3
97378	Ballston, 120	D 3
97458	Bancroft, 25	C 4
97411	Bandon, 1,832	C 4
97106	Banks, 430	A 1
97003	Barlow, 105	B 2
† 97009	Barton, 100	B 2
† 97136	Bar View, 75	C 2
97817	Bates, 430	J 3
97107	Bay City, 898	D 2
97621	Beatty, 50	F 5
97108	Beaver, 450	D 2
97004	Beavercreek, 708	B 2
97005	Beaverton, 18,577	A 2
97456	Bellfountain, 50	D 3
† 97701	Bend◎, 13,710	F 3
† 97058	Biggs, 50	G 2
97016	Birkenfeld, 45	D 1
97412	Blachly, 425	D 3
† 97108	Blaine, 150	D 2
97326	Blodgett, 150	D 3
97413	Blue River, 350	E 3
97622	Bly, 500	F 5
97008	Bonneville, 130	C 2
97009	Boring, 150	B 2
97002	Boyd, 26	F 2
97818	Boardman, 192	H 2
97623	Bonanza, 450	F 5
97342	Breitenbush, 50	F 3
97458	Bridge, 250	C 4
97010	Bridal Veil, 155	E 2
† 97458	Bridge, 250	D 4
97819	Bridgeport, 45	K 3
† 97136	Bar View, 75	C 2
97001	Brightwood, 420	E 2
† 97032	Broadacres, 80	A 1
97414	Broadbent, 265	C 4
97903	Brogan, 140	K 3
97415	Brookings, 2,720	C 5
97305	Brooks, 490	A 3
† 97840	Brownlee, 50	L 3
97524	Brownsboro, 150	E 5
97327	Brownsville, 1,034	E 3
97351	Buena Vista, 90	D 3
97420	Bunker Hill, 1,549	C 4
† 97720	Burns◎, 3,293	H 4
97522	Butte Falls, 358	E 5
97002	Butteville, 385	A 2
97109	Buxton, 163	D 2
97416	Camas Valley, 665	D 4
97730	Camp Sherman, 87	F 3
97493	Canary, 50	D 4
97013	Canby, 3,813	B 2
97110	Cannon Beach, 779	D 2
97820	Canyon City◎, 600	J 3
97417	Canyonville, 940	D 5
97111	Carlton, 1,126	D 2
† 97415	Carpenterville, 30	C 5
† 97015	Carver, 500	B 2
97014	Cascade Locks, 574	E 2
97329	Cascadia, 150	E 3
97523	Cave Junction, 415	D 5
97821	Cayuse, 300	J 2
97822	Cecil, 75	H 2
97225	Cedar Hills, 2,900	A 2
† 97005	Cedar Mill, 1,500	A 2
97058	Celilo, 50	F 2
97501	Central Point, 4,004	D 5
97420	Charleston, 500	C 4
97306	Chemawa, 900	A 3
97731	Chemult, 580	F 4
† 97058	Chenoweth, 2,329	F 2
97119	Cherry Grove, 200	D 2
† 97055	Cherryville, 80	E 2
97624	Chiloquin, 826	F 5
97015	Clackamas, 6,000	B 2
97016	Clatskanie, 1,286	D 1
97112	Cloverdale, 151	D 2
97401	Coburg, 665	E 3
97017	Colton, 305	B 2

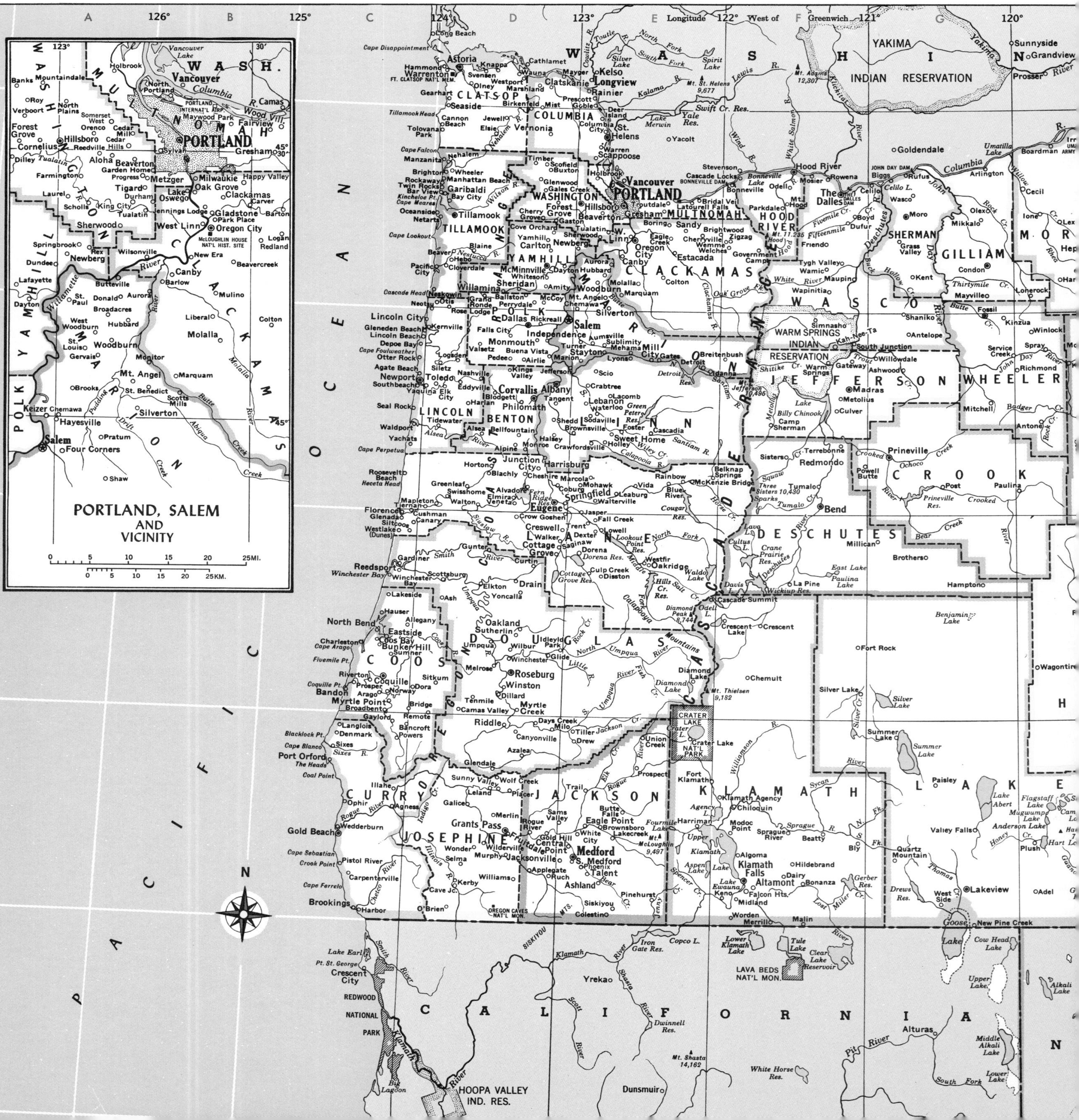

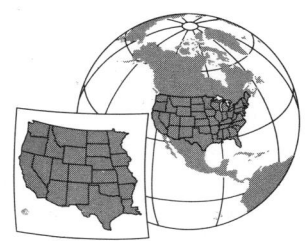

AREA 96,981 sq. mi.
POPULATION 2,091,385 ('70); 2,632,663 ('80)
CAPITAL Salem
LARGEST CITY Portland
HIGHEST POINT Mt. Hood 11,235 ft.
SETTLED IN 1810
ADMITTED TO UNION February 14, 1859
POPULAR NAME Beaver State
STATE FLOWER Oregon Grape
STATE BIRD Western Meadowlark

Topography

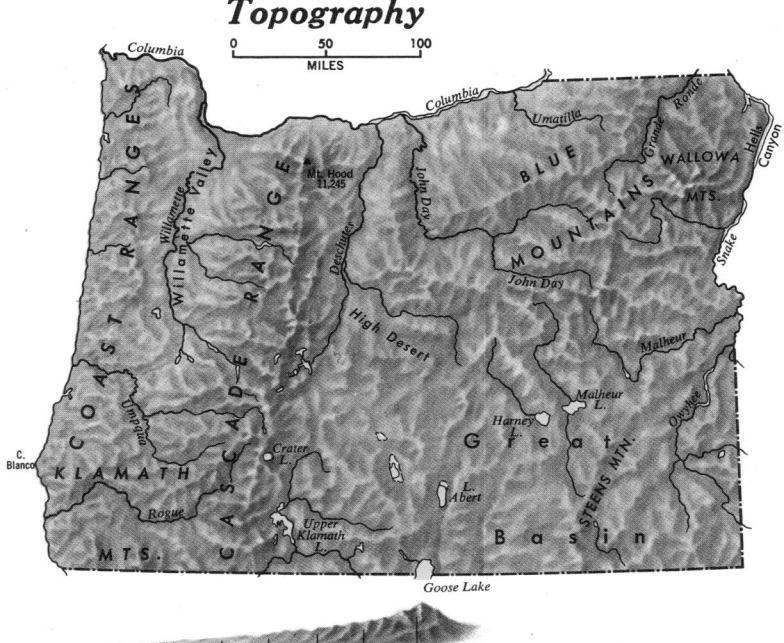

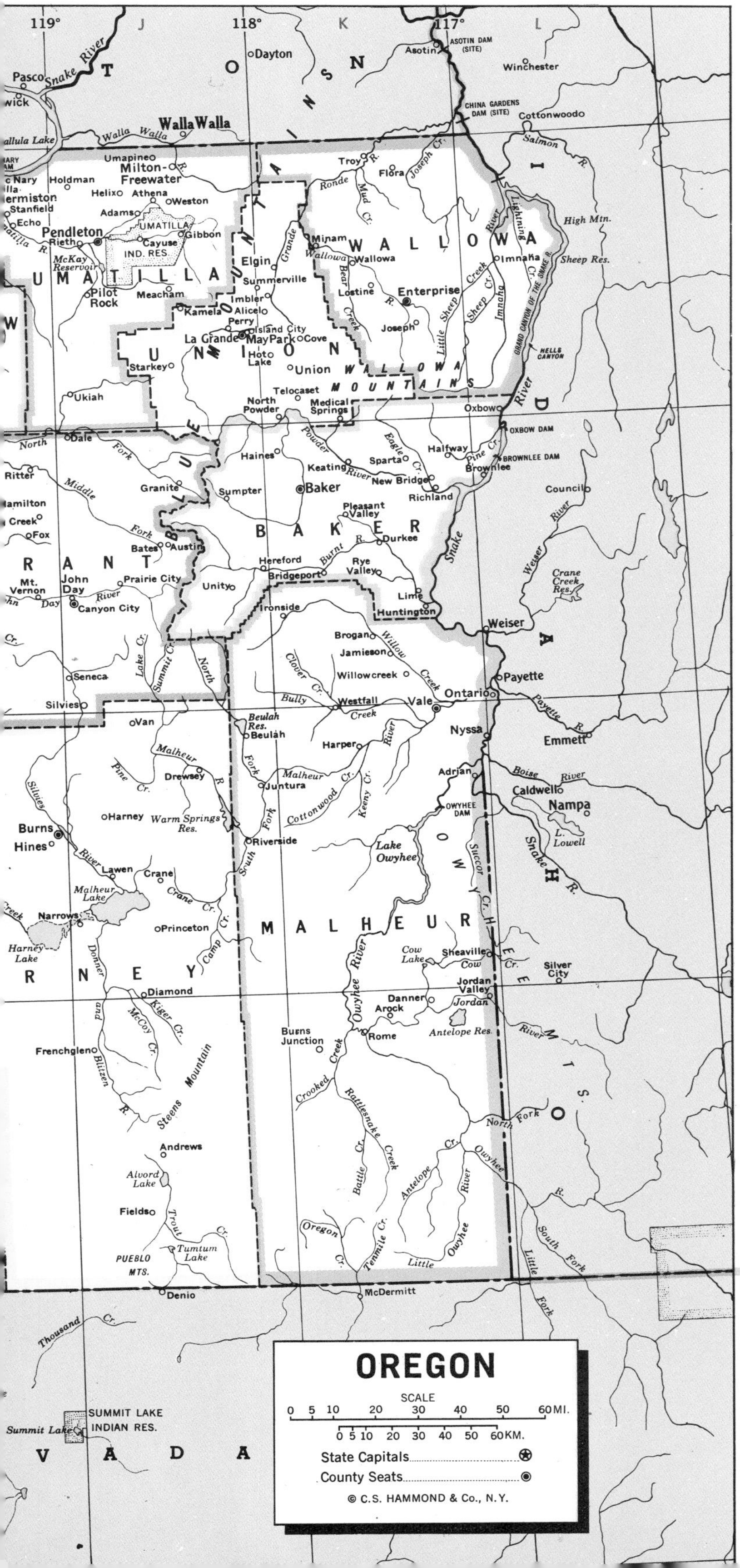

(continued on following page)

OREGON

SCALE

0 5 10 20 30 40 50 60 MI.

0 5 10 20 30 40 50 60 KM.

State Capitals .... ⊛

County Seats .... ⊙

© C.S. HAMMOND & Co., N.Y.

Agriculture, Industry and Resources

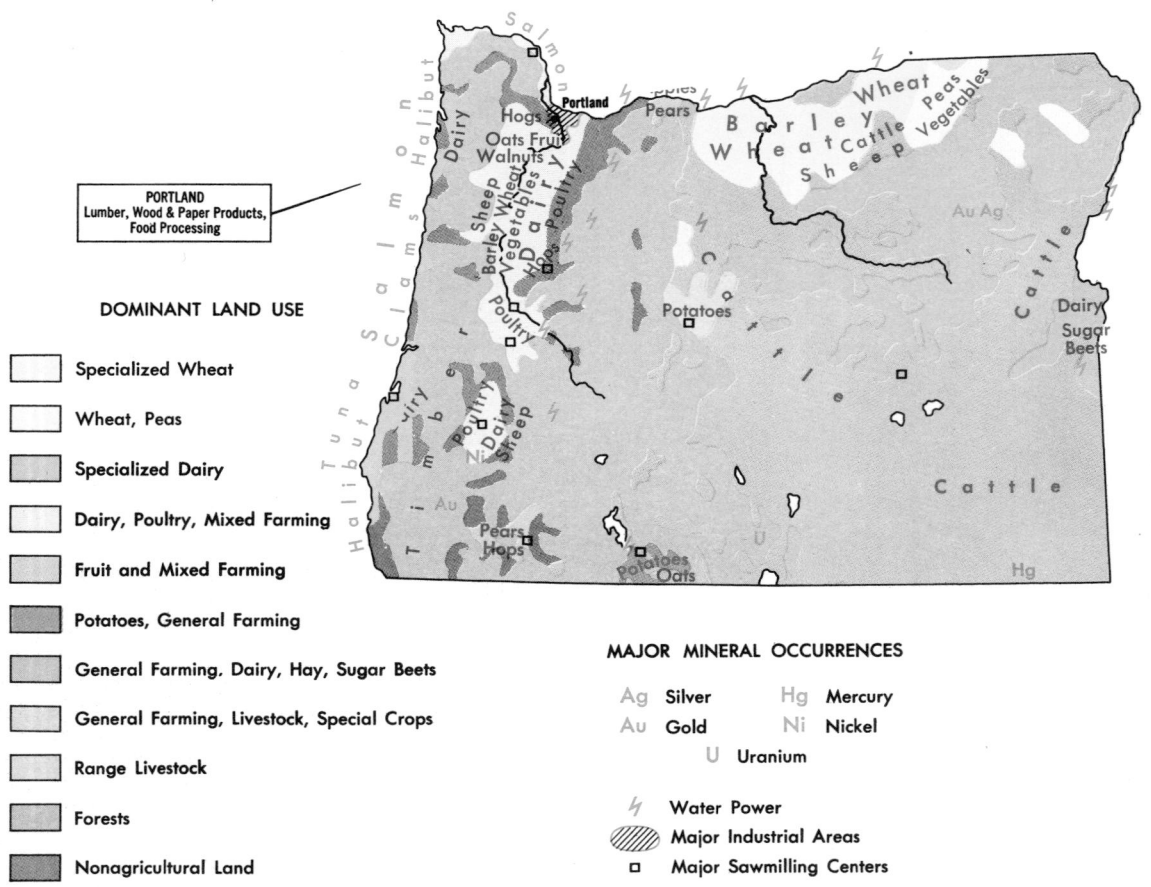

PORTLAND
Lumber, Wood & Paper Products,
Food Processing

DOMINANT LAND USE

- Specialized Wheat
- Wheat, Peas
- Specialized Dairy
- Dairy, Poultry, Mixed Farming
- Fruit and Mixed Farming
- Potatoes, General Farming
- General Farming, Dairy, Hay, Sugar Beets
- General Farming, Livestock, Special Crops
- Range Livestock
- Forests
- Nonagricultural Land

MAJOR MINERAL OCCURRENCES

Ag Silver   Hg Mercury
Au Gold   Ni Nickel
        U Uranium

⚡ Water Power
▨ Major Industrial Areas
□ Major Sawmilling Centers

Oregon's magnificently rugged coastline — sandy beaches interspersed with rock fragments ("stacks") torn from the cliffs.

Oregon State Highway Department

Agriculture, Industry and Resources

DOMINANT LAND USE

- Specialized Dairy
- Dairy, General Farming
- Fruit and Mixed Farming
- Fruit, Truck and Mixed Farming
- General Farming, Livestock, Tobacco
- General Farming, Livestock, Fruit, Tobacco
- Forests
- Urban Areas

AREA 45,333 sq. mi.
POPULATION 11,793,909 ('70); 11,866,728 ('80)
CAPITAL Harrisburg
LARGEST CITY Philadelphia
HIGHEST POINT Mt. Davis 3,213 ft.
SETTLED IN 1682
ADMITTED TO UNION December 12, 1787
POPULAR NAME Keystone State
STATE FLOWER Mountain Laurel
STATE BIRD Ruffed Grouse

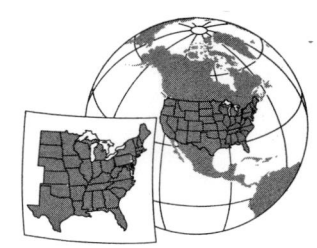

MAJOR MINERAL OCCURRENCES

C	Coal	G	Natural Gas	Sl	Slate
Cl	Clay	Ls	Limestone	Ss	Sandstone
Co	Cobalt	O	Petroleum	Zn	Zinc
Fe	Iron Ore				

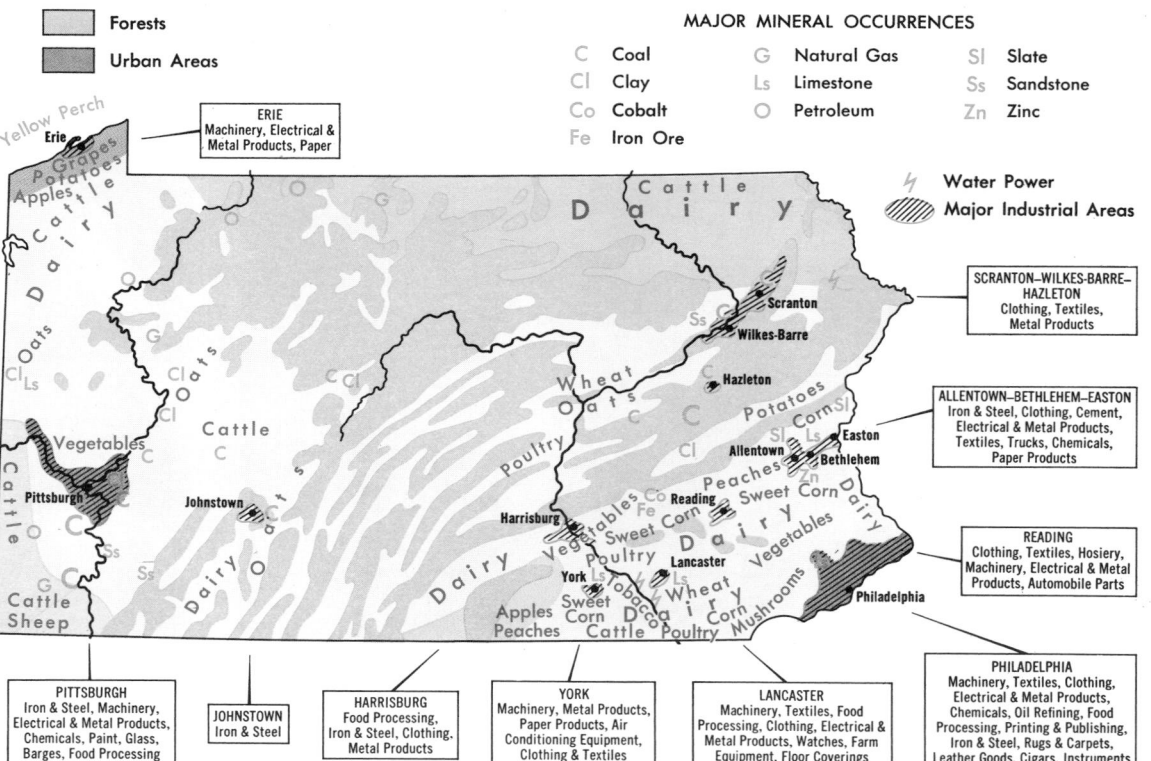

Water Power
Major Industrial Areas

ERIE Machinery, Electrical & Metal Products, Paper

SCRANTON–WILKES-BARRE–HAZLETON Clothing, Textiles, Metal Products

ALLENTOWN–BETHLEHEM–EASTON Iron & Steel, Clothing, Cement, Electrical & Metal Products, Textiles, Trucks, Chemicals, Paper Products

READING Clothing, Textiles, Hosiery, Machinery, Electrical & Metal Products, Automobile Parts

PHILADELPHIA Machinery, Textiles, Clothing, Electrical & Metal Products, Chemicals, Oil Refining, Food Processing, Printing & Publishing, Iron & Steel, Rugs & Carpets, Leather Goods, Cigars, Instruments

PITTSBURGH Iron & Steel, Machinery, Electrical & Metal Products, Chemicals, Paint, Glass, Barges, Food Processing

JOHNSTOWN Iron & Steel

HARRISBURG Food Processing, Iron & Steel, Clothing, Metal Products

YORK Machinery, Metal Products, Paper Products, Air Conditioning Equipment, Clothing & Textiles

LANCASTER Machinery, Textiles, Food Processing, Clothing, Electrical & Metal Products, Watches, Farm Equipment, Floor Coverings

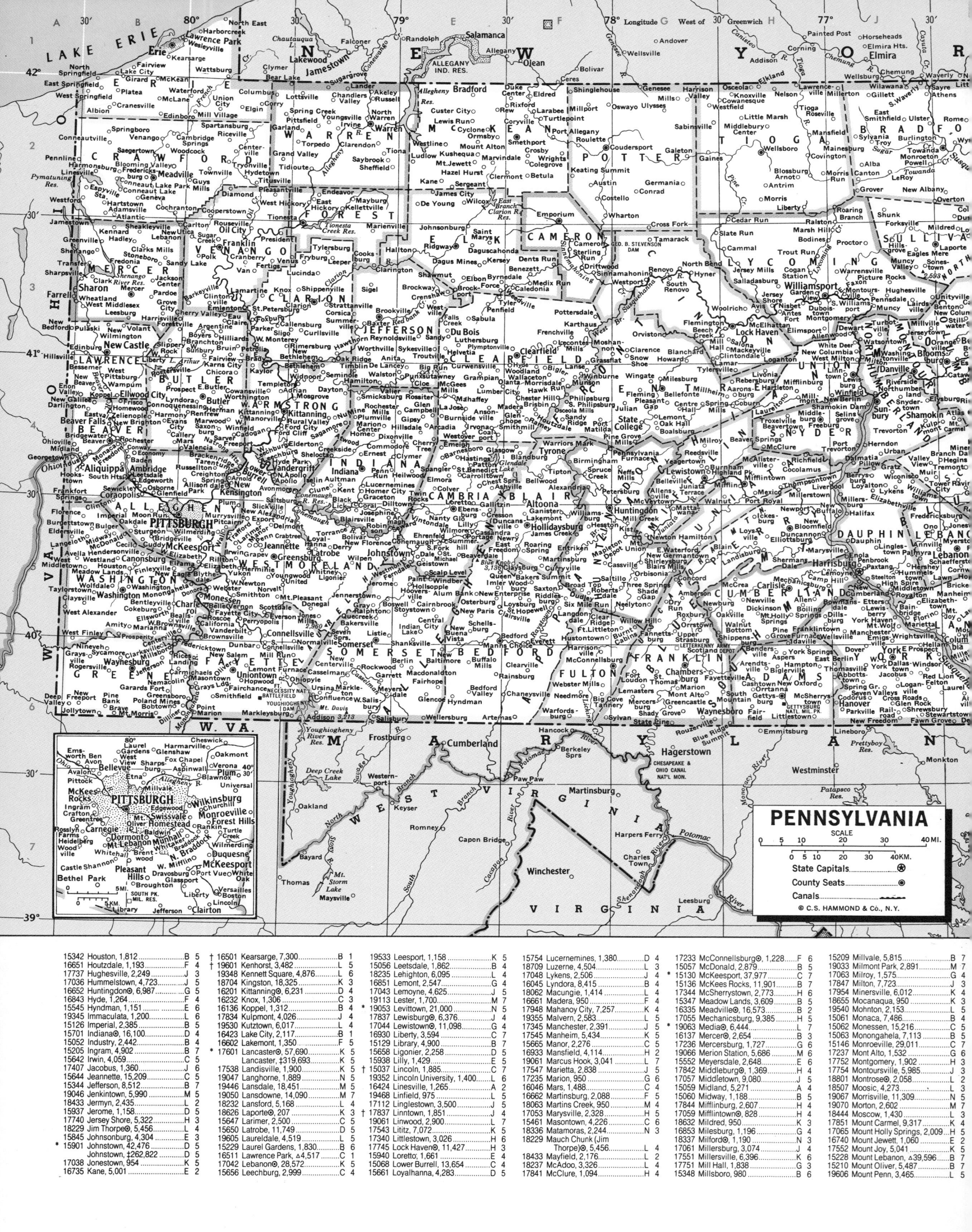

PENNSYLVANIA

SCALE
0 5 10   20   30   40 MI.
0 5 10 20 30 40 KM.

State Capitals .... ⊛
County Seats .... ⊙
Canals ....

© C.S. HAMMOND & Co., N.Y.

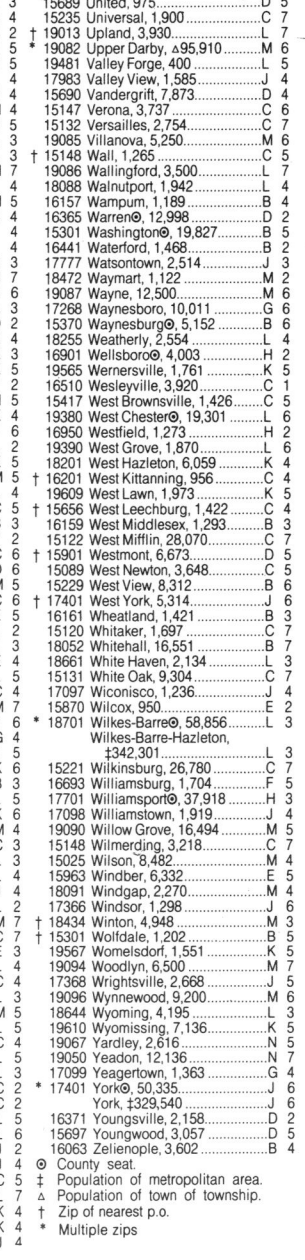

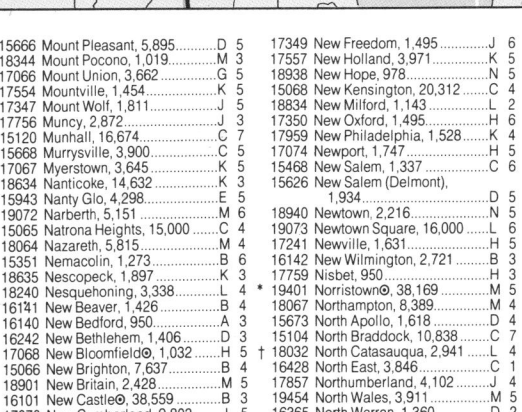

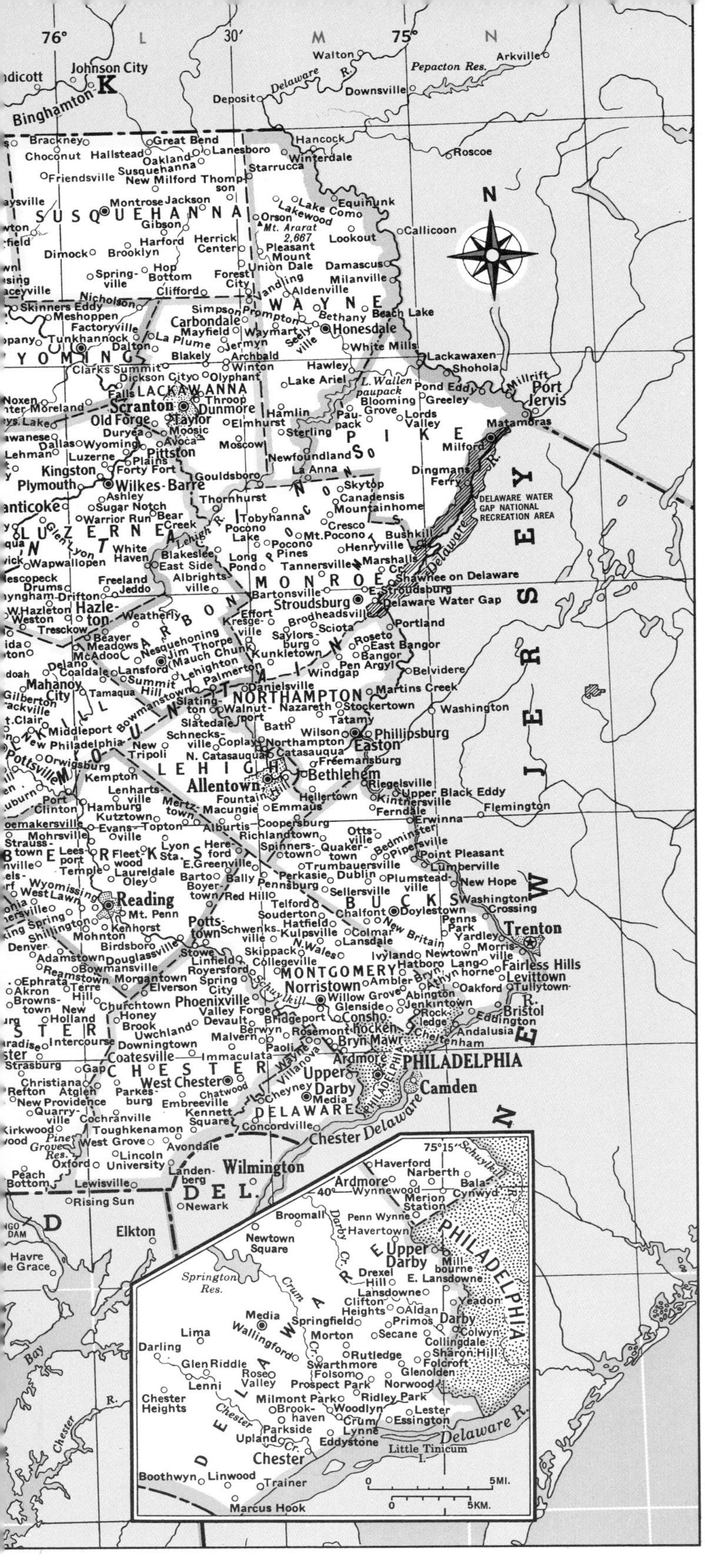

Zip	Place	Grid
19074	Norwood, 7,229	M 7
18636	Noxen, 950	K 3
18241	Nuremberg, 950	K 4
15071	Oakdale, 1,614	B 5
†19047	Oakford, 3,800	G 6
15139	Oakmont, 7,550	C 6
†15059	Ohioville, 3,918	B 4
16301	Oil City, 15,033	C 3
18518	Old Forge, 9,522	L 3
15472	Oliver, 3,091	C 5
18447	Olyphant, 5,422	L 3
17961	Orwigsburg, 2,661	K 4
16666	Osceola Mills, 1,671	F 4
19363	Oxford, 3,658	K 6
18071	Palmerton, 5,620	L 4
17078	Palmyra, 7,615	J 5
19301	Paoli, 5,835	M 5
17562	Paradise, 975	L 6
19365	Parkesburg, 2,701	L 5
†19013	Parkside, 2,343	M 7
†17331	Parkville, 5,120	J 6
16668	Patton, 2,762	E 4
17111	Paxtang, 2,160	J 5
18072	Pen Argyl, 3,668	M 4
17103	Penbrook, 3,379	J 5
18073	Pennsburg, 2,260	M 5
†19003	Penn Wynne, 6,038	M 6
18944	Perkasie, 5,451	M 5
15473	Perryopolis, 2,043	C 5
*19101	Philadelphia⊙, 1,948,609	N 6
	Philadelphia, ‡4,817,914	N 6
16866	Philipsburg, 3,700	F 4
19460	Phoenixville, 14,823	L 5
17963	Pine Grove, 2,197	K 4
16868	Pine Grove Mills, 950	G 4
15140	Pitcairn, 4,741	C 5
*15201	Pittsburgh⊙, 520,117	B 7
	Pittsburgh, ‡2,401,245	B 7
*18640	Pittston, 11,113	L 3
18705	Plains, 6,606	L 3
16823	Pleasant Gap, 1,773	G 4
15236	Pleasant Hills, 10,409	B 7
16341	Pleasantville, 1,005	C 2
15239	Plum, 21,932	C 5
18651	Plymouth, 9,536	K 3
†16830	Plymptonville, 1,040	E 3
15474	Point Marion, 1,750	C 6
16342	Polk, 3,673	C 2
15946	Portage, 4,151	E 5
16743	Port Allegany, 2,703	F 2
17965	Port Carbon, 2,717	K 4
15133	Port Vue, 5,862	C 7
19464	Pottstown, 25,355	L 5
17901	Pottsville⊙, 19,715	K 4
19018	Primos, 3,900	M 7
16052	Prospect, 973	B 4
19076	Prospect Park, 7,250	M 7
15767	Punxsutawney, 7,792	D 4
18951	Quakertown, 7,276	M 5
17566	Quarryville, 1,571	K 6
15485	Rankin, 3,817	C 7
†19601	Reading⊙, 87,643	L 5
	Reading, ‡415,056	L 5
17567	Reamstown, 1,050	K 5
18076	Red Hill, 1,201	L 5
17356	Red Lion, 5,645	J 6
17084	Reedsville, 950	G 4
17764	Renovo, 2,620	G 3
15851	Reynoldsville, 2,771	D 3
17087	Richland, 1,444	K 5
15853	Ridgway⊙, 6,022	E 3
19078	Ridley Park, 9,025	M 7
18077	Riegelsville, 1,050	M 4
15678	Rillton, 975	C 5
16248	Rimersburg, 1,146	D 3
17868	Riverside, 1,685	J 4
19551	Robesonia, 1,685	K 5
15949	Robinson, 975	D 5
15074	Roscoe, 1,176	C 5
19010	Rosemont, 4,900	M 5
19111	Rockledge, 2,564	M 7
15557	Rockwood, 1,051	C 6
15477	Roscoe, 1,176	C 5
18013	Roseto, 1,538	M 4
17250	Rouzerville, 1,419	G 6
†17067	Royalton, 1,040	J 5
19468	Royersford, 4,235	L 5
16249	Rural Valley, 962	D 4
16345	Russell, 950	D 2
15076	Russellton, 1,597	C 4
19070	Rutledge, 1,167	M 7
16433	Saegertown, 1,348	B 2
17970	Saint Clair, 4,576	K 4
15857	Saint Marys, 7,470	E 3
15951	Saint Michael, 1,248	E 5
15681	Saltsburg, 1,037	C 4
†15801	Sandy, 2,000	E 3
16056	Saxonburg, 1,191	C 4
18840	Sayre, 7,473	K 2
15963	Scalp Level, 1,353	E 5
17088	Schaefferstown, 1,027	K 5
18078	Schnecksville, 1,550	L 4
17972	Schuylkill Haven, 6,125	K 4
18354	Sciota, 950	M 4
15683	Scottdale, 5,818	C 5
*18501	Scranton⊙, 103,564	L 3
	Scranton, ‡234,107	L 3
19018	Secane, 5,700	M 7
17870	Selinsgrove, 5,116	J 4
18960	Sellersville, 4,389	M 5
15143	Sewickley, 5,660	B 4
17872	Shamokin, 11,719	J 4
17876	Shamokin Dam, 1,562	J 4
16146	Sharon, 22,653	A 3
19079	Sharon Hill, 7,464	N 7
15215	Sharpsburg, 5,499	B 6
16150	Sharpsville, 6,126	A 3
16347	Sheffield, 1,564	D 2
17976	Shenandoah, 8,287	K 4
18655	Shickshinny, 1,685	K 3
19607	Shillington, 6,249	K 5
16748	Shinglehouse, 1,320	F 2
17257	Shippensburg, 6,536	H 5
19555	Shoemakersville, 1,427	K 4
17361	Shrewsbury, 1,716	J 6
18407	Simpson, 1,900	L 2
19608	Sinking Spring, 2,862	K 5
19474	Skippack, 975	M 5
18080	Slatington, 4,687	L 4
15684	Slickville, 1,066	C 5
16057	Slippery Rock, 4,949	B 3
16749	Smethport, 1,883	F 2
15478	Smithfield, 969	C 6
15501	Somerset⊙, 6,269	D 6
18964	Souderton, 6,380	M 5
15425	South Connellsville, 2,385	C 6
15956	South Fork, 1,661	E 5
14892	South Waverly, 1,307	J 2
17701	South Williamsport, 7,153	J 3
15775	Spangler, 3,109	E 4
19475	Spring City, 3,578	L 5
15144	Springdale, 5,202	C 4
19064	Springfield, △2,446	M 7
17362	Spring Grove, 1,969	J 6
16801	State College, 33,778	G 4
17113	Steelton, 8,556	J 5
17363	Stewartstown, 1,157	K 6
16153	Stoneboro, 1,129	B 3
19464	Stowe, 3,596	L 5
17579	Strasburg, 1,887	K 6
18360	Stroudsburg⊙, 5,451	M 4
16323	Sugarcreek, 5,944	C 3
18706	Sugar Notch, 1,333	L 3
18250	Summit Hill, 3,811	L 4
17801	Sunbury⊙, 13,025	J 4
18847	Susquehanna, 2,319	L 2
19081	Swarthmore, 6,156	M 7
15218	Swissvale, 13,821	C 7
15865	Sykesville, 1,311	E 3
18252	Tamaqua, 9,246	L 4
15084	Tarentum, 7,379	C 4
18517	Taylor, 6,977	L 3
18969	Telford, 3,409	M 5
19560	Temple, 1,667	K 5
16259	Templeton, 950	D 4
17581	Terre Hill, 1,129	L 5
18512	Throop, 4,307	L 3
16353	Tionesta⊙, 711	C 2
16354	Titusville, 7,331	C 2
19562	Topton, 1,744	L 5
19374	Toughkenamon, 1,233	L 6
18848	Towanda⊙, 4,224	J 2
17980	Tower City, 1,774	J 4
15085	Trafford, 4,383	C 5
†19013	Trainer, 2,336	M 7
17981	Tremont, 1,833	K 4
18254	Tresckow, 1,146	K 4
17881	Trevorton, 2,196	J 4
16947	Troy, 1,315	J 2
19007	Tullytown, 2,194	N 5
18657	Tunkhannock⊙, 2,251	L 2
15145	Turtle Creek, 8,308	C 7
15960	Twin Rocks, 975	E 4
16686	Tyrone, 7,072	F 4
16438	Union City, 3,631	C 2
15401	Uniontown⊙, 16,282	C 6
15689	United, 975	D 5
15235	Universal, 1,900	C 7
†19013	Upland, 3,930	M 7
19082	Upper Darby, △95,910	M 6
19481	Valley Forge, 400	L 5
17983	Valley View, 1,585	J 4
15690	Vandergrift, 7,873	D 4
15147	Verona, 3,737	C 7
15132	Versailles, 2,754	C 7
19085	Villanova, 5,250	M 6
15148	Wall, 1,265	C 7
19086	Wallingford, 3,500	L 4
18088	Walnutport, 1,942	L 4
16157	Wampum, 1,189	B 3
16365	Warren⊙, 12,998	D 2
15301	Washington⊙, 19,827	B 5
16441	Waterford, 1,468	B 2
17777	Watsontown, 2,514	J 3
18472	Waymart, 1,122	M 2
19087	Wayne, 12,500	M 5
17268	Waynesboro, 10,011	G 6
15370	Waynesburg⊙, 5,152	B 6
18255	Weatherly, 2,554	L 4
16901	Wellsboro⊙, 4,003	H 2
19565	Wernersville, 1,761	K 5
16510	Wesleyville, 3,920	C 1
15417	West Brownsville, 1,426	C 5
19380	West Chester⊙, 19,301	L 6
16950	Westfield, 1,273	H 2
19390	West Grove, 1,870	L 6
18201	West Hazleton, 6,059	K 4
16201	West Kittanning, 956	C 4
19609	West Lawn, 1,973	K 5
15656	West Leechburg, 1,422	C 4
16159	West Middlesex, 1,293	B 3
15122	West Mifflin, 28,070	C 7
†15901	Westmont, 6,673	D 5
15089	West Newton, 3,648	C 5
15229	West View, 8,312	B 6
17401	West York, 5,314	J 6
16161	Wheatland, 1,421	B 3
15120	Whitaker, 1,697	C 7
18052	Whitehall, 16,551	L 4
18661	White Haven, 2,134	L 3
15131	White Oak, 9,304	C 7
17097	Wiconisco, 1,236	J 4
15870	Wilcox, 950	E 2
*18701	Wilkes-Barre⊙, 58,856	L 3
	Wilkes-Barre-Hazleton, ‡342,301	L 3
15221	Wilkinsburg, 26,780	C 7
16693	Williamsburg, 1,704	F 4
17701	Williamsport⊙, 37,918	H 3
17098	Williamstown, 1,919	J 4
19090	Willow Grove, 16,494	M 5
15148	Wilmerding, 3,218	C 7
15025	Wilson, 8,482	M 4
15963	Windber, 6,332	E 5
18091	Windgap, 2,270	M 4
17366	Windsor, 1,298	J 6
†18434	Winton, 4,948	M 3
†15301	Wolfdale, 1,202	B 5
15501	Womelsdorf, 1,551	K 5
19094	Woodlyn, 6,500	M 7
17368	Wrightsville, 2,668	J 6
19096	Wynnewood, 9,200	M 6
18644	Wyoming, 4,195	L 3
19610	Wyomissing, 7,136	K 5
19067	Yardley, 2,616	N 5
19050	Yeadon, 12,136	M 7
17099	Yeagertown, 1,363	G 4
*17401	York⊙, 50,335	J 6
	York, ‡329,540	J 6
16371	Youngsville, 2,158	D 2
15697	Youngwood, 3,057	D 5
16063	Zelienople, 3,602	B 4

⊙ County seat.
‡ Population of metropolitan area.
△ Population of town or township.
† Zip of nearest p.o.
* Multiple zips

Zip	Place	Grid
15666	Mount Pleasant, 5,895	D 5
18344	Mount Pocono, 1,019	M 3
17066	Mount Union, 3,662	G 5
17554	Mountville, 1,454	K 5
17347	Mount Wolf, 1,811	J 6
17756	Muncy, 2,872	J 3
15120	Munhall, 16,674	C 7
15668	Murrysville, 3,900	C 4
17067	Myerstown, 3,645	K 5
18634	Nanticoke, 14,632	K 3
15943	Nanty Glo, 4,298	E 5
19072	Narberth, 5,151	M 6
15065	Natrona Heights, 15,000	C 4
18064	Nazareth, 5,815	M 4
15351	Nemacolin, 1,273	B 6
18635	Nescopeck, 1,897	K 3
18240	Nesquehoning, 3,338	L 4
†16141	New Beaver, 1,426	B 4
16140	New Bedford, 950	A 3
16242	New Bethlehem, 1,406	D 3
17068	New Bloomfield⊙, 1,032	H 5
15066	New Brighton, 7,637	B 4
18901	New Britain, 2,428	M 5
*16101	New Castle⊙, 38,559	B 3
17070	New Cumberland, 9,803	J 5
15067	New Eagle, 2,497	B 5
17349	New Freedom, 1,495	J 6
17557	New Holland, 3,971	K 5
18938	New Hope, 978	N 5
15068	New Kensington, 20,312	C 4
18834	New Milford, 1,143	L 2
17350	New Oxford, 1,495	H 6
17959	New Philadelphia, 1,528	K 4
17074	Newport, 1,747	H 5
15468	New Salem, 1,337	C 6
15626	New Salem (Delmont), 1,934	D 5
18940	Newtown, 2,216	N 5
19073	Newtown Square, 16,000	L 6
17241	Newville, 1,631	H 5
16142	New Wilmington, 2,721	B 3
17759	Nisbet, 950	H 3
*19401	Norristown⊙, 38,169	M 5
18067	Northampton, 8,389	L 4
15673	North Apollo, 1,618	D 4
15104	North Braddock, 10,838	C 7
16428	North East, 3,846	C 1
17857	Northumberland, 4,102	J 4
19454	North Wales, 3,911	M 5
16365	North Warren, 1,360	D 2
15674	Norvelt, 2,588	C 5

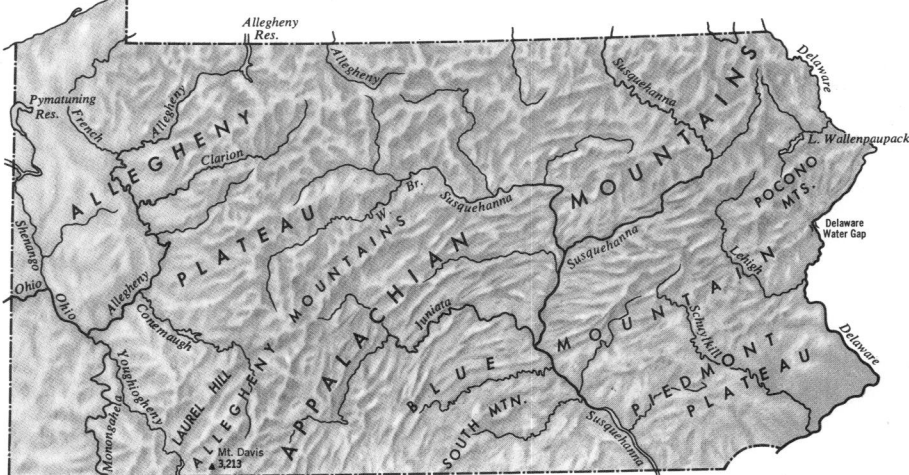

Topography

0   30   60
MILES

| 5,000 m. 16,404 ft. | 2,000 m. 6,562 ft. | 1,000 m. 3,281 ft. | 500 m. 1,640 ft. | 200 m. 656 ft. | 100 m. 328 ft. | Sea Level | Below |

SOUTH CAROLINA

SCALE
0 5 10 20 30 40 MI.
0 5 10 20 30 40 KM.
State Capitals..............⊛
County Seats..............◉
Canals..............

© C.S. HAMMOND & Co., N.Y.

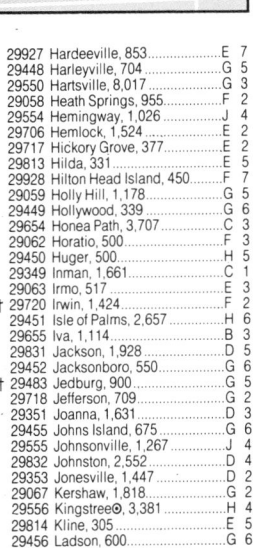

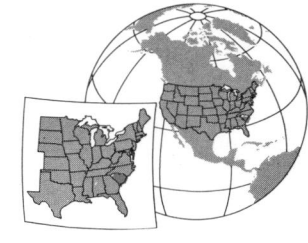

Agriculture, Industry and Resources

DOMINANT LAND USE

- Tobacco, Cotton
- Specialized Cotton
- Cotton, General Farming
- General Farming, Forest Products, Truck Farming, Cotton
- Forests
- Swampland, Limited Agriculture

MAJOR MINERAL OCCURRENCES

Cl Clay
Mi Mica

GREENVILLE-SPARTANBURG-PIEDMONT
Textiles, Clothing

NORTH AUGUSTA-AIKEN COUNTY
Textiles

Major Industrial Areas
Water Power
Major Textile Centers

AREA 31,055 sq. mi.
POPULATION 2,590,516 ('70); 3,119,208 ('80)
CAPITAL Columbia
LARGEST CITY Columbia
HIGHEST POINT Sassafras Mtn. 3,560 ft.
SETTLED IN 1670
ADMITTED TO UNION May 23, 1788
POPULAR NAME Palmetto State
STATE FLOWER Yellow Jessamine
STATE BIRD Carolina Wren

◉ County seat.
◉ Population of metropolitan area.
† Zip of nearest p.o.
* Multiple zips

Colorful materials being Sanforized in a South Carolina textile mill. Textiles are by far the most important of the state's industries.

A. D'Arazien — Shostal Associates

Topography

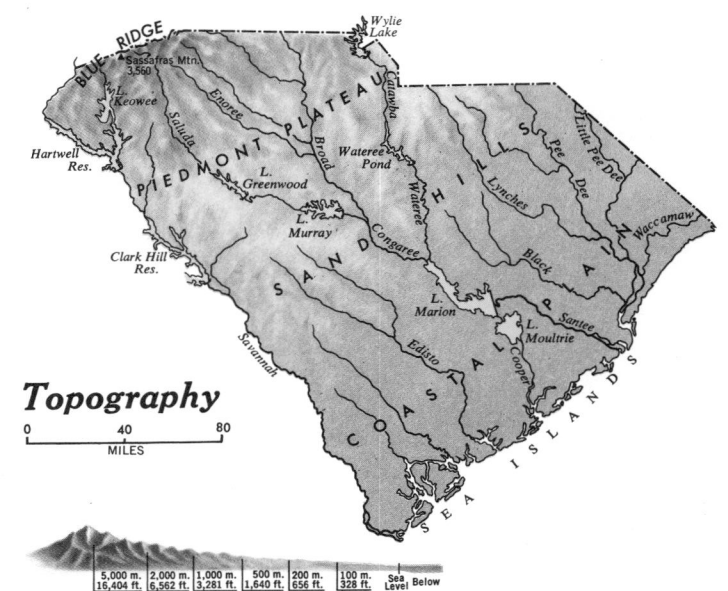

0   40   80
MILES

| 5,000 m. | 2,000 m. | 1,000 m. | 500 m. | 200 m. | 100 m. | Sea Level | Below |
| 16,404 ft. | 6,562 ft. | 3,281 ft. | 1,640 ft. | 656 ft. | 328 ft. | | |

298 South Dakota

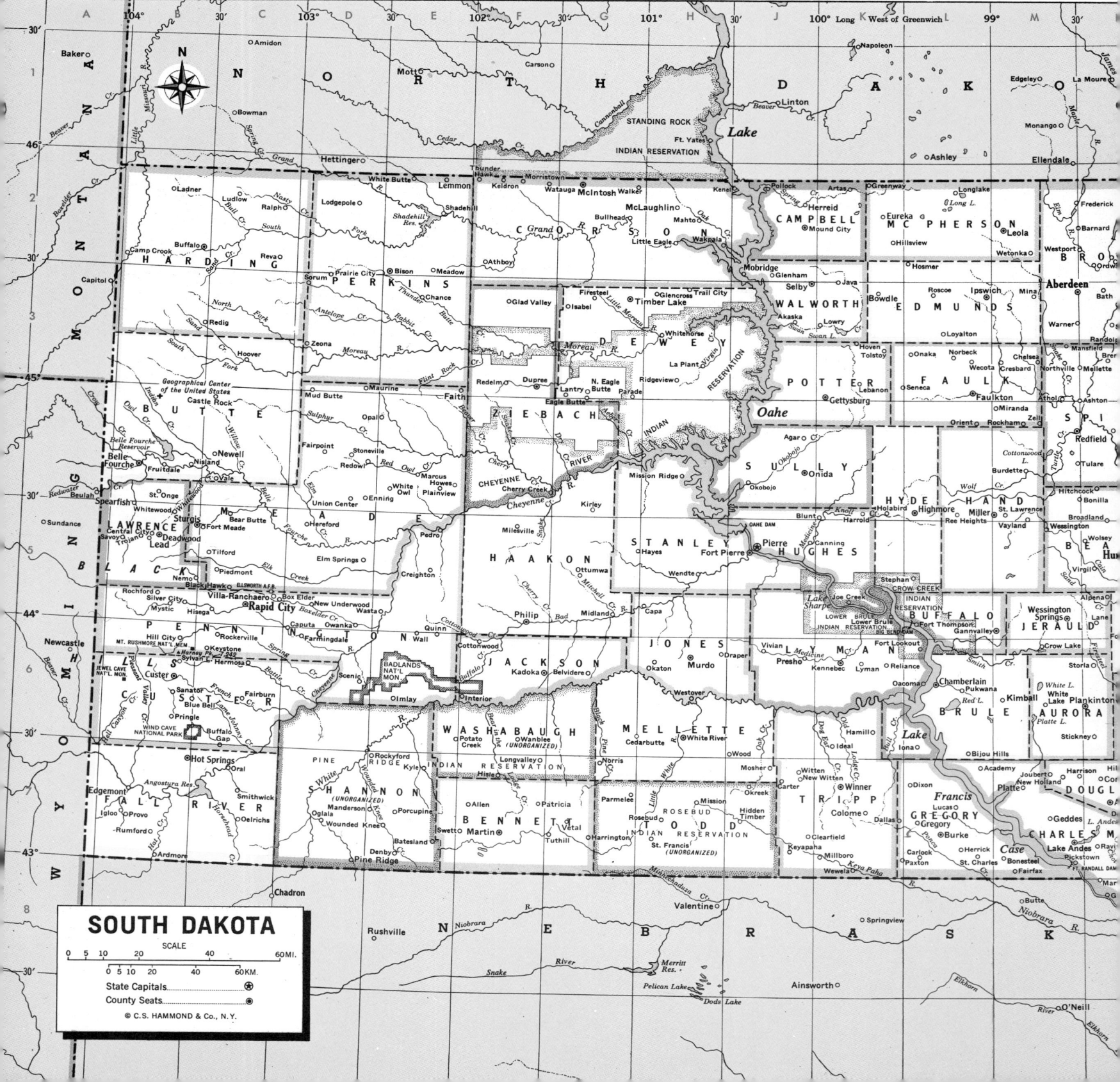

SOUTH DAKOTA

SCALE

0 5 10   20   40   60 MI.

0 5 10   20   40   60 KM.

State Capitals ....⊛
County Seats ....◉

© C. S. HAMMOND & Co., N.Y.

(continued on following page)

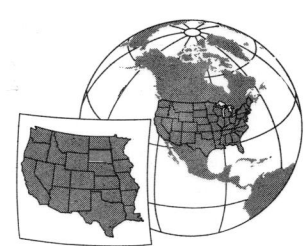

AREA 77,047 sq. mi.
POPULATION 666,257 ('70); 690,178 ('80)
CAPITAL Pierre
LARGEST CITY Sioux Falls
HIGHEST POINT Harney Pk. 7,242 ft.
SETTLED IN 1856
ADMITTED TO UNION November 2, 1889
POPULAR NAME Coyote State; Sunshine State
STATE FLOWER Pasqueflower
STATE BIRD Ring-necked Pheasant

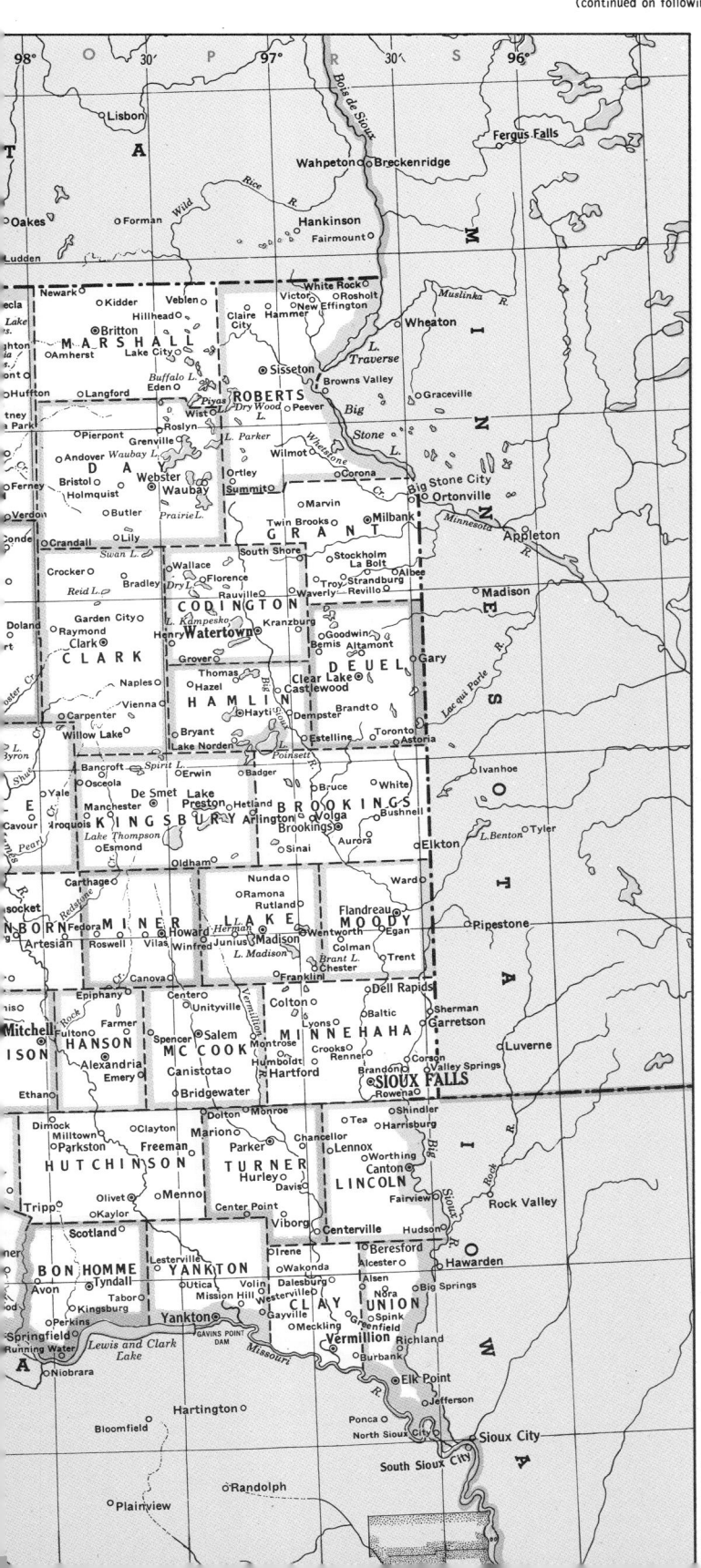

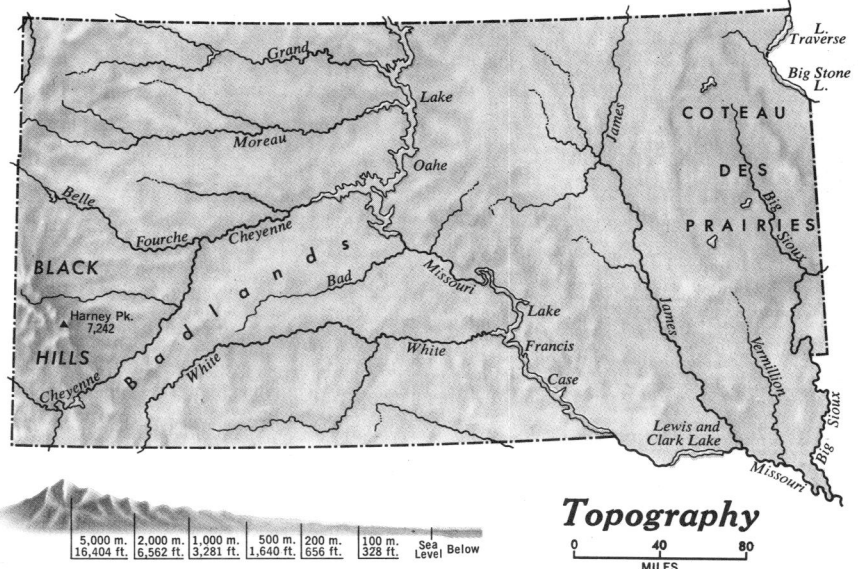

Topography

5,000 m.	2,000 m.	1,000 m.	500 m.	200 m.	100 m.	Sea	Below
16,404 ft.	6,562 ft.	3,281 ft.	1,640 ft.	656 ft.	328 ft.	Level	

0   40   80
MILES

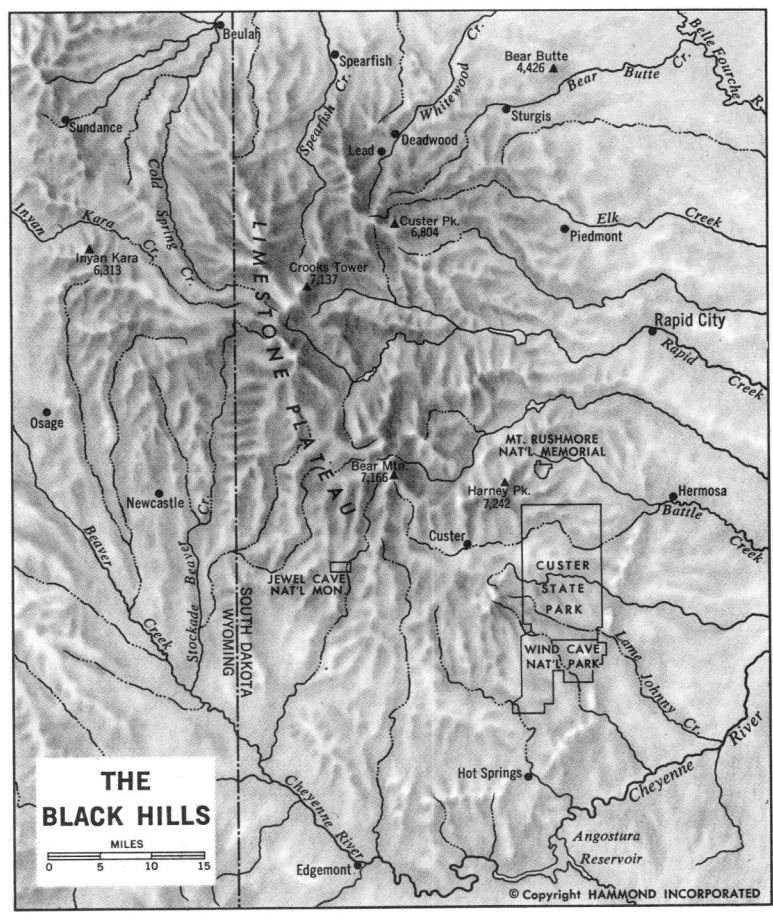

THE BLACK HILLS

MILES
0   5   10   15

© Copyright HAMMOND INCORPORATED

Agriculture, Industry and Resources

DOMINANT LAND USE

Specialized Wheat

Wheat, General Farming

Wheat, Range Livestock

Cattle Feed, Hogs

Livestock, Cash Grain

General Farming, Livestock, Special Crops

Range Livestock

Forests

⚡ Water Power

MAJOR MINERAL OCCURRENCES

Ag Silver   Mi Mica

Au Gold   O Petroleum

Be Beryl   U Uranium

Gn Granite   V Vanadium

E. C. Werner — Shostal Associates

Beds of fossils await paleontologists in the vast, semi-arid buttes of the Badlands, east of the Black Hills of South Dakota.

Texas 301

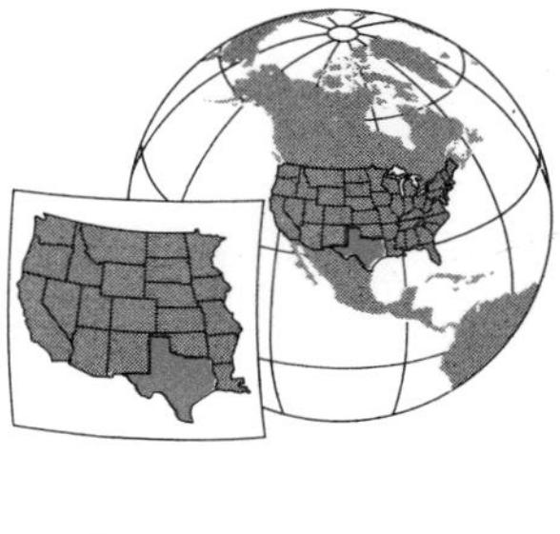

AREA 267,339 sq. mi.
POPULATION 11,196,730 ('70); 14,228,383 ('80)
CAPITAL Austin
LARGEST CITY Houston
HIGHEST POINT Guadalupe Pk. 8,751 ft.
SETTLED IN 1686
ADMITTED TO UNION December 29, 1845
POPULAR NAME Lone Star State
STATE FLOWER Bluebonnet
STATE BIRD Mockingbird

COUNTIES

Name/Pop.	Key
Anderson, 27,789	J 6
Andrews, 10,372	B 5
Angelina, 49,349	K 6
Aransas, 8,902	H 10
Archer, 5,759	F 4
Armstrong, 1,895	C 3
Atascosa, 18,696	F 9
Austin, 13,831	H 8
Bailey, 8,487	B 3
Bandera, 4,747	E 8
Bastrop, 17,297	G 7
Baylor, 5,221	E 4
Bee, 22,737	G 9
Bell, 124,483	G 6
Bexar, 830,460	F 8
Blanco, 3,567	F 7
Borden, 888	C 5
Bosque, 10,966	G 6
Bowie, 67,813	K 4
Brazoria, 108,312	J 8
Brazos, 57,978	H 7
Brewster, 7,780	A 8
Briscoe, 2,794	C 3
Brooks, 8,005	F 11
Brown, 25,877	F 6
Burleson, 9,999	H 7
Burnet, 11,420	F 7
Caldwell, 21,178	G 8
Calhoun, 17,831	H 9
Callahan, 8,205	E 5
Cameron, 140,368	G 11
Camp, 8,005	K 5
Carson, 6,358	C 2
Cass, 24,133	K 4
Castro, 10,394	B 3
Chambers, 12,187	K 8
Cherokee, 32,008	J 6
Childress, 6,605	D 3
Clay, 8,079	F 4
Cochran, 5,326	B 4
Coke, 3,087	D 6
Coleman, 10,288	E 6
Collin, 66,920	H 4
Collingsworth, 4,755	D 3
Colorado, 17,638	H 8
Comal, 24,165	F 8
Comanche, 11,898	F 5
Concho, 2,937	E 6
Cooke, 23,471	G 4
Coryell, 35,311	G 6
Cottle, 3,204	D 3
Crane, 4,172	B 6
Crockett, 3,885	C 7
Crosby, 9,085	C 4
Culberson, 3,429	C 11
Dallam, 6,012	B 1
Dallas, 1,327,321	H 5
Dawson, 16,604	C 5
Deaf Smith, 18,999	B 3
Delta, 4,927	J 4
Denton, 75,633	G 4
De Witt, 18,660	G 9
Dickens, 3,737	D 4
Dimmit, 9,039	E 9
Donley, 3,641	D 2
Duval, 11,722	F 10
Eastland, 18,092	F 5
Ector, 91,805	B 6
Edwards, 2,107	D 7
Ellis, 46,638	H 5
El Paso, 359,291	A 10
Erath, 18,141	F 5
Falls, 17,300	H 6
Fannin, 22,705	H 4
Fayette, 17,650	H 8
Fisher, 6,344	D 5
Floyd, 11,044	C 3
Foard, 2,211	E 3
Fort Bend, 52,314	J 8
Franklin, 5,291	J 4
Freestone, 11,116	H 6
Frio, 11,159	E 9
Gaines, 11,593	B 5
Galveston, 169,812	K 8
Garza, 5,289	C 4
Gillespie, 10,553	F 7
Glasscock, 1,155	C 6
Goliad, 4,869	G 9
Gonzales, 16,375	G 8
Gray, 26,949	D 2
Grayson, 83,225	H 4
Gregg, 75,929	K 5
Grimes, 11,855	J 7
Guadalupe, 33,554	G 8
Hale, 34,137	C 3
Hall, 6,015	D 3
Hamilton, 7,198	F 6
Hansford, 6,351	C 1
Hardeman, 6,795	E 3
Hardin, 29,996	K 7
Harris, 1,741,912	J 8
Harrison, 44,841	K 5
Hartley, 2,782	B 2
Haskell, 8,512	E 4
Hays, 27,642	F 7
Hemphill, 3,084	D 2
Henderson, 26,466	J 5
Hidalgo, 181,535	F 11
Hill, 22,596	G 5
Hockley, 20,396	B 4
Hood, 6,368	G 5
Hopkins, 20,710	J 4
Houston, 17,855	J 6
Howard, 37,796	C 5
Hudspeth, 2,392	B 10
Hunt, 47,948	H 4
Hutchinson, 24,443	C 2
Irion, 1,070	C 6
Jack, 6,711	F 4
Jackson, 12,975	H 9
Jasper, 24,692	K 7
Jeff Davis, 1,527	C 11
Jefferson, 244,773	K 8
Jim Hogg, 4,654	F 11
Jim Wells, 33,032	F 10
Johnson, 45,769	G 5
Jones, 16,106	E 5
Karnes, 13,462	G 9
Kaufman, 32,392	H 5
Kendall, 6,964	F 8
Kenedy, 678	G 11
Kent, 1,434	D 4
Kerr, 19,454	E 7
Kimble, 3,904	E 7
King, 464	D 4
Kinney, 2,006	D 8
Kleberg, 33,166	G 10
Knox, 5,972	E 4
Lamar, 36,062	J 4
Lamb, 17,770	B 3
Lampasas, 9,323	F 6
La Salle, 5,014	E 9
Lavaca, 17,903	H 8
Lee, 8,048	H 7
Leon, 8,738	J 6
Liberty, 33,014	K 7
Limestone, 18,100	H 6
Lipscomb, 3,486	D 1
Live Oak, 6,697	F 9
Llano, 6,979	F 7
Loving, 164	D 10
Lubbock, 179,295	C 4
Lynn, 9,107	C 4
Madison, 7,693	J 6
Marion, 8,517	K 5
Martin, 4,774	C 5
Mason, 3,356	E 7
Matagorda, 27,913	H 9
Maverick, 18,093	D 9
McCulloch, 8,571	E 6
McLennan, 147,553	G 6
McMullen, 1,095	F 9
Medina, 20,249	E 8
Menard, 2,646	E 7
Midland, 65,433	B 6
Milam, 20,028	H 7
Mills, 4,212	F 6
Mitchell, 9,073	D 5
Montague, 15,326	G 4
Montgomery, 49,479	J 7
Moore, 14,060	C 2
Morris, 12,310	K 4
Motley, 2,178	D 3
Nacogdoches, 36,362	K 6
Navarro, 31,150	H 5
Newton, 11,657	L 7
Nolan, 16,220	D 5
Nueces, 237,544	G 10
Ochiltree, 9,704	D 1
Oldham, 2,258	B 2
Orange, 71,170	L 7
Palo Pinto, 28,962	F 5
Panola, 15,894	K 5
Parker, 33,888	G 5
Parmer, 10,509	B 3
Pecos, 13,748	B 7
Polk, 14,457	K 7
Potter, 90,511	C 2
Presidio, 4,842	C 12
Rains, 3,752	J 5
Randall, 53,885	C 2
Reagan, 3,239	C 6
Real, 2,013	E 8
Red River, 14,298	J 4
Reeves, 16,526	D 11
Refugio, 9,494	G 9
Roberts, 967	D 2
Robertson, 14,389	H 6
Rockwall, 7,046	H 5
Runnels, 12,108	E 6
Rusk, 34,102	K 5
Sabine, 7,187	L 6
San Augustine, 7,858	K 6
San Jacinto, 6,702	J 7
San Patricio, 47,288	G 10
San Saba, 5,540	F 6
Schleicher, 2,277	D 7
Scurry, 15,760	D 5
Shackelford, 3,323	E 5
Shelby, 19,672	K 6
Sherman, 3,657	C 1
Smith, 97,096	J 5
Somervell, 2,793	G 5
Starr, 17,707	F 11
Stephens, 8,414	F 5
Sterling, 1,056	C 6
Stonewall, 2,397	D 4
Sutton, 3,175	D 7
Swisher, 10,373	C 3
Tarrant, 716,317	G 5
Taylor, 97,853	E 5
Terrell, 1,940	B 7
Terry, 14,118	B 4
Throckmorton, 2,205	E 4
Titus, 16,702	K 4
Tom Green, 71,047	D 6
Travis, 295,516	G 7
Trinity, 7,628	J 6
Tyler, 12,417	K 7
Upshur, 20,976	K 5
Upton, 4,697	B 6
Uvalde, 17,348	E 8
Val Verde, 27,471	C 8
Van Zandt, 22,155	J 5
Victoria, 53,766	H 9
Walker, 27,680	J 7
Waller, 14,285	J 8
Ward, 13,019	A 6
Washington, 18,842	H 7
Webb, 72,859	E 10
Wharton, 36,729	H 8
Wheeler, 6,434	D 2
Wichita, 121,862	F 3
Wilbarger, 15,355	E 3
Willacy, 15,570	G 11
Williamson, 37,305	G 7
Wilson, 13,041	F 8
Winkler, 9,640	A 6
Wise, 19,687	G 4
Wood, 18,589	J 5
Yoakum, 7,344	B 4
Young, 15,400	F 4
Zapata, 4,352	E 11
Zavala, 11,370	E 9

CITIES ana TOWNS

	Zip	Name/Pop.	Key
	79311	Abernathy, 2,625	B 4
*	79601	Abilene⊙, 89,653	E 5
		Abilene, ‡113,959	E 5
	78516	Alamo, 4,291	F 11
	78209	Alamo Heights, 6,933	F 8
	76430	Albany⊙, 1,978	E 5
	78332	Alice⊙, 20,121	F 10
	79830	Alpine⊙, 5,971	D 11
	77510	Alta Loma, 1,536	K 3
	75925	Alto, 1,045	J 6
	76009	Alvarado, 2,129	G 5
	77511	Alvin, 10,671	J 3
*	79101	Amarillo⊙, 127,010	C 2
		Amarillo, ‡144,396	C 2
	77514	Anahuac⊙, 1,881	K 8
	77830	Anderson⊙, 500	J 7
	79714	Andrews⊙, 8,625	B 5
	77515	Angleton⊙, 9,770	J 8
	79501	Anson⊙, 2,615	E 5
	88021	Anthony, 2,154	A 10
	79313	Anton, 1,034	B 4
	78336	Aransas Pass, 5,813	G 10
	77517	Arcadia, 1,200	K 3
	76351	Archer City⊙, 1,722	F 4
*	76010	Arlington, 90,643	F 2
	78827	Asherton, 1,645	E 9
	79502	Aspermont⊙, 1,198	D 4
	75751	Athens⊙, 9,582	J 5
	75551	Atlanta, 5,007	K 4
*	78701	Austin (cap.)⊙, 251,808	G 7
		Austin, ‡295,516	G 7
	76020	Azle, 4,493	E 1
	77518	Bacliff, 1,900	K 2
	79504	Baird⊙, 1,538	E 5
	75149	Balch Springs, 10,464	H 2
	76821	Ballinger⊙, 4,203	E 6
	78003	Bandera⊙, 891	F 8
	76823	Bangs, 1,214	E 6
	77532	Barrett, 2,750	K 1
	76511	Bartlett, 1,622	G 7
	78602	Bastrop⊙, 3,112	G 7
	77414	Bay City⊙, 11,733	H 9
	77520	Baytown, 43,980	L 2
	77701	Beaumont⊙, 115,919	K 7
		Beaumont-Port Arthur-Orange, ‡315,943	K 7
	76021	Bedford, 10,049	F 2
	78102	Beeville⊙, 13,506	G 9
	77401	Bellaire, 19,009	J 2
	76705	Bellmead, 7,698	H 6
	77418	Bellville⊙, 2,371	H 8
	76513	Belton⊙, 8,696	G 7
	78341	Benavides, 2,112	F 10
	76126	Benbrook, 8,169	E 2
	79505	Benjamin⊙, 308	E 4
	76932	Big Lake⊙, 2,489	C 6
	79720	Big Spring⊙, 28,735	C 5
	78343	Bishop, 3,466	G 10
	77951	Bloomington, 1,676	H 9
	76131	Blue Mound, 1,283	F 1
	78006	Boerne⊙, 2,432	F 8
	75417	Bogata, 1,287	J 4
	75418	Bonham⊙, 7,698	H 4
	79007	Borger, 14,195	C 2
	75557	Boston⊙, 500	K 4
	79009	Bovina, 1,428	A 3
	76230	Bowie, 5,185	G 4
	78832	Brackettville⊙, 1,539	D 8
	76825	Brady⊙, 5,557	E 6
	77422	Brazoria, 1,681	J 9
	76024	Breckenridge⊙, 5,944	F 5
	77833	Brenham⊙, 8,922	H 7
	77611	Bridge City, 8,164	L 7
	76026	Bridgeport, 3,614	G 4
	77423	Brookshire, 1,683	J 8
	77581	Brookside Village, 1,507	J 2
	79316	Brownfield⊙, 9,647	B 4
	78520	Brownsville⊙, 52,522	G 12
		Brownsville-Harlingen-San Benito, ‡140,368	G 12
	76801	Brownwood⊙, 17,368	F 6
	77801	Bryan⊙, 33,719	H 7
		Bryan-College Station, ‡57,978	H 7
	75831	Buffalo, 1,242	J 6
	77612	Buna, 1,649	L 7
†	79007	Bunavista, 1,402	C 2
†	77001	Bunker Hill Village, 3,977	J 1
	76354	Burkburnett, 9,230	F 3
	76028	Burleson, 7,713	F 2
	78611	Burnet⊙, 2,864	F 7
	77836	Caldwell⊙, 2,308	H 7
	77837	Calvert, 2,072	H 7
	76520	Cameron⊙, 5,546	H 7
	79014	Canadian⊙, 2,292	D 2
	75103	Canton⊙, 2,283	J 5
	79835	Canutillo, 1,588	A 10
	79015	Canyon⊙, 8,333	C 3

(continued on following page)

Agriculture, Industry and Resources

DOMINANT LAND USE

- Wheat, Grain Sorghums, Range Livestock
- Cotton, Wheat
- Specialized Cotton
- Cotton, General Farming
- Cotton, Forest Products
- Cotton, Range Livestock
- Rice, General Farming
- Peanuts, General Farming
- General Farming, Livestock, Cash Grain
- General Farming, Forest Products, Truck Farming, Cotton
- Fruit, Truck and Mixed Farming
- Range Livestock
- Forests
- Swampland, Limited Agriculture
- Nonagricultural Land
- Urban Areas

MAJOR MINERAL OCCURRENCES

- At Asphalt
- Cl Clay
- Fe Iron Ore
- G Natural Gas
- Gn Granite
- Gp Gypsum
- Gr Graphite
- He Helium
- Ls Limestone
- Na Salt
- O Petroleum
- S Sulfur
- Tc Talc
- U Uranium

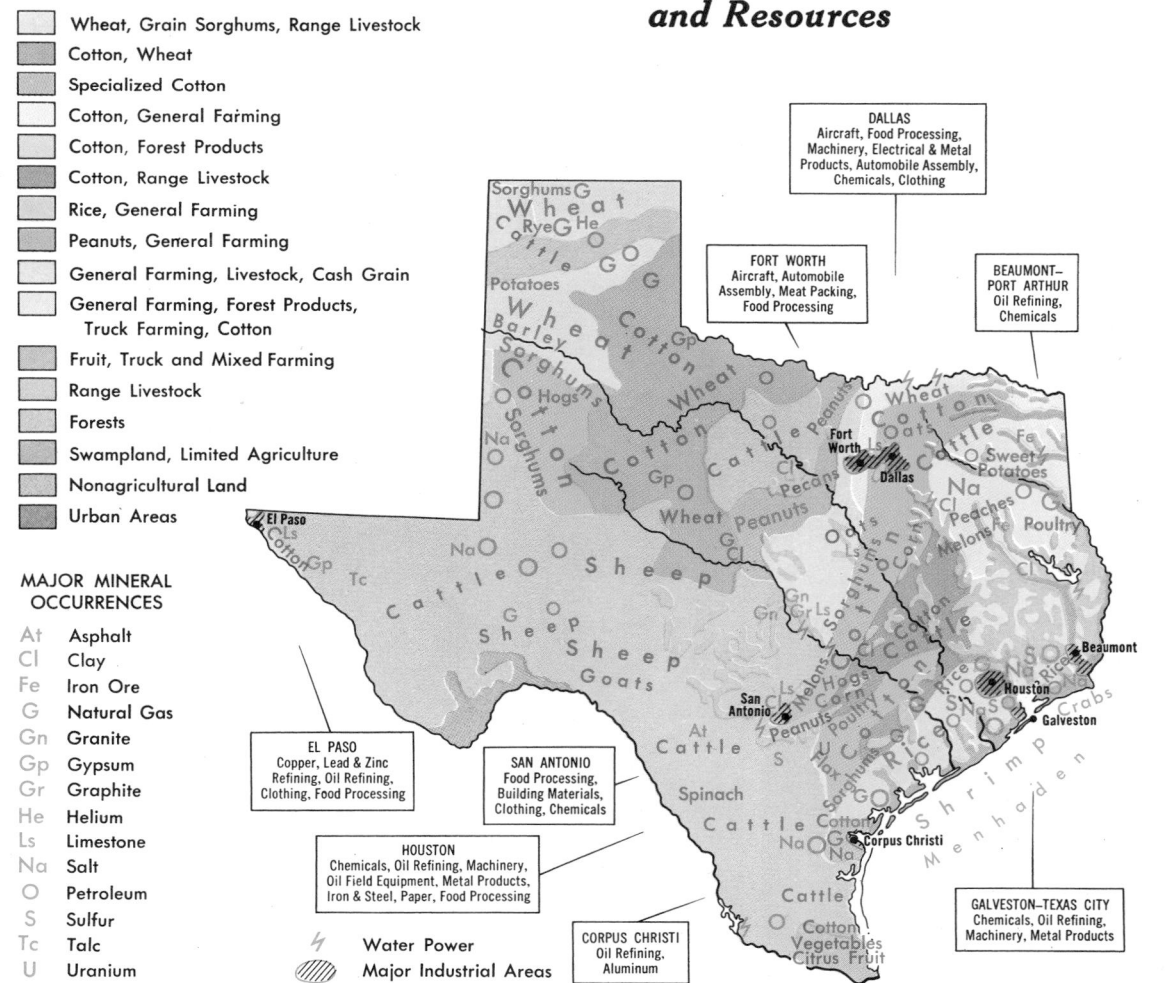

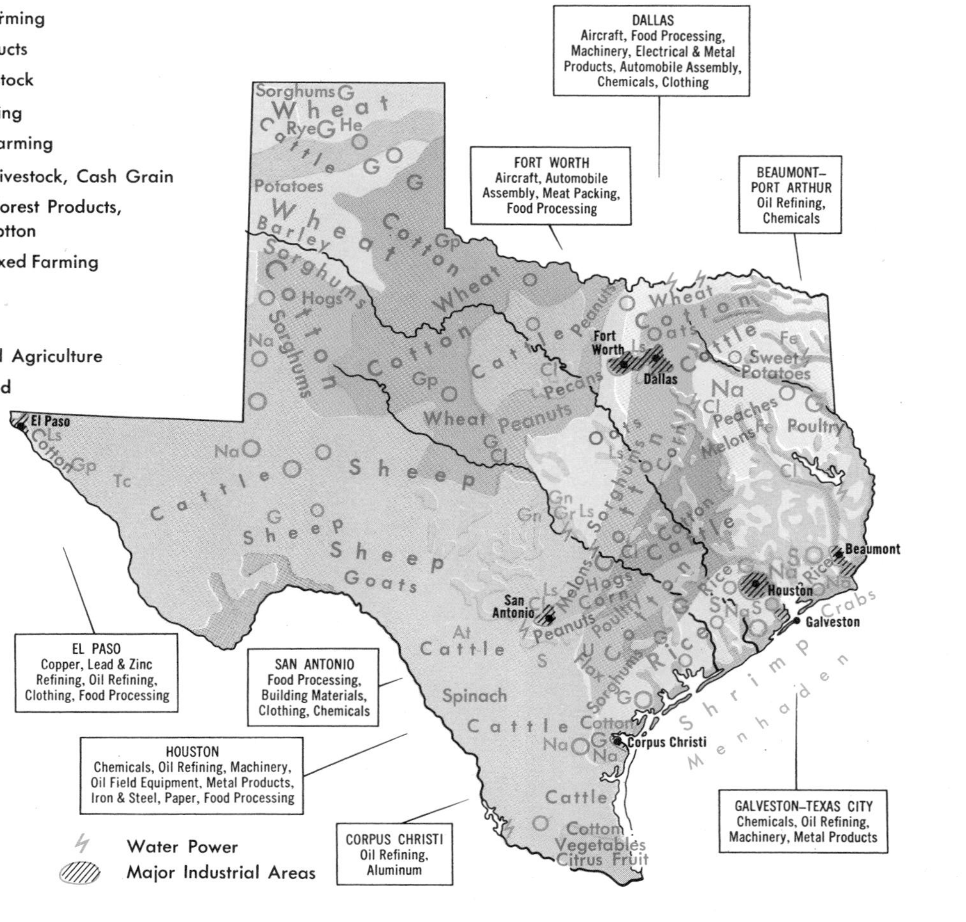
DALLAS
Aircraft, Food Processing, Machinery, Electrical & Metal Products, Automobile Assembly, Chemicals, Clothing
FORT WORTH
Aircraft, Automobile Assembly, Meat Packing, Food Processing
BEAUMONT–PORT ARTHUR
Oil Refining, Chemicals
EL PASO
Copper, Lead & Zinc Refining, Oil Refining, Clothing, Food Processing
SAN ANTONIO
Food Processing, Building Materials, Clothing, Chemicals
HOUSTON
Chemicals, Oil Refining, Machinery, Oil Field Equipment, Metal Products, Iron & Steel, Paper, Food Processing
CORPUS CHRISTI
Oil Refining, Aluminum
GALVESTON–TEXAS CITY
Chemicals, Oil Refining, Machinery, Metal Products
El Paso
Fort Worth
Dallas
San Antonio
Houston
Galveston
Beaumont
Corpus Christi
Wheat
Sorghums
Cattle
Potatoes
Barley
Cotton
Hogs
Sheep
Goats
Peanuts
Pecans
Oats
Sweet Potatoes
Peaches
Poultry
Melons
Rice
Corn
Flax
Spinach
Vegetables
Citrus Fruit
Crabs
Shrimp
Menhaden

- Water Power
- Major Industrial Areas

TEXAS

State Capitals ⊛
County Seats ⊙

© C.S. HAMMOND & Co., N.Y.

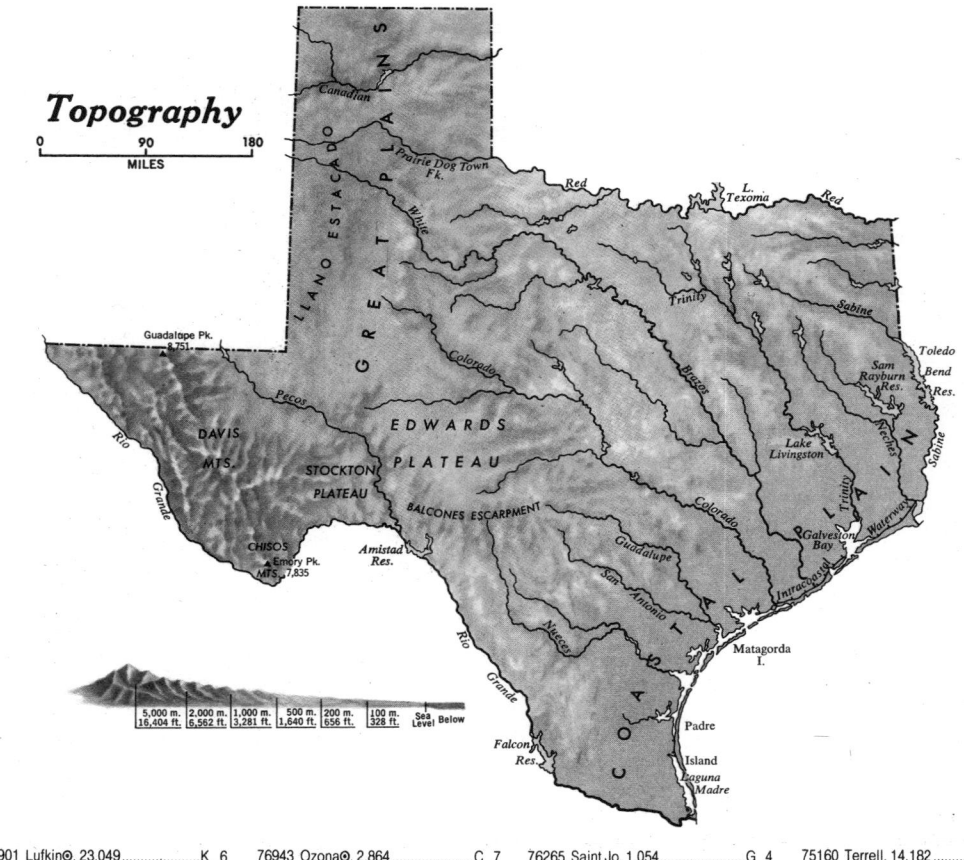

Topography

0   90   180
MILES

5,000 m. / 16,404 ft. — 2,000 m. / 6,562 ft. — 1,000 m. / 3,281 ft. — 500 m. / 1,640 ft. — 200 m. / 656 ft. — 100 m. / 328 ft. — Sea Level — Below

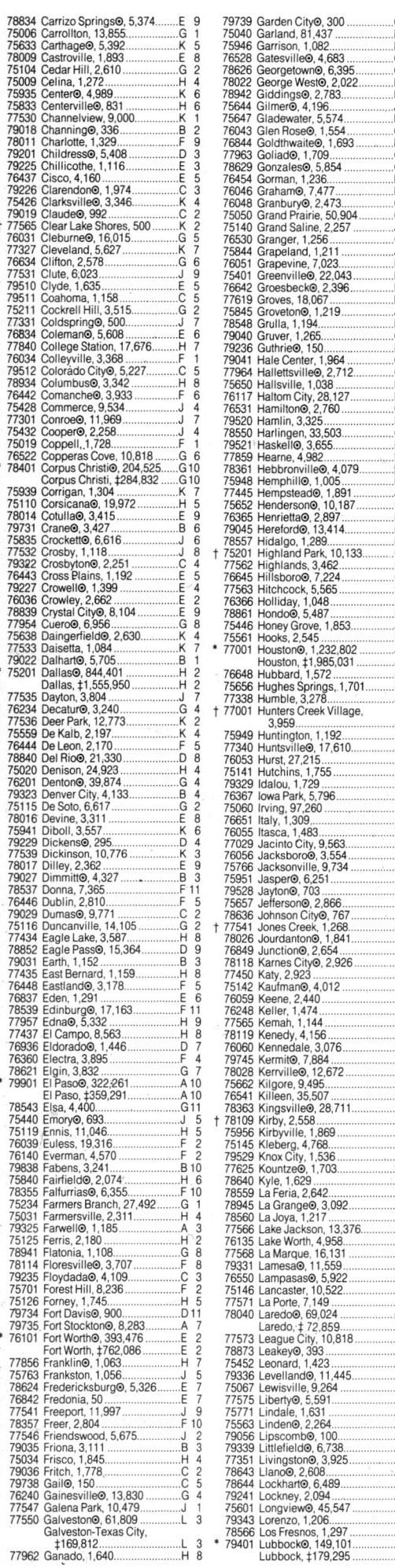

78834 Carrizo Springs⊙, 5,374....E 9
75006 Carrollton, 13,855....G 1
75633 Carthage⊙, 5,392....K 5
78009 Castroville, 1,893....E 8
75104 Cedar Hill, 2,610....G 2
75009 Celina, 1,272....H 4
75935 Center⊙, 4,989....K 6
75833 Centerville⊙, 831....H 6
77530 Channelview, 9,000....K 1
79018 Channing, 336....B 2
78011 Charlotte, 1,329....F 9
79201 Childress⊙, 5,408....D 3
79629 Chillicothe, 1,116....E 3
76437 Cisco, 4,160....E 5
79226 Clarendon⊙, 1,974....C 3
75426 Clarksville⊙, 3,346....K 4
79019 Claude⊙, 992....C 2
† 77565 Clear Lake Shores, 500....K 2
76031 Cleburne⊙, 16,015....G 5
77327 Cleveland, 5,627....K 7
76634 Clifton, 2,578....G 6
77531 Clute, 6,023....J 9
75510 Clyde, 1,635....E 5
79511 Coahoma, 1,158....C 5
75211 Cockrell Hill, 3,515....G 2
77331 Coldspring⊙, 500....J 7
76834 Coleman⊙, 5,608....E 6
77840 College Station, 17,676....H 7
76034 Colleyville, 3,368....F 1
79512 Colorado City⊙, 5,227....C 5
78934 Columbus⊙, 3,342....H 8
76442 Comanche⊙, 3,933....F 6
75428 Commerce, 9,534....J 4
77301 Conroe⊙, 11,969....J 7
75432 Cooper⊙, 2,258....J 4
75019 Coppell, 1,728....F 1
76522 Copperas Cove, 10,818....G 6
* 78401 Corpus Christi⊙, 204,525....G10
    Corpus Christi, ‡284,832....G10
75939 Corrigan, 1,304....K 7
75110 Corsicana⊙, 19,972....H 5
78014 Cotulla⊙, 3,415....E 9
79731 Crane⊙, 3,427....B 6
75835 Crockett⊙, 6,616....J 6
77532 Crosby, 1,118....J 8
79322 Crosbyton⊙, 2,251....C 4
76443 Cross Plains, 1,192....E 5
79227 Crowell⊙, 1,399....E 3
76036 Crowley, 2,662....F 2
78839 Crystal City⊙, 8,104....E 9
77954 Cuero⊙, 6,956....G 8
75638 Daingerfield⊙, 2,630....K 4
77533 Daisetta, 1,084....K 7
79022 Dalhart⊙, 5,705....B 1
* 75201 Dallas⊙, 844,401....H 2
    Dallas, ‡1,555,950....H 2
77535 Dayton, 3,804....J 7
76234 Decatur⊙, 3,240....G 4
77536 Deer Park, 12,773....K 2
75559 De Kalb, 2,197....K 4
76444 De Leon, 2,170....F 5
78840 Del Rio⊙, 21,330....D 8
75020 Denison, 24,923....H 4
76201 Denton⊙, 39,874....G 4
79323 Denver City, 4,133....B 4
75115 De Soto, 6,617....G 2
78016 Devine, 3,311....E 8
75941 Diboll, 3,557....K 6
79229 Dickens⊙, 295....D 4
77539 Dickinson, 10,776....K 3
78017 Dilley, 2,362....E 9
79027 Dimmitt⊙, 4,327....B 3
78537 Donna, 7,365....F 11
76446 Dublin, 2,810....F 5
79029 Dumas⊙, 9,771....C 2
75116 Duncanville, 14,105....G 2
77434 Eagle Lake, 3,587....H 8
78852 Eagle Pass⊙, 15,364....D 9
79031 Earth, 1,152....B 3
77435 East Bernard, 1,159....H 8
76448 Eastland⊙, 3,178....F 5
76837 Eden, 1,291....E 6
78539 Edinburg⊙, 17,163....F 11
77957 Edna⊙, 5,332....H 8
77437 El Campo, 8,563....H 8
76936 Eldorado⊙, 1,446....D 7
76360 Electra, 3,895....F 4
78621 Elgin, 3,832....G 7
* 79901 El Paso⊙, 322,261....A 10
    El Paso, ‡359,291....A 10
78543 Elsa, 4,400....G 11
75440 Emory⊙, 693....J 5
75119 Ennis, 11,046....H 5
76039 Euless, 19,316....F 2
76140 Everman, 4,570....F 2
79838 Fabens, 3,241....B 10
75840 Fairfield⊙, 2,074....H 6
78355 Falfurrias⊙, 6,355....F 10
75234 Farmers Branch, 27,492....G 1
75031 Farmersville, 2,311....H 4
79325 Farwell⊙, 1,185....A 3
75125 Ferris, 2,180....H 2
78941 Flatonia, 1,108....G 8
78114 Floresville⊙, 3,707....F 8
79235 Floydada⊙, 4,109....C 3
75701 Forest Hill, 8,236....F 2
75126 Forney, 1,745....H 2
79734 Fort Davis⊙, 900....D 11
79735 Fort Stockton⊙, 8,283....A 7
* 76101 Fort Worth⊙, 393,476....E 2
    Fort Worth, ‡762,086....E 2
77856 Franklin⊙, 1,063....H 7
75763 Frankston, 1,056....J 5
78624 Fredericksburg⊙, 5,326....E 7
76842 Fredonia, 50....E 7
77541 Freeport, 11,997....J 9
78357 Freer, 2,804....F 10
77546 Friendswood, 5,675....J 2
79035 Friona, 3,111....B 3
75034 Frisco, 1,845....H 2
79036 Fritch, 1,778....C 2
79738 Gail⊙, 150....C 5
76240 Gainesville⊙, 13,830....G 4
77547 Galena Park, 10,479....J 1
77550 Galveston⊙, 61,809....L 3
    Galveston-Texas City, ‡169,812....L 3
77962 Ganado, 1,640....H 8

79739 Garden City⊙, 300....C 6
75040 Garland, 81,437....H 1
75946 Garrison, 1,082....K 6
76528 Gatesville⊙, 4,683....G 6
78626 Georgetown⊙, 6,395....G 7
78022 George West⊙, 2,022....F 9
78942 Giddings⊙, 2,783....H 7
75644 Gilmer⊙, 4,196....J 5
75647 Gladewater, 5,574....K 5
76043 Glen Rose⊙, 1,554....G 5
76844 Goldthwaite⊙, 1,693....F 6
77963 Goliad⊙, 1,709....G 9
78629 Gonzales⊙, 5,854....G 8
76454 Gorman, 1,236....F 5
76046 Graham⊙, 7,477....F 4
76048 Granbury⊙, 2,473....G 5
75050 Grand Prairie, 50,904....G 2
75140 Grand Saline, 2,257....J 5
76530 Granger, 1,256....G 7
75844 Grapeland, 1,211....J 6
76051 Grapevine, 7,023....F 1
75401 Greenville⊙, 22,043....H 4
76642 Groesbeck⊙, 2,396....H 6
77619 Groves, 18,067....L 8
75845 Groveton⊙, 1,219....J 7
78548 Grulla, 1,194....F 11
79040 Gruver, 1,265....C 1
79236 Guthrie⊙, 150....D 4
79041 Hale Center, 1,964....C 3
77964 Hallettsville⊙, 2,712....G 8
75650 Hallsville, 1,038....K 5
76117 Haltom City, 28,127....F 2
76531 Hamilton⊙, 2,760....G 6
79520 Hamlin, 3,325....E 5
78550 Harlingen, 33,503....G11
79521 Haskell⊙, 3,655....E 4
77859 Hearne, 4,982....H 7
78361 Hebbronville⊙, 4,079....F 10
75948 Hemphill⊙, 1,005....L 6
77445 Hempstead⊙, 1,891....J 7
75652 Henderson⊙, 10,187....K 5
76365 Henrietta⊙, 2,897....F 4
79045 Hereford⊙, 13,414....B 3
78557 Hidalgo⊙, 1,289....F 11
† 75201 Highland Park, 10,133....G 2
77562 Highlands, 3,462....K 1
76645 Hillsboro⊙, 7,224....G 5
77563 Hitchcock, 5,565....K 3
76366 Holliday, 1,048....F 4
78861 Hondo⊙, 5,487....E 8
75446 Honey Grove, 1,853....J 4
75561 Hooks, 2,545....K 4
* 77001 Houston⊙, 1,232,802....J 2
    Houston, ‡1,985,031....J 2
76648 Hubbard, 1,572....H 6
75656 Hughes Springs, 1,701....K 5
78338 Humble, 3,278....J 7
† 77001 Hunters Creek Village, 3,959....J 1
75949 Huntington, 1,192....K 6
77340 Huntsville⊙, 17,610....J 7
76053 Hurst, 27,215....F 2
75141 Hutchins, 1,755....G 2
79329 Idalou, 1,729....C 4
76367 Iowa Park, 5,796....F 4
75060 Irving, 97,260....G 2
76651 Italy, 1,309....H 5
76055 Itasca, 1,483....G 5
77029 Jacinto City, 9,563....J 1
76056 Jacksboro⊙, 3,554....F 4
75766 Jacksonville, 9,734....J 5
75951 Jasper⊙, 6,251....L 7
79528 Jayton⊙, 703....D 4
75657 Jefferson⊙, 2,866....K 5
76836 Johnson City⊙, 767....F 7
† 77541 Jones Creek, 1,268....J 9
78026 Jourdanton⊙, 1,841....F 9
76849 Junction⊙, 2,654....E 7
78118 Karnes City⊙, 2,926....G 9
77450 Katy, 2,923....J 8
75142 Kaufman⊙, 4,012....H 5
76059 Keene, 2,440....G 5
76248 Keller, 1,474....F 1
77565 Kemah, 1,144....K 2
78119 Kenedy, 4,156....G 9
76060 Kennedale, 3,076....F 2
79745 Kermit⊙, 7,884....B 6
78028 Kerrville⊙, 12,672....E 7
75662 Kilgore, 9,495....K 5
76541 Killeen, 35,507....G 6
78363 Kingsville⊙, 28,711....G10
† 78109 Kirby, 2,558....F 8
75956 Kirbyville, 1,869....K 7
75145 Kleberg, 4,768....H 2
79529 Knox City, 1,536....E 4
77625 Kountze⊙, 1,703....K 7
78640 Kyle, 1,629....G 8
78559 La Feria, 2,642....G11
78945 La Grange⊙, 3,092....G 8
78560 La Joya, 1,217....F 11
77566 Lake Jackson, 13,376....J 8
76135 Lake Worth, 4,958....E 2
77568 La Marque, 16,131....K 3
79331 Lamesa⊙, 11,559....C 5
76550 Lampasas⊙, 5,922....F 6
75146 Lancaster, 10,522....G 2
77571 La Porte, 7,149....K 2
78040 Laredo⊙, 69,024....E 10
    Laredo, ‡72,859....E 10
77573 League City, 10,818....K 2
78873 Leakey⊙, 393....E 8
75452 Leonard, 1,423....H 4
79336 Levelland⊙, 11,445....B 4
75067 Lewisville, 9,264....G 1
77575 Liberty⊙, 5,591....K 7
75771 Lindale, 1,631....J 5
75563 Linden⊙, 2,264....K 4
79339 Littlefield⊙, 6,738....B 3
77351 Livingston⊙, 3,925....K 7
78643 Llano⊙, 2,608....F 7
78644 Lockhart⊙, 6,489....G 8
79351 Lockney, 1,965....C 3
75601 Longview⊙, 45,547....K 5
79343 Lorenzo, 1,206....C 4
78566 Los Fresnos, 1,297....G11
* 79401 Lubbock⊙, 149,101....C 4
    Lubbock, ‡179,295....C 4

75901 Lufkin⊙, 23,049....K 6
78648 Luling, 4,719....G 8
78569 Lyford, 1,425....G11
78052 Lytle, 1,271....F 8
75147 Mabank, 1,239....H 5
77864 Madisonville⊙, 2,881....J 7
75148 Malakoff, 2,045....H 5
76063 Mansfield, 3,658....F 2
78654 Marble Falls, 2,209....F 7
79843 Marfa⊙, 2,647....C 12
76661 Marlin⊙, 6,351....H 6
75670 Marshall⊙, 22,937....K 5
76664 Mart, 2,183....H 6
76856 Mason⊙, 1,806....E 7
79244 Matador⊙, 1,091....D 3
78368 Mathis, 5,351....G 9
75567 Maud, 1,107....K 4
78501 McAllen, 37,636....F 11
    McAllen-Pharr-Edinburg, ‡181,535....F 11
79752 McCamey, 2,647....B 6
76657 McGregor, 4,365....G 6
75069 McKinney⊙, 15,193....H 4
79057 McLean, 1,183....D 2
77520 McNair, 2,039....K 1
79245 Memphis⊙, 3,227....D 3
76859 Menard⊙, 1,740....E 7
79754 Mentone⊙, 50....B 6
78570 Mercedes, 9,355....F 12
76665 Meridian⊙, 1,162....G 6
79536 Merkel, 2,163....E 5
76941 Mertzon⊙, 513....D 6
75149 Mesquite, 55,131....H 2
76667 Mexia, 5,943....H 6
79059 Miami⊙, 611....D 2
79701 Midland⊙, 59,463....C 6
    Midland, ‡65,433....C 6
76065 Midlothian, 2,322....G 5
75773 Mineola, 3,926....J 5
76067 Mineral Wells, 18,411....F 5
78572 Mission, 13,043....F 11
77459 Missouri City, 4,136....J 2
77756 Monahans⊙, 8,333....B 6
76251 Montague⊙, 490....G 4
77580 Mont Belvieu, 1,144....L 1
76557 Moody, 1,286....G 6
79346 Morton⊙, 2,738....B 4
75455 Mount Pleasant⊙, 8,877....K 4
75457 Mount Vernon⊙, 1,806....J 4
76252 Muenster, 1,411....G 4
79347 Muleshoe⊙, 4,525....B 3
76371 Munday, 1,726....E 4
75961 Nacogdoches⊙, 22,544....J 6
75568 Naples, 1,726....K 4
75569 Nash, 1,961....K 4
78059 Natalia, 1,296....E 8
77868 Navasota, 5,111....J 7
77627 Nederland, 16,810....L 8
77461 Needville, 1,024....J 8
75570 New Boston, 3,699....K 4
78130 New Braunfels⊙, 17,859....F 8
75966 Newton⊙, 1,529....L 7
78140 Nixon, 1,925....G 8
76255 Nocona, 2,871....G 4
† 76118 North Richland Hills, 16,514....F 1
79760 Odessa⊙, 78,380....B 6
    Odessa, ‡91,805....B 6
79351 O'Donnell, 1,148....C 5
79831 Olney, 3,624....F 4
79104 Olton, 1,782....C 3
77630 Orange⊙, 24,457....L 7
78372 Orange Grove, 1,075....F10
75684 Overton, 2,084....K 5

76943 Ozona⊙, 2,864....C 7
79248 Paducah⊙, 2,052....D 4
76866 Paint Rock⊙, 193....E 6
77465 Palacios, 3,642....H 9
75801 Palestine⊙, 14,525....J 6
76072 Palo Pinto⊙, 250....F 5
79065 Pampa⊙, 21,726....D 2
79068 Panhandle⊙, 2,141....C 2
75460 Paris⊙, 23,441....J 4
* 77501 Pasadena, 89,277....J 2
77581 Pearland, 6,444....J 2
78061 Pearsall⊙, 5,545....E 9
79772 Pecos⊙, 12,682....D 10
79070 Perryton⊙, 7,810....D 1
79250 Petersburg, 1,300....C 4
78577 Pharr, 15,829....F 11
79071 Phillips, 2,515....C 2
76258 Pilot Point, 1,663....H 4
75968 Pineland, 1,127....L 6
† 77001 Piney Point Village, 2,548....J 1
75686 Pittsburg⊙, 3,844....J 4
79355 Plains⊙, 1,087....B 4
79072 Plainview⊙, 19,096....C 3
75074 Plano, 17,872....H 4
78064 Pleasanton, 5,407....F 9
77978 Point Comfort, 1,446....H 9
78373 Port Aransas, 1,218....H10
77640 Port Arthur⊙, 57,371....K 8
77365 Porter, 1,900....J 7
77578 Port Isabel, 3,067....G11
78374 Portland, 7,302....G10
77979 Port Lavaca⊙, 10,491....H 9
77651 Port Neches, 10,894....K 7
79356 Post⊙, 3,854....C 4
78065 Poteet, 3,013....F 8
78147 Poth, 1,296....F 8
77445 Prairie View, 3,589....J 7
78375 Premont, 3,282....F 10
79845 Presidio, 850....C 12
79252 Quanah⊙, 3,948....E 3
75572 Queen City, 1,227....L 4
75783 Quitman⊙, 1,494....J 5
79357 Ralls, 1,962....C 4
79778 Rankin⊙, 1,105....B 6
76470 Ranger, 3,094....F 5
78580 Raymondville⊙, 7,987....G11
78377 Refugio⊙, 2,941....G 9
75080 Richardson, 48,582....G 1
76118 Richland Hills, 8,865....F 2
77469 Richmond⊙, 5,777....J 2
78582 Rio Grande City⊙, 5,676....F 11
77583 Rio Hondo, 1,167....G11
77019 River Oaks, 8,193....E 2
76945 Robert Lee⊙, 1,119....D 6
78380 Robstown, 11,217....G10
79543 Roby⊙, 784....D 5
76567 Rockdale, 4,655....G 7
78382 Rockport⊙, 3,879....H 9
78880 Rocksprings⊙, 1,221....D 7
75087 Rockwall⊙, 3,121....H 4
76569 Rogers, 1,030....G 6
78584 Roma-Los Saenz, 2,154....E 11
79545 Roscoe, 1,580....D 5
76570 Rosebud, 1,597....G 7
77471 Rosenberg, 12,098....J 2
79546 Rotan, 2,404....D 5
78664 Round Rock, 2,811....G 6
75088 Rowlett, 1,696....H 1
75089 Royse City, 1,535....H 4
78151 Runge, 1,297....G 8
75785 Rusk⊙, 4,914....J 6
76574 Saginaw, 2,382....E 1

76265 Saint Jo, 1,054....G 4
76901 San Angelo⊙, 63,884....D 6
    San Angelo, ‡71,047....D 6
* 78201 San Antonio⊙, 654,153....F 8
    San Antonio, ‡864,014....F 8
75972 San Augustine⊙, 2,539....K 6
78586 San Benito, 15,176....G12
79848 Sanderson⊙, 1,229....B 7
78384 San Diego⊙, 4,490....F 10
78266 Sanger, 1,603....G 4
78289 San Juan, 5,070....F 11
77539 San Leon, 1,500....L 2
78666 San Marcos⊙, 18,860....F 8
76877 San Saba⊙, 2,555....F 6
† 76101 Sansom Park Village, 4,771....E 2
78389 Santa Anna, 1,310....E 6
78385 Sarita⊙, 250....G10
78154 Schertz, 4,061....F 8
78956 Schulenburg, 2,294....H 8
77586 Seabrook, 3,811....K 2
77983 Seadrift, 1,092....H 9
75159 Seagoville, 4,390....H 2
79359 Seagraves, 2,440....B 5
77474 Sealy, 2,685....H 8
78155 Seguin⊙, 15,934....G 8
79360 Seminole⊙, 5,007....B 5
76380 Seymour⊙, 3,469....E 4
79079 Shamrock, 2,644....D 2
79363 Shallowater, 1,339....B 4
† 77001 Sheldon, 1,665....K 1
75090 Sherman⊙, 29,061....H 4
    Sherman-Denison, ‡83,225....H 4
77984 Shiner, 2,102....G 8
† 77551 Shore Acres, 1,872....K 2
79851 Sierra Blanca⊙, 900....B 11
77656 Silsbee, 7,271....K 7
79257 Silverton⊙, 1,026....C 3
78387 Sinton⊙, 5,563....G 9
79364 Slaton, 6,583....C 4
78957 Smithville, 2,959....G 7
79549 Snyder⊙, 11,171....C 5
77879 Somerville, 1,250....H 7
76950 Sonora⊙, 2,149....D 7
77659 Sourlake, 1,694....K 7
77587 South Houston, 11,527....J 2
76051 Southlake, 2,031....F 1
† 77001 Southside Place, 1,466....J 2
79081 Spearman⊙, 3,435....C 1
77373 Spring, 1,900....J 1
76082 Springtown, 1,194....G 5
† 77001 Spring Valley, 3,170....J 1
79370 Spur, 1,747....D 4
77477 Stafford, 2,906....J 2
79553 Stamford, 4,558....E 5
79782 Stanton⊙, 2,117....C 5
76401 Stephenville⊙, 9,277....F 5
76951 Sterling City⊙, 780....D 6
79083 Stinnett⊙, 2,014....C 2
78160 Stockdale, 1,132....G 8
79084 Stratford⊙, 2,139....C 1
77478 Sugar Land, 3,318....J 2
75482 Sulphur Springs⊙, 10,642....J 4
79372 Sundown, 1,129....B 4
79086 Sunray, 1,947....C 2
77480 Sweeny, 3,191....J 2
79556 Sweetwater⊙, 12,020....D 5
78390 Taft, 3,274....G 9
79373 Tahoka⊙, 2,956....C 4
76574 Taylor, 9,616....G 7
75860 Teague, 2,867....H 6
76501 Temple, 33,431....G 6
75974 Tenaha, 1,094....K 6
79852 Terlingua, 100....D 12

75160 Terrell, 14,182....H 5
† 78201 Terrell Hills, 5,225....F 8
75501 Texarkana, 30,497....L 4
    Texarkana, ‡101,198....L 4
77590 Texas City, 38,908....K 3
73949 Texhoma, 356....C 1
76577 Thorndale, 1,031....G 7
78071 Three Rivers, 1,761....F 9
76083 Throckmorton⊙, 1,105....F 4
78072 Tilden⊙, 600....F 9
75975 Timpson, 1,256....K 6
77375 Tomball, 2,734....J 1
75163 Trinidad, 1,079....J 5
75862 Trinity, 2,512....J 7
75789 Troup, 1,668....J 5
79088 Tulia⊙, 5,294....C 3
75701 Tyler⊙, 57,770....J 5
    Tyler, ‡97,096....J 5
78228 University Park, 23,498....H 2
78801 Uvalde⊙, 10,764....E 8
75790 Van, 1,593....J 5
75095 Van Alstyne, 1,981....H 4
79855 Van Horn⊙, 2,240....C11
79092 Vega⊙, 839....B 2
76384 Vernon⊙, 11,454....E 3
77901 Victoria⊙, 41,349....H 9
77662 Vidor, 9,738....L 7
* 76701 Waco⊙, 95,326....G 6
    Waco, ‡147,553....G 6
78959 Waelder, 1,054....G 8
75501 Wake Village, 2,408....K 4
77485 Wallis, 1,028....H 8
75692 Waskom, 1,460....L 5
75165 Waxahachie⊙, 13,452....H 5
76086 Weatherford⊙, 11,750....F 5
77598 Webster, 2,231....K 2
78962 Weimar, 2,104....H 8
79095 Wellington⊙, 2,884....D 3
78596 Weslaco, 15,313....G11
76691 West, 2,406....G 6
77486 West Columbia, 3,335....J 8
77630 West Orange, 4,787....L 7
† 77001 West University Place, 13,317....J 2
† 76101 Westworth, 4,578....E 2
77488 Wharton⊙, 7,881....J 8
79096 Wheeler⊙, 1,116....D 2
79097 White Deer, 1,092....C 2
76273 Whitesboro, 2,927....H 4
76108 White Settlement, 13,449....E 2
75491 Whitewright, 1,742....H 4
76692 Whitney, 1,371....G 6
* 76301 Wichita Falls⊙, 97,564....F 4
    Wichita Falls, ‡127,621....F 4
75378 Willis, 1,727....J 7
75169 Wills Point, 2,636....H 5
75172 Wilmer, 1,922....H 2
77665 Winnie, 1,542....K 8
75494 Winnsboro, 3,064....J 5
79567 Winters, 2,904....E 6
75496 Wolfe City, 1,433....J 4
79382 Wolfforth, 1,090....C 4
78393 Woodsboro, 1,839....G 9
75979 Woodville⊙, 2,662....K 7
76693 Wortham, 1,036....H 6
75098 Wylie, 2,675....H 1
77995 Yoakum, 5,755....G 8
78164 Yorktown, 2,411....G 8
78076 Zapata⊙, 2,102....E 11

⊙ County seat.
‡ Population of metropolitan area.
† Zip of nearest p.o.
* Multiple zips

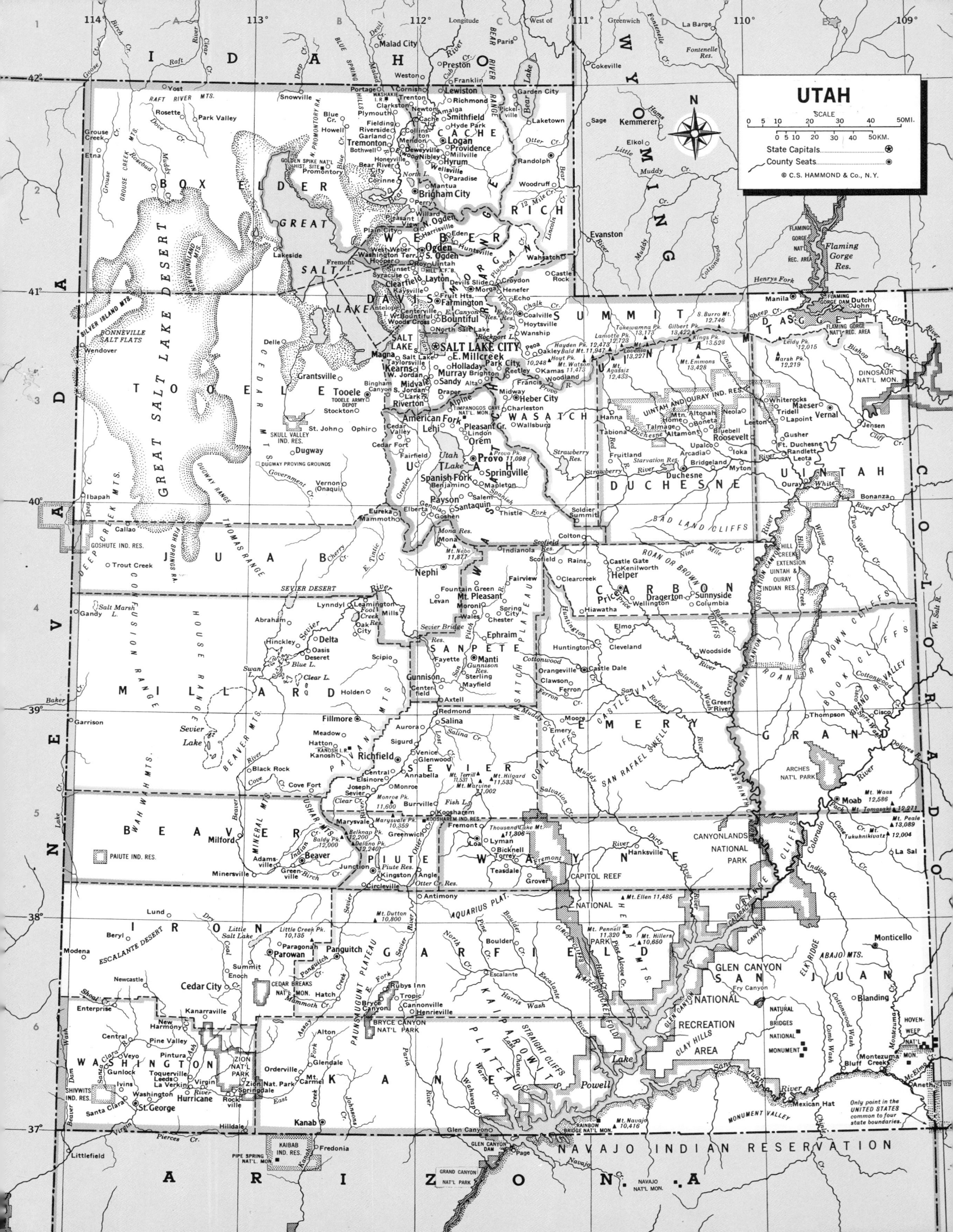

UTAH

SCALE

0 5 10   20   30   40   50 MI.

0 5 10   20   30   40   50 KM.

State Capitals.............⍟

County Seats.............◉

© C.S. HAMMOND & Co., N.Y.

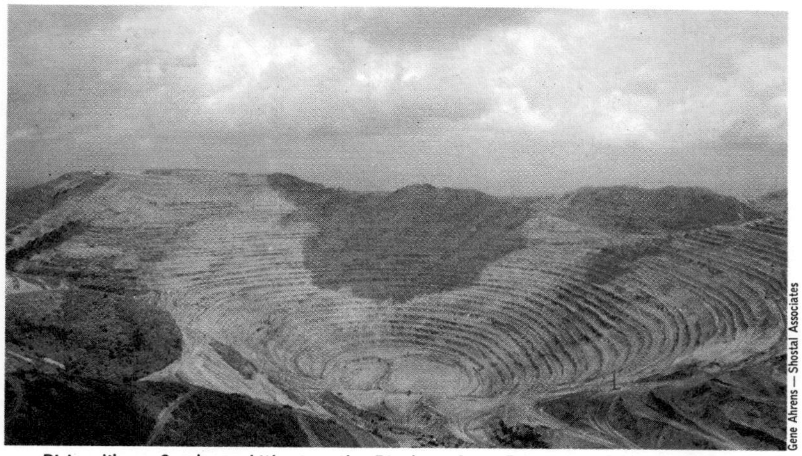

Gene Ahrens — Shostal Associates

Rising like a Greek amphitheater, the Bingham Open Pit Copper Mine in Utah is constantly changing as giant electric shovels remove seven tons of earth at a time.

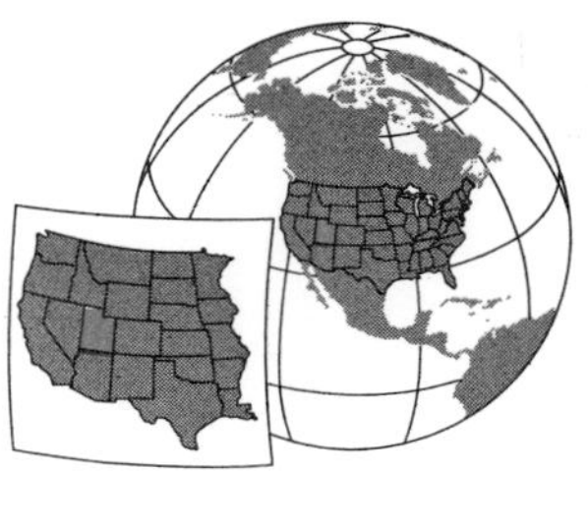

AREA 84,916 sq. mi.
POPULATION 1,059,273 ('70); 1,461,037 ('80)
CAPITAL Salt Lake City
LARGEST CITY Salt Lake City
HIGHEST POINT Kings Pk. 13,528 ft.
SETTLED IN 1847
ADMITTED TO UNION January 4, 1896
POPULAR NAME Beehive State
STATE FLOWER Sego Lily
STATE BIRD Sea Gull

COUNTIES

Name/Pop.	Key
Beaver, 3,800	A 5
Box Elder, 28,129	A 2
Cache, 42,331	C 2
Carbon, 15,647	D 4
Daggett, 666	E 3
Davis, 99,028	B 3
Duchesne, 7,299	D 3
Emery, 5,137	D 4
Garfield, 3,157	C 6
Grand, 6,688	E 5
Iron, 12,177	A 6
Juab, 4,574	A 4
Kane, 2,421	B 6
Millard, 6,988	A 4
Morgan, 3,983	C 2
Piute, 1,164	B 5
Rich, 1,615	C 2
Salt Lake, 458,607	B 3
San Juan, 9,606	E 6
Sanpete, 10,976	C 4
Sevier, 10,103	C 5
Summit, 5,879	D 3
Tooele, 21,545	A 3
Uintah, 12,684	E 3
Utah, 137,776	C 3
Wasatch, 5,863	C 3
Washington, 13,669	A 6
Wayne, 1,483	C 5
Weber, 126,278	B 2

CITIES and TOWNS

	Zip	*Name/Pop.*	*Key*
†	84003	Alpine, 1,047	C 3
	84001	Altamont, 129	D 3
	84002	Altonah, 225	D 3
†	84335	Amalga, 207	C 2
	84003	American Fork, 7,713	C 3
	84510	Aneth, 250	E 6
	84711	Annabella, 221	B 5
	84712	Antimony, 113	C 5
	84005	Arcadia, 150	D 3
	84620	Aurora, 493	B 5
	84621	Axtell, 150	C 4
	84301	Bear River City, 445	B 2
	84713	Beaver⊙, 1,453	B 5
†	84660	Benjamin, 503	C 3
	84715	Bicknell, 264	C 5
	84511	Blanding, 2,250	E 6
	84007	Bluebell, 210	D 3
	84512	Bluff, 300	E 6
	84008	Bonanza, 150	E 3
†	84337	Bothwell, 300	B 2
	84716	Boulder, 93	C 6
	84010	Bountiful, 27,853	C 3
	84012	Bridgeland, 150	D 3
	84302	Brigham City⊙, 14,007	C 2
	84117	Brighton, 150	C 3
	84717	Bryce Canyon, 229	B 6
	84718	Cannonville, 113	B 6
	84513	Castle Dale⊙, 541	D 4
	84514	Castle Gate, 205	D 4
	84720	Cedar City, 8,946	A 6
†	84013	Cedar Fort, 188	B 3
	84013	Cedar Valley, 290	B 3
	84622	Centerfield, 419	C 4
	84014	Centerville, 3,268	C 3
	84722	Central, 154	B 5
†	84032	Charleston, 196	C 3
	84623	Chester, 130	C 4
	84723	Circleville, 443	B 5
	84305	Clarkston, 420	B 2
	84516	Clawson, 95	C 4
	84015	Clearfield, 13,316	B 2
	84518	Cleveland, 244	D 4
	84017	Coalville⊙, 864	C 3
	84519	Columbia, 380	D 4
	84307	Corinne, 471	B 2
	84308	Cornish, 173	B 2
	84018	Croydon, 90	C 2
	84624	Delta, 1,610	B 4
	84625	Deseret, 215	B 4
	84309	Deweyville, 248	B 2
	84520	Dragerton, 1,614	D 4
	84020	Draper, 4,000	C 3
	84021	Duchesne⊙, 1,094	D 3
	84022	Dugway, 2,357	B 3
	84023	Dutch John, 263	E 3
†	84101	East Millcreek, 26,579	C 3
	84310	Eden, 421	C 2
	84626	Elberta, 325	B 4
	84521	Elmo, 141	D 4
	84724	Elsinore, 357	B 5
†	84337	Elwood, 294	B 2
	84522	Emery, 216	C 5
†	84720	Enoch, 120	A 6
	84725	Enterprise, 844	A 6
	84627	Ephraim, 2,127	C 4
	84726	Escalante, 638	C 6
	84628	Eureka, 753	B 4
	84629	Fairview, 696	C 4
	84025	Farmington⊙, 2,526	C 3
	84630	Fayette, 93	C 4
	84523	Ferron, 663	C 4
	84311	Fielding, 254	B 2
	84631	Fillmore⊙, 1,411	B 5
	84026	Fort Duchesne, 300	E 3
	84632	Fountain Green, 467	C 4
†	84036	Francis, 268	C 3
	84727	Fremont, 160	C 5
†	84037	Fruit Heights, 800	C 2
	84028	Garden City, 134	C 2
	84312	Garland, 1,187	B 2
†	84655	Genola, 424	C 4
	84729	Glendale, 200	B 6
	84730	Glenwood, 212	C 5
	84633	Goshen, 459	C 4
	84029	Grantsville, 2,931	B 3
	84525	Green River, 1,033	D 4
	84731	Greenville, 97	B 5
	84313	Grouse Creek, 100	A 2
	84733	Gunlock, 93	A 6
	84634	Gunnison, 1,073	C 4
	84030	Gusher, 125	E 3
	84734	Hanksville, 224	D 5
	84031	Hanna, 135	D 3
†	84401	Harrisville, 603	C 2
	84735	Hatch, 139	B 6
	84032	Heber City⊙, 3,245	C 3
	84526	Helper, 1,964	D 4
	84033	Henefer, 446	C 2
	84736	Henrieville, 145	C 6
	84527	Hiawatha, 166	D 4
†	84767	Hilldale, 480	B 6
	84635	Hinckley, 400	B 4
	84636	Holden, 351	B 4
	84117	Holladay, 23,014	C 3
	84314	Honeyville, 640	B 2
	84315	Hooper, 1,705	B 2
	84316	Howell, 146	B 2
†	84017	Hoytsville, 500	C 3
	84528	Huntington, 857	C 4
	84317	Huntsville, 553	C 2
	84737	Hurricane, 1,408	A 6
	84318	Hyde Park, 1,025	C 2
	84319	Hyrum, 2,340	C 2
	84034	Ibapah, 135	A 3
†	84052	Ioka, 115	D 3
	84738	Ivins, 137	A 6
	84035	Jensen, 360	E 3
	84739	Joseph, 125	B 5
	84740	Junction⊙, 135	B 5
	84036	Kamas, 806	C 3
	84741	Kanab⊙, 1,381	B 6
	84742	Kanarraville, 204	A 6
	84637	Kanosh, 319	B 5
	84037	Kaysville, 6,192	B 2
	84118	Kearns, 17,071	B 3
	84529	Kenilworth, 500	D 4
	84743	Kingston, 114	B 5
	84744	Koosharem, 141	C 5
	84038	Laketown, 208	C 2
	84039	Lapoint, 335	E 3
	84040	Lark, 728	B 3
	84530	La Sal, 200	E 5
	84745	La Verkin, 463	A 6
	84041	Layton, 13,603	C 2
	84638	Leamington, 112	B 4
	84746	Leeds, 151	A 6
	84043	Lehi, 4,659	C 3
	84639	Levan, 376	C 4
	84320	Lewiston, 1,244	C 2
†	84062	Lindon, 1,644	C 3
	84747	Loa⊙, 324	C 5
	84321	Logan⊙, 22,333	C 2
	84749	Lyman, 180	C 5
	84640	Lynndyl, 111	B 4
†	84078	Maeser, 1,248	E 3
	84044	Magna, 5,509	B 3
	84046	Manila⊙, 226	E 3
	84642	Manti⊙, 1,803	C 4
†	84302	Mantua, 413	C 2
†	84663	Mapleton, 1,980	C 3
	84750	Marysvale, 289	B 5
	84643	Mayfield, 267	C 4
	84644	Meadow, 238	B 5
	84325	Mendon, 345	B 2
	84531	Mexican Hat, 100	E 6
	84047	Midvale, 7,840	B 3
	84049	Midway, 804	C 3
	84751	Milford, 1,304	A 5
	84326	Millville, 441	C 2
	84752	Minersville, 448	A 5
	84532	Moab⊙, 4,793	E 5
	84645	Mona, 309	C 4
	84754	Monroe, 918	B 5
	84534	Montezuma Creek, 500	E 6
	84535	Monticello⊙, 1,431	E 6
	84050	Morgan⊙, 1,586	C 2
	84646	Moroni, 894	C 4
	84051	Mountain Home, 140	D 3
	84647	Mount Pleasant, 1,516	C 4
	84107	Murray, 21,206	C 3
	84052	Myton, 322	D 3
	84053	Neola, 600	D 3
	84648	Nephi⊙, 2,699	C 4
	84756	Newcastle, 150	A 6
	84327	Newton, 444	C 2
†	84321	Nibley, 367	C 2
†	84401	North Ogden, 5,257	C 2
	84054	North Salt Lake, 2,143	C 3
	84649	Oak City, 278	B 4
	84055	Oakley, 265	C 3
	84650	Oasis, 150	B 4
*	84401	Ogden⊙, 69,478	C 2
		Ogden, ‡126,278	C 4
†	84080	Onaqui (Vernon), 541	B 3
	84537	Orangeville, 511	C 4
	84758	Orderville, 399	B 6
	84057	Orem, 25,729	C 3
	84059	Ouray, 100	E 3
	84759	Panguitch⊙, 1,318	B 6
	84328	Paradise, 399	C 2
	84760	Paragonah, 275	B 6
	84060	Park City, 1,193	C 3
	84329	Park Valley, 100	A 2
	84761	Parowan⊙, 1,423	B 6
	84651	Payson, 4,501	C 3
	84061	Peoa, 230	C 3
†	84302	Perry, 909	C 2
†	84028	Pickleville, 106	C 2
†	84401	Plain City, 1,543	B 2
	84062	Pleasant Grove, 5,327	C 3
†	84401	Pleasant View, 2,028	B 2
	84330	Plymouth, 203	B 2
	84331	Portage, 144	B 2
	84501	Price⊙, 6,218	D 4
	84332	Providence, 1,608	C 2
	84601	Provo⊙, 53,131	C 3
		Provo-Orem, ‡137,776	C 3
	84063	Randlett, 350	E 3
	84064	Randolph⊙, 500	C 2
	84652	Redmond, 409	C 4
	84701	Richfield⊙, 4,471	B 5
	84333	Richmond, 1,000	C 2
	84334	Riverside, 290	B 2
	84065	Riverton, 2,820	B 3
	84763	Rockville, 110	A 6
	84066	Roosevelt, 2,005	D 3
	84067	Roy, 14,356	C 2
	84770	Saint George⊙, 7,097	A 6
	84069	Saint John, 200	B 3
	84653	Salem, 1,081	C 3
	84654	Salina, 1,494	C 5
*	84101	Salt Lake City (cap.)⊙, 175,885	B 3
		Salt Lake City, ‡557,635	B 3
	84070	Sandy, 6,438	C 3
	84765	Santa Clara, 271	A 6
	84655	Santaquin, 1,236	C 4
	84656	Scipio, 264	B 4
	84657	Sigurd, 291	B 5
	84335	Smithfield, 3,342	C 2
	84336	Snowville, 174	B 2
†	84065	South Jordan, 2,942	B 3
†	84401	South Ogden, 9,991	C 2
	84115	South Salt Lake, 7,810	C 3
	84660	Spanish Fork, 7,284	C 3
	84662	Spring City, 456	C 4
	84767	Springdale, 172	B 6
	84663	Springville, 8,790	C 3
	84665	Sterling, 144	C 4
	84071	Stockton, 469	B 3
	84772	Summit, 150	B 6
	84539	Sunnyside, 485	D 4
†	84015	Sunset, 6,268	B 2
†	84041	Syracuse, 1,843	B 2
	84072	Tabiona, 125	D 3
	84073	Talmage, 140	D 3
†	84101	Taylorsville, 12,522	B 3
	84773	Teasdale, 160	C 5
	84074	Tooele⊙, 12,539	B 3
	84774	Toquerville, 185	A 6
	84337	Tremonton, 2,794	B 2
	84338	Trenton, 390	B 2
	84076	Tridell, 212	E 3
	84776	Tropic, 329	B 6
†	84401	Uintah, 400	C 2
†	84007	Upalco, 150	D 3
	84777	Venice, 220	C 5
	84078	Vernal⊙, 3,908	E 3
	84080	Vernon, 541	B 3
†	84722	Veyo, 144	A 6
	84779	Virgin, 119	A 6
	84082	Wallsburg, 211	C 3
†	84017	Wanship, 175	C 3
	84780	Washington, 750	A 6
†	84401	Washington Terrace, 7,241	B 2
	84542	Wellington, 922	D 4
	84339	Wellsville, 1,267	C 2
	84083	Wendover, 781	A 3
†	84087	West Bountiful, 1,246	B 3
	84084	West Jordan, 4,221	B 3
†	84401	West Weber, 750	B 2
	84085	Whiterocks, 600	E 3
	84340	Willard, 1,045	C 2
†	84036	Woodland, 190	C 3
	84086	Woodruff, 173	C 2
	84087	Woods Cross, 3,124	B 3

⊙ County seat.
‡ Population of metropolitan area.
† Zip of nearest p.o.
* Multiple zips

Agriculture, Industry and Resources

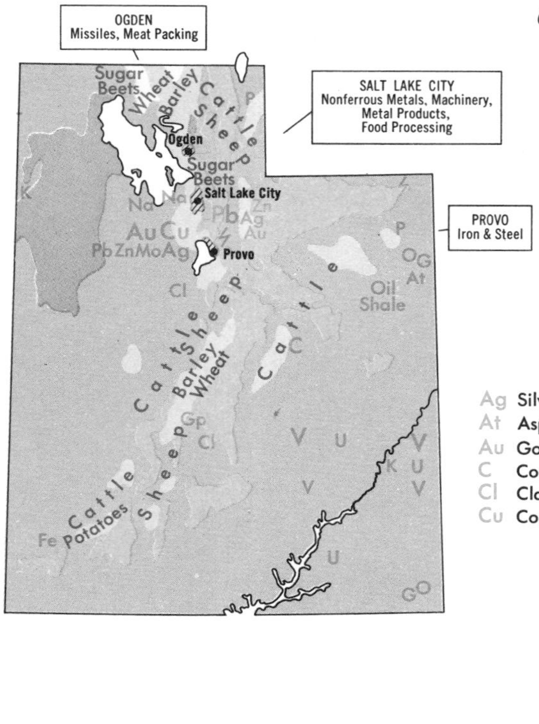
OGDEN
Missiles, Meat Packing
SALT LAKE CITY
Nonferrous Metals, Machinery, Metal Products, Food Processing
PROVO
Iron & Steel
Sugar Beets
Wheat
Barley
Cattle
Sheep
Ogden
Salt Lake City
Provo
Oil Shale

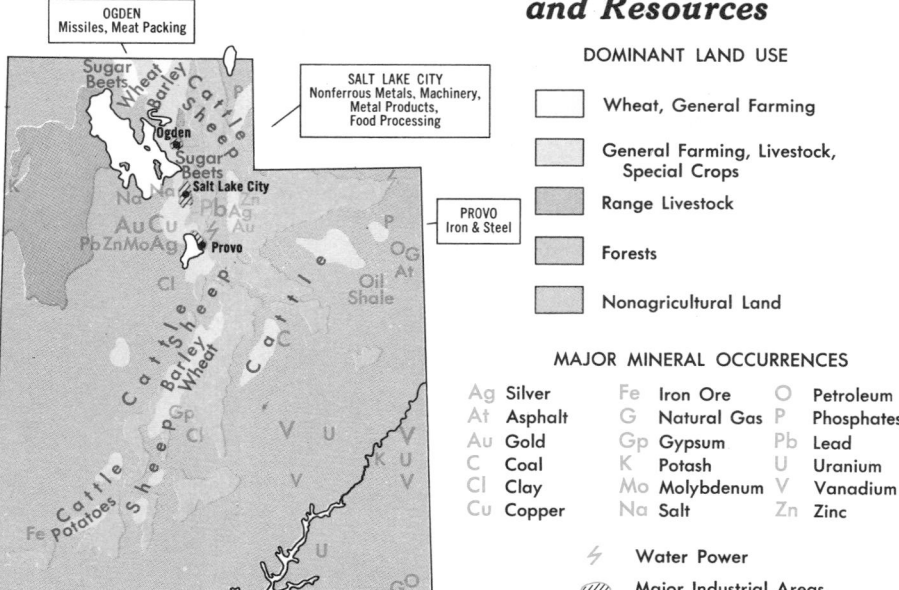

DOMINANT LAND USE

- Wheat, General Farming
- General Farming, Livestock, Special Crops
- Range Livestock
- Forests
- Nonagricultural Land

MAJOR MINERAL OCCURRENCES

Ag	Silver	Fe	Iron Ore	O	Petroleum
At	Asphalt	G	Natural Gas	P	Phosphates
Au	Gold	Gp	Gypsum	Pb	Lead
C	Coal	K	Potash	U	Uranium
Cl	Clay	Mo	Molybdenum	V	Vanadium
Cu	Copper	Na	Salt	Zn	Zinc

Water Power
Major Industrial Areas

Topography

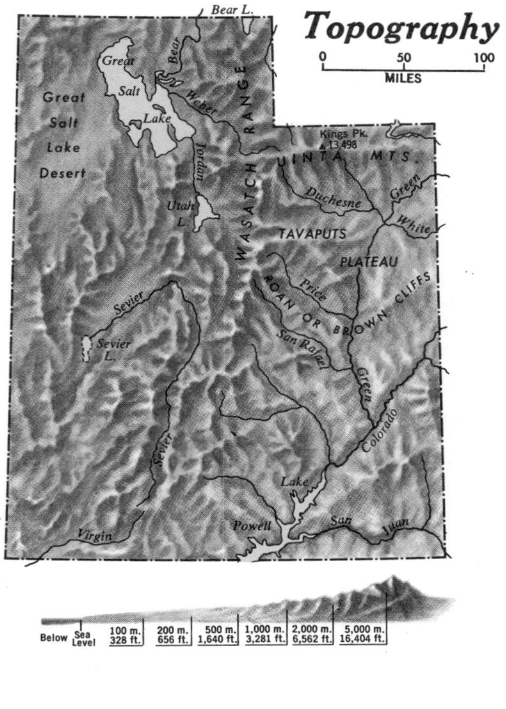
0 50 100
MILES
Bear L.
Great Salt Lake
Great Salt Lake Desert
Bear
Weber
WASATCH RANGE
Kings Pk. 13,498
UINTA MTS.
Jordan
Utah L.
Duchesne
Green
White
TAVAPUTS PLATEAU
Price
ROAN OR BROWN CLIFFS
San Rafael
Sevier
Sevier L.
Green
Colorado
Sevier
Lake Powell
San Juan
Virgin
Below Sea Level
100 m. 328 ft.
200 m. 656 ft.
500 m. 1,640 ft.
1,000 m. 3,281 ft.
2,000 m. 6,562 ft.
5,000 m. 16,404 ft.

Topography

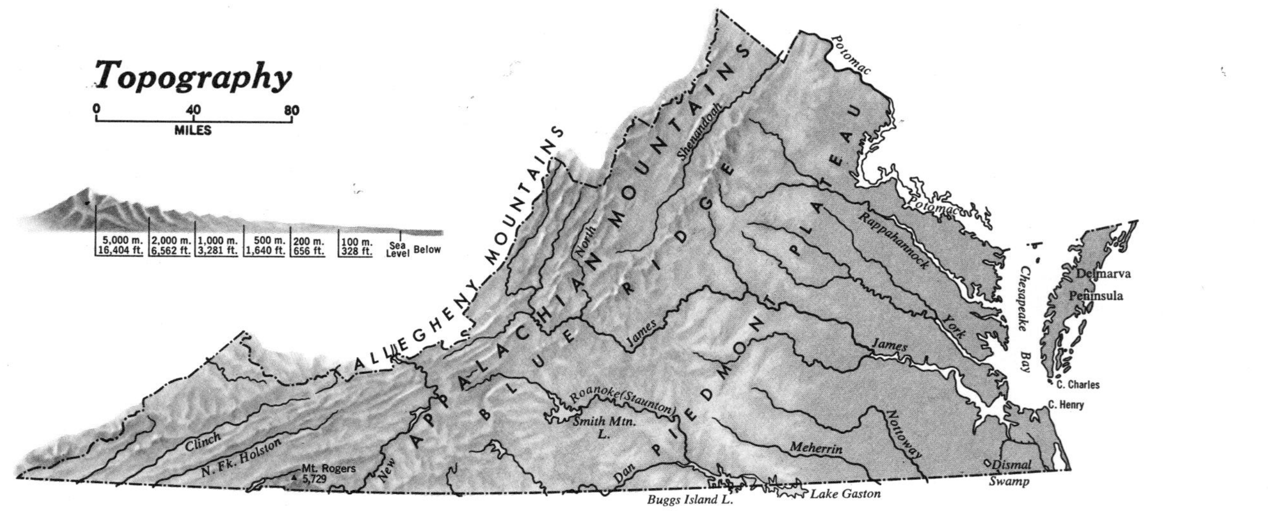

COUNTIES

Name/Pop.	Key
Accomack, 29,004	S 5
Albemarle, 37,780	L 5
Alleghany, 12,461	H 5
Amelia, 7,592	M 6
Amherst, 26,072	K 5
Appomattox, 9,784	L 6
Arlington, 174,284	O 3
Augusta, 44,220	K 4
Bath, 5,192	J 4
Bedford, 26,728	J 6
Bland, 5,423	F 6
Botetourt, 18,193	J 5
Brunswick, 16,172	N 7
Buchanan, 32,071	D 6
Buckingham, 10,597	L 5
Campbell, 43,319	K 6
Caroline, 13,925	O 4
Carroll, 23,092	G 7
Charles City, 6,158	O 6
Charlotte, 11,551	L 6
Chesterfield, 76,855	N 6
Clarke, 8,102	M 2
Craig, 3,524	H 6
Culpeper, 18,218	M 3
Cumberland, 6,179	M 6
Dickenson, 16,077	D 6
Dinwiddie, 25,046	N 6
Essex, 7,099	P 5
Fairfax, 455,021	O 3
Fauquier, 26,375	N 3
Floyd, 9,775	H 7
Fluvanna, 7,621	M 5
Franklin, 26,858	J 6
Frederick, 28,893	M 2
Giles, 16,741	G 6
Gloucester, 14,059	P 6
Goochland, 10,069	N 5
Grayson, 15,439	F 7
Greene, 5,248	M 4
Greensville, 9,604	N 7
Halifax, 30,076	L 7
Hanover, 37,479	N 5
Henrico, 154,364	O 6
Henry, 50,901	J 7
Highland, 2,529	J 4
Isle of Wight, 18,285	P 7
James City, 17,853	P 6
King and Queen, 5,491	P 5
King George, 8,039	O 4
King William, 7,497	O 5
Lancaster, 9,126	R 5
Lee, 20,321	B 7
Loudoun, 37,150	N 2
Louisa, 14,004	N 5
Lunenburg, 11,687	M 7
Madison, 8,638	M 4
Mathews, 7,168	R 6
Mecklenburg, 29,426	M 7
Middlesex, 6,295	R 5
Montgomery, 47,157	H 6
Nansemond, 35,166	P 7
Nelson, 11,702	L 5
New Kent, 5,300	P 5
Northampton, 14,442	S 6
Northumberland, 9,239	R 5
Nottoway, 14,260	M 6
Orange, 13,792	M 4
Page, 16,581	M 3
Patrick, 15,282	H 7
Pittsylvania, 58,789	K 7
Powhatan, 7,696	N 5
Prince Edward, 14,379	M 6
Prince George, 29,092	O 6
Prince William, 111,102	O 3
Pulaski, 29,564	G 6
Rappahannock, 5,199	M 3
Richmond, 5,841	P 5
Roanoke, 67,339	H 6
Rockbridge, 16,637	K 5
Rockingham, 47,890	L 4
Russell, 24,533	D 7
Scott, 24,376	C 7
Shenandoah, 22,852	L 3
Smyth, 31,349	E 7
Southampton, 18,582	O 7
Spotsylvania, 16,424	N 4
Stafford, 24,587	O 4
Surry, 5,882	P 6
Sussex, 11,464	O 7
Tazewell, 39,816	E 6
Warren, 15,301	M 3
Washington, 40,835	D 7
Westmoreland, 12,142	P 4
Wise, 35,947	C 6
Wythe, 22,139	F 7
York, 33,203	P 6

INDEPENDENT CITIES

	Zip	Name/Pop.	Key
*	22301	Alexandria, 110,938	P 3
	24523	Bedford⊙, 6,011	J 6
	24201	Bristol, 14,857	D 7
	24416	Buena Vista, 6,425	K 5
*	22901	Charlottesville⊙, 38,880	M 4
*	23320	Chesapeake, 89,580	R 7
	24422	Clifton Forge, 5,501	J 5
	23834	Colonial Heights, 15,097	O 6
	24426	Covington⊙, 10,060	H 5
	24541	Danville, 46,391	J 7
	23847	Emporia⊙, 5,300	N 7
	22030	Fairfax⊙, 21,970	O 3
*	22040	Falls Church, 10,772	O 3
	23851	Franklin, 6,880	P 7
	22401	Fredericksburg, 14,450	N 4
	24333	Galax, 6,278	G 7
*	23360	Hampton, 120,779	R 6
	22801	Harrisonburg⊙, 14,605	K 4
	23860	Hopewell, 23,471	O 6
	24450	Lexington⊙, 7,597	J 5
*	24501	Lynchburg, 54,083	K 6
	24112	Martinsville⊙, 19,653	J 7
*	23601	Newport News, 138,177	P 6
*	23501	Norfolk, 307,951	R 7
	24273	Norton, 4,001	C 7
	23803	Petersburg, 36,103	N 6
*	23701	Portsmouth⊙, 110,963	R 7
	24141	Radford, 11,596	G 6
*	23201	Richmond (cap.)⊙, 249,621	O 5
*	24001	Roanoke, 92,115	H 6
	24153	Salem⊙, 21,982	H 6
	24592	South Boston, 6,889	L 7
	24401	Staunton⊙, 24,504	K 4
	23434	Suffolk⊙, 9,858	P 7
*	23450	Virginia Beach, 172,106	S 7
	22980	Waynesboro, 16,707	K 4
	23185	Williamsburg⊙, 9,069	P 6
	22601	Winchester⊙, 14,643	M 2

CITIES and TOWNS

	Zip	Name/Pop.	Key
	24210	Abingdon⊙, 4,376	D 7
	23301	Accomac⊙, 373	S 5
	23001	Achilles, 525	R 6
	22920	Afton, 525	L 4
†	22959	Alberene, 200	L 5
	23821	Alberta, 466	N 7
	24310	Allisonia, 325	G 7
	24517	Altavista, 2,708	K 6
	24520	Alton, 250	K 7
	23002	Amelia Court House⊙, 537	N 6
	24521	Amherst⊙, 1,108	K 5
	22002	Amissville, 150	M 3
	24601	Amonate, 500	E 6
	24215	Andover, 300	C 7
	22003	Annandale, 27,428	O 3
	24216	Appalachia, 2,161	C 7
	24522	Appomattox⊙, 1,400	L 6
	24053	Ararat, 500	G 7
*	22201	Arlington⊙, 174,284	P 3
	22922	Arrington, 350	L 5
	23004	Arvonia, 300	M 5
	22011	Ashburn, 345	O 2
	23005	Ashland, 2,934	N 5
	24311	Atkins, 500	F 7
	24411	Augusta Springs, 400	K 4
	24312	Austinville, 750	F 7
	24054	Axton, 540	J 7
	23009	Aylett, 300	O 5
	24602	Bandy, 500	E 6
	24231	Banner, 350	D 7
	22923	Barboursville, 207	M 4
	24313	Barren Springs, 150	G 7
	24055	Bassett, 3,058	J 7
	24314	Bastian, 450	F 6
	22924	Batesville, 450	L 5
	23016	Beaverlett, 178	R 6
†	23201	Bellbluff, 3,900	N 6
	23306	Belle Haven, 504	S 5
	22307	Belleview, 8,299	O 3
	24218	Ben Hur, 300	B 7
	24059	Bent Mountain, 140	H 6
	22610	Bentonville, 700	M 3
	22811	Bergton, 150	L 3
	22611	Berryville⊙, 1,569	M 2
	24526	Big Island, 500	K 5
	24603	Big Rock, 350	D 6
	24219	Big Stone Gap, 4,153	C 7
	24220	Birchleaf, 650	D 6
	23307	Birdsnest, 250	S 6
	24604	Bishop, 400	E 6
	23916	Blackridge, 140	M 7
	24060	Blacksburg, 9,384	H 6
	23824	Blackstone, 3,412	N 6
	24221	Blackwater, 205	B 7
	24527	Blairs, 500	K 7
	24315	Bland⊙, 950	F 6
	23308	Bloxom, 391	S 5
	24605	Bluefield, 5,286	F 6
	22012	Bluemont, 310	N 2
	24064	Blue Ridge, 926	J 6
	24606	Boissevain, 975	F 6
	23235	Bon Air, 10,562	N 5
	24065	Boones Mill, 363	J 6
	22427	Bowling Green⊙, 528	O 4
	22620	Boyce, 378	M 2
	23917	Boydton⊙, 541	M 7
	23827	Boykins, 742	O 7
	23828	Branchville, 189	O 7
	22714	Brandy Station, 530	N 4
	24607	Breaks, 500	D 6
	23022	Bremo Bluff, 200	M 5
	22812	Bridgewater, 2,828	K 4
	22715	Brightwood, 250	M 4
	24316	Broadford, 850	E 7
	22815	Broadway, 887	L 3
	23920	Brodnax, 569	N 7
	22430	Brooke, 275	O 4
	24528	Brookneal, 1,037	L 6
	24415	Brownsburg, 200	K 5
	22610	Browntown, 175	M 3
	22622	Brucetown, 150	M 2
†	22810	Bryce Mountain, 205	L 3
	24066	Buchanan, 1,326	J 5
	23921	Buckingham⊙, 200	L 5
	22432	Burgess, 300	R 5
	24608	Burkes Garden, 275	F 6
	23922	Burkeville, 703	M 6
	24420	Burnsville, 138	J 4
	22435	Callao, 500	P 5
	24067	Callaway, 191	H 7
	22016	Calverton, 200	N 3
	24317	Cana, 168	G 7
	23310	Cape Charles, 1,689	R 6
	23313	Capeville, 300	R 6
	23829	Capron, 314	O 7
†	23039	Cardwell, 200	N 5
	23315	Carrsville, 375	P 7
	23830	Carson, 275	O 6
	22017	Casanova, 200	N 3
	24069	Cascade, 835	J 7
	24224	Castlewood, 799	D 7
	22019	Catlett, 500	N 3
	24609	Cedar Bluff, 1,050	E 6
†	24368	Cedar Springs, 200	F 7
†	22630	Cedarville, 150	M 3
	22437	Center Cross, 360	P 5
	22438	Champlain, 160	O 4
	22021	Chantilly, 620	O 3
	23030	Charles City⊙, 5	O 6
	23923	Charlotte Court House⊙, 539	L 6
	23924	Chase City, 2,909	M 7
	24531	Chatham⊙, 1,801	K 7
	23316	Cheriton, 655	R 6
	23831	Chester, 5,556	O 6
	23832	Chesterfield⊙, 950	N 6
	22623	Chester Gap, 450	M 3
	24319	Chilhowie, 1,317	E 7
	23336	Chincoteague, 1,867	T 5
	24073	Christiansburg⊙, 7,857	H 6
	23339	Chuckatuck, 500	P 7
	23032	Church View, 200	P 5
	24421	Churchville, 250	K 4
	22928	Cismont, 400	M 4
	23899	Claremont, 383	P 6
	23927	Clarksville, 1,641	M 7
	24076	Claudville, 180	H 7
†	23061	Clay Bank, 200	P 6
	24225	Cleveland, 357	D 7
	24533	Clifford, 160	K 5
	24321	Clinchburg, 250	E 7
	24226	Clinchco, 900	D 6
	24227	Clinchport, 286	C 7
	24228	Clintwood⊙, 1,320	D 6

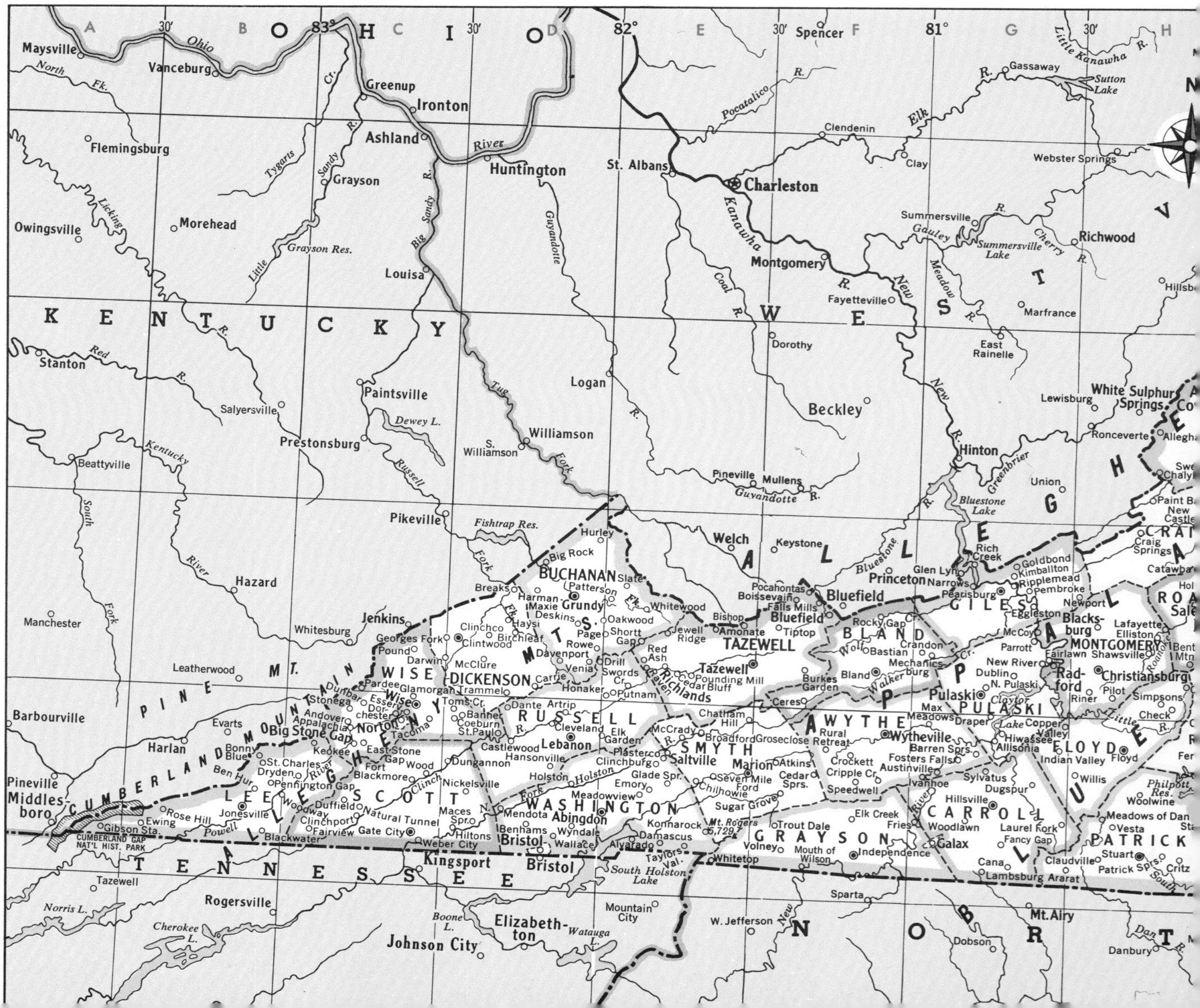

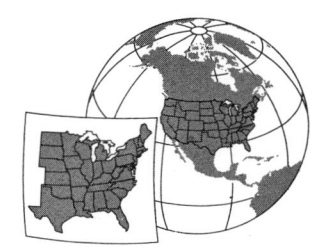

AREA 40,817 sq. mi.
POPULATION 4,648,494 ('70); 5,346,279 ('80)
CAPITAL Richmond
LARGEST CITY Norfolk
HIGHEST POINT Mt. Rogers 5,729 ft.
SETTLED IN 1607
ADMITTED TO UNION June 26, 1788
POPULAR NAME Old Dominion
STATE FLOWER Dogwood
STATE BIRD Cardinal

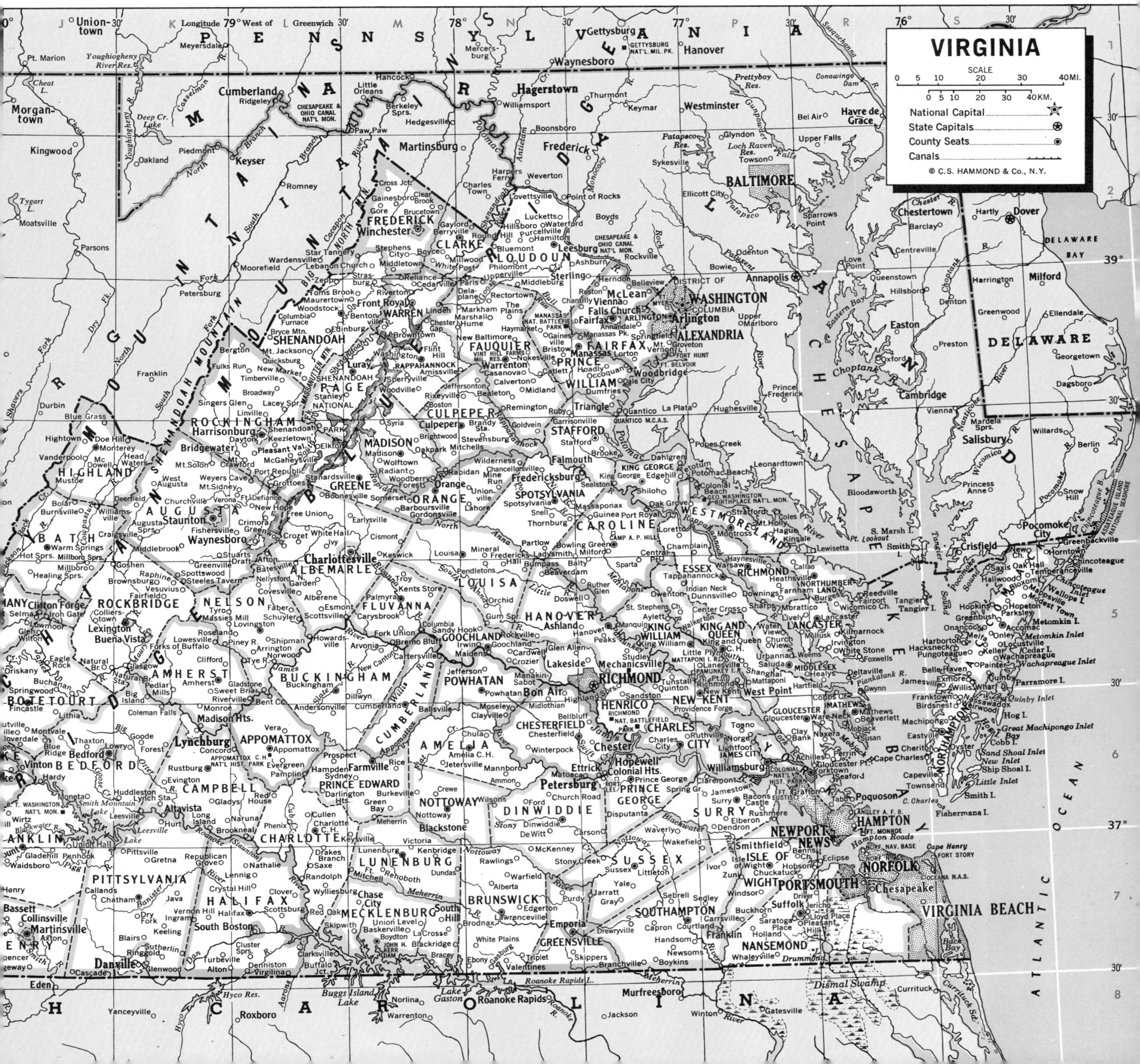

VIRGINIA

SCALE
0 5 10 20 30 40 MI.
0 5 10 20 30 40 KM.

National Capital ★
State Capitals ⊛
County Seats ⊙
Canals

© C.S. HAMMOND & Co., N.Y.

Agriculture, Industry and Resources

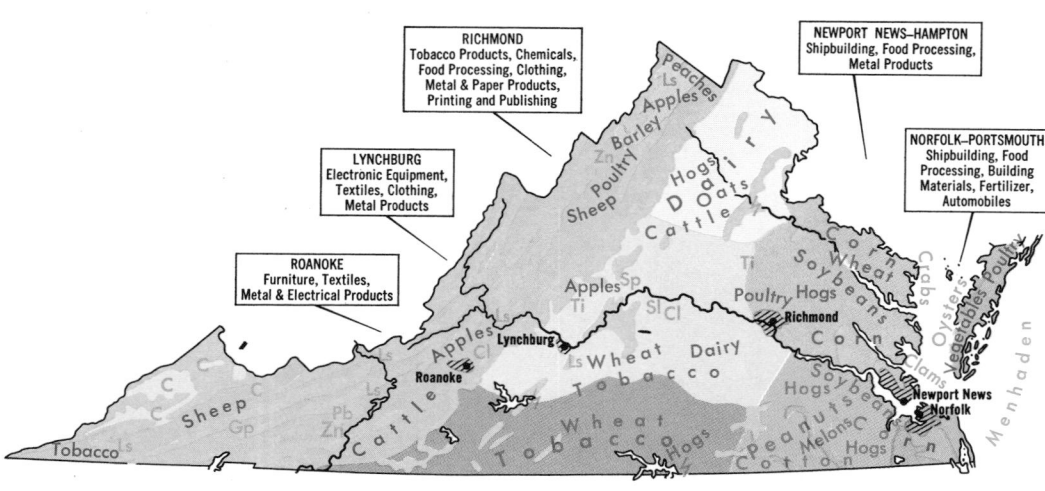

RICHMOND
Tobacco Products, Chemicals, Food Processing, Clothing, Metal & Paper Products, Printing and Publishing

LYNCHBURG
Electronic Equipment, Textiles, Clothing, Metal Products

ROANOKE
Furniture, Textiles, Metal & Electrical Products

NEWPORT NEWS–HAMPTON
Shipbuilding, Food Processing, Metal Products

NORFOLK–PORTSMOUTH
Shipbuilding, Food Processing, Building Materials, Fertilizer, Automobiles

MAJOR MINERAL OCCURRENCES

C	Coal	Sl	Slate
Cl	Clay	Sp	Soapstone
Gp	Gypsum	Ti	Titanium
Ls	Limestone	Zn	Zinc
Pb	Lead		

⚡ Water Power
▨ Major Industrial Areas

DOMINANT LAND USE

- Dairy, General Farming
- General Farming, Livestock, Dairy
- General Farming, Livestock, Tobacco
- General Farming, Livestock, Fruit, Tobacco
- General Farming, Truck Farming, Tobacco, Livestock
- Tobacco, General Farming
- Peanuts, General Farming
- Fruit and Mixed Farming
- Truck and Mixed Farming
- Forests
- Swampland, Limited Agriculture

Eric Carle — Shostal Associates

The Governor's Palace in Williamsburg, Virginia, typifies the splendor enjoyed by the royal governors in residence from 1720 to 1780.

⊙ County seat.
* Population of metropolitan area.
‡ Zip of nearest p.o.
† Multiple zips

Agriculture, Industry and Resources

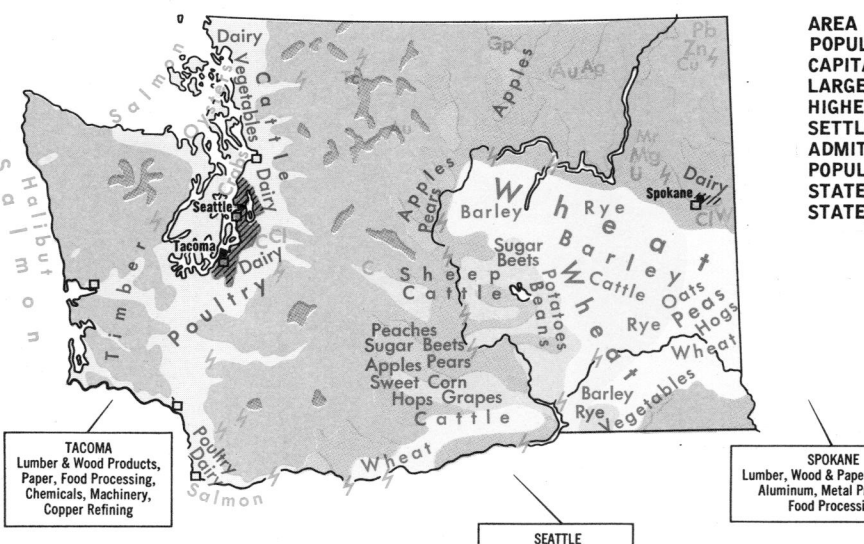

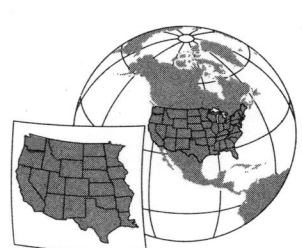

AREA 68,192 sq. mi.
POPULATION 3,409,169 ('70); 4,130,163 ('80)
CAPITAL Olympia
LARGEST CITY Seattle
HIGHEST POINT Mt. Rainier 14,410 ft.
SETTLED IN 1811
ADMITTED TO UNION November 11, 1889
POPULAR NAME Evergreen State
STATE FLOWER Coast Rhododendron
STATE BIRD Willow Goldfinch

TACOMA
Lumber & Wood Products, Paper, Food Processing, Chemicals, Machinery, Copper Refining

SEATTLE
Aircraft, Lumber, Wood & Paper Products, Food Processing, Metal Products

SPOKANE
Lumber, Wood & Paper Products, Aluminum, Metal Products, Food Processing

DOMINANT LAND USE

- Specialized Wheat
- Wheat, Peas
- Dairy, Poultry, Mixed Farming
- Fruit and Mixed Farming
- General Farming, Dairy, Range Livestock
- General Farming, Livestock, Special Crops
- Range Livestock
- Forests
- Urban Areas
- Nonagricultural Land

MAJOR MINERAL OCCURRENCES

Ag	Silver		Mr	Marble
Au	Gold		Pb	Lead
C	Coal		Tc	Talc
Cl	Clay		U	Uranium
Cu	Copper		W	Tungsten
Gp	Gypsum		Zn	Zinc
Mg	Magnesium			

⚡ Water Power
▨ Major Industrial Areas
□ Major Sawmilling Centers

Pulpwood being rafted to the mills is a familiar sight in the Northwest, the region which leads the country in lumber production.

Warren Dick — Shostal Associates

COUNTIES

Adams, 12,014 ....G 3
Asotin, 13,799 ....H 4
Benton, 67,540 ....F 4
Chelan, 41,355 ....E 3
Clallam, 34,770 ....B 2
Clark, 128,454 ....C 5
Columbia, 4,439 ....H 4
Cowlitz, 68,616 ....C 4
Douglas, 16,787 ....F 3
Ferry, 3,655 ....G 2
Franklin, 25,816 ....G 4
Garfield, 2,911 ....H 4
Grant, 41,881 ....F 3
Grays Harbor, 59,533 ....B 3
Island, 27,011 ....C 2
Jefferson, 10,661 ....B 3
King, 1,156,633 ....D 3
Kitsap, 101,732 ....C 3
Kittitas, 25,039 ....E 3
Klickitat, 12,138 ....E 5
Lewis, 45,467 ....C 4
Lincoln, 9,572 ....G 3
Mason, 20,918 ....B 3
Okanogan, 25,867 ....F 2
Pacific, 15,796 ....B 4
Pend Oreille, 6,025 ....H 2
Pierce, 411,027 ....C 3
San Juan, 3,856 ....C 2
Skagit, 52,381 ....D 2
Skamania, 5,845 ....D 5
Snohomish, 265,236 ....D 2
Spokane, 287,487 ....H 3
Stevens, 17,405 ....H 2
Thurston, 76,894 ....C 4
Wahkiakum, 3,592 ....B 4
Walla Walla, 42,176 ....G 4
Whatcom, 81,950 ....D 2
Whitman, 37,900 ....H 4
Yakima, 144,971 ....E 4

CITIES and TOWNS

Zip	Name/Pop.	Key
98520	Aberdeen, 18,489	B 3
98220	Acme, 170	C 2
99101	Addy, 141	H 2
98522	Adna, 150	B 4
98810	Aeneas, 85	F 2
99001	Airway Heights, 744	H 3
99102	Albion, 687	H 4
98301	Alder, 300	C 4
98002	Algona, 1,276	C 3
98524	Allyn, 850	C 3
99103	Almira, 376	G 3
98525	Aloha, 140	A 3
† 98643	Altoona, 66	B 4
98526	Amanda Park, 495	A 3
99002	Amber, 32	H 3
98601	Amboy, 480	C 5
98221	Anacortes, 7,701	C 2
99401	Anatone, 70	H 4
98602	Appleton, 40	D 5
† 99114	Arden, 30	H 2
98811	Ardenvoir, 350	E 3
98603	Ariel, 386	C 5
98223	Arlington, 2,261	C 2
98304	Ashford, 415	C 4
99402	Asotin⊙, 637	H 4
98002	Auburn, 21,817	C 3
† 98348	Ayer, 70	G 4
98816	Azwell, 152	F 3
98110	Bainbridge Island-Winslow, 1,461	A 2
98224	Baring, 75	D 3
98604	Battle Ground, 1,438	C 5
98527	Bay Center, 350	A 4
† 98520	Bay City, 58	B 4
† 98004	Beaux Arts, 475	B 2
98305	Beaver, 450	A 2
98528	Belfair, 500	C 3
* 98004	Bellevue, 61,102	B 2
98225	Bellingham⊙, 39,375	C 2
99104	Belmont, 59	H 3
99105	Benge, 45	G 4
99320	Benton City, 1,070	F 4
99321	Beverly, 86	F 4
99322	Bickleton, 200	E 5
† 98273	Biglake, 105	C 2
98605	Bingen, 671	D 5
98010	Black Diamond, 1,160	D 3
98230	Blaine, 1,955	C 2
98231	Blanchard, 200	C 2
99106	Bluecreek, 40	H 2
† 98382	Blyn, 350	B 3
† 98532	Boistfort, 55	B 4
† 98390	Bonney Lake, 2,313	C 3
† 99126	Bossburg, 66	H 2
98011	Bothell, 4,883	B 1
98232	Bow, 975	C 2
98107	Boyds, 68	G 2
98310	Bremerton, 35,307	A 2
98812	Brewster, 1,059	F 2
98813	Bridgeport, 952	F 3
98036	Brier, 3,093	C 3
98320	Brinnon, 500	B 3

Zip	Name/Pop.	Key
† 98537	Brooklyn, 50	B 4
98920	Brownstown, 80	E 4
98310	Brownsville, 50	A 2
98606	Brush Prairie, 200	C 5
† 98101	Bryn Mawr, 4,589	B 2
98321	Buckley, 3,446	C 3
98530	Bucoda, 421	C 4
98921	Buena, 590	E 4
99323	Burbank, 800	G 4
98166	Burien, 2,000	A 2
98322	Burley, 200	C 3
98233	Burlington, 3,138	C 2
98013	Burton, 650	C 3
98607	Camas, 5,790	C 5
98323	Carbonado, 394	D 3
98324	Carlsborg, 500	B 2
98814	Carlton, 120	F 2
98014	Carnation, 530	D 3
98609	Carrolls, 400	C 4
98610	Carson, 500	D 5
98815	Cashmere, 1,976	E 3
98611	Castle Rock, 1,647	B 4
98612	Cathlamet⊙, 647	B 4
† 98045	Cedar Falls, 200	D 3
98613	Centerville, 100	D 5
98531	Centralia, 10,054	C 4
98520	Central Park, 2,720	B 3
99003	Chattaroy, 250	H 3
98532	Chehalis⊙, 5,727	C 4
98816	Chelan, 2,430	E 3
98817	Chelan Falls, 200	E 3
99004	Cheney, 6,358	H 3
98818	Chesaw, 32	G 2
99109	Chewelah, 1,365	H 2
98325	Chimacum, 275	C 3
98614	Chinook, 445	B 4
98533	Cinebar, 35	C 4
98326	Clallam Bay, 750	A 2
99403	Clarkston, 6,312	H 4
99110	Clayton, 204	H 3
98235	Clearlake, 750	C 2
98399	Clearwater, 155	A 3
† 98922	Cle Elum, 1,725	E 3
† 98937	Cliffdell, 50	E 4
98236	Clinton, 500	C 3
98244	Clipper, 25	C 2
† 99402	Cloverland, 80	H 4
98004	Clyde Hill, 2,987	B 2
† 98055	Colfield, 500	B 2
99005	Colbert, 225	H 3
† 98366	Colby, 150	A 2
99111	Colfax⊙, 2,664	H 4
99324	College Place, 4,510	G 4
99113	Colton, 279	H 4
† 98632	Columbia Heights, 1,572	C 4
99114	Colville⊙, 3,742	H 2
98819	Conconully, 122	F 2
98237	Concrete, 573	D 2
99326	Connell, 1,161	G 4
98238	Conway, 120	C 2
98605	Cook, 240	D 5
98535	Copalis Beach, 481	A 3
98536	Copalis Crossing, 200	B 3
98537	Cosmopolis, 1,599	B 4
98616	Cougar, 76	C 4
99115	Coulee City, 558	F 3
99116	Coulee Dam, 1,425	G 3
98239	Coupeville⊙, 678	C 2
98923	Cowiche, 150	E 4
99117	Creston, 325	G 3
98015	Cumberland, 250	D 3
99118	Curlew, 200	G 2
98538	Curtis, 200	B 4
99119	Cusick, 257	H 2
98240	Custer, 315	C 2
98617	Dallesport, 400	D 5
99121	Danville, 108	G 2
98241	Darrington, 1,094	D 2
99122	Davenport⊙, 1,363	G 3
99328	Dayton⊙, 2,596	H 4
† 99010	Deepcreek, 73	H 3
98618	Deep River, 500	B 4
98243	Deer Harbor, 200	B 2
99006	Deer Park, 1,295	H 3
98244	Deming, 250	C 2
99006	Denison, 100	H 3
98188	Des Moines, 3,871	B 2
98283	Diablo, 200	D 2
99111	Diamond, 49	H 4
99213	Dishman, 9,079	H 3
99329	Dixie, 200	G 4
98279	Doebay, 100	C 2
98951	Donald, 100	E 4
98539	Doty, 210	B 4
† 98858	Douglas, 27	F 3
98821	Dryden, 550	E 3
† 98382	Dungeness, 675	B 2
98327	Du Pont, 384	C 3
98019	Duvall, 607	D 3
98540	East Olympia, 300	B 4
98925	Easton, 300	D 3
98245	Eastsound, 800	B 2
98801	East Wenatchee, 913	F 3
98328	Eatonville, 2,446	C 4
98246	Edison, 250	C 2
98020	Edmonds, 23,998	C 3

(continued on following page)

Topography

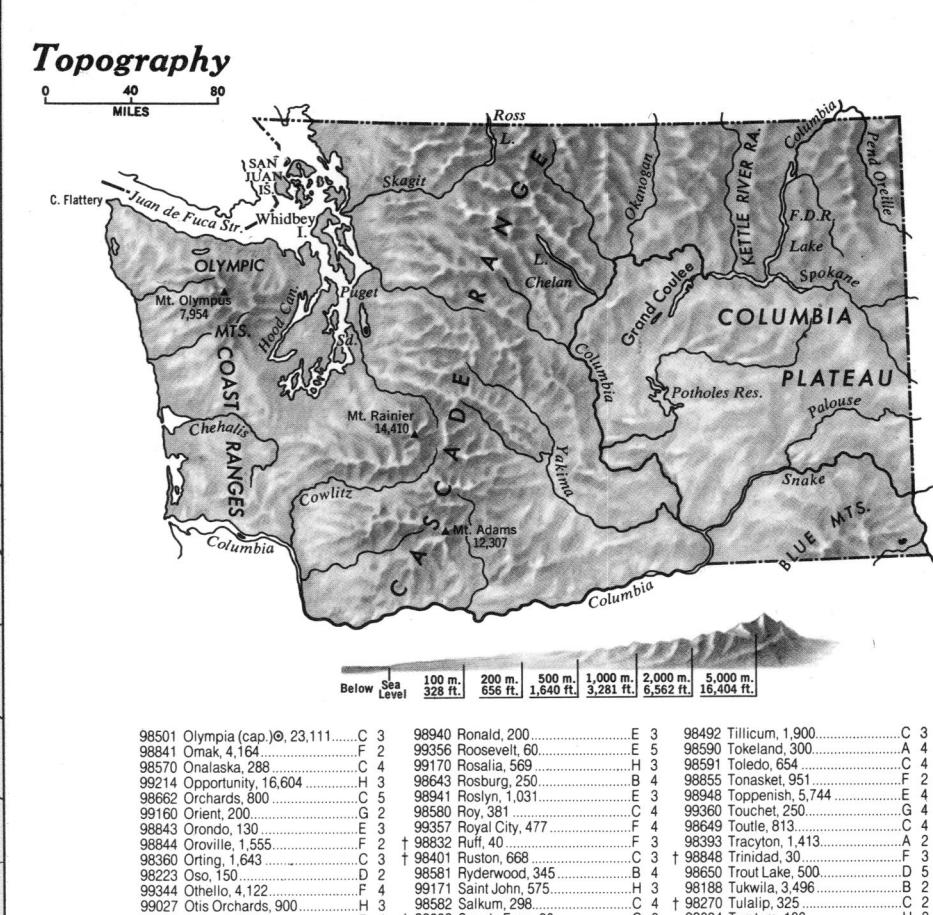

Below Sea Level	100 m. 328 ft.	200 m. 656 ft.	500 m. 1,640 ft.	1,000 m. 3,281 ft.	2,000 m. 6,562 ft.	5,000 m. 16,404 ft.

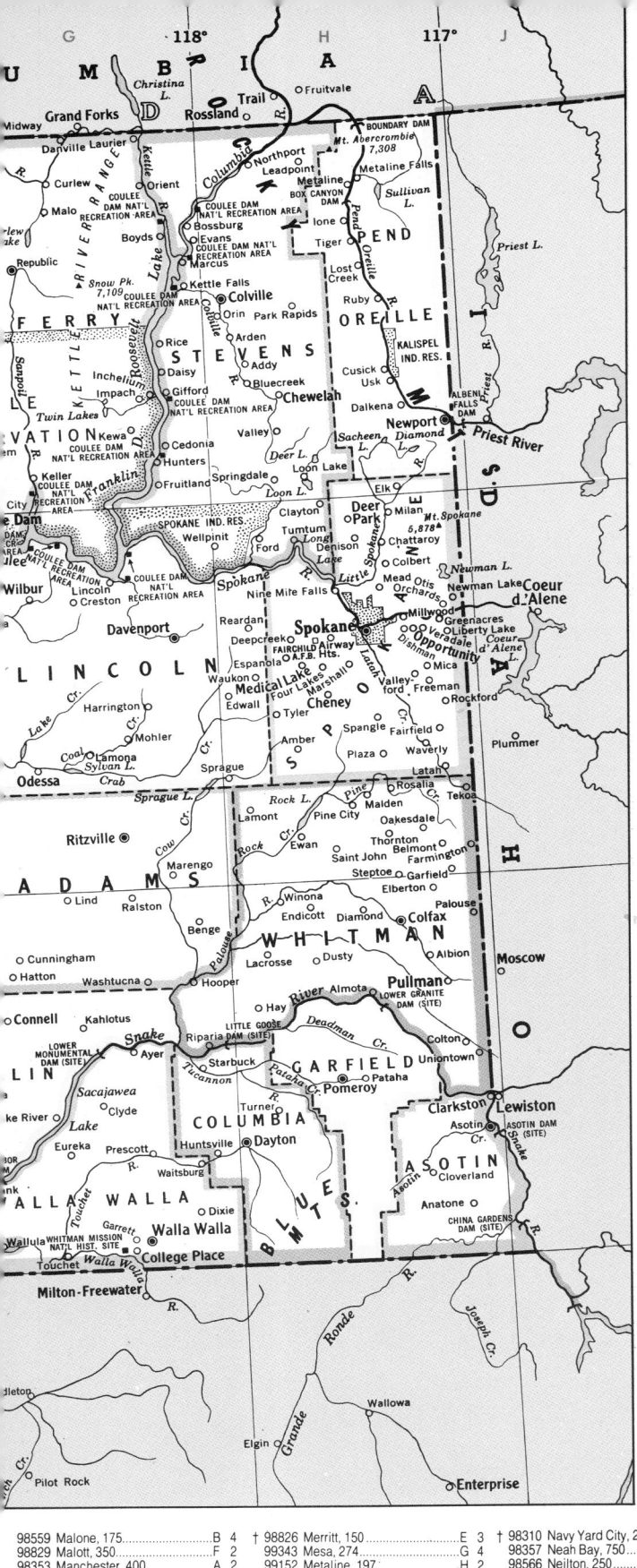

98501 Olympia (cap.)⊙, 23,111......C 3
98841 Omak, 4,164................F 2
98570 Onalaska, 288.............C 4
99214 Opportunity, 16,604.......H 3
98662 Orchards, 800.............C 5
99160 Orient, 200...............G 2
98843 Orondo, 130...............E 3
98844 Oroville, 1,555...........F 2
98360 Orting, 1,643 ....C 3
98223 Oso, 150..................D 2
99344 Othello, 4,122............F 4
99171 Otis Orchards, 900........H 3
98938 Outlook, 300..............E 4
98641 Oysterville, 86...........A 4
† 98326 Ozette, 50...............A 2
98047 Pacific, 1,831............C 3
98571 Pacific Beach, 975........A 3
98361 Packwood, 800.............D 4
98845 Palisades, 90.............E 3
98048 Palmer, 250...............D 3
99161 Palouse, 948..............H 4
98398 Paradise Inn, 200.........D 4
98939 Parker, 700...............E 4
98444 Parkland, 21,012..........C 3
99301 Pasco⊙, 13,920............F 4
98284 Pateros, 472..............E 2
99345 Paterson, 50..............F 5
98572 Pe Ell, 582...............B 4
98847 Peshastin, 90.............E 3
99162 Pine City, 48.............H 3
† 98826 Plain, 75................E 3
99346 Plymouth, 89..............F 5
98281 Point Roberts, 400........B 2
98347 Pomeroy⊙, 1,823...........H 4
98362 Port Angeles⊙, 16,367.....B 2
98110 Port Blakely, 600.........B 3
98573 Porter, 200...............B 4
98364 Port Gamble, 425..........C 2
98365 Port Ludlow, 200..........C 2
98366 Port Orchard⊙, 3,904......A 2
98368 Port Townsend⊙, 5,241.....C 2
98574 Potlatch, 350.............B 3
98370 Poulsbo, 1,856............A 2
99348 Prescott, 242.............G 4
98050 Preston, 500..............D 3
† 98250 Prevost, 25..............B 2
99350 Prosser⊙, 2,954...........F 4
99163 Pullman, 20,509...........H 4
98371 Puyallup, 14,742..........C 3
† 98399 Queets, 180..............A 3
98376 Quilcene, 800.............B 3
98575 Quinault, 340.............B 3
98848 Quincy, 3,237.............E 3
98576 Rainier, 382..............C 4
99165 Ralston, 35...............G 4
98377 Randle, 950...............D 4
98051 Ravensdale, 400...........D 3
98577 Raymond, 3,126............B 4
99029 Reardan, 389..............H 3
98052 Redmond, 11,031...........B 1
98054 Redondo, 950..............A 2
98055 Renton, 25,258............B 2
99166 Republic⊙, 862............G 2
98378 Retsil, 419...............A 2
99352 Richland, 26,290..........F 4
98160 Richmond Beach, 2,550.....A 1
98133 Richmond Highlands,
6,854.....................A 1
98642 Ridgefield, 1,004.........C 5
99169 Ritzville⊙, 1,876.........G 3
98849 Riverside, 228............F 2
† 98188 Riverton, 23,160.........B 2
98188 Riverton Heights, 34,800..B 2
† 98252 Robe, 175................D 2
98250 Roche Harbor, 175.........B 2
98579 Rochester, 325............C 4
99030 Rockford, 327.............H 3
† 98801 Rock Island, 191.........E 3
98283 Rockport, 350.............D 2
† 98626 Rocky Point, 1,733.......C 5
98061 Rollingbay, 950...........A 2

98940 Ronald, 200...............E 3
99356 Roosevelt, 60.............E 5
99170 Rosalia, 569..............H 3
98643 Rosburg, 250..............B 4
98941 Roslyn, 1,031.............E 3
98580 Roy, 381..................C 3
99357 Royal City, 477...........F 4
† 98832 Ruff, 40.................F 3
† 98401 Ruston, 668..............C 3
98581 Ryderwood, 345............B 4
98582 Salkum, 298...............C 4
98583 San de Fuca, 80..........B 2
98379 Sappho, 200...............A 2
98583 Satsop, 300...............B 3
98047 Sauk, 50..................D 2
† 98370 Scandia, 75..............A 2
† 99321 Schawana, 100............F 4
98380 Seabeck, 200..............C 3
98110 Seabold, 250..............A 1
98062 Seahurst, 3,000...........A 2
* 98101 Seattle⊙, 530,831........A 2
Seattle-Everett, ‡1,421,869..A 2
98644 Seaview, 950..............A 4
98284 Sedro-Woolley, 4,598......C 2
98381 Sekiu, 500................A 2
98942 Selah, 3,070..............E 4
98064 Selleck, 300..............D 3
98382 Sequim, 1,549.............B 2
98286 Shaw Island, 95...........B 2
98584 Shelton⊙, 6,515..........B 3
98585 Silver Creek, 382.........C 4
98383 Silverdale, 950...........A 2
98645 Silverlake, 42............C 4
98252 Silverton, 65.............D 2
98646 Skamania, 200.............C 5
98647 Skamokawa, 500............B 4
98288 Skykomish, 283............D 3
† 98357 Smyrna, 70...............F 4
98290 Snohomish, 5,174..........D 3
98065 Snoqualmie, 1,260.........D 3
98066 Snoqualmie Falls, 250.....D 3
98851 Soap Lake, 1,064..........F 3
98586 South Bend⊙, 1,795.......B 4
98901 South Broadway, 3,298.....E 4
98943 South Cle Elum, 374.......D 3
98384 South Colby, 450..........A 2
98385 South Prairie, 206........D 3
98386 South Worth, 425..........A 2
98387 Spanaway, 5,768...........C 3
99031 Spangle, 278..............H 3
* 99201 Spokane⊙, 170,516........H 3
Spokane, ‡287,487...........H 3
99032 Sprague, 550..............G 3
99173 Springdale, 215...........H 2
98292 Stanwood, 1,347...........C 2
99359 Starbuck, 216.............G 4
98293 Startup, 450..............D 3
98852 Stehekin, 40..............E 2
98388 Steilacoom, 2,850.........C 3
98648 Stevenson⊙, 916..........C 5
98853 Stratford, 160............F 3
98294 Sultan, 1,119.............D 3
98295 Sumas, 689................C 2
98390 Sumner, 4,325.............C 3
† 98101 Sunnydale, 1,850.........B 2
98944 Sunnyside, 6,751..........F 4
98392 Suquamish, 950............A 2
* 98401 Tacoma⊙, 154,581.........C 3
Tacoma, ‡411,027............C 3
98587 Taholah, 900..............A 3
98588 Tahuya, 260...............B 3
99033 Tekoa, 808................H 4
98826 Telma, 70.................E 3
98580 Tenino, 962...............C 4
98901 Terrace Heights, 1,033....E 4
99176 Thornton, 97..............H 3
98946 Thorp, 350................E 3
98947 Tieton, 415...............E 4
99177 Tiger, 69.................H 2

98492 Tillicum, 1,900...........C 3
98590 Tokeland, 300.............A 4
98591 Toledo, 654...............C 4
98855 Tonasket, 951.............F 2
98948 Toppenish, 5,744..........E 4
99360 Touchet, 250..............G 4
98649 Toutle, 813...............C 4
98393 Tracyton, 1,413...........A 2
† 98848 Trinidad, 30.............F 3
98650 Trout Lake, 500...........D 5
98188 Tukwila, 3,496............B 2
† 98270 Tulalip, 325.............C 2
99034 Tumtum, 100...............H 3
98501 Tumwater, 5,373...........B 3
† 99328 Turner, 25...............H 4
98856 Twisp, 756................E 2
99035 Tyler, 25.................H 3
98651 Underwood, 500............D 5
98592 Union, 380................B 3
98903 Union Gap, 2,040..........E 4
99179 Uniontown, 310............H 4
99180 Usk, 250..................H 2
98593 Valor, 387................B 4
99181 Valley, 156...............H 2
99183 Valleyford, 250...........H 3
* 98660 Vancouver⊙, 42,493.......C 5
98950 Vantage, 125..............E 4
99244 Van Zandt, 25.............C 2
98070 Vashon, 350...............A 2
98394 Vaughn, 600...............C 3
99037 Veradale, 5,320...........H 3
98670 Wahkiacus, 65.............D 5
99361 Waitsburg, 953............G 4
98297 Waldron, 75...............B 2
99362 Walla Walla⊙, 23,619.....G 4
99363 Wallula, 89...............G 4
98951 Wapato, 2,841.............E 4
99347 Warden, 1,254............F 4
† 98292 Warm Beach, 225..........C 2
98871 Washougal, 3,388..........C 5
99371 Washtucna, 316............G 4
98858 Waterville⊙, 919.........E 3
99038 Waukon, 41................H 3
98395 Wauna, 300................C 3
99039 Waverly, 48...............H 3
99040 Wellpinit, 125............H 2
98801 Wenatchee⊙, 16,912.......E 3
† 98837 Westlake, 258............F 3
98595 Westport, 1,364...........A 4
99352 West Richland, 1,107......F 4
98801 West Wenatchee, 2,134.....E 3
† 98837 Wheeler, 75..............F 3
98146 White Center, 17,300......B 2
98541 Whites, 70................B 3
98672 White Salmon, 1,585.......D 5
98952 White Swan, 270...........E 4
98285 Wickersham, 200...........C 2
99185 Wilbur, 1,074.............G 3
99906 Wiley City, 250...........E 4
98396 Wilkeson, 317.............D 3
† 98577 Willapa, 300.............B 4
98860 Wilson Creek, 184.........F 3
† 98848 Winchester, 70...........F 3
98596 Winlock, 990..............C 4
99186 Winona, 51................H 4
† 98110 Winslow (Bainbridge Island-
Winslow), 1,461...........A 2
98682 Winthrop, 371.............E 2
98673 Wishram, 575..............D 5
98863 Withrow, 200..............E 3
98072 Woodinville, 2,900........B 1
98674 Woodland, 1,622...........C 5
98020 Woodway, 879..............C 3
98587 Yacolt, 488...............C 5
* 98901 Yakima⊙, 45,588..........E 4
* 98604 Yarrow Point, 1,103......B 1
98597 Yelm, 628.................C 4
98188 Zenith, 1,900.............B 2
98953 Zillah, 1,138.............E 4

⊙ County seat.
‡ Population of metropolitan area.
* Zip of nearest p.o.
* Multiple zips

98559 Malone, 175..............B 4
98829 Malott, 350..............F 2
98353 Manchester, 400..........A 2
98830 Mansfield, 273...........F 3
98831 Manson, 220..............E 3
98266 Maple Falls, 90..........D 2
98038 Maple Valley, 2,900......D 3
98267 Marblemount, 387.........D 2
99151 Marcus, 142..............H 2
98268 Marietta, 300............C 2
* 98520 Markham, 180............B 4
98832 Marlin, 52...............F 3
99020 Marshall, 150............H 3
98620 Maryhill, 90.............E 5
98270 Marysville, 4,343........C 2
99344 Mattawa, 180.............F 4
98557 McCleary, 1,265..........B 4
98558 McKenna, 250.............C 3
† 98273 McMurray, 62............C 2
99021 Mead, 1,099..............H 3
99022 Medical Lake, 3,529......H 3
98039 Medina, 3,455............B 2
† 98563 Melbourne, 200..........B 4
98561 Menlo, 200...............B 4
98040 Mercer Island (city), 19,047..B 2

† 98826 Merritt, 150............E 3
99343 Mesa, 274................G 4
99152 Metaline, 197............H 2
99153 Metaline Falls, 307......H 2
98834 Methow, 84...............E 2
† 98283 Newhalem, 350...........D 2
99023 Mica, 130................H 3
99024 Milan, 84................H 3
99212 Millwood, 1,770..........H 3
98354 Milton, 2,607............C 3
98355 Mineral, 500.............D 4
98562 Moclips, 650.............A 3
98836 Monitor, 75..............E 3
98272 Monroe, 2,687............D 3
† 98812 Monse, 29...............F 2
98563 Montesano⊙, 2,847.......B 4
98356 Morton, 1,134............C 4
98564 Mossyrock, 409...........C 4
98043 Mountlake Terrace, 16,600..B 1
98273 Mount Vernon⊙, 8,804....C 2
98936 Moxee City, 600..........E 4
98275 Mukilteo, 1,369..........C 3
98937 Naches, 666..............E 4
98537 Nahcotta, 200............A 4
98565 Napavine, 377............C 4
98638 Naselle, 500.............B 4

† 98310 Navy Yard City, 2,827....A 2
98357 Neah Bay, 750............A 2
98566 Neilton, 250.............B 3
99155 Nespelem, 323............G 2
98283 Newhalem, 350............D 2
99025 Newman Lake, 102.........J 3
99156 Newport⊙, 1,418.........H 2
99026 Nine Mile Falls, 150.....H 3
† 98501 Nisqually, 500..........C 3
98276 Nooksack, 322............C 2
98562 Nordland, 500............C 2
† 98100 Normandy Park, 4,208....A 2
98045 North Bend, 1,625........D 3
98639 North Bonneville, 459....C 5
† 98590 North Cove, 50..........A 4
99157 Northport, 423...........H 2
99158 Oakesdale, 447...........H 3
98277 Oak Harbor, 9,167........C 2
98568 Oakville, 460............B 4
98569 Ocean City, 300..........A 3
98640 Ocean Park, 918..........A 4
† 98520 Ocosta, 300.............B 4
99159 Odessa, 1,074............G 3
98840 Okanogan⊙, 2,015........F 2
98359 Olalla, 800..............A 2
98279 Olga, 150................C 2

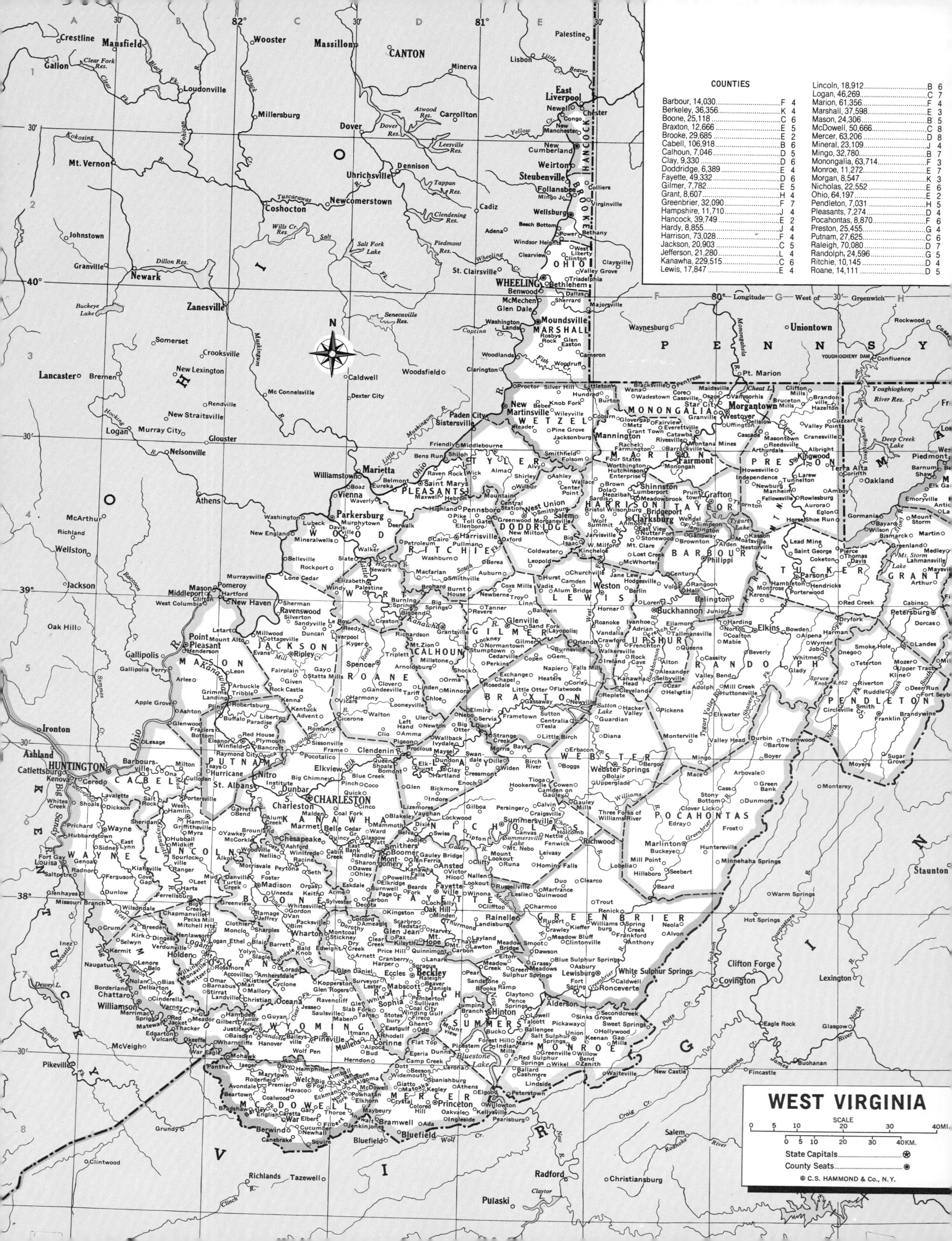

WEST VIRGINIA

COUNTIES

Barbour, 14,030	F 4	Lincoln, 18,912	B 6
Berkeley, 36,356	K 4	Logan, 46,269	C 7
Boone, 25,118	C 6	Marion, 61,356	F 4
Braxton, 12,666	E 5	Marshall, 37,598	E 3
Brooke, 29,685	E 2	Mason, 24,306	B 5
Cabell, 106,918	B 6	McDowell, 50,666	C 8
Calhoun, 7,046	D 5	Mercer, 63,206	D 8
Clay, 9,330	D 6	Mineral, 23,109	J 4
Doddridge, 6,389	E 4	Mingo, 32,780	B 7
Fayette, 49,332	D 6	Monongalia, 63,714	F 3
Gilmer, 7,782	E 5	Monroe, 11,272	E 7
Grant, 8,607	H 4	Morgan, 8,547	K 3
Greenbrier, 32,090	F 7	Nicholas, 22,552	E 6
Hampshire, 11,710	J 4	Ohio, 64,197	E 3
Hancock, 39,749	E 2	Pendleton, 7,031	H 5
Hardy, 8,855	J 4	Pleasants, 7,274	D 4
Harrison, 73,028	F 4	Pocahontas, 8,870	F 6
Jackson, 20,903	C 5	Preston, 25,455	G 4
Jefferson, 21,280	L 4	Putnam, 27,625	C 6
Kanawha, 229,515	C 6	Raleigh, 70,080	D 7
Lewis, 17,847	E 4	Randolph, 24,596	G 5
		Ritchie, 10,145	D 4
		Roane, 14,111	D 5

SCALE

0 5 10 20 30 40 MI.

0 5 10 20 30 40 KM.

State Capitals................⊛

County Seats.................◉

Summers, 13,213.......................E 7
Taylor, 13,878.........................F 4
Tucker, 7,447..........................G 4
Tyler, 9,929............................E 4
Upshur, 19,092........................F 5
Wayne, 37,581.........................B 6
Webster, 9,809.........................F 6
Wetzel, 20,314.........................E 3
Wirt, 4,154.............................D 4
Wood, 86,818..........................D 4
Wyoming, 30,095.....................C 7

CITIES and TOWNS

Zip	Name/Pop.	Key
25606	Accoville, 975	C 7
† 24701	Ada, 250	D 8
† 26288	Addison (Webster Springs)◉, 1,038	F 6
26210	Adrian, 500	E 5
26519	Albright, 319	G 3
24910	Alderson, 1,278	E 7
24807	Algoma, 400	D 8

25501 Alkol, 500.............................C 6
26320 Alma, 296.............................D 3
24710 Alpoca, 200...........................D 7
25003 Alum Creek, 900.....................C 6
25410 Bakerton, 250........................L 4
25004 Ameagle, 210.........................D 7
25607 Amherstdale, 1,602.................C 4
24808 Anawalt, 801..........................D 8
26323 Anmoore, 944........................F 4
25812 Ansted, 1,511.........................D 7
24915 Arbovale, 300.........................G 6
25006 Arbuckle, 300.........................C 6
26324 Arden, 200............................G 4
25007 Arnett, 300............................D 7
25234 Arnoldsburg, 175...................D 4
26816 Arthur, 200...........................H 4
26520 Arthurdale, 950......................G 3
24916 Asbury, 280...........................E 7
24809 Asco, 200..............................C 8
25009 Ashford, 400..........................C 6
24712 Athens, 967...........................E 8
26704 Augusta, 550.........................J 4
26705 Aurora, 275...........................G 3
24811 Avondale, 250........................C 8

24812 Baileysville, 800.....................C 7
25608 Baisden, 500.........................C 7
26801 Baker, 200............................J 4
25410 Bakerton, 250........................L 4
25010 Bald Knob, 356......................C 7
24918 Ballard, 220..........................E 8
25011 Bancroft, 446.........................C 6
25504 Barboursville, 2,279...............B 6
25609 Barnabus, 750........................C 7
26559 Barrackville, 1,596.................F 3
25013 Barrett, 950..........................C 7
24813 Bartley, 600..........................C 8
† 25411 Bath, 944.............................K 3
26707 Bayard, 475..........................H 3
† 26629 Bays, 186.............................E 5
25014 Beards Fork, 350....................D 6
24814 Beartown, 500........................C 8
25813 Beaver (Glen Hedrick), 1,711.....D 7
25801 Beckley◉, 19,884...................D 7
26030 Beech Bottom, 544.................E 2
24714 Beeson, 250..........................D 8
26250 Belington, 1,567.....................F 5

AREA, POPULATION, etc.

AREA 24,181 sq. mi.
POPULATION 1,744,237 ('70); 1,949,644 ('80)
CAPITAL Charleston
LARGEST CITY Huntington
HIGHEST POINT Spruce Knob 4,862 ft.
SETTLED IN 1774
ADMITTED TO UNION June 20, 1863
POPULAR NAME Mountain State
STATE FLOWER Rhododendron
STATE BIRD Cardinal

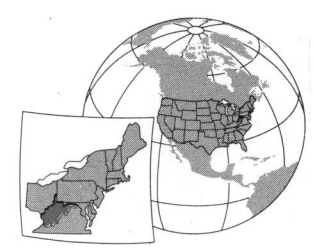

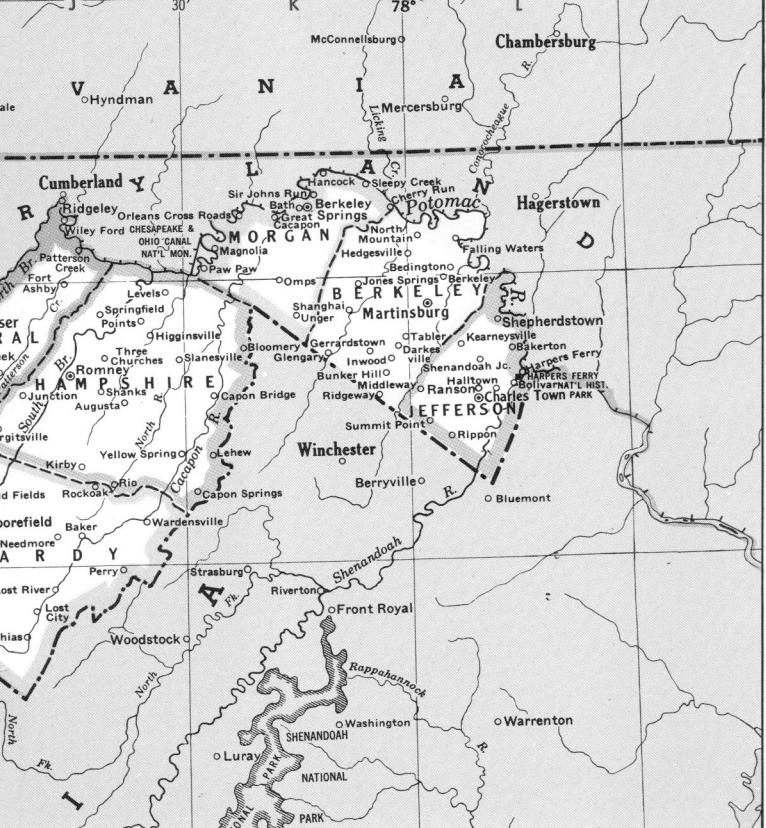

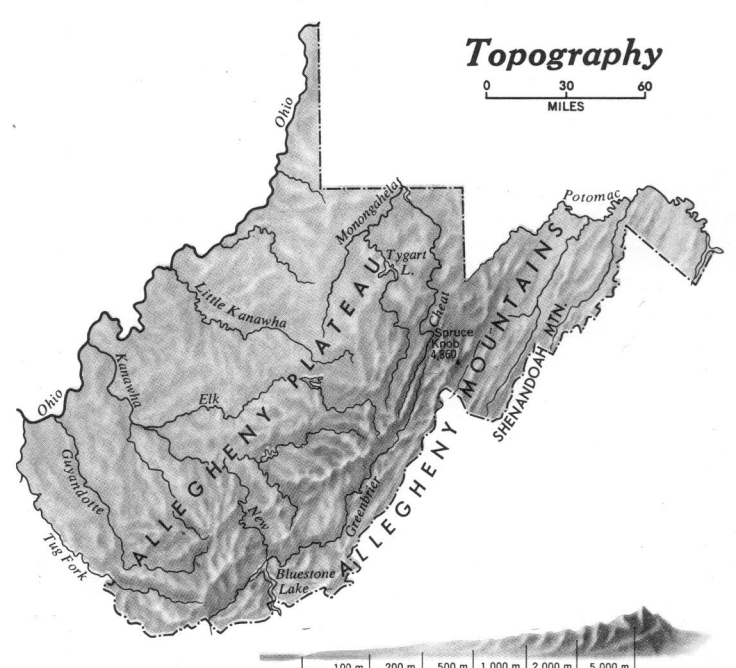

Topography

0   30   60
MILES

Below Sea Level | 100 m. 328 ft. | 200 m. 656 ft. | 500 m. 1,640 ft. | 1,000 m. 3,281 ft. | 2,000 m. 6,562 ft. | 5,000 m. 16,404 ft.

25015 Belle, 1,786..........................C 6
26134 Belmont, 802........................D 4
26656 Belva, 550............................D 6
26031 Benwood, 2,737....................E 2
26298 Bergoo, 260..........................F 6
† 25401 Berkeley, 600........................K 3
25411 Berkeley Springs◉, 2,200.......K 3
24815 Berwind, 675.........................C 8
26032 Bethany, 602........................E 2
† 26003 Bethlehem, 2,461..................E 2
26253 Beverly, 470.........................G 5
25019 Bickmore, 375......................D 6
25302 Big Chimney, 450..................C 6
25505 Big Creek, 500......................B 7
† 24853 Big Four, 200........................C 7
25021 Bim, 395..............................C 7
26610 Birch River, 650....................E 5
26521 Blacksville, 264....................F 3
25022 Blair, 700.............................C 7
25023 Blakeley, 260........................D 6
25026 Blue Creek, 300....................D 6
24701 Bluefield, 15,921...................D 8
26288 Bolair, 450...........................F 6
25426 Bolivar, 943..........................L 4
25030 Bomont, 412.........................D 6
25031 Boomer, 1,261......................D 6
25665 Borderland, 250....................B 7
24817 Bradshaw, 1,048...................C 8
24715 Bramwell, 1,125....................D 8
26802 Brandywine, 187...................H 5
25666 Breeden, 300........................B 7
26330 Bridgeport, 4,777..................F 4
† 25314 Brounland, 900.....................C 6
26334 Brownton, 700......................F 4
26525 Bruceton Mills, 209...............G 3
26201 Buckhannon◉, 7,261............F 5
24716 Bud, 400..............................D 7
25033 Buffalo, 831..........................C 5
25413 Bunker Hill, 500....................K 4
26710 Burlington, 338.....................J 4
26335 Burnsville, 591......................E 5
26562 Burton, 250...........................F 3
25035 Cabin Creek, 900...................C 6
26855 Cabins, 300..........................H 4
26337 Cairo, 412............................D 4
24925 Caldwell, 425........................F 7
26660 Calvin, 200...........................E 6
26208 Camden on Gauley, 243.........E 6
26033 Cameron, 1,537....................E 3
25820 Camp Creek, 200..................D 7
24819 Canebrake, 250....................C 8
26662 Canvas, 300..........................E 6
26711 Capon Bridge, 211................K 4
26823 Capon Springs, 250...............K 4
25037 Carbon, 200.........................D 6
24821 Caretta, 650.........................C 8
26527 Cassville, 800........................F 3
26564 Catawba, 186.......................F 3
25039 Cedar Grove, 1,275...............D 6
26340 Central Station, 275...............E 4
26214 Century, 239.........................F 4
25507 Ceredo, 1,583.......................B 6
25508 Chapmanville, 1,175..............B 7
* 25301 Charleston (cap.)◉, 71,505....C 6
    Charleston, ‡229,515............C 6
25414 Charles Town◉, 3,023...........L 4
25958 Charmco, 900.......................E 7
25667 Chattaroy, 1,145...................B 7
25315 Chesapeake, 2,428................C 6
26034 Chester, 3,614.......................E 1
25306 Cinco, 500............................D 6
26804 Circleville, 180......................H 5
26301 Clarksburg◉, 24,864.............F 4
25043 Clay◉, 479...........................D 6
25044 Clear Creek, 300...................D 7
† 26003 Clearview, 512......................E 2
25045 Clendenin, 1,438...................D 5
25237 Clifton, 358..........................B 5
† 25854 Clifty, 250............................E 6
† 26058 Clinton, 350..........................E 2
25046 Clio, 300..............................D 6
25047 Clothier, 950.........................C 7
25238 Clover, 350...........................C 5
24929 Clover Lick, 250....................F 6
25823 Coal City, 1,089....................D 7
25306 Coal Fork, 950......................C 6
26257 Coalton, 234.........................G 5
24824 Coalwood, 650......................C 8
26565 Coburn, 230..........................E 7
25048 Colcord, 600.........................D 7
26035 Colliers, 500..........................E 2
† 24740 Colored Hill, 1,031.................D 8
26615 Copen, 312...........................E 5
25826 Corinne, 1,090......................C 7
26713 Corinth, 195..........................H 4
25051 Costa, 500............................D 6
25239 Cottageville, 500...................C 5
25509 Cove Gap, 650......................E 6
26206 Cowen, 467...........................E 6
26205 Craigsville, 300......................E 6
25828 Cranberry, 297......................D 7
25669 Crum, 300............................B 7
24826 Cucumber, 275......................C 8
25510 Culloden, 1,033.....................B 6
24827 Cyclone, 500.........................C 7
25832 Daniels, 950..........................D 7
25053 Danville, 580.........................C 6
† 25428 Darkesville, 375....................L 4
26260 Davis, 868............................H 4
26142 Davisville, 200.......................C 4
24828 Davy, 993.............................C 8

25054 Dawes, 800...........................D 6
24932 Decota, 800..........................E 7
25055 Decota, 800..........................D 7
25670 Delbarton, 903......................B 7
26531 Dellslow, 500........................G 3
26217 Diana, 600............................F 5
25535 Dickson, 200........................B 6
24815 Dille, 300..............................E 6
25671 Dingess, 600.........................B 7
25059 Dixie, 800............................D 6
† 26386 Dola, 200.............................F 4
26835 Dorcas, 250...........................H 5
25060 Dorothy, 450.........................D 7
25062 Dry Creek, 290......................D 7
26263 Dryfork, 208..........................H 5
25063 Duck, 500.............................E 5
25064 Dunbar, 9,151.......................C 6
24934 Dunmore, 200.......................G 6
26264 Durbin, 347...........................G 5
25067 East Bank, 1,025...................D 6
25835 Eastgulf, 300.........................D 7
25512 East Lynn, 500......................B 6
† 26301 East View, 1,618...................F 4
25836 Eccles, 1,105........................D 7
24829 Eckman, 850.........................C 8
25672 Edgarton, 415........................B 7
† 24954 Edray, 175............................F 6
24830 Elbert, 400............................C 8
25070 Eleanor, 1,035......................C 5
26143 Elizabeth◉, 821....................D 4
26241 Elkins◉, 8,287......................G 5
24868 Elkridge, 500.........................D 8
25071 Elkview, 1,486.......................C 6
26267 Ellamore, 400........................F 5
26346 Ellenboro, 267.......................D 4
25965 Elton, 320.............................E 7
24832 English, 500..........................D 8
26568 Enterprise, 975......................F 4
26203 Erbacon, 350........................E 5
25075 Eskdale, 500.........................D 6
25076 Ethel, 450............................C 7
25241 Evans, 400............................C 5
26533 Everettville, 200.....................F 3
26554 Fairmont◉, 26,093...............F 4
† 25271 Fairplain, 200........................C 5
26570 Fairview, 640........................F 3
† 24966 Falling Springs (Renick), 255...F 6
26571 Farmington, 595....................F 3
25840 Fayetteville◉, 1,712..............D 6
26202 Fenwick, 500.........................E 6
25513 Ferrellsburg, 300....................B 6
25823 Fireco, 300............................D 7
26818 Fisher, 250............................H 4
25841 Flat Top, 550.........................D 7
26621 Flatwoods, 220......................E 5
26347 Flemington, 458....................F 4
26037 Follansbee, 3,883..................E 2
26348 Folsom, 325..........................F 4
24935 Forest Hill, 314......................E 7
26719 Fort Ashby, 1,225.................J 4
25514 Fort Gay, 792........................A 6
26806 Fort Seybert, 208..................H 5
24936 Fort Spring, 250.....................E 7
26572 Four States, 300.....................F 4
25071 Frame, 200...........................C 5
26623 Frametown, 600....................E 5
24938 Frankford, 200.......................F 7
26807 Franklin◉, 695......................H 5
26218 French Creek, 200..................F 5
26219 Frenchton, 212......................F 5
26146 Friendly, 190.........................D 3
25515 Gallipolis Ferry, 325...............B 5
26349 Galloway, 289.......................F 4
24836 Gary, 850.............................C 8
25243 Gandeeville, 271....................D 5
26624 Gassaway, 1,253...................E 5
25085 Gauley Bridge, 1,800.............D 6
25420 Gerrardstown, 258................K 4
25843 Ghent, 450...........................D 7
† 24736 Giatto, 400............................D 8
25621 Gilbert, 778...........................C 7
26671 Gilboa, 375...........................E 6
25086 Glasgow, 904........................D 6
26038 Glen Dale, 2,150...................E 3
25844 Glen Daniel, 300....................D 7
25090 Glen Ferris, 275.....................D 6
† 25813 Glen Hedrick (Beaver), 1,711...D 7
25846 Glen Jean, 1,510....................D 7
25848 Glen Rogers, 500...................D 7
26351 Glenville◉, 2,183..................E 5
25849 Glen White, 600.....................D 7
25520 Glenwood, 400......................B 5
25093 Gordon, 500.........................D 7
26720 Gormania, 250......................H 4
26354 Grafton◉, 6,433...................G 4
26147 Grantsville◉, 795..................D 5
26574 Grant Town, 946....................F 3
26534 Granville, 1,027.....................F 3
25422 Great Cacapon, 750..............K 3
25966 Green Sulphur Springs, 300....E 7
† 25166 Greenview, 250......................C 6
26360 Greenwood, 460....................F 4
25521 Griffithsville, 300....................B 6
25095 Grimms Landing, 350............B 5
26221 Guardian, 200.......................F 5
25423 Guyan, 800...........................C 5
25423 Halltown, 325........................L 4
26269 Hambleton, 328.....................G 4

25523 Hamlin◉, 1,024....................B 6
25623 Hampden, 251.......................C 7
25102 Handley, 500.........................C 6
24839 Hanover, 300.........................C 7
† 26250 Harding, 200..........................G 5
25851 Harper, 300...........................D 7
25425 Harpers Ferry, 423.................L 4
26362 Harrisville◉, 1,464................E 4
25247 Hartford, 527........................C 5
25852 Harvey, 500...........................D 7
24841 Havaco, 329..........................C 8
26627 Heaters, 343.........................E 5
25427 Hedgesville, 274....................K 3
26224 Helvetia, 269.........................F 5
24842 Hemphill, 785........................C 8
25106 Henderson, 496.....................B 5
26271 Hendricks, 317.......................G 4
25624 Henlawson, 900.....................B 7
26369 Hepzibah, 600.......................F 4
24726 Herndon, 200.........................D 7
25854 Hico, 750..............................D 6
24946 Hillsboro, 267........................F 6
25951 Hinton◉, 4,503.....................E 7
26262 Holcomb, 500........................E 6
25625 Holden, 2,325........................B 7
† 26651 Hookersville, 250...................E 6
26575 Hundred, 475........................E 3
* 25701 Huntington◉, 74,315...........A 6
    Huntington-Ashland, ‡253,743.....A 6
25526 Hurricane, 3,491...................C 6
24844 Iaeger, 822...........................C 8
25111 Indore, 200...........................D 6
25112 Institute, 3,100......................C 6
25428 Inwood, 600..........................K 4
24847 Itmann, 500..........................D 7
25113 Ivydale, 700...........................D 5
26377 Jacksonburg, 735...................E 3
26378 Jane Lew, 397.......................F 4
† 26462 Jarvisville, 250.......................F 4
25114 Jeffrey, 900...........................C 7
24848 Jenkinjones, 800....................C 8
26674 Jodie, 300.............................D 6
25969 Jumping Branch, 297.............E 7
26275 Junior, 513............................G 5
24851 Justice, 600...........................C 7
25430 Kearneysville, 250.................L 4
24731 Kegley, 450...........................D 8
24732 Kellysville, 200......................E 8
25248 Kenna, 380...........................C 5
25530 Kenova, 4,860.......................A 6
25674 Kermit, 716..........................B 7
26726 Keyser◉, 6,586....................J 4
24852 Keystone, 1,008....................D 8
25859 Kilsyth, 450...........................D 7
24853 Kimball, 962.........................C 8
26537 Kingwood◉, 2,550...............G 4
† 25671 Kirk, 400..............................B 7
25628 Kistler, 750...........................C 7
24854 Kopperston, 900....................C 7
25860 Lanark, 375...........................D 7
† 25831 Landisburg, 250.....................E 7
25629 Landville, 600........................D 8
25535 Lavalette, 600........................B 6
25864 Layland, 455..........................E 7
† 26430 Layopolis (Sand Fork), 252.....E 5
25251 Left Hand, 200......................D 5
26676 Leivasy, 450..........................E 6
25676 Lenore, 800...........................B 7
25123 Leon, 192.............................C 5
25971 Lerona, 350...........................E 8
25537 Lesage, 600...........................B 6
25972 Leslie, 500.............................E 6
25865 Lester, 507............................D 7
25253 Letart, 250............................C 5
24901 Lewisburg◉, 2,407...............E 7
24951 Lindside, 225.........................E 8
26384 Linn, 212..............................E 5
26629 Little Birch, 180.....................E 5
† 26624 Little Otter, 250......................E 5
26581 Littleton, 333.........................F 3
25125 Lizemores, 400......................D 6
26677 Lockwood, 300......................E 6
25601 Logan◉, 3,311......................B 7
25868 Lookout, 200.........................D 6
25630 Lorado, 400...........................C 7
26385 Lost Creek, 571.....................F 4
† 26101 Lubeck, 500..........................C 4
26386 Lumberport, 957....................F 4
25631 Lundale, 700.........................C 7
25870 Maben, 200...........................D 7
† 26278 Mabie, 366............................G 5
25871 Mabscott, 1,254....................D 7
25873 MacArthur, 1,614..................D 7
25130 Madison◉, 2,342..................C 6
26541 Maidsville, 485......................F 3
25306 Malden, 900..........................C 6
25634 Mallory, 1,240.......................C 7
25132 Mammoth, 576......................D 6
25635 Man, 1,201...........................C 7
26582 Mannington, 2,747................F 3
25975 Marfrance, 240......................E 7
24954 Marlinton◉, 1,286................F 6
25315 Marmet, 2,339......................C 6
25401 Martinsburg◉, 14,626..........K 4
25260 Mason, 1,319........................B 4
26542 Masontown, 868....................G 3
25678 Matewan, 651.......................B 7
24736 Matoaka, 608........................D 8
24861 Maybeury, 850.......................D 8

(continued on following page)

Agriculture, Industry and Resources

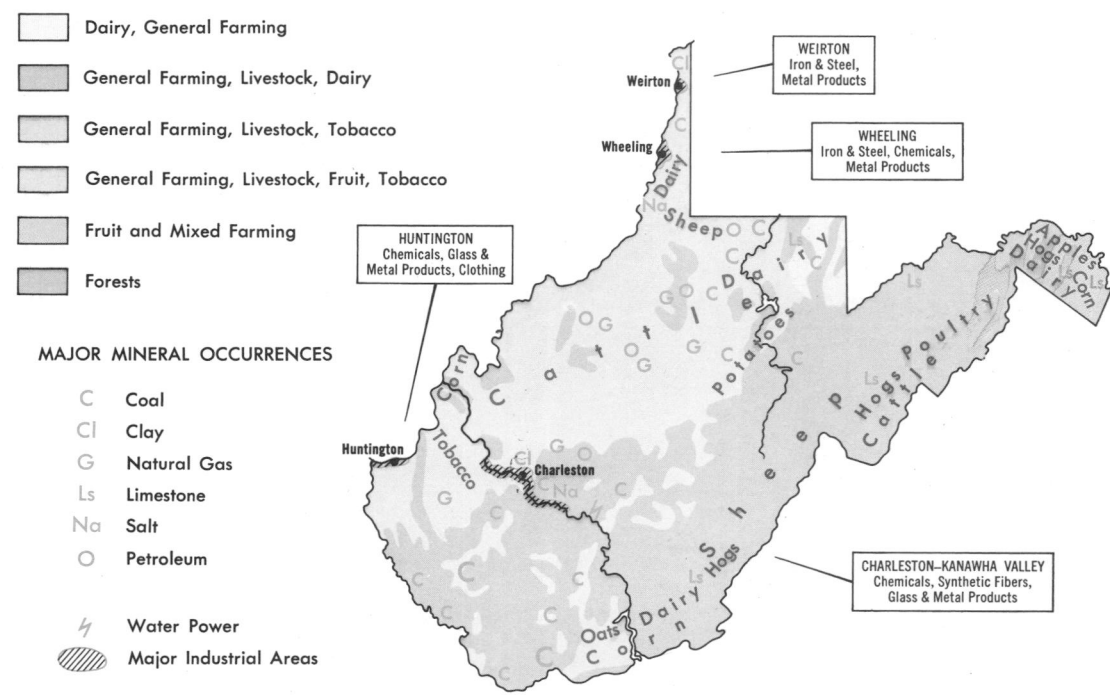

DOMINANT LAND USE

- Dairy, General Farming
- General Farming, Livestock, Dairy
- General Farming, Livestock, Tobacco
- General Farming, Livestock, Fruit, Tobacco
- Fruit and Mixed Farming
- Forests

WEIRTON
Iron & Steel,
Metal Products

WHEELING
Iron & Steel, Chemicals,
Metal Products

HUNTINGTON
Chemicals, Glass &
Metal Products, Clothing

CHARLESTON–KANAWHA VALLEY
Chemicals, Synthetic Fibers,
Glass & Metal Products

MAJOR MINERAL OCCURRENCES

- C   Coal
- Cl   Clay
- G   Natural Gas
- Ls   Limestone
- Na   Salt
- O   Petroleum

- ⚡   Water Power
- 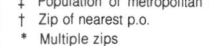   Major Industrial Areas

At one of Clarksburg, West Virginia's glass plants, liquid glass is poured into a machine and becomes beautifully textured stained-glass panels.

A. D'Arazien — Shostal Associates

AREA 56,154 sq. mi.
POPULATION 4,417,933 ('70); 4,705,335 ('80)
CAPITAL Madison
LARGEST CITY Milwaukee
HIGHEST POINT Timms Hill 1,952 ft.
SETTLED IN 1670
ADMITTED TO UNION May 29, 1848
POPULAR NAME Badger State
STATE FLOWER Wood Violet
STATE BIRD Robin

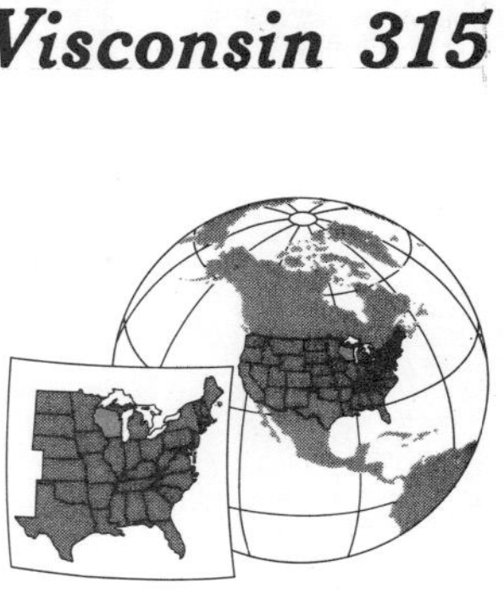

COUNTIES

Adams, 9,234 G 8
Ashland, 16,743 E 3
Barron, 33,955 C 5
Bayfield, 11,683 D 3
Brown, 158,244 L 7
Buffalo, 13,743 C 7
Burnett, 9,276 B 4
Calumet, 27,604 K 7
Chippewa, 47,717 D 5
Clark, 30,361 E 6
Columbia, 40,150 H 9
Crawford, 15,252 E 9
Dane, 290,272 H 9
Dodge, 69,004 J 9
Door, 20,106 M 6
Douglas, 44,657 C 3
Dunn, 29,154 C 6
Eau Claire, 67,219 D 6
Florence, 3,298 K 4
Fond du Lac, 84,567 K 8
Forest, 7,691 J 4
Grant, 48,398 E 10
Green, 26,714 G 10
Green Lake, 16,878 H 8
Iowa, 19,306 F 9
Iron, 6,533 F 3
Jackson, 15,325 E 7
Jefferson, 60,060 J 9
Juneau, 18,455 F 8
Kenosha, 117,917 K 10
Kewaunee, 18,961 L 6
La Crosse, 80,468 D 8
Lafayette, 17,456 F 10
Langlade, 19,220 H 5
Lincoln, 23,499 G 5
Manitowoc, 82,294 L 7
Marathon, 97,457 G 6
Marinette, 35,810 K 5
Marquette, 8,865 H 8
Menominee, 2,607 J 5
Milwaukee, 1,054,063 L 9
Monroe, 31,610 E 8
Oconto, 25,553 K 6
Oneida, 24,427 G 4
Outagamie, 119,356 K 7
Ozaukee, 54,421 L 9
Pepin, 7,319 C 6
Pierce, 26,652 B 6
Polk, 26,666 B 5
Portage, 47,541 G 6
Price, 14,520 F 4
Racine, 170,838 K 10
Richland, 17,079 F 9
Rock, 131,970 H 10
Rusk, 14,238 D 5
Saint Croix, 34,354 B 5
Sauk, 39,057 G 9
Sawyer, 9,670 D 4
Shawano, 32,650 J 6
Sheboygan, 96,660 L 8
Taylor, 16,958 E 5
Trempealeau, 23,344 D 7
Vernon, 24,557 E 8
Vilas, 10,958 G 3
Walworth, 63,444 J 10
Washburn, 10,601 C 4
Washington, 63,839 K 9
Waukesha, 231,365 K 9
Waupaca, 37,780 J 6
Waushara, 14,795 H 7
Winnebago, 129,931 J 7
Wood, 65,362 F 7

CITIES and TOWNS

Zip *Name/Pop.* *Key*
54405 Abbotsford, 1,375 F 6
54101 Abrams, 300 L 6
53910 Adams, 1,440 G 8
53001 Adell, 380 L 8
53501 Afton, 250 H 10
53502 Albany, 875 G 10
† 53534 Albion, 250 H 10
54201 Algoma, 4,023 M 6
53002 Allenton, 584 K 9
† 54301 Allouez, 13,753 L 7
54610 Alma⊙, 956 C 7
54611 Alma Center, 495 E 7
54805 Almena, 423 B 5
54909 Almond, 440 G 7
54720 Altoona, 2,842 C 6
49936 Alvin, 160 J 4
54102 Amberg, 711 K 5
54001 Amery, 2,126 B 5
54406 Amherst, 585 H 7
† 54162 Angelica, 200 K 6
54408 Aniwa, 233 H 6
54409 Antigo⊙, 9,005 H 5
54911 Appleton⊙, 57,143 J 7
Appleton-Oshkosh, ‡276,893 J 7
54510 Arbor Vitae, 950 G 4
54612 Arcadia, 2,159 D 7
53503 Arena, 377 G 9
54511 Argonne, 400 J 4
53504 Argyle, 673 G 10
54721 Arkansaw, 350 B 6
53911 Arlington, 379 H 9
54103 Armstrong Creek, 555 K 4
54410 Arpin, 355 G 6
53003 Ashippun, 400 H 1
54806 Ashland⊙, 9,615 E 2
54304 Ashwaubenon, 9,323 K 7
54411 Athens, 856 G 5
54412 Auburndale, 468 F 6
54722 Augusta, 1,242 D 6
54920 Auroraville, 250 H 7
53506 Avoca, 421 F 9
† 53520 Avon, 600 H 10
54413 Babcock, 260 F 7
53801 Bagley, 271 D 10
54202 Baileys Harbor, 900 M 5
54002 Baldwin, 1,399 B 6
54810 Balsam Lake⊙, 648 B 5
54921 Bancroft, 150 G 7
54614 Bangor, 974 E 8
53913 Baraboo⊙, 7,931 G 9
† 54873 Barnes, 450 D 3
53507 Barneveld, 528 F 10
54812 Barron⊙, 2,337 C 5
† 53001 Batavia, 160 K 8
54723 Bay City, 317 B 6
54814 Bayfield, 874 E 2
† 53201 Bayside, 4,461 M 1
54922 Bear Creek, 520 J 6
53916 Beaver Dam, 14,265 J 9
53802 Beetown, 170 E 10
53004 Belgium, 809 L 8
53508 Belleville, 1,063 G 10
53510 Belmont, 688 F 10
53511 Beloit, 35,729 H 10
54815 Bennett, 350 C 3
53803 Benton, 873 F 10
54923 Berlin, 5,338 H 8
† 53401 Berryville, 150 M 3
† 54410 Bethel, 210 F 6
† 54440 Bevent, 200 H 6
53103 Big Bend, 1,148 K 2
54817 Birchwood, 394 C 4
54414 Birnamwood, 632 H 6
† 54494 Biron, 771 G 7
54106 Black Creek, 921 K 7
53515 Black Earth, 1,114 G 9
54615 Black River Falls⊙, 3,273 E 7
† 54541 Blackwell, 350 J 4
54616 Blair, 1,036 D 7
53516 Blanchardville, 671 G 10
54724 Bloomer, 3,143 D 5
53804 Bloomington, 719 E 10
53517 Blue Mounds, 261 G 9
53518 Blue River, 369 E 9
54107 Bonduel, 995 K 6
53805 Boscobel, 2,510 E 9
54512 Boulder Junction, 500 G 3
54416 Bowler, 272 J 6
54725 Boyceville, 725 C 5
54726 Boyd, 574 E 6
54203 Branch, 225 L 7
53919 Brandon, 872 J 8
54513 Brantwood, 500 F 4
53920 Briggsville, 250 H 8
54110 Brillion, 2,588 L 7
53520 Brodhead, 2,515 G 10
54417 Brokaw, 312 G 5
53005 Brookfield, 32,140 K 1
53521 Brooklyn, 565 H 10
† 53201 Brown Deer, 12,622 L 1
† 53105 Browns Lake, 1,669 K 3
53006 Brownsville, 374 J 8
53522 Browntown, 253 G 10
54819 Bruce, 799 D 5
54820 Brule, 675 C 2
54204 Brussels, 306 L 6
† 54622 Buffalo, 671 C 7
53105 Burlington, 7,479 K 10
53922 Burnett, 241 J 9
53007 Butler, 2,261 K 1
54514 Butternut, 453 E 3
54821 Cable, 281 D 3
54727 Cadott, 977 D 6
53923 Cambria, 631 H 8
53523 Cambridge, 689 H 9
54822 Cameron, 893 C 5
† 53019 Campbellsport, 1,681 K 8
54618 Camp Douglas, 547 F 8
53109 Camp Lake, 1,898 K 10
54928 Caroline, 450 J 6
53011 Cascade, 603 K 8
54205 Casco, 481 L 6
54619 Cashton, 824 E 8
53806 Cassville, 1,343 E 10
54515 Catawba, 215 E 4
53924 Cazenovia, 335 F 8
54111 Cecil, 369 K 6
53012 Cedarburg, 7,697 L 9
53013 Cedar Grove, 1,276 L 8
54824 Centuria, 632 A 5
54621 Chaseburg, 224 D 8
† 53029 Chenequa, 642 J 1
54728 Chetek, 1,630 C 5
54420 Chili, 205 F 6
53014 Chilton⊙, 3,030 K 7
54729 Chippewa Falls⊙, 12,351 D 6
54004 Clayton, 306 B 5
54005 Clear Lake, 721 B 5
54518 Clearwater Lake, 200 H 4
53015 Cleveland, 761 L 8
53525 Clinton, 1,333 J 10
54929 Clintonville, 4,600 J 6
53016 Clyman, 328 J 9
53526 Cobb, 410 F 10
54622 Cochrane, 506 C 7
54421 Colby, 1,178 F 6
54112 Coleman, 683 L 5
54730 Colfax, 1,026 C 6
54930 Coloma, 336 H 7
53925 Columbus, 3,789 H 9
54113 Combined Locks, 2,734 K 7
† 53147 Como, 1,132 K 10
† 53066 Concord, 200 H 1
54519 Conover, 500 H 3
54623 Coon Valley, 596 E 8
54732 Cornell, 1,616 D 5
54827 Cornucopia, 250 D 2
54520 Crandon⊙, 1,582 H 4
54114 Crivitz, 985 L 5
53528 Cross Plains, 1,478 G 9
53807 Cuba City, 1,993 F 10
53110 Cudahy, 22,078 M 2
54829 Cumberland, 1,839 C 4
54931 Dale, 410 J 7
54733 Dallas, 359 C 5
53926 Dalton, 320 H 8
54830 Danbury, 350 B 3
53529 Dane, 486 G 9
53114 Darien, 839 J 10
53530 Darlington⊙, 2,351 F 10
53531 Deerfield, 1,067 H 9
54007 Deer Park, 217 B 5
53532 De Forest, 1,911 H 9
53018 Delafield, 3,182 J 1
53115 Delavan, 5,526 J 10
† 53115 Delavan Lake, 2,124 J 10
54856 Delta, 180 D 3
54208 Denmark, 1,364 L 7
54115 De Pere, 13,309 K 7
† 54663 De Soto, 295 D 9
53808 Dickeyville, 1,057 E 10
54625 Dodge, 204 D 7
53533 Dodgeville⊙, 3,255 F 10
54425 Dorchester, 491 F 5
53118 Dousman, 451 J 1
54734 Downing, 215 B 5
53928 Doylestown, 265 H 9
54009 Dresser, 533 A 5
54736 Durand⊙, 2,103 C 6
† 54217 Dyckesville, 300 L 6
53119 Eagle, 745 H 2
54521 Eagle River⊙, 1,326 H 4
54626 Eastman, 319 D 9
53120 East Troy, 1,711 J 2
54701 Eau Claire⊙, 44,619 D 6
53019 Eden, 376 K 8
54426 Edgar, 928 G 6
53534 Edgerton, 4,118 H 10
54209 Egg Harbor, 184 M 5
54427 Eland, 229 H 6
54428 Elcho, 500 H 5
54429 Elderon, 185 H 6
54932 Eldorado, 200 J 8
54738 Eleva, 574 D 6
53020 Elkhart Lake, 787 L 8
53121 Elkhorn⊙, 3,992 J 10
54739 Elk Mound, 471 C 6
54011 Ellsworth⊙, 1,983 A 6
53122 Elm Grove, 7,201 K 1
54740 Elmwood, 737 B 6
† 53401 Elmwood Park, 456 M 3
53929 Elroy, 1,513 F 8
54430 Elton, 250 J 5
54933 Embarrass, 472 J 6
53930 Endeavor, 328 G 8
54211 Ephraim, 236 M 5
54627 Ettrick, 463 D 7
54934 Eureka, 300 J 7
53536 Evansville, 2,992 H 10
54835 Exeland, 189 D 4
54741 Fairchild, 562 D 6
53931 Fair Water, 373 J 8
54742 Fall Creek, 825 D 6
53932 Fall River, 633 H 9
54120 Fence, 187 K 4
53809 Fennimore, 1,861 E 9
54628 Ferryville, 183 D 9
54524 Fifield, 287 F 4
54212 Fish Creek, 275 M 5
54121 Florence⊙, 800 K 4
54935 Fond du Lac⊙, 35,515 K 8
53125 Fontana, 1,464 J 10
53537 Footville, 698 H 10
54123 Forest Junction, 255 K 7
54213 Forestville, 349 L 6
53538 Fort Atkinson, 9,164 J 10
54629 Fountain City, 1,017 C 7
54836 Foxboro, 950 B 2
53933 Fox Lake, 1,242 J 8
53217 Fox Point, 7,937 M 1
54214 Francis Creek, 492 L 7
53132 Franklin, 12,247 L 2
53126 Franksville, 375 M 3
54837 Frederic, 908 B 4
53021 Fredonia, 1,045 L 8
54940 Fremont, 598 J 7
53934 Friendship⊙, 641 G 8
53935 Friesland, 301 H 8
54630 Galesville, 1,162 D 7
54631 Gays Mills, 623 E 9
† 53127 Genesee, 375 J 2
53127 Genesee Depot, 425 J 2
54632 Genoa, 305 D 8
53128 Genoa City, 1,085 K 11
53022 Germantown, 6,974 K 1
† 53085 Gibbsville, 408 L 8
54525 Gile, 450 F 3
54124 Gillett, 1,288 K 6
54433 Gilman, 328 E 5
54743 Gilmanton, 200 C 7
54435 Gleason, 300 G 5
53023 Glenbeulah, 496 L 8
† 53201 Glendale, 13,436 M 1
53810 Glen Haven, 250 E 10
54013 Glenwood City, 822 B 5
54527 Glidden, 860 E 3
54125 Goodman, 800 K 4
54838 Gordon, 350 C 3
53540 Gotham, 175 F 9
53024 Grafton, 5,998 L 9
53936 Grand Marsh, 200 G 8
54839 Grand View, 350 D 3
54436 Granton, 288 E 6
54840 Grantsburg⊙, 930 A 4
53541 Gratiot, 249 F 10
* 54301 Green Bay⊙, 87,809 K 6
Green Bay, ‡158,244 K 6
53129 Greendale, 15,089 L 2
53220 Greenfield, 24,424 L 2
54941 Green Lake⊙, 1,109 H 8
54126 Greenleaf, 350 L 7
54942 Greenville, 900 J 7
54437 Greenwood, 1,036 E 6
54128 Gresham, 448 J 6
53130 Hales Corners, 7,771 K 2
† 54729 Hallie, 1,223 D 6
54438 Hamburg, 170 G 5
54015 Hammond, 768 A 6
54943 Hancock, 404 G 7
54529 Harshaw, 200 G 4
53027 Hartford, 6,499 K 9
53029 Hartland, 2,763 J 1
54440 Hatley, 315 H 6
54841 Haugen, 246 C 4
54530 Hawkins, 385 E 4
54843 Hayward⊙, 1,457 D 3
53811 Hazel Green, 982 F 11
54531 Hazelhurst, 334 G 4
† 53538 Hebron, 190 J 10
53137 Helenville, 230 J 10
54844 Herbster, 250 D 2
54441 Hewitt, 300 F 6
53543 Highland, 785 F 9
54129 Hilbert, 896 K 7
54533 Hiles, 260 J 4
54634 Hillsboro, 1,231 F 8
53031 Hingham, 210 K 8
54635 Hixton, 300 E 7
54745 Holcombe, 200 D 5
53544 Hollandale, 256 G 10
54636 Holmen, 1,081 D 8
53138 Honey Creek, 350 J 3
53032 Horicon, 3,356 J 9
54944 Hortonville, 1,524 J 7
† 55082 Houlton, 400 A 5
54303 Howard, 4,911 K 6
† 53081 Howards Grove-Millersville, 998 L 8
53033 Hubertus, 600 K 1
54016 Hudson⊙, 5,049 A 6
54746 Humbird, 219 E 6
54534 Hurley⊙, 2,418 F 3
53034 Hustisford, 789 J 9
54637 Hustler, 190 F 8
† 54450 Hutchins, 409 H 6
54747 Independence, 1,036 D 7
54945 Iola, 900 H 6
54536 Iron Belt, 425 F 3
53035 Iron Ridge, 480 K 9
54847 Iron River, 800 D 2
53938 Ironton, 195 F 8
† 53177 Ives Grove, 250 L 3
53036 Ixonia, 300 H 1
53037 Jackson, 561 K 9
54236 Jacksonport, 180 M 6
53545 Janesville⊙, 46,426 J 10
53549 Jefferson⊙, 5,429 J 10
54748 Jim Falls, 310 D 5
53038 Johnson Creek, 790 J 9
53550 Juda, 500 H 10
54443 Junction City, 396 G 6
53039 Juneau⊙, 2,043 J 9
53139 Kansasville, 300 L 3
54130 Kaukauna, 11,292 K 7
† 53050 Kekoskee, 233 J 8
54215 Kellnersville, 250 L 7
54638 Kendall, 468 F 8
54537 Kennan, 167 F 5
53140 Kenosha⊙, 78,805 M 3
Kenosha, ‡117,917 M 3
54135 Keshena⊙, 980 J 6
53040 Kewaskum, 1,926 K 8
54216 Kewaunee⊙, 2,901 M 7
53042 Kiel, 2,848 L 8
53812 Kieler, 653 E 10
54136 Kimberly, 6,131 K 7
54946 King, 1,040 H 7
53939 Kingston, 343 H 8
54749 Knapp, 369 B 6
53044 Kohler, 1,738 L 8
53147 Krakow, 315 K 6
54538 Lac du Flambeau, 500 G 4
† 53066 Lac La Belle, 227 H 1
54601 La Crosse⊙, 51,153 D 8
La Crosse, ‡80,468 D 8
54848 Ladysmith⊙, 3,674 D 5
54639 La Farge, 748 E 8
53940 Lake Delton, 1,059 G 8
53147 Lake Geneva, 4,890 K 10
53551 Lake Mills, 3,556 H 9
54849 Lake Nebagamon, 523 C 3
54539 Lake Tomahawk, 555 H 4
† 54494 Lake Wazeecha, 1,285 G 7
† 54729 Lake Wissota, 1,419 D 6
54138 Lakewood, 300 K 5
† 53065 Lamartine, 190 J 8
53813 Lancaster⊙, 3,756 E 10
54540 Land O'Lakes, 786 H 3
53046 Lannon, 1,056 K 1
54541 Laona, 1,500 J 4
54850 La Pointe, 300 E 2
53941 La Valle, 411 F 8
53047 Lebanon, 250 H 1
54139 Lena, 569 K 6
† 54656 Leon, 160 E 8
† 53190 Lima Center, 175 J 10
53942 Limeridge, 203 F 9
53553 Linden, 408 F 10
54140 Little Chute, 5,365 K 7
54141 Little Suamico, 190 L 6
53554 Livingston, 503 E 10
53555 Lodi, 1,831 G 9
53943 Loganville, 199 F 9
† 54970 Lohrville, 195 H 7
53048 Lomira, 1,084 J 8
† 53523 London, 317 H 9
53556 Lone Rock, 506 F 9
54852 Loretta, 200 E 4
53557 Lowell, 322 J 9
54446 Loyal, 1,126 E 6
54853 Luck, 848 B 4
54217 Luxemburg, 853 L 6
53944 Lyndon Station, 533 F 8
53148 Lyons, 550 K 10
* 53701 Madison (cap.)⊙, 173,258 H 9
Madison, ‡290,272 H 9
54750 Maiden Rock, 172 B 6
54949 Manawa, 1,105 J 7
54220 Manitowoc⊙, 33,430 L 7
54226 Maplewood, 192 M 6
54448 Marathon, 1,214 G 6
54855 Marengo, 350 E 3
54227 Maribel, 316 L 7
54143 Marinette⊙, 12,696 L 5
54950 Marion, 1,218 J 6
53946 Markesan, 1,378 J 8
53947 Marquette, 161 H 8
53559 Marshall, 1,043 H 9
54449 Marshfield, 15,619 F 6
54450 Mattoon, 377 J 5
53948 Mauston⊙, 3,466 F 8
53050 Mayville, 4,139 K 9
53560 Mazomanie, 1,217 G 9
53558 McFarland, 2,386 H 10
54543 McNaughton, 350 H 4
54451 Medford⊙, 3,454 F 5
54546 Mellen, 1,168 E 3
54642 Melrose, 505 E 7
54952 Menasha, 14,905 J 7
53051 Menomonee Falls, 31,697 K 1
54751 Menomonie⊙, 11,275 C 6
53092 Mequon, 12,110 L 1
54547 Mercer, 1,100 F 3
54452 Merrill⊙, 9,502 G 5
54754 Merrillan, 612 E 7
53561 Merrimac, 376 G 9
53056 Merton, 646 K 1
54148 Middle Inlet, 200 K 5
53562 Middleton, 8,286 G 9
54857 Mikana, 215 C 4
54454 Milladore, 229 G 6
54643 Millston, 200 E 7
54858 Milltown, 634 B 4
53563 Milton, 3,699 J 10
* 53201 Milwaukee⊙, 717,099 M 1
Milwaukee, ‡1,403,887 M 1
54644 Mindoro, 230 D 7
53565 Mineral Point, 2,305 F 10
54548 Minocqua, 950 G 4
54859 Minong, 420 C 3
54228 Mishicot, 938 L 7
54755 Mondovi, 2,338 C 6
54549 Monico, 285 H 4
53716 Monona, 10,420 H 9
53566 Monroe⊙, 8,654 G 10
53949 Montello⊙, 1,082 H 8
53569 Montfort, 518 E 10
53570 Monticello, 870 G 10
54550 Montreal, 877 F 3

(continued on following page)

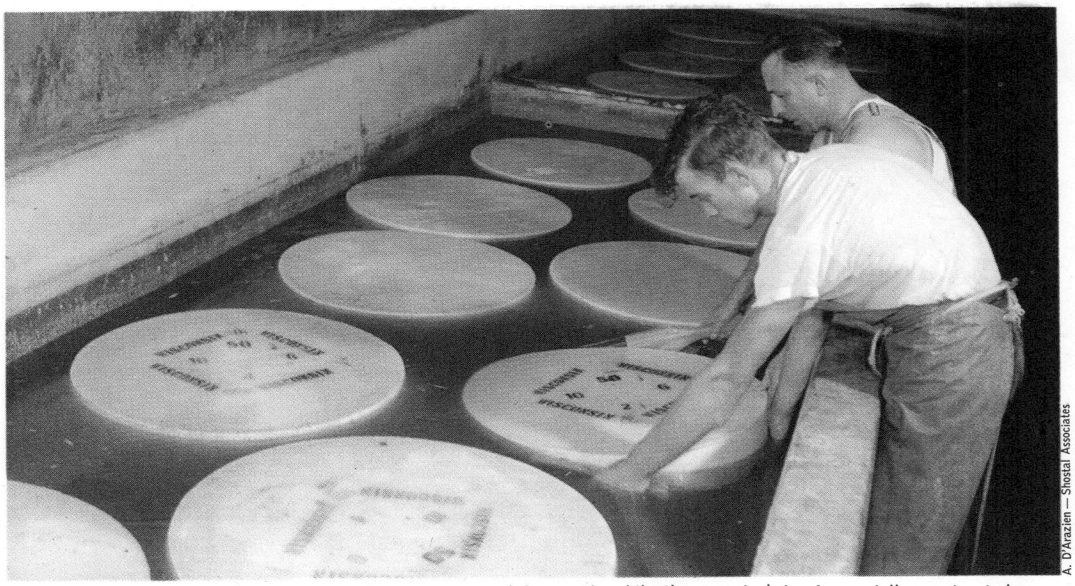

A. D'Arazien — Shostal Associates

"America's Dairyland"— Wisconsin cheeses are turned frequently while they age in brine in specially constructed rooms. Temperature and humidity control are vital for proper ripening.

⊙ County seat.
‡ Population of metropolitan area.
† Zip of nearest p.o.
* Multiple zips

Topography

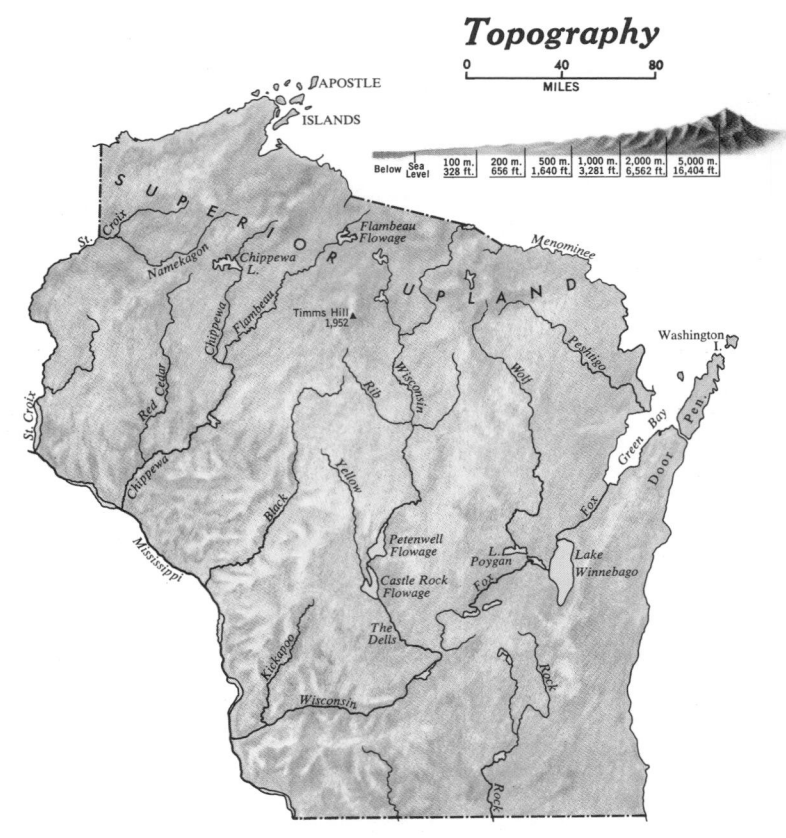

APOSTLE ISLANDS

SUPERIOR UPLAND

Below Sea Level	100 m. 328 ft.	200 m. 656 ft.	500 m. 1,640 ft.	1,000 m. 3,281 ft.	2,000 m. 6,562 ft.	5,000 m. 16,404 ft.

0   40   80
MILES

Agriculture, Industry and Resources

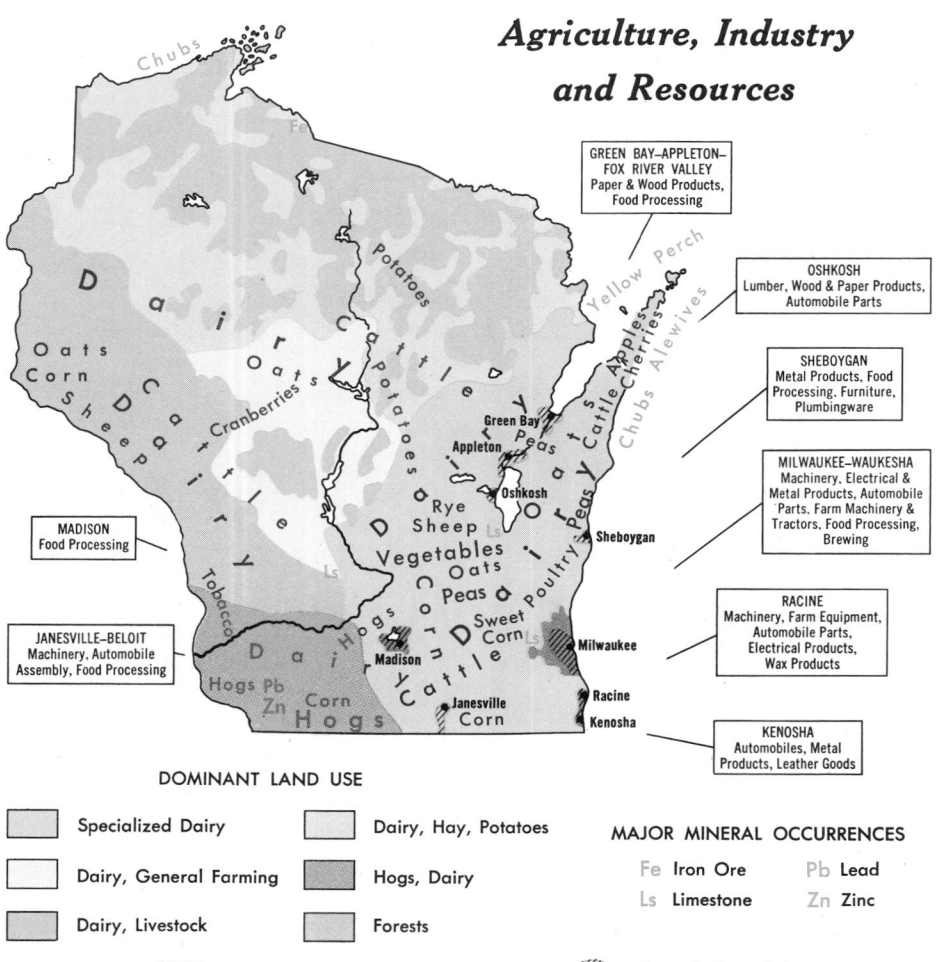

GREEN BAY–APPLETON–FOX RIVER VALLEY
Paper & Wood Products, Food Processing

OSHKOSH
Lumber, Wood & Paper Products, Automobile Parts

SHEBOYGAN
Metal Products, Food Processing, Furniture, Plumbingware

MILWAUKEE–WAUKESHA
Machinery, Electrical & Metal Products, Automobile Parts, Farm Machinery & Tractors, Food Processing, Brewing

MADISON
Food Processing

JANESVILLE–BELOIT
Machinery, Automobile Assembly, Food Processing

RACINE
Machinery, Farm Equipment, Automobile Parts, Electrical Products, Wax Products

KENOSHA
Automobiles, Metal Products, Leather Goods

DOMINANT LAND USE

- Specialized Dairy
- Dairy, General Farming
- Dairy, Livestock
- Dairy, Hay, Potatoes
- Hogs, Dairy
- Forests
- Urban Areas

MAJOR MINERAL OCCURRENCES

Fe Iron Ore Pb Lead
Ls Limestone Zn Zinc

⫽⫽⫽ Major Industrial Areas

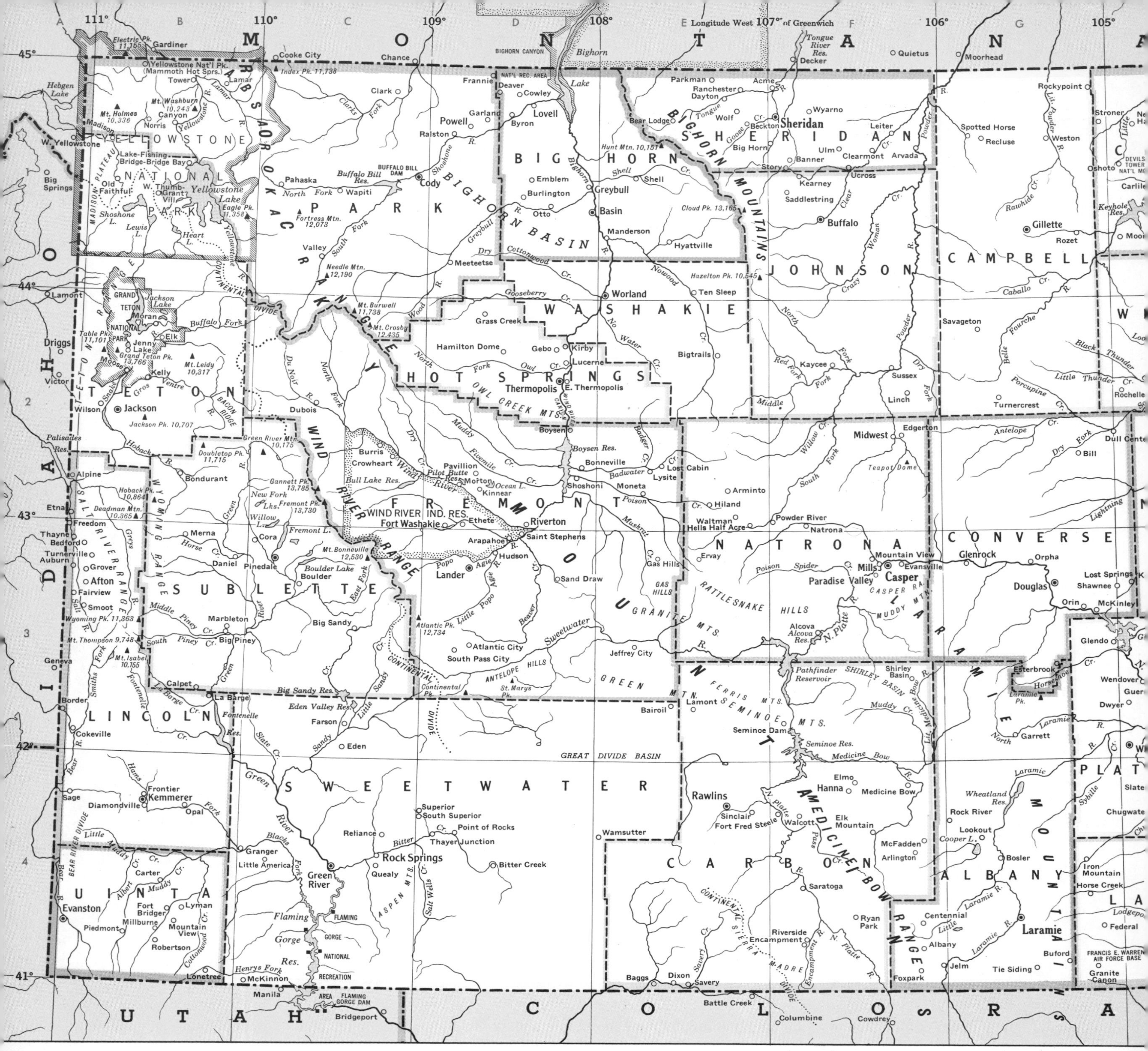

Agriculture, Industry and Resources

DOMINANT LAND USE

- ☐ Specialized Wheat
- ☐ Specialized Dairy
- ☐ General Farming, Livestock, Special Crops
- ☐ Sugar Beets, Dry Beans, Livestock, General Farming
- ☐ Range Livestock
- ☐ Forests
- ☐ Nonagricultural Land

MAJOR MINERAL OCCURRENCES

C Coal	G Natural Gas	P Phosphates
Cl Clay	O Petroleum	U Uranium
Fe Iron Ore		V Vanadium

⚡ Water Power

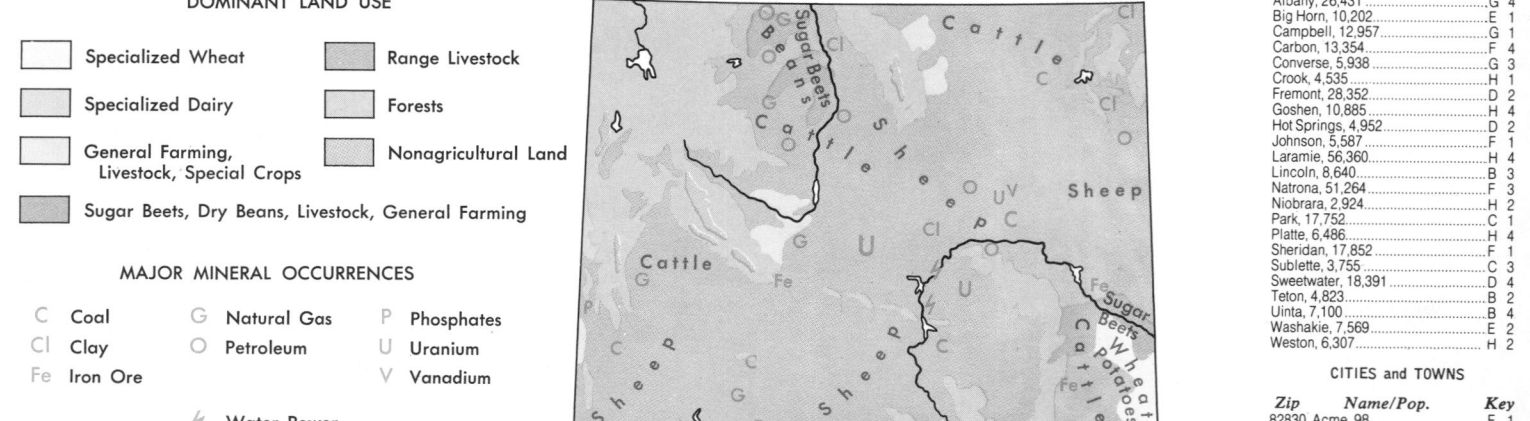

COUNTIES

Albany, 26,431	G 4
Big Horn, 10,202	E 1
Campbell, 12,957	G 1
Carbon, 13,354	F 4
Converse, 5,938	G 3
Crook, 4,535	H 1
Fremont, 28,352	D 2
Goshen, 10,885	H 4
Hot Springs, 4,952	D 2
Johnson, 5,587	F 1
Laramie, 56,360	H 4
Lincoln, 8,640	B 3
Natrona, 51,264	F 3
Niobrara, 2,924	H 2
Park, 17,752	C 1
Platte, 6,486	H 4
Sheridan, 17,852	F 1
Sublette, 3,755	C 3
Sweetwater, 18,391	B 4
Teton, 4,823	B 2
Uinta, 7,100	B 4
Washakie, 7,569	E 2
Weston, 6,307	H 2

CITIES and TOWNS

Zip	Name/Pop.	Key
82830	Acme, 98	E 1
83110	Afton, 1,290	B 3

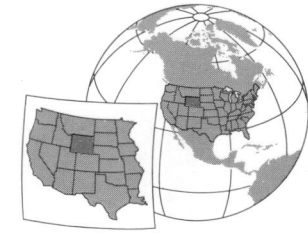

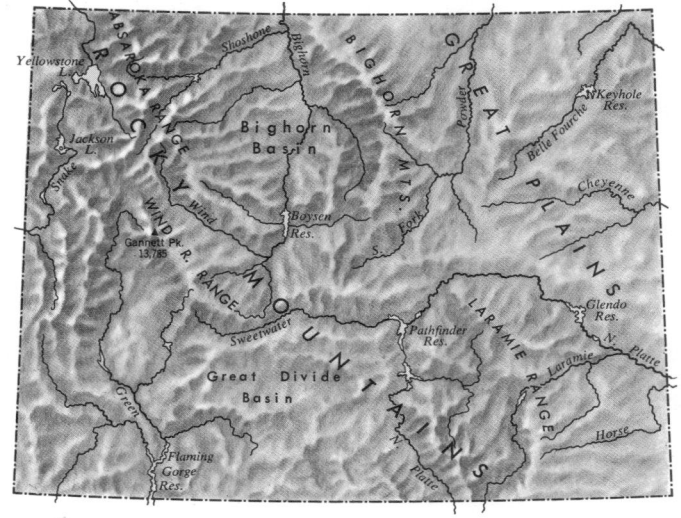

WYOMING

SCALE
0 5 10 20 30 40 MI.
0 5 10 20 30 40 KM.

State Capitals ⊛
County Seats ⊛

© C.S. HAMMOND & Co., N.Y.

Topography

5,000 m. 2,000 m. 1,000 m. 500 m. 200 m. 100 m. Sea Level Below
16,404 ft. 6,562 ft. 3,281 ft. 1,640 ft. 656 ft. 328 ft.

0 50 100
MILES

AREA 97,914 sq. mi.
POPULATION 332,416 ('70); 470,816 ('80)
CAPITAL Cheyenne
LARGEST CITY Cheyenne
HIGHEST POINT Gannett Pk. 13,785 ft.
SETTLED IN 1834
ADMITTED TO UNION July 10, 1890
POPULAR NAME Equality State
STATE FLOWER Indian Paintbrush
STATE BIRD Meadowlark

Intrepid mountain climbers are challenged by the sheer granite cliffs of Wyoming's Teton Range. Lowland meadows and trails attract less ambitious sportsmen.

Jack Zehrt—Shostal Associates

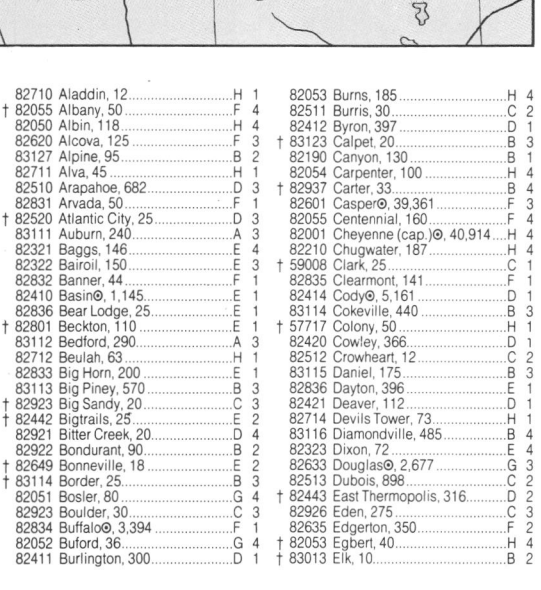

82710 Aladdin, 12	H 1
† 82055 Albany, 50	F 4
82050 Albin, 118	H 4
82620 Alcova, 125	F 3
83127 Alpine, 95	B 2
82711 Alva, 45	H 1
82510 Arapahoe, 682	D 3
82831 Arvada, 50	F 1
83111 Auburn, 240	A 3
82321 Baggs, 146	E 4
82322 Bairoil, 150	E 3
82832 Banner, 44	F 1
82410 Basin◉, 1,145	E 1
82836 Bear Lodge, 25	E 1
† 82801 Beckton, 110	E 1
83112 Bedford, 290	A 3
82712 Beulah, 63	H 1
82833 Big Horn, 200	E 1
83113 Big Piney, 570	B 3
† 82923 Big Sandy, 20	C 3
82921 Bitter Creek, 20	D 4
82922 Bondurant, 90	B 3
82649 Bonneville, 18	E 2
† 83114 Border, 25	B 3
82051 Bosler, 80	G 4
82923 Boulder, 30	C 3
82834 Buffalo◉, 3,394	F 1
82052 Buford, 36	G 4
82411 Burlington, 300	D 1
82053 Burns, 185	H 4
82511 Burris, 30	C 2
82412 Byron, 397	D 1
† 83123 Calpet, 20	B 3
82190 Canyon, 130	B 1
82054 Carpenter, 100	H 4
† 82937 Carter, 33	C 4
82601 Casper◉, 39,361	F 3
82055 Centennial, 160	F 4
82001 Cheyenne (cap.)◉, 40,914	H 4
82210 Chugwater, 187	G 4
† 59008 Clark, 25	C 1
82637 Clearmont, 141	F 1
82934 Granger, 137	C 4
82414 Cody◉, 5,161	D 1
83114 Cokeville, 440	B 3
† 57717 Colony, 50	H 1
82420 Cowley, 366	D 1
82512 Crowheart, 12	C 2
83115 Daniel, 175	B 3
82836 Dayton, 396	E 1
82421 Deaver, 112	D 1
82714 Devils Tower, 73	H 1
83116 Diamondville, 485	B 4
82323 Dixon, 72	E 4
82215 Dubois, 898	C 2
82633 Douglas◉, 2,677	G 3
82513 Dubois, 898	C 2
82443 East Thermopolis, 316	D 2
82635 Edgerton, 350	F 2
† 82053 Egbert, 40	H 4
83013 Elk, 10	B 2
82324 Elk Mountain, 127	F 4
† 82327 Elmo, 53	F 4
82422 Emblem, 250	D 1
82325 Encampment, 321	F 4
82520 Ethete, 30	D 2
83118 Etna, 400	A 2
82930 Evanston◉, 4,462	B 4
82636 Evansville, 832	F 3
83119 Fairview, 245	B 3
82932 Farson, 210	C 3
† 82001 Federal, 15	G 4
82933 Fort Bridger, 150	B 4
† 82301 Fort Fred Steele, 15	E 4
82212 Fort Laramie, 197	H 3
82514 Fort Washakie, 140	C 2
† 82001 Fox Farm, 1,329	H 4
82057 Foxpark, 110	F 4
82423 Frannie, 95	D 1
83120 Freedom, 497	B 3
83121 Frontier, 246	B 4
82424 Garland, 57	D 1
82058 Garrett, 10	G 3
82501 Gas Hills, 200	E 3
† 82430 Gebo, 15	D 2
82716 Gillette◉, 7,194	G 1
82213 Glendo, 210	G 3
82637 Glenrock, 1,515	G 3
82059 Granite Canon, 72	G 4
82425 Grass Creek, 125	D 2
82935 Green River◉, 4,196	C 4
82426 Greybull, 1,953	E 1
83122 Grover, 120	B 3
82214 Guernsey, 793	H 3
82427 Hamilton Dome, 106	D 2
† 82701 Hampshire, 23	H 2
82327 Hanna, 460	F 4
82215 Hartville, 246	H 3
82217 Hawk Springs, 125	H 4
82060 Hillsdale, 160	H 4
82061 Horse Creek, 225	G 4
82515 Hudson, 38	D 3
82720 Hulett, 318	H 1
82218 Huntley, 50	H 4
83115 Merna, 25	A 3
82428 Hyattville, 73	E 1
82062 Iron Mountain, 12	G 4
83001 Jackson◉, 2,101	B 2
82219 Jay Em, 25	H 3
82310 Jeffrey City, 702	E 3
82063 Jelm, 29	G 4
† 83012 Jenny Lake, 10	B 2
82639 Kaycee, 272	F 2
82832 Kearney, 49	F 1
82220 Keeline, 30	H 3
83011 Kelly, 35	B 2
83101 Kemmerer◉, 2,292	B 4
82516 Kinnear, 44	D 2
82430 Kirby, 75	D 2
83123 La Barge, 375	B 3
83124 Opal, 34	B 4
† 82190 Lake-Fishing Bridge-Bridge Bay, 167	B 1
† 82190 Lamar, 27	B 1
82328 Lamont, 30	E 3
82222 Lance Creek, 175	H 2
82520 Lander◉, 7,125	D 3
82070 Laramie◉, 23,143	G 4
82837 Leiter, 100	F 1
82640 Linch, 185	F 2
82223 Lingle, 446	H 3
82929 Little America, 47	C 4
82051 Lookout, 20	G 4
† 82642 Lost Cabin, 20	E 2
82431 Lovell, 2,371	D 1
† 82443 Lucerne, 140	D 2
82225 Lusk◉, 1,495	H 3
82937 Lyman, 643	B 4
82642 Lysite, 25	E 2
82431 Madison, 42	B 1
† 82190 Mammoth Hot Springs (Yellowstone Nat'l Park), 162	B 1
82432 Manderson, 117	E 1
82227 Manville, 92	H 3
† 83113 Marbleton, 223	B 3
82080 McFadden, 150	F 4
82938 McKinnon, 135	C 4
82329 Medicine Bow, 455	F 4
82433 Meeteetse, 459	D 1
82643 Midwest, 743	F 2
† 82933 Millburne, 54	B 4
82644 Mills, 1,724	F 3
82721 Moorcroft, 981	H 1
83012 Moose, 115	B 2
83013 Moran, 600	B 2
† 82701 Morrisey, 28	H 2
82522 Morton, 35	D 2
82939 Mountain View, 1,641	F 3
82939 Mountain View, 500	B 4
† 57735 Mule Creek, 10	H 2
82701 Newcastle◉, 3,432	H 1
82722 New Haven, 35	H 1
† 82190 Norris, 20	B 1
82430 Old Faithful, 134	B 1
† 82001 Orchard Valley, 1,015	H 4
82652 Orin, 20	G 3
† 82633 Orpha, 12	G 3
82723 Osage, 346	H 2
82434 Otto, 75	D 1
82414 Pahaska, 75	C 1
† 82601 Paradise Valley, 1,764	F 3
82838 Parkman, 30	E 1
82523 Pavillion, 181	D 2
82082 Pine Bluffs, 937	H 4
82941 Pinedale◉, 948	C 3
82942 Point of Rocks, 20	D 4
82648 Powder River, 75	F 2
82435 Powell, 4,807	D 1
82440 Ralston, 85	D 1
82839 Ranchester, 208	E 1
82301 Rawlins◉, 7,855	E 4
82725 Recluse, 25	G 1
82943 Reliance, 425	C 4
82325 Riverside, 46	F 4
82501 Riverton, 7,995	D 2
82944 Robertson, 30	B 4
† 82701 Rochelle, 23	H 2
82083 Rock River, 344	G 4
82901 Rock Springs, 11,657	C 4
82726 Rockypoint, 22	G 1
82727 Rozet, 10	H 1
82330 Ryan Park, 18	F 4
82840 Saddlestring, 100	F 1
83125 Sage, 45	B 4
82524 Saint Stephens, 100	D 3
82501 Sand Draw, 40	D 3
82331 Saratoga, 1,181	F 4
† 82716 Savageton, 30	G 2
82332 Savery, 29	E 4
† 82720 Seely, 10	H 1
82333 Seminoe Dam, 40	E 3
82229 Shawnee, 11	G 3
82441 Shell, 50	E 1
82801 Sheridan◉, 10,856	F 1
82601 Shirley Basin, 700	F 3
82649 Shoshoni, 562	D 2
82334 Sinclair, 445	E 4
83126 Smoot, 200	A 3
† 82945 South Superior, 197	D 4
82842 Story, 637	F 1
82729 Sundance◉, 1,056	H 1
82215 Sunrise, 80	H 3
82945 Superior, 2	D 4
82639 Sussex, 200	F 2
82442 Ten Sleep, 320	E 1
82901 Thayer Junction, 15	D 4
83127 Thayne, 195	A 2
82443 Thermopolis◉, 3,063	D 2
82240 Torrington◉, 4,237	H 3
† 82190 Tower, 24	B 1
83112 Turnerville, 25	A 3
† 82835 Ucross, 17	F 1
82835 Ulm, 25	F 1
82730 Upton, 947	H 1
82242 Van Tassell, 21	H 3
82243 Veteran, 35	H 4
82335 Walcott, 20	F 4
82648 Waltman, 20	F 2
82336 Wamsutter, 139	E 4
82450 Wapiti, 92	C 1
† 82190 West Thumb-Grant Village, 64	B 1
82201 Wheatland◉, 2,498	H 3
83014 Wilson, 550	B 2
82844 Wolf, 30	E 1
82401 Worland◉, 5,055	E 1
82845 Wyarno, 97	F 1
82190 Yellowstone Nat'l Park, 162	B 1
82244 Yoder, 101	H 4

◉ County seat.
† Zip of nearest p.o.

ACQUISITIONS OF TERRITORY

OREGON COUNTRY 1846 — OREGON Treaty with Great Britain

MEXICAN CESSION 1848

GADSDEN PURCHASE 1853

LOUISIANA — Purchased from France 1803

RED RIVER — Title Established 1818

TEXAS — Annexed in 1845

UNITED STATES 1783

FLORIDA 1819 — Treaty with Spain

ALASKA 1867 Purchased from Russia

HAWAII — Annexed in 1898

The United States in 1783 comprised the thirteen original states and included lands acquired by conquest during the Revolution and by the Treaty of 1783.

RANK BY AREA

RANK BY POPULATION 1970

YEAR OF ADMISSION TO THE UNION

State	Year
DELAWARE	1787
PENNSYLVANIA	1788
NEW JERSEY	1788
GEORGIA	1788
CONNECTICUT	1788
MASSACHUSETTS	1788
MARYLAND	1788
SOUTH CAROLINA	1788
NEW HAMPSHIRE	1788
VIRGINIA	1788
NEW YORK	1788
NORTH CAROLINA	1789
RHODE ISLAND	1790
VERMONT	1791
KENTUCKY	1792
TENNESSEE	1796
OHIO	1803
LOUISIANA	1812
INDIANA	1816
MISSISSIPPI	1817
ILLINOIS	1818
ALABAMA	1819
MAINE	1820
MISSOURI	1821

1959 HAWAII / ALASKA

1912 ARIZONA / NEW MEXICO

1907 OKLAHOMA

UTAH — 1896
WYOMING — 1890
IDAHO / MONTANA / WASHINGTON — 1889
NORTH DAKOTA / SOUTH DAKOTA
COLORADO — 1876
NEBRASKA — 1867
NEVADA — 1864
WEST VIRGINIA — 1863
KANSAS — 1861
MINNESOTA — 1858
OREGON — 1859
CALIFORNIA — 1850
WISCONSIN — 1848
IOWA — 1846
FLORIDA / TEXAS — 1845
MICHIGAN — 1837
ARKANSAS — 1836

© Copyright
HAMMOND INCORPORATED

INDEX OF THE WORLD

Introduction

This index contains a complete alphabetical listing of more than one hundred thousand names shown on all the maps included in this atlas. Names not found in the individual indexes accompanying the maps appear here. The user who is unfamiliar with the location of a country, town, or physical feature, or who is in doubt as to which country, state or province a place belongs will find the answers to his questions in this index. Entries are indexed to all maps or insets showing the place.

The name of the feature sought will be found in its proper alphabetical sequence, followed by the name of the political division in which it is located, the page number of the map on which it will be found, and the key reference necessary for finding its location on the map. After noting the key reference letter-number combination for the place name, turn to the page number indicated. The place name will be found within the square formed by the two lines of latitude and the two lines of longitude which enclose the co-ordinates—i.e., the marginal letters and numbers.

Certain symbols will be found in this index. A double dagger (‡) after the name indicates that the name will not be found on the map because of scale limitations, but that the place is located within the designated square. A triangle (⏃) after the name signifies a township — better known as a town — in the northeastern U.S.

All index entries for cities and towns in the United States are followed by a five-digit postal ZIP code number applying to the community. This useful feature permits the reader to address his mail so that it will be routed and delivered more efficiently and quickly by the U.S. Postal Service. A dagger (†) designates those places that do not possess a post office. The ZIP code number listed in such cases refers to that of the nearest post office. An asterisk (*) marks those larger cities which are divided into multiple ZIP code areas. Using the single ZIP code number listed in such cases will direct your letter to the proper city with dispatch. However, if the precise ZIP code number of the address within the city is needed, it is suggested that the reader refer to the ZIP code zone maps of the largest U.S. cities appearing on the pages following the index. For other multi-ZIP code cities it is suggested that the reader refer to the latest National ZIP Code Directory at his local post office. This detailed guide lists every street in a multiple ZIP code city with the proper ZIP code for the street.

Because of limitations of space on the map, place names do not always appear in their complete form on the map. The complete forms are, however, given in the index. Variant spellings of names and alternate names are also given in this index. The alternate form or spelling of the name appears first, followed in parentheses by the name as it appears on the map. Physical features are usually listed under their proper names and not according to their generic terms; that is to say, Rio Negro will be found under Negro and not under Rio Negro. Exceptions are familiar names such as Rio Grande.

The abbreviations for the political division names and geographical features are explained on page XVI of the atlas. In addition, reference can be made to the Gazetteer-Index appearing on pages IX through XIII in which area, population, capital, map reference and population source data may be found for all major political and physical divisions of the world. Population figures for most entries are also included in the comprehensive individual indexes accompanying each map.

A

Aa (riv.), Switz. 39/F3
Aabenraa, Den. 18/F9
Aabenraa, Den. 21/C7
Aabenraa-Sønderborg (co.), Den. 21/C8
Aabybro, Den. 21/C3
Aachen, W. Ger., 7/E3
Aachen, W. Ger. 22/B3
Aadorf, Switz. 39/G2
Aakirkeby, Den. 21/F9
Aalborg, Den., 7/E3
Aalborg, Den. 18/G8
Aalborg (co.), Den. 21/D4
Aalborg, Den. 21/D4
Aalborg (bay), Den. 21/D4
Aalen, W. Ger. 22/D4
Aalestrup, Den. 21/C4
Aalsmeer, Neth. 27/F4
Aalst, Belg. 27/D7
Aalst, Neth. 27/G6
Aalten, Neth. 27/K5
Aalter, Belg. 27/C6
Äänekoski, Fin. 18/O5
Aarau, Switz. 39/F2
Aarberg, Switz. 39/D2
Aarburg, Switz. 39/E2
Aardenburg, Neth. 27/C6
Aare (riv.), Switz. 39/E3
Aargau (canton), Switz. 39/F2
Aarhus, Den., 7/E3
Aarhus, Den. 18/F8
Aarhus (co.), Den. 21/D5
Aarhus, Den. 21/D5
Aarlen (Arlon), Belg. 27/H9
Aarø (isl.), Den. 21/C7
Aarons (creek), Va. 307/L7
Aaronsburg, Pa. (16820) 294/H4
Aarøsund, Den. 21/C7
Aars, Den. 21/C4
Aarschot, Belg. 27/F7
Aarup, Den. 21/D7
Aat (Ath), Belg. 27/D7
Aba, Hung. 41/E3
Aba, Nigeria 106/F7
Aba, Dem. Rep. of the Congo. 115/F3
Abacaxis (riv.), Braz. 132/B4
Abadan, Iran, 54/H6
Abadan, Iran 59/E3
Abadan, Iran 66/F5
Abadeh, Iran 59/F3
Abadeh, Iran 66/H5
Abadla, Alg. 106/D2
Abádszalók, Hung. 41/F3
Abaeté, Braz. 132/E7
Abaetetuba, Braz. 132/D3
Abaiang (atoll), Gilb. and Ell., 87/H5
'Abaila, Saudi Ar. 59/F5
Abajo (mts.), Utah 304/E6
Abakan, U.S.S.R. 48/J4
Abalos (pt.), Cuba 158/A2
Abana, Turkey 63/F2
Abancay, Peru 128/F9
Abanda, Ala. (†36274) 194/H4
Abapó, Bol. 136/D6
Abarquh, Iran 59/F3
Abarquh, Iran 66/H5
Abashiri, Japan 81/M1
Abashiri (riv.), Japan 81/M1
Abau, Papua 85/C7
Abaújszántó, Hung. 41/F2
Abaya (lake), Eth. 111/G6
Abbai (riv.), Eth. 111/G5
Abbaye (pt.), Mich. 250/B2
Abbe (lake), Afars Issas 111/H5
Abbeville, Ala. (36310) 194/H7
Abbeville, France 28/D2
Abbeville, Ga. (31001) 216/F7
Abbeville, La. (70510) 238/F7
Abbeville, Miss. (38601) 256/F2
Abbeville (co.), S.C. 296/B3
Abbeville, S.C. (29620) 296/C3
Abbey, Sask. 181/C5
Abbey (head), Scot. 15/J10
Abbeydorney, Ire. 17/B7
Abbeyfeale, 10/B4
Abbeyfeale, Ire. 17/C7
Abbeylara, Ire. 17/F4
Abbeyleix, Ire. 17/G6
Abbotsford, Br. Col. 184/L3
Abbotsford, Scot. 15/L8
Abbotsford, Wis. (54405) 317/F6
Abbott, Ark. (72920) 203/B3
Abbott, N. Mex. (†87747) 274/E2
Abbott, Texas (76621) 302/G6
Abbottabad, Pak. 59/K3
Abbottabad, Pak. 68/C2
Abbottsburg, N.C. (28321) 281/M5
Abbottsford, Ga. (†30240) 216/B4
Abbottstown, Pa. (17301) 294/J6
Abbot Village▵, Maine (04406) 242/D5
Abbyville, Kans. (67510) 232/D4
'Abdul 'Aziz, Jebel (mts.), Syria 63/J4
Abdulino, U.S.S.R. 52/H4
Abécher, Chad 111/D5
Abécher, 102/E3
Abee, Alta. 182/D2
Abell, Md. (20606) 245/M8
Abemama (atoll), Gilb. and Ell., 87/H5
Abengourou, Ivory Coast 106/D7
Abeokuta, 102/C4
Abeokuta, Niger 106/E7
Aberaeron, 10/D4
Aberaeron, Wales 13/C5
Aberchirder, Scot. 15/L4
Abercorn, Que. 172/E4
Abercorn (Mbala), Zambia 115/F5
Abercrombie, N. Dak. (58001) 283/S7
Abercrombie (mt.), Wash. 310/H2
Aberdare, 10/E5
Aberdare, Wales 13/D6
Aberdaron, Wales 13/C5
Aberdeen, Idaho (83210) 220/F7
Aberdeen, Ky. (42201) 237/H6
Aberdeen, 10/F2
Aberdeen, Md. (21001) 245/O2
Aberdeen, Miss. (39730) 256/H3
Aberdeen, N.C. (28315) 281/L4
Aberdeen, N.S.W. 97/F3
Aberdeen (lake), N.W.T. 187/J3
Aberdeen, Ohio (45101) 284/C8
Aberdeen, S. Africa 118/C6
Aberdeen, S. Dak., 146/H5
Aberdeen, S. Dak., 188/G1
Aberdeen, S. Dak. (57401) 298/M3
Aberdeen, Sask. 181/E3
Aberdeen, Scot., 7/D3
Aberdeen (co.), Scot. 15/L5
Aberdeen, Scot. 15/N5
Aberdeen, Wash., 188/B1
Aberdeen, Wash. (98520) 310/B3
Aberdeen Proving Ground, Md. 245/N3
Aberfeldy, 10/D2
Aberfeldy, Scot. 15/J6
Aberfoyle, Scot. 15/H7
Abergavenny, 10/E5
Abergavenny, Wales 13/E6
Abergele, Wales 13/D4
Aberlour, Scot. 15/K5
Abermain, N.S.W. 97/F3
Abernant, Ala. (35440) 194/D4
Abernathy, Sask. 181/H5
Abernathy, Texas (79311) 302/B4
Abernethy, Scot. 15/K7
Aberporth, Wales 13/C5
Abert (lake), Oreg., 188/C2
Abert (lake), Oreg. 291/G5
Abertillery, 10/E5
Abertillery, Wales 13/E6
Aberystwyth, 10/D4
Aberystwyth, Wales 13/C5
Abez', U.S.S.R. 52/K1
Abha, Saudi Ar. 59/D6
Abhar, Iran 66/F2
Abiad, Ras el (Blanc) (cape), Tun. 106/G1
Abibe, Serranía de (mts.), Col. 126/B3
'Abidiya, Sudan 59/B6
Ab-i-Diz (riv.), Iran 66/F4
Abidjan (cap.), Ivory Coast, 3/J5
Abidjan (cap.), Ivory Coast, 106/D7
Abidjan (cap.), Ivory Coast, 102/B4
Abie, Nebr. (68001) 264/H3
Abilene, Alta. 182/E2
Abilene, Kans. (67410) 232/E3
Abilene, Texas, 146/J6
Abilene, Texas, 188/G4
Abilene, Texas (*79601) 302/E5
Abingdon, 10/F5
Abingdon, Eng. 13/F6
Abingdon, Ill. (61410) 222/C3
Abingdon, Iowa (†52533) 229/J6
Abingdon, Md. (21009) 245/N3
Abingdon, Queens. 95/B3
Abingdon, Va. (24210) 307/D7
Abington, Conn. (06230) 210/G1
Abington, Ind. (†47330) 227/H5
Abington▵, Mass. (02351) 249/L4
Abington, Mass. (02351) 249/L4
Abington, Pa. (19001) 294/M5
Abiqua (creek), Oreg. 291/B3
Abiquiu, N. Mex. (87510) 274/C2
Abisko, Sweden 18/L2
Abita Springs, La. (70420) 238/L6
Abitibi (lake), 163/J6
Abitibi (riv.), 163/H5
Abitibi (co.), Que. 174/B2
Abitibi (dist.), Que. 174/B3
Abitibi (lake), Ont. 175/E3
Abitibi (riv.), Ont. 175/D2
Abitibi (riv.), Ont. 177/J5
Abkhaz A.S.S.R., U.S.S.R. 48/E5
Abkhaz A.S.S.R., U.S.S.R. 52/F6
Abminga, S. Aust. 94/D2
Abner, N.C. (†27371) 281/K4
Abnûb, U.A.R. 111/J4
Åbo (Turku), Fin. 18/N6
Aboisso, Ivory Coast 106/D7
Aboite, Ind. (†46783) 227/G3
Abomey, Dahomey 106/E7
Abong-Mbang, Cameroon 115/B3
Abony, Hung. 41/E3
Abor (hills), India 68/G3
Aborlan, Phil. 82/B6
Abou Deia, Chad 111/C5
Aboyne, Scot. 15/L5
Abqaiq, Saudi Ar. 59/E4
Abra (prov.), Phil. 82/C2
Abra (riv.), Phil. 82/C2
Abraham (mt.), Maine 242/C5
Abraham, Utah (†84635) 304/B4
Abraham (mt.), Vt. 268/B3
Abraham Lincoln Birthplace Nat'l Hist. Site, Ky. 237/K5
Abrams, Wis. (54101) 317/L6
Abrantes, Port. 33/B3
Abra Pampa, Arg. 143/C1
Abreus, Cuba 158/D2
Abricots, Haiti 158/A6
Abruzzi (reg.), Italy 34/D3
Absaraka, N. Dak. (58002) 283/P6
Absaroka (range), Mont. 262/F5
Absaroka (range), Wyo. 319/C1
Absarokee, Mont. (59001) 262/G5
Absecon, N.J. (08201) 273/D5
Absecon (inlet), N.J. 273/E5
Abu, India 68/C4
Abu 'Arish, Saudi Ar. 59/D6
Abu Dara, Ras (cape), Sudan 59/C5
Abu Dara, Ras (cape), Sudan 111/G3
Abu Deleiq, Sudan 59/B6
Abu Dhabi (cap.), Trucial States 59/F5
Abu Dhabi, Trucial States, 54/J7
Abu ed Duhur, Syria 63/G5
Abu Habl, Wadi (dry riv.), Sudan 111/F5
Abu Hadriya, Saudi Ar. 59/E4
Abu Hamed, 102/F3
Abu Hamed, Sudan 59/B6
Abu Hamed, Sudan 111/F4
Abuja, Niger 106/F7
Abu Kemal, Syria 59/D3
Abu Kemal, Syria 63/J5
Abukuma (riv.), Japan 81/K4
Abu-Mad, Ras (cape), Saudi Ar. 59/C5
Abu Matariq, Sudan 111/E5
Abumombazi, Dem. Rep. of the Congo. 115/D3
Abunã (riv.), 120/D4
Abunã (riv.), Braz. 132/G10
Abu Qir (bay), U.A.R. 111/J2
Abu Qurqâs, U.A.R. 111/J4
Abu Road, India 68/C4
Abu Rujmein, Jebel (mts.), Syria 63/H5
Abu Shagara, Ras (cape), Sudan 59/C5
Abu Shagara, Ras (cape), Sudan 111/G3
Abut (head), N.Z. 101/B5
Abu Tabari (well), Sudan 111/E4
Abuyog, Phil. 82/E5
Abu Zabad, Sudan 59/A7
Abu Zabad, Sudan 111/E5
Abwong, Sudan 111/F6
Aby (lag.), Ivory Coast 106/D8
Abydos (ruins), Turkey 63/B6
Abydos (ruins), U.A.R. 111/F2
Abyei, Sudan 111/E6
Acacías, Col. 126/D6
Academy, S. Dak. (57310) 298/M7
Acadia (par.), La. 238/F6
Acadia Nat'l Park, Maine 242/G7
Acadia Valley, Alta. 182/E4
Acadie Siding, N. Br. 170/E2
Acadieville, N. Br. 170/E2
Acahay, Par. 144/B7
Acajutla, El Salv. 154/B4
Acala, Texas (79828) 302/B10
Acámbaro, Mex. 150/J7
Acampo, Calif. (95220) 204/C9
Acandí, Col. 126/B3
Acaponeta, Mex. 150/G5
Acapulco de Juárez, Mex., 146/H8
Acapulco de Juárez, Mex. 150/K8
Acaraí (mts.), 120/E2
Acaraú, Braz. 132/F3
Acaray (riv.), Par. 144/E5
Acarí (range), Braz. 132/B2
Acarí, Peru 128/E10
Acarí (riv.), Peru 128/E10
Acarigua, Ven. 124/D3
Acatlán de Osorio, Mex. 150/K7
Acatzingo de Hidalgo, Mex. 150/N2
Acayucan, Mex. 150/M8
Acchilla, Bol. 136/C7
Accident, Md. (21520) 245/A2
Accokeek, Md. (20607) 245/L6
Accomac, Va. (23301) 307/S5
Accomack (co.), Va. 307/S5
Accord, Mass. (02018) 249/E8
Accord, N.Y. (12404) 276/M7
Accoville, W. Va. (25606) 313/C7
Accra (cap.), Ghana, 3/J5
Accra (cap.), Ghana 106/D7
Accra (cap.), Ghana 102/B4
Accrington, 10/G1
Accrington, Eng. 13/E4
Acebal, Arg. 143/F6
Aceguá, Urug. 145/E2
Acequia, Idaho (83310) 220/E7
Acevedo, Arg. 143/F6
Achacachi, Bol. 136/A5
Achaguas, Ven. 124/D4
Achalpur, India 68/D4
Achao, Chile 138/D4
Achar, Urug. 145/C3
Acharacle, Scot. 15/E6
Achchik Kol (lake), China 77/C4
Achégour (well), Niger 106/G5
Achenkirch, Austria 41/A3
Achikulak, U.S.S.R. 52/G6
Achill (head), 10/A4
Achill (isl.), 10/A4
Achill (head), Ire. 17/A4
Achill (isl.), Ire. 17/A4
Achille, Okla. (74720) 288/O7
Achilles, Va. (23001) 307/R6
Achill Sound, Ire. 17/B4
Achiltibuie, Scot. 15/F3
Achmore, Scot. 15/C3
Achnasheen, 10/D2
Achnasheen, Scot. 15/F4
Achourat (well), Mali 106/D4
A'Chralaig (mt.), Scot. 15/F5
Aci (lake), Turkey 63/C4
Acigöl, Turkey 63/F3
Acipayam, Turkey 63/C4
Acireale, Italy 34/E6
Ackerly, Texas (79713) 302/C5
Ackerman, Miss. (39735) 256/F4
Ackerville, Ala. (†36778) 194/E6
Ackley, Iowa (50601) 229/G3
Acklins (isl.), Bah. Is., 146/L7
Acklins (isl.), Bah. Is. 156/C2
Ackworth, Iowa (50001) 229/G6
Aclare, Ire. 17/D3
Acme, Alta. 182/D4
Acme, La. (71316) 238/G4
Acme, Mich. (49610) 250/D4
Acme, Texas (†79252) 302/E3
Acme, W. Va. (†25122) 313/D6
Acme, Wash. (98220) 310/C2
Acme, Wyo. (82830) 319/E1
Acoaxet, Mass. (02701) 249/K7
Acobamba, Peru 128/E9
Acolla, Peru 128/E8
Acoma, N. Mex. (†87049) 274/B4
Acomayo, Cuzco, Peru 128/G9
Acomayo, Huánuco, Peru 128/E7
Acomita, N. Mex. (†87049) 274/B3
Acona, Miss. (†39095) 256/D4
Aconcagua (mt.), 120/D6
Aconcagua, Cerro (mt.), Arg. 143/C3
Aconcagua (prov.), Chile 138/A9
Aconcagua (riv.), Chile 138/F2
Aconchi, Mex. 150/D2
Acopiara, Braz. 132/G4
Acora, Peru 128/H11
Acorizal, Braz. 132/C6
Acoyapa, Nic. 154/E5
Acquarossa, Switz. 39/G4
Acqui Terme, Italy 34/B2
Acraman (lake), S. Aust. 94/D5
Acre (state), Braz. 132/G10
Acre (riv.), Braz. 132/G10
Acre, Israel 65/C2
Acree, Ga. (†31791) 216/D7
Acri, Italy 34/F5
Ács, Hung. 41/E3
Actinolite, Ont. 177/G3
Acton, Ont. 177/D4
Acton▵, Maine (04001) 242/B8
Acton, Maine (04001) 242/B8
Acton▵, Mass. (01720) 249/J3
Acton, Mont. (59002) 262/H5
Acton Vale, Que. 172/E4
Actopan, Mex. 150/Q1
Açu, Braz. 132/G4
Aculeo, Chile 138/G4
Aculeo (lag.), Chile 138/G4
Acuña, Arg. 143/G5
Acuracay, Peru 128/F5
Acworth, Ga. (30101) 216/C2
Acworth▵, N.H. (03601) 268/C5
Acworth, N.H. (03601) 268/C5
Acy, La. (†70774) 238/L3
Ada (co.), Idaho 220/B6
Ada, Kans. (67414) 232/E2
Ada, Minn. (56510) 254/B3
Ada, Ohio (45810) 284/C4
Ada, Okla., 188/G4
Ada, Okla. (74820) 288/N5
Ada, Sask. 181/E5
Ada, W. Va. (†24701) 313/D8
Adadle, Somalia 115/H2
Adafer (reg.), Mauritania 106/B5
Ada Foah, Ghana 106/E7
Adair, Ill. (61411) 222/C3
Adair (co.), Iowa 229/E6
Adair, Iowa (50002) 229/D6
Adair (co.), Ky. 237/L6
Adair (co.), Mo. 261/G2
Adair (cape), N.W.T. 187/L2
Adair (co.), Okla. 288/S3
Adair, Okla. (74330) 288/R2
Adair, Tenn. (†38301) 237/D9
Adairsville, Ga. (30103) 216/C2
Adairville, Ky. (42202) 237/H7
Adaja (riv.), Spain 33/D2
Adak (isl.), Alaska 196/L4
Adak (str.), Alaska 196/K4
Adako, N.C. (†28611) 281/F3
Adalar (isl.), Turkey 63/D6
Adalia (Antayla), Turkey 63/D4
Adam, Oman 59/G5
Adamawa (reg.), Nigeria 106/G7
Adamawa (reg.), Cameroon 115/B2
Adaminaby, N.S.W. 97/E5
Adams (lake), Br. Col. 184/H4
Adams (riv.), Br. Col. 184/H4
Adams (co.), Colo. 208/L3
Adams (mt.), Colo. 208/H6
Adams (co.), Idaho 220/B5
Adams (co.), Ill. 222/B4
Adams (co.), Ind. 227/H3
Adams, Ind. (47240) 227/F6
Adams (co.), Iowa 229/D6
Adams, Kans. (†67128) 232/E4
Adams, Ky. (41201) 237/R4
Adams▵, Mass. (01220) 249/B2
Adams, Mass. (01220) 249/B2
Adams, Minn. (55909) 254/F7
Adams (co.), Miss. 256/B8
Adams (co.), N. Dak. 283/F7
Adams, N. Dak. (58210) 283/O3
Adams (mt.), N.H. 268/E3
Adams, N.Y. (13605) 276/J3
Adams (co.), Nebr. 264/F4
Adams, Nebr. (68301) 264/H4
Adam's (peak), Ceylon 68/E7
Adams (co.), Ohio 284/D8
Adams, Okla. (73901) 288/D1
Adams, Oreg. (97810) 291/J2
Adams (co.), Pa. 294/H6
Adams, Sask. 181/G5
Adams, Tenn. (37010) 237/G7
Adams (co.), Wash. 310/G3
Adams (mt.), Wash. 310/D4
Adams (co.), Wis. 317/G8
Adams, Wis. (53910) 317/G8
Adamsboro, Ind. (†46947) 227/E3
Adam's Bridge (shoals), Ceylon 68/D7
Adams's Bridge (sound), India 68/D7
Adamsburg‡, Pa. (15611) 294/C5
Adamsburg, S.C. (29380) 296/D2
Adams Center, N.Y. (13606) 276/H3
Adams Lake, Br. Col. 184/G5
Adams Mills, Ohio (43801) 284/G5
Adams Nat'l Hist. Site, Mass. 249/D7
Adamson, Okla. (74520) 288/P5
Adams Run, S.C. (29426) 296/G6
Adamstown, Md. (21710) 245/H3
Adamstown, Pa. (19501) 294/K5
Adamstown (cap.), Pitcairn Is., 87/N8
Adamsville, Ala. (35005) 194/D3
Adamsville, Que. 172/E4
Adamsville, N. Br. 170/E2
Adamsville, Ohio (43802) 284/G5
Adamsville, Pa. (16110) 294/B2
Adamsville, R.I. (02801) 249/K6
Adamsville, Tenn. (38310) 237/E10
Adamsville, Texas (76510) 302/F6
Adamsville, Utah (†84713) 304/B5
Adana, Turkey 59/C2
Adana (prov.), Turkey 63/F4
Adana, Turkey 63/F4
Adana, Turkey, 54/G6
Adanac, Sask. 181/B3
Adapazari, Turkey 59/B1
Adapazari, Turkey 63/D2
Adarama, Sudan 59/C6
Adarama, Sudan 111/G4
Adare (cape), Ant., 3/T10
Adare (cape), Ant. 5/B9
Adare, Ire. 17/D6
Adar Qaga, Jebel (mt.), Sudan 59/C5
Adaut, Indon. 85/J7
Adavale, Queens. 95/C5
Adaza, Iowa (†50050) 229/E4
Adda (riv.), Italy 34/B2
Adda (riv.), Sudan 111/D6
Addanki, India 68/D5
Addieville, Ill. (62214) 222/D5
Addington, Okla. (73520) 288/L6
Addis, La. (70710) 238/J2
Addis Ababa (cap.), Eth., 3/L5
Addis Ababa (cap.), Eth. 111/G6
Addis Ababa (cap.), Eth. 102/F4
Addis Alam, Eth. 111/G6
Addison, Ala. (35540) 194/D2
Addison, Conn. (†06033) 210/E2
Addison, Ill. (60101) 222/A2
Addison▵, Maine (04606) 242/H6
Addison, Maine (04606) 242/H6
Addison, Mich. (49220) 250/E7
Addison, N.Y. (14801) 276/F6
Addison, Ohio (45610) 284/F8
Addison, Pa. (15411) 294/D6
Addison, Texas (75001) 302/G1
Addison (co.), Vt. 268/A3
Addison▵, Vt. (†05491) 268/A3
Addison, Vt. (†05491) 268/A3
Addison (Webster Springs), W. Va. (†26288) 313/F6
Addi Ugri, Eth. 59/C7
Ad Diwaniya, Iraq 66/D5
Addo Nat'l Park, S. Africa 118/D6
Addor, N.C. (†28373) 281/L4
Addy, Wash. (99101) 310/H2
Addyston, Ohio (45001) 284/B9
Ade, Ind. (†47922) 227/C3
Adel, Ga. (31620) 216/F8
Adel, Iowa (50003) 229/E5
Adel, Oreg. (97620) 291/H5
Adelaida, Cuba 158/F2
Adelaide (isl.), Ant. 5/C15
Adelaide, Australia, 3/S7
Adelaide (cap.), S. Aust., 88/D7
Adelaide (cap.), S. Aust., 94/B6
Adelaide (pen.), N.W.T. 187/J3
Adelaide, S. Africa 118/D6
Adelaide River, Aust. 88/E2
Adelaide River, No. Terr. 93/B2
Adelanto, Calif. (92301) 204/H9
Adelboden, Switz. 39/E3
Adele (isl.), Aust. 88/C3
Adele (isl.), W. Aust. 92/C1
Adélie Coast (reg.), Ant. 5/C7
Adeline, Ill. (†61047) 222/D1
Adeline, La. (†70544) 238/G7
Adell, Wis. (53001) 317/L8
Adelong, N.S.W. 97/D4
Adelphi, Jam. 158/H5
Adelphi, Ohio (43101) 284/E7
Adelphia, N.J. (07710) 273/E3
Aden (gulf), 3/M5
Aden (gulf), 54/H8
Aden (gulf), 102/G3
Aden (gulf), Afars Issas 111/J5
Aden (gulf), Somalia 115/J1
Aden (cap.), P.D.R. Yemen 59/E7
Aden (cap.), P.D.R. Yemen, 54/H8
Aden, Alta. 182/E5
Adena, Ohio (43901) 284/J5
Adenau, W. Ger. 22/B3
Adger, Ala. (35006) 194/D4
Adhaim (riv.), Iraq 66/D3
Adi (isl.), Indon. 85/J6
Adícora, Ven. 124/D2
Adige (riv.), Italy 34/C2
Adigrat, Eth. 111/G5
Adilabad, India 68/D5
Adilcevaz, Turkey 63/K3
Adimi, U.S.S.R. 48/O5
Adin, Calif. (96006) 204/E2
Adinkerke, Belg. 27/A6
Adin Khel, Afgh. 59/J3
Adirondack, N.Y. (12808) 276/N3
Adirondack (mts.), N.Y. 276/M3
Adi Ugri, Eth. 111/G5
Adiyaman (prov.), Turkey 63/H4
Adiyaman, Turkey 63/H4
Adjuntas, P. Rico 156/F1
Adjuntas, P. Rico 161/B2
Adlatok (bay), Newf. 166/B2
Adlavik (isls.), Newf. 166/C2
Admiral, Sask. 181/C6
Admiral's Beach, Newf. 166/D2
Admiralty (inlet), 163/H1
Admiralty (isl.), Alaska 196/M1
Admiralty (gulf), Aust. 88/C2
Admiralty (isls.), N.S.W. 97/J1
Admiralty (inlet), N.W.T. 187/K2
Admiralty (gulf), W. Aust. 92/D1
Admiralty (isls.), Terr. N.G., 87/E6
Admiralty (inlet), Wash. 310/B2
Admire, Kans. (66830) 232/F3
Admont, Austria 41/C3
Adna, Wash. (98522) 310/B4
Ado, Nigeria 106/E7
Adok, Sudan 111/F6
Adola, Eth. 111/G6
Adolfo Alsina, Arg. 143/D4
Adolph, Minn. (55701) 254/F4
Adolph, W. Va. (26247) 313/F5
Adolphus, Ky. (42120) 237/J7
Adona, Ark. (72001) 203/E3
Adonara (isl.), Indon. 85/G7
Adoni, India 68/D5
Adony, Hung. 41/E3
Adorf, E. Ger. 22/E3
Adour (riv.), France 28/C6
Adra, Spain 33/E4
Adrano, Italy 34/E6
Adrar, Alg. 106/D3
Adrar (reg.), Mauritania 106/B4
Adrar, 102/B2
Adrar des Iforas (plat.), Alg. 106/E5
Adrar des Iforas (plat.), Mali 106/E5
Adré, Chad 111/D5
Adria, Italy 34/D2
Adrian, Ga. (31002) 216/G5
Adrian, Ill. (62310) 222/B3
Adrian, Mich. (49221) 250/F7
Adrian, Minn. (56110) 254/C7
Adrian, Mo. (64720) 261/D6
Adrian, N. Dak. (58410) 283/O6
Adrian, Ohio (44801) 284/D3
Adrian, Oreg. (97901) 291/K4
Adrian, Pa. (16210) 294/D4
Adrian, S.C. (†29526) 296/J4
Adrian, Texas (79001) 302/B2
Adrian, W. Va. (26210) 313/F5
Adriatic (sea), 7/F4
Adriatic (sea), Alb. 45/B4
Adriatic (sea), Italy 34/E3
Adriatic (sea), Yugo. 45/B4
Aduwa, Eth. 59/C7
Advance, Ind. (46102) 227/D5
Advance, Mich. (†49712) 250/D3
Advance, Mo. (63730) 261/N8
Advance, N.C. (27006) 281/J3
Advent, W. Va. (25231) 313/C5
Adventure (bay), Chile 138/D5
Adventure, Guyana 131/B2
Advocate Harbour, N.S. 169/D3
Adwa, Eth. 111/G5
Adwa, 102/F3
Adygey Aut. Obl., U.S.S.R. 48/D5
Adygey Aut. Obl., U.S.S.R. 52/F6
Adzhar A.S.S.R., U.S.S.R. 48/E5
Adzhar A.S.S.R., U.S.S.R. 52/F6
Aeber (creek), S. Dak. 298/G4
Aegean (sea), 54/F6
Aegean (sea), Greece, 7/G5
Aegean (sea), Greece 45/G6
Aegean (sea), Turkey 63/A3
Aegean Islands (reg.), Greece 45/G6
Aeneas, Wash. (98810) 310/F2
Aennofield, Br. Col. 184/G2
AErø (isl.), Den. 21/D8
AErøskøbing, Den. 21/D8
Aesch, Switz. 39/F2
Aeschi bei Spiez, Switz. 39/E3
Aetna, Alta. 182/D5
Aetna, Tenn. (†37033) 237/G9
'Afaq, Iraq 66/D4
AFARS AND ISSAS, TERR. OF THE, 111/H5
Afars and Issas, Terr. of the, 3/L5
AFARS and ISSAS, TERR. OF THE, 102/G3
Afflolé (reg.), Mauritania 106/B5
Affoltern am Albis, Switz. 39/F2
Affoltern im Emmental, Switz. 39/E2
Affric (lake), Scot. 15/G5
Affton, Mo. (63123) 261/P3
Afghanistan, 3/N4
Afghanistan, 54/K6
AFGHANISTAN, 59/H3
AFGHANISTAN, 68/A2
Afgoi, Somalia 115/J3
Afikpo, Nigeria 106/F7
Afiqim, Israel 65/D2
Åfjord, Norway 18/G5
Aflex, Ky. (41510) 237/S5
Afmadu, Somalia 115/H3
Afognak (isl.), Alaska 196/H3
Africa, 3/K4
AFRICA, 102
Afşin, Turkey 63/G3
Afton, Iowa (50830) 229/E6
Afton, La. (†71282) 238/H2
Afton, Mich. (49705) 250/E3
Afton, Minn. (55001) 254/F6
Afton, N.Y. (13730) 276/J6
Afton, Okla. (74331) 288/S1
Afton, Tenn. (37616) 237/R8
Afton, Texas (79220) 302/D4
Afton, Va. (22920) 307/L4
Afton, Wis. (53501) 317/H10
Afton, Wyo. (83110) 319/B3
Afuá, Braz. 132/D3
'Afula, Israel 65/C2
Afyon, Turkey 59/B2
Afyon, Turkey 63/D3
Afyonkarahisar (prov.), Turkey 63/D3
Agadem, 102/D3
Agadem (well), Niger 106/G5
Agadès, 102/C3
Agadès, Niger 106/F5
Agadir, 102/A1
Agadir, Mor. 106/C2
Agaña (cap.), Guam, 87/E4
Agano (riv.), Japan 81/J4
Agar, S. Dak. (57520) 298/J4
Agartala, India 68/G4
Agassiz (peak), Ariz. 198/D3
Agassiz, Br. Col. 184/M3
Agassiz (mt.), Utah 304/D3
Agate, Colo. (80101) 208/M4
Agate, N. Dak. (58310) 283/L2
Agate, Nebr. (†69346) 264/A2
Agate Beach, Oreg. (97320) 291/C3
Agate Fossil Beds Nat'l Mon., Nebr. 264/A2
Agats, Indon. 85/K7
Agatti (isl.), India 68/C6
Agattu (isl.), Alaska 196/J3
Agattu (str.), Alaska 196/J3
Agawa Bay, Ont. 175/D3
Agawa Bay, Ont. 177/J5
Agawam▵, Mass. (01001) 249/D4
Agawam (riv.), Mass. 249/M5
Agboville, Ivory Coast 106/D7
Agdam, U.S.S.R. 52/G6
Agde, France 28/E6
Agen, France 28/D5
Agency, Iowa (52530) 229/J7
Agency, Mo. (64401) 261/C3
Agency (lake), Oreg. 291/E5
Agenda, Kans. (66930) 232/E2
Ageo, Japan 81/O2
Ägeri (lake), Switz. 39/G2
Agger, Den. 21/B4
Aghadoe, Ire. 17/C7
Aghadowey, N. Ire. 17/H1
Aghagower, Ire. 17/C4
Agha Jari, Iran 66/F5
Aginsk Nat'l Okr., U.S.S.R. 48/M4
Aginskoye, U.S.S.R. 48/M4
Agiobampo (bay), Mex. 150/E3
Agira, Italy 34/E6
Ağlasun, Turkey 63/D4
Ağli, Turkey 63/E2
Agmar (well), Mauritania 106/B3
Agness, Oreg. (97406) 291/C5
Agno, Phil. 82/B2
Agnone, Italy 34/E4
Agnos, Ark. (72510) 203/G1
Agoo, Phil. 82/C2
Agordat, Eth. 59/C6
Agordat, Eth. 111/G4
Agra, India, 54/L7
Agra, India 68/D3
Agra, Kans. (67621) 232/C2
Agra, Okla. (74824) 288/N3
Agraciada, Urug. 145/A4
Agrado, Col. 126/C6
Agramonte, Cuba 158/D1
Ágreda, Spain 33/E2
Ağri (prov.), Turkey 63/K3
Ağri (Karaköse), Turkey 63/K3
Agricola, Kans. (66831) 232/G3
Agricola, Miss. (†39452) 256/G9
Agrigento (prov.), Italy 34/D6
Agrigento, Italy 34/D6
Agrihan (isl.), Pac. Is., 87/E4
Agrínion, Greece 45/E6
Agropoli, Italy 34/E4
Agryz, U.S.S.R. 52/H3
Agua Caliente, Ariz. (†85333) 198/B6

Alexandretta 323

Agua Caliente Ind. Res., Calif. 204/J10
Aguachica, Col. 126/D3
Aguada, P. Rico 161/A1
Aguada de Pasajeros, Cuba 158/D2
Aguada Grande, Ven. 124/D2
Aguadas, Col. 126/C5
Agua de Dios, Col. 126/C5
Aguadilla, P. Rico 156/F1
Aguadilla (dist.), P. Rico 161/A1
Aguadilla, P. Rico 161/A1
Aguadilla (bay), P. Rico 161/A1
Agua Dulce, Mex. 150/M7
Aguadulce, Pan. 154/G6
Agua Dulce, Texas (78330) 302/F10
Agua Fria (riv.), Ariz. 198/C5
Agua Fría, Ven. 124/D2
Agualeguas, Mex. 150/J3
Agua Linda, Ven. 124/E5
Aguán (riv.), Hond. 154/D3
Aguanaval (riv.), Mex. 150/H4
Aguanish, Que. 174/E2
Aguanus (riv.), Que. 174/E2
Aguanus (riv.), Newf. 166/B3
Agua Prieta, Mex. 150/E1
Aguaray-guazú (riv.), Par. 144/C5
Aguarico (riv.), Col. 126/B7
Aguarico (riv.), Ec. 128/D3
Aguasay, Ven. 124/G3
Aguas Blancas, Chile 138/B4
Aguas Buenas, P. Rico 161/E2
Aguas Calientes, Cerro (mt.), Chile 138/C4
Aguascalientes, Mex., 146/H7
Aguascalientes (state), Mex. 150/H6
Aguascalientes, Mex. 150/H6
Aguas Corrientes, Urug. 145/A6
Aguaytía (riv.), Peru 128/E7
Agudos, Braz. 135/B3
Águeda, Port. 33/B2
Agueda (riv.), Port. 33/C2
Agueda (riv.), Spain 33/C2
Agueraktem (well), Mali 106/C4
Agueraktem (well), Mauritania 106/C4
Aguila, Ariz. (85320) 198/B5
Aguilar, Colo. (81020) 208/K8
Aguilar, Spain 33/D4
Aguilares, Arg. 143/C2
Águilas, Spain 33/F4
Aguililla, Mex. 150/H7
Aguja, La (cape), Col. 126/C2
Aguja (pt.), Peru, 3/E6
Aguja (pt.), Peru, 120/B3
Aguja (pt.), Peru 128/B5
Agulhas (cape), 102/D8
Agulhas (cape), S. Africa 118/B6
Agusan (prov.), Phil. 82/E6
Agusan (riv.), Phil. 82/E6
Agusan Canyon, Phil. 82/E6
Agustín Codazzi, Col. 126/D3
Agutaya, Phil. 82/C5
Agutaya (isl.), Phil. 82/C5
Ahaggar (range), Alg. 106/F4
Ahaggar (range), 102/C2
Ahar, Iran 66/E1
Ahascragh, Ire. 17/E5
Ahau, Fiji, 87/H7
Ahaura, N.Z. 101/C5
Ahaus, W. Ger. 22/B2
Aherlow (riv.), Ire. 17/E7
Ah-Gwah-Ching, Minn. (56430) 254/D3
Ahipara, N.Z. 101/D1
Ahlat, Turkey 63/K3
Ahlbeck, E. Ger. 22/F2
Ahlen, W. Ger. 22/B3
Ahmadabad, India, 3/N4
Ahmadabad, India, 54/K7
Ahmadabad, India 68/C4
Ahmadnagar, India 68/C5
Ahmadpur East, Pak. 68/C3
Ahmeek, Mich. (49901) 250/A1
Ahmic (lake), Ont. 177/E2
Ahoghill, N. Ire. 17/J2
Ahoskie, N.C. (27910) 281/P2
Ahousat, Br. Col. 184/D5
Ahpa, China 77/F5
Ahrensburg, W. Ger. 22/D2
Ahsahka, Idaho (83520) 220/B3
Ahtanum (creek), Wash. 310/D4
Ähtäri, Fin. 18/N5
Ahua (pt.), Hawaii 218/B4
Ahuacatlán, Mex. 150/G6
Ahuachapán, El Salv. 154/B4
Ahuás, Hond. 154/E3
Ahurei, Fr. Poly., 87/M8
Åhus, Sweden 18/J9
Ahuzzam, Israel 65/B4
Ahvaz, Iran 66/M4
Ahvenanmaa (prov.), Fin. 18/L6
Ahwa, India 68/C4
Ahwahnee, Calif. (93601) 204/F6
Ahwar, P.D.R. Yemen 59/E7
Ahwaz, Iran 59/E3
Ahwaz, Iran 66/F5
Ai-Ais, S.W. Afr. 118/B5
Aialik (bay), Alaska 196/C1
Aiama (lake), Braz. 132/H9
Aibonito, P. Rico 161/D2
Aicheng, China 77/G8
Aichi (pref.), Japan 81/H6
Aid, Mo. (†63825) 261/M9
Aid, Ohio (†45645) 284/F8
Aiea, Hawaii (96701) 218/B3
Aigen, Austria 41/B2
Aigle, Switz. 39/C4
Aiguá, Urug. 145/E5
Aiguá (riv.), Urug. 145/E4
Aiguille d'Argentière (mt.), Switz. 39/C5
Aigun, China, 54/R5
Aigun, China 77/L1
Aihui (Aigun), China 77/L1
Aija, Peru 128/D7
Aijal, India 68/G4
Aikawa, Japan 81/H4
Aiken (co.), S.C. 296/D4
Aiken, S.C. (29801) 296/D4
Aikens (lake), Man. 179/G3
Aikin, Md. (†21903) 245/O2
Aileron, No. Terr. 93/C7
Ailey, Ga. (30410) 216/G6
Ailinglapalap (atoll), Pac. Is., 87/G5
Aillon (lake), Que. 172/C2
Ailsa Craig, Ont. 177/C4
Ailsa Craig (isl.), Scot. 15/F9
Ailuk (atoll), Pac. Is., 87/H4
Aimogasta, Arg. 143/C2
Aimwell, La. (71401) 238/G3
Ain (dept.), France 28/F4
Ain (riv.), France 28/F4
Ainabo, Somalia 115/J2
Aina Haina, Hawaii (96821) 218/F2
'Ain al Mubarrak, Saudi Ar. 59/C5
Ainaži, U.S.S.R. 53/C2
Aïn-Béïda, Alg. 106/F1
Aïn ben Tili (well), Mauritania 106/C3
Aïn Dawa (well), Libya 111/D3
'Ain el 'Arab, Syria 63/H4
Ain-Galakka, Chad 111/C4
Aïn-Sefra, Alg. 106/D2
Ainsworth, Br. Col. 184/J5
Ainsworth, Iowa (52201) 229/K6
Ainsworth, Nebr. (69210) 264/D2
Aïn-Témouchent, Alg. 106/D1
Aïoun el Atrous, Mauritania 106/C5
Aipe, Col. 126/C6
Aiquile, Bol. 136/C6
Aiquina, Chile 138/B3
Air (plat.), 102/C3
Air (mts.), Niger 106/F5
Aird (pt.), Scot. 15/D4
Airdrie, Alta. 182/C4
Airdrie, 10/B1
Airdrie, Scot. 15/D2
Aire (riv.), Eng. 13/F4
Aire (riv.), 10/F4
Aire-sur-l'Adour. France 28/C6
Airey, Md. (†21613) 245/O6
Air Force (isl.), N.W.T. 187/L3
Air Force Academy, Colo. 208/K5
Airlie, Oreg. (†97361) 291/D3
Airolo, Switz. 39/G3
Airport Drive, Mo. (†64836) 261/C8
Airville, Pa. (17302) 294/K6
Airway Heights, Wash. (99001) 310/H3
Aisén (prov.), Chile 138/D6
Aishihik, Yukon 187/E3
Aišiškes, U.S.S.R. 53/C3
Aisne (dept.), France 28/E3
Aisne (riv.), France 28/E3
Aitape, Terr. N.G. 85/B6
Aitape, Terr. N.G., 87/E6
Aitkin (co.), Minn. 254/E4
Aitkin, Minn. (56431) 254/E4
Aitutaki (atoll), Cook Is., 87/K7
Aiud, Rum. 45/F2
Aix (mt.), Wash. 310/D4
Aix-en-Provence, France 28/F6
Aix-les-Bains, France 28/G5
Aiyansh, Br. Col. 184/C2
Aíyina, Greece 45/F7
Aíyion, Greece 45/F6
Aizpute, U.S.S.R. 53/A2
Aizuwakamatsu, Japan 81/J5
Ajaccio, France, 7/E4
Ajaccio, France 28/B7
Ajaccio (gulf), France 28/B7
Ajalpan, Mex. 150/L7
Ajana, Aust. 88/B5
Ajana, W. Aust. 92/A5
Ajanta, India 68/D4
Ajax, Ont. 177/F4
Ajax, La. (†71450) 238/D3
Ajedabia, Libya 111/D1
Aji Chai (riv.), Iran 66/E1
Ajigasawa, Japan 81/J3
'Ajja, Jordan 65/C3
Ajka, Hung. 41/D3
'Ajlun (dist.), Jordan 65/D3
'Ajlun, Jordan 65/D3
'Ajlun (range), Jordan 65/D3
'Ajman (cap.), Trucial States 59/G4
Ajmer, India, 54/L7
Ajmer, India 68/C3
Ajo, Ariz. (85321) 198/C6
Ajoewa, Sur. 131/C4
Ajoupa-Bouillon, Mart. 161/C5
Aju (isls.), Indon. 85/J5
Ak (mts.), Turkey 63/G3
Akabira, Japan 81/K2
Akan Nat'l Park, Japan 81/M2
Akarai (mts.), Guyana 131/B5
Akaroa, N.Z. 101/D5
Akashi, Japan 81/H8
Akaska, S. Dak. (57420) 298/J3
Akçaabat, Turkey 63/H2
Akçadağ, Turkey 63/G3
Akçakale, Turkey 63/H4
Akçakoca, Turkey 63/D2
Akçay, Turkey 63/C4
Akçay (riv.), Turkey 63/C4
Akdağ (mt.), Turkey 59/A2
Ak Dağ (mts.), Turkey 59/C2
Akdağ (mt.), Turkey 63/C4
Akdağ (mt.), Turkey 63/E4
Akdağmadeni, Turkey 63/F3
Akeley, Minn. (56433) 254/D3
Akeley, Pa. (†16345) 294/D2
Aken, E. Ger. 22/D3
Akers, La. (70421) 238/N2
Akershus (co.), Norway 18/D4
Aketi, Dem. Rep. of the Congo. 115/D3
Akhaltsikhe, U.S.S.R. 52/F6
Akhdar, Jebel (range), Oman 59/G5
Akhdar, Saudi Ar. 59/C4
Akhdar, Jebel (mts.), Libya 111/D1
Akhiok, Alaska (99615) 196/H3
Akhisar, Turkey 63/B3
Akhmim, U.A.R. 59/B4
Akhmim, U.A.R. 111/F2
Akhtopol, Bulg. 45/H4
Akhtubinsk, U.S.S.R. 52/G5
Akhty, U.S.S.R. 52/G6
Akhtyrka, U.S.S.R. 52/E4
Aki, Japan 81/F7
Akiachak, Alaska (99551) 196/F2
Akiak, Alaska (99552) 196/F2
Akimiski (isl.), 163/H5
Akim Oda, Ghana 106/D7
Akin, Ill. (62805) 222/E6
Akins, Okla. (†74955) 288/S3
Akita, Japan, 54/S6
Akita (pref.), Japan 81/J4
Akita, Japan 81/J4
Akitio, N.Z. 101/F4
Akjoujt, Mauritania 106/B5
Akkerman (Belgorod-Dnestrovskiy), U.S.S.R. 52/D5
Akkeshi, Japan 81/M2
Akko (Acre), Israel 65/C2
Akkrum, Neth. 27/H2
Aklan (prov.), Phil. 82/D5
Aklavik, 163/C2
Aklavik, Canada, 4/C16
Aklavik, N.W.T. 187/E3
Aklavik, Yukon, 146/E3
Akmolinsk (Tselinograd), U.S.S.R. 48/H4
Akobo (riv.), Eth. 111/F6
Akobo, Sudan 111/F6
Akobo (riv.), Sudan 111/F6
Akola, India 68/D4
Akolmiut (Kasigluk), Alaska (†99609) 196/F2
Akpatok (isl.), 163/K3
Akpatok (isl.), N.W.T. 187/M3
Akpazar, Turkey 63/H3
Akpinar, Turkey 63/D5
Akra, N. Dak. (58211) 283/P2
Akranes, Ice. 21/B1
Akreïjit, Mauritania 106/C5
Akrítas (cape), Greece 45/E7
Akron, Ala. (35441) 194/C5
Akron, Colo. (80720) 208/N2
Akron, Ind. (46910) 227/E2
Akron, Iowa (51001) 229/A3
Akron, Mich. (48701) 250/F5
Akron, N.Y. (14001) 276/C4
Akron, Ohio, 188/K2
Akron, Ohio (*44301) 284/G3
Akron, Pa. (17501) 294/K5
Aksaray, Turkey 63/F3
Akşehir, Turkey 59/B2
Akşehir, Turkey 63/D3
Akşehir (lake), Turkey 63/D3
Akseki, Turkey 63/D4
Aksha, U.S.S.R. 48/M4
Aksu (riv.), Turkey 63/D4
Aksum, Eth. 59/C7
Aksum, Eth. 111/G5
Aktí (pen.), Greece 45/G5
Aktyubinsk, U.S.S.R. 48/F4
Aktyubinsk, U.S.S.R., 54/J5
Aku, Nigeria 106/F7
Akun (isl.), Alaska 196/E4
Akune, Japan 81/E7
Akure, Nigeria 106/F7
Akureyri, Ice., 4/C10
Akureyri, Ice., 7/C2
Akureyri, Ice. 21/C1
Akutan, Alaska (99553) 196/E4
Akutan (isl.), Alaska 196/E4
Akutan (passg.), Alaska 196/E4
Akviran, Turkey 63/E4
Akyazi, Turkey 63/D2
Ål, Norway 18/F6
Ala (riv.), Phil. 82/E7
Alabam, Ark. (†72740) 203/C1
Alabama, 188/J4
ALABAMA, 194
Alabama (riv.), Ala., 146/K6
Alabama (riv.), Ala., 188/J4
Alabama (riv.), Ala. 194/D6
Alabama (state), U.S., 146/K6
Alabama and Coushatta Ind. Res., Texas 302/K7
Alabaster, Ala. (35007) 194/E4
Alabaster, Mich. (48764) 250/F4
Alabat, Phil. 82/D3
Alabat (isl.), Phil. 82/D3
Alaca, Turkey 63/F2
Alacahan, Turkey 63/G3
Alaçam, Turkey 63/F2
Alachua (co.), Fla. 212/D2
Alachua, Fla. (32615) 212/D2
Alacrán (reef), Mex. 150/P5
Alacranes, Cuba 158/D1
Aladağ (mt.), Turkey 63/F4
Aladagh, Kuh-i- (mt.), Iran 59/G2
Aladagh, Kuh-i- (mts.), Iran 66/K2
Ala Dağlari (mts.), Turkey 63/F4
Aladdin, Wyo. (82710) 319/H1
Alaejos, Spain 33/D2
Alagir, U.S.S.R. 52/F6
Alagoa Grande, Braz. 132/H4
Alagoas (state), Braz. 132/G5
Alagoinhas, Braz., 120/G4
Alagoinhas, Braz. 132/G6
Alagón, Spain 33/F2
Alagón (riv.), Spain 33/C2
Al Ahqaf (Bahr es Safi) (des.), Saudi Ar. 59/E6
Al 'Ain, Saudi Ar. 59/C4
Alajuela, C. Rica 154/E6
Alakanuk, Alaska (99554) 196/E2
Alakol' (lake), U.S.S.R. 48/J5
Alakol' (lake), U.S.S.R., 54/M5
Al 'Ala, Saudi Ar. 59/C4
Alalakeiki (chan.), Hawaii 218/J3
Alalapadu, Sur. 131/C4
Alamagan (isl.), Pac. Is., 87/E4
Alamance (co.), N.C. 281/L3
Alamance, N.C. (27201) 281/K2
Alameda, Calif., 188/B3
Alameda (co.), Calif. 204/D6
Alameda, Calif. (94501) 204/J2
Alameda (creek), Calif. 204/K3
Alameda, N. Mex. (87114) 274/C3
Alameda, Sask. 181/J6
Alamikamba, Nic. 154/E4
Alamo (res.), Ariz. 198/B4
Alamo (riv.), Calif. 204/K10
Alamo, Ga. (30411) 216/G6
Alamo, Ind. (47916) 227/C5
Alamo, Mex. 150/L6
Alamo, N. Dak. (58830) 283/D2
Alamo, Nev. (89001) 266/F5
Alamo, Tenn. (38001) 237/C9
Alamo, Texas (78516) 302/F11
Alamo-Danville, Calif. (94507) 204/K2
Alamogordo, N. Mex. (88310) 274/C6
Alamogordo (dam), N. Mex. 274/E4
Alamogordo (res.), N. Mex. 274/E4
Alamo Heights, Texas (78209) 302/F8
Alamos, Mex. 150/E3
Alamosa (co.), Colo. 208/H7
Alamosa, Colo. (81101) 208/H8
Alamosa (creek), Colo. 208/G8
Alamosa (riv.), N. Mex. 274/B5
Alamota, Kans. (67830) 232/B3
Åland (isls.), Fin. 18/L6
Alanje, Pan. 154/F6
Alanreed, Texas (79002) 302/D2
Alanson, Mich. (49706) 250/E3
Alanthus Grove, Mo. (†64489) 261/D2
Alanya, Turkey 59/B2
Alanya, Turkey 63/D4
Alaotra (lake), Malag. Rep. 118/H3
Alapaha (riv.), Fla. 212/C1
Alapaha, Ga. (31622) 216/F8
Alapaha (riv.), Ga. 216/F7
Alaqua (creek), Fla. 212/C6
Alargate (reef), Nic. 154/F3
Alarka, N.C. (†28713) 281/C4
Alas (str.), Indon. 85/F7
Alaşehir, Turkey 63/C3
Alashan (des.), China 77/F4
Alaska (state), 4/C17
Alaska, 188/C5
ALASKA, 196
Alaska (pen.), Alaska, 146/C4
Alaska (gulf), Alaska, 188/D6
Alaska (pen.), Alaska, 188/C6
Alaska (range), Alaska, 188/C6
Alaska (gulf), Alaska 196/K3
Alaska (range), Alaska 196/H2
Alaska (pen.), Alaska 196/G3
Alaska, Mich. (†49316) 250/D6
Alaska (state), U.S., 3/B2
Alaska (gulf), U.S., 4/D17
Alaska (mts.), U.S., 4/C17
Alaska (pen.), U.S., 4/D18
Alaska (state), U.S., 146/C4
Alaska Highway, Alaska 196/K2
Alaska Highway, Br. Col. 184/F1
Alaska Highway, Yukon 187/E3
Alassio, Italy 34/A2
Alatna, Alaska (†99720) 196/H1
Alatna (riv.), Alaska 196/H1
Alatri, Italy 34/D4
Alatyr', U.S.S.R. 52/G4
Al 'Auda, Saudi Ar. 59/E4
Alausí, Ec. 128/C4
Álava (prov.), Spain 33/E1
Alava (cape), Wash., 188/A1
Alava (cape), Wash. 310/A2
Alavus, Fin. 18/N5
Alayor, Spain 33/J3
Al 'Azair, Iraq 66/E5
Al'Aziziya, Iraq 59/E3
Al 'Aziziya, Iraq 66/D4
Alba, Italy 34/B2
Alba, Mich. (49611) 250/E4
Alba, Mo. (64830) 261/D8
Alba, N.S. 169/H3
Alba, Pa. (16910) 294/J2
Alba, Texas (75410) 302/J5
Albacete, Spain, 7/D5
Albacete (prov.), Spain 33/E3
Albacete, Spain 33/F3
Alba de Tormes, Spain 33/D2
Albaida, Spain 33/F3
Alba Iulia, Rum. 45/F2
Albalate del Arzobispo, Spain 33/F2
Alban, Ont. 177/D1
Albanel, Que. 172/E1
Albanel (lake), Que. 174/C2
Albania, 3/K3
Albania, 7/G4
ALBANIA, 45/E5
Albano (lake), Italy 34/F7
Albano Laziale, Italy 34/F7
Albany, Australia, 87/B9
Albany, Aust. 88/B6
Albany (riv.), 163/H5
Albany, Calif. (94706) 204/J2
Albany, Jam. 158/J6
Albany (riv.), Ont. 175/C2
Albany, Ga. (*31701) 216/D7
Albany, Ill. (61230) 222/C2
Albany, Ind. (47320) 227/G4
Albany, Ky. (42602) 237/L7
Albany, La. (70711) 238/M1
Albany, Minn. (56307) 254/D5
Albany, Mo. (64402) 261/D2
Albany△, N.H. (†03864) 268/E4
Albany, N.H. (†03864) 268/E4
Albany (cap.), N.Y., 146/L5
Albany (cap.), N.Y., 188/M2
Albany (co.), N.Y. 276/M5
Albany (cap.), N.Y. (*12201) 276/N5
Albany, N.Z. 101/B1
Albany, W. Aust. 92/B6
Albany, Ohio (45710) 284/F7
Albany, Okla. (74721) 288/O7
Albany (riv.), Ont., 146/K4
Albany, Oreg., 188/B2
Albany, Oreg. (97321) 291/D3
Albany, P.E.I. 169/E2
Albany, Texas (76430) 302/E5
Albany△, Vt. (05820) 268/C2
Albany, Vt. (05820) 268/C2
Albany, Wis. (53502) 317/G10
Albany (co.), Wyo. 319/G4
Albany, Wyo. (†82055) 319/F4
Albany N.A.S., Ga. 216/E7
Albarracín, Spain 33/F2
Albatross (bay), Aust. 88/G2
Albatross (pt.), N.Z. 101/E3
Albatross (bay), Queens. 95/B2
Albay (prov.), Phil. 82/D4
Albay (gulf), Phil. 82/D4
Albee, S. Dak. (57210) 298/S3
Albemarle (pt.), Ec. 128/B9
Albemarle (sound), N.C., 188/L3
Albemarle, N.C. (28001) 281/J4
Albemarle (sound), N.C. 281/S2
Albemarle (co.), Va. 307/L5
Albenga, Italy 34/B3
Albeni Falls (dam), Idaho 220/B1
Alberdi, Par. 144/D6
Alberene, Va. (†22959) 307/L5
Alberga, Aust. 88/E5
Alberga, S. Aust. 94/D2
Alberga, The (riv.), Aust. 88/E5
Alberga, The (riv.), S. Aust. 94/D2
Alberhill, Calif. (†92330) 204/E11
Alberni, Br. Col. 184/H3
Alberni (inlet), Br. Col. 184/H3
Albers, Ill. (62215) 222/D5
Albert (canal), Belg. 27/F6
Albert (lake), 102/E4
Albert (lake), Que. 172/C3
Albert, France 28/E2
Albert, Kans. (67511) 232/C3
Albert (co.), N. Br. 170/F3
Albert, N. Mex. (87733) 274/F3
Albert, N.S.W. 97/D3
Albert (lake), Dem. Rep. of the Congo. 115/F3
Albert (lake), Uganda 115/F3
Albert, Okla. (73001) 288/K4
Albert (creek), Wyo. 319/B4
Alberta (mt.), 163/E5
ALBERTA, 182
Alberta, Ala. (36720) 194/D6
Alberta (mt.), Alta. 182/B3
Alberta (prov.), Canada, 146/G4
Alberta, La. (†71016) 238/D2
Alberta, Minn. (56207) 254/B5
Alberta, Va. (23821) 307/N7
Alberta Beach, Alta. 182/C3
Albert Canyon, Br. Col. 184/J4
Albert City, Iowa (50510) 229/C3
Albert Edward (bay), N.W.T. 187/H3
Alberti, Arg. 143/G7
Albertirsa, Hung. 41/E3
Albert Lea, Minn. (56007) 254/E7
Albert Mines, N. Br. 170/F3
Albert Nat'l Park, Dem. Rep. of the Congo. 115/E4
Alberton, Mont. (59820) 262/B3
Alberton, P.E.I. 169/E2
Alberton, S. Africa 118/H6
Albertson‡, N.Y. (11507) 276/R7
Albert Town, Jam. 158/H6
Albertville, Ala. (35950) 194/F2
Albertville, Que. 172/B2
Albertville, France 28/G5
Albertville, Minn. (55301) 254/E5
Albertville, Sask. 181/F2
Albeuve, Switz. 39/D3
Albi, France 28/E6
Albia, Iowa (52531) 229/H6
Albin, Wyo. (82050) 319/H4
Albina, Sur. 131/D3
Albino, Italy 34/B2
Albion, Calif. (95410) 204/B4
Albion, Idaho (83311) 220/E7
Albion (mts.), Idaho 220/E7
Albion, Ill. (62806) 222/E5
Albion, Ind. (46701) 227/G2
Albion, Iowa (50005) 229/H4
Albion△, Maine (04910) 242/E6
Albion, Mich. (49224) 250/E6
Albion, Mont. (†59311) 262/M5
Albion, N.Y. (14411) 276/D4
Albion, Nebr. (68620) 264/F3
Albion, Okla. (74521) 288/R5
Albion, Pa. (16401) 294/B2
Albion, R.I. (02802) 249/H5
Albion, Wash. (99102) 310/H4
Albion, Wis. (†53534) 317/H10
Albocácer, Spain 33/F2
Alborán (isl.), Spain 33/E5
Alborn, Minn. (55702) 254/F4
Albox, Spain 33/E4
Albreda, Br. Col. 184/H4
Albright, Alta. 182/A2
Albright, W. Va. (26519) 313/G3
Albrightsville, Pa. (18210) 294/L3
Albristhorn (mt.), Switz. 39/D4
Albufeira, Port. 33/B4
Albuñol, Spain 33/E4
Albuquerque (cays), Col. 126/A10
Albuquerque, N.Mex., 146/H6
Albuquerque, N. Mex. (*87101) 274/C3
Alburg△, Vt. (05440) 268/A2
Alburg, Vt. (05440) 268/A2
Alburnett, Iowa (52202) 229/K4
Alburquerque, Spain 33/C3
Alburtis, Pa. (18011) 294/L5
Albury, Australia, 87/E9
Albury, Aust. 88/H7
Albury, N.S.W. 97/D5
Albury, N.Z. 101/C6
Alby, Sweden 18/J5
Alca, Peru 128/F10
Alcácer do Sal, Port. 33/B3
Alcalá, Bol. 136/C6
Alcalá de Chivert, Spain 33/G2
Alcalá de Guadaira, Spain 33/D4
Alcalá de Henares, Spain 33/G4
Alcalá de los Gazules, Spain 33/D4
Alcalá la Real, Spain 33/E4
Alcalde, N. Mex. (87511) 274/C2
Alcamo, Italy 34/D6
Alcanar, Spain 33/G2
Alcañices, Spain 33/C2
Alcañiz, Spain 33/F2
Alcântara, Port. 33/A1
Alcántara, Spain 33/C3
Alcantarilla, Spain 33/F4
Alcaraz, Arg. 143/G5
Alcaraz, Spain 33/E3
Alcaraz (range), Spain 33/E3
Alcatraz (isl.), Calif. 204/J2
Alcaudete, Spain 33/D4
Alcázar de San Juan, Spain 33/E3
Alcester, Eng. 13/F5
Alcester, S. Dak. (57001) 298/R7
Alcida, N. Br. 170/E1
Alcira, Spain 33/F3
Alco, Ark. (72610) 203/F2
Alco, La. (71402) 238/D4
Alcoa, Tenn. (37701) 237/N9
Alcobaça, Braz., 120/E3
Alcobaça, Braz. 132/G7
Alcobaça, Port. 33/B3
Alcolu, S.C. (29001) 296/G4
Alcomdale, Alta. 182/C3
Alcona (co.), Mich. 250/F4
Alcona Beach, Ont. 177/E3
Alcones, Chile 138/F5
Alcony, Ohio (†45373) 284/B5
Alcora, Spain 33/F2
Alcorisa, Spain 33/F2
Alcorn, Ky. (40401) 237/O5
Alcorn (co.), Miss. 256/G1
Alcorn College, Miss. (39096) 256/B7
Alcorta, Arg. 143/F6
Alcoutim, Port. 33/C4
Alcova, Wyo. (82620) 319/F3
Alcova (res.), Wyo. 319/F3
Alcoy, Spain 33/F3
Alcudia (bay), Spain 33/H3
Alda, Nebr. (68810) 264/F4
Aldabra (isls.), 102/G6
Aldama, Chihuahua, Mex. 150/G2
Aldama, Tamaulipas, Mex. 150/L5
Aldan, U.S.S.R. 48/N4
Aldan (plat.), U.S.S.R. 48/N4
Aldan (riv.), U.S.S.R. 48/O3
Aldan, Pa. (19018) 294/M7
Aldan (riv.), U.S.S.R., 54/S4
Aldan, U.S.S.R., 54/R4
Aldbrough, Eng. 13/H4
Aldeburgh, 10/G4
Aldeburgh, Eng. 13/J5
Aldeia Nova de São Bento, Port. 33/C4
Alden, Ill. (60001) 222/E1
Alden, Iowa (50006) 229/G4
Alden, Kans. (67512) 232/D3
Alden, Mich. (49612) 250/D4
Alden, Minn. (56009) 254/E7
Alden, N.Y. (14004) 276/C5
Alden Bridge, La. (†71006) 238/C1
Aldenville, Pa. (18401) 294/M2
Alder, Mont. (59710) 262/D5
Alder, Wash. (98301) 310/C4
Alder (lake), Wash. 310/C4
Alder Creek, N.Y. (13301) 276/K4
Alder Flats, Alta. 182/C3
Aldergrove, Br. Col. 184/L3
Alderley, Wis. (†53066) 317/J1
Alderney (isl.), Chan. Is. 13/E8
Alderney (isl.), 10/E6
Alderpoint, Calif. (95411) 204/B3
Alder Point, N.S. 169/H2
Aldershot, 10/F5
Aldershot, Eng. 13/G6
Aldershot, N.S. 169/D3
Alderson, Alta. 182/E4
Alderson, Okla. (74522) 288/P5
Alderson, W. Va. (24910) 313/E7
Aldersville, N.S. 169/D4
Aldersyde, Alta. 182/C4
Aldine, Ind. (†46366) 227/D2
Aldora, Ga. (†30204) 216/D4
Aldouane, N. Br. 170/E2
Aldrich, Ala. (†35115) 194/E4
Aldrich, Minn. (56434) 254/C4
Aldrich, Mo. (65601) 261/F7
Aldridge-Brownhills, 10/G3
Aledo, Ill. (61231) 222/C2
Aledo, Texas (76008) 302/G5
Aleg, Mauritania 106/B5
Alegre, Braz. 132/F8
Alegre, Braz. 135/F2
Alegre (riv.), Par. 144/C3
Alegrete, Braz. 132/B10
'Aleih, Leb. 63/F6
Alejandra, Arg. 143/F5
Alejandría, Bol. 136/C3
Aleknagik, Alaska (99555) 196/G3
Aleksandriya, U.S.S.R. 52/D5
Aleksandrov, U.S.S.R. 52/E3
Aleksandrov Gay, U.S.S.R. 52/G4
Aleksandrovsk-Sakhalinskiy, U.S.S.R. 48/P5
Aleksandrovsk-Sakhalinskiy, U.S.S.R., 54/T4
Aleksandrów Kujawski, Poland 47/D2
Aleksandrów Łódzki, Poland 47/D3
Alekseyevka, U.S.S.R. 52/E4
Aleksin, U.S.S.R. 52/E4
Aleksinac, Yugo. 45/E4
Além Paraíba, Braz. 135/E2
Alençon, France 28/D3
Alenquer, Braz. 132/C3
Alenuihaha (chan.), Hawaii 218/E7
Aleppo, Syria 59/C2
Aleppo (prov.), Syria 63/G4
Aleppo, Syria 63/G4
Aleppo, Syria, 54/G6
Aléria, France 28/B6
Alert, 163/N3
Alert, Canada, 4/A12
Alert, Ind. (†47283) 227/F6
Alert, N.C. (†27589) 281/N2
Alert, N.W.T. 187/M1
Alert (pt.), N.W.T. 187/K1
Alert Bay, Br. Col. 184/D5
Alès, France 28/E5
Alessandria (prov.), Italy 34/B2
Alessandria, Italy 34/B2
Ålesund, Norway 18/D5
Ålesund, Norway, 7/E2
Aletschhorn (mt.), Switz. 39/F4
Aleutian (isls.), Alaska, 188/D6
Aleutian (isls.), Alaska 196/D4
Aleutian (range), Alaska 196/G3
Aleutian (isls.), U.S., 3/A3
Aleutian (isls.), U.S., 4/D18
Alex, Okla. (73002) 288/L5
Alexander (arch.), Alaska, 146/E4
Alexander (arch.), Alaska 196/L1
Alexander (isl.), Ant. 5/B15
Alexander, Ark. (72002) 203/F4
Alexander (lake), Conn. 210/H1
Alexander, Ga. (30801) 216/J4
Alexander (co.), Ill. 222/D6
Alexander, Ill. (62601) 222/D4
Alexander, Iowa (50420) 229/G3
Alexander, Kans. (67513) 232/C3
Alexander△, Maine (†04610) 242/H5
Alexander, Man. 179/B5
Alexander (co.), N.C. 281/G3
Alexander, N.C. (28701) 281/D3
Alexander, N. Dak. (58831) 283/C4
Alexander, N.Y. (14005) 276/D5
Alexander (arch.), U.S., 4/D16
Alexander, W. Va. (26211) 313/F5
Alexander Bay, S. Africa 118/B5
Alexander City, Ala. (35010) 194/G5
Alexander Mills‡, N.C. (28043) 281/F4
Alexandra (falls), N.W.T. 187/G3
Alexandra, N.Z. 101/B6
Alexandra, S. Africa 118/H6
Alexandra, Vic. 97/C5
Alexandra Fiord, 163/N3
Alexandra Fiord, Canada, 4/A13
Alexandra Fiord, N.W.T. 187/L2
Alexandra Land (isl.), U.S.S.R. 48/E1
Alexandra Land (isl.), U.S.S.R., 4/A8
Alexandretta (Iskenderun), Turkey 63/G4
Alexandretta (gulf), Turkey 63/F4

Annville 325

Amargosa, Braz. 132/F6
Amarillas, Cuba 158/D2
Amarillo, Texas, 146/H6
Amarillo, Texas, 188/F3
Amarillo, Texas (*79101) 302/C2
Amarillo A.F.B., Texas 302/C2
Amasa, Mich. (49903) 250/G2
Amasra, Turkey 63/E2
Amasya, Turkey 59/C1
Amasya (prov.), Turkey 63/F2
Amasya, Turkey 63/G2
Amatignak (isl.), Alaska 196/K4
Amatitlán, Guat. 154/B3
Amatlán de los Reyes, Mex. 150/P2
Amay, Belg. 27/G7
Amazon (riv.), 3/G6
Amazon (riv.), Braz., 120/E3
Amazon (riv.), Col. 126/E9
Amazon (riv.), Braz. 132/C3
Amazon (riv.), Peru 128/F4
Amazon, Sask. 181/F4
Amazonas (Amazon) (riv.), Braz., 120/E3
Amazonas (comm.), Col. 126/D8
Amazonas (state), Braz. 132/G9
Amazonas (dept.), Peru 128/C5
Amazonas (terr.), Ven. 124/E5
Amazonia, Mo. (64421) 261/C3
Ambala, India 68/D2
Ambalavao, Malag. Rep. 118/H4
Ambanja, Malag. Rep. 118/H2
Ambarchik, U.S.S.R. 48/R3
Ambarchik, U.S.S.R., 4/B1
Ambato, Ec. 128/C3
Ambato Boina, Malag. Rep. 118/H3
Ambatofinandrahana, Malag. Rep. 118/H4
Ambatolampy, Malag. Rep. 118/H3
Ambatomainty, Malag. Rep. 118/H3
Ambatondrazaka, Malag. Rep. 118/H3
Ambelau (isl.), Indon. 85/H6
Amber, Iowa (52204) 229/L4
Amber (cape), 102/G6
Amber (cape), Malag. Rep. 118/H2
Amber, Okla. (73004) 288/L4
Amber, Wash. (99002) 310/H3
Amberg, W. Ger. 22/D4
Amberg, Wis. (54102) 317/K5
Ambergris (cay), Br. Hond. 154/D1
Ambergris (cay), Turks Caicos Is. 156/D2
Ambérieu-en-Bugey, France 28/F5
Amberley, N.Z. 101/D5
Amberley, Ohio (†45201) 284/C9
Amberson, Pa. (17210) 294/G5
Ambert, France 28/E5
Amber Valley, Alta. 182/D2
Ambia, Ind. (47917) 227/C4
Ambikapur, India 68/E4
Ambil (isl.), Phil. 82/C4
Ambilobe, Malag. Rep. 118/H2
Amble, Eng. 13/F2
Amble, Mich. (†49329) 250/D5
Ambler, Alaska (99786) 196/G1
Ambler, Pa. (19002) 294/M5
Ambleside, 10/E3
Ambleside, Eng. 13/E3
Ambo, Peru 128/D8
Amboasary, Malag. Rep. 118/H4
Ambodifototra, Malag. Rep. 118/J3
Ambohimahasoa, Malag. Rep. 118/H4
Amboina, Indon., 54/R10
Amboina, Indon. 85/H6
Amboise, France 28/D4
Ambon (Amboina), Indon. 85/H6
Amboró, Bol. 136/D6
Ambositra, Malag. Rep. 118/H4
Ambovombe, Malag. Rep. 118/H5
Amboy, Calif. (92304) 204/K9
Amboy, Ga. (†31714) 216/E7
Amboy, Ill. (61310) 222/D2
Amboy, Ind. (46911) 227/F3
Amboy, Minn. (56010) 254/D7
Amboy, W. Va. (26701) 313/G4
Amboy, Wash. (98601) 310/C5
Amboyna (cay), Asia 85/E4
Ambri, Switz. 39/G4
Ambridge, Pa. (15003) 294/B4
Ambriz, Angola 115/B5
Ambriz, 102/D5
Ambrizete, Angola 115/B5
Ambrizete, 102/D5
Ambrose, Ga. (31512) 216/G7
Ambrose, N. Dak. (58833) 283/D2
Ambrym (isl.), New Hebr., 87/G7
Ambunti, Terr. N.G. 85/B6
Amburgey, Ky. (41801) 237/R6
Amchitka (isl.), Alaska, 188/D6
Amchitka (isl.), Alaska 196/K4
Amchitka (passg.), Alaska 196/K4
Am-Dam, Chad 111/D5
Amderma, U.S.S.R. 48/F3
Amderma, U.S.S.R. 52/K1
Ameagle, W. Va. (25004) 313/D7
Amealco, Mex. 150/K6
Ameca, Mex. 150/H6
Amecameca de Juárez, Mex. 150/L1
Amedika Akuse, Ghana 106/E7
Ameghino, Arg. 143/D3
Ameland (isl.), Neth. 27/H2
Amelia (isl.), Fla. 212/E1
Amelia, Italy 34/D3
Amelia, La. (70340) 238/H7
Amelia, Nebr. (68711) 264/F2
Amelia, Ohio (45102) 284/D10
Amelia (co.), Va. 307/M6
Amelia City, Fla. (†32034) 212/E1
Amelia Court House, Va. (23002) 307/N6
Amenia, N. Dak. (58004) 283/R6
Amenia, N.Y. (12501) 276/N7
America, Ill. (†62996) 222/D6
America, Okla. (†71821) 288/S7
American (highlands), Ant., 3/N10
American (riv.), Calif. 204/C8
Americana, Braz. 135/C3
American Corner, Md. (†21632) 245/P5
American Falls (res.), Idaho, 188/D2
American Falls, Idaho (83211) 220/E7
American Falls (res.), Idaho 220/F6
American Fork, Utah (84003) 304/C3
American Highland, Ant. 5/B4
American Samoa, 3/A6
American Samoa, 87/J7
Americus, Ga. (31709) 216/D6
Americus, Ind. (†47901) 227/D3
Americus, Kans. (66835) 232/F3
Americus, Mo. (†65069) 261/J5
Amersfoort, Neth. 27/G4
Amersham, Eng. 13/G6
Amery, 163/G4
Amery, Man. 179/J2
Amery, Wis. (54001) 317/B5
Amery Ice Shelf, Ant., 3/N9
Amery Ice Shelf, Ant. 5/C4
Ames, Iowa (50010) 229/F4
Ames, Kans. (66931) 232/E2
Ames, N.Y. (13317) 276/L5
Ames, Okla. (73718) 288/K2
Amesbury, Alta. 182/D2
Amesbury, Eng. 13/F6
Amesbury△, Mass. (01913) 249/L1
Amesbury, Mass. (01913) 249/L1
Amesville, Conn. (†06031) 210/B1
Amesville, Ohio (45711) 284/F7
Amfilokhía, Greece 45/E6
Ámfissa, Greece 45/F6
Amga, U.S.S.R. 48/O3
Amguid, Alg. 106/F3
Amhara (reg.), Eth. 111/G5
Amherst, 163/K6
Amherst, Colo. (80721) 208/P1
Amherst (isl.), Ont. 177/H3
Amherst△, Maine (†04408) 242/G6
Amherst△, Mass. (01002) 249/E3
Amherst, Mass. (01002) 249/E3
Amherst△, N.H. (03031) 268/D6
Amherst, N.H. (03810) 268/D6
Amherst, N.S. 169/D3
Amherst, Nebr. (68812) 264/E4
Amherst, Burma 72/C3
Amherst (mt.), W. Aust. 92/D2
Amherst, Ohio (44001) 284/F3
Amherst, S. Dak. (57421) 298/O2
Amherst, Texas (79312) 302/B4
Amherst (co.), Va. 307/K5
Amherst, Va. (24521) 307/K5
Amherst, Wis. (54406) 317/H7
Amherstburg, Ont. 177/A5
Amherstdale, W. Va. (25607) 313/C4
Amherst Junction, Wis. (54407) 317/H7
Amherst View, Ont. 177/H3
Amidon, N. Dak. (58620) 283/D7
Amiens, France, 7/E4
Amiens, France 28/D3
Amiens, Sask. 181/D2
Amindivi (isls.), India 68/C6
Aminga, Arg. 143/C2
Amini (isl.), India 68/C6
'Amir, Ras (cape), Libya 111/D1
Amiret, Minn. (56112) 254/C6
Amisk, Alta. 182/E3
Amisk (lake), Sask. 181/M4
Amissville, Va. (22002) 307/M3
Amistad (res.), Mex. 150/J2
Amistad, N. Mex. (88410) 274/F3
Amistad (dam), Texas 302/C8
Amistad (res.), Texas 302/C8
Amistad Nat'l Rec. Area, Texas 302/C8
Amite, La. (70422) 238/K5
Amite (riv.), La. 238/L2
Amite (co.), Miss. 256/C8
Amite (riv.), Miss. 256/C9
Amity, Ark. (71921) 203/D5
Amity, Ga. (†30817) 216/G3
Amity, Ind. (†46131) 227/E6
Amity, Mo. (64422) 261/D3
Amity, Oreg. (97101) 291/D2
Amity, Pa. (15311) 294/B5
Amityville, N.Y. (11701) 276/O9
Åmli, Norway 18/F7
Amlia (isl.), Alaska 196/L4
Amlia (passg.), Alaska 196/L4
Amlikon, Switz. 39/G1
Amlwch, 10/D4
Amlwch, Wales 13/C4
Amma, W. Va. (25005) 313/D5
Amman (cap.), Jordan, 54/G6
Amman (cap.), Jordan 59/C3
Amman (dist.), Jordan 65/D4
Amman (cap.), Jordan 65/D4
Ammanford, Wales 13/C6
Ammersee (lake), W. Ger. 22/D4
Ammie, Ky. (†40933) 237/O6
Ammon, Idaho (83401) 220/G6
Ammon, Va. (23822) 307/N6
Ammonoosuc (riv.), N.H. 268/D3
Amnat, Thai. 72/E4
Amne Machin (mts.), China 77/F5
Amo, Ind. (46103) 227/D5
Amonate, Va. (24601) 307/E6
Amor, Minn. (†56515) 254/C4
Amora, Port. 33/A1
Amorbach, W. Ger. 22/C4
Amoret, Mo. (64722) 261/C6
Amorgós (isl.), Greece 45/G7
Amorita, Okla. (†73723) 288/K1
Amory, Miss. (38821) 256/H3
Amos, 163/J6
Amos, Que. 174/B3
Åmotfors, Sweden 18/H7
Amoy, China, 54/P7
Amoy, China 77/J7
Amozoc de Mota, Mex. 150/N2
Ampana, Indon. 85/G6
Ampanihy, Malag. Rep. 118/G4
Amparo, Braz. 135/C3
Amper (riv.), W. Ger. 22/D4
Amphitrite (isls.), China 85/E2
Amposta, Spain 33/G2
Ampthill, Eng. 13/G5
Amqui, Que. 172/B2
'Amran, Yemen Arab Rep., 59/D6
'Amran, Yemen Arab Rep., 54/H8
'Amrani, Iran 66/L3
Amravati, India 68/D4
Amreli, India 68/C4
Amriswil, Switz. 39/H1
'Amrit, Syria 63/F5
Amritsar, India, 54/L6
Amritsar, India 68/C2
Amrum (isl.), W. Ger. 22/C1
Amsden, Ohio (44803) 284/D3
Amsteg, Switz. 39/G3
Amstelveen, Neth. 27/B5
Amsterdam (isl.), 3/N7
Amsterdam (isl.), 54/L13
Amsterdam, Ga. (31734) 216/D9
Amsterdam, Mo. (64723) 261/D6
Amsterdam, Mont. (†59741) 262/E5
Amsterdam, N.Y. (12010) 276/M5
Amsterdam (cap.), Neth., 7/E3
Amsterdam (cap.), Neth. 27/B4
Amsterdam, Ohio (43903) 284/J5
Amsterdam, Sask. 181/J4
Amstetten, Austria 41/C2
Amston, Conn. (06231) 210/F2
Am-Timan, Chad 111/D5
Amuay, Ven. 124/C2
Amu-Dar'ya (riv.), 3/N3
Amu-Dar'ya (riv.), U.S.S.R. 48/G5
Amu-Dar'ya (riv.), U.S.S.R., 54/K5
Amukta (isl.), Alaska 196/D4
Amukta (passg.), Alaska 196/D4
Amuku (mts.), Guyana 131/B4
Amul, Iran 59/F2
Amul, Iran 66/H2
Amulet, Sask. 181/G6
Amund Ringnes (isl.), 163/M3
Amund Ringnes (isl.), N.W.T. 187/J2
Amundsen (sea), 3/D10
Amundsen (gulf), 163/D1
Amundsen (bay), Ant. 5/C3
Amundsen (sea), Ant. 5/B13
Amundsen (gulf), Canada, 4/B16
Amundsen (gulf), N.W.T., 146/F2
Amundsen (gulf), N.W.T. 187/F2
Amuntai, Indon. 85/F6
Amur (riv.), 3/R3
Amur (riv.), U.S.S.R. 48/O4
Amur (riv.), China 77/L2
'Amur, Wadi (dry riv.), Sudan 111/G4
Amur (riv.), U.S.S.R., 54/R4
Amurang, Indon. 85/G5
Amy, Kans. (†67850) 232/B3
Amya (pass), Burma 72/C4
Amya (pass), Thai. 72/C4
Amyun, Leb. 63/F5
An, Burma 72/B3
'Ana, Iraq 59/D3
'Ana, Iraq 66/B3
Anaa (atoll), Fr. Poly., 87/M7
Anabel, Mo. (63431) 261/H3
Ana Branch, Darling (riv.), N.S.W. 97/A3
'Anabta, Jordan 65/C3
Anacapa (isl.), Calif. 204/F10
Anaco, Ven. 124/F3
Anacoco, La. (71403) 238/D4
Anacoco (lake), La. 238/D4
Anaconda, Mont., 188/D1
Anaconda, Mont. (59711) 262/C4
Anacortes, Wash. (98221) 310/C2
Anacostia, D.C. (20020) 245/F5
Anacostia (riv.), D.C. 245/F5
Anacostia Naval Air Station, D.C. 245/F5
Anadarko, Okla. (73719) 288/K4
Anadolufeneri, Turkey 63/D5
Anadoluhisari, Turkey 63/D6
Anadyr', U.S.S.R. 48/S3
Anadyr' (gulf), U.S.S.R. 48/T3
Anadyr' (range), U.S.S.R. 48/S3
Anadyr' (riv.), U.S.S.R. 48/S3
Anadyr', (gulf), U.S.S.R., 54/X3
Anadyr', U.S.S.R, 3/T2
Anadyr' (gulf), U.S.S.R., 4/C18
Anadyr' (river), U.S.S.R., 4/C1
Anadyr', U.S.S.R., 4/C1
Anadyr' (riv.), U.S.S.R., 54/W3
Anadyr', U.S.S.R., 54/W3
Anáfi (isl.), Greece 45/G7
Anagance, N. Br. 170/E3
Anaheim, Calif. (*92801) 204/D11
Anahim Lake, Br. Col. 184/E4
Anahola, Hawaii (96703) 218/C1
Anahuac, Texas (77514) 302/K8
Anai (well), Libya 111/B3
Anai Mudi (mt.), India 68/D6
'Anaiza, Saudi Ar. 59/D4
'Anaiza, Saudi Ar., 54/H7
Anak, N. Korea 81/B4
Anakapalle, India 68/E5
Anaktalik Brook (riv.), Newf. 166/B2
Anaktuvuk Pass, Alaska (99721) 196/H1
Analalava, Malag. Rep. 118/H2
Anama Bay, Man. 179/D3
Ana María (gulf), Cuba 158/F3
Anambas (isls.), Indon. 85/D5
Anamoose, N. Dak. (58710) 283/K4
Anamosa, Iowa (52205) 229/L4
Anamur (cape), Turkey 59/B2
Anamur, Turkey 63/E4
Anamur (cape), Turkey 63/E5
Anan, Japan 81/G7
Anandale, La. (†71301) 238/F4
Ananea, Bol. 136/A4
Anantapur, India 68/D6
Anantnag, India 68/D2
Anapa, U.S.S.R. 52/E6
Anápolis, Braz., 120/F4
Anápolis, Braz. 132/D7
Anar, Iran 59/G3
Anar, Iran 66/J5
Anarak, Iran 59/F3
Anarak, Iran 66/H4
Anardarra, Afgh. 59/H3
Anardarra, Afgh. 68/A2
Añasco, P. Rico 156/F1
Añasco, P. Rico 161/A1
Añasco (bay), P. Rico 161/A1
Anatahan (isl.), Pac. Is., 87/E4
Anatolia (reg.), Turkey 63/D3
Anatone, Wash. (99401) 310/H4
Añatuya, Arg. 143/D2
Anauá (riv.), Braz. 132/B2
Anawalt, W. Va. (24808) 313/D8
Anaye (well), Niger 106/G5
Ancash (dept.), Peru 128/D7
Anceney, Mont. (†59741) 262/E5
Ancenis, France 28/C4
Anchieta, Braz. 132/F8
Ancho (chan.), Chile 138/D8
Ancho, N. Mex. (88313) 274/D5
Anchor, Ill. (61720) 222/E3
Anchorage, Alaska, 146/C3
Anchorage, Alaska, 188/D6
Anchorage, Alaska (*99501) 196/B1
Anchorage, Ky. (40223) 237/K4
Anchorage, U.S., 3/B2
Anchorage, U.S., 4/D17
Anchor Bay Gardens‡, Mich. (†48047) 250/G6
Anchorena, Arg. 143/C4
Anchor Point, Alaska (99556) 196/B2
Anchorville, Mich. (48004) 250/G6
Anchovy, Jam. 158/H5
Anclitas (cay), Cuba 158/F3
Anclote (keys), Fla. 212/D3
Anco, Ky. (41711) 237/P6
Ancohuma, Nevada (mt.), Bol. 136/A4
Ancón, Peru 128/D8
Ancona, Ill. (61311) 222/E2
Ancona, Italy, 7/F4
Ancona (prov.), Italy 34/D3
Ancona, Italy 34/D3
Ancón de Sardinas (bay), Col. 126/A7
Ancón de Sardinas (bay), Ec. 128/C2
Ancoraimes, Bol. 136/A4
Ancram, N.Y. (12502) 276/N6
Ancud, Chile, 120/C7
Ancud, Chile 138/D4
Ancud (gulf), Chile 138/D4
Andacollo, Arg. 143/B4
Andacollo, Chile 138/A8
Andado, No. Terr. 93/D8
Andahuaylas, Peru 128/F9
Andale, Kans. (67001) 232/E4
Andalgalá, Arg. 143/C2
Åndalsnes, Norway 18/F5
Andalusia, Ala. (36420) 194/E8
Andalusia, Ill. (61232) 222/C2
Andalusia, Pa. (19020) 294/N5
Andalusia (reg.), Spain 33/D4
Andaman (sea), 54/N9
Andaman (isls.), 3/P5
Andaman (isls.), India, 54/M8
Andaman (isls.), India 68/G6
Andaman (sea), India 68/G6
Andaman (sea), Burma 72/B4
Andaman and Nicobar Isls. (terr.), India 68/G6
Andamarca, Bol. 136/B6
Andamarca, Peru 128/E8
Andamooka, S. Aust. 94/E4
Andapa, Malag. Rep. 118/H2
Andaraí, Braz. 132/F6
Andau, Austria 41/D3
Andeer, Switz. 39/H3
Andenne, Belg. 27/G8
Anderlecht, Belg. 27/B9
Anderlues, Belg. 27/E8
Andermatt, Switz. 39/G3
Andernach, W. Ger. 22/B3
Anderson (riv.), 163/D2
Anderson, Ala. (35610) 194/D1
Anderson, Alaska (†99760) 196/H2
Anderson, Arg. 143/F7
Anderson, Calif. (96007) 204/C3
Anderson, Ind., 188/J2
Anderson, Ind. (*46011) 227/F4
Anderson (riv.), Ind. 227/D8
Anderson, Iowa (†51652) 229/B7
Anderson (co.), Kans. 232/G3
Anderson (co.), Ky. 237/M5
Anderson (lake), Man. 179/D2
Anderson (pt.), Man. 179/F3
Anderson, Mo. (64831) 261/D9
Anderson (riv.), N.W.T. 187/F3
Anderson (lake), Oreg. 291/G5
Anderson, S.C., 188/K4
Anderson (co.), S.C. 296/B2
Anderson, S.C. (29621) 296/B2
Anderson (co.), Tenn. 237/N8
Anderson, Tenn. (†37376) 237/K10
Anderson (co.), Texas 302/J6
Anderson, Texas (77830) 302/J7
Anderson Ranch (res.), Idaho 220/C6
Andersonville, Ga. (31711) 216/D6
Andersonville, Ind. (†47024) 227/G5
Andersonville, Tenn. (37705) 237/O8
Andersonville, Va. (23911) 307/L6
Anderstorp, Sweden 18/H8
Andes (range), 120/C26
Andes, Cordillera de los (mts.), Arg. 143/C2
Andes, Cordillera de los (mts.), Chile 138/3E3
Andes, Cordillera de los (mts.), Peru 128/F10
Andes, Col. 126/C5
Andes, Mont. (†59218) 262/M3
Andes, N.Y. (13731) 276/L6
Andes (lake), S. Dak. 298/N7
Andes de Patagonia (range), 120/C7
Andheri, India 68/B7
Andhra Pradesh (state), India 68/D5
Andijk, Neth. 27/G3
Andikíthira (isl.), Greece 45/F8
Andilamena, Malag. Rep. 118/H3
Andimeshk, Iran 66/F4
Anding, Miss. (†39040) 256/D5
Andirin, Turkey 63/G4
Ándissa, Greece 45/H6
Andizhan, U.S.S.R. 48/H5
Andizhan, U.S.S.R., 54/L5
Andkhui, Afgh. 59/J2
Andkhui, Afgh. 68/B1
Andoas Nuevo, Ec. 128/D4
Andong, S. Korea 81/D5
Andorra, 7/E4
ANDORRA, 33/G1
Andorra, Spain 33/F2
Andorra la Vella (cap.), And. 33/G1
Andover, 10/F5
Andover△, Conn. (06232) 210/F2
Andover, Eng. 13/F6
Andover, Ill. (61233) 222/C2
Andover, Iowa (52701) 229/N5
Andover, Kans. (67002) 232/E4
Andover△, Maine (04216) 242/B6
Andover, Maine (04216) 242/B6
Andover△, Mass. (01810) 249/K2
Andover, N. Br. 170/C2
Andover△, N.H. (03216) 268/D5
Andover, N.H. (03216) 268/D5
Andover, N.J. (07821) 273/D2
Andover, N.Y. (14806) 276/E6
Andover, Ohio (44003) 284/J2
Andover, S. Dak. (57422) 298/O3
Andover, Va. (24215) 307/C7
Andover△, Vt. (†05143) 268/B5
Andover, Vt. (†05143) 268/B5
Andøy (isl.), Norway 18/J2
Andraitx, Spain 33/H3
Andravídha, Greece 45/E6
Andre (lake), Newf. 166/A3
Andreafski (Saint Marys), Alaska (†99658) 196/F2
Andreanof (isls.), Alaska 196/L4
Andreas (cape), Cyprus 63/F5
Andrelândia, Braz. 135/D2
Andrés, Nic. 154/F3
Andréville, Que. 172/H2
Andrew, Alta. 182/D3
Andrew, Iowa (52030) 229/M4
Andrew, La. (†70548) 238/F6
Andrew (co.), Mo. 261/C3
Andrew Johnson Nat'l Hist. Site, Tenn. 237/R8
Andrews, Ind. (46702) 227/F3
Andrews, N.C. (28901) 281/B4
Andrews, Oreg. (†97732) 291/J5
Andrews, S.C. (29510) 296/H5
Andrews (co.), Texas 302/B5
Andrews, Texas (79714) 302/B5
Andrews A.F.B., Md. 245/G5
Andreyevka, U.S.S.R. 52/H4
Andria, Italy 34/F4
Androka, Malag. Rep. 118/G5
Andros (isl.), Bah. Is., 146/L7
Andros (isl.), Bah. Is. 156/B1
Ándros, Greece 45/G7
Ándros (isl.), Greece 45/G7
Androscoggin (co.), Maine 242/C7
Androscoggin (riv.), Maine 242/C7
Androscoggin (riv.), N.H. 268/E2
Androth (isl.), India 68/C6
Andsfjord (fjord), Norway 18/K2
Andújar, Spain 33/D3
Andul, India 68/F2
Andulo, Angola 115/C6
Andulo, 102/D6
Anécho, Togo 106/E7
Anéfis, Mali 106/E5
Anegada (passg.), St. Chr.-N.-A. 156/F3
Anegada (isl.), V.I. (Br.) 156/H1
Anegada (passg.), V.I. (Br.) 156/F3
Aneityum (isl.), New Hebr., 87/H8
'Aneiza, Jebel (mt.), Iraq 59/C3
'Aneiza, Jebel (mt.), Iraq 66/A4
'Aneiza, Jebel (mt.), Jordan 59/C3
'Aneiza, Jebel (mt.), Saudi Ar. 59/C3
Añelo, Arg. 143/C4
Anerley, Sask. 181/D4
Aneroid, Sask. 181/D6
Aneta, N. Dak. (58212) 283/P4
Aneth, Utah (84510) 304/E6
Aneto (mt.), Spain 33/G1
Angaki, Phil. 82/C2
Angamos (isl.), Chile 138/D8
Angamos (pt.), Chile 138/A4
Angara (riv.), U.S.S.R. 48/L4
Angara (riv.), U.S.S.R., 54/N4
Angarsk, U.S.S.R. 48/L4
Angas Downs, No. Terr. 93/C8
Angaston, S. Aust. 94/F6
Angaur (isl.), Pac. Is., 87/D5
Ånge, Sweden 18/J5
Angedeva (isl.), India 68/C6
Ange-Gardien-de-Rouville, Que. 172/E4
Angel (isl.), Calif. 204/J2
Angel (fall), Ven. 124/G5
Angela, Mont. (59312) 262/K4
Ángel de la Guarda (isl.), Mex. 150/C2
Ángeles, P. Rico 161/B2
Angeles, Phil. 82/C3
Ängelholm, Sweden 18/H8
Angélica, Arg. 143/E5
Angelica, N.Y. (14709) 276/E6
Angelica, Wis. (†54162) 317/K6
Angelina (co.), Texas 302/K6
Angelina (riv.), Texas 302/K6
Angelito, Par. 144/D4
Angelo, Wis. (†54656) 317/E8
Angels Camp, Calif. (95222) 204/E5
Angelus, S.C. (†29718) 296/G2
Angerman (riv.), Sweden, 7/F2
Angermanälven (riv.), Sweden 18/K5
Angermünde, E. Ger. 22/E2
Angers, Que. 172/B4
Angers, France, 7/D4
Angers, France 28/C4
Angicos, Braz. 132/G4
Angie, La. (70426) 238/L5
Angier, N.C. (27501) 281/M4
Angijak (isl.), N.W.T. 187/M3
Angikuni (lake), N.W.T. 187/J3
Angkor Wat (ruins), Cambodia, 54/O8
Angkor Wat (ruins), Cambodia 72/E4
Angle, Utah (†84712) 304/C5
Angle Inlet, Minn. (56711) 254/C1
Anglem (mt.), N.Z. 101/A7
Anglesey (isl.), 10/D4
Anglesey (co.), Wales 13/C4
Anglesey (isl.), Wales 13/C4
Angleton, Texas (77515) 302/J8
Anglia, Sask. 181/C4
Angliers, Que. 174/B3
Angmagssalik, Greenl., 4/C11
Angmagssalik, Greenl., 146/P3
Ango, Dem. Rep. of the Congo. 115/E3
Angoche (isl.), Moz. 118/G3
Angol, Chile 138/D1
Angola, 3/K6
ANGOLA, 115/C6
ANGOLA, 102/D6
Angola, Del. (†19951) 245/T6
Angola, Ind. (46703) 227/G1
Angola, Kans. (67331) 232/G4
Angola, La. (70712) 238/G5
Angola (swamp), N.C. 281/O5
Angola, N.Y. (14006) 276/C5
Angola on the Lake, N.Y. (†14006) 276/B5
Angoon, Alaska (99820) 196/M1
Angora, Minn. (55703) 254/F3
Angora, Nebr. (69331) 264/A3
Angoram, Terr. N.G. 85/B6
Angostura (falls), Col. 126/E6
Angostura, Mex. 150/E4
Angostura, Par. 144/A6
Angostura (res.), S. Dak. 298/B7
Angoulême, France 28/D5
Angra dos Reis, Braz., 120/F5
Angra dos Reis, Braz. 135/D3
Ang Thong, Thai. 72/D4
Anguil, Arg. 143/D4
Anguilla (isl.), St. Chr.-N.-A. 156/F3
Anguilla, Miss. (38721) 256/C5
Anguilla (isl.), St. Chr.-N.-A., 146/M8
Anguillara Sabazia, Italy 34/F6
Anguille (cape), Newf. 166/C4
Angul, India 68/F4
Angus, Ont. 177/E3
Angus, Iowa (†50220) 229/E5
Angus, Minn. (56712) 254/B2
Angus, Nebr. (68921) 264/F4
Angus (co.), Scot. 15/K6
Angusville, Man. 179/A4
Angwin, Calif. (94508) 204/C5
Anholt (isl.), Den. 18/G8
Anholt, Den. 21/E4
Anholt (isl.), Den. 21/E4
Anhwei (prov.), China 77/J5
Aniak, Alaska (99557) 196/G2
Aniakchak (vol.), Alaska 196/G3
Anicuns, Braz. 132/D7
Aniene (riv.), Italy 34/F6
Animas (riv.), Colo. 208/D8
Animas, N. Mex. (88020) 274/A7
Animas (riv.), N. Mex. 274/B1
Añimbo, Bol. 136/C7
'Anin, Jordan 65/C2
Anin, Burma 72/C4
Anina, Rum. 45/E3
Anita, Iowa (50020) 229/D6
Anita, Pa. (15711) 294/D3
Aniwa, Wis. (54408) 317/H6
'Anjara, Jordan 65/D3
Anjidiv (Angedeva) (isl.), India 68/C6
Anjou, Que. 172/H4
Anjouan (isl.), Comoro Is. 118/G2
Anjouan (isl.), 102/G6
Anju, N. Korea 81/B4
Anjum, Neth. 27/J2
Ankang, China 77/G5
Ankara (cap.), Turkey 59/B2
Ankara (prov.), Turkey 63/E3
Ankara (cap.), Turkey 63/E3
Ankara (riv.), Turkey 63/D3
Ankara (cap.), Turkey, 3/L4
Ankara (cap.), Turkey, 54/G5
Ankazoabo, Malag. Rep. 118/G4
Ankeny, Iowa (50021) 229/F5
Anker (riv.), 10/G3
Ankerton, Alta. 182/D3
An Khe, S. Vietnam 72/F4
Ankhor, Somalia 115/J1
Anking, China, 54/P6
Anking, China 77/J5
Anklam, E. Ger. 22/E2
Ankober, Eth. 111/H6
Ankober, 102/F4
Ankona, Fla. (†33450) 212/F4
An Loc, S. Vietnam 72/E5
Anmoore, W. Va. (26323) 313/F4
Ann (cape), Mass. 249/M2
Anna, Ill. (62906) 222/D6
Anna, Ky. (†42270) 237/J6
Anna, Ohio (45302) 284/B5
Anna, Texas (75003) 302/H4
Annaba, Alg. 106/F1
Annaba, 102/C1
Annabella, Utah (84711) 304/B5
Annaberg-Buchholz, E. Ger. 22/E3
Anna Creek, Aust. 88/F5
Anna Creek, S. Aust. 94/D3
Annada, Mo. (63330) 261/L4
Annadel, Tenn. (†37770) 237/M8
Annagassan, Ire. 17/J4
Annaheim, Sask. 181/G3
Annai, Guyana 131/B4
An Najaf, Iraq 59/D3
An Najaf, Iraq 66/D5
Annalee (riv.), Ire. 17/G3
Annalong, N. Ire. 17/K3
Annaly (bay), V.I.(U.S.) 161/E3
Anna Maria, Fla. (33501) 212/D4
Annan, 10/E3
Annan, Scot. 15/K10
Annan (riv.), Scot. 15/K9
Annandale, Minn. (55302) 254/D5
Annandale, N.J. (08801) 273/D2
Annandale, Va. (22003) 307/O3
Annandale-on-Hudson, N.Y. (12504) 276/N6
Anna Plains, W. Aust. 92/C2
Annapolis, Calif. (95412) 204/B5
Annapolis, Ill. (62413) 222/F4
Annapolis (cap.), Md., 188/L3
Annapolis (cap.), Md. (*21401) 245/M5
Annapolis, Mo. (63620) 261/L8
Annapolis (co.), N.S. 169/C4
Annapolis Junction, Md. (20701) 245/M4
Annapolis Royal, N.S. 169/C4
Annapurna (mt.), Nepal 68/E3
Ann Arbor, Mich. (*48103) 250/F6
Anna Regina, Guyana 131/B2
Annascaul, Ire. 17/B7
An Nasiriya, Iraq 59/E3
An Nasiriya, Iraq 66/D5
Annaville, Que. 172/E3
Annawan, Ill. (61234) 222/C2
Anne Arundel (co.), Md. 245/M4
Annecy, France 28/G5
Annemanie, Ala. (36721) 194/D6
Anner (riv.), Ire. 17/F7
Anneta, Ky. (42710) 237/J6
Annette, Alaska (99920) 196/N2
Annieopsquotch (mts.), Newf. 166/C4
Anniston, Ala., 188/J4
Anniston, Ala. (36201) 194/G3
Anniston, Mo. (63820) 261/O9
Anniston Army Depot, Ala. 194/F3
Annobón (isl.), 102/C5
Annona, Texas (75550) 302/K4
Annonay, France 28/F5
Annotto Bay, Jam. 156/C3
Annotto Bay, Jam. 158/K6
Annville, Ky. (40402) 237/O6

Aswân 327

Argentino (lake), Arg. 143/B7
Argenton-sur-Creusot, France 28/D4
Argeş (riv.), Rum. 45/G3
Argo, Ala. (†35173) 194/E3
Argo, Sudan 59/B6
Argo, Sudan 111/F4
Argo, Sask. 181/C3
Argolis (gulf), Greece 45/F7
Argonia, Kans. (67004) 232/E4
Argonne, Wis. (54511) 317/J4
Argonne Nat'l Laboratory, Ill. 222/A2
Árgos, Greece 45/F7
Argos, Ind. (46501) 227/E2
Argos (cape), N.S. 169/G3
Argostólion, Greece 45/E6
Arguello (pt.), Calif. 204/E9
Arguin (bay), Mauritania 106/A4
Argun (riv.), 54/P5
Argun' (riv.), U.S.S.R. 48/M4
Argun (riv.), China 77/J1
Argungu, Nigeria 106/E6
Argus (range), Calif. 204/H7
Argusville, N. Dak. (58005) 283/R5
Argyle, Fla. (32422) 212/C6
Argyle, Ga. (31623) 216/G8
Argyle, Iowa (52619) 229/K7
Argyle, Maine (†04468) 242/F5
Argyle, Man. 179/E4
Argyle, Mich. (48410) 250/G5
Argyle, Minn. (56713) 254/B2
Argyle, Mo. (65001) 261/J6
Argyle, N. Br. 170/C2
Argyle, N.S. 169/C5
Argyle, N.Y. (12809) 276/O4
Argyle‡, Texas (76226) 302/G4
Argyle, Wis. (53504) 317/G10
Argyle Downs, W. Aust. 92/E2
Argyll (co.), Scot. 15/F7
Argyll (dist.), Scot. 15/F7
Arhavi, Turkey 63/J2
Aria, N.Z. 101/E3
Ariah Park, N.S.W. 97/D4
Ariail, S.C. (29640) 296/B2
Ariano Irpino, Italy 34/E4
Ariari (riv.), Col. 126/D6
Aribinda, Upp. Volta 106/D6
Arica, Chile, 120/C4
Arica, Chile 138/A1
Arica, Col. 126/E9
Aricagua, Ven. 124/C3
Ariccia, Italy 34/F7
Arichat, N.S. 169/H3
Arichuna, Ven. 124/E4
Arichuna (riv.), Ven. 124/D4
Arid (cape), Aust. 88/C6
Arid (cape), W. Aust. 92/C6
Ariège (dept.), France 28/D6
Ariel, Wash. (98603) 310/C5
Arigna, 10/B3
Ariguaní (riv.), Col. 126/D3
'Ariha (Jericho), Jordan 65/C4
Arikaree (riv.), Colo. 208/O3
Arima, Trinidad Tobago 156/G5
Arima, Trinidad Tobago 161/B10
Arimo, Idaho (83214) 220/F7
Arinagour, Scot. 15/C6
Arinos (riv.), Braz., 120/E4
Arinos (riv.), Braz. 132/B5
Arion, Iowa (51520) 229/B5
Aripao, Ven. 124/F4
Aripeka, Fla. (33502) 212/D3
Aripine, Ariz. (†85901) 198/E4
Aripo, El Cerro del (mt.), Trinidad Tobago 161/B10
Ariporo (riv.), Col. 126/E4
Aripuanã (riv.), Braz., 120/E3
Aripuanã, Braz. 132/B5
Aripuanã (riv.), Braz. 132/A4
Arisaig, N.S. 169/F3
Arisaig, Scot. 15/E6
Arisaig (dist.), Scot. 15/E6
Arisaig (sound), Scot. 15/E6
Arismendi, Ven. 124/D3
Arispe, Iowa (50831) 229/E7
Aristazabal (isl.), Br. Col. 184/C4
Aritao, Phil. 82/C2
Ariton, Ala. (36311) 194/G7
Arivaca, Ariz. (85601) 198/D7
Arivonimamo, Malag. Rep. 118/H3
Ariza, Spain 33/E2
Arizaro, Salar de (salt dep.), Arg. 143/C2
Arizona, 188/D4
ARIZONA, 198
Arizona (plat.), Ariz. 198/D3
Arizona (state), U.S., 146/G6
Arizpe, Mex. 150/D1
Årjäng, Sweden 18/H7
Arjay, Ky. (40902) 237/O7
Arjona, Col. 126/C2
Arkabutla, Miss. (38602) 256/D1
Arkabutla (dam), Miss. 256/D1
Arkabutla (lake), Miss. 256/E1
Arkadelphia, Ala. (35033) 194/E3
Arkadelphia, Ark. (71923) 203/D5
Arkaig (lake), 10/D2
Arkaig (lake), Scot. 15/F6
Arkalyk, U.S.S.R. 48/G4
Arkansas, 188/H3
Arkansas (riv.), 188/H3
ARKANSAS, 203
Arkansas (co.), Ark. 203/H5
Arkansas (riv.), Ark. 203/G5
Arkansas (riv.), Colo. 208/P6
Arkansas (riv.), Kans. 232/D3
Arkansas (riv.), Okla. 288/S4
Arkansas (riv.), U.S., 3/E4
Arkansas (riv.), U.S., 146/J6
Arkansas City, Ark. (71630) 203/H6
Arkansas City, Kans., 188/G3
Arkansas City, Kans. (67005) 232/E4
Arkansas Divide (mts.), Colo. 208/L4
Arkansas Post, Ark. (†72055) 203/H5
Arkansas Post Nat'l Mem., Ark. 203/H5
Arkansas (state) U.S., 146/J6
Arkansaw, Wis. (54721) 317/B6
Arkdale, Wis. (54613) 317/G7
Arkhángelos, Greece 45/J7
Arkhipo-Osipovka, U.S.S.R. 52/E6
Arkinda, Ark. (71821) 203/B6
Arklow, 10/C4
Arklow, Ire. 17/J6
Arklow (bank), Ire. 17/K6
Arkoe, Mo. (†64468) 261/C2
Arkoma, Okla. (74901) 288/T4
Arkona, Ont. 177/C4
Arkona (cape), E. Ger. 22/E1
Arkport, N.Y. (14807) 276/E6
Arkticheskiy Institut (isls.), U.S.S.R. 48/H2
Arkville, N.Y. (12406) 276/L6
Arkwright, S.C. (†29301) 296/C2
Arlecdon, Eng. 13/D3
Arlee, Mont. (59821) 262/B3
Arlee, W. Va. (†25106) 313/B5
Arlene, Mich. (†49663) 250/D4
Arles, France 28/F6
Arlesheim, Switz. 39/E2
Arley, Ala. (35541) 194/D2
Arlington, Ala. (36722) 194/C6
Arlington, Ariz. (85322) 198/C5
Arlington, Colo. (81021) 208/N6
Arlington, Ga. (31713) 216/C8
Arlington, Ill. (61312) 222/D2
Arlington, Ind. (46104) 227/F5
Arlington, Iowa (50606) 229/K3
Arlington, Kans. (67514) 232/D4
Arlington, Ky. (42021) 237/D7
Arlington▵, Mass. (02174) 249/C6
Arlington, Minn. (55307) 254/D6
Arlington, N.C. (†28642) 281/H2
Arlington, N.Y. (12603) 276/N7
Arlington, Nebr. (68002) 264/H3
Arlington, Ohio (45814) 284/C4
Arlington, Oreg. (97812) 291/G2
Arlington, S. Dak. (57212) 298/P5
Arlington, Tenn. (38002) 237/B10
Arlington, Texas (*76010) 302/F2
Arlington (lake), Texas 302/F2
Arlington (co.), Va. 307/O3
Arlington, Va. (*22201) 307/P3
Arlington▵, Vt. (05250) 268/A5
Arlington, Vt. (05250) 268/A5
Arlington, Wash. (98223) 310/C2
Arlington, Wis. (53911) 317/H9
Arlington, Wyo. (†82080) 319/F4
Arlington Heights, Ill. (*60004) 222/A1
Arlington Heights, Ohio (†45201) 284/C9
Arlington Heights-Pocono Park‡, Pa. (†18360) 294/M3
Arlon, Belg. 27/H9
Arltunga, No. Terr. 93/D7
Arm (riv.), Sask. 181/F5
Arma, Kans. (66712) 232/H4
Arma (plat.), Saudi Ar. 59/E4
Armada, Alta. 182/D4
Armada, Mich. (48005) 250/G6
Armadale, Aust. 88/B2
Armadale, 10/B1
Armadale, W. Aust. 92/A1
Armadale, Scot. 15/E2
Armagh, Que. 172/G3
Armagh (co.), N. Ire. 17/H3
Armagh, N. Ire. 17/H3
Armagh, Pa. (15920) 294/E5
Armagh, 10/C3
Armathwaite, Tenn. (38506) 237/M8
Armavir, U.S.S.R. 48/E5
Armavir, U.S.S.R. 52/F5
Armavir, U.S.S.R., 7/J4
Armdale, N.S. 169/E4
Armena, Alta. 182/D3
Armenia, Col. 126/B5
Armenian S.S.R., U.S.S.R. 48/E6
Armenian S.S.R., U.S.S.R. 52/F6
Armenian S.S.R., U.S.S.R., 7/J4
Armentières, France 28/E2
Armeria, Mex. 150/G7
Armero, Col. 126/C5
Armidale, Australia, 87/F9
Armidale, Aust. 88/J6
Armidale, N.S.W. 97/F2
Armington, Ill. (61721) 222/D3
Armington, Mont. (†59412) 262/F3
Arminto, Wyo. (82630) 319/E2
Armistead, La. (†71019) 238/D3
Armit (lake), Man. 179/A2
Armit, Sask. 181/K3
Armley, Sask. 181/G2
Armona, Calif. (93202) 204/F7
Armorel, Ark. (72310) 203/L2
Armour, S. Dak. (57313) 298/N7
Armourdale, N. Dak. (†58365) 283/M2
Armoy, N. Ire. 17/J1
Armstrong, Br. Col. 184/H5
Armstrong, Ont. 175/C2
Armstrong, Ill. (61812) 222/F3
Armstrong, Ind. (†47708) 227/B8
Armstrong, Iowa (50514) 229/D2
Armstrong, Mo. (65230) 261/G4
Armstrong (co.), Pa. 294/D4
Armstrong (co.), Texas 302/C3
Armstrong, Texas (78338) 302/G11
Armstrong Creek, Wis. (54103) 317/K4
Armstrongs Mills, Ohio (43904) 284/J6
Armstrong Station, 163/H5
Armuchee, Ga. (30105) 216/B2
Army Chemical Center, Md. 245/O3
Army Map Service, Md. 245/E4
Arnala, Greece 45/F5
Arnaud (riv.), Que. 174/F1
Arnaud, Man. 179/E5
Arnaudville, La. (70512) 238/G6
Arnauti (cape), Cyprus 59/B2
Arnauti (cape), Cyprus 63/E5
Arnavutköy, Turkey 63/D6
Arnedo, Spain 33/E1
Arnegard, N. Dak. (58835) 283/D4
Årnes, Norway 18/G6
Arnes, Man. 179/E4
Arnett, Okla. (73832) 288/G2
Arnett, W. Va. (25007) 313/D7
Arney (riv.), N. Ire. 17/F3
Arnheim, Mich. (†49958) 250/G1
Arnhem (cape), Australia, 87/D7
Arnhem (cape), Aust. 88/F2
Arnhem, Neth. 27/H5
Arnhem (cape), No. Terr. 93/E2
Arnhem Land (reg.), Australia, 87/D7
Arnhem Land (reg.), Aust. 88/E2
Arnhem Land (reg.), No. Terr. 93/D2
Arno (riv.), Italy 34/C3
Arno (atoll), Pac. Is., 87/H5
Arnold, Calif. (95223) 204/E5
Arnold, Eng. 13/F4
Arnold, Kans. (67515) 232/B3
Arnold, Mich. (49819) 250/B2
Arnold, Minn. (†55801) 254/F4
Arnold, Mo. (63010) 261/P4
Arnold, Nebr. (69120) 264/D3
Arnold (riv.), No. Terr. 93/D3
Arnold, Pa. (15068) 294/C4
Arnold Mills, R.I. (†02864) 249/J5
Arnoldsburg, W. Va. (25234) 313/D5
Arnold's Cove, Newf. 166/C2
Arnolds Park, Iowa (51331) 229/C2
Arnoldstein, Austria 41/B3
Arnoldsville, Ga. (30619) 216/F3
Arnot, Pa. (16911) 294/H2
Arnøy (isl.), Norway 18/M1
Arnprior, Ont. 177/H2
Arnsberg, W. Ger. 22/C3
Arnstadt, E. Ger. 22/D3
Aro (riv.), Ven. 124/F4
Aroa, Ven. 124/D2
Aroab, S.W. Afr. 118/B5
Aroche, Spain 33/C4
Arock, Oreg. (97902) 291/K5
Arolla, Switz. 39/E4
Arolsen, W. Ger. 22/C3
Aroma, Bol. 136/B5
Aroma, Sudan 111/G4
Aroma Park, Ill. (60910) 222/F2
Aromas, Calif. (95004) 204/D7
Arona‡, Pa. (15617) 294/C5
Aroostook (co.), Maine 242/F2
Aroostook (riv.), Maine 242/G2
Arorae (atoll), Gilb. and Ell., 87/H6
Aroroy, Phil. 82/D4
Arosa, Ria de (est.), Spain 33/B1
Arosa, Switz. 39/J3
Aroser Rothorn (mt.), Switz. 39/J3
Arouca, Trinidad Tobago 161/B10
Arp, Ga. (†31783) 216/F7
Arp, Texas (75750) 302/J5
Arpa (riv.), Turkey 63/K2
Arpin, Wis. (54410) 317/G6
Arque, Bol. 136/B5
'Arraba, Jordan 65/C3
'Arrabe, Israel 65/C2
Arrah, India 68/E3
Ar Rahhaliya, Iraq 59/D3
Ar Rahhaliya, Iraq 66/C4
Arraias, Braz. 132/E6
Arran, Fla. (†32327) 212/B1
Arran, Sask. 181/K4
Arran (isl.), 10/D3
Arran (isl.), Scot. 15/F8
Arras, Br. Col. 184/G2
Arras, France 28/E2
Arrecifal, Col. 126/F6
Arrecife, Spain 33/C4
Arrecife, Spain 106/B3
Arrecifes, Arg. 143/F7
Arrecifes (riv.), Arg. 143/G6
Arrey, N. Mex. (87930) 274/B6
Arriaga, Mex. 150/N8
Arriba, Colo. (80804) 208/N4
Arribeños, Arg. 143/F7
Ar Rimal (des.), Saudi Ar., 54/H7
Arrington, Kans. (66001) 232/G2
Arrington, Tenn. (37014) 237/H9
Arrington, Va. (22922) 307/L5
Arriola, Colo. (†81323) 208/B8
Arrochar, Scot. 15/G7
Arronches, Port. 33/C3
Arrow (lake), Ire. 17/E3
Arrow (creek), Mont. 262/F3
Arrow Canyon (range), Nev. 266/G6
Arrow Creek, Mont. (†59424) 262/F3
Arrowhead, Br. Col. 184/H5
Arrowhead Mountain (lake), Vt. 268/A2
Arrow Park, Br. Col. 184/H5
Arrow River, Man. 179/B4
Arrowrock (res.), Idaho 220/C6
Arrow Rock, Mo. (65320) 261/F4
Arrowsmith, Ill. (61722) 222/E3
Arrowtown, N.Z. 101/B6
Arrowwood, Alta. 182/D4
Arrowwood (lake), N. Dak. 283/N5
Arroyas, Los (lake), Bol. 136/C3
Arroyo, P. Rico 156/G1
Arroyo, P. Rico 161/E3
Arroyo de la Luz, Spain 33/C3
Arroyo del Valle (dry riv.), Calif. 204/L3
Arroyo Grande, Bol. 136/A2
Arroyo Grande, Calif. (93420) 204/E8
Arroyo Hondo (dry riv.), Calif. 204/L3
Arroyo Hondo, N. Mex. (87513) 274/D2
Arroyo Mocho (dry riv.), Calif. 204/L2
Arroyos de Mantua, Cuba 158/A2
Arroyo Seco, Arg. 143/F6
Arroyo Seco (dry riv.), Calif. 204/K10
Arroyo Seco, N. Mex. (87514) 274/D2
Arroyos y Esteros, Par. 144/B6
Ar Rumaila, Iraq 66/E5
Ars-en-Ré, France 28/C4
Arsin, Turkey 63/H2
Árta, Greece, 7/G5
Árta, Greece 45/E6
Artá, Spain 33/H3
Artas, S. Dak. (57423) 298/K2
Artawiya, Saudi Ar. 59/E4
Arteaga, Mex. 150/H7
Artem, U.S.S.R. 48/O5
Artemas, Pa. (17211) 294/E6
Artemisa, Cuba 156/A2
Artemisa, Cuba 158/B1
Artemovsk, U.S.S.R. 52/E5
Artemovskiy, U.S.S.R. 48/M4
Artemus, Ky. (40903) 237/O7
Artena, Italy 34/F7
Artesia, Calif. (90701) 204/C11
Artesia, Miss. (39736) 256/G4
Artesia, N. Mex. (88210) 274/E6
Artesian, S. Dak. (57314) 298/O6
Artesia Wells, Texas (78001) 302/E9
Arth, Switz. 39/F2
Arthabaska (co.), Que. 172/E4
Arthabaska, Que. 172/F3
Arthur, Ont. 177/D4
Arthur, Ill. (61911) 222/E4
Arthur, Ind. (†47598) 227/C8
Arthur, Iowa (51431) 229/C4
Arthur, N. Dak. (58006) 283/R5
Arthur (range), N.Z. 101/D4
Arthur (co.), Nebr. 264/C3
Arthur, Nebr. (69121) 264/C3
Arthur (riv.), W. Aust. 92/B2
Arthur (lake), Pa. 294/B4
Arthur, Tenn. (37707) 237/O7
Arthur, W. Va. (26816) 313/H4
Arthurdale, W. Va. (26520) 313/G3
Arthurette, N. Br. 170/C2
Arthur Kill (str.), N.J. 273/B3
Arthur's (pass), N.Z. 101/C5
Arthurstown, Ire. 17/H7
Artibonite (dept.), Haiti 158/C5
Artibonite (riv.), Haiti 158/C5
Artigas (dept.), Urug. 145/B1
Artigas, Urug. 145/C1
Artillery (lake), N.W.T. 187/H3
Artland, Sask. 181/B3
Artois, Calif. (95913) 204/C4
Artova, Turkey 63/G3
Artvin, Turkey 59/D1
Artvin (prov.), Turkey 63/J2
Artvin, Turkey 63/J2
Aru (isls.), Indon. 85/K7
Arua, Uganda 115/F3
Aruba (isl.), Neth. Ant. 156/E4
Aruba (isl.), Neth. Ant. 161/E9
Arucas, Spain 33/B5
Arundel, 10/F5
Arundel, Que. 172/C4
Arundel, Eng. 13/G7
Aruppukkottai, India 68/D7
'Arura, Jordan 65/C3
Arus, P. Rico 161/C3
Arus (cape), Indon. 85/G5
Arusha, 102/F5
Arusha (reg.), Tanz. 115/G3
Arusha, Tanz. 115/G4
Arusi (prov.), Eth. 111/G6
Aruwimi (riv.), Dem. Rep. of the Congo. 115/E3
Arva, Ont. 177/C4
Arva, Ire. 17/F4
Arvada, Colo. (80002) 208/J3
Arvada, Wyo. (82831) 319/F1
Arvel, Ky. (40303) 237/O5
Arvi, India 68/D4
Arvida, Que. 172/F1
Arvidsjaur, Sweden 18/L4
Arvika, Sweden 18/H7
Arvilla, N. Dak. (58214) 283/P4
Arvin, Calif. (93203) 204/G8
Arvonia, Va. (23004) 307/M5
Arzamas, U.S.S.R. 48/E4
Arzamas, U.S.S.R. 52/F3
Arzier, Switz. 39/B4
Arzúa, Spain 33/B1
As, Belg. 27/H6
Aš, Czech. 41/B1
Asaa, Den. 21/D3
Asaba, Nigeria 106/F7
Asadabad, Iran 66/F3
Asahan (riv.), Indon. 85/B5
Asahi, Japan 81/K6
Asahi (mt.), Japan 81/J4
Asahikawa, Japan 81/L2
Asama (mt.), Japan 81/J5
Asansol, India 68/F4
Åsarna, Sweden 18/J5
Asbestos, Que. 172/F4
Asbury, Iowa (†52001) 229/M4
Asbury, Mo. (64832) 261/C8
Asbury, N.J. (08802) 273/C2
Asbury, W. Va. (24916) 313/E7
Asbury Park, N.J. (07712) 273/F3
As Busaiya, Iraq 66/E5
Ascención, Bol. 136/D4
Ascensión, Arg. 143/F7
Ascension, Neth. Ant. 161/F8
Ascension (par.), La. 238/J6
Ascensión, Mex. 150/F1
Ascension (isl.), 102/A5
Ascension (isl.), St. Helena, 3/J6
Aschaffenburg, W. Ger. 22/C4
Aschendorf, W. Ger. 22/B2
Aschersleben, E. Ger. 22/D3
Asco, W. Va. (24809) 313/C8
Ascoli Piceno (prov.), Italy 34/D3
Ascoli Piceno, Italy 34/D3
Ascona, Switz. 39/G4
Ascope, Peru 128/C6
Ascot, Queens. 95/E2
Ascotán, Chile 138/B3
Ascotán, Salar de (salt dep.), Chile 138/B3
Ascot Corner, Que. 172/F4
Ascrib (isls.), Scot. 15/C4
Ascutney, Vt. (05030) 268/C5
Ascutney (mt.), Vt. 268/C5
Åseda, Sweden 18/J8
Åsele, Sweden 18/K4
Asenovgrad, Bulg. 45/G5
Ash (riv.), Minn. 254/F2
Ash, N.C. (28420) 281/N6
Ash, Oreg. (†97473) 291/D4
Ash (creek), Utah 304/A6
'Ashaira, Saudi Ar. 59/D5
Ashanti (reg.), Ghana 106/D7
Ashanti (reg.), 102/B4
Asharoken‡, N.Y. (†11768) 276/O9
Ashaway, R.I. (02804) 249/G7
Ashboro, Ind. (†47840) 227/C6
Ashbourne, Eng. 13/F4
Ashburn, Ga. (31714) 216/E7
Ashburn, Mo. (63433) 261/K3
Ashburn, Va. (22011) 307/O2
Ashburnham▵, Mass. (01430) 249/G2
Ashburnham, Mass. (01430) 249/G2
Ashburton (riv.), Australia, 87/B8
Ashburton (riv.), Aust. 88/B4
Ashburton, Eng. 13/D7
Ashburton, N.Z. 101/C5
Ashburton (riv.), W. Aust. 92/A3
Ashburton Downs, W. Aust. 92/B3
Ashby, Ala. (†35035) 194/E4
Ashby▵, Mass. (01431) 249/G2
Ashby, Minn. (56309) 254/C4
Ashby, Nebr. (69333) 264/C2
Ashbyburg, Ky. (†42456) 237/G5
Ashby de la Zouch, Eng. 13/F5
Ashcamp, Ky. (41512) 237/S6
Ash Creek, Minn. (†56173) 254/B7
Ashcroft, Br. Col. 184/G5
Ashdale, Maine (†04565) 242/D8
Ashdod, Israel 65/B4
Ashdot Ya'aqov, Israel 65/D2
Ashdown, Ark. (71822) 203/B6
Ashe (co.), N.C. 281/F2
Ashe (isl.), N.C. 281/P6
Asheboro, N.C. (27203) 281/K3
Ashepoo, S.C. (†29446) 296/G6
Ashepoo (riv.), S.C. 296/F6
Asher, Okla. (74826) 288/N5
Ashern, Man. 179/D3
Asherton, Texas (78827) 302/E9
Asherville, Ind. (†47834) 227/C6
Asherville, Kans. (67415) 232/D2
Asheville, N.C., 188/K3
Asheville, N.C. (*28801) 281/D3
Asheweig (riv.), Ont. 175/C2
Ashfield▵, Mass. (01330) 249/C2
Ashfield, N.S.W. 97/J3
Ash Flat, Ark. (72513) 203/G1
Ashford, 10/G5
Ashford, Ala. (36312) 194/H8
Ashford▵, Conn. (†06250) 210/G1
Ashford, Eng. 13/H6
Ashford, Ire. 17/J5
Ashford, N.C. (28603) 281/F3
Ashford, N.S.W. 97/F1
Ashford, W. Va. (25009) 313/C6
Ashford, Wash. (98304) 310/C4
Ash Fork, Ariz. (86320) 198/C3
Ash Grove, Kans. (†67455) 232/D2
Ash Grove, Mo. (65604) 261/E8
Ashhurst, N.Z. 101/E4
Ashibetsu, Japan 81/L2
Ashikaga, Japan 81/J5
Ashington, 10/F3
Ashington, Eng. 13/F2
Ashippun, Wis. (53003) 317/H1
Ashiya, Japan 81/H8
Ashizuri (cape), Japan 81/F7
Ashkhabad, U.S.S.R. 48/F6
Ashkhabad, U.S.S.R., 54/J6
Ashkum, Ill. (60911) 222/F3
Ash Lake, Minn. (†55771) 254/F2
Ashland, Ala. (36251) 194/G4
Ashland, Calif. (†94578) 204/K2
Ashland, Ga. (†30521) 216/F2
Ashland, Ill. (62612) 222/C4
Ashland, Kans. (67831) 232/C4
Ashland, Ky., 188/K3
Ashland, Ky. (41101) 237/R4
Ashland, La. (71002) 238/D2
Ashland▵, Maine (04732) 242/G2
Ashland, Maine (04732) 242/G2
Ashland▵, Mass. (01721) 249/J3
Ashland, Miss. (38603) 256/F1
Ashland, Mo. (65010) 261/H5
Ashland, Mont. (59003) 262/K5
Ashland▵, N.H. (03217) 268/D4
Ashland, N.H. (03217) 268/D4
Ashland, N.J. (†08033) 273/B3
Ashland, N.Y. (12407) 276/M6
Ashland, Nebr. (68003) 264/H3
Ashland (co.), Ohio 284/F4
Ashland, Ohio (44805) 284/F4
Ashland, Okla. (74524) 288/O5
Ashland, Oreg. (97520) 291/E5
Ashland, Pa. (17921) 294/K4
Ashland, Va. (23005) 307/N5
Ashland (co.), Wis. 317/E3
Ashland, Wis. (54806) 317/E2
Ashland City, Tenn. (37015) 237/G8
Ashley (co.), Ark. 203/G7
Ashley, Ill. (62808) 222/D5
Ashley, Ind. (46705) 227/G1
Ashley, Mich. (48806) 250/E5
Ashley, Mo. (†63334) 261/K4
Ashley (lake), Mont. 262/B2
Ashley, N. Dak. (58413) 283/M7
Ashley, N.S.W. 97/E1
Ashley, Ohio (43003) 284/E5
Ashley, Pa. (18706) 294/L3
Ashley (riv.), S.C. 296/G6
Ashley, W. Va. (†26339) 313/E4
Ashley Falls, Mass. (01222) 249/A4
Ashmere (lake), Mass. 249/B3
Ashmont, Alta. 182/E2
Ashmore (isls.), Aust. 88/C2
Ashmore, Ill. (61912) 222/F4
ASHMORE and CARTIER ISLANDS, 88/C2
Ashokan, N.Y. (†12491) 276/M7
Ashokan (res.), N.Y. 276/M7
Ashport, Tenn. (38003) 237/B9
Ashqelon, Israel 65/A4
Ash Shabicha, Iraq 66/C5
Ashtabula (lake), N. Dak. 283/P5
Ashtabula (co.), Ohio 284/J2
Ashtabula, Ohio (44004) 284/J2
Ashton, Idaho (83420) 220/G5
Ashton, Ill. (61006) 222/D2
Ashton, Iowa (51232) 229/B2
Ashton, Kans. (67001) 232/E4
Ashton, Mich. (†49677) 250/D5
Ashton, Nebr. (68817) 264/F3
Ashton, R.I. (02864) 249/J5
Ashton, S.C. (†29082) 296/E5
Ashton, S. Dak. (57424) 298/N3
Ashton, W. Va. (25503) 313/B5
Ashton-under-Lyne, 10/G2
Ashuanipi (lake), Newf. 166/A3
Ashuanipi (riv.), Newf. 166/A3
Ashuelot, N.H. (03441) 268/C6
Ashuelot (riv.), N.H. 268/C6
Ash Valley, Kans. (†67550) 232/C3
Ashville, Ala. (35953) 194/F3
Ashville, Maine (04607) 242/G7
Ashville, Man. 179/B3
Ashville, Ohio (43103) 284/E6
Ashville, Pa. (16613) 294/F4
Ashwaubenon, Wis. (54304) 317/K7
Ashwood, Oreg. (97711) 291/G3
'Asi (riv.), Syria 59/C2
'Asi (riv.), Syria 63/G5
Asia, 3/P3
ASIA, 54
Asia (isls.), Indon. 85/J5
Asid (gulf), Phil. 82/D4
Asidonhoppo, Sur. 131/D4
Asilah, Mor. 106/C1
Asinara (gulf), Italy 34/B4
Asinara (isl.), Italy 34/B4
Asino, U.S.S.R. 48/J4
'Asir (prov.), Saudi Ar. 59/D6
Aşkale, Turkey 63/J3
Askeaton, Ire. 17/D6
Askew, Miss. (38604) 256/D1
Askewville, N.C. (†27983) 281/R2
Askim, Norway 18/E4
Aski Mosul, Iraq 66/C2
Askival (mt.), Scot. 15/D6
Askov, Minn. (55704) 254/F4
Askov, Den. 21/C7
Askrigg, Eng. 13/E3
Askvoll, Norway 18/D6
Aslanköy, Turkey 63/F4
Asmara, Eth. 59/C6
Asmara, Eth. 111/G4
Asmara, 102/F3
Asnaes, Den. 21/E6
Åsnen (lake), Sweden 18/J8
Asnières, France 28/A1
Aso (mt.), Japan 81/E7
Aso Nat'l Park, Japan 81/E7
Asosa, Eth. 111/F5
Asoteriba, Jebel (mt.), Sudan 111/G3
Asotin (co.), Wash. 310/H4
Asotin, Wash. (99402) 310/H4
Asotin (creek), Wash. 310/H4
Asotin (dam), Wash. 310/J4
Aspang, Austria 41/D3
Aspatria, Eng. 13/D3
Aspe, Spain 33/F3
Aspelund, Minn. (†55946) 254/F6
Aspen, Colo. (81611) 208/F4
Aspen, N.S. 169/F3
Aspen (lake), Oreg. 291/E5
Aspen (mts.), Wyo. 319/C4
Aspen Grove, Br. Col. 184/G5
Aspen Hill, Md. (†20015) 245/K4
Aspermont, Texas (79502) 302/D4
Aspers, Pa. (17304) 294/H6
Aspetuck, Conn. (†06880) 210/B4
Aspetuck (res.), Conn. 210/B4
Aspetuck (riv.), Conn. 210/B3
Aspinwall, Iowa (51432) 229/C5
Aspinwall, Pa. (15215) 294/C6
Aspiring (mt.), N.Z. 101/B6
Aspry (bay), N.S. 169/H2
Asquith, Sask. 181/D3
Assab, Eth. 59/D7
Assab, Eth. 111/H5
Assaba (reg.), Mauritania 106/B5
Assabet (riv.), Mass. 249/H3
Assakarai (dry riv.), Niger 106/F5
Assale (lake), Eth. 111/H5
As Salman, Iraq 59/E3
As Salman, Iraq 66/D5
Assam (state), India 68/G3
Assapan (riv.), Man. 179/G2
Assaria, Kans. (67416) 232/E3
Assateague Island Nat'l Seashore, Va. 307/T4
Assawompset (pond), Mass. 249/L5
Assay (creek), Utah 304/B6
Asse, Belg. 27/E7
Assebroek, Belg. 27/C6
Asselar (well), Mali 106/D5
Asselle, Eth. 111/G6
Assen, Neth. 27/K3
Assens, Den. 21/D7
Assens, Den. 21/D4
Assesse, Belg. 27/G8
Assiniboia, Sask. 181/E6
Assiniboine (mt.), Alta. 182/C4
Assiniboine (mt.), Br. Col. 184/K5
Assiniboine (riv.), Man. 179/C5
Assiniboine (riv.), Sask. 181/J3
Assinica (lake), Que. 174/C3
Assinika (lake), Man. 179/G2
Assinika (riv.), Man. 179/G2
Assinippi, Mass. (02339) 249/E8
Assis, Braz. 132/D8
Assis, Braz. 135/A3
Assisi, Italy 34/D3
Assonet, Mass. (02702) 249/K5
Assumption, Alta. 182/A5
Assumption, Ill. (62510) 222/E4
Assumption (par.), La. 238/H7
Assumption, Ohio (†43540) 284/B2
Assumption (isl.), Seych. 118/H1
Assynt (dist.), Scot. 15/F3
Assynt (lake), Scot. 15/G3
Assyria, Mich. (†49021) 250/D6
Astara, U.S.S.R. 52/G7
Astatula, Fla. (32705) 212/E3
Asten, Neth. 27/H6
Asterabad (Gurgan), Iran 59/F2
Asterabad (Gurgan), Iran 66/J2
Asti, Calif. (95413) 204/C5
Asti (prov.), Italy 34/B2
Asti, Italy 34/B2
Astillero, Peru 128/H9
Astipalaia, Greece 45/H7
Astipálaia (isl.), Greece 45/H7
Astle, N. Br. 170/D2
Aston (bay), N.W.T. 187/J2
Aston-Junction, Que. 172/E3
Astor, Fla. (32002) 212/E2
Astorga, Spain 33/C1
Astoria, Ill. (61501) 222/C3
Astoria, Oreg., 188/B1
Astoria, Oreg. (97103) 291/D1
Astoria, S. Dak. (57213) 298/S4
Astorville, Ont. 177/E1
Astove (isl.), Seych. 118/H2
Astra, Arg. 143/C6
Astrakhan', U.S.S.R. 48/E5
Astrakhan', U.S.S.R. 52/G5
Astrakhan', U.S.S.R., 7/J4
Astray (lake), Newf. 166/A3
Astudillo, Spain 33/D1
Asturias (reg.), Spain 33/D1
Asunción, Bol. 136/B2
Asuncion (passg.), Phil. 82/D5
Asuncion (isl.), Pac. Is., 87/E4
Asunción (cap.), Par., 3/F7
Asunción (cap.), Par., 120/E5
Asunción (cap.), Par. 144/A6
Asunción Mita, Guat. 154/C3
Asunción Nochixtlán, Mex. 150/L8
Asunta, Bol. 136/B5
Aswad, Ras al (cape), Saudi Ar. 59/C5
Aswân, 102/F2

Ballenstedt 329

Ayvalik, Turkey 63/B3
Aywaille, Belg. 27/H8
Azalea, Oreg. (97410) 291/D5
Azalea Park‡, Fla. (32807) 212/E3
Azalia, Ind. (†47232) 227/F6
Azalia, Mich. (48110) 250/F6
Azamgarh, India 68/E3
Azángaro, Peru 128/H10
Azángaro (riv.), Peru 128/G10
Azaoua (reg.), Niger 106/E5
Azaouad (reg.), Mali 106/D5
Azaouak (dry riv.), Mali 106/E5
Azapa, Chile 138/A1
Azapa, Quebrada (riv.), Chile 138/B1
Azare, Nigeria 106/G6
Azarshahr, Iran 66/D2
A'zaz, Syria 63/G4
Azbine (Air) (plat.), 102/C3
Azbine (Air) (mts.), Niger 106/F5
Azcapotzalco, Mex. 150/L1
Azemmour, Mor. 106/C2
Azerbaidzhan S.S.R., U.S.S.R. 48/E5
Azerbaidzhan S.S.R., U.S.S.R. 52/G6
Azerbaidzhan S.S.R., U.S.S.R., 7/J4
Azerbaijan, East (prov.), Iran 66/E1
Azerbaijan, West (prov.), Iran 66/D1
Aziscoos (lake), Maine 242/A5
Azle, Texas (76020) 302/E1
Azna, Iran 66/F4
Azogues, Ec. 128/C4
Azor, Israel 65/B3
Azores (isls.), Port., 3/H4
Azov (sea), U.S.S.R. 48/D5
Azov, U.S.S.R. 52/E5
Azov (sea), U.S.S.R. 52/E5
Azov (sea), U.S.S.R., 7/H4
Azoyú, Mex. 150/K8
Azpeitia, Spain 33/E1
Azrou, Mor. 106/C2
Aztec, Ariz. (†85333) 198/B6
Aztec, N. Mex. (87410) 274/B2
Aztec Ruins Nat'l Mon., N. Mex. 274/A2
Azua, Dom. Rep. 156/D3
Azua (prov.), Dom. Rep. 158/D6
Azua, Dom. Rep. 158/D6
Azuaga, Spain 33/D3
Azuara, Spain 33/F2
Azuay (prov.), Ec. 128/C4
Azuero (pen.), Pan. 154/G7
Azul, Arg. 143/E4
Azul (riv.), Guat. 154/C2
Azul, Cordillera (mts.), Peru 128/E7
Azurduy, Bol. 136/C6
Azure (lake), Br. Col. 184/G4
Azusa, Calif. (91702) 204/D10
Azwell, Wash. (98816) 310/F3
Azzel Mati, Sebkra (lake), Alg. 106/E3
Az Zubair, Iraq 66/E5

B

Baa, Indon. 85/G8
Baagø (isl.), Den. 21/C7
Ba'albek, Leb. 63/G5
Baan Baa, N.S.W. 97/E2
Baar, Switz. 39/F2
Baarle-Nassau, Neth. 27/F6
Baarn, Neth. 27/G4
Baba, Ec. 128/C3
Baba (cape), Turkey 63/A3
Baba (cape), Turkey 63/D2
Babadağ, Turkey 63/C4
Babadag, Rum. 45/J3
Babaeski, Turkey 63/B2
Baba Hatim, China 77/B4
Babahoyo, Ec. 128/C3
Babanusa, 102/E3
Babanusa, Sudan 111/E5
Babar (isl.), Indon. 85/H7
Babar (isls.), Indon. 85/H7
Babati, Tanz. 115/G4
Babayevo, U.S.S.R. 52/E3
Babb, Mont. (59411) 262/C2
Babbie, Ala. (†36420) 194/F8
Babbitt, Minn. (55706) 254/G3
Babbitt, Nev. (89416) 266/C4
Babcock, Wis. (54413) 317/F7
Babel (isls.), Tas. 99/E1
Bab el Mandeb (str.), 111/H5
Bab el Mandeb (str.), 102/G3
Babelthuap (isl.), Pac. Is., 87/D5
Babia (riv.), Mex. 150/J2
Babine (lake), 163/D5
Babine, Br. Col. 184/D2
Babine (lake), Br. Col. 184/E3
Babine (riv.), Br. Col. 184/D2
Babo, Indon. 85/K7
Babol, Iran, 54/J6
Babol, Iran 59/F2
Babol, Iran 66/H2
Baboquivari (mts.), Ariz. 198/D7
Baboua, Centr. Afr. Rep. 115/C2
Babson Park, Fla. (33827) 212/E4
Babulsar, Iran 66/H2
Babuyan (chan.), Phil. 82/C1
Babuyan (isl.), Phil. 82/B2
Babuyan (isls.), Phil. 82/A2
Babuyan (isls.), Phil. 85/G2
Babuyan (isls.), Phil., 54/R8
Babylon, N.Y. (*11702) 276/O9
Babylon (ruins), Iraq 66/D4
Baca (co.), Colo. 208/O8
Bacabal, Braz., 120/E3
Bacabal, Braz. 132/E4
Bacadéhuachi, Mex. 150/E2
Bacalar, Mex. 150/P7
Bacalar (lake), Mex. 150/P7
Bacanora, Mex. 150/E2
Bacarra, Phil. 82/C1
Bacău, Rum. 45/H2
Baccalieu (isl.), Newf. 166/D2
Bac Can, N. Vietnam 72/E2
Baccaro (pt.), N.S. 169/C5
Bacchus Marsh, Aust. 88/L6
Bacchus Marsh, Vic. 97/C5
Bacerac, Mex. 150/E1
Bach, Mich. (48704) 250/F5
Bachaquero, Ven. 124/C3
Bache (pen.), N.W.T. 187/L2
Bache, Okla. (74526) 288/P5
Bachelor (brook), Mass. 249/D3
Bachelor, N.C. (†28532) 281/R5
Bach Long Vi, Dao (isl.), N. Vietnam 72/F2
Back (riv.), 163/G2
Back (riv.), Md. 245/N4
Back (lake), N.H. 268/E1
Back (riv.), N.W.T. 187/J3
Back (bay), India 68/B7
Back (bay), Va. 307/S7
Back (creek), Va. 307/J4
Bačka Topola, Yugo. 45/D3
Back Bay, N. Br. 170/D3
Backbone (mt.), Md. 245/A3
Backnang, W. Ger. 22/C4
Backoo, N. Dak. (58215) 283/P2
Backus, Minn. (56435) 254/D4
Backway, The (inlet), Newf. 166/C3
Bac Lieu (Vinh Loi), S. Vietnam 72/E5
Bacliff, Texas (77518) 302/K2
Bac Ninh, N. Vietnam 72/E2
Baco (mt.), Phil. 82/C4
Bacolod, Phil. 82/D5
Bacolod, Phil. 85/G3
Bacon (co.), Ga. 216/G7
Bacone, Okla. (74420) 288/R3
Bacon Ridge (mts.), Wyo. 319/B2
Bacons, Del. (†19940) 245/R6
Bacons Castle, Va. (†23883) 307/P6
Baconton, Ga. (31716) 216/D8
Bácsalmás, Hung. 41/E3
Bács-Kiskun (co.), Hung. 41/E3
Bácum, Mex. 150/D3
Bacuna, Neth. Ant. 161/E8
Bacup, 10/G1
Bad (riv.), Mich. 250/E5
Bad (riv.), S. Dak. 298/G5
Bad (lake), Sask. 181/C4
Badachro, Scot. 15/E4
Badacsonytomaj, Hung. 41/D3
Badagara, India 68/D6
Bad Aibling, W. Ger. 22/D5
Badajoz, Spain, 7/D5
Badajoz (prov.), Spain 33/C3
Badajoz, Spain 33/C3
Badalona, Spain 33/H2
Bad Aussee, Austria 41/B3
Bad Axe, Mich. (48413) 250/G5
Bad Berneck, W. Ger. 22/D3
Bad Bramstedt, W. Ger. 22/C2
Badcall, Scot. 15/F3
Baddeck, N.S. 169/H2
Baddeck (riv.), N.S. 169/H2
Bad Doberan, E. Ger. 22/D1
Bad Driburg, W. Ger. 22/C3
Bad Dürkheim, W. Ger. 22/C4
Bad Dürrenberg, E. Ger. 22/D3
Bad Ems, W. Ger. 22/B3
Baden, Austria 41/D2
Baden, Ont. 177/D4
Baden, Man. 179/A2
Baden, Md. (†20613) 245/M6
Baden, Pa. (15005) 294/B4
Baden, Switz. 39/F2
Baden-Baden, W. Ger. 22/C4
Badenoch (dist.), Scot. 15/H6
Badenweiler, W. Ger. 22/B5
Baden-Württemberg (state), W. Ger. 22/C4
Bad Freienwalde, E. Ger. 22/F2
Bad Gandersheim, W. Ger. 22/D3
Badgastein, Austria 41/B3
Badger (peak), Idaho 220/E7
Badger, Iowa (50516) 229/E3
Badger, Man. 179/G5
Badger, Minn. (56714) 254/B2
Badger, Newf. 166/C4
Badger (creek), Oreg. 291/H3
Badger, S. Dak. (57214) 298/P5
Badger (creek), Wyo. 319/E2
Badger's Quay, Newf. 166/D4
Bad Goisern, Austria 41/B3
Badham, S.C. (†29471) 296/F5
Bad Harzburg, W. Ger. 22/D3
Bad Heart, Alta. 182/A2
Bad Hersfeld, W. Ger. 22/C3
Badhoevedorp, Neth. 27/B5
Bad Hofgastein, Austria 41/B3
Bad Homburg, W. Ger. 22/C3
Bad Honnef, W. Ger. 22/B3
Badian, Phil. 82/D6
Badin, N.C. (28009) 281/J4
Badin, Pak. 68/B4
Badiraguato, Mex. 150/F4
Bad Ischl, Austria 41/B3
Bad Kissingen, W. Ger. 22/D3
Bad Kreuznach, W. Ger. 22/B4
Bad Land (cliffs), Utah 304/D4
Bad Lands (reg.), N. Dak. 283/C7
Badlands Nat'l Mon., S. Dak. 298/E6
Bad Langensalza, E. Ger. 22/D3
Bad Lauterberg, W. Ger. 22/D3
Bad Liebenwerda, E. Ger. 22/E3
Bad Lippspringe, W. Ger. 22/C3
Bad Mergentheim, W. Ger. 22/C4
Bad Münster-Ebernburg, W. Ger. 22/B4
Bad Münstereifel, W. Ger. 22/B3
Bad Muskau, E. Ger. 22/F3
Bad Nauheim, W. Ger. 22/C3
Bad Nenndorf, W. Ger. 22/C2
Bad Neuenahr-Ahrweiler, W. Ger. 22/B3
Bad Neustadt, W. Ger. 22/D3
Bado, Mo. (†65447) 261/H8
Bad Oeynhausen, W. Ger. 22/C2
Bad Oldesloe, W. Ger. 22/D2
Ba Don, N. Vietnam 72/E3
Bad Orb, W. Ger. 22/C3
Badougou, Mali 106/C6
Bad Pyrmont, W. Ger. 22/C3
Badr, Saudi Ar. 59/C5
Badra, Iraq 66/D4
Bad Ragaz, Switz. 39/H2
Bad Reichenhall, W. Ger. 22/E5
Bad River Ind. Res., Wis. 317/E2
Bad Sachsa, W. Ger. 22/D3
Bad Salzschlirf, W. Ger. 22/C3
Bad Salzuflen, W. Ger. 22/C2
Bad Salzungen, E. Ger. 22/C3
Bad Sankt Leonhard, Austria 41/C3
Bad Schwartau, W. Ger. 22/D2
Bad Segeberg, W. Ger. 22/D2
Bad Tölz, W. Ger. 22/D5
Baduen, Somalia 115/J2
Badulla, Ceylon 68/E7
Bad Vilbel, W. Ger. 22/C3
Bad Waldsee, W. Ger. 22/C5
Badwater (creek), Wyo. 319/E2
Bad Wildungen, W. Ger. 22/C3
Bad Wimpfen, W. Ger. 22/C4
Baelum, Den. 21/D4
Baena, Spain 33/D4
Baerle-Duc, Belg. 27/F6
Báez, Cuba 158/E2
Baeza, Ec. 128/D3
Baeza, Spain 33/E4
Bafa (lake), Turkey 63/B4
Baffin (bay), 4/B13
Baffin (bay), 146/L2
Baffin (bay), 163/K1
Baffin (isl.), 163/J2
Baffin (bay), Canada, 3/F2
Baffin (isl.), Canada, 3/F2
Baffin (isl.), Canada, 4/C13
Baffin (isl.), N.W.T., 146/L2
Baffin (bay), N.W.T. 187/M2
Baffin (isl.), N.W.T. 187/L2
Baffin (bay), Texas 302/G10
Bafia, Cameroon 115/B3
Bafing (riv.), Guinea 106/B6
Bafing (riv.), Mali 106/B6
Bafoulabé, Mali 106/B6
Bafoussam, Cameroon 115/B2
Bafq, Iran 59/G3
Bafq, Iran 66/J5
Bafra, Turkey 59/C1
Bafra (cape), Turkey 59/C1
Bafra, Turkey 63/F2
Bafra (cape), Turkey 63/G2
Baft, Iran 59/G4
Baft, Iran 66/K6
Baga, Nigeria 106/G6
Bagabag, Phil. 82/C2
Bagac, Phil. 82/C3
Bagaces, C. Rica 154/E5
Bagadó, Col. 126/B5
Bagalkot, India 68/D5
Bagam (well), Niger 106/F5
Bagamoyo, 102/F5
Bagamoyo, Tanz. 115/G5
Bagañga, Phil. 82/F7
Baganian (pen.), Phil. 82/D7
Bagansiapiapi, Indon. 85/C5
Bagata, Dem. Rep. of the Congo. 115/C4
Bagdad, Ariz. (86321) 198/B4
Bagdad, Fla. (32530) 212/B6
Bagdad, Ky. (40003) 237/L4
Bagdad, Tas. 99/D4
Bagdarin, U.S.S.R. 48/M4
Bagé, Braz., 120/E6
Bagé, Braz. 132/C10
Bagenalstown, 10/C4
Bagenalstown (Muinebeag), Ire. 17/H6
Bagenkop, Den. 21/D8
Baggs, Wyo. (82321) 319/E4
Bagh Baqu, Iran 66/M3
Baghdad (cap.), Iraq, 3/M4
Baghdad (cap.), Iraq, 54/H6
Baghdad (cap.), Iraq 59/E3
Baghdad (prov.), Iraq 66/C3
Baghdad (cap.), Iraq 66/D4
Baghlan, Afgh. 59/J2
Baghlan, Afgh. 68/B1
Baghu, Iran 66/K7
Bağirpaşa Daği (mt.), Turkey 59/D2
Bağirpaşa Daği (mt.), Turkey 63/J3
Bagley, Iowa (50026) 229/E5
Bagley, Minn. (56621) 254/C3
Bagley, N.C. (†27542) 281/N3
Bagley, Wis. (53801) 317/D10
Bagnell, Mo. (†65026) 261/G6
Bagnell (dam), Mo. 261/G6
Bagnères-de-Bigorre, France 28/D6
Bagnères-de-Luchon, France 28/D6
Bagneria, Italy 34/D5
Bagnolet, France 28/B2
Bagnols-sur-Cèze, France 28/F5
Bagoé (riv.), Ivory Coast 106/C6
Bagoé (riv.), Mali 106/C6
Bagot (co.), Que. 172/E4
Bagot, Man. 179/D5
Bagotville, Que. 172/G1
Bagraband, Kuh-i- (mts.), Iran 66/M8
Bagrach Kol (lake), China 77/C3
Bagtic, Phil. 82/D6
Bagua, Peru 128/C5
Báguanos, Cuba 158/J3
Baguio, Phil. 82/C2
Baguio, Phil. 85/G2
Baguio, Phil., 54/P8
Baguirmi (reg.), Chad 111/C5
Bagwell, Texas (75412) 302/J4
Bahama (isls.), 3/F4
Bahama, N.C. (27503) 281/M2
Bahama Islands, 146/L7
BAHAMA ISLANDS, 156/C1
Bahariya (oasis), U.A.R. 59/A4
Bahariya (oasis), U.A.R. 111/E2
Bahawalnagar, Pak. 68/C2
Bahawalpur, Pak. 59/K4
Bahawalpur, Pak. 68/C3
Bahçe, Turkey 63/G4
Bahia (Salvador), Braz., 120/G4
Bahia (state), Braz. 132/F6
Bahia (Salvador), Braz. 132/G6
Bahía (isls.), Hond. 154/D2
Bahía Blanca, Arg., 3/F7
Bahía Blanca, Arg., 120/D6
Bahía Blanca, Arg. 143/D4
Bahía Bustamante, Arg. 143/C6
Bahía de Caráquez, Ec. 128/B3
Bahía Honda, Cuba 158/B1
Bahía Kino, Mex. 150/C2
Bahía Negra, Par. 144/C3
Bahía San Blas, Arg. 143/D5
Bahía Thetis, Arg. 143/C7
Bahía Tortugas, Mex. 150/B3
Bahomamey, P. Rico 161/A1
Bahoruco (Baoruco) (prov.), Dom. Rep. 158/D6
Bahraich, India 68/E3
Bahramabad, Iran 59/G3
Bahramabad, Iran 66/K5
Bahr Azoum (riv.), Sudan 111/D5
Bahrein, 54/J7
BAHREIN, 59/F4
Bahr el 'Arab (riv.), Sudan 111/E6
Bahr el Ghazal (dry riv.), Chad 111/C5
Bahr el Ghazal (prov.), Sudan 111/E6
Bahr es Safi (des.), Saudi Ar. 59/E6
Bahr ez Zeraf (riv.), Sudan 111/F6
Bahr Yusef (stream), U.A.R. 111/J4
Bai, China 77/B3
Baia de Aramă, Rum. 45/F3
Baía dos Tigres, Angola 115/B7
Baia Farta, Angola 115/B6
Baia Mare, Rum. 45/F2
Baião, Braz. 132/D3
Baibiene, Arg. 143/G4
Baibokoum, Chad 111/C6
Baida (prov.), Libya 111/D1
Baida (cap.), Libya 111/D1
Baidoa, 102/G4
Baidoa, Somalia 115/H3
Baidyabati, India 68/F1
Baie-Comeau, Que. 172/A1
Baie-Comeau, Que. 174/D3
Baie-de-Henne, Haiti 158/B5
Baie-de-Shawinigan, Que. 172/E3
Baie-des-Moutons, Que. 174/F2
Baie-des-Rochers, Que. 172/H2
Baie-des-Sables, Que. 172/A1
Baie de Wasai, Mich. (†49783) 250/E2
Baie-d'Urfé, Que. 172/G4
Baie-du-Vieux-Fort, Que. 174/F2
Baie-Johan-Beetz, Que. 174/E2
Baie-Mahault, Guad. 161/A6
Baiersbronn, W. Ger. 22/C4
Baie-Sainte-Catherine, Que. 172/H1
Baie-Saint-Paul, 163/J6
Baie-Saint-Paul, Que. 172/G2
Baie-Saint-Paul, Que. 174/C3
Baie-Trinité, Que. 172/B1
Baie Verte, N. Br. 170/F2
Baie Verte, Newf. 166/C4
Baieville, Que. 172/E3
Baigorrita, Arg. 143/F7
Baiji, Iraq 66/C3
Baildon, Sask. 181/F5
Baile Átha Cliath (Dublin) (cap.), Ire. 10/C4
Baile Átha Cliath (Dublin) (cap.), Ire. 17/K5
Bailén, Spain 33/E3
Băileşti, Rum. 45/F3
Bailey, Colo. (80421) 208/H4
Bailey, Iowa (†50455) 229/H2
Bailey, Mich. (49303) 250/D5
Bailey, Miss. (39320) 256/G6
Bailey, N. Br. 170/D3
Bailey, N.C. (27807) 281/N3
Bailey (co.), Texas 302/B3
Bailey‡, Texas (75413) 302/H4
Baileyboro, Texas (†79371) 302/B3
Bailey Island, Maine (04003) 242/D8
Bailey Lakes, Ohio (†44805) 284/B4
Bailey's Crossroads‡, Va. (22041) 307/O3
Baileys Harbor, Wis. (54202) 317/M5
Baileys Prairie‡, Texas (†77515) 302/J8
Baileysville, W. Va. (24812) 313/C7
Baileyton, Ala. (35019) 194/E2
Baileyton, Tenn. (37743) 237/R8
Baileyville, Conn. (†06455) 210/E2
Baileyville, Ill. (61007) 222/D1
Baileyville, Kans. (66404) 232/F2
Bailieborough, Ire. 17/G4
Baillie (isls.), N.W.T. 187/F2
Baillif, Guad. 161/A7
Bainbridge (isl.), Alaska 196/C1
Bainbridge, Ga. (31717) 216/C9
Bainbridge, Ind. (46105) 227/D5
Bainbridge, N.Y. (13733) 276/J6
Bainbridge, Ohio (45612) 284/D7
Bainbridge, Pa. (17502) 294/J5
Bainbridge (isl.), Wash. 310/A2
Bainbridge Island-Winslow, Wash. (98110) 310/A2
Bainbridge N.T.C., Md. 245/O2
Bainet, Haiti 158/B6
Bains, La. (70713) 238/H5
Bainville, Mont. (59212) 262/M2
Baird (inlet), Alaska 196/F2
Baird (mts.), Alaska 196/F1
Baird, Miss. (38724) 256/C4
Baird (pen.), N.W.T. 187/L3
Baird, Texas (79504) 302/E5
Bairdstown, Ohio (†45872) 284/C3
Bairdsville, N. Br. 170/C2
Baire, Cuba 158/H4
Bairiki (cap.), Gilb. and Ell., 87/H5
Bairnsdale, Aust. 88/H7
Bairnsdale, Vic. 97/D5
Bairoil, Wyo. (82322) 319/E3
Baisden, W. Va. (25608) 313/C7
Baïse (riv.), France 28/D6
Baishintu, Mong. 77/H2
Baitadi, Nepal 68/E3
Bait al Faqih, Yemen Arab Rep. 59/D7
Bai Thuong, N. Vietnam 72/E3
Baixa de Banheira, Port. 33/B3
Baixa Verde, Braz. 132/G4
Baixo (isl.), Port. 33/B2
Baixo Alentejo (prov.), Port. 33/B4
Baixo Guandu, Braz. 132/F7
Baja, Hung. 41/E3
Baja California (state), Mex. 150/B1
Baja California Sur (terr.), Mex. 150/C3
Bajadero, P. Rico 161/C1
Bajgiran, Iran 66/L2
Bajo Boquete, Pan. 154/F6
Bajo Nuevo (shoal), Col. 126/C8
Bajos de Haina, Dom. Rep. 158/E6
Bajram Cur, Alb. 45/D4
Bakala, Centr. Afr. Rep. 115/D2
Bakalar A.F.B., Ind. 227/E6
Bakanas, U.S.S.R. 48/H5
Bakar, Yugo. 45/B3
Bakel, 102/A3
Bakel, Sen. 106/B6
Baker (lake), 163/G3
Baker (isl.), Alaska 196/M2
Baker, Calif. (92309) 204/J8
Baker (riv.), Chile 138/D7
Baker (mt.), Colo. 208/H2
Baker (co.), Fla. 212/D1
Baker, Fla. (32531) 212/C5
Baker (co.), Ga. 216/D8
Baker, Idaho (83461) 220/E4
Baker, La. (70714) 238/K1
Baker (lake), Maine 242/D3
Baker, Minn. (56513) 254/B4
Baker‡, Mo. (†63846) 261/N9
Baker, Mont. (59313) 262/M4
Baker, N. Dak. (58312) 283/L3
Baker (riv.), N.H. 268/D4
Baker (lake), N.W.T. 187/J3
Baker, Nev. (89311) 266/G3
Baker, Okla. (73930) 288/D1
Baker, Oreg., 188/C2
Baker (co.), Oreg. 291/K3
Baker, Oreg. (97814) 291/K3
Baker (isl.), Pacific, 87/J5
Baker (creek), Utah 304/A4
Baker, W. Va. (26801) 313/J4
Baker (lake), Wash. 310/D2
Baker (mt.), Wash. 310/D2
Baker (riv.), Wash. 310/D2
Baker Brook, N. Br. 170/B1
Baker Butte (mt.), Ariz. 198/D4
Baker Hill, Ala. (36004) 194/H7
Baker Lake, 163/G3
Baker Lake, N.W.T. 187/J3
Bakers (isl.), Mass. 249/F5
Bakersfield, Calif., 188/C3
Bakersfield, Calif. (*93301) 204/F8
Bakersfield, Mo. (65609) 261/H9
Bakersfield, Texas (79717) 302/B7
Bakersfield△, Vt. (05441) 268/B2
Bakersfield, Vt. (05441) 268/B2
Bakers Summit, Pa. (16614) 294/F5
Bakersville, Conn. (†06057) 210/C1
Bakersville, N.C. (28705) 281/E2
Bakersville, Ohio (43803) 284/G5
Bakersville, Pa. (†15501) 294/D5
Bakerton, Ky. (42711) 237/L7
Bakerton, W. Va. (25410) 313/L4
Bakerville, Tenn. (37185) 237/F9
Bakewell, 10/G2
Bakewell, Eng. 13/F4
Bakewell, Tenn. (37304) 237/L10
Bakharz, Kuh-i- (mt.), Iran 66/M3
Bakhchisaray, U.S.S.R. 52/D6
Bakhmach, U.S.S.R. 52/D4
Bakhtegan (lake), Iran 66/J6
Bakhtiari (governorate), Iran 66/F4
Bakhun, Kuh-i- (mt.), Iran 66/K6
Bakhuys (mts.), Sur. 131/C3
Bakirköy, Turkey 63/D6
Baklan, Turkey 63/C4
Bako, Eth. 111/G6
Bakony (mts.), Hung. 41/D3
Bakoy (riv.), Guinea 106/B6
Bakoy (riv.), Mali 106/B6
Baktalórántháza, Hung. 41/G2
Baktu (Paektu) (mt.), N. Korea 81/C3
Baku, U.S.S.R. 48/F5
Baku, U.S.S.R. 52/H6
Baku, U.S.S.R., 3/M3
Baku, U.S.S.R., 7/K4
Bala, Ont. 177/E2
Bala, Kans. (†66531) 232/F2
Bala, 10/E4
Balâ, Turkey 63/E3
Bala, Wales 13/D5
Balabac, Phil. 82/A7
Balabac (isl.), Phil. 82/A7
Balabac (str.), Phil. 82/A7
Balabac (isl.), Phil. 85/F4
Balabac (str.) Phil. 85/F4
Balabalangan (isls.), Indon. 85/F7
Balaclava, Jam. 158/H6
Bala-Cynwyd, Pa. (19004) 294/N6
Balad, Somalia 115/J3
Balaghat, India 68/E4
Balaguer, Spain 33/G2
Balaitous (mt.), Spain 33/F1
Balakhna, U.S.S.R. 52/F3
Balakhna, U.S.S.R., 7/J3
Balaklava, U.S.S.R. 52/D6
Balaklava, S. Aust. 94/F6
Balakovo, U.S.S.R. 52/G4
Bal'ama, Jordan 65/E3
Balambangan (isl.), Malaysia 85/F4
Bala Murghab, Afgh. 59/H2
Bala Murghab, Afgh. 68/A1
Balana, Hond. 154/E3
Balancán de Domínguez, Mex. 150/O8
Balandra (pt.), Dom. Rep. 158/F5
Balanga, Phil. 82/C3
Balangala, Dem. Rep. of the Congo. 115/D3
Balangan (isls.), Indon. 85/F6
Balangiga, Phil. 82/E5
Balao, Ec. 128/C4
Balashi, Neth. Ant. 161/E10
Balashov, U.S.S.R. 48/E4
Balashov, U.S.S.R. 52/F4
Balasore, India 68/F4
Balassagyarmat, Hung. 41/E2
Balaton (lake), Hung., 7/F4
Balaton (lake), Hung. 41/D3
Balaton, Minn. (56115) 254/C6
Balatonfüred, Hung. 41/D3
Balatonszentgyörgy, Hung. 41/D3
Balayan (bay), Phil. 82/C4
Balboa, C.Z. 154/H6
Balbriggan, 10/C4
Balbriggan, Ire. 17/J4
Balcarce, Arg. 143/E4
Balcarres, Sask. 181/H5
Balchik, Bulg. 45/H4
Balch Springs, Texas (75149) 302/H2
Balclutha, N.Z. 101/B7
Balcones Escarpment (plat.), Texas 302/E8
Balcones Heights‡, Texas (†78201) 302/F8
Bald (head), Aust. 88/B7
Bald (mt.), Colo. 208/H4
Bald (hill), Conn. 210/G1
Bald (mt.), Idaho 220/D5
Bald (mt.), N. Br. 170/C1
Bald (mts.), N.C. 281/D3
Bald (head), W. Aust. 92/B6
Bald (mts.), Tenn. 237/R9
Bald (mt.), Utah 304/C3
Bald (mt.), Vt. 268/D2
Bald Eagle (lake), Minn. 254/G3
Bald Eagle (lake), Minn. 254/G5
Baldeggersee (lake), Switz. 39/F2
Baldhill (Ashtabula) (res.), N. Dak. 283/P5
Bald Hill Branch (riv.), Md. 245/G4
Bald Knob, Ark. (72010) 203/G3
Bald Knob, W. Va. (25010) 313/C7
Baldonnel, Br. Col. 184/G2
Baldur, Man. 179/C5
Baldwin (co.), Ala. 194/C9
Baldwin, Fla. (32234) 212/E1
Baldwin (co.), Ga. 216/F4
Baldwin, Ga. (30511) 216/E2
Baldwin, Ill. (62217) 222/D5
Baldwin, Iowa (52207) 229/M4
Baldwin, La. (70514) 238/H7
Baldwin, Mich. (49304) 250/D5
Baldwin, N. Dak. (58521) 283/J5
Baldwin, N.Y. (11510) 276/R7
Baldwin, Pa. (†15201) 294/B7
Baldwin, W. Va. (26326) 313/E5
Baldwin, Wis. (54002) 317/B6
Baldwin-Aragon Mills, S.C. (29706) 296/E2
Baldwin City, Kans. (66006) 232/G3
Baldwin Park, Calif. (91706) 204/D10
Baldwinsville, N.Y. (13027) 276/H4
Baldwinton, Sask. 181/B3
Baldwinville, Mass. (01436) 249/F2
Baldwyn, Miss. (38824) 256/G2
Baldy (peak), Ariz. 198/F5
Baldy (mt.), Man. 179/B3
Baldy (peak), N. Mex. 274/D3
Baldy (peak), Utah 304/B5
Bale (mt.), Eth. 111/G6
Baleares (prov.), Spain 33/H3
Balearic (isls.), Spain, 7/E5
Balearic (Baleares) (isls.), Spain 33/H3
Baleine (riv.), 163/K4
Baleine (riv.), Que. 174/D1
Baleine, Grand Rivière de la (riv.), Que. 174/B1
Baleine, Petite Rivière de la (riv.), Que. 174/B1
Baleine, Grande Rivière de la (riv.), 163/J5
Balen, Belg. 27/G6
Baler, Phil. 82/C3
Baler (bay), Phil. 82/C3
Balerna, Switz. 39/G5
Baleshare (isl.), Scot. 15/A4
Balestrand, Norway 18/E6
Balfate, Hond. 154/D3
Balfour, N.C. (28706) 281/E4
Balfour, N. Dak. (58712) 283/J4
Balfours, N.C. (†27203) 281/K3
Balgonie, Sask. 181/G5
Balhaf, P.D.R. Yemen 59/E7
Bal Harbour, Fla. (†33101) 212/C4
Bali (isl.), Indon., 54/P10
Bali (isl.), Indon. 85/F7
Bali (sea), Indon. 85/F7
Bali (str.), Indon. 85/E7
Bali, Cameroon 115/A2
Baliangao, Phil. 82/D6
Balicuatro (isls.), Phil. 82/E4
Balige, Indon. 85/B5
Balik (lake), Turkey 63/G2
Balikesir, Turkey 59/A2
Balikesir (prov.), Turkey 63/B3
Balikesir, Turkey 63/B3
Balikpapan, Indon. 85/F6
Balimbing, Phil. 82/C8
Baling, Malaysia 72/D6
Balingasag, Phil. 82/E6
Balingen, W. Ger. 22/C4
Balintang (chan.), Phil. 82/A2
Balintang (isls.), Phil. 82/A2
Baljennie, Sask. 181/C3
Balkan (mts.), Bulg. 45/G4
Balkan, Ky. (40804) 237/O7
Balkans (mts.), 7/G4
Balkány, Hung. 41/G3
Balkar (mts.), Leb. 63/F4
Balkbrug, Neth. 27/J3
Balkh, Afghan., 54/K6
Balkh, Afgh. 59/J2
Balkh, Afgh. 68/B1
Balkhash, U.S.S.R. 48/H5
Balkhash (lake), U.S.S.R. 48/H5
Balkhash (lake), U.S.S.R., 3/N3
Balkhash (lake), U.S.S.R., 54/L5
Balko, Okla. (73931) 288/E1
Ball (bay), Aust. 88/M5
Ball (mt.), Conn. 210/C1
Ball (pond), Conn. 210/A3
Ball, La. (71405) 238/F4
Balla, Ire. 17/C4
Balla Balla, Rhod. 118/D4
Ballachulish, Scot. 15/F6
Balladonia, W. Aust. 92/D6
Ballaghaderreen, Ire. 17/E4
Ballaigues, Switz. 39/B3
Ballantine, Mont. (59006) 262/J5
Ballantrae, Scot. 15/F9
Ballantyne (str.), N.W.T. 187/G2
Ballantynes Cove, N.S. 169/F3
Ballarat, Australia, 87/E9
Ballarat, Aust. 88/G7
Ballarat, Vic. 97/C5
Ballard (co.), Ky. 237/C6
Ballard, Mo. (†64730) 261/D6
Ballard (cape), Newf. 166/D2
Ballard, W. Va. (24918) 313/E8
Ballardsville, Miss. (†38801) 256/H2
Ballardvale, Mass. (01810) 249/K2
Ballater, 10/E2
Ballater, Scot. 15/K5
Ball Club, Minn. (56622) 254/E3
Ballenas (bay), Mex. 150/C3
Ballenero (chan.), Chile 138/E11
Ballengee, W. Va. (24919) 313/E7
Ballens, Switz. 39/B3
Ballenstedt, E. Ger. 22/D3

330 Ballentine

Ballentine, S.C. (29002) 296/E3
Balleny (isls.), Ant., 3/S9
Balleny (isls.), Ant. 5/C9
Ballerup, Den. 21/F6
Ballesteros, Phil. 82/C1
Balleza, Mex. 150/F3
Ball Ground, Ga. (30107) 216/D2
Ballground, Miss. (†39156) 256/C5
Ballia, India 68/E3
Ballidu, Aust. 88/B6
Ballidu, W. Aust. 92/B5
Ballina, Aust. 88/J5
Ballina, 10/B3
Ballina, Ire. 17/C3
Ballina, N.S.W. 97/G1
Ballinagh, Ire. 17/G4
Ballinakill, Ire. 17/G6
Ballinamore, Ire. 17/F3
Ballinasloe, 10/B4
Ballinasloe, Ire. 17/E5
Ballincollig, Ire. 17/D8
Ballindine, Ire. 17/C4
Ballingarry, Limerick, Ire. 17/D7
Ballingarry, Tipperary, Ire. 17/F6
Ballinger, Texas (76821) 302/E6
Ballinlough, Ire. 17/D4
Ballinrobe, 10/B4
Ballinrobe, Ire. 17/C4
Ballinskelligs (bay), Ire. 17/A8
Ballintober, Ire. 17/E4
Ballintra, Ire. 17/E2
Ballisodare, Ire. 17/E3
Ballivián, Par. 144/B4
Ballouville, Conn. (06233) 210/H1
Ballston, Oreg. (†97378) 291/D2
Ballston Spa, N.Y. (12020) 276/N5
Ballsville, Va. (23010) 307/M6
Balltown, Iowa (†52073) 229/M3
Ballum, Den. 21/B7
Ballville, Ohio (†43420) 284/D3
Ballwin, Mo. (63011) 261/O3
Bally, India 68/F1
Bally, Pa. (19503) 294/L5
Ballybay, Ire. 17/G3
Ballybofey, Ire. 17/F2
Ballybunion, 10/B4
Ballybunion, Ire. 17/B7
Ballycanew, Ire. 17/J6
Ballycarney, Ire. 17/J6
Ballycastle, Ire. 17/C3
Ballycastle, N. Ire. 17/J1
Ballycastle, 10/C3
Ballyclare, N. Ire. 17/J2
Ballyconnell, Ire. 17/F3
Ballycotton, Ire. 17/F8
Ballycotton (bay), Ire. 17/F8
Ballydehob, Ire. 17/C8
Ballydesmond, Ire. 17/C7
Ballyduff, Ire. 17/B7
Ballygally, N. Ire. 17/K2
Ballygar, Ire. 17/E4
Ballygawley, N. Ire. 17/G3
Ballyhaunis, Ire. 17/D4
Ballyheige (bay), Ire. 17/B7
Ballyheigue, Ire. 17/B7
Ballyhoura (hills), Ire. 17/E7
Ballyjamesduff, Ire. 17/G4
Ballykelly, N. Ire. 17/G1
Ballylanders, Ire. 17/E7
Ballylongford, Ire. 17/B6
Ballymahon, Ire. 17/F4
Ballymakeery-Ballyvourney, Ire. 17/C8
Ballymena, N. Ire. 17/J2
Ballymena, 10/C3
Ballymoney, N. Ire. 17/J1
Ballymoney, 10/C3
Ballymore, Ire. 17/F5
Ballymore Eustace, Ire. 17/J5
Ballymote, 10/B3
Ballymote, Ire. 17/D3
Ballynacargy, Ire. 17/G4
Ballynahinch, N. Ire. 17/J3
Ballynakill (harb.), Ire. 17/A4
Ballynure, N. Ire. 17/K2
Ballyporeen, Ire. 17/E7
Ballyragget, Ire. 17/G6
Ballyroan, Ire. 17/G6
Ballysadare (bay), Ire. 17/D3
Ballyshannon, 10/B3
Ballyshannon, Ire. 17/E3
Ballyteige (bay), Ire. 17/H7
Ballytore, Ire. 17/H5
Ballyvaughan, Ire. 17/C5
Ballywalter, N. Ire. 17/K2
Balmaceda, Chile 138/E6
Balmaha, Scot. 15/C1
Balmazújváros, Hung. 41/F3
Balmertown, Ont. 175/B2
Balmhorn (mt.), Switz. 39/E4
Balmoral, Man. 179/E4
Balmoral, Minn. (†56515) 254/C4
Balmoral, N. Br. 170/D1
Balmoral, W. Aust. 92/B3
Balmoral, Queens. 95/E2
Balmoral, Vic. 97/A5
Balmoral Castle, 10/E2
Balmoral Castle, Scot. 15/K5
Balmorhea, Texas (79718) 302/D11
Balmville, N.Y. (†12550) 276/M7
Balnearia, Arg. 143/D3
Balneario El Tesoro, Urug. 145/E5
Balneario La Barra, Urug. 145/E5
Balneario Solís, Urug. 145/D5
Balonne (riv.), Aust. 88/H5
Balonne (riv.), Queens. 95/D6
Balotra, India 68/C3
Balovale, Zambia 115/D6
Baloy (mt.), Phil. 82/D5
Balpunga, N.S.W. 97/A3
Balquhidder, Scot. 15/H7
Balrampur, India 68/E3
Balranald, Aust. 88/G6
Balranald, N.S.W. 97/B4
Balrothery, Ire. 17/J4
Balş, Rum. 45/G3
Balsam (lake), Ont. 177/F3
Balsam, N.C. (28707) 281/C4
Balsam Creek, Ont. 177/E1
Balsam Lake, Wis. (54810) 317/B5
Balsapuerto, Peru 128/D5
Balsas, Braz. 132/E4
Balsas (riv.), Braz. 132/E5
Balsas (riv.), Mex. 150/J7
Bålsta, Sweden 18/G1
Balsthal, Switz. 39/E2
Balta, N. Dak. (58313) 283/K3
Baltanás, Spain 33/D2
Baltasar Brum, Urug. 145/B1
Baltasound, Scot. 15/M2
Baltic (sea), 3/K3
Baltic (sea), 7/F3
Baltic, Conn. (06330) 210/G2
Baltic (sea), Fin. 18/K9
Baltic (sea), Sweden 18/K9
Baltic (sea), U.S.S.R. 48/B4
Baltic (sea), U.S.S.R. 52/B3
Baltic (sea), E. Ger. 22/E1
Baltic, Mich. (49907) 250/G1
Baltic, Ohio (43804) 284/G5
Baltic (sea), Poland 47/B1
Baltic, S. Dak. (57003) 298/R6
BALTIC STATES, 53
Baltimore, 10/B5
Baltimore, Ire. 17/C9
Baltimore, Md., 146/L6
Baltimore, Md., 188/L3
Baltimore (co.), Md. 245/M3
Baltimore (city county), Md. 245/M3
Baltimore, Md. (*21201) 245/M3
Baltimore, Ohio (43105) 284/E6
Baltinglass, Ire. 17/H6
Baltistan (reg.), India 68/D1
Baltit, India 68/C1
Baltiysk, U.S.S.R. 52/A4
Baltra (isl.), Ec. 128/B9
Baltrum (isl.), W. Ger. 22/B2
Balturino, U.S.S.R. 48/K4
Balty, Va. (†22546) 307/O5
Baluchistan (reg.), Iran 66/M7
Baluchistan (prov.), Pak. 68/B3
Baluchistan (reg.), Pak. 59/J4
Baluchistan (reg.), Pak. 68/B3
Balvi, U.S.S.R. 53/D2
Balya, Turkey 63/B3
Balzac, Alta. 182/C4
Balzar, Ec. 128/C3
Bam, Iran, 54/J7
Bam, Iran 59/G4
Bam, Iran 66/L6
Bama, Nigeria 106/G6
Bamako (cap.), Mali, 102/B3
Bamako (cap.), Mali, 3/J5
Bamako (cap.), Mali 106/C6
Bamba, Mali 106/D5
Bambamarca, Peru 128/C6
Bamban, Phil. 82/C3
Bambang, Phil. 82/C2
Bambari, Centr. Afr. Rep. 115/D2
Bamberg (co.), S.C. 296/E5
Bamberg, S.C. (29003) 296/E5
Bamberg, W. Ger. 22/D4
Bambesa, Dem. Rep. of the Congo. 115/E3
Bambili, Dem. Rep. of the Congo. 115/E3
Bamble, Norway 18/F7
Bamboo, Aust. 88/C4
Bamboo, W. Aust. 92/C3
Bambui, Braz. 132/E8
Bambuí, Braz. 135/C2
Bamburgh, Eng. 13/F2
Bamenda, Cameroon 115/B2
Bamfield, Br. Col. 184/E6
Bamian, Afgh. 59/J3
Bamian, Afgh. 68/B2
Bamingui (riv.), Centr. Afr. Rep. 115/C2
Bamoa, Mex. 150/E4
Bampton, Devon, Eng. 13/D7
Bampton, Oxford, Eng. 13/F6
Bampur, Iran 59/H4
Bampur, Iran 66/M7
Bampur (riv.), Iran 66/M7
Bam Tso (lake), China 77/D5
Bañado de Medina, Urug. 145/E3
Bañado de Ovanta, Arg. 143/C2
Bañado de Rocha, Urug. 145/C2
Banagher, Ire. 17/F5
Banagüises, Cuba 158/D1
Banahao (mt.), Phil. 82/C3
Banalia, Dem. Rep. of the Congo. 115/E3
Banam, Cambodia 72/E5
Banana (riv.), Fla. 212/F3
Banana, Dem. Rep. of the Congo. 115/B5
Bananal (isl.), Braz., 120/E4
Bananal (isl.), Braz. 132/D5
Bananier, Guad. 161/A7
Banao, Cuba 158/G2
Ban Aranyaprathet, Thai. 72/D4
Banas (riv.), India 68/D3
Bânâs, Ras (cape), U.A.R. 59/C5
Bânâs, Ras (cape), U.A.R. 111/G3
Banaue, Phil. 82/C2
Banavie, Scot. 15/F6
Banaz, Turkey 63/C3
Banaz (riv.), Turkey 63/C3
Banbridge, N. Ire. 17/J3
Ban Bung Sai, Laos 72/E4
Banbury, 10/F4
Banbury, Eng. 13/F5
Bancalan (isl.), Phil. 82/A6
Bancannia (lake), N.S.W. 97/A2
Banchory, 10/E2
Banchory, Scot. 15/M5
Bancoran (isl.), Phil. 82/B7
Bancroft, Ont. 177/G2
Bancroft, Idaho (83217) 220/G7
Bancroft, Iowa (50517) 229/E2
Bancroft, Kans. (†66428) 232/G2
Bancroft, La. (†70653) 238/C5
Bancroft△, Maine (04409) 242/H4
Bancroft, Maine (04409) 242/H4
Bancroft, Mich. (48414) 250/E6
Bancroft, Nebr. (68004) 264/H2
Bancroft (Chililabombwe), Zambia 115/E6
Bancroft, Oreg. (†97458) 291/D5
Bancroft, S. Dak. (57316) 298/O4
Bancroft, W. Va. (25011) 313/C5
Bancroft, Wis. (54921) 317/G7
Bancroft, Zambia, 115/E6
Banda, India 68/D3
Banda (isls.), Indon. 85/H6
Banda (sea), Indon. 85/H7
Banda, Gabon 115/B4
Banda Atjeh, Indon., 54/N9
Banda Atjeh, Indon. 85/A4
Bandai (mt.), Japan 81/K5
Bandai-Asahi Nat'l Park, Japan 81/J4
Bandama (riv.), Ivory Coast 106/C7
Bandana, Ky. (42022) 237/D6
Bandanaira, Indon. 85/H6
Bandar (Machilipatnam), India, 54/M8
Bandar 'Abbas, Iran, 54/J7
Bandar 'Abbas, Iran 59/G4
Bandar 'Abbas, Iran 66/J7
Bandar Dilam, Iran 66/G5
Bandar Maharani, Malaysia 72/D7
Bandar Ma'shur, Iran 66/F5
Bandar Penggaram, Malaysia 72/D7
Bandar Rig, Iran 59/F4
Bandar Rig, Iran 66/G6
Bandar Seri Begawan, Brunei 85/E4
Bandar Shah, Iran 59/F2
Bandar Shah, Iran 66/H2
Bandar Shahpur, Iran 59/E3
Bandar Shahpur, Iran 66/F5
Bandawe, Malawi 115/F6
Bande, Spain 33/B1
Bandeira (mt.), Braz. 132/F8
Bandeira (mt.), Braz. 135/E2
Bandelier Nat'l Mon., N. Mex. 274/C3
Bandera, Arg. 143/D2
Bandera (co.), Texas 302/E8
Bandera, Texas (78003) 302/F8
Banderas (bay), Mex. 150/G6
Bandholm, Den. 21/E8
Bandiagara, 102/B3
Bandiagara, Mali 106/D6
Bandirma, Turkey 59/A1
Bandirma, Turkey 63/B2
Bandjarmasin, Indon., 54/P10
Bandjarmasin, Indon. 85/E6
Bandon, 10/B5
Bandon, Ire. 17/D8
Bandon (riv.), Ire. 17/D8
Bandon, Oreg. (97411) 291/C4
Bandra, India 68/B7
Bandundu, 102/D5
Bandundu (prov.), Dem. Rep. of the Congo. 115/C4
Bandundu, Dem. Rep. of the Congo. 115/C4
Bandung, Indon., 54/O10
Bandung, Indon. 85/H2
Bandy, Va. (24602) 307/E6
Bandya, W. Aust. 92/C4
Banes, Cuba 156/C2
Banes, Cuba 158/J3
Banff, Alta. 182/C4
Banff, 10/E2
Banff (co.), Scot. 15/K5
Banff, Scot. 15/L4
Banff Nat'l Park, 163/E5
Banff Nat'l Park, Alta. 182/B4
Banfora, Upp. Volta 106/D6
Bangalore, India, 3/N5
Bangalore, India, 54/L8
Bangalore, India 68/D6
Bangalow, N.S.W. 97/G1
Bangar, Phil. 82/C2
Bangassou, Centr. Afr. Rep. 115/D3
Banggai, Indon. 85/G6
Banggai (arch.), Indon. 85/G6
Banggi (isl.), Malaysia 85/F4
Bangil, Indon. 85/K2
Bangka (isl.), Indon., 54/O10
Bangka (isl.), Indon. 85/D6
Bangka (str.), Indon. 85/C6
Bangkalan, Indon. 85/K2
Bangkok (cap.), Thai., 3/P5
Bangkok (cap.), Thai., 54/N8
Bangkok (cap.), Thai., 72/D4
Bang Lamung, Thai. 72/D4
Bangor, Calif. (95914) 204/D4
Bangor, 10/D4
Bangor, Maine, 146/M5
Bangor, Maine, 188/N2
Bangor, Maine (04401) 242/F6
Bangor, Mich. (49013) 250/C6
Bangor, N. Ire. 17/K2
Bangor, N.Y. (12966) 276/M1
Bangor, Pa. (18013) 294/M4
Bangor, Sask. 181/J5
Bangor, Wales 13/C4
Bangor, Wis. (54614) 317/E8
Bangs, Texas (76823) 302/E6
Bang Saphan, Thai. 72/C5
Bangued, Phil. 82/C2
Bangued, Phil. 85/G2
Banguezane (mt.), Niger 106/F5
Bangui, Phil. 82/C1
Bangui (bay), Phil. 82/C1
Bangui, Phil. 85/G2
Bangui (cap.), Cent. Afr. Rep., 3/K5
Bangui (cap.), Centr. Afr. Rep. 115/C3
Bangui (cap.), Centr. Afr. Rep. 102/D4
Bangweulu (lake), 102/F6
Bangweulu (lake), Zambia 115/F6
Baní, Dom. Rep. 156/D3
Baní, Dom. Rep. 158/E6
Bani (riv.), Mali 106/C6
Bani, Jebel (mts.), Mor. 106/C3
Bani, Phil. 82/B2
Bania, Centr. Afr. Rep. 115/C3
Baniara, Papua 85/C7
Bánica, Dom. Rep. 156/D3
Bánica, Dom. Rep. 158/D5
Banida, Idaho (83264) 220/G7
Banister (riv.), Va. 307/K7
Baniyas, Syria 63/F5
Banjak (isls.), Indon. 85/B5
Banja Luka, Yugo., 7/F4
Banja Luka, Yugo. 45/C3
Banjumas, Indon. 85/J2
Banjuwangi, Indon. 85/L2
Bank, S. Africa 118/G7
Banka Banka, No. Terr. 93/C5
Ban Kantang, Thai. 72/C6
Ban Kapong, Thai. 72/C5
Bankend, Sask. 181/H4
Bankhead (lake), Ala. 194/D4
Ban Khlong Yai, Thai. 72/D5
Bankot, India 68/C5
Banks (isl.), 163/D1
Banks, Ala. (36005) 194/G7
Banks (pt.), Alaska 196/H3
Banks, Ark. (71631) 203/F6
Banks (str.), Aust. 88/H8
Banks (isl.), Br. Col. 184/B3
Banks (isl.), Canada, 3/C2
Banks (isl), Canada, 4/B16
Banks (bay), Ec. 128/B9
Banks (co.), Ga. 216/E2
Banks (lake), Ga. 216/F9
Banks, Idaho (83602) 220/B5
Banks, Miss. (†38664) 256/D1
Banks (cape), N.S.W. 97/K4
Banks (isl.), N.W.T., 146/F2
Banks (isl.), N.W.T. 187/F2
Banks (pen.), N.Z. 101/D5
Banks (isls.), New Hebr., 87/G7
Banks (isl.), Queens. 95/B1
Banks, Oreg. (97106) 291/A1
Banks (str.), Tasmania 99/D2
Banks (lake), Wash. 310/F3
Bankston, Ala. (35542) 194/C3
Bankston, Iowa (†52045) 229/L3
Bankstown, Aust. 88/L3
Bankstown, N.S.W. 97/J3
Ban Kui Nua, Thai. 72/D4
Bankura, India 68/F4
Ban Me Thuot, S. Vietnam 72/F4
Bann (riv.), Ire. 17/J6
Bann (riv.), N. Ire. 17/H2
Bannack, Mont. (†59725) 262/C5
Banner, Ill. (†61520) 222/D3
Banner, Ky. (41603) 237/R5
Banner, Miss. (38913) 256/F2
Banner, Mo. (†63623) 261/L7
Banner (co.), Nebr. 264/A3
Banner, Va. (24231) 307/D7
Banner, Wyo. (82832) 319/F1
Banner Elk‡, N.C. (28604) 281/F2
Banner Hill, Tenn. (†37650) 237/R8
Bannerman, Man. 179/C5
Banner Springs, Tenn. (38557) 237/M8
Bannertown, N.C. (†27030) 281/H1
Ban Ngon, Thai. 72/D3
Banning, Calif. (92220) 204/J10
Banning, Ga. (†30185) 216/C3
Bannister, Mich. (48807) 250/E5
Bannock (co.), Idaho 220/F7
Bannock (creek), Idaho 220/F7
Bannock (peak), Idaho 220/F7
Bannock (range), Idaho 220/F7
Bannockburn, Ont. 177/G3
Bannockburn‡, Ill. (†60015) 222/F1
Bannockburn, 10/B1
Bannockburn, Scot. 15/D1
Bannow, Ire. 17/H7
Bannu, Pak. 59/K3
Bannu, Pak. 68/C2
Bañolas, Spain 33/H1
Bánovce, Czech. 41/E2
Ban Pak Phanang, Thai. 72/D5
Banphot Phisai, Thai. 72/C3
Ban Pua, Thai. 72/D3
Banquo, Ind. (†46940) 227/F3
Ban Sattahip, Thai. 72/D4
Bansberia, India 68/F1
Banská Bystrica, Czech. 41/E2
Banská Štiavnica, Czech. 41/E2
Bansko, Bulg. 45/F5
Banstead, 10/B6
Bansud, Phil. 82/C4
Banswara, India 68/C4
Bantam, Conn. (06750) 210/B2
Bantam (lake), Conn. 210/C2
Bantam (riv.), Conn. 210/B2
Bantayan, Phil. 82/D5
Bantayan (isl.), Phil. 82/D5
Ban Tha Uthen, Thai. 72/D3
Banton, Phil. 82/D4
Banton (isl.), Phil. 82/D4
Bantry, 10/B5
Bantry (bay), 10/A5
Bantry, Ire. 17/C8
Bantry (bay), Ire. 17/B8
Bantry, N. Dak. (58713) 283/J3
Bantul, Indon. 85/J2
Bañuelo (mt.), Spain 33/D3
Banyo, Cameroon 115/B2
Banzare Coast (reg.), Ant. 5/C7
Banzyville, Dem. Rep. of the Congo 115/D3
Bao Ha, N. Vietnam 72/D2
Bao Lac, N. Vietnam 72/E2
Baoruco (prov.), Dom. Rep. 158/D6
Baoruco, Sierra de (mts.), Dom. Rep. 158/D6
Baoulé (riv.), Ivory Coast 106/C6
Baoulé (dry riv.), Mali 106/C6
Baoulé (riv.), Mali 106/C6
Bapaume, Sask. 181/D2
Bapchule, Ariz. (85221) 198/D5
Bapsfontein, S. Africa 118/J6
Baptist, La. (†70401) 238/M1
Baptiste (lake), Ont. 177/G2
Baptistown, N.J. (08803) 273/D2
Ba'quba, Iraq 59/D3
Ba'quba, Iraq 66/D4
Baquedano, Chile 138/A4
Baqura, Jordan 65/D2
Bar, Yugo. 45/D4
Bara, Sudan 59/B7
Bara, Sudan 111/F5
Barabai, Indon. 85/F6
Barabinsk, U.S.S.R. 48/H4
Barabinsk, U.S.S.R., 54/L4
Baraboo, Wis. (53913) 317/G9
Barachois (pt.), N.S. 169/G4
Barachois-de-Malbaie, Que. 172/D1
Baracoa, Cuba 156/C2
Baracoa, Cuba 158/K4
Barada, Nebr. (†68457) 264/J4
Baradères, Haiti 158/B6
Baradères (bay), Haiti 158/B6
Baradero, Arg. 143/G6
Baradine, N.S.W. 97/E2
Baradine (creek), N.S.W. 97/E2
Baraga (co.), Mich. 250/A2
Baraga, Mich. (49908) 250/G1
Baragoi, Kenya 115/G3
Baragua, Ven. 124/D2
Barahona, Dom. Rep. 156/D3
Barahona (prov.), Dom. Rep. 158/D6
Barahona, Dom. Rep. 158/D6
Barajas, Spain 33/F4
Barak, Turkey 63/G4
Baraka (riv.), Sudan 59/C6
Baraka (riv.), Eth. 111/G4
Baraka (riv.), Sudan 111/G4
Baraka, Dem. Rep. of the Congo. 115/E4
Bara Khel, Afgh. 59/J3
Baralzon (lake), Man. 179/J1
Barama (riv.), Guyana 131/A2
Baramanni, Guyana 131/B2
Baramati, India 68/C5
Baramita, Guyana 131/A2
Baramula, India 68/D2
Barankwa, Sudan 59/B7
Baranoa, Col. 126/C2
Baranof, Alaska (99822) 196/M1
Baranof (isl.), Alaska 196/M1
Baranovichi, U.S.S.R. 48/C4
Baranovichi, U.S.S.R. 52/C4
Baranya (co.), Hung. 41/E4
Barão de Cocais, Braz. 135/E1
Baras, Phil. 82/E4
Barasat, India 68/F1
Baratang (isl.), India 68/G6
Barataria, La. (70036) 238/K7
Barataria (bay), La. 238/L8
Barataria (passg.), La. 238/L8
Barawa (Brava), Somalia 115/H3
Baraya, Col. 126/C6
Barbacan (Roxas), Phil. 82/B5
Barbacena, Braz., 120/F5
Barbacena, Braz. 132/F8
Barbacena, Braz. 135/E2
Barbacoas, Col. 126/A7
Barbacoas, Ven. 124/E3
Barbados, 3/G5
Barbados, 146/M8
BARBADOS, 156/G4
BARBADOS, 161/B8
Barbar (isls.), Indon. 85/J7
Barbas (cape), Sp. Sahara 106/A4
Barbastro, Spain 33/F1
Barbate (riv.), Spain 33/D4
Bărbătești, Rum. 45/F3
Barbeau, Mich. (49710) 250/E2
Barbeau (peak), N.W.T. 187/L1
Barber, Ark. (72922) 203/B3
Barber (co.), Kans. 232/D4
Barber, Mont. (†59074) 262/G4
Barber, N.C. (27008) 281/H3
Barbers (pt.), Hawaii 218/E2
Barbers Point Housing, Hawaii (†96706) 218/E2
Barbers Point Nav. Air Sta., Hawaii 218/E2
Barberton, Ohio (44203) 284/G4
Barberton, S. Africa 118/E5
Barberville, Fla. (32005) 212/E2
Barbezieux, France 28/C5
Barbizon, France 28/E3
Barbosa, Col. 126/D5
Barbour (co.), Ala. 194/H7
Barbour (co.), W. Va. 313/F4
Barbourmeade‡, Ky. (†40201) 237/K4
Barboursville, Va. (22923) 307/M4
Barboursville, W. Va. (25504) 313/B6
Barbourville, Ky. (40906) 237/O7
Barbuda (isl.), Antigua, 146/M8
Barbuda (isl.), Antigua 156/G3
Barcaldine, Aust. 88/G4
Barcaldine, Queens. 95/C4
Barcarrota, Spain 33/C3
Barce (El Marj), Libya 111/D1
Barcellona Pozzo di Gotto, Italy 34/E5
Barcelona, Spain, 7/E4
Barcelona (prov.), Spain 33/G2
Barcelona, Spain 33/H2
Barcelona, Ven., 120/D2
Barcelona, Ven. 124/F2
Barceloneta, P. Rico 161/C1
Barcelonnette, France 28/G5
Barcelos, Braz., 120/D3
Barcelos, Braz. 132/H9
Barcelos, Port. 33/B2
Barclay, Md. (21607) 245/P4
Barco, N.C. (27917) 281/T2
Barcoo (creek), Aust. 88/F5
Barcoo (creek), S. Aust. 94/F3
Barcoo (creek), Queens. 95/B5
Barcos (pt.), Cuba 158/B2
Barcs, Hung. 41/D4
Bard, Calif. (92222) 204/L11
Bard, N. Mex. (88411) 274/F3
Bardai, Chad 111/C3
Bardejov, Czech. 41/F2
Bardera, 102/G4
Bardera, Somalia 115/H3
Bardolph, Ill. (61416) 222/C3
Bardon (lake), Wis. 317/C3
Bardsey (isl.), Wales 13/C5
Bardstown, Ky. (40004) 237/L5
Bardu (riv.), Norway 18/L2
Bardwell, Ky. (42023) 237/D7
Bardwell, Texas (75101) 302/H5
Bareilly, India, 54/M7
Bareilly, India 68/D3
Barellan, N.S.W. 97/D4
Bärenhorn (mt.), Switz. 39/H3
Barents (sea), 3/L2
Barents (sea), 4/B8
Barents (sea), 7/H1
Barents (sea), U.S.S.R. 48/D2
Barents (sea), U.S.S.R. 52/E1
Barentsburg, Norway 18/C2
Barentsøya (isl.), Norway 18/D2
Bäretswil, Switz. 39/G2
Barfield, Ark. (†72315) 203/L2
Barfleur, France 28/C3
Barfleur (pt.), France 28/C3
Barford, Sask. 181/H3
Bargal, Somalia 115/K1
Bargamin (creek), Idaho 220/C4
Bargersville, Ind. (46106) 227/E5
Bargo, Aust. 88/K4
Bargo, N.S.W. 97/F4
Barguzin, U.S.S.R., 54/P4
Barham, N.S.W. 97/C4
Bar Harbor△, Maine (04609) 242/G7
Bar Harbor, Maine (04609) 242/G7
Bar Haven, Newf. 166/C2
Bari, Italy, 7/F4
Bari (prov.), Italy 34/F4
Bari, Italy 34/F4
Baria (riv.), Ven. 124/E7
Barich, Alta. 182/D2
Barichara, Col. 126/D4
Barida, Ras (cape), Saudi Ar. 59/C5
Barima (riv.), Guyana 131/B2
Barinas (state), Ven. 124/D3
Barinas, Ven. 124/C3
Baring, Maine (04610) 242/J5
Baring, Mo. (63531) 261/H2
Baring (cape), N.W.T. 187/G3
Baring (head), N.Z. 101/B3
Baring, Sask. 181/J5
Baring, Wash. (98224) 310/D3
Barinitas, Ven. 124/C3
Baripada, India 68/F4
Bariri, Braz. 135/B3
Bâris, U.A.R. 111/F3
Barisal, Pak. 68/G4
Barisan (mts.), Indon. 85/C6
Barito (riv.), Indon. 85/E6
Bark (lake), Ont. 177/G2
Barker, N.Y. (14012) 276/C4
Barker Heights, N.C. (†28739) 281/D4
Barkers Point, N. Br. 170/D3
Barkerville, Br. Col. 184/G3
Barkeyville, Pa. (†16038) 294/C3
Barkha, China 77/B5
Barkhamsted△, Conn. (†06063) 210/D1
Barkhamsted (res.), Conn. 210/D1
Barkhan, Pak. 59/J4
Barkhan, Pak. 68/B3
Barkhatu, China 77/B4
Barking, 10/C5
Barkley (sound), Br. Col. 184/E6
Barkley (dam), Ky. 237/E6
Barkley (lake), Ky. 237/F7
Barkley (lake), Tenn. 237/F7
Barkly Downs, Queens. 95/A4
Barkly East, S. Africa 118/D6
Barkly Tableland (plat.), Australia, 87/D7
Barkly Tableland, Aust. 88/F3
Barkly Tableland, No. Terr. 93/D4
Barkly Tableland, Queens. 95/A4
Barkmere, Que. 172/C3
Barkol, China 77/D3
Bark River, Mich. (49807) 250/B3
Barksdale, Texas (78828) 302/D8
Barksdale A.F.B., La. 238/C2
Bar-le-Duc, France 28/F3
Barlee (lake), Australia, 87/B8
Barlee (lake), Aust. 88/C5
Barlee (lake), W. Aust. 92/B5
Barletta, Italy 34/F4
Barling, Ark. (72923) 203/B3
Barlow, Ky. (42024) 237/D6
Barlow, Miss. (†39083) 256/C7
Barlow, N. Dak. (†58421) 283/M4
Barlow, Ohio (45612) 284/G7
Barlow, Oreg. (97003) 291/B2
Barlow Bend, Ala. (36506) 194/C8
Barmedman, N.S.W. 97/D4
Barmer, India 68/C3
Barmera, S. Aust. 94/G6
Bar Mills, Maine (04004) 242/C8
Barmouth, 10/D4
Barmouth, Wales 13/C5
Barna, Ire. 17/C5
Barnabus, W. Va. (25609) 313/C7
Barnaby (riv.), N. Br. 170/E2
Barnaby River, N. Br. 170/E2
Barnagore, India 68/F1
Barnard, Kans. (67418) 232/D2
Barnard, Mo. (64423) 261/C2
Barnard, N.C. (†28753) 281/D3
Barnard, S. Dak. (57426) 298/N2
Barnard△, Vt. (05031) 268/B4
Barnard, Vt. (05031) 268/B4
Barnard Castle, Eng. 13/F3
Barnardsville, N.C. (28709) 281/E3
Barnaul, U.S.S.R. 48/J4
Barnaul, U.S.S.R., 54/M4
Barn Bluff (mt.), Tas 99/B3
Barnegat, Alta. 182/E2
Barnegat, N.J. (08005) 273/E4
Barnegat (bay), N.J. 273/E4
Barnegat (inlet), N.J. 273/E4
Barnegat Light, N.J. (08006) 273/E4
Barnes (sound), Fla. 212/F6
Barnes, Kans. (66933) 232/F2
Barnes (co.), N. Dak. 283/O5
Barnes, Wis. (†54873) 317/D3
Barnesboro, Pa. (15714) 294/E4
Barnes City, Iowa (50027) 229/H6
Barnes Corners, N.Y. (13610) 276/J3
Barneston, Nebr. (68309) 264/H4
Barnesville, Colo. (†80624) 208/L2
Barnesville, Ga. (30204) 216/D4
Barnesville, Md. (20703) 245/J4
Barnesville, Minn. (56514) 254/B4
Barnesville, N. Br. 170/E3
Barnesville, N.C. (28319) 281/L6
Barnesville, Ohio (43713) 284/H6
Barnet, 10/B5
Barnet, Eng. 13/G6
Barnet△, Vt. (05821) 268/C3
Barnet, Vt. (05821) 268/C3
Barnett, Ga. (30804) 216/G3
Barnett, Miss. (†39347) 256/G7
Barnett, Mo. (65011) 261/G6
Barnetteville, N. Br. 170/E2
Barneveld, N.Y. (13304) 276/K4
Barneveld, Neth. 27/H4
Barneveld, Wis. (53507) 317/F10
Barneville-Carteret, France 28/C3
Barney, Ga. (31625) 216/E8
Barney, N. Dak. (58008) 283/S7
Barnhart, Texas (76930) 302/C6
Barnhill, Ohio (†44663) 284/H5
Barnrock, Ky. (†41219) 237/R5
Barnsdall, Okla. (74002) 288/O1
Barnsley, 10/F4
Barnsley, Eng. 13/F4
Barnstable (co.), Mass. 249/N6
Barnstable△, Mass. (02630) 249/N6
Barnstaple, 10/E5
Barnstaple, Eng. 13/C6
Barnstaple (bay), Eng. 13/C6
Barnstaple (bay), 10/D5
Barnstead△, N.H. (03218) 268/E5
Barnstead, N.H. (03218) 268/E5
Barnum, Iowa (50518) 229/E3
Barnum, Minn. (55707) 254/F4
Barnum, W. Va. (26706) 313/H4
Barnum, Wis. (†54631) 317/E9
Barnwell, Ala. (†36532) 194/C10

Beacon 331

Barnwell, Alta. 182/D5
Barnwell (co.), S.C. 296/E5
Barnwell, S.C. (29812) 296/E5
Baro, 102/C4
Baro, Nigeria 106/F7
Baro (riv.), Eth. 111/G6
Baroda, India, 54/L7
Baroda, Mich. (49101) 250/C7
Baroda, India 68/C4
Baroghil (pass), Afgh. 68/C1
Baroghil (pass), Pak. 68/C1
Baron, Okla. (†74965) 288/S3
Baron Bluff (prom.), V.I.(U.S.) 161/E3
Barons, Alta. 182/D4
Barooga, N.S.W. 97/C4
Barossa (res.), S. Aust. 94/C6
Barotseland (reg.), Zambia 115/D7
Barpeta, India 68/G3
Barques (pt.), Mich. 250/C3
Barquisimeto, Ven., 120/D2
Barquisimeto, Ven. 124/D2
Barr, Scot. 15/G9
Barr, Tenn. (†38040) 237/B9
Barra, Braz. 132/F5
Barra (head), 10/C2
Barra (isl.), 10/C2
Barra (isls.), 10/C2
Barra (head), Scot. 15/A6
Barra (isl.), Scot. 15/A5
Barra (isls.), Scot. 15/B6
Barra (passg.), Scot. 15/B6
Barra (sound), Scot. 15/A5
Barraba, Aust. 88/J6
Barraba, N.S.W. 97/F2
Barrackpore, India 68/F1
Barrackville, W. Va. (26559) 313/F3
Barra de Río Grande, Nic. 154/F4
Barra-do-Bugres, Braz. 132/B6
Barra-do-Corda, Braz. 132/E4
Barra-do-Piraí, Braz. 132/E8
Barra do Piraí, Braz. 135/E3
Barra Mansa, Braz. 135/D3
Barranca, Lima, Peru 128/C8
Barranca, Loreto, Peru 128/D5
Barrancabermeja, Col. 126/C4
Barranca de Upía, Col. 126/D5
Barrancas, Arg. 143/F6
Barrancas (riv.), Arg. 143/G5
Barrancas, Chile 138/G3
Barrancas, Col. 126/D2
Barrancas, Barinas, Ven. 124/C3
Barrancas, Monagas, Ven. 124/G3
Barranco de Loba, Col. 126/C3
Barrancos, Cerro (mt.), Chile 138/D7
Barrancos, Port. 33/C3
Barranqueras, Arg. 143/E2
Barranquilla, Col., 120/C1
Barranquilla, Col. 126/C2
Barranquitas, P. Rico 161/D2
Barras (riv.), Bol. 136/B6
Barras, Col. 126/D8
Barras, Braz. 132/F4
Barraute, Que. 174/B3
Barre▵, Mass. (01005) 249/F3
Barre, Mass. (01005) 249/F3
Barre, Vt. (05641) 268/C3
Barreal, Arg. 143/C3
Barreau (pt.), N. Br. 170/F1
Barre Center, N.Y. (†14411) 276/D4
Barreiras, Braz. 132/E6
Barreirinha, Braz. 132/B3
Barreirinhas, Braz. 132/F3
Barreiro, Port. 33/B1
Barreiros, Braz. 132/H5
Barren (isls.), Alaska 196/B2
Barren (co.), Ky. 237/K7
Barren (riv.), Ky. 237/H6
Barren (isls.), Malag. Rep. 118/G3
Barren (isl.), N.S. 169/G4
Barren (isl.), India 68/G6
Barren (cape), Tas. 99/E2
Barren Plains, Tenn. (†37172) 237/H7
Barren River (res.), Ky. 237/J7
Barren Springs, Va. (24313) 307/G7
Barre Plains, Mass. (01006) 249/F3
Barrera, Bol. 136/B3
Barretos, Braz. 132/D8
Barretos, Braz. 135/B2
Barrett, Minn. (56311) 254/B5
Barrett, Texas (77532) 302/K1
Barrett, W. Va. (25013) 313/C7
Barretts, Ga. (†31601) 216/F8
Barrhead, Alta. 182/C2
Barrhead, 10/A1
Barrhead, Scot. 15/C2
Barrie, Ont. 177/E3
Barrie (isl.), Ont. 177/B1
Barrie Island, Ont. 177/B2
Barriere, Br. Col. 184/H4
Barrineau Park, Fla. (†32533) 212/B6
Barrington, Ill. (60010) 222/E1
Barrington▵, N.H. (†03825) 268/F5
Barrington, N.H. (03825) 268/F5
Barrington, N.J. (08007) 273/B3
Barrington, N.S. 169/C5
Barrington (bay), N.S. 169/C5
Barrington▵, R.I. (02806) 249/J6
Barrington, R.I. (02806) 249/J6
Barrington, Tas. 99/C3
Barrington Hills‡, Ill. (†60010) 222/E1
Barrington Passage, N.S. 169/C5
Barrington P.O. (East Barrington), N.H. (03825) 268/F5
Barrington Tops (mt.), N.S.W. 97/F2
Barringun, N.S.W. 97/C1
Barron (co.), Wis. 317/C5
Barron, Wis. (54812) 317/C5
Barronett, Wis. (54813) 317/B4
Barrouallie, St. Vincent 161/A9
Barroui, Dominica 161/E6
Barrow (str.), 163/G1
Barrow (isl.), Australia, 87/B8
Barrow, Alaska, 146/C2
Barrow, Alaska, 188/C5
Barrow, Alaska (99723) 196/G1
Barrow (pt.), Alaska 196/G1
Barrow (isl.), Aust. 88/A4
Barrow (bay), Ont. 177/C2
Barrow (riv.), 10/C4
Barrow (co.), Ga. 216/E2
Barrow (riv.), Ire. 17/H7
Barrow (str.), N.W.T. 187/J2
Barrow (isl.), W. Aust. 92/A3
Barrow (pt.), U.S., 3/B2
Barrow (pt.), U.S., 4/B18
Barrow, U.S., 4/B17
Barrow Bay, Ont. 177/C3
Barrow Creek, Aust. 88/E4
Barrow Creek, No. Terr. 93/D6
Barrow-in-Furness, 10/E3
Barrow-in-Furness, Eng. 13/D3
Barrows, Man. 179/A2
Barrowsville, Mass. (02710) 249/K5
Barr Smith (mt.), Ant. 5/C5
Barruelo de Santullán, Spain 33/D1
Barry, Ill. (62312) 222/B4
Barry, 10/E5
Barry (co.), Mich. 250/D6
Barry, Minn. (56210) 254/B5
Barry (co.), Mo. 261/E9
Barry‡, Texas (75102) 302/H5
Barry (mts.), Vic. 97/D5
Barry, Wales 13/D6
Barry's Bay, Ont. 177/G2
Barryton, Mich. (49305) 250/D5
Barryville, N.Y. (12719) 276/L8
Barsi, India 68/D5
Barss Corners, N.S. 169/D4
Barstow, Calif. (92311) 204/H9
Barstow, Md. (20610) 245/M6
Barstow, Texas (79719) 302/A6
Bar-sur-Aube, France 28/F3
Bar-sur-Seine, France 28/F3
Bartelso, Ill. (62218) 222/D5
Barter Island (Kaktovik), Alaska (†99747) 196/K1
Barterville, Ky. (40304) 237/N4
Barth, E. Ger. 22/E1
Barth, Fla. (32532) 212/B6
Barthel, Sask. 181/B2
Bartholomew (bayou), Ark. 203/G6
Bartholomew (co.), Ind. 227/F6
Bartibog (riv.), N. Br. 170/E1
Bartica, Guyana 131/B2
Bartin, Turkey 63/E2
Bartle, Cuba 158/H3
Bartle Frere (mt.), Queens. 95/C3
Bartlesville, Okla. (74003) 288/O1
Bartlett (dam), Ariz. 198/D5
Bartlett (res.), Ariz. 198/D5
Bartlett‡, Ill. (60103) 222/E1
Bartlett, Iowa (51655) 229/B7
Bartlett, Kans. (67332) 232/G4
Bartlett, N. Dak. (58314) 283/N3
Bartlett▵, N.H. (03812) 268/E3
Bartlett, N.H. (03812) 268/E3
Bartlett, Nebr. (68622) 264/F3
Bartlett, Ohio (45713) 284/G7
Bartlett, Tenn. (38005) 237/B10
Bartlett, Texas (76511) 302/G7
Bartlett Deep, Cayman Is. 156/B3
Bartletts Ferry (dam), Ala. 194/H5
Bartletts Ferry (dam), Ga. 216/B5
Bartley, N.J. (†07930) 273/D2
Bartley, Nebr. (69020) 264/D4
Bartley, W. Va. (24813) 313/C8
Barto, Pa. (19504) 294/L5
Bartolomeu Dias, Moz. 118/F4
Barton, Ala. (35614) 194/C1
Barton, Ark. (72312) 203/J4
Barton (co.), Kans. 232/D3
Barton, Md. (21521) 245/B2
Barton (co.), Mo. 261/D7
Barton, N. Dak. (58315) 283/K2
Barton, Ohio (43905) 284/J5
Barton, Oreg. (†97009) 291/B2
Barton▵, Vt. (05822) 268/C2
Barton, Vt. (05822) 268/C2
Barton (riv.), Vt. 268/C2
Barton City, Mich. (48705) 250/F4
Barton-on-Humber, 10/F4
Bartonsville, Pa. (18321) 294/M4
Bartonsville, Vt. (05140) 268/B5
Barton-upon-Humber, Eng. 13/G4
Bartonville, Ill. (61607) 222/D3
Bartoszyce, Poland 47/E1
Bartow, Fla. (33830) 212/E4
Bartow (co.), Ga. 216/C2
Bartow, Ga. (30413) 216/G5
Bartow, W. Va. (24920) 313/G5
Bartra Antiguo, Peru 128/E4
Bartra Nuevo, Peru 128/E4
Barú (isl.), Col. 126/C2
Barus, Indon. 85/B5
Baruun Urta, Mong. 77/H2
Barvas, 10/C1
Barvas, Scot. 15/D3
Barvaux, Belg. 27/H8
Bar View, Oreg. (†97136) 291/C2
Barview‡, Oreg. (†97136) 291/C4
Barville, Que. 174/B3
Barwani, India 68/D4
Barwick, Ont. 175/B3
Barwick, Ont. 177/F5
Barwick, Ga. (31720) 216/E9
Barwon (riv.), Aust. 88/H5
Barwon (riv.), N.S.W. 97/D2
Barysh, U.S.S.R. 52/G4
Baryulgil, N.S.W. 97/G1
Basalt, Colo. (81621) 208/E4
Basalt, Idaho (83218) 220/F6
Basankusu, Dem. Rep. of the Congo 115/C3
Basavilbaso, Arg. 143/G6
Bascharage, Lux. 27/H9
Basco, Ill. (62313) 222/B3
Basco, Phil. 82/A2
Bascom, Fla. (32423) 212/A1
Bascom, Ohio (44809) 284/D3
Bascuñán (cape), Chile 138/A7
Basècles, Belg. 27/D7
Basehor, Kans. (66007) 232/G2
Basel, Switz. 7/E4
Basel, Switz. 39/E1
Baselland (canton), Switz. 39/E2
Baselstadt (canton), Switz. 39/E1
Basey, Phil. 82/E5
Bashan, Conn. (†06423) 210/F2
Bashan (lake), Conn. 210/F3
Bashaw, Alta. 182/D3
Basher‡, Alaska (†99501) 196/C1
Bashi, Ala. (†36784) 194/C7
Bashi (chan.), China 77/K7
Bashi (chan.), Phil. 82/A1
Bashkir A.S.S.R., U.S.S.R. 48/F4
Bashkir A.S.S.R., U.S.S.R. 52/J4
Basht, Iran 66/G5
Basic, Miss. (†39330) 256/G6
Basilan, Phil. 82/C7
Basilan (isl.), Phil. 82/D7
Basilan (str.), Phil. 82/C7
Basilan (isl.), Phil. 85/G4
Basildon, 10/G5
Basildon, Eng. 13/H6
Basile, La. (70515) 238/E5
Basilicata (reg.), Italy 34/F4
Basim, India 68/D4
Basin, Mont. (59613) 262/D4
Basin (lake), Sask. 181/F3
Basin, Wyo. (82410) 319/E1
Basinger, Fla. (33428) 212/F4
Basingstoke, 10/F5
Basingstoke, Eng. 13/F6
Basirhat, India 68/F4
Basit (cape), Syria 63/F5
Baskahegan (lake), Maine 242/H5
Başkale, Turkey 63/K3
Baskatong (lake), Que. 172/B3
Baskatong (lake), 163/J6
Baskerville, Va. (23915) 307/M7
Basket (lake), Man. 179/C3
Baskett, Ky. (42402) 237/F5
Baskin, La. (71219) 238/G2
Basking Ridge, N.J. (07920) 273/D2
Başmakçi, Turkey 63/D4
Basodino (mt.), Switz. 39/G4
Basoko, 102/E4
Basoko, Dem. Rep. of the Congo. 115/D3
Basom, N.Y. (14013) 276/D4
Basongo, Dem. Rep. of the Congo. 115/D4
Basora (pt.), Neth. Ant. 161/E10
Basra, Iraq, 3/M4
Basra, Iraq, 54/H7
Basra, Iraq 59/E3
Basra (prov.), Iraq 66/E5
Basra, Iraq 66/E5
Bas-Rhin (dept.), France 28/G3
Bass (str.), Australia, 87/E9
Bass (str.), Aust. 88/H7
Bass (isls.), Fr. Poly., 87/M8
Bass, Ind. (†46534) 227/D2
Bass (lake), Ind. 227/D2
Bass (str.), Tasmania 99/C1
Bass (str.), Vic. 97/D6
Bassano, Alta. 182/D4
Bassano del Grappa, Italy 34/C2
Bassas da India (isl.), Réunion 118/F4
Basse, Gambia 106/B6
Bassecourt, Switz. 39/D2
Bassein, Burma, 54/N8
Bassein, India 68/C5
Bassein, Burma 72/B3
Basse-Pointe, Mart. 161/C5
Basses-Alpes (dept.), France 28/G5
Basse-Terre (cap.), Guad. 156/F4
Basseterre (cap.), St. Chr.-N.-A. 156/F3
Basse-Terre (cap.), Guad. 161/A7
Basse-Terre (isl.), Guad. 161/A6
Basseterre (cap.), St. Chr.-N.-A. 161/C10
Basse Terre, Trinidad Tobago 161/B11
Bassett, Ark. (72313) 203/K2
Bassett, Iowa (†50645) 229/J2
Bassett, Kans. (†66749) 232/G4
Bassett, Nebr. (68714) 264/E2
Bassett, Va. (24055) 307/J7
Bassfield, Miss. (39421) 256/E8
Bass Harbor, Maine (04653) 242/G7
Bassikounou, Mauritania 106/C5
Bassin-Bleu, Haiti 158/B5
Bass River, N. Br. 170/E2
Bass River, N.S. 169/E3
Bassum, W. Ger. 22/C2
Basswood (lake), Ont. 175/B3
Basswood, Man. 179/B4
Basswood (lake), Minn. 254/G2
Båstad, Sweden 18/H8
Bastak, Iran 66/J7
Bastar, India 68/E5
Bastelica, France 28/B6
Bastenaken (Bastogne), Belg. 27/H9
Bastia, France 28/B6
Bastian, Va. (24314) 307/F6
Bastimentos (isl.), Pan. 154/G6
Bastogne, Belg. 27/H9
Bastrop, La. (71220) 238/G1
Bastrop (co.), Texas 302/G7
Bastrop, Texas (78602) 302/G7
Bastuträsk, Sweden 18/L4
Bata, Eq. Guin. 115/B3
Bata, 102/D4
Bataan (prov.), Phil. 82/C3
Batabanó, Cuba 156/A2
Batabanó (gulf), Cuba 156/A2
Batabanó (gulf), Cuba 158/C2
Batag (isl.), Phil. 82/E4
Batala, India 68/D2
Batalha, Braz. 132/F3
Batalha, Port. 33/B3
Batama, Dem. Rep. of the Congo 115/E3
Batan, Albay (isl.), Phil. 82/E4
Batan, Batanes (isl.), Phil. 82/B2
Batan (isls.), Phil. 82/A2
Batan (isls.), Phil. 85/G1
Batan (isls.), Phil., 54/R7
Batanes (prov.), Phil. 82/A2
Batang, China, 54/N6
Batang, China 77/E6
Batang, Indon. 85/J2
Batangafo, Centr. Afr. Rep. 115/C2
Batangan (cape), S. Vietnam 72/F4
Batangas (prov.), Phil. 82/C4
Batangas, Phil. 82/C4
Batangas, Phil. 85/G3
Batas (isl.), Phil. 82/B5
Bátaszék, Hung. 41/E3
Batatais, Braz. 135/C2
Batavia, Arg. 143/C3
Batavia, Ill. (60510) 222/E2
Batavia (Djakarta) (cap.), Indon., 54/O10
Batavia, Iowa (52533) 229/J7
Batavia, Mich. (†49036) 250/D7
Batavia, N.Y. (14020) 276/D5
Batavia (Djakarta) (cap.), Indon. 85/H1
Batavia, Ohio (45103) 284/B7
Batavia, Wis. (†53001) 317/K8
Bataysk, U.S.S.R. 52/E5
Bat Cave, N.C. (28710) 281/E4
Batchelor, La. (70715) 238/G5
Batchelor, No. Terr. 93/B2
Batchtown, Ill. (62006) 222/C4
Batchwana Bay, Ont. 177/J5
Bateman, Sask. 181/E5
Batemans Bay-Batehaven, N.S.W. 97/F4
Bates, Ark. (72924) 203/B4
Bates, Mich. (†49690) 250/D4
Bates (co.), Mo. 261/D6
Bates, Oreg. (97817) 291/J3
Batesburg, S.C. (29006) 296/D4
Bates City, Mo. (64011) 261/E5
Batesland, S. Dak. (57716) 298/E7
Batesville, Ala. (†36018) 194/H6
Batesville, Ark. (72501) 203/G2
Batesville, Ind. (47006) 227/G6
Batesville, Miss. (38606) 256/E2
Batesville, Ohio (43715) 284/H6
Batesville, Texas (78829) 302/E9
Batesville, Va. (22924) 307/L5
Bath, 10/E5
Bath, Jam. 158/K6
Bath, Ont. 177/H3
Bath, Eng. 13/E6
Bath, Ill. (62617) 222/C3
Bath, Ind. (47010) 227/H5
Bath (co.), Ky. 237/O4
Bath, Maine (04530) 242/D8
Bath, Mich. (48808) 250/E6
Bath, N. Br. 170/C2
Bath, N.C. (27808) 281/R4
Bath▵, N.H. (03740) 268/D3
Bath, N.H. (03740) 268/D3
Bath, N.Y. (14810) 276/F6
Bath, Neth. 27/E6
Bath, Pa. (18014) 294/M4
Bath, S.C. (29816) 296/D5
Bath, S. Dak. (57427) 298/N3
Bath (co.), Va. 307/J4
Bath, W. Va. (†25411) 313/K3
Batha (riv.), Chad 111/C5
Bathgate, 10/C1
Bathgate, N. Dak. (58216) 283/P2
Bathgate, Scot. 15/J8
Bathsheba, Barb. 161/B8
Bath Springs, Tenn. (38311) 237/E10
Bathurst, 163/K6
Bathurst (cape), 163/D1
Bathurst (isls.), 163/M3
Bathurst (isl.), Australia, 87/C7
Bathurst, Aust. 88/H6
Bathurst (isl.), Aust. 88/D2
Bathurst (isl.), Canada, 4/B15
Bathurst (cap.), Gambia 102/A3
Bathurst (cap.), Gambia 106/A6
Bathurst, N. Br. 170/E1
Bathurst (Nepisiguit) (lakes), N. Br. 170/D1
Bathurst, N.S.W. 97/E3
Bathurst (isl.), N.W.T., 146/H2
Bathurst (cape), N.W.T. 187/F2
Bathurst (inlet), N.W.T. 187/H3
Bathurst (isl.), N.W.T. 187/H2
Bathurst (isl.), No. Terr. 93/A1
Bathurst (harbor), Tas. 99/C5
Bathurst Inlet, 163/E2
Bathurst Inlet, Canada, 4/C15
Bathurst Inlet, N.W.T. 187/H3
Bathurst Island Mission, No. Terr. 93/B1
Bathurst Mines, N. Br. 170/E1
Batié, Upp. Volta 106/D7
Bati Firat (riv.), Turkey 63/H3
Batin, Wadi al (dry riv.), Iraq 59/E4
Batin, Wadi al (dry riv.), Saudi Ar. 59/E4
Batin, Wadi al (dry riv.), Iraq 66/E6
Batina (reg.), Oman 59/G5
Batiscan, Que. 172/E3
Batiscan (lake), Que. 172/E2
Batiscan (riv.), Que. 172/E2
Batjan (isls.), Indon. 85/H6
Batley, Eng. 13/F4
Batlow, N.S.W. 97/E4
Batman, Turkey 63/J4
Batna, Alg. 106/F1
Bato, Catanduanes, Phil. 82/E4
Bato, Leyte, Phil. 82/E5
Batobato, Phil. 82/E7
Batoche, Sask. 181/E3
Baton Rouge (cap.), La., 146/J6
Baton Rouge (cap.), La., 188/H4
Baton Rouge (cap.), La. (*70801) 238/K2
Batopilas, Mex. 150/F3
Batouri, Cameroon 115/B3
Batovi, Urug. 145/D2
Batrun, Leb. 63/F5
Bat Shelomo, Israel 65/B2
Batson, Texas (77519) 302/K7
Batsto, N.J. (08037) 273/D4
Batsto (riv.), N.J. 273/D4
Battambang, Cambodia 72/D4
Batteau, Newf. 166/C3
Batten Kill (riv.), N.Y. 276/O4
Batten Kill (riv.), Vt. 268/A5
Batterbee (cape), Ant., 3/N9
Batterbee (cape), Ant. 5/C3
Bätterkinden, Switz. 39/E2
Battersea, Ont. 177/H3
Batticaloa, Ceylon 68/E7
Battiest, Okla. (74722) 288/S6
Batti Malv (isl.), India 68/G7
Battle, 10/G5
Battle (riv.), 163/E5
Battle (riv.), Alta. 182/D3
Battle, Eng. 13/H7
Battle (creek), Idaho 220/B7
Battle (riv.), Minn. 254/D3
Battle (creek), Mont. 262/G1
Battle (creek), Oreg. 291/K5
Battle (creek), S. Dak. 298/C6
Battle (creek), Sask. 181/B6
Battle (riv.), Sask. 181/B3
Battlebend, Alta. 182/E3
Battleboro, N.C. (27809) 281/O2
Battle Creek, Iowa (51006) 229/B4
Battle Creek, Mich., 188/J2
Battle Creek, Mich. (*49014) 250/D6
Battle Creek, Nebr. (68715) 264/G3
Battle Creek, Sask. 181/B6
Battlefield, Mo. (†65619) 261/F8
Battleford, 163/F5
Battleford, Sask. 181/C3
Battle Ground, Ind. (47920) 227/D3
Battle Ground, Wash. (98604) 310/C5
Battle Harbour, 163/L5
Battle Harbour, Newf. 166/C3
Battle Heights, Sask. 181/H2
Battle Lake, Alta. 182/C3
Battle Lake, Minn. (56515) 254/C4
Battle Mountain, Nev. (89820) 266/E2
Battles Wharf, Ala. (36533) 194/C10
Battletown, Ky. (40104) 237/J4
Battleview, N. Dak. (58714) 283/E2
Battock (mt.), Scot. 15/L6
Battonya, Hung. 41/F3
Battrum, Sask. 181/C5
Batu (isls.), Indon. 85/B6
Batuc, Mex. 150/D2
Batuco, Chile 138/G3
Batu Gajah, Malaysia 72/D6
Batulaki, Phil. 82/E8
Batumi, U.S.S.R. 48/E5
Batumi, U.S.S.R. 52/F6
Batumi, U.S.S.R., 7/J4
Baturadja, Indon. 85/C6
Baturité, Braz. 132/G4
Batusangkar, Indon. 85/C6
Bat Yam, Israel 65/B3
Bauang, Phil. 82/C2
Baubau, Indon. 85/G7
Bauchi, 102/D3
Bauchi, Nigeria 106/F6
Baudette, Minn. (56623) 254/D2
Baudette (riv.), Minn. 254/D2
Baudh, India 68/E4
Baudó (riv.), Col. 126/B5
Baudó, Serranía de (mts.), Col. 126/B5
Baudouinville, Dem. Rep. of the Congo. 115/E5
Baugé, France 28/D4
Bauld (cape), 163/L5
Bauld (cape), Newf. 166/C3
Bauline, Newf. 166/D2
Baulkham Hills, N.S.W. 97/H3
Baulmes, Switz. 39/C3
Bauma, Switz. 39/G2
Baumann (fjord), N.W.T. 187/K2
Baume-les-Dames, France 28/G4
Baunt, U.S.S.R. 48/M4
Baures, Bol. 136/D3
Baures (riv.), Bol. 136/D3
Baurtregaum (mt.), Ire. 17/A7
Bauru, Braz. 132/D8
Bauru, Braz. 135/B3
Bauska, U.S.S.R. 53/B2
Bauta, Cuba 158/C1
Bauta (riv.), P. Rico 161/C2
Bautzen, E. Ger. 22/F3
Bauxite, Ark. (72011) 203/F4
Bavaria, Kans. (67419) 232/E3
Bavaria (state), W. Ger. 22/D4
Bavarian (mts.), Austria 41/A3
Bavarian (for.), W. Ger. 22/E4
Bavarian Alps (range), W. Ger. 22/D5
Baviácora, Mex. 150/E2
Bavispe, Mex. 150/E1
Bavispe (riv.), Mex. 150/E1
Bawean (isl.), Indon. 85/K1
Bawku, Ghana 106/D6
Bawlf, Alta. 182/D3
Bawtry, Eng. 13/F4
Baxley, Ga. (31513) 216/H7
Baxter (co.), Ark. 203/F1
Baxter, Iowa (50028) 229/G5
Baxter, Minn. (†56401) 254/D4
Baxter, Miss. (†39343) 256/F6
Baxter, Pa. (†15829) 294/D3
Baxter, Tenn. (38544) 237/K8
Baxter Estates‡, N.Y. (†11050) 276/R7
Baxter Springs, Kans. (66713) 232/H4
Baxterville, Miss. (†39455) 256/E8
Bay, Ark. (72411) 203/J2
Bay (co.), Fla. 212/C6
Bay (co.), Mich. 250/E5
Bay, Mo. (65041) 261/J5
Bay (lag.), Phil. 82/C3
Bayag, Phil. 82/C1
Bayaguana, Dom. Rep. 158/E6
Bayamo, Cuba 156/C2
Bayamo, Cuba 158/H4
Bayamón, P. Rico 156/G1
Bayamón (dist.), P. Rico 161/D1
Bayamón, P. Rico 161/D1
Bayamón (riv.), P. Rico 161/D1
Bayang, Phil. 82/E7
Bayan Kara Shan (range), China 77/E5
Bayan Khongor (prov.), Mong. 77/E2
Bayan Khongor, Mong. 77/F2
Bayan Tumen (Choibalsan), Mong. 77/H2
Bayan Ulegei (prov.), Mong. 77/C2
Bayan Ulegei, Mong. 77/D2
Bayard, Del. (†19945) 245/T6
Bayard, Iowa (50029) 229/D5
Bayard, N. Mex. (88023) 274/A6
Bayard, Nebr. (69334) 264/A3
Bayard, Sask. 181/F5
Bayard, W. Va. (26707) 313/H4
Bayat, Turkey 63/F2
Bayate, Cuba 158/J4
Baybay, Phil. 82/E5
Baybay, Phil. 85/H3
Bayboro, N.C. (28515) 281/R4
Bay Bulls, Newf. 166/D2
Bayburt, Turkey 59/D1
Bayburt, Turkey 63/H2
Bay Center, Wash. (98527) 310/A4
Bay City (J.F. Kennedy City)‡, Alaska (†99501) 196/J2
Bay City, Mich., 188/K2
Bay City, Mich. (48706) 250/F5
Bay City, Oreg. (97107) 291/D2
Bay City, Texas (77414) 302/H9
Bay City, Wash. (†98520) 310/B4
Bay City, Wis. (54723) 317/B6
Baydarata (bay), U.S.S.R. 52/L1
Bay de Verde, Newf. 166/D2
Bay du Vin (riv.), N. Br. 170/E2
Bayeux, France 28/C3
Bayfield, Colo. (81122) 208/D8
Bayfield, Ont. 177/C4
Bayfield (sound), Ont. 177/B2
Bayfield, N. Br. 170/G2
Bayfield (co.), Wis. 317/D3
Bayfield, Wis. (54814) 317/E2
Bay Harbour Islands, Fla. (†33101) 212/B4
Bay Head, N.J. (08742) 273/E3
Bayindir, Turkey 63/B3
Bayinhot, China 77/F4
Bayir, Turkey 63/B6
Baykal (lake), U.S.S.R. 48/L4
Baykal (range), U.S.S.R. 48/L4
Baykal (lake), U.S.S.R., 3/Q3
Baykal (lake), U.S.S.R., 54/P4
Baykit, U.S.S.R. 48/K3
Baykonur, U.S.S.R. 48/G5
Bay Lake, Fla. (†32786) 212/E3
Bay Lake, Minn. (†56444) 254/E4
Bay L'Argent, Newf. 166/D4
Baylis, Ill. (62314) 222/C4
Baylor (co.), Texas 302/E4
Bay Minette, Ala. (36507) 194/C9
Baynes Lake, Br. Col. 184/K5
Bayombong, Phil. 82/C2
Bayombong, Phil. 85/G2
Bayonne, France, 7/D4
Bayonne, France 28/C6
Bayonne, N.J. (07002) 273/B2
Bayonne Military Ocean Terminal, N.J. 273/B2
Bayou, Ky. (†42081) 237/E6
Bayou Barbary, La. (†70754) 238/M2
Bayou Bodcau (res.), Ark. 203/C7
Bayou Bodcau (res.), La. 238/D1
Bayou Cane, La. (†70360) 238/J7
Bayou Chicot, La. (†70586) 238/F5
Bayou Clear (lake), La. 238/C2
Bayou Current, La. (†71353) 238/G5
Bayou D'Arbonne (lake), La. 238/E1
Bayou Des Arc (riv.), Ark. 203/G3
Bayou Goula, La. (70716) 238/J3
Bayou La Batre, Ala. (36509) 194/B10
Bayou Meto, Ark. (†72160) 203/H5
Bayou Vista, La. (70380) 238/H7
Bayóvar, Peru 128/B5
Bay Pines, Fla. (33504) 212/B3
Bay Point, Maine (†04548) 242/D8
Bay Point (isl.), S.C. 296/F7
Bayport, Fla. (†33512) 212/D3
Bay Port, Mich. (48720) 250/F5
Bayport, Minn. (55003) 254/F5
Bayport, N.Y. (11705) 276/O9
Bayport Park-Lakeside‡, Mich. (†48451) 250/F6
Bayram-Ali, U.S.S.R. 48/G6
Bayramiç, Turkey 63/B3
Bayreuth, W. Ger. 22/D4
Bay Ridges, Ont. 177/K4
Bayrischzell, W. Ger. 22/E5
Bay Roberts, Newf. 166/D2
Bays (lake), Ont. 177/F2
Bays, Ky. (41310) 237/P5
Bays, W. Va. (†26629) 313/E5
Bay Saint Lawrence, N.S. 169/H1
Bay Saint Louis, Miss. (39520) 256/F10
Bayshore, Fla. (†33902) 212/E5
Bayshore, Mich. (49711) 250/D3
Bay Shore, N.Y. (11706) 276/O9
Bayshore Gardens‡, Fla. (33505) 212/D4
Bayside, Calif. (95524) 204/B3
Bayside, Ont. 177/G3
Bayside, Maine (04915) 242/F7
Bayside, Texas (78340) 302/G9
Bayside, Wis. (†53201) 317/M1
Bay Springs, Fla. (†36502) 212/B6
Bay Springs, Miss. (39422) 256/F7
Baysville, Ont. 177/E2
Bayswater, Vic. 97/K5
Baytown, Texas (77520) 302/L2
Bay Trail, Sask. 181/F3
Bay Tree, Alta. 182/A2
Bayuca, Spain 33/B1
Bayugan, Phil. 82/E6
Bayview, Calif. (†95501) 204/A3
Bayview‡, Fla. (†32401) 212/C6
Bayview, Idaho (83803) 220/B2
Bayview, Md. (†21901) 245/P2
Bay View, Mich. (49770) 250/E3
Bay View, N.Z. 101/F3
Bay View, Ohio (†44870) 284/E3
Bayview, Texas (†78566) 302/G11
Bay View Gardens‡, Ill. (†61611) 222/D3
Bay Village, Ohio (44140) 284/G9
Bayville, N.J. (08721) 273/E4
Bayville, N.Y. (11709) 276/R6
Baywood, La. (†70739) 238/K1
Baywood Park-Los Osos, Calif. (†93401) 204/E8
Baza, Spain 33/E4
Bazaar, Kans. (66837) 232/F3
Bazaruto (isl.), Moz. 118/F4
Bazas, France 28/C5
Bazile Mills, Nebr. (†68729) 264/G2
Bazine, Kans. (67516) 232/C3
Bazman, Kuh-i- (mt.), Iran 59/H4
Bazman, Iran 66/M7
Bazman, Kuh-i- (mt.), Iran 66/H4
Bazqush, Kuh-i- (mts.), Iran 66/E2
Beach (pond), Conn. 210/H2
Beach, Ga. (†31554) 216/G8
Beach, N. Dak. (58621) 283/C6
Beachburg, Ont. 177/H2
Beach City, Ohio (44608) 284/G4
Beach City, Texas (†77520) 302/L2
Beach Haven, N.J. (08008) 273/E4
Beach Haven (inlet), N.J. 273/E4
Beach Haven Crest, N.J. (†08008) 273/E4
Beach Haven Terrace, N.J. (†08008) 273/E4
Beach Lake, Pa. (18405) 294/M2
Beach Meadows, N.S. 169/D4
Beachport, Aust. 88/F7
Beachport, S. Aust. 94/F7
Beachton, Ga. (†31792) 216/D9
Beachville, Ont. 177/D4
Beachwood, N.J. (08722) 273/E4
Beachwood, Ohio (†44101) 284/J9
Beachy (head), Eng. 13/H7
Beachy (head), 10/G5
Beacon, Iowa (52534) 229/H6
Beacon, N.Y. (12508) 276/N7

334 Bethlehem

Bethlehem, Iowa (†50238) 229/G7
Bethlehem, Ky. (40007) 237/L4
Bethlehem, Md. (21609) 245/P6
Bethlehem, Miss. (†38659) 256/F1
Bethlehem△, N.H. (03574) 268/D3
Bethlehem, N.H. (03574) 268/D3
Bethlehem, Jordan 65/C4
Bethlehem, Pa. (*18015) 294/M4
Bethlehem, 102/E7
Bethlehem, S. Africa 118/D5
Bethlehem, W. Va. (†26003) 313/E2
Bethpage‡, N.Y. (11714) 276/O9
Bethpage, Tenn. (37022) 237/J7
Bethune, Colo. (80805) 208/P4
Béthune, France 28/E2
Bethune, S.C. (29009) 296/G3
Bethune, Sask. 181/F5
Betijoque, Ven. 124/C3
Betim, Braz. 135/D2
Betioky, Malag. Rep. 118/G4
Betoota, Aust. 88/G5
Betoota, Queens. 95/B5
Bet-Pak-Dala (des.), U.S.S.R. 48/H5
Bet Qama, Israel 65/B5
Betroka, Malag. Rep. 118/H4
Bet She'an, Israel 65/D3
Bet Shemesh, Israel 65/B4
Betsiamites (riv.), Que. 174/C2
Betsiamites (riv.), 163/K5
Betsiboka (riv.), Malag. Rep. 118/H3
Betsy (riv.), Mich. 250/D2
Betsy Layne, Ky. (41605) 237/R5
Bette (peak), Libya 111/C3
Bettendorf, Iowa (52722) 229/N5
Betteravia, Calif. (†93454) 204/E9
Betterton, Md. (21610) 245/O3
Bettiah, India 68/E3
Bettles, Alaska (†99726) 196/H1
Bettles Field, Alaska (99726) 196/H1
Bettsville, Ohio (44815) 284/D3
Bettyhill, Scot. 15/H3
Betul, India 68/D4
Betula, Pa. (†16749) 294/F2
Betwa (riv.), India 68/D4
Between, Ga. (†30655) 216/E3
Betws-y-Coed, Wales 13/C4
Betzdorf, W. Ger. 22/B3
Beulah, Ala. (†36872) 194/H5
Beulah, Colo. (81023) 208/K6
Beulah, Man. 179/A4
Beulah, Mich. (49617) 250/C4
Beulah, Miss. (38726) 256/B3
Beulah, Mo. (65436) 261/J7
Beulah, N. Dak. (58523) 283/G5
Beulah, Oreg. (†97911) 291/J4
Beulah (res.), Oreg. 291/J4
Beulah, Vic. 97/B4
Beulah (lake), Wis. 317/J2
Beulah, Wyo. (82712) 319/H1
Beulaker Wijde (lake), Neth. 27/H3
Beulaville, N.C. (28518) 281/O5
Bevans, N.J. (†07851) 273/D1
Bevent, Wis. (†54440) 317/H6
Beveren, Belg. 27/E6
Beverin (mt.), Switz. 39/H3
Beverley, 10/F4
Beverley, Aust. 88/B2
Beverley, Eng. 13/G4
Beverley, W. Aust. 92/B1
Beverley, Sask. 181/C5
Beverly, C. Rica 154/F6
Beverly, Kans. (67423) 232/E2
Beverly, Ky. (40913) 237/P7
Beverly, Mass. (01915) 249/E5
Beverly, Mo. (†64079) 261/O4
Beverly, N.J. (08010) 273/D3
Beverly (lake), N.W.T. 187/H3
Beverly, Ohio (45715) 284/G6
Beverly, W. Va. (26253) 313/G5
Beverly, Wash. (99321) 310/F4
Beverly Beach, Fla. (†32036) 212/E2
Beverly Hills, Calif. (*90210) 204/B10
Beverly Hills‡, Mich. (†48008) 250/B6
Beverly Hills‡, Mo. (†63101) 261/P3
Beverly Hills‡, Texas (75211) 302/G6
Beverly Shores, Ind. (46301) 227/C1
Beverwijk, Neth. 27/F4
Bevier, Mo. (63532) 261/G3
Bevil Oaks‡, Texas (†77701) 302/K7
Bevington, Iowa (50033) 229/F6
Bewdley, 10/F3
Bewdley, Ont. 177/F3
Bex, Switz. 39/D4
Bexar, Ala. (35547) 194/B2
Bexar (co.), Texas 302/F8
Bexhill, Eng. 13/H7
Bexhill-on-Sea, 10/G5
Bexley, 10/C5
Bexley, Miss. (39453) 256/G9
Bexley, Ohio (43209) 284/E6
Bey (mts.), Turkey 63/D4
Bey el Kebir, Wadi (dry riv.), Libya 111/B1
Beykoz, Turkey 63/D5
Beyla, Guinea 106/C7
Beylerbei, Turkey 63/D6
Beynon, Alta. 182/D4
Beyoğlu, Turkey 63/D6
Beypazari, Turkey 59/B1
Beypazari, Turkey 63/D2
Beyşehir, Turkey 59/B2
Beyşehir, Turkey 63/D4
Beyşehir (lake), Turkey 63/D4
Beytüşşebap, Turkey 63/K4
Bezanson, Alta. 182/A2
Bezdružice, Czech. 41/B2
Bezhetsk, U.S.S.R. 52/E3
Béziers, France 28/E6
Bezwada (Vijayawada), India, 54/L8
Bhadrak, India 68/F4
Bhadravati, India 68/D6
Bhadreswar, India 68/F1
Bhag, Pak. 59/J4
Bhag, Pak. 68/B3
Bhagalpur, India, 54/M7
Bhagalpur, India 68/F4
Bhaktapur, Nepal 68/F3
Bhamo, Burma, 54/N7
Bhamo, Burma 72/C1
Bhandara, India 68/E4
Bhandup, India 68/B7
Bharatpur, India 68/D3
Bhatinda, India 68/C2
Bhatkal, India 68/C6
Bhatpara, India 68/F1
Bhaujanagar, India 68/E4
Bhavnagar, India, 54/K7
Bhavnagar, India 68/C4
Bhawanipatna, India 68/E5
Bhera, Pak 68/C2
Bheri (riv.), Nepal 68/E3
Bhilai, India 68/E4
Bhilwara, India 68/C3
Bhima (riv.), India 68/D5
Bhimavaram, India 68/E5
Bhir (Bir), India 68/D5
Bhiwandi, India 68/C5
Bhiwani, India 68/D3
Bhojpur, Nepal 68/F3
Bhopal, India, 54/L7
Bhopal, India 68/D4
Bhor, India 68/C5
Bhubaneswar, India 68/F4
Bhuj, India 68/B4
Bhusawal, India 68/D4
Bhutan (prot.), India, 54/M7
Bhutan (prot.), India 68/G3
Biafra (bight), Nigeria 106/F8
Biafra (bight), Cameroon 115/A3
Biafra (bight), Eq. Guin. 115/A3
Biak, Indon. 85/K6
Biak (isl.), Indon. 85/K6
Biała Podlaska, Poland 47/F2
Białogard, Poland 47/B2
Białystok, Poland, 7/G3
Białystok (prov.), Poland 47/F2
Białystok, Poland 47/F2
Biancavilla, Italy 34/E6
Biarritz, France, 7/D4
Biarritz, France 28/C6
Bias, W. Va. (†25661) 313/B7
Biasca, Switz. 39/H4
Biba, U.A.R. 111/J4
Bibai, Japan 81/L2
Bibb (co.), Ala. 194/D5
Bibb (co.), Ga. 216/E5
Bibb City, Ga. (31904) 216/B5
Bibbenluke, N.S.W. 97/E5
Biberach, W. Ger. 22/C4
Biberist, Switz. 39/D2
Bible Grove, Ill. (62813) 222/E5
Bic (isl.), Que. 172/J1
Bicas, Braz. 135/E2
Bicester, Eng. 13/F6
Biche (lake), Alta. 182/E2
Biche, Trinidad Tobago 161/B10
Bicheno, Tas. 99/E3
Bickerdike, Alta. 182/B3
Bickerton (isl.), No. Terr. 93/E2
Bickerton West, N.S. 169/G3
Bickleigh, Sask. 181/C4
Bickleton, Wash. (99322) 310/E5
Bickmore, W. Va. (25019) 313/D6
Bicknell, Ind. (47512) 227/C7
Bicknell, Utah (84715) 304/C5
Bicske, Hung. 41/E3
Bida, Nigeria 106/F7
Bidar, India 68/D5
Biddeford, Maine, 188/N2
Biddeford, Maine (04005) 242/B9
Biddeford Pool, Maine (04006) 242/C9
Biddle, Mont. (59314) 262/L5
Biddu, Jordan 65/C4
Bideford, 10/D5
Bideford, Eng. 13/C6
Bidon 5 (Poste Maurice Cordier), Alg. 106/E4
Bidukht, Iran 66/L3
Bidwell, Ohio (45614) 284/F8
Bidyadhari (riv.), India 68/F2
Bié (dist.), Angola 115/C6
Bieber, Calif. (96009) 204/D2
Biel, Switz. 39/D2
Biel (lake), Switz. 39/D2
Bielawa, Poland 47/C3
Bield, Man. 179/A3
Bielefeld, W. Ger. 22/C2
Bieler (lake), N.W.T. 187/L2
Biella, Italy 34/B2
Bielsko-Biała, Poland 47/D4
Bielsk Podlaski, Poland 47/F2
Bienfait, Sask. 181/J6
Bien Hoa, S. Vietnam 72/E5
Bienne (Biel), Switz. 39/D2
Bienvenue, Fr. Gui. 131/E4
Bienville (lake), Que. 174/C2
Bienville (lake), 163/J5
Bienville (par.), La. 238/D2
Bienville, La. (71008) 238/D2
Bière, Switz. 39/D3
Bietigheim, W. Ger. 22/C4
Bietschorn (mt.), Switz. 39/E4
Bièvres, France 28/A2
Big (isl.), Alta. 182/B5
Big (creek), Idaho 220/C4
Big (creek), Ind. 227/B8
Big (brook), Maine 242/E2
Big (lake), Maine 242/H5
Big (pond), Mass. 249/B4
Big (riv.), Mo. 261/L6
Big (lake), Mont. 262/G5
Big (isl.), N.W.T. 187/L3
Big (bay), Newf. 166/B2
Big (isl.), Newf. 166/B2
Big (riv.), Newf. 166/C3
Biga, Turkey 63/B2
Bigadiç, Turkey 63/C3
Bigali, Turkey 63/B6
Big Annemessex (riv.), Md. 245/P8
Big Arm, Mont. (59910) 262/B3
Big Bald (mt.), N. Br. 170/D1
Big Bar, Calif. (96010) 204/B3
Big Bar Creek, Br. Col. 184/F4
Big Basin, Calif. (95006) 204/J4
Big Bay, Mich. (49808) 250/B2
Big Bay (pt.), Mich. 250/B2
Big Bay de Noc (bay), Mich. 250/C3
Big Bear City, Calif. (92314) 204/J9
Big Bear Lake, Calif. (92315) 204/J9
Big Beaver‡, Pa. (†15010) 294/B4
Big Beaver, Sask. 181/F6
Bigbee, Ala. (36510) 194/B7
Bigbee Valley, Miss. (39738) 256/H4
Big Bell, Aust. 88/B5
Big Bell, W. Aust. 92/B4
Big Belt (mts.), Mont. 262/E4
Big Bend (res.), Alta. 182/C3
Big Bend, N. Dak. (†58531) 283/H5
Big Bend (dam), S. Dak. 298/K5
Bigbend, W. Va. (26136) 313/D5
Big Bend, Wis. (53103) 317/K2
Big Bend City, Minn. (†56262) 254/C5
Big Bend National Park, Texas (79834) 302/A8
Big Bend Nat'l Park, Texas 302/A8
Big Black (riv.), Maine 242/D2
Big Black (riv.), Miss. 256/C4
Big Black (creek), S.C. 296/G2
Big Blue (riv.), Ind. 227/F5
Big Blue (riv.), Kans. 232/F1
Big Blue (riv.), Nebr. 264/H4
Big Bow, Kans. (67832) 232/A4
Big Bras d'Or, N.S. 169/H2
Big Bureau (riv.), Ill. 222/D2
Big Burro (mts.), N. Mex. 274/A6
Bigbury (bay), Eng. 13/C7
Big Cabin, Okla. (74332) 288/R1
Big Canoe (creek), Ala. 194/F3
Big Chimney, W. Va. (25302) 313/C6
Big Clifty, Ky. (42712) 237/J5
Big Cove Tannery, Pa. (17212) 294/F6
Big Creek, Br. Col. 184/F4
Big Creek, Calif. (93605) 204/F6
Big Creek, Idaho (†83677) 220/C4
Big Creek, Ky. (40914) 237/O6
Big Creek, Miss. (38914) 256/F3
Big Creek, W. Va. (25505) 313/B7
Big Cypress (swamp), Fla. 212/E5
Big Delta, Alaska (†99737) 196/J2
Big Dry (creek), Mont. 262/K3
Big Eau Pleine (res.), Wis. 317/G6
Big Elk (peak), Idaho 220/G6
Bigelow, Ark. (72016) 203/E3
Bigelow (brook), Conn. 210/G1
Bigelow (bight), Maine 242/C9
Bigelow (mt.), Maine 242/C5
Bigelow (bight), Mass. 249/M1
Bigelow, Minn. (56117) 254/C7
Bigelow, Mo. (64425) 261/B2
Big Falls, Minn. (56627) 254/E2
Big Falls, Wis. (54926) 317/H6
Bigflat, Ark. (72617) 203/F1
Big Flat (brook), N.J. 273/D1
Big Flats, N.Y. (14814) 276/G6
Bigfoot, Texas (78005) 302/F9
Big Fork, Ark. (71928) 203/B5
Bigfork, Minn. (56628) 254/E3
Big Fork (riv.), Minn. 254/E2
Bigfork, Mont. (59911) 262/C2
Big Four, W. Va. (†24853) 313/C8
Bigga, N.S.W. 97/E4
Biggar, 10/E3
Biggar, 163/F5
Biggar, Sask. 181/C3
Biggar, Scot. 15/J8
Bigge (isl.), W. Aust. 92/D1
Bigge (range), Queens. 95/D5
Biggers, Ark. (72413) 203/J1
Biggleswade, 10/F4
Biggleswade, Eng. 13/G5
Big Grizzly (creek), Colo. 208/G1
Biggs, Calif. (95917) 204/D4
Biggs, Oreg. (†97058) 291/G2
Biggs A.F.B., Texas 302/A10
Biggsville, Ill. (61418) 222/C3
Big Hole (mts.), Idaho 220/G6
Big Hole (riv.), Mont. 262/C5
Big Hole Nat'l Battlefield, Mont. 262/C5
Bighorn (riv.), 188/E2
Big Horn (mts.), Ariz. 198/B5
Big Horn (co.), Mont. 262/J5
Bighorn, Mont. (59010) 262/J4
Bighorn (lake), Mont. 262/H5
Bighorn (riv.), Mont. 262/J4
Big Horn (co.), Wyo. 319/E1
Big Horn, Wyo. (82833) 319/E1
Bighorn (basin), Wyo. 319/D1
Bighorn (lake), Wyo. 319/D1
Bighorn (mts.), Wyo. 319/E1
Bighorn (riv.), Wyo. 319/D1
Bighorn Canyon Nat'l Rec. Area, Mont. 262/H5
Bighorn Canyon Nat'l Rec. Area, Wyo. 319/D1
Big Indian, N.Y. (12410) 276/M6
Big Isaac, W. Va. (†26426) 313/E4
Big Island, Ont. 177/G3
Big Island, Va. (24526) 307/K5
Big Lake, Alaska (†99726) 196/J1
Big Lake, Alaska (†99687) 196/B1
Big Lake, Minn. (55309) 254/E5
Big Lake, Texas (76932) 302/C6
Biglake, Wash. (†98273) 310/C2
Bigler, Pa. (16825) 294/F4
Biglerville, Pa. (17307) 294/H6
Big Lick, Tenn. (†38555) 237/L9
Big Lost (riv.), Idaho 220/E6
Big Maumelle (lake), Ark. 203/E4
Big Moose, N.Y. (13307) 276/L3
Big Moose (lake), N.Y. 276/L3
Big Muddy (riv.), Ill. 222/D6
Big Muddy (riv.), Mont. 262/M2
Big Muddy, Sask. 181/G6
Big Muddy (lake), Sask. 181/G6
Big Muskego (lake), Wis. 317/L2
Bignasco, Switz. 39/G4
Bignona, Sen. 106/A6
Big North (mt.), Va. 307/L2
Big Oak Flat, Calif. (95305) 204/E6
Bigosovo, U.S.S.R., 7/G3
Big Otter (riv.), Va. 307/K6
Big Otter, W. Va. (25020) 313/D5
Big Pine, Calif. (93513) 204/G6
Big Pine (key), Fla. 212/E7
Big Pine (creek), Ind. 227/C3
Big Pine, N.C. (†28753) 281/D3
Big Piney, Mo. (65468) 261/H7
Big Piney, Wyo. (83113) 319/B3
Big Pipe (creek), Md. 245/K2
Big Plain, Ohio (†43140) 284/D6
Bigpoint, Miss. (†39567) 256/H9
Big Pond, N.S. 169/H3
Big Pool, Md. (21711) 245/F2
Big Porcupine (creek), Mont. 262/J4
Big Port Walter, Alaska (†99833) 196/M2
Big Prairie, Ohio (44611) 284/F4
Big Raccoon (creek), Ind. 227/C5
Big Rapids, Mich. (49307) 250/D5
Big Rib (riv.), Wis. 317/G5
Big River, 163/F5
Big River, Sask. 181/D2
Big Rock, Ill. (60511) 222/E2
Big Rock, Iowa (52725) 229/M5
Big Rock, Tenn. (37023) 237/F7
Big Rock, Va. (24603) 307/D6
Big Run, Pa. (15715) 294/E4
Big Sable (pt.), Mich. 250/C4
Big Sable (riv.), Mich. 250/C4
Big Sage (res.), Calif. 204/E2
Big Salmon (riv.), N. Br. 170/E3
Big Sandy (riv.), Ariz. 198/B4
Big Sandy (creek), Colo. 208/N4
Big Sandy (riv.), Ky. 237/R4
Big Sandy (lake), Minn. 254/E4
Big Sandy, Mont. (59520) 262/G2
Big Sandy, Tenn. (38221) 237/E8
Big Sandy (riv.), Tenn. 237/E9
Big Sandy, Texas (75755) 302/J5
Big Sandy (riv.), W. Va. 313/A6
Big Sandy, Wyo. (†82923) 319/C3
Big Sandy (res.), Wyo. 319/C3
Big Sioux (riv.), Iowa 229/A3
Big Sioux (riv.), S. Dak., 188/G2
Big Sioux (riv.), S. Dak. 298/S7
Big Smoky (valley), Nev. 266/D4
Big Southern (butte), Idaho 220/E6
Big Spencer (mt.), Maine 242/E4
Big Spring, Ga. (†30240) 216/C5
Big Spring, Ky. (40106) 237/J5
Big Spring, Md. (21712) 245/G2
Big Spring, Tenn. (37323) 237/M10
Big Spring, Texas, 188/F4
Big Spring, Texas (79720) 302/C5
Big Springs, Idaho (†83420) 220/G5
Big Springs, Nebr. (69122) 264/B3
Big Springs, S. Dak. (†57001) 298/S8
Big Springs, W. Va. (26137) 313/D5
Big Star (lake), Mich. 250/C5
Bigstick (lake), Sask. 181/B5
Big Stone, Alta. 182/E4
Bigstone (pt.), Man. 179/E2
Bigstone (lake), Man. 179/J3
Bigstone (riv.), Man. 179/J3
Big Stone (co.), Minn. 254/B5
Big Stone (lake), Minn. 254/B5
Big Stone (lake), S. Dak. 298/R3
Big Stone City, S. Dak. (57216) 298/S3
Big Stone Gap, Va. (24219) 307/C7
Big Sur, Calif. (93920) 204/D7
Big Thompson (riv.), Colo. 208/H2
Big Timber, Mont. (59011) 262/G5
Big Timber (creek), N.J. 273/C4
Big Tracadie (riv.), N. Br. 170/E1
Bigtrails, Wyo. (†82442) 319/E2
Big Trout (lake), Ont. 175/B2
Big Trout (lake), Ont. 177/F2
Big Valley, Alta. 182/D3
Big Walnut (creek), Ind. 227/D5
Big Walnut (creek), Ohio 284/E5
Big Wells, Texas (78830) 302/E9
Big Wood (riv.), Idaho 220/D6
Bihać, Yugo. 45/B3
Bihar (state), India 68/F4
Bihar, India 68/F3
Biharamulo, Tanz. 115/F4
Biharkeresztes, Hung. 41/F3
Biharnagybajom, Hung. 41/F3
Bijagós (isls.), 102/A3
Bijagós (isls.), Port. Guin. 106/A6
Bijagual, Cuba 158/J4
Bijapur, India 68/D5
Bijapur, India 68/E5
Bijar, Iran 66/E3
Bijawar, India 68/D4
Bijeljina, Yugo. 45/D3
Bijelo Polje, Yugo. 45/D4
Bijistan, Iran 59/G3
Bijistan, Iran 66/K3
Bijnor, India 68/D3
Bijou (creek), Colo. 208/L3
Bijou Hills, S. Dak. (†57310) 298/L6
Bikaner, India, 54/L7
Bikaner, India 68/C3
Bikar (atoll), Pac. Is., 87/H4
Bikini (atoll), Pac. Is., 87/G4
Bikoro, Dem. Rep. of the Congo. 115/C4
Bilaspur, India 68/E4
Bilauktaung (range), Burma 72/C4
Bilauktaung (range), Thai. 72/C4
Bilbao, Spain, 7/D4
Bilbao, Spain 33/E1
Bileća, Yugo. 45/D4
Bilecik, Turkey 59/A1
Bilecik (prov.), Turkey 63/D2
Bilecik, Turkey 63/D2
Biłgoraj, Poland 47/F3
Bilibino, U.S.S.R. 48/R3
Bilin, Burma 72/C3
Bílina, Czech. 41/B1
Biliran (isl.), Phil. 82/E5
Bill, Wyo. (82631) 319/G2
Billate (riv.), Eth. 111/G6
Billerica△, Mass. (01821) 249/J2
Billimun, Sask. 181/D6
Billings (lake), Conn. 210/H2
Billings, Mo. (65610) 261/F8
Billings, Mont., 146/H5
Billings, Mont., 188/E1
Billings, Mont. (*59101) 262/H5
Billings (co.), N. Dak. 283/D5
Billings, Okla. (74630) 288/M1
Billingsgate (isl.), Mass. 249/O5
Billingsley, Ala. (36006) 194/E5
Billington Heights‡, N.Y. (†14052) 276/C5
Billiton (isl.), Indon., 54/O10
Billiton (isl.), Indon. 85/D6
Bill Williams (riv.), Ariz. 198/B4
Billy Chinook (lake), Oreg. 291/F3
Bilma, 102/D3
Bilma, Niger 106/G5
Biloela, Aust. 88/J4
Biloela, Queens. 95/D5
Biloku, Guyana 131/B5
Biloxi, Miss., 188/J4
Biloxi, Miss. (*39530) 256/G10
Biloxi-Gulfport, Miss. 256/G10
Biltine, Chad 111/D5
Biltmore Forest, N.C. (†28803) 281/E3
Bilwaskarma, Nic. 154/F3
Bilzen, Belg. 27/G7
Bim, W. Va. (25021) 313/C7
Biminis, The (isls.), Bah. Is. 156/B1
Bimlipatam, India 68/E5
Bina, India 68/D4
Binalbagan, Phil. 82/D5
Binboğa (mts.), Turkey 63/G3
Binche, Belg. 27/E8
Binda, N.S.W. 97/E4
Bindjai, Indon. 85/B5
Bindloss, Alta. 182/E4
Bindoon, W. Aust. 92/B1
Bindura, Rhod. 118/E3
Binéfar, Spain 33/G2
Binevenagh (mt.), N. Ire. 17/H1
Binford, N. Dak. (58416) 283/O4
Binga (mt.), Moz. 118/E3
Bingara, Aust. 88/H5
Bingara, N.S.W. 97/F1
Bingen, W. Ger. 22/B4
Bingen, Wash. (98605) 310/D5
Binger, Okla. (73009) 288/K4
Bingerville, Ivory Coast 106/D7
Bingerville, 102/B4
Bingham (co.), Idaho 220/F6
Bingham, Ill. (62011) 222/D4
Bingham△, Maine (04920) 242/D5
Bingham, Maine (04920) 242/D5
Bingham, N. Mex. (87815) 274/C5
Bingham, Nebr. (69335) 264/B2
Bingham, S.C. (†29565) 296/H3
Bingham Farms‡, Mich. (†48008) 250/B6
Bingham Lake, Minn. (56118) 254/C7
Binghamton, N.Y., 188/L2
Binghamton, N.Y. (*13901) 276/J6
Bingöl (prov.), Turkey 63/J3
Bingöl (Capakçur), Turkey 63/J3
Bingöl Dağlari (mts.), Turkey 63/J3
Binh Dinh, S. Vietnam 72/F4
Binh Son, S. Vietnam 72/F4
Binn, Switz. 39/F4
Binnalong, N.S.W. 97/E4
Binnaway, N.S.W. 97/E2
Binningen, Switz. 39/D1
Binongko (isl.), Indon. 85/G7
Binscarth, Man. 179/A4
Bintan (isl.), Indon. 85/C5
Bintuhan, Indon. 85/C6
Bintulu, Malaysia 85/E5
Binyamina, Israel 65/B2
Bío-Bío (prov.), Chile 138/D1
Bío-Bío (riv.), Chile 138/E2
Biograd, Yugo. 45/B4
Biola, Calif. (93606) 204/E7
Bippus, Ind. (46713) 227/F3
Bir, Iran 59/G4
Bir, Iran 66/L8
Bir, India 68/D5
Bira, U.S.S.R., 54/S5
Bir 'Ali, P.D.R. Yemen 59/E7
Birama (pt.), Cuba 158/G4
Birao, Centr. Afr. Rep. 115/D2
Biratnagar, Nepal 68/F3
Biratori, Japan 81/L2
Bir Bidea, Syria 63/J4
Birch (creek), Alaska 196/J1
Birch (hills), Alta. 182/A2
Birch (lake), Alta. 182/E3
Birch (mts.), Alta. 182/B5
Birch (riv.), Alta. 182/B5
Birch (creek), Idaho 220/F5
Birch (isl.), Man. 179/C2
Birch (lake), Minn. 254/G3
Birch (creek), Mont. 262/D2
Birch (lake), Sask. 181/C2
Birch (creek), Utah 304/B5
Birch (pt.), Wash. 310/C2
Bircham, Alta. 182/D4
Birch Creek, Alaska (†99740) 196/J1
Birch Creek (valley), Idaho 220/E5
Birchdale, Minn. (56629) 254/D2
Birch Harbor, Maine (04613) 242/H7
Birch Hills, Sask. 181/F3
Birchip, Vic. 97/B4
Birch Island, Br. Col. 184/H4
Birch Lake, Sask. 181/D2
Birchleaf, Va. (24220) 307/D6
Birch River, Man. 179/A2
Birch River, W. Va. (26610) 313/E6
Birch Run, Mich. (48415) 250/F5
Birchtown, N.S. 169/C5
Birch Tree, Mo. (65438) 261/K9
Birchwood, Alaska (†99567) 196/C1
Birchwood‡, Minn. (†55110) 254/F5
Birchwood, Tenn. (37308) 237/M10
Birchwood, Wis. (54817) 317/C4
Birchwood City‡, Md. (†20031) 245/L5
Bird, Alaska (†99501) 196/C1
Bird (isl.), Aust. 88/K4
Bird (Aves) (isl.), Ven. 156/F4
Bird (isl.), La. 238/M8
Bird (creek), Okla. 288/O1
Bird City, Kans. (67731) 232/A2
Bird Island, Minn. (55310) 254/D6
Birds, Ill. (62415) 222/F5
Birdsboro, Pa. (19508) 294/L5
Birdseye, Ind. (47513) 227/D8
Birdsnest, Va. (23307) 307/S6
Birdsong, Ark. (†72386) 203/K3
Birdsville, Aust. 88/F5
Birdsville, Ky. (†42081) 237/D6
Birdsville, Queens. 95/A5
Birdtail, Man. 179/B4
Birdum, No. Terr. 93/C3
Birdwood, S. Aust. 94/C7
Birecik, Turkey 63/H4
Bir el Khzaim (well), Mauritania 106/C4
Bireuen, Indon. 85/B4
Birg, Kuh-i- (mt.), Iran 66/M7
Bir Ganduz (well), Sp. Sahara 106/A4
Birganj, Nepal 68/F3
Bir Hakeim, Libya 111/D1
Birigui, Braz. 135/A2
Birikao (Bur Gavo), Somalia 115/H4
Birjand, Iran, 54/J6
Birjand, Iran 59/G3
Birjand, Iran 66/L4
Birken, Br. Col. 184/F5
Birkenfeld, Oreg. (97016) 291/D1
Birkenfeld, W. Ger. 22/B4
Birkenhead, 10/F2
Birkenhead, Eng. 13/D4
Birkenhead, N.Z. 101/B1
Birkerød, Den. 21/F6
Birket Qârûn (lake), U.A.R. 111/J3
Bir Ksaib Ounane (well), Mali 106/C4
Birksgate (range), Aust. 88/D5
Birksgate (range), S. Aust. 94/A2
Bîrlad, Rum. 45/H2
Bîrlad (riv.), Rum. 45/H2
Birmingham, 10/G3
Birmingham, Ala., 146/K6
Birmingham, Ala., 188/J4
Birmingham, Ala. (*35201) 194/D3
Birmingham, Eng., 7/D3
Birmingham, Eng. 13/F5
Birmingham, Iowa (52535) 229/K7
Birmingham, Mich. (*48008) 250/B6
Birmingham, Mo. (†64068) 261/P5
Birmingham, N.J. (08011) 273/D4
Birmingham, Ohio (44816) 284/F3
Birmingham, Pa. (†16686) 294/F4
Birmingham, Sask. 181/H5
Birmitrapur, India 68/E4
Bir-Mogrein, Mauritania 106/B4
Birnamwood, Wis. (54414) 317/H6
Birney, Mont. (59012) 262/K5
Birnie, Man. 179/C4
Birnin Kebbi, Nigeria 106/E6
Birni-N'Konni, Niger 106/E6
Bir Nzaran (well), Sp. Sahara 106/B4
Birobidzhan, U.S.S.R. 48/O5
Biron, Wis. (†54494) 317/G7
Bir Ounane (well), Mali 106/D4
Birqin, Jordan 65/C3
Birr, 10/B4
Birr, Ire. 17/F5
Birregurra, Vic. 97/B6
Birrie (riv.), N.S.W. 97/D1
Birrimbah, No. Terr. 93/C3
Birrindudu, No. Terr. 93/A5
Birriwa, N.S.W. 97/E3
Birs (riv.), Switz. 39/D2
Birsay, 10/E1
Birsay, Sask. 181/D4
Birsay, Scot. 15/K1
Birsk, U.S.S.R. 52/J3
Birta, Ark. (†72853) 203/D3
Bir Taba, U.A.R. 59/B4
Bir Taba (well), U.A.R. 111/F2
Birtle, Man. 179/B4
Biruaca, Ven. 124/E4
Biržai, U.S.S.R. 53/C2
Bir Zeit, Jordan 65/C4
Bisbee, Ariz., 188/E4
Bisbee, Ariz. (85603) 198/F7
Bisbee, N. Dak. (58317) 283/M2
Biscarrosse (lag.), France 28/C5
Biscay (bay), 3/J3
Biscay (bay), 7/D4
Biscay (bay), France 28/B5
Biscay, Minn. (†55336) 254/D6
Biscay (bay), Spain 33/E1
Biscay Bay (riv.), Newf. 166/D2
Biscayne (bay), Fla. 212/F6
Biscayne (key), Fla. 212/B5
Biscayne Nat'l Mon., Fla. 212/F6
Biscayne Park, Fla. (33152) 212/B4
Bisceglie, Italy 34/F4
Bischofshofen, Austria 41/B3
Bischofswerda, E. Ger. 22/F3
Bischofszell, Switz. 39/H1
Biscoe (isls.), Ant. 5/C15
Biscoe, Ark. (72017) 203/H4
Biscoe, N.C. (27209) 281/K4
Biscotasing, Ont. 175/D3
Biscotasing, Ont. 177/J5
Biscucuy, Ven. 124/D3
Bisha, Saudi Ar. 59/D5
Bisha, Wadi (dry riv.), Saudi Ar. 59/D5
Bishiara (well), Libya 111/D3
Bishop, Calif. (93514) 204/G6
Bishop, Ga. (30621) 216/F3
Bishop, Md. (†21813) 245/S7
Bishop, Texas (78343) 302/G10
Bishop (creek), Utah 304/E3
Bishop, Va. (24604) 307/E6
Bishop Auckland, 10/E3
Bishop Auckland, Eng. 13/E3
Bishopbriggs, Scot. 15/D2
Bishop Hill, Ill. (61419) 222/C2
Bishopric, Sask. 181/F5
Bishops (creek), Nev. 266/F1
Bishop's Castle, 10/E4
Bishop's Castle, Eng. 13/E5
Bishop's Falls, Newf. 166/C4
Bishops Head, Md. (21611) 245/O7
Bishops Mitre (mt.), Newf. 166/B2
Bishop's Stortford, 10/G5
Bishop's Stortford, Eng. 13/H6
Bishop's Waltham, Eng. 13/F7
Bishopton, Que. 172/F4
Bishopville, Md. (21813) 245/T7
Bishopville, S.C. (29010) 296/G3
Bishri, Jebel el (mts.), Syria 63/H5
Biskra, Alg. 106/F2
Biskra, 102/B1
Biskupiec, Poland 47/E2
Bislig, Phil. 82/F6
Bislig, Phil. 85/H4
Bismarck, Ark. (71929) 203/D5
Bismarck, Ill. (61814) 222/F3
Bismarck, Mo. (63624) 261/L7
Bismarck (cap.), N. Dak., 146/H5
Bismarck (cap.), N. Dak., 188/G1
Bismarck (cap.), N. Dak. (58501) 283/J6
Bismarck (arch.), Terr. N.G., 87/E6
Bismarck (arch.), Terr. N.G., 3/S6
Bismarck, W. Va. (†26739) 313/H4
Bismil, Turkey 63/J4
Bison (lake), Alta. 182/B1
Bison, Kans. (67520) 232/C3
Bison, Okla. (73720) 288/L2
Bison, S. Dak. (57620) 298/E2
Bispgården, Sweden 18/K5
Bissau (cap.), Port. Guin. 102/A3
Bissau (cap.), Port. Guin. 106/A6
Bissett, Man. 179/G4
Bistineau (lake), La. 238/D2
Bistrița, Rum. 45/G2

Boca Grande 335

Bita (riv.), Col. 126/F5
Bitagron, Sur. 131/C3
Bitam, Gabon 115/B3
Bitburg, W. Ger. 22/B4
Bitely, Mich. (49309) 250/D5
Bithlo, Fla. (†32801) 212/E3
Bitlis, Turkey 59/D2
Bitlis (prov.), Turkey 63/J3
Bitlis, Turkey 63/J3
Bitola, Yugo., 7/G4
Bitola (Bitolj), Yugo. 45/E5
Bitonto, Italy 34/F4
Bitter (lakes), U.A.R. 111/K3
Bitter (lake), Sask. 181/B5
Bitter (creek), Wyo. 319/C4
Bitter Creek, Wyo. (82921) 319/D4
Bitterfeld, E. Ger. 22/E3
Bitterfontein, S. Africa 118/B6
Bittern (lake), Alta. 182/D3
Bittern Lake, Alta. 182/D3
Bitterroot (range), 188/D1
Bitterroot (range), Idaho 220/D3
Bitterroot (range), Mont. 262/B4
Bitterroot (riv.), Mont. 262/B4
Bitterroot (range), U.S., 146/G5
Bitti, Italy 34/B4
Bitumount, Alta. 182/E1
Bitung, Indon. 85/H5
Biu, Nigeria 106/G6
Bivalve, Md. (21814) 245/P7
Bivalve, N.J. (08301) 273/C5
Bivolari, Rum. 45/H2
Biwa (lake), Japan 81/H6
Biwabik, Minn. (55708) 254/F3
Bixby, Minn. (55916) 254/E7
Bixby, Mo. (65439) 261/K7
Bixby, Okla. (74008) 288/P3
Biysk, U.S.S.R. 48/J4
Bizcocho, Urug. 145/B4
Bizerte, 102/C1
Bizerte, Tun. 106/F1
Bjargtangar (pt.), Ice. 21/A1
Bjelovar, Yugo. 45/C3
Bjerringbro, Den. 21/C5
Bjorkdale, Sask. 181/H3
Bjørna (fjord), Norway 18/D6
Bjorne (pen.), N.W.T. 187/K2
Bjornøya (isl.), Norway 18/D3
Blaavands (pt.), Den. 21/A6
Blabon, N. Dak. (†58046) 283/P5
Blachly, Oreg. (97412) 291/D3
Black (sea), 3/L3
Black (sea), 7/H4
Black (sea), 54/G5
Black, Ala. (36314) 194/G8
Black (riv.), Alaska 196/K1
Black (mesa), Ariz. 198/E2
Black (mts.), Ariz. 198/E5
Black (riv.), Ariz. 198/A3
Black (riv.), Ark. 203/H2
Black (sea), Bulg. 45/J4
Black (pond), Conn. 210/G1
Black (pt.), Conn. 210/G3
Black (sea), U.S.S.R. 48/D5
Black (sea), U.S.S.R. 52/D6
Black (riv.), Jam. 158/H6
Black (riv.), Ont. 177/E3
Black (creek), Fla. 212/E1
Black (head), Ire. 17/C5
Black (mt.), Ky. 237/R7
Black (lake), La. 238/D3
Black (pond), Maine 242/D3
Black (isl.), Man. 179/F3
Black (riv.), Man. 179/F4
Black (lake), Mich. 250/E3
Black (riv.), Mich. 250/E3
Black (riv.), Mich. 250/G5
Black (riv.), Minn. 254/D2
Black (creek), Miss. 256/F8
Black, Mo. (63625) 261/L7
Black (riv.), Mo. 261/L10
Black (riv.), N.C. 281/N5
Black (mt.), N. Mex. 274/A6
Black (range), N. Mex. 274/B5
Black (lake), N.Y. 276/J1
Black (riv.), N.Y. 276/K3
Black (sea), Turkey 63/E1
Black (riv.), N. Vietnam 72/D2
Black (riv.), China 77/F7
Black (riv.), Ohio 284/F3
Black (sea), Rum. 45/J4
Black (riv.), S.C. 296/H4
Black (lake), Sask. 181/M2
Black (creek), Vt. 268/B2
Black (riv.), Vt. 268/B5
Black (riv.), Vt. 268/C2
Black (for.), W. Ger. 22/C4
Black (riv.), Wis. 317/E7
Black (riv.), Yukon 187/D3
Blackall, Australia, 87/E8
Blackall, Aust. 88/G4
Blackall, Queens. 95/C5
Black Bear (creek), Okla. 288/M2
Blackberry (riv.), Conn. 210/B1
Blackbird, Del. (†19734) 245/R3
Black Branch, Nulhegan (riv.), Vt. 268/D2
Blackburn, 10/G1
Blackburn (mt.), Alaska 196/K2
Blackburn, Eng. 13/E4
Blackburn, La. (†71038) 238/D1
Blackburn, Mo. (65321) 261/F4
Blackburn, Okla. (74058) 288/N2
Blackburne (pt.), Aust. 88/M5
Black Butte (res.), Calif. 204/C4
Black Canyon City, Ariz. (85324) 198/C4
Black Canyon of the Gunnison Nat'l Mon., Colo. 208/D5
Black Cape, Que. 172/C2
Black Creek, Br. Col. 184/E5
Black Creek, N.C. (27813) 281/O3
Black Creek, Wis. (54106) 317/K7
Black Diamond, Alta. 182/C4
Black Diamond, Wash. (98010) 310/D3
Black Duck (riv.), Ont. 175/C1
Blackduck, Minn. (56630) 254/D3
Black Eagle, Mont. (59414) 262/E3
Black Earth, Wis. (53515) 317/G9
Black Elster (riv.), E. Ger. 22/E3
Blackey, Ky. (41804) 237/R6
Blackfalds, Alta. 182/D3
Blackfeet Ind. Res., Mont. 262/D2
Blackfoot, Alta. 182/E3
Blackfoot, Idaho (83221) 220/F6
Blackfoot (riv.), Idaho 220/G6
Blackfoot, Mont. (59415) 262/D2
Blackfoot (riv.), Mont. 262/C4
Blackfoot River (res.), Idaho 220/G7
Blackford (co.), Ind. 227/G4
Blackford, Ky. (42403) 237/F6
Black Forest, Colo. (80908) 208/K4
Blackfork, Ohio (45615) 284/E8
Black Fork, Mohican (riv.), Ohio 284/F4
Blackgum, Okla. (†74962) 288/S3
Black Hall, Conn. (†06371) 210/F3
Black Hawk, Colo. (80422) 208/J3
Blackhawk, Ind. (†47866) 227/C6
Black Hawk (co.), Iowa 229/J4
Black Hawk, Miss. (38918) 256/E4
Black Hawk, S. Dak. (57718) 298/C5
Blackhead, Newf. 166/D2
Blackhead (bay), Newf. 166/D2
Black Hills (mts.), 188/F2
Black Hills (mts.), S. Dak. 298/B5
Blackie, Alta. 182/D4
Black Isle (dist.), Scot. 15/H4
Black Jack, Mo. (†63031) 261/P2
Black Lake, Que. 172/F3
Black Lake (bayou), La. 238/D1
Black Lake, Sask. 181/M2
Blackledge (riv.), Conn. 210/F2
Black Lick, Pa. (15716) 294/D4
Blacklick Estates‡, Ohio (43004) 284/E6
Blacklock (pt.), Oreg. 291/C5
Black Mesa (mt.), Okla. 288/A1
Blackmore (mt.), Mont. 262/F5
Black Mountain, N.C. (28711) 281/E3
Black Oak, Ark. (72414) 203/K2
Blackoak, Ind. (†46401) 227/C1
Black Pine (mts.), Idaho 220/E7
Black Pine (peak), Idaho 220/E7
Black Pine (creek), S. Dak. 298/G6
Black Pines, Br. Col. 184/G4
Black Point, Calif. (†94947) 204/J1
Black Point, Conn. (†06333) 210/G3
Black Point, N. Br. 170/D1
Blackpool, 10/F1
Blackpool, Eng. 13/D4
Blackridge, Va. (23916) 307/M7
Black River, Jam. 156/B3
Black River, Jam. 158/H6
Black River (bay), Jam. 158/G6
Black River, Mich. (48721) 250/F4
Black River, N. Br. 170/E3
Black River, N.Y. (13612) 276/J3
Black River (pond), Newf. 166/C2
Black River Bridge, N. Br. 170/E2
Black River Falls, Wis. (54615) 317/E7
Black Rock, Ark. (72415) 203/H1
Black Rock (des.), Nev. 266/B2
Black Rock (range), Nev. 266/B1
Black Rock, Utah (†84751) 304/B5
Blacksburg, S.C. (29702) 296/D1
Blacksburg, Va. (24060) 307/H6
Blacks Fork, Green (riv.), Wyo. 319/C4
Blacks Harbour, N. Br. 170/D3
Blackshear, Ga. (31516) 216/H8
Blackshear (lake), Ga. 216/E7
Blacksher, Ala. (†36507) 194/C8
Blacksod (bay), Ire. 17/A3
Black Springs, Ark. (71930) 203/C5
Black Springs, Nev. (89508) 266/B3
Black Squirrel (creek), Colo. 208/L5
Blackstairs (mt.), Ire. 17/H6
Blackstock, Ont. 177/F3
Blackstock, S.C. (29014) 296/E2
Blackstone▵, Mass. (01504) 249/H4
Blackstone (riv.), Mass. 249/G3
Blackstone, Va. (23824) 307/N6
Blacksville, W. Va. (26521) 313/F3
Black Thunder (creek), Wyo. 319/G2
Black Tickle, Newf. 166/C3
Blackton, Ark. (†72069) 203/H4
Blacktown, Aust. 88/K3
Blacktown, N.S.W. 97/H3
Blackville, N. Br. 170/E2
Blackville, S.C. (29817) 296/E5
Black Volta (riv.), 102/B4
Black Volta (riv.), Ghana 106/D6
Black Volta (riv.), Ivory Coast 106/D6
Black Volta (riv.), Upp. Volta 106/D6
Black Warrior (riv.), Ala. 194/C5
Blackwater (riv.), Eng. 13/J6
Blackwater (riv.), Fla. 212/B6
Blackwater (riv.), 10/B4
Blackwater, Ire. 17/J7
Blackwater (riv.), Ire. 17/D7
Blackwater (riv.), Ire. 17/H4
Blackwater, Mo. (65322) 261/G5
Blackwater (res.), N.H. 268/D5
Blackwater (riv.), N. Ire. 17/H3
Blackwater (res.), Scot. 15/G6
Blackwater, Va. (24221) 307/B7
Blackwater (riv.), Va. 307/J6
Blackwater (riv.), Va. 307/O6
Blackwell, Ark. (72019) 203/E3
Blackwell (brook), Conn. 210/H1
Blackwell, Okla. (74631) 288/M1
Blackwell, Texas (79506) 302/D5
Blackwell, Wis. (†54541) 317/J4
Blackwood, N.J. (08012) 273/C4
Blackwood (Ngundju) (cape), Indon. 85/F8
Blackwood, Sask. 181/H5
Bladen (co.), N.C. 281/M5
Bladen, Nebr. (68928) 264/F4
Bladenboro, N.C. (28320) 281/M5
Bladensburg, Md. (20710) 245/G4
Bladensburg, Ohio (43005) 284/F5
Blades, Del. (†19973) 245/R6
Bladon Springs, Ala. (36902) 194/B7
Bladworth, Sask. 181/E4
Blaeberry, Br. Col. 184/J4
Blagodarnoye, U.S.S.R. 52/F5
Blagoveshchensk, U.S.S.R. 48/N4
Blagoveshchensk, U.S.S.R., 54/P4
Blagoyevgrad, Bulg. 45/F5
Blain, France 28/C4
Blain, Pa. (17006) 294/H5
Blaine, Ga. (†30175) 216/C1
Blaine (co.), Idaho 220/D6
Blaine, Kans. (66410) 232/F2
Blaine, Ky. (41124) 237/R4
Blaine▵, Maine (04734) 242/H2
Blaine, Mich. (†48032) 250/G5
Blaine, Minn. (†55303) 254/G5
Blaine, Miss. (38727) 256/C3
Blaine (co.), Mont. 262/G2
Blaine (co.), Nebr. 264/E3
Blaine, Ohio (43909) 284/J5
Blaine (co.), Okla. 288/K3
Blaine, Oreg. (†97108) 291/D2
Blaine, Tenn. (37709) 237/O8
Blaine, Wash. (98230) 310/C2
Blaine Lake, Sask. 181/D3
Blaine-Mars Hill, Maine (04734) 242/H2
Blair, Kans. (†66090) 232/H2
Blair, Nebr. (68008) 264/H3
Blair, Okla. (73526) 288/H5
Blair (co.), Pa. 294/F4
Blair, S.C. (29015) 296/E3
Blair, W. Va. (25022) 313/C7
Blair, Wis. (54616) 317/D7
Blair Athol, Aust. 88/H4
Blair Athol, Queens. 95/C4
Blair-Atholl, 10/E2
Blair-Atholl, Scot. 15/J6
Blairgowrie and Rattray, 10/E2
Blairgowrie and Rattray, Scot. 15/J6
Blairmore, Alta. 182/C5
Blairs, Va. (24527) 307/K7
Blairsburg, Iowa (50034) 229/F4
Blairsden, Calif. (96103) 204/E4
Blairs Mills, Ky. (41402) 237/P4
Blairs Mills, Pa. (17213) 294/G5
Blairstown, Iowa (52209) 229/J5
Blairstown, Mo. (64726) 261/E5
Blairstown, N.J. (07825) 273/C2
Blairsville, Ga. (30512) 216/E1
Blairsville, Pa. (15717) 294/D5
Blaisdell, N. Dak. (58720) 283/F3
Blaj, Rum. 45/F2
Blake (pt.), Mich. 250/E1
Blakeley, Minn. (†56011) 254/E6
Blakeley, W. Va. (25023) 313/D6
Blakely, Ga. (31723) 216/C8
Blakely, Pa. (18447) 294/L2
Blakeney, Eng. 13/J5
Blakesburg, Iowa (52536) 229/H7
Blakeslee, Ohio (43505) 284/A2
Blakeslee, Pa. (18610) 294/L3
Blaketown, Newf. 166/D2
Blalock, Ala. (†36773) 194/D6
Blalock, Ga. (†30525) 216/E1
Blalock (isl.), Wash. 310/F5
Blanc (cape), 3/J4
Blanc (cape), 102/A2
Blanc (mt.), France 28/G5
Blanc (mt.), Italy 34/A2
Blanc (cape), 102/A2
Blanc (cape), Mauritania 106/A4
Blanc (cape), Sp. Sahara 106/A4
Blanc (cape), Tun. 106/G1
Blanca (bay), Arg., 120/E6
Blanca (bay), Arg. 143/D4
Blanca (pt.), C. Rica 154/F5
Blanca (lag.), Chile 138/E10
Blanca (peak), Colo., 188/F3
Blanca, Colo. (81123) 208/H8
Blanca (peak), Colo. 208/H7
Blanca, Cordillera (mts.), Peru 128/D7
Blanch, N.C. (27212) 281/L2
Blanchard, Idaho (83804) 220/A1
Blanchard, Iowa (51630) 229/C7
Blanchard, La. (71009) 238/C1
Blanchard▵, Maine (†04406) 242/D5
Blanchard, Mich. (49310) 250/D5
Blanchard, N. Dak. (58009) 283/R5
Blanchard (riv.), Ohio 284/C4
Blanchard, Okla. (73010) 288/L4
Blanchard, Pa. (16826) 294/G3
Blanchard, Wash. (98231) 310/C2
Blanchardville, Wis. (53516) 317/G10
Blanche (lake), Aust. 88/G5
Blanche (riv.), Que. 172/E2
Blanche, Ky. (†40902) 237/O7
Blanche (lake), S. Aust. 94/F3
Blanche, Tenn. (†38488) 237/H10
Blanche Marie (fall), Sur. 131/C3
Blanchester, Ohio (45107) 284/B7
Blanchisseuse, Trinidad Tobago 161/B10
Blanco (riv.), Arg. 143/C2
Blanco (riv.), Bol. 136/D4
Blanco (cape), C. Rica 154/E6
Blanco (peak), C. Rica 154/F6
Blanco (lake), Chile 138/F10
Blanco (riv.), Mex. 150/Q2
Blanco, N. Mex. (87412) 274/B2
Blanco (creek), N. Mex. 274/F4
Blanco, Okla. (74528) 288/P5
Blanco (cape), Oreg., 188/A2
Blanco (cape), Oreg. 291/C5
Blanco (cape), Peru 128/B5
Blanco (riv.), Peru 128/F6
Blanco (co.), Texas 302/F7
Blanco, Texas (78606) 302/F7
Blanc-Sablon, Que. 174/F2
Bland, Mo. (65014) 261/J6
Bland (co.), Va. 307/F6
Bland, Va. (24315) 307/F6
Blandburg, Pa. (16619) 294/F4
Blandford (Blandford Forum), 10/E5
Blandford (Blandford Forum), Eng. 13/F7
Blandford▵, Mass. (01008) 249/C4
Blandford, N.S. 169/D4
Blanding, Utah (84511) 304/E6
Blandinsville, Ill. (61420) 222/C3
Blandon‡, Pa. (19510) 294/L5
Blandville, Ky. (42026) 237/D7
Blanes, Spain 33/H2
Blaney Park, Mich. (49809) 250/D2
Blanford, Ind. (47831) 227/B5
Blankenberge, Belg. 27/C6
Blankenburg, E. Ger. 22/D3
Blanket, Texas (76432) 302/F6
Blanquillo, Urug. 145/D3
Blansko, Czech. 41/D2
Blanton, Ala. (†36872) 194/H5
Blanton, Fla. (†33525) 212/D3
Blantyre, 102/F6
Blantyre, Malawi 115/F7
Blantyre, Scot. 15/D2
Blarney, 10/B5
Blarney, Ire. 17/D8
Blas (mt.), Switz. 39/G3
Blasdell, N.Y. (14219) 276/C5
Blasket (isls.), 10/A4
Blasket (isls.), Ire. 17/A7
Blatná, Czech. 41/B2
Blatten, Switz. 39/E4
Blaubeuren, W. Ger. 22/C4
Blauvelt‡, N.Y. (10913) 276/N8
Blawenburg, N.J. (08504) 273/D3
Blawnox, Pa. (15238) 294/C6
Blaydon, Eng. 13/F3
Blaydon-on-Tyne, 10/F3
Blaye, France 28/C5
Blayney, N.S.W. 97/E3
Blaze (pt.), Aust. 88/D2
Blaze (pt.), No. Terr. 93/A2
Bleckley (co.), Ga. 216/F6
Bled, Yugo. 45/A2
Bledsoe (co.), Tenn. 237/L9
Bledsoe, Texas (79314) 302/A4
Bleecker, Ala. (†36874) 194/H5
Blejeşti, Rum. 45/G3
Blekinge (co.), Sweden 18/J8
Blencoe, Iowa (51523) 229/A5
Blende, Colo. (†81001) 208/K6
Blenheim, Ont. 177/C5
Blenheim, N.Z. 101/D4
Blenheim, S.C. (29516) 296/H2
Blenker, Wis. (54415) 317/F6
Blennerhassett (isl.), Ohio 284/G7
Blerick, Neth. 27/J6
Blesbok (riv.), S. Africa 118/J7
Blessing, Texas (77419) 302/H9
Blessington, Ire. 17/J5
Bletchley, 10/F4
Bletchley, Eng. 13/G5
Blevins, Ark. (71825) 203/C6
Blewett, Sask. 181/H6
Blewett, Texas (†78801) 302/D8
Blida, Alg. 106/E1
Bligh (sound), N.Z. 101/A6
Blind Channel, Br. Col. 184/E5
Blind River, 163/H6
Blind River, Ont. 175/D3
Blind River, Ont. 177/J5
Blinman, S. Aust. 94/F4
Blinnenhorn (mt.), Switz. 39/F4
Bliss, Idaho (83314) 220/D7
Bliss, N.Y. (14024) 276/D5
Blissfield, Mich. (49228) 250/F7
Blissfield, N. Br. 170/D2
Blissfield, Ohio (43805) 284/G5
Blisworth, Eng. 13/F5
Blitar, Indon. 85/K2
Blitchton, Ga. (†31308) 216/J6
Blocher, Ind. (47170) 227/F7
Block (isl.), R.I. 249/H8
Blocker, Okla. (74529) 288/P4
Block House, N.S. 169/D4
Block Island (sound), N.Y. 276/S8
Block Island, R.I. (02807) 249/H8
Block Island (sound), R.I. 249/H8
Blockton, Iowa (50836) 229/D7
Blodgett, Mo. (63824) 261/O8
Blodgett, Oreg. (97326) 291/D3
Blodgett Landing, N.H. (03255) 268/D5
Bloedel, Br. Col. 184/E5
Bloemendaal, Neth. 27/E4
Bloemfontein, 102/E7
Bloemfontein, S. Africa 118/C5
Blois, France 28/D4
Blokzijl, Neth. 27/H3
Blomkest, Minn. (56216) 254/D6
Bloodroot (mt.), Vt. 268/B4
Bloodsworth (isl.), Md. 245/O8
Bloodvein (riv.), Ont. 175/A2
Bloodvein (riv.), Man. 179/F3
Bloody Foreland (prom.), 10/B3
Bloody Foreland (prom.), Ire. 17/E1
Bloom, Kans. (67833) 232/C4
Bloom, N. Dak. (†58401) 283/N6
Blomburg, Texas (75556) 302/L4
Bloom City, Wis. (54617) 317/E8
Bloomdale, Ohio (44817) 284/D3
Bloomer, Ark. (†72933) 203/B3
Bloomer, Wis. (54724) 317/D5
Bloomery, W. Va. (26817) 313/K4
Bloomfield, Sierra (mts.), Bol. 136/D4
Bloomfield▵, Conn. (06002) 210/E1
Bloomfield, Conn. (06002) 210/E1
Bloomfield, Ont. 177/G4
Bloomfield, Ind. (47424) 227/D6
Bloomfield, Iowa (52537) 229/J7
Bloomfield, Ky. (40008) 237/L5
Bloomfield, Mo. (63825) 261/M9
Bloomfield, Mont. (59315) 262/M3
Bloomfield, N.J. (07003) 273/B2
Bloomfield, N. Mex. (87413) 274/A2
Bloomfield, Nebr. (68718) 264/G2
Bloomfield, Newf. 166/D2
Bloomfield (New Bloomfield), Pa. (15224) 294/H5
Bloomfield▵, Vt. (†03590) 268/D2
Bloomfield, Vt. (†03590) 268/D2
Bloomfield Hills, Mich. (48013) 250/B6
Bloomfield Ridge, N. Br. 170/D2
Bloomfield Station, N. Br. 170/E3
Blooming, Sask. 181/G6
Bloomingburg, N.Y. (12721) 276/L7
Bloomingburg, Ohio (43106) 284/D6
Bloomingdale, Ga. (31302) 216/K6
Bloomingdale‡, Ill. (60108) 222/E1
Bloomingdale, Ind. (47832) 227/C5
Bloomingdale, Mich. (49026) 250/C6
Bloomingdale, N.J. (07403) 273/E1
Bloomingdale, N.Y. (12913) 276/M2
Bloomingdale, Ohio (43910) 284/J5
Bloomingdale, Tenn. (37660) 237/R7
Bloomingdale, Wis. (†54667) 317/E8
Blooming Grove, Ind. (†47012) 227/G5
Blooming Grove, Pa. (†18428) 294/M3
Blooming Grove, Texas (76626) 302/H5
Bloomingport, Ind. (†47355) 227/G5
Blooming Prairie, Minn. (55917) 254/E7
Bloomington, Calif. (92316) 204/E10
Bloomington, Idaho (83223) 220/G7
Bloomington, Ill., 188/J2
Bloomington, Ill. (61701) 222/D3
Bloomington, Ind. (47401) 227/D6
Bloomington, Md. (21523) 245/B3
Bloomington, Minn. (55420) 254/G6
Bloomington, Nebr. (68929) 264/F4
Bloomington, Texas (77951) 302/H9
Bloomington, Wis. (53804) 317/E10
Bloomington Springs, Tenn. (38545) 237/K8
Blooming Valley, Pa. (†16335) 294/B2
Bloomsburg, Pa. (17815) 294/J3
Bloomsbury, Alta. 182/C2
Bloomsbury, N.J. (08804) 273/C2
Bloomsdale, Mo. (63627) 261/M6
Bloomville, N.Y. (13739) 276/L6
Bloomville, Ohio (44818) 284/D3
Blora, Indon. 85/K2
Blossburg, Pa. (16912) 294/H2
Blossom, Texas (75416) 302/J4
Bloubergstrand, S. Africa 118/E6
Blount (co.), Ala. 194/E2
Blount (co.), Tenn. 237/O9
Blounts Creek, N.C. (27814) 281/P4
Blount Springs, Ala. (†35079) 194/E3
Blountstown, Fla. (32424) 212/A1
Blountsville, Ala. (35031) 194/E2
Blountsville, Ind. (†47360) 227/G4
Blountville, Tenn. (37617) 237/S7
Blovice, Czech. 41/B2
Blowing Rock, N.C. (28605) 281/F2
Bloxom, Va. (23308) 307/S5
Blucher, Sask. 181/E3
Bludenz, Austria 41/A3
Blue, Ariz. (85922) 198/F5
Blue (riv.), Ariz. 198/F5
Blue (mt.), Colo. 208/B2
Blue (riv.), Colo. 208/G3
Blue (mts.), Jam. 158/K6
Blue (riv.), Ind. 227/E8
Blue (mt.), Maine 242/C6
Blue (hills), Mass. 249/C8
Blue (mt.), N. Br. 170/D1
Blue (mt.), N.H. 268/E2
Blue (mts.), N.S.W. 97/F3
Blue (creek), Nebr. 264/B3
Blue, Okla. (74725) 288/O7
Blue (riv.), Okla. 288/O6
Blue (mts.), Oreg. 291/J3
Blue (mt.), Pa. 294/G5
Blue (creek), Utah 304/B2
Blue (lake), Utah 304/B4
Blue (lake), Wash. 310/F3
Blue (mts.), Wash. 310/H4
Blue Ash, Ohio (†45201) 284/C9
Blue Ball, Ark. (†72866) 203/C4
Blue Bell, N. Br. 170/C2
Blue Bell, S. Dak. (†57773) 298/C6
Bluebell, Utah (84007) 304/D3
Blueberry Mountain, Alta. 182/A2
Blue Cove, N. Br. 170/E1
Blue Creek, Ohio (45616) 284/D8
Blue Creek, Utah (†84337) 304/B2
Blue Creek, W. Va. (25026) 313/D6
Bluecreek, Wash. (99106) 310/H2
Blue Cypress (lake), Fla. 212/F4
Blue Diamond, Ky. (41718) 237/P6
Blue Earth (co.), Minn. 254/D6
Blue Earth, Minn. (56013) 254/D7
Blue Earth (riv.), Minn. 254/D7
Blue Eye, Ark. (†65611) 203/D1
Blue Eye, Mo. (65611) 261/F9
Bluefield, Va. (24605) 307/F6
Bluefield, W. Va., 188/K3
Bluefield, W. Va. (24701) 313/D8
Bluefields, Jam. 158/H6
Bluefields, Nic. 154/F4
Bluegrass, Ind. (†46939) 227/E3
Blue Grass, Iowa (52726) 229/M5
Blue Grass, Minn. (†56477) 254/C4
Blue Grass, Va. (24413) 307/J3
Blue Heron, Sask. 181/E2
Blue Hill▵, Maine (04614) 242/F7
Blue Hill, Maine (04614) 242/F7
Blue Hill (bay), Maine 242/G7
Blue Hill, Nebr. (68930) 264/F4
Blue Hill Falls, Maine (04615) 242/F7
Blue Hills, Conn. (06112) 210/E1
Blue Island, Ill. (60406) 222/B2
Bluejacket, Okla. (74333) 288/R1
Blue Jay, Calif. (92317) 204/H9
Blue Knob (mt.), Pa. 294/E5
Blue Lake, Calif. (95525) 204/A3
Blue Mesa (res.), Colo. 208/E5
Bluemont, Va. (22012) 307/N2
Blue Mound, Ill. (62513) 222/D4
Blue Mound, Kans. (66010) 232/H3
Blue Mound, Texas (76131) 302/F1
Blue Mounds, Wis. (53517) 317/G9
Blue Mountain, Ala. (36201) 194/G3
Blue Mountain, Ark. (72826) 203/C3
Blue Mountain (lake), Ark. 203/C3
Blue Mountain (peak), Jam. 156/C3
Blue Mountain (peak), Jam. 158/K6
Blue Mountain, Miss. (38610) 256/G1
Blue Mountain (lake), N.Y. 276/M3
Blue Mountain Lake, N.Y. (12812) 276/M3
Blue Mountains, Australia, 87/E9
Blue Mountains, Aust. 88/H6
Blue Mountains, N.S.W. 97/F3
Blue Nile (riv.), 102/F3
Blue Nile (riv.), Sudan 59/B6
Blue Nile (Abbai) (riv.), Eth. 111/G5
Blue Nile (prov.), Sudan 111/F5
Blue Nile (riv.), Sudan 111/F5
Blue Nile (riv.), 102/F3
Blue Nose (mt.), Idaho 220/D4
Bluenose (lake), N.W.T. 187/G3
Blue Rapids, Kans. (66411) 232/F2
Blue Ridge, Alta. 182/C2
Blue Ridge, Ga. (30513) 216/D1
Blue Ridge (lake), Ga. 216/D1
Blue Ridge (mts.), Ga. 216/E1
Blue Ridge, Ind. (†46176) 227/F5
Blue Ridge (mts.), Md. 245/H3
Blue Ridge (mts.), N.C. 281/E3
Blue Ridge (mts.), S.C. 296/B1
Blue Ridge‡, Texas (75004) 302/H4
Blue Ridge, Va. (24064) 307/J6
Blue Ridge (mts.), Va. 307/J6
Blue Ridge Manor‡, Ky. (†40201) 237/K4
Blue Ridge Summit, Pa. (17214) 294/G6
Blue River, Br. Col. 184/H4
Blue River, Colo. (†80424) 208/G4
Blue River, Oreg. (97413) 291/E3
Blue River, Wis. (53518) 317/E9
Blue Rock (Gaysport), Ohio (43720) 284/G6
Blue Rocks, N.S. 169/D4
Bluesky, Alta. 182/A1
Blue Spring (hills), Utah 304/B1
Blue Springs, Ala. (†36017) 194/G7
Blue Springs, Miss. (38828) 256/G2
Blue Springs, Mo. (64015) 261/R6
Blue Springs, Nebr. (68318) 264/H4
Blue Stack (mts.), Ire. 17/E2
Bluestone (res.), Va. 307/G5
Bluestone (lake), W. Va. 313/E7
Blue Sulphur Springs, W. Va. (†25545) 313/E7
Blue Summit, Mo. (†64101) 261/R5
Bluevale, Ont. 177/C4
Bluewater, N. Mex. (87005) 274/A3
Bluewater (creek), N. Mex. 274/B4
Bluewater (creek), N. Mex. 274/D6
Bluewater (lake), N. Mex. 274/A3
Bluewing, Man. 179/A3
Bluff, Alaska (†99784) 196/F2
Bluff, N.C. (†28743) 281/D3
Bluff, N.Z. 101/B7
Bluff (cape), Newf. 166/C3
Bluff, Utah (84512) 304/E6
Bluff City, Ark. (71722) 203/D6
Bluff City, Ill. (†62624) 222/E5
Bluff City, Kans. (67018) 232/E4
Bluff City, Tenn. (37618) 237/S8
Bluff Dale, Texas (76433) 302/F5
Bluff Knoll (mt.), W. Aust. 92/B6
Bluff Park, Ala. (35226) 194/E4
Bluffs, Ill. (62621) 222/C4
Bluffsprings, Fla. (†32535) 212/B5
Bluffton, Alta. 182/C3
Bluffton, Ark. (72827) 203/C4
Bluffton, Ga. (31724) 216/C7
Bluffton, Ind. (46714) 227/G3
Bluffton, Minn. (56518) 254/C4
Bluffton, Ohio (45817) 284/C4
Bluffton, S.C. (29910) 296/F7
Bluford, Ill. (62814) 222/E5
Blum, Texas (76627) 302/G5
Blumenau, Braz. 132/D9
Blumenfeld, Man. 179/D5
Blumenhof, Sask. 181/D5
Blumenort, Man. 179/E5
Blumenort, Man. 179/F5
Blumenstein, Switz. 39/E3
Blümlisalp (mt.), Switz. 39/E3
Blunt, S. Dak. (57522) 298/J4
Bly, Oreg. (97622) 291/F5
Blying (sound), Alaska 196/C1
Blyn, Wash. (†98382) 310/B3
Blyth, 10/F3
Blyth, Ont. 177/C4
Blyth, Eng. 13/F2
Blythe, Calif. (92225) 204/L10
Blythe, Ga. (30805) 216/H4
Blythedale, Md. (†21904) 245/O2
Blythedale, Mo. (64426) 261/E2
Blythedale, Pa. (15013) 294/C5
Blytheswood, Ont. 177/B5
Blytheville, Ark., 188/H3
Blytheville, Ark. (72315) 203/L2
Blytheville A.F.B., Ark. 203/K2
Blythewood, S.C. (29016) 296/E3
Bo, S. Leone 106/B7
Boac, Phil. 82/C4
Boaco, Nic. 154/E4
Boa Esperança, Braz. 135/D2
Boalsburg, Pa. (16827) 294/G4
Boano (isl.), Indon. 85/H6
Board Camp, Ark. (71932) 203/B4
Boardman (riv.), Mich. 250/D4
Boardman, N.C. (†28438) 281/M6
Boardman, Ohio (44512) 284/J3
Boardman, Oreg. (97818) 291/H2
Boardman, Wis. (†54016) 317/A5
Boardmans Bridge, Conn. (†06776) 210/B2
Boas (riv.), N.W.T. 187/K3
Boat Basin, Br. Col. 184/D5
Boat Harbour, Tas. 99/B2
Boa Vista, Braz., 120/D2
Boa Vista (isl.), C. Verde Is. 106/B8
Boa Vista, Braz. 132/H8
Boa Vista (isl.), 102/G8
Boayan (isl.), Phil. 82/B5
Boaz, Ala. (35957) 194/F2
Boaz, Ky. (42027) 237/D7
Boaz, Mo. (†65631) 261/F8
Boaz, W. Va. (†26187) 313/D4
Boaz, Wis. (†53581) 317/E9
Bobadah, N.S.W. 97/D3
Bobare, Ven. 124/D2
Bobbili, India 68/F5
Bobbitt, N.C. (†27544) 281/N2
Bobcaygeon, Ont. 177/F3
Bobigny, France 28/B1
Böblingen, W. Ger. 22/C4
Bobo, Miss. (38728) 256/C2
Bobo-Dioulasso, 102/B3
Bobo-Dioulasso, Upp. Volta 106/D6
Bobolice, Poland 47/C2
Bobon, Phil. 82/F7
Bobonaza (riv.), Ec. 128/D3
Bobonong, Botswana 118/D4
Bobotov Kuk (mt.), Yugo. 45/D4
Bobrinets, U.S.S.R. 52/D5
Bobruysk, U.S.S.R. 48/C4
Bobruysk, U.S.S.R. 52/C4
Bobs (lake), Ont. 177/H3
Bobtown, Pa. (15315) 294/B6
Bobures, Ven. 124/C3
Boby, Pic (mt.), Malag. Rep. 118/H4
Bocabec, N. Br. 170/C3
Boca Chica, Dom. Rep. 158/E6
Boca Chica (key), Fla. 212/E7
Boca Ciega (bay), Fla. 212/B3
Boca de Aroa, Ven. 124/D2
Boca del Mangle, Ven. 124/D2
Boca del Pao, Ven. 124/F3
Boca del Pepé, Col. 126/B5
Boca del Río, Mex. 150/Q2
Boca del Soco, Dom. Rep. 158/F6
Bôca do Acre, Braz. 132/G10
Boca Grande (passg.), Trinidad Tobago 161/A10
Boca Grande, Fla. (33921) 212/D5
Boca Grande (key), Fla. 212/D7
Boca Grande (gulf), Ven. 124/H3

336 Bocaiúva

Bocaiúva, Braz. 132/E7
Bocaranga, Centr. Afr. Rep. 115/C2
Boca Raton, Fla. (33432) 212/F5
Bocas del Toro, Pan. 154/F6
Bocay, Nic. 154/E3
Bochnia, Poland 47/E4
Bocholt, Belg. 27/H6
Bocholt, W. Ger. 22/B3
Bochov, Czech. 41/B1
Bochum, W. Ger. 22/B3
Bock, Minn. (56313) 254/E5
Boco, Chile 138/F2
Boconó, Ven. 124/C3
Böda, Sweden 18/K8
Boda, Centr. Afr. Rep. 115/C3
Bodalla, N.S.W. 97/F5
Bodaybo, U.S.S.R. 48/M4
Bodaybo, U.S.S.R., 54/P4
Bodcau (bayou), La. 238/C1
Bodcaw, Ark. (†71858) 203/D6
Boddam, Scot. 15/N5
Boddington, W. Aust. 92/B2
Bode, Iowa (50519) 229/E3
Bodega (bay), Calif. 204/B5
Bodega (head), Calif. 204/B5
Bodega Bay, Calif. (94923) 204/B5
Bodegraven, Neth. 27/F4
Bodélé (depr.), Chad 111/C4
Boden, Sweden 18/N4
Bodensee (Constance) (lake), Austria 41/A3
Bodensee (Constance) (lake), Switz. 39/H1
Bodensee (Constance) (lake), W. Ger. 22/C5
Boderg (lake), Ire. 17/E4
Bodfish, Calif. (93205) 204/G8
Bodhan, India 68/D5
Bodinayakkanur, India 68/D6
Bodines, Pa. (17722) 294/H3
Bodio, Switz. 39/G4
Bodjonegoro, Indon. 85/J2
Bodkin (pt.), Md. 245/N4
Bodmin, 10/D5
Bodmin, Eng. 13/C7
Bodmin, Sask. 181/D2
Bodo, Alta. 182/E3
Bodø, Norway 18/J3
Bodrum, Turkey 59/A2
Bodrum, Turkey 63/B4
Bodum, Minn. (†55040) 254/E5
Bódvaszilas, Hung. 41/F2
Boelus, Nebr. (68820) 264/F3
Boende, Dem. Rep. of the Congo. 115/D4
Boerne, Texas (78006) 302/F8
Boeuf (lake), La. 238/J7
Boeuf (riv.), La. 238/G1
Boffa, Guinea 106/B6
Bog (lake), Maine 242/H6
Bogalusa, La., 188/H4
Bogalusa, La. (70427) 238/L5
Bogan (riv.), N.S.W. 97/D2
Bogandé, Upp. Volta 106/E6
Bogan Gate, N.S.W. 97/D3
Bogantungan, Queens. 95/C4
Bogard, Mo. (64622) 261/E4
Bogart, Ga. (30622) 216/E3
Bogata, Texas (75417) 302/J4
Bogatynia, Poland 47/B3
Boğazliyan, Turkey 63/F3
Bogdan (mt.), Bulg. 45/G4
Bogda Ula (mts.), China 77/C3
Bogen, W. Ger. 22/E4
Bogenfels, S.W. Afr. 118/B5
Bogense, Den. 21/D6
Boger City, N.C. (28092) 281/G4
Boggabilla, N.S.W. 97/F1
Boggabri, N.S.W. 97/F2
Boggeragh (mts.), Ire. 17/D7
Boggs, W. Va. (26299) 313/E6
Boggstown, Ind. (46110) 227/F5
Boggy (peak), Antigua 161/D11
Boggy Creek, Man. 179/A3
Boggy Depot, Okla. (†74525) 288/O6
Boghé, Mauritania 106/B5
Bogia, Terr. N.G. 85/B6
Bognor Regis, 10/F5
Bognor Regis, Eng. 13/G7
Bogo, Phil. 82/E5
Bogong (mt.), Vic. 97/D5
Bogor, Indon. 85/H2
Bogoslof (isl.), Alaska 196/E4
Bogotá (cap.), Col., 3/F5
Bogotá (cap.), Col., 120/C2
Bogotá (cap.), Col. 126/D5
Bogota, Ill. (62416) 222/E5
Bogota, N.J. (07603) 273/B2
Bogota, Tenn. (38007) 237/C8
Bogra, Pak. 68/F4
Boguchar, U.S.S.R. 52/F5
Bogue, Kans. (67625) 232/C2
Bogue, N.C. (†28570) 281/R5
Bogue (inlet), N.C. 281/P5
Bogue (sound), N.C. 281/R5
Bogue Chitto, Miss. (39629) 256/D8
Bogue Chitto (riv.), Miss. 256/D8
Bogue Homo (lake), Miss. 256/F7
Bog Walk, Jam. 158/J6
Boharm, Sask. 181/F5
Bohemia (reg.), Czech. 41/C2
Bohemia‡, N.Y. (11716) 276/O9
Bohemian (for.), Czech. 41/B2
Bohemian (for.), W. Ger. 22/E4
Bohemian-Moravian Heights (hills), Czech. 41/C2
Bohners Lake‡, Wis. (†53105) 317/K10
Bohol (prov.), Phil. 82/E6
Bohol (isl.), Phil. 82/E6
Bohol (isl.), Phil. 85/G4
Bohol (str.), Phil. 82/D6
Böhönye, Hung. 41/D3
Bohotleh, Somalia 115/J2
Boiaçu, Braz. 132/H8
Boicourt, Kans. (†66075) 232/H3
Boiestown, N. Br. 170/D2
Boiling Spring Lakes, N.C. (28461) 281/N7
Boiling Springs, N.C. (28017) 281/F4
Boiling Springs, Pa. (17007) 294/H5
Boiling Springs-Dixie Acres‡, Ill. (†61832) 222/F3
Bois (isl.), Newf. 166/C4
Bois Blanc (isl.), Mich. 250/E3
Boischatel, Que. 172/J3
Boisdale, N.S. 169/H2
Boisdale (inlet), Scot. 15/B5
Bois D'Arc, Mo. (65612) 261/F8
Bois de Sioux (riv.), Minn. 254/B4
Bois de Sioux (riv.), S. Dak. 298/R1
Boise (co.), Idaho 220/C6
Boise (cap.), Idaho, 146/G5
Boise (cap.), Idaho, 188/C2
Boise (cap.), Idaho (*83701) 220/B6
Boise (mts.), Idaho 220/B6
Boise (riv.), Idaho 220/B6
Boise City, Okla. (73933) 288/B1
Boissevain, 163/G6
Boissevain, Man. 179/C5
Boissevain, Va. (24606) 307/F6
Boistfort, Wash. (†98532) 310/B4
Boisvert (pt.), Que. 172/J1
Boizenburg, E. Ger. 22/D2
Bojador (cape), 102/A2
Bojador (cape), Sp. Sahara 106/B3
Bojeador (cape), Phil. 82/C1
Bojkovice, Czech. 41/D2
Bokchito, Okla. (74726) 288/O6
Boké, Guinea 106/B6
Bokeelia, Fla. (33922) 212/D5
Bokel (cay), Br. Hond. 154/D2
Bokhara (riv.), N.S.W. 97/D1
Bokhoma, Okla. (†71821) 288/S7
Boknafjord (fjord), Norway 18/D7
Boko, Rep. of Congo 115/B4
Bokoro, Chad 111/C5
Bokoshe, Okla. (74930) 288/S4
Bokote, Dem. Rep. of the Congo. 115/D4
Bokpyin, Burma 72/C5
Boksburg, S. Africa 118/J6
Bokungu, Dem. Rep. of the Congo. 115/D4
Bol, Chad 111/B5
Bolair, W. Va. (26288) 313/F6
Bolama, Port. Guin. 106/A6
Bolan (pass), Pak. 68/B3
Bolangir, India 68/E4
Bolar, Va. (24414) 307/J4
Bolatusha, Miss. (†39160) 256/E5
Bolayir, Turkey 63/C5
Bolbec, France 28/D3
Bolckow, Mo. (64427) 261/C2
Bolderslev, Den. 21/C8
Bolding, Ark. (†71747) 203/F7
Boldman, Ky. (†41501) 237/R5
Bole, Ghana 106/D7
Boles, Ark. (72926) 203/B4
Bolesławiec, Poland 47/B3
Boley, Okla. (74829) 288/O4
Bolgatanga, Ghana 106/D6
Boligee, Ala. (35443) 194/C5
Bolinao, Phil. 82/B2
Bolinao (cape), Phil. 82/B2
Bolinas, Calif. (94924) 204/H1
Boling, Texas (77420) 302/H8
Bolingbroke, Ga. (31004) 216/E5
Bolingbrook‡, Ill. (60439) 222/E2
Bolinger, Ala. (36903) 194/B7
Bolinger, La. (†71064) 238/C1
Bolivar, Arg. 143/D4
Bolivar, Bol. 136/B3
Bolívar, Antioquia, Col. 126/C5
Bolívar, Cauca, Col. 126/B7
Bolívar (dept.), Col. 126/C3
Bolívar (prov.), Ec. 128/C3
Bolívar, Ec. 128/C2
Bolivar (co.), Miss. 256/C3
Bolivar, Mo. (65613) 261/F7
Bolivar, N.Y. (14715) 276/D6
Bolivar, Ohio (44612) 284/G4
Bolivar, Pa. (15923) 294/D5
Bolivar, Peru 128/D6
Bolivar, Tenn. (38008) 237/C10
Bolivar (pen.), Texas 302/K8
Bolívar (state), Ven. 124/F7
Bolívar, Cerro (mt.), Ven. 124/G4
Bolívar, Pico (peak), Ven. 124/C3
Bolivar, W. Va. (25426) 313/L4
Bolivia, 3/F6
Bolivia, 120/D4
BOLIVIA, 136
Bolivia, N.C. (28422) 281/N6
Bolkhov, U.S.S.R. 52/E4
Bolligen, Switz. 39/E3
Bolling, Ala. (36007) 194/E7
Bolling A.F.B., D.C. 245/E5
Bollinger (co.), Mo. 261/M8
Bollington, 10/G2
Bollnäs, Sweden 18/K6
Bollon, Queens. 95/C6
Bolmen (lake), Sweden 18/H8
Bolney, Sask. 181/B2
Bolobo, Dem. Rep. of the Congo. 115/C4
Bologna, Italy, 7/F4
Bologna (prov.), Italy 34/C2
Bologna, Italy 34/C2
Bolognesi, Peru 128/F6
Bolognesi, Peru 128/F8
Bologoye, U.S.S.R. 52/D3
Bolomba, Dem. Rep. of the Congo. 115/C3
Bolonchén de Rejón, Mex. 150/O7
Bolondrón, Cuba 156/B2
Bolondrón, Cuba 158/D1
Bolovens (plat.), Laos 72/E4
Boipebra, Bol. 136/A2
Bolsena (lake), Italy 34/C3
Bol'shevik (isl.), U.S.S.R. 48/K2
Bol'shevik (isl.), U.S.S.R., 4/A4
Bol'shevik (isl.), U.S.S.R., 54/O2
Bol'shoy Lyakhov (isl.), U.S.S.R. 48/P2
Bol'shoy Lyakhov (isl.),U.S.S.R., 54/T2
Bolsover, Eng. 13/F4
Bolsters Mills, Maine (†04040) 242/B7
Bolsward, Neth. 27/H2
Boltaña, Spain 33/F1
Boltigen, Switz. 39/D3
Bolton, 10/G2
Bolton▵, Conn. (06040) 210/F1
Bolton, Ont. 177/J4
Bolton, Eng. 13/E4
Bolton▵, Mass. (01740) 249/H3
Bolton, Miss. (39041) 256/D6
Bolton, N.C. (28423) 281/N6
Bolton▵, Vt. (†05466) 268/B3
Bolton, Vt. (†05477) 268/B3
Bolton (mt.), Vt. 268/B3
Bolton Landing, N.Y. (12814) 276/N3
Bolton-Sud, Que. 172/E4
Bolu, Turkey 59/B1
Bolu (prov.), Turkey 63/D2
Bolu, Turkey 63/D2
Bolus (head), Ire. 17/A8
Bolvadin, Turkey 63/D3
Bolvanskiy Nos (cape), U.S.S.R. 48/G2
Bolvanskiy Nos (cape), U.S.S.R. 52/K1
Bolzano, Italy, 7/F4
Bolzano (prov.), Italy 34/C1
Bolzano, Italy 34/C1
Boma, 102/D5
Boma, Dem. Rep. of the Congo. 115/B5
Bomaderry-Nowra, N.S.W. 97/F4
Bomarton, Texas (76353) 302/E4
Bomba (gulf), Libya 111/D1
Bombala, Aust. 88/H7
Bombala, N.S.W. 97/E5
Bombardopolis, Haiti 158/B5
Bombay, India, 3/N5
Bombay, India, 54/L8
Bombay, India 68/B7
Bombay (harb.), India 68/B7
Bombay, Minn. (†55946) 254/F6
Bombay, N.Y. (12914) 276/M1
Bomboma, Dem. Rep. of the Congo. 115/C3
Bom Conselho, Braz. 132/G5
Bom Despacho, Braz. 132/E7
Bom Despacho, Braz. 135/D1
Bomi Hills, Liberia 106/B7
Bom Jesus, Braz. 132/E5
Bom Jesus da Lapa, Braz. 132/F6
Bomongo, Dem. Rep. of the Congo. 115/C3
Bomont, W. Va. (25030) 313/D6
Bomoseen, Vt. (05732) 268/A4
Bomoseen (lake), Vt. 268/A4
Bom Retiro, Braz. 132/D10
Bom Sucesso, Braz. 135/D2
Bomu (riv.), Centr. Afr. Rep. 115/D3
Bomu (riv.), Dem. Rep. of the Congo. 115/D3
Bon (cape), 102/D1
Bon (cape), Tun. 106/G1
Bona (mt.), Alaska 196/K2
Bonabéri, Cameroon 115/A3
Bonacca (Guanaja) (isl.), Hond. 154/E2
Bon-Accord, Alta. 182/D3
Bon Air, Ala. (35032) 194/F4
Bonair, Iowa (†52155) 229/J2
Bon Air, Tenn. (†38583) 237/L9
Bon Air, Va. (23235) 307/N5
Bonaire (isl.), Neth. Ant. 156/E4
Bonaire (isl.), Neth. Ant. 161/E9
Bonalbo, N.S.W. 97/G1
Bonanza, Alta. 182/A2
Bonanza, Ark. (†72901) 203/B3
Bonanza, Colo. (†81155) 208/G6
Bonanza, Nic. 154/E4
Bonanza, Oreg. (97623) 291/F5
Bonanza, Utah (84008) 304/E3
Bonanza (peak), Wash. 310/E2
Bonao, Dom. Rep. 158/E6
Bonaparte, Iowa (52620) 229/K7
Bonaparte (lake), N.Y. 276/K2
Bonaparte (arch.), W. Aust. 92/D1
Bonaparte (creek), Wash. 310/F2
Bonaparte (mt.), Wash. 310/F2
Bon Aqua, Tenn. (37025) 237/G9
Bonar Bridge, Scot. 15/H4
Bonaventure (co.), Que. 172/C2
Bonaventure, Que. 172/C2
Bonaventure (riv.), Que. 172/C1
Bonaventure (co.), Que. 174/D3
Bonaventure (cape), Newf. 166/D2
Bonavista, 163/L6
Bonavista, Newf. 166/D2
Bonavista (bay), Newf. 166/D1
Bonavista (cape), Newf. 166/D1
Bonbon, Haiti 158/A6
Boncarbo, Colo. (81024) 208/K8
Boncourt, Switz. 39/C2
Bond, Colo. (80423) 208/F3
Bond (co.), Ill. 222/D5
Bond, Ky. (40437) 237/N6
Bond, Miss. (39550) 256/F9
Bond (mt.), N.H. 268/E3
Bondeno, Italy 34/C2
Bond Falls (res.), Mich. 250/G2
Bondi, N.S.W. 97/K3
Bondi (beach), N.S.W. 97/K3
Bondiss, Alta. 182/D2
Bondo, 102/E4
Bondo, Dem. Rep. of the Congo. 115/D3
Bondoukou, Ivory Coast 106/D7
Bondowoso, Indon. 85/L2
Bondsville, Mass. (01009) 249/E4
Bonduel, Wis. (54107) 317/K6
Bondurant, Iowa (50035) 229/G5
Bondurant, Wyo. (82922) 319/B2
Bondville, Ill. (61815) 222/E3
Bondville, Ky. (40308) 237/M5
Bondville, Vt. (05340) 268/B5
Bondy, France 28/B1
Bône (Annaba), 102/C1
Bône (Annaba), Alg. 106/F1
Bone, Idaho (†83401) 220/G6
Bone (gulf), Indon., 54/R10
Bone (gulf), Indon. 85/G7
Bone Cave, Tenn. (38546) 237/L9
Bone Gap, Ill. (62815) 222/F5
Bo'ness, 10/C1
Bo'ness, Scot. 15/J7
Bonesteel, S. Dak. (57317) 298/M7
Bonet (riv.), Ire. 17/E3
Boneta, Utah (†84051) 304/D3
Bonete (dam), Urug. 145/C3
Bonetraill, N. Dak. (58836) 283/C3
Boneville, Ga. (30806) 216/G4
Bonfield, Ont. 177/E1
Bonfield, Ill. (60913) 222/E2
Bonfol, Switz. 39/D2
Bong (mts.), Liberia 106/B7
Bongabon, Phil. 82/C3
Bongabong, Phil. 82/C4
Bongandanga, Dem. Rep. of the Congo. 115/D3
Bongao, Phil. 82/B8
Bongo (isl.), Phil. 82/D7
Bongor, Chad 111/C5
Bong Son, S. Vietnam 72/F4
Bonham, Texas (75418) 302/H4
Bonhill, Scot. 15/B2
Bon Homme (co.), S. Dak. 298/O7
Bonifacio, France 28/B7
Bonifacio (str.), France 28/B7
Bonifacio (str.), Italy 34/B4
Bonifay, Fla. (32425) 212/C5
Bönigen, Switz. 39/E3
Bonilla, S. Dak. (57318) 298/N4
Bonin (isls.), Japan, 87/E3
Bonin (isls.), Japan, 3/S4
Bonin (isls.), Japan 81/M3
Bonita, Ariz. (†85643) 198/E6
Bonita (pt.), Calif. 204/H2
Bonita, La. (71223) 238/G1
Bonita, Miss. (39321) 256/G6
Bonita Springs, Fla. (33923) 212/E5
Bonlee, N.C. (27213) 281/L3
Bonn (cap.), W. Ger., 7/E3
Bonn (cap.), W. Ger. 22/B3
Bonne (bay), Newf. 166/C4
Bonneau, S.C. (29431) 296/H5
Bonneauville‡, Pa. (†17325) 294/H6
Bonner (co.), Idaho 220/B1
Bonner, Mont. (59823) 262/C4
Bonners Ferry, Idaho (83805) 220/B1
Bonner Springs, Kans. (66012) 232/H2
Bonnet (lake), Man. 179/G4
Bonnétable, France 28/D3
Bonnet Carré Spillway and Floodway, La. 238/N3
Bonne Terre, Mo. (63628) 261/L7
Bonnet Plume (riv.), Yukon 187/E3
Bonneville, France 28/G4
Bonneville (co.), Idaho 220/G6
Bonneville, Oreg. (97008) 291/F2
Bonneville (dam), Oreg. 291/E2
Bonneville (dam), Wash. 310/D5
Bonneville (lake), Wash. 310/D5
Bonneville, Wyo. (†82649) 319/E2
Bonneville (mt.), Wyo. 319/C3
Bonneville Flats (salt dep.), Utah 304/A3
Bonney Lake, Wash. (†98390) 310/C3
Bonnie, Ill. (62816) 222/E5
Bonnieville, Ky. (42713) 237/K6
Bonnots Mill, Mo. (65016) 261/J5
Bonny (res.), Colo. 208/P3
Bonny, Nigeria 106/F8
Bonnybridge, Scot. 15/D2
Bonnyman, Ky. (41719) 237/P6
Bonnyrigg, N.S.W. 97/H3
Bonnyrigg and Lasswade, 10/C1
Bonnyrigg and Lasswade, Scot. 15/K8
Bonny River, N. Br. 170/D3
Bonnyview‡, Calif. (†96001) 204/C3
Bonnyville, Alta. 182/E2
Bono, Ark. (72416) 203/J2
Bono, Ohio (43401) 284/D2
Bonorva, Italy 34/B4
Bonpas (creek), Ill. 222/F5
Bonpland (mt.), N.Z. 101/A6
Bon Secour, Ala. (36511) 194/C10
Bon Secour (bay), Ala. 194/C10
Bonsecours, Que. 172/E4
Bonsecours, Que. 172/G4
Bonshaw, P.E.I. 169/E2
Bonthain, Indon. 85/F7
Bonthe, S. Leone 106/B7
Bontoc, Phil. 82/C2
Bontoc, Phil. 85/G2
Bon Wier, Texas (75928) 302/L7
Bonyhád, Hung. 41/E3
Boody, Ill. (62514) 222/D4
Book (cliffs), Utah 304/E4
Booker, Texas (79005) 302/D1
Booker T. Washington Nat'l Mon., Va. 307/J6
Boolaloo, W. Aust. 92/B3
Booligal, N.S.W. 97/C3
Boom, Belg. 27/E6
Boom, Tenn. (†38573) 237/L7
Boomer, N.C. (28606) 281/G2
Boomer, W. Va. (25031) 313/D6
Boomi, N.S.W. 97/E1
Boon (pt.), Antigua 161/E11
Boon, Mich. (49618) 250/D4
Boone (co.), Ark. 203/D1
Boone, Colo. (81025) 208/L6
Boone (co.), Ill. 222/E1
Boone (co.), Ind. 227/E4
Boone (co.), Iowa 229/F5
Boone, Iowa (50036) 229/F4
Boone (co.), Ky. 237/M3
Boone, Ky. (40408) 237/N5
Boone (co.), Mo. 261/H4
Boone, N.C. (28607) 281/F2
Boone (co.), Nebr. 264/F3
Boone, Nebr. (68625) 264/F3
Boone (lake), Tenn. 237/S8
Boone (co.), W. Va. 313/C6
Boone Grove, Ind. (46302) 227/C2
Boonesboro, Mo. (†65250) 261/G4
Boones Mill, Va. (24065) 307/J6
Boonesville, Va. (22925) 307/M4
Booneville, Ark. (72927) 203/C3
Booneville, Ky. (41314) 237/O6
Booneville, Miss. (38829) 256/G1
Boonsboro, Md. (21713) 245/H2
Boonton, N.J. (07005) 273/E2
Boonton (res.), N.J. 273/E2
Boonville, Calif. (95415) 204/B5
Boonville, Ind. (47601) 227/C8
Boonville, Mo. (65233) 261/G5
Boonville, N.C. (27011) 281/H2
Boonville, N.Y. (13309) 276/K4
Boopi (riv.), Bol. 136/B4
Booroorban, N.S.W. 97/C4
Boorowa, N.S.W. 97/E4
Boort, Vic. 97/B5
Booth, Ala. (36008) 194/E6
Booth, Sask. 181/G4
Boothbay▵, Maine (04537) 242/D8
Boothbay, Maine (04537) 242/D8
Boothbay Harbor, Maine (04538) 242/D8
Boothia (gulf), 163/H2
Boothia (isth.), 163/G2
Boothia (pen.), 163/G1
Boothia (gulf), Canada, 4/B14
Boothia (pen.), Canada, 4/B14
Boothia (gulf), N.W.T., 146/K2
Boothia (pen.), N.W.T., 146/J2
Boothia (gulf), N.W.T. 187/K3
Boothia (pen.), N.W.T. 187/J2
Boothville, La. (70038) 238/M8
Boothwyn, Pa. (19061) 294/L7
Bootle, 10/F2
Bootle, Cumberland, Eng. 13/D3
Bootle, Lancashire, Eng. 13/D4
Booué, Gabon 115/B3
Booué, 102/D4
Boppard, W. Ger. 22/B3
Boquerón, Cuba 156/C3
Boquerón, Cuba 158/K4
Boquerón, P. Rico 156/F1
Boquerón, P. Rico 161/A3
Boquerón (bay), P. Rico 161/A3
Boquerón (dept.), Par. 144/B3
Boquerón, El (pass), Peru 128/E7
Bor, Czech. 41/B2
Bor, Turkey 63/F4
Bor, Sudan 111/F6
Bor, Yugo. 45/E3
Bora-Bora (isl.), Fr. Poly., 87/L7
Borah (peak), Idaho, 188/D2
Borah (peak), Idaho 220/E5
Borama, Somalia 115/H2
Borås, Sweden 18/H8
Borås, Sweden, 7/F3
Borazjun, Iran 59/F4
Borazjun, Iran 66/G6
Borba, Braz., 120/E3
Borba, Braz. 132/H9
Borba, Port. 33/C3
Borbón, Ven. 124/F4
Borçka, Turkey 63/J2
Borculo, Neth. 27/J4
Bordeaux (mt.), V.I.(U.S.) 161/C4
Bordeaux, France, 7/D4
Bordeaux, France 28/C5
Bordeaux, S.C. (†29835) 296/C4
Bordelonville, La. (71320) 238/G4
Borden (isl.), 163/M3
Borden, Aust. 88/B6
Borden (isl.), Canada, 4/B15
Borden, Ind. (47106) 227/F8
Borden (isl.), N.W.T., 146/F2
Borden (isl.), N.W.T. 187/G2
Borden (pen.), N.W.T. 187/K2
Borden, W. Aust. 92/B6
Borden, P.E.I. 169/E2
Borden, S.C. (29017) 296/G3
Borden, Sask. 181/D3
Borden (co.), Texas 302/C5
Borden Shaft, Md. (†21532) 245/B2
Borden Springs, Ala. (36252) 194/H3
Bordentown, N.J. (08505) 273/D3
Border, Minn. (†56623) 254/D2
Border, Wyo. (†83114) 319/B3
Borderland, W. Va. (25665) 313/B7
Bordertown, Aust. 88/G7
Bordertown, S. Aust. 94/G7
Bordighera, Italy 34/A3
Bordj-Bou-Arréridj, Alg. 106/E1
Bordj Fly Sainte-Marie, Alg. 106/D3
Bordulac, N. Dak. (58417) 283/N5
Boree Creek, N.S.W. 97/D4
Boreing, Ky. (40723) 237/N6
Boreray (isl.), Scot. 15/B4
Boreray (isl.), Scot. 15/B8
Borgå, Fin. 18/O6
Borge, Norway 18/H2
Borger, Neth. 27/K3
Borger, Texas, 188/F3
Borger, Texas (79007) 302/C2
Borgerhout, Belg. 27/E6
Borgholm, Sweden 18/K8
Borghorst, W. Ger. 22/B2
Borgloon, Belg. 27/G7
Borgne (lake), La. 238/L7
Borgne (riv.), Switz. 39/D4
Borgo, Italy 34/C1
Borgomanero, Italy 34/B2
Borgo San Lorenzo, Italy 34/C2
Borgworm (Waremme), Belg. 27/G7
Borikhane, Laos 72/D3
Boring, Md. (21020) 245/L2
Boring, Oreg. (97009) 291/E2
Borinquen (pt.), P. Rico 156/F1
Borinquen (pt.), P. Rico 161/A1
Borislav, U.S.S.R. 52/B5
Borisoglebsk, U.S.S.R. 48/E4
Borisoglebsk, U.S.S.R. 52/F4
Borisov, U.S.S.R. 52/C4
Borisovka, U.S.S.R. 52/E4
Boris Vil'kitskiy (str.), U.S.S.R. 48/L2
Boris Vil'kitskiy (str.), U.S.S.R., 4/B4
Bo River Post, Sudan 111/E6
Borja, Par. 144/C7
Borja, Peru 128/D5
Borja, Spain 33/F2
Borjas Blancas, Spain 33/G2
Borken, W. Ger. 22/B3
Børkop, Den. 21/C6
Borku (reg.), Chad 111/C4
Borkum, W. Ger. 22/B2
Borkum (isl.), W. Ger. 22/B2
Borlänge, Sweden 18/J6
Borna, E. Ger. 22/E3
Borndiep (chan.), Neth. 27/H2
Borne, Neth. 27/K4
Borneo (isl.), 3/O6
Borneo (isl.), Indon., 54/P9
Borneo (isl.), Indon. 85/E5
Borneo (Kalimantan) (reg.), Indon. 85/E5
Borneo (isl.), Malaysia 85/E5
Bornholm (isl.), Den., 7/F3
Bornholm (isl.), Den. 18/J9
Bornholm (co.), Den. 21/F9
Bornholm (isl.), Den. 21/F9
Bor Nor (lake), China 77/J2
Bor Nor (lake), Mong. 77/J2
Bornova, Turkey 63/B3
Bornu (reg.), Nigeria 106/G6
Borocay (isl.), Phil. 82/D5
Borojó, Ven. 124/C2
Boron, Calif. (93516) 204/H8
Borongan, Phil. 82/E5
Borot Kidod (well), Israel 65/C5
Borovichi, U.S.S.R. 52/D3
Borradaile, Alta. 182/E3
Borre, Norway 18/D4
Borrego Springs, Calif. (92004) 204/J10
Borris, Ire. 17/H6
Borrisokane, Ire. 17/E6
Borroloola, Aust. 88/F3
Borroloola, No. Terr. 93/E4
Borsod-Abaúj-Zemplén (co.), Hung. 41/F2
Bort-les-Orgues, France 28/E5
Boruca, C. Rica 154/F6
Borup, Minn. (56519) 254/B3
Borup, Den. 21/E7
Borzhomi, U.S.S.R. 52/F6
Börzsöny (mts.), Hung. 41/E3
Borzya, U.S.S.R. 48/M4
Bosa, Italy 34/B4
Bošáca, Czech. 41/D2
Bosanska Dubica, Yugo. 45/C3
Bosanska Gradiška, Yugo. 45/C3
Bosanska Kostajnica, Yugo. 45/B3
Bosanska Krupa, Yugo. 45/C3
Bosanski Brod, Yugo. 45/D3
Bosanski Novi, Yugo. 45/C3
Bosanski Petrovac, Yugo. 45/C3
Bosanski Šamac, Yugo. 45/D3
Bosaso, 102/G3
Bosaso, Somalia 115/J1
Boscawen▵, N.H. (03301) 268/D5
Boscawen, N.H. (03301) 268/D5
Bosch, van den (cape), Indon. 85/J6
Bosco, La. (71224) 238/F2
Boscobel, Wis. (53805) 317/E9
Böser Faulen (mt.), Switz. 39/G3
Boskoop, Neth. 27/F4
Boskovice, Czech. 41/D2
Bosler, Wyo. (82051) 319/G4
Bosna (riv.), Yugo. 45/D3
Bosnia and Hercegovina (rep.), Yugo. 45/C3
Boso (pen.), Japan 81/K6
Bosobolo, Dem. Rep. of the Congo. 115/D3
Bosporus (str.), Turkey 59/A1
Bosporus (str.), Turkey 63/C2
Bosporus (str.), Turkey, 7/G4
Bosque, N. Mex. (87006) 274/C4
Bosque (co.), Texas 302/G6
Boss, Mo. (65440) 261/K7
Bossangoa, Centr. Afr. Rep. 115/C2
Bossburg, Wash. (†99126) 310/H2
Bossé, N. Br. 170/B1
Bossembele, Centr. Afr. Rep. 115/C2
Bossier (par.), La. 238/C1
Bossier City, La. (71010) 238/C1
Bosso, Niger 106/G6
Bostan, Iran 66/F5
Bostan, Pak. 68/B2
Bostic‡, N.C. (28018) 281/F4
Boston, 10/F4
Boston (mts.), Ark. 203/B2
Boston, Eng. 13/H5
Boston, Ga. (31626) 216/E9
Boston, Ind. (47324) 227/H5
Boston, Ky. (40107) 237/K5
Boston (cap.), Mass., 146/L5
Boston (cap.), Mass., 188/M2
Boston (cap.), Mass. (*02101) 249/D7
Boston (bay), Mass. 249/E6
Boston (harb.), Mass. 249/D7
Boston, Mo. (64727) 261/D8
Boston, N.Y. (14025) 276/C5
Boston (mts.), Okla. 288/S3
Boston, Pa. (15135) 294/C7
Boston, Tenn. (†37064) 237/G9
Boston, Texas (75557) 302/K4
Boston, U.S., 3/F3
Boston, Va. (22713) 307/M3
Boston Army Base, Mass. 249/D7
Boston Heights, Ohio (†44264) 284/J10
Bostonnais (isl.), Que. 172/E2
Bostonnais (riv.), Que. 172/E2
Bostwick, Fla. (32007) 212/E2
Bostwick, Ga. (30623) 216/E3
Bostwick, Nebr. (†68978) 264/F4
Boswell, Pa. (72516) 203/F1
Boswell, Br. Col. 184/J5
Boswell, Ind. (47921) 227/C3
Boswell, Okla. (74727) 288/P6
Boswell, Pa. (15531) 294/E5
Boswell Bay, Alaska (†99574) 196/J2
Boswil, Switz. 39/F2
Bosworth, Mo. (64723) 261/F4
Bot (riv.), S. Africa 118/G7
Botany, Aust. 88/L3
Botany, N.S.W. 97/J4
Botany (bay), Aust. 88/L3
Botany (bay), N.S.W. 97/J4
Botene, Laos 72/D3
Botetourt (co.), Va. 307/J5
Botevgrad, Bulg. 45/F4
Botha, Alta. 182/D3
Botha (riv.), Alta. 182/B1
Bothell, Wash. (98011) 310/B1
Bothnia (gulf), 7/G2
Bothnia (gulf), Fin. 18/M5
Bothnia (gulf), Sweden 18/N4
Bothwell, Ont. 177/C5
Bothwell, Miss. (†39456) 256/G8
Bothwell, Utah (†84337) 304/B2
Botkins, Ohio (45306) 284/B5
Botna, Iowa (†51454) 229/C5
Botoşani, Rum. 45/H2
Botrange (mt.), Belg. 27/J8
Botrivier, S. Africa 118/F7
Botsford, Conn. (06404) 210/C3
Botswana, 3/L7
BOTSWANA, 118/C4
BOTSWANA, 102/E7
Bottineau (co.), N. Dak. 283/J2
Bottineau, N. Dak. (58318) 283/J2
Bottrel, Alta. 182/C4
Bottrop, W. Ger. 22/B3

Brežice 337

Botucatu, Braz. 132/D8
Botucatu, Braz. 135/B3
Botwood, Newf. 166/C4
Bouaflé, Ivory Coast 106/C7
Bouaké, Ivory Coast 106/D7
Bouaké, 102/B4
Bouali, Centr. Afr. Rep. 115/C3
Bouar, Centr. Afr. Rep. 115/C2
Bouârfa, Mor. 106/D2
Bouca, Centr. Afr. Rep. 115/C2
Boucaut (bay), Aust. 88/E2
Boucaut (bay), No. Terr. 93/D1
Boucherville, Que. 172/J4
Boucherville (isls.), Que. 172/J4
Bouches-du-Rhône (dept.), France 28/F6
Bouchette, Que. 172/A3
Bouckville, N.Y. (13310) 276/J5
Bou Djebeha, Mali 106/D5
Boudreau (bay), La. 238/M7
Boudreaux, La. (†70353) 238/J8
Boudreaux (lake), La. 238/J8
Boudry, Switz. 39/C3
Boufarik, Alg. 106/E1
Bougainville (reef), Aust. 88/H3
Bougainville (cape), Aust. 88/D2
Bougainville (cape), W. Aust. 92/D1
Bougainville (isl.), Terr. N.G., 87/F6
Bougaroun (cape), Alg. 106/F1
Boughton (isl.), P.E.I. 169/F2
Bougie (Béjaïa), Alg. 106/F1
Bougouni, Mali 106/C6
Bouillante, Guad. 161/A6
Bouillon, Belg. 27/G9
Bou-Izakarn, Mor. 106/C3
Boujad, Mor. 106/C2
Boularderie (isl.), N.S. 169/H2
Boulder, Australia, 87/C9
Boulder, Aust. 88/C6
Boulder, Colo., 146/H5
Boulder, Colo., 188/E2
Boulder (co.), Colo. 208/J2
Boulder, Colo. (*80301) 208/J2
Boulder (creek), Idaho 220/B7
Boulder (mts.), Idaho 220/D6
Boulder, Mont. (59632) 262/E4
Boulder (lake), N. Mex. 274/C2
Boulder, W. Aust. 92/C5
Boulder, Utah (84716) 304/C6
Boulder (creek), Utah 304/C6
Boulder, Wyo. (82923) 319/C3
Boulder (lake), Wyo. 319/C3
Boulder City, Nev. (89005) 266/G7
Boulder Creek, Calif. (95006) 204/J4
Boulder Junction, Wis. (54512) 317/G3
Boulevard, Calif. (92005) 204/J11
Boulevard Heights, Md. (†20027) 245/F5
Boulia, Aust. 88/G4
Boulia, Queens. 95/A4
Boulogne, Fla. (†32046) 212/E1
Boulogne, France, 7/E3
Boulogne-Billancourt, France 28/A2
Boulogne-sur-Mer, France 28/D2
Bouna, Ivory Coast 106/D7
Boundary (co.), Idaho 220/B1
Boundary (peak), Nev. 266/C5
Boundary (bay), Wash. 310/C1
Boundary (dam), Wash. 310/H2
Boundary Bend, Vic. 97/B4
Bound Brook, N.J. (08805) 273/D2
Boundiali, Ivory Coast 106/C7
Boun Neua, Laos 72/D2
Boun Tai, Laos 72/D2
Bountiful, Utah (84010) 304/C3
Bounty (isls.), N.Z., 87/H10
Bounty (isls.), N.Z., N.Z. 101/H10
Bounty, Sask. 181/D4
Bourail, New Cal., 87/G8
Bourbon, Ill. (†61953) 222/E4
Bourbon, Ind. (46504) 227/E2
Bourbon (co.), Kans. 232/H4
Bourbon (co.), Ky. 237/N4
Bourbon, Miss. (38729) 256/C4
Bourbon, Mo. (65441) 261/K6
Bourbonnais, Ill. (60914) 222/F2
Bourem, Mali 106/E5
Bourg, La. (70343) 238/J7
Bourganeuf, France 28/D5
Bourg-des-Saintes, Guad. 161/A7
Bourg-en-Bresse, France 28/F4
Bourges, France 28/E4
Bourget, Ont. 177/J2
Bourg-Léopold (Leopoldsburg), Belg. 27/G6
Bourgoin-Jallieu, France 28/F5
Bourg Saint-Pierre, Switz. 39/D5
Bourke, Aust. 88/H6
Bourke, N.S.W. 97/D2
Bourlamaque, Que. 174/B3
Bourne, Eng. 13/G5
Bourne△, Mass. (02532) 249/M6
Bourne, Mass. (02532) 249/M6
Bournedale, Mass. (†02532) 249/M5
Bournemouth, 10/F5
Bournemouth, Eng. 13/F7
Bourneville, Ohio (45617) 284/D7
Bou-Saâda, Alg. 106/E1
Bouse, Ariz. (85325) 198/A5
Bouse Wash (dry riv.), Ariz. 198/A4
Boussac, France 28/D4
Bousso, Chad 111/C5
Boussu, Belg. 27/D8
Boutilimit, Mauritania 106/B5
Bouton, Iowa (50039) 229/E5
Boutte, La. (70039) 238/N4
Bouvard (cape), Aust. 88/B2
Bouvard (cape), W. Aust. 92/A2
Bouveret, Switz. 39/C4
Bouvet (isl.), Ant. 5/D1
Boven Bolivia, Neth. Ant. 161/E8
Boves, Italy 34/A2
Bovey, Minn. (55709) 254/E3
Bovigny, Belg. 27/H8
Bovill, Idaho (83806) 220/B3
Bovina, Miss. (†39180) 256/C6
Bovina, Texas (79009) 302/A3
Bovril, Arg. 143/G5
Bow (riv.), 163/E5
Bow (riv.), Alta. 182/D4
Bow (lake), N.H. 268/E5
Bow, Wash. (98232) 310/C2
Bowbells, N. Dak. (58721) 283/F2
Bowden, Alta. 182/C4
Bowden, Jam. 158/K6
Bowden, W. Va. (26254) 313/G5
Bowdens, N.C. (28322) 281/N4
Bowdle, S. Dak. (57428) 298/K3
Bowdoin (lake), Mont. 262/J2
Bowdoinham△, Maine (04008) 242/D7
Bowdon, Ga. (30108) 216/B3
Bowdon, N. Dak. (58418) 283/L5
Bowdon Junction, Ga. (30109) 216/B3
Bowell, Alta. 182/E4
Bowen, Australia, 87/E7
Bowen, Aust. 88/H3
Bowen, Ill. (62316) 222/B3
Bowen, Ky. (40309) 237/O5
Bowen, Queens. 95/D3
Bowen Island, Br. Col. 184/K3
Bowens, Md. (†20678) 245/M6
Bowerbank△, Maine (04481) 242/E5
Bowers, Del. (†19962) 245/S4
Bowers, Ind. (†47940) 227/D4
Bowers Mill, Mo. (†64848) 261/E8
Bowerston, Ohio (44695) 284/H5
Bowersville, Ga. (30516) 216/G2
Bowersville, Ohio (44695) 284/C6
Bowes, Eng. 13/F3
Bowesmont, N. Dak. (58217) 283/R2
Bowie, Ariz. (85605) 198/F6
Bowie, Colo. (†81428) 208/D5
Bowie, Md. (20715) 245/L4
Bowie (creek), Miss. 256/E7
Bowie (co.), Texas 302/K4
Bowie, Texas (76230) 302/G4
Bow Island, Alta. 182/E5
Bowlegs, Okla. (74830) 288/N4
Bowler, Wis. (54416) 317/J6
Bowling Green (cape), Aust. 88/H3
Bowling Green, Fla. (33834) 212/E4
Bowling Green, Ind. (47833) 227/D6
Bowling Green, Ky., 188/J3
Bowling Green, Ky. (42101) 237/H7
Bowling Green, Mo. (63334) 261/K4
Bowling Green (cape), Queens. 95/C3
Bowling Green, Ohio (43402) 284/C3
Bowling Green, S.C. (29703) 296/E1
Bowling Green, Va. (22427) 307/O4
Bowlus, Minn. (56314) 254/D5
Bowman (bay), 163/J3
Bowman, Calif. (95707) 204/C8
Bowman, Ga. (30624) 216/G2
Bowman (co.), N. Dak. 283/C7
Bowman, N. Dak. (58623) 283/D7
Bowman (bay), N.W.T. 187/L3
Bowman, S.C. (29018) 296/F5
Bowmansdale, Pa. (17008) 294/J5
Bowmanstown, Pa. (18030) 294/L4
Bowmansville, Pa. (17507) 294/L5
Bowmanville, Ont. 177/F4
Bow Mar‡, Colo. (†80120) 208/J3
Bow Mills△, N.H. (†03301) 268/D5
Bowmont, Idaho (†83651) 220/B6
Bowmore, 10/C3
Bowmore, Scot. 15/D8
Bowness, Eng. 13/D3
Bowral, N.S.W. 97/F4
Bowraville, N.S.W. 97/G2
Bowring, Okla. (74009) 288/O1
Bowron Lake Prov. Park, Br. Col. 184/G3
Bowser, Br. Col. 184/H2
Bowser (lake), Br. Col. 184/C2
Bowsman, Man. 179/A2
Bowstring, Minn. (56631) 254/E3
Bowstring (lake), Minn. 254/E3
Boxborough△, Mass. (†01720) 249/H3
Box Butte (co.), Nebr. 264/A2
Box Butte (res.), Nebr. 264/A2
Box Canyon (dam), Wash. 310/H2
Boxelder (creek), Colo. 208/K4
Box Elder, Mont. (59521) 262/F2
Boxelder (creek), Mont. 262/H3
Boxelder (creek), Mont. 262/M5
Box Elder, S. Dak. (57719) 298/D5
Boxelder (creek), S. Dak. 298/D5
Box Elder (co.), Utah 304/A2
Boxford△, Mass. (01921) 249/L2
Boxford, Mass. (01921) 249/L2
Box Hill, Vic. 97/J5
Boxholm, Iowa (50040) 229/E4
Boxley, Ark. (†72742) 203/D2
Boxmeer, Neth. 27/H5
Box Springs, Ga. (31801) 216/C5
Boxtel, Neth. 27/G5
Boyabat, Turkey 63/F2
Boyacá (dept.), Col. 126/D5
Boyanup, W. Aust. 92/A2
Boyce, La. (71409) 238/E4
Boyce, Va. (22620) 307/M2
Boyceville, Wis. (54725) 317/C5
Boyd, Ala. (†35470) 194/B5
Boyd, Fla. (†32347) 212/C1
Boyd (co.), Ky. 237/R4
Boyd, Minn. (56218) 254/C6
Boyd, Mont. (59013) 262/G5
Boyd (co.), Nebr. 264/F2
Boyd, Okla. (†73931) 288/E1
Boyd, Oreg. (†97021) 291/F2
Boyd, Texas (76023) 302/G4
Boyd, Wis. (54726) 317/E6
Boydell, Ark. (71632) 203/H7
Boyden, Iowa (51234) 229/B2
Boyden Arbor, S.C. (†29201) 296/F3
Boyd Lake, Maine (†04463) 242/F5
Boyds, Md. (20720) 245/J4
Boyds, Wash. (99107) 310/G2
Boydton, Va. (23917) 307/M7
Boyer (riv.), Alta. 182/A5
Boyer, Iowa (†51448) 229/C4
Boyer (riv.), Iowa 229/B5
Boyer, W. Va. (†24915) 313/G5
Boyer Ahmedi and Kohkiluye (governorate), Iran 66/F4
Boyero, Colo. (80806) 208/N5
Boyers, Pa. (16020) 294/C3
Boyertown, Pa. (19512) 294/L5
Boyes, Mont. (59316) 262/M5
Boyes Hot Spring‡, Calif. (95416) 204/C5
Boykin, Ga. (†31737) 216/C8
Boykin, S.C. (29019) 296/F3
Boykins, Va. (23827) 307/O7
Boyle, Alta. 182/D2
Boyle, 10/B3
Boyle, Ire. 17/E4
Boyle (co.), Ky. 237/M5
Boyle, Miss. (38730) 256/C3
Boyleston, Ind. (†46057) 227/E4
Boylston (lake), Mont. (36110) 194/F6
Boylston△, Mass. (01505) 249/H3
Boylston, N.S. 169/G3
Boyne (riv.), Ire. 17/J4
Boyne City, Mich. (49712) 250/E3
Boyne Falls, Mich. (49713) 250/E3
Boynton, Okla. (74422) 288/P3
Boynton Beach, Fla. (33435) 212/F5
Boy River, Minn. (56632) 254/D3
Boysen, Wyo. (†82649) 319/D2
Boysen (res.), Wyo. 319/D2
Boysen Bay‡, N.Y. (†13029) 276/H4
Boys Ranch, Texas (79010) 302/B2
Boys Town, Nebr. (68010) 264/H3
Boyuibe, Bol. 136/D7
Bozcaada (isl.), Turkey 63/A3
Bozdoğan, Turkey 63/C4
Bozeman, Mont., 188/D1
Bozeman, Mont. (59715) 262/E5
Bozkir, Turkey 63/E4
Bozkurt, Turkey 63/F2
Bozman, Md. (21612) 245/N5
Bozoum, Centr. Afr. Rep. 115/C2
Bozova, Turkey 63/H4
Bozüyük, Turkey 59/B2
Bozüyük, Turkey 63/C3
Bra, Italy 34/A2
Brabant (prov.), Belg. 27/F7
Brabrand, Den. 21/C5
Brač (isl.), Yugo. 45/C4
Bracadale, Scot. 15/D5
Bracadale (inlet), Scot. 15/C5
Bracciano, Italy 34/C3
Bracciano (lake), Italy 34/D3
Bracebridge, Ont. 177/E2
Braceville, Ill. (60407) 222/E2
Bracey, Va. (23919) 307/M7
Bräcke, Sweden 18/J5
Bracken (co.), Ky. 237/N3
Bracken, Sask. 181/C6
Brackendale, Br. Col. 184/F5
Brackenridge, Pa. (15014) 294/C4
Brackett, Wis. (†54742) 317/D6
Brackettville, Texas (78832) 302/D8
Brackley, 10/F4
Brackley, Eng. 13/F5
Bracknell, Eng. 13/G6
Brackney, Pa. (18812) 294/K2
Brackwede, W. Ger. 22/C3
Braço Maior do Araguaia (riv.), Braz. 132/D5
Braço Menor do Araguaia (riv.), Braz. 132/D6
Brad, Rum. 45/F2
Bradbury, Calif. (91010) 204/D10
Braddock, N. Dak. (58524) 283/K6
Braddock, Pa. (15104) 294/C7
Braddock, Sask. 181/D5
Braddock Hills‡, Pa. (†15201) 294/C7
Braddyville, Iowa (51631) 229/D7
Braden, Okla. (†74959) 288/S4
Braden, Tenn. (38010) 237/B10
Bradenton, Fla. (33505) 212/D4
Bradenton Beach, Fla. (33510) 212/D4
Bradford, 10/H1
Bradford, Ark. (72020) 203/G3
Bradford, Ont. 177/E3
Bradford, Eng. 13/F4
Bradford (co.), Fla. 212/D2
Bradford, Ill. (61421) 222/D2
Bradford, Ind. (47107) 227/E8
Bradford, Iowa (50041) 229/G3
Bradford, Ky. (†41043) 237/N3
Bradford△, Maine (04410) 242/F5
Bradford, Maine (04410) 242/F5
Bradford△, N.H. (03221) 268/D5
Bradford, Ohio (45308) 284/B5
Bradford (co.), Pa. 294/J2
Bradford, Pa. (16701) 294/E2
Bradford, R.I. (02808) 249/H7
Bradford, Tenn. (38316) 237/D8
Bradford△, Vt. (05033) 268/C3
Bradford, Vt. (05033) 268/C3
Bradford Center, Maine (†04410) 242/F5
Bradford-on-Avon, Eng. 13/E6
Bradfordsville, Ky. (40009) 237/L6
Bradfordwoods‡, Pa. (15015) 294/B4
Bradgate, Iowa (50520) 229/E3
Bradley (co.), Ark. 203/F7
Bradley, Ark. (71826) 203/C7
Bradley, Calif. (93426) 204/E8
Bradley, Fla. (33835) 212/D4
Bradley, Ga. (†31032) 216/E4
Bradley, Ill. (60915) 222/F2
Bradley△, Maine (04411) 242/F6
Bradley, Miss. (†39759) 256/G4
Bradley, Ohio (†43917) 284/J5
Bradley, Okla. (73011) 288/L5
Bradley, S.C. (29819) 296/C3
Bradley, S. Dak. (57217) 298/O3
Bradley (co.), Tenn. 237/M10
Bradley, Wis. (†54487) 317/G4
Bradley Beach, N.J. (07720) 273/F3
Bradleyton, Ala. (†36041) 194/F7
Bradleyville, Mo. (65614) 261/F9
Bradner, Ohio (43406) 284/C3
Bradshaw, Nebr. (68319) 264/G4
Bradshaw, Texas (†79567) 302/D5
Bradshaw, W. Va. (24817) 313/C8
Bradwardine, Man. 179/B5
Bradwell, Sask. 181/E4
Brady (glac.), Alaska 196/M1
Brady, Mont. (59416) 262/E2
Brady, Nebr. (69123) 264/D3
Brady (mt.), S. Aust. 94/D3
Brady, Texas (76825) 302/E6
Brady Lake, Ohio (44211) 284/H3
Bradyville, Tenn. (37026) 237/J9
Braedstrup, Den. 21/C6
Braemar, 10/E2
Braemar, Scot. 15/K5
Braemar (dist.), Scot. 15/K5
Braemar-Hampton, Tenn. (37658) 237/S8
Braeside, Ont. 177/H2
Braeside, W. Aust. 92/C3
Braga, Port., 7/D4
Braga, Port. 33/B2
Bragado, Arg. 143/F7
Bragança, Braz., 120/F3
Bragança, Braz. 132/E3
Bragança, Port. 33/C2
Bragança Paulista, Braz. 132/E8
Bragança Paulista, Braz. 135/C3
Braggadocio, Mo. (63826) 261/N10
Bragg City, Mo. (63827) 261/N10
Bragg Creek, Alta. 182/C4
Braggs, Ala. (36761) 194/E6
Braggs, Okla. (74423) 288/R3
Bragman's Bluff (Puerto Cabezas), Nic. 154/F3
Braham, Minn. (55006) 254/E5
Brahmaputra (riv.), 54/N7
Brahmaputra (riv.), India 68/G3
Brahmaputra (riv.), Pak. 68/G3
Brahmaputra (riv.), China 77/D6
Braich-y-Pwll (prom.), 10/D4
Braich-y-Pwll (prom.), Wales 13/C5
Braidwood, Ill. (60408) 222/E2
Braidwood, N.S.W. 97/E4
Brăila, Rum., 7/G4
Brăila, Rum. 45/H3
Brăila (marshes), Rum. 45/H3
Brainard, Nebr. (68626) 264/G3
Brainards, N.J. (08865) 273/C2
Braine-l'Alleud, Belg. 27/E7
Braine-le-Comte, Belg. 27/D7
Brainerd, Minn., 188/H1
Brainerd, Minn. (56401) 254/D4
Braintree△, Mass. (02184) 249/D8
Braintree△, Vt. (05646) 268/B4
Braintree and Bocking, 10/G5
Braintree and Bocking, Eng. 13/H6
Braithwaite, La. (70040) 238/P4
Brak, Libya 111/B2
Brak, 102/D2
Brake, W. Ger. 22/C2
Brakna (reg.), Mauritania 106/B5
Brakpan, S. Africa 118/J6
Bralorne, Br. Col. 184/F5
Bramalea, Ont. 177/J4
Braman, Okla. (74632) 288/M1
Bramber, N.S. 169/D3
Bramberg, Austria 41/B3
Bramble (bay), Aust. 88/K2
Bramble (bay), Queens. 95/E2
Bramhapuri, India 68/E4
Bramminge, Den. 21/B7
Bramon, Ven. 124/B4
Brampton, Ont. 177/J4
Brampton, Eng. 13/E3
Brampton, Mich. (49810) 250/B3
Brampton, N. Dak. (58010) 283/P7
Bramsche, W. Ger. 22/B2
Bramwell, W. Va. (24715) 313/D8
Bran (falls), Scot. 15/J6
Brancepeth, Sask. 181/F2
Branch, Ark. (72928) 203/C3
Branch, La. (70516) 238/F6
Branch (co.), Mich. 250/D7
Branch, Mich. (49402) 250/D5
Branch, Minn. (†55056) 254/F5
Branch, Mo. (†65786) 261/G7
Branch, Newf. 166/D2
Branch (riv.), Newf. 166/C2
Branch, Wis. (54203) 317/L7
Branch Dale, Pa. (17923) 294/K4
Branchport, N.Y. (14418) 276/F5
Branchton, Pa. (16021) 294/C3
Branchville, Ala. (†35120) 194/F3
Branchville, Conn. (†06829) 210/B3
Branchville, Ind. (47514) 227/D8
Branchville, N.J. (07826) 273/D1
Branchville, S.C. (29432) 296/F5
Branchville, Va. (23828) 307/O7
Branco (riv.), Braz., 120/B3
Branco (riv.), Braz. 132/H8
Brandberg (mt.), S.W. Afr. 118/A4
Brande, Den. 21/C6
Brandenburg, E. Ger. 22/E2
Brandenburg (reg.), E. Ger. 22/E2
Brandenburg, Ky. (40108) 237/J4
Brandon, 163/F6
Brandon, Colo. (81026) 208/P6
Brandon, Fla. (33511) 212/D4
Brandon, Iowa (52210) 229/K4
Brandon (bay), Ire. 17/A7
Brandon (head), Ire. 17/A7
Brandon (mt.), Ire. 17/A7
Brandon, Man., 146/H5
Brandon, Man. 179/C5
Brandon, Minn. (56315) 254/C5
Brandon, Miss. (39042) 256/E6
Brandon, Nebr. (69102) 264/C4
Brandon, Ohio (†43050) 284/F5
Brandon, S. Dak. (57005) 298/R6
Brandon‡, Texas (76628) 302/G5
Brandon△, Vt. (05733) 268/A4
Brandon, Vt. (05733) 268/A4
Brandon, Wis. (53919) 317/J8
Brandon and Byshottles, 10/F3
Brandon and Byshottles, Eng. 13/F3
Brandon Gap (pass), Vt. 268/B4
Brandonville, W. Va. (26523) 313/G3
Brandreth (lake), N.Y. 276/L3
Brandsville, Mo. (65688) 261/J9
Brandt, Ohio (†45371) 284/B6
Brandt, S. Dak. (57218) 298/R4
Brandvlei, S. Africa 118/B6
Brandýs nad Labem-Stará Boleslav, Czech. 41/C1
Brandy Station, Va. (22714) 307/N4
Brandywine, Md. (20613) 245/L6
Brandywine, W. Va. (26802) 313/H5
Brandywine Village‡, Pa. (†19406) 294/M5
Branford△, Conn. (06405) 210/D3
Branford, Conn. (06405) 210/D3
Branford (harb.), Conn. 210/D4
Branford (riv.), Conn. 210/D3
Branford, Fla. (32008) 212/D2
Braniewo, Poland 47/E1
Brannock (isls.), Ire. 17/A5
Bransfield (str.), Ant. 5/C16
Branson, Colo. (81027) 208/M8
Branson, Mo. (65616) 261/F9
Brant, Alta. 182/D4
Brant (co.), Ont. 177/D4
Brant, Mich. (48614) 250/E5
Brant, N.Y. (14027) 276/B5
Brant (lake), N.Y. 276/N3
Brant (lake), S. Dak. 298/R6
Brant Beach, N.J. (†08008) 273/E4
Brantford, Ont. 177/D4
Brantford, Kans. (†66938) 232/E2
Brantford, N. Dak. (58419) 283/N4
Brant Lake, N.Y. (12815) 276/N3
Brantley, Ala. (36009) 194/F7
Brantley (co.), Ga. 216/J8
Brant Rock, Mass. (02020) 249/M4
Brantville, N. Br. 170/E1
Brantwood, Wis. (54513) 317/F4
Branxholme, Vic. 97/A5
Branxton-Greta, N.S.W. 97/F3
Bras-d'Apic, Que. 172/G3
Bras d'Or, N.S. 169/H2
Bras d'Or (lake), N.S. 169/H3
Braselton, Ga. (30517) 216/E2
Brasfield, Ark. (†72017) 203/H4
Brashear, Mo. (63533) 261/H2
Brasher, Mo. (†63830) 261/N10
Brasher Falls, N.Y. (13613) 276/L1
Brasiléia, Braz. 132/G10
Brasília (cap.), Braz., 3/G6
Brasília (cap.), Braz., 120/F4
Brasília (cap.), Braz. 132/D6
Brasília, Braz. 132/F7
Brașov, Rum., 7/G4
Brașov, Rum. 45/G3
Brass (isls.), V.I.(U.S.) 161/A4
Brass, Nigeria 106/F8
Brassey (range), W. Aust. 92/C4
Brasstown Bald (mt.), Ga. 216/E1
Brassua (lake), Maine 242/D4
Braswell, Ga. (†30153) 216/C3
Brate, Norway 18/G7
Bratenahl, Ohio (†44101) 284/H9
Bratislava, Czech., 7/F4
Bratislava, Czech. 41/D2
Bratsk, U.S.S.R. 48/L4
Bratsk (res.), U.S.S.R. 48/L4
Brattleboro△, Vt. (05301) 268/B6
Brattleboro, Vt. (05301) 268/B6
Braunau, Austria 41/B2
Braunlage, W. Ger. 22/D3
Braunschweig (Brunswick), W. Ger. 22/D2
Brava (isl.), C. Verde Is. 106/B8
Brava, 102/G4
Brava, Somalia 115/H3
Brava (isl.), 102/G9
Brava (pt.), Urug. 145/B7
Brave, Pa. (15316) 294/B6
Bravo (riv.), Chile 138/D7
Bravo (Grande) (riv.), Mex. 150/G2
Brawley, Calif., 188/C4
Brawley, Calif. (92227) 204/K11
Braxton, Miss. (39044) 256/D6
Braxton (co.), W. Va. 313/E5
Bray, 10/C4
Bray, Ire. 17/K5
Bray (head), Ire. 17/A8
Bray (isl.), N.W.T. 187/L3
Bray, Okla. (73012) 288/L5
Braymer, Mo. (64624) 261/E3
Brayton, Iowa (50042) 229/D5
Brazeau (mt.), Alta. 182/B3
Brazeau (riv.), Alta. 182/B3
Brazeau (Nordegg), Alta. 182/B3
Brazil, 3/F6
Brazil, 120/E4
BRAZIL, 132
Brazil, Ind. (47834) 227/C5
Brazil, Miss. (38956) 256/D2
Brazil, Tenn. (†38382) 237/C9
Brazilton, Kans. (†66743) 232/H4
Brazito, Mo. (†65101) 261/H6
Brazoria (co.), Texas 302/J8
Brazoria, Texas (77422) 302/J9
Brazos (peak), N. Mex. 274/C2
Brazos (riv.), Texas, 146/J6
Brazos (riv.), Texas, 188/G4
Brazos (co.), Texas 302/H7
Brazos (riv.), Texas 302/H7
Brazo Sur, Pilcomayo (riv.), Arg. 143/E1
Brazzaville (cap.), Rep. of Congo 115/C4
Brazzaville (cap.), Rep. of Congo, 3/K6
Brazzaville (cap.), Rep. of Congo. 102/D5
Brčko, Yugo. 45/D3
Brda (riv.), Poland 47/C2
Brea, Calif. (92621) 204/D11
Breadalbane (dist.), Scot. 15/H7
Bread Loaf, Vt. (05753) 268/B4
Bread Loaf (mt.), Vt. 268/A3
Breakabeen, N.Y. (†12122) 276/M5
Breaks, Va. (24607) 307/D6
Breaksea (sound), N.Z. 101/A6
Bream (bay), N.Z. 101/E1
Breathitt (co.), Ky. 237/P5
Breau-Village, N. Br. 170/F2
Breaux Bridge, La. (70517) 238/G6
Brebes, Indon. 85/H2
Brébeuf, Que. 172/C3
Brechin, Ont. 177/E3
Brechin, 10/E2
Brechin, Scot. 15/L6
Breckenridge, Colo. (80424) 208/G4
Breckenridge, Mich. (48615) 250/E5
Breckenridge, Minn. (56520) 254/B4
Breckenridge, Mo. (64625) 261/E3
Breckenridge, Texas (76024) 302/F5
Breckenridge Hills, Mo. (†63101) 261/O2
Breckinridge (co.), Ky. 237/H5
Breckinridge, Okla. (73721) 288/L2
Brecknock, 10/E5
Brecknock, Wales 13/D6
Brecksville, Ohio (44141) 284/H10
Břeclav, Czech. 41/D2
Brecon Beacons (mt.), Wales 13/D6
Breconshire (co.), Wales 13/D6
Breda, Iowa (51436) 229/C4
Breda, Neth. 27/F5
Bredasdorp Nat'l Park, S. Africa 118/C6
Bredbo, N.S.W. 97/E4
Bredenbury, Sask. 181/K5
Bredene, Belg. 27/B6
Bredstedt, W. Ger. 22/C1
Bree, Belg. 27/H6
Breed, Wis. (†54174) 317/K5
Breeden, W. Va. (25666) 313/B7
Breeding, Ky. (42715) 237/L7
Breedsville, Mich. (49027) 250/C6
Breese, Ill. (62230) 222/D5
Breesport, N.Y. (14816) 276/G6
Breezand, Neth. 27/F3
Breezy Point Village, Minn. (†56472) 254/D4
Bregenz, Austria 41/A3
Bregovo, Bulg. 45/F3
Breidhafjördhur (fjord), Ice. 21/B1
Breien, N. Dak. (58525) 283/H7
Breil-Brigels, Switz. 39/H3
Breil-sur-Roya, France 28/G6
Breisach, W. Ger. 22/B4
Breisgau (reg.), W. Ger. 22/B5
Breitenbach, Switz. 39/E2
Breitenbush, Oreg. (†97342) 291/F3
Breithorn (mt.), Switz. 39/E5
Breithorn (mt.), Switz. 39/E4
Brejo, Braz. 132/F3
Bremanger (isl.), Norway 18/D6
Bremen, Ala. (35033) 194/E3
Bremen, Ga. (30110) 216/B3
Bremen, Ill. (†62233) 222/D6
Bremen, Ind. (46506) 227/E2
Bremen, Kans. (66412) 232/F2
Bremen, Ky. (42325) 237/G6
Bremen, N. Dak. (58319) 283/M4
Bremen, Ohio (43107) 284/F6
Bremen, Sask. 181/F3
Bremen, W. Ger., 7/E3
Bremen (state), W. Ger. 22/C2
Bremen, W. Ger. 22/C2
Bremer (riv.), Aust. 88/E8
Bremer (co.), Iowa 229/J3
Bremer, Iowa (50610) 229/J3
Bremerhaven, W. Ger. 22/C2
Bremerton, Wash., 188/B1
Bremerton, Wash. (98310) 310/A2
Bremervörde, W. Ger. 22/C2
Bremgarten, Switz. 39/F2
Bremo Bluff, Va. (23022) 307/M5
Bremond, Texas (76629) 302/H6
Brenham, Texas (77833) 302/H7
Brenner (pass), Austria 41/A3
Brenner (pass), Italy 34/C1
Brent, 10/B5
Brent, Ala. (35034) 194/D5
Brent, Ont. 177/F1
Brentford, S. Dak. (57429) 298/N3
Brenton (pt.), R.I. 249/J7
Brentwood, 10/C5
Brentwood, Ark. (†72959) 203/B2
Brentwood, Calif. (94513) 204/L2
Brentwood, Eng. 13/H6
Brentwood, Md. (20722) 245/F4
Brentwood, Mo. (63144) 261/P3
Brentwood△, N.H. (†03833) 268/E6
Brentwood, N.Y. (11717) 276/O9
Brentwood, Pa. (15227) 294/B7
Brentwood, Tenn. (37027) 237/H8
Bresaylor, Sask. 181/C3
Brescia, Italy, 7/E4
Brescia (prov.), Italy 34/C2
Brescia, Italy 34/C2
Breskens, Neth. 27/C6
Breslau (Wrocław), Poland, 7/F3
Bressanone, Italy 34/C1
Bressay (isl.), 10/G1
Bressay (isl.), Scot. 15/N3
Bressuire, France 28/C4
Brest, U.S.S.R. 48/C4
Brest, U.S.S.R. 52/B4
Brest, France, 7/D4
Brest, France 28/A3
Brest, Ga. (†31716) 216/D8
Brest, U.S.S.R., 7/G3
Bretaña, Peru 128/E5
Brethren, Mich. (49619) 250/D4
Breton, Alta. 182/C3
Breton (isl.), La. 238/M8
Breton (sound), La. 238/M7
Breton (cape), N.S. 169/J3
Breton Woods, N.J. (08723) 273/E3
Brett (cape), N.Z. 101/E1
Bretten, W. Ger. 22/C4
Bretton Woods, N.H. (03575) 268/E3
Brevard (co.), Fla. 212/F3
Brevard, N.C. (28712) 281/D4
Breves, Braz. 132/D3
Brevig Mission, Alaska (99785) 196/E1
Brevik, Minn. (†56655) 254/D3
Brevoort (lake), Mich. 250/D3
Brevoort (isl.), N.W.T. 187/M3
Brevort, Mich. (†49760) 250/E2
Brewarrina, Aust. 88/H5
Brewarrina, N.S.W. 97/D1
Brewer, Maine (04412) 242/F6
Brewer, Mo. (†63775) 261/N7
Brewer, Sask. 181/J4
Brewers, Ky. (†42025) 237/E7
Brewersville, Ind. (†47265) 227/F6
Brewerton, N.Y. (13029) 276/H4
Brewood, 10/G2
Brewster (pond), Conn. 210/F2
Brewster, Kans. (67732) 232/A2
Brewster△, Mass. (02631) 249/O5
Brewster (isls.), Mass. 249/E7
Brewster, Minn. (56119) 254/C7
Brewster (lake), N.S.W. 97/D3
Brewster, N.Y. (10509) 276/N8
Brewster, Nebr. (68821) 264/D3
Brewster, Ohio (44613) 284/G4
Brewster, Cerro (mt.), Pan. 154/H6
Brewster (co.), Texas 302/A8
Brewster, Wash. (98812) 310/F2
Brewster Heights‡, N.Y. (†10509) 276/N8
Brewster Hills‡, N.Y. (†10509) 276/N8
Brewton, Ala. (36426) 194/D8
Breynat, Alta. 182/D4
Brežice, Yugo. 45/B3

Burnside 339

Bruno, Sask. 181/F3
Brunot, Mo. (†63636) 261/M8
Brunsbüttelkoog, W. Ger. 22/C2
Brunson, S.C. (29911) 296/E6
Brunsville, Iowa (51008) 229/A3
Brunswick (bay), Aust. 88/C3
Brunswick (pen.), Chile 138/E10
Brunswick, Ga., 188/K4
Brunswick, Ga. (31520) 216/K8
Brunswick▵, Maine (04011) 242/C8
Brunswick, Maine (04011) 242/C8
Brunswick, Md. (21716) 245/H3
Brunswick, Minn. (†55051) 254/E5
Brunswick, Miss. (†39180) 256/C5
Brunswick, Mo. (65236) 261/F4
Brunswick (co.), N.C. 281/N6
Brunswick, N.C. (28424) 281/M6
Brunswick, Nebr. (68720) 264/G2
Brunswick (bay), W. Aust. 92/D1
Brunswick, Ohio (44212) 284/G3
Brunswick, Tenn. (38014) 237/B10
Brunswick (co.), Va. 307/N7
Brunswick, Vic. 97/H5
Brunswick, W. Ger., 7/E3
Brunswick, W. Ger. 22/D2
Brunswick Heads, N.S.W. 97/G1
Brunswick Junction, W. Aust. 92/A2
Bruntál, Czech. 41/D2
Brus (lag.), Hond. 154/E2
Brusett, Mont. (59318) 262/J3
Brush, Colo. (80723) 208/M2
Brushart, Ky. (†41184) 237/P3
Brush Creek, Minn. (†56014) 254/E7
Brush Creek, Mo. (†65536) 261/G7
Brush Creek, Tenn. (38547) 237/J8
Brush Prairie, Wash. (98606) 310/C5
Brushton, N.Y. (12916) 276/L1
Brushy Prairie, Ind. (†46761) 227/G1
Brusio, Switz. 39/K4
Brus Laguna, Hond. 154/E3
Brusly, La. (70719) 238/J2
Brusque, Braz. 132/D9
Brussels (cap.), Belg., 7/E3
Brussels (cap.), Belg., 27/E7
Brussels, Ont. 177/C4
Brussels, Ill. (62013) 222/C5
Brussels, Wis. (54204) 317/L6
Brute (lake), Que. 172/C3
Bruthen, Vic. 97/D5
Bruton, Eng. 13/E6
Brutus, Mich. (49716) 250/E3
Bruxelles (Brussels) (cap.), Belg. 27/E7
Bruxelles, Man. 179/C5
Bruzual, Ven. 124/D3
Bryan (co.), Ga. 216/K6
Bryan, Ohio (43506) 284/A3
Bryan (co.), Okla. 288/O7
Bryan, Texas, 188/G4
Bryan, Texas (77801) 302/H7
Bryansk, U.S.S.R. 48/D4
Bryansk, U.S.S.R. 52/D4
Bryansk, U.S.S.R., 7/H3
Bryanston, Ont. 177/C4
Bryant, Ala. (35958) 194/G1
Bryant, Ark. (72022) 203/F4
Bryant, Fla. (33439) 212/F5
Bryant (lake), Fla. 212/E2
Bryant, Ill. (61519) 222/C3
Bryant, Ind. (47326) 227/G3
Bryant, Iowa (52727) 229/N5
Bryant, Okla. (†74437) 288/P4
Bryant, S. Dak. (57221) 298/P4
Bryant, Sask. 181/H6
Bryant, Wis. (54418) 317/J5
Bryant Pond, Maine (04219) 242/B7
Bryantsburg, Ind. (†47250) 227/G7
Bryantsville, Ky. (40410) 237/M5
Bryantville, Mass. (02327) 249/L4
Bryce (mt.), Br. Col. 184/J4
Bryce Canyon, Utah (84717) 304/B6
Bryce Canyon Nat'l Park, Utah 304/B6
Bryceland, La. (71014) 238/E2
Bryce Mountain, Va. (†22810) 307/L3
Bryceville, Fla. (32009) 212/D1
Bryn Athyn, Pa. (19009) 294/M5
Brynmawr, 10/E5
Bryn Mawr, Pa. (19010) 294/M5
Brynmawr, Wales 13/D6
Bryn Mawr, Wash. (†98101) 310/B2
Byrup, Den. 21/C5
Bryson, Texas (76027) 302/F4
Bryson City, N.C. (28713) 281/C4
Bryte-Broderick, Calif. (95605) 204/B8
Brzeg, Poland 47/C3
Brześć Kujawski, Poland 47/D2
Brzesko, Poland 47/E4
Brzeziny Śląskie, Poland 47/B4
Brzozów, Poland 47/E4
B-Say-Tah, Sask. 181/G5
Bua Chum, Thai. 72/D4
Buad (isl.), Phil. 82/E5
Buayan, Phil. 82/E7
Buba, Port. Guin. 106/B6
Bubali, Neth. Ant. 161/D10
Bubaque, Port. Guin. 106/A6
Bubendorf, Switz. 39/E2
Bubikon, Switz. 39/G2
Bubiyan (isl.), Kuwait 59/E4
Bubwith, Eng. 13/G4
Bucaramanga, Col., 120/C2
Bucaramanga, Col. 126/D4
Bucareli (bay), Alaska 196/M2
Bucas Grande (isl.), Phil. 82/F6
Buccaneer (arch.), Aust. 88/C3
Buccaneer (arch.), W. Aust. 92/C2
Buchan (gulf), N.W.T. 187/L2
Buchan (dist.), Scot. 15/M4
Buchanan, Ga. (30113) 216/B3
Buchanan (co.), Iowa 229/K4
Buchanan, Iowa (†52772) 229/L5
Buchanan, Ky. (41205) 237/R4
Buchanan, Liberia 106/B7
Buchanan, Mich. (49107) 250/C7
Buchanan (co.), Mo. 261/C3
Buchanan, N. Dak. (58420) 283/N5
Buchanan, N.Y. (10511) 276/N8
Buchanan, 102/A4
Buchanan, Sask. 181/J4
Buchanan, Tenn. (38222) 237/E8
Buchanan (lake), Texas 302/F7
Buchanan (co.), Va. 307/D6
Buchanan, Va. (24066) 307/J5
Buchan Ness (prom.), Scot. 15/N5
Buchans, Newf. 166/C4
Bucharest (cap.), Rum., 3/L3
Bucharest (cap.), Rum., 7/G4
Bucharest (cap.), Rum. 45/G3
Buchegg (mts.), Switz. 39/D2
Buchholz, W. Ger. 22/C2
Buchon (pt.), Calif. 204/D8
Buchs, Switz. 39/H2
Buchtel, Ohio (45716) 284/F7
Buck (isl.), V.I.(U.S.) 161/G3
Buck (creek), Ind. 227/E8
Buck (creek), S.C. 296/J3
Buck (creek), Texas 302/D3
Buck, W. Va. (†24935) 313/E7
Buckatunna, Miss. (39322) 256/G7
Buck Creek, Alta. 182/C3
Buck Creek, Ind. (47924) 227/D4
Bückeburg, W. Ger. 22/C2
Buckeye, Ariz. (85326) 198/C5
Buckeye, Iowa (50043) 229/G4
Buckeye, La. (71321) 238/F4
Buckeye, N. Mex. (88212) 274/F6
Buckeye (lake), Ohio 284/F6
Buckeye, W. Va. (24924) 313/F6
Buckeye Lake, Ohio (43008) 284/F6
Buckeystown, Md. (21717) 245/J3
Buckfastleigh, Eng. 13/D7
Buckfield▵, Maine (04220) 242/C7
Buck Grove, Iowa (†51442) 229/C5
Buckhannon, W. Va. (26201) 313/F5
Buckhannon (riv.), W. Va. 313/F5
Buckhaven and Methil, 10/E2
Buckhaven and Methil, Scot. 15/L7
Buckhead, Ga. (30625) 216/F3
Buck Hollow (creek), Oreg. 291/G2
Buckholts, Texas (76518) 302/H7
Buckhorn, Ont. 177/F3
Buckhorn (lake), Ont. 177/F3
Buckhorn (res.), Ky. 237/O6
Buckhorn, Mo. (†63655) 261/M8
Buckhorn, N. Mex. (88025) 274/A5
Buckhorn, Va. (†23391) 307/P7
Buckie, 10/E2
Buckie, Scot. 15/L4
Buckingham, 10/F5
Buckingham, Colo. (†80742) 208/L1
Buckingham, Conn. (†06033) 210/E2
Buckingham, Que. 172/B4
Buckingham, Eng. 13/G5
Buckingham, Ill. (60917) 222/E2
Buckingham, Iowa (50612) 229/J4
Buckingham, Texas (†75080) 302/G1
Buckingham (co.), Va. 307/L5
Buckingham, Va. (23921) 307/L5
Buckinghamshire (co.), Eng. 13/G6
Buck Island (chan.), V.I.(U.S.) 161/F3
Buck Island Reef Nat'l Mon., V.I.(U.S.) 161/G3
Buck Lake, Alta. 182/C3
Buckland, Alaska (99727) 196/F1
Buckland, Conn. (06040) 210/E1
Buckland, Que. 172/G3
Buckland▵, Mass. (01338) 249/C2
Buckland, Ohio (45819) 284/B4
Buckleboo, Aust. 88/F6
Buckley, Ill. (60918) 222/F3
Buckley, Mich. (49620) 250/D4
Buckley, Wash. (98321) 310/C3
Bucklin, Kans. (67834) 232/C4
Bucklin, Mo. (64631) 261/G3
Buckman, Minn. (56317) 254/D5
Buckner, Ark. (71827) 203/D7
Buckner, Ill. (62819) 222/E6
Buckner, Ky. (40010) 237/L4
Buckner, Mo. (64016) 261/R5
Bucks, Ala. (36512) 194/B8
Bucks (co.), Pa. 294/M5
Bucks Harbor, Maine (04618) 242/J6
Buckskin (mts.), Ariz. 198/B4
Buckskin, Ind. (47517) 227/C8
Bucksport▵, Maine (04416) 242/F6
Bucksport, Maine (04416) 242/F6
Bucksport, S.C. (29527) 296/J4
Bucktail, Nebr. (69155) 264/C3
Buckville, Ark. (71934) 203/D4
Bucoda, Mo. (†63876) 261/M10
Bucoda, Wash. (98530) 310/C4
Bučovice, Czech. 41/D2
Buco-Zau, Angola 115/B4
Buctouche, N. Br. 170/F2
Buctouche (harb.), N. Br. 170/F2
Buctouche (riv.), N. Br. 170/F2
București (Bucharest) (cap.), Rum. 45/G3
Bucyrus, Kans. (66013) 232/H3
Bucyrus, Mo. (65444) 261/H8
Bucyrus, N. Dak. (58624) 283/E7
Bucyrus, Ohio (44820) 284/E4
Bud, Ind. (†46131) 227/E6
Bud, W. Va. (24716) 313/D7
Buda, Ill. (61314) 222/D2
Buda, Texas (78610) 302/G7
Budafok, Hung. 41/E3
Budaörs, Hung. 41/E3
Budapest (cap.), Hung., 7/G4
Budapest (cap.), Hung. 41/E3
Budaun, India 68/D3
Budd (lake), N.J. 273/D2
Budd Coast (reg.), Ant. 5/C6
Budd Lake, N.J. (07828) 273/D2
Buddon Ness (prom.), Scot. 15/L7
Bude, Miss. (39630) 256/C8
Bude-Stratton, Eng. 13/C7
Budge-Budge, India 68/F2
Budia, Spain 33/E2
Büdingen, W. Ger. 22/C3
Budišov, Czech. 41/D2
Budjala, Dem. Rep. of the Congo. 115/C3
Bu Dop, S. Vietnam 72/E4
Budrio, Italy 34/C2
Buea, Cameroon 115/A3
Buea, 102/C4
Buechel, Ky. (40218) 237/K4
Buel (lake), Mass. 249/A4
Buell, Mo. (63361) 261/K4
Buellton, Calif. (93427) 204/E9
Buena, N.J. (08310) 273/D4
Buena, Wash. (98921) 310/E4
Buena Hora, Bol. 136/E4
Buena Park, Calif. (90620) 204/D11
Buenaventura, Col., 120/C2
Buenaventura, Col. 126/B6
Buenaventura (bay), Col. 126/B6
Buenaventura, Mex. 150/F2
Buena Vista, Ala. (36430) 194/D7
Buena Vista, Arg. 143/F5
Buena Vista, Ark. (†71764) 203/D7
Buena Vista, Pando, Bol. 136/B2
Buena Vista, Santa Cruz, Bol. 136/D5
Buena Vista (lake), Calif. 204/F8
Buena Vista, Colo. (81211) 208/G5
Buena Vista (chan.), Cuba 158/F2
Buena Vista‡, Fla. (†33552) 212/D3
Buena Vista, Ga. (31803) 216/C6
Buena Vista (co.), Iowa 229/C3
Buena Vista, Miss. (†38851) 256/G3
Buena Vista, N. Mex. (87712) 274/D3
Buenavista, Phil. 82/E6
Buena Vista, Ohio (†45684) 284/D8
Buena Vista, Oreg. (†97351) 291/D3
Buena Vista, Par. 144/E5
Buena Vista, Tenn. (38318) 237/E9
Buena Vista, Urug. 145/E3
Buena Vista, Va. (24416) 307/K5
Buena Vista, Anzoátegui, Ven. 124/F3
Buena Vista, Apure, Ven. 124/D4
Buena Vista, Falcón, Ven. 124/D2
Bueno (riv.), Chile 138/D3
Buenos Aires (lake), 120/C7
Buenos Aires (cap.), Arg., 3/F7
Buenos Aires (cap.), Arg., 120/D6
Buenos Aires (prov.), Arg. 143/D4
Buenos Aires (cap.), Arg. 143/H7
Buenos Aires (lake), Arg. 143/B6
Buenos Aires, C. Rica 154/F6
Buenos Aires (lake), Chile 138/E6
Buenos Aires, Amazonas, Col. 126/F9
Buenos Aires, Caquetá, Col. 126/D7
Buesaco, Col. 126/B7
Bueycito, Cuba 158/H4
Bueyeros, N. Mex. (88412) 274/F3
Buffalo, Ala. (†36862) 194/H5
Buffalo, Alta. 182/E4
Buffalo (lake), Alta. 182/D3
Buffalo (riv.), Ark. 203/E2
Buffalo, Ill. (62515) 222/D4
Buffalo, Ind. (47925) 227/D3
Buffalo, Iowa (52728) 229/M6
Buffalo, Kans. (66717) 232/G4
Buffalo, Ky. (42716) 237/K6
Buffalo (bay), Man. 179/G5
Buffalo, Minn. (55313) 254/E5
Buffalo (riv.), Minn. 254/B4
Buffalo, Mo. (65622) 261/F7
Buffalo, Mont. (59418) 262/G4
Buffalo, N. Dak. (58011) 283/R6
Buffalo, N.Y., 146/L5
Buffalo, N.Y., 188/L2
Buffalo, N.Y. (*14201) 276/B5
Buffalo (co.), Nebr. 264/E4
Buffalo (creek), Nev. 266/B2
Buffalo, Ohio (43722) 284/G6
Buffalo, Okla. (73834) 288/G1
Buffalo, S.C. (29321) 296/D2
Buffalo (co.), S. Dak. 298/L5
Buffalo, S. Dak. (57720) 298/B2
Buffalo (creek), S. Dak. 298/F6
Buffalo (lake), S. Dak. 298/P2
Buffalo (riv.), Tenn. 237/F9
Buffalo, Texas (75831) 302/J6
Buffalo, W. Va. (25033) 313/C5
Buffalo (co.), Wis. 317/C7
Buffalo, Wis. (†54622) 317/C7
Buffalo, Wyo. (82834) 319/F1
Buffalo Bill (dam), Wyo. 319/C1
Buffalo Bill (res.), Wyo. 319/C1
Buffalo Center, Iowa (50424) 229/F2
Buffalo City, Ark. (†72653) 203/E1
Buffalo City, N.C. (†27931) 281/T3
Buffalo Creek, Br. Col. 184/G4
Buffalo Creek, Colo. (80425) 208/J4
Buffalo Fork, Snake (riv.), Wyo. 319/B2
Buffalo Gap, S. Dak. (57722) 298/C6
Buffalo Gap, Texas (79508) 302/E5
Buffalo Grove‡, Ill. (60090) 222/F1
Buffalo Head (hills), Alta. 182/B5
Buffalo Head Prairie, Alta. 182/B5
Buffalo Junction, Va. (24529) 307/L7
Buffalo Lake, Alta. 182/A2
Buffalo Lake, Minn. (55314) 254/D6
Buffalo Lodge (lake), N. Dak. 283/J3
Buffalo Mills, Pa. (15534) 294/E6
Buffalo Narrows, Sask. 181/L3
Buffalo Springs, N. Dak. (†58623) 283/D7
Buffalo Valley, Tenn. (38548) 237/K8
Buffaloville, Ind. (47518) 227/D8
Buff Bay, Jam. 158/K6
Buford, Alta. 182/D3
Buford, Ga. (30518) 216/D2
Buford, N. Dak. (58837) 283/C3
Buford, Ohio (45110) 284/C7
Buford, Wyo. (82052) 319/G4
Bug (riv.), 7/G3
Bug (riv.), U.S.S.R. 52/B4
Bug (riv.), U.S.S.R. 52/D5
Bug (riv.), Poland 47/F2
Buga, Col. 126/B6
Bugaldie, N.S.W. 97/E2
Bugasong, Phil. 82/C5
Buggs Island (lake), N.C. 281/M1
Buggs Island (lake), Va. 307/M7
Bugio (isl.), Port. 33/B2
Bugojno, Yugo. 45/C3
Bugrino, U.S.S.R. 52/G1
Bugsuk (isl.), Phil. 82/A6
Bugsuk (isl.), Phil. 85/F4
Bugui (pt.), Phil. 82/D4
Bugul'ma, U.S.S.R. 48/F4
Bugul'ma, U.S.S.R. 52/H4
Buguruslan, U.S.S.R. 52/H4
Buhl, Ala. (35446) 194/C4
Buhl, Idaho (83316) 220/D7
Buhl, Minn. (55713) 254/F3
Bühl, W. Ger. 22/C4
Buhler, Kans. (67522) 232/E3
Buhuşi, Rum. 45/H2
Buies, N.C. (†28377) 281/L5
Buies Creek, N.C. (27506) 281/M4
Buiksloot, Neth. 27/B4
Builth Wells, 10/E4
Builth Wells, Wales 13/D5
Buin, Chile 138/G4
Buin (peak), Switz. 39/K3
Bujalance, Spain 33/D4
Buje, Yugo. 45/A3
Bujnurd, Iran 59/G2
Bujnurd, Iran 66/K2
Bujumbura (cap.), Burundi, 102/F5
Bujumbura (cap.), Burundi, 115/E4
Bukama, 102/E5
Bukama, Dem. Rep. of the Congo. 115/E5
Bukan, Iran 66/D2
Bukavu, 102/E5
Bukavu, Dem. Rep. of the Congo. 115/E4
Bukene, Tanz. 115/F4
Bukhara, U.S.S.R. 48/G5
Bukhara, U.S.S.R., 54/K6
Bukidnon (prov.), Phil. 82/E6
Bukittinggi, Indon. 85/B6
Bükk (mts.), Hung. 41/F2
Bukoba, Tanz. 115/F4
Bul, Kuh-i- (mt.), Iran 66/H5
Bula, Indon. 85/J6
Bula, Texas (79320) 302/B4
Bulacan (prov.), Phil. 82/C3
Bülach, Switz. 39/G1
Bulagan (prov.), Mong. 77/F2
Bulagan, Mong. 77/F2
Bulahdelah, N.S.W. 97/G3
Bulak, China 77/B2
Bulalacao, Phil. 82/C4
Bulan, Ky. (41722) 237/P6
Bulan, Phil. 82/D4
Bulancak, Turkey 63/H2
Bulanik, Turkey 63/K3
Bûlaq, U.A.R. 59/B4
Bûlaq, U.A.R. 111/F2
Bulawayo, 102/E7
Bulawayo, Rhod. 118/D3
Buldan, Turkey 59/A2
Buldan, Turkey 63/C3
Buldibuyo, Peru 128/D7
Buldir (isl.), Alaska 196/J3
Bulgaria, 3/L3
Bulgaria, 7/G4
BULGARIA, 45/G4
Bulger, Pa. (15019) 294/B5
Bulgroo, Aust. 88/G5
Bulgroo, Queens. 95/B5
Bulhar, Somalia 115/H2
Buli, Indon. 85/H5
Buliluyan (cape), Phil. 82/A6
Buliluyan (cape), Phil. 85/F4
Bulimba (creek), Queens. 95/E3
Bulkley (riv.), Br. Col. 184/D2
Bull, The (isl.), Ire. 17/A8
Bull (isl.), Newf. 166/D2
Bull (isl.), S.C. 296/H6
Bull (creek), S. Dak. 298/C2
Bull (creek), S. Dak. 298/K6
Bullard, Ga. (†31020) 216/F5
Bullard, Texas (75757) 302/J5
Bull Arm (inlet), Newf. 166/D2
Bullas, Spain 33/F4
Bulldog (isl.), Newf. 166/C3
Bulle, Switz. 39/D3
Bullen (bay), Neth. Ant. 161/F8
Buller (riv.), N.Z. 101/D4
Buller (mt.), Vic. 97/D5
Bullfinch, Aust. 88/B6
Bullfinch, W. Aust. 92/B5
Bull Harbour, Br. Col. 184/C5
Bullhead, S. Dak. (57621) 298/G2
Bullhead City, Ariz. (86430) 198/A3
Bulli, Aust. 88/L4
Bullitt (co.), Ky. 237/K5
Bull Lake (res.), Wyo. 319/C2
Bulloch (co.), Ga. 216/J6
Bullock (co.), Ala. 194/G6
Bullock, N.C. (27507) 281/M2
Bullock (creek), S.C. 296/E2
Bulloo (lake), Aust. 88/G5
Bulloo (riv.), Aust. 88/G5
Bulloo (lake), Queens. 95/B6
Bulloo (riv.), Queens. 95/B6
Bull Run (creek), Va. 307/N3
Bulls, N.Z. 101/E4
Bulls (bay), S.C. 296/H6
Bulls Bridge, Conn. (†06785) 210/B2
Bulls Gap, Tenn. (37711) 237/P8
Bull Shoals, Ark. (72619) 203/E1
Bull Shoals (lake), Ark. 203/E1
Bull Shoals (lake), Mo. 261/G10
Bully (creek), Oreg. 291/K3
Bulnes, Chile 138/E1
Bulo Burti, Somalia 115/J3
Bulolo, Terr. N.G. 85/B7
Bulpitt, Ill. (62517) 222/D4
Bulsar, India 68/C4
Bulusan (lake), Phil. 82/E7
Bulukumba, Indon. 85/G7
Bulun, U.S.S.R. 48/N2
Bulun, U.S.S.R., 4/B3
Bulun, U.S.S.R., 54/R2
Bulusan, Phil. 82/E4
Bulusan (vol.), Phil. 82/D4
Bulwark, Alta. 182/E3
Bulwer, Aust. 88/L1
Bulwer, Que. 172/F4
Bulyea, Sask. 181/G5
Bumba, Dem. Rep. of the Congo. 115/D3
Bumble Bee, Ariz. (85327) 198/C4
Bumiaju, Indon. 85/H2
Bumpass, Va. (23024) 307/N5
Bumping (lake), Wash. 310/D4
Bumpus Mills, Tenn. (37028) 237/F7
Bumthang, India 68/G3
Buna, Papua 85/C7
Buna, Kenya 115/G3
Buna, Texas (77612) 302/L7
Bunavista, Texas (†79007) 302/C2
Bunawan, Phil. 82/E6
Bunbury, Australia, 87/B9
Bunbury, Aust. 88/A6
Bunbury, W. Aust. 92/A2
Buncetón, Mo. (65237) 261/G5
Bunch, Iowa (†52552) 229/H7
Bunch, Okla. (74931) 288/S3
Bunche Park, Fla. (†33054) 212/B4
Bunclody-Carrickduff, Ire. 17/H6
Buncombe, Ill. (62912) 222/E6
Buncombe (co.), N.C. 281/D3
Buncrana, 10/C3
Buncrana, Ire. 17/G1
Bundaberg, Australia, 87/E8
Bundaberg, Aust. 88/J5
Bundaberg, Queens. 95/D5
Bundanoon, N.S.W. 97/F4
Bundarra, N.S.W. 97/F2
Bundi, India 68/D3
Bundick (lake), La. 238/D5
Bundooma, Aust. 88/F4
Bundooma, No. Terr. 93/D8
Bundoora, Vic. 97/J4
Bundoran, Ire. 17/E3
Bunessan, Scot. 15/D7
Bunga (pt.), Phil. 82/E4
Bungay, 10/G4
Bungay, Eng. 13/J5
Bungee (brook), Conn. 210/G1
Bu Ngem, Libya 111/C1
Bungendore, N.S.W. 97/E4
Bungo (str.), Japan 81/F7
Bunguran (Great Natuna) (isl.), Indon. 85/D5
Bunguran (Natuna) (isls.), Indon. 85/D5
Bunia, Dem. Rep. of the Congo. 115/E3
Bunji, India 68/C1
Bunju (isl.), Indon. 85/F5
Bunker, Mo. (63629) 261/K8
Bunker Group (isls.), Queens. 95/E4
Bunker Hill, Ill. (62014) 222/D4
Bunker Hill, Ind. (46914) 227/E3
Bunker Hill, Kans. (67626) 232/D3
Bunker Hill, Oreg. (†97420) 291/C4
Bunker Hill, W. Va. (25413) 313/K4
Bunker Hill Village, Texas (†77001) 302/J1
Bunkerville, Nev. (89007) 266/G6
Bunkeya, Dem. Rep. of the Congo. 115/E6
Bunkie, La. (71322) 238/F5
Bunmahon, Ire. 17/G7
Bunn, N.C. (27508) 281/N3
Bunnell, Fla. (32010) 212/E2
Bunnlevel, N.C. (28323) 281/M4
Bunny Run‡, Mich. (†48035) 250/F6
Buntok, Indon. 85/F6
Bünyan, Turkey 63/G3
Bunyan's Cove, Newf. 166/C2
Buochs, Switz. 39/F3
Buol, Indon. 85/G5
Buq, Iran 66/M6
Bura, Kenya 115/H4
Bur Acaba, Somalia 115/H3
Buraida, Saudi Ar. 59/D4
Buraida, Saudi Ar., 54/E7
Buraimi, Asia 59/G5
Buram, 102/E3
Buram, Sudan 111/E5
Burao, 102/G4
Burao, Somalia 115/J2
Buras-Triumph, La. (70041) 238/L8
Burauen, Phil. 82/E5
Burbank, Calif. (*91501) 204/C10
Burbank, Ohio (44214) 284/F4
Burbank, Okla. (74633) 288/N1
Burbank, S. Dak. (57010) 298/R8
Burbank, Wash. (99323) 310/G4
Burchard, Minn. (†56115) 254/C6
Burchard, Nebr. (68323) 264/H4
Burcher, N.S.W. 97/D3
Burchinal, Iowa (50425) 229/G2
Burchun, China 77/C2
Burdekin (riv.), Aust. 88/H3
Burdekin (riv.), Queens. 95/C3
Burden, Kans. (67019) 232/F4
Burdett, Alta. 182/E5
Burdett, Kans. (67523) 232/C3
Burdett, N.Y. (14818) 276/G6
Burdette, Ark. (72321) 203/L2
Burdette, S. Dak. (†57476) 298/M4
Burdick, Kans. (66838) 232/F3
Burdur, Turkey 59/A2
Burdur (prov.), Turkey 63/D4
Burdur, Turkey 63/D4
Burdur (lake), Turkey 63/D4
Burdwan, India 68/F4
Burea, Sweden 18/M4
Bureau (co.), Ill. 222/D2
Bureau, Ill. (61315) 222/D2
Burei, Eth. 111/G6
Büren, W. Ger. 22/C3
Büren an der Aare, Switz. 39/D2
Bures, Sask. 181/G6
Burford, Ont. 177/D4
Burford (lake), N. Mex. 274/C2
Burfordville, Mo. (63739) 261/N8
Burg, E. Ger. 22/D2
Burg, W. Ger. 22/D1
Burgas, Bulg., 7/G4
Burgas, Bulg. 45/H4
Bur Gavo, Somalia 115/H4
Burgaw, N.C. (28425) 281/N5
Burgaz, Turkey 63/B6
Burgaz (isl.), Turkey 63/D6
Burgdorf, Switz. 39/E2
Burgenland (prov.), Austria 41/D3
Burgeo, Newf. 166/C4
Burgersdorp, S. Africa 118/D6
Burgess, Mo. (†66756) 261/C7
Burgess, S.C. (29517) 296/J4
Burgess, Va. (22432) 307/R5
Burgess (mt.), Yukon 187/D3
Burgess Hill, Eng. 13/G7
Burgessville, Ont. 177/D4
Burgettstown, Pa. (15021) 294/A5
Burghausen, W. Ger. 22/E4
Burghead, 10/E2
Burghead, Scot. 15/J4
Burghill, Ohio (44404) 284/J3
Burgin, Ky. (40310) 237/M5
Burgis, Sask. 181/J4
Bürglen, Thurgau, Switz. 39/H1
Bürglen, Uri, Switz. 39/G3
Burglengenfeld, W. Ger. 22/D4
Burgoon, Ohio (43407) 284/D3
Burgos, Mex. 150/K4
Burgos, Spain, 7/D4
Burgos (prov.), Spain 33/E1
Burgos, Spain 33/E1
Burg Stargard, E. Ger. 22/E2
Burgsteinfurt, W. Ger. 22/B2
Burgsvik, Sweden 18/K8
Burhaniye, Turkey 63/B3
Burhanpur, India 68/D4
Buri, Braz. 135/B3
Buri (pen.), Eth. 111/H4
Burias (isl.), Phil. 82/D4
Burias (passg.), Phil. 82/D4
Burica (pt.), C. Rica 154/F6
Burica (pt.), Pan. 154/F6
Burien, Wash. (98166) 310/A2
Burin, Newf. 166/C4
Burin (pen.), Newf. 166/C4
Buriram, Thai. 72/D4
Buriti, Braz. 132/F3
Buriti Alegre, Braz. 132/D7
Buriti dos Lopes, Braz. 132/F3
Burkburnett, Texas (76354) 302/F3
Burke (chan.), Br. Col. 184/D4
Burke (co.), Ga. 216/J4
Burke, Idaho (83807) 220/C2
Burke (co.), N.C. 281/F3
Burke (co.), N. Dak. 283/E2
Burke, N.Y. (12917) 276/M1
Burke, S. Dak. (57523) 298/L7
Burke, Texas (75941) 302/K6
Burke▵, Vt. (†05871) 268/D2
Burke, Vt. (†05871) 268/D2
Burke (mt.), Vt. 268/D2
Bürkelkopf (mt.), Switz. 39/K3
Burkes Garden, Va. (24608) 307/F6
Burkesville, Ky. (42717) 237/L7
Burket, Ind. (46508) 227/F2
Burketown, Aust. 88/F3
Burketown, Queens. 95/A3
Burkett, Texas (76828) 302/E5
Burkettsville, Ohio (45310) 284/A5
Burkettville, Maine (04540) 242/E7
Burkeville, Texas (75932) 302/L7
Burkeville, Va. (23922) 307/M6
Burkittsville, Md. (21718) 245/H3
Burkley, Ky. (†42021) 237/C7
Burk's Falls, Ont. 177/E2
Burkville, Ala. (36725) 194/E6
Burl, Ala. (†36753) 194/D7
Burleigh (co.), N. Dak. 283/J6
Burleson (co.), Texas 302/H7
Burleson, Texas (76028) 302/F2
Burley, Idaho (83318) 220/E7
Burley, Wash. (98322) 310/C3
Burlingame, Calif. (94010) 204/J2
Burlingame, Kans. (66413) 232/G3
Burlington, Colo. (80807) 208/P4
Burlington▵, Conn. (06085) 210/D1
Burlington, Conn. (06085) 210/D1
Burlington, Ont. 177/E4
Burlington, Ill. (60109) 222/E1
Burlington, Ind. (46915) 227/E4
Burlington, Iowa, 188/H2
Burlington, Iowa (52601) 229/L7
Burlington, Kans. (66839) 232/G3
Burlington, Ky. (41005) 237/R3
Burlington▵, Maine (04417) 242/G5
Burlington▵, Mass. (01803) 249/C5
Burlington, Mich. (49029) 250/D6
Burlington, N.C. (27215) 281/K2
Burlington, N. Dak. (58722) 283/H3
Burlington (co.), N.J. 273/D4
Burlington, N.J. (08016) 273/D3
Burlington, Newf. 166/C4
Burlington, Ohio (†45680) 284/F9
Burlington, Okla. (73722) 288/K1
Burlington, Pa. (18814) 294/J2
Burlington, Vt., 188/M2
Burlington, Vt. (05401) 268/A3
Burlington, W. Va. (26710) 313/J4
Burlington, Wash. (98233) 310/C2
Burlington, Wis. (53105) 317/K10
Burlington, Wyo. (82411) 319/D1
Burlington Flats, N.Y. (13315) 276/K5
Burlington Junction, Mo. (64428) 261/B2
Burlison, Tenn. (38015) 237/B9
Burma, 3/P4
Burma, 54/N7
BURMA, 72
Burmis, Alta. 182/C5
Burna, Ky. (42028) 237/E6
Burnaby, Br. Col. 184/K3
Burnaby (isl.), Br. Col. 184/B4
Burnet (co.), Texas 302/F7
Burnet, Texas (78611) 302/F7
Burnett, Minn. (55714) 254/F4
Burnett (co.), Wis. 317/B4
Burnett, Wis. (53922) 317/J9
Burnettown, S.C. (†29834) 296/D5
Burnettsville, Ind. (47926) 227/D3
Burney, Calif. (96013) 204/D3
Burney (mt.), Chile 138/D9
Burney, Ind. (47222) 227/F6
Burneyville, Okla. (73430) 288/M7
Burnham, Ill. (†60601) 222/B2
Burnham▵, Maine (04922) 242/E6
Burnham, Mo. (†65793) 261/J9
Burnham, Pa. (17009) 294/H4
Burnham Market, Eng. 13/H4
Burnham-on-Crouch, Eng. 13/H6
Burnham-on-Sea, Eng. 13/D6
Burnie, Aust. 88/H8
Burnie, Tasmania 99/B3
Burning Springs, Ky. (40922) 237/O6
Burning Springs, W. Va. (26139) 313/D5
Burnips, Mich. (49314) 250/D6
Burnley, 10/G1
Burnley, Eng. 13/E4
Burns, Colo. (80426) 208/F3
Burns, Kans. (66840) 232/F3
Burns, Miss. (†39153) 256/E6
Burns, N.S.W. 97/A3
Burns, Oreg. (97720) 291/H4
Burns, Tenn. (37029) 237/G8
Burns, Wyo. (82053) 319/H4
Burns City, Ind. (47553) 227/D7
Burns Flat, Okla. (73624) 288/H4
Burns Harbor, Ind. (†46401) 227/C1
Burnside, Conn. (†06108) 210/E1
Burnside, Ill. (62318) 222/B3
Burnside, Iowa (50521) 229/E4
Burnside, Ky. (42519) 237/M6
Burnside, La. (70738) 238/L3
Burnside, Miss. (†39350) 256/F5
Burnside (riv.), N.W.T. 187/G3
Burnside, S. Aust. 94/B8
Burnside, Pa. (15721) 294/E4

340 Burnside

Burnside, Sur. 131/C2
Burns Junction, Oreg. (†97902) 291/K5
Burns Lake, 163/D5
Burns Lake, Br. Col. 184/D3
Burnstad, N. Dak. (58526) 283/L7
Burnsville, Ala. (†36701) 194/E6
Burnsville, Ind. (†47201) 227/F6
Burnsville, Minn. (55378) 254/E6
Burnsville, Miss. (38833) 256/H1
Burnsville, N. Br. 170/E1
Burnsville, N.C. (28714) 281/E3
Burnsville, Va. (24420) 307/J4
Burnsville, W. Va. (26335) 313/E5
Burnt (lakes), Alta. 182/C1
Burnt (lake), Que. 174/E2
Burnt (riv.), Ont. 177/F3
Burnt (lake), Newf. 166/B3
Burnt (riv.), Oreg. 291/K3
Burnt Cabins, Pa. (17215) 294/G5
Burnt Corn, Ala. (36431) 194/D7
Burnt Fort, Ga. (†31568) 216/J9
Burnt House, W. Va. (26336) 313/D4
Burnt Island (lake), Ont. 177/F2
Burntisland, 10/C1
Burntisland, Scot. 15/K7
Burnt Islands, Newf. 166/C4
Burnt Prairie, Ill. (62820) 222/E5
Burnt River, Ont. 177/F3
Burntroot (lake), Ont. 177/F2
Burntside (lake), Minn. 254/F3
Burntwood, 10/G2
Burntwood (lake), Man. 179/H3
Burntwood (riv.), Man. 179/J2
Burnwell, W. Va. (25034) 313/D6
Burqa, Jordan 65/C3
Burr (pond), Conn. 210/C1
Burr, Minn. (†56220) 254/B6
Burr, Nebr. (68324) 264/H4
Burr, Sask. 181/F3
Burra, S. Aust. 94/F5
Burraboi, N.S.W. 97/C4
Burramurra, No. Terr. 93/E6
Burravoe, Scot. 15/N2
Burrel, Alb. 45/D5
Burren Junction, N.S.W. 97/E2
Burriana, Spain 33/G3
Burrinjuck (res.), N.S.W. 97/E4
Burris, Wyo. (82511) 319/C2
Burro (creek), Ariz. 198/B4
Burro (mts.), Mex. 150/J2
Burr Oak, Ind. (46509) 227/E2
Burr Oak, Iowa (52131) 229/K2
Burr Oak, Kans. (66936) 232/D2
Burr Oak, Mich. (49030) 250/D7
Burro-Burro (riv.), Guyana 131/B3
Burrow (head), Scot. 15/H10
Burrows, Ind. (46916) 227/E3
Burrows, Sask. 181/K5
Burr Ridge, Ill. (†60558) 222/A2
Burrsville, Md. (†21629) 245/P5
Burrton, Kans. (67020) 232/E3
Burrville, Conn. (†06790) 210/C1
Burrville, Tenn. (37712) 237/M8
Burrville, Utah (†84701) 304/C5
Burrwood, La. (†70091) 238/M8
Burry Port, Wales 13/C6
Bursa, Turkey 59/A1
Bursa (prov.), Turkey 63/C2
Bursa, Turkey 63/C2
Bursa, Turkey, 54/F6
Bur Sa'id (Port Said), U.A.R. 59/B3
Bur Sa'id (Port Said), U.A.R. 111/K2
Burstall, Sask. 181/B5
Burt, Iowa (50522) 229/E2
Burt, Mich. (48417) 250/F5
Burt (lake), Mich. 250/E3
Burt, N. Dak. (58527) 283/F7
Burt, N.Y. (14028) 276/C4
Burt (co.), Nebr. 264/H3
Burta, N.S.W. 97/A3
Burt Lake, Mich. (49717) 250/E3
Burton, Br. Col. 184/H5
Burton (lake), Ga. 216/E1
Burton, Ky. (†41612) 237/R6
Burton, N. Br. 170/D3
Burton, Nebr. (68721) 264/E2
Burton, Ohio (44021) 284/H3
Burton, S.C. (29902) 296/F7
Burton, Texas (77835) 302/H7
Burton, W. Va. (26562) 313/F3
Burton, Wash. (98013) 310/C3
Burtonport, 10/B3
Burtonport, Ire. 17/E2
Burtonsville, Md. (20730) 245/L4
Burton-upon-Trent, 10/G2
Burton-upon-Trent, Eng. 13/F5
Burtonville, Ky. (†41179) 237/P4
Burtonwood, 10/G2
Burträsk, Sweden 18/M4
Burtrum, Minn. (56318) 254/D5
Burtts Corner, N. Br. 170/D2
Buru (isl.), Indon., 54/R10
Buru (isl.), Indon. 85/H6
Buru (sea), Indon. 85/H6
Burujird, Iran 59/E3
Burujird, Iran 66/F4
Burundi, 3/L6
BURUNDI, 115/E4
BURUNDI, 102/F5
Bururi, Burundi 115/F4
Burutu, Nigeria 106/F7
Burwash Landing, Yukon 187/D3
Burwell, Nebr. (68823) 264/E3
Burwell (mt.), Wyo. 319/C2
Burwood, N.S.W. 97/J3
Bury, 10/G2
Bury, Que. 172/F4
Bury, Eng. 13/E4
Buryat A.S.S.R., U.S.S.R. 48/M4
Burye, Eth. 111/G5
Bury Saint Edmunds, 10/G4
Bury Saint Edmunds, Eng. 13/H5
Busanga, Dem. Rep. of the Congo. 115/D6
Busby, Alta. 182/C3
Busby, Mont. (59016) 262/J5
Buseno, Switz. 39/H4
Bush, Ill. (†62924) 222/D6
Bush, Ky. (40724) 237/O6
Bush, La. (70431) 238/L5
Bush (creek), Md. 245/J3
Bush (riv.), N. Ire. 17/H1
Bush (riv.), S.C. 296/D3
Bush City, Kans. (†66032) 232/G3
Bushey, 10/B5
Bushire, Iran, 54/J7
Bushire, Iran 59/F4
Bushire, Iran 66/G6
Bushiribana, Neth. Ant. 161/E10
Bush Island, N.S. 169/D4
Bushkill, Pa. (18324) 294/M3
Bushland, Texas (79012) 302/B2
Bushman Land (reg.), S. Africa 118/B5
Bushmills, N. Ire. 17/J1
Bushnell, Fla. (33513) 212/D3
Bushnell, Ill. (61422) 222/C3
Bushnell, Nebr. (69128) 264/A3
Bushnell, S. Dak. (57011) 298/R5
Bushong, Kans. (66841) 232/F3
Bushton, Ill. (†61920) 222/E4
Bushton, Kans. (67427) 232/D3
Bushwood, Md. (20618) 245/L7
Bushyhead, Okla. (†74016) 288/P2
Busick, N.C. (†28714) 281/E3
Businga, Dem. Rep. of the Congo. 115/D3
Buskerud (co.), Norway 18/F6
Buskirk, Ky. (41406) 237/P5
Busko Zdrój, Poland 47/E3
Busra, Syria 63/G6
Busselton, Aust. 88/A6
Busselton, W. Aust. 92/A6
Busseron (creek), Ind. 227/C7
Bussey, Iowa (50044) 229/H6
Bussigny-près-Lausanne, Switz. 39/B3
Bussum, Neth. 27/G4
Bustam, Iran 66/J2
Bustanabad, Iran 66/E2
Bustard (isls.), Ont. 177/C2
Busti, N.Y. (†14701) 276/B6
Bustinza, Arg. 143/F6
Busto Arsizio, Italy 34/B2
Busuanga (isl.), Phil. 82/B4
Busuanga (isl.), Phil. 85/F3
Busu-Djanoa, Dem. Rep. of the Congo. 115/D3
Büsum, W. Ger. 22/C1
Buta, 102/E4
Buta, Dem. Rep. of the Congo. 115/D3
Butare, Rwanda 115/E4
Butaritari (atoll), Gilb. and Ell., 87/H5
Butcher (isl.), India 68/B7
Bute (inlet), Br. Col. 184/E5
Bute (co.), Scot. 15/F8
Bute (isl.), Scot. 15/F8
Bute (sound), Scot. 15/F8
Butedale, Br. Col. 184/C3
Butembo, Dem. Rep. of the Congo. 115/E3
Butiaba, Uganda 115/F3
Butler (co.), Ala. 194/E7
Butler, Ala. (36904) 194/B6
Butler (bay), V.I.(U.S.) 161/E4
Butler, Ga. (31006) 216/D5
Butler, Ill. (62015) 222/D4
Butler, Ind. (46721) 227/H2
Butler (co.), Iowa 229/H3
Butler (co.), Kans. 232/F4
Butler (co.), Ky. 237/H6
Butler, Ky. (41006) 237/N3
Butler, Man. 179/A5
Butler, Md. (21023) 245/M2
Butler, Minn. (†56567) 254/C4
Butler (co.), Mo. 261/M9
Butler, Mo. (64730) 261/D6
Butler, N.J. (07405) 273/E2
Butler (co.), Nebr. 264/G3
Butler (co.), Ohio 284/A7
Butler, Ohio (44822) 284/F4
Butler, Okla. (73625) 288/H3
Butler (co.), Pa. 294/C4
Butler, Pa. (16001) 294/C4
Butler, S. Dak. (57222) 298/O3
Butler, Tenn. (37640) 237/T8
Butler, Wis. (53007) 317/K1
Butler Springs, Ala. (†36030) 194/E7
Butlerville, Ark. (†72176) 203/G4
Butlerville, Ind. (47223) 227/F6
Butlerville, Ohio (†45162) 284/B7
Butner, N.C. (27509) 281/M2
Bütschelegg (mt.), Switz. 39/D3
Bütschwil, Switz. 39/H2
Butthatchee (riv.), Miss. 256/H3
Butte‡, Alaska (†99645) 196/C1
Butte (co.), Calif. 204/D4
Butte (co.), Idaho 220/E6
Butte, Mont., 146/G5
Butte, Mont., 188/D1
Butte, Mont. (59701) 262/D5
Butte, N. Dak. (58723) 283/J4
Butte, Nebr. (68722) 264/F2
Butte (mts.), Nev. 266/F3
Butte (creek), Oreg. 291/G2
Butte (creek), Oreg. 291/B3
Butte (co.), S. Dak. 298/B4
Butte City, Calif. (95920) 204/C4
Butte City, Idaho (†83213) 220/E6
Butte-d'Or, N. Br. 170/E1
Butte Falls, Oreg. (97522) 291/E5
Butter (creek), Oreg. 291/H2
Butterfield, Ark. (†72104) 203/E5
Butterfield, Minn. (56120) 254/D7
Butterfield, Mo. (65623) 261/E9
Butterfield (lake), N.Y. 276/J2
Butternut, Mich. (†48811) 250/E5
Butternut, Wis. (54514) 317/E3
Butternut (lake), Wis. 317/J4
Butter Pot Prov. Park, Newf. 166/D2
Butters, N.C. (28324) 281/M5
Butterworth, Malaysia 72/D6
Butterworth, S. Africa 118/D6
Buttes, Switz. 39/C3
Butte-Saint-Pierre, Sask. 181/B2
Buttevant, Ire. 17/D7
Butteville, Oreg. (†97002) 291/A2
Butt of Lewis (prom.), Scot. 15/D3
Button (isls.), N.W.T. 187/M3
Buttonwillow, Calif. (93206) 204/F8
Buttress, Sask. 181/F5
Butts (co.), Ga. 216/E4
Buttzville, N. Dak. (†58054) 283/P6
Buttzville, N.J. (07829) 273/D2
Butuan, Phil. 82/E6
Butuan, Phil. 85/H4
Butuan (bay), Phil. 82/E6
Butung (isl.), Indon. 85/G6
Buturlinovka, U.S.S.R. 52/F4
Butzbach, W. Ger. 22/C3
Bützow, E. Ger. 22/E2
Buxtehude, W. Ger. 22/C2
Buxton, 10/G2
Buxton, Eng. 13/F4
Buxton△, Maine (†04093) 242/C8
Buxton, N.C. (27920) 281/U4
Buxton, N. Dak. (58218) 283/R4
Buxton, Oreg. (97109) 291/D2
Buxton Center, Maine (†04093) 242/B8
Buy, U.S.S.R. 52/F3
Buyck, Minn. (55771) 254/F2
Buynaksk, U.S.S.R. 52/G6
Büyükada, Turkey 63/D6
Büyük Ağri (Ararat) (mt.), Turkey 59/D2
Büyük Ağri (Ararat) (mt.), Turkey 63/L3
Büyükanafarta, Turkey 63/B6
Büyükdere, Turkey 63/D5
Büyük Kemikli (cape), Turkey 63/B6
Buzău, Rum. 45/H3
Buzău (riv.), Rum. 45/H3
Buzeima, Libya 111/D3
Buziaş, Rum. 45/E3
Buzios (cape), Braz. 135/F3
Buzuluk, U.S.S.R. 48/F4
Buzuluk, U.S.S.R. 52/H4
Buzzard Roost (dam), S.C. 296/D3
Buzzards (bay), Mass. 249/L7
Buzzards Bay, Mass. (02532) 249/M5
Byala, Bulg. 45/G4
Byala Slatina, Bulg. 45/F4
Byam Martin (chan.), N.W.T. 187/H2
Byam Martin (isl.), N.W.T. 187/H2
Byars, Okla. (74831) 288/N5
Bybee, Tenn. (37713) 237/P8
Bydgoszcz, Poland, 7/F3
Bydgoszcz (prov.), Poland 47/D2
Bydgoszcz, Poland 47/D2
Byemoor, Alta. 182/D4
Byers, Colo. (80103) 208/L3
Byers, Kans. (67021) 232/D4
Byers, Texas (76357) 302/F3
Byesville, Ohio (43723) 284/G6
Byfield, Mass. (01922) 249/L1
Bygland, Norway 18/F7
Bygland, Minn. (†56723) 254/B3
Byhalia, Miss. (38611) 256/E1
Bykhov, U.S.S.R. 52/C4
Bylas, Ariz. (85530) 198/E5
Bylot (isl.), 163/J1
Bylot (isl.), N.W.T., 146/L2
Bylot (isl.), N.W.T. 187/L2
Byng, Okla. (†74820) 288/N5
Byng Inlet, Ont. 175/D3
Byng Inlet, Ont. 177/D2
Bynum, Mont. (59419) 262/D3
Bynum (res.), Mont. 262/D2
Bynum, N.C. (27228) 281/L3
Bynumville, Mo. (65238) 261/G3
Byram, Conn. (10573) 210/A4
Byram (pt.), Conn. 210/A4
Byram (riv.), Conn. 210/A4
Byram, Miss. (†39205) 256/D6
Byrd Station, Ant. 5/A12
Byrdstown, Tenn. (38549) 237/L7
Byrnedale, Pa. (15827) 294/E3
Byrock, Aust. 88/H6
Byrock, N.S.W. 97/D2
Byromville, Ga. (31007) 216/E6
Byron (cape), Aust. 88/J5
Byron, Calif. (94514) 204/L2
Byron (isl.), Chile 138/D7
Byron, Ga. (31008) 216/E5
Byron, Ill. (61010) 222/D1
Byron, Ind. (†46371) 227/C5
Byron△, Maine (†04275) 242/B6
Byron, Maine (†04275) 242/B6
Byron, Mich. (48418) 250/E6
Byron, Minn. (55920) 254/F6
Byron (cape), N.S.W. 97/G1
Byron, N.Y. (14422) 276/D4
Byron, Nebr. (68325) 264/G4
Byron (bay), Newf. 166/C3
Byron, Okla. (73723) 288/K1
Byron (lake), S. Dak. 298/N4
Byron, Wis. (53009) 317/K8
Byron, Wyo. (82412) 319/D1
Byron Bay, N.S.W. 97/G1
Byron Center, Mich. (49315) 250/D6
Byrum, Den. 21/E3
Byskeälv (riv.), Sweden 18/L4
Bystřice nad Pernštejnem, Czech. 41/D2
Bystřice pod Hostýnem, Czech. 41/D2
Bystrzyca Kłodzka, Poland 47/C3
Byt'ča, Czech. 41/E2
Bytom, Poland 47/B4
Bytów, Poland 47/C1
Bzura (riv.), Poland 47/D2

C

Caacupé, Par. 144/B6
Caaguazú (dept.), Par. 144/E5
Caaguazú, Par. 144/E5
Caamaño (sound), Br. Col. 184/C4
Caapucú, Par. 144/D6
Caatingas (for.), Braz., 120/F3
Caazapá (dept.), Par. 144/D6
Caazapá, Par. 144/D6
Caba, Phil. 82/C2
Cabadbaran, Phil. 82/E6
Cabaiguán, Cuba 158/E2
Cabalasan (mt.), Phil. 82/E5
Cabalian, Phil. 82/E5
Caballero, Par. 144/B6
Caballo, N. Mex. (87931) 274/B6
Caballo (res.), N. Mex. 274/B6
Caballo (creek), Wyo. 319/G1
Caballococha, Peru 128/G4
Caballones (chan.), Cuba 158/F3
Caballos, Cuba 158/F2
Cabana, Peru 128/C7
Cabañaquinta, Spain 33/D1
Cabañas, Cuba 158/B1
Cabanatuan, Phil. 82/C3
Cabanatuan, Phil. 85/G2
Cabanes, Spain 33/F2
Cabano, Que. 172/J2
Cabaret, Haiti 158/C6
Cabarrus (co.), N.C. 281/H4
Cabazon, Calif. (92230) 204/J10
Cabbage Tree (creek), Queens. 95/D2
Cabedelo, Braz. 132/H4
Cabell (co.), W. Va. 313/B6
Cabery, Ill. (60919) 222/E3
Cabet, Pitons du (mt.), Mart. 161/C6
Cabeza del Buey, Spain 33/D3
Cabezas, Bol. 136/D6
Cabezas, Cuba 158/D1
Cabildo, Chile 138/A9
Cabimas, Ven. 124/C2
Cabin Creek, W. Va. (25035) 313/C6
Cabinda (dist.), Angola 115/B5
Cabinda, Angola 115/B5
Cabinda, 102/D5
Cabinet (mts.), Mont. 262/A2
Cabin John, Md. (20731) 245/E4
Cabin John (creek), Md. 245/E4
Cabins, W. Va. (26855) 313/H4
Cable, Minn. (†56301) 254/D5
Cable, Ohio (43009) 284/C5
Cable, Wis. (54821) 317/D3
Cable Station, Aust. 88/L5
Cabo Blanco, Peru 128/B5
Cabo de las Vírgenes, Arg. 143/C7
Cabo Delgado (dist.), Moz. 118/F2
Cabo Frio, Braz. 132/F8
Cabo Frio, Braz. 135/F3
Cabo Gracias a Dios, Nic. 154/F3
Cabonga (res.), Que. 174/B3
Cabonico, Cuba 158/J3
Cabool, Mo. (65689) 261/H8
Caboolture, Aust. 88/K1
Caborn, Ind. (†47620) 227/B9
Cabo Rojo, P. Rico 161/A2
Cabot (str.), 163/K6
Cabot, Ark. (72023) 203/F4
Cabot (str.), Canada, 146/M5
Cabot (head), Ont. 177/C2
Cabot (mt.), N.H. 268/E2
Cabot (lake), Newf. 166/B2
Cabot (str.), Newf. 166/B4
Cabot△, Vt. (05647) 268/C3
Cabot, Vt. (05647) 268/C3
Cabra, Spain 33/D4
Cabra del Santo Cristo, Spain 33/E4
Cabral, Dom. Rep. 158/D6
Cabrera, Dom. Rep. 158/E5
Cabrera (isl.), Spain 33/H3
Cabri (isl.), Mart. 161/D7
Cabri, Sask. 181/C5
Cabri (lake), Sask. 181/B4
Cabrillo Nat'l Mon., Calif. 204/H11
Cabrón (cape), Dom. Rep. 158/F5
Cabruta, Ven. 124/E4
Cabudare, Ven. 124/D3
Cabugao, Phil. 82/C2
Cabulauan (isls.), Phil. 82/C5
Cabullón (pt.), P. Rico 161/C3
Caburai (mt.), Guyana 131/A3
Cabure, Ven. 124/D2
Caçador, Braz. 132/D9
Čačak, Yugo. 45/E4
Caça Nat'l Park, Moz. 118/E3
Caçapava, Braz. 135/D3
Caçapava do Sul, Braz. 132/C10
Cacapon (riv.), W. Va. 313/J4
Cáceres (mts.), Bol. 136/F6
Cáceres, Col. 126/C4
Cáceres, Braz. 132/B7
Cáceres (prov.), Spain 33/C3
Cáceres, Spain 33/C3
Cachapoal (riv.), Chile 138/G5
Cache (riv.), Ark. 203/H3
Cache (riv.), Ill. 222/D6
Cache, Okla. (73527) 288/J5
Cache (creek), Okla. 288/K6
Cache (co.), Utah 304/C2
Cache Bay, Ont. 177/D1
Cache Creek, Br. Col. 184/G5
Cache Junction, Utah (84304) 304/C2
Cache la Poudre (riv.), Colo. 208/H1
Cacheu, Port. Guin. 106/A6
Cachi, Arg. 143/C2
Cachina, Quebrada (riv.), Chile 138/A5
Cachipo, Ven. 124/E3
Cachoeira, Braz., 120/F4
Cachoeira, Braz. 132/G6
Cachoeira do Arari, Braz. 132/D3
Cachoeira do Sul, Braz. 132/C10
Cachoeiro de Itapemirim, Braz. 132/G8
Cachorras, Col. 126/D8
Cachos (pt.), Chile 138/A6
Cachuela Esperanza, Bol. 136/C2
Cachuma (lake), Calif. 204/F9
Cacocum, Cuba 156/C2
Cacocum, Cuba 158/H3
Cacolo, Angola 115/C6
Caconda, Angola 115/B6
Cactus (range), Nev. 266/E5
Cactus, Texas (79013) 302/C1
Cactus Lake, Sask. 181/B3
Cacuri, Ven. 124/F5
Cacuso, Angola 115/C5
Čadca, Czech. 41/E2
Caddo (riv.), Ark. 203/D5
Caddo (par.), La. 238/C1
Caddo (lake), La. 238/B1
Caddo (co.), Okla. 288/K4
Caddo, Okla. (74729) 288/O6
Caddo, Texas (76029) 302/F5
Caddo (lake), Texas 302/L5
Caddo Gap, Ark. (71935) 203/C5
Caddo Mills‡, Texas (75005) 302/H4
Cade, La. (70519) 238/G6
Cadereyta de Montes, Mex. 150/K6
Cadereyta Jiménez, Mex. 150/K4
Cader Idris (mts.), Wales 13/D5
Cades, S.C. (29518) 296/H4
Cades, Tenn. (38319) 237/D9
Cades Cove, Tenn. (†37882) 237/O9
Cadet, Mo. (63630) 261/L6
Cadibarrawirracanna (lake), S. Aust. 94/D3
Cadillac, Que. 174/B3
Cadillac, Mich. (49601) 250/D4
Cadillac, Sask. 181/D6
Cadiz, Calif. (92319) 204/K9
Cadiz (lake), Calif. 204/K9
Cadiz, Ind. (†47362) 227/G5
Cadiz, Ky. (42211) 237/F7
Cadiz, Phil. 82/D5
Cadiz, Ohio (43907) 284/J5
Cádiz (gulf), Port. 33/C4
Cádiz (gulf), Spain, 7/D5
Cádiz, Spain, 7/D5
Cádiz (prov.), Spain 33/D4
Cádiz, Spain 33/C4
Cádiz (gulf), Spain 33/C4
Cadogan, Alta. 182/E3
Cadogan△, Pa. (16212) 294/C4
Cadomin, Alta. 182/B3
Cadott, Wis. (54727) 317/D6
Cadotte (lake), Alta. 182/B1
Cadotte (riv.), Alta. 182/B1
Cadotte Lake, Alta. 182/B1
Cadron (creek), Ark. 203/F3
Caduruan (pt.), Phil. 82/D5
Cadwell, Ga. (31009) 216/G6
Cadyville, N.Y. (12918) 276/N1
Caen, France 28/C3
Caerleon, Wales 13/E6
Caernarvon, 10/D4
Caernarvon (bay), 10/D4
Caernarvon, Wales 13/C4
Caernarvon (bay), Wales 13/C4
Caernarvonshire (co.), Wales 13/C5
Caerphilly, 10/E5
Caerphilly, Wales 13/D6
Caesar, Miss. (†39466) 256/E9
Caesars Head, S.C. (†29635) 296/B1
Caeté, Braz. 135/E1
Caetité, Braz. 132/F6
Cafayate, Arg. 143/C2
Cafelândia, Braz. 135/B2
Cagayan (prov.), Phil. 82/C1
Cagayan (isls.), Phil. 82/C6
Cagayan (riv.), Phil. 82/C2
Cagayan (isls.), Phil. 85/F4
Cagayancillo, Phil. 82/C6
Cagayan de Oro, Phil. 82/E6
Cagayan de Oro, Phil. 85/G4
Cagayan Sulu (isl.), Phil. 82/B7
Cagayan Sulu (isl.), Phil. 85/F4
Cagle, Tenn. (†37327) 237/L10
Cagli, Italy 34/D3
Cagliari, Italy, 7/E5
Cagliari (prov.), Italy 34/B5
Cagliari, Italy 34/B5
Cagliari (gulf), Italy 34/B5
Cagua (vol.), Phil. 82/D1
Cagua, Ven. 124/E2
Caguán (riv.), Col. 126/C7
Caguas, P. Rico 156/G1
Caguas, P. Rico 161/E2
Caha (mts.), Ire. 17/B8
Cahaba, Ala. (†36767) 194/D6
Cahaba (riv.), Ala. 194/D5
Cahabón, Guat. 154/C3
Cahir, 10/B4
Cahir, Ire. 17/F7
Cahirciveen, 10/A5
Cahirciveen, Ire. 17/A8
Cahokia, Ill. (62206) 222/B6
Cahone, Colo. (81320) 208/B7
Cahore (pt.), Ire. 17/J6
Cahors, France 28/D5
Cahuapanas, Peru 128/D5
Cahuilla Ind. Res., Calif. 204/J10
Cahuinari (riv.), Col. 126/E8
Cahuita (pt.), C. Rica 154/F6
Caiapônia, Braz. 132/C7
Caibarién, Cuba 156/B2
Caibarién, Cuba 158/F2
Caibiran, Phil. 82/E5
Caicara, Ven. 124/G3
Caicara de Orinoco, Ven. 124/E4
Caicedonia, Col. 126/C5
Caicó, Braz. 132/G4
Caicos (passg.), Bah. Is. 156/D2
Caicos (bank), Turks Caicos Is. 156/D2
Caicos (isls.), Turks Caicos Is. 156/D2
Caicos (passg.), Turks Caicos Is. 156/D2
Caile, Miss. (†38754) 256/C4
Cailloma, Peru 128/G10
Caillou (bay), La. 238/J8
Caimanera, Cuba 156/C3
Caimanera, Cuba 158/J4
Cain (creek), S. Dak. 298/N5
Cainde, Angola 115/B7
Cains (riv.), N. Br. 170/D2
Cains Store, Ky. (42520) 237/M6
Cainsville, Mo. (64632) 261/E2
Cainsville, Tenn. (†37085) 237/J9
Caird Coast (reg.), Ant. 5/B17
Cairnbrook, Pa. (15924) 294/E5
Cairn Gorm (mt.), Scot. 15/J5
Cairngorm (mts.), Scot. 15/J5
Cairn Mor (mt.), Scot. 15/K5
Cairnryan, Scot. 15/G10
Cairns, Australia, 87/E7
Cairns, Aust. 88/H3
Cairns, Queens. 95/C3
Cairnsmore (mt.), Scot. 15/H9
Cairn Toul (mt.), Scot. 15/J5
Cairo, Ga. (31728) 216/D9
Cairo, Ill., 188/J3
Cairo, Ill. (62914) 222/D6
Cairo, Kans. (†67035) 232/D4
Cairo, Mo. (65239) 261/H4
Cairo, N.Y. (12413) 276/M6
Cairo, Nebr. (68824) 264/F3
Cairo (cap.), U.A.R. 102/E2
Cairo (cap.), U.A.R. 59/B4
Cairo (cap.), U.A.R. 111/J3
Cairo (cap.), U.A.R., 3/L4
Cairo, Ohio (45820) 284/B4
Cairo, Okla. (†74538) 288/O5
Cairo, W. Va. (26337) 313/D4
Caissie (pt.), N. Br. 170/F2
Caissie-Village, N. Br. 170/F2
Caister-on-Sea, Eng. 13/J5
Caistor, Eng. 13/G4
Caithness (co.), Scot. 15/J3
Caiundo, Angola 115/D6
Caiza, Bol. 136/C7
Cajabamba, Ec. 128/C3
Cajabamba, Peru 128/C6
Cajacay, Peru 128/D8
Caja de Muertos (isl.), P. Rico 161/C3
Cajamarca, Peru, 120/C3
Cajamarca (dept.), Peru 128/C6
Cajamarca, Peru 128/C6
Cajatambo, Peru 128/D8
Cajàzeiras, Braz., 120/F3
Cajàzeiras, Braz. 132/G4
Cajidiocan, Phil. 82/D4
Cajuata, Bol. 136/B5
Cajuru, Braz. 135/C2
Çal, Turkey 63/C3
Çala, Turkey 63/K2
Calabar, Nigeria 106/F7
Calabazar de Sagua, Cuba 158/E1
Calabogie, Ont. 177/H2
Calabozo, Ven. 124/E3
Calabria (reg.), Italy 34/F5
Cala Burras (pt.), Spain 33/D4
Calaceite, Spain 33/G2
Calacoto, Bol. 136/A5
Caladesi (isl.), Fla. 212/B2
Calafat, Rum. 45/F3
Calafquén (lake), Chile 138/E3
Calagnaan (isl.), Phil. 82/D5
Calagua (isls.), Phil. 82/D3
Calahoo, Alta. 182/D3
Calahorra, Spain 33/E1
Calais, Alta. 182/B2
Calais, France 28/D2
Calais (Dover) (str.), France 28/D2
Calais, Maine, 188/N1
Calais, Maine (04619) 242/J5
Calais△, Vt. (05648) 268/B3
Calais, Vt. (05648) 268/B3
Calais, France, 7/E3
Calama, Chile, 120/D5
Calama, Chile 138/B3
Calamar, Bolívar, Col. 126/C2
Calamar, Vaupés, Col. 126/D7
Calamarca, Bol. 136/A5
Calamba, Laguna, Phil. 82/C3
Calamba, Misamis Occ., Phil. 82/D6
Calamian Group (isls.), Phil. 82/B4
Calamian Group (isls.), Phil. 85/F3
Calamine, Ark. (72418) 203/H1
Calamocha, Spain 33/F2
Calamus, Iowa (52729) 229/M5
Calancasca (riv.), Switz. 39/H4
Calanda, Spain 33/F2
Calansho, Serir (des.), Libya 111/D2
Calansho Sand Sea (des.), Libya 111/D2
Calapan, Phil. 82/C4
Calapan, Phil. 85/G3
Calapooia (riv.), Oreg. 291/E3
Calapooya (mts.), Oreg. 291/E4
Călăraşi, Rum. 45/H3
Calarcá, Col. 126/C5
Calasparra, Spain 33/F3
Calatayud, Spain 33/F2
Calatorao, Spain 33/F2
Calauag, Phil. 82/D4
Calaveras (co.), Calif. 204/E5
Calaveras (res.), Calif. 204/L3
Calavite (cape), Phil. 82/C4
Calayan, Phil. 82/A2
Calayan (isl.), Phil. 82/A2
Calbayog, Phil. 82/E4
Calbe, E. Ger. 22/D3
Calbuco, Chile 138/D4
Calca, Peru 128/G9
Calcasieu (par.), La. 238/D6
Calcasieu, La. (71433) 238/E4
Calcasieu (lake), La. 238/D7
Calcasieu (passg.), La. 238/D7
Calcasieu (riv.), La. 238/E5
Calceta, Ec. 128/C3
Calcha, Bol. 136/C7
Calcha, Bol. 136/B7
Calchaquí, Arg. 143/F5
Calcis, Ala. (35039) 194/F4
Calcutta, India, 3/P4
Calcutta, India, 54/M7
Calcutta, India 68/F2
Calcutta, Ohio (43920) 284/J4
Calcutta, Sur. 131/C3
Caldas (dept.), Col. 126/C5
Caldas da Rainha, Port. 33/B3
Caldas Novas, Braz. 132/D7
Calder, Idaho (83808) 220/B2
Calder, Sask. 181/K4
Caldera, Chile, 120/C5
Caldera, Chile 138/A6
Calderas (bay), Dom. Rep. 158/D6
Calderas, Ven. 124/E3
Calderbank, Sask. 181/E5
Calderwood, Tenn. (†37801) 237/N9
Çaldiran, Turkey 63/K3
Caldwell, Ark. (72322) 203/J3
Caldwell, Idaho, 188/C2
Caldwell, Idaho (83605) 220/B6
Caldwell, Kans. (67022) 232/E4
Caldwell (co.), Ky. 237/F6
Caldwell (par.), La. 238/F2
Caldwell (co.), Mo. 261/E3
Caldwell (co.), N.C. 281/F3
Caldwell, N.J. (07006) 273/B2
Caldwell, Ohio (43724) 284/G6
Caldwell (co.), Texas 302/G8
Caldwell, Texas (77836) 302/H7
Caldwell, W. Va. (24925) 313/F7
Caldwell, Wis. (†53149) 317/J2
Caldy (isl.), Wales 13/C6
Cale, Ark. (71828) 203/D6
Cale, Ind. (†47544) 227/D7
Caledon, N. Ire. 17/H3
Caledon, S. Africa 118/G7
Caledon East, Ont. 177/E4
Caledonia, Ala. (†36753) 194/D7
Caledonia, Ont. 177/E4
Caledonia, Ill. (61011) 222/E1
Caledonia, Mich. (49316) 250/D6
Caledonia, Minn. (55921) 254/G7
Caledonia, Miss. (39740) 256/H3
Caledonia, Mo. (63631) 261/L7
Caledonia, N. Dak. (58219) 283/S5
Caledonia, N.S. 169/C4
Caledonia, N.S. 169/F3
Caledonia, N.Y. (14423) 276/E5
Caledonia, Ohio (43314) 284/D4
Caledonia, Pa. (†15868) 294/F3
Caledonia (co.), Vt. 268/C2
Caledonia, Wis. (53108) 317/L2

Canton 341

Caledonian (canal), Scot. 15/G5
Calella, Spain 33/H2
Calenzana, France 28/B6
Calera, Ala. (35040) 194/E4
Calera, Okla. (74730) 288/O7
Calera de Tango, Chile 138/G4
Calera Victor Rosales, Mex. 150/H5
Caleta Barquito, Chile 138/A6
Caleta Clarencia, Chile 138/E10
Caleta Olivia, Arg. 143/C6
Caleta Pan de Azúcar, Chile 138/A5
Caleu, Chile 138/G2
Caleufú, Arg. 143/C4
Calexico, Calif. (92231) 204/K11
Calf of Man (isl.), I. of Man 13/B3
Calgary, 163/E5
Calgary, Alta., 146/G4
Calgary, Alta. 182/C4
Calgary, Canada, 3/D3
Calhan, Colo. (80808) 208/L4
Calheta, Port. 33/A2
Calhoun (co.), Ala. 194/G3
Calhoun, Ala. (36012) 194/F6
Calhoun (co.), Ark. 203/E6
Calhoun (co.), Fla. 212/D6
Calhoun (co.), Ga. 216/C7
Calhoun, Ga. (30701) 216/C1
Calhoun (co.), Ill. 222/C4
Calhoun, Ill. (62419) 222/E5
Calhoun (co.), Iowa 229/D4
Calhoun, Ky. (42327) 237/G5
Calhoun, La. (71225) 238/F2
Calhoun (co.), Mich. 250/D6
Calhoun (co.), Miss. 256/F3
Calhoun, Mo. (65323) 261/E6
Calhoun (co.), S.C. 296/F4
Calhoun, Tenn. (37309) 237/M10
Calhoun (co.), Texas 302/H9
Calhoun (co.), W. Va. 313/D5
Calhoun City, Miss. (38916) 256/F3
Calhoun Falls, S.C. (29628) 296/B3
Cali, Col., 120/C2
Cali, Col. 126/B6
Calicito, Cuba 158/H4
Calicoan (isl.), Phil. 82/E5
Calico Rock, Ark. (72519) 203/F1
Calicut (Kozhikode), India 68/D6
Caliente, Nev. (89008) 266/G5
Caliento, Man. 179/F5
Califon, N.J. (07830) 273/D2
California, 188/B3
CALIFORNIA, 204
California, Trinidad Tobago 161/A11
California, Ky. (41007) 237/N3
California, Md. (20619) 245/M7
California (gulf), Mex., 146/G7
California (gulf), Mex. 150/D3
California, Mo. (65018) 261/H5
California, Pa. (15419) 294/C5
California (state), U.S., 146/F6
California Aqueduct, Calif. 204/E7
California City, Calif. (93501) 204/H8
California Hot Springs, Calif. (93207) 204/G8
California Junction, Iowa (†51555) 229/B5
Calimete, Cuba 158/D1
Calio, N. Dak. (58322) 283/N2
Calion, Ark. (71724) 203/E7
Calipatria, Calif. (92233) 204/K10
Calistoga, Calif. (94515) 204/C5
Calixa-Lavallée, Que. 172/J4
Calkiní, Mex. 150/O6
Call, Texas (75933) 302/L7
Callabonna (lake), S. Aust. 94/F3
Callafo, Eth. 111/H6
Callahan, Calif. (96014) 204/C2
Callahan, Fla. (32011) 212/E1
Callahan (co.), Texas 302/E5
Callalli, Peru 128/G10
Callan, 10/C4
Callan, Ire. 17/G7
Callander, 163/H6
Callander, Ont. 177/E1
Callander, 10/D2
Callander, Scot. 15/H7
Callands, Va. (24530) 307/J7
Callantsoog, Neth. 27/F3
Callao, Mo. (63534) 261/G3
Callao, Peru, 3/F6
Callao, Peru, 120/C4
Callao, Peru 128/D9
Callao (prov.), Peru 128/D9
Callao, Utah (†84034) 304/A4
Callao, Va. (22435) 307/P5
Callapa, Bol. 136/A5
Callaway, Fla. (32401) 212/D6
Callaway, Minn. (56521) 254/C3
Callaway (co.), Mo. 261/J5
Callaway, Nebr. (68825) 264/D3
Callaway, Va. (24067) 307/H7
Calle Larga, Chile 138/G2
Callender, Iowa (50523) 229/E4
Callensburg, Pa. (16213) 294/D3
Callery, Pa. (16024) 294/C4
Calleuque, Chile 138/F5
Calliaqua, St. Vincent 161/A9
Callicoon, N.Y. (12723) 276/K7
Callicoon Center, N.Y. (12724) 276/L7
Calliham, Texas (78007) 302/F9
Calling (lake), Alta. 182/D2
Calling Lake, Alta. 182/D2
Callington, Eng. 13/C7
Callis, Somalia 115/J2
Callison, S.C. (29820) 296/C3
Callosa de Ensarria, Spain 33/G3
Calloway (co.), Ky. 237/E7
Calmar, Alta. 182/D3
Calmar, Iowa (52132) 229/K2
Calmer, Ark. (†71665) 203/F6
Calne, Eng. 13/F6
Calobre, Pan. 154/G6
Caloosahatchee (riv.), Fla. 212/E5
Caloundra, Queens. 95/E5
Čalovo, Czech. 41/D3
Calpella, Calif. (95418) 204/B4
Calpet, Wyo. (†83123) 319/B3
Calpulálpan, Mex. 150/M1
Caltagirone, Italy 34/E6
Caltanissetta (prov.), Italy 34/D6
Caltanissetta, Italy 34/D6
Caluire-et-Cuire, France 28/F5
Calulo, Angola 115/C6
Calumet, Que. 172/C4
Calumet (lake), Ill. 222/B2
Calumet, Iowa (51009) 229/B3
Calumet, La. (†70538) 238/H7
Calumet, Mich., 188/J1
Calumet, Mich. (49913) 250/A1
Calumet, Minn. (55716) 254/E3
Calumet, Okla. (73014) 288/K3
Calumet (co.), Wis. 317/K7
Calumet City, Ill. (60409) 222/B2
Calumet Park, Ill. (†60601) 222/B2
Calumetville, Wis. (†53049) 317/K8
Caluquembe, Angola 115/B6
Calva, Ariz. (†85530) 198/E5
Calvados (dept.), France 28/C3
Calvary, Ga. (31729) 216/D9
Calvary, Ky. (†40033) 237/L6
Calvert, Ala. (36513) 194/B8
Calvert (isl.), Br. Col. 184/C4
Calvert, Kans. (†67622) 232/C2
Calvert (co.), Md. 245/M6
Calvert, Md. (†21911) 245/O2
Calvert, Newf. 166/D2
Calvert, Texas (77837) 302/H7
Calvert City, Ky. (42029) 237/E6
Calvert Hills, No. Terr. 93/E4
Calverton, Md. (†20705) 245/L4
Calverton, Va. (22016) 307/N3
Calverton Park‡, Mo. (†63101) 261/P2
Calvertville, Ind. (†47424) 227/D6
Calvi, France 28/B6
Calvillo, Mex. 150/H6
Calvin, Ky. (40813) 237/O7
Calvin, La. (71410) 238/E3
Calvin, N. Dak. (58323) 283/N2
Calvin, Okla. (74531) 288/O5
Calvin, W. Va. (26660) 313/E6
Calvinia, 102/D8
Calvinia, S. Africa 118/B6
Calwa, Calif. (93745) 204/F7
Calypso, N.C. (28325) 281/N4
Calzada de Calatrava, Spain 33/E3
Camacho, Bol. 136/C7
Camaguán, Ven. 124/E3
Camagüey, Cuba, 146/K7
Camagüey, Cuba 156/B2
Camagüey (prov.), Cuba 158/G2
Camagüey, Cuba 158/G3
Camagüey (arch.), Cuba 158/G2
Camaiore, Italy 34/C3
Camajuaní, Cuba 158/E2
Camak, Ga. (30807) 216/G4
Camaná, Peru 128/F11
Camanche (res.), Calif. 204/C9
Camanche, Iowa (52730) 229/N5
Camano (isl.), Wash. 310/C2
Camanongue, Angola 115/D6
Camaquã, Braz. 132/C10
Câmara de Lobos, Port. 33/A2
Camargo, Bol. 136/C7
Camargo, Ill. (61919) 222/E4
Camargo, Okla. (73835) 288/H2
Camarillo, Calif. (93010) 204/F9
Camarillo Heights‡, Calif. (†93010) 204/F9
Camarines Norte (prov.), Phil. 82/D3
Camarines Sur (prov.), Phil. 82/D4
Camarón (cape), Hond. 154/E2
Camarones, Arg., 120/D7
Camarones, Arg. 143/C5
Camarones, Chile 138/B2
Camarones (riv.), Chile 138/A2
Camas (co.), Idaho 220/D6
Camas, Idaho (†83425) 220/F5
Camas (creek), Idaho 220/D5
Camas (creek), Idaho 220/D6
Camas (creek), Idaho 220/F5
Camas, Wash. (98607) 310/C5
Camas Prairie, Mont. (†59857) 262/B3
Camas Valley, Oreg. (97416) 291/D4
Camatagua, Ven. 124/E3
Camatindi, Bol. 136/D7
Ca Mau (pt.), S. Vietnam 72/E5
Cambará, Braz. 132/B8
Cambará, Braz. 135/A3
Cambay, India 68/C4
Cambay (gulf), India 68/C4
Camberwell, Aust. 88/M7
Camberwell, Vic. 97/J5
Cambo, Angola 115/C5
Cambo (riv.), Angola 115/C5
Cambodia, 3/Q5
Cambodia, 54/O8
CAMBODIA, 72
Camborne-Redruth, 10/D5
Camborne-Redruth, Eng. 13/B7
Cambra, Pa. (18611) 294/K3
Cambrai, France 28/E2
Cambria, Alta. 182/D4
Cambria, Calif. (93428) 204/D8
Cambria, Ill. (62915) 222/D6
Cambria, Ind. (†46041) 227/D4
Cambria, Iowa (50045) 229/G7
Cambria, Mich. (†49242) 250/E7
Cambria, Minn. (†56073) 254/D6
Cambria (co.), Pa. 294/E4
Cambria, Wis. (53923) 317/H8
Cambrian (mts.), Wales 13/D5
Cambrian Heights‡, Calif. (†95101) 204/K3
Cambridge, 10/G4
Cambridge, Jam. 158/H6
Cambridge, Eng. 13/H5
Cambridge, Idaho (83610) 220/B5
Cambridge, Ill. (61238) 222/C2
Cambridge, Iowa (50046) 229/G5
Cambridge, Kans. (67023) 232/F4
Cambridge‡, Ky. (†40201) 237/K4
Cambridge▵, Maine (04923) 242/E5
Cambridge, Mass. (†02138) 249/C7
Cambridge (res.), Mass. 249/B6
Cambridge, Md. (21613) 245/O6
Cambridge, Minn. (55008) 254/E5
Cambridge, N. Br. 170/E3
Cambridge, N.Y. (12816) 276/O4
Cambridge, N.Z. 101/E2
Cambridge, Nebr. (69022) 264/D4
Cambridge, Ohio (43725) 284/G5
Cambridge, Tas. 99/D4
Cambridge▵, Vt. (05444) 268/B2
Cambridge, Vt. (05444) 268/B2
Cambridge, Wis. (53523) 317/H9
Cambridge Bay, 163/F2
Cambridge Bay, Canada, 4/B15
Cambridge Bay, N.W.T. 187/H3
Cambridge City, Ind. (47327) 227/G5
Cambridgeport, Vt. (05141) 268/B5
Cambridgeshire and Isle of Ely (co.), Eng. 13/H5
Cambridge Springs, Pa. (16403) 294/C2
Cambulo, Angola 115/D5
Cambuslang, Scot. 15/D2
Camden, 10/B5
Camden, Ala. (36726) 194/D7
Camden (bay), Alaska 196/K1
Camden, Ark. (71701) 203/E6
Camden, Aust. 88/K4
Camden, Del. (19934) 245/R4
Camden (co.), Ga. 216/J9
Camden, Ill. (62319) 222/C3
Camden, Ind. (46917) 227/D3
Camden▵, Maine (04843) 242/F7
Camden, Maine (04843) 242/F7
Camden, Mich. (49232) 250/E7
Camden, Miss. (39045) 256/E5
Camden (co.), Mo. 261/G6
Camden, Mo. (64017) 261/D4
Camden (co.), N.C. 281/S2
Camden, N.C. (27921) 281/S2
Camden, N.J., 188/M3
Camden (co.), N.J. 273/D4
Camden, N.J. (*08101) 273/B3
Camden, N.S.W. 97/F4
Camden, N.Y. (13316) 276/J4
Camden, Ohio (45311) 284/A6
Camden, S.C. (29020) 296/F3
Camden, Tenn. (38320) 237/E8
Camden, Texas (75934) 302/K7
Camden, W. Va. (26338) 313/E4
Camden on Gauley, W. Va. (26208) 313/E6
Camden Park, St. Vincent 161/A9
Camden Point, Mo. (64018) 261/C4
Camdenton, Mo. (65020) 261/G6
Cameia, Angola 115/D6
Camelford, Eng. 13/C7
Çameli, Turkey 63/C4
Camels Hump (mt.), Vt. 268/B3
Cameo, Sask. 181/E2
Camerino, Italy 34/D3
Cameron, Ariz. (86020) 198/D3
Cameron (peak), Colo. 208/H1
Cameron, Ill. (61423) 222/C3
Cameron (par.), La. 238/D7
Cameron, La. (70631) 238/D7
Cameron, Mo. (64429) 261/D3
Cameron, Mont. (59720) 262/E5
Cameron, N.C. (28326) 281/L4
Cameron (isl.), N.W.T. 187/H2
Cameron, N.Y. (14819) 276/F6
Cameron (mts.), N.Z. 101/A7
Cameron, Ohio (43914) 284/J6
Cameron, Okla. (74932) 288/T4
Cameron (co.), Pa. 294/F3
Cameron, Pa. (†15834) 294/F3
Cameron, S.C. (29030) 296/F4
Cameron (co.), Texas 302/G11
Cameron, Texas (76520) 302/H7
Cameron, W. Va. (26033) 313/E3
Cameron, Wis. (54822) 317/C5
Cameron Falls, Ont. 177/H5
Cameron Highlands, Malaysia 72/D6
Cameroon, 3/K5
CAMEROON, 115/B2
CAMEROON, 102/D4
Cameroon (mt.), Cameroon 115/A3
Cameroon (mt.), 102/D4
Camerota, Italy 34/E4
Cametá, Braz., 120/E3
Cametá, Braz. 132/D3
Camiguin, Cagayan (isl.), Phil. 82/B3
Camiguin, Misamis Or. (isl.), Phil. 82/E6
Camiling, Phil. 82/C3
Camilla, Ga. (31730) 216/D8
Camillus, N.Y. (13031) 276/H4
Camiña, Chile 138/B2
Camiña, Quebrada (riv.), Chile 138/B2
Caminha, Port. 33/B2
Camino, Calif. (95709) 204/E5
Camiri, Bol. 136/D7
Camlachie, Ont. 177/B4
Çamlidere, Turkey 63/E2
Cammack, Ind. (†47302) 227/G4
Cammack Village, Ark. (†72201) 203/E4
Cammal, Pa. (17723) 294/H3
Camoapa, Nic. 154/E4
Camocim, Braz., 120/F3
Camocim, Braz. 132/F3
Camooweal, Aust. 88/F4
Camooweal, Queens. 95/A3
Camopi, Fr. Gui. 131/E4
Camopi (riv.), Fr. Gui. 131/E4
Camorta (isl.), India 68/G7
Camoruco, Col. 126/E4
Camotes (isls.), Phil. 82/E5
Camotes (sea), Phil. 82/E5
Camp (creek), Ind. 227/E6
Camp (creek), Oreg. 291/J4
Camp (co.), Texas 302/K5
Campaign, Tenn. (38550) 237/K9
Campamento, Urug. 145/C1
Campana, Arg. 143/G6
Campana (isl.), Chile, 120/C7
Campana (isl.), Chile 138/D7
Campanario, Cerro (mt.), Arg. 143/C4
Campanario, Cerro (mt.), Chile 138/A10
Campanario, Spain 33/D3
Campanha, Braz. 135/D2
Campania, Ga. (†30814) 216/H4
Campania (reg.), Italy 34/E4
Camp A. P. Hill, Va. 307/O4
Campaspe (riv.), Vic. 97/C5
Campbell, Ala. (36727) 194/C7
Campbell‡, Alaska (†99901) 196/N2
Campbell, Calif. (95008) 204/K3
Campbell (co.), Ky. 237/N3
Campbell, Minn. (56522) 254/B4
Campbell, Mo. (63933) 261/M9
Campbell, N.Y. (14821) 276/F6
Campbell (cape), N.Z. 101/E4
Campbell, Nebr. (68932) 264/F4
Campbell, Ohio (44405) 284/J3
Campbell (hill), Ohio 284/C5
Campbell (co.), S. Dak. 298/J2
Campbell (co.), Tenn. 237/N8
Campbell (co.), Va. 307/K6
Campbell (co.), Wyo. 319/G1
Campbell (mt.), Yukon 187/E3
Campbellford, Ont. 177/G3
Campbell Hall, N.Y. (10916) 276/M8
Campbell Hill, Ill. (62916) 222/D6
Campbell Island, Br. Col. 184/C4
Campbellpore, Pak. 68/C2
Campbell River, Br. Col. 184/E5
Campbells (lake), Oreg. 291/H5
Campbellsburg, Ind. (47108) 227/E7
Campbellsburg, Ky. (40011) 237/L3
Campbellsport, Wis. (†53019) 317/K8
Campbell Station, Ark. (†72473) 203/H2
Campbellsville, Ky. (42718) 237/L6
Campbellton, 163/K6
Campbellton, Fla. (32426) 212/D5
Campbellton, Mo. (†63068) 261/K5
Campbellton, N. Br. 170/D1
Campbellton, Newf. 166/D4
Campbellton, P.E.I. 169/D2
Campbellton, Texas (78008) 302/F9
Campbelltown, 163/E5
Campbelltown, Aust. 88/L3
Campbelltown, N.S.W. 97/F4
Campbelltown, S. Aust. 94/B7
Campbelltown‡, Pa. (17010) 294/J5
Campbell Town, Tas. 99/D3
Campbeltown, 10/C3
Campbeltown, Scot. 15/E9
Camp Creek, Alta. 182/C2
Camp Creek, W. Va. (25820) 313/D7
Camp Crook, S. Dak. (57724) 298/B2
Camp Dennison, Ohio (45111) 284/D9
Camp Dix, Ky. (41127) 237/P3
Camp Douglas, Wis. (54618) 317/F8
Campeche (bay), Mex., 146/J7
Campeche (state), Mex. 150/O7
Campeche, Mex. 150/O7
Campeche (bank), Mex. 150/O6
Campeche (bay), Mex. 150/N7
Campechuela, Cuba 158/G4
Camper, Man. 179/D3
Camperdown, Vic. 97/C6
Camperville, Man. 179/B2
Camp Grove, Ill. (61424) 222/D2
Camp Hale, Colo. 208/G4
Camp Hill, Ala. (36850) 194/G5
Camp Hill, Queens. 95/E3
Camp Hill, Pa. (17011) 294/H5
Campiglia Marittima, Italy 34/C3
Campillo de Altobuey, Spain 33/F3
Campillos, Spain 33/D4
Campina Grande, Braz. 132/G4
Campinas, Braz., 120/F5
Campinas, Braz. 132/E8
Campinas, Braz. 135/C3
Campina Verde, Braz. 132/D7
Camp Lake, Wis. (53109) 317/K10
Camp Lejeune, N.C. 281/P5
Campli, Italy 34/D3
Camp Mackall, N.C. 281/K5
Camp Morton, Man. 179/F4
Camp Nelson, Calif. (93208) 204/G7
Campo, Calif. (92006) 204/J11
Campo, Colo. (81029) 208/O8
Campo, Cameroon 115/B3
Campoalegre, Col. 126/C6
Campobasso (prov.), Italy 34/E4
Campobasso, Italy 34/E4
Campobello (isl.), N. Br. 170/D4
Campobello, S.C. (29322) 296/C1
Campo Belo, Braz. 132/E8
Campo Belo, Braz. 135/D2
Campo Claro, Ven. 124/G2
Campo de Criptana, Spain 33/E3
Campo de la Cruz, Col. 126/C2
Campo Florido, Braz. 135/B1
Campo Formoso, Braz. 132/F5
Campo Gallo, Arg. 143/D2
Campo Grande, Braz., 120/E5
Campo Grande, Braz. 132/C8
Campo Ind. Res., Calif. 204/J11
Campo Largo, Braz. 135/B4
Campo Maior, Braz. 132/F4
Campo Maior, Port. 33/C3
Campos, Braz., 120/F5
Campos (reg.), Braz., 120/F4
Campos, Braz. 132/F8
Campos, Braz. 135/F2
Campos Altos, Braz. 135/C1
Campo Seco, Calif. (95226) 204/D9
Campo-Tencia (peak), Switz. 39/G4
Campo Tures, Italy 34/C1
Camp-Perrin, Haiti 158/A6
Camp Point, Ill. (62320) 222/B3
Camp Sherman, Oreg. (97730) 291/F3
Campsie, Alta. 182/C2
Camp Springs, Md. (20031) 245/G6
Campti, La. (71411) 238/D3
Campton, Ga. (30626) 216/E3
Campton, Ky. (41301) 237/O5
Campton▵, N.H. (03223) 268/D4
Campton, N.H. (03223) 268/D4
Camptown, Pa. (18815) 294/K2
Campus, Ill. (60920) 222/E2
Camp Verde, Ariz. (86322) 198/D4
Campville, Fla. (†32640) 212/D2
Camp Wood, Texas (78833) 302/D8
Cam Ranh, S. Vietnam 72/F5
Cam Ranh (bay), S. Vietnam 72/F5
Camrose, 163/E5
Camrose, Alta. 182/D3
Camsell (riv.), N.W.T. 187/G3
Camsell Portage, Sask. 181/L2
Camuy, P. Rico 156/F1
Camuy, P. Rico 161/B1
Camuy (riv.), P. Rico 161/B1
Çan, Turkey 63/B2
Čaňa, Czech. 41/F2
Cana (pt.), Dom. Rep. 158/F6
Cana, Sask. 181/J5
Cana, Va. (24317) 307/G7
Canaan▵, Conn. (06018) 210/B1
Canaan, Conn. (06018) 210/B1
Canaan (mt.), Conn. 210/B1
Canaan, Ind. (47224) 227/G7
Canaan▵, Maine (04924) 242/D6
Canaan, Miss. (38612) 256/F1
Canaan (riv.), N. Br. 170/E2
Canaan▵, N.H. (03741) 268/C4
Canaan, N.H. (03741) 268/C4
Canaan, N.Y. (12029) 276/O6
Canaan▵, Vt. (05903) 268/D2
Canaan, Vt. (05903) 268/D2
Canaan Center, N.H. (†03741) 268/C4
Canaan Road, N. Br. 170/E2
Canaan Station, N. Br. 170/E2
Canada, 3/D3
Canada, 4/C14
Canada, 146/G4
CANADA, 163
Canada, La (mt.), Cuba 158/B2
Canada, Ky. (41519) 237/S5
Canada (bay), Newf. 166/C3
Cañada de Gómez, Arg. 143/F6
Cañada Honda, Arg. 143/C3
Cañada Nieto, Urug. 145/B4
Cañada Oruro, Par. 144/A3
Canadensis, Pa. (18325) 294/M3
Canadian (riv.), 188/F3
Canadian (riv.), N. Mex. 274/F3
Canadian (co.), Okla. 288/K3
Canadian, Okla. (74425) 288/P4
Canadian (riv.), Okla. 288/O4
Canadian, Texas (79014) 302/D2
Canadian (riv.), Texas 302/B2
Canadian (riv.), U.S., 146/J6
Canadice (lake), N.Y. 276/E5
Canadys, S.C. (29433) 296/F5
Canagua (riv.), Ven. 124/C3
Canajoharie, N.Y. (13317) 276/L5
Çanakkale, Turkey 59/A2
Çanakkale (prov.), Turkey 63/B2
Çanakkale, Turkey 63/B6
Çanakkale Boğazi (str.), Turkey 59/A2
Çanakkale Boğazi (Dardanelles) (str.), Turkey 63/B6
Canal (creek), Alta. 182/E5
Canal Flats, Br. Col. 184/K5
Canal Fulton, Ohio (44614) 284/H4
Canalou, Mo. (63828) 261/N9
Canal Point, Fla. (33438) 212/F5
Canals, Arg. 143/D3
Canal Winchester, Ohio (43110) 284/E6
Canal Zone, 146/L8
CANAL ZONE, 154/G6
Canandaigua, N.Y. (14424) 276/F5
Canandaigua (lake), N.Y. 276/F5
Cananea, Mex. 150/D1
Cananéia, Braz. 132/E9
Cananéia, Braz. 135/C4
Cananova, Cuba 158/K3
Cañar (prov.), Ec. 128/C4
Cañar, Ec. 128/C4
Canaries, St. Lucia 161/G6
Canaries, Piton (mt.), St. Lucia 161/G6
Canarreos, Los (arch.), Cuba 158/C2
Canary (isls.), 102/A2
Canary, Oreg. (†97493) 291/D4
Canary (isls.), Spain, 3/H4
Canary (isls.), Spain 33/B4
Canary (isls.), Spain 106/A3
Cañas, Bol. 136/C8
Cañas, C. Rica 154/E5
Cañas, Cuba 158/B1
Cañas (range), Urug. 145/C2
Canaseraga, N.Y. (14822) 276/E6
Cañasgordas, Col. 126/B4
Canastota, N.Y. (13032) 276/J4
Canatlán, Mex. 150/G4
Canaveral (Kennedy) (cape), Fla., 188/L5
Canaveral (Kennedy) (cape), Fla. 212/F3
Canavieiras, Braz. 132/G6
Cañazas, Pan. 154/G6
Canbelego, N.S.W. 97/D2
Canberra (cap.), Australia, 87/F9
Canberra (cap.), Australia, 88/H6
Canberra (cap.), Australia, A.C.T. 97/E4
Canberra (cap.), Australia, 3/S7
Canby, Calif. (96015) 204/E2
Canby, Minn. (56220) 254/B6
Canby, Oreg. (97013) 291/B2
Cancún, Mex. 150/Q6
Candala, Somalia 115/J1
Candarave, Peru 128/G11
Çandarli (gulf), Turkey 63/B3
Candás, Spain 33/D1
Candela, Mex. 150/J3
Candelaria, Bol. 136/F5
Candelaria (riv.), Bol. 136/F5
Candelaria, Cuba 158/B1
Candelaria (riv.), Mex. 150/O8
Candelaria, Phil. 82/B3
Candelaria, Texas (†79843) 302/C12
Candelaria, Ven. 124/F4
Candeleda, Spain 33/D2
Candelero (pt.), P. Rico 161/F2
Candia (Iráklion), Greece 45/G8
Candia▵, N.H. (03034) 268/E5
Candia, N.H. (03034) 268/E5
Candiac, Que. 172/J4
Candiac, Sask. 181/H5
Cândido Mendes, Braz. 132/E3
Çandir, Turkey 63/F3
Candle (lake), Sask. 181/F2
Candle Lake, Sask. 181/F2
Candler, Fla. (†32624) 212/E2
Candler (co.), Ga. 216/H6
Candler, N.C. (28715) 281/D3
Candlewood (lake), Conn. 210/A2
Candlewood, N.J. (†08701) 273/E3
Cando, N. Dak. (58324) 283/M3
Cando, Sask. 181/C3
Candon, Phil. 82/C2
Candor, N.C. (27229) 281/K4
Candor, N.Y. (13743) 276/H6
Cane (creek), Utah 304/E5
Canea (Khaniá), Greece 45/G8
Caneadea, N.Y. (14717) 276/D6
Canebay, V.I.(U.S.) 161/E3
Cane Beds, Ariz. (†86022) 198/B2
Canebrake, W. Va. (24819) 313/C8
Caneel (bay), V.I.(U.S.) 161/B4
Canehill, Ark. (72717) 203/B2
Canelones (dept.), Urug. 145/D5
Canelones, Urug. 145/B6
Canelos, Ec. 128/D3
Cañete, Chile 138/D2
Cañete, Spain 33/F2
Cane Valley, Ky. (42720) 237/L6
Caney, Cuba 158/J4
Caney, Kans. (67333) 232/G4
Caney, Ky. (41407) 237/P5
Caney, Okla. (74533) 288/O6
Caney (riv.), Okla. 288/O1
Caney Fork (riv.), Tenn. 237/L9
Caneyville, Ky. (42721) 237/J6
Canfield, Ark. (71829) 203/C7
Canfield, Ont. 177/E4
Canfield, Ohio (44406) 284/J3
Canford, Br. Col. 184/G5
Cangallo, Peru 128/E9
Cangamba, Angola 115/C6
Cangamba, 102/D6
Cangas, Spain 33/B1
Cangas de Narcea, Spain 33/C1
Cangas de Onís, Spain 33/D1
Canguaretama, Braz. 132/H4
Caniapiscau (lake), Que. 174/D2
Caniapiscau (riv.), Que. 174/D1
Caniapiscau (riv.), 163/K4
Caniçado, Moz. 118/E4
Canicatti, Italy 34/E6
Canigao (chan.), Phil. 82/E5
Canik (mts.), Turkey 63/G2
Caniles, Spain 33/E4
Canim (lake), Br. Col. 184/G4
Canim Lake, Br. Col. 184/G4
Canindé, Braz. 132/G4
Canistear (res.), N.J. 273/E1
Canisteo, N.Y. (14823) 276/E6
Canisteo (riv.), N.Y. 276/F6
Canistota, S. Dak. (57012) 298/P6
Cañitas de Felipe Pescador, Mex. 150/H5
Canjáyar, Spain 33/E4
Canje (riv.), Guyana 131/C2
Canjilon, N. Mex. (87515) 274/C2
Çankaya, Turkey 63/E3
Çankiri, Turkey 59/B1
Çankiri (prov.), Turkey 63/E2
Çankiri, Turkey 63/E2
Cankton, La. (†70584) 238/F6
Canlaon (peak), Phil. 82/D5
Canmer, Ky. (42722) 237/K6
Canmore, Alta. 182/C4
Canna (isl.), 10/C2
Canna (isl.), Scot. 15/C5
Canna (sound), Scot. 15/C6
Cannalville, Ohio (†43777) 284/F6
Cannanore, India 68/C6
Cannelburg, Ind. (47519) 227/C7
Cannel City, Ky. (41408) 237/P5
Cannelles (pt.), St. Lucia 161/G7
Cannelles (riv.), St. Lucia 161/G6
Cannelton, Ind. (47520) 227/D9
Cannes, France 28/G6
Cannich, Scot. 15/G5
Canning (riv.), Alaska 196/J1
Canning, N.S. 169/D3
Canning, S. Dak. (57524) 298/K5
Cannington, Ont. 177/E3
Cannock, 10/G2
Cannock, Eng. 13/E5
Cannon, Del. (19935) 245/R6
Cannon (co.), Tenn. 237/J9
Cannon A.F.B., N. Mex. 274/F4
Cannon Ball, N. Dak. (58528) 283/J7
Cannonball (riv.), N. Dak. 283/G7
Cannon Beach, Oreg. (97110) 291/D2
Cannondale, Conn. (†06897) 210/B4
Cannon Falls, Minn. (55009) 254/F6
Cannonsburg, Miss. (†39120) 256/B7
Cannonsville (res.), N.Y. 276/K6
Cannonville, Utah (84718) 304/B6
Cann River, Vic. 97/E5
Caño (isl.), C. Rica 154/F6
Canoas, Braz. 132/D10
Canobie Lake, N.H. (†03079) 268/E6
Caño Capure (riv.), Ven. 124/H3
Canoe, Ala. (36514) 194/D8
Canoe, Br. Col. 184/H5
Canoe (riv.), Br. Col. 184/H4
Canoe (lake), Sask. 181/L3
Canoga Park, Calif. (*91303) 204/B10
Canoinhas, Braz. 132/D9
Caño Macareo (riv.), Ven. 124/H3
Caño Mánamo (riv.), Ven. 124/G3
Canon, Ga. (30520) 216/F2
Canonbie, Scot. 15/K9
Canonchet, R.I. (†02833) 249/H7
Canon City, Colo. (81212) 208/J6
Canones, N. Mex. (87516) 274/C2
Canonsburg, Pa. (15317) 294/B5
Canoochee, Ga. (30416) 216/H5
Canoose (lake), N. Br. 170/C3
Canopus, Sask. 181/E6
Canora, Sask. 181/J4
Canosa di Puglia, Italy 34/E4
Canouan (isl.), St. Vincent 156/G4
Canova, S. Dak. (57321) 298/O6
Canóvanas (riv.), P. Rico 161/E1
Canowindra, N.S.W. 97/E3
Canquella, Bol. 136/A7
Cansa (str.), N.S. 169/G3
Canso, N.S. 169/H3
Canso (cape), N.S. 169/H3
Canta, Peru 128/D8
Cantabrian (range), Spain 33/D1
Cantagalo, Braz. 135/E3
Cantal (dept.), France 28/E5
Cantalejo, Spain 33/D2
Cantanhede, Port. 33/B2
Cantaura, Ven. 124/F3
Canterbury, 10/G5
Canterbury▵, Conn. (06331) 210/H2
Canterbury, Del. (†19943) 245/R4
Canterbury, Eng. 13/J6
Canterbury, N. Br. 170/C3
Canterbury▵, N.H. (03224) 268/D5
Canterbury, N.S.W. 97/J3
Canterbury (bight), N.Z. 101/D6
Canterbury (prov. dist.), N.Z. 101/C5
Can Tho, S. Vietnam 72/E5
Cantil, Calif. (93519) 204/H8
Cantiles (cay), Cuba 158/C3
Cantillana, Alto de (mt.), Chile 138/G4
Cantin (cape), Mor. 106/C2
Canto del Agua, Chile 138/A7
Canto do Buriti, Braz. 132/F5
Canton, China, 3/Q4
Canton, China, 54/P7
Canton, China 77/H7
Canton▵, Conn. (06019) 210/D1
Canton (isl.), Gilb. and Ell., 87/J6

Cedar 343

Carryville, Ark. (†72454) 203/K1
Çarşamba, Turkey 63/G2
Carseland, Alta. 182/D4
Carson, Ala. (†36548) 194/C8
Carson, Calif. (90744) 204/C11
Carson, Iowa (51525) 229/C6
Carson, Miss. (39427) 256/E7
Carson, N. Dak. (58529) 283/H7
Carson, N. Mex. (87517) 274/D2
Carson (lake), Nev. 266/C3
Carson (riv.), Nev. 266/B3
Carson (sink), Nev. 266/C3
Carson (co.), Texas 302/C2
Carson, Va. (23830) 307/O6
Carson, Wash. (98610) 310/D5
Carson City, Mich. (48811) 250/E5
Carson City (city) (co.), Nev. 266/D3
Carson City (cap.), Nev., 146/G6
Carson City (cap.), Nev., 188/C3
Carson City (cap.), Nev., (89701) 266/B3
Carson Lake, Ark. (†72370) 203/K2
Carson Sink (depr.), Nev., 188/C3
Carsonville, Ga. (†31827) 216/D5
Carsonville, Mich. (48419) 250/G5
Carsphairn, Scot. 15/H9
Carstairs, Alta. 182/D4
Carstairs Junction, Scot. 15/J8
Carswell A.F.B., Texas 302/E2
Cartagena, Chile 138/F3
Cartagena, Col., 120/C1
Cartagena, Col. 126/C2
Cartagena, Cuba 158/D2
Cartagena, Spain, 7/D5
Cartagena, Spain 33/F4
Cartago, C. Rica 154/F6
Cartago, Calif. (93520) 204/G7
Cartago, Col. 126/B5
Carta Valley, Texas (78835) 302/D8
Cartaxo, Port. 33/B3
Cartecay, Ga. (†30540) 216/D1
Carter (co.), Ky. 237/P4
Carter, Ky. (41128) 237/P4
Carter (co.), Mo. 261/L9
Carter (co.), Mont. 262/M5
Carter, Mont. (59420) 262/E3
Carter (co.), Okla. 288/M6
Carter, Okla. (73627) 288/H4
Carter, S. Dak. (57526) 298/J7
Carter (co.), Tenn. 237/S8
Carter, Tenn. (†37643) 237/S8
Carter, Wis. (†54566) 317/J5
Carter, Wyo. (†82937) 319/B4
Carter Dome (mt.), N.H. 268/E3
Carteret (co.), N.C. 281/R5
Carteret, N.J. (07008) 273/E2
Carter Fell (mt.), Eng. 13/E2
Carter Lake, Iowa (†68101) 229/B6
Carter Nine, Okla. (†74633) 288/N1
Carters, Ga. (30704) 216/C1
Carters (res.), Ga. 216/C1
Cartersburg, Ind. (46114) 227/E5
Cartersville, Ga. (30120) 216/C2
Cartersville, Iowa (†50469) 229/G2
Cartersville, Mont. (†59347) 262/K4
Cartersville, Okla. (74934) 288/S4
Cartersville, S.C. (†29161) 296/H3
Cartersville, Va. (23027) 307/M5
Carterton, N.Z. 101/E4
Carterville, Ill. (62918) 222/D6
Carterville, Mo. (64835) 261/D8
Carthage, Ark. (71725) 203/E5
Carthage, Ill. (62321) 222/B3
Carthage, Ind. (46115) 227/F5
Carthage▵, Maine (†04224) 242/C6
Carthage, Maine (†04224) 242/C6
Carthage, Miss. (39051) 256/E5
Carthage, Mo. (64836) 261/D8
Carthage, N.C. (28327) 281/K4
Carthage, N.Y. (13619) 276/J3
Carthage, S. Dak. (57323) 298/O5
Carthage, Tenn. (37030) 237/K8
Carthage, Texas (75633) 302/K5
Cartier (isl.), Aust. 88/C2
Cartier, Ont. 177/J5
Cartwright, 163/L5
Cartwright, Man. 179/C5
Cartwright, N. Dak. (58838) 283/C4
Cartwright, Newf. 166/C3
Caruai (riv.), Ven. 124/H5
Caruaru, Braz. 132/H5
Carumás, Peru 128/G11
Carúpano, Ven., 120/D1
Carúpano, Ven. 124/G2
Carurú, Col. 126/E7
Carutapera, Braz. 132/E3
Caruth, Mo. (†63857) 261/N10
Caruthers, Calif. (93609) 204/E7
Caruthersville, Mo. (63830) 261/N10
Carver▵, Mass. (02330) 249/M5
Carver (bay), Mich. 250/G1
Carver (co.), Minn. 254/E6
Carver, Minn. (55315) 254/E6
Carver, Oreg. (†97015) 291/B2
Carver Ranch Estates‡, Fla. (†33009) 212/B4
Carville, La. (70721) 238/K3
Carvoeiro (cape), Port. 33/B3
Cary, Ill. (60013) 222/E1
Cary▵, Maine (†04465) 242/H4
Cary, Miss. (39054) 256/C5
Cary, N.C. (27511) 281/M3
Caryapundy (swamp), N.S.W. 97/B1
Caryapundy (swamp), Queens. 95/B6
Carysbrook, Va. (22927) 307/M5
Caryville, Fla. (32427) 212/C6
Caryville, Mass. (02024) 249/J4
Caryville, Tenn. (37714) 237/N8
Casa, Ark. (72025) 203/D3
Casa Agapito, Col. 126/D6
Casablanca, Chile 138/F3
Casablanca, Estero de (riv.), Chile 138/F3
Casablanca, 102/B1
Casablanca, Mor., 3/J4
Casablanca, Mor. 106/C2
Casa Blanca, N. Mex. (87007) 274/B4
Casa Branca, Braz. 135/C2
Casa Cruz (cape), Trinidad Tobago 161/B11
Casa Grande, Ariz. (85222) 198/D6
Casa Grande Ruins Nat'l Mon., Ariz. 198/D6
Casale Monferrato, Italy 34/B2
Casalmaggiore, Italy 34/C2
Casamance (riv.), Sen. 106/A6
Casanare (riv.), Col. 126/E4
Casanay, Ven. 124/G2
Casa Nova, Braz. 132/F5
Casanova, Va. (22017) 307/N3
Casa Piedra, Texas (†79843) 302/C12
Casar, N.C. (28020) 281/F3
Casar de Cáceres, Spain 33/C3
Casas Grandes (riv.), Mex. 150/F1
Casas-Ibáñez, Spain 33/F3
Cascade (range), 188/B1
Cascade, Aust. 88/L5
Cascade (bay), Aust. 88/L5
Cascade, Br. Col. 184/H6
Cascade (range), Calif. 204/D1
Cascade, Colo. (80809) 208/K5
Cascade, Jam. 158/G6
Cascade, Idaho (83611) 220/C5
Cascade (res.), Idaho 220/C5
Cascade, Iowa (52033) 229/L4
Cascade (co.), Mont. 262/E3
Cascade, Mont. (59421) 262/E3
Cascade, N.H. (†03581) 268/E3
Cascade (pt.), N.Z. 101/B6
Cascade (head), Oreg. 291/C2
Cascade (range), Oreg. 291/E4
Cascade, Seych. 118/H5
Cascade (range), U.S., 146/F5
Cascade, Va. (24069) 307/J7
Cascade, W. Va. (26526) 313/G3
Cascade (pass), Wash. 310/D2
Cascade (range), Wash. 310/D4
Cascade (riv.), Wash. 310/D2
Cascade, Wis. (53011) 317/K8
Cascade Locks, Oreg. (97014) 291/E2
Cascade Summit, Oreg. (97418) 291/F4
Cascadia, Oreg. (97329) 291/E3
Cascais, Port. 33/B3
Cascajal, Cuba 158/E1
Cascapédia (riv.), Que. 172/C1
Cascas, Peru 128/C6
Cascatinha, Braz. 135/E3
Cascavel, Braz. 132/G4
Cascilla, Miss. (38920) 256/D3
Cascina-Navacchio, Italy 34/C3
Casco▵, Maine (04015) 242/B7
Casco, Maine (04015) 242/B7
Casco (bay), Maine 242/C8
Casco, Wis. (54205) 317/L6
Cascorro, Cuba 158/H3
Cascumpeque (bay), P.E.I. 169/E2
Case-Pilote, Mart. 161/C6
Caseros, Arg. 143/F7
Caserta (prov.), Italy 34/E4
Caserta, Italy 34/E4
Caseville, Mich. (48725) 250/F5
Casey (key), Fla. 212/D4
Casey, Ill. (62420) 222/F4
Casey, Iowa (50048) 229/D5
Casey (co.), Ky. 237/M6
Casey Creek, Ky. (42723) 237/L6
Caseyville, Ill. (62232) 222/B6
Caseyville, Ky. (†42459) 237/E5
Cash, Ark. (72421) 203/J2
Cashel, 10/C4
Cashel, Ire. 17/F7
Cashiers, N.C. (28717) 281/C4
Cashion, Ariz. (85329) 198/C5
Cashion, Okla. (73016) 288/L3
Cashmere, W. Va. (24926) 313/E8
Cashmere, Wash. (98815) 310/E3
Cashton, Wis. (54619) 317/E8
Cashtown, Pa. (17310) 294/H6
Cashville, S.C. (†29388) 296/C2
Casigua, Falcón, Ven. 124/C2
Casigua, Zulia, Ven. 124/B3
Casiguran, Phil. 82/D2
Casiguran (sound), Phil. 82/C2
Casilda, Arg. 143/F6
Casilda, Cuba 158/E2
Casilda (pt.), Cuba 158/E2
Casino. Aust. 88/J5
Casino, N.S.W. 97/G1
Casiquiare, Brazo (riv.), Ven. 124/E6
Casitas Springs, Calif. (†93001) 204/F9
Caslan, Alta. 182/D2
Čáslav, Czech. 41/C2
Casma, Peru 128/C7
Casma (riv.), Peru 128/C7
Casmalia, Calif. (93429) 204/E9
Casnovia, Mich. (49318) 250/D5
Caspaco, Br. Col. 184/B3
Caspar, Calif. (95420) 204/B4
Caspe, Spain 33/G2
Casper, Wyo., 146/H5
Casper, Wyo., 188/E2
Casper, Wyo. (82601) 319/F3
Casper (range), Wyo. 319/F3
Caspian (sea), 3/M3
Caspian (sea), 54/H5
Caspian (sea), U.S.S.R. 48/F6
Caspian (sea), U.S.S.R. 52/G6
Caspian, Mich. (49915) 250/G2
Caspian (sea), Iran 66/G1
Caspian (sea), U.S.S.R., 7/J4
Caspian (lake), Vt. 268/C2
Caspiana, La. (71015) 238/C2
Cass, Ark. (†72949) 203/C2
Cass (co.), Ill. 222/C4
Cass (co.), Ind. 227/E3
Cass, Ind. (†47882) 227/C6
Cass (co.), Iowa 229/D6
Cass (co.), Mich. 250/C7
Cass (riv.), Mich. 250/F5
Cass (co.), Minn. 254/D4
Cass (lake), Minn. 254/D3
Cass (co.), Mo. 261/D5
Cass (co.), N. Dak. 283/R5
Cass (co.), Nebr. 264/H4
Cass (co.), Texas 302/K4
Cass, W. Va. (24927) 313/G6
Cassadaga, Fla. (32706) 212/E3
Cassadaga, N.Y. (14718) 276/B6
Cassá de la Selva, Spain 33/H2
Cassai, Angola 115/D6
Cassamba, Angola 115/D6
Cassandra, Ga. (†30727) 216/B1
Cassandra, Pa. (15925) 294/E5
Cassano allo Ionio, Italy 34/F5
Cassatt, S.C. (29032) 296/G3
Cass City, Mich. (48726) 250/F5
Casscoe, Ark. (72026) 203/H4
Casselberry, Fla. (32707) 212/E3
Casselman, Ont. 177/J2
Casselman (riv.), Md. 245/B2
Casselman, Pa. (†15557) 294/D6
Casselman (riv.), Pa. 294/D6
Casselton, N. Dak. (58012) 283/R6
Cássia, Braz. 135/C2
Cassia (co.), Idaho 220/E7
Cassiar, Br. Col. 184/K2
Cassiar (mts.), Br. Col. 184/K2
Cassiar (mts.), Yukon 187/E3
Cassidy, Br. Col. 184/J3
Cassilis, N.S.W. 97/E3
Cassils, Alta. 182/D4
Cassinga, Angola 115/C7
Cassino, Italy 34/E4
Cassiporé (cape), Braz. 132/D2
Cassity, W. Va. (†26278) 313/F5
Cass Lake, Minn. (56633) 254/D3
Cassoday, Kans. (66842) 232/F3
Cassopolis, Mich. (49031) 250/C7
Casstown, Ohio (45312) 284/B5
Cassville, Ga. (30123) 216/C2
Cassville, Ind. (†46901) 227/E4
Cassville, Mo. (65625) 261/E9
Cassville, Pa. (16623) 294/G5
Cassville, W. Va. (26527) 313/F3
Cassville, Wis. (53806) 317/E10
Castagnola, Switz. 39/G4
Castaic, Calif. (91310) 204/G9
Castalia, Iowa (52133) 229/K2
Castalia, N. Br. 170/D4
Castalia, N.C. (27816) 281/O2
Castalia, Ohio (44824) 284/E3
Castalian Springs, Tenn. (37031) 237/J8
Castana, Iowa (51010) 229/B4
Castanhal, Braz. 132/E3
Castelfranco Veneto, Italy 34/D2
Castel Gandolfo, Italy 34/F7
Casteljaloux, France 28/D5
Castella, Calif. (96017) 204/C2
Castellammare (gulf), Italy 34/D5
Castellammare del Golfo, Italy 34/D5
Castellammare di Stabia, Italy 34/E4
Castellane, France 28/G6
Castellanos, Urug. 145/B6
Castelli, Buenos Aires, Arg. 143/H7
Castelli, Chaco, Arg. 143/D2
Castellón (prov.), Spain 33/G2
Castellón de la Plana, Spain 33/G3
Castellote, Spain 33/F2
Castell San Pietro Terme, Italy 34/C2
Castelnaudary, France 28/E6
Castelo, Braz. 132/F8
Castelo Branco, Port. 33/C3
Castelo de Vide, Port. 33/C3
Castelo do Piauí, Braz. 132/F4
Castelsarrasin, France 28/D6
Castelvetrano, Italy 34/D6
Casterton, Aust. 88/G7
Casterton, Vic. 97/A5
Castiglione del Lago, Italy 34/C3
Castiglion Fiorentino, Italy 34/C3
Castile, N.Y. (14427) 276/D5
Castilla, Peru 128/B5
Castilletes, Ven. 124/C2
Castillo, Cerro (mt.), Chile 138/E6
Castillo, Dom. Rep. 158/E5
Castillo de Jagua, Cuba 158/D2
Castillo de San Marcos Nat'l Mon., Fla. 212/E2
Castillos, Urug. 145/F5
Castillos (lag.), Urug. 145/F5
Castine▵, Maine (04421) 242/F7
Castine, Ohio (45313) 284/A6
Castle (mt.), Br. Col. 184/A2
Castle (peak), Colo. 208/F5
Castle (harb.), Berm. 156/H2
Castle (creek), Idaho 220/B7
Castle (peak), Idaho 220/D5
Castle (pt.), N.Z. 101/F4
Castle, Okla. (74833) 288/O4
Castle (valley), Utah 304/D4
Castle A.F.B., Calif. 204/E6
Castlebar, 10/B4
Castlebar, Ire. 17/C4
Castlebay, Scot. 15/B6
Castlebellingham, Ire. 17/J4
Castleberry, Ala. (36432) 194/D8
Castleblayney, 10/C3
Castleblayney, Ire. 17/H3
Castlebridge, Ire. 17/J7
Castle Bromwich, 10/G3
Castle Bruce, Dominica 161/F6
Castlecomer-Donaguile, 10/C4
Castlecomer-Donaguile, Ire. 17/G6
Castle Dale, Utah (84513) 304/D4
Castle Danger, Minn. (†56616) 254/G3
Castledawson, N. Ire. 17/H2
Castlederg, N. Ire. 17/F2
Castledermot, Ire. 17/H6
Castle Dome (mts.), Ariz. 198/A5
Castle Douglas, 10/D3
Castle Douglas, Scot. 15/H10
Castlefin, Ire. 17/F2
Castleford, Eng. 13/F4
Castleford, Idaho (83321) 220/C7
Castlegar, Br. Col. 184/J5
Castle Gate, Utah (84514) 304/D4
Castlegregory, 10/B4
Castlegregory, Ire. 17/A7
Castle Hayne, N.C. (28429) 281/O6
Castle Hills‡, Texas (†78213) 302/F8
Castle Hot Springs, Ariz. (†85342) 198/C5
Castleisland, Ire. 17/B7
Castlemaine, Ire. 17/B7
Castlemaine, Vic. 97/C5
Castle Park, Mich. (49422) 250/C6
Castle Point, Man. 179/C5
Castlepollard, Ire. 17/G4
Castlerea, 10/B4
Castlerea, Ire. 17/D4
Castlereagh (riv.), N.S.W. 97/E2
Castle Rising, Eng. 13/H5
Castle Rock, Colo. (80104) 208/K4
Castle Rock, Minn. (55010) 254/E6
Castle Rock, S. Dak. (57726) 298/B4
Castle Rock, Utah (†82930) 304/C2
Castle Rock, Wash. (98611) 310/B4
Castle Rock Flowage (res.), Wis. 317/G8
Castle Shannon, Pa. (15234) 294/B7
Castleton, Jam. 158/J6
Castleton, Ont. 177/F3
Castleton, Ill. (61426) 222/D2
Castleton, Md. (†21034) 245/N2
Castleton▵, Vt. (05735) 268/A4
Castleton, Vt. (05735) 268/A4
Castleton-on-Hudson, N.Y. (12033) 276/N5
Castletown, I. of Man 13/C3
Castletown, Ire. 17/F6
Castletownbere, Ire. 17/B8
Castletownroche, Ire. 17/D7
Castletownshend, Ire. 17/C9
Castlewellan, N. Ire. 17/K3
Castlewood, S. Dak. (57223) 298/R4
Castlewood, Va. (24224) 307/D7
Castolon, Texas (†79852) 302/D12
Castor, Alta. 182/D3
Castor, La. (71016) 238/D2
Castorland, N.Y. (13620) 276/J3
Castres, France 28/E6
Castries (cap.), St. Lucia 156/G4
Castries (cap.), St. Lucia 161/G6
Castro, Braz., 120/E5
Castro, Chile, 120/C7
Castro, Chile 138/D4
Castro, Braz. 132/D9
Castro, Braz. 135/B2
Castro, Spain 33/C1
Castro (co.), Texas 302/B3
Castro Alves, Braz. 132/G6
Castro Daire, Port. 33/C2
Castro del Río, Spain 33/D4
Castrojeriz, Spain 33/E1
Castro Marim, Port. 33/C4
Castropol, Spain 33/C1
Castroreale, Italy 34/E5
Castro-Urdiales, Spain 33/E1
Castro Valley, Calif. (94546) 204/K2
Castro Verde, Port. 33/C4
Castrovillari, Italy 34/F5
Castroville, Calif. (95012) 204/D7
Castroville, Texas (78009) 302/E8
Castrovirreyna, Peru 128/E9
Castuera, Spain 33/D3
Casuarito, Col. 126/G5
Casupá, Urug. 145/D5
Caswell, Alaska (†99688) 196/B1
Caswell (co.), N.C. 281/L2
Cat (isl.), Bah. Is., 146/L7
Cat (isl.), Bah. Is. 156/C1
Cat (isl.), Miss. 256/F10
Çat, Turkey 63/J3
Cat (isl.), Wis. 317/E1
Catacamas, Hond. 154/E3
Catacaos, Peru 128/B5
Catacocha, Ec. 128/C5
Catadupa, Jam. 158/H6
Cataguases, Braz. 135/E2
Catahoula (par.), La. 238/G3
Catahoula (lake), La. 238/F4
Cataíñgan, Phil. 82/E5
Catalão, Braz. 132/D7
Çatalca, Turkey 63/C2
Cataldo, Idaho (83810) 220/B2
Catalina, Chile 138/B5
Catalina (pt.), Chile 138/F10
Catalina (isl.), Dom. Rep. 158/F6
Catalina, Newf. 166/D2
Catalone, N.S. 169/H3
Catalonia (reg.), Spain 33/G2
Catalpa (creek), Miss. 256/G4
Catamarca, Arg., 120/D5
Catamarca (prov.), Arg. 143/C2
Catamarca, Arg. 143/C2
Catamayo, Ec. 128/C4
Catanauan, Phil. 82/D4
Catanduanes (prov.), Phil. 82/E4
Catanduanes (isl.), Phil. 82/E4
Catanduanes (isl.), Phil. 85/H3
Catanduva, Braz. 132/D8
Catanduva, Braz. 135/B2
Catania, Italy, 7/F5
Catania (prov.), Italy 34/E6
Catania, Italy 34/E6
Cataño, P. Rico 156/G1
Cataño, P. Rico 161/D1
Catanzaro, Italy, 7/F5
Catanzaro (prov.), Italy 34/F5
Catanzaro, Italy 34/F5
Cataouatche (lake), La. 238/N4
Cataract (creek), Ariz. 198/C3
Cataract, Ind. (†47460) 227/D6
Cataract (lake), Ind. 227/D6
Cataract (canyon), Utah 304/D5
Cataract, Wis. (54620) 317/E7
Catarama, Ec. 128/C3
Cataricahua, Bol. 136/B6
Catarina, Texas (78836) 302/E9
Catarman, Phil. 82/E4
Catarman (range), Phil. 82/F7
Catasauqua, Pa. (18032) 294/M4
Catastrophe (cape), S. Aust. 94/D6
Catatumbo (riv.), Col. 126/D3
Catatumbo (riv.), Ven. 124/B3
Cataula, Ga. (31804) 216/C5
Cataumet, Mass. (02534) 249/M6
Catawba (co.), N.C. 281/G3
Catawba, N.C. (28609) 281/G3
Catawba (lake), N.C. 281/G4
Catawba (riv.), N.C. 281/H5
Catawba, Ohio (43010) 284/C6
Catawba, S.C. (29704) 296/F2
Catawba (riv.), S.C. 296/F2
Catawba, Va. (24070) 307/H6
Catawba, W. Va. (26564) 313/F3
Catawba, Wis. (54515) 317/E4
Catawba Ind. Res., S.C. 296/F2
Catawba Island, Ohio (†43452) 284/E2
Catawissa, Mo. (63015) 261/N4
Catawissa, Pa. (17820) 294/K4
Cat Ba, Dao (isl.), N. Vietnam 72/E2
Catbalogan, Phil. 82/E5
Catbalogan, Phil. 85/H3
Cat Creek, Mont. (59017) 262/H3
Cateechee, S.C. (29629) 296/B2
Cateel, Phil. 82/F7
Cateel, Phil. 85/H4
Catemaco, Mex. 150/M7
Catemu, Chile 138/G2
Caterham and Warlingham, 10/B6
Caterham and Warlingham, Eng. 13/G6
Cates, Ind. (47927) 227/C4
Catete, Angola 115/B5
Catfish (lake), Ont. 177/F2
Catfish (lake), N.C. 281/P5
Catfish (creek), S.C. 296/J3
Cathance (lake), Maine 242/J6
Catharine, Kans. (67627) 232/C3
Catharine Lake, N.C. (†28754) 281/O5
Cathay, N. Dak. (58422) 283/M4
Cathedral (mt.), Texas 302/D12
Cathedral City, Calif. (92234) 204/J10
Catherine, Ala. (36728) 194/D6
Catherine (lake), Ark. 203/E5
Catherwood, Sask. 181/D4
Catheys Valley, Calif. (95306) 204/E6
Cathlamet, Wash. (98612) 310/B4
Cat Island (chan.), La. 238/M6
Cat Island (passg.), La. 238/J8
Catlett, Va. (22019) 307/N3
Catlettsburg, Ky. (41129) 237/R4
Catlin, Ill. (61817) 222/F3
Catlin, Ind. (†47872) 227/C5
Catmon, Phil. 82/E5
Cato (isl.), Australia, 87/F8
Cato, Ark. (†72076) 203/F4
Cato (isl.), Aust. 88/K4
Cato, Ind. (†47598) 227/C8
Cato, N.Y. (13033) 276/G4
Cato, Wis. (54206) 317/L7
Catoche (cape), Mex. 150/Q6
Catoctin (creek), Md. 245/H3
Catoctin Furnace, Md. (†21788) 245/J2
Catolé do Rocha, Braz. 132/G4
Catonsville, Md. (21228) 245/M3
Catoosa (co.), Ga. 216/B1
Catoosa, Okla. (74015) 288/P2
Catriló, Arg. 143/D4
Catron, Mo. (63833) 261/N9
Catron (co.), N. Mex. 274/A4
Catskill, N.Y. (12414) 276/N6
Catskill (mts.), N.Y. 276/L6
Cattaraugus (co.), N.Y. 276/C6
Cattaraugus, N.Y. (14719) 276/C6
Cattaraugus (creek), N.Y. 276/C6
Cattaraugus Ind. Res., N.Y. 276/C5
Catumbela, Angola 115/B6
Cauayan, Isabela, Phil. 82/C2
Cauayan, Negros Occ., Phil. 82/D6
Cauca (riv.), Col., 120/C2
Cauca (riv.), Col. 126/C4
Cauca (dept.), Col. 126/B6
Caucagua, Ven. 124/E2
Caucasia, Col. 126/C4
Caucasus (mts.), U.S.S.R. 48/E5
Caucasus (mts.), U.S.S.R. 52/F6
Caucasus (mts.), U.S.S.R., 7/J4
Caucedo (cape), Dom. Rep. 158/E6
Caucomgomoc (lake), Maine 242/D3
Caudete, Spain 33/F3
Caughnawaga, Que. 172/H4
Cauit (range), Phil. 82/F6
Caulfield, Aust. 88/M7
Caulfield, Mo. (65626) 261/H9
Caulfield, Vic. 97/J5
Caulksville, Ark. (†72951) 203/C3
Caulonia, Italy 34/F5
Caúngula, Angola 115/C5
Cauquenes, Chile 138/A11
Caura (riv.), Ven., 120/D2
Caura (riv.), Ven. 124/F5
Causapscal, Que. 172/B2
Causey, N. Mex. (88113) 274/F5
Causses (reg.), France 28/D5
Cauterets, France 28/C6
Cauthron, Ark. (72929) 203/B4
Cautín (prov.), Chile 138/E2
Cauto, Cuba 158/H4
Cauto (riv.), Cuba 158/H3
Cauto del Embarcadero, Cuba 158/H4
Cauto del Paso, Cuba 158/H3
Caux, Switz. 39/C4
Cava de'Tirreni, Italy 34/E4
Cavaillon, Haiti 158/A6
Cavaillon, France 28/F6
Cavalcante, Braz. 132/D6
Cavalier (co.), N. Dak. 283/N2
Cavalier, N. Dak. (58220) 283/P2
Cavalier, Sask. 181/E1
Cavalli (isls.), N.Z. 101/E1
Cavallo (passg.), Texas 302/H9
Cavally (riv.), Ivory Coast 106/C7
Cavally (riv.), Liberia 106/C7
Cavan, Ont. 177/F3
Cavan, 10/C4
Cavan (co.), Ire. 17/G4
Cavan, Ire. 17/G3
Cavanaugh (lake), Wash. 310/D2
Cavari, Bol. 136/B5
Cavarzere, Italy 34/D2
Cave City, Ark. (72521) 203/G2
Cave City, Ky. (42127) 237/K6
Cave Creek, Ariz. (85331) 198/D5
Cave Hill, Barb. 161/B9
Cave in Rock, Ill. (62919) 222/E6
Cave Junction, Oreg. (97523) 291/D5
Cavell, Sask. 181/C3
Cavendish, Alta. 182/E4
Cavendish, Idaho (†83550) 220/B3
Cavendish, Newf. 166/D2
Cavendish▵, Vt. (05142) 268/B5
Cavendish, Vt. (05142) 268/B5
Cave Spring, Ga. (30124) 216/B2
Cave Springs, Ark. (72718) 203/B1
Cavetown, Md. (21720) 245/H2
Caviana (isl.), Braz., 120/F2
Caviana (isl.), Braz. 132/D2
Cavili (isl.), Phil. 82/C6
Cavinas, Bol. 136/B3
Cavite (prov.), Phil. 82/C3
Cavite, Phil. 82/C3
Cavite, Phil. 85/G3
Cavour, S. Dak. (57324) 298/N5
Cavour, Wis. (54516) 317/J4
Cawdor, Scot. 15/J5
Cawker City, Kans. (67430) 232/D2
Cawndilla (lake), N.S.W. 97/A3
Cawnpore (Kanpur), India, 54/L7
Cawnpore (Kanpur), India 68/E3
Cawood, Ky. (40815) 237/P7
Cawston, Br. Col. 184/H5
Cawston, Eng. 13/J5
Caxambu, Braz. 132/E8
Caxambu, Braz. 135/D2
Caxias, Braz., 120/F3
Caxias, Braz. 132/F4
Caxias do Sul, Braz., 120/E5
Caxias do Sul, Braz. 132/D10
Caxito, Angola 115/B5
Çay, Turkey 63/D3
Cayacoa, Dom. Rep. 158/E6
Cayamas (cay), Cuba 158/C2
Cayambe, Ec. 128/D3
Cayambe (mt.), Ec. 128/D2
Cayasta, Arg. 143/F5
Cayastacito, Arg. 143/F5
Cayce, Ky. (†42041) 237/C7
Cayce, S.C. (29033) 296/E4
Caycuse, Br. Col. 184/J3
Çayeli, Turkey 63/J2
Cayenne (cap.), Fr. Gui., 3/G5
Cayenne (cap.), Fr. Gui., 120/E2
Cayenne (dist.), Fr. Gui. 131/E3
Cayenne (cap.), Fr. Gui. 131/E3
Cayer, Man. 179/D3
Cayes-Jacmel, Haiti 158/C6
Cayeux-sur-Mer, France 28/D2
Cayey, P. Rico 156/G1
Cayey, P. Rico 161/D2
Cayey, Sierra de (mts.), P. Rico 161/D2
Çayiralan, Turkey 63/F3
Cayley, Alta. 182/D4
Cayman Brac (isl.), Cayman Is. 156/B3
CAYMAN ISLANDS, 156/B3
Cayo, Br. Hond. 154/C2
Cayo Mambí, Cuba 158/K3
Cayon, St. Chr.-N.-A. 161/C10
Cay Sal (bank), Bah. Is. 156/B2
Cayucos, Calif. (93430) 204/E8
Cayuga, Ont. 177/E5
Cayuga, Ind. (47928) 227/C5
Cayuga, N. Dak. (58013) 283/R7
Cayuga (co.), N.Y. 276/G4
Cayuga, N.Y. (13034) 276/G5
Cayuga (lake), N.Y. 276/G5
Cayuga, Texas (75832) 302/J6
Cayuga Heights, N.Y. (†14850) 276/H6
Cayuse, Oreg. (97821) 291/J2
Cayuta (creek), N.Y. 276/G6
Cazadero, Calif. (95421) 204/B5
Cazalla de la Sierra, Spain 33/D4
Cazaux (lag.), France 28/C5
Cazenovia, N.Y. (13035) 276/J5
Cazenovia, Wis. (53924) 317/F8
Cazin, Yugo. 45/B3
Cazis, Switz. 39/H3
Cazma (riv.), Yugo. 45/C3
Cazombo, Angola 115/D6
Cazombo, 102/E6
Cazones (gulf), Cuba 158/C2
Cazorla, Spain 33/E4
Cazorla, Ven. 124/E3
Cazot, Urug. 145/B6
Cazueleja, Cerro (mt.), Col. 126/C6
Ceanannus Mór, 10/C4
Ceanannus Mór, Ire. 17/G4
Ceará (Fortaleza), Braz., 120/G3
Ceará (state), Braz. 132/G4
Ceará (Fortaleza), Braz. 132/G3
Ceará-Mirim, Braz. 132/H4
Ceba, Sask. 181/J2
Cébaco (isl.), Pan. 154/G7
Ceballos, Mex. 150/H3
Cebeci, Turkey 63/E3
Cebolla (creek), Colo. 208/E6
Cebolla, N. Mex. (87518) 274/C2
Cebollatí, Urug. 145/F4
Cebollatí (riv.), Urug. 145/F4
Cebreros, Spain 33/D2
Cebu (prov.), Phil. 82/D5
Cebu, Phil. 82/D5
Cebu (isl.), Phil. 82/D6
Cebu, Phil. 85/G3
Cebu (isl.), Phil. 85/G3
Cebu, Phil., 3/R5
Cebu, Phil., 54/R9
Cecebe, Ont. 177/E2
Cecelia, La. (70521) 238/G6
Cecil, Ala. (36013) 194/F6
Cecil, Ark. (72930) 203/C3
Cecil, Ga. (31627) 216/F8
Cecil (co.), Md. 245/P2
Cecil, Ohio (45821) 284/A3
Cecil, Oreg. (97822) 291/H2
Cecil, Pa. (15321) 294/B5
Cecil, Wis. (54111) 317/K6
Cecil Field N.A.S., Fla. 212/E1
Cecilia, Ky. (42724) 237/K5
Cecil Lake, Br. Col. 184/G2
Cecilton, Md. (21913) 245/P3
Cecilville, Calif. (96018) 204/B2
Cecina, Italy 34/C3
Ceclavín, Spain 33/C3
Cedar (pt.), Ala. 194/B10
Cedar, Br. Col. 184/J3
Cedar (creek), Colo. 208/M1
Cedar (lake), Conn. 210/E3
Cedar (lake), Que. 172/E2
Cedar (lake), Ont. 177/F1
Cedar (creek), Ind. 227/G2
Cedar (co.), Iowa 229/L5
Cedar, Iowa (52543) 229/H6
Cedar (riv.), Iowa, 188/H2
Cedar (riv.), Iowa 229/K4
Cedar, Kans. (67628) 232/D2
Cedar (lake), Man. 179/B1
Cedar (pt.), Md. 245/N7
Cedar, Mich. (49621) 250/D4
Cedar (lake), Mich. 250/F4

346 Chevroux

Chevroux, Switz. 39/C3
Chevy Chase, Md. (20015) 245/E4
Chevy Chase Heights‡, Pa. (†15701) 294/D4
Chevy Chase Section Four‡, Md. (†20015) 245/E4
Chevy Chase Village‡, Md. (†20015) 245/E4
Chewack (riv.), Wash. 310/E2
Chewalla, Tenn. (38393) 237/D10
Chewelah, Wash. (99109) 310/H2
Chewsville, Md. (21721) 245/H2
Chexbres, Switz. 39/C3
Cheyenne (riv.), 188/F2
Cheyenne (co.), Colo. 208/O5
Cheyenne (co.), Kans. 232/A2
Cheyenne (co.), Nebr. 264/A3
Cheyenne, Okla. (73628) 288/G3
Cheyenne (riv.), S. Dak. 298/F4
Cheyenne (riv.), U.S., 146/H5
Cheyenne (cap.), Wyo., 146/H5
Cheyenne (cap.), Wyo., 188/E2
Cheyenne (cap.), Wyo. (82001) 319/H4
Cheyenne (riv.), Wyo. 319/H2
Cheyenne Bottoms (lake), Kans. 232/D3
Cheyenne River Ind. Res., S. Dak. 298/F4
Cheyenne Wells, Colo. (80810) 208/P5
Cheyne (bay), W. Aust. 92/B6
Cheyney, Pa. (19319) 294/M6
Cheyres, Switz. 39/C3
Chhatarpur, India 68/D4
Chhindwara, India 68/D4
Chhlong, Cambodia 72/E4
Chi, Mae Nam (riv.), Thai. 72/D3
Chiai, China 77/K7
Chiamboni, Ras (cape), Kenya 115/H4
Chiamboni, Ras (cape), Somalia 115/H4
Chiang Dao, Thai. 72/C3
Chiange, Angola 115/B7
Chiang Khan, Thai. 72/D3
Chiang Rai, Thai. 72/C3
Chiang Saen, Thai. 72/C2
Chiapa de Corzo, Mex. 150/N8
Chiapas (state), Mex. 150/N8
Chiari, Italy 34/C2
Chiasso, Switz. 39/G5
Chiatura, U.S.S.R. 52/F6
Chiautempan, Mex. 150/N1
Chiavari, Italy 34/B2
Chiba (pref.), Japan 81/P2
Chiba, Japan 81/P2
Chiblow (lake), Ont. 177/A1
Chibougamau, 163/J6
Chibougamau, Que. 174/C3
Chibukak (cape), Alaska 196/D2
Chibuto, Moz. 118/E4
Chibwe, Zambia 115/E6
Chicago, Ill., 146/J5
Chicago, Ill., 188/J2
Chicago, Ill. (*60601) 222/B2
Chicago, U.S., 3/E3
Chicago Heights, Ill. (60411) 222/B3
Chicago Portage Nat'l Hist. Site, Ill. 222/A2
Chicago Ridge, Ill. (60415) 222/A2
Chicama, Peru 128/C6
Chicamacomico (riv.), Md. 245/P7
Chicamocha (riv.), Col. 126/D4
Chicanán (riv.), Ven. 124/H4
Chicapa (riv.), Angola 115/D5
Chicapa (riv.), Dem. Rep. of the Congo. 115/D5
Chichagof (isl.), Alaska 196/M1
Chichagof (isl.) Alaska, 188/D6
Chichén-Itzá (ruin), Mex. 150/P6
Chichester, 10/F5
Chichester, Eng. 13/G7
Chichester▵, N.H. (†03258) 268/E5
Chichester, N.H. (†03258) 268/E5
Chichester, N.Y. (12416) 276/M6
Chichi (isl.), Japan, 87/E3
Chichi (isl.), Japan 81/M3
Chichibu, Japan 81/J6
Chichibu-Tama Nat'l Park, Japan 81/J6
Chichicaste, Hond. 154/E3
Chichicastenango, Guat. 154/B3
Chichigalpa, Nic. 154/D4
Chichiriviche, Ven. 124/D2
Chickalah, Ark. (†72833) 203/D3
Chickaloon, Alaska (†99645) 196/C1
Chickamauga, Ga. (30707) 216/B1
Chickamauga (lake), Tenn., 188/J3
Chickamauga (dam), Tenn. 237/L10
Chickamauga (lake), Tenn. 237/L10
Chickamauga and Chattanooga Nat'l Mil. Park, Ga. 216/B1
Chickamaw Beach, Minn. (†56474) 254/D4
Chickasaw, Ala. (36611) 194/B9
Chickasaw (co.), Iowa 229/J2
Chickasaw (co.), Miss. 256/G3
Chickasaw, Ohio (45826) 284/A5
Chickasawhay (riv.), Miss. 256/G7
Chickasaw Unit, Natchez Trace Pkwy, Miss. 256/G2
Chickasha, Okla., 188/G4
Chickasha, Okla. (73018) 288/L4
Chickashe (lake), Okla. 288/K4
Chicken, Alaska (99732) 196/K2
Chiclana de la Frontera, Spain 33/C4
Chiclayo, Peru, 120/B3
Chiclayo, Peru 128/C6
Chico (riv.), Arg., 120/D7
Chico (riv.), Arg. 143/C5
Chico (riv.), Arg. 143/C6
Chico, Calif. (95926) 204/D4
Chico, Mont. (†59027) 262/F5
Chico (riv.), Phil. 82/C2
Chico, Texas (76030) 302/G4
Chicoa, Moz. 118/E3
Chicoana, Arg. 143/C2
Chicoloapan de Juárez, Mex. 150/M1
Chicopee, Kans. (†66762) 232/H4
Chicopee, Mass. (*01013) 249/D4
Chicopee (riv.), Mass. 249/D4
Chicora, Miss. (†39322) 256/G7
Chicora, Pa. (16025) 294/C4
Chicot (co.), Ark. 203/H7
Chicot, Ark. (†71640) 203/H7
Chicot (pt.), La. 238/M7
Chicoutimi, 163/J6
Chicoutimi (co.), Que. 172/G1
Chicoutimi, Que. 172/G1
Chicoutimi (riv.), Que. 172/F2
Chicoutimi (co.), Que. 174/C2
Chicoutimi, Que. 174/C3
Chicoutimi, Que., 146/L5
Chicoutimi-Nord, Que. 172/G1
Chidambaram, India 68/E6
Chidester, Ark. (71726) 203/D6
Chidley (cape), 163/K3
Chidley (cape), Canada, 146/M3
Chidley (cape), N.W.T. 187/M3
Chidley (cape), Newf. 166/B1
Chief Joseph (dam), Wash. 310/F3
Chiefland, Fla. (32626) 212/D2
Chiefs (pt.), Ont. 177/C3
Chiehmo (Cherchen), China 77/C4
Chiemsee (lake), W. Ger. 22/E5
Chiengmai, Thai. 72/C3
Chiengmai, Thai., 54/N8
Chienti (riv.), Italy 34/D3
Chieri, Italy 34/A2
Chieti (prov.), Italy 34/E3
Chieti, Italy 34/E3
Chietla, Mex. 150/M2
Chièvres, Belg. 27/D7
Chigasaki, Japan 81/O3
Chiginagak (mt.), Alaska 196/G3
Chignahuapan, Mex. 150/N1
Chignautla, Mex. 150/O1
Chignecto (bay), N. Br. 170/F3
Chignecto (bay), N.S. 169/D3
Chignecto (cape), N.S. 169/C3
Chignecto (isth.), N.S. 169/D3
Chignik, Alaska (99564) 196/G3
Chignik (bay), Alaska 196/G3
Chignik Lagoon, Alaska (99565) 196/G3
Chignik Lake, Alaska (†99564) 196/G3
Chiguana, Bol. 136/A7
Chigubo, Moz. 118/E4
Chigwell, 10/C5
Chihfeng, China 77/J3
Chihli (gulf), China 77/K4
Chihshui, China 77/G6
Chihtan, China 77/G4
Chihuahua, Mex., 146/H7
Chihuahua (state), Mex. 150/F2
Chihuahua, Mex. 150/F2
Chikaskia (riv.), Kans. 232/E4
Chik Ballapur, India 68/D6
Chikmagalur, India 68/D6
Chilanga, Zambia 115/E7
Chilapa de Álvarez, Mex. 150/K8
Chilas, India 68/C1
Chilca (Pucusana), Peru 128/D9
Chilcoot, Calif. (96105) 204/E4
Chilcotin (riv.), Br. Col. 184/E4
Childersburg, Ala. (35044) 194/F4
Childress (co.), Texas 302/D3
Childress, Texas (79201) 302/D3
Childs (lake), Man. 179/A3
Childs, Md. (21916) 245/P2
Childwold, N.Y. (12922) 276/L2
Chile, 3/F7
Chile, 120/C6
CHILE, 138/C4
Chile Chico, Chile 138/E6
Chilecito, Arg., 120/D5
Chilecito, Arg. 143/C2
Chiles, Col. 126/A7
Chilesburg, Ky. (†40507) 237/N4
Chilete, Peru 128/C6
Chilga, Eth. 111/G5
Chilhowee, Mo. (64733) 261/E5
Chilhowee, Tenn. (†37901) 237/O9
Chilhowee (mt.), Tenn. 237/O9
Chilhowie, Va. (24319) 307/E7
Chili, Ind. (46926) 227/F3
Chili, Wis. (54420) 317/F6
Chililabombwe, Zambia 115/E6
Chilili, N. Mex. (†87059) 274/C4
Chilka (lake), India 68/F5
Chilko (lake), Br. Col. 184/F4
Chilko (riv.), Br. Col. 184/E4
Chilkoot (pass), Alaska 196/M1
Chilkoot (pass), Br. Col. 184/J1
Chillán, Chile, 120/C6
Chillán, Chile 138/A11
Chillicothe, Ill. (61523) 222/D3
Chillicothe, Iowa (52548) 229/J6
Chillicothe, Mo. (64601) 261/E3
Chillicothe, Ohio (45601) 284/E7
Chillicothe, Texas (79225) 302/E3
Chilliwack, 163/D6
Chilliwack, Br. Col. 184/M3
Chillum, Md. (20783) 245/F4
Chilmark▵, Mass. (02535) 249/M7
Chilo, Ohio (45112) 284/B8
Chilocco, Okla. (74635) 288/M1
Chiloé (isl.), Chile, 120/C7
Chiloé (prov.), Chile 138/D4
Chiloé (isl.), Chile 138/D4
Chiloquin, Oreg. (97624) 291/F5
Chilpancingo de los Bravos, Mex. 150/K8
Chilton (co.), Ala. 194/E5
Chilton, Texas (76632) 302/G6
Chilton, Wis. (53014) 317/K7
Chiltonville, Mass. (†02360) 249/M5
Chilumbe, Malawi 115/F6
Chilwa (lake), Moz. 118/F3
Chilwa (lake), Malawi 115/G7
Chimacum, Wash. (98325) 310/C3
Chimaltenango, Guat. 154/B3
Chimán, Pan. 154/H6
Chimantá-tepuí (mt.), Ven. 124/G5
Chimay, Belg. 27/E8
Chimayo, N. Mex. (87522) 274/D3
Chimbarongo, Chile 138/A10
Chimbay, U.S.S.R. 48/F5
Chimborazo (mt.), Ec., 120/B3
Chimborazo (prov.), Ec. 128/C3
Chimborazo (mt.), Ec. 128/C3
Chimbote, Peru, 120/B3
Chimbote, Peru 128/C7
Chimbote (bay), Peru 128/C7
Chimichaqua, Col. 126/D3
Chimkent, U.S.S.R. 48/G5
Chimney Point, Vt. (†05491) 268/A3
Chimney Rock, Colo. (81127) 208/E8
Chimney Rock Nat'l Hist. Site, Nebr. 264/A3
Chimunai, China 77/C2
Chin, Alta. 182/D5
Chin (cape), Ont. 177/C2
Chin (hills), Burma 72/B2
China, 3/P4
China, 54/O6
CHINA, 77
China▵, Maine (04926) 242/E7
China, Maine (04926) 242/E7
China, Mex. 150/K4
Chinácota, Col. 126/D4
China Gardens (dam), Wash. 310/J4
China Grove, Ala. (†36081) 194/G7
China Grove, N.C. (28023) 281/H3
China Grove‡, Texas (†78201) 302/F8
Chinaja, Guat. 154/B2
China Lake, Calif. (93555) 204/H8
Chinameca, El Salv. 154/C4
Chinandega, Nic. 154/D4
Chinati (mts.), Texas 302/C12
Chinati (peak), Texas 302/C12
Chincha (isls.), Peru 128/D9
Chincha Alta, Peru 128/D9
Chinchaga (riv.), Alta. 182/A5
Chinchilla, Aust. 88/J5
Chinchilla de Monte Aragón, Spain 33/F3
Chinchiná, Col. 126/C5
Chinchón, Spain 33/G5
Chinchoua, Gabon 115/A4
Chinchow, Kwangsi Chuang, China 77/G7
Chinchow, Liaoning, China 77/J3
Chincoteague (bay), Md. 245/S8
Chincoteague, Va. (23336) 307/T5
Chincoteague (bay), Va. 307/T4
Chincoteague (inlet), Va. 307/T5
Chindamani Suma, Mong. 77/E2
Chindwin (riv.), Burma 72/B2
Chinese Camp, Calif. (95309) 204/E6
Chingleput, India 68/E6
Chingola, Zambia 115/E6
Chinguar, Angola 115/C6
Chinguetti, 102/A3
Chinguetti, Mauritania 106/B4
Chinhae, S. Korea 81/D6
Chin Hills (special div.), Burma 72/B2
Chiniak (cape), Alaska 196/H3
Chiñijo, Bol. 136/A4
Chiniot, Pak. 68/C2
Chínipas, Mex. 150/E3
Chinju, S. Korea 81/D6
Chinkapin Knob (mt.), Ark. 203/E2
Chinkiang, China, 54/R6
Chinkiang, China 77/K5
Chinle, Ariz. (86503) 198/F2
Chinle (creek), Ariz. 198/F2
Chinle (valley), Ariz. 198/F2
Chinle (creek), Utah 304/E6
Chinnur, India 68/D5
Chino (creek), Ariz. 198/C3
Chino, Calif. (91710) 204/D10
Chinon, France 28/D4
Chinook, Alta. 182/E4
Chinook, Mont. (59523) 262/G2
Chinook, Wash. (98614) 310/B4
Chinook (pass), Wash. 310/D4
Chinook Cove, Br. Col. 184/G4
Chinook Valley, Alta. 182/B1
Chino Valley, Ariz. (86323) 198/C4
Chinquapin, N.C. (28521) 281/O5
Chinsali, Zambia 115/F6
Chinsi, China 77/K3
Chinteche, Malawi 115/F6
Chinú, Col. 126/C3
Chinwangtao, China 77/K4
Chioggia, Italy 34/D2
Chios (Khíos) (isl.), Greece 45/G6
Chipamanu (riv.), Bol. 136/A2
Chipata, 102/F6
Chipata, Zambia 115/F6
Chipewyan, Alta., 146/G4
Chipewyan (lake), Alta. 182/D1
Chipewyan (riv.), Alta. 182/D1
Chipewyan Lake, Alta. 182/D1
Chipindo, Angola 115/B7
Chipinga, Rhod. 118/E4
Chip Lake, Alta. 182/C3
Chipley, Fla. (32428) 212/D6
Chiplun, India 68/C5
Chipman, Alta. 182/D3
Chipman, N. Br. 170/E2
Chipman (riv.), Sask. 181/M2
Chipman Brook, N.S. 169/D3
Chipoka, Malawi 115/F6
Chipola (riv.), Fla. 212/D6
Chipola, La. (†70441) 238/J5
Chippawa, Ont. 177/F4
Chippenham, 10/F5
Chippenham, Eng. 13/F6
Chippewa (co.), Mich. 250/E2
Chippewa (riv.), Mich. 250/E5
Chippewa (co.), Minn. 254/C5
Chippewa (riv.), Minn. 254/C5
Chippewa (riv.), Wis., 188/H1
Chippewa (co.), Wis. 317/D5
Chippewa (lake), Wis. 317/D4
Chippewa (riv.), Wis. 317/B7
Chippewa Falls, Wis. (54729) 317/D6
Chippewa Lake, Mich. (49320) 250/D5
Chippewa on the Lake‡, Ohio (44215) 284/G3
Chipping Campden, Eng. 13/F5
Chipping Norton, Eng. 13/F6
Chipping Sodbury, Eng. 13/E6
Chiputneticook (lakes), Maine 242/H4
Chiputneticook (lakes), N. Br. 170/C3
Chiquián, Peru 128/D8
Chiquimula, Guat. 154/C3
Chiquinquirá, Col., 120/C2
Chiquinquirá, Col. 126/C5
Chiquita (lake), Arg., 120/D6
Chir (riv.), U.S.S.R. 52/F5
Chira (riv.), Ec. 128/B5
Chira, China 77/B4
Chirala, India 68/E5
Chireno, Texas (75937) 302/K6
Chirfa, Niger 106/G4
Chiri (mt.), S. Korea 81/C6
Chiribiquete, Sierra de (mts.), Col. 126/D7
Chiricahua (mts.), Ariz. 198/F6
Chiricahua Nat'l Mon., Ariz. 198/F6
Chiriguaná, Col. 126/D3
Chirikof (isl.), Alaska 196/G3
Chirinos, Peru 128/C5
Chiriquí (gulf), Pan. 154/F7
Chiriquí (lag.), Pan. 154/G6
Chiriquí (vol.), Pan. 154/F6
Chiriquí Grande, Pan. 154/F6
Chirmiri, India 68/E4
Chirnside, Scot. 15/M8
Chiromo, Malawi 115/F7
Chironico, Switz. 39/G4
Chirpan, Bulg. 45/G4
Chirripó Grande (mt.), C. Rica 154/F6
Chirundu, Rhod. 118/D3
Chisago (co.), Minn. 254/F5
Chisago City, Minn. (55013) 254/E5
Chisamba, Zambia 115/E6
Chisana, Alaska (†99566) 196/K2
Chisec, Guat. 154/B3
Chisel Lake, Man. 179/H3
Chisholm, Maine (04222) 242/C7
Chisholm, Minn. (55719) 254/E3
Chisholm Mills, Alta. 182/C2
Chişineu Criş, Rum. 45/E2
Chismville, Ark. (†72943) 203/C3
Chisos (mts.), Texas 302/A8
Chistochina, Alaska (†99586) 196/K2
Chistopol', U.S.S.R. 52/H3
Chiswick, Ont. 177/E1
Chita, U.S.S.R. 48/M4
Chita, U.S.S.R., 54/P4
Chitado, Angola 115/B7
Chitado, S.W. Afr. 118/A3
Chitek (lake), Man. 179/C2
Chitek (lake), Sask. 181/D2
Chitek Lake, Sask. 181/D2
Chitembo, Angola 115/C6
Chitina, Alaska (99566) 196/K2
Chitina (riv.), Alaska 196/K2
Chitipa, Malawi 115/F5
Chitorgarh, India 68/C4
Chitose, Japan 81/K2
Chitradurga, India 68/D6
Chitral, Pak. 59/K2
Chitral, Pak. 68/C1
Chitré, Pan. 154/G7
Chittagong, Pak. 68/G4
Chittagong, Pak., 54/N7
Chittenango, N.Y. (13037) 276/J4
Chittenden (co.), Vt. 268/A3
Chittenden▵, Vt. (05737) 268/B4
Chittenden, Vt. (05737) 268/B4
Chittenden (res.), Vt. 268/B4
Chittoor, India 68/D6
Chiva, Spain 33/F3
Chivacoa, Ven. 124/D2
Chivapure (riv.), Ven. 124/E4
Chivasso, Italy 34/A2
Chivato (mesa), N. Mex. 274/B3
Chivay, Peru 128/G10
Chivé, Bol. 136/A3
Chivilcoy, Arg., 120/D6
Chivilcoy, Arg. 143/F7
Chivington, Colo. (81031) 208/O6
Chiwawa (riv.), Wash. 310/E2
Chixoy (riv.), Guat. 154/B2
Chixoy (riv.), Mex. 150/O8
Chizha, U.S.S.R. 52/F1
Chkalov (Orenburg), U.S.S.R. 52/J4
Chkalov (Orenburg), U.S.S.R., 7/K3
Chloe, W. Va. (25235) 313/D5
Chloride, Ariz. (86431) 198/A3
Chloride, Mo. (†63646) 261/L8
Chlumec, Czech. 41/C1
Chmielnik, Poland 47/E3
Choapa, Chile 138/A9
Choapa (riv.), Chile 138/A9
Chobe (riv.), Botswana 118/C3
Chobe (riv.), S.W. Afr. 118/C3
Choc, St. Lucia 161/G5
Choc (bay), St. Lucia 161/G5
Chocalán, Chile 138/F4
Chocaya, Bol. 136/B7
Choccolocco, Ala. (36254) 194/G3
Choceň, Czech. 41/D1
Choch'iwŏn, S. Korea 81/C5
Chocó (bay), Col. 126/B6
Chocó (dept.), Col. 126/B6
Chocolate (mts.), Ariz. 198/A5
Chocolate (mts.), Calif. 204/K10
Chocomán, Mex. 150/P2
Choconut, Pa. (†18818) 294/K2
Chocorua, N.H. (03817) 268/E4
Chocorua (mt.), N.H. 268/E4
Chocowinity, N.C. (27817) 281/P4
Choctaw (co.), Ala. 194/B6
Choctaw, Ala. (36905) 194/B6
Choctaw, Ark. (72028) 203/F2
Choctaw (co.), Miss. 256/F4
Choctaw (co.), Okla. 288/P6
Choctaw, Okla. (73020) 288/M3
Choctaw Bluff, Ala. (†36545) 194/C8
Choctawhatchee (riv.), Ala. 194/H8
Choctawhatchee (bay), Fla. 212/C6
Choctawhatchee (riv.), Fla. 212/C6
Chodov, Czech. 41/B1
Chodzież, Poland 47/C2
Choele-Choel, Arg. 143/C4
Choestoe, Ga. (†30512) 216/E1
Chofu, Japan 81/O2
Choibalsan, Mong. 77/H2
Choiceland, Sask. 181/G2
Choiren, Mong. 77/G2
Choiseul (isl.), Br. Sol. Is., 87/F6
Choiseul, St. Lucia 161/F7
Choisy-le-Roi, France 28/B2
Choix, Mex. 150/E3
Chojna, Poland 47/B2
Chojnice, Poland 47/C2
Chojnów, Poland 47/B3
Chokai (mt.), Japan 81/J4
Chokio, Minn. (56221) 254/B5
Chokoloskee, Fla. (33925) 212/E6
Chokurdakh, U.S.S.R. 48/P2
Chokurdakh, U.S.S.R., 4/B2
Cholame, Calif. (93431) 204/E8
Cholet, France 28/C4
Cholo, Malawi 115/F7
Choloma, Hond. 154/C3
Cholula de Rivadavia, Mex. 150/M1
Choluteca, Hond. 154/D4
Choluteca (riv.), Hond. 154/D4
Choma, Zambia 115/E7
Chomes, C. Rica 154/E5
Chomo Dzong, China 77/D6
Chomo Lhari (mt.), India 68/F3
Chomutov, Czech. 41/B1
Ch'ŏnan, S. Korea 81/C5
Chon Buri, Thai. 72/D4
Chonchi, Chile 138/D4
Chone, Ec. 128/B3
Ch' ŏngjin, N. Korea, 54/S5
Ch'ŏngjin, N. Korea 81/E3
Chŏngju, N. Korea 81/B4
Ch'ŏngju, S. Korea 81/C5
Chong Kal, Cambodia 72/D4
Chong Pak Phra (cape), Thai. 72/C5
Chŏngŭp, S. Korea 81/C6
Chŏnju, S. Korea 81/C6
Chon May (bay), S. Vietnam 72/F3
Chonos (arch.), Chile, 120/C7
Chonos (arch.), Chile 138/D6
Chopin, La. (71412) 238/E4
Choptank (riv.), Del. 245/P5
Choptank, Md. (†21655) 245/P6
Choptank (riv.), Md. 245/O6
Choquecota, Bol. 136/A6
Chorley, 10/G2
Chorley, Eng. 13/E4
Choroní, Ven. 124/E2
Choros (cape), Chile 138/A7
Choros, Los (riv.), Chile 138/A7
Chorrera, Pan. 154/H6
Chorrillos, Bol. 136/B7
Chorrillos, Peru 128/D9
Chortkov, U.S.S.R. 52/B5
Ch'ŏrwŏn, S. Korea 81/C4
Chorzów, Poland 47/B4
Ch'osan, N. Korea 81/C3
Choshi, Japan 81/K6
Chosica, Peru 128/D8
Chos-Malal, Arg. 143/C4
Choszczno, Poland 47/B2
Chota, Peru 128/C6
Choteau, Mont. (59422) 262/D3
Choteau (creek), S. Dak. 298/N7
Chotěboř, Czech. 41/C2
Choudrant, La. (71227) 238/F1
Chouteau (co.), Mont. 262/F3
Chouteau, Okla. (74337) 288/R2
Chovoreca, Cerro (mt.), Bol. 136/F6
Chovoreca, Cerro (mt.), Par. 144/C2
Chowan (co.), N.C. 281/R2
Chowan (riv.), N.C. 281/R2
Chowchilla, Calif. (93610) 204/E6
Chrastava, Czech. 41/C1
Chriesman, Texas (77838) 302/H7
Chrisman, Ill. (61924) 222/F4
Chrisney, Ind. (47611) 227/C8
Christchurch, 10/F5
Christchurch, Eng. 13/F7
Christchurch, N.Z., 3/T8
Christchurch, N. Z., 87/H10
Christchurch, N.Z. 101/D5
Christian, Alaska (†99740) 196/J1
Christian (sound), Alaska 196/M2
Christian (isl.), Ont. 177/D3
Christian (co.), Ill. 222/D4
Christian (co.), Ky. 237/F7
Christian (co.), Mo. 261/F9
Christian (cape), N.W.T. 187/M2
Christian, W. Va. (†25635) 313/C7
Christiana, Del. (19702) 245/R2
Christiana, Jam. 158/H6
Christiana, Pa. (17509) 294/K6
Christiana, S. Africa 118/D5
Christiana, Tenn. (37037) 237/J9
Christianburg-Wismar-Mackenzie, Guyana 131/B2
Christiansburg, Ohio (45389) 284/C5
Christiansburg, Va. (24073) 307/H6
Christiansfeld, Den. 21/C7
Christiansted, V.I. (U.S.) 156/H2
Christiansted, V.I.(U.S.) 161/F4
Christiansted Nat'l Hist. Site, V.I.(U.S.) 161/F4
Christie, Okla. (†74965) 288/S3
Christina (lake), Alta. 182/E2
Christina (riv.), Alta. 182/E1
Christina (lake), Minn. 254/C4
Christina, Mont. (59423) 262/G3
Christine, N. Dak. (58015) 283/S6
Christine, Texas (78012) 302/F9
Christmas, Ariz. (†85292) 198/E5
Christmas (isl.), Australia, 3/Q6
Christmas (isl.), Australia, 54/O11
Christmas, Fla. (32709) 212/E3
Christmas (isl.), Gilb. and Ell., 87/L5
Christmas, Mich. (49862) 250/C2
Christmas Creek, W. Aust. 92/D2
Christmas Island, N.S. 169/H3
Christopher, Ill. (62822) 222/D6
Christopher Lake, Sask. 181/F2
Christoval, Texas (76935) 302/D6
Chromo, Colo. (81128) 208/F8
Chrudim, Czech. 41/C2
Chrudimka (riv.), Czech. 41/C2
Chrysler, Ala. (36520) 194/C8
Chrzanów, Poland 47/D3
Chu (riv.), U.S.S.R. 48/H5
Chualar, Calif. (93925) 204/D7
Chüanchow, Fukien, China 77/J7
Chüanchow, Kwangsi Chuang, China 77/G6
Chuathbaluk‡, Alaska (†99559) 196/G2
Chubbuck, Idaho (83201) 220/F7
Chubu-Sangaku Nat'l Park, Japan 81/H5
Chubut (riv.), Arg., 120/D7
Chubut (prov.), Arg. 143/C5
Chubut (riv.), Arg. 143/C5
Chucheng, China 77/J4
Chuchi (lake), Br. Col. 184/E2
Chuchow, China 77/H6
Chu Chua, Br. Col. 184/H4
Chuckatuck, Va. (23339) 307/P7
Chuckey, Tenn. (37641) 237/R8
Chucunaque (riv.), Pan. 154/J6
Chudleigh, Eng. 13/D7
Chudovo, U.S.S.R. 52/D3
Chugach (isls.), Alaska 196/B2
Chugach (mts.), Alaska 196/C1
Chugiak, Alaska (99567) 196/C1
Chuginadak (isl.), Alaska 196/D4
Chuguchak, China 77/B2
Chugwater, Wyo. (82210) 319/H4
Chugwater (creek), Wyo. 319/H4
Chühsien, China 77/J6
Chukai, Malaysia 72/D6
Chukchi (sea), 4/C18
Chukchi (sea), Alaska 196/E1
Chukchi (pen.), U.S.S.R. 48/T3
Chukchi (sea), U.S.S.R. 48/T2
Chukchi (pen.), U.S.S.R., 4/C18
Chukchi (pen.), U.S.S.R., 54/X3
Chukchi Nat'l Okr., U.S.S.R. 48/R3
Chukhloma, U.S.S.R. 52/F3
Chula, Ark. (†72857) 203/C4
Chula, Ga. (31733) 216/E7
Chula, Mo. (64635) 261/F3
Chula, Va. (†23002) 307/N6
Chula Vista, Calif. (*92010) 204/J11
Chul'man, U.S.S.R. 48/N4
Chulucanas, Peru 128/B5
Chulumani, Bol. 136/B5
Chulym (riv.), U.S.S.R. 48/J4
Chuma, Bol. 136/A4
Chumar (riv.), China 77/D4
Chumatien, China 77/H5
Chumbicha, Arg. 143/C2
Chumikan, U.S.S.R. 48/O4
Chumikan, U.S.S.R., 54/S4
Chumphon, Thai. 72/C5
Chuna (riv.), U.S.S.R. 48/K4
Chunchi, Ec. 128/C4
Ch'unch'ŏn, S. Korea 81/D5
Chunchula, Ala. (36521) 194/B9
Chunghsin, China 77/K7
Ch'ungju, S. Korea 81/C5
Chungking, China, 3/P4
Chungking, China, 54/O7
Chungking, China 77/G6
Chungning, China 77/G4
Chŭngsan, N. Korea 81/B4
Chungshan, China 77/H7
Chungtien, China 77/E6
Chunky, Miss. (39323) 256/G6
Chunya (riv.), U.S.S.R. 48/K3
Chunya, Tanz. 115/F5
Chupaca, Peru 128/E9
Chupadera (mesa), N. Mex. 274/C5
Chupara (pt.), Trinidad Tobago 161/B10
Chuquibamba, Peru 128/F10
Chuquibambilla, Peru 128/F9
Chuquicamata, Chile 138/B3
Chuquichambi, Bol. 136/B5
Chuquisaca (dept.), Bol. 136/C6
Chur, Switz. 39/J3
Church, Iowa (†52151) 229/L2
Churchbridge, Sask. 181/J5
Church Creek, Md. (21622) 245/O6
Church Hill, Md. (21623) 245/O4
Church Hill, Miss. (39055) 256/B7
Church Hill, Tenn. (37642) 237/R7
Churchill (riv.), 163/F4
Churchill (peak), 163/D4
Churchill, 163/G4
Churchill (cape), 163/G4
Churchill (riv.), 163/K5
Churchill (peak), Br. Col. 184/L2
Churchill, Man., 146/J4
Churchill (riv.), Man., 146/J4
Churchill, Man. 179/K2
Churchill (cape), Man. 179/K2
Churchill (riv.), Man. 179/J2
Churchill (co.), Nev. 266/C3
Churchill (falls), Newf. 166/B3
Churchill (riv.), Newf. 166/B3
Churchill‡, Ohio (†44501) 284/J3
Churchill, Pa. (†15201) 294/C7
Churchill (riv.), Sask. 181/M3
Churchill Falls, Newf. 166/B3
Churchman (mt.), W. Aust. 92/B5
Church Point, La. (70525) 238/F6
Church Point, N.S. 169/B4
Church Road, Va. (23833) 307/N6
Church's Ferry, N. Dak. (58325) 283/M3
Church Stretton, Eng. 13/E5
Churchton, Md. (20733) 245/N5
Churchtown, Pa. (17510) 294/L5
Church View, Va. (23032) 307/P5
Churchville, Md. (21028) 245/N2
Churchville, N.Y. (14428) 276/E4
Churchville, Va. (24421) 307/K4
Churchville, W. Va. (†26338) 313/E4
Churdan, Iowa (50050) 229/D4
Churfirsten (mt.), Switz. 39/H2
Churín, Peru 128/D8
Churu, India 68/D3
Churubusco, Ind. (46723) 227/G2
Churubusco, N.Y. (12923) 276/N1
Churuguara, Ven. 124/D2
Churwalden, Switz. 39/J3
Chushan (arch.), China 77/K5
Chushul, India 68/D2
Chushul, China 77/D5
Chuska (mts.), N. Mex. 274/A2
Chusovoy, U.S.S.R. 52/J3
Chute-à-Blondeau, Ont. 177/K2
Chute-aux-Outardes, Que. 172/A1
Chuŭronjang, N. Korea 81/E2
Chuvash A.S.S.R., U.S.S.R. 48/E4
Chuvash A.S.S.R., U.S.S.R. 52/G3
Chuy, Urug. 145/F4
Chu Yang Sin (mt.), S. Vietnam 72/F4
Chvalšiny, Czech. 41/C2
Ciales, P. Rico 161/C1
Ciampino, Italy 34/F7
Cibecue, Ariz. (85901) 198/E4
Cibolo‡, Texas (78108) 302/F8
Cibolo (creek), Texas 302/C12
Cicero, Ill. (60650) 222/B2
Cicero, Ind. (46034) 227/E4
Cicero, N.Y. (13039) 276/H4
Cícero Dantas, Braz. 132/G5
Cicerone, W. Va. (†25243) 313/D5
Ciconcine (lake), Que. 172/D2
Cid, N.C. (†27292) 281/J3

Clinton 347

Cide, Turkey 63/E2
Cidlina (riv.), Czech. 41/C1
Cidra, Cuba 158/D1
Cidra, P. Rico 161/D2
Ciechanów, Poland 47/E2
Ciechocinek, Poland 47/D2
Ciego de Ávila, Cuba 156/B2
Ciego de Ávila, Cuba 158/F2
Ciempozuelos, Spain 33/F5
Ciénaga, Col., 120/C1
Ciénaga, Col. 126/C2
Ciénaga de Oro, Col. 126/C3
Cienfuegos, Cuba, 146/K7
Cienfuegos, Cuba 156/B2
Cienfuegos, Cuba 158/D2
Cienfuegos (bay), Cuba 158/D2
Cieplice Śląskie-Zdrój, Poland 47/B3
Čierny Balog, Czech. 41/E2
Cieszyn, Poland 47/D4
Cieza, Spain 33/F3
Çifteler, Turkey 63/D3
Cifuentes, Spain 33/E2
Cigánd, Hung. 41/F2
Cihanbeyli, Turkey 63/E3
Cihuatlán, Mex. 150/G7
Çildir, Turkey 63/K2
Çildir (lake), Turkey 63/K2
Cilleros, Spain 33/C2
Cilo Daği (mt.), Leb. 63/K4
Cima, Calif. (92323) 204/K8
Cimarron (riv.), 188/G3
Cimarron, Colo. (81220) 208/D6
Cimarron, Kans. (87835) 232/B4
Cimarron (riv.), Kans. 232/B4
Cimarron, N. Mex. (87714) 274/E2
Cimarron (riv.), N. Mex. 274/E2
Cimarron (co.), Okla. 288/A1
Cimarron (riv.), Okla. 288/N2
Cimin, Turkey 63/H3
Cimone (mt.), Italy 34/C2
Cîmpeni, Rum. 45/F2
Cîmpia Turzii, Rum. 45/F2
Cîmpina, Rum. 45/H3
Cîmpulung, Rum. 45/G3
Cîmpulung Moldovenesc, Rum. 45/G2
Cinaruco (riv.), Col. 126/F4
Cinaruco (riv.), Ven. 124/D4
Cinca (riv.), Spain 33/G2
Cincinnati, Ark. (†72769) 203/B1
Cincinnati, Iowa (52549) 229/G7
Cincinnati, Ohio, 146/K6
Cincinnati, Ohio, 188/K3
Cincinnati, Ohio (*45201) 284/B9
Cincinnatus, N.Y. (13040) 276/H5
Cinclare, La. (†70767) 238/J2
Cinco, W. Va. (25306) 313/D6
Cinco Balas (cay), Cuba 158/E3
Cinco Bayou, Fla. (†32548) 212/B6
Cinco Saltos, Arg. 143/C4
Cinderella, W. Va. (†25661) 313/B7
Çine, Turkey 63/B4
Cinebar, Wash. (98533) 310/C4
Ciney, Belg. 27/G8
Cintalapa de Figueroa, Mex. 150/N8
Cinto (mt.), France 28/B6
Cipolletti, Arg. 143/C4
Circeo (cape), Italy 34/D4
Circle, Alaska (99733) 196/K1
Circle, Mont. (59215) 262/L3
Circle (cliffs), Utah 304/C6
Circle Back, Texas (†79371) 302/B3
Circle Pines, Minn. (55014) 254/G5
Circle Springs, Alaska (†99730) 196/K1
Circleville, Kans. (66416) 232/G2
Circleville, Ohio (43113) 284/D6
Circleville, Utah (84723) 304/B5
Circleville, W. Va. (26804) 313/H5
Cirencester, 10/F5
Cirencester, Eng. 13/F6
Cirque (mt.), Newf. 166/B2
Cisco, Ga. (30708) 216/C1
Cisco, Ill. (61830) 222/E3
Cisco, Texas (76437) 302/E5
Cisco, Utah (84515) 304/E5
Cisco Springs Wash (creek), Utah 304/E4
Cismont, Va. (22928) 307/M4
Cisnădie, Rum. 45/G3
Cisne, Ill. (62823) 222/E5
Cisneros, Col. 126/C4
Cisnes (riv.), Chile 138/E5
Cispus (pass), Wash. 310/D4
Cispus (ridge), Wash. 310/D4
Cissna Park, Ill. (60924) 222/F3
Cité de Cansado, Mauritania 106/A4
Citlaltépetl (mt.), Mex. 150/O2
Citra, Fla. (32627) 212/D2
Citronelle, Ala. (36522) 194/B8
Citrus (co.), Fla. 212/D3
Citrus Center, Fla. (†33471) 212/E5
Citrus Heights, Calif. (95610) 204/C8
Cittadella, Italy 34/C2
Città di Castello, Italy 34/C3
Cittanova, Italy 34/F5
City Mills, Mass. (†02056) 249/J4
City of Refuge Nat'l Hist. Park, Hawaii 218/G6
City Point, Fla. (†32922) 212/F3
City Point, Wis. (54466) 317/F7
City View, Ont. 177/J2
City View, S.C. (29611) 296/C2
Ciudad Acuña, Mex. 150/J2
Ciudad Altamirano, Mex. 150/J7
Ciudad Bolívar, Ven., 120/D2
Ciudad Bolívar, Ven. 124/G3
Ciudad Bolivia, Ven. 124/C3
Ciudad Camargo, Chihuahua, Mex. 150/G3
Ciudad Camargo, Tamaulipas, Mex. 150/K3
Ciudad Darío, Nic. 154/D4
Ciudad Delicias, Mex. 150/G2
Ciudad del Maíz, Mex. 150/K5
Ciudad de Nutrias, Ven. 124/D3
Ciudad de Valles, Mex. 150/K5
Ciudadela, Spain 33/H2
Ciudad Guayana, Ven. 124/G3
Ciudad Guerrero, Mex. 150/F2
Ciudad Guzmán, Mex. 150/H7
Ciudad Juárez, Mex., 146/H6
Ciudad Juárez, Mex. 150/F1
Ciudad Lerdo, Mex. 150/H4
Ciudad Madero, Mex. 150/L5
Ciudad Mante, Mex. 150/K5
Ciudad Mendoza, Mex. 150/O2
Ciudad Miguel Alemán, Mex. 150/K3
Ciudad Obregón, Mex. 150/E3
Ciudad Ojeda, Ven. 124/C2
Ciudad Piar, Ven. 124/G4
Ciudad Quesada, C. Rica 154/E5
Ciudad Real (prov.), Spain 33/D3
Ciudad Real, Spain 33/D3
Ciudad Río Bravo, Mex. 150/K4
Ciudad Rodrigo, Spain 33/C2
Ciudad Serdán, Mex. 150/O2
Ciudad Victoria, Mex. 150/K5
Civa (cape), Turkey 63/G2
Cividale del Friuli, Italy 34/D1
Civitavecchia, Italy 34/C3
Civitella del Tronto, Italy 34/D3
Civray, France 28/D4
Civril, Turkey 63/C3
Cizre, Turkey 63/J4
Clackamas (co.), Oreg. 291/E2
Clackamas, Oreg. (97015) 291/B2
Clackamas (riv.), Oreg. 291/E2
Clackmannan, 10/B1
Clackmannan (co.), Scot. 15/J7
Clackmannan, Scot. 15/J7
Clacton, Eng. 13/J6
Clacton-on-Sea, 10/G5
Claflin, Kans. (67525) 232/D3
Claiborne, Ala. (36434) 194/D7
Claiborne (par.), La. 238/D1
Claiborne (lake), La. 238/E1
Claiborne, Md. (21624) 245/N5
Claiborne (co.), Miss. 256/C7
Claiborne (co.), Tenn. 237/O8
Clair (lake), Que. 172/E2
Clair, N. Br. 170/B1
Clair, Sask. 181/G3
Claire (lake), 163/E4
Claire (lake), Alta. 182/B5
Claire City, S. Dak. (57224) 298/P2
Clairemont, Texas (79509) 302/D4
Clair Engle (lake), Calif. 204/C3
Clairette, Texas (76441) 302/F5
Clairfield, Tenn. (37715) 237/O7
Clair Haven‡, Mich. (†48043) 250/B6
Clairmont, Alta. 182/A2
Clairmont Springs, Ala. (†35160) 194/G4
Clairton, Pa. (15025) 294/C7
Clallam (co.), Wash. 310/B2
Clallam Bay, Wash. (98326) 310/A2
Clam (bay), N.S. 169/F4
Clam (lake), Wis. 317/B4
Clam (riv.), Wis. 317/A4
Clamart, France 28/A2
Clamecy, France 28/E4
Clam Falls, Wis. (54825) 317/B4
Clam Gulch, Alaska (99568) 196/B1
Clam Lake, Wis. (54517) 317/E3
Clan Alpine (mts.), Nev. 266/D3
Clancy, Mont. (59634) 262/E4
Clandeboye, Ont. 177/C4
Clandeboye, Man. 179/E4
Clandonald, Alta. 182/E3
Clanton, Ala. (35045) 194/E5
Clanwilliam, Man. 179/C4
Clanwilliam, S. Africa 118/B6
Clapperton (isl.), Ont. 177/B1
Clàr, nan (lake), Scot. 15/J3
Clara 10/C4
Clara, Ire. 17/F5
Clara, Miss. (39324) 256/G7
Clara, Urug. 145/D3
Clara City, Minn. (56222) 254/C6
Claravale, No. Terr. 93/B3
Clare, Ill. (60111) 222/E1
Clare, Ind. (†46060) 227/F4
Clare, Iowa (50524) 229/E3
Clare (co.), Ire. 17/D6
Clare (riv.), Ire. 17/D5
Clare (co.), Mich. 250/E5
Clare, Mich. (48617) 250/E5
Clare, N.S.W. 97/B3
Clare. S. Aust. 94/F5
Claregalway, Ire. 17/D5
Claremont, Calif. (91711) 204/D10
Claremont, Jam. 158/J6
Claremont, Ont. 177/K3
Claremont, Ill. (62421) 222/F5
Claremont, Minn. (55924) 254/E6
Claremont, N.C. (28610) 281/G3
Claremont, N.H. (03743) 268/C5
Claremont, S. Dak. (57432) 298/N2
Claremont, Va. (23899) 307/P6
Claremore, Okla. (74017) 288/R2
Claremorris, 10/B4
Claremorris. Ire. 17/C4
Clarence (str.), Alaska 196/N2
Clarence (str.), Aust. 88/E2
Clarence (isl.), Chile, 120/C8
Clarence (isl.), Chile 138/E10
Clarence, Iowa (52216) 229/M5
Clarence, La. (71414) 238/E3
Clarence, Mo. (63437) 261/H3
Clarence (riv.), N.S.W. 97/G1
Clarence (cape), N.W.T. 187/K2
Clarence (head), N.W.T. 187/L2
Clarence, N.Y. (14031) 276/C5
Clarence (riv.), N.Z. 101/E5
Clarence (str.), No. Terr. 93/B2
Clarence, Pa. (16829) 294/G3
Clarence Bridge, N.Z. 101/E5
Clarence Center‡, N.Y. (14032) 276/C5
Clarence Creek, Ont. 177/J2
Clarenceville, Que. 172/D4
Clarendon, Ark. (72029) 203/H4
Clarendon (lake), Ont. 177/G3
Clarendon, N.C. (28432) 281/M6
Clarendon, Pa. (16313) 294/D2
Clarendon (co.), S.C. 296/G4
Clarendon, Texas (79226) 302/C3
Clarendon△, Vt. (†05759) 268/A4
Clarendon, Vt. (†05759) 268/A4
Clarendon Hills, Ill. (60514) 222/A2
Clarens, Switz. 39/C4
Clarenville, Newf. 166/C2
Claresholm, Alta. 182/D4
Clare with Inishturk (isls.), 10/A4
Clare with Inishturk (isls.), Ire. 17/A4
Claridenstock (mt.), Switz. 39/G3
Clarie Coast (reg.), Ant. 5/C7
Clarinda, Iowa (51632) 229/C7
Clarines, Ven. 124/F3
Clarington, Ohio (43915) 284/J6
Clarington, Pa. (15828) 294/D3
Clarion, Iowa (50525) 229/F3
Clarión (isl.), Mex. 150/B7
Clarion, Mich. (†49796) 250/E3
Clarion (co.), Pa. 294/D3
Clarion, Pa. (16214) 294/D3
Clarion (riv.), Pa. 294/D3
Clarion River, East Branch (res.), Pa. 294/E2
Clarissa, Minn. (56440) 254/C4
Clarita, Okla. (74535) 288/O6
Clark (lake), Alaska 196/H2
Clark (co.), Ark. 203/D5
Clark, Colo. (80428) 208/F1
Clark (pt.), Ont. 177/C3
Clark (co.), Idaho 220/F5
Clark (co.), Ill. 222/F4
Clark (co.), Ind. 227/F8
Clark (co.), Kans. 232/C4
Clark (co.), Ky. 237/N4
Clark (co.), Mo. 261/J2
Clark, Mo. (65243) 261/H4
Clark, N.C. (†28560) 281/P4
Clark (buttes), N. Dak. 283/G7
Clark△, N.J. (07066) 273/A3
Clark (co.), Nev. 266/F6
Clark (co.), Ohio 284/C6
Clark, Ohio (43810) 284/G5
Clark, Pa. (16113) 294/B3
Clark (co.), S. Dak. 298/O4
Clark, S. Dak. (57225) 298/O4
Clark (co.), Wash. 310/C5
Clark (co.), Wis. 317/E6
Clark, Wyo. (†59008) 319/C1
Clark Bridge, Sask. 181/F6
Clark Center, Ill. (†62441) 222/F4
Clarkdale, Ariz. (86324) 198/C4
Clarke (co.), Ala. 194/C7
Clarke, Arg. 143/F6
Clarke (co.), Ga. 216/F3
Clarke (co.), Iowa 229/F6
Clarke (co.), Miss. 256/G6
Clarke (range), Queens. 95/C4
Clarke (co.), Va. 307/M2
Clarke City, Que. 174/D2
Clarkedale, Ark. (72325) 203/K3
Clarke's Beach, Newf. 166/D2
Clarkesville, Ga. (30523) 216/F1
Clarkfield, Minn. (56223) 254/C6
Clark Fork, Idaho (83811) 220/B1
Clark Fork (riv.), Mont., 188/D1
Clark Fork (riv.), Mont. 262/A3
Clark Hill (res.), Ga. 216/H3
Clark Hill (dam), S.C. 296/C4
Clark Hill (res.), S.C. 296/C4
Clarkia, Idaho (83812) 220/B2
Clark Island, Maine (†04859) 242/E8
Clarklake, Mich. (49234) 250/E6
Clarkleigh, Man. 179/D4
Clark Mills‡, N.Y. (13321) 276/K4
Clarkrange, Tenn. (38553) 237/L8
Clarks, La. (71415) 238/F2
Clarks, Nebr. (68628) 264/G3
Clarksboro, N.J. (08020) 273/C4
Clarksburg, Calif. (95612) 204/B9
Clarksburg, Ont. 177/D3
Clarksburg, Ind. (47225) 227/G6
Clarksburg, Md. (20734) 245/J4
Clarksburg, Mo. (65025) 261/G5
Clarksburg, N.J. (08510) 273/E3
Clarksburg, Ohio (43115) 284/D7
Clarksburg, Tenn. (38324) 237/E9
Clarksburg, W. Va., 188/K3
Clarksburg, W. Va. (26301) 313/F4
Clarks Corner, Conn. (†06256) 210/G1
Clarksdale, Miss., 188/J4
Clarksdale, Miss. (38614) 256/D2
Clarksdale, Mo. (64430) 261/D3
Clarks Falls, Conn. (†06359) 210/H3
Clarks Fork, Yellowstone (riv.), Mont. 262/G6
Clarks Fork (riv.), Wyo. 319/C1
Clarks Green‡, Pa. (†18411) 294/L3
Clarks Grove, Minn. (56016) 254/E7
Clark's Harbour, N.S. 169/C5
Clarks Hill, Ind. (47930) 227/D4
Clarks Hill, S.C. (29821) 296/C4
Clarks Mill, Maine (†04847) 242/B8
Clarks Mills, Pa. (16114) 294/B3
Clarkson, Ky. (42726) 237/J6
Clarkson, Miss. (†39752) 256/F3
Clarkson, N.Y. (14430) 276/E4
Clarkson, Nebr. (68629) 264/G3
Clarkson Valley, Alta. 182/B2
Clarkson Valley, Mo. (†63017) 261/N3
Clarks Point, Alaska (99569) 196/G3
Clarks Summit, Pa. (18411) 294/L3
Clarkston, Ga. (30021) 216/D3
Clarkston, Mich. (48016) 250/F6
Clarkston, Utah (84305) 304/B2
Clarkston, Wash. (99403) 310/H4
Clark's Town, Jam. 158/H6
Clarksville, Ark. (72830) 203/D3
Clarksville, Del. (19937) 245/T6
Clarksville, Fla. (32430) 212/D6
Clarksville, Ind. (47130) 227/F8
Clarksville, Iowa (50619) 229/H3
Clarksville, Md. (21029) 245/L4
Clarksville, Mich. (48815) 250/D6
Clarksville, Mo. (63336) 261/K4
Clarksville△, N.H. (†05902) 268/E1
Clarksville, N.H. (†05902) 268/E1
Clarksville, N.Y. (12041) 276/M5
Clarksville, Ohio (45113) 284/C7
Clarksville, Pa. (15322) 294/B6
Clarksville (Clark), Pa. (16113) 294/B3
Clarksville, Tenn., 188/J3
Clarksville, Tenn. (37040) 237/G7
Clarksville, Texas (75426) 302/K4
Clarksville, Va. (23927) 307/M7
Clarksville City‡, Texas (†75647) 302/K5
Clarkton, Mo. (63837) 261/M10
Clarkton, N.C. (28433) 281/M6
Clarkville, Colo. (†80731) 208/P2
Clarno, Wis. (†53566) 317/G10
Claro (riv.), Bol. 136/A3
Claro (riv.), Chile 138/G5
Claro (riv.), Braz. 132/D7
Claro, Switz. 39/G4
Clashmoor, Sask. 181/H3
Clashmore, Ire. 17/F8
Clatonia, Nebr. (68328) 264/H4
Clatskanie, Oreg. (97016) 291/D1
Clatsop (co.), Oreg. 291/D1
Claud, Ala. (†36024) 194/F5
Claude, Texas (79019) 302/C2
Claudell, Kans. (†66951) 232/C2
Claudville, Va. (24076) 307/H7
Claudy, N. Ire. 17/G2
Claunch, N. Mex. (87011) 274/C4
Claussen, S.C. (†29501) 296/H3
Clausthal-Zellerfeld, W. Ger. 22/D3
Claverack, N.Y. (12513) 276/N6
Claveria, Phil. 82/C1
Clavet, Sask. 181/E4
Clawson, Mich. (48017) 250/B6
Clawson, Utah (84516) 304/C4
Claxton, Ga. (30417) 216/J6
Clay (co.), Ala. 194/G4
Clay (co.), Ark. 203/K1
Clay, Calif. (†95638) 204/C9
Clay (creek), Colo. 208/O7
Clay (co.), Fla. 212/E2
Clay (co.), Ga. 216/B7
Clay (co.), Ill. 222/E5
Clay (co.). Ind. 227/C6
Clay (co.), Iowa 229/C2
Clay (co.), Kans. 232/E2
Clay (co.), Ky. 237/O6
Clay, Ky. (42404) 237/F6
Clay, La. (71228) 238/E2
Clay (co.), Minn. 254/B4
Clay (co.), Miss. 256/G3
Clay (co.), Mo. 261/D4
Clay (co.), N.C. 281/B4
Clay (co.), Nebr. 264/F4
Clay (co.), S. Dak. 298/P8
Clay (co.), Tenn. 237/K7
Clay (co.), Texas 302/F4
Clay (hills), Utah 304/D6
Clay (co.), W. Va. 313/D6
Clay, W. Va. (25043) 313/D6
Claybank, Sask. 181/F5
Clay Bank, Va. (†23061) 307/P6
Clayburn, Br. Col. 184/L3
Clay Center, Kans. (67432) 232/E2
Clay Center, Nebr. (68933) 264/F4
Clay Center, Ohio (43408) 284/D2
Clay City, Ill. (62824) 222/E5
Clay City, Ind. (47841) 227/C6
Clay City, Ky. (40312) 237/O5
Claycomo, Mo. (64119) 261/P5
Clay Cross, Eng. 13/F4
Claydon, Sask. 181/B6
Claymont, Del. (19703) 245/S1
Claymour, Ky. (†42220) 237/G7
Clayoquot, Br. Col. 184/D5
Clayoquot (sound), Br. Col. 184/D5
Claypool, Ariz. (85532) 198/E5
Claypool, Ind. (46510) 227/F2
Claypool, Ky. (†42101) 237/J7
Claysburg, Pa. (16625) 294/F5
Clay Springs, Ariz. (†85934) 198/E4
Claysville, Ohio (43729) 284/G6
Claysville, Pa. (15323) 294/B5
Clayton, Ala. (36015) 194/G7
Clayton, Calif. (94517) 204/K2
Clayton, Del. (19938) 245/R3
Clayton (co.), Ga. 216/D3
Clayton, Ga. (30525) 216/F1
Clayton, Idaho (83227) 220/D5
Clayton, Ill. (62324) 222/B3
Clayton, Ind. (46118) 227/D5
Clayton (co.), Iowa 229/L3
Clayton, Iowa (†52049) 229/L3
Clayton, Kans. (67629) 232/B2
Clayton, La. (71326) 238/H3
Clayton (lake), Maine 242/D2
Clayton, Mich. (49235) 250/E7
Clayton, Miss. (†38626) 256/D1
Clayton, Mo. (63105) 261/P3
Clayton, N.C. (27520) 281/N3
Clayton, N.J. (08312) 273/C4
Clayton, N. Mex. (88415) 274/F2
Clayton, N.Y. (13624) 276/H2
Clayton, Ohio (45315) 284/B6
Clayton, Okla. (74536) 288/R5
Clayton, S. Dak. (†57332) 298/O7
Clayton, Vic. 97/J5
Clayton, W. Va. (†24910) 313/E7
Clayton, Wash. (99110) 310/H3
Clayton, Wis. (54004) 317/B5
Clayton Lake, Maine (04018) 242/E2
Claytonville, Ill. (60926) 222/F3
Clayton, Sask. 181/F2
Claytor (lake), Va 307/G6
Clayville, N.Y. (13322) 276/K5
Clayville, R.I. (02815) 249/H5
Clayville, Va. (23034) 307/N6
Clear, Alaska (99704) 196/J2
Clear (cape), Alaska 196/D1
Clear (hills), Alta. 182/A1
Clear (creek), Ariz. 198/D4
Clear (lake), Calif., 188/B3
Clear (lake), Calif. 204/C4
Clear (lake), Ont. 177/F3
Clear (lake), Ont. 177/G2
Clear (cape), 10/B5
Clear (lake), Iowa 229/G2
Clear (cape), Ire., 7/C3
Clear (cape), Ire. 17/B9
Clear (isl.), Ire. 17/C9
Clear (lake), La. 238/D3
Clear (lake), Man. 179/C4
Clear (creek), Utah 304/B5
Clear (lake), Utah 304/B4
Clear (creek), Wyo. 319/F1
Clear Boggy (creek), Okla. 288/O6
Clearbrook, Minn. (56634) 254/C3
Clear Brook, Va. (22624) 307/M2
Clearco, W. Va. (25959) 313/F6
Clear Creek, Calif. (†96039) 204/B2
Clear Creek (co.), Colo. 208/H3
Clear Creek, Ind. (47426) 227/E6
Clearcreek, Utah (†84538) 304/C4
Clear Creek, W. Va. (25044) 313/D7
Clearfield, Iowa (50840) 229/D7
Clearfield, Ky. (40313) 237/P4
Clearfield (co.), Pa. 294/F3
Clearfield, Pa. (16830) 294/F3
Clearfield, S. Dak. (57581) 298/K7
Clearfield, Sask. 181/H6
Clearfield, Utah (84015) 304/B2
Clear Fork (res.), Ohio 284/E4
Clear Fork, Mohican (riv.), Ohio 284/F4
Clear Fork, Brazos (riv.), Texas 302/D5
Clear Fork, Guyandotte (riv.), W. Va. 313/C7
Clear Hills, Alta. 182/B1
Clear Lake (res.), Calif. 204/D2
Clear Lake‡, Ill. (†62701) 222/D4
Clear Lake, Ind. (†46737) 227/H1
Clear Lake, Iowa (50428) 229/G2
Clear Lake, La. (†71414) 238/E3
Clear Lake, Minn. (55319) 254/E5
Clear Lake, S. Dak. (57226) 298/R4
Clear Lake, Sask. 181/B3
Clearlake, Wash. (98235) 310/C2
Clear Lake, Wis. (54005) 317/B5
Clear Lake City, Texas (†77598) 302/K2
Clearlake Highlands, Calif. (95422) 204/C5
Clearlake Oaks, Calif. (95423) 204/C4
Clear Lake Shores, Texas (†77565) 302/K2
Clearmont, Mo. (64431) 261/C1
Clearmont, Wyo. (82835) 319/F1
Clear Prairie, Alta. 182/A1
Clear Ridge, Pa. (†17229) 294/F5
Clearsite, Sask. 181/B6
Clear Spring, Ind. (†47220) 227/E7
Clear Spring, Md. (21722) 245/G2
Clearview, Okla. (74835) 288/O4
Clearview, W. Va. (†26003) 313/E2
Clearville, Pa. (15535) 294/F6
Clearwater (riv.), Alta. 182/C4
Clearwater (riv.), Alta. 182/E1
Clearwater, Br. Col. 184/G4
Clearwater (lake), Br. Col. 184/G4
Clearwater (riv.), Br. Col. 184/G4
Clearwater, Fla. (*33515) 212/B2
Clearwater (co.), Idaho 220/C3
Clearwater, Idaho (83521) 220/C3
Clearwater (mts.), Idaho 220/C3
Clearwater (riv.), Idaho 220/B3
Clearwater, Kans. (67026) 232/E4
Clearwater, Man. 179/D5
Clearwater (co.), Minn. 254/C3
Clearwater, Minn. (55320) 254/D5
Clearwater (riv.), Minn. 254/C3
Clearwater (lake), Mo. 261/L8
Clearwater (brook), N. Br. 170/D2
Clearwater, Nebr. (68726) 264/F2
Clearwater, S.C. (29822) 296/D4
Clearwater (riv.), Sask. 181/L3
Clearwater, Wash. (98399) 310/A3
Clearwater Beach (isl.), Fla. 212/B2
Clearwater Lake, Wis. (54518) 317/H4
Clearwater Prov. Park, Man. 179/H3
Cleator Moor, Eng. 13/D3
Cleburne (co.), Ala. 194/G3
Cleburne (co.), Ark. 203/F2
Cleburne, Texas, 188/G4
Cleburne, Texas (76031) 302/G5
Cle Elum, Wash. (98922) 310/E3
Cle Elum (lake), Wash. 310/E3
Cleethorpes, 10/F4
Cleethorpes, Eng. 13/H4
Cleeves, Sask. 181/C2
Cleghorn, Iowa (51014) 229/B3
Cleghorn, Wis. (†54738) 317/C6
Clem, Ga. (30128) 216/B3
Clemenceau, Ariz. (†86326) 198/C4
Clemenceau, Sask. 181/J3
Clément, Fr. Gui. 131/E4
Clemente (isl.), Chile 138/D6
Clementon, N.J. (08021) 273/D4
Clements, Calif. (95227) 204/C9
Clements, Kans. (66844) 232/F3
Clements, Md. (20624) 245/L7
Clements, Minn. (56224) 254/D6
Clementson, Minn. (56623) 254/D2
Clementsport, N.S. 169/C4
Clementsvale, N.S. 169/C4
Clementsville, N. Dak. (†58492) 283/O5
Clemmons, N.C. (27012) 281/J2
Clemons, Iowa (50051) 229/G4
Clemscot, Okla. (†73437) 288/L6
Clemson, S.C. (29631) 296/B2
Clendenin, W. Va. (25045) 313/D5
Clendening (res.), Ohio 284/H5
Cleona‡, Pa. (17042) 294/K5
Cleopatra Needle (mt.), Phil. 82/B5
Cleora, Okla. (†74331) 288/S1
Cleo Springs, Okla. (73729) 288/K2
Clerf (riv.), Lux. 27/J8
Clermont, Aust. 88/H4
Clermont, Que. 172/G2
Clermont, Fla. (32711) 212/E3
Clermont, France 28/E3
Clermont, Ga. (30527) 216/E2
Clermont, Iowa (52135) 229/K3
Clermont, Ky. (40110) 237/K5
Clermont, N.Y. (†12526) 276/N6
Clermont, Queens. 95/C4
Clermont (co.), Ohio 284/B7
Clermont, Pa. (16722) 294/E2
Clermont-Ferrand, France, 7/E4
Clermont-Ferrand, France 28/E5
Clermont Harbor, Miss. (39551) 256/F10
Clervaux, Lux. 27/J8
Cleve, S. Aust. 94/E5
Clevedon, Eng. 13/E6
Cleveland, Ala. (35049) 194/E3
Cleveland (co.), Ark. 203/F6
Cleveland, Ark. (72030) 203/E3
Cleveland, Aust. 88/K2
Cleveland, Fla. (†33950) 212/E5
Cleveland, Ga. (30528) 216/E1
Cleveland, Idaho (†83263) 220/G7
Cleveland‡, Ill. (†61254) 222/C2
Cleveland, Minn. (56017) 254/E6
Cleveland, Miss. (38732) 256/C3
Cleveland, Mo. (64734) 261/C5
Cleveland, Mont. (†59523) 262/G2
Cleveland (co.), N.C. 281/F4
Cleveland, N.C. (27013) 281/H3
Cleveland, N. Dak. (58424) 283/M6
Cleveland, N. Mex. (87715) 274/D2
Cleveland, N.Y. (13042) 276/J4
Cleveland, Ohio, 146/K5
Cleveland, Ohio, 188/K2
Cleveland, Ohio (*44101) 284/H9
Cleveland (co.), Okla. 288/M4
Cleveland, Okla. (74020) 288/O2
Cleveland, S.C. (29635) 296/C1
Cleveland, Tenn. (37311) 237/M10
Cleveland, Texas (77327) 302/K7
Cleveland, Utah (84518) 304/D4
Cleveland, Va. (24225) 307/D7
Cleveland, W. Va. (26215) 313/F5
Cleveland, Wis. (53015) 317/L8
Cleveland Heights, Ohio (44118) 284/H9
Cleveland-Hopkins Mun. Airport, Ohio 284/G9
Clevelândia do Norte, Braz. 132/D2
Cleveland Park, D.C. (20008) 245/E4
Clever, Mo. (65631) 261/F8
Cleves, Iowa (†50601) 229/G4
Cleves, Ohio (45002) 284/B9
Clew (bay), 10/B4
Clew (bay), Ire. 17/B4
Clewiston, Fla. (33440) 212/E5
Clichy, France 28/B1
Clicquot-Millis, Mass. (†02054) 249/A8
Clifden, 10/B4
Clifden, Ire. 17/B5
Cliff‡, Mo. (†64801) 261/D8
Cliff, N. Mex. (88028) 274/A6
Cliff (cape), N.S. 169/C3
Cliff (creek), Utah 304/E3
Cliffdell, Wash. (†98937) 310/E4
Cliff Island, Maine (04019) 242/C8
Clifford, Ont. 177/D4
Clifford, Ind. (47226) 227/F6
Clifford, Ky. (41208) 237/S4
Clifford (lake), Maine 242/H5
Clifford, Mich. (48727) 250/F5
Clifford, N. Dak. (58016) 283/R5
Clifford, Pa. (18413) 294/L2
Clifford, Va. (24533) 307/K5
Clifford, Wis. (†54564) 317/F4
Cliffordvale, N. Br. 170/C2
Cliffside, N.C. (28024) 281/F4
Cliffside Park, N.J. (07010) 273/C2
Clifftop, W. Va. (25822) 313/E6
Cliffwood, N.J. (07721) 273/E3
Clifton, Ariz. (85533) 198/F5
Clifton, Colo. (81520) 208/C4
Clifton, Eng. 13/E3
Clifton, Idaho (83228) 220/F7
Clifton, Ill. (60927) 222/F3
Clifton, Kans. (66937) 232/E2
Clifton, La. (†70438) 238/K5
Clifton△, Maine (†04428) 242/G6
Clifton, N. Br. 170/E1
Clifton, N.J. (*07011) 273/B2
Clifton, Ohio (45316) 284/C6
Clifton, S.C. (29324) 296/D2
Clifton, Tenn. (38425) 237/F10
Clifton, Texas (76634) 302/G6
Clifton‡, Va. (22024) 307/O3
Clifton, W. Va. (25237) 313/B5
Clifton, Wis. (†54618) 317/F8
Clifton City, Mo. (†65348) 261/G5
Clifton Forge, Va. (24422) 307/J5
Clifton Heights, Pa. (19018) 294/M7
Clifton Hill, Mo. (65244) 261/G4
Clifton Hills, S. Aust. 94/F2
Clifton Knolls‡, N.Y. (†12118) 276/N5
Clifton Mills, W. Va. (†26525) 313/G3
Clifton Park△, N.Y. (†12118) 276/N5
Clifton Royal, N. Br. 170/E3
Clifton Springs, N.Y. (14432) 276/F4
Cliftonville, Miss. (39742) 256/H4
Clifty, Ark. (72720) 203/C1
Clifty, Ind. (†47240) 227/F6
Clifty (creek), Ind. 227/F6
Clifty, Ky. (42216) 237/G7
Clifty, Tenn. (†38583) 237/L9
Clifty, W. Va. (†25854) 313/E6
Climax, Colo. (80429) 208/G4
Climax, Ga. (31734) 216/D9
Climax, Kans. (67027) 232/F4
Climax, Ky. (40413) 237/N6
Climax, Mich. (49034) 250/D6
Climax, Minn. (56523) 254/B3
Climax, N.C. (27233) 281/K3
Climax, Sask. 181/C6
Climax Springs, Mo. (65324) 261/G6
Climbing Hill, Iowa (51015) 229/B4
Clinch (co.), Ga. 216/G9
Clinch (riv.), Tenn. 237/N9
Clinch (riv.), Va. 307/C7
Clinchburg, Va. (24321) 307/E7
Clinchco, Va. (24226) 307/D6
Clinchfield, Ga. (31013) 216/E6
Clinchmore, Tenn. (†37714) 237/N8
Clinchport, Va. (24227) 307/C7
Clingmans Dome (mt.), N.C. 281/C3
Clingmans Dome (mt.), Tenn. 237/P9
Clint, Texas (79836) 302/B10
Clinton, Ala. (35448) 194/C5
Clinton, Ark. (72031) 203/F2
Clinton, Br. Col. 184/G4
Clinton△, Conn. (06413) 210/E3
Clinton, Conn. (06413) 210/E3
Clinton, Ont. 177/C4
Clinton (co.), Ill. 222/D5
Clinton, Ill. (61727) 222/E3
Clinton (co.), Ind. 227/E4
Clinton, Ind. (47842) 227/C5
Clinton, Iowa, 188/J2
Clinton (co.), Iowa 229/M5
Clinton, Iowa (52732) 229/N5
Clinton (co.), Ky. 237/L7
Clinton, Ky. (42031) 237/D7
Clinton, La. (70722) 238/J5
Clinton△, Maine (04927) 242/D6
Clinton, Maine (04927) 242/D6
Clinton△, Mass. (01510) 249/H3
Clinton, Md. (20735) 245/G6
Clinton (co.), Mich. 250/E6
Clinton, Mich. (49236) 250/F6
Clinton, Minn. (56225) 254/B5
Clinton, Miss. (39056) 256/D6

350 Coolibah

Coolibah, Aust. 88/E3
Coolibah, No. Terr. 93/B3
Coolidge, Ariz. (85228) 198/D6
Coolidge (dam), Ariz. 198/E5
Coolidge, Ga. (31738) 216/E8
Coolidge, Kans. (67836) 232/A3
Coolidge, Texas (76635) 302/H6
Coolidge Dam, Ariz. (†85542) 198/E5
Coolin, Idaho (83821) 220/B1
Cool Spring, Del. (†19951) 245/T6
Cool Valley‡, Mo. (†63101) 261/P2
Coolville, Ohio (45723) 284/G7
Cooma, Aust. 88/H7
Cooma, N.S.W. 97/E5
Coombs, Br. Col. 184/H3
Coonabarabran, N.S.W. 97/E2
Coonamble, Aust. 88/H6
Coonamble, N.S.W. 97/E2
Coondapoor, India 68/C6
Coon Rapids, Iowa (50058) 229/D5
Coon Rapids, Minn. (55433) 254/G5
Coon Valley, Wis. (54623) 317/E8
Cooper, Ala. (36019) 194/E5
Cooper (pt.), Calif. 204/D7
Cooper, Iowa (50059) 229/E5
Cooper, Ky. (42609) 237/M7
Cooper▵, Maine (†04638) 242/H6
Cooper, Maine (†04638) 242/H6
Cooper (co.), Mo. 261/G5
Cooper (riv.), N.J. 273/B3
Cooper, S.C. (†29560) 296/H4
Cooper (riv.), S.C. 296/H6
Cooper, Texas (75432) 302/J4
Cooper (lake), Wyo. 319/G4
Co-Operative, Ky. (42610) 237/M7
Cooper City, Fla. (33314) 212/F5
Cooper Creek, Br. Col. 184/J5
Cooperdale, Ohio (†43842) 284/F5
Cooper Landing, Alaska (99572) 196/C1
Cooper Road‡, La. (71101) 238/C1
Coopers (creek), Australia, 87/D8
Coopers (Barcoo) (creek), Aust. 88/F5
Coopers (Barcoo) (creek), S. Aust. 94/F3
Coopers (Barcoo) (creek), Queens. 95/B5
Coopersburg, Pa. (18036) 294/M5
Coopers Mills, Maine (04341) 242/E7
Coopers Plains, N.Y. (14827) 276/F6
Coopers Plains, Queens. 95/D3
Cooperstown, N. Dak. (58425) 283/O5
Cooperstown, N.Y. (13326) 276/L5
Cooperstown, Pa. (16317) 294/C2
Coopersville, Ky. (42611) 237/M7
Coopersville, Mich. (49404) 250/C5
Cooperton, Okla. (73023) 288/J5
Co-op Point, Sask. 181/N3
Coorabie, S. Aust. 94/B4
Coorong, The (lag.), S. Aust. 94/F6
Coorow, W. Aust. 92/B5
Coos (co.), N.H. 268/E2
Coos (co.), Oreg. 291/C4
Coos (riv.), Oreg. 291/D4
Coosa (co.), Ala. 194/F5
Coosa (riv.), Ala. 194/F4
Coosa, Ga. (30129) 216/B2
Coosa (riv.), Ga. 216/A2
Coosada, Ala. (36020) 194/F5
Coosaw (riv.), S.C. 296/G7
Coosawattee (riv.), Ga. 216/C1
Coosawhatchie, S.C. (29912) 296/F6
Coosawhatchie (riv.), S.C. 296/E6
Coos Bay, Oreg., 188/A2
Coos Bay, Oreg. (97420) 291/C4
Cootamundra, Aust. 88/H6
Cootamundra, N.S.W. 97/D4
Cootehill, 10/C3
Cootehill, Ire. 17/G3
Cooter, Mo. (63839) 261/N10
Copacabana, Arg. 143/C2
Copacabana, Bol. 136/A5
Copake, N.Y. (12516) 276/N6
Copake Falls, N.Y. (12517) 276/N6
Copalis Beach, Wash. (98535) 310/A3
Copalis Crossing, Wash. (98536) 310/B3
Copán, Hond. 154/C3
Copan, Okla. (74022) 288/P1
Copano (bay), Texas 302/G9
Copco (lake), Calif. 204/C2
Cope, Colo. (80812) 208/O3
Cope, Ind. (†46151) 227/E6
Cope, S.C. (29038) 296/E5
Copea (cape), Spain 33/F4
Copeau, Sask. 181/H3
Copeland, Ala. (†36558) 194/B7
Copeland, Fla. (33926) 212/E6
Copeland, Idaho (83822) 220/B1
Copeland, Kans. (67837) 232/B4
Copeland (isl.), N. Ire. 17/K2
Copeland, Sask. 181/G4
Copemish, Mich. (49625) 250/D4
Copen, W. Va. (26615) 313/E5
Copenhagen (city county), Den. 21/F6
Copenhagen (cap.), Den., 7/E3
Copenhagen (cap.), Den. 18/G9
Copenhagen (co.), Den. 21/F6
Copenhagen (cap.), Den. 21/F6
Copenhagen, N.Y. (13626) 276/J3
Copere, Bol. 136/D6
Copiague‡, N.Y. (11726) 276/O9
Copiah (co.), Miss. 256/D7
Copiapó, Chile, 120/C5
Copiapó, Chile 138/B6
Copiapó (bay), Chile 138/A6
Copiapó (riv.), Chile 138/A6
Copinsay (isl.), Scot. 15/L2
Coplay, Pa. (18037) 294/L4
Copley, S. Aust. 94/F4
Copmanhurst, N.S.W. 97/G1
Coporito, Ven. 124/H3
Coporolo (riv.), Angola 115/B6
Coppell, Ont. 175/D3
Coppell, Texas (75019) 302/F1
Coppename (riv.), Sur. 131/C3
Copper (riv.), Alaska 196/J2
Copper (mts.), Ariz. 198/B6
Copperas Cove, Texas (76522) 302/G6
Copper Center, Alaska (99573) 196/J2
Copper City, Mich. (49917) 250/A1
Copper Cliff, Ont. 175/D3
Copper Cliff, Ont. 177/J5
Copperfield, W. Aust. 92/B5
Copper Harbor, Mich. (49918) 250/B1
Copperhill, Tenn. (37317) 237/N10
Copper Hill, Va. (24079) 307/H6
Coppermine, 163/E2
Coppermine (riv.), 163/E2
Coppermine, Canada, 4/C15
Coppermine, N.W.T. 187/G3
Coppermine (riv.), N.W.T. 187/G3
Copper Mountain, Br. Col. 184/G5
Copper River Highway, Alaska 196/K2
Copper Valley, Va. (24080) 307/G7
Coppet, Switz. 39/B4
Coppock, Iowa (†52654) 229/K6
Coquet (riv.), Eng. 13/F2
Coquí, P. Rico 161/D3
Coquille, Oreg. (97423) 291/C4
Coquille (pt.), Oreg. 291/C4
Coquimbo, Chile, 120/C6
Coquimbo (prov.), Chile 138/A8
Coquimbo, Chile 138/A8
Coquitlam, Br. Col. 184/K3
Cora, Ill. (†62280) 222/D6
Cora, Wyo. (82925) 319/C3
Corabia, Rum. 45/G4
Coracora, Peru 128/F10
Corail, Haiti 158/A6
Coraki, N.S.W. 97/G1
Coral (sea), 3/S6
Coral (sea), 87/F7
Coral (sea), Aust. 88/H2
Coral (bay), V.I.(U.S.) 161/C4
Coral, Ont. 175/D2
Coral, Ont. 177/J4
Coral, Mich. (49322) 250/D5
Coral (bay), Phil. 82/A6
Coral (sea), Papua 85/B7
Coral (sea), Queens. 95/C1
Coral, Pa. (15731) 294/D5
Coral Cove, Fla. (†83559) 212/D4
Coral Gables, Fla. (33134) 212/B5
Coral Harbour, 163/H3
Coral Harbour, N.W.T. 187/K3
Coral Hills, Md. (†20027) 245/G5
Coralillo, Cuba 158/D1
CORAL SEA ISLANDS TERRITORY, 88/J3
Coral Springs‡, Fla. (33060) 212/F5
Coralville, Iowa (52240) 229/K5
Coralville (res.), Iowa 229/K5
Coram, Mont. (59913) 262/C2
Corangamite (lake), Vic. 97/B6
Corantijn (riv.), Sur. 131/C3
Coraopolis, Pa. (15108) 294/B4
Corapeake, N.C. (27926) 281/R1
Corato, Italy 34/F4
Corberrie, N.S. 169/C4
Corbigny, France 28/E4
Corbin, Kans. (67032) 232/E4
Corbin, Ky. (40701) 237/N7
Corbin, La. (†70785) 238/L1
Corbin City, N.J. (†08270) 273/D5
Corby, Eng. 13/G5
Corcelles-près-Payerne, Switz. 39/C3
Corcoran, Calif. (93212) 204/F7
Corcoran, Minn. (†55340) 254/F5
Corcovado (gulf), Chile, 120/C7
Corcovado (gulf), Chile 138/D4
Corcovado (vol.), Chile 138/D5
Corcubión, Spain 33/B1
Cord, Ark. (72524) 203/H2
Cordaville, Mass. (†01772) 249/H3
Cordele, Ga. (31015) 216/E7
Cordelia, Calif. (†94585) 204/K1
Cordell, Okla. (73632) 288/H4
Cordell Hull (res.), Tenn. 237/K8
Corder, Mo. (64021) 261/E4
Cordesville, S.C. (29434) 296/H5
Cordillera (dept.), Par. 144/D5
Cordillo Grounds, S. Aust. 94/G2
Córdoba, Arg., 3/F7
Córdoba, Arg., 120/D6
Córdoba (prov.), Arg. 143/D3
Córdoba, Arg. 143/D3
Córdoba (dept.), Col. 126/C3
Córdoba, Mex. 150/P2
Córdoba, Spain, 7/D5
Córdoba (prov.), Spain 33/D3
Córdoba, Spain 33/D4
Cordobés (riv.), Urug. 145/D3
Cordova, Ala. (35550) 194/D3
Cordova, Alaska, 146/D3
Cordova, Alaska, 188/D6
Cordova, Alaska (99574) 196/D1
Cordova (bay), Alaska 196/M2
Cordova, Ill. (61242) 222/C2
Cordova, Man. 179/C4
Cordova, Md. (21625) 245/O5
Cordova, N. Mex. (87523) 274/D2
Cordova, Nebr. (68330) 264/G4
Córdova, Peru 128/E10
Cordova, S.C. (29039) 296/F5
Cordova, Tenn. (38018) 237/B10
Cordova, U.S., 4/C17
Cordova Mines, Ont. 177/G3
Core (banks), N.C. 281/S5
Core (sound), N.C. 281/S5
Core, W. Va. (26529) 313/F3
Corea, Maine (04624) 242/H7
Coredó (Humboldt) (bay), Col. 126/B4
Coree South, N.S.W. 97/C4
Corella, Spain 33/F1
Corey, La. (†71201) 238/F2
Corfe Castle, Eng. 13/E7
Corfield, Aust. 88/G4
Corfield, Queens. 95/B4
Corfu (Kérkira) (isl.), Greece 45/D6
Corfu, N.Y. (14036) 276/D5
Corgémont, Switz. 39/D2
Cori, Italy 34/F7
Coria, Spain 33/C3
Coria del Río, Spain 33/C4
Coriander, Sask. 181/D6
Corigliano Calabro, Italy 34/F5
Corinda, Aust. 88/K2
Corinda, Queens. 95/A3
Corinda, Queens. 95/D3
Coringa (islets), Australia, 87/F7
Coringa (isls.), Aust. 88/H3
Corinna▵, Maine (04928) 242/E6
Corinne, Okla. (†74751) 288/R6
Corinne, Sask. 181/G5
Corinne, Utah (84307) 304/B2
Corinne, W. Va. (25826) 313/D7
Corinth, Ga. (†30230) 216/B4
Corinth, Greece, 7/G5
Corinth, Greece 45/F7
Corinth (gulf), Greece 45/F6
Corinth, Ky. (41010) 237/M3
Corinth, Miss. (38834) 256/G1
Corinth, N. Dak. (†58830) 283/D2
Corinth, N.Y. (12822) 276/N4
Corinth‡, Texas (†76201) 302/G4
Corinth▵, Vt. (05039) 268/C3
Corinth, Vt. (05039) 268/C3
Corinth, W. Va. (26713) 313/H4
Corinto, Col. 126/B6
Corinto, Braz. 132/E7
Corinto, Nic. 154/D4
Corio, Aust. 88/L7
Corio (bay), Aust. 88/L7
Coriolei, Somalia 115/H3
Coripata, Bol. 136/B5
Corisco (isl.), Eq. Guin. 115/A3
Cork, 10/B5
Cork (harb.), 10/B5
Cork, Ire., 7/D3
Cork (co.), Ire. 17/D7
Cork, Ire. 17/E8
Cork (harb.), Ire. 17/E8
Corker (cay), Br. Hond. 154/D2
Corleone, Italy 34/D6
Corley, Iowa (†51537) 229/C5
Corley, W. Va. (26616) 313/E5
Çorlu, Turkey 63/B2
Cormorant, Man. 179/H3
Cormorant (lake), Man. 179/H3
Cormorant, Minn. (†56572) 254/B4
Corn (creek), Ariz. 198/E3
Corn, Okla. (73024) 288/J4
Cornaca, Bol. 136/C7
Corncake (inlet), N.C. 281/O7
Cornelia, Ga. (30531) 216/E1
Cornélio Procópio, Braz. 132/D8
Cornelius, N.C. (28031) 281/H4
Cornelius, Oreg. (97113) 291/A2
Cornell, Ill. (61319) 222/E3
Cornell, Mich. (49818) 250/B3
Cornell, Wis. (54732) 317/D5
Corner (inlet), Vic. 97/D6
Corner Brook, 163/L6
Corner Brook, Newf. 166/C4
Cornerstone, Ark. (†72004) 203/G5
Cornersville, Md. (†21613) 245/O6
Cornersville, Miss. (†38659) 256/F1
Cornersville, Tenn. (37047) 237/H10
Cornerville, Ark. (†71667) 203/G6
Cornettes de Bise (mts.), Switz. 39/C4
Cornfield (pt.), Conn. 210/F3
Cornfields, Ariz. (†86505) 198/F3
Cornhill, N. Br. 170/E3
Corning, Ark. (72422) 203/J1
Corning, Calif. (96021) 204/C4
Corning, Iowa (50841) 229/D7
Corning, Kans. (66417) 232/F2
Corning, Mo. (64435) 261/B2
Corning, N.Y. (14830) 276/F6
Corning, Ohio (43730) 284/F6
Corning, Sask. 181/J6
Cornish, Colo. (80611) 208/L2
Cornish▵, Maine (04020) 242/B8
Cornish, Okla. (†73456) 288/L6
Cornish, Utah (84308) 304/B2
Cornish Flat, N.H. (03746) 268/C4
Cornish Heights (hills), Eng. 13/B7
Cornishville, Ky. (40314) 237/M5
Cornland, Ill. (62519) 222/D4
Cornlea, Nebr. (68630) 264/G3
Corno (mt.), Italy 34/D3
Cornucopia, Wis. (54827) 317/D2
Cornville, Ariz. (86325) 198/D4
Cornville▵, Maine (†04976) 242/D6
Cornwall (isl.), 163/M3
Cornwall, 163/J7
Cornwall▵, Conn. (06753) 210/B1
Cornwall, Conn. (06753) 210/B1
Cornwall (co.), Jam. 158/H6
Cornwall, Ont. 177/K2
Cornwall (co.), Eng. 13/C7
Cornwall (cape), Eng. 13/B7
Cornwall (isl.), N.W.T. 187/J2
Cornwall, N.Y. (12518) 276/M8
Cornwall, Pa. (17016) 294/K5
Cornwall▵, Vt. (†05753) 268/A4
Cornwall, Vt. (†05753) 268/A4
Cornwall Bridge, Conn. (06754) 210/B1
Cornwall Center, Conn. (†06796) 210/B1
Cornwall Hollow, Conn. (†06031) 210/B1
Cornwallis (isl.), 163/M3
Cornwallis (isl.), N.W.T. 187/J2
Cornwell, Fla. (33836) 212/E4
Coro, Ven., 120/D1
Coro, Ven. 124/D2
Coroatá, Braz. 132/F3
Corocoro, Bol. 136/A5
Corofin, Ire. 17/C6
Coroico, Bol. 136/B5
Corolla, N.C. (27927) 281/T2
Coroma, Bol. 136/B6
Coromandel, Braz. 132/E7
Coromandel, N.Z. 101/E2
Coromandel (pen.), N.Z. 101/F2
Coromandel (range), N.Z. 101/E2
Coromandel Coast (reg.), India 68/E6
Coron, Phil. 82/C4
Coron (isl.), Phil. 82/C5
Corona, Ala. (†35546) 194/C3
Corona, Calif. (91720) 204/E11
Corona, N. Mex. (88318) 274/D4
Corona, S. Dak. (57227) 298/R3
Coronaca, S.C. (†29646) 296/C3
Coronach, Sask. 181/F6
Coronado (bay), C. Rica 154/F6
Coronado, Alta. 182/D3
Coronado, Calif. (92118) 204/H11
Coronado (pt.), Phil. 82/C7
Coronado Nat'l Memorial, Ariz. 198/E7
Coronados (gulf), Chile 138/D4
Coronation (gulf), 163/E2
Coronation (isl.), Alaska 196/M2
Coronation, Alta. 182/E3
Coronation (isl.), Ant. 5/C16
Coronation (gulf), N.W.T. 187/G3
Coronda, Arg. 143/F6
Coronel, Chile 138/D1
Coronel Bogado, Arg. 143/F6
Coronel Bogado, Par. 144/E6
Coronel Brandsen, Arg. 143/H7
Coronel Dorrego, Arg. 143/D4
Coronel Martínez, Par. 144/C6
Coronel Moldes, Arg. 143/C2
Coronel Oviedo, Par. 144/C6
Coronel Pringles, Arg. 143/D4
Coronel Suárez, Arg. 143/D4
Corongo, Peru 128/D7
Coronie, Sur., 120/E2
Coronie (dist.), Sur. 131/C3
Coropuna, Nudo (mt.), Peru 128/F10
Cororooke, Vic. 97/B6
Çorovodë, Alb. 45/E5
Corowa, N.S.W. 97/D4
Corozal, Br. Hond. 154/C1
Corozal, Col. 126/C3
Corozal, P. Rico 161/D1
Corozo Pando, Ven. 124/E3
Corpach, Scot. 15/F6
Corpus Christi, Texas, 146/J7
Corpus Christi (bay), Texas, 188/G5
Corpus Christi, Texas, 188/G5
Corpus Christi, Texas (*78401) 302/G10
Corpus Christi (lake), Texas 302/F9
Corpus Christi (passg.), Texas 302/G10
Corpus Christi N.A.S., Texas 302/G10
Corque, Bol. 136/B6
Corquín, Hond. 154/C3
Corral, Chile 138/D3
Corral, Idaho (83322) 220/D6
Corral de Almaguer, Spain 33/E3
Corral de Bustos, Arg. 143/D3
Corrales, N. Mex. (87048) 274/C3
Corralitos, Calif. (95076) 204/L4
Corral Viejo, P. Rico 161/C2
Correct, Ind. (†47042) 227/G7
Correctionville, Iowa (51016) 229/B4
Correggio, Italy 34/C2
Corregidor (isl.), Phil. 82/C3
Correll, Minn. (56227) 254/B5
Corrente, Braz. 132/E5
Corrente (riv.), Braz. 132/E6
Correntina, Braz. 132/E6
Corrèze (dept.), France 28/D5
Corrib (lake), 10/B4
Corrib (lake), Ire. 17/C5
Corridon, Mo. (63635) 261/L8
Corrientes, Arg., 120/E5
Corrientes (prov.), Arg. 143/E2
Corrientes, Arg. 143/E2
Corrientes (riv.), Arg. 143/E2
Corrientes (cape), Col., 120/C2
Corrientes (cape), Col. 126/B5
Corrientes (cape), Cuba 158/A2
Corrientes (inlet), Cuba 158/A2
Corrientes (cape), Mex., 146/H7
Corrientes (cape), Mex. 150/F6
Corrientes (riv.), Peru 128/E4
Corrigan, Texas (75939) 302/K7
Corriganville, Md. (21524) 245/C2
Corrigin, Aust. 88/B6
Corrigin, W. Aust. 92/B6
Corrimal, Aust. 88/L4
Corry, Pa. (16407) 294/C2
Corryong, Vic. 97/D5
Corryton, Tenn. (37721) 237/O8
Corryvreckan (gulf), Scot. 15/E7
Corse (Corsica) (isl.), France, 7/E4
Corse (cape), France 28/B6
Corsewall (pt.), Scot. 15/F9
Corsica (isl.), France, 7/E4
Corsica (dept.), France 28/B6
Corsica (isl.), France 28/B6
Corsica, Pa. (15829) 294/D3
Corsica, S. Dak. (57328) 298/N7
Corsicana, Texas, 188/G4
Corsicana, Texas (75110) 302/H5
Corso, Mo. (63337) 261/K4
Corson (inlet), N.J. 273/D5
Corson (co.), S. Dak. 298/G2
Corson, S. Dak. (57019) 298/R6
Cortaro, Ariz. (85230) 198/D6
Corte, France 28/B6
Corte Madera, Calif. (94925) 204/J2
Cortés, Cuba 158/A2
Cortés (inlet), Cuba 158/B2
Cortez, Colo. (81321) 208/B8
Cortez, Fla. (33522) 212/D4
Cortez (mts.), Nev. 266/E2
Cortina d'Ampezzo, Italy 34/D1
Cortland, Ill. (60112) 222/E2
Cortland, Ind. (47228) 227/F7
Cortland (co.), N.Y. 276/H5
Cortland, N.Y. (13045) 276/H5
Cortland, Nebr. (68331) 264/H4
Cortland, Ohio (44410) 284/J3
Cortona, Italy 34/C3
Coruche, Port. 33/B3
Çoruh (riv.), Turkey 59/D1
Çoruh (riv.), Turkey 63/J2
Çorum, Turkey 59/B1
Çorum (prov.), Turkey 63/F2
Çorum, Turkey 63/F2
Çorum (riv.), Turkey 63/F2
Corumbá, Braz., 120/E4
Corumbá, Braz. 132/B7
Corunna, Ont. 177/B5
Corunna, Ind. (46730) 227/G2
Corunna, Mich. (48817) 250/E6
Corvallis, Mont. (59828) 262/C4
Corvallis, Oreg., 188/B2
Corvallis, Oreg. (97330) 291/D3
Corvuso, Minn. (†56228) 254/D6
Corwen, 10/E4
Corwen, Wales 13/D4
Corwin, Kans. (†67061) 232/D4
Corwin, Ohio (†45068) 284/B6
Corwin Springs, Mont. (59021) 262/F5
Corwith, Iowa (50430) 229/F3
Cory, Ind. (47846) 227/C6
Corydon, Ind. (47112) 227/E8
Corydon, Iowa (50060) 229/G7
Corydon, Ky. (42406) 237/F5
Coryell (co.), Texas 302/G6
Coryville, Pa. (16723) 294/F2
Cosalá, Mex. 150/F4
Cosamaloapan de Carpio, Mex. 150/M7
Cosapa, Bol. 136/A6
Cosautlán de Carvajal, Mex. 150/P1
Cosby, Mo. (64436) 261/C3
Cosby, Tenn. (37722) 237/P9
Cos Cob, Conn. (06807) 210/A4
Coscomatepec de Bravo, Mex. 150/P2
Coseguina (pt.), Nic. 154/D4
Cosenza (prov.), Italy 34/F5
Cosenza, Italy 34/F5
Coshocton (co.), Ohio 284/G5
Coshocton, Ohio (43812) 284/G5
Cosine, Sask. 181/A3
Coslo, Mex. 150/H5
Cosmoledo (isls.), Seych. 118/H1
Cosmopolis, Wash. (98537) 310/B4
Cosmos, Minn. (56228) 254/D6
Cosne-sur-Loire, France 28/E4
Cosoleacaque, Mex. 150/M7
Cosperville, Ind. (†46794) 227/F1
Cosquín, Arg. 143/D3
Cossonay, Switz. 39/C3
Costa, W. Va. (25051) 313/C6
Costa Azul, Urug. 145/E5
Costa Brava (reg.), Spain 33/H2
Costa da Caparica, Port. 33/A1
Costa de Sola (reg.), Spain 33/D4
Costa Mesa, Calif. (*92626) 204/D11
Costa Rica, 146/K8
COSTA RICA, 154/E5
Costa Rica, Bol. 136/A2
Costa Rica, Mex. 150/F4
Costello, Pa. (†16720) 294/G2
Costigan, Maine (04423) 242/F5
Costilla (co.), Colo. 208/J8
Costilla, N. Mex. (87524) 274/D2
Costilla (peak), N. Mex. 274/D2
Cosumnes (riv.), Calif. 204/C9
Coswig, Dresden, E. Ger. 22/E3
Coswig, Halle, E. Ger. 22/E3
Cotabato (prov.), Phil. 82/E7
Cotabato, Phil. 82/D7
Cotabato, Phil. 85/G4
Cotacajes (riv.), Bol. 136/B5
Cotagaita, Bol. 136/C7
Cotahuasi, Peru 128/F10
Cotati‡, Calif. (94928) 204/C5
Côte, Sask. 181/K4
Coteau, N. Dak. (58728) 283/F2
Coteau, The (hills), Sask. 181/D4
Coteau du Missouri (plain), N. Dak. 283/G3
Coteau-Landing, Que. 172/C4
Coteau-Station, Que. 172/C4
Côteaux, Haiti 158/A6
Côte-d'Or (dept.), France 28/F4
Côte-d'Or (mts.), France 28/F4
Cotentin (pen.), France 28/C3
Côte-Saint-Luc, Que. 172/H4
Côtes-de-Fer, Haiti 158/B6
Côtes-du-Nord (dept.), France 28/B3
Cotesfield, Nebr. (68829) 264/F3
Cotham, Sask. 181/J5
Cotija de la Paz, Mex. 150/H7
Cotile (res.), La. 238/E4
Coto, Arg. 143/D2
Cotoca, Bol. 136/D5
Coto Laurel, P. Rico 161/C2
Cotonou, Dahomey 106/E7
Cotonou, 102/C4
Cotopaxi, Colo. (81223) 208/H6
Cotopaxi (mt.), Ec., 120/C3
Cotopaxi (prov.), Ec. 128/C3
Cotopaxi (mt.), Ec. 128/C3
Cotswold (hills), Eng. 13/E6
Cottage City, Md. (†20722) 245/F4
Cottage Grove, Ala. (35088) 194/F5
Cottage Grove, Ind. (†47353) 227/H5
Cottage Grove, Minn. (55016) 254/F6
Cottage Grove, Oreg. (97424) 291/D4
Cottage Grove (res.), Oreg. 291/E4
Cottage Grove, Tenn. (38224) 237/E8
Cottage Grove‡, Wis. (53527) 317/H9
Cottagehill, Fla. (32533) 212/B6
Cottage Hills, Ill. (62018) 222/B6
Cottageville, S.C. (29435) 296/G6
Cottageville, W. Va. (25239) 313/C5
Cottam, Ont. 177/B5
Cottbus (dist.), E. Ger. 22/F3
Cottbus, E. Ger. 22/F3
Cotter, Ark. (72626) 203/E1
Cotter, Iowa (52221) 229/L6
Cottian Alps (range), France 28/G5
Cottian Alps (range), Italy 34/A2
Cottica, Sur. 131/D4
Cottica (riv.), Sur. 131/D3
Cottle, Ky. (41412) 237/P5
Cottle (co.), Texas 302/D3
Cottleville, Mo. (63338) 261/N2
Cotton, Ga. (31739) 216/D8
Cotton, Minn. (55724) 254/F3
Cotton (co.), Okla. 288/K6
Cottonburg, Ky. (40418) 237/N5
Cotton Center, Texas (79021) 302/C4
Cottondale, Ala. (35453) 194/D4
Cottondale, Fla. (32431) 212/D6
Cotton Ground, St. Chr.-N.-A. 161/C11
Cotton Plant, Ark. (72036) 203/H3
Cottonport, La. (71327) 238/F5
Cottonton, Ala. (36851) 194/H6
Cottontown, Tenn. (37048) 237/H8
Cotton Valley, La. (71018) 238/D1
Cottonwood, Ala. (36320) 194/H8
Cottonwood, Ariz. (86326) 198/D4
Cottonwood (cliffs), Ariz. 198/B3
Cottonwood, Br. Col. 184/G3
Cottonwood, Calif. (96022) 204/C3
Cottonwood (creek), Calif. 204/C3
Cottonwood, Idaho (83522) 220/B3
Cottonwood (butte), Idaho 220/C4
Cottonwood (riv.), Kans. 232/F3
Cottonwood (co.), Minn. 254/C6
Cottonwood, Minn. (56229) 254/C6
Cottonwood (riv.), Minn. 254/C6
Cottonwood (creek), Mont. 262/E2
Cottonwood (creek), Oreg. 291/K4
Cottonwood, S. Dak. (57728) 298/F6
Cottonwood (creek), S. Dak. 298/E5
Cottonwood (lake), S. Dak. 298/M4
Cottonwood, Texas (79504) 302/D5
Cottonwood‡, Utah (†84101) 304/C3
Cottonwood (creek), Utah 304/C4
Cottonwood (creek), Utah 304/E4
Cottonwood (creek), Wyo. 319/B4
Cottonwood Draw (creek), Texas 302/C10
Cottonwood Falls, Kans. (66845) 232/F3
Cottonwood Wash (dry riv.), Ariz. 198/E4
Cottonwood Wash (creek), Utah 304/E6
Cotuí, Dom. Rep. 158/E5
Cotuit, Mass. (02635) 249/N6
Cotulla, Texas (78014) 302/E9
Couch, Mo. (65690) 261/K9
Couchiching (lake), Ont. 177/E3
Couchwood, La. (†71018) 238/D1
Coudekerque-Branche, France 28/E2
Couderay, Wis. (54828) 317/D4
Coudersport, Pa. (16915) 294/G2
Coudres (isl.), Que. 172/G2
Cougar (res.), Oreg. 291/E3
Cougar, Wash. (98616) 310/C4
Couillet, Belg. 27/E8
Coulee, N. Dak. (58729) 283/F2
Coulee City, Wash. (99115) 310/F3
Coulee Dam, Wash. (99116) 310/G3
Coulee Dam Nat'l Rec. Area, Wash. 310/G2
Coulihaut, Dominica 161/E6
Coulommiers, France 28/E3
Coulter, Iowa (50431) 229/G3
Coulter, Man. 179/B5
Coulterville, Calif. (95311) 204/E6
Coulterville, Ill. (62237) 222/D5
Counamama, Fr. Gui. 131/E3
Counce, Tenn. (38326) 237/E10
Council, Alaska (†99784) 196/F2
Council, Ga. (†31631) 216/G9
Council, Idaho (83612) 220/B5
Council, N.C. (28434) 281/M6
Council Bluffs, Iowa (51501) 229/B6
Council Grove, Kans. (66846) 232/F3
Council Grove (res.), Kans. 232/F3
Council Hill, Okla. (74428) 288/P3
Countess, Alta. 182/D4
Country (harb.), N.S. 169/G3
Country Club Heights‡, Ind. (†46011) 227/F4
Country Club Hills, Ill. (60477) 222/B3
Country Club Hills‡, Mo. (†63101) 261/P3
Country Club Village, Mo. (†64501) 261/C3
Country Estates‡, Fla. (†33552) 212/D3
Country Harbour Mines, N.S. 169/G3
Country Knolls‡, N.Y. (†12118) 276/N5
Country Life Acres‡, Mo. (†63101) 261/O3
Countryside, Ill. (†60525) 222/A2
Countryside‡, Kans. (†66222) 232/H2
County Line, Ala. (†35172) 194/E3
Countyline, Okla. (73025) 288/L6
Coupar Angus, 10/E2
Coupar Angus, Scot. 15/K6
Coupeville, Wash. (98239) 310/C2
Courantyne (riv.), 120/E2
Courantyne (riv.), Guyana 131/C3
Courbevoie, France 28/A1
Courcelles, Belg. 27/E8
Courcelles, Que. 172/G4
Courgenay, Switz. 39/D2
Courmayeur, Italy 34/A2
Courroux, Switz. 39/D2
Court, Switz. 39/D2
Courtdale‡, Pa. (†18704) 294/L3
Courtelary, Switz. 39/C2
Courtenay, 163/D6
Courtenay, Br. Col. 184/E5
Courtenay, N. Dak. (58426) 283/N5
Courtételle, Switz. 39/D2
Courtice, Ont. 177/F4
Courtland, Ala. (35618) 194/D1
Courtland, Calif. (95615) 204/B9
Courtland, Ont. 177/D5
Courtland, Kans. (66939) 232/E2
Courtland, Minn. (56021) 254/D6
Courtland, Miss. (38620) 256/E2
Courtland, Va. (23837) 307/O7
Courtmacsherry, Ire. 17/D8
Courtmacsherry (bay), Ire. 17/D8
Courtney, Mo. (†64051) 261/R5
Courtney, Okla. (†73456) 288/L7
Courtois, Mo. (65451) 261/K7
Courtown (Este Sudeste) (cays), Col. 126/A10
Courtown Harbour-Riverchapel, Ire. 17/J6
Courtrai, Belg. 27/C7
Courtright, Ont. 177/B5
Courval, Sask. 181/E5
Courville, Que. 172/J3
Coushatta, La. (71019) 238/D2
Coutances, France 28/C3
Coutras, France 28/C5
Coutts, Alta. 182/D5
Coutts (inlet), N.W.T. 187/L2
Couva, Trinidad Tobago 161/B10
Couvet, Switz. 39/C3
Couvin, Belg. 27/F8
Cova da Piedade, Port. 33/A1
Cove, Ark. (71937) 203/B5
Cove (isl.), Ont. 177/C2
Cove (pt.), Md. 245/N7
Cove, Minn. (†56359) 254/E4
Cove, Ohio (†45640) 284/E8
Cove, Oreg. (97824) 291/K2
Cove (creek), Utah 304/B5
Cove and Kilcreggan, Scot. 15/B1
Cove City, N.C. (28523) 281/P4
Cove City‡, Texas (†77630) 302/L7
Cove Creek, N.C. (†28786) 281/D3
Covedale, Ohio (†45201) 284/B10
Cove Fort, Utah (†84713) 304/B5
Cove Gap, W. Va. (25509) 313/B6
Covelo, Calif. (95428) 204/B4
Covena, Ga. (30422) 216/H6
Covendo, Bol. 136/B4
Cove Neck, N.Y. (†11771) 276/O9
Coventry, 10/F4
Coventry▵, Conn. (06238) 210/F1
Coventry, Conn. (06238) 210/F1
Coventry, Eng. 13/F5
Coventry▵, R.I. (02816) 249/H6
Coventry, R.I. (02816) 249/H6
Coventry▵, Vt. (05825) 268/C2
Coventry, Vt. (05825) 268/C2

Çubuk 351

Coventry Center, R.I. (02816) 249/H6
Cove Orchard, Oreg. (†97148) 291/D2
Coverdale, Ont. 177/F4
Coverdale, Ga. (†31714) 216/E7
Covert, Mich. (49043) 250/C6
Covesville, Va. (22931) 307/L5
Covilhã, Port. 33/C2
Covin, Ala. (†35555) 194/C3
Covina, Calif. (91722) 204/D10
Covington (co.), Ala. 194/F8
Covington, Ga. (30209) 216/E3
Covington, Ind. (47932) 227/C4
Covington, Iowa (†52324) 229/K5
Covington, Ky. (*41011) 237/S2
Covington, La. (70433) 238/K5
Covington, Mich. (49919) 250/G2
Covington (co.), Miss. 256/E7
Covington, Ohio (45318) 284/B5
Covington, Okla. (73730) 288/L2
Covington, Pa. (16917) 294/J2
Covington, Tenn. (38019) 237/B9
Covington, Va. (24426) 307/H5
Cow (creek), Mont. 262/G2
Cow (creek), Oreg. 291/K4
Cow (lake), Oreg. 291/K4
Cow (creek), Wash. 310/G3
Cowal (lake), N.S.W. 97/D3
Cowal (dist.), Scot. 15/F7
Cowan (lake), Aust. 88/C6
Cowan, Ind. (†47302) 227/G4
Cowan, Ky. (†41039) 237/O4
Cowan, Man. 179/B2
Cowan (lake), W. Aust. 92/C5
Cowan (lake), Sask. 181/D2
Cowan, Tenn. (37318) 237/K10
Cowanesque, Pa. (16918) 294/H2
Cowangie, Vic. 97/A4
Cowansville, Que. 172/E4
Cowansville, Pa. (16218) 294/C4
Cowaramup, W. Aust. 92/A6
Coward, S.C. (29530) 296/H4
Coward Springs, S. Aust. 94/E3
Cowarie, S. Aust. 94/F2
Cowarts, Ala. (36321) 194/H8
Cowbridge, Wales 13/D6
Cowcreek, Ky. (†41314) 237/O6
Cowden, Ill. (62422) 222/E4
Cowdenbeath, 10/C1
Cowdenbeath, Scot. 15/K7
Cowdrey, Colo. (80434) 208/G1
Cowell, S. Aust. 94/E5
Cowen, W. Va. (26206) 313/E6
Cowes, 10/F5
Cowes, Eng. 13/F7
Coweta (co.), Ga. 216/C4
Coweta, Okla. (74429) 288/P3
Cowgill, Mo. (64637) 261/E3
Cow Head, Newf. 166/C4
Cowichan (lake), Br. Col. 184/J3
Cowiche, Wash. (98923) 310/E4
Cowikee, North Fork (creek), Ala. 194/H6
Cow Island, La. (†70510) 238/F7
Cowles, N. Mex. (87525) 274/D3
Cowles, Nebr. (†68930) 264/F4
Cowlesville, N.Y. (14037) 276/D5
Cowley, Alta. 182/D5
Cowley (co.), Kans. 232/F4
Cowley, Wyo. (82420) 319/D1
Cowlington, Okla. (†74934) 288/S4
Cowlitz (co.), Wash. 310/C4
Cowlitz (pass), Wash. 310/D4
Cowlitz (riv.), Wash. 310/C4
Cowpasture (riv.), Va. 307/J4
Cowpens, S.C. (29330) 296/D1
Cowpens Nat'l Battlefield Site, S.C. 296/D1
Cowra, Aust. 88/H6
Cowra, N.S.W. 97/E3
Coxburg, Miss. (†39095) 256/D5
Coxby, Sask. 181/F2
Cox City, Okla. (73082) 288/L5
Coxim, Braz. 132/C7
Coxsackie, N.Y. (12051) 276/N6
Cox's Bazar (Maheshkhali), Pak. 68/G4
Cox's Cove, Newf. 166/C4
Coxs Mills, W. Va. (26342) 313/E4
Cox Station (Bel Alton), Md. (†20611) 245/L7
Coxton, Ky. (40831) 237/P7
Coy, Ala. (36435) 194/D7
Coy, Ark. (72037) 203/G4
Coyame, Mex. 150/G2
Coyle (riv.), Arg. 143/B7
Coyle, Okla. (73027) 288/M3
Coylton, Scot. 15/H9
Coyoacán, Mex. 150/L1
Coyote (creek), Calif. 204/L3
Coyote (res.), Calif. 204/L4
Coyote, N. Mex. (87012) 274/C2
Coyotepec, Mex. 150/L1
Coyuca (riv.), Mex. 150/O1
Coyuca de Benítez, Mex. 150/J8
Coyuca de Catalán, Mex. 150/J7
Coyutla, Mex. 150/L6
Coyville, Kans. (66727) 232/G4
Cozad, Nebr. (69130) 264/E4
Cozumel (isl.), Mex., 146/K7
Cozumel, Mex. 150/Q6
Cozumel (isl.), Mex. 150/Q6
Crab (creek), Wash. 310/F3
Crab Hill, Barb. 161/B8
Crab Orchard (lake), Ill. 222/E6
Crab Orchard, Ky. (40419) 237/M6
Crab Orchard, Nebr. (68332) 264/H4
Crab Orchard, Tenn. (37723) 237/M9
Crab Orchard‡, W. Va. (25827) 313/D7
Crabtree, Que. 172/D4
Crabtree, Oreg. (97335) 291/E3
Crabtree, Pa. (15624) 294/D5
Cracknell, Man. 179/A4
Cracow, Poland, 7/G3
Cracow (prov.), Poland 47/D4
Cracow, Poland 47/E4
Cradock, 102/E8
Cradock, S. Africa 118/D6
Crafton, Pa. (15205) 294/B7
Craftsbury▵, Vt. (05826) 268/C2
Craftsbury, Vt. (05826) 268/C2
Craftsbury Common, Vt. (05827) 268/C2
Cragford, Ala. (36255) 194/G4
Craggy Dome (mt.), N.C. 281/D3
Craig, Alaska (99921) 196/M2
Craig, Colo. (81625) 208/D2
Craig (mts.), Idaho 220/B4
Craig, Iowa (51017) 229/A3
Craig, Mo. (64437) 261/B2
Craig, Mont. (†59648) 262/D3
Craig, Nebr. (68019) 264/H3
Craig (co.), Okla. 288/R1
Craig (co.), Va. 307/H6
Craig (creek), Va. 307/H5
Craig Air Force Base, Ala. 194/E6
Craigavon, 10/C3
Craig Beach, Ohio (†44429) 284/H3
Craigend, Alta. 182/E2
Craig Harbour, Canada, 4/B13
Craighead (co.), Ark. 203/J2
Craiglands, Sask. 181/B4
Craigleath, Ont. 177/D3
Craigmont, Idaho (83523) 220/B3
Craigmyle, Alta. 182/D4
Craignish (hills), N.S. 169/G3
Craignure, Scot. 15/E7
Craigs, Man. 179/F5
Craig Springs, Va. (†24127) 307/H6
Craigsville, Va. (24430) 307/J4
Craigsville, W. Va. (26205) 313/E6
Craigville, Ind. (46731) 227/G3
Craigville, Minn. (†56639) 254/E3
Craik, Sask. 181/F4
Crail, 10/E2
Crail, Scot. 15/L7
Crailsheim, W. Ger. 22/D4
Crainville‡, Ill. (†62918) 222/D6
Craiova, Rum., 7/G4
Craiova, Rum. 45/F3
Cramersburg, Sask. 181/C5
Cramerton, N.C. (28032) 281/G4
Crammond, Alta. 182/C3
Cranberry (lake), N. Dak. 283/L3
Cranberry (lake), N.Y. 276/L2
Cranberry, Pa. (16319) 294/C3
Cranberry, W. Va. (25828) 313/D7
Cranberry Isles▵, Maine (04625) 242/G7
Cranberry Isles, Maine (04625) 242/G7
Cranberry Lake, N.J. (07821) 273/D2
Cranberry Lake, N.Y. (12927) 276/L2
Cranberry Portage, Man. 179/H3
Cranbrook, 163/E6
Cranbrook, Br. Col. 184/K5
Cranbrook, Eng. 13/H6
Cranbrook, W. Aust. 92/B6
Cranbury, Conn. (†06856) 210/B4
Cranbury, N.J. (08512) 273/E3
Crandall, Ga. (30711) 216/C1
Crandall, Ind. (47114) 227/E8
Crandall, Man. 179/B4
Crandall, S. Dak. (57228) 298/O3
Crandall, Texas (75114) 302/H5
Crandon, Va. (†24315) 307/G6
Crandon, Wis. (54520) 317/H4
Crane, Barb. 161/C9
Crane, Ind. (47522) 227/D7
Crane, Mo. (65633) 261/E9
Crane, Mont. (59217) 262/M3
Crane, Oreg. (97732) 291/J4
Crane (creek), Oreg. 291/J4
Crane (lake), Sask. 181/B5
Crane (co.), Texas 302/B6
Crane, Texas (79731) 302/B6
Crane Creek (res.), Idaho 220/B5
Crane Hill, Ala. (35053) 194/D2
Crane Lake, Minn. (55725) 254/F2
Crane Naval Amm. Depot, Ind. 227/D7
Crane Nest, Ky. (40928) 237/O7
Crane Prairie (res.), Oreg. 291/F4
Crane River, Man. 179/C3
Canesville, Pa. (16410) 294/B2
Cranesville, W. Va. (†26764) 313/G3
Crane Valley, Sask. 181/F6
Cranfield, Miss. (†39120) 256/B7
Cranfills Gap, Texas (76637) 302/G6
Cranford▵, N.J. (07016) 273/E2
Cransac, France 28/E5
Cranston, Iowa (52741) 229/L6
Cranston, R.I. (02910) 249/J5
Crapo, Md. (21626) 245/O7
Crary, N. Dak. (58327) 283/N3
Crater (lake), Oreg. 291/E5
Crater Lake, Oreg. (†97601) 291/E5
Crater Lake Nat'l Park, Oreg. 291/E5
Craters of the Moon Nat'l Mon., Idaho 220/E6
Crateús, Braz., 120/G3
Crateús, Braz. 132/F4
Crati (riv.), Italy 34/F5
Crato, Braz. 132/G4
Crato, Port. 33/C3
Crauford (cape), N.W.T. 187/K2
Craven (co.), N.C. 281/P4
Craven, Sask. 181/G5
Cravens, La. (†70656) 238/E5
Cravo Norte, Col. 126/F4
Cravo Norte (riv.), Col. 126/E4
Cravo Sur (riv.), Col. 126/E5
Crawford (co.), Ark. 203/B2
Crawford, Colo. (81415) 208/D5
Crawford (co.), Ga. 216/E5
Crawford, Ga. (30630) 216/F3
Crawford (co.), Ill. 222/F4
Crawford (co.), Ind. 227/E8
Crawford (co.), Iowa 229/C4
Crawford (co.), Kans. 232/H4
Crawford, Kans. (†67444) 232/E3
Crawford▵, Maine (†04610) 242/H5
Crawford (lake), Maine 242/H5
Crawford (co.), Mich. 250/E4
Crawford, Miss. (39743) 256/G4
Crawford (co.), Mo. 261/K7
Crawford, Nebr. (69339) 264/A2
Crawford (co.), Ohio 284/E4
Crawford, Okla. (73638) 288/G3
Crawford (co.), Pa. 294/B2
Crawford, Scot. 15/J9
Crawford, Tenn. (38554) 237/L8
Crawford, Texas (76638) 302/G6
Crawford, W. Va. (26343) 313/F5
Crawford (co.), Wis. 317/E9
Crawford Bay, Br. Col. 184/J5
Crawford House, N.H. (03577) 268/E3
Crawford Notch (pass), N.H. 268/E3
Crawfordsville, Ark. (72327) 203/K3
Crawfordsville, Ind. (47933) 227/D4
Crawfordsville, Iowa (52621) 229/K6
Crawfordsville, Oreg. (97336) 291/E3
Crawfordville, Fla. (32327) 212/B1
Crawfordville, Ga. (30631) 216/G3
Crawley, Eng. 13/G6
Crawley, W. Va. (24931) 313/E7
Cray, Wales 13/D6
Crayne, Ky. (42033) 237/E6
Crazy (peak), Mont. 262/F4
Crazy Woman (creek), Wyo. 319/F1
Creagerstown, Md. (†21788) 245/J2
Creag Meagaidh (mt.), Scot. 15/G6
Creal Springs, Ill. (62922) 222/E6
Cream (hill), Conn. 210/B1
Cream, Wis. (†54610) 317/C7
Creamridge, N.J. (08514) 273/E3
Crean (lake), Sask. 181/E1
Crediton, 10/E5
Crediton, Ont. 177/C4
Crediton, Eng. 13/D7
Cree (lake), 163/F4
Cree (lake), Sask. 181/L3
Cree (riv.), Sask. 181/M2
Cree (riv.), Scot. 15/G9
Creede, Colo. (81130) 208/E7
Creedmoor, N.C. (27522) 281/M2
Creek (co.), Okla. 288/O3
Creekside, Pa. (15732) 294/D4
Creek Stand, Ala. (†36070) 194/G6
Creekville, Ky. (40929) 237/P6
Cree Lake, Sask. 181/L3
Creelman, Sask. 181/H6
Creelsboro, Ky. (†42629) 237/L7
Creemore, Ont. 177/D3
Creetown, Scot. 15/H10
Creighton, Ont. 177/B5
Creighton, Mo. (64739) 261/D6
Creighton, Nebr. (68729) 264/G2
Creighton, Pa. (15030) 294/C4
Creighton, S. Dak. (57729) 298/E5
Creighton, Sask. 181/N4
Creil, France 28/E3
Crellin, Md. (21525) 245/A3
Crema, Italy 34/B2
Cremona, Alta. 182/C4
Cremona (prov.), Italy 34/B2
Cremona, Italy 34/B2
Crenshaw (co.), Ala. 194/F7
Crenshaw, Miss. (38621) 256/D2
Crenshaw, Pa. (†15824) 294/E3
Creola, Ala. (36525) 194/B9
Creola, Ohio (45622) 284/E7
Creole, La. (70632) 238/D7
Crepori, Braz. 132/B4
Crépy-en-Valois, France 28/E3
Creran (inlet), Scot. 15/F7
Cres (isl.), Yugo. 45/B3
Cresaptown, Md. (21502) 245/C2
Cresbard, S. Dak. (57435) 298/M3
Crescent (lake), Fla. 212/E2
Crescent, Iowa (51526) 229/B6
Crescent, La. (†70764) 238/J2
Crescent, Mo. (63018) 261/N3
Crescent (valley), Nev. 266/E2
Crescent (isls.), China 85/E2
Crescent, Okla. (73028) 288/L3
Crescent, Oreg. (97733) 291/F4
Crescent (lake), Wash. 310/B3
Crescent Beach, Conn. (†06537) 210/G3
Crescent City, Calif. (95531) 204/A2
Crescent City, Fla. (32012) 212/E2
Crescent City, Ill. (60928) 222/F3
Crescent Lake, Maine (†04015) 242/C7
Crescent Lake, Oreg. (97425) 291/F4
Crescent Lake, Sask. 181/J4
Crescent Mills, Calif. (95934) 204/E3
Crescent Park, Ont. 177/E4
Crescent Park‡, Ky. (†41017) 237/S2
Crescent Springs, Ky. (†41016) 237/R2
Cresciente (isl.), Mex. 150/D5
Cresco, Iowa (52136) 229/J2
Cresco, Pa. (18326) 294/M3
Crespo, Arg. 143/F5
Cresskill, N.J. (07626) 273/C1
Cressmont, W. Va. (†25074) 313/E6
Cresson, Pa. (16630) 294/E5
Cresson, Texas (76035) 302/G5
Cressona, Pa. (17929) 294/K4
Cressy, Tas. 99/C3
Crest, France 28/F5
Crest, Ga. (†30286) 216/D5
Crest, Sask. 181/H2
Crested Butte, Colo. (81224) 208/E5
Crest Hill, Ill. (60435) 222/E2
Crestline, Calif. (92325) 204/H9
Crestline, Kans. (66728) 232/H4
Crestline, Ohio (44827) 284/E4
Creston, Br. Col. 184/J5
Creston, Calif. (93432) 204/E8
Creston, Ill. (60113) 222/D2
Creston, Ind. (†46356) 227/C2
Creston, Iowa (50801) 229/E6
Creston, Ky. (42524) 237/L6
Creston, La. (71020) 238/E3
Creston, Mont. (59902) 262/C2
Creston, Nebr. (68631) 264/G3
Creston, Newf. 166/C4
Creston, Ohio (44217) 284/G3
Creston, S.C. (†29030) 296/F4
Creston, W. Va. (26141) 313/D5
Creston, Wash. (99117) 310/G3
Crestone, Colo. (81131) 208/H7
Crestone (peak), Colo. 208/H7
Crestview, Fla. (32536) 212/C6
Crestview, Ky. (†41076) 237/S2
Crestview Hills, Ky. (†41017) 237/R3
Crestwood, Ill. (60445) 222/B2
Crestwood, Ky. (40014) 237/L4
Crestwood, Mo. (†63101) 261/O3
Crestwynd, Sask. 181/F5
Creswell, N.C. (27928) 281/S3
Creswell (bay), N.W.T. 187/J2
Creswell, Oreg. (97426) 291/D4
Creswell Downs, No. Terr. 93/E4
Creswick, Vic. 97/B5
Crete (isl.), Greece, 7/G5
Crete (reg.), Greece 45/G8
Crete (isl.), Greece 45/G8
Crete (sea), Greece 45/G7
Crete, Ill. (60417) 222/F2
Crete, N. Dak. (58020) 283/P7
Crete, Nebr. (68333) 264/G4
Créteil, France 28/B2
Creus (cape), Spain 33/H1
Creuse (dept.), France 28/D4
Creuse (riv.), France 28/D4
Creve Coeur, Ill. (61611) 222/D3
Creve Coeur, Mo. (63141) 261/O3
Crevillente, Spain 33/F3
Crewe, 10/G2
Crewe, Eng. 13/E4
Crewe, Va. (23930) 307/M6
Crewkerne, 10/E5
Crewkerne, Eng. 13/E7
Crews, Ala. (†35586) 194/B3
Criccieth, 10/D4
Criccieth, Wales 13/C5
Crichton, Sask. 181/D6
Criciúma, Braz. 132/D10
Cricklade, Eng. 13/F6
Crider, Ky. (†42445) 237/F6
Cridersville, Ohio (45806) 284/B4
Crieff, 10/E2
Crieff, Scot. 15/J7
Criehaven, Maine (†04851) 242/F8
Crillon (mt.), Alaska 196/L1
Crimea (pen.), U.S.S.R. 48/D5
Crimea (pen.), U.S.S.R. 52/D5
Crimea (pen.), U.S.S.R., 7/H4
Crimean Oblast, U.S.S.R. 52/D6
Crimmitschau, E. Ger. 22/E3
Crimora, Va. (24431) 307/L4
Crinan, Scot. 15/E7
Cripple Creek, Colo., 188/F3
Cripple Creek, Colo. (80813) 208/J5
Cripple Creek, Va. (24322) 307/F7
Crisfield, Md. (21817) 245/P9
Crisp (co.), Ga. 216/E7
Crisp (pt.), Mich. 250/D2
Crisp, N.C. (27852) 281/O3
Crissolo, Italy 34/A2
Cristal, Sierra del (mts.), Cuba 158/J4
Cristalina, Braz. 132/E7
Cristo, Cuba 158/J4
Cristobal, C.Z. 154/G6
Cristóbal (pt.), Ec. 128/B9
Cristóbal Colón, Pico (peak), Col. 126/D2
Crişul Alb (riv.), Rum. 45/F2
Crişul Repede (riv.), Rum. 45/F2
Crittenden (co.), Ark. 203/K3
Crittenden (co.), Ky. 237/E6
Crittenden, Ky. (41030) 237/M3
Critz, Va. (24082) 307/H7
Crivitz, Wis. (54114) 317/L5
Croagh Patrick (mt.), Ire. 17/C4
Croatan (sound), N.C. 281/T3
Croatia (rep.), Yugo. 45/C3
Croche (riv.), Que. 172/E2
Crocheron, Md. (21627) 245/O8
Crochu, Grenada 161/D8
Crocker, Mo. (65452) 261/H7
Crocker, S. Dak. (57229) 298/O3
Crockett, Calif. (94525) 204/J1
Crockett (co.), Tenn. 237/C9
Crockett (co.), Texas 302/C7
Crockett, Texas (75835) 302/J6
Crockett, Va. (24323) 307/F7
Crockett Mills, Tenn. (38021) 237/C9
Crocketts Bluff, Ark. (72038) 203/H5
Crocketville, S.C. (29913) 296/E6
Crocodile (riv.), S. Africa 118/H6
Croft, Kans. (†67028) 232/D4
Crofton, Br. Col. 184/J3
Crofton, Ky. (42217) 237/G6
Crofton, Md. (21113) 245/M4
Crofton, Nebr. (68730) 264/G2
Croghan, N.Y. (13327) 276/K3
Croix-des-Bouquets, Haiti 158/C6
Croker (cape), Ont. 177/D3
Croker (bay), N.W.T. 187/K2
Croker (cape), No. Terr. 93/C1
Croker Island Mission, Aust. 88/E2
Croker Island Mission, No. Terr. 93/C1
Croll, Man. 179/B5
Cromarty, 10/D2
Cromarty, Scot. 15/J4
Cromarty (firth), Scot. 15/H4
Cromer, 10/G4
Cromer, Eng. 13/J5
Cromer, Man. 179/A5
Cromwell, Ala. (36906) 194/B6
Cromwell▵, Conn. (06416) 210/E2
Cromwell, Ind. (46732) 227/F2
Cromwell, Iowa (50842) 229/E6
Cromwell, Ky. (42333) 237/H6
Cromwell, Minn. (55726) 254/F4
Cromwell, N.Z. 101/B6
Cromwell, Okla. (74837) 288/N4
Cronulla, N.S.W. 97/J4
Crook, Colo. (80726) 208/O1
Crook (co.), Oreg. 291/G3
Crook (pt.), Oreg. 291/C5
Crook (co.), Wyo. 319/H1
Crook and Willington, Eng. 13/F3
Crooked (isl.), Bah. Is. 156/D2
Crooked (lake), Fla. 212/E4
Crooked (creek), Ind. 227/D2
Crooked (creek), Kans. 232/B4
Crooked (creek), Minn. 254/F4
Crooked (lake), Minn. 254/G2
Crooked (lake), N. Dak. 283/J4
Crooked (creek), Oreg. 291/K5
Crooked (riv.), Oreg. 291/G3
Crooked (creek), S.C. 296/H2
Crooked Creek, Alaska (99575) 196/G2
Crooked Creek, Alta. 182/B2
Crooked Island (passg.), Bah. Is. 156/C2
Crooked River, Sask. 181/H3
Crookhaven, Ire. 17/B9
Crooks, S. Dak. (57020) 298/R6
Crookston, Minn., 188/G1
Crookston, Minn. (56716) 254/B3
Crookston, Nebr. (69212) 264/D2
Crooksville, Ohio (43731) 284/F6
Crookwell, N.S.W. 97/E4
Croom, Ire. 17/D6
Cropper, Ky. (40015) 237/L4
Cropsey, Ill. (61731) 222/E3
Cropwell, Ala. (35054) 194/F3
Crosby, 10/F2
Crosby, Ala. (†36343) 194/H8
Crosby, Minn. (56441) 254/D4
Crosby, Miss. (39633) 256/B8
Crosby, N. Dak. (58730) 283/D2
Crosby, Pa. (16724) 294/F2
Crosby (co.), Texas 302/C4
Crosby, Texas (77532) 302/J8
Crosby (mt.), Wyo. 319/C2
Crosbyton, Texas (79322) 302/C4
Crosland, Ga. (†31771) 216/E8
Cross (sound), Alaska 196/L1
Cross (co.), Ark. 203/J3
Cross (lake), La. 238/C2
Cross (isl.), Maine 242/J6
Cross (lake), Maine 242/G1
Cross (bay), Man. 179/C1
Cross (lake), Man. 179/J3
Cross (isl.), N.S. 169/D4
Cross (riv.), Nigeria 106/F7
Cross (riv.), Cameroon 115/A2
Cross, S.C. (29436) 296/G5
Cross (cape), S.W. Afr. 118/A4
Cross, Sask. 181/B6
Cross Anchor, S.C. (29331) 296/D2
Cross City, Fla. (32628) 212/C2
Cross Creek, N. Br. 170/D2
Crossett, Ark. (71635) 203/G7
Crossfarnoge (pt.), Ire. 17/J7
Cross Fell (mt.), Eng. 13/E3
Crossfield, Alta. 182/C4
Cross Fork, Pa. (17729) 294/G3
Crossgar, N. Ire. 17/K3
Crosshaven, Ire. 17/E8
Cross Hill, S.C. (29332) 296/D3
Cross Junction, Va. (22625) 307/M2
Cross Keys, S.C. (†29379) 296/D2
Cross Lake, Man. 179/J3
Crosslake, Minn. (56442) 254/E4
Crossley (mt.), N.Z. 101/D5
Crossmaglen, N. Ire. 17/H3
Crossmolina, Ire. 17/C3
Cross Plains, Ind. (47017) 227/G7
Cross Plains, Tenn. (37049) 237/H7
Cross Plains, Texas (76443) 302/E5
Cross Plains, Wis. (53528) 317/G9
Cross Point, Que. 172/C2
Cross Roads, Calif. (†92242) 204/L9
Crossroads, N. Mex. (88114) 274/F5
Cross Roads, P.E.I. 169/F2
Cross Roads, Pa. (†17322) 294/J6
Cross Roads Ohio, N.S. 169/F3
Cross Timbers, Mo. (65634) 261/F6
Crosstown, Mo. (†63775) 261/N7
Cross Village, Mich. (49723) 250/D3
Crossville, Ala. (35962) 194/G2
Crossville, Ill. (62827) 222/F5
Crossville, Tenn. (38555) 237/L9
Crosswicks, N.J. (08515) 273/D3
Crosswicks (creek), N.J. 273/D3
Croswell, Mich. (48422) 250/G5
Crotch (lake), Ont. 177/H3
Crothersville, Ind. (47229) 227/F7
Croton, Ohio (43013) 284/E5
Crotone, Italy 34/F5
Croton Falls, N.Y. (10519) 276/N8
Croton-on-Hudson, N.Y. (10520) 276/N8
Crouch, Idaho (†83622) 220/B5
Crouse, N.C. (28033) 281/G4
Crouseville, Maine (04738) 242/G2
Crow (creek), Colo. 208/L1
Crow (riv.), Minn. 254/F5
Crow, Oreg. (†97401) 291/D4
Crow (creek), S. Dak. 298/A4
Crow (creek), Wyo. 319/H4
Crow Agency, Mont. (59022) 262/J5
Crow Creek Ind. Res., S. Dak. 298/L5
Crowder, Miss. (38622) 256/D2
Crowder, Mo. (†63801) 261/N9
Crowder, Okla. (74430) 288/P4
Crow Duck (lake), Man. 179/G4
Crowdy (head), N.S.W. 97/G2
Crowell, Texas (79227) 302/E4
Crowfoot, Alta. 182/D4
Crowheart, Wyo. (82512) 319/C2
Crow Ind. Res., Mont. 262/H5
Crowl (creek), N.S.W. 97/C2
Crow Lake, S. Dak. (†57382) 298/M6
Crowle, Eng. 13/G4
Crowley (lake), Calif. 204/G6
Crowley (co.), Colo. 208/M6
Crowley, Colo. (81033) 208/M6
Crowley, La. (70526) 238/F6
Crowley, Texas (76036) 302/E2
Crowleys Ridge (mt.), Ark. 203/J2
Crown (mt.), V.I.(U.S.) 161/A4
Crown, Minn. (†55005) 254/E5
Crown City, Ohio (45623) 284/F8
Crown King, Ariz. (86333) 198/C4
Crown Point, Ind. (46307) 227/C2
Crownpoint, N. Mex. (87313) 274/A3
Crown Point, N.Y. (12928) 276/N3
Crown Prince Frederik (isl.), N.W.T. 187/K3
Crownsville, Md. (21032) 245/M4
Crows Landing, Calif. (95313) 204/D6
Crowsnest (pass), Alta. 182/C5
Crowsnest, Br. Col. 184/K5
Crowsnest (pass), Br. Col. 184/K5
Crowville, La. (71230) 238/G2
Crow Wing (co.), Minn. 254/D4
Crow Wing (riv.), Minn. 254/D4
Croydon, 10/B6
Croydon, Aust. 88/G3
Croydon, Eng. 13/G6
Croydon▵, N.H. (†03753) 268/C5
Croydon (peak), N.H. 268/C5
Croydon, Queens. 95/B3
Croydon, Utah (84018) 304/C2
Croydon, Vic. 97/K5
Croydon Branch, Sugar (riv.), N.H. 268/C5
Crozet (isls.), 3/M8
Crozet, Va. (22932) 307/L4
Crozier (chan.), N.W.T. 187/G2
Crozier, Va. (23039) 307/N5
Cruces, Cuba 156/B2
Cruces, Cuba 158/E2
Cruden Bay, Scot. 15/N5
Cruger, Miss. (38924) 256/D4
Cruillas, Mex. 150/K4
Crum (creek), Pa. 294/M7
Crum, W. Va. (25669) 313/B7
Crumlin, N. Ire. 17/J2
Crum Lynne, Pa. (19022) 294/M7
Crummies, Ky. (40821) 237/P7
Crump, Mich. (†48634) 250/E5
Crump, Tenn. (38327) 237/E10
Crumpton (pt.), Dominica 161/F5
Crumpton, Md. (21628) 245/P4
Crumrod, Ark. (72328) 203/H5
Crumstown, Ind. (†46554) 227/E1
Crusheen, Ire. 17/D6
Cruso, N.C. (†28716) 281/D4
Cruta, Hond. 154/F3
Crutchfield, Ky. (42034) 237/D7
Crutwell, Sask. 181/E2
Cruz (cape), Cuba 156/C3
Cruz (cape), Cuba 158/G4
Cruz Alta, Braz., 120/E5
Cruz Alta, Braz. 132/C10
Cruz Bay, V.I.(U.S.) 161/C4
Cruz del Eje, Arg. 143/C3
Cruz de Piedra, Urug. 145/E3
Cruz de San Pedro, Urug. 145/E2
Cruzeiro, Braz. 135/D3
Cruzeiro do Sul, Braz. 132/G10
Cruz Grande, Chile 138/A7
Crysler, Ont. 177/J2
Crystal (lake), Conn. 210/F1
Crystal (pond), Conn. 210/G1
Crystal (bay), Fla. 212/D3
Crystal, Ind. (†47527) 227/D8
Crystal▵, Maine (†04747) 242/G4
Crystal, Mich. (48818) 250/E5
Crystal (lake), Mich. 250/C4
Crystal, Minn. (†55401) 254/G5
Crystal, N. Dak. (58222) 283/P2
Crystal, N.H. (†03591) 268/E2
Crystal (lake), N.H. 268/E5
Crystal, N. Mex. (†86504) 274/A2
Crystal (mts.), Rep. of Congo 115/B4
Crystal (mts.), Gabon 115/B4
Crystal (lake), Vt. 268/C2
Crystal, W. Va. (†24747) 313/D8
Crystal Bay, Minn. (55323) 254/F5
Crystal Bay, Nev. (89402) 266/A3
Crystal Beach, Ont. 177/E5
Crystal Brook, S. Aust. 94/E5
Crystal City, Man. 179/C5
Crystal City, Mo. (63019) 261/M6
Crystal City, Texas (78839) 302/E9
Crystal Falls, Ont. 177/D1
Crystal Falls, Mich. (49920) 250/A2
Crystal Hill, Sask. 181/F6
Crystal Hill, Va. (24539) 307/L7
Crystal Lake, Conn. (†06066) 210/F1
Crystal Lake, Fla. (32463) 212/D6
Crystal Lake, Ill. (60014) 222/E1
Crystal Lake, Iowa (50432) 229/F2
Crystal Lake Park‡, Mo. (†63101) 261/P3
Crystal Lakes, Ohio (†45341) 284/C6
Crystal River, Fla. (32629) 212/D3
Crystal Springs, Ark. (71938) 203/D5
Crystal Springs (res.), Calif. 204/J3
Crystal Springs, Fla. (33524) 212/D3
Crystal Springs, Ga. (†30105) 216/B2
Crystal Springs, Kans. (67033) 232/D4
Crystal Springs, Miss. (39059) 256/D7
Crystal Springs, N. Dak. (58427) 283/L6
Crystal Springs, Sask. 181/F3
Crystal Valley, Mich. (†49420) 250/C5
Csabrendek, Hung. 41/D3
Csákvár, Hung. 41/E3
Csanádpalota, Hung. 41/F3
Csenger, Hung. 41/G3
Csepel, Hung. 41/E3
Csepelsziget (isl.), Hung. 41/E3
Csepreg, Hung. 41/D3
Csongrád (co.), Hung. 41/F3
Csongrád, Hung. 41/E3
Csorna, Hung. 41/D3
Csorvás, Hung. 41/F3
Csurgó, Hung. 41/D3
Ctesiphon (ruins), Iraq 66/D4
Cúa, Ven. 124/E2
Cuadro Nacional, Arg. 143/C3
Cuando Cubango (dist.), Angola 115/C7
Cuangar, Angola 115/C7
Cuango, Angola 115/C5
Cuango (riv.), Angola 115/C6
Cuanza (riv.), Angola 115/C5
Cuanza-Norte (dist.), Angola 115/B5
Cuanza-Sul (dist.), Angola 115/B6
Cuao (riv.), Ven. 124/E5
Cua Rao, N. Vietnam 72/E3
Cuareim (riv.), Urug. 145/B1
Cuaró, Urug. 145/D2
Cuarto (riv.), Arg. 143/D3
Cuatrociénagas de Carranza, Mex. 150/H3
Cuatro Compañeros, Cuba 158/G3
Cuatro Ojos, Bol. 136/D5
Cuauhtémoc, Mex. 150/F2
Cuautitlán de Romero Rubio, Mex. 150/L1
Cuautla Morelos, Mex. 150/L2
Cub (creek), Utah 304/C1
Cub (creek), Va. 307/L6
Cuba, 3/E4
Cuba, 146/L7
CUBA, 156/B2
CUBA, 158
Cuba, Ala. (36907) 194/B6
Cuba, Ill. (61427) 222/C3
Cuba, Ind. (†47460) 227/D6
Cuba, Kans. (66940) 232/E2
Cuba, Mo. (65453) 261/K6
Cuba, N. Mex. (87013) 274/B2
Cuba, N.Y. (14727) 276/D6
Cuba (chan.), N.Z. 101/D7
Cuba, Ohio (45114) 284/C7
Cuba, Port. 33/C3
Cuba City, Wis. (53807) 317/F10
Cubage, Ky. (40822) 237/O7
Cubagua (isl.), Ven. 124/F2
Cuballing, W. Aust. 92/B2
Cubango (riv.), Angola 115/C7
Cubango (riv.), S.W. Afr. 118/B3
Cubatão, Braz. 135/C3
Cube (mt.), N.H. 268/D4
Cubero, N. Mex. (87014) 274/B3
Cubiro, Ven. 124/D3
Cub Run, Ky. (42729) 237/J6
Çubuk, Turkey 63/E2

Deer Park 353

Dama, Poulo (isls.), S. Vietnam 72/D5
Daman, India, 54/L7
Daman (dist.), India 68/C4
Damanhur, U.A.R. 59/A3
Damanhur, U.A.R. 111/J3
Damar, Kans. (67632) 232/C2
Damar (isl.), Indon. 85/H7
Damar (isls.), Indon. 85/H7
Damara, Centr. Afr. Rep. 115/C2
Damaraland (reg.), S.W. Afr. 118/B4
Damariscotta△, Maine (04543) 242/E7
Damariscotta-Newcastle, Maine (04543) 242/E7
Damascus, Ark. (72039) 203/F3
Damascus, Ga. (31741) 216/C8
Damascus, Md. (20750) 245/K3
Damascus (prov.), Syria 63/G6
Damascus (cap.), Syria, 54/G6
Damascus (cap.), Syria 59/C3
Damascus (cap.), Syria 63/G6
Damascus, Ohio (44619) 284/J4
Damascus, Pa. (18415) 294/M2
Damascus, Va. (24236) 307/E7
Damba, Angola 115/B5
Dam Doi, S. Vietnam 72/E5
Dame-Marie (cape), Haiti 156/C3
Dame-Marie, Haiti 158/A6
Dame-Marie (cape), Haiti 158/A6
Dameron, Md. (20628) 245/N8
Dames Ferry, Ga. (†31046) 216/E4
Dames Quarter, Md. (21820) 245/P8
Damghan, Iran 59/F2
Damghan, Iran 66/J2
Damietta, 102/F1
Damietta, U.A.R. 59/B3
Damietta, U.A.R. 111/J3
Damiya, Jordan 65/D3
Dammam, Saudi Ar. 59/F4
Dammastock (mt.), Switz. 39/F3
Damodar (riv.), India 68/F4
Damoh, India 68/D4
Damongo, Ghana 106/D7
Dampier (arch.), Aust. 88/B4
Dampier (str.), Terr. N.G. 85/C7
Dampier (str.), Indon. 85/J6
Dampier, W. Aust. 92/B3
Dampier (arch.), W. Aust. 92/B3
Dampier Downs, W. Aust. 92/C2
Dampier Land (reg.), Aust. 88/C3
Dampier Land (reg.), W. Aust. 92/C2
Damqut, P.D.R. Yemen 59/F6
Damvant, Switz. 39/C2
Dan (riv.), N.C. 281/L1
Dan, Israel 65/D1
Dan (riv.), Va. 307/K7
Dana, Ill. (61321) 222/E3
Dana, Ind. (47847) 227/C5
Dana, Iowa (50064) 229/E4
Dana, Jordan 65/E5
Dana, Sask. 181/F3
Danakil (reg.), Eth. 111/H5
Danané, Ivory Coast 106/C7
Da Nang, S. Vietnam 72/E3
Da Nang, S. Vietnam, 54/O8
Danao, Phil. 82/D5
Dana Point, Calif. (92629) 204/H10
Danburg, Ga. (30632) 216/G3
Danbury, Conn. (06810) 210/B3
Danbury, Iowa (51019) 229/B4
Danbury, N.C. (27016) 281/J2
Danbury△, N.H. (03230) 268/D4
Danbury, N.H. (03230) 268/D4
Danbury, Nebr. (69026) 264/D4
Danbury, Sask. 181/J4
Danbury, Texas (77534) 302/J8
Danbury, Wis. (54830) 317/B3
Danbury P.O. (South Danbury), N.H. (03230) 268/D5
Danby (lake), Calif. 204/K9
Danby, Que. 172/E4
Danby△, Vt. (05739) 268/A5
Danby, Vt. (05739) 268/B5
Dancing (pt.), Man. 179/D2
Dancy, Ala. (†35442) 194/B4
Dancy, Miss. (†39751) 256/F3
Dancy, Wis. (†54455) 317/G6
Dancyville, Tenn. (†38069) 237/C10
Dand, Man. 179/B5
Dandaragan, W. Aust. 92/A5
Dandenong, Aust. 88/M7
Dandenong (creek), Aust. 88/M7
Dandenong, Vic. 97/K5
Dandenong (creek), Vic. 97/K5
Dandenong (mt.), Vic. 97/K5
Danderyd, Sweden 18/H1
Dandridge, Tenn. (37725) 237/O8
Dane (co.), Wis. 317/H9
Dane, Wis. (53529) 317/G9
Daneborg, Greenl., 4/B10
Danforth, Ill. (60930) 222/E3
Danforth△, Maine (04424) 242/H4
Danforth, Maine (04424) 242/H4
Danger (Pukapuka) (atoll), Cook Is., 87/K7
Dangila, Eth. 111/G5
Dang Raek, Phanom (mts.), Cambodia 72/D4
Dang Raek, Phanom (mts.), Thai. 72/D4
Dania, Fla. (33004) 212/B4
Daniel (mt.), Wash. 310/D3
Daniel, Wyo. (83115) 319/B3
Daniel Boone, Ky. (†42442) 237/G6
Daniels, Md. (21033) 245/L3
Daniels (co.), Mont. 262/L2
Daniels, W. Va. (25832) 313/D7
Daniel's Harbour, Newf. 166/C3
Danielson, Conn. (06239) 210/H1
Daniel's Point, Newf. 166/D2
Danielstown, Guyana 131/B2
Danielsville, Ga. (30633) 216/F2
Danielsville, Pa. (18038) 294/M4
Danilov, U.S.S.R. 52/E3
Dankhar Gömpa, India 68/D2
Danlí, Hond. 154/D3
Danmarkshavn, Greenl., 4/B10
Dannebrog, Nebr. (68831) 264/F3
Dannemora, Sweden 18/K6
Dannemora, N.Y. (12929) 276/N1
Dannenberg, W. Ger. 22/D2
Danner, Oreg. (†97910) 291/K5
Dannevirke, N.Z. 101/F4
Dan Sai, Thai. 72/D3
Dansville, Mich. (48819) 250/E6
Dansville, N.Y. (14437) 276/E5
Dante (Hafun), Somalia 115/K1
Dante, S. Dak. (57329) 298/N7
Dante, Va. (24237) 307/D7
Danube (riv.), 7/G4
Danube (riv.), Austria 41/C2
Danube (riv.), Bulg. 45/H4
Danube (riv.), Czech. 41/C2
Danube (riv.), Hung. 41/E3
Danube, Minn. (56230) 254/C6
Danube (delta), Rum. 45/J3
Danube (riv.), Rum. 45/H4
Danube (riv.), W. Ger. 22/C4
Danube (riv.), Yugo. 45/E5
Danubyu, Burma 72/B3
Danvers, Ill. (61732) 222/D3
Danvers△, Mass. (01923) 249/D5
Danvers, Minn. (56231) 254/C5
Danvers, Mont. (59629) 262/G3
Danversport, Mass. (†01923) 249/E5
Danville, Ala. (35619) 194/D2
Danville, Ark. (72833) 203/D3
Danville, Que. 172/E4
Danville, Ga. (31017) 216/F5
Danville, Ill., 188/J3
Danville, Ill. (61832) 222/F3
Danville, Ind. (46122) 227/D5
Danville, Iowa (52623) 229/L7
Danville, Kans. (67036) 232/E4
Danville, Ky. (40422) 237/M5
Danville, La. (†71008) 238/E2
Danville, Mo. (†63361) 261/J5
Danville△, N.H. (03819) 268/E6
Danville, N.H. (03819) 268/E6
Danville, Ohio (43014) 284/F5
Danville, Pa. (17821) 294/J4
Danville, Va., 146/K6
Danville, Va., 188/L3
Danville, Va. (24541) 307/J7
Danville△, Vt. (05828) 268/C3
Danville, Vt. (05828) 268/C3
Danville, W. Va. (25053) 313/C6
Danville, Wash. (99121) 310/G2
Danville, Wis. (†53925) 317/J9
Danville-Alamo, Calif. (94526) 204/K2
Danzig (gulf), Poland 47/D1
Dao Bach Long Vi (isl.), N. Vietnam 72/F2
Dao Phu Quoc (isl.), S. Vietnam 72/D5
Dapa, Phil. 82/E6
Daphne, Ala. (36526) 194/C9
Daphne, Sask. 181/G3
Dapitan, Phil. 82/D6
Dapoli, India 68/C5
Dapp, Alta. 182/C2
Darab, Iran 59/G4
Darab, Iran 66/J6
Darabani, Rum. 45/H1
Dar al Hamra, Saudi Ar. 59/C4
Daram (isl.), Phil. 82/E5
Daran, Iran 66/G4
Darbandikhan (dam), Iraq 66/D3
Darbhanga, India 68/F3
Darbun, Miss. (†39643) 256/D8
Darby (cape), Alaska 196/F2
Darby, Mont. (59829) 262/B4
Darby (creek), Ohio 284/D5
Darby, Pa. (19023) 294/M7
Darby (creek), Pa. 294/M6
Darby, Vic. 97/D6
Darbydale, Ohio (43123) 284/D6
Darbyville, Ohio (†43164) 284/D6
D'Arcy, Br. Col. 184/F5
D'Arcy, Sask. 181/C4
Dardanelle, Ark. (72834) 203/D3
Dardanelle (res.), Ark. 203/D3
Dardanelles (str.), Turkey 59/A2
Dardanelles (str.), Turkey 63/B6
Dardanelles (str.), Turkey, 7/G5
Darden, Tenn. (38328) 237/E9
Dardenne, Mo. (†63366) 261/N2
Dare (co.), N.C. 281/T3
Dar-el-Beida (Casablanca), Mor. 106/C2
Darende, Turkey 63/G3
Dar es Salaam (cap.), Tanz., 102/F5
Dar es Salaam (cap.), Tanz. 115/G5
Dar es Salaam (cap.), Tanz., 3/M6
Daretown, N.J. (†08318) 273/C4
Darfur, Minn. (56022) 254/D6
Darfur (prov.), Sudan 111/D5
Dargan, Md. (†25425) 245/H3
Dargaville, N.Z. 101/D1
Dar Hamid (reg.), Sudan 111/F5
Darien△, Conn. (06820) 210/B4
Darien, Ga. (31305) 216/K8
Darien‡, Ill. (†60515) 222/A2
Darien, N.Y. (†14040) 276/D5
Darién, Sierra del (mts.), Pan. 154/J6
Darien, Wis. (53114) 317/J10
Darien Center, N.Y. (14040) 276/D5
Dariense, Cordillera (range), Nic. 154/E4
Darjeeling, India, 54/M7
Darjeeling, India 68/F3
Dark (head), St. Vincent 161/A8
Darkan, W. Aust. 92/B2
Dark Canyon (creek), N. Mex. 274/E6
Dark Cove, Newf. 166/D4
Darke (co.), Ohio 284/A5
Darkesville, W. Va. (†25428) 313/L4
Darkhan, Mong. 77/G2
Darkharbor, Maine (†04848) 242/F7
Darlac (plat.), S. Vietnam 72/F4
Darling (river), Australia, 87/E9
Darling (riv.), Aust. 88/G6
Darling (range), Aust. 88/B6
Darling, Miss. (38623) 256/D2
Darling (lake), N. Dak. 283/G2
Darling (riv.), N.S.W. 97/B3
Darling (range), W. Aust. 92/A1
Darling, Pa. (19063) 294/L7
Darling Downs, Queens. 95/D5
Darlingford, Man. 179/D5
Darlington, 10/F3
Darlington, Ala. (36730) 194/D7
Darlington, Eng. 13/F3
Darlington, Fla. (†32464) 212/C5
Darlington, Idaho (83231) 220/E6
Darlington, Ind. (47940) 227/D4
Darlington, La. (†70441) 238/J5
Darlington, Md. (21034) 245/N2
Darlington, Mo. (64438) 261/D2
Darlington, Pa. (16115) 294/A4
Darlington (co.), S.C. 296/H3
Darlington, S.C. (29532) 296/H3
Darlington, Wis. (53530) 317/F10
Darlington Heights, Va. (23935) 307/L6
Darlington Point, N.S.W. 97/C4
Darliston, Jam. 158/H6
Darłowo, Poland 47/C1
Dar Masalit (reg.), Sudan 111/D5
Darmody, Sask. 181/E5
Darmstadt, Ill. (†62255) 222/D5
Darmstadt, W. Ger. 22/C4
Darnell, La. (71231) 238/G1
Darnestown, Md. (20760) 245/J4
Darnick, N.S.W. 97/B3
Darnley (cape), Ant. 5/C4
Darnley (bay), N.W.T. 187/F3
Daroca, Spain 33/F2
Darr, Nebr. (†69130) 264/E4
Darreh Gaz, Iran 66/L2
Darrington, Wash. (98241) 310/D2
Dar Rounga (reg.), Centr. Afr. Rep. 115/D2
Darrouzett, Texas (79024) 302/D1
Darrow, La. (70725) 238/K3
Darrtown, Ohio (†45056) 284/A7
Darsser Ort (pt.), E. Ger. 22/E1
Därstetten, Switz. 39/D3
Dart (cape), Ant. 5/B12
Dartford, 10/C5
Dartmoor (for.), Eng. 13/C7
Dartmoor, Vic. 97/A5
Dartmouth, 10/E5
Dartmouth, 163/K7
Dartmouth (riv.), Que. 172/D1
Dartmouth, Eng. 13/D7
Dartmouth△, Mass. (02714) 249/K6
Dartmouth, N.S. 169/E4
Dartuch (cape), Spain 33/H3
Daru, Papua 85/B7
Daru, Papua 87/E6
Darvel, Scot. 15/H8
Darwell, Alta. 182/C3
Darwen, 10/G1
Darwin, Australia, 87/D7
Darwin, Aust. 88/E2
Darwin, Australia, 3/R6
Darwin, Calif. (93522) 204/H7
Darwin (bay), Chile 138/D6
Darwin, Cordillera (mts.), Chile 138/D8
Darwin, Cordillera (mts.), Chile 138/E11
Darwin (Culpepper) (isl.), Ec. 128/B8
Darwin, Ill. (†62477) 222/F4
Darwin, Minn. (55324) 254/D5
Darwin (cap.), No. Terr. 93/B2
Darwin, Okla. (†74523) 288/P6
Das (isl.), Trucial States 59/F4
Dash, Ben (hill), Ire. 17/D6
Dashan, Ras (mt.), Eth. 59/C7
Dasher, Ga. (31601) 216/F9
Dasht (riv.), Pak. 59/H4
Dasht (riv.), Pak. 68/A3
Dashtiari, Iran 59/H4
Dashtiari, Iran 66/M8
Dashwood, Ont. 177/C4
Dasol (bay), Phil. 82/B3
Dassel, Minn. (55325) 254/D5
Datça, Turkey 63/B4
Dateland, Ariz. (85333) 198/B6
Datia, India 68/D3
Datil, N. Mex. (87821) 274/B4
Datil (mts.), N. Mex. 274/B4
Datto, Ark. (72424) 203/J1
Datu Piang, Phil. 82/E7
Daufuskie Island, S.C. (29915) 296/F7
Daugava (Western Dvina) (riv.), U.S.S.R. 53/D2
Daugavpils, U.S.S.R. 48/C4
Daugavpils, U.S.S.R. 52/C3
Daugavpils, U.S.S.R. 53/D3
Daugavpils, U.S.S.R., 7/G3
Daulatabad, Afgh. 59/H3
Daulatabad, Iran 66/K6
Daulatabad, Iran 66/M2
Daulatabad (Malayer), Iran 66/F3
Daulatabad, Afgh. 68/A2
Daulat Yar, Afgh. 59/J3
Daulat Yar, Afgh. 68/B2
Daule, Ec. 128/B3
Daulnay, N. Br. 170/E1
Daun, W. Ger. 22/B3
Dauphin, 163/F5
Dauphin, St. Lucia 161/G5
Dauphin, Man. 179/B3
Dauphin (lake), Man. 179/C3
Dauphin (riv.), Man. 179/D3
Dauphin (cape), N.S. 169/H2
Dauphin (co.), Pa. 294/J5
Dauphin, Pa. (17018) 294/J5
Dauphin Island, Ala. (36528) 194/B10
Daus, Tenn. (37320) 237/L10
Davangere, India 68/D6
Davant, La. (70046) 238/L7
Davao (prov.), Phil. 82/E7
Davao, Phil. 82/E7
Davao (gulf), Phil. 82/E7
Davao, Phil. 85/H4
Davao (gulf), Phil. 85/H4
Davao, Phil., 3/R5
Davao, Phil., 54/R9
Daveluyville, Que. 172/E3
Davenport, Calif. (95017) 204/K4
Davenport, Fla. (33837) 212/E3
Davenport, Iowa, 188/H2
Davenport, Iowa (*52801) 229/M5
Davenport, N. Dak. (58021) 283/R6
Davenport, N.Y. (13750) 276/L6
Davenport, Nebr. (68335) 264/G4
Davenport (mt.), No. Terr. 93/B7
Davenport, Okla. (74026) 288/N3
Davenport, Va. (24239) 307/D6
Davenport, Wash. (99122) 310/G3
Davenport-Rock Island-Moline, Iowa 229/M5
Daventry, Eng. 13/F5
Davey, Nebr. (68336) 264/H4
Davey, Port (inlet), Aust. 88/G8
Davey, Port (inlet), Tasmania 99/B5
David (pt.), Grenada 161/D8
David, Ky. (41616) 237/R5
David, Pan. 154/F6
David City, Nebr. (68632) 264/G3
Davidson (mts.), Alaska 196/K1
Davidson, Maine (†04782) 242/F4
Davidson (co.), N.C. 281/J3
Davidson, N.C. (28036) 281/H4
Davidson, Okla. (73530) 288/J6
Davidson, Sask. 181/E4
Davidson (co.), Tenn. 237/H8
Davidson (mts.), Yukon 187/D3
Davidsonville, Md. (21035) 245/M5
Davie, Fla. (33314) 212/B4
Davie (co.), N.C. 281/H3
Daviess (co.), Ind. 227/C7
Daviess (co.), Ky. 237/G5
Daviess (co.), Mo. 261/E3
Davik, Norway 18/D6
Davilla, Texas (76523) 302/G7
Davin, Sask. 181/H5
Daviot, Scot. 15/H5
Davis (str.), 3/G2
Davis (strait), 4/C12
Davis (str.), 146/N3
Davis (str.), 163/L2
Davis (sea), Ant. 5/C5
Davis (dam), Ariz. 198/A3
Davis, Calif. (95616) 204/B8
Davis (isl.), Fla. 212/C3
Davis, Ill. (61019) 222/D1
Davis (co.), Iowa 229/J7
Davis, N.C. (28524) 281/R5
Davis (str.), N.W.T. 187/M3
Davis (dam), Nev. 266/G7
Davis, Okla. (73030) 288/M5
Davis (lake), Oreg. 291/F4
Davis (mt.), Pa. 294/D6
Davis, S. Dak. (57021) 298/P7
Davis, Sask. 181/F2
Davis (mts.), Texas 302/C11
Davis (co.), Utah 304/B3
Davis, W. Va. (26260) 313/H4
Davisboro, Ga. (31018) 216/G5
Davis City, Iowa (50065) 229/F7
Davis Cove, Newf. 166/D4
Davis Creek, Calif. (96108) 204/E2
Davis Dam, Ariz. (†86430) 198/A3
Davis Inlet, Newf. 166/B2
Davis Junction, Ill. (61020) 222/D1
Davis-Monthan A.F.B., Ariz. 198/E6
Davison, Mich. (48423) 250/F5
Davison (co.), S. Dak. 298/N6
Davisson (lake), Wash. 310/C4
Davis Station, Ant. 5/C4
Davis Station, S.C. (29041) 296/G4
Daviston, Ala. (36256) 194/G4
Davisville, Mo. (65456) 261/K7
Davisville, R.I. (02854) 249/H6
Davisville, W. Va. (26142) 313/C4
Davlekanovo, U.S.S.R. 52/H4
Davos (valley), Switz. 39/J3
Davos (Dorf and Platz), Switz. 39/J3
Davy, W. Va. (24828) 313/C8
Davyroyd, Sask. 181/F6
Dawa (riv.), Eth. 111/H7
Dawa (riv.), Kenya 115/H3
Dawasir, Wadi (dry riv.), Saudi Ar. 59/E5
Dawasir, Hadhb (range), Saudi Ar. 59/D5
Dawes (co.), Nebr. 264/A2
Dawes, W. Va. (25054) 313/D6
Dawley, Eng. 13/E5
Dawlish, Eng. 13/D7
Dawn, Mo. (64638) 261/E3
Dawn, Texas (79025) 302/B3
Dawna (range), Burma 72/C3
Dawson, Ala. (35963) 194/G2
Dawson (riv.), Aust. 88/H4
Dawson, Canada, 4/C16
Dawson (isl.), Chile 138/E10
Dawson (co.), Ga. 216/D2
Dawson, Ga. (31742) 216/D7
Dawson, Ill. (62520) 222/D4
Dawson, Iowa (50066) 229/E5
Dawson, 163/C3
Dawson (bay), Man. 179/B2
Dawson, Minn. (56232) 254/B6
Dawson, Mo. (†65548) 261/H8
Dawson (co.), Mont. 262/M3
Dawson, N. Dak. (58428) 283/L6
Dawson (inlet), N.W.T. 187/J3
Dawson (co.), Nebr. 264/E4
Dawson, Nebr. (68337) 264/J4
Dawson (riv.), Queens. 95/D5
Dawson‡, Pa. (15428) 294/C5
Dawson (co.), Texas 302/C5
Dawson, Texas (76639) 302/H6
Dawson, W. Va. (24932) 313/E7
Dawson, Yukon, 146/E3
Dawson, Yukon 187/E3
Dawson Creek, 163/D4
Dawson Creek, Br. Col. 184/G2
Dawson Landing, N.W.T. 187/G3
Dawson Springs, Ky. (42408) 237/F6
Dawsonville, Ga. (30534) 216/D2
Dawsonville, N. Br. 170/C1
Dax, France 28/C6
Day, Fla. (32013) 212/C1
Day, Minn. (†55006) 254/E5
Day (co.), S. Dak. 298/O3
Day Book, N.C. (†28714) 281/E3
Dayboro, Aust. 88/K1
Daykin, Nebr. (68338) 264/G4
Daylesford, Aust. 88/G7
Daylesford, Vic. 97/C5
Daylight, Ind. (†47708) 227/B8
Daylight, Tenn. (†37110) 237/K9
Daymán, Urug. 145/B2
Daymán (range), Urug. 145/B2
Daymán (riv.), Urug. 145/B2
Days Creek, Oreg. (97429) 291/D5
Daysland, Alta. 182/D3
Daysville, Ky. (†42276) 237/G7
Dayton, Ala. (36731) 194/C6
Dayton, Idaho (83232) 220/F7
Dayton, Ill. (†61350) 222/E2
Dayton, Ind. (47941) 227/D4
Dayton, Iowa (50530) 229/E4
Dayton, Ky. (41074) 237/T2
Dayton, Mich. (†49113) 250/C7
Dayton, Minn. (55327) 254/E5
Dayton, Mont. (59914) 262/B3
Dayton, N.Y. (14041) 276/C6
Dayton, Nev. (89403) 266/B3
Dayton, Ohio, 146/K6
Dayton, Ohio, 188/K3
Dayton, Ohio (*45401) 284/B6
Dayton, Oreg. (97114) 291/A3
Dayton, Pa. (16222) 294/D4
Dayton, Tenn. (37321) 237/L9
Dayton, Texas (77535) 302/J7
Dayton, Va. (22821) 307/L4
Dayton, Wash. (99328) 310/H4
Dayton, Wis. (†53508) 317/H10
Dayton, Wyo. (82836) 319/E1
Daytona Beach, Fla., 188/K5
Daytona Beach, Fla. (*32014) 212/F2
Daytona Beach Shores, Fla. (32016) 212/F2
Dayville△, Conn. (06241) 210/H1
Dayville, Oreg. (97825) 291/H3
Dazey, N. Dak. (58429) 283/O5
De Aar, 102/E8
De Aar, S. Africa 118/C6
Dead (lake), Fla. 212/D6
Dead (riv.), Maine 242/C5
Dead (riv.), Mich. 250/B2
Dead (lake), Minn. 254/C4
Dead (sea), Israel 59/C3
Dead (sea), Jordan 59/C3
Dead (sea), Israel 65/C4
Dead (sea), Jordan 65/C4
Deadman (creek), Wash. 310/H4
Deadman (mt.), Wyo. 319/B2
Deadwood, Alta. 182/B1
Deadwood (res.), Idaho 220/C5
Deadwood (riv.), Idaho 220/C5
Deadwood, S. Dak. (57732) 298/B5
Deaf Smith (co.), Texas 302/B3
Deal, 10/G5
Deal, Eng. 13/J6
Deal, N.J. (07723) 273/F3
Deal (isl.), Tas. 99/D1
Deale, Md. (20751) 245/M5
Deal Island, Md. (21821) 245/P8
Dean (chan.), Br. Col. 184/D4
Dean (riv.), Br. Col. 184/D4
Dean, Mont. (†59028) 262/G5
Dean, N.S. 169/F3
Deán Funes, Arg. 143/D3
Deanville, Texas (77852) 302/H7
Dearborn (co.), Ind. 227/H6
Dearborn, Mich. (*48120) 250/B7
Dearborn, Mo. (64439) 261/C3
Dearborn Heights, Mich. (48127) 250/B7
Dearing, Ga. (30808) 216/H4
Dearing, Kans. (67340) 232/G4
De Armanville, Ala. (36257) 194/G3
Deary, Idaho (83823) 220/B3
Dease (str.), 163/F2
Dease (inlet), Alaska 196/H1
Dease (lake), Br. Col. 184/K2
Dease (riv.), Br. Col. 184/K2
Dease (str.), N.W.T., 146/H3
Dease (str.), N.W.T. 187/H3
Dease Arm (inlet), N.W.T. 187/F3
Dease Lake, Br. Col. 184/K2
Death (valley), Calif. 204/H7
Death Valley (depr.), Calif., 188/C3
Death Valley, Calif. (92328) 204/J7
Death Valley Nat'l Mon., Calif. 204/H7
Death Valley Nat'l Mon., Nev. 266/E6
Deatsville, Ala. (36022) 194/F5
Deauville, Que. 172/E4
Deauville, France 28/C3
Deaver, Wyo. (82421) 319/D1
Deavertown, Ohio (†43731) 284/G6
Debaba, Saudi Ar. 59/D6
De Baca (co.), N. Mex. 274/E4
Deba Habe, Nigeria 106/G6
Debar, Yugo. 45/E5
De Bary, Fla. (32713) 212/E3
Debden, Sask. 181/E2
Débé, Trinidad Tobago 161/B11
Debec Junction, N. Br. 170/C2
De Beque, Colo. (81630) 208/C4
Deberai (pen.), Indon. 85/J6
De Berry, Texas (75639) 302/L5
Debert, N.S. 169/E3
Dębica, Poland 47/E3
DeBilt, Neth. 27/G4
Dęblin, Poland 47/E3
Deblois△, Maine (†04622) 242/H6
Dębno, Poland 47/B2
Debo (lake), Mali 106/D5
Debolt, Alta. 182/B2
De Borgia, Mont. (59830) 262/A3
Debra Birhan, Eth. 111/G6
Debra Markos, Eth. 111/G5
Debra Markos, 102/F3
Debra Tabor, Eth. 111/G5
Debra Tabor, 102/F3
Debrecen, Hung., 7/G4
Debrecen, Hung. 41/F3
Decatur, Ala. (35601) 194/D1
Decatur, Ark. (72722) 203/A1
Decatur (co.), Ga. 216/C9
Decatur, Ga. (*30030) 216/D3
Decatur, Ill., 188/J3
Decatur, Ill. (*62521) 222/E4
Decatur (lake), Ill. 222/E4
Decatur (co.), Ind. 227/G6
Decatur, Ind. (46733) 227/H3
Decatur (co.), Iowa 229/F7
Decatur, Iowa (50067) 229/F7
Decatur (co.), Kans. 232/B2
Decatur, Mich. (49045) 250/C6
Decatur, Miss. (39327) 256/F6
Decatur, Nebr. (68020) 264/H2
Decatur, Ohio (45115) 284/C8
Decatur (co.), Tenn. 237/E9
Decatur, Tenn. (37322) 237/M9
Decatur, Texas (76234) 302/G4
Decaturville, Tenn. (38329) 237/E9
Decazeville, France 28/E5
Deccan (plat.), India 68/D6
Deception (bay), Aust. 88/K2
Decherd, Tenn. (37324) 237/J10
Děčín, Czech. 41/C1
Decision (cape), Alaska 196/M2
Decize, France 28/E4
Decker, Ind. (47524) 227/B7
Decker, Man. 179/B4
Decker, Mich. (48426) 250/F5
Decker, Mont. (59025) 262/K5
Decker Lake, Br. Col. 184/E3
Deckers, Colo. (†80135) 208/J4
Deckerville, Ark. (†72386) 203/K3
Deckerville, Mich. (48427) 250/G5
Declo, Idaho (83323) 220/E7
Decorah, Iowa (52101) 229/K2
Decota, W. Va. (25055) 313/D6
Decoy, Ky. (41321) 237/P5
Deddington, Eng. 13/F5
Dedegöl Tepesi (mt.), Turkey 63/D4
Dedemsvaart, Neth. 27/J3
Dederick, Mo. (†64744) 261/D7
Dedham, Iowa (51440) 229/D5
Dedham△, Maine (†04429) 242/F6
Dedham, Maine (†04429) 242/F6
Dedham△, Mass. (02026) 249/C7
Dédougou, Upp. Volta 106/D6
Dedza, Malawi 115/F6
Dee (riv.), Eng. 13/D4
Dee (riv.), Ire. 17/H4
Dee (riv.), 10/E2
Dee (riv.), 10/E4
Dee (riv.), Scot. 15/H9
Dee (riv.), Scot. 15/M5
Dee (riv.), Wales 13/D4
Deedsville, Ind. (46921) 227/E3
Deel (riv.), Ire. 17/C3
Deel (riv.), Ire. 17/D7
Deel (riv.), Ire. 17/G4
Deele (riv.), Ire. 17/F2
Deemston‡, Pa. (†15333) 294/B5
Deenwood, Ga. (†31501) 216/H8
Deep (creek), Idaho 220/B7
Deep (creek), Idaho 220/F7
Deep (riv.), N.C. 281/K3
Deep (riv.), N. Dak. 283/H2
Deep (inlet), Newf. 166/B2
Deep (creek), S.C. 296/B2
Deep (creek), Texas 302/C5
Deep (creek), Utah 304/A4
Deep (creek), Utah 304/B1
Deep Brook, N.S. 169/C4
Deep Creek (mts.), Idaho 220/F7
Deep Creek (lake), Md. 245/A3
Deep Creek (mts.), Utah 304/A4
Deepcreek, Wash. (†99010) 310/H3
Deepdale, Man. 179/A3
Deep Fork, North Canadian (riv.), Okla. 288/N3
Deep Gap, N.C. (28618) 281/F2
Deephaven, Minn. (55391) 254/G5
Deep River△, Conn. (06417) 210/F3
Deep River, Conn. (06417) 210/F3
Deep River (res.), Conn. 210/F2
Deep River, Ont. 175/E3
Deep River, Ont. 177/G1
Deep River, Iowa (52222) 229/J5
Deep River, Wash. (98618) 310/B4
Deep Run, N.C. (28525) 281/O4
Deep Springs, Calif. (†93513) 204/H6
Deepstep, Ga. (31082) 216/G4
Deep Valley, Pa. (15352) 294/A6
Deep Water (pt.), Del. 245/S4
Deepwater, Mo. (64740) 261/E6
Deepwater, N.J. (08023) 273/C4
Deepwater, N.S.W. 97/F1
Deer (isl.), Alaska 196/F4
Deer, Ariz. (72628) 198/D2
Deer (creek), Ind. 227/E3
Deer (creek), Ind. 227/D5
Deer (isl.), Maine 242/F7
Deer (isl.), Mass. 249/E7
Deer (creek), Md. 245/N2
Deer (riv.), Mich. 250/A2
Deer (lake), Minn. 254/E3
Deer (creek), Miss. 256/C4
Deer (isl.), N. Br. 170/D4
Deer (riv.), N.Y. 276/J3
Deer (riv.), N.Y. 276/L1
Deer (harb.), Newf. 166/D2
Deer (creek), Ohio 284/D6
Deer (lake), Wash. 310/H2
Deerbrook, Miss. (†39739) 256/G4
Deerbrook, Wis. (54424) 317/H5
Deer Creek, Ill. (61733) 222/D3
Deer Creek, Ind. (†46917) 227/E3
Deer Creek, Minn. (56527) 254/C4
Deer Creek, Okla. (74636) 288/L1
Deer Creek, Sask. 181/B2
Deerfield, Ill. (60015) 222/F1
Deerfield, Ind. (†47380) 227/H4
Deerfield, Kans. (67838) 232/A4
Deerfield△, Mass. (01342) 249/D2
Deerfield (riv.), Mass. 249/C2
Deerfield, Mich. (49238) 250/F7
Deerfield, Mo. (64741) 261/D7
Deerfield△, N.H. (03037) 268/E5
Deerfield, N.H. (03037) 268/E5
Deerfield, Ohio (44411) 284/H3
Deerfield, Va. (24432) 307/K4
Deerfield (riv.), Vt. 268/B6
Deerfield, Wis. (53531) 317/H9
Deerfield Beach, Fla. (33441) 212/F5
Deerfield Street, N.J. (08313) 273/C4
Deerford, La. (†70791) 238/K1
Deer Grove, Ill. (61243) 222/D2
Deer Harbor, Wash. (98243) 310/B2
Deerhorn, Man. 179/E4
Deering, Alaska (99736) 196/F1
Deering, Mo. (63840) 261/N10
Deering, N. Dak. (58731) 283/J3
Deering△, N.H. (†03244) 268/D5
Deer Island, Oreg. (97054) 291/E2
Deer Isle△, Maine (04627) 242/F7
Deer Isle, Maine (04627) 242/F7
Deer Lake, Ont. 175/B2
Deer Lake, Newf. 166/C4
Deer Lake‡, Pa. (†17961) 294/K4
Deer Lodge (co.), Mont. 262/C5
Deer Lodge, Mont. (59722) 262/D4
Deer Lodge, Tenn. (37726) 237/M8
Deer Park, Ala. (36529) 194/B8
Deer Park, Calif. (94576) 204/C5
Deer Park, Fla. (†32901) 212/F3
Deer Park‡, Ill. (†60010) 222/E1
Deer Park, Md. (21550) 245/A3
Deer Park, N.Y. (11729) 276/O9
Deer Park, Ohio (45236) 284/C9

Donnelly 355

Dhankuta, Nepal 68/F3
Dhar, India 68/C4
Dharma, Saudi Ar. 59/E5
Dharmsala, India 68/D2
Dharwar, India 68/C5
Dhaulagiri (mt.), Nepal 68/E3
Dhidhimótikhon, Greece 45/H5
Dhíkaia, Greece 45/H5
Dhimitsána, Greece 45/F7
Dhira', Jordan 65/C5
Dhofar (reg.), Oman 59/F6
Dholpur, India 68/D3
Dhomokós, Greece 45/F6
Dhond, India 68/C5
Dhoraji, India 68/C4
Dhrépanon (cape), Greece 45/G6
Dhubri, India 68/G3
Dhuheartach (isl.), Scot. 15/C7
Dhulia, India 68/C4
Día (isl.), Greece 45/G8
Diable (pt.), Mart. 161/D5
Diablerets (mt.), Switz. 39/D4
Diablo (canyon), Ariz. 198/D4
Diablo, Calif. (94528) 204/K2
Diablo, Sierra (mts.), Texas 302/C10
Diablo, Wash. (†98283) 310/D2
Diablo (dam), Wash. 310/D2
Diablo (lake), Wash. 310/D2
Diablotin, Morne (mt.), Dominica 161/E6
Diagonal, Iowa (50845) 229/E7
Dial, Ga. (30536) 216/D1
Diamant, Mart. 161/D7
Diamant, Rocher du (isl.), Mart. 161/C7
Diamante, Arg. 143/F6
Diamante (riv.), Arg. 143/C3
Diamantina (riv.), Aust. 88/G4
Diamantina, Braz., 120/F4
Diamantina, Braz. 132/F7
Diamantina (riv.), Queens. 95/B4
Diamantina Lakes, Queens. 95/B4
Diamantino, Braz., 120/E4
Diamantino, Braz. 132/B6
Diamond (lake), Conn. 210/F2
Diamond, V.I.(U.S.) 161/F4
Diamond (head), Hawaii 218/C5
Diamond (peak), Idaho 220/E5
Diamond‡, Ill. (†60416) 222/E2
Diamond, Ind. (†47874) 227/C5
Diamond, La. (70048) 238/L7
Diamond, Mo. (64840) 261/D9
Diamond (pt.), Indon. 85/B4
Diamond, Ohio (44412) 284/H3
Diamond, Oreg. (97722) 291/J4
Diamond (lake), Oreg. 291/E4
Diamond (peak), Oreg. 291/E4
Diamond, Pa. (†16354) 294/C2
Diamond, Wash. (†99111) 310/H4
Diamond (lake), Wash. 310/H2
Diamond Bar‡, Calif. (91766) 204/D10
Diamond Bluff, Wis. (†54014) 317/A6
Diamond City, Alta. 182/D5
Diamond City, Ark. (72644) 203/E1
Diamond Coast (reg.), S.W. Afr. 118/A5
Diamond Lake‡, Ill. (†60060) 222/E1
Diamond Lake, Oreg. (97731) 291/E4
Diamond Point, N.Y. (12824) 276/N4
Diamond Springs, Calif. (95619) 204/D8
Diamondville, Wyo. (83116) 319/B4
Diana, W. Va. (26217) 313/F5
Diano Marina, Italy 34/B3
Dianópolis, Braz. 132/E5
Diapaga, Upp. Volta 106/E6
Dias Creek, N.J. (†08210) 273/D5
Díaz, Arg. 143/F6
Diaz, Ark. (72043) 203/H2
Dibaya, Dem. Rep. of the Congo. 115/D5
Dibaya-Lubue, Dem. Rep. of the Congo. 115/C4
Dibble, Okla. (73031) 288/L4
Dibeng, S. Africa 118/C5
D'Iberville, Miss. (39532) 256/G10
Dibete, Botswana 118/D4
Diboll, Texas (75941) 302/K6
Dibrugarh, India 68/G3
Dibulla, Col. 126/D2
Dickens, Iowa (51333) 229/C2
Dickens, Nebr. (69132) 264/C4
Dickens (pt.), R.I. 249/H8
Dickens (co.), Texas 302/D4
Dickens, Texas (79229) 302/D4
Dickenson (co.), Va. 307/D6
Dickerson, Md. (20753) 245/J4
Dickey, Ga. (†31746) 216/C7
Dickey (co.), N. Dak. 283/N7
Dickey, N. Dak. (58431) 283/N6
Dickeyville, Wis. (53808) 317/E10
Dickinson, Ala. (36436) 194/C7
Dickinson (co.), Iowa 229/C2
Dickinson (co.), Kans. 232/E3
Dickinson (co.), Mich. 250/B2
Dickinson, N. Dak., 188/F1
Dickinson, N. Dak. (58601) 283/E6
Dickinson, Pa. (17218) 294/H5
Dickinson, Texas (77539) 302/K3
Dickinson Center, N.Y. (12930) 276/M1
Dick's Head (Chiamboni) (cape), Kenya 115/H4
Dick's Head (Chiamboni) (cape), Somalia 115/H4
Dickson, Alta. 182/C3
Dickson (lake), Ont. 177/F2
Dickson, Okla. (†73401) 288/M6
Dickson (co.), Tenn. 237/G8
Dickson, Tenn. (37055) 237/G8
Dickson, W. Va. (†25535) 313/B6
Dickson City, Pa. (18519) 294/L3
Dicle, Turkey 63/J3
Dicle (riv.), Turkey 63/J4
Didcot, Eng. 13/F6
Dido, La. (†70656) 238/E5
Didsbury, 163/E5
Didsbury, Alta. 182/C4
Die, France 28/F5
Diefenbaker (lake), Sask. 181/E4
Diegem, Belg. 27/C9
Diego de Almagro (isl.), Chile 138/D9
Diego Garcia (isls.), Br. Ind. Ocean Terr., 54/L10
Diego Lamas, Urug. 145/C1
Diego Pérez (cay), Cuba 158/C2
Diégo-Suarez, 102/G6
Diégo Suarez (prov.), Malag. Rep. 118/H2
Diégo-Suarez, Malag. Rep. 118/H2
Diehlstadt, Mo. (63834) 261/N9
Diekirch, Lux. 27/J9
Diemen, Neth. 27/C5
Diemtigen, Switz. 39/D3
Dien Bien Phu, N. Vietnam 72/D2
Diep (riv.), S. Africa 118/F6
Diepholz, W. Ger. 22/C2
Dieppe, France 28/D3
Dieppe, N. Br. 170/F2
Dieppe Bay, St. Chr.-N.-A. 161/C10
Dieren, Neth. 27/J4
Dierks, Ark. (71833) 203/B5
Diessenhofen, Switz. 39/G1
Diest, Belg. 27/F7
Dieterich, Ill. (62424) 222/E4
Dietikon, Switz. 39/F2
Dietrich, Idaho (83324) 220/D7
Diever, Neth. 27/J3
Diez y Nueve de Abril, Urug. 145/E5
Diez y Ocho de Julio, Urug. 145/F4
Dif, Somalia 115/H3
Diffa, Niger 106/G6
Differdange, Lux. 27/H9
Difficult, Tenn. (†37145) 237/K8
Difficult (mt.), Vic. 97/B5
Digby (co.), N.S. 169/C4
Digby, N.S. 169/C4
Digby Gut (inlet), N.S. 169/C4
Digby Neck (pen.), N.S. 169/B4
Digdeguash (riv.), N. Br. 170/C3
Digges (isls.), N.W.T. 187/L3
Diggins, Mo. (65636) 261/G8
Dighton, Kans. (67839) 232/B3
Dighton▵, Mass. (02715) 249/K5
Dighton, Mich. (†49688) 250/D4
Digne, France 28/G5
Digoin, France 28/F4
Digor, Turkey 63/K2
Digos, Phil. 82/E7
Digul (riv.), Indon. 85/K7
Dijon, France, 7/E4
Dijon, France 28/F4
Dike, Iowa (50624) 229/H4
Dikhil, Afars Issas 111/H5
Dikili, Turkey 63/B3
Diksmuide, Belg. 27/B6
Dikson, U.S.S.R. 48/J2
Dikson, U.S.S.R., 4/B5
Dikwa, 102/D3
Dikwa, Nigeria 106/G6
Dilam, Saudi Ar. 59/E5
Dilaram, Afgh. 59/H3
Dilaram, Afgh. 68/A2
Dilbeek, Belg. 27/B9
Dildo, Newf. 166/D2
Dili (cap.), Port. Timor 85/H7
Dili (cap.), Port. Timor, 54/R10
Dilia, N. Mex. (†87711) 274/D3
Diligent River, N.S. 169/D3
Di Linh, S. Vietnam 72/F5
Dilke, Sask. 181/F5
Dilkon, Ariz. (†86047) 198/E3
Dilla, Eth. 111/G6
Dillard, Ga. (30537) 216/F1
Dillard, Mo. (65458) 261/K7
Dillard, Oreg. (97432) 291/D4
Dill City, Okla. (73641) 288/H4
Dille, W. Va. (26617) 313/E6
Dillenburg, W. Ger. 22/C3
Diller, Nebr. (68342) 264/H4
Dilley, Oreg. (†97116) 291/A2
Dilley, Texas (78017) 302/E9
Dillia (dry riv.), Niger 106/G5
Dilliner, Pa. (15327) 294/B6
Dilling, Sudan 111/E5
Dillingen, W. Ger. 22/D4
Dillingham, Alaska, 188/C6
Dillingham, Alaska (99576) 196/G3
Dillingham A.F.B., Hawaii 218/D1
Dillon (riv.), Alta. 182/E2
Dillon, Colo. (80435) 208/H3
Dillon, Kans. (†67451) 232/E3
Dillon, Mont. (59725) 262/D5
Dillon (res.), Ohio 284/F5
Dillon (co.), S.C. 296/J3
Dillon, S.C. (29536) 296/J3
Dillonvale, Ohio (43917) 284/J5
Dillsboro, Ind. (47018) 227/G6
Dillsboro, N.C. (28725) 281/C4
Dillsburg, Pa. (17019) 294/J5
Dilltown, Pa. (15929) 294/E5
Dillwyn, Va. (23936) 307/M5
Dilolo, Dem. Rep. of the Congo. 115/D6
Dilworth, Minn. (56529) 254/B4
Dimas, Cuba 158/A2
Dimbelenge, Dem. Rep. of the Congo. 115/D5
Dimbokro, Ivory Coast 106/D7
Dimboola, Vic. 97/B5
Dime Box, Texas (77853) 302/H7
Dimishq (Damascus) (cap.), Syria 59/C3
Dimishq (Damascus) (cap.), Syria 63/G6
Dimitrovgrad, Bulg. 45/G4
Dimitrovgrad, Yugo. 45/F4
Dimmit (co.), Texas 302/E9
Dimmitt, Texas (79027) 302/B3
Dimock, Pa. (18816) 294/L2
Dimock, S. Dak. (57331) 298/O7
Dimona, Israel 65/D4
Dimondale, Mich. (48821) 250/E6
Dimsdale, Alta. 182/A2
Dinagat, Phil. 82/E5
Dinagat (isl.), Phil. 82/E5
Dinagat (sound), Phil. 82/E5
Dinagat (isl.), Phil. 85/H3
Dinajpur, Pak. 68/F3
Dinan, France 28/B3
Dinant, Belg. 27/G8
Dinar, Turkey 63/D3
Dinar, Kuh-i- (mts.), Iran 66/G5
Dinard, France 28/B3
Dinaric Alps (mts.), Yugo. 45/B3
Dinas Powis, Wales 13/D6
Dinder (riv.), Sudan 59/B7
Dinder (riv.), Eth. 111/F5
Dinder (riv.), Sudan 111/F5
Dindigul, India 68/D6
Dingalan (bay), Phil. 82/C3
Dingess, W. Va. (25671) 313/B7
Dingle, 10/A4
Dingle, Idaho (83233) 220/G7
Dingle, Ire. 17/A7
Dingle (bay), Ire. 17/A7
Dingle (bay), 10/A4
Dingmans Ferry, Pa. (18328) 294/N3
Dingolfing, W. Ger. 22/E4
Dinguiraye, Guinea 106/B6
Dingwall, 10/D2
Dingwall, N.S. 169/H2
Dingwall, Scot. 15/H4
Dinkelsbühl, W. Ger. 22/D4
Dinkey Creek, Calif. (93617) 204/F6
Dinnebito Wash (dry riv.), Ariz. 198/E3
Dinokwe, Botswana 118/D4
Dinosaur, Colo. (81610) 208/B2
Dinosaur Nat'l Mon., Colo. 208/B2
Dinosaur Nat'l Mon., Utah 304/E3
Dinsdale, Iowa (†50669) 229/H4
Dinsmore, Sask. 181/D4
Dinsor, Somalia 115/H3
Dinuba, Calif. (93618) 204/F7
Dinwiddie (co.), Va. 307/N6
Dinwiddie, Va. (23841) 307/N6
Dinxperlo, Neth. 27/K5
Diogo (isl.), Phil. 82/B2
Dioila, Mali 106/C6
Diomede, Alaska (†99762) 196/E1
Diourbel, 102/A3
Diourbel, Sen. 106/A6
Diphu, India 68/G3
Dipilto, Cordillera (range), Nic. 154/D4
Diplo, Pak. 68/B4
Dipolog, Phil. 82/D6
Dipper Harbour, N. Br. 170/D3
Dir, Pak. 59/K2
Dir, Pak. 68/C1
Dire, Mali 106/D5
Direction (cape), Aust. 88/G2
Direction (cape), Queens. 95/B2
Dire Dawa, Eth. 111/H6
Dire Dawa, 102/G4
Diriamba, Nic. 154/D5
Dirico, Angola 115/D7
Dirico, S.W. Afr. 118/C3
Dirk Hartogs (isl.), Australia, 87/B8
Dirk Hartogs (isl.), Aust. 88/A5
Dirk Hartogs (isl.), W. Aust. 92/A4
Dirksland, Neth. 27/E5
Dirmil, Turkey 63/C4
Dirranbandi, Aust. 88/H5
Dirranbandi, Queens. 95/D6
Dirty Devil (riv.), Utah 304/D5
Disappointment (lake), Australia, 87/C8
Disappointment (lake), Aust. 88/C4
Disappointment (creek), Colo. 208/B7
Disappointment (isls.), Fr. Poly., 87/N7
Disappointment (lake), Newf. 166/B3
Disappointment (lake), W. Aust. 92/C3
Disappointment (cape), Wash., 188/A1
Disappointment (cape), Wash. 310/A4
Discovery (bay), Aust. 88/G7
Discovery, N.W.T. 187/G3
Discovery (bay), Vic. 97/A6
Discovery Bay, Jam. 158/J5
Disentis-Mustér, Switz. 39/G3
Dishman, Wash. (99213) 310/H3
Disko (isl.), Greenl., 4/C12
Disko (isl.), Greenl., 146/N2
Disko, Ind. (†46982) 227/E2
Disley, Sask. 181/F5
Dismal (swamp), N.C. 281/S1
Dismal (riv.), Nebr. 264/C3
Dismal (swamp), Va. 307/R8
Disney, Okla. (74340) 288/S2
Dison, Belg. 27/H7
Disputanta, Va. (23842) 307/O6
Disraëli, Que. 172/F4
Disraeli (bay), N.W.T. 187/L1
Diss, 10/G4
Diss, Eng. 13/J5
Disston (lake), Fla. 212/E2
Disston, Oreg. (97433) 291/E4
District Heights, Md. (20028) 245/G5
District of Columbia, 146/L6
DISTRICT OF COLUMBIA, 245
Distrito Especial, Col. 126/C5
Distrito Federal, Arg. 143/H7
Distrito Federal, Mex. 150/L1
Distrito Federal, Par. 144/A6
Distrito Federal, Ven. 124/E2
Distrito Nacional, Dom. Rep. 158/E6
Disûq, U.A.R. 111/J3
Dittmer, Mo. (63023) 261/L6
Ditton Park, Sask. 181/H2
Diu, India, 54/L7
Diu (dist.), India 68/C4
Diuata (mts.), Phil. 82/E6
Divernon, Ill. (62530) 222/D4
Divide, Colo. (80814) 208/J5
Divide, Mont. (59727) 262/D5
Divide (co.), N. Dak. 283/C2
Divide, Sask. 181/B6
Dividing (creek), Md. 245/R8
Dividing Creek, N.J. (08315) 273/C5
Divinópolis, Braz. 132/E8
Divinópolis, Braz. 135/D2
Divis (mt.), N. Ire. 17/J2
Division (peak), Nev. 266/B1
Divnoye, U.S.S.R. 52/F5
Divriği, Turkey 59/C2
Divriği, Turkey 63/H3
Diwaniya (prov.), Iraq 66/D5
Dix, Ill. (62830) 222/E5
Dix (riv.), Ky. 237/M5
Dix, Nebr. (69133) 264/A3
Dixfield▵, Maine (04224) 242/C6
Dixfield, Maine (04224) 242/C6
Dix Hills‡, N.Y. (†11743) 276/O9
Dixie, Ala. (†36420) 194/E8
Dixie (co.), Fla. 212/C2
Dixie, Ga. (31629) 216/E9
Dixie, Idaho (83525) 220/C4
Dixie, La. (71022) 238/C1
Dixie, W. Va. (25059) 313/D6
Dixie, Wash. (99329) 310/G4
Dixie Inn, La. (†71055) 238/D1
Dixmont▵, Maine (04932) 242/E6
Dixmont, Maine (04932) 242/E6
Dixmoor, Ill. (†60469) 222/B2
Dixmude (Diksmuide), Belg. 27/B6
Dixon, Calif. (95620) 204/B9
Dixon, Ill. (61021) 222/D2
Dixon, Iowa (52745) 229/M5
Dixon, Ky. (42409) 237/F5
Dixon, Miss. (†39350) 256/F5
Dixon, Mo. (65459) 261/H6
Dixon, Mont. (59831) 262/B3
Dixon, N.C. (†28445) 281/O5
Dixon, N. Mex. (87527) 274/D2
Dixon (co.), Nebr. 264/H2
Dixon, Nebr. (68732) 264/H2
Dixon, Ohio (†46773) 284/A4
Dixon, S. Dak. (57530) 298/L7
Dixon, Wyo. (82323) 319/E4
Dixon Entrance (chan.), 146/E4
Dixon Entrance (chan.), 163/C5
Dixon Entrance (chan.), Alaska 196/M2
Dixon Entrance (chan.), Br. Col. 184/A3
Dixons Mills, Ala. (36736) 194/C6
Dixon Springs, Ill. (†62911) 222/E6
Dixon Springs, Tenn. (37057) 237/J8
Dixonville, Ala. (†36426) 194/E8
Dixonville, Alta. 182/B1
Dixonville, Pa. (15734) 294/D4
Dixville, Que. 172/F4
Dixville (peak), N.H. 268/E2
Dixville Notch, N.H. (†03576) 268/E2
Dixville Notch (pass), N.H. 268/E2
Diyadin, Turkey 63/K3
Diyala (prov.), Iraq 66/D4
Diyala (riv.), Iraq 66/D4
Diyarbakir, Turkey 59/C2
Diyarbakir (prov.), Turkey 63/H4
Diyarbakir, Turkey 63/H4
Diyarbakir, Turkey, 54/H6
Diz, Ab-i- (riv.), Iran 59/E3
Dizful, Iran, 54/H6
Dizful, Iran 59/E3
Dizful, Iran 66/F4
Dja (riv.), Cameroon 115/B3
Dja (riv.), Rep. of Congo 115/B3
Djado, 102/D2
Djado (plat.), 102/D2
Djado, Niger 106/G4
Djado (plat.), Niger 106/G4
Djailolo, Indon. 85/H5
Djaja (mt.), Indon. 85/K6
Djajapura, Indon. 85/L6
Djajawidjaja (range), Indon. 85/K6
Djakarta (cap.), Indon., 3/Q6
Djakarta (cap.), Indon., 54/O10
Djakarta (cap.), Indon. 85/H1
Djakovica, Yugo. 45/E4
Djakovo, Yugo. 45/D3
Djamaâ, Alg. 106/F2
Djambala, Rep. of Congo 115/B4
Djambi (Telanaipura), Indon. 85/C6
Djanet, Alg. 106/F4
Djanet, 102/C2
Djelfa, Alg. 106/E2
Djéma, Centr. Afr. Rep. 115/E2
Djemadja (isl.), Indon. 85/D5
Djember, Indon. 85/K2
Djeneponto, Indon. 85/F7
Djenné, 102/B3
Djenné, Mali 106/D6
Djepara, Indon. 85/J2
Djerba (isl.), Tun. 106/G2
Djerid, Shott el (salt lake), Tun. 106/F2
Djibo, Upp. Volta 106/D6
Djibouti (cap.), Afars Issas 111/H5
Djibouti (cap.), Afars Issas 102/G3
Djidjelli, Alg. 106/F1
Djokjakarta, Indon., 54/O10
Djokjakarta, Indon. 85/J2
Djolu, Dem. Rep. of the Congo. 115/D3
Djombang, Indon. 85/K2
Djouf, El (des.), Mauritania 106/C4
Djougou, Dahomey 106/E7
Djoum, Cameroon 115/B3
Djugu, Dem. Rep. of the Congo. 115/F3
Djuma, Dem. Rep. of the Congo. 115/C4
Djursholm, Sweden 18/H1
D'Lo, Miss. (39062) 256/E7
Dmitriy Laptev (str.), U.S.S.R. 48/O2
Dmitriy Laptev (str.), U.S.S.R., 4/B2
Dmitrov, U.S.S.R. 52/E3
Dmitrovsk-Orlovskiy, U.S.S.R. 52/D4
Dneprodzerzhinsk, U.S.S.R. 52/D5
Dneprodzerzhinsk, U.S.S.R., 7/H4
Dnepropetrovsk, U.S.S.R. 48/D5
Dnepropetrovsk, U.S.S.R. 52/D5
Dnepropetrovsk, U.S.S.R., 7/H4
Dnieper (riv.), U.S.S.R. 48/D5
Dnieper (riv.), U.S.S.R. 52/D5
Dnieper (Dnepr) (riv.), U.S.S.R., 7/H3
Dniester (riv.), U.S.S.R. 48/C5
Dniester (riv.), U.S.S.R. 52/C5
Dniester (Dnestr) (riv.), U.S.S.R., 7/G4
Dno, U.S.S.R. 52/D3
Doagh, N. Ire. 17/J2
Doaghbeg, Ire. 17/F1
Doaktown, N. Br. 170/D2
Doans, Ind. (47428) 227/D7
Doba, Chad 111/C6
Dobbie (mt.), No. Terr. 93/E7
Dobbin (bay), N.W.T. 187/L2
Dobbins A.F.B., Ga. 216/D3
Dobbs Ferry, N.Y. (10522) 276/O6
Dobbyn, Aust. 88/F3
Dobbyn, Queens. 95/A3
Dobele, U.S.S.R. 53/B2
Döbeln, E. Ger. 22/E3
Doblas, Arg. 143/D4
Dobo, Indon. 85/J7
Doboy (sound), Ga. 216/K8
Dobřany, Czech. 41/B2
Dobrich (Tolbukhin), Bulg. 45/H4
Dobříš, Czech. 41/C2
Dobrush, U.S.S.R. 52/D4
Dobruška, Czech. 41/D1
Dobšiná, Czech. 41/F2
Dobson, N.C. (27017) 281/H2
Doce (riv.), Braz. 132/F7
Doce (riv.), Braz. 135/E2
Doce Leguas (cays), Cuba 158/F3
Docena‡, Ala. (35060) 194/E3
Dockery, N.C. (†28685) 281/G2
Dock Junction (Arco), Ga. (†31520) 216/J8
Doctor Arroyo, Mex. 150/K5
Doctors Inlet, Fla. (32030) 212/E1
Doctortown, Ga. (†31545) 216/J7
Dodd City‡, Texas (75438) 302/H4
Doddridge, Ark. (71834) 203/C7
Doddridge (co.), W. Va. 313/E4
Dodds, Alta. 182/D3
Doddsville, Miss. (38736) 256/C3
Dodecanese (isls.), Greece 45/H8
Dodge (co.), Ga. 216/F6
Dodge, Mass. (†01507) 249/G4
Dodge (co.), Minn. 254/F7
Dodge, N. Dak. (58625) 283/F5
Dodge (co.), Nebr. 264/H3
Dodge, Nebr. (68633) 264/H3
Dodge, Texas (77334) 302/J7
Dodge (co.), Wis. 317/J9
Dodge, Wis. (54625) 317/D7
Dodge Center, Minn. (55927) 254/F6
Dodge City, Kans. (67801) 232/B4
Dodgeville, Wis. (53533) 317/F10
Dodgingtown, Conn. (†06470) 210/B3
Dodoma, 102/F5
Dodoma (reg.), Tanz. 115/G4
Dodoma, Tanz. 115/G5
Dods (lake), Nebr. 264/D2
Dodsland, Sask. 181/C4
Dodson, La. (71422) 238/E2
Dodson, Mont. (59524) 262/H2
Dodson, Texas (79230) 302/D3
Doe (lake), Ont. 177/E2
Doebay, Wash. (†98279) 310/C2
Doe Hill, Va. (24433) 307/K4
Doel, Belg. 27/E6
Doering, Wis. (†54435) 317/G5
Doe River, Br. Col. 184/G2
Doerun, Ga. (31744) 216/E8
Doe Run, Mo. (63637) 261/M7
Doesburg, Neth. 27/J4
Doetinchem, Neth. 27/J5
Dog (pond), Conn. 210/C1
Dog (lake), Ont. 177/G5
Dog (isl.), Fla. 212/B2
Dog (lake), Man. 179/D3
Dog (isl.), Newf. 166/B2
Doğanbey, Turkey 63/B4
Doğanhisar, Turkey 63/D3
Doğanşehir, Turkey 63/G3
Dog Creek, Br. Col. 184/G4
Dog Ear (creek), S. Dak. 298/K6
Döger, Turkey 63/D3
Dogo (isl.), Japan 81/F5
Dogondoutchi, Niger 106/E6
Dogpatch, Ark. (72648) 203/D1
Dog Pound, Alta. 182/D4
Dogskin (lake), Man. 179/G3
Doğubeyazit, Turkey 63/K3
Dogwood (pt.), St. Chr.-N.-A. 161/D11
Doha (cap.), Qatar 59/F4
Dohad, India 68/C4
Doheny, Que. 172/E2
Dohuk (prov.), Iraq 66/C2
Dohuk, Iraq 66/C2
Doi Inthanon (mt.), Thai. 72/C3
Doi Pha Hom Pok (mt.), Thai. 72/C2
Doi Pia Fai (mt.), Thai. 72/D4
Dois Córregos, Braz. 135/B3
Dois Irmãos (range), Braz. 132/F5
Dokkum, Neth. 27/H2
Doksy, Czech. 41/C1
Dokterstuin, Neth. Ant. 161/F8
Dola, Ohio (45835) 284/C4
Dola, W. Va. (†26386) 313/F4
Dolak (isl.), Indon. 85/K7
Dolan, Ind. (†47401) 227/E6
Doland, S. Dak. (57436) 298/N4
Dolavon, Arg. 143/C5
Dolbeau, Que. 172/E1
Dolbeau, Que. 174/C3
Doldenhorn (mt.), Switz. 39/E4
Dôle, France 28/F4
Dolega, Pan. 154/F6
Dolent (mt.), Switz. 39/C5
Doles, Ga. (†31791) 216/E7
Dolgellau, 10/E4
Dolgellau, Wales 13/D5
Dolgeville, N.Y. (13329) 276/L4
Dolgiy (isl.), U.S.S.R. 52/J1
Dolinsk, U.S.S.R. 48/P5
Dolisie, Rep. of Congo 115/B4
Dollar, 10/B1
Dollar Bay, Mich. (49922) 250/G1
Dollard, Que. 172/H4
Dollard, Sask. 181/C6
Dollart (bay), Neth. 27/L2
Dollart (est.), W. Ger. 22/B2
Dollarville, Mich. (†49868) 250/D2
Dolliver, Iowa (50531) 229/D2
Dolní Kralovice, Czech. 41/C2
Dolný Kubín, Czech. 41/E2
Dolo, Eth. 111/H7
Dolomite, Ala. (35061) 194/D4
Dolomite Alps (range), Italy 34/C1
Dolores, Arg., 120/E6
Dolores, Arg. 143/E4
Dolores (co.), Colo. 208/C7
Dolores, Colo. (81323) 208/C8
Dolores (riv.), Colo. 208/B5
Dolores, Guat. 154/C2
Dolores, Phil. 82/E4
Dolores, Spain 33/F3
Dolores, Urug. 145/A4
Dolores (riv.), Utah 304/E5
Dolores, Ven. 124/D3
Dolphin and Union (str.), N.W.T. 187/G3
Dölsach, Austria 41/B3
Dolton, Ill. (60419) 222/B2
Dolton, S. Dak. (57023) 298/P7
Dom (mt.), Switz. 39/E4
Domain, Man. 179/E5
Domar (dry riv.), Chad 111/C4
Domažlice, Czech. 41/B2
Dombås, Norway 18/F5
Dombe Grande, Angola 115/B6
Dombóvár, Hung. 41/E3
Dombrád, Hung. 41/F2
Dombresson, Switz. 39/C2
Domburg, Neth. 27/C5
Domburg, Sur. 131/D3
Dome, Ariz. (†85364) 198/A6
Dome Creek, Br. Col. 184/G3
Domeiko, Chile 138/A7
Domel (isl.), Burma 72/C5
Domeyko, Cordillera (mts.), Chile 138/B4
Dominguez‡, Calif. (†90501) 204/C11
Dominica (isl.), 146/M8
DOMINICA, 156/G4
DOMINICA, 161/E7
Dominica (passg.), Dominica 161/E5
Dominican Republic, 3/F4
Dominican Republic, 146/L8
DOMINICAN REPUBLIC, 156/D3
DOMINICAN REPUBLIC, 158
Dominion, N.S. 169/J2
Dominion (cape), N.W.T. 187/L3
Dominion (lake), Newf. 166/B3
Dominion City, Man. 179/E5
Dömitz, E. Ger. 22/D2
Domjor, India 68/F1
Dommel (riv.), Neth. 27/H6
Domo, Eth. 111/J6
Domodossola, Italy 34/A1
Dom Pedrito, Braz. 132/C10
Dompu, Indon. 85/F7
Domremy, Sask. 181/F3
Domrémy-la-Pucelle, France 28/F3
Dömsöd, Hung. 41/E3
Domuyo (vol.), Arg. 143/B4
Don (riv.), Ont. 177/J4
Don (riv.), Eng. 13/F4
Don (riv.), 10/E2
Don (riv.), 10/F4
Don (riv.), Scot. 15/L5
Don (riv.), U.S.S.R., 7/J4
Don (riv.), U.S.S.R. 48/E5
Don (riv.), U.S.S.R. 52/F5
Dona Ana, Moz. 118/F3
Dona Ana (co.), N. Mex. 274/C6
Dona Ana, N. Mex. (88032) 274/C6
Donabate, Ire. 17/J5
Donaghadee, N. Ire. 17/K2
Donahue, Iowa (52746) 229/M5
Donald, Br. Col. 184/J4
Donald, Oreg. (97020) 291/A3
Donald, Vic. 97/B5
Donald, Wash. (†98951) 310/E4
Donald, Wis. (†54433) 317/E5
Donalda, Alta. 182/D3
Donalds, S.C. (29638) 296/C3
Donaldson, Ark. (71941) 203/E5
Donaldson, Ind. (46513) 227/E2
Donaldson, Minn. (56720) 254/B2
Donaldson A.F.B., S.C. 296/C2
Donaldsonville, La. (70346) 238/K3
Donalsonville, Ga. (31745) 216/C8
Donansburg, Ky. (†42743) 237/K6
Donath, Switz. 39/H3
Donatville, Alta. 182/D2
Donau (Danube) (riv.), Austria 41/D2
Donau (Danube) (riv.), W. Ger. 22/C4
Donaueschingen, W. Ger. 22/C5
Donauwörth, W. Ger. 22/D4
Donavon, Sask. 181/D4
Donbar, Queens. 95/B3
Don Benito, Spain 33/C3
Doncaster, 10/F4
Doncaster, Eng. 13/G4
Doncaster, Md. (†20646) 245/K7
Doncaster and Templestowe, Vic. 97/J5
Doncrest, Sask. 181/J3
Dondo, Angola 115/B5
Dondra (head), Ceylon, 54/M9
Dondra (head), Ceylon 68/E7
Donegal, 10/B3
Donegal (bay), 10/B3
Donegal (bay), Ire., 7/C3
Donegal (bay), Ire. 17/D3
Donegal (co.), Ire. 17/K2
Donegal, Ire. 17/F2
Donegal (harb.), Ire. 17/E2
Donegal (pt.), Ire. 17/B6
Donegal, Pa. (15628) 294/D5
Donegal, Sask. 181/B3
Donel, Hond. 154/E3
Donelson, Tenn. (37214) 237/H8
Donerail, Ky. (40505) 237/N4
Doneraile, Ire. 17/D7
Doneraile, S.C. (†29532) 296/H3
Donets (riv.), U.S.S.R. 48/D5
Donets (riv.), U.S.S.R. 52/E5
Donets (riv.), U.S.S.R., 7/H4
Donetsk, U.S.S.R. 48/D5
Donetsk, U.S.S.R. 52/E5
Donetsk, U.S.S.R., 7/H4
Donga, Nigeria 106/G7
Donga (riv.), Nigeria 106/G7
Donga (riv.), Cameroon 115/B2
Dongara, Aust. 88/A5
Dongara, W. Aust. 92/A5
Dongen, Neth. 27/F5
Donggala, Indon. 85/F6
Dong Hoi, N. Vietnam 72/E3
Dongio, Switz. 39/H4
Dongo, Dem. Rep. of the Congo. 115/C3
Dongola, 102/F3
Dongola, Ill. (62926) 222/D6
Dongola, Sudan 59/B6
Dongola, Sudan 111/F4
Dongou, Rep. of Congo 115/C3
Dongwe (riv.), Zambia 115/D6
Donie, Texas (75838) 302/H6
Doñihue, Chile 138/G5
Doniphan (co.), Kans. 232/G2
Doniphan, Mo. (63935) 261/L9
Doniphan, Nebr. (68832) 264/F4
Donji Vakuf, Yugo. 45/C3
Donkin, N.S. 169/J2
Donlands, Sask. 181/H2
Donley (co.), Texas 302/D2
Dønna (isl.), Norway 18/H3
Donna, Texas (78537) 302/F11
Donnacona, Que. 172/F3
Donnan, Iowa (51339) 229/K3
Donnellson, Ill. (62019) 222/D4
Donnellson, Iowa (52625) 229/K7
Donnelly, Alaska (†99737) 196/J2
Donnelly, Alta. 182/B2

East Glacier Park 357

Dunbar, W. Va. (25064) 313/C6
Dunbar, Wis. (54119) 317/K4
Dunbarton▵, N.H. (†03301) 268/D5
Dunbarton, N.H. (†03301) 268/D5
Dunbarton, N. Ire. 17/J3
Dunbarton (co.), Scot. 15/G7
Dunbarton Center, N.H. (†03301) 268/D5
Dunbeath, Scot. 15/K3
Dunblane, 10/D2
Dunblane, Sask. 181/D4
Dunblane, Scot. 15/D1
Dunboyne, Ire. 17/H5
Dunbridge, Ohio (43414) 284/C3
Duncairn, Sask. 181/D5
Duncan, Ariz. (85534) 198/F6
Duncan, Br. Col. 184/J3
Duncan (riv.), Br. Col. 184/J5
Duncan (lake), Que. 174/B2
Duncan, Ill. (†61559) 222/D3
Duncan, Miss. (38740) 256/C2
Duncan, Nebr. (68634) 264/G3
Duncan (passg.), India 68/G6
Duncan (isls.), China 85/E2
Duncan, Okla. (73533) 288/L5
Duncan, S.C. (29334) 296/C2
Duncan, W. Va. (25240) 313/C5
Duncan Falls, Ohio (43734) 284/G6
Duncannon, Ire. 17/H7
Duncannon, Pa. (17020) 294/H5
Duncans, Jam. 158/H5
Duncans Bridge, Mo. (†63437) 261/H3
Duncansby (head), 10/E1
Duncansby (head), Scot. 15/L2
Duncansville, Pa. (16635) 294/F5
Duncanville, Ala. (35456) 194/D4
Duncanville, Texas (75116) 302/G2
Dunchurch, Ont. 177/E2
Duncombe (bay), Aust. 88/L5
Duncombe, Iowa (50532) 229/E4
Dundaga, U.S.S.R. 53/B2
Dundalk, Ont. 177/D3
Dundalk, 10/C4
Dundalk, Ire., 7/D3
Dundalk, Ire. 17/H3
Dundalk (bay), Ire. 17/J4
Dundalk, Md. (21222) 245/N3
Dundalk (bay), 10/C4
Dundarrach, N.C. (†28386) 281/L5
Dundas (str.), Aust. 88/E2
Dundas (lake), Aust. 88/C6
Dundas (isl.), Br. Col. 184/B3
Dundas, Ill. (62425) 222/E5
Dundas, Minn. (55019) 254/E6
Dundas (pen.), N.W.T. 187/G2
Dundas (lake), W. Aust. 92/C6
Dundas (str.), No. Terr. 93/B1
Dundas, Ohio (45625) 284/E7
Dundas (co.), Ont. 177/J2
Dundas, Ont. 177/D4
Dundas, Va. (23938) 307/M7
Dundas Harbour, Canada, 4/B14
Dundee, Fla. (33838) 212/E3
Dundee (East and West Dundee), Ill. (60118) 222/E1
Dundee, Ind. (†47348) 227/F4
Dundee, Iowa (52038) 229/L3
Dundee, Ky. (42338) 237/H5
Dundee, 10/E2
Dundee, Mich. (48131) 250/F7
Dundee, Minn. (56126) 254/C7
Dundee, Miss. (38626) 256/D1
Dundee, N. Br. 170/D1
Dundee, N.Y. (14837) 276/F5
Dundee, Oreg. (97115) 291/A2
Dundee, S. Africa 118/E5
Dundee, Scot., 7/D3
Dundee, Scot. 15/K7
Dundee, Texas (76358) 302/F4
Dundon, W. Va. (†25043) 313/D6
Dundonald, Scot. 15/H8
Dundrum, N. Ire. 17/K3
Dundrum (bay), N. Ire. 17/K3
Dundurn, Sask. 181/E4
Dundy (co.), Nebr. 264/C4
Dune Acres, Ind. (†46304) 227/C1
Dunedin, Fla. (33528) 212/B2
Dunedin, N.Z., 3/T8
Dunedin, N.Z., 87/H10
Dunedin, N.Z. 101/C6
Dunedoo, N.S.W. 97/E3
Dunellen, N.J. (08812) 273/D2
Dunes (Westlake), Oreg. (†97493) 291/C4
Dunfanaghy, Ire. 17/F1
Dunfee, Ind. (†46802) 227/G2
Dunfermline, Ill. (61524) 222/D3
Dunfermline, 10/C1
Dunfermline, Scot. 15/J7
Dungalear Station, N.S.W. 97/D1
Dungannon, Ont. 177/C4
Dungannon, N. Ire. 17/H3
Dungannon, Va. (24245) 307/D7
Dunganstown, Ire. 17/G7
Dungarpur, India 68/C4
Dungarvan, 10/C4
Dungarvan, Ire. 17/F7
Dungarvan (harb.), Ire. 17/G7
Dungarvan (harb.), 10/C4
Dungarvon (riv.), N. Br. 170/D2
Dungeness (pt.), Arg. 143/C7
Dungeness (pt.), Chile 138/F10
Dungeness (prom.), Eng. 13/J7
Dungeness (prom.), 10/G5
Dungeness, Wash. (†98382) 310/B2
Dungiven, N. Ire. 17/H2
Dungloe, Ire. 17/E2
Dungog, N.S.W. 97/F3
Dungowan, N.S.W. 97/F2
Dungu, Dem. Rep. of the Congo. 115/E3
Dungunab, Sudan 59/C5
Dungunab, Sudan 111/G3
Dunham, Que. 172/E4
Dunkeld, Queens. 95/D5
Dunkeld, Scot. 15/J6
Dunkeld, Vic. 97/B5
Dunkellin (riv.), Ire. 17/D5
Dunkerque (Dunkirk), France 28/E2
Dunkerton, Iowa (50626) 229/J3
Dunkery Beacon (mt.), Eng. 13/D6
Dunkineely, Ire. 17/E2
Dunkirk (riv.), Alta. 182/D1
Dunkirk, France 28/E2
Dunkirk, Ind. (47336) 227/G4
Dunkirk, N.Y. (14048) 276/B5
Dunkirk, Ohio (45836) 284/C4
Dunkirk, Sask. 181/F5
Dunklin (co.), Mo. 261/M10
Dunkwa, Ghana 106/D7
Dún Laoghaire, 10/D4
Dún Laoghaire, Ire. 17/K5
Dunlap, Ill. (61525) 222/D3
Dunlap, Ind. (†46514) 227/F1
Dunlap, Iowa (51529) 229/B5
Dunlap, Kans. (66848) 232/F3
Dunlap, Mo. (†64683) 261/F2
Dunlap, Tenn. (37327) 237/L10
Dunlavin, Ire. 17/H5
Dunleath, Sask. 181/K4
Dunleer, Ire. 17/J4
Dunleith, Miss. (†38756) 256/C4
Dunlevy‡, Pa. (15432) 294/C5
Dunlow, W. Va. (25511) 313/B6
Dunmanus (bay), Ire. 17/B8
Dunmanway, 10/B5
Dunmanway, Ire. 17/C8
Dunmor, Ky. (42339) 237/G6
Dunmore, Alta. 182/E4
Dunmore, Ire. 17/D4
Dunmore, Pa. (18512) 294/L3
Dunmore (lake), Vt. 268/A4
Dunmore, W. Va. (24934) 313/G6
Dunmore East, Ire. 17/G7
Dunn, La. (71236) 238/G2
Dunn, N.C. (28334) 281/M4
Dunn (co.), N. Dak. 283/E5
Dunn, Texas (79516) 302/D5
Dunn (co.), Wis. 317/C6
Dunnamanagh, N. Ire. 17/G2
Dunn Center, N. Dak. (58626) 283/E5
Dunnegan, Mo. (65640) 261/E7
Dunnell, Minn. (56127) 254/D7
Dunnellon, Fla. (32630) 212/D2
Dunnet (head), 10/E1
Dunnet, Scot. 15/K2
Dunnet (bay), Scot. 15/J2
Dunnet (head), Scot. 15/J2
Dunnigan, Calif. (95937) 204/C5
Dunning, Nebr. (68833) 264/D3
Dunning, Sask. 181/G6
Dunnottar, Man. 179/E4
Dunns, W. Va. (25834) 313/D7
Dunnsville, Va. (22454) 307/P5
Dunnville, Ont. 177/E5
Dunnville, Ky. (42528) 237/M6
Du Noir (riv.), Wyo. 319/C2
Dunolly, Vic. 97/B5
Dunoon, 10/A1
Dunoon, Scot. 15/A2
Dunphy, Nev. (†89821) 266/E2
Dunrea, Man. 179/C5
Dunreith, Ind. (47337) 227/F5
Duns, 10/E3
Duns, Scot. 15/M86
Dunscore, Scot. 15/J9
Dunseith, N. Dak. (58329) 283/K2
Dunshaughlin, Ire. 17/H5
Dunsmuir, Calif. (96025) 204/C2
Dunstable, 10/F5
Dunstable, Eng. 13/G6
Dunstable▵, Mass. (01827) 249/J2
Dunster, Br. Col. 184/G3
Dunvegan, Alta. 182/A2
Dunvegan, N.S. 169/F4
Dunvegan, Scot. 15/D5
Dunvegan (head), Scot. 15/C4
Dunvegan (inlet), Scot. 15/C4
Dunville, Newf. 166/D2
Dunwich, Eng. 13/J5
Duo, W. Va. (†25984) 313/E6
Duong Dong, S. Vietnam 72/E5
Du Page (co.), Ill. 222/E2
Du Page (riv.), Ill. 222/E2
Duparquet, Que. 174/B3
Duplessis, La. (70728) 238/K2
Duplin (co.), N.C. 281/O5
Dupo, Ill. (62239) 222/A6
Du Pont, Ga. (31630) 216/G9
Dupont, Ind. (47231) 227/G7
Dupont, Ohio (45837) 284/B3
Dupont‡, Pa. (18641) 294/L3
Du Pont, Wash. (98327) 310/C3
Dupont Manor, Del. (†19901) 245/R4
Dupree, S. Dak. (57623) 298/F3
Dupuis Corner, N. Br. 170/F2
Dupuy, Que. 174/B3
Dupuyer, Mont. (59432) 262/D2
Duque de Bragança, Angola 115/C5
Duque de Caxias, Braz. 135/E3
Duque de York (isl.), Chile 138/C9
Duquesne, Mo. (†64801) 261/D8
Duquesne, Pa. (15110) 294/C7
Duquette, Minn. (55729) 254/F4
Du Quoin, Ill. (62832) 222/D5
Duquoin, Kans. (67040) 232/D4
Dura, Jordan 65/C4
Duran, N. Mex. (88319) 274/D4
Durance (riv.), France 28/F6
Durand, Ga. (†31830) 216/C5
Durand, Ill. (61024) 222/D1
Durand, Mich. (48429) 250/E6
Durand, Wis. (54736) 317/C6
Durango, Colo., 188/E3
Durango, Colo. (81301) 208/D8
Durango, Iowa (52039) 229/M3
Durango, Mex., 146/H7
Durango (state), Mex. 150/G4
Durango, Mex. 150/G4
Durango, Spain 33/E1
Duranillin, W. Aust. 92/B2
Durant, Iowa (52747) 229/M5
Durant, Miss. (39063) 256/E4
Durant, Okla., 188/G4
Durant, Okla. (74701) 288/O6
Duratón (riv.), Spain 33/E2
Durazno (dept.), Urug. 145/C3
Durazno, Urug. 145/C4
Durazno, Grande del (range), Urug. 145/D4
Durban, Man. 179/A3
Durban, 102/F7
Durban, S. Afr., 3/L7
Durban, S. Africa 118/E5
Durbanville, S. Africa 118/F6
Durbe, U.S.S.R. 53/A2
Durbin, Ind. (†46060) 227/F4
Durbin, N. Dak. (58023) 283/R6
Durbin, W. Va. (26264) 313/G5
Durbuljin, China 77/B2
Düren, W. Ger. 22/B3
Durfee (hill), R.I. 249/G5
Durg, India 68/E4
Durga Nor (lake), Mong. 77/D2
Durgapur, India, 68/F4
Durgerdam, Neth. 27/C4
Durham, 10/F3
Durham, Ark. (†72701) 203/C2
Durham, Calif. (95938) 204/D4
Durham▵, Conn. (06422) 210/E3
Durham, Conn. (06422) 210/E3
Durham (co.), Eng. 13/F3
Durham, Eng. 13/F3
Durham, Kans. (67438) 232/E3
Durham, Mo. (63438) 261/J3
Durham, N.C., 188/L3
Durham (co.), N.C. 281/M3
Durham, N.C. (*27701) 281/M2
Durham▵, N.H. (03824) 268/F5
Durham, N.H. (03824) 268/F5
Durham (pt.), N.Z. 101/D7
Durham, Okla. (73642) 288/G3
Durham (co.), Ont. 177/F3
Durham, Ont. 177/D3
Durham, Oreg. (†97233) 291/A2
Durham Bridge, N. Br. 170/D2
Durham Center, Conn. (†06422) 210/E3
Durham Centre, N. Br. 170/D1
Durham Downs, Queens. 95/B5
Durham-Sud, Que. 172/E4
Durhamville, N.Y. (13054) 276/J4
Duri, N.S.W. 97/F2
Durkee, Oreg. (97905) 291/K3
Durness, Scot. 15/G2
Durness, Kyle of (inlet), Scot. 15/G2
Durnford (pt.), Sp. Sahara 106/A4
Dürnten, Switz. 39/G2
Durrell, Newf. 166/D4
Dürrenroth, Switz. 39/E2
Durrës, Alb., 7/F4
Durrës (Durazzo), Alb. 45/D5
Durrow, Laoighis, Ire. 17/G6
Durrow, Westmeath, Ire. 17/F5
Dursey (isl.), Ire. 17/A8
Dursunbey, Turkey 63/C3
Duruh, Iran 59/H3
Duruh, Iran 66/M4
D'Urville (isl.), N.Z. 101/D4
Duryea, Pa. (18642) 294/L3
Dusa Mareb, Somalia 115/J2
Dûsh, U.A.R. 59/B5
Dûsh, U.A.R. 111/F3
Dushanbe, U.S.S.R. 48/G6
Dushanbe, U.S.S.R., 3/N4
Dushore, Pa. (18614) 294/K2
Dusky (sound), N.Z. 101/A6
Duson, La. (70529) 238/F6
Düsseldorf, W. Ger., 7/E3
Düsseldorf, W. Ger. 22/B3
Dustin, Okla. (74839) 288/O4
Dusty, N. Mex. (87934) 274/B5
Dusty, Wash. (†99143) 310/H4
Dutch (creek), Ark. 203/C4
Dutch Cap (cay), V.I.(U.S.) 161/A4
Dutchess (co.), N.Y. 276/N7
Dutch Flat, Calif. (95714) 204/E4
Dutch Guiana (Surinam), 120/E2
Dutch Harbor, Alaska (†99685) 196/E4
Dutch John, Utah (84023) 304/E3
Dutch Mills, Ark. (†72744) 203/B2
Dutch Neck, N.J. (†08550) 273/D3
Dutchtown, Mo. (63745) 261/N8
Dutton, Ala. (35744) 194/G1
Dutton, Ark. (72726) 203/C2
Dutton (mt.), Conn. 210/C1
Dutton, Ont. 177/C5
Dutton, Mont. (59433) 262/E3
Dutton (mt.), Utah 304/B5
Duval (co.), Fla. 212/E1
Duval, Sask. 181/G4
Duval (co.), Texas 302/F10
Duvall, Wash. (98019) 310/D3
Duved, Sweden 18/H5
Duvergé, Dom. Rep. 158/D6
Duvernay, Alta. 182/E3
Duwadami, Saudi Ar. 59/D5
Duxbury (pt.), Calif. 204/H2
Duxbury▵, Mass. (02332) 249/M4
Duxbury, Mass. (02332) 249/M4
Duxbury▵, Vt. (†05676) 268/B3
Duxbury, Vt. (†05676) 268/B3
Düzce, Turkey 63/D2
Duzdab (Zahidan), Iran 59/H4
Duzdab (Zahidan), Iran 66/M6
Dvina (bay), U.S.S.R. 52/E2
Dvina, Northern (riv.), U.S.S.R. 48/E3
Dvina, Northern (riv.), U.S.S.R. 52/F2
Dvina, Northern (riv.), U.S.S.R., 7/J2
Dvina, Northern (river), U.S.S.R., 4/C7
Dvina, Western (riv.), U.S.S.R. 48/C4
Dvina, Western (riv.), U.S.S.R. 52/C3
Dvina, Western (riv.), U.S.S.R. 53/C2
Dvinsk (Daugavpils), U.S.S.R. 52/C3
Dvory, Czech. 41/E3
Dvůr Králové nad Labem, Czech. 41/C1
Dwale, Ky. (41621) 237/R5
Dwarka, India 68/B4
Dwellingup, W. Aust. 92/B2
Dwight, Ont. 177/E2
Dwight, Ill. (60420) 222/E2
Dwight, Kans. (66849) 232/F3
Dwight, N. Dak. (58024) 283/S7
Dwight, Nebr. (68635) 264/G3
Dworshak (res.), Idaho 220/C3
Dwyer, N. Mex. (†88034) 274/B6
Dwyer, Wyo. (82211) 319/G3
Dyas, Ala. (†36507) 194/C9
Dybvad, Den. 21/D3
Dyce, Scot. 15/M5
Dyckesville, Wis. (†54217) 317/L6
Dycusburg, Ky. (42037) 237/E6
Dyer (cape), 163/K2
Dyer, Ark. (72935) 203/B3
Dyer, Ind. (46311) 227/C1
Dyer, Ky. (40116) 237/J5
Dyer (cape), N.W.T. 187/M3
Dyer, Nev. (89010) 266/C5
Dyer (co.), Tenn. 237/C8
Dyer, Tenn. (38330) 237/D8
Dyer Brook▵, Maine (†04747) 242/G3
Dyersburg, Tenn. (38024) 237/C8
Dyersville, Iowa (52040) 229/L3
Dyess‡, Ark. (72330) 203/K2
Dyess A.F.B., Texas 302/D5
Dyje (riv.), Czech. 41/D2
Dyke (lake), Newf. 166/A3
Dykh-Tau (mt.), U.S.S.R. 52/F6
Dyle (riv.), Belg. 27/F7
Dysart, Iowa (52224) 229/J4
Dysart, Sask. 181/H5
Dysartsville, N.C. (†28761) 281/F3
Dzabkhan (prov.), Mong. 77/E2
Dzabkhan (riv.), Mong. 77/D2
Dza Chu (riv.), China 77/E5
Dzamyn Ude, Mong. 77/G3
Dzaoudzi, Comoro Is. 118/H2
Dzerzhinsk, U.S.S.R. 48/E4
Dzerzhinsk, U.S.S.R. 52/F3
Dzerzhinsk, U.S.S.R., 7/J3
Dzhalal-Abad, U.S.S.R. 48/H5
Dzhalinda, U.S.S.R. 48/N4
Dzhambul, U.S.S.R. 48/H5
Dzhankoy, U.S.S.R. 52/D5
Dzhelinda, U.S.S.R. 48/M2
Dzhelinda, U.S.S.R., 54/P2
Dzhetygara, U.S.S.R. 48/G4
Dzhezkazgan, U.S.S.R. 48/G5
Dzhugdzhur (range), U.S.S.R. 48/O4
Dzhul'fa, U.S.S.R. 52/G7
Dzhul'fa, U.S.S.R., 7/J5
Działdowo, Poland 47/E2
Dzibichaltún (ruin), Mex. 150/P6
Dzierżoniów, Poland 47/C3
Dzilam de Bravo, Mex. 150/P6
Dzitbalché, Mex. 150/P6
Dzungaria (reg.), China 77/C3
Dzun Modo, Mong. 77/G2

E

Eabamet (lake), Ont. 175/C2
Eads, Colo. (81036) 208/O6
Eads, Tenn. (38028) 237/B10
Eadytown, S.C. (†29468) 296/G5
Eagan, Tenn. (37730) 237/O7
Eagar, Ariz. (85925) 198/F4
Eagarville, Ill. (62023) 222/D4
Eagle, Alaska, 188/D5
Eagle, Alaska (99738) 196/K2
Eagle (creek), Ariz. 198/F5
Eagle (lake), Calif. 204/E3
Eagle (peak), Calif. 204/E2
Eagle (co.), Colo. 208/F3
Eagle, Colo. (81631) 208/F3
Eagle (riv.), Colo. 208/E3
Eagle (mt.), V.I.(U.S.) 161/E4
Eagle (riv.), Que. 172/A3
Eagle (lake), Ont. 177/F5
Eagle (lake), Ont. 177/E2
Eagle, Idaho (83616) 220/B6
Eagle (creek), Ind. 227/E4
Eagle (lake), Iowa 229/F2
Eagle (creek), Ky. 237/M3
Eagle (lake), Maine 242/E3
Eagle (lake), Maine 242/F1
Eagle, Mich. (48822) 250/E6
Eagle (lake), Maine 242/F2
Eagle (mt.), Minn. 254/G2
Eagle (mt.), W. Va. (25067) 313/D6
Eagle, Nebr. (68347) 264/H4
Eagle (riv.), Newf. 166/C3
Eagle (creek), Oreg. 291/K3
Eagle (hills), Sask. 181/C3
Eagle (peak), Texas 302/C11
Eagle, Wis. (53119) 317/H2
Eagle (lake), Wis. 317/H2
Eagle (lake), Wis. 317/K3
Eagle (peak), Wyo. 319/B1
Eagle Bay, N.Y. (13331) 276/L3
Eagle Bend, Minn. (56446) 254/D4
Eagle Bridge, N.Y. (12057) 276/O5
Eagle Butte, Alta. 182/E5
Eagle Butte, S. Dak. (57625) 298/G4
Eagle City, Okla. (73643) 288/J3
Eagle Crags (mt.), Calif. 204/J8
Eagle Creek, Oreg. (97022) 291/E2
Eagle Grove, Iowa (50533) 229/F3
Eagle Harbor, Md. (†20608) 245/M6
Eagle Harbor, Mich. (49951) 250/A1
Eaglehawk, Vic. 97/C5
Eagle Hill, Alta. 182/C4
Eaglehill (creek), Sask. 181/D4
Eagle Lake, Fla. (33839) 212/E4
Eagle Lake▵, Maine (04739) 242/F1
Eagle Lake, Maine (04739) 242/F1
Eagle Lake, Minn. (56024) 254/E6
Eagle Lake, Texas (77434) 302/H8
Eagle Mills, Ark. (71729) 203/E6
Eagle Mountain, Calif. (92241) 204/K10
Eagle Mountain (lake), Texas 302/E1
Eagle Nest, N. Mex. (87718) 274/D2
Eagle Nest (lake), N. Mex. 274/D2
Eagle Pass, Texas (78852) 302/D9
Eagle Point, Oreg. (97524) 291/E5
Eagle River, Alaska (99577) 196/C1
Eagle River, Mich. (49924) 250/A1
Eagle River, Wis. (54521) 317/H4
Eagle Rock, Mo. (65641) 261/E9
Eagle Rock, Va. (24085) 307/J5
Eaglesham, Alta. 182/B2
Eagles Mere, Pa. (17731) 294/J3
Eagle Springs, N.C. (27242) 281/K4
Eagleton, Tenn. (†37801) 237/O9
Eagletown, Ind. (†46074) 227/E4
Eagletown, Okla. (74734) 288/S6
Eagleville, Calif. (96110) 204/E2
Eagleville, Conn. (†06268) 210/F1
Eagleville, Mo. (64442) 261/D2
Eagleville, Tenn. (37060) 237/H9
Eakly, Okla. (73033) 288/K4
Ealing, 10/B5
Ealing, Eng. 13/G6
Ear (lake), Sask. 181/B3
Eardley (lake), Man. 179/F2
Ear Falls, Ont. 175/B2
Earl (lake), Calif. 204/A2
Earl, N.C. (28038) 281/F4
Earl, Wis. (54833) 317/C4
Earle, Ark. (72331) 203/K3
Earleigh Heights, Md. (†21146) 245/M4
Earle Naval Amm. Depot, N.J. 273/E3
Earleton, Fla. (32631) 212/D2
Earleville, Md. (21919) 245/P3
Earleysville, Va. (22936) 307/M4
Earl Grey, Sask. 181/G5
Earlham, Iowa (50072) 229/E6
Earlimart, Calif. (93219) 204/F8
Earling, Iowa (51530) 229/C5
Earlington, Ky. (42410) 237/F6
Earl Park, Ind. (47942) 227/C3
Earlsboro, Okla. (74840) 288/N4
Earlston, Scot. 15/L8
Earlton, Kans. (66731) 232/G4
Earltown, N.S. 169/E3
Earlville, Ill. (60518) 222/E2
Earlville, Iowa (52041) 229/L4
Earlville, N.Y. (13332) 276/J5
Early (co.), Ga. 216/C8
Early, Iowa (50535) 229/C4
Early‡, Texas (†76801) 302/F6
Early Branch, S.C. (29916) 296/F6
Earn (lake), Scot. 15/H7
Earn (riv.), Scot. 15/J7
Earnslaw (mt.), N.Z. 101/B6
Earp, Calif. (92242) 204/L9
Earth, Texas (79031) 302/B3
Earthquake (lake), Mont. 262/E6
Easby, N. Dak. (†58249) 283/O2
Easingwold, Eng. 13/F3
Eask (lake), Ire. 17/E2
Easky, Ire. 17/D3
Easley, S.C. (29640) 296/B2
East (cape), Alaska 196/K4
East (riv.), Conn. 210/E3
East (pt.), V.I.(U.S.) 161/G4
East (cape), Fla. 212/E6
East (bay), La. 238/M8
East (pt.), Mass. 249/E6
East (bay), N.S. 169/H3
East (riv.), N.S. 169/F3
East (pt.), N.S.W. 97/J2
East (riv.), N.Y. 276/N9
East (cape), N.Z., 87/H9
East (cape), N.Z. 101/G2
East (range), Nev. 266/D2
East (lake), Oreg. 291/F4
East (pt.), P.E.I. 169/G2
East (Dezhnev) (cape), U.S.S.R., 4/C18
Eastaboga, Ala. (36260) 194/F3
Eastabuchie, Miss. (39436) 256/F8
East Albany, Vt. (†05820) 268/C2
East Alburg, Vt. (†05440) 268/A2
East Alliance‡, Ohio (†44601) 284/J3
East Alligator (riv.), No. Terr. 93/C2
East Alton, Ill. (62024) 222/B6
East Andover, Maine (04226) 242/B6
East Andover, N.H. (03231) 268/D5
East Anglian Heights (hills), Eng. 13/H5
East Angus, Que. 172/F4
Eastanollee, Ga. (30538) 216/F1
East Arlington, Vt. (05252) 268/A5
East Arrow Park, Br. Col. 184/J5
East Aspetuck (riv.), Conn. 210/B2
East Auburndale‡, Fla. (†33823) 212/E3
East Aurora, N.Y. (14052) 276/C5
East Baldwin, Maine (04024) 242/B8
East Bangor, Pa. (18013) 294/M4
East Bank, W. Va. (25067) 313/D6
East Barnet, Vt. (†05821) 268/C3
East Barre, Vt. (05649) 268/C3
East Barrington, N.H. (03825) 268/F5
East Baton Rouge (par.), La. 238/K1
East Bay, N.S. 169/H2
East Bay (hills), N.S. 169/H3
East Bend, N.C. (27018) 281/H2
East Berbice (dist.), Guyana 131/C3
East Berkshire, Vt. (05447) 268/B2
East Berlin, Conn. (06023) 210/E2
East Berlin, Pa. (17316) 294/J6
East Bernard, Texas (77435) 302/H8
East Bernstadt, Ky. (40729) 237/N6
East Berwick, Pa. (†18603) 294/K3
East Bethany, N.Y. (14054) 276/D5
East Bethel, Minn. (†55005) 254/E5
East Bethel, Vt. (†05032) 268/B4
East Blackstone, Mass. (†01504) 249/H4
East Bloomfield, N.Y. (14443) 276/E5
East Blue Hill, Maine (04629) 242/G7
East Blythe, Calif. (†92225) 204/L10
East Boothbay, Maine (04544) 242/D8
Eastborough, Kans. (†67201) 232/E4
Eastbourne, 10/G5
Eastbourne, Eng. 13/H7
Eastbourne, N.Z. 101/B3
East Brady, Pa. (16028) 294/C3
East Braintree, Man. 179/G5
East Braintree, Mass. (†02184) 249/D8
East Braintree, Vt. (†05060) 268/B3
East Branch, Lièvre (riv.), Que. 172/C2
East Branch, Pemigewasset (riv.), N.H. 268/D3
East Branch, N.Y. (13756) 276/K7
East Branch, Rocky (riv.), Ohio 284/G10
East Branch, Nulhegan (riv.), Vt. 268/D2
East Brewster, Mass. (02640) 249/O5
East Brewton, Ala. (36426) 194/E8
East Bridgewater▵, Mass. (02333) 249/L4
East Brisbane, Queens. 95/E3
Eastbrook, Sask. 181/C6
East Brookfield▵, Mass. (01515) 249/G4
East Brookfield, Mass. (01515) 249/G4
East Brookfield, Vt. (†05036) 268/C3
East Brooklyn, Conn. (†06239) 210/H1
East Brooklyn‡, Ill. (†60474) 222/E2
East Broughton, Que. 172/F3
East Broughton Station, Que. 172/F3
East Brownfield, Maine (†04010) 242/B8
East Brunswick▵, N.J. (08816) 273/E3
East Burke, Vt. (05832) 268/D2
East Butler, Pa. (16029) 294/C4
East Calais, Vt. (05650) 268/C3
East Camden, Ark. (71701) 203/E6
East Canaan, Conn. (06024) 210/B1
East Candia, N.H. (03040) 268/E5
East Canon, Colo. (†81212) 208/J6
East Canton, Ohio (44730) 284/H4
East Canyon (res.), Utah 304/C3
East Carondelet, Ill. (62240) 222/A6
East Carroll (par.), La. 238/H1
East Cayuga Heights‡, N.Y. (†14850) 276/H6
East-Central (state), Nigeria 106/F7
East Chain, Minn. (†56031) 254/D7
East Charleston, Vt. (05833) 268/D2
East Chester, N.S. 169/D4
Eastchester‡, N.Y. (10709) 276/O7
East Chezzetcook, N.S. 169/E4
East Chicago, Ind. (46312) 227/C1
East Chicago Heights, Ill. (†60411) 222/B3
East China (sea), 54/R6
East China (sea), China 77/L6
East China (sea), Japan 81/C8
East China (sea), Ryukyu Is. 81/C8
East China (sea), S. Korea 81/C8
East Chop (pt.), Mass. 249/M7
East Claridon, Ohio (44033) 284/H2
East Cleveland, Ohio (44112) 284/H9
East Cleveland, Tenn. (†37311) 237/M10
East Coast Bays, N.Z. 101/B1
East Compton‡, Calif. (90220) 204/C11
East Concord, Vt. (05834) 268/D3
East Conemaugh, Pa. (15909) 294/E5
East Corinth, Maine (04427) 242/F5
East Corinth, Vt. (05040) 268/C3
East Coulée, Alta. 182/D4
East Craftsbury, Vt. (†05826) 268/C2
East Dedham, Mass. (02026) 249/C8
East Demerara (dist.), Guyana 131/B2
East Dennis, Mass. (02641) 249/O5
East Dereham, 10/G4
East Dereham, Eng. 13/J5
East Derry, N.H. (03041) 268/E6
East Detroit, Mich. (48021) 250/B6
East Devils (lake), N. Dak. 283/N4
East Dixfield, Maine (04227) 242/C6
East Dixmont, Maine (†04932) 242/E6
East Dorset, Vt. (05253) 268/A5
East Douglas, Mass. (01516) 249/G4
East Dover, Vt. (05341) 268/B6
East Dublin, Ga. (31021) 216/G5
East Dubuque, Ill. (61025) 222/C1
East Duke, Okla. (†73532) 288/H5
East Dundee (Dundee), Ill. (†60118) 222/E1
East Durham, N.Y. (12423) 276/M6
East Eddington, Maine (04428) 242/F6
East Ellijay, Ga. (30539) 216/C1
East Ely, Nev. (89315) 266/G3
Eastend, V.I.(U.S.) 161/D4
Eastend, Sask. 181/C6
East Enterprise, Ind. (47019) 227/H7
Easter (isl.), Chile, 87/Q8
Easter (isl.), Chile, 3/D7
Eastern (pt.), Conn. 210/G3
Eastern (pt.), Mass. 249/M2
Eastern (bay), Md. 245/N5
Eastern (creek), N.S.W. 97/H3
Eastern (prov.), Saudi Ar. 59/E4
Eastern (prov.), Mong. 77/H2
Eastern (Arabian) (des.), U.A.R. 111/F2
Eastern (prov.), Kenya 115/G4
Eastern Ghats (mts.), India 68/D6
Eastern Passage, N.S. 169/E4
Eastern Scheldt (est.), Neth. 27/D5
Eastern Taurus (mts.), Turkey 63/J3
Easterville, Man. 179/C1
East Fairfield, Vt. (05448) 268/B2
East Fairwell, Sask. 181/B6
East Falkland (isl.), Falk. Is., 120/E8
East Falmouth, Mass. (02536) 249/M6
East Falmouth P.O. (Teaticket), Mass. (02536) 249/M6
East Farmington, Wis. (†54020) 317/A5
East Farnham, Que. 172/E4
East Faxon, Pa. (†17701) 294/J3
East Feliciana (par.), La. 238/H5
East Ferry, N.S. 169/B4
East Flanders (prov.), Belg. 27/D7
East Flat Rock, N.C. (28726) 281/E4
East Flevoland Polder, Neth. 27/H4
East Florenceville, N. Br. 170/C2
Eastford▵, Conn. (06242) 210/G1
East Fork, Chandalar (riv.), Alaska 196/J1
East Fork, White (riv.), Ind. 227/C7
East Fork, Clarks (riv.), Ky. 237/E7
East Fork, Humboldt (riv.), Nev. 266/F1
East Fork, Little Miami (riv.), Ohio 284/C7
East Fork, Sevier (riv.), Utah 304/B6
East Fork, Virgin (riv.), Utah 304/B6
East Fork, Green (riv.), Wyo. 319/C3
East Foxboro, Mass. (†02035) 249/K4
East Franklin, Maine (†04634) 242/G6
East Franklin, Vt. (†05457) 268/B2
East Freedom, Pa. (16637) 294/E5
East Freetown, Mass. (02717) 249/L5
East Friesland (reg.), W. Ger. 22/B2
East Frisian (isls.), W. Ger. 22/B2
East Gaffney, S.C. (†29340) 296/D1
East Galesburg, Ill. (61430) 222/C3
East Gary, Ind. (46405) 227/C1
Eastgate, Nev. (†89406) 266/D3
East Georgia, Vt. (†05455) 268/A2
East Germantown (Pershing), Ind. (†47370) 227/G5
East Germany, 7/F3
EAST GERMANY, 22/E2
East Gillespie, Ill. (†62033) 222/D4
East Glacier Park, Mont. (59434) 262/C2

358 East Glastonbury

East Glastonbury, Conn. (06025) 210/E2
East Glenville‡, N.Y. (†12301) 276/N5
East Gobi (prov.), Mong. 77/G3
East Grafton, N.H. (†03240) 268/D4
East Granby△, Conn. (06026) 210/E1
East Grand Forks, Minn. (56721) 254/B3
East Grand Rapids, Mich. (†49506) 250/D6
East Granville, Vt. (†05669) 268/B3
East Greenbush, N.Y. (12061) 276/N5
East Greenville, Ohio (†44666) 284/G4
East Greenville, Pa. (18041) 294/L5
East Greenwich△, R.I. (02818) 249/H6
East Griffin‡, Ga. (†30223) 216/D4
East Grinstead, 10/G5
East Grinstead, Eng. 13/G6
Eastgulf, W. Va. (25835) 313/D7
East Gull Lake, Minn. (†56401) 254/D4
East Haddam△, Conn. (06423) 210/F3
East Half Hollow Hills‡, N.Y. (†11743) 276/O9
Eastham△, Mass. (02642) 249/O5
East Hampstead, N.H. (03826) 268/E6
East Hampton△, Conn. (06424) 210/E2
East Hampton, Conn. (06424) 210/E2
Easthampton△, Mass. (01027) 249/D3
East Hampton, N.Y. (11937) 276/R9
East Hanover△, N.J. (07936) 273/E2
East Hardin, Ill. (†62031) 222/C4
East Hardwick, Vt. (05836) 268/C2
East Harling, Eng. 13/J5
East Hartford△, Conn. (06108) 210/E1
East Hartland, Conn. (06027) 210/D1
East Harwich, Mass. (02645) 249/O6
East Haven, Conn. (06512) 210/D3
East Haven△, Vt. (05837) 268/D2
East Haven, Vt. (05837) 268/D2
East Haverhill, N.H. (†03780) 268/D3
East Hazelcrest, Ill. (†60429) 222/B2
East Hebron, N.H. (03232) 268/D4
East Helena, Mont. (59635) 262/E4
East Hereford, Que. 172/F4
East Herkimer, N.Y. (†13350) 276/L4
East Hickory, Pa. (16321) 294/D2
East Hills, N.Y. (†11576) 276/R7
East Hiram, Maine (04026) 242/B8
East Hodge, La. (†71247) 238/E2
East Holden, Maine (04429) 242/F6
East Hope, Idaho (†83836) 220/B1
East Irvine, Calif. (92650) 204/D11
East Islip‡, N.Y. (11730) 276/O9
East Jackson, Maine (†04986) 242/E6
East Jamaica, Vt. (†05343) 268/B5
East Jordan, Mich. (49727) 250/D3
East Juliette, Ga. (†31046) 216/E4
East Keansburg, N.J. (07734) 273/E3
East Kelowna, Br. Col. 184/H5
East Kent, Conn. (†06785) 210/B2
East Kilbride, Scot. 15/C2
East Kildonan, Man. 179/E5
East Killingly, Conn. (06243) 210/H1
East Kingsford, Mich. (†49801) 250/A3
East Kingston△, N.H. (03827) 268/F6
East Kingston, N.H. (03827) 268/F6
East Knox, Maine (†04921) 242/E7
East Korea (bay), N. Korea 81/D4
Eastlake, Mich. (49626) 250/C4
East Lake, Minn. (†55760) 254/E4
East Lake, N.C. (27931) 281/S3
Eastlake, Ohio (44094) 284/J8
East Lake-Orient Park, Fla. (†33601) 212/C2
East La Mirada‡, Calif. (†90638) 204/D11
Eastland, Tenn. (†38583) 237/L9
Eastland (co.), Texas 302/F5
Eastland, Texas (76448) 302/F5
East Lansdowne, Pa. (†19050) 294/M7
East Lansing, Mich. (48823) 250/E6
East Laport, N.C. (†28723) 281/C4
East Las Vegas, Nev. (89112) 266/F6
East Laurinburg, N.C. (28352) 281/L5
Eastlawn Gardens‡, Pa. (†18064) 294/M4
East Layton‡, Utah (†84041) 304/C2
East Lebanon, Maine (04027) 242/B9
East Lee, Mass. (†01238) 249/B3
Eastleigh, 10/F5
Eastleigh, Eng. 13/F7
Eastleigh, Sask. 181/E5
East Lempster, N.H. (03605) 268/C5
East Limington, Maine (†04049) 242/B8
East Linton, Scot. 15/L7
East Litchfield, Conn. (†06759) 210/C1
East Livermore, Maine (04228) 242/C7
East Liverpool, Ohio (43920) 284/J4
East Loch (inlet), Hawaii 218/B3
East Loch Tarbert (inlet), Scot. 15/C4
East London, 102/E8
East London, S. Africa 118/D6
East Longmeadow△, Mass. (01028) 249/E4
East Los Angeles, Calif. (90804) 204/C10
East Lothian (co.), Scot. 15/L8
East Lowell, Maine (†04433) 242/G5
East Lyme△, Conn. (06333) 210/G3
East Lynn, Ill. (60932) 222/F3
East Lynn, W. Va. (25512) 313/B6
East Lynne, Mo. (64743) 261/D5
East Machias△, Maine (04630) 242/J6
East Machias, Maine (04630) 242/J6
East Machias (riv.), Maine 242/H6
East Madison, Maine (†04950) 242/D6
East Madison, N.H. (03828) 268/E4
East-Main, 163/J5
East-Main, Que. 174/B2
Eastmain (riv.), Que. 174/B2
East-Main (riv.), 163/J5
Eastmain (riv.), Que., 146/L4
Eastman, Que. 172/E4
Eastman, Ga. (31023) 216/F6
Eastman, Wis. (54626) 317/D9
East Marion, N.C. (†28752) 281/F3
East Massapequa‡, N.Y. (†11758) 276/O9
East McKeesport‡, Pa. (15035) 294/C7
East Meadow, N.Y. (11554) 276/R7
East Meredith, N.Y. (13757) 276/L6
East Middlebury, Vt. (05740) 268/A4
East Middletown‡, N.Y. (†10940) 276/M8
East Millcreek, Utah (†84101) 304/C3
East Millinocket△, Maine (04430) 242/F4
East Millinocket, Maine (04430) 242/F4
East Millstone, N.J. (08873) 273/D3
East Milton, Mass. (†02186) 249/D7
East Mines, N.S. 169/E3
East Moline, Ill. (61244) 222/C2
East Montpelier△, Vt. (05651) 268/B3
East Montpelier, Vt. (05651) 268/B3
East Moriches, N.Y. (11940) 276/P9
East Morris, Conn. (†06763) 210/C2
East Musquash (lake), Maine 242/H5
East Naples, Fla. (†33940) 212/E5
East Neck‡, N.Y. (†11721) 276/O9
East Newark, N.J. (07100) 273/B2
East New Market, Md. (21631) 245/P6
East Newnan, Ga. (†30263) 216/C4
East New Portland, Maine (†04954) 242/D6
East Nishnabotna (riv.), Iowa 229/C6
East Northfield, Mass. (01360) 249/E2
East Northport, N.Y. (11731) 276/O9
East Norton, Mass. (†02766) 249/K5
East Norwalk, Conn. (06856) 210/B4
East Olympia, Wash. (98540) 310/B4
Easton, Calif. (93706) 204/F7
Easton△, Conn. (06425) 210/B4
Easton, Conn. (06425) 210/B4
Easton (res.), Conn. 210/B3
Easton, Ill. (62633) 222/D3
Easton, Kans. (66020) 232/G2
Easton, La. (70530) 238/F5
Easton△, Maine (04740) 242/H2
Easton△, Mass. (02334) 249/K4
Easton, Md. (21601) 245/O5
Easton, Minn. (56025) 254/E7
Easton, Mo. (64443) 261/C3
Easton△, N.H. (†03580) 268/D3
Easton, N.H. (†03580) 268/D3
Easton, Pa. (18042) 294/M4
Easton‡, Texas (75641) 302/K5
Easton, Wash. (98925) 310/D3
Easton, Wis. (†53936) 317/G8
Eastondale, Mass. (02335) 249/K4
East Orange, N.J. (*07017) 273/B2
East Orland, Maine (04431) 242/F6
East Orleans, Mass. (02643) 249/P5
East Otis, Mass. (01029) 249/B4
East Otisfield, Maine (†04270) 242/B7
East Otto, N.Y. (14729) 276/C6
Eastover, S.C. (29044) 296/F4
East Pakistan (prov.), Pak. 68/G4
East Palatka, Fla. (32031) 212/E2
East Palestine, Ohio (44413) 284/J4
East Palo Alto‡, Calif. (94303) 204/K3
East Park (res.), Calif. 204/C4
East Parsonfield, Maine (04028) 242/B8
East Patchogue‡, N.Y. (11772) 276/P9
East Paterson, N.J. (07407) 273/B2
East Peacham, Vt. (†05821) 268/C3
East Pembroke, Mass. (02336) 249/M4
East Pembroke, N.Y. (14056) 276/D5
East Peoria, Ill. (61611) 222/D3
East Pepperell, Mass. (01437) 249/H2
East Peru (Peru), Iowa (†50222) 229/F6
East Peru, Maine (04229) 242/C7
East Petersburg, Pa. (17520) 294/K5
East Pine, Br. Col. 184/G2
East Pittsburgh‡, Pa. (15112) 294/C7
East Pleasant Plain, Iowa (52541) 229/K6
Eastpoint, Fla. (32328) 212/B2
East Point, Ga. (30344) 216/C3
East Point, Ky. (41216) 237/R5
East Point, La. (71025) 238/D2
East Poland, Maine (04230) 242/C7
East Poplar, Sask. 181/F6
Eastport, Idaho (83826) 220/B1
Eastport, Maine, 188/N2
Eastport, Maine (04631) 242/K6
Eastport, Mich. (49627) 250/D3
Eastport, N.Y. (11941) 276/P9
Eastport, Newf. 166/D1
East Porterville‡, Calif. (†93257) 204/G7
East Poultney, Vt. (05741) 268/A4
East Prairie, Mo. (63845) 261/O9
East Prospect, Pa. (17317) 294/J6
East Providence, R.I. (02914) 249/J5
East Putnam, Conn. (†06260) 210/H1
East Quogue‡, N.Y. (11942) 276/P9
East Randolph, N.Y. (14730) 276/C6
East Randolph, Vt. (05041) 268/B4
East Retford, 10/F4
East Retford, Eng. 13/G4
East Richford, Vt. (†05476) 268/B2
East Ridge, Tenn. (37412) 237/L11
East Rindge, N.H. (03461) 268/D6
East River, Conn. (†06443) 210/E3
East River, Saint Marys, N.S. 169/F3
East Rochester, N.Y. (14445) 276/F4
East Rochester, Ohio (44625) 284/H4
East Rochester‡, Pa. (†15074) 294/B4
East Rockaway, N.Y. (11518) 276/R7
East Rockingham‡, N.C. (28379) 281/F5
East Rutherford, N.J. (07073) 273/B2
East Ryegate, Vt. (05042) 268/C3
East Saint Louis, Ill., 188/J3
East Saint Louis, Ill. (*62201) 222/B6
East Sandwich, Mass. (02537) 249/N6
East Saugus, Mass. (†01906) 249/D6
East Sebago, Maine (04029) 242/B8
East Selkirk, Man. 179/F4
East Shoal (lake), Man. 179/E4
East Siberian (sea), U.S.S.R. 48/S2
East Siberian (sea), U.S.S.R., 4/B1
Eastside, Oreg. (97420) 291/C4
East Side, Pa. (18634) 294/L3
East Sister (peak), Idaho 220/C2
East Smithfield, Pa. (18817) 294/J2
Eastsound, Wash. (98245) 310/B2
East Sparta, Ohio (44626) 284/H4
East Spencer, N.C. (28039) 281/J3
East Springfield, N.Y. (13333) 276/L5
East Springfield, Pa. (16411) 294/A2
East Stone Gap, Va. (24246) 307/C7
East Stoneham, Maine (04231) 242/B7
East Stroudsburg, Pa. (18301) 294/M4
East Sullivan, Maine (04632) 242/G6
East Sullivan, N.H. (03445) 268/C6
East Sumner, Maine (04232) 242/C7
East Swan (riv.), Minn. 254/F3
East Swanzey, N.H. (03446) 268/C6
East Syracuse, N.Y. (13057) 276/H4
East Tawakoni‡, Texas (†75472) 302/J5
East Tawas, Mich. (48730) 250/F4
East Templeton, Mass. (01438) 249/G2
East Thermopolis, Wyo. (†82443) 319/D2
East Thetford, Vt. (05043) 268/C4
East Thompson, Conn. (†06255) 210/H1
East Tintic (creek), Utah 304/B4
East Tohopekaliga (lake), Fla. 212/E3
East Troy, Wis. (53120) 317/J2
East Union, Maine (†04862) 242/E7
East Uniontown‡, Pa. (†15401) 294/C6
Eastvale, Pa. (†15010) 294/B4
East Vandergrift‡, Pa. (15629) 294/C4
East Vassalboro, Maine (04935) 242/D7
East Verde (riv.), Ariz. 198/D4
East Vestal‡, N.Y. (†13850) 276/H6
Eastview, Sask. 181/F5
Eastview, Tenn. (†38367) 237/D10
East View, W. Va. (†26301) 313/F4
East Village, Conn. (†06468) 210/C3
Eastville, Ga. (†30677) 216/E3
Eastville, Va. (23347) 307/R6
East Wakefield, N.H. (03830) 268/E4
East Walker (riv.), Nev. 266/B4
East Wallingford, Vt. (05742) 268/B5
East Walpole, Mass. (02032) 249/C8
East Wareham, Mass. (02538) 249/M5
East Washington, Pa. (†15301) 294/B5
East Waterboro, Maine (04030) 242/B8
East Waterford, Pa. (17021) 294/G5
East Weissport‡, Pa. (†18235) 294/L4
East Wellington, Br. Col. 184/J3
East Wenatchee, Wash. (98801) 310/E3
East Weymouth, Mass. (†02189) 249/E8
East Whately, Mass. (†01373) 249/D3
East Williamson, N.Y. (14449) 276/F4
East Willington, Conn. (†06279) 210/G1
East Williston‡, N.Y. (11596) 276/R7
East Wilton, Maine (04234) 242/C6
East Windsor△, Conn. (†06088) 210/E1
East Windsor Hill, Conn. (06028) 210/E1
East Winn, Maine (†04495) 242/G5
East Winter Haven‡, Fla. (†33880) 212/E3
East Wolf (isl.), N. Br. 170/D4
East Wolfeboro, N.H. (†03894) 268/E4
Eastwood, Ont. 177/D4
Eastwood, Mich. (†49001) 250/D6
Eastwood, N.S.W. 97/J3
East Woodstock, Conn. (06244) 210/H1
East Worcester, N.Y. (12064) 276/L5
East York, Ont. 177/K4
Easyford, Alta. 182/C3
Eaton, Colo. (80615) 208/K1
Eaton, Ill. (†62454) 222/F4
Eaton, Ind. (47338) 227/G4
Eaton, Maine (04432) 242/H4
Eaton (co.), Mich. 250/E6
Eaton, N.Y. (13334) 276/J5
Eaton, Ohio (45320) 284/A6
Eaton, Tenn. (38331) 237/C9
Eaton Center△, N.H. (03832) 268/E4
Eaton Center, N.H. (03832) 268/E4
Eaton Estates, Ohio (†44035) 284/G3
Eatonia, Sask. 181/B4
Eaton Rapids, Mich. (48827) 250/E6
Eatonton, Ga. (31024) 216/F4
Eatontown, N.J. (07724) 273/E3
Eatonville‡, Fla. (32751) 212/E3
Eatonville, Wash. (98328) 310/C4
Eau-Claire (lake), Que. 174/C1
Eau-Claire (lake), 163/J4
Eau Claire, Mich. (49111) 250/C6
Eau Claire, Pa. (16030) 294/C3
Eau Claire, Wis., 188/H2
Eau Claire (co.), Wis. 317/D6
Eau Claire, Wis. (54701) 317/D6
Eau Claire (riv.), Wis. 317/D6
Eau Galle, Wis. (54737) 317/B6
Eauripik (atoll), Pac. Is., 87/E5
Ebal (mt.), Jordan 65/C3
Ebb, Fla. (†32331) 212/C1
Ebb and Flow (lake), Man. 179/C3
Ebbw Vale, 10/E5
Ebbw Vale, Wales 13/D6
Ebeltoft, Den. 18/G8
Ebeltoft, Den. 21/D5
Ebenezer, Miss. (39064) 256/D5
Ebenezer, Sask. 181/J4
Ebenfurth, Austria 41/D3
Eben Junction, Mich. (49825) 250/B2
Ebensburg, Pa. (15931) 294/E5
Ebensee, Austria 41/B3
Eberbach, W. Ger. 22/C4
Ebersbach, E. Ger. 22/F3
Eberswalde, E. Ger. 22/E2
Ebetsu, Japan 81/K2
Ebingen, W. Ger. 22/C4
Ebi Nor (lake), China 77/B2
Ebnat-Kappel, Switz. 39/H2
Eboli, Italy 34/E4
Ebolowa, Cameroon 115/B3
Ebolowa, 102/D4
Ebon (atoll), Pac. Is., 87/G5
Ebony, Va. (23845) 307/N7
Ebor, Man. 179/A5
Ebrach, W. Ger. 22/D4
Ebrié (lag.), Ivory Coast 106/D8
Ebro, Fla. (32437) 212/C6
Ebro, Minn. (56638) 254/C3
Ebro (riv.), Spain, 7/D4
Ebro (riv.), Spain 33/G2
Ecaussinnes-d'Enghien, Belg. 27/E7
Ecclefechan, Scot. 15/K9
Eccles, 10/G2
Eccles, W. Va. (25836) 313/D7
Ecclesfield, Eng. 13/F4
Ecclesville, Trinidad Tobago 161/B11
Eceabat, Turkey 63/B6
Echallens, Switz. 39/C3
Echarate, Peru 128/F9
Echeconnee, Ga. (†31008) 216/E5
Echo, Ala. (†36360) 194/G8
Echo (cliffs), Ariz. 198/D2
Echo, La. (71330) 238/F4
Echo, Minn. (56237) 254/C6
Echo (lake), N.J. 273/E1
Echo, Oreg. (97826) 291/H2
Echo, Utah (84024) 304/C3
Echo (res.), Utah 304/C3
Echo (lake), Vt. 268/D2
Echo Bay, Ont. 175/D3
Echo Bay, Ont. 177/J5
Echola, Ala. (35457) 194/C4
Echo Lake, N.J. (†07435) 273/E1
Echols (co.), Ga. 216/G9
Echols, Ky. (42340) 237/H6
Echt, Neth. 27/H6
Echternach, Lux. 27/J9
Echuca, Aust. 88/G7
Echuca, Vic. 97/C5
Echunga, Aust. 88/E8
Écija, Spain 33/D4
Eck (lake), Scot. 15/F7
Eckelson, N. Dak. (58432) 283/O6
Eckerman, Mich. (49728) 250/E2
Eckernförde, W. Ger. 22/D1
Eckert, Colo. (81418) 208/C5
Eckerty, Ind. (47116) 227/D8
Eckhart Mines, Md. (21528) 245/C2
Eckley, Colo. (80727) 208/P2
Eckman, N. Dak. (†58760) 283/H2
Eckman, W. Va. (24829) 313/C8
Eckville, Alta. 182/C3
Eclectic, Ala. (36024) 194/F5
Eclipse (sound), N.W.T. 187/L2
Eclipse (harb.), Newf. 166/B2
Eclipse, Va. (23349) 307/R7
Economy, Ind. (47339) 227/G5
Economy, N.S. 169/D3
Economy, Pa. (†15005) 294/B4
Écorce (lake), Que. 172/A2
Écorces (riv.), Que. 172/F1
Ecorse, Mich. (48229) 250/B7
Écrins, Les (mt.), France 28/G5
Ecru, Miss. (38841) 256/F2
Ector (co.), Texas 302/B6
Ector‡, Texas (75439) 302/H4
Ecuador, 3/D6
Ecuador, 120/C3
ECUADOR, 128
Ecum Secum, N.S. 169/F3
Ecum Secum West, N.S. 169/F4
Edam, Neth. 27/G4
Edam, Sask. 181/C2
Eday (isl.), 10/E1
Eday (isl.), Scot. 15/L1
Edberg, Alta. 182/D3
Edcouch‡, Texas (78538) 302/G11
Edd, Eth. 59/D7
Edd, Eth. 111/H5
Ed Da'ein, 102/E3
Ed Da'ein, Sudan 111/E5
Ed Damer, 102/F3
Ed Damer, Sudan 59/B6
Ed Damer, Sudan 111/F4
Ed Debba, Sudan 59/B6
Ed Debba, Sudan 111/F4
Edderton, Scot. 15/H4
Eddiceton, Miss. (39634) 256/C8
Eddington△, Maine (†04428) 242/F6
Eddington, Maine (†04428) 242/F6
Eddington, Pa. (19020) 294/N5
Eddleston, Scot. 15/K8
Eddrachillis (bay), Scot. 15/F3
Ed Dueim, 102/F3
Ed Dueim, Sudan 59/B7
Ed Dueim, Sudan 111/F5
Eddy (co.), N. Dak. 283/N4
Eddy (co.), N. Mex. 274/E6
Eddy, Texas (76524) 302/G6
Eddystone (pt.), Aust. 88/H8
Eddystone (rocks), 10/D5
Eddystone (rocks), Eng. 13/C7
Eddystone, Man. 179/C3
Eddystone, Pa. (19013) 294/M7
Eddystone (pt.), Tasmania 99/E2
Eddyville, Ill. (62928) 222/E6
Eddyville, Iowa (52553) 229/H6
Eddyville, Ky. (42038) 237/F6
Eddyville, Nebr. (68834) 264/E3
Eddyville, Oreg. (97343) 291/D3
Ed Dzong, China 77/D5
Ede, Neth. 27/H4
Ede, Nigeria 106/E7
Edéa, Cameroon 115/B3
Edelény, Hung. 41/F2
Edelstein, Ill. (61526) 222/D3
Eden, Ariz. (85535) 198/F6
Eden, Ont. 177/D5
Edén, Ec. 128/E3
Eden (riv.), Eng. 13/E3
Eden, Ga. (31307) 216/K6
Eden, Idaho (83325) 220/D7
Eden, Ind. (†46140) 227/F5
Eden, Man. 179/C4
Eden, Md. (21822) 245/R7
Eden, Miss. (39065) 256/D5
Eden, Mont. (†59401) 262/E3
Eden, N.C. (27288) 281/K1
Eden, N.S.W. 97/E5
Eden, N.Y. (14057) 276/C5
Eden (riv.), 10/E3
Eden, S. Dak. (57232) 298/P2
Eden (riv.), Scot. 15/L7
Eden, Texas (76837) 302/E6
Eden, Utah (84310) 304/C2
Eden△, Vt. (05652) 268/B2
Eden, Vt. (05652) 268/B2
Eden, Wis. (53019) 317/K8
Eden, Wyo. (82926) 319/C3
Edenburg, S. Africa 118/D5
Edendale, S. Africa 118/D5
Edenderry, 10/C4
Edenderry, Ire. 17/G5
Edenhope, Vic. 97/A5
Eden Mills, Vt. (05653) 268/C2
Eden Prairie, Minn. (55343) 254/G6
Edenton, N.C. (27932) 281/R2
Edenton, Ohio (45117) 284/C7
Edenvale, S. Africa 118/H6
Eden Valley, Minn. (55329) 254/D5
Eden Valley (res.), Wyo. 319/C3
Edenville, Mich. (48620) 250/E5
Edenwold, Sask. 181/G5
Edenwold, Tenn. (†37115) 237/H8
Eder (res.), W. Ger. 22/C3
Eder (riv.), W. Ger. 22/C3
Ederny, N. Ire. 17/F2
Edgar (co.), Ill. 222/F4
Edgar, Mont. (59026) 262/H5
Edgar, Nebr. (68935) 264/F4
Edgar, Wis. (54426) 317/G6
Edgard, La. (70049) 238/M3
Edgar Springs, Mo. (65462) 261/J7
Edgarton, W. Va. (25672) 313/B7
Edgartown△, Mass. (02539) 249/M7
Edgartown, Mass. (02539) 249/M7
Edge (isl.), Norway, 4/B8
Edgecliff, Texas (†76101) 302/E2
Edgecomb△, Maine (04545) 242/D8
Edgecombe (co.), N.C. 281/O3
Edgecumbe (cape), Alaska 196/L1
Edgecumbe, N.Z. 101/F2
Edgefield, La. (†71019) 238/D2
Edgefield (co.), S.C. 296/D4
Edgefield, S.C. (29824) 296/C4
Edge Hill, Ga. (†30810) 216/G4
Edgehill, Va. (†22485) 307/O4
Edgeley, N. Dak. (58433) 283/N7
Edgell (isl.), N.W.T. 187/M3
Edgell, Sask. 181/B6
Edgely, Sask. 181/H5
Edgemere, Idaho (†83856) 220/B1
Edgemere, Md. (†21219) 245/N4
Edgemont, Ark. (72044) 203/F2
Edgemont, S. Dak. (57735) 298/B7
Edgemoor, Del. (†19801) 245/S1
Edgemoor, S.C. (29712) 296/E2
Edgeøya (isl.), Norway 18/E2
Edgerly, La. (†70669) 238/C6
Edgerton, Alta. 182/E3
Edgerton, Ind. (†46797) 227/H2
Edgerton, Kans. (66021) 232/H3
Edgerton, Minn. (56128) 254/B7
Edgerton, Mo. (64444) 261/C4
Edgerton, Ohio (43517) 284/A3
Edgerton, Va. (†23868) 307/N7
Edgerton, Wis. (53534) 317/H10
Edgerton, Wyo. (82635) 319/F2
Edgewater, Br. Col. 184/J5
Edgewater, Colo. (80214) 208/J3
Edgewater, Fla. (32032) 212/F3
Edgewater, N.J. (07020) 273/C2
Edgewater, Wis. (54834) 317/D4
Edgewater Gulf Beach‡, Fla. (32401) 212/C6
Edgewater Park△, N.J. (†08010) 273/D3
Edgewood, Br. Col. 184/H5
Edgewood, Calif. (96094) 204/C2
Edgewood, Fla. (†32801) 212/E3
Edgewood, Ill. (62426) 222/E5
Edgewood, Ind. (†46011) 227/F4
Edgewood, Iowa (52042) 229/K3
Edgewood, Ky. (†41017) 237/S3
Edgewood, Md. (21040) 245/N3
Edgewood, N. Mex. (87015) 274/C3
Edgewood, Ohio (44004) 284/J2
Edgewood, Pa. (†15201) 294/B7
Edgewood‡, Pa. (†17872) 294/J4
Edgewood‡, Texas (75117) 302/J5
Edgeworth, Pa. (†15143) 294/B4
Edgington, Ill. (†61284) 222/C2
Édhessa, Greece 45/F5
Edievale, N.Z. 101/B6
Edina, Minn. (55424) 254/G5
Edina, Mo. (63537) 261/H2
Edinbain, Scot. 15/D5
Edinboro, Pa. (16412) 294/B2
Edinburg, Ill. (62531) 222/D4
Edinburg, Ind. (46124) 227/E6
Edinburg, Miss. (†39051) 256/F5
Edinburg, Mo. (†64683) 261/E2
Edinburg, N. Dak. (58227) 283/P3
Edinburg, Pa. (16116) 294/B3
Edinburg, Texas (78539) 302/F11
Edinburg, Va. (22824) 307/M3
Edinburgh (cap.), Scot. 10/C1
Edinburgh (cap.), Scot., 7/D3
Edinburgh (cap.), Scot. 15/K8
Edingen (Enghien), Belg. 27/D7
Edirne, Turkey 59/A1
Edirne (prov.), Turkey 63/B2
Edirne, Turkey 63/B2
Edirne, Turkey, 7/G4
Edison (lake), Calif. 204/F6
Edison, Ga. (31746) 216/C7
Edison△, N.J. (08817) 273/E2
Edison, Nebr. (68936) 264/E4
Edison, Ohio (43320) 284/E4
Edison, Wash. (98246) 310/C2
Edison Nat'l Hist. Site, N.J. 273/A2
Edisto (isl.), S.C. 296/G7
Edisto (riv.), S.C. 296/G7
Edisto Island, S.C. (29438) 296/G6
Edith, Ga. (†31631) 216/G9
Edithburgh, Aust. 88/F6
Edithburgh, S. Aust. 94/E6
Edith Ronne Ice Shelf, Ant., 3/G11
Edith Ronne Ice Shelf, Ant. 5/B16
Ediz Hook (pen.), Wash. 310/B2
Edjeleh, Alg. 106/F3
Edmeston, N.Y. (13335) 276/K5
Edmond, Fr. Gui. 131/E3
Edmond, Kans. (67636) 232/C2
Edmond, Okla. (73034) 288/M3
Edmonds, Wash. (98020) 310/C3
Edmondson, Ark. (72332) 203/K3
Edmonson (co.), Ky. 237/J6
Edmonson, Texas (79032) 302/C3
Edmonston, Md. (†20781) 245/F4
Edmonton (cap.), Alta. 163/E5
Edmonton (cap.), Alta., 146/G4
Edmonton (cap.), Alta. 182/D3
Edmonton, Canada, 3/D3
Edmonton, Ky. (42129) 237/K7
Edmore, Mich. (48829) 250/E5
Edmore, N. Dak. (58330) 283/O3
Edmore, Sask. 181/H4
Edmund, Wis. (53535) 317/F9
Edmunds, Maine (†04628) 242/J6
Edmunds, N. Dak. (58434) 283/M5
Edmunds (co.), S. Dak. 298/L3
Edmundson‡, Mo. (†63101) 261/P2
Edmundston, 163/K6
Edmundston, N. Br. 170/B1
Edna, Ala. (†36922) 194/B6
Edna, Iowa (†51246) 229/A2
Edna, Kans. (67342) 232/G4
Edna, Texas (77957) 302/H9
Edna Bay, Alaska (†99901) 196/M2
Edo (riv.), Japan 81/P2
Edolo, Italy 34/C1
Edom, Texas (75756) 302/J5
Edon, Ohio (43518) 284/A2
Édouard (lake), Que. 172/E2
Edrans, Man. 179/C4
Edray, W. Va. (†24954) 313/F6
Edremit, Turkey 59/A2
Edremit, Turkey 63/B3
Edremit (gulf), Turkey 63/B3
Edri, Libya 111/B2
Edsbyn, Sweden 18/J6
Edson, 163/E5
Edson, Alta. 182/B3
Edson, Kans. (67733) 232/A2
Eduardo Castex, Arg. 143/D4
Edwall, Wash. (99008) 310/H3
Edwand, Alta. 182/D2
Edward (lake), 102/E5
Edward, N.C. (27821) 281/R4
Edward (lake), Dem. Rep. of the Congo. 115/E4
Edward (lake), Uganda 115/E4
Edward A. Patterson (lake), N. Dak. 283/E6
Edward MacDowell (res.), N.H. 268/D6
Edwards, Calif. (93523) 204/G9
Edwards, Colo. (81632) 208/F3
Edwards (co.), Ill. 222/E5
Edwards, Ill. (61528) 222/D3
Edwards (riv.), Ill. 222/C2
Edwards (co.), Kans. 232/C4
Edwards, Miss. (39066) 256/C6
Edwards, Mo. (65326) 261/F6
Edwards, N.Y. (13635) 276/K2
Edwards (co.), Texas 302/D7
Edwards (plat.), Texas 302/C7
Edwards A.F.B., Calif. 204/H9
Edwardsburg, Mich. (49112) 250/C7
Edwardsport, Ind. (47528) 227/C7
Edwardsville, Ala. (36261) 194/H3
Edwardsville, Ill. (62025) 222/B6
Edwardsville, Ind. (†47150) 227/F8
Edwardsville, Kans. (66022) 232/H2
Edwardsville‡, Pa. (18704) 294/L3
Edward VII (pen.), Ant. 5/B11
Edward VIII (bay), Ant. 5/C4
Edwight, W. Va. (†25189) 313/C7
Edwin, Ala. (†36317) 194/H7
Edwin, Man. 179/D5
Edzell, Scot. 15/L6
Eefde, Neth. 27/J4
Eek, Alaska (99578) 196/F2
Eeklo, Belg. 27/D6
Eel (riv.), Calif. 204/B4
Eel (riv.), Ind. 227/C6
Eel (riv.), Ind. 227/F3
Eel River Bridge, N. Br. 170/F1
Eel River Crossing, N. Br. 170/D1
Eernegem, Belg. 27/B6
Eersterivier, S. Africa 118/F6
Efate (isl.), New Hebr., 87/G7
Eferding, Austria 41/B2
Effie, La. (71331) 238/F4
Effie, Minn. (56639) 254/E3
Effigy Mounds Nat'l Mon., Iowa 229/L2
Effingham (co.), Ga. 216/K6
Effingham (co.), Ill. 222/E4
Effingham, Ill. (62401) 222/E4
Effingham, Kans. (66023) 232/G2
Effingham, S.C. (29541) 296/H3
Effingham Falls, N.H. (†03814) 268/E4
Effort, Pa. (18330) 294/M4
Efland, N.C. (27243) 281/L2
Eflâni, Turkey 63/E2
Egadi (isls.), Italy 34/C6
Egan, Ill. (61026) 222/D1
Egan (range), Nev. 266/G4
Egan, S. Dak. (57024) 298/R6
Egaña, Urug. 145/B4
Eganville, Ont. 177/G2
Egbert, Wyo. (†82053) 319/H4
Ege, Ind. (†46763) 227/G2
Egegik, Alaska (99579) 196/G3
Ege-Khaya, U.S.S.R. 48/O3
Egeland, N. Dak. (58331) 283/M2
Eger, Hung. 41/F3
Egeria, W. Va. (†25902) 313/D7
Egernsund, Den. 21/C8
Egerton (mt.), W. Aust. 92/B4
Egg (isl.), Man. 179/E3
Egg (creek), N. Dak. 283/H3
Egg, Switz. 39/G2
Eggenburg, Austria 41/C2
Eggertsville, N.Y. (†14226) 276/C5
Egg Harbor, Wis. (54209) 317/M5
Egg Harbor City, N.J. (08215) 273/D4
Egg Island (pt.), N.J. 273/C5
Eggiwil, Switz. 39/E3
Egg Lake, Alta. 182/D2
Eggleston, Va. (24086) 307/G6
Egham, 10/B5
Egilsay (isl.), Scot. 15/L1
Egin (riv.), Mong. 77/F2
Eglin A.F.B., Fla. 212/C6
Eglington (isl.), 163/L3

Elmira Heights 359

Eglinton (cape), N.W.T. 187/M2
Eglinton (isl.), N.W.T. 187/F2
Eglisau, Switz. 39/G1
Eglon, W. Va. (26716) 313/G4
Egmond aan Zee, Neth. 27/E3
Egmondville, Ont. 177/C4
Egmont (key), Fla. 212/D4
Egmont (cape), N.S. 169/H2
Egmont (cape), N.Z. 101/D3
Egmont (mt.), N.Z. 101/D3
Egmont (bay), P.E.I. 169/D2
Egmont (cape), P.E.I. 169/D2
Egnach, Switz. 39/H1
Egnar, Colo. (81325) 208/B7
Egremont, Alta. 182/D2
Egremont, Eng. 13/D3
Eğridir (lake), Turkey 59/B2
Eğridir, Turkey 63/D4
Eğridir (lake), Turkey 63/D4
Egtved, Den. 21/C6
Egyek, Hung. 41/F3
Egypt (United Arab Republic), 3/L4
EGYPT (UNITED ARAB REP.), 102/E2
EGYPT (UNITED ARAB REP.), 111/E2
EGYPT (UNITED ARAB REP.), 59/A4
Egypt, Ga. (†31329) 216/K6
Egypt, Mass. (†02066) 249/F8
Egypt, Miss. (38842) 256/G3
Egypt Lake, Fla. (†33601) 212/C2
Eha Amufu, Nigeria 106/F7
Ehime (pref.), Japan 81/F7
Ehingen, W. Ger. 22/C4
Eholt, Br. Col. 184/H5
Ehrenberg (range), No. Terr. 93/B7
Ehrenburg, Ariz. (85334) 198/A5
Ehrenfeld, Pa. (15933) 294/E5
Ehrhardt, S.C. (29081) 296/E5
Ehrwald, Austria 41/A3
Eiao (isl.), Fr. Poly., 87/M6
Eibar, Spain 33/E1
Eichstätt, W. Ger. 22/D4
Eider (riv.), W. Ger. 22/C1
Eidfjord, Norway 18/E6
Eidsfoss, Norway 18/C4
Eidson, Tenn. (37731) 237/P7
Eidsvold, Aust. 88/J5
Eidsvold, Queens. 95/D5
Eidsvoll, Norway 18/G6
Eielson A.F.B., Alaska 196/J2
Eiffel Flats, Rhod. 118/E3
Eigenbrakel (Braine-l'Alleud), Belg. 27/E7
Eigersund, Norway 18/D7
Eigg (isl.), 10/C2
Eigg (mt.), N.S. 169/F3
Eigg (isl.), Scot. 15/D6
Eigg (sound), Scot. 15/D6
Eighteen Mile (peak), Idaho 220/E5
Eight Mile (brook), Conn. 210/C3
Eight Mile (riv.), Conn. 210/F3
Eights Coast (reg.), Ant. 5/B14
Eighty Eight, Ky. (42130) 237/K7
Eighty Mile (beach), Aust. 88/C3
Eighty Mile (beach), W. Aust. 92/C2
Eijerlandsche Gat (str.), Neth. 27/F2
Eil, 102/G4
Eil, Somalia 115/J2
Eil (inlet), Scot. 15/F6
Eildon, Vic. 97/C5
Eildon (lake), Vic. 97/C5
Eileen (lake), 163/F3
Eileen, Ill. (†60416) 222/E2
Eilenburg, E. Ger. 22/E3
Eilerts de Haan (mts.), Sur. 131/C4
Eina, Norway 18/G6
'Einat, P.D.R. Yemen 59/E6
Einbeck, W. Ger. 22/C3
Eindhoven, Neth. 27/G6
'Ein Gedi (well), Israel 65/C5
'Ein Harod, Israel 65/C2
'Ein Netafim (well), Israel 65/D5
Einsiedeln, Switz. 39/G2
Eirunepé, Braz., 120/C3
Eirunepé, Braz. 132/G10
Eisenach, E. Ger. 22/D3
Eisenberg, E. Ger. 22/D3
Eisenerz, Austria 41/C3
Eisenhower (mt.), Alta. 182/C4
Eisenhüttenstadt, E. Ger. 22/F2
Eisenkappel, Austria 41/C3
Eisenstadt, Austria 41/D3
Eiserfeld, W. Ger. 22/C3
Eishort (inlet), Scot. 15/D5
Eisleben, E. Ger. 22/D3
Eisling (mts.), Lux. 27/H9
Eitzen, Minn. (55931) 254/G7
Ejby, Den. 21/D7
Ejea de los Caballeros, Spain 33/F1
Ejido, Ven. 124/C3
Ejstrup, Den. 21/C6
Ejutla de Crespo, Mex. 150/L8
Ekalaka, Mont. (59324) 262/M5
Ekenäs, Fin. 18/N6
Ekeren, Belg. 27/E6
Eketahuna, N.Z. 101/E4
Ekibastuz, U.S.S.R. 48/H4
Ekibin, Queens. 95/D3
Ekimchan, U.S.S.R. 48/O4
Ekin, Ind. (†46072) 227/E4
Eklutna, Alaska (†99645) 196/C1
Ekonk, Conn. (†06384) 210/H2
Ekron, Ky. (40117) 237/J5
Eksjö, Sweden 18/J8
Ekuk, Alaska (†99569) 196/G3
Ekwan (riv.), 163/H5
Ekwan (riv.), Ont. 175/C2
Ekwok, Alaska (99580) 196/G3
El Aaiún (cap.), Sp. Sahara 102/A2
El Aaiún (cap.), Sp. Sahara 106/B3
El Abbasiya, Sudan 111/F5
El Abiar, Libya 111/D1
El Abiod-Sidi-Cheikh, Alg. 106/E2
El Agheila, Libya 111/C1
Elaine, Ark. (72333) 203/J5
El 'Al, Jordan 65/D4
El 'Alamein, U.A.R. 59/A3
El 'Alamein, U.A.R. 111/E1
El Almacén, Ven. 124/G4
El Amparo de Apure, Ven. 124/C4
Elams, N.C. (†23919) 281/O1
Elamton, Ky. (41420) 237/P5
Elamville, Ala. (†36311) 194/G7
Eland, Wis. (54427) 317/H6
El Ángel, Ec. 128/C2
El Arahal, Spain 33/D4
El Arco, Mex. 150/C2
El 'Arish, U.A.R. 59/B3
El 'Arish, U.A.R. 111/F1
El Asiento, Bol. 136/B6
El Asnam, Alg. 106/E1
Elassón, Greece 45/F6
Elath, Israel 59/B4
Elath (Elat), Israel 65/D5
El Athale (Itala), Somalia 115/J3
Elato (atoll), Pac. Is., 87/E5
El 'Atrun (oasis), Sudan 111/E4
El 'Auja, Israel 65/D5
Elâziğ, Turkey 59/C2
Elâziğ (prov.), Turkey 63/H3
Elâziğ, Turkey 63/H3
El Azizia, Libya 111/B1
El Azúcar (res.), Mex. 150/K3
Elba, Ala. (36323) 194/F8
Elba, Idaho (83326) 220/E7
Elba (isl.), Italy, 7/E4
Elba (isl.), Italy 34/C3
Elba, Mich. (†48446) 250/F5
Elba, Minn. (†55910) 254/F6
Elba, N.Y. (14058) 276/D4
Elba, Nebr. (68835) 264/F3
Elba, Ohio (45728) 284/H6
El Bab, Syria 63/G4
El Balqa (dist.), Jordan 65/D4
El Banco, Col. 126/D3
El Barco, Spain 33/C1
El Barco de Ávila, Spain 33/D2
El Bardi, Libya 111/D1
El Barkat, Libya 111/B3
Elbasan, Alb. 45/E5
El Baúl, Ven. 124/D3
El Bawiti, U.A.R. 59/A4
El Bawiti, U.A.R. 111/E2
El Bayadh, Alg. 106/E2
Elbe (riv.), 7/F3
Elbe (riv.), E. Ger. 22/D2
Elbe (riv.), W. Ger. 22/C2
Elbe, Wash. (98330) 310/C4
El Beni (dept.), Bol. 136/C3
Elberfeld, Ind. (47613) 227/C8
Elberon, Iowa (52225) 229/J4
Elberon, N.J. (07740) 273/F3
Elberon, Va. (23846) 307/P6
Elbert (mt.), Colo., 188/E3
Elbert (co.), Colo. 208/L4
Elbert, Colo. (80106) 208/L4
Elbert (mt.), Colo. 208/G4
Elbert (co.), Ga. 216/G2
Elbert, Texas (76359) 302/E4
Elbert, W. Va. (24830) 313/C8
Elberta, Ala. (36530) 194/C10
Elberta, Ga. (†31093) 216/E5
Elberta, Mich. (49628) 250/C4
Elberta, Utah (84626) 304/B4
Elberton, Ga. (30635) 216/G2
Elberton, Wash. (†99130) 310/H4
Elbeuf, France 28/D3
Elbing, Kans. (67041) 232/E3
El Bira, Jordan 65/C4
Elbistan, Turkey 63/G3
Elbląg, Poland 47/D1
El Bolsón, Arg. 143/B5
Elbon, Pa. (†15823) 294/E3
El Bonillo, Spain 33/E3
El Boquerón (pass), Peru 128/E7
Elbow (riv.), Alta. 182/C4
Elbow (lake), Man. 179/G4
Elbow (lake), Minn. 254/C3
Elbow, Sask. 181/E4
Elbow Lake, Minn. (56531) 254/B5
Elbridge, N.Y. (13060) 276/G5
Elbridge, Tenn. (38227) 237/C8
El'brus (mt.), U.S.S.R. 52/F6
El'brus (mt.), U.S.S.R., 7/J4
El Bur, Somalia 115/J3
Elburg, Neth. 27/H4
El Burgo de Osma, Spain 33/E2
Elburn, Ill. (60119) 222/E2
Elburz (range), Iran 59/F2
Elburz (range), Iran 66/G2
El Cajon, Calif. (*92020) 204/J11
El Calafate, Arg. 143/B7
El Callao, Ven. 124/G4
El Calvario, Ven. 124/E3
El Cambio, Guat. 154/C2
El Campo, Texas (77437) 302/H8
El Carmen, El Beni, Bol. 136/D3
El Carmen, Santa Cruz, Bol. 136/F6
El Carmen, Ñuble, Chile 138/A11
El Carmen, O'Higgins, Chile 138/F5
El Carmen, Chocó, Col. 126/B5
El Carmen, Nariño, Col. 126/A6
El Carmen, Norte de Santander, Col. 126/D3
El Carmen, Mex. 150/O1
El Carmen, Ven. 124/E7
El Carmen de Bolívar, Col. 126/C3
El Carre, Eth. 111/H6
El Centro, Calif., 188/C4
El Centro, Calif. (92243) 204/K11
El Centro, Col. 126/D4
El Cercado, Dom. Rep. 158/D6
El Cerrito, Calif. (94530) 204/J2
El Cerrito, Col. 126/B6
El Cerro, Bol. 136/E5
El Chaparro, Ven. 124/F3
Elche, Spain 33/F3
Elche de la Sierra, Spain 33/E3
Elcho (isl.), Aust. 88/F2
Elcho (isl.), No. Terr. 93/D1
Elcho, Wis. (54428) 317/H5
El Chocón (res.), Arg. 143/C4
Elcho Island Mission, No. Terr. 93/D1
El Choro, Bol. 136/B6
El Chorro, Arg. 143/D1
Elco, Ill. (62929) 222/D6
Elco‡, Pa. (15434) 294/C5
El Cobre, Chile 138/A4
El Cocuy, Col. 126/D4
El Convento, Chile 138/F4
El Corazón, Ec. 128/C3
El Cristo, Ven. 124/G4
El Crucero, Mex. 150/D4
El Cuey, Dom. Rep. 158/F6
Elda, Spain 33/F3
El Dara, Ill. (62333) 222/B4
Elde (riv.), E. Ger. 22/D2
Elden (mt.), Ariz. 198/D3
El Der, Eth. 111/H6
Elderbank, N.S. 169/E4
El Dere, Somalia 115/J3
Elderon, Wis. (54429) 317/H6
Eldersburg, Md. (†21784) 245/L3
Eldersley, Sask. 181/H3
Elderslie, Scot. 15/C2
Eldersville, Pa. (15036) 294/A5
Elderton, Pa. (15736) 294/D4
El Desemboque, Mex. 150/C1
El Diente (peak), Colo. 208/C7
El'dikan, U.S.S.R. 48/O3
Eldivan, Turkey 63/E2
El Diviso, Col. 126/A7
El Djem, Tun. 106/G1
El Djezair (Algiers) (cap.), Alg. 106/E1
Eldon, Iowa (52554) 229/J7
Eldon, Mo. (65026) 261/G6
Eldon, Wash. (†98555) 310/B3
Eldora, Colo. (80437) 208/H3
Eldora, Iowa (50627) 229/G4
Eldora, N.J. (†08270) 273/D5
Eldorado, Arg. 143/F2
El Dorado, Ark., 188/H4
El Dorado, Ark. (71730) 203/E7
Eldorado, Braz. 135/B4
El Dorado (co.), Calif. 204/E5
El Dorado, Calif. (95623) 204/C8
Eldorado, Ill. (62930) 222/E6
Eldorado, Iowa (52175) 229/K2
El Dorado, Kans. (67042) 232/F4
Eldorado, Md. (†21659) 245/P6
El Dorado, Mex. 150/F4
Eldorado, Miss. (†39156) 256/C5
Eldorado, N.C. (†27371) 281/K4
Eldorado, Ohio (45321) 284/A6
Eldorado, Okla. (73537) 288/G6
Eldorado, Sask. 181/L2
Eldorado, Texas (76936) 302/D7
El Dorado, Ven. 124/H4
Eldorado, Wis. (54932) 317/J8
El Dorado Hills, Calif. (95630) 204/C8
El Dorado Springs, Mo. (64744) 261/E7
Eldorena, Alta. 182/D2
Eldorendo, Ga. (31717) 216/C8
Eldoret, Kenya 115/G3
Eldred, Ill. (62027) 222/C4
Eldred, Minn. (56532) 254/B3
Eldred, Pa. (16731) 294/F2
Eldridge, Ala. (35554) 194/C3
Eldridge, Iowa (52748) 229/M5
Eldridge, Mo. (65463) 261/G7
Eldridge, N. Dak. (58435) 283/N6
El Dulce Nombre, Hond. 154/E3
Eleanor, W. Va. (25070) 313/C5
El Ebano, Mex. 150/K5
Electra, Texas (76360) 302/F4
Electric (peak), Mont. 262/F6
Electric City, Wash. (99123) 310/F3
Electric Mills, Miss. (39329) 256/G5
Electron, Wash. (†98360) 310/C4
Eleele, Hawaii (96705) 218/C2
Elefantes (gulf), Chile 138/D6
Elek, Hung. 41/F3
El Empedrado, Ven. 124/C3
Elena, Bulg. 45/G4
El Encanto Heights‡, Calif. (†93017) 204/F9
Elephant (isl.), Ant. 5/D16
Elephant (riv.), S.W. Afr. 118/B5
Elephant (mt.), Texas 302/D12
Elephanta (isl.), India 68/B7
Elephant Butte (res.), N. Mex., 188/E4
Elephant Butte, N. Mex. (87935) 274/B5
Elephant Butte (res.), N. Mex. 274/B5
El Ergh, Libya 111/D2
Eleroy, Ill. (61027) 222/D1
Eleşkirt, Turkey 63/K3
El Espinar, Spain 33/D2
Eleuthera (isl.), Bah. Is., 146/L7
Eleuthera (isl.), Bah. Is. 156/C1
Eleva, Wis. (54738) 317/D6
Eleven Mile Canyon (res.), Colo. 208/H5
Elevtheroupolis, Greece 45/G5
El Faiyûm, 102/E2
El Faiyûm, U.A.R. 59/B4
El Faiyûm, U.A.R. 111/J3
El Fasher, 102/E3
El Fasher, Sudan 111/E5
El Fashn, U.A.R. 111/J4
El Ferrol, Spain, 7/D4
El Ferrol del Caudillo, Spain 33/B1
Elfers, Fla. (33531) 212/D3
El Fifi, Sudan 111/D5
Elfin Cove, Alaska (99825) 196/M1
El Fogaha, Libya 111/C2
Elfrida, Ariz. (†85617) 198/F7
Elfros, Sask. 181/H4
El Fuerte, Mex. 150/E3
El Furat (riv.), Syria 63/H4
El Gallo, Nic. 154/E4
El Gatrun, Libya 111/B3
El Gatrun, 102/D2
El Geteina, Sudan 59/B7
El Geteina, Sudan 111/F5
El Gezira, Libya 111/D2
Elgg, Switz. 39/G2
El Gheria esh Sherqia, Libya 111/B1
El Ghor (reg.), Jordan 65/C5
Elgin, Ariz. (†85637) 198/E7
Elgin, Ill., 188/J2
Elgin, Ill. (60120) 222/E1
Elgin, Iowa (52141) 229/K3
Elgin, Kans. (67361) 232/F4
Elgin, 10/E2
Elgin, Man. 179/B5
Elgin, Minn. (55932) 254/F6
Elgin, N. Br. 170/E3
Elgin, N. Dak. (58533) 283/G7
Elgin, Nebr. (68636) 264/F3
Elgin, Nev. (†89009) 266/G5
Elgin, Ohio (45838) 284/A4
Elgin, Okla. (73538) 288/K5
Elgin (co.), Ont. 177/C5
Elgin, Ont. 177/H3
Elgin, Oreg. (97827) 291/K2
Elgin, Pa. (16413) 294/C2
Elgin, S.C. (29045) 296/F3
Elgin, Scot. 15/K4
Elgin, Tenn. (37732) 237/M8
Elgin, Texas (78621) 302/G7
El Goléa, Alg. 106/E2
El Goléa, 102/C1
Elgon (mt.), Kenya 115/F3
Elgon (mt.), Uganda 115/F3
Elgon (mt.), 102/F4
Elgood, W. Va. (24723) 313/E8
El Granada, Calif. (94018) 204/H3
El Guapo, Ven. 124/F2
El Guayabo, Dom. Rep. 158/E5
El Hamad (des.), Iraq 59/D3
El Hammam, Syria 63/H5
El Hammam, U.A.R. 59/A3
El Hammam, U.A.R. 111/E1
El Hamurre, Somalia 115/J2
El Haseke, Syria 59/D2
El Haseke, Syria 63/J4
El Hilla, Sudan 111/E5
El Huecu, Arg. 143/B4
El Husn, Jordan 65/D3
Eli, Nebr. (69213) 264/C2
Elias, Ky. (40431) 237/O6
Elías Piña (prov.), Dom. Rep. 158/D5
Elías Piña, Dom. Rep. 158/C6
Elida, N. Mex. (88116) 274/F5
Elida, Ohio (45807) 284/B4
Elie, Man. 179/E5
Elie and Earlsferry, Scot. 15/L7
Elihu, Ky. (42530) 237/M6
Elijah, Mo. (65642) 261/H9
Elila, Dem. Rep. of the Congo. 115/E4
Elila (riv.), Dem. Rep. of the Congo. 115/E4
Elim, Alaska (99739) 196/F2
Elimsport, Pa. (†17810) 294/H3
El Indio, Texas (78860) 302/D9
Elin Pelin, Bulg. 45/F4
Eliot▲, Maine (03903) 242/B9
Eliot (mt.), Newf. 166/B2
Elisa, Arg. 143/F5
Eliska, Ala. (†36480) 194/C8
El Iskandariya (Alexandria), U.A.R. 59/A3
El Iskandariya (Alexandria), U.A.R. 111/J2
Elista, U.S.S.R. 48/E5
Elista, U.S.S.R. 52/F5
Elista, U.S.S.R., 7/J4
Eliza (mt.), Aust. 88/M7
Elizabeth, Ark. (72531) 203/F1
Elizabeth (reef), Aust. 88/K5
Elizabeth, Aust. 88/D7
Elizabeth, Colo. (80107) 208/K4
Elizabeth, Ga. (30060) 216/C2
Elizabeth, Ill. (61028) 222/C1
Elizabeth, Ind. (47117) 227/F8
Elizabeth, La. (70638) 238/E5
Elizabeth (cape), Maine 242/C8
Elizabeth (isls.), Mass. 249/L7
Elizabeth, Minn. (56533) 254/B4
Elizabeth, Miss. (38742) 256/C4
Elizabeth (mt.), N. Br. 170/D1
Elizabeth, N.J. (*07201) 273/D2
Elizabeth, S. Aust. 94/B7
Elizabeth, Pa. (15037) 294/C5
Elizabeth, W. Va. (26143) 313/D4
Elizabeth City, N.C. (27909) 281/S2
Elizabethton, Tenn. (37643) 237/S8
Elizabethtown, Ill. (62931) 222/E6
Elizabethtown, Ind. (47232) 227/F6
Elizabethtown, Ky. (42701) 237/K5
Elizabethtown, N.C. (28337) 281/M5
Elizabethtown, N.Y. (12932) 276/N2
Elizabethtown, Ohio (†45052) 284/A9
Elizabethtown, Pa. (17022) 294/J5
Elizabethville, Pa. (17023) 294/J4
Elizaville, Ind. (†46052) 227/E4
Elizaville, Ky. (41037) 237/O4
Elizondo, Spain 33/F1
El Jadida, 102/B1
El Jadida, Mor. 106/C2
El Jauf, Libya 111/D3
El Jauf, 102/E2
El Jicaral, Nic. 154/D4
El Jícaro, Nic. 154/E4
Elk (riv.), Ala. 194/D1
Elk (riv.), Br. Col. 184/K5
Elk, Calif. (95432) 204/B4
Elk (riv.), Colo. 208/F1
Elk (co.), Kans. 232/F4
Elk (riv.), Kans. 232/F4
Elk (isl.), Man. 179/F4
Elk (riv.), Md. 245/P3
Elk (lake), Mich. 250/D4
Elk, N. Mex. (†88210) 274/D6
Elk (creek), Okla. 288/H4
Elk (creek), Oreg. 291/E5
Elk (co.), Pa. 294/E3
Ełk, Poland 47/F2
Elk (creek), S. Dak. 298/C5
Elk (riv.), Tenn. 237/H10
Elk (ridge), Utah 304/E6
Elk (riv.), W. Va. 313/D6
Elk, Wash. (99009) 310/H2
Elk, Wyo. (†83013) 319/B2
Elkader, Iowa (52043) 229/L3
El Kamlin, Sudan 59/B7
El Karak, Jordan 59/C3
El Karak (dist.), Jordan 65/E5
El Karak, Jordan 65/E4
El Karnak, U.A.R. 59/B4
El Karnak, U.A.R. 111/F2
Elkatawa, Ky. (41322) 237/P5
Elk City, Idaho (83525) 220/C4
Elk City, Kans. (67344) 232/G4
Elk City (res.), Kans. 232/F4
Elk City, Okla. (73644) 288/G4
Elk City, Oreg. (†97391) 291/D3
Elk Creek, Calif. (95939) 204/C4
Elk Creek, Ky. (†40071) 237/L4
Elk Creek, Mo. (65464) 261/H8
Elk Creek, Nebr. (68348) 264/H4
Elk Creek, Va. (24326) 307/F7
Elk Creek, Wis. (†54747) 317/C7
El Kef, Tun. 106/F1
El Kelâa des Srarhna, Mor. 106/C2
Elk Falls, Kans. (67345) 232/F4
Elkfork, Ky. (41421) 237/P5
Elk Garden, Va. (†24266) 307/E7
Elk Garden, W. Va. (26717) 313/H4
Elk Grove, Calif. (95624) 204/B9
Elk Grove Village, Ill. (60007) 222/A1
El Khalil (Hebron), Jordan 65/C4
El Khandaq, Sudan 59/B6
El Khandaq, Sudan 111/E4
El Khârga, 102/E2
El Khârga, U.A.R. 59/B4
El Khârga, U.A.R. 111/F2
Elkhart, Ill. (62634) 222/D3
Elkhart, Ind., 188/J2
Elkhart (co.), Ind. 227/F1
Elkhart, Ind. (46514) 227/F1
Elkhart (riv.), Ind. 227/F1
Elkhart, Iowa (50073) 229/F5
Elkhart, Kans. (67950) 232/A4
Elkhart, Texas (75839) 302/J6
Elkhart Lake, Wis. (53020) 317/L8
Elkhead, Mo. (65753) 261/G8
Elk Hill, Sask. 181/G2
Elk Horn, Iowa (51531) 229/C5
Elkhorn, Man. 179/A5
Elkhorn, Nebr. (68022) 264/H3
Elkhorn (riv.), Nebr. 264/G3
Elkhorn, W. Va. (24831) 313/D8
Elkhorn, Wis. (53121) 317/J10
Elkhorn City, Ky. (41522) 237/S6
Elkhovo, Bulg. 45/H4
Elkhurst, W. Va. (†25043) 313/D6
Elkin, N.C. (28621) 281/H2
Elkins, Ark. (72727) 203/C1
Elkins, N. Mex. (88117) 274/E5
Elkins, W. Va. (26241) 313/G5
Elkinsville, Ind. (†47448) 227/E6
Elk Island Nat'l Park, 163/E5
Elk Island Nat'l Park, Alta. 182/D3
El Kitta, Jordan 65/D3
Elk Lake, Ont. 175/D3
Elk Lake, Ont. 177/K5
Elkland, Mo. (65644) 261/F8
Elkland, Pa. (16920) 294/H1
Elk Mills, Md. (21920) 245/P2
Elkmont, Ala. (35620) 194/E1
Elkmont, Tenn. (†37862) 237/O9
Elk Mound, Wis. (54739) 317/C6
Elk Mountain, Wyo. (82324) 319/F4
Elk Neck, Md. (†21901) 245/P2
Elko, Br. Col. 184/K5
Elko, Ga. (31025) 216/E6
Elko, Minn. (55020) 254/E6
Elko, Nev., 146/G5
Elko, Nev., 188/C2
Elko (co.), Nev. 266/F1
Elko, Nev. (89801) 266/F2
Elko, S.C. (29826) 296/E5
Elk Park, Mont. (†59701) 262/D4
Elk Park, N.C. (28622) 281/F2
Elk Point, Alta. 182/E3
Elk Point, S. Dak. (57025) 298/R8
Elkport, Iowa (52044) 229/L3
Elk Ranch, Man. 179/C4
Elk Rapids, Mich. (49629) 250/D4
Elkridge, Md. (21227) 245/M4
Elkridge, W. Va. (†24868) 313/D6
Elk River, Idaho (83827) 220/B3
Elk River, Minn. (55330) 254/E5
Elk Run Heights, Iowa (†50700) 229/J4
Elk Springs, Colo. (81633) 208/C2
Elkton, Alta. 182/C4
Elkton, Fla. (32033) 212/E2
Elkton, Ky. (42220) 237/G7
Elkton, Md. (21921) 245/P2
Elkton, Mich. (48731) 250/F5
Elkton, Minn. (55933) 254/F7
Elkton, Mo. (†65650) 261/F7
Elkton, Oreg. (97436) 291/D4
Elkton, S. Dak. (57026) 298/S5
Elkton, Tenn. (38455) 237/H10
Elkton, Va. (22827) 307/L4
Elk Valley, Tenn. (37734) 237/N7
Elkview, W. Va. (25071) 313/C6
Elkville, Ill. (62932) 222/D6
Elkwater, Alta. 182/E5
Elkwater, W. Va. (†26273) 313/G5
Ellabell, Ga. (31308) 216/K6
El Ladhiqiya (Latakia), Syria 59/C2
El Ladhiqiya (Latakia), Syria 63/F5
Ellamar, Alaska (†99677) 196/D1
Ellamore, W. Va. (26267) 313/F5
Ellaville, Fla. (†32060) 212/C1
Ellaville, Ga. (31806) 216/D6
Ellef Ringnes (isl.), 163/M3
Ellef Ringnes (isl.), Canada, 4/B15
Ellef Ringnes (isl.), N.W.T. 187/H2
Ellen (mt.), Utah 304/D5
Ellen (mt.), Vt. 268/B3
Ellenboro, N.C. (28040) 281/F4
Ellenboro, W. Va. (26346) 313/D4
Ellenboro, Wis. (†53813) 317/E10
Ellenburg Center, N.Y. (12934) 276/N1
Ellenburg Depot, N.Y. (12935) 276/N1
Ellendale, Del. (19941) 245/S5
Ellendale, Minn. (56026) 254/E7
Ellendale, N. Dak. (58436) 283/N7
Ellendale, W. Aust. 92/D2
Ellendale, Tenn. (38029) 237/B10
Ellensburg, Wash. (98926) 310/E3
Ellenton‡, Fla. (33532) 212/D4
Ellenton, Ga. (31747) 216/E8
Ellenville, N.Y. (12428) 276/M7
Ellerbe, N.C. (28338) 281/K4
Ellershouse, N.S. 169/D4
Ellerslie, Ga. (31807) 216/C5
Ellerslie, Md. (21529) 245/C2
Ellerslie, N.Z. 101/C1
Ellerslie, P.E.I. 169/D2
Ellerton, Barb. 161/B9
Ellerton, Md. (†21773) 245/H2
Ellery, Ill. (62833) 222/E5
Ellesmere (isl.), 163/N3
Ellesmere (isl.), Canada, 3/F1
Ellesmere (isl.), Canada, 4/B14
Ellesmere, Eng. 13/E5
Ellesmere (isl.), N.W.T., 146/K2
Ellesmere (isl.), N.W.T. 187/K2
Ellesmere (lake), N.Z. 101/D5
Ellesmere Port, 10/F2
Ellesmere Port, Eng. 13/E4
Ellettsville, Ind. (47429) 227/D6
Ellezelles, Belg. 27/D7
Ellice (isls.), 3/T6
Ellice (isls.), Gilb. and Ell., 87/H6
Ellice (riv.), N.W.T. 187/H3
Ellicott City, Md. (21043) 245/L3
Ellicottville, N.Y. (14731) 276/C6
Ellijay, Ga. (30540) 216/C1
El Limón, Nic. 154/E4
Ellington▲, Conn. (06029) 210/F1
Ellington, Mo. (63638) 261/L8
Ellington, N.Y. (14732) 276/B6
Ellington A.F.B., Texas 302/K2
Ellinwood, Kans. (67526) 232/D3
Elliot (lake), Man. 179/G2
Elliot, S. Africa 118/D6
Elliot Lake, Ont. 175/D3
Elliot Lake, Ont. 177/B1
Elliott, Ark. (†71701) 203/E7
Elliott (key), Fla. 212/F6
Elliott, Ill. (60933) 222/E3
Elliott, Iowa (51532) 229/C6
Elliott (co.), Ky. 237/P4
Elliott, Md. (21823) 245/P7
Elliott, Miss. (38926) 256/E3
Elliott, N. Dak. (58025) 283/P7
Elliott, No. Terr. 93/C4
Elliott, S.C. (29046) 296/G3
Elliottsburg, Pa. (17024) 294/H5
Elliottville, Ky. (40317) 237/P4
Ellis, Idaho (83235) 220/D5
Ellis (co.), Kans. 232/C3
Ellis, Kans. (67637) 232/C3
Ellis (pond), Maine 242/B6
Ellis (riv.), Maine 242/B6
Ellis (riv.), N.H. 268/E3
Ellis (co.), Okla. 288/G2
Ellis (co.), Texas 302/H5
El Lisan (pen.), Jordan 65/C5
Ellisboro, Sask. 181/H5
Ellisburg, N.Y. (13636) 276/H3
Ellisgrove, Ill. (62241) 222/D5
Ellison Bay, Wis. (54210) 317/M5
Elliston, Aust. 88/F6
Elliston, Mont. (59728) 262/D4
Elliston, Newf. 166/D2
Elliston, S. Aust. 94/D5
Elliston, Ohio (43415) 284/D2
Elliston, Va. (24087) 307/H6
Ellisville, Ill. (61431) 222/C3
Ellisville, Miss. (39437) 256/F7
Ellisville, Mo. (63011) 261/N3
Ellisville, Wis. (†54217) 317/L7
Ellon, 10/E2
Ellon, Scot. 15/M5
Elloree, S.C. (29047) 296/F4
Ellport‡, Pa. (16117) 294/B4
Ells (riv.), Alta. 182/D1
Ellscott, Alta. 182/D2
Ellsinore, Mo. (63937) 261/L9
Ellston, Iowa (50074) 229/E7
Ellsworth (hill), Conn. 210/B1
Ellsworth, Ill. (61737) 222/E3
Ellsworth, Iowa (50075) 229/F4
Ellsworth (co.), Kans. 232/D3
Ellsworth, Kans. (67439) 232/D3
Ellsworth, Maine (04605) 242/F6
Ellsworth, Mich. (49729) 250/D3
Ellsworth, Minn. (56129) 254/C7
Ellsworth▲, N.H. (†03264) 268/D4
Ellsworth, N.H. (†03264) 268/D4
Ellsworth, Nebr. (69340) 264/B2
Ellsworth (lake), Okla. 288/K5
Ellsworth, Pa. (15331) 294/B5
Ellsworth, Wis. (54011) 317/A6
Ellsworth A.F.B., S. Dak. 298/C5
Ellsworth Land (reg.), Ant. 5/B14
Ellwangen, W. Ger. 22/D4
Ellwood City, Pa. (16117) 294/B4
Elm (riv.), N. Dak. 283/N8
Elm (riv.), N. Dak. 283/R5
Elm (creek), S. Dak. 298/O4
Elm (riv.), S. Dak. 298/M2
Elm, Switz. 39/H3
Elma, Iowa (50628) 229/J2
Elma, Man. 179/G5
Elma, N.Y. (14059) 276/C5
Elma, Wash. (98541) 310/B4
El Macao, Dom. Rep. 158/F6
El Madwar, Jordan 65/E3
El Mafraq, Jordan 65/E3
El Mahalla el Kubra, U.A.R. 111/J3
El Maitén, Arg. 143/B5
El Majdal, Jordan 65/D3
Elmali, Turkey 63/C4
El Mansûra, U.A.R. 59/B3
El Mansûra, U.A.R. 111/K3
El Manteco, Ven. 124/G4
El Manzano, Chile 138/F5
El Marj, Libya 111/D1
El Marmol, Mex. 150/B2
Elm City, N.C. (27822) 281/O3
Elm Creek, Man. 179/E5
Elm Creek, Nebr. (68836) 264/E4
Elmdale, Kans. (66850) 232/F3
Elmdale, Minn. (†56314) 254/D5
Elmendorf, Texas (78112) 302/F8
Elmendorf A.F.B., Alaska 196/B1
Elmer, La. (71424) 238/E4
Elmer, Minn. (55730) 254/F3
Elmer, Mo. (63538) 261/G3
Elmer, N.J. (08318) 273/C4
Elmer, Okla. (73539) 288/H6
Elmer City, Wash. (99124) 310/G2
Elm Fork, Trinity (riv.), Texas 302/G1
Elm Grove, La. (†71051) 238/C2
Elm Grove, Wis. (53122) 317/K1
Elmhurst, Ill. (60126) 222/A2
Elmhurst, Pa. (18416) 294/M3
Elmhurst, Sask. 181/C2
El Miamo, Ven. 124/H4
Elmina, Ghana 106/D8
El Minya, 102/E2
El Minya, U.A.R. 59/B4
El Minya, U.A.R. 111/J4
Elmira, Ont. 177/D4
Elmira, Ill. (†61483) 222/D2
Elmira, Mich. (49730) 250/E3
Elmira, Mo. (†64062) 261/D3
Elmira, N.Y., 188/L2
Elmira, N.Y. (*14901) 276/G6
Elmira, Oreg. (97437) 291/D3
Elmira, P.E.I. 169/F2
Elmira, W. Va. (26618) 313/E5
El Mirage, Ariz. (85335) 198/C5
Elmira Heights, N.Y. (14903) 276/G6

360 El Misti

El Misti (mt.), Peru 128/G11
Elmo, Kans. (†67451) 232/E3
Elmo, Mo. (64445) 261/B1
Elmo, Mont. (59915) 262/B3
Elmo, Texas (75118) 302/H5
Elmo, Utah (84521) 304/D4
Elmo, Wyo. (†82327) 319/F4
Elmodel, Ga. (31748) 216/D8
Elmont, Kans. (†66603) 232/G2
Elmont, N.Y. (11003) 276/R7
El Monte, Calif. (*91731) 204/D10
El Monte, Chile 138/G4
Elmora, Pa. (15737) 294/E4
Elmore (co.), Ala. 194/F5
Elmore, Ala. (36025) 194/F5
Elmore (co.), Idaho 220/C6
Elmore, Minn. (56027) 254/D7
Elmore, Ohio (43416) 284/D3
Elmore City, Okla. (73035) 288/M5
El Morro, N. Mex. (†87321) 274/A3
El Morro Nat'l Mon., N. Mex. 274/A3
Elm Park, La. (†70775) 238/H5
El-Mraiti (well), Mali 106/D5
El Mrayer (well), Mauritania 106/C4
El Mreïti (well), Mauritania 106/C4
Elmrock, Ky. (41624) 237/P6
Elmsdale, N.S. 169/E4
Elmsdale, P.E.I. 169/D2
Elmsford, N.Y. (10523) 276/P6
Elmshorn, W. Ger. 22/C2
Elm Springs, Ark. (72728) 203/B1
Elm Springs, S. Dak. (57736) 298/D5
Elm Springs, Sask. 181/F6
Elmsvale, N.S. 169/E3
Elmvale, Ont. 177/E3
Elmville, Conn. (†06239) 210/H1
Elmwood, Conn. (06110) 210/D2
Elmwood, Ont. 177/C3
Elmwood, Ill. (61529) 222/D3
Elmwood, Mass. (02337) 249/L4
Elmwood, N. Br. 170/C2
Elmwood, N.C. (†28677) 281/H3
Elmwood, Nebr. (68349) 264/H4
Elmwood, Okla. (73935) 288/F1
Elmwood, Wis. (54740) 317/B6
Elmwood Park, Ill. (60635) 222/B2
Elmwood Park, Wis. (†53401) 317/M3
Elmwood Place, Ohio (45216) 284/B9
Elmworth, Alta. 182/A2
Elne, France 28/E6
El Nido, Calif. (95317) 204/E6
El Nido, Phil. 82/B5
El Ñilhue, Chile 138/G2
Elnora, Alta. 182/D3
Elnora, Ind. (47529) 227/C7
El Obeid, 102/E3
El Obeid, Sudan 59/B7
El Obeid, Sudan 111/E5
Elobey (isls.), Eq. Guin. 115/A3
El Odaiya, Sudan 111/E5
Eloff, S. Africa 118/J6
Eloi (bay), La. 238/M7
Eloise‡, Fla. (33880) 212/E4
Elon, Ala. (†35760) 194/F1
Elon College, N.C. (27244) 281/L2
Elora, Ont. 177/D4
Elora, Tenn. (37328) 237/J10
El Oro (prov.), Ec. 128/C4
El Oro, Mex. 150/G4
El Oro de Hidalgo, Mex. 150/K7
Elortondo, Arg. 143/F6
Elorza, Ven. 124/D4
El Oso, Ven. 124/H5
El Oued, Alg. 106/F2
Eloy, Ariz. (85231) 198/D6
El Pájaro, Col. 126/D2
El Palmar, Chuquisaca, Bol. 136/D7
El Palmar, Santa Cruz, Bol. 136/D5
El Palmar, Tarija, Bol. 136/D7
El Palmar, Ven. 124/G4
El Pao, Anzoátegui, Ven. 124/F3
El Pao, Bolívar, Ven. 124/G3
El Pao, Cojedes, Ven. 124/D3
El Paraíso, Col. 126/C7
El Paraíso, Copán, Hond. 154/C3
El Paraíso, El Paraíso, Hond. 154/D4
El Pardo, Spain 33/F4
El Paso, Ark. (72045) 203/F3
El Paso (co.), Colo. 208/K5
El Paso, Ill. (61738) 222/D3
El Paso, Texas, 146/H6
El Paso, Texas, 188/E4
El Paso (co.), Texas 302/A10
El Paso, Texas (*79901) 302/A10
El Paso, U.S., 3/D4
El Pato, Col. 126/C6
El Perú, Bol. 136/B3
El Perú, Ven. 124/H4
Elphin, Ire. 17/E4
Elphinstone, Man. 179/B4
Elphinstone (isl.), Burma 72/C4
El Pilar, Cuba 158/G3
El Pilar, Ven. 124/G2
El Pintado, Arg. 143/D1
El Piquete, Arg. 143/D1
El Portal, Calif. (95318) 204/F6
El Portal, Fla. (†33101) 212/B4
El Portugués, Peru 128/C7
El Porvenir, Guat. 154/B2
El Porvenir, Hond. 154/D3
El Porvenir, N. Mex. (†87731) 274/D3
El Potosí, Mex. 150/J4
El Pozo, Dom. Rep. 158/E5
El Prado, N. Mex. (87529) 274/D2
El Progreso, Ec. 128/C9
El Progreso, Guat. 154/B3
El Progreso, Hond. 154/D3
El Puente, Santa Cruz, Bol. 136/D5
El Puente, Tarija, Bol. 136/C7
El Puerto de Santa María, Spain 33/C4
El Pun, Ec. 128/D2
El Qadmus, Syria 63/F5
El Qâhira (Cairo) (cap.), U.A.R. 59/B4
El Qâhira (Cairo) (cap.), U.A.R. 111/J3
El Qantara, U.A.R. 59/B3
El Qantara, U.A.R. 111/K3
El Qaryatein, Syria 63/G5
El Qasr, U.A.R. 59/A4
El Qasr, U.A.R. 111/E2
El Quebrachal, Arg. 143/D2
Elqui (riv.), Chile 138/A8
El Quisco, Chile 138/E3
El Quneitra (prov.), Syria 63/F6
El Quneitra, Syria 63/F6
El Quseir, Syria 63/G5
El Quseir, 102/F2
El Quseir, U.A.R. 59/B4
El Quseir, U.A.R. 111/F2
El Quweira, Jordan 65/E5
Elrama, Pa. (15038) 294/C5
El Ranchero Village-Golf Lake Estates‡, Fla. (†33558) 212/D4
El Rashid, Syria 59/C2
El Rashid, Syria 63/H5
El Rastro, Ven. 124/E3
El Real, Pan. 154/J6
El Reno, Okla. (73036) 288/K3
El Rio, Calif. (93030) 204/F9
El Rito, N. Mex. (87530) 274/C2
El Rito (riv.), N. Mex. 274/C2
Elrod, Ala. (35458) 194/C4
Elrod, Ind. (†47018) 227/G6
El Roque, Ven. 124/E2
Elrosa, Minn. (56325) 254/C5
El Rosario, Estero (riv.), Chile 138/F3
Elrose, Sask. 181/D4
Elroy, Wis. (53929) 317/F8
Elsa, Texas (78543) 302/G11
Elsa, Yukon 187/E3
Elsah, Ill. (62028) 222/C5
El Salado, Dom. Rep. 158/F6
El Salto, Mex. 150/G5
El Salvador, 3/E5
El Salvador, 146/J8
EL SALVADOR, 154/C4
El Salvador, C. Rica 154/F5
El Samán de Apure, Ven. 124/D4
El Sauce, Nic. 154/D4
Elsberry, Mo. (63343) 261/L4
El Segundo, Calif. (90245) 204/B11
El Seibo (prov.), Dom. Rep. 158/F6
El Seibo, Dom. Rep. 158/F6
Elsey, Mo. (†65633) 261/E9
Elsie, Mich. (48831) 250/E5
Elsie, Nebr. (69134) 264/C4
Elsie, Oreg. (†97138) 291/D2
Elsinore, Calif. (92330) 204/F11
Elsinore (lake), Calif. 204/E11
Elsinore (Helsingør), Den. 18/H8
Elsinore (Helsingør), Den. 21/F6
Elsinore, Utah (84724) 304/B5
Elsmere, Del. (†19801) 245/R2
Elsmere, Ky. (†41018) 237/R3
Elsmere, Nebr. (69135) 264/D2
Elsmore, Kans. (66732) 232/G4
El Socorro, Ven. 124/F3
El Sombrero, Ven. 124/E3
Elst, Neth. 27/H5
Elster, Black (riv.), E. Ger. 22/E3
Elster, White (riv.), E. Ger. 22/E3
Elston, Ind. (†47901) 227/D4
Elston, Mo. (65029) 261/H5
Elstow, Sask. 181/E4
El Tabo, Chile 138/F3
El Tambo, Col. 126/B6
El Teleno (mt.), Spain 33/C1
Eltham, N.Z. 101/E3
Eltham, Vic. 97/J4
El Tiemblo, Spain 33/D2
El Tigre, Ven. 124/F3
El Tocuyo, Ven. 124/C3
El Tofo, Chile 138/A7
El'ton, U.S.S.R. 52/G5
Elton, La. (70532) 238/E6
Elton, W. Va. (25965) 313/E7
Elton, Wis. (54430) 317/J5
Eltopia, Wash. (99330) 310/G4
El Toro, Calif. (92630) 204/E11
El Toro (mt.), P. Rico 161/F2
El Toro, Ven. 124/H3
El Toro Marine Air Sta., Calif. 204/D11
El Tránsito, Chile 138/B7
El Triunfo, Hond. 154/D4
El Tucuche (mt.), Trinidad Tobago 161/B10
El Tûr, U.A.R. 59/B4
El Tûr, U.A.R. 111/F2
El Turbio, Arg., 120/C8
Eluru, India 68/E5
Elva, Man. 179/A5
Elva, U.S.S.R. 53/D1
El Vado, N. Mex. (†87575) 274/C2
Elvanfoot, Scot. 15/J9
Elvas, Port. 33/C3
Elvaston, Ill. (62334) 222/B3
El Verano‡, Calif. (95433) 204/C5
Elverson, Pa. (19520) 294/L5
Elverum, Norway 18/G6
El Viejo, Nic. 154/D4
El Vigía, Ven. 124/C3
El Vínculo, Ven. 124/D1
Elvins, Mo. (63639) 261/L7
Elvira, Iowa (†52732) 229/N5
Elvira (isl.), N.W.T. 187/H2
El Volcán, Chile 138/B10
El Wak, Kenya 115/H3
El War (well), Niger 106/G4
El Wasta, U.A.R. 111/J3
Elwell, Mich. (48832) 250/E5
Elwha (riv.), Wash. 310/B3
Elwood, Ill. (60421) 222/E2
Elwood, Ind. (46036) 227/F4
Elwood, Iowa (52226) 229/M4
Elwood, Kans. (66024) 232/H2
Elwood, N.J. (08217) 273/D4
Elwood‡, N.Y. (11731) 276/O9
Elwood, Nebr. (68937) 264/E4
Elwood, Utah (†84337) 304/B2
Ely, 10/G4
Ely, Eng. 13/H5
Ely, Iowa (52227) 229/K5
Ely, Minn. (55731) 254/G3
Ely, Nev., 188/D3
Ely, Nev. (89301) 266/G3
Ely (range), Nev. 266/G4
Ely, Vt. (05044) 268/C4
El Yaduda, Jordan 65/D4
El Yagual, Ven. 124/D4
Elyakim, Israel 65/C2
Elyashiv, Israel 65/B3
Elyria, Kans. (†67460) 232/E3
Elyria, Nebr. (68837) 264/E3
Elyria, Ohio (*44035) 284/F3
Elysburg, Pa. (17824) 294/K4
Elysian, Minn. (56028) 254/E6
Elysian Fields, Texas (75642) 302/L5
Elysian Grove, Tenn. (†37185) 237/F8
El Yunque (mt.), P. Rico 161/F1
Elze, W. Ger. 22/C2
Emådalen, Sweden 18/J6
Emanguk (Emmonak), Alaska (99581) 196/E2
Emanuel (co.), Ga. 216/H5
Emba (riv.), U.S.S.R. 48/F5
Embarcación, Arg., 120/D5
Embarcación, Arg. 143/D1
Embarras (riv.), Ill. 222/E4
Embarras Portage, Alta. 182/C5
Embarrass, Minn. (55732) 254/F3
Embarrass, Wis. (54933) 317/J6
Embden (pond), Maine 242/D6
Embden, N. Dak. (†58079) 283/R6
Emblem, Wyo. (82422) 319/D1
Emboscada, Par. 144/B6
Embreeville, Pa. (†19320) 294/L6
Embreeville Junction, Tenn. (†37601) 237/R8
Embro, Ont. 177/C4
Embrun, Ont. 177/J2
Embrun, France 28/G5
Embu, Kenya 115/G4
Embudo, N. Mex. (87531) 274/C2
Emden, Ill. (62635) 222/D3
Emden, Mo. (63439) 261/J3
Emden, W. Ger. 22/B2
Emeigh, Pa. (15738) 294/E4
Emelle, Ala. (35459) 194/B5
Emerado, N. Dak. (58228) 283/R4
Emerald, Aust. 88/H4
Emerald (isl.), N.W.T. 187/G2
Emerald, Queens. 95/C4
Emerald, Wis. (54012) 317/B5
Emerald Isle, N.C. (†28557) 281/P5
Emero (riv.), Bol. 136/B3
Emerson, 163/G6
Emerson, Ark. (71740) 203/D7
Emerson, Ga. (30137) 216/C2
Emerson, Iowa (51533) 229/C6
Emerson, Man. 179/E5
Emerson, N.C. (28437) 281/M6
Emerson, N.J. (07630) 273/B1
Emerson, Nebr. (68733) 264/H2
Emery, S. Dak. (57332) 298/O6
Emery (co.), Utah 304/D4
Emery, Utah (84522) 304/C5
Emery Mills, Maine (04031) 242/B8
Emeryville, Calif. (94608) 204/J2
Emet, Turkey 63/C3
Emhouse‡, Texas (75110) 302/H5
Emida, Idaho (83828) 220/B2
Emigrant, Mont. (59027) 262/F5
Emigrant (peak), Mont. 262/F5
Emigrant (peak), Nev. 266/C5
Emigsville, Pa. (17318) 294/J5
Emi Koussi (mt.), Chad 111/C4
Emi Koussi (mt.), 102/D3
Emilia-Romagna (reg.), Italy 34/C2
Emilio Ayarza, Arg. 143/F7
Emily, Minn. (56447) 254/E4
Emily (lake), Minn. 254/C5
Emine (cape), Bulg. 45/J4
Eminence, Ind. (46125) 227/D5
Eminence, Ky. (40019) 237/L4
Eminence, Mo. (65466) 261/K8
Emington, Ill. (60934) 222/E3
Emirdağ, Turkey 63/D3
Emirgazi, Turkey 63/E4
Emiroğlu Tepesi (mt.), Turkey 59/B2
Emiroğlu Tepesi (mt.), Turkey 63/D3
Emison, Ind. (47530) 227/C7
Emlenton, Pa. (16373) 294/C3
Emlyn, Ky. (40730) 237/N7
Emma, Ill. (62834) 222/E6
Emma, Ind. (†46571) 227/F1
Emma, Ky. (41625) 237/R5
Emma, Mo. (65327) 261/F5
Emma (range), Sur. 131/C4
Emmaboda, Sweden 18/J8
Emma Lake, Sask. 181/F2
Emmalane, Ga. (†30442) 216/H5
Emmastad, Neth. Ant. 161/F9
Emmaus, V.I.(U.S.) 161/C4
Emmaus, Pa. (18049) 294/M4
Emmaville, N.S.W. 97/F1
Emmeloord, Neth. 27/H3
Emmen, Neth. 27/K3
Emmen, Switz. 39/F2
Emmendingen, W. Ger. 22/B4
Emmental (riv.), Switz. 39/E3
Emmerich, W. Ger. 22/B3
Emmet, Ark. (71835) 203/D6
Emmet (co.), Iowa 229/D2
Emmet (co.), Mich. 250/E3
Emmet, N. Dak. (58534) 283/G4
Emmet, Nebr. (68734) 264/F2
Emmet, Queens. 95/C5
Emmetsburg, Iowa (50536) 229/D2
Emmett, Idaho (83617) 220/B6
Emmett, Kans. (66422) 232/F2
Emmett, Mich. (48022) 250/G6
Emmitsburg, Md. (21727) 245/J2
Emmonak, Alaska (99581) 196/E2
Emmons, Minn. (56029) 254/E7
Emmons (co.), N. Dak. 283/K7
Emmons (mt.), Utah 304/D3
Emo, Ont. 175/B3
Emo, Ont. 177/F5
Emőd, Hung. 41/F3
Emory (riv.), Tenn. 237/M8
Emory, Texas (75440) 302/J5
Emory (peak), Texas 302/A8
Emory, Va. (24327) 307/E7
Emory Gap, Tenn. (37735) 237/M9
Emoryville, W. Va. (26717) 313/H4
Empalme, Mex. 150/D2
Empalme Olmos, Urug. 145/B6
Empangeni, S. Africa 118/E5
Empedrado, Arg. 143/E2
Empedrado, Chile 138/A11
Empexa (salt dep.), Bol. 136/A7
Empire, Ala. (35063) 194/D3
Empire, Calif. (95319) 204/D6
Empire, Colo. (80438) 208/H3
Empire (res.), Colo. 208/L2
Empire, Ga. (31026) 216/F6
Empire, La. (70050) 238/L8
Empire, Mich. (49630) 250/C4
Empire, Ohio (43926) 284/J5
Empire, Okla. (†73529) 288/K6
Empoli, Italy 34/C3
Emporia, Fla. (†32080) 212/E2
Emporia, Ind. (†46056) 227/F5
Emporia, Kans., 188/G3
Emporia, Kans. (66801) 232/F3
Emporia, Va. (23847) 307/N7
Emporium, Pa. (15834) 294/F2
Empress, Alta. 182/E4
Emrick, N. Dak. (58437) 283/L4
Ems (riv.), W. Ger. 22/B2
Emsdale, Ont. 177/E2
Emsworth, Pa. (15202) 294/B6
Emu (creek), Aust. 88/L6
Emyvale, Ire. 17/G3
Enard (bay), Scot. 15/F3
Enarotali, Indon. 85/K6
Enaville, Idaho (83829) 220/B2
Encampment, Wyo. (82325) 319/F4
Encampment (riv.), Wyo. 319/F4
Encarnación, Par., 120/E5
Encarnación, Par. 144/E6
Encarnación de Díaz, Mex. 150/H6
Enchant, Alta. 182/D4
Encinal, Texas (78019) 302/E9
Encinitas, Calif. (92024) 204/H10
Encino, Calif. (91316) 204/B10
Encino, N. Mex. (87531) 274/D4
Encino, Texas (78353) 302/F11
Enciso, Col. 126/E7
Encontrados, Ven. 124/B3
Encounter (bay), Aust. 88/F7
Encounter (bay), S. Aust. 94/F6
Encrucijada, Cuba 158/E1
Endako, Br. Col. 184/E3
Endcliffe, Man. 179/A4
Endeavor, Pa. (16322) 294/D2
Endeavor, Wis. (53930) 317/G8
Endeavour (str.), Aust. 88/G2
Endeavour (str.), Queens. 95/B1
Endeavour, Sask. 181/J3
Endee, N. Mex. (†88411) 274/F3
Endeh, Indon. 85/G7
Endelave (isl.), Den. 21/D6
Enderbury (isl.), Gilb. and Ell., 87/J6
Enderby, Br. Col. 184/H5
Enderby Land (reg.), Ant., 3/M9
Enderby Land (reg.), Ant. 5/B3
Enderlin, N. Dak. (58027) 283/P6
Enders, Nebr. (69027) 264/C4
Enders (res.), Nebr. 264/C4
Endiang, Alta. 182/D4
Endicott (mts.), Alaska 196/H1
Endicott, N.Y. (13760) 276/H6
Endicott, Nebr. (68350) 264/G4
Endicott, S. Africa 118/J6
Endicott, Wash. (99125) 310/H4
Endless (lake), Maine 242/F5
Endrőd, Hung. 41/F3
Endwell, N.Y. (13760) 276/H6
Ene (riv.), Peru 128/E8
Energy, Ill. (62933) 222/E6
Enetai, Wash. (†98310) 310/A2
Enez, Turkey 63/B2
Enfield, 10/B5
Enfield▵, Conn. (06082) 210/E1
Enfield, Ill. (62835) 222/E5
Enfield▵, Maine (04433) 242/F5
Enfield, Maine (04433) 242/F5
Enfield, Minn. (†55362) 254/E5
Enfield, N.C. (27823) 281/O2
Enfield▵, N.H. (03748) 268/C4
Enfield, N.H. (03748) 268/C4
Enfield, N.S. 169/E4
Enfield, S. Aust. 94/B7
Enfield Center, N.H. (03749) 268/C4
Enfield P.O. (Thompsonville), Conn. (06082) 210/E1
Engadine, Mich. (49827) 250/D2
Engadine (valley), Switz. 39/K3
Engaño (cape), Dom. Rep. 158/F5
Engaño (cape), Phil. 82/D1
Engaño (cape), Phil., 54/R8
Engelberg, Switz. 39/F3
Engelhard, N.C. (27824) 281/T3
Engelhartszell, Austria 41/B2
Engel's, U.S.S.R. 48/E4
Engel's, U.S.S.R. 52/G4
Engel's, U.S.S.R., 7/J3
Engen, Br. Col. 184/E3
Enggano (isl.), Indon. 85/C7
Enghien, Belg. 27/D7
Engi, Switz. 39/H3
ENGLAND, 10/F5
ENGLAND, 13
England, U.K., 7/D3
England, Ark. (72046) 203/G4
England A.F.B., La. 238/E4
Engle, N. Mex. (†87935) 274/B5
Englee, Newf. 166/C3
Englefeld, Sask. 181/G3
Englehart, 163/H6
Englehart, Ont. 175/E3
Englehart, Ont. 177/K5
Englevale, Kans. (†66756) 232/H4
Englevale, N. Dak. (58028) 283/P7
Englewood, Colo. (80110) 208/K3
Englewood, Fla. (33533) 212/D5
Englewood‡, Ind. (†47421) 227/D7
Englewood, Kans. (67840) 232/C4
Englewood, N.J. (*07631) 273/C2
Englewood, Ohio (45322) 284/B6
Englewood, Tenn. (37329) 237/M10
Englewood Cliffs, N.J. (07632) 273/C2
English (chan.), 7/D3
English (riv.), Ont. 175/B2
English (chan.), Eng. 13/D8
English (chan.), France 28/B3
English, Ind. (47118) 227/E8
English, Ky. (†41008) 237/L3
English (chan.), 10/E6
English, W. Va. (24832) 313/C8
English Bay, Alaska (†99603) 196/B2
English Bazar, Pak. 68/F3
English Coast (reg.), Ant. 5/B15
English Creek, N.J. (†08330) 273/D5
English Harbour, Newf. 166/D2
English Harbour West, Newf. 166/C4
English Lake, Ind. (46366) 227/D2
Englishman (bay), Maine 242/J6
Englishtown, N.J. (07726) 273/E3
Englishtown, N.S. 169/H2
Enguera, Spain 33/F3
Enid, Miss. (38927) 256/E2
Enid (lake), Miss. 256/E2
Enid, Mont. (59220) 262/M3
Enid (mt.), W. Aust. 92/B3
Enid, Okla., 188/G3
Enid, Okla. (73701) 288/L2
Enid, Sask. 181/H4
Enigma, Ga. (31749) 216/F8
Enilda, Alta. 182/B2
Eniwetok (atoll), Pac. Is., 87/G4
Enka, N.C. (28728) 281/D3
Enkeldoorn, Rhod. 118/E3
Enkhuizen, Neth. 27/G3
Enköping, Sweden 18/G1
Enkyi, Ghana 106/D7
Enloe‡, Texas (75441) 302/J4
Enmore, Guyana 131/C2
Enna (prov.), Italy 34/E6
Enna, Italy 34/E6
Ennadai, 163/F3
Ennadai, N.W.T. 187/H3
Ennadai (lake), N.W.T. 187/H3
En Nahud, Sudan 111/E5
En Naqura, Leb. 63/F6
En Nebk, Syria 59/C3
En Nebk, Syria 63/G5
Ennedi (plat.), Chad 111/D4
Ennell (lake), Ire. 17/G5
Ennenda, Switz. 39/H2
Enngonia, N.S.W. 97/C1
Enning, S. Dak. (57737) 298/E4
Ennis, 10/B4
Ennis, Ire. 17/D6
Ennis, Ky. (†42337) 237/H6
Ennis, Mont. (59729) 262/E5
Ennis (lake), Mont. 262/E5
Ennis, Texas (75119) 302/H5
Enniscorthy, 10/C4
Enniscorthy, Ire. 17/J7
Enniskerry, Ire. 17/J5
Enniskillen, N. Ire. 17/F3
Enniskillen, 10/C3
Enniskillen Station, N. Br. 170/D3
Ennistymon, 10/B4
Ennistymon, Ire. 17/C6
Enns, Austria 41/C2
Enns (riv.), Austria 41/C3
Enoch, Utah (†84720) 304/A6
Enoch, W. Va. (25074) 313/E6
Enochs, Texas (79324) 302/B4
Enoggera (creek), Queens. 95/D2
Enola, Ark. (72047) 203/F3
Enola, Pa. (17025) 294/J5
Enon, Mo. (†65074) 261/G6
Enon, Ohio (45323) 284/C6
Enontekiö, Fin. 18/N2
Enon Valley, Pa. (16120) 294/B4
Enoree, S.C. (29335) 296/D2
Enoree (riv.), S.C. 296/C2
Enos, Ind. (†47963) 227/C2
Enosburg Falls, Vt. (05450) 268/B2
Enrage (cape), N. Br. 170/F3
Enrile, Phil. 82/C2
Enrique Carbó, Arg. 143/G6
Enriquillo, Dom. Rep. 156/D3
Enriquillo, Dom. Rep. 158/D7
Enriquillo (lake), Dom. Rep. 158/C6
Ens, Sask. 181/F3
Enschede, Neth. 27/K4
Ensenada, Arg. 143/H7
Ensenada, P. Rico 161/B3
Ensenada, Mex. 150/A1
Enshih, China 77/G5
Ensign, Alta. 182/D4
Ensign, Kans. (67841) 232/B4
Ensign, Mich. (†49878) 250/C3
Ensival, Belg. 27/H7
Ensley, Fla. (32504) 212/B6
Ent A.F.B., Colo. 208/K5
Entebbe, 102/F5
Entebbe, Uganda 115/F4
Enterprise, Ala. (36330) 194/G8
Enterprise, Calif. (96001) 204/C3
Enterprise, Ont. 177/H3
Enterprise, Kans. (67441) 232/E3
Enterprise, La. (71425) 238/G3
Enterprise, Miss. (39330) 256/G6
Enterprise, Ohio (†43138) 284/F6
Enterprise, Okla. (†74561) 288/R4
Enterprise, Oreg. (97828) 291/K2
Enterprise, Utah (84725) 304/A6
Enterprise, W. Va. (26568) 313/F4
Entiat, Wash. (98822) 310/E3
Entiat (lake), Wash. 310/E3
Entiat (mts.), Wash. 310/E2
Entiat (riv.), Wash. 310/E3
Entlebuch, Switz. 39/F3
Entrance, Alta. 182/B3
Entrance Island, Alaska (†99801) 196/N1
Entrejo, Neth. Ant. 161/E8
Entre Ríos (prov.), Arg. 143/E3
Entre Ríos, Bol. 136/C7
Entre-Rios, Moz. 118/F2
Entriken, Pa. (16638) 294/F5
Entwistle, Alta. 182/C3
Enugu, 102/C4
Enugu, Nigeria 106/F7
Enumclaw, Wash. (98022) 310/D3
Envigado, Col. 126/C4
Enville, Tenn. (38332) 237/E10
Enwarak (mt.), Guyana 131/B3
Enying, Hung. 41/E3
Enzeli (Pahlevi), Iran 59/E2
Enzeli (Pahlevi), Iran 66/F2
Eola, La. (71332) 238/F5
Eola, Texas (76937) 302/E6
Eolia, Ky. (40826) 237/R6
Eolia, Mo. (63344) 261/L4
Eoline, Ala. (35042) 194/D4
Epe, Neth. 27/H4
Epéme, Togo 106/E7
Epéna, Rep. of Congo 115/C3
Epenarra, No. Terr. 93/D6
Épendes, Switz. 39/C3
Épernay, France 28/E3
Epes, Ala. (35460) 194/B5
Ephesus, Ga. (†30217) 216/B4
Ephesus (ruins), Turkey 63/B4
Ephraim, Utah (84627) 304/C4
Ephraim, Wis. (54211) 317/M5
Ephrata, Pa. (17522) 294/K5
Ephrata, Wash. (98823) 310/F3
Ephratah, N.Y. (†13339) 276/L4
Épinal, France 28/G3
Épinay-sur-Seine, France 28/B1
Epiphany, S. Dak. (†57321) 298/O6
Epira, Guyana 131/C3
Epirus (reg.), Greece 45/E6
Episkopi, Cyprus 63/E5
Eport (inlet), Scot. 15/B4
Epoufette, Mich. (49731) 250/D2
Epping, 10/C5
Epping, Eng. 13/H6
Epping, N. Dak. (58843) 283/D3
Epping▵, N.H. (03042) 268/E5
Epping, N.H. (03042) 268/E5
Epps, La. (71237) 238/G1
Epsie, Mont. (59325) 262/L5
Epsom, Ind. (†47568) 227/C7
Epsom▵, N.H. (03234) 268/E5
Epsom, N.H. (03234) 268/E5
Epsom and Ewell, 10/B6
Epukiro, S.W. Afr. 118/B4
Epworth, Ga. (30541) 216/D1
Epworth, Iowa (52045) 229/M4
Equality, Ala. (36026) 194/F5
Equality, Ill. (62934) 222/E6
Equateur (prov.), Dem. Rep. of the Congo. 115/D3
Equateur, Dem. Rep. of the Congo. 115/C3
Equator, 3/H5
Equatoria (prov.), Sudan 111/E6
Equatorial Guinea, 3/K5
EQUATORIAL GUINEA, 115/A3
EQUATORIAL GUINEA, 102/C4
Equinox (mt.), Vt. 268/A5
Equinunk, Pa. (18417) 294/M2
Era, Ohio (†43143) 284/D6
Era, Texas (76238) 302/G4
Eran, Phil. 82/A6
Erath, La. (70533) 238/F7
Erath (co.), Texas 302/F5
Erbaa, Turkey 63/G2
Erbach, W. Ger. 22/C4
Erbacon, W. Va. (26203) 313/E5
Erbil, Iraq 59/D2
Erbil (prov.), Iraq 66/D3
Erbil, Iraq 66/D2
Erçek (lake), Turkey 63/K3
Ercilla, Chile 138/E2
Erciş, Turkey 59/D2
Erciş, Turkey 63/K3
Erciyas Dağı (mt.), Leb. 63/F3
Ercsi, Hung. 41/E3
Érd, Hung. 41/E3
Erdahl, Minn. (†56531) 254/C5
Erdek, Turkey 63/B2
Erdemli, Turkey 63/F4
Erdeni Dzuu, Mong. 77/F2
Erdőtelek, Hung. 41/F3
Erebato (riv.), Ven. 124/F5
Erechim, Braz. 132/C9
Ereğli, Turkey 59/B2
Ereğli, Turkey 63/D2
Ereğli, Turkey 63/F4
Erenköy, Turkey 63/D6
Erepecuru (riv.), Braz., 120/E3
Erepecuru (riv.), Braz. 132/B3
Eresma (riv.), Spain 33/D2
Erfoud, Mor. 106/D2
Erfurt, E. Ger., 7/F3
Erfurt (dist.), E. Ger. 22/D3
Erfurt, E. Ger. 22/D3
Ergani, Turkey 63/H3
Ergene (riv.), Turkey 63/B2
Ergli, U.S.S.R. 53/C2
Erhard, Minn. (56534) 254/B4
Erh Hai (lake), China 77/F6
Erhlien, China 77/H3
Eriboll, Scot. 15/G3
Eriboll (inlet), Scot. 15/G2
Erica, Neth. 27/K3
Erica, Vic. 97/D5
Erice, Italy 34/D5
Ericeira, Port. 33/B3
Erichsen (lake), N.W.T. 187/K2
Ericht (lake), Scot. 15/H6
Erick, Okla. (73645) 288/G4
Erickson, Br. Col. 184/J5
Erickson, Man. 179/C4
Ericsburg, Minn. (56640) 254/E2
Ericson, Nebr. (68637) 264/F3
Erie (lake), 146/K5
Erie (lake), 163/H7
Erie (lake), 188/K2
Erie, Colo. (80516) 208/K2
Erie (lake), Ont. 177/E5
Erie, Ill. (61250) 222/C2
Erie, Kans. (66733) 232/G4
Erie, Mich. (48133) 250/F7
Erie (lake), Mich. 250/G7
Erie, N. Dak. (58029) 283/R5
Erie (co.), N.Y. 276/C5
Erie (lake), N.Y. 276/A5
Erie (co.), Ohio 284/E3
Erie (lake), Ohio 284/H1
Erie, Pa., 146/L5
Erie, Pa., 188/K2
Erie (co.), Pa. 294/B2
Erie, Pa. (*16501) 294/B1
Erie (lake), Pa. 294/B1
Erie, Tenn. (37736) 237/M9
Erieau, Ont. 177/C5
Erie Beach, Ont. 177/B5
Erieville, N.Y. (13061) 276/J5
Erigavo, Somalia 115/J1
Eriksdale, Man. 179/D4
Erimo (cape), Japan 81/L3
Erin (bay), Trinidad Tobago 161/A11
Erin (pt.), Trinidad Tobago 161/A11
Erin, Ont. 177/D4
Erin, Tenn. (37061) 237/F8
Erinferry, Sask. 181/D2
Erinview, Man. 179/E4
Eriskay (isl.), Scot. 15/B5
Erisort (inlet), Scot. 15/D3
Eritrea (reg.), Eth. 59/C6
Eritrea (prov.), Eth. 111/G4
Eritrea (reg.), 102/F3
Erivan, U.S.S.R. 48/E6
Erivan, U.S.S.R. 52/F6
Erivan, U.S.S.R., 7/J4
Erkelenz, W. Ger. 22/B3
Erkilet, Turkey 63/F3
Erkina (riv.), Ire. 17/G6
Erlach, Switz. 39/D2
Erlandson (lake), Que. 174/D1
Erlands Point, Wash. (†98310) 310/A2
Erlangen, W. Ger. 22/D4
Erlanger, Ky. (41018) 237/R3
Erldunda, No. Terr. 93/C8

Fachi 361

Erlenbach im Simmental, Switz. 39/E3
Erling (lake), Ark. 203/C7
Ermatingen, Switz. 39/H1
Ermelo, Neth. 27/H4
Ermelo, S. Africa 118/E5
Ermenek, Turkey 63/E4
Ermeran Station, N.S.W. 97/D3
Ermine, Sask. 181/B4
Ermoúpolis, Greece 45/G7
Ernabella, Aust. 88/E5
Ernabella, S. Aust. 94/C2
Ernakulam, India 68/D6
Erne (riv.), Ire. 17/E3
Erne (lake), N. Ire. 17/F3
Erne (lake), 10/C3
Ernée, France 28/C3
Ernen, Switz. 39/F4
Ernest, Pa. (15739) 294/D4
Ernfold, Sask. 181/D5
Ernul, N.C. (28527) 281/P4
Erode, India 68/D6
Eromanga, Aust. 88/G5
Eromanga, Queens. 95/B5
Eros, La. (71238) 238/F2
Erquelinnes, Belg. 27/E8
Err (mt.), Switz. 39/J3
Er Rafid, Jordan 65/D2
Er Rahad, Sudan 59/B7
Er Rahad, Sudan 111/F5
Er Ramtha, Jordan 65/E2
Er Ras, Saudi Ar. 59/D4
Errata, Miss. (†39440) 256/F7
Errego, Moz. 118/F3
Er Rif (range), Mor. 106/D2
Errigal (mt.), Ire. 17/E1
Er Rihiya, Jordan 65/C5
Erris (head), Ire. 17/A3
Erris (head), 10/A3
Errol△, N.H. (03579) 268/E2
Errol, N.H. (03579) 268/E2
Errol, Scot. 15/K7
Erromanga (isl.), New Hebr., 87/H7
Er Roseires, 102/F3
Er Roseires, Sudan 111/F5
Er Rumman, Jordan 65/D3
Er Ruseifa, Jordan 65/E3
Ersekë, Alb. 45/E5
Erskine, Alta. 182/D3
Erskine, Minn. (56535) 254/B3
Erstein, France 28/G3
Erstfeld, Switz. 39/G3
Ertil', U.S.S.R. 52/F4
Eruh, Turkey 63/K4
Erval, Braz. 132/C11
Ervay, Wyo. (†82638) 319/E3
Erving△, Mass. (01344) 249/E2
Erwin, N.C. (28339) 281/M4
Erwin, S. Dak. (57233) 298/P5
Erwin, Tenn. (37650) 237/S8
Erwinna, Pa. (18920) 294/N5
Erwinville, La. (70729) 238/H5
Erwood, Sask. 181/J3
Erzgebirge (mts.), Czech. 41/B1
Erzgebirge (mts.), E. Ger. 22/E3
Erzin, Turkey 63/G4
Erzincan, Turkey 59/C2
Erzincan (prov.), Turkey 63/H3
Erzincan, Turkey 63/H3
Erzurum, Turkey 59/D2
Erzurum (prov.), Turkey 63/J3
Erzurum, Turkey 63/J3
Erzurum, Turkey, 54/H5
Esan (pt.), Japan 81/K3
Esashi, Hokkaido, Japan 81/L1
Esashi, Hokkaido, Japan 81/J3
Esashi, Iwate, Japan 81/K4
Esbjerg, Den., 7/E3
Esbjerg, Den. 18/F9
Esbjerg, Den. 21/B7
Esbon, Kans. (66941) 232/D2
Escabosa, N. Mex. (†87059) 274/C4
Escalante, Phil. 82/D5
Escalante, Utah (84726) 304/C6
Escalante (des.), Utah 304/A6
Escalante (riv.), Utah 304/C6
Escalon, Calif. (95320) 204/E6
Escalona, Spain 33/D2
Escambia (co.), Ala. 194/D8
Escambia (creek), Ala. 194/D8
Escambia (riv.), Ala. 194/D8
Escambia (co.), Fla. 212/B6
Escambia (riv.), Fla. 212/B6
Escanaba, Mich. (49829) 250/C3
Escanaba (riv.), Mich. 250/B2
Escatawpa, Ala. (†36584) 194/B8
Escatawpa, Miss. (39552) 256/G10
Eschenbach, Switz. 39/G2
Escholzmatt, Switz. 39/E3
Esch-sur-Alzette, Lux. 27/J9
Esch-sur-Sauer, Lux. 27/H9
Eschwege, W. Ger. 22/C3
Eschweiler, W. Ger. 22/B3
Escobar, Arg. 143/G7
Escobar, Par. 144/B6
Escocesa (bay), Dom. Rep. 158/E5
Escoma, Bol. 136/A4
Escondido, Calif. (92025) 204/J10
Escondido (riv.), Nic. 154/F4
Escoumins, Que. 172/H1
Escudo de Veraguas (isl.), Pan. 154/G6
Escuinapa de Hidalgo, Mex. 150/G5
Escuintla, Guat. 154/B3
Escuintla, Mex. 150/N9
Escuminac, N. Br. 170/F1
Escuminac (bay), N. Br. 170/D1
Escuminac (pt.), N. Br. 170/F1
Esdaile, Wis. (†54723) 317/A6
Eséka, Cameroon 115/B3
Eşen, Turkey 63/C4
Esher, 10/B6
Eshowe, S. Africa 118/E5
Esk (riv.), Eng. 13/D2
Esk, Queens. 95/E5
Esk, Sask. 181/G4
Esk (riv.), Scot. 15/L9
Eska, Alaska (†99674) 196/B1
Eskbank, Sask. 181/E5
Eskdale, W. Va. (25075) 313/D6
Eskilstuna, Sweden 18/K7
Eskilstuna, Sweden, 7/F3
Eskimalatya, Turkey 63/H3
Eskimo (lakes), N.W.T. 187/E3
Eskimo Point, 163/G3
Eskimo Point, N.W.T. 187/J3
Eskipazar, Turkey 63/E2
Eskişehir, Turkey 59/B2
Eskişehir (prov.), Turkey 63/D3
Eskişehir, Turkey 63/D3
Esko, Minn. (55733) 254/F4
Eskridge, Kans. (66423) 232/F3
Eskutassis (pond), Maine 242/G5
Esla (riv.), Spain 33/D2
Eslöv, Sweden 18/H9
Eşme, Turkey 63/C3
Esme, Sask. 181/D6
Esmeralda (isl.), Chile 138/C8
Esmeralda, Cuba 158/G1
Esmeralda (co.), Nev. 266/D5
Esmeraldas, Ec., 120/B2
Esmeraldas (prov.), Ec. 128/C2
Esmeraldas, Ec. 128/B2
Esmeraldas (riv.), Ec. 128/C2
Esmond, Ill. (60129) 222/E1
Esmond, N. Dak. (58332) 283/L3
Esmond, R.I. (02917) 249/H5
Esmond, S. Dak. (57333) 298/O5
Esmont, Va. (22937) 307/L5
Esmoraca, Bol. 136/B7
Esneux, Belg. 27/H7
Esom Hill, Ga. (30138) 216/B3
Espada (pt.), Col. 126/E1
Espada (pt.), Dom. Rep. 158/F6
Espagnol (pt.), St. Vincent 161/A8
Espaillat (prov.), Dom. Rep. 158/E5
Espalion, France 28/E5
Espanola, Ont. 175/D3
Espanola, Ont. 177/J5
Española (isl.), Ec. 128/C10
Espanola, Fla. (†32010) 212/E2
Espanola, N. Mex. (87532) 274/C3
Espanola, Wash. (99010) 310/H3
Espanong (Lake Hopatcong), N.J. (07849) 273/D2
Espargos, 102/G8
Esparta, C. Rica 154/E5
Esparto, Calif. (95627) 204/C5
Espejo, Chile 138/G3
Espejo, Spain 33/D4
Espelkamp, W. Ger. 22/C2
Espenberg (cape), Alaska 196/F1
Esperança, Braz. 132/G4
Esperance, Australia, 87/C9
Esperance, Aust. 88/C6
Esperance, N.Y. (12066) 276/M5
Esperance, W. Aust. 92/C6
Esperance (bay), W. Aust. 92/C6
Esperanza, Arg. 143/F5
Esperanza, Br. Col. 184/D5
Esperanza, Cuba 158/E2
Esperanza, Dom. Rep. 158/D5
Esperanza, P. Rico 161/G2
Esperanza, Sierra de (mts.), Hond. 154/E3
Esperanza, Peru 128/G7
Esperanza, Texas (79841) 302/B11
Esperanza, Ven. 124/E6
Espichel (cape), Port. 33/B3
Espigão Mestre (Geral) (range), Braz. 132/E6
Espinal, Col. 126/C5
Espinhaço (range), Braz. 132/F7
Espinho, Port. 33/B2
Espinillo (pt.), Urug. 145/A7
Espino, Ven. 124/F3
Espírito Santo (state), Braz. 132/F7
Espírito Santo (state), Braz. 135/F2
Espiritu Santo (isl.), Mex. 150/D4
Espiritu Santo (isl.), New Hebr., 87/G7
Espiritu Santo (cape), Phil. 82/E4
Espiritu Santo (cape), Phil. 85/H3
Espita, Mex. 150/Q6
Espiye, Turkey 63/H2
Esplanada, Braz. 132/G5
Espluga de Francoli, Spain 33/G2
Espoir (bay), Newf. 166/C4
Espoo, Fin. 18/O6
Esprit-Saint, Que. 172/J1
Espungabera, Moz. 118/E4
Espy, Pa. (17815) 294/K4
Espyville Station, Pa. (16414) 294/B2
Esquel, Arg. 143/B5
Esquimalt, Br. Col. 184/K4
Esquina, Arg. 143/G5
Esquipulas, Nic. 154/E4
Es Sahab, Jordan 65/E4
Es Salt, Jordan 59/C3
Es Salt, Jordan 65/D3
Essaouira, 102/A1
Essaouira, Mor. 106/B2
Essen, Belg. 27/F6
Essen, W. Ger., 7/E3
Essen, W. Ger. 22/B3
Essendon, Aust. 88/L6
Essendon, Vic. 97/H5
Essequibo (riv.), Guyana, 120/E2
Essequibo (dist.), Guyana 131/B2
Essequibo (riv.), Guyana 131/B3
Essequibo Islands (dist.), Guyana 131/B2
Esserville, Va. (24274) 307/G2
Essex, Calif. (92332) 204/K9
Essex△, Conn. (06426) 210/F3
Essex, Conn. (06426) 210/F3
Essex (co.), Eng. 13/H6
Essex, Ill. (60935) 222/E2
Essex, Iowa (51638) 229/C7
Essex (co.), Mass. 249/L2
Essex△, Mass. (02112) 249/L2
Essex, Md. (21221) 245/N3
Essex, Mo. (63846) 261/N9
Essex, Mont. (59916) 262/C2
Essex (co.), N.J. 273/E2
Essex (co.), N.Y. 276/N2
Essex, N.Y. (12936) 276/O2
Essex (co.), Ont. 177/B5
Essex, Ont. 177/B5
Essex (co.), Va. 307/P5
Essex (co.), Vt. 268/D2
Essex△, Vt. (05451) 268/A2
Essex, Vt. (05451) 268/A2
Essex Fells, N.J. (07021) 273/B2
Essex Junction, Vt. (05452) 268/A3
Essexville, Mich. (48732) 250/F5
Essie, Ky. (40827) 237/P6
Essig, Minn. (56030) 254/D6
Essington, Pa. (19029) 294/M7
Esslingen, W. Ger. 22/C4
Essonne (dept.), France 28/E3
Es Sukhna, Jordan 65/E3
Es Sukhne, Syria 59/C3
Es Sukhne, Syria 63/H5
Es Suki, Sudan 59/B7
Es Suweida, Syria 59/C3
Es Suweida (prov.), Syria 63/G6
Es Suweida, Syria 63/G6
Est (pt.), Haiti 158/C4
Est (lake), Que. 172/H2
Estacada, Oreg. (97023) 291/E2
Estaca de Vares (pt.), Spain 33/C1
Estación Atlántida, Urug. 145/B6
Estación Cuaró, Urug. 145/C1
Estación General Campero, Bol. 136/A5
Estación J.J. Castro, Urug. 145/C4
Estación José Ignacio, Urug. 145/E5
Estación La Floresta, Urug. 145/C7
Estación Lasala, Urug. 145/C7
Estación Laureles, Urug. 145/C2
Estación Margat, Urug. 145/B6
Estación Migues, Urug. 145/C6
Estación Pampa, Urug. 145/C3
Estación Rincón, Urug. 145/F3
Estación Salus, Urug. 145/D5
Estación Sosa Díaz, Urug. 145/C6
Estación Tapia, Urug. 145/C6
Estación Villasboas, Urug. 145/C4
Estación Yi, Urug. 145/C4
Estados (isl.), Arg., 120/D8
Estados, Los (isl.), Arg. 143/D7
Estahbanat, Iran 59/F4
Estahbanat, Iran 66/J6
Estaire, Ont. 177/D1
Estância, Braz. 132/G5
Estancia, N. Mex. (87016) 274/D4
Estancia Caleta Josefina, Chile 138/F10
Estancia Laguna Blanca, Chile 138/E9
Estancia Morro Chico, Chile 138/E9
Estancia Punta Delgada, Chile 138/E9
Estancia San Gregorio, Chile 138/E9
Estancia Springhill (Cerro Manantiales), Chile 138/F10
Estanzuela, Urug. 145/B5
Estanzuelas, El Salv. 154/C4
Estarca, Bol. 136/C7
Estats (mt.), Spain 33/G1
Estavayer-le-Lac, Switz. 39/C3
Estcourt, Que. 172/H2
Estcourt, S. Africa 118/D5
Este (pt.), Cuba 158/C3
Este (pt.), P. Rico 161/G2
Este, Italy 34/C2
Este (pt.), Urug. 145/D6
Esteban Rams, Arg. 143/F5
Estelí, Nic. 154/D4
Estella, Spain 33/E1
Estelline, S. Dak. (57234) 298/R4
Estelline, Texas (79233) 302/D3
Estell Manor, N.J. (08319) 273/D5
Estepa, Spain 33/D4
Estepona, Spain 33/D4
Ester, Alaska (99725) 196/J2
Esterbrook, Wyo. (†82633) 319/G3
Esterhazy, Sask. 181/K5
Estero (bay), Calif. 204/D8
Estero (pt.), Calif. 204/D8
Estero, Fla. (33928) 212/E5
Estero (isl.), Fla. 212/E5
Esteros, Par. 144/B4
Estes Park, Colo. (80517) 208/J2
Este Sudeste (cays), Col. 126/A10
Estevan, 163/F6
Estevan, Sask. 181/J6
Estevan Point, Br. Col. 184/D5
Estey, Mich. (†48652) 250/E5
Esther (isl.), Alaska 196/C1
Esther, Alta. 182/E4
Esther, La. (†70510) 238/F7
Esther, Mo. (†63601) 261/M7
Estherville, Iowa (51334) 229/D2
Estherwood, La. (70534) 238/F6
Estill (co.), Ky. 237/O5
Estill, Miss. (†38748) 256/C4
Estill, S.C. (29918) 296/E6
Estillfork, Ala. (35745) 194/F1
Estill Springs, Tenn. (37330) 237/J10
Estlin, Sask. 181/G5
Esto, Fla. (32425) 212/C5
Eston, 163/F5
Eston, Sask. 181/C4
ESTONIA, 53/C1
Estonian S.S.R., U.S.S.R. 48/C4
Estonian S.S.R., U.S.S.R. 52/C3
Estonian S.S.R., U.S.S.R., 7/G3
Estoril, Port. 33/B3
Estral Beach, Mich. (†48166) 250/F7
Estrela, Serra da (mts.), Port. 33/C2
Estrella (riv.), Calif. 204/E8
Estremadura (prov.), Port. 33/B3
Estremadura (reg.), Spain 33/C3
Estremoz, Port. 33/C3
Estrondo (mts.), Braz., 120/F3
Estrondo (range), Braz. 132/D4
Estuary, Sask. 181/B5
Esztergom, Hung. 41/E3
Etadunna, S. Aust. 94/F3
Etalle, Belg. 27/H9
Étampes, France 28/E3
Étaples, France 28/D2
Etawah, India 68/D3
Etawney (lake), Man. 179/J2
Etchojoa, Mex. 150/E3
Ethan, S. Dak. (57334) 298/N6
Ethel, Ark. (72048) 203/H5
Ethel (mt.), Colo. 208/F1
Ethel, Ont. 177/C4
Ethel, La. (70730) 238/H5
Ethel, Miss. (39067) 256/F4
Ethel, Mo. (63539) 261/G3
Ethel, W. Va. (25076) 313/C7
Ethel, Wash. (98542) 310/C4
Ethelbert, Man. 179/B3
Ethel Creek, W. Aust. 92/C3
Ethelsville, Ala. (35461) 194/B4
Ethelton, Sask. 181/G3
Ether, N.C. (27247) 281/K4
Ethete, Wyo. (82520) 319/D2
Ethiopia, 3/L5
ETHIOPIA, 111/G5
ETHIOPIA, 102/F4
Ethridge, Mont. (59435) 262/D2
Ethridge, Tenn. (38456) 237/G10
Etive (inlet), Scot. 15/F7
Etiwanda, Calif. (91739) 204/E10
Etna, Calif. (96027) 204/C2
Etna, Ind. (†46725) 227/F2
Etna (vol.), Italy, 7/F5
Etna (vol.), Italy 34/E6
Etna△, Maine (04434) 242/E6
Etna, N.H. (03750) 268/C4
Etna, Ohio (43018) 284/E6
Etna, Pa. (15223) 294/B6
Etna, Utah (†84313) 304/A2
Etna, Wyo. (83118) 319/A2
Etna Green, Ind. (46524) 227/E2
Etoile, Ky. (42131) 237/K7
Etoile, Dem. Rep. of the Congo. 115/E6
Etolin (isl.), Alaska 196/N2
Etolin (str.), Alaska 196/E2
Etomami (riv.), Man. 179/F2
Etomami (riv.), Sask. 181/J3
Eton, 10/F5
Eton, Aust. 88/H4
Eton, Ga. (30724) 216/C1
Eton, Queens. 95/D4
Etosha (salt dep.), 102/D6
Etosha Pan (salt pan), S.W. Afr. 118/B3
Etoumbi, Rep. of Congo 115/B3
Etowah (co.), Ala. 194/F2
Etowah, Ark. (72428) 203/K2
Etowah (riv.), Ga. 216/C2
Etowah, N.C. (28729) 281/D4
Etowah, Tenn. (37331) 237/M10
Étretat, France 28/D3
Etta, Miss. (38627) 256/F2
Etta (lake), N. Dak. 283/L6
Et Tafila, Jordan 65/E5
Et Taiyiba, Jordan 65/D2
Ettelbruck, Lux. 27/J9
Et Tell el Abyad, Syria 63/H4
Etten, Neth. 27/F5
Etter, Minn. (†55033) 254/F6
Etterbeek, Belg. 27/C9
Etters, Pa. (17319) 294/J5
Ettington, Sask. 181/F6
Ettlingen, W. Ger. 22/C4
Ettrick, Scot. 15/K9
Ettrick, Va. (23803) 307/O6
Ettrick, Wis. (54627) 317/D7
Ettrick Pen (mt.), Scot. 15/K9
Etty, Ky. (41523) 237/R6
Etzikom, Alta. 182/E5
Etzikom Coulee (riv.), Alta. 182/E5
Eu, France 28/D3
Euabalong, N.S.W. 97/D3
Eubank, Ky. (42567) 237/M6
Euboea (isl.), Greece, 7/G5
Euboea (isl.), Greece 45/G6
Eucha, Okla. (74342) 288/S2
Eucla, Aust. 88/D6
Eucla, W. Aust. 92/E5
Euclid, Minn. (56722) 254/B3
Euclid, Ohio (44117) 284/J9
Eucumbene (lake), N.S.W. 97/E5
Eucutta, Miss. (†39360) 256/G7
Eudora, Ark. (71640) 203/H7
Eudora, Kans. (66025) 232/G3
Eudora, Miss. (†38632) 256/D1
Eudora, Mo. (65645) 261/E7
Eufaula, Ala. (36027) 194/H7
Eufaula (lake), Ala. 194/H7
Eufaula (lake), Ga. 216/B7
Eufaula (res.), Ohio 284/L4
Eufaula, Okla. (74432) 288/P4
Eufaula (res.), Okla. 288/P4
Eugene, Ind. (†47928) 227/B5
Eugene, Mo. (65032) 261/H6
Eugene, Oreg., 146/F5
Eugene, Oreg., 188/B2
Eugene, Oreg. (*97401) 291/D3
Eugowra, N.S.W. 97/E3
Euless, Texas (76039) 302/F2
Eulo, Aust. 88/G5
Eulo, Queens. 95/C6
Eulonia, Ga. (†31331) 216/K7
Eumungerie, N.S.W. 97/E2
Eunice, La. (70535) 238/F6
Eunice, N. Mex. (88231) 274/F6
Eunola, Ala. (†36340) 194/G8
Eupen, Belg. 27/J7
Euphrates (riv.), 54/H6
Euphrates (riv.), Iran 59/E3
Euphrates (riv.), Iraq 59/E3
Euphrates (riv.), Iraq 66/D4
Euphrates (riv.), Syria 59/E3
Euphrates (El Furat) (riv.), Syria 63/H4
Euphrates (Firat) (riv.), Turkey 63/G4
Eupora, Miss. (39744) 256/F3
Eure (dept.), France 28/D3
Eure (riv.), France 28/D3
Eure, N.C. (27935) 281/R2
Eure-et-Loir (dept.), France 28/D3
Eureka, 163/N3
Eureka, Calif., 146/F5
Eureka, Calif., 188/B2
Eureka, Calif. (95501) 204/A3
Eureka, Canada, 4/A14
Eureka, Colo. (†81433) 208/D7
Eureka (res.), Fla. 212/E2
Eureka, Ill. (61530) 222/D3
Eureka, Ind. (†47635) 227/C9
Eureka, Kans. (67045) 232/F4
Eureka, Mich. (48833) 250/E5
Eureka, Mo. (63025) 261/L6
Eureka, Mont. (59917) 262/B2
Eureka, N.C. (27830) 281/O3
Eureka, N.S. 169/F3
Eureka, N.W.T. 187/K2
Eureka (sound), N.W.T. 187/K2
Eureka (co.), Nev. 266/E3
Eureka, Nev. (89316) 266/E3
Eureka, S.C. (†29847) 296/D4
Eureka (Hemlock), S.C. (†29706) 296/E2
Eureka, S. Dak. (57437) 298/K2
Eureka, Utah (84628) 304/B4
Eureka, W. Va. (26144) 313/D4
Eureka, Wash. (†99348) 310/G4
Eureka, Wis. (54934) 317/J7
Eureka Lodge, Alaska (†99588) 196/C1
Eureka River, Alta. 182/A1
Eureka Springs, Ark. (72632) 203/C1
Euroa, Vic. 97/C5
Europa (pt.), Gibr. 33/D4
Europa (isl.), Réunion 118/G4
Europe, 3/K3
EUROPE, 7
Europoort, Neth. 27/E5
Eusebio Ayala, Par. 144/B6
Euskirchen, W. Ger. 22/B3
Eustace, Texas (75124) 302/H5
Eustis, Fla. (32726) 212/E3
Eustis△, Maine (04936) 242/B5
Eustis, Maine (04936) 242/B5
Eustis, Nebr. (69028) 264/D4
Euston, N.S.W. 97/B4
Eutaw, Ala. (35462) 194/C5
Eutawville, S.C. (29048) 296/G5
Eutin, W. Ger. 22/D1
Eutsuk (lake), Br. Col. 184/D3
Eva, Ala. (35621) 194/E2
Eva (lake), Alta. 182/B5
Eva, La. (†71354) 238/G4
Eva, Okla. (73936) 288/C1
Eva, Tenn. (38333) 237/E8
Evadale, Texas (77615) 302/L7
Eva Downs, No. Terr. 93/D5
Evan (lake), Que. 174/B2
Evan, Minn. (56238) 254/D6
Evandale, N. Br. 170/D3
Evangeline (par.), La. 238/F5
Evangeline, La. (70537) 238/F6
Evangeline, N. Br. 170/F1
Evans (str.), 163/H3
Evans, Colo. (80620) 208/K2
Evans (mt.), Colo. 208/H3
Evans (co.), Ga. 216/J6
Evans, Ga. (30809) 216/H3
Evans, La. (70639) 238/D5
Evans (head), N.S.W. 97/G1
Evans (str.), N.W.T. 187/K3
Evans, W. Va. (25241) 313/C5
Evans, Wash. (99126) 310/H2
Evansburg, Alta. 182/C3
Evans Center, N.Y. (†14006) 276/B5
Evans City, Pa. (16033) 294/B4
Evansdale, Iowa (50707) 229/J4
Evans Head, N.S.W. 97/G1
Evans Mills, N.Y. (13637) 276/J2
Evansport, Ohio (43519) 284/B3
Evanston, Ill. (*60201) 222/B1
Evanston, Ind. (47531) 227/D8
Evanston, Wyo., 188/D2
Evanston, Wyo. (82930) 319/B4
Evansville, Ark. (72729) 203/B2
Evansville, Ill. (62242) 222/D5
Evansville, Ind., 146/K6
Evansville, Ind., 188/J3
Evansville, Ind. (*47701) 227/C9
Evansville, Minn. (56326) 254/C4
Evansville, Miss. (†38676) 256/D1
Evansville, Pa. (19521) 294/L5
Evansville, Wis. (53536) 317/H10
Evansville, Wyo. (82636) 319/F3
Evant, Texas (76525) 302/G6
Evanton, Scot. 15/H4
Evart, Mich. (49631) 250/D5
Evarts, Ky. (40828) 237/P7
Evaton, S. Africa 118/H7
Evaz Iran 66/J7
Eveleth, Minn. (55734) 254/F3
Evelyn, La. (†71052) 238/D3
Evendale, Ohio (†45201) 284/C9
Evening Shade, Ark. (72532) 203/G1
Eveningshade, Mo. (†65552) 261/H7
Evenki Nat'l Okr., U.S.S.R. 48/K3
Evensk, U.S.S.R. 48/Q3
Evensville, Tenn. (37332) 237/M9
Even Yehuda, Israel 65/B3
Everard (lake), Aust. 88/E6
Everard (lake), S. Aust. 94/D4
Everard (ranges), S. Aust. 94/C2
Evere, Belg. 27/C9
Everest, Kans. (66424) 232/G2
Everest, N. Dak. (†58023) 283/R6
Everest (mt.), 54/M7
Everest (mt.), China 77/C6
Everest (mt.), Nepal 68/F3
Everett, Ont. 177/E3
Everett, Ga. (31536) 216/J8
Everett, Mass. (02149) 249/D6
Everett (mt.), Mass. 249/A4
Everett (dam), N.H. 268/D5
Everett (mts.), N.W.T. 187/M3
Everett, Pa. (15537) 294/F5
Everett, Wash., 188/B1
Everett, Wash. (98201) 310/C3
Everetts, N.C. (27825) 281/P3
Everettville, W. Va. (26533) 313/F3
Evergem, Belg. 27/D6
Everglades, The (swamp), Fla. 212/F6
Everglades, The (swamp), Fla., 188/K5
Everglades City, Fla. (33929) 212/E6
Everglades Nat'l Park, Fla. 212/F6
Evergreen, Ala. (36401) 194/E8
Evergreen, Colo. (80439) 208/J3
Evergreen, La. (71333) 238/F5
Evergreen, N.C. (28438) 281/M6
Evergreen, Va. (23939) 307/L6
Evergreen Park, Ill. (60642) 222/B2
Everly, Iowa (51338) 229/C2
Everman, Texas (76140) 302/F2
Everson, Pa. (15631) 294/C5
Everson, Wash. (98247) 310/C2
Eversonville, Mo. (†64688) 261/F3
Everton, Ark. (72633) 203/E1
Everton, Ind. (†47331) 227/G5
Everton, Mo. (65646) 261/E8
Evesham, 10/F4
Evesham, Eng. 13/F5
Evesham, Sask. 181/B3
Evington, Va. (24550) 307/K6
Evolène, Switz. 39/D4
Évora, Port., 7/D5
Évora, Port. 33/C3
Évreux, France 28/D3
Évros (riv.), Greece 45/H5
Évry, France 28/E3
Ewa, Hawaii (96706) 218/A4
Ewab (isls.), Indon. 85/J7
Ewa Beach, Hawaii (96706) 218/A4
Ewan, N.J. (08025) 273/C4
Ewan, Wash. (99127) 310/H3
Ewaninga, Aust. 88/E4
Ewaninga, No. Terr. 93/D8
Ewart, Iowa (†50171) 229/H5
Ewart, Man. 179/A5
Ewarton, Jam. 156/C3
Ewarton, Jam. 158/J6
Ewauna (lake), Oreg. 291/F5
Ewe (inlet), Scot. 15/E4
Ewell, Md. (21824) 245/O9
Ewen, Mich. (49925) 250/F2
Ewes, Scot. 15/K9
Ewing, Ill. (62836) 222/E5
Ewing, Ky. (41039) 237/O4
Ewing, Mo. (63440) 261/J2
Ewing, Nebr. (68735) 264/F2
Ewing (mt.), No. Terr. 93/E7
Ewing, Va. (24248) 307/B7
Ewings, Br. Col. 184/H5
Ewington, Ohio (45627) 284/F8
Ewo, Rep. of Congo 115/B4
Exaltación, El Beni, Bol. 136/C3
Exaltación, Pando, Bol. 136/B2
Excel, Ala. (36439) 194/D8
Excel, Alta. 182/E4
Excello, Mo. (65247) 261/H3
Excello, Ohio (45042) 284/B7
Excelsior, Ark. (†72936) 203/B3
Excelsior, Minn. (55331) 254/E6
Excelsior (mts.), Nev. 266/C4
Excelsior, Wis. (†53518) 317/E9
Excelsior Springs, Mo. (64024) 261/R4
Exchange, W. Va. (26619) 313/E5
Excursion Inlet, Alaska (†99826) 196/M1
Exe (riv.), Eng. 13/D7
Exe (riv.), 10/E5
Executive Committee (range), Ant. 5/B12
Exeland, Wis. (54835) 317/D4
Exeter, 10/E5
Exeter, Calif. (93221) 204/F7
Exeter, Conn. (†06249) 210/F2
Exeter, Ont. 177/C4
Exeter, Eng. 13/D7
Exeter, Ill. (†62694) 222/C4
Exeter△, Maine (04435) 242/E6
Exeter, Maine (04435) 242/E6
Exeter, Mo. (65647) 261/D9
Exeter△, N.H. (03833) 268/F6
Exeter, N.H. (03833) 268/F6
Exeter (riv.), N.H. 268/E6
Exeter (sound), N.W.T. 187/M3
Exeter, Nebr. (68351) 264/G4
Exeter‡, Pa. (18643) 294/L3
Exeter△, R.I. (02822) 249/H6
Exeter, R.I. (02822) 249/H6
Exira, Iowa (50076) 229/D5
Exline, Iowa (52555) 229/H7
Exminster, Eng. 13/D7
Exmoor (for.), Eng. 13/D6
Exmore, Va. (23350) 307/S5
Exmouth, 10/E5
Exmouth (gulf), Aust. 88/A4
Exmouth, Eng. 13/D7
Exmouth (gulf), W. Aust. 92/A3
Exmouth Gulf, Aust. 88/A4
Exmouth Gulf, W. Aust. 92/A3
Experiment, Ga. (30212) 216/D4
Exploits (bay), Newf. 166/C4
Exploits (riv.), Newf. 166/C4
Export, Pa. (15632) 294/C5
Exshaw, Alta. 182/D4
Extension, Br. Col. 184/J3
Extension, La. (71239) 238/G3
Exu, Braz. 132/G4
Exuma (cays), Bah. Is. 156/C1
Exuma (sound), Bah. Is. 156/C1
Eyasi (lake), Tanz. 115/F4
Eye, 10/G4
Eye, Eng. 13/J5
Eye (pen.), Scot. 15/D3
Eyebrow, Sask. 181/E5
Eyebrow (lake), Sask. 181/E5
Eyehill (creek), Sask. 181/B3
Eyemouth, 10/F3
Eyemouth, Scot. 15/M8
Eynesil, Turkey 63/H2
Eynhallow (sound), Scot. 15/K1
Eynort (inlet), Scot. 15/B5
Eyota, Minn. (55934) 254/F7
Eyre (lake), Australia, 87/D8
Eyre (lake), Aust. 88/F5
Eyre (pen.), Aust. 88/F6
Eyre, Aust. 88/D6
Eyre (bay), Chile 138/D8
Eyre (mts.), N.Z. 101/B6
Eyre, W. Aust. 92/D6
Eyre (pen.), S. Aust. 94/D5
Eyre, Sask. 181/B4
Eyrecourt, Ire. 17/E5
Eyre North (lake), S. Aust. 94/E3
Eyre South (lake), S. Aust. 94/E3
Eysturoy (isl.), Den. 21/B3
Eyüp, Turkey 63/D6
Ezel, Ky. (41425) 237/P5
Ezbider, Turkey 63/H2
Ezine, Turkey 63/B3
Ez Zababida, Jordan 65/C3
Ez Zarqa', Jordan 65/E3
Ez Zuetina, Libya 111/D1

F

Faaborg, Den. 18/G9
Faaborg, Ribe, Den. 21/B6
Faaborg, Svendborg, Den. 21/D7
Fabens, Texas (79838) 302/B10
Faber (lake), N.W.T. 187/G3
Faber, Va. (22938) 307/L5
Fabius, Ala. (35965) 194/G1
Fabius, N.Y. (13063) 276/J5
Fabriano, Italy 34/D3
Fabyan, Alta. 182/E3
Fabyan, Conn. (06245) 210/H1
Fabyan House, N.H. (03595) 268/E3
Facatativá, Col. 126/C5
Faceville, Ga. (†31717) 216/C9
Fachi, Niger 106/G5

362 Fackler

Fackler, Ala. (35746) 194/G1
Factoryville, Pa. (18419) 294/L2
Fada, Chad 111/D4
Fada-N'Gourma, Upp. Volta 106/E6
Faddeyevskiy (isl.), U.S.S.R. 48/P2
Faddeyevskiy (isl.), U.S.S.R., 4/B2
Faenza, Italy 34/D2
Faerøe (isls.), Den., 7/D2
Faerøe (isls.), Den. 21/B2
Fafan (riv.), Eth. 111/H6
Fafe, Port. 33/B2
Fagan, Ky. (†40322) 237/O5
Făgăraş, Rum. 45/G3
Fagernes, Norway 18/F6
Fagersta, Sweden 18/J6
Fagnano (lake), Arg. 143/C7
Fagnano (lake), Chile 138/F11
Faguibine (lake), Mali 106/D5
Fagus, Mo. (63938) 261/M9
Fahan, Ire. 17/G1
Fahrej (Iranshahr), Iran 59/H4
Fahrej (Iranshahr), Iran 66/M7
Faid, Saudi Ar. 59/D4
Faido, Switz. 39/G4
Fair (isl.), 10/F1
Fair (head), N. Ire. 17/J1
Fair (isl.), Scot. 15/L3
Fairacres, N. Mex. (88033) 274/C6
Fairbank, Ariz. (85612) 198/E7
Fairbank, Iowa (50629) 229/K3
Fairbank, Md. (†21671) 245/N6
Fairbanks, Alaska, 146/D3
Fairbanks, Alaska, 188/D5
Fairbanks, Alaska (99701) 196/J2
Fairbanks, Fla. (†32601) 212/D2
Fairbanks, Ind. (47849) 227/B6
Fairbanks, La. (71240) 238/F1
Fairbanks, Maine (†04938) 242/C6
Fairbanks, Minn. (†55602) 254/G3
Fairbanks, U.S., 3/C2
Fairbanks, U.S., 4/C17
Fair Bluff, N.C. (28439) 281/M6
Fairborn, Ohio (45324) 284/B6
Fairburn, Ga. (30213) 216/C3
Fairburn, S. Dak. (57738) 298/C6
Fairbury, Ill. (61739) 222/E3
Fairbury, Nebr. (68352) 264/G4
Fairchance, Pa. (15436) 294/C6
Fairchild, Wis. (54741) 317/D6
Fairchild A.F.B., Wash. 310/H3
Fairdale, Ill. (†60146) 222/E1
Fairdale, Ky. (40118) 237/K4
Fairdale, N. Dak. (58229) 283/O3
Fairdale‡, Pa. (†15320) 294/C6
Fairdealing, Mo. (63939) 261/L9
Fairfax, Ala. (36854) 194/H5
Fairfax, Calif. (94930) 204/H1
Fairfax, Iowa (52228) 229/K5
Fairfax, Man. 179/B5
Fairfax, Minn. (55332) 254/D6
Fairfax, Mo. (64446) 261/B2
Fairfax, Ohio (†45201) 284/C9
Fairfax, Okla. (74637) 288/N1
Fairfax, S.C. (29827) 296/E6
Fairfax, S. Dak. (57335) 298/M7
Fairfax (co.), Va. 307/O3
Fairfax, Va. (22030) 307/O3
Fairfax△, Vt. (05454) 268/B2
Fairfax, Vt. (05454) 268/B2
Fairfax, Wash. (†98323) 310/C4
Fairfield, Ala. (35064) 194/E3
Fairfield, Calif. (94533) 204/K1
Fairfield (co.), Conn. 210/B3
Fairfield△, Conn. (06430) 210/B4
Fairfield, Fla. (32634) 212/D2
Fairfield, Idaho (83327) 220/D6
Fairfield, Ill. (62837) 222/E5
Fairfield, Iowa (52556) 229/J6
Fairfield, Ky. (40020) 237/L5
Fairfield△, Maine (04937) 242/D6
Fairfield, Maine (04937) 242/D6
Fairfield, Mont. (59436) 262/D3
Fairfield, N.C. (27826) 281/S3
Fairfield, N. Dak. (58627) 283/D5
Fairfield, N.J. (07006) 273/A2
Fairfield, N.S.W. 97/H3
Fairfield, N.Z. 101/C6
Fairfield, Nebr. (68938) 264/G4
Fairfield (co.), Ohio 284/E6
Fairfield, Ohio (45014) 284/A7
Fairfield, Pa. (17320) 294/H6
Fairfield (co.), S.C. 296/E3
Fairfield, Tenn. (†37183) 237/J9
Fairfield, Texas (75840) 302/H6
Fairfield, Utah (†84013) 304/B3
Fairfield, Va. (24435) 307/K5
Fairfield△, Vt. (05455) 268/B2
Fairfield, Vt. (05455) 268/B2
Fairfield (pond), Vt. 268/A2
Fairfield, Wash. (99012) 310/H3
Fairfield Center, Maine (†04937) 242/D6
Fairford, Ala. (36531) 194/B8
Fairford, Man. 179/D3
Fairgrange, Ill. (†61920) 222/E4
Fairgrove, Mich. (48733) 250/F5
Fair Grove, Mo. (65648) 261/F8
Fair Harbour, Br. Col. 184/D5
Fairhaven△, Mass. (02719) 249/L6
Fairhaven, Mich. (48023) 250/G6
Fairhaven, Minn. (55383) 254/D5
Fairhaven, N. Br. 170/C4
Fair Haven, N.J. (07701) 273/E3
Fair Haven, N.Y. (13064) 276/G4
Fairhaven, Ohio (†45003) 284/A6
Fair Haven△, Vt. (05743) 268/A4
Fair Haven, Vt. (05743) 268/A4
Fair Hill, Md. (†21921) 245/P2
Fairholme, Sask. 181/C2
Fairhope, Ala. (36532) 194/C10
Fairhope, Pa. (15538) 294/E6
Fairhope-Arnold City‡, Pa. (15538) 294/C5
Fairland, Ind. (46126) 227/F5
Fairland, Okla. (74343) 288/S1
Fair Lawn, N.J. (07410) 273/B1
Fairlawn, Ohio (44313) 284/G3
Fairlawn, Va. (24141) 307/G6
Fairlee, Md. (†21620) 245/O4
Fairlee△, Vt. (05045) 268/C4
Fairlee, Vt. (05045) 268/C4
Fairless Hills, Pa. (19030) 294/N5
Fairlie, N.Z. 101/C6
Fairlight, Sask. 181/K6
Fairmead, Calif. (†93610) 204/E6
Fairmeade‡, Ky. (†40201) 237/K4
Fairmont, Ill. (†62002) 222/A6
Fairmont, Minn. (56031) 254/D7
Fairmont, Mo. (†63474) 261/J2
Fairmont, N.C. (28340) 281/L6
Fairmont, Nebr. (68354) 264/G4
Fairmont, Okla. (73736) 288/L2
Fairmont, W. Va., 188/K3
Fairmont, W. Va. (26554) 313/F4
Fairmont City, Ill. (†62201) 222/B6
Fairmont Heights, Md. (†20027) 245/G5
Fairmont Hot Springs, Br. Col. 184/J5
Fairmount, Ga. (30139) 216/C2
Fairmount, Ill. (61841) 222/F3
Fairmount, Ind. (46928) 227/F4
Fairmount, Md. (21871) 245/P8
Fairmount, N. Dak. (58030) 283/S7
Fairmount‡, N.Y. (†13209) 276/H4
Fairmount, Sask. 181/B4
Fair Oaks, Ark. (72397) 203/J3
Fair Oaks, Calif. (95628) 204/C8
Fair Oaks, Ind. (47943) 227/C2
Fair Oaks, Okla. (†74080) 288/P2
Fair Plain, Mich. (49022) 250/C6
Fairplain, W. Va. (†25271) 313/C5
Fairplay, Colo. (80440) 208/H4
Fairplay, Ky. (42735) 237/L7
Fair Play, Mo. (65649) 261/E7
Fair Play, S.C. (29643) 296/A2
Fairpoint, Ohio (43927) 284/J5
Fairpoint, S. Dak. (57339) 298/D4
Fairport, Iowa (†52761) 229/M6
Fairport, Kans. (†67665) 232/C2
Fairport, Mo. (64447) 261/D2
Fairport, N.Y. (14450) 276/F4
Fairport, Va. (†22539) 307/R5
Fairport Harbor, Ohio (44077) 284/H2
Fairton, N.J. (08320) 273/C5
Fairvale, N. Br. 170/E3
Fairview, Ala. (35208) 194/E2
Fairview, Alta. 182/A1
Fairview, Ill. (61432) 222/C3
Fairview, Ind. (†46127) 227/G5
Fairview, Ind. (†47018) 227/G7
Fairview, Kans. (66425) 232/G2
Fairview, Ky. (42221) 237/G7
Fairview, Ky. (†41000) 237/S3
Fairview, Mich. (48621) 250/F4
Fairview, Mo. (64842) 261/D9
Fairview, Mont. (59221) 262/M3
Fairview, N.C. (28730) 281/D3
Fairview, N.J. (07022) 273/C2
Fairview, N.Y. (†12601) 276/N7
Fairview, Ohio (43736) 284/H5
Fairview, Okla. (73737) 288/J2
Fairview, Oreg. (97024) 291/B2
Fairview, Pa. (16415) 294/B1
Fairview, Pa. (†16041) 294/C3
Fairview, S. Dak. (57027) 298/R7
Fairview, Tenn. (37062) 237/G9
Fairview‡, Texas (†75002) 302/H4
Fairview, Utah (84629) 304/C4
Fairview, W. Va. (26570) 313/F3
Fairview, Wash. (†98901) 310/E4
Fairview, Wyo. (83119) 319/B3
Fairview Acres‡, Mo. (†63601) 261/M7
Fairview-Ferndale‡, Pa. (16415) 294/J4
Fairview Heights, Ill. (62232) 222/B6
Fairview Park, Ind. (†47842) 227/C5
Fairview Park, Ohio (44126) 284/G9
Fairvilla, Fla. (‡32804) 212/E3
Fair Water, Wis. (53931) 317/J8
Fairway‡, Kans. (†66101) 232/H2
Fairweather (mt.), 163/C4
Fairweather (cape), Alaska 196/L1
Fairweather (mt.), Alaska 196/L1
Fairweather (mt.), Br. Col. 184/H1
Fairy Glen, Sask. 181/G2
Fairy Hill, Sask. 181/G5
Fais (isl.), Pac. Is., 87/E5
Faison, N.C. (28341) 281/N4
Faith, Alta. 182/E5
Faith, Minn. (†56584) 254/B3
Faith, N.C. (28041) 281/J3
Faith, S. Dak. (57626) 298/E4
Faithorn, Mich. (†49892) 250/B3
Faizabad, Afghan., 54/K6
Faizabad, Afgh. 59/K2
Faizabad, Afgh. 68/C1
Faizabad, India 68/E3
Fajami, Syria 63/J5
Fajardo, P. Rico 161/F1
Fajardo (riv.), P. Rico 161/F1
Fajou (isl.), Guad. 161/A6
Fakaofo (isl.), Tokelau Is., 87/J5
Fakarava (atoll), Fr. Poly., 87/M7
Fakenham, Eng. 13/H5
Fakfak, Indon. 85/J6
Fakili, Turkey 63/F3
Fakse, Den. 21/F7
Fakse (bay), Den. 21/F7
Fakse Ladeplads, Den. 21/F7
Falaise, France 28/C3
Falam, Burma 72/B2
Falama, Jordan 65/C3
Fălciu, Rum. 45/J2
Falcon, Ky. (41426) 237/P5
Falcon (lake), Man. 179/G5
Falcón (res.), Mex. 150/K3
Falcon, Miss. (38628) 256/D2
Falcon, N.C. (28342) 281/M4
Falcon (cape), Oreg. 291/C2
Falcon (res.), Texas, 188/G5
Falcon (dam), Texas 302/E11
Falcon (res.), Texas 302/E11
Falcón (state), Ven. 124/D2
Falcone (cape), Italy 34/B4
Falconer, N.Y. (14733) 276/B6
Falcon Heights, Minn. (55113) 254/G5
Falcon Heights, Oreg. (†97601) 291/F5
Falcon Lake, Man. 179/G5
Falémé (riv.), Mali 106/B6
Falémé (riv.), Sen. 106/B6
Falfurrias, Texas (78355) 302/F10
Falher, Alta. 182/B2
Falkenberg, Sweden 18/H8
Falkensee, E. Ger. 22/E3
Falkenstein, E. Ger. 22/E3
Falkirk, 10/B1
Falkirk, N. Dak. (†58577) 283/H5
Falkirk, Scot. 15/E1
Falkland (isls.), 3/G8
Falkland Islands, 120/E8
Falkland, Br. Col. 184/H5
Falkland, N.C (27827) 281/O3
Falkner, Miss. (38629) 256/G1
Falknov (Sokolov), Czech. 41/B1
Falköping, Sweden 18/H7
Falkville, Ala. (35622) 194/E2
Fall (riv.), Kans. 232/G4
Falla, Cuba 158/F2
Fall Branch, Tenn. (37656) 237/R8
Fallbrook, Calif. (92028) 204/H10
Fall City, Wash. (98024) 310/D3
Fall Creek, Oreg. (97438) 291/E4
Fall Creek, Wis. (54742) 317/D6
Falling Springs (Renick), W. Va. (†24966) 313/F6
Falling Waters, W. Va. (25419) 313/L3
Fallis, Okla. (†74881) 288/M3
Fall Mills, Tenn. (†37345) 237/J10
Fallon (co.), Mont. 262/M4
Fallon, Mont. (59326) 262/L4
Fallon, Nev. (89406) 266/C3
Fallon Ind Res., Nev. 266/C3
Fallon N.A.A.S., Nev. 266/C3
Fall River, Kans. (67047) 232/G4
Fall River (res.), Kans. 232/F4
Fall River, Mass., 188/M2
Fall River, Mass. (*02720) 249/K6
Fall River (co.), S. Dak. 298/B7
Fall River, Tenn. (†38468) 237/G10
Fall River, Wis. (53932) 317/H9
Fall River Mills, Calif. (96028) 204/D3
Falls (riv.), Mass. 249/D2
Falls, Pa. (18615) 294/L3
Falls (co.), Texas 302/H6
Falls Church, Va. (*22040) 307/O3
Falls City, Nebr. (68355) 264/J4
Falls City, Oreg. (97344) 291/D3
Falls City, Texas (78113) 302/G9
Falls Creek, Pa. (15840) 294/E3
Falls Mill, W. Va. (26620) 313/E5
Falls Mills, Va. (24613) 307/F6
Falls of Rough, Ky. (40119) 237/J5
Fallston, Md. (21047) 245/N2
Fallston‡, Pa. (†15066) 294/B4
Falls Village, Conn. (06031) 210/B1
Fallsville, Ark. (†72861) 203/D2
Falmouth, 10/D5
Falmouth, Antigua 156/F3
Falmouth, Antigua 161/E11
Falmouth, Eng. 13/C7
Falmouth (bay), Eng. 13/C7
Falmouth, Ind. (46127) 227/G5
Falmouth, Jam. 156/C3
Falmouth, Jam. 158/H5
Falmouth, Ky. (41040) 237/N3
Falmouth△, Maine (04105) 242/C8
Falmouth, Maine (04105) 242/C8
Falmouth△, Mass. (*02540) 249/M6
Falmouth, Mass. (*02540) 249/M6
Falmouth, Mich. (49632) 250/E4
Falmouth, N.S. 169/D3
Falmouth, Va. (22401) 307/O4
Falmouth Foreside (Falmouth), Maine (†04105) 242/C8
Falsa (cape), Hond. 154/F3
False (pt.), India 68/F4
False (bay), S. Africa 118/F7
False Detour (chan.), Mich. 250/F3
False Divi (pt.), India 68/E5
False Pass, Alaska (99583) 196/F4
Falso (cape), Dom. Rep. 158/C7
Falso (cape), Mex. 150/D5
Falster (isl.), Den. 21/E8
Fălticeni, Rum. 45/H2
Falun, Sweden 18/J6
Falun, Kans. (67442) 232/E3
Falun, Sweden, 7/F2
Falun, Wis. (†54840) 317/A4
Famagusta, Cyprus 59/B3
Famagusta, Cyprus 63/F5
Famagusta (bay), Cyprus 63/F5
Famaka, 102/F3
Famaka, Sudan 111/F5
Famatina, Arg. 143/C2
Famatina, Sierra de (mts.), Arg. 143/C2
Family (lake), Man. 179/G3
Famoso, Calif. (†93280) 204/F8
Fan (lake), N. Dak. 283/L2
Fanad (head), Ire. 17/F1
Fancy Farm, Ky. (42039) 237/D7
Fancy Gap, Va. (24328) 307/G7
Fancy Prairie, Ill. (62637) 222/D4
Fandriana, Malag. Rep. 118/H4
Fangak, Sudan 111/F6
Fannettsburg, Pa. (17221) 294/G5
Fannich (lake), Scot. 15/F4
Fannin (co.), Ga. 216/D1
Fannin, Miss. (†39042) 256/E6
Fannin (co.), Texas 302/H4
Fannin, Texas (77960) 302/G9
Fanning (isl.), 3/B5
Fanning (isl.), Gilb. and Ell., 87/L5
Fannystelle, Man. 179/E5
Fanø (isl.), Den. 18/F9
Fanø (isl.), Den. 21/B7
Fano, Italy 34/D3
Fanshaw, Alaska (†99833) 196/N1
Fanshawe, Okla. (74935) 288/S5
Fan Si Pan (mt.), N. Vietnam 72/D2
Fantasque (pt.), Haiti 158/B6
Fanwood, N.J. (07023) 273/E2
Fao, Iraq 66/F6
Faradje, Dem. Rep. of the Congo. 115/E3
Farafangana, 102/G7
Farafangana, Malag. Rep. 118/H4
Farâfra (oasis), U.A.R. 59/A4
Farâfra (oasis), U.A.R. 111/E2
Farah, Afgh. 59/H3
Farah, Afgh. 68/A2
Farah Rud (riv.), Afgh. 59/H3
Farah Rud (riv.), Afgh. 68/A2
Farallon (isls.), Calif. 204/B6
Farallon de Pajaros (isl.), Pac. Is., 87/E3
Farallons, The (gulf), Calif. 204/H2
Faranah, Guinea 106/B6
Farasan (isls.), Saudi Ar. 59/D6
Farasan (isls.), Saudi Ar., 54/H8
Faraulep (atoll), Pac. Is., 87/E5
Farber, Mo. (63345) 261/J4
Fardale (Farwell), Nebr. (†68838) 264/F3
Fareham, 10/F5
Fareham, Eng. 13/F7
Farewell, Alaska (†99629) 196/H2
Farewell (cape), Greenl., 4/D12
Farewell (cape), Greenl., 146/O4
Farewell (cape), N.Z. 101/D4
Farfa, Italy 34/D3
Farfán, Ec. 128/D2
Fargo, Ark. (72049) 203/H4
Fargo, Ga. (31631) 216/G9
Fargo, Mich. (†48006) 250/G5
Fargo, N.Dak., 146/J5
Fargo, N. Dak., 188/G1
Fargo, N. Dak. (58102) 283/S6
Fargo, Okla. (73840) 288/G2
Fargo, Texas (†76384) 302/E3
Far Hills, N.J. (07931) 273/D2
Faribault, Minn., 188/H2
Faribault (co.), Minn. 254/D7
Faribault, Minn. (55021) 254/E6
Faridpur, Pak. 68/F4
Fariman, Iran 66/L3
Farina, Aust. 88/F5
Farina, Ill. (62838) 222/E5
Faringdon, Eng. 13/F6
Farisita, Colo. (81037) 208/J7
Fariston, Ky. (†40741) 237/N6
Färjestaden, Sweden 18/K8
Farler, Ky. (41742) 237/P6
Farley, Iowa (52046) 229/L4
Farley, Mo. (64028) 261/O4
Farley, N. Mex. (87720) 274/E2
Farlin, Iowa (50077) 229/E4
Farlington, Kans. (66734) 232/H4
Farm (riv.), Conn. 210/D3
Farmdale, Ohio (44417) 284/J3
Farmer, N.C. (27203) 281/K3
Farmer (isl.), N.W.T. 187/K4
Farmer, Ohio (43520) 284/A3
Farmer, S. Dak. (57336) 298/O6
Farmer City, Ill. (61842) 222/E3
Farmers, Ky. (40319) 237/P4
Farmers Branch, Texas (75234) 302/G1
Farmersburg, Ind. (47850) 227/C6
Farmersburg, Iowa (52047) 229/L3
Farmersville, Ala. (36737) 194/E6
Farmersville, Calif. (93223) 204/F7
Farmersville, Ill. (62533) 222/D4
Farmersville, Mo. (†64683) 261/E3
Farmersville, Ohio (45325) 284/A6
Farmersville, Texas (75031) 302/H4
Farmerville, La. (71241) 238/F1
Farmhaven, Miss. (†39046) 256/E5
Farmill (riv.), Conn. 210/C3
Farmingdale△, Maine (†04345) 242/D7
Farmingdale, Maine (†04345) 242/D7
Farmingdale, N.J. (07727) 273/E3
Farmingdale, N.Y. (11735) 276/N9
Farmingdale, S. Dak. (57740) 298/D6
Farmingdale, Sask. 181/H3
Farmington, Ark. (72730) 203/B1
Farmington, Br. Col. 184/G2
Farmington, Calif. (95230) 204/E6
Farmington△, Conn. (06032) 210/D2
Farmington (riv.), Conn. 210/D1
Farmington, Del. (19942) 245/R5
Farmington, Ga. (30638) 216/F3
Farmington, Ill. (61531) 222/C3
Farmington, Iowa (52626) 229/K7
Farmington, Ky. (42040) 237/D7
Farmington△, Maine (04938) 242/C6
Farmington, Maine (04938) 242/C6
Farmington, Md. (†21911) 245/O2
Farmington, Mich. (48024) 250/F6
Farmington, Minn. (55024) 254/E6
Farmington, Mo. (63640) 261/M7
Farmington, N.C. (†27028) 281/H3
Farmington△, N.H. (03835) 268/E5
Farmington, N.H. (03835) 268/E5
Farmington, N. Mex. (87401) 274/A2
Farmington, Oreg. (†97123) 291/A2
Farmington, Tenn. (†37091) 237/H9
Farmington, Utah (84025) 304/C3
Farmington, W. Va. (26571) 313/F3
Farmington, Wash. (99128) 310/H3
Farmington Falls, Maine (04940) 242/C6
Farmland, Ind. (47340) 227/G4
Farmville, N.C. (27828) 281/O3
Farmville, Va. (23901) 307/M6
Farnam, Nebr. (69029) 264/D4
Farnams, Mass. (†01225) 249/B2
Farnborough, Eng. 13/G6
Farner, Tenn. (37333) 237/N10
Farnham, 10/F5
Farnham, Que. 172/E4
Farnham, Eng. 13/G6
Farnham, N.Y. (14061) 276/B6
Farnham, Va. (22460) 307/P5
Farnhamville, Iowa (50538) 229/D4
Farnsworth, Texas (79033) 302/C1
Farnumsville, Mass. (†01560) 249/H4
Faro, Braz. 132/B3
Faro, Port. 33/B4
Fårö (isl.), Sweden 18/L8
Faro, Yukon 187/E3
Fårösund, Sweden 18/L8
Farquhar (cape), Aust. 88/A4
Farquhar (cape), W. Aust. 92/A3
Farr (bay), Ant. 5/C5
Farragut, Iowa (51639) 229/C7
Farrar, Ga. (31027) 216/E4
Farrar, Iowa (50161) 229/G5
Farrar, Mo. (63740) 261/N7
Farrar (riv.), Scot. 15/G5
Farrashband, Iran 66/G6
Farrell (lake), Alta. 182/D4
Farrell, Miss. (38630) 256/C2
Farrell, Pa. (16121) 294/A3
Farris, Okla. (74542) 288/P6
Fars (prov.), Iran 66/H6
Fársala, Greece 45/F6
Farsi, Afgh. 59/H3
Farsi (isl.), Iran 66/G7
Farsi, Afgh. 68/A2
Farsø, Den. 21/C4
Farson, Iowa (†52563) 229/J6
Farson, Wyo. (82932) 319/C3
Farsund, Norway 18/E7
Fartak, Ras (cape), P.D.R. Yemen 59/F6
Farum, Den. 21/F6
Farwell, Mich. (48622) 250/E5
Farwell, Minn. (56327) 254/C5
Farwell, Nebr. (68838) 264/F3
Farwell, Texas (79325) 302/A3
Fasa, Iran 59/F4
Fasa, Iran 66/H6
Fasano, Italy 34/F4
Fashoda (Kodok), Sudan 111/F6
Fassett, Que. 172/C4
Fastnet Rock (isl.), Ire. 17/B9
Fastov, U.S.S.R. 52/C4
Fatagar Tuting (cape), Indon. 85/J6
Fate‡, Texas (75032) 302/H5
Fatehgarh, India 68/D3
Fatehpur, Rajasthan, India 68/C3
Fatehpur, Uttar Pradesh, India 68/E3
Father Point, Que. 172/J1
Fatih, Turkey 63/D6
Fátima, Port. 33/B3
Fatsa, Turkey 63/G2
Fatshan, China, 54/P7
Fatshan, China 77/H7
Fatuhiva (isl.), Fr. Poly., 87/N7
Faubush, Ky. (42532) 237/M6
Faucett, Mo. (64448) 261/C3
Faucilles (mts.), France 28/G3
Fauldhouse, 10/C1
Faulk (co.), S. Dak. 298/L3
Faulkner (co.), Ark. 203/F3
Faulkner, Iowa (†50601) 229/G3
Faulkner, Man. 179/D3
Faulkton, S. Dak. (57438) 298/L3
Faunsdale, Ala. (36738) 194/C6
Fauquier, Ont. 175/D3
Fauquier, Ont. 177/J5
Fauquier (co.), Va. 307/N3
Faust, Alta. 182/C2
Favara, Italy 34/D6
Faversham, 10/G5
Faversham, Eng. 13/J6
Favignana (isl.), Italy 34/D6
Fawcett, Alta. 182/C2
Fawley, Eng. 13/F7
Fawn (lake), 163/H5
Fawn (riv.), Ont. 175/C2
Fawn (riv.), Ind. 227/G1
Fawn (riv.), Mich. 250/D7
Fawn Grove, Pa. (17321) 294/J6
Fawnskin, Calif. (92333) 204/J9
Faxaflói (bay), Ice. 21/B1
Faxon, Okla. (73540) 288/J6
Faxon‡, Pa. (†17701) 294/J3
Fay, Ill. (†61285) 222/C2
Fay, Okla. (73646) 288/J3
Faya (Largeau), Chad 111/C4
Fayette (co.), Ala. 194/C3
Fayette, Ala. (35555) 194/C3
Fayette (co.), Ga. 216/C4
Fayette (co.), Ill. 222/D4
Fayette (co.), Ind. 227/G5
Fayette, Ind. (†46052) 227/E5
Fayette (co.), Iowa 229/K3
Fayette, Iowa (52142) 229/K3
Fayette (co.), Ky. 237/N4
Fayette△, Maine (04344) 242/C7
Fayette, Miss. (39069) 256/B7
Fayette, Mo. (65248) 261/G4
Fayette, N. Dak. (†58642) 283/E5
Fayette (co.), Ohio 284/D6
Fayette, Ohio (43521) 284/B2
Fayette (co.), Pa. 294/C6
Fayette (co.), Tenn. 237/C10
Fayette (co.), Texas 302/H8
Fayette, Utah (84630) 304/C4
Fayette (co.), W. Va. 313/D6
Fayette City, Pa. (15438) 294/C5
Fayetteville, Ala. (†35150) 194/F4
Fayetteville, Ark., 188/H3
Fayetteville, Ark. (72701) 203/B1
Fayetteville, Ga. (30214) 216/C4
Fayetteville, Ill. (†62258) 222/D5
Fayetteville, Ind. (†47421) 227/D7
Fayetteville, Mo. (†64093) 261/E5
Fayetteville, N.C., 188/L3
Fayetteville, N.C. (*28301) 281/M4
Fayetteville, N.Y. (13066) 276/J4
Fayetteville, Ohio (45118) 284/C7
Fayetteville, Pa. (17222) 294/G6
Fayetteville, Tenn. (37334) 237/H10
Fayetteville, Texas (78940) 302/H8
Fayetteville, W. Va. (25840) 313/D6
Fayville, Mass. (01745) 249/H3
Faywood, N. Mex. (88034) 274/B6
F'Dérick, Mauritania 106/B4
Feakle, Ire. 17/D6
Feale (riv.), Ire. 17/C7
Fear (cape), N.C., 188/L4
Fear (cape), N.C. 281/O7
Fearer, Md. (†21531) 245/A2
Fearn, Scot. 15/J4
Fearns Springs, Miss. (†39339) 256/G4
Feather (riv.), Calif. 204/D4
Feather Falls, Calif. (95940) 204/D4
Featherston, N.Z. 101/E4
Featherston, Okla. (†74561) 288/P4
Fécamp, France 28/D3
Fédala (Mohammedia), Mor. 106/C2
Federación, Arg. 143/G5
Federal, Alta. 182/E3
Federal (dist.), Braz., 120/F4
Federal, Wyo. (†82001) 319/G4
Federal Dam, Minn. (56641) 254/D3
Federal District, Braz. 132/E6
Federal Heights, Colo. (†80030) 208/J3
Federalsburg, Md. (21632) 245/P6
Fedora, S. Dak. (57337) 298/O5
Fedscreek, Ky. (41524) 237/S6
Feeagh (lake), Ire. 17/B4
Feeding Hills, Mass. (01030) 249/D4
Feeny, N. Ire. 17/H2
Feesburg, Ohio (45119) 284/B8
Fegyvernek, Hung. 41/F3
Fehérgyarmat, Hung. 41/G3
Fehmarn (str.), Den. 21/E8
Fehmarn (isl.), W. Ger. 22/D1
Fehmarn (str.), W. Ger. 22/D1
Feia (lag.), Braz. 135/F3
Feilding, N.Z. 101/E4
Feio (riv.), Braz. 135/B2
Feira, Zambia 115/E7
Feira, Port. 33/B2
Feira de Santana, Braz. 132/G5
Fejér (co.), Hung. 41/E3
Feke, Turkey 63/F4
Felanitx, Spain 33/H3
Felch, Mich. (49831) 250/B3
Felchville (Reading), Vt. (†05062) 268/B5
Felda, Fla. (33930) 212/E5
Feldbach, Austria 41/C3
Feldberg (mt.), W. Ger. 22/C5
Feldkirch, Austria 41/A3
Feldkirchen in Kärnten, Austria 41/B3
Feliciano (riv.), Arg. 143/G5
Felicidad, Cuba 158/K4
Felicité (isl.), Seych. 118/J5
Felicity, Ohio (45120) 284/B8
Felipe Carillo Puerto, Mex. 150/P7
Felix (cape), N.W.T. 187/J3
Felixstowe, 10/G5
Felixstowe, Eng. 13/J6
Fellbach, W. Ger. 22/C4
Fellers Heights, Br. Col. 184/G2
Felletin, France 28/E5
Fellows, Calif. (93224) 204/F8
Fellowsville, W. Va. (†26410) 313/G4
Fellsburg, Kans. (67048) 232/C4
Fellsburg‡, Pa. (†15012) 294/C5
Fellsmere, Fla. (32948) 212/F4
Fels, Austria 41/C2
Felsenthal, Ark. (†71747) 203/F7
Felt, Idaho (83424) 220/G6
Felt, Okla. (73937) 288/A1
Felton, Ark. (†72360) 203/J4
Felton, Calif. (95018) 204/K4
Felton, Del. (19943) 245/R4
Felton, Ga. (30140) 216/B3
Felton, Minn. (56536) 254/B3
Felton, Pa. (17322) 294/J6
Feltre, Italy 34/C1
Felts Mills, N.Y. (13638) 276/J3
Felty, Ky. (40933) 237/O6
Femme Osage, Mo. (†63332) 261/M3
Femund (lake), Norway 18/G5
Fence (riv.), Mich. 250/A2
Fence, Wis. (54120) 317/K4
Fence Lake, N. Mex. (87315) 274/A4
Fender, Ga. (31794) 216/E8
Fenelon Falls, Ont. 177/F3
Fénérive, Malag. Rep. 118/H3
Fengfeng, China 77/H4
Fenghsien, China 77/G5
Fengkieh, China, 54/O6
Fengkieh, China 77/G5
Fengning, China 77/J3
Fen Ho (riv.), China 77/H4
Fenholloway (riv.), Fla. 212/C1
Fenimore (passg.), Alaska 196/L4
Fenit, Ire. 17/B7
Fenn, Alta. 182/D3
Fenn, Idaho (83531) 220/B4
Fenner, Calif. (92334) 204/K9
Fennimore, Wis. (53809) 317/E9
Fennville, Mich. (49408) 250/C6
Fenoarivo, Malag. Rep. 118/H4
Fenton (riv.), Conn. 210/G1
Fenton, Ill. (61251) 222/C2
Fenton, Iowa (50539) 229/E2
Fenton, La. (70640) 238/E6
Fenton, Mich. (48430) 250/F6
Fenton, Mo. (63026) 261/P3
Fenton, Sask. 181/F2
Fentress (co.), Tenn. 237/M8
Fenwick, Conn. (†06475) 210/F3
Fenwick, Mich. (48834) 250/D5
Fenwick, N.S. 169/D3
Fenwick, W. Va. (26202) 313/E6
Fenwick Island, Del. (19944) 245/T7
Fenwood, Sask. 181/D6
Fenwood, Wis. (54431) 317/F6
Fenyang, China 77/H4
Feodosiya, U.S.S.R. 52/D5
Ferbane, Ire. 17/F5
Ferdig, Mont. (59437) 262/E2
Ferdinand, Idaho (83526) 220/B3
Ferdinand, Ind. (47532) 227/D8
Ferfer, Somalia 115/J2
Fergana, U.S.S.R. 48/H5
Fergus, Ont. 177/D4
Fergus (riv.), Ire. 17/D6
Fergus (co.), Mont. 262/G3
Fergus, Mont. (59438) 262/H3
Fergus Falls, Minn. (56537) 254/B4
Ferguson, Br. Col. 184/J5
Ferguson, Iowa (50078) 229/H5
Ferguson, Ky. (42533) 237/M6
Ferguson, Mo. (63135) 261/P2
Ferguson, N.C. (28624) 281/G2
Ferguson, W. Va. (†25511) 313/B6
Ferguson Lake, N.W.T. 187/J3
Ferintosh, Alta. 182/D3
Ferkessédougou, Ivory Coast 106/D7
Ferlach, Austria 41/C3
Ferland, Sask. 181/D6
Ferlo (reg.), Sen. 106/B6
Fermanagh (co.), N. Ire. 17/F3
Ferme-Neuve, Que. 172/B3
Fermeuse, Newf. 166/D2
Fermo, Italy 34/D3
Fermoselle, Spain 33/C2
Fermoy, 10/B4
Fermoy, Ire. 17/E7
Fernald, Iowa (50201) 229/G4
Fernández, Arg. 143/D2
Fernandina (isl.), Ec. 128/B9
Fernandina Beach, Fla. (32034) 212/E1
Fernando de la Mora, Par. 144/A6
Fernando de Noronha (isl.), Braz., 120/G3
Fernando Po (terr.), Eq. Guin. 115/A3
Fernando Po (isl.), Eq. Guin. 115/A3
Fernando Po (terr.), 102/C4
Fernando Po (isl.), 102/C4
Fernandópolis, Braz. 135/A2
Fernan Lake‡, Idaho (†83814) 220/B2
Fernbank, Ala. (35558) 194/B3
Fern Crest Village, Fla. (†33301) 212/B4
Ferndale, Calif. (95536) 204/A3
Ferndale, Md. (21061) 245/M4
Ferndale, Mich. (48220) 250/B6

Folsom **363**

Ferndale, Pa. (18921) 294/E5
Ferndale, Pa. (18921) 294/M4
Ferndale, Wash. (98248) 310/C2
Ferney, S. Dak. (57439) 298/N3
Fernie, 163/E6
Fernie, Br. Col. 184/K5
Fernley, Nev. (89408) 266/B3
Fern Ridge (res.), Oreg. 291/D3
Ferns, Ire. 17/J6
Fern Tree Gully, Vic. 97/K5
Fernwood, Idaho (83830) 220/B2
Fernwood, Miss. (39635) 256/D8
Fernwood, N.Y. (†13142) 276/H4
Fernwood, N.Y. (†12801) 276/N4
Ferolle (pt.), Newf. 166/C3
Ferozepore, India 68/C2
Ferrandina, Italy 34/F4
Ferrara, Italy, 7/F4
Ferrara (prov.), Italy 34/C2
Ferrara, Italy 34/C2
Ferré (cape), Mart. 161/E7
Ferreira do Alentejo, Port. 33/B3
Ferreira Gomes, Braz. 132/D2
Ferrellsburg, W. Va. (25513) 313/B6
Ferrelo (cape), Oreg. 291/C5
Ferrelview‡, Mo. (64163) 261/O4
Ferreñafe, Peru 128/C6
Ferriday, La. (71334) 238/G3
Ferris, Ont. 177/E1
Ferris, Ill. (62336) 222/B3
Ferris, Texas (75125) 302/H2
Ferris (mts.), Wyo. 319/E3
Ferrisburg∆, Vt. (05456) 268/A3
Ferrisburg, Vt. (05456) 268/A3
Ferrol (pen.), Peru 128/C7
Ferron, Utah (84523) 304/C4
Ferron (creek), Utah 304/C4
Ferros, Braz. 132/F7
Ferrum, Va. (24088) 307/H7
Ferry, Alaska (†99760) 196/J2
Ferry, Guad. 161/A6
Ferry, Mich. (49455) 250/C5
Ferry (co.), Wash. 310/G2
Ferryland, Newf. 166/D2
Ferryland (cape), Newf. 166/D2
Ferry Road, N. Br. 170/E1
Ferrysburg, Mich. (49409) 250/C5
Ferryville, Wis. (54628) 317/D9
Fertigs, Pa. (†16364) 294/C3
Fertile, Iowa (50434) 229/G2
Fertile, Minn. (56540) 254/B3
Fertile, Sask. 181/K6
Fertilia, Italy 34/B4
Fertő tó (Neusiedler) (lake), Austria 41/D3
Fertő tó (Neusiedler) (lake), Hung. 41/D3
Feshi, Dem. Rep. of the Congo. 115/C5
Fessenden, N. Dak. (58438) 283/L4
Festina, Iowa (52143) 229/K2
Festus, Mo. (63028) 261/M6
Feteşti, Rum. 45/H3
Fethard, Tipperary, Ire. 17/F7
Fethard, Wexford, Ire. 17/H7
Fethiye, Turkey 59/A2
Fethiye, Turkey 63/C4
Fetlar (isl.), 10/H1
Fetlar (isl.), Scot. 15/N2
Fetteresso, Scot. 15/M6
Feudal, Sask. 181/D4
Feuilles (riv.), Que. 174/C1
Feuilles (riv.), 163/J4
Feversham, Ont. 177/D3
Fevzipaşa, Turkey 63/G4
Fez, 102/B1
Fez, Mor. 106/D2
Fezzan (reg.), Libya 111/B2
Fezzan (reg.), 102/D2
Ffestiniog, 10/E4
Ffestiniog, Wales 13/D5
Fiambalá, Arg. 143/C2
Fianarantsoa, 102/G7
Fianarantsoa (prov.), Malag. Rep. 118/H3
Fianarantsoa, Malag. Rep. 118/H4
Fianga, Chad 111/C6
Fiat, Ind. (†47326) 227/G3
Fiatt, Ill. (61433) 222/C3
Fichtelberg (mt.), E. Ger. 22/E3
Fichtelgebirge (range), W. Ger. 22/D3
Fickle, Ind. (†46035) 227/D4
Ficklin, Ga. (†30673) 216/G3
Ficksburg, S. Africa 118/D5
Fidalgo (isl.), Wash. 310/C2
Fiddown, Ire. 17/G7
Fidelity, Ill. (62030) 222/C4
Fidelity‡, Mo. (†64836) 261/D8
Fidenza, Italy 34/B2
Fieberbrunn, Austria 41/B3
Field, Br. Col. 184/J4
Field, Ont. 177/E1
Field, Ky. (40934) 237/O7
Fieldale, Va. (24089) 307/H7
Field Creek, Texas (76838) 302/F7
Fielding, Sask. 181/D3
Fielding, Utah (84311) 304/B2
Fieldon, Ill. (62031) 222/C4
Fields, La. (70641) 238/C5
Fields (lake), La. 238/J7
Fields, Oreg. (97710) 291/J5
Fieldsboro, N.J. (†08505) 273/D3
Fieldton, Texas (79326) 302/B3
Fier, Alb. 45/D5
Fierro, N. Mex. (†88041) 274/A6
Fiesch, Switz. 39/F4
Fiesole, Italy 34/C3
Fife (lake), Sask. 181/E6
Fife (co.), Scot. 15/K7
Fife, Wash. (98424) 310/C3
Fife Lake, Mich. (49633) 250/D4
Fife Lake, Sask. 181/F6
Fife Ness (prom.), Scot. 15/L7
Fifield, N.S.W. 97/D3
Fifield, Wis. (54524) 317/F4
Fifteenmile (creek), Oreg. 291/F2
Fifteenmile Arroyo (creek), N. Mex. 274/D4
Fifth (lake), Maine 242/H5
Fifth Cataract, Sudan, 102/F3
Fifth Cataract, Sudan 59/B6
Fifth Cataract, Sudan 111/F4
Fifty Lakes, Minn. (56448) 254/D4
Fig (riv.), Newf. 166/B3
Figeac, France 28/D5
Figueira da Foz, Port. 33/B2
Figueras, Spain 33/H1
Figuig, 102/B1
Figuig, Mor. 106/D2
Figuras (pt.), P. Rico 161/E3
Fiji, 3/A6
Fiji, 87/H8
Filadelfia, Bol. 136/A2
Filadelfia, C. Rica 154/E5
Filadelfia, Par. 144/C4
Fil'akovo, Czech. 41/E2
Filbert, S.C. (†29745) 296/E1
Filbert, W. Va. (24835) 313/D8
Filchner Ice Shelf, Ant., 3/H10
Filchner Ice Shelf, Ant. 5/B16
Fildi Remia (peak), Switz. 39/H4
File (hills), Sask. 181/H5
Filer, Idaho (83328) 220/D7
Filer City, Mich. (49634) 250/C4
Filey, 10/F3
Filey, Eng. 13/G3
Filiátes, Greece 45/E6
Filiatrá, Greece 45/E7
Filicudi (isl.), Italy 34/E5
Filingué, Niger 106/E6
Filion, Mich. (48432) 250/G5
Filipstad, Sweden 18/H7
Filisur, Switz. 39/J3
Filley, Nebr. (68357) 264/H4
Fillmore, Calif. (93015) 204/G9
Fillmore, Ill. (62032) 222/D4
Fillmore, Ind. (46128) 227/D5
Fillmore (co.), Minn. 254/F7
Fillmore, Minn. (†55990) 254/F7
Fillmore, Mo. (64449) 261/C2
Fillmore, N. Dak. (58333) 283/L3
Fillmore, N.Y. (14735) 276/D6
Fillmore (co.), Nebr. 264/G4
Fillmore, Okla. (73434) 288/N6
Fillmore, Sask. 181/H6
Fillmore, Utah (84631) 304/B5
Filtu, Eth. 111/H6
Filyos (riv.), Turkey 63/D2
Fimi (riv.), Dem. Rep. of the Congo. 115/C4
Finale Emilia, Italy 34/C2
Finale Ligure, Italy 34/B2
Fiñana, Spain 33/E4
Fincastle, Ind. (†46172) 227/D5
Fincastle, Va. (24090) 307/J6
Finch, Ont. 177/J2
Finch, Mont. (†59076) 262/K4
Finchburg, Ala. (36440) 194/D7
Finchville, Ky. (40022) 237/L4
Findhorn, Scot. 15/K4
Findhorn (riv.), Scot. 15/J5
Findikli, Turkey 63/J2
Findlater, Sask. 181/F5
Findlay, Ill. (62534) 222/E4
Findlay, Man. 179/B5
Findlay, Ohio (45840) 284/C3
Findley Lake, N.Y. (14736) 276/A6
Findochty, Scot. 15/K4
Findon, Mont. (†59053) 262/F4
Findon, Scot. 15/M5
Fine, N.Y. (13639) 276/K2
Finesville, N.J. (†08865) 273/C2
Fingal, Ont. 177/C5
Fingal, N. Dak. (58031) 283/P6
Fingal, Tas. 99/E3
Finger (lake), Ont. 175/B2
Finger, Tenn. (38334) 237/D10
Fingerville, S.C. (29338) 296/D1
Fingoè, Moz. 118/E2
Finhaut, Switz. 39/C4
Finike, Turkey 63/D4
Finistère (dept.), France 28/A3
Finisterre (cape), Spain, 7/C4
Finisterre (cape), Spain 33/B1
Finke (riv.), Aust. 88/E5
Finke (riv.), No. Terr. 93/C8
Finke (riv.), S. Aust. 94/C1
Finksburg, Md. (21048) 245/L3
Finland, 3/L2
Finland, 4/C8
Finland, 7/G2
FINLAND, 18
Finland (gulf), 7/G3
Finland (gulf), Fin. 18/P7
Finland (gulf), U.S.S.R. 48/C4
Finland (gulf), U.S.S.R. 52/C3
Finland (gulf), U.S.S.R. 53/D1
Finland, Minn. (55603) 254/G3
Finlay (riv.), 163/D4
Finlay (riv.), Br. Col. 184/E1
Finlay (mts.), Texas 302/B10
Finlay Forks, Br. Col. 184/F2
Finlayson, Minn. (55735) 254/F4
Finley, Ky. (42736) 237/L6
Finley, N. Dak. (58230) 283/P4
Finley, N.S.W. 97/C4
Finley, Okla. (74543) 288/R6
Finley, Tenn. (38030) 237/B8
Finley, Wash. (99336) 310/F4
Finleyson, Ga. (†31071) 216/F6
Finleyville, Pa. (15332) 294/B5
Finly, Ind. (46129) 227/F5
Finmoore, Br. Col. 184/F3
Finn (riv.), Ire. 17/F2
Finn (riv.), Ire. 17/G3
Finnegan, Alta. 182/E4
Finney (co.), Kans. 232/B3
Finnmark (co.), Norway 18/O2
Finschhafen, Terr. N.G. 85/C7
Finspång, Sweden 18/J7
Finsteraarhorn (mt.), Switz. 39/F3
Finstermünz (pass), Switz. 39/K3
Finsterwalde, E. Ger. 22/E3
Fintona, N. Ire. 17/G3
Fionn (lake), Scot. 15/F4
Fionnay, Switz. 39/D4
Fir (riv.), Sask. 181/J2
Firat (riv.), Turkey 63/G4
Fircrest, Wash. (98466) 310/C3
Firdale, Man. 179/C5
Firdaus, Iran (pt.), Syo 66/J3
Firdaus, Iran 66/K3
Fire (isl.), Alaska 196/B1
Firebag (riv.), Alta. 182/E1
Firebaugh, Calif. (93622) 204/E7
Firebrick, Ky. (41137) 237/P3
Fireco, W. Va. (25823) 313/D7
Fire Island (beach), N.Y. 276/O9
Fire Island National Seashore, N.Y. 276/P9
Fire Lake‡, Alaska (†99501) 196/C1
Firenze (Florence), Italy, 7/F4
Fire Steel (riv.), Mich. 250/G1
Firesteel, S. Dak. (57628) 298/G3
Firesteel (creek), S. Dak. 298/N6
Firestone, Colo. (80520) 208/K2
Firmat, Arg. 143/F6
Firminy, France 28/F5
Fir Mountain, Sask. 181/E6
Firozabad, India 68/D3
Fir Ridge, Sask. 181/F2
First (lake), N. Br. 170/B1
First Branch, White (riv.), Vt. 268/B4
First Cataract, U.A.R. 59/B5
First Connecticut (lake), N.H. 268/E1
First Eel (lake), N. Br. 170/C3
Firstview, Colo. (†80810) 208/O5
Firth (riv.), Alaska 196/K1
Firth, Idaho (83236) 220/F6
Firth, Nebr. (68358) 264/H4
Firth (riv.), Yukon 187/D3
Firthcliffe‡, N.Y. (†12518) 276/M8
Firuzabad, Iran 66/H6
Firuzkuh, Iran 66/H3
Fischot Island, Newf. 166/C3
Fish (creek), Ind. 227/H2
Fish (riv.), Maine 242/F2
Fish (creek), Oreg. 291/E4
Fish (riv.), S.W. Afr. 118/B5
Fish (lake), Utah 304/C5
Fish (creek), W. Va. 313/E3
Fish Camp, Calif. (93623) 204/F6
Fish Creek (res.), Idaho 220/E6
Fish Creek (mts.), Nev. 266/D2
Fish Creek, Sask. 181/E3
Fish Creek, Wis. (54212) 317/M5
Fisher (str.), 163/H3
Fisher, Ark. (72429) 203/J2
Fisher, Aust. 88/E6
Fisher (isl.), Fla. 212/B5
Fisher, Ill. (61843) 222/E3
Fisher, La. (71426) 238/D4
Fisher (bay), Man. 179/E3
Fisher (riv.), Man. 179/E3
Fisher, Minn. (56723) 254/B3
Fisher (lake), N.S. 169/C4
Fisher (str.), N.W.T. 187/K3
Fisher, S. Aust. 94/B4
Fisher (co.), Texas 302/D5
Fisher, W. Va. (26818) 313/H4
Fisher Bay, Man. 179/E3
Fisher Branch, Man. 179/E3
Fisher-Eldora‡, Pa. (†15063) 294/C5
Fisher Home, Alta. 182/C3
Fishermans (isl.), Va. 307/S6
Fishers, Ind. (46038) 227/E5
Fishers (isl.), N.Y. 276/S8
Fishers Island, N.Y. (06390) 276/R8
Fishersville, Va. (22939) 307/K4
Fisherville, Ont. 177/E5
Fishguard and Goodwick, 10/D5
Fishguard and Goodwick, Wales 13/B6
Fish Haven, Idaho (83261) 220/G7
Fishing (lake), Man. 179/G2
Fishing (bay), Md. 245/O7
Fishing (creek), N.C. 281/O2
Fishing Creek, Md. (21634) 245/N7
Fishing River, Man. 179/C3
Fishkill, N.Y. (12524) 276/N7
Fish Lake, Alaska (†99676) 196/B1
Fish River (lake), Maine 242/F2
Fishs Eddy, N.Y. (13774) 276/K8
Fish Springs (range), Utah 304/A4
Fishtail, Mont. (59028) 262/G5
Fishtrap, Ky. (41525) 237/S6
Fishtrap (res.), Ky. 237/S6
Fisk, Mo. (63940) 261/M9
Fiskdale, Mass. (01518) 249/F4
Fiske, Sask. 181/C4
Fiskeville, R.I. (02823) 249/H6
Fitch Bay, Que. 172/E4
Fitchburg, Mass. (01420) 249/G2
Fitchville, Conn. (06334) 210/G2
Fitchville, Ohio (†44851) 284/E3
Fithian, Ill. (61844) 222/F3
Fitler, Miss. (39070) 256/B5
Fittri (lake), Chad 111/C5
Fittstown, Okla. (74842) 288/N5
Fitzcarrald, Peru 128/G8
Fitzgerald, Ga. (31750) 216/F7
Fitzhugh (sound), Br. Col. 184/D4
Fitzhugh, Okla. (74843) 288/N5
Fitzmaurice (riv.), No. Terr. 93/B3
Fitzmaurice, Sask. 181/H4
Fitzpatrick, Ala. (36029) 194/G6
Fitzpatrick, Que. 172/E2
Fitzpatrick, Ga. (†31044) 216/F5
Fitzroy (riv.), Australia, 87/C7
Fitzroy (riv.), Aust. 88/H4
Fitzroy (riv.), Aust. 88/C3
Fitz Roy (Chaltel) (mt.), Chile 138/E8
Fitzroy (riv.), W. Aust. 92/D2
Fitzroy, No. Terr. 93/B4
Fitzroy (riv.), Queens. 95/D4
Fitzroy, Vic. 97/H5
Fitzroy Crossing, Aust. 88/D3
Fitzroy Crossing, W. Aust. 92/D2
Fitzroy Harbor, Ont. 177/H2
Fitzwilliam (isl.), Ont. 177/C2
Fitzwilliam∆, N.H. (03447) 268/C6
Fitzwilliam, N.H. (03447) 268/C6
Fitzwilliam Depot, N.H. (03447) 268/C6
Fiume (Rijeka), Yugo., 7/F4
Fiume (Rijeka), Yugo. 45/B3
Fiumicino, Italy 34/F7
Five (isls.), N.S. 169/D3
Five Island (lake), Iowa 229/D2
Five Islands, Maine (04546) 242/D8
Five Islands, N.S. 169/D3
Five Mile (riv.), Conn. 210/H1
Fivemile (creek), Oreg. 291/F2
Fivemile (pt.), Oreg. 291/C4
Fivemile (creek), Wyo. 319/D2
Fivemiletown, N. Ire. 17/G3
Five Points, Ala. (36855) 194/H4
Five Points‡, Fla. (32922) 212/D1
Five Points, Ohio (†43143) 284/D6
Five Points, Tenn. (38457) 237/G10
Fives Lille, Arg. 143/F5
Five Stars, Guyana 131/A2
Fivizzano, Italy 34/B2
Fizi, Dem. Rep. of the Congo. 115/E4
Fjällbacka, Sweden 18/G7
Fjällnäs, Sweden 18/H5
Fjerritslev, Den. 21/C3
Fladdachuain (isl.), Scot. 15/D4
Flagler, Colo. (80815) 208/N4
Flagler (co.), Fla. 212/E2
Flagler Beach, Fla. (32036) 212/E2
Flag Pond, Tenn. (37657) 237/R8
Flagstaff, Ariz., 188/D3
Flagstaff, Ariz. (86001) 198/D3
Flagstaff (lake), Maine 242/C5
Flagstaff (lake), Oreg. 291/H5
Flagtown, N.J. (08821) 273/D2
Flambeau (riv.), Wis. 317/E4
Flambeau Flowage (res.), Wis. 317/F3
Flamborough (head), Eng. 13/H3
Flamborough (head), 10/G3
Flamenco de San Pedro, Cuba 158/F3
Flaming Gorge (dam), Utah 304/E3
Flaming Gorge (res.), Utah 304/E3
Flaming Gorge (res.), Wyo. 319/C4
Flaming Gorge Nat'l Rec. Area, Utah 304/E3
Flaming Gorge Nat'l Rec. Area, Wyo. 319/C4
Flamingo (cay), Bah. Is. 156/C2
Flanagan (passg.), V.I. (Br.) 161/D4
Flanagan (passg.), V.I.(U.S.) 161/D4
Flanagan, Ill. (61740) 222/E3
Flanagin Town, Trinidad Tobago 161/B10
Flanders, Conn. (†06757) 210/B1
Flanders, Ont. 175/B3
Flanders, N.J. (07836) 273/D2
Flanders, N.Y. (†11901) 276/P9
Flandreau, S. Dak. (57028) 298/R5
Flanigan, Nev. (†89501) 266/B2
Flannan (isls.), 10/C1
Flannan (isls.), Scot. 15/A3
Flasher, N. Dak. (58535) 283/H7
Flat (cays), V.I.(U.S.) 161/A4
Flat, Ky. (41325) 237/O5
Flat, Mo. (†65550) 261/J7
Flat (isl.), Asia 85/F3
Flat, Texas (76526) 302/G6
Flat (creek), Va. 307/M6
Flat Bay, Newf. 166/C4
Flatbrookville, N.J. (†07832) 273/D1
Flatbush, Alta. 182/C2
Flat Creek, Tenn. (†37160) 237/H10
Flat Creek-Wegra, Ala. (†35129) 194/D3
Flat Fork, Ky. (41427) 237/P5
Flatgap, Ky. (41219) 237/R5
Flathead, Br. Col. 184/K5
Flathead (riv.), Br. Col. 184/K6
Flathead (lake), Mont., 188/D1
Flathead (co.), Mont. 262/B2
Flathead (lake), Mont. 262/C3
Flathead (riv.), Mont. 262/B3
Flathead Ind. Res., Mont. 262/B3
Flat Lake, Alta. 182/E2
Flatlands, N. Br. 170/D1
Flat Lick, Ky. (40935) 237/O7
Flatonia, Texas (78941) 302/G8
Flat River, Mo. (63601) 261/M7
Flat Rock, Ala. (35966) 194/G1
Flat Rock, Ill. (62427) 222/F5
Flat Rock, Ind. (47234) 227/F6
Flatrock (creek), Ind. 227/F5
Flat Rock, Ky. (†42634) 237/M7
Flat Rock, Mich. (48134) 250/F6
Flat Rock, N.C. (28731) 281/E4
Flat Rock‡, N.C. (28731) 281/H2
Flat Rock, Newf. 166/D2
Flat Rock, Ohio (44828) 284/E3
Flats, N.C. (†28781) 281/B4
Flats, Nebr. (69136) 264/C3
Flattery (cape), Aust. 88/H2
Flattery (cape), Queens. 95/C2
Flattery (cape), Wash., 146/F5
Flattery (cape), Wash., 188/A1
Flattery (cape), Wash. 310/A2
Flat Top, W. Va. (25841) 313/D7
Flatwillow (creek), Mont. 262/H4
Flatwood, Ala. (36739) 194/C6
Flatwoods, Ky. (41139) 237/R4
Flatwoods, La. (71427) 238/E4
Flat Woods, Tenn. (38458) 237/F10
Flatwoods, W. Va. (26621) 313/E5
Flawil, Switz. 39/H2
Flaxcombe, Sask. 181/B4
Flaxman (isl.), Alaska 196/J1
Flaxton, N. Dak. (58737) 283/F2
Flaxville, Mont. (59222) 262/L2
Fleet, Alta. 182/E3
Fleet, Eng. 13/G6
Fleet (inlet), Scot. 15/J4
Fleetwood, 10/E4
Fleetwood, Eng. 13/D4
Fleetwood, Okla. (†73569) 288/L7
Fleetwood, Pa. (19522) 294/L5
Fleischmanns, N.Y. (12430) 276/L6
Flekkefjord, Norway 18/F7
Flémalle-Haute, Belg. 27/G7
Fleming, Colo. (80728) 208/O1
Fleming, Ga. (31309) 216/K7
Fleming (co.), Ky. 237/O4
Fleming, Ky. (41816) 237/R6
Fleming, Mo. (†64077) 261/D4
Fleming, Pa. (16835) 294/G4
Fleming, Sask. 181/K5
Flemingsburg, Ky. (41041) 237/O4
Flemington, Ga. (†31313) 216/K7
Flemington, Mo. (65650) 261/F7
Flemington, N.J. (08822) 273/D2
Flemington, Pa. (17745) 294/G3
Flemington, W. Va. (26347) 313/F4
Flen, Sweden 18/K7
Flensburg, Minn. (56328) 254/D5
Flensburg, W. Ger., 7/E3
Flensburg, W. Ger. 22/C1
Flers, France 28/C3
Flesherton, Ont. 177/D3
Flesk (riv.), Ire. 17/C7
Fleta, Ala. (†36043) 194/F6
Fletcher (pond), Mich. 250/F4
Fletcher, Mo. (63030) 261/L6
Fletcher, N.C. (28732) 281/E4
Fletcher, Ohio (45326) 284/B5
Fletcher, Okla. (73541) 288/K5
Fletcher∆, Vt. (†05444) 268/B2
Fletcher, Vt. (†05444) 268/B2
Fletschhorn (mt.), Switz. 39/F4
Fleurance, France 28/D6
Fleur de Lys, Newf. 166/C3
Fleur-de-Mai (lake), Newf. 166/B3
Fleurier, Switz. 39/C3
Fleurus, Belg. 27/F8
Flims, Switz. 39/H3
Flinders (riv.), Australia, 87/E7
Flinders (reef), Aust. 88/H3
Flinders (riv.), Aust. 88/G3
Flinders (range), Aust. 88/F6
Flinders (isl.), Aust. 88/H7
Flinders (bay), Aust. 88/A6
Flinders (bay), W. Aust. 92/A6
Flinders (range), S. Aust. 94/F4
Flinders (riv.), Queens. 95/B3
Flinders (isl.), Tasmania 99/D1
Flin Flon, 163/F4
Flin Flon, Man. 179/H3
Flint (riv.), Ga., 188/K4
Flint, Ga. (†31716) 216/D8
Flint (riv.), Ga. 216/D8
Flint, Ind. (†46703) 227/G1
Flint, Mich., 146/K5
Flint, Mich., 188/K2
Flint, Mich. (*48501) 250/F6
Flint (riv.), Mich. 250/F5
Flint (lake), N.W.T. 187/L3
Flint (isl.), Pacific, 87/L7
Flint, Wales 13/D4
Flint City, Ala. (†35601) 194/D1
Flinthill, Mo. (63346) 261/M2
Flint Hill, Va. (22627) 307/M3
Flintoft, Sask. 181/E6
Flint Rock (creek), S. Dak. 298/E3
Flintshire (co.), Wales 13/D4
Flintstone, Ga. (30725) 216/B1
Flintstone (lake), Man. 179/G4
Flintstone, Md. (21530) 245/D2
Flintville, Tenn. (37335) 237/H10
Flippen, Ark. (72634) 203/E1
Flippen, Ga. (30215) 216/D3
Flippin, Ky. (42132) 237/K7
Flix, Spain 33/G2
Flom, Minn. (56541) 254/B3
Flomaton, Ala. (36441) 194/D8
Flomot, Texas (79234) 302/D3
Flood, Br. Col. 184/M3
Floodwood, Minn. (55736) 254/E4
Flora, Norway 18/D6
Flora, Ill. (62839) 222/E5
Flora, Ind. (46929) 227/E3
Flora, La. (71428) 238/D3
Flora, Miss. (39071) 256/D5
Flora, N. Dak. (58334) 283/M4
Flora (riv.), No. Terr. 93/B3
Flora, Oreg. (†97828) 291/K2
Florac, France 28/E5
Florahome, Fla. (32635) 212/E2
Floral, Ark. (72534) 203/G2
Florala, Ala. (36442) 194/F8
Floral City, Fla. (32636) 212/D3
Floral Park, Mont. (†59701) 262/D5
Floral Park, N.Y. (*11001) 276/R7
Floraville, Aust. 88/F3
Floraville, Queens. 95/B3
Flora Vista, N. Mex. (87415) 274/A2
Flordell Hills‡, Mo. (†63101) 261/P2
Floreana, Ec. 128/B10
Floreana (Santa María) (isl.), Ec. 128/B10
Florence, Ala., 188/J4
Florence, Ala. (35630) 194/C1
Florence, Ariz. (85232) 198/D5
Florence, Ark. (†71655) 203/G6
Florence (lake), Calif. 204/G6
Florence, Colo. (81226) 208/J6
Florence, Ont. 177/B5
Florence, Ill. (†62363) 222/C4
Florence, Ind. (47020) 227/H7
Florence, Italy, 7/F4
Florence (prov.), Italy 34/C3
Florence, Italy 34/C3
Florence, Kans. (66851) 232/E3
Florence, Ky. (41042) 237/R3
Florence, Minn. (56130) 254/B6
Florence, Miss. (39073) 256/D6
Florence, Mo. (65329) 261/G5
Florence, Mont. (59833) 262/B4
Florence, N.C. (†28556) 281/R4
Florence, N.S. 169/H2
Florence, N.Y. (†13316) 276/J4
Florence, Oreg. (97439) 291/C4
Florence, Pa. (15040) 294/A5
Florence, S.C., 188/L4
Florence (co.), S.C. 296/H3
Florence, S.C. (29501) 296/H3
Florence, S. Dak. (57235) 298/P3
Florence, Tenn. (†37130) 237/H9
Florence, Texas (76527) 302/G7
Florence, Vt. (05744) 268/A4
Florence (co.), Wis. 317/K4
Florence, Wis. (54121) 317/K4
Florence-Graham‡, Calif. (†90001) 204/C11
Florence Junction, Ariz. (85233) 198/D5
Florence-Roebling, N.J. (08518) 273/D3
Florenceville, N. Br. 170/C2
Florencia, Col. 126/C7
Florennes, Belg. 27/F8
Florenton, Minn. (†55792) 254/F3
Florenville, Belg. 27/G9
Flores, Las (riv.), Arg. 143/G7
Flores (isl.), Br. Col. 184/D5
Flores, Braz. 132/G4
Flores, Guat. 154/C2
Flores (sea), Indon., 3/Q6
Flores (isl.), Indon., 54/R10
Flores (sea), Indon., 54/R10
Flores (isl.), Indon. 85/G7
Flores (sea), Indon. 85/F7
Flores (dept.), Urug. 145/C4
Flores (isl.), Urug. 145/D5
Floresville, Texas (78114) 302/F8
Florey, Texas (79732) 302/B5
Florham Park, N.J. (07932) 273/E2
Floriano, Braz. 132/F4
Florianópolis, Braz., 120/F5
Florianópolis, Braz. 132/E9
Florida (strs.), 146/K7
Florida, 188/K5
FLORIDA, 212
Florida, El Beni, Bol. 136/C2
Florida, Santa Cruz, Bol. 136/D6
Florida (strs), Cuba 156/B1
Florida, Cuba 158/G3
Florida (keys), Fla., 146/K7
Florida (bay), Fla., 188/K6
Florida (keys), Fla., 188/K6
Florida (strs.), Fla., 188/K6
Florida (bay), Fla. 212/F6
Florida (cape), Fla. 212/F6
Florida (keys), Fla. 212/E7
Florida (strs), Fla. 212/F7
Florida∆, Mass. (†01247) 249/B2
Florida, Mass. (†01247) 249/B2
Florida, Mo. (†65283) 261/J4
Florida (mts.), N. Mex. 274/B7
Florida, N.Y. (10921) 276/M8
Florida, Ohio (†43545) 284/B3
Florida, P. Rico 161/C1
Florida (state), U.S., 146/K7
Florida, Urug., 120/E6
Florida (dept.), Urug. 145/D4
Florida, Urug. 145/C5
Florida City, Fla. (33030) 212/F6
Florida Ridge‡, Fla. (†32960) 212/F4
Floridatown, Fla. (†32570) 212/B6
Floridia, Italy 34/E6
Florien, La. (71429) 238/D4
Florin, Calif. (95828) 204/B8
Florin, Pa. (†17552) 294/J5
Flórina, Greece 45/E5
Floris, Iowa (52560) 229/J7
Florissant, Colo. (80816) 208/J5
Florissant, Mo. (*63031) 261/P2
Florissant Fossil Beds Nat'l Mon., Colo. 208/J5
Florosa, Fla. (†32569) 212/B6
Flossmoor, Ill. (60422) 222/B3
Flourtown‡, Pa. (19031) 294/M3
Flovilla, Ga. (30216) 216/E4
Floweree, Mont. (59440) 262/E3
Flower Hill‡, N.Y. (†11051) 276/R7
Flower Mound‡, Texas (†75067) 302/G4
Flowerpot (isl.), Ont. 177/C2
Flowers (bay), Newf. 166/B2
Flower's Cove, Newf. 166/C3
Flower Station, Ont. 177/H2
Flowery Branch, Ga. (30542) 216/E2
Flowing Well, Sask. 181/E5
Flowood, Miss. (†39201) 256/D6
Floyd (co.), Ga. 216/B2
Floyd (co.), Ind. 227/F8
Floyd (co.), Iowa 229/H2
Floyd, Iowa (50435) 229/H2
Floyd (riv.), Iowa 229/A3
Floyd (co.), Ky. 237/R5
Floyd, La. (†71266) 238/H1
Floyd, N. Mex. (88118) 274/F4
Floyd (co.), Texas 302/C3
Floyd (co.), Va. 307/H7
Floyd, Va. (24091) 307/H7
Floydada, Texas (79235) 302/C3
Floyd Dale, S.C. (29542) 296/J3
Floyds Knobs, Ind. (47119) 227/F8
Fluchthorn (mt.), Switz. 39/K3
Flüela (pass), Switz. 39/J3
Flüelen, Switz. 39/G3
Fluhberg (mt.), Switz. 39/G2
Fluker, La. (70436) 238/K5
Flums, Switz. 39/H2
Flushing, Mich. (48433) 250/F5
Flushing, Neth. 27/C6
Flushing, Ohio (43977) 284/J5
Fluvanna, Texas (79517) 302/D5
Fluvanna (co.), Va. 307/M5
Fly, Ohio (45730) 284/H6
Fly (riv.), Papua 85/A7
Fly (riv.), Papua, 87/E6
Fly Creek, N.Y. (13337) 276/K5
Flying H, N. Mex. (88322) 274/E5
Flynns Lick, Tenn. (†38562) 237/K8
Foam Lake, Sask. 181/H4
Foard (co.), Texas 302/E3
Foça, Turkey 63/B3
Foča, Yugo. 45/D4
Fochabers, Scot. 15/K4
Focşani, Rum. 45/H3
Foge (isl.), Nigeria 106/E6
Foggia, Italy, 7/F4
Foggia (prov.), Italy 34/E4
Foggia, Italy 34/E4
Fogo (isl.), 102/G9
Fogo (isl.), C. Verde Is. 106/B8
Fogo (isl.), 163/L6
Fogo, Newf. 166/D4
Fogo (isl.), Newf. 166/D4
Fohnsdorf, Austria 41/C3
Föhr (isl.), W. Ger. 22/C1
Foia (mt.), Port. 33/B4
Foinaven (mt.), Scot. 15/G3
Foisy, Alta. 182/E3
Foix, France 28/D6
Fojnica, Yugo. 45/C4
Folcroft, Pa. (19032) 294/M7
Folda (fjord), Norway 18/G4
Folda (fjord), Norway 18/J3
Földeák, Hung. 41/F3
Foley, Ala. (36535) 194/C10
Foley, Fla. (†32347) 212/C1
Foley, Minn. (56329) 254/D5
Foley, Mo. (63347) 261/L4
Foley (isl.), N.W.T. 187/L3
Foleyet, Ont. 175/D3
Foleyet, Ont. 177/J5
Folgares, Angola 115/C6
Foligno, Italy 34/D3
Folkestone, 10/G5
Folkestone, Eng. 13/J6
Folkston, Ga. (31537) 216/H9
Folkstone, N.C. (†28445) 281/O5
Follansbee, W. Va. (26037) 313/E2
Follett, Texas (79034) 302/D1
Folly Beach, S.C. (29439) 296/H6
Folsom, Calif. (95630) 204/C8
Folsom (lake), Calif. 204/C8
Folsom, La. (70437) 238/K5
Folsom, N.J. (†08037) 273/D4
Folsom, N. Mex. (88419) 274/F2

364 Folsom

Folsom, Pa. (19033) 294/M7
Folsom, W. Va. (26348) 313/E4
Folsomville, Ind. (47614) 227/C8
Folteşti, Rum. 45/H3
Fomboni, Comoro Is. 118/G2
Fomento, Cuba 158/E2
Fonda, Iowa (50540) 229/D3
Fonda, N. Dak.-(†58366) 283/K2
Fonda, N.Y. (12068) 276/M5
Fond d'Or (bay), St. Lucia 161/G6
Fond-du-Lac (riv.), 163/F4
Fond du Lac, Sask. 181/L2
Fond du Lac (riv.), Sask. 181/M2
Fond du Lac, Wis., 188/J2
Fond du Lac (co.), Wis. 317/K8
Fond du Lac, Wis. (54935) 317/K8
Fond du Lac Ind. Res., Minn. 254/F4
Fonde, Ky. (40937) 237/O7
Fondi, Italy 34/D4
Fond-Lahaye, Mart. 161/C6
Fond-Saint-Denis, Mart. 161/C6
Fond-Verrettes, Haiti 158/C6
Fonehill, Sask. 181/J4
Fongafale, Gilb. and Ell., 87/H6
Fonsagrada, Spain 33/C1
Fonseca, Col. 126/D2
Fonseca (gulf), El Salv. 154/D4
Fonseca (gulf), Hond. 154/D4
Fonseca (gulf), Nic. 154/D4
Fontaine, N. Br. 170/F2
Fontainebleau, Que. 172/F4
Fontainebleau, France 28/E3
Fontana, Calif. (92335) 204/E10
Fontana, Kans. (66026) 232/H3
Fontana (lake), N.C. 281/B4
Fontana, Wis. (53125) 317/J10
Fontanelle, Iowa (50846) 229/E6
Fontanet, Ind. (47851) 227/C5
Fontas (riv.), Br. Col. 184/M2
Fonte Boa, Braz. 132/G9
Fontein, Neth. Ant. 161/E8
Fontenay-le-Comte, France 28/C4
Fontenay-sous-Bois, France 28/C2
Fonteneau (lake), Newf. 166/B3
Fontenelle, Que. 172/D1
Fontenelle (creek), Wyo. 319/B3
Fontenelle (res.), Wyo. 319/B3
Fonthill, Ont. 177/E4
Fontibón, Col. 126/C5
Fontur (prom.), Ice. 21/D1
Fonyód, Hung. 41/D3
Foochow, China, 54/P7
Foochow, China 77/J6
Fool Creek (res.), Utah 304/B4
Foosland, Ill. (61845) 222/E3
Foothills, Alta. 182/B3
Footscray, Aust. 88/L7
Footscray, Vic. 97/H5
Footville, Ohio (†44084) 284/J2
Footville, Wis. (53537) 317/H10
Forada, Minn. (†56308) 254/C5
Foraker (mt.), Alaska 196/H2
Foraker, Ind. (46525) 227/F1
Foraker, Ohio (†45812) 284/C4
Foraker, Okla. (74638) 288/O1
Forbach, France 28/G3
Forbes (mt.), Alta. 182/B4
Forbes, Aust. 88/H6
Forbes (lake), Que. 172/C3
Forbes (isl.), Fla. 212/A2
Forbes, Minn. (55738) 254/F3
Forbes, Mo. (64450) 261/B3
Forbes, N. Dak. (58439) 283/N8
Forbes, N.S.W. 97/E3
Forbes A.F.B., Kans. 232/G3
Forbing, La. (71026) 238/C2
Forbus, Tenn. (38561) 237/M7
Forcados, Nigeria 106/E7
Forcalquier, France 28/F6
Force, Pa. (15841) 294/E3
Forchheim, W. Ger. 22/D4
Ford (ranges), Ant. 5/B11
Ford (cape), Aust. 88/D2
Ford (isl.), Hawaii 218/B3
Ford (co.), Ill. 222/E3
Ford (co.), Kans. 232/C4
Ford, Kans. (67842) 232/C4
Ford, Ky. (40320) 237/N5
Ford (riv.), Mich. 250/B2
Ford (cape), No. Terr. 93/A2
Ford, Scot. 15/F7
Ford, Va. (23850) 307/N6
Ford, Wash. (99013) 310/H3
Ford City, Calif. (†93268) 204/F8
Ford City, Mo. (†64463) 261/C2
Ford City, Pa. (16226) 294/D4
Ford Cliff, Pa. (16228) 294/D4
Ford Island Nav. Air Sta., Hawaii 218/B3
Fordland, Mo. (65652) 261/G8
Fordlândia, Braz., 120/E3
Fordlândia, Braz. 132/C3
Fordoche, La. (70732) 238/G5
Fordoun, Scot. 15/M6
Fords, N.J. (08863) 273/E2
Fords Bridge, N.S.W. 97/C1
Fords Prairie, Wash. (†98531) 310/B4
Fordsville, Ky. (42343) 237/H5
Fordville, N. Dak. (58231) 283/P3
Fordwich, Ont. 177/C4
Fordyce, Ark. (71742) 203/F6
Fordyce, Nebr. (68736) 264/G2
Forécariah, Guinea 106/B7
Foreman, Ark. (71836) 203/B6
Foremost, Alta. 182/E5
Foresman, Ind. (†47922) 227/C3
Forest, Belg. 27/B9
Forest, Ont. 177/C4
Forest, Ind. (46039) 227/E4
Forest, La. (71242) 238/H1
Forest, Miss. (39074) 256/F6
Forest (riv.), N. Dak. 283/P3
Forest, Ohio (45843) 284/C4
Forest (co.), Pa. 294/D2
Forest, Va. (24551) 307/K6
Forest (co.), Wis. 317/J4
Forest Acres, S.C. (29206) 296/F3
Forest Beach, S.C. (†29928) 296/F7
Forestburg, Alta. 182/E3
Forestburg, S. Dak. (57338) 298/N5
Forestburg, Texas (76239) 302/G4
Forest City, Ill. (61532) 222/D3
Forest City, Iowa (50436) 229/F2
Forest City, Maine (04436) 242/H4
Forest City, Mo. (64451) 261/B3
Forest City, N. Br. 170/C3
Forest City, N.C. (28043) 281/E4
Forest City, Pa. (18421) 294/L2
Forestdale, Ala. (35214) 194/E3
Forestdale, R.I. (02824) 249/H5
Forest Dale, Vt. (05745) 268/A4
Forester, Mich. (†48419) 250/G5
Foresters Falls, Ont. 177/G2
Forest Farm, Sask. 181/K5
Forest Gate, Sask. 181/F2
Forest Glen, Ga. (†31001) 216/F7
Forest Glen, Md. (†20907) 245/F4
Forest Green, Mo. (65249) 261/G4
Forest Grove, Br. Col. 184/G4
Forestgrove, Mont. (59441) 262/H3
Forest Grove, Oreg. (97116) 291/A2
Forest Heights, Md. (†20001) 245/F5
Foresthill, Calif. (†95703) 204/E4
Forest Hill, Ind. (†47240) 227/F6
Forest Hill, La. (71430) 238/E4
Forest Hill, Md. (21050) 245/N2
Forest Hill, Tenn. (38031) 237/B10
Forest Hill, Texas (75701) 302/F2
Forest Hill, W. Va. (24935) 313/E7
Forest Hills‡, Fla. (†33552) 212/D3
Forest Hills‡, Ky. (41527) 237/K4
Forest Hills, Pa. (15221) 294/C7
Forest Hills, Tenn. (†37201) 237/H8
Forest Home, Ala. (36030) 194/E7
Forest Homes, Ill. (†62018) 222/B6
Forest Junction, Wis. (54123) 317/K7
Forest Knolls, Calif. (94933) 204/H1
Forest Lake, Mich. (49832) 250/C2
Forest Lake, Minn. (55025) 254/F5
Forest Lake‡, S.C. (†29201) 296/F3
Foreston, Minn. (56330) 254/E5
Foreston, S.C. (29049) 296/G4
Forest Park, Ga. (30050) 216/D3
Forest Park, Ill. (60130) 222/B2
Forest Park, Ohio (45405) 284/B9
Forest Park, Okla. (†73101) 288/M3
Forestport, N.Y. (13338) 276/K4
Forest River, N. Dak. (58233) 283/P3
Forest Station, Maine (†04413) 242/H4
Forest View, Ill. (†60402) 222/B2
Forestville, Conn. (†06010) 210/D2
Forestville, Que. 172/H1
Forestville, Que. 174/D3
Forestville, Md. (†20028) 245/G5
Forestville, Mich. (48434) 250/G5
Forestville, N.Y. (14062) 276/B6
Forestville, Ohio (†45202) 284/C10
Forestville, Pa. (16035) 294/B3
Forestville, Wis. (54213) 317/L6
Forez (mts.), France 28/E5
Forfar, 10/E2
Forfar, Scot. 15/L6
Forfar (Angus) (co.), Scot. 15/K6
Forgan, Okla. (73938) 288/E1
Forgan, Sask. 181/D4
Forget, Sask. 181/J6
Forge Village, Mass. (01828) 249/H2
Foristell, Mo. (63348) 261/M2
Fork, N.C. (†27028) 281/J3
Fork, S.C. (29543) 296/J3
Forked (lake), N.Y. 276/L3
Forked Deer (riv.), Tenn. 237/C9
Forked River, N.J. (08731) 273/E4
Fork Lake, Alta. 182/E2
Forkland, Ala. (36740) 194/C5
Fork Mountain, Tenn. (†37728) 237/N8
Fork River, Man. 179/B3
Forks, Wash. (98331) 310/A3
Forks of Buffalo, Va. (†24521) 307/K5
Forks of Elkhorn, Ky. (†40601) 237/M4
Forks of Salmon, Calif. (96031) 204/B2
Forksville, Pa. (18616) 294/J3
Fork Union, Va. (23055) 307/M5
Forkville, Miss. (39076) 256/E6
Forlì (prov.), Italy 34/D2
Forlì, Italy 34/D2
Forman, N. Dak. (58032) 283/P7
Formartine (dist.), Scot. 15/M5
Formby, 10/F2
Formby (head), Eng. 13/D4
Formentera (isl.), Spain 33/G3
Formentor (cape), Spain 33/H2
Formia, Italy 34/D4
Formiga, Braz. 132/E8
Formiga, Braz. 135/D2
Formosa, Arg., 120/E5
Formosa (prov.), Arg. 143/D1
Formosa, Arg. 143/E2
Formosa, Ark. (†72031) 203/E3
Formosa (Taiwan) (isl.), China, 3/R4
Formosa (Taiwan) (isl.), China, 54/R7
Formosa (Taiwan) (isl.), China 77/K7
Formosa (Taiwan) (str.), China 77/J7
Formosa, Braz. 132/E6
Formosa (range), Braz. 132/C5
Formosa, Ont. 177/C3
Formosa (bay), Kenya 115/H4
Formoso, Kans. (66942) 232/D2
Forney, Ala. (†30124) 194/H2
Forney, Texas (75126) 302/H5
Forney (res.), Texas 302/H2
Forres, 10/E2
Forres, Scot. 15/K4
Forrest, Aust. 88/D6
Forrest (lakes), Aust. 88/D5
Forrest, Ill. (61741) 222/E3
Forrest (co.), Miss. 256/F8
Forrest, N. Mex. (†88401) 274/F4
Forrest, W. Aust. 92/D5
Forrest (lake), Sask. 181/L3
Forrest City, Ark. (72335) 203/J3
Forreston, Ill. (61030) 222/D1
Forrest River Mission, W. Aust. 92/D1
Forrest Station, Man. 179/C5
Forsan, Texas (79733) 302/C5
Forsayth, Aust. 88/G3
Forsayth, Queens. 95/B3
Forshaga, Sweden 18/H7
Forshee, Alta. 182/C3
Forssa, Fin. 18/N6
Forst, E. Ger. 22/F3
Forster, N.S.W. 97/G3
Forsyth (co.), Ga. 216/D2
Forsyth, Ga. (31029) 216/E4
Forsyth, Ill. (62535) 222/D4
Forsyth, Mo. (65653) 261/F9
Forsyth, Mont. (59327) 262/K4
Forsyth (co.), N.C. 281/J2
Fort (pt.), St. Chr.-N.-A. 161/C11
Fort (mt.), Switz. 39/D4
Fort Adams, Miss. (39636) 256/B8
Fort à la Corne, Sask. 181/G2
Fort Albany, 163/H5
Fort Albany, Ont. 175/D2
Fort Albany, Ont., 146/K4
Fort Alexander, Man. 179/F4
Fortaleza, Bol. 136/B3
Fortaleza, Braz., 3/H6
Fortaleza, Braz., 120/G3
Fortaleza, Braz. 132/G3
Fortaleza de Santa Teresa, Urug. 145/F5
Fort Ann, N.Y. (12827) 276/N4
Fort Apache, Ariz. (85926) 198/F5
Fort Apache Ind. Res., Ariz. 198/E5
Fort-Archambault, Chad 111/C6
Fort-Archambault, 102/D4
Fort Ashby, W. Va. (26719) 313/J4
Fort Assiniboine, Alta. 182/C2
Fort Atkinson, Iowa (52144) 229/J2
Fort Atkinson, Wis. (53538) 317/J10
Fort Augustus, 10/D2
Fort Augustus, Scot. 15/G5
Fort Baker, Calif. 204/J2
Fort Bayard, N. Mex. (88036) 274/A6
Fort Beaufort, S. Africa 118/D6
Fort Beauséjour Nat'l Hist. Park, N. Br. 170/F3
Fort Belknap, Mont. (†59526) 262/H2
Fort Belknap Ind. Res., Mont. 262/H2
Fort Belvoir, Va. 307/O3
Fort Bend (co.), Texas 302/J8
Fort Benjamin Harrison, Ind. 227/E5
Fort Benning, Ga. 216/B6
Fort Benton, Mont. (59442) 262/F3
Fort Berthold Ind. Res., N. Dak. 283/E4
Fort Bidwell, Calif. (96112) 204/E2
Fort Bidwell Ind. Res. Calif. 204/E2
Fort Blackmore, Va. (24250) 307/C7
Fort Bliss, Texas 302/A10
Fort Bowie Nat'l Hist. Site, Ariz. 198/F6
Fort Bragg, Calif. (95437) 204/B4
Fort Bragg, N.C. 281/M4
Fort Branch, Ind. (47533) 227/B8
Fort Bridger, Wyo. (82933) 319/B4
Fort Calhoun, Nebr. (68023) 264/J3
Fort Campbell, Ky. 237/G7
Fort Campbell, Tenn. 237/G7
Fort Caroline Nat'l Mem., Fla. 212/E1
Fort Carson, Colo. 208/K5
Fort-Chambly, Que. 172/J4
Fort Chimo, 163/K4
Fort-Chimo, Que. 174/F2
Fort Chipewyan, 163/F4
Fort Chipewyan, Alta. 182/C5
Fort Clark, N. Dak. (†58571) 283/H5
Fort Clatsop Nat'l Mem., Oreg. 291/C1
Fort Cobb, Okla. (73038) 288/K4
Fort Cobb (res.), Okla. 288/J4
Fort Collins, Colo., 188/E2
Fort Collins, Colo. (80521) 208/J1
Fort Covington, N.Y. (12937) 276/M1
Fort-Crampel, Centr. Afr. Rep. 115/C2
Fort-Crampel, 102/D4
Fort-Dauphin, 102/G7
Fort-Dauphin, Malag. Rep. 118/H5
Fort Davis, Ala. (36031) 194/G6
Fort Davis, Alaska 196/E2
Fort Davis, Texas (79734) 302/D11
Fort Davis Nat'l Hist. Site, Texas 302/D11
Fort Defiance, Ariz. (86504) 198/F3
Fort Defiance, Va. (24437) 307/L4
Fort-de-France (cap.), Mart. 156/G4
Fort-de-France (cap.), Mart. 161/C6
Fort-de-France (bay), Mart. 161/C6
Fort Denaud, Fla. (†33935) 212/E5
Fort Deposit, Ala. (36032) 194/E7
Fort-de-Possel, Centr. Afr. Rep. 115/C2
Fort-Desaix, Mart. 161/D6
Fort Devens, Mass. 249/H2
Fort Dick, Calif. (95538) 204/A2
Fort Dix, N.J. 273/D3
Fort Dodge, Iowa, 188/H2
Fort Dodge, Iowa (50501) 229/E3
Fort Dodge, Kans. (67843) 232/C4
Fort Donelson Nat'l Mil. Park, Tenn. 237/F8
Fort Drum, Fla. (†33472) 212/F4
Fort Duchesne, Utah (84026) 304/E3
Forteau, Newf. 166/C3
Fort Edward, N.Y. (12828) 276/O4
Forte República, Angola 115/C5
Fort Erie, Ont. 177/E5
Fortescue (riv.), Aust. 88/B4
Fortescue, Mo. (64452) 261/B2
Fortescue, N.J. (08321) 273/C5
Fortescue (riv.), W. Aust. 92/B3
Fort Eustis, Va. 307/P6
Fort Fairfield▵, Maine (04742) 242/H2
Fort Fairfield, Maine (04742) 242/H2
Fort Fitzgerald, 163/E4
Fort Fitzgerald, Alta. 182/C4
Fort Foote, Md. (†20013) 245/F6
Fort-Foureau, Cameroon 115/B1
Fort Frances, 163/G6
Fort Frances, Ont. 175/B3
Fort Frances, Ont. 177/F5
Fort Franklin, 163/D2
Fort Franklin, N.W.T. 187/F3
Fort Fraser, Br. Col. 184/E3
Fort Frederica Nat'l Mon., Ga. 216/K8
Fort Fred Steele, Wyo. (†82301) 319/E4
Fort Gaines, Ala. 194/B10
Fort Gaines, Ga. (31751) 216/C7
Fort Garland, Colo. (81133) 208/J8
Fort Garry, Man. 179/E5
Fort Gates‡, Texas (†76528) 302/G6
Fort Gay, W. Va. (25514) 313/A6
Fort George, Br. Col. 184/F3
Fort George, 163/J5
Fort-George, Que. 174/B2
Fort-George, Que., 146/L4
Fort George G. Meade, Md. 245/L4
Fort Gibson, Okla. (74434) 288/R3
Fort Gibson (res.), Okla. 288/R2
Fort Glenn, Alaska (†99638) 196/E4
Fort Good Hope, 163/D2
Fort Good Hope, N.W.T. 187/F3
Fort Gordon, Ga. 216/H4
Fort Grahame, Br. Col. 184/E2
Fort Grant, Ariz. (85643) 198/E6
Fort Greely, Alaska 196/J2
Fort Green, Fla. (33834) 212/E4
Forth (firth), 10/E2
Forth (riv.), 10/C1
Forth (firth), Scot. 15/L7
Forth (riv.), Scot. 15/H7
Forth Tas. 99/C3
Fort Hall, Idaho (83203) 220/F6
Fort Hall, Kenya 115/G4
Fort Hall, 102/F5
Fort Hall Ind. Res., Idaho 220/F6
Fort Hancock, N.J. 273/F3
Fort Hancock, Texas (79839) 302/B11
Forth and Clyde (canal), 10/B1
Forth and Clyde (canal), Scot. 15/H8
Fort Hertz (Putao), Burma 72/C1
Fort Holabird, Md. 245/M3
Fort Hood, Texas 302/G6
Fort Hope, Ont. 175/C2
Fort Huachuca, Ariz. (85613) 198/E7
Fort Huachuca, Ariz. 198/E7
Fort Hunt, Va. 307/O3
Fortier, Man. 179/E5
Fortierville, Que. 172/F3
Fortín Alta Vista, Bol. 136/F6
Fortín Ávalos Sánchez, Par. 144/B4
Fortín Ayacucho, Par. 144/B2
Fortín Boquerón, Par. 144/C4
Fortín Buenos Aires, Par. 144/B4
Fortín Campero, Bol. 136/C8
Fortín Carlos Antonio López, Par. 144/C3
Fortín Coronel Bogado, Par. 144/C3
Fortín Coroneles Sánchez, Par. 144/B2
Fortín de las Flores, Mex. 150/P2
Fort Independence Ind. Res., Calif. 204/G7
Fortine, Mont. (59918) 262/A2
Fortín Falcón, Par. 144/B4
Fortín Florida, Par. 144/C3
Fortín Gabino Mendoza, Par. 144/B3
Fortingall, Scot. 15/H6
Fortín Galpón, Par. 144/C2
Fortín Garrapatal, Par. 144/B3
Fortín General Aquino, Par. 144/C5
Fortín General Bruguez, Par. 144/C5
Fortín General Caballero, Par. 144/C5
Fortín General Díaz, Boquerón, Par. 144/B4
Fortín General Díaz, Olimpo, Par. 144/C3
Fortín General Pando, Par. 144/C2
Fortín Guachalla, Par. 144/A4
Fortín Hernandarias, Par. 144/B3
Fortín Ingavi, Par. 144/B2
Fortín Juan de Zalazar, Par. 144/C4
Fortín Junín, Par. 144/B3
Fortín Linares, Par. 144/B4
Fortín Madrejón, Par. 144/B3
Fortín Max Paredes, Bol. 136/F6
Fortín Mayor Rodríguez, Par. 144/B4
Fortín Mutum, Bol. 136/F6
Fortín Orihuela, Par. 144/C4
Fortín Patria, Par. 144/C2
Fortín Presidente Ayala, Par. 144/C4
Fortín Ravelo, Bol. 136/E6
Fortín Salto Palmar, Par. 144/C5
Fortín Suárez Arana, Bol. 136/F6
Fortín Tinfunqué, Par. 144/B4
Fortín Toledo, Par. 144/B4
Fortín Torres, Par. 144/C3
Fortín Valois Rivarola, Par. 144/C4
Fortín Vanguardia Primero, Bol. 136/F6
Fort Irwin, Calif. 204/J8
Fort Jackson, N.Y. (12938) 276/L1
Fort Jackson, S.C. 296/F4
Fort Jefferson Nat'l Mon., Fla. 212/C7
Fort Jennings, Ohio (45844) 284/B4
Fort Jesup, La. (†71449) 238/C3
Fort Johnson, N.Y. (12070) 276/M5
Fort Johnston, 102/F6
Fort Johnston, Malawi 115/G6
Fort Jones, Calif. (96032) 204/C2
Fort Kent, Alta. 182/E2
Fort Kent▵, Maine (04743) 242/F1
Fort Kent, Maine (04743) 242/F1
Fort Kent Mills, Maine (04744) 242/F1
Fort Klamath, Oreg. (97626) 291/E5
Fort Knox, Ky. (40121) 237/K5
Fort-Lallemand, Alg. 106/F2
Fort Lamar, Ga. (†30633) 216/F2
Fort-Lamy (cap.), Chad, 3/K5
Fort-Lamy (cap.), Chad 111/C5
Fort-Lamy (cap.), Chad 102/D3
Fort Langley, Br. Col. 184/L3
Fort Laramie, Wyo. (82212) 319/H3
Fort Laramie Nat'l Hist. Site, Wyo. 319/H3
Fort Larned Nat'l Hist. Site, Kans. 232/C3
Fort Lauderdale, Fla. (*33301) 212/C4
Fort Lawn, S.C. (29714) 296/F2
Fort Lawrence, N.S. 169/D3
Fort Lawton, Wash. 310/A2
Fort Leavenworth, Kans. (66027) 232/H2
Fort Lee, N.J. (07024) 273/C2
Fort Lee, Va. 307/O6
Fort Leonard Wood, Mo. 261/H7
Fort Lesley J. McNair, D.C. 245/E5
Fort Lewis, Wash. 310/C3
Fort Liard, 163/D3
Fort Liard, N.W.T., 146/F3
Fort Liard, N.W.T. 187/F3
Fort-Liberté, Haiti 156/D3
Fort-Liberté, Haiti 158/C5
Fort Littleton, Pa. (17223) 294/F5
Fort Logan, Mont. (†59645) 262/E4
Fort Lookout, S. Dak. (†57548) 298/K6
Fort Loramie, Ohio (45845) 284/B5
Fort Loudon, Pa. (17224) 294/G6
Fort Loudoun (lake), Tenn. 237/N9
Fort Lupton, Colo. (80621) 208/K2
Fort Lyon, Colo. (81038) 208/N6
Fort MacArthur, Calif. 204/C11
Fort Macleod, 163/E6
Fort Macleod, Alta. 182/D5
Fort-Mac-Mahon, Alg. 106/E3
Fort Madison, Iowa, 188/H2
Fort Madison, Iowa (52627) 229/L7
Fort Matanzas Nat'l Mon., Fla. 212/E2
Fort McClellan Mil. Res., Ala. 194/G3
Fort McCoy, Fla. (32637) 212/E2
Fort McDowell Ind. Res., Ariz. 198/D5
Fort McHenry Nat'l Mon., Md. 245/M3
Fort McKavett, Texas (76841) 302/E7
Fort McKay, 163/E4
Fort McKay, Alta. 182/E1
Fort McKenzie, 163/K4
Fort McKinley, Ohio (†45401) 284/B6
Fort McMurray, 163/E4
Fort McMurray, Alta., 146/H4
Fort McMurray, Alta. 182/E1
Fort McPherson, Ga. 216/D3
Fort McPherson, 163/C2
Fort McPherson, N.W.T., 146/E3
Fort McPherson, N.W.T. 187/E3
Fort Meade, Fla. (33841) 212/E4
Fort Mill, S.C. (29715) 296/F1
Fort-Miribel, Alg. 106/E3
Fort Mitchell, Ala. (36856) 194/H6
Fort Mitchell, Ky. (41017) 237/S3
Fort Mitchell, Va. (23941) 307/M7
Fort Mohave Ind. Res., Ariz. 198/A4
Fort Mohave Ind. Res., Calif. 204/L9
Fort Mohave Ind. Res., Nev. 266/G7
Fort Monmouth, N.J. 273/E3
Fort Monroe, Va. 307/R6
Fort Morgan, Ala. 194/C10
Fort Morgan, Colo. (80701) 208/M2
Fort Motte, S.C. (29050) 296/F4
Fort Myer, Va. 307/O3
Fort Myers, Fla., 188/K5
Fort Myers, Fla. (*33901) 212/E5
Fort Myers Beach, Fla. (33931) 212/E5
Fort Myers Villas-Pine Manor‡, Fla. (†33901) 212/E5
Fort Necessity, La. (71243) 238/G2
Fort Necessity Nat'l Battlefield, Pa. 294/C6
Fort Nelson, 163/D4
Fort Nelson, Br. Col., 146/F4
Fort Nelson, Br. Col. 184/M2
Fort Nelson (riv.), Br. Col. 184/M2
Fort Niagara, N.Y. 276/C4
Fort Norman, 163/D2
Fort Norman, N.W.T., 146/F3
Fort Norman, N.W.T. 187/F3
Fort Ogden, Fla. (33842) 212/E4
Fort Oglethorpe, Ga. (30741) 216/B1
Fort Ord, Calif. 204/D7
Fort Payne, Ala. (35967) 194/G2
Fort Peck (res.), Mont., 146/H5
Fort Peck (res.), Mont., 188/E1
Fort Peck, Mont. (59223) 262/K2
Fort Peck (dam), Mont. 262/K3
Fort Peck (res.), Mont. 262/K3
Fort Pelly, Sask. 181/J4
Fort Pierce, Fla. (33450) 212/F4
Fort Pierre, S. Dak. (57532) 298/H5
Fort Pillow, Tenn. (38032) 237/B9
Fort Pitt, Sask. 181/B2
Fort Plain, N.Y. (13339) 276/L5
Fort Polk, La. 238/D4
Fort Portal, Uganda 115/F3
Fort Providence, 163/E3
Fort Providence, N.W.T. 187/G3
Fort Pulaski Nat'l Mon., Ga. 216/L6
Fort Qu'Appelle, Sask. 181/H5
Fort Raleigh Nat'l Hist. Site, N.C. 281/T3
Fort Randall (dam), S. Dak. 298/N7
Fort Ransom, N. Dak. (58033) 283/P6
Fort Recovery, Ohio (45846) 284/A5
Fort Reliance, 163/F3
Fort Reliance, N.W.T. 187/H3
Fort Resolution, 163/E3
Fort Resolution, N.W.T., 146/G3
Fort Resolution, N.W.T. 187/G3
Fortress (mt.), Wyo. 319/C1
Fort Rice, N. Dak. (58537) 283/J6
Fort Richardson, Alaska 196/C1
Fort Riley, Kans. 232/F2
Fort Ripley, Minn. (56449) 254/D4
Fort Ritchie, Md. 245/H2
Fort Ritner, Ind. (47430) 227/E7
Fort Robinson, Nebr. (†69339) 264/A2
Fort Rock, Oreg. (97735) 291/G4
Fort Rodman, Mass. 249/L6
Fortrose, 10/D2
Fortrose, Scot. 15/H4
Fort Rosebery (Mansa), Zambia 115/E6
Fort-Rousset, Rep. of Congo 115/C4
Fort Rucker, Ala. 194/G8
Fort-Rupert, 163/J5
Fort-Rupert, Que. 174/B2
Fort-Rupert, Que., 146/L4
Fort-Saint, Tun. 106/F2
Fort Saint James, 163/D5
Fort Saint James, Br. Col. 184/E3
Fort Saint John, 163/D4
Fort Saint John, Br. Col. 184/G2
Fort Saint Philip, La. (†70041) 238/M8
Fort Salonga‡, N.Y. (†11787) 276/O9
Fort Sandeman, Pak. 59/J3
Fort Sandeman, Pak. 68/B2
Fort Saskatchewan, 163/E5
Fort Saskatchewan, Alta. 182/D3
Forts Barry and Cronkhite, Calif. 204/H2
Fort Scott, Kans., 188/H3
Fort Scott, Kans. (66701) 232/H4
Fort Selkirk, 163/C3
Fort Selkirk, Yukon 187/E3
Fort Seneca, Ohio (44829) 284/D3
Fort Seward, Calif. (95438) 204/B3
Fort Seybert, W. Va. (26806) 313/H5
Fort Shafter, Hawaii 218/C3
Fort Shaw, Mont. (59443) 262/E3
Fort Shawnee, Ohio (†45801) 284/B4
Fort Sheridan, Ill. 222/F1
Fort Shevchenko, U.S.S.R. 48/F5
Fort-Sibut, Centr. Afr. Rep. 115/C2
Fort Sill Mil. Res., Okla. 288/K5
Fort Simpson, 163/D3
Fort Simpson, Canada, 4/C15
Fort Simpson, N.W.T., 146/F3
Fort Simpson, N.W.T. 187/F3
Fort Smith, Ark., 146/J6
Fort Smith, Ark., 188/H3
Fort Smith, Ark. (72901) 203/B3
Fort Smith, Mont. (†59075) 262/J5
Fort Smith, N.W.T., 146/H3
Fort Smith, N.W.T., 163/E3
Fort Smith, N.W.T. 187/G3
Fort Smith Nat'l Hist. Site, Ark. 203/B3
Fortson, Ga. (31808) 216/C5
Fort Spring, W. Va. (24936) 313/E7
Fort Stanton, N. Mex. (88323) 274/D5
Fort Stanwix Nat'l Mon., N.Y. 276/J4
Fort Steele, Br. Col. 184/K5
Fort Stewart, Ont. 177/G2
Fort Stewart, Ga. 216/J7
Fort Stockton, Texas (79735) 302/A7
Fort Story, Va. 307/S7
Fort Sumner, N. Mex. (88119) 274/E4
Fort Sumter Nat'l Mon., S.C. 296/H6
Fort Supply, Okla. (73841) 288/G1
Fort Supply (res.), Okla. 288/G1
Fort Thomas, Ariz. (85536) 198/E5
Fort Thomas, Ky. (41075) 237/S2
Fort Thompson, S. Dak. (57339) 298/L5
Fort Ticonderoga, N.Y. (†12883) 276/O3
Fort Tilden, N.Y. 276/N9
Fort Totten, N. Dak. (58335) 283/M4
Fort Totten, N.Y. 276/N9
Fort Totten Ind. Res., N. Dak. 283/N4
Fort Towson, Okla. (74735) 288/R7
Fortuna, Calif. (95540) 204/A3
Fortuna, Mo. (65034) 261/G5
Fortuna, N. Dak. (58844) 283/C2
Fortuna, Spain 33/F3
Fortuna Ledge, Alaska (99585) 196/F2
Fortune, Newf. 166/C4
Fortune (bay), Newf. 166/C4
Fort Union Nat'l Mon., N. Mex. 274/E3
Fort Union Trading Post Nat'l Hist. Site, N. Dak. 283/B3
Fort Valley, Ga. (31030) 216/E5
Fort Vancouver Nat'l Hist. Site, Wash. 310/C5
Fort Vermilion, 163/E4
Fort Vermilion, Alta., 146/G4
Fort Vermilion, Alta. 182/B5
Fort Victoria, 102/F7
Fort Victoria, Rhod. 118/E4
Fortville, Ind. (46040) 227/F5
Fort Wainwright, Alaska 196/J1
Fort Walton Beach, Fla. (32548) 212/C6
Fort Washakie, Wyo. (82514) 319/C2
Fort Washington, Md. (†20735) 245/L6
Fort Wayne, Ind., 188/J2
Fort Wayne, Ind. (*46801) 227/G2
Fort White, Fla. (32038) 212/D2
Fort William, 10/D2
Fort William, Scot. 15/F6
Fort Winfield Scott, Calif. 204/J2
Fort Wingate, N. Mex. (87316) 274/A3
Fort Wingate Army Depot, N. Mex. 274/A3
Fort Worden, Wash. 310/C2
Fort Worth, Texas, 146/J6
Fort Worth, Texas, 188/G4
Fort Worth, Texas (*76101) 302/E2
Fort Wright-Lookout Heights, Ky. (†41011) 237/S3
Fort Yates, N. Dak. (58538) 283/J7
Forty Fort, Pa. (18704) 294/L3
Forty Mile, 163/C3
Forty Mile (pt.), Mich. 250/F3
Forty Mile, Yukon 187/D3
Fort Yukon, Alaska, 146/D3
Fort Yukon, Alaska, 188/D5
Fort Yukon, Alaska (99740) 196/J1
Fort Yukon, U.S., 4/C17
Forum, Ark. (72731) 203/C1
Fosforescente (bay), P. Rico 161/A3
Fosheim (pen.), N.W.T. 187/K1
Foss, Okla. (73647) 288/H4
Foss (res.), Okla. 288/H3
Fossano, Italy 34/A2
Fosses-la-Ville, Belg. 27/F8
Fossil (creek), Ariz. 198/D4
Fossil, Oreg. (97830) 291/G2
Fossombrone, Italy 34/D3
Fosston, Minn. (56542) 254/C3
Fosston, Sask. 181/H3
Foster, Que. 172/E4
Foster, Ind. (†47932) 227/C4
Foster, Ky. (41043) 237/N3
Foster, Mo. (64745) 261/D6
Foster (co.), N. Dak. 283/N5
Foster, Nebr. (68737) 264/G2
Foster, Okla. (73039) 288/M5
Foster, Oreg. (97345) 291/E3
Foster▵, R.I. (02825) 249/H5
Foster (creek), S. Dak. 298/N4
Foster (riv.), Sask. 181/M3
Foster, W. Va. (25081) 313/C6
Foster, Wis. (†54758) 317/D6
Foster Center (Foster P.O.), R.I. (†02825) 249/H5
Foster City, Calif. (94404) 204/J2
Foster City, Mich. (49834) 250/B3
Fosters, Ala. (35463) 194/C4
Fosters, Mich. (†48415) 250/F5
Fosters Falls, Va. (24329) 307/G7
Fosterton, Sask. 181/C5
Foster Village, Hawaii (†96701) 218/B3
Fosterville, N. Br. 170/C3
Fosterville, Tenn. (37063) 237/J9
Fostoria, Ala. (†36737) 194/E6
Fostoria, Iowa (51340) 229/C2
Fostoria, Kans. (66426) 232/F2
Fostoria, Mich. (48435) 250/F5
Fostoria, Ohio (44830) 284/D3
Fougères, France 28/C3
Fouke, Ark. (71837) 203/C7
Foul (sound), Ire. 17/B5
Foul (bay), U.A.R. 111/G3
Foula (isl.), 10/G1
Foula (isl.), Scot. 15/L3
Foules, La. (†71326) 238/G3
Foulness (isl.), Eng. 13/J6
Foulpointe, Malag. Rep. 118/H3
Foulsham, Eng. 13/H5

366 Fuerte

Fuerte (isl.), Col. 126/B3
Fuerte (riv.), Mex. 150/E3
Fuerte Bulnes, Chile 138/E10
Fuerte Olimpo, Par. 144/D3
Fuerteventura (isl.), 102/A2
Fuerteventura (isl.), Spain 33/C4
Fuerteventura (isl.), Spain 106/B3
Fuga (isl.), Phil. 82/C1
Fuglebjerg, Den. 21/E7
Fuhai, China 77/C2
Fuik, Neth. Ant. 161/G9
Fujairah (cap.), Trucial States 59/G4
Fuji (mt.), Japan, 54/S6
Fuji, Japan 81/J6
Fuji (mt.), Japan 81/J6
Fuji (riv.), Japan 81/J6
Fujieda, Japan 81/J6
Fuji-Hakone-Izu Nat'l Park, Japan 81/H6
Fujisawa, Japan 81/O3
Fukien (prov.), China 77/J6
Fukuchiyama, Japan 81/G6
Fukue, Japan 81/D7
Fukui (pref.), Japan 81/G5
Fukui, Japan 81/G5
Fukuoka, Japan, 54/R6
Fukuoka (pref.), Japan 81/D7
Fukuoka, Japan 81/D7
Fukushima (pref.), Japan 81/K5
Fukushima, Japan 81/K5
Fukuyama, Japan 81/F6
Fulbright, Texas (75436) 302/J4
Fulda, Ind. (47536) 227/D8
Fulda, Minn. (56131) 254/C7
Fulda, Sask. 181/F3
Fulda, W. Ger. 22/C3
Fulda (riv.), W. Ger. 22/C3
Fulford, Eng. 13/F4
Fulford Harbour, Br. Col. 184/K3
Fulks Run, Va. (22830) 307/L3
Fullarton, Trinidad Tobago 161/A11
Fullerton, Calif. (*92631) 204/D11
Fullerton, Ky. (†41175) 237/P3
Fullerton, La. (70642) 238/D4
Fullerton, N. Dak. (58441) 283/O7
Fullerton, Nebr. (68638) 264/F3
Fullerton‡, Pa. (18052) 294/M4
Fully, Switz. 39/D4
Fulnek, Czech. 41/D2
Fulpmes, Austria 41/A3
Fulton, Ala. (36446) 194/C7
Fulton (co.), Ark. 203/G1
Fulton, Ark. (71838) 203/C6
Fulton (co.), Ga. 216/D3
Fulton (co.), Ill. 222/C3
Fulton, Ill. (61252) 222/C2
Fulton (co.), Ind. 227/E2
Fulton, Ind. (46931) 227/E3
Fulton, Iowa (†52060) 229/M4
Fulton, Kans. (66738) 232/H4
Fulton (co.), Ky. 237/C7
Fulton, Ky. (42041) 237/D7
Fulton, Mich. (49052) 250/D6
Fulton, Miss. (38843) 256/H2
Fulton, Mo. (65251) 261/J5
Fulton (co.), N.Y. 276/M4
Fulton, N.Y. (13069) 276/H4
Fulton (co.), Ohio 284/B2
Fulton, Ohio (43321) 284/E5
Fulton (co.), Pa. 294/F6
Fulton, S. Dak. (57340) 298/O6
Fulton, Tenn. (38035) 237/B9
Fulton‡, Texas (78358) 302/G9
Fulton Chain (lakes), N.Y. 276/K3
Fultondale, Ala. (35068) 194/E3
Fultonham, Ohio (43738) 284/F6
Fultonville, N.Y. (12072) 276/M5
Fults, Ill. (62244) 222/C5
Fulwood, 10/G1
Fumen, Iran 66/F2
Funabashi, Japan 81/P2
Funafuti (atoll), Gilb. and Ell., 87/H6
Funchal (cap.), Madeira, Port. 102/A1
Funchal (cap.), Madeira, Port. 33/A2
Funchal (cap.), Madeira, Port. 106/A2
Fundación, Col. 126/C2
Fundão, Port. 33/C2
Fundy (bay), 163/K7
Fundy (bay), N. Br. 170/E3
Fundy (bay), N.S. 169/C3
Fundy Nat'l Park, N. Br. 170/E3
Funhalouro, Moz. 118/E4
Funk, Nebr. (68940) 264/E4
Funk (isl.), Newf. 166/D4
Funkley, Minn. (†56630) 254/D3
Funkstown, Md. (21734) 245/H2
Funston, Ga. (31753) 216/E8
Funter, Alaska (†99801) 196/M1
Funtua, Nigeria 106/F6
Fuquay-Varina, N.C. (27526) 281/M3
Furancungo, Moz. 118/E2
Furka (pass), Switz. 39/F3
Furman, Ala. (36741) 194/E6
Furman, S.C. (29921) 296/E6
Furmanov, U.S.S.R. 52/F3
Furnace, Ky. (40433) 237/O5
Furnace, Mass. (†01031) 249/F3
Furnas (dam), Braz. 135/C2
Furnas (co.), Nebr. 264/E4
Furneaux Group (isls.), Australia, 87/E9
Furneaux Group (isls.), Aust. 88/H8
Furneaux Group (isls.), Tasmania 99/E1
Furnes (Veurne), Belg. 27/B6
Furness, Sask. 181/B2
Fürstenberg, E. Ger. 22/E2
Fürstenfeld, Austria 41/C3
Fürstenfeldbruck, W. Ger. 22/D4
Fürstenwalde, E. Ger. 22/F2
Fürth, W. Ger. 22/D4
Furth, W. Ger. 22/E4
Furukawa, Japan 81/K4
Fury and Hecla (str.), 163/H2
Fury and Hecla (str.), N.W.T. 187/K3
Fusagasugá, Col. 126/C5
Fushun, China 77/K3
Fusilier, Sask. 181/B4
Fusin, China 77/K3
Fusingchen, China 77/F7
Fusio, Switz. 39/G4
Füssen, W. Ger. 22/D5
Futa Jallon (mts.), Guinea 106/B6
Futaleufú, Chile 138/E4
Futrono, Chile 138/E3
Futtsu, Japan 81/O3
Fuyü, China 77/L2
Fuyüan, China 77/M2
Füzesabony, Hung. 41/F3
Füzesgyarmat, Hung. 41/F3
Fyffe, Ala. (35971) 194/G2
Fyn (isl.), Den. 18/G9
Fyn (isl.), Den. 21/D7
Fyne (inlet), 10/D2
Fyne (inlet), Scot. 15/F8
Fyns (prom.), Den. 21/D6
Fyzabad, Trinidad Tobago 161/A11

G

Gaastra, Mich. (49927) 250/G2
Gabarouse, N.S. 169/H3
Gabarus (bay), N.S. 169/H3
Gâbarus (cape), N.S. 169/J3
Gabbettville, Ga. (31809) 216/B5
Gabbro (lake), Newf. 166/A3
Gabbs, Nev. (89409) 266/D4
Gabčíkovo, Czech. 41/D3
Gabela, Angola 115/B6
Gabès, 102/D1
Gabès, Tun. 106/F2
Gabès (gulf), Tun. 106/G2
Gabgaba, Wadi (dry riv.), Sudan 111/F3
Gable, S.C. (29051) 296/G4
Gabon, 3/K6
GABON, 115/B4
GABON, 102/D5
Gaborone (cap.), Botswana, 3/L7
Gaborone (cap.), Botswana 118/D4
Gaborone (cap.), Botswana, 102/E7
Gabras, Sudan 111/E5
Gabredarre, Eth. 111/H6
Gabriel (str.), N.W.T. 187/M3
Gabrig (riv.), Iran 66/L7
Gabriola Island, Br. Col. 184/J3
Gabrovo, Bulg. 45/G4
Gachalá, Col. 126/D5
Gach Saran, Iran 59/F3
Gach Saran, Iran 66/G5
Gackle, N. Dak. (58442) 283/M6
Gacko, Yugo. 45/D4
Gadag, India 68/D5
Gäddede, Sweden 18/J4
Gadebusch, E. Ger. 22/D2
Gadmen, Switz. 39/F3
Gadsby, Alta. 182/D3
Gadsden, Ala., 188/J4
Gadsden, Ala. (*35901) 194/G2
Gadsden, Ariz. (85336) 198/A6
Gadsden (co.), Fla. 212/B1
Gadsden, S.C. (29052) 296/F4
Gadsden, Tenn. (38337) 237/D9
Gads Hill, Mo. (†63957) 261/L8
Gadston (pt.), Fla. 212/C3
Gadwal, India 68/D5
Gadyach, U.S.S.R. 52/D4
Găeşti, Rum. 45/G3
Gaeta, Italy 34/D4
Gaeta (gulf), Italy 34/D4
Gaferut (isl.), Pac. Is., 87/E5
Gaffney, S.C. (29340) 296/D1
Gafsa, Tun. 106/F2
Gagarin, U.S.S.R. 52/D3
Gage, Alta. 182/A1
Gage, N. Mex. (88037) 274/A6
Gage (co.), Nebr. 264/H4
Gage, Okla. (73843) 288/G2
Gages Lake-Wildwood‡, Ill. (60030) 222/F1
Gagetown, Mich. (48735) 250/F5
Gagetown, N. Br. 170/D3
Gaggenau, W. Ger. 22/C4
Gagnoa, Ivory Coast 106/C7
Gagnon, 163/K5
Gagnon, Que. 174/D2
Gagny, France 28/C1
Gagra, U.S.S.R. 52/E6
Gahanna, Ohio (43230) 284/E5
Gaiba (lag.), Bol. 136/G5
Gail, Saudi Ar. 59/E5
Gail, Texas (79738) 302/C5
Gaillac, France 28/D6
Gaillard (lake), Conn. 210/D3
Gaillard, Ga. (†31078) 216/D5
Gaima, Papua 85/B7
Gaiman, Arg. 143/C5
Gaines, Mich. (48436) 250/F6
Gaines, Pa. (16921) 294/G2
Gaines (co.), Texas 302/B5
Gainesboro, Tenn. (38562) 237/K8
Gainesboro, Va. (22636) 307/M2
Gainestown, Ala. (36540) 194/C8
Gainesville, Ala. (35464) 194/B5
Gainesville, Fla., 188/K5
Gainesville, Fla. (32601) 212/D2
Gainesville, Ga. (30501) 216/E2
Gainesville, Mo. (65655) 261/G9
Gainesville, N.Y. (14066) 276/D5
Gainesville, Texas (76240) 302/G4
Gainesville, Va. (22065) 307/N3
Gainesville Cotton Mills‡, Ga. (†30501) 216/E2
Gainford, Alta. 182/C3
Gainsborough, 10/F4
Gainsborough, Eng. 13/G4
Gainsborough, Sask. 181/K6
Gair (inlet), Scot. 15/E4
Gairdner (lake), Australia, 87/D9
Gairdner (lake), Aust. 88/F6
Gairdner (lake), S. Aust. 94/D4
Gairloch, Scot. 15/E4
Gairloch (dist.), Scot. 15/E4
Gais, Switz. 39/H2
Gaithersburg, Md. (20760) 245/K4
Gajdel, Czech. 41/E2
Gakona, Alaska (99586) 196/K2
Galadi, Eth. 111/J6
Galahad, Alta. 182/E3
Galana (riv.), Kenya 115/G4
Galand, Iran 66/J2
Galanta, Czech. 41/D2
Galápagos (isls.), Ec. 128/C8
Galápagos (isls.), Ecuador, 3/E6
Galashiels, 10/E3
Galashiels, Scot. 15/L8
Galata, Mont. (59444) 262/E2
Galata, Turkey 63/C6
Galaţi, Rum., 7/G4
Galaţi, Rum. 45/H3
Galatia, Ill. (62935) 222/E6
Galatia, Kans. (67528) 232/D3
Galatina, Italy 34/G4
Galatone, Italy 34/F4
Galax, Va. (24333) 307/G7
Galbally, Ire. 17/E7
Galbraith, La. (†71447) 238/E4
Galchutt, N. Dak. (58034) 283/S7
Gale, Ill. (62936) 222/D6
Gale (riv.), N.H. 268/D3
Galeana, Chihuahua, Mex. 150/F1
Galeana, Nuevo León, Mex. 150/J4
Galela, Indon. 85/H5
Galen, Mont. (†59722) 262/D4
Galena, Alaska (99741) 196/G2
Galena, Ill. (61036) 222/C1
Galena, Ind. (†47119) 227/F8
Galena, Kans. (66739) 232/H4
Galena, Md. (21635) 245/P3
Galena, Mo. (65656) 261/F9
Galena, Ohio (43021) 284/E5
Galena Park, Texas (77547) 302/J1
Galeota (pt.), Trinidad Tobago 161/B11
Galera (pt.), Chile 138/D3
Galera (pt.), Trinidad Tobago 156/G5
Galera (pt.), Trinidad Tobago 161/C10
Galera (pt.), Ec. 128/B2
Galesburg, Ill., 188/H2
Galesburg, Ill. (61401) 222/C3
Galesburg, Kans. (66740) 232/G4
Galesburg, Mich. (49053) 250/D6
Galesburg, N. Dak. (58035) 283/R5
Gales Creek, Oreg. (97117) 291/D2
Gales Ferry, Conn. (06335) 210/G3
Galestown, Md. (†19973) 245/P6
Galesville, Md. (20765) 245/M5
Galesville, Wis. (54630) 317/D7
Galeton, Colo. (80622) 208/K1
Galeton, Pa. (16922) 294/G2
Galetta, Ont. 177/H2
Galgenberg (hill), Neth. 27/H4
Galiano (isl.), Br. Col. 184/K3
Galiano Island, Br. Col. 184/K3
Galice, Oreg. (†97532) 291/D5
Galich, U.S.S.R. 52/F3
Galicia (reg.), Spain 33/B1
Galien, Mich. (49113) 250/C7
Galilee, Sea of (lake), Israel 59/C3
Galilee, Sea of (Tiberias) (lake), Israel 65/D2
Galilee (reg.), Israel 65/C2
Galilee (lake), Queens. 95/C4
Galilee, Sask. 181/F6
Galina (pt.), Jam. 158/J6
Galion (bay), Mart. 161/D6
Galion, Ohio (44833) 284/E4
Galisteo, N. Mex. (†87540) 274/D3
Galiuro (mts.), Ariz. 198/E6
Galivants Ferry, S.C. (29544) 296/J3
Galkayu, Somalia 115/J2
Gallabat, Sudan 111/G5
Gallan (head), Scot. 15/B3
Gallant, Ala. (35972) 194/F2
Gallarate, Italy 34/B2
Gallatin (co.), Ill. 222/E6
Gallatin (co.), Ky. 237/M3
Gallatin, Mo. (64640) 261/E3
Gallatin (co.), Mont. 262/E5
Gallatin (peak), Mont. 262/E5
Gallatin (riv.), Mont. 262/E5
Gallatin, Tenn. (37066) 237/H8
Gallatin Gateway, Mont. (59730) 262/E5
Gallaway, Tenn. (38036) 237/B10
Galle, Ceylon, 54/L9
Galle, Ceylon 68/D7
Gallegos (riv.), Arg. 143/B7
Gallegos, N. Mex. (†87733) 274/F3
Galley (head), Ire. 17/D9
Gallia (co.), Ohio 284/F8
Galliano, La. (70354) 238/K8
Gallina, N. Mex. (87017) 274/C2
Gallinas (pt.), Col., 120/C1
Gallinas (pt.), Col. 126/E1
Gallinas (mts.), N. Mex. 274/B4
Gallinas (riv.), N. Mex. 274/E3
Gallion, Ala. (36742) 194/C6
Gallion, La. (†71223) 238/G1
Gallipoli, Italy 34/F4
Gallipoli, Turkey 59/A1
Gallipoli (Gelibolu), Turkey 63/C5
Gallipolis, Ohio (45631) 284/F8
Gallipolis Ferry, W. Va. (25515) 313/B5
Gallitzin, Pa. (16641) 294/E4
Gällivare, Sweden 18/M3
Gällivare, Sweden, 7/F2
Gallman, Miss. (39077) 256/D7
Gallo (pt.), Chile 138/E3
Gallo (mt.), Dom. Rep. 158/D5
Galloo (isl.), N.Y. 276/H3
Galloway, Ark. (†72114) 203/F4
Galloway, Br. Col. 184/K5
Galloway, Mull of (prom.), 10/D3
Galloway (dist.), Scot. 15/H10
Galloway, Mull of (prom.), Scot. 15/G10
Galloway, W. Va. (26349) 313/F4
Galloway, Wis. (54432) 317/H6
Gallup, N. Mex., 188/E3
Gallup, N. Mex. (87301) 274/A3
Gallur, Spain 33/F2
Galmiz, Switz. 39/D3
Gal'on, Israel 65/B4
Galston, 10/D3
Galston, Scot. 15/H8
Galt, Calif. (95632) 204/C9
Galt, Ont. 177/D4
Galt, Iowa (50101) 229/F3
Galt, Mo. (64641) 261/F2
Galtee (mts.), Ire. 17/E7
Galtymore (mt.), Ire. 17/E7
Galva, Ill. (61434) 222/D2
Galva, Iowa (51020) 229/C4
Galva, Kans. (67443) 232/E3
Galvarino, Chile 138/D2
Galveston, Ind. (46932) 227/E3
Galveston, Texas, 146/J7
Galveston (bay), Texas, 188/H5
Galveston, Texas, 188/H5
Galveston (co.), Texas 302/K8
Galveston, Texas (77550) 302/L3
Galveston (bay), Texas 302/L2
Galveston (isl.), Texas 302/K8
Gálvez, Rosario, Arg. 143/F6
Gálvez, Santa Fe, Arg. 143/F6
Galvez, La. (†70769) 238/L2
Gálvez, Spain 33/D3
Galvin, Wash. (98544) 310/B4
Galway, 10/B4
Galway, Ire., 7/D3
Galway (co.), Ire. 17/D5
Galway, Ire. 17/C5
Galway (bay), Ire. 17/C5
Galway (bay), 10/B4
Galway, N.Y. (12074) 276/N4
Gamaliel, Ky. (42140) 237/K7
Gamarra, Col. 126/D3
Gamas Ab (riv.), Iran 66/E3
Gamay, Phil. 82/E4
Gamay (bay), Phil. 82/E4
Gambaga, Ghana 106/D6
Gambela, Eth. 111/F6
Gambela, 102/F4
Gambell, Alaska (99742) 196/D2
Gamber, Md. (†21048) 245/L3
Gambia, 3/J5
GAMBIA, 106/A6
GAMBIA, 102/A3
Gambia (riv.), Gambia 106/B6
Gambia (riv.), Sen. 106/B6
Gambier (isls.), Fr. Poly., 87/N8
Gambier, Ohio (43022) 284/F5
Gambo, Newf. 166/D4
Gamboma, Rep. of Congo 115/C4
Gamboma, 102/D5
Gambrills, Md. (21054) 245/M4
Gamerco, N. Mex. (87317) 274/A3
Gaming, Austria 41/C3
Gamleby, Sweden 18/J8
Gammon (riv.), Man. 179/G3
Gammon (pt.), Mass. 249/N6
Gampel, Switz. 39/E4
Gamu-Gofa (prov.), Eth. 111/G6
Gamvik, Norway 18/Q1
Ganado, Ariz. (86505) 198/F3
Ganado, Texas (77962) 302/H8
Ganale Dorya (riv.), Eth. 111/H6
Gananoque, Ont. 177/H3
Ganassi, Phil. 82/D7
Ganaveh, Iran 66/G6
Gandajika, Dem. Rep. of the Congo. 115/D5
Gándara, Arg. 143/H7
Gandara, Phil. 82/E4
Gándara, Spain 33/C1
Gandava, Pak. 59/J4
Gandava, Pak. 68/B3
Gandeeville, W. Va. (25243) 313/D5
Gander, 163/L6
Gander, Newf. 166/D4
Gander (lake), Newf. 166/D4
Gander (riv.), Newf. 166/D4
Gandesa, Spain 33/G2
Gandhinagar, India 68/C4
Gandía, Spain 33/F3
Gandy, Nebr. (69137) 264/D3
Gandy, Utah (†84728) 304/A4
Gandzha (Kirovabad), U.S.S.R. 52/G6
Ganga (Ganges) (riv.), India 68/F3
Gan Gan, Arg. 143/C5
Ganganagar, India 68/C3
Gangara, Niger 106/F6
Gangaw, Burma 72/B2
Ganges, Br. Col. 184/K3
Ganges (riv.), 3/P4
Ganges (riv.), India, 54/M7
Ganges (riv.), India 68/F3
Ganges, Mouths of the (delta), India 68/F4
Ganges, Mouths of the (delta), Pak. 68/F4
Ganges (riv.), Pak. 68/F3
Gang Mills‡, N.Y. (†14870) 276/F6
Gang Ranch, Br. Col. 184/F4
Gangtok, India 68/F3
Gani, Indon. 85/H6
Ganister, Pa. (16642) 294/F5
Ganmain, N.S.W. 97/D4
Gann (Brinkhaven), Ohio (†43006) 284/F5
Gannat, France 28/E4
Gannett, Idaho (†83313) 220/D6
Gannett (peak), Wyo., 188/D2
Gannett (peak), Wyo. 319/C2
Gannvalley, S. Dak. (57341) 298/L5
Gans, Okla. (74936) 288/S4
Gänserndorf, Austria 41/D2
Gansevoort, N.Y. (12831) 276/N4
Ganshoren, Belg. 27/B9
Gansville, La. (†71422) 238/E2
Gantt, Ala. (36038) 194/E8
Gantt, S.C. (†29601) 296/C2
Gantts Quarry, Ala. (35069) 194/F4
Gan Yavne, Israel 65/B4
Gao, 102/C3
Gao, Mali 106/E5
Gao (mt.), Centr. Afr. Rep. 115/C2
Gaoua, Upp. Volta 106/D6
Gaoual, Guinea 106/B6
Gap, France 28/G5
Gap, Pa. (17527) 294/L6
Gap (creek), Sask. 181/B6
Gapan, Phil. 82/C3
Gapcreek, Ky. (†42603) 237/M7
Gap Mills, W. Va. (24941) 313/F7
Gara (lake), Ire. 17/D4
Gara (lake), 10/B4
Garachiné, Pan. 154/H6
Garad, Somalia 115/J2
Garadice (lake), Ire. 17/F3
Garah, N.S.W. 97/E1
Garamba Nat'l Park, Dem. Rep. of the Congo. 115/E3
Garanhuns, Braz. 132/G5
Garapan (cap.), Pac. Is., 87/E4
Garards Fort, Pa. (15334) 294/B6
Garba Tula, Kenya 115/G3
Garber, Iowa (52048) 229/L3
Garber, Okla. (73738) 288/M2
Garberville, Calif. (95440) 204/B3
Garbitt, Br. Col. 184/F2
Garbosh, Kuh-i- (mt.), Iran 66/G4
Garça, Braz. 135/B3
Garcia, Colo. (81134) 208/J8
García de la Cadena, Mex. 150/H6
Garcitas, Ven. 124/C3
Gard (dept.), France 28/F6
Gard (riv.), France 28/F5
Garda (lake), Italy 34/C2
Gardanne, France 28/F6
Gardar, N. Dak. (58234) 283/P2
Gardelegen, E. Ger. 22/D2
Garden (isl.), Aust. 88/B6
Garden, Mich. (49835) 250/C3
Garden (isl.), Mich. 250/D3
Garden (pen.), Mich. 250/C3
Garden (co.), Nebr. 264/B3
Garden (isl.), W. Aust. 92/A1
Gardena, Calif. (*90247) 204/C11
Gardena, Idaho (83621) 220/B5
Gardena, N. Dak. (58739) 283/J2
Garden Acres‡, Calif. (†95201) 204/D6
Garden City, Ala. (35070) 194/E2
Garden City‡, Colo. (†80631) 208/K2
Garden City, Cuba 158/G2
Garden City, Ga. (31408) 216/K6
Garden City, Idaho (83704) 220/B6
Garden City, Iowa (50102) 229/G4
Garden City, Kans., 188/F3
Garden City, Kans. (67846) 232/B4
Garden City, La. (70540) 238/H7
Garden City‡, Mich. (48135) 250/B7
Garden City, Minn. (56034) 254/D6
Garden City, Mo. (64747) 261/D5
Garden City, N.Y. (11530) 276/R7
Garden City, S. Dak. (57236) 298/O4
Garden City, Texas (79739) 302/C6
Garden City, Utah (84028) 304/C2
Garden City Beach, S.C. (29576) 296/K4
Garden City Park‡, N.Y. (†11530) 276/R7
Gardendale, Ala. (35071) 194/E3
Garden Grove, Calif. (*92640) 204/D11
Garden Grove, Iowa (50103) 229/F7
Garden Head, Sask. 181/C6
Garden Home, Oreg. (97223) 291/A2
Garden Island (bay), La. 238/M8
Garden Plain, Kans. (67050) 232/E4
Garden Prairie, Ill. (61038) 222/E1
Garden Reach, India 68/F2
Gardenstown, Scot. 15/M4
Gardenton, Man. 179/F5
Garden Valley, Idaho (83622) 220/C5
Garden View, Pa. (†17701) 294/H3
Gardez, Afgh. 59/J3
Gardez, Afgh. 68/B2
Gardi, Ga. (†31545) 216/J7
Gardiner, Maine (04345) 242/D7
Gardiner, Mont. (59030) 262/F5
Gardiner, Oreg. (97441) 291/C4
Gardiner, Wash. (98334) 310/B2
Gardiners (bay), N.Y. 276/R8
Gardiners (isl.), N.Y. 276/R8
Gardner (canal), Br. Col. 184/C3
Gardner, Colo. (81040) 208/J7
Gardner (lake), Conn. 210/G2
Gardner, Fla. (†33890) 212/E4
Gardner (isl.), Gilb. and Ell., 87/J6
Gardner, Ill. (60424) 222/E2
Gardner, Kans. (66030) 232/H3
Gardner (lake), Maine 242/J6
Gardner, Mass. (01440) 249/G2
Gardner, N. Dak. (58036) 283/R5
Gardner, Tenn. (†38237) 237/D8
Gardner (mt.), Wash. 310/E2
Gardner Creek, N. Br. 170/E3
Gardner Pinnacles (isls.), Hawaii, 87/K3
Gardner Pinnacles (isls.), Hawaii, 188/F6
Gardner Pinnacles (isls.), Hawaii 218/C6
Gardnertown‡, N.Y. (†12550) 276/M7
Gardnerville, Nev. (89410) 266/B4
Gardo, Somalia 115/J2
Gardula, Eth. 111/G6
Gardula, 102/F4
Garelochhead, 10/A1
Garelochhead, Scot. 15/A1
Gareloi (isl.), Alaska 196/K4
Garessio, Italy 34/A2
Garfield, Ark. (72732) 203/C1
Garfield (co.), Colo. 208/C3
Garfield, Colo. (81227) 208/G5
Garfield, Ga. (30425) 216/H5
Garfield, Kans. (67529) 232/C3
Garfield, Ky. (40140) 237/J5
Garfield, Minn. (56332) 254/C5
Garfield (co.), Mont. 262/J3
Garfield, N.J. (07026) 273/B2
Garfield, N. Mex. (87936) 274/B6
Garfield (co.), Nebr. 264/E3
Garfield (co.), Okla. 288/L2
Garfield (co.), Utah 304/C6
Garfield (co.), Wash. 310/H4
Garfield, Wash. (99130) 310/H3
Garfield Heights, Ohio (44125) 284/J9
Gargaliánoi, Greece 45/E7
Garibaldi, Br. Col. 184/F5
Garibaldi, Oreg. (97118) 291/D2
Garibaldi Prov. Park, Br. Col. 184/L2
Garies, S. Africa 118/B6
Garioch (dist.), Scot. 15/L5
Garissa, Kenya 115/G4
Garita, N. Mex. (88421) 274/E3
Garland, Ala. (36448) 194/E7
Garland (co.), Ark. 203/D4
Garland, Ark. (71839) 203/C7
Garland, Kans. (66741) 232/H4
Garland, Maine (04939) 242/E5
Garland, Maine (04939) 242/E5
Garland, Man. 179/B3
Garland, N.C. (28441) 281/N5
Garland, Nebr. (68360) 264/G4
Garland, Pa. (16416) 294/C2
Garland, Tenn. (†38019) 237/B9
Garland, Texas (75040) 302/H1
Garland, Utah (84312) 304/B2
Garland, Wyo. (82424) 319/D1
Garlandville, Miss. (†39345) 256/F6
Garlin, Ky. (42739) 237/L6
Garmisch-Partenkirchen, W. Ger. 22/D5
Garmsar, Iran 59/F2
Garmsar, Iran 66/H3
Garnavillo, Iowa (52049) 229/L3
Garneill, Mont. (59445) 262/G4
Garner, Ark. (72052) 203/G3
Garner, Iowa (50438) 229/F2
Garner (lake), Man. 179/G4
Garner, N.C. (27529) 281/M3
Garnet, Mich. (49734) 250/D2
Garnet, Mont. (†59832) 262/C4
Garnet (bay), N.W.T. 187/L3
Garnett, Kans. (66032) 232/G3
Garnett, S.C. (29922) 296/E6
Garnish, Newf. 166/C4
Garoe, Somalia 115/J2
Garonne (riv.), France, 7/D4
Garonne (riv.), France 28/C5
Garoua, Cameroon 115/B2
Garoua, 102/D4
Garrard (co.), Ky. 237/M5
Garretson, S. Dak. (57030) 298/S6
Garrett, Ill. (61927) 222/E4
Garrett, Ind. (46738) 227/G2
Garrett, Ky. (41630) 237/R6
Garrett (co.), Md. 245/A2
Garrett, Pa. (15542) 294/D6
Garrett‡, Texas (75119) 302/H5
Garrett, Wash. (†99362) 310/G4
Garrett, Wyo. (82058) 319/G3
Garrett Park, Md. (20766) 245/E3
Garretts Bend, W. Va. (†25523) 313/C6
Garrettsville, Ohio (44231) 284/H3
Garrick, Sask. 181/G2
Garrison, Iowa (52229) 229/J4
Garrison, Ky. (41141) 237/P3
Garrison, Md. (21055) 245/L3
Garrison, Minn. (56450) 254/E4
Garrison, Mo. (65657) 261/F9
Garrison, Mont. (59731) 262/D4
Garrison, N. Dak. (58540) 283/H4
Garrison (dam), N. Dak. 283/H5
Garrison, N.Y. (10524) 276/N8
Garrison, Nebr. (68639) 264/G3
Garrison, Texas (75946) 302/K6
Garrison, Utah (84728) 304/A5
Garrisonville, Va. (22463) 307/N4
Garron (pt.), N. Ire. 17/K1
Garrovillas, Spain 33/C3
Garry (lake), 163/G2
Garry (lake), Canada, 4/C14
Garry (lake), N.W.T. 187/H3
Garry (lake), Scot. 15/G5
Garry (riv.), Scot. 15/J6
Garry Lake, N.W.T. 187/H3
Garryowen, Mont. (59031) 262/J5
Garsen, Kenya 115/G4
Garske, N. Dak. (†58382) 283/N3
Garson (lake), Alta. 182/E1
Garson, Ont. 177/D1
Garson, Man. 179/F4
Garstang, Eng. 13/E4
Gartan (lake), Ire. 17/F2
Gartok, China, 54/M6
Gartok, China 77/B5
Garulia, India 68/F1
Garut, Indon. 85/H2
Garvagh, N. Ire. 17/H2
Garvan (isls.), Ire. 17/G1
Garvin, Minn. (56132) 254/C6
Garvin (co.), Okla. 288/M5
Garvin, Okla. (74736) 288/S7
Garwin, Iowa (50632) 229/H4
Garwolin, Poland 47/E3
Garwood, Mo. (†63965) 261/L8
Garwood, N.J. (07027) 273/E2
Garwood, Texas (77442) 302/H8
Gary, Ind., 146/K5
Gary, Ind., 188/J2
Gary, Ind. (*46401) 227/C1
Gary, Minn. (56545) 254/B3
Gary, S. Dak. (57237) 298/S4
Gary, Texas (75643) 302/K5
Gary, W. Va. (24836) 313/C8
Garysburg, N.C. (27831) 281/O2
Garyville, La. (70051) 238/M3
Garza (co.), Texas 302/C4
Garzón, Col. 126/C6
Garzón, Urug. 145/E5
Garzón (lag.), Urug. 145/E5
Gas, Kans. (66742) 232/G4
Gas (hills), Wyo. 319/E3
Gasan-Kuli, U.S.S.R. 48/F6
Gasburg, Va. (23857) 307/N7
Gas City, Ind. (46933) 227/F4
Gasconade (co.), Mo. 261/J6
Gasconade, Mo. (65036) 261/J5
Gasconade (riv.), Mo. 261/H7
Gascons, Que. 172/D2
Gascoyne (riv.), Australia, 87/B8
Gascoyne (riv.), Aust. 88/A4
Gascoyne, N. Dak. (58629) 283/D7
Gascoyne (riv.), W. Aust. 92/B4
Gascoyne Junction, W. Aust. 92/A4
Gashaka, Nigeria 106/G7
Gas Hills, Wyo. (82501) 319/E3
Gashun Nor (lake), China 77/E3
Gasker (isl.), Scot. 15/B4
Gaskiers, Newf. 166/D2
Gaspar, Cuba 158/F2
Gaspar Hernández, Dom. Rep. 158/E5
Gasparilla (isl.), Fla. 212/D5
Gaspé, 163/K6
Gaspé, Que. 172/D1
Gaspé (bay), Que. 172/D1
Gaspé (cape), Que. 172/D1
Gaspé (pen.), Que. 172/D2
Gaspé, Que. 174/E3
Gaspé-Est (co.), Que. 172/D1
Gaspé-Est (co.), Que. 174/E3
Gaspé-Ouest (co.), Que. 172/C1
Gaspé-Ouest (co.), Que. 174/D3

368 Gillett

Gillett, Wis. (54124) 317/K6
Gillette, N.J. (07933) 273/E2
Gillette, Wyo. (82716) 319/G1
Gillett Grove, Iowa (51341) 229/C2
Gillham, Ark. (71841) 203/B5
Gilliam, La. (71029) 238/C1
Gilliam, Mo. (65330) 261/F4
Gilliam (co.), Oreg. 291/G2
Gillingham, Dorset, Eng. 13/E6
Gillingham, Kent, Eng. 13/H6
Gillis (range), Nev. 266/C4
Gillisonville, S.C. (†29936) 296/E6
Gillsburg, Miss. (†39657) 256/C8
Gillsville, Ga. (30543) 216/E2
Gilly, Belg. 27/E8
Gilly, Switz. 39/B4
Gilman, Colo. (81634) 208/G3
Gilman, Conn. (06336) 210/G2
Gilman, Ill. (60938) 222/E3
Gilman, Ind. (†46001) 227/F4
Gilman, Iowa (50106) 229/H5
Gilman, Minn. (56333) 254/E5
Gilman, Vt. (05904) 268/D3
Gilman, Wis. (54433) 317/E5
Gilman City, Mo. (64642) 261/D2
Gilmanton∆, N.H. (03237) 268/E5
Gilmanton, N.H. (03237) 268/E5
Gilmanton, Wis. (54743) 317/C7
Gilmanton Iron Works, N.H. (03837) 268/E5
Gilmer (co.), Ga. 216/D1
Gilmer, Texas (75644) 302/J5
Gilmer (co.), W. Va. 313/E5
Gilmer, W. Va. (26350) 313/E5
Gilmore, Ark. (72339) 203/K3
Gilmore, Mo. (†63385) 261/N2
Gilmore City, Iowa (50541) 229/D3
Gilpin (co.), Colo. 208/H3
Gilroy, Calif. (95020) 204/D6
Gilroy, Sask. 181/E5
Gilson, Ill. (61436) 222/C3
Gilsum∆, N.H. (03448) 268/C5
Gilsum, N.H. (03448) 268/C5
Gilt Edge, Tenn. (†38015) 237/B9
Giltner, Nebr. (68841) 264/F4
Gilwood, Alta. 182/B2
Gimco City‡, Ind. (†46001) 227/F4
Gimel, Switz. 39/B4
Gimie (mt.), St. Lucia 161/G6
Gimlet, Ky. (†41164) 237/P4
Gimli, Man. 179/F4
Gimo, Sweden 18/K6
Gingerland, St. Chr.-N.-A. 161/D11
Gingin, Aust. 88/B1
Gingin, W. Aust. 92/A1
Gingoog, Phil. 82/E6
Gingoog (bay), Phil. 82/E6
Gings, Ind. (†46173) 227/G5
Ginir, Eth. 111/H6
Ginnosar, Israel 65/D2
Ginzo de Limia, Spain 33/C1
Gioia del Colle, Italy 34/F4
Gioiosa Ionica, Italy 34/F5
Giornico, Switz. 39/G4
Giovinazzo, Italy 34/F4
Gi-Paraná (riv.), Braz. 132/H10
Gippsland (reg.), Vic. 97/D6
Gipsy (lake), Alta. 182/E1
Gipsy, Mo. (63750) 261/M8
Gipsy, Pa. (15741) 294/E4
Giraltovce, Czech. 41/F2
Girard, Ga. (30426) 216/J4
Girard, Kans. (66743) 232/H4
Girard, La. (71244) 238/G2
Girard, Mich. (†49036) 250/E6
Girard, Ohio (44420) 284/J3
Girard, Pa. (16417) 294/B2
Girard, Texas (79518) 302/D4
Girardot, Col. 126/C5
Girardville, Pa. (17935) 294/K4
Girdle Ness (prom.), Scot. 15/N5
Girdler, Ky. (40943) 237/O7
Girdletree, Md. (21829) 245/S8
Girdwood, Alaska (99587) 196/C1
Girenbad bei Turbenthal, Switz. 39/G2
Giresun, Turkey 59/C1
Giresun (prov.), Turkey 63/H2
Giresun, Turkey 63/H2
Girga, U.A.R. 59/B4
Girga, U.A.R. 111/F2
Giri (riv.), Dem. Rep. of the Congo. 115/C3
Girilambone, N.S.W. 97/D2
Girishk, Afgh. 59/H3
Girishk, Afgh. 68/A2
Girón, Ec. 128/C4
Gironde (dept.), France 28/C5
Gironde (riv.), France 28/C5
Giroux, Man. 179/F5
Girouxville, Alta. 182/B2
Girvan, 10/D3
Girvan, Scot. 15/G9
Girvin, Sask. 181/F4
Girvin, Texas (79740) 302/B6
Gisborne (mt.), Aust. 88/L6
Gisborne, N. Z., 87/H9
Gisborne, N.Z. 101/G3
Giscome, Br. Col. 184/F3
Gisenyi, Rwanda 115/E4
Gisors, France 28/D3
Giswil, Switz. 39/F3
Gitega, Burundi 115/F4
Giubiasco, Switz. 39/H4
Giulianova, Italy 34/E3
Giurgiu, Rum. 45/G3
Giv'atayim, Israel 65/B3
Giv'at Brenner, Israel 65/B4
Giv'at Hayyim, Israel 65/B3
Give, Den. 21/C6
Given, W. Va. (25245) 313/C5
Givet, France 28/F2
Givhans, S.C. (†29472) 296/G5
Givors, France 28/F5
Giza, U.A.R. 59/B4
Giza, U.A.R. 111/J3
Gizhiga, U.S.S.R. 48/R3
Gizhiga, U.S.S.R., 54/V3
Giżycko, Poland 47/E1
Gjerlev, Den. 21/D4
Gjerrild (prom.), Den. 21/D5
Gjirokastër, Alb. 45/D5
Gjoa Haven, 163/G2
Gjoa Haven, N.W.T. 187/J3
Gjøvik, Norway 18/G6
Glace Bay, 163/L6
Glace Bay, N.S. 169/J2
Glacier (bay), Alaska 196/M1
Glacier, Br. Col. 184/J4
Glacier (co.), Mont. 262/C2
Glacier, Wash. (98244) 310/D2
Glacier (peak), Wash. 310/D2
Glacier Bay Nat'l Mon., Alaska 196/M1
Glacier Creek, Yukon 187/D3
Glacier Nat'l Park, 163/D5
Glacier Nat'l Park, Br. Col. 184/J4
Glacier Nat'l Park, Mont., 188/D1
Glacier Nat'l Park, Mont. 262/C2
Gladbrook, Iowa (50635) 229/H4
Glade, Kans. (67639) 232/C2
Glade, La. (†71374) 238/G4
Gladehill, Va. (24092) 307/J7
Glade Park, Colo. (81523) 208/B5
Glades (co.), Fla. 212/E5
Glade Spring, Va. (24340) 307/E7
Glade Valley, N.C. (28627) 281/G2
Gladeville, Tenn. (37071) 237/J8
Gladewater, Texas (75647) 302/K5
Gladmar, Sask. 181/G6
Gladstone, Aust. 88/J4
Gladstone, Aust. 88/F6
Gladstone, Ill. (61437) 222/B3
Gladstone, Man. 179/D4
Gladstone, Mich. (49837) 250/C3
Gladstone, Mo. (64118) 261/P5
Gladstone, N. Dak. (58630) 283/F6
Gladstone, N. Mex. (88422) 274/F2
Gladstone, Nebr. (68363) 264/G4
Gladstone, S. Aust. 94/F5
Gladstone, Queens. 95/D4
Gladstone, Oreg. (97027) 291/B2
Gladstone, Va. (24553) 307/L5
Glad Valley, S. Dak. (57629) 298/F3
Gladwin (co.), Mich. 250/E4
Gladwin, Mich. (48624) 250/E5
Glady, W. Va. (26268) 313/G5
Gladys, Va. (24554) 307/K6
Glamis, Calif. (92248) 204/K11
Glamis, Sask. 181/D4
Glamis, Scot. 15/L6
Glamoč, Yugo. 45/C3
Glamorganshire (co.), Wales 13/D6
Glamsbjerg, Den. 21/D7
Glan, Phil. 82/E8
Glan, Phil. 85/G4
Glancy, Miss. (†39083) 256/C7
Gland, Switz. 39/B4
Glandore, Ire. 17/C8
Glandore (harb.), Ire. 17/C9
Glandorf, Ohio (45848) 284/B3
Glâne (riv.), Switz. 39/C3
Glarnisch (mt.), Switz. 39/H2
Glarus (canton), Switz. 39/H3
Glarus, Switz. 39/H2
Glarus Alps (mts.), Switz. 39/H3
Glasco, Kans. (67445) 232/E2
Glasco, N.Y. (12432) 276/M6
Glascock (co.), Ga. 216/G4
Glasford, Ill. (61533) 222/D3
Glasgo, Conn. (06337) 210/H2
Glasgow, Del. (†19711) 245/R2
Glasgow, Ill. (†62610) 222/C4
Glasgow, Ky. (42141) 237/J7
Glasgow, 10/B1
Glasgow, Mo. (65254) 261/G4
Glasgow, Mont. (59230) 262/K2
Glasgow, Pa. (16644) 294/E4
Glasgow‡, Pa. (16644) 294/B4
Glasgow, Scot., 7/D3
Glasgow, Scot. 15/D2
Glasgow, Va. (24555) 307/K5
Glasgow, W. Va. (25086) 313/D6
Glasier (lake), N. Br. 170/A1
Glaslyn, Sask. 181/C2
Glas Maol (mt.), Scot. 15/K6
Glasnevin, Sask. 181/F6
Glass (lake), Scot. 15/G4
Glass (riv.), Scot. 15/G5
Glass (mts.), Texas 302/A7
Glassboro, N.J. (08028) 273/C4
Glasscock (co.), Texas 302/C6
Glassport, Pa. (15045) 294/C7
Glasston, N. Dak. (58236) 283/R2
Glassville, N. Br. 170/C2
Glastenbury (mt.), Vt. 268/A6
Glastonbury, 10/E5
Glastonbury∆, Conn. (06033) 210/E2
Glastonbury, Eng. 13/E6
Glatt (riv.), Switz. 39/G2
Glattfelden, Switz. 39/F1
Glauchau, E. Ger. 22/E3
Glazier, Texas (79037) 302/D2
Glazov, U.S.S.R. 52/H3
Gleason, Tenn. (38229) 237/D8
Gleason, Wis. (54435) 317/G5
Gleasondale, Mass. (01749) 249/J3
Gledhow, Sask. 181/E4
Gleeson, Ariz. (†85617) 198/F7
Gleichen, Alta. 182/D4
Gleisdorf, Austria 41/C3
Glemsford, Eng. 13/H5
Glen (lake), Ire. 17/F1
Glen (lake), Mich. 250/C4
Glen, Minn. (†56431) 254/E4
Glen, Miss. (38846) 256/H1
Glen, Mont. (†59725) 262/D5
Glen, N.H. (03838) 268/E3
Glen (canyon), Utah 304/D6
Glen, W. Va. (25088) 313/D6
Glenada, Oreg. (†97439) 291/C4
Glenaire, Mo. (†64068) 261/R5
Glen Alice, Tenn. (†37854) 237/M9
Glen Allan, Miss. (38744) 256/B4
Glen Allen, Ala. (35559) 194/C3
Glenallen, Mo. (63751) 261/M8
Glen Allen, Va. (23060) 307/N5
Glen Almond, Que. 172/B4
Glen Alpine, N.C. (28628) 281/F3
Glen Alps‡, Alaska (†99501) 196/B1
Glen Arbor, Mich. (49636) 250/C4
Glenarden, Md. (20801) 245/G4
Glenarm, N. Ire. 17/J2
Glenavon, Sask. 181/F5
Glen Avon Heights, Calif. (†92501) 204/E10
Glenavy, N. Ire. 17/J2
Glenavy, N.Z. 101/C6
Glen Bain, Sask. 181/E6
Glenbarr, Scot. 15/E8
Glenbeulah, Wis. (53023) 317/L8
Glenboro, Man. 179/C5
Glenbrook, Nev. (89413) 266/B3
Glenburn∆, Maine (†04401) 242/F6
Glenburn, N. Dak. (58740) 283/H2
Glen Burnie, Md. (21061) 245/M4
Glenbush, Sask. 181/D2
Glencairn, Man. 179/C4
Glen Campbell, Pa. (15742) 294/E4
Glen Canyon (dam), Ariz. 198/D2
Glen Canyon, Utah (84741) 304/C6
Glen Canyon Nat'l Rec. Area, Utah 304/D6
Glen Canyon Nat'l Recr. Area, Ariz. 198/D1
Glen Carbon, Ill. (62034) 222/B6
Glencliff, N.H. (03238) 268/D4
Glencoe, Ala. (35905) 194/G3
Glencoe, Ont. 177/C5
Glencoe, Ill. (60022) 222/F1
Glencoe, Ky. (41046) 237/M3
Glencoe, La. (†70538) 238/G7
Glencoe, Minn. (55336) 254/D6
Glencoe, Mo. (63038) 261/N3
Glencoe, N. Br. 170/D1
Glencoe, N. Mex. (88324) 274/D5
Glencoe, Ohio (43928) 284/J6
Glencoe, Okla. (74032) 288/M2
Glencoe, Pa. (15543) 294/E6
Glencoe, S. Africa 118/E5
Glencolumbkille, Ire. 17/D2
Glen Cove, Maine (04846) 242/E7
Glen Cove, N.Y. (11542) 276/R6
Glencross, S. Dak. (57630) 298/H3
Glencullen, Ire. 17/J5
Glendale, Ariz. (85301) 198/C5
Glendale, Calif., 188/C4
Glendale, Calif. (*91201) 204/C10
Glendale‡, Colo. (†80201) 208/K3
Glendale, Fla. (†32433) 212/C5
Glendale, Ind. (†47558) 227/C7
Glendale, Kans. (†67425) 232/E3
Glendale, Ky. (42740) 237/K5
Glendale, Mass. (01229) 249/A3
Glendale, Mo. (63122) 261/P3
Glendale, N.H. (†03246) 268/E4
Glendale, N.S. 169/G3
Glendale, Nev. (†89025) 266/G6
Glendale, Ohio (45246) 284/C9
Glendale, Oreg. (97442) 291/D5
Glendale (lake), Pa. 294/F4
Glendale, R.I. (02826) 249/H5
Glendale, S.C. (29346) 296/D2
Glendale, Utah (84729) 304/B6
Glen Dale, W. Va. (26038) 313/E3
Glendale, Wis. (†53201) 317/M1
Glendale Heights‡, Ill. (†60137) 222/E2
Glen Daniel, W. Va. (25844) 313/D7
Glen Dean, Ky. (40141) 237/G5
Glendevey, Colo. (80485) 208/H1
Glendive, Mont. (59330) 262/M3
Glendo, Wyo. (82213) 319/G3
Glendo (res.), Wyo. 319/H3
Glendon, Alta. 182/E2
Glendon, N.C. (27251) 281/L4
Glendon‡, Pa. (†18042) 294/M4
Glendora, Calif. (91740) 204/D10
Glendora, Miss. (38928) 256/D3
Glendora, N.J. (08029) 273/B4
Glendower, Sask. 181/G2
Glen Easton, W. Va. (26039) 313/E3
Glen Echo, Md. (20768) 245/E4
Glen Echo Heights, Md. (†20013) 245/E4
Glen Echo Park‡, Mo. (†63101) 261/P3
Glen Eden, N.Z. 101/B1
Gleneden Beach, Oreg. (97388) 291/C3
Glen Elder, Kans. (67446) 232/D2
Glen Elder (res.), Kans. 232/D2
Glenelg, 10/D2
Glenelg, Md. (21737) 245/L3
Glenelg, S. Aust. 94/A8
Glenelg, Scot. 15/E5
Glenelg (dist.), Scot. 15/E5
Glenelg (riv.), Vic. 97/A5
Glenella, Man. 179/C4
Glen Ellen‡, Calif. (95442) 204/C5
Glenellen, Sask. 181/C4
Glen Ellyn, Ill. (60137) 222/F2
Glenevis, Alta. 182/C3
Glen Ewen, Sask. 181/K6
Glen Ferris, W. Va. (25090) 313/D6
Glenfield, N. Dak. (58443) 283/N5
Glenfield, N.Y. (13343) 276/K3
Glenfield, N.Z. 101/B1
Glenfield, Pa. (†15143) 294/B4
Glen Flora, Texas (77443) 302/H8
Glen Flora, Wis. (54526) 317/E4
Glenford, Ohio (43739) 284/F6
Glen Gardner, N.J. (08826) 273/D2
Glengarriff, Ire. 17/C8
Glengarry (co.), Ont. 177/K2
Glengarry, Mont. (†59457) 262/G3
Glengary, W. Va. (25421) 313/K4
Glenham‡, N.Y. (12527) 276/N7
Glenham, S. Dak. (57631) 298/J2
Glen Haven, Colo. (80532) 208/H2
Glen Haven, Mich. (†49621) 250/C4
Glen Haven, Wis. (53810) 317/E10
Glenhayes, W. Va. (25519) 313/A6
Glen Head, N.Y. (11545) 276/R7
Glen Hedrick (Beaver), W. Va. (†25813) 313/D7
Glenhope, Pa. (16645) 294/F4
Glen Innes, Aust. 88/J5
Glen Innes, N.S.W. 97/F1
Glenisla, Scot. 15/K6
Glen Jean, W. Va. (25846) 313/D7
Glen Kerr, Sask. 181/D5
Glenlea, Man. 179/E5
Glen Livet, N. Br. 170/D1
Glenluce, Scot. 15/G10
Glen Lyn, Va. (24093) 307/G6
Glen Lyon, Pa. (18617) 294/K3
Glen Mary, Sask. 181/F2
Glenmary, Tenn. (37740) 237/M8
Glen McPherson, Sask. 181/D6
Glenmont, Ohio (44628) 284/F4
Glenmora, La. (71433) 238/E5
Glenmorgan, Aust. 88/H5
Glenmorgan, Queens. 95/D5
Glenn (co.), Calif. 204/C4
Glenn, Ga. (30219) 216/B4
Glenn, Mich. (49416) 250/C6
Glennallen, Alaska (99588) 196/D1
Glenn Heights‡, Texas (†75115) 302/G2
Glenn Highway, Alaska 196/J2
Glennie, Mich. (48737) 250/F4
Glenns Ferry, Idaho (83623) 220/C7
Glenn Springs, S.C. (29347) 296/D2
Glennville, Calif. (93226) 204/G8
Glennville, Ga. (30427) 216/J7
Glenolden, Pa. (19036) 294/M7
Glenoma, Wash. (98336) 310/C4
Glenora, Br. Col. 184/K2
Glenora, Man. 179/C5
Glenorchy, Tas. 99/D4
Glenormiston, Queens. 95/A4
Glen Park, N.Y. (†13601) 276/J3
Glenpool, Okla. (74033) 288/P3
Glen Raven, N.C. (27215) 281/L2
Glenreagh, N.S.W. 97/G2
Glen Riddle, Pa. (19037) 294/L7
Glen Ridge‡, Fla. (†33401) 212/F5
Glen Ridge, N.J. (07028) 273/B2
Glenrio, N. Mex. (88434) 274/F3
Glen Robertson, Ont. 177/K2
Glen Rock, N.J. (07452) 273/B1
Glen Rock, Pa. (17327) 294/J6
Glenrock, Wyo. (82637) 319/G3
Glen Rogers, W. Va. (25848) 313/D7
Glen Rose, Texas (76043) 302/G5
Glenrothes, Scot. 15/K7
Glen Roy, Ohio (†45692) 284/E7
Glen Saint Mary, Fla. (32040) 212/D1
Glens Falls, N.Y. (12801) 276/N4
Glens Fork, Ky. (42741) 237/L6
Glenshaw, Pa. (15116) 294/C6
Glenside, N.Z. 101/B2
Glenside, Pa. (19038) 294/M5
Glenside, Sask. 181/E4
Glensted, Mo. (†65084) 261/G5
Glentana, Mont. (59240) 262/K2
Glenties, 10/B3
Glenties, Ire. 17/E2
Glentworth, Sask. 181/E6
Glen Ullin, N. Dak. (58631) 283/G6
Glenview, Ill. (60025) 222/B1
Glenview Nav. Air. Sta., Ill. 222/A1
Glenvil, Nebr. (68941) 264/F4
Glenville, Conn. (†06830) 210/A4
Glenville, Ire. 17/E7
Glenville, Minn. (56036) 254/E7
Glenville, N.C. (28736) 281/C4
Glenville, W. Va. (26351) 313/E5
Glen Walter, Ont. 177/K2
Glen White, W. Va. (25849) 313/D7
Glen Williams, Ont. 177/D4
Glenwillow, Ohio (†44139) 284/J10
Glen Wilton, Va. (24438) 307/J5
Glenwood, Ala. (36034) 194/F7
Glenwood, Alta. 182/D5
Glenwood, Ark. (71943) 203/C5
Glenwood, Fla. (32722) 212/E2
Glenwood, Ga. (30428) 216/G6
Glenwood, Ill. (60425) 222/B3
Glenwood, Ind. (47343) 227/G5
Glenwood, Iowa (51534) 229/B6
Glenwood, Mich. (†49047) 250/C6
Glenwood, Minn. (56334) 254/C5
Glenwood, Mo. (63541) 261/G1
Glenwood, N.C. (28737) 281/E3
Glenwood, N.J. (07418) 273/D1
Glenwood, N. Mex. (88039) 274/A5
Glenwood, Newf. 166/D4
Glenwood, Oreg. (97120) 291/D2
Glenwood, Utah (84730) 304/C5
Glenwood, Va. (†24541) 307/K7
Glenwood, W. Va. (25520) 313/B5
Glenwood, Wash. (98619) 310/D4
Glenwood City, Wis. (54013) 317/B5
Glenwood Springs, Colo. (81601) 208/E4
Gletsch, Switz. 39/F3
Glezen, Ind. (†47567) 227/C8
Glidden, Iowa (51443) 229/D4
Glidden, Sask. 181/B4
Glidden, Wis. (54527) 317/E3
Glide, Oreg. (97443) 291/D4
Glin, Ire. 17/C6
Glittertind (mt.), Norway 18/F6
Gliwice, Poland 47/A4
Globe, Ariz., 188/D4
Globe, Ariz. (85501) 198/E5
Gloggnitz, Austria 41/D3
Głogów, Poland 47/B3
Glomawr, Ky. (†41701) 237/P6
Glomfjord, Norway 18/J3
Glomma (lake), Norway 18/E4
Glomma (riv.), Norway 18/G6
Glória, Braz. 132/G5
Gloria (bay), Cuba 158/G2
Gloria Glens Park‡, Ohio (†44215) 284/G3
Glorieta, N. Mex. (87535) 274/D3
Glorioso (isls.), Réunion 118/H2
Glory, Minn. (†56431) 254/E4
Glory of Russia (cape), Alaska 196/D2
Glossop, 10/G4
Glossop, Eng. 13/F4
Gloster, La. (71030) 238/C2
Gloster, Miss. (39638) 256/B8
Glostrup, Den. 21/F6
Gloucester, 10/E5
Gloucester, Eng. 13/E6
Gloucester, Mass. (01930) 249/M2
Gloucester (co.), N. Br. 170/E1
Gloucester (co.), N.C. (28528) 281/S5
Gloucester (co.), N.J. 273/C4
Gloucester, N.S.W. 97/F2
Gloucester (co.), Va. 307/P6
Gloucester, Va. (23061) 307/P6
Gloucester City, N.J. (08030) 273/B3
Gloucester Point, Va. (23062) 307/R6
Gloucestershire (co.), Eng. 13/E6
Glouster, Ohio (45732) 284/F6
Glover, Mo. (63646) 261/L8
Glover, N. Dak. (†58474) 283/O7
Glover (isl.), Newf. 166/C4
Glover, Okla. (74728) 288/S6
Glover∆, Vt. (05839) 268/C2
Glover, Vt. (05839) 268/C2
Glovergap, W. Va. (†26585) 313/F3
Glovers (reef), Br. Hond. 154/D2
Gloversville, N.Y. (12078) 276/M4
Glovertown, Newf. 166/D2
Gloverville, S.C. (29828) 296/D4
Głowno, Poland 47/D3
Głubczyce, Poland 47/D3
Glubokoye, U.S.S.R. 52/C3
Głuchołazy, Poland 47/C3
Glücksburg, W. Ger. 22/C1
Gluckstadt, Miss. (†39110) 256/D5
Glückstadt, W. Ger. 22/C2
Glukhov, U.S.S.R. 52/D4
Glumso, Den. 21/E7
Glyde (riv.), Ire. 17/H4
Glynco Nav. Air Sta., Ga. 216/J8
Glyndon, Minn. (56547) 254/B4
Glyndon-Reisterstown, Md. (21071) 245/L3
Glyngore, Den. 21/C4
Glynn (co.), Ga. 216/J8
Glynn, La. (70736) 238/H5
Glynn, N. Ire. 17/K2
Gmünd, Carinthia, Austria 41/B3
Gmünd, Lower Austria, Austria 41/C2
Gmunden, Austria 41/B3
Gnadenhutten, Ohio (44629) 284/G5
Gnaw Bone, Ind. (†47448) 227/E6
Gnesta, Sweden 18/G2
Gniezno, Poland 47/C2
Gnjilane, Yugo. 45/E4
Gnowangerup, W. Aust. 92/B6
Goa, Daman and Diu (terr.), India 68/C4
Goa (dist.), India 68/C5
Goalpara, India 68/G3
Goascorán, Hond. 154/D4
Goat Fell (mt.), Scot. 15/F8
Goat Rock (dam), Ala. 194/H5
Goat Rock (lake), Ala. 194/H5
Goat Rock (dam), Ga. 216/B5
Goat Rock (lake), Ga. 216/B5
Goat Rocks (mt.), Wash. 310/D4
Goba, Moz. 118/E5
Goba, Eth. 111/H6
Gobabis, 102/D7
Gobabis, S.W. Afr. 118/B4
Gobernador Crespo, Arg. 143/F5
Gobernador Gregores, Arg. 143/C6
Gobernador Mansilla, Arg. 143/G6
Gobi (des.), Mong., 54/O5
Gobi (des.), China 77/G3
Gobi (des.), Mong. 77/G3
Gobi-Altay (prov.), Mong. 77/D2
Goble, Oreg. (97048) 291/E1
Gobler, Mo. (63849) 261/N10
Gobles, Mich. (49055) 250/D6
Gobo, Japan 81/G7
Gobwen, Somalia 115/H4
Goch, W. Ger. 22/B3
Go Cong, S. Vietnam 72/E5
Godahl, Minn. (†56081) 254/D6
Godalming, 10/F5
Godalming, Eng. 13/G6
Godavari (riv.), India, 54/L8
Godavari (riv.), India 68/D5
Godbout, Que. 172/B1
Godbout, Que. 174/D3
Goddard, Kans. (67052) 232/E4
Godech, Bulg. 45/F4
Goderich, Ont. 177/C4
Godfrey, Ont. 177/H3
Godfrey, Ga. (30650) 216/F4
Godfrey, Ill. (62035) 222/A6
Godhavn, Greenl., 4/C12
Godhavn, Greenl., 146/N3
Godhra, India 68/C4
Godley‡, Ill. (†60407) 222/E2
Godley‡, Texas (76044) 302/G5
Gödöllő, Hung. 41/E3
Godoy Cruz, Arg. 143/C3
Gods (lake), 163/G5
Gods (riv.), 163/G4
Gods (lake), Man. 179/K3
Gods (riv.), Man. 179/K3
Gods Lake, Man. 179/K3
Gods Mercy (bay), N.W.T. 187/K3
Gods River, Man. 179/K3
Godthaab (cap.), Greenl., 3/G2
Godthaab (cap.), Greenl., 4/C12
Godthaab (cap.), Greenl., 146/N3
Godwin, N.C. (28344) 281/M4
Godwin Austen (K2) (mt.), India 68/D1
Godwinsville, Ga. (†31023) 216/F6
Goehner, Nebr. (68364) 264/G4
Goéland (lake), Que. 174/B3
Goélands (lake), Que. 174/E1
Goeree (isl.), Neth. 27/D5
Goes, Neth. 27/D6
Goessel, Kans. (67053) 232/E3
Goetzville, Mich. (49736) 250/E2
Goff, Kans. (66428) 232/G2
Goff (creek), Okla. 288/C1
Goffstown∆, N.H. (03045) 268/D5
Goffstown, N.H. (03045) 268/D5
Gogama, Ont. 175/D3
Gogama, Ont. 177/J5
Gogebic (co.), Mich. 250/F2
Gogebic (lake), Mich. 250/F2
Göggingen, W. Ger. 22/D4
Gogrial, Sudan 111/E6
Goiana, Braz. 132/H4
Goiandira, Braz. 132/E7
Goiânia, Braz., 120/E4
Goiânia, Braz. 132/D7
Goiás, Braz., 120/E4
Goiás (state), Braz. 132/D6
Goiás, Braz. 132/D6
Goin, Tenn. (†37825) 237/O8
Goirle, Neth. 27/G5
Góis, Port. 33/B2
Gojjam (prov.), Eth. 111/G5
Gokirmak (riv.), Turkey 63/E2
Göksu (riv.), Turkey 63/E4
Göksun, Turkey 63/G3
Gokteik, Burma 72/C2
Gol, Norway 18/F6
Gola (isl.), Ire. 17/E1
Gölbaşi, Turkey 63/G4
Golburn, Sask. 181/H3
Gol'chikha, U.S.S.R. 48/J2
Gol'chikha, U.S.S.R., 54/M2
Golconda, Ill. (62938) 222/E6
Golconda, Nev. (89414) 266/D2
Golconda (ruins), India 68/D5
Gölcük, Turkey 63/C2
Golčův Jeníkov, Czech. 41/C2
Gold (riv.), N.S. 169/D4
Gołdap, Poland 47/F1
Goldau, Switz. 39/G2
Gold Bar, Wash. (98251) 310/D3
Gold Beach, Oreg. (97444) 291/C5
Goldbond, Va. (24094) 307/G6
Goldboro, N.S. 169/G3
Gold Bridge, Br. Col. 184/F5
Gold Coast, Aust. 88/J5
Gold Coast (reg.), Ghana 106/D8
Gold Coast, Queens. 95/E6
Goldcreek, Mont. (59733) 262/D4
Golden, Br. Col. 184/J4
Golden, Colo. (80401) 208/J3
Golden (lake), Ont. 177/G2
Golden, Idaho (†83530) 220/C4
Golden, Ill. (62339) 222/B3
Golden, Ire. 17/F7
Golden, Miss. (38847) 256/H2
Golden, Mo. (65658) 261/E9
Golden, N. Mex. (†87047) 274/C3
Golden (bay), N.Z. 101/D4
Golden, Okla. (74737) 288/S6
Golden (lake), Wis. 317/H1
Golden Beach, Fla. (33160) 212/C4
Golden City, Mo. (64748) 261/D8
Goldendale, Wash. (98620) 310/E5
Golden Gate (chan.), Calif., 188/B3
Golden Gate (chan.), Calif. 204/H2
Golden Gate, Fla. (33940) 212/E5
Goldengate, Ill. (62843) 222/E5
Golden Gate (range), Nev. 266/F5
Golden Grove, Jam. 158/K6
Golden Hill, Md. (†21622) 245/O7
Golden Lake, Ont. 177/G2
Golden Meadow, La. (70357) 238/K8
Golden Prairie, Sask. 181/B5
Golden Rock, St. Chr.-N.-A. 161/C10
Golden's Bridge, N.Y. (10526) 276/N8
Golden Spike, Alta. 182/D3
Golden Spike Nat'l Hist. Site, Utah 304/B2
Golden Stream, Man. 179/D4
Golden Vale (plain), Ire. 17/E7
Golden Valley, Ont. 177/E2
Golden Valley, Minn. (55427) 254/G5
Golden Valley (co.), Mont. 262/G4
Golden Valley (co.), N. Dak. 283/C5
Goldenvalley, N. Dak. (58541) 283/F5
Goldenville, N.S. 169/F3
Goldfield, Iowa (50542) 229/F3
Goldfield, Nev., 188/C3
Goldfield, Nev. (89013) 266/D5
Gold Hill, Ala. (†36879) 194/G5
Gold Hill, N.C. (28071) 281/J3
Gold Hill, Nev. (†89440) 266/B3
Gold Hill, Oreg. (97525) 291/D5
Goldman, Ark. (†72160) 203/G5
Goldonna, La. (71031) 238/D2
Gold Point, N.C. (†27871) 281/P3
Gold Point, Nev. (†89013) 266/D5
Gold River, Br. Col. 184/D5
Gold River, N.S. 169/D4
Goldsberry, Mo. (63542) 261/G3
Goldsboro, Md. (21636) 245/P4
Goldsboro, N.C., 188/L3
Goldsboro, N.C. (27530) 281/O4
Goldsboro (Etters), Pa. (17319) 294/J5
Goldsby, Okla. (†73093) 288/M4
Goldsmith, Ind. (46045) 227/E4
Goldsmith, Texas (79741) 302/B5
Goldston, N.C. (27252) 281/L3
Goldstone (mt.), Idaho 220/E4
Goldstream, Br. Col. 184/J3
Goldsworthy (mt.), W. Aust. 92/C3
Goldthwaite, Texas (76844) 302/F6
Goldvein, Va. (22720) 307/N4
Göle, Turkey 63/K2
Goleniów, Poland 47/B2
Goleta, Calif. (93017) 204/F9
Golf, Fla. (†33444) 212/F5
Golf, Ill. (60029) 222/A1
Golfito, C. Rica 154/F6
Golf Manor, Ohio (†45201) 284/C9
Golfview‡, Fla. (†33401) 212/F5
Gol Gol, N.S.W. 97/B4
Gölhisar, Turkey 63/C4
Goliad (co.), Texas 302/G9
Goliad, Texas (77963) 302/G9
Gölköy, Turkey 63/G2
Gollier, Sask. 181/E6
Golling an der Salzach, Austria 41/B3
Gölmarmara, Turkey 63/C3
Golmo, China 77/D4
Golo (riv.), France 28/B6
Golo (isl.), Phil. 82/C4
Golovin, Alaska (99762) 196/F2
Gölpazari, Turkey 63/D2
Golshan (Tabas), Iran 66/K4
Golspie, Scot. 15/H4
Goltry, Okla. (73739) 288/K1
Golts, Md. (21637) 245/P3
Golungo Alto, Angola 115/B5
Golva, N. Dak. (58632) 283/C6
Goma, Dem. Rep. of the Congo. 115/E4
Gombari, Dem. Rep. of the Congo. 115/E3
Gombe, Nigeria 106/G6
Gombe (riv.), Tanz. 115/F4
Gomel', U.S.S.R. 48/D4
Gomel', U.S.S.R. 52/D4
Gomel', U.S.S.R., 7/H3
Gomer, Ohio (45809) 284/B4
Gomera (isl.), Spain 33/B5
Gomera (isl.), Spain 106/A3
Gomez, Fla. (†33455) 212/F4
Gómez Farías, Mex. 150/F2
Gómez Palacio, Mex. 150/G4
Goms (valley), Switz. 39/F4
Gona, Papua 85/C7
Gonaïves, Haiti 156/D3
Gonaïves, Haiti 158/B5
Gonâve (isl.), Haiti 156/D3
Gonâve (gulf), Haiti 158/B5
Gonâve (isl.), Haiti 158/B6
Gönc, Hung. 41/F2
Gonda, India 68/E3
Gondal, India 68/C4
Gondar, Eth. 59/C7

Grand River 369

Gondar, Eth. 111/G5
Gondar, 102/F3
Gondo, Switz. 39/F4
Gondomar, Port. 33/B2
Gönen, Turkey 63/B2
Gongola (riv.), Nigeria 106/G6
Gongolgon, N.S.W. 97/D2
Góngora (mt.), C. Rica 154/E5
Goñi, Urug. 145/C4
Gonvick, Minn. (56644) 254/C3
Gonzaga, Phil. 82/D1
Gonzales, Calif. (93926) 204/D7
Gonzales, La. (70737) 238/L2
Gonzales (co.), Texas 302/G8
Gonzales, Texas (78629) 302/G8
Gonzalez, Fla. (32560) 212/B6
González, Mex. 150/K5
González (riv.), Par. 144/C4
Goobies, Newf. 166/D2
Goochland (co.), Va. 307/N5
Goochland, Va. (23063) 307/N5
Goodbee, La. (†70433) 238/K6
Goode (mt.), Alaska 196/C1
Goode, Va. (24556) 307/K6
Goodell, Iowa (50439) 229/F3
Goodenough (cape), Ant. 5/C7
Gooderham, Ont. 177/F3
Goodeve, Sask. 181/H4
Goodfare, Alta. 182/A2
Goodfellow A.F.B., Texas 302/D6
Goodfellow Terrace‡, Mo. (†63101) 261/P3
Goodfield, Ill. (61742) 222/D3
Goodfish Lake, Alta. 182/D2
Good Harbor (bay), Mich. 250/D3
Good Hart, Mich. (49737) 250/D3
Good Hope, Ala. (†36024) 194/E2
Goodhope (bay), Alaska 196/F1
Good Hope, Ga. (30641) 216/E3
Good Hope, Ill. (61438) 222/C3
Good Hope, La. (70079) 238/N3
Good Hope, Miss. (†39094) 256/E5
Good Hope (cape), Indon. 85/J5
Good Hope, Ohio (43121) 284/D7
Good Hope (cape), 102/D8
Good Hope (cape), S. Afr., 3/K7
Good Hope (cape), S. Africa 118/E7
Goodhue (co.), Minn. 254/F6
Goodhue, Minn. (55027) 254/F6
Gooding (co.), Idaho 220/D6
Gooding, Idaho (83330) 220/D7
Goodland, Fla. (33933) 212/E6
Goodland, Ind. (47948) 227/C3
Goodland, Kans. (67735) 232/A2
Goodland, Minn. (55742) 254/E3
Goodlands, Man. 179/B5
Goodlettsville, Tenn. (37072) 237/H8
Good Luck, Md. (†20715) 245/G4
Goodman, Miss. (39079) 256/E5
Goodman, Mo. (63843) 261/C9
Goodman, Wis. (54125) 317/K4
Goodman Heights‡, Mo. (†64843) 261/D9
Goodna, Aust. 88/K2
Goodnews Bay, Alaska (99589) 196/F3
Goodnight, Texas (†79226) 302/C3
Goodnoe Hills, Wash. (†99356) 310/E5
Goodooga, N.S.W. 97/D1
Good Pine, La. (71337) 238/F3
Goodrich, Colo. (80625) 208/M2
Goodrich, Mich. (48438) 250/F6
Goodrich, N. Dak. (58444) 283/K5
Goodrich, Wis. (†54451) 317/G5
Goodridge, Alta. 182/E2
Goodridge, Minn. (56725) 254/C2
Goodsoil, Sask. 181/L4
Goodson, Mo. (65659) 261/F7
Good Spirit (lake), Sask. 181/J4
Goodspirit Prov. Park, Sask. 181/J4
Goodspring, Tenn. (38460) 237/G10
Goodsprings, Ala. (35560) 194/D3
Goodsprings, Nev. (89019) 266/F7
Good Thunder, Minn. (56037) 254/D6
Goodview, Minn. (55027) 254/G6
Goodwater, Ala. (35072) 194/F4
Goodwater, Okla. (†74740) 288/S7
Goodwater, Sask. 181/H6
Goodway, Ala. (36449) 194/D8
Goodwell, Okla. (73939) 288/C1
Goodwin, Alta. 182/A2
Goodwin, Ark. (72340) 203/J4
Goodwin, S. Dak. (57238) 298/R4
Goodwins Mills, Maine (†04005) 242/B8
Goodwood, Ont. 177/E3
Goodwood, S. Africa 118/F6
Goodyear, Ariz. (85338) 198/C5
Goole, 10/F4
Goole, Eng. 13/G4
Goolgowi, N.S.W. 97/C3
Gooloogong, N.S.W. 97/E3
Goomalling, Aust. 88/B1
Goomalling, W. Aust. 92/B1
Goombalie, N.S.W. 97/C1
Goondiwindi, Aust. 88/H5
Goondiwindi, Queens. 95/D6
Goor, Neth. 27/K4
Goose (lake), 188/B2
Goose (lake), Calif. 204/E1
Goose (creek), Idaho 220/E7
Goose (riv.), N. Dak. 283/P4
Goose (isl.), N.S. 169/F4
Goose (isl.), N.S. 169/G3
Goose (riv.), Newf. 166/B3
Goose (lake), Oreg. 291/G5
Goose (creek), Va. 307/J6
Goose (creek), Va. 307/N3
Goose (creek), Wyo. 319/E1
Goose Bay (Goose Airport), 163/K5
Goose Bay, Newf. 166/B3
Gooseberry (creek), Wyo. 319/D1
Goose Cove, Newf. 166/C3
Goose Creek (mts.), Idaho 220/E7
Goose Creek, S.C. (29445) 296/H6
Gooselake, Iowa (52750) 229/N5
Gooseprairie, Wash. (98929) 310/D4
Gooserock, Ky. (40944) 237/O6
Goose Rocks Beach, Maine (†04046) 242/C9
Gopalpur, India 68/F5
Goppenstein, Switz. 39/E4
Göppingen, W. Ger. 22/C4
Go Quao, S. Vietnam 72/E5
Góra, Poland 47/C3
Gorakhpur, India 68/E3
Gorchs, Arg. 143/G7
Gorda (pt.), Cuba 158/C2
Gorda (bank), Hond. 154/F3
Gorda (cay), Hond. 154/F3
Gorda (pt.), Nic. 154/F5
Gorda (pt.), Pan. 154/H6
Gördes, Turkey 63/C3
Gording, Den. 21/B7
Gordo, Ala. (35466) 194/C4
Gordola, Switz. 39/G4
Gordon, Ala. (36343) 194/H8
Gordon, Alaska (†99747) 196/K1
Gordon (lake), Alta. 182/E1
Gordon (riv.), Br. Col. 184/H3
Gordon (isl.), Chile 138/E11
Gordon (co.), Ga. 216/C2
Gordon, Ga. (31031) 216/F5
Gordon, Kans. (†67010) 232/F4
Gordon, N.S.W. 97/J3
Gordon, Nebr. (69343) 264/B2
Gordon, Ohio (45329) 284/B6
Gordon‡, Pa. (17936) 294/K4
Gordon (riv.), Tas. 99/B4
Gordon, Texas (76543) 302/F5
Gordon, W. Va. (25093) 313/C7
Gordon, Wis. (54838) 317/C3
Gordondale, Alta. 182/A2
Gordon Downs, W. Aust. 92/E2
Gordon's Bay, S. Africa 118/F7
Gordonsburg, Tenn. (†38462) 237/F9
Gordonsville, Ala. (†36040) 194/E6
Gordonsville, Minn. (†56036) 254/E7
Gordonsville, Tenn. (38563) 237/K8
Gordonsville, Va. (22942) 307/M4
Gordonvale, Queens. 95/C3
Gordonville, Mo. (63752) 261/N8
Gore (pt.), Alaska 196/C2
Gore (range), Colo. 208/G3
Gore, N.S. 169/E3
Gore, N.Z. 101/B7
Goré, Chad 111/C6
Gore, Eth. 111/G6
Gore, Ohio (43123) 284/F6
Gore, Okla. (74435) 288/R3
Gore, Va. (22637) 307/M2
Gore (mt.), Vt. 268/D2
Gore Bay, Ont. 177/B2
Gorebridge, 10/C1
Goree, Texas (76363) 302/E4
Goregaon, India 68/B7
Görele, Turkey 63/H2
Gore Springs, Miss. (38929) 256/E3
Goreville, Ill. (62939) 222/E6
Gorey, Chan. Is. 13/F8
Gorey, 10/C4
Gorey, Ire. 17/J6
Gorgas, Ala. (35561) 194/D3
Gorgol (reg.), Mauritania 106/B5
Gorgona (isl.), Col. 126/A6
Gorgona (isl.), Italy 34/B3
Gorham, Ill. (62940) 222/D6
Gorham, Kans. (67640) 232/D3
Gorham▵, Maine (04038) 242/C8
Gorham, Maine (04038) 242/C8
Gorham, N. Dak. (58633) 283/D5
Gorham▵, N.H. (03581) 268/E3
Gorham, N.H. (03581) 268/E3
Gorham, N.Y. (14461) 276/F5
Gori, U.S.S.R. 52/F6
Gorin, Mo. (63543) 261/H2
Gorinchem, Neth. 27/G5
Gorizia (prov.), Italy 34/D2
Gorizia, Italy 34/D2
Gorki, U.S.S.R. 52/D4
Gor'kiy, U.S.S.R. 48/E4
Gor'kiy, U.S.S.R. 52/F3
Gor'kiy, U.S.S.R., 3/M3
Gor'kiy, U.S.S.R., 7/J3
Gorlev, Den. 21/E7
Gorlice, Poland 47/E4
Görlitz, E. Ger. 22/F3
Gorlitz, Sask. 181/J4
Gorlovka, U.S.S.R. 52/E5
Gorman, Calif. (93534) 204/G9
Gorman, Tenn. (†37101) 237/F8
Gorman, Texas (76454) 302/F5
Gormania, W. Va. (26720) 313/H4
Gormley, Ont. 177/J3
Gorna Dzhumaya (Blagoyevgrad), Bulg. 45/F5
Gorna Oryakhovitsa, Bulg. 45/G4
Gornji Vakuf, Yugo. 45/C4
Gorno-Altay Aut. Obl., U.S.S.R. 48/J4
Gorno-Altaysk, U.S.S.R. 48/J4
Gorno-Altaysk, U.S.S.R., 54/M4
Gorno-Badakhshan Aut. Obl., U.S.S.R. 48/H6
Gornyatskiy, U.S.S.R. 52/K1
Gorodets, U.S.S.R. 52/F3
Gorodok, U.S.S.R. 52/D3
Goroka, Terr. N.G. 85/B7
Goroke, Vic. 97/A5
Gorong (isl.), Indon. 85/J6
Gorong (isls.), Indon. 85/J6
Gorontalo, Indon. 85/G5
Gorrahei, Eth. 111/H6
Gorredijk, Neth. 27/J2
Gorrie, Ont. 177/C4
Gorst, Wash. (98337) 310/C3
Gort, 10/B4
Gort, Ire. 17/D5
Gortin, N. Ire. 17/G2
Gorum, La. (71434) 238/E4
Gorumna (isl.), Ire. 17/B5
Goryn' (riv.), U.S.S.R. 52/C4
Gorzów Wielkopolski, Poland 47/B2
Göschenen, Switz. 39/G3
Gose, Japan 81/J8
Gosen, Japan 81/J5
Gosford, N.S.W. 97/F3
Goshen, Ala. (36035) 194/F7
Goshen, Ark. (72735) 203/C1
Goshen, Calif. (93227) 204/F7
Goshen▵, Conn. (06756) 210/C1
Goshen (pt.), Conn. 210/G3
Goshen, Ind. (46526) 227/F1
Goshen, Ky. (40026) 237/K4
Goshen▵, Mass. (01032) 249/C3
Goshen▵, N.H. (03752) 268/C5
Goshen, N.J. (08218) 273/D5
Goshen, N.S. 169/G3
Goshen, N.Y. (10924) 276/M8
Goshen, Ohio (45122) 284/B7
Goshen, Oreg. (97401) 291/D4
Goshen, Utah (84633) 304/C4
Goshen, Va. (24439) 307/K5
Goshen (co.), Wyo. 319/H4
Goshen Springs, Miss. (†39042) 256/E6
Gosh Halav (Jish), Israel 65/C1
Goshogawara, Japan 81/K3
Goshute (mts.), Nev. 266/G2
Goshute Ind. Res., Nev. 266/G3
Goshute Ind. Res., Utah 304/A4
Gosier, Guad. 161/B6
Goslar, W. Ger. 22/D3
Gosnell, Ark. (†72315) 203/K2
Gosnells, W. Aust. 92/A1
Gosper (co.), Nebr. 264/E4
Gospić, Yugo. 45/B3
Gosport, 10/F5
Gosport, Ala. (36450) 194/C7
Gosport, Eng. 13/F7
Gosport, Ind. (47433) 227/D6
Goss, Miss. (†39429) 256/E8
Gossau, Switz. 39/H2
Gosselies, Belg. 27/E8
Gossville, N.H. (03239) 268/E5
Gostivar, Yugo. 45/E5
Gostyń, Poland 47/C3
Gostynin, Poland 47/D2
Göta (canal), Sweden 18/J7
Göta (riv.), Sweden 18/H7
Gotebo, Okla. (73041) 288/J4
Göteborg, Sweden 18/G8
Göteborg, Sweden, 7/F3
Göteborg och Bohus (co.), Sweden 18/G7
Gotha, E. Ger. 22/D3
Gotham, Wis. (53540) 317/F9
Gothenburg, Nebr. (69138) 264/D4
Gothic (mesa), Ariz. 198/F2
Gotland (co.), Sweden 18/L8
Gotland (isl.), Sweden 18/L8
Gotland, (isl.), Sweden, 7/F3
Goto (lake), Neth. Ant. 161/D8
Goto (isls.), Japan 81/D7
Gotse Delchev, Bulg. 45/F5
Gotska Sandön (isl.), Sweden 18/L7
Gotsu, Japan 81/F6
Göttingen, W. Ger. 22/D3
Gottwaldov, Czech. 41/D2
Götzis, Austria 41/A3
Goubéré, Centr. Afr. Rep. 115/E2
Gouda, Neth. 27/F4
Goudeau, La. (71338) 238/G5
Goudreau, Ont. 175/C3
Gough (lake), Alta. 182/D3
Gough, Ga. (30811) 216/H4
Gough (isl.), St. Helena, 3/J8
Gouin (res.), Que. 174/C3
Gouin (res.), 163/J6
Goulburn, Aust. 88/J7
Goulburn (isls.), Aust. 88/E2
Goulburn, N.S.W. 97/E4
Goulburn (isls.), No. Terr. 93/C1
Goulburn (riv.), Vic. 97/C5
Gould, Ark. (71643) 203/G6
Gould, Colo. (80445) 208/G2
Gould, Que. 172/F4
Gould, Okla. (73544) 288/G5
Gould City, Mich. (49838) 250/D2
Goulding, Fla. (†32502) 212/B6
Goulds, Fla. (33170) 212/F6
Gouldsboro▵, Maine (04636) 242/H7
Gouldsboro, Maine (04636) 242/H7
Gouldsboro, Pa. (18424) 294/L3
Gouldtown, Sask. 181/D5
Goulmima, Mor. 106/C2
Goumbou, Mali 106/C6
Gounamitz (riv.), N. Br. 170/C1
Goundam, 102/B3
Goundam, Mali 106/D5
Gourara (oasis), Alg. 106/E3
Gourbeyre, Guad. 161/A7
Gourdon, France 28/D5
Gouré, Niger 106/G6
Gourma-Rharous, Mali 106/D5
Gournay-en-Bray, France 28/D3
Gouro, Chad 111/C4
Gourock, 10/A1
Gourock, Scot. 15/B2
Gouveia, Port. 33/C2
Gouverneur, N.Y. (13642) 276/K2
Gouyave (passages), Grenada 156/F4
Gouyave, Grenada 161/C8
Govan, S.C. (†29843) 296/E5
Govan, Sask. 181/G4
Gove (co.), Kans. 232/B3
Gove, Kans. (67736) 232/B3
Gove (Nhulunbuy), No. Terr. 93/E2
Govenlock, Sask. 181/B6
Governador Valadares, Braz. 132/F7
Government (mt.), Ariz. 198/C3
Government (peak), Mich. 250/F1
Government (creek), Utah 304/B3
Government Camp, Oreg. (97028) 291/F2
Governor (lake), N.S. 169/F3
Gowan, Minn. (55743) 254/F4
Gowanda, N.Y. (14070) 276/B6
Gowen, Mich. (49326) 250/D5
Gowen, Okla. (74545) 288/R5
Gowensville, S.C. (†29356) 296/C1
Gower, Mo. (64454) 261/C3
Gower (isl.), N.S.W. 97/J2
Gower (mt.), N.S.W. 97/J2
Gower (pen.), Wales 13/C6
Gowna (lake), Ire. 17/G4
Gowran, Ire. 17/G6
Gowrie, Iowa (50543) 229/E4
Goya, Arg. 143/G4
Goyave, Guad. 161/A6
Goyder (riv.), No. Terr. 93/D2
Goyders (lag.), Aust. 88/G5
Goyders (lag.), S. Aust. 94/F2
Göynük, Turkey 63/D2
Gozo (isl.), Malta 34/E6
Goz Regeb, Sudan 111/G4
Graaff-Reinet, 102/E8
Graaff-Reinet, S. Africa 118/C6
Graal-Müritz, E. Ger. 22/E1
Graasten, Den. 21/C8
Graauw, Neth. 27/E6
Grabill, Ind. (46741) 227/H2
Grabouw, S. Africa 118/F7
Grabs, Switz. 39/H2
Gračac, Yugo. 45/B3
Gračanica, Yugo. 45/D3
Grace, Idaho (83241) 220/G7
Grace (mt.), Mass. 249/E2
Grace, Miss. (38745) 256/C5
Grace (pt.), R.I. 249/H8
Grace City, N. Dak. (58445) 283/N4
Gracefield, Que. 172/A3
Graceham, Md. (†21788) 245/J2
Gracemont, Okla. (73042) 288/K4
Graceton, Minn. (56645) 254/D2
Graceton, Pa. (15743) 294/D4
Graceville, Fla. (32440) 212/D5
Graceville, Minn. (56240) 254/B5
Gracewood, Ga. (30812) 216/H4
Gracey, Ky. (42232) 237/F7
Gracias, Hond. 154/C3
Gracias a Dios (cape), 146/K8
Gracias a Dios (cape), Nic. 154/F3
Gradačac, Yugo. 45/D3
Gradaús (range), Braz. 132/D4
Grado, Spain 33/D1
Grady, Ala. (36036) 194/F7
Grady, Ark. (71644) 203/G5
Grady (co.), Ga. 216/D9
Grady, N. Mex. (88120) 274/F4
Grady (isl.), Newf. 166/C3
Grady (co.), Okla. 288/L5
Grady, Okla. (73545) 288/L6
Gradyville, Ky. (42742) 237/L6
Graeagle, Calif. (96103) 204/E4
Graehl‡, Alaska (†99701) 196/J2
Graested, Den. 21/F5
Graettinger, Iowa (51342) 229/D2
Graf, Iowa (†52039) 229/M3
Grafenau, W. Ger. 22/E4
Grafenwöhr, W. Ger. 22/D4
Graff, Mo. (65660) 261/H8
Graford, Texas (76045) 302/F5
Grafton, Australia, 87/F8
Grafton, Aust. 88/J5
Grafton (isls.), Chile 138/D10
Grafton, Ont. 177/G4
Grafton, Ill. (62037) 222/C5
Grafton, Ind. (†47620) 227/B9
Grafton, Iowa (50440) 229/G2
Grafton▵, Mass. (01519) 249/H4
Grafton, N. Br. 170/C2
Grafton, N. Dak. (58237) 283/R3
Grafton (co.), N.H. 268/D4
Grafton▵, N.H. (03240) 268/D4
Grafton, N.H. (03240) 268/D4
Grafton, N.S.W. 97/G1
Grafton, N.Y. (12082) 276/N5
Grafton, Nebr. (68365) 264/G4
Grafton, Ohio (44044) 284/F3
Grafton, Va. (23490) 307/P6
Grafton▵, Vt. (05146) 268/B5
Grafton, Vt. (05146) 268/B5
Grafton, W. Va. (26354) 313/G4
Grafton, Wis. (53024) 317/L9
Grafton Center, N.H. (†03240) 268/D4
Graham (isl.), 163/D5
Graham, Ala. (36263) 194/H4
Graham (lake), Alta. 182/C1
Graham (co.), Ariz. 198/E6
Graham (mt.), Ariz. 198/F6
Graham (isl.), Br. Col. 184/A3
Graham (peak), Colo. 208/E8
Graham, Ont. 175/B3
Graham, Ont. 177/G5
Graham, Fla. (32042) 212/D2
Graham, Ga. (†31513) 216/H7
Graham (creek), Ind. 227/F7
Graham (co.), Kans. 232/C2
Graham, Ky. (42344) 237/G6
Graham (lake), Maine 242/G6
Graham, Mo. (64455) 261/C2
Graham (co.), N.C. 281/B4
Graham, N.C. (27253) 281/L2
Graham (isl.), N.W.T. 187/J2
Graham, Okla. (73437) 288/M6
Graham, Texas (76046) 302/F4
Graham Bell (isl.), U.S.S.R. 48/G1
Graham Bell (isl.), U.S.S.R., 4/A6
Grahamdale, Man. 179/D3
Graham Heights‡, W. Va. (†26554) 313/F4
Graham Land (reg.), Ant., 3/G9
Graham Land (reg.), Ant. 5/C15
Graham Reach (chan.), Br. Col. 184/C3
Grahamstown, 102/E8
Grahamstown, S. Africa 118/D6
Grahamsville, N.Y. (12740) 276/L7
Grahn, Ky. (41142) 237/P4
Graian Alps (range), France 28/G5
Graian Alps (range), Italy 34/A2
Grain Coast (reg.), Liberia 106/B8
Grainfield, Kans. (67737) 232/B2
Grainger, Alta. 182/D4
Grainger (co.), Tenn. 237/O8
Graingers, N.C. (†28501) 281/O4
Grainola, Okla. (74639) 288/N1
Grainton, Nebr. (69139) 264/C4
Grain Valley, Mo. (64029) 261/S6
Grajaú, Braz. 132/E4
Grajaú (riv.), Braz. 132/E4
Grajewo, Poland 47/F2
Gram, Den. 21/C7
Gramalote, Col. 126/D4
Gramat, France 28/D5
Grambling, La. (71245) 238/E1
Gramercy, La. (70052) 238/M3
Gramling, S.C. (29348) 296/C1
Grammer, Ind. (47236) 227/F6
Grammont (Geraardsbergen), Belg. 27/D7
Grampian, Pa. (16838) 294/E4
Grampian (mts.), Scot. 15/G6
Gramsbergen, Neth. 27/K3
Gran, Norway 18/G6
Granada, Colo. (81041) 208/P6
Granada, Minn. (56039) 254/D7
Granada, Nic. 154/E5
Granada, Spain, 7/D5
Granada (prov.), Spain 33/E4
Granada, Spain 33/E4
Granada Hills, Calif. (91344) 204/B10
Granados, Mex. 150/E2
Granard, Ire. 17/F4
Granbury, Texas (76048) 302/G5
Granby, Colo. (80446) 208/H2
Granby (lake), Colo. 208/G2
Granby▵, Conn. (06035) 210/D1
Granby, Que. 172/E4
Granby▵, Mass. (01033) 249/E3
Granby, Mass. (01033) 249/E3
Granby, Mo. (64844) 261/D9
Granby▵, Vt. (05840) 268/D2
Gran Chaco (reg.), 120/D5
Gran Chaco (reg.), Arg. 143/D1
Gran Chaco (reg.), Par. 144/B4
Gran Couva, Trinidad Tobago 161/B11
Grand, Le (cape), Aust. 88/C6
Grand (canal), China, 54/P6
Grand (canal), China 77/J4
Grand (co.), Colo. 208/G2
Grand (bay), Dominica 161/F7
Grand (riv.), Ont. 177/D4
Grand (canal), Ire. 17/G5
Grand (lake), La., 188/H4
Grand (lake), La. 238/E7
Grand (lake), La. 238/H8
Grand (riv.), La. 238/H6
Grand (lake), Maine 242/H4
Grand (isl.), Mich. 250/C2
Grand (lake), Mich. 250/F3
Grand (riv.), Mich. 250/D6
Grand (riv.), Mo. 261/F3
Grand (bay), N. Br. 170/D3
Grand (lake), N. Br. 170/C3
Grand (lake), N. Br. 170/D3
Grand (riv.), N. Br. 170/C1
Grand (isl.), N.Y. 276/B5
Grand (lake), Newf. 166/B3
Grand (lake), Newf. 166/C4
Grand (riv.), Ohio 284/H2
Grand (riv.), S. Dak. 298/F2
Grand (co.), Utah 304/E5
Grand Anse, Grenada 161/C9
Grand Bahama (isl.), Bah. Is., 146/L7
Grand Bahama (isl.), Bah. Is. 156/B1
Grand Bank, Newf. 166/C4
Grand Bassa (Buchanan), Liberia 106/B7
Grand-Bassam, Ivory Coast 106/D7
Grand Bay, Ala. (36541) 194/B10
Grand Bay, Dominica 161/F7
Grand Bay, N. Br. 170/D3
Grand Bayou, La. (†71052) 238/C2
Grand Beach, Mich. (†49117) 250/C7
Grand Bend, Ont. 177/C4
Grand Blanc, Mich. (48439) 250/F6
Grand-Bourg, Guad. 161/B7
Grand Bruit, Newf. 166/C4
Grand Caicos (isl.), Turks Caicos Is. 156/D2
Grand Caille (pt.), St. Lucia 161/F6
Grand Canary (isl.), 102/A2
Grand Canary (isl.), Spain 33/B5
Grand Canary (isl.), Spain 106/A3
Grand Cane, La. (71032) 238/C2
Grand Canyon, Ariz., 188/D3
Grand Canyon, Ariz. (86023) 198/C2
Grand Canyon, Snake R. (canyon) Oreg. 291/L2
Grand Canyon Nat'l Mon., Ariz. 198/C2
Grand Canyon Nat'l Park, Ariz., 188/D3
Grand Canyon Nat'l Park, Ariz. 198/C2
Grand Canyon of the Snake River (canyon), Idaho 220/B4
Grand Cayman (isl.), Cayman Is., 146/K8
Grand Cayman (isl.), Cayman Is. 156/B3
Grand Centre, Alta. 182/E2
Grand Cess, Liberia 106/C8
Grand Chain, Ill. (62941) 222/E6
Grand Chenier, La. (70643) 238/E7
Grand Combin (mt.), Switz. 39/D5
Grand Comoro (isl.), Comoro Is. 118/G2
Grand Comoro (isl.), 102/G6
Grand Coteau, La. (70541) 238/G6
Grand Coulee, Sask. 181/G5
Grand Coulee, Wash. (99133) 310/G3
Grand Coulee (canyon), Wash. 310/F3
Grand Coulee (dam), Wash. 310/F3
Grand Cul de Sac (riv.), St. Lucia 161/G6
Grand Cul-de-Sac Marin (bay), Guad. 161/A6
Grand Desert, N.S. 169/E4
Grand Detour, Ill. (†61021) 222/D2
Grande (bay), Arg., 120/D8
Grande (bay), Arg. 143/C7
Grande (falls), Arg. 143/E3
Grande (riv.), Arg. 143/C4
Grande (riv.), Bol., 120/D4
Grande (marsh), Bol. 136/F5
Grande (riv.), Bol. 136/C4
Grande (riv.), Bol. 136/C6
Grande (riv.), Braz., 120/F5
Grande (riv.), Braz. 132/E5
Grande (riv.), Braz. 132/D8
Grande (isl.), Braz. 135/D3
Grande (riv.), Braz. 135/B1
Grande (isl.), Chile 138/A6
Grande (riv.), Chile 138/F10
Grande, Salar (salt dep.), Chile 138/B3
Grande (isl.), Col. 126/B4
Grande, Salto (falls), Col. 126/D8
Grande (riv.), Jam. 158/K6
Grande (riv.), Mex. 150/G2
Grande (riv.), Mex. 150/N8
Grande (riv.), Nic. 154/E4
Grande (riv.), Peru 128/E10
Grande (range), Urug. 145/D4
Grande, Arroyo (riv.), Urug. 145/B4
Grande-Anse, N. Br. 170/E1
Grande Cache, Alta. 182/A3
Grande-Cascapédia, Que. 172/C2
Grande Cayemite (isl.), Haiti 158/B6
Grande Clairière, Man. 179/B5
Grande de Añasco (riv.), P. Rico 161/B2
Grande de Arecibo (riv.), P. Rico 161/C1
Grande de Lípez (riv.), Bol. 136/B7
Grande de Loíza (riv.), P. Rico 161/E1
Grande de Manatí (riv.), P. Rico 161/C1
Grande de Santiago (riv.), Mex. 150/G6
Grande de Tierra del Fuego (isl.), Arg 143/C7
Grande de Tierra del Fuego (isl.), Chile 138/E11
Grande-Digue, N. Br. 170/F2
Grande Dixence (dam), Switz. 39/D4
Grande-Grève, Que. 172/D1
Grande Inferior (range), Urug. 145/C4
Grande-Ligne, Que. 172/D4
Grande Prairie, 163/E4
Grande-Prairie, Alta. 182/A2
Grande-Prairie, Br. Col., 146/F4
Grande-Rivière, Mart. 161/C5
Grande Rivière, Trinidad Tobago 161/B10
Grande-Rivière, Que. 172/D2
Grande-Rivière, La (riv.), Que. 174/B2
Grande-Rivière, La (riv.), 163/J5
Grande Rivière de la Baleine (riv.), 163/J5
Grande Rivière de la Baleine (riv.), Que., 146/L4
Grande-Rivière-du-Nord, Haiti 158/C5
Grande Ronde (riv.), Oreg. 291/K2
Grande Ronde (riv.), Wash. 310/H5
Grande-Saline, Haiti 158/B5
Grandes-Bergeronnes, Que. 172/H1
Grandes-Piles, Que. 172/E3
Grand-Étang, N.S. 169/G2
Grande-Terre (isl.), Guad. 161/B6
Grande-Vallée, Que. 172/D1
Grande Vigie (pt.), Guad. 161/B5
Grand Falls, 163/L6
Grand Falls (lake), Maine 242/H5
Grand Falls, N. Br. 170/C1
Grand Falls, Newf., 146/N5
Grand Falls, Newf. 166/C4
Grandfalls, Texas (79742) 302/B6
Grand Falls Hill, N. Br. 170/C1
Grandfield, Okla. (73546) 288/J6
Grand Forks, Br. Col. 184/H6
Grand Forks, N. Dak., 146/J5
Grand Forks, N. Dak., 188/G1
Grand Forks (co.), N. Dak. 283/P3
Grand Forks, N. Dak. (58201) 283/R4
Grand Forks A.F.B., N. Dak. 283/R4
Grand Glaise, Ark. (72056) 203/G3
Grand-Goâve, Haiti 158/B6
Grand Gorge, N.Y. (12434) 276/L6
Grand-Gosier, Haiti 158/C6
Grand Gulf, Miss. (†39150) 256/B6
Grand Harbour, N. Br. 170/D4
Grand Haven, Mich. (49417) 250/C5
Grand-Îlet (isl.), Guad. 161/A7
Grandin, Alta. 182/D3
Grandin, Fla. (32638) 212/E2
Grandin, Mo. (63943) 261/L9
Grandin, N. Dak. (58038) 283/R5
Grand Island, N.Y. (14072) 276/B5
Grand Island, Nebr., 146/J5
Grand Island, Nebr., 188/G2
Grand Island, Nebr. (68801) 264/F4
Grand Isle, La. (70358) 238/L8
Grand Isle▵, Maine (04746) 242/G1
Grand Isle, Maine (04746) 242/G1
Grand Isle (co.), Vt. 268/A2
Grand Isle▵, Vt. (05458) 268/A2
Grand Isle, Vt. (05458) 268/A2
Grand Junction, Colo., 188/E3
Grand Junction, Colo. (81501) 208/B4
Grand Junction, Iowa (50107) 229/E4
Grand Junction, Mich. (49056) 250/C6
Grand Junction, Tenn. (38039) 237/C10
Grand-Lahou, Ivory Coast 106/C8
Grand Lake, Ark. (†71640) 203/H7
Grand Lake, Colo. (80447) 208/H2
Grand Lake, La. (†70601) 238/D6
Grand Lake Seboeis (lake), Maine 242/F3
Grand Lake Stream▵, Maine (04637) 242/H5
Grand Lake Towne, Okla. (†74349) 288/S1
Grand Ledge, Mich. (48837) 250/E6
Grand-Lieu (lake), France 28/C4
Grandmaison, N. Br. 170/B1
Grand Manan (chan.), Maine 242/K6
Grand Manan (chan.), N. Br. 170/C4
Grand Manan (isl.), N. Br. 170/D4
Grand-Marais, Man. 179/F4
Grand Marais, Mich. (49839) 250/D2
Grand Marais, Minn. (55604) 254/G2
Grand Marsh, Wis. (53936) 317/G8
Grand Meadow, Minn. (55936) 254/F7
Grand Mère, Que. 172/E3
Grand Mound, Iowa (52751) 229/M5
Grand Mound, Wash. (†98531) 310/C4
Grand Muveran (mt.), Switz. 39/D4
Grand Narrows, N.S. 169/H3
Grândola, Port. 33/B3
Grandora, Sask. 181/E3
Grand Pass, Mo. (65331) 261/F4
Grand-Popo, Dahomey 106/E7
Grand Portage, Minn. (55605) 254/G2
Grand Portage Ind. Res., Minn. 254/G2
Grand Portage Nat'l Mon., Minn. 254/G2
Grand Prairie, Texas (75050) 302/G2
Grand Pré, N.S. 169/D3
Grand Rapids, Man. 179/C1
Grand Rapids, Mich., 146/K5
Grand Rapids, Mich., 188/K2
Grand Rapids, Mich. (*49501) 250/D5
Grand Rapids, Minn. (55744) 254/E3
Grand Rapids, N. Dak. (58446) 283/N7
Grand Rapids, Ohio (43522) 284/C3
Grand Ridge, Fla. (32442) 212/A1
Grand Ridge, Ill. (61325) 222/E2
Grand River, Iowa (50108) 229/F7
Grand River, N.S. 169/H3

372 Gumma

Gumma (pref.), Japan 81/J5
Gummersbach, W. Ger. 22/B3
Gummi, Nigeria 106/F6
Gum Spring, Va. (23065) 307/N5
Gum Springs, Ark. (†71923) 203/D5
Gümüş, Turkey 63/F2
Gümüşhaciköy, Turkey 63/F2
Gümüşhane, Turkey 59/C1
Gümüşhane (prov.), Turkey 63/H2
Gümüşhane, Turkey 63/H2
Gun (cay), Bah. Is. 156/B1
Gun (lake), Mich. 250/D6
Guna, India 68/D4
Gunabad, Iran 59/G3
Gunabad, Iran 66/L3
Gunbad-i-Qabus, Iran 66/J2
Gunbadli, Iran 66/M2
Gunbower, Vic. 97/C4
Gundagai, N.S.W. 97/D4
Gunderbooka (ranges), N.S.W. 97/C2
Gündoğmuş, Turkey 63/D4
Güney, Turkey 63/C3
Gunflint Trail, Minn. (†55604) 254/F1
Gungu, Dem. Rep. of the Congo. 115/C5
Gunisao (lake), Man. 179/J3
Gunlock, Utah (84733) 304/A6
Gunna (isl.), Scot. 15/C6
Gunna (sound), Scot. 15/C6
Gunnbjørn (mt.), Greenl., 4/C11
Gunn City, Mo. (†64760) 261/D5
Gunnedah, Aust. 88/H6
Gunnedah, N.S.W. 97/F2
Gunning, N.S.W. 97/E4
Gunningsville, N. Br. 170/F2
Gunnison (co.), Colo. 208/E5
Gunnison, Colo. (81230) 208/E5
Gunnison (riv.), Colo. 208/C5
Gunnison (tunnel), Colo. 208/D6
Gunnison, Miss. (38746) 256/C3
Gunnison, Utah (84634) 304/C4
Gunnison (res.), Utah 304/C4
Gunnworth, Sask. 181/C4
Gunpowder (riv.), Md. 245/N3
Gunpowder Falls (creek), Md. 245/M2
Guntakal, India 68/D5
Gunter, Ont. 177/G3
Gunter, Oreg. (†97436) 291/D4
Gunter‡, Texas (75058) 302/H4
Gunter Air Force Base, Ala. 194/F6
Guntersville, Ala. (35976) 194/F2
Guntersville (dam), Ala. 194/F2
Guntersville (lake), Ala. 194/F2
Gunton, Man. 179/E4
Guntown, Miss. (38849) 256/G2
Guntur, India 68/D5
Gunungapi (isl.), Indon. 85/H7
Gunungsitoli, Indon. 85/B5
Günzburg, W. Ger. 22/D4
Gunzenhausen, W. Ger. 22/D4
Gurabo, P. Rico 161/E2
Gurais, India 68/D2
Gurau, Kuh-i- (mt.), Iran 59/F3
Gurau, Kuh-i- (mt.), Iran 66/F3
Gurdon, Ark. (71743) 203/D6
Gurgan, Iran, 54/J6
Gurgan, Iran 59/F2
Gurgan (riv.), Iran 59/F2
Gurgan, Iran 66/J2
Gurgan (riv.), Iran 66/J2
Gurgueia (riv.), Braz. 132/E5
Guri, Ven. 124/G4
Guri (dam), Ven. 124/G4
Guri (res.), Ven. 124/G4
Gurk, Austria 41/C3
Gurk (riv.), Austria 41/D2
Gurla Mandhata (mt.), China 77/B5
Gurley, Ala. (35748) 194/F1
Gurley, La. (†70730) 238/H5
Gurley, N.S.W. 97/E1
Gurley, Nebr. (69141) 264/B3
Gurley, S.C. (†29569) 296/J3
Gurleyville, Conn. (†06268) 210/G1
Gurnee, Ill. (60031) 222/F1
Gurnet (pt.), Mass. 249/M4
Gurney, Wis. (54528) 317/F3
Gurneyville, Alta. 182/E2
Gurtnellen, Switz. 39/G3
Gürün, Turkey 63/G3
Gurupá, Braz. 132/D3
Gurupi (riv.), Braz., 120/F3
Gurupi, Braz. 132/D5
Gurupi (range), Braz. 132/E4
Gurupi (riv.), Braz. 132/E3
Gur'yev, U.S.S.R. 48/F5
Gur'yev, U.S.S.R., 54/J5
Gus, Ky. (†42365) 237/H6
Gusau, Nigeria 106/F6
Gusher, Utah (84030) 304/E3
Gusht, Iran 66/M7
Gusinje, Yugo. 45/D4
Gusinoözersk, U.S.S.R. 48/L4
Gus-Khrustal'nyy, U.S.S.R. 52/F3
Güssing, Austria 41/D3
Gustavus, Alaska (99826) 196/M1
Gustavus, Ohio (†44417) 284/J3
Gustine, Calif. (95322) 204/D6
Gustine, Texas (76455) 302/F6
Guston, Ky. (40142) 237/J5
Güstrow, E. Ger. 22/E2
Gutenberg, Arg. 143/D2
Gütersloh, W. Ger. 22/C3
Guthrie, Ind. (†47421) 227/D7
Guthrie (co.), Iowa 229/D5
Guthrie, Ky. (42234) 237/G7
Guthrie, Minn. (56451) 254/D3
Guthrie, Mo. (†65063) 261/H5
Guthrie, Okla., 188/G3
Guthrie, Okla. (73044) 288/M3
Guthrie, Texas (79236) 302/D4
Guthrie Center, Iowa (50115) 229/D5
Gutiérrez, Bol. 136/D6
Gutiérrez Zamora, Mex. 150/L6
Guttannen, Switz. 39/F3
Guttenberg, Iowa (52052) 229/L3
Guttenberg, N.J. (07093) 273/C2
Gu-Win, Ala. (†35563) 194/C3
Guy, Alta. 182/B2
Guy, Ark. (72061) 203/F3
Guyan, W. Va. (24838) 313/C7
Guyana, 3/G5
Guyana, 120/E2
GUYANA, 131/B3
Guyandotte (riv.), W. Va. 313/B6
Guymon, Okla. (73942) 288/D1
Guynemer, Man. 179/C3
Guyot (glac.), Alaska 196/K2
Guyot (mt.), N.C. 281/C3
Guyot (mt.), Tenn. 237/P9
Guyra, N.S.W. 97/F2
Guys, Tenn. (38339) 237/D10
Guysborough (co.), N.S. 169/F3
Guysborough, N.S. 169/G3
Guysborough (riv.), N.S. 169/G3
Guys Mills, Pa. (16327) 294/C2
Guysville, Ohio (45735) 284/G7
Guyton, Ga. (31312) 216/K6
Guzmán (lake), Mex. 150/F1
Guzmán Blanco, Ven. 124/E6
Guzmanes (cay), Cuba 158/B2
Gwa, Burma 72/B3
Gwaai, Rhod. 118/D3
Gwabegar, Aust. 88/H6
Gwabegar, N.S.W. 97/E2
Gwadabawa, Nigeria 106/F6
Gwadar, Pak. 59/H5
Gwadar, Pak. 68/A4
Gwadar, Pak., 54/K7
Gwalia, W. Aust. 92/C5
Gwalior, India 68/D3
Gwanda, Rhod. 118/D4
Gwätar, Iran 59/H4
Gwatar, Iran 66/M8
Gwda (riv.), Poland 47/C2
Gweebarra (bay), Ire. 17/D2
Gweebarra (riv.), Ire. 17/E2
Gwelo, 102/E6
Gwelo, Rhod. 118/D3
Gwinn, Mich. (49841) 250/B2
Gwinner,‡N. Dak. (58040) 283/P7
Gwinnett (co.), Ga. 216/D2
Gwydir (riv.), N.S.W. 97/E1
Gwynn, Va. (23066) 307/R5
Gwynne, Alta. 182/D3
Gwynneville, Ind. (46144) 227/F5
Gyangtse, China, 54/N7
Gyangtse, China 77/C6
Gyasikan, Ghana 106/D7
Gyatsa Dzong, China 77/D6
Gyda (pen.), U.S.S.R. 48/H2
Gyda (pen.), U.S.S.R., 4/C6
Gydan (Kolyma) (range), U.S.S.R. 48/Q3
Gydy, U.S.S.R. 48/H2
Gylling, Den. 21/D6
Gympie, Australia, 87/F8
Gympie, Aust. 88/J5
Gympie, Queens. 95/E5
Gyobingauk, Burma 72/C3
Gyoma, Hung. 41/F3
Gyöngyös, Hung. 41/E3
Gyönk, Hung. 41/E3
Győr, Hung., 7/F4
Győr, Hung. 41/D3
Győr-Sopron (co.), Hung. 41/D3
Gypsum, Colo. (81637) 208/F3
Gypsum, Kans. (67448) 232/E3
Gypsum (lake), Man. 179/D3
Gypsum, Ohio (43433) 284/E2
Gypsumville, Man. 179/D3
Gyrfalcon (isls.), N.W.T. 187/M4
Gyula, Hung. 41/F3

H

Haacht, Belg. 27/F7
Haag, Austria 41/C2
Haakon (co.), S. Dak. 298/F5
Haamstede, Neth. 27/D5
Ha'apai Group (isls.), Tonga, 87/J8
Haapajärvi, Fin. 18/O5
Haapamäki, Fin. 18/O5
Haapsalu, U.S.S.R. 53/B1
Haar, W. Ger. 22/D4
Haarby, Den. 21/D7
Haarlem, Neth. 27/F4
Haarlemmermeer (Hoofddorp), Neth. 27/F4
Haarlemmermeer Polder, Neth. 27/B5
Haarlev, Den. 21/F7
Haast, N.Z. 101/B5
Haast (pass), N.Z. 101/B6
Haast (riv.), N.Z. 101/B5
Haasts Bluff, No. Terr. 93/B7
Hab (riv.), Pak. 59/J4
Hab (riv.), Pak. 68/B3
Habay, Alta. 182/A5
Habban, P.D.R. Yemen 59/E7
Habbaniya, Iraq 59/D3
Habbaniya, Iraq 66/C4
Habbaniya, Hor al (lake), Iraq 66/C4
Habersham (co.), Ga. 216/E1
Habersham, Ga. (30544) 216/F1
Habersham, Tenn. (†37766) 237/N8
Habiganj, Pak. 68/G4
Habikino, Japan 81/J8
Habomai (isls.), Japan 81/N2
Habonim, Israel 65/B2
Haboro, Japan 81/K1
Hachenburg, W. Ger. 22/B3
Hachinohe, Japan 81/K3
Hachioji, Japan 81/O2
Hachiro (mts.), Japan 81/J3
Hachita, N. Mex. (88040) 274/A7
Hacibektaş, Turkey 63/F3
Hacienda, Fla. (†33301) 212/B4
Hacienda Heights‡, Calif. (91745) 204/D11
Hacilar, Turkey 63/F3
Hack (mt.), S. Aust. 94/F4
Hackberry, Ariz. (86401) 198/B3
Hackberry, La. (70645) 238/D7
Hackensack, Minn. (56452) 254/D4
Hackensack, N.J. (*07601) 273/B2
Hackensack (riv.), N.J. 273/C1
Hacker Valley, W. Va. (26222) 313/F5
Hacketstown, Ire. 17/H6
Hackett, Alta. 182/D3
Hackett, Ark. (72937) 203/B3
Hacketts Cove, N.S. 169/E4
Hackettstown, N.J. (07840) 273/D2
Hacking, Port (inlet), Aust. 88/L3
Hackleburg, Ala. (35564) 194/C2
Hackleman, Ind. (†46928) 227/F4
Hackney, 10/B5
Hacksneck, Va. (23358) 307/S5
Hacoda, Ala. (†36442) 194/F8
Hadama, Eth. 111/G6
Hadar, Nebr. (68738) 264/G2
Hadarba, Ras (cape), Sudan 111/G3
Hadashville, Man. 179/G5
Hadd, Ras al (cape), Oman 59/G5
Hadd, Ras al (cape), Oman, 54/K7
Haddam△, Conn. (06438) 210/E3
Haddam, Conn. (06438) 210/E3
Haddam, Kans. (66944) 232/E2
Haddam Neck, Conn. (†06424) 210/E2
Haddar, Saudi Ar. 59/E5
Haddington, 10/E3
Haddington, Scot. 15/L8
Haddix, Ky. (41331) 237/P6
Haddock, Alta. 182/B3
Haddock, Ga. (31033) 216/F4
Haddonfield, N.J. (08033) 273/B3
Haddon Heights, N.J. (08035) 273/B3
Hadejia, Nigeria 106/G6
Hadejia (riv.), Nigeria 106/F6
Hadensville, Ky. (†42234) 237/G7
Hadera, Israel 65/B3
Hadera (dry riv.), Israel 65/B3
Haderslev, Den. 18/F9
Haderslev (co.), Den. 21/C7
Haderslev, Den. 21/C7
Hadhar, Iraq 66/C3
Hadhramaut (dist.), P.D.R. Yemen 59/E7
Hadhramaut, Wadi (dry riv.), P.D.R. Yemen 59/F7
Hadhramaut (des.), P.D.R. Yemen, 54/H8
Hadibu, P.D.R. Yemen 59/F7
Hadibu, P.D.R. Yemen, 54/J8
Hadim, Turkey 63/E4
Haditha, Iraq 59/D3
Haditha, Iraq 66/C3
Hadiya, Saudi Ar. 59/C4
Hadleigh, Eng. 13/J6
Hadley, Ind. (†46122) 227/D5
Hadley, Ky. (42235) 237/H6
Hadley△, Mass. (01035) 249/D3
Hadley, Mich. (48440) 250/F6
Hadley, Minn. (56133) 254/C7
Hadley (bay), N.W.T. 187/H2
Hadley, N.Y. (12835) 276/N4
Hadley, Pa. (16130) 294/B3
Hadlock, Wash. (98339) 310/C2
Hadlyme, Conn. (06439) 210/F3
Hadsel (fjord), Norway 18/J2
Hadsten, Den. 21/C5
Hadsund, Den. 21/D4
Hadu, Kenya 115/G4
Haedo (range), Urug. 145/C2
Haeju, N. Korea 81/B4
Haena, Hawaii (†96714) 218/C1
Haena (pt.), Hawaii 218/C1
Hafar al Batin, Saudi Ar. 59/E4
Haffe, Syria 63/G5
Hafford, Sask. 181/D3
Hafik, Turkey 63/G3
Haflong, India 68/G3
Hafnarfjördhur, Ice. 21/B1
Haft Kel, Iran 66/F5
Hafun, Somalia 115/K1
Hafun, Ras (cape), Somalia 115/K1
Hafun, Ras (cape), 102/G3
Hagaman, N.Y. (12086) 276/M5
Hagan, Ga. (30429) 216/J6
Hagari (riv.), India 68/D6
Hagarstown, Ill. (62247) 222/D5
Hagarville, Ark. (72839) 203/D2
Hagemeister (isl.), Alaska 196/F3
Hagen, Sask. 181/F3
Hagen, W. Ger. 22/B3
Hagenow, E. Ger. 22/D2
Hagensborg, Br. Col. 184/D4
Hager City, Wis. (54014) 317/A6
Hagerman, Idaho (83332) 220/D7
Hagerman, N. Mex. (88232) 274/E5
Hagerstown, Ind. (47346) 227/G5
Hagerstown, Md., 188/L3
Hagerstown, Md. (21740) 245/G2
Hagersville, Ont. 177/D5
Hagfors, Sweden 18/H6
Hagi, Japan 81/E6
Ha Giang, N. Vietnam 72/E2
Hagood, S.C. (†29128) 296/F3
Hags (head), Ire. 17/B6
Hague, Fla. (†32601) 212/D2
Hague (cape), France 28/C3
Hague, N. Dak. (58542) 283/L7
Hague, N.Y. (12836) 276/N3
Hague, Sask. 181/E3
Hague, The (cap.), Neth. 27/E4
Hague, The (cap.), Neth., 7/E3
Hague, Va. (22469) 307/P4
Haguenau, France 28/G3
Ha! Ha! (lake), Que. 172/G1
Ha! Ha! (riv.), Que. 172/G1
Haha (isl.), Japan, 87/E3
Haha (isl.), Japan 81/M3
Hahatonka, Mo. (†65020) 261/G7
Hahira, Ga. (31632) 216/F9
Hahndorf, Aust. 88/E8
Hahndorf, S. Aust. 94/C8
Hahnville, La. (70057) 238/N4
Hai, Iraq 59/E3
Hai, Iraq 66/E4
Haibak, Afgh. 59/J2
Haibak, Afgh. 68/B1
Haifa, Israel 59/B3
Haifa (dist.), Israel 65/C2
Haifa, Israel 65/B2
Haifa (bay), Israel 65/C2
Haig (lake), Alta. 182/B1
Haight, Alta. 182/D3
Haigler, Nebr. (69030) 264/C4
Haikow (Hoihow), China 77/H7
Haiku, Hawaii (96708) 218/J2
Hail, Saudi Ar. 59/D4
Hail, Saudi Ar., 54/F7
Hailar, China 77/J2
Haile, La. (71246) 238/F1
Hailesboro, N.Y. (13645) 276/K2
Hailey, Idaho (83333) 220/D6
Haileybury, Ont. 175/D3
Haileybury, Ont. 177/K5
Haileyville, Okla. (74546) 288/P5
Hailsham, Eng. 13/H7
Hailun, China 77/L2
Hailung, China 77/L3
Hailuoto, Fin. 18/O4
Hailuoto (isl.), Fin. 18/O4
Haina, Hawaii (96709) 218/H3
Hainan (isl.), China, 3/O5
Hainan (isl.), China, 54/P8
Hainan (isl.), China 77/G8
Hainault (prov.), Belg. 27/D7
Hainburg, Austria 41/D2
Haines, Alaska (99827) 196/M1
Haines, Oreg. (97833) 291/J3
Hainesburg, N.J. (†07832) 273/C2
Haines City, Fla. (33844) 212/E3
Haines Highway, Alaska 196/L2
Haines Junction, Yukon 187/E3
Haines Landing, Maine (†04964) 242/B6
Hainesport△, N.J. (08036) 273/D4
Hainesville‡, Ill. (†60030) 222/E1
Hainesville, N.J. (†07826) 273/D1
Hainfeld, Austria 41/C2
Haiphong, N. Vietnam, 54/O7
Haiphong, N. Vietnam 72/E2
Hairy Hill, Alta. 182/D3
Haiti, 3/F5
Haiti, 146/L8
HAITI, 156/D3
HAITI, 158
Haiwee, Calif. 204/H7
Haiya Junction, 102/F3
Haiya Junction, Sudan 59/C6
Haiya Junction, Sudan 111/G4
Hajara, Al (plain), Iraq 66/D5
Hajarain, P.D.R. Yemen 59/E6
Hajdú-Bihar (co.), Hung. 41/F3
Hajdúböszörmény, Hung. 41/F3
Hajdúdorog, Hung. 41/F3
Hajdúhadház, Hung. 41/F3
Hajdúnánás, Hung. 41/F3
Hajdúsámson, Hung. 41/F3
Hajdúszoboszló, Hung. 41/F3
Haji Ibraham (mt.), Iraq 66/D2
Hajla (mt.), Yugo. 45/E4
Hajnowka, Poland 47/F2
Hajós, Hung. 41/E3
Haka, Burma 72/B2
Hakalau, Hawaii (96710) 218/J4
Hakkâri (mts.), Leb. 63/K4
Hakkâri (prov.), Turkey 63/K4
Hakkâri (Çölemerik), Turkey 63/K4
Hakken (mt.), Japan 81/H6
Hakodate, Japan, 54/T5
Hakodate, Japan 81/K3
Haku (mt.), Japan 81/H5
Hakui, Japan 81/H5
Hakusan Nat'l Park, Japan 81/H5
Hal (Halle), Belg. 27/E7
Halabja, Iraq 66/D3
Halachó, Mex. 150/O6
Halaib, Sudan 59/C5
Halaib, Sudan 111/G3
Halalii (lake), Hawaii 218/A2
Halaula, Hawaii, 188/G5
Halaula, Hawaii (96711) 218/G3
Halawa, Hawaii (†96711) 218/G3
Halawa, Hawaii (†96748) 218/H1
Halawa (bay), Hawaii 218/H1
Halawa (cape), Hawaii 218/H1
Halawa (stream), Hawaii 218/B3
Halawa Heights, Hawaii (†96701) 218/B3
Halberstadt, E. Ger. 22/D3
Halbrite, Sask. 181/H6
Halbstadt, Man. 179/E5
Halbur, Iowa (51444) 229/D4
Halcon (mt.), Phil. 82/C4
Halcyon Dale, Ga. (†30467) 216/J5
Halcyon Hot Springs, Br. Col. 184/J5
Haldane, Ill. (†61030) 222/D1
Haldeman, Ky. (40329) 237/P4
Halden, Norway 18/G7
Halden, Norway, 7/F3
Haldensleben, E. Ger. 22/D2
Haldenstein, Switz. 39/H3
Haldimand (co.), Ont. 177/E5
Hale (co.), Ala. 194/C5
Hale, Arg. 143/F7
Hale (mt.), Aust. 88/B5
Hale, Colo. (80730) 208/P3
Hale, Camp, Colo. 208/G4
Hale, Iowa (52230) 229/L4
Hale, Mich. (48739) 250/F4
Hale, Mo. (64643) 261/F3
Hale (mt.), W. Aust. 92/B4
Hale (riv.), No. Terr. 93/D8
Hale (co.), Texas 302/C3
Haleakala (crater), Hawaii 218/K2
Haleakala Nat'l Park, Hawaii 218/K2
Haleb (Aleppo), Syria 59/C2
Haleb (Aleppo), Syria 63/G4
Haleburg, Ala. (†36319) 194/H8
Hale Center, Texas (79041) 302/C3
Haledon, N.J. (07508) 273/B1
Haleiwa, Hawaii (96712) 218/E1
Halen, Belg. 27/G7
Hales Corners, Wis. (53130) 317/K2
Halesowen, 10/G3
Hales Point, Tenn. (†38040) 237/B9
Halesworth, Eng. 13/J5
Haley, N. Dak. (†58629) 283/D8
Haley Station, Ont. 177/H2
Haleyville, Ala. (35565) 194/C2
Haleyville, N.J. (†08349) 273/C5
Half Assini, Ghana 106/D8
Halfeti, Turkey 63/H4
Half Hollow Hills‡, N.Y. (†11743) 276/O9
Half Island Cove, N.S. 169/G3
Half Moon (cay), Br. Hond. 154/D2
Half Moon (reefs), Hond. 154/F3
Halfmoon Bay, Br. Col. 184/J2
Half Moon Bay, Calif. (94019) 204/H3
Halfmoon Bay, N.Z. 101/B7
Halfmoon Junction‡, N.Y. (†12118) 276/N5
Halford, Kans. (†67701) 232/B2
Halfway (riv.), Br. Col. 184/F2
Halfway, Ky. (42150) 237/J7
Halfway, Md. (†21740) 245/G2
Half Way, Mo. (65663) 261/F7
Halfway, Oreg. (97834) 291/K3
Halfway House, Hawaii (†96718) 218/H6
Halfweg, Neth. 27/A4
Halhul, Jordan 65/C4
Haliburton (co.), Ont. 177/F2
Haliburton, Ont. 177/F2
Haliburton (lake), Ont. 177/F2
Halibut Cove‡, Alaska (99603) 196/C2
Halieli, Turkey 63/B6
Halifax, 10/G1
Halifax (bay), Aust. 88/H3
Halifax, Canada, 3/F3
Halifax (harb.), Grenada 161/C8
Halifax, Eng. 13/F4
Halifax△, Mass. (02338) 249/L5
Halifax (co.), N.C. 281/O2
Halifax, N.C. (27839) 281/O2
Halifax (co.), N.S. 169/E4
Halifax (harb.), N.S. 169/E4
Halifax (cap.), N.S. 169/E4
Halifax (cap.), N.S., 146/M5
Halifax (cap.), N.S. 163/K7
Halifax (bay), Queens. 95/C3
Halifax, Pa. (17032) 294/J5
Halifax (co.), Va. 307/L7
Halifax, Va. (24558) 307/L7
Halifax△, Vt. (†05358) 268/B6
Halifax Center, Vt. (†05358) 268/B6
Haliimaile, Hawaii (96787) 218/J2
Halin, Somalia 115/J2
Haliri (riv.), Iran 59/G4
Halkett (cape), Alaska 196/H1
Halkirk, Alta. 182/D3
Halkirk, 10/E1
Halkirk, Scot. 15/K3
Hall (pen.), 163/K3
Hall (isl.), Alaska 196/D2
Hall (riv.), Que. 172/C2
Hall (co.), Ga. 216/E2
Hall, Ind. (46145) 227/D5
Hall, Ky. (41820) 237/R6
Hall, Md. (†20716) 245/L5
Hall, Mont. (59837) 262/C4
Hall (basin), N.W.T. 187/M1
Hall (lake), N.W.T. 187/K3
Hall (pen.), N.W.T. 187/M3
Hall (co.), Nebr. 264/F4
Hall (isls.), Pac. Is., 87/F5
Hall (co.), Texas 302/D3
Hall, W. Va. (†26201) 313/F4
Halla (mt.), S. Korea 81/C7
Halladale (riv.), Scot. 15/J3
Hallam, Nebr. (68368) 264/H4
Hallam, Vic. 97/K5
Halland (co.), Sweden 18/H8
Hallandale, Fla. (33009) 212/B4
Hallaniya (isl.), P.D.R. Yemen 59/G6
Hallau, Switz. 39/F1
Hallboro, Man. 179/C4
Halle, Belg. 27/E7
Halle, E. Ger., 7/F3
Halle (dist.), E. Ger. 22/D3
Halle, E. Ger. 22/D3
Halleck, Nev. (89824) 266/F2
Hällefors, Sweden 18/J7
Hallein, Austria 41/B3
Hallett, Okla. (74034) 288/N2
Hallettsville, Texas (77964) 302/G8
Halley, Ark. (71645) 203/H6
Halli, Saudi Ar. 59/D6
Halliday, N. Dak. (58636) 283/F5
Hallie, Wis. (†54729) 317/D6
Halligen (isls.), W. Ger. 22/C1
Hall Lake, N.W.T. 187/K3
Hall Meadow (brook), Conn. 210/C1
Hall Mills, Ont. 177/H2
Hällnäs, Sweden 18/L4
Hallock, Minn. (56728) 254/A2
Hallonquist, Sask. 181/D5
Hallowell, Kans. (66744) 232/H4
Hallowell, Maine (04347) 242/D7
Hall Park‡, Okla. (†73069) 288/M4
Halls (stream), N.H. 268/E1
Halls, Tenn. (38040) 237/C9
Halls (creek), Utah 304/D6
Hallsberg, Sweden 18/J7
Hallsboro, N.C. (28442) 281/M6
Halls Creek, Australia, 87/C7
Halls Creek, Aust. 88/D3
Halls Creek, W. Aust. 92/D2
Hallson, N. Dak. (†58220) 283/P2
Halls Summit, Kans. (†66871) 232/G3
Hallstahammar, Sweden 18/K7
Hallstatt, Austria 41/B3
Hallstavik, Sweden 18/L6
Hallstead, Pa. (18822) 294/L2
Hall Summit, La. (71034) 238/D2
Hallsville, Ill. (†61727) 222/D3
Hallsville, Mo. (65255) 261/H4
Hallsville, Ohio (45633) 284/E7
Hallsville, Texas (75650) 302/K5
Hallton, Pa. (15842) 294/E3
Halltown, Mo. (65664) 261/E8
Halltown, W. Va. (25423) 313/L4
Hallum, Neth. 27/H2
Hallwilersee (lake), Switz. 39/F2
Hallwood, Va. (23359) 307/S5
Halma, Minn. (56729) 254/B2
Halmahera (isl.), Indon., 54/R9
Halmahera (isl.), Indon. 85/H5
Halmahera (sea), Indon. 85/H5
Halmstad, Sweden 18/H8
Halpine, Md. (†20850) 245/K4
Halq el Oued, Tun. 106/G1
Hals, Den. 21/D3
Halsell, Ala. (36909) 194/B6
Halsey, Nebr. (69142) 264/D3
Halsey, Oreg. (97348) 291/D3
Hälsingborg, Sweden 18/H8
Hälsingborg, Sweden, 7/F3
Halstad, Minn. (56548) 254/B3
Halstead, 10/G5
Halstead, Eng. 13/H6
Halstead, Kans. (67056) 232/E4
Haltdalen, Norway 18/G5
Haltemprice, 10/F4
Haltemprice, Eng. 13/G4
Haltern, W. Ger. 22/B3
Haltia (mt.), Fin. 18/M2
Haltia (mt.), Norway 18/M2
Haltom City, Texas (76117) 302/F2
Halton (co.), Ont. 177/E4
Haltwhistle, Eng. 13/E3
Halvorgate, Sask. 181/E5
Ham, Chad 111/C5
Ham, France 28/E3
Hama, Syria 59/C2
Hama (prov.), Syria 63/G5
Hama, Syria 63/G5
Hamada, Jebel (mt.), U.A.R. 59/B5
Hamada, Japan 81/E6
Hamadan, Iran, 54/H6
Hamadan, Iran 59/E3
Hamadan (governorate), Iran 66/F3
Hamadan, Iran 66/F3
Hamamatsu, Japan 81/H6
Hamar, Norway 18/G6
Hamar, N. Dak. (58336) 283/N4
Hamar, Saudi Ar. 59/E5
Hambantota, Ceylon 68/E7
Hamberg, N. Dak. (58337) 283/L4
Hamber Prov. Park, Br. Col. 184/J4
Hamblen (co.), Tenn. 237/P8
Hambleton, W. Va. (26269) 313/G4
Hamburg, Ark. (71646) 203/G7
Hamburg, Conn. (†06371) 210/F3
Hamburg, Ill. (62045) 222/C4
Hamburg, Iowa (51640) 229/B7
Hamburg, Mich. (48139) 250/F6
Hamburg, Minn. (55339) 254/D6
Hamburg, Miss. (†39661) 256/B7
Hamburg, N.J. (07419) 273/D1
Hamburg, N.Y. (14075) 276/C5
Hamburg, Pa. (19526) 294/L4
Hamburg, W. Ger., 7/F3
Hamburg (state), W. Ger. 22/D2
Hamburg, W. Ger. 22/D2
Hamburg, Wis. (54438) 317/G5
Hamden△, Conn. (06514) 210/D3
Hamden, N.Y. (13782) 276/K6
Hamden, Ohio (45634) 284/F7
Häme (prov.), Fin. 18/O6
Hämeenlinna, Fin. 18/O6
Hamel, Ill. (62046) 222/B6
Hamel, Minn. (55340) 254/F5
Hamelin Pool, W. Aust. 92/A4
Hameln, W. Ger. 22/C2
Hamer, Idaho (83425) 220/F6
Hamer, S.C. (29547) 296/J3
Hamersley (range), Aust. 88/B4
Hamersley (range), W. Aust. 92/B3
Hamersville, Ohio (45130) 284/C8
Hamhŭng, N. Korea 81/C4
Hami, China, 54/N5
Hami, China 77/D3
Hamill, S. Dak. (57534) 298/K6
Hamilton (inlet), 163/L5
Hamilton, 163/H7
Hamilton, Ala. (35570) 194/C2
Hamilton (lake), Ark. 203/D5
Hamilton, Aust. 88/G7
Hamilton (cap.), Berm. 156/G3
Hamilton (mt.), Calif. 204/L3
Hamilton, Colo. (81638) 208/D2
Hamilton, Ont. 177/E4
Hamilton (co.), Fla. 212/D1
Hamilton, Ga. (31811) 216/C5
Hamilton (co.), Ill. 222/E5
Hamilton, Ill. (62341) 222/B3
Hamilton (co.), Ind. 227/E4
Hamilton, Ind. (46742) 227/H1
Hamilton (co.), Iowa 229/F4
Hamilton, Iowa (50116) 229/H6
Hamilton (co.), Kans. 232/A3
Hamilton, Kans. (66853) 232/F4
Hamilton△, Mass. (01936) 249/L2
Hamilton, Mich. (49419) 250/C6
Hamilton, Miss. (39746) 256/H3
Hamilton, Mo. (64644) 261/E3
Hamilton, Mont. (59840) 262/B4
Hamilton, N.C. (27840) 281/P3
Hamilton, N. Dak. (58238) 283/R2
Hamilton (co.), N.Y. 276/L3
Hamilton, N.Y. (13346) 276/J5
Hamilton, N.Z. 101/E2
Hamilton, N. Z., 87/H9
Hamilton (co.), Nebr. 264/F4
Hamilton (inlet), Newf., 146/N4
Hamilton (inlet), Newf. 166/C3
Hamilton (sound), Newf. 166/D4
Hamilton, The (riv.), S. Aust. 94/D2
Hamilton (riv.), Queens. 95/B4
Hamilton, Ohio, 188/K3
Hamilton (co.), Ohio 284/A7
Hamilton, Ohio (*45011) 284/A7
Hamilton, Ont., 146/K5
Hamilton, Oreg. (†97856) 291/H3
Hamilton, Pa. (15744) 294/D4
Hamilton, R.I. (†02852) 249/J6
Hamilton, 10/B1
Hamilton, Scot. 15/D2
Hamilton (co.), Tenn. 237/L10
Hamilton (co.), Texas 302/F6
Hamilton, Texas (76531) 302/G6
Hamilton, Va. (22068) 307/N2
Hamilton, Vic. 97/B5
Hamilton, Wash. (98255) 310/D2
Hamilton A.F.B., Calif. 204/J1
Hamilton City, Calif. (95951) 204/C4
Hamilton Dome, Wyo. (82427) 319/D2
Hamilton Square, N.J. (08690) 273/D3
Hamina, Fin. 18/P6
Hamiota, Man. 179/B4
Hamler, Ohio (43524) 284/B3
Hamlet, Ind. (46532) 227/D2
Hamlet, N.C. (28345) 281/K5
Hamlet, N. Dak. (58742) 283/E2
Hamlet, N.Y. (†14138) 276/B6
Hamlet, Nebr. (69031) 264/C4
Hamlet, Ohio (†45102) 284/B8
Hamletsburg, Ill. (62944) 222/E6
Hamlin, Alta. 182/D2
Hamlin, Iowa (50117) 229/D5
Hamlin, Kans. (66430) 232/G2
Hamlin, Ky. (42046) 237/E7
Hamlin△, Maine (†04785) 242/H1
Hamlin (lake), Mich. 250/C4
Hamlin, N.Y. (14464) 276/E4
Hamlin, Pa. (18427) 294/M3
Hamlin (co.), S. Dak. 298/P4
Hamlin, Texas (79520) 302/E5
Hamlin, W. Va. (25523) 313/B6
Hamm, W. Ger. 22/B3
Hammamet (gulf), Tun. 106/G1
Hammar, Hor al (lake), Iraq 66/E5

Haslemere **373**

Hamme, Belg. 27/E6
Hammel, Den. 21/C5
Hammelburg, W. Ger. 22/C3
Hammer, S. Dak. (57240) 298/R2
Hammerfest, Norway 18/N1
Hammerfest, Norway, 4/B9
Hammerfest, Norway, 7/G1
Hammersmith, 10/B5
Hammerum, Den. 21/C5
Hammett, Idaho (83627) 220/C7
Hammon, Okla. (73650) 288/H3
Hammonasset (pt.), Conn. 210/E3
Hammonasset (res.), Conn. 210/E3
Hammonasset (riv.), Conn. 210/E3
Hammond, Ill. (61929) 222/E4
Hammond, Ind. (*46320) 227/B1
Hammond, Ky. (40947) 237/O7
Hammond, La. (70401) 238/N1
Hammond, Minn. (55938) 254/F6
Hammond, Mo. (65665) 261/G9
Hammond, Mont. (59332) 262/M5
Hammond (riv.), N. Br. 170/E3
Hammond, N.Y. (13646) 276/J2
Hammond, Oreg. (97121) 291/C1
Hammond, Wis. (54015) 317/A6
Hammondsport, N.Y. (14840) 276/F6
Hammondsville, Ohio (43930) 284/J4
Hammondville, Ala. (†35989) 194/G1
Hammonton, N.J. (08037) 273/D4
Hamner, Ala. (†35459) 194/B5
Ham-Nord, Que. 172/F4
Hamoa, Hawaii (†96713) 218/K2
Hamont, Belg. 27/H6
Hampden▵, Maine (04444) 242/F6
Hampden, Maine (04444) 242/F6
Hampden (co.), Mass. 249/D4
Hampden▵, Mass. (01036) 249/E4
Hampden, N. Dak. (58338) 283/N2
Hampden, N.Z. 101/C6
Hampden, Newf. 166/C4
Hampden, W. Va. (25623) 313/C7
Hampden Highlands, Maine (04445) 242/F6
Hampden-Sydney, Va. (23943) 307/L6
Hampshire (Hants, Southampton) (co.), Eng. 13/F6
Hampshire, Ill. (60140) 222/E1
Hampshire (co.), Mass. 249/D3
Hampshire, Tenn. (38461) 237/G9
Hampshire (co.), W. Va. 313/J4
Hampshire, Wyo. (†82701) 319/H2
Hampstead, Dominica 161/E5
Hampstead, Md. (21074) 245/L2
Hampstead, N. Br. 170/D3
Hampstead, N.C. (28443) 281/O6
Hampstead▵, N.H. (03841) 268/E6
Hampstead, N.H. (03841) 268/E6
Hampton, Ark. (71744) 203/F6
Hampton▵, Conn. (06247) 210/G1
Hampton, Ont. 177/F4
Hampton, Fla. (32044) 212/D2
Hampton, Ga. (30228) 216/D4
Hampton, Ill. (61256) 222/C2
Hampton, Iowa (50441) 229/G3
Hampton, Ky. (42047) 237/E6
Hampton, Minn. (55031) 254/E6
Hampton, Miss. (†38744) 256/B4
Hampton, N. Br. 170/E3
Hampton▵, N.H. (03842) 268/F6
Hampton, N.H. (03842) 268/F6
Hampton, N.J. (08827) 273/D2
Hampton, N.S. 169/C4
Hampton, N.Y. (12837) 276/O3
Hampton, Nebr. (68843) 264/G4
Hampton, Oreg. (†97712) 291/G4
Hampton, Pa. (17330) 294/H6
Hampton (co.), S.C. 296/E6
Hampton, S.C. (29924) 296/E6
Hampton, Va. (*23360) 307/R6
Hampton Bays, N.Y. (11946) 276/R9
Hampton Beach, N.H. (03842) 268/F6
Hampton-Braemar, Tenn. (37658) 237/S8
Hampton Falls▵, N.H. (03844) 268/F6
Hampton Nat'l Hist. Site, Md. 245/M3
Hampton Park, Vic. 97/K6
Hampton Roads (est.), Va. 307/R7
Hampton Springs, Fla. (†32347) 212/C1
Hampton Station, N. Br. 170/E3
Hamptonville, N.C. (27020) 281/H2
Hamrin, Jabal (mts.), Iraq 66/D3
Hams Bluff (prom.), V.I.(U.S.) 161/E3
Hams Fork (riv.), Wyo. 319/B4
Ham-Sud, Que. 172/F4
Ham Tan, S. Vietnam 72/E5
Hamton, Sask. 181/J4
Hamtramck, Mich. (48212) 250/B6
Hamur, Turkey 63/K3
Han (riv.), S. Korea 81/C5
Hana, Hawaii, 188/F5
Hana, Hawaii (96713) 218/K2
Hanaford (Logan), Ill. (†62856) 222/E6
Hanagita (peak), Alaska 196/K2
Hanahan, S.C. (29410) 296/H6
Hanakiya, Saudi Ar. 59/D5
Hanalei, Hawaii (96714) 218/C1
Hanalei (bay), Hawaii 218/C1
Hanalei (riv.), Hawaii 218/C1
Hanamaki, Japan 81/K4
Hanamalo (pt.), Hawaii 218/F7
Hanamaulu, Hawaii (96715) 218/C1
Hanapepe, Hawaii (96716) 218/C2
Hanapepe (bay), Hawaii 218/C2
Hanau, W. Ger. 22/C3
Hanawa, Japan 81/K3
Hanceville, Ala. (35077) 194/E2
Hanceville, Br. Col. 184/F4
Hanchung, China, 54/O6
Hanchung, China 77/G5
Hancock, Conn. (†06786) 210/C2
Hancock (co.), Ga. 216/G4
Hancock (co.), Ill. 222/B3
Hancock (co.), Ind. 227/F5
Hancock (co.), Iowa 229/F2
Hancock, Iowa (51536) 229/C6
Hancock (co.), Ky. 237/H5
Hancock (co.), Maine 242/G6
Hancock▵, Maine (04640) 242/G6
Hancock▵, Mass. (01237) 249/A2
Hancock, Md. (21750) 245/F2
Hancock, Mich. (49930) 250/G1
Hancock, Minn. (56244) 254/C5
Hancock (co.), Miss. 256/E10
Hancock, Mo. (†65452) 261/H7
Hancock▵, N.H. (03449) 268/C6
Hancock (mt.), N.H. 268/D3
Hancock, N.Y. (13783) 276/K7
Hancock (co.), Ohio 284/C3
Hancock (co.), Tenn. 237/P7
Hancock▵, Vt. (05748) 268/B4
Hancock, Vt. (05748) 268/B4
Hancock (co.), W. Va. 313/E2
Hancock, W. Va. (25424) 313/K3
Hancock, Wis. (54943) 317/G7
Hancocks Bridge, N.J. (08038) 273/C4
Hand (co.), S. Dak. 298/L4
Handa (isl.), Scot. 15/F3
Handel, Sask. 181/C3
Handeni, Tanz. 115/G5
Handies (peak), Colo. 208/E7
Handley, W. Va. (25102) 313/D6
Handlová, Czech. 41/E2
Handsom, Va. (23859) 307/O7
Handsworth, Sask. 181/J6
Haney, Br. Col. 184/L3
Hanford, Calif. (93230) 204/F7
Hanford Atomic Energy Res., Wash. 310/F4
Hangchow, China, 54/R7
Hangchow, China 77/J5
Hangchow (bay), China 77/K5
Hanging Rock, Ohio (45635) 284/E8
Hangklip (cape), S. Africa 118/F7
Hangö, Fin. 18/N7
Hangö, Fin., 7/G3
Hangöudd (prom.), Fin. 18/N7
Hani, Turkey 63/J3
Haniqra (cape), Israel 65/C1
Hanish (isls.), Yemen Arab Rep 59/D7
Hanjam (isl.), Iran 66/J7
Han Kiang (riv.), China 77/H5
Hankinson, N. Dak. (58041) 283/S7
Hanko (Hangö), Fin. 18/N7
Hankow (in Wuhan), China 77/H5
Hanks, N. Dak. (†58856) 283/C2
Hanksville, Utah (84734) 304/D5
Hanle, India 68/D2
Hanley, Sask. 181/E4
Hanley Falls, Minn. (56245) 254/C6
Hanley Hills‡, Mo. (†63101) 261/P3
Hanlontown, Iowa (50444) 229/G2
Hanmer, N.Z. 101/D5
Hann (mt.), W. Aust. 92/D1
Hanna, 163/E5
Hanna, Alta. 182/E4
Hanna, Ind. (46340) 227/D2
Hanna, La. (71035) 238/D3
Hannå, Okla. (74845) 288/P4
Hanna, Utah (84031) 304/D3
Hanna, Wyo. (82327) 319/F4
Hanna City, Ill. (61536) 222/D3
Hannaford, N. Dak. (58448) 283/O5
Hannah (bay), Ont. 175/D2
Hannah, N. Dak. (58239) 283/N2
Hannawa Falls, N.Y. (13647) 276/L1
Hannibal, Mo., 188/H3
Hannibal, Mo. (63401) 261/K3
Hannibal, N.Y. (13074) 276/G4
Hannibal, Ohio (43931) 284/J6
Hannibal, Wis. (54439) 317/E5
Hanno, Japan 81/O2
Hannover, N. Dak. (58543) 283/H5
Hannover, W. Ger., 7/E3
Hannover, W. Ger. 22/C2
Hannut (Hannuit), Belg. 27/G7
Hanöbukten (bay), Sweden 18/J9
Hanoi (cap.), N. Vietnam, 3/Q4
Hanoi (cap.), N. Vietnam, 54/O7
Hanoi (cap.), N. Vietnam 72/E2
Hanover (isl.), Chile, 120/C8
Hanover (isl.), Chile 138/D9
Hanover, Conn. (06350) 210/G2
Hanover, Ont. 177/C3
Hanover, Ill. (61041) 222/C1
Hanover, Ind. (47243) 227/F7
Hanover, Kans. (66945) 232/F2
Hanover▵, Maine (04237) 242/B7
Hanover▵, Mass. (02339) 249/L4
Hanover, Md. (21201) 245/M4
Hanover, Mich. (49241) 250/E6
Hanover, Minn. (55341) 254/E5
Hanover, Mont. (†59457) 262/G3
Hanover▵, N.H. (03755) 268/C4
Hanover, N.H. (03755) 268/C4
Hanover, N. Mex. (88041) 274/A6
Hanover, Ohio (†43055) 284/F5
Hanover, Pa. (17331) 294/J6
Hanover (co.), Va. 307/N5
Hanover, Va. (23069) 307/O5
Hanover, W. Va. (24839) 313/C7
Hanover Park‡, Ill. (60103) 222/E1
Hanoverton, Ohio (44423) 284/J4
Hansboro, N. Dak. (58339) 283/M2
Hansell, Iowa (50640) 229/G3
Hansen, Idaho (83334) 220/D7
Hansford (co.), Texas 302/C1
Hanska, Minn. (56041) 254/D6
Hans Lollik (isls.), V.I.(U.S.) 161/B4
Hanson, Ky. (42413) 237/G6
Hanson▵, Mass. (02341) 249/L4
Hanson (bay), N.Z. 101/E7
Hanson (riv.), No. Terr. 93/C6
Hanson, Okla. (†74955) 288/S4
Hanson (co.), S. Dak. 298/O6
Hansonville, Va. (†24266) 307/D7
Hansted, Den. 21/B3
Hanston, Kans. (67849) 232/C3
Hansville, Wash. (98340) 310/C3
Hantan, China 77/H4
Hants (co.), N.S. 169/D4
Hant's Harbour, Newf. 166/D2
Hantsport, N.S. 169/D3
Hantzsch (riv.), N.W.T. 187/L3
Hanwood, N.S.W. 97/C4
Hanyang (in Wuhan), China 77/H5
Hao (atoll), Fr. Poly., 87/N7
Haouach, Wadi (dry riv.), Chad 111/C4
Haparanda, Sweden 18/N4
Haparanda, Sweden, 7/G2
Hapeville, Ga. (30354) 216/D3
Happy, Ky. (41746) 237/P6
Happy, Texas (79042) 302/C3
Happy Adventure, Newf. 166/D2
Happy Camp, Calif. (96039) 204/B2
Happy Jack, Ariz. (86024) 198/D4
Happy Jack, La. (†70083) 238/L7
Happy Valley, Newf. 166/B3
Happy Valley, Oreg. (†97222) 291/B2
Haql, Saudi Ar. 59/C4
Haradh, Saudi Ar. 59/E5
Harahan, La. (70123) 238/N4
Haraja, Saudi Ar. 59/D6
Haralson (co.), Ga. 216/B3
Haralson, Ga. (30229) 216/C4
Haramachi, Japan 81/K5
Harar (prov.), Eth. 111/H6
Harar, Eth. 111/H6
Harar, 102/G4
Harardera, Somalia 115/J3
Harbeson, Del. (19951) 245/S6
Harbin, China, 3/R3
Harbin, China, 54/R5
Harbin, China 77/L2
Harbine, Nebr. (68369) 264/G4
Harbinger, N.C. (27941) 281/T2
Harbor, Oreg. (97415) 291/C5
Harbor Beach, Mich. (48441) 250/G5
Harbor City, Calif. (90710) 204/C11
Harborcreek, Pa. (16421) 294/C1
Harbor Springs, Mich. (49740) 250/D3
Harborton, Va. (23389) 307/S5
Harbor View, Ohio (43434) 284/C2
Harbour (isl.), Bah. Is. 156/C1
Harbour Breton, Newf. 166/C4
Harbour Buffett, Newf. 166/C2
Harbour Grace, 163/L6
Harbour Grace, Newf. 166/D2
Harbour Main, Newf. 166/D2
Harbourton, N.J. (†08530) 273/D3
Harbourview, N.S. 169/G3
Harbourville, N.S. 169/D3
Harburg-Wilhelmsburg, W. Ger. 22/C2
Harco, Ill. (62945) 222/E6
Harcourt, Iowa (50544) 229/E4
Harcourt, N. Br. 170/E2
Harcus, Man. 179/D4
Harcuvar (mts.), Ariz. 198/B5
Harda, India 68/D4
Hardanger (fjord), Norway 18/D7
Hardanger (fjord), Norway, 7/E3
Hardanger (mts.), Norway 18/E6
Hardaway, Ala. (36039) 194/G6
Hardburly, Ky. (41747) 237/P6
Hardee (co.), Fla. 212/E4
Hardee, Miss. (†39177) 256/C5
Hardeeville, S.C. (29927) 296/E7
Hardeman (co.), Tenn. 237/C10
Hardeman (co.), Texas 302/E3
Hardenberg, Neth. 27/J3
Harden City, Okla. (74846) 288/N5
Harderwijk, Neth. 27/H4
Hardesty, Okla. (73944) 288/D1
Hardieville, Alta. 182/D5
Hardin (co.), Ill. 222/E6
Hardin, Ill. (62047) 222/C4
Hardin (co.), Iowa 229/G4
Hardin (co.), Ky. 237/K5
Hardin, Ky. (42048) 237/E7
Hardin, Mo. (64035) 261/E4
Hardin, Mont. (59034) 262/J5
Hardin (co.), Ohio 284/C4
Hardin (co.), Tenn. 237/E10
Hardin (co.), Texas 302/K7
Harding (lake), Ala. 194/H5
Harding (lake), Ga. 216/B5
Harding, Man. 179/B5
Harding, Minn. (56364) 254/E4
Harding (co.), N. Mex. 274/F3
Harding (pt.), N.S. 169/D5
Harding (co.), S. Dak. 298/B2
Harding, W. Va. (†26250) 313/G5
Harding Icefield, Alaska 196/C2
Hardingville, N.J. (†08343) 273/C4
Hardinsburg, Ind. (47125) 227/E8
Hardinsburg, Ky. (40143) 237/H5
Hardin Springs, Ky. (†42712) 237/J5
Hardinville, Ill. (†62449) 222/F5
Hardinxveld, Neth. 27/G5
Hardisty, Alta. 182/E3
Hardisty (lake), N.W.T. 187/G3
Hardman, Oreg. (†97836) 291/H2
Hardoi, India 68/E3
Hardshell, Ky. (41348) 237/P6
Hardt (mts.), W. Ger. 22/C4
Hardtner, Kans. (67057) 232/D4
Hardwar, India 68/D2
Hardwick, Ga. (31034) 216/F4
Hardwick▵, Mass. (01037) 249/F3
Hardwick, Minn. (56134) 254/B7
Hardwick▵, Vt. (05843) 268/C2
Hardwick, Vt. (05843) 268/C2
Hardwick (lake), Vt. 268/C2
Hardwicke Island, Br. Col. 184/E5
Hardwood Ridge, N. Br. 170/D2
Hardy, Ark. (72542) 203/H1
Hardy (pen.), Chile 138/F11
Hardy, Iowa (50545) 229/E3
Hardy, Ky. (41531) 237/S5
Hardy, Miss. (†38901) 256/E3
Hardy, Nebr. (68943) 264/G4
Hardy, Okla. (†74641) 288/N1
Hardy, Sask. 181/G6
Hardy, Va. (24101) 307/J6
Hardy (co.), W. Va. 313/J4
Hardyville, Ky. (42746) 237/K6
Hare (fjord), N.W.T. 187/K1
Hare (bay), Newf. 166/C3
Hare Bay, Newf. 166/D4
Harelbeke, Belg. 27/C7
Harfleur, France 28/D3
Harford (co.), Md. 245/N2
Harford, N.Y. (13784) 276/H6
Harford, Pa. (18823) 294/L2
Harghessa, 102/G4
Harghessa, Somalia 115/H2
Hargill, Texas (78549) 302/F11
Hargrave, Man. 179/A5
Hari (riv.), Indon. 85/C6
Harib, Yemen Arab Rep 59/E6
Haricha Hamada (des.), Mali 106/D4
Harim, Syria 63/G4
Harima, Jordan 65/D2
Harima (sea), Japan 81/G6
Haringey, 10/B5
Haringvliet (str.), Neth. 27/E5
Hariq, Saudi Ar. 59/E5
Hari Rud (riv.), Afgh. 59/H3
Hari Rud (riv.), Iran 66/M3
Hari Rud (riv.), Afgh. 68/A1
Haris, Jordan 65/C3
Harjavalta, Fin. 18/M6
Harjo, Okla. (†74854) 288/N4
Harkaway, Vic. 97/K5
Harker Heights‡, Texas (76541) 302/G7
Harkers Island, N.C. (28531) 281/R5
Harkiko, Eth. 111/G4
Harlan, Ind. (46743) 227/H2
Harlan, Iowa (51537) 229/C5
Harlan, Kans. (67641) 232/D2
Harlan (co.), Ky. 237/P7
Harlan, Ky. (40831) 237/P7
Harlan (co.), Nebr. 264/E4
Harlan, Oreg. (†97343) 291/D3
Harlan, Sask. 181/B2
Harlan County (res.), Nebr. 264/E5
Harlech, 10/E4
Harlech, Wales 13/D5
Harlem, Fla. (33440) 212/F5
Harlem, Ga. (30814) 216/H4
Harlem, Mont. (59526) 262/H2
Harlem Springs, Ohio (44631) 284/J4
Harleton, Texas (75651) 302/K5
Harleysville‡, Pa. (19438) 294/M5
Harleyville, S.C. (29448) 296/G5
Harlingen, N.J. (†08502) 273/D3
Harlingen, Neth. 27/G2
Harlingen, Texas, 188/G5
Harlingen, Texas (78550) 302/G11
Harlow, Eng. 13/H6
Harlow, N. Dak. (58340) 283/M3
Harlowton, Mont. (59036) 262/F4
Harman, W. Va. (26270) 313/G5
Harmancik, Turkey 63/C3
Harman-Maxie, Va. (24618) 307/D6
Harmans, Md. (21077) 245/M4
Harmarville, Pa. (†15201) 294/C6
Harmattan, Alta. 182/C4
Harmon, Ill. (61042) 222/D2
Harmon (co.), Okla. 288/H5
Harmon, Okla. (73845) 288/G2
Harmonsburg, Pa. (16422) 294/B2
Harmon Valley, Alta. 182/B1
Harmony, Ark. (†72830) 203/D2
Harmony, Ind. (47853) 227/C5
Harmony▵, Maine (04942) 242/D6
Harmony, Maine (04942) 242/D6
Harmony, Minn. (55939) 254/F7
Harmony, N.C. (28634) 281/H3
Harmony, Pa. (16037) 294/B4
Harmony, R.I. (02829) 249/H5
Harmony, W. Va. (25246) 313/D5
Harms, Tenn. (†37334) 237/H10
Harned, Ky. (40144) 237/J5
Harnett (co.), N.C. 281/M4
Harney (lake), Fla. 212/F3
Harney, Md. (†21787) 245/K2
Harney (lake), Oreg., 188/C2
Harney (co.), Oreg. 291/H4
Harney, Oreg. (†97720) 291/J4
Harney (lake), Oreg. 291/H4
Harney (peak), S. Dak. 298/B6
Härnösand, Sweden 18/L5
Haro, Spain 33/E1
Haro (str.), Wash. 310/B2
Harold, Fla. (32563) 212/B6
Harold, Ky. (41635) 237/R5
Harp (lake), Newf. 166/B2
Harper, Ill. (†61030) 222/D1
Harper, Iowa (52231) 229/J6
Harper (co.), Kans. 232/D4
Harper, Kans. (67058) 232/D4
Harper, Liberia 106/C8
Harper (co.), Okla. 288/G1
Harper, Oreg. (97906) 291/K4
Harper, Texas (78631) 302/E7
Harper, W. Va. (25851) 313/D7
Harper, Wash. (98341) 310/A2
Harpers Ferry, Iowa (52146) 229/L2
Harpers Ferry, W. Va. (25425) 313/L4
Harpers Ferry Nat'l Hist. Park, Md. 245/G3
Harpers Ferry Nat'l Hist. Park, W. Va. 313/L4
Harpersville, Ala. (35078) 194/F4
Harperville, Miss. (39080) 256/E6
Harper Woods, Mich. (48236) 250/B6
Harpeth (riv.), Tenn. 237/G8
Harpster, Idaho (†83521) 220/C4
Harpster, Ohio (43323) 284/D4
Harpswell▵, Maine (†04011) 242/D8
Harpswell Center, Maine (†04011) 242/D8
Harptree, Sask. 181/F6
Harpursville, N.Y. (13787) 276/J6
Harput, Turkey 63/H3
Harquahala (mts.), Ariz. 198/B5
Harrah, Okla. (73045) 288/M4
Harrah, Wash. (98933) 310/E4
Harran, Turkey 63/H4
Harrell, Ark. (71745) 203/F7
Harrells, N.C. (28444) 281/N5
Harrellsville, N.C. (27942) 281/R2
Harricanaw (riv.), Que. 174/B2
Harriet, Ark. (72939) 203/E2
Harrietta, Mich. (49638) 250/D4
Harriettsville, Ohio (†45745) 284/H6
Harrigan Cove, N.S. 169/F4
Harriman, N.Y. (10926) 276/M8
Harriman, Oreg. (†97601) 291/E5
Harriman, Tenn. (37748) 237/M9
Harriman (res.), Vt. 268/B6
Harrington, Del. (19952) 245/R5
Harrington (sound), Berm. 156/G3
Harrington▵, Maine (04643) 242/H6
Harrington (lake), Maine 242/E4
Harrington, S. Dak. (57535) 298/G7
Harrington, Wash. (99134) 310/G3
Harrington Harbour, Que. 174/F2
Harrington Park, N.J. (07640) 273/C1
Harris (lake), Aust. 88/E6
Harris, Calif. (95447) 204/B3
Harris (co.), Ga. 216/C5
Harris, Iowa (51345) 229/C2
Harris, Kans. (66034) 232/G3
Harris, Mich. (49845) 250/B3
Harris, Minn. (55032) 254/F5
Harris, Mo. (64645) 261/F2
Harris (lake), S. Aust. 94/D4
Harris, Okla. (74739) 288/S7
Harris, Sask. 181/D4
Harris (dist.), Scot. 15/C4
Harris (dist.), 10/C2
Harris (sound), 10/C2
Harris (sound), Scot. 15/B4
Harris (Tarbert), Scot. 15/C4
Harris, Tenn. (†38261) 237/C8
Harris (co.), Texas 302/J8
Harrisburg, Ark. (72432) 203/J2
Harrisburg, Ill. (62946) 222/E6
Harrisburg, Ind. (†47331) 227/G5
Harrisburg, Mo. (65256) 261/H4
Harrisburg, N.C. (28075) 281/H4
Harrisburg, Nebr. (69345) 264/A3
Harrisburg, Ohio (43126) 284/D6
Harrisburg, Oreg. (97446) 291/D3
Harrisburg (cap.), Pa., 146/L5
Harrisburg (cap.), Pa., 188/L2
Harrisburg (cap.), Pa. (*17101) 294/H5
Harrisburg, S. Dak. (57032) 298/R7
Harrismith, S. Africa 118/D5
Harrison (cape), 163/L5
Harrison (bay), Alaska 196/H1
Harrison, Ark. (72601) 203/D1
Harrison (lake), Br. Col. 184/M2
Harrison, Ga. (31035) 216/G5
Harrison, Idaho (83833) 220/B2
Harrison, Ill. (†61072) 222/D1
Harrison (co.), Ind. 227/E8
Harrison (co.), Iowa 229/B5
Harrison (co.), Ky. 237/N4
Harrison▵, Maine (04040) 242/B7
Harrison, Mich. (48625) 250/E4
Harrison (co.), Miss. 256/F10
Harrison (co.), Mo. 261/E2
Harrison, Mont. (59735) 262/E5
Harrison, N.J. (07029) 273/B2
Harrison, N.Y. (10528) 276/P7
Harrison, Nebr. (69346) 264/A2
Harrison (cape), Newf. 166/C3
Harrison (co.), Ohio 284/E4
Harrison, Ohio (45030) 284/A9
Harrison, S. Dak. (57344) 298/M7
Harrison, Tenn. (37341) 237/L10
Harrison (co.), Texas 302/K5
Harrison (co.), W. Va. 313/F4
Harrison, Wis. (†54435) 317/G5
Harrisonburg, La. (71340) 238/G3
Harrisonburg, Va. (22801) 307/K4
Harrison Hot Springs, Br. Col. 184/M3
Harrison Valley, Pa. (16927) 294/G2
Harrisonville, Ill. (†62295) 222/C5
Harrisonville, Mo. (64701) 261/D5
Harrisonville, N.J. (08039) 273/C4
Harrisonville, Ohio (45737) 284/F7
Harrisonville, Pa. (17228) 294/F6
Harriston, Ont. 177/D4
Harriston, Miss. (39081) 256/C7
Harristown, Ill. (62537) 222/D4
Harrisville, Ind. (†47390) 227/H4
Harrisville, Mich. (48740) 250/F4
Harrisville, Miss. (39082) 256/D7
Harrisville▵, N.H. (03450) 268/C6
Harrisville, N.H. (03450) 268/C6
Harrisville, N.Y. (13648) 276/K2
Harrisville, Ohio (43974) 284/J5
Harrisville, Pa. (16038) 294/B3
Harrisville, R.I. (02830) 249/H5
Harrisville, Utah (†84401) 304/C2
Harrisville, W. Va. (26362) 313/E4
Harris Wash (creek), Utah 304/C6
Harrod, Ohio (45850) 284/C4
Harrodsburg, Ind. (47434) 227/D6
Harrodsburg, Ky. (40330) 237/M5
Harrods Creek, Ky. (40027) 237/K4
Harrogate, 10/F4
Harrogate, Br. Col. 184/J5
Harrogate, Eng. 13/F4
Harrogate, Tenn. (37752) 237/O8
Harrold, S. Dak. (57536) 298/K4
Harrold, Texas (76364) 302/F3
Harrop (lake), Man. 179/G2
Harrow, 10/B5
Harrow, Ont. 177/B5
Harrow, Vic. 97/A5
Harrowby, Man. 179/A4
Harrowsmith, Ont. 177/H3
Harry Strunk (lake), Nebr. 264/D4
Harsens Island, Mich. (48028) 250/G6
Harshaw, Wis. (54529) 317/G4
Harstad, Norway 18/K2
Hart (lake), Fla. 212/E3
Hart (co.), Ga. 216/G2
Hart (co.), Ky. 237/K6
Hart, Mich. (49420) 250/C5
Hart (lake), Oreg. 291/H5
Hart (mt.), Oreg. 291/H5
Hart, Texas (79043) 302/B3
Hart (riv.), Yukon 187/E3
Hartbees (riv.), S. Africa 118/C5
Hartberg, Austria 41/C3
Harte, Man. 179/C4
Harte (mt.), Man. 179/A2
Hartell, Alta. 182/C4
Hartfield, Va. (23071) 307/R5
Hartford, Ala. (36344) 194/G8
Hartford, Ark. (72938) 203/B3
Hartford (cap.), Conn., 146/L5
Hartford (cap.), Conn., 188/M2
Hartford (co.), Conn. 210/D1
Hartford (cap.), Conn. (*06101) 210/E1
Hartford, Ill. (62048) 222/B6
Hartford, Iowa (50118) 229/G6
Hartford, Kans. (66854) 232/F3
Hartford, Ky. (42347) 237/H6
Hartford▵, Maine (†04221) 242/C7
Hartford, Mich. (49057) 250/C6
Hartford, N.J. (†08057) 273/D4
Hartford, N.Y. (12838) 276/O4
Hartford, Ohio (44424) 284/J3
Hartford (Croton), Ohio (†43013) 284/E5
Hartford, S. Dak. (57033) 298/P6
Hartford, Tenn. (37753) 237/P9
Hartford▵, Vt. (05047) 268/C4
Hartford, Vt. (05047) 268/C4
Hartford, W. Va. (25247) 313/C4
Hartford, Wis. (53027) 317/K9
Hartford City, Ind. (47348) 227/G4
Hartington, Nebr. (68739) 264/G2
Hartland▵, Conn. (†06091) 210/D1
Hartland, Eng. 13/C7
Hartland (pt.), 10/D5
Hartland (pt.), Eng. 13/C6
Hartland▵, Maine (04943) 242/D6
Hartland, Maine (04943) 242/D6
Hartland, Mich. (48029) 250/F6
Hartland, Minn. (56042) 254/E7
Hartland, N. Br. 170/C2
Hartland, N. Dak. (†58725) 283/G3
Hartland▵, Vt. (05047) 268/C4
Hartland, Vt. (05048) 268/C4
Hartland, W. Va. (†25043) 313/D6
Hartland, Wis. (53029) 317/J1
Hartland Four Corners, Vt. (05049) 268/C4
Hartlepool, 10/F3
Hartlepool, Eng. 13/F3
Hartleton, Pa. (17829) 294/H4
Hartley, Iowa (51346) 229/C2
Hartley, Rhod. 118/E3
Hartley (co.), Texas 302/B2
Hartley, Texas (79044) 302/B2
Hartley Bay, Br. Col. 184/C3
Hartleyville, Alta. 182/D5
Hartline, Wash. (99135) 310/F3
Hartly, Del. (19953) 245/R4
Hartman, Ark. (72840) 203/C3
Hartman, Colo. (81043) 208/P6
Hartney, Man. 179/B5
Harts, W. Va. (25524) 313/B6
Harts (pass), Wash. 310/E2
Hartsburg, Ill. (62643) 222/D3
Hartsburg, Mo. (65039) 261/H5
Hartsdale‡, N.Y. (10530) 276/O7
Hartsel, Colo. (80449) 208/H4
Hartselle, Ala. (35640) 194/E2
Hartsfield, Ga. (31756) 216/E8
Hartsgrove, Ohio (†44085) 284/J2
Hartshorn, Mo. (65479) 261/J8
Hartshorne, Okla. (74547) 288/R5
Harts Range, Aust. 88/E4
Harts Range, No. Terr. 93/D7
Hartstown, Pa. (16131) 294/B2
Hartsville, Ind. (47244) 227/F6
Hartsville, Mass. (†01230) 249/B4
Hartsville, S.C. (29550) 296/G3
Hartsville, Tenn. (37074) 237/J8
Hartville, Mo. (65667) 261/G8
Hartville, Ohio (44632) 284/H4
Hartville, Wyo. (82215) 319/H3
Hartwell, Ga. (30643) 216/G2
Hartwell (dam), Ga. 216/G2
Hartwell (res.), Ga. 216/G2
Hartwell (dam), S.C. 296/B3
Hartwell (res.), S.C. 296/A3
Hartwick, Iowa (52232) 229/J5
Hartwick, N.Y. (13348) 276/K5
Harty, Ont. 177/J5
Harug el Asued, El (mts.), Libya 111/C2
Haruniye, Turkey 63/G4
Harvard (mt.), Colo. 208/G5
Harvard, Idaho (83834) 220/B3
Harvard, Ill. (60033) 222/E1
Harvard, Iowa (†50008) 229/G7
Harvard▵, Mass. (01451) 249/H2
Harvard, Nebr. (68944) 264/F4
Harvel, Ill. (62538) 222/D4
Harvest, Ala. (35749) 194/E1
Harvey, Ill. (60426) 222/B2
Harvey, Iowa (50119) 229/H6
Harvey (co.), Kans. 232/E3
Harvey, La. (70058) 238/O4
Harvey, N. Br. 170/F3
Harvey, N. Br. 170/C3
Harvey (lake), N. Br. 170/C3
Harvey (mt.), N. Br. 170/D3
Harvey, N. Dak. (58341) 283/L4
Harvey, W. Aust. 92/A2
Harvey, W. Va. (25852) 313/D7
Harvey Cedars, N.J. (08008) 273/E4
Harveys (lake), Vt. 268/C3
Harveysburg, Ohio (45032) 284/C7
Harveys Lake, Pa. (18618) 294/K3
Harveyton, Ky. (†41718) 237/P6
Harveyville, Kans. (66431) 232/F3
Harviell, Mo. (63945) 261/M9
Harwich, 10/G5
Harwich, Eng. 13/J6
Harwich▵, Mass. (02645) 249/O6
Harwich, Mass. (02645) 249/O6
Harwich Port, Mass. (02646) 249/O6
Harwill, Man. 179/E3
Harwinton▵, Conn. (06790) 210/C1
Harwood, Ont. 177/F3
Harwood, Mo. (64750) 261/D7
Harwood, N. Dak. (58042) 283/S6
Harwood, Texas (78632) 302/G8
Harwood Heights, Ill. (60656) 222/B1
Harwood Island, N.S.W. 97/G1
Haryana (state), India 68/D3
Harz (mts.), E. Ger. 22/D3
Harz (mts.), W. Ger. 22/D3
Harzgerode, E. Ger. 22/D3
Hasa, Wadi (dry riv.), Jordan 65/E5
Hasan Daği (mt.), Turkey 63/E3
Hasbrouck Heights, N.J. (07604) 273/B2
Hase (riv.), W. Ger. 22/B2
Haseke (prov.), Syria 63/J4
Haselünne, W. Ger. 22/B2
Hasenkamp, Arg. 143/F5
Hashtadan (reg.), Iran 66/M3
Hashtpar, Iran 66/F2
Haskeir (isls.), Scot. 15/A4
Haskell, Ark. (72062) 203/E4
Haskell (co.), Kans. 232/B4
Haskell (co.), Okla. 288/R4
Haskell, Okla. (74436) 288/P3
Haskell (co.), Texas 302/E4
Haskell, Texas (79521) 302/E4
Haskins, Iowa (†52201) 229/K6
Haskins, Ohio (43525) 284/C3
Haslach an der Muhl, Austria 41/C2
Hasle, Den. 21/F8
Haslemere, 10/F5

Hirsch 375

Henley Harbour, Newf. 166/C3
Henley on Klip, S. Africa 118/H7
Henley-on-Thames, Eng. 13/F6
Henlopen (cape), Del. 245/T5
Henne, Den. 21/B6
Hennebont, France 28/B4
Hennef, W. Ger. 22/B3
Hennepin, Ill. (61327) 222/D2
Hennepin (co.), Minn. 254/E5
Hennepin, Okla. (73046) 288/M5
Hennessey, Okla. (73742) 288/L2
Hennigsdorf, E. Ger. 22/E3
Henniker▵, N.H. (03242) 268/D5
Henniker, N.H. (03242) 268/D5
Henning, Ill. (61848) 222/F3
Henning, Minn. (56551) 254/C4
Henning, Tenn. (38041) 237/B9
Henribourg, Sask. 181/F2
Henrico (co.), Va. 307/O6
Henrietta, Mo. (64036) 261/E4
Henrietta, N.Y. (14467) 276/E4
Henrietta, Texas (76365) 302/F4
Henrietta-Avondale, N.C. (28076) 281/F4
Henrietta Maria (cape), 163/H4
Henrietta Maria (cape), Ont. 175/D1
Henriette, Minn. (55036) 254/E5
Henrieville, Utah (84736) 304/C6
Henrique de Carvalho, Angola 115/D5
Henrique de Carvalho, 102/E5
Henry (co.), Ala. 194/H7
Henry (co.), Ga. 216/D4
Henry, Idaho (†83230) 220/G7
Henry (co.), Ill. 222/C2
Henry, Ill. (61537) 222/D2
Henry (co.), Ind. 227/G5
Henry (co.), Iowa 229/K6
Henry (co.), Ky. 237/L4
Henry (co.), Mo. 261/E6
Henry (isl.), N.S. 169/G3
Henry, Nebr. (69349) 264/A2
Henry (co.), Ohio 284/B3
Henry, S.C. (†29554) 296/J4
Henry, S. Dak. (57243) 298/P4
Henry (co.), Tenn. 237/E8
Henry, Tenn. (38231) 237/E8
Henry (mts.), Utah 304/D6
Henry (co.), Va. 307/J7
Henry, Va. (24102) 307/J7
Henry (cape), Va. 307/R7
Henryetta, Okla. (74437) 288/O4
Henry House, Alta. 182/B3
Henry Kater (cape), N.W.T. 187/M3
Henrys (lake), Idaho 220/G5
Henrys Fork, Snake (riv.), Idaho 220/G5
Henrys Fork, Green (riv.), Wyo. 319/C4
Henryton, Md. (21080) 245/L3
Henryville, Que. 172/D4
Henryville, Ind. (47126) 227/F7
Henryville, Pa. (18332) 294/M3
Henryville, Tenn. (†38483) 237/G10
Hensall, Ont. 177/C4
Hensel, N. Dak. (58241) 283/P2
Henshaw, Ky. (†42459) 237/F5
Hensler, N. Dak. (58547) 283/H5
Hensley, Ark. (72065) 203/F4
Henson (creek), Md. 245/F6
Henty, N.S.W. 97/D4
Henzada, Burma 54/N8
Henzada, Burma 72/B3
Hepburn, Iowa (†51632) 229/C7
Hepburn, Ohio (†43326) 284/D4
Hepburn, Sask. 181/E3
Hephzibah, Ga. (30815) 216/H4
Hepler, Kans. (66746) 232/H4
Heppner, Oreg. (97836) 291/H2
Hepworth, Ont. 177/C3
Hepzibah, W. Va. (26369) 313/F4
Herald, Calif. (95638) 204/C9
Herat, Afghan., 54/K6
Herat, Afgh. 59/H3
Herat, Afgh. 68/A2
Herauabad, Iran 66/F2
Hérault (dept.), France 28/E6
Hérault (riv.), France 28/E6
Herbert, Ala. (†36401) 194/E8
Herbert, Sask. 181/D5
Herbert Hoover Nat'l Hist. Site, Iowa 229/L5
Herbes (isl.), Ala. 194/B10
Herbeumont, Belg. 27/G9
Herb Lake, Man. 179/H3
Herborn, W. Ger. 22/C3
Herbst, Ind. (†46952) 227/F3
Herbster, Wis. (54844) 317/D2
Hercegnovi, Yugo. 45/D4
Herchmer, 163/G4
Herchmer, Man. 179/K2
Herculaneum, Mo. (63048) 261/M6
Hercules, Alta. 182/D3
Hercules, Calif. (94547) 204/J1
Herd, Okla. (†74056) 288/O1
Heredia, C. Rica 154/E5
Hereford, Ariz. (85615) 198/E7
Hereford, Colo. (80732) 208/L1
Hereford, 10/E4
Hereford, Eng. 13/E5
Hereford, Md. (†21111) 245/M2
Hereford (inlet), N.J. 273/D5
Hereford, Oreg. (97837) 291/K3
Hereford, Pa. (18056) 294/L5
Hereford, S. Dak. (57743) 298/D5
Hereford, Texas (79045) 302/B3
Herefordshire (co.), Eng. 13/E5
Hérémence, Switz. 39/D4
Herencia, Spain 33/E3
Herentals, Belg. 27/F6
Heretaunga-Pinehaven, N.Z. 101/C2
Herford, W. Ger. 22/C2
Héricourt, France 28/G4
Heringsdorf, E. Ger. 22/F1
Herington, Kans. (67449) 232/E3
Herisau, Switz. 39/H2
Herkimer, Kans. (66433) 232/F2
Herkimer (co.), N.Y. 276/L4
Herkimer, N.Y. (13350) 276/L4
Herlong, Calif. (96113) 204/E3
Herm (isl.), Chan. Is. 13/E8
Hermagor, Austria 41/B3
Herman, Mich. (49846) 250/A2
Herman, Minn. (56248) 254/B5
Herman, Nebr. (68029) 264/H3
Herman, Pa. (16039) 294/C4
Herman (lake), S. Dak. 298/P5
Hermance, Switz. 39/B4
Herma Ness (prom.), Scot. 15/M2
Hermann, Mo. (65041) 261/K5
Hermannsburg Mission, Aust. 88/E4
Hermannsburg Mission, No. Terr. 93/C7
Hermansverk, Norway 18/E6
Hermansville, Mich. (49847) 250/B3
Hermanus, S. Africa 118/G7
Hermanville, Miss. (39086) 256/C7
Hermidale, N.S.W. 97/D2
Hermil, Leb. 63/G5
Herminie, Pa. (15637) 294/C5
Hermiston, Oreg. (97838) 291/H2
Hermitage, Ark. (71647) 203/F7
Hermitage, Grenada 161/D8
Hermitage, Mo. (65668) 261/F7
Hermitage, Newf. 166/C4
Hermitage (bay), Newf. 166/C4
Hermitage, Tenn. (37076) 237/H8
Hermitage Springs, Tenn. (†37150) 237/K7
Hermite (isls.), Chile 138/F11
Hermleigh, Texas (79526) 302/D5
Hermon, Ill. (†61458) 222/C3
Hermon▵, Maine (†04401) 242/F6
Hermon, N.Y. (13652) 276/K2
Hermon (mt.), Syria 63/F6
Hermosa (peak), Colo. 208/D7
Hermosa, S. Dak. (57744) 298/C6
Hermosa Beach, Calif. (90254) 204/B11
Hermosillo, Mex., 146/G7
Hermosillo, Mex. 150/D2
Hermsdorf, W. Ger. 22/E3
Hernád (riv.), Hung. 41/F2
Hernandarias, Par. 144/E5
Hernández, Arg. 143/F6
Hernandez, N. Mex. (87537) 274/C2
Hernando, Arg. 143/D3
Hernando (co.), Fla. 212/D3
Hernando, Fla. (32642) 212/D3
Hernando, Miss. (38632) 256/E1
Herndon, Ga. (30430) 216/H5
Herndon, Iowa (50121) 229/E5
Herndon, Kans. (67739) 232/B2
Herndon, Ky. (42236) 237/G7
Herndon, Pa. (17830) 294/J4
Herndon, Va. (22070) 307/O3
Herndon, W. Va. (24726) 313/D7
Herne, W. Ger. 22/B3
Herne Bay, Eng. 13/J6
Herning, Den. 18/F8
Herning, Den. 21/B5
Herod, Ga. (†31742) 216/D7
Herod, Ill. (62947) 222/E6
Heroica Caborca, Mex. 150/C1
Heroica Huamantla, Mex. 150/N1
Heroica Nogales, Mex. 150/D1
Heron (lake), Minn. 254/C7
Heron, Mont. (59844) 262/A2
Heron (isl.), N. Br. 170/D1
Heron Bay, Ont. 175/C3
Heron Bay, Ont. 177/H5
Heron Lake, Minn. (56137) 254/C7
Hérouxville, Que. 172/E3
Herradura, Arg. 143/E2
Herreid, S. Dak. (57632) 298/K2
Herrera, Arg. 143/D2
Herrera del Duque, Spain 33/D3
Herrera de Pisuerga, Spain 33/D1
Herrero (pt.), Mex. 150/Q7
Herrick, Ill. (62431) 222/D4
Herrick, S. Dak. (57538) 298/L7
Herrick Center, Pa. (18430) 294/L2
Herricks‡, N.Y. (†11040) 276/R7
Herrin, Ill. (62948) 222/E6
Herring Cove‡, Alaska (†99901) 196/N2
Herring Cove, N.S. 169/E4
Herrings, N.Y. (13653) 276/J2
Herrington (lake), Ky. 237/M5
Herron, Mich. (49744) 250/F3
Herronton, Alta. 182/D4
Hersbruck, W. Ger. 22/D4
Herschel, Sask. 181/C4
Herschel, Yukon 187/E3
Herschel (isl.), Yukon 187/E3
Herscher, Ill. (60941) 222/E2
Herselt, Belg. 27/F6
Hersey, Mich. (49639) 250/D5
Hersey, Wis. (†54027) 317/B6
Hershey, Nebr. (69143) 264/D3
Hershey, Pa. (17033) 294/J5
Hersman, Ill. (62342) 222/C4
Herstal, Belg. 27/H7
Hertel, Wis. (54845) 317/B4
Hertford, 10/G5
Hertford, Eng. 13/G6
Hertford (co.), N.C. 281/P2
Hertford, N.C. (27944) 281/S2
Hertfordshire (co.), Eng. 13/G6
Hervás, Spain 33/D2
Herve, Belg. 27/H7
Hervey (bay), Aust. 88/J4
Hervey (bay), Queens. 95/E5
Herzberg, E. Ger. 22/E3
Herzel, Sask. 181/H4
Herzeliyya, Israel 65/B3
Herzogenbuchsee, Switz. 39/E2
Herzogenburg, Austria 41/C2
Hespeler, Ont. 177/D4
Hesper, Iowa (†52101) 229/K2
Hesper, N. Dak. (†58348) 283/L4
Hesperange, Lux. 27/J9
Hesperia, Calif. (92345) 204/H9
Hesperia, Mich. (49421) 250/D5
Hespero, Alta. 182/C3
Hesperus, Colo. (81326) 208/C8
Hesperus (peak), Colo. 208/C8
Hess, Okla. (†73539) 288/H6
Hess (riv.), Yukon 187/E3
Hesse (state), W. Ger. 22/C3
Hessel, Mich. (49745) 250/E2
Hessmer, La. (71341) 238/F4
Hesston, Kans. (67062) 232/E3
Hesston, Pa. (16647) 294/F5
Hester, La. (70743) 238/L3
Hester, Okla. (†73554) 288/H5
Hesterville, Miss. (†39192) 256/E4
Hetch Hetchy (res.), Calif. 204/F6
Heth, Ark. (72346) 203/K3
Het IJ (est.), Neth. 27/C4
Hetland, S. Dak. (57244) 298/P5
Hettick, Ill. (62649) 222/C4
Hettinger (co.), N. Dak. 283/E7
Hettinger, N. Dak. (58639) 283/E8
Hetton, Eng. 13/F3
Hettstedt, E. Ger. 22/D3
Heusden, Neth. 27/G5
Heuvelton, N.Y. (13654) 276/K1
Heves (co.), Hung. 41/F3
Heves, Hung. 41/F3
Heward, Sask. 181/H6
Hewins, Kans. (67024) 232/F4
Hewitt, Minn. (56453) 254/C4
Hewitt, N.J. (07421) 273/E1
Hewitt‡, Texas (76643) 302/G6
Hewitt, Wis. (54441) 317/F6
Hewitt Landing, Sask. 181/A2
Hewlett, N.Y. (11557) 276/R7
Hewlett Bay Park‡, N.Y. (†11557) 276/R7
Hewlett Harbor, N.Y. (†11557) 276/N9
Hewlett Neck‡, N.Y. (†11557) 276/R7
Hexham, 10/E3
Hexham, Eng. 13/E3
Hext, Texas (76848) 302/E7
Heybeli (isl.), Turkey 63/D6
Heyburn, Idaho (83336) 220/E7
Heyburn (res.), Okla. 288/O3
Heyfield, Vic. 97/D6
Heywood (chan.), Burma 72/B3
Heywood, Vic. 97/A6
Heyworth, Ill. (61745) 222/E3
Hialeah, Fla. (*33010) 212/B4
Hialeah Gardens, Fla. (†33010) 212/B4
Hiattville, Kans. (66747) 232/H4
Hiawassee, Ga. (30546) 216/E1
Hiawatha, Iowa (52233) 229/K4
Hiawatha, Kans. (66434) 232/G2
Hiawatha, Mich. (†49854) 250/C2
Hiawatha, Utah (84527) 304/D4
Hibbard, Ind. (†46511) 227/E2
Hibbing, Minn., 188/H1
Hibbing, Minn. (55746) 254/F3
Hibernia, N.J. (07842) 273/E2
Hibuson (isl.), Phil. 82/E5
Hicacos (pen.), Cuba 158/D1
Hicacos (pt.), Cuba 158/D1
Hickam A.F.B., Hawaii 218/B4
Hickam Housing, Hawaii (96824) 218/B4
Hickman, Ark. (†72315) 203/L2
Hickman, Del. (†21629) 245/R5
Hickman (co.), Ky. 237/C7
Hickman, Ky. (42050) 237/D7
Hickman, Nebr. (68372) 264/H4
Hickman (co.), Tenn. 237/G9
Hickman, Tenn. (38567) 237/K8
Hickman's Harbour, Newf. 166/D2
Hickok, Kans. (†67880) 232/A4
Hickory, Ky. (42051) 237/D7
Hickory, Miss. (39332) 256/F6
Hickory (co.), Mo. 261/F7
Hickory, N.C. (28601) 281/G3
Hickory, Okla. (†73086) 288/N5
Hickory Corners, Mich. (49060) 250/D6
Hickory Creek‡, Texas (†75423) 302/G4
Hickory Flat, Ala. (†36274) 194/H4
Hickory Flat, Miss. (38633) 256/F1
Hickory Grove, S.C. (29717) 296/E2
Hickory Hills, Ill. (60457) 222/B2
Hickory Plains, Ark. (72066) 203/G3
Hickory Ridge, Ark. (72347) 203/J3
Hickory Valley, Tenn. (38042) 237/C10
Hickory Withe, Tenn. (38043) 237/B10
Hickox, Ga. (†31553) 216/H8
Hicks, La. (71437) 238/E4
Hickson, Ont. 177/D4
Hickson, N. Dak. (58044) 283/S6
Hicksville, N.Y. (*11801) 276/R7
Hicksville, Ohio (43526) 284/A3
Hico, La. (†71235) 238/E1
Hico, Texas (76457) 302/F6
Hico, W. Va. (25854) 313/D6
Hida (riv.), Japan 81/H6
Hidalgo, Ill. (62432) 222/E4
Hidalgo (state), Mex. 150/K6
Hidalgo, Mex. 150/K4
Hidalgo (co.), N. Mex. 274/A7
Hidalgo (co.), Texas 302/F11
Hidalgo, Texas (78557) 302/F11
Hidden Hills, Calif. (†91302) 204/B10
Hiddenite, N.C. (28636) 281/G3
Hiddensee (isl.), E. Ger. 22/E1
Hidden Timber, S. Dak. (†69501) 298/J7
Hieflau, Austria 41/C3
Hierro (isl.), Spain 33/A5
Hierro (isl.), Spain 106/A3
Higashiosaka, Japan 81/J8
Higbee, Mo. (65257) 261/H4
Higden, Ark. (72067) 203/F2
Higdon, Ala. (35979) 194/G1
Higganum, Conn. (06441) 210/E2
Higgins (lake), Mich. 250/E4
Higgins, Texas (79046) 302/D1
Higgins Lake, Mich. (48627) 250/E4
Higginson, Ark. (72068) 203/G3
Higginsport, Ohio (45131) 284/C8
Higginsville, Mo. (64037) 261/E4
Higginsville, W. Va. (†25437) 313/J4
Higgston, Ga. (30410) 216/G6
High, Iowa (†52203) 229/K5
High (isl.), Ire. 17/A4
High (isl.), Mich. 250/D3
High Atlas (ranges), Mor. 106/C2
High Bluff, Man. 179/D4
High Bridge, Ky. (40333) 237/M5
High Bridge, N.J. (08829) 273/D2
High Bridge, Wis. (54846) 317/E3
Highbury, W. Aust. 92/B2
Highfalls, N.C. (27259) 281/K4
High Falls, N.Y. (12440) 276/M7
Highfield, Md. (21753) 245/J2
Highfield‡, Pa. (†16045) 294/C4
Highfill, Ark. (†72734) 203/B1
Highgate, Jam. 158/J6
Highgate, Ont. 177/C5
Highgate, Sask. 181/C3
Highgate▵, Vt. (†05459) 268/B2
Highgate Center, Vt. (05459) 268/B2
Highgate Falls, Vt. (†05459) 268/A2
Highgate Springs, Vt. (05460) 268/A2
Highgrove, Calif. (92507) 204/E10
High Hill, Mo. (63350) 261/K5
High Hill, Sask. 181/H3
High Island, Texas (77623) 302/K8
Highland, Calif. (92346) 204/H9
Highland (lake), Conn. 210/C1
Highland (pt.), Fla. 212/E6
Highland, Ill. (62249) 222/D5
Highland, Ind. (46322) 227/B1
Highland, Kans. (66035) 232/G2
Highland (lake), N.H. 268/C5
Highland, N.Y. (12528) 276/M7
Highland (peak), Nev. 266/G5
Highland (co.), Ohio 284/C7
Highland, Ohio (45132) 284/C7
Highland‡, Texas (†75067) 302/G4
Highland (co.), Va. 307/J4
Highland, W. Va. (26371) 313/D4
Highland, Wis. (53543) 317/F9
Highland Beach, Fla. (33444) 212/F5
Highland Beach, Md. (†21401) 245/M5
Highland Center, Iowa (52564) 229/J6
Highland City, Fla. (33846) 212/E4
Highland Falls, N.Y. (10928) 276/M8
Highland Heights, Ky. (41076) 237/T3
Highland Heights, Ohio (†44143) 284/J9
Highland Home, Ala. (36041) 194/F7
Highland Lake‡, Ala. (†35013) 194/F3
Highland Lake, Maine (†04082) 242/C8
Highland Park, Alta. 182/A1
Highland Park, Conn. (†06040) 210/F1
Highland Park, Fla. (32401) 212/E4
Highland Park, Ill. (60035) 222/F1
Highland Park, Mich. (48203) 250/B6
Highland Park, N.J. (08904) 273/D2
Highland Park, Pa. (†17044) 294/H4
Highland Park‡, Pa. (†18042) 294/M4
Highland Park, Texas (†75201) 302/G2
Highlands (co.), Fla. 212/E4
Highlands, N.C. (28741) 281/C4
Highlands, N.J. (07732) 273/F3
Highlands, Texas (77562) 302/K1
Highland Springs, Va. (23075) 307/O5
Highlandville, Iowa (52149) 229/K2
Highlandville, Mo. (65669) 261/F9
High Level, Alta. 182/A5
Highley Heights‡, Mo. (†63601) 261/L7
Highmore, S. Dak. (57345) 298/L4
High Mountain Sheep (res.), Idaho 220/B4
High Mountain Sheep (res.), Oreg. 291/L2
Highpine, Maine (†04090) 242/B9
High Plateaus (ranges), Alg. 106/D2
High Point, Fla. (†33515) 212/B3
Highpoint, Miss. (†39339) 256/F4
High Point, Mo. (65042) 261/G5
High Point, N.C., 188/K3
High Point, N.C. (*27260) 281/J3
High Point (mt.), N.J. 273/D1
High Point, Sask. 181/D5
High Prairie, Alta. 182/B2
Highridge, Alta. 182/D2
High Ridge, Mo. (63049) 261/O4
High River, 163/E5
High River, Alta. 182/D4
High Rock, N.C. (27239) 281/J3
High Rock (lake), N.C. 281/J3
High Rock (creek), Nev. 266/B1
High Rolls Mountain Park, N. Mex. (88325) 274/D5
High Shoals, N.C. (28077) 281/G4
High Spire, Pa. (17034) 294/J5
Highsplint, Ky. (40841) 237/P7
High Springs, Fla. (32643) 212/D2
High Tatra (range), Poland 47/D4
Hightower, Ala. (†36264) 194/H3
Hightown, Va. (24444) 307/J4
Hightstown, N.J. (08520) 273/D3
Highvale, Alta. 182/C3
Highview, Sask. 181/J6
Highway, Alta. 182/C3
Highway, Ky. (†42602) 237/L7
High Willhays (mt.), Eng. 13/C7
Highwood (riv.), Alta. 182/C4
Highwood, Ill. (60040) 222/B1
Highwood, Mont. (59450) 262/F3
High Wycombe, 10/F5
High Wycombe, Eng. 13/G6
Higley, Ariz. (85236) 198/D5
Higuerote, Ven. 124/F2
Hiiumaa (isl.), U.S.S.R. 48/C4
Hiiumaa (isl.), U.S.S.R. 52/B3
Hiiumaa (isl.), U.S.S.R. 53/B1
Hiiumaa (isl.), U.S.S.R., 7/G3
Híjar, Spain 33/F2
Hijuelas, Chile 138/F2
Hiko, Nev. (89017) 266/F5
Hikone, Japan 81/H6
Hikueru (atoll), Fr. Poly., 87/M7
Hikurangi, N.Z. 101/E1
Hikurangi (mt.), N.Z. 101/G2
Hiland, Wyo. (82638) 319/E2
Hiland Park, Fla. (32401) 212/C6
Hilbert, Wis. (54129) 317/K7
Hilbre, Man. 179/D3
Hilda, Alta. 182/E4
Hilda, S.C. (29813) 296/E5
Hildburghausen, E. Ger. 22/D3
Hildebran, N.C. (28637) 281/F3
Hildebrand, Oreg. (†97625) 291/F5
Hilden, N.S. 169/E3
Hildesheim, W. Ger. 22/D2
Hildreth, Nebr. (68947) 264/E4
Hiles, Wis. (54533) 317/J4
Hilgard (mt.), Utah 304/C5
Hilger, Mont. (59451) 262/G3
Hilham, Tenn. (38568) 237/L8
Hill (riv.), Minn. 254/C3
Hill (co.), Mont. 262/F2
Hill▵, N.H. (03243) 268/D4
Hill (co.), Texas 302/G5
Hill (creek), Utah 304/E4
Hilla, Iraq 59/D3
Hilla (prov.), Iraq 66/D4
Hilla, Iraq 66/D4
Hillaby (mt.), Barb. 161/B8
Hill A.F.B., Utah 304/C2
Hillandale, Md. (†20901) 245/F4
Hillandale, Sask. 181/D6
Hill Bank, Br. Hond. 154/C2
Hillburn, N.Y. (10931) 276/M8
Hill City, Idaho (83337) 220/D6
Hill City, Kans. (67642) 232/C2
Hill City, Minn. (55748) 254/E4
Hill City, S. Dak. (57745) 298/B6
Hill Country Village‡, Texas (†78201) 302/F8
Hill Creek Ext., Uintah and Ouray Ind. Res., Utah 304/E4
Hillcrest, Alta. 182/C5
Hillcrest, Ill. (61244) 222/D2
Hillcrest, N.J. (07502) 273/C2
Hillcrest‡, N.Y. (†10977) 276/M8
Hillcrest‡, Pa. (15102) 294/B3
Hill Crest‡, Texas (†77511) 302/J2
Hillcrest Heights, Fla. (†33827) 212/E4
Hillcrest Heights, Md. (†20001) 245/F5
Hilldale, Utah (†84767) 304/B6
Hillegom, Neth. 27/E4
Hillemann, Ark. (†72101) 203/H3
Hill End, N.S.W. 97/E3
Hiller‡, Pa. (15444) 294/C6
Hillerød, Den. 18/H9
Hillerød, Den. 21/F6
Hillers (mt.), Utah 304/D6
Hillery-Batestown‡, Ill. (†61832) 222/F3
Hillesden, Sask. 181/J5
Hillham, Ind. (†47432) 227/D7
Hillhead, S. Dak. (†57270) 298/O2
Hillhouse, Miss. (38747) 256/C2
Hillhouse Addition‡, Mo. (†65556) 261/H7
Hilliard, Alta. 182/D3
Hilliard, Fla. (32046) 212/E1
Hilliard, Ohio (43026) 284/D5
Hilliards, Pa. (16040) 294/C3
Hilliardville, Fla. (†32327) 212/B1
Hillingdon, 10/B5
Hillis‡, N.Y. (†12601) 276/N7
Hillisburg, Ind. (46046) 227/E4
Hill Island (lake), N.W.T. 187/H3
Hillman, Mich. (49746) 250/F3
Hillman, Minn. (56338) 254/E4
Hillmond, Sask. 181/B2
Hillrose, Colo. (80733) 208/N2
Hills, Iowa (52235) 229/K5
Hills, Minn. (56138) 254/B7
Hills and Dales‡, Ohio (†44701) 284/G4
Hillsboro, Ala. (35643) 194/D1
Hillsboro, Ga. (31038) 216/E4
Hillsboro, Ill. (62049) 222/D4
Hillsboro, Ind. (47949) 227/C4
Hillsboro, Iowa (52630) 229/K7
Hillsboro, Kans. (67063) 232/E3
Hillsboro, Ky. (41049) 237/O4
Hillsboro, Md. (21641) 245/P5
Hillsboro, Miss. (39087) 256/E6
Hillsboro, Mo. (63050) 261/L6
Hillsboro, N. Dak. (58045) 283/S5
Hillsboro (co.), N.H. 268/D6
Hillsboro▵, N.H. (03244) 268/D5
Hillsboro, N.H. (03244) 208/D5
Hillsboro, N. Mex. (88042) 274/B6
Hillsboro, Ohio (45133) 284/C7
Hillsboro, Oreg. (97123) 291/A2
Hillsboro, Tenn. (37342) 237/K10
Hillsboro, Texas (76645) 302/G5
Hillsboro, Va. (22132) 307/N2
Hillsboro, W. Va. (24946) 313/F6
Hillsboro, Wis. (54634) 317/F8
Hillsboro Beach, Fla. (†33060) 212/F5
Hillsboro Lower Village, N.H. (†03244) 268/D5
Hillsborough‡, Calif. (94010) 204/J2
Hillsborough (co.), Fla. 212/D4
Hillsborough (bay), Fla. 212/C3
Hillsborough (canal), Fla. 212/F5
Hillsborough (riv.), Fla. 212/C2
Hillsborough, N. Br. 170/F3
Hillsborough, N.C. (27278) 281/L2
Hillsborough, N. Ire. 17/J3
Hillsborough (bay), P.E.I. 169/E2
Hillsboro Upper Village, N.H. (†03244) 268/D5
Hillsburgh, Ont. 177/D4
Hillsburn, N.S. 169/C4
Hills Creek (res.), Oreg. 291/E4
Hillsdale, Ont. 177/E3
Hillsdale, Ill. (61257) 222/C2
Hillsdale, Ind. (47854) 227/C5
Hillsdale, Kans. (66036) 232/H3
Hillsdale (co.), Mich. 250/E7
Hillsdale, Mich. (49242) 250/E7
Hillsdale‡, Mo. (†63101) 261/P3
Hillsdale, N. Br. 170/E3
Hillsdale, N.J. (07642) 273/B1
Hillsdale, N.Y. (12529) 276/O6
Hillsdale, Okla. (73743) 288/K1
Hillsdale, Pa. (15746) 294/E4
Hillsdale, Wis. (54744) 317/C5
Hillsdale, Wyo. (82060) 319/H4
Hillsgrove, Pa. (18619) 294/J3
Hillsgrove, R.I. (†02887) 249/J6
Hillside, Ariz. (†86301) 198/B4
Hillside, Colo. (81232) 208/H6
Hillside, Ill. (60162) 222/A2
Hillside▵, N.J. (07205) 273/B2
Hillside, S. Dak. (†57328) 298/N7
Hillside Beach, Man. 179/F4
Hill Spring, Alta. 182/D5
Hillston, Aust. 88/G6
Hillston, N.S.W. 97/C3
Hillsview, S. Dak. (†57437) 298/L2
Hillsville, Pa. (16132) 294/A4
Hillsville, Va. (24343) 307/G7
Hillswick, Scot. 15/M2
Hilltonia, Ga. (30467) 216/J5
Hilltop, Ariz. (†85632) 198/F6
Hilltop‡, Minn. (†55401) 254/G5
Hilltown, N. Ire. 17/J3
Hillview, Ill. (62050) 222/C4
Hillview, Minn. (†56477) 254/C4
Hillview, Newf. 166/D2
Hilmar, Calif. (95324) 204/E6
Hilo, Hawaii, 87/L4
Hilo, Hawaii 188/G6
Hilo, Hawaii (96720) 218/J5
Hilo (bay), Hawaii 218/J5
Hilongos, Phil. 82/E5
Hilshire Village, Texas (†77001) 302/J1
Hilt, Calif. (96043) 204/C2
Hilton, Ga. (31758) 216/C8
Hilton, Man. 179/C5
Hilton, N.Y. (14468) 276/E4
Hilton Beach, Ont. 177/J5
Hilton Head (isl.), S.C. 296/F7
Hilton Head Island, S.C. (29928) 296/F7
Hilton Inlet (bay), Ant. 5/B16
Hiltons, Va. (24258) 307/D7
Hilvan, Turkey 63/H4
Hilvarenbeek, Neth. 27/G6
Hilversum, Neth. 27/G4
Hima, Ky. (40951) 237/O6
Himachal Pradesh (state), India 68/D2
Himalaya (mts.), 54/L6
Himalaya (mts.), China 77/BD6
Himalaya (mts.), India 68/D2
Himalaya (mts.), Nepal 68/D2
Himanka, Fin. 18/N5
Himeji, Japan 81/G6
Himi, Japan 81/H5
Himlerville (Beauty), Ky. (†41203) 237/S5
Himrod, N.Y. (14842) 276/F5
Himyar, Ky. (40952) 237/O7
Hinatuan, Phil. 82/F6
Hinchcliff, Miss. (†38646) 256/D2
Hinche, Haiti 156/D3
Hinche, Haiti 158/C5
Hinchinbrook (isl.), Alaska 196/D1
Hinchinbrook (isl.), Aust. 88/H3
Hinchinbrook (isl.), Queens. 95/C3
Hinchinbrook Entrance (chan.), Alaska 196/J3
Hinchliffe, Sask. 181/J3
Hinckley, 10/F4
Hinckley, Eng. 13/F5
Hinckley, Ill. (60520) 222/E2
Hinckley, Maine (04944) 242/D6
Hinckley, Minn. (55037) 254/E4
Hinckley, N.Y. (13352) 276/K4
Hinckley (res.), N.Y. 276/K4
Hinckley, Ohio (44233) 284/G3
Hinckley, Utah (84635) 304/B4
Hindarabi (isl.), Iran 66/H7
Hindeloopen, Neth. 27/G3
Hinderwell, Eng. 13/G3
Hindiya, Iraq 66/C4
Hindman, Ky. (41822) 237/R6
Hindmarsh, Aust. 88/D7
Hindmarsh, S. Aust. 94/A7
Hindmarsh (lake), Vic. 97/A5
Hindon, Eng. 13/E6
Hinds (co.), Miss. 256/D6
Hinds, N.Z. 101/C6
Hindsboro, Ill. (61930) 222/E4
Hindsville, Ark. (72738) 203/C1
Hindubagh, Pak. 68/B2
Hindu Kush (mts.), 54/K6
Hindu Kush (mts.), Afgh. 59/J2
Hindu Kush (mts.), Afgh. 68/B1
Hindu Kush (mts.), Pak. 68/B1
Hindupur, India 68/D6
Hi-Nella, N.J. (†08083) 273/B4
Hines, Minn. (56647) 254/D3
Hines, Oreg. (97738) 291/H4
Hinesburg▵, Vt. (05461) 268/A3
Hinesburg, Vt. (05461) 268/A3
Hines Creek, 163/E4
Hines Creek, Alta. 182/A1
Hineston, La. (71438) 238/E4
Hinesville, Ga. (31313) 216/J7
Hinganghat, India 68/D4
Hingham▵, Mass. (02043) 249/E8
Hingham (bay), Mass. 249/E7
Hingham, Mont. (59528) 262/F2
Hingham, Wis. (53031) 317/K8
Hingi, China 77/G6
Hingoli, India 68/D5
Hinigaran, Phil. 82/D5
Hinis, Turkey 63/J3
Hinkley, Calif. (92347) 204/H9
Hinkston (creek), Ky. 237/N4
Hinlopen (str.), Norway 18/C1
Hinnerup, Den. 21/D5
Hinnøy (isl.), Norway 18/K2
Hinojosa del Duque, Spain 33/D3
Hinsdale (co.), Colo. 208/E7
Hinsdale, Ill. (60521) 222/A2
Hinsdale▵, Mass. (01235) 249/B3
Hinsdale, Mont. (59241) 262/K2
Hinsdale▵, N.H. (03451) 268/C6
Hinsdale, N.H. (03451) 268/C6
Hinsdale, N.Y. (14743) 276/D6
Hinson, Fla. (†32333) 212/B1
Hinsonton, Ga. (31779) 216/D8
Hinterrhein, Switz. 39/H3
Hinterrhein (riv.), Switz. 39/H3
Hinton, Alta. 182/B3
Hinton, Iowa (51024) 229/A3
Hinton, Mo. (†65201) 261/H4
Hinton, Okla. (73047) 288/K4
Hinton, W. Va. (25951) 313/E7
Hintonville, Miss. (†39462) 256/F8
Hinwil, Switz. 39/G2
Hinze, Miss. (†39108) 256/F4
Hippolytushoef, Neth. 27/G3
Hirakata, Japan 81/J7
Hiram, Ga. (30141) 216/C3
Hiram, Ky. (†40823) 237/P7
Hiram▵, Maine (04041) 242/B8
Hiram, Maine (04041) 242/B8
Hiram, Mo. (63967) 261/M8
Hiram, Ohio (44234) 284/H3
Hiran (prov.), Somalia 115/J3
Hirara, Ryukyu Is. 81/L7
Hirata, Japan 81/F6
Hiratsuka, Japan 81/O3
Hîrlău, Rum. 45/H2
Hiroo, Japan 81/L2
Hirosaki, Japan 81/K3
Hiroshima, Japan, 54/S6
Hiroshima (pref.), Japan 81/E6
Hiroshima, Japan 81/E6
Hirsch, Sask. 181/J6

Huntington Bay 377

Hopwood, Pa. (15445) 294/C6
Hoquiam, Wash., 188/B1
Hoquiam, Wash. (98550) 310/A3
Horace, Kans. (†67879) 232/A3
Horace, N. Dak. (58047) 283/S6
Horasan, Turkey 63/K2
Horatio, Ark. (71842) 203/B6
Horatio, S.C. (29062) 296/F3
Horažďovice, Czech. 41/B2
Horche, Spain 33/E2
Horconcitos, Pan. 154/F6
Hordaland (co.), Norway 18/E6
Hordio, Somalia 115/K1
Hordville, Nebr. (68846) 264/G3
Horgen, Switz. 39/G2
Horice, Czech. 41/C1
Horicon, Wis. (53032) 317/J9
Horine, Mo. (†63070) 261/M6
Horizon, Sask. 181/F6
Hormigüeros, P. Rico 161/A2
Hormuz, Iran 66/J7
Hormuz (isl.), Iran 66/K7
Hormuz (str.), Iran 66/K7
Horn (cape), 3/F8
Horn, Austria 41/C2
Horn (cape), Chile, 120/D8
Horn (cape), Chile 138/F11
Horn (cape), Ice. 21/B1
Horn (head), Ire. 17/E1
Horn (isl.), Miss. 256/G10
Horn (mts.), N.W.T. 187/G3
Horn (riv.), N.W.T. 187/G3
Horn, W. Ger. 22/C3
Hornád (riv.), Czech. 41/F2
Hornaday (riv.), N.W.T. 187/F3
Hornafjördhur (fjord), Ice., 7/C2
Hornafjördhur (fjord), Ice. 21/D1
Horná Štubňa, Czech. 41/E2
Hornbeak, Tenn. (38232) 237/C8
Hornbeck, La. (71439) 238/D4
Hornbrook, Calif. (96044) 204/C2
Hornby (bay), N.W.T. 187/G3
Hornby, N.Z. 101/D5
Hornby Island, Br. Col. 184/H2
Horncastle, 10/F4
Horncastle, Eng. 13/G4
Horndean, Man. 179/E5
Hornell, N.Y. (14843) 276/E6
Hornepayne, Ont. 175/C3
Hornepayne, Ont. 177/J5
Horner, W. Va. (26372) 313/F5
Hornerstown, N.J. (†08514) 273/E3
Hornersville, Mo. (63855) 261/M10
Horní Benešov, Czech. 41/D2
Hornick, Iowa (51026) 229/A4
Horní Libina, Czech. 41/D2
Hornings Mills, Ont. 177/D3
Hornitos, Calif. (95325) 204/E6
Horn Lake, Miss. (38637) 256/D1
Hornli (mt.), Switz. 39/G2
Hornos (Horn) (cape), Chile, 120/D8
Hornos, Falso (cape), Chile 138/F11
Hornsby, N.S.W. 97/J3
Hornsby, Tenn. (38044) 237/D10
Hornsea, 10/F4
Hornsea, Eng. 13/G4
Hornslandet (pen.), Sweden 18/K6
Hornslet, Den. 21/D5
Hornsund (bay), Norway 18/C2
Horntown, Va. (23395) 307/T5
Hornu, Belg. 27/D8
Hornum, Den. 21/C4
Horod, Man. 179/B4
Hořovice, Czech. 41/C2
Horqueta, Par. 144/D4
Horry (co.), S.C. 296/J4
Horse (lake), Calif. 204/E3
Horse (creek), Colo. 208/M5
Horse (creek), Fla. 212/E4
Horse (isls.), Newf. 166/C3
Horse (creek), Oreg. 291/F3
Horse (creek), Wyo. 319/B3
Horse (creek), Wyo. 319/H4
Horse Branch, Ky. (42349) 237/H6
Horse Cave, Ky. (42749) 237/K6
Horse Chops (chan.), Newf. 166/D2
Horse Creek, Calif. (96045) 204/C2
Horse Creek (res.), Colo. 208/N6
Horse Creek, Sask. 181/E6
Horse Creek, Wyo. (82061) 319/G4
Horsefly, Br. Col. 184/G4
Horsefly (lake), Br. Col. 184/G4
Horsehead (lake), N. Dak. 283/L5
Horsehead (creek), S. Dak. 298/C7
Horse Head, Sask. 181/C2
Horseheads, N.Y. (14845) 276/G6
Horse Islands, Newf. 166/C3
Horsens, Den. 18/F9
Horsens, Den. 21/C6
Horsens (fjord), Den. 21/D6
Horseshoe (lake), Ariz. 198/D5
Horse Shoe (pt.), St. Chr.-N.-A. 161/C11
Horseshoe (pt.), Fla. 212/C2
Horseshoe (lake), Man. 179/G2
Horseshoe (creek), Wyo. 319/G3
Horseshoe Beach, Fla. (32648) 212/C2
Horseshoe Bend, Ark. (72536) 203/G1
Horseshoe Bend, Idaho (83629) 220/B6
Horseshoe Bend Nat'l Mil. Park, Ala. 194/G5
Horseshoe Lake, Ont. 177/E2
Horse Shoe Run, W. Va. (26769) 313/G4
Horse Springs, N. Mex. (87822) 274/A5
Horsetooth (res.), Colo. 208/J1
Horsham, 10/F5
Horsham, Aust. 88/G7
Horsham, Eng. 13/G6
Horsham, Sask. 181/B5
Horsham, Vic. 97/B5
Hørsholm, Den. 21/F6
Horšovský Týn, Czech. 41/B2
Horst, Neth. 27/H6
Hortaleza, Spain 33/G4
Horten, Norway 18/D4
Hortens (fjord), Norway 18/G4
Hortense, Ga. (31543) 216/J8
Horton, Ala. (35980) 194/F2
Horton, Iowa (†50677) 229/J3
Horton, Kans. (66439) 232/G2
Horton, Man. 179/B5
Horton, Mich. (49246) 250/E6
Horton, Mo. (64751) 261/D7
Horton (riv.), N.S.W. 97/F2
Horton (riv.), N.W.T. 187/F3
Horton, Oreg. (97448) 291/D3
Horton Bay, Mich. (†49712) 250/D3
Hortonia (lake), Vt. 268/A4
Hortonville, Ind. (†46069) 227/E4
Hortonville, Mass. (†02777) 249/K5
Hortonville, Wis. (54944) 317/J7
Hørve, Den. 21/E6
Hoschton, Ga. (30548) 216/E2
Hosenofu (well), Libya 111/D3
Hosford, Fla. (32334) 212/B1
Hoshab, Pak. 59/H4
Hoshab, Pak. 68/A3
Hoshangabad, India 68/D4
Hoskins, Nebr. (68740) 264/G2
Hosmer, Br. Col. 184/K5
Hosmer, S. Dak. (57448) 298/L2
Hospental, Switz. 39/F3
Hospers, Iowa (51238) 229/B2
Hospet, India 68/D5
Hospital, Chile 138/G4
Hospital, Ire. 17/E7
Hospitalet, Spain 33/H2
Hosseina, Eth. 111/G6
Hosston, La. (71043) 238/C1
Hoste (isl.), Chile, 120/D8
Hoste (isl.), Chile 138/F11
Hostinné, Czech. 41/C1
Hot, Thai. 72/C3
Hotagen, Sweden 18/J5
Hotchkiss, Alta. 182/B1
Hotchkiss, Colo. (81419) 208/D5
Hotchkissville, Conn. (†06798) 210/C2
Hot Creek (range), Nev. 266/E4
Hot Creek (valley), Nev. 266/E4
Hotevilla, Ariz. (86030) 198/E3
Hotham (inlet), Alaska 196/F1
Hotham (riv.), Aust. 88/B2
Hotien (Khotan), China 77/A4
Hoting, Sweden 18/K4
Hot Lake, Oreg. (†97850) 291/K2
Hotso, China 77/F5
Hot Spring (co.), Ark. 203/E5
Hot Springs, Mont. (59845) 262/B3
Hot Springs, N.C. (28743) 281/D3
Hot Springs (Truth or Consequences), N. Mex. (87901) 274/B5
Hot Springs, S. Dak., 188/F2
Hot Springs, S. Dak. (57747) 298/C7
Hot Springs, Va. (24445) 307/J4
Hot Springs (co.), Wyo. 319/D2
Hot Springs Cove, Br. Col. 184/D5
Hot Springs National Park, Ark., 188/H4
Hot Springs National Park, Ark. (71901) 203/D4
Hot Springs Nat'l Park, Ark. 203/D4
Hot Sulphur Springs, Colo. (80451) 208/H2
Hottah (lake), 163/E2
Hottah (lake), N.W.T. 187/G3
Hottentot (bay), S.W. Afr. 118/A5
Hou, Nam (riv.), Laos 72/D2
Houck, Ariz. (86506) 198/F3
Houcktown, Ohio (†45840) 284/C4
Houei Sai, Laos 72/D2
Houffalize, Belg. 27/H8
Houghton, Iowa (52631) 229/K7
Houghton, Maine (†04275) 242/B6
Houghton, Mich., 188/J1
Houghton (co.), Mich. 250/G1
Houghton, Mich. (49931) 250/G1
Houghton (lake), Mich. 250/E4
Houghton, N.Y. (14744) 276/D6
Houghton, S. Dak. (57449) 298/N2
Houghton Lake, Mich. (48629) 250/E4
Houghton Lake Heights, Mich. (48630) 250/E4
Houhoek, S. Africa 118/F7
Houlka, Miss. (38850) 256/G2
Houlton, Maine, 188/N1
Houlton△, Maine (04730) 242/H3
Houlton, Maine (04730) 242/H3
Houlton, Wis. (†55082) 317/A5
Houma, La. (70360) 238/J7
Houndé, Upp. Volta 106/D6
Hounslow, 10/B5
Hourn (inlet), Scot. 15/F5
Housatonic (riv.), Conn. 210/C3
Housatonic, Mass. (01236) 249/A3
Housatonic (riv.), Mass. 249/A4
House (mt.), Alta. 182/C2
House (riv.), Alta. 182/D2
House, N. Mex. (88121) 274/F4
House (range), Utah 304/A4
House Springs, Mo. (63051) 261/O4
Houston, Ala. 194/H8
Houston (co.), Ala. (35572) 194/D2
Houston, Alaska (†99687) 196/B1
Houston, Ark. (72070) 203/E3
Houston, Br. Col. 184/D3
Houston, Del. (19954) 245/S5
Houston, Fla. (†32060) 212/D1
Houston (co.), Ga. 216/E6
Houston, Ind. (†47235) 227/E6
Houston (co.), Minn. 254/G7
Houston, Minn. (55943) 254/G7
Houston, Miss. (38851) 256/G3
Houston, Mo. (65483) 261/J8
Houston, Ohio (45333) 284/B5
Houston, Pa. (15342) 294/B5
Houston (co.), Tenn. 237/F8
Houston, Texas, 146/J7
Houston, Texas, 188/G5
Houston (co.), Texas 302/J6
Houston, Texas (*77001) 302/J2
Houston (lake), Texas 302/J8
Houston, U.S., 3/E4
Houston Acres‡, Ky. (†40201) 237/K4
Houstonia, Mo. (65333) 261/F5
Houston Lake‡, Mo. (†64152) 261/O5
Houston Ship (chan.), Texas 302/K2
Hout (bay), S. Africa 118/E6
Houtman Abrolhos (isls.), Aust. 88/A5
Houtman Abrolhos (isls.), W. Aust. 92/A5
Houtrak Polder, Neth. 27/A4
Houtzdale, Pa. (16651) 294/F4
Hov, Den. 21/D6
Hove, 10/F5
Hove, Eng. 13/G7
Hoven, S. Dak. (57450) 298/K3
Hovenweep Nat'l Mon., Colo. 208/A8
Hovenweep Nat'l Mon., Utah 304/E6
Hoving, N. Dak. (†58060) 283/P7
Hovland, Minn. (55606) 254/G2
Howar, Wadi (dry riv.), Sudan 111/E4
Howard (pass), Alaska 196/G1
Howard (co.), Ark. 203/C5
Howard, Colo. (81233) 208/H6
Howard, Ga. (31039) 216/D5
Howard (co.), Ind. 227/E4
Howard (co.), Iowa 229/J2
Howard, Kans. (67349) 232/F4
Howard (co.), Md. 245/L4
Howard (co.), Mo. 261/G4
Howard, N. Br. 170/E2
Howard (co.), Nebr. 264/F3
Howard, Ohio (43028) 284/F5
Howard, Pa. (16841) 294/G3
Howard, S. Dak. (57349) 298/P5
Howard (co.), Texas 302/C5
Howard (creek), Texas 302/C7
Howard, Wis. (54303) 317/K6
Howard A. Hanson (res.), Wash. 310/D3
Howard City, Mich. (49329) 250/D5
Howard City (Boelus), Nebr. (†68820) 264/F3
Howard Lake, Minn. (55349) 254/D5
Howards Grove-Millersville, Wis. (†53081) 317/L8
Howards Ridge, Mo. (65673) 261/H9
Howardstown, Ky. (40028) 237/K5
Howardsville, Va. (24562) 307/L5
Howardville‡, Mo. (63869) 261/N9
Howden, Eng. 13/G4
Howe (cape), Australia, 87/F9
Howe (cape), Aust. 88/J7
Howe (pt.), Aust. 88/L5
Howe (sound), Br. Col. 184/K2
Howe, Idaho (83244) 220/F6
Howe, Ind. (46746) 227/G1
Howe (cape), N.S.W. 97/F5
Howe, Okla. (74940) 288/S5
Howe‡, Texas (75059) 302/H4
Howell, Ark. (72071) 203/H3
Howell, Ga. (†31636) 216/F9
Howell, Mich. (48843) 250/E6
Howell (co.), Mo. 261/J9
Howell△, N.J. (07727) 273/E3
Howell, Tenn. (37344) 237/H10
Howell, Utah (84316) 304/B2
Howells, Nebr. (68641) 264/H3
Howes, S. Dak. (57748) 298/E4
Howesville, Ind. (†47438) 227/C6
Howesville, W. Va. (†26444) 313/G4
Howey In The Hills, Fla. (32737) 212/E3
Howick, Que. 172/D4
Howick, N.Z. 101/C1
Howick, S. Africa 118/E5
Howison, Miss. (†39574) 256/F9
Howland△, Maine (04448) 242/F5
Howland, Maine (04448) 242/F5
Howland (isl.), Pacific, 87/J5
Howland Ridge, N. Br. 170/C2
Howley, Newf. 166/C4
Howlong, N.S.W. 97/D4
Howmore, Scot. 15/A5
Howrah, India, 54/M7
Howrah, India 68/F2
Howser, Br. Col. 184/J5
Howth, 10/D4
Hoxeyville, Mich. (49641) 250/D4
Hoxie, Ark. (72433) 203/H1
Hoxie, Kans. (67740) 232/B2
Höxter, W. Ger. 22/C3
Hoy (isl.), 10/E1
Hoy (isl.), Scot. 15/K2
Hoy (sound), Scot. 15/K2
Hoyerswerda, E. Ger. 22/F3
Hoylake, 10/F2
Hoylake, Eng. 13/D4
Hoyleton, Ill. (62803) 222/D5
Hoyos, Spain 33/C2
Hoyran (lake), Turkey 63/D3
Hoyt, Colo. (80641) 208/L2
Hoyt, Kans. (66440) 232/G2
Hoyt, N. Br. 170/D3
Hoyt, Okla. (74440) 288/R4
Hoyt (peak), Utah 304/C3
Hoyt Lakes, Minn. (55750) 254/F3
Hoytsville, Utah (†84017) 304/C3
Hoytville, Ohio (43529) 284/C3
Hozat, Turkey 59/C2
Hozat, Turkey 63/H3
Hradec Králové, Czech. 41/C1
Hranice, Czech. 41/D2
Hron (riv.), Czech. 41/E2
Hronov, Czech. 41/D1
Hrubieszów, Poland 47/F3
Hrušovany, Czech. 41/D2
Hsenwi, Burma 72/C2
Hsipaw, Burma 72/C2
Hsüchang, China 77/H5
Hsünkow, China 77/L2
Htawgaw, Burma 72/C1
Huacaraje, Bol. 136/D3
Huacareta, Bol. 136/C7
Huacas (pt.), Peru, 120/C4
Huacaya, Bol. 136/D7
Huachacalla, Bol. 136/A6
Huachipato, Chile 138/D1
Huacho, Peru, 120/C4
Huacho, Peru 128/D8
Huachuca (peak), Ariz. 198/E7
Huachuca City, Ariz. (85616) 198/E7
Huacrachuco, Peru 128/D7
Hua Hin, Thai. 72/D4
Huahine (isl.), Fr. Poly., 87/L7
Huajuapan de León, Mex. 150/L8
Hualaihué, Chile 138/E4
Hualalai (mt.), Hawaii 218/G5
Hualañé, Chile 138/A10
Hualapai (mts.), Ariz. 198/B4
Hualapai (peak), Ariz. 198/B3
Hualapai Ind. Res., Ariz. 198/B3
Hualgayoc, Peru 128/C6
Hualla, Peru 128/E10
Huallaga (riv.), Peru 128/D5
Huallanca, Ancash, Peru 128/D7
Huallanca, Huánuco, Peru 128/D7
Huallen, Alta. 182/A2
Huamachuco, Peru 128/D6
Huambo (dist.), Angola 115/C6
Hua Muong, Laos 72/D2
Huanaqui, Bol. 136/A7
Huancabamba, Peru 128/C5
Huancané, Bol. 136/B6
Huancané, Peru 128/H10
Huancapi, Peru 128/E9
Huancavelica (dept.), Peru 128/E9
Huancavelica, Peru 128/E9
Huancayo, Peru 128/E9
Huanchaca, Bol. 136/B7
Huanchaca (mt.), Bol. 136/B7
Huanchaca, Serranía de (mts.), Bol. 136/E4
Huanchaco, Peru 128/C7
Huanqueros, Arg. 143/F5
Huanta, Peru 128/E9
Huánuco (dept.), Peru 128/D7
Huánuco, Peru 128/E7
Huanuni, Bol. 136/B6
Huapai, N.Z. 101/B1
Huapí (mts.), Nic. 154/E4
Huaquechula, Mex. 150/M2
Huara, Chile 138/B2
Huaral, Peru 128/D8
Huaráz, Peru, 120/C3
Huaráz, Peru 128/D7
Huari, Bol. 136/B6
Huari, Peru 128/D7
Huariaca, Peru 128/E8
Huarina, Bol. 136/A5
Huarmey, Peru 128/C8
Huarochirí, Peru 128/D9
Huarocondo, Peru 128/F9
Huásabas, Mex. 150/E2
Huasaga (riv.), Peru 128/D4
Huascarán (mt.), Peru, 120/C3
Huascarán (mt.), Peru 128/D7
Huasco, Chile, 120/C5
Huasco, Chile 138/A7
Huasco (riv.), Chile 138/A7
Huatabampo, Mex. 150/D3
Huatunas (lag.), Bol. 136/B3
Huatusco de Chicuellar, Mex. 150/P2
Huauchinango, Mex. 150/L6
Huaura, Peru 128/D8
Huautla de Jiménez, Mex. 150/L7
Huayabamba (riv.), Peru 128/D6
Huaylas, Peru 128/C7
Huayllas, Bol. 136/C6
Hub, Miss. (†39429) 256/E8
Hubball, W. Va. (†25506) 313/B6
Hubbard, Iowa (50122) 229/G4
Hubbard (lake), Mich. 250/F4
Hubbard (co.), Minn. 254/D3
Hubbard, Minn. (†56470) 254/C4
Hubbard, Nebr. (68741) 264/H2
Hubbard, Ohio (44425) 284/J3
Hubbard, Oreg. (97032) 291/A3
Hubbard, Sask. 181/H4
Hubbard, Texas (76648) 302/H6
Hubbard Creek (res.), Texas 302/F5
Hubbard Lake, Mich. (49747) 250/F4
Hubbards, N.S. 169/D4
Hubbardston△, Mass. (01452) 249/F3
Hubbardston, Mich. (48845) 250/E5
Hubbardstown, W. Va. (†25555) 313/A6
Hubbardsville, N.Y. (13355) 276/J5
Hubbardton△, Vt. (05749) 268/A4
Hubbardton, Vt. (05749) 268/A4
Hubbart (pt.), Man. 179/K2
Hubbell, Mich. (49934) 250/A1
Hubbell, Nebr. (68375) 264/G4
Hubbell Trading Post Nat'l Hist. Site, Ariz. 198/F3
Hub City, Wis. (†53581) 317/F9
Huberdeau, Que. 172/C4
Huber Heights, Ohio (45424) 284/B6
Hubert, N.C. (28539) 281/P5
Hubertus, Wis. (53033) 317/K1
Hubli, India 68/C5
Huch'ang, N. Korea 81/C3
Hucknall, Eng. 13/F4
Huddersfield, 10/G2
Huddersfield, Eng. 13/F4
Huddleston, Va. (24104) 307/K6
Huddy, Ky. (41535) 237/S5
Hudiksvall, Sweden 18/K6
Hudson (bay), 163/H3
Hudson (str.), 163/J3
Hudson (bay), Canada, 3/E3
Hudson (bay), Canada, 146/K3
Hudson (str.), Canada, 146/L3
Hudson, Colo. (80642) 208/K2
Hudson, Fla. (33568) 212/D3
Hudson, Ill. (61748) 222/E3
Hudson, Ind. (46747) 227/G1
Hudson, Iowa (50643) 229/H4
Hudson, Kans. (67545) 232/D3
Hudson, Ky. (40145) 237/J5
Hudson△, Maine (04449) 242/F5
Hudson (bay), Man. 179/K2
Hudson△, Mass. (01749) 249/H3
Hudson, Mass. (01749) 249/H3
Hudson, Md. (†21613) 245/N6
Hudson, Mich. (49247) 250/E7
Hudson, N.C. (28638) 281/G3
Hudson△, N.H. (03051) 268/E6
Hudson, N.H. (03051) 268/E6
Hudson (co.), N.J. 273/E2
Hudson (riv.), N.J. 273/C1
Hudson (bay), N.W.T. 187/K3
Hudson (str.), N.W.T. 187/L3
Hudson, N.Y. (12534) 276/N6
Hudson (riv.), N.Y. 276/N7
Hudson, Ohio (44236) 284/H3
Hudson (lake), Okla. 288/R2
Hudson, Ont. 175/B2
Hudson (bay), Ont. 175/D1
Hudson, Ont. 177/G4
Hudson, Que. 172/C4
Hudson (bay), Que. 174/A1
Hudson (str.), Que. 174/F1
Hudson, S. Dak. (57034) 298/R7
Hudson‡, Texas (†75901) 302/K6
Hudson, Wis. (54016) 317/A6
Hudson, Wyo. (82515) 319/D3
Hudson Bay, Sask. 181/J3
Hudson Falls, N.Y. (12839) 276/O4
Hudson Hope, Br. Col. 184/F2
Hudson Lake, Ind. (46552) 227/D1
Hudsonville, Mich. (49426) 250/D6
Hudspeth (co.), Texas 302/B10
Hudwin (lake), Man. 179/G1
Hue, S. Vietnam 72/E3
Hue, S. Vietnam, 54/O8
Hueco (mts.), N. Mex. 274/D6
Hueco (mts.), Texas 302/B10
Huedin, Rum. 45/F2
Huehue, Hawaii (†96740) 218/G5
Huehuetenango, Guat. 154/B3
Huehuetlán el Chico, Mex. 150/M2
Huejotzingo, Mex. 150/M1
Huejutla de Reyes, Mex. 150/K6
Huelma, Spain 33/E4
Huelva (prov.), Spain 33/C4
Huelva, Spain 33/C4
Huelva (riv.), Spain 33/C4
Huentelauquén, Chile 138/A8
Huercal-Overa, Spain 33/F4
Huerfano (co.), Colo. 208/K7
Huerfano (riv.), Colo. 208/L7
Huesca (prov.), Spain 33/F1
Huesca, Spain 33/F1
Huéscar, Spain 33/E4
Huetamo de Nuñez, Mex. 150/J7
Huete, Spain 33/E2
Huetter, Idaho (†83854) 220/B2
Huey, Ill. (62252) 222/D5
Hueyotlipan de Hidalgo, Mex. 150/M1
Hueytown, Ala. (35020) 194/D4
Huff, N. Dak. (58555) 283/J6
Huffman, Ark. (†72315) 203/L2
Huffton, S. Dak. (†57432) 298/N2
Huger, S.C. (29450) 296/H5
Huggins, Mo. (65484) 261/H8
Hugh Butler (lake), Nebr. 264/D4
Hughenden, Alta. 182/E3
Hughenden, Australia, 87/E8
Hughenden, Aust. 88/G4
Hughenden, Queens. 95/B4
Hughes, Alaska (99745) 196/H1
Hughes, Ark. (72348) 203/J4
Hughes, Aust. 88/D6
Hughes, S. Aust. 94/A4
Hughes (co.), Okla. 288/O4
Hughes (co.), S. Dak. 298/J5
Hughes (riv.), W. Va. 313/D4
Hughes Springs, Texas (75656) 302/K5
Hughestown‡, Pa. (†18640) 294/L3
Hughesville, Md. (20637) 245/L6
Hughesville, Mo. (65334) 261/F5
Hughesville, Pa. (17737) 294/J3
Hughson, Calif. (95326) 204/E6
Hughton, Sask. 181/D4
Hugh Town, Eng. 13/A8
Hugo, Colo. (80821) 208/N4
Hugo, Minn. (55038) 254/E5
Hugo, Okla. (74743) 288/R6
Hugoton, Kans. (67951) 232/A4
Huhehot, China, 54/P5
Huhehot, China 77/H3
Huiarau (range), N.Z. 101/F3
Hŭich'ŏn, N. Korea 81/C3
Huila (dist.), Angola 115/B7
Huila (mt.), Col., 120/C2
Huila (dept.), Col. 126/C6
Huila, Nevado del (mt.), Col. 126/C6
Huimanguillo, Mex. 150/N8
Huinca Renancó, Arg. 143/D3
Huissen, Neth. 27/J5
Huitzuco de los Figueroa, Mex. 150/K7
Huixtla, Mex. 150/N9
Huizen, Neth. 27/G4
Hulaco, Ala. (†35087) 194/E2
Hulah (res.), Kans. 232/F5
Hulah, Okla. (†67333) 288/O1
Hulah (res.), Okla. 288/O1
Hulatt, Br. Col. 184/F3
Hulbert, Ark. (72349) 203/K3
Hulbert, Mich. (49748) 250/D2
Hulbert, Okla. (74441) 288/R3
Hulberton, N.Y. (14473) 276/D4
Hulett, Wyo. (82720) 319/H1
Hull, 10/F4
Hull, Eng., 7/E3
Hull, Eng. 13/G4
Hull, Fla. (†33842) 212/E4
Hull (isl.), Gilb. and Ell., 87/J6
Hull, Ga. (30646) 216/F2
Hull, Ill. (62343) 222/B4
Hull, Iowa (51239) 229/A2
Hull△, Mass. (02045) 249/E7
Hull, N. Dak. (†58542) 283/K7
Hull, 163/J6
Hull (co.), Que. 172/B4
Hull, Que. 172/B4
Hull, Texas (77564) 302/K7
Hulls Cove, Maine (04644) 242/G7
Hulmeville‡, Pa. (19047) 294/N5
Hulst, Neth. 27/E6
Hultsfred, Sweden 18/K8
Hulun Nor (lake), China 77/J2
Huma, China 77/L1
Humacao, P. Rico 156/G1
Humacao (dist.), P. Rico 161/E2
Humacao, P. Rico 161/E2
Humacao (riv.), P. Rico 161/E2
Humahuaca, Arg. 143/C1
Humaitá, Bol. 136/B2
Humaitá, Braz., 120/D3
Humaitá, Braz. 132/H10
Humaitá, Par. 144/C6
Humansdorp, S. Africa 118/C6
Humansville, Mo. (65674) 261/E7
Humarock, Mass. (02047) 249/M4
Humber (riv.), Ont. 177/J3
Humber (riv.), Eng. 13/H4
Humber (riv.), Newf. 166/C4
Humber (riv.), 10/G4
Humberto, Arg. 143/F5
Humbird, Wis. (54746) 317/E6
Humble, Texas (77338) 302/J7
Humble City, N. Mex. (88251) 274/F6
Humboldt, Ariz. (86329) 198/C4
Humboldt (co.), Calif. 204/B3
Humboldt (bay), Calif. 204/A3
Humboldt (bay), Col. 126/B4
Humboldt, Ill. (61931) 222/E4
Humboldt (co.), Iowa 229/E3
Humboldt, Iowa (50548) 229/E3
Humboldt, Kans. (66748) 232/G4
Humboldt, 163/F5
Humboldt, Minn. (56731) 254/A2
Humboldt, Nebr. (68376) 264/J4
Humboldt (riv.), Nev., 188/C2
Humboldt (co.), Nev. 266/C1
Humboldt, Nev. (†89418) 266/C2
Humboldt (range), Nev. 266/C2
Humboldt (riv.), Nev. 266/E2
Humboldt (sink), Nev. 266/C2
Humboldt, S. Dak. (57035) 298/P6
Humboldt, Sask. 181/F3
Humboldt, Tenn. (38343) 237/D9
Humboldt Salt (marsh), Nev. 266/D3
Hume, Ill. (61932) 222/F4
Hume, Mo. (64752) 261/C6
Hume (lake), N.S.W. 97/D4
Hume, N.Y. (14745) 276/D5
Hume, Sask. 181/H6
Hume, Va. (22639) 307/N3
Hume (lake), Vic. 97/D4
Humenné, Czech. 41/G2
Humeston, Iowa (50123) 229/G7
Humlum, Den. 21/B5
Hummelstown, Pa. (17036) 294/J5
Humnoke, Ark. (72072) 203/G4
Humphrey (pt.), Alaska 196/K1
Humphrey, Ark. (72073) 203/G5
Humphrey, Idaho (†83446) 220/F5
Humphrey, Nebr. (68642) 264/G3
Humphreys (peak), Ariz. 198/D3
Humphreys, La. (†70356) 238/J7
Humphreys (co.), Miss. 256/C4
Humphreys, Mo. (64646) 261/F2
Humphreys, Okla. (†73521) 288/H5
Humphreys (co.), Tenn. 237/F8
Humpolec, Czech. 41/C2
Humptulips, Wash. (98552) 310/A3
Humptulips (riv.), Wash. 310/B3
Humpty Doo, No. Terr. 93/B2
Húnaflói (bay), Ice., 7/B2
Húnaflói (bay), Ice. 21/B1
Hunan (prov.), China 77/H6
Hunchun, China 77/M3
Hundested, Den. 21/E6
Hundred, W. Va. (26575) 313/E3
Hunedoara, Rum. 45/F3
Hünfeld, W. Ger. 22/C3
Hungary, 7/F4
HUNGARY, 41
Hunger (mt.), Vt. 268/B3
Hungerford, Aust. 88/G5
Hungerford, Queens. 95/B6
Hŭngnam, N. Korea 81/C4
Hungry Horse, Mont. (59919) 262/C2
Hungry Horse (res.), Mont. 262/C2
Hungshui Ho (riv.), China 77/G6
Hungtow (isl.), China 77/K7
Hungtse (lake), China 77/J5
Hunker (Hunkers)‡, Pa. (15639) 294/C5
Hunkiang, China 77/L3
Hunnewell, Kans. (67141) 232/E4
Hunnewell, Mo. (63443) 261/J3
Hunse (riv.), Neth. 27/K3
Hunsrück (mts.), W. Ger. 22/B4
Hunstanton, 10/G4
Hunstanton, Eng. 13/H4
Hunt, Ill. (†62480) 222/E4
Hunt (co.), Texas 302/H4
Hunt (mt.), Wyo. 319/E1
Hunte (riv.), W. Ger. 22/C2
Hunter, Ark. (72074) 203/H3
Hunter (isls.), Aust. 88/G8
Hunter (isl.), Br. Col. 184/C4
Hunter (peak), Idaho 220/D3
Hunter, Kans. (67452) 232/D2
Hunter, Mo. (63948) 261/L9
Hunter, N. Dak. (58048) 283/R5
Hunter (riv.), N.S.W. 97/F3
Hunter, N.Y. (12442) 276/M6
Hunter (mt.), N.Y. 276/M6
Hunter (mts.), N.Z. 101/A6
Hunter, Okla. (74640) 288/L1
Hunter (isls.), Tasmania 99/B2
Hunterdon (co.), N.J. 273/D2
Hunter Liggett Mil. Res., Calif. 204/D8
Hunters, Wash. (99137) 310/G2
Hunters Creek Village, Texas (†77001) 302/J1
Hunters Hill, N.S.W. 97/J3
Hunters River, P.E.I. 169/E2
Huntersville, Ky. (†42602) 237/L7
Huntersville, Minn. (†56464) 254/D4
Huntersville, N.C. (28078) 281/H4
Huntersville, W. Va. (24954) 313/G6
Huntertown, Ind. (46748) 227/G2
Hunterville, N.Z. 101/E3
Hunting (riv.), N.C. 281/H2
Hunting (isl.), S.C. 296/G7
Huntingburg, Ind. (47542) 227/D8
Huntingdon, Br. Col. 184/L3
Huntingdon (co.), Que. 172/C4
Huntingdon, Que. 172/C4
Huntingdon (isl.), Newf. 166/C3
Huntingdon (co.), Pa. 294/F5
Huntingdon, Pa. (16652) 294/G5
Huntingdon, Tenn. (38344) 237/E8
Huntingdon and Godmanchester, 10/F4
Huntingdon and Godmanchester, Eng. 13/G5
Huntingdon and Peterborough (co.), Eng. 13/G5
Huntington, Ark. (72940) 203/B3
Huntington, Conn. (†06484) 210/C3
Huntington (co.), Ind. 227/G3
Huntington, Ind. (46750) 227/G3
Huntington (res.), Ind. 227/F3
Huntington, Iowa (†51334) 229/D2
Huntington△, Mass. (01050) 249/C4
Huntington, N.J. (†08865) 273/C2
Huntington, N.Y. (11743) 276/O9
Huntington (creek), Nev. 266/F2
Huntington, Oreg. (97907) 291/K3
Huntington, Texas (75949) 302/K6
Huntington, Utah (84528) 304/C4
Huntington (creek), Utah 304/C4
Huntington‡, Va. (†22301) 307/O3
Huntington△, Vt. (05462) 268/B3
Huntington, Vt. (05462) 268/B3
Huntington, W. Va., 188/K3
Huntington, W. Va. (*25701) 313/A6
Huntington Bay‡, N.Y. (†11743) 276/O9

378 Huntington Beach

Huntington Beach, Calif. (*92646) 204/C11
Huntington Center, Vt. (05462) 268/B3
Huntington Park, Calif. (90255) 204/C11
Huntington Station, N.Y. (11746) 276/O9
Huntington Woods‡, Mich. (48070) 250/B6
Huntingtown, Md. (20639) 245/M6
Hunting Valley, Ohio (†44022) 284/J9
Huntland, Tenn. (37345) 237/J10
Huntleigh‡, Mo. (†63101) 261/P3
Huntley, Ill. (60142) 222/E1
Huntley, Minn. (56047) 254/D7
Huntley, Mont. (59037) 262/H5
Huntley, Nebr. (68951) 264/E4
Huntley, Wyo. (82218) 319/H4
Huntly, 10/E2
Huntly, N.Z. 101/E2
Huntly, Scot. 15/L5
Huntoon, Sask. 181/H6
Huntsburg, Ohio (44046) 284/H2
Hunts Point, N.S. 169/D5
Hunts Point‡, Wash. (†98004) 310/C3
Huntsville, Ala., 188/J4
Huntsville, Ala. (*35801) 194/E1
Huntsville, Ark. (72740) 203/C1
Huntsville, Conn. (†06031) 210/B1
Huntsville, Ont. 175/E3
Huntsville, Ont. 177/E2
Huntsville, Ind. (†47358) 227/F4
Huntsville, Ind. (†46064) 227/G4
Huntsville, Ky. (42251) 237/H6
Huntsville, Mo. (65259) 261/H4
Huntsville, Ohio (43324) 284/C5
Huntsville, Tenn. (37756) 237/N8
Huntsville, Texas (77340) 302/J7
Huntsville, Utah (84317) 304/C2
Huntsville, Wash. (†99328) 310/G4
Hunucmá, Mex. 150/O6
Hunza (Baltit), India 68/C1
Huocheng, China 77/B3
Huon (isls.), New Cal., 87/G7
Huon (riv.), Tas. 99/C5
Huon (gulf), Terr. N.G. 85/C7
Huon (gulf), Terr. N.G., 87/E6
Huong Khe, N. Vietnam 72/E3
Huonville-Ranelagh, Tas. 99/C4
Huot, Minn. (†56716) 254/B3
Hupei (prov.), China 77/H5
Hurbanovo, Czech. 41/E3
Hurd (cape), Ont. 177/C2
Hurdland, Mo. (63547) 261/H2
Hurdle Mills, N.C. (27541) 281/L2
Hurdsfield, N. Dak. (58451) 283/L5
Hureidha, P.D.R. Yemen 59/E6
Hurghada, U.A.R. 59/B4
Hurghada, U.A.R. 111/F2
Hurlburt‡, Fla. (†32548) 212/C6
Hurlbut, Ind. (†46341) 227/C2
Hurley, Miss. (39555) 256/H9
Hurley, Mo. (65675) 261/F9
Hurley, N. Mex. (88043) 274/A6
Hurley, N.Y. (12443) 276/M7
Hurley, S. Dak. (57036) 298/P7
Hurley, Va. (24620) 307/D6
Hurley, Wis. (54534) 317/F3
Hurleyville, N.Y. (12747) 276/L7
Hurlford, Scot. 15/H8
Hurlock, Md. (21643) 245/P6
Huron (lake), 146/K5
Huron (lake), 163/H7
Huron, Calif. (93234) 204/E7
Huron (lake), Ont. 175/D3
Huron (co.), Ont. 177/C4
Huron (lake), Ont. 177/B3
Huron, Ind. (47437) 227/D7
Huron, Kans. (66038) 232/G2
Huron (lake), Mich., 188/K2
Huron (co.), Mich. 250/F5
Huron (bay), Mich. 250/A2
Huron (lake), Mich. 250/G4
Huron (riv.), Mich. 250/F6
Huron (co.), Ohio 284/E3
Huron, Ohio (44839) 284/E3
Huron (riv.), Ohio 284/E3
Huron, S. Dak., 188/G2
Huron, S. Dak. (57350) 298/N5
Huron, Tenn. (38345) 237/E9
Huron City, Mich. (†48467) 250/G4
Huron Mountain, Mich. (†49808) 250/B2
Huron River (pt.), Mich. 250/B2
Huronville, Sask. 181/H5
Hurricane, Ala. (†36507) 194/C9
Hurricane (mt.), Mont. 262/D2
Hurricane, Utah (84737) 304/A6
Hurricane, W. Va. (25526) 313/C6
Hurricane Deck, Mo. (†65079) 261/G6
Hurricane Ledge, Ariz. 198/B2
Hurricane Mills, Tenn. (37078) 237/F9
Hursley Station (Stockton), Md. (†21864) 245/S8
Hurst, Ga. (30561) 216/D1
Hurst, Ill. (62949) 222/D6
Hurst, Texas (76053) 302/F2
Hurst, W. Va. (26373) 313/E4
Hurstbourne Acres‡, Ky. (†40201) 237/L4
Hurstbridge, Aust. 88/M6
Hurstville, Aust. 88/L3
Hurstville, Iowa (†52060) 229/M4
Hurstville, N.S.W. 97/J4
Hurt, Va. (24563) 307/K6
Hürth, W. Ger. 22/B3
Hurtsboro, Ala. (36860) 194/H6
Hurunui (riv.), N.Z. 101/D5
Hurup, Den. 21/B4
Husavick, Man. 179/F4
Húsavík, Ice. 21/C1
Husher, Wis. (†53108) 317/L2
Hushpuckena, Miss. (†38774) 256/C2
Huşi, Rum. 45/J2
Husk, N.C. (28639) 281/F1
Huskisson, N.S.W. 97/F4
Huskvarna, Sweden 18/J8
Huslia, Alaska (99746) 196/G1
Huson, Mont. (59846) 262/B3
Hussar, Alta. 182/D4
Hustisford, Wis. (53034) 317/J9
Hustler, Wis. (54637) 317/F8
Hustontown, Pa. (17229) 294/F5
Hustonville, Ky. (40437) 237/M6
Hustopeče, Czech. 41/D2
Husum, W. Ger. 22/C1
Husum, Wash. (98623) 310/D5
Hutchins (mt.), N.H. 268/E2
Hutchins, Texas (75141) 302/G2
Hutchins, Wis. (†54450) 317/H6
Hutchinson, Kans., 146/J6
Hutchinson, Kans., 188/G3
Hutchinson, Kans. (67501) 232/D3
Hutchinson, Minn. (55350) 254/D6
Hutchinson (co.), S. Dak. 298/O7
Hutchinson (co.), Texas 302/C2
Hutchinson, W. Va. (25627) 313/F4
Huth, Yemen Arab Rep. 59/D6
Hutsonville, Ill. (62433) 222/F4
Hutt (riv.), N.Z. 101/C2
Hutt (Upper and Lower), N. Z., 101/B2
Hüttenberg, Austria 41/C3
Hüttental, W. Ger. 22/C3
Hutte-Sauvage (lake), Que. 174/E1
Huttig, Ark. (71747) 203/F7
Hutto, Texas (78634) 302/G7
Hutton, La. (†71402) 238/D4
Hutton, Md. (†21550) 245/A3
Hutton, Scot. 15/K9
Huttonsville, W. Va. (26273) 313/G5
Hutton Valley, Mo. (†65793) 261/J9
Huttwil, Switz. 39/E2
Huumula, Hawaii (†96743) 218/H5
Huutokoski, Fin. 18/P5
Huwelijkszorg, Sur. 131/C2
Huxford, Ala. (36543) 194/D8
Huxley, Alta. 182/D4
Huxley, Iowa (50124) 229/F5
Huxley, Texas (†75973) 302/L6
Huy, Belg. 27/G8
Hvannadalshnúkur (mt.), Ice. 21/C1
Hvar (isl.), Yugo. 45/C4
Hvidbjerg, Den. 21/B4
Hviding, Den. 21/B7
Hvitá (riv.), Ice. 21/B1
Hwainan, China 77/J5
Hwaiteh, China 77/K3
Hwangchung, China 77/F4
Hwang Ho (riv.), China, 3/Q4
Hwang Ho (riv.), China, 54/P6
Hwang Ho (riv.), China 77/H5
Hwangju, N. Korea 81/C4
Hwangling, China 77/G4
Hwangshih, China 77/J5
Hwangyüan, China 77/F4
Hweili, China 77/F6
Hwohsien, China 77/H4
Hyak, Wash. (98026) 310/D3
Hyalite (peak), Mont. 262/E5
Hyannis, Mass. (02601) 249/N6
Hyannis, Nebr. (69350) 264/C3
Hyannis Port, Mass. (02647) 249/N6
Hyas, Sask. 181/J4
Hyattstown, Md. (20734) 245/J3
Hyattsville, Md. (*20780) 245/F4
Hyattville, Wyo. (82428) 319/E1
Hybart, Ala. (36452) 194/D7
Hyco (riv.), N.C. 281/L2
Hyco (riv.), Va. 307/K8
Hydaburg, Alaska (99922) 196/M2
Hyde, 10/G2
Hyde (co.), N.C. 281/S3
Hyde, N.Z. 101/C6
Hyde, Pa. (16843) 294/F4
Hyde (co.), S. Dak. 298/K4
Hyde, Sask. 181/J5
Hyden, Aust. 88/B6
Hyden, Ky. (41749) 237/P6
Hyden, W. Aust. 92/B6
Hyde Park, Mass. (02136) 249/C7
Hyde Park, N.Y. (12538) 276/N6
Hyde Park, Pa. (15641) 294/D4
Hyde Park, Utah (84318) 304/C2
Hyde Park‡, Vt. (05655) 268/B2
Hyde Park, Vt. (05655) 268/B2
Hyder, Alaska (99923) 196/P2
Hyderabad, India, 3/N5
Hyderabad, India, 54/L8
Hyderabad, Pak. 59/J4
Hyderabad, India 68/D5
Hyderabad, Pak. 68/B3
Hyderabad, Pak., 54/K7
Hydesville, Calif. (95547) 204/B3
Hydetown, Pa. (16328) 294/C2
Hydeville, Vt. (05750) 268/A4
Hydraulic, Br. Col. 184/F4
Hydro, Okla. (73048) 288/J3
Hye, Texas (78635) 302/F7
Hyères, France 28/G6
Hyères (isls.), France 28/G6
Hyesan, N. Korea 81/D3
Hygiene, Colo. (80533) 208/J2
Hyland (riv.), Yukon 187/F3
Hylo, Alta. 182/D2
Hyman, S.C. (†29583) 296/H4
Hymer, Kans. (†66869) 232/F3
Hymera, Ind. (47855) 227/C6
Hyndman (peak), Idaho 220/D6
Hyndman, Pa. (15545) 294/E6
Hyner, Pa. (17738) 294/G3
Hynish (bay), Scot. 15/C7
Hyogo (pref.), Japan 81/H7
Hypoluxo, Fla. (†33460) 212/F5
Hyrra Banda, Centr. Afr. Rep. 115/D2
Hyrum, Utah (84319) 304/C2
Hyrynsalmi, Fin. 18/Q4
Hysham, Mont. (59038) 262/J4
Hyskier (isl.), Scot. 15/C6
Hythe, 10/G5
Hythe, 163/E5
Hythe, Alta. 182/A2
Hythe, Eng. 13/H6
Hytop, Ala. (35753) 194/F1
Hyuga, Japan 81/E7
Hyvinkää, Fin. 18/O6

I

Iaco (riv.), Braz., 120/D3
Iaeger, W. Va. (24844) 313/C8
Ialomiţa (marshes), Rum. 45/J3
Ialomiţa (riv.), Rum. 45/H3
Iamonia (lake), Fla. 212/B1
Iantha, Mo. (64753) 261/D8
Iara, Rum. 45/F2
Iar Connaught (dist.), Ire. 17/C5
Iaşi, Rum., 7/G4
Iaşi, Rum. 45/H2
Iatan, Mo. (†64098) 261/C4
Iatt (lake), La. 238/E3
Iba, Phil. 82/B3
Iba, Phil. 85/F2
Ibadan, 102/C4
Ibadan, Nigeria, 3/K5
Ibadan, Nigeria 106/E7
Ibagué, Col., 120/C2
Ibagué, Col. 126/C5
Ibaiti, Braz. 135/A3
Ibapah, Utah (84034) 304/A3
Ibar (riv.), Yugo. 45/E4
Ibaraki (pref.), Japan 81/K5
Ibaraki, Japan 81/J7
Ibarra, Ec., 120/C2
Ibarra, Ec. 128/D2
Ibarreta, Arg. 143/D2
Ibb, Yemen Arab Rep. 59/D7
Ibbenbüren, W. Ger. 22/B2
'Ibbin, Jordan 65/D3
Iberia (par.), La. 238/G7
Iberia, Mo. (65486) 261/H6
Iberia, Ohio (43325) 284/E4
Iberia, Peru 128/F5
Iberville (co.), Que. 172/D4
Iberville, Que. 172/D4
Iberville (lake), Que. 174/C1
Iberville (par.), La. 238/H6
Iberville, La. (70746) 238/K2
Ibi, Nigeria 106/F7
Ibiá, Braz. 132/E7
Ibibobo, Bol. 136/D7
Ibicuí (riv.), Braz. 132/C10
Ibicuy, Arg. 143/G6
Ibipetuba, Braz. 132/F5
Ibitinga, Braz. 135/B2
Ibiza (isl.), Spain, 7/E5
Ibiza, Spain 33/G3
Ibiza (isl.), Spain 33/G3
Ibo, Bol. 136/D7
Ibo, Moz. 118/G2
Ibounzi (mt.), Gabon 115/B4
Ibra, Oman 59/G5
Ibra, Wadi (dry riv.), Sudan 111/D5
'Ibri, Oman 59/G5
Iburg, W. Ger. 22/C2
Ibusuki, Japan 81/E8
Içá (riv.), Braz., 120/D3
Içá (riv.), Braz. 132/G9
Ica, Peru, 120/C4
Ica (dept.), Peru 128/E10
Ica, Peru 128/E10
Ica (riv.), Peru 128/E10
Icabarú, Ven. 124/H5
Icabarú (riv.), Ven. 124/G5
Icacos (pt.), Trinidad Tobago 161/A11
Icaño, Catamarca, Arg. 143/C2
Icaño, Santiago del Estero, Arg. 143/D2
Icard, N.C. (28666) 281/G3
Ice Harbor (dam), Wash. 310/G4
Içel (prov.), Turkey 63/F4
Içel (Mersin), Turkey 63/F4
Iceland, 3/J2
Iceland, 4/C10
Iceland, 7/C2
ICELAND, 21/B1
Ichang, China, 54/P6
Ichang, China 77/H5
Ichchapuram, India 68/F5
Ichhapur, India 68/F1
Ichihara, Japan 81/P2
Ichikawa, Japan 81/P2
Ichilo (riv.), Bol. 136/C5
Ichinohe, Japan 81/K3
Ichinomiya, Japan 81/H6
Ichinoseki, Japan 81/K4
Ichnya, U.S.S.R. 52/D4
Ichoa (riv.), Bol. 136/C4
Ichoca, Bol. 136/B5
Ichun, China 77/L2
Ichuña, Peru 128/G11
Icicle (creek), Wash. 310/E3
Ickesburg, Pa. (17037) 294/H5
Icla, Bol. 136/C6
Içme, Turkey 63/H3
Icó, Braz. 132/G4
Iconium, Mo. (†64776) 261/E6
Icoraci, Braz. 132/D3
Icy (bay), Alaska 196/K3
Icy (cape), Alaska 196/F1
Icy (cape), Alaska 196/K3
Icy (pt.), Alaska 196/L1
Icy (str.), Alaska 196/M1
Ida (co.), Iowa 229/C4
Ida, La. (71044) 238/C1
Ida, Mich. (48140) 250/F7
Idabel, Okla. (74745) 288/S7
Ida Grove, Iowa (51445) 229/B4
Idaho, 188/D2
IDAHO, 220
Idaho (co.), Idaho 220/C4
Idaho, Ohio (45661) 284/D7
Idaho (state), U.S., 146/G5
Idaho City, Idaho (83631) 220/C6
Idaho Falls, Idaho, 188/D2
Idaho Falls, Idaho (83401) 220/F6
Idaho Springs, Colo. (80452) 208/H3
Idahue, Chile 138/F5
Idalia, Colo. (80735) 208/P3
Idalou, Texas (79329) 302/C4
Idana, Kans. (67453) 232/E2
Idanha, Oreg. (97350) 291/E3
Idanha-a-Nova, Port. 33/C3
Idar-Oberstein, W. Ger. 22/B4
Idaville, Ind. (47950) 227/D3
Idaville, Pa. (17337) 294/H5
Iddan, Somalia 115/J2
Iddesleigh, Alta. 182/E4
Ide, Japan 81/J7
Ideal, Ga. (31041) 216/D6
Ideal, S. Dak. (57541) 298/K6
Idehan (des.), Libya 111/B2
Idehan Murzuk (des.), Libya 111/B2
Idelès, Alg. 106/F4
Idenburg (riv.), Indon. 85/K6
Ider, Ala. (35981) 194/G1
Ider (riv.), Mong. 77/E2
Idfu, U.A.R. 59/B5
Idfu, U.A.R. 111/F3
Ídhi (mt.), Greece 45/G8
Ídhra, Greece 45/F7
Idi, Indon. 85/B4
Idil, Turkey 63/J4
Idiofa, Dem. Rep. of the Congo. 115/C4
Idlewild, Mich. (49642) 250/D5
Idlewild, Tenn. (38346) 237/D8
Idleyld Park, Oreg. (97447) 291/D4
Idlib (prov.), Syria 63/G5
Idlib, Syria 63/G5
Idna, Jordan 65/B4
Idyllwild, Calif. (92349) 204/J10
Ie (isl.), Ryukyu Is. 81/N6
Ieper, Belg. 27/B7
Ierápetra, Greece 45/G8
Ierhsieh, China 77/J2
Iesi, Italy 34/D3
Iet, Somalia 115/H3
Ifakara, Tanz. 115/G5
Ifalik (atoll), Pac. Is., 87/E5
Ifanadiana, Malag. Rep. 118/H4
Ife, Nigeria 106/E7
Iférouane, 102/C3
Iférouane, Niger 106/F5
Iffley, Sask. 181/C3
Igal, Hung. 41/D3
Igara-Paraná (riv.), Col. 126/D8
Igarapava, Braz. 135/C2
Igarapé-Miri, Braz. 132/D3
Igarka, U.S.S.R. 48/J3
Igarka, U.S.S.R., 4/C5
Igarka, U.S.S.R., 54/M3
Iğdir, Turkey 63/K3
Ighil-Izane, Alg. 106/E1
Igis, Switz. 39/J3
Igiugig, Alaska (†99625) 196/G3
Iglesia, Arg. 143/C3
Iglesias, Italy, 7/E5
Iglesias, Italy 34/B5
Igli, Alg. 106/D2
Igloo, Alaska (†99778) 196/E1
Igloo, S. Dak. (†57774) 298/B7
Igloolik, 163/H2
Igloolik, Canada, 4/B14
Igloolik, N.W.T. 187/K3
Iglosiatik (isl.), Newf. 166/B2
Ignace, 163/G6
Ignace, Ont. 175/B3
Ignace, Ont. 177/G5
Ignacio, Calif. (94947) 204/H1
Ignacio, Colo. (81137) 208/D8
Ignacio de la Llave, Mex. 150/Q2
Iğneada (cape), Turkey 63/C2
Igoumenítsa, Greece 45/E6
Iguaçu (riv.), 120/E5
Iguaçu (riv.), Braz. 132/C9
Igualada, Spain 33/G2
Iguala de la Independencia, Mex. 150/K7
Iguape, Braz. 135/C4
Iguassú (falls), Braz. 132/C9
Iguatu, Braz., 120/F3
Iguatu, Braz. 132/G4
Iguazú, Arg. 143/F2
Iguazú (falls), Arg. 143/F2
Iguazú Nat'l Park, Arg. 143/E2
Iguéla, Gabon 115/A4
Iguidi (des.), 102/B2
Iguidi Erg (des.), Alg. 106/C3
Iguidi Erg (des.), 102/B2
Iguidi Erg (des.), Mauritania 106/C3
Iheya (isl.), Ryukyu Is. 81/N6
Ihlen, Minn. (56140) 254/B7
Ihosy, Malag. Rep. 118/H4
Ihu, Papua 85/B7
Ii (riv.), Fin. 18/O4
Iida, Japan 81/H6
Iisalmi, Fin. 18/P5
Iizuta, Japan 81/E7
Ijamsville, Md. (21754) 245/J3
Ijebu-Ode, Nigeria 106/E7
IJlst, Neth. 27/H2
IJmeer (bay), Neth. 27/C4
IJmuiden, Neth. 27/D4
IJssel (riv.), Neth. 27/J4
IJsselmeer (lake), Neth. 27/G3
IJsselstein, Neth. 27/F4
Ijuí, Braz. 132/C10
IJzendijke, Neth. 27/D6
Ikaalinen, Fin. 18/N6
Ikaría (isl.), Greece 45/G7
Ikast, Den. 21/C5
Ikeda, Hokkaido, Japan 81/L2
Ikeda, Osaka, Japan 81/H7
Ikela, Dem. Rep. of the Congo. 115/D4
Ikelemba, Rep. of Congo 115/C3
Ikhtiman, Bulg. 45/F4
Iki (isl.), Japan 81/D7
Ikom, Nigeria 106/F7
Ikopa (riv.), Malag. Rep. 118/H3
Ikpik (Thom Bay), N.W.T. 187/J2
Ikpikpuk (riv.), Alaska 196/H1
Ikryanoye, U.S.S.R. 52/G5
Iksal, Israel 65/C2
Ikuno, Japan 81/G6
Ila, Ga. (30647) 216/F2
Ilagan, Phil. 82/C2
Ilam (governorate), Iran 66/E4
Ilam, Iran 66/E4
Ilam, Nepal 68/F3
Ilanskiy, U.S.S.R. 48/K4
Ilanz, Switz. 39/H3
Ilasco, Mo. (†63401) 261/K3
Ilava, Czech. 41/E2
Ilave, Peru 128/H11
Iława, Poland 47/D2
Ilchester, Eng. 13/E6
Ilderton, Ont. 177/C4
Île-à-la-Crosse, Sask. 181/L3
Île-à-la-Crosse (lake), Sask. 181/L3
Île-Bizard, Que. 172/H4
Île-des-Chênes, Man. 179/F5
Ilek (riv.), U.S.S.R. 52/J4
Île-Perrot, Que. 172/H4
Îles (lake), Que. 172/B3
Îles (lake), Que. 172/E2
Ilesha, Nigeria 106/F7
Ilfeld, N. Mex. (87538) 274/D3
Ilfis (riv.), Switz. 39/E3
Ilford, Man. 179/J2
Ilford, N.S.W. 97/E3
Ilfracombe, 10/D5
Ilfracombe, Eng. 13/C6
Ilgaz, Turkey 63/E2
Ilgaz (mts.), Turkey 63/E2
Ilgin, Turkey 63/D3
Ilha Grande (bay), Braz. 135/D3
Ílhavo, Port. 33/B2
Ilhéus, Braz., 120/G4
Ilhéus, Braz. 132/G6
Ili (riv.), U.S.S.R. 48/H5
Ili (riv.), U.S.S.R., 54/L5
Iliamna (lake), Alaska, 146/C4
Iliamna (lake), Alaska, 188/C6
Iliamna, Alaska (99606) 196/G3
Iliamna (lake), Alaska 196/G3
Iliamna (vol.), Alaska 196/H2
Iliang, China 77/F7
Iliç, Turkey 63/H3
Ilica, Turkey 63/J3
Iliff, Colo. (80736) 208/N1
Iligan, Phil. 82/E6
Iligan (bay), Phil. 82/E6
Ilin (isl.), Phil. 82/C4
Ilio (pt.), Hawaii 218/G1
Ilion, N.Y. (13357) 276/K5
Ilium (ruins), Turkey 63/B6
Ilkeston, 10/F4
Ilkeston, Eng. 13/F5
Ilkley, Eng. 13/F4
Illabo, N.S.W. 97/D4
Illahe, Oreg. (†97406) 291/C5
Illampu (mt.), Bol., 120/D4
Illampu, Nevada (mt.), Bol. 136/A4
Illana (bay), Phil. 82/D7
Illana, Spain 33/E2
Illapel, Chile 138/A8
Ille-et-Vilaine (dept.), France 28/C3
Iller (riv.), W. Ger. 22/D4
Illerbrun, Sask. 181/C6
Illescas, Spain 33/D2
Illescas, Urug. 145/D4
Ille-sur-Têt, France 28/E6
Illimani, Nevada (mt.), Bol. 136/B5
Illinois, 188/J3
ILLINOIS, 222
Illinois (bayou), Ark. 203/D3
Illinois (riv.), Colo. 208/G1
Illinois (riv.), Ill., 188/H2
Illinois (riv.), Ill. 222/C4
Illinois (riv.), Okla. 288/S3
Illinois (riv.), Oreg. 291/D5
Illinois (state), U.S., 146/K5
Illinois-Mississippi (canal), Ill. 222/C2
Illiopolis, Ill. (62539) 222/D4
Illizi, Alg. 106/F3
Illmo, Mo. (63754) 261/O8
Illnau, Switz. 39/G2
Illora, Spain 33/E4
Il'men (lake), U.S.S.R. 52/D3
Il'men (lake), U.S.S.R., 7/H3
Ilmenau, E. Ger. 22/D3
Ilmenau (riv.), W. Ger. 22/D2
Ilminster, Eng. 13/E7
Ilo, Peru, 120/C4
Ilo, Peru 128/G11
Ilobasco, El Salv. 154/C4
Ilocos Norte (prov.), Phil. 82/C1
Ilocos Sur (prov.), Phil. 82/C2
Iloilo (prov.), Phil. 82/D5
Iloilo, Phil. 82/D5
Iloilo (str.), Phil. 82/D5
Iloilo, Phil. 85/G3
Iloilo, Phil., 54/R8
Ilomantsi, Fin. 18/R5
Ilorin, 102/C4
Ilorin, Nigeria 106/E7
Ilpendam, Neth. 27/C4
Ilsley, Ky. (†42408) 237/F6
Ilubabor (prov.), Eth. 111/F6
Ilūkste, U.S.S.R. 53/D3
Ilwaco, Wash. (98624) 310/A4
Imabari, Japan 81/F6
Iman, U.S.S.R. 48/O5
Imandra (lake), U.S.S.R. 48/D3
Imandra (lake), U.S.S.R. 52/D1
Imari, Japan 81/D7
Imataca, Serranía (mts.), Ven. 124/H4
Imatra, Fin. 18/Q6
Imazu, Japan 81/G6
Imbâba, U.A.R. 111/J3
Imbabura (prov.), Ec. 128/C2
Imbaimadai, Guyana 131/A3
Imbert, Dom. Rep. 158/D5
Imbituba, Braz. 132/D10
Imbituva, Braz. 135/A4
Imbler, Oreg. (97841) 291/J2
Imboden, Ark. (72434) 203/H1
Imeri, Sierra (mts.), Ven. 124/F7
Imese, Dem. Rep. of the Congo. 115/C3
Imi, Eth. 111/H6
Imías, Cuba 158/K4
Imielin, Poland 47/B4
Imilac, Chile 138/B4
Imlay, Nev. (89418) 266/C2
Imlay, S. Dak. (†57780) 298/E6
Imlay City, Mich. (48444) 250/F5
Imlaystown, N.J. (08526) 273/D3
Imler, Pa. (16655) 294/E5
Immaculata, Pa. (19345) 294/L6
Immenstadt, W. Ger. 22/C5
Immingham, Eng. 13/G4
Immokalee, Fla. (33934) 212/E5
Imnaha, Oreg. (97842) 291/L2
Imnaha (riv.), Oreg. 291/L2
Imogene, Iowa (51645) 229/C7
Imola, Italy 34/C2
Impach, Wash. (†99138) 310/G2
Impact‡, Texas (†79601) 302/E5
Imperatriz, Braz. 132/E4
Imperia (prov.), Italy 34/B3
Imperia, Italy 34/B3
Imperial (dam), Ariz. 198/A6
Imperial (res.), Ariz. 198/A6
Imperial (co.), Calif. 204/K10
Imperial, Calif. (92251) 204/K11
Imperial (dam), Calif. 204/L11
Imperial (res.), Calif. 204/L10
Imperial (valley), Calif. 204/K10
Imperial (riv.), Chile 138/D2
Imperial, Mo. (63052) 261/P4
Imperial, Nebr. (69033) 264/C4
Imperial, Pa. (15126) 294/B5
Imperial, Peru 128/D9
Imperial, Sask. 181/F4
Imperial, Texas (79743) 302/B6
Imperial Beach, Calif. (92032) 204/H11
Imperial Mills, Alta. 182/E2
Impfondo, Rep. of Congo 115/C3
Impfondo, 102/D4
Imphal, India, 54/N7
Imphal, India 68/G4
Impora, Bol. 136/C7
Imrali (isl.), Turkey 63/C2
Imranli, Turkey 63/H2
Imroz (isl.), Turkey 59/A1
Imroz, Turkey 63/B2
Imroz (isl.), Turkey 63/A2
Imst, Austria 41/A3
Imuris, Mex. 150/D1
Imuruan (bay), Phil. 82/B5
Imuruk (basin), Alaska 196/E1
'Imwas, Jordan 65/C4
Ina, Ill. (62846) 222/E5
Ina, Japan 81/H6
Ina (riv.), Japan 81/H7
Inaha, Ga. (†31790) 216/E7
Inala, Queens. 95/D3
Inambari, Peru 128/H9
Inambari (riv.), Peru 128/H9
In-Amenas, Alg. 106/F3
In-Amguel, Alg. 106/E4
Inangahua, N.Z. 101/C4
Iñapari, Peru 128/H8
Inari, Fin. 18/P2
Inari (lake), Fin. 18/P2
Inari (lake), Fin., 7/G2
Inavale, Nebr. (68952) 264/F4
Inawashiro (lake), Japan 81/K5
In-Azaoua (well), Niger 106/F4
Inca, Spain 33/H3
Incacamachi, Cerro (mt.), Bol. 136/A6
Inca de Oro, Chile 138/B6
Incaguasi, Nevada (mt.), Chile 138/C6
Incahuasi, Cerro de (mt.), Arg. 143/C2
Ince (cape), Turkey 63/F1
Incekum (cape), Turkey 63/F4
Incesu, Turkey 63/F3
Inchard (inlet), Scot. 15/F3
Inchcape (Bell Rock) (isl.), Scot. 15/M7
Inchelium, Wash. (99138) 310/G2
Inchigeela, Ire. 17/C8
Inchiri (reg.), Mauritania 106/A5
Inchkeith, Sask. 181/J5
Inchkeith (isl.), Scot. 15/K7
Inch'ŏn, S. Korea 81/C5
Inch'ŏn, S. Korea, 54/R6
Indaal (inlet), Scot. 15/D8
In Dagouber (well), Mali 106/D4
Indalsälven (riv.), Sweden 18/H5
Indawgyi (lake), Burma 72/C1
Indé, Mex. 150/G4
Independence (co.), Ark. 203/G2
Independence, Calif. (93526) 204/H7
Independence, Ind. (†47918) 227/C4
Independence, Iowa (50644) 229/K4
Independence, Kans. (67301) 232/G4
Independence, Ky. (41051) 237/M3
Independence, La. (70443) 238/M1
Independence (lake), Mich. 250/B2
Independence, Minn. (†55359) 254/F5
Independence (lake), Minn. 254/F5
Independence, Miss. (38638) 256/E1
Independence, Mo. (*64050) 261/R5
Independence (mts.), Nev. 266/E1
Independence, Ohio (44131) 284/H9
Independence, Oreg. (97351) 291/D3
Independence, Va. (24348) 307/F7
Independence, W. Va. (26374) 313/G4
Independence, Wis. (54747) 317/D7
Independencia, Bol. 136/B5
Independencia (prov.), Dom. Rep. 158/D6
Independencia (bay), Peru 128/D10
Independencia, Ven. 124/B4
Index, Wash. (98256) 310/D3
Index (peak), Wyo. 319/C1
India, 3/N4
India, 54/L7
INDIA, 68/D4
Indiahoma, Okla. (73552) 288/J5
Indialantic, Fla. (32901) 212/F3
India Muerta (riv.), Urug. 145/E4
Indian (mt.), Conn. 210/B1
Indian (pond), Conn. 210/A1
Indian (riv.), Del. 245/S6
Indian (riv.), Fla. 212/F3
Indian (creek), Idaho 220/C5
Indian (creek), Ind. 227/E8
Indian (creek), Ind. 227/D6
Indian (riv.), Md. 245/G4
Indian (lake), Mich. 250/C2
Indian (stream), N.H. 268/E1
Indian (harb.), N.S. 169/G3
Indian (lake), N.Y. 276/M3
Indian (lake), Ohio 284/C5
Indian (creek), S. Dak. 298/B4
Indian (creek), Utah 304/E5
Indian (creek), Utah 304/B5
Indiana, 188/J3
INDIANA, 227
Indiana (co.), Pa. 294/D4
Indiana, Pa. (15701) 294/D4
Indiana (state), U.S., 146/K6
Indiana Dunes Nat'l Lakeshore, Ind. 227/C1
Indianapolis (cap.), Ind., 146/K5
Indianapolis (cap.), Ind., 188/J3
Indianapolis (cap.), Ind. (*46201) 227/E5
Indian Bay, Man. 179/G5
Indian Brook, N.S. 169/H2
Indian Cabins, Alta. 182/B4
Indian Creek, Fla. (†33139) 212/B4
Indian Creek‡, Ill. (†60069) 222/E1
Indian Harbour, N.S. 169/E4
Indian Harbour Beach, Fla. (32935) 212/F3
Indian Head, 163/F5
Indian Head, Md. (20640) 245/K6
Indian Head, Sask. 181/H5

Isle Pierre 379

Indian Head Park‡, Ill. (†60525) 222/A1
Indian Hill, Ohio (†45201) 284/C9
Indian Hills‡, Ky. (†40201) 237/K4
Indian Hills, N.C. (†28719) 281/C4
Indian Hills Cherokee Section‡, Ky. (†40201) 237/K4
Indian Lake, N.Y. (12842) 276/M3
Indian Lake, Pa. (†15560) 294/E5
Indian Mills, W. Va. (24949) 313/E7
Indian Mound, Tenn. (37079) 237/F7
Indian Neck, Conn. (†06405) 210/D3
Indian Neck, Va. (23077) 307/O5
Indian Ocean, 3/N6
Indian Ocean, 54/L10
Indian Ocean, Ant. 5/C3
Indian Ocean, Indon. 85/E8
Indian Ocean, W. Aust. 92/A5
Indian Ocean, S. Aust. 94/E7
Indian Ocean, Vic. 97/B6
Indianola, Ill. (61850) 222/F4
Indianola, Iowa (50125) 229/F6
Indianola, Miss. (38751) 256/C4
Indianola, Nebr. (69034) 264/D4
Indianola, Okla. (74442) 288/P4
Indianola, Utah (†84629) 304/C4
Indianola, Wash. (98342) 310/A1
Indian Pond (lake), Maine 242/D4
Indian River (bay), Del. 245/T6
Indian River (inlet), Del. 245/T6
Indian River, Ont. 177/F3
Indian River (co.), Fla. 212/F4
Indian River, Maine (†04649) 242/H6
Indian River, Mich. (49749) 250/E3
Indian River Shores, Fla. (†32960) 212/F4
Indian Rocks Beach, Fla. (33535) 212/B3
Indian Rocks Beach South Shore, Fla. (†33535) 212/B3
Indian Springs, Ga. (30231) 216/E4
Indian Springs, Ind. (47544) 227/D7
Indian Springs, Man. 179/D5
Indian Springs, Nev. (89018) 266/F6
Indiantown, Fla. (33456) 212/F4
Indian Trail, N.C. (28079) 281/H4
Indian Valley, Idaho (83632) 220/B5
Indian Valley, Va. (24105) 307/G7
Indian Village, Ind. (†46601) 227/E1
Indian Village, La. (†70764) 238/H6
Indian Wells, Ariz. (86031) 198/E3
Indian Wells‡, Calif. (92260) 204/J10
Indiga, U.S.S.R. 48/E3
Indiga, U.S.S.R. 52/G1
Indigirka (riv.), U.S.S.R. 48/P3
Indigirka (river), U.S.S.R., 4/C2
Indigirka (riv.), U.S.S.R., 54/T3
Indigo (creek), Oreg. 291/D5
Indio, Calif. (92201) 204/J10
Indios (chan.), Cuba 158/B2
Indochina (reg.), 54/O8
Indochina (pen.), 72/E3
Indonesia, 3/Q6
Indonesia, 54/P10
INDONESIA, 85
Indooroopilly, Queens. 95/D3
Indore, India, 54/L7
Indore, India 68/D4
Indore, W. Va. (25111) 313/D6
Indramaju, Indon. 85/H2
Indramaju (pt.), Indon. 85/H1
Indravati (riv.), India 68/E5
Indre (dept.), France 28/D4
Indre (riv.), France 28/D4
Indre-et-Loire (dept.), France 28/D4
Indus (riv.), 3/N4
Indus (riv.), 54/K7
Indus, Alta. 182/D4
Indus, Minn. (56648) 254/E2
Indus (riv.), Pak. 59/J4
Indus (riv.), India 68/B3
Indus, Mouths of the (delta), Pak. 68/B4
Indus (riv.), Pak. 68/B3
Indus (riv.), China 77/A5
Industry‡, Calif. (†91744) 204/D10
Industry, Ill. (61440) 222/C3
Industry, Kans. (†67410) 232/E2
Industry, Pa. (15052) 294/B4
Industry, Texas (78944) 302/H7
Inebolu, Turkey 59/B1
Inebolu, Turkey 63/E2
Inegöl, Turkey 63/C2
In-Eker, Alg. 106/F4
Ineu, Rum. 45/E2
Inez, Ky. (41224) 237/S5
Inez, N.C. (27589) 281/N2
Inezgane, Mor. 106/C2
In-Ezzane (well), Alg. 106/G4
Infanta, Phil. 82/C3
Infieles (pt.), Chile 138/A6
Infiesto, Spain 33/D1
In-Gall, Niger 106/F5
Ingalls, Ark. (71648) 203/F7
Ingalls (mt.), Calif. 204/E3
Ingalls, Ind. (46048) 227/F5
Ingalls, Kans. (67853) 232/B4
Ingalls, Mich. (49848) 250/B3
Ingalls Park, Ill. (†60431) 222/F2
Ingavi, Bol. 136/B2
Ingelmunster, Belg. 27/C7
Ingelow, Man. 179/C5
Ingenbohl, Switz. 39/G2
Ingende, Dem. Rep. of the Congo. 115/C4
Ingeniero Huergo, Arg. 143/C4
Ingeniero Jacobacci, Arg. 143/C5
Ingeniero Luiggi, Arg. 143/D4
Ingeniero Montero Hoyos (Tocomechi), Bol. 136/D5
Ingersoll, Ont. 177/C4
Ingersoll, Okla. (†73728) 288/K1
Ingham, Aust. 88/H3
Ingham (co.), Mich. 250/E6
Ingham, Queens. 95/C3
Inglefield, Ind. (47618) 227/B8
Inglés (pt.), Cuba 158/G4
Inglesa (bay), Chile 138/A6
Ingleside, Ont. 177/J2
Ingleside‡, Ill. (60041) 222/E1
Ingleside, Md. (21644) 245/P4
Ingleside‡, Texas (78362) 302/G10
Ingleside, W. Va. (24730) 313/E8
Inglewood, Calif. (*90301) 204/B11
Inglewood, Ont. 177/E4
Inglewood, N.Z. 101/E3
Inglewood, Nebr. (†68025) 264/H3
Inglewood, Tenn. (†37201) 237/H8
Inglewood, Vic. 97/B5
Inglis, Fla. (32649) 212/D2
Inglis, Man. 179/A4
Ingold, N.C. (28446) 281/N5
Ingoldsby, Ont. 177/F3
Ingolstadt, W. Ger. 22/D4
Ingomar, Miss. (†38652) 256/F2
Ingomar, Mont. (59039) 262/J4
Ingomar, N.S. 169/C5
Ingonish, N.S. 169/H2
Ingonish, North (bay), N.S. 169/H2
Ingonish Beach, N.S. 169/H2
Ingornachoix (bay), Newf. 166/C3
Ingraham (lake), Fla. 212/E6
Ingraham, Ill. (62434) 222/E5
Ingram, Pa. (15205) 294/B7
Ingram, Texas (78025) 302/E7
Ingram, Va. (24564) 307/K7
Ingram, Wis. (54535) 317/E5
Ingre, Bol. 136/D7
In-Guezzam (well), Alg. 106/F5
Ingwavuma, S. Africa 118/E5
Inhambane, 102/F7
Inhambane (dist.), Moz. 118/E4
Inhaminga, Moz. 118/F3
Inharrime, Moz. 118/F4
Inhumas, Braz. 132/D7
Iniesta, Spain 33/F3
Ining (Kuldja), China 77/B3
Inini (dist.), Fr. Gui., 120/E2
Inini (dist.), Fr. Gui. 131/E4
Inini, Fr. Gui. 131/E4
Inini (riv.), Fr. Gui. 131/E4
Inírida (riv.), Col. 126/F6
Inishbofin (isl.), Ire. 17/A4
Inishbofin (isl.), Ire. 17/E1
Inishbofin (isl.), 10/A4
Inisheer (isl.), Ire. 17/B5
Inishmaan (isl.), Ire. 17/C5
Inishmore (isl.), Ire. 17/B5
Inishmurray (isl.), Ire. 17/D3
Inishowen (head), Ire. 17/H1
Inishowen (pen.), Ire. 17/G1
Inishshark (isl.), Ire. 17/A4
Inishtrahull (isl.), Ire. 17/G1
Inishtrahull (sound), Ire. 17/G1
Inishturk with Clare (isls.), Ire. 17/A4
Inishturk with Clare (isls.), 10/A4
Injune, Aust. 88/H5
Injune, Queens. 95/D5
Inkerman, N. Br. 170/F1
Inklin (riv.), Br. Col. 184/J2
Inkom, Idaho (83245) 220/F7
Inkster, Mich. (48141) 250/B7
Inkster, N. Dak. (58244) 283/P3
Inland (lake), Ala. 194/E3
Inland (lake), Alaska 196/G1
Inland, Alta. 182/D3
Inland (lake), Man. 179/C2
Inland, Nebr. (68954) 264/F4
Inle (lake), Burma 72/C2
Inlet, N.Y. (13360) 276/L3
Inman, Ga. (30232) 216/D4
Inman, Kans. (67546) 232/E3
Inman, Nebr. (68742) 264/F2
Inman, S.C. (29349) 296/C1
Inman Mills‡, S.C. (†29349) 296/C1
Inn (riv.), Austria 41/B2
Inn (riv.), Switz. 39/K3
Inn (riv.), W. Ger. 22/E4
Innamincka, S. Aust. 94/G2
Inner (sound), 10/D2
Inner (sound), Scot. 15/E5
Inner Hebrides (isls.), Scot. 15/D5
Innerkip, Ont. 177/D4
Innerleithen, 10/E3
Innerleithen, Scot. 15/K8
Inner Mongolia (reg.), China, 54/O5
Inner Mongolia (reg.), China 77/H3
Inner Mongolian (aut. reg.), China 77/G3
Innertkirchen, Switz. 39/F3
Innes (lake), N.S.W. 97/G2
Innis, La. (70747) 238/G5
Innis, Sask. 181/H6
Inniscrone, Ire. 17/C3
Innisfail, Alta. 182/D3
Innisfail, Aust. 88/H3
Innisfail, Queens. 95/C3
Innisfree, Alta. 182/E3
Innisville, Ont. 177/H2
Innoko (riv.), Alaska 196/G2
Innsbruck, Austria, 7/F4
Innsbruck, Austria 41/A3
Innuit (mt.), Newf. 166/B2
Inny (riv.), Ire. 17/A8
Inny (riv.), Ire. 17/F4
Inola, Okla. (74036) 288/P2
Inongo, 102/D5
Inongo, Dem. Rep. of the Congo. 115/C4
Inönü, Turkey 63/D3
Inoucdjouac, 163/J4
Inoucdjouac, Que. 174/E1
Inowrocław, Poland 47/C2
Inquisivi, Bol. 136/B5
In-Rhar, Alg. 106/E3
Ins, Switz. 39/D2
In Salah, Alg. 106/E3
In Salah, 102/C2
Insch, Scot. 15/L5
Insein, Burma 72/C3
Inset, Norway 18/G5
Insh, Scot. 15/J5
Insinger, Sask. 181/H4
Inspiration, Ariz. (85537) 198/D5
Institute, W. Va. (25112) 313/C6
Instow, Sask. 181/C6
Inta, U.S.S.R. 48/G3
Inta, U.S.S.R. 52/K1
Intake, Mont. (59335) 262/M3
Intelewa, Sur. 131/D4
Intendente Alvear, Arg. 143/D4
Intepe, Turkey 63/B6
Intercession City, Fla. (33848) 212/E3
Intercourse, Pa. (17534) 294/K5
Interior, S. Dak. (57750) 298/F6
Interlachen, Fla. (32048) 212/E2
Interlaken, Mass. (†01266) 249/A3
Interlaken, N.J. (†07712) 273/E3
Interlaken, N.Y. (14847) 276/G5
Interlaken, Switz. 39/E3
Interlochen, Mich. (49643) 250/D4
International Falls, Minn., 188/H1
International Falls, Minn. (56649) 254/E2
International Peace Garden, Man. 179/B5
International Peace Garden, N. Dak. 283/K1
Intervale, N.H. (03845) 268/E3
Interview (isl.), India 68/G6
Inthanon, Doi (mt.), Thai. 72/C3
Intipucá, El Salv. 154/D4
Intracoastal Waterway, S.C. 296/H5
Intracoastal Waterway, Texas 302/J9
Intragna, Switz. 39/G4
Intutu, Peru 128/E4
Inubo (cape), Japan 81/K6
Inútil (bay), Chile 138/E10
Inuvik, 163/C2
Inuvik, Canada, 4/C16
Inuvik, N.W.T., 146/E3
Inuvik, N.W.T. 187/E3
Inver (bay), Ire. 17/E2
Inver (inlet), Scot. 15/F3
Inveraray, 10/D2
Inveraray, Scot. 15/F7
Inverbervie, 10/E2
Inverbervie, Scot. 15/M6
Invercargill, N. Z., 87/H10
Invercargill, N.Z. 101/B7
Inverell, Aust. 88/J5
Inverell, N.S.W. 97/F1
Invergordon, 10/D2
Invergordon, Scot. 15/H4
Inver Grove Heights, Minn. (55075) 254/E6
Inverie, Scot. 15/E5
Inverkeilor, Scot. 15/M6
Inverkeithing, 10/C1
Inverkeithing, Scot. 15/K7
Invermay, Sask. 181/J4
Invermere, Br. Col. 184/J5
Inverness, 163/K6
Inverness, Ala. (†36089) 194/G6
Inverness, Calif. (94937) 204/B5
Inverness, Que. 172/F3
Inverness, Fla. (32650) 212/D3
Inverness‡, Ill. (†60067) 222/E1
Inverness, 10/D2
Inverness, Miss. (38753) 256/C4
Inverness, Mont. (59530) 262/F2
Inverness (co.), N.S. 169/G2
Inverness, N.S. 169/G2
Inverness, Scot., 7/D3
Inverness (co.), Scot. 15/G5
Inverness, Scot. 15/H5
Inverurie, 10/E2
Inverurie, Scot. 15/M5
Inverway, No. Terr. 93/A4
Investigator (str.), Aust. 88/F7
Investigator (shoal), Asia 85/E4
Investigator (str.), S. Aust. 94/E6
Investigator Group (isls.), Aust. 88/E6
Investigator Group (isls.), S. Aust. 94/D5
Inwood, Ont. 177/C5
Inwood, Ind. (46533) 227/E2
Inwood, Iowa (51240) 229/A2
Inwood, Man. 179/E4
Inwood, N.Y. (11696) 276/R7
Inwood, W. Va. (25428) 313/K4
Inyanga, Rhod. 118/E3
Inyanga Nat'l Park, Rhod. 118/E3
Inyan Kara (creek), Wyo. 319/H1
Inyan Kara (mt.), Wyo. 319/H1
Inyo (co.), Calif. 204/H7
Inyo (mts.), Calif. 204/G6
Inyokern, Calif. (93527) 204/H8
Inyokern Nav. Ordnance Test Sta., Calif. 204/H8
Inza, U.S.S.R. 52/G4
Inzana (lake), Br. Col. 184/E3
Ioánnina, Greece, 7/G4
Ioánnina, Greece 45/E6
Ioco, Br. Col. 184/K3
Ioka, Utah (†84052) 304/D3
Iola, Ill. (62847) 222/E5
Iola, Kans. (66749) 232/G4
Iola, Texas (77861) 302/H7
Iola, Wis. (54945) 317/H6
Iolotan', U.S.S.R. 48/G6
Ioma, Papua 85/C7
Iona, Ont. 177/C5
Iona, Idaho (83427) 220/G6
Iona, Minn. (56141) 254/C7
Iona, N.J. (†08322) 273/C4
Iona, N.S. 169/H3
Iona (isls.), Newf. 166/C2
Iona, Angola 115/B7
Iona (isl.), 10/C2
Iona, S. Dak. (57542) 298/L6
Iona (isl.), Scot. 15/D7
Iona (sound), Scot. 15/D7
Ione, Ark. (†72927) 203/B3
Ione, Calif. (95640) 204/C9
Ione, Nev. (†89310) 266/D4
Ione, Oreg. (97843) 291/H2
Ione, Wash. (99139) 310/H2
Ionia, Iowa (50645) 229/J2
Ionia, Kans. (66947) 232/D2
Ionia (co.), Mich. 250/D6
Ionia, Mich. (48846) 250/D6
Ionia, Mo. (65335) 261/F6
Ionian (sea), 7/F5
Ionian (isls.), Greece, 7/F5
Ionian (sea), Greece 45/D7
Ionian (sea), Italy 34/F6
Ionian Islands (reg.), Greece 45/D6
Íos (isl.), Greece 45/G7
Iosco (co.), Mich. 250/F4
Iosegun (lake), Alta. 182/B2
Iosegun (riv.), Alta. 182/B2
Iota, La. (70543) 238/E6
Iowa, 188/H2
IOWA, 229
Iowa (riv.), Iowa, 188/H2
Iowa (co.), Iowa 229/J5
Iowa (riv.), Iowa 229/H4
Iowa, La. (70647) 238/D6
Iowa (state), U.S., 146/J5
Iowa (co.), Wis. 317/F9
Iowa City, Iowa, 188/H2
Iowa City, Iowa (52240) 229/L5
Iowa Colony, Texas (†77583) 302/J2
Iowa Falls, Iowa (50126) 229/G3
Iowa Park, Texas (76367) 302/F4
Iowa Point, Kans. (†66035) 232/G2
Ipala, Guat. 154/C3
Ipameri, Braz. 132/E7
Iparia, Peru 128/E7
Ipava, Ill. (61441) 222/C3
Ipel' (riv.), Czech. 41/E2
Iphigenia (bay), Alaska 196/M2
Ipiales, Col. 126/B7
Ipiaú, Braz. 132/G6
Ipil, Phil. 82/D7
Ipin, China, 54/O7
Ipin, China 77/F6
Ipitá, Bol. 136/D6
Ipoh, Malaysia, 54/O9
Ipoh, Malaysia 72/D6
Ipoly (riv.), Hung. 41/E2
Ipperwash Prov. Park, Ont. 177/C4
Ippy, Centr. Afr. Rep. 115/D2
Ipsala, Turkey 63/B2
Ipsile, Turkey 63/G2
Ipswich, 10/G4
Ipswich, Australia, 87/F8
Ipswich, Aust. 88/K2
Ipswich, Jam. 158/H6
Ipswich, Eng. 13/J5
Ipswich△, Mass. (01938) 249/L2
Ipswich, Mass. (01938) 249/L2
Ipswich (riv.), Mass. 249/L2
Ipswich, Queens. 95/E5
Ipswich, S. Dak. (57451) 298/L3
Ipu, Braz. 132/F4
Iquique, Chile, 120/C5
Iquique, Chile 138/A2
Iquitos, Peru, 120/C3
Iquitos, Peru 128/F4
Ira, Iowa (50127) 229/G5
Ira, Mo. (†65463) 261/G7
Ira, N.Y. (†13033) 276/G4
Ira, Texas (79527) 302/C5
Ira△, Vt. (†05777) 268/A4
Ira, Vt. (†05777) 268/A4
Iraan, Texas (79744) 302/B7
Iracoubo, Fr. Gui. 131/E3
Iráklion, Greece, 7/G5
Iráklion, Greece 45/G8
Irala, Par. 144/E5
Iran, 3/M4
Iran, 54/J6
IRAN, 59/F3
IRAN, 66
Iran (mts.), Malaysia 85/E5
Iranshahr, Iran 59/H4
Iranshahr, Iran 66/M7
Irapa, Ven. 124/G2
Irapuato, Mex. 150/J6
Iraq, 3/M4
Iraq, 54/H6
IRAQ, 59/D3
IRAQ, 66
Irasburg△, Vt. (05845) 268/C2
Irasburg, Vt. (05845) 268/C2
Irati, Braz. 132/D9
Irati, Braz. 135/A4
Irawan, Phil. 82/B6
Irazú (mt.), C. Rica 154/F6
Irbid, Jordan 65/D2
Irby, Wash. (99159) 310/G3
Ircalaya, Bol. 136/C7
Iredell (co.), N.C. 281/H3
Iredell, Texas (76649) 302/G6
Ireland, 3/J3
Ireland, 7/C3
IRELAND, 10/B4
IRELAND, 17
Ireland (isl.), Berm. 156/G3
Ireland, Ind. (47545) 227/C8
Ireland, Texas (76536) 302/F6
Ireland, W. Va. (26376) 313/F5
Ireland's Eye (isl.), Ire. 17/K5
Ireland's Eye, Newf. 166/D2
Irene, S. Africa 118/H6
Irene, S. Dak. (57037) 298/P7
Ireng (riv.), Guyana 131/B3
Ireton, Iowa (51027) 229/A3
Irharhar, Wadi (dry riv.), Alg. 106/F3
Iri, S. Korea 81/C6
Iriga, Phil. 82/D4
Irigoyen, Arg. 143/F6
Iringa (reg.), Tanz. 115/G4
Iringa, Tanz. 115/G5
Iriomote (isl.), Ryukyu Is. 81/K7
Irion (co.), Texas 302/C6
Iriona, Hond. 154/E2
Iriri (riv.), Braz., 120/E3
Iriri (riv.), Braz. 132/C4
Irish (sea), 7/D3
Irish (sea), 10/D4
Irish (sea), Eng. 13/C4
Irish (sea), Ire. 17/K4
Irishtown, N. Br. 170/F2
Irish Vale, N.S. 169/H3
Irkutsk, U.S.S.R. 48/L4
Irkutsk, U.S.S.R., 3/Q3
Irkutsk, U.S.S.R., 54/O4
Irma, Alta. 182/E3
Irma, Wis. (54442) 317/G5
Irmo, S.C. (29063) 296/E3
Iro (cape), Japan 81/J6
Irois (cape), Haiti 158/A6
Iron (mt.), Fla. 212/E4
Iron (co.), Mich. 250/G2
Iron (riv.), Mich. 250/F1
Iron, Minn. (55751) 254/F3
Iron (co.), Mo. 261/L7
Iron (mts.), Tenn. 237/S8
Iron (co.), Utah 304/A6
Iron (co.), Wis. 317/F3
Iron Belt, Wis. (54536) 317/F3
Ironbound (isls.), Newf. 166/C2
Iron Bridge, Ont. 177/A1
Iron City, Ga. (31759) 216/C8
Iron City, Tenn. (38463) 237/F10
Irondale, Ala. (35210) 194/E3
Irondale, Mo. (63648) 261/L7
Irondale, Ohio (43932) 284/J4
Irondequoit△, N.Y. (14617) 276/E4
Iron Gate (res.), Calif. 204/C2
Iron Gate (canyon), Rum., 7/G4
Iron Gate, Va. (24448) 307/J5
Iron Gates‡, Mo. (†64801) 261/D8
Ironia, N.J. (07845) 273/D2
Iron Knob, Aust. 88/F6
Iron Knob, S. Aust. 94/E5
Iron Mountain, Mich. (49801) 250/B3
Iron Mountain, Wyo. (82062) 319/G4
Iron Range, Queens. 95/B2
Iron Ridge, Wis. (53035) 317/K9
Iron River, Alta. 182/E2
Iron River, Mich. (49935) 250/G2
Iron River, Wis. (54847) 317/D2
Irons, Mich. (49644) 250/D4
Ironshire, Md. (†21811) 245/T7
Ironside, Oreg. (97908) 291/K3
Ironspring (creek), Sask. 181/G3
Iron Springs, Alta. 182/D5
Iron Springs, Ariz. (86330) 198/C4
Iron Station, N.C. (28080) 281/G4
Ironton, Colo. (81427) 208/D7
Ironton, Minn. (56455) 254/D4
Ironton, Mo. (63650) 261/L7
Ironton, Ohio (45638) 284/E8
Ironton, Wis. (53938) 317/F8
Ironwood, Mich. (49938) 250/F2
Iroquois, Ont. 177/J3
Iroquois (co.), Ill. 222/F3
Iroquois, Ill. (60945) 222/F3
Iroquois (riv.), Ill. 222/F3
Iroquois (riv.), Ind. 227/B3
Iroquois, N. Br. 170/B1
Iroquois, S. Dak. (57353) 298/O5
Iroquois (lake), Vt. 268/A3
Iroquois Falls, 163/H6
Iroquois Falls, Ont. 175/D3
Iroquois Falls, Ont. 177/J5
Iroquois Point, Hawaii (†96706) 218/A4
'Irqa, P.D.R. Yemen 59/E7
Irrara (creek), N.S.W. 97/C1
Irrawaddy (riv.), Burma, 54/N7
Irrawaddy (div.), Burma 72/B3
Irrawaddy (riv.), Burma 72/B3
Irrawaddy, Mouths of the (delta), Burma 72/B4
Irricana, Alta. 182/D4
Irrigon, Oreg. (97844) 291/H2
Irtysh (riv.), U.S.S.R. 48/H4
Irtysh (riv.), U.S.S.R., 54/K4
Irumu, 102/E4
Irumu, Dem. Rep. of the Congo. 115/E3
Irún, Spain 33/F1
Irupana, Bol. 136/B5
Iruya, Arg. 143/D1
Irvine, Alta. 182/E5
Irvine, Ky. (40336) 237/O5
Irvine, 10/D3
Irvine (lake), N. Dak. 283/M3
Irvine, Pa. (16329) 294/D2
Irvine, Scot. 15/G8
Irvinestown, N. Ire. 17/F3
Irving, Ill. (62051) 222/D4
Irving, Iowa (†52225) 229/J5
Irving, N.Y. (14081) 276/B5
Irving, Texas (75060) 302/G2
Irvington, Ala. (36544) 194/B9
Irvington, Ill. (62848) 222/D5
Irvington, Iowa (50550) 229/E3
Irvington, Ky. (40146) 237/J5
Irvington, N.J. (07111) 273/B2
Irvington, N.Y. (10533) 276/O6
Irvington, Va. (22480) 307/R5
Irvin's (bay), Grenada 161/D8
Irvona, Pa. (16656) 294/E4
Irwin (co.), Ga. 216/F7
Irwin, Idaho (83428) 220/G6
Irwin‡, Ill. (†60901) 222/E2
Irwin, Iowa (51446) 229/C5
Irwin, Mo. (64754) 261/D7
Irwin, Ohio (43029) 284/D5
Irwin, Pa. (15642) 294/C5
Irwin, S.C. (†29720) 296/F2
Irwin, Va. (23078) 307/N5
Irwindale‡, Calif. (91706) 204/D10
Irwinton, Ga. (31042) 216/F5
Irwinville, Ga. (31760) 216/F7
Isa, Nigeria 106/F6
Isaac (lake), Br. Col. 184/G3
Isaacs (riv.), Aust. 88/H4
Isaacs (riv.), Queens. 95/D4
Isaac's Harbour, N.S. 169/G3
Isabel (bay), Ec. 128/B9
Isabel, Kans. (67065) 232/D4
Isabel, La. (†70427) 238/K5
Isabel, S. Dak. (57633) 298/G3
Isabel (mt.), Wyo. 319/B3
Isabela, P. Rico 156/F1
Isabela (pt.), Dom. Rep. 158/D5
Isabela (cape), Dom. Rep. 158/D5
Isabela, P. Rico 161/A1
Isabela (isl.), Ec. 128/B9
Isabela (prov.), Phil. 82/C2
Isabela de Sagua, Cuba 158/E1
Isabelia, Cordillera (range), Nic. 154/E4
Isabella (res.), Calif. 204/G8
Isabella, Man. 179/B4
Isabella (co.), Mich. 250/E5
Isabella, Mich. (†49878) 250/C3
Isabella, Minn. (55607) 254/G3
Isabella (lake), Minn. 254/G3
Isabella (riv.), Minn. 254/G3
Isabella (bay), N.W.T. 187/M3
Isabella, Okla. (73747) 288/K2
Isabella, Tenn. (37346) 237/N10
Isabel María, Cuba 158/A2
Isabel Rubio, Cuba 158/A2
Isabel Segunda, P. Rico 161/G2
Isaccea, Rum. 45/J3
Isachsen, Canada, 4/B15
Isachsen, N.W.T., 146/G2
Isachsen, N.W.T. 187/H2
Isachsen (cape), N.W.T. 187/H2
Ísafjördhur, Ice. 21/B1
Ísafjördhur (fjord), Ice. 21/B1
Isahaya, Japan 81/D7
Isana (riv.), Col. 126/F7
Isangi, Dem. Rep. of the Congo. 115/D3
Isangila, Dem. Rep. of the Congo. 115/B5
Isanti (co.), Minn. 254/E5
Isanti, Minn. (55040) 254/E5
Isar (riv.), W. Ger. 22/E4
Isarog (mt.), Phil. 82/D4
Isbell, Ala. (†35653) 194/C2
Iscar, Spain 33/D2
Ischia (isl.), Italy 34/D4
Ischua, N.Y. (14746) 276/D6
Iscuandé, Col. 126/A6
Ise (fjord), Den. 21/E6
Ise, Japan 81/H6
Ise (bay), Japan 81/H6
Iselin, N.J. (08830) 273/E2
Iselin, Pa. (15681) 294/D4
Isenthal, Switz. 39/F3
Iseo (lake), Italy 34/C2
Isère (dept.), France 28/F5
Isère (riv.), France 28/F5
Iserlohn, W. Ger. 22/B3
Isernia, Italy 34/E4
Ise-Shima Nat'l Park, Japan 81/H6
Iseyin, Nigeria 106/E7
Isfahan, Iran, 54/J6
Isfahan, Iran 59/F3
Isfahan (prov.), Iran 66/H4
Isfahan, Iran 66/G4
Isfandak, Iran 66/N7
Isfi Maidan, Afgh. 59/J2
Isfi Maidan, Afgh. 68/B1
Isfjorden (fjord), Norway 18/C2
Isham, Sask. 181/C4
Ishan, China 77/G7
Ishigaki, Ryukyu Is. 81/L7
Ishigaki (isl.), Ryukyu Is. 81/L7
Ishige, Japan 81/P2
Ishikari (bay), Japan 81/K2
Ishikari (riv.), Japan 81/L2
Ishikawa (pref.), Japan 81/H5
Ishim, U.S.S.R. 48/H4
Ishim (riv.), U.S.S.R. 48/G4
Ishim (riv.), U.S.S.R., 54/K4
Ishimbay, U.S.S.R. 48/F4
Ishimbay, U.S.S.R. 52/J4
Ishinomaki, Japan 81/K4
Ishioka, Japan 81/K5
Ishizuchi (mt.), Japan 81/F7
Ishkashim, Afgh. 59/K2
Ishpeming, Mich. (49849) 250/B2
Isiboro (riv.), Bol. 136/C5
Isil'-Kul', U.S.S.R. 48/H4
Isimu, Indon. 85/G5
Isiolo, Kenya 115/G3
Isiro, Dem. Rep. of the Congo. 115/E3
Isisford, Queens. 95/C5
Iskenderun, Turkey 59/C2
Iskenderun, Turkey 63/G4
Iskilip, Turkey 63/F2
Iskŭr (riv.), Bulg. 45/G4
Iskut (riv.), Br. Col. 184/B2
Isla, Salar de la (salt dep.), Chile 138/B5
Isla (riv.), Scot. 15/K6
Isla Alta, Par. 144/D6
Isla Cristina, Spain 33/C4
Isla de Aguada, Mex. 150/O7
Isla de Maipo, Chile 138/G4
Islâhiye, Turkey 63/G4
Islamabad (cap.), Pak. 68/C2
Islamabad (cap.), Pak., 3/N4
Islamabad (cap.), Pak., 54/K6
Islamorada, Fla. (33036) 212/F7
Isla Mujeres, Mex. 150/Q6
Island (lake), 163/G5
Island, Ky. (42350) 237/G6
Island (lake), Man. 179/K3
Island (lake), N. Dak. 283/L2
Island (beach), N.J. 273/E4
Island (bay), Phil. 82/B6
Island (lag.), S. Aust. 94/E4
Island (pond), Vt. 268/D2
Island (co.), Wash. 310/C2
Island City, Oreg. (97851) 291/K2
Island Creek, Md. (†20685) 245/M7
Island Falls, Ont. 175/D3
Island Falls△, Maine (04747) 242/G3
Island Grove, Fla. (32654) 212/D2
Island Heights, N.J. (08732) 273/E4
Islandia, Fla. (†33101) 212/F6
Island Lake, Ill. (60042) 222/E1
Island Lake, Man. 179/J3
Island Lake, Wis. (†54757) 317/D5
Island Park, Idaho (83429) 220/G5
Island Park (res.), Idaho 220/G5
Island Park, N.Y. (11558) 276/R8
Island Park, R.I. (†02871) 249/J6
Island Pond, Vt. (05846) 268/D2
Islands (bay), N.Z. 101/E1
Islands (bay), Newf. 166/C2
Islands (bay), Newf. 166/C4
Islandton, S.C. (29929) 296/F6
Island View, Minn. (†56649) 254/E2
Isla Patrulla, Urug. 145/E3
Isla Pucú, Par. 144/B6
Isla Umbú, Par. 144/C6
Isla Vista, Calif. (93017) 204/E9
Islay, Alta. 182/E3
Islay (isl.), 10/C3
Islay (isl.), Scot. 15/D8
Islay (sound), Scot. 15/D8
Isle (riv.), France 28/D5
Isle, Minn. (56342) 254/E4
Isle au Haut△, Maine (04645) 242/F7
Isle-aux-Coudres, Que. 172/G2
Isle-aux-Grues, Que. 172/G2
Isle aux Morts, Newf. 166/C4
Isle La Motte△, Vt. (05463) 268/A2
Isle La Motte, Vt. (05463) 268/A2
Isle of Hope, Ga. (31406) 216/K7
ISLE OF MAN, 13/C3
ISLE OF MAN, 10/D3
Isle of Palms, S.C. (29451) 296/H6
Isle of Wight (co.), Eng. 13/F7
Isle of Wight (co.), Va. 307/P7
Isle of Wight, Va. (23397) 307/P7
Isle Pierre, Br. Col. 184/F3

Julian 381

Jay▵, Maine (04239) 242/C7
Jay, Maine (04239) 242/C7
Jay, N.Y. (12941) 276/N2
Jay, Okla. (74346) 288/S2
Jay▵, Vt. (†05859) 268/C2
Jay, Vt. (†05859) 268/C2
Jay (peak), Vt. 268/B2
Jayanca, Peru 128/B6
Jay Em, Wyo. (82219) 319/H3
Jayess, Miss. (39641) 256/D8
Jayton, Texas (79528) 302/D4
Jayuya, P. Rico 156/G1
Jayuya, P. Rico 161/C2
Jaz-Murian, Hamun-i- (marsh), Iran 59/G4
Jaz Murian, Hamun-i- (marsh), Iran 66/L7
Jean, Nev. (89019) 266/F7
Jean, Texas (†76374) 302/F4
Jean Coté, Alta. 182/B2
Jeanerette, La. (70544) 238/G7
Jeanette (bay), Newf. 166/C3
Jean Marie, N.W.T. 187/F3
Jeanne Mance, N. Br. 170/E1
Jeannette, Pa. (15644) 294/C5
Jean-Rabel, Haiti 158/B5
Jean-Rabel (pt.), Haiti 158/B5
Jebba, Nigeria 106/E7
Jebel Abyad (plat.), Sudan 111/E4
Jebel Aulia (dam), Sudan 111/F4
Jebel Dhanna, Trucial States 59/F5
Jeberos, Peru 128/D5
Jeble, Syria 63/F5
Jechiang (Charkhliq), China 77/C4
Jedburg, S.C. (†29483) 296/G5
Jedburgh, 10/E3
Jedburgh, Sask. 181/J4
Jedburgh, Scot. 15/M9
Jeddito, Ariz. (†86025) 198/E3
Jeddo, Mich. (48032) 250/G5
Jeddo, Pa. (†18224) 294/L3
Jeddore (cape), N.S. 169/E4
Jeddore (harb.), N.S. 169/F4
Jeddore Oyster Ponds, N.S. 169/F4
Jędrzejów, Poland 47/E3
Jedway, Br. Col. 184/B4
Jefara (reg.), Libya 111/B1
Jefara (reg.), Tun. 106/G2
Jeff, Ala. (†35804) 194/E1
Jeff, Ky. (41751) 237/P6
Jeff Davis (co.), Ga. 216/G7
Jeff Davis (co.), Texas 302/C11
Jeffers, Minn. (56145) 254/C6
Jeffers, Mont. (59737) 262/E5
Jefferson (co.), Ala. 194/E3
Jefferson, Ala. (36745) 194/C6
Jefferson (co.), Ark. 203/G5
Jefferson, Ark. (72079) 203/F5
Jefferson (co.), Colo. 208/J3
Jefferson, Colo. (80456) 208/H4
Jefferson (co.), Fla. 212/C1
Jefferson (co.), Ga. 216/H4
Jefferson, Ga. (30549) 216/F2
Jefferson (co.), Idaho 220/F6
Jefferson (co.), Ill. 222/E5
Jefferson (co.), Ind. 227/G7
Jefferson, Ind. (†46041) 227/D4
Jefferson (co.), Iowa 229/K6
Jefferson, Iowa (50129) 229/E4
Jefferson (co.), Kans. 232/G2
Jefferson (co.), Ky. 237/K4
Jefferson (par.), La. 238/K7
Jefferson▵, Maine (04348) 242/D7
Jefferson, Mass. (01522) 249/G3
Jefferson, Md. (21755) 245/J3
Jefferson (co.), Miss. 256/B7
Jefferson (co.), Mo. 261/L6
Jefferson (co.), Mont. 262/D4
Jefferson (riv.), Mont. 262/D5
Jefferson, N.C. (28640) 281/G2
Jefferson▵, N.H. (03583) 268/D3
Jefferson, N.H. (03583) 268/E3
Jefferson (mt.), N.H. 268/E3
Jefferson (co.), N.Y. 276/J2
Jefferson, N.Y. (12093) 276/L6
Jefferson (co.), Nebr. 264/G4
Jefferson (co.), Ohio 284/J5
Jefferson, Ohio (44047) 284/J2
Jefferson (West Jefferson), Ohio (†43162) 284/D6
Jefferson (co.), Okla. 288/L6
Jefferson, Okla. (73748) 288/L1
Jefferson (co.), Oreg. 291/F3
Jefferson, Oreg. (97352) 291/D3
Jefferson (mt.), Oreg. 291/F3
Jefferson (co.), Pa. 294/D3
Jefferson, Pa. (†15025) 294/B7
Jefferson, Pa. (15344) 294/B6
Jefferson (Codorus), Pa. (17311) 294/J6
Jefferson, S.C. (29718) 296/G2
Jefferson, S. Dak. (57038) 298/S8
Jefferson (co.), Tenn. 237/P8
Jefferson (co.), Texas 302/K8
Jefferson, Texas (75657) 302/K5
Jefferson, Va. (†23139) 307/N5
Jefferson‡, Va. (22303) 307/O3
Jefferson (co.), W. Va. 313/L4
Jefferson (co.), Wash. 310/B3
Jefferson (co.), Wis. 317/J9
Jefferson, Wis. (53549) 317/J10
Jefferson City (cap.), Mo., 146/J6
Jefferson City (cap.), Mo., 188/H3
Jefferson City (cap.), Mo. (65101) 261/H5
Jefferson City, Mont. (59638) 262/E4
Jefferson City, Tenn. (37760) 237/P8
Jefferson Davis (par.), La. 238/E6
Jefferson Davis (co.), Miss. 256/E7
Jefferson Heights, La. (70121) 238/O4
Jefferson Island, Mont. (†59721) 262/E5
Jefferson Nat'l Expansion Mem., Mo. 261/R3
Jefferson Proving Ground, Ind. 227/G7
Jeffersonton, Va. (22724) 307/N3
Jeffersontown, Ky. (40299) 237/L4
Jefferson-Trooper‡, Pa. (†19401) 294/M5
Jeffersonville, Ga. (31044) 216/F5
Jeffersonville, Ind. (47130) 227/F8
Jeffersonville, Ky. (40337) 237/O5
Jeffersonville, N.Y. (12748) 276/L7
Jeffersonville, Ohio (43128) 284/C6
Jeffersonville, Vt. (05464) 268/B2
Jeffrey, N. Br. 170/E3
Jeffrey (res.), Nebr. 264/D4
Jeffrey, W. Va. (25114) 313/C7
Jeffrey City, Wyo. (82310) 319/E3
Jeffrey's, Newf. 166/C4
Jef Jef (plat.), Chad 111/D3
Jega, Nigeria 106/E6
Jegenstorf, Switz. 39/D2
Jeinemeni, Cerro (mt.), Chile 138/E6
Jeisyville, Ill. (†62568) 222/D4
Jejui-guazú (riv.), Par. 144/D5
Jēkabpils, U.S.S.R. 52/C3
Jēkabpils, U.S.S.R. 53/C2
Jekyll (isl.), Ga. 216/K8
Jelenia Góra, Poland 47/B3
Jelgava, U.S.S.R. 52/B3
Jelgava, U.S.S.R. 53/B2
Jelgava, U.S.S.R., 7/G3
Jelib, Somalia 115/H3
Jellico, Tenn. (37762) 237/N7
Jellico Creek, Ky. (†40769) 237/N7
Jellicoe, Br. Col. 184/G5
Jellicoe, Ont. 177/H5
Jelling, Den. 21/C6
Jelloway, Ohio (†43014) 284/F4
Jelm, Wyo. (82063) 319/G4
Jelšava, Czech. 41/E2
Jemappes, Belg. 27/D8
Jemeppe, Belg. 27/G7
Jemez (riv.), N. Mex. 274/C3
Jemez Canyon (res.), N. Mex. 274/C3
Jemez Pueblo, N. Mex. (87024) 274/C3
Jemez Springs, N. Mex. (87025) 274/C3
Jemison, Ala. (35085) 194/E5
Jemnice, Czech. 41/C2
Jemseg, N. Br. 170/D3
Jemtland, Maine (†04783) 242/G1
Jena, E. Ger. 22/D3
Jena, La. (71342) 238/F3
Jenaz, Switz. 39/J3
Jenbach, Austria 41/A3
Jendouba, Tun. 106/F1
Jenera, Ohio (45841) 284/C4
Jenifer, Ala. (†36268) 194/G3
Jenin, Jordan 65/C3
Jenison, Mich. (49428) 250/D6
Jenkinjones, W. Va. (24848) 313/D8
Jenkins (co.), Ga. 216/J5
Jenkins, Ky. (41537) 237/R6
Jenkins, Minn. (56456) 254/D4
Jenkins, Mo. (65677) 261/E9
Jenkinsburg, Ga. (30234) 216/E4
Jenkinsville, S.C. (29065) 296/E3
Jenkintown, Pa. (19046) 294/M5
Jenks, Okla. (74037) 288/P2
Jenner, Alta. 182/E4
Jennersdorf, Austria 41/C3
Jennerstown, Pa. (15547) 294/D5
Jennie, Ark. (71649) 203/H7
Jennings, Antigua 161/D11
Jennings, Fla. (32053) 212/C1
Jennings (co.), Ind. 227/F7
Jennings, Kans. (67643) 232/B2
Jennings, La. (70546) 238/E6
Jennings, Md. (†21536) 245/B2
Jennings, Mich. (†49651) 250/D4
Jennings, Mo. (63136) 261/P2
Jennings, Okla. (74038) 288/N2
Jennings Lodge, Oreg. (97267) 291/B2
Jenny (creek), Oreg. 291/E5
Jenny Lake, Wyo. (†83012) 319/B2
Jenny Lind, Ark. (†72901) 203/B3
Jenny Lind, Calif. (†95252) 204/C9
Jenny Lind (isl.), N.W.T. 187/H3
Jenolan Caves, N.S.W. 97/E3
Jensen, Utah (84035) 304/E3
Jensen Beach, Fla. (33457) 212/F4
Jens Munk (isl.), 163/J2
Jens Munk (isl.), N.W.T. 187/K3
Jequié, Braz., 120/F4
Jequié, Braz. 132/F6
Jequitinhonha, Braz. 132/F7
Jequitinhonha (riv.), Braz. 132/F7
Jerablus, Syria 63/G4
Jerada, Mor. 106/D2
Jerauld (co.), S. Dak. 298/M5
Jérémie, Haiti 156/C3
Jérémie, Haiti 158/A6
Jeremoabo, Braz. 132/G5
Jeremy (riv.), Conn. 210/F2
Jerez, Spain, 7/D5
Jerez de García Salinas, Mex. 150/H5
Jerez de la Frontera, Spain 33/C4
Jerez de los Caballeros, Spain 33/C3
Jericho, Ark. (†72327) 203/K3
Jericho, Aust. 88/H4
Jericho, N.Y. (11753) 276/S7
Jericho, Jordan 65/C4
Jericho, Queens 95/C4
Jericho, Va. (†23434) 307/P7
Jericho▵, Vt. (05465) 268/B3
Jericho, Vt. (05465) 268/A2
Jericho Center, Vt. (05465) 268/B3
Jerico Springs, Mo. (64756) 261/E7
Jeriel, Ky. (41151) 237/R4
Jerilderie, N.S.W. 97/C4
Jerimoth (hill), R.I. 249/G5
Jermyn, Pa. (18433) 294/L2
Jermyn, Texas (76057) 302/F4
Jerome, Ariz. (86331) 198/C4
Jerome, Ark. (71650) 203/G7
Jerome (co.), Idaho 220/D7
Jerome, Idaho (83338) 220/D7
Jerome, Ill. (†62701) 222/D4
Jerome, Mo. (65529) 261/J7
Jerome, Pa. (15937) 294/D5
Jeromesville, Ohio (44840) 284/F4
Jerry City, Ohio (43437) 284/C3
Jerrys Plains, N.S.W. 97/F3
Jersey, Ark. (71651) 203/F7
Jersey (isl.), 10/E6
Jersey (isl.), Chan. Is. 13/E8
Jersey (bay), V.I.(U.S.) 161/B4
Jersey, Ga. (30235) 216/E3
Jersey (co.), Ill. 222/C4
Jersey, Ohio (†43062) 284/E5
Jersey City, N.J. (*07301) 273/B2
Jersey Mills, Pa. (17739) 294/H3
Jersey Shore, Pa. (17740) 294/H3
Jerseyside, Newf. 166/B3
Jerseytown, Pa. (†17815) 294/J3
Jersey Village, Texas (†77001) 302/J1
Jerseyville, Ill. (62052) 222/C4
Jerslev, Den. 21/D3
Jerumenha, Braz. 132/F4
Jerusalem, Ark. (72080) 203/E3
Jerusalem (cap.), Israel, 54/G6
Jerusalem, Jordan, 54/G6
Jerusalem (cap.), Israel 59/C3
Jerusalem, Jordan 59/C3
Jerusalem (dist.), Israel 65/B4
Jerusalem (cap.), Israel 65/C4
Jerusalem (dist.), Jordan 65/C4
Jerusalem, Jordan 65/C4
Jerusalem, Ohio (43747) 284/H6
Jervis (inlet), Br. Col. 184/E5
Jervis (mt.), Chile 138/D8
Jervis Bay, A.C.T. 97/F4
Jesenice, Yugo. 45/A2
Jeseník, Czech. 41/D1
Jeseníky (mts.), Czech. 41/D1
Jesenské, Czech. 41/F2
Jessamine (co.), Ky. 237/M5
Jesse, W. Va. (24849) 313/C7
Jessie, N. Dak. (58452) 283/O4
Jessieville, Ark. (71949) 203/D4
Jessnitz, E. Ger. 22/E3
Jessore, Pak. 68/F4
Jesterville, Md. (†21814) 245/P7
Jesuit Bend, La. (†70113) 238/K7
Jesup, Ga. (31545) 216/J7
Jesup, Iowa (50648) 229/J4
Jésus (isl.), Que. 172/H4
Jesús, Par. 144/E6
Jesús de Machaca, Bol. 136/A5
Jesús de Otoro, Hond. 154/C3
Jesús María, Arg. 143/D3
Jesús María (reef), Mex. 150/L4
Jet, Okla. (73749) 288/K1
Jetersville, Va. (23083) 307/M6
Jetmore, Kans. (67854) 232/B3
Jett, Ky. (40338) 237/M4
Jette, Belg. 27/B9
Jetts Creek, Ky. (†41382) 237/O6
Jever, W. Ger. 22/B2
Jevíčko, Czech. 41/D2
Jewel Cave Nat'l Mon., S. Dak. 298/B6
Jewell, Ga. (31045) 216/G4
Jewell, Iowa (50130) 229/F4
Jewell (co.), Kans. 232/D2
Jewell, Kans. (66949) 232/D2
Jewell, Ohio (43530) 284/B3
Jewell, Oreg. (†97138) 291/D2
Jewell Ridge, Va. (24622) 307/E6
Jewett, Ill. (62436) 222/E4
Jewett, Ohio (43986) 284/H5
Jewett, Texas (75846) 302/H6
Jewett City, Conn. (06351) 210/H2
Jewish Aut. Obl., U.S.S.R. 48/O5
Jeypore, India 68/E5
Jhalawar, India 68/D4
Jhal Jhao, Pak. 59/H4
Jhal Jhao, Pak. 68/B3
Jhang Maghiana, Pak. 59/K3
Jhang-Maghiana, Pak. 68/C2
Jhansi, India 68/D3
Jhelum, Pak. 59/K3
Jhelum (riv.), India 68/C2
Jhelum, Pak. 68/C2
Jhelum (riv.), Pak. 68/C2
Jhudo, Pak. 68/B3
Jhunjhunu, India 68/D3
Jibaro, Cuba 158/F2
Jibhalanta (Uliassutai), Mong. 77/E2
Jibsh, Ras (cape), Oman 59/G5
Jicarilla, N. Mex. (†88313) 274/D5
Jicarilla Ind. Res., N. Mex. 274/B2
Jicaron (isl.), Pan. 154/F7
Jičín, Czech. 41/C1
Jico, Mex. 150/P1
Jidda, Saudi Ar. 59/C5
Jidda, Saudi Ar., 54/G7
Jifna, Jordan 65/C4
Jigger, La. (71249) 238/G2
Jiggitai Tso (lake), China 77/C4
Jiggs, Nev. (89827) 266/F2
Jiguaní, Cuba 158/H4
Jiguero (pt.), P. Rico 156/F1
Jiguero (pt.), P. Rico 161/A1
Jigüey (bay), Cuba 158/G2
Jihlava, Czech. 41/C2
Jihlava (riv.), Czech. 41/D2
Jihočeský (reg.), Czech. 41/C2
Jihomoravský (reg.), Czech. 41/D2
Jijia (riv.), Rum. 45/H2
Jijiga, Eth. 111/H6
Jijona, Spain 33/F3
Jilemnice, Czech. 41/C1
Jilotepec de Abasolo, Mex. 150/K7
Jim (lake), N. Dak. 283/N5
Jima Abajo, Dom. Rep. 158/E5
Jimaní, Dom. Rep. 158/C6
Jimbolia, Rum. 45/E3
Jimena de la Frontera, Spain 33/D4
Jiménez, Chihuahua, Mex. 150/G3
Jiménez, Coahuila, Mex. 150/J2
Jim Falls, Wis. (54748) 317/D5
Jim Hogg (co.), Texas 302/F11
Jimma, Eth. 111/G6
Jimma, 102/F4
Jimpond, Maine (†04936) 242/B5
Jim Thorpe, Pa. (18229) 294/L4
Jim Wells (co.), Texas 302/F10
Jim Woodruff (dam), Ga. 216/C9
Jind, India 68/D3
Jindabyne, N.S.W. 97/E5
Jindabyne (res.), N.S.W. 97/E5
Jindalee, N.S.W. 97/E4
Jindřichuv Hradec, Czech. 41/C2
Jingellic, N.S.W. 97/D4
Jinja, 102/F4
Jinja, Uganda 115/F3
Jinotega, Nic. 154/E4
Jinotepe, Nic. 154/D5
Jintotolo (chan.), Phil. 82/D5
Jipijapa, Ec. 128/B3
Jiquí, Cuba 158/G2
Jiran, Eth. 111/G6
Jirgalanta (Kobdo), Mong. 77/D2
Jirira, Bol. 136/B6
Jirkov, Czech. 41/B1
Jish, Israel 65/C1
Jisr esh Shughur, Syria 63/G5
Jiu (riv.), Rum. 45/F3
Jizera (riv.), Czech. 41/C1
Joaçaba, Braz. 132/D9
Joachimsthal, E. Ger. 22/E2
Joanico, Urug. 145/B6
Joanna, S.C. (29351) 296/D3
João Belo, 102/F7
João Belo, Moz. 118/E5
João Pessoa, Braz., 120/G3
João Pessoa, Braz. 132/H4
João Pinheiro, Braz. 132/E7
Joaquim Távora, Braz. 135/B3
Joaquin, Texas (75954) 302/L5
Joaquín Suárez, Canelones, Urug. 145/B6
Joaquín Suárez, Colonia, Urug. 145/B5
Joaquín V. González, Arg. 143/D2
Job (peak), Nev. 266/C3
Job, W. Va. (26274) 313/G5
Jobabo, Cuba 158/H3
Jobos, P. Rico 161/D3
Jobos (bay), P. Rico 161/D3
Job's Cove, Newf. 166/D2
Jobson, Arg. 143/F5
Jobstown, N.J. (08041) 273/D3
Joch (pass), Switz. 39/E3
Jódar, Spain 33/E4
Jo Daviess (co.), Ill. 222/C1
Jodhpur, India 68/C3
Jodie, W. Va. (26674) 313/D6
Jodoigne, Belg. 27/F7
Joe Batt's Arm, Newf. 166/D4
Joe Creek, S. Dak. (†57548) 298/K5
Joelton, Tenn. (37080) 237/H8
Joensuu, Fin. 18/R5
Joensuu, Fin., 7/H2
Joes, Colo. (80822) 208/O3
Joes (brook), Vt. 268/C3
Joffre, Alta. 182/D3
Jofra (oasis), Libya 111/C2
Jõgeva, U.S.S.R. 53/D1
Joggins, N.S. 169/D3
Johannesburg, Calif. (93528) 204/H8
Johannesburg, Mich. (49751) 250/E4
Johannesburg, 102/E7
Johannesburg, S. Afr., 3/L7
Johannesburg, S. Africa 118/H6
Johanngeorgenstadt, E. Ger. 22/E3
Johar, Somalia 115/J3
John (riv.), Alaska 196/H1
John (cape), N.S. 169/E3
John Day, Oreg. (97845) 291/J3
John Day (dam), Oreg. 291/G2
John Day (riv.), Oreg. 291/G2
John Day (dam), Wash. 310/E5
Johnetta, Ky. (40439) 237/N6
John F. Kennedy Nat'l Hist. Site, Mass. 249/C7
John F. Kennedy Space Center, Fla. 212/F3
John Hart Highway, Br. Col. 184/F2
John H. Kerr (dam), Va. 307/M7
John Jay (mt.), Br. Col. 184/B2
John Martin (res.), Colo. 208/N6
John Muir Nat'l Hist. Site, Calif. 204/K1
John O'Groats, Scot. 15/K2
John Redmond (res.), Kans. 232/G3
Johns, Ala. (35086) 194/D4
Johns, Miss. (†39042) 256/E6
Johns, N.C. (†28352) 281/K5
Johns (isl.), S.C. 296/G6
Johnsburg, Minn. (†55909) 254/F7
Johnsburg, N.Y. (12843) 276/M3
Johnshaven, Scot. 15/M6
Johns Island, S.C. (29455) 296/G6
Johnson (co.), Ark. 203/C2
Johnson, Ark. (72741) 203/B1
Johnson (isl.), Chile 138/D5
Johnson (co.), Ga. 216/G5
Johnson (creek), Idaho 220/C5
Johnson (co.), Ill. 222/E6
Johnson (co.), Ind. 227/E6
Johnson, Ind. (†47565) 227/B8
Johnson (co.), Iowa 229/K5
Johnson (co.), Kans. 232/H3
Johnson, Kans. (67855) 232/A4
Johnson (co.), Ky. 237/R5
Johnson, Minn. (56250) 254/B5
Johnson (co.), Mo. 261/E5
Johnson (co.), Nebr. 264/H4
Johnson, Nebr. (68378) 264/J4
Johnson (res.), Nebr. 264/E4
Johnson (co.), Tenn. 237/T7
Johnson (co.), Texas 302/G5
Johnson (draw), Texas 302/C7
Johnson▵, Vt. (05656) 268/B2
Johnson, Vt. (05656) 268/B2
Johnson (co.), Wyo. 319/F1
Johnsonburg, N.J. (07846) 273/D2
Johnsonburg, Pa. (15845) 294/E3
Johnson City, N.Y. (13790) 276/J6
Johnson City, Tenn. (37601) 237/S8
Johnson City, Texas (78636) 302/F7
Johnson Creek, Wis. (53038) 317/J9
Johnsondale, Calif. (93236) 204/G8
Johnsons (creek), Utah 304/B6
Johnsons Bayou, La. (†70631) 238/C7
Johnsons Landing, Br. Col. 184/J5
Johnsons Point, Antigua 161/D11
Johnsonville, Ill. (62850) 222/E5
Johnsonville, N.Y. (12094) 276/O5
Johnsonville, S.C. (29555) 296/J4
Johnston (key), Fla. 212/E7
Johnston, Iowa (50131) 229/F5
Johnston (co.), N.C. 281/N4
Johnston, The (lakes), W. Aust. 92/C6
Johnston (co.), Okla. 288/N6
Johnston (atoll), Pacific, 87/K4
Johnston, S.C. (29832) 296/D4
Johnston City, Ill. (62951) 222/E6
Johnstone (str.), Br. Col. 184/D5
Johnstone, 10/A1
Johnstone, Scot. 15/B2
Johnstons Station, Miss. (39642) 256/D8
Johnstown, Colo. (80534) 208/K2
Johnstown, Ont. 177/J3
Johnstown, Ire. 17/G6
Johnstown, N. Dak. (58245) 283/R3
Johnstown, N.Y. (12095) 276/M4
Johnstown, Nebr. (69214) 264/D2
Johnstown, Ohio (43031) 284/E5
Johnstown, Pa., 188/L2
Johnstown, Pa. (*15901) 294/D5
Johnsville, Ark. (†71648) 203/F7
Johnsville, Md. (†21791) 245/K2
Johnville, N. Br. 170/C2
Johor (state), Malaysia 72/D7
Johor (riv.), Malaysia 72/F5
Johor Baharu, Malaysia 72/F5
Johore (str.), Malaysia 72/E6
Joice, Iowa (50446) 229/G2
Joigny, France 28/E3
Joiner, Ark. (72350) 203/K3
Joinville (isl.), Ant. 5/C16
Joinville, Braz., 120/E5
Joinville, Braz. 132/D9
Joinville, Braz. 132/D9
Jojutla de Juárez, Mex. 150/L2
Jokkmokk, Sweden 18/L3
Jökulsá (riv.), Ice. 21/C1
Joli (pt.), N.S. 169/D5
Joliet, Ill., 188/J2
Joliet, Ill. (*60431) 222/E2
Joliet, Mont. (59041) 262/G5
Joliette (co.), Que. 172/C3
Joliette, Que. 172/D3
Joliette (co.), Que. 174/B3
Joliette, N. Dak. (58246) 283/R2
Jolietville, Ind. (†46074) 227/E4
Jolley, Iowa (50551) 229/D4
Jollytown, Pa. (†15352) 294/B6
Jolo, Phil. 82/C8
Jolo (isl.), Phil. 82/C7
Jolo (isl.), Phil. 85/G4
Jolon, Calif. (93928) 204/D7
Jomalig (isl.), Phil. 82/D3
Jo-Mary (lakes), Maine 242/E4
Jona, Switz. 39/G2
Jonacatepec, Mex. 150/M2
Jonava, U.S.S.R. 53/C3
Joncs (plain), Cambodia 72/E5
Joncs (plain), S. Vietnam 72/E5
Jones (sound), 163/M3
Jones, Ala. (36749) 194/E5
Jones (isls.), Alaska 196/J1
Jones (co.), Ga. 216/E5
Jones (co.), Iowa 229/L4
Jones, La. (71250) 238/G1
Jones, Mich. (49061) 250/D7
Jones (co.), Miss. 256/F7
Jones (co.), N.C. 281/P4
Jones (sound), N.W.T., 146/K2
Jones (sound), N.W.T. 187/K2
Jones (beach), N.Y. 276/S8
Jones, Okla. (73049) 288/M3
Jones (co.), S. Dak. 298/H6
Jones, Tenn. (†38006) 237/C9
Jones (co.), Texas 302/E5
Jonesboro, Ark., 188/H3
Jonesboro, Ark. (72401) 203/J2
Jonesboro, Ga. (30236) 216/D4
Jonesboro, Ill. (62952) 222/D6
Jonesboro, Ind. (46938) 227/F4
Jonesboro, La. (71251) 238/E2
Jonesboro▵, Maine (04648) 242/J6
Jonesboro, Tenn. (37659) 237/R8
Jonesborough, N. Ire. 17/J3
Jonesburg, Mo. (63351) 261/K5
Jones Creek, Texas (†77541) 302/J9
Jonesdale, Wis. (†53565) 317/F10
Jones Mill, Ark. (72105) 203/E5
Jones Mills, Pa. (15646) 294/D5
Jonesport▵, Maine (04649) 242/H6
Jonesport, Maine (04649) 242/H6
Jones Springs, W. Va. (25429) 313/K4
Jonestown, Miss. (38639) 256/D2
Jonestown, Pa. (17038) 294/K5
Jonesville, Alaska (†99674) 196/B1
Jonesville, Ind. (47247) 227/F6
Jonesville, Ky. (41052) 237/M3
Jonesville, La. (71343) 238/G3
Jonesville, Mich. (49250) 250/E6
Jonesville, N.C. (28642) 281/H2
Jonesville, S.C. (29353) 296/D2
Jonesville, Va. (24263) 307/B7
Jonesville, Vt. (05466) 268/B3
Joniškis, U.S.S.R. 53/B2
Jönköping (co.), Sweden 18/H8
Jönköping, Sweden 18/H8
Jönköping, Sweden, 7/F3
Jonquière, 163/J6
Jonquière, Que. 172/F1
Jonquière, Que. 174/C3
Jonuta, Mex. 150/N7
Jonzac, France 28/C5
Joplin, Mo., 188/H3
Joplin, Mo. (64801) 261/C8
Joplin, Mont. (59531) 262/F2
Joppa, Ala. (35087) 194/E2
Joppa, Ill. (62953) 222/E6
Joppa, Tenn. (†37861) 237/O8
Joppatowne, Md. (†21101) 245/N3
Jorat (mt.), Switz. 39/C3
Jordan, 3/L4
Jordan, 54/G6
JORDAN, 59/C3
JORDAN, 65/D3
Jordan (dam), Ala. 194/F5
Jordan, Iowa (†50036) 229/F4
Jordan, Minn. (55352) 254/E6
Jordan, Mont. (59337) 262/J3
Jordan (bay), N.S. 169/C5
Jordan (lake), N.S. 169/C4
Jordan (riv.), N.S. 169/C5
Jordan, N.Y. (13080) 276/H4
Jordan (riv.), Israel 65/D3
Jordan (riv.), Jordan 65/D3
Jordan (riv.), Oreg. 291/K5
Jordan, S.C. (†29102) 296/G4
Jordan (riv.), Utah 304/C3
Jordan Falls, N.S. 169/C5
Jordan River, Sask. 181/H2
Jordan Valley, Oreg. (97910) 291/K5
Jorge Montt (isl.), Chile 138/D9
Jorhat, India 68/G3
Jormsjö (lake), Sweden 18/J4
Jörn, Sweden 18/M4
Jornada del Muerto (valley), N. Mex. 274/C5
Jorquera (riv.), Chile 138/B6
Jõrva-Jaani, U.S.S.R. 53/D1
Jos, 102/C4
Jos, Nigeria 106/F7
Jose Abad Santos, Phil. 82/E8
José Agustín Palacios, Bol. 136/B3
José Batlle y Ordóñez, Urug. 145/D4
José de San Martín, Arg. 143/B5
José Enrique Rodó, Urug. 145/B4
José Ignacio (lag.), Urug. 145/E5
José M. Micheo, Arg. 143/G7
Jose Pañganiban, Phil. 82/D3
José Pedro Varela, Urug. 145/E4
Joseph (lake), Ont. 177/E2
Joseph (lake), Newf. 166/B3
Joseph, Oreg. (97846) 291/K2
Joseph (creek), Oreg. 291/K2
Joseph, Utah (84739) 304/B5
Joseph Bonaparte (gulf), Australia, 87/C7
Joseph Bonaparte (gulf), Aust. 88/D2
Joseph Bonaparte (gulf), W. Aust. 92/E1
Joseph Bonaparte (gulf), No. Terr. 93/A3
Joseph City, Ariz. (86032) 198/E4
Josephine, Ala. (†36530) 194/C10
Josephine (co.), Oreg. 291/D5
Josephine, Pa. (15750) 294/D5
Josephine‡, Texas (75064) 302/H4
Josephville, Mo. (†63385) 261/N2
Joshinetsu-Kogen Nat'l Park, Japan 81/J5
Joshua (pt.), Conn. 210/E4
Joshua‡, Texas (76058) 302/G5
Joshua Tree, Calif. (92252) 204/J9
Joshua Tree Nat'l Mon., Calif. 204/J10
Jostedal, Norway 18/E6
Jostedals (glac.), Norway 18/E6
Jost Van Dyke (isl.), V.I. (Br.) 156/G1
Jost Van Dyke (isl.), V.I. (Br.) 161/C3
Joubert, S. Dak. (†57344) 298/M7
Jourdanton, Texas (78026) 302/F9
Joure, Neth. 27/H3
Jourimain (isl.), N. Br. 170/G2
Joussard, Alta. 182/B2
Joux (lake), Switz. 39/B3
Jovellanos, Cuba 156/B2
Jovellanos, Cuba 158/D1
Joy, Ill. (61260) 222/C2
Joy, Ky. (†42047) 237/E6
Joyce, La. (71440) 238/E3
Joyce, Wash. (98343) 310/B2
Joyce's Country (dist.), Ire. 17/B4
Joynes, N.C. (†28685) 281/G2
Joyo, Japan 81/J7
Juab (co.), Utah 304/A4
Juana Díaz, P. Rico 161/C2
Juan Aldama, Mex. 150/H4
Juan B. Arruabarrena, Arg. 143/G5
Juan B. Molina, Arg. 143/F6
Juan de Fuca (str.), 146/F5
Juan de Fuca (str.), 163/D6
Juan de Fuca (str.), Br. Col. 184/J4
Juan de Fuca (str.), Wash., 188/A1
Juan de Fuca (str.), Wash. 310/B2
Juan de Mena, Par. 144/D5
Juan de Nova (isl.), Réunion 118/G3
Juan D. Jackson, Urug. 145/C4
Juan Fernández (isls.), Chile, 3/E7
Juan Fernández (isls.), Chile, 120/C6
Juangriego, Ven. 124/G2
Juani (isl.), Tanz. 115/G5
Juanita, N. Dak. (58453) 283/N4
Juanita, Wash. (98033) 310/B1
Juanjuí, Peru 128/D6
Juan L. Lacaze, Urug. 145/B5
Juan Ortíz, Arg. 143/F6
Juan Pujol, Arg. 143/G5
Juan Stuven (isl.), Chile 138/D7
Juárez, Arg. 143/D4
Juárez, Mex. 150/J3
Juàzeiro, Braz., 120/G3
Juàzeiro, Braz. 132/G5
Juàzeiro do Norte, Braz., 120/G3
Juàzeiro do Norte, Braz. 132/F4
Juba, 102/F4
Juba, Sudan 111/F7
Juba (riv.), Somalia 115/H3
Jubail, Saudi Ar. 59/F4
Jubba, Saudi Ar. 59/D4
Jubbulpore, India, 54/M7
Jubbulpore (Jabalpur), India 68/D4
Juby (cape), Mor. 106/B3
Júcar (riv.), Spain 33/F3
Júcaro, Cuba 158/F2
Juchipila Mex. 150/H6
Juchique de Ferrer, Mex. 150/Q1
Juchitán de Zaragoza, Mex. 150/M8
Jucuarán, El Salv. 154/C4
Jud, N. Dak. (58454) 283/N6
Juda, Wis. (53550) 317/H10
Judaea (reg.), Jordan 65/C4
Judas (pt.), C. Rica 154/E6
Judea (reg.), Israel 65/B5
Judenburg, Austria 41/C3
Judibana, Ven. 124/C2
Judique, N.S. 169/G3
Judith (riv.), Mont. 262/G3
Judith (pt.), R.I. 249/J7
Judith Basin (co.), Mont. 262/F4
Judith Gap, Mont. (59453) 262/G4
Judson, Ind. (47856) 227/C5
Judson, Minn. (56049) 254/D6
Judson, N. Dak. (58548) 283/H6
Judsonia, Ark. (72081) 203/G3
Judyville, Ind. (†47993) 227/C4
Juelsminde, Den. 21/D6
Juhu, India 68/B7
Juian, China 77/K6
Juigalpa, Nic. 154/E4
Juikin, China 77/J6
Juist (isl.), W. Ger. 22/B2
Juiz de Fora, Braz., 120/F5
Juiz de Fora, Braz. 132/F8
Juiz de Fora, Braz. 135/E2
Jujuy, Arg., 120/D5
Jujuy (prov.), Arg. 143/C1
Jujuy, Arg. 143/C1
Jukskei (riv.), S. Africa 118/H6
Julesburg, Colo. (80737) 208/P1
Juli, Peru 128/H11
Julia (riv.), Switz. 39/J3
Juliaca, Peru, 120/C4
Juliaca, Peru 128/G10
Julia Creek, Queens. 95/B4
Juliaetta, Idaho (83535) 220/B3
Julian, Calif. (92036) 204/J10
Julian, N.C. (27283) 281/K3
Julian, Nebr. (68379) 264/J4

K

Kempston 383

Kapuas (riv.), Indon. 85/D6
Kapulena, Hawaii (†96758) 218/H4
Kapunda, S. Aust. 94/F6
Kapuskasing, 163/H6
Kapuskasing, Ont. 175/D3
Kapuskasing (riv.), Ont. 175/D3
Kapuskasing, Ont. 177/J5
Kapuskasing (riv.), Ont. 177/J5
Kapuvár, Hung. 41/D3
Kapydzhik (mt.), U.S.S.R. 52/G7
Kara (sea), U.S.S.R. 48/G2
Kara (sea), U.S.S.R. 52/K1
Kara (sea), U.S.S.R., 4/B6
Kara (sea), U.S.S.R., 54/K2
Karabekaul, U.S.S.R. 48/G6
Kara-Bogaz-Gol (gulf), U.S.S.R. 48/F5
Karabük, Turkey 63/E2
Karaburun, Turkey 63/B3
Karacabey, Turkey 63/C2
Karaca Dağ (mt.), Turkey 63/H4
Karachay-Cherkess Aut. Obl., U.S.S.R. 48/E5
Karachay-Cherkess Aut. Obl., U.S.S.R. 52/F6
Karachayevsk, U.S.S.R. 52/F6
Karachayevsk, U.S.S.R., 7/J4
Karachev, U.S.S.R. 52/E4
Karachi, Pak. 59/J5
Karachi, Pak. 68/B4
Karachi, Pak., 3/N4
Karachi, Pak., 54/K7
Karád, Hung. 41/D3
Karad, India 68/C5
Kara Dağ (mt.), Turkey 59/B2
Kara Dağ (mt.), Turkey 63/E4
Karadeniz Boğazi (Bosporus) (str.), Turkey 59/A1
Karadeniz Boğazi (Bosporus) (str.), Turkey 63/C2
Karaganda, U.S.S.R. 48/H5
Karaganda, U.S.S.R., 3/N3
Karaganda, U.S.S.R., 54/K5
Karaginskiy (isl.), U.S.S.R. 48/R4
Karahalli, Turkey 63/C3
Karaikudi, India 68/D7
Karaj, Iran 66/G3
Kara-Kalpak A.S.S.R., U.S.S.R. 48/G5
Karakelong (isl.), Indon. 85/H5
Karakhoto (ruins), China 77/F3
Karakoçan, Turkey 63/H3
Karakoram (mts.), India 68/D1
Karakoram (mts.), China 77/A4
Karakorum (ruins), Mong., 54/O5
Karakorum (ruins), Mong. 77/F2
Karaköse, Turkey 59/D2
Karaköse, Turkey 63/K3
Kara-Kum (canal), U.S.S.R. 48/G6
Kara-Kum (des.), U.S.S.R. 48/F5
Karakuwisa, S.W. Afr. 118/B3
Karamai, China 77/B2
Karaman, Turkey 59/B2
Karaman, Turkey 63/E4
Karamanli, Turkey 63/C4
Karamea, N.Z. 101/C4
Karamea (bight), N.Z. 101/C4
Karangasem, Indon. 85/F7
Karanja, India 68/D4
Kara Nor (lake), China 77/E4
Karapelit, Bulg. 45/H4
Karapinar, Turkey 63/E4
Karas, S.W. Afr. 118/B5
Karasabai, Guyana 131/B4
Karasburg, S.W. Afr. 118/B5
Karasjok, Norway 18/O2
Karasu, Turkey 63/D2
Karasu (riv.), Turkey 63/J3
Karasu-Aras (mts.), Turkey 63/J3
Karasuk, U.S.S.R. 48/H4
Karataş, Turkey 63/F4
Karataş (cape), Turkey 63/F4
Karathuri, Burma 72/C5
Karatsu, Japan 81/D7
Karauli, India 68/D3
Karawanken (range), Austria 41/C3
Karayaka, Turkey 63/F4
Karayazi, Turkey 63/J3
Karbala, Iraq, 54/H6
Karbala', Iraq 59/D3
Karbala' (prov.), Iraq 66/C4
Karbala', Iraq 66/C4
Karbers Ridge, Ill. (62955) 222/E6
Karby, Den. 21/B4
Karcag, Hung. 41/F3
Kardeljevo, Yugo. 45/C4
Kardhítsa, Greece 45/E6
Kärdla, U.S.S.R. 53/B1
Karelian A.S.S.R., U.S.S.R. 48/D3
Karelian A.S.S.R., U.S.S.R. 52/D2
Karema, Tanz. 115/F5
Karesuando, Sweden 18/M2
Kargi, Turkey 63/F2
Kargil, India 68/D2
Kargiz, Kuh-i- (mt.), Iran 66/G4
Kargopol', U.S.S.R. 52/E2
Kariá, Greece 45/E6
Karial, Greece 45/G5
Kariba (lake), 102/E6
Kariba (mt.), Japan 81/K2
Kariba (dam), Zambia 115/E7
Kariba (lake), Zambia 115/E7
Kariba, Rhod. 118/D3
Kariba (dam), Rhod. 118/D3
Kariba (lake), Rhod. 118/D3
Karibib, S.W. Afr. 118/B4
Karikal, India, 54/M8
Karikal, India 68/E6
Karikari (cape), N.Z. 101/D1
Karima, Sudan 59/B6
Karima, Sudan 111/F4
Karimata (str.), Indon., 54/O10
Karimata (arch.), Indon. 85/D6
Karimata (isl.), Indon. 85/D6
Karimata (str.), Indon. 85/D6
Karimundjawa (isls.), Indon. 85/J1
Karin, Somalia 115/J1
Karis, Fin. 18/N6
Karise, Den. 21/F7
Karisimbi (mt.), Dem. Rep. of the Congo. 115/E4
Karisimbi (mt.), Rwanda 115/E4
Káristos, Greece 45/G6
Kariz, Iran 66/M3
Karjaa (Karis), Fin. 18/N6
Karkabat, Eth. 111/G4
Karkal, India 68/C6
Karkar (isl.), Terr. N.G. 85/B6
Karkaralinsk, U.S.S.R. 48/H5
Karkheh (riv.), Iran 66/E4
Karkkila, Fin. 18/N6
Karkur, Israel 65/C3
Karliova, Turkey 63/J3
Karl-Marx-Stadt, E. Ger., 7/F3
Karl-Marx-Stadt (dist.), E. Ger. 22/E3
Karl-Marx-Stadt, E. Ger. 22/E3
Karlö (Hailuoto) (isl.), Fin. 18/O4
Karlovac, Yugo. 45/B3
Karlovy Vary, Czech. 41/B1
Karlshamn, Sweden 18/J8
Karlskoga, Sweden 18/J7
Karlskrona, Sweden 18/K8
Karlskrona, Sweden, 7/F3
Karlsruhe, N. Dak. (58744) 283/J3
Karlsruhe, W. Ger., 7/E4
Karlsruhe, W. Ger. 22/C4
Karlstad, Minn. (56732) 254/B2
Karlstad, Sweden 18/H7
Karlstad, Sweden, 7/F3
Karlstadt, W. Ger. 22/C4
Karluk, Alaska (99608) 196/H3
Karmøy (isl.), Norway 18/D7
Karnak, Ill. (62956) 222/E6
Karnak, N. Dak. (†58448) 283/O5
Karnal, India 68/D3
Karnes (co.), Texas 302/G9
Karnes City, Texas (78118) 302/G9
Karns, Tenn. (37921) 237/N9
Karns City, Pa. (16041) 294/C4
Karonga, 102/F5
Karonga, Malawi, 115/F5
Karora, Sudan 111/G4
Karoro, N.Z. 101/C5
Karosa, Indon. 85/F6
Karpakora, N.S.W. 97/B3
Kárpathos (isl.), Greece 45/H8
Karpenísion, Greece 45/E6
Karpogory, U.S.S.R. 52/F2
Kars, Turkey 59/D1
Kars (prov.), Turkey 63/K2
Kars, Turkey 63/K2
Kärsava, U.S.S.R. 53/D2
Karshi, U.S.S.R. 48/G6
Karşiyaka, Turkey 63/B3
Karskiye Vorota (str.), U.S.S.R. 48/F2
Karskiye Vorota (str.), U.S.S.R. 52/J1
Karskiye Vorota (str.), U.S.S.R., 4/B7
Kart, Iran 66/M3
Kartal, Turkey 63/D6
Karthaus, Pa. (16845) 294/F3
Karumba, Queens. 95/B3
Karun (riv.), Iran 59/E3
Karun (riv.), Iran 66/F5
Karungu, Kenya 115/F4
Karunjie, W. Aust. 92/D2
Karunki, Fin. 18/O4
Karup, Den. 21/C5
Karur, India 68/D6
Karval, Colo. (80823) 208/N5
Karviná, Czech. 41/E2
Karwar, India 68/C6
Kaş, Turkey 63/C4
Kasaan, Alaska (99924) 196/N2
Kasabonika, Ont. 175/C2
Kasai (riv.), 102/E5
Kasai (riv.), Angola 115/D5
Kasai (riv.), Dem. Rep. of the Congo. 115/C4
Kasai-Occidental (prov.), Dem. Rep. of the Congo. 115/D4
Kasai-Oriental (prov.), Dem. Rep. of the Congo. 115/D5
Kasaji, Dem. Rep. of the Congo. 115/D6
Kasama, 102/F5
Kasama, Zambia 115/F6
Kasane, Botswana 118/D3
Kasanga, 102/F5
Kasanga, Tanz. 115/F5
Kasangulu, Dem. Rep. of the Congo. 115/C4
Kasar, Ras (cape), Sudan 59/C6
Kasar, Ras (cape), Eth. 111/G4
Kasar, Ras (cape), Sudan 111/G4
Kasaragod, India 68/C6
Kasba (lake), 163/F3
Kasba (lake), N.W.T. 187/H3
Kasbeer, Ill. (61328) 222/D2
Kaseda, Japan 81/D8
Kasempa, 102/E6
Kasempa, Zambia 115/E6
Kasenga, Dem. Rep. of the Congo. 115/E6
Kasenyi, Dem. Rep. of the Congo. 115/E3
Kasese, Dem. Rep. of the Congo. 115/E4
Kasese, Uganda 115/F3
Kasganj, India 68/D3
Kashaf Rud (riv.), Iran 66/M2
Kashan, Iran, 54/J6
Kashan, Iran 59/F3
Kashan, Iran 66/G3
Kashegelok, Alaska (†99668) 196/G2
Kasheshibaw (lake), Newf. 166/B3
Kashgar, China, 54/L6
Kashgar, China 77/A4
Kashihara, Japan 81/J8
Kashin, U.S.S.R. 52/E3
Kashing, China 77/K5
Kashiwa, Japan 81/P2
Kashiwazaki, Japan 81/J5
Kashmar, Iran 59/G2
Kashmar, Iran 66/L3
Kashmor, Pak. 68/C3
Kashum Tso (lake), China 77/C5
Kashunuk (riv.), Alaska 196/F2
Kasigluk, Alaska (99609) 196/F2
Kasilof, Alaska (99610) 196/B1
Kasimov, U.S.S.R. 52/F4
Kaskaskia, Ill. (†63673) 222/C6
Kaskaskia (riv.), Ill. 222/E4
Kaskinen (Kaskö), Fin. 18/M5
Kaskö, Fin. 18/M5
Kas Kong (isl.), Cambodia 72/D5
Kaslo, 163/E6
Kaslo, Br. Col. 184/J5
Kasongo, 102/E5
Kasongo, Dem. Rep. of the Congo. 115/E4
Kasongo-Lunda, Dem. Rep. of the Congo. 115/C5
Kásos (isl.), Greece 45/H8
Kasota, Minn. (56050) 254/D6
Kašperské Hory, Czech. 41/B2
Kaspiysk, U.S.S.R. 52/G6
Kaspiyskiy, U.S.S.R. 52/G5
Kassala, 102/F3
Kassala, Sudan 59/C6
Kassala (prov.), Sudan 111/G4
Kassala, Sudan 111/G4
Kassándra (pen.), Greece 45/F6
Kassel, W. Ger., 7/E3
Kassel, W. Ger. 22/C3
Kasserine, Tun. 106/F1
Kasson, Minn. (55944) 254/F6
Kasson, W. Va. (26380) 313/G4
Kastamonu, Turkey 59/B1
Kastamonu (prov.), Turkey 63/E2
Kastamonu, Turkey 63/F2
Kas Tang (isl.), Cambodia 72/D5
Kastav, Yugo. 45/B3
Kastéllion, Greece 45/F8
Kastéllion, Greece 45/G8
Kastoría, Greece 45/E5
Kastornoye, U.S.S.R. 52/E4
Kastrup, Den. 18/H9
Kastrup, Den. 21/F6
Kasugai, Japan 81/H6
Kasukabe, Japan 81/O2
Kasulu, Tanz. 115/F4
Kasumiga (mts.), Japan 81/K5
Kasungu, Malawi 115/F6
Kasur, Pak. 59/K3
Kasur, Pak. 68/C2
Katahdin (mt.), Maine 242/F4
Katako-Kombe, Dem. Rep. of the Congo. 115/D4
Katákolon, Greece 45/E7
Katana, Dem. Rep. of the Congo. 115/E4
Katanga (reg.), 102/E5
Katanga (prov.), Dem. Rep. of the Congo. 115/E5
Katanino, Zambia 115/E6
Katanning, Aust. 88/B6
Katanning, W. Aust. 92/B6
Katarnian Ghat, India 68/E3
Katchall (isl.), India 68/G7
Katemcy, Texas (76850) 302/E7
Katenga, Dem. Rep. of the Congo. 115/E5
Katepwa Beach, Sask. 181/H5
Kateríni, Greece 45/F5
Kates Needle (mt.), Alaska 196/N1
Kates Needle (mt.), Br. Col. 184/A1
Katha, Burma 72/C1
Katherina, Jebel (mt.), U.A.R. 59/B4
Katherina, Jebel (mt.), U.A.R. 111/F2
Katherine, Australia, 87/D7
Katherine, Aust. 88/E2
Katherine, No. Terr. 93/B3
Katherine (riv.), No. Terr. 93/C3
Katherine Landing, Ariz. (†86401) 198/A3
Kathleen, Alta. 182/B2
Kathleen, Fla. (33849) 212/D3
Kathleen, Ga. (31047) 216/E6
Kathryn, Alta. 182/D4
Kathryn, N. Dak. (58049) 283/P6
Kati, Mali 106/C6
Katihar, India 68/F3
Katima Mulilo, S.W. Afr. 118/C3
Katimík (lake), Man. 179/C2
Katiola, Ivory Coast 106/C7
Katipunan, Phil. 82/D6
Katmai (vol.), Alaska 196/H3
Katmai Nat'l Mon., Alaska 196/H3
Katmandu (cap.), Nepal, 54/M7
Katmandu (cap.), Nepal 68/E3
Katni (Murwara), India 68/E4
Katonah, N.Y. (10536) 276/N8
Katowice, Poland, 7/F4
Katowice (prov.), Poland 47/D3
Katowice, Poland 47/B4
Katrime, Man. 179/D4
Katrine, Ont. 177/E2
Katrine (lake), Scot. 15/G7
Katrineholm, Sweden 18/K7
Katsina, 102/C3
Katsina, Nigeria 106/F6
Katsina Ala, Nigeria 106/F7
Katsuta, Japan 81/K5
Katsuura, Japan 81/K6
Kattegat (str.), 7/F3
Kattegat (str.), Den. 18/G8
Kattegat (str.), Sweden 18/G8
Kattegat (str.), Den. 21/E4
Katwe, Uganda 115/F4
Katwijk aan Zee, Neth. 27/E4
Katy, Texas (77450) 302/J8
Kau (des.), Hawaii 218/J6
Kau, Indon. 85/H5
Kauai (isl.), Hawaii, 87/L3
Kauai (isl.), Hawaii, 188/E5
Kauai (co.), Hawaii 218/A1
Kauai (chan.), Hawaii 218/E6
Kauai (isl.), Hawaii 218/C1
Kaufbeuren, W. Ger. 22/D5
Kaufman (co.), Texas 302/H5
Kaufman, Texas (75142) 302/H5
Kauhola (pt.), Hawaii 218/G3
Kauiki (head), Hawaii 218/K2
Kaukauna, Wis. (54130) 317/K7
Kaukauveld (mts.), Botswana 118/C3
Kaukauveld (mts.), S.W. Afr. 118/C3
Kaula (isl.), Hawaii, 188/F6
Kaula (isl.), Hawaii 218/D6
Kaulakahi (chan.), Hawaii 218/B2
Kauliranta, Fin. 18/O3
Kaumajet (mts.), Newf. 166/B2
Kaumakani, Hawaii (96747) 218/C2
Kauna (pt.), Hawaii 218/G7
Kaunakakai, Hawaii (96748) 218/G1
Kaunakakai (harb.), Hawaii 218/G1
Kaunas, U.S.S.R. 48/C4
Kaunas, U.S.S.R. 52/B4
Kaunas, U.S.S.R. 53/C3
Kaunas, U.S.S.R., 7/G3
Kaunuopou (pt.), Hawaii 218/B2
Kaupakulua, Hawaii (†96708) 218/K2
Kaupo, Hawaii (†96713) 218/K2
Kaura Namoda, 102/C3
Kaura Namoda, Nigeria 106/F6
Kauswagan, Phil. 82/E6
Kautokeino, Norway 18/N2
Kauttua, Fin. 18/M6
Kavadarci, Yugo. 45/E5
Kavajë, Alb. 45/D5
Kavak, Çanakkale, Turkey 63/C5
Kavak, Samsun, Turkey 63/F2
Kavalga (isl.), Alaska 196/K4
Kavali, India 68/E6
Kavála, Greece, 7/G4
Kavála, Greece 45/G5
Kavanagh, Alta. 182/D3
Kavanayen, Ven. 124/H5
Kavaratti, India 68/C6
Kavarna, Bulg. 45/J4
Kaveri (riv.), India 68/D6
Kavieng, Terr. N.G., 87/E6
Kavir, Dasht-i- (salt des.), Iran 59/G3
Kavir, Dasht-i- (salt des.), Iran 66/J3
Kavir-i-Namak (salt des.), Iran 59/G3
Kavirondo (gulf), Kenya 115/F4
Kaw, Fr. Gui. 131/E3
Kaw, Okla. (74641) 288/N1
Kawachi, Japan 81/J8
Kawachinagano, Japan 81/J8
Kawagama (lake), Ont. 177/F2
Kawagoe, Japan 81/O2
Kawaguchi, Japan 81/O2
Kawaihae, Hawaii (96743) 218/G4
Kawaihae (bay), Hawaii 218/G4
Kawaihoa (cape), Hawaii 218/A2
Kawaikini (peak), Hawaii 218/C1
Kawailoa, Hawaii (†96712) 218/E1
Kawakawa, N.Z. 101/E1
Kawambwa, Zambia 115/E5
Kawanishi, Japan 81/H7
Kawardha, India 68/E4
Kawasaki, Japan 81/O2
Kawau (isl.), N.Z. 101/E2
Kawerau, N.Z. 101/F3
Kawhia, N.Z. 101/E3
Kawhia (harb.), N.Z. 101/E3
Kawi (mt.), Indon. 85/K2
Kawich (peak), Nev. 266/E5
Kawich (range), Nev. 266/E5
Kawinaw (lake), Man. 179/C2
Kawio (isls.), Indon. 85/G5
Kawkawlin, Mich. (48631) 250/F5
Kawlin, Burma 72/B2
Kawludo, Burma 72/C3
Kawthoolei (state), Burma 72/C3
Kay (co.), Okla. 288/M1
Kaya, Upp. Volta 106/D6
Kayah (state), Burma 72/C3
Kayak (isl.), Alaska 196/K3
Kaycee, Wyo. (82639) 319/F2
Kayenta, Ariz. (86033) 198/E2
Kayes, 102/A3
Kayes, Mali 106/B6
Kayes, Rep. of Congo 115/B4
Kayjay, Ky. (40906) 237/O7
Kaylor, Pa. (16042) 294/C4
Kaylor, S. Dak. (57354) 298/O7
Kayser (mts.), Sur. 131/C4
Kayseri, Turkey 59/C2
Kayseri (prov.), Turkey 63/F3
Kayseri, Turkey 63/F3
Kayseri, Turkey, 54/G6
Kaysville, Utah (84037) 304/B2
Kayville, Sask. 181/F6
Kazabazua, Que. 172/A4
Kazach'ye, U.S.S.R. 48/O2
Kazach'ye, U.S.S.R., 4/C3
Kazakh S.S.R., U.S.S.R. 48/G5
Kazakh S.S.R., U.S.S.R., 54/J5
Kazalinsk, U.S.S.R. 48/G5
Kazalinsk, U.S.S.R., 54/K5
Kazan (riv.), 163/F3
Kazan', U.S.S.R. 48/F4
Kazan', U.S.S.R. 52/G3
Kazan (riv.), N.W.T. 187/H3
Kazan', U.S.S.R., 7/J3
Kazandzhik, U.S.S.R. 48/F6
Kazanli, Turkey 63/F4
Kazanlŭk, Bulg. 45/G4
Kazan-retto (Volcano) (isls.), Japan 81/M4
Kazatin, U.S.S.R. 52/C5
Kazbek (mt.), U.S.S.R. 52/F6
Kazerun, Iran 59/F4
Kazerun, Iran 66/G6
Kazimierza Wielka, Poland 47/E3
Kazimierz Dolny, Poland 47/E3
Kazimkarabekir, Turkey 63/E4
Kazincbarcika, Hung. 41/F2
Kazlu-Rūda, U.S.S.R. 53/B3
Kazumba, Dem. Rep. of the Congo. 115/D5
Kazusa, Japan 81/P3
Kazvin, Iran, 54/H6
Kazvin, Iran 59/E2
Kazvin, Iran 66/F2
Kdyně, Czech. 41/B2
Kéa, Greece 45/G7
Kéa (isl.), Greece 45/G7
Keaau, Hawaii, 188/G6
Keaau, Hawaii (96749) 218/J5
Keady, N. Ire. 17/H3
Keahi (pt.), Hawaii 218/E2
Keahole (pt.), Hawaii 218/F5
Keal, na (inlet), Scot. 15/D7
Kealaikahiki (chan.), Hawaii 218/H3
Kealaikahiki (pt.), Hawaii 218/H3
Kealakekua, Hawaii (96750) 218/G5
Kealakekua (bay), Hawaii 218/F6
Kealapuali, Hawaii (†96725) 218/G5
Kealey Springs, Sask. 181/B6
Kealia, Hawaii (96751) 218/D1
Kealia, Hawaii (96751) 218/G6
Keams Canyon, Ariz. (86034) 198/E3
Keanae, Hawaii (†96708) 218/K2
Keanapapa (pt.), Hawaii 218/G2
Keansburg, N.J. (07734) 273/E3
Kearney, Ont. 177/E2
Kearney, Mo. (64060) 261/D4
Kearney, Nebr., 188/G2
Kearney (co.), Nebr. 264/F4
Kearney, Nebr. (68847) 264/E4
Kearney, Wyo. (†82832) 319/F1
Kearneysville, W. Va. (25430) 313/L4
Kearns, Utah (84118) 304/B3
Kearny, Ariz. (85237) 198/E5
Kearny (co.), Kans. 232/A3
Kearny, N.J. (07032) 273/B2
Kearsarge, N.H. (03847) 268/E3
Kearsarge (mt.), N.H. 268/D5
Kearsarge, Pa. (†16501) 294/B1
Keasbey, N.J. (08832) 273/E2
Keatchie, La. (71046) 238/C2
Keating, Oreg. (97847) 291/K3
Keating Summit, Pa. (16737) 294/F2
Keaton, Ky. (41226) 237/P5
Keats (mt.), Aust. 88/B2
Keats, Kans. (†66502) 232/F2
Keats (mt.), W. Aust. 92/A2
Keavy, Ky. (40737) 237/N6
Keawekaheka (pt.), Hawaii 218/F5
Keban, Turkey 63/H3
Kebang, India 68/G3
Kebang (mt.), S. Korea 81/D5
Ke Bao, N. Vietnam 72/E2
Kebbi (riv.), Nigeria 106/E6
Kebnekaise (mt.), Sweden 18/L3
Kebock (head), Scot. 15/D3
Kebumen, Indon. 85/J2
Kecel, Hung. 41/E3
Kechi, Kans. (67067) 232/E4
Kechika (riv.), Br. Col. 184/L2
Keçiborlu, Turkey 63/D4
Kecskemét, Hung., 7/G4
Kecskemét, Hung. 41/E3
Kedah (state), Malaysia 72/D6
Kedainiai, U.S.S.R. 53/C3
Keddie, Calif. (95952) 204/E3
Kedges (strs), Md. 245/O8
Kedgwick, N. Br. 170/C1
Kedgwick (riv.), N. Br. 170/C1
Kedgwick Ouest, N. Br. 170/C1
Kedgwick River, N. Br. 170/C1
Kediri, Indon. 85/K2
Kédougou, Sen. 106/B6
Kedron (brook), Queens. 95/D2
Kedzierzyn, Poland 47/C3
Keechelus (lake), Wash. 310/D3
Keedysville, Md. (21756) 245/H3
Keefers, Br. Col. 184/G5
Keefeton, Okla. (†74401) 288/R3
Keegan, Maine (04748) 242/G1
Keego Harbor, Mich. (48030) 250/F6
Keehi (lag.), Hawaii 218/B4
Keel, Ire. 17/A4
Keele (riv.), N.W.T. 187/F3
Keele (peak), Yukon 187/E3
Keeler, Calif. (93530) 204/H7
Keeler, Sask. 181/F5
Keeline, Wyo. (82220) 319/H3
Keeling (cocos) (isls.), Australia, 54/N11
Keeling, Va. (24566) 307/K7
Keels, Newf. 166/D1
Keelung, China 77/K6
Keenan, W. Va. (†24983) 313/F7
Keenan Siding, N. Br. 170/E2
Keene, Calif. (93531) 204/G8
Keene, Ont. 177/F3
Keene, Ky. (40339) 237/M5
Keene, N. Dak. (58847) 283/E4
Keene, N.H. (03431) 268/C6
Keene, N.Y. (12942) 276/N2
Keene, Ohio (43828) 284/G5
Keene, Texas (76059) 302/G5
Keeneland‡, Ky. (†40223) 237/K4
Keener, Ala. (†35954) 194/G2
Keenes, Ill. (62851) 222/E5
Keenesburg, Colo. (80643) 208/L2
Keene Valley, N.Y. (12943) 276/N2
Keensburg, Ill. (62852) 222/F5
Keeny (creek), Oreg. 291/K4
Keeper (hill), Ire. 17/E6
Keerweer (cape), Aust. 88/G2
Keerweer (cape), Queens. 95/B2
Keeseville, N.Y. (12944) 276/O2
Keesler A.F.B., Miss. 256/G10
Keetley, Utah (†84060) 304/C3
Keetmanshoop, 102/D7
Keetmanshoop, S.W. Afr. 118/B5
Keewatin, Ont. 175/A3
Keewatin, Ont. 177/F5
Keewatin, Minn. (55753) 254/E3
Keewatin (dist.), 163/G2
Keewatin (dist.), N.W.T. 187/J3
Keewong, N.S.W. 97/C3
Keezletown, Va. (22832) 307/L4
Kefallinía (isl.), Greece 45/E6
Kefar Atta, Israel 65/C2
Kefar Blum, Israel 65/D1
Kefar Gil'adi, Israel 65/C1
Kefar Ruppin, Israel 65/D3
Kefar Sava, Israel 65/B3
Kefar Vitkin, Israel 65/B3
Kefar Yona, Israel 65/B3
Kefar Zekharya, Israel 65/B4
Keffi, Nigeria 106/F7
Keflavík, Ice. 21/B1
Ke Ga (pt.), S. Vietnam 72/F5
Kegaska, Que. 174/E2
Kegley, W. Va. (24731) 313/D8
Kegonsa (lake), Wis. 317/H10
Keg River, Alta. 182/A5
Kegworth, Sask. 181/J5
Kehl, W. Ger. 22/B4
Kehoe, Ky. (†41144) 237/P4
Kehra, U.S.S.R. 53/C1
Ke-hsi Mansam, Burma 72/C2
Keighley, 10/H1
Keighley, Eng. 13/F4
Keila, U.S.S.R. 53/C1
Keilor, Vic. 97/H5
Keimoes, S. Africa 118/C5
Keirn, Miss. (†38924) 256/D4
Keiser, Ark. (72351) 203/K2
Keiss, Scot. 15/K2
Keitele (lake), Fin. 18/O5
Keith, 10/E2
Keith (co.), Nebr. 264/C3
Keith, S. Aust. 94/G7
Keith, Scot. 15/L4
Keith, W. Va. (†25148) 313/C6
Keith Arm (inlet), N.W.T. 187/F3
Keithley Creek, Br. Col. 184/G4
Keithsburg, Ill. (61442) 222/B2
Keithville, La. (71047) 238/C2
Keizer, Oreg. (97303) 291/A3
Kejimkujik (lake), N.S. 169/C4
Kejimkujik Nat'l Park, N.S. 169/C4
Kekaa (pt.), Hawaii 218/H2
Kekaha, Hawaii, 188/E5
Kekaha, Hawaii (96752) 218/C2
Kekertaluk (isl.), N.W.T. 187/M3
Kékes (mt.), Hung. 41/E3
Kekoskee, Wis. (†53050) 317/J8
Kelang, Malaysia 72/D7
Kelantan (state), Malaysia 72/D6
Kelantan (riv.), Malaysia 72/D6
Keldron, S. Dak. (57634) 298/F2
Kelfield, Sask. 181/C4
Kelford, N.C. (27847) 281/P2
Kelheim, W. Ger. 22/D4
Kelkit (riv.), Turkey 59/C1
Kelkit, Turkey 63/H2
Kelkit (riv.), Turkey 63/G2
Kell, Ill. (62853) 222/E5
Kellé, Rep. of Congo 115/B4
Keller (lake), N.W.T. 187/F3
Keller, Texas (76248) 302/F1
Keller, Va. (23401) 307/S5
Keller, Wash. (99140) 310/G2
Kellerberrin, W. Aust. 92/B5
Kellerman, Ala. (35468) 194/D4
Kellerton, Iowa (50133) 229/E7
Kellerville, Texas (79049) 302/D2
Kellett (cape), 163/D1
Kellett (cape), N.W.T. 187/F2
Kellett (str.), N.W.T. 187/G2
Kellettville, Pa. (†16353) 294/D2
Kelley, Iowa (50134) 229/F5
Kelley (creek), Nev. 266/D1
Kelleys (isl.), Ohio 284/E2
Kelleys Island, Ohio (43438) 284/E2
Kelligrews, Newf. 166/D2
Kelliher, Minn. (56650) 254/D3
Kelliher, Sask. 181/H4
Kellnersville, Wis. (54215) 317/L7
Kelloe, Man. 179/B4
Kellogg (mt.), Ariz. 198/E6
Kellogg, Idaho (83837) 220/B2
Kellogg, Iowa (50135) 229/H5
Kellogg, Minn. (55945) 254/G6
Kelloggsville, Ohio (†44048) 284/J2
Kelloselkä, Fin. 18/Q3
Kells, Ire. 17/G7
Kells (Ceanannus Mór), Ire. 17/G4
Kells, N. Ire. 17/J2
Kelly‡, Ala. (†36322) 194/G8
Kelly, Ga. (31048) 216/E4
Kelly (creek), Idaho 220/C3
Kelly, Kans. (66446) 232/G2
Kelly, Ky. (†42240) 237/G7
Kelly, La. (71441) 238/F3
Kelly, N.C. (28448) 281/N6
Kelly, Wyo. (83011) 319/B2
Kelly A.F.B., Texas 302/F8
Kelly Lake, Minn. (55754) 254/F3
Kellys, N. Dak. (†58201) 283/R4
Kellysville, W. Va. (24732) 313/E8
Kellyton, Ala. (35089) 194/F5
Kellyville, Okla. (74039) 288/O3
Kelmė, U.S.S.R. 53/B3
Kélo, Chad 111/C6
Kelowna, 163/E6
Kelowna, Br. Col. 184/H5
Kelpin (Koping), China 77/A3
Kelsey, Alta. 182/D3
Kelsey, Minn. (55755) 254/F3
Kelsey Bay, Br. Col. 184/D5
Kelseyville, Calif. (95451) 204/C5
Kelso, Ark. (†71674) 203/H6
Kelso, Calif. (92351) 204/K8
Kelso, 10/E3
Kelso, Mo. (63758) 261/O8
Kelso, N. Dak. (†58045) 283/R5
Kelso, Sask. 181/K6
Kelso, Scot. 15/M8
Kelso, Tenn. (37348) 237/J10
Kelso, Wash., 188/B1
Kelso, Wash. (98626) 310/C4
Kelstern, Sask. 181/E5
Kelston West, N.Z. 101/B1
Keltie (cape), Ant. 5/C7
Keltner, Ky. (42750) 237/K6
Kelton, S.C. (†29353) 296/D2
Kelty, 10/C1
Keluang, Malaysia 72/D7
Kelvington, Sask. 181/H3
Kelwood, Man. 179/C4
Kem', U.S.S.R. 48/D3
Kem', U.S.S.R. 52/D2
Kem', U.S.S.R., 4/C8
Kem', U.S.S.R., 7/H2
Ké-Macina, Mali 106/C6
Kemah, Turkey 63/H3
Kemah, Texas (77565) 302/K2
Kemaliye, Turkey 63/H3
Kemalpaşa, Turkey 63/J2
Kemano, Br. Col. 184/D3
Kemasik, Malaysia 72/D6
Kembé, Centr. Afr. Rep. 115/D3
Kemboma, Gabon 115/B3
Kembuchi, Japan 81/L1
Kemecse, Hung. 41/F2
Kemer, Turkey 63/D4
Kemerburgaz, Turkey 63/D5
Kemerovo, U.S.S.R. 48/J4
Kemerovo, U.S.S.R., 54/M4
Kemi, Fin. 18/O4
Kemi (lake), Fin. 18/Q3
Kemi (riv.), Fin. 18/O3
Kemijärvi, Fin. 18/P3
Kemirhisar, Turkey 63/F3
Kemmerer, Wyo. (83101) 319/B4
Kemnay, Man. 179/B5
Kemp, Ill. (†61910) 222/E4
Kemp, Okla. (74747) 288/O7
Kemp, Texas (75143) 302/H5
Kemp (lake), Texas 302/E4
Kemp City (Hendrix), Okla. (†74741) 288/O7
Kemp Coast (reg.), Ant. 5/C3
Kemper, Ill. (62055) 222/C4
Kemper (co.), Miss. 256/G5
Kemp Mill‡, Md. (†20901) 245/F4
Kempsey, Aust. 88/J6
Kempsey, N.S.W. 97/G2
Kempster, Wis. (54444) 317/H5
Kempston, Eng. 13/G5

Kleinlützel 385

Killala, Ire. 17/C3
Killala (bay), Ire. 17/C3
Killaloe, 10/B4
Killaloe, Ire. 17/D6
Killaloe Station, Ont. 177/G2
Killaly, Sask. 181/J5
Killam, Alta. 182/E3
Killams Mills, N. Br. 170/E2
Killarney, 163/G6
Killarney, Ont. 177/C2
Killarney, 10/B4
Killarney, Ire. 17/C7
Killarney (lakes), 10/B4
Killarney, Man. 179/C5
Killarney, No. Terr. 93/B4
Killary (harb.), Ire. 17/A4
Killavullen, Ire. 17/D7
Killbear Point Prov. Park, Ont. 177/D2
Kill Buck, N.Y. (14748) 276/C6
Killbuck, Ohio (44637) 284/G5
Killbuck (creek), Ohio 284/G4
Killdeer, N. Dak. (58640) 283/E5
Killdeer, Sask. 181/E6
Kill Devil Hills, N.C. (27948) 281/T3
Killduff, Iowa (50137) 229/H5
Killeen, Texas (76541) 302/G6
Killen, Ala. (35645) 194/D1
Killenaule, Ire. 17/F6
Killeshandra, Ire. 17/F3
Killeter, N. Ire. 17/F2
Killian, La. (†70462) 238/M2
Killimor, Ire. 17/E5
Killin, Scot. 15/H7
Killinaboy, Ire. 17/C6
Killinglyᐃ, Conn. (†06241) 210/H1
Killington, Vt. (05751) 268/B4
Killington (peak), Vt. 268/B4
Killingworthᐃ, Conn. (†06413) 210/E3
Killona, La. (70066) 238/M3
Killorglin, Ire. 17/B7
Killough, N. Ire. 17/K3
Killucan-Rathwire, Ire. 17/G4
Kill Van Kull (str.), N.J. 273/B2
Killybegs, Ire. 17/E2
Killyleagh, N. Ire. 17/K3
Kilmacolm, Scot. 15/B2
Kilmacrennan, Ire. 17/F1
Kilmacthomas, Ire. 17/G7
Kilmallock, Ire. 17/D7
Kilmarnock, 10/D3
Kilmarnock, Scot. 15/G8
Kilmarnock, Va. (22482) 307/R5
Kilmeaden, Ire. 17/G7
Kilmelford, Scot. 15/F7
Kilmichael, Miss. (39747) 256/E4
Kilmihill, Ire. 17/C6
Kilmore, Scot. 15/F7
Kilmore, Vic. 97/C5
Kilmory, 10/D3
Kilmory, Scot. 15/F9
Kilmuir, Scot. 15/D5
Kiln, Miss. (39556) 256/F10
Kilnaleck, Ire. 17/G4
Kilo, Dem. Rep. of the Congo. 115/E3
Kilombero (riv.), Tanz. 115/G5
Kilómetro 642, Arg. 143/D1
Kilosa, Tanz. 115/G5
Kilpis (lake), Fin. 18/M2
Kilpis (lake), Sweden 18/M2
Kilrea, N. Ire. 17/H2
Kilrenny and Anstruther, 10/E2
Kilrenny and Anstruther, Scot. 15/L7
Kilronan, Ire. 17/B5
Kilronan, Sask. 181/B2
Kilrush, 10/B4
Kilrush, Ire. 17/C6
Kilsheelan, Ire. 17/F7
Kilsyth, Ont. 177/D3
Kilsyth, 10/B1
Kilsyth, Scot. 15/D2
Kilsyth, W. Va. (25859) 313/D7
Kiltan (isl.), India 68/C6
Kiltimagh, Ire. 17/C4
Kilwa, Dem. Rep. of the Congo. 115/E5
Kilwa Kivinje, 102/G5
Kilwa Kivinje, Tanz. 115/G5
Kilwa Masoko, Tanz. 115/G5
Kilworth, Ire. 17/E7
Kilyos, Turkey 63/D5
Kim, Colo. (81049) 208/N8
Kimba, S. Aust. 94/E5
Kimball (mt.), Alaska 196/K2
Kimball, Alta. 182/D5
Kimball, Kans. (†66733) 232/G4
Kimball, Minn. (55353) 254/D5
Kimball (co.), Nebr. 264/A3
Kimball, Nebr. (69145) 264/A3
Kimball, S. Dak. (57355) 298/M6
Kimball, Tenn. (†34347) 237/K10
Kimball, W. Va. (24853) 313/C8
Kimballton, Iowa (51543) 229/D5
Kimballton, Va. (24107) 307/G6
Kimberley (plat.), Aust. 88/D3
Kimberley, Br. Col. 184/K5
Kimberley, Ont. 177/D3
Kimberley (plat.), W. Aust. 92/D2
Kimberley, 102/E7
Kimberley, S. Africa 118/C5
Kimberley Research Station, W. Aust. 92/E1
Kimberlin Heights, Tenn. (37920) 237/O9
Kimberly, Ala. (35091) 194/E3
Kimberly, Idaho (83341) 220/D7
Kimberly, Minn. (56457) 254/E4
Kimberly, Oreg. (97848) 291/H3
Kimberly, Wis. (54136) 317/K7
Kimble (co.), Texas 302/E7
Kimbolton, Ohio (43749) 284/G5
Kimbrough, Ala. (36746) 194/C6
Kimchaek, N. Korea 81/D3
Kimch'ŏn, S. Korea 81/D5
Kimesville, N.C. (†27298) 281/L3
Kími, Greece 45/F6
Kimiwan (lake), Alta. 182/B2
Kimmell, Ind. (46760) 227/F2
Kimmins, Tenn. (37081) 237/F9
Kimmswick, Mo. (63053) 261/M6
Kimovsk, U.S.S.R. 52/E4
Kimry, U.S.S.R. 52/E3
Kimsquit, Br. Col. 184/D4
Kinabalu (mt.), Malaysia 85/F4
Kinali (isl.), Turkey 63/D6
Kinalung, N.S.W. 97/B3
Kinard, Fla. (32449) 212/D6
Kinards, S.C. (29355) 296/D3
Kinbrae, Minn. (56148) 254/C7
Kincaid, Ill. (62540) 222/D4
Kincaid, Kans. (66039) 232/G3
Kincaid, Sask. 181/D6
Kincardine, Ont. 177/C3
Kincardine, 10/B1
Kincardine (co.), Scot. 15/M6
Kincardine, Scot. 15/H4
Kincardine O'Neil, Scot. 15/L5
Kincheloe (pt.), Oreg. 291/C2
Kincheloe, W. Va. (†26378) 313/E4
Kincheloe A.F.B., Mich. 250/E2
Kincolith, Br. Col. 184/B2
Kindberg, Austria 41/C3
Kinde, Mich. (48445) 250/G5
Kinder, La. (70648) 238/E6
Kinderhook, Ill. (62345) 222/B4
Kinderhook, N.Y. (12106) 276/N6
Kindersley, 163/F5
Kindersley, Sask. 181/B4
Kindia, Guinea 106/B6
Kindred, N. Dak. (58051) 283/R6
Kindu-Port Empain, 102/E5
Kindu-Port Empain, Dem. Rep. of the Congo. 115/E4
Kinel', U.S.S.R. 52/H4
Kinel' (riv.), U.S.S.R. 52/H4
Kineo, Maine (†04478) 242/D4
Kineshma, U.S.S.R. 52/F3
King (isl.), Australia, 87/E10
King (isl.), Aust. 88/G7
King (sound), Aust. 88/C3
King (isl.), Br. Col. 184/D4
King (isl.), Burma 72/C4
King, Ky. (†40906) 237/O7
King, N.C. (27021) 281/J2
King (pt.), N.S.W. 97/J2
King (isl.), Newf. 166/C2
King (cays), Nic. 154/F4
King (sound), W. Aust. 92/C2
King (isl.), Tasmania 99/A1
King (co.), Texas 302/D4
King (co.), Wash. 310/D3
King, Wis. (54946) 317/H7
King and Queen (co.), Va. 307/P5
King and Queen Court House, Va. (23085) 307/P5
Kingaroy, Aust. 88/J5
Kingaroy, Queens. 95/D5
King Christian (isl.), N.W.T. 187/H2
King Christian IX Land (reg.), Greenl., 4/C11
King Christian IX Land (reg.), Greenl., 146/P3
King Christian X Land (reg.), Greenl., 4/B11
King Christian X Land (reg.), Greenl., 146/R2
King City, Calif. (93930) 204/D7
King City, Ont. 177/J3
King City, Mo. (64463) 261/D2
King City, Oreg. (†97123) 291/A2
Kingcome Inlet, Br. Col. 184/D4
King Cove, Alaska (99612) 196/F4
Kingdom City, Mo. (†65262) 261/H5
King Ferry, N.Y. (13081) 276/G5
Kingfieldᐃ, Maine (04947) 242/C6
Kingfisher (co.), Okla. 288/L3
Kingfisher, Okla. (73750) 288/L3
King Frederik VIII Land (reg.), Greenl., 4/B11
King Frederik VIII Land (reg.), Greenl., 146/O1
King George (isl.), Ant. 5/C16
King George (isls.), N.W.T. 187/L4
King George (co.), Va. 307/O4
King George, Va. (22485) 307/O4
King George's (falls), S. Africa 118/B5
King Hill, Idaho (83633) 220/C6
Kinghung, China 77/E7
Kingisepp, U.S.S.R. 52/C3
Kingisepp, U.S.S.R., 7/G3
King Island, Alaska (†99762) 196/E1
Kingku, China 77/F7
King Leopold (range), Aust. 88/D3
King Leopold (range), W. Aust. 92/D2
Kingman, Alta. 182/D3
Kingman, Ariz. (86401) 198/A3
Kingman, Ind. (47952) 227/C5
Kingman (co.), Kans. 232/D4
Kingman, Kans. (67068) 232/D4
Kingman, Maine (04451) 242/G4
Kingman (reef), Pacific, 87/K5
Kingoonya, Aust. 88/E6
Kingoonyah, S. Aust. 94/D4
Kingpeng, China 77/J3
Kings (co.), Calif. 204/F8
Kings (riv.), Calif. 204/F7
King's (co.), N. Br. 170/E3
Kings (co.), N.S. 169/D4
Kings (co.), N.Y. 276/N9
Kings (Brooklyn) (borough)ᐃ, N.Y. (*11201) 276/N9
Kings (riv.), Nev. 266/C1
Kings (co.), P.E.I. 169/F2
Kings (peak), Utah 304/D3
King Salmon, Alaska (99613) 196/G3
Kings Beach, Calif. (95719) 204/F4
Kingsbridge, Eng. 13/D7
Kingsburg, Calif. (93631) 204/F7
Kingsburg, S.C. (†29555) 296/H4
Kingsburg, S. Dak. (†57062) 298/O8
Kingsbury, Que. 172/E4
Kingsbury, Ind. (46345) 227/D1
Kingsburyᐃ, Maine (†04990) 242/D5
Kingsbury (pond), Maine 242/D5
Kingsbury (co.), S. Dak. 298/O5
Kingsbury, Texas (78638) 302/G8
Kings Canyon Nat'l Park, Calif. 204/G7
Kingsclear, N. Br. 170/D3
Kingsclere, Eng. 13/F6
Kingscliff-Fingal, N.S.W. 97/G1
Kingscote, Aust. 88/F7
Kingscote, S. Aust. 94/E6
Kingscourt, 10/C4
Kingscourt, Ire. 17/H4
King's Cove, Newf. 166/D1
Kings Creek, N.C. (†28645) 281/G3
Kings Creek, Ohio (†43078) 284/C5
Kings Creek, S.C. (29719) 296/E1
Kingsdale, Minn. (†55015) 254/F4
Kingsdown, Kans. (67858) 232/C4
Kingsey Falls, Que. 172/E4
Kingsford, Mich. (49801) 250/A3
Kingsford, Sask. 181/J6
Kingsford Heights, Ind. (46346) 227/D2
Kingsford-Smith Airport, N.S.W. 97/J4
Kingsgate, Br. Col. 184/K5
Kingshill, V.I.(U.S.) 161/F4
Kingsland, Ark. (71652) 203/F6
Kingsland, Ga. (31548) 216/J9
Kingsland, Sask. 181/C4
Kingsland, Texas (78639) 302/F7
Kings Landing, Ala. (†36775) 194/D6
Kingsley (lake), Fla. 212/E2
Kingsley, Iowa (51028) 229/A3
Kingsley‡, Ky. (†40201) 237/K4
Kingsley, Mich. (49649) 250/D4
Kingsley (dam), Nebr. 264/C3
King's Lynn, 10/G4
King's Lynn, Eng. 13/H5
Kingsmere (lake), Sask. 181/E1
Kingsmill, Texas (†79065) 302/D2
Kings Mills, Ohio (45034) 284/B7
Kings Mountain, Ky. (40442) 237/M6
Kings Mountain, N.C. (28086) 281/G4
Kings Mountain Nat'l Mil. Park, S.C. 296/E1
Kings Park, N.Y. (11754) 276/O9
Kings Point, N.Y. (11024) 276/R7
King's Point, Newf. 166/C4
Kingsport, N.S. 169/D3
Kingsport, Tenn. (*37660) 237/R7
Kingston, 163/J7
Kingston, Australia, 87/G8
Kingston, Ark. (72742) 203/C1
Kingston, Aust. 88/L5
Kingston, Aust. 88/F7
Kingston, Ont. 177/H3
Kingston, Ga. (30145) 216/C2
Kingston, Ill. (60145) 222/E1
Kingston, Ind. (†47240) 227/G6
Kingston, Iowa (†52637) 229/L7
Kingston (cap.), Jam., 146/L8
Kingston (cap.), Jam. 156/C3
Kingston (cap.), Jam. 158/K6
Kingston, La. (†71032) 238/C2
Kingstonᐃ, Mass. (02360) 249/M5
Kingston, Mass. (02360) 249/M5
Kingston, Md. (21834) 245/R8
Kingston, Mich. (48741) 250/F5
Kingston, Minn. (55326) 254/D5
Kingston, Mo. (64650) 261/E3
Kingston, N. Br. 170/D3
Kingstonᐃ, N.H. (03848) 268/E6
Kingston, N.J. (08528) 273/D3
Kingston, N. Mex. (†88042) 274/B6
Kingston, N.S. 169/D4
Kingston, N.Y. (12401) 276/M7
Kingston, N.Z. 101/B6
Kingston, S. Aust. 94/G7
Kingston, Ohio (45644) 284/E7
Kingston, Okla. (73439) 288/N7
Kingston, Pa. (18704) 294/K3
Kingston, R.I. (02881) 249/J7
Kingston, Tenn. (37763) 237/N9
Kingston, Utah (84743) 304/B5
Kingston, W. Va. (25120) 313/D7
Kingston, Wash. (98346) 310/C3
Kingston, Wis. (53939) 317/H8
Kingston Mines, Ill. (61539) 222/D3
Kingston Springs, Tenn. (37082) 237/G8
Kingston-upon-Hull (Hull), 10/F4
Kingston-upon-Hull (Hull), Eng. 13/G4
Kingston-upon-Thames, 10/B6
Kingston-upon-Thames, Eng. 13/G6
Kingstown (cap.), St. Vincent 156/G4
Kingstown (cap.), St. Vincent 161/A9
Kingstown (bay), St. Vincent 161/A9
Kingstown (Dún Laoghaire), Ire. 17/K5
Kingstown, N.S.W. 97/F2
Kingstree, S.C. (29556) 296/H4
Kings Valley, Oreg. (97353) 291/D3
Kingsville, Ont. 177/B6
Kingsville, Md. (21087) 245/N3
Kingsville, Mo. (64061) 261/D5
Kingsville, Ohio (44048) 284/J2
Kingsville, Texas (78363) 302/G10
Kingsville N.A.S., Texas 302/G10
Kingswood, Eng. 13/E6
Kingswood, Ky. (†40144) 237/J5
Kingtehchen, China 77/J6
Kington, 10/E4
Kington, Eng. 13/E5
Kingurutik (lake), Newf. 166/B2
Kingussie, 10/D2
Kingussie, Scot. 15/H5
Kingville, S.C. (†29052) 296/F4
Kingwell, Newf. 166/C2
King William (isl.), 163/G2
King William (isl.), N.W.T. 187/J3
King William (co.), Va. 307/O5
King William, Va. (23086) 307/O5
King William's Town, 102/E8
King William's Town, S. Africa 118/D6
Kingwood, W. Va. (26537) 313/G4
Kingyang, China 77/G4
Kinhwa, China 77/J6
Kiniama, Dem. Rep. of the Congo. 115/E6
Kinik, Turkey 63/B3
Kinistino, Sask. 181/F3
Kinkala, Rep. of Congo 115/B4
Kinkora, P.E.I. 169/E2
Kinley, Sask. 181/D3
Kinloch, Mo. (63140) 261/P2
Kinloch, Sask. 181/H3
Kinlochbervie, Scot. 15/G3
Kinlochleven, Scot. 15/G6
Kinloch Rannoch, Scot. 15/H6
Kinlough, Ire. 17/E3
Kinmount, Ont. 177/F3
Kinmount, Minn. (†55771) 254/F2
Kinmundy, Ill. (62854) 222/E5
Kinna, Sweden 18/H8
Kinnaird, Br. Col. 184/J5
Kinnairds (head), 10/F2
Kinnairds (head), Scot. 15/N4
Kinnear, Wyo. (82516) 319/D2
Kinnears Mills, Que. 172/F3
Kinnegad, Ire. 17/G5
Kinnelon, N.J. (07405) 273/E2
Kinneret, Israel 65/D2
Kinney, Minn. (55758) 254/F3
Kinney (co.), Texas 302/D8
Kinnitty, Ire. 17/F5
Kino (riv.), Japan 81/G6
Kinochisona (lake), Que. 172/B2
Kinosota, Man. 179/D4
Kinross, Iowa (52250) 229/J6
Kinross, 10/E2
Kinross (co.), Scot. 15/K7
Kinross, Scot. 15/K7
Kinsale, 10/B5
Kinsale, Ire. 17/D8
Kinsale (harb.), Ire. 17/E8
Kinsale, Old Head of (head), Ire. 17/E8
Kinsale, Va. (22488) 307/P4
Kinsella, Alta. 182/E3
Kinsey, Ala. (†36301) 194/H8
Kinsey, Mont. (59338) 262/L4
Kinshasa (prov.), Dem. Rep. of the Congo. 115/C4
Kinshasa (cap.), Dem. Rep. of the Congo, 3/K6
Kinshasa (cap.), Dem. Rep. of the Congo, 102/D5
Kinshasa (cap.), Dem. Rep. of the Congo. 115/C4
Kinsley, Kans. (67547) 232/C4
Kinsman, Ill. (60437) 222/E2
Kinsman (mt.), N.H. 268/D3
Kinsman, Ohio (44428) 284/J3
Kinsman Notch (pass), N.H. 268/D3
Kinston, Ala. (36453) 194/F8
Kinston, N.C. (28501) 281/O4
Kinta, China 77/E3
Kinta, Okla. (74552) 288/R4
Kintampo, Ghana 106/D7
Kintnersville, Pa. (18930) 294/M4
Kintore, Scot. 15/M5
Kintyre, N. Dak. (58549) 283/L6
Kintyre (dist.), Scot. 15/E9
Kintyre, Mull of (prom.), Scot. 15/E9
Kinuso, Alta. 182/C2
Kinvara, Ire. 17/D5
Kinwow (bay), Man. 179/E2
Kinyangiri, Tanz. 115/F4
Kinyeti (mt.), Sudan 111/F7
Kinzel Springs, Tenn. (†37882) 237/O9
Kinzua, Oreg. (97849) 291/H3
Kioga (lake), 102/F4
Kioga (lake), Uganda 115/F3
Kiona, Wash. (99340) 310/F4
Kiosk, Ont. 177/F1
Kiowa (co.), Colo. 208/O6
Kiowa, Colo. (80117) 208/L4
Kiowa (creek), Colo. 208/L3
Kiowa (co.), Kans. 232/C4
Kiowa, Kans. (67070) 232/D4
Kiowa (co.), Okla. 288/J5
Kiowa, Okla. (74553) 288/P5
Kiowa (creek), Okla. 288/F1
Kiowa (creek), Texas 302/D1
Kipahulu, Hawaii (†96713) 218/K2
Kiparissía, Greece 45/E7
Kiparissía (gulf), Greece 45/E7
Kipawa, Que. 174/B3
Kipili, Tanz. 115/F5
Kipini, Kenya 115/H4
Kipling, N.C. (27543) 281/M4
Kipling, Sask. 181/J5
Kipnuk, Alaska (99614) 196/F2
Kipp, Alta. 182/D5
Kipp, Kans. (†67401) 232/E3
Kippel, Switz. 39/E4
Kippen, Ont. 177/C4
Kippens, Newf. 166/C4
Kippure (mt.), Ire. 17/J5
Kipton, Ohio (44049) 284/F3
Kipushi, Dem. Rep. of the Congo. 115/E6
Kiput, Phil. 82/C8
Kirazli, Turkey 63/C6
Kirby, Ark. (71950) 203/C5
Kirby, Mont. (59042) 262/J5
Kirby, Ohio (43330) 284/D4
Kirby, Texas (†78109) 302/F8
Kirby, W. Va. (26729) 313/J4
Kirby, Wyo. (82430) 319/D2
Kirby Moorside, Eng. 13/G3
Kirbyville, Texas (75956) 302/K7
Kirchberg, Bern, Switz. 39/E2
Kirchberg, St. Gallen, Switz. 39/G2
Kirchdorf an der Krems, Austria 41/C3
Kirchheim, W. Ger. 22/C4
Kircubbin, N. Ire. 17/K3
Kirensk, U.S.S.R. 48/L4
Kirensk, U.S.S.R., 54/P4
Kirghiz S.S.R., U.S.S.R. 48/H5
Kirghiz S.S.R., U.S.S.R., 54/L5
Kirgis Nor (lake), Mong. 77/D2
Kiri, Dem. Rep. of the Congo. 115/C4
Kirigalpota (mt.), Ceylon 68/E7
Kirikhan, Turkey 63/G4
Kirikkale, Turkey 63/E3
Kirillov, U.S.S.R. 52/E2
Kirin, China, 54/R5
Kirin (prov.), China 77/L3
Kirin, China 77/L3
Kirishima-Yaku Nat'l Park, Japan 81/E7
Kiriwina (isl.), Papua 85/C7
Kirk (pt.), Aust. 88/L7
Kirk, Colo. (80824) 208/P3
Kirk, Ky. (†40143) 237/H5
Kirk, W. Va. (†25671) 313/B7
Kirkağaç, Turkey 63/B3
Kirkbride, Eng. 13/D3
Kirkby, 10/F2
Kirkby-in-Ashfield, Eng. 13/F4
Kirkby Lonsdale, Eng. 13/E3
Kirkby Stephen, Eng. 13/E3
Kirkcaldy, Alta. 182/D4
Kirkcaldy, 10/C1
Kirkcaldy, Scot. 15/K7
Kirkcolm, Scot. 15/F10
Kirkcowan, Scot. 15/G10
Kirkcudbright, 10/E3
Kirkcudbright (co.), Scot. 15/H9
Kirkcudbright, Scot. 15/H10
Kirkee, India 68/C5
Kirkella, Man. 179/A4
Kirkenes, Norway 18/Q2
Kirkersville, Ohio (43033) 284/E6
Kirkfield, Ont. 177/E3
Kirkham, 10/F1
Kirkham, Eng. 13/D4
Kirkintilloch, 10/B1
Kirkintilloch, Scot. 15/C2
Kirkland, Ariz. (86332) 198/C4
Kirkland, Ga. (†31642) 216/G8
Kirkland, Ill. (60146) 222/E1
Kirkland, N. Br. 170/C3
Kirkland, Tenn. (†37046) 237/H9
Kirkland, Texas (79238) 302/D3
Kirkland, Wash. (98033) 310/B2
Kirkland Lake, 163/H6
Kirkland Lake, Ont. 175/D3
Kirkland Lake, Ont. 177/K5
Kirklareli (prov.), Turkey 63/B2
Kirklareli, Turkey 63/B2
Kirklin, Ind. (46050) 227/E4
Kirkman, Iowa (51447) 229/C5
Kirkmansville, Ky. (†42216) 237/G6
Kirkoswald, Scot. 15/G9
Kirkpatrick (lake), Alta. 182/E4
Kirkpatrick (mt.), Ant. 5/A8
Kirkpatrick, Ind. (†47955) 227/D4
Kirkpatrick, Ohio (†43302) 284/D4
Kirkpatrick Fleming, Scot. 15/K9
Kirksey, Ky. (42054) 237/E7
Kirksville, Ind. (†47401) 227/D6
Kirksville, Ky. (40443) 237/N5
Kirksville, Mo. (63501) 261/H2
Kirkuk, Iraq, 54/H6
Kirkuk, Iraq 59/D2
Kirkuk (prov.), Iraq 66/D3
Kirkuk, Iraq 66/D3
Kirkville, Iowa (52566) 229/H6
Kirkville, Miss. (†38856) 256/H2
Kirkwall, 10/E1
Kirkwall, Scot., 7/D3
Kirkwall, Scot. 15/K2
Kirkwood, Del. (19708) 245/R2
Kirkwood, Ill. (61447) 222/C3
Kirkwood, Mo. (63122) 261/O3
Kirkwood, N.J. (08043) 273/B4
Kirkwood, N.Y. (13795) 276/J6
Kirkwood, Pa. (17536) 294/K6
Kirkwood, Tanz. 118/D6
Kirley, S. Dak. (57546) 298/G4
Kirmasti (riv.), Turkey 63/C3
Kirn, W. Ger. 22/B4
Kiron, Iowa (51448) 229/C4
Kirov, U.S.S.R. 48/E4
Kirov, U.S.S.R. 52/D4
Kirov, U.S.S.R. 52/G3
Kirov, U.S.S.R., 7/J3
Kirovabad, U.S.S.R. 48/E5
Kirovabad, U.S.S.R. 52/G6
Kirovakan, U.S.S.R. 52/G6
Kirovo-Chepetsk, U.S.S.R. 52/H3
Kirovograd, U.S.S.R. 48/D5
Kirovograd, U.S.S.R. 52/D5
Kirovograd, U.S.S.R., 7/H4
Kirovsk, U.S.S.R. 52/D1
Kirovsk, U.S.S.R., 7/H2
Kirriemuir, Alta. 182/E4
Kirriemuir, 10/E2
Kirriemuir, Scot. 15/L6
Kirsanov, U.S.S.R. 52/F4
Kirşehir, Turkey 59/B2
Kirşehir (prov.), Turkey 63/F3
Kirşehir, Turkey 63/F3
Kirte, Turkey 63/B6
Kirtland, N. Mex. (87417) 274/A2
Kirtland, Ohio (44094) 284/H2
Kirtland A.F.B., N. Mex. 274/C3
Kirtland Hills, Ohio (†44094) 284/H2
Kiruna, Sweden 18/L3
Kiruna, Sweden, 4/C8
Kirundu, Dem. Rep. of the Congo. 115/E4
Kirvin‡, Texas (75848) 302/H6
Kirwan, Newf. 166/D2
Kirwin, Kans. (67644) 232/C2
Kirwin (res.), Kans. 232/C2
Kiryu, Japan 81/J5
Kisa, Sweden 18/J8
Kisangani, 102/E4
Kisangani, Dem. Rep. of the Congo. 115/E3
Kisar (isl.), Indon. 85/H7
Kisarazu, Japan 81/P3
Kisatchie, La. (71442) 238/D4
K.I. Sawyer A.F.B., Mich. 250/B2
Kisbér, Hung. 41/D3
Kisbey, Sask. 181/J6
Kiselevsk, U.S.S.R. 48/J4
Kishangarh, India 68/D3
Kishinev, U.S.S.R. 48/C5
Kishinev, U.S.S.R. 52/C5
Kishinev, U.S.S.R., 7/G4
Kishiwada, Japan 81/J8
Kishorganj, Pak. 68/G4
Kishow, China 77/G6
Kishtwar, India 68/D2
Kisi, China 77/M2
Kisii, Kenya 115/F4
Kisiju, Tanz. 115/G5
Kiska (isl.), Alaska, 188/D6
Kiska (isl.), Alaska 196/J4
Kiska (vol.), Alaska 196/J4
Kiskatinaw (riv.), Br. Col. 184/G2
Kiskissink, Que. 172/E2
Kiskőrös, Hung. 41/E3
Kiskundorozsma, Hung. 41/E3
Kiskunfélegyháza, Hung. 41/E3
Kiskunhalas, Hung. 41/E3
Kiskunmajsa, Hung. 41/E3
Kislovodsk, U.S.S.R. 52/F6
Kislovodsk, U.S.S.R., 7/J4
Kismayu, 102/G5
Kismayu, Somalia 115/H4
Kismet, Kans. (67859) 232/B4
Kispest, Hung. 41/E3
Kissee Mills, Mo. (65680) 261/G9
Kissidougou, Guinea 106/B7
Kissimmee, Fla. (32741) 212/E3
Kissimmee (lake), Fla. 212/E4
Kissimmee (riv.), Fla. 212/E4
Kississing, Man. 179/H3
Kississing (lake), Man. 179/H3
Kistelek, Hung. 41/E3
Kisten (pass), Switz. 39/H3
Kistler, Pa. (†17066) 294/G5
Kistler, W. Va. (25628) 313/C7
Kistna (riv.), India, 54/L8
Kistna (Krishna) (riv.), India 68/D5
Kistrand, Norway 18/O1
Kisújszállás, Hung. 41/F3
Kisumu, Kenya 115/F4
Kisumu, 102/F5
Kisvárda, Hung. 41/G2
Kita, 102/B3
Kita, Mali 106/C6
Kitai, China 77/C3
Kitaibaraki, Japan 81/K5
Kita Iwo (isl.), Japan, 87/D3
Kita Iwo (isl.), Japan 81/M4
Kitakami (riv.), Japan 81/K4
Kitakata, Japan 81/J5
Kitakyushu, Japan, 3/R4
Kitakyushu, Japan, 54/S6
Kitakyushu, Japan 81/E6
Kitale, Kenya 115/G3
Kitami, Japan 81/L2
Kit Carson (co.), Colo. 208/O4
Kit Carson, Colo. (80825) 208/O5
Kit Carson (mt.), Colo. 208/H7
Kitchel, Ind. (†47353) 227/H5
Kitchener (mt.), Alta. 182/B3
Kitchener, 163/H7
Kitchener, Br. Col. 184/J5
Kitchener, Ont. 177/D4
Kite, Ga. (31049) 216/G5
Kite, Ky. (41828) 237/R6
Kitgum, Uganda 115/F3
Kíthira, Greece 45/F7
Kíthira (isl.), Greece 45/F7
Kíthnos (isl.), Greece 45/G7
Kitim, Jordan 65/D3
Kitimat, 163/D5
Kitimat, Br. Col. 184/C3
Kitinen (riv.), Fin. 18/P3
Kitsap (co.), Wash. 310/C3
Kitscoty, Alta. 182/E3
Kitt (peak), Ariz. 198/D7
Kittanning, Pa. (16201) 294/D4
Kittanning Heights‡, Pa. (†16201) 294/C4
Kittatinny (mts.), N.J. 273/D1
Kitteryᐃ, Maine (03904) 242/B9
Kittery, Maine (03904) 242/B9
Kittery Point, Maine (03905) 242/B9
Kittilä, Fin. 18/O3
Kittitas (co.), Wash. 310/E3
Kittitas, Wash. (98934) 310/E4
Kittrell, N.C. (27544) 281/M2
Kitts, Ky. (40848) 237/P7
Kitts Hill, Ohio (45645) 284/E8
Kittson (co.), Minn. 254/B2
Kitty Hawk, N.C. (27949) 281/T2
Kitui, Kenya 115/G4
Kitunda, Tanz. 115/F5
Kitwanga, Br. Col. 184/D2
Kitwe, Zambia 115/E6
Kitzbühel, Austria 41/B3
Kitzingen, W. Ger. 22/C4
Kitzmiller, Md. (21538) 245/B3
Kiuchüan, China, 54/N5
Kiuchüan, China 77/E4
Kiukiang, China 77/J6
Kiunga, Papua 85/B7
Kiungchow (str.), China 77/G7
Kiungshan, China 77/H8
Kivalina, Alaska (99750) 196/E1
Kivertsy, U.S.S.R. 52/C4
Kivi (lake), Fin. 18/O5
Kiviõli, U.S.S.R. 53/D1
Kivu (prov.), Dem. Rep. of the Congo. 115/E4
Kivu (lake), 102/E5
Kivu (lake), Dem. Rep. of the Congo. 115/E4
Kivu (lake), Rwanda 115/E4
Kiyiu (lake), Sask. 181/C4
Kizel', U.S.S.R. 48/F4
Kizel', U.S.S.R. 52/J3
Kizilcahamam, Turkey 63/E2
Kizil Dağ (mt.), Turkey 63/E4
Kizilhisar, Turkey 63/C4
Kizilirmak (riv.), Turkey 59/B1
Kizilirmak (riv.), Turkey 63/F2
Kiziltepe, Turkey 63/J4
Kiziltoprak, Turkey 63/D6
Kizilviran, Turkey 63/E4
Kizimkazi, Tanz. 115/G5
Kizlyar, U.S.S.R. 52/G6
Kizu, Japan 81/J7
Kizyl-Arvat, U.S.S.R. 48/F6
Kjeller, Norway 18/E3
Kjellerup, Den. 21/C5
Kjölen (mts.), 7/F2
Kjölen (mts.), Norway 18/K3
Kjölen (mts.), Sweden 18/K3
Kladanj, Yugo. 45/D3
Kladno, Czech. 41/B1
Klagenfurt, Austria 41/C3
Klagetoh, Ariz. (†86505) 198/F3
Klaipėda, U.S.S.R. 48/B4
Klaipėda, U.S.S.R. 52/B3
Klaipėda, U.S.S.R. 53/A3
Klaipėda, U.S.S.R., 7/F3
Klaksvík, Den. 21/B2
Klamath (riv.), Calif., 188/B2
Klamath, Calif. (95548) 204/B2
Klamath (riv.), Calif. 204/B2
Klamath (co.), Oreg. 291/F5
Klamath (riv.), Oreg. 291/E6
Klamath Agency, Oreg. (97624) 291/F5
Klamath Falls, Oreg., 146/F5
Klamath Falls, Oreg., 188/B2
Klamath Falls, Oreg. (97601) 291/F5
Klapmuts, S. Africa 118/F6
Klarälv (riv.), Sweden 18/H6
Klaten, Indon. 85/J2
Klatovy, Czech. 41/B2
Klausen (pass), Switz. 39/G3
Klawock, Alaska (99925) 196/M2
Kleberg (co.), Texas 302/G10
Kleberg, Texas (75145) 302/H2
Kleefeld, Man. 179/F5
Kleena Kleene, Br. Col. 184/E4
Klein (isl.), Neth. Ant. 161/E8
Klein, Mont. (†59072) 262/H4
Kleinburg, Ont. 177/J4
Kleine Emme (riv.), Switz. 39/F3
Klein Karas, S.W. Afr. 118/B5
Kleinlützel, Switz. 39/D2

Lafayette Hills 387

Krosno, Poland 47/E4
Krosno Odrzanskie, Poland 47/B2
Krotoszyn, Poland 47/C3
Krotz Springs, La. (70750) 238/G5
Krško, Yugo. 45/B3
Kru Coast (reg.), Liberia 106/C8
Kruë, Alb. 45/D5
Kruger Nat'l Park, S. Africa 118/E4
Krugersdorp, S. Africa 118/H6
Krugloi (pt.), Alaska 196/J3
Kruis (riv.), S. Africa 118/F6
Krum, Texas (76249) 302/G4
Krumbach, W. Ger. 22/D4
Krumovgrad, Bulg. 45/G5
Krung Thep (Bangkok) (cap.), Thai., 72/D4
Krupina, Czech. 41/E2
Krupka, Czech. 41/B1
Krupp, Sask. 181/B5
Krupp (Marlin), Wash. (†98832) 310/F3
Krusenstern (cape), Alaska 196/F1
Krusenstern (cape), N.W.T. 187/G3
Kruševac, Yugo. 45/E4
Krušné Hory (Erzgebirge) (mts.), Czech. 41/B1
Kruzof (isl.), Alaska 196/M1
Krydor, Sask. 181/D3
Krymsk, U.S.S.R. 52/E6
Krynica, Poland 47/E4
Krypton, Ky. (41754) 237/P6
Krzyż, Poland 47/C2
Ksar-el-Boukhari, Alg. 106/E1
Ksar-el-Kebir, Mor. 106/C2
Ksar-es-Souk, Mor. 106/D2
Ktima, Cyprus 63/E5
Kuala Besut, Malaysia 72/D6
Kuala Dungun, Malaysia 72/D6
Kualakapuas, Indon. 85/E6
Kuala Kerai, Malaysia 72/D6
Kualakurun, Indon. 85/E6
Kuala Lipis, Malaysia 72/D6
Kuala Lumpur (cap.), Malaysia, 3/P5
Kuala Lumpur (cap.), Malaysia, 54/O9
Kuala Lumpur (cap.), Malaysia 72/D7
Kualapembuang, Indon. 85/E6
Kuala Pilah, Malaysia 72/D7
Kualapuu, Hawaii (96757) 218/G1
Kuala Rompin, Malaysia 72/D7
Kuala Selangor, Malaysia 72/D7
Kuala Terengganu, Malaysia 72/D6
Kuantan, Malaysia 72/D7
Kuba, U.S.S.R. 52/G6
Kubaisa, Iraq 66/C4
Kuban' (riv.), U.S.S.R. 52/E5
Kubbum, Sudan 111/D5
Kubeno (lake), U.S.S.R. 52/E3
Küblis, Switz. 39/J3
Kubrat, Bulg. 45/H4
Kucha, China 77/B3
Kuching, Malaysia, 54/O9
Kuching, Malaysia 85/E5
Kuchino (isl.), Japan 81/O4
Kuçovë (Stalin), Alb. 45/D5
Küçükköy, Turkey 63/C6
Kudarebe (pt.), Neth. Ant. 161/D9
Kudat, Malaysia 85/F4
Kudus, Indon. 85/J2
Kudymkar, U.S.S.R. 48/F4
Kudymkar, U.S.S.R. 52/H3
Kueitun, China 77/C3
Kuest, Sask. 181/B5
Kufra (oasis), Libya 111/D3
Kufra (oasis), 102/E2
Kufrinja, Jordan 65/D3
Kufrinja, Wadi (dry riv.), Jordan 65/D3
Kufstein, Austria 41/A3
Kuh (cape), Iran 66/K8
Kuhak, Iran 66/N7
Kühlungsborn, E. Ger. 22/D1
Kuhmo, Fin. 18/Q4
Kuhpayeh, Iran 66/H4
Kuhsan, Afgh. 59/H3
Kuhsan, Afgh. 68/A2
Kuilsrivier, S. Africa 118/F6
Kuiseb (riv.), S.W. Afr. 118/B4
Kuiu (isl.), Alaska 196/M2
Kuivaniemi, Fin. 18/O4
Kuji, Japan 81/K3
Kuju (mt.), Japan 81/E7
Kuk (riv.), Alaska 196/G1
Kukaiau, Hawaii (†96775) 218/H4
Kukaklek (lake), Alaska 196/G3
Kukalaya (riv.), Nic. 154/F4
Kukawa, Nigeria 106/G6
Kukës, Alb. 45/E4
Kuki, Japan 81/O2
Kukpowruk (riv.), Alaska 196/F1
Kukui (riv.), Guyana 131/A3
Kukuihaele, Hawaii (96758) 218/H3
Kula, Bulg. 45/F4
Kula, Hawaii (96790) 218/J2
Kula, Turkey 63/C3
Kulai, Malaysia 72/F5
Kula Kangri (mt.), India 68/G3
Kulang, China 77/F4
Kuldiga, U.S.S.R. 53/A2
Kuldja, China, 54/M5
Kuldja, China 77/B3
Kulebaki, U.S.S.R. 52/F3
Kulen Vakuf, Yugo. 45/B3
Kulgera, Aust. 88/E5
Kulgera, No. Terr. 93/C8
Kulkyne (creek), N.S.W. 97/C1
Kulm, N. Dak. (58456) 283/N7
Kulmbach, W. Ger. 22/D3
Kulp, Turkey 63/J3
Kulpmont, Pa. (17834) 294/J4
Kulpsville, Pa. (19443) 294/M5
Kul'sary, U.S.S.R. 48/F5
Kultala, Fin. 18/P2
Kulu, Turkey 63/E3
Kulu, India 68/D2
Kŭm (riv.), S. Korea 81/C5
Kuma (riv.), U.S.S.R. 48/E5
Kuma (riv.), U.S.S.R. 52/G5
Kumagaya, Japan 81/J5
Kumai, Indon. 85/E6
Kumaka, Guyana 131/B4
Kumamoto, Japan, 54/S6
Kumamoto (pref.), Japan 81/E7
Kumamoto, Japan 81/E7
Kumano, Japan 81/H7
Kumanovo, Yugo. 45/E4
Kumara, N.Z. 101/C5
Kumara (riv.), China 77/K1
Kumasi, Ghana 106/D7
Kumba, Cameroon 115/A3
Kumbakonam, India 68/D6
Kumbi Saleh (ruins), Mauritania 106/C5
Kumbo, Cameroon 115/B2
Kume (isl.), Ryukyu Is. 81/M6
Kumertau, U.S.S.R. 52/J4
Kumgang (mt.), N. Korea 81/D4
Kumiyama, Japan 81/J7
Kumkale, Turkey 63/B6
Kumköy, Turkey 63/B6
Kumla, Sweden 18/J7
Kumluca, Turkey 63/D4
Kummerowersee (lake), E. Ger. 22/E2
Kumo, Nigeria 106/G7
Kumphawapi, Thai. 72/D3
Kumta, India 68/C6
Kumukahi (cape), Hawaii 218/K5
Kuna, Idaho (83634) 220/B6
Kunágota, Hung. 41/F3
Kunar (riv.), Afgh. 59/K2
Kunar (riv.), Afgh. 68/C1
Kunar (riv.), Pak. 68/C1
Kunda, U.S.S.R. 52/C3
Kunda, U.S.S.R. 53/D1
Kundl, Austria 41/A3
Kunduz (riv.), Afgh. 59/J2
Kunduz (riv.), Afgh. 68/B1
Kungälv, Sweden 18/G8
Kunghit (isl.), Br. Col. 184/B4
Kungliu, China 77/B3
Kungsbacka, Sweden 18/G8
Kungu, Dem. Rep. of the Congo. 115/C3
Kungur, U.S.S.R. 48/F4
Kungur, U.S.S.R. 52/J3
Kungwe (mt.), Tanz. 115/F5
Kunhegyes, Hung. 41/F3
Kunia, Hawaii (96759) 218/E2
Kuningan, Indon. 85/H2
Kunkle, Ohio (43531) 284/A2
Kunkletown, Pa. (18058) 294/M4
Kunlong, Burma 72/C2
Kunlun (range), China, 54/M6
Kunlun (range), India 68/D1
Kunlun (range), China 77/C4
Kunmadaras, Hung. 41/F3
Kunming, China, 3/Q4
Kunming, China, 54/O7
Kunming, China 77/F6
Kunsan, S. Korea 81/C6
Kunszentmárton, Hung. 41/F3
Kunszentmiklós, Hung. 41/E3
Kuolayarvi, U.S.S.R. 52/D1
Kuopio (prov.), Fin. 18/P5
Kuopio, Fin. 18/Q5
Kuopio, Fin., 7/G2
Kupang, Indon., 54/R11
Kupang, Indon. 85/G8
Kuparuk (riv.), Alaska 196/H1
Kupino, U.S.S.R. 48/H4
Kupiškis, U.S.S.R. 53/C3
Kupreanof (isl.), Alaska 196/N1
Kupreanof (pt.), Alaska 196/G3
Kupyansk, U.S.S.R. 52/E5
Kur (isl.), Indon. 85/J7
Kura (riv.), U.S.S.R. 48/E6
Kura (riv.), U.S.S.R. 52/G6
Kuraiyima, Jordan 65/D3
Kurang (riv.), Iran 66/G4
Kurashiki, Japan 81/F6
Kurayoshi, Japan 81/F6
Kurdistan (reg.), Iran 59/D2
Kurdistan (reg.), Iraq 59/D2
Kurdistan (reg.), Turkey 59/D2
Kurdistan (reg.), Turkey 63/K4
Kurdistan (prov.), Iran 66/E3
Kurdistan (reg.), Iran 66/D2
Kurdistan (reg.), Iraq 66/C2
Kurd Kui, Iran 66/J2
Kŭrdzhali, Bulg. 45/G5
Kure (isl.), Hawaii, 87/J3
Kure (isl.), Hawaii 218/A5
Kure, Japan, 54/S6
Küre, Turkey 63/E2
Küre (mts.), Turkey 63/E2
Kure, Japan 81/F6
Kure Beach, N.C. (28449) 281/O7
Kuressaare, U.S.S.R. 52/B3
Kuressaare, U.S.S.R. 53/B1
Kurgan, U.S.S.R. 48/G4
Kurgan-Tyube, U.S.S.R. 48/G6
Kuria Muria (isls.), Oman 59/G6
Kuria Muria (isls.), Oman, 54/J8
Kurikka, Fin. 18/M5
Kuril (isls.), U.S.S.R. 48/P5
Kuril (isls.), U.S.S.R., 3/S3
Kuril (isls.), U.S.S.R., 54/T5
Kuril'sk, U.S.S.R. 48/P5
Kuring Kuru, S.W. Afr. 118/B3
Kurla, India 68/B7
Kurla, China 77/C3
Kurmuk, Sudan 111/F5
Kurnell (pen.), N.S.W. 97/J4
Kurnool, India 68/D5
Kurnub, Israel 65/C5
Kuroki, N. Dak. (†58711) 283/H2
Kuroki, Sask. 181/H4
Kurow, N.Z. 101/C6
Kurrajong, N.S.W. 97/F3
Kurri Kurri-Weston, N.S.W. 97/F3
Kur Rud (riv.), Iran 66/H6
Kuršėnai, U.S.S.R. 53/B2
Kursk, U.S.S.R. 48/D4
Kursk, U.S.S.R. 52/E4
Kursk, U.S.S.R., 7/H3
Kurşunlu, Turkey 63/E2
Kurtalan, Turkey 63/J3
Kurthwood, La. (71443) 238/D4
Kurtistown, Hawaii (96760) 218/J5
Kurtz, Ind. (47249) 227/E7
Kuruçasile, Turkey 63/E2
Kuruman, S. Africa 118/C5
Kurume, Japan 81/E7
Kurundi, No. Terr. 93/D6
Kurunegala, Ceylon 68/E7
Kurungiku (mts.), Guyana 131/B3
Kurupukari, Guyana 131/B3
Kuşada (gulf), Turkey 63/B4
Kuşadasi, Turkey 63/B4
Kusaie (isl.), Pac. Is., 87/G5
Kushchevskaya, U.S.S.R. 52/E5
Kushequa, Pa. (†16735) 294/E2
Kushikino, Japan 81/E8
Kushima, Japan 81/E8
Kushimoto, Japan 81/G7
Kushiro, Japan, 54/T5
Kushiro, Japan 81/M2
Kushk, Afgh. 59/H3
Kushk, Afgh. 68/A1
Kushka, U.S.S.R. 48/G6
Kushog (lake), Ont. 177/F2
Kuskokwim (riv.), Alaska, 146/B3
Kuskokwim (riv.), Alaska, 188/C6
Kuskokwim (bay), Alaska 196/F3
Kuskokwim (mts.), Alaska 196/G2
Kuskokwim (riv.), Alaska 196/G2
Kuskokwim (riv.), U.S., 4/C17
Küsnacht, Switz. 39/G2
Kusŏng, N. Korea 81/B4
Küssnacht, Switz. 39/F2
Kustanay, U.S.S.R. 48/G4
Kustanay, U.S.S.R., 54/K4
Kustatan, Alaska (†99682) 196/B1
Kut, Iraq 59/E3
Kut (prov.), Iraq 66/D4
Kut, Iraq 66/D4
Kut, Ko (isl.), Thai. 72/D5
Kuta, Nigeria 106/F7
Kütahya, Turkey 59/B2
Kütahya (prov.), Turkey 63/C3
Kütahya, Turkey 63/C3
Kutaisi, U.S.S.R. 48/E5
Kutaisi, U.S.S.R. 52/F6
Kutaisi, U.S.S.R., 7/J4
Kutaradja (Banda Atjeh), Indon. 85/A4
Kutari (riv.), Guyana 131/C4
Kutari (riv.), Sur. 131/C4
Kutch, Colo. (80826) 208/M5
Kutch (reg.), India, 54/L7
Kutch, Rann of (salt lake), Pak. 59/K5
Kutch (gulf), India 68/B4
Kutch, Rann of (salt marsh), India 68/B4
Kutch, Rann of (salt marsh), Pak. 68/B4
Kutchan, Japan 81/K2
Kutcharo (lake), Japan 81/M2
Kutná Hora, Czech. 41/C2
Kutno, Poland 47/D2
Kutoardjo, Indon. 85/J2
Kütsing, China 77/F6
Kuttawa, Ky. (42055) 237/E6
Küttigen, Switz. 39/F2
Kutu, Dem. Rep. of the Congo. 115/C4
Kutum, Sudan 111/D5
Kůty, Czech. 41/D2
Kutztown, Pa. (19530) 294/L4
Kuŭp-tong, N. Korea 81/C3
Kuusamo, Fin. 18/Q4
Kuusamo (lake), Fin. 18/Q4
Kuvandyk, U.S.S.R. 52/J4
Kuwait, 3/M4
Kuwait, 54/H7
KUWAIT, 59/E4
Kuyang, China 77/G3
Kuybyshev, U.S.S.R. 48/F4
Kuybyshev (res.), U.S.S.R. 48/F4
Kuybyshev, U.S.S.R. 52/H4
Kuybyshev (res.), U.S.S.R. 52/G4
Kuybyshev, U.S.S.R., 3/M3
Kuybyshev (res.), U.S.S.R., 7/K3
Kuybyshev, U.S.S.R., 7/K3
Kuyto (lake), U.S.S.R. 52/D2
Kuyüan, China 77/G4
Kuyucat, Turkey 63/C4
Kuyuwini (riv.), Guyana 131/B4
Kuznetsk, U.S.S.R. 52/G4
Kuzomen', U.S.S.R. 52/E1
Kvaenangen (fjord), Norway 18/N2
Kvaerndrup, Den. 21/D7
Kvaløy (isl.), Norway 18/O1
Kvarner (gulf), Yugo. 45/B3
Kvichak, Alaska (†99625) 196/G3
Kvichak (bay), Alaska 196/G3
Kvikkjokk, Sweden 18/K3
Kvinnherad, Norway 18/E6
Kviteseid, Norway 18/F7
Kwa (riv.), Dem. Rep. of the Congo. 115/C4
Kwajalein (atoll), Pac. Is., 87/G5
Kwakoegron, Sur. 131/D3
Kwakwani, Guyana 131/C3
Kwale, Kenya 115/G4
Kwamouth, Dem. Rep. of the Congo. 115/C4
Kwando (riv.), Angola 115/D7
Kwando (riv.), Zambia 115/D7
Kwanghwa, China 77/H5
Kwangju, S. Korea 81/C6
Kwangnan, China 77/G7
Kwango (riv.), Dem. Rep. of the Congo. 115/C5
Kwangsi Chuang (aut. reg.), China 77/G7
Kwangtung (prov.), China 77/H7
Kwanmo (mt.), N. Korea 81/D3
Kwara (state), Nigeria 106/E7
Kwatta, Sur. 131/D2
Kweichow (prov.), China 77/G6
Kweilin, China, 54/P7
Kweilin, China 77/G6
Kweiping, China 77/H7
Kweisui (Huhehot), China 77/H3
Kweiyang, China, 54/O7
Kweiyang, Hunan, China 77/H6
Kweiyang, Kweichow, China 77/G6
Kwethluk, Alaska (99621) 196/F2
Kwidzin, Poland 47/D2
Kwigillingok, Alaska (99622) 196/F3
Kwilu (riv.), Angola 115/C5
Kwilu (riv.), Dem. Rep. of the Congo. 115/C5
Kwinana, Aust. 88/B2
Kwinana, W. Aust. 92/A1
Kwinhagak (Quinhagak), Alaska (†99655) 196/F3
Kwinitsa, Br. Col. 184/C3
Kwitaro (riv.), Guyana 131/B4
Kyabé, Chad 111/C6
Kyabram, Vic. 97/C5
Kyaikto, Burma 72/C3
Kyakhta, U.S.S.R. 48/L4
Kyakhta, U.S.S.R., 54/O4
Kyalite, N.S.W. 97/B4
Kyana, Ind. (47549) 227/D8
Kyancutta, S. Aust. 94/D5
Kyangin, Burma 72/B3
Kyaring Tso (lake), China 77/C5
Kyaring Tso (lake), China 77/E4
Kyaukpadaung, Burma 72/B2
Kyaukpyu, Burma 72/B3
Kyaukse, Burma 72/C2
Kybartai, U.S.S.R. 53/B3
Kyeburn, N.Z. 101/C6
Kyger, Ohio (†45620) 284/F8
Kyger, W. Va. (†25270) 313/D5
Kyjov, Czech. 41/D2
Kyle, S. Dak. (57752) 298/E7
Kyle, Sask. 181/C5
Kyle (dist.), Scot. 15/H9
Kyle, Texas (78640) 302/G8
Kylemore, Sask. 181/H4
Kyle of Lochalsh, Scot. 15/E5
Kyles Ford, Tenn. (37765) 237/R7
Kymi (prov.), Fin. 18/Q6
Kyneton, Vic. 97/C5
Kynšperk, Czech. 41/B1
Kynuna, Queens. 95/B4
Kyogle, N.S.W. 97/G1
Kyonan, Japan 81/O3
Kyŏngju, S. Korea 81/D6
Kyoto, Japan, 54/S6
Kyoto (pref.), Japan 81/J7
Kyoto, Japan 81/J7
Kyrenia, Cyprus 63/E5
Kyritz, E. Ger. 22/E2
Kysucké Nové Mesto, Czech. 41/E2
Kythrea, Cyprus 63/E5
Kyuquot, Br. Col. 184/D5
Kyuquot (sound), Br. Col. 184/C5
Kyushu (isl.), Japan, 3/R4
Kyushu (isl.), Japan, 54/S6
Kyushu (isl.), Japan 81/E7
Kyustendil, Bulg. 45/F4
Kyusyur, U.S.S.R. 48/N2
Kywebwe, Burma 72/C3
Kyzyl, U.S.S.R. 48/K4
Kyzyl, U.S.S.R., 54/N4
Kyzyl-Kum (des.), U.S.S.R. 48/G5
Kzyl-Orda, U.S.S.R. 48/G5
Kzyl-Orda, U.S.S.R., 54/K5

L

Laa an der Thaya, Austria 41/D2
La Aduana, Ven. 124/D3
Laager, Tenn. (37349) 237/K10
La Aguja (cape), Col. 126/C2
Laakirchen, Austria 41/B3
La Almunia de Doña Godina, Spain 33/F2
La Altagracia (prov.), Dom. Rep. 158/F6
La Anna, Pa. (†18326) 294/M3
La Asunción, Ven. 124/G2
Laau (pt.), Hawaii 218/G1
La Babia, Mex. 150/H2
Labadie, Mo. (63055) 261/N3
Labadieville, La. (70372) 238/K4
La Banda, Arg. 143/D2
La Bandera (pt.), P. Rico 161/F1
La Bañeza, Spain 33/C1
La Barca, Mex. 150/H6
La Barge, Wyo. (83123) 319/B3
La Barge (creek), Wyo. 319/B3
Labasheeda, Ire. 17/C6
La Baule-Escoublac, France 28/B4
L'Abbaye, Switz. 39/B3
Labe (riv.), Czech. 41/C1
Labé, Guinea 106/B6
Łabedy, Poland 47/A4
Labelle (co.), Que. 172/B3
Labelle, Que. 172/C3
Labelle (lake), Que. 172/C3
La Belle, Fla. (33935) 212/E5
La Belle, Mo. (63447) 261/J2
La Belle (lake), Wis. 317/H1
Laberge (lake), Yukon 187/E3
Laberinto de las Doce Leguas (cay), Cuba 158/F3
La Berra (mt.), Switz. 39/D3
Labette (co.), Kans. 232/G4
Labette, Kans. (67350) 232/G4
Labinsk, U.S.S.R. 52/F6
La Bisbal, Spain 33/H1
La Blanquilla (isl.), Ven. 124/F2
Labo, Phil. 82/D3
Labo (mt.), Phil. 82/D3
La Bolsa, Urug. 145/C1
La Bolt, S. Dak. (57246) 298/R3
La Boquilla (res.), Mex. 150/G3
Laborec (riv.), Czech. 41/F2
Laborie, St. Lucia 161/G7
Labougle, Arg. 143/G5
Laboulaye, Arg. 143/D3
Labrador (sea), 146/N4
Labrador (reg.), 163/K5
Labrador (reg.), Canada, 3/G3
Labrador (reg.), Newf., 146/M4
Labrador (reg.), Newf. 166/B2
Labrador (sea), Newf. 166/C2
Labrador City, Newf. 166/A3
La Branche, Mich. (†49873) 250/B3
Lábrea, Braz., 120/D3
Lábrea, Braz. 132/G10
La Brea, Trinidad Tobago 161/A11
Labrieville, Que. 174/C3
La Broquerie, Man. 179/F5
Labuan (isl.), Malaysia, 54/P9
Labuan, Indon. 85/G2
Labuan (isl.), Malaysia 85/E4
Labuha, Indon. 85/H6
Labuk (bay), Malaysia 85/F4
Labutta, Burma 72/B3
Labyrinth (canyon), Utah 304/D5
Labytnangi, U.S.S.R. 48/G3
Lac (bay), Neth. Ant. 161/D9
Lac-à-Beauce, Que. 172/E2
Lacadena, Sask. 181/C5
L'Acadie, Que. 172/J4
La Cahouane, Haiti 158/A6
Lac-à-la-Croix, Que. 172/F1
La Calera, Chile 138/F2
Lacamp, La. (71444) 238/E4
La Canada, Calif. (91011) 204/C10
Lacanau (lag.), France 28/C5
La Canoa, Ven. 124/G3
La Carlota, Phil. 82/D5
La Carlota, Spain 33/D4
La Carolina, Spain 33/E3
Lacassine, La. (70650) 238/E6
La Castellana, Phil. 82/D5
Lac-au-Saumon, Que. 172/B2
Lac-aux-Sables, Que. 172/E3
La Cayoba, Bol. 136/C3
Lac Baker, N. Br. 170/B1
Lac-Beauport, Que. 172/F3
Lac-Bouchette, Que. 172/E1
Laccadive (isls.), India, 54/K8
Laccadive, Minicoy and Amindivi Isls. (terr.), India 68/C6
Laccadive (isls.), India 68/C6
Lac-Carré, Que. 172/C3
Lac-Cayamant, Que. 172/A3
Lac-Chat, Que. 172/E2
Lac Court Oreilles Ind. Res., Wis. 317/D4
Lac de Gras (lake), N.W.T. 187/G3
Lac-des-Écorces, Que. 172/B3
Lac-des-Îles, Que. 172/B3
Lac du Bonnet, Man. 179/G4
Lac du Flambeau, Wis. (54538) 317/G4
Lac du Flambeau Ind. Res., Wis. 317/G3
Lac-Édouard, Que. 172/E2
La Ceiba, Hond., 146/K8
La Ceiba, Hond. 154/D3
La Ceiba, Apure, Ven. 124/C4
La Ceiba, Trujillo, Ven. 124/C3
La Cenia, Spain 33/G2
La Center, Ky. (42056) 237/C6
La Center, Wash. (98629) 310/C5
Lacepede (bay), Aust. 88/F7
Lacepede (isls.), Aust. 88/C3
Lacepede (isls.), W. Aust. 92/C2
Lacepede (bay), S. Aust. 94/F7
La Cerbatana, Serranía de (mts.), Ven. 124/E4
Lac-Etchemin, Que. 172/G3
Lacey, Ark. (†71655) 203/G7
Lacey, Wash. (98501) 310/C3
Lacey Spring, Va. (22833) 307/L3
Laceys Spring, Ala. (35754) 194/E1
Laceyville, Pa. (18623) 294/K2
Lac-Frontière, Que. 172/H3
Lacha (lake), U.S.S.R. 52/E2
La Charité-sur-Loire, France 28/E4
La Châtre, France 28/D4
La Chaux-de-Fonds, Switz. 39/C2
Lachay (pt.), Peru 128/D8
Lachen, Switz. 39/G2
Lachine, Que. 172/H4
Lachine, Mich. (49753) 250/F3
Lachlan (riv.), Aust. 88/G6
Lachlan (range), N.S.W. 97/C3
Lachlan (riv.), N.S.W. 97/C3
La Chorrera, Col. 126/D8
Lac-Humqui, Que. 172/B2
Lachute, Que. 172/C4
La Ciénaga, Dom. Rep. 158/D6
La Ciotat, France 28/F6
Lack, N. Ire. 17/F2
Lackawanna, N.Y. (14218) 276/B5
Lackawanna (co.), Pa. 294/L3
Lackawaxen, Pa. (18435) 294/N3
Lackey, Ky. (41643) 237/R6
Lac La Belle, Wis. (†53066) 317/H1
Lac La Biche, 163/E5
Lac La Biche, Alta. 182/E2
Lac La Hache, Br. Col. 184/G4
Lac la Martre, N.W.T. 187/G3
La Clarita, Arg. 143/G5
Lac La Ronge Prov. Park, Sask. 181/M3
Laclede, Idaho (83841) 220/B1
La Clede, Ill. (62437) 222/E5
Laclede (co.), Mo. 261/G7
Laclede, Mo. (64651) 261/F3
Lac-Mégantic, Que. 172/G4
Lacolle, Que. 172/D4
La Coloma, Cuba 158/B2
La Colonia, Chile 138/D7
Lacomb, Oreg. (97354) 291/E3
Lacombe, 163/E5
Lacombe, Alta. 182/D3
Lacombe, La. (70445) 238/L6
Lacon, Ill. (61540) 222/D2
Lacona, Iowa (50139) 229/G6
Lacona, N.Y. (13083) 276/J3
La Concepción, Hond. 154/E3
La Concepción, Pan. 154/F6
La Concepción, Ven. 124/B2
La Concepción, Ven. 124/C2
La Conception, Que. 172/C3
La Concordia, Mex. 150/N9
Laconia, Ind. (47135) 227/E8
Laconia, N.H. (03246) 268/E4
Laconia, Tenn. (38045) 237/C10
La Conner, Wash. (98257) 310/C2
La Conquista, Nic. 154/D5
Lacoochee, Fla. (33537) 212/D3
La Corey, Alta. 182/E2
La Coronilla, Urug. 145/F4
La Coruña, Spain, 7/D4
La Coruña (prov.), Spain 33/B1
La Coruña, Spain 33/B1
Lacosta (isl.), Fla. 212/D5
La Coste, Texas (78039) 302/E8
La Courneuve France 28/B1
Lacovia, Jam. 158/H6
Lac qui Parle (co.), Minn. 254/B6
Lac qui Parle, Minn. (†56265) 254/B5
Lac qui Parle (lake), Minn. 254/C5
Lac qui Parle (riv.), Minn. 254/B6
Lacre (pt.), Neth. Ant. 161/E9
Lac-Rémi, Que. 172/C3
La Crescent, Minn. (55947) 254/G7
La Crescenta-Montrose, Calif. (91214) 204/C10
La Crete, Alta. 182/B5
La Croix (lake), Minn. 254/F2
La Crosse, Fla. (32658) 212/D2
La Crosse, Ga. (†31806) 216/D6
La Crosse, Ind. (46348) 227/D2
La Crosse, Kans. (67548) 232/C3
La Crosse, Va. (23950) 307/M7
Lacrosse, Wash. (99143) 310/H4
La Crosse, Wis., 188/H2
La Crosse (co.), Wis. 317/D8
La Crosse, Wis. (54601) 317/D8
La Cruz, Chile 138/F2
La Cruz, Col. 126/B7
La Cruz, Chihuahua, Mex. 150/G3
La Cruz, Sinaloa, Mex. 150/F5
La Cruz, Nic. 154/E4
La Cruz, Urug. 145/C4
Lac-Saguay, Que. 172/B3
Lac-Sainte-Marie, Que. 172/A4
Lac-Saint-Jean-Est (co.), Que. 172/F1
Lac-Saint-Jean-Est (co.), Que. 174/C3
Lac-Saint-Jean-Ouest (co.), Que. 172/E1
Lac-Saint-Jean-Ouest (co.), Que. 174/C2
Lac-Saint-Paul, Que. 172/B3
Lac Seul, Ont. 175/B2
La Cuchilla, Urug. 145/F3
La Cueva, N. Mex. (†87712) 274/D3
La Cumbre, Arg. 143/C3
La Cure, Switz. 39/B4
Lacuy (pen.), Chile 138/D4
Lac Vert, Sask. 181/G3
La Cygne, Kans. (66040) 232/H3
Lacy-Lakeview‡, Texas (†76701) 302/G6
Ladakh (reg.), India 68/D2
Ladd, Ill. (61329) 222/D2
Ladder (creek), Kans. 232/A3
Ladder Valley, Sask. 181/E2
Laddonia, Mo. (63352) 261/J4
Ladelle, Ark. (†71655) 203/G7
Ladera Heights‡, Calif. (†90001) 204/C11
Ladgasht, Pak. 59/H4
Ladgasht, Pak. 68/A3
Ladiesburg, Md. (21759) 245/J2
La Digue (isl.), Seych. 118/J5
Lâdik, Turkey 63/F2
Ladis, Iran 66/M6
Ladispoli, Italy 34/E6
Ladner, S. Dak. (57753) 298/B2
Lado, Sudan 111/F6
Ladoga (lake), U.S.S.R. 48/D3
Ladoga (lake), U.S.S.R. 52/D2
Ladoga, Ind. (47954) 227/D5
Ladoga (lake), U.S.S.R., 7/H2
La Dôle (mt.), Switz. 39/B4
Ladonia, Texas (75449) 302/J4
Ladora, Iowa (52251) 229/J5
La Dorada, Col. 126/C5
Ladrillero (gulf), Chile 138/C8
Ladrillero (mt.), Chile 138/E10
Ladrillo (pt.), Cuba 158/E3
Ladron (mts.), N. Mex. 274/B4
Ladrones (isls.), Pan. 154/F7
Ladson, S.C. (29456) 296/G6
La Due, Mo. (64758) 261/E6
Ladue, Mo. (†64758) 261/P3
La Durantaye, Que. 172/G3
Lady (pond), Newf. 166/D2
Lady Ann (str.), N.W.T. 187/K2
Ladybrand, S. Africa 118/D5
Lady Franklin (bay), N.W.T. 187/M1
Lady Franklin (isl.), N.W.T. 187/M3
Lady Lake, Fla. (32659) 212/E3
Lady Lake, Sask. 181/J3
Lady's Island Lake (inlet), Ire. 17/J7
Ladysmith, Br. Col. 184/J3
Ladysmith, 102/F7
Ladysmith, S. Africa 118/D5
Ladysmith, Va. (22501) 307/N4
Ladysmith, Wis. (54848) 317/D5
Ladywood, Man. 179/F4
Lae, Thai. 72/D3
Lae, Terr. N.G. 85/B7
Lae, Terr. N.G., 87/E6
Laem Pho (cape), Thai. 72/D6
Laem Talumphuk (cape), Thai. 72/D5
Laerdal, Norway 18/E6
La Esmeralda, Arg. 143/G5
La Esmeralda, Bol. 136/D8
La Esmeralda, Par. 144/A4
La Esmeralda, Ven. 124/F6
Laesø (isl.), Den. 18/G8
Laesø (isl.), Den. 21/D3
La Esperanza, Arg. 143/B7
La Esperanza, Bol. 136/D4
La Esperanza, Hond. 154/C3
La Esperanza, Ven. 124/H3
La Estrada, Spain 33/B1
La Estrella, Bol. 136/D5
La Estrella, Chile 138/F5
La Estrelleta (prov.), Dom. Rep. 158/C5
La Falda, Arg. 143/D3
La Farge, Wis. (54639) 317/E8
La Fargeville, N.Y. (13656) 276/J2
Lafayette, Ala. (36862) 194/H5
Lafayette (co.), Ark. 203/C7
Lafayette, Calif. (94549) 204/K2
Lafayette, Colo. (80026) 208/K3
Lafayette (co.), Fla. 212/C2
La Fayette, Ga. (30728) 216/B1
La Fayette, Ill. (61449) 222/C2
Lafayette, Ind., 188/J2
Lafayette, Ind. (*47901) 227/D4
La Fayette, Ky. (42254) 237/F7
Lafayette (par.), La. 238/F6
Lafayette, La. (70501) 238/F6
Lafayette, Minn. (56054) 254/D6
Lafayette (co.), Miss. 256/E2
Lafayette (co.), Mo. 261/E4
Lafayette (mt.), N.H. 268/D3
Lafayette, N.J. (07848) 273/D1
La Fayette, N.Y. (13084) 276/H5
Lafayette, Ohio (45854) 284/C4
Lafayette, Oreg. (97127) 291/A2
Lafayette, R.I. (†02852) 249/H6
Lafayette, Tenn. (37083) 237/J7
Lafayette, Va. (24108) 307/H6
Lafayette (co.), Wis. 317/F10
Lafayette Hills-Youth Meeting‡, Pa. (19444) 294/M5

388 Lafayette Springs

Lafayette Springs, Miss. (38640) 256/F2
Lafe, Ark. (72436) 203/J1
La Fé, Cuba 158/A2
La Feria, Texas (78559) 302/G11
La Ferté-Macé, France 28/C3
Lafferty, Ohio (43951) 284/H5
Lafia, Nigeria 106/F7
Lafiagi, Nigeria 106/F7
Lafitte, La. (70067) 238/K7
Laflèche, Que. 172/J4
La Flèche, France 28/C4
Lafleche, Sask. 181/E6
Laflin‡, Pa. (†18701) 294/L3
La Florencia, Arg. 143/D1
La Floresta, Urug. 145/C7
La Florestal, Par. 144/C3
La Follette, Tenn. (37766) 237/N8
Lafond, Alta. 182/E3
La Fontaine, Ind. (46940) 227/F3
Lafontaine, Kans. (66750) 232/G4
Lafourche (par.), La. 238/K7
Lafourche, La. (†70301) 238/J7
Lafourche (bayou), La. 238/K8
La France, S.C. (29656) 296/B2
La Fría, Ven. 124/B3
Laful, India 68/G7
Lagacéville, N. Br. 170/E1
La Gallareta, Arg. 143/F5
Lagan, La. (†70086) 238/L4
Lagan (riv.), N. Ire. 17/K2
Lagarfljot (stream), Ice. 21/C1
La Garita, Colo. (81139) 208/G7
La Garita (mts.), Colo. 208/F7
Lagarto (Nuevo Chagres), Pan. 154/G6
Lagayan, Phil. 82/C2
Lage, W. Ger. 22/C3
Lågen (riv.), Norway 18/G6
Laggan, 10/D2
Laggan, N.S.W. 97/E4
Laggan, Scot. 15/H5
Laggan (bay), Scot. 15/D8
Laggan (lake), Scot. 15/H6
Laghey, Ire. 17/E2
Laghouat, Alg. 106/E2
Laghouat, 102/C1
La Gineta, Spain 33/E3
La Glace, Alta. 182/A2
La Gloria, Col. 126/D3
La Gloria, Cuba 158/G2
Lagoa, Port. 33/B4
Lago Argentino (El Calafate), Arg. 143/B7
La Goleta, Col. 126/B3
La Gomera, Guat. 154/B3
Lagonegro, Italy 34/E4
Lagonoy (gulf), Phil. 82/E4
Lago Ranco, Chile 138/E3
Lagos (state), Nigeria 106/E7
Lagos (cap.), Nigeria 102/C4
Lagos (cap.), Nigeria, 3/K5
Lagos (cap.), Nigeria, 106/E7
Lagos, Port. 33/B4
Lagos de Moreno, Mex. 150/J6
Lagosta (Lastovo) (isl.), Yugo. 45/C4
Lago Verde, Chile 138/E5
La Grand-Combe, France 28/E5
La Grande, Oreg., 188/C1
La Grande, Oreg. (97850) 291/J2
La Grande, Wash. (98348) 310/C4
La Grande Rivière (riv.), Que., 146/L4
La Grange, Australia, 87/C7
La Grange, Ark. (72352) 203/J4
La Grange, Aust. 88/C4
La Grange, Calif. (95329) 204/E6
La Grange, Ga., 188/K4
La Grange, Ga. (30240) 216/B4
La Grange, Ill. (60525) 222/A2
Lagrange (co.), Ind. 227/G1
Lagrange, Ind. (46761) 227/F1
La Grange, Ky. (40031) 237/L4
La Grange▵, Maine (04453) 242/F5
La Grange, Maine (04453) 242/F5
La Grange, Mo. (63448) 261/K2
La Grange, N.C. (28551) 281/O4
La Grange, W. Aust. 92/C2
Lagrange, Ohio (44050) 284/F3
La Grange, Tenn. (38046) 237/C10
La Grange, Texas (78945) 302/G8
Lagrange, Wyo. (82221) 319/H4
La Grange Highlands‡, Ill. (60525) 222/A2
La Grange Park, Ill. (60525) 222/A2
La Granja (San Ildefonso), Spain 33/E2
La Gran Sabana (plain), Ven. 124/G5
La Grita, Ven. 124/C3
Lagro, Ind. (46941) 227/F3
La Grue (bayou), Ark. 203/H5
La Guadeloupe, Que. 172/F4
La Guaira, Ven., 120/D1
La Guaira, Ven. 124/E2
La Guajira (dept.), Col. 126/D2
La Guardia, Bol. 136/D5
La Guardia, Spain 33/B2
Laguardia, Spain 33/E1
La Guata, Hond. 154/D3
Laguna (dam), Ariz. 198/A6
Laguna (res.), Ariz. 198/A6
Laguna, Braz., 120/F5
Laguna, Braz. 132/D10
Laguna (res.), Calif. 204/L11
Laguna, N. Mex. (87026) 274/B3
Laguna (prov.), Phil. 82/C3
Laguna Beach, Calif. (*92651) 204/G10
Laguna de Perlas, Nic. 154/F4
Laguna Hills, Calif. (92653) 204/D11
Laguna Larga, Cuba 158/G2
Laguna Niguel, Calif. (92677) 204/H10
Laguna Paiva, Arg. 143/F5
Lagunas, Chile 138/B3
Lagunas, Peru 128/E5
Laguna Vista‡, Texas (†78578) 302/G11
Lagunetas, Ven. 124/C3
Lagunillas, Bol. 136/D6
Lagunillas, Chile 138/F3
Lagunillas, Ven. 124/C2
Lagunitas, Calif. (94938) 204/H1
La Habana (prov.), Cuba 158/C1
La Habra, Calif. (90631) 204/D11
Lahad Datu, Malaysia 85/F5
Lahaina, Hawaii, 188/F5
Lahaina, Hawaii (96761) 218/H2
Laham, Indon. 85/F5
Lahan, Nong (lake), Thai. 72/D3
La Harpe, Ill. (61450) 222/C3
La Harpe, Kans. (66751) 232/G4
Lahat, Indon. 85/C6
La Have, N.S. 169/D4
Lahave (isl.), N.S. 169/D4
Lahave (riv.), N.S. 169/D4
Lahej, P.D.R. Yemen 59/E7
La Higuera, Chile 138/A7
Lahijan, Iran 66/G2
Lahinch, Ire. 17/C6
Lahmansville, W. Va. (26731) 313/H4
Lahn (riv.), W. Ger. 22/C3
Laholm, Sweden 18/H8
Lahoma, Okla. (73754) 288/K2
La Honda, Calif. (94020) 204/J3
Lahontan (res.), Nev. 266/B3
Lahore, Pak. 59/K3
Lahore, Pak. 68/C2
Lahore, Pak., 54/L6
Lahore, Va. (22502) 307/N4
La Horqueta, Ven. 124/G3
Lahr, W. Ger. 22/B4
Lahri, Pak. 68/B3
Lahti, Fin. 18/O6
La Huaca, Peru 128/B5
Lai, Chad 111/C6
Lai, 102/D4
Lai Chau, N. Vietnam 72/D2
Laidlaw, Br. Col. 184/M3
Laie, Hawaii (96762) 218/E1
L'Aigle, France 28/D3
Lai-hka, Burma 72/C2
Laila, Saudi Ar. 59/E5
Laila, Saudi Ar., 54/H7
Lailan, Iraq 66/D3
La Inglesa, Ven. 124/G3
Laings, Ohio (43752) 284/J6
Laingsburg, Mich. (48848) 250/E6
Lainioälv (riv.), Sweden 18/N3
Lair, Ky. (†41031) 237/N4
Laird, Colo. (80739) 208/P2
Laird, Sask. 181/E3
Lairdsville, Pa. (17742) 294/J3
Lairg, 10/D1
Lairg, Scot. 15/H3
Lais, Phil. 82/E7
Laisamis, Kenya 115/G3
La Isla, Texas (†79838) 302/A10
Laiwui, Indon. 85/H6
Laiyang, China 77/K4
Laja (riv.), Chile 138/E1
La Jalca, Peru 128/D6
La Jara, Colo. (81140) 208/H8
La Jara, N. Mex. (87027) 274/B2
Lajas, P. Rico 161/A2
Lajes, Braz. 132/D9
La Jolla, Calif. (92037) 204/H11
La Jolla Ind. Res., Calif. 204/J10
Lajord, Sask. 181/G5
La Jose, Pa. (15753) 294/E4
Lajosmizse, Hung. 41/E3
La Joya, Bol. 136/B5
Lajoya, N. Mex. (87028) 274/C4
La Joya, Peru 128/G11
La Joya, Texas (78560) 302/F11
La Junta, Colo., 188/F3
La Junta, Colo. (81050) 208/M7
La Junta, Mex. 150/F2
Lak Dera (dry riv.), Kenya 115/H3
Lak Dera (dry riv.), Somalia 115/H3
Lake (co.), Calif. 204/C4
Lake (co.), Colo. 208/G4
Lake (co.), Fla. 212/E3
Lake, Ga. (†30260) 216/D3
Lake (co.), Ill. 222/E1
Lake (co.), Ind. 227/C2
Lake, Ky. (†40741) 237/O6
Lake (co.), Mich. 250/D5
Lake, Mich. (48632) 250/E5
Lake (co.), Minn. 254/G3
Lake, Miss. (39092) 256/F6
Lake (co.), Mont. 262/B3
Lake‡, N.Y. (†10990) 276/M8
Lake (co.), Ohio 284/H2
Lake (co.), Oreg. 291/G5
Lake (creek), Oreg. 291/J3
Lake (co.), S. Dak. 298/P5
Lake (co.), Tenn. 237/B8
Lake (creek), Utah 304/A5
Lake (creek), Wash. 310/G3
Lake Alfred, Fla. (33850) 212/E3
Lake Alma, Sask. 181/G6
Lake Alpine, Calif. (95235) 204/F5
Lake Aluma‡, Okla. (†73101) 288/M3
Lake Andes, S. Dak. (57356) 298/M7
Lake Angelus‡, Mich. (†48053) 250/F6
Lake Ann, Mich. (49650) 250/D4
Lake Ariel, Pa. (18436) 294/M3
Lake Arrowhead, Calif. (92352) 204/H9
Lake Arthur, La. (70549) 238/E6
Lake Arthur, N. Mex. (88253) 274/E5
Lake Barbara‡, Texas (†77531) 302/J9
Lake Barcroft‡, Va. (†22040) 307/O3
Lake Barrington‡, Ill. (†60010) 222/E1
Lake Benton, Minn. (56149) 254/B6
Lake Beulah, Wis. (†53120) 317/J2
Lake Bluff, Ill. (60044) 222/F1
Lake Boga, Vic. 97/B4
Lake Bolac, Vic. 97/B5
Lake Bronson, Minn. (56734) 254/B2
Lake Bruce, Ind. (†46939) 227/E2
Lake Buena Vista, Fla. (†32741) 212/E3
Lake Butler, Fla. (32054) 212/D1
Lake Butte des Morts‡, Wis. (†54901) 317/J7
Lake Cargelligo, Aust. 88/H6
Lake Cargelligo, N.S.W. 97/D3
Lake Carmel, N.Y. (10512) 276/N8
Lake Carroll, Fla. (†33601) 212/C2
Lake Catherine, Ill. (†60002) 222/E1
Lake Charles, La., 188/H4
Lake Charles, La. (70601) 238/D6
Lake Church, Wis. (†53004) 317/L9
Lake Cicott, Ind. (46942) 227/D3
Lake City, Ark. (72437) 203/K2
Lake City, Calif. (96115) 204/E2
Lake City, Colo. (81235) 208/E6
Lake City, Fla. (32055) 212/D1
Lake City, Ill. (61935) 222/E4
Lake City, Iowa (51449) 229/D4
Lake City, Kans. (67071) 232/D4
Lake City, Mich. (49651) 250/D4
Lake City, Minn. (55041) 254/F6
Lake City, Pa. (16423) 294/B1
Lake City, S.C. (29560) 296/H4
Lake City, S. Dak. (57247) 298/O2
Lake City, Tenn. (37769) 237/N8
Lake City Arsenal, Mo. 261/R5
Lake Clarke Shores‡, Fla. (†33401) 212/F5
Lake Clear, N.Y. (12945) 276/M2
Lake Como, Fla. (32057) 212/E2
Lake Como, Miss. (†39422) 256/F7
Lake Como, Pa. (18437) 294/M2
Lake Cormorant, Miss. (38641) 256/D1
Lake Cowichan, Br. Col. 184/J3
Lakecreek, Oreg. (†97524) 291/E5
Lake Crystal, Minn. (56055) 254/D6
Lake Dallas‡, Texas (75065) 302/G4
Lake Delton, Wis. (53940) 317/G8
Lake Dunmore, Vt. (†05769) 268/A4
Lake Eliza, Alta. 182/E3
Lake Elmo, Minn. (55042) 254/F6
Lake Elmore, Vt. (05657) 268/B2
Lake End, La. (†71019) 238/D3
Lake Erie Beach, N.Y. (†14006) 276/B5
Lakefield, Ont. 177/F3
Lakefield, Minn. (56150) 254/C7
Lake-Fishing Bridge-Bridge Bay, Wyo. (†82190) 319/B1
Lake Forest‡, Fla. (32208) 212/B4
Lake Forest, Ill. (60045) 222/F1
Lake Forest Park, Wash. (†98101) 310/B1
Lake Fork, Gunnison (riv.), Colo. 208/E6
Lake Fork, Idaho (83635) 220/B5
Lake Fork, Ill. (62541) 222/D4
Lake Frances, Ark. (†72761) 203/B1
Lake Francis, Man. 179/E4
Lake Fremont (Zimmerman), Minn. (†55398) 254/E5
Lake Geneva, Wis. (53147) 317/K10
Lake George, Colo. (80827) 208/J5
Lake George, Mich. (48633) 250/E5
Lake George, Minn. (56458) 254/D3
Lake George, N.Y. (12845) 276/N4
Lake Grace, Aust. 88/B6
Lake Grace, W. Aust. 92/B6
Lake Grove‡, N.Y. (11755) 276/P9
Lake Hamilton‡, Fla. (33851) 212/E3
Lake Harbor, Fla. (33459) 212/F5
Lake Harbour, 163/K3
Lake Harbour, N.W.T. 187/L3
Lake Havasu City, Ariz. (86403) 198/A4
Lakehead, Calif. (96051) 204/C3
Lake Helen, Fla. (32744) 212/E3
Lake Henry, Minn. (†56362) 254/D5
Lake Hiawatha, N.J. (07034) 273/E2
Lake Hills-Murray Hills, Tenn. (37416) 237/L10
Lake Holloway‡, Fla. (†33801) 212/E3
Lake Hopatcong, N.J. (07849) 273/D2
Lake Hubert, Minn. (56459) 254/D4
Lake Hughes, Calif. (93532) 204/G9
Lake Huntington, N.Y. (12752) 276/L7
Lakehurst, N.J. (08733) 273/E3
Lakehurst Naval Air Sta., N.J. 273/E3
Lake in the Hills‡, Ill. (†60102) 222/E1
Lake Isabella, Calif. (93240) 204/G8
Lake Itasca, Minn. (56460) 254/C3
Lake Jackson, Texas (77566) 302/J8
Lake James, Ind. (†46703) 227/H1
Lake Jem, Fla. (32745) 212/E3
Lake Katrine, N.Y. (12449) 276/M7
Lakeland, Fla., 188/K5
Lakeland, Fla. (*33801) 212/D3
Lakeland, Ga. (31635) 216/F8
Lakeland, La. (70752) 238/H5
Lakeland, Man. 179/D4
Lakeland, Mich. (48143) 250/F6
Lakeland, Minn. (55043) 254/E1
Lake Landing, N.C. (†27824) 281/T4
Lakeland Shores‡, Minn. (†55043) 254/F6
Lakeland Village, Calif. (†92330) 204/E11
Lake Leelanau, Mich. (49653) 250/D4
Lake Lenore, Sask. 181/G3
Lake Lillian, Minn. (56253) 254/C6
Lake Linden, Mich. (49945) 250/A1
Lakeline, Ohio (†44094) 284/J8
Lake Lotawana, Mo. (64063) 261/R6
Lake Louise, 163/E5
Lake Louise, Alta. 182/C4
Lake Louisvilla‡, Ky. (†40014) 237/K4
Lake Lure, N.C. (28746) 281/E4
Lake Luzerne, N.Y. (12846) 276/N4
Lake Madge, Sask. 181/K4
Lake Magdalene, Fla. (†33601) 212/D3
Lake Mary, Fla. (32746) 212/E3
Lake McDonald, Mont. (59921) 262/B2
Lake Mead Nat'l Rec. Area, Nev. 266/G6
Lake Mead Nat'l Rec. Area, Ariz. 198/A2
Lake Michigan Beach, Mich. (†49039) 250/C6
Lake Mills, Iowa (50450) 229/F2
Lake Mills, Wis. (53551) 317/H9
Lake Minchumina, Alaska (99623) 196/H2
Lake Mohawk, N.J. (†07871) 273/D1
Lake Monroe, Fla. (32747) 212/E3
Lakemont, Ga. (30552) 216/F1
Lakemont, Pa. (16602) 294/F5
Lakemoor‡, Ill. (†60050) 222/E1
Lakemore, Ohio (44250) 284/H3
Lake Moxie, Maine (†04985) 242/D5
Lake Nash, No. Terr. 93/E6
Lake Nebagamon, Wis. (54849) 317/C3
Lakenheath, Sask. 181/E6
Lake Norden, S. Dak. (57248) 298/P4
Lake Odessa, Mich. (48849) 250/D6
Lake of the Woods (lake), 163/G6
Lake of the Woods (lake), Ont. 175/B3
Lake of the Woods (lake), Ont. 177/F5
Lake of the Woods (lake), Man. 179/H5
Lake of the Woods (co.), Minn. 254/D2
Lake of the Woods (lake), Minn. 254/D1
Lake Orion Heights‡, Mich. (†48035) 250/F6
Lake Oswego, Oreg. (97034) 291/B2
Lake Ozark, Mo. (65049) 261/G6
Lake Park, Fla. (33403) 212/F5
Lake Park, Ga. (31636) 216/F9
Lake Park, Iowa (51347) 229/C2
Lake Park, Minn. (56554) 254/B4
Lake Placid, Fla. (33852) 212/E4
Lake Placid, N.Y. (12946) 276/N2
Lake Pleasant, N.Y. (12108) 276/M4
Lake Pocotopaug, Conn. (†06424) 210/F2
Lakeport, Calif. (95453) 204/C4
Lakeport, Ont. 177/G4
Lakeport, Fla. (†33471) 212/E5
Lakeport‡, Texas (†75641) 302/K5
Lake Preston, S. Dak. (57249) 298/P5
Lake Providence, La. (71254) 238/H1
Lake Saint Croix Beach, Minn. (†55043) 254/F6
Lake Saint Peter, Ont. 177/F2
Lakes Entrance, Vic. 97/E5
Lake Ship Heights‡, Fla. (†33839) 212/E4
Lakeshire‡, Mo. (†63101) 261/P3
Lake Shore, Minn. (†56401) 254/D4
Lakeshore, Miss. (39558) 256/F10
Lakeside, Ariz. (85929) 198/E4
Lakeside‡, Calif. (92040) 204/J11
Lakeside‡, Colo. (80201) 208/J3
Lakeside, Conn. (06758) 210/B2
Lakeside, Iowa (50588) 229/C3
Lakeside‡, Mo. (†65049) 261/G6
Lakeside, Mont. (59922) 262/B2
Lakeside, Nebr. (69351) 264/B2
Lakeside, Ohio (43440) 284/E2
Lakeside, Oreg. (97449) 291/C4
Lakeside‡, Texas (†76101) 302/E2
Lakeside‡, Texas (†76366) 302/F4
Lakeside, Utah (†84401) 304/B2
Lakeside, Va. (23228) 307/N5
Lakeside Park, Ky. (†41017) 237/R3
Lake Spring, Mo. (65532) 261/J7
Lake Stevens, Wash. (98258) 310/D3
Lake Success, N.Y. (11040) 276/R7
Lake Superior Prov. Park, Ont. 175/D3
Lake Superior Prov. Park, Ont. 177/J5
Lakesville, Md. (†21622) 245/O7
Lake Tapawingo, Mo. (†64015) 261/R6
Lake Tomahawk, Wis. (54539) 317/H4
Laketon, Ind. (46943) 227/F3
Laketon, N. Br. 170/E2
Laketown, Utah (84038) 304/C2
Lake Toxaway, N.C. (28747) 281/D4
Lake Valley, Sask. 181/E5
Lakeview‡, Ala. (†35974) 194/G2
Lakeview, Ark. (72642) 203/E1
Lake View, Iowa (51480) 229/C4
Lakeview‡, Ky. (†41017) 237/S2
Lake View▵, Maine (†04463) 242/F5
Lakeview, Mich. (48850) 250/D5
Lakeview‡, Mich. (†49014) 250/D6
Lake View, Miss. (†38680) 256/D1
Lakeview, Mont. (†59744) 262/E6
Lakeview, N.C. (28350) 281/L4
Lake View, N.Y. (14085) 276/B5
Lakeview‡, N.Y. (†11565) 276/R7
Lakeview, Ohio (43331) 284/C4
Lakeview, Oreg. (97630) 291/G5
Lake View, S.C. (29563) 296/J3
Lakeview‡, Texas (†77647) 302/L7
Lakeview, Texas (79239) 302/D3
Lakeview Heights, Mo. (†65338) 261/F6
Lake Villa‡, Ill. (60046) 222/F1
Lake Village, Ark. (71653) 203/H7
Lake Village, Ind. (46349) 227/C2
Lakeville, Conn. (06039) 210/B1
Lakeville, Ind. (46536) 227/E1
Lakeville▵, Mass. (02346) 249/L5
Lakeville, Mass. (02346) 249/L5
Lakeville, Minn. (55044) 254/E6
Lakeville, N. Br. 170/C2
Lakeville, N.Y. (14480) 276/E5
Lakeville, Ohio (44638) 284/F4
Lake Waccamaw, N.C. (28450) 281/M6
Lake Walcott (res.), Idaho 220/E7
Lake Wales, Fla. (33853) 212/E4
Lake Waukomis‡, Mo. (†64152) 261/P5
Lake Wawasee, Ind. (†46567) 227/F2
Lake Way, W. Aust. 92/C4
Lake Wazeecha, Wis. (†54494) 317/G7
Lake Williams, N. Dak. (58457) 283/L5
Lake Wilson, Minn. (56151) 254/B7
Lake Winnebago, Mo. (†64034) 261/R6
Lake Wissota, Wis. (†54729) 317/D6
Lakewood, Calif. (*90712) 204/C11
Lakewood, Colo. (80215) 208/J3
Lakewood, Fla. (32566) 212/C5
Lakewood‡, Ill. (†60014) 222/E1
Lakewood, Ill. (62438) 222/E4
Lakewood, N.J. (08701) 273/E3
Lakewood, N. Mex. (88254) 274/E6
Lakewood, N.Y. (14750) 276/B6
Lakewood, Ohio (44107) 284/G9
Lakewood, Pa. (18439) 294/M2
Lakewood, Tenn. (†37138) 237/H8
Lakewood, Wash. (98259) 310/C2
Lakewood, Wis. (54138) 317/K5
Lakewood Club, Mich. (†49440) 250/C5
Lake Worth, Fla. (33460) 212/G5
Lake Worth, Texas (76135) 302/E2
Lake Zurich, Ill. (60047) 222/E1
Lakhdenpokh'ya, U.S.S.R. 52/C2
Lakhish, Wadi (dry riv.), Israel 65/B4
Lakin, Kans. (67860) 232/A4
Lakolk, Den. 21/B7
Lakonía (gulf), Greece 45/F7
Lakor (isl.), Indon. 85/H7
Lakota, Iowa (50451) 229/E2
Lakota, N. Dak. (58344) 283/O3
Lakse (fjord), Norway 18/P1
Lakselv, Norway 18/O2
La Laguna, Chile 138/F2
La Laguna, Spain 106/A3
La Laja (mts.), Chile 138/E1
La Lande, N. Mex. (†88119) 274/E4
Lalara, Gabon 115/B3
La Lata, Urug. 145/E2
Lalehzar, Kuh-i- (mt.), Iran 59/G4
Lalehzar, Kuh-i- (mt.), Iran 66/K6
La Leona, Ven. 124/G3
Lalibela, Eth. 111/G5
La Libertad, Ec. 128/B4
La Libertad, El Salv. 154/C4
La Libertad, Guat. 154/B2
La Libertad, Nic. 154/E4
La Libertad (dept.), Peru 128/C6
La Ligua, Chile 138/A9
La Ligua (riv.), Chile 138/A9
Lalín, Spain 33/C1
La Línea, Spain 33/D4
Lalitpur, Nepal 68/E3
La Loche, Sask. 181/L3
La Loma, Bol. 136/C7
La Louvière, Belg. 27/E8
La Lune, Trinidad Tobago 161/B11
La Luz, N. Mex. (88337) 274/C6
La Luz, Ven. 124/D3
La Macarena, Serranía de (mts.), Col. 126/D6
La Macaza, Que. 172/C3
La Maddalena, Italy 34/B4
La Madera, N. Mex. (87539) 274/C2
Lamag, Malaysia 85/F4
Lama-Kara, Togo 106/E7
La Malbaie, Que. 172/C2
Lamaline, Newf. 166/C4
Lamar (co.), Ala. 194/B3
Lamar, Ark. (72846) 203/D3
Lamar, Colo. (81052) 208/O6
Lamar (co.), Ga. 216/D4
Lamar, Ind. (47550) 227/D8
Lamar, Kans. (†67436) 232/E2
Lamar, La. (†71232) 238/G2
Lamar (co.), Miss. 256/E8
Lamar, Miss. (38642) 256/F1
Lamar, Mo. (64759) 261/D8
Lamar, Nebr. (69035) 264/C4
Lamar, Okla. (74850) 288/O4
Lamar, Pa. (16848) 294/H4
Lamar, S.C. (29069) 296/G3
Lamar (co.), Texas 302/J4
Lamar, Wyo. (†82190) 319/B1
Lamar (riv.), Wyo. 319/B1
La Margarita, Ven. 124/H3
Lamar Heights‡, Mo. (†64759) 261/D8
La Marque, Texas (77568) 302/K3
Lamartine, Pa. (16375) 294/C3
Lamartine, Wis. (†53065) 317/J8
La Martre (lake), N.W.T., 146/F3
La Martre (lake), N.W.T. 187/G3
Lamas, Peru 128/D6
Lamasco, Ky. (†42038) 237/F7
La Maya, Cuba 158/J4
Lamb, Ind. (†47043) 227/G7
Lamb (co.), Texas 302/B3
Lambach, Austria 41/C2
Lamballe, France 28/B3
Lambaré, Par. 144/B6
Lambaréné, Gabon 115/B4
Lambari, Braz. 135/D2
Lambay (isl.), Ire. 17/K5
Lambayeque (dept.), Peru 128/B6
Lambayeque, Peru 128/B6
Lambert, Ark. (71929) 203/D5
Lambert, Miss. (38643) 256/D2
Lambert, Mo. (†63736) 261/O8
Lambert, Mont. (59243) 262/M3
Lambert, Okla. (73728) 288/J1
Lambert Lake, Maine (04454) 242/H4
Lamberton, Minn. (56152) 254/C6
Lambert's Bay, S. Africa 118/B6
Lambertville, Mich. (48144) 250/F7
Lambertville, N. Br. 170/C3
Lambertville, N.J. (08530) 273/D3
Lambeth, 10/B5
Lambeth, Ont. 177/C5
Lambourn, Eng. 13/F6
Lambric, Ky. (41340) 237/P5
Lamb's (head), Ire. 17/A8
Lambsburg, Va. (24351) 307/G7
Lambs Grove, Iowa (†50208) 229/G5
Lambton, Que. 172/F4
Lambton (co.), Ont. 177/B5
Lambton (cape), N.W.T. 187/F2
Lame Deer, Mont. (59043) 262/K5
Lamego, Port. 33/C2
Lame Johnny (creek), S. Dak. 298/C6
Lamentin, Guad. 161/A6
Lamentin, Mart. 161/D6
Lamèque, N. Br. 170/F1
La Merced, Bol. 136/C8
Lameroo, S. Aust. 94/G6
La Mesa, Calif. (92041) 204/H11
La Mesa, N. Mex. (88044) 274/C6
Lamesa, Texas (79331) 302/C5
Lamía, Greece, 7/G5
Lamía, Greece 45/F6
La Minerve, Que. 172/C3
Lamington, N.J. (†08876) 273/D2
Lamington (riv.), N.J. 273/D2
La Mirada, Calif. (90638) 204/D11
Lamison, Ala. (36747) 194/C6
Lamitan, Phil. 82/D7
Lamkin, Texas (76460) 302/F6
Lamlash, Scot. 15/F8
Lammermuir (hills), Scot. 15/L8
Lamming Hills, Br. Col. 184/G3
La Moille, Ill. (61330) 222/D2
La Moille, Iowa (†50158) 229/G4
Lamoille, Minn. (55948) 254/G6
Lamoille, Nev. (89828) 266/F2
Lamoille (co.), Vt. 268/B2
Lamoille (riv.), Vt. 268/A2
La Moine (riv.), Ill. 222/C3
Lamoine▵, Maine (†04605) 242/G7
Lamon (bay), Phil. 82/C3
Lamona, Wash. (99144) 310/G3
Lamongan, Indon. 85/K2
Lamoni, Iowa (50140) 229/E7
Lamont, Alta. 182/D3
Lamont, Calif. (93241) 204/G8
Lamont, Fla. (32336) 212/C1
Lamont, Idaho (83430) 220/G6
Lamont, Iowa (50650) 229/K3
Lamont, Kans. (66855) 232/F3
Lamont, Miss. (38755) 256/B3
Lamont, Okla. (74643) 288/L1
Lamont, Wash. (99017) 310/H3
Lamont, Wis. (†53530) 317/G10
Lamont, Wyo. (82328) 319/E3
La Monte, Mo. (65337) 261/F5
Lamotrek (atoll), Pac. Is., 87/E5
La Motte, Iowa (52054) 229/M4
Lamotte (peak), Utah 304/D3
La Moure (co.), N. Dak. 283/N7
La Moure, N. Dak. (58458) 283/O7
Lampa, Chile 138/G3
Lampa, Peru 128/G10
Lampang, Thai. 72/C3
Lampasas (co.), Texas 302/F6
Lampasas, Texas (76550) 302/F6
Lampasas (riv.), Texas 302/G6
Lampe, Mo. (65681) 261/F9
Lampedusa (isl.), Italy 34/D7
Lampertheim, W. Ger. 22/C4
Lampeter, 10/D4
Lampeter, Pa. (17537) 294/K6
Lampeter, Wales 13/C5
Lamphun, Thai. 72/C3
Lampman, Sask. 181/J6
Lamprey (riv.), N.H. 268/E5
Lampson, Wis. (†54888) 317/C3
Lamu, Burma 72/B3
Lamu, Kenya 115/H4
Lamu, 102/G5
Lamud, Peru 128/C6
Lamy, N. Mex. (87540) 274/D3
Lanagan, Mo. (64847) 261/C9
Lanai (isl.), Hawaii, 87/L3
Lanai (isl.), Hawaii, 188/F5
Lanai (isl.), Hawaii 218/H2
Lanai City, Hawaii, 188/F5
Lanai City, Hawaii (96763) 218/H2
Lanaihale (mt.), Hawaii 218/H2
Lanaken, Belg. 27/H7
Lanao (lake), Phil. 82/E7
Lanao del Norte (prov.), Phil. 82/E6
Lanao del Sur (prov.), Phil. 82/E7
Lanark (co.), Ont. 177/H3
Lanark, Ont. 177/H2
Lanark, Ill. (61046) 222/D1
Lanark, 10/E3
Lanark (co.), Scot. 15/J8
Lanark, Scot. 15/J8
Lanark, W. Va. (25860) 313/D7
Lancashire (co.), Eng. 13/E4
Lancaster, 10/E3
Lancaster (sound), 163/M4
Lancaster, Calif. (93534) 204/G9
Lancaster (sound), Canada, 4/B14
Lancaster, Ont. 177/K2
Lancaster, Eng. 13/E3
Lancaster, Ill. (62855) 222/F5
Lancaster, Ind. (†47250) 227/F7
Lancaster, Kans. (66041) 232/G2
Lancaster, Ky. (40444) 237/M5
Lancaster▵, Mass. (01523) 249/H3
Lancaster, Minn. (56735) 254/B2
Lancaster, Mo. (63548) 261/H1
Lancaster▵, N.H. (03584) 268/D3
Lancaster, N.H. (03584) 268/D3
Lancaster (sound), N.W.T., 146/K2
Lancaster (sound), N.W.T. 187/K2
Lancaster, N.Y. (14086) 276/C5
Lancaster (co.), Nebr. 264/H4
Lancaster, Ohio (43130) 284/E6
Lancaster, Pa., 188/L2
Lancaster (co.), Pa. 294/K5
Lancaster, Pa. (*17601) 294/K5
Lancaster (co.), S.C. 296/F2
Lancaster, S.C. (29720) 296/F2
Lancaster, Texas (75146) 302/G2
Lancaster (co.), Va. 307/R5
Lancaster, Va. (22503) 307/R5
Lancaster, Wis. (53813) 317/E10
Lancaster Mills, S.C. (†29720) 296/F2
Lance (creek), Wyo. 319/H2
Lance Cove, Newf. 166/D2
Lance Creek, Wyo. (82222) 319/H2
Lancer, Sask. 181/C5
Lanchow, China, 3/P4
Lanchow, China, 54/O6
Lanchow, China 77/F4
Lanciano, Italy 34/E3
Lancing, Tenn. (37770) 237/M8
Lanco, Chile 138/D2
Łancut, Poland 47/F3
Land, Ala. (†36904) 194/B6
Landa, N. Dak. (58749) 283/J2
Landaff▵, N.H. (†03585) 268/D3
Landaff, N.H. (†03585) 268/D3
Landau, Bavaria, W. Ger. 22/E4
Landau, Rhineland-Palatinate, W. Ger. 22/C4
Land Between The Lakes Nat'l Rec. Area, Ky. 237/E7
Landeck, Austria 41/A3
Landeck, Ohio (†45833) 284/B4
Landen, Belg. 27/G7
Landenberg, Pa. (19350) 294/L6
Lander (dry riv.), Aust. 88/E4
Lander (co.), Nev. 266/D3
Lander (riv.), No. Terr. 93/C6
Lander, Pa. (†16350) 294/D2
Lander, Wyo., 188/E2
Lander, Wyo. (82520) 319/D3
Landerneau, France 28/B3
Landersville, Ala. (†35650) 194/D2
Landeryd, Sweden 18/H8
Landes (dept.), France 28/C5
Landes, W. Va. (26832) 313/H5
Landess, Ind. (46944) 227/F3
Landfall‡, Minn. (†55101) 254/F6
Landfall (isl.), India 68/G6
Landhi, Pak. 59/J4
Landhi, Pak. 68/B4
Landi Muhammad Amin Khan, Afgh. 59/H3
Landi Muhammad Amin Khan, Afgh. 68/A2
Landing, N.J. (07850) 273/D2
Landing (creek), N.J. 273/D4
Landingville‡, Pa. (17942) 294/K4
Landis, N.C. (28088) 281/H3
Landis, Sask. 181/C3

La Vega 389

Landisburg, Pa. (17040) 294/H5
Landisburg, W. Va. (†25831) 313/E7
Landisville, Pa. (17538) 294/K5
Lando, S.C. (29724) 296/E2
Land O'Lakes, Fla. (33539) 212/D3
Land O'Lakes, Wis. (54540) 317/H3
Landonville, Alta. 182/E3
Landover, Md. (20785) 245/G4
Landover Hills, Md. (20784) 245/G4
Landquart (riv.), Switz. 39/J3
Landrum, S.C. (29356) 296/C1
Landry, N. Br. 170/E1
Landsberg, W. Ger. 22/D4
Land's End (prom.), 10/D5
Land's End (prom.), Eng., 7/D4
Land's End (prom.), Eng. 13/B7
Lands End (cape), N.W.T. 187/F2
Landshut, W. Ger. 22/E4
Landskron, Austria 41/B3
Landskrona, Sweden 18/H9
Landsman (creek), Colo. 208/P4
Landsmeer, Neth. 27/C4
Landstuhl, W. Ger. 22/B4
Landusky, Mont. (59533) 262/H3
Landville, W. Va. (25629) 313/C7
Lane, Ill. (61750) 222/E3
Lane (co.), Kans. 232/B3
Lane, Kans. (66042) 232/G3
Lane, Okla. (74555) 288/O6
Lane (co.), Oreg. 291/E4
Lane, S.C. (29564) 296/H5
Lane, S. Dak. (57358) 298/N5
Lane, Tenn. (38234) 237/C8
Laneburg, Ark. (71844) 203/D6
Lane Cove, N.S.W. 97/J3
Lane Cove (riv.), N.S.W. 97/J3
Lanes (creek), N.C. 281/J5
Lanesboro, Iowa (51451) 229/D4
Lanesboro▵, Mass. (01237) 249/A2
Lanesboro, Minn. (55949) 254/G7
Lanesboro, Pa. (18827) 294/L2
Lanesborough-Ballyleague, Ire. 17/E4
Lanes Prairie, Mo. (†65013) 261/J6
Lanesville, Ind. (47136) 227/E8
Lanesville, Va. (23088) 307/P5
Lanett, Ala. (36863) 194/H5
La Neuveville, Switz. 39/D2
Lanfine, Alta. 182/E4
Lanford, S.C. (†29335) 296/C2
Lang (glac.), Ice. 21/B1
Lang, Sask. 181/G6
Langaa, Den. 21/C5
Langadhás, Greece 45/F5
Langanes (prom.), Ice., 7/C2
Langara (isl.), Br. Col. 184/A3
Langavat (lake), Scot. 15/C3
Langbank, Sask. 181/J5
Lang Bay, Br. Col. 184/E5
Lang Bian (mts.), S. Vietnam 72/E4
Langdale, Ala. (36864) 194/H5
Langdon, Alta. 182/D4
Langdon, Iowa (51348) 229/C2
Langdon, Kans. (67549) 232/D4
Langdon, Mo. (64464) 261/A2
Langdon, N. Dak. (58249) 283/O2
Langdon▵, N.H. (†03602) 268/C5
Langdondale, Pa. (16658) 294/F5
Langeac, France 28/E5
L'Ange-Gardien, Que. 172/F3
Langeland (isl.), Den. 21/D8
Langelands Baelt (chan.), Den. 21/D8
Längelmä (lake), Fin. 18/O6
Langeloth, Pa. (15054) 294/A5
Langemark, Belg. 27/B7
Langen, W. Ger. 22/C4
Langenburg, Sask. 181/K5
Längenfeld, Austria 41/B4
Langenhagen, W. Ger. 22/C2
Langenlois, Austria 41/C2
Langenthal, Switz. 39/E2
Langenwang, Austria 41/C3
Langeoog (isl.), W. Ger. 22/B2
Langford, Miss. (†39042) 256/E6
Langford, S. Dak. (57454) 298/O2
Langham, Sask. 181/E3
Langholm, 10/E3
Langholm, Scot. 15/K9
Langhorne, Pa. (19047) 294/N5
Langhorne Manor‡, Pa. (15665) 294/N5
Langkawi, Pulau (isl.), Malaysia 72/C6
Langlade (co.), Wis. 317/H5
Langley, Ark. (71952) 203/C5
Langley, Br. Col. 184/L3
Langley, Okla. (74350) 288/R2
Langley, S.C. (29834) 296/D4
Langley, Wash. (98260) 310/C2
Langley A.F.B., Va. 307/R6
Langley Park, Md. (20787) 245/F4
Langleyville, Ill. (62542) 222/D4
Langlois, Oreg. (97450) 291/C5
Lang Mo, N. Vietnam 72/E3
Langnau, Switz. 39/E3
Langnau am Albis, Switz. 39/G2
Langness (prom.), I. of Man 13/C3
Langogne, France 28/E5
Langon, France 28/C5
Langøy (isl.), Norway 18/J2
Langport, Eng. 13/E6
Langres, France 28/F4
Langres (plat.), France 28/F4
Langruth, Man. 179/D4
Langsa, Indon. 85/B5
Långsele, Sweden 18/K5
Långshyttan, Sweden 18/K6
Lang Son, N. Vietnam 72/E2
Langston, Ala. (35755) 194/G1
Langston, Okla. (73050) 288/M3
Lang Suan, Thai. 72/C5
Langsville, Ohio (45741) 284/F7
Langtao, Burma 72/C1
Langton, Ont. 177/D5
Langtry, Texas (78871) 302/C8
L'Anguille (riv.), Ark. 203/J3
Languiñeo, Arg. 143/B5
Langwies, Switz. 39/J3
Langworthy, Iowa (52252) 229/L4
Lanham, Nebr. (†68415) 264/H4
Lanham-Seabrook, Md. (20801) 245/G4
Lanier (co.), Ga. 216/F8
Lanigan, Sask. 181/F4
Lanigan (creek), Sask. 181/F4
Lanín (vol.), Arg. 143/B4
Lanín (vol.), Chile 138/E2
Lanín Nat'l Park, Arg. 143/B4
Lankin, N. Dak. (58250) 283/P3
Lanlacuni Bajo, Peru 128/G9
Lannion, France 28/B3
Lannon, Wis. (53046) 317/K1
L'Annonciation, Que. 172/C3
Lanoka Harbor, N.J. (08734) 273/E4
Lanoraie, Que. 172/D4
Lansdale, Pa. (19446) 294/M5
Lansdowne, Ont. 177/H3
Lansdowne, Md. (21227) 245/M3
Lansdowne, India 68/D3
Lansdowne, Pa. (19050) 294/M7
Lansdowne House, Ont. 175/C2
L'Anse, Mich. (49946) 250/G1
Lanse, Pa. (16849) 294/F4
L'Anse-Amour, Newf. 166/C3
L'Anse-au-Beaufils, Que. 172/D1
L'Anse-au-Clair, Newf. 166/C3
L'Anse-au-Loup, Newf. 166/C3
L'Anse-au-Meadow, Newf. 166/C3
L'Anse Ind. Res., Mich. 250/A2
L'Anse-Saint-Jean, Que. 172/G1
Lansford, N. Dak. (58750) 283/H2
Lansford, Pa. (18232) 294/L4
Lansing, Ill. (60438) 222/B3
Lansing, Iowa (52151) 229/L2
Lansing, Kans. (66043) 232/H2
Lansing (cap.), Mich., 146/K5
Lansing (cap.), Mich., 188/K2
Lansing (cap.), Mich. (*48901) 250/E6
Lansing, Minn. (55950) 254/F7
Lansing, N.C. (28643) 281/F1
Lansing, Ohio (43934) 284/J5
Lanškroun, Czech. 41/D2
Lanta, Ko (isl.), Thai. 72/C6
Lantana, Fla. (33460) 212/F5
Lanton, Mo. (65792) 261/J9
Lantry, S. Dak. (57636) 298/G3
Lantsang, China 77/E7
Lantsch-Lenz, Switz. 39/J3
Lantz, Md. (21760) 245/J2
Lantzville, Br. Col. 184/J3
Lanús, Arg. 143/H7
Lanusei, Italy 34/B5
Lanuvio, Italy 34/F7
Lanuza, Phil. 82/F6
Lanuza (bay), Phil. 82/F6
Lanyon, Iowa (50544) 229/E4
Lanza, Bol. 136/B5
Lanzarote (isl.), Spain 33/C4
Lanzarote (isl.), Spain 106/B3
Laoag, Phil. 82/C1
Laoag, Phil. 85/F2
Laoag, Phil., 54/P8
Laoang, Phil. 82/E4
Lao Cai, N. Vietnam 72/E2
Laoighis (co.), Ire. 17/G6
Laon, France 28/E3
Laona, Wis. (54541) 317/J4
La Orchila (isl.), Ven. 124/F2
La Orotava, Spain 33/B4
La Oroya, Peru, 120/C4
La Oroya, Peru 128/D8
Laos, 3/Q5
Laos, 54/O8
LAOS, 72
Laotto, Ind. (46763) 227/G2
Lapa, Braz. 132/D9
Lapa, Phil. 82/C8
Lapalisse, France 28/E4
La Pallice, France 28/C4
La Palma‡, Calif. (90620) 204/C11
La Palma (isl.), 102/A2
La Palma, Col. 126/C5
La Palma, El Salv. 154/C3
La Palma, Pan. 154/H6
La Palma (isl.), Spain 33/A4
La Palma (isl.), Spain 106/A3
La Palma de Condado, Spain 33/C4
La Paloma, Urug. 145/F5
La Pampa (prov.), Arg. 143/C4
La Paragua, Ven. 124/G4
Laparan (isl.), Phil. 82/B8
Laparan (isls.), Phil. 82/B8
La Passe, Ont. 177/H2
La Patrie, Que. 172/F4
La Paz, Entre Ríos, Arg. 143/G5
La Paz, Mendoza, Arg. 143/C3
La Paz (cap.), Bol., 3/F6
La Paz (cap.), Bol., 120/D4
La Paz (dept.), Bol. 136/A4
La Paz (cap.), Bol. 136/B5
La Paz, Hond. 154/D3
Lapaz, Ind. (46537) 227/E2
La Paz, Mex. 150/D5
La Paz (bay), Mex. 150/D4
La Paz, Phil. 82/E6
La Paz, Canelones, Urug. 145/B6
La Paz, Colonia, Urug. 145/B5
La Paz Central, Nic. 154/D4
La Paz de Oriente, Nic. 154/E5
La Pedrera, Col. 126/F8
La Pedrera, Urug. 145/F5
Lapeer (co.), Mich. 250/F5
Lapeer, Mich. (48446) 250/F5
Lapeer Heights‡, Mich. (†48501) 250/F6
Lapel, Ind. (46051) 227/F4
La Pelada, Arg. 143/F5
La Pérade, Que. 172/E3
La Pérouse (str.), 54/T5
La Pérouse (str.), U.S.S.R. 48/P5
La Perouse, N.S.W. 97/J4
La Piedad Cavadas, Mex. 150/H6
Lapine, Ala. (36046) 194/F7
La Pine, Oreg. (97739) 291/F4
Lapinin (isl.), Phil. 82/E5
Lapithos, Cyprus 63/E5
La Place, Ill. (61936) 222/E4
Laplace, La. (70068) 238/N3
La Plaine, Dominica 161/F6
La Plaine, Sask. 181/E3
Lapland (reg.), Fin. 18/O2
Lapland (reg.), Norway 18/K2
Lapland (reg.), Sweden 18/M2
Lapland (reg.), U.S.S.R. 52/D1
La Plant, S. Dak. (57637) 298/H3
La Plante, N. Br. 170/E1
La Plata (isl.), Ec. 128/E6
La Plata, Arg., 120/E6
La Plata, Arg. 143/H7
La Plata, Río de (est.), Arg. 143/E4
La Plata, Col. 126/C6
La Plata (co.), Colo. 208/D8
La Plata (peak), Colo. 208/G4
La Plata (riv.), Colo. 208/C8
La Plata, Md. (20646) 245/L6
La Plata, Mo. (63549) 261/H2
La Plata, N. Mex. (87418) 274/A2
La Plata (riv.), N. Mex. 274/A1
Laplaza, Spain 33/E1
La Plume, Pa. (18440) 294/L2
La Pobla de Lillet, Spain 33/G1
La Pocatière, Que. 172/H2
La Poile, Newf. 166/C4
La Poile (bay), Newf. 166/C4
Lapoint, Utah (84039) 304/E3
La Pointe, Wis. (54850) 317/E2
La Porte, Calif. (95981) 204/D4
Laporte, Colo. (80535) 208/J1
LaPorte (co.), Ind. 227/D1
LaPorte, Ind. (46350) 227/D1
Laporte, Mich. (†48623) 250/E5
Laporte, Minn. (56461) 254/D3
Laporte, Pa. (18626) 294/K3
Laporte, Sask. 181/B4
La Porte, Texas (77571) 302/K2
La Porte City, Iowa (50651) 229/J4
Lappa (lake), Fin. 18/O5
Lappajärvi, Fin. 18/O5
Lappeenranta, Fin. 18/P6
Lappi (prov.), Fin. 18/P3
Laprairie (co.), Que. 172/H4
La Prairie, Que. 172/J4
Laprairie (basin), Que. 172/H4
La Prairie, Ill. (62346) 222/B3
La Prairie, Minn. (†55744) 254/E3
La Protección, Hond. 154/D3
La Providence, Que. 172/E4
La Pryor, Texas (78872) 302/E9
Lapseki, Turkey 63/C6
Laptev (sea), U.S.S.R. 48/N2
Laptev (sea), U.S.S.R., 4/B3
Laptev (sea), U.S.S.R., 54/R2
Lapuan (riv.), Fin. 18/N5
La Puebla, Spain 33/H3
La Puebla de Montalbán, Spain 33/D3
La Puente, Calif. (*91744) 204/D10
La Puntilla (cape), Ec. 128/B4
La Purísima, Mex. 150/D3
La Push, Wash. (98350) 310/A3
Lapwai, Idaho (83540) 220/B3
Łapy, Poland 47/F2
Laqiya 'Umran (well), Sudan 111/E3
Laquey, Mo. (65534) 261/H7
La Quiaca, Arg., 120/D5
La Quiaca, Arg. 143/C1
L'Aquila (prov.), Italy 34/D3
L'Aquila, Italy 34/D3
Lar, Iran 59/F4
Lar, Iran 66/J7
Lara (state), Ven. 124/C2
Larabee, Pa. (†16731) 294/F2
Larache, Mor. 106/C1
Laracor, Ire. 17/H4
Larak (isl.), Iran 66/K7
La Rambla, Spain 33/D4
Laramie (mts.), Colo. 208/H1
Laramie (riv.), Colo. 208/H1
Laramie, Wyo., 188/E2
Laramie (co.), Wyo. 319/H4
Laramie, Wyo. (82070) 319/G4
Laramie (mts.), Wyo. 319/G3
Laramie (peak), Wyo. 319/G3
Laramie (riv.), Wyo. 319/G4
Laranjeiras, Braz. 132/G5
Laranjeiras do Sul, Braz. 132/C9
Larantuka, Indon. 85/G7
Larat (isl.), Indon. 85/J7
Larbert, 10/B1
Larbert, Scot. 15/D1
Lärbro, Sweden 18/L8
Larchmont, N.Y. (10538) 276/P7
Larchwood, Iowa (51241) 229/A2
Lardeau, Br. Col. 184/J5
Larder Lake, Ont. 175/E3
L'Ardoise West, N.S. 169/H3
Laredo (sound), Br. Col. 184/C4
Laredo, Mo. (64652) 261/E2
Laredo, Mont. (†59501) 262/G2
Laredo, Spain 33/E1
Laredo, Texas, 146/J7
Laredo, Texas, 188/G5
Laredo, Texas (78040) 302/E10
Laredo A.F.B., Texas 302/E10
Laren, Neth. 27/G4
Larena, Phil. 82/D6
La Réole, France 28/C5
Lares, P. Rico 156/F1
Lares, P. Rico 161/B2
La Retuca, Chile 138/F3
Larew, W. Va. (†26537) 313/G4
Largeau, Chad 111/C4
Largentière, France 28/F5
Largo (cay), Cuba 156/B2
Largo (cay), Cuba 158/D2
Largo, Neth. Ant. 161/E10
Largo, Fla. (33540) 212/B3
Largo (key), Fla. 212/F6
Largo, Md. (†208/0) 245/G5
Largo, Canon (creek), N. Mex. 274/B2
Largoen, Neth. Ant. 161/F8
Largs, 10/A1
Largs, Scot. 15/B2
Lariat, Texas (79335) 302/B3
Larimer (co.) Colo. 208/H1
Larimer, Pa. (15647) 294/C5
Larimore, N. Dak. (58251) 283/P4
Larino, Italy 34/E4
La Rioja, Arg., 120/D5
La Rioja (prov.), Arg. 143/C2
La Rioja, Arg. 143/C2
La Rioja, Cuba 158/H3
Lárisa, Greece, 7/G5
Lárisa, Greece 45/F6
Laristan (reg.), Iran 66/J7
La Rivière, Man. 179/D5
Lark, N. Dak. (58550) 283/H7
Lark, Utah (84040) 304/B3
Larkana, Pak. 59/J4
Larkana, Pak. 68/B3
Larkhall, 10/B1
Larkhall, Scot. 15/D2
Lark Harbour, Newf. 166/C4
Larkinburg, Kans. (†66436) 232/G2
Larkinsville, Ala. (†35768) 194/F1
Larkspur, Calif. (94939) 204/H1
Larkspur, Colo. (80118) 208/K4
Larksville‡, Pa. (†18704) 294/L3
Larnaca, Cyprus 59/B3
Larnaca, Cyprus 63/E5
Larnaca (bay), Cyprus 63/E5
Larne, N. Ire. 17/K2
Larne (inlet), N. Ire. 17/K2
Larne, 10/D3
Larned, Kans. (67550) 232/C3
La Robla, Spain 33/D1
La Roche, Switz. 39/D3
La Roche-en-Ardenne, Belg. 27/G8
La Rochelle, France, 7/D4
La Rochelle, France 28/C4
La Rochelle, Man. 179/F5
La Roche-sur-Yon, France 28/C4
La Roda, Spain 33/E3
La Romana, Dom. Rep. 156/E3
La Romana (prov.), Dom. Rep. 158/F6
La Romana, Dom. Rep. 158/F6
La Ronge, Sask. 181/L3
La Ronge (lake), Sask. 181/M3
La Rose, Ill. (61541) 222/D3
Larose, La. (70373) 238/K7
Larouche, Que. 172/F1
Larrabee, Iowa (51029) 229/B3
Larrimah, Aust. 88/E3
Larrimah, No. Terr. 93/C3
Larry's River, N.S. 169/G3
Larsen (sound), N.W.T. 187/J2
Larsen Bay, Alaska (99624) 196/H3
Larsen Ice Shelf, Ant., 3/F9
Larsen Ice Shelf, Ant., 5/C16
Larslan, Mont. (59244) 262/K2
Larsmont, Minn. (55610) 254/G4
Larson, N. Dak. (58751) 283/E2
Larto, La. (71344) 238/G4
Larue (co.), Ky. 237/K5
La Rue, Ohio (43332) 284/D4
Laruns, France 28/C6
La Russell, Mo. (64848) 261/D8
Larvik, Norway 18/C4
Larvik, Norway, 7/E3
Larwill, Ind. (46764) 227/F2
La Sal, Utah (84530) 304/E5
La Salle, Colo. (80645) 208/K2
La Salle, Que. 172/H4
La Salle (co.), Ill. 222/E2
La Salle, Ill. (61301) 222/E2
La Salle (par.), La. 238/F3
La Salle, Man. 179/E5
La Salle, Mich. (48145) 250/F7
La Salle, Minn. (56056) 254/D6
La Salle (co.), Texas 302/E9
Las Animas (co.), Colo. 208/L8
Las Animas, Colo. (81054) 208/N6
Las Animas (creek), N. Mex. 274/B5
Las Anod, Somalia 115/J2
La Sarraz, Switz. 39/C3
La Sarre, 163/J6
La Sarre, Que. 174/B3
Lasauces, Colo. (†81151) 208/H8
Las Aves (isls.), Ven. 124/E2
Las Bonitas, Ven. 124/F4
Las Breas, Chile 138/B7
Lasca, Ala. (†36784) 194/C6
Las Cabras, Chile 138/F5
Lascahobas, Haiti 156/D3
Lascahobas, Haiti 158/C6
Lascano, Urug. 145/E4
Las Carreras, Bol. 136/C7
Lascassas, Tenn. (37085) 237/J9
L'Ascension, Que. 172/C3
L'Ascension, Que. 172/F1
La Scie, Newf. 166/C4
Las Cruces, Chile 138/F3
Las Cruces, N. Mex., 188/E4
Las Cruces, N. Mex. (88001) 274/C6
Las Dureh, Somalia 115/J1
La Selle (peak), Haiti 158/C6
La Selva Beach, Calif. (95076) 204/K4
La Serena, Chile, 120/C5
La Serena, Chile 138/A8
La Seyne-sur-Mer, France 28/F6
Las Flores, Arg. 143/E4
Las Flores, Urug. 145/D5
Lashburn, Sask. 181/B2
Lashio, Burma 72/C2
La Sierra, Urug. 145/D5
L'Asile, Haiti 158/B6
Las Juntas, C. Rica 154/E5
Las Juntas, Col. 126/E6
Lasker, N.C. (27848) 281/P2
La Skhirra, Tun. 106/G2
Las Khoreh, Somalia 115/J1
Las Lajas, Arg. 143/B4
Las Lajitas, Ven. 124/F4
Las Lomitas, Arg. 143/D1
Las Marias, P. Rico 161/B2
Las Martinas, Cuba 158/A2
Las Matas de Farfán, Dom. Rep. 156/D3
Las Matas de Farfán, Dom. Rep. 158/D6
Las Mercedes, Ven. 124/E3
Las Navas del Marqués, Spain 33/D2
La Solana, Spain 33/E3
La Sorcière (mt.), St. Lucia 161/G6
La Souterraine, France 28/D4
Las Palmas, Arg. 143/E2
Las Palmas (cap.), Canary Is., 102/A2
Las Palmas, Pan. 154/G6
Las Palmas (prov.), Spain 33/C4
Las Palmas de Gran Canaria, Spain 33/B4
Las Palmas de Gran Canaria, Spain 106/B3
Las Pampitas, Bol. 136/C3
Las Parejas, Arg. 143/F6
Las Pedroñeras, Spain 33/E3
Las Petas, Bol. 136/F5
La Spezia, Italy, 7/E4
La Spezia (prov.), Italy 34/B2
La Spezia, Italy 34/B2
Las Piedras, Bol. 136/B2
Las Piedras, P. Rico 161/E2
Las Piedras, Peru 128/H9
Las Piedras, Urug. 145/B6
Las Piedras, Falcón, Ven. 124/C2
Las Piedras, Zulia, Ven. 124/B2
Las Plumas, Arg., 120/D7
Las Plumas, Arg. 143/C5
Lasqueti Island, Br. Col. 184/J2
Las Rosas, Arg. 143/F6
Lassen (co.), Calif. 204/E3
Lassen (peak), Calif. 204/D3
Lassen Volcanic Nat'l Park, Calif. 204/D3
L'Assomption (co.), Que. 172/D4
L'Assomption, Que. 172/D4
L'Assomption (riv.), Que. 172/D3
Las Tablas, N. Mex. (87541) 274/C2
Las Tablas, Pan. 154/G7
Lastarria (vol.), Chile 138/B5
Last Chance (creek), Utah 304/C6
Last Mountain (lake), Sask. 181/F4
Las Toscas, Urug. 145/E3
Lastoursville, Gabon 115/B4
Lastoursville, 102/D5
Lastovo (isl.), Yugo. 45/C4
Las Trincheras, Ven. 124/F4
Lastrup, Minn. (56344) 254/D4
Las Varillas, Arg. 143/D3
Las Vegas, N. Mex., 188/E3
Las Vegas (city), N. Mex. (87701) 274/D3
Las Vegas (town)‡, N. Mex. (87701) 274/D3
Las Vegas, Nev., 188/C3
Las Vegas, Nev. (*89101) 266/F6
Las Vegas (range), Nev. 266/F6
Las Vegas, Ven. 124/D3
Las Vegas Bombing and Gunnery Range, Nev. 266/E5
Las Vigas, Mex. 150/P1
Las Villas (prov.), Cuba 158/E2
Las Yaras, Peru 128/G11
Las Yungas (reg.), Bol. 136/B5
La Tabatière, Que. 174/F2
Latacunga, Ec. 128/C3
La Tagua, Col. 126/C8
Latah (co.), Idaho 220/B3
Latah, Wash. (99018) 310/H3
Latah (creek), Wash. 310/H3
Latakia, Syria 59/C2
Latakia (prov.), Syria 63/G5
Latakia, Syria 63/F5
La Taste, Grenada 161/D8
Latchford, Ont. 177/K5
Laterrière, Que. 172/F1
Latexo, Texas (75849) 302/J6
Latham, Ala. (†36579) 194/C8
Latham, Ill. (62543) 222/D4
Latham, Kans. (67072) 232/F4
Latham, Mo. (65050) 261/G5
Latham‡, N.Y. (12110) 276/N5
Latham, Ohio (45646) 284/D7
Latham, Tenn. (†38225) 237/D8
Latheron, Scot. 15/K3
Lathrop, Calif. (95330) 204/D6
Lathrop, Mich. (†49880) 250/B2
Lathrop, Mo. (64465) 261/D3
Lathrup Village‡, Mich. (48075) 250/B6
La Tigra, Ven. 124/H4
Latimer, Iowa (50452) 229/G3
Latimer, Kans. (†67449) 232/F3
Latimer (co.), Okla. 288/R5
Latimers (brook), Conn. 210/G3
Latina (prov.), Italy 34/D4
Latina, Italy 34/D4
La Tina, Peru 128/B5
Latium (reg.), Italy 34/D3
La Tola, Ec. 128/C2
La Toma, Arg. 143/C3
Laton, Calif. (93242) 204/F7
Latonia Lakes‡, Ky. (†41011) 237/N3
Latorica (riv.), Czech. 41/F2
La Tortuga (isl.), Ven. 124/F2
Latouche Treville (cape), Aust. 88/C3
Latouche Treville (cape), W. Aust. 92/C2
Latour, Mo. (64760) 261/D5
La Tour-de-Peilz, Switz. 39/C4
La Tour-du-Pin, France 28/F5
Latourell Falls, Oreg. (†97060) 291/E2
La Trinidad, Nic. 154/D4
La Trinidad, Ven. 124/D3
La Trinidad de Arauca, Ven. 124/D4
La Trinidad de Orichuna, Ven. 124/D4
La Trinitaria, Mex. 150/N9
Latrobe, Pa. (15650) 294/D5
Latrobe, Tas. 99/C3
Latta, S.C. (29565) 296/J3
Lattimore, N.C. (28089) 281/F4
Lattingtown, N.Y. (†11560) 276/R6
Latty, Ohio (45855) 284/A3
La Tuque, 163/J6
La Tuque, Que. 172/E2
La Tuque, Que. 174/C3
Latur, India 68/D5
LATVIA, 53/B2
Latvian S.S.R., U.S.S.R. 48/C4
Latvian S.S.R., U.S.S.R. 52/B3
Latvian S.S.R., U.S.S.R., 7/G3
Lauca (riv.), Bol. 136/A6
Lauca (riv.), Chile 138/B1
Lauchhammer, E. Ger. 22/E3
Laud, Ind. (†46725) 227/G2
Laudat, Dominica 161/E6
Lauder, 10/E3
Lauder, Man. 179/B5
Lauder, Scot. 15/L8
Lauderdale (co.), Ala. 194/C1
Lauderdale, Minn. (†55101) 254/G5
Lauderdale (co.), Miss. 256/G6
Lauderdale, Miss. (39335) 256/G5
Lauderdale, Tas. 99/D4
Lauderdale (co.), Tenn. 237/B9
Lauderdale-by-the-Sea, Fla. (33308) 212/C3
Lauderdale Lakes, Fla. (†33301) 212/B4
Lauderhill, Fla. (33313) 212/B4
Lauenburg, W. Ger. 22/D2
Lauenen, Switz. 39/D4
Lauf, W. Ger. 22/D4
Läufelfingen, Switz. 39/E2
Laufen, Switz. 39/D2
Laufen, W. Ger. 22/E5
Laufenburg, Switz. 39/F1
Laufen-Uhwiesen, Switz. 39/G1
Laufnitz (riv.), Austria 41/D3
Laugharne, Wales 13/C6
Laughery (creek), Ind. 227/G6
Laughing Fish (pt.), Mich. 250/B2
Laughlin A.F.B., Texas 302/D8
Lau Group (isls.), Fiji, 87/J7
Lauingen, W. Ger. 22/D4
Launceston, 10/D5
Launceston, Australia, 87/E10
Launceston, Aust. 88/H8
Launceston, Eng. 13/C7
Launceston, Tasmania 99/C3
Laune (riv.), Ire. 17/B7
Launglon Bok (isls.), Burma 72/C4
La Unión, Chile 138/D3
La Unión, Col. 126/B7
La Unión, El Salv. 154/D4
La Union, N. Mex. (†88021) 274/C7
La Union (prov.), Phil. 82/C2
La Unión, Peru 128/D7
La Unión, Spain 33/F4
La Unión, Ven. 124/E3
Laupahoehoe, Hawaii (96764) 218/J4
Laupen, Switz. 39/D3
Lauperswil, Switz. 39/E3
Laura, Aust. 88/G3
Laura, Ill. (61451) 222/D3
Laura, S. Aust. 94/F5
Laura, Queens. 95/C2
Laura, Ohio (45337) 284/B6
Laura, Sask. 181/D4
La Urbana, Ven. 124/E4
Laurel, Del. (19956) 245/R6
Laurel, Ind. (47024) 227/G6
Laurel, Iowa (50141) 229/H5
Laurel (co.), Ky. 237/N6
Laurel, Md. (20810) 245/L4
Laurel, Miss., 188/J4
Laurel, Miss. (39440) 256/F7
Laurel, Mont. (59044) 262/H5
Laurel, Nebr. (68745) 264/G2
Laurel, Oreg. (†97123) 291/A2
Laurel, Pa. (†17322) 294/K6
Laurel (mt.), W. Va. 313/G4
Laurel, Wash. (98630) 310/D5
Laurel Bloomery, Tenn. (37680) 237/T7
Laureldale, Pa. (19605) 294/L5
Laurel Dale, W. Va. (†26743) 313/H4
Laureles, Par. 144/D6
Laurel Fork, Va. (24352) 307/G7
Laurel Gardens, Pa. (15229) 294/B6
Laurel Hill, Fla. (32567) 212/C5
Laurel Hill, N.C. (28351) 281/K5
Laurel Hill (mt.), Pa. 294/D5
Laurel Hollow‡, N.Y. (†11791) 276/R7
Laurel-Nokomis, Fla. (33545) 212/D4
Laurel Park, N.C. (†28739) 281/D4
Laurel River (res.), Ky. 237/N6
Laurel Run‡, Pa. (†18701) 294/L3
Laurel Springs, N.J. (08021) 273/B4
Laurelton, Pa. (17835) 294/H4
Laurelville, Ohio (43135) 284/E7
Laurence G. Hanscom Field, Mass. 249/B6
Laurence Harbor, N.J. (08879) 273/E3
Laurencekirk, 10/E2
Laurencekirk, Scot. 15/M6
Laurens (co.), Ga. 216/G6
Laurens, Iowa (50554) 229/D3
Laurens, N.Y. (13796) 276/K5
Laurens (co.), S.C. 296/D2
Laurens, S.C. (29360) 296/C3
Laurentides, Que. 172/D4
Laurentides Prov. Park, Que. 172/F2
Laurentides Prov. Park, Que. 174/C3
Lauria, Italy 34/E4
Laurie (lake), Man. 179/A3
Laurie‡, Mo. (65038) 261/G6
Laurier, Man. 179/C4
Laurier, Wash. (99146) 310/G2
Laurier-Station, Que. 172/F3
Laurierville, Que. 172/F3
Laurieton, N.S.W. 97/G2
Laurin, Mont. (59738) 262/D5
Laurinburg, N.C. (28352) 281/K5
Laurium, Mich. (49913) 250/A1
Laurot (Laut Ketjil) (isls.), Indon. 85/E7
Lausanne, Switz., 7/E4
Lausanne, Switz. 39/C3
Lauscha, E. Ger. 22/D3
Laut (isl.), Indon. 85/F6
Laut (North Natuna) (isl.), Indon. 85/D5
Lautaro, Chile 138/E2
Lauterbach, W. Ger. 22/C3
Lauterbrunnen, Switz. 39/E3
Lauterique, Hond. 154/D4
Laut Ketjil (isls.), Indon. 85/E7
Lauwers (chan.), Neth. 27/J1
Lauwers Zee (bay), Neth. 27/J2
Lauzon, Que. 172/J3
Lava (lake), Oreg. 291/F4
Lava Beds Nat'l Mon., Calif. 204/D2
Lavaca, Ala. (36911) 194/B6
Lavaca, Ark. (72941) 203/B3
Lavaca (co.), Texas 302/H8
Lavaca (bay), Texas 302/H9
Lava Hot Springs, Idaho (83246) 220/F7
Laval (co.), Que. 172/H4
Laval (bay), Que. 172/J1
Laval, France 28/C3
Laval, Que. 172/H4
La Vale-Narrows Park, Md. (21502) 245/C2
Lavalette, W. Va. (25535) 313/B6
Lavalle, Arg. 143/G4
La Valle, Wis. (53941) 317/F8
Lavalleja (dept.), Urug. 145/D5
Lavallette, N.J. (08735) 273/E4
Lavalley, Colo. (†81153) 208/J8
Lavaltrie, Que. 172/D4
Lavamünd, Austria 41/C3
Lavant Station, Ont. 177/H2
Lavapié (pt.), Chile 138/D1
Lavaur, France 28/D6
La Vecilla de Curueno, Spain 33/D1
Laveen, Ariz. (85339) 198/C5
La Vega, Dom. Rep. 156/D3
La Vega (prov.), Dom. Rep. 158/D6
La Vega, Dom. Rep. 158/E5
La Vega, Spain 33/C1

Lincolnton 391

Le Prese, Switz. 39/K4
Leptis Magna (ruins), Libya 111/B1
Le Puy, France 28/F5
Lequille, N.S. 169/C4
Lequire, Okla. (74943) 288/R4
Le Raimeux (mt.), Switz. 39/D2
Le Raysville, Pa. (18829) 294/K2
Lerdal, Minn. (†56007) 254/E7
Lere, Nigeria 106/F7
Léré, Chad 111/B6
Leribe, Lesotho 118/D5
Lerici, Italy 34/B2
Lérida, Col. 126/E7
Lérida (prov.), Spain 33/G2
Lérida, Spain 33/G2
Lerín, Spain 33/F1
Lerma, Spain 33/E2
Lerna, Ill. (62440) 222/E4
Lerona, W. Va. (25971) 313/D8
Léros (isl.), Greece 45/H7
Leross, Sask. 181/H4
Leroux Wash (dry riv.), Ariz. 198/E3
Leroy, Ala. (36548) 194/B8
Le Roy, Ill. (61752) 222/E3
Leroy, Ind. (46355) 227/C2
Le Roy, Iowa (50123) 229/F7
Le Roy, Kans. (66857) 232/G3
Leroy, La. (†70555) 238/F6
Le Roy, Mich. (49655) 250/D4
Le Roy, Minn. (55951) 254/F7
Leroy, N. Dak. (58252) 283/P2
Le Roy, N.Y. (14482) 276/E5
Leroy, Ohio (44251) 284/G3
Le Roy, Pa. (17743) 294/J2
Leroy, Sask. 181/G4
Leroy, Texas (76654) 302/G6
Le Roy, W. Va. (25252) 313/C5
Leroy Anderson (res.), Calif. 204/L4
Lerwick, 10/G1
Lerwick, Scot., 7/D2
Lerwick, Scot. 15/N3
Léry, Que. 172/H4
Les Abymes, Guad. 161/B6
Lesage, W. Va. (25537) 313/B5
Les Andelys, France 28/D3
Les Anglais, Haiti 158/A6
Les Avants, Switz. 39/C4
Les Becquets, Que. 172/E3
Les Bois, Switz. 39/C2
Les Cayes, Haiti 156/C3
Les Cayes, Haiti 158/B6
Les Diablerets, Switz. 39/D4
Les Éboulements, Que. 172/G2
Le Sentier, Switz. 39/B3
Le Sépey, Switz. 39/D4
Les Étroits, Que. 172/J2
Leshara, Nebr. (68035) 264/H3
Les Haudères, Switz. 39/E4
Les Hauteurs-de-Rimouski, Que. 172/A1
Leshukonskoye, U.S.S.R. 52/G2
Lesina (lake), Italy 34/E3
Les Irois, Haiti 158/A6
Lesja, Norway 18/F5
Lesko, Poland 47/F4
Leskovac, Yugo. 45/E4
Leskovik, Alb. 45/E5
Leslie, Ark. (72645) 203/E2
Leslie, Ga. (31764) 216/D7
Leslie, Idaho (83249) 220/E6
Leslie (co.), Ky. 237/P6
Leslie, Mich. (49251) 250/E6
Leslie, Mo. (63056) 261/K6
Leslie, Sask. 181/H4
Leslie, Scot. 15/K7
Leslie, W. Va. (25972) 313/E6
Leslie, Wis. (†53510) 317/F10
Leslieville, Alta. 182/C3
Lesmahagow, Scot. 15/H8
Les Mayens-de-Sion, Switz. 39/D4
Les Méchins, Que. 172/B1
Lesnoy, U.S.S.R. 52/D1
Lesotho, 3/L7
LESOTHO, 118/D5
LESOTHO, 102/E7
Lesozavodsk, U.S.S.R. 48/O5
Lesozavodskiy, U.S.S.R. 52/D1
Lesparre-Médoc, France 28/C5
Les Ponts-de-Martel, Switz. 39/C2
Les Sables-d'Olonne, France 28/B4
Lesse (riv.), Belg. 27/F8
Lessen (Lessines), Belg. 27/D7
Lesser Slave (lake), 163/E4
Lesser Slave (lake), Alta. 182/C2
Lessines, Belg. 27/D7
Lessley, Miss. (39644) 256/B8
Losslie, S.C. (29734) 296/E2
Les Tantes (isls.), Grenada 161/D7
Lester, Ala. (35647) 194/D1
Lester, Iowa (51242) 229/A2
Lester, Pa. (19113) 294/M7
Lester, W. Va. (25865) 313/D7
Lester, Wash. (98035) 310/D3
Lester Prairie, Minn. (55354) 254/D6
Lesterville, Mo. (63654) 261/L8
Lesterville, S. Dak. (57040) 298/O7
Lesti (lake), Fin. 18/O5
Lestock, Sask. 181/G4
Le Sueur (co.), Minn. 254/E6
Le Sueur, Minn. (56058) 254/E6
Les Verrières, Switz. 39/B3
Lésvos (isl.), Greece, 7/G5
Lésvos (isl.), Greece 45/G6
Leszno, Poland 47/C3
Letart, W. Va. (25253) 313/C5
Letart Falls, Ohio (†45771) 284/F8
Letcher (co.), Ky. 237/R6
Letcher, S. Dak. (57359) 298/N6
Letchworth, Eng. 13/G6
Le Teil, France 28/F5
Letellier, Man. 179/E5
Letenye, Hung. 41/D3
Letha, Idaho (83636) 220/B6
Lethbridge, 163/E6
Lethbridge, Alta., 146/G5
Lethbridge, Alta. 182/D5
Lethbridge, Newf. 166/D2
Lethem, Guyana 131/B4
Leti (isls.), Indon. 85/H7
Leticia, Col., 120/D3
Leticia, Col. 126/F10
L'Etivaz, Switz. 39/D4
Letka, U.S.S.R. 52/H3
Leto, Fla. (†33601) 212/C2
Letohatchee, Ala. (36047) 194/E6
Leton, La. (†71072) 238/D1
Letona, Ark. (72085) 203/G3
Letong, Indon. 85/D5
Le Touquet-Paris-Plage, France 28/D2
Letpadan, Burma 72/C3
Le Tréport, France 28/D2
Lette, N.S.W. 97/B4
Letterkenny, 10/B3
Letterkenny, Ire. 17/F2
Letterkenny Army Depot, Pa. 294/G6
Lettermullan (isl.), Ire. 17/B5
Letts, Ind. (†47240) 227/F6
Letts, Iowa (52754) 229/L6
Lettsworth, La. (70753) 238/G5
Leucadia, Calif. (92024) 204/H10
Leucate (lag.), France 28/E6
Leuchars, Scot. 15/L7
Leuk, Switz. 39/E4
Leukerbad, Switz. 39/E4
Leupp, Ariz. (86035) 198/E3
Leuser (mt.), Indon. 85/B5
Leuven (Louvain), Belg. 27/F7
Leuze, Belg. 27/D7
Levack, Ont. 175/D3
Levack, Ont. 177/J5
Levádhia, Greece 45/F6
Levallois-Perret, France 28/A1
Levan, Utah (84639) 304/C4
Levanger, Norway 18/G5
Levant, Kans. (67743) 232/A2
Levant∆, Maine (04456) 242/F6
Levanzo (isl.), Italy 34/D5
Levasy, Mo. (64066) 261/S5
Levee, Ky. (†40337) 237/O5
Level, Md. (†21078) 245/O2
Level Green, Ky. (†40456) 237/N6
Level Land, S.C. (†29655) 296/C3
Levelland, Texas (79336) 302/B4
Levelock, Alaska (99625) 196/G3
Level Park-Oak Park‡, Mich. (†49014) 250/D6
Level Plains, Ala. (†36322) 194/G8
Levels, W. Va. (25431) 313/J4
Lévél-sur-Québillon, Que. 174/B3
Leven, 10/E2
Leven, Scot. 15/L7
Leven (inlet), Scot. 15/F6
Leven (lake), Scot. 15/K7
Leven (riv.), Tasmania 99/B3
Lévêque (cape), Australia, 87/C7
Lévêque (cape), Aust. 88/C3
L'Évêque (cape), N.Z. 101/D7
Lévêque (cape), W. Aust. 92/C2
Leverburgh, Scot. 15/C4
Le Verdon-sur-Mer, France 28/C5
Leverett∆, Mass. (01054) 249/E3
Levering, Mich. (49755) 250/E3
Leverkusen, W. Ger. 22/B3
Levice, Czech. 41/E2
Levick (mt.), Ant. 5/B8
Levie, France 28/B7
Le Vigan, France 28/E5
Levin, N.Z. 101/E4
Lévis (co.), Que. 172/J3
Lévis, Que. 172/J3
Lévis, Que. 174/C3
Levisa Fork (riv.), Va. 307/D6
Levítha (isl.), Greece 45/H7
Levittown, P. Rico 161/D1
Levittown, N.Y. (11756) 276/S7
Levittown, Pa. (*19053) 294/N5
Levkás, Greece 45/E6
Levkás (isl.), Greece 45/E6
Levoča, Czech. 41/F2
Lévrier (bay), Mauritania 106/A4
Levskigrad, Bulg. 45/G4
Levuka, Fiji, 87/H7
Levy (co.), Fla. 212/D2
Levy (lake), Fla. 212/D2
Levy, N. Mex. (†87752) 274/E2
Lewe, Burma 72/B3
Lewellen, Nebr. (69147) 264/B3
Lewes, 10/G5
Lewes, Del. (19958) 245/T5
Lewes, Eng. 13/H7
Lewis, Butt of (prom.), 10/C1
Lewis, Butt of (prom.), Scot. 15/D3
Lewis, Colo. (81327) 208/B8
Lewis (isl.), Fla. 212/B3
Lewis (co.), Idaho 220/B3
Lewis, Ind. (47858) 227/C6
Lewis, Iowa (51544) 229/C6
Lewis, Kans. (67552) 232/C4
Lewis (co.), Ky. 237/P3
Lewis, Man. 179/F5
Lewis (lake), Man. 179/G2
Lewis (co.), Mo. 261/J2
Lewis, Mo. (†64735) 261/E6
Lewis (range), Mont. 262/C2
Lewis (co.), N.Y. 276/K3
Lewis, N.Y. (12950) 276/N2
Lewis (dist.), 10/C1
Lewis (dist.), Scot. 15/C3
Lewis, S.C. (†29706) 296/E2
Lewis (co.), Tenn. 237/F9
Lewis (creek), Vt. 268/A3
Lewis (co.), W. Va. 313/E4
Lewis (co.), Wash. 310/C4
Lewis (riv.), Wash. 310/C5
Lewis, Wis. (54851) 317/B4
Lewis (lake), Wyo. 319/B1
Lewis and Clark (co.), Mont. 262/D3
Lewis and Clark (lake), Nebr. 264/G2
Lewis and Clark (lake), S. Dak. 298/O8
Lewisberry, Pa. (17339) 294/J5
Lewisburg, Ky. (42256) 237/G6
Lewisburg, La. (†70525) 238/F6
Lewisburg, Ohio (45338) 284/A6
Lewisburg, Pa. (17837) 294/J4
Lewisburg, Tenn. (37091) 237/H10
Lewisburg, W. Va. (24901) 313/E7
Lewis Center, Ohio (43035) 284/D5
Lewis Creek, Ind. (†47234) 227/F6
Lewisetta, Va. (22505) 307/R4
Lewisham, 10/B5
Lewisport, Ky. (42351) 237/H5
Lewisporte, Newf. 166/C4
Lewis Run, Pa. (16738) 294/E2
Lewiston, Calif. (96052) 204/C3
Lewiston, Idaho, 188/C1
Lewiston, Idaho (83501) 220/A3
Lewiston, Maine, 188/N2
Lewiston, Maine (04240) 242/C7
Lewiston, Mich. (49756) 250/E4
Lewiston, Minn. (55952) 254/G7
Lewiston, N.C. (27849) 281/P2
Lewiston, N.Y. (14092) 276/B4
Lewiston, Nebr. (68380) 264/H4
Lewiston, Utah (84320) 304/C2
Lewiston, Vt. (†05055) 268/C4
Lewistown, Ill. (61542) 222/C3
Lewistown, Md. (21701) 245/J2
Lewistown, Mo. (63452) 261/J2
Lewistown, Mont. (59457) 262/G3
Lewistown, Ohio (43333) 284/C5
Lewistown, Pa. (17044) 294/G4
Lewisville, Ark. (71845) 203/C7
Lewisville, Idaho (83431) 220/F6
Lewisville, Ind. (47352) 227/G5
Lewisville, Minn. (56060) 254/D7
Lewisville, N. Br. 170/F2
Lewisville, Ohio (43754) 284/H6
Lewisville, Pa. (19351) 294/L6
Lewisville (Ulysses), Pa. (16948) 294/G2
Lewisville, Texas (75067) 302/G5
Lewvan, Sask. 181/H5
Lexa, Ark. (72355) 203/J4
Lexie, Miss. (†39667) 256/D8
Lexington, Ala. (35648) 194/D1
Lexington, Ark. (†72153) 203/F2
Lexington, Ga. (30648) 216/F3
Lexington, Ill. (61753) 222/E3
Lexington, Ind. (47138) 227/F7
Lexington, Ky., 146/K6
Lexington, Ky., 188/K3
Lexington, Ky. (*40501) 237/N4
Lexington∆, Mass. (02173) 249/B6
Lexington, Mich. (48450) 250/G5
Lexington, Minn. (†55014) 254/G5
Lexington, Miss. (39095) 256/D4
Lexington, Mo. (64067) 261/E4
Lexington, N.C. (27292) 281/J3
Lexington, N.Y. (12452) 276/M6
Lexington, Nebr. (68850) 264/E4
Lexington, Ohio (44904) 284/E4
Lexington, Okla. (73051) 288/M4
Lexington, Oreg. (97839) 291/H2
Lexington (co.), S.C. 296/E4
Lexington, S.C. (29072) 296/E4
Lexington, Tenn. (38351) 237/E9
Lexington, Texas (78947) 302/G7
Lexington, Va. (24450) 307/J5
Lexington Blue Grass Army Depot, Ky. 237/N5
Lexington Park, Md. (20653) 245/M7
Lexsy, Ga. (30432) 216/H6
Leyba, N. Mex. (87542) 274/D3
Leyburn, Eng. 13/F3
Leyden∆, Mass. (†01301) 249/D2
Leyland, 10/F1
Leyland, Alta. 182/B3
Leyland, Eng. 13/E4
Leyond (riv.), Man. 179/F3
Leysin, Switz. 39/C4
Leyte (prov.), Phil. 82/E5
Leyte (gulf), Phil. 82/E5
Leyte (isl.), Phil. 82/E5
Leyte (isl.), Phil. 85/H3
Leyte (isl.), Phil., 54/R8
Leżajsk, Poland 47/F3
Lezama, Arg. 143/H7
Lézarde (riv.), Mart. 161/D6
Lezh, Alb. 45/D5
Lézignan-Corbières, France 28/E6
Lezuza, Spain 33/E3
L'gov, U.S.S.R. 52/E4
Lhakang Dzong, China 77/D6
Lhasa, China, 3/P4
Lhasa, China, 54/N6
Lhasa, China 77/D6
Lhatse Dzong, China 77/C6
Lhokseumawe, Indon. 85/B4
Lhuntse Dzong, China 77/D6
Lianga, Phil. 82/E6
Lianga (bay), Phil. 82/F6
Liangtang, China 77/G5
Liao Ho (riv.), China 77/J3
Liaoning (prov.), China 77/K3
Liaotung (pen.), China 77/K4
Liaoyang, China 77/K3
Liaoyüan, China 77/L3
Liard (riv.), 163/D4
Liard (riv.), Br. Col. 184/L2
Liard (riv.), N.W.T., 146/F3
Liard (riv.), N.W.T. 187/F4
Liard (riv.), Yukon 187/E3
Liard River, Br. Col. 184/L2
Libáň, Czech. 41/C1
Líbano, Col. 126/C5
Libau, Man. 179/F4
Libby, Minn. (†55760) 254/E4
Libby, Mont. (59923) 262/A2
Libenge, 102/D4
Libenge, Dem. Rep. of the Congo. 115/C3
Liberador General San Martín, Arg. 143/D1
Liberal, Kans. (67901) 232/B4
Liberal, Mo. (64762) 261/D7
Liberal, Oreg. (†97042) 291/B3
Liberec, Czech. 41/C1
Liberia, 3/J5
LIBERIA, 102/B4
LIBERIA, 106/C7
Liberia, C. Rica 154/E5
Liberta, Antigua 161/E11
Libertad, Urug. 145/C5
Libertad, Barinas, Ven. 124/D3
Libertad, Cojedes, Ven. 124/D3
Liberty, Ariz. (†85326) 198/C5
Liberty (co.), Fla. 212/B1
Liberty (co.), Ga. 216/J7
Liberty, Ill. (62347) 222/B4
Liberty (Burnt Prairie), Ill. (†62820) 222/E5
Liberty, Ind. (47353) 227/H5
Liberty, Kans. (67351) 232/G4
Liberty, Ky. (42539) 237/M6
Liberty∆, Maine (04949) 242/E7
Liberty, Maine (04949) 242/E7
Liberty, Miss. (39645) 256/C8
Liberty, Mo. (64068) 261/R5
Liberty (co.), Mont. 262/E2
Liberty, N.C. (27298) 281/K3
Liberty (mt.), N.H. 268/D3
Liberty, N.Y. (12754) 276/L7
Liberty, Nebr. (68381) 264/H4
Liberty, Pa. (†15100) 294/C7
Liberty, Pa. (16930) 294/H3
Liberty, S.C. (29657) 296/B2
Liberty, Sask. 181/F4
Liberty, Tenn. (37095) 237/K8
Liberty (co.), Texas 302/K7
Liberty, Texas (77575) 302/K7
Liberty, W. Va. (25124) 313/C5
Liberty, Wash. (†98922) 310/E3
Liberty Center, Ind. (46766) 227/G3
Liberty Center, Iowa (50145) 229/F6
Liberty Center, Ohio (43532) 284/B3
Liberty Corner, N.J. (07938) 273/D2
Liberty Grove, Md. (21931) 245/O2
Liberty Hill, Conn. (†06249) 210/G2
Liberty Hill, La. (†71008) 238/E2
Liberty Hill, S.C. (29074) 296/F3
Liberty Hill, Texas (78642) 302/F7
Liberty Lake, Wash. (99019) 310/J3
Liberty Mills, Ind. (46946) 227/F2
Liberty Pole, Wis. (†54665) 317/D8
Libertytown, Md. (21762) 245/J3
Libertyville‡, Ala. (†36420) 194/F8
Libertyville, Ill. (60048) 222/F1
Libertyville, Iowa (52567) 229/K7
Libochovice, Czech. 41/B1
Libon, Phil. 82/D4
Libong, Ko (isl.), Thai. 72/C6
Libourne, France 28/C5
Libramont, Belg. 27/G9
Library, Pa. (15129) 294/B7
Libres, Mex. 150/O1
Libreville (cap.), Gabon, 3/K6
Libreville (cap.), Gabon 115/A3
Libreville (cap.), Gabon, 102/C4
Libuse, La. (71348) 238/F4
Libya, 3/K4
LIBYA, 111/B2
LIBYA, 102/D2
Libyan (des.), 102/E2
Libyan (des.), Libya 111/D2
Libyan (plat.), Libya 111/D1
Libyan (des.), Sudan 111/E3
Libyan (des.), U.A.R. 111/E2
Libyan (plat.), U.A.R. 111/E1
Libyan (des.), 102/E2
Licancábur, Cerro (mt.), Chile 138/B4
Licantén, Chile 138/A10
Licata, Italy 34/D6
Lice, Turkey 63/J3
Lichfield, 10/G2
Lichfield, Eng. 13/F5
Lichtenberg, E. Ger. 22/F4
Lichtenfels, W. Ger. 22/D3
Lichtenrade, W. Ger. 22/F4
Lichterfelde, W. Ger. 22/E4
Lichtervelde, Belg. 27/C6
Lick (creek), Tenn. 237/R8
Lick Creek, Ill. (†62912) 222/D6
Licking (riv.), Ky. 237/N3
Licking, Mo. (65542) 261/J8
Licking (co.), Ohio 284/F5
Licking (riv.), Ohio 284/F5
Licking (creek), Pa. 294/F6
Licosa (cape), Italy 34/E4
Lida, U.S.S.R. 52/C4
Lida, Ky. (40739) 237/O6
Lida (lake), Minn. 254/C4
Lidcombe, N.S.W. 97/J3
Liddel Water (riv.), Eng. 13/E2
Liddel Water (riv.), Scot. 15/L9
Lidderdale, Iowa (51452) 229/D4
Liddes, Switz. 39/D5
Liddon (gulf), N.W.T. 187/G4
Lidgerwood, N. Dak. (58053) 283/R7
Lidice, Czech. 41/C1
Lidingö, Sweden 18/H1
Lidköping, Sweden 18/H7
Lido di Ostia, Italy 34/F7
Lido di Venezia, Italy 34/D2
Lidzbark Warmiński, Poland 47/E1
Liebenthal, Kans. (67553) 232/C3
Liechtenstein, 7/F4
LIECHTENSTEIN, 39/J2
Liedekerke, Belg. 27/D7
Liège (riv.), Alta. 182/D1
Liège, Belg., 7/E3
Liège (prov.), Belg. 27/H7
Liège, Belg. 27/H7
Liege, Mo. (†63333) 261/K5
Lieksa, Fin. 18/R5
Lienartville, Dem. Rep. of the Congo. 115/E3
Lienyünkang, China 77/J5
Lienz, Austria 41/B3
Liepāja, U.S.S.R. 48/B4
Liepāja, U.S.S.R. 52/B3
Liepāja, U.S.S.R. 53/A2
Liepāja, U.S.S.R., 7/F3
Lier, Belg. 27/F6
Lierneux, Belg. 27/H8
Lierre (Lier), Belg. 27/F6
Liestal, Switz. 39/E2
Liévin, France 28/E2
Lièvre (riv.), Que. 172/B4
Lièvres (isl.), Que. 172/H2
Liezen, Austria 41/C3
Liffey (riv.), Ire. 17/H5
Liffey (riv.), 10/C4
Lifford, 10/C3
Lifford, Ire. 17/F2
Lifu (isl.), New Cal., 87/G8
Ligao, Phil. 82/D4
Ligatne, U.S.S.R. 53/C2
Liggett, Ky. (40852) 237/P7
Lighten Tso (lake), China 77/B5
Lightfoot, Va. (23090) 307/P6
Lighthouse (pt.), Fla. 212/B2
Light House (pt.), Mich. 250/D3
Lighthouse Point, Fla. (33064) 212/F5
Lightning (creek), Oreg. 291/L2
Lightning (creek), Wyo. 319/G2
Lightning Ridge, N.S.W. 97/E1
Lightsville, Ohio (†45362) 284/A5
Lightwoods, Sask. 181/G3
Lignières, Switz. 39/D2
Lignite, Alaska (†99743) 196/J2
Lignite, N. Dak. (58752) 283/F2
Ligon, Ky. (41646) 237/R6
Ligonha (riv.), Moz. 118/F3
Ligonier, Ind. (46767) 227/F2
Ligonier, Pa. (15658) 294/D5
Liguasan (marsh), Phil. 82/E7
Liguria (reg.), Italy 34/E2
Ligurian (sea), Italy 34/B3
Lihou (cays), Aust. 88/J3
Lihou (reef), Aust. 88/J3
Lihsien, China 77/H6
Lihue, Hawaii, 188/E5
Lihue, Hawaii (96766) 218/C2
Lihula, U.S.S.R. 53/C1
Likasi, 102/E6
Likasi, Dem. Rep. of the Congo. 115/E6
Likati, Dem. Rep. of the Congo. 115/D3
Likely, Br. Col. 184/G4
Likely, Calif. (96116) 204/E2
Likhoslavl', U.S.S.R. 52/E3
Likiang, China, 54/O7
Likiang, China 77/F6
Lila (lake), N.Y. 276/L2
Lilbourn, Mo. (63862) 261/N9
Lilburn, Ga. (30247) 216/D3
L'Île-Rousse, France 28/B6
Liles (pt.), Chile 138/F2
Lilesville, N.C. (28091) 281/K5
Lilienfeld, Austria 41/C3
Lille, France, 7/E3
Lille, France 28/E2
Lille, Maine (04749) 242/G1
Lilleaa (riv.), Den. 21/B5
Lille Baelt (chan.), Den. 21/C7
Lillehammer, Norway 18/F6
Lillehammer, Norway, 7/E2
Lillesand, Norway 18/F7
Lillestrøm, Norway 18/E3
Lillestrom, Sask. 181/E5
Lillian, Ala. (36549) 194/D10
Lillie, La. (71256) 238/E1
Lillington, N.C. (27546) 281/M4
Lillinonah (lake), Conn. 210/B3
Lilliwaup, Wash. (98555) 310/B3
Lillo, Spain 33/E3
Lillooet, 163/D5
Lillooet, Br. Col. 184/G5
Lillooet (riv.), Br. Col. 184/F5
Lilly, Ga. (31051) 216/E6
Lilly, Ill. (†61755) 222/D3
Lilly, Pa. (15938) 294/E5
Lilly Chapel, Ohio (†43162) 284/D6
Lillydale, Tasmania 99/D3
Lillydale, Vic. 97/J4
Lilly Grove‡, W. Va. (†24740) 313/D8
Lilongwe, Malawi 115/F6
Liloy, Phil. 82/D6
Lily, Ky. (40740) 237/N6
Lily, S. Dak. (57250) 298/O3
Lily, Wis. (54445) 317/J5
Lilydale, Minn. (†55050) 254/G5
Lily Dale, N.Y. (14752) 276/B6
Lilydale, Sask. 181/B3
Lily Plain, Sask. 181/E2
Lim (fjord), Den. 18/E8
Lim (fjord), Den. 21/A3
Lim (fjord), Den. 21/D4
Lim (riv.), Yugo. 45/D4
Lima (pt.), P. Rico 161/F2
Lima, Ill. (62348) 222/B3
Lima (lake), Ill. 222/B3
Lima, Mont. (59739) 262/D6
Lima (res.), Mont. 262/D6
Lima, N.Y. (14485) 276/E5
Lima, Pulau (isl.), Malaysia 72/F6
Lima, Ohio, 188/K2
Lima, Ohio (*45801) 284/B4
Lima (New Lima), Okla. (†74858) 288/D4
Lima, Pa. (19060) 294/L7
Lima, Par. 144/D4
Lima (cap.), Peru, 3/F6
Lima (cap.), Peru, 120/C4
Lima (dept.), Peru 128/D8
Lima (cap.), Peru 128/D8
Lima (riv.), Port. 33/B2
Lima (riv.), Spain 33/B2
Lima Center, Wis. (†53190) 317/J10
Limache, Chile 138/F2
Lima Duarte, Braz. 135/E2
Limanowa, Poland 47/E4
Limarí (riv.), Chile 138/A8
Limasawa (isl.), Phil. 82/E6
Limassol, Cyprus 59/B3
Limassol, Cyprus 63/E5
Limavady, N. Ire. 17/H1
Limavady, 10/C3
Limaville, Ohio (44640) 284/H4
Limay (riv.), Arg. 143/C4
Limbach-Oberfrohna, E. Ger. 22/E3
Limbani, Peru 128/H10
Limbaži, U.S.S.R. 53/C2
Limbé, Haiti 158/C5
Limbourg, Belg. 27/J7
Limbunya, No. Terr. 93/B4
Limburg (prov.), Belg. 27/G7
Limburg (Limbourg), Belg. 27/J7
Limburg (prov.), Neth. 27/H6
Limburg, W. Ger. 22/C3
Lime, Oreg. (†97907) 291/K3
Lime Creek, Minn. (56154) 254/C7
Limedsforsen, Sweden 18/H6
Lime Hall, Jam. 158/J6
Limeira, Braz. 132/E8
Limeira, Braz. 135/C3
Lime Kiln, Md. (21763) 245/J3
Limenária, Greece 45/G5
Limerick, 10/B4
Limerick, Ire., 7/D3
Limerick (co.), Ire. 17/D7
Limerick, Ire. 17/D6
Limerick∆, Maine (04048) 242/B8
Limerick, Sask. 181/E6
Limeridge, Wis. (53942) 317/F9
Lime Rock, Conn. (†06039) 210/B1
Lime Springs, Iowa (52155) 229/J2
Limestone (co.), Ala. 194/E1
Limestone, Ark. (72646) 203/D2
Limestone, Fla. (†33865) 212/E4
Limestone∆, Maine (04750) 242/H2
Limestone, Maine (04750) 242/H2
Limestone, Mont. (†59028) 262/F5
Limestone, N.Y. (14753) 276/C6
Limestone, Tenn. (37681) 237/R8
Limestone (co.), Texas 302/H6
Lime Village‡, Alaska (†99673) 196/G2
Limington∆, Maine (04049) 242/B8
Limington, Maine (04049) 242/B8
Limín Vathéos, Greece 45/H7
Limmat (riv.), Switz. 39/F2
Limmen (bight), Aust. 88/F2
Limmen (bight), No. Terr. 93/D3
Limmen Bight (riv.), Aust. 88/F3
Limmen Bight (riv.), No. Terr. 93/D4
Límni, Greece 45/F6
Límnos (isl.), Greece 45/G6
Limoeiro, Braz. 132/H4
Limoeiro do Norte, Braz. 132/G4
Limoges, Ont. 177/J2
Limoges, France, 7/E4
Limoges, France 28/D5
Limón, C.Rica, 146/K9
Limón, C. Rica 154/F6
Limon, Colo. (80828) 208/M4
Limón, Hond. 154/E3
Limonade, Haiti 158/C5
Limonar, Cuba 158/D1
Limoquije, Bol. 136/C4
Limousin (reg.), France 28/D5
Limoux, France 28/E6
Limpio, Par. 144/B6
Limpopo (riv.), Botswana 118/D4
Limpopo (riv.), 102/E6
Limpopo (riv.), Moz. 118/E4
Limpopo (riv.), S. Africa 118/D4
Lim Rock, Ala. (†35776) 194/F1
Linapacan (isl.), Phil. 82/B5
Linapacan (str.), Phil. 82/B5
Linard (mt.), Switz. 39/K3
Linares (prov.), Chile 138/A11
Linares, Chile 138/A11
Linares, Mex. 150/K4
Linares, Spain 33/E3
Linaria, Alta. 182/C2
Linch, Wyo. (82640) 319/F2
Linchwan, China 77/J6
Lincklaen, N.Y. (†13052) 276/J5
Lincoln (sea), 4/A12
Lincoln, 10/F4
Lincoln (sea), 146/M1
Lincoln, Ala. (35096) 194/F3
Lincoln, Arg. 143/F7
Lincoln (co.), Ark. 203/G6
Lincoln, Ark. (72744) 203/B2
Lincoln, Calif. (95648) 204/B8
Lincoln (isl.), China 85/E2
Lincoln (co.), Colo. 208/M5
Lincoln (mt.), Colo. 208/G4
Lincoln, Del. (19960) 245/S5
Lincoln (co.), Ont. 177/E4
Lincoln, Eng. 13/G4
Lincoln (co.), Ga. 216/H3
Lincoln (co.), Idaho 220/D6
Lincoln, Ill. (62656) 222/D3
Lincoln, Ind. (†46994) 227/E3
Lincoln, Iowa (50652) 229/H4
Lincoln (co.), Kans. 232/D2
Lincoln, Kans. (67455) 232/D2
Lincoln (co.), Ky. 237/M6
Lincoln (par.), La. 238/E1
Lincoln (co.), Maine 242/D7
Lincoln∆, Maine (04457) 242/G5
Lincoln, Maine (04457) 242/G5
Lincoln∆, Mass. (01773) 249/B6
Lincoln, Mass. (01773) 249/B6
Lincoln, Mich. (48742) 250/F4
Lincoln (co.), Minn. 254/B6
Lincoln (co.), Miss. 256/D8
Lincoln (co.), Mo. 261/L4
Lincoln, Mo. (65338) 261/F6
Lincoln (co.), Mont. 262/A2
Lincoln, Mont. (59639) 262/D4
Lincoln (co.), N.C. 281/G3
Lincoln∆, N.H. (03251) 268/D3
Lincoln, N.H. (03251) 268/D3
Lincoln (mt.), N.H. 268/D3
Lincoln (co.), N. Mex. 274/D5
Lincoln, N. Mex. (88338) 274/D5
Lincoln (sea), N.W.T. 187/M1
Lincoln (cap.), Nebr., 146/J5
Lincoln (cap.), Nebr., 188/G2
Lincoln (co.), Nebr. 264/D4
Lincoln (cap.), Nebr. (*68501) 264/H4
Lincoln (co.), Nev. 266/F5
Lincoln‡, Ohio (44905) 284/D6
Lincoln (co.), Okla. 288/N3
Lincoln (co.), Oreg. 291/D3
Lincoln, Pa. (†15037) 294/C7
Lincoln (co.), S. Dak. 298/R7
Lincoln (co.), Tenn. 237/H10
Lincoln, Texas (78948) 302/H7
Lincoln (creek), Utah 304/C2
Lincoln∆, Vt. (†05443) 268/B3
Lincoln, Vt. (†05443) 268/B3
Lincoln (co.), W. Va. 313/B6
Lincoln (co.), Wash. 310/G3
Lincoln, Wash. (99147) 310/G3
Lincoln (co.), Wis. 317/G5
Lincoln (co.), Wyo. 319/B3
Lincoln Beach, Oreg. (†97341) 291/C3
Lincoln Boyhood Nat'l Mem., Ind. 227/C8
Lincoln Center, Maine (04458) 242/G5
Lincoln Center, Mass. (01773) 249/B6
Lincoln City, Ind. (47552) 227/C8
Lincoln City, Oreg. (97367) 291/C3
Lincoln Gap (pass), Vt. 268/B3
Lincoln Heights (hills), Eng. 13/G4
Lincoln Heights, Ohio (†45201) 284/C9
Lincolnia‡, Va. (22312) 307/O3
Lincoln Park, Colo. (†81212) 208/J6
Lincoln Park, Ga. (†30286) 216/D5
Lincoln Park, Mich. (48146) 250/B7
Lincoln Park, N.J. (07035) 273/A1
Lincoln Park‡, N.Y. (14223) 276/M7
Lincolnshire‡, Ill. (†60015) 222/F1
Lincolnshire‡, Ky. (†40201) 237/K4
Lincolnshire-Holland (co.), Eng. 13/G5
Lincolnshire-Kesteven (co.), Eng. 13/G5
Lincolnshire-Lindsey (co.), Eng. 13/G4
Lincolnton, Ga. (30817) 216/G3

Los Teques **393**

Lock, S. Aust. 94/D5
Lockatong (creek), N.J. 273/C3
Lockbourne, Ohio (43137) 284/E6
Locke, Calif. (†95690) 204/B9
Locke, N.Y. (13092) 276/H5
Locke (mt.), Texas 302/D11
Lockeford, Calif. (95237) 204/C9
Locke Mills, Maine (04255) 242/B7
Lockeport, Br. Col. 184/A4
Lockeport, N.S. 169/C5
Lockerbie, 10/E3
Lockerbie, Scot. 15/K9
Lockesburg, Ark. (71846) 203/B6
Lockhart, Ala. (36455) 194/F8
Lockhart‡, Fla. (32810) 212/E3
Lockhart, Minn. (56555) 254/B3
Lockhart (mt.), Mont. 262/D3
Lockhart, N.S.W. 97/D4
Lockhart (riv.), N.W.T. 187/H3
Lockhart, S.C. (29364) 296/E2
Lockhart, Texas (78644) 302/G8
Lock Haven, Pa. (17745) 294/H3
Lockington, Ohio (†45356) 284/B5
Lockland, Ohio (45215) 284/C9
Lockney, Texas (79241) 302/C3
Lockney, W. Va. (25258) 313/E5
Lockport, Ill. (60441) 222/F2
Lockport, Ky. (40036) 237/M4
Lockport, La. (70374) 238/K7
Lockport, Man. 179/E4
Lockport, N.Y. (14094) 276/C4
Lockridge, Iowa (52635) 229/K7
Lock Springs, Mo. (64654) 261/E3
Lockwood, Mo. (65682) 261/E8
Lockwood, Mont. (†59101) 262/H5
Lockwood, Sask. 181/G4
Lockwood, W. Va. (26677) 313/D6
Loc Ninh, S. Vietnam 72/E5
Loco, Okla. (73442) 288/L6
Loco Hills, N. Mex. (88255) 274/F6
Locumba, Peru 128/G11
Locumba (riv.), Peru 128/G11
Locust, N.C. (28097) 281/J4
Locust Bayou, Ark. (†71701) 203/E6
Locust Fork (riv.), Ala. 194/E3
Locust Grove, Ark. (72550) 203/G2
Locust Grove, Ga. (30248) 216/D4
Locust Grove‡, N.Y. (†11791) 276/R7
Locust Grove, Ohio (†45660) 284/D8
Locust Grove, Okla. (74352) 288/R2
Locust Hill, Ky. (40151) 237/J5
Locustville, Va. (23404) 307/S5
Lod (Lydda), Israel 65/B4
Loda, Ill. (60948) 222/E3
Lodar, P.D.R. Yemen 59/E7
Loddon (riv.), Vic. 97/B5
Lodève, France 28/E6
Lodeynoye Pole, U.S.S.R. 52/D2
Lodge (creek), Mont. 262/G1
Lodge, S.C. (29082) 296/F5
Lodge (creek), Sask. 181/B6
Lodge Grass, Mont. (59050) 262/J5
Lodge Hill, Barb. 161/B8
Lodgepole, Alta. 182/C3
Lodgepole, Mont. (†59524) 262/H2
Lodgepole, Nebr. (69149) 264/B3
Lodgepole (creek), Nebr. 264/A3
Lodgepole, S. Dak. (57640) 298/D2
Lodgepole (creek), Wyo. 319/H2
Lodgepole (creek), Wyo. 319/H4
Lodi, Calif., 188/B3
Lodi, Calif. (95240) 204/C9
Lodi, Italy 34/B2
Lodi, Miss. (†39767) 256/E3
Lodi, Mo. (63950) 261/M8
Lodi, N.J. (07644) 273/B2
Lodi, N.Y. (14860) 276/G5
Lodi, Ohio (44254) 284/F3
Lodi, Texas (75564) 302/K5
Lodi, Wis. (53555) 317/G9
Lødingen, Norway 18/J2
Lodja, Dem. Rep. of the Congo. 115/D4
Lodosa, Spain 33/E1
Lodrino, Switz. 39/G4
Lodwar, Kenya 115/G3
Łódź, Poland, 7/F3
Łódź (prov.), Poland 47/D3
Łódź, Poland 47/D3
Łódź (city), Poland 47/D3
Loei, Thai. 72/D3
Loen, Norway 18/E6
Lofer, Austria 41/B3
Lofoten (isls.), Norway 18/H2
Lofoten (isls.), Norway, 4/C9
Lofoten (isls.), Norway, 7/F2
Loftus, 10/F3
Loftus, Eng. 13/G3
Lofty (mt.), Aust. 88/D8
Lofty (mt.), S. Aust. 94/B8
Logan, Ala. (35098) 194/E2
Logan (lake), Alta. 182/E2
Logan (co.), Ark. 203/C3
Logan (riv.), Aust. 88/K2
Logan (mt.), Canada, 4/C17
Logan (co.), Colo. 208/N1
Logan (co.), Ill. 222/D3
Logan, Ill. (62856) 222/E6
Logan, Ind. (†45030) 227/H6
Logan, Iowa (51546) 229/B5
Logan (co.), Kans. 232/A3
Logan, Kans. (67646) 232/C2
Logan (co.), Ky. 237/H7
Logan, Mont. (59763) 262/E5
Logan (co.), N. Dak. 283/L7
Logan, N. Dak. (†58701) 283/H3
Logan, N. Mex. (88426) 274/F3
Logan (co.), Nebr. 264/D3
Logan (creek), Nebr. 264/H2
Logan (co.), Ohio 284/C5
Logan, Ohio (43138) 284/F6
Logan (co.), Okla. 288/M3
Logan, Okla. (73849) 288/F1
Logan, Oreg. (†97405) 291/B2
Logan, Utah, 188/D2
Logan, Utah (84321) 304/C2
Logan (co.), W. Va. 313/C7
Logan, W. Va. (25601) 313/B7
Logan (mt.), Wash. 310/E2
Logan (mt.), 163/C3
Logan (mt.), Yukon 187/D3
Logan (mts.), Yukon 187/F3
Logandale, Nev. (89021) 266/G6
Logan Internat'l Airport, Mass. 249/D7
Logan Martin (lake), Ala. 194/F4
Logansport, Ind. (46947) 227/E3
Logansport, Ky. (42258) 237/H6
Logansport, La. (71049) 238/C3
Loganton, Pa. (17747) 294/H3
Loganville, Ga. (30249) 216/E3
Loganville, Pa. (17342) 294/J6
Loganville, Wis. (53943) 317/F9
Loge (riv.), Angola 115/B5
Loggieville, N. Br. 170/E1
Logierait, Scot. 15/J6
Log Lane Village, Colo. (†80701) 208/M2
Logone (riv.), Chad 111/C5
Logone (riv.), Cameroon 115/C2
Logroño (prov.), Spain 33/E1
Logroño, Spain 33/E1
Logrosán, Spain 33/D3
Logsden, Oreg. (97357) 291/D3
Løgstør, Den. 18/F8
Løgstør, Den. 21/C4
Løgstør Bredning (fjord), Den. 21/C4
Løgumkloster, Den. 21/B7
Log Valley, Sask. 181/D5
Lohals, Den. 21/E7
Lohardaga, India 68/E4
Lohatlha, S. Africa 118/C5
Lohman, Mo. (65053) 261/H5
Lohman, Mont. (†59523) 262/G2
Lohn, Texas (76852) 302/E6
Loho, China 77/H5
Lo Ho (riv.), China 77/G4
Lohr, W. Ger. 22/C4
Lohrville, Iowa (51453) 229/D4
Lohrville, Wis. (†54970) 317/H7
Loica, Chile 138/F4
Loi-kaw, Burma 72/C3
Loi Leng (mt.), Burma 72/C2
Loimaa, Fin. 18/N6
Loir (riv.), France 28/D4
Loire (riv.), France, 7/E4
Loire (dept.), France 28/F5
Loire (riv.), France 28/C4
Loire-Atlantique (dept.), France 28/C4
Loiret (dept.), France 28/E4
Loir-et-Cher (dept.), France 28/D4
Loíza, P. Rico 161/E1
Loíza Aldea, P. Rico 161/E1
Loja, Ec., 120/C3
Loja (prov.), Ec. 128/C4
Loja, Ec. 128/C4
Loja, Spain 33/D4
Løjt Kirkeby, Den. 21/C7
Loka, Sudan 111/F7
Lokeren, Belg. 27/D6
Lokitaung, Kenya 115/G3
Lokka (res.), Fin. 18/Q3
Løkken, Norway 18/F5
Løkken, Den. 21/C3
Lokoja, 102/C4
Lokoja, Nigeria 106/F7
Lokolama, Dem. Rep. of the Congo. 115/D4
Lokoro (riv.), Dem. Rep. of the Congo. 115/C4
Lökösháza, Hung. 41/F3
Loksa, U.S.S.R. 53/C1
Loks Land (isl.), N.W.T. 187/M3
Lol (dry riv.), Sudan 111/E6
Lola, Ky. (42059) 237/E6
Loleta, Calif. (95551) 204/A3
Lolgorien, Kenya 115/G4
Lolita, Texas (77971) 302/H9
Lolland (isl.), Den. 18/G9
Lolland (isl.), Den. 21/E8
Lollie, Ga. (30433) 216/G6
Lolo (creek), Idaho 220/C3
Lolo (pass), Idaho 220/D3
Lolo, Mont. (59847) 262/B4
Lolo, Dem. Rep. of the Congo. 115/D3
Lolo Hot Springs, Mont. (†59847) 262/B4
Lom, Bulg. 45/F4
Lom (riv.), Bulg. 45/H4
Lom, Norway 18/F6
Lom (riv.), Cameroon 115/B2
Loma, Colo. (81524) 208/B4
Loma, Mont. (59460) 262/F3
Loma, N. Dak. (†58311) 283/O2
Loma (mts.), S. Leone 106/B7
Loma Alta, Bol. 136/B2
Loma Bonita, Mex. 150/M7
Loma Escobar, Pan. 154/G6
Loma Linda, Calif. (92354) 204/F10
Loma Mar, Calif. (94021) 204/J3
Lomami (riv.), Dem. Rep. of the Congo. 115/D4
Loman, Minn. (56654) 254/E2
Lomas, Peru, 120/C4
Lomas, Peru 128/E10
Lomas de Zamora, Arg. 143/G7
Lomax, Ala. (†35045) 194/E5
Lomax, Ill. (61454) 222/B3
Lomax, Texas (†77571) 302/K2
Lombard, Ill. (60148) 222/A2
Lombard, Mont. (†59643) 262/E4
Lombardville, Ill. (†61421) 222/D2
Lombardy, Ont. 177/H3
Lombardy (reg.), Italy 34/B2
Lombez, France 28/D6
Lomblen (isl.), Indon. 85/G7
Lombok (isl.), Indon., 54/P11
Lombok (isl.), Indon. 85/F7
Lombok (str.), Indon. 85/E7
Lomé (cap.), Togo 102/C4
Lomé (cap.), Togo 106/E7
Lomela, Dem. Rep. of the Congo. 115/D4
Lomela (riv.), Dem. Rep. of the Congo. 115/D4
Lometa, Texas (76853) 302/F6
Lomié, Cameroon 115/B3
Lomira, Wis. (53048) 317/J8
Lo Miranda, Chile 138/G5
Lomita, Calif. (90717) 204/C11
Lommel, Belg. 27/G6
Lomnice, Czech. 41/C2
Lomond, Alta. 182/D4
Lomond (lake), 10/A1
Lomond, Loch (lake), N.S. 169/H3
Lomond (lake), Scot. 15/G7
Lompoc, Calif. (93436) 204/E9
Lom Sak, Thai. 72/D3
Łomża, Poland 47/F2
Lonaconing, Md. (21539) 245/C2
Loncoche, Chile 138/D2
Loncopué, Arg. 143/B4
London, 163/H7
London, Ark. (72847) 203/D3
London, Ont. 177/C5
London (cap.), Eng., 7/D3
London (cap.), Eng. 13/G6
London, Ind. (†46126) 227/F5
London, Ky. (40741) 237/N6
London, Minn. (56061) 254/E7
London, Ohio (43140) 284/C6
London, Ont., 146/K5
London, Texas (76854) 302/E7
London (cap.), U.K., 3/J3
London (cap.), U.K., 10/B5
London, Wis. (†53523) 317/H9
Londonderry (cape), Aust. 88/D2
Londonderry (isl.), Chile 138/E11
LondonderryΔ, N.H. (03053) 268/E6
Londonderry (co.), N. Ire. 17/H2
Londonderry, 10/C3
Londonderry, N. Ire. 17/G2
Londonderry, N.S. 169/E3
Londonderry (cape), W. Aust. 92/D1
Londonderry, Ohio (45647) 284/E7
LondonderryΔ, Vt. (05148) 268/B5
Londonderry, Vt. (05148) 268/B5
Londonderry Station, N.S. 169/E3
London Mills, Ill. (61544) 222/C3
Londontowne, Md. (†21037) 245/M4
Londrina, Braz., 120/E5
Londrina, Braz. 132/D8
Lone (mt.), Mont. 262/E5
Lone (mt.), Nev. 266/D4
Lone Butte, Br. Col. 184/G4
Lone Cedar, W. Va. (†26153) 313/C4
Lone Cone (mt.), Colo. 208/C7
Lone Elm, Kans. (†66039) 232/G3
Lone Grove, Okla. (73443) 288/M6
Lone Jack, Mo. (64070) 261/S6
Lonely (isl.), Ont. 177/C2
Lonely (lake), Man. 179/C3
Lone Mountain, Tenn. (37773) 237/O8
Lone Oak, Ga. (†30230) 216/C4
Lone Oak, Ky. (42001) 237/D6
Lone Oak, Texas (75453) 302/H5
Lone Pine, Alta. 182/C2
Lone Pine, Calif. (93545) 204/H7
Lone Pine (peak), Idaho 220/D5
Lonepine, La. (†71367) 238/F5
Lonepine, Mont. (59848) 262/B3
Lone Rock, Iowa (50559) 229/E2
Lonerock, Oreg. (†97823) 291/H2
Lone Rock, Sask. 181/A2
Lone Rock, Wis. (53556) 317/F9
Lonesome Butte, Sask. 181/E6
Lone Star, S.C. (29077) 296/F4
Lone Star‡, Texas (75668) 302/K4
Lone Tree (creek), Colo. 208/K1
Lone Tree, Iowa (52755) 229/L6
Lonetree, N. Dak. (†58718) 283/G3
Lonetree, Wyo. (82936) 319/B4
Lone Wolf, Okla. (73655) 288/H5
Long, Alaska (†99768) 196/G2
Long (isl.), Alaska 196/M2
Long (reef), Aust. 88/D2
Long (isl.), Bah. Is., 146/L7
Long (mt.), Conn. 210/B2
Long (pond), Conn. 210/H3
Long (cay), Bah. Is. 156/C2
Long (isl.), Bah. Is. 156/C2
Long (bay), Jam. 158/H7
Long (isl.), Antigua 161/E11
Long (bay), Barb. 161/B9
Long (isl.), Mart. 161/D6
Long (pt.), V.I.(U.S.) 161/B4
Long (pt.), V.I.(U.S.) 161/E4
Long (lake), Que. 172/C2
Long (lake), Que. 172/B3
Long (lake), Que. 172/E3
Long (lake), Ont. 175/C3
Long (lake), Ont. 177/H5
Long (pt.), Ont. 177/D5
Long (key), Fla. 212/B3
Long (key), Fla. 212/F7
Long (pond), Fla. 212/D2
Long (co.), Ga. 216/J7
Long, Loch (inlet), 10/A1
Long (lake), Maine 242/B7
Long (lake), Maine 242/E2
Long (lake), Maine 242/G1
Long (pond), Maine 242/D4
Long (pond), Maine 242/D6
Long (pond), Maine 242/E5
Long (lake), Man. 179/G4
Long (pt.), Man. 179/D1
Long (pt.), Man. 179/D4
Long (isl.), Mass. 249/E7
Long (pt.), Mass. 249/O4
Long (pond), Mass. 249/L5
Long (lake), Mich. 250/F3
Long (lake), Minn. 254/D4
Long (lake), Minn. 254/F3
Long, Miss. (†38828) 256/C4
Long (isl.), N. Br. 170/D3
Long (lake), N. Br. 170/D1
Long (lake), N.C. 281/P5
Long (lake), N. Dak. 283/J4
Long (lake), N. Dak. 283/K6
Long (lake), N. Dak. 283/L2
Long (mt.), N.H. 268/E2
Long (beach), N.J. 273/E4
Long (isl.), N.S. 169/B4
Long (isl.), N.Y., 188/M2
Long (isl.), N.Y. 276/O9
Long (lake), N.Y. 276/M2
Long (isl.), N.Z. 101/A7
Long (valley), Nev. 266/B1
Long (isl.), Newf. 166/C2
Long (isl.), Newf. 166/D2
Long (lake), Newf. 166/B3
Long (lake), Newf. 166/A3
Long (pt.), Newf. 166/C4
Long (isl.), Terr. N.G. 85/B7
Long (reef), W. Aust. 92/D1
Long (lake), S. Dak. 298/L2
Long (creek), Sask. 181/H6
Long (inlet), Scot. 15/B1
Long (isl.), Wash. 310/A4
Long (lake), Wash. 310/F3
Long (lake), Wash. 310/H3
Long (lake), Wis. 317/C4
Longa (isl.), Scot. 15/E4
Longaví, Chile 138/A11
Long Beach, Calif., 188/C4
Long Beach, Calif. (*90801) 204/C11
Long Beach (pen.), Conn. 210/C4
Long Beach, Ind. (†46360) 227/D1
Long Beach, Minn. (†56334) 254/C5
Long Beach, Miss. (39560) 256/F10
Long Beach, N.C. (28461) 281/N7
Long Beach, N.Y. (11561) 276/R8
Long Beach, Wash. (98631) 310/A4
Long Beach Resort‡, Fla. (†32401) 212/C6
Longboat (key), Fla. 212/D4
Longboat Key, Fla. (33548) 212/D4
Long Bottom, Ohio (45743) 284/G7
Long Branch, N.J. (08008) 273/F3
Long Branch, Ont. 177/J4
Long Branch‡, Pa. (†15423) 294/C5
Long Branch‡, Va. (†22003) 307/O3
Longbranch, Wash. (98351) 310/C3
Long Cove, Maine (†04857) 242/E8
Long Creek, Oreg. (97856) 291/H3
Longcreek, S.C. (29658) 296/A2
Longdale, Okla. (73755) 288/K2
Long Eaton, Eng. 13/F5
Long Eddy, N.Y. (12760) 276/K7
Long Falls (dam), Maine 242/C5
Longfellow (mts.), Maine 242/B6
Longford, V.I.(U.S.) 161/F4
Longford, Ont. 177/E3
Longford, 10/C4
Longford (co.), Ire. 17/F4
Longford, Ire. 17/F4
Longford, Kans. (67458) 232/E2
Longford, Tas. 99/C3
Long Green, Md. (21092) 245/M3
Long Grove‡, Ill. (60047) 222/E1
Long Grove, Iowa (52756) 229/M5
Long Harbour, Newf. 166/D2
Long Hill, Conn. (†06611) 210/C3
Longhope, Sask. 181/E3
Longhurst, N.C. (27548) 281/L2
Longido, Tanz. 115/G4
Longiram, Indon. 85/F5
Long Island‡, Alaska (†99687) 196/J2
Long Island (sound), Conn. 210/C4
Long Island (bay), Ire. 17/B9
Long Island, Kans. (67647) 232/C2
Long Island, Maine (04050) 242/C8
Longisland, N.C. (28648) 281/H3
Long Island (sound), N.Y. 276/P8
Long Island, Tenn. (†37662) 237/S7
Long Island, Va. (24569) 307/K6
Long Key, Fla. (33001) 212/F7
Longlac, Ont. 175/C3
Longlac, Ont. 177/H5
Long Lake, Man. 179/G4
Long Lake, Mich. (48743) 250/F4
Long Lake, Minn. (55356) 254/F5
Long Lake, N.Y. (12847) 276/L3
Longlake, S. Dak. (57457) 298/L2
Long Lake, Wis. (54542) 317/J4
Long Lane, Mo. (65590) 261/G7
Longleaf, La. (71448) 238/E4
Long Meadow (pond), Conn. 210/C2
LongmeadowΔ, Mass. (01106) 249/D4
Long Melford, Eng. 13/H5
Longmire, Wash. (98397) 310/D4
Longmont, Colo., 188/E2
Longmont, Colo. (80501) 208/J2
Longnawan, Indon. 85/F5
Long Neck (pt.), Conn. 210/B4
Long Pine, Nebr. (69217) 264/E2
Long Point, Ont. 177/D5
Long Point (bay), Ont. 177/D5
Long Point, Ill. (61333) 222/E3
Long Point, N. Br. 170/E3
Long Point, N.S. 169/G3
Long Pond, Maine (†04945) 242/C4
Long Pond, Newf. 166/D2
Long Pond, Pa. (18334) 294/L3
Longport, N.J. (08403) 273/D5
Long Prairie, Minn. (56347) 254/D5
Long Prairie (riv.), Minn. 254/D4
Long Range (mts.), Newf. 166/C4
Long Rapids, Mich. (†49753) 250/F3
Longreach, Australia, 87/E8
Longreach, Aust. 88/G4
Long Reach (inlet), N. Br. 170/D3
Longreach, Queens. 95/B4
Long Reef (pt.), N.S.W. 97/K3
Longridge, 10/G1
Longridge, Eng. 13/E4
Longs (peak), Colo. 208/H2
Longs, S.C. (29568) 296/K4
Long Sault, Ont. 177/K2
Long Siding, Minn. (†55371) 254/E5
Long Society, Conn. (†06360) 210/G2
Longstreet, La. (71050) 238/B2
Long Sutton, Eng. 13/G5
Longton, Kans. (67352) 232/F4
Longtown, Eng. 13/E2
Longtown, Miss. (†38665) 256/D1
Longtown, Mo. (†63775) 261/N7
Longtown, S.C. (†29130) 296/F3
Longueuil, Que. 172/J4
Long Valley, N.J. (07853) 273/D2
Longvalley, S. Dak. (57547) 298/F7
Longview, Ala. (†35137) 194/E4
Longview, Alta. 182/C4
Longview, Colo. (†80135) 208/J4
Longview, Ill. (61852) 222/E4
Longview, Miss. (39749) 256/G4
Long View, N.C. (28601) 281/F3
Longview, Texas, 188/G4
Longview, Texas (75601) 302/K5
Longview, Wash., 188/B1
Longview, Wash. (98632) 310/B4
Longville, La. (70652) 238/D5
Longville, Minn. (56655) 254/D4
Longwood, Fla. (32750) 212/E3
Longwood, Mo. (†65301) 261/F5
Longwood, N.C. (28452) 281/N6
Longwood Park, N.C. (†28345) 281/K5
Longworth, Br. Col. 184/G3
Longworth, Texas (79531) 302/D5
Longwy, France 28/F3
Long Xuyen, S. Vietnam 72/E5
Long Xuyen, S. Vietnam, 54/O8
Longyearbyen, Norway 18/D2
Longyearbyen, Norway, 4/B8
Loni Beach, Man. 179/F4
Lonigo, Italy 34/C2
Lonneker, Neth. 27/L4
Lonoke (co.), Ark. 203/G4
Lonoke, Ark. (72086) 203/G4
Lonquimay, Chile 138/E2
Lonsdale, Ark. (72087) 203/E4
Lonsdale, Minn. (55046) 254/E6
Lonsdale, R.I. (†02864) 249/J5
Lons-le-Saunier, France 28/F4
Lonton, Burma 72/B1
Looe, Eng. 13/C7
Loogootee, Ind. (47553) 227/D7
Lookeba, Okla. (73053) 288/K4
Lookingglass (riv.), Mich. 250/E6
Lookout (mt.), Ala. 194/G2
Lookout (ridge), Alaska 196/G1
Lookout, Calif. (96054) 204/D2
Lookout (mt.), Idaho 220/D5
Lookout (mt.), Idaho 220/F5
Lookout, Ky. (41542) 237/S6
Lookout (pt.), Md. 245/N8
Lookout (cape), N.C., 188/L4
Lookout (cape), N.C. 281/S5
Lookout, Okla. (73850) 288/H1
Lookout (cape), Oreg., 188/B1
Lookout (cape), Oreg. 291/C2
Lookout, Pa. (†18417) 294/M2
Lookout, W. Va. (25868) 313/E6
Lookout, Wyo. (†82051) 319/G4
Lookout Mountain, Ga. (†30741) 216/B1
Lookout Mountain, Tenn. (37350) 237/L11
Lookout Point (res.), Oreg. 291/E4
Looma, Alta. 182/D3
Loomis, Calif. (95650) 204/C8
Loomis, Nebr. (68958) 264/E4
Loomis, S. Dak. (57360) 298/N6
Loomis, Wash. (98827) 310/F2
Loomis, Wis. (54158) 317/K5
Loon (lake), Alta. 182/C1
Loon (riv.), Alta. 182/C1
Loon (lake), Ont. 177/F3
Loon (lake), Maine 242/D3
Loon (creek), Sask. 181/G4
Loon (lake), Wash. 310/H2
Looneyville, W. Va. (25259) 313/D5
Loon Lake, Maine (†04970) 242/B5
Loon Lake, N.Y. (12951) 276/M1
Loon Lake, Sask. 181/B1
Loon Lake, Wash. (99148) 310/H2
Loon op Zand, Neth. 27/G5
Loon Strait, Man. 179/F3
Loop (head), Ire. 17/A6
Loop (head), 10/A4
Loop, Texas (79342) 302/B5
Loos, Br. Col. 184/G3
Loosahatchie (riv.), Tenn. 237/B10
Loose Creek, Mo. (65054) 261/J5
Lo Ovalle, Chile 138/F3
Looxahoma, Miss. (†38668) 256/E1
Looz (Borgloon), Belg. 27/G7
Lopatka (cape), U.S.S.R. 48/Q4
Lopatka (cape), U.S.S.R., 54/V4
Lop Buri, Thai. 72/D4
Lopeno, Texas (78564) 302/E11
Lopez (pt.), Calif. 204/D7
Lopez (cape), Gabon 115/A4
Lopez, Pa. (18628) 294/K3
Lopez (cape), 102/C5
Lopez, Wash. (98261) 310/C2
Lopez (isl.), Wash. 310/C2
Lopi, Rep. of Congo 115/C3
Lop Nor (basin), China, 54/M5
Lop Nor (dry lake), China 77/D3
Lopphavet (bay), Norway 18/M1
Lora (riv.), Afgh. 59/J3
Lora (riv.), Afgh. 68/B2
Lora, Hamun-i- (swamp), Pak. 59/J4
Lora, Hamun-i- (swamp), Pak. 68/B3
Lora del Río, Spain 33/D4
Lorado, W. Va. (25630) 313/C7
Lorain (co.), Ohio 284/F3
Lorain, Ohio (*44052) 284/F3
Lorain‡, Pa. (†15901) 294/E5
Loraine, Ill. (62349) 222/B3
Loraine, N. Dak. (58753) 283/G2
Loraine, Texas (79532) 302/D5
Loraine, Wis. (†54825) 317/B4
Loralai, Pak. 59/J3
Loralai, Pak. 68/B2
Loramie (lake), Ohio 284/B5
Loranger, La. (70446) 238/N1
Lorca, Spain, 7/D5
Lorca, Spain 33/F4
Lord Howe (isl.), Australia, 87/G9
Lord Howe (isl.), Aust. 88/K6
Lord Howe (isl.), Australia, 3/T7
Lord Howe (Ontong Java) (isl.), Br. Sol. Is., 87/G6
Lord Howe (isl.), N.S.W. 97/J2
Lord Mayor (bay), N.W.T. 187/J3
Lordsburg, N. Mex. (88045) 274/A6
Lords Point, Conn. (†06378) 210/H3
Lords Valley, Pa. (†18428) 294/M3
Loreauville, La. (70552) 238/G6
Loreburn, Sask. 181/D4
Lore City, Ohio (43755) 284/H6
Lorena, Braz. 135/D3
Lorena, Miss. (†39153) 256/F6
Lorena‡, Texas (76655) 302/G6
Lorentz, W. Va. (26229) 313/F4
Lorenzo, Idaho (83432) 220/G6
Lorenzo, Sask. 181/D2
Lorenzo, Texas (79343) 302/C4
Lorenzo Geyres, Urug. 145/B3
Lorenz Park‡, N.Y. (†12534) 276/N6
Loreto, Bol. 136/C4
Loreto, Col., 120/C3
Loreto, Col. 126/C5
Loreto, Ec. 128/D3
Loreto, Baja California, Mex. 150/D4
Loreto, Zacatecas, Mex. 150/J5
Loreto, Agusan, Phil. 82/E6
Loreto, Surigao del Norte, Phil. 82/E5
Loreto, Par. 144/D4
Loreto (dept.), Peru 128/E5
Loretta, Kans. (†67520) 232/C3
Loretta, Wis. (54852) 317/E4
Lorette, Man. 179/F5
Loretteville, Que. 172/H3
Loretto, Ky. (40037) 237/L5
Loretto, Mich. (49852) 250/B3
Loretto, Minn. (55357) 254/F5
Loretto, Nebr. (68646) 264/F3
Loretto, Pa. (15940) 294/E4
Loretto, Tenn. (38469) 237/G10
Loretto, Va. (22509) 307/O4
Lorian (swamp), Kenya 115/G3
Lorica, Col. 126/C3
Lorida, Fla. (33857) 212/E4
Lorient, France 28/B4
L'Orignal, Ont. 177/K2
Lorimor, Iowa (50149) 229/E6
Lőrinci, Hung. 41/E3
Loring, Alaska (†99901) 196/N2
Loring, Ont. 177/D2
Loring, Mont. (59537) 262/J2
Loring A.F.B., Maine 242/H2
Loris, S.C. (29569) 296/K3
Lorlie, Sask. 181/H5
Lorman, Miss. (39096) 256/B7
Lorne (firth), 10/D2
Lorne, N. Br. 170/D1
Lorne (dist.), Scot. 15/F7
Lorne (firth), Scot. 15/E7
Loros (pt.), Chile 138/E3
Lörrach, W. Ger. 22/B5
Lorrain, Mart. 161/D5
Lorrain (riv.), Mart. 161/D5
Lorraine, Kans. (67459) 232/D3
Lorraine, N.Y. (13659) 276/J3
Lorrha, Ire. 17/E5
Lorton, Nebr. (68382) 264/H4
Lorton, Va. (22079) 307/O3
Lorze (riv.), Switz. 39/F2
Los (isls.), Guinea 106/B7
Losada (riv.), Col. 126/C6
Los Alamitos, Calif. (90720) 204/D11
Los Alamos, Calif. (93440) 204/E9
Los Alamos, N.Mex., 188/E3
Los Alamos (co.), N. Mex. 274/C3
Los Alamos, N. Mex. (87544) 274/C3
Los Alerces Nat'l Park, Arg. 143/C5
Los Algodones, Mex. 150/B1
Los Altos, Calif. (94022) 204/K3
Los Altos Hills, Calif. (94022) 204/J3
Los Amates, Guat. 154/C3
Los Andes, Chile 138/B9
Los Andes, Col. 126/B7
Los Angeles, Calif., 146/G6
Los Angeles, Calif., 188/C4
Los Angeles (co.), Calif. 204/G9
Los Angeles, Calif. (*90001) 204/C10
Los Ángeles, Chile 138/D1
Los Angeles, Texas (78051) 302/F9
Los Angeles, U.S., 3/D4
Los Angeles Aqueduct, Calif. 204/G8
Los Antiguos, Arg. 143/B6
Losantville, Ind. (47354) 227/G4
Los Arabos, Cuba 158/E1
Los Banos, Calif. (93635) 204/E6
Los Barcos (pt.), Cuba 158/B2
Los Canarreos (arch.), Cuba 158/C2
Los Caños, Cuba 158/K4
Los Castillos, Ven. 124/G3
Los Choros (riv.), Chile 138/A7
Los Colorados (arch.), Cuba 158/A1
Los Coyotes Ind. Res., Calif. 204/J10
Los Cusis, Bol. 136/D4
Los Estados (isl.), Arg. 143/D7
Los Frailes (isl.), Dom. Rep. 158/C7
Los Fresnos, Texas (78566) 302/G11
Los Gatos, Calif. (95030) 204/K4
Los Glaciares Nat'l Park, Arg. 143/B6
Loshan, China 77/F6
Los Hermanos (isls.), Ven. 124/F2
Łosice, Poland 47/F2
Los Indios, Cuba 158/B2
Lošinj (isl.), Yugo. 45/B3
Los Lagos, Chile 138/D3
Los Llanos, Dom. Rep. 158/F6
Los Loros, Chile 138/B6
Los Lunas, N. Mex. (87031) 274/C4
Los Menucos, Arg. 143/C5
Los Mochis, Mex. 150/E4
Los Molinos, Calif. (96055) 204/D3
Los Monjes (isls.), Ven. 124/C1
Los Muermos, Chile 138/D3
Los Navalmorales, Spain 33/D3
Los Navalucillos, Spain 33/D3
Los Negros, Cuba 158/F2
Løsning, Den. 21/C6
Los Novillos, Urug. 145/D2
Los Olivos, Calif. (93441) 204/E9
Los Olmos (creek), Texas 302/F10
Los Olmos (creek), Texas 302/F11
Los Osos-Baywood Park, Calif. (†93401) 204/E8
Los Palacios, Cuba 156/A2
Los Palacios, Cuba 158/B1
Los Perales de Tapihue, Chile 138/F3
Los Pinos (riv.), Colo. 208/D8
Los Pinos (riv.), Colo. 208/G8
Los Pinos (riv.), N. Mex. 274/B2
Los Ranchos de Albuquerque, N. Mex. (†87101) 274/C3
Los Reyes de Salgado, Mex. 150/H7
Los Ríos (prov.), Ec. 128/C3
Los Roques (isls.), Ven. 124/E2
Los Santos, Pan. 154/G7
Los Santos de Maimona, Spain 33/C3
Los Sauces, Chile 138/D2
Losser, Neth. 27/L4
Lossiemouth and Branderburgh, 10/E2
Lossiemouth and Branderburgh, Scot. 15/K4
Lost (riv.), Calif. 204/D1
Lost (riv.), Ind. 227/D7
Lost (riv.), Minn. 254/C3
Lost (riv.), Oreg. 291/F5
Lost (creek), Utah 304/C5
Lostallo, Switz. 39/H4
Lostant, Ill. (61334) 222/D2
Los Taques, Ven. 124/C2
Lost Cabin, Wyo. (†82642) 319/E2
Lost City, W. Va. (26810) 313/J5
Lost Creek, Ky. (41348) 237/P6
Lost Creek, W. Va. (26385) 313/F4
Lost Creek, Wash. (†99180) 310/H2
Los Teques, Ven. 124/E2

Magnolia 395

Luzon (isl.), Phil., 3/R5
Luzon (isl.), Phil., 54/R8
Luz-Saint-Sauveur, France 28/C6
L'vov, U.S.S.R. 48/C4
L'vov, U.S.S.R. 52/B5
L'vov, U.S.S.R., 7/G4
Lwów (L'vov), U.S.S.R. 52/B5
Lyakhov (isls.), U.S.S.R., 4/B3
Lyal (isl.), Ont. 177/C3
Lyallpur, Pak. 59/K3
Lyallpur, Pak. 68/C2
Lyalta, Alta. 182/D4
Lybster, 10/E1
Lybster, Scot. 15/K3
Lycan, Colo. (81056) 208/P7
Lycksele, Sweden 18/L4
Lycoming, N.Y. (13093) 276/H3
Lycoming (co.), Pa. 294/H3
Lycoming (creek), Pa. 294/H3
Lydallville, Conn. (†06040) 210/F1
Lydd, Eng. 13/H7
Lydda, Israel 65/B4
Lydden, Sask. 181/C4
Lydenburg, S. Africa 118/E4
Lydia, Minn. (†55352) 254/E6
Lydia, S.C. (29079) 296/G3
Lydia Mills, S.C. (29325) 296/D3
Lydiatt, Man. 179/F5
Lydick, Ind. (†46601) 227/E1
Lydney, Eng. 13/E6
Lyell (mt.), Alta. 182/B4
Lyell (isl.), Br. Col. 184/B4
Lyell (mt.), Br. Col. 184/J4
Lyell (mt.), Tas. 99/B4
Lyerly, Ga. (30730) 216/B2
Lyford, Ind. (†47874) 227/C5
Lyford, Texas (78569) 302/G11
Lykens, Pa. (17048) 294/J4
Lyle, Minn. (55953) 254/F7
Lyle, Wash. (98635) 310/D5
Lyles, Tenn. (37098) 237/G9
Lyleton, Man. 179/A5
Lyman, Miss. (†39501) 256/F10
Lyman△, N.H. (†03585) 268/D3
Lyman, N.H. (†03585) 268/D3
Lyman, Nebr. (69352) 264/A3
Lyman, S.C. (29365) 296/C2
Lyman (co.), S. Dak. 298/J6
Lyman, S. Dak. (†57569) 298/K6
Lyman, Utah (84749) 304/C5
Lyman, Wash. (98263) 310/D2
Lyman, Wyo. (82937) 319/B4
Lyman Park-Thompson Park‡, Va. (†22172) 307/O3
Lymburn, Alta. 182/A2
Lyme (bay), Eng. 13/E7
Lyme△, N.H. (03768) 268/C4
Lyme, N.H. (03768) 268/C4
Lyme (bay), 10/E5
Lyme Center, N.H. (03769) 268/C4
Lyme Regis, 10/E5
Lyme Regis, Eng. 13/E7
Lymington, 10/F5
Lymington, Eng. 13/F7
Lymm, 10/G2
Lyn, Ont. 177/J3
Łyna (riv.), Poland 47/E1
Lynbrook, N.Y. (11563) 276/R7
Lynch, Ky. (40855) 237/R7
Lynch, Md. (21646) 245/O3
Lynch, Nebr. (68746) 264/F2
Lynchburg, Mo. (65543) 261/H7
Lynchburg, N. Dak. (†58023) 283/R6
Lynchburg, Ohio (45142) 284/C7
Lynchburg, S.C. (29080) 296/G3
Lynchburg, Tenn. (37352) 237/J10
Lynchburg, Va., 146/L6
Lynchburg, Va., 188/L3
Lynchburg, Va. (*24501) 307/K6
Lynches (riv.), S.C. 296/H3
Lynch Station, Va. (24571) 307/K6
Lynd, Aust. 88/H3
Lynd, Minn. (56157) 254/C6
Lynd, Queens. 95/C3
Lyndeboro△, N.H. (†03082) 268/D6
Lyndeboro, N.H. (†03082) 268/D6
Lynden, Ont. 177/D4
Lynden, Wash. (98264) 310/C2
Lyndhurst, Ont. 177/H3
Lyndhurst△, N.J. (07071) 273/B2
Lyndhurst, N.S.W. 97/E3
Lyndhurst, S. Aust. 94/E4
Lyndhurst, Ohio (44124) 284/J9
Lyndoch, S. Aust. 94/C6
Lyndon, Ill. (61261) 222/D2
Lyndon, Kans. (66451) 232/G3
Lyndon‡, Ky. (40222) 237/K4
Lyndon, W. Aust. 92/A3
Lyndon, Ohio (45649) 284/D7
Lyndon△, Vt. (05849) 268/C2
Lyndon, Vt. (05849) 268/C2
Lyndon B. Johnson Nat'l Hist. Site, Texas 302/F7
Lyndon Center, Vt. (05850) 268/C2
Lyndon Station, Wis. (53944) 317/F8
Lyndonville, N.Y. (14098) 276/D4
Lyndonville, Vt. (05851) 268/D2
Lyndora, Pa. (16045) 294/B4
Lyngby, Den. 21/F6
Lynn, Ala. (35575) 194/C2
Lynn (canal), Alaska 196/M1
Lynn, Ark. (72440) 203/H2
Lynn, Ind. (47355) 227/H4
Lynn, Mass. (*01901) 249/D6
Lynn, N.C. (28750) 281/E4
Lynn (co.), Texas 302/C4
Lynn, Wis. (†54436) 317/F6
Lynn Center, Ill. (61262) 222/C2
Lynn Creek, Br. Col. 184/K3
Lynn Creek, Miss. (†39739) 256/G4
Lynndyl, Utah (84640) 304/B4
Lynnfield△, Mass. (01940) 249/D5
Lynnfield Center (Lynnfield P.O.), Mass. (†01940) 249/C5
Lynn Grove, Ky. (42062) 237/E7
Lynn Haven, Fla. (32444) 212/C6
Lynn Lake, 163/F4
Lynn Lake, Man. 179/H2
Lynnview, Ky. (†40201) 237/K4
Lynnville, Ill. (†62650) 222/C4
Lynnville, Ind. (47619) 227/C8
Lynnville, Iowa (50153) 229/H5
Lynnville, Ky. (42063) 237/D7
Lynnville, Tenn. (38472) 237/G10
Lynnwood, Wash. (98036) 310/C3
Lynnwood-Pricedale‡, Pa. (19150) 294/C5
Lynton, 10/E5
Lynton, Eng. 13/D6
Lynwood, Calif. (90262) 204/C11
Lynwood, Ill. (†60411) 222/B3
Lynx (lake), N.W.T. 187/H3
Lynxville, Wis. (54640) 317/D9
Lyon, France, 7/E4
Lyon, France 28/F5
Lyon (co.), Iowa 229/A2
Lyon (co.), Kans. 232/F3
Lyon (co.), Ky. 237/E6
Lyon (co.), Minn. 254/C6
Lyon, Miss. (38645) 256/D2
Lyon (inlet), N.W.T. 187/K3
Lyon (co.), Nev. 266/B3
Lyon (riv.), Scot. 15/H6
Lyon Mountain, N.Y. (12952) 276/N1
Lyons (riv.), Aust. 88/B4
Lyons, Colo. (80540) 208/J2
Lyons, Ga. (30436) 216/H6
Lyons, Ill. (60534) 222/B2
Lyons, Ind. (47443) 227/C7
Lyons, Kans. (67554) 232/D3
Lyons, Ky. (†40051) 237/K5
Lyons, Mich. (48851) 250/E6
Lyons, N.J. (07939) 273/D2
Lyons, N.Y. (14489) 276/F4
Lyons, Nebr. (68038) 264/H3
Lyons (riv.), W. Aust. 92/A4
Lyons, Ohio (43533) 284/B2
Lyons, Oreg. (97358) 291/E3
Lyons (Lyon Station), Pa. (19536) 294/L5
Lyons, S. Dak. (57041) 298/R6
Lyons, Wis. (53148) 317/K10
Lyons Falls, N.Y. (13368) 276/K3
Lyons Plain, Conn. (†06880) 210/B4
Lyon Station, Pa. (19536) 294/L5
Lys (riv.), Belg. 27/B7
Lys (riv.), France 28/E2
Lysá, Czech. 41/C1
Lysaker, Norway 18/D3
Lysander, N.Y. (13094) 276/H4
Lysekil, Sweden 18/G7
Lysite, Wyo. (82642) 319/E2
Lyskovo, U.S.S.R. 52/F3
Lyss, Switz. 39/D2
Lyster, Que. 172/F3
Lysterfield, Vic. 97/K5
Lys'va, U.S.S.R. 48/F4
Lys'va, U.S.S.R. 52/J3
Lytham Saint Anne's, 10/F1
Lytham Saint Anne's, Eng. 13/D4
Lytle, Texas (78052) 302/F8
Lyttelton, N.Z. 101/D5
Lytton, Br. Col. 184/G5
Lytton, Iowa (50561) 229/D4
Lyubotin, U.S.S.R. 52/E4
Lyudinovo, U.S.S.R. 52/D4

M

Ma'ad, Jordan 65/D2
Maalaea, Hawaii (†96753) 218/J2
Maalaea (bay), Hawaii 218/J2
Ma'an, Jordan 59/C3
Ma'an (dist.), Jordan 65/D5
Ma'an, Jordan 65/E5
Maarianhamina (Mariehamn), Fin. 18/M7
Maarssen, Neth. 27/F4
Maas (riv.), Neth. 27/G5
Maasbree, Neth. 27/H6
Maaseik, Belg. 27/H6
Maasin, Phil. 82/E5
Maassluis, Neth. 27/E5
Maastricht, Neth. 27/H7
Mababe (depr.), Botswana 118/C3
Mabalane, Moz. 118/E4
Mabank, Texas (75147) 302/H5
Mabaruma, Guyana 131/B1
Mabel (lake), Br. Col. 184/H5
Mabel, Minn. (55954) 254/G7
Mabel Lake, Br. Col. 184/H5
Mabelvale, Ark. (72103) 203/F4
Maben, Miss. (39750) 256/F3
Maben, W. Va. (25870) 313/D7
Maberly, Ont. 177/H3
Mabie, W. Va. (26278) 313/G5
Mabille (lake), Newf. 166/B3
Mabini, Phil. 82/E6
Mablethorpe and Sutton, 10/G4
Mablethorpe and Sutton, Eng. 13/H4
Mableton, Ga. (30059) 216/C3
Mabote, Moz. 118/E4
Mabou, N.S. 169/G2
Mabou (inlet), N.S. 169/G2
Mabou Highlands (hills), N.S. 169/G2
Mabrouk, Mali 106/D5
Mabscott, W. Va. (25871) 313/D7
Mabton, Wash. (98935) 310/E4
Macá (mt.), Chile 138/D5
Macachín, Arg. 143/D4
Macaé, Braz. 132/F8
Macaé, Braz. 135/F3
Macajalar (bay), Phil. 82/E6
Macalister, Br. Col. 184/F4
MacAlpine (lake), N.W.T. 187/H3
Macamic, Que. 174/B3
Macanao (pen.), Ven. 124/F2
Macao, 3/Q4
Macao, 54/P7
MACAO, 77/H7
Macao (cap.), Macao 77/H7
Mação, Port. 33/B3
Macapá, Braz., 120/E2
Macapá, Braz. 132/D2
Macará, Ec. 128/C5
Macaranaima, Col. 126/E7
Macarena, Serranía de La (mts.), Col. 126/D6
Macareo Santo Niño, Ven. 124/H3
Macarthur, Vic. 97/A6
MacArthur, W. Va. (25873) 313/D7
Macas, Ec. 128/D4
Macau, Braz. 132/G4
Macaúbas, Braz. 132/F6
Macaya (mt.), Haiti 158/A6
Macbeth, S.C. (†29431) 296/H5
Maccan, N.S. 169/D3
Maccarese, Italy 34/F6
Macclenny, Fla. (32063) 212/D1
Maccles (lake), Newf. 166/C1
Macclesfield, 10/G2
Macclesfield, Eng. 13/F4
Macclesfield, N.C. (27852) 281/O3
Macdiarmid, Ont. 177/H5
MacDill A.F.B., Fla. 212/C3
Macdoel, Calif. (96058) 204/D2
Macdonald (lake), Aust. 88/D4
Macdonald, Man. 179/D4
Macdonald (lake), W. Aust. 92/E3
Macdonald (lake), No. Terr. 93/B7
Macdonaldton, Pa. (15530) 294/E6
Macdonnell (ranges), Australia, 87/D8
Macdonnell (ranges), Aust. 88/E4
Macdonnell (ranges), No. Terr. 93/C7
Macdowall, Sask. 181/E2
Macduff, 10/E2
Macduff, Scot. 15/M4
Mace, Ind. (†47933) 227/D4
Mace, W. Va. (26279) 313/F6
Macedon, N.Y. (14502) 276/F4
Macedonia, Ark. (†71753) 203/D7
Macedonia, Conn. (†06757) 210/A2
Macedonia (reg.), Greece 45/F5
Macedonia, Ill. (62860) 222/E5
Macedonia, Iowa (51549) 229/C6
Macedonia, Ohio (44056) 284/J10
Macedonia (rep.), Yugo. 45/E5
Maceió, Braz., 120/G3
Maceió, Braz. 132/H5
Macel, Miss. (†38950) 256/D3
Macenta, Guinea 106/C7
Maceo, Cuba 158/H3
Maceo, Ky. (42355) 237/H5
Macerata (prov.), Italy 34/D3
Macerata, Italy 34/D3
Maces (bay), N. Br. 170/D3
Maces Bay, N. Br. 170/D3
Macfarlan, W. Va. (26148) 313/D4
Macfarlane (lake), S. Aust. 94/E5
Macgillicuddy's Reeks (mts.), Ire. 17/B7
MacGregor, Man. 179/D5
Mach, Pak. 59/J4
Mach, Pak. 68/B3
Macha, Bol. 136/B6
Machacamarca, Bol. 136/B5
Machachi, Ec. 128/C3
Machado, Braz. 135/C2
Machakos, Kenya 115/G4
Machala, Ec. 128/B4
Machalí, Chile 138/G5
Machalilla, Ec. 128/B3
Machaneng, Botswana 118/D4
Machanga, Moz. 118/F4
Machareti, Bol. 136/D7
Machattie (lake), Queens. 95/B5
Machaze, Moz. 118/E4
Machelen, Belg. 27/C9
Machens, Mo. (†63373) 261/P2
Machias△, Maine (04654) 242/J6
Machias, Maine (04654) 242/J6
Machias (bay), Maine 242/J6
Machias (riv.), Maine 242/F2
Machias (riv.), Maine 242/H6
Machias, N.Y. (14101) 276/D6
Machiasport△, Maine (04655) 242/H6
Machiasport, Maine (04655) 242/H6
Machias Seal (isl.), Maine 242/J7
Machico, Port. 33/A2
Machida, Japan 81/O2
Machilipatnam, India, 54/M8
Machilipatnam, India 68/E5
Machipongo, Va. (23405) 307/S6
Machiques, Ven. 124/B3
Macho, Arroyo del (creek), N. Mex. 274/D5
Ma Chu (riv.), China 77/E5
Machupicchu, Peru 128/F9
Machupo (riv.), Bol. 136/C3
Machynlleth, 10/D4
Machynlleth, Wales 13/D5
Macia, Moz. 118/E4
Maciel, Arg. 143/F6
Maciel, Par. 144/D6
Maciel, Arroyo (riv.), Urug. 145/C4
Macina (depr.), Mali 106/D6
Macintyre (riv.), N.S.W. 97/E1
Macintyre (riv.), Queens. 95/D6
Mack, Colo. (81525) 208/B4
Mack, Ohio (†45202) 284/B9
Mackay, Australia, 87/F8
Mackay (lake), Australia, 87/D8
MacKay, Alta. 182/C3
MacKay (riv.), Alta. 182/D1
Mackay (lake), Aust. 88/E4
Mackay, Aust. 88/H4
Mackay, Idaho (83251) 220/E6
Mackay (res.), Idaho 220/E6
MacKay (lake), N.W.T. 187/G3
Mackay (lake), W. Aust. 92/E3
Mackay (lake), No. Terr. 93/A7
Mackay, Queens. 95/D4
Mackay North, Queens. 95/D4
Mackenzie (riv.), 163/C2
Mackenzie (bay), 163/C2
Mackenzie (dist.), 163/E3
Mackenzie (bay), Ant. 5/C4
Mackenzie, Br. Col. 184/F2
Mackenzie (riv.), Canada, 3/C2
Mackenzie (bay), Canada, 4/B16
Mackenzie (mts.), Canada, 4/C16
Mackenzie (river), Canada, 4/C16
Mackenzie (riv.), Canada, 146/E3
Mackenzie‡, Mo. (†63101) 261/P3
Mackenzie (dist.), N.W.T. 187/G3
Mackenzie (bay), N.W.T. 187/E3
Mackenzie (mts.), N.W.T. 187/E3
Mackenzie (riv.), N.W.T. 187/F3
Mackenzie (lake), Newf. 166/B3
Mackenzie (bay), Yukon 187/E3
Mackenzie (mts.), Yukon 187/E3
Mackenzie Highway, Alta. 182/B1
Mackenzie King (isl.), 163/M3
Mackenzie King (isl.), Canada, 4/B15
Mackenzie King (isl.), N.W.T. 187/G2
Mackey, Ind. (47554) 227/C8
Mackeys, N.C. (27951) 281/R3
Mackeyville, Pa. (17750) 294/H3
Mackinac (co.), Mich. 250/D2
Mackinac (isl.), Mich. 250/E3
Mackinac (str.), Mich. 250/E3
Mackinac Island, Mich. (49757) 250/E3
Mackinaw, Ill. (61755) 222/D3
Mackinaw (riv.), Ill. 222/E3
Mackinaw City, Mich. (49701) 250/E3
Macklin, Sask. 181/A3
Macks, Ark. (72113) 203/H2
Macksburg, Iowa (50155) 229/E6
Macksburg, Ohio (45746) 284/G6
Macks Creek, Mo. (65786) 261/G7
Macks Inn, Idaho (83433) 220/G5
Macksville, Kans. (67557) 232/D4
Macksville, N.S.W. 97/G2
Mackville, Ky. (40040) 237/L5
Maclean, N.S.W. 97/G1
Maclean (str.), N.W.T. 187/H2
Maclear, S. Africa 118/D6
Maclear (cape), S. Africa 118/F7
Macmillan (pass), N.W.T. 187/F3
Macmillan (pass), Yukon 187/F3
Macmillan (riv.), Yukon 187/E3
Macnean (lake), Ire. 17/F3
Macnean (lake), N. Ire. 17/F3
MacNutt, Sask. 181/K4
Macomb, Ill. (61455) 222/C3
Macomb (co.), Mich. 250/G6
Macomb, Okla. (74852) 288/M4
Macomer, Italy 34/B4
Macomia, Moz. 118/F2
Macon (co.), Ala. 194/G6
Mâcon, France 28/F4
Macon, Ga., 146/K6
Macon, Ga., 188/K4
Macon (co.), Ga. 216/D6
Macon, Ga. (*31201) 216/E5
Macon (co.), Ill. 222/E4
Macon, Ill. (62544) 222/E4
Macon (bayou), La. 238/H1
Macon, Miss. (39341) 256/G4
Macon (co.), Mo. 261/G3
Macon, Mo. (63552) 261/H3
Macon (co.), N.C. 281/B4
Macon, N.C. (27551) 281/N2
Macon, Nebr. (†68939) 264/E4
Macon, Ohio (45143) 284/C8
Macon (co.), Tenn. 237/J7
Macon, Tenn. (38048) 237/B10
Macondo, Angola 115/D6
Macorís (cape), Dom. Rep. 158/E5
Macotera, Spain 33/D2
Macouba, Mart. 161/C5
Macoun, Sask. 181/H6
Macoupin (co.), Ill. 222/D4
Macoupin (riv.), Ill. 222/C4
Macouria (Tonate), Fr. Gui. 131/E3
Macquarie (harb.), Aust. 88/G8
Macquarie (lake), N.S.W. 97/F3
Macquarie (riv.), N.S.W. 97/D2
Macquarie (harb.), Tasmania 99/B4
Mac-Robertson Land (reg.), Ant. 5/B4
Macroom, 10/B5
Macroom, Ire. 17/C8
Macrorie, Sask. 181/E4
Mactan (isl.), Phil. 82/E5
MacTier, Ont. 177/E2
Macumba (riv.), Aust. 88/F5
Macumba, The (riv.), S. Aust. 94/E2
Macungie, Pa. (18062) 294/L4
Macurijes (pt.), Cuba 158/F3
Macuro, Ven. 124/H2
Macusani, Peru 128/G10
Macuspana, Mex. 150/N8
Macuto, Ven. 124/E2
Macwahoc△, Maine (†04451) 242/G4
Macworth, Sask. 181/E6
Macy, Ind. (46951) 227/E3
Macy, Nebr. (68039) 264/H2
Mad (riv.), Calif. 204/B3
Mad (riv.), Conn. 210/C1
Mad (riv.), Conn. 210/C2
Mad (riv.), N.H. 268/D4
Mad (riv.), Ohio 284/C6
Mad (riv.), Vt. 268/B3
Ma'daba, Jordan 65/D4
Madadi, Chad 111/D4
Madagascal (pond), Maine 242/G5
Madagascar (isl.), 102/G7
Madagascar (isl.), Malag. Rep. 118/G4
Madaket, Mass. (†02554) 249/N7
Madama, Niger 106/G4
Madame (isl.), N.S. 169/H3
Madang, Terr. N.G. 85/B7
Madang, Terr. N.G. 86/F6
Madaoua, Niger 106/F6
Madaras, Hung. 41/E3
Madaripur, Pak. 68/G4
Madauk, Burma 72/C3
Madawaska, Ont. 177/F2
Madawaska (riv.), Ont. 177/G2
Madawaska△, Maine (04756) 242/G1
Madawaska, Maine (04756) 242/G1
Madawaska (co.), N. Br. 170/B1
Madawaska (riv.), N. Br. 170/B1
Madbury△, N.H. (†03820) 268/F5
Maddela, Phil. 82/C2
Madden, Alta. 182/C4
Madden, Miss. (39109) 256/F5
Maddock, N. Dak. (58348) 283/L4
Maddy (inlet), Scot. 15/B4
Madeira (riv.), Braz., 3/F6
Madeira (riv.), Braz., 120/D3
Madeira (riv.), Braz. 132/A4
Madeira (isl.), 102/A1
Madeira (isls.), 102/A1
Madeira, Ohio (45243) 284/C9
Madeira (isls.), Port., 3/H4
Madeira (isl.), Port. 33/A2
Madeira (prov.), Port. 33/A2
Madeira (isl.), Port. 33/A2
Madeira (isls.), Port. 106/A2
Madeira (isl.), Port. 106/A2
Madeira Beach, Fla. (33738) 212/B3
Madeira Park, Br. Col. 184/E5
Madeleine (cape), Que. 172/D1
Madelia, Minn. (56062) 254/D6
Madeline, Calif. (96119) 204/E2
Madeline (isl.), Wis. 317/E2
Maden, Turkey 63/H3
Madera (co.), Calif. 204/F6
Madera, Calif. (93637) 204/E7
Madera, Mex. 150/F2
Madera, Pa. (16661) 294/F4
Madera Canyon, Ariz. (†85637) 198/E7
Madh, India 68/B7
Madhubani, India 68/F3
Madhya Pradesh (state), India 68/D4
Madidi (riv.), Bol. 136/A3
Madill, Okla. (73446) 288/N6
Madimba, Dem. Rep. of the Congo. 115/C5
Madinat ash Sha'b (cap.), P.D.R. Yemen 59/E7
Madinat ash Sha'b (cap.), P.D.R. Yemen, 54/H8
Madingo, Rep. of Congo 115/B4
Madingou, Rep. of Congo 115/B4
Madirovalo, Malag. Rep. 118/H3
Madison (co.), Ala. 194/E1
Madison, Ala. (35758) 194/E1
Madison (co.), Ark. 203/C1
Madison, Ark. (72359) 203/J4
Madison, Calif. (95653) 204/D5
Madison△, Conn. (06443) 210/E3
Madison, Conn. (06443) 210/E3
Madison (co.), Fla. 212/C1
Madison, Fla. (32340) 212/C1
Madison (co.), Ga. 216/F2
Madison, Ga. (30650) 216/F3
Madison (co.), Idaho 220/G6
Madison (co.), Ill. 222/D5
Madison, Ill. (62060) 222/B6
Madison (co.), Ind. 227/F4
Madison, Ind. (47250) 227/G7
Madison (co.), Iowa 229/E6
Madison, Kans. (66860) 232/F3
Madison (co.), Ky. 237/N5
Madison (par.), La. 238/H2
Madison△, Maine (04950) 242/D6
Madison, Maine (04950) 242/D6
Madison, Md. (21648) 245/O6
Madison, Minn. (56256) 254/B5
Madison (co.), Miss. 256/D5
Madison, Miss. (39110) 256/D6
Madison (co.), Mo. 261/M8
Madison, Mo. (65263) 261/H4
Madison (co.), Mont. 262/D5
Madison (riv.), Mont. 262/E5
Madison (co.), N.C. 281/D3
Madison, N.C. (27025) 281/J2
Madison△, N.H. (03849) 268/E4
Madison, N.H. (03849) 268/E4
Madison (mt.), N.H. 268/E3
Madison, N.J. (07940) 273/E2
Madison (co.), N.Y. 276/J5
Madison, N.Y. (13402) 276/J5
Madison (co.), Nebr. 264/G3
Madison, Nebr. (68748) 264/G3
Madison (co.), Ohio 284/D6
Madison, Ohio (44057) 284/H2
Madison‡, Pa. (15663) 294/C5
Madison, S.C. (29660) 296/B2
Madison‡, S.C. (†29829) 296/D4
Madison, S. Dak. (57042) 298/P6
Madison (lake), S. Dak. 298/P6
Madison, Sask. 181/B4
Madison (co.), Tenn. 237/D9
Madison, Tenn. (37115) 237/H8
Madison (co.), Texas 302/J6
Madison (co.), Va. 307/M4
Madison, Va. (22727) 307/M4
Madison, W. Va. (25130) 313/C6
Madison (cap.), Wis., 146/K5
Madison (cap.), Wis., 188/H2
Madison (cap.), Wis. (*53701) 317/H9
Madison, Wyo. (†82190) 319/B1
Madison (plat.), Wyo. 319/B1
Madisonburg, Ohio (†44691) 284/G4
Madison Heights, Mich. (48071) 250/F6
Madison Heights, Va. (24572) 307/K6
Madison Lake, Minn. (56063) 254/E6
Madison Mills, Ohio (†43143) 284/D6
Madisonville, Ky. (42431) 237/F6
Madisonville, La. (70447) 238/K6
Madisonville, Tenn. (37354) 237/N9
Madisonville, Texas (77864) 302/J7
Madiun, Indon. 85/K2
Madjalengka, Indon. 85/H2
Madjene, Indon. 85/F6
Madley, Eng. 13/E5
Madley (mt.), W. Aust. 92/D4
Madoc, Ont. 177/G3
Madoc, Mont. (†59222) 262/L2
Madona, U.S.S.R. 52/C3
Madona, U.S.S.R. 53/C2
Madone (mt.), Switz. 39/F4
Madonna, Md. (†21161) 245/M2
Madraka, Ras (cape), Oman 59/G6
Madran, N. Br. 170/E1
Madras, India, 3/P5
Madras, India, 54/M8
Madras, India 68/E6
Madras, Oreg. (97741) 291/F3
Madre (lag.), Mex. 150/L4
Madre (lag.), Texas, 188/G5
Madre (lag.), Texas 302/G11
Madre de Dios (riv.), Bol. 136/A3
Madre de Dios (isl.), Chile, 120/C8
Madre de Dios (isl.), Chile 138/D8
Madre de Dios (riv.), Peru 128/G8
Madre de Dios, Peru 128/G9
Madre de Dios (riv.), Peru 128/G9
Madre del Sur, Sierra (mts.), Mex. 150/K8
Madre Occidental (mts.), Mex., 146/H7
Madre Occidental, Sierra (mts.), Mex. 150/F3
Madre Oriental, Sierra (mts.), Mex. 150/J4
Madrid, Ala. (36348) 194/H8
Madrid, Iowa (50156) 229/F5
Madrid△, Maine (†04966) 242/B6
Madrid, N. Mex. (†87010) 274/C3
Madrid, N.Y. (13660) 276/K1
Madrid, Nebr. (69150) 264/C4
Madrid (cap.), Spain, 3/J4
Madrid (cap.), Spain, 7/D4
Madrid (prov.), Spain 33/E2
Madrid (cap.), Spain 33/F4
Madridejos, Spain 33/E3
Madrigal de las Altas Torres, Spain 33/D2
Madrigalejo, Spain 33/D3
Madrisahorn (mt.), Switz. 39/J3
Madroñera, Spain 33/D3
Madugula, India 68/E5
Madura (Madurai), India, 54/L9
Madura (isl.), Indon., 54/P10
Madura (isl.), Indon. 85/K2
Madura (str.), Indon. 85/K2
Madura, W. Aust. 92/D5
Madurai, India, 54/L9
Madurai, India 68/D7
Madvar, Kuh-i- (mt.), Iran 59/F3
Madvar, Kuh-i- (mt.), Iran 66/F3
Maebashi, Japan 81/J5
Mae Hong Son, Thai. 72/C3
Mae Klong, Mae Nam (riv.), Thai. 72/C4
Mael, Norway 18/F6
Maella, Spain 33/G2
Maerhkang, China 77/F5
Maeser, Utah (†84078) 304/E3
Maestra, Sierra (mts.), Cuba 158/H4
Maevatanana, 102/G6
Maevatanana, Malag. Rep. 118/H3
Maeystown, Ill. (62256) 222/C5
Mafeking, Man. 179/B2
Mafeking, 102/E7
Mafeking, S. Africa 118/C5
Mafeteng, Lesotho 118/D5
Maffin (bay), Indon. 85/K6
Maffra, Vic. 97/D5
Mafia (isl.), 102/G5
Mafia (isl.), Tanz. 115/H5
Mafra, Braz. 132/D9
Mafra, Port. 33/B3
Magadan, U.S.S.R. 48/P4
Magadan, U.S.S.R., 3/S3
Magadan, U.S.S.R., 54/U3
Magadi, Kenya 115/G4
Magaguadavic, N. Br. 170/C3
Magaguadavic (lake), N. Br. 170/C3
Magaguadavic (riv.), N. Br. 170/C3
Magalia, Calif. (95954) 204/D4
Magalie, Sur. 131/D4
Magaliesburg, S. Africa 118/G6
Magallanes (prov.), Chile 138/E10
Magallanes (Magellan) (str.), Chile 138/D10
Magallanes, Phil. 82/D4
Magallenes (Magellan) (str.), Arg. 143/C7
Magangué, Col. 126/C3
Mağara, Turkey 63/G3
Magarabomba, Cuba 158/G2
Magaria, Niger 106/F6
Magariños, Par. 144/B4
Magazine, Ark. (72943) 203/C3
Magazine (mt.), Ark. 203/C3
Magdagachi, U.S.S.R. 48/N4
Magdala, Eth. 111/G5
Magdalen (isls.), 163/K6
Magdalena, Arg. 143/H7
Magdalena, Bol. 136/C3
Magdalena (isl.), Chile 138/D5
Magdalena (riv.), Col., 120/C2
Magdalena (riv.), Col. 126/C3
Magdalena (dept.), Col. 126/D3
Magdalena, Mex. 150/D1
Magdalena (bay), Mex. 150/C4
Magdalena, N. Mex. (87825) 274/B4
Magdalena (mts.), N. Mex. 274/B4
Magdeburg, E. Ger., 7/F3
Magdeburg (dist.), E. Ger. 22/D2
Magdeburg, E. Ger. 22/D2
Magdelaine (cays), Aust. 88/J3
Magé, Braz. 135/E3
Magee, Miss. (39111) 256/E7
Magee, Island (pen.), N. Ire. 17/K2
Magelang, Indon. 85/J2
Magellan (str.), 3/F8
Magellan (str.), 120/D8
Magellan (str.), Arg. 143/C7
Magellan (str.), Chile 138/D10
Magen, Israel 65/A5
Magens (bay), V.I.(U.S.) 161/B4
Magerøy (isl.), Norway 18/P1
Magerrain (mt.), Switz. 39/H2
Magetan, Indon. 85/K2
Maggia, Switz. 39/G4
Maggia (riv.), Switz. 39/G4
Maggie, N.C. (28751) 281/C3
Maggiore (lake), Fla. 212/B3
Maggiore (lake), Italy 34/B1
Maggiore (lake), Switz. 39/G5
Maggotty, Jam. 158/H6
Maghâgha, U.A.R. 59/B4
Maghâgha, U.A.R. 111/J4
Maghama, Mauritania 106/B5
Maghera, N. Ire. 17/H2
Magherafelt, N. Ire. 17/H2
Magherafelt, 10/C3
Magic (res.), Idaho 220/D6
Magilligan (pt.), N. Ire. 17/H1
Maglaj, Yugo. 45/D3
Magley, Ind. (†46733) 227/G3
Maglie, Italy 34/G4
Magna, Utah (84044) 304/B3
Magna Bay, Br. Col. 184/H4
Magness, Ark. (72553) 203/H2
Magnet, Ark. (†72104) 203/E5
Magnet, Ind. (47555) 227/D8
Magnet, Man. 179/C3
Magnet, Nebr. (68749) 264/G2
Magnetawan, Ont. 177/E2
Magnetawan (riv.), Ont. 177/D2
Magnetic Springs, Ohio (43036) 284/D5
Magnitogorsk, U.S.S.R. 48/G4
Magnitogorsk, U.S.S.R., 54/J4
Magnolia, Ala. (36754) 194/C6
Magnolia, Ark. (71753) 203/D7
Magnolia, Del. (19962) 245/R4
Magnolia, Ill. (61336) 222/D2
Magnolia, Iowa (51550) 229/B5
Magnolia, Minn. (56158) 254/B7
Magnolia, Miss. (39652) 256/D8
Magnolia, N.C. (28453) 281/O5
Magnolia, N.J. (08049) 273/B3
Magnolia, Ohio (44643) 284/H4
Magnolia, Texas (77355) 302/J7
Magnolia, W. Va. (†25422) 313/K3

Market Weighton 397

Manitou (lake), Ont. 177/C2
Manitou, Ky. (42436) 237/F6
Manitou, Man. 179/D5
Manitou (isl.), Mich. 250/B1
Manitou, Minn. (56656) 254/D2
Manitou, N. Dak. (†58776) 283/E3
Manitou, Okla. (73555) 288/J5
Manitou Beach, Sask. 181/F4
Manitou Beach-Devils Lake‡, Mich. (49253) 250/E7
Manitoulin (isl.), 163/H6
Manitoulin (co.), Ont. 175/D3
Manitoulin (isl.), Ont. 175/D3
Manitoulin (co.), Ont. 177/B2
Manitoulin (isl.), Ont. 177/B2
Manitou Springs, Colo. (80829) 208/J5
Manitouwadge, Ont. 175/C3
Manitouwadge, Ont. 177/H5
Manitowaning, Ont. 177/C2
Manitowish, Wis. (†54547) 317/F3
Manitowoc (co.), Wis. 317/L7
Manitowoc, Wis. (54220) 317/L7
Maniwaki, Que. 172/B3
Maniwaki, Que. 174/B3
Manizales, Col., 120/C2
Manizales, Col. 126/C5
Manja, Malag. Rep. 118/G4
Manja, Jordan 65/D4
Manjacaze, Moz. 118/E5
Manjimup, W. Aust. 92/B6
Mankato, Kans. (66956) 232/D2
Mankato, Minn., 188/H2
Mankato, Minn. (56001) 254/E6
Mankota, Sask. 181/D6
Mankoya, Zambia 115/D6
Manley, Nebr. (68403) 264/H4
Manley Hot Springs, Alaska (99756) 196/H2
Manlius, Ill. (61338) 222/D2
Manlius, N.Y. (13104) 276/J5
Manlleu, Spain 33/H1
Manly, Aust. 88/L3
Manly, Aust. 88/K2
Manly, Iowa (50456) 229/G2
Manly, N.C. (†28387) 281/L4
Manly, N.S.W. 97/K3
Manmad, India 68/C4
Manmanoc (mt.), Phil. 82/C2
Mann (riv.), No. Terr. 93/D2
Manna, Indon. 85/C6
Mannahill, S. Aust. 94/F5
Mannar (gulf), 54/L9
Mannar, Ceylon 68/E7
Mannar (gulf), Ceylon 68/D7
Mannar (gulf), India 68/D7
Mannargudi, India 68/E6
Mannboro, Va. (23105) 307/N6
Männedorf, Switz. 39/G2
Mannersdorf, Austria 41/D3
Manners Sutton, N. Br. 170/D3
Mannford, Okla. (74044) 288/O2
Mannheim, W. Ger., 7/E4
Mannheim, W. Ger. 22/C4
Manning, Alta. 182/B1
Manning, Ark. (71757) 203/E5
Manning, E.C., Prov. Park, Br. Col. 184/G5
Manning, Iowa (51455) 229/C5
Manning, Kans. (†67871) 232/B3
Manning, N. Dak. (58642) 283/E5
Manning (riv.), N.S.W. 97/F2
Manning (cape), N.W.T. 187/F2
Manning (Wanning), China 77/H8
Manning, S.C. (29102) 296/G4
Mannington, Ky. (42260) 237/G6
Mannington, W. Va. (26582) 313/F3
Männlifluh (mt.), Switz. 39/E3
Manns Choice, Pa. (15550) 294/E6
Manns Harbor, N.C. (27953) 281/T3
Mannsville, Ky. (42758) 237/L6
Mannsville, N.Y. (13661) 276/H3
Mannsville, Okla. (73447) 288/N6
Mannu (riv.), Italy 34/B5
Mannum, S. Aust. 94/F6
Mannville, Alta. 182/E3
Mano (riv.), Liberia 106/B7
Mano (riv.), S. Leone 106/B7
Manoa, Bol. 136/C1
Manokin, Md. (21836) 245/P8
Manokin (riv.), Md. 245/P8
Manokotak, Alaska (99628) 196/G3
Manokwari, Indon. 85/J6
Manola, Alta. 182/C2
Manombo, Malag. Rep. 118/G4
Manomet, Mass. (02345) 249/M5
Manomet (pt.), Mass. 249/N5
Manono, Dem. Rep. of the Congo. 115/E5
Manor, Ga. (31550) 216/G8
Manor, Pa. (15665) 294/C5
Manor, Sask. 181/K6
Manor, Texas (78653) 302/G7
Manorhamilton, Ire. 17/E3
Manorhaven‡, N.Y. (†11050) 276/R7
Manori, India 68/B6
Manori (creek), India 68/B7
Manorville, N.Y. (11949) 276/P9
Manorville, Pa. (16238) 294/C4
Manosque, France 28/G6
Manotick, Ont. 177/J2
Manouane (lake), Que. 174/C2
Manp'o, N. Korea 81/B3
Manquin, Va. (23106) 307/O5
Manra (Sydney) (isl.), Gilb. and Ell., 87/K6
Manresa, Spain 33/G2
Mansa, 102/E6
Mansa, Zambia 115/E6
Mansalay, Phil. 82/C4
Mansavillagra, Urug. 145/D4
Manseau, Que. 172/E3
Mansel (isl.), 163/H3
Mansel (isl.), N.W.T., 146/K3
Mansel (isl.), N.W.T. 187/K3
Mansel'ka (mts.), U.S.S.R. 52/C1
Mansfield, 10/F4
Mansfield, Ark. (72944) 203/B3
MansfieldΔ, Conn. (†06250) 210/F1
Mansfield, Eng. 13/F4
Mansfield, Ga. (30255) 216/E4
Mansfield, Ill. (61854) 222/E3
Mansfield, Ind. (†47872) 227/C5
Mansfield (res.), Ind. 227/C5
Mansfield, La. (71052) 238/C2
MansfieldΔ, Mass. (02048) 249/J4
Mansfield, Mass. (02048) 249/J4
Mansfield, Minn. (†56009) 254/E7
Mansfield, Mo. (65704) 261/G8
Mansfield, Ohio, 188/K2
Mansfield, Ohio (*44901) 284/F4
Mansfield, Pa. (16933) 294/H2
Mansfield, S. Dak. (57460) 298/N3
Mansfield, Tenn. (38236) 237/E8
Mansfield, Texas (76063) 302/F2
Mansfield, Vic. 97/D5
Mansfield (mt.), Vt. 268/B2
Mansfield, Wash. (98830) 310/F3
Mansfield Center, Conn. (06250) 210/G1
Mansfield Depot, Conn. (06251) 210/F1
Mansilla de las Mulas, Spain 33/D1
Manso (riv.), Braz. 132/C6
Manso (riv.), Chile 138/E4
Manson, Ind. (†46041) 227/D4
Manson, Iowa (50563) 229/D3
Manson, Man. 179/A4
Manson, N.C. (27553) 281/N2
Manson, Wash. (98831) 310/E3
Manson Creek, Br. Col. 184/E2
Mansonville, Que. 172/E4
Mansura, La. (71350) 238/G4
Manta, Ec., 120/B3
Manta, Ec. 128/B3
Manta (bay), Ec. 128/B3
Mantachie, Miss. (38855) 256/H2
Mantador, N. Dak. (58058) 283/R7
Mantagao (lake), Man. 179/E3
Mantagao (riv.), Man. 179/E3
Mantalingajan (mt.), Phil. 82/A6
Mantario, Sask. 181/B4
Mantaro (riv.), Peru 128/E8
Mantas (well), Niger 106/E5
Manteca, Calif. (95336) 204/D6
Mantecal, Apure, Ven. 124/D4
Mantecal, Bolívar, Ven. 124/F4
Mantee, Miss. (39751) 256/F3
Manteigas, Port. 33/C2
Manteno, Ill. (60950) 222/F2
Manteo, N.C. (27954) 281/T3
Manter, Kans. (67862) 232/A4
Mantes-la-Jolie, France 28/D3
Manti, Utah (84642) 304/C4
Mantiqueira (range), Braz. 135/D3
Manto, Hond. 154/D3
Mantoloking, N.J. (08738) 273/E3
Manton, Calif. (96059) 204/D3
Manton, Mich. (49663) 250/D4
Manton, R.I. (†02904) 249/J5
Mantorville, Minn. (55955) 254/F6
Mänttä, Fin. 18/O6
Mantua, Ala. (35472) 194/C4
Mantua, Cuba 158/A2
Mantua (prov.), Italy 34/C2
Mantua, Italy 34/C2
Mantua, N.J. (08051) 273/C4
Mantua, Ohio (44255) 284/H3
Mantua, Utah (†84302) 304/C2
Mantua‡, Va. (†22030) 307/O3
Manturovo, U.S.S.R. 52/F3
Manú, Peru 128/G9
Manú (riv.), Peru 128/G8
Manua (isls.), Amer. Samoa, 87/K7
Manuae (atoll), Cook Is., 87/L7
Manucho, Arg. 143/F5
Manuel Benavides, Mex. 150/H2
Manuelito, N. Mex. (87318) 274/A3
Manuel Rodríguez (isl.), Chile 138/D10
Manuels, N. Br. 170/F1
Manui (isl.), Indon. 85/G6
Manukan, Phil. 82/D6
Manukau, N.Z. 101/C1
Manukau (harb.), N.Z. 101/B1
Manulla, Ire. 17/C4
Manumuskin (riv.), N.J. 273/D5
Manunui, N.Z. 101/E3
Manuripi (riv.), Bol. 136/B2
Manus (isl.), Terr. N.G., 87/E6
Manutuke, N.Z. 101/F3
Manvel, N. Dak. (58256) 283/R3
Manvel, Texas (77578) 302/J3
Manville, N.J. (08835) 273/D2
Manville, R.I. (02838) 249/H5
Manville, Wyo. (82227) 319/H3
Many, La. (71449) 238/C3
Manyara (lake), Tanz. 115/G4
Manyas (lake), Turkey 63/B2
Manyberries, Alta. 182/E5
Manych-Gudilo (lake), U.S.S.R. 52/F5
Many Farms, Ariz. (86503) 198/F2
Manyoni, 102/F5
Manyoni, Tanz. 115/G5
Manzai, Pak. 59/K3
Manzanar, Chile 138/F2
Manzanares, Spain 33/E3
Manzanares (riv.), Spain 33/F4
Manzanillo, Cuba 156/C2
Manzanillo, Cuba 158/H4
Manzanillo (bay), Dom. Rep. 158/A2
Manzanillo (bay), Haiti 158/C5
Manzanillo, Mex., 146/H8
Manzanillo, Mex. 150/G7
Manzanillo (pt.), Pan. 154/H6
Manzanita, Oreg. (97130) 291/C2
Manzanita Ind. Res., Calif. 204/J11
Manzano, N. Mex. (†87016) 274/C4
Manzano (mts.), N. Mex. 274/C4
Manzano (peak), N. Mex. 274/C4
Manzanola, Colo. (81058) 208/M6
Manzini, Swaz. 118/E5
Mao, Chad 111/C5
Mao, 102/D3
Maoke (mts.), Indon. 85/K6
Mapai, Moz. 118/E4
Mapararí, Ven. 124/D2
Mapastepec, Mex. 150/N9
Mapes, N. Dak. (58349) 283/O3
Mapia (isls.), Indon. 85/J5
Mapimí, Mex. 150/G4
Mapimí (depr.), Mex. 150/G3
Mapire, Ven. 124/F4
Mapiri, Bol. 136/B4
Mapiripán (lag.), Col. 126/E6
Maple (peak), Ariz. 198/F5
Maple, Ont. 177/J4
Maple (riv.), Mich. 250/E5
Maple (lake), Minn. 254/B3
Maple (riv.), Minn. 254/E7
Maple (riv.), N. Dak. 283/O8
Maple (riv.), N. Dak. 283/R6
Maple (riv.), S. Dak. 298/M1
Maple (creek), Sask. 181/B5
Maple, Wis. (54854) 317/C2
Maple Bay, Br. Col. 184/J3
Maple Bay, Minn. (†56736) 254/B3
Maple Bluff‡, Wis. (†53701) 317/H9
Maple City, Kans. (67102) 232/F4
Maple City, Mich. (49664) 250/D4
Maple Creek, 163/F6
Maple Creek, Sask. 181/B6
Maple Falls, Wash. (98266) 310/D2
Maple Grove, Que. 172/H4
Maple Grove, Ont. 177/F4
Maple Grove, Minn. (†55369) 254/F5
Maple Heights, Ohio (44137) 284/H9
Maple Hill, Iowa (50564) 229/D2
Maple Hill, Kans. (66507) 232/F2
Maple Hill, N.C. (28454) 281/O5
Maple Island, Minn. (†55082) 254/E7
Maple Lake, Minn. (55358) 254/D5
Maple Park, Ill. (60151) 222/E2
Maple Plain, Minn. (55359) 254/F5
Maple Rapids, Mich. (48853) 250/E5
Maple River, Iowa (†51401) 229/D4
Maples, Ind. (†46802) 227/H2
Maples, Mo. (†65542) 261/J7
Maple ShadeΔ, N.J. (08052) 273/B3
Maplesville, Ala. (36750) 194/E5
Mapleton‡, Ill. (61547) 222/D3
Mapleton, Iowa (51034) 229/B4
Mapleton, Kans. (66754) 232/H3
MapletonΔ, Maine (04757) 242/G2
Mapleton, Mich. (†49684) 250/D4
Mapleton, Minn. (56065) 254/E7
Mapleton, N.C. (†27855) 281/P2
Mapleton, N. Dak. (58059) 283/R6
Mapleton, Oreg. (97453) 291/C3
Mapleton (Mapleton Depot), Pa. (17052) 294/F5
Mapleton, Utah (†84663) 304/C3
Mapleton, Wis. (†53066) 317/J1
Mapleton Depot, Pa. (17052) 294/F5
Maple Valley, Wash. (98038) 310/C3
Mapleview, Minn. (†55912) 254/E7
Mapleview, N. Br. 170/C2
Mapleville, Md. (†21713) 245/H2
Mapleville, R.I. (02839) 249/H5
Maplewood, La. (70663) 238/D6
Maplewood, Minn. (55109) 254/G5
Maplewood, Mo. (63143) 261/P3
Maplewood, N.H. (†03574) 268/D3
MaplewoodΔ, N.J. (07040) 273/E2
Maplewood, Ohio (45340) 284/B5
Maplewood, Wis. (54226) 317/M6
Mapocho (riv.), Chile 138/G3
Mapoon Mission Station, Queens. 95/B1
Maporal, Ven. 124/C4
Mapova, Alta. 182/D2
Mappsville, Va. (23407) 307/T5
Mapuera (riv.), Braz., 120/E3
Mapuera (riv.), Braz. 132/B3
Maqatin, P.D.R. Yemen 59/E7
Maqil, Iraq 66/E5
Maqna, Saudi Ar. 59/C4
Maquapit (lake), N. Br. 170/D3
Maqueda (chan.), Phil. 82/D3
Maquela do Zombo, Angola 115/C5
Maquela do Zombo, 102/D5
Maquereau (pt.), Que. 172/D2
Maquinchao, Arg. 143/C5
Maquoketa, Iowa (52060) 229/M4
Maquon, Ill. (61458) 222/C3
Mar (mts.), Braz., 120/F5
Mar (range), Braz. 132/E9
Mar (range), Braz. 135/C4
Mar (dist.), Scot. 15/L5
Mara, Br. Col. 184/H5
Mara, Guyana 131/C2
Mara (reg.), Tanz. 115/F3
Mara (reg.), Tanz. 115/F3
Marabá, Braz. 120/E3
Marabá, Braz. 132/D4
Marabahan, Indon. 85/E6
Marabella, Trinidad Tobago 161/A11
Maracá (isl.), Braz., 120/F2
Maracá (isl.), Braz. 132/D2
Maracaibo (lake), Ven., 120/C2
Maracaibo, Ven., 120/C1
Maracaibo, Ven. 124/C2
Maracaibo (lake), Ven. 124/C3
Maracaju, Braz. 132/C8
Maracay, Ven. 124/E2
Marada, Libya 111/C2
Maradi, Niger 106/F6
Maragheh, Iran 59/E2
Maragheh, Iran 66/E2
Maragogipe, Braz. 132/G6
Maraira (pt.), Phil. 82/C1
Marais des Cygnes (riv.), Kans. 232/H3
Marajó (isl.), Braz., 120/F3
Marajó (bay), Braz. 132/E2
Marajó (isl.), Braz. 132/D3
Maralal, Kenya 115/G3
Maralbashi, China 77/A4
Maralinga and Woomera, Aust. 88/E5
Maralinga and Woomera, S. Aust. 94/B3
Maramag, Phil. 82/E7
Maramec, Okla. (74045) 288/N2
Marana, Ariz. (85238) 198/D6
Marand, Iran 59/E2
Marand, Iran 66/D1
Marandellas, Rhod. 118/E3
Marang, Malaysia 72/D6
Maranguape, Braz. 132/G3
Maranhão (state), Braz. 132/E4
Maranoa (riv.), Queens. 95/C5
Marañón (riv.), Peru, 120/C3
Marañón (riv.), Peru 128/E5
Marapanim, Braz. 132/E3
Maraş, Turkey 59/C2
Maraş (prov.), Turkey 63/G4
Maraş, Turkey 63/G4
Maras (mt.), Indon. 85/D6
Marathon, Fla. (33050) 212/E7
Marathón, Greece 45/G6
Marathon, Iowa (50565) 229/C3
Marathon, N.Y. (13803) 276/J6
Marathon, Ohio (45145) 284/C7
Marathon, 163/H6
Marathon, Ont. 175/C3
Marathon, Ont. 177/H5
Marathon, Texas (79842) 302/A7
Marathon (co.), Wis. 317/G6
Marathon, Wis. (54448) 317/G6
Maratua (isl.), Indon. 85/F5
Maravillas, Bol. 136/B2
Maravillas (creek), Texas 302/A7
Marawi, Phil. 82/E6
Marawi, Phil. 85/G4
Marazion, Eng. 13/B7
Marbach, Switz. 39/E3
Marbach, W. Ger. 22/C4
Marbella, Spain 33/D4
Marble (isl.), 163/G3
Marble, Ark. (72746) 203/C1
Marble, Colo. (†81623) 208/E4
Marble, Minn. (55764) 254/E3
Marble, N.C. (28905) 281/B4
Marble (isl.), N.W.T. 187/J3
Marble Bar, Australia, 87/C8
Marble Bar, Aust. 88/C4
Marble Bar, W. Aust. 92/C3
Marble Canyon, Ariz. (86036) 198/D2
Marble Canyon Nat'l Mon., Ariz. 198/D2
Marble City, Okla. (74945) 288/S3
Marble Cliff‡, Ohio (†43201) 284/D6
Marble Dale, Conn. (06761) 210/B2
Marble Falls, Texas (78654) 302/F7
Marblehead, Ill. (62350) 222/B4
MarbleheadΔ, Mass. (01945) 249/E7
Marblehead (neck), Mass. 249/F6
Marblehead, Ohio (†43440) 284/E2
Marblehill, Ga. (30148) 216/D2
Marble Hill, Mo. (63764) 261/N8
Marblemount, Wash. (98267) 310/D2
Marble Mountain, N.S. 169/G3
Marble Rock, Iowa (50653) 229/H3
Marbleton, Que. 172/F4
Marbleton, Wyo. (†83113) 319/B3
Marble Valley, Ala. (†35150) 194/F4
Marburg, W. Ger. 22/C3
Marbury, Ala. (36051) 194/E5
Marbury, Md. (20658) 245/K6
Marcala, Hond. 154/C3
Marcali, Hung. 41/D3
Marcapata, Peru 128/G9
Marcelin, Sask. 181/E3
Marceline, Mo. (64658) 261/F3
Marcell, Minn. (56657) 254/E3
Marcella, Ark. (72555) 203/G2
Marcella, N.J. (†07866) 273/E2
Marcelline, Ill. (†62376) 222/B3
Marcellus, Mich. (49067) 250/D6
Marcellus, N.Y. (13108) 276/H5
Marcelville, N. Br. 170/E2
March, 10/G4
March (riv.), Austria 41/D2
March, Eng. 13/H5
March A.F.B., Calif. 204/E11
Marchand, Man. 179/F5
Marchantgrove, Sask. 181/E2
Marche, Ark. (†72114) 203/F4
Marche (reg.), Italy 34/D3
Marche-en-Famenne, Belg. 27/G8
Marchegg, Austria 41/D2
Marchena (isl.), Ec. 128/B9
Marchena, Spain 33/D4
Marchfield, Barb. 161/B9
Marchigüe, Chile 138/F5
Marchin, Belg. 27/G8
Mar Chiquita (lake), Arg. 143/D3
Marchwell, Sask. 181/K5
Marcinelle, Belg. 27/E8
Marco, Fla. (33937) 212/E6
Marco (isl.), Fla. 212/E6
Marco, Ind. (†47443) 227/C7
Marco, La. (†71447) 238/E3
Marco, Man. 179/B4
Marcola, Oreg. (97454) 291/E3
Marcona, Peru 128/E10
Marcos Juárez, Arg. 143/D3
Marcos Paz, Arg. 143/G7
Marcus, Iowa (51035) 229/B3
Marcus (isl.), Japan, 87/F3
Marcus, S. Dak. (57757) 298/E4
Marcus, Wash. (99151) 310/H2
Marcus Baker (mt.), Alaska 196/C1
Marcus Hook, Pa. (19061) 294/L7
Marcy, N.Y. (13403) 276/K4
Marcy (mt.), N.Y. 276/N2
Mardan, Pak. 59/K3
Mardan, Pak. 68/C2
Mardela Springs, Md. (21837) 245/P7
Mar del Plata, Arg., 120/E6
Mar del Plata, Arg. 143/E4
Mardin, Turkey 59/D2
Mardin (prov.), Turkey 63/J4
Mardin, Turkey 63/J4
Mardvasht, Iran 66/H6
Maré (isl.), New Cal., 87/G8
Marechal-Deodoro, Braz. 132/H5
Maree (lake), Scot. 15/E4
Maree (lake), 10/D2
Mareeba, Aust. 88/H3
Mareeba, Queens. 95/C3
Mare Island Navy Yard, Calif. 204/J1
Marek, Somalia 115/J3
Marengo (co.), Ala. 194/C6
Marengo, Ala. (†36736) 194/C6
Marengo, Ill. (60152) 222/E1
Marengo, Ind. (47140) 227/E8
Marengo, Iowa (52301) 229/J5
Marengo, Ohio (43334) 284/E5
Marengo, Sask. 181/B4
Marengo, Wash. (†99004) 310/G3
Marengo, Wis. (54855) 317/E3
Marenisco, Mich. (49947) 250/F2
Marennes, France 28/C5
Mareth, Tun. 106/F2
Marettimo (isl.), Italy 34/C6
Marfa, Texas (79843) 302/C12
Marfield, N.S.W. 97/C3
Marfrance, W. Va. (25975) 313/E6
Marganets, U.S.S.R. 52/E5
Margao, India 68/C5
Margaree, N.S. 169/G2
Margaree (isl.), N.S. 169/F4
Margaree Centre, N.S. 169/H2
Margaree Forks, N.S. 169/G2
Margaree Harbour, N.S. 169/G2
Margaree Valley, N.S. 169/H2
Margaret, Ala. (35112) 194/F3
Margaret (lake), Alta. 182/B5
Margaret, Man. 179/C5
Margaret, Texas (†79227) 302/E3
Margaret Bay, Br. Col. 184/D4
Margaret River, W. Aust. 92/D2
Margaret River, W. Aust. 92/A6
Margaretsville, N.S. 169/C3
Margarettsville, N.C. (27853) 281/P1
Margaretville, N.Y. (12455) 276/L6
Margarita, Arg. 143/F5
Margarita (isl.), Ven., 120/D1
Margarita (isl.), Ven. 124/F2
Margarítion, Greece 45/E6
Margate, 10/G5
Margate, Eng. 13/J6
Margate, Fla. (33063) 212/F5
Margate, S. Africa 118/E6
Margate, Tas. 99/D4
Margate City, N.J. (08402) 273/E5
Margelan, U.S.S.R., 54/L5
Margento, Col. 126/C4
Margerum, Ala. (†35616) 194/B1
Margherita (mt.), Dem. Rep. of the Congo. 115/E3
Margherita (Jamama), Somalia 115/H3
Margherita (mt.), Uganda 115/E3
Margie, Minn. (56658) 254/E2
Margo, Dasht-i- (des.), Afgh. 59/H3
Margo, Dasht-i- (des.), Afgh. 68/A2
Margo, Sask. 181/H4
Margona Village‡, Mo. (†63101) 261/P3
Margos, Peru 128/D8
Margosatubig, Phil. 82/D7
Margraten, Neth. 27/H7
Margret, Ga. (†30536) 216/D1
Margrethe (lake), Mich. 250/E4
Marguerite (bay), Ant. 5/C15
Marguerite, Br. Col. 184/F4
Maria (lake), Alta. 182/C1
Maria (isl.), St. Lucia 161/G7
Maria, Que. 172/C2
Maria (isl.), Fr. Poly., 87/L8
Maria (creek), Ind. 227/C7
Maria (isl.), Tas. 99/E4
María Albina, Urug. 145/E4
María Cleófas (isl.), Mex. 150/F6
María Elena, Chile 138/B3
Mariager, Den. 18/G8
Mariager, Den. 21/D4
Mariager (fjord), Den. 21/D4
María Grande, Arg. 143/F5
Mariah Hill, Ind. (47556) 227/D8
María Madre (isl.), Mex. 150/F6
María Magdalena (isl.), Mex. 150/F6
Marian (lake), Fla. 212/E4
Marian (lake), N.W.T. 187/G3
Mariana, Braz. 135/E2
Mariana (isls.), Pac. Is., 87/E4
Mariana (isls.), Pac. IS., 3/S5
Marianao, Cuba 156/A2
Marianao, Cuba 158/C1
Mariana Trench, 87/E4
Marianna, Ark. (72360) 203/J4
Marianna, Fla. (32446) 212/A1
Marianna, Pa. (15345) 294/B5
Mariánské Lázně, Czech. 41/B2
María Pinto, Chile 138/G3
Mariapolis, Man. 179/C5
Marias (riv.), Mont., 188/D1
Marias (riv.), Mont. 262/D2
Mari A.S.S.R., U.S.S.R. 48/E4
Mari A.S.S.R., U.S.S.R. 52/G3
Maria Stein, Ohio (45860) 284/A5
Mariato (pt.), Pan. 154/G7
María Trinidad Sánchez (prov.), Dom. Rep. 158/E5
Maria van Diemen (cape), N.Z. 101/D1
Mariazell, Austria 41/C3
Marib, Yemen Arab Rep. 59/D6
Mariba, Ky. (40345) 237/O5
Maribel, Wis. (54227) 317/L7
Maribo (co.), Den. 21/E8
Maribo, Den. 21/E8
Maribor, Yugo., 7/F4
Maribor, Yugo. 45/B2
Maribyrnong (riv), Vic. 97/H5
Maricao, P. Rico 161/B2
Maricopa (co.), Ariz. 198/C5
Maricopa, Ariz. (85239) 198/C5
Maricopa (mts.), Ariz. 198/C5
Maricopa, Calif. (93252) 204/F8
Maricopa Ind. Res., Ariz. 198/C6
Maricourt, 163/J3
Maricourt, Que. 174/F1
Maricunga, Salar de (salt dep.), Chile 138/B6
Maridi, Sudan 111/E7
Marie (lake), Alta. 182/E2
Marie, Ark. (†72395) 203/K2
Marie, W. Va. (†24910) 313/E7
Marie Byrd Land (reg.), Ant., 3/D10
Marie Byrd Land (reg.), Ant. 5/B13
Mariefred, Sweden 18/F1
Marie-Galante (isl.), Guad. 156/G4
Marie-Galante (isl.), Guad. 161/B7
Mariehamn, Fin. 18/M7
Mariel, Cuba 158/B1
Mariembourg, Belg. 27/E8
Mariemont, Ohio (45227) 284/C9
Marienberg, Terr. N.G. 85/B6
Marienburg, Sur. 131/D2
Mariental, S.W. Afr. 118/B4
Marienthal, Kans. (67863) 232/A3
Marienthal, Sask. 181/H6
Marienville, Pa. (16239) 294/D3
Marie-Reine, Alta. 182/B1
Maries (co.), Mo. 261/J6
Mariestad, Sweden 18/H7
Marietta, Ga. (30060) 216/D3
Marietta, Ill. (61459) 222/C3
Marietta, Ind. (†46176) 227/F6
Marietta, Minn. (56257) 254/B5
Marietta, Miss. (38856) 256/H2
Marietta, N.C. (28362) 281/L6
Marietta, Ohio (45750) 284/G7
Marietta, Okla. (73448) 288/M7
Marietta, Pa. (17547) 294/J5
Marietta, Wash. (98268) 310/C2
Marietta-Slater, S.C. (29661) 296/C1
Marieval, Sask. 181/J5
Marie-Victorin (mts.), Que. 174/C2
Marieville, Que. 172/D4
Marigot, Haiti 158/C6
Marigot, Dominica 161/F6
Marigot, Mart. 161/D5
Marigot, St. Lucia 161/G6
Marigüitar, Ven. 124/G2
Marihatag, Phil. 82/F6
Marília, Braz. 132/D8
Marília, Braz. 135/A3
Marilla, N.Y. (14102) 276/C5
Marin (co.), Calif. 204/C5
Marin, Mart. 161/D7
Marín, Spain 33/B1
Marina‡, Calif. (94123) 204/D7
Marinduque (prov.), Phil. 82/C4
Marinduque (isl.), Phil. 82/C4
Marine, Ill. (62061) 222/D5
Marine City, Mich. (48039) 250/G6
Marineland, Fla. (†32084) 212/E2
Marine on Saint Croix, Minn. (55047) 254/F5
Marinette (co.), Wis. 317/K5
Marinette, Wis. (54143) 317/L5
Maringá, Braz. 132/D8
Maringouin, La. (70757) 238/G6
Marinha Grande, Port. 33/B3
Marinhas, Port. 33/B2
Marino, Italy 34/F7
Marino Alejandro Selkirk (isl.), Chile, 120/C6
Marinwood, Calif. (†94901) 204/H1
Marion (co.), Ala. 194/C2
Marion, Ala. (36756) 194/D5
Marion (lake), Alta. 182/D3
Marion (co.), Ark. 203/E1
Marion, Ark. (72364) 203/K3
Marion (reef), Aust. 88/J3
Marion, Aust. 88/D8
Marion, Conn. (06444) 210/D2
Marion (co.), Fla. 212/D2
Marion (co.), Ga. 216/C6
Marion (co.), Ill. 222/E5
Marion, Ill. (62059) 222/E6
Marion, Ind., 188/J2
Marion (co.), Ind. 227/E5
Marion, Ind. (46952) 227/F3
Marion (co.), Iowa 229/G6
Marion, Iowa (52302) 229/K4
Marion (co.), Kans. 232/E3
Marion, Kans. (66861) 232/F3
Marion (res.), Kans. 232/E3
Marion (co.), Ky. 237/L5
Marion, Ky. (42064) 237/E6
Marion, La. (71260) 238/F1
MarionΔ, Mass. (02738) 249/L6
Marion, Mass. (02738) 249/L6
Marion, Mich. (49665) 250/D4
Marion (co.), Miss. 256/E8
Marion, Miss. (39342) 256/G6
Marion (co.), Mo. 261/J3
Marion, Mont. (59925) 262/B2
Marion, N.C. (28752) 281/E3
Marion, N. Dak. (58466) 283/O6
Marion, N.Y. (14505) 276/F4
Marion, S. Aust. 94/A8
Marion, Ohio, 188/K2
Marion (co.), Ohio 284/D4
Marion, Ohio (43302) 284/D4
Marion (co.), Oreg. 291/E3
Marion, Oreg. (97359) 291/D3
Marion, Pa. (17235) 294/G6
Marion (lake), S.C., 188/K4
Marion (co.), S.C. 296/J3
Marion, S.C. (29571) 296/J3
Marion (lake), S.C. 296/G5
Marion, S. Dak. (57043) 298/P7
Marion (co.), Tenn. 237/K10
Marion (co.), Texas 302/K5
Marion‡, Texas (78124) 302/F8
Marion, Va. (24354) 307/E7
Marion (co.), W. Va. 313/F4
Marion, Wis. (54950) 317/J6
Marion Center, Pa. (15759) 294/D4
Marion Heights‡, Pa. (†17832) 294/K4
Marion Junction, Ala. (36759) 194/D6
Marion Station, Md. (21838) 245/R8
Marionville, Mo. (65705) 261/E8
Maripa, Fr. Gui. 131/E4
Maripa, Ven. 124/F4
Maripasoula, Fr. Gui. 131/D4
Mariposa (co.), Calif. 204/E6
Mariposa, Calif. (95338) 204/F6
Mariscala, Urug. 145/E5
Mariscal Estigarribia, Par., 120/D5
Mariscal Estigarribia, Par. 144/B4
Marismas, Las (marsh), Spain 33/C4
Marissa, Ill. (62257) 222/D5
Maritime Alps (range), France 28/G5
Maritime Alps (range), Italy 34/A2
Maritsa, Bulg. 45/H4
Maritsa (riv.), Bulg. 45/G4
Mariupol' (Zhdanov), U.S.S.R. 52/E5
Marius, Man. 179/D4
Marivan (Dezh-i-Shahpur), Iran 66/E3
Mariveles, Phil. 82/C3
Märjamaa, U.S.S.R. 53/C1
Mark (riv.), Belg. 27/F6
Mark, Ill. (61340) 222/D2
Mark (riv.), Neth. 27/F6
Markaryd, Sweden 18/H8
Mark Center, Ohio (43536) 284/A3
Markdale, Ont. 177/D3
Marked Tree, Ark. (72365) 203/K2
Marken (isl.), Neth. 27/G4
Markerwaard Polder, Neth. 27/G3
Markesan, Wis. (53946) 317/J8
Market Bosworth, Eng. 13/F5
Market Drayton, 10/E4
Market Drayton, Eng. 13/E5
Markethill, N. Ire. 17/H3
Market Rasen, Eng. 13/G4
Market Weighton, Eng. 13/G4

398 Markha

Markha (riv.), U.S.S.R. 48/M3
Markham (mt.), Ant. 5/A8
Markham, Ont. 177/K4
Markham, Ill. (60426) 222/B2
Markham (bay), N.W.T. 187/L3
Markham (inlet), N.W.T. 187/L1
Markham, Va. (22643) 307/N3
Markham, Wash. (†98520) 310/B4
Markham Dzong, China 77/E6
Markinch, Sask. 181/G5
Markinch, Scot. 15/K7
Markkleeberg, E. Ger. 22/E3
Markland, Ind. (†47020) 227/G7
Markland, Newf. 166/D2
Markle, Ind. (46770) 227/G3
Markleeville, Calif. (96120) 204/F5
Marklesburg (James Creek), Pa. (15459) 294/F5
Markleton, Pa. (15551) 294/D6
Markleville, Ind. (46056) 227/F5
Markleysburg, Pa. (15459) 294/C6
Markovo, U.S.S.R. 48/S3
Markovo, U.S.S.R., 4/C1
Marks, U.S.S.R. 52/G4
Marks, Miss. (38646) 256/D2
Markstay, Ont. 177/D1
Marksville, La. (71351) 238/G4
Marktredwitz, W. Ger. 22/E4
Markville, Minn. (55048) 254/F4
Marl, W. Ger. 22/B3
Marland, Okla. (74644) 288/M1
Marlbank, Ont. 177/G3
Marlboro, Alta. 182/B3
Marlboro, N.J. (07746) 273/E3
Marlboro, N.Y. (12542) 276/M7
Marlboro (co.), S.C. 296/H2
Marlboro▵, Vt. (05344) 268/B6
Marlboro, Vt. (05344) 268/B6
Marlborough, 10/F5
Marlborough▵, Conn. (†06424) 210/F2
Marlborough, Eng. 13/F6
Marlborough, Mass. (01752) 249/H3
Marlborough‡, Mo. (†63101) 261/P3
Marlborough▵, N.H. (03455) 268/C6
Marlborough, N.H. (03455) 268/C6
Marlborough (prov. dist.), N.Z. 101/D4
Marlborough, Queens. 95/D4
Marlette, Mich. (48453) 250/G5
Marlin, Sask. 181/C2
Marlin, Texas (76661) 302/H6
Marlin, Wash. (98832) 310/F3
Marlinton, W. Va. (24954) 313/F6
Marlow, Ala. (†36580) 194/C10
Marlow, Eng. 13/G6
Marlow, Ga. (†31312) 216/K6
Marlow▵, N.H. (03456) 268/C5
Marlow, N.H. (03456) 268/C5
Marlow, Okla. (73055) 288/K5
Marlton, N.J. (08053) 273/D4
Marmaduke, Ark. (72443) 203/K1
Marmagao, India 68/C5
Marmande, France 28/C5
Marmara (sea), Turkey 59/A1
Marmara (isl.), Turkey 63/B2
Marmara (sea), Turkey 63/C2
Marmara (sea), Turkey, 7/G4
Marmaris, Turkey 63/C4
Marmarth, N. Dak. (58643) 283/B7
Mar Menor (lag.), Spain 33/F4
Marmet, W. Va. (25315) 313/C6
Marmolada (mt.), Italy 34/C1
Marmon, N. Dak. (†58801) 283/C3
Marmontana (mt.), Switz. 39/H4
Marmora, Ont. 177/G3
Marmora, N.J. (08223) 273/D5
Marmot (bay), Alaska 196/H3
Marmot (isl.), Alaska 196/H3
Marne (riv.), France, 7/E4
Marne (dept.), France 28/F3
Marne (riv.), France 28/C2
Marne, Iowa (51552) 229/C6
Marne, Mich. (49435) 250/D5
Marne, W. Ger. 22/C2
Maro (reef), Hawaii, 188/F6
Maro (reef), Hawaii 218/C6
Maro (dry riv.), Chad 111/C4
Maroa, Ill. (61756) 222/E3
Maroa, Ven. 124/E6
Maroantsetra, Malag. Rep. 118/J3
Marolambo, Malag. Rep. 118/H4
Maromokotro (mt.), Malag. Rep. 118/H2
Maroni (riv.), 120/E2
Maroni (riv.), Braz. 132/C1
Maroni (riv.), Fr. Gui. 131/D3
Maroon (peak), Colo. 208/F4
Maroon Town, Jam. 158/H6
Maros (riv.), Hung. 41/F3
Maros, Indon. 85/F6
Maroua, Cameroon 115/B1
Maroubra, N.S.W. 97/K3
Marouini (riv.), Fr. Gui. 131/D4
Marovoay, 102/G6
Marovoay, Malag. Rep. 118/H3
Marowijne (dist.), Sur. 131/D4
Marowijne (riv.), Sur. 131/D3
Marple, 10/G2
Marquam, Oreg. (97362) 291/B3
Marquand, Mo. (63655) 261/M8
Marquesas (keys), Fla. 212/D7
Marquesas (isls.), Fr. Poly., 87/N6
Marquesas (isls.), Fr. Poly., 3/B6
Marques de Valença, Braz. 135/D3
Marquette, Iowa (52158) 229/L2
Marquette, Kans. (67464) 232/E3
Marquette, Man. 179/E4
Marquette, Mich., 146/K5
Marquette, Mich., 188/J1
Marquette (co.), Mich. 250/B2
Marquette, Mich. (49855) 250/B2
Marquette (isl.), Mich. 250/E3
Marquette, Nebr. (68854) 264/G4
Marquette (co.), Wis. 317/H8
Marquette, Wis. (53947) 317/H8
Marquette Heights, Ill. (†61554) 222/D3
Marquez, Texas (77865) 302/H6
Marquis, Grenada 161/D8
Marquis, St. Lucia 161/G6
Marquis, Sask. 181/F5
Marra (creek), N.S.W. 97/D2
Marra, Jebel (mt.), Sudan 111/D5
Marrakech, 102/B1
Marrakech, Mor. 106/C2
Marree, Aust. 88/E5
Marree. S. Aust. 94/E3
Marrero, La. (70072) 238/O4
Marrickville, N.S.W. 97/J3
Marriott, Sask. 181/D4
Marromeu, Moz. 118/F3
Marrowbone, Ky. (42759) 237/K7
Marrowie (creek), N.S.W. 97/C3
Marrupa, Moz. 118/F2
Mars (riv.), Que. 172/G1
Mars, Pa. (16046) 294/C4
Marsabit, Kenya 115/G3
Marsabit, 102/F4
Marsa el Awegia, Libya 111/C1
Marsa el Brega, Libya 111/D1
Marsa el Hariga, Libya 111/D1
Marsala, Italy 34/D6
Marsa Oseif, Sudan 111/G3
Marsa Susa, Libya 111/D1
Mars Bluff, S.C. (†29501) 296/H3
Marsciano, Italy 34/D3
Marsden, N.S.W. 97/D3
Marsden, Sask. 181/B3
Marsdiep (chan.), Neth. 27/F3
Marseille, France, 7/E4
Marseille, France 28/F6
Marseilles, Ill. (61341) 222/E2
Marseilles, Ohio (†43351) 284/D4
Marsh (creek), Idaho 220/F7
Marsh (isl.), La. 238/G7
Marsh (lake), Minn. 254/B5
Marsh, Mont. (†59326) 262/M4
Marsh (peak), Utah 304/E3
Marshall (co.), Ala. 194/F2
Marshall (Fortuna Ledge), Alaska (†99585) 196/F2
Marshall, Ark. (72650) 203/E2
Marshall (co.), Ill. 222/D2
Marshall, Ill. (62441) 222/F4
Marshall (co.), Ind. 227/E2
Marshall, Ind. (47859) 227/C5
Marshall (co.), Iowa 229/G4
Marshall (co.), Kans. 232/F2
Marshall (co.), Ky. 237/E7
Marshall, Liberia 106/B7
Marshall (isl.), Maine 242/G7
Marshall, Mich. (49068) 250/E6
Marshall (co.), Minn. 254/B2
Marshall, Minn. (56258) 254/C6
Marshall (co.), Miss. 256/E1
Marshall, Mo. (65340) 261/F4
Marshall, N.C. (28753) 281/D3
Marshall, N. Dak. (58644) 283/F5
Marshall (riv.), No. Terr. 93/D7
Marshall, Ohio (†45133) 284/C7
Marshall (co.), Okla. 288/N6
Marshall, Okla. (73056) 288/L2
Marshall (isls.), Pac. Is., 87/G4
Marshall (isls.), Pac. Is., 3/T5
Marshall (co.), S. Dak. 298/O2
Marshall, Sask. 181/B2
Marshall (co.), Tenn. 237/H10
Marshall, Texas, 188/H4
Marshall, Texas (75670) 302/K5
Marshall, Va. (22115) 307/N3
Marshall (co.), W. Va. 313/E3
Marshall, Wash. (99020) 310/H3
Marshall, Wis. (53559) 317/H9
Marshallberg, N.C. (28553) 281/S5
Marshall Hall, Md. (†20616) 245/K6
Marshalls Creek, Pa. (18335) 294/M3
Marshallton, Del. (19808) 245/R2
Marshallton‡, Pa. (†17872) 294/J4
Marshalltown, Iowa, 188/H2
Marshalltown, Iowa (50158) 229/G4
Marshallville, Ga. (31057) 216/D6
Marshallville, Ohio (44645) 284/G4
Marshes Siding, Ky. (42631) 237/M7
Marshfield, Ind. (47956) 227/C4
Marshfield▵, Mass. (02050) 249/M4
Marshfield, Mass. (02050) 249/M4
Marshfield, Mo. (65706) 261/G8
Marshfield▵, Vt. (05658) 268/C3
Marshfield, Vt. (05658) 268/C3
Marshfield, Wis. (54449) 317/F6
Marshfield Hills, Mass. (02051) 249/M4
Marsh Hill, Pa. (†17722) 294/H3
Mars Hill▵, Maine (04758) 242/H2
Mars Hill, N.C. (28754) 281/D3
Mars Hill-Blaine, Maine (04758) 242/H2
Marshland, Oreg. (†97016) 291/D1
Marshville, N.C. (28103) 281/J4
Marshy (lake), Man. 179/B5
Marshyhope (creek), Md. 245/P6
Marsing, Idaho (83639) 220/B6
Marsland, Nebr. (69354) 264/A2
Marsoui, Que. 172/C1
Marstal, Den. 21/D8
Marston, Mo. (63866) 261/N9
Marston, N.C. (28363) 281/K5
Marstons Mills, Mass. (02648) 249/N6
Marstrand, Sweden 18/G8
Mart, Texas (76664) 302/H6
Martaban (gulf), Burma, 54/N8
Martaban, Burma 72/C3
Martaban (gulf), Burma 72/C4
Martapura, Indon. 85/F6
Martel, Ohio (43335) 284/E4
Martel, Tenn. (†37771) 237/N9
Martelange, Belg. 27/H9
Martell, Calif. (95654) 204/C9
Martell, Wis. (†54767) 317/B6
Martelle, Iowa (52305) 229/L4
Marten (mt.), Alta. 182/C2
Martensdale, Iowa (50160) 229/F6
Martensville, Sask. 181/E3
Martha, Ky. (41159) 237/R4
Martha, Okla. (73556) 288/H5
Martha, Tenn. (†37087) 237/J8
Marthaguy (creek), N.S.W. 97/D2
Marthasville, Mo. (63357) 261/L5
Martha's Vineyard (isl.), Mass., 188/N2
Martha's Vineyard (isl.), Mass. 249/M7
Marthaville, La. (71450) 238/D3
Martí, Cuba 156/C2
Martí, Camagüey, Cuba 158/G3
Martí, Matanzas, Cuba 158/D1
Martigny, Switz. 39/C4
Martigues, France 28/F6
Martin (dam), Ala. 194/G5
Martin (lake), Ala. 194/G5
Martin, Czech. 41/E2
Martin, Ont. 175/B3
Martin, Ont. 177/G5
Martin (co.), Fla. 212/F4
Martin, Ga. (30557) 216/F2
Martin (co.), Ind. 227/D7
Martin (co.), Ky. 237/R5
Martin, Ky. (41649) 237/R5
Martin, Mich. (49070) 250/D6
Martin (co.), Minn. 254/D7
Martin (head), N. Br. 170/E3
Martin (co.), N.C. 281/P3
Martin, N. Dak. (58758) 283/K4
Martin, N.H. (†03101) 268/E5
Martin, Ohio (43445) 284/D2
Martin, S.C. (29836) 296/D5
Martin, S. Dak. (57551) 298/F7
Martin, Tenn. (38237) 237/D8
Martin (co.), Texas 302/C5
Martin, W. Va. (†26702) 313/H4
Martina Franca, Italy 34/F4
Martinborough, N.Z. 101/E4
Martín Chico, Urug. 145/A5
Martinez, Calif. (94553) 204/K1
Martinez, Ga. (30907) 216/H3
Martínez de la Torre, Mex. 150/L6
Martín García (isl.), Arg. 143/H6
Martinique (isl.), 146/M8
MARTINIQUE, 156/G4
MARTINIQUE, 161/D5
Martinique (passg.), Dominica 161/E7
Martinique (passg.), Mart. 161/C5
Martinsburg, Ind. (†47165) 227/E8
Martinsburg, Iowa (52568) 229/J6
Martinsburg, Mo. (65264) 261/J4
Martinsburg, N.Y. (13404) 276/J3
Martinsburg, Nebr. (†68770) 264/H2
Martinsburg, Ohio (43037) 284/F5
Martinsburg, Pa. (16662) 294/F5
Martinsburg, W. Va. (25401) 313/K4
Martins Creek, Pa. (18063) 294/M4
Martinsdale, Mont. (59053) 262/F4
Martins Ferry, Ohio (43935) 284/J5
Martins Mills, Tenn. (†38471) 237/F10
Martinsville, Ill. (62442) 222/F4
Martinsville, Ind. (46151) 227/D6
Martinsville, Miss. (†39083) 256/D7
Martinsville, Mo. (64467) 261/D2
Martinsville, N.J. (08836) 273/D2
Martinsville, Ohio (45146) 284/C7
Martinsville, Va. (24112) 307/J7
Martinton, Ill. (60951) 222/F3
Martintown, Ont. 177/K2
Martinville, Ark. (†72039) 203/F3
Martinville, Que. 172/F4
Martofte, Den. 21/D6
Marton, N.Z. 101/E4
Martos, Spain 33/E4
Martre (lake), 163/E3
Martwick, Ky. (42330) 237/H6
Marty, S. Dak. (57361) 298/N8
Marudi (mts.), Guyana 131/B5
Marudi, Malaysia 85/E5
Maruf, Afgh. 59/J3
Maruf, Afgh. 68/B2
Marulan, N.S.W. 97/E4
Marulas, Phil. 82/C3
Marungu (mts.), Dem. Rep. of the Congo. 115/E5
Marutea (atoll), Fr. Poly., 87/N8
Marvejols, France 28/E5
Marvel, Ala. (35113) 194/D4
Marvel, Colo. (81329) 208/C8
Marvell, Ark. (72366) 203/J4
Marvin, S. Dak. (57251) 298/R3
Marvindale, Pa. (†16749) 294/E2
Marvine (mt.), Utah 304/C5
Marvyn, Ala. (†36801) 194/H6
Marwayne, Alta. 182/E3
Marwood, Pa. (16047) 294/C4
Mary, U.S.S.R. 48/G6
Mary, Ky. (41350) 237/O5
Mary (lake), Minn. 254/C5
Mary (riv.), Queens. 95/E5
Mary, U.S.S.R., 54/K6
Maryborough, Australia, 87/F8
Maryborough, Aust. 88/J5
Maryborough, Aust. 88/G7
Maryborough (Portlaoighise), 10/C4
Maryborough (Portlaoighise), Ire. 17/G5
Maryborough, Queens. 95/E5
Maryborough, Vic. 97/B5
Marydel, Md. (21649) 245/P4
Marydell, Miss. (†39051) 256/F5
Mary Esther, Fla. (32569) 212/B6
Maryfield, Sask. 181/K6
Maryhill, Wash. (†98620) 310/E5
Mary Hill Estates‡, Ky. (†40201) 237/K4
Mary Kathleen, Aust. 88/F4
Mary Kathleen, Queens. 95/A4
Marykirk, Scot. 15/M6
Maryland, 188/L3
MARYLAND, 245
Maryland, N.Y. (12116) 276/L5
Maryland (state), U.S., 146/L6
Maryland City‡, Md. (†21113) 245/M4
Maryland Heights‡, Mo. (63043) 261/P3
Maryland Line, Md. (21105) 245/M2
Maryneal, Texas (79535) 302/D5
Maryport, 10/E3
Maryport, Eng. 13/D3
Mary Ridge‡, Mo. (†63101) 261/P2
Marys Ronan (lake), Mont. 262/B3
Marys (creek), Idaho 220/C7
Marys (riv.), Nev. 266/F1
Marysburg, Sask. 181/G3
Mary's Harbour, Newf. 166/C3
Marystown, Newf. 166/D4
Marysvale, Utah (84750) 304/B5
Marysvale (peak), Utah 304/B5
Marysville, Br. Col. 184/K5
Marysville, Calif., 188/B3
Marysville, Calif. (95901) 204/D4
Marysville, Ind. (47141) 227/F7
Marysville, Iowa (†50116) 229/G6
Marysville, Kans. (66508) 232/F2
Marysville, Mich. (48040) 250/G6
Marysville, Mont. (59640) 262/D4
Marysville, N. Br. 170/D2
Marysville, Ohio (43040) 284/D5
Marysville, Pa. (17053) 294/H5
Marysville, Wash. (98270) 310/C2
Marytown, W. Va. (†24889) 313/C8
Maryvale, Queens. 95/C3
Maryville, Ill. (62062) 222/B6
Maryville, Mo. (64468) 261/C2
Maryville, Tenn. (37801) 237/O9
Marzo (pt.), Col. 126/B4
Masagua, Guat. 154/B3
Masahim, Kuh-i- (mt.), Iran 66/J5
Masai (steppe), Tanz. 115/G4
Masaka, Uganda 115/F4
Masalima (isls.), Indon. 85/F7
Masamba, Indon. 85/G6
Masan, S. Korea 81/D6
Masardis▵, Maine (04759) 242/G3
Masaryktown, Fla. (33512) 212/D3
Masasi, 102/F6
Masasi, Tanz. 115/G6
Masatepe, Nic. 154/D5
Masaya, Nic. 154/D5
Masbate (prov.), Phil. 82/D4
Masbate, Phil. 82/D4
Masbate (isl.), Phil. 82/D4
Masbate (isl.), Phil. 85/G3
Mascara, Alg. 106/D1
Mascarene (isls.), Mauritius 118/F5
Mascarene (isls.), Réunion 118/F5
Mascoma, N.H. (†03748) 268/C4
Mascoma (lake), N.H. 268/C4
Mascot, Tenn. (37806) 237/O8
Mascota, Mex. 150/G6
Mascotte, Fla. (32753) 212/E3
Mascouche, Que. 172/H4
Mascoutah, Ill. (62258) 222/D5
Masefield, Sask. 181/D6
Masela (isl.), Indon. 85/H7
Maseru (cap.), Lesotho 118/D5
Maseru (cap.), Lesotho 102/E8
Mash' Abbe Sade, Israel 65/B6
Mashabi (isl.), Saudi Ar. 59/C4
Masham, Eng. 13/F3
Mashapaug, Conn. (†06076) 210/G1
Mashapaug (lake), Conn. 210/G1
Mashash, Wadi (dry riv.), Jordan 65/C4
Mashike, Japan 81/K2
Mashkel (riv.), Iran 59/H4
Mashkel, Hamun-i- (swamp), Pak. 59/H4
Mashkel (riv.), Iran 66/N7
Mashkel (riv.), Pak. 68/A3
Mashkel, Hamun-i- (swamp), Pak. 68/A3
Mashonaland (reg.), Rhod. 118/E3
Mashpee▵, Mass. (02649) 249/M6
Mashulaville, Miss. (†39341) 256/G4
Masi-Manimba, Dem. Rep. of the Congo. 115/C4
Masindi, Uganda 115/F3
Masinloc, Phil. 82/B3
Masio (cay), Cuba 158/C2
Masira (gulf), Oman 59/G6
Masira (isl.), Oman 59/G5
Masira (isl.), Oman, 54/J7
Masisea, Peru 128/E7
Masisi, Dem. Rep. of the Congo. 115/E4
Masjid-i-Sulaiman, Iran 66/F5
Mask (lake), Ire. 17/C4
Mask (lake), 10/B4
Maskell, Nebr. (68751) 264/H2
Maskinongé (co.), Que. 172/D3
Maskinongé, Que. 172/E3
Maskinongé (riv.), Que. 172/D3
Maskinongé (co.), Que. 174/C3
Masoala (pen.), Malag. Rep. 118/J3
Masoller, Urug. 145/C2
Mason (co.), Ill. 222/D3
Mason, Ill. (62443) 222/E5
Mason (co.), Ky. 237/O3
Mason, Ky. (41054) 237/M3
Mason (co.), Mich. 250/C4
Mason, Mich. (48854) 250/E6
Mason (bay), N.Z. 101/A7
Mason, Nev. (†89447) 266/B4
Mason (peak), Nev. 266/F1
Mason, Ohio (45040) 284/B7
Mason, Okla. (74853) 288/O3
Mason, Tenn. (38049) 237/B10
Mason (co.), Texas 302/E7
Mason, Texas (76856) 302/E7
Mason (co.), W. Va. 313/B5
Mason, W. Va. (25260) 313/B4
Mason (co.), Wash. 310/B3
Mason, Wis. (54856) 317/D3
Mason City, Ill. (62664) 222/D3
Mason City, Iowa, 188/H2
Mason City, Iowa (50401) 229/G2
Mason City, Nebr. (68855) 264/E3
Mason Hall, Tenn. (†38233) 237/C8
Masons (isl.), Conn. 210/H3
Mason Springs, Md. (†20640) 245/K6
Masontown, Pa. (15461) 294/C6
Masontown, W. Va. (26542) 313/G3
Masonville, Colo. (80541) 208/J2
Masonville, Iowa (50654) 229/K4
Masonville, N.J. (08054) 273/D4
Masonville, N.Y. (13804) 276/K6
Mass, Mich. (49948) 250/G1
Massa, Italy 34/C2
Massabesic (lake), N.H. 268/E6
Massac (co.), Ill. 222/E6
Massa-Carrara (prov.), Italy 34/C2
Massachusetts, 188/M2
MASSACHUSETTS, 249
Massachusetts (bay), Mass. 249/M4
Massachusetts (state), U.S., 146/L5
Massacre (lake), Nev. 266/B1
Massafra, Italy 34/F4
Massakori, Chad 111/C5
Massa Marittima, Italy 34/C3
Massangena, Moz. 118/E4
Massango (Forte República), Angola 115/C5
Massanutten (mt.), Va. 307/L3
Massapê, Braz. 132/G3
Massapeag, Conn. (†06382) 210/G3
Massapequa, N.Y. (11758) 276/O9
Massapequa Park, N.Y. (11762) 276/O9
Massaponax, Va. (†22553) 307/O4
Massawa, Eth. 59/C6
Massawa, Eth. 111/G4
Massawa, 102/F3
Massbach, Ill. (†61028) 222/C1
Massena, Iowa (50853) 229/D6
Massena, N.Y. (13662) 276/L1
Massénya, Chad 111/C5
Masset, Br. Col. 184/B3
Masset (inlet), Br. Col. 184/A3
Massey, Ont. 177/C1
Massey, Md. (21650) 245/P3
Massey, N.Z. 101/B1
Massies Mill, Va. (22954) 307/K5
Massillon, Ala. (†36759) 194/D6
Massillon, Iowa (†52255) 229/L5
Massillon, Ohio (44646) 284/H4
Massinga, Moz. 118/F4
Massive (mt.), Colo. 208/F4
Masslo, Eth. 111/G6
Masson, Que. 172/B4
Massueville, Que. 172/E4
Mastaba, Saudi Ar. 59/C5
Mastens Corner, Del. (†19943) 245/R5
Masters, Colo. (†80649) 208/L2
Masterton, N.Z. 101/E4
Mastic Beach, N.Y. (11950) 276/P9
Mastuj, Pak. 59/J4
Mastung, Pak. 59/J4
Mastung, Pak. 68/B3
Mastura, Saudi Ar. 59/C5
Masuda, Japan 81/E6
Masury, Ohio (44438) 284/J3
Masyaf, Syria 63/G5
Matabeleland (reg.), Rhod. 118/D3
Matachewan, Ont. 175/D3
Matachewan, Ont. 177/J5
Mata de São João, Braz. 132/G6
Matadi, 102/D5
Matadi, Dem. Rep. of the Congo. 115/B5
Matador, Sask. 181/D5
Matador, Texas (79244) 302/D3
Matagalpa, Nic. 154/E4
Matagami, Que. 174/B3
Matagorda (bay), Texas, 188/G5
Matagorda (co.), Texas 302/H9
Matagorda, Texas (77457) 302/J9
Matagorda (bay), Texas 302/H9
Matagorda (isl.), Texas 302/H9
Matagorda (pen.), Texas 302/J9
Matagorda Isl. Bombing and Gunnery Range, Texas 302/H9
Matakana (isl.), N.Z. 101/F2
Matam, Sen. 106/B5
Matamoras, Pa. (18336) 294/N3
Matamoros, Coahuila, Mex. 150/H4
Matamoros, Tamaulipas, Mex. 150/L4
Matane (co.), Que. 172/B1
Matane, Que. 172/B1
Matane (riv.), Que. 172/B1
Matane (co.), Que. 174/D3
Matane, Que. 174/D3
Matanuska, Alaska (†99645) 196/C1
Matanuska (riv.), Alaska 196/C1
Matanza, Col. 126/D4
Matanzas, Cuba, 146/K7
Matanzas, Cuba 156/B2
Matanzas (prov.), Cuba 158/D1
Matanzas, Cuba 158/C1
Matanzas (bay), Cuba 158/D1
Matanzas (inlet), Fla. 212/E2
Mata Palacio, Dom. Rep. 158/F6
Matapalo (cape), C. Rica 154/F6
Matapan (Taínaron) (cape), Greece 45/F7
Matapédia (co.), Que. 172/B2
Matapédia, Que. 172/B2
Matapédia (lake), Que. 172/B1
Matapédia (riv.), Que. 172/B2
Matapédia (co.), Que. 174/D3
Mataquito (riv.), Chile 138/A10
Matara, Ceylon 68/E7
Mataram, Indon. 85/F7
Matarani, Peru, 120/C4
Matarani, Peru 128/F11
Mataranka, Aust. 88/E2
Mataranka, No. Terr. 93/C3
Matarinao (bay), Phil. 82/E5
Mataró, Spain 33/H2
Matatiele, S. Africa 118/D6
Matatindoc (pt.), Phil. 82/D6
Mataura, N.Z. 101/B7
Mataura (riv.), N.Z. 101/B6
Matautu (cap.), Wallis and Futuna, 87/J7
Matawai, N.Z. 101/F3
Matawan, Minn. (56066) 254/E7
Matawan, N.J. (07747) 273/E3
Matawin (res.), Que. 172/D3
Mateare, Nic. 154/D4
Mateguá, Bol. 136/D3
Matehuala, Mex. 150/J5
Matelot, Trinidad Tobago 161/B10
Matera (prov.), Italy 34/F4
Matera, Italy 34/F4
Maternillos (pt.), Cuba 158/H2
Mátészalka, Hung. 41/G3
Matetsi, Rhod. 118/D3
Mateur, Tun. 106/F1
Matewan, W. Va. (25678) 313/B7
Matfield Green, Kans. (66862) 232/F3
Mather, Man. 179/C5
Mather, Wis. (54641) 317/F7
Mather A.F.B., Calif. 204/C8
Matherville, Ill. (61263) 222/C2
Matherville, Miss. (†39360) 256/G7
Matheson, Colo. (80830) 208/M4
Matheson, Ont. 177/K5
Matheson Island, Man. 179/E3
Mathews, Ala. (36052) 194/F6
Mathews (lake), Calif. 204/E11
Mathews, La. (70375) 238/J7
Mathews (co.), Va. 307/R6
Mathews, Va. (23109) 307/R6
Mathias, W. Va. (26812) 313/J5
Mathis, Texas (78368) 302/G9
Mathiston, Miss. (39752) 256/F3
Mathoura, N.S.W. 97/C4
Mathry, Wales 13/C6
Mathura, India 68/D3
Mati, Phil. 82/F7
Mati, Phil. 85/H4
Matías de Gálvez, Guat. 154/C3
Matías Romero, Mex. 150/M8
Matinecock‡, N.Y. (†11560) 276/R7
Matinenda (lake), Ont. 177/B1
Matinicus, Maine (04851) 242/F8
Matinicus Rock (isl.), Maine 242/F8
Matjan (isls.), Indon. 85/G7
Matlock, 10/F4
Matlock, Eng. 13/F4
Matlock, Iowa (51244) 229/A2
Matlock, Man. 179/F4
Matlock, Wash. (98560) 310/B3
Mato, China 77/E4
Matoaca, Va. (23803) 307/N6
Matoaka, W. Va. (24736) 313/D8
Matochkin Shar (str.), U.S.S.R. 48/F2
Matochkin Shar, U.S.S.R., 4/B7
Mato Grosso, Braz., 120/E4
Mato Grosso (plat.), Braz., 120/E4
Mato Grosso (state), Braz. 132/B6
Mato Grosso, Braz. 132/B6
Mato Grosso (plat.), Braz. 132/B6
Matopos, Rhod. 118/D4
Matosinhos, Port. 33/B2
Mátra (mts.), Hung. 41/E3
Matrah, Oman 59/G5
Matrah, Oman, 54/J7
Matrei, Austria 41/B3
Matrûh, 102/E1
Matrûh, U.A.R. 59/A3
Matrûh, U.A.R. 111/E1
Matson, Mo. (63358) 261/N3
Matsqui, Br. Col. 184/L3
Matsu (isl.), China 77/K6
Matsubara, Japan 81/H8
Matsudo, Japan 81/P2
Matsue, Japan 81/F6
Matsumae, Japan 81/J3
Matsumoto, Japan 81/H5
Matsunaga, Japan 81/F6
Matsusaka, Japan 81/H6
Matsuto, Japan 81/H5
Matsuyama, Japan 81/F7
Matt, Switz. 39/H3
Mattabesset (riv.), Conn. 210/E2
Mattagami (lake), Que. 174/B3
Mattagami (riv.), Ont. 175/D3
Mattagami (riv.), Ont. 177/J5
Mattamiscontis (lake), Maine 242/F4
Mattamuskeet (lake), N.C. 281/S3
Mattancheri, India 68/D7
Mattapan, Mass. (02126) 249/C7
Mattapoisett▵, Mass. (02739) 249/L6
Mattapoisett, Mass. (02739) 249/L6
Mattaponi, Va. (23110) 307/P5
Mattaponi (riv.), Va. 307/O5
Mattaponi Ind. Res., Va. 307/P5
Mattawa, 163/J6
Mattawa, Ont. 175/E3
Mattawa, Ont. 177/F1
Mattawa, Wash. (99344) 310/F4
Mattawamkeag▵, Maine (04459) 242/G5
Mattawamkeag (lake), Maine 242/G4
Mattawamkeag (riv.), Maine 242/G4
Mattawan, Mich. (49071) 250/D6
Mattawana, Pa. (17054) 294/G5
Mattawatchan, Ont. 177/G2
Mattawin (lake), Que. 172/C3
Mattawin (riv.), Que. 172/D3
Mattawoman (creek), Md. 245/K6
Matterhorn (mt.), Switz. 39/E4
Mattersburg, Austria 41/D3
Mattes, Sask. 181/E2
Matteson, Ill. (60443) 222/B3
Matthew, Ky. (41454) 237/P5
Matthews, Ga. (30818) 216/H4
Matthews, Ind. (46957) 227/F4
Matthews, Mo. (63857) 261/N9
Matthews, N.C. (28105) 281/H4
Mattice, Ont. 175/D3
Mattice, Ont. 177/J5
Mattighofen, Austria 41/B2
Mattituck, N.Y. (11952) 276/P9
Mattoon, Ill. (61938) 222/E4
Mattoon, Wis. (54450) 317/J5
Mattson, Miss. (38758) 256/C2
Mattydale‡, N.Y. (13211) 276/H4
Matu, Ven. 124/F4
Matucana, Peru 128/D8
Matún, Cuba 158/D2
Matun, Afgh. 59/J3
Matun, Afgh. 68/B2
Matura, Trinidad Tobago 161/B10
Matura (bay), Trinidad Tobago 161/B10
Maturín, Ven. 124/G3
Matutum (mt.), Phil. 82/E7
Matutum (mt.), Phil. 85/G4
Matveyev (isl.), U.S.S.R. 52/J1
Mau, India 68/E3
Maúa, Moz. 118/F2
Maubeuge, France 28/F2
Ma-ubin, Burma 72/B2
Mauch Chunk (Jim Thorpe), Pa. (18229) 294/L4
Mauchline, Scot. 15/H8
Mauckport, Ind. (47142) 227/E8
Maud, Ala. (†35616) 194/B1
Maud, Ky. (40042) 237/L5
Maud, Miss. (†38626) 256/D1
Maud, Ohio (45069) 284/B7
Maud, Okla. (74854) 288/N4
Maud, Texas (75567) 302/K4
Maude, N.S.W. 97/C4
Maudlow, Mont. (59742) 262/E4
Mauerkirchen, Austria 41/B2
Maués, Braz. 132/B3
Maués Guaçu (riv.), Braz. 132/B4
Maugansville, Md. (21767) 245/H2
Mauger (cay), Br. Hond. 154/D2
Maugerville, N. Br. 170/D3
Maui (isl.), Hawaii, 87/L3
Maui (isl.), Hawaii, 188/F5
Maui (co.), Hawaii 218/J1
Maui (isl.), Hawaii 218/J2
Mauk, Ga. (31058) 216/D6
Mauke (isl.), Cook Is., 87/L8
Mauldin, S.C. (29662) 296/C2
Maule (prov.), Chile 138/A11
Maule (riv.), Chile 138/A11
Mauléon-Licharre, France 28/C6
Maullín, Chile 138/D4
Maullín (riv.), Chile 138/D3
Maumakeogh (mt.), Ire. 17/C3
Maumee (riv.), Ind. 227/H2

400 Medford

Medford, Oreg., 146/F5
Medford, Oreg., 188/B2
Medford, Oreg. (97501) 291/E5
Medford, Wis. (54451) 317/F5
Medford Center, Maine (†04453) 242/F5
Medford Lakes, N.J. (08055) 273/D4
Medgidia, Rum. 45/J3
Medgun (creek), N.S.W. 97/E1
Media, Ill. (61460) 222/C3
Media, Pa. (*19063) 294/L7
Media Luna, Cuba 158/G4
Mediapolis, Iowa (52637) 229/L6
Mediaş, Rum. 45/G2
Medical Lake, Wash. (99022) 310/H3
Medical Springs, Oreg. (97860) 291/K2
Medicine (lake), Mont. 262/M2
Medicine (creek), Nebr. 264/D4
Medicine (creek), S. Dak. 298/J6
Medicine Bow (range), Colo. 208/G1
Medicine Bow, Wyo. (82329) 319/F4
Medicine Bow (range), Wyo. 319/F4
Medicine Bow (riv.), Wyo. 319/F3
Medicine Creek (dam), Nebr. 264/D4
Medicine Hat, 163/E5
Medicine Hat, Alta. 182/E4
Medicine Hat, Alta. 146/H5
Medicine Knoll (creek), S. Dak. 298/J5
Medicine Lake, Minn. (55427) 254/G5
Medicine Lake, Mont. (59247) 262/M2
Medicine Lodge (creek), Idaho 220/F5
Medicine Lodge, Kans. (67104) 232/D4
Medicine Lodge (riv.), Kans. 232/D4
Medicine Mound, Texas (†79252) 302/E3
Medicine Park, Okla. (73557) 288/J5
Medika, Man. 179/G5
Medill, Mo. (63455) 261/J2
Medina, Col. 126/D5
Medina (Hamel), Minn. (†55340) 254/F5
Medina, N. Dak. (58467) 283/M6
Medina, N.Y. (14103) 276/D4
Medina (co.), Ohio 284/G3
Medina, Ohio (44256) 284/G3
Medina, Saudi Ar., 54/H7
Medina, Saudi Ar. 59/D5
Medina, Tenn. (38355) 237/D9
Medina (co.), Texas 302/E8
Medina, Texas (78055) 302/E8
Medina (lake), Texas 302/E8
Medina (riv.), Texas 302/F8
Medina, Wash. (98039) 310/B2
Medinaceli, Spain 33/E2
Medina del Campo, Spain 33/D2
Medina de Rioseco, Spain 33/D2
Medina-Sidonia, Spain 33/D4
Mediodía, Col. 126/D8
Mediterranean (sea), 3/K4
Mediterranean (sea), 7/E5
Mediterranean (sea), 54/F6
Mediterranean (sea), 102/D1
Mediterranean (sea), Alg. 106/E1
Mediterranean (sea), France 28/E7
Mediterranean (sea), Italy 34/B6
Mediterranean (sea), Mor. 106/D1
Mediterranean (sea), Libya 111/C1
Mediterranean (sea), U.A.R. 111/E1
Mediterranean (sea), Tun. 106/F1
Medix Run, Pa. (†15868) 294/F3
Medjerda (riv.), Alg. 106/F1
Medjerda (riv.), Tun. 106/F1
Medley, Fla. (†33101) 212/B4
Medley, W. Va. (26734) 313/H4
Mednogorsk, U.S.S.R. 48/F4
Mednogorsk, U.S.S.R. 52/J4
Médoc (reg.), France 28/C5
Medon, Tenn. (38356) 237/D10
Medora, Ill. (62063) 222/C4
Medora, Ind. (47260) 227/E7
Medora, Kans. (67558) 232/E3
Medora, Man. 179/B5
Medora, N. Dak. (58645) 283/C6
Medstead, Sask. 181/C2
Meductic, N. Br. 170/C3
Medveditsa (riv.), U.S.S.R. 52/F4
Medvezhiy Yar, U.S.S.R. 48/K2
Medvezh'yegorsk, U.S.S.R. 48/D3
Medvezh'yegorsk, U.S.S.R. 52/D2
Medway▵, Maine (04460) 242/G4
Medway▵, Mass. (02053) 249/J4
Medway, Mass. (02053) 249/J4
Medway (harb.), N.S. 169/D4
Medway (riv.), N.S. 169/C4
Medzilaborce, Czech. 41/F2
Meehan, Miss. (†39301) 256/G6
Meekatharra, Australia, 87/B8
Meekatharra, Aust. 88/B5
Meekatharra, W. Aust. 92/B4
Meeker, Colo. (81641) 208/D2
Meeker, La. (71346) 238/F4
Meeker (co.), Minn. 254/D5
Meeker, Ohio (†43302) 284/D4
Meeker, Okla. (74855) 288/N4
Meeks, Ga. (†31049) 216/G5
Meerane, E. Ger. 22/E3
Meerhout, Belg. 27/G6
Meerle, Belg. 27/F6
Meers, Okla. (73558) 288/J5
Meersburg, W. Ger. 22/C5
Meerssen, Neth. 27/H7
Meerut, India, 54/L7
Meerut, India 68/D3
Meeteetse, Wyo. (82433) 319/D1
Meeting Creek, Alta. 182/D3
Meeting Lake, Sask. 181/D2
Mega (isl.), Indon. 85/C6
Mega, Eth. 111/G7
Megalópolis, Greece 45/E7
Megan, Sask. 181/H2
Mégantic (co.), Que. 172/F3
Mégantic (lake), Que. 172/G4
Mégara, Greece 45/F6
Megargel, Ala. (36457) 194/D8
Megargel, Texas (76370) 302/F4
Meggett, S.C. (29460) 296/G6
Megiddo, Israel 65/C2
Megion, U.S.S.R. 48/H3
Mehadia, Rum. 45/F3
Mehama, Oreg. (97384) 291/E3
Mehan, Okla. (†74074) 288/M2
Meherrin (riv.), N.C. 281/P1
Meherrin, Va. (23954) 307/M6
Meherrin (riv.), Va. 307/M7
Mehetia (isl.), Fr. Poly., 87/M7
Mehoopany, Pa. (18629) 294/K2
Mehran (riv.), Iran 59/F4
Mehran, Iran 66/F4
Mehran (riv.), Iran 66/J7
Mehsana, India 68/C4
Mehun-sur-Yèvre, France 28/E4
Meifa, P.D.R. Yemen 59/E7
Meiganga, Cameroon 115/B2
Meighen (isl.), 163/M3
Meighen (isl.), N.W.T. 187/H1
Meigle, Scot. 15/K6
Meigs, Ga. (31765) 216/D8
Meigs (co.), Ohio 284/F7
Meigs (co.), Tenn. 237/M9
Meihsien, China 77/J7
Meikle (riv.), Alta. 182/A1
Meiktila, Burma 72/B2
Meilen, Switz. 39/G2
Meiners Oaks, Calif. (93023) 204/F9
Meiningen, E. Ger. 22/D3
Meire Grove, Minn. (†56352) 254/C5
Meiringen, Switz. 39/F3
Meiron (mt.), Israel 65/C1
Meissen, E. Ger. 22/E3
Mejillones, Chile 138/A4
Mejillones del Sur (bay), Chile 138/A4
Mekambo, Gabon 115/B3
Mekerhane, Sebkra (salt lake), Alg. 106/E3
Mekili, Libya 111/D1
Mékinac (lake), Que. 172/E2
Mekinock, N. Dak. (58258) 283/R4
Meknès, 102/B1
Meknès, Mor. 106/C2
Mekong (riv.), 3/Q4
Mekong (riv.), 54/O8
Mekong (riv.), Burma 72/D2
Mekong (riv.), Cambodia 72/E4
Mekong (riv.), Laos 72/D3
Mekong (riv.), Thai. 72/E3
Mekong, Mouths of the (delta), S. Vietnam 72/E5
Mekong (riv.), China 77/F7
Mekoryuk, Alaska (99630) 196/E2
Melaka, Malaysia, 54/O9
Melaka (state), Malaysia 72/D7
Melaka, Malaysia 72/D7
Melanesia (reg.), Pacific, 87/E5
Melaval, Sask. 181/E6
Melba, Idaho (83641) 220/B6
Melber, Ky. (42069) 237/D7
Melbern, Ohio (†43506) 284/A3
Melbeta, Nebr. (69355) 264/A3
Melbourn, Eng. 13/H5
Melbourne, Ark. (72556) 203/G1
Melbourne, Australia, 3/R7
Melbourne, Aust., 87/E9
Melbourne, Que. 172/E4
Melbourne, Ont. 177/C5
Melbourne, Fla. (32901) 212/F3
Melbourne, Iowa (50162) 229/G5
Melbourne, Ky. (41059) 237/T3
Melbourne, Man. 179/C5
Melbourne, Mo. (†64642) 261/E2
Melbourne (isl.), N.W.T. 187/H3
Melbourne (cap.), Vic., 88/M6
Melbourne (cap.), Vic., 97/H5
Melbourne, Wash. (†98563) 310/B4
Melbourne Beach, Fla. (32951) 212/F3
Melbourne Village‡, Fla. (†32901) 212/F3
Melby, Minn. (56351) 254/C4
Melcher, Hond. 154/D3
Melcher, Iowa (50163) 229/G6
Melchnau, Switz. 39/E2
Melchor (isl.), Chile 138/D6
Melchor Múzquiz, Mex. 150/H3
Melchor Ocampo, Mex. 150/H4
Melchor Ocampo del Balsas, Mex. 150/H8
Melder, La. (71451) 238/E4
Meldorf, W. Ger. 22/C1
Meldrim, Ga. (31318) 216/K6
Meldrum Bay, Ont. 177/A2
Meldrum Creek, Br. Col. 184/F4
Meleb, Man. 179/E4
Melekess, U.S.S.R. 48/F4
Melekess, U.S.S.R. 52/G4
Melenki, U.S.S.R. 52/F3
Meleuz, U.S.S.R. 52/J4
Mélèzes (riv.), Que. 174/C1
Melfa, Va. (23410) 307/S5
Melfi, Italy 34/E4
Melfi, Chad 111/C5
Melfort, 163/F5
Melfort, Sask. 181/G3
Melgar de Fernamental, Spain 33/D1
Melhus, Norway 18/G5
Melide, Switz. 39/G5
Meligalá, Greece 45/F7
Melilla, 102/B1
Melilla, Spain, 7/D5
Melilla, Spain 106/D1
Melimoyu (mt.), Chile 138/D5
Melinca, Chile 138/D5
Melipilla, Chile 138/F4
Melita, Man. 179/A5
Melitopol', U.S.S.R. 52/D5
Melitota, Md. (†21620) 245/O4
Melk, Austria 41/C2
Melksham, 10/E5
Melksham, Eng. 13/F6
Mellansel, Sweden 18/L5
Melle, W. Ger. 22/C2
Mellen, Wis. (54546) 317/E3
Mellerud, Sweden 18/H7
Mellette (co.), S. Dak. 298/H6
Mellette, S. Dak. (57461) 298/N3
Mellingen, Switz. 39/F2
Mellott, Ind. (47958) 227/C4
Mellwood, Ark. (72367) 203/H5
Melmore, Ohio (44845) 284/D3
Melo, Urug., 120/E6
Melo, Urug. 145/E3
Melocheville, Que. 172/C4
Melozitna (riv.), Alaska 196/H1
Melrhir, Shott (salt lake), Alg. 106/F2
Melrose, Conn. (06049) 210/E1
Melrose, Fla. (32666) 212/D2
Melrose, Iowa (52569) 229/G7
Melrose, La. (71452) 238/E3
Melrose, Mass. (02176) 249/D6
Melrose, Md. (†21102) 245/L2
Melrose, Minn. (56352) 254/D5
Melrose, Mont. (59743) 262/D5
Melrose, N. Br. 170/F2
Melrose, N. Mex. (88124) 274/F4
Melrose, N.S.W. 97/D3
Melrose, Newf. 166/D2
Melrose, Ohio (45861) 284/B3
Melrose, Oreg. (†97470) 291/D4
Melrose, 10/E3
Melrose, Scot. 15/L8
Melrose, Wis. (54642) 317/E7
Melrose Park, Fla. (†33301) 212/B4
Melrose Park, Ill. (*60160) 222/A2
Melrose Park, N.Y. (†13021) 276/G5
Melrude, Minn. (55766) 254/F3
Mels, Switz. 39/H2
Melsbroek, Belg. 27/D9
Melsetter, Rhod. 118/E3
Melstone, Mont. (59054) 262/H4
Melsungen, W. Ger. 22/C3
Melton Hill (lake), Tenn. 237/N9
Melton Mowbray, 10/F4
Melton Mowbray, Eng. 13/G5
Meltonville, Iowa (†50472) 229/G2
Melun, France 28/E3
Melut, Sudan 111/F5
Melvaig, Scot. 15/E4
Melvern, Kans. (66510) 232/G3
Melvern Square, N.S. 169/C3
Melvich, Scot. 15/H2
Melville (lake), 163/L5
Melville (isl.), 163/M3
Melville (pen.), 163/H2
Melville (isl.), Australia, 87/D7
Melville (bay), Aust. 88/F2
Melville (isl.), Aust. 88/E2
Melville (cape), Aust. 88/G2
Melville (isl.), Canada, 4/B15
Melville (pen.), Canada, 4/C14
Melville (bay), Greenl., 4/B13
Melville, 163/F5
Melville, La. (71353) 238/G5
Melville, Mont. (59055) 262/F4
Melville, N. Dak. (†58421) 283/M5
Melville (isl.), N.W.T., 146/G2
Melville (pen.), N.W.T., 146/K3
Melville (isl.), N.W.T. 187/G2
Melville (pen.), N.W.T. 187/K3
Melville‡, N.Y. (11746) 276/O9
Melville (lake), Newf. 166/C3
Melville (bay), No. Terr. 93/E2
Melville (isl.), No. Terr. 93/B1
Melville (cape), Queens. 95/C2
Melville, Sask. 181/J5
Melvin, Ala. (36913) 194/B7
Melvin, Ill. (60952) 222/E3
Melvin, Iowa (51350) 229/B2
Melvin (lake), Ire. 17/E3
Melvin (lake), 10/B3
Melvin, Mich. (48454) 250/G5
Melvin, Minn. (†56540) 254/B3
Melvin, Texas (76858) 302/E6
Melvina, Wis. (54619) 317/E8
Melvindale, Mich. (48122) 250/B7
Melvin Mills, N.H. (†03278) 268/D5
Melvin Village, N.H. (03850) 268/E4
Mélykút, Hung. 41/E3
Memaliaj, Alb. 45/D5
Memba, Moz. 118/G2
Membij, Syria 63/G4
Memel (Klaipėda), U.S.S.R. 52/B3
Memel (Klaipėda), U.S.S.R. 53/A3
Memel (Klaipėda), U.S.S.R., 7/F3
Memmingen, W. Ger. 22/D5
Mempawah, Indon. 85/D5
Memphis, Fla. (†33561) 212/D4
Memphis, Ind. (47143) 227/F8
Memphis, Mich. (48041) 250/G6
Memphis, Mo. (63555) 261/H2
Memphis, Nebr. (68042) 264/H3
Memphis (ruins), U.A.R. 111/J3
Memphis, Tenn., 146/K6
Memphis, Tenn., 188/J3
Memphis, Tenn. (*38101) 237/B10
Memphis, Texas (79245) 302/D3
Memphis Army Depot, Tenn. 237/A10
Memphis Naval Air Sta., Tenn. 237/B10
Memphremagog (lake), Que. 172/E4
Memphremagog (lake), Vt. 268/C1
Memramcook, N. Br. 170/F2
Mena, Ark. (71953) 203/B4
Mena, U.S.S.R. 52/D4
Menafra, Urug. 145/B3
Menahga, Minn. (56464) 254/C4
Menai (str.), Wales 13/C4
Menai Bridge, Wales 13/C4
Menaik, Alta. 182/D3
Ménaka, Mali 106/E5
Menan, Idaho (83434) 220/F6
Menands, N.Y. (†12201) 276/N5
Menarandra (riv.), Malag. Rep. 118/H4
Menard (co.), Ill. 222/D3
Menard (co.), Texas 302/E7
Menard, Texas (76859) 302/E7
Menasalbas, Spain 33/D3
Menasha, Wis. (54952) 317/J7
Mencué, Arg. 143/C5
Mendak, Saudi Ar. 59/D5
Mende, France 28/E5
Mendebo (prov.), Eth. 111/H6
Mendenhall (cape), Alaska 196/E3
Mendenhall, Miss. (39114) 256/E7
Menderes (riv.), Turkey 59/A2
Menderes (riv.), Turkey 63/C4
Mendes, Ga. (†30427) 216/H7
Méndez, Ec. 128/C4
Mendham, N.J. (07945) 273/D2
Mendham, Sask. 181/B5
Mendi, Papua 85/B7
Mendi, Eth. 111/G6
Mendip (hills), Eng. 13/E6
Mendocino (cape), Calif., 146/F5
Mendocino (cape), Calif., 188/A2
Mendocino (co.), Calif. 204/B4
Mendocino, Calif. (95460) 204/B4
Mendocino (cape), Calif. 204/A3
Mendon, Ill. (62351) 222/B3
Mendon▵, Mass. (01756) 249/H4
Mendon, Mich. (49072) 250/D7
Mendon, Mo. (64660) 261/F3
Mendon, N.Y. (14506) 276/E4
Mendon, Ohio (45862) 284/A4
Mendon, Utah (84325) 304/B2
Mendon▵, Vt. (†05701) 268/B4
Mendon, Vt. (†05701) 268/B4
Mendong Gomba, China 77/C5
Mendooran, N.S.W. 97/E2
Mendota, Calif. (93640) 204/E7
Mendota, Ill. (61342) 222/D2
Mendota, Minn. (55050) 254/G5
Mendota, Va. (24270) 307/D7
Mendota (lake), Wis. 317/H9
Mendota Heights, Minn. (†55050) 254/G6
Mendoza, Arg., 120/D6
Mendoza (prov.), Arg. 143/C4
Mendoza, Arg. 143/C3
Mendoza (riv.), Arg. 143/C3
Mendoza, Bol. 136/C5
Mendoza, Peru 128/D6
Mendoza, Urug. 145/C5
Mendrisio, Switz. 39/G5
Mene de Mauroa, Ven. 124/C2
Mene Grande, Ven. 124/C3
Menemen, Turkey 63/B3
Menemsha, Mass. (02552) 249/L7
Menen, Belg. 27/C7
Meneses, Cuba 158/F2
Menfi, Italy 34/D6
Menfro, Mo. (63765) 261/N7
Mengen, Turkey 63/D2
Menggala, Indon. 85/D6
Mengtsz, China, 54/O7
Menifee, Ark. (72107) 203/E3
Menifee (co.), Ky. 237/O5
Menihek, Newf. 166/A3
Menihek (lakes), Newf. 166/A3
Menin (Menen), Belg. 27/C7
Menindee, Aust. 88/G6
Menindee, N.S.W. 97/B3
Menindee (lake), N.S.W. 97/B3
Meningie, S. Aust. 94/F6
Menisino, Man. 179/F5
Menistouc (lake), Newf. 166/A3
Menlo, Ga. (30731) 216/B2
Menlo, Iowa (50164) 229/E5
Menlo, Kans. (67746) 232/B2
Menlo, Wash. (98561) 310/B4
Menlo Park, Calif. (94025) 204/J3
Menlo Park, N.J. (08817) 273/E2
Menneval, N. Br. 170/C1
Menno, S. Dak. (57045) 298/P7
Meno, Okla. (73760) 288/K2
Menoken, N. Dak. (58558) 283/J6
Menominee, Ill. (†61025) 222/C1
Menominee (co.), Mich. 250/B3
Menominee, Mich. (49858) 250/B3
Menominee (riv.), Mich. 250/B3
Menominee (co.), Wis. 317/J5
Menominee (riv.), Wis. 317/L5
Menomonee Falls, Wis. (53051) 317/K1
Menomonie, Wis. (54751) 317/C6
Menor, Mar (lag.), Spain 33/F4
Menorca (Minorca) (isl.), Spain 33/J2
Mentasta (pass), Alaska 196/K2
Mentasta Lake, Alaska (†99586) 196/K2
Mentawai (isls.), Indon., 54/N10
Mentawai (isls.), Indon. 85/B6
Mentmore, N. Mex. (87319) 274/A3
Menton, France 28/G6
Mentone, Ala. (35984) 194/G1
Mentone, Calif. (92359) 204/H9
Mentone, Ind. (46539) 227/E2
Mentone, Texas (79754) 302/D10
Mentor, Kans. (67465) 232/E3
Mentor, Ky. (41060) 237/N3
Mentor, Minn. (56736) 254/B3
Mentor, Ohio (44060) 284/H2
Mentor-on-the-Lake, Ohio (44060) 284/G2
Menunketesuck (riv.), Conn. 210/E3
Menye, Turkey 63/C3
Menyüan, China 77/F4
Menza, U.S.S.R. 48/L5
Menzel-Bourguiba, Tun. 106/F1
Menzel-Temime, Tun. 106/G1
Menzie, Man. 179/B4
Menzies, Aust. 88/C5
Menzies, W. Aust. 92/C5
Menzingen, Switz. 39/G2
Menznau, Switz. 39/E2
Me'ona, Israel 65/C1
Meoqui, Mex. 150/G2
Meota, Sask. 181/C2
Meppel, Neth. 27/J3
Meppen, W. Ger. 22/B2
Mequon, Wis. (53092) 317/L1
Mera, Ec. 128/C3
Merabéllou (gulf), Greece 45/H8
Meraia (reg.), Mauritania 106/C5
Merak, Indon. 85/G1
Meråker, Norway 18/G5
Meramangye (lake), S. Aust. 94/C3
Meramec (riv.), Mo. 261/M4
Merano, Italy 34/C1
Merasheen, Newf. 166/D4
Merasheen (isl.), Newf. 166/C2
Merauke, Indon. 85/K7
Merbein, Vic. 97/A4
Mercaderes, Col. 126/B7
Mercara, India 68/D6
Merced (co.), Calif. 204/E6
Merced, Calif. (95340) 204/E6
Merced (riv.), Calif. 204/E6
Mercedario (mt.), 120/C6
Mercedario, Cerro (mt.), Arg. 143/B3
Mercedes, Arg., 120/D6
Mercedes, Buenos Aires, Arg. 143/G7
Mercedes, Corrientes, Arg. 143/G4
Mercedes, San Luis, Arg. 143/C3
Mercedes, Texas (78570) 302/F12
Mercedes, Urug., 120/E6
Mercedes, Urug. 145/B4
Merceditas, Chile 138/B7
Mercer (co.), Ill. 222/C2
Mercer (co.), Ky. 237/M5
Mercer▵, Maine (04957) 242/D6
Mercer (co.), Mo. 261/E2
Mercer, Mo. (64661) 261/F2
Mercer (co.), N. Dak. 283/G5
Mercer, N. Dak. (58559) 283/J5
Mercer (co.), N.J. 273/D3
Mercer, N.Z. 101/E2
Mercer (co.), Ohio 284/A4
Mercer, Ohio (†45862) 284/A4
Mercer (co.), Pa. 294/B3
Mercer, Pa. (16137) 294/B3
Mercer, Tenn. (38392) 237/D10
Mercer (co.), W. Va. 313/D8
Mercer, Wis. (54547) 317/F3
Mercer Island (city), Wash. (98040) 310/B2
Mercer Island (town)‡, Wash. (98040) 310/B2
Mercersburg, Pa. (17236) 294/G6
Mercerville, N.J. (08619) 273/D3
Merchantville, N.J. (08109) 273/B3
Merchtem, Belg. 27/E7
Mercier, Bol. 136/B2
Mercier (dam), Que. 172/A3
Mercier, Kans. (66511) 232/G2
Mercoal, Alta. 182/B3
Mercury (bay), N.Z. 101/F2
Mercury (isls.), N.Z. 101/F2
Mercury, Nev. (89023) 266/E6
Mercury, Texas (76880) 302/E6
Mercy (bay), N.W.T. 187/G2
Mercy (cape), N.W.T. 187/M3
Meredith, Colo. (81642) 208/F4
Meredith (lake), Colo. 208/M6
Meredith▵, N.H. (03253) 268/D4
Meredith, N.H. (03253) 268/D4
Meredith (lake), Texas 302/C2
Meredith Center, N.H. (†03253) 268/D4
Meredosia, Ill. (62665) 222/C4
Merefa, U.S.S.R. 52/E5
Merelbeke, Belg. 27/D7
Merevari (riv.), Ven. 124/F5
Mergui, Burma, 54/N8
Mergui, Burma 72/C4
Mergui (arch.), Burma 72/C5
Meriç (riv.), Turkey 63/B2
Merid, Sask. 181/B4
Mérida, Mex., 146/K7
Mérida, Mex. 150/P6
Mérida, Spain 33/C3
Mérida, Ven., 120/C2
Mérida (state), Ven. 124/C3
Mérida, Ven. 124/C3
Mérida, Cordillera de (range), Ven. 124/C3
Meriden, Conn. (06450) 210/D2
Meriden, Iowa (51037) 229/B3
Meriden, Kans. (66512) 232/G2
Meriden, Minn. (56067) 254/E6
Meriden, N.H. (03770) 268/C4
Meriden, Wyo. (82081) 319/H4
Meridian, Ga. (31319) 216/K8
Meridian, Idaho (83642) 220/B6
Meridian, Miss., 146/K6
Meridian, Miss., 188/J4
Meridian, Miss. (39301) 256/G6
Meridian, N.Y. (13113) 276/G4
Meridian, Okla. (73058) 288/M3
Meridian‡, Pa. (16001) 294/C4
Meridian, Texas (76665) 302/G6
Meridian N.A.A.S., Miss. 256/G6
Meridianville, Ala. (35759) 194/F1
Merigold, Miss. (38759) 256/C3
Merigomish, N.S. 169/F3
Merigomish (harb.), N.S. 169/F3
Merimbula, N.S.W. 97/F5
Merino, Colo. (80741) 208/N2
Merino, Vic. 97/A5
Merino Jarpa (isl.), Chile 138/D7
Merinos, Urug. 145/C3
Merino Village, Mass. (†01570) 249/G4
Merionethshire (co.), Wales 13/D5
Merion Station, Pa. (19066) 294/M6
Merir (isl.), Pac. Is., 87/D5
Meriwether (co.), Ga. 216/C4
Meriwether Unit, Natchez Trace Pkwy., Tenn. 237/F9
Merj 'Uyun, Leb. 63/F6
Merka, Somalia 115/H3
Merkel, Texas (79536) 302/E5
Merket, China 77/A4
Merksem, Belg. 27/E6
Merksplas, Belg. 27/F6
Merle, Sask. 181/H3
Merlin, Ont. 177/B5
Merlin, Oreg. (97532) 291/D5
Merlo, Arg. 143/G7
Mermentau, La. (70556) 238/E6
Mermentau (riv.), La. 238/E7
Merna, Nebr. (68856) 264/E3
Merna, Wyo. (†83115) 319/B3
Meroe (ruins), Sudan 111/F4
Merom, Ind. (47861) 227/B6
Merowe, 102/F3
Merowe, Sudan 59/B6
Merowe, Sudan 111/F4
Merredin, Aust. 88/B6
Merredin, W. Aust. 92/B5
Merriam, Ind. (†46701) 227/G2
Merriam, Kans. (66203) 232/H3
Merrick, N.Y. (11566) 276/S7
Merrick (co.), Nebr. 264/F3
Merrick (mt.), Scot. 15/H9
Merrickville, Ont. 177/J3
Merricourt, N. Dak. (58469) 283/N7
Merridale, Man. 179/A3
Merriewold Lake‡, N.Y. (†10992) 276/M8
Merrifield, Minn. (56465) 254/D4
Merrifield, N. Dak. (†58201) 283/R4
Merrifield (bay), Newf. 166/B2
Merrill (pass), Alaska 196/H2
Merrill, Iowa (51038) 229/A3
Merrill, Mich. (48637) 250/E5
Merrill, Miss. (39452) 256/G9
Merrill, N.Y. (12955) 276/N1
Merrill, Oreg. (97633) 291/F5
Merrill, Wis. (54452) 317/G5
Merrillan, Wis. (54754) 317/E7
Merrillville, Ga. (†31792) 216/E9
Merrillville, Ind. (46410) 227/C2
Merrimac▵, Mass. (01860) 249/L1
Merrimac, W. Va. (25661) 313/B7
Merrimac, Wis. (53561) 317/G9
Merrimack, Ky. (†40009) 237/L6
Merrimack (riv.), Mass. 249/K1
Merrimack (co.), N.H. 268/D5
Merrimack▵, N.H. (03054) 268/D6
Merrimack, N.H. (03054) 268/D6
Merrimack (riv.), N.H. 268/D5
Merrimacport, Mass. (†01860) 249/L1
Merriman, Nebr. (69218) 264/C2
Merrimon, N.C. (†28516) 281/R5
Merrionette Park, Ill. (†60601) 222/B2
Merritt, 163/D5
Merritt, Br. Col. 184/G5
Merritt (isl.), Fla. 212/F3
Merritt, Ill. (†62650) 222/C4
Merritt, Mich. (49667) 250/D4
Merritt (res.), Nebr. 264/D2
Merritt, Wash. (†98826) 310/E3
Merritt Island, Fla. (32952) 212/F3
Merriwa, N.S.W. 97/F3
Merriwagga, N.S.W. 97/C3
Merriweather, Mich. (49949) 250/F1
Mer Rouge, La. (71261) 238/G1
Merrow, Conn. (06253) 210/F1
Merryall, Conn. (†06776) 210/B2
Merryflat, Sask. 181/B6
Merry Hill, N.C. (27957) 281/R2
Merrymeeting (lake), N.H. 268/E5
Merry Oaks, N.C. (†27559) 281/L3
Merryville, La. (70653) 238/D5
Mersa Fatma, Eth. 111/H5
Mersch, Lux. 27/J9
Mersea (isl.), Eng. 13/J6
Merseburg, E. Ger. 22/D3
Mersey (riv.), N.S. 169/C4
Mersey (riv.), 10/F2
Mersey (riv.), Tas. 99/C3
Mershon, Ga. (31551) 216/H8
Mersin, Turkey 59/B2
Mersin, Turkey 63/F4
Mersing, Malaysia 72/E7
Měrsrags, U.S.S.R. 53/B2
Mertens‡, Texas (76666) 302/G6
Mertert, Lux. 27/J9
Merthyr Tydfil, 10/E5
Merthyr Tydfil, Wales 13/D6
Mértola, Port. 33/C4
Merton, 10/B5
Merton, Wis. (53056) 317/K1
Mertz Glacier Tongue, Ant. 5/C8
Mertzon, Texas (76941) 302/C6
Mertztown, Pa. (19539) 294/L4
Meru, Kenya 115/G3
Meru (mt.), Tanz. 115/G4
Merv (Mary), U.S.S.R., 54/K6
Merville, Br. Col. 184/E5
Mervin, Sask. 181/C2
Merwin, Mo. (†64723) 261/C6
Merwin (lake), Wash. 310/C5
Merzifon, Turkey 63/F2
Merzig, W. Ger. 22/B4
Mesa, Ariz., 188/D4
Mesa, Ariz. (*85201) 198/D5
Mesa (co.), Colo. 208/B5
Mesa, Colo. (81005) 208/C4
Mesa, Idaho (83643) 220/B5
Mesa, Miss. (†39667) 256/D8
Mesa‡, Texas (†79838) 302/A10
Mesa, Wash. (99343) 310/G4
Mesabi (range), Minn. 254/E3
Mesa Bolívar, Ven. 124/C3
Mesachie Lake, Br. Col. 184/J3
Mesagne, Italy 34/G4
Mesai (riv.), Col. 126/D7
Mesará (gulf), Greece 45/G8
Mesa Verde National Park, Colo. (81330) 208/C8
Mesa Verde Nat'l Park, Colo. 208/C8
Mescalero, N. Mex. (88340) 274/D5
Mescalero (ridge), N. Mex. 274/F6
Mescalero (valley), N. Mex. 274/F5
Mescalero Apache Ind. Res., N. Mex. 274/D5
Meschede, W. Ger. 22/C3
Mesena, Ga. (30819) 216/G4
Meservey, Iowa (50457) 229/G3
Meshed, Iran, 54/J6
Meshed, Iran 59/H2
Meshed, Iran 66/L2
Meshed-i-Sar (Babulsar), Iran 66/H2
Meshik, Alaska (†99579) 196/G3
Meshkinshahr, Iran 66/F1
Meshoppen, Pa. (18630) 294/L2
Meshra' er Req, Sudan 111/E6
Mesick, Mich. (49668) 250/D4
Mesilla, N. Mex. (88046) 274/C6
Mesilla Park, N. Mex. (88047) 274/C6
Mesita, Colo. (81142) 208/H8
Meskanaw, Sask. 181/F3
Meskene, Syria 59/C2
Meskene, Syria 63/H5
Mesocco, Switz. 39/H4
Mesolóngion, Greece 45/E6
Mesopotamia (reg.), Iraq 59/D3
Mesopotamia (reg.), Iraq 66/B3
Mesopotamia, Ohio (44439) 284/J3
Mesquite, N. Mex. (88048) 274/C6
Mesquite, Nev. (89024) 266/G6
Mesquite, Texas (75149) 302/H2
Messancy, Belg. 27/H9
Messina, Italy, 7/F5
Messina (prov.), Italy 34/E5
Messina, Italy 34/E5
Messina (str.), Italy 34/E6
Messina, S. Africa 118/D4
Messines, Que. 172/B3
Messíni, Greece 45/E7
Messíni (gulf), Greece 45/F7
Mesta (riv.), Bulg. 45/F5
Město Teplá, Czech. 41/B2
Mestre, Italy 34/D2
Mesudiye, Turkey 63/F4
Meta (riv.), Col. 126/E5
Meta (dept.), Col. 126/D6
Meta, Ky. (41501) 237/S5
Meta, Mo. (65058) 261/H6
Meta (riv.), Ven. 124/E4
Métabetchouan (riv.), Que. 172/F1

Milltown 401

Metairie, La. (*70001) 238/O4
Metaline, Wash. (99152) 310/H2
Metaline Falls, Wash. (99153) 310/H2
Metamma, Eth. 111/G5
Metamora, Ill. (61548) 222/D3
Metamora, Ind. (47030) 227/G6
Metamora, Mich. (48455) 250/F6
Metamora, Ohio (43540) 284/C2
Metán, Arg. 143/D2
Metangula, Moz. 118/F2
Metapán, El Salv. 154/C3
Metaskuak (lake), Que. 172/F2
Metasville, Ga. (†30673) 216/G3
Metauro (riv.), Italy 34/D3
Metcalf, Ga. (†31792) 216/E9
Metcalf, Ill. (61940) 222/F4
Metcalfe, Ont. 177/J2
Metcalfe (co.), Ky. 237/K7
Metcalfe, Miss. (38760) 256/B4
Metchin (riv.), Newf. 166/B3
Metchosin, Br. Col. 184/K4
Metea, Ind. (†46950) 227/E3
Metedeconk (riv.), N.J. 273/E3
Meteghan, N.S. 169/B4
Meteghan Centre, N.S. 169/B4
Meteghan River, N.S. 169/B4
Meteor (crater), Ariz. 198/E3
Meteor, Sask. 181/H2
Metepec, Mex. 150/M2
Methley, Man. 179/C3
Methlick, Scot. 15/M5
Methow, Wash. (98834) 310/E2
Methow (riv.), Wash. 310/E2
Methuen, Mass. (01844) 249/K2
Methven, N.Z. 101/C5
Methven, Scot. 15/J7
Metica (riv.), Col. 126/D6
Metigoshe (lake), N. Dak. 283/K2
Metinic (isl.), Maine 242/E8
Metiskow, Alta. 182/E3
Métis-sur-Mer, Que. 172/A1
Metlakatla, Alaska (99926) 196/N2
Metlakatla, Br. Col. 184/B3
Metlili Chaamba, Alg. 106/E2
Meto (bayou), Ark. 203/H5
Metolius, Oreg. (97742) 291/F3
Metolius (riv.), Oreg. 291/F3
Metomkin (inlet), Va. 307/T5
Metomkin (isl.), Va. 307/T5
Metonga (lake), Wis. 317/J4
Metropolis, Ill. (62960) 222/E6
Metropolitan, Mich. (†49381) 250/A3
Métsovon, Greece 45/E6
Mettawa‡, Ill. (†60048) 222/E1
Mettawee (riv.), Vt. 268/A5
Metter, Ga. (30439) 216/H6
Mettet, Belg. 27/F8
Metuchen, N.J. (08840) 273/E2
Metula, Israel 65/D1
Metz, France 28/G3
Metz, Ind. (†46703) 227/H1
Metz, Mich. (49758) 250/F3
Metz, Mo. (64765) 261/C6
Metz, W. Va. (26585) 313/F3
Metzger, Oreg. (†97223) 291/A2
Metzingen, W. Ger. 22/C4
Meudon, France 28/A2
Meulaboh, Indon. 85/B5
Meulebeke, Belg. 27/C7
Meung-sur-Loire, France 28/D4
Meurthe-et-Moselle (dept.), France 28/G3
Meuse (riv.), Belg. 27/F8
Meuse (dept.), France 28/F3
Meuse (riv.), France 28/F3
Meuselwitz, E. Ger. 22/E3
Mexia, Ala. (36458) 194/D8
Mexia, Texas (76667) 302/H6
Mexiana (isl.), Braz. 132/D2
Mexicali, Mex. 150/B1
Mexican Hat, Utah (84531) 304/E6
Mexican Springs, N. Mex. (87320) 274/A3
Mexico, 3/D4
Mexico, 146/H7
MEXICO, 150
Mexico (gulf), 3/E4
Mexico (gulf), 146/J7
Mexico (gulf), 188/J5
Mexico (gulf), Ala. 194/E10
Mexico (gulf), Cuba 158/A1
Mexico (gulf), Fla. 212/C4
Mexico, Ind. (46958) 227/E3
Mexico, Ky. (†42411) 237/E6
Mexico (gulf), La. 238/F8
Mexico△, Maine (04257) 242/B6
Mexico, Maine (04257) 242/B6
México (state), Mex. 150/K7
Mexico (gulf), Mex. 150/N4
Mexico, Mo. (65265) 261/J4
Mexico, N.Y. (13114) 276/H4
Mexico, Pa. (17056) 294/H4
Mexico (gulf), Texas 302/K9
Mexico Beach, Fla. (32410) 212/D6
Mexico City (cap.), Mex., 3/E5
Mexico City (cap.), Mex., 146/J7
Mexico City (cap.), Mex. 150/L1
Meyadin, Syria 59/C3
Meyadin, Syria 63/J5
Meyer, Iowa (†50455) 229/H2
Meyers Bay‡, Ill. (†60020) 222/E1
Meyers Chuck, Alaska (99903) 196/N2
Meyersdale, Pa. (15552) 294/E6
Meyers Lake, Ohio (†44701) 284/H4
Meyerton, S. Africa 118/H7
Meyronne, Sask. 181/E6
Mezen', U.S.S.R. 48/E3
Mezen' (riv.), U.S.S.R. 48/E3
Mezen', U.S.S.R. 52/F1
Mezen' (bay), U.S.S.R. 52/F1
Mezen' (riv.), U.S.S.R. 52/G1
Mezen', U.S.S.R., 4/C7
Mezen' (bay), U.S.S.R., 7/J2
Mezen' (riv.), U.S.S.R., 7/J2
Mezen', U.S.S.R., 7/J2
Mézenc (mt.), France 28/E5
Mezhdusharskiy (isl.), U.S.S.R. 52/G1
Meziadin (lake), Br. Col. 184/C2
Mézin, France 28/D5
Mezőberény, Hung. 41/F3
Mezőcsát, Hung. 41/F3
Mezőfalva, Hung. 41/E3
Mezőhegyes, Hung. 41/F3
Mezőkövesd, Hung. 41/F3
Mezőszilas, Hung. 41/E3
Mezőtúr, Hung. 41/F3
Mezquital, Mex. 150/G5
Mezquital (riv.), Mex. 150/G5
Mhor (lake), Scot. 15/H5
Mhow, India 68/D4
Miacatlán, Mex. 150/K2
Miajadas, Spain 33/D3
Miami, Ariz. (85539) 198/E5
Miami, Fla., 146/K7
Miami, Fla., 188/K5
Miami, Fla. (*33101) 212/B5
Miami (canal), Fla. 212/F5
Miami (riv.), Fla. 212/B5
Miami (co.), Ind. 227/E3
Miami, Ind. (46959) 227/E3
Miami (co.), Kans. 232/H3
Miami, Man. 179/D5
Miami, Mo. (65344) 261/F4
Miami, N. Mex. (87729) 274/E2
Miami (co.), Ohio 284/B5
Miami (riv.), Ohio 284/B6
Miami, Okla. (74354) 288/S1
Miami, Texas (79059) 302/D2
Miami, U.S., 3/F4
Miami Beach, Fla., 188/L5
Miami Beach, Fla. (33139) 212/C5
Miami Lakes, Fla. (†33101) 212/B4
Miamisburg, Ohio (45342) 284/B6
Miami Shores, Fla. (33153) 212/B4
Miami Springs, Fla. (33166) 212/B5
Miamitown, Ohio (45041) 284/A9
Miamiville, Ohio (45147) 284/D9
Miandrivazo, Malag. Rep. 118/G3
Mianeh, Iran 59/E2
Mianeh, Iran 66/E2
Mianus, Conn. (†06830) 210/A4
Mianus (riv.), Conn. 210/A4
Mianwali, Pak. 59/K3
Mianwali, Pak. 68/C2
Miastko, Poland 47/C1
Miazal, Ec. 128/D4
Mica, Wash. (99023) 310/H3
Mica Creek, Br. Col. 184/H4
Micanopy, Fla. (32667) 212/D2
Micawber, Okla. (†74882) 288/N3
Micay, Col. 126/B6
Micco, Fla. (†32960) 212/F4
Miccosukee, Fla. (32309) 212/B1
Miccosukee (lake), Fla. 212/B1
Michael, I. of Man 13/C3
Michael (lake), Newf. 166/C3
Michalovce, Czech. 41/G2
Michaud (pt.), N.S. 169/H3
Michel, Br. Col. 184/K5
Michelago, N.S.W. 97/E4
Michelson (mt.), Alaska 196/K1
Michelstadt, W. Ger. 22/C4
Miches, Dom. Rep. 158/F6
Michiana, Mich. (†49117) 250/C7
Michiana Shores‡, Ind. (†49117) 227/D1
Michichi, Alta. 182/D4
Michie, Tenn. (38357) 237/E10
Michigamme, Mich. (49861) 250/B2
Michigamme (lake), Mich. 250/A2
Michigamme (res.), Mich. 250/B2
Michigamme (riv.), Mich. 250/A2
Michigan (lake), 146/K5
Michigan, 188/J1
Michigan (lake), 188/J2
MICHIGAN, 250
Michigan (lake), Ill. 222/F1
Michigan (lake), Ind. 227/C1
Michigan (lake), Mich. 250/B5
Michigan, N. Dak. (58259) 283/O3
Michigan (state), U.S., 146/K5
Michigan (isl.), Wis. 317/F2
Michigan (lake), Wis. 317/M9
Michigan Bar, Calif. (†95683) 204/C8
Michigan Center, Mich. (49254) 250/E6
Michigan City, Ind. (46360) 227/C1
Michigan City, Miss. (38647) 256/F1
Michigantown, Ind. (46057) 227/E4
Michigan Valley, Kans. (†66528) 232/G3
Michikamats (lake), Newf. 166/B3
Michikamau (lake), 163/K5
Michikamau (lake), Newf. 166/B3
Michipicoten (isl.), Ont. 175/C3
Michipicoten (isl.), Ont. 177/H5
Michipicoten Harbour, Ont. 175/C3
Michipicoten Harbour, Ont. 177/H5
Michoacán (state), Mex. 150/H7
Michurin, Bulg. 45/H4
Michurinsk, U.S.S.R. 48/E4
Michurinsk, U.S.S.R. 52/F4
Michurinsk, U.S.S.R., 7/H3
Mickleton, N.J. (08056) 273/C4
Micotrin (mt.), Dominica 161/F6
Micoud, St. Lucia 161/G6
Micro, N.C. (27555) 281/N3
Micronesia (reg.), Pacific, 87/E4
Midale, Sask. 181/H6
Midas, Nev. (†89414) 266/E1
Middelburg, Neth. 27/C6
Middelburg, C. of Good Hope, S. Africa 118/D6
Middelburg, Transvaal, S. Africa 118/D5
Middelfart, Den. 18/G9
Middelfart, Den. 21/C7
Middelharnis, Neth. 27/E5
Middelvlei, S. Africa 118/G7
Middenmeer, Neth. 27/F3
Middle (riv.), Conn. 210/F1
Middle (cape), Fla. 212/E6
Middle, Iowa (52307) 229/K5
Middle (riv.), Minn. 254/B2
Middle Alkali (lake), Calif. 204/E2
Middle Andaman (isl.), India 68/G6
Middle Atlas (ranges), Mor. 106/C2
Middle Bass, Ohio (43446) 284/E2
Middle Bass (isl.), Ohio 284/E2
Middle Beaver (creek), Kans. 232/A2
Middleboro△, Mass. (02346) 249/L5
Middleboro, Mass. (02346) 249/L5
Middleboro (McKean), Pa. (16426) 294/B2
Middlebourne, W. Va. (26149) 313/E3
Middlebranch, Ohio (44652) 284/H4
Middlebro, Man. 179/G5
Middlebrook, Va. (24459) 307/K4
Middleburg, Fla. (32068) 212/E1
Middleburg, Ky. (42541) 237/M6
Middleburg, Md. (21768) 245/K2
Middleburg, N.C. (27556) 281/N2
Middleburg, N.Y. (12122) 276/M5
Middleburg, Ohio (43336) 284/C5
Middleburg, Pa. (17842) 294/H4
Middleburg, Va. (22117) 307/N3
Middleburg Heights, Ohio (†44017) 284/G10
Middlebury△, Conn. (06762) 210/C2
Middlebury, Ind. (46540) 227/F1
Middlebury△, Vt. (05753) 268/A3
Middlebury, Vt. (05753) 268/A3
Middlebury Center, Pa. (16935) 294/H2
Middlebury Gap (pass), Vt. 268/B4
Middlebush, N.J. (08874) 273/D3
Middle Concho (riv.), Texas 302/C6
Middledam, Maine (†04216) 242/B6
Middle Falls, N.Y. (12848) 276/O4
Middlefield△, Conn. (06455) 210/E2
Middlefield△, Mass. (01243) 249/B3
Middlefield, Ohio (44062) 284/H3
Middle Fork (peak), Idaho 220/D5
Middlefork, Ind. (†46039) 227/E4
Middle Fork, Willamette (riv.), Oreg. 291/E4
Middle Fork, Forked Deer (riv.), Tenn. 237/C9
Middle Fork, Obion (riv.), Tenn. 237/D8
Middle Fork, Powder (riv.), Wyo. 319/F2
Middle Gobi (prov.), Mong. 77/G2
Middle Granville, N.Y. (12849) 276/O4
Middlegrove, Ill. (61549) 222/C3
Middle Grove, Mo. (†65263) 261/H4
Middle Haddam, Conn. (06456) 210/E2
Middleham, Eng. 13/F3
Middle Harbour (creek), N.S.W. 97/J3
Middle Hope, N.Y. (12550) 276/M7
Middle Inlet, Wis. (54148) 317/K5
Middle Lake, Sask. 181/F3
Middle Loch (inlet), Hawaii 218/A3
Middle Loup (riv.), Nebr. 264/D3
Middlemarch, N.Z. 101/B6
Middle Musquodoboit, N.S. 169/E3
Middle Patuxent (riv.), Md. 245/L3
Middle Piney (creek), Wyo. 319/B3
Middle Point, Ohio (45863) 284/B4
Middleport, N.Y. (14105) 276/C4
Middleport, Ohio (45760) 284/F7
Middleport, Pa. (17953) 294/K4
Middle River, Md. (21220) 245/N3
Middle River, Minn. (56737) 254/B2
Middle River, N.S. 169/G2
Middle Sackville, N. Br. 170/F3
Middle Saranac (lake), N.Y. 276/M2
Middlesboro, Ky., 188/K3
Middlesboro, Ky. (40965) 237/O7
Middlesex (co.), Conn. 210/E3
Middlesex (co.), Jam. 158/J6
Middlesex (co.), Ont. 177/C4
Middlesex (co.), Mass. 249/J3
Middlesex, N.C. (27557) 281/N3
Middlesex (co.), N.J. 273/E3
Middlesex, N.J. (08846) 273/E2
Middlesex, N.Y. (14507) 276/F5
Middlesex (co.), Va. 307/R5
Middlesex△, Vt. (†05602) 268/B3
Middlesex, Vt. (†05602) 268/B3
Middle Stewiacke, N.S. 169/E3
Middleton, 10/G2
Middleton (isl.), Alaska 196/J3
Middleton (reef), Aust. 88/K5
Middleton, Eng. 13/E3
Middleton, Ga. (†30635) 216/G2
Middleton, Idaho (83644) 220/B6
Middleton△, Mass. (01949) 249/K2
Middleton, Mich. (48856) 250/E5
Middleton△, N.H. (†03887) 268/E5
Middleton, N.S. 169/C4
Middleton, Tenn. (38052) 237/D10
Middleton, Wis. (53562) 317/G9
Middleton-in-Teesdale, Eng. 13/E3
Middletown, Calif. (95461) 204/C5
Middletown, Conn. (06457) 210/E2
Middletown, Del. (19709) 245/R3
Middletown, Ill. (62666) 222/D3
Middletown, Ind. (47356) 227/F4
Middletown, Iowa (52638) 229/L7
Middletown, Ky. (40243) 237/L4
Middletown, Md. (21769) 245/J3
Middletown, Mo. (63359) 261/J4
Middletown, N.C. (27824) 281/T4
Middletown, N. Ire. 17/H3
Middletown△, N.J. (07748) 273/E3
Middletown, N.Y. (10940) 276/L8
Middletown, Ohio (45042) 284/A6
Middletown, Pa. (17057) 294/J5
Middletown△, R.I. (02840) 249/J6
Middletown, Va. (22645) 307/M2
Middletown Springs△, Vt. (05757) 268/A5
Middletown Springs, Vt. (05757) 268/A5
Middle Valley, N.J. (†07853) 273/D2
Middleville, Ont. 177/H2
Middleville, Mich. (49333) 250/D6
Middleville, N.J. (07855) 273/D1
Middleville, N.Y. (13406) 276/K4
Middle Water, Texas (79060) 302/B2
Middleway, W. Va. (†25430) 313/K4
Middle West Pubnico, N.S. 169/C5
Middlewich, 10/G2
Middlewich, Eng. 13/E4
Middlewood, N.S. 169/D4
Midfield, Ala. (35228) 194/E4
Midgic, N. Br. 170/F3
Midhurst, Ont. 177/E3
Midhurst, Eng. 13/G6
Midian (dist.), Saudi Ar. 59/C4
Midkiff, W. Va. (25540) 313/B6
Midland, Ark. (72945) 203/B3
Midland, Aust. 88/B2
Midland, Ont. 177/D3
Midland, Ga. (31820) 216/C5
Midland, Ind. (47445) 227/C6
Midland, La. (70557) 238/F6
Midland, Md. (21542) 245/C2
Midland (co.), Mich. 250/E5
Midland, Mich. (48640) 250/E5
Midland, N.C. (28107) 281/J4
Midland, W. Aust. 92/A1
Midland, Ohio (45148) 284/C7
Midland, Oreg. (97634) 291/F5
Midland, Pa. (15059) 294/A4
Midland, S. Dak. (57552) 298/G5
Midland (co.), Texas 302/B6
Midland, Texas (79701) 302/C6
Midland, Va. (22728) 307/N3
Midland City, Ala. (36350) 194/H8
Midland Park, N.J. (07432) 273/B1
Midlandvale, Alta. 182/D4
Midleton, 10/B5
Midleton, Ire. 17/E8
Midlothian, Ill. (60445) 222/B2
Midlothian (co.), Scot. 15/K8
Midlothian, Texas (76065) 302/G5
Midlothian, Va. (23113) 307/N6
Midnapore, India 68/F4
Midnight, Miss. (39115) 256/C4
Midnight Lake, Sask. 181/C2
Midongy Sud, Malag. Rep. 118/H4
Midstate Mill, N.C. (†28377) 281/L5
Midvale, Idaho (83645) 220/B5
Midvale, Ohio (44653) 284/H5
Midvale, Utah (84047) 304/B3
Midville, Ga. (30441) 216/H5
Midway, Ala. (36053) 194/H6
Midway, Br. Col. 184/H5
Midway, Del. (†19971) 245/T6
Midway, Fla. (32343) 212/B1
Midway, Ga. (31320) 216/K7
Midway, Ind. (†47635) 227/C8
Midway, Ky. (40347) 237/M4
Midway‡, Mo. (65201) 261/D9
Midway (Sedalia), Ohio (†43151) 284/D6
Midway, Pa. (15060) 294/B5
Midway‡, Pa. (†17331) 294/H6
Midway, Tenn. (37809) 237/P8
Midway (isls.), U.S., 87/J3
Midway (isls.), 188/E6
Midway, Utah (84049) 304/C3
Midway-Canaan‡, Fla. (32343) 212/E3
Midway City, Calif. (92655) 204/D11
Midway Park, N.C. (28544) 281/O5
Midwest, Wyo. (82643) 319/F2
Midwest City, Okla. (73110) 288/M4
Mid-Western (state), Nigeria 106/F7
Midyat, Turkey 63/J4
Midye, Turkey 63/C2
Mid Yell, Scot. 15/N2
Midzhur (mt.), Bulg. 45/F4
Midzhur (mt.), Yugo. 45/F4
Mie (pref.), Japan 81/H6
Miechów, Poland 47/E3
Międzychód, Poland 47/B2
Międzyrzec Podlaski, Poland 47/F3
Międzyrzecz, Poland 47/B2
Mielec, Poland 47/E3
Mienning, China 77/F6
Mienyang, China 77/G5
Mier, Ind. (†46919) 227/F3
Mier, Mex. 150/K3
Miercurea Ciuc, Rum. 45/G2
Mieres, Spain 33/D1
Miesso, Eth. 111/H6
Miesville, Minn. (†55033) 254/F6
Miette, Alta. 182/B3
Mifflin, Ohio (†44805) 284/F4
Mifflin (co.), Pa. 294/G4
Mifflin, Pa. (17058) 294/H4
Mifflin, Wis. (†53580) 317/F10
Mifflinburg, Pa. (17844) 294/H4
Mifflintown, Pa. (17059) 294/H4
Mifflinville‡, Pa. (18631) 294/K3
Miflin, Ala. (†36530) 194/C10
Migdal, Israel 65/C2
Mignon, Ala. (†35150) 194/F4
Miguel Alves, Braz. 132/F4
Miguel Azua, Mex. 150/H4
Miguel de la Borda, Pan. 154/G6
Miguelete, Urug. 145/B5
Migues, Urug. 145/C6
Mihaliççik, Turkey 63/D3
Mihara, Japan 81/F6
Mijirtein (prov.), Somalia 115/J2
Mikado, Mich. (48745) 250/F4
Mikado, Sask. 181/J4
Mikana, Wis. (54857) 317/C4
Mikhaylovgrad, Bulg. 45/F4
Mikhaylovka, U.S.S.R. 52/F4
Mikhmoret, Israel 65/B3
Miki, Japan 81/H7
Mikínai, Greece 45/F7
Mikkalo, Oreg. (97861) 291/G2
Mikkeli (prov.), Fin. 18/P6
Mikkeli, Fin. 18/P6
Mikkwa (riv.), Alta. 182/B5
Mikołów, Poland 47/B4
Míkonos (isl.), Greece 45/G7
Mikulov, Czech. 41/D2
Mikun', U.S.S.R. 52/H2
Mikuni, Japan 81/G5
Milaca, Minn. (56353) 254/E5
Milagro, Arg. 143/C3
Milagro, Ec. 128/C4
Milagros, Phil. 82/D4
Milam (co.), Texas 302/H7
Milam, Texas (75959) 302/L6
Milam, W. Va. (26838) 313/H5
Milan, Que. 172/F4
Milan, Ga. (31060) 216/G6
Milan, Ill. (61264) 222/C2
Milan, Ind. (47031) 227/G6
Milan, Italy, 3/K3
Milan, Italy, 7/E4
Milan (prov.), Italy 34/B2
Milan, Italy 34/B2
Milan, Kans. (67105) 232/E4
Milan, Mich. (48160) 250/F6
Milan, Minn. (56262) 254/C5
Milan, Mo. (63556) 261/F2
Milan△, N.H. (03588) 268/E2
Milan, N.H. (03588) 268/E2
Milan, N. Mex. (87020) 274/B3
Milan, Ohio (44846) 284/E3
Milan, Tenn. (38358) 237/D9
Milan, Wash. (99024) 310/H3
Milan, Wis. (54453) 317/F6
Milange, Moz. 118/F3
Milano, Texas (76556) 302/H7
Milanville, Pa. (18443) 294/M2
Milâs, Turkey 63/B4
Milazzo, Italy 34/E5
Milbank, S. Dak. (57252) 298/R3
Milbanke (sound), Br. Col. 184/C4
Milberger, Kans. (†67665) 232/D3
Milbridge△, Maine (04658) 242/H6
Milburn, Ky. (42070) 237/D7
Milburn, Nebr. (68857) 264/E3
Milburn, Okla. (73450) 288/O6
Milden, Sask. 181/D4
Mildenhall, Eng. 13/H5
Mildmay, Ont. 177/C3
Mildred, Kans. (66055) 232/G3
Mildred, Mont. (59341) 262/M4
Mildred, Pa. (18632) 294/K3
Mildred, Sask. 181/D2
Mildred Lake, Alta. 182/E1
Mildura, Aust. 88/G6
Mildura, Vic. 97/A4
Miles, Iowa (52064) 229/N4
Miles, Texas (76861) 302/D6
Milesburg, Pa. (16853) 294/G4
Miles City, Mont., 188/E1
Miles City, Mont. (59301) 262/L4
Milestone, Sask. 181/G5
Milesville, S. Dak. (57553) 298/F5
Milevsko, Czech. 41/C2
Miley, S.C. (29933) 296/E6
Milfay, Okla. (74046) 288/N3
Milford, Calif. (96121) 204/E3
Milford, Conn. (06460) 210/C4
Milford (pt.), Conn. 210/C4
Milford, Del. (19963) 245/S5
Milford, Ga. (†31762) 216/C8
Milford, Ill. (60953) 222/F3
Milford, Ind. (46542) 227/F2
Milford (Clifty), Ind. (†47240) 227/F6
Milford, Iowa (51351) 229/C2
Milford, Ire. 17/F1
Milford, Kans. (66514) 232/F2
Milford (res.), Kans. 232/E2
Milford, Ky. (41061) 237/N3
Milford△, Maine (04461) 242/F6
Milford, Maine (04461) 242/F6
Milford△, Mass. (01757) 249/H4
Milford, Mass. (01757) 249/H4
Milford, Mich. (48042) 250/F6
Milford, Mo. (64766) 261/D7
Milford△, N.H. (03055) 268/D6
Milford, N.H. (03055) 268/D6
Milford, N.J. (08848) 273/C2
Milford, N.Y. (13807) 276/K5
Milford (sound), N.Z. 101/A6
Milford, Nebr. (68405) 264/H4
Milford, Ohio (45150) 284/D9
Milford, Pa. (18337) 294/N3
Milford, Texas (76670) 302/H5
Milford, Utah (84751) 304/A5
Milford, Va. (22514) 307/O4
Milford, Wis. (†53038) 317/J9
Milford Bay, Ont. 177/E2
Milford Center, Ohio (43045) 284/D5
Milford Haven, 10/D5
Milford Haven (inlet), 10/D5
Milford Haven, Wales 13/B6
Milford Haven (inlet), Wales 13/B6
Milford Station, N.S. 169/E3
Milh, Bahr al (lake), Iraq 66/C4
Mili (atoll), Pac. Is., 87/H5
Miliana, Alg. 106/E1
Milicz, Poland 47/C3
Milieu (riv.), Que. 172/C3
Mililani, Hawaii (†96786) 218/E2
Milingimbi Mission, No. Terr. 93/D2
Milk (riv.), 146/H5
Milk (riv.), 163/F6
Milk (riv.), Alta. 182/D5
Milk (riv.), Mont., 188/D1
Milk (riv.), Mont. 262/J2
Milk, Wadi el (dry riv.), Sudan 59/A6
Milk, Wadi el (dry riv.), Sudan 111/E4
Milk River, Alta. 182/D5
Mill (creek), Calif. 204/D3
Mill (riv.), Conn. 210/D3
Mill (riv.), Conn. 210/B4
Mill (creek), Ind. 227/D5
Mill (riv.), Mass. 249/C3
Mill (riv.), Mass. 249/D3
Mill (creek), Mich. 250/G5
Mill (creek), N.J. 273/E4
Mill (isl.), N.W.T. 187/L3
Mill (riv.), Vt. 268/B4
Mill (creek), W. Va. 313/C5
Milladore, Wis. (54454) 317/G6
Millard, Ky. (41501) 237/S6
Millard, Mo. (†63501) 261/G2
Millard, Nebr. (68137) 264/H3
Millard (co.), Utah 304/A4
Millardale, Sask. 181/B4
Millarton, N. Dak. (58470) 283/N6
Millarville, Alta. 182/C4
Millau, France 28/E5
Millbank, Ont. 177/D4
Mill Bay, Br. Col. 184/C2
Millboro, S. Dak. (57554) 298/K7
Millboro, Va. (24460) 307/J5
Millboro Springs, Va. (24460) 307/J4
Millbourne, Pa. (†19082) 294/M6
Millbrae, Calif. (94030) 204/J2
Millbridge, Ont. 177/G3
Millbrook, Ala. (36054) 194/F6
Millbrook, Ont. 177/F3
Millbrook, Ill. (60536) 222/E2
Millbrook, Mass. (†02332) 249/M4
Millbrook, Mich. (49334) 250/D5
Millbrook, N.C. (27558) 281/M3
Millbrook, N.Y. (12545) 276/N7
Millburn△, N.J. (07041) 273/E2
Millburne, Wyo. (†82933) 319/B4
Millbury△, Mass. (01527) 249/H4
Millbury, Ohio (43447) 284/D2
Mill City, Nev. (†89418) 266/D2
Mill City, Oreg. (97360) 291/E3
Mill Cove, N. Br. 170/D3
Millcreek, Ill. (62961) 222/D6
Mill Creek, Ind. (46365) 227/D1
Millcreek, Mo. (63658) 261/M7
Mill Creek, Okla. (74856) 288/N6
Mill Creek, Pa. (17060) 294/G5
Mill Creek, W. Va. (26280) 313/G5
Milldale, Conn. (06467) 210/D2
Mille Coquins (lake), Mich. 250/D2
Milledgeville, Ga. (31061) 216/F4
Milledgeville, Ill. (61051) 222/D1
Milledgeville, Ohio (43142) 284/C6
Milledgeville, Tenn. (38359) 237/E10
Mille-Îles (riv.), Que. 172/H4
Mille Lac Ind. Res., Minn. 254/E4
Mille Lacs (lake), Ont. 175/B3
Mille Lacs (lake), Ont. 177/G5
Mille Lacs (lake), Minn., 188/H1
Mille Lacs (co.), Minn. 254/E5
Mille Lacs (lake), Minn. 254/E4
Millen, Ga. (30442) 216/J5
Miller (peak), Ariz. 198/E7
Miller (co.), Ark. 203/C7
Miller (co.), Ga. 216/C8
Miller, Iowa (50438) 229/F2
Miller, Kans. (†66868) 232/F3
Miller, Miss. (†38654) 256/E1
Miller (co.), Mo. 261/H6
Miller, Mo. (65707) 261/E8
Miller, Nebr. (68858) 264/E4
Miller, Ohio (†45623) 284/F8
Miller (creek), Oreg. 291/F5
Miller, S. Dak. (57362) 298/L4
Miller City, Ohio (45864) 284/B3
Miller House, Alaska (99730) 196/J1
Millerovo, U.S.S.R. 48/E5
Millerovo, U.S.S.R. 52/F5
Millerovo, U.S.S.R., 7/J4
Millers (riv.), Mass. 249/E2
Millers, Md. (21107) 245/L2
Millersburg, Ind. (46543) 227/F1
Millersburg, Iowa (52308) 229/J5
Millersburg, Ky. (40348) 237/N4
Millersburg, Mich. (49759) 250/F3
Millersburg, Ohio (44654) 284/F4
Millersburg, Pa. (17061) 294/J4
Millers Falls, Mass. (01349) 249/E2
Millers Ferry, Ala. (36760) 194/D6
Millers Ferry, Fla. (†32437) 212/C6
Millersport, Ohio (43046) 284/E6
Millerstown, Ky. (†42754) 237/J6
Millerstown, Pa. (17062) 294/H4
Millersview, Texas (76862) 302/E6
Millersville, Md. (21108) 245/M4
Millersville, Ohio (43448) 284/D3
Millersville, Pa. (17551) 294/K6
Millerton (lake), Calif. 204/F6
Millerton, Iowa (50165) 229/G7
Millerton, N. Br. 170/E2
Millerton, N.Y. (12546) 276/O7
Millerton, Okla. (74750) 288/S7
Millerton, Pa. (16936) 294/J2
Millertown, Newf. 166/C4
Millerville, Ala. (36267) 194/G4
Millerville, Minn. (†56315) 254/C4
Millet, Alta. 182/D3
Milleton, Sask. 181/B2
Millett, Texas (†78014) 302/E9
Millettville, S.C. (†29836) 296/D5
Millgrove, Ind. (†47348) 227/G4
Mill Grove, Mo. (64662) 261/E2
Mill Hall, Pa. (17751) 294/G3
Millhaven, Ga. (†30467) 216/J5
Millheim, Pa. (16854) 294/G4
Millhousen, Ind. (47261) 227/G6
Millican, Oreg. (†97701) 291/F4
Millicent, Alta. 182/E4
Millicent, S. Aust. 94/F7
Milligan, Fla. (32537) 212/C6
Milligan, Ind. (†47856) 227/C5
Milligan, Nebr. (68406) 264/G4
Milligan College, Tenn. (37682) 237/S8
Milliken, Colo. (80543) 208/K2
Milliken, Ont. 177/J4
Millikin, La. (†71254) 238/H1
Millingen aan den Rijn, Neth. 27/J5
Millington, Conn. (†06423) 210/F3
Millington, Ill. (60537) 222/E2
Millington, Md. (21651) 245/P3
Millington, Mich. (48746) 250/F5
Millington, N.J. (07946) 273/D2
Millington, Tenn. (38053) 237/B10
Millinocket△, Maine (04462) 242/F4
Millinocket, Maine (04462) 242/F4
Millinocket (lake), Maine 242/F4
Millinocket (lake), Maine 242/F3
Million, Man. 179/C3
Mill Iron, Mont. (59342) 262/M5
Millis△, Mass. (02054) 249/A8
Millis-Clicquot, Mass. (02054) 249/A8
Millisle, N. Ire. 17/K2
Millmerran, Queens. 95/D5
Millmont, Pa. (17845) 294/H4
Mill Neck, N.Y. (11765) 276/R6
Millom, Eng. 13/D3
Mill Plain, Conn. (†06810) 210/A3
Mill Point, W. Va. (24959) 313/F6
Millport, Ala. (35576) 194/B3
Millport, 10/A1
Millport, N.Y. (14864) 276/G6
Millport, Pa. (16739) 294/F2
Millport, Scot. 15/A2
Millrift, Pa. (18340) 294/N3
Mill River, Mass. (01244) 249/A4
Millrose, W. Aust. 92/C4
Mill Run, Pa. (15464) 294/C6
Millry, Ala. (36558) 194/B7
Mills (co.), Iowa 229/B6
Mills, Ky. (40970) 237/O7
Mills, N. Mex. (87730) 274/E2
Mills (lake), N.W.T. 187/G3
Mills, Nebr. (68753) 264/E2
Mills, Pa. (16937) 294/G2
Mills (co.), Texas 302/F6
Mills, Utah (†84639) 304/B4
Mills, Wyo. (82644) 319/F3
Millsap, Texas (76066) 302/G5
Millsboro, Del. (19966) 245/S6
Millsboro, Pa. (15348) 294/B6
Mill Shoals, Ill. (62862) 222/E5
Mill Spring, Mo. (63952) 261/L8
Mill Springs, Ky. (42632) 237/M7
Millstadt, Ill. (62260) 222/B6
Millston, Wis. (54643) 317/E7
Millstone, Ky. (41838) 237/R6
Millstone, N.J. (08849) 273/D2
Millstone (riv.), N.J. 273/D3
Millstone, W. Va. (25261) 313/D5
Millstream, N. Br. 170/E3
Millstreet, Ire. 17/D7
Millthorpe, N.S.W. 97/E5
Milltown, Ala. (†36855) 194/H4
Milltown, Ind. (47145) 227/E8

402 Milltown

Milltown, Ky. (42761) 237/L6
Milltown, Mont. (59851) 262/C4
Milltown, N. Br. 170/C3
Milltown, N.J. (08850) 273/E3
Milltown, Newf. 166/C4
Milltown, S. Dak. (†57366) 298/O7
Milltown, Wis. (54858) 317/B4
Millungera, Queens. 95/B3
Millvale, Pa. (15209) 294/B7
Mill Valley, Calif. (94941) 204/H2
Mill Village, N.S. 169/D4
Mill Village, Pa. (16427) 294/C2
Millville, Del. (19967) 245/T6
Millville, Ind. (†47362) 227/G5
Millville, Iowa (†52052) 229/L3
Millville△, Mass. (01529) 249/H4
Millville, Mass. (01529) 249/H4
Millville, Minn. (55957) 254/F6
Millville, N. Br. 170/C2
Millville, N.J. (08332) 273/C5
Millville, Ohio (45013) 284/A7
Millville, Pa. (17846) 294/J3
Millville, Utah (84326) 304/C2
Millwood (res.), Ark. 203/C6
Millwood, Ga. (31552) 216/G8
Millwood, Ky. (42762) 237/J6
Millwood, Man. 179/A4
Millwood, Ohio (†43014) 284/F5
Millwood, Va. (22646) 307/N2
Millwood, W. Va. (25262) 313/C5
Millwood, Wash. (99212) 310/H3
Milly, Sask. 181/E6
Milly Milly, W. Aust. 92/B4
Milmay, N.J. (08340) 273/D5
Milmine, Ill. (61855) 222/E4
Milmont Park, Pa. (19033) 294/M7
Milne (inlet), N.W.T. 187/K2
Milne (bay), Papua 85/C8
Milner, Br. Col. 184/L3
Milner, Colo. (80477) 208/F2
Milner, Ga. (30257) 216/D4
Milner Ridge, Man. 179/F4
Milnesand, N. Mex. (88125) 274/F5
Milnes Landing, Br. Col. 184/J4
Milngavie, 10/B1
Milngavie, Scot. 15/C2
Milnor, N. Dak. (58060) 283/R7
Milo, Alta. 182/D4
Milo (riv.), Guinea 106/C7
Milo, Iowa (50166) 229/G6
Milo, Ky. (41235) 237/R5
Milo△, Maine (04463) 242/F5
Milo, Maine (04463) 242/F5
Milo, Mo. (64767) 261/D7
Milo, Okla. (73451) 288/M6
Milo, Oreg. (97455) 291/E5
Milo, Tenn. (†37381) 237/L9
Milolii, Hawaii (†96704) 218/G6
Mílos, Greece 45/G7
Mílos (isl.), Greece 45/G7
Milpa, N.S.W. 97/B2
Milparinka, N.S.W. 97/A1
Milperra, N.S.W. 97/H4
Milpitas, Calif. (95035) 204/L3
Milroy, Ind. (46156) 227/G6
Milroy, Minn. (56263) 254/C6
Milroy, Pa. (17063) 294/G4
Milstead, Ala. (†36075) 194/G6
Milstead, Ga. (30207) 216/D3
Milton (res.), Colo. 208/K2
Milton, Conn. (†06759) 210/C1
Milton, Del. (19968) 245/S5
Milton, Ont. 177/E4
Milton, Fla. (32570) 212/B6
Milton, Ill. (62352) 222/C4
Milton, Ind. (47357) 227/G5
Milton, Iowa (52570) 229/J7
Milton, Kans. (67106) 232/E4
Milton, Ky. (40045) 237/L3
Milton, La. (70558) 238/F6
Milton△, Mass. (02186) 249/D7
Milton, N.C. (27305) 281/L1
Milton, N. Dak. (58260) 283/O2
Milton△, N.H. (03851) 268/F5
Milton, N.H. (03851) 268/F5
Milton, N.J. (07438) 273/D1
Milton, N.S. 169/D4
Milton, N.S.W. 97/F4
Milton, N.Y. (12547) 276/M7
Milton, N.Y. (†12020) 276/N4
Milton, N.Z. 101/B7
Milton, Newf. †66/C2
Milton, Okla. (†74944) 288/S4
Milton, Pa. (17847) 294/J3
Milton, Tenn. (37118) 237/J9
Milton△, Vt. (05468) 268/A2
Milton, Vt. (05468) 268/A2
Milton, W. Va. (25541) 313/B6
Milton, Wash. (98354) 310/C3
Milton, Wis. (53563) 317/J10
Miltona, Minn. (56354) 254/C4
Miltona (lake), Minn. 254/C4
Milton Center, Ohio (43541) 284/C3
Milton-Freewater, Oreg. (97862) 291/J2
Milton Mills, N.H. (03852) 268/F4
Miltonsburg, Ohio (†43793) 284/H6
Miltonvale, Kans. (67466) 232/E2
Miltown Malbay, Ire. 17/C6
Milverton, Ont. 177/D4
Milwaukee, N.C. (27854) 281/P2
Milwaukee, Wis., 146/K5
Milwaukee, Wis., 188/J2
Milwaukee (co.), Wis. 317/L9
Milwaukee, Wis. (*53201) 317/M1
Milwaukie, Oreg. (97222) 291/B2
Mima, Ky. (41456) 237/P5
Mimbres, N. Mex. (88049) 274/B6
Mimbres (mts.), N. Mex. 274/B6
Mimbres (riv.), N. Mex. 274/B6
Mimінegash, P.E.I. 169/D2
Mimizan, France 28/C5
Mimoň, Czech. 41/C1
Mimongo, Gabon 115/B4
Mimosa Park‡, La. (†70070) 238/N4
Mimoso do Sul, Braz. 135/F2
Mims, Fla. (32754) 212/F3
Mina (mt.), Mali 106/C6
Mina, Nev. (89422) 266/C4
Mina, S. Dak. (57462) 298/M3
Mina al Ahmadi, Kuwait 59/E4
Mina al Fahal, Oman 59/G5
Minab, Iran 59/G2
Minab, Iran 66/K7
Minaki, Ont. 175/A3
Minaki, Ont. 177/F4
Minam, Oreg. (†97827) 291/K2
Minamata, Japan 81/E7
Minami Iwo (isl.), Japan 81/M5
Minami Iwo (isl.), Japan, 87/D3
Minapasuk, Phil. 82/D5
Minard, Ire. 17/A7
Minas, Cuba 158/G2
Minas (mts.), Guat. 154/C3
Minas (basin), N.S. 169/D3
Minas (chan.), N.S. 169/D3
Minas, Urug. 145/D5
Mina Sa'ud, Saudi Ar. 59/E4
Minas-cué, Par. 144/C4
Minas de Corrales, Urug. 145/D2
Minas de Matahambre, Cuba 158/A1
Minas de Riotinto, Spain 33/C4
Minas de Santa Lucía, Cuba 158/A1
Minas Gerais (state), Braz. 132/E7
Minas Gerais (state), Braz. 135/D2
Minas Novas, Braz., 120/F4
Minas Novas, Braz. 132/F7
Minatare, Nebr. (69356) 264/A3
Minatare (lake), Nebr. 264/A3
Minatitlán, Mex. 150/M8
Minbu, Burma 72/B2
Minburn, Alta. 182/E3
Minburn, Iowa (50167) 229/E5
Minbya, Burma 72/B2
Minch, The (str.), Scot., 7/D3
Mincha, Chile 138/A8
Minchinmávida (vol.), Chile 138/E4
Mincio (riv.), Italy 34/C2
Minco, Okla. (73059) 288/L4
Mindanao (isl.), Phil. 82/D7
Mindanao (riv.), Phil. 82/E7
Mindanao (sea), Phil. 82/D6
Mindanao (isl.), Phil. 85/H4
Mindanao (sea), Phil. 85/G4
Mindanao (isl.), Phil., 3/R5
Mindanao (isl.), Phil., 54/R9
Mindelheim, W. Ger. 22/D4
Mindelo, C. Verde Is. 106/A7
Mindemoya, Ont. 177/B2
Mindemoya (lake), Ont. 177/B2
Minden, Ont. 177/F3
Minden, Iowa (51553) 229/C6
Minden, La. (71055) 238/D1
Minden, Nebr. (68959) 264/F4
Minden, Nev. (89423) 266/B4
Minden, Texas (75680) 302/K5
Minden, W. Ger. 22/C2
Minden, W. Va. (25879) 313/D7
Minden City, Mich. (48456) 250/G5
Mindenmines, Mo. (64769) 261/D8
Mindiptana, Indon. 85/L7
Mindoro (isl.), Phil. 82/C4
Mindoro (str.), Phil. 82/C4
Mindoro (isl.), Phil. 85/G3
Mindoro (str.), Phil. 85/F3
Mindoro (isl.), Phil., 54/P8
Mindoro, Wis. (54644) 317/D7
Mindouli, Rep. of Congo 115/B4
Mindszent, Hung. 41/F3
Mine (head), Ire. 17/F8
Mine Center, Ont. 175/B3
Mine Center, Ont. 177/G5
Minehead, 10/E5
Minehead, Eng. 13/D6
Mine Hill△, N.J. (†07801) 273/D2
Mineiros, Braz. 132/C7
Mine La Motte, Mo. (63659) 261/M7
Mineola, Iowa (51554) 229/B6
Mineola, Mo. (63360) 261/J5
Mineola, N.Y. (11501) 276/R7
Mineola, Texas (75773) 302/J5
Miner, Mo. (†63801) 261/N9
Miner, Mont. (†59027) 262/E5
Miner (co.), S. Dak. 298/O5
Mineral, Calif. (96063) 204/D3
Mineral (co.), Colo. 208/F7
Mineral, Ill. (61344) 222/D2
Mineral (co.), Mont. 262/B3
Mineral (co.), Nev. 266/C4
Mineral, Ohio (†45766) 284/F7
Mineral, Texas (78125) 302/G9
Mineral (mts.), Utah 304/B5
Mineral, Va. (23117) 307/N4
Mineral (co.), W. Va. 313/J4
Mineral, Wash. (98355) 310/C4
Mineral Bluff, Ga. (30559) 216/D1
Mineral Center, Minn. (†55605) 254/G2
Mineral City, Ohio (44656) 284/H4
Mineral del Monte, Mex. 150/K6
Mineral Hills, Mich. (†49935) 250/G2
Mineral'nye Vody, U.S.S.R. 52/F6
Mineral Point, Mo. (63660) 261/L7
Mineral Point, Wis. (53565) 317/F10
Mineral Ridge, Ohio (44440) 284/J3
Mineral Springs, Ark. (71851) 203/C6
Mineral Springs, N.C. (28108) 281/H5
Mineral Wells, Miss. (38648) 256/E1
Mineral Wells, Texas (76067) 302/F5
Mineralwells, W. Va. (26150) 313/C4
Minersville, Ohio (45763) 284/G7
Minersville, Pa. (17954) 294/K4
Minersville, Utah (84752) 304/A5
Mine Run, Va. (22568) 307/N4
Minerva, Ky. (41062) 237/O3
Minerva, N.Y. (12851) 276/N3
Minerva, Ohio (44657) 284/H4
Minerva (reefs), Tonga, 87/J8
Minerva Park, Ohio (†43201) 284/E5
Minetto, N.Y. (13115) 276/H4
Mineville-Witherbee, N.Y. (12956) 276/O2
Minford, Ohio (45653) 284/E8
Mingan, 163/K5
Mingan, Que. 174/E2
Mingan (Jacques-Cartier) (pass), Que. 174/E3
Mingechaur, U.S.S.R. 52/G6
Mingenew, Aust. 88/B5
Mingenew, W. Aust. 92/A5
Minginish (dist.), Scot. 15/D5
Minglanilla, Spain 33/F3
Mingo, Iowa (50168) 229/G5
Mingo, Kans. (†67701) 232/B2
Mingo (lake), N.W.T. 187/L3
Mingo, Ohio (43047) 284/C5
Mingo (co.), W. Va. 313/B7
Mingo, W. Va. (26281) 313/F5
Mingo Junction, Ohio (43938) 284/J5
Mingulay (isl.), Scot. 15/A6
Mingus, Texas (76463) 302/F5
Minhla, Burma 72/B3
Minho (riv.), Jam. 158/J6
Minho (prov.), Port. 33/B2
Minho (riv.), Port. 33/B2
Minhsien, China 77/F5
Minicoy (isl.), India 68/C7
Minidoka (co.), Idaho 220/E7
Minidoka, Idaho (83343) 220/E7
Minier, Ill. (61759) 222/D3
Minigwal (lake), W. Aust. 92/C5
Minilya, W. Aust. 92/A4
Miniota, Man. 179/B4
Minipi (lake), Newf. 166/B3
Minipi (riv.), Newf. 166/B3
Ministikwan (lake), Sask. 181/B1
Ministre (pt.), St. Lucia 161/G7
Minitonas, Man. 179/B2
Min Kiang (riv.), China 77/F5
Min Kiang (riv.), China 77/J6
Minlaton, S. Aust. 94/E6
Minna, 102/C4
Minna, Nigeria 106/F7
Minneapolis, Kans. (67467) 232/E2
Minneapolis, Minn., 146/J5
Minneapolis,Minn., 188/H1
Minneapolis, Minn. (*55401) 254/G5
Minneapolis, U.S., 3/E3
Minneapolis-Saint Paul Airport, Minn. 254/G5
Minnechaduza (creek), S. Dak. 298/H7
Minnedosa, Man. 179/B4
Minnedosa (riv.), Man. 179/B4
Minnehaha (co.), S. Dak. 298/R6
Minnehaha Springs, W. Va. (24960) 313/G6
Minneiska, Minn. (55958) 254/G6
Minneola, Fla. (32755) 212/E3
Minneola, Kans. (67865) 232/C4
Minneota, Minn. (56264) 254/C6
Minnesota, 188/H1
MINNESOTA, 254
Minnesota (riv.), Minn., 188/G2
Minnesota (riv.), Minn. 254/E6
Minnesota (riv.), S. Dak. 298/S3
Minnesota (state), U.S., 146/J5
Minnesota City, Minn. (55959) 254/G6
Minnesota Lake, Minn. (56068) 254/E7
Minnetonka, Minn. (55343) 254/G5
Minnetonka (lake), Minn. 254/F5
Minnetonka Beach‡, Minn. (55361) 254/F5
Minnetrista, Minn. (†55364) 254/F5
Minnewaska (lake), Minn. 254/C5
Minnewaukan, N. Dak. (58351) 283/M3
Minnie Lake, Sask. 181/D5
Minnipa, S. Aust. 94/D5
Minnitaki (lake), Ont. 177/G4
Minnith, Mo. (63673) 261/M7
Minnora, W. Va. (25263) 313/D5
Miño (riv.), Spain, 7/D4
Miño (riv.), Spain 33/B1
Minoa‡, N.Y. (13116) 276/J4
Minobu, Japan 81/J6
Minocqua, Wis. (54548) 317/G4
Miñones, Arg. 143/G5
Minong, Wis. (54859) 317/C3
Minonk, Ill. (61760) 222/D3
Minoo, Japan 81/J7
Minooka, Ill. (60447) 222/E2
Minorca (isl.), Spain, 7/E5
Minorca (isl.), Spain 33/J2
Minor Hill, Tenn. (38473) 237/G10
Minor Lane Heights‡, Ky. (†40201) 237/K4
Minortown, Conn. (†06798) 210/C2
Minot△, Maine (04258) 242/C7
Minot, Maine (04258) 242/C7
Minot, Mass. (02055) 249/F8
Minot, N. Dak., 188/F1
Minot, N. Dak. (58701) 283/H3
Minot A.F.B., N. Dak. 283/H3
Min Shan (range), China 77/F5
Minsk, U.S.S.R. 48/C4
Minsk, U.S.S.R. 52/C4
Minsk, U.S.S.R., 3/L3
Minsk, U.S.S.R., 7/G3
Mińsk Mazowiecki, Poland 47/E2
Minster, Ohio (45865) 284/B5
Minstrel Island, Br. Col. 184/D5
Minter, Ala. (36761) 194/D6
Minter (Lollie), Ga. (30433) 216/G6
Minter City, Miss. (38944) 256/D3
Mint Hill, N.C. (28212) 281/H4
Minto, Alaska (99758) 196/J2
Minto (lake), Que. 174/E2
Minto (lake), 163/J4
Minto, Man. 179/B5
Minto, N. Br. 170/D2
Minto, N. Dak. (58261) 283/R3
Minto (inlet), N.W.T. 187/G2
Minto Mine, Br. Col. 184/F5
Minton, Sask. 181/G6
Mintsin, China 77/F4
Minturn, Ark. (72445) 203/H2
Minturn, Colo. (81645) 208/G3
Minturn, Maine (04659) 242/G7
Minturn, S.C. (29573) 296/J2
Minturno, Italy 34/D4
Minûf, U.A.R. 111/J3
Minusinsk, U.S.S.R. 48/K4
Minusinsk, U.S.S.R., 54/N4
Minusio, Switz. 39/G4
Minutang, India 68/H3
Minute Man Nat'l Hist. Park, Mass. 249/B6
Minvoul, Gabon 115/B3
Minya Konka (mt.), China 77/F6
Minyip, Vic. 97/B5
Mio, Mich. (48647) 250/E4
Miocene, Br. Col. 184/G4
Miquihuana, Mex. 150/J5
Miquillo (pt.), P. Rico 161/F1
Mira (riv.), Col. 126/A7
Mira (riv.), Ec. 128/C2
Mira, La. (71059) 238/C1
Mira, N.S. 169/H2
Mira (bay), N.S. 169/J2
Mira (riv.), N.S. 169/H3
Mira, Port. 33/B2
Mira (riv.), Port. 33/B4
Mirabad, Afgh. 59/H3
Mirabad, Afgh. 68/A2
Mirabile, Mo. (†64671) 261/D3
Miracema, Braz. 132/F8
Miracema, Braz. 135/E2
Mirador, Braz. 132/E4
Mirador Nacional (mt.), Urug. 145/D5
Miraflores, Boyacá, Col. 126/D5
Miraflores, Vaupés, Col. 126/D7
Miraflores, Peru 128/G11
Miragoâne, Haiti 156/D3
Miragoâne, Haiti 158/B6
Miraj, India 68/D5
Miraje, Salar del (salt dep.), Chile 138/B3
Mira Loma, Calif. (91752) 204/E10
Miramar (General Alvarado), Arg. 143/E4
Miramar, C. Rica 154/E5
Miramar, Fla. (33023) 212/B4
Miramar, Pan. 154/H6
Miramichi (bay), N. Br. 170/E1
Miram Shah, Pak. 68/C2
Miranda, Col. 126/B6
Miranda, Braz. 132/C8
Miranda (riv.), Braz. 132/B8
Miranda, Cuba 158/J4
Miranda, S. Dak. (57463) 298/M4
Miranda (state), Ven. 124/E2
Miranda de Ebro, Spain 33/E1
Miranda do Corvo, Port. 33/B2
Miranda do Douro, Port. 33/C2
Mirande, France 28/D6
Mirandela, Port. 33/C2
Mirando City, Texas (78369) 302/E10
Mirandola, Italy 34/C2
Mirani, Aust. 88/H4
Mirani, Queens. 95/D4
Mira Por Vos (cays), Bah. Is. 156/C2
Mirassol, Braz. 135/B2
Mira Taglio, Italy 34/D2
Mirebalais, Haiti 156/D3
Mirebalais, Haiti 158/C6
Mirecourt, France 28/G3
Mirgorod, U.S.S.R. 52/D5
Miri, Malaysia, 54/P9
Miri (hills), India 68/G3
Miri, Malaysia 85/E5
Mirik (Timiris) (cape), Mauritania 106/A5
Mirim (lag.), 120/E6
Mirim (lag.), Braz. 132/C11
Mirim (lag.), Urug. 145/F4
Mirimire, Ven. 124/D2
Mírina, Greece 45/G6
Miritiparaná (riv.), Col. 126/E8
Mirjawa, Iran 59/H4
Mirjawa, Iran 66/M6
Mirnyy, Ant. 5/C5
Mirnyy, U.S.S.R. 48/M3
Mirpur, India 68/C2
Mirpur Khas, Pak. 68/B3
Mirror, Alta. 182/D3
Mirror Lake, N.H. (03853) 268/E4
Mirtóön (sea), Greece 45/F7
Miryang, S. Korea 81/D6
Mirzapur, India 68/E4
Misamis Occidental (prov.), Phil. 82/D6
Misamis Oriental (prov.), Phil. 82/E6
Misantla, Mex. 150/P1
Misawa, Japan 81/K3
Miscou (isl.), N. Br. 170/F1
Miscou (pt.), N. Br. 170/F1
Miscou Centre, N. Br. 170/F1
Miscouche, P.E.I. 169/D2
Miscou Harbour, N. Br. 170/F1
Misenheimer, N.C. (28109) 281/J4
Misery (mt.), St. Chr.-N.-A. 161/C10
Misery (riv.), Mich. 250/G1
Misgar, India 68/C1
Misha'ab, Ras (cape), Saudi Ar. 59/E4
Mishagua, Peru 128/F8
Mishan, China 77/M2
Mishaum (pt.), Mass. 249/L6
Mishawaka, Ind. (46544) 227/E1
Misheguk (mt.), Alaska 196/F1
Mishicot, Wis. (54228) 317/L7
Mishima, Japan 81/J7
Mishmar Hanegev, Israel 65/B5
Mishmar Hayarden, Israel 65/D1
Mishmi (hills), India 68/H3
Misima (isl.), Papua 85/C8
Misiones (prov.), Arg. 143/F2
Misiones (dept.), Par. 144/D6
Miskito (cays), Nic. 154/F3
Miskolc, Hung., 7/F4
Miskolc, Hung. 41/F2
Misool (isl.), Indon. 85/J6
Mispec, N. Br. 170/E3
Mispillion (riv.), Del. 245/S5
Misquah (hills), Minn. 254/F2
Missaukee (co.), Mich. 250/D4
Missinaibi (riv.), 163/H6
Missinaibi, Ont. 175/D3
Missinaibi (lake), Ont. 175/D3
Missinaibi (riv.), Ont. 175/D2
Missinaibi, Ont. 177/J5
Missinaibi (riv.), Ont. 177/J5
Mission, Kans. (66222) 232/H2
Mission (range), Mont. 262/C3
Mission, S. Dak. (57555) 298/H7
Mission, Texas (78572) 302/F11
Mission City, Br. Col. 184/L3
Mission Hill, S. Dak. (57046) 298/P8
Mission Hills‡, Kans. (†66101) 232/H2
Mission Ridge, S. Dak. (57557) 298/H4
Mission Viejo, Calif. (92675) 204/D11
Mission Woods‡, Kans. (†66101) 232/H2
Missisa (lake), Ont. 175/D2
Missisquoi (co.), Que. 172/D4
Missisquoi (riv.), Vt. 268/B2
Missisagi (riv.), Ont. 177/A1
Missisagi (str.), Ont. 177/A2
Mississauga, Ont. 177/J4
Mississinewa (res.), Ind. 227/F3
Mississinewa (riv.), Ind. 227/F3
Mississippi, 188/J4
Mississippi (riv.), 188/H4
MISSISSIPPI, 256
Mississippi (sound), Ala. 194/B10
Mississippi (co.), Ark. 203/K2
Mississippi (riv.), Ark. 203/H7
Mississippi (lake), Ont. 177/H2
Mississippi (riv.), Ill. 222/C5
Mississippi (riv.), Iowa 229/L7
Mississippi (riv.), Ky. 237/A10
Mississippi (delta), La., 146/K7
Mississippi (delta), La., 188/J5
Mississippi (delta), La. 238/N8
Mississippi (riv.), La. 238/H3
Mississippi (sound), La. 238/M6
Mississippi (riv.), Minn. 254/D4
Mississippi (riv.), Miss. 256/A8
Mississippi (sound), Miss. 256/G10
Mississippi (co.), Mo. 261/O9
Mississippi (riv.), Mo. 261/L4
Mississippi (riv.), Tenn. 237/A10
Mississippi (riv.), U.S., 3/E4
Mississippi (riv.), U.S., 146/J6
Mississippi (state), U.S., 146/K6
Mississippi (riv.), Wis. 317/D10
Mississippi River Gulf Outlet (canal), La. 238/L7
Missolonghi (Mesolóngion), Greece 45/E6
Missoula, Mont., 146/G5
Missoula, Mont., 188/D1
Missoula (co.), Mont. 262/C3
Missoula, Mont (59801) 262/C4
Missouri, 188/H3
Missouri (riv.), 188/H3
MISSOURI, 261
Missouri (riv.), Iowa 229/A4
Missouri (riv.), Kans. 232/G1
Missouri (riv.), Mo. 261/H5
Missouri (riv.), Mont. 262/L3
Missouri (riv.), N. Dak. 283/H5
Missouri (riv.), Nebr. 264/H3
Missouri (riv.), S. Dak. 298/P8
Missouri (riv.), U.S., 3/D3
Missouri (riv.), U.S., 146/J5
Missouri (state), U.S., 146/J6
Missouri Branch, W. Va. (†25511) 313/A7
Missouri City, Mo. (64072) 261/R5
Missouri City, Texas (77459) 302/J2
Missouri Coteau (hills), Sask. 181/F6
Missouri Valley, Iowa (51555) 229/B5
Mist, Ark. (†71646) 203/G7
Mist, Oreg. (97016) 291/D1
Mistake (bay), N.W.T. 187/J3
Mistake Creek, No. Terr. 93/A4
Mistaken (pt.), Newf. 166/D2
Mistassibi (riv.), Que. 174/C3
Mistassibi (riv.), 163/J6
Mistassini, Que. 172/E1
Mistassini (dist.) (co.), Que. 174/B2
Mistassini, Que. 174/C3
Mistassini (lake), Que. 174/C2
Mistassini (lake), 163/J5
Mistassini (lake), Que., 146/L4
Mistastin (lake), Newf. 166/B2
Mistastin (riv.), Newf. 166/B2
Mistatim, Sask. 181/H3
Mistehae (lake), Alta. 182/C2
Místek-Frýdek, Czech. 41/E2
Mistelbach an der Zaya, Austria 41/D2
Misteriosa (bank), Cayman Is. 156/A3
Misti, El (mt.), Peru, 120/C4
Misti, El (mt.), Peru 128/G11
Mistinippi (lake), Newf. 166/B3
Miston, Tenn. (38056) 237/B8
Mistretta, Italy 34/E6
Misurata (prov.), Libya 111/C1
Misurata, Libya 111/C1
Misurata, 102/D1
Mita (pt.), Mex. 150/G6
Mitaka, Japan 81/O2
Mitcham, Aust. 88/D8
Mitcham, S. Aust. 94/B8
Mitchell (lake), Ala., 188/J4
Mitchell (dam), Ala. 194/E5
Mitchell, Ark. (†72583) 203/G1
Mitchell, Aust. 88/H5
Mitchell (riv.), Aust. 88/G3
Mitchell, Ont. 177/C4
Mitchell (co.), Ga. 216/D8
Mitchell, Ga. (30820) 216/G4
Mitchell, Ind. (47446) 227/E7
Mitchell (co.), Iowa 229/H2
Mitchell, Iowa (50485) 229/H2
Mitchell (co.), Kans. 232/D2
Mitchell, La. (71453) 238/C3
Mitchell (mt.), N.C., 188/K3
Mitchell (co.), N.C. 281/E2
Mitchell (mt.), N.C. 281/E3
Mitchell, Nebr. (69357) 264/A3
Mitchell, Queens. 95/C5
Mitchell (riv.), Queens. 95/B2
Mitchell, Oreg. (97750) 291/G3
Mitchell, S. Dak., 188/G2
Mitchell, S. Dak. (57301) 298/N6
Mitchell (creek), S. Dak. 298/G5
Mitchell (co.), Texas 302/D5
Mitchell (riv.), Vic. 97/D5
Mitchell Heights, W. Va. (†25601) 313/B7
Mitchells, Va. (22729) 307/N4
Mitchellsburg, Ky. (40452) 237/M5
Mitchellsville, Ill. (†62946) 222/E6
Mitchellton, Kans. 181/F6
Mitchellville, Ark. (†71639) 203/H6
Mitchellville, Iowa (50169) 229/G5
Mitchellville, Tenn. (37119) 237/J7
Mitchelstown, 10/B4
Mitchelstown, Ire. 17/E7
Mitchelton, Queens. 95/D2
Mithcinamekus (lake), Que. 172/C2
Mithi, Pak. 68/C4
Mithimna, Greece 45/G6
Mitiaro, Cook Is., 87/L7
Mitilíni, Greece 45/H6
Mitkof (isl.), Alaska 196/N2
Mitla (ruin), Mex. 150/M8
Mito, Japan 81/K5
Mitrofania (isl.), Alaska 196/G3
Mitsamiouli, Comoro Is. 118/G2
Mitsinjo, Malag. Rep. 118/H3
Mitsukaido, Japan 81/P2
Mittagong, N.S.W. 97/F4
Mitta Mitta (riv.), Vic. 97/D5
Mittenwald, W. Ger. 22/D5
Mittersill, Austria 41/B3
Mittie, La. (70654) 238/E5
Mittweida, E. Ger. 22/E3
Mitú, Col. 126/E7
Mituas, Col. 126/F6
Mitwaba, Dem. Rep. of the Congo. 115/E5
Mitzic, Gabon 115/B3
Miura, Japan 81/O3
Miura (pen.), Japan 81/O3
Mivtahim, Israel 65/A5
Mix, La. (70758) 238/G5
Miyagi (pref.), Japan 81/F4
Miyako, Japan 81/L4
Miyako (isl.), Ryukyu Is. 81/L7
Miyako (isls.), Ryukyu Is. 81/L7
Miyakonojo, Japan 81/E8
Miyanduab, Iran 66/E2
Miyazaki (pref.), Japan 81/E8
Miyazaki, Japan 81/E8
Miyazu, Japan 81/G6
Miyoshi, Japan 81/F6
Mizda, Libya 111/B1
Mize, Ga. (†30577) 216/F2
Mize, Miss. (39116) 256/E7
Mizen (head), Ire. 17/B9
Mizen (head), Ire. 17/K6
Mizen (head), 10/A5
Mizil, Rum. 45/H3
Mizpah, Minn. (56660) 254/D3
Mizpah, N.J. (08342) 273/D5
Mizpe Ramon, Israel 65/D5
Mizque, Bol. 136/C5
Mizque (riv.), Bol. 136/C6
Mizusawa, Japan 81/K4
Mjölby, Sweden 18/J7
Mkokotoni, Tanz. 115/G5
Mladá Boleslav, Czech. 41/C1
Mladá Vožice, Czech. 41/C2
Mladenovac, Yugo. 45/E3
Mlanje (mt.), 102/F6
Mlanje (mt.), Malawi 115/G7
Mława, Poland 47/E2
Mljet (isl.), Yugo. 45/C4
Mnichovo Hradiště, Czech. 41/C1
Mo, Norway 18/J3
Mo, Norway, 7/F2
Moa (riv.), Guinea 106/B7
Moa (isl.), Indon. 85/H7
Moa (riv.), S. Leone 106/B7
Moab, Utah (84532) 304/E5
Moak Lake, Man. 179/J2
Moama, N.S.W. 97/C5
Moamba, Moz. 118/E5
Moanalua (stream), Hawaii 218/B3
Moanda, Dem. Rep. of the Congo. 115/B5
Moanda, Gabon 115/B4
Moapa, Nev. (89025) 266/G6
Moapa River Ind. Res., Nev. 266/G6
Moar (lake), Man. 179/G2
Moark, Ark. (†72422) 203/J1
Moate, Ire. 17/F5
Moatize, Moz. 118/E3
Moatsville, W. Va. (26405) 313/G4
Moba, Dem. Rep. of the Congo. 115/E5
Mobara, Japan 81/K6
Mobaye, Centr. Afr. Rep. 115/D3
Mobeetie, Texas (79061) 302/D2
Moberly (lake), Br. Col. 184/F2
Moberly, Mo., 188/H3
Moberly, Mo. (65270) 261/G4
Mobile, Ala., 146/K6
Mobile, Ala., 188/J4
Mobile (bay), Ala., 188/J5
Mobile (co.), Ala. 194/B9
Mobile, Ala. (*36601) 194/B9
Mobile (bay), Ala. 194/B10
Mobile (pt.), Ala. 194/B10
Mobile (riv.), Ala. 194/C9
Mobile, Ariz. (†85239) 198/C5
Mobile, Newf. 166/D2
Mobile Big (pond), Newf. 166/D2
Mobjack, Va. (23118) 307/R6
Mobjack (bay), Va. 307/R6
Mobridge, S. Dak. (57601) 298/J2
Moca, Dom. Rep. 156/D3
Moca, Dom. Rep. 158/D5
Moca, P. Rico 161/A1
Mocajuba, Braz. 132/D3
Moçambique, 102/G6
Moçambique (dist.), Moz. 118/F2
Moçâmedes (dist.), Angola 115/B7
Moçâmedes, Angola 115/B7
Moçâmedes, 102/D6
Mocanaqua, Pa. (18655) 294/K3
Moccasin, Ariz. (86022) 198/C2
Moccasin, Mont. (59462) 262/F3
Mocha (isl.), Chile 138/B2
Mocha, Yemen Arab Rep. 59/D7
Mocha, Yemen Arab Rep., 54/H8
Moc Hoa, S. Vietnam 72/E5
Mochudi, Botswana 118/D4
Mocímboa da Praia, Moz. 118/G2
Mociu, Rum. 45/G2
Mockingbird Valley‡, Ky. (†40201) 237/K4
Mocksville, N.C. (27028) 281/H3
Moclips, Wash. (98562) 310/A3
Moco (mt.), Angola 115/C6
Mocoa, Col. 126/B7
Mococa, Braz. 135/C2
Mocodome (cape), N.S. 169/G3
Mocomoco, Bol. 136/A4
Mocorito, Mex. 150/F4
Moctezuma (riv.), Mex. 150/K6
Moctezuma, San Luis Potosí, Mex. 150/J5
Moctezuma, Sonora, Mex. 150/E2
Mocuba, Moz. 118/F3
Modale, Iowa (51556) 229/B5
Modane, France 28/G5
Modasa, India 68/C4
Modderfontein, S. Africa 118/H6
Mode, Ill. (62444) 222/E4
Model, Colo. (81059) 208/L8
Modena, Italy, 7/E4
Modena (prov.), Italy 34/C2
Modena, Italy 34/C2
Modena, Mo. (64663) 261/E2
Modena‡, Pa. (19358) 294/L6
Modena, Utah (84753) 304/A6
Modena, Wis. (†54755) 317/C7
Modeste, La. (70376) 238/K3

Montpelier 403

Modesto, Calif., 188/B3
Modesto, Calif. (*95350) 204/D6
Modesto, Ill. (62667) 222/D4
Modest Town, Va. (23412) 307/T5
Modica, Italy 34/E6
Modjokerto, Indon. 85/K2
Mödling, Austria 41/D2
Modoc (co.), Calif. 204/E2
Modoc, Ga. (†30401) 216/H5
Modoc, Ill. (62261) 222/C5
Modoc, Ind. (47358) 227/G4
Modoc, Kans. (67866) 232/A3
Modoc, S.C. (29838) 296/C4
Modoc Point, Oreg. (†97624) 291/F5
Modra, Czech. 41/D2
Modriča, Yugo. 45/D3
Modrý Kameň, Czech. 41/E2
Mo Duc, S. Vietnam 72/F4
Moe, Vic. 97/D6
Moen (isl.), Pac. Is., 87/F5
Moencopi (plat.), Ariz. 198/D3
Moengo, Sur. 131/D3
Moenkopi Wash (dry riv.), Ariz. 198/D2
Moerai, Fr. Poly., 87/L8
Moerdijk, Neth. 27/F5
Moerewa, N.Z. 101/E1
Moesa (riv.), Switz. 39/H4
Moeskron (Mouscron), Belg. 27/C7
Moffat (co.), Colo. 208/C1
Moffat, Colo. (81143) 208/H6
Moffat, 10/E3
Moffat, Sask. 181/H5
Moffat, Scot. 15/K9
Moffett, Okla. (74946) 288/S4
Moffett Nav. Air Sta., Calif. 204/K3
Moffit, N. Dak. (58560) 283/K6
Mogadishu (cap.), Somalia 102/G4
Mogadishu (cap.), Somalia 115/J3
Mogadishu (cap.), Somalia, 3/M5
Mogador (Essaouira), 102/A1
Mogador (Essaouira), Mor. 106/B2
Mogadore, Ohio (44260) 284/H3
Mogadouro, Port. 33/C2
Mogami (riv.), Japan 81/K4
Mogaung, Burma 72/C1
Møgeltønder, Den. 21/B8
Mogi das Cruzes, Braz. 132/E9
Mogi das Cruzes, Braz. 135/C3
Mogilev, U.S.S.R. 48/D4
Mogilev, U.S.S.R. 52/C4
Mogilev-Podol'skiy, U.S.S.R. 52/C5
Mogil Mogil, N.S.W. 97/E1
Mogilno, Poland 47/C2
Mogi-Mirim, Braz. 135/C3
Mogincual, Moz. 118/G3
Mogocha, U.S.S.R. 48/N4
Mogok, Burma 72/C2
Mogollon (mesa), Ariz. 198/D4
Mogollon, N. Mex. (88050) 274/A5
Mogollon (mts.), N. Mex. 274/A5
Mogollon Baldy (peak), N. Mex. 274/A5
Mogollon Rim (cliffs), Ariz. 198/F5
Mogororo, Chad 111/D5
Mogotes (pt.), Arg. 143/E4
Moguer, Spain 33/C4
Mohács, Hung. 41/E4
Mohaka (riv.), N.Z. 101/F3
Mohaleshoek, Lesotho 118/D6
Mohall, N. Dak. (58761) 283/G2
Mohammadia, Alg. 106/D1
Mohammedia, Mor. 106/C2
Mohave (co.), Ariz. 198/A3
Mohave (lake), Ariz. 198/A4
Mohave (mts.), Ariz. 198/A4
Mohave (lake), Nev. 266/G7
Mohawk (mts.), Ariz. 198/B6
Mohawk (mt.), Conn. 210/B1
Mohawk, Ind. (†46140) 227/F5
Mohawk, Mich. (49950) 250/A1
Mohawk (riv.), N.H. 268/E2
Mohawk (lake), N.J. 273/D1
Mohawk, N.Y. (13407) 276/L4
Mohawk (riv.), N.Y. 276/L5
Mohawk, Oreg. (†97477) 291/E3
Mohawk, Tenn. (37810) 237/P8
Mohawk, W. Va. (24862) 313/C7
Mohegan, Conn. (†06382) 210/G3
Mohéli (isl.), Comoro Is. 118/G2
Mohéli (isl.), 102/G6
Mohelnice, Czech. 41/D2
Mohenjo Daro (ruins), Pak. 68/B3
Moher (cliffs), Ire. 17/B6
Mohican (cape), Alaska 196/E2
Mohican (riv.), Ohio 284/F4
Mohill, Ire. 17/F4
Mohler, Wash. (99154) 310/G3
Möhlin, Switz. 39/E1
Mohn (cape), Norway 18/E1
Mohnton, Pa. (19540) 294/L5
Mohnyin, Burma 72/C1
Moho, China 77/K1
Moho, Peru 128/H10
Mohoro, Tanz. 115/G5
Mohrsville, Pa. (19541) 294/K5
Moi, Norway 18/E7
Moidart (dist.), Scot. 15/E6
Moiese, Mont. (59824) 262/B3
Moineşti, Rum. 45/H2
Moingona, Iowa (†50036) 229/F4
Moira, N. Ire. 17/J3
Moira, N.Y. (12957) 276/M1
Moirones, Urug. 145/E2
Mõisaküla, U.S.S.R. 53/C1
Moisés Ville, Arg. 143/E5
Moisie (riv.), Canada, 146/M4
Moisie, Que. 174/D2
Moisie (riv.), Que. 174/D2
Moisie (riv.), 163/K5
Moissac, France 28/D5
Moissala, Chad 111/C6
Moitaco, Ven. 124/F4
Mojácar, Spain 33/F4
Mojave, Calif. (93501) 204/G8
Mojave (des.), Calif. 204/H9
Mojave (riv.), Calif. 204/J9
Moji Guaçu (riv.), Braz. 135/C2
Mojo, Bol. 136/C7
Mojocoya, Bol. 136/C6
Mokane, Mo. (65059) 261/J5
Mokapu, Hawaii (†96734) 218/F2
Mokapu (pen.), Hawaii 218/F2
Mokau (riv.), N.Z. 101/E3
Mokelumne (riv.), Calif. 204/C9
Mokelumne Hill, Calif. (95245) 204/E5
Mokena, Ill. (60448) 222/F2
Mokil (atoll), Pac. Is., 87/G5
Moknine, Tun. 106/G1
Mokohinau (isl.), N.Z. 101/E1
Mokolo, Cameroon 115/B1
Mokp'o, S. Korea 81/C6
Mokp'o, S. Korea, 54/R6
Moksha (riv.), U.S.S.R. 52/F4
Mokuaweoweo (crater), Hawaii 218/H6
Mokuhooniki (isl.), Hawaii 218/J1
Mokuleia, Hawaii (†96791) 218/D1
Mol, Belg. 27/G6
Mola di Bari, Italy 34/F4
Molalla, Oreg. (97038) 291/B3
Molalla (riv.), Oreg. 291/B3
Moland, Minn. (†55946) 254/E6
Molanosa, Sask. 181/M4
Moláoi, Greece 45/F7
Molare (mt.), Switz. 39/G3
Mold, Wales 13/D4
Moldau (Vltava) (riv.), Czech. 41/C2
Moldava, Czech. 41/F2
Moldavian S.S.R., U.S.S.R. 48/C5
Moldavian S.S.R., U.S.S.R. 52/C5
Moldavian S.S.R., U.S.S.R., 7/G4
Molde, Norway 18/E5
Moldova Nouă, Rum. 45/E3
Moldoveanul (mt.), Rum. 45/G3
Môle (cape), Haiti 158/B5
Molega (lake), N.S. 169/D4
Molena, Ga. (30258) 216/D4
Molenbeek-Saint-Jean, Belg. 27/B9
Molepolole, Botswana 118/C4
Molepolole, 102/E7
Môle-Saint-Nicolas, Haiti 158/B5
Molfetta, Italy 34/F4
Molina, Chile 138/A10
Molina, Colo. (81646) 208/D4
Molina, Spain 33/F2
Molinas, Arg. 143/C2
Moline, Ill., 188/J2
Moline, Ill. (61265) 222/C2
Moline, Kans. (67353) 232/F4
Moline, Man. 179/B4
Moline, Mich. (49335) 250/D6
Moline Acres‡, Mo. (†63101) 261/P2
Molinicos, Spain 33/E3
Molinière (pt.), Grenada 161/C8
Molino, Fla. (32577) 212/B6
Molinos (pt.), P. Rico 161/G1
Moliro, Dem. Rep. of the Congo. 115/E5
Molise (reg.), Italy 34/E4
Mollebjerg (mt.), Den. 21/C6
Mollendo, Peru, 120/C4
Mollendo, Peru 128/F11
Mollerusa, Spain 33/G2
Molles (pt.), Chile 138/A9
Mollis, Switz. 39/H2
Mölln, W. Ger. 22/D2
Mollusk, Va. (22517) 307/P5
Mollys Falls (pond), Vt. 268/C3
Mölndal, Sweden 18/H8
Moloaa, Hawaii (†96703) 218/D1
Molodechno, U.S.S.R. 48/C4
Molodechno, U.S.S.R. 52/C4
Molokai (isl.), Hawaii, 87/L3
Molokai (isl.), Hawaii, 188/F5
Molokai (isl.), Hawaii 218/G1
Molokini (isl.), Hawaii 218/J2
Molong, N.S.W. 97/E3
Molopo (riv.), Botswana 118/C5
Molopo (riv.), S. Africa 118/C5
Molotov (Perm'), U.S.S.R. 52/J3
Molotov (Perm'), U.S.S.R., 7/K3
Molotovsk (Nolinsk), U.S.S.R. 52/H3
Molotovsk (Severodvinsk), U.S.S.R. 52/E2
Moloundou, Cameroon 115/C3
Molson, Man. 179/F4
Molson (lake), Man. 179/J3
Molson, Wash. (†98844) 310/F2
Molt, Mont. (59057) 262/H5
Molteno, S. Africa 118/D6
Molucca (isls.), Indon., 54/R9
Molucca (sea), Indon., 54/R10
Molucca (sea), Indon. 85/H6
Moluccas (isls.), Indon. 85/H6
Molunkus (lake), Maine 242/G4
Moma, Moz. 118/F3
Mombasa, Kenya 115/G4
Mombasa, 102/G5
Mombetsu, Japan 81/L1
Mombo, Tanz. 115/G4
Momchilgrad, Bulg. 45/G5
Momence, Ill. (60954) 222/F2
Momeyer, N.C. (†27856) 281/N3
Mominabad, India 68/D5
Momostenango, Guat. 154/B3
Mompog (passg.), Phil. 82/D4
Mompós, Col., 120/C2
Mompós, Col. 126/C3
Møn (isl.), Den. 18/H9
Møn (isl.), Den. 21/F8
Mon (riv.), Burma 72/B2
Mona (passg.), 146/M8
Mona (passg.), Dom. Rep. 156/E3
Mona (isl.), P. Rico 156/E3
Mona (passg.), P. Rico 156/E3
Mona (passg.), Dom. Rep. 158/F6
Mona (passg.), P. Rico 161/A2
Mona, Utah (84645) 304/C4
Mona (res.), Utah 304/C4
Monaca, Pa. (15061) 294/B4
Monach (isls.), Scot. 15/A4
Monach (sound), Scot. 15/A4
Monaco, 7/E4
MONACO, 28/G6
Monadhliath (mts.), Scot. 15/H5
Monadnock (mt.), N.H. 268/C6
Monagas (state), Ven. 124/G3
Monaghan, 10/C3
Monaghan (co.), Ire. 17/H3
Monaghan, Ire. 17/G3
Monahans, Texas (79756) 302/B6
Monango, N. Dak. (58471) 283/N7
Monar (lake), Scot. 15/F5
Monarch, Alta. 182/D5
Monarch, Mont. (59463) 262/F3
Monarch Mills, S.C. (†29379) 296/D2
Monarda, Maine (†04776) 242/G4
Monaro (range), N.S.W. 97/E5
Monashee (mts.), Br. Col. 184/H4
Monasterevan, Ire. 17/H5
Monasterio, Spain 33/C3
Monastery, N.S. 169/G3
Monastir, Tun. 106/G1
Mona Vale, N.S.W. 97/K2
Monaville, W. Va. (25636) 313/B7
Monavullagh (mts.), Ire. 17/F7
Moncalieri, Italy 34/A2
Monção, Port. 33/B1
Mon Cay, N. Vietnam 72/E2
Moncayo (mt.), Spain 33/F2
Moncayo (range), Spain 33/F2
Monchegorsk, U.S.S.R. 48/C3
Monchegorsk, U.S.S.R. 52/D1
Mönchengladbach, W. Ger. 22/B3
Monches, Wis. (†53029) 317/J1
Monchique, Port. 33/B4
Monchique, Serra de (mts.), Port. 33/B4
Monchouche (lake), Que. 172/G1
Monchy, Sask. 181/D6
Monción, Dom. Rep. 158/D5
Moncks Corner, S.C. (29461) 296/G5
Monclo, W. Va. (†25183) 313/C7
Monclova, Mex. 150/J3
Monclova, Ohio (43542) 284/C2
Moncton, 163/K6
Moncton, N. Br., 146/M5
Moncton, N. Br. 170/F2
Moncure, N.C. (27559) 281/L3
Mondamin, Iowa (51557) 229/B5
Monday (riv.), Par. 144/E5
Mondego (cape), Port. 33/B2
Mondego (riv.), Port. 33/C2
Mondéjar, Spain 33/E2
Mondonak (lake), Que. 172/D2
Mondoñedo, Spain 33/C1
Mondou, Sask. 181/D4
Mondovi, Wis. (54755) 317/C6
Mondovì Breo, Italy 34/A2
Mondragon, Phil. 82/E4
Mondragon, Phil. 85/H3
Mondsee, Austria 41/B3
Moneague, Jam. 158/J6
Monee, Ill. (60449) 222/F2
Monero, N. Mex. (†87547) 274/C2
Monessen, Pa. (15062) 294/C5
Moneta, Iowa (51352) 229/C2
Moneta, Va. (24121) 307/J6
Moneta, Wyo. (82645) 319/E2
Monett, Mo. (65708) 261/E9
Monetta, S.C. (29105) 296/D4
Monette, Ark. (72447) 203/K2
Money, Miss. (38945) 256/D3
Money (isl.), China 85/E2
Moneygall, Ire. 17/F6
Moneymore, N. Ire. 17/H2
Monfalcone, Italy 34/D2
Monforte, Port. 33/C3
Monforte, Spain 33/C1
Monga, Dem. Rep. of the Congo. 115/D3
Mongalla, 102/F4
Mongalla, Sudan 111/F6
Mong Hsat, Burma 72/C2
Monghyr, India 68/F3
Mong Mau, Burma 72/C3
Mongo, Ind. (46771) 227/G1
Mongo, Chad 111/C5
Mongolia, 3/P3
Mongolia, 54/O5
MONGOLIA, 77
Möng Pan, Burma 72/C2
Mong Si, Burma 72/C2
Mongu, 102/E6
Mongu, Zambia 115/D7
Monhegan△, Maine (04852) 242/E8
Monhegan (isl.), Maine 242/E8
Moniac, Ga. (†31646) 216/H9
Moniaive, 10/D3
Moniaive, Scot. 15/J9
Monica, Ill. (61559) 222/D3
Monico, Wis. (54549) 317/H4
Monida, Mont. (†59739) 262/D6
Monie, Md. (†21853) 245/P8
Monifieth, Scot. 15/L7
Moniquirá, Col. 126/D5
Moniteau (co.), Mo. 261/G5
Monitor, Alta. 182/E4
Monitor, Ind. (†47901) 227/D4
Monitor (range), Nev. 266/E4
Monitor, Oreg. (97072) 291/B3
Monitor, Wash. (98836) 310/E3
Monivea, Ire. 17/D5
Monkayo, Phil. 82/E7
Monkey (hill), St. Chr.-N.-A. 161/C10
Monkey (pt.), Nic. 154/F5
Monkey River, Br. Hond. 154/C2
Monkoto, Dem. Rep. of the Congo. 115/D4
Monkton, Ont. 177/C4
Monkton, Md. (21111) 245/M2
Monkton△, Vt. (05469) 268/A3
Monkton, Vt. (05469) 268/A3
Monkton Ridge, Vt. (†05473) 268/A3
Monmouth, Ill. (61462) 222/C3
Monmouth, Ind. (†46733) 227/H3
Monmouth, Iowa (52309) 229/M4
Monmouth, 10/E5
Monmouth△, Maine (04259) 242/D7
Monmouth, Maine (04259) 242/D7
Monmouth (co.), N.J. 273/E3
Monmouth, Oreg. (97361) 291/D3
Monmouth, Wales 13/E6
Monmouth Beach, N.J. (07750) 273/F3
Monmouth Junction, N.J. (08852) 273/D3
Monmouthshire (co.), Wales 13/E6
Monnikendam, Neth. 27/C4
Mono (lake), Calif., 188/C3
Mono (co.), Calif. 204/F5
Mono (lake), Calif. 204/G5
Mono (riv.), Dahomey 106/E7
Mono (riv.), Togo 106/E7
Monocacy (riv.), Md. 245/J3
Mono Lake, Calif. (†93541) 204/F5
Monolith, Calif. (93548) 204/G8
Monólithos, Greece 45/H7
Mono Mills, Ont. 177/D4
Monomonac (lake), Mass. 249/G2
Monomoy (isl.), Mass. 249/O6
Monomoy (pt.), Mass. 249/O6
Monon, Ind. (47959) 227/D3
Monona (co.), Iowa 229/B4
Monona, Iowa (52159) 229/L2
Monona, Wis. (53716) 317/H9
Monongah, W. Va. (26554) 313/F4
Monongahela, Pa. (15063) 294/B5
Monongahela (riv.), Pa. 294/C6
Monongahela (riv.), W. Va. 313/G3
Monongalia (co.), W. Va. 313/F3
Monopoli, Italy 34/F4
Monor, Hung. 41/E3
Monos (isl.), Trinidad Tobago 161/A10
Monóvar, Spain 33/F3
Monoville, Tenn. (37121) 237/K8
Monowi, Nebr. (68754) 264/F2
Monreal del Campo, Spain 33/F2
Monreale, Italy 34/D5
Monroe (co.), Ala. 194/D7
Monroe (co.), Ark. 203/H4
Monroe, Ark. (72108) 203/H4
Monroe△, Conn. (06468) 210/C3
Monroe (co.), Fla. 212/E7
Monroe (lake), Fla. 212/E3
Monroe (co.), Ga. 216/E4
Monroe, Ga. (30655) 216/E3
Monroe (co.), Ill. 222/C5
Monroe (co.), Ind. 227/D6
Monroe, Ind. (46772) 227/H3
Monroe (res.), Ind. 227/E6
Monroe (co.), Iowa 229/H7
Monroe, Iowa (50170) 229/G5
Monroe (co.), Ky. 237/K7
Monroe, La., 146/J6
Monroe, La., 188/H4
Monroe, La. (71201) 238/F1
Monroe△, Maine (04951) 242/E6
Monroe (co.), Mich. 250/F7
Monroe, Mich. (48161) 250/F7
Monroe (co.), Miss. 256/H3
Monroe (co.), Mo. 261/H3
Monroe, N.C. (28110) 281/J5
Monroe△, N.H. (03771) 268/C3
Monroe, N.H. (03771) 268/C3
Monroe (mt.), N.H. 268/E3
Monroe△, N.J. (07434) 273/E3
Monroe (co.), N.Y. 276/E4
Monroe, N.Y. (10950) 276/M8
Monroe, Nebr. (68647) 264/G3
Monroe (co.), Ohio 284/H6
Monroe, Ohio (45050) 284/B7
Monroe, Okla. (74947) 288/S4
Monroe, Oreg. (97456) 291/D3
Monroe (co.), Pa. 294/M3
Monroe (Monroeton), Pa. (18832) 294/J2
Monroe, S. Dak. (57047) 298/P7
Monroe (co.), Tenn. 237/N10
Monroe, Tenn. (38573) 237/L8
Monroe, Utah (84754) 304/B5
Monroe (peak), Utah 304/B5
Monroe, Va. (24574) 307/K6
Monroe (co.), W. Va. 313/E7
Monroe, Wash. (98272) 310/D3
Monroe (co.), Wis. 317/E8
Monroe, Wis. (53566) 317/G10
Monroe Bridge, Mass. (01350) 249/C2
Monroe Center, Ill. (61052) 222/E1
Monroe City, Ind. (47557) 227/C7
Monroe City, Mo. (63456) 261/J3
Monroe P.O. (Stepney), Conn. (06468) 210/B3
Monroeton, Pa. (18832) 294/J2
Monroeville, Ala. (36460) 194/D7
Monroeville, Ind. (46773) 227/H3
Monroeville, N.J. (08343) 273/C4
Monroeville, Ohio (44847) 284/E3
Monroeville, Pa. (15146) 294/C7
Monrovia, Ala. (†35804) 194/E1
Monrovia, Calif. (91016) 204/D10
Monrovia, Ind. (46157) 227/E5
Monrovia (cap.), Liberia, 3/J5
Monrovia (cap.), Liberia, 102/A4
Monrovia (cap.), Liberia 106/B7
Monrovia, Md. (21770) 245/J3
Mons, Belg. 27/E8
Møns (point), Den. 21/F8
Monsanto, Port. 33/C2
Monsanto (mt.), Port. 33/A1
Monschau, W. Ger. 22/B3
Monse, Wash. (†98812) 310/F2
Monsefú, Peru 128/C6
Monselice, Italy 34/C2
Monserrate (isl.), Mex. 150/D4
Monsey‡, N.Y. (10952) 276/M8
Monson△, Maine (04464) 242/E5
Monson△, Mass. (01057) 249/E4
Monson, Mass. (01057) 249/E4
Mönsterås, Sweden 18/K8
Montagne-de-la-Croix, N. Br. 170/C1
Montagu, S. Africa 118/C6
Montague (isl.), Alaska 196/D1
Montague (str.), Alaska 196/D1
Montague (sound), Aust. 88/C2
Montague, Calif. (96064) 204/C2
Montague△, Mass. (01351) 249/E2
Montague (isl.), Mex. 150/B1
Montague, Mich. (49437) 250/C5
Montague, Mont. (†59442) 262/F3
Montague, N.C. (†28435) 281/N6
Montague, N.J. (†12771) 273/D1
Montague (sound), W. Aust. 92/D1
Montague, P.E.I. 169/F2
Montague (co.), Texas 302/G4
Montague, Texas (76251) 302/G4
Montague City, Mass. (†01351) 249/D2
Montague Village‡, Texas (†76522) 302/G6
Montalba, Texas (75853) 302/J6
Montalbán, Spain 33/F2
Montalcino, Italy 34/C3
Mont Alto, Pa. (17237) 294/G6
Montalto Uffugo, Italy 34/E5
Montalvão, Port. 33/C3
Montalvo, Calif. (93003) 204/F9
Montana, 188/E1
MONTANA, 262
Montana, Alaska (†99676) 196/B1
Montaña, La (reg.), Peru 128/F8
Montana (state), U.S., 146/H5
Montana Mines, W. Va. (26586) 313/F3
Montana-Vermala, Switz. 39/E4
Montánchez, Spain 33/D3
Montanja di Reij, Neth. Ant. 161/G9
Montara, Calif. (94037) 204/H3
Montargil, Port. 33/B3
Montargis, France 28/E3
Montauban, Que. 172/E3
Montauban, France, 7/E4
Montauban, France 28/D5
Montauk, Mo. (65545) 261/J8
Montauk, N.Y. (11954) 276/S8
Montauk (pt.), N.Y. 276/S8
Montbard, France 28/F4
Montbéliard, France 28/G4
Mont Belvieu, Texas (77580) 302/L1
Montblanch, Spain 33/G2
Montbrison, France 28/E5
Montbrook, Fla. (†32696) 212/D2
Montcalm (co.), Que. 172/C3
Montcalm (co.), Que. 174/B3
Montcalm (co.), Mich. 250/D5
Montcalm (lake), China 77/C5
Montceau-les-Mines, France 28/F4
Mont Cenis (tunnel), France 28/G5
Mont Cenis (tunnel), Italy 34/A2
Montcerf, Que. 172/A3
Montclair, Calif. (91763) 204/D10
Montclair, N.J. (*07042) 273/B2
Mont Clare‡, Pa. (19453) 294/M5
Montclare, S.C. (†29532) 296/H3
Montcoal, W. Va. (25135) 313/D7
Mont-de-Marsan, France 28/C6
Montdidier, France 28/E3
Mont-Dore, France 28/E5
Monte, Arg. 143/G7
Monteagle, Tenn. (37356) 237/K10
Monteagudo, Bol. 136/D6
Monte Alegre, Braz. 132/C3
Montealegre del Castillo, Spain 33/F3
Monte Alegre de Minas, Braz. 132/D7
Monte Aprazível, Braz. 135/A2
Monte Azul, Braz. 132/F6
Monte Bello (isls.), Australia, 87/B8
Monte Bello (isls.), Aust. 88/A4
Montebello, Calif. (90640) 204/C10
Montebello, Que. 172/B4
Monte Bello (isls.), W. Aust. 92/A3
Montebelluna, Italy 34/D2
Monte Carlo, Monaco 28/G6
Monte Caseros, Arg. 143/G5
Montecito, Calif. (93103) 204/F9
Monte Comán, Arg. 143/C3
Monte Creek, Br. Col. 184/G5
Montecristi, Dom. Rep. 156/D2
Montecristi (prov.), Dom. Rep. 158/D5
Montecristi, Dom. Rep. 158/C5
Montecristi, Ec. 128/B3
Monte Cristo, Bol. 136/E4
Montecristo (isl.), Italy 34/C3
Monte Cristo (range), Nev. 266/D4
Montefiascone, Italy 34/D3
Montefrío, Spain 33/D4
Montegnée, Belg. 27/G7
Montego (bay), Jam. 158/G5
Montego Bay, Jam. 156/B3
Montego Bay, Jam. 158/H5
Montego Bay (pt.), Jam. 158/G5
Montegut, La. (70377) 238/J8
Montehermoso, Spain 33/C2
Monteiro, Braz. 132/G4
Monteith, Iowa (†50115) 229/D5
Montejinni, No. Terr. 93/C4
Monte Lake, Br. Col. 184/G5
Montélimar, France 28/F5
Monte Lindo (riv.), Par. 144/D4
Montellano, Spain 33/D4
Montello, Nev. (89830) 266/G1
Montello, Wis. (53949) 317/H8
Montemayor (plat.), Arg. 143/C5
Montemorelos, Mex. 150/K4
Montemor-o-Novo, Port. 33/B3
Montemor-o-Velho, Port. 33/B2
Monte Ne, Ark. (†72756) 203/B1
Montenegro, Chile 138/G2
Montenegro, Braz. 132/D10
Montenegro (rep.), Yugo. 45/D4
Monte Patria, Chile 138/A8
Monte Plata, Dom. Rep. 158/E6
Montepuez, Moz. 118/F2
Montepulciano, Italy 34/C3
Monte Quemado, Arg. 143/D2
Monterey, Ala. (†36030) 194/E7
Monterey (bay), Calif., 188/B3
Monterey, Calif., 188/B3
Monterey (co.), Calif. 204/D7
Monterey, Calif. (93940) 204/D7
Monterey (bay), Calif. 204/K4
Monterey, Ind. (46960) 227/D2
Monterey, Ky. (†40359) 237/M4
Monterey, La. (71354) 238/G4
Monterey△, Mass. (01245) 249/B4
Monterey, Tenn. (38574) 237/L8
Monterey, Va. (24465) 307/K4
Monterey, Wis. (†53066) 317/J1
Monterey Park, Calif. (91754) 204/C10
Montería, Col. 126/B3
Monte Rio, Calif. (95462) 204/B5
Montero, Bol. 136/D5
Monteros, Arg. 143/C2
Monterotondo, Italy 34/F6
Monterrey, Mex., 3/D4
Monterrey, Mex., 146/J7
Monterrey, Mex. 150/J4
Monterville, W. Va. (26282) 313/F5
Montes, Urug. 145/D5
Montesano, Wash. (98563) 310/B4
Monte Sant'Angelo, Italy 34/F4
Monte Santo, Braz. 132/G5
Montes Claros, Braz., 120/F4
Montes Claros, Braz. 132/E7
Monte Sereno, Calif. (95030) 204/K4
Montevallo, Ala. (35115) 194/E4
Montevallo, Mo. (†64767) 261/D7
Montevarchi, Italy 34/C3
Montevideo, Minn. (56265) 254/C6
Montevideo, Urug., 3/G7
Montevideo (cap.), Urug., 120/E6
Montevideo (dept.), Urug. 145/B7
Montevideo (cap.), Urug. 145/B7
Monteview, Idaho (83435) 220/F6
Monte Vista, Colo. (81144) 208/G7
Montezuma (co.), Colo. 208/B8
Montezuma, Colo. (80464) 208/H3
Montezuma (peak), Colo. 208/F8
Montezuma, Ga. (31063) 216/E6
Montezuma, Ind. (47862) 227/C5
Montezuma, Iowa (50171) 229/H5
Montezuma, Kans. (67867) 232/B4
Montezuma, N. Mex. (87731) 274/D3
Montezuma, Ohio (45866) 284/A4
Montezuma, Tenn. (38360) 237/D10
Montezuma (creek), Utah 304/E6
Montezuma Castle Nat'l Mon., Ariz. 198/D4
Montezuma Creek, Utah (84534) 304/E6
Montfoort, Neth. 27/G4
Montfort, France 28/C3
Montfort, Wis. (53569) 317/E10
Montgomery (cap.), Ala., 146/K6
Montgomery (cap.), Ala., 188/J4
Montgomery (co.), Ala. 194/F6
Montgomery (cap.), Ala. (*36101) 194/F6
Montgomery (co.), Ark. 203/C4
Montgomery (co.), Ga. 216/G6
Montgomery (co.), Ill. 222/D4
Montgomery, Ill. (60538) 222/E2
Montgomery (co.), Ind. 227/D4
Montgomery, Ind. (47558) 227/C7
Montgomery (co.), Iowa 229/C6
Montgomery, Iowa (51353) 229/C2
Montgomery (co.), Kans. 232/G4
Montgomery (co.), Ky. 237/O4
Montgomery, La. (71454) 238/E3
Montgomery, 10/E4
Montgomery (co.), Md. 245/J4
Montgomery, Mich. (49255) 250/E7
Montgomery, Minn. (56069) 254/E6
Montgomery (co.), Miss. 256/E4
Montgomery (co.), Mo. 261/K5
Montgomery (co.), N.C. 281/K4
Montgomery (co.), N.Y. 276/M5
Montgomery, N.Y. (12549) 276/M7
Montgomery, Pak. 59/K3
Montgomery, Pak. 68/C2
Montgomery (co.), Ohio 284/B6
Montgomery, Ohio (45242) 284/C9
Montgomery (co.), Pa. 294/M5
Montgomery, Pa. (17752) 294/H3
Montgomery (co.), Tenn. 237/G8
Montgomery (co.), Texas 302/J7
Montgomery, Texas (77356) 302/J7
Montgomery (co.), Va. 307/H6
Montgomery△, Vt. (05470) 268/B2
Montgomery, Vt. (05470) 268/B2
Montgomery, W. Va. (25136) 313/D6
Montgomery, Wales 13/D5
Montgomery Center, Vt. (05471) 268/B2
Montgomery City, Mo. (63361) 261/K5
Montgomeryshire (co.), Wales 13/D5
Monthey, Switz. 39/C4
Monticello, Ark. (71655) 203/G6
Monticello, Fla. (32344) 212/C1
Monticello, Ga. (31064) 216/E4
Monticello, Ill. (61856) 222/E3
Monticello, Ind. (47960) 227/D3
Monticello, Iowa (52310) 229/L4
Monticello, Ky. (42633) 237/M7
Monticello△, Maine (04760) 242/H3
Monticello, Minn. (55362) 254/E5
Monticello, Miss. (39654) 256/D7
Monticello, Mo. (63457) 261/J2
Monticello, N. Mex. (87939) 274/B5
Monticello, N.Y. (12701) 276/L7
Monticello, Ohio (†45887) 284/B4
Monticello, S.C. (29106) 296/E3
Monticello, Utah (84535) 304/E6
Monticello, Wis. (53570) 317/G10
Mont Ida, Kans. (†66091) 232/G3
Montier, Mo. (65546) 261/J8
Montignies-sur-Sambre, Belg. 27/F8
Montigny-les-Metz, France 28/G3
Montijo, Pan. 154/G6
Montijo (gulf), Pan. 154/G7
Montijo, Port. 33/B3
Montijo, Spain 33/C3
Montilla, Spain 33/D4
Montjoie (lake), Que. 172/B3
Mont-Joli, 163/K6
Mont-Joli, Que. 172/J1
Mont-Joli, Que. 174/D3
Mont-Laurier, 163/J6
Mont-Laurier, Que. 172/B3
Mont-Laurier, Que. 174/B3
Mont-Louis, Que. 172/C1
Montluçon, France 28/E4
Montmagny (co.), Que. 172/G3
Montmagny, Que. 172/G3
Montmagny, Que. 174/C3
Montmartre, Sask. 181/H5
Montmédy, France 28/F3
Montmorenci, Ind. (47962) 227/D4
Montmorenci, S.C. (29839) 296/D4
Montmorency, Que. 172/J3
Montmorency (riv.), Que. 172/F2
Montmorency (co.), Que. 174/C3
Montmorency (co.), Mich. 250/E3
Montmorency, Vic. 97/J4
Montmorency No. 1 (co.), Que. 172/F2
Montmorency No. 2 (co.), Que. 172/G3
Montmorillon, France 28/D4
Mont Nebo, Sask. 181/E2
Montney, Br. Col. 184/G2
Monto, Queens. 95/D5
Montoire-sur-le-Loir, France 28/D4
Montoro, Spain 33/D3
Montosa (mesa), N. Mex. 274/E3
Montour, Idaho (83646) 220/B6
Montour, Iowa (50173) 229/H5
Montour (co.), Pa. 294/J3
Montour Falls, N.Y. (14865) 276/G6
Montoursville, Pa. (17754) 294/J3
Montowese, Conn. (†06473) 210/D3
Montoya, N. Mex. (88428) 274/F3
Montz (mt.), Switz. 39/D2
Montpelier, Jam. 158/H6
Montpelier, Idaho, 188/D2
Montpelier, Idaho (83254) 220/G7
Montpelier, Ind. (47359) 227/G3
Montpelier, Iowa (52759) 229/M6

404 Montpelier

Montpelier, La. (70422) 238/M1
Montpelier, Miss. (39754) 256/G3
Montpelier, N. Dak. (58472) 283/N6
Montpelier, Ohio (43543) 284/A2
Montpelier (cap.), Vt., 146/L5
Montpelier (cap.), Vt., 188/M2
Montpelier (cap.), Vt. (05602) 268/B3
Montpellier, Que. 172/B4
Montpellier, France, 7/E4
Montpellier, France 28/E6
Montreal (riv.), Mich. 250/F1
Montreal, Mo. (65591) 261/G7
Montréal, Que., 146/L5
Montréal, 163/J6
Montréal, Canada, 3/F3
Montréal, Que. 172/H4
Montréal (isl.), Que. 172/H4
Montreal (lake), Sask. 181/F1
Montreal, Wis. (54550) 317/F3
Montreal (riv.), Wis. 317/F2
Montréal-Est, Que. 172/J4
Montréal-Nord, Que. 172/H4
Montreal River Harbor, Ont. 177/J5
Montreat, N.C. (28757) 281/E3
Montreuil, Pas-de-Calais, France 28/D2
Montreuil, Seine-Saint-Denis, France 28/B2
Montreux-Le Châtelard, Switz. 39/C4
Montricher, Switz. 39/B3
Mont-Rolland, Que. 172/C4
Montrose, Ala. (36559) 194/C9
Montrose, Ark. (71658) 203/H7
Montrose, Br. Col. 184/J5
Montrose (co.), Colo. 208/C6
Montrose, Colo. (81401) 208/D6
Montrose, Ga. (31065) 216/F5
Montrose, Ill. (62445) 222/E4
Montrose, Iowa (52639) 229/L7
Montrose, Kans. (66957) 232/D2
Montrose, 10/E2
Montrose, La. (†71457) 238/D3
Montrose, Md. (†20850) 245/K4
Montrose, Mich. (48457) 250/F5
Montrose, Minn. (55363) 254/E5
Montrose, Miss. (39343) 256/F6
Montrose, Mo. (64770) 261/E6
Montrose, Pa. (18801) 294/L2
Montrose, S. Dak. (57048) 298/P6
Montrose, Scot. 15/M6
Montrose, Vic. 97/K5
Montrose, W. Va. (26283) 313/G4
Montrose-La Crescenta, Calif. (91020) 204/C10
Montross, Va. (22520) 307/P4
Montrouge, France 28/B2
Mont Rouge, Pic de (mt.), Spain 33/G1
Mont-Royal, Que. 172/H4
Monts (pt.), Que. 172/B1
Mont-Saint-Hilaire, Que. 172/D4
Mont-Saint-Michel, Que. 172/B3
Mont-Saint-Michel, France 28/C3
Mont-Saint-Pierre, Que. 172/C1
MONTSERRAT, 156/G3
Montserrat (mt.), Spain 33/G2
Montsinéry, Fr. Gui. 131/E3
Mont-Tremblant, Que. 172/C3
Mont-Tremblant Prov. Park, Que. 172/C3
Mont-Tremblant Prov. Park, Que. 174/C3
Montvale, N.J. (07645) 273/B1
Montvale, Va. (24122) 307/J6
Montverde, Fla. (32756) 212/E3
Mont Vernon△, N.H. (03057) 268/D6
Montville△, Conn. (06353) 210/C2
Montville, Conn. (06353) 210/G3
Montville△, Maine (†04941) 242/E7
Montville, Maine (†04941) 242/E7
Montville, Mass. (†01255) 249/B4
Montville, N.J. (07045) 273/E2
Montville, Ohio (44064) 284/H2
Montz, La. (†70068) 238/M3
Monument, Colo. (80132) 208/K4
Monument (peak), Idaho 220/B4
Monument, Kans. (67747) 232/A2
Monument, N. Mex. (88265) 274/F6
Monument, Oreg. (97864) 291/H3
Monument (valley), Utah 304/D6
Monument Beach, Mass. (02553) 249/M6
Monveda, Dem. Rep. of the Congo. 115/D3
Monywa, Burma 72/B2
Monza, Italy 34/B2
Monze, Zambia 115/E7
Monzón, Spain 33/G2
Mooar, Iowa (†52632) 229/L8
Moodie (isl.), N.W.T. 187/M3
Moodus, Conn. (06469) 210/F2
Moodus (res.), Conn. 210/F2
Moody, Ala. (†35125) 194/F3
Moody, Maine (04054) 242/B9
Moody, Mo. (65770) 261/J9
Moody (co.), S. Dak. 298/R5
Moody, Texas (76557) 302/G6
Moody A.F.B., Ga. 216/F9
Moodys, Okla. (74444) 288/S2
Moodyville, Tenn. (†38549) 237/L7
Mooers, N.Y. (12958) 276/N1
Mooka, Japan 81/K5
Mooleyville, Ky. (40154) 237/H4
Mooloo Downs, W. Aust. 92/B4
Moomin (creek), N.S.W. 97/E1
Moon (lake), Calif. 204/E2
Moon (lake), Nebr. 264/E2
Moon, Okla. (†71821) 288/S7
Moonachie, N.J. (07074) 273/B2
Moonah (creek), Queens. 95/A4
Moonbeam, Ont. 177/J5
Mooncoin, Ire. 17/G7
Moon Hills, Sask. 181/D2
Moonie (riv.), N.S.W. 97/E1
Moonie, Queens. 95/D6
Moon Lake, Alta. 182/C3
Moon Run, Pa. (†15244) 294/B5
Moonta, Aust. 88/F6
Moonta, S. Aust. 94/E5
Moora, Aust. 88/B6
Moora, W. Aust. 92/B5
Moorabbin, Vic. 97/J5
Moorcroft, Wyo. (82721) 319/H1
Moore (lake), Aust. 88/B5
Moore (riv.), Aust. 88/B1
Moore, Idaho (83255) 220/E6
Moore, Mont. (59464) 262/G4
Moore (co.), N.C. 281/L4
Moore (dam), N.H. 268/D3
Moore (lake), W. Aust. 92/B5
Moore, Okla. (73060) 288/M4
Moore, S.C. (29369) 296/D2
Moore (co.), Tenn. 237/J10
Moore (co.), Texas 302/C2
Moore, Texas (78057) 302/E9
Moore, Utah (†84523) 304/C5
Moore (dam), Vt. 268/D3
Moorea (isl.), Fr. Poly., 87/L7
Moore Dale, Man. 179/C3
Moorefield, Ark. (72558) 203/G2
Moorefield, Ont. 177/D4
Moorefield, Ind. (†47043) 227/G7
Moorefield, Ky. (40350) 237/O4
Moorefield, Nebr. (69039) 264/D4
Moorefield, W. Va. (26836) 313/J4
Moore Haven, Fla. (33471) 212/E5
Mooreland, Ind. (47360) 227/G5
Mooreland, Okla. (73852) 288/H2
Moorepark, Man. 179/C4
Mooresboro, N.C. (28114) 281/F4
Moores Bridge, Ala. (†35458) 194/C4
Mooresburg, Tenn. (37811) 237/P8
Moores Creek, Ky. (40453) 237/O6
Moores Creek Nat'l Mil. Park, N.C. 281/N6
Moores Hill, Ind. (47032) 227/G6
Moores Mills, N. Br. 170/C3
Moorestown, Mich. (49651) 250/D4
Moorestown, N.J. (08057) 273/B3
Mooresville, Ala. (35649) 194/E1
Mooresville, Ind. (46158) 227/E5
Mooresville, Mo. (64664) 261/E3
Mooresville, N.C. (28115) 281/H3
Mooreton, N. Dak. (58061) 283/S7
Moore Town, Jam. 158/K6
Mooretown, Ont. 177/B5
Mooreville, Miss. (38857) 256/G2
Moorhead, Iowa (51558) 229/B5
Moorhead, Minn. 188/G1
Moorhead, Minn. (56560) 254/B4
Moorhead, Miss. (38761) 256/C4
Mooringsport, La. (71060) 238/B1
Moorland, Iowa (50566) 229/E4
Moorland‡, Ky. (†40223) 237/K4
Moorman, Ky. (42357) 237/G6
Moorooka, Aust. 88/K2
Moorooka, Queens. 95/D3
Mooroopna, Vic. 97/C5
Moorpark, Calif. (93021) 204/G9
Moorreesburg, S. Africa 118/B6
Moosburg, W. Ger. 22/D4
Moose (creek), Idaho 220/D3
Moose (pond), Maine 242/B7
Moose (riv.), Maine 242/D4
Moose (isl.), Man. 179/E3
Moose (riv.), Minn. 254/C2
Moose (riv.), N.Y. 276/K3
Moose (mt.), Sask. 181/J6
Moose (riv.), Vt. 268/D2
Moose (lake), Wis. 317/E3
Moose (lake), Wis. 317/F3
Moose, Wyo. (83012) 319/B2
Moose Bay, Man. 179/C3
Moose Creek, Ont. 177/K2
Moosedale, Sask. 181/H2
Moose Factory, Ont. 175/D2
Moosehead, Maine (†04478) 242/D4
Moosehead (lake), Maine 242/D4
Mooseheart, Ill. (60539) 222/E2
Moose Heights, Br. Col. 184/F3
Moosehorn, Man. 179/D3
Moose Jaw, 163/F6
Moose Jaw, Sask., 146/H4
Moose Jaw, Sask. 181/F5
Moose Jaw (riv.), Sask. 181/G5
Moose Lake, Man. 179/H3
Moose Lake, Minn. (55767) 254/F4
Mooseland, N.S. 169/F4
Mooseleuk (stream), Maine 242/F2
Mooselookmeguntic (lake), Maine 242/B6
Moose Mountain (creek), Sask. 181/J6
Moose Mountain Prov. Park, Sask. 181/J6
Moose Pass, Alaska (99631) 196/C1
Moose Range, Sask. 181/H2
Moose River△, Maine (†04945) 242/C4
Moose Valley, Sask. 181/J5
Moosic, Pa. (18507) 294/L3
Moosilauke (mt.), N.H. 268/D3
Moosomin, 163/F5
Moosomin, Sask. 181/K5
Moosonee, 163/H5
Moosonee, Ont. 175/D2
Moosonee, Ont., 146/K4
Moosup, Conn. (06354) 210/H2
Moosup (riv.), Conn. 210/H2
Mopang (lake), Maine 242/H6
Mopeia, Moz. 118/F3
Mopti, Mali 106/D6
Moqatta, Sudan 59/C7
Moquah, Wis. (†54806) 317/D2
Moquegua, Peru, 120/C4
Moquegua (dept.), Peru 128/G11
Moquegua, Peru 128/G11
Mór, Hung. 41/E3
Mora, Sweden 18/J6
Mora, La. (71455) 238/E4
Mora, Minn. (56266) 254/E5
Mora, Mo. (65345) 261/F5
Mora (co.), N. Mex. 274/E3
Mora, N. Mex. (87732) 274/D3
Mora (riv.), N. Mex. 274/E3
Mora, India 68/B7
Mora, Port. 33/B3
Mora, Spain 33/E3
Morada‡, Calif. (†95201) 204/D5
Moradabad, India, 54/L7
Moradabad, India 68/D3
Mora de Rubielos, Spain 33/F2
Morado, Quebrado (riv.), Chile 138/A6
Morafenobe, Malag. Rep. 118/G3
Morag, Poland 47/D2
Moraga, Calif. (94556) 204/K2
Moraine, Ohio (45439) 284/B6
Morais, N. Br. 170/F1
Moraleda (chan.), Chile 138/D5
Morales, Guat. 154/C3
Morales, Peru 128/D6
Moramanga, Malag. Rep. 118/H3
Moran, Ind. (†46041) 227/D4
Moran, Kans. (66755) 232/G4
Moran, Mich. (49760) 250/E2
Moran, Texas (76464) 302/E5
Moran, Wyo. (83013) 319/B2
Morane (isl.), Fr. Poly., 87/N8
Morant (pt.), Jam. 156/C3
Morant Bay, Jam. 158/K7
Morar (dist.), Scot. 15/E6
Morar (lake), Scot. 15/E6
Morat (lake), Switz. 39/D3
Morata de Tajuña, Spain 33/G4
Moratalla, Spain 33/E3
Morattico, Va. (22523) 307/P5
Moratuwa, Ceylon 68/D7
Morava (riv.), Czech. 41/D2
Morava (riv.), Yugo., 7/G4
Morava (riv.), Yugo. 45/E3
Moravia (reg.), Czech. 41/D2
Moravia, Iowa (52571) 229/H7
Moravia, N.Y. (13118) 276/H5
Moravian Falls, N.C. (28654) 281/G2
Moravská Třebová, Czech. 41/D2
Moravské Budějovice, Czech. 41/D2
Moravský Krumlov, Czech. 41/D2
Morawa, Aust. 88/B5
Morawa, W. Aust. 92/B5
Morawhanna, Guyana, 120/E2
Morawhanna, Guyana 131/B1
Moray (firth), Scot., 7/D3
Moray (co.), Scot. 15/K5
Moray (firth), Scot. 15/J4
Moray (firth), 10/E2
Morayfield, Aust. 88/K1
Morazán, Hond. 154/D3
Morbihan (dept.), France 28/B4
Morden, 163/G6
Morden, Man. 179/D5
Mordialloc, Aust. 88/M7
Mordialloc, Vic. 97/J6
Mordvinian A.S.S.R., U.S.S.R. 48/E4
Mordvinian A.S.S.R., U.S.S.R. 52/G4
More (lake), Scot. 15/G3
Morea, Vic. 97/A5
Moreau (riv.), S. Dak. 298/G3
Moreauville, La. (71355) 238/G4
Morecambe, Alta. 182/E3
Morecambe (bay), Eng. 13/D3
Morecambe (bay), 10/E3
Morecambe and Heysham, 10/E3
Morecambe and Heysham, Eng. 13/E3
Moree, Aust. 88/H5
Moree, N.S.W. 97/E1
Morehead, Kans. (†66776) 232/G4
Morehead, Ky. (40351) 237/P4
Morehead City, N.C. (28557) 281/R5
Morehouse (par.), La. 238/G1
Morehouse, Mo. (63868) 261/N9
Moreland, Ark. (72849) 203/E3
Moreland, Ga. (30259) 216/C4
Moreland, Idaho (83256) 220/F6
Moreland, Ky. (40454) 237/M6
Moreland, Sask. 181/G6
Moreland Hills, Ohio (†44022) 284/J9
Morelia, Mex., 146/H8
Morelia, Mex. 150/J7
Morell, P.E.I. 169/F2
Morella, Queens. 95/B4
Morella, Spain 33/F2
Morelos (state), Mex. 150/K7
Morelos, Mex. 150/J2
Morelos Cañada, Mex. 150/O2
Morena, Sierra (mts.), Spain, 7/D5
Morena, Sierra (range), Spain 33/E3
Morenci, Ariz. (85540) 198/F5
Morenci, Mich. (49256) 250/E7
Moreni, Rum. 45/G3
Moreno, Calif. (92360) 204/H10
Moreno (bay), Chile 138/A4
Møre og Romsdal (co.), Norway 18/E5
Mores (creek), Idaho 220/C6
Moresby, Br. Col. 184/B3
Moresby (isl.), Br. Col. 184/B4
Moreton (bay), Aust. 88/L2
Moreton (cape), Aust. 88/L1
Moreton (isl.), Aust. 88/L1
Moreton (bay), Queens. 95/E5
Moreton (isl.), Queens. 95/E5
Moretonhampstead, Eng. 13/C7
Moretown△, Vt. (05660) 268/B3
Moretown, Vt. (05660) 268/B3
Morewood, Ont. 177/J2
Morgan (co.), Ala. 194/E2
Morgan (co.), Colo. 208/M2
Morgan (pt.), Conn. 210/D4
Morgan (co.), Ga. 216/F3
Morgan, Ga. (31766) 216/C7
Morgan (co.), Ill. 222/C4
Morgan (co.), Ind. 227/E6
Morgan (co.), Ky. 237/P5
Morgan, Ky. (†41040) 237/N3
Morgan, Minn. (56266) 254/D6
Morgan (co.), Mo. 261/G6
Morgan, Mo. (65709) 261/G7
Morgan (co.), Ohio 284/G6
Morgan (co.), Tenn. 237/M8
Morgan, Texas (76671) 302/G5
Morgan (co.), Utah 304/C2
Morgan, Utah (84050) 304/C2
Morgan△, Vt. (05853) 268/D2
Morgan, Vt. (05853) 268/D2
Morgan (co.), W. Va. 313/K3
Morgan Center, Vt. (05854) 268/D2
Morgan City, La. (70380) 238/H7
Morgan City, Miss. (38946) 256/D4
Morganfield, Ky. (42437) 237/E5
Morgan Hill, Calif. (95037) 204/L4
Morganito, Ven. 124/E5
Morgans Point, Texas (†77571) 302/K2
Morgansville, W. Va. (†26456) 313/E4
Morganton, Ark. (72109) 203/F3
Morganton, Ga. (30560) 216/D1
Morganton, N.C. (28655) 281/F3
Morgantown, Ind. (46160) 227/E6
Morgantown, Ky. (42261) 237/H6
Morgantown, Miss. (39484) 256/E8
Morgantown‡, Miss. (39484) 256/B7
Morgantown‡, N.C. (†27215) 281/L2
Morgantown, Ohio (†45612) 284/D7
Morgantown, Pa. (19543) 294/L5
Morgantown, W. Va. (26505) 313/G3
Morganville, Ala. (†36043) 194/F6
Morganville, Kans. (67468) 232/E2
Morganza, La. (70759) 238/G5
Morges, Switz. 39/B3
Morgins, Switz. 39/C4
Morguilla (pt.), Chile 138/D1
Mori, Japan 81/K2
Moriah, N.Y. (12960) 276/N2
Moriah Center, N.Y. (12961) 276/N2
Moriarty, N. Mex. (87035) 274/D4
Morice (lake), Br. Col. 184/D3
Morice (riv.), Br. Col. 184/D3
Morichal, Col. 126/F6
Morichal Largo (riv.), Ven. 124/G3
Morien (cape), N.S. 169/J2
Moriguchi, Japan 81/J7
Morin (lake), Que. 172/C3
Morin Creek, Sask. 181/C1
Morin Heights, Que. 172/C4
Morinville, Alta. 182/D3
Morioka, Japan 81/K4
Moriston (riv.), Scot. 15/G5
Morjärv, Sweden 18/N3
Morlaix, France 28/B3
Morland, Kans. (67650) 232/B2
Morley, Alta. 182/C4
Morley, Eng. 13/F4
Morley, Iowa (52312) 229/L4
Morley, Mich. (49336) 250/D5
Morley, Mo. (63767) 261/N8
Morley, N.Y. (13617) 276/K1
Morley, Tenn. (37812) 237/O7
Mormon (lake), Ariz. 198/D4
Mormon (mt.), Idaho 220/D4
Mormon (mts.), Nev. 266/G5
Mormon Lake, Ariz. (86038) 198/D4
Morne-à-l'Eau, Guad. 161/A6
Morne-Rouge, Mart. 161/C5
Morne Seychellois (mt.), Seych. 118/H5
Morne-Vert, Mart. 161/C6
Morningside, Alta. 182/D3
Morningside, Md. (†20028) 245/G5
Morningside Park, Conn. (†06385) 210/G3
Morning Sun, Iowa (52640) 229/L6
Morning Sun, Ohio (†45311) 284/A6
Mornington (isl.), Aust. 88/G3
Mornington, Aust. 88/M7
Mornington (isl.), Chile 138/D8
Mornington (isl.), Queens. 95/A3
Mornington, Vic. 97/C6
Mornington (pen.), Vic. 97/C6
Morning View, Ky. (41063) 237/N3
Moro, Ark. (72368) 203/H4
Moro (creek), Ark. 203/F7
Moro (gulf), Phil. 82/D7
Moro (gulf), Phil. 85/G4
Moro, Oreg. (97039) 291/G2
Moro (mt.), Switz. 39/E5
Moro Bay, Ark. (†71651) 203/F7
Morobe, Terr. N.G. 85/C7
Morobe, Terr. N.G., 87/E6
Morocco, 3/J4
MOROCCO, 102/B1
MOROCCO, 106/C2
Morocco, Ind. (47963) 227/C3
Morocelí, Hond. 154/D3
Morochata, Bol. 136/B5
Morococha, Peru 128/D8
Morogoro, 102/F5
Morogoro (reg.), Tanz. 115/G4
Morogoro, Tanz. 115/G5
Moroka, S. Africa 118/H6
Moroleón, Mex. 150/J6
Morombe, Malag. Rep. 118/G4
Moromoro, Bol. 136/C6
Morón, Arg. 143/G7
Morón, Cuba 156/B2
Morón, Cuba 158/F2
Moron, Haiti 158/A6
Moron (mt.), Switz. 39/D2
Morón, Ven. 124/D2
Morona, Ec. 128/D4
Morona (riv.), Peru 128/D5
Morona-Santiago (prov.), Ec. 128/C4
Morondava, 102/G6
Morondava, Malag. Rep. 118/G4
Morón de la Frontera, Spain 33/D4
Morongo Ind. Res., Calif. 204/J10
Moroni (cap.), Comoro Is. 118/G2
Moroni (cap.), Comoro Is. 102/G6
Moroni, Utah (84646) 304/C4
Morotai (isl.), Indon. 85/H5
Moroto, Uganda 115/F3
Morovis, P. Rico 161/D1
Morozovsk, U.S.S.R. 52/F5
Morpeth, 10/F3
Morpeth, Ont. 177/C5
Morpeth, Eng. 13/F2
Morphou, Cyprus 63/E5
Morphou (bay), Cyprus 63/E5
Morral, Ohio (43337) 284/D4
Morrice, Mich. (48857) 250/E6
Morrill, Kans. (66515) 232/G2
Morrill△, Maine (04952) 242/E7
Morrill, Minn. (†56329) 254/E5
Morrill (co.), Nebr. 264/A3
Morrill, Nebr. (69358) 264/A3
Morrilton, Ark. (72110) 203/E3
Morrin, Alta. 182/D4
Morrinhos, Braz. 132/D7
Morrinsville, N.Z. 101/E2
Morris, Ala. (35116) 194/E3
Morris (res.), Calif. 204/D10
Morris△, Conn. (06763) 210/C2
Morris, Ga. (31767) 216/C7
Morris, Ill. (60450) 222/E2
Morris, Ind. (47033) 227/G6
Morris (co.), Kans. 232/F3
Morris, Man. 179/E5
Morris, Minn. (56267) 254/C5
Morris (co.), N.J. 273/D2
Morris, N.Y. (13808) 276/K5
Morris (mt.), S. Aust. 94/B2
Morris, Okla. (74445) 288/P3
Morris, Pa. (16938) 294/H2
Morris (isl.), S.C. 296/H6
Morris (co.), Texas 302/K4
Morris, W. Va. (†26639) 313/E5
Morrisburg, Ont. 177/J3
Morris Chapel, Tenn. (38361) 237/E10
Morrisdale, N. Br. 170/D3
Morrisdale, Pa. (16858) 294/F4
Morrisey, Wyo. (†82701) 319/H2
Morris Fork, Ky. (41353) 237/O6
Morris Jesup (cape), Greenl., 4/A11
Morrison, Colo. (80465) 208/J3
Morrison, Ill. (61270) 222/C2
Morrison, Iowa (50657) 229/H4
Morrison (lake), Man. 179/C1
Morrison (co.), Minn. 254/D4
Morrison, Mo. (65061) 261/J5
Morrison, Okla. (73061) 288/M2
Morrison, Tenn. (37357) 237/K9
Morrison Bluff, Ark. (†72863) 203/D3
Morrison City, Tenn. (†37660) 237/R7
Morrisonville, Ill. (62546) 222/D4
Morrisonville, N.Y. (12962) 276/N1
Morrisonville, Wis. (53571) 317/G9
Morris Plains, N.J. (07950) 273/D2
Morris Run, Pa. (16939) 294/J2
Morriston, Ark. (72559) 203/G1
Morriston, Fla. (32668) 212/D2
Morristown, Ariz. (85342) 198/C5
Morristown, Ill. (†61101) 222/D1
Morristown, Ind. (46161) 227/F5
Morristown, Minn. (55052) 254/E6
Morristown, N.J. (07960) 273/D2
Morristown, N.Y. (13664) 276/J1
Morristown, Ohio (43759) 284/H5
Morristown, S. Dak. (57645) 298/F2
Morristown, Tenn. (37814) 237/P8
Morristown△, Vt. (†05661) 268/B2
Morristown, Vt. (†05661) 268/B2
Morristown Nat'l Hist. Park, N.J. 273/D2
Morrisvale, W. Va. (25542) 313/C6
Morrisville, Mo. (65710) 261/F8
Morrisville, N.C. (27560) 281/M3
Morrisville, N.Y. (13408) 276/J5
Morrisville, Pa. (19067) 294/N5
Morrisville‡, Pa. (19067) 294/B6
Morrisville, Vt. (05661) 268/B2
Morrito, Nic. 154/E5
Morro (pt.), Chile 138/A6
Morro Bay, Calif. (93442) 204/D8
Morro do Chapéu, Braz. 132/F5
Morropón, Peru 128/C5
Morros, Braz. 132/F3
Morrosquillo (gulf), Col. 126/C3
Morrow, Ark. (72749) 203/B2
Morrow‡, Ga. (30260) 216/D3
Morrow, La. (71356) 238/F5
Morrow (co.), Ohio 284/E4
Morrow, Ohio (45152) 284/B7
Morrow (co.), Oreg. 291/H2
Morrow Point (res.), Colo. 208/E6
Morrowville, Kans. (66958) 232/E2
Morrumbala, Moz. 118/F3
Morrumbene, Moz. 118/F4
Mors (isl.), Den. 21/B4
Morse (res.), Ind. 227/E4
Morse, La. (70559) 238/F6
Morse, Sask. 181/D5
Morse, Texas (79062) 302/C1
Morse, Wis. (†54527) 317/E3
Morse Bluff, Nebr. (68648) 264/H3
Morse Mill, Mo. (63066) 261/L6
Morses Line, Vt. (†05459) 268/A2
Morshansk, U.S.S.R. 52/F4
Mortagne-au-Perche, France 28/D3
Mortara, Italy 34/B2
Morte (pt.), Eng. 13/C6
Morteau, France 28/G4
Morteros, Arg. 143/D3
Mortes (riv.), Braz., 120/E4
Mortes (Manso) (riv.), Braz. 132/D6
Mortes (lake), N. Dak. 283/M3
Mortimer, N.C. (†28645) 281/F2
Mortlach, Sask. 181/E5
Mortlake, Vic. 97/B6
Morton, Ont. 177/H3
Morton, Ill. (61550) 222/D3
Morton (co.), Kans. 232/A4
Morton, Minn. (56270) 254/C6
Morton, Miss. (39117) 256/E6
Morton (co.), N. Dak. 283/H6
Morton, Pa. (19070) 294/M7
Morton, Texas (79346) 302/B4
Morton, Wash. (98356) 310/C4
Morton, Wyo. (82522) 319/D2
Morton Grove, Ill. (60053) 222/B1
Morton Mills, Iowa (†50864) 229/C6
Mortons Gap, Ky. (42440) 237/F6
Mortsel, Belg. 27/E6
Moruga, Trinidad Tobago 161/B11
Moruka (riv.), Guyana 131/B2
Morundah, N.S.W. 97/D4
Moruya, N.S.W. 97/F4
Morvan (plat.), France 28/F4
Morven, Ga. (31638) 216/E9
Morven, N.C. (28119) 281/J5
Morven, N.Z. 101/C6
Morven, Queens. 95/C5
Morven (dist.), Scot. 15/E6
Morven (mt.), Scot. 15/J3
Morvi, India 68/C4
Morvin, Ala. (36762) 194/C7
Morwell, Vic. 97/D6
Mosbach, W. Ger. 22/C4
Mosby, Mo. (64073) 261/R4
Mosby, Mont. (59058) 262/J4
Mosca, Colo. (81146) 208/H7
Moscavide, Port. 33/A1
Mosconi, Arg. 143/F7
Moscow, Ark. (71659) 203/G5
Moscow, Idaho, 188/C1
Moscow, Idaho (83843) 220/B3
Moscow, Ind. (†46156) 227/F6
Moscow, Iowa (52760) 229/L5
Moscow, Kans. (67952) 232/A4
Moscow, Ky. (†42031) 237/D7
Moscow, Miss. (†39328) 256/G5
Moscow, Ohio (45153) 284/B8
Moscow, Pa. (18444) 294/L3
Moscow, Tenn. (38057) 237/C10
Moscow (cap.), U.S.S.R., 3/L3
Moscow (cap.), U.S.S.R., 7/H3
Moscow (cap.), U.S.S.R. 48/D4
Moscow (cap.), U.S.S.R. 52/E3
Moscow, Vt. (05662) 268/B3
Moscow Mills, Md. (†21521) 245/B2
Moscow Mills, Mo. (63362) 261/M1
Mosel (riv.), Lux. 27/J9
Mosel (riv.), W. Ger. 22/B3
Moseley, Va. (23120) 307/N6
Moselle (dept.), France 28/G3
Moselle (riv.), France 28/G3
Moselle, Miss. (39459) 256/F8
Moselle, Mo. (63067) 261/M4
Mosers River, N.S. 169/F4
Moses (lake), Wash. 310/F3
Moses Coulee (canyon), Wash. 310/F3
Moses Lake, Wash. (98837) 310/F3
Moses Point, Alaska (†99762) 196/F2
Mosetenes, Cordillera de (range), Bol. 136/B5
Mosgiel, N.Z. 101/C6
Mosgrove, Pa. (†16259) 294/D4
Moshannon, Pa. (16859) 294/F3
Mosheim, Tenn. (37818) 237/R8
Mosher, Ont. 177/J5
Mosher, S. Dak. (57558) 298/J7
Moshi, 102/F5
Moshi, Tanz. 115/G4
Mosi-Ao-Tunya (Victoria) (falls), 102/E6
Mosi-Ao-Tunya (Victoria) (falls), Zambia 115/E7
Mosi-Ao-Tunya (Victoria) (falls), Rhod. 118/C3
Mosier, Oreg. (97040) 291/F2
Mosinee, Wis. (54455) 317/G6
Mosjøen, Norway 18/H4
Moskenesøy (isl.), Norway 18/H3
Moskva (Moscow) (cap.), U.S.S.R. 52/E3
Moskva (riv.), U.S.S.R. 52/E3
Mosman, N.S.W. 97/J3
Mosonmagyaróvár, Hung. 41/D3
Mosquera, Col. 126/A6
Mosquero, N. Mex. (87733) 274/F3
Mosquik (lake), Que. 172/C3
Mosquito (lag.), Fla. 212/F3
Mosquito (gulf), Pan. 154/G6
Mosquito Coast (reg.), Hond. 154/E4
Mosquito Coast (reg.), Nic. 154/E4
Mosquito Creek (res.), Ohio 284/J3
Moss, Norway 18/D4
Moss, Miss. (39460) 256/F7
Moss, Tenn. (38575) 237/K7
Mossaka, Rep. of Congo 115/C4
Mossbank, Sask. 181/E6
Moss Beach, Calif. (94038) 204/H3
Mossel Bay, 102/E8
Mossel Bay, S. Africa 118/C6
Mossendjo, Rep. of Congo 115/B4
Mossgiel, N.S.W. 97/C4
Mosside, Alta. 182/C2
Moss Landing, Calif. (95039) 204/C7
Mossleigh, Alta. 182/D4
Mossman, Aust. 88/G3
Mossman, Queens. 95/C3
Mossoró, Braz. 132/G4
Moss Point, Miss. (39563) 256/G10
Mossuril, Moz. 118/G2
Moss Vale, N.S.W. 97/F4
Mossville, Ill. (61552) 222/D3
Mossy (riv.), Man. 179/C3
Mossy (riv.), Sask. 181/H1
Mossy Head, Fla. (32434) 212/C6
Mossyrock, Wash. (98564) 310/C4
Most, Czech. 41/B1
Mostaganem, Alg. 106/D1
Mostaganem, 102/B1
Mostar, Yugo., 7/H3
Mostar, Yugo., 7/F4
Mostar, Yugo. 45/D4
Mosty, U.S.S.R. 52/B4
Mosul, Iraq, 54/H6
Mosul, Iraq 59/D2
Mosul (prov.), Iraq 66/C2
Mosul, Iraq 66/C2
Motacucito, Bol. 136/E5
Mota del Cuervo, Spain 33/E3
Motagua (riv.), Guat. 154/C3
Motala, Sweden 18/J7
Motherwell and Wishaw, 10/B1
Motherwell and Wishaw, Scot. 15/D2
Motilla del Palancar, Spain 33/E3
Motiti (isl.), N.Z. 101/F2
Motley, Minn. (56466) 254/D4
Motley (co.), Texas 302/D3
Moto, Dem. Rep. of the Congo. 115/E3
Motobu, Ryukyu Is. 81/N6
Motozintla de Mendoza, Mex. 150/N9
Motril, Spain 33/E4
Motsuta (cape), Japan 81/J2
Mott, N. Dak. (58646) 283/F7
Motu (riv.), N.Z. 101/F3
Motueka, N.Z. 101/D4
Motuhora (isl.), N.Z. 101/F2
Motuihe (isl.), N.Z. 101/C1
Motul de Felipe Carillo Puerto, Mex. 150/P6
Motupe, Peru 128/C6
Motutapu (isl.), N.Z. 101/C1
Motygino, U.S.S.R. 48/K4
Mouchoir (passg.), Turks Caicos Is. 156/D2
Moúdhros, Greece 45/G6
Moudjéria, Mauritania 106/B5
Moudon, Switz. 39/C3
Mouila, Gabon 115/B4
Mouka, Centr. Afr. Rep. 115/D2
Moulamein, N.S.W. 97/C4
Moulamein (creek), N.S.W. 97/C4
Mould Bay, Canada, 4/B16
Mould Bay, N.W.T. 187/F2
Moule à Chique (cape), St. Lucia 161/G7
Moulins, France 28/E4
Moulmein, Burma, 54/N8
Moulmein, Burma 72/C3
Moulouya (riv.), Mor. 106/D2
Moulton, Ala. (35650) 194/D2
Moulton, Iowa (52572) 229/H7
Moulton, Mont. (†59423) 262/G3
Moulton, Texas (77975) 302/H8
Moultonboro△, N.H. (03254) 268/E4
Moultonboro, N.H. (03254) 268/E4
Moultrie, Fla. (†32084) 212/E2

406 Muonio

Muonio (riv.), Fin. 18/M2
Muonioälv (riv.), Sweden 18/M2
Muota (riv.), Switz. 39/G3
Muotathal, Switz. 39/G3
Mup'yŏng-ni, N. Korea 81/C3
Muqaddam, Wadi (dry riv.), Sudan 111/F4
Muqdadiyah, Iraq 66/D4
Muqeible, Israel 65/C2
Muqui, Braz. 132/F8
Mur (riv.), Austria 41/C3
Mur (riv.), Yugo. 45/B2
Mura (riv.), Hung. 41/D3
Muradiye, Turkey 63/K3
Murakami, Japan 81/J4
Murallón, Cerro (mt.), Arg. 143/B6
Murallón, Cerro (mt.), Chile 138/D8
Murashi, U.S.S.R. 52/G3
Murat, France 28/E5
Murat (riv.), Turkey 59/C2
Murat (riv.), Turkey 63/H3
Murat Daği (mt.), Turkey 63/C3
Murau, Austria 41/C3
Murbat, Oman 59/G6
Murchison (range), Aust. 88/E4
Murchison (riv.), Aust. 88/B5
Murchison, N.Z. 101/D4
Murchison (mt.), W. Aust. 92/B4
Murchison (riv.), W. Aust. 92/B4
Murchison (range), No. Terr. 93/D6
Murchison (falls), Uganda 115/F3
Murchison‡, Texas (75778) 302/J5
Murcia, Spain, 7/D5
Murcia (prov.), Spain 33/F4
Murcia, Spain 33/F4
Murcia (reg.), Spain 33/F3
Murderers (creek), Oreg. 291/H3
Murderkill (riv.), Del. 245/R5
Murdo, S. Dak. (57559) 298/H6
Murdochville, Que. 172/C1
Murdock, Fla. (33938) 212/D4
Murdock, Ill. (61941) 222/E4
Murdock, Kans. (67111) 232/E4
Murdock, Minn. (56271) 254/C5
Murdock, Nebr. (68407) 264/H4
Muren, Mong. 77/F2
Mureş (riv.), Rum. 45/E2
Muret, France 28/D6
Muretto (pass), Switz. 39/J4
Murfreesboro, Ark. (71958) 203/C5
Murfreesboro, N.C. (27855) 281/R2
Murfreesboro, Tenn. (37130) 237/J9
Murg (riv.), Switz. 39/G1
Murgab, U.S.S.R. 48/H6
Murgab (riv.), U.S.S.R. 48/G6
Murgash (mt.), Bulg. 45/F4
Murghab (riv.), Afgh. 59/H2
Murgon, Queens. 95/D5
Murgoo, W. Aust. 92/B4
Muri, Switz. 39/F2
Muriaé, Braz. 132/F8
Muriaé, Braz. 135/E2
Murias de Paredes, Spain 33/C1
Muri bei Bern, Switz. 39/E3
Muriel (lake), Alta. 182/E2
Murindó, Col. 126/B4
Müritzee (lake), E. Ger. 22/E2
Murjek, Sweden 18/M3
Murjo (mt.), Indon. 85/J2
Murl, Ky. (†42633) 237/M7
Murle, Eth. 111/G6
Murmansk, U.S.S.R. 48/D3
Murmansk, U.S.S.R. 52/D1
Murmansk, U.S.S.R., 3/L2
Murmansk, U.S.S.R., 4/C8
Murmansk, U.S.S.R., 7/H2
Murnau, W. Ger. 22/D5
Murnpeowie, S. Aust. 94/F3
Murom, U.S.S.R. 52/F3
Murongo, Tanz. 115/F4
Muroran, Japan 81/K2
Muros, Spain 33/B1
Muroto, Japan 81/G7
Muroto (pt.), Japan 81/G7
Murphy, Idaho (83650) 220/B6
Murphy, Miss. (†38748) 256/C4
Murphy, Mo. (†63088) 261/O4
Murphy, N.C. (28906) 281/B4
Murphy, Oreg. (97533) 291/D5
Murphy (isl.), S.C. 296/J5
Murphy‡, Texas (†75074) 302/H4
Murphys, Calif. (95247) 204/E5
Murphysboro, Ill. (62966) 222/D6
Murphytown, W. Va. (†26142) 313/D4
Murra Murra, Queens. 95/C6
Murray (river), Australia, 87/E9
Murray (riv.), Aust. 88/G6
Murray (riv.), Aust. 88/B2
Murray (riv.), Br. Col. 184/G3
Murray (co.), Ga. 216/C1
Murray, Idaho (83874) 220/C2
Murray, Ind. (†46714) 227/G3
Murray, Iowa (50174) 229/F6
Murray, Ky. (42071) 237/E7
Murray (co.), Minn. 254/C6
Murray (riv.), N.S.W. 97/A4
Murray, Nebr. (68409) 264/J4
Murray (lake), Papua 85/B7
Murray (riv.), W. Aust. 92/A2
Murray (riv.), S. Aust. 94/F6
Murray (co.), Okla. 288/M6
Murray (lake), Okla. 288/M6
Murray (lake), S.C., 188/K4
Murray (lake), S.C. 296/D4
Murray, Utah, 188/D2
Murray, Utah (84107) 304/C3
Murray (riv.), Vic. 97/A4
Murray Bridge, Aust. 88/F7
Murray Bridge, S. Aust. 94/F6
Murray City, Ohio (43144) 284/F6
Murraydale, Sask. 181/B6
Murray Downs, No. Terr. 93/D6
Murray Harbour, P.E.I. 169/F2
Murray River, P.E.I. 169/F2
Murraysville, W. Va. (26153) 313/C4
Murrayville, Br. Col. 184/L3
Murrayville, Ga. (30564) 216/E2
Murrayville, Ill. (62668) 222/C4
Murrayville, Vic. 97/A4
Murree, Pak. 68/C2
Murrells Inlet, S.C. (29576) 296/K4
Mürren, Switz. 39/E3
Murrieta, Calif. (92362) 204/H10
Murringo, N.S.W. 97/E4
Murrumbidgee (riv.), Aust. 88/G6
Murrumbidgee (riv.), N.S.W. 97/C4
Murrumburrah, N.S.W. 97/E4
Murrurundi, N.S.W. 97/F2
Murrycross, Ala. (†35902) 194/G2
Murrysville, Pa. (15668) 294/C5
Murtaröl (mt.), Switz. 39/K3
Murtaugh, Idaho (83344) 220/D7
Murten, Switz. 39/D3
Murtle (lake), Br. Col. 184/H4
Murtoa, Vic. 97/B5
Murud, India 68/C5
Murupara, N.Z. 101/F3
Mururoa (isl.), Fr. Poly., 87/M8
Murwara, India 68/E4
Murwillumbah, Aust. 88/J5
Murwillumbah, N.S.W. 97/G1
Mürz (riv.), Austria 41/C3
Murzuk, Libya 111/B2
Murzuk, 102/D2
Mürzzuschlag, Austria 41/C3
Muş, Turkey 59/D2
Muş (prov.), Turkey 63/J3
Muş, Turkey 63/J3
Musa Khel Bazar, Pak. 59/K3
Musa Khel Bazar, Pak. 68/B2
Musala (mt.), Bulg. 45/F4
Musan, N. Korea 81/D2
Musandam, Ras (cape), Oman 59/G4
Musashino, Japan 81/O2
Muscadine, Ala. (36269) 194/H3
Muscat (cap.), Oman 59/G5
Muscat (cap.), Oman, 3/M4
Muscat (cap.), Oman, 54/J7
Muscatatuck (riv.), Ind. 227/E7
Muscatine, Iowa, 188/H2
Muscatine (co.), Iowa 229/L5
Muscatine, Iowa (52761) 229/L6
Muscle Shoals, Ala. (35660) 194/C1
Muscoda, Wis. (53573) 317/F9
Muscogee (co.), Ga. 216/C6
Musconetcong (riv.), N.J. 273/C2
Muscongus (bay), Maine 242/E8
Muscotah, Kans. (66058) 232/G2
Muscow, Sask. 181/G5
Muscoy, Calif. (92405) 204/E10
Muse, Okla. (74949) 288/S5
Muse‡, Pa. (15350) 294/B5
Musella, Ga. (31066) 216/E5
Musgrave (ranges), Australia, 87/D8
Musgrave (ranges), Aust. 88/E5
Musgrave (ranges), S. Aust. 94/B2
Musgrave, Queens. 95/B2
Musgravetown, Newf. 166/C2
Mushaboom, N.S. 169/F4
Mushandike Nat'l Park, Rhod. 118/D4
Mushie, Dem. Rep. of the Congo. 115/C4
Mushin, Nigeria 106/E7
Musi (riv.), Indon. 85/C6
Musidora, Alta. 182/E3
Muskeegan, Sask. 181/H3
Muskeg (bay), Man. 179/G6
Muskeg (bay), Minn. 254/C2
Muskeget (chan.), Mass. 249/N7
Muskeget (isl.), Mass. 249/N7
Muskego, Wis. (53150) 317/K2
Muskegon, Mich., 188/J2
Muskegon (co.), Mich. 250/C5
Muskegon, Mich. (*49440) 250/C5
Muskegon (riv.), Mich. 250/C5
Muskegon Heights, Mich. (49444) 250/C5
Muskingum (co.), Ohio 284/G5
Muskingum (riv.), Ohio 284/G6
Muskogee, Okla., 146/J6
Muskogee, Okla., 188/H3
Muskogee (co.), Okla. 288/R3
Muskogee, Okla. (74401) 288/R3
Muskoka (co.), Ont. 177/E3
Muskoka (lake), Ont. 177/E2
Muskrat (creek), Wyo. 319/E2
Muskwa (lake), Alta. 182/C1
Muskwa (riv.), Alta. 182/C1
Muskwa (riv.), Br. Col. 184/M2
Muslimiya, Syria 63/G4
Musmar, Sudan 111/G4
Musoma, Tanz. 115/F4
Musquacook (lakes), Maine 242/E2
Musquash, N. Br. 170/D3
Musquash (harb.), N. Br. 170/D3
Musquodoboit (riv.), N.S. 169/E4
Musquodoboit Harbour, N.S. 169/E4
Musselburgh, 10/C1
Musselburgh, Scot. 15/L8
Musselshell (riv.), 188/E1
Musselshell (co.), Mont. 262/H4
Musselshell, Mont. (59059) 262/H4
Musselshell (riv.), Mont. 262/J3
Mustafa Kemalpaşa, Turkey 63/C3
Mustahil, Eth. 111/H6
Müstair, Switz. 39/K3
Mustang, Nepal 68/E3
Mustang, Okla. (73064) 288/L4
Mustang (creek), Texas 302/A1
Mustang Draw (creek), Texas 302/B5
Musters (lake), Arg. 143/C6
Mustinka (riv.), Minn. 254/B5
Mustoe, Va. (24468) 307/J4
Mustvee, U.S.S.R. 53/D1
Muswellbrook, Aust. 88/J6
Muswellbrook, N.S.W. 97/F3
Mût, U.A.R. 59/A4
Mût, U.A.R. 111/E2
Mut, Turkey 63/E4
Mutankiang, China 77/M3
Mutelet, Mong. 77/E2
Muthill, Scot. 15/J7
Muting, Indon. 85/K7
Mutsamudu, Comoro Is. 118/G2
Mutshatsha, Dem. Rep. of the Congo. 115/D6
Mutsu, Japan 81/K3
Mutsu (bay), Japan 81/K3
Muttaburra, Queens. 95/C4
Muttalip, Turkey 63/D3
Muttenz, Switz. 39/E1
Muttler (mt.), Switz. 39/K3
Mutton (isl.), Ire. 17/B6
Mutton Bird (isl.), N.S.W. 97/J2
Muttontown‡, N.Y. (†11791) 276/R7
Muttonville, Mich. (†48062) 250/G6
Mutual, Ohio (†43078) 284/C5
Mutual, Okla. (73853) 288/H2
Muwailih, Saudi Ar. 59/C4
Muwale, Tanz. 115/F5
Muxima, Angola 115/B5
Muya, U.S.S.R. 48/M4
Muy Muy, Nic. 154/E4
Muy Muy Viejo, Nic. 154/E4
Muynak, U.S.S.R. 48/F5
Muyumba, Dem. Rep. of the Congo. 115/E5
Muyuquiri, Bol. 136/C7
Muzaffarabad, India 68/B2
Muzaffarnagar, India 68/D3
Muzaffarpur, India 68/E3
Muzambinho, Braz. 135/C2
Muzo, Col. 126/D5
Muzon (cape), Alaska 196/M2
Muztagh (mt.), China 77/B4
Muztagh Ata (mt.), China 77/A4
M'Vouti, Rep. of Congo 115/B4
Mwadingusha, Dem. Rep. of the Congo. 115/E6
Mwadui, Tanz. 115/F4
Mwanza, 102/F5
Mwanza, Dem. Rep. of the Congo. 115/E5
Mwanza (reg.), Tanz. 115/F3
Mwanza, Tanz. 115/F4
Mwaya, Tanz. 115/F5
Mweelrea (mt.), Ire. 17/B4
Mweenish (isl.), Ire. 17/B5
Mweka, Dem. Rep. of the Congo. 115/D4
Mwene Ditu, Dem. Rep. of the Congo. 115/D5
Mwenga, Dem. Rep. of the Congo. 115/E4
Mweru (lake), 102/E5
Mweru (lake), Dem. Rep. of the Congo. 115/E5
Mweru (lake), Zambia 115/E5
Mwesi, Tanz. 115/F5
Mwinilunga, Zambia 115/D6
Mya, Wadi (dry riv.), Alg. 106/E2
Myadhi, Gabon 115/B3
Myakka (riv.), Fla. 212/D4
Myakka City, Fla. (33551) 212/D4
Myall (lake), N.S.W. 97/G3
Myanaung, Burma 72/B3
Myaungmya, Burma 72/B3
Myebon, Burma 72/B2
Myers, Ky. (40311) 237/O4
Myers, Mont. (59060) 262/J4
Myers Corner‡, N.Y. (†12590) 276/N7
Myerstown, Pa. (17067) 294/K5
Myersville, Jam. 158/H6
Myersville, Md. (21773) 245/H3
Myingyan, Burma 72/B2
Myitkyina, Burma, 54/N7
Myitkyina, Burma 72/C1
Myitnge, Burma 72/C2
Myitnge (riv.), Burma 72/C2
Myjava, Czech. 41/D2
Mylo, N. Dak. (58353) 283/L2
Mymensingh, Pak. 68/G4
Myohaung, Burma 72/B2
Myohyang (mt.), N. Korea 81/C3
Myŏngch'ŏn, N. Korea 81/D3
Myra, Texas (76253) 302/G4
Myra, W. Va. (25544) 313/B6
Myricks, Mass. (†02780) 249/K5
Myrleville, Miss. (†39040) 256/D5
Myrnam, Alta. 182/E3
Myrtle, Idaho (†83540) 220/B3
Myrtle, Man. 179/E5
Myrtle, Minn. (56070) 254/E7
Myrtle, Miss. (38650) 256/F1
Myrtle, Mo. (65778) 261/K9
Myrtle (lake), N. Dak. 283/L5
Myrtle Beach, S.C. (29577) 296/K4
Myrtle Beach A.F.B., S.C. 296/K4
Myrtle Creek, Oreg. (97457) 291/D4
Myrtleford, Vic. 97/D5
Myrtle Grove, Fla. (32506) 212/B6
Myrtle Grove, La. (†70083) 238/K7
Myrtle Point, Oreg. (97458) 291/C4
Myrtlewood, Ala. (36763) 194/C6
Mysen, Norway 18/G7
Myślenice, Poland 47/E4
Myślibórz, Poland 47/B2
Mysłowice, Poland 47/C4
Mysore, India, 54/L8
Mysore (state), India 68/D6
Mysore, India 68/D6
Mystery Lake, Alta. 182/C2
Mystic, Conn. (06355) 210/H3
Mystic (riv.), Conn. 210/H3
Mystic, Ga. (31769) 216/E7
Mystic, Iowa (52574) 229/H7
Mystic (lake), Mass. 249/C6
Mystic (riv.), Mass. 249/C6
Mystic, S. Dak. (†57778) 298/B5
Mystic Islands, N.J. (†08087) 273/E4
Myszków, Poland 47/D3
My Tho, S. Vietnam 72/E5
Myton, Utah (84052) 304/D3
Mzab (oasis), Alg. 106/E2
Mže (riv.), Czech. 41/B2
Mzimba, Malawi 115/F6

N

Naab (riv.), W. Ger. 22/E4
Naafkopf (mt.), Liecht. 39/J2
Naafkopf (mt.), Switz. 39/J2
Naaldwijk, Neth. 27/E4
Naalehu, Hawaii, 188/G6
Naalehu, Hawaii (96772) 218/H7
Naantali, Fin. 18/M6
Naarden, Neth. 27/G4
Naas, 10/C4
Naas, Ire. 17/H5
Naba, Burma 72/B1
Nababiep, S. Africa 118/B5
Naband, Iran 59/F4
Naband, Iran 66/H7
Nabari, Gilb. and Ell., 87/J6
Nabb, Ind. (47147) 227/F7
Nabburg, W. Ger. 22/E4
Naberezhnye Chelny, U.S.S.R. 52/H3
Nabesna, Alaska (†99764) 196/K2
Nabeul, Tun. 106/G1
Nabiac, N.S.W. 97/G3
Nabire, Indon. 85/K6
Nablus (dist.), Jordan 65/C3
Nablus (Nabulus), Jordan 65/C3
Nabnasset, Mass. (01861) 249/J2
Nabua, Phil. 82/D4
Nacala, 102/F6
Nacala, Moz. 118/G2
Nacaome, Hond. 154/D4
Naches, Wash. (98937) 310/E4
Naches (pass), Wash. 310/D3
Naches (riv.), Wash. 310/E4
Nachikatsuura, Japan 81/H7
Nachingwea, Tanz. 115/G6
Náchod, Czech. 41/D1
Nachū, China 77/D5
Nachusa, Ill. (61057) 222/D2
Nachvak (fjord), Newf. 166/B2
Nacimiento (riv.), Calif. 204/D8
Nacimiento, Chile 138/D1
Nacimiento (mts.), N. Mex. 274/C3
Nacimiento (peak), N. Mex. 274/C2
Nacka, Sweden 18/H1
Nacmine, Alta. 182/D4
Naco, Alta. 182/E4
Naco, Ariz. (85620) 198/E7
Naco, Mex. 150/D1
Nacogdoches (co.), Texas 302/K6
Nacogdoches, Texas (75961) 302/J6
Nacozari de García, Mex. 150/E1
Ñacunday, Par. 144/E6
Nadadores, Mex. 150/H3
Nadawah, Ala. (†36726) 194/D7
Nadeau, Mich. (49863) 250/B3
Naden (harb.), Br. Col. 184/A3
Nadiad, India 68/C4
Nadina River, Br. Col. 184/D3
Nădlac, Rum. 45/E2
Nador, Mor. 106/D1
Nádudvar, Hung. 41/F3
Nadym (riv.), U.S.S.R. 48/H3
Naestved, Den. 18/G9
Naestved, Den. 21/E7
Naf, Idaho (83345) 220/E7
Näfels, Switz. 39/H2
Naft-i-Shah, Iran 66/D4
Naft Kaneh, Iraq 66/D3
Naga, Phil. 82/D4
Naga, Phil. 85/G3
Nagahama, Ehime, Japan 81/F7
Nagahama, Shiga, Japan 81/H6
Nagai (isl.), Alaska 196/F4
Nagaland (state), India 68/G3
Nagano (pref.), Japan 81/J5
Nagano, Japan 81/J5
Nagaoka, Kyoto, Japan 81/J7
Nagaoka, Niigata, Japan 81/J5
Nagapattinam, India 68/E6
Nagar, India 68/D1
Nagarote, Nic. 154/D4
Nagar Parkar, Pak. 68/C4
Nagasaki, Japan, 54/R6
Nagasaki (pref.), Japan 81/D7
Nagasaki, Japan 81/D7
Nagato, Japan 81/E6
Nagaur, India 68/C3
Nagawicka (lake), Wis. 317/J1
Nagele, Neth. 27/H3
Nagercoil, India 68/D7
Nagina, India 68/D3
Nagishot, Sudan 111/F7
Nagles (mts.), Ire. 17/E7
Nago, Ryukyu Is. 81/N6
Nagold, W. Ger. 22/C4
Nagorno-Karabakh Aut. Obl., U.S.S.R. 48/E5
Nagorno-Karabakh Aut. Obl., U.S.S.R. 52/G7
Nagornyy, U.S.S.R. 48/N4
Nagoya, Japan, 3/R4
Nagoya, Japan, 54/S6
Nagoya, Japan 81/H6
Nagpur, India, 54/L7
Nagpur, India 68/D4
Nags Head, N.C. (27959) 281/T3
Nagua, Dom. Rep. 158/E5
Naguabo, P. Rico 156/G1
Naguabo, P. Rico 161/F2
Nagyatád, Hung. 41/D3
Nagybajom, Hung. 41/D3
Nagyecsed, Hung. 41/G3
Nagyhalász, Hung. 41/F2
Nagykálló, Hung. 41/F3
Nagykanizsa, Hung. 41/D3
Nagykáta, Hung. 41/E3
Nagykőrös, Hung. 41/E3
Nagyléta, Hung. 41/G3
Nagyszénás, Hung. 41/F3
Naha (cap.), Ryukyu Is. 81/N6
Naha (cap.), Ryukyu Is., 54/R7
Nahan, India 68/D2
Nahanni Butte, N.W.T. 187/F3
Nahant∆, Mass. (01908) 249/E6
Nahant (bay), Mass. 249/E6
Nahariyya, Israel 65/C1
Nahcotta, Wash. (98537) 310/A4
Nahhalin, Jordan 65/C4
Nahiku, Hawaii (†96713) 218/K2
Nahma, Mich. (49864) 250/C3
Nahmakanta (lake), Maine 242/E4
Nahuel Huapi (lake), Arg. 143/B5
Nahuel Huapi Nat'l Park, Arg. 143/B5
Nahunta, Ga. (31553) 216/H8
Naibandan, Iran 59/G3
Naibandan, Iran 66/K4
Naicam, Sask. 181/G3
Naihati, India 68/F1
Nailsworth, Eng. 13/E6
Na'in, Iran 59/F3
Na'in, Iran 66/H4
Nain, 163/K4
Nain, Newf. 166/B2
Naini Tal, India 68/D3
Nainpur, India 68/E4
Naipo (isl.), Col. 126/F6
Nairn, 10/E2
Nairn, La. (70077) 238/L8
Nairn (co.), Scot. 15/J5
Nairn, Scot. 15/J5
Nairn (riv.), Scot. 15/J5
Nairne, Aust. 88/E8
Nairne, S. Aust. 94/C8
Nairobi (dist.), Kenya 115/G4
Nairobi (cap.), Kenya 3/L6
Nairobi (cap.), Kenya 115/G4
Nairobi (cap.), Kenya 102/F5
Naisberry, Sask. 181/G3
Naivasha, Kenya 115/G4
Naivasha, Kenya 102/F5
Najayo Abajo, Dom. Rep. 158/E6
Najin, N. Korea 54/S5
Najin, N. Korea 81/E2
Najouoland (lake), Que. 172/E2
Najran, Saudi Ar. 59/D6
Naka (riv.), Japan 81/K5
Nakalele (pt.), Hawaii 218/J1
Nakaminato, Japan 81/K5
Nakamti, Eth. 111/G4
Nakamura, Japan 81/F7
Nakanna, U.S.S.R. 48/L3
Nakasato, Japan 81/K3
Nakatsu, Japan 81/E7
Na Keal (inlet), Scot. 15/D7
Naked (isl.), Alaska 196/D1
Nakfa, Eth. 111/G4
Nakhichevan', U.S.S.R. 48/E6
Nakhichevan', U.S.S.R. 52/F7
Nakhichevan, U.S.S.R. 7/J5
Nakhichevan' A.S.S.R., U.S.S.R., 48/E6
Nakhichevan' A.S.S.R., U.S.S.R., 52/F7
Nakhodka, U.S.S.R. 48/05
Nakhon Nayok, Thai. 72/D4
Nakhon Pathom, Thai. 72/C4
Nakhon Phanom, Thai. 72/D3
Nakhon Ratchasima, Thai. 72/D4
Nakhon Sawan, Thai. 72/D4
Nakhon Si Thammarat, Thai. 72/D5
Nakina, 163/H5
Nakina, Ont. 175/C2
Nakina, Ont. 177/H4
Nakina, N.C. (28455) 281/M6
Nakło nad Notecia, Poland 47/C2
Naknek, Alaska (99633) 196/G3
Naknek (lake), Alaska 196/G3
Nakonde, Zambia 115/F5
Nakop, S.W. Afr. 118/B5
Nakoso, Japan 81/K5
Nakskov, Den. 18/G9
Nakskov, Den. 21/E8
Naktong (riv.), S. Korea 81/D6
Nakuru, Kenya 115/G4
Nakusp, Br. Col. 184/J5
Nal, Pak. 59/J4
Nal, Pak. 68/B3
Nal (riv.), Pak. 59/J4
Nal (riv.), Pak. 68/B3
Nalaikha, Mong. 77/G2
Nalcayec (isl.), Chile 138/D6
Nal'chik, U.S.S.R. 48/E5
Nal'chik, U.S.S.R. 52/F6
Nalgonda, India 68/D5
Nallen, W. Va. (26680) 313/E6
Nallihan, Turkey 63/D2
Nalut, Libya 111/B1
Namacurra, Moz. 118/F3
Namak, Darya-yi- (salt lake), Iran 59/F3
Namak, Darya-yi- (salt lake), Iran 66/G3
Namaka, Alta. 182/D4
Namaksar (salt lake), Afgh. 59/H3
Namaksar (salt lake), Iran 59/H3
Namaksar (lake), Iran 66/M4
Namaksar (salt lake), Afgh. 68/A2
Namakzar (marsh), Iran 59/G3
Namakzar (marsh), Iran 66/L5
Namanga, Kenya 115/G4
Namangan, U.S.S.R. 48/H5
Namangan, U.S.S.R., 54/K5
N'amaniya, Iraq 66/D4
Namapa, Moz. 118/F2
Namarrói, Moz. 118/F3
Namasagali, Uganda 115/F3
Namasigüe, Hond. 154/D4
Namatanai, Terr. N.G., 87/F6
Nambe, N. Mex. (†87501) 274/D3
Nambour, Queens. 95/E5
Nambucca Heads, N.S.W. 97/G2
Namcha Barwa (mt.), China 77/E6
Nam Dinh, N. Vietnam 72/E2
Namekagon (lake), Wis. 317/D3
Namekagon (res.), Wis. 317/C3
Namen (Namur), Belg. 27/F8
Námestovo, Czech. 41/E2
Nametil, Moz. 118/F3
Nam Hka (riv.), Burma 72/C2
Namhkam, Burma 72/C2
Nam Hou (riv.), Laos 72/D2
Namib (des.), S.W. Afr. 118/A3
Naminga, U.S.S.R. 48/M4
Namlan, Burma 72/C2
Namlea, Indon. 85/H6
Namoi (riv.), N.S.W. 97/E2
Namonuito (atoll), Pac. Is., 87/E5
Namorik (atoll), Pac. Is., 87/G5
Nampa, Alta. 182/B1
Nampa, Idaho, 188/C2
Nampa, Idaho (83651) 220/B6
Nampala, Mali 106/C5
Nam Pawn (riv.), Burma 72/C2
Namp'o, N. Korea 81/B4
Nampo-Shoto (isls.), Japan 81/M3
Nampula, 102/G6
Nampula, Moz., 118/F3
Namsen (riv.), Norway 18/H4
Namsos, Norway 18/G4
Namsos, Norway, 7/F2
Nam Teng (riv.), Burma 72/C2
Nam Tha, Laos 72/D2
Nam Tha (riv.), Laos 72/D2
Nam Tram (cape), S. Vietnam 72/F4
Nam Tso (lake), China, 54/N6
Nam Tso (lake), China 77/D5
Namtu, Burma 72/C2
Namu, Br. Col. 184/D4
Namuac, Phil. 82/C1
Namuli (mt.), 102/E6
Namuli (mt.), Moz. 118/F3
Namur (lake), Alta. 182/D1
Namur (prov.), Belg. 27/F8
Namur, Belg. 27/F8
Namur, Que. 172/C4
Namutoni, S.W. Afr. 118/B3
Namwala, Zambia 115/E7
Namwŏn, S. Korea 81/C6
Namysłów, Poland 47/C3
Nan, Thai. 72/D3
Nan, Mae Nam (riv.), Thai. 72/D3
Nanacamilpa, Mex. 150/M1
Nana Candundo, Angola 115/D6
Nanafalia, Ala. (36764) 194/B6
Nanaimo, 163/D6
Nanaimo, Br. Col., 146/F5
Nanaimo, Br. Col. 184/J3
Nanakuli, Hawaii (96792) 218/D2
Nanam, N. Korea 81/D3
Nanao, Japan 81/H5
Nanay (riv.), Peru 128/E4
Nancagua, Chile 138/F6
Nance (co.), Nebr. 264/F3
Nanchang, China, 54/P7
Nanchang, China 77/H6
Nancheng, China 77/J6
Nanchung, China 77/G5
Nan Clàr (lake), Scot. 15/J3
Nancowry (isl.), India 68/G7
Nancy, France, 7/E4
Nancy, France 28/G3
Nancy, Ky. (42544) 237/M6
Nanda Devi (mt.), India 68/D2
Nandaime, Nic. 154/E5
Nander, India 68/D5
Nandi, Fiji, 87/H7
Nando, Urug. 145/F3
Nandurbar, India 68/C4
Nandyal, India 68/D5
Nanga Parbat (mt.), India 68/D1
Nangapinoh, Indon. 85/E6
Nangatajap, Indon. 85/E6
Nangnim-sanmaek (range), N. Korea 81/C3
Nang Rong, Thai. 72/D4
Nangtsien, China 77/E5
Nangwarry, S. Aust. 94/G7
Nanhsiung, China 77/H6
Nanika (dam), Br. Col. 184/D3
Nanika (lake), Br. Col. 184/D3
Nanjemoy, Md. (20662) 245/K7
Nanking, China, 3/Q4
Nanking, China, 54/P6
Nanking, China 77/J5
Nankipooh, Ga. (†31808) 216/C5
Nankoku, Japan 81/F7
Nan Ling (mts.), China 77/H7
Nannine, Aust. 88/B5
Nannine, W. Aust. 92/B4
Nanning, China, 54/O7
Nanning, China 77/G7
Nannup, Aust. 88/A6
Nannup, W. Aust. 92/B6
Nanoose Bay, Br. Col. 184/J3
Nanortalik, Greenl., 4/D12
Nanping, China 77/J6
Nansei-Shoto (isls.), Ryukyu Is. 81/M6
Nansemond (co.), Va. 307/P7
Nansen (sound), N.W.T. 187/J1
Nan Shan (range), China 77/E4
Nanson, N. Dak. (58354) 283/L2
Nantahala, N.C. (†28702) 281/B4
Nantahala (lake), N.C. 281/B4
Nantai (mt.), Japan 81/J5
Nantasket Beach, Mass. (†02045) 249/E7
Nanterre, France 28/A1
Nantes, Que. 172/F4
Nantes, France, 7/D4
Nantes, France 28/C4
Nanticoke (riv.), Del. 245/R6
Nanticoke, Ont. 177/E5
Nanticoke, Md. (21840) 245/P7
Nanticoke (riv.), Md. 245/P7
Nanticoke, Pa. (18634) 294/K3
Nanton, Alta. 182/D4
Nantua, France 28/F4
Nantucket (isl.), Mass., 188/N2
Nantucket (co.), Mass. 249/O7
Nantucket∆, Mass. (02554) 249/O7
Nantucket, Mass. (02554) 249/O7
Nantucket (isl.), Mass. 249/O8
Nantucket (sound), Mass. 249/N6
Nantwich, 10/G2
Nantwich, Eng. 13/E4
Nanty Glo, Pa. (15943) 294/E5
Nanuet‡, N.Y. (10954) 276/M8
Nanuktok (isls.), Newf. 166/C2
Nanumea (atoll), Gilb. and Ell., 87/H6
Nanyang, China 77/H5
Nanyuki, Kenya 115/G3
Nao (cape), Spain 33/G3
Naococane (lake), Que. 174/C2
Naoetsu, Japan 81/H5
Naolinco de Victoria, Mex. 150/P1
Naomi, Ky. (†42544) 237/M6
Náousa, Greece 45/F5
Napa, Calif., 188/B3
Napa (co.), Calif. 204/C5
Napa, Calif. (94558) 204/C5
Napadogan, N. Br. 170/D2
Napaiskak, Alaska (†99559) 196/F2
Napa Junction, Calif. (†94590) 204/J1
Napakiak, Alaska (99634) 196/F2
Napaktok (bay), Newf. 166/B2
Napamute, Alaska (†99557) 196/G2
Napanee, Ont. 177/G3
Napanoch, N.Y. (12458) 276/M7
Napas, U.S.S.R. 48/J4
Napata (ruins), Sudan 111/F4
Napavine, Wash. (98565) 310/C4
Napé, Laos 72/E3
Naper, Nebr. (68755) 264/E2
Naperville, Ill. (60540) 222/E2
Napf (mt.), Switz. 39/E3
Napier, Ky. (40859) 237/P7
Napier, N. Z., 87/H9
Napier, N.Z. 101/F3
Napier (mt.), No. Terr. 93/A4
Napier, W. Va. (26631) 313/E5
Napierville (co.), Que. 172/D4
Napierville, Que. 172/D4
Napinka, Man. 179/B5

Neuberg an der Mürz 407

Naplate, Ill. (†61350) 222/E2
Naples, Alta. 182/C2
Naples, Fla. (33940) 212/E5
Naples, Idaho (83847) 220/B1
Naples, Ill. (62669) 222/C4
Naples, Italy, 7/F4
Naples (prov.), Italy 34/E4
Naples, Italy 34/E4
Naples▵, Maine (04055) 242/B8
Naples, N.Y. (14512) 276/F5
Naples, S. Dak. (57254) 298/O4
Naples, Texas (75568) 302/K4
Naples Park, Fla. (†33940) 212/E5
Napo (riv.), 120/C3
Napo (prov.), Ec. 128/D3
Napo, Ec. 128/D3
Napo (riv.), Ec. 128/D3
Napo (riv.), Peru 128/F4
Napoleon, Ind. (47034) 227/G6
Napoleon, Mich. (49261) 250/E6
Napoleon, Mo. (64074) 261/E4
Napoleon, N. Dak. (58561) 283/L6
Napoleon, Ohio (43545) 284/B3
Napoleonville, La. (70390) 238/K4
Napoli (Naples), Italy, 7/F4
Naponee, Nebr. (68960) 264/E4
Nappamerry, Queens. 95/B5
Nappanee, Ind. (46550) 227/F2
Napperby, No. Terr. 93/C7
Napton, Mo. (65346) 261/F4
Naqa (ruins), Sudan 111/F4
Nara, Mali 106/C5
Nara (pref.), Japan 81/J8
Nara, Japan 81/J8
Naracoorte, Aust. 88/F7
Naracoorte, S. Aust. 94/G7
Naradhan, N.S.W. 97/D3
Naramata, Br. Col. 184/H5
Naranja, Fla. (33030) 212/F6
Naranjal (riv.), Ec. 128/C4
Naranjito, P. Rico 161/D1
Naranjito, Hond. 154/C3
Naranjos, Mex. 150/L6
Naraq, Iran 66/G3
Narashino, Japan 81/P2
Narathiwat, Thai. 72/D6
Nara Visa, N. Mex. (88430) 274/F3
Narayanganj, Pak. 68/G4
Narayanpet, India 68/D5
Narberth, Pa. (19072) 294/M6
Narberth, Wales 13/C6
Narbonne, France 28/E6
Narcissa, Okla. (†74354) 288/S1
Narcisse, Man. 179/E4
Narcondam (isl.), India 68/G6
Narcoossee, Fla. (†32769) 212/E3
Narcosli Creek, Br. Col. 184/F4
Nardin, Okla. (74646) 288/M1
Nardò, Italy 34/F4
Naré, Arg. 143/F5
Nare, Col. 126/C4
Nares (str.), 146/L2
Nares (str.), 163/N3
Nares (str.), N.W.T. 187/L2
Narew (riv.), Poland 47/E2
Naricual, Ven. 124/F2
Nariño (dept.), Col. 126/B7
Nariva (swamp), Trinidad Tobago 161/B10
Narka, Kans. (66960) 232/E2
Narmada (riv.), India, 54/L7
Narmada (riv.), India 68/D4
Narman, Turkey 63/J2
Narnaul, India 68/D3
Narni, Italy 34/D3
Naro, Italy 34/D6
Narodnaya (mt.), U.S.S.R. 48/G3
Narodnaya (mt.), U.S.S.R. 52/J1
Naro-Fominsk, U.S.S.R. 52/E3
Narok, Kenya 115/G4
Narooma, N.S.W. 97/F5
Narrabeen, N.S.W. 97/K3
Narrabri, Aust. 88/H6
Narrabri, N.S.W. 97/E2
Narragansett▵, R.I. (02882) 249/J7
Narragansett, R.I. (02882) 249/J7
Narragansett (bay), R.I. 249/J6
Narran (lake), N.S.W. 97/D1
Narran (riv.), N.S.W. 97/D1
Narrandera, Aust. 88/H6
Narrandera, N.S.W. 97/D4
Narre Warren, Vic. 97/K5
Narre Warren North, Vic. 97/K5
Narrogin, Aust. 88/B6
Narrogin, W. Aust. 92/B2
Narromine, Aust. 88/H6
Narromine, N.S.W. 97/E3
Narrows, The (str.), St. Chr.-N.-A. 161/D11
Narrows, The (str.), V.I. (Br.) 161/C4
Narrows, The (str.), V.I.(U.S.) 161/C4
Narrows, Ky. (42358) 237/H5
Narrows, N. Br. 170/E3
Narrows, Oreg. (†97721) 291/H4
Narrows, Va. (24124) 307/G6
Narrowsburg, N.Y. (12764) 276/L7
Narrows Park-La Vale, Md. (†21502) 245/C2
Narsinghgarh, India 68/D4
Narsinghpur, India 68/D4
Narssaq, Greenl., 4/C12
Naruna, Va. (24576) 307/L6
Narva, U.S.S.R. 52/C3
Narva, U.S.S.R. 53/E1
Narva (res.), U.S.S.R. 53/D1
Narva, U.S.S.R., 7/G3
Narvik, Norway 18/K2
Narvik, Norway, 4/C9
Narvik, Norway, 7/F2
Nary, Minn. (†56601) 254/D3
Nar'yan-Mar, U.S.S.R. 48/F3
Nar'yan-Mar, U.S.S.R. 52/H1
Nar'yan-Mar, U.S.S.R., 4/C7
Nar'yan-Mar, U.S.S.R., 7/K2
Narym, U.S.S.R., 54/L4
Naryn, U.S.S.R. 48/H5
Nasarawa, Nigeria 106/F7
N.A.S.A. Space Ctr., Texas 302/K2
Năsăud, Rum. 45/G2
Naseby, N.Z. 101/C6
Naselle, Wash. (98638) 310/B4
Naselle (riv.), Wash. 310/B4
Nash (co.), N.C. 281/O2
Nash, N. Dak. (58264) 283/P3
Nash (stream), N.H. 268/E2
Nash, Okla. (73761) 288/K1
Nash, Texas (75569) 302/K4
Nashawena (isl.), Mass. 249/L7
Nash Creek, N. Br. 170/D1
Nash Harbor, Alaska (†99630) 196/E2
Nashoba, Okla. (74558) 288/R6
Nashotah, Wis. (53058) 317/J1
Nashport, Ohio (43830) 284/F5
Nashua, Iowa (50658) 229/J3
Nashua (riv.), Mass. 249/H3
Nashua, Minn. (56565) 254/B4
Nashua, Mont. (59248) 262/K2
Nashua, N.H., 188/M2
Nashua, N.H. (03060) 268/D6
Nashville, Ark. (71852) 203/C6
Nashville, Ga. (31639) 216/F8
Nashville, Ill. (62263) 222/D5
Nashville, Ind. (47448) 227/E6
Nashville, Kans. (67112) 232/D4
Nashville, Mich. (49073) 250/D6
Nashville, Mo. (†64855) 261/D8
Nashville, N.C. (27856) 281/O3
Nashville, Ohio (44661) 284/F4
Nashville, Oreg. (97370) 291/D3
Nashville (cap.), Tenn., 146/K6
Nashville (cap.), Tenn., 188/J3
Nashville (cap.), Tenn. (*37201) 237/H8
Nashwaak, N. Br. 170/D2
Nashwaak (riv.), N. Br. 170/D2
Nashwaak Bridge, N. Br. 170/D2
Nashwaaksis, N. Br. 170/D3
Nashwauk, Minn. (55769) 254/E3
Näsi (lake), Fin. 18/O6
Našice, Yugo. 45/C3
Nasik, India 68/C4
Nasir, Sudan 111/F6
Nasirabad, India 68/C3
Nasiriya (prov.), Iraq 66/E5
Naskaupi (riv.), Newf. 166/B3
Naso (pt.), Phil. 82/C5
Nason, Ill. (62866) 222/D5
Nasonville, R.I. (†02830) 249/H5
Nasratabad (Zabul), Iran 59/H3
Nasratabad (Zabul), Iran 66/M5
Nasratabad Sipi, Iran 66/L6
Nass (riv.), Br. Col. 184/C2
Nassau (cap.), Bah. Is., 146/L7
Nassau (cap.), Bah. Is. 156/C1
Nassau (bay), Chile, 120/D8
Nassau (bay), Chile 138/F11
Nassau (isl.), Cook Is., 87/K7
Nassau, Del. (19969) 245/T6
Nassau (co.), Fla. 212/E1
Nassau (riv.), Fla. 212/E1
Nassau (sound), Fla. 212/E1
Nassau, Minn. (56272) 254/B5
Nassau (co.), N.Y. 276/N9
Nassau, N.Y. (12123) 276/N5
Nassawadox, Va. (23413) 307/S6
Nassawango (creek), Md. 245/S8
Nasser (lake), 102/F2
Nasser (lake), U.A.R. 59/F3
Nasser (lake), U.A.R. 111/F3
Nasser (lake), Sudan 111/F3
Nassereith, Austria 41/A3
Nass Harbour, Br. Col. 184/C3
Nässjö, Sweden 18/J8
Nasty (creek), S. Dak. 298/C2
Nasu (mt.), Japan 81/J5
Nasugbu, Phil. 82/C3
Natá, Pan. 154/G6
Natagaima, Col. 126/C6
Natal, Braz., 3/H6
Natal, Braz., 120/G3
Natal, Braz. 132/H4
Natal (prov.), 102/F7
Natal (prov.), S. Africa 118/E5
Natalbany, La. (70451) 238/N1
Natalia, Texas (78059) 302/F8
Natalicio Talavera, Par. 144/D5
Natanz, Iran 59/F3
Natanz, Iran 66/H4
Natashquan, Que. 174/E3
Natashquan (riv.), Que. 174/E2
Natashquan (riv.), 163/K5
Natashquan (riv.), Newf. 166/B3
Natashquan-Est (riv.), Newf. 166/B3
Natchaug (riv.), Conn. 210/G1
Natchez, Ala. (†36425) 194/D7
Natchez, La. (71456) 238/D3
Natchez, Miss., 188/H4
Natchez, Miss. (39120) 256/B7
Natchitoches (par.), La. 238/D3
Natchitoches, La. (71457) 238/D3
Naters, Switz. 39/E4
Nathalia, Vic. 97/C5
Nathalie, Va. (24577) 307/L7
Nathan, Mich. (†49821) 250/B3
Nathrop, Colo. (81236) 208/H5
Natick▵, Mass. (01760) 249/A7
Natick, R.I. (†02887) 249/H6
Natimuk, Vic. 97/A5
Nation (riv.), Br. Col. 184/F2
National Agricultural Research Center, Md. 245/G3
National City, Calif. (92050) 204/J11
National City, Mich. (48748) 250/F4
National Gardens, Fla. (†32074) 212/E2
National Mills, Man. 179/A2
National Mine, Mich. (49865) 250/B2
National Park, N.J. (08063) 273/B3
National Park, Switz. 39/K3
National Reactor Testing Sta. (U.S.A.E.C. Res.), Idaho 220/F6
National Stock Yards, Ill. (62071) 222/B6
Natitingou, Dahomey 106/E6
Natividade, Braz. 132/E5
Natmauk, Burma 72/B2
Natoma, Kans. (67651) 232/D2
Natron (lake), Kenya 115/G4
Natron (lake), Tanz. 115/G4
Natrona (co.), Wyo. 319/F3
Natrona, Wyo. (82646) 319/F2
Natrona Heights, Pa. (15065) 294/C4
Natuna (isls.), Indon., 54/O9
Natuna (isls.), Indon. 85/D5
Natural Bridge, Ala. (35577) 194/C2
Natural Bridge, N.Y. (13665) 276/K2
Natural Bridge, Va. (24578) 307/J5
Natural Bridges Nat'l Mon., Utah 304/E6
Natural Bridge Station, Va. (24579) 307/K5
Natural Dam, N.Y. (†13642) 276/J2
Naturaliste (cape), Aust. 88/A6
Naturaliste (chan.), Aust. 88/A5
Naturaliste (cape), W. Aust. 92/A6
Naturaliste (chan.), W. Aust. 92/A4
Natural Steps, Ark. (†72135) 203/F4
Naturita, Colo. (81422) 208/B6
Naubinway, Mich. (49762) 250/D2
Naubuc, Conn. (†06033) 210/E2
Naucalpan de Juárez, Mex. 150/L1
Nauders, Austria 41/A3
Nauen, E. Ger. 22/E2
Naugatuck, Conn. (06770) 210/C3
Naugatuck (riv.), Conn. 210/C3
Naugatuck, W. Va. (25685) 313/B7
Nauhcampatépetl (mt.), Mex. 150/O1
Naujan (lake), Phil. 82/C4
Naumburg, E. Ger. 22/D3
Na'ur, Jordan 65/D4
Nauru, 3/T6
Nauru, 87/G6
Naushahr, Iran 66/G2
Naushon (isl.), Mass. 249/L7
Naustdal, Norway 18/E6
Nauta, Peru 128/F5
Nautla, Mex. 150/L6
Nauvoo, Ala. (35578) 194/D3
Nauvoo, Ill. (62354) 222/B3
Nauwigewauk, N. Br. 170/E3
Nauzad, Afgh. 59/H3
Nauzad, Afgh. 68/A2
Nava, Mex. 150/J2
Nava del Rey, Spain 33/D2
Navajo (co.), Ariz. 198/E3
Navajo, Ariz. (86509) 198/F3
Navajo (creek), Ariz. 198/D2
Navajo (peak), Colo. 208/F8
Navajo (res.), Colo. 208/E8
Navajo, Mont. (†59222) 262/M2
Navajo, N. Mex. (87328) 274/A3
Navajo (dam), N. Mex. 274/B2
Navajo (res.), N. Mex. 274/B2
Navajo (mt.), Utah 304/D6
Navajo Ind. Res., Ariz. 198/F2
Navajo Ind. Res., N. Mex. 274/A2
Navajo Ind. Res., Utah 304/D7
Navajo Nat'l Mon., Ariz. 198/E2
Navajo Ord. Depot, Ariz. 198/D3
Naval Academy, U.S., Md. 245/N5
Naval Base, S.C. (29408) 296/G6
Navalcarnero, Spain 33/F4
Naval Gun Factory, D.C. 245/F5
Naval Medical Center, Md. 245/E4
Navalmoral de la Mata, Spain 33/D3
Naval Oceanographic Office, Md. 245/F5
Naval Ordnance Laboratory, Md. 245/F3
Naval Ordnance Sta., U.S., Md. 245/K6
Naval Submarine Base, Conn. 210/G3
Navan (An Uaimh), Ire. 17/H4
Navarin (cape), U.S.S.R. 48/T3
Navarin (cape), U.S.S.R., 4/C18
Navarino (isl.), Chile 138/F11
Navarino, Wis. (54108) 317/J6
Navarra (prov.), Spain 33/F1
Navarre, Kans. (67469) 232/E3
Navarre, Ohio (44662) 284/H4
Navarro, Arg. 143/G7
Navarro, Calif. (95463) 204/B4
Navarro (riv.), Calif. 204/B4
Navarro (co.), Texas 302/H5
Navasota, Texas (77868) 302/J7
Navasota (riv.), Texas 302/H7
Navassa (isl.), W. Indies 156/C3
Naver (lake), Scot. 15/H3
Naver (riv.), Scot. 15/H3
Navesink, N.J. (07752) 273/E3
Navesink (riv.), N.J. 273/E3
Navia (riv.), Spain 33/C1
Navidad, Chile 138/A10
Navidad (riv.), Texas 302/H8
Navojoa, Mex. 150/E3
Navolato, Mex. 150/E4
Návpaktos, Greece 45/F7
Návplion, Greece 45/F7
Navrongo, Ghana 106/D6
Navsari, India 68/C4
Navy Board (inlet), N.W.T. 187/K2
Navy Yard City, Wash. (†98310) 310/A2
Nawabganj, Pak. 68/F4
Nawabshah, Pak. 59/J4
Nawabshah, Pak. 68/B3
Nawiliwili (bay), Hawaii 218/D2
Naxera, Va. (23122) 307/R6
Náxos, Greece 45/G7
Náxos (isl.), Greece 45/G7
Naya, Col. 126/B6
Nayarit (state), Mex. 150/G6
Nayarit, Sierra (mts.), Mex. 150/G5
Naylor, Ga. (31641) 216/F9
Naylor, Mo. (63953) 261/L9
Nayoro, Japan 81/L1
Naytahwaush, Minn. (56566) 254/C3
Nazaré, Braz. 132/G6
Nazaré, Port. 33/B3
Nazareth, Israel 65/C2
Nazareth, Pa. (18064) 294/M4
Nazareth, Texas (79063) 302/B3
Nazas, Mex. 150/G4
Nazas (riv.), Mex. 150/G4
Nazca, Peru 128/E10
Naze, The (prom.), Eng. 13/J6
Naze, Japan 81/O5
Nazilli, Turkey 63/C4
Nazimabad, Pak. 68/B3
Nazko, Br. Col. 184/F3
Nchanga, Zambia 115/E6
Ncheu, Malawi 115/F6
Ndélé, Centr. Afr. Rep. 115/D2
N'Dendé, Gabon 115/B4
Ndeni (isl.), Br. Sol. Is., 87/G7
N'Djolé, Gabon 115/B4
N'Dogo (lag.), Gabon 115/B4
Ndola, 102/E6
Ndola, Zambia 115/E6
Nead, Ind. (†46970) 227/E3
Néa Filippiás, Greece 45/E6
Neagh (lake), 10/C3
Neagh (lake), N. Ire. 17/J2
Neah Bay, Wash. (98357) 310/A2
Neal, Kans. (66863) 232/F4
Neale (lake), No. Terr. 93/A8
Neales, The (riv.), S. Aust. 94/E3
Neápolis, Greece 45/F7
Neapolis, Ohio (43547) 284/C3
Near (isls.), Alaska 196/H3
Neath, 10/E5
Neath, Wales 13/D6
Neave (isl.), Scot. 15/H2
Neavitt, Md. (21652) 245/N6
Nebikon, Switz. 39/F2
Nebish, Minn. (†56667) 254/D3
Nebit-Dag, U.S.S.R. 48/F6
Neblina (peak), Braz. 132/G8
Neblina, Pico da (peak), Braz., 120/D2
Neblina (Phelps) (peak), Ven. 124/E7
Nebo (mt.), Ark. 203/D3
Nebo (mt.), Aust. 88/K2
Nebo, Ill. (62355) 222/C4
Nebo, Ky. (42441) 237/F6
Nebo, La. (†71342) 238/F3
Nebo, Mo. (65471) 261/H7
Nebo (mt.), Jordan 65/D4
Nebo (mt.), Utah 304/C4
Nebo, W. Va. (25141) 313/D5
Nebo Center‡, Calif. (†92311) 204/J9
Nebraska, 188/F2
NEBRASKA, 264
Nebraska, Ind. (47262) 227/F6
Nebraska (state), U.S., 146/H5
Nebraska City, Nebr. (68410) 264/J4
Necedah, Wis. (54646) 317/F7
Nechako (riv.), Br. Col. 184/E3
Neche, N. Dak. (58265) 283/P2
Neches, Texas (75779) 302/J6
Neches (riv.), Texas 302/K6
Nechí (riv.), Col. 126/C4
Neckar (riv.), W. Ger. 22/C4
Neckarsulm, W. Ger. 22/C4
Neck City, Mo. (64849) 261/C8
Necker (isl.), Hawaii, 87/K3
Necker (isl.), Hawaii 188/F6
Necker (isl.), Hawaii 218/D6
Necochea, Arg. 143/E4
Necum Teuch (harb.), N.S. 169/F4
Ned, Ky. (41355) 237/P6
Neded, Czech. 41/D2
Nederland, Colo. (80466) 208/H3
Nederland, Texas (77627) 302/K8
Nedgera (creek), N.S.W. 97/E2
Nedlands, Aust. 88/B2
Nedlands, W. Aust. 92/A1
Neeb, Sask. 181/C1
Neebish (isl.), Mich. 250/E2
Neede, Neth. 27/K4
Needham, Ala. (36915) 194/B7
Needham, Ind. (46162) 227/E5
Needham▵, Mass. (02192) 249/B7
Needham Heights, Mass. (02194) 249/B7
Needle (mt.), Wyo. 319/C1
Needles, Br. Col. 184/H5
Needles, Calif., 188/C4
Needles, Calif. (92363) 204/L9
Needles (pt.), N.Z. 101/E2
Needmore, Ind. (†47421) 227/E7
Needmore, N.C. (†28713) 281/B4
Needmore, Pa. (17238) 294/F6
Needmore, W. Va. (†26801) 313/J4
Needville, Texas (77461) 302/J8
Neelin, Man. 179/C5
Neely, Miss. (39461) 256/G8
Neelys Landing, Mo. (†63755) 261/O7
Neelyton, Pa. (17239) 294/G5
Neelyville, Mo. (63954) 261/M9
Ñeembucú (dept.), Par. 144/D6
Neenah, Wis. (54956) 317/J7
Neepawa, Man. 179/C4
Neerlandia, Alta. 182/C2
Neerlinter, Belg. 27/G7
Neerpelt, Belg. 27/G6
Neeses, S.C. (29107) 296/E4
Nee Soon, Sing. 72/F6
Neffs, Ohio (43940) 284/J5
Neffs Mills, Pa. (†16669) 294/G4
Nefta, Tun. 106/F2
Neftekamsk, U.S.S.R. 52/J3
Neftelensk, U.S.S.R. 48/M4
Nefud (des.), Saudi Ar. 59/D4
Nefud Dahi (des.), Saudi Ar. 59/D5
Nefusa, Jebel (mts.), Libya 111/B1
Nefyn, Wales 13/C5
Negage, Angola 115/C5
Negara, Indon. 85/E7
Negaunee, Mich. (49866) 250/B2
Negba, Israel 65/B4
Negelli, Eth. 111/G6
Negeri Sembilan (state), Malaysia 72/D7
Negev (reg.), Israel 65/D5
Negley, Ohio (44441) 284/J4
Negoiul (mt.), Rum. 45/G3
Negomano, Moz. 118/F2
Negombo, Ceylon 68/D7
Negoreloye, U.S.S.R., 7/G3
Negotin, Yugo. 45/F3
Negra (pt.), P. Rico 161/G2
Negra (pt.), Peru 128/B6
Negra, Cordillera (mts.), Peru 128/D7
Negra (lag.), Urug. 145/F5
Negra (range), Urug. 145/D2
Negrais (cape), Burma 72/B3
Negreet, La. (71460) 238/C4
Negreiros, Chile 138/B2
Negrești, Rum. 45/H2
Negril, Jam. 158/G6
Negrillos, Bol. 136/A6
Negritos, Peru 128/B5
Negro (riv.), 3/F5
Negro (riv.), Arg., 120/D6
Negro (riv.), Arg. 143/D4
Negro (riv.), Bol. 136/D4
Negro (riv.), Braz., 120/D3
Negro (riv.), Col. 126/G7
Negro (riv.), Braz. 132/H9
Negro (cape), N.S. 169/C5
Negro (harb.), N.S. 169/C5
Negro (cape), Angola 115/B7
Negro (bay), Somalia 115/J2
Negro (riv.), Par. 144/D5
Negro (riv.), Urug. 145/B4
Negro, Arroyo (riv.), Urug. 145/B3
Negro (riv.), Ven. 124/E7
Negro Bay, V.I.(U.S.) 161/E4
Negros (isl.), Phil. 82/D6
Negros (isl.), Phil. 85/G4
Negros (isl.), Phil., 54/R9
Negros Occidental (prov.), Phil. 82/D6
Negros Oriental (prov.), Phil. 82/D6
Neguac, N. Br. 170/E1
Neh, Iran 59/G3
Neh, Iran 66/M5
Nehalem, Oreg. (97131) 291/D2
Nehalem (riv.), Oreg. 291/D2
Nehavend, Iran 59/E3
Nehavend, Iran 66/F3
Nehawka, Nebr. (68413) 264/H4
Neheim-Hüsten, W. Ger. 22/C3
Neiafu, Tonga, 87/J7
Neiba, Dom. Rep. 156/D3
Neiba, Dom. Rep. 158/D6
Neiba (bay), Dom. Rep. 158/D6
Neiba, Sierra de (mts.), Dom. Rep. 158/D6
Neidpath, Sask. 181/D5
Neiges (lake), Que. 172/F2
Neigette, Que. 172/J1
Neihart, Mont. (59465) 262/F4
Neikiang, China 77/F6
Neilburg, Sask. 181/B3
Neil Harbour, N.S. 169/H2
Neillsville, Wis. (54456) 317/E6
Neilston, Scot. 15/C2
Neilton, Wash. (98566) 310/B3
Neisse (riv.), E. Ger. 22/F3
Neisse (Nysa Łużycka) (riv.), Poland 47/B3
Neist (pt.), Scot. 15/C5
Neiva, Col., 120/C2
Neiva, Col. 126/C6
Nejafabad, Iran 59/F3
Nejafabad, Iran 66/G4
Nejanilini (lake), Man. 179/J1
Nejapa, Guat. 154/B3
Nejd (prov.), Saudi Ar. 59/D4
Nejdek, Czech. 41/B1
Nejo, Eth. 111/G6
Nekoma, Kans. (67559) 232/C3
Nekoma, N. Dak. (58355) 283/O2
Nekoosa, Wis. (54457) 317/G7
Neksø, Den. 18/J9
Neksø, Den. 21/F9
Nelagoney, Okla. (†74056) 288/O1
Nelas, Port. 33/C2
Nelchina, Alaska (†99588) 196/C1
Nelidovo, U.S.S.R. 52/D3
Neligh, Nebr. (68756) 264/G2
Nel'kan, U.S.S.R. 48/O4
Nel'kan, U.S.S.R., 54/S4
Nellie, Ohio (†43844) 284/F5
Nellis, W. Va. (25142) 313/C6
Nellis A.F.B., Nev. 266/F6
Nelliston, N.Y. (13410) 276/L5
Nellore, India 68/E6
Nellysford, Va. (22958) 307/L5
Nelma, Wis. (†49935) 317/J3
Nelse, Ky. (41550) 237/R6
Nelson, 10/G1
Nelson, 163/E6
Nelson (riv.), 163/G4
Nelson (isl.), Alaska 196/E2
Nelson, Alta., 146/G5
Nelson, Ariz. (†86434) 198/B3
Nelson, Br. Col. 184/J5
Nelson (str.), Chile 138/D9
Nelson, Eng. 13/E4
Nelson, Ga. (30151) 216/D2
Nelson, Ill. (61058) 222/D2
Nelson (co.), Ky. 237/K5
Nelson, Ky. (†42330) 237/G6
Nelson (riv.), Man., 146/J4
Nelson (riv.), Man. 179/J2
Nelson, Minn. (56355) 254/C5
Nelson, Mo. (65347) 261/F4
Nelson (res.), Mont. 262/J2
Nelson (co.), N. Dak. 283/O4
Nelson▵, N.H. (†03457) 268/C5
Nelson, N.H. (†03457) 268/C5
Nelson (prov. dist.), N.Z. 101/D4
Nelson, N. Z., 87/H10
Nelson, N.Z. 101/D4
Nelson, Nebr. (68961) 264/F4
Nelson, Nev. (†89046) 266/G7
Nelson (creek), Nev. 266/G2
Nelson, Pa. (16940) 294/H2
Nelson (co.), Va. 307/L5
Nelson (cape), Vic. 97/A6
Nelson, Wis. (54756) 317/C7
Nelson Forks, Br. Col. 184/M2
Nelson Head (prom.), N.W.T. 187/F2
Nelson House, Man. 179/J2
Nelson Lagoon, Alaska (†99571) 196/F3
Nelson-Miramichi, N. Br. 170/E2
Nelsonville, Ark. (†72569) 203/H1
Nelsonville, Ky. (†40051) 237/K5
Nelsonville, N.Y. (10516) 276/N8
Nelsonville, Ohio (45764) 284/F7
Nelsonville, Wis. (54458) 317/H7
Nelspruit, S. Africa 118/E5
Néma, Mauritania 106/C5
Nemacolin, Pa. (15351) 294/B6
Nemadji (riv.), Minn. 254/F4
Nemaha, Iowa (50567) 229/C3
Nemaha (co.), Kans. 232/F2
Nemaha (riv.), Kans. 232/G1
Nemaha (co.), Nebr. 264/J4
Nemaha, Nebr. (68414) 264/J4
Neméa, Greece 45/F7
Nemi, Italy 34/F7
Nemiscau, Que. 174/B2
Nemiskam, Alta. 182/E5
Nemo, S. Dak. (57759) 298/B5
Nemours, France 28/E3
Nemrut Daği (mt.), Turkey 63/J3
Nemunas (Niemen) (riv.), U.S.S.R. 53/A3
Nemuro, Japan 81/M2
Nemuto (str.), Japan 81/M1
Nen (riv.), China 77/K2
Nenagh, 10/B4
Nenagh, Ire. 17/E6
Nenagh (riv.), Ire. 17/E6
Nenana, Alaska (99760) 196/J2
Nene (riv.), Eng. 13/H5
Nene (riv.), 10/F4
Nenets Nat'l Okr., U.S.S.R. 48/F3
Nenets Nat'l Okr., U.S.S.R. 52/H1
Nenkiang, China 77/L2
Nenzel, Nebr. (69219) 264/C2
Neodesha, Kans. (66757) 232/G4
Neoga, Ill. (62447) 222/E4
Neola, Iowa (51559) 229/B6
Neola, Sask. 181/D3
Neola, Utah (84053) 304/D3
Neola, W. Va. (24961) 313/F7
Neon, Ky. (41840) 237/R6
Néon Karlóvasi, Greece 45/H7
Neopit, Wis. (54150) 317/J6
Neópolis, Braz. 132/G5
Neosho (riv.), 188/G3
Neosho (co.), Kans. 232/G4
Neosho (riv.), Kans. 232/G4
Neosho, Mo. (64850) 261/D9
Neosho (riv.), Okla. 288/R2
Neosho, Wis. (53059) 317/J9
Neosho Falls, Kans. (66758) 232/G3
Neosho Rapids, Kans. (66864) 232/F3
Neotsu, Oreg. (97364) 291/C2
Nepa, U.S.S.R. 48/L4
Nepal, 3/P4
Nepal, 54/M7
NEPAL, 68
Nepalganj, Nepal 68/E3
Nepaug (res.), Conn. 210/D1
Nepaug (riv.), Conn. 210/C1
Nepean (riv.), Aust. 88/K3
Nepean (isl.), Aust. 88/M5
Nephi, Utah (84648) 304/C4
Nephin (mt.), Ire. 17/C3
Nephin Beg (mt.), Ire. 17/B3
Nephton, Ont. 177/G3
Nepisiguit (bay), N. Br. 170/E1
Nepisiguit (lakes), N. Br. 170/D1
Nepisiguit (riv.), N. Br. 170/D1
Nepomuk, Czech. 41/B2
Neponset, Ill. (61345) 222/D2
Neponset, Mass. (†02122) 249/D7
Neponset (riv.), Mass. 249/C8
Nepton, Ky. (†41039) 237/O4
Neptune▵, N.J. (07753) 273/E3
Neptune (isls.), S. Aust. 94/D6
Neptune, Ohio (†45822) 284/A4
Neptune, Sask. 181/G6
Neptune Beach, Fla. (32233) 212/E1
Neptune City, N.J. (07753) 273/E3
Nera (riv.), Italy 34/D3
Nérac, France 28/D5
Nerchinsk, U.S.S.R. 48/M4
Nerchinsk, U.S.S.R., 54/P4
Nerekhta, U.S.S.R. 52/F3
Nerepis (riv.), N. Br. 170/D3
Neresheim, W. Ger. 22/D4
Nereta, U.S.S.R. 53/C2
Neretva (riv.), Yugo. 45/D4
Neriga, U.S.S.R. 52/B3
Neriquinha, Angola 115/D7
Nerja, Spain 33/E4
Nerka (lake), Alaska 196/G3
Ñermete (pt.), Peru 128/B5
Nerpio, Spain 33/E3
Nerriga, N.S.W. 97/F4
Nerstrand, Minn. (55053) 254/E6
Nerva, Spain 33/C4
Nes, Neth. 27/H2
Nes (Neskaupstadhur), Ice. 21/D1
Nesbit, Miss. (38651) 256/D1
Nesbitt, Man. 179/C5
Nesbitt‡, Texas (†75688) 302/K5
Nesconset‡, N.Y. (11767) 276/O9
Nescopeck, Pa. (18635) 294/K3
Nesebŭr, Bulg. 45/H4
Neshanic, N.J. (†08853) 273/D3
Nesher, Israel 65/C2
Neshkoro, Wis. (54960) 317/H8
Neshoba (co.), Miss. 256/F5
Neshoba, Miss. (39344) 256/F5
Neskaupstadhur, Ice. 21/D1
Neskowin, Oreg. (97149) 291/D2
Nesmith, S.C. (29580) 296/H4
Nespelem, Wash. (99155) 310/G2
Nesquehoning, Pa. (18240) 294/L4
Ness (co.), Kans. 232/C3
Ness (lake), Scot. 15/H5
Ness (riv.), Scot. 15/H5
Ness (lake), 10/D2
Ness City, Kans. (67560) 232/C3
Nesselrode (mt.), Alaska 196/N1
Nesselwang, W. Ger. 22/D5
Nesslau, Switz. 39/H2
Neston, 10/F2
Nestor, Trinidad Tobago 161/B10
Nestoria, Mich. (49867) 250/A2
Nestórion, Greece 45/E5
Nestorville, W. Va. (†26380) 313/G4
Néstos (riv.), Greece 45/G5
Nestow, Alta. 182/D2
Nesttun, Norway 18/D6
Nestucca (riv.), Oreg. 291/D2
Nesvady, Czech. 41/E3
Nes Ziyyona, Israel 65/B4
Net (riv.), Mich. 250/G2
Netanya, Israel 65/B3
Netarts, Oreg. (97143) 291/C2
Netawaka, Kans. (66516) 232/G2
Netcong, N.J. (07857) 273/D2
Nethe (riv.), Belg. 27/F6
Netherhill, Sask. 181/C4
Netherlands, 3/K3
Netherlands, 7/E3
NETHERLANDS, 27/G4
Netherlands Antilles, 120/D1
Netherlands Antilles, 146/L8
NETHERLANDS ANTILLES, 156/E4
NETHERLANDS ANTILLES, 161
Netley, Man. 179/E4
Netolice, Czech. 41/C2
Netstal, Switz. 39/H2
Nett (lake), Minn. 254/E2
Nettie, W. Va. (26681) 313/E6
Nettilling (lake), 163/K2
Nettilling (lake), Canada, 4/C13
Nettilling (lake), N.W.T., 146/L3
Nettilling (fjord), N.W.T. 187/M3
Nettilling (lake), N.W.T. 187/L3
Nett Lake, Minn. (55772) 254/E2
Nett Lake Ind. Res., Minn. 254/E2
Nettleton, Miss. (38858) 256/G2
Nettuno, Italy 34/D4
Neuanlage, Sask. 181/E3
Neuberg an der Mürz, Austria 41/C3

Nyudo 411

North Raymond, Maine (†04274) 242/C8
North Reading△, Mass. (01864) 249/C5
North Redington Beach, Fla. (†33708) 212/B3
North Redwood, Minn. (56275) 254/D6
North Renous (riv.), N. Br. 170/D2
North Rhine-Westphalia (state), W. Ger. 22/B3
North Richland Hills, Texas (†76118) 302/F1
Northridge, Ohio (45414) 284/C6
North Ridgeville, Ohio (44035) 284/F3
North Rim, Ariz. (86022) 198/C2
North River, N.S. 169/D4
North River, N.Y. (12856) 276/M3
North Riverside, Ill. (60546) 222/B2
North Robinson, Ohio (44856) 284/E4
North Ronaldsay (firth), Scot. 15/M1
North Ronaldsay (isl.), Scot. 15/M1
North Ronaldsay (isl.), 10/E1
Northrop, Minn. (56075) 254/D7
North Rose, N.Y. (14516) 276/G4
North Royalton, Ohio (44133) 284/H10
North Rustico, P.E.I. 169/E2
North Rutland, Mass. (01543) 249/G3
North Saanich, Br. Col. 184/K3
North Saint Paul, Minn. (55109) 254/E5
North Salem, Ind. (46165) 227/D5
North Salem, N.H. (03073) 268/E6
North Salt Lake, Utah (84054) 304/C3
North Sandwich, N.H. (03259) 268/E4
North San Juan, Calif. (95960) 204/E4
North San Pedro‡, Texas (†78380) 302/G10
North Santiam (riv.), Oreg. 291/E3
North Saskatchewan (riv.), 163/E5
North Saskatchewan (riv.), Alta. 182/E3
North Saskatchewan (riv.), Sask. 181/D3
North Scituate, Mass. (02060) 249/F8
North Scituate, R.I. (02857) 249/H5
North Sea (canal), Neth. 27/F4
North Seal (riv.), Man. 179/H2
North Searsmont, Maine (†04973) 242/E7
North Sentinel (isl.), India 68/G6
North Sevogle (riv.), N. Br. 170/D1
North Shapleigh, Maine (04060) 242/B8
North Shoal (lake), Man. 179/E4
Northside, N.C. (27564) 281/M2
Northside, Sask. 181/F2
North Sioux City, S. Dak. (57049) 298/R8
North Skunk (riv.), Iowa 229/H5
North Somercotes, 10/G4
North Somercotes, Eng. 13/H4
North Somers, Conn. (†06071) 210/F1
North Spectacle (lake), Conn. 210/B2
North Springfield, Pa. (16430) 294/A1
North Springfield, Va. (22151) 307/O3
North Springfield, Vt. (05150) 268/B5
North Star, Alta. 182/B1
North Star, Mich. (48862) 250/E5
North Star, Ohio (45350) 284/A5
North Stonington△, Conn. (06359) 210/H3
North Stradbroke (isl.), Aust. 88/L2
North Stratford, N.H. (03590) 268/D2
North Sullivan, Maine (04664) 242/G6
North Sunderland, Eng. 13/F2
North Sutton, N.H. (03260) 268/D5
North Swansea, Mass. (†02777) 249/K5
North Sydney, N.S. 169/H2
North Sydney, N.S.W. 97/J3
North Syracuse, N.Y. (13212) 276/H4
North Takoma Park‡, Md. (†20012) 245/F4
North Taranaki (bight), N.Z. 101/D3
North Tarrytown, N.Y. (10591) 276/O6
North Terre Haute, Ind. (47805) 227/C5
North Thetford, Vt. (05054) 268/C4
North Thompson (riv.), Br. Col. 184/G4
North Tiverton, R.I. (†02722) 249/K6
North Tonawanda, N.Y. (14120) 276/C4
North Trap (isl.), N.Z. 101/B7
North Troy, Vt. (05859) 268/C2
North Truchas (peak), N. Mex. 274/D3
North Truro, Mass. (02652) 249/O4
North Tunbridge, Vt. (†05077) 268/C4
North Turner, Maine (04266) 242/C7
North Twin (mt.), N.H. 268/D3
North Tyne (riv.), Eng. 13/E2
North Uist (isl.), Scot. 15/A4
North Uist (isl.), 10/C2
Northumberland (cape), Aust. 88/F7
Northumberland (co.), Ont. 177/G3
Northumberland (co.), Eng. 13/E2
Northumberland (co.), N. Br. 170/D2
Northumberland (str.), N. Br. 170/F2
Northumberland△, N.H. (†03582) 268/D2
Northumberland, N.H. (†03582) 268/D2
Northumberland (str.), N.S. 169/E2
Northumberland (cape), S. Aust. 94/F8
Northumberland (isls.), Queens. 95/D4
Northumberland (str.), P.E.I. 169/D2
Northumberland (co.), Pa. 294/J4
Northumberland, Pa. (17857) 294/J4
Northumberland (co.), Va. 307/R5
North Umpqua (riv.), Oreg. 291/E4
North Ural (mts.), U.S.S.R. 52/K1
North Utica (Utica), Ill. (†61373) 222/E2
North Uxbridge, Mass. (01538) 249/H4
Northvale, N.J. (07647) 273/F1
North Valley Stream‡, N.Y. (†11580) 276/R7
North Vancouver, 163/D6
North Vancouver, Br. Col. 184/K3
North Vandergrift‡, Pa. (†15690) 294/C4
North Vassalboro, Maine (04962) 242/D7
North Vermilion, Alta. 182/B5
North Vernon, Ind. (47265) 227/F6
NORTH VIETNAM, 72/E3
Northview, Mo. (65716) 261/G8
Northville, Alta. 182/C3
Northville, Conn. (†06776) 210/B2
Northville, Mich. (48167) 250/F6
Northville, N.Y. (12134) 276/M4
Northville, S. Dak. (57465) 298/M3
North Wabasca (lake), Alta. 182/D1
North Wakefield, N.H. (†03872) 268/E4
North Waldoboro, Maine (†04572) 242/E7
North Wales, Pa. (19454) 294/M5
North Walpole, N.H. (†03608) 268/C5
North Walsham, 10/G4
North Walsham, Eng. 13/J5
North Wantagh‡, N.Y. (†11793) 276/N9
North Warren, Pa. (16365) 294/D2
North Washington, Iowa (50661) 229/J2
North Waterboro, Maine (04061) 242/B8
North Waterford, Maine (04267) 242/B7
Northway, Alaska (99764) 196/K2
North Wayne, Maine (†04284) 242/C7
North Weare, N.H. (†03281) 268/D5
North Webster, Ind. (46555) 227/F2
North West (cape), Australia, 87/B8
North West (cape), Aust. 88/A4
North West (pt.), Jam. 158/G5
Northwest (cape), Fla. 212/E6
North West (dist.), Guyana 131/A2
North West (cape), W. Aust. 92/A3
North-West (prov.), Somalia 115/H2
North West Arm (inlet), Newf. 166/D2
North West Brook, Newf. 166/C2
North West Brook (riv.), Newf. 166/D2
North Westchester, Conn. (06474) 210/F2
Northwestern (sen. dist.), Alaska 196/E2
Northwestern (gov.), Alaska 196/E2
North-Western (state), Nigeria 106/F6
North-West Frontier (prov.), Pak. 68/C2
North West Gander (riv.), Newf. 166/C4
North Westminster, Vt. (†05101) 268/B5
Northwest Miramichi (riv.), N. Br. 170/D1
Northwest Oromocto (riv.), N. Br. 170/D3
North Westport, Mass. (†02790) 249/K6
North West Providence (chan.), Bah. Is. 156/B1
North West River, Newf. 166/B3
NORTHWEST TERRITORIES, 187
Northwest Territories (terr.), Canada, 146/G3
Northwest Upsalquitch (riv.), N. Br. 170/D1
North Weymouth, Mass. (†02191) 249/D8
North Whitefield, Maine (04353) 242/D7
Northwich, 10/G2
Northwich, Eng. 13/E4
North Wilbraham, Mass. (01067) 249/E4
North Wildwood, N.J. (08260) 273/D6
North Wilkesboro, N.C. (28659) 281/G2
North Williston, Vt. (†05495) 268/A3
North Wilton, Conn. (†06897) 210/B4
North Windham, Conn. (06256) 210/G1
North Windham, Maine (04062) 242/C8
North Winter Haven‡, Fla. (†33880) 212/E3
North Wolcott, Vt. (†05680) 268/C2
Northwood, Iowa (50459) 229/G2
Northwood, N. Dak. (58267) 283/P4
Northwood△, N.H. (03261) 268/E5
Northwood, N.H. (03261) 268/E5
Northwood, Ohio (†43601) 284/D2
North Woodbury, Conn. (†06798) 210/C2
Northwood Center, N.H. (†03261) 268/E5
Northwood Narrows, N.H. (†03261) 268/E5
Northwoods, Mo. (†63101) 261/P2
North Woodstock, Conn. (06257) 210/G1
North Woodstock, Maine (†04219) 242/B7
North Woodstock, N.H. (03262) 268/D3
Northwye, Mo. (†65401) 261/J7
North Yarmouth△, Maine (†04096) 242/C8
North Yarmouth, Maine (†04096) 242/C8
North York, Ont. 177/J4
North York‡, Pa. (†17401) 294/J5
North Zanesville, Ohio (†43701) 284/G6
Norton (sound), Alaska, 146/B3
Norton (sound), Alaska, 188/C5
Norton (bay), Alaska 196/F2
Norton (sound), Alaska 196/E2
Norton, Eng. 13/G3
Norton (peak), Idaho 220/D6
Norton (co.), Kans. 232/C2
Norton, Kans. (67654) 232/C2
Norton (res.), Kans. 232/C2
Norton△, Mass. (02766) 249/K5
Norton, Mass. (02766) 249/K5
Norton, N. Br. 170/E3
Norton, N. Dak. (†35210) 283/O3
Norton, Ohio (44203) 284/G4
Norton, Texas (76865) 302/E6
Norton (sound), U.S., 4/C18
Norton, Va. (24273) 307/C7
Norton△, Vt. (05907) 268/D2
Norton, Vt. (05907) 268/D2
Norton (pond), Vt. 268/D2
Norton, W. Va. (26285) 313/G5
Norton A.F.B., Calif. 204/F10
Norton-Radstock, Eng. 13/E6
Norton Shores, Mich. (†49444) 250/C5
Nortonville, Kans. (66060) 232/G2
Nortonville, Ky. (42442) 237/G6
Nortonville, N. Dak. (58473) 283/N6
Norumbega, Arg. 143/F7
Norval, Ont. 177/E4
Norvegia (cape), Ant. 5/B18
Norvell, Ark. (†72386) 203/K3
Norvelt, Pa. (15674) 294/C5
Norwalk, Calif. (90650) 204/C11
Norwalk, Conn. (*06850) 210/B4
Norwalk (isls.), Conn. 210/B4
Norwalk (riv.), Conn. 210/B4
Norwalk, Iowa (50211) 229/F6
Norwalk, Mich. (†49660) 250/C4
Norwalk, Ohio (44857) 284/E3
Norwalk, Wis. (54648) 317/E8
Norway, 3/K2
Norway, 4/C9
Norway, 7/E2
NORWAY, 18
Norway, Ind. (†47960) 227/D3
Norway, Iowa (52318) 229/K5
Norway, Kans. (66961) 232/E2
Norway△, Maine (04268) 242/B7
Norway, Maine (04268) 242/B7
Norway, Mich. (49870) 250/B3
Norway (bay), N.W.T. 187/H2
Norway, Oreg. (97460) 291/C4
Norway, S.C. (29113) 296/E5
Norway House, 163/G5
Norway House, Man. 179/J3
Norway Lake, Maine (†04268) 242/B7
Norwegian (sea), 4/C10
Norwegian (sea), 7/D2
Norwegian (sea), Norway 18/F3
Norwegian (bay), N.W.T. 187/J2
Norwell△, Mass. (02061) 249/F8
Norwich, 10/G4
Norwich, Conn. (06360) 210/G2
Norwich, Ont. 177/D5
Norwich, Eng. 13/J5
Norwich, Kans. (67118) 232/E4
Norwich, N. Dak. (58768) 283/J3
Norwich, N.Y. (13815) 276/J5
Norwich, Ohio (43767) 284/G6
Norwich△, Vt. (05055) 268/C4
Norwich, Vt. (05055) 268/C4
Norwichtown, Conn. (†06360) 210/G2
Norwood, Colo. (81423) 208/C6
Norwood, Ont. 177/F3
Norwood, Fla. (†33054) 212/B4
Norwood, Ga. (30821) 216/G4
Norwood‡, Ill. (60031) 222/D3
Norwood, La. (70761) 238/H5
Norwood△, Mass. (02062) 249/B8
Norwood, Minn. (55368) 254/E6
Norwood, Mo. (65717) 261/H8
Norwood, N.C. (28128) 281/J4
Norwood, N.J. (07648) 273/C1
Norwood, N.Y. (13668) 276/L1
Norwood, Ohio (45212) 284/C9
Norwood, Pa. (19074) 294/M7
Norwood, R.I. (†02887) 249/J6
Norwood, Va. (24581) 307/L5
Norwood Court‡, Mo. (†63101) 261/P3
Nosbonsing (lake), Ont. 177/E1
Nose, Japan 81/J7
Noshappu (pt.), Japan 81/N2
Noshiro, Japan 81/J3
Nosovka, U.S.S.R. 52/D4
Noss (head), Scot. 15/L3
Nossa Senhora do Livramento, Braz. 132/B6
Nossi-Bé (isl.), Malag. Rep. 118/H2
Nossob (riv.), Botswana 118/B4
Nossob (riv.), S.W. Afr. 118/B4
Nosy-Varika, Malag. Rep. 118/H4
Notakun (lake), Que. 172/B2
Notasulga, Ala. (36866) 194/G5
Noteć (Netze) (riv.), Poland 47/B2
Notikewin, Alta. 182/B1
Notikewin (riv.), Alta. 182/A1
Noto, Italy 34/E6
Noto, Japan 81/H5
Noto (pen.), Japan 81/H5
Notodden, Norway 18/F7
Notre Dame, Ind. (46556) 227/E1
Notre-Dame, N. Br. 170/F2
Notre Dame (bay), Newf. 166/C4
Notre-Dame-de-Ham, Que. 172/F4
Notre-Dame-de-la-Doré, Que. 172/E1
Notre-Dame-de-la-Paix, Que. 172/C4
Notre-Dame-de-la-Salette, Que. 172/B4
Notre-Dame-de-Lorette, Que. 172/H3
Notre-Dame-de-Lourdes, Man. 179/D5
Notre-Dame-de-Pierreville, Que. 172/D3
Notre-Dame-de-Rimouski, Que. 172/J1
Notre-Dame-des-Anges, Que. 172/E3
Notre-Dame-des-Bois, Que. 172/G4
Notre-Dame-des-Monts, Que. 172/G2
Notre-Dame-de-Stanbridge, Que. 172/D4
Notre-Dame-d'Hébertville, Que. 172/F1
Notre-Dame-du-Bon-Conseil, Que. 172/E4
Notre-Dame-du-Lac, Que. 172/J2
Notre-Dame-du-Laus, Que. 172/B3
Nottawa, Ont. 177/D3
Nottawasaga (bay), Ont. 177/D3
Nottawasaga (riv.), Ont. 177/E3
Nottaway (riv.), Que. 174/B2
Nottaway (riv.), 163/J5
Nottaway (riv.), Que., 146/L4
Nottely (lake), Ga. 216/D1
Nøtterøy, Norway 18/D4
Nottingham, 10/F4
Nottingham (isl.), 163/J3
Nottingham, Ala. (†35014) 194/F4
Nottingham, Eng. 13/F5
Nottingham△, N.H. (03290) 268/E5
Nottingham, N.H. (03290) 268/E5
Nottingham, Sask. 181/K6
Nottingham Island, N.W.T. 187/L3
Nottinghamshire (co.), Eng. 13/F4
Nottinghill, Mo. (65718) 261/G9
Nottoway (co.), Va. 307/M6
Nottoway, Va. (23955) 307/M6
Nottoway (riv.), Va. 307/O7
Notukeu (creek), Sask. 181/D6
Notus, Idaho (83656) 220/B6
Nouadhibou, 102/A2
Nouadhibou, Mauritania 106/A4
Nouakchott (cap.), Mauritania 102/A3
Nouakchott (cap.), Mauritania, 3/J5
Nouakchott (cap.), Mauritania 106/A5
Nouméa (cap.), New Cal., 87/G8
Nouméa (cap.), New Cal., 3/T7
Nounan, Idaho (†83254) 220/G7
Noup (head), Scot. 15/K1
Noupoort, S. Africa 118/C6
Nouveau-Québec (dist.), Que. 174/E1
Nouveau-Québec (crater), Que. 174/F1
Nouveaux-Comptoir, Que. 174/B2
Nouvelle, Que. 172/C2
Nouvelle (riv.), Que. 172/C2
Nouvelle-Anvers, 102/D4
Nouvelle-Anvers, Dem. Rep. of the Congo. 115/C3
Nouvelle-France (cape), Que. 174/F1
Nouvelle-Ouest, Que. 172/C2
Nova, Hung. 41/D3
Nova, Ohio (44859) 284/F3
Nová Baňa, Czech. 41/E2
Nová Bystrica, Czech. 41/E2
Nová Bystřice, Czech. 41/C2
Nova Chaves, Angola 115/D6
Nova Cruz, Braz. 132/H4
Nova Era, Braz. 135/E1
Nova Freixo, Moz. 118/F2
Nova Friburgo, Braz. 132/F8
Nova Friburgo, Braz. 135/E3
Nova Gaia, Angola 115/C5
Nova Goa (Panjim), India 54/L8
Nova Goa (Panjim), India 68/C5
Nova Gradiška, Yugo. 45/C3
Nova Granada, Braz. 135/B2
Nova Iguaçu, Braz. 132/F8
Nova Iguaçu, Braz. 135/E3
Nova Iorque, Braz. 132/E4
Nova Lima, Braz. 135/E2
Nova Lisboa, Angola, 3/K6
Nova Lisboa, Angola 115/C6
Nova Lisboa, 102/D6
Nova Luzitânia, Moz. 118/E3
Nova Mambone, 102/F7
Nova Mambone, Moz. 118/F4
Novar, Ont. 177/E2
Novara (prov.), Italy 34/B2
Novara, Italy 34/B2
Nova Russas, Braz. 132/F4
NOVA SCOTIA, 169
Nova Scotia (prov.), Canada, 146/M5
Nova Sofala, 102/F7
Nova Sofala, Moz. 118/F4
Novato, Calif. (94947) 204/H1
Novaya Kakhovka, U.S.S.R. 52/D5
Novaya Kazanka, U.S.S.R. 48/F5
Novaya Sibir' (isl.), U.S.S.R. 48/Q2
Novaya Zemlya (isls.), U.S.S.R. 48/F2
Novaya Zemlya (isls.), U.S.S.R. 52/H1
Novaya Zemlya (isl.), U.S.S.R., 3/L2
Novaya Zemlya (isls.), U.S.S.R., 4/B7
Nova Zagora, Bulg. 45/H4
Nové Hrady, Czech. 41/C2
Novelda, Spain 33/F3
Novelty, Mo. (63460) 261/H2
Nové Město nad Váhom, Czech. 41/D2
Nové Město na Moravě, Czech. 41/D2
Nové Strašecí, Czech. 41/B1
Nové Zámky, Czech. 41/D3
Novgorod, U.S.S.R. 48/D4
Novgorod, U.S.S.R. 52/D3
Novgorod-Severskiy, U.S.S.R. 52/D4
Novi, Mich. (48050) 250/F6
Novi, Yugo. 45/B3
Novice, Texas (79538) 302/E5
Novi Ligure, Italy 34/B2
Novinger, Mo. (63559) 261/G2
Novi Pazar, Bulg. 45/H4
Novi Pazar, Yugo. 45/E4
Novi Sad, Yugo., 7/F4
Novi Sad, Yugo. 45/D3
Nóvita, Col. 126/B5
Novoanninskiy, U.S.S.R. 52/F4
Novocherkassk, U.S.S.R. 52/F5
Novograd-Volynskiy, U.S.S.R. 52/C4
Novogrudok, U.S.S.R. 52/C4
Novo Hamburgo, Braz. 132/D10
Novo Horizonte, Braz. 135/B2
Novokuybyshevsk, U.S.S.R. 52/G4
Novokuznetsk, U.S.S.R. 48/J4
Novokuznetsk, U.S.S.R., 54/M4
Novo Mesto, Yugo. 45/B3
Novomoskovsk, U.S.S.R. 48/E4
Novomoskovsk, U.S.S.R. 52/E4
Novopolotsk, U.S.S.R. 52/C3
Novo Redondo, Angola 115/B6
Novo Redondo, 102/D6
Novorossiysk, U.S.S.R. 48/D5
Novorossiysk, U.S.S.R. 52/E6
Novorossiysk, U.S.S.R., 7/H4
Novoshakhtinsk, U.S.S.R. 52/E5
Novosibirsk, U.S.S.R. 48/J4
Novosibirsk, U.S.S.R., 3/P3
Novosibirsk, U.S.S.R., 54/L4
Novotroitsk, U.S.S.R. 52/J4
Novoukrainka, U.S.S.R. 52/D5
Novouzensk, U.S.S.R. 48/E4
Novouzensk, U.S.S.R. 52/G4
Novovolynsk, U.S.S.R. 52/B4
Novozybkov, U.S.S.R. 48/D4
Novozybkov, U.S.S.R. 52/D4
Novra, Man. 179/B2
Novska, Yugo. 45/C3
Nový Bohumín, Czech. 41/E2
Nový Bor, Czech. 41/C1
Nový Bydžov, Czech. 41/C1
Nový Hrozenkov, Czech. 41/E2
Nový Jičín, Czech. 41/E2
Novyy Bug, U.S.S.R. 52/D5
Novyy Port, U.S.S.R. 48/G3
Novyy Port, U.S.S.R., 4/C6
Nowa Huta, Poland 47/E3
Nowa Nowa, Vic. 97/E5
Nowa Ruda, Poland 47/C3
Nowa Sól, Poland 47/B3
Nowata (co.), Okla. 288/P1
Nowata, Okla. (74048) 288/P1
No Water (creek), Wyo. 319/E2
Nowe Miasto Lubawskie, Poland 47/D2
Nowendoc, N.S.W. 97/F2
Nowgong, India 68/G3
Nowitna (riv.), Alaska 196/H2
Nowogard, Poland 47/B2
Nowogród, Poland 47/E2
Nowood (creek), Wyo. 319/E1
Nowra, Aust. 88/J6
Nowra-Bomaderry, N.S.W. 97/F4
Nowshera, Pak. 59/K3
Nowshera, Pak. 68/C2
Nowy Dwór Gdański, Poland 47/D1
Nowy Dwór Mazowiecki, Poland 47/E3
Nowy Sącz, Poland 47/E4
Nowy Targ, Poland 47/E4
Nowy Tomyśl, Poland 47/C2
Noxapater, Miss. (39346) 256/F5
Noxen, Pa. (18636) 294/K3
Noxon, Mont. (59853) 262/A3
Noxubee (co.), Miss. 256/G4
Noxubee (riv.), Miss. 256/G4
Noya, Spain 33/B1
Noyan, Mong. 77/F3
Noyes (isl.), Alaska 196/M2
Noyes, Minn. (56740) 254/A2
Noyes (pt.), R.I. 249/H7
Noyo (riv.), Calif. 204/B4
Noyon, France 28/E3
Nsanje, 102/F6
Nsanje, Malawi 115/G7
Nsukka, Nigeria 106/F7
Nuanetsi, Rhod. 118/E4
Nuangola‡, Pa. (18637) 294/L3
Nuba (mts.), Sudan 111/E5
Nubanusit (lake), N.H. 268/C5
Nuberg, Ga. (†30634) 216/G2
Nubian (des.), 102/F2
Nubian (des.), Sudan 59/B5
Nubian (des.), Sudan 111/F3
Nubieber, Calif. (96068) 204/D2
Ñuble (prov.), Chile 138/E1
Nuckolls (co.), Nebr. 264/F4
Nuckols, Ky. (42360) 237/G5
Nucla, Colo. (81424) 208/B6
Nueces (riv.), Texas, 188/G5
Nueces (co.), Texas 302/G10
Nueces (riv.), Texas 302/F9
Nueltin (lake), 163/G3
Nueltin (lake), Man. 179/H1
Nueltin (lake), N.W.T. 187/H3
Nuestra Señora (bay), Chile 138/A5
Nueva (isl.), Arg. 143/C8
Nueva (isl.), Chile 138/F11
Nueva Alejandría, Peru 128/F5
Nueva Antioquia, Col. 126/F5
Nueva Armenia, Hond. 154/D4
Nueva Casas Grandes, Mex. 150/F1
Nueva Ciudad Guerrero, Mex. 150/K3
Nueva Ecija (prov.), Phil. 82/C3
Nueva Esparta (state), Ven. 124/G2
Nueva Germania, Par. 144/D4
Nueva Gerona, Cuba 156/A2
Nueva Gerona, Cuba 158/B2
Nueva Helvecia, Urug. 145/B5
Nueva Imperial, Chile 138/D2
Nueva Manoa, Bol. 136/C1
Nueva Ocotepeque, Hond. 154/C3
Nueva Palmira, Urug. 145/A4
Nueva Pompeya, Arg. 143/D2
Nueva Rosita, Mex. 150/J2
Nueva San Salvador (Santa Tecla), El Salv. 154/C4
Nueva Vizcaya (prov.), Phil. 82/C2
Nueve de Julio, Arg. 143/F7
Nuevitas, Cuba 156/C2
Nuevitas, Cuba 158/G2
Nuevitas (bay), Cuba 158/H2
Nuevo (gulf), Arg. 143/D5
Nuevo (cay), Mex. 150/O6
Nuevo Berlín, Urug. 145/B3
Nuevo Chagres, Pan. 154/G6
Nuevo Juncal, Chile 138/B5
Nuevo Laredo, Mex. 150/J3
Nuevo León (state), Mex. 150/K4
Nuevo Mamo, Ven. 124/G3
Nuevo Morelos, Mex. 150/K5
Nuevo Mundo, Bol. 136/B2
Nuevo Rocafuerte, Ec. 128/E3
Nugget (pt.), N.Z. 101/C7
Nugrus, Jebel (mt.), U.A.R. 59/B4
Nuhurowa (isl.), Indon. 85/J7
Nuhutjut (isl.), Indon. 85/J7
Nui (atoll), Gilb. and Ell., 87/H6
Nui Ba Den (mt.), S. Vietnam 72/E5
Nuka (bay), Alaska 196/C2
Nuka (isl.), Alaska 196/C2
Nukey Bluff (mt.), S. Aust. 94/D5
Nukheila (oasis), Sudan 111/E4
Nuku'alofa (cap.), Tonga, 87/J8
Nukuhiva (isl.), Fr. Poly., 87/M6
Nukulaelae (atoll), Gilb. and Ell., 87/H6
Nukumanu (atoll), Terr. N.G., 87/F6
Nukunonu (atoll), Tokelau Is., 87/J6
Nukuoro (atoll), Pac. Is., 87/F5
Nukus, U.S.S.R. 48/G5
Nulato, Alaska (99765) 196/G2
Nules, Spain 33/F3
Nulhegan (riv.), Vt. 268/D2
Nullagine, Aust. 88/C4
Nullagine, W. Aust. 92/C3
Nullarbor (plain), Australia, 87/C9
Nullarbor (plain), Aust. 88/D6
Nullarbor (plain), W. Aust. 92/D5
Nullarbor, S. Aust. 94/B4
Nullarbor (plain), S. Aust. 94/A4
Nulliberg (mt.), V.I.(U.S.) 161/B4
Nulltown, Ind. (†47331) 227/G5
Numa, Iowa (52575) 229/G7
Numan, Nigeria 106/G7
Numancia, Phil. 82/D5
Numansdorp, Neth. 27/E5
Numata, Japan 81/J5
Numazu, Japan 81/J6
Numbulwar, No. Terr. 93/D3
Numfoor (isl.), Indon. 85/J6
Ñumí, Par. 144/D5
Nu Mine, Pa. (16244) 294/D4
Numurkah, Vic. 97/C5
Nunaksaluk (isl.), Newf. 166/B2
Nunapitchuk, Alaska (99641) 196/F2
Nunawading, Vic. 97/J5
Nunchía, Col. 126/D5
Nunda, N.Y. (14517) 276/E5
Nunda, S. Dak. (57050) 298/P5
Nundah, Queens. 95/E2
Nundle, N.S.W. 97/F2
Nuneaton, 10/F4
Nuneaton, Eng. 13/F5
Nunebor, Sask. 181/A3
Núñez (isl.), Chile 138/D10
Nunez, Ga. (30448) 216/H5
Nungarin, W. Aust. 92/B5
Nungesser (lake), Ont. 175/B2
Nunivak (isl.), Alaska, 146/B4
Nunivak (isl.), Alaska, 188/C6
Nunivak (isl.), Alaska 196/E3
Nunivak (isl.), U.S., 4/D18
Nunley, Ark. (†71953) 203/B4
Nunn, Colo. (80648) 208/K1
Nunnelly, Tenn. (37137) 237/G9
Nunningen, Switz. 39/E2
Nuñoa, Peru 128/G10
Nunspeet, Neth. 27/H4
Nuoro (prov.), Italy 34/B4
Nuoro, Italy 34/B4
Nuqub, P.D.R. Yemen 59/E6
Nuquí, Col. 126/B5
Nura, China 77/B4
Nuremberg, Pa. (18241) 294/K4
Nuremberg, W. Ger., 7/F4
Nuremberg, W. Ger. 22/D4
Nurhak, Turkey 63/G4
Nurhak Daği (mt.), Turkey 63/G3
Nuri, Mex. 150/E3
Nuri (ruins), Sudan 111/F4
Nuria, Sierra de (mts.), Ven. 124/H4
Nuriootpa, S. Aust. 94/F6
Nurmes, Fin. 18/Q5
Nürnberg (Nuremberg), W. Ger. 22/D4
Nurrari (lakes), S. Aust. 94/B3
Nursery, Texas (77976) 302/H9
Nürtingen, W. Ger. 22/C4
Nus, Ras (cape), Oman 59/G6
Nusa Barung (isl.), Indon. 85/K3
Nusaybin, Turkey 63/J4
Nushagak, Alaska (†99569) 196/G3
Nushagak (bay), Alaska 196/G3
Nushagak (riv.), Alaska 196/G2
Nushki, Pak. 59/J4
Nushki, Pak. 68/B3
Nutak, 163/K4
Nutak, Newf., 146/M4
Nutley, N.J. (07110) 273/B2
Nut Mountain, Sask. 181/H3
Nutrioso, Ariz. (85932) 198/F5
Nuttby (mt.), N.S. 169/E3
Nutter Fort, W. Va. (26301) 313/F4
Nutting Lake, Mass. (01865) 249/B5
Nutwood Downs, No. Terr. 93/D3
Nuuanu (stream), Hawaii 218/C4
Nuwara Eliya, Ceylon 68/E7
Nuyakuk (lake), Alaska 196/F3
Nuyts (cape), Aust. 88/E6
Nuyts (arch.), S. Aust. 94/C5
Nuyts (cape), S. Aust. 94/C5
Nyabisindu, Rwanda 115/F4
Nyack, Mont. (†59936) 262/C2
Nyack, N.Y. (10960) 276/N8
Nyah, Vic. 97/B4
Nyah West, Vic. 27/H4
Nyala, 102/E3
Nyala, Sudan 111/E5
Ny-Ålesund, Norway 18/C2
Nyamlell, Sudan 111/E6
Nyandoma, U.S.S.R. 48/E3
Nyandoma, U.S.S.R. 52/F2
Nyandoma, U.S.S.R., 7/J2
Nyanga, Gabon 115/A4
Nyanza (prov.), Kenya 115/F4
Nyasa (lake), 3/L6
Nyasa (lake), 102/F6
Nyasa (lake), Moz. 118/E2
Nyasa (lake), Malawi 115/F6
Nyasa (lake), Tanz. 115/F6
Nyaunglebin, Burma 72/C3
Nyborg, Den. 18/G9
Nyborg, Den. 21/D7
Nybro, Sweden 18/J8
Nyda, U.S.S.R. 48/H3
Nye, Mont. (59061) 262/G5
Nye (co.), Nev. 266/E4
Nyenchen Tanglha (range), China 77/C6
Nyeri, Kenya 115/G4
Nyerol, Sudan 111/F6
Nyira (mt.), Kenya 115/G3
Nyírábrány, Hung. 41/G3
Nyírádony, Hung. 41/G3
Nyírbátor, Hung. 41/G3
Nyíregyháza, Hung. 41/F3
Nyírmada, Hung. 41/F2
Nykarleby, Fin. 18/N5
Nykøbing, Holbaek, Den. 18/G9
Nykøbing, Maribo, Den. 18/H9
Nykøbing, Thisted, Den. 18/F8
Nykøbing, Holbaek, Den. 21/E6
Nykøbing, Maribo, Den. 21/F8
Nykøbing, Thisted, Den. 21/B4
Nyköping, Sweden 18/K7
Nylstroom, S. Africa 118/D4
Nymagee, Aust. 88/H6
Nymagee, N.S.W. 97/D3
Nymboida, N.S.W. 97/G1
Nymboida (riv.), N.S.W. 97/G1
Nymburk, Czech. 41/C1
Nynäshamn, Sweden 18/L7
Nyngan, Aust. 88/H6
Nyngan, N.S.W. 97/D2
Nyon, Switz. 39/B4
Nyons, France 28/F5
Nýřany, Czech. 41/B2
Nyrob, U.S.S.R. 52/J2
Nýrsko, Czech. 41/B2
Nysa, Poland 47/C3
Nysa Kłodzka (riv.), Poland 47/C3
Nysa Łużycka (riv.), Poland 47/B3
Nyssa, Oreg. (97913) 291/K4
Nysted, Den. 21/E8
Nyudo (cape), Japan 81/J4

Oregon 413

Okovango (basin), 102/E6
Okovango (riv.), 102/D6
Okoyo, Rep. of Congo 115/C4
Okreek, S. Dak. (57563) 298/J7
Oksino, U.S.S.R. 52/H1
Oktaha, Okla. (74450) 288/R3
Oktibbeha (co.), Miss. 256/G4
Oktyabr'sk, U.S.S.R. 52/G4
Oktyabr'skiy, U.S.S.R. 52/H4
Okushiri (isl.), Japan 81/J2
Ola, Ark. (72853) 203/D3
Ola, Ga. (†30253) 216/E4
Ola, Idaho (83657) 220/B5
Olá, Pan. 154/G6
Ólafsfjördhur, Ice. 21/C1
Ola Grande (pt.), P. Rico 161/D3
Olalla, Br. Col. 184/H5
Olalla, Wash. (98359) 310/A2
Olamon, Maine (04467) 242/F5
Olancha, Calif. (93549) 204/H7
Olanchito, Hond. 154/D3
Öland (isl.), Sweden 18/K8
Öland (isl.), Sweden, 7/F3
Olanta, Pa. (16863) 294/F4
Olanta, S.C. (29114) 296/H4
Olar, S.C. (29843) 296/E5
Olary, Aust. 88/F6
Olary, S. Aust. 94/G5
Olathe, Colo. (81425) 208/D5
Olathe, Kans. (66061) 232/H3
Olathe Nav. Air. Sta., Kans. 232/H3
Olavarría, Arg. 143/D4
Oława, Poland 47/C3
Olberg, Ariz. (†85247) 198/D5
Olbernhau, E. Ger. 22/E3
Olbia, Italy, 7/E4
Olbia, Italy 34/B4
Olcott, N.Y. (14126) 276/C4
Old (riv.), Calif. 204/L1
Old (stream), Maine 242/H6
Oldany (isl.), Scot. 15/F3
Old Appleton, Mo. (63770) 261/N7
Old Bahama (chan.), Bah. Is. 156/B2
Old Bahama (chan.), Cuba 156/B2
Old Bahama (chan.), Cuba 158/G1
Old Bennington, Vt. (†05201) 268/A6
Old Bethpage‡, N.Y. (11804) 276/N9
Old Bonaventure, Newf. 166/D2
Old Bridge, N.J. (08857) 273/E3
Old Brookville‡, N.Y. (†11545) 276/R7
Old Castile (reg.), Spain 33/D2
Oldcastle, 10/C4
Oldcastle, Ire. 17/G4
Old Crow, Yukon 187/E3
Olden, Norway 18/E6
Olden, Mo. (†65789) 261/J9
Olden, Texas (76466) 302/F5
Oldenburg, Ind. (47036) 227/G6
Oldenburg, Miss. (†39661) 256/C7
Oldenburg, Lower Saxony, W. Ger. 22/C2
Oldenburg, Schleswig-Holstein, W. Ger. 22/D1
Old England, Jam. 158/H6
Oldenzaal, Neth. 27/K4
Old Faithful, Wyo. (82190) 319/B1
Oldfield, La. (†70754) 238/L1
Old Field‡, N.Y. (†11733) 276/O9
Old Fields, W. Va. (26845) 313/J4
Old Fletton, Eng. 13/G5
Old Forge, N.Y. (13420) 276/L3
Old Forge, Pa. (18518) 294/L3
Old Fort, N.C. (28762) 281/E3
Old Fort, Ohio (44861) 284/D3
Oldfort, Tenn. (37362) 237/M10
Old Fort Nelson, Br. Col. 184/M2
Old Glory, Texas (79540) 302/D4
Old Greenwich, Conn. (06870) 210/A4
Oldham, 10/G2
Oldham, Eng. 13/E4
Oldham (co.), Ky. 237/L4
Oldham, N.S. 169/E4
Oldham, S. Dak. (57051) 298/P5
Oldham (co.), Texas 302/B2
Old Harbor, Alaska (99643) 196/H3
Old Harbour, Jam. 158/J6
Old Harbour (bay), Jam. 158/J6
Old Harbour Bay, Jam. 158/J6
Old Hickory, Tenn. (37138) 237/H8
Old Hickory (dam), Tenn. 237/H8
Old Hickory (lake), Tenn. 237/J8
Old Landing, Ky. (41358) 237/O5
Old Leighlin, Ire. 17/G6
Old Lodge (creek), S. Dak. 298/K6
Old Lyme▵, Conn. (06371) 210/F3
Old Lyme, Conn. (06371) 210/F3
Oldman (riv.), Alta. 182/D5
Oldman (riv.), Sask. 181/L2
Oldmans (creek), N.J. 273/C4
Old Marissa, Ill. (†62257) 222/D5
Old Marsh Bed, No. Terr. 93/B6
Old Meldrum, 10/E2
Old Meldrum, Scot. 15/M5
Old Mill Creek‡, Ill. (†60083) 222/F1
Old Mission, Mich. (49673) 250/D4
Old Monroe, Mo. (63369) 261/N1
Old Mystic, Conn. (06372) 210/H3
Old Orchard Beach▵, Maine (04064) 242/C9
Old Orchard Beach, Maine (04064) 242/C9
Old Perlican, Newf. 166/D2
Old Rhine (riv.), Neth. 27/E4
Old Rhodes (key), Fla. 212/F6
Old Ripley, Ill. (†62275) 222/D5
Old Road, Antigua 161/D11
Old Road, St. Chr.-N.-A. 161/C10
Olds, Alta. 182/D4
Olds, Iowa (52647) 229/K6
Old Saybrook▵, Conn. (06475) 210/F3
Old Saybrook, Conn. (06475) 210/F3
Old Shawneetown, Ill. (†62984) 222/E6
Oldsmar, Fla. (33557) 212/B2
Old Spring Hill, Ala. (†36742) 194/C6
Old Sturbridge Village, Mass. (†01566) 249/F4
Old Tampa (bay), Fla. 212/B3
Old Tappan, N.J. (07675) 273/C1
Old Town, Fla. (32680) 212/C2
Oldtown, Idaho (†99156) 220/A1
Old Town, Iowa (†51351) 229/C2
Oldtown, Ky. (41163) 237/R4
Old Town, Maine (04468) 242/F6
Oldtown, Md. (21555) 245/D2
Old Trap, N.C. (27961) 281/T2
Olduvai Gorge (canyon), Tanz. 115/G4
Old Washington, Ohio (43768) 284/H5
Old Westbury‡, N.Y. (11568) 276/R7
Oldwick, N.J. (08858) 273/D2
Old Wives, Sask. 181/E5
Old Wives (lake), Sask. 181/E5
Old Woman (creek), Wyo. 319/H3
Olean, Mo. (65064) 261/G6
Olean, N.Y. (14760) 276/D6
O'Leary (peak), Ariz. 198/D3
O'Leary, P.E.I. 169/D2
Olecko, Poland 47/F2
Oleiros, Port. 33/B3
Olekma (riv.), U.S.S.R. 48/N4
Olekma (riv.), U.S.S.R., 54/R4
Olëkminsk, U.S.S.R. 48/N3
Olëkminsk, U.S.S.R., 54/R4
Olema, Calif. (94950) 204/H1
Olenegorsk, U.S.S.R. 52/D1
Olënek, U.S.S.R. 48/M3
Olënek (bay), U.S.S.R. 48/N2
Olënek (riv.), U.S.S.R. 48/M3
Olenek, U.S.S.R., 4/C4
Olentangy (riv.), Ohio 284/D4
Oléron (isl.), France, 7/D4
Oléron (isl.), France 28/C5
Oleśnica, Poland 47/C3
Oleta, Okla. (74751) 288/R6
Olex, Oreg. (97812) 291/G2
Oley, Pa. (19547) 294/L5
Olga, N. Dak. (†58221) 283/O2
Olga (mt.), No. Terr. 93/B8
Olga, Sask. 181/B6
Olga, Wash. (98279) 310/C2
Ølgod, Den. 21/B6
Olha, Man. 179/B4
Olhão, Port. 33/C4
Oliena, Italy 34/B4
Olifants (riv.), Moz. 118/D4
Olifants (riv.), S. Africa 118/D4
Olimar, Urug. 145/E3
Olimar Grande (riv.), Urug. 145/E4
Olimbía, Greece 45/E7
Olímpia, Braz. 135/B2
Olimpo (dept.), Par. 144/C3
Olin, Iowa (52320) 229/L5
Olin, Ky. (†40447) 237/N6
Olin, N.C. (28660) 281/H3
Olinda, Braz. 132/H4
Olinda, Calif. (96007) 204/C3
Olinda, Vic. 97/K5
Oliva, Arg. 143/D3
Oliva, Spain 33/F3
Oliva de la Frontera, Spain 33/C3
Olivais, Port. 33/A1
Olivar Alto, Chile 138/G5
Olivares, Cerro de (mt.), Arg. 143/B3
Olivares, Cerro de (mt.), Chile 138/B8
Olive, Mont. (59343) 262/L5
Olive, Okla. (†74030) 288/O2
Olive Branch, Ill. (62969) 222/D6
Olive Branch, Miss. (38654) 256/E1
Olive Branch, Ohio (†45103) 284/D10
Olive Hill, Ky. (41164) 237/P4
Olivehill, Tenn. (38475) 237/E10
Olivehurst‡, Calif. (95961) 204/D4
Oliveira, Braz. 132/E8
Oliveira, Braz. 135/D2
Olivenza, Spain 33/C3
Oliver (dam), Ala. 194/J5
Oliver, Br. Col. 184/H5
Oliver, Ga. (30449) 216/J5
Oliver (dam), Ga. 216/B6
Oliver (lake), Ga. 216/B5
Oliver, Ind. (†47620) 227/B8
Oliver (co.), N. Dak. 283/H5
Oliver, Pa. (15472) 294/C6
Oliver, Wis. (†54880) 317/B2
Oliver Springs, Tenn. (37840) 237/N8
Olivet, Ill. (61860) 222/F4
Olivet, Kans. (66519) 232/G3
Olivet, Md. (†20657) 245/N7
Olivet, Mich. (49076) 250/E6
Olivet, S. Dak. (57052) 298/O7
Olivet, Wis. (†54767) 317/B6
Olivette, Mo. (63132) 261/P3
Olivia, Minn. (56277) 254/C6
Olivia, N.C. (28368) 281/L4
Olivier, La. (†70560) 238/G7
Olivone, Switz. 39/G3
Olkusz, Poland 47/D3
Olla, La. (71465) 238/F3
Ollachea, Peru 128/G9
Ollagüe (vol.), Bol. 136/B7
Ollagüe, Chile, 120/D5
Ollagüe, Chile 138/B3
Ollantaytambo, Peru 128/F9
Ollie, Iowa (52576) 229/J6
Ollie, Mont. (†59313) 262/M4
Ollon, Switz. 39/D4
Olmedo, Spain 33/D2
Olmitz, Kans. (67564) 232/D3
Olmos, Arg. 143/F4
Olmos, Peru 128/C5
Olmos Park‡, Texas (78212) 302/F8
Olmstead, Ky. (42265) 237/H7
Olmstead, N. Dak. (†58331) 283/M2
Olmsted, Ill. (62970) 222/D6
Olmsted (co.), Minn. 254/F7
Olmsted Falls, Ohio (44138) 284/G9
Olmstedville, N.Y. (12857) 276/N3
Olmué, Chile 138/F2
Olney, Eng. 13/G5
Olney, Ill. (62450) 222/E5
Olney, Md. (20832) 245/K4
Olney, Mo. (63370) 261/K4
Olney, Mont. (59927) 262/B2
Olney, Okla. (†74538) 288/O6
Olney, Oreg. (†97103) 291/D1
Olney, Texas (76374) 302/F4
Olney Springs, Colo. (81062) 208/M6
Olofström, Sweden 18/J8
Oloh, Miss. (†39482) 256/E8
Olomouc, Czech., 7/F4
Olomouc, Czech. 41/D2
Olonets, U.S.S.R. 52/D2
Oloron-Sainte-Marie, France 28/C6
Olot, Spain 33/H1
Olowalu, Hawaii (†96761) 218/H2
Olpe, Kans. (66865) 232/F3
Olsburg, Kans. (66520) 232/F2
Olst, Neth. 27/J4
Olsztyn, Poland, 7/G4
Olsztyn (prov.), Poland 47/E2
Olsztyn, Poland 47/E2
Olt (riv.), Rum., 7/G4
Olt (riv.), Rum. 45/G3
Olta, Arg. 143/C3
Olten, Switz. 39/E2
Oltenita, Rum. 45/H3
Olton, Texas (79064) 302/B3
Oltu, Turkey 63/J2
Olur, Turkey 63/K2
Olustee, Fla. (32072) 212/D1
Olustee (riv.), Fla. 212/D1
Olustee, Okla. (73560) 288/H5
Olutanga (isl.), Phil. 82/D7
Olutanga (isl.), Phil. 85/G4
Olvera, Spain 33/D4
Olvey, Ark. (†72601) 203/E1
Olwanpi (cape), China 77/K7
Olympia, Ky. (40358) 237/O4
Olympia (cap.), Wash., 146/F5
Olympia (cap.), Wash., 188/B1
Olympia (cap.), Wash. (98501) 310/C3
Olympia Fields, Ill. (60461) 222/B3
Olympic (mts.), Wash. 310/B3
Olympic Nat'l Park, Wash., 188/A1
Olympic Nat'l Park, Wash. 310/B3
Olympic Valley, Calif. (95730) 204/E4
Olympus (mt.), Greece 45/F5
Olympus (mt.), Wash. 310/B3
Olyphant, Ark. (72020) 203/H3
Olyphant, Pa. (18447) 294/L3
Olyphic, N.C. (†28463) 281/M7
Olyutorskiy, U.S.S.R. 48/S3
Olyutorskiy (cape), U.S.S.R. 48/S4
Olyutorskiy, U.S.S.R., 54/V3
Oma, Miss. (39142) 256/D7
Oma (cape), Japan 81/K3
Omagari, Japan 81/K4
Omagh, N. Ire. 17/G2
Omagh, 10/C3
Omaguas, Peru 128/F5
Omaha, Ala. (†36274) 194/H4
Omaha, Ark. (72662) 203/D1
Omaha (beach), France 28/C3
Omaha, Ga. (31821) 216/C6
Omaha, Ill. (62871) 222/E6
Omaha, Nebr., 146/J5
Omaha, Nebr., 188/G2
Omaha, Nebr. (*68101) 264/J3
Omaha‡, Texas (75571) 302/K4
Omaha Ind. Res., Nebr. 264/H2
Omaja, Cuba 158/H3
Omak, Wash. (98841) 310/F2
Omak (lake), Wash. 310/F2
O'Malley, Sask. 181/E4
Oman, 3/M5
Oman, 54/J8
OMAN, 59/G6
Oman (gulf), 54/J7
Oman (gulf), Iran 59/G5
Oman (gulf), Oman 59/G5
Oman (reg.), Oman 59/G5
Oman (gulf), Trucial States 59/G5
Oman (gulf), Iran 66/M8
Omar, W. Va. (25638) 313/C7
Omaruru, S.W. Afr. 118/B4
Omas, Peru 128/D9
Omatako (riv.), S.W. Afr. 118/B3
Omate, Peru 128/G11
Ombai (str.), Indon. 85/H7
Omboué, Gabon 115/A4
Ombrone (riv.), Italy 34/C3
Ombúes de Lavalle, Urug. 145/B4
Ombúes de Oribe, Urug. 145/C4
Omdurman, 102/F3
Omdurman, Sudan 59/B6
Omdurman, Sudan 111/F4
Omega, Ala. (†36081) 194/G7
Omega, Ga. (31775) 216/E8
Omega, Ind. (†46030) 227/F4
Omega, Ohio (†45690) 284/E7
Omega, Okla. (73764) 288/K3
Omemee, Ont. 177/F3
Omemee, N. Dak. (†58739) 283/K2
Omena, Mich. (49674) 250/D3
Omeo, Vic. 97/D5
Omer, Mich. (48749) 250/F4
'Omer, Israel 65/B5
Ömerli, Turkey 63/J4
Omerville, Que. 172/E4
Ometepe (isl.), Nic. 154/E5
Ometepec, Mex. 150/K8
Omey (isl.), Ire. 17/A5
Omin (Durbuljin), China 77/B2
Ominato, Japan 81/K3
Omineca (mts.), Br. Col. 184/E2
Omineca (riv.), Br. Col. 184/E2
Omiš, Yugo. 45/C4
Omiya, Japan 81/O2
Ommaney (cape), Alaska 196/M2
Ommanney (bay), N.W.T. 187/H2
Omme (riv.), Den. 21/B6
Ommen, Neth. 27/J3
Omo (riv.), Eth. 111/G6
Omoa, Hond. 154/C3
Omolon (riv.), U.S.S.R. 48/Q3
Omolon (river), U.S.S.R., 4/C1
Omolon (riv.), U.S.S.R., 54/U3
Omono (riv.), Japan 81/J4
Ompah, Ont. 177/H2
Omps, W. Va. (25433) 313/K4
Omro, Wis. (54963) 317/J7
Omsk, U.S.S.R. 48/H4
Omsk, U.S.S.R., 3/N3
Omsk, U.S.S.R., 54/L4
Omu, Japan 81/L1
Omul (mt.), Rum. 45/G3
Omura, Bonin Is., Japan 81/M3
Omura, Nagasaki, Japan 81/E7
Omurtag, Bulg. 45/H4
Omuta, Japan 81/E7
Omutninsk, U.S.S.R. 48/F4
Omutninsk, U.S.S.R. 52/H3
Ona, Fla. (33865) 212/E4
Ona, W. Va. (25545) 313/B6
Onaga, Kans. (66521) 232/F2
Onagawa, Japan 81/K4
Onaka, S. Dak. (57466) 298/L3
Onalaska, Texas (77360) 302/J7
Onalaska, Wash. (98570) 310/C4
Onalaska, Wis. (54650) 317/D8
Onaman (lake), Ont. 177/H4
Onamia, Minn. (56359) 254/E4
Onancock, Va. (23417) 307/S5
Onangué (lake), Gabon 115/A4
Onanole, Man. 179/C4
Onaping, Ont. 175/D3
Onaqui (Vernon), Utah (†84080) 304/B3
Onarga, Ill. (60955) 222/F3
Onawa, Iowa (51040) 229/A4
Onawa, Maine (04470) 242/E5
Onawa (lake), Maine 242/E5
Onaway, Idaho (†83855) 220/B3
Onaway, Mich. (49765) 250/E3
Onbekend, S. Africa 118/J6
Onchan, I. of Man 13/C3
Onchiota, N.Y. (12968) 276/M2
Oncócua, Angola 115/B7
Onda, Spain 33/F3
Ondangua, S.W. Afr. 118/B3
Ondava (riv.), Czech. 41/F2
Ondo, Nigeria 106/F7
Öndverdharnes (mt.), Ice. 21/A1
O'Neals, Calif. (93645) 204/F6
Oneco, Conn. (06373) 210/H2
Oneco, Fla. (33558) 212/D4
Onefour, Alta. 182/E5
Onega, U.S.S.R. 48/D3
Onega (lake), U.S.S.R. 48/D3
Onega (riv.), U.S.S.R. 48/D3
Onega, U.S.S.R. 52/E2
Onega (bay), U.S.S.R. 52/E2
Onega (lake), U.S.S.R. 52/E2
Onega (riv.), U.S.S.R. 52/E2
Onega (lake), U.S.S.R., 7/H2
Onega (riv.), U.S.S.R., 7/H2
Onega, U.S.S.R., 7/H2
Onego, W. Va. (26886) 313/H5
One Hundred and Fifty Mile House, Br. Col. 184/G4
One Hundred Mile House, Br. Col. 184/G4
Onehunga, N.Z. 101/B1
Oneida, Ark. (72369) 203/J5
Oneida (co.), Idaho 220/F7
Oneida, Ill. (61467) 222/C2
Oneida, Iowa (†52057) 229/L3
Oneida, Kans. (66522) 232/G2
Oneida, Ky. (40972) 237/O6
Oneida (co.), N.Y. 276/J4
Oneida, N.Y. (13421) 276/J4
Oneida (lake), N.Y. 276/J4
Oneida, Pa. (18242) 294/K4
Oneida, Tenn. (37841) 237/N7
Oneida (co.), Wis. 317/G4
Oneida, Wis. (54155) 317/K7
Oneida Castle‡, N.Y. (†13421) 276/J4
O'Neill, Nebr. (68763) 264/F2
Onekama, Mich. (49675) 250/C4
Oneonta, Ala. (35121) 194/E3
Oneonta, N.Y. (13820) 276/K6
One Tree Hill, N.Z. 101/B1
Ong, Nebr. (68452) 264/G4
Ongjin, N. Korea 81/B5
Ongole, India 68/E5
Onguday, U.S.S.R. 48/J4
Oni, U.S.S.R. 52/F6
Oniad Lake‡, N.Y. (†12590) 276/N7
Onida, S. Dak. (57564) 298/K4
Onilahy (riv.), Malag. Rep. 118/G4
Onima, Neth. Ant. 161/E8
Onion Lake, Sask. 181/B2
Onitsha, Nigeria 106/F7
Onkaparinga (riv.), Aust. 88/D8
Onkaparinga (riv.), S. Aust. 94/B8
Onkivesi (lake), Fin. 18/P5
Onley, Va. (23418) 307/S5
Only, Tenn. (37140) 237/F9
Ono, Calif. (96072) 204/C3
Ono, Japan 81/H6
Ono (riv.), Japan 81/E7
Ono, Pa. (17077) 294/J5
Onoda, Japan 81/E6
Onomea, Hawaii (†96781) 218/J4
Onomichi, Japan 81/F6
Onon, Mong. 77/H2
Onon (riv.), Mong. 77/H2
Onondaga, Mich. (49264) 250/E6
Onondaga (co.), N.Y. 276/H5
Onondaga Ind. Res., N.Y. 276/H5
Onota (lake), Mass. 249/A3
Onoto, Ven. 124/F3
Onotoa (atoll), Gilb. and Ell., 87/H6
Onoville, N.Y. (†14783) 276/B6
Onoway, Alta. 182/C3
Onrusrivier, S. Africa 118/G7
Onset, Mass. (02558) 249/M6
Onslow, Australia, 87/B8
Onslow, Aust. 88/B4
Onslow, Iowa (52321) 229/M4
Onslow (co.), N.C. 281/P5
Onslow (bay), N.C. 281/P6
Onslow, W. Aust. 92/A3
Onsong, N. Korea 81/E2
Onsted, Mich. (49265) 250/E6
Onstwedde, Neth. 27/K2
Ontake (mt.), Japan 81/H6
Ontario (lake), 146/L5
Ontario (lake), 163/J7
Ontario, Calif. (*91761) 204/D10
Ontario (prov.), Canada, 146/K4
ONTARIO, 177
Ontario (co.), Ont. 177/E3
Ontario (lake), Ont. 177/G4
Ontario, Ind. (†46746) 227/G1
Ontario, Iowa (†50010) 229/F4
Ontario (lake), N.Y., 188/L2
Ontario (co.), N.Y. 276/F5
Ontario, N.Y. (14519) 276/F4
Ontario (lake), N.Y. 276/F3
Ontario, Ohio (44862) 284/E4
Ontario, Oreg. (97914) 291/K3
Ontario, Wis. (54651) 317/E8
Onteniente, Spain 33/F3
Onton, Ky. (42443) 237/G5
Ontonagon (co.), Mich. 250/F1
Ontonagon, Mich. (49953) 250/F1
Ontonagon (riv.), Mich. 250/G1
Ontonagon Ind. Res., Mich. 250/F1
Ontong Java (isl.), Br. Sol. Is., 87/G6
Onward, Ind. (46967) 227/E3
Onward, Miss. (39143) 256/C5
Onward, Sask. 181/B4
Onyx, Ark. (†72860) 203/D4
Onyx, Calif. (93255) 204/G8
Oobagooma, W. Aust. 92/D2
Oodnadatta, Australia, 87/D8
Oodnadatta, Aust. 88/E5
Oodnadatta, S. Aust. 94/D2
Ookala, Hawaii (96774) 218/J4
Oola, Ire. 17/E6
Ooldea, Aust. 88/E6
Ooldea, S. Aust. 94/B4
Oolitic, Ind. (47451) 227/E7
Oologah, Okla. (74053) 288/P2
Oologah (res.), Okla. 288/R1
Ooltewah, Tenn. (37363) 237/M10
Oona River, Br. Col. 184/C3
Oostanaula, Ga. (†30701) 216/B1
Oostanaula (riv.), Ga. 216/B2
Oostburg, Neth. 27/C6
Oostburg, Wis. (53070) 317/L8
Oostende (Ostend), Belg. 27/B6
Ooster Eems (chan.), Neth. 27/K1
Oosterend, Neth. 27/G2
Oosterhout, Neth. 27/F5
Oostkamp, Belg. 27/C6
Oostmahorn, Neth. 27/J2
Oost-Vlieland, Neth. 27/F2
Oostzaan, Neth. 27/C4
Oostzaan Polder, Neth. 27/B4
Ootacamund, India 68/D6
Ootmarsum, Neth. 27/K4
Ootsa (lake), Br. Col. 184/D3
Ootsa Lake, Br. Col. 184/E3
Opal, Alta. 182/D3
Opal, S. Dak. (57765) 298/D4
Opal, Wyo. (83124) 319/B4
Opala, Dem. Rep. of the Congo 115/D4
Opal Cliffs, Calif. (95060) 204/K4
Opa-locka, Fla. (33054) 212/B4
Opalton, Aust. 88/G4
Opalton, Queens. 95/B4
Opari, Sudan 111/F7
Oparino, U.S.S.R. 52/G3
Opasatika, Ont. 175/D3
Opatija, Yugo. 45/A3
Opatów, Poland 47/E3
Opava, Czech. 41/E2
Opazatika (riv.), Ont. 175/D3
Opdyke, Ill. (62872) 222/E5
Opelika, Ala. (36801) 194/H5
Opelousas, La. (70570) 238/G5
Openshaw, Sask. 181/J6
Opeongo (lake), Ont. 177/F2
Opheim, Ill. (61468) 222/C2
Opheim, Mont. (59250) 262/K2
Ophir, Colo. (81426) 208/D7
Ophir, Man. 179/G5
Ophir, Oreg. (97464) 291/C5
Ophir, Utah (†84074) 304/B3
Ophoven, Belg. 27/H6
Opihikao, Hawaii (†96778) 218/K6
Opinaca (riv.), Que. 174/B2
Opinaca (riv.), 163/J5
Opine, Ala. (†36784) 194/C7
Opinnagau (riv.), Ont. 175/D2
Opiscotéo (lake), Que. 174/D2
Opladen, W. Ger. 22/B3
Opochka, U.S.S.R. 52/C3
Opoco, Bol. 136/B6
Opoczno, Poland 47/E3
Opodepe, Mex. 150/D2
Opole, Minn. (†56340) 254/D5
Opole (prov.), Poland 47/C3
Opole, Poland 47/C3
Opole Lubelskie, Poland 47/F3
Opolis, Kans. (66760) 232/H4
Oporto, Port., 7/D4
Oporto, Port. 33/B2
Opotiki, N.Z. 101/F3
Opp, Ala. (36467) 194/F8
Oppdal, Norway 18/F5
Oppelo, Ark. (†72110) 203/E3
Oppenheim, W. Ger. 22/C4
Oppland (co.), Norway 18/F6
Opportunity, Wash. (99214) 310/H3
Oppy, Ky. (†25685) 237/S5
Optima, Okla. (73948) 288/D1
Optima (res.), Okla. 288/D1
Opua, N.Z. 101/D1
Opunake, N.Z. 101/D3
Opuntia (lake), Sask. 181/C4
Oputo, Mex. 150/E1
Opwijk, Belg. 27/E7
'Oqair, Saudi Ar. 59/E4
Oquawka, Ill. (61469) 222/C3
Oquossoc, Maine (04964) 242/B6
Ora, Ind. (46968) 227/D2
Ora, Miss. (†39428) 256/E7
Ora, S.C. (29371) 296/D2
Oracabessa, Jam. 158/J5
Oracle, Ariz. (85623) 198/E6
Oradea, Rum., 7/G4
Oradea, Rum. 45/E2
Oradell, N.J. (07649) 273/B1
Oradell (res.), N.J. 273/B1
Orai, India 68/D3
Oraibi, Ariz. (86039) 198/E3
Oraibi Wash (dry riv.), Ariz. 198/E3
Oral, S. Dak. (57766) 298/C7
Orán, Alg. 106/D1
Orán, Arg., 120/D5
Orán, Arg. 143/D1
Oran, Iowa (50664) 229/J3
Oran, Mo. (63771) 261/N8
Oran, 102/B1
Orange (riv.), 3/K7
Orange, Australia, 87/E9
Orange, Aust. 88/H6
Orange (riv.), Botswana 118/B5
Orange (co.), Calif. 204/H10
Orange, Calif. (*92666) 204/D11
Orange▵, Conn. (06477) 210/C3
Orange (cape), Braz. 132/D1
Orange (co.), Fla. 212/E3
Orange, Fla. (†32321) 212/B1
Orange (lake), Fla. 212/D2
Orange, France 28/F5
Orange, Ga. (†30114) 216/D2
Orange (co.), Ind. 227/E7
Orange, Ind. (†47343) 227/G5
Orange▵, Mass. (01364) 249/E2
Orange, Mass. (01364) 249/E2
Orange (co.), N.C. 281/L2
Orange▵, N.H. (†03741) 268/D4
Orange, N.H. (†03741) 268/D4
Orange, N.J. (*07050) 273/B2
Orange, N.S.W. 97/E3
Orange (co.), N.Y. 276/M8
Orange (canal), Neth. 27/K3
Orange, Ohio (†44101) 284/J9
Orange (riv.), 102/D7
Orange (riv.), S. Africa 118/B5
Orange (mts.), Sur. 131/D4
Orange (co.), Texas 302/L7
Orange, Texas (77630) 302/L7
Orange (cliffs), Utah 304/D5
Orange (co.), Va. 307/M4
Orange, Va. (22960) 307/M4
Orange (co.), Vt. 268/C3
Orange▵, Vt. (†05649) 268/C3
Orange, Vt. (†05649) 268/C3
Orange Beach, Ala. (36561) 194/C10
Orangeburg (co.), S.C. 296/F5
Orangeburg, S.C. (29115) 296/F4
Orange City, Fla. (32763) 212/E3
Orange City, Iowa (51041) 229/A2
Orange Cove, Calif. (93646) 204/F7
Orangedale, N.S. 169/G3
Orange Free State (prov.), 102/E7
Orange Free State (prov.), S. Africa 118/D4
Orange Grove, Miss. (†39501) 256/H10
Orange Grove, Texas (78372) 302/F10
Orange Lake, Fla. (32681) 212/D2
Orange Lake‡, N.Y. (†12550) 276/M8
Orange Park, Fla. (32073) 212/E1
Orange Springs, Fla. (32682) 212/E2
Orangevale‡, Calif. (95662) 204/C8
Orangeville, Ont. 177/D4
Orangeville, Ill. (61060) 222/D1
Orangeville, Ind. (†47452) 227/D7
Orangeville, Mich. (†49344) 250/D6
Orangeville, Ohio (44453) 284/J3
Orangeville, Pa. (17859) 294/K3
Orangeville, Utah (84537) 304/C4
Orange Walk, Br. Hond. 154/C1
Oranienburg, E. Ger. 22/E2
Oranjemund, S.W. Afr. 118/B5
Oranjestad, Neth. Ant. 156/D4
Oranjestad (cap.), Aruba, Neth. Ant. 161/D10
Oranmore, Ire. 17/D5
Oras, Alta. 182/C3
Oras, Phil. 82/E4
Orăştie, Rum. 45/F3
Oraşul Gheorghe Gheorghiu-Dej, Rum. 45/H2
Orava (res.), Czech. 41/E2
Orava (riv.), Czech. 41/E2
Orava (res.), Poland 47/D4
Oraville, Ill. (62971) 222/D6
Oravita, Rum. 45/E3
Orb (riv.), France 28/E6
Orbe, Switz. 39/C3
Orbe (riv.), Switz. 39/B3
Orbetello, Italy 34/C3
Órbigo (riv.), Spain 33/D1
Orbisonia, Pa. (17243) 294/G5
Orbost, Aust. 88/H7
Orbost, Vic. 97/E5
Örbyhus, Sweden 18/K6
Orca, Alaska (†99574) 196/J2
Orcadia, Sask. 181/J4
Orcas (isl.), Wash. 310/C2
Orcera, Spain 33/E3
Orchard, Colo. (80649) 208/L2
Orchard, Iowa (50460) 229/H2
Orchard, Nebr. (68764) 264/F2
Orchard Beach, Md. (†21122) 245/M4
Orchard City (Eckert), Colo. (†81418) 208/C5
Orchard Farm, Mo. (†63301) 261/O2
Orchard Hill, Ga. (30266) 216/D4
Orchard Hills‡, Pa. (†15613) 294/C4
Orchard Lake, Mich. (48033) 250/F6
Orchard Lake, Minn. (†55044) 254/E6
Orchard Mesa, Colo. (†81501) 208/C4
Orchard Park, N.Y. (14127) 276/C5
Orchards, Wash. (98662) 310/C5
Orchard Valley, Wyo. (†82001) 319/H4
Orchid‡, Fla. (†32970) 212/F4
Orchid, Va. (23117) 307/N5
Orchy (riv.), Scot. 15/G7
Orcotuna, Peru 128/E8
Orcutt, Calif. (93454) 204/E9
Orcuttville, Conn. (†06076) 210/F1
Ord (mt.), Ariz. 198/D5
Ord (riv.), Australia, 87/C7
Ord (riv.), Aust. 88/D3
Ord, Nebr. (68862) 264/F3
Ord (mt.), W. Aust. 92/D2
Ord (riv.), W. Aust. 92/E2
Ordale, Sask. 181/E2
Órdenes, Spain 33/B1
Orderville, Utah (84758) 304/B6
Ordoqui, Arg. 143/F7
Ordos (des.), China 77/G4
Ord River, Aust. 88/D3
Ord River, W. Aust. 92/E2
Ordu, Turkey 59/C1
Ordu (prov.), Turkey 63/G2
Ordu, Turkey 63/G2
Ordway, Colo. (81063) 208/M6
Ordway, S. Dak. (†57433) 298/N2
Ordzhonikidze, U.S.S.R. 48/E5
Ordzhonikidze, U.S.S.R. 52/F6
Ordzhonikidze, U.S.S.R., 7/J4
Orealla, Guyana 131/C3
Öreälv (riv.), Sweden 18/L4
Oreana, Idaho (83659) 220/B6
Oreana, Ill. (62554) 222/E4
Oreana, Nev. (†89419) 266/C2
Orebank, Tenn. (†37660) 237/R7
Örebro (co.), Sweden 18/J7
Örebro, Sweden 18/J7
Örebro, Sweden, 7/F3
Ore City, Texas (75683) 302/K5
Oregon, 188/B2
OREGON, 291
Oregon, Ill. (61061) 222/D1
Oregon (co.), Mo. 261/K9
Oregon, Mo. (64473) 261/B2
Oregon (inlet), N.C. 281/U3
Oregon, Ohio (43616) 284/D2
Oregon (creek), Oreg. 291/K5
Oregon (state), U.S., 146/F5
Oregon, Wis. (53575) 317/H10

414 Oregon Caves Nat'l Mon.

Oregon Caves Nat'l Mon., Oreg. 291/D5
Oregon City, Oreg., 188/B1
Oregon City, Oreg. (97045) 291/B2
Oregon Coast (range), Oreg. 291/D4
Oregonia, Ohio (45054) 284/B7
öregrund, Sweden 18/L6
Orekhovo-Zuyevo, U.S.S.R. 52/E3
Orekhovo-Zuyevo, U.S.S.R., 7/H3
Orel, U.S.S.R. 48/D4
Orel, U.S.S.R. 52/E4
Orel, U.S.S.R., 7/H3
Oreland‡, Pa. (19075) 294/M5
Orellana, Peru 128/E6
Orellana la Vieja, Spain 33/D3
Orem, Utah (84057) 304/C3
Orenburg, U.S.S.R. 48/F4
Orenburg, U.S.S.R. 52/J4
Orenburg, U.S.S.R., 7/K3
Orenco, Oreg. (†97123) 291/A2
Orense (prov.), Spain 33/C1
Orense, Spain 33/C1
Orestes, Ind. (46063) 227/F4
Orestiás, Greece 45/H5
øresund (sound), Den. 18/H9
øresund (sound), Den. 21/F6
öresund (sound), Sweden 18/H9
Oreti (riv.), N.Z. 101/B6
Oretta, La. (†70660) 238/D5
Orewa, N.Z. 101/E2
Oreway, Newf. 166/A3
Orford, Eng. 13/J5
Orford△, N.H. (03777) 268/C4
Orford, N.H. (03777) 268/C4
Orfordness (prom.), Eng. 13/J5
Orfordville, N.H. (03778) 268/C4
Orfordville, Wis. (53576) 317/H10
Organ, N. Mex. (88052) 274/C6
Organobo, Fr. Gui. 131/E3
Organ Pipe Cactus Nat'l Mon., Ariz. 198/C6
Orgãos (range), Braz. 135/E3
Orgas, W. Va. (25148) 313/C6
Orgaz, Spain 33/E3
Orgeyev, U.S.S.R. 52/C5
Orhaneli, Turkey 63/C3
Oria, Spain 33/E4
Orick, Calif. (95555) 204/A2
Orient, Ill. (62874) 222/E6
Orient, Iowa (50858) 229/E6
Orient△, Maine (04471) 242/H4
Orient, N.Y. (11957) 276/R8
Orient (pt.), N.Y. 276/R8
Orient, Ohio (43146) 284/D6
Orient, S. Dak. (57467) 298/L4
Orient, Wash. (99160) 310/G2
Orienta, Okla. (73765) 288/J2
Oriental, Cordillera (range), Bol. 136/C5
Oriental, Cordillera (range), Col. 126/D5
Oriental, Cordillera (range), Dom. Rep. 158/F6
Oriental, Cordillera (range), Peru 128/H10
Oriental, Mex. 150/O1
Oriental, N.C. (28571) 281/R4
Orientale (prov.), Dem. Rep. of the Congo. 115/E3
Oriental Mindoro (prov.), Phil. 82/C4
Oriente (prov.), Cuba 158/H4
Orihuela, Spain 33/F3
Orihvesi (lake), Fin. 18/Q5
Orillia, Ont. 177/E3
Orin, Wash. (†99114) 310/H2
Orin, Wyo. (82652) 319/G3
Orinda, Calif. (94563) 204/J2
Orinoca, Bol. 136/B6
Orinoco (riv.), 3/F5
Orinoco (riv.), 120/D2
Orinoco (riv.), Col. 126/G5
Orinoco (delta), Ven. 124/H3
Orinoco (riv.), Ven. 124/G3
Oriole, Md. (21848) 245/P8
Orion, Ala. (†36081) 194/F7
Orion, Alta. 182/E5
Orion, Ill. (61273) 222/C2
Oriska, N. Dak. (58063) 283/P6
Oriskany, N.Y. (13424) 276/K4
Oriskany, Va. (24130) 307/J5
Oriskany Falls, N.Y. (13425) 276/J5
Orissa (state), India 68/E5
Oristano, Italy 34/B5
Oristano (gulf), Italy 34/B5
Orituco (riv.), Ven. 124/E3
Oriximiná, Braz. 132/C3
Orizaba, Mex., 146/J8
Orizaba, Mex. 150/P2
Orizaba (Citlaltépetl) (mt.), Mex. 150/O2
órjiva, Spain 33/E4
Orkanger, Norway 18/F5
örkény, Hung. 41/E3
Orkhon (riv.), Mong. 77/F2
Orkney (isls.), 10/E1
Orkney, Sask. 181/D6
Orkney (isls.), Scot., 7/D3
Orkney (co.), Scot. 15/K1
Orkney (isls.), Scot. 15/J1
Orla, Texas (79770) 302/D10
Orland, Calif. (95963) 204/C4
Orland, Ind. (46776) 227/G1
Orland△, Maine (04472) 242/F6
Orland, Maine (04472) 242/F6
Orlândia, Braz. 135/C2
Orlando, Fla., 146/K7
Orlando, Fla., 188/K5
Orlando, Fla. (*32801) 212/E3
Orlando, Ky. (40460) 237/N6
Orlando, Okla. (73073) 288/M2
Orlando, S. Africa 118/H6
Orlando, W. Va. (26412) 313/E5
Orlando N.T.C., Fla. 212/E3
Orland Park, Ill. (60462) 222/A2
Orleães, Braz. 132/D10
Orleans, Calif. (95556) 204/B2
Orléans (isl.), Que. 172/F3
Orleans, Ont. 177/J2
Orléans, France, 7/E4
Orléans, France 28/D3
Orleans, Ind. (47452) 227/D7
Orleans, Iowa (†51360) 229/C2
Orleans (par.), La. 238/L6
Orleans△, Mass. (02653) 249/O5
Orleans, Minn. (56743) 254/B2
Orleans (co.), N.Y. 276/D4
Orleans, Nebr. (68966) 264/E4
Orleans (co.), Vt. 268/C2
Orleans, Vt. (05860) 268/C2
Orleans Cross Roads, W. Va. (†25422) 313/K3
Orléansville (El Asnam), Alg. 106/E1
Orley, Sask. 181/H3
Orlice (riv.), Czech. 41/D1
Orlická (res.), Czech. 41/C2
Orlik, U.S.S.R. 48/K4
Orlinda, Tenn. (37141) 237/H7
Orlová, Czech. 41/E2
Orly, France 28/B2
Orma, W. Va. (25268) 313/D5
Ormara, Pak. 59/J4
Ormara, Pak. 68/A3
Orme, Tenn. (35740) 237/K10
Ormea, Italy 34/A2
Ormeaux, Sask. 181/D2
Ormiston, Sask. 181/F6
Ormoc, Phil. 82/E5
Ormoc (bay), Phil. 82/E5
Ormond Beach, Fla. (32074) 212/E2
Ormont-Dessous, Switz. 39/D4
Ormsby, Ont. 177/G3
Ormsby, Minn. (56162) 254/D7
Ormsby, Pa. (16741) 294/E2
Ormside, Sask. 181/J3
Ormskirk, 10/F2
Ormskirk, Eng. 13/E4
Ormstown, Que. 172/D4
Orne (dept.), France 28/C3
Orne (riv.), France 28/C3
Orneta, Poland 47/E1
Ornö (isl.), Sweden 18/J2
örnsköldsvik, Sweden 18/L5
Orobayaya, Bol. 136/D3
Orochen, U.S.S.R. 48/N4
Orocovis, P. Rico 161/C2
Orocué, Col. 126/E5
Orofino, Idaho (83544) 220/B3
Orofino (creek), Idaho 220/C3
Oro Grande, Calif. (92368) 204/H9
Orogrande, Idaho (†83525) 220/C4
Orogrande, N. Mex. (88342) 274/D6
Oro Ingenio, Bol. 136/C7
Orolow, Sask. 181/D3
Oroluk (atoll), Pac. Is., 87/F5
Oromocto, N. Br. 170/D3
Oromocto (lake), N. Br. 170/C3
Oromocto (riv.), N. Br. 170/D3
Oron, Nigeria 106/F8
Oron, Israel 65/C6
Orona (Hull) (isl.), Gilb. and Ell., 87/J6
Orondo, Wash. (98843) 310/E3
Orongorongo (riv.), N.Z. 101/B3
Oron-la-Ville, Switz. 39/C3
Orono, Ont. 177/F4
Orono△, Maine (04473) 242/F6
Orono, Maine (04473) 242/F6
Orono (Crystal Bay), Minn. (†55323) 254/F5
Oronoco, Minn. (55960) 254/F6
Oronogo, Mo. (64855) 261/D8
Oronsay (isl.), Scot. 15/D7
Oronsay (passg.), Scot. 15/D7
Orontes ('Asi) (riv.), Syria 59/C2
Orontes ('Asi) (riv.), Syria 63/G5
Oropesa, Spain 33/D3
Oropuche (riv.), Trinidad Tobago 161/B10
Oroquieta, Phil. 82/D6
Oroquieta, Phil. 85/G4
Orosei (gulf), Italy 34/B4
Orosháza, Hung. 41/F3
Orosi, Calif. (93647) 204/F7
Oroszlány, Hung. 41/E3
Orotina, C. Rica 154/E6
Orovada, Nev. (89425) 266/D1
Oroville, Calif. (95965) 204/D4
Oroville (res.), Calif. 204/D4
Oroville, Wash. (98844) 310/F2
Orozco, Cuba 158/B1
Orpha, Wyo. (†82633) 319/G3
Orr, Minn. (55771) 254/F2
Orr, N. Dak. (58268) 283/P3
Orr, Okla. (†73456) 288/M6
Orrefors, Sweden 18/J8
Orrick, Mo. (64077) 261/D4
Orrin, N. Dak. (58359) 283/K3
Orrin (riv.), Scot. 15/G5
Orrington△, Maine (04474) 242/F6
Orrington, Maine (04474) 242/F6
Orroroo, S. Aust. 94/F5
Orrs Island, Maine (04066) 242/D8
Orrstown, Pa. (17244) 294/G5
Orrtanna, Pa. (17353) 294/H6
Orrum, N.C. (28369) 281/L6
Orrville, Ala. (36767) 194/D6
Orrville, Ont. 177/E2
Orrville, Ohio (44667) 284/G4
Orsa, Sweden 18/J6
Orsainville, Que. 172/H3
Orsha, U.S.S.R. 52/C4
Orsières, Switz. 39/D4
Orsk, U.S.S.R. 48/F4
Orsk, U.S.S.R. 52/J4
Orson, Pa. (18449) 294/M2
Orsonnens, Switz. 39/D3
Orşova, Rum. 45/F3
ørsted, Den. 21/D5
Orta, Turkey 63/E2
Ortaca, Turkey 63/C4
Ortakaraviran, Turkey 63/E4
Ortaköy, Corum, Turkey 63/F2
Ortaköy, Niğde, Turkey 63/F4
Ortega, Col. 126/C6
Ortegal (cape), Spain 33/B1
Orteguaza (riv.), Col. 126/C7
Orthez, France 28/C6
Ortigueira, Spain 33/C1
Orting, Wash. (98360) 310/C3
Ortiz, Colo. (†81120) 208/H8
Ortiz, Ven. 124/E3
Ortles (range), Italy 34/C1
Ortley, S. Dak. (57256) 298/P3
Ortoire (riv.), Trinidad Tobago 161/B11
Ortón (riv.), Bol. 136/B2
Ortona, Italy 34/E3
Ortonville, Mich. (48462) 250/F6
Ortonville, Minn. (56278) 254/B5
Oruro, Bol., 120/D4
Oruro (dept.), Bol. 136/A6
Oruro, Bol. 136/B5
Orvieto, Italy 34/D3
Orville, Ky. (40057) 237/M4
Orviston, Pa. (16864) 294/G3
Orwell, N.Y. (13426) 276/J3
Orwell, Ohio (44076) 284/J2
Orwell△, Vt. (05760) 268/A4
Orwell, Vt. (05760) 268/A4
Orwigsburg, Pa. (17961) 294/K4
Oryakhovo, Bulg. 45/F4
Osa, U.S.S.R. 52/J3
Osage (riv.), 188/H3
Osage, Ark. (72664) 203/D1
Osage, Iowa (50461) 229/H2
Osage (co.), Kans. 232/G3
Osage, Minn. (56570) 254/C4
Osage (co.), Mo. 261/J6
Osage (riv.), Mo. 261/E6
Osage, Okla. (74054) 288/O2
Osage, Sask. 181/H6
Osage, W. Va. (26543) 313/F3
Osage, Wyo. (82723) 319/H2
Osage Beach, Mo. (65065) 261/G6
Osage City, Kans. (66523) 232/G3
Osage Ind. Res., Okla. 288/O1
Osaka, Japan, 3/R4
Osaka, Japan, 54/S6
Osaka (pref.), Japan 81/J8
Osaka, Japan 81/J8
Osaka (bay), Japan 81/H8
Osakis, Minn. (56360) 254/C5
Osawatomie, Kans. (66064) 232/H3
Osborn, Miss. (†39759) 256/G3
Osborn, Mo. (64474) 261/D3
Osborn, S.C. (29426) 296/G6
Osborne (co.), Kans. 232/D2
Osborne, Kans. (67473) 232/D2
Osborne, Man. 179/E5
Osborne, Pa. (†15143) 294/B4
Osbornsville, N.J. (08723) 273/E3
Osburn, Idaho (83849) 220/B2
Oscar, Fr. Gui. 131/E4
Oscar, La. (70762) 238/H5
Oscar, Okla. (73561) 288/L7
Oscar Lake, Sask. 181/D3
Oscarville, Alaska (†99559) 196/F2
Osceola, Ark. (72370) 203/K2
Osceola (co.), Fla. 212/E3
Osceola, Ind. (46561) 227/E1
Osceola (co.), Iowa 229/B2
Osceola, Iowa (50213) 229/F6
Osceola (co.), Mich. 250/D5
Osceola, Mo. (64776) 261/E6
Osceola (mt.), N.H. 268/E3
Osceola, N.Y. (†13316) 276/J3
Osceola, Nebr. (68651) 264/G3
Osceola, Pa. (16942) 294/H2
Osceola, S. Dak. (†57353) 298/O5
Osceola, Wis. (54020) 317/A5
Osceola Mills, Pa. (16666) 294/F4
Oschatz, E. Ger. 22/E3
Oschersleben, E. Ger. 22/D2
Oscoda (co.), Mich. 250/E4
Oscoda-Au Sable, Mich. (48750) 250/F4
Oscuro, N. Mex. (†88301) 274/C5
ösel (Saaremaa) (isl.), U.S.S.R. 52/B3
Osel (Saaremaa) (isl.), U.S.S.R., 7/G3
Osgood, Ind. (47037) 227/G6
Osgood, Mo. (†63556) 261/F2
Osgood, Ohio (45351) 284/A5
Osgoode, Ont. 177/J2
Osh, U.S.S.R. 48/H5
Osha (peak), N. Mex. 274/C4
Oshakati, S.W. Afr. 118/B3
Oshawa, Ont. 177/F4
Oshikango, S.W. Afr. 118/A3
Oshima (isl.), Japan 81/J6
Oshkosh, Nebr. (69154) 264/B3
Oshkosh, Wis., 188/J2
Oshkosh, Wis. (54901) 317/J8
Oshogbo, Nigeria 106/F7
Oshoto, Wyo. (82724) 319/G1
Oshwe, Dem. Rep. of the Congo. 115/C4
Osierfield, Ga. (†31798) 216/F7
Osijek, Yugo. 45/D3
Osimo, Italy 34/D3
Osipenko (Berdyansk), U.S.S.R. 52/E5
Osipovichi, U.S.S.R. 52/C4
Oskaloosa, Iowa, 188/H2
Oskaloosa, Iowa (52577) 229/H6
Oskaloosa, Kans. (66066) 232/G2
Oskaloosa, Mo. (†66711) 261/D7
Oskarshamn, Sweden 18/K8
Oskelaneo, Que. 174/C3
Oslavany, Czech. 41/D2
Osler, Sask. 181/E3
Oslo, Minn. (56744) 254/A2
Oslo (city county), Norway 18/D3
Oslo (cap.), Norway 18/D3
Oslo (cap.), Norway, 3/K2
Oslo (cap.), Norway, 7/E2
Oslo (fjord), Norway 18/D4
Osmanabad, India 68/D5
Osmancik, Turkey 63/F2
Osmaniye, Turkey 63/G4
Osmond, Nebr. (68765) 264/G2
Osnabrock, N. Dak. (58269) 283/O2
Osnabrück, W. Ger. 22/C2
Oso, Wash. (98223) 310/D2
Osogna, Switz. 39/H4
Osorno (prov.), Chile 138/D3
Osorno, Chile 138/D3
Osorno, Spain 33/D1
Osoyoos, Br. Col. 184/H5
Osoyoos (lake), Wash. 310/F1
Ospino, Ven. 124/D3
Osprey (reef), Aust. 88/H2
Osprey, Fla. (33559) 212/D4
Oss, Neth. 27/H5
óssa (mt.), Greece 45/F6
Ossa, Serra da (mts.), Port. 33/C3
Ossabaw (isl.), Ga. 216/K7
Ossabaw (sound), Ga. 216/K7
Osse (riv.), Nigeria 106/F7
Osseo, Mich. (49266) 250/E7
Osseo, Minn. (55369) 254/G5
Osseo, Wis. (54758) 317/D6
Ossian, Ind. (46777) 227/G3
Ossian, Iowa (52161) 229/K2
Ossineke, Mich. (49766) 250/F4
Ossining, N.Y. (10562) 276/N8
Ossipee△, N.H. (03864) 268/E4
Ossipee, N.H. (03864) 268/E4
Ossipee (lake), N.H. 268/E4
Ossipee (mts.), N.H. 268/E4
Ossipee (riv.), N.H. 268/F4
Ossokmanuan (lake), Newf. 166/B3
Ostashkov, U.S.S.R. 52/D3
Oste (riv.), W. Ger. 22/C2
Osteen, Fla. (32764) 212/E3
Ostend, Belg. 27/B6
Ostenfeld, Man. 179/F5
Osterburg, Pa. (16667) 294/E5
österdalälven (riv.), Sweden 18/H6
Osterdock, Iowa (†52035) 229/L3
östergötland (co.), Sweden 18/J7
Osterholz-Scharmbeck, W. Ger. 22/C2
Osterode, W. Ger. 22/D3
östersund, Sweden 18/J5
östersund, Sweden, 7/F2
Osterville, Mass. (02655) 249/N6.
øster Vraa, Den. 21/D3
Osterwick, Man. 179/D5
østfold (co.), Norway 18/D4
östhammar, Sweden 18/L6
Ostia Antica, Italy 34/F7
Ostrander, Minn. (55961) 254/F7
Ostrander, Ohio (43061) 284/D5
Ostrava, Czech., 7/F4
Ostrava, Czech. 41/E2
Ostróda, Poland 47/D2
Ostrogozhsk, U.S.S.R. 48/D4
Ostrogozhsk, U.S.S.R. 52/E4
Ostrołęka, Poland 47/E2
Ostrov, Czech. 41/B1
Ostrov, U.S.S.R. 52/C3
Ostrowiec Świętokrzyski, Poland 47/E3
Ostrów Mazowiecka, Poland 47/E2
Ostrów Wielkopolski, Poland 47/C3
Ostrzeszów, Poland 47/C3
Ostuni, Italy 34/F4
O'Sullivan (dam), Wash. 310/F4
Osŭm (riv.), Bulg. 45/G4
Osumi (isls.), Japan 81/E8
Osumi (pen.), Japan 81/E8
Osumi (str.), Japan 81/E8
Osuna, Spain 33/D4
Oswayo, Pa. (16915) 294/G2
Oswegatchie, N.Y. (13670) 276/K2
Oswegatchie (riv.), N.Y. 276/K2
Oswego, Ill. (60543) 222/E2
Oswego, Ind. (†46538) 227/F2
Oswego, Kans. (67356) 232/G4
Oswego, Mont. (59251) 262/L2
Oswego (riv.), N.J. 273/E4
Oswego, N.Y., 188/L2
Oswego (co.), N.Y. 276/H4
Oswego, N.Y. (13126) 276/G4
Oswego (riv.), N.Y. 276/H4
Oswego, S.C. (29121) 296/G3
Oswestry, 10/E4
Oswestry, Eng. 13/E5
Oświęcim, Poland 47/D3
Osyka, Miss. (39657) 256/D8
Ota, Japan 81/J5
Otago (harb.), N.Z. 101/C6
Otago (pen.), N.Z. 101/C6
Otago (Otago Part) (prov. dist.), N.Z. 101/B6
Otago (Southland) (land dist.), N.Z. 101/A6
Otahuhu, N.Z. 101/C1
Otaki, N.Z. 101/E4
Otakine (mt.), Japan 81/K5
Otaru, Japan, 54/S5
Otaru, Japan 81/K2
Otautau, N.Z. 101/B7
Otava (riv.), Czech. 41/B2
Otavalo, Ec. 128/C2
Otavi, S.W. Afr. 118/B3
Otawara, Japan 81/K5
Otay-Castle Park‡, Calif. (†92010) 204/H11
O.T. Downs, No. Terr. 93/D4
Oteen, N.C. (28805) 281/E3
Otego, N.Y. (13825) 276/K6
Otematata, N.Z. 101/B6
Otero (co.), Colo. 208/M7
Otero (co.), N. Mex. 274/D6
Othello, Wash. (99344) 310/F4
Otho, Iowa (50569) 229/E4
Oti (riv.), Ghana 106/E7
Oti (riv.), Togo 106/E7
Oti (riv.), Upp. Volta 106/E7
Otira, N.Z. 101/C5
Otis, Colo. (80743) 208/O2
Otis, Ind. (46367) 227/D1
Otis, Kans. (67565) 232/C3
Otis, La. (71466) 238/E4
Otis△, Mass. (01253) 249/B4
Otis (res.), Mass. 249/B4
Otis, N. Br. 170/C3
Otis, N. Mex. (†88220) 274/E6
Otis, Oreg. (97368) 291/D2
Otis A.F.B., Mass. 249/M6
Otisco, Ind. (47163) 227/F7
Otisco, Minn. (56077) 254/E7
Otisco (lake), N.Y. 276/H5
Otisfield△, Maine (†04270) 242/B7
Otisfield, Maine (†04270) 242/B7
Otis Orchards, Wash. (99027) 310/H3
Otisville, Mich. (48463) 250/F5
Otisville, N.Y. (10963) 276/L8
Otjiwarongo, S.W. Afr. 118/B4
Otley, Eng. 13/F4
Otley, Iowa (50214) 229/G6
Oto, Iowa (51044) 229/B4
Otoe (co.), Nebr. 264/H4
Otoe, Nebr. (68417) 264/H4
Otorohanga, N.Z. 101/E3
Otoskwin (riv.), Ont. 175/B2
Otosquen, Sask. 181/J2
Otrabanda, Neth. Ant. 161/F9
Otradnyy, U.S.S.R. 52/H4
Otranto (str.), Alb. 45/D5
Otranto, Iowa (†50472) 229/H2
Otranto, Italy 34/G4
Otranto (str.), Italy 34/G5
Otrokovice-Kvítkovice, Czech. 41/D2
Otsego (co.), Mich. 250/E3
Otsego, Mich. (49078) 250/D6
Otsego (lake), Mich. 250/E4
Otsego (co.), N.Y. 276/K5
Otsego (lake), N.Y. 276/L5
Otsego, Ohio (†43762) 284/G5
Otsego Lake, Mich. (†49735) 250/E4
Otselic (riv.), N.Y. 276/J5
Otsu, Japan 81/J7
Otta, Norway 18/F6
Ottauquechee (riv.), Vt. 268/B4
Ottawa (riv.), 163/J6
Ottawa (isls.), 163/H4
Ottawa (cap.), Canada, 163/J6
Ottawa (cap.), Canada, 3/F3
Ottawa (cap.), Canada, 146/L5
Ottawa, Ont. (cap.), Canada 177/J2
Ottawa (riv.), Canada, 146/L5
Ottawa (riv.), Que. 172/B4
Ottawa (riv.), Que. 174/B3
Ottawa (riv.), Ont. 175/E3
Ottawa (riv.), Ont. 177/H2
Ottawa, Ill. (61350) 222/E2
Ottawa (co.), Kans. 232/E2
Ottawa, Kans. (66067) 232/G3
Ottawa (co.), Mich. 250/C6
Ottawa, Minn. (†56058) 254/E6
Ottawa (isls.), N.W.T., 146/K4
Ottawa (isls.), N.W.T. 187/K4
Ottawa (co.), Ohio 284/D2
Ottawa, Ohio (45875) 284/B3
Ottawa (co.), Okla. 288/S1
Ottawa Beach, Mich. (†49423) 250/C6
Ottawa Hills, Ohio (†43601) 284/C2
Ottawa Lake, Mich. (49267) 250/F7
Ottenby, Sweden 18/K8
Otter (isl.), Alaska 196/D3
Otter (lake), Alta. 182/B1
Otter (riv.), Norway 18/E7
Otter, Mont. (59062) 262/K5
Otter (creek), Utah 304/C5
Otter (creek), Utah 304/C2
Otter (creek), Vt. 268/A3
Otterbein, Ind. (47970) 227/C4
Otterburn, Eng. 13/E2
Otterburne, Man. 179/E5
Otter Creek, Fla. (32683) 212/D2
Otter Creek, Maine (04665) 242/G7
Otter Creek (res.), Utah 304/C5
Otter Lake, Ont. 177/E2
Otter Lake, Mich. (48464) 250/F5
Otterlo, Neth. 27/H4
Otterøy (isl.), Norway 18/E5
Otter River, Mass. (†01440) 249/F2
Otter Rock, Oreg. (97369) 291/C3
Otter Tail (co.), Minn. 254/C4
Ottertail, Minn. (56571) 254/C4
Otter Tail (lake), Minn. 254/C4
Otter Tail (riv.), Minn. 254/B4
Otterup, Den. 21/D7
Otterville, Ont. 177/D5
Otterville, Ill. (†62052) 222/C4
Otterville, Iowa (†50644) 229/K3
Otterville, Mo. (65348) 261/G5
Ottery Saint Mary, 10/E5
Ottery Saint Mary, Eng. 13/D7
Otthon, Sask. 181/J4
Ottleys (creek), N.S.W. 97/F1
Otto, Ind. (†47162) 227/G7
Otto, Mo. (63052) 261/M6
Otto, N.C. (28763) 281/C4
Otto (fjord), N.W.T. 187/K1
Otto, N.Y. (14766) 276/C6
Otto, Wyo. (82434) 319/D1
Ottosen, Iowa (50570) 229/E3
Ottoville, Ohio (45876) 284/B4
Ottsville, Pa. (18942) 294/M5
Ottumwa, Iowa, 188/H2
Ottumwa, Iowa (52501) 229/J6
Ottumwa, S. Dak. (57565) 298/G5
Otumba de Gómez Farías, Mex. 150/M1
Otuquis (riv.), Bol. 136/F6
Otuzco, Peru 128/C6
Otway (cape), Aust. 88/G7
Otway (bay), Chile 138/D10
Otway (sound), Chile 138/E10
Otway, Ohio (45657) 284/D8
Otway (cape), Vic. 97/B6
Otwell, Ark. (†72401) 203/J2
Otwell, Ind. (47564) 227/C8
Otwock, Poland 47/E2
ötztal Alps (range), Austria 41/A3
ötztal Alps (range), Italy 34/C1
Ouachita (riv.), 188/H4
Ouachita (co.), Ark. 203/E6
Ouachita, Ark. (†71763) 203/E6
Ouachita (lake), Ark. 203/C4
Ouachita (mts.), Ark. 203/C4
Ouachita (riv.), Ark. 203/E7
Ouachita (par.), La. 238/F2
Ouachita (riv.), La. 238/F1
Ouachita (mts.), Okla. 288/R5
Ouadane, Mauritania 106/B4
Ouadda, Centr. Afr. Rep. 115/D2
Ouagadougou (cap.), Upp. Volta 102/B3
Ouagadougou (cap.), Upp. Volta 106/D6
Ouahigouya, 102/B3
Ouahigouya, Upp. Volta 106/D6
Oualata, 102/B3
Oualata, Mauritania 106/C5
Ouallene, Alg. 106/E4
Ouanaminthe, Haiti 158/C5
Ouanary, Fr. Gui. 131/F3
Ouanda-Djalé, Centr. Afr. Rep. 115/D2
Ouango, Centr. Afr. Rep. 115/D3
Ouaqui, Fr. Gui. 131/D4
Ouarane (reg.), Mauritania 106/B4
Ouareau (lake), Que. 172/D3
Ouareau (riv.), Que. 172/D3
Ouargla, Alg. 106/F2
Ouargla, 102/C1
Ouarzazate, Mor. 106/C2
Ouchy, Switz. 39/C4
Oud-Beijerland, Neth. 27/E5
Ouddorp, Neth. 27/D5
Oudenaarde, Belg. 27/D7
Oudenbosch, Neth. 27/E5
Oude-Pekela, Neth. 27/K2
Oudeschild, Neth. 27/F2
Oude-Tonge, Neth. 27/E5
Oudewater, Neth. 27/F4
Oudtshoorn, 102/E8
Oudtshoorn, S. Africa 118/C6
Oud-Turnhout, Belg. 27/F6
Oued-Zem, Mor. 106/C2
Ouelle (riv.), Que. 172/H2
Ouellette, Maine (†04743) 242/G1
Ouémé (riv.), Dahomey 106/E7
Ouessant (isl.), France 28/A3
Ouesso, Rep. of Congo 115/C3
Ouesso, 102/D4
Ouest (dept.), Haiti 158/C6
Ouest (pt.), Haiti 158/B4
Ouest (pt.), Haiti 158/B6
Ouezzane, Mor. 106/C2
Oughter (lake), Ire. 17/G3
Oughterard, Ire. 17/C5
Ougrée, Belg. 27/H7
Ouiatchouan, Que. 172/E1
Ouidah, Dahomey 106/E7
Oujaf, Mauritania 106/C5
Oujda, 102/B1
Oujda, Mor. 106/D2
Oujeft, Mauritania 106/B4
Oulainen, Fin. 18/O4
Ouled-Djellal, Alg. 106/F2
Oullins, France 28/F5
Oulu (prov.), Fin. 18/P4
Oulu, Fin. 18/O4
Oulu (lake), Fin. 18/P4
Oulu (riv.), Fin. 18/O4
Oulu, Fin., 7/G2
Oulu (lake), Fin., 7/G2
Oum Chalouba, Chad 111/D4
Oum el Asel (well), Mali 106/D4
Oum Hadjer, Chad 111/D5
Ounas (riv.), Fin. 18/O3
Oundle, Eng. 13/G5
Ou Neua, Laos 72/D2
Oungre, Sask. 181/H6
Ounianga-Kébir, Chad 111/D4
Our (riv.), Lux. 27/J9
Our (riv.), W. Ger. 22/B3
Ouray (co.), Colo. 208/D6
Ouray, Colo. (81427) 208/D6
Ouray (peak), Colo. 208/G6
Ouray, Utah (84059) 304/E3
Ourinhos, Braz. 132/D8
Ourinhos, Braz. 135/B3
Ourique, Port. 33/B4
Ouro Fino, Braz. 132/E8
Ouro Fino, Braz. 135/C3
Ouro Prêto, Braz., 120/F5
Ouro Prêto, Braz. 132/F8
Ouro Prêto, Braz. 135/E2
Ourthe (riv.), Belg. 27/H8
Ouse (riv.), Eng. 13/F3
Ouse (riv.), Eng. 13/H5
Ouse (riv.), 10/G4
Ousley, Ga. (†31601) 216/F9
Outagamie (co.), Wis. 317/K7
Outardes (riv.), Que. 174/D2
Outer (isl.), Wis. 317/F1
Outer Harbor, Aust. 88/D7
Outer Harbor, S. Aust. 94/A7
Outer Hebrides (isls.), Scot. 15/A5
Outer Santa Barbara (passg.), Calif. 204/G10
Outing, Minn. (56662) 254/E4
Outjo, 102/D6
Outjo, S.W. Afr. 118/B4
Outlook, Mont. (59252) 262/M2
Outlook, Sask. 181/E4
Outlook, Wash. (98938) 310/E4
Outokumpu, Fin. 18/Q5
Outram, Sask. 181/H6
Outremont, Que. 172/H4
Ouyen, Vic. 97/B4
Ouzinkie, Alaska (99644) 196/H3
Ovacik, Içel, Turkey 63/E4
Ovacik, Tunceli, Turkey 63/H3
Ovalle, Chile, 120/C6
Ovalle, Chile 138/A8
Ovamboland (reg.), S.W. Afr. 118/B3
Ovando, Mont. (59854) 262/C3
Ovar, Port. 33/B2
Ovens (riv.), Vic. 97/D5
Overall, Tenn. (†37130) 237/J9
Overbrook, Kans. (66524) 232/G3
Overbrook, Okla. (73453) 288/M6
Overflakkee (isl.), Neth. 27/E5
Overflow (bay), Man. 179/A1
Overflowing (riv.), Man. 179/A1
Overflowing (riv.), Sask. 181/K2
Overflowing River, Man. 179/A1
Overgaard, Ariz. (85933) 198/E4
Overhills, N.C. (28370) 281/L4
Overijse, Belg. 27/F7
Overijssel (prov.), Neth. 27/J4
Overisel, Mich. (†49423) 250/C6
Overland, Mo. (63114) 261/P3
Overland, Sask. 181/G6
Overland Park, Kans. (66204) 232/H3
Overlea, Md. (21206) 245/N3
Overlook-Page Manor‡, Ohio (45431) 284/B6
Overloon, Neth. 27/H5
Overly, N. Dak. (58360) 283/K2
Overpelt, Belg. 27/G6
Overstreet, Fla. (32453) 212/D6
Overton, Man. 179/D4
Overton, Nebr. (68863) 264/E4
Overton, Nev. (89040) 266/G6
Overton, Pa. (18833) 294/K2
Overton (co.), Tenn. 237/L8
Overton, Texas (75684) 302/K5
övertorneå, Sweden 18/N3
överum, Sweden 18/K7
Ovett, Miss. (39464) 256/F8
Ovid, Colo. (80744) 208/P1
Ovid, Idaho (83260) 220/G7
Ovid, Mich. (48866) 250/E5
Ovid, N.Y. (14521) 276/G5
Oviedo, Dom. Rep. 158/D7
Oviedo, Fla. (32765) 212/E3
Oviedo, Spain, 7/D4
Oviedo (prov.), Spain 33/C1
Oviedo, Spain 33/C1
Ovilla, Texas (†76065) 302/G2
Ovoca (riv.), Ire. 17/J6
øvre-Sirdal, Norway 18/E7
Ovtrup, Den. 21/B6
Owaka, N.Z. 101/B7
Owaneco, Ill. (62555) 222/D4
Owanka, S. Dak. (57767) 298/D5

Panarukan 415

Owasa, Iowa (†50627) 229/G4
Owasco, N.Y. (13130) 276/G5
Owasco (lake), N.Y. 276/G5
Owase, Japan 81/H6
Owassa, Ala. (36468) 194/E8
Owassa (lake), N.J. 273/D1
Owasso, Okla. (74055) 288/P2
Owatonna, Minn. (55060) 254/E6
Owego, N.Y. (13827) 276/H6
Owell (lake), Ire. 17/G4
Owen (chan.), Ont. 177/C2
Owen (sound), Ont. 177/D3
Owen (co.), Ind. 227/D6
Owen (co.), Ky. 237/M3
Owen (mt.), N.Z. 101/D4
Owen, Wis. (54460) 317/F6
Owen (lake), Wis. 317/D3
Owendale, Alta. 182/D5
Owendale, Mich. (48754) 250/F5
Owendo, Gabon 115/A3
Owen Falls (dam), Uganda 115/F3
Owenga, N.Z. 101/E7
Owenkillew (riv.), N. Ire. 17/G2
Owenmore (riv.), Ire. 17/B3
Owenmore (riv.), Ire. 17/D3
Owens (lake), Calif., 188/C3
Owens (lake), Calif. 204/H7
Owens (peak), Calif. 204/H8
Owens (riv.), Calif. 204/G6
Owensboro, Ky., 188/J3
Owensboro, Ky. (42301) 237/G5
Owensburg, Ind. (47453) 227/D7
Owens Cross Roads, Ala. (35763) 194/E1
Owen Sound, 163/H7
Owen Sound, Ont. 177/D3
Owensville, Ark. (†72087) 203/E4
Owensville, Ind. (47565) 227/B8
Owensville, Mo. (65066) 261/K6
Owensville, Ohio (45160) 284/B7
Owenton, Ky. (40359) 237/M4
Owenton, Va. (†23077) 307/O5
Owey (isl.), Ire. 17/D1
Owia (bay), St. Vincent 161/A8
Owikeno (lake), Br. Col. 184/D4
Owings, Md. (20836) 245/M6
Owings, S.C. (29668) 296/C2
Owings Mills, Md. (21117) 245/L3
Owingsville, Ky. (40360) 237/O4
Owl (creek), Colo. 208/K1
Owl (riv.), Man. 179/K2
Owl (creek), S. Dak. 298/B4
Owl, North Fork (creek), Wyo. 319/D2
Owl Creek (mts.), Wyo. 319/D2
Owl River, Alta. 182/E2
Owlseye Lake, Alta. 182/E2
Owls Head▵, Maine (04854) 242/F7
Owo, Nigeria 106/F7
Owosso, Mich. (48867) 250/E5
Owpu, China 77/L1
Owsley (co.), Ky. 237/O6
Owyhee (riv.), 188/C2
Owyhee (co.), Idaho 220/B7
Owyhee (mts.), Idaho 220/B6
Owyhee (riv.), Idaho 220/B7
Owyhee, Nev. (89832) 266/F1
Owyhee (riv.), Nev. 266/E1
Owyhee (dam), Oreg. 291/K4
Owyhee (lake), Oreg. 291/K4
Owyhee (mts.), Oreg. 291/K5
Owyhee (riv.), Oreg. 291/K5
Ox (Slieve Gamph) (mts.), Ire. 17/D3
Oxapampa, Peru 128/E8
Oxarat, Sask. 181/B6
Oxbow (dam), Idaho 220/B5
Oxbow▵, Maine (04764) 242/G3
Oxbow, Oreg. (97840) 291/L2
Oxbow (dam), Oreg. 291/L3
Oxbow, Sask. 181/J6
Oxelösund, Sweden 18/K7
Oxford, 10/F5
Oxford, Ala. (36201) 194/G3
Oxford, Ark. (72565) 203/G1
Oxford▵, Conn. (06483) 210/C3
Oxford, Conn. (06483) 210/C3
Oxford (co.), Ont. 177/D4
Oxford, Eng. 13/F6
Oxford, Fla. (32684) 212/D3
Oxford, Ga. (30267) 216/E3
Oxford, Idaho (†83263) 220/F7
Oxford, Ind. (47971) 227/C3
Oxford, Iowa (52322) 229/K5
Oxford, Kans. (67119) 232/E4
Oxford, La. (71062) 238/C3
Oxford (co.), Maine 242/B7
Oxford▵, Maine (04270) 242/B7
Oxford, Maine (04270) 242/B7
Oxford (lake), Man. 179/J3
Oxford▵, Mass. (01540) 249/G4
Oxford, Mass. (01540) 249/G4
Oxford, Md. (21654) 245/O6
Oxford, Mich. (48051) 250/F6
Oxford, Miss. (38655) 256/E2
Oxford, N.C. (27565) 281/M2
Oxford, N.J. (07863) 273/C2
Oxford, N.S. 169/E3
Oxford, N.Y. (13830) 276/J6
Oxford, N.Z. 101/D5
Oxford, Nebr. (68967) 264/E4
Oxford, Ohio (45056) 284/A6
Oxford, Pa. (19363) 294/K6
Oxford, W. Va. (26414) 313/E4
Oxford, Wis. (53952) 317/H8
Oxford House, Man. 179/J3
Oxford Junction, Iowa (52323) 229/M4
Oxford Junction, N.S. 169/E3
Oxford Mills, Ont. 177/J3
Oxford Mills, Iowa (†52323) 229/L5
Oxfordshire (co.), Eng. 13/F6
Oxkutzcab, Mex. 150/P7
Oxley, N.S.W. 97/C4
Oxley (creek), Queens. 95/D3
Oxly, Mo. (63955) 261/L9
Oxnard, Calif. (93030) 204/F9
Oxnard A.F.B., Calif. 204/F9
Oxon Hill, Md. (20021) 245/F6
Oxon Run (riv.), Md. 245/F5
Oxtongue Lake, Ont. 177/E2
Oyabe, Japan 81/H5
Oyahue (vol.), Chile 138/C3
Oyama, Br. Col. 184/H5
Oyama, Japan 81/J5
Oyapock (riv.), 120/E2
Oyapock (riv.), Braz. 132/C2
Oyapock (riv.), Fr. Gui. 131/E4
Oyem, Gabon 115/B3
Oyem, 102/D4
Oyen, Alta. 182/E4
Oyens, Iowa (51045) 229/A3
Oykel Bridge, Scot. 15/G4
Oykell (riv.), Scot. 15/G4
Oylen, Minn. (†56481) 254/D4
Oymyakon, U.S.S.R. 48/O3
Oymyakon, U.S.S.R., 4/C2
Oyo, 102/C4
Oyo, Nigeria 106/E7
Oyón, Peru 128/D8
Oyonnax, France 28/F4
Oyster (bay), Aust. 88/H8
Oyster (bay), Tasmania 99/E4
Oyster, Va. (23419) 307/S6
Oyster Bay, N.Y. (11771) 276/S6
Oyster Bay Cove‡, N.Y. (†11771) 276/R7
Oyster River (pt.), Conn. 210/D4
Oysterville, Wash. (98641) 310/A4
Ozada, Alta. 182/C4
özalp, Turkey 63/K3
Ozamiz, Phil. 82/D6
Ozan, Ark. (71855) 203/C6
Ozark (mts.), 188/H3
Ozark, Ala. (36360) 194/G8
Ozark, Ark. (72949) 203/C3
Ozark (plat.), Ark. 203/C1
Ozark, Ill. (62972) 222/E6
Ozark (co.), Mo. 261/H9
Ozark, Mo. (65721) 261/F8
Ozark (plat.), Mo. 261/F9
Ozarks (lake), Mo. 261/G6
Ozaukee (co.), Wis. 317/L9
Ozawkie, Kans. (66070) 232/G2
özd, Hung. 41/F2
Ozerna, Man. 179/B4
Ozernoy (cape), U.S.S.R. 48/R4
Ozette, Wash. (†98326) 310/A2
Ozette (lake), Wash. 310/A2
Ozette Ind. Res., Wash. 310/A2
Ozieri, Italy 34/B4
Ozona, Fla. (33560) 212/D3
Ozona, Texas (76943) 302/C7
Ozone, Ark. (72854) 203/D2
Ozone, Tenn. (37842) 237/M9
Ozorków, Poland 47/D2
Ozu, Japan 81/F7
Ozuluama, Mex. 150/L6
Ozumba de Alzate, Mex. 150/M1

P

Pa-an, Burma 72/C3
Paarden (bay), Neth. Ant. 161/D10
Paarl, 102/D8
Paarl, S. Africa 118/F6
Paauhau, Hawaii (96775) 218/H4
Paauilo, Hawaii (96776) 218/H4
Paavola, Fin. 18/O4
Pabbay (isl.), Scot. 15/A6
Pabbay (isl.), Scot. 15/B4
Pabianice, Poland 47/D3
Pablo, Mont. (59855) 262/B3
Pabna, Pak. 68/F4
Pabos, Que. 172/D2
Pabos Mills, Que. 172/D2
Pabrade, U.S.S.R. 53/C3
Pacajá Grande (riv.), Braz. 132/D4
Pacaraima (mts.), 120/D2
Pacaraima (mts.), Braz. 132/H8
Pacaraima, Sierra (mts.), Ven. 124/G5
Pacasmayo, Peru, 120/B3
Pacasmayo, Peru 128/C6
Pace, Fla. (32570) 212/B6
Pace, Miss. (38764) 256/C3
Pachaug, Conn. (†06351) 210/H2
Pachaug (pond), Conn. 210/H2
Pachaug (riv.), Conn. 210/H2
Pachen, China 77/D5
Pachino, Italy 34/E6
Pachitea (riv.), Peru 128/E7
Pachiza, Peru 128/D6
Pachmarhi, India 68/D4
Pacho, Col. 126/C5
Pachu (Maralbashi), China 77/A4
Pachuca de Soto, Mex. 150/K6
Pachung, China 77/G5
Pachuta, Miss. (39347) 256/G6
Pacific, Br. Col. 184/C3
Pacific, Mo. (63069) 261/N4
Pacific (co.), Wash. 310/B4
Pacific, Wash. (98047) 310/C3
Pacifica, Calif. (94044) 204/H2
Pacific Beach, Calif. (92109) 204/H11
Pacific Beach, Wash. (98571) 310/A3
Pacific City, Oreg. (97135) 291/C2
Pacific Grove, Calif. (93950) 204/C7
Pacific Heights, Hawaii (†96801) 218/C4
Pacific Islands, Terr. of the, 87/F5
Pacific Islands, Territory of the, 3/S5
Pacific Junction, Iowa (51561) 229/B6
PACIFIC OCEAN, 87
Pacific Palisades, Hawaii (†96782) 218/E2
Pack (riv.), Idaho 220/B1
Pack (creek), Utah 304/E5
Packanack Lake, N.J. (07470) 273/B1
Packertown, Ind. (†46510) 227/F2
Packerville, Conn. (†06331) 210/H2
Packs Harbour, Newf. 166/C3
Packsville, W. Va. (25151) 313/C7
Packwaukee, Wis. (53953) 317/G8
Packwood, Iowa (52580) 229/J6
Packwood, Wash. (98361) 310/D4
Paco, Phil. 82/C2
Pacoa, Col. 126/E7
Paço de Arcos, Port. 33/A1
Pacolet, S.C. (29372) 296/D2
Pacolet (riv.), S.C. 296/D1
Pacolet Mills, S.C. (29373) 296/D2
Pacolet Park‡, S.C. (†29372) 296/D2
Pacov, Czech. 41/C2
Pacsa, Hung. 41/D3
Pacsan (mt.), Phil. 82/C2
Pactolus, N.C. (27858) 281/P3
Padada, Phil. 82/E7
Padang, Indon., 54/O10
Padang, Indon. 85/B6
Padangpandjang, Indon. 85/B6
Padangsidimpuan, Indon. 85/B5
Padany, U.S.S.R. 52/D2
Padborg, Den. 21/C8
Padcaya, Bol. 136/C7
Paddle Prairie, Alta. 182/A5
Paddock Lake, Wis. (†53168) 317/K10
Paddockwood, Sask. 181/F2
Paden, Miss. (38861) 256/H1
Paden, Okla. (74860) 288/N3
Paden City, W. Va. (26159) 313/D3
Paderborn, W. Ger. 22/C3
Padgett, S.C. (†29481) 296/F5
Padilla, Bol. 136/C6
Padilla, Mex. 150/K5
Padilla (creek), N. Mex. 274/D5
Padilla (bay), Wash. 310/C2
Padlei, 163/G3
Padlei, N.W.T. 187/J3
Padloping (isl.), 163/K2
Padloping Island, N.W.T. 187/M3
Padoue, Que. 172/A1
Padre (isl.), Texas, 188/G5
Padre (isl.), Texas 302/G10
Padre Island Nat'l Seashore, Texas 302/G11
Padre Las Casas, Dom. Rep. 158/D6
Padrón, Spain 33/B1
Padroni, Colo. (80745) 208/N1
Padstow, 10/D5
Padstow, Eng. 13/B7
Padua, Italy, 7/F4
Padua (prov.), Italy 34/C2
Padua, Italy 34/C2
Padua, Minn. (†56378) 254/C5
Paducah, Ky., 188/J3
Paducah, Ky. (42001) 237/D6
Paducah, Texas (79248) 302/D4
Padul, Spain 33/E4
Paekakariki, N.Z. 101/E4
Paekam, N. Korea 81/D3
Paektu (mt.), N. Korea 81/C3
Paeroa, N.Z. 101/E2
Páez, Col. 126/C6
Pafúri, Moz. 118/E4
Pag, Yugo. 45/B3
Pag (isl.), Yugo. 45/B3
Pagadian, Phil. 82/D7
Pagan, Burma 72/B2
Pagan (isl.), Pac. Is., 87/E4
Page, Ariz. (86040) 198/D2
Page (co.), Iowa 229/C7
Page, Minn. (†56353) 254/E5
Page, N. Dak. (58064) 283/P5
Page, Nebr. (68766) 264/F2
Page, Okla. (74950) 288/S5
Page (co.), Va. 307/M3
Page, W. Va. (25152) 313/D6
Page City, Kans. (67750) 232/A2
Pagedale, Mo. (†63101) 261/P3
Pageland, S.C. (29728) 296/G2
Pagoda (peak), Colo. 208/E2
Pago Pago (cap.), Amer. Samoa, 87/J7
Pagosa Junction, Colo. (†81147) 208/E8
Pagosa Springs, Colo. (81147) 208/E8
Pagoua (bay), Dominica 161/F6
Paguate, N. Mex. (87040) 274/B3
Pagwa River, Ont. 175/D3
Pagwa River, Ont. 177/J5
Pahala, Hawaii, 188/G6
Pahala, Hawaii (96777) 218/H6
Pahang (state), Malaysia 72/D7
Pahang (riv.), Malaysia 72/D7
Pahaska, Wyo. (82414) 319/C1
Pahiatua, N.Z. 101/F4
Pahlevi, Iran 54/H6
Pahlevi, Iran 59/E2
Pahlevi, Iran 66/F2
Pahoa, Hawaii (96778) 218/J5
Pahokee, Fla. (33476) 212/F5
Pahranagat (range), Nev. 266/F5
Pahrock (range), Nev. 266/F5
Pah-rum (peak), Nev. 266/B2
Pahrump, Nev. (89041) 266/E6
Pahrump (valley), Nev. 266/F6
Pahsimeroi (riv.), Idaho 220/E5
Pahute (mesa), Nev. 266/E5
Pahute (peak), Nev. 266/B1
Paia, Hawaii (96779) 218/J2
Paicheng, Kirin, China 77/K2
Paicheng (Bai), Sinkiang-Uigur, China 77/B3
Paicines, Calif. (95043) 204/D7
Paide, U.S.S.R. 53/C1
Paige, Texas (78659) 302/G7
Paignton, 10/E5
Paihia, N.Z. 101/D1
Paihuano, Chile 138/B8
Paiján, Peru 128/C6
Päijänne (lake), Fin. 18/O6
Pailin, Cambodia 72/D4
Pailingmiao, China, 54/P5
Pailingmiao, China 77/H3
Paillaco, Chile 138/D3
Pailolo (chan.), Hawaii 218/H1
Paimboeuf, France 28/C4
Paimpol, France 28/B3
Painan, Indon. 85/C6
Paincourt, Ont. 177/B5
Paincourtville, La. (70391) 238/K3
Paine, Chile 138/G4
Paine, Cerro (mt.), Chile 138/D9
Painesdale, Mich. (49955) 250/G1
Painesville, Ohio (44077) 284/H2
Painswick, Ont. 177/E3
Paint (lake), Man. 179/J2
Paint (riv.), Mich. 250/A2
Paint (creek), Ohio 284/D7
Paint, Pa. (†15963) 294/E5
Paint Bank, Va. (24131) 307/H5
Paint Branch (riv.), Md. 245/F4
Painted (des.), Ariz. 198/D2
Painted Desert Section (Petrified Forest Nat'l Park), Ariz. 198/F3
Painted Post, N.Y. (14870) 276/F6
Painted Rock (dam), Ariz. 198/C5
Painter, Ala. (†35962) 194/F2
Painter (mt.), Aust. 88/F6
Painter, Va. (23420) 307/S5
Painter Ridge (hills), Conn. 210/B2
Painters Hill, Fla. (†32036) 212/B2
Paintersville, Ohio (†45335) 284/C6
Paint Lick, Ky. (40461) 237/N5
Paint Lick (riv.), Ky. 237/M5
Paint Rock, Ala. (35764) 194/F1
Paint Rock (riv.), Ala. 194/F1
Paint Rock, Texas (76866) 302/E6
Paintsville, Ky. (41240) 237/R5
Paipa, Col. 126/D5
Paipote, Chile 138/B6
Paipote, Quebrada de (riv.), Chile 138/B6
Paisley, Ont. 177/C3
Paisley, 10/A1
Paisley, Oreg. (97636) 291/G5
Paisley, Scot. 15/C2
Paisley Brook, Sask. 181/F6
Paita, Peru, 120/B3
Paita, Peru 128/B5
Paita (bay), Peru 128/B5
Paiute Ind. Res., Calif. 204/G6
Paiute Ind. Res., Utah 304/A5
Paiyin, China 77/F4
Paiyü, China 77/E5
Pajakumbuh, Indon. 85/C6
Pajala, Sweden 18/N3
Paján, Ec. 128/B3
Pajarito (creek), N. Mex. 274/A2
Pajaro, Calif. (†95076) 204/D7
Pájaros (isls.), Chile 138/A7
Pakan, Alta. 182/D2
Pakanbaru, Indon. 85/C5
Pakaraima (mts.), Guyana 131/A3
Pakawau, N.Z. 101/D4
Pak Beng, Laos 72/D3
Pakchan (riv.), Burma 72/C5
Pakchan (riv.), Thai. 72/C5
Pakch'ŏn, N. Korea 81/B4
Pakenham, Ont. 177/H2
Pak Hin Boun, Laos 72/E3
Pakhoi, China 77/G7
Pakistan, 3/NP4
Pakistan, 54/L6
Pakistan, 54/N7
PAKISTAN, 59/J4
PAKISTAN, 68
Paklay, Laos 72/D3
Pakokku, Burma 72/B2
Pakowki (lake), Alta. 182/E5
Paks, Hung. 41/E3
Pak Sane, Laos 72/D3
Pakse, Laos 72/E4
Pakwach, Uganda 115/F3
Pala, Chad 111/B6
Palacios, Texas (77465) 302/H9
Palafrugell, Spain 33/H2
Pala Ind. Res., Calif. 204/H10
Palama, Hawaii (†96801) 218/C4
Palamós, Spain 33/H2
Palana, U.S.S.R. 48/R4
Palanan, Phil. 82/D2
Palanan (bay), Phil. 82/D2
Palanan, Phil. 85/G2
Palanda, Ec. 128/C5
Palanga, U.S.S.R. 53/A3
Palangkaraja, Indon. 85/E6
Palanpur, India 68/C4
Palaoa (pt.), Hawaii 218/G2
Palapag, Phil. 82/E4
Palapye, Botswana 118/D4
Palas de Rey, Spain 33/C1
Palatine, Ill. (60067) 222/E1
Palatine Bridge‡, N.Y. (13428) 276/L5
Palatka, Ark. (†72422) 203/J1
Palatka, Fla. (32077) 212/E2
Palau (isls.), Pac. Is., 87/D5
Palaw, Burma 72/C4
Palawan (prov.), Phil. 82/B6
Palawan (isl.), Phil. 82/B6
Palawan (isl.), Phil. 85/F4
Palawan (isl.), Phil., 3/Q5
Palawan (isl.), Phil., 54/P8
Palaya, Bol. 136/A6
Palayankottai, India 68/D7
Palazzolo Acreide, Italy 34/E6
Palca, Bol. 136/A5
Palco, Kans. (67657) 232/C2
Paldiski, U.S.S.R. 52/B3
Paldiski, U.S.S.R. 53/B1
Palel, India 68/G4
Paleleh, Indon. 85/G5
Palembang, Indon., 54/O10
Palembang, Indon. 85/D6
Palena, Chile 138/E5
Palena (lake), Chile 138/E5
Palena (riv.), Chile 138/D5
Palencia (prov.), Spain 33/D1
Palencia, Spain 33/D1
Palenque (pt.), Dom. Rep. 158/E6
Palenque, Mex. 150/O8
Palenque (ruin), Mex. 150/O8
Palenville, N.Y. (12463) 276/M6
Palermo, Calif. (95968) 204/D4
Palermo, Italy, 7/F5
Palermo (prov.), Italy 34/D5
Palermo, Italy 34/D5
Palermo▵, Maine (04354) 242/E7
Palermo, N. Dak. (58769) 283/F3
Palermo, N.J. (†08226) 273/D5
Palermo, Urug. 145/D4
Palestina, Chile 138/B4
Palestine, Ala. (†36252) 194/H3
Palestine, Ark. (72372) 203/J4
Palestine, Ill. (62451) 222/F4
Palestine, Ind. (†46508) 227/F2
Palestine, Ohio (45352) 284/A5
Palestine, Texas 188/H4
Palestine, Texas (75801) 302/J6
Palestine, W. Va. (26160) 313/D4
Palestrina, Italy 34/F7
Paletwa, Burma 72/B2
Palghat, India 68/D6
Palgrave, Ont. 177/E4
Palha, Mar da (bay), Port. 33/A1
Pali, India 68/C3
Palidoro, Italy 34/F6
Palimé, Togo 106/E7
Paliocabe (Payocabe), Chile 138/F4
Palisade, Colo. (81526) 208/C4
Palisade, Minn. (56469) 254/E4
Palisade, Nebr. (69040) 264/C4
Palisade, Nev. (†89822) 266/E2
Palisades, Idaho (83437) 220/G6
Palisades (res.), Idaho 220/G6
Palisades, N.J. 273/C1
Palisades, Wash. (98845) 310/E3
Palisades (res.), Wyo. 319/A2
Palisades Park, N.J. (07650) 273/C2
Palizada, Mex. 150/O7
Palk (str.), Ceylon 68/D7
Palk (str.), India 68/D7
Pallamallawa, N.S.W. 97/F1
Palling, Br. Col. 184/D3
Palliser (bay), N.Z. 101/C3
Palliser (cape), N.Z. 101/E4
Pall Mall, Tenn. (38577) 237/M7
Palm (beach), Neth. Ant. 161/D10
Palma (bay), Alaska 196/L1
Palma (riv.), Braz., 120/F4
Palma, Moz. 118/G2
Palma, Spain, 7/E5
Palma, Spain 33/H3
Palma (bay), Spain 33/H3
Palma, La (isl.), Spain 33/A4
Palma del Río, Spain 33/D4
Palma di Montechiaro, Italy 34/D6
Palmar de Bravo, Mex. 150/O2
Palmarejo, Ven. 124/C2
Palmares, C. Rica 154/F6
Palmares, Braz. 132/H5
Palmarito, Cuba 158/J4
Palmarito, Apure, Ven. 124/D4
Palmarito, Guárico, Ven. 124/F3
Palmarito, Mérida, Ven. 124/C3
Palmarola (isl.), Italy 34/D4
Palmas, Braz. 132/C9
Palmas (cape), Liberia 106/C8
Palmas (cape), 102/B4
Palmas, Las (prov.), Spain 33/C4
Palmas Altas (pt.), P. Rico 161/C1
Palma Sola‡, Fla. (33505) 212/D4
Palma Soriano, Cuba 158/J4
Palm Bay, Fla. (32901) 212/F3
Palm Beach, Fla., 188/L5
Palm Beach (co.), Fla. 212/F5
Palm Beach, Fla. (33480) 212/G4
Palm Beach Gardens‡, Fla. (†33403) 212/F5
Palm Beach Shores, Fla. (†33404) 212/G5
Palm City, Fla. (33490) 212/F4
Palmdale, Calif. (93550) 204/G9
Palmdale, Fla. (33944) 212/E5
Palmdale‡, Pa. (†17078) 294/J5
Palm Desert, Calif. (92260) 204/J10
Palmeira, Braz. 132/D9
Palmeira, Braz. 135/B4
Palmeira das Missões, Braz. 132/C9
Palmeiras, Braz. 132/F6
Palmeiras de Goiás, Braz. 132/D7
Palmeirinhas (pt.), Angola 115/B5
Palmer, Alaska, 188/D5
Palmer, Alaska (99645) 196/C1
Palmer (arch.), Ant. 5/C15
Palmer, P. Rico 161/F1
Palmer, Ill. (62556) 222/D4
Palmer, Ind. (†46307) 227/C2
Palmer, Iowa (50571) 229/D3
Palmer, Kans. (66962) 232/E2
Palmer▵, Mass. (01069) 249/E4
Palmer, Mass. (01069) 249/E4
Palmer, Mich. (49871) 250/B2
Palmer (head), N.Z. 101/B3
Palmer, Nebr. (68864) 264/F3
Palmer (riv.), Queens. 95/B2
Palmer, Sask. 181/E6
Palmer, Tenn. (37365) 237/K10
Palmer‡, Texas (75152) 302/H5
Palmer, Wash. (98048) 310/D3
Palmer (lake), Wash. 310/F2
Palmer Lake, Colo. (80133) 208/J4
Palmerland (reg.), Ant., 3/F9
Palmer Land (reg.), Ant. 5/B15
Palmer Park‡, Md. (20785) 245/G4
Palmer Rapids, Ont. 177/G2
Palmers, Minn. (†55801) 254/G4
Palmers Crossing, Miss. (†39401) 256/F8
Palmer Station, Ant. 5/C15
Palmerston (atoll), Cook Is., 87/K7
Palmerston, Ont. 177/D4
Palmerston, N.Z. 101/C6
Palmerston North, N. Z., 87/H10
Palmerston North, N.Z. 101/E4
Palmersville, Tenn. (38241) 237/D8
Palmerton, Pa. (18071) 294/L4
Palmerville, Aust. 88/G3
Palmerville, Queens. 95/B3
Palmetto (pt.), St. Chr.-N.-A. 161/C10
Palmetto, Fla. (33561) 212/D4
Palmetto, Ga. (30268) 216/C3
Palmetto, La. (71358) 238/G5
Palm Harbor, Fla. (33563) 212/D3
Palmhurst‡, Texas (†78572) 302/F11
Palmi, Italy 34/E5
Palmiet (riv.), S. Africa 118/F7
Palmilla, Chile 138/F6
Palmillas (pt.), Dom. Rep. 158/F6
Palmillas, Mex. 150/K5
Palmira, Col. 126/B6
Palmira, Cuba 158/E2
Palmitas, Urug. 145/B4
Palmito de la Virgen (isl.), Mex. 150/F5
Palmito del Verde (isl.), Mex. 150/F5
Palm River-Clair Mel, Fla. (33619) 212/C3
Palms, Mich. (48465) 250/G5
Palms, Isle of (isl.), S.C. 296/H6
Palm Shores, Fla. (32935) 212/F3
Palm Springs, Calif., 188/C4
Palm Springs, Calif. (92262) 204/J10
Palm Springs, Fla. (33460) 212/F5
Palmyra (isl.), 3/A5
Palmyra, Ill. (62674) 222/C4
Palmyra, Ind. (47164) 227/E8
Palmyra▵, Maine (04965) 242/E6
Palmyra, Mich. (49268) 250/E7
Palmyra, Mo. (63461) 261/J3
Palmyra, N.C. (27859) 281/P2
Palmyra, N.J. (08065) 273/B3
Palmyra, N.Y. (14522) 276/F4
Palmyra, Nebr. (68418) 264/H4
Palmyra (Tadmor), Syria 59/C3
Palmyra (Tadmor), Syria 63/H5
Palmyra (isl.), Pacific, 87/K5
Palmyra, Pa. (17078) 294/J5
Palmyra, Tenn. (37142) 237/G8
Palmyra, Va. (22963) 307/M5
Palmyra, Wis. (53156) 317/H2
Palmyras (pt.), India 68/F4
Palni, India 68/D6
Palo, Iowa (52324) 229/K4
Palo, Mich. (48870) 250/E5
Palo, Minn. (†55705) 254/F3
Palo, Phil. 82/E5
Palo Alto, Calif., 188/B3
Palo Alto, Calif. (*94301) 204/K3
Palo Alto, Cuba 158/F3
Palo Alto (co.), Iowa 229/D2
Palo Alto (lake), Iowa 229/D2
Palo Alto‡, Pa. (†17901) 294/K4
Palo Duro (creek), Texas 302/B2
Palo Duro (creek), Texas 302/C1
Paloemeu (riv.), Sur. 131/D4
Palolo (stream), Hawaii 218/D4
Paloma, Ill. (62359) 222/B3
Palomar (mt.), Calif. 204/J10
Palomas, Urug. 145/B2
Palombara Sabina, Italy 34/F6
Palometas, Bol. 136/D5
Palompon, Phil. 82/E5
Palo Pinto (co.), Texas 302/F5
Palo Pinto, Texas (76072) 302/F5
Palopo, Indon. 85/F6
Palos (cape), Spain 33/F4
Palo Santo, Arg. 143/E2
Palo Seco, P. Rico 161/D1
Palo Seco, Trinidad Tobago 161/A11
Palos Heights, Ill. (60463) 222/A2
Palos Hills, Ill. (60465) 222/A2
Palos Park, Ill. (60464) 222/A2
Palos Verdes Estates, Calif. (90274) 204/B11
Palos Verdes Peninsula‡, Calif. (90274) 204/B11
Palouse (riv.), Idaho 220/B3
Palouse, Wash. (99161) 310/H4
Palouse (riv.), Wash. 310/G4
Palo Verde, Ariz. (85343) 198/C5
Palo Verde, Calif. (92266) 204/L10
Palpa, Nepal 68/E3
Palpa, Peru 128/E10
Palsagua, Nic. 154/E4
Palsen (riv.), Man. 179/G2
Palu, Indon. 85/F6
Palu, Turkey 63/H3
Paluan, Phil. 82/C4
Pama, Upp. Volta 106/E6
Pamangkat, Indon. 85/D5
Pamar, Col. 126/E8
Pambrun, Sask. 181/D6
Pambula, N.S.W. 97/E5
Pamdenic, N. Br. 170/D3
Pamekasan, Indon. 85/L2
Pameungpeuk, Indon. 85/H2
Pamiers, France 28/D6
Pamir (plat.), 54/L6
Pamlico (sound), N.C., 188/L3
Pamlico (co.), N.C. 281/R4
Pamlico (riv.), N.C. 281/R4
Pamlico (sound), N.C. 281/S4
Pampa, Texas, 188/F3
Pampa, Texas (79065) 302/D2
Pampa Aullagas, Bol. 136/B6
Pampachiri, Peru 128/F10
Pampacolca, Peru 128/F10
Pampa de la Salina (salt dep.), Arg. 143/C3
Pampa de las Tres Hermanas (plain), Arg. 143/C6
Pampa del Chañar, Arg. 143/C2
Pampa del Infierno, Arg. 143/D2
Pampa Grande, Bol. 136/D6
Pampanga (prov.), Phil. 82/C3
Pampas (plain), Arg., 120/D6
Pampas (plain), Arg. 143/D4
Pampas, Peru 128/E9
Pampas (riv.), Peru 128/E9
Pampilhosa da Serra, Port. 33/C3
Pamplico, S.C. (29583) 296/H4
Pamplin, Va. (23958) 307/L6
Pamplona, Col., 120/C2
Pamplona, Col. 126/D4
Pamplona, Spain 33/F1
Pamunkey (riv.), Va. 307/O5
Pamunkey Ind. Res., Va. 307/P5
Pana, Ill. (62557) 222/D4
Panabo, Phil. 82/E7
Panaca, Nev. (89042) 266/G5
Panacachi, Bol. 136/B6
Panacea, Fla. (32346) 212/B1
Panache (lake), Ont. 177/C1
Panagyurishte, Bulg. 45/F4
Panaitan (isl.), Indon. 85/C7
Panama, 3/E5
Panama (canal), 3/E5
Panama, 146/K9
Panamá (gulf), 146/L9
PANAMA, 154/G6
Panama, Ill. (62077) 222/D4
Panama, Iowa (51562) 229/B5
Panama, N.Y. (14767) 276/A6
Panama, Nebr. (68419) 264/H4
Panama, Okla. (74951) 288/S4
Panamá (cap.), Pan., 146/L9
Panamá (gulf), Pan. 154/H7
Panamá (cap.), Pan. 154/H6
Panama City, Fla., 188/K4
Panama City, Fla. (32401) 212/C6
Panama City Beach‡, Fla. (32401) 212/C6
Panamint (range), Calif. 204/H7
Panamint (valley), Calif. 204/H7
Panao, Peru 128/E7
Panaon (isl.), Phil. 82/E5
Panarea (isl.), Italy 34/E5
Panaro (riv.), Italy 34/C2
Panarukan, Indon. 85/K2

416 Panay

Panay (isl.), Phil. 82/D5
Panay (isl.), Phil. 85/G3
Panay (isl.), Phil., 54/R8
Pancake (range), Nev. 266/F4
Pančevo, Yugo. 45/E3
Panchia (lake), Newf. 166/B3
Panchor, Malaysia 72/F5
Panchur, India 68/F2
Panciu, Rum. 45/H3
Pancoastburg, Ohio (†43160) 284/D6
Panda, Moz. 118/E4
Panda, Dem. Rep. of the Congo. 115/E6
Pandale, Texas (76944) 302/C7
Pandan, Antique, Phil. 82/C5
Pandan, Catanduanes, Phil. 82/E3
Pan de Azúcar, Quebrado (riv.), Chile 138/B5
Pan de Azúcar, Urug. 145/D5
Pandeglang, Indon. 85/G1
Pandharpur, India 68/D5
Pandie Pandie, S. Aust. 94/F2
Pando (dept.), Bol. 136/B2
Pando, Cerro (mt.), Pan. 154/F6
Pando, Urug. 145/B6
Pando (riv.), Urug. 145/B6
Pandora, Ohio (45877) 284/C4
Pandrup, Den. 21/C3
Panevėžys, U.S.S.R. 52/B3
Panevėžys, U.S.S.R. 53/C3
Panevėžys, U.S.S.R., 7/G3
Panfilov, U.S.S.R. 48/H5
Panfilov, U.S.S.R., 54/L5
Pangai, Tonga, 87/J7
Pangala, Rep. of Congo 115/B4
Pangani, Tanz. 115/G5
Pangani (riv.), Tanz. 115/G4
Panganiban, Phil. 82/E4
Pangasinan (prov.), Phil. 82/C3
Pangburn, Ark. (72121) 203/G3
Pangi, Dem. Rep. of the Congo. 115/E4
Pangkalanberandan, Indon. 85/B5
Pangkalanbuun, Indon. 85/E6
Pangkalpinang, Indon. 85/D6
Pangkiang, China 77/H3
Pangkor, Pulau (isl.), Malaysia 72/D6
Panglao (isl.), Phil. 82/D6
Pangman, Sask. 181/G6
Pangnirtung, 163/K3
Pangnirtung, Canada, 4/C13
Pangnirtung, N.W.T. 187/M3
Pangong Tso (lake), India 68/D2
Pangong Tso (lake), China 77/A5
Pangsau (pass), Burma 72/B1
Panguipulli, Chile 138/E2
Panguitch, Utah (84759) 304/B6
Panguitch (creek), Utah 304/B6
Pangutaran, Phil. 82/C7
Pangutaran (isl.), Phil. 82/C7
Pangutaran Group (isls.), Phil. 82/C7
Pangutaran Group (isls.), Phil. 85/G4
Panhandle, Texas (79068) 302/C2
Paniau (peak), Hawaii 218/A2
Panihati, India 68/F1
Panipat, India 68/D3
Paniqui, Phil. 82/C3
Panjao, Afgh. 59/J3
Panjao, Afgh. 68/B2
Panjgur, Pak. 59/H4
Panjgur, Pak. 68/A3
Panjim, India, 54/L8
Panjim, India 68/C5
Pankow, E. Ger. 22/F3
Pankshin, Nigeria 106/F7
P'anmunjŏm, Korea 81/C5
Panmure (isl.), P.E.I. 169/F2
Panna, India 68/E4
Pannonhalma, Hung. 41/D3
Panny (riv.), Alta. 182/C1
Panola, Ala. (35477) 194/B5
Panola, Ill. (†61738) 222/E3
Panola (co.), Miss. 256/E2
Panola, Okla. (74559) 288/R5
Panola (co.), Texas 302/K5
Panora, Iowa (50216) 229/E5
Panorama Park, Iowa (†52722) 229/N5
Panquehue, Chile 138/G2
Panruti, India 68/D6
Pansey, Ala. (36370) 194/H8
Pantar (isl.), Indon. 85/G7
Pantego, N.C. (27860) 281/R3
Pantego, Texas (†76101) 302/F2
Pantelleria (isl.), Italy, 7/F5
Pantelleria, Italy 34/C6
Pantelleria (isl.), Italy 34/D6
Pantha, Burma 72/B2
Panther (creek), Idaho 220/D4
Panther (creek), Ky. 237/G5
Panther, W. Va. (24872) 313/C8
Panther Burn, Miss. (38765) 256/C4
Pantin, France 28/B1
Pantoja, Peru 128/E3
Pantonᴧ, Vt. (†05491) 268/A3
Panton, Vt. (†05491) 268/A3
Pánuco, Mex. 150/K6
Pánuco (riv.), Mex. 150/K5
Panuke (lake), N.S. 169/D4
Panyam, Nigeria 106/F7
Panzós, Guat. 154/C3
Pao (riv.), Ven. 124/D3
Pao (riv.), Ven. 124/F3
Paochang, China 77/H3
Paoki, China 77/G5
Paola, Italy 34/E5
Paola, Kans. (66071) 232/H3
Paoli, Colo. (80746) 208/P1
Paoli, Ind. (47454) 227/E7
Paoli, Okla. (73074) 288/M5
Paoli, Pa. (19301) 294/M5
Paoli, Wis. (†53508) 317/G10
Paonia, Colo. (81428) 208/D5
Paoshan, China, 54/O7
Paoshan, China 77/E7
Paoting, China, 54/P6
Paoting, China 77/J4
Paotow, China, 54/O5
Paotow, China 77/G3
Paoua, Centr. Afr. Rep. 115/C2
Papa, Hawaii (†96704) 218/G6
Pápa, Hung. 41/D3
Papaaloa, Hawaii (96780) 218/J4
Papagaio (riv.), Braz. 132/B6
Papagayo (gulf), C. Rica 154/E5
Papago Ind. Res., Ariz. 198/C6
Papaikou, Hawaii, 188/G6
Papaikou, Hawaii (96781) 218/J5
Papakura, N.Z. 101/E2
Papallacta, Ec. 128/D3
Papanoa, Mex. 150/J8
Papantla de Olarte, Mex. 150/L6
Papar, Malaysia 85/F4
Papa Stour (isl.), 10/G1
Papa Stour (isl.), Scot. 15/L3
Papatoetoe, N.Z. 101/C1
Papa Westray (isl.), 10/E1
Papa Westray (isl.), Scot. 15/L1
Papeete (cap.), Fr. Poly., 87/M7
Papeete (cap.), Fr. Poly., 3/B6
Papelón, Ven. 124/D3
Papenburg, W. Ger. 22/B2
Paphos, Cyprus 63/E5
Papillion, Nebr. (68046) 264/J3
Papineau (co.), Que. 172/B4
Papineau (lake), Que. 172/C4
Papineau (lake), Ont. 177/G2
Papineau, Ill. (60956) 222/F3
Papineauville, Que. 172/C4
Paposo, Chile 138/A5
Papradno, Czech. 41/E2
Paps, The (mt.), Ire. 17/C7
Paps of Jura (peaks), Scot. 15/E8
Papua, 3/S6
Papua, 87/E6
PAPUA, 85/B7
Papua (gulf), Papua 85/B7
Papua (gulf), Papua, 87/E6
Papudo, Chile 138/A9
Papun, Burma 72/C3
Papunáua (riv.), Col. 126/E6
Papurí (riv.), Col. 126/F7
Paquera, C. Rica 154/E6
Paquette, Que. 172/F4
Paquetville, N. Br. 170/E1
Pará (est.), Braz., 120/F2
Pará (state), Braz. 132/C4
Pará (Belém), Braz. 132/E3
Pará (riv.), Braz. 132/D3
Para (dist.), Sur. 131/D3
Paracale, Phil. 82/D3
Paracas (pen.), Peru 128/D9
Paracatu, Braz. 132/E7
Paracatu (riv.), Braz. 132/E7
Paracel (isls.), China 85/E2
Parachilna, Aust. 88/F6
Parachilna, S. Aust. 94/F4
Parachinar, Pak. 68/B2
Paraćin, Yugo. 45/E4
Parada Esperanza, Urug. 145/B3
Parada Liebigs, Urug. 145/A4
Parada Rivas, Urug. 145/B2
Parade, S. Dak. (57647) 298/G3
Pará de Minas, Braz. 132/E7
Pará de Minas, Braz. 135/D1
Paradis, La. (70080) 238/M4
Paradise, Ariz. (†85632) 198/F7
Paradise, Calif. (95969) 204/D4
Paradise, Guyana 131/C3
Paradise, Kans. (67658) 232/D2
Paradise, Mich. (49768) 250/D2
Paradise (lake), Mich. 250/E3
Paradise, Mo. (†64089) 261/D4
Paradise, Mont. (59856) 262/B3
Paradise, N.S. 169/C4
Paradise (lake), N.S. 169/C4
Paradise, Nev. (†89101) 266/F6
Paradise (riv.), Newf. 166/C3
Paradise, Pa. (17562) 294/K5
Paradise, Texas (76073) 302/G5
Paradise, Utah (84328) 304/C2
Paradise, W. Va. (†25124) 313/C5
Paradise Hill, Sask. 181/B2
Paradise Inn, Wash. (98398) 310/D4
Paradise Valley, Alta. 182/E3
Paradise Valley‡, Ariz. (85253) 198/D5
Paradise Valley, Nev. (89426) 266/D1
Paradise Valley, Wyo. (†82601) 319/F3
Paradisino (peak), Switz. 39/K4
Paradox, Colo. (81429) 208/B6
Paragon, Ind. (46166) 227/D6
Paragonah, Utah (84760) 304/B6
Paragould, Ark. (72450) 203/J1
Paraguá (riv.), Bol. 136/E4
Paragua (riv.), Ven. 124/G4
Paraguaçu (riv.), Braz. 132/F6
Paraguaçu Paulista, Braz. 132/D8
Paraguai (riv.), Braz. 132/B8
Paraguaipoa, Ven. 124/C2
Paraguaná (pen.), Ven. 124/C1
Paraguarí (dept.), Par. 144/D6
Paraguarí, Par. 144/B6
Paraguay, 3/F7
Paraguay, 120/E5
Paraguay (riv.), 120/E4
PARAGUAY, 144
Paraguay (riv.), Arg. 143/E1
Paraguay (riv.), Bol. 136/F7
Paraguay (riv.), Par. 144/D5
Paraíba (state), Braz. 132/G4
Paraíba (riv.), Braz. 135/E2
Paraíba (João Pessoa) Braz., 120/G3
Paraíba do Sul, Braz. 135/E3
Paraíso, C. Rica 154/F6
Paraíso, Dom. Rep. 158/D7
Paraíso, Mex. 150/N7
Paraíso de Chabasquén, Ven. 124/D3
Parakou, Dahomey 106/E7
Parallel, Kans. (†66933) 232/F2
Paraloma, Ark. 203/B6
Paramaribo (cap.), Sur., 3/G5
Paramaribo (cap.), Sur., 120/E2
Paramaribo (dist.), Sur. 131/D2
Paramaribo (cap.), Sur. 131/D2
Paramithiá, Greece 45/E6
Paramonga, Peru 128/C8
Paramount, Calif. (90723) 204/C11
Paramus, N.J. (07652) 273/B1
Paramushir (isl.), U.S.S.R., 54/U4
Paran, Wadi (dry riv.), Israel 65/D5
Paraná (riv.), 3/G7
Paraná (riv.), 120/E5
Paraná, Arg. 120/E6
Paraná, Arg. 143/F5
Paraná (riv.), Arg. 143/E2
Paranã, Braz., 120/F4
Paranã (riv.), Braz., 120/F4
Paraná (state), Braz. 132/D9
Paranã, Braz. 132/E6
Paraná (riv.), Braz. 132/C8
Paranã (riv.), Braz. 132/E6
Paraná (state), Braz. 135/B4
Paraná, Alto (riv.), Par. 144/D6
Paranaguá, Braz., 120/F5
Paranaguá, Braz. 132/E9
Paranaguá, Braz. 135/B4
Paranaíba (riv.), Braz., 120/F4
Paranaíba, Braz. 132/D7
Paranam, Sur. 131/D3
Paranapanema (riv.), Braz. 132/C8
Paranapanema (riv.), Braz. 135/B3
Paranapiacaba (range), Braz. 135/B4
Paranatinga (riv.), Braz. 132/C6
Parang, Cotabato, Phil. 82/E7
Parang, Sulu, Phil. 82/C8
Parao (riv.), Urug. 145/E3
Parapetí (riv.), Bol. 136/D6
Para Station, N.S.W. 97/B3
Parati, Braz. 135/D3
Paratinga, Braz. 132/F6
Paray-le-Monial, France 28/F4
Parbhani, India 68/D5
Parbold, 10/G2
Parchim, E. Ger. 22/D2
Parchman, Miss. (38738) 256/D3
Parchment, Mich. (49004) 250/D6
Parczew, Poland 47/F3
Pardee (res.), Calif. 204/C9
Pardee, Va. (†24285) 307/C6
Pardeeville, Wis. (53954) 317/H8
Pardes Hanna, Israel 65/B2
Pardo (riv.), Braz., 120/F4
Pardo (riv.), Braz. 132/D8
Pardo (riv.), Braz. 132/C8
Pardo (riv.), Braz. 132/F6
Pardo (riv.), Braz. 135/B2
Pardoe, Pa. (†16137) 294/B3
Pardones, Chile 138/A10
Pardoo, Aust. 88/B4
Pardoo, W. Aust. 92/B3
Pardubice, Czech. 41/C1
Pare, Indon. 85/K2
Parece Vela (isl.), Japan, 87/D3
Parece Vela (isl.), Japan, 54/S7
Parecis (mts.), Braz., 120/D4
Parecis (range), Braz. 132/B6
Paredes de Nava, Spain 33/D1
Paremata-Plimmerton, N.Z. 101/B2
Parent, Que. 174/C3
Pareora, N.Z. 101/C6
Parepare, Indon. 85/F6
Parguera, P. Rico 161/A3
Parham, Antigua 161/E11
Parham, Ont. 177/H3
Parhams, La. (†71343) 238/G4
Paria (gulf), 120/D1
Paria (plat.), Ariz. 198/D2
Paria (riv.), Ariz. 198/D1
Paria, Bol. 136/B5
Paria (gulf), Trinidad Tobago 156/G5
Paria (gulf), Trinidad Tobago 161/A11
Paria (riv.), Utah 304/B6
Paria (gulf), Ven. 124/H2
Paria (pen.), Ven. 124/G2
Pariaguán, Ven. 124/F3
Pariaman, Indon. 85/B6
Parícutin (vol.), Mex. 150/H7
Parida (isl.), Pan. 154/F6
Parika, Guyana 131/B2
Parikkala, Fin. 18/Q6
Parima (mts.), 120/D2
Parima, Sierra (mts.), Ven. 124/F6
Parinacochas (lake), Peru 128/F10
Parinacota, Cerro (mt.), Chile 138/B1
Parinari, Peru 128/E5
Pariñas (pt.), Peru 128/B5
Parintins, Braz., 120/E3
Parintins, Braz. 132/B3
Paris, Ark. (72855) 203/C3
Paris (dept.), France 28/B2
Paris (cap.), France, 3/J3
Paris (cap.), France, 7/E4
Paris (cap.), France 28/B2
Paris, Idaho (83261) 220/G7
Paris, Ill. (61944) 222/F4
Paris, Iowa (†52214) 229/K4
Paris, Ky. (40361) 237/N4
Parisᴧ, Maine (04271) 242/B7
Paris, Mich. (49338) 250/D5
Paris, Miss. (38949) 256/F2
Paris, Mo. (65275) 261/J4
Paris, Ohio (44669) 284/H4
Paris, Ont. 177/D4
Paris, Tenn. (38242) 237/E8
Paris, Texas, 188/G4
Paris, Texas (75460) 302/J4
Paris, Va. (22130) 307/N3
Paris Crossing, Ind. (47270) 227/F7
Parish, N.Y. (13131) 276/H4
Parish, Urug. 145/C3
Parishville, N.Y. (13672) 276/L1
Parisville, Que. 172/F3
Parisville, Mich. (†48470) 250/G5
Parita, Pan. 154/G6
Parita (gulf), Pan. 154/G6
Park (co.), Colo. 208/H4
Park (range), Colo. 208/F1
Park (riv.), Conn. 210/E2
Park, Kans. (67751) 232/B2
Park (co.), Mont. 262/F5
Park (riv.), N. Dak. 283/R3
Park (dist.), Scot. 15/C3
Park (co.), Wyo. 319/C1
Parkano, Fin. 18/N6
Parkbeg, Sask. 181/E5
Park City‡, Ill. (†60085) 222/F1
Park City, Kans. (67219) 232/E4
Park City, Ky. (42160) 237/J6
Park City, Mont. (59063) 262/H5
Park City, Utah (84060) 304/C3
Parkdale, Ark. (71661) 203/H7
Parkdale, Colo. (81238) 208/H6
Parkdale‡, Mo. (†63049) 261/L6
Parkdale, Oreg. (97047) 291/F2
Parkdale, P.E.I. 169/E2
Parke (co.), Ind. 227/C5
Parker, Ariz. (85344) 198/A4
Parker (dam), Ariz. 198/A4
Parker, Colo. (80134) 208/K4
Parker, Fla. (32401) 212/C6
Parker, Idaho (83438) 220/G6
Parker, Ind. (47368) 227/G4
Parker, Kans. (66072) 232/H3
Parker, Pa. (16049) 294/C3
Parker, S. Dak. (57053) 298/P7
Parker (lake), S. Dak. 298/P3
Parker (co.), Texas 302/G5
Parker‡, Texas (†75069) 302/H4
Parker, Wash. (98939) 310/E4
Parker Dam, Calif. (92267) 204/L9
Parkersburg, Ill. (62452) 222/F5
Parkersburg, Ind. (†47954) 227/D5
Parkersburg, Iowa (50665) 229/H3
Parkersburg, N.C. (†28441) 281/N5
Parkersburg, W. Va., 188/K3
Parkersburg, W. Va. (26101) 313/D4
Parkers Cove, N.S. 169/C4
Parkers Lake, Ky. (42634) 237/M7
Parkers Prairie, Minn. (56361) 254/C4
Parkertown, N.J. (†08087) 273/E4
Parkerview, Sask. 181/H4
Parkerville, Kans. (†66846) 232/F3
Parkes, Aust. 88/H6
Parkes, N.S.W. 97/E3
Parkesburg, Pa. (19365) 294/L6
Park Falls, Wis. (54552) 317/F4
Park Forest, Ill. (60466) 222/B3
Park Forest South‡, Ill. (60466) 222/F2
Park Hall, Md. (20667) 245/N8
Parkhill, Ont. 177/C4
Park Hill, Okla. (74451) 288/R3
Park Hills, Ky. (†41011) 237/S2
Parkin, Ark. (72373) 203/J3
Parkland, Alta. 182/D4
Parkland‡, Fla. (†33441) 212/F5
Parkland, Okla. (†74824) 288/N3
Parkland, Wash. (98444) 310/C3
Parkmanᴧ, Maine (†04443) 242/D5
Parkman, Ohio (44080) 284/H3
Parkman, Sask. 181/K6
Parkman, Wyo. (82838) 319/E1
Parknasilla, Ire. 17/B8
Park Place, Oreg. (†97045) 291/B2
Park Rapids, Minn. (56470) 254/D4
Park Rapids, Wash. (†99114) 310/H2
Park Ridge, Ill. (60068) 222/A1
Park Ridge, N.J. (07656) 273/B1
Park Ridge, Wis. (†54481) 317/H6
Park River, N. Dak. (58270) 283/P3
Parks, Ariz. (86001) 198/C3
Parks, Ark. (72950) 203/B4
Parks, La. (70582) 238/G6
Parks, Nebr. (69041) 264/C4
Parkside, Pa. (†19013) 294/M7
Parkside, Sask. 181/E2
Parksley, Va. (23421) 307/S5
Parkston, S. Dak. (57366) 298/O7
Parksville, Br. Col. 184/J3
Parksville, Ky. (40464) 237/M5
Parksville, N.Y. (12768) 276/L7
Parksville, S.C. (29844) 296/C4
Parkton, Md. (21120) 245/M2
Parkton, N.C. (28371) 281/M5
Park Valley, Sask. 181/E2
Park Valley, Utah (84329) 304/A2
Parkview (mt.), Colo. 208/G2
Park View, N. Mex. (87551) 274/C2
Parkview, Nebr. (†68801) 264/F4
Parkville, Md. (21234) 245/M3
Parkville, Mo. (64152) 261/O5
Parkville, Pa. (†17331) 294/J6
Parkville, Vic. 97/H5
Parkway‡, Mo. (64130) 261/L6
Parkway Village‡, Ky. (†40201) 237/K4
Parkwood‡, N.C. (27707) 281/M3
Parlakhemundi, India 68/E5
Parlier, Calif. (93648) 204/F7
Parlin, Colo. (81239) 208/F6
Parlin (pond), Maine 242/C4
Parma, Idaho (83660) 220/B6
Parma, Italy, 7/E4
Parma (prov.), Italy 34/C2
Parma, Italy 34/C2
Parma (riv.), Italy 34/C2
Parma, Mich. (49269) 250/E6
Parma, Mo. (63870) 261/N9
Parma, Ohio (44129) 284/H9
Parmachenee (lake), Maine 242/B5
Parma Heights, Ohio (†44129) 284/G9
Parmana, Ven. 124/F4
Parmele, N.C. (27861) 281/P3
Parmelee, S. Dak. (57566) 298/G7
Parmer (co.), Texas 302/B3
Parnaguá, Braz. 132/E5
Parnaíba, Braz., 120/F3
Parnaíba (riv.), Braz., 120/F3
Parnaíba, Braz. 132/F3
Parnaíba (riv.), Braz. 132/E5
Parnamirim, Braz. 132/F4
Parnassus (mt.), Greece 45/F6
Parnassus, N.Z. 101/D5
Parndana, S. Aust. 94/E6
Parnell, Iowa (52325) 229/J5
Parnell, Mo. (64475) 261/C2
Pärnu, U.S.S.R. 48/C4
Pärnu, U.S.S.R. 52/C3
Pärnu, U.S.S.R. 53/C1
Pärnu, U.S.S.R., 7/G3
Paro Dzong, India 68/F3
Paron, Ark. (72132) 203/E4
Paroo (riv.), Aust. 88/G5
Paroo (chan.), N.S.W. 97/B2
Paroo (riv.), N.S.W. 97/C1
Paroo (riv.), Queens. 95/C6
Paropamisus (range), Afgh. 59/H3
Paropamisus (range), Afgh. 68/A2
Páros (isl.), Greece 45/G7
Parow, S. Africa 118/F6
Parowan, Utah (84761) 304/B6
Parpan, Switz. 39/J3
Parr, Ind. (†47978) 227/C2
Parr, S.C. (29066) 296/E3
Parral, Chile 138/A11
Parral, Mex. 150/G3
Parral, Ohio (†44622) 284/G4
Parramatta, Aust. 88/K3
Parramatta, N.S.W. 97/H3
Parramatta (riv.), N.S.W. 97/J3
Parramore (isl.), Va. 307/S5
Parran, Md. (†20639) 245/M6
Parras de la Fuente, Mex. 150/H4
Parrett (riv.), Eng. 13/E6
Parrish, Ala. (35580) 194/D3
Parrish, Fla. (33564) 212/D4
Parrish, Wis. (†54435) 317/H5
Parris Island Marine Base, S.C. 296/F7
Parrott, Ga. (31777) 216/D7
Parrott, Va. (24132) 307/G6
Parrottsville, Tenn. (37843) 237/P8
Parrsboro, N.S. 169/D3
Parr View, Sask. 181/K3
Parry (chan.), 146/H2
Parry (chan.), 163/E1
Parry (isls.), 163/M3
Parry (isl.), Ont. 177/D2
Parry (sound), Ont. 177/D2
Parry (bay), N.W.T. 187/K3
Parry (cape), N.W.T. 187/F2
Parry (chan.), N.W.T. 187/G2
Parry (isls.), N.W.T. 187/G2
Parry (pen.), N.W.T. 187/F2
Parry, Sask. 181/G6
Parry Sound, 163/J6
Parry Sound (co.), Ont. 175/E3
Parry Sound, Ont. 175/D3
Parry Sound (co.), Ont. 177/D2
Parry Sound, Ont. 177/E2
Parryville‡, Pa. (18244) 294/L4
Parseierspitze (mt.), Austria 41/A3
Parshall, Colo. (80468) 208/G2
Parshall, N. Dak. (58770) 283/F4
Parsippanyᴧ, N.J. (07054) 273/E2
Parsnip (riv.), Br. Col. 184/F2
Parson, Br. Col. 184/J4
Parsons, Kans., 188/G3
Parsons, Kans. (67357) 232/G4
Parsons, Tenn. (38363) 237/E9
Parsons, W. Va. (26287) 313/G4
Parsonsburg, Md. (21849) 245/R7
Parson's Pond, Newf. 166/C3
Partanna, Italy 34/D6
Partapgarh, India 68/C4
Parthenay, France 28/C4
Partinico, Italy 34/D5
Partizánske, Czech. 41/E2
Partlow, Va. (22534) 307/N4
Partridge, Kans. (67566) 232/D4
Partridge (riv.), Minn. 254/G3
Partridge (bay), Newf. 166/C3
Partridge (pt.), Newf. 166/C3
Partry (mts.), Ire. 17/C4
Paru (riv.), Braz. 132/C3
Paruro, Peru 128/F9
Parvatipuram, India 68/E5
Parys, S. Africa 118/D5
Pas (riv.), Que. 174/D1
Pasacao, Phil. 82/D4
Pasadena, Calif., 188/C4
Pasadena, Calif. (*91101) 204/C10
Pasadena, Md. (21122) 245/M4
Pasadena, Newf. 166/C4
Pasadena, Texas (*77501) 302/J2
Pasadena Hills‡, Mo. (†63101) 261/P2
Pasadena Park‡, Mo. (†63101) 261/P3
Pasado (cape), Ec. 128/B3
Pasaje, Ec. 128/C4
Pa Sak, Mae Nam (riv.), Thai. 72/D4
Pasangkaju, Indon. 85/F6
Pasargadae (ruins), Iran 66/H5
Pasatiempo, Calif. (†95060) 204/K4
Pasawng, Burma 72/C3
Pasayten (riv.), Wash. 310/E2
Pascagoula, Miss. (39567) 256/G10
Pascagoula (riv.), Miss. 256/G9
Pascal, Sask. 181/D2
Paşcani, Rum. 45/H2
Paschall, N.C. (†27589) 281/N1
Pasco (co.), Fla. 212/D3
Pasco (dept.), Peru 128/E8
Pasco, Wash. (99301) 310/F4
Pascoag, R.I. (02859) 249/H5
Pascola, Mo. (63871) 261/N10
Pascua (riv.), Chile 138/D7
Pas-de-Calais (dept.), France 28/E2
Pasewalk, E. Ger. 22/F2
Pashley, Alta. 182/E5
Pasig, Phil. 82/C3
Pasighat, India 68/G3
Pasinler, Turkey 63/J3
Pasión (riv.), Guat. 154/B2
Paskenta, Calif. (96074) 204/C4
Pasłek, Poland 47/D1
Pasley (bay), N.W.T. 187/J2
Pasni, Pak. 59/H4
Pasni, Pak. 68/A3
Paso Ataques, Urug. 145/D2
Paso Barreto, Par. 144/D4
Paso de Andrés Pérez, Urug. 145/B3
Paso de Indios, Arg. 143/C5
Paso de la Laguna, Salto, Urug. 145/B2
Paso de la Laguna, Tacuarembó, Urug. 145/D3
Paso de las Piedras, Urug. 145/C2
Paso del Borracho, Urug. 145/D2
Paso del Cerro, Urug. 145/C2
Paso de León, Urug. 145/B1
Paso del Horno, Urug. 145/C2
Paso de los Libres, Arg. 143/E2
Paso de los Toros, Urug. 145/C3
Paso del Parque, Urug. 145/B2
Paso de Patria, Par. 144/C6
Paso de Ramos, Urug. 145/C1
Paso de Uleste, Urug. 145/B3
Paso Flores, Arg. 143/C5
Paso Hondo, Urug. 145/B4
Paso Potrero, Urug. 145/C2
Pasorapa, Bol. 136/C6
Paso Real, Hond. 154/E3
Paso Real de San Diego, Cuba 158/B1
Paso Robles, Calif. (93446) 204/E8
Paspébiac, Que. 172/D2
Pasqua, Sask. 181/F5
Pasque (isl.), Mass. 249/L7
Pasquia (hills), Sask. 181/J2
Pasquia (riv.), Sask. 181/K2
Pasquotank (co.), N.C. 281/S2
Pass (creek), Wyo. 319/F4
Passaconaway (mt.), N.H. 268/E4
Passadumkeagᴧ, Maine (04475) 242/F5
Passage (isl.), Mich. 250/E1
Passage East, Ire. 17/G7
Passagem Franca, Braz. 132/E4
Passage West, 10/B5
Passage West, Ire. 17/E8
Passaic, Mo. (64777) 261/D6
Passaic (co.), N.J. 273/E1
Passaic, N.J. (*07055) 273/E2
Passaic (riv.), N.J. 273/E2
Passamaquoddy (bay), Maine 242/J5
Passamaquoddy (bay), N. Br. 170/C3
Passamaquoddy Ind. Res., Maine 242/J5
Passau, W. Ger. 22/E4
Pass Christian, Miss. (39571) 256/F10
Passekeag, N. Br. 170/E3
Passero (cape), Italy 34/E6
Passes (lake), Que. 172/F2
Passi, Phil. 82/D5
Passo Fundo, Braz. 132/D10
Passos, Braz. 132/E8
Passos, Braz. 135/C2
Passumpsic, Vt. (05861) 268/D3
Passumpsic (riv.), Vt. 268/D2
Pastaza (prov.), Ec. 128/D3
Pastaza (riv.), Ec. 128/D4
Pastaza (riv.), Peru 128/D5
Pasto, Col., 120/C2
Pasto, Col. 126/B7
Pastol (bay), Alaska 196/F2
Pastora (peak), Ariz. 198/F2
Pastos Bons, Braz. 132/E4
Pas Trail, Sask. 181/H2
Pastrana, Spain 33/E2
Pastura, N. Mex. (88435) 274/E4
Pasuquin, Phil. 82/C1
Pasuruan, Indon. 85/K2
Pasvalys, U.S.S.R. 53/C2
Pasvik (riv.), Fin. 18/Q2
Pasvik (riv.), Norway 18/Q2
Paswegin, Sask. 181/H4
Pásztó, Hung. 41/E3
Pata, Bol. 136/A4
Patacamaya, Bol. 136/B5
Patagonia (reg.), Arg., 120/D7
Patagonia (reg.), Arg. 143/C5
Patagonia, Ariz. (85624) 198/E7
Pataguanset (lake), Conn. 210/G3
Pataha, Wash. (†99347) 310/H4
Pataha (creek), Wash. 310/H4
Pata-Kesar, Afgh. 59/J2
Patan, India 68/C4
Patapédia (riv.), Que. 172/B2
Patapédia (riv.), N. Br. 170/C1
Patapsco, Md. (21127) 245/L2
Patapsco (res.), Md. 245/L3
Patapsco (riv.), Md. 245/M4
Pataskala, Ohio (43062) 284/E5
Pataz, Peru 128/D6
Patchewollock, Aust. 88/G7
Patchewollock, Vic. 97/A4
Patch Grove, Wis. (53817) 317/D10
Patchogue, N.Y. (11772) 276/P9
Patea, N.Z. 101/E3
Paternion, Austria 41/B3
Paterno, Italy 34/E6
Pateros, Wash. (98846) 310/E2
Pateros (lake), Wash. 310/F2
Paterson, N.J., 188/L2
Paterson, N.J. (*07501) 273/B2
Paterson, Wash. (99345) 310/F5
Patesville, Ky. (†42364) 237/H5
Pathfinder (res.), Wyo., 188/E2
Pathfinder (res.), Wyo. 319/F3
Pathiu, Thai. 72/C5
Pathlow, Sask. 181/G3
Pati, Indon. 85/J2
Patía, Col. 126/B6
Patía (riv.), Col. 126/B6
Patiala, India 68/D2
Patillas, P. Rico 161/E2
Patillas (lake), P. Rico 161/E2
Patiño, Estero (swamp), Par. 144/B5
Pativilca (riv.), Peru 128/D8
Patjitan, Indon. 85/J2
Patmos, Ark. (71856) 203/C7
Pátmos (isl.), Greece 45/H7
Patna, India, 54/M7
Patna, India 68/F3
Patnanongan (isl.), Phil. 82/D3
Patnos, Turkey 63/K3
Patoka, Ill. (62875) 222/D5
Patoka, Ind. (47566) 227/B8
Patoka (riv.), Ind. 227/C8
Paton, Iowa (50217) 229/E4
Patos (lag.), Braz., 120/F6
Patos, Braz. 132/G4
Patos (lag.), Braz. 132/D10
Patos de Minas, Braz. 132/E7
Patoutville, La. (†70544) 238/G7
Patquía, Arg. 143/C3
Pátrai, Greece, 7/G5
Pátrai, Greece 45/E6
Patricia, Alta. 182/E4
Patricia, S. Dak. (†57551) 298/G7
Patricia, Texas (79352) 302/B5
Patricio Lynch (isl.), Chile 138/D7
Patrick, Neth. Ant. 161/F8
Patrick, S.C. (29584) 296/G2
Patrick (co.), Va. 307/H7
Patrick A.F.B., Fla. 212/F3
Patricksburg, Ind. (47455) 227/D6
Patrick's Cove, Newf. 166/C2
Patrick Springs, Va. (24133) 307/H7
Patrickswell, Ire. 17/D6
Patriot, Ind. (47038) 227/H7
Patriot, Ohio (45658) 284/F8
Patrocínio, Braz. 132/E7
Patronville, Ind. (†47635) 227/C9
Patroon, Texas (75967) 302/L6
Patsaliga (creek), Ala. 194/F7
Patsburg, Ala. (36059) 194/F7
Patta (isl.), Kenya 115/H4
Pattani, Thai. 72/D6
Pattenᴧ, Maine (04765) 242/F4
Patten, Maine (04765) 242/F4
Pattenburg, N.J. (08860) 273/C2
Patterdale, Eng. 13/E3
Patterson, Ark. (72123) 203/H3
Patterson, Calif. (95363) 204/D6
Patterson, Ga. (31557) 216/H8
Patterson, Idaho (†83253) 220/E5
Patterson, Ill. (62078) 222/C4
Patterson, Iowa (50218) 229/F6
Patterson, La. (70392) 238/H7
Patterson (pt.), Mich. 250/D3
Patterson, Mo. (63956) 261/L8
Patterson, N.C. (28661) 281/F3
Patterson, N.Y. (12563) 276/N7

Percé 417

Patterson, Ohio (45878) 284/C4
Patterson, Va. (24633) 307/D6
Patterson (creek), W. Va. 313/J4
Patterson Creek, W. Va. (26746) 313/J3
Patterson Gardens‡, Mich. (†48161) 250/F7
Patterson Heights‡, Pa. (†15010) 294/B4
Pattersonville, N.Y. (12137) 276/M5
Patti, Italy 34/E5
Pattison, Miss. (39144) 256/C7
Patton, Mo. (63662) 261/M7
Patton, Pa. (16668) 294/E4
Patton‡, Texas (†77372) 302/J7
Pattonsburg, Mo. (64670) 261/D2
Patuca, Hond. 154/E3
Patuca (pt.), Hond. 154/E3
Patuca (riv.), Hond. 154/E3
Patuha (mt.), Indon. 85/H2
Pătulele, Rum. 45/F3
Patutahi, N.Z. 101/F3
Patuxent (riv.), Md. 245/M7
Patuxent Nav. Air Test Ctr., Md. 245/N7
Patzau, Wis. (†54836) 317/B3
Pátzcuaro, Mex. 150/J7
Pátzcuaro (lake), Mex. 150/J7
Pau, France 28/C6
Paucarbamba, Peru 128/E9
Paucartambo, Cuzco, Peru 128/G9
Paucartambo, Pasco, Peru 128/E8
Paudash (lake), Ont. 177/F3
Pau dos Ferros, Braz. 132/G4
Pauillac, France 28/C5
Paukaa, Hawaii (†96781) 218/J5
Paul, Ala. (36469) 194/E8
Paul, Idaho (83347) 220/E7
Paul (isl.), Newf. 166/B2
Paul (stream), Vt. 268/D2
Paulatuk, 163/D2
Paulatuk, N.W.T. 187/F3
Paulaya (riv.), Hond. 154/E3
Paulden, Ariz. (86334) 198/C4
Paulding (co.), Ga. 216/C3
Paulding, Miss. (39348) 256/F6
Paulding (co.), Ohio 284/A3
Paulding, Ohio (45879) 284/A3
Paulette, Miss. (39349) 256/H4
Paulina, La. (70763) 238/L3
Paulina, Oreg. (97751) 291/G3
Paulina (lake), Oreg. 291/F4
Pauline, Kans. (66619) 232/G3
Pauline, Nebr. (†68941) 264/F4
Pauline, S.C. (29374) 296/D2
Paulins Kill (riv.), N.J. 273/D1
Paul Isnard, Fr. Gui. 131/E3
Paulistana, Braz., 120/F3
Paulistana, Braz. 132/F4
Paullina, Iowa (51046) 229/B3
Paulo de Faria, Braz. 135/B2
Pauloff Harbor, Alaska (99646) 196/F4
Paulsboro, N.J. (08066) 273/C4
Paul Smiths, N.Y. (12970) 276/M2
Paul Spur, Ariz. (†85607) 198/F7
Pauls Valley, Okla. (73075) 288/M5
Paungassi, Man. 179/G2
Paungde, Burma 72/B3
Paunsaugunt (plat.), Utah 304/B6
Paupack, Pa. (18451) 294/M3
Paute, Ec. 128/C4
Pauto (riv.), Col. 126/E5
Pauwalu (pt.), Hawaii 218/K2
Pauwela, Hawaii (†96708) 218/K2
Pavant (mts.), Utah 304/B5
Pavia (prov.), Italy 34/B2
Pavia, Italy 34/B2
Pavilion, Br. Col. 184/G5
Pavilion (key), Fla. 212/E6
Pavilion, N.Y. (14525) 276/D5
Pavillion, Wyo. (82523) 319/D2
Pāvilosta, U.S.S.R. 52/B3
Pāvilosta, U.S.S.R. 53/A2
Pavlodar, U.S.S.R. 48/H4
Pavlof (bay), Alaska 196/F3
Pavlof (vol.), Alaska 196/F3
Pavlovo, U.S.S.R. 52/F3
Pavlovsk, U.S.S.R. 52/F4
Pavo, Ga. (31778) 216/E9
Pavón, Col. 126/D6
Pavullo nel Frignano, Italy 34/C2
Pawcatuck, Conn. (02891) 210/H3
Pawcatuck (riv.), Conn. 210/H3
Pawcatuck (riv.), R.I. 249/G7
Pawhuska, Okla. (74056) 288/O1
Pawhuska (lake), Okla. 288/O1
Pawlet▵, Vt. (05761) 268/A5
Pawlet, Vt. (05761) 268/A5
Pawleys Island, S.C. (29585) 296/J5
Pawling, N.Y. (12564) 276/N7
Pawn, Nam (riv.), Burma 72/C2
Pawnee (creek), Colo. 208/M1
Pawnee, Ill. (62558) 222/D4
Pawnee (co.), Kans. 232/C3
Pawnee (riv.), Kans. 232/B3
Pawnee (co.), Nebr. 264/H4
Pawnee (co.), Okla. 288/N2
Pawnee, Okla. (74058) 288/N2
Pawnee City, Nebr. (68420) 264/H4
Pawnee Rock, Kans. (67567) 232/D3
Pawpaw, Ill. (61353) 222/E2
Paw Paw, Mich. (49079) 250/D6
Paw Paw (riv.), Mich. 250/C6
Paw Paw, W. Va. (25434) 313/K3
Paw Paw Lake, Mich. (†49038) 250/C6
Pawtuckaway (pond), N.H. 268/E5
Pawtucket, R.I. (*02860) 249/J5
Pax, W. Va. (25904) 313/D7
Paxico, Kans. (66526) 232/F2
Paxoí (isl.), Greece 45/D6
Paxson, Alaska (99737) 196/J2
Paxson, Alta. 182/D2
Paxtang, Pa. (17111) 294/J5
Paxton, Fla. (32538) 212/C5
Paxton, Ill. (60957) 222/E3
Paxton, Ind. (47865) 227/C6
Paxton▵, Mass. (01612) 249/G3
Paxton, Mass. (01612) 249/G3
Paxton, Nebr. (69155) 264/C3
Paxton, S. Dak. (†57529) 298/L7
Paxville, S.C. (29102) 296/G4
Paya Lebar, Sing. 72/F6
Payerne, Switz. 39/C3
Payette (co.), Idaho 220/B5
Payette, Idaho (83661) 220/B5
Payette (lake), Idaho 220/C4
Payette (mts.), Idaho 220/B5
Payette (riv.), Idaho 220/B6
Payne, Ga. (†31201) 216/E5
Payne (lake), 163/J4
Payne, Minn. (55774) 254/F3
Payne, Ohio (45880) 284/A3
Payne (co.), Okla. 288/N2
Payne (Bellin), 163/J3
Payne (Bellin), Que. 174/F1
Payne (lake), Que. 174/E1
Payneham, S. Aust. 94/B7
Paynes, Miss. (†38920) 256/D3
Paynes Creek, Calif. (96075) 204/D3
Paynes Find, W. Aust. 92/B5
Paynesville, Ind. (†47250) 227/F7
Paynesville, Mich. (†49912) 250/G2
Paynesville, Minn. (56362) 254/D5
Paynesville, Mo. (63371) 261/L4
Payneville, Ky. (40157) 237/J5
Paynton, Sask. 181/B2
Paysandú, Urug., 120/E6
Paysandú (dept.), Urug. 145/B3
Paysandú, Urug. 145/A3
Payson, Ariz. (85541) 198/D4
Payson, Ill. (62360) 222/B4
Payson, Utah (84651) 304/C3
Pay-Yer (mt.), U.S.S.R. 52/K1
Paz, Arg. 143/F6
Pazanun, Iran 66/F5
Pazar, Rize, Turkey 63/J2
Pazar, Tokat, Turkey 63/F4
Pazarcik, Turkey 63/G4
Pazardzhik, Bulg. 45/G4
Pazaryer, Turkey 63/C3
Paz de Ariporo, Col. 126/E5
Paz de Río, Col. 126/D4
Pazña, Bol. 136/B6
Pea (riv.), Ala. 194/F8
Peabody, Kans. (66866) 232/E3
Peabody, Ky. (40974) 237/O6
Peabody, Mass. (01960) 249/E5
Peace (riv.), 163/E4
Peace (riv.), Alta. 182/B1
Peace (riv.), Br. Col. 184/F2
Peace (riv.), Canada, 146/G4
Peace (riv.), Fla. 212/E4
Peace Dale-Wakefield, R.I. (02883) 249/J7
Peace Point, Alta. 182/B5
Peace River, 163/E4
Peace River, Alta., 146/G4
Peace River, Alta. 182/B1
Peace Valley, Mo. (65788) 261/J9
Peach (co.), Ga. 216/E5
Peacham▵, Vt. (05862) 268/C3
Peacham, Vt. (05862) 268/C3
Peach Bottom, Pa. (17563) 294/K6
Peachburg, Ala. (†36089) 194/G6
Peachland, Br. Col. 184/G5
Peachland, N.C. (28133) 281/J5
Peach Orchard, Ark. (72453) 203/J1
Peach Orchard, Mo. (63872) 261/N10
Peach Springs, Ariz. (86434) 198/B3
Peachtree City, Ga. (†30214) 216/C4
Peacock, Mich. (†49938) 250/D4
Peacock, Texas (79542) 302/D4
Peahi, Hawaii (†96708) 218/K2
Peak, The (mt.), Eng. 13/F4
Peak (range), Queens. 95/C4
Peak, S.C. (29122) 296/E3
Peak Hill, N.S.W. 97/E3
Peak Hill, W. Aust. 92/B4
Peaks, Va. (†23069) 307/O5
Peale (mts.), Idaho 220/G7
Peale (mt.), Utah 304/E5
Peapack-Gladstone, N.J. (07977) 273/D2
Pear, W. Va. (†25955) 313/E7
Pearblossom, Calif. (93553) 204/H9
Pearce, Alta. 182/D5
Pearce, Ariz. (85625) 198/F7
Pearcy, Ark. (71964) 203/D5
Peard (bay), Alaska 196/G1
Pea Ridge, Ark. (72751) 203/B1
Pea Ridge Nat'l Mil. Park, Ark. 203/B1
Pearisburg, Va. (24134) 307/G6
Pearl (riv.), 188/J4
Pearl (harb.), Hawaii, 188/F5
Pearl (harb.), Hawaii 218/A3
Pearl, Idaho (†83616) 220/B6
Pearl, Ill. (62361) 222/C4
Pearl (riv.), La. 238/L5
Pearl, Miss. (39208) 256/D6
Pearl (riv.), Miss. 256/D8
Pearl (cays), Nic. 154/F4
Pearl (creek), S. Dak. 298/N5
Pearl, Texas (76563) 302/F6
Pearland, Texas (77581) 302/J2
Pearl and Hermes (reef), Hawaii, 188/E5
Pearl and Hermes (reef), Hawaii 218/B5
Pearl Beach, Mich. (48052) 250/G6
Pearl City, Hawaii (96782) 218/B3
Pearl City, Ill. (61062) 222/D1
Pearlington, Miss. (39572) 256/E10
Pearl River, La. (70452) 238/L6
Pearl River (co.), Miss. 256/E9
Pearl River, N.Y. (10965) 276/M8
Pear Ridge‡, Texas (77640) 302/L8
Pearsall, Texas (78061) 302/E9
Pearse (canal), Alaska 196/N2
Pearson, Ark. (†72131) 203/F3
Pearson, Ga. (31642) 216/G8
Pearson, Okla. (74861) 288/N4
Pearson, Wis. (54462) 317/H5
Peary (chan.), N.W.T. 187/H2
Peary Land (reg.), Greenl., 4/A11
Peary Land (reg.), Greenl., 146/O1
Pease, Minn. (56363) 254/E5
Pease (riv.), Texas 302/D3
Pease A.F.B., N.H. 268/F5
Peasleeville, N.Y. (†12972) 276/N1
Peason, La. (†71429) 238/D4
Pebane, Moz. 118/F3
Pebble Beach, Calif. (93953) 204/C7
Pebworth, Ky. (41359) 237/O5
Peć, Yugo. 45/E4
Pecan Gap‡, Texas (75469) 302/J4
Peçanha, Braz. 132/F7
Pecan Island, La. (†70548) 238/F7
Pecan Point, Ark. (†72350) 203/L3
Pecatonica, Ill. (61063) 222/D1
Pecatonica (riv.), Wis. 317/H11
Peccia, Switz. 39/G4
Pechea, Rum. 45/H3
Pechenga, U.S.S.R. 48/D2
Pechenga, U.S.S.R. 52/D1
Pechenga, U.S.S.R., 4/C8
Pechenga, U.S.S.R., 7/H2
Pechora, U.S.S.R. 48/F3
Pechora (riv.), U.S.S.R. 48/F3
Pechora, U.S.S.R. 52/J1
Pechora (riv.), U.S.S.R. 52/H1
Pechora (river), U.S.S.R., 4/C7
Pechora (riv.), U.S.S.R., 7/K2
Pecica, Rum. 45/E2
Peck, Idaho (83545) 220/B3
Peck, Kans. (67120) 232/E4
Peck, La. (†71368) 238/G3
Peck, Mich. (48466) 250/G5
Peckerwood (lake), Ark. 203/G4
Peckham, Okla. (74648) 288/M1
Pecks Mill, W. Va. (25547) 313/B7
Peconic, N.Y. (11958) 276/P8
Peconic (bay), N.Y. 276/R9
Pecos (riv.), 188/F4
Pecos, N. Mex. (87552) 274/D3
Pecos (riv.), N. Mex. 274/E5
Pecos (co.), Texas 302/B7
Pecos, Texas (79772) 302/D10
Pecos (riv.), Texas 302/C7
Pecos (riv.), U.S., 146/H6
Pecos Nat'l Mon., N. Mex. 274/D3
Pécs, Hung., 7/F4
Pécs, Hung. 41/E3
Pécsvárad, Hung. 41/E3
Peculiar, Mo. (64078) 261/D5
Pedasí, Pan. 154/G7
Pedee, Oreg. (†97361) 291/D3
Pedernal, Arg. 143/G5
Pedernal, Par. 144/D4
Pedernales, Salar de (salt dep.), Chile 138/B5
Pedernales (prov.), Dom. Rep. 158/D7
Pedernales, Dom. Rep. 158/C7
Pedernales, Ec. 128/B2
Pedernales (riv.), Texas 302/F7
Pedernales, Ven. 124/G3
Pederneiras, Braz. 135/B3
Pedersborg, Den. 21/E7
Pedlar Mills, Va. (†24574) 307/K5
Pedra Azul, Braz. 132/F6
Pedraza, Col. 126/C2
Pedregal, Ven. 124/C2
Pedreiras, Braz. 132/E4
Pedrera, Urug. 145/C6
Pedricktown, N.J. (08067) 273/C4
Pedrika, S. Aust. 94/D2
Pedro (bank), Jam. 156/B3
Pedro (cays), Jam. 156/C3
Pedro, Ohio (45659) 284/E8
Pedro (pt.), Ceylon 68/E6
Pedro, S. Dak. (†57729) 298/E5
Pedro Afonso, Braz. 132/E5
Pedro Antonio Santos, Mex. 150/Q7
Pedro Bay, Alaska (99647) 196/H3
Pedro Betancourt, Cuba 158/D1
Pedro Chico, Col. 126/E7
Pedro de Valdivia, Chile 138/B4
Pedro Díaz Colodrero, Arg. 143/G5
Pedro González, Par. 144/C6
Pedro Juan Caballero, Par. 144/E4
Pedro Montoya, Mex. 150/K6
Pedro Segundo, Braz. 132/F4
Peduyim, Israel 65/B5
Peebles, 10/E3
Peebles, Ohio (45660) 284/D8
Peebles, Sask. 181/J5
Peebles (co.), Scot. 15/K8
Peebles, Scot. 15/K8
Pee Dee, N.C. (†28091) 281/K5
Pee Dee (riv.), N.C. 281/K5
Peedee, S.C. (29586) 296/H3
Pee Dee (riv.), S.C. 296/J4
Peekskill, N.Y. (10566) 276/N8
Peeksville, N.S. (†54514) 317/E3
Peel (sound), 163/G1
Peel (isl.), Austr. 88/L2
Peel (inlet), Austr. 88/B2
Peel (co.), Ont. 177/E4
Peel, 10/D3
Peel, I. of Man 13/C3
Peel (riv.), 163/C2
Peel, N. Br. 170/C2
Peel (sound), N.W.T. 187/J2
Peel (inlet), W. Aust. 92/A2
Peel (riv.), Yukon 187/E3
Peel Fell (mt.), Eng. 13/E2
Peel Fell (mt.), Scot. 15/L9
Pe Ell, Wash. (98572) 310/B4
Peene (riv.), E. Ger. 22/E2
Peenemünde, E. Ger. 22/E1
Peer, Belg. 27/G6
Peera Peera Poolanna (lake), Aust. 88/F5
Peera Peera Poolanna (lake), S. Aust. 94/F2
Peerless (lake), Alta. 182/C1
Peerless, Mont. (59253) 262/L2
Peerless, Sask. 181/L4
Peerless Park, Mo. (†63088) 261/O3
Peers, Alta. 182/B3
Peers, Mo. (†63357) 261/K5
Peery (lake), N.S.W. 97/B2
Peesane, Sask. 181/H3
Peetz, Colo. (80747) 208/N1
Peever, S. Dak. (57257) 298/R2
Pefferlaw, Ont. 177/E3
Pegasus (bay), N.Z. 101/D5
Pegasus, Port (inlet), N.Z. 101/B7
Peggs, Okla. (74452) 288/R2
Pegnitz, W. Ger. 22/D4
Pego, Spain 33/F3
Pegram, Tenn. (37143) 237/H8
Pegu (div.), Burma 72/C3
Pegu, Burma 72/C3
Pegun (isl.), Indon. 85/J5
Pegu Yoma (mts.), Burma 72/B3
Pehan, China 77/L2
Pehuajó, Arg. 143/D4
Peihai (Pakhoi), China 77/G7
Peine, W. Ger. 22/D2
Peiping (Peking) (cap.), China, 54/P5
Peiping (Peking) (cap.), China 77/J3
Peipus (lake), U.S.S.R. 48/C4
Peipus (lake), U.S.S.R. 52/C3
Peipus (lake), U.S.S.R. 53/D1
Peipus (lake), U.S.S.R., 7/G3
Peixoto (dam), Braz. 135/C2
Pejepscot, Maine (04067) 242/D8
Pejivalle, C. Rica 154/F6
Pekalongan, Indon. 85/J2
Pekan, Malaysia 72/D7
Pekan Nanas, Malaysia 72/E5
Pekelmeer (lake), Neth. Ant. 161/E9
Pekin, Ill. (61554) 222/D3
Pekin, Ind. (47165) 227/E7
Pekin, N. Dak. (58361) 283/O4
Peking (cap.), China, 54/P5
Peking (cap.), China, 3/Q3
Peking (cap.), China 77/J3
Pekisko, Alta. 182/C4
Pelabuhan Ratu (bay), Indon. 85/G2
Pelagie (isls.), Italy 34/D7
Pelagruž (Pelagosa) (isl.), Yugo. 45/C4
Pelahatchie, Miss. (39145) 256/E6
Peleaga (mt.), Rum. 45/F3
Pelechuco, Bol. 136/A4
Peleduy, U.S.S.R. 48/M4
Peleduy, U.S.S.R., 54/O4
Pelée (vol.), Mart. 156/G4
Pelée (vol.), Mart. 161/C5
Pelee (pt.), Ont. 177/B5
Peleliu (isl.), Pac. Is., 87/D5
Peleng (isl.), Indon. 85/G6
Pelequén, Chile 138/G5
Pelham, Ala. (35124) 194/E4
Pelham, Ga. (31779) 216/D8
Pelham▵, Mass. (†01002) 249/E3
Pelham, Mass. (†01002) 249/E3
Pelham, N.C. (27311) 281/L1
Pelham▵, N.H. (03076) 268/E6
Pelham‡, N.Y. (10803) 276/O7
Pelham, Queens. 95/B3
Pelham, Tenn. (37366) 237/K10
Pelham Manor, N.Y. (†10803) 276/O7
Pelhřimov, Czech. 41/C2
Pelican, Alaska (99832) 196/M1
Pelican (lake), Alta. 182/D2
Pelican (mt.), Alta. 182/D2
Pelican (mts.), Alta. 182/D2
Pelican (isl.), Barb. 161/B9
Pelican, La. (71063) 238/C3
Pelican (bay), Man. 179/B2
Pelican (lake), Man. 179/B2
Pelican (lake), Man. 179/B5
Pelican (lake), Minn. 254/C4
Pelican (lake), Minn. 254/E4
Pelican (lake), Minn. 254/F2
Pelican (riv.), Minn. 254/B4
Pelican (riv.), Minn. 254/F2
Pelican (lake), Nebr. 264/D2
Pelican (lake), Sask. 181/E5
Pelican (lake), Wis. 317/H4
Pelican Lake, Wis. (54463) 317/H4
Pelican Lakes (Breezy Point Village), Minn. (†56472) 254/D4
Pelican Narrows, Sask. 181/N3
Pelican Portage, Alta. 182/D2
Pelican Rapids, Man. 179/B2
Pelican Rapids, Minn. (56572) 254/B4
Pelileo, Ec. 128/C3
Pelion, S.C. (29123) 296/E4
Pelkie, Mich. (49958) 250/G1
Pelkosenniemi, Fin. 18/P3
Pella, Iowa (50219) 229/H6
Pella, Wis. (†54950) 317/J6
Pell City, Ala. (35125) 194/F3
Pellegrini, Arg. 143/D4
Pelletiers Mills, N. Br. 170/B1
Pell Lake‡, Wis. (53157) 317/K10
Pello, Fin. 18/O3
Pellston, Mich. (49769) 250/E3
Pellville, Ky. (42364) 237/H5
Pellworm (isl.), W. Ger. 22/C1
Pelly (riv.), Canada, 146/E3
Pelly (riv.), 163/C3
Pelly (bay), N.W.T. 187/J3
Pelly (lake), N.W.T. 187/H3
Pelly, Sask. 181/K4
Pelly (mts.), Yukon 187/E3
Pelly (riv.), Yukon 187/E3
Pelly Bay, 163/G2
Pelly Bay, N.W.T. 187/K3
Pelly Crossing, Yukon 187/E3
Peloncillo (mts.), Ariz. 198/F6
Peloncillo (mts.), N. Mex. 274/A6
Pelopónnisos (reg.), Greece 45/F7
Pelotas, Braz., 120/E6
Pelotas, Braz. 132/C10
Pelsor, Ark. (72856) 203/D2
Pelzer, Ind. (†47601) 227/C8
Pelzer, S.C. (29669) 296/B2
Pemadumcook (lake), Maine 242/E4
Pemalang, Indon. 85/J2
Pemaquid, Maine (04558) 242/E8
Pematangsiantar, Indon. 85/B5
Pemba (isl.), 102/G5
Pemba (reg.), Tanz. 115/H4
Pemba (isl.), Tanz. 115/H5
Pemberton, Br. Col. 184/F5
Pemberton, Minn. (56078) 254/E7
Pemberton, N.J. (08068) 273/D4
Pemberton, W. Aust. 92/A6
Pemberton, Ohio (45353) 284/B5
Pemberton, W. Va. (25905) 313/D7
Pemberton Meadows, Br. Col. 184/F5
Pemberville, Ohio (43450) 284/C3
Pembina (riv.), Alta. 182/C3
Pembina (mt.), Man. 179/D5
Pembina (riv.), Man. 179/E5
Pembina (co.), N. Dak. 283/P2
Pembina, N. Dak. (58271) 283/R2
Pembina (riv.), N. Dak. 283/O1
Pembine, Wis. (54156) 317/L4
Pembroke, 163/J6
Pembroke, Ont. 175/E2
Pembroke, Ont. 177/G2
Pembroke, Ga. (31321) 216/J6
Pembroke, Ky. (42266) 237/G7
Pembroke, 10/D5
Pembroke▵, Maine (04666) 242/J6
Pembroke, Maine (04666) 242/J6
Pembroke▵, Mass. (02359) 249/L4
Pembroke, N.C. (28372) 281/L5
Pembroke▵, N.H. (†03275) 268/E5
Pembroke, Va. (24136) 307/G6
Pembroke, Wales 13/B6
Pembroke Park, Fla. (†33023) 212/B4
Pembroke Pines, Fla. (33023) 212/B4
Pembrokeshire (co.), Wales 13/C6
Pembuang (riv.), Indon. 85/E6
Pemigewasset (riv.), N.H. 268/D4
Pemiscot (co.), Mo. 261/N10
Pemmican Portage, Sask. 181/J2
Pemuco, Chile 138/E1
Peña, Dom. Rep. 158/D5
Peñablanca, Chile 138/F2
Penablanca, N. Mex. (87041) 274/C3
Penafiel, Port. 33/B2
Peñafiel, Spain 33/E2
Peñaflor, Chile 138/G4
Peñal, Trinidad Tobago 161/B11
Peñalara (mt.), Spain 33/E2
Penalosa, Kans. (67121) 232/D4
Penalva, Braz. 132/E3
Penamacor, Port. 33/C2
Penápolis, Braz. 135/A2
Peñaranda de Bracamonte, Spain 33/D2
Pen Argyl, Pa. (18072) 294/M4
Peñarroya (peak), Spain 33/F2
Peñarroya-Pueblonuevo, Spain 33/D3
Penarth, Wales 13/D6
Penas (gulf), Chile, 120/C7
Penas (gulf), Chile 138/D7
Peñas (cape), Spain 33/D1
Penasco, N. Mex. (87553) 274/D2
Penbrook, Pa. (17103) 294/J5
Pencarrow (head), N.Z. 101/B3
Pence, Ind. (47973) 227/C4
Pence, Wis. (54553) 317/F3
Pencer, Minn. (56746) 254/C2
Pence Springs, W. Va. (24962) 313/E7
Pencilan (head), Wales 13/C5
Pencil Bluff, Ark. (71965) 203/C4
Penco, Chile 138/D1
Pencoyd‡, Pa. (†19004) 294/N6
Pendant d'Oreille, Alta. 182/E5
Pendé (riv.), Chad 111/C6
Pendé (riv.), Centr. Afr. Rep. 115/C2
Pendembu, 102/A4
Pendembu, S. Leone 106/B7
Pender (co.), N.C. 281/O5
Pender, Nebr. (68047) 264/H2
Pendergrass, Ga. (30567) 216/E2
Pendleton, Camp, Calif. 204/H10
Pendleton, Ind. (46064) 227/F5
Pendleton (co.), Ky. 237/N3
Pendleton, N.C. (27862) 281/P2
Pendleton, N.Y. (†14094) 276/C4
Pendleton, Oreg., 188/C1
Pendleton, Oreg. (97801) 291/J2
Pendleton, S.C. (29670) 296/B2
Pendleton (co.), W. Va. 313/H5
Pendletons, Va. (23117) 307/N5
Pend Oreille (riv.), Br. Col. 184/J6
Pend Oreille (lake), Idaho, 188/C1
Pend Oreille (lake), Idaho 220/B1
Pend Oreille (mt.), Idaho 220/B1
Pend Oreille (riv.), Idaho 220/A1
Pend Oreille (co.), Wash. 310/H2
Pend Oreille (riv.), Wash. 310/H2
Pendroy, Mont. (59467) 262/D2
Pendryl, Alta. 182/C3
Penedo, Braz. 132/G5
Penelope‡, Texas (76676) 302/H6
Penetanguishene, Ont. 177/D3
Penfield, Ga. (30658) 216/F3
Penfield, Ill. (61862) 222/F3
Penfield, N.Y. (14526) 276/F4
Penfield, Pa. (15849) 294/E3
Penganga (riv.), India 68/D5
Penge, Dem. Rep. of the Congo. 115/D5
Penghu (isls.), China 77/J7
Pengilly, Minn. (55775) 254/E3
Penglai, China 77/K4
Pengpu, China 77/J5
Penhold, Alta. 182/D3
Penhook, Va. (24137) 307/J7
Penibética (range), Spain 33/E4
Peniche, Port. 33/B3
Penicuik, 10/C1
Penicuik, Scot. 15/K8
Peninsula (pt.), Mich. 250/C3
Peninsula (pt.), N.Y. 276/H3
Peninsula, Ohio (44264) 284/G3
Peninsula Point‡, Alaska (†99901) 196/N2
Peñíscola, Spain 33/G2
Penitente (range), Braz. 132/E5
Pénjamo, Mex. 150/J6
Penju (isls.), Indon. 85/H7
Penk (riv.), 10/G2
Penki, China 77/K3
Penkill, Sask. 181/C4
Penmaenmawr, Wales 13/C4
Penmarch (pt.), France 28/A4
Penn, N. Dak. (58362) 283/M3
Penn, Pa. (15675) 294/C5
Penn, Sask. 181/D2
Pennant (pt.), N.S. 169/E4
Pennant, Sask. 181/C5
Penndel‡, Pa. (19047) 294/N5
Penne, Italy 34/D3
Pennell (mt.), Utah 304/D6
Pennellville, N.Y. (13132) 276/H4
Penner (riv.), India 68/D6
Penney Farms, Fla. (32079) 212/E2
Pennfield, N. Br. 170/D3
Pennine (range), Eng. 13/E3
Pennine Alps (range), Italy 34/A2
Pennine Alps (range), Switz. 39/E5
Pennington, Ala. (36916) 194/B6
Pennington (co.), Minn. 254/B2
Pennington, Minn. (56663) 254/D3
Pennington, N.J. (08534) 273/D3
Pennington (co.), S. Dak. 298/C6
Pennington, Texas (75856) 302/J6
Pennington Gap, Va. (24277) 307/C7
Pennline, Pa. (†16424) 294/A2
Pennock, Minn. (56279) 254/C5
Pennock Island‡, Alaska (†99901) 196/N2
Penn Run, Pa. (15765) 294/D4
Pennsauken▵, N.J. (08110) 273/B3
Pennsauken (creek), N.J. 273/B3
Pennsboro, Mo. (†65752) 261/E8
Pennsboro, W. Va. (26415) 313/E4
Pennsburg, Pa. (18073) 294/M5
Pennsdale, Pa. (17761) 294/J3
Penns Grove, N.J. (08069) 273/C4
Penns Park, Pa. (18943) 294/N5
Penn Square-Plymouth Valley‡, Pa. (†19401) 294/M5
Pennsuco, Fla. (†33010) 212/B4
Pennsville, N.J. (08070) 273/C4
Pennsville, Ohio (43770) 284/G6
Pennsylvania, 188/L2
PENNSYLVANIA, 294
Pennsylvania (state), U.S., 146/L5
Pennsylvania Furnace, Pa. (16865) 294/G4
Pennville, Ind. (47369) 227/G4
Pennville‡, Pa. (†17331) 294/J6
Penn Wynne, Pa. (†19003) 294/M6
Penny, Br. Col. 184/G3
Penny (str.), N.W.T. 187/J2
Penn Yan, N.Y. (14527) 276/F5
Penobscot (co.), Maine 242/F5
Penobscot▵, Maine (04476) 242/F7
Penobscot, Maine (04476) 242/F7
Penobscot (bay), Maine 242/F7
Penobscot (lake), Maine 242/C4
Penobscot (riv.), Maine 242/F5
Penobscot Ind. Res., Maine 242/F6
Penobsquis, N. Br. 170/E3
Penokee, Kans. (67659) 232/C2
Penola, S. Aust. 94/G7
Peñón (pt.), P. Rico 161/B1
Peñón Blanco, Mex. 150/H4
Penong, Aust. 88/E6
Penong, S. Aust. 94/C4
Penonomé, Pan. 154/G6
Penrhyn (Tongareva) (atoll), Cook Is., 87/L6
Penrith, 10/E3
Penrith, Eng. 13/E3
Penrith, N. S. W., 88/K3
Penrith, N.S.W. 97/F3
Penrod, Ky. (42365) 237/G6
Penrose, Colo. (81240) 208/K6
Penrose, N.C. (28766) 281/D4
Penryn, Calif. (95663) 204/C8
Penryn, Eng. 13/B7
Pensacola, Fla., 146/K7
Pensacola, Fla., 188/J4
Pensacola, Fla. (*32501) 212/B6
Pensacola (bay), Fla. 212/B6
Pensacola, Okla. (†74301) 288/R2
Pensacola N.A.S., Fla. 212/B6
Pensamiento, Bol. 136/E4
Pensaukee, Wis. (†54153) 317/L6
Pense, Sask. 181/G5
Penshurst, Vic. 97/B5
Penticton, Br. Col. 184/H5
Pentland (firth), 10/E1
Pentland (firth), Scot., 7/D3
Pentland (firth), Scot. 15/K2
Penton, Miss. (†38664) 256/D1
Pentress, W. Va. (26544) 313/F3
Pentwater, Mich. (49449) 250/C5
Peñuelas, Chile 138/F3
Peñuelas (lake), Chile 138/F2
Peñuelas, P. Rico 161/B2
Penwell, Texas (79776) 302/B6
Penza, U.S.S.R. 48/E4
Penza, U.S.S.R. 52/F4
Penza, U.S.S.R., 7/J3
Penzance, 10/D5
Penzance, Eng. 13/B7
Penzance, Sask. 181/F4
Penzberg, W. Ger. 22/D5
Penzhina (bay), U.S.S.R. 48/R3
Peoa, Utah (84061) 304/C3
Peonan (pt.), Man. 179/D3
Peoples, Ky. (40467) 237/N6
Peoria, Alta. 182/A2
Peoria, Ariz. (85345) 198/C5
Peoria, Ill., 146/J5
Peoria, Ill., 188/J2
Peoria (co.), Ill. 222/D3
Peoria, Ill. (*61601) 222/D3
Peoria, Iowa (†50219) 229/H6
Peoria, Kans. (†66067) 232/G3
Peoria, Miss. (†39645) 256/C8
Peoria, Ohio (†43067) 284/D5
Peoria, Okla. (†66713) 288/S1
Peoria Heights, Ill. (61614) 222/D3
Peosta, Iowa (52068) 229/M4
Peotone, Ill. (60468) 222/F2
Pep, N. Mex. (88126) 274/F5
Pepacton (res.), N.Y. 276/L6
Pepe (cape), Cuba 158/B3
Pepeekeo, Hawaii (96783) 218/J4
Pepeekeo (pt.), Hawaii 218/J4
Pepel, S. Leone 106/B7
Pepin (lake), Minn. 254/F6
Pepin (co.), Wis. 317/C6
Pepin, Wis. (54759) 317/B7
Pepin (lake), Wis. 317/B7
Pepperell▵, Mass. (01463) 249/H2
Pepperell, Mass. (01463) 249/H2
Pepper Pike, Ohio (44124) 284/J9
Pepperwood, Calif. (†95569) 204/A3
Peqin, Alb. 45/D5
Pequabuck, Conn. (06781) 210/C2
Pequabuck (riv.), Conn. 210/D2
Pequaming, Mich. (†49946) 250/A2
Pequannock, N.J. (07440) 273/B1
Pequea, Pa. (17565) 294/K6
Pequest (riv.), N.J. 273/D2
Pequiri (riv.), Braz. 132/C7
Pequiri (riv.), Braz. 132/C9
Pequonnock (riv.), Conn. 210/C3
Pequop (mts.), Nev. 266/G2
Pequot Lakes, Minn. (56472) 254/D4
Pera (head), Aust. 88/G2
Pera (Beyoğlu), Turkey 63/D6
Pera (head), Queens. 95/B2
Perahbumulih, Indon. 85/C6
Peraitepuí, Ven. 124/H5
Perak (state), Malaysia 72/D6
Perak, Gunong (mt.), Malaysia 72/D6
Perales (riv.), Spain 33/F4
Peralta, Dom. Rep. 158/D6
Peralta, N. Mex. (87042) 274/C4
Peralta, Spain 33/F1
Peralta, Urug. 145/C3
Peravia (prov.), Dom. Rep. 158/E6
Percé, Que. 172/D1
Percé, Que. 174/E3

Plavinas 419

Pietersburg, 102/E7
Pietersburg, S. Africa 118/D4
Pie Town, N. Mex. (87827) 274/A4
Pietrasanta, Italy 34/B3
Piet Retief, S. Africa 118/D5
Pietrosul (mt.), Rum. 45/G2
Pigádhia, Greece 45/H8
Pigeon (creek), Ala. 194/E7
Pigeon (lake), Alta. 182/D3
Pigeon, Guad. 161/A6
Pigeon (isl.), St. Lucia 161/G5
Pigeon (cays), Hond. 154/F3
Pigeon (creek), Ind. 227/C8
Pigeon (riv.), Ind. 227/F1
Pigeon (riv.), Man. 179/F2
Pigeon, Mich. (48755) 250/F5
Pigeon (riv.), Mich. 250/D7
Pigeon (riv.), Mich. 250/E3
Pigeon (riv.), Minn. 254/G1
Pigeon (riv.), N.C. 281/C3
Pigeon, W. Va. (25155) 313/D5
Pigeon (creek), W. Va. 313/B7
Pigeon Cove, Mass. (01966) 249/M2
Pigeon Creek, Ala. (36063) 194/E7
Pigeon Falls, Wis. (54760) 317/D7
Pigeon Forge, Tenn. (37862) 237/O9
Pigeon Hill, N. Br. 170/F1
Pigeonroost, Ky. (40976) 237/O6
Pigg (riv.), Va. 307/J7
Piggott, Ark. (72454) 203/K1
Pignon, Haiti 158/C5
Pigs (Cochinos) (bay), Cuba 158/D2
Pigüé, Arg. 143/D4
Piippola, Fin. 18/P4
Pija, Sierra de (mts.), Hond. 154/D3
Pijijiapan, Mex. 150/N9
Pik, Iran 66/G3
Pike (co.), Ala. 194/G7
Pike (co.), Ark. 203/C5
Pike (co.), Ga. 216/D4
Pike (co.), Ill. 222/C4
Pike (co.), Ind. 227/C8
Pike (co.), Ky. 237/S6
Pike (riv.), Minn. 254/F3
Pike (co.), Miss. 256/D8
Pike (co.), Mo. 261/K4
Pike, N.H. (03780) 268/C3
Pike, N.Y. (14130) 276/D5
Pike (co.), Ohio 284/D7
Pike (co.), Pa. 294/M3
Pike, W. Va. (†26346) 313/D4
Pike City, Ark. (†71940) 203/C5
Pike Lake, Sask. 181/E4
Pike Road, Ala. (36064) 194/F6
Pike Road, N.C. (27860) 281/R3
Pikes (peak), Colo., 188/E3
Pikes (peak), Colo. 208/J5
Pikes Peak, Ind. (†47201) 227/E6
Pikes Peak, Sask. 181/B2
Pikesville, Md. (21208) 245/M3
Piketberg, S. Africa 118/B6
Piketon, Ohio (45661) 284/E7
Pike View, Ky. (42770) 237/K6
Pikeville, Ind. (†47590) 227/C8
Pikeville, Ky. (41501) 237/S6
Pikeville, N.C. (27863) 281/N4
Pikeville, Tenn. (37367) 237/L9
Pikiang, China 77/E6
Pikwitonei, Man. 179/J3
Pila, Arg. 143/H7
Piła, Poland 47/C2
Pilão Arcado, Braz. 132/F5
Pilar, Arg. 143/F5
Pilar, Braz. 132/H5
Pilar, Par. 144/C6
Pilas (isl.), Phil. 82/C7
Pilate, Haiti 158/C5
Pilatus (mt.), Switz. 39/F3
Pilaya (riv.), Bol. 136/C7
Pilcomayo (riv.), 120/D5
Pilcomayo (riv.), Arg. 143/E1
Pilcomayo (riv.), Bol. 136/D7
Pilcomayo (riv.), Par. 144/C5
Pilger, Nebr. (68768) 264/G2
Pilger, Sask. 181/F3
Pilgrim, Ky. (41250) 237/S5
Pilibhit, India 68/D3
Pilica (riv.), Poland 47/E3
Pilis, Hung. 41/E3
Pilisvörösvár, Hung. 41/E3
Pillager, Minn. (56473) 254/D4
Pillar (cape), Aust. 88/H8
Pillar (pt.), Calif. 204/H3
Pillar (cape), Tasmania 99/E5
Pillar (pt.), Wash. 310/A2
Pillaro, Ec. 128/C3
Pilliga, N.S.W. 97/E2
Pillow, Pa. (17080) 294/J4
Pillsbury (lake), Calif. 204/C4
Pillsbury (sound), V.I.(U.S.) 161/B4
Pillsbury, N. Dak. (58065) 283/P5
Pilmaiquén (riv.), Chile 138/D3
Pílos, Greece 45/E7
Pilot (peak), Idaho 220/C4
Pilot (peak), Idaho 220/C6
Pilot, Ky. (40469) 237/O5
Pilot (peak), Nev. 266/C4
Pilot, Va. (24138) 307/H6
Pilot Butte, Sask. 181/G5
Pilot Butte (res.), Wyo. 319/D2
Pilote (riv.), Mart. 161/D7
Pilot Grove, Iowa (52648) 229/L7
Pilot Grove, Minn. (†56027) 254/D7
Pilot Grove, Mo. (65276) 261/G5
Pilot Knob (mt.), Idaho 220/C4
Pilot Knob, Ind. (†47118) 227/E8
Pilot Knob, Mo. (63663) 261/L7
Pilot Mound, Iowa (50223) 229/F4
Pilot Mound, Man. 179/D5
Pilot Mound, Minn. (†55923) 254/F7
Pilot Mountain, N.C. (27041) 281/H2
Piloto Juan Fernández (isl.), Chile, 120/B6
Pilotos, Cuba 158/B1
Pilot Point, Alaska (99649) 196/G3
Pilot Point, Texas (76258) 302/H4
Pilot Rock, Oreg. (97868) 291/J2
Pilot Station, Alaska (99650) 196/F2
Pilottown, La. (70081) 238/M8
Pilsen, Wis. (†54217) 317/L7
Piltene, U.S.S.R. 53/A2
Pima (co.), Ariz. 198/D6
Pima, Ariz. (85543) 198/F6
Pimentel, Dom. Rep. 158/E5
Pimentel, Peru 128/B6
Pimento, Ind. (47866) 227/C6
Pimichín, Ven. 124/E6
Pimville, S. Africa 118/H6
Pina, Cuba 158/F2
Pina de Ebro, Spain 33/F2
Pinal (co.), Ariz. 198/D6
Pinal (peak), Ariz. 198/E5
Pinaleno (mts.), Ariz. 198/F6
Pinamalayan, Phil. 82/C4
Pinang, Malaysia, 54/N9
Pinang (state), Malaysia 72/D6
Pinang, Malaysia 72/C6
Pinang (Pulau) (isl.), Malaysia 72/C6
Pinarbaşi, Turkey 63/G3
Pinar del Río, Cuba, 146/K7
Pinar del Río, Cuba 156/A2
Pinar del Río (prov.), Cuba 158/A1
Pinar del Río, Cuba 158/B2
Pinarhisar, Turkey 63/B2
Piñas, Ec. 128/C4
Piñas (pt.), Pan. 154/H7
Pinatubo (mt.), Phil. 82/C3
Pinawa, Man. 179/G4
Pinch, W. Va. (25156) 313/D6
Pincher, Alta. 182/C5
Pincher Creek, 163/E6
Pincher Creek, Alta. 182/D5
Pinchi (lake), Br. Col. 184/E3
Pinckard, Ala. (36371) 194/G8
Pinckney, Mich. (48169) 250/F6
Pinckneyville, Ill. (62274) 222/D5
Pinckneyville, Miss. (39658) 256/B8
Pinconning, Mich. (48650) 250/F5
Pińczów, Poland 47/E3
Pindall, Ark. (72669) 203/E1
Pindamonhangaba, Braz. 135/D3
Pindi Gheb, Pak. 68/C2
Pindo (riv.), Ec. 128/D3
Pindus (mts.), Greece 45/E6
Pine, Ariz. (85544) 198/D4
Pine (riv.), Br. Col. 184/G2
Pine (creek), Calif. 204/D3
Pine, Colo. (80470) 208/J4
Pine (brook), Conn. 210/E2
Pine (isl.), Fla. 212/D5
Pine (pt.), Fla. 212/C2
Pine, Idaho (†83647) 220/C6
Pine (mt.), Ky. 237/O7
Pine (lake), Mich. 250/F4
Pine (riv.), Mich. 250/D4
Pine (riv.), Mich. 250/E5
Pine (co.), Minn. 254/F4
Pine, Mo. (63958) 261/K9
Pine (riv.), N.H. 268/E4
Pine (creek), Nev. 266/E2
Pine (cape), Newf. 166/D2
Pine (creek), Oreg. 291/L3
Pine (creek), Oreg. 291/J4
Pine (creek), Pa. 294/H2
Pine (creek), Utah 304/C6
Pine (creek), Wash. 310/H3
Pine (lake), Wis. 317/J1
Pine Alcove (creek), Utah 304/D6
Pine Apple, Ala. (36768) 194/E7
Pine Bank, Pa. (15354) 294/B6
Pine Beach, N.J. (08741) 273/E4
Pine Bluff, Ark., 188/H4
Pine Bluff, Ark. (71601) 203/F5
Pinebluff, N.C. (28373) 281/K4
Pine Bluff Arsenal, Ark. 203/F5
Pine Bluffs, Wyo. (82082) 319/H4
Pine Brook, N.J. (07058) 273/E2
Pine Bush, N.Y. (12566) 276/M7
Pine City, Ark. (†72069) 203/H4
Pine City, Minn. (55063) 254/F5
Pine City, Wash. (99162) 310/H3
Pinecliffe, Colo. (80471) 208/J3
Pinecraft‡, Fla. (33578) 212/D4
Pine Creek, Aust. 88/E2
Pine Creek (pt.), Conn. 210/C4
Pinecreek, Minn. (56747) 254/C2
Pine Creek, No. Terr. 93/C2
Pine Creek (res.), Okla. 288/R6
Pinecrest, Calif. (95364) 204/F5
Pinedale, Ariz. (85934) 198/E4
Pinedale, Calif. (93650) 204/F7
Pinedale, Wyo. (82941) 319/C3
Pine Dock, Man. 179/F3
Pine Falls, Man. 179/F4
Pine Flat (res.), Calif. 204/F7
Pine Forest (range), Nev. 266/C1
Pine Forest‡, Texas (†77662) 302/L7
Pinega, U.S.S.R. 52/F2
Pinega (riv.), U.S.S.R. 52/G2
Pine Grove, Ark. (†71763) 203/E6
Pine Grove, Ont. 177/J4
Pine Grove, Ga. (†31513) 216/H7
Pine Grove, Ky. (40470) 237/N5
Pine Grove, La. (70453) 238/J5
Pine Grove, Pa. (17963) 294/K4
Pine Grove (res.), Pa. 294/K6
Pine Grove, W. Va. (26419) 313/E3
Pine Grove Furnace, Pa. (†17324) 294/H5
Pine Grove Mills, Pa. (16868) 294/G4
Pine Hall, N.C. (27042) 281/K2
Pinehaven (Heretaunga-Pinehaven), N.Z. 101/C2
Pine Hill, Ala. (36769) 194/C7
Pine Hill, Ky. (40364) 237/N6
Pine Hill, N.J. (08021) 273/D4
Pine Hill, N.Y. (12465) 276/M6
Pine Hills‡, Fla. (32808) 212/E3
Pine House, Sask. 181/M3
Pinehurst (lake), Alta. 182/E2
Pinehurst, Ga. (31071) 216/E6
Pinehurst, Idaho (83850) 220/B2
Pinehurst, Mass. (01866) 249/B5
Pinehurst, N.C. (28374) 281/K4
Pinehurst, Oreg. (†97520) 291/E5
Pinehurst‡, Texas (77362) 302/L7
Pinehurst-Sheppard Park‡, S.C. (†29483) 296/G5
Pine Island (bay), Ant. 5/C13
Pine Island (sound), Fla. 212/D5
Pine Island, Minn. (55963) 254/F6
Pine Island, N.Y. (10969) 276/L8
Pine Knot, Ky. (42635) 237/M7
Pine Lake, Alta. 182/D3
Pine Lake‡, Ga. (30072) 216/D3
Pine Lake, Ind. (†46350) 227/D1
Pineland, Fla. (33945) 212/D5
Pineland, S.C. (29934) 296/E6
Pineland, Texas (75968) 302/L6
Pinelands, S. Africa 118/E6
Pine Lawn, Mo. (63120) 261/P3
Pine Level, Ala. (36065) 194/F6
Pine Level, N.C. (27568) 281/N4
Pinellas (co.), Fla. 212/D4
Pinellas (pt.), Fla. 212/C3
Pinellas Park, Fla. (33565) 212/B3
Pine Log (creek), Fla. 212/C6
Pine Log, Ga. (30152) 216/C2
Pine Meadow, Conn. (06061) 210/D1
Pine Mountain, Ga. (31822) 216/C5
Pine Neck-West Tiana‡, N.Y. (†11946) 276/R9
Pineola, N.C. (28662) 281/F2
Pineora, Ga. (†31312) 216/K6
Pine Orchard, Conn. (†06405) 210/D3
Pine Park, Ga. (†31728) 216/D9
Pine Plains, N.Y. (12567) 276/N7
Pine Point, Maine (†04064) 242/C8
Pine Point, N.W.T. 187/G3
Pine Prairie, La. (70576) 238/E5
Piñera, Urug. 145/C3
Pine Ridge, Ark. (71966) 203/C4
Pine Ridge, Miss. (†39120) 256/B7
Pineridge, S.C. (†29169) 296/E4
Pine Ridge, S. Dak. (57770) 298/E7
Pine Ridge Ind. Res., S. Dak. 298/D7
Pine River, Man. 179/B3
Pine River, Minn. (56474) 254/D4
Pine River, Wis. (54965) 317/H7
Pinerolo, Italy 34/A2
Pines (Pinos) (isl.), Cuba 156/A2
Pines (isl.), Cuba 158/B3
Pines, Isle of (isl.), Cuba, 146/K7
Pines (lake), N.J. 273/B1
Pines (isl.), New Cal., 87/G8
Pine Shores‡, Fla. (†33577) 212/D4
Pine Springs‡, Minn. (†55109) 254/G5
Pine Springs, Texas (†88220) 302/C10
Pinetop, Ariz. (85935) 198/F4
Pinetops, N.C. (27864) 281/O3
Pinetown, N.C. (27865) 281/R3
Pinetown, S. Africa 118/E5
Pinetta, Fla. (32350) 212/C1
Pine Valley, Calif. (92062) 204/J11
Pine Valley, N.J. (†08021) 273/C4
Pine Valley, N.Y. (14872) 276/G6
Pine Valley, Utah (†84722) 304/A6
Pineview, Ga. (31071) 216/F6
Pineview, N.C. (†27330) 281/L4
Pine Village, Ind. (47975) 227/C4
Pineville, Ky. (40977) 237/O7
Pineville, La. (71360) 238/F4
Pineville, Miss. (†39074) 256/F6
Pineville, Mo. (64856) 261/D9
Pineville, N.C. (28134) 281/H4
Pineville, S.C. (29468) 296/H5
Pineville, W. Va. (24874) 313/C7
Pinewood, Minn. (56664) 254/C3
Pinewood, S.C. (29125) 296/G4
Piney, Ark. (†72847) 203/D3
Piney (isl.), Fla. 212/B1
Piney (pt.), Fla. 212/C2
Piney, Man. 179/F5
Piney Flats, Tenn. (37686) 237/S8
Piney Fork, Ohio (43941) 284/J5
Piney Park, Mo. (†63077) 261/L6
Piney Point, Md. (20674) 245/M8
Piney Point Village, Texas (†77001) 302/J1
Piney River, Va. (22964) 307/L5
Piney Woods, Miss. (39148) 256/D6
Ping, Mae Nam (riv.), Thai. 72/C3
Pingchüan, China 77/J3
Pingelap (atoll), Pac. Is., 87/G5
Pingelly, Aust. 88/B2
Pingelly, W. Aust. 92/B2
Pingelly West, W. Aust. 92/B2
Pinger (pt.), N.W.T. 187/K3
Pingliang, China 77/G4
Pinglo, China 77/H7
Pingree, Idaho (83262) 220/F6
Pingree, N. Dak. (58476) 283/N5
Pingree Grove‡, Ill. (†60140) 222/E1
Pingsiang, Kiangsi, China 77/H6
Pingsiang, Kwangsi Chuang, China 77/G7
Pingtung, China 77/K7
Pingwu, China, 54/O6
Pingwu, China 77/F5
Pingyao, China 77/H4
Pinhal, Braz. 135/C3
Pinheiro, Braz. 132/E3
Pinhel, Port. 33/C2
Piniós (riv.), Greece 45/E6
Pinjarra, Aust. 88/B6
Pinjarra, W. Aust. 92/A2
Pink (cliffs), Ariz. 198/E4
Pinkafeld, Austria 41/C3
Pinkegat (chan.), Neth. Ant. 27/H2
Pinkham, Sask. 181/B4
Pinkham Notch (pass), N.H. 268/E3
Pink Hill, N.C. (28572) 281/O4
Pink Mountain, Br. Col. 184/F1
Pinkstaff, Ill. (62453) 222/F5
Pinnacle, N.C. (27043) 281/J2
Pinnacles Nat'l Mon., Calif. 204/D7
Pinnaroo, Aust. 88/G7
Pinnaroo, S. Aust. 94/G6
Pinneberg, W. Ger. 22/C2
Pinnebog, Mich. (†48445) 250/F5
Pinola, Miss. (39149) 256/E7
Pinole, Calif. (94564) 204/J1
Pinon, Ariz. (86510) 198/E2
Pinon, Colo. (†81001) 208/K6
Pinon, N. Mex. (88344) 274/D6
Pinopolis, S.C. (29469) 296/G5
Pinopolis (dam), S.C. 296/G5
Pinos Altos, N. Mex. (88053) 274/A6
Pinos-Puente, Spain 33/E4
Pinquén, Peru 128/G9
Pinrang, Indon. 85/F6
Pins (pt.), Ont. 177/C5
Pinsk, U.S.S.R. 48/C4
Pinsk, U.S.S.R. 52/C4
Pinsk, U.S.S.R., 7/G3
Pinson, Ala. (35126) 194/E3
Pinson, Tenn. (38366) 237/D10
Pinta (isl.), Ec. 128/B9
Pintada, N. Mex. (†88435) 274/D4
Pintada (creek), N. Mex. 274/E4
Pintado, Artigas, Urug. 145/C1
Pintado, Florida, Urug. 145/C4
Pintados, Chile 138/B2
Pintados, Salar de (salt dep.), Chile 138/B2
Pinto, Chile 138/A11
Pinto, Md. (21556) 245/C2
Pinto, Sask. 181/J6
Pinto (creek), Sask. 181/D6
Pintura, Utah (84762) 304/A6
Pintuyan, Phil. 82/E6
Pintwater (range), Nev. 266/F6
Pinware, Newf. 166/C3
Pinware (riv.), Newf. 166/C3
Pinyang, China 77/G7
Pinyon (peak), Idaho 220/C5
Pinzón (isl.), Ec. 128/B9
Pioche, Nev. (89043) 266/G5
Piombino, Italy 34/C3
Pioneer, Alta. 182/B3
Pioneer (mts.), Idaho 220/D6
Pioneer, Iowa (50572) 229/E3
Pioneer, La. (71266) 238/H1
Pioneer, Mo. (†65734) 261/E9
Pioneer, Ohio (43554) 284/A2
Pioneer, Tenn. (37847) 237/N8
Pioneer Mine, Br. Col. 184/F5
Pioner (isl.), U.S.S.R. 48/J2
Pionki, Poland 47/E3
Piopio, N.Z. 101/E3
Piopolis, Que. 172/F4
Piotrków Trybunalski, Poland 47/D3
Piotta, Switz. 39/G3
Piove di Sacco, Italy 34/C2
Pipe (creek), Ind. 227/F4
Piper (peak), Nev. 266/D5
Piper City, Ill. (60959) 222/E3
Pipersville, Pa. (18947) 294/M5
Pipe Spring Nat'l Mon., Ariz. 198/C2
Pipestem (riv.), N. Dak. 283/M5
Pipestem, W. Va. (25979) 313/E7
Pipestone (riv.), Ont. 175/B2
Pipestone, Man. 179/B5
Pipestone (creek), Man. 179/A5
Pipestone (co.), Minn. 254/B6
Pipestone, Minn. (56164) 254/B7
Pipestone (creek), Sask. 181/K6
Pipestone (riv.), Sask. 181/L2
Pipestone Nat'l Mon., Minn. 254/B6
Pipines, Arg. 143/H7
Pipinui (pt.), N.Z. 101/B2
Pipmouacane (res.), Que. 174/D3
Piqua, Kans. (66761) 232/G4
Piqua, Ohio (45356) 284/B5
Piquete, Braz. 135/D3
Piracambu (range), Braz. 132/E3
Piracanjuba, Braz. 132/D7
Piracicaba, Braz. 132/E8
Piracicaba, Braz. 135/C3
Piracuruca, Braz. 132/F3
Piraí do Sul, Braz. 132/D9
Piraí do Sul, Braz. 135/B4
Piraiévs, Greece, 7/G5
Piraiévs (Piraeus), Greece 45/F7
Piraju, Braz. 135/B3
Pirajuí, Braz. 135/B2
Pirámide, Cerro (mt.), Chile 138/D8
Piran, Yugo. 45/A3
Piraré, Arg. 143/E2
Pirapora, Braz., 120/F4
Pirapora, Braz. 132/E7
Piraraja, Urug. 145/E4
Pirassununga, Braz. 135/C3
Pirata (mt.), P. Rico 161/F2
Pirates Cove, Fla. (†33042) 212/E7
Piray (riv.), Bol. 136/D5
Pirayú, Par. 144/B6
Pirdop, Bulg. 45/G4
Pirenópolis, Braz. 132/D6
Pires do Rio, Braz. 132/D7
Pírgos, Greece, 7/G5
Pírgos, Crete, Greece 45/G8
Pírgos, Pelopónnisos, Greece 45/E7
Piriápolis, Urug. 145/D5
Piribebuy, Par. 144/B6
Piribebuy (riv.), Par. 144/B6
Piripiri, Braz. 132/F4
Píritu, Anzoátegui, Ven. 124/F2
Píritu, Falcón, Ven. 124/D2
Píritu, Portuguesa, Ven. 124/D3
Pirmasens, W. Ger. 22/B4
Pirna, E. Ger. 22/E3
Piro (Kumgang) (mt.), N. Korea 81/D4
Pirongia (mt.), N.Z. 101/E3
Pirot, Yugo. 45/F4
Piru, Calif. (93040) 204/G9
Piru, Indon. 85/H6
Piryatin, U.S.S.R. 52/D4
Piryí, Greece 45/G6
Pisa (prov.), Italy 34/C3
Pisa, Italy 34/C3
Pisac, Peru 128/G9
Pisagua, Chile, 120/C4
Pisagua, Chile 138/A2
Piscadera (bay), Neth. Ant. 161/F9
Piscataqua (riv.), Maine 242/B9
Piscataqua (riv.), N.H. 268/F5
Piscataquis (co.), Maine 242/E4
Piscataquis (riv.), Maine 242/E5
Piscataquog (riv.), N.H. 268/D5
Piscataway, Md. (†20735) 245/L6
Piscataway (creek), Md. 245/G6
Piscataway△, N.J. (08854) 273/D2
Piscatosin (lake), Que. 172/B3
Pisco, Peru, 120/C4
Pisco, Peru 128/D9
Pisco (bay), Peru 128/D9
Pisco (riv.), Peru 128/D9
Piseco, N.Y. (12139) 276/L4
Piseco (lake), N.Y. 276/M4
Písek, Czech. 41/C2
Pisek, N. Dak. (58273) 283/P3
Pisgah, Ala. (35765) 194/G1
Pisgah, Iowa (51564) 229/B5
Pisgah, Md. (20640) 245/K6
Pisgah Forest, N.C. (28768) 281/D4
Pishan (Guma), China 77/A4
Pishin, Pak. 59/J3
Pishin, Iran 66/M7
Pishin, Pak. 68/B2
Pishkun (res.), Mont. 262/D3
Pisinimo, Ariz. (85634) 198/C6
Pismo Beach, Calif. (93449) 204/E8
Piso Firme, Bol. 136/D3
Pisoniano, Italy 34/F6
Pissis (mt.), Arg. 143/C2
Pistapaug (pond), Conn. 210/E3
Pisticci, Italy 34/F4
Pistoia (prov.), Italy 34/C2
Pistoia, Italy 34/C2
Pistolet (bay), Newf. 166/C3
Pistol River, Oreg. (97444) 291/C5
Pisz, Poland 47/E2
Pit (riv.), Calif. 204/D2
Pitalito, Col. 126/B7
Pitangui, Braz. 135/D1
Pitarpunga (lake), N.S.W. 97/B4
Pitcairn (isl.), 3/C7
Pitcairn (isl.), 87/O8
Pitcairn, Pa. (15140) 294/C5
Pitch (lake), Trinidad Tobago 161/A11
Piteå, Sweden 18/M4
Piteälv (riv.), Sweden 18/M4
Pitești, Rum. 45/G3
Píthion, Greece 45/H5
Pithiviers, France 28/E3
Pitiquito, Mex. 150/D1
Pitkas Point, Alaska (†99658) 196/F2
Pitkin (co.), Colo. 208/F4
Pitkin, Colo. (81241) 208/F5
Pitkin, La. (70656) 238/E5
Pitlochry, 10/E2
Pitlochry, Scot. 15/J6
Pitman, N.J. (08071) 273/C4
Pitman, Sask. 181/G5
Pitogo, Phil. 82/C4
Piton des Neiges (mt.), Réunion 118/G5
Pitrufquén, Chile 138/D2
Pitsburg, Ohio (45358) 284/A6
Pitt (mt.), Aust. 88/M5
Pitt (isl.), Br. Col. 184/C3
Pitt (lake), Br. Col. 184/L2
Pitt, Minn. (56665) 254/D2
Pitt (co.), N.C. 281/P3
Pitt (isl.), N.Z. 101/E7
Pitt (str.), N.Z. 101/E7
Pittenweem, Scot. 15/L7
Pitti (isl.), India 68/C6
Pittock, Pa. (15141) 294/B7
Pitts, Ark. (†72421) 203/J2
Pitts, Ga. (31072) 216/E7
Pittsboro, Ind. (46167) 227/D5
Pittsboro, Miss. (38951) 256/F3
Pittsboro, N.C. (27312) 281/L3
Pittsburg, Calif. (94565) 204/L1
Pittsburg, Ill. (62974) 222/E6
Pittsburg, Ind. (†46923) 227/D3
Pittsburg, Kans. (66762) 232/H4
Pittsburg, Ky. (40755) 237/N6
Pittsburg, Mo. (65724) 261/F7
Pittsburg△, N.H. (03592) 268/E1
Pittsburg, N.H. (03592) 268/E1
Pittsburg (co.), Okla. 288/P5
Pittsburg, Okla. (74560) 288/P5
Pittsburg, Texas (75686) 302/J4
Pittsburgh, Pa., 146/K5
Pittsburgh, Pa., 188/L2
Pittsburgh, Pa. (*15201) 294/B7
Pittsfield, Ill. (62363) 222/C4
Pittsfield△, Maine (04967) 242/E6
Pittsfield, Maine (04967) 242/E6
Pittsfield, Mass., 188/M2
Pittsfield, Mass. (01201) 249/A3
Pittsfield△, N.H. (03263) 268/E5
Pittsfield, N.H. (03263) 268/E5
Pittsfield, Pa. (16340) 294/D2
Pittsfield△, Vt. (05762) 268/B4
Pittsfield, Vt. (05762) 268/B4
Pittsford, Mich. (49271) 250/E7
Pittsford, N.Y. (14534) 276/E4
Pittsford△, Vt. (05763) 268/A4
Pittsford, Vt. (05763) 268/A4
Pittston△, Maine (†04345) 242/D7
Pittston, Pa. (*18640) 294/L3
Pittstown, N.J. (08867) 273/C2
Pittsview, Ala. (36871) 194/H6
Pittsville, Md. (21850) 245/S7
Pittsville, Mo. (†64040) 261/E5
Pittsville, Va. (24139) 307/K7
Pittsville, Wis. (54466) 317/F7
Pittsylvania (co.), Va. 307/K7
Pittville, Calif. (†96056) 204/E2
Pittwood, Ill. (†60970) 222/F3
Piuí, Braz. 132/E8
Piuí, Braz. 135/D2
Piura, Peru, 120/B3
Piura (dept.), Peru 128/B5
Piura, Peru 128/B5
Piura (riv.), Peru 128/B5
Piute (co.), Utah 304/B5
Piute (res.), Utah 304/B5
Pivijay, Col. 126/C2
Pixley, Calif. (93256) 204/F8
Piyas (lake), S. Dak. 298/P2
Pizacoma, Peru 128/H11
Pizarro, Col. 126/B5
Place, Ky. (†40734) 237/N7
Placentia, Calif. (92670) 204/D11
Placentia, Newf. 166/C2
Placentia (bay), Newf. 166/C2
Placentia (sound), Newf. 166/C2
Placer (co.), Calif. 204/E4
Placer, Phil. 82/E6
Placer, Oreg. (†97478) 291/D5
Placerville, Calif. (95667) 204/C8
Placerville, Colo. (81430) 208/D6
Placerville, Idaho (83666) 220/C6
Placetas, Cuba 158/E2
Placid (lake), Fla. 212/E4
Placid (lake), N.Y. 276/N2
Placida, Fla. (33946) 212/D5
Placilla, Chile 138/F6
Placilla de Caracoles, Chile 138/B4
Placilla de Peñuelas, Chile 138/F2
Placitas, N. Mex. (87043) 274/C3
Plad, Mo. (†65764) 261/G7
Pladda (isl.), Scot. 15/F9
Pladju, Indon. 85/D6
Plain, Wash. (†98826) 310/E3
Plain, Wis. (53577) 317/F9
Plain City, Ohio (43064) 284/D5
Plain City, Utah (†84401) 304/B2
Plain Dealing, La. (71064) 238/C1
Plainedge‡, N.Y. (†11714) 276/R7
Plainfield, Ark. (†71740) 203/D7
Plainfield△, Conn. (06374) 210/H2
Plainfield, Conn. (06374) 210/H2
Plainfield, Ga. (31073) 216/F6
Plainfield, Ill. (60544) 222/E2
Plainfield, Ind. (46168) 227/E5
Plainfield, Iowa (50666) 229/J3
Plainfield△, Mass. (01070) 249/C2
Plainfield△, N.H. (03781) 268/C4
Plainfield, N.H. (03781) 268/C4
Plainfield, N.J. (*07060) 273/E2
Plainfield, Ohio (43836) 284/G5
Plainfield△, Vt. (05667) 268/C3
Plainfield, Vt. (05667) 268/C3
Plainfield, Wis. (54966) 317/G7
Plain Lake, Alta. 182/E3
Plains, Ga. (31780) 216/D6
Plains, Kans. (67869) 232/B4
Plains, Mont. (59859) 262/B3
Plains, Pa. (18705) 294/L3
Plains, Texas (79355) 302/B4
Plainsboro, N.J. (08536) 273/D3
Plainview, Ark. (72857) 203/D4
Plainview, Ill. (62676) 222/C4
Plain View, Iowa (†52773) 229/M5
Plainview, Minn. (55964) 254/F6
Plainview, N.Y. (11803) 276/O9
Plainview, Nebr. (68769) 264/G2
Plainview, S. Dak. (57771) 298/E4
Plain View, Sask. 181/J4
Plainview, Texas (79072) 302/C3
Plainville△, Conn. (06062) 210/D2
Plainville, Ga. (30733) 216/C2
Plainville, Ill. (62365) 222/B4
Plainville, Ind. (47568) 227/C7
Plainville, Kans. (67663) 232/C2
Plainville△, Mass. (02762) 249/J4
Plainwell, Mich. (49080) 250/D6
Plaisance, Haiti 158/C5
Plaisance, Que. 172/B4
Plaisted, Maine (04767) 242/F1
Plaistow△, N.H. (03865) 268/E6
Plaistow, N.H. (03865) 268/E6
Plamondon, Alta. 182/D2
Planá, Czech. 41/B2
Plana (cays), Bah. Is. 156/D2
Planada, Calif. (95365) 204/E6
Planaltina, Braz. 132/E6
Plandome‡, N.Y. (11030) 276/R7
Plandome Heights‡, N.Y. (†11030) 276/R7
Plandome Manor‡, N.Y. (†11030) 276/R7
Planeta Rica, Col. 126/C3
Plánice, Czech. 41/B2
Plankinton, S. Dak. (57368) 298/N6
Plano, Ill. (60545) 222/E2
Plano, Iowa (52581) 229/G7
Plano, Texas (75074) 302/H4
Plant, Tenn. (†37054) 237/F9
Plantagenet, Ont. 177/K2
Plantation, Fla. (33314) 212/B4
Plantation (key), Fla. 212/F7
Plantation‡, Ky. (†40201) 237/K4
Plant City, Fla. (33566) 212/D3
Plantersville, Ala. (36758) 194/E5
Plantersville, Miss. (38862) 256/G2
Plantersville, S.C. (29441) 296/J4
Plantsite, Ariz. (†85540) 198/F5
Plantsville, Conn. (06479) 210/D2
Plaquemine, La. (70764) 238/J2
Plaquemines (par.), La. 238/L8
Plasencia, Spain 33/C2
Plasselb, Switz. 39/D3
Plaster City, Calif. (92269) 204/K11
Plaster Rock, N. Br. 170/C2
Plasy, Czech. 41/B2
Plat, Wis. (†53017) 317/K1
Plata, Río de la (est.), Arg. 143/E4
Plata (riv.), P. Rico 161/D2
Plata, La (riv.), Urug. 145/B5
Platanal, Ven. 124/F6
Platanilla, C. Rica 154/F6
Platea, Pa. (†16417) 294/B2
Plateau (creek), Colo. 208/C4
Plateau, N.S. 169/H2
Plateau City, Colo. (†81624) 208/D4
Plate Cove, Newf. 166/D2
Platen (cape), Norway 18/D1
Platina, Calif. (96076) 204/B3
Platinum, Alaska (99651) 196/F3
Platner, Colo. (†80743) 208/N2
Plato, Col. 126/C3
Plato, Minn. (55370) 254/D6
Plato, Mo. (65552) 261/H8
Plato, Sask. 181/C4
Platoro (res.), Colo. 208/F8
Platte (riv.), Iowa 229/D8
Platte (lake), Mich. 250/C4
Platte (co.), Mo. 261/C4
Platte (riv.), Mo. 261/C3
Platte (riv.), Nebr., 188/G2
Platte (co.), Nebr. 264/G3
Platte (riv.), Nebr. 264/E4
Platte, S. Dak. (57369) 298/M7
Platte (lake), S. Dak. 298/M6
Platte (riv.), U.S., 146/H5
Platte (co.), Wyo. 319/H4
Platte Center, Nebr. (68653) 264/G3
Platte City, Mo. (64079) 261/C4
Plattenville, La. (70393) 238/K4
Platter, Okla. (74753) 288/O7
Platteville, Colo. (80651) 208/K2
Platteville, Wis. (53818) 317/F10
Platte Woods, Mo. (†64152) 261/O5
Platt Nat'l Park, Okla. 288/N6
Plattsburg, Mo. (64477) 261/D3
Plattsburgh, N.Y. (12901) 276/O1
Plattsburgh A.F.B., N.Y. 276/N1
Plattsmouth, Nebr. (68048) 264/J3
Plattsville, Ont. 177/D4
Plau, E. Ger. 22/F2
Plaucheville, La. (71362) 238/G5
Plauen, E. Ger., 7/F3
Plauen, E. Ger. 22/E3
Plauersee (lake), E. Ger. 22/E2
Plav, Yugo. 45/D4
Plavinas, U.S.S.R. 53/C2

Prairie 421

Portage, Mich. (49081) 250/D6
Portage (isl.), N. Br. 170/F1
Portage (co.), Ohio 284/H3
Portage, Ohio (43451) 284/C3
Portage (riv.), Ohio 284/D3
Portage, Pa. (15946) 294/E5
Portage, Utah (84331) 304/B2
Portage (co.), Wis. 317/G6
Portage, Wis. (53901) 317/G8
Portage Des Sioux, Mo. (63373) 261/P2
Portage la Prairie, 163/G5
Portage la Prairie, Man. 179/D4
Portageville, Mo. (63873) 261/N10
Portageville, N.Y. (14536) 276/D5
Portal, Ariz. (85632) 198/F7
Portal, Ga. (30450) 216/J5
Portal, N. Dak. (58772) 283/E2
Portalban, Switz. 39/C3
Port Alberni, Br. Col. 184/H3
Port Albert, Aust. 88/H7
Port Albert, Vic. 97/D6
Port Albion, Br. Col. 184/E6
Portalegre, Port. 33/C3
Portales, N. Mex., 188/F4
Portales, N. Mex. (88130) 274/F4
Port Alexander, Alaska (99834) 196/M2
Port Alexander, Ont. 177/G1
Port-Alfred, Que. 172/G1
Port Alfred, S. Africa 118/D6
Port Alice, Br. Col. 184/D5
Port Allegany, Pa. (16743) 294/F2
Port Allen, La. (70767) 238/J2
Port Alma, Ont. 177/B5
Port Althorp, Alaska (†99825) 196/M1
Port Angeles, Wash., 188/B1
Port Angeles, Wash. (98362) 310/B2
Port Angeles Ind. Res., Wash. 310/B2
Port Anson, Ont. 177/E2
Port Antonio, Jam. 156/C3
Port Antonio, Jam. 158/K6
Port-à-Piment, Haiti 158/A6
Port Appin, Scot. 15/F6
Port Aransas, Texas (78373) 302/H10
Portarlington, Aust. 88/L7
Portarlington, 10/C4
Portarlington, Ire. 17/G5
Port Arthur (in Lüta), China 77/K4
Port Arthur, Texas, 188/H5
Port Arthur, Texas (77640) 302/K8
Port Ashton, Alaska (99654) 196/C1
Portaskaig, Scot. 15/D8
Port Augusta, Australia, 87/D9
Port Augusta, Aust. 88/F6
Port Augusta, S. Aust. 94/E5
Port-au-Persil, Que. 172/G2
Port-au Port, Newf. 166/C4
Port au Port (bay), Newf. 166/C4
Port au Port (pen.), Newf. 166/C4
Port-au-Prince (cap.), Haiti 156/D3
Port-au-Prince (cap.), Haiti 158/C6
Port-au-Prince (cap.), Haiti, 146/L8
Port Austin, Mich. (48467) 250/F4
Port aux Basques-Channel, 163/L6
Port aux Basques-Channel, Newf. 166/C4
Portavogie, N. Ire. 17/K3
Port Barre, La. (70577) 238/G5
Port-Bergé, Malag. Rep. 118/H3
Port Blair, India, 54/N8
Port Blair, India 68/G6
Port Blakely, Wash. (98110) 310/A2
Port Blandford, Newf. 166/C2
Port Bolivar, Texas (77650) 302/L3
Port-Bou, Spain 33/H1
Port-Bouet, Ivory Coast 106/D7
Port Broughton, S. Aust. 94/F5
Port Bruce, Ont. 177/D5
Port Burwell, Ont. 177/D5
Port Burwell, N.W.T. 187/M3
Port Byron, Ill. (61275) 222/C2
Port Byron, N.Y. (13140) 276/G4
Port Carbon, Pa. (17965) 294/K4
Port Carling, Ont. 177/E2
Port-Cartier, Que. 174/D2
Port-Cartier-Ouest 163/K6
Port-Cartier-Ouest, Que. 174/D3
Port Castries (harb.), St. Lucia 161/G6
Port Chalmers, N.Z. 101/C6
Port Charlotte, Fla. (33950) 212/D5
Port Chester, N.Y. (10573) 276/P7
Port Chilkoot, Alaska (†99827) 196/N1
Port Clarence (inlet), Alaska 196/E1
Port Clements, Br. Col. 184/B3
Port Clinton, Ohio (43452) 284/E2
Port Clinton, Pa. (19549) 294/K4
Port Clyde, Maine (04855) 242/E8
Port Colborne, Ont. 177/E5
Port Coquitlam, Br. Col. 184/L3
Port Costa, Calif. (94569) 204/J1
Port Darwin (inlet), No. Terr. 93/B2
Port Davey (inlet), Tas. 99/B5
Port-de-Bouc, France 28/F6
Port-de-Paix, Haiti 156/D3
Port-de-Paix, Haiti 158/B5
Port Deposit, Md. (21904) 245/O2
Port Dickinson, N.Y. (†13901) 276/J6
Port Dickson, Malaysia 72/D7
Port Dinorwic, Wales 13/C4
Port Dover, Ont. 177/D5
Port Dufferin, N.S. 169/F4
Porteau, Br. Col. 184/K2
Porte des Morts (str.), Wis. 317/N5
Port Edward, Br. Col. 184/B3
Port Edwards, Wis. (54469) 317/G7
Portel, Braz. 132/D3
Port Elgin, Ont. 177/C3
Port Elgin, N. Br. 170/F2
Port Elizabeth, N.J. (08348) 273/D5
Port Elizabeth, 102/E8
Port Elizabeth, S. Africa 118/D6
Port Ellen, Scot. 15/D8
Porter (pt.), St. Vincent 161/A8
Porter (co.), Ind. 227/C2
Porter, Ind. (46304) 227/C1
Porter△, Maine (04068) 242/B8
Porter, Maine (04068) 242/B8
Porter, Minn. (56280) 254/B6
Porter (lake), N.S. 169/E4
Porter, Ohio (†45614) 284/F8
Porter, Okla. (74454) 288/R3
Porter, Texas (77365) 302/J7
Porter, Wash. (98573) 310/B4
Porterdale, Ga. (30270) 216/E3
Porterfield, Wis. (54159) 317/L5
Port Erin, I. of Man 13/C3
Portersville, Ala. (35985) 194/G2
Portersville, Ind. (†47546) 227/C8
Portersville, Pa. (16051) 294/B4
Portersville, W. Va. (†25571) 313/B6
Porterville, Calif. (93257) 204/G7
Porterville, Miss. (39352) 256/G5
Porterwood, W. Va. (†26283) 313/G4
Port Essington, Br. Col. 184/C3
Port Everglades (harb.), Fla. 212/C4
Port Ewen, N.Y. (12466) 276/N7
Port Fairy, Aust. 88/G7
Port Fairy, Vic. 97/B6
Port-Félix, N.S. 169/G3
Port-Francqui, 102/E5
Port-Francqui, Dem. Rep. of the Congo. 115/D4
Port Franks, Ont. 177/C4
Port Fuad, U.A.R. 111/K3
Port Gamble, Wash. (98364) 310/C3
Port Gamble Ind. Res., Wash. 310/C3
Port-Gentil, Gabon 115/A4
Port-Gentil, 102/C5
Port Gibson, Miss. (39150) 256/B7
Port Glasgow, 10/A1
Port Glasgow, Scot. 15/B2
Portglenone, N. Ire. 17/H2
Port Graham, Alaska (†99603) 196/B2
Port Hamilton (So) (isl.), S. Korea 81/C6
Port Hammond, Br. Col. 184/L3
Port Harcourt, 102/C4
Port Harcourt, Nigeria 106/F8
Port Hardy, Br. Col. 184/D5
Port-Harrison (Inoucdjouac), 163/J4
Port-Harrison (Inoucdjouac), Que. 174/E1
Port Hastings, N.S. 169/G3
Port Hawkesbury, N.S. 169/G3
Porthcawl, Wales 13/D6
Port Hebert (harb.), N.S. 169/D5
Port Hedland, Australia, 87/B7
Port Hedland, Aust. 88/B3
Port Hedland, Australia, 3/R7
Port Hedland, W. Aust. 92/B3
Port Heiden, Alaska (†99579) 196/G3
Port Heiden (inlet), Alaska 196/G3
Port Henry, N.Y. (12974) 276/O2
Port Higgins‡, Alaska (†99901) 196/N2
Porthill, Idaho (83853) 220/B1
Port Hood, N.S. 169/G2
Port Hood (isl.), N.S. 169/G2
Port Hope, Ont. 177/F4
Port Hope, Mich. (48468) 250/G5
Port Hope Simpson, Newf. 166/C3
Port Houghton (inlet), Alaska 196/N1
Port Howe, N.S. 169/E3
Port Hudson, La. (†70791) 238/J1
Port Hueneme, Calif. (93041) 204/F9
Port Huron, Mich., 188/K2
Port Huron, Mich. (48060) 250/G6
Portia, Ark. (72457) 203/H1
Portimão, Port. 33/B4
Portis, Kans. (67474) 232/D2
Port Isabel, Texas (78578) 302/G11
Portishead, Eng. 13/E6
Port Jackson (inlet), N.S.W. 97/J3
Port Jefferson, N.Y. (11777) 276/P9
Port Jefferson, Ohio (†45360) 284/C5
Port Jefferson Station‡, N.Y. (11777) 276/O9
Port Jervis, N.Y. (12771) 276/L8
Port Joli (harb.), N.S. 169/D5
Port Kaiser, Jam. 158/H7
Port Kaituma, Guyana 131/B2
Port Keats Mission, No. Terr. 93/A3
Port Kembla, Aust. 88/K4
Port Kembla, N.S.W. 97/F4
Port Kenny, S. Aust. 94/D5
Port Kent, N.Y. (12975) 276/O1
Portknockie, Scot. 15/L4
Port Lambton, Ont. 177/B5
Portland (canal), 163/D4
Portland (canal), Alaska 196/N2
Portland, Ark. (71663) 203/H7
Portland, Aust. 88/G7
Portland (bay), Aust. 88/G7
Portland (canal), Br. Col. 184/B2
Portland (inlet), Br. Col. 184/C3
Portland, Colo. (†81226) 208/K6
Portland, Colo. (†81427) 208/D6
Portland△, Conn. (06480) 210/E2
Portland (pt.), Jam. 156/C3
Portland (pt.), Jam. 158/J7
Portland, Barb. 161/B8
Portland, Ont. 177/H3
Portland, Eng. 13/E7
Portland (pen.), Eng. 13/E7
Portland, Fla. (†32439) 212/C6
Portland, Ind. (47371) 227/H4
Portland (prom.), 163/J4
Portland, Maine, 146/M5
Portland, Maine, 188/N2
Portland, Maine (*04101) 242/C8
Portland, Mich. (48875) 250/E6
Portland, Mo. (65067) 261/J5
Portland, N. Dak. (58274) 283/R5
Portland, N.S.W. 97/E3
Portland, N.Y. (14769) 276/B6
Portland, N.Z. 101/E1
Portland (isl.), N.Z. 101/G3
Portland, Ohio (45770) 284/G7
Portland, Oreg., 146/F5
Portland, Oreg., 188/B1
Portland, Oreg. (*97201) 291/B2
Portland, Pa. (18351) 294/M4
Portland (pen.), 10/E5
Portland, Tenn. (37148) 237/H7
Portland, Texas (78374) 302/G10
Portland, U.S., 3/C3
Portland, Vic. 97/A6
Portland (bay), Vic. 97/A6
Portland Bill (prom.), Eng. 13/E7
Portland Bill (prom.), 10/E5
Portland Creek (pond), Newf. 166/C3
Portland Int'l Airport, Oreg. 291/B2
Portlaoighise, 10/C4
Portlaoighise, Ire. 17/G5
Port Lavaca, Texas (77979) 302/H9
Portlaw, Ire. 17/G7
Portlethen, Scot. 15/M5
Port Leyden, N.Y. (13433) 276/K3
Port Lincoln, Australia, 87/D9
Port Lincoln, Aust. 88/E6
Port Lincoln, S. Aust. 94/C6
Port Lions, Alaska (99550) 196/H3
Portlock, Alaska (†99603) 196/C2
Port Loko, S. Leone 106/B7
Port Loring, Ont. 177/E2
Port Lorne, N.S. 169/C4
Port-Louis, Guad. 156/G3
Port-Louis, Guad. 161/B5
Port-Louis, France 28/B4
Port Louis (cap.), Mauritius 118/G5
Port Ludlow, Wash. (98365) 310/C3
Port-Lyautey (Kénitra), 102/B1
Port-Lyautey (Kénitra), Mor. 106/C2
Port Macquarie, Aust. 88/J6
Port Macquarie, N.S.W. 97/G2
Port Madison Ind. Res., Wash. 310/A1
Portmadoc, 10/D4
Portmadoc, Wales 13/C5
Portmahomack, Scot. 15/J4
Port Maitland, Ont. 177/E5
Port Maitland, N.S. 169/B5
Port Manvers (harb.), Newf. 166/B2
Port-Margot, Haiti 158/C5
Port Maria, Jam. 156/C3
Port Maria, Jam. 158/J6
Portmarnock, Ire. 17/J5
Port Matilda, Pa. (16870) 294/F4
Port Mayaca, Fla. (†33438) 212/F5
Port McNeill, Br. Col. 184/D5
Port McNicoll, Ont. 177/E3
Port Medway, N.S. 169/D4
Port Melbourne, Aust. 88/L7
Port Melbourne, Vic. 97/H5
Port Mellon, Br. Col. 184/K2
Port Menier, 163/K6
Port Menier, Que. 174/E3
Port Moller, Alaska (†99571) 196/F3
Port Moller (inlet), Alaska 196/F3
Port Monmouth, N.J. (07758) 273/E3
Port Moody, Br. Col. 184/L3
Port Morant, Jam. 158/K6
Port Moresby (cap.), Papua 85/B7
Port Moresby (cap.), Papua, 87/E6
Port Morien, N.S. 169/H3
Port Morris, N.J. (†07850) 273/D2
Port Mouton, N.S. 169/D5
Port Mouton (harb.), N.S. 169/D5
Port Murray, N.J. (07865) 273/D2
Port Neches, Texas (77651) 302/K7
Port Nellie Juan, Alaska (†99501) 196/C1
Port Nelson, 163/G4
Port Nelson, Man., 146/J4
Portneuf (co.), Que. 172/E3
Portneuf, Que. 172/F3
Portneuf (riv.), Que. 172/H1
Portneuf, Que. 174/E3
Portneuf (res.), Idaho 220/F7
Portneuf (riv.), Idaho 220/F7
Portneuf-sur-Mer, Que. 172/H1
Port Neville, Br. Col. 184/E5
Port Nicholson (inlet), N.Z. 101/B3
Port Nolloth, 102/D7
Port Nolloth, S. Africa 118/B5
Port Norris, N.J. (08349) 273/C5
Port-Nouveau-Québec, 163/K4
Port-Nouveau-Québec, Que. 174/F2
Pôrto, Braz. 132/F3
Porto (Oporto), Port., 7/D4
Porto (Oporto), Port. 33/B2
Pôrto Alegre, Braz., 3/G7
Pôrto Alegre, Braz., 120/E5
Pôrto Alegre, Braz. 132/D10
Porto Alexandre, Angola 115/B7
Porto Alexandre, 102/D6
Porto Amboim, Angola 115/B6
Porto Amélia, 102/G6
Porto Amélia, Moz., 118/G2
Portobello, 10/C1
Portobello, Scot. 15/K8
Portobelo, Pan. 154/H6
Porto Civitanova, Italy 34/D3
Port O'Connor, Texas (77982) 302/H9
Pôrto de Mós, Port. 33/B3
Pôrto de Moz, Braz. 132/D3
Porto Empedocle, Italy 34/D6
Pôrto Esperança, Braz., 120/E4
Pôrto Esperança, Braz. 132/B7
Pôrto Feliz, Braz. 135/C3
Portoferraio, Italy 34/C3
Portofino, Italy 34/B2
Port of Ness, Scot. 15/D3
Pôrto Franco, Braz. 132/E4
Port-of-Spain (cap.), Trinidad Tobago 156/G5
Port-of-Spain (cap.), Trinidad Tobago 161/A10
Porto Grande, 102/G8
Portogruaro, Italy 34/D2
Portola, Calif. (96122) 204/E4
Portola Valley, Calif. (94025) 204/J3
Portomaggiore, Italy 34/C2
Pôrto Mendes, Braz., 120/E5
Porto Moniz, Port. 33/A2
Pôrto Murtinho, Braz. 132/B8
Pôrto Nacional, Braz., 120/F4
Pôrto Nacional, Braz. 132/E5
Porto-Novo (cap.), Dahomey 102/C4
Porto-Novo (cap.), Dahomey 106/E7
Porto Novo, India 68/E6
Port Orange, Fla. (32019) 212/F2
Port Orchard, Wash. (98366) 310/A2
Porto Recanati, Italy 34/D3
Port Orford, Oreg. (97465) 291/C5
Pôrto Santana, Braz. 132/D3
Porto Santo, Port. 33/A2
Porto Santo (isl.), 102/A1
Porto Santo (isl.), Port. 33/B2
Porto Santo (isl.), Port. 106/A2
Pôrto Seguro, Braz. 132/G7
Pôrto Tibiriça, Braz., 120/E5
Porto Tolle, Italy 34/D2
Porto Torres, Italy 34/B4
Pôrto União, Braz. 132/D9
Porto-Vecchio, France 28/B7
Pôrto Velho, Braz., 120/D3
Pôrto Velho, Braz. 132/H10
Portoviejo, Ec. 128/B3
Portpatrick, 10/D3
Portpatrick, Scot. 15/F10
Port Pegasus (inlet), N.Z. 101/B7
Port Penn, Del. (19731) 245/R2
Port Perry, Ont. 177/E3
Port Phillip (bay), Aust. 88/M7
Port Phillip (bay), Vic. 97/C6
Port Pirie, Australia, 87/D9
Port Pirie, Aust. 88/F6
Port Pirie, S. Aust. 94/E5
Port Praslin (bay), St. Lucia 161/G6
Port Radium, 163/E3
Port Radium, Canada, 4/C15
Port Radium, N.W.T., 146/G3
Port Radium, N.W.T. 187/G3
Port Reading, N.J. (07064) 273/E2
Portree, 10/C2
Portree, Scot. 15/D5
Portreeve, Sask. 181/B5
Port Renfrew, Br. Col. 184/J3
Port Republic, Md. (20676) 245/N6
Port Republic, N.J. (08241) 273/D4
Port Republic, Va. (24471) 307/L4
Port Rexton, Newf. 166/D2
Port Rhoades, Jam. 158/J6
Port Richey, Fla. (33568) 212/D3
Port Richmond, Va. (23181) 307/P5
Port Rowan, Ont. 177/D5
Port Royal, Jam. 158/J6
Port Royal, Ky. (40058) 237/L3
Port Royal, Pa. (17082) 294/H4
Port Royal, S.C. (29935) 296/F7
Port Royal (sound), S.C. 296/F7
Port Royal, Va. (22535) 307/O4
Portrush, N. Ire. 17/H1
Portrush, 10/C3
Port Ryerse, Ont. 177/D5
Port Safâga, U.A.R. 59/B4
Port Safâga, U.A.R. 111/F2
Port Said, 102/F1
Port Said, U.A.R. 59/B3
Port Said, U.A.R. 111/K2
Port Saint Joe, Fla. (32456) 212/D6
Port Saint Johns, S. Africa 118/D6
Port-Saint-Louis-du-Rhône, France 28/F6
Port Saint Lucie, Fla. (33450) 212/F4
Port Saint Mary, I. of Man 13/C3
Port Salerno, Fla. (33492) 212/F4
Port-Salut, Haiti 158/A6
Port Sanilac, Mich. (48469) 250/G5
Port Saunders, Newf. 166/C3
Pörtschach, Austria 41/C3
Port Shepstone, 102/F8
Port Shepstone, S. Africa 118/E6
Port Simpson, Br. Col. 184/B3
Portslade-by-Sea, Eng. 13/G7
Portsmouth, 10/F5
Portsmouth, Dominica 156/G4
Portsmouth, Dominica 161/E5
Portsmouth, Eng., 7/D3
Portsmouth, Eng. 13/G7
Portsmouth, Iowa (51565) 229/C5
Portsmouth, N.C. (†27960) 281/S4
Portsmouth (isl.), N.C. 281/T5
Portsmouth, N.H., 188/N2
Portsmouth, N.H. (*03801) 268/F5
Portsmouth, Ohio, 188/K3
Portsmouth, Ohio (45662) 284/D8
Portsmouth△, R.I. (02871) 249/J6
Portsmouth, R.I. (02871) 249/J6
Portsmouth, Va., 188/L3
Portsmouth, Va. (*23701) 307/R7
Portsoy, Scot. 15/L4
Port Stanley, Ont. 177/C5
Port Stephens (inlet), N.S.W. 97/G3
Portstewart, N. Ire. 17/H1
Port Sudan, 102/F3
Port Sudan, Sudan 59/C6
Port Sudan, Sudan 111/G4
Port Sulphur, La. (70083) 238/L8
Port Swettenham, Malaysia 72/D7
Port Sydney, Ont. 177/E2
Port Talbot, Ont. 177/C5
Port Talbot, 10/E5
Port Talbot, Wales 13/D6
Port Tampa (harb.), Fla. 212/B3
Port Taufiq, U.A.R. 111/K3
Port Tobacco, Md. (20677) 245/K6
Port Townsend, Wash. (98368) 310/C2
Port Trevorton, Pa. (17864) 294/J4
Portugal, 3/J3
Portugal, 7/D5
PORTUGAL, 33/B3
Portugal Cove, Newf. 166/D2
Portugal Cove South, Newf. 166/D2
Portugalete, Bol. 136/B7
Portugalete, Spain 33/E1
Portugália, Angola 115/D5
Portuguesa (state), Ven. 124/D3
Portuguesa (riv.), Ven. 124/D3
Portuguese Guinea, 3/H5
PORTUGUESE GUINEA, 106/A6
PORTUGUESE GUINEA, 102/A3
Portuguese Timor, 54/R10
PORTUGUESE TIMOR, 85
Portumna, Ire. 17/E5
Port Union, Newf. 166/D2
Port-Vendres, France 28/E6
Port Victoria, Kenya 115/F3
Portville, N.Y. (14770) 276/D6
Port Vincent, La. (†70726) 238/L2
Port Vue, Pa. (15133) 294/C7
Port Washington, N.Y. (11050) 276/R6
Port Washington, Ohio (43837) 284/G5
Port Washington, Wis. (53074) 317/L9
Port Washington North‡, N.Y. (†11050) 276/R7
Port Weld, Malaysia 72/D6
Port Wells (inlet), Alaska 196/C1
Port Wentworth, Ga. (31407) 216/K6
Port William, Ohio (45164) 284/C6
Port William, Scot. 15/H10
Port Williams, N.S. 169/D3
Port Wing, Wis. (54865) 317/D2
Poruba, Czech. 41/D2
Porum, Okla. (74455) 288/R4
Porus, Jam. 158/H6
Porvenir, Pando, Bol. 136/A2
Porvenir, Santa Cruz, Bol. 136/E4
Porvenir, Chile 138/E10
Porvenir, Peru 128/E5
Porvenir, Urug. 145/B3
Porvoo (Borgå), Fin. 18/O6
Porz, W. Ger. 22/B3
Posadas, Arg., 120/E5
Posadas, Arg. 143/E2
Posadas, Spain 33/D4
Poschiavo, Switz. 39/J4
Poschiavo (riv.), Switz. 39/K4
Poschiavo (valley), Switz. 39/K4
Poseh, China 77/G7
Posen, Ill. (60469) 222/B2
Posen, Mich. (49776) 250/F3
Posey (co.), Ind. 227/B8
Poseyville, Ind. (47633) 227/B8
Posio, Fin. 18/Q3
Poskin, Wis. (54866) 317/C5
Poso, Indon. 85/G6
Posof, Turkey 63/K2
Posŏng, S. Korea 81/C6
Posorja, Ec. 128/B4
Posse, Braz. 132/E6
Pössneck, E. Ger. 22/D3
Possum Kingdom (lake), Texas 302/F5
Post (riv.), Que. 172/D3
Post, Oreg. (97752) 291/G3
Post, Texas (79356) 302/C4
Postavy, U.S.S.R. 52/C3
Poste-de-la-Baleine, 163/J4
Poste-de-la-Baleine, Que. 174/B1
Poste-de-Mistassini, Que. 174/C2
Postelle, Ark. (72375) 203/J4
Postelle, Tenn. (37368) 237/N10
Poste Maurice Cordier, Alg. 106/E4
Poste Weygand, Alg. 106/D4
Post Falls, Idaho (83854) 220/A2
Postiljon (isls.), Indon. 85/F7
Postmasburg, S. Africa 118/C5
Post Mills, Vt. (05058) 268/C4
Postoak, Mo. (†64761) 261/E5
Postoak, Texas (76260) 302/F4
Postojna, Yugo. 45/B3
Poston, Ariz. (85371) 198/A4
Poston, S.C. (29588) 296/J4
Postrervalle, Bol. 136/D6
Postville, Iowa (52162) 229/K2
Postville, Newf. 166/B3
Pot (creek), Colo. 208/A1
Pot (mt.), Idaho 220/C3
Pot (creek), Utah 304/E3
Potagannissing (bay), Mich. 250/F2
Potam, Mex. 150/D3
Potapovo, U.S.S.R. 48/J3
Potaro (riv.), Guyana 131/B3
Potato Creek, S. Dak. (†57750) 298/F6
Potawatomi Ind. Res., Kans. 232/G2
Potchefstroom, S. Africa 118/D5
Poteau (mt.), Ark. 203/B4
Poteau, Okla. (74953) 288/S4
Poteau (riv.), Okla. 288/S5
Poteca, Nic. 154/E4
Poteet, Texas (78065) 302/F8
Potenza (prov.), Italy 34/E4
Potenza, Italy 34/E4
Potes, Spain 33/D1
Potgietersrus, S. Africa 118/D4
Poth, Texas (78147) 302/F8
Potholes (res.), Wash. 310/F3
Poti, U.S.S.R. 52/F6
Potlatch, Idaho (83855) 220/A3
Potlatch (riv.), Idaho 220/B3
Potlatch, Wash. (98574) 310/B3
Poto, Peru 128/H10
Potomac (riv.), 188/L3
Potomac, Ill. (61865) 222/F3
Potomac (riv.), Md. 245/M8
Potomac (Potomac Valley), Md. (20854) 245/K4
Potomac, Mont. (59862) 262/C4
Potomac (riv.), Va. 307/O4
Potomac (riv.), W. Va. 313/L3
Potomac Beach, Va. (†22443) 307/P4
Potomac Heights, Md. (20640) 245/K6
Potomac Park, Md. (†21502) 245/C2
Potosí, Bol., 120/D4
Potosí (dept.), Bol. 136/B7
Potosí, Bol. 136/B6
Potosí, Col. 126/C7
Potosi, Mo. (63664) 261/L7
Potosi (mt.), Nev. 266/F7
Potosi, Wis. (53820) 317/E10
Potrerillo (peak), Cuba 158/E2
Potrerillos, Chile 138/B6
Potrerillos, Pan. 154/F6
Potrero, Calif. (92063) 204/J11
Potrillo (mts.), N. Mex. 274/B7
Potro, Cerro del (mt.), Arg. 143/C2
Potro, Cerro del (mt.), Chile 138/B7
Potsdam (dist.), E. Ger. 22/E2
Potsdam, E. Ger. 22/E2
Potsdam, Minn. (†55932) 254/F6
Potsdam, N.Y. (13676) 276/K1
Potsdam, Ohio (45361) 284/B6
Pottawatomie (co.), Kans. 232/F2
Pottawatomie (co.), Okla. 288/N4
Pottawattamie (co.), Iowa 229/B6
Pottawattamie Park, Ind. (†46360) 227/C1
Potter, Kans. (66077) 232/G2
Potter, Nebr. (69156) 264/A3
Potter (co.), Pa. 294/G2
Potter (co.), S. Dak. 298/J3
Potter (co.), Texas 302/C2
Potter, Wis. (54160) 317/K7
Potter Hill, R.I. (†02891) 249/H7
Potters Bar, 10/B5
Pottersdale, Pa. (16871) 294/F3
Pottersville, Mass. (†02726) 249/K6
Pottersville, Mo. (65790) 261/H9
Pottersville, N.J. (07979) 273/D2
Pottersville, N.Y. (12860) 276/N3
Potter Valley, Calif. (95469) 204/B4
Potterville, Mich. (48876) 250/E6
Potts (creek), W. Va. 313/F7
Pottsboro, Texas (75076) 302/H4
Potts Camp, Miss. (38659) 256/F1
Pottstown, Pa. (19464) 294/L5
Pottsville, Ark. (72858) 203/D3
Pottsville, Pa. (17901) 294/K4
Pottsville, Texas (76565) 302/F6
Potwin, Kans. (67123) 232/F4
Pouce Coupé, Br. Col. 184/G2
Pouch Cove, Newf. 166/D2
Poudre d'Or, Mauritius 118/G5
Poughkeepsie, Ark. (72569) 203/H1
Poughkeepsie, N.Y. (*12601) 276/N7
Pouillon, France 28/C6
Poulan, Ga. (31781) 216/E8
Poulet Cove (bay), N.S. 169/H2
Poulo Dama (isls.), S. Vietnam 72/D5
Poulo Way (isls.), S. Vietnam 72/D5
Poulsbo, Wash. (98370) 310/A1
Poultney△, Vt. (05764) 268/A4
Poultney, Vt. (05764) 268/A4
Poultney (riv.), Vt. 268/A4
Poulton le Fylde, 10/F1
Pound, Va. (24279) 307/C6
Pound, Wis. (54161) 317/L5
Pounding Mill, Va. (24637) 307/E6
Pouso Alegre, Braz. 132/E8
Pouso Alegre, Braz. 135/D3
Považská Bystrica, Czech. 41/E2
Povenets, U.S.S.R. 52/E2
Poverty (isl.), Mich. 250/C3
Poverty (bay), N.Z. 101/G3
Povoa de Varzim, Port. 33/B2
Povorino, U.S.S.R. 52/F4
Povungnituk, 163/J3
Povungnituk, Que. 174/E1
Powassan, Ont. 177/E1
Poway, Calif. (92064) 204/J11
Powder (riv.), 188/E2
Powder (riv.), Mont. 262/L4
Powder (riv.), Oreg. 291/K3
Powder (riv.), U.S., 146/H5
Powder (riv.), Wyo. 319/F2
Powderhorn, Colo. (81243) 208/E6
Powderly, Ky. (42367) 237/G6
Powderly, Texas (75473) 302/J4
Powder River (co.), Mont. 262/L5
Powder River, Wyo. (82648) 319/F2
Powder Springs, Ga. (30073) 216/C3
Powder Springs, Tenn. (37848) 237/O8
Powderville, Mont. (59345) 262/L5
Powe, Mo. (†63822) 261/M9
Powell (lake), 188/D3
Powell (lake), Ariz. 198/E1
Powell (co.), Ky. 237/O5
Powell (co.), Mont. 262/D4
Powell, Nebr. (68425) 264/G4
Powell, Ohio (43065) 284/D5
Powell, Pa. (†18832) 294/J2
Powell, Tenn. (37849) 237/N8
Powell (riv.), Tenn. 237/P8
Powell‡, Texas (75153) 302/H5
Powell (lake), Utah 304/D6
Powell (riv.), Va. 307/B7
Powell, Wyo. (82435) 319/D1
Powell Butte, Oreg. (97753) 291/G3
Powell Creek, Aust. 88/E3
Powell Creek, No. Terr. 93/C5
Powell River, Br. Col. 184/E5
Powells Point, N.C. (27966) 281/T2
Powellsville, N.C. (27967) 281/R2
Powellton, W. Va. (25161) 313/D6
Powellville, Md. (21852) 245/S7
Powelton, Ga. (†31059) 216/G4
Power (co.), Idaho 220/F7
Power, Mont. (59468) 262/E3
Power, W. Va. (26054) 313/E2
Powers (lake), Conn. 210/G3
Powers, Mich. (49874) 250/B3
Powers, Oreg. (97466) 291/D5
Powersburg, Ky. (42636) 237/M7
Powers Lake, N. Dak. (58773) 283/E2
Powersville, Ga. (31074) 216/E5
Powersville, Iowa (†50636) 229/H3
Powersville, Mo. (64672) 261/F1
Powerview, Man. 179/F4
Poweshiek (co.), Iowa 229/H5
Powhatan, Ark. (72458) 203/H1
Powhatan, La. (71066) 238/D3
Powhatan (co.), Va. 307/N5
Powhatan, Va. (23139) 307/N5
Powhatan, W. Va. (24877) 313/D8
Powhatan Point, Ohio (43942) 284/J6
Powhattan, Kans. (66527) 232/G2
Pownal△, Maine (04069) 242/C8
Pownal△, Vt. (05261) 268/A6
Pownal, Vt. (05261) 268/A6
Pownal Center, Vt. (†05261) 268/A6
Powwow River, N.H. (†03827) 268/E6
Poxoréu, Braz. 132/C6
Poyang (lake), China, 54/P7
Poyang (lake), China 77/J6
Poyen, Ark. (72128) 203/E5
Poygan (lake), Wis. 317/J7
Poynette, Wis. (53955) 317/G9
Poynor, Mo. (63959) 261/L9
Poynor, Texas (75782) 302/J5
Poysdorf, Austria 41/D2
Poy Sippi, Wis. (54967) 317/J7
Pozanti, Turkey 63/F4
Požarevac, Yugo. 45/E3
Poza Rica de Hidalgo, Mex. 150/L6
Požega, Yugo. 45/C3
Poznań, Poland, 7/F3
Poznań (prov.), Poland 47/C2
Poznań, Poland 47/C2
Pozo Almonte, Chile 138/B2
Pozoblanco, Spain 33/D3
Pozo Hondo, Arg. 143/D2
Pozohondo, Spain 33/F3
Pozuelo de Alarcón, Spain 33/D2
Pozuelos, Ven. 124/F2
Pozuzo, Peru 128/E8
Pozzallo, Italy 34/E6
Pozzuoli, Italy 34/D4
Prabuty, Poland 47/D2
Prachatice, Czech. 41/B2
Prachin Buri, Thai. 72/D4
Prachuap Khiri Khan, Thai. 72/D5
Pradera, Col. 126/B6
Prades, France 28/E6
Praestø (co.), Den. 21/F7
Praestø, Den. 21/E7
Pragel (pass), Switz. 39/G2
Prague (cap.), Czech., 7/F3
Prague (city), Czech. 41/C1
Prague (Praha) (cap.), Czech. 41/C1
Prague, Nebr. (68050) 264/H3
Prague, Okla. (74864) 288/N4
Praha (Prague) (cap.), Czech., 7/F3
Prahran, Vic. 97/J5
Praia (cap.), C. Verde Is. 106/B8
Praia (cap.), C. Verde Is. 102/G9
Prainha, Braz., 120/E3
Prainha, Braz. 132/C3
Prairie, Ala. (36771) 194/D6
Prairie (co.), Ark. 203/G4

Rabch **423**

Puerto Toledo, Col. 126/C8
Puerto Torno, Bol. 136/C5
Puerto Vallarta, Mex. 150/G6
Puerto Varas, Chile 138/E3
Puerto Velarde, Bol. 136/D5
Puerto Victoria, Peru 128/E7
Puerto Villaroel, Bol. 136/C5
Puerto Villazón, Bol. 136/D3
Puerto Vita, Cuba 158/J4
Puerto Wilches, Col. 126/D4
Puerto Williams, Chile 138/F11
Puerto Yartou, Chile 138/E10
Puerto Ybapobó, Par. 144/D4
Puesto Estrella, Par. 144/A3
Pueyrredón (lake), Arg. 143/B6
Puffin (isl.), Ire. 17/A8
Pugachev, U.S.S.R. 52/G4
Puget (isl.), Wash. 310/B4
Puget (sound), Wash. 310/C3
Puget Sound Navy Yard, Wash. 310/A2
Pugwash, N.S. 169/E3
Pugwash (harb.), N.S. 169/E3
Puha, N.Z. 101/F3
Puhi, Hawaii (96766) 218/C2
Puigcerdá, Spain 33/G1
Puigmal (mt.), Spain 33/H1
Puina, Bol. 136/A4
Puinagua, Canal de (riv.), Peru 128/E5
Pujada (bay), Phil. 82/F7
Pujehun, S. Leone 106/B7
Pujili, Ec. 128/C3
Pukaki (lake), N.Z. 101/B6
Pukalani, Hawaii (96788) 218/J2
Pukapuka (atoll), Cook Is., 87/K7
Puka-Puka (atoll), Fr. Poly., 87/N7
Pukatawagan, Man. 179/H2
Pukch'ŏng, N. Korea 81/C3
Pukë, Alb. 45/E4
Pukekohe, N.Z. 101/E2
Pukerua Bay, N.Z. 101/E4
Pukoo, Hawaii (†96748) 218/H1
Puksubaek (mt.), N. Korea 81/C3
Pukwana, S. Dak. (57370) 298/L6
Pula, Yugo. 45/A3
Pulacayo, Bol. 136/B7
Pulai (riv.), Malaysia 72/E5
Pulanduta (pt.), Phil. 82/D5
Pulangi (riv.), Phil. 82/E7
Pulap (atoll), Pac. Is., 87/E5
Púlar, Cerro (mt.), Chile 138/B4
Pulaski (co.), Ark. 203/F4
Pulaski (co.), Ga. 216/E6
Pulaski, Ga. (30451) 216/J6
Pulaski (co.), Ill. 222/D6
Pulaski, Ill. (62976) 222/D6
Pulaski (co.), Ind. 227/D2
Pulaski, Ind. (†46996) 227/D3
Pulaski, Iowa (52584) 229/J7
Pulaski (co.), Ky. 237/M6
Pulaski, Ky. (42550) 237/M6
Pulaski, Miss. (39152) 256/E6
Pulaski (co.), Mo. 261/H7
Pulaski, N.Y. (13142) 276/H3
Pulaski, Ohio (†43506) 284/A2
Pulaski, Pa. (16143) 294/B3
Pulaski, Tenn. (38478) 237/G10
Pulaski (co.), Va. 307/G6
Pulaski, Va. (24301) 307/G6
Pulaski, Wis. (54162) 317/K6
Pulau (isl.), Malaysia 72/C6
Puławy, Poland 47/F3
Pulborough, Eng. 13/G7
Pulcifer, Wis. (54164) 317/K6
Pulehu, Hawaii (†96788) 218/J2
Pulicat (lake), India 68/E6
Pull (pt.), V.I.(U.S.) 161/F3
Pullman, Mich. (49450) 250/C6
Pullman, W. Va. (26421) 313/D4
Pullman, Wash. (99163) 310/H4
Pully, Switz. 39/C4
Pulo Anna (isl.), Pac. Is., 87/D5
Pulpit Harbor, Maine (†04853) 242/F7
Pulp River, Man. 179/B3
Pulteney, N.Y. (14874) 276/F5
Pulteneyville, N.Y. (14538) 276/F4
Pułtusk, Poland 47/E2
Pülümür, Turkey 63/H3
Pulusuk (atoll), Pac. Is., 87/F5
Puluwat (atoll), Pac. Is., 87/E5
Pumanque, Chile 138/F9
Pumphrey‡, Md. (†21090) 245/M4
Pumpkin (creek), Nebr. 264/A3
Pumpville, Texas (78876) 302/C8
Puna, Bol. 136/C6
Puná (isl.), Ec. 128/B4
Puna de Atacama (reg.), Arg. 143/C2
Punakha, India 68/G3
Punaluu, Hawaii (†96777) 218/H7
Punaluu (harb.), Hawaii 218/H7
Punata, Bol. 136/C5
Punch, India 68/C2
Punchaw, Br. Col. 184/F3
Punchbowl (hill), Hawaii 218/C4
Punchestown, Ire. 17/H5
Pungo, N.C. (†27860) 281/R3
Pungo (lake), N.C. 281/S3
Pungo (riv.), N.C. 281/R4
Pungoteague, Va. (23422) 307/S5
P'ungsan, N. Korea 81/D3
Punia, Dem. Rep. of the Congo. 115/E4
Punitaqui, Chile 138/A8
Punjab (state), India 68/D2
Punjab (prov.), Pak. 68/C2
Punjab (reg.), Pak. 68/C2
Punk (isl.), Man. 179/F3
Punnichy, Sask. 181/G4
Puno, Peru, 120/C4
Puno (dept.), Peru 128/G10
Puno, Peru 128/G10
Punta, Cerro de (mt.), P. Rico 161/C2
Punta Alta, Arg. 143/D4
Punta Arenas, Chile, 120/D8
Punta Arenas, Chile 138/E10
Punta Cardón, Ven. 124/C2
Punta de Bombón, Peru 128/F11
Punta de Díaz, Chile 138/B7
Punta del Este, Urug. 145/E6
Punta de Mata, Ven. 124/G3
Punta de Piedras, Ven. 124/F2
Punta Gorda, Br. Hond. 154/C2
Punta Gorda (pt.), Calif. 204/A3
Punta Gorda, Fla. (33950) 212/E5
Punta Moreno, Peru 128/C6
Punta Negra, Salar de (salt dep.), Chile 138/B5
Punta Prieta, Mex. 150/B2
Puntarenas, C. Rica 154/E6
Punta Santiago (Playa de Humacao), P. Rico 161/F2
Puntas de Maciel, Urug. 145/C4
Punto Fijo, Ven. 124/D2
Punxsutawney, Pa. (15767) 294/E4
Puolanka, Fin. 18/P4
Puolo (pt.), Hawaii 218/C2
Pupiales, Col. 126/B7
Puposky, Minn. (56667) 254/C3
Pupuke (lake), N.Z. 101/B1
Pupuya, Nevada (mt.), Bol. 136/A4
Puquina, Peru 128/G11
Puquintica, Cerro (mt.), Bol. 136/A6
Puquintica, Cerro (mt.), Chile 138/B1
Puquio, Peru 128/F10
Puquios, Chile 138/B1
Pur (riv.), U.S.S.R. 48/H3
Puracé (vol.), Col. 126/B6
Purbeck, Isle of (pen.), Eng. 13/F7
Purbolinggo, Indon. 85/J2
Purcell (mts.), Br. Col. 184/J5
Purcell (mts.), Idaho 220/B1
Purcell, Kans. (†66038) 232/G2
Purcell, Mo. (64857) 261/D8
Purcell (mts.), Mont. 262/A2
Purcell, Okla. (73080) 288/M4
Purcellville, Va. (22132) 307/N2
Purchase, N.Y. (10577) 276/P7
Purdin, Mo. (64674) 261/F3
Purdon‡, Texas (76679) 302/H5
Purdum, Nebr. (69157) 264/D2
Purdy, Mo. (65734) 261/E9
Purdy, Va. (23847) 307/N7
Pure Air, Mo. (†63559) 261/G2
Purén, Chile 138/D2
Purgatoire (riv.), Colo. 208/M8
Purgitsville, W. Va. (26852) 313/J4
Puri, India 68/F5
Purificación, Col. 126/C6
Purificación, Mex. 150/G7
Purmerend, Neth. 27/F4
Purnea, India 68/F3
Purple Springs, Alta. 182/E5
Purranque, Chile 138/D3
Pursat, Cambodia 72/D4
Puru (lake), Fin. 18/Q6
Puruándiro, Mex. 150/J7
Puruey, Ven. 124/F4
Puruktjahu, Indon. 85/E6
Purulia, India 68/F4
Puruname, Ven. 124/E6
Puruni (riv.), Guyana 131/B2
Purus (riv.), Braz., 120/D3
Purus (riv.), Braz. 132/H9
Purus (riv.), Peru 128/G8
Purves, Man. 179/D5
Purvis, Miss. (39475) 256/F8
Purwakarta, Indon. 85/H2
Purwodadi, Indon. 85/J2
Purwokerto, Indon. 85/H2
Purworedjo, Indon. 85/J2
Puryear, Tenn. (38251) 237/E8
Pusan, S. Korea 81/D6
Pusan, S. Korea, 54/S6
Pushaw (lake), Maine 242/F6
Pushkin, U.S.S.R. 48/C4
Pushkin, U.S.S.R. 52/D3
Pushmataha, Ala. (36917) 194/B6
Pushmataha (co.), Okla. 288/R6
Pushthrough, Newf. 166/C4
Pusht-i-Kuh (mts.), Iran 66/E4
Püspökladány, Hung. 41/F3
Pustunich, Mex. 150/O7
Putaendo, Chile 138/A9
Putao, Burma 72/C1
Putaruru, N.Z. 101/E3
Putbus, E. Ger. 22/E1
Puteau, France 28/A2
Putien, China 77/J6
Putignano, Italy 34/F4
Putina, Peru 128/H10
Put-in-Bay, Ohio (43456) 284/E2
Puting, Borneo (cape), Indon. 85/E6
Puting, Sumatra (cape), Indon. 85/C7
Putla de Guerrero, Mex. 150/L8
Putnam, Ala. (36772) 194/B6
Putnam▵, Conn. (06260) 210/H1
Putnam, Conn. (06260) 210/H1
Putnam (co.), Fla. 212/E2
Putnam (co.), Ga. 216/F4
Putnam, Ga. (†31803) 216/D6
Putnam (co.), Ill. 222/D2
Putnam, Ill. (61560) 222/D2
Putnam (co.), Ind. 227/D5
Putnam (co.), Mo. 261/F2
Putnam (co.), N.Y. 276/N8
Putnam (co.), Ohio 284/B3
Putnam, Okla. (73659) 288/J3
Putnam (co.), Tenn. 237/K8
Putnam, Texas (76469) 302/E5
Putnam (co.), W. Va. 313/C6
Putnam Heights, Conn. (†06260) 210/H1
Putnam Lake‡, N.Y. (†10509) 276/N7
Putnam Valley▵, N.Y. (10579) 276/N8
Putnamville, Ind. (46170) 227/D5
Putney, Ga. (31782) 216/D8
Putney, S. Dak. (57402) 298/N2
Putney▵, Vt. (05346) 268/B6
Putney, Vt. (05346) 268/B6
Putnok, Hung. 41/F2
Putre, Chile 138/B1
Puttalam, Ceylon 68/E7
Putte, Belg. 27/F6
Putten, Neth. 27/H4
Puttgarden, W. Ger. 22/D1
Puttur, India 68/D6
Putumayo (riv.), 120/C3
Putumayo (riv.), Col. 126/E9
Putumayo (comm.), Col. 126/C7
Putumayo, Ec. 128/E3
Putumayo (riv.), Ec. 128/E2
Putumayo (riv.), Peru 128/G4
Pütürge, Turkey 63/H3
Putussibau, Indon. 85/E5
Puuanahulu, Hawaii (†96740) 218/G4
Puuiki, Hawaii (†96713) 218/K2
Puu Keahiakahoe (mt.), Hawaii 218/D3
Puu Konahuanui (mt.), Hawaii 218/D3
Puu Kukui (mt.), Hawaii 218/J2
Puula (lake), Fin. 18/P5
Puu Lanihuli (mt.), Hawaii 218/D3
Puunene, Hawaii (96784) 218/J2
Puunui, Hawaii (†96801) 218/C4
Puuwaawaa, Hawaii (†96740) 218/G5
Puuwai, Hawaii (†96769) 218/A2
Puxico, Mo. (63960) 261/M9
Puyallup, Wash., 188/B1
Puyallup, Wash. (98371) 310/C3
Puyallup (riv.), Wash. 310/C4
Puy-de-Dôme (dept.), France 28/E5
Puy-de-Dôme (mt.), France 28/E5
Puyehue, Chile 138/E3
Puyehue (lake), Chile 138/E3
Puyo, Ec. 128/D3
Puysegur (pt.), N.Z. 101/A7
Pweto, Dem. Rep. of the Congo. 115/E5
Pwllheli, 10/D4
Pwllheli, Wales 13/C5
Pyandzh (riv.), Afgh. 59/K2
Pyapon, Burma 72/B3
Pyasina (riv.), U.S.S.R. 48/J2
Pyatigorsk, U.S.S.R. 52/F6
Pyatigorsk, U.S.S.R., 7/J4
Pyatikhatki, U.S.S.R. 52/D5
Pyatt, Ark. (72672) 203/E1
Pye (isls.), Alaska 196/C2
Pye, Burma, 54/N8
Pye, Burma 72/B3
Pyhä (lake), Fin. 18/O5
Pyhä (lake), Fin. 18/M6
Pyinmana, Burma 72/C3
Pyland, Miss. (†38851) 256/F3
Pymatuning (res.), Ohio 284/J2
Pymatuning (res.), Pa. 294/A2
P'yŏnggang, N. Korea 81/C4
P'yŏngsan, N. Korea 81/C4
P'yŏngyang (cap.), N. Korea, 54/R5
P'yŏngyang (cap.), N. Korea 81/C4
Pyote, Texas (79777) 302/A6
Pyramid (peak), Idaho 220/E4
Pyramid, Ky. (41656) 237/R5
Pyramid (isl.), N.Z. 101/E7
Pyramid, Nev. (†89501) 266/B2
Pyramid (lake), Nev. 266/B2
Pyramid Lake Ind. Res., Nev. 266/B2
Pyramids (ruins), U.A.R. 111/J3
Pyrenees (range), 7/D4
Pyrenees (range), France 28/C6
Pyrenees (range), Spain 33/G1
Pyrénées-Atlantiques (dept.), France 28/C6
Pyrénées-Orientales (dept.), France 28/E6
Pyrites, N.Y. (13677) 276/K1
Pyriton, Ala. (†36266) 194/G4
Pyrzyce, Poland 47/B2
Pyshchug, U.S.S.R. 52/G3
Pysht, Wash. (†98362) 310/A2
Pyskowice, Poland 47/A4
Pytalovo, U.S.S.R. 52/C3
Pyu, Burma 72/C3
Pyuthan, Nepal 68/E3

Q

Qabalan, Jordan 65/C3
Qabatiya, Jordan 65/C3
Qadhima, Saudi Ar. 59/C5
Qadima, Israel 65/B3
Qafar, Saudi Ar. 59/D4
Qaffin, Jordan 65/C3
Qain, Iran 59/G3
Qain, Iran 66/L4
Qais (isl.), Iran 59/F4
Qais (isl.), Iran 66/J7
Qala Panja, Afgh. 59/K2
Qala Panja, Afgh. 68/C1
Qal'a Sharqat, Iraq 59/D2
Qal'a Sharqat, Iraq 66/C3
Qa'lat Diza, Iraq 66/D2
Qal'at es Salihiye, Syria 63/J5
Qaleh-i-Kang, Afgh. 59/H3
Qaleh-i-Kang, Afgh. 68/A2
Qal'eh-i-Mura (riv.), Iran 66/J3
Qalqiliya, Jordan 65/C3
Qalyub, U.A.R. 111/J3
Qamishliye, Syria 63/J4
Qamr (bay), P.D.R. Yemen 59/F6
Qarajeh Dagh (mts.), Iran 66/E1
Qaranqu (riv.), Iran 66/E2
Qara Qash, China 77/B4
Qaraqum, China 77/C3
Qara Shahr, China 77/C3
Qara Su (riv.), Iran 66/E1
Qara Su (riv.), Iran 66/G3
Qara Su (riv.), Iran 66/K2
Qarghaliq, China 77/A4
Qarn (riv.), Israel 65/C1
Qasr al Haiyanya, Saudi Ar. 59/D4
Qasr al Khubbaz, Iraq 66/B4
Qasr Farâfra, 102/E2
Qasr Farâfra, U.A.R. 59/A4
Qasr Farâfra, U.A.R. 111/E2
Qasr-i-Shirin, Iran 66/E3
Qasrqand (Nikshahr), Iran 66/M7
Qatar, 54/J7
QATAR, 59/F4
Qatif, Saudi Ar. 59/E4
Qattâra (depr.), U.A.R. 59/A4
Qattâra (depr.), U.A.R. 111/E2
Qazian, Iran 66/F2
Qedma, Israel 65/B4
Qena, 102/F2
Qena, U.A.R. 59/B4
Qena, U.A.R. 111/F2
Qibya, Jordan 65/C4
Qina (Qena), U.A.R. 59/B4
Qiryat Bialik, Israel 65/C2
Qiryat Gat, Israel 65/B4
Qiryat Haayin, Israel 65/C2
Qiryat Motzkin, Israel 65/C2
Qiryat Shemona, Israel 65/C1
Qiryat Tivo'n, Israel 65/C2
Qiryat Yam, Israel 65/C2
Qishm, Iran 59/G4
Qishm (isl.), Iran 66/J7
Qishn, P.D.R. Yemen 59/F6
Qishon (riv.), Israel 65/C2
Qizan, Saudi Ar. 59/D6
Qizil-Qala, Afgh. 59/J2
Qizil Uzun (riv.), Iran 59/E2
Qizil Uzun (riv.), Iran 66/F2
Quabbin (res.), Mass. 249/E3
Quaboag (riv.), Mass. 249/F4
Quaco (head), N. Br. 170/E3
Quaddick, Conn. (†06277) 210/H1
Quaddick (res.), Conn. 210/H1
Quadeville, Ont. 177/G2
Quaduck (brook), Conn. 210/H1
Quail, Texas (79251) 302/D3
Quairading, W. Aust. 92/B1
Quajote Wash (dry riv.), Ariz. 198/D6
Quakenbrück, W. Ger. 22/C2
Quaker City, Ohio (43773) 284/H6
Quaker Farms, Conn. (†06483) 210/C3
Quaker Hill, Conn. (06375) 210/G3
Quakers Hill-Marayong, N.S.W. 97/H3
Quakertown‡, Mich. (†48024) 250/F6
Quakertown, N.J. (08868) 273/D2
Quakertown, Pa. (18951) 294/M5
Qualicum Beach, Br. Col. 184/J3
Quality, Ky. (42268) 237/H6
Quamba, Minn. (55064) 254/E5
Quambatook, Vic. 97/B4
Quambone, N.S.W. 97/E2
Quanah, Texas (79252) 302/E3
Quandary (peak), Colo. 208/G4
Quandialla, N.S.W. 97/D4
Quang Khe, N. Vietnam 72/E3
Quang Nam, S. Vietnam 72/E4
Quang Ngai, S. Vietnam 72/F4
Quang Tri, S. Vietnam 72/E3
Quang Yen, N. Vietnam 72/E2
Quan Long, S. Vietnam 72/E5
Quantico, Md. (21856) 245/R7
Quantico, Va. (22134) 307/O3
Quantico Marine Corps Air Sta., Va. 307/O4
Quapaw, Okla. (74363) 288/S1
Qu'Appelle, Sask. 181/H5
Qu'Appelle (riv.), Sask. 181/J5
Quaraí, Braz. 132/C10
Quaregnon, Belg. 27/D8
Quarryville, N. Br. 170/E2
Quarryville, Pa. (17566) 294/K6
Quartu Sant'Elena, Italy 34/B5
Quartz (peak), Calif. 204/L11
Quartz Hill, Calif. (93534) 204/G9
Quartz Mountain, Oreg. (†97630) 291/G5
Quartzsite, Ariz. (85346) 198/A5
Quasqueton, Iowa (52326) 229/K4
Quassapaug (pond), Conn. 210/C2
Quatervals (mt.), Switz. 39/K3
Quathiaski Cove, Br. Col. 184/E5
Quatre Bornes, Mauritius 118/G5
Quatsino, Br. Col. 184/D5
Quatsino (sound), Br. Col. 184/C5
Quay (co.), N. Mex. 274/F3
Quay, N. Mex. (88433) 274/F4
Quay, Okla. (†74085) 288/N2
Quchan, Iran 59/G2
Quchan, Iran 66/L2
Quealy, Wyo. (†82901) 319/C4
Queanbeyan, N.S.W. 97/E4
Québec (prov.), Canada, 146/L4
QUÉBEC, 172
Québec, Canada, 3/F3
Québec (co.), Que. 172/F3
Québec (co.), Que. 174/C3
Québec (cap.), Que. 146/L5
Québec (cap.), Que. 163/J6
Québec (cap.), Que. 172/H3
Québec (cap.), Que. 174/C3
Quebeck, Tenn. (38579) 237/K9
Québec-Ouest, Que. 172/J3
Quebracho, Urug. 145/B2
Quebracho Coto, Arg. 143/D2
Quebrada de Alvarado, Chile 138/F2
Quebradillas, P. Rico 161/B1
Quechee, Vt. (05059) 268/C4
Quechisla, Bol. 136/C7
Quecholac, Mex. 150/O2
Quecreek, Pa. (15555) 294/D5
Quedlinburg, E. Ger. 22/D3
Queen (cape), N.W.T. 187/L3
Queen, Pa. (16670) 294/E5
Queen Anne, Md. (21657) 245/O5
Queen Annes (co.), Md. 245/P4
Queen Charlotte (isls.), 163/C5
Queen Charlotte (sound), 163/D5
Queen Charlotte (isls.), Br. Col. 146/E4
Queen Charlotte, Br. Col. 184/A3
Queen Charlotte (isls.), Br. Col. 184/B3
Queen Charlotte (sound), Br. Col. 184/C4
Queen Charlotte (str.), Br. Col. 184/D5
Queen City, Mo. (63561) 261/H2
Queen City, Texas (75572) 302/L4
Queen Creek, Ariz. (85242) 198/D5
Queen Elizabeth (isls.), 163/M2
Queen Elizabeth (isls.), Canada, 3/C2
Queen Elizabeth (isls.), Canada, 4/B15
Queen Elizabeth (isls.), N.W.T., 146/H2
Queen Elizabeth (isls.), N.W.T. 187/H1
Queen Elizabeth Nat'l Park, Uganda 115/F4
Queen Mary Coast (reg.), Ant. 5/C5
Queen Maud (gulf), 163/F2
Queen Maud (gulf), N.W.T. 187/H3
Queen Maud Land (reg.), Ant., 3/K10
Queen Maud Land (reg.), Ant. 5/B1
Queens (sound), Br. Col. 184/C4
Queen's (co.), N. Br. 170/D3
Queens (co.), N.S. 169/C4
Queens (chan.), N.W.T. 187/J2
Queens (co.), N.Y. 276/N9
Queens (borough)▵, N.Y. (*11101) 276/N9
Queens (co.), P.E.I. 169/E2
Queens, W. Va. (26231) 313/F5
Queensberry (mt.), Scot. 15/J9
Queensborough, Ont. 177/G3
Queensborough-in-Sheppey, 10/G5
Queenscliff, Aust. 88/L8
Queensferry, 10/C1
Queensferry, Scot. 15/K8
Queen Shoals, W. Va. (†25045) 313/D6
Queensland (state), Australia, 87/E8
QUEENSLAND, 88/G4
QUEENSLAND, 95
Queensport, N.S. 169/G3
Queenstown, Alta. 182/D4
Queenstown, Aust. 88/G8
Queenstown, Guyana 131/B2
Queenstown (Cóbh), 10/B5
Queenstown (Cóbh), Ire. 17/E8
Queenstown, Md. (21658) 245/O5
Queenstown, N. Br. 170/D3
Queenstown, N.Z. 101/B6
Queenstown, 102/E8
Queenstown, S. Africa 118/D6
Queenstown, Tasmania 99/B4
Queens Village, N.Y. (11429) 276/R7
Queensville, Ind. (†47265) 227/F6
Queets, Wash. (†98399) 310/A3
Queets (riv.), Wash. 310/A3
Queilén, Chile 138/D4
Queimadas, Braz. 132/F5
Quela, Angola 115/C5
Quelimane, 102/F6
Quelimane, Moz., 118/F3
Quelpart (Cheju) (isl.), S. Korea 81/C7
Queluz, Port. 33/A1
Quemado (pt.), Cuba 158/K4
Quemado, N. Mex. (87829) 274/A4
Quemado, Texas (78877) 302/D9
Quemado de Güines, Cuba 158/E1
Quemchi, Chile 138/D4
Quemoy (isl.), China 77/J7
Quemú-Quemú, Arg. 143/D4
Quendale, Scot. 15/M3
Quenemo, Kans. (66528) 232/G3
Quentin, Miss. (39660) 256/C8
Quepos, C. Rica 154/E6
Quequay Chico (riv.), Urug. 145/B3
Quequay Grande (riv.), Urug. 145/B3
Que Que, Rhod. 118/D3
Quequén, Arg., 120/E6
Quequén, Arg. 143/E4
Querecotillo, Peru 128/B5
Querétara, Mex., 146/J7
Querétaro (state), Mex. 150/J6
Querétaro, Mex. 150/J6
Quesada, Spain 33/E4
Quesnel, 163/D5
Quesnel (lake), 163/D5
Quesnel, Br. Col. 184/F4
Quesnel (lake), Br. Col. 184/G4
Quesnel (riv.), Br. Col. 184/F4
Quesnel (lake), Man. 179/G4
Questa, N. Mex. (87556) 274/D2
Queteña, Bol. 136/B8
Quetico Prov. Park, Ont. 175/B3
Quetico Prov. Park, Ont. 177/G5
Quetta, Pak. 59/J3
Quetta, Pak. 68/B2
Quetta, Pak., 54/K6
Queule, Chile 138/D2
Quevedo, Ec. 128/C3
Quezaltenango, Guat. 154/B3
Quezaltepeque, Guat. 154/C3
Quezon (prov.), Phil. 82/C3
Quezon City (cap.), Phil. 82/C3
Quezon City (cap.), Phil. 85/G3
Quezon City (cap.), Phil., 54/R8
Quibala, Angola 115/C6
Quibaxe, Angola 115/B5
Quibdó, Col. 126/B5
Quiberon, France 28/B4
Quibor, Ven. 124/D3
Quicacha, Peru 128/F10
Quick, Br. Col. 184/D3
Quick, W. Va. (25045) 313/D6
Quicksand, Ky. (41363) 237/P5
Quicksburg, Va. (22847) 307/L3
Quiebra Hacha, Cuba 158/B1
Quiévrain, Belg. 27/D8
Quigley, Alta. 182/E1
Quiindy, Par. 144/B7
Quijotoa, Ariz. (†85634) 198/C6
Quilalí, Nic. 154/E4
Quilán (cape), Chile 138/D4
Quilán (isl.), Chile 138/D5
Quilca, Peru 128/F11
Quilcene, Wash. (98376) 310/B3
Quilchena, Br. Col. 184/G5
Quilengues, Angola 115/B6
Quilicura, Chile 138/G3
Quill (lakes), Sask. 181/G4
Quillabamba, Peru 128/F9
Quillacas, Bol. 136/B6
Quillacollo, Bol. 136/B5
Quillagua, Chile 138/B3
Quillaicillo, Chile 138/A8
Quillan, France 28/E6
Quillayute Ind. Res., Wash. 310/A3
Quilleco, Chile 138/E1
Quill Lake, Sask. 181/G3
Quillota, Chile 138/F2
Quilon, India 68/D7
Quilpie, Aust. 88/G5
Quilpie, Queens. 95/C5
Quilpué, Chile 138/F2
Quilty, Ire. 17/C6
Quimby, Iowa (51049) 229/B3
Quimby, Maine (04770) 242/F2
Quime, Bol. 136/B5
Quimili, Arg. 143/D2
Quimper, France 28/A4
Quimper, Sask. 181/D6
Quimperlé, France 28/B4
Quinan, N.S. 169/C5
Quinault, Wash. (98575) 310/B3
Quinault (lake), Wash. 310/B3
Quinault (riv.), Wash. 310/A3
Quinault Ind. Res., Wash. 310/A3
Quinby, S.C. (†29501) 296/H3
Quinby, Va. (23423) 307/S5
Quinby (inlet), Va. 307/S6
Quince Mil, Peru 128/G9
Quincy, Calif. (95971) 204/E4
Quincy, Fla. (32351) 212/B1
Quincy, Ill., 188/H3
Quincy, Ill. (62301) 222/B4
Quincy, Ind. (47456) 227/D6
Quincy, Kans. (66867) 232/F4
Quincy, Ky. (41166) 237/P3
Quincy, Mass. (†02169) 249/D7
Quincy (bay), Mass. 249/D7
Quincy, Mich. (49082) 250/E7
Quincy, Miss. (†38848) 256/H3
Quincy, Mo. (65735) 261/E6
Quincy, N.H. (†03266) 268/D4
Quincy, Ohio (43343) 284/C5
Quincy, W. Va. (25016) 313/C6
Quincy, Wash. (98848) 310/F3
Quindío (dept.), Col. 126/C5
Quinebaug, Conn. (06262) 210/H1
Quinebaug (riv.), Conn. 210/H2
Quinebaug (riv.), Mass. 249/F4
Quines, Arg. 143/C3
Quinhagak, Alaska (99655) 196/F3
Qui Nhon, S. Vietnam 72/F4
Qui Nhon, S. Vietnam, 54/P8
Quiniluban (isls.), Phil. 82/C5
Quinlan, Okla. (†73852) 288/J2
Quinlan, Texas (75474) 302/H5
Quinn (riv.), Nev. 266/D1
Quinn, S. Dak. (57775) 298/E5
Quinn Canyon (range), Nev. 266/F4
Quinnesec, Mich. (49876) 250/A3
Quinnimont, W. Va. (25910) 313/D7
Quinnipiac, Conn. (†06492) 210/D3
Quinnipiac (riv.), Conn. 210/D3
Quinta de Tilcoco, Chile 138/G5
Quintana de la Serena, Spain 33/D3
Quintanar de la Orden, Spain 33/E3
Quintana Roo (terr.), Mex. 150/P7
Quintay, Chile 138/F3
Quinter, Kans. (67752) 232/B2
Quintero, Chile 138/F2
Quinto (riv.), Arg. 143/D3
Quinto, Spain 33/F2
Quinto, Switz. 39/G3
Quinton, Ky. (†42518) 237/M7
Quinton, N.J. (08072) 273/C4
Quinton, Okla. (74561) 288/R4
Quinton, Sask. 181/G4
Quinton, Va. (23141) 307/O5
Quinwood, W. Va. (25981) 313/E6
Quinzau, Angola 115/B5
Quionga, Moz. 118/G2
Quipapá, Braz. 132/G5
Quirey, Col. 126/F5
Quirihue, Chile 138/E1
Quirindi, Aust. 88/H6
Quirindi, N.S.W. 97/F2
Quiriquire, Ven. 124/G3
Quirke (lake), Ont. 177/B1
Quiroga, Arg. 143/F7
Quiroga, Bol. 136/C6
Quiroga, Spain 33/C1
Quirusillas, Bol. 136/D6
Quisiro, Ven. 124/C2
Quissanga, Moz. 118/G2
Quissett, Mass. (†02540) 249/M6
Quissico, Moz. 118/F4
Quitaque, Texas (79255) 302/C3
Quitasueño (bank), Col. 126/A8
Quitilipi, Arg. 143/D2
Quitman, Ark. (72131) 203/F3
Quitman (co.), Ga. 216/B7
Quitman, Ga. (31643) 216/E9
Quitman, La. (71268) 238/E2
Quitman (co.), Miss. 256/D2
Quitman, Miss. (39355) 256/G6
Quitman, Mo. (64478) 261/C2
Quitman, Texas (75783) 302/J5
Quitman (mts.), Texas 302/B11
Quito (cap.), Ec., 120/C3
Quito (cap.), Ec. 128/C3
Quito (cap.), Ecuador, 3/F6
Quixadá, Braz. 132/G4
Quixeramobim, Braz. 132/F4
Quilin, Mo. (63961) 261/M9
Qum, Iran 59/F3
Qum, Iran 66/G3
Qumeim, Jordan 65/D2
Qunfidha, Saudi Ar. 59/D6
Quogue, N.Y. (11959) 276/P9
Quoich (riv.), N.W.T. 187/J3
Quoich (lake), Scot. 15/F5
Quonnipaug (lake), Conn. 210/E3
Quonset Point Nav. Air Sta., R.I. 249/J6
Quorn, Aust. 88/F6
Quorn, S. Aust. 94/F5
Qurveh, Iran 66/E3
Quryat, Oman 59/G5
Qusaiba, Saudi Ar. 59/D4
Quteife, Syria 63/G6
Qutur, Iran 66/D1
Quyquyhó, Par. 144/D6

R

Raab (riv.), Austria 41/C3
Raabs, Austria 41/C2
Raahe, Fin. 18/O4
Raalte, Neth. 27/J4
Ra'anana, Israel 65/B3
Raanes (pen.), N.W.T. 187/K2
Raasay (isl.), Scot. 15/D5
Raasay (sound), Scot. 15/D5
Rab, Yugo. 45/B3
Rab (isl.), Yugo. 45/B3
Rába (riv.), Hung. 41/D3
Raba, Indon. 85/F7
Rabat (cap.), Mor. 102/B1
Rabat (cap.), Mor., 3/J4
Rabat (cap.), Mor. 106/C2
Rabaul, Terr. N.G., 87/F6
Rabbit (riv.), Mich. 250/D6
Rabbit (isl.), N.S.W. 97/J2
Rabbit (creek), S. Dak. 298/E3
Rabbit Ears (peak), Colo. 208/G2
Rabbit Ears (range), Colo. 208/F2
Rabbithash, Ky. (†41091) 237/M3
Rabbit Lake, Sask. 181/D2
Rabch (riv.), Iran 66/L8

424 Rabey

Rabey, Minn. (†55752) 254/E4
Rabigh, Saudi Ar. 59/C5
Rabinal, Guat. 154/B3
Rabocheostrovsk, U.S.S.R. 52/D1
Rabun, Ala. (†36507) 194/C8
Rabun (co.), Ga. 216/F1
Rabun (lake), Ga. 216/E1
Rabun Gap, Ga. (30568) 216/F1
Rača, Yugo. 45/E3
Raccoon (pt.), Fla. 212/D3
Raccoon, Ind. (†46172) 227/D5
Raccoon (riv.), Iowa 229/D4
Raccoon (pt.), La. 238/H8
Raccoon (creek), N.J. 273/C4
Raccoon (creek), Ohio 284/F8
Race (cape), 163/L6
Race (pt.), Mass. 249/N4
Race (cape), Newf., 146/N5
Race (cape), Newf. 166/D2
Raceland, Ky. (41169) 237/R3
Raceland, La. (70394) 238/J7
Racepond, Ga. (†31537) 216/H8
Rachel, W. Va. (26587) 313/F3
Rach Gia, S. Vietnam 72/E5
Racibórz, Poland 47/C3
Racine, Que. 172/E4
Racine, Minn. (55967) 254/F7
Racine, Mo. (64858) 261/C9
Racine, Ohio (45771) 284/G8
Racine, W. Va. (25165) 313/C6
Racine, Wis., 188/J2
Racine (co.), Wis. 317/K10
Racine, Wis. (*53401) 317/M3
Ráckeve, Hung. 41/E3
Rackham, Man. 179/B4
Rackwick, Scot. 15/K2
Raco, Mich. (49778) 250/E2
Racola, Mo. (†63630) 261/L6
Radama (isls.), Malag. Rep. 118/H2
Rădăuţi, Rum. 45/G2
Radbuza (riv.), Czech. 41/B2
Radcliff, Ky. (40160) 237/K5
Radcliff, Ohio (45670) 284/F7
Radcliffe, Iowa (50230) 229/G4
Radeberg, E. Ger. 22/E3
Radebeul, E. Ger. 22/E3
Radeče, Yugo. 45/B2
Radenthein, Austria 41/B3
Rader, Tenn. (†37743) 237/R8
Radersburg, Mont. (59641) 262/E4
Radford, Va. (24141) 307/G6
Radhanpur, India 68/C4
Radiant, Va. (22732) 307/M4
Radisson, Sask. 181/D3
Radisson, Wis. (54867) 317/D4
Radium, Colo. (80472) 208/G3
Radium, Kans. (67571) 232/D3
Radium, Minn. (56749) 254/B2
Radium Hill, Aust. 88/G6
Radium Hill, S. Aust. 94/G5
Radium Hot Springs, Br. Col. 184/J5
Radium Springs, N. Mex. (88054) 274/B6
Radja Ampat Group (isls.), Indon. 85/H6
Radkersburg, Austria 41/C3
Radley, Ind. (†46938) 227/F4
Radnice, Czech. 41/B2
Radnor, Ind. (46981) 227/D3
Radnor, Ohio (43066) 284/D5
Radnor, W. Va. (25556) 313/A6
Radnorshire (co.), Wales 13/D5
Radolfzell, W. Ger. 22/C5
Radom, Ill. (62876) 222/D5
Radom, Poland, 7/F3
Radom, Poland 47/E3
Radomir, Bulg. 45/F4
Radomsko, Poland 47/D3
Radomyshl', U.S.S.R. 52/C4
Radoviš, Yugo. 45/F5
Radstadt, Austria 41/B3
Radviliškis, U.S.S.R. 53/B3
Radville, 163/F6
Radville, Sask. 181/G6
Radway, Alta. 182/D2
Radziejów, Poland 47/D2
Radzymin, Poland 47/E2
Radzyń Podlaski, Poland 47/F3
Rae, 163/E3
Rae (isth.), 163/H2
Rae, N.W.T. 187/G3
Rae (isth.), N.W.T. 187/K3
Rae (riv.), N.W.T. 187/G3
Rae (str.), N.W.T. 187/J3
Raeford, N.C. (28376) 281/L5
Raeren, Belg. 27/J7
Raeside (lake), Aust. 88/C5
Raeside (lake), W. Aust. 92/C5
Raetihi, N.Z. 101/E3
Raeville, Nebr. (68656) 264/F3
Rafaela, Arg. 143/F5
Rafai, Centr. Afr. Rep. 115/D2
Rafid, Jordan 65/D2
Rafidiya, Jordan 65/C3
Rafsenjan (Bahramabad), Iran 66/K5
Raft (riv.), Idaho 220/E7
Raft (riv.), Utah 304/A1
Raft River (mts.), Utah 304/A2
Rafz, Switz. 39/G1
Raga, Sudan 111/E6
Ragan, Nebr. (68969) 264/E4
Ragang (vol.), Phil. 82/E7
Ragay (gulf), Phil. 82/D4
Ragged (isl.), Bah. Is. 156/C2
Ragged (pt.), Barb. 161/C8
Ragged (isl.), Maine 242/F8
Ragged (lake), Maine 242/E4
Ragged (isls.), Newf. 166/C2
Raglan, N.Z. 101/E2
Raglan (harb.), N.Z. 101/E2
Ragland, Ala. (35131) 194/F3
Ragley, La. (70657) 238/D5
Rago, Kans. (67128) 232/D4
Ragsdale, Ind. (47573) 227/C7
Ragunda, Sweden 18/J5
Ragusa (prov.), Italy 34/E6
Ragusa, Italy 34/E6
Ragusa (Dubrovnik), Yugo., 7/F4
Ragusa (Dubrovnik), Yugo. 45/C4
Raha, Indon. 85/G6
Rahaeng (Tak), Thai. 72/C3
Rahan, Ire. 17/F5
Rahimyar Khan, Pak. 68/C3
Rahotu, N.Z. 101/D3
Rahue (riv.), Chile 138/D3
Rahway, N.J. (*07065) 273/E2
Rai, Iran 66/G3
Raiatea (isl.), Fr. Poly., 87/L7
Raíces, Arg. 143/G6
Raichur, India 68/D5
Raiford, Fla. (32083) 212/D1
Raigarh, India 68/E4
Railley (mt.), Mont. 262/C3
Railroad (valley), Nev. 266/F4
Railroad, Pa. (17355) 294/J6
Railroad Canyon (res.), Calif. 204/E11
Railton, Tas. 99/C3
Rainbow (plat.), Ariz. 198/D2
Rainbow, Conn. (†06095) 210/E1
Rainbow (mt.), Idaho 220/C4
Rainbow (lake), Maine 242/E4
Rainbow, Oreg. (†97413) 291/E3
Rainbow, Vic. 97/A4
Rainbow Bridge Nat'l Mon., Utah 304/C6
Rainbow City, Ala. (35901) 194/F3
Rainbow Lake, Alta. 182/A5
Rainelle, W. Va. (25962) 313/E7
Rainier, Alta. 182/E4
Rainier, Oreg. (97048) 291/E1
Rainier (mt.), Wash., 188/B1
Rainier, Wash. (98576) 310/C4
Rainier (mt.), Wash. 310/D4
Rains, S.C. (29589) 296/J3
Rains (co.), Texas 302/J5
Rainsboro, Ohio (45165) 284/C7
Rainsburg, Pa. (†15522) 294/F6
Rainsville, Ala. (35986) 194/G2
Rainsville, Ind. (†47918) 227/C4
Rainsville, N. Mex. (87736) 274/D2
Rainy (lake), 163/G6
Rainy (lake), Ont. 175/B3
Rainy (lake), Ont. 177/G5
Rainy (lake), Minn., 188/H1
Rainy (riv.), Minn., 188/H1
Rainy (lake), Minn. 254/E2
Rainy (riv.), Minn. 254/D2
Rainy River, 163/G6
Rainy River (co.), Ont. 175/B3
Rainy River, Ont. 175/A3
Rainy River (co.), Ont. 177/G5
Rainy River, Ont. 177/F5
Raipur, India 68/E4
Rairakhol, India 68/E4
Raisin, Calif. (93652) 204/E7
Raisin (riv.), Mich. 250/F7
Raith, Ont. 175/C3
Raith, Ont. 177/G5
Raivavae (isl.), Fr. Poly., 87/M8
Raja (mt.), Indon. 85/E6
Rajahmundry, India 68/E5
Rajang (riv.), Malaysia 85/E5
Rajapalaiyam, India 68/D7
Rajapur, India 68/C5
Rajasthan (state), India 68/C3
Rajec, Czech. 41/E2
Rajgarh, India 68/D4
Rajka, Hung. 41/D3
Rajkot, India 68/C4
Rajnandgaon, India 68/E4
Rajpipla, India 68/C4
Rajpur, India 68/F2
Rajpura, India 68/D2
Rajshahi, Pak. 68/F4
Rak, Sask. 181/E3
Rakahanga (atoll), Cook Is., 87/K7
Rakaia, N.Z. 101/C5
Rakaia (riv.), N.Z. 101/C5
Rakamaz, Hung. 41/F2
Rakan, Ras (cape), Qatar 59/F4
Rakaposhi (mt.), India 68/C1
Rakata (isl.), Indon. 85/C7
Rake, Iowa (50465) 229/F2
Rakhov, U.S.S.R. 52/B5
Rakino (isl.), N.Z. 101/C1
Rakitu (isl.), N.Z. 101/E2
Rakkestad, Norway 18/G7
Rakof (isls.), Alaska 196/M1
Rákospalota, Hung. 41/E3
Rakovník, Czech. 41/B1
Rakvere, U.S.S.R. 52/C3
Rakvere, U.S.S.R. 53/D1
Raleigh, Fla. (†32696) 212/D2
Raleigh, Ga. (†30293) 216/C5
Raleigh, Ill. (62977) 222/E6
Raleigh, Ind. (†46173) 227/G5
Raleigh, Miss. (39153) 256/F6
Raleigh (cap.), N.C., 146/L6
Raleigh (cap.), N.C., 188/L3
Raleigh (bay), N.C. 281/S5
Raleigh (cap.), N.C. (*27601) 281/M3
Raleigh, N. Dak. (58564) 283/H7
Raleigh, Newf. 166/C3
Raleigh, Tenn. (38128) 237/B10
Raleigh (co.), W. Va. 313/D7
Raleigh, W. Va. (25911) 313/D7
Ralik Chain (isls.), Pac. Is., 87/G5
Ralls (co.), Mo. 261/J3
Ralls, Texas (79357) 302/C4
Ralph, Ala. (35480) 194/C4
Ralph, Mich. (49877) 250/B2
Ralph, S. Dak. (57650) 298/C2
Ralph, Sask. 181/H6
Ralphton, Pa. (†15563) 294/D5
Ralston, Alta. 182/E4
Ralston, Iowa (51459) 229/D4
Ralston, N.J. (†07945) 273/D2
Ralston, Nebr. (68127) 264/J3
Ralston, Okla. (74650) 288/N2
Ralston, Pa. (17763) 294/H2
Ralston, Tenn. (†38237) 237/D8
Ralston, Wash. (99165) 310/G4
Ralston, Wyo. (82440) 319/D1
Ram (head), V.I.(U.S.) 161/C5
Rama, Nic. 154/E4
Rama, Sask. 181/H4
Ramadi, Iraq 59/D3
Ramadi (prov.), Iraq 66/C4
Ramadi, Iraq 66/C4
Ramage, W. Va. (25166) 313/C7
Ramah, Colo. (80832) 208/L4
Ramah, N. Mex. (87321) 274/A3
Ramah (bay), Newf. 166/B2
Ramallah, Jordan 65/C4
Ramallo, Arg. 143/F6
Ramapo (riv.), N.J. 273/E1
Ramat Gan, Israel 65/B3
Ramat Hasharon, Israel 65/B3
Ramblewood, N.J. (†08057) 273/D4
Rambouillet, France 28/D3
Rame, Israel 65/C2
Ramea, Newf. 166/C4
Ramea (isls.), Newf. 166/C4
Ramechhap, Nepal 68/F3
Ramelton, Ire. 17/F1
Ramer, Ala. (36069) 194/F6
Ramer, Tenn. (38367) 237/D10
Rameswaram, India 68/D7
Ramey, Minn. (†56329) 254/E5
Ramey, Pa. (16671) 294/F4
Ramey A.F.B., P. Rico 161/A1
Ram Hormuz, Iran 66/F5
Ramhurst, Ga. (†30705) 216/C1
Ramièrs (isl.), Mart. 161/C6
Ramla, Israel 65/B4
Ramm, Jebel (mt.), Jordan 65/D5
Ramme, Den. 21/B5
Rammun, Jordan 65/C4
Ramnäs, Sweden 18/J7
Ramon, N. Mex. (†88136) 274/D4
Ramon (mt.), Israel 65/D5
Ramona, Calif. (92065) 204/J10
Ramona, Kans. (67475) 232/E3
Ramona, Okla. (74061) 288/P1
Ramona, S. Dak. (57054) 298/P5
Ramón Castilla, Peru 128/G5
Ramón de las Yaguas, Cuba 158/J4
Ramón Santana, Dom. Rep. 158/F6
Ramón Trigo, Urug. 145/E3
Ramor (lake), Ire. 17/G4
Ramos (riv.), Mex. 150/G4
Ramos Arizpe, Mex. 150/J4
Ramosch, Switz. 39/K3
Ramotswa, Botswana 118/C4
Ramp, W. Va. (†25985) 313/E7
Rampart, Alaska (99767) 196/H1
Ramparts (riv.), N.W.T. 187/E3
Rampur, India 68/D2
Rampur, India 68/D3
Ramree (isl.), Burma 72/B3
Ramsar, Iran 66/G2
Ramsay, Mich. (49959) 250/F2
Ramsay, Mont. (59748) 262/D4
Ramsele, Sweden 18/K5
Ramsen, Switz. 39/G1
Ramseur, N.C. (27316) 281/K3
Ramsey, 10/F4
Ramsey, Eng. 13/G5
Ramsey, 10/D3
Ramsey, I. of Man 13/C3
Ramsey, Ill. (62080) 222/D4
Ramsey, Ind. (47166) 227/E8
Ramsey (co.), Minn. 254/E5
Ramsey (co.), N. Dak. 283/N3
Ramsey, N.J. (07446) 273/B1
Ramsey (isl.), Wales 13/B6
Ramsgate, 10/G5
Ramsgate, Eng. 13/J6
Ramsjö, Sweden 18/J5
Ramtha, Jordan 65/E2
Ramu (riv.), Terr. N.G. 85/B7
Ramunia, Tanjong (pt.), Malaysia 72/F6
Ramville (isl.), Mart. 161/D6
Ran (fjord), Norway 18/H3
Rana (riv.), Norway 18/J3
Ranau, Malaysia 85/F4
Ranburne, Ala. (36273) 194/H3
Rancagua, Chile 138/G5
Rance, Belg. 27/E8
Ranches of Taos, N. Mex. (87557) 274/D2
Ranchester, Wyo. (82839) 319/E1
Ranchi, India 68/F4
Rancho Cordova, Calif. (95670) 204/C8
Rancho Mirage‡, Calif. (92270) 204/J10
Rancho Rinconada‡, Calif. (†95101) 204/K3
Ranchos, Arg. 143/H7
Rancho Santa Clarita, Calif. (†91321) 204/G9
Rancho Santa Fe, Calif. (92067) 204/H10
Rancho Veloz, Cuba 158/D1
Ranchuelo, Cuba 158/E2
Ranco (lake), Chile 138/E3
Rancocas, N.J. (08073) 273/D3
Rancocas (creek), N.J. 273/D3
Rand, Colo. (80473) 208/G2
Randalia, Iowa (52164) 229/K3
Randall, Iowa (50231) 229/F4
Randall, Kans. (66963) 232/D2
Randall, Minn. (56475) 254/D4
Randall (co.), Texas 302/C2
Randallstown, Md. (21133) 245/L3
Randalstown, N. Ire. 17/J2
Randbøl, Den. 21/C6
Randers, Den. 18/G8
Randers (co.), Den. 21/D5
Randers, Den. 21/C5
Randfontein, S. Africa 118/G6
Randle, Wash. (98377) 310/D4
Randleman, N.C. (27317) 281/K3
Randles, Mo. (†63740) 261/N8
Randlett, Okla. (73562) 288/K6
Randlett, Utah (84063) 304/E3
Randolph (co.), Ala. 194/H4
Randolph, Ala. (36792) 194/E5
Randolph, Ariz. (85243) 198/D6
Randolph (co.), Ark. 203/H1
Randolph (co.), Ga. 216/C7
Randolph (co.), Ill. 222/D5
Randolph (co.), Ind. 227/G4
Randolph, Iowa (51649) 229/B7
Randolph, Kans. (66554) 232/F2
Randolph▵, Maine (†04345) 242/D7
Randolph, Maine (†04345) 242/D7
Randolph, Man. 179/F5
Randolph▵, Mass. (02368) 249/D8
Randolph, Md. (†20853) 245/K4
Randolph, Minn. (55065) 254/E6
Randolph, Miss. (38864) 256/F2
Randolph (co.), Mo. 261/G3
Randolph, Mo. (†64101) 261/P5
Randolph (co.), N.C. 281/K3
Randolph▵, N.H. (03593) 268/E3
Randolph, N.H. (03593) 268/E3
Randolph, N.Y. (14772) 276/C6
Randolph, Nebr. (68771) 264/G2
Randolph, Ohio (44265) 284/H3
Randolph, S. Dak. (†57474) 298/N3
Randolph, Utah (84064) 304/C2
Randolph, Va. (23962) 307/L7
Randolph▵, Vt. (05060) 268/B4
Randolph, Vt. (05060) 268/B4
Randolph (co.), W. Va. 313/G5
Randolph, Wis. (53956) 317/H8
Randolph Center, Vt. (05061) 268/B4
Random (isl.), Newf. 166/D2
Random (sound), Newf. 166/D2
Randsburg, Calif. (93554) 204/H8
Randwick, Aust. 88/L3
Randwick, N.S.W. 97/J3
Ranfurly, Alta. 182/E3
Ranfurly, N.Z. 101/B6
Rangamati, Pak. 68/G4
Rangatira (isl.), N.Z. 101/E7
Range, Ala. (36473) 194/D8
Range (creek), Utah 304/D4
Rangeley▵, Maine (04970) 242/B6
Rangeley, Maine (04970) 242/B6
Rangeley (lake), Maine 242/B6
Rangely, Colo. (81648) 208/B2
Ranger, Ga. (30734) 216/C2
Ranger (peak), Idaho 220/D3
Ranger, N.C. (†28906) 281/A4
Ranger, Sask. 181/D2
Ranger, Texas (76470) 302/F5
Ranger, W. Va. (25557) 313/B6
Rangeview, Sask. 181/B6
Rangiauria (Pitt) (isl.), N.Z. 101/E7
Rangiora, N.Z. 101/D5
Rangiroa (atoll), Fr. Poly., 87/M7
Rangitaiki (riv.), N.Z. 101/F3
Rangitata (riv.), N.Z. 101/C5
Rangitikei (riv.), N.Z. 101/E3
Rangitoto (isl.), N.Z. 101/C1
Rangkasbitung, Indon. 85/G2
Rangoon (cap.), Burma, 3/P5
Rangoon (cap.), Burma, 54/N8
Rangoon (cap.), Burma 72/C3
Rangoon, W. Va. (26232) 313/F4
Rangpur, Pak. 68/F3
Rang Saint Sauveur, N. Br. 170/E1
Rania, Iraq 66/D2
Ranier, Minn. (56668) 254/E2
Raniwara, India 68/C4
Ranken (riv.), No. Terr. 93/E6
Rankin, Ill. (60960) 222/F3
Rankin (co.), Miss. 256/E6
Rankin, Pa. (†15104) 294/C7
Rankin, Texas (79778) 302/B6
Rankine Store, No. Terr. 93/E5
Rankin Inlet, N.W.T. 187/J3
Rankins Springs, N.S.W. 97/D3
Rankovićevo, Yugo. 45/E4
Rankweil, Austria 41/A3
Ranlo, N.C. (28052) 281/G4
Rannoch (lake), 10/D2
Rannoch (dist.), Scot. 15/H6
Rannoch (lake), Scot. 15/H6
Ranong, Thai. 72/C5
Ransiki, Indon. 85/J6
Ransom, Ill. (60470) 222/E2
Ransom, Kans. (67572) 232/B3
Ransom (co.), N. Dak. 283/P7
Ransomville, N.Y. (14131) 276/C4
Ranson, W. Va. (25438) 313/L4
Rantauprapat, Indon. 85/C5
Rantekombola (mt.), Indon. 85/F6
Rantis, Jordan 65/C3
Rantoul, Ill. (61866) 222/E3
Rantoul, Kans. (66079) 232/G3
Ranua, Fin. 18/P4
Ranui, N.Z. 101/B1
Ranum, Den. 21/C4
Ranya, Wadi (dry riv.), Saudi Ar. 59/D5
Rao Co (mt.), Laos 72/E3
Rao Co (mt.), N. Vietnam 72/E3
Raoui Erg (des.), Alg. 106/D3
Raoul (isl.), N.Z., 87/J8
Rapa (isl.), Fr. Poly., 87/M8
Rapallo, Italy 34/B2
Rapa Nui (Easter) (isl.), Chile, 87/Q8
Rapel, Chile 138/F4
Rapel (riv.), Chile 138/F4
Rapelje, Mont. (59067) 262/G5
Raper (cape) 163/K2
Raper (cape), N.W.T. 187/M3
Raphine, Va. (24472) 307/K5
Raphoe, Ire. 17/F2
Rapid (riv.), Mich. 250/B2
Rapid (riv.), Minn. 254/D2
Rapidan, Va. (22733) 307/M4
Rapidan (riv.), Va. 307/M4
Rapid City, Man. 179/B4
Rapid City, Mich. (49676) 250/D4
Rapid City, S. Dak., 188/F2
Rapid City, S. Dak. (57701) 298/C5
Rapide-Blanc, Que. 174/C3
Rapides (par.), La. 238/E4
Rapid River, Mich. (49878) 250/C3
Rapids City, Ill. (61278) 222/C2
Rapid View, Sask. 181/C1
Räpina, U.S.S.R. 53/D1
Raposos, Braz. 135/E2
Rappahannock (co.), Va. 307/M3
Rappahannock (riv.), Va. 307/P4
Rapperswil, Switz. 39/G2
Rápulo (riv.), Bol. 136/C4
Rapu-Rapu (isl.), Phil. 82/E4
Raqqa (El Rashid), Syria 63/H5
Raquette (lake), N.Y. 276/L3
Raquette (riv.), N.Y. 276/L1
Raquette Lake, N.Y. (13436) 276/L3
Raraka (atoll), Fr. Poly., 87/M7
Rarden, Ohio (45671) 284/D8
Rardin, Ill. (61948) 222/E4
Raritan, Ill. (61471) 222/C3
Raritan, N.J. (08869) 273/D2
Raritan (bay), N.J. 273/E3
Raritan (riv.), N.J. 273/D2
Raroia (atoll), Fr. Poly., 87/M7
Raron, Switz. 39/E4
Rarotonga (isl.), Cook Is., 87/K8
Rasa (isl.), Phil. 82/B6
Ras al Khaimah (cap.), Trucial States 59/G4
Rasar, Tenn. (†37878) 237/O9
Ras Dashan (mt.), Eth. 111/G5
Ras Dashan (mt.), 102/F3
Raseiniai, U.S.S.R. 53/B3
Ras' en Naqb, Jordan 65/E5
Ras Ghârib, U.A.R. 111/F2
Rashad, Sudan 111/F5
Rasharkin, N. Ire. 17/J2
Rasheiya, Leb. 63/F6
Rashid (prov.), Syria 63/H5
Rashid (Rosetta), U.A.R. 59/B3
Rashid (Rosetta), U.A.R. 111/J2
Rask, Iran 66/M7
Raška, Yugo. 45/E4
Ras Lanuf, Libya 111/C1
Rason (lake), W. Aust. 92/D5
Rasskazovo, U.S.S.R. 52/F4
Ras Tanura, Saudi Ar. 59/F4
Rastatt, W. Ger. 22/C4
Rastede, W. Ger. 22/C2
Rat (isls.), Alaska 196/K4
Rat (riv.), Que. 172/D2
Rat (riv.), Man. 179/F5
Ratak Chain (isls.), Pac. Is., 87/G5
Ratangarh, India 68/C3
Rat Buri, Thai. 72/C4
Ratcliff, Ark. (72951) 203/C3
Ratcliff, Texas (75858) 302/J6
Ratcliffe, Sask. 181/G6
Rathangan, Ire. 17/G5
Rathbun, Iowa (52545) 229/H7
Rathbun (res.), Iowa 229/G7
Rathcormac, Ire. 17/E7
Rathdowney, Ire. 17/F6
Rathdrum, Idaho (83858) 220/A2
Rathdrum, Ire. 17/J6
Rathedaung, Burma 72/B2
Rathenow, E. Ger. 22/E2
Rathfriland, N. Ire. 17/J3
Rathgormuck, Ire. 17/F7
Rathkeale, 10/B4
Rathkeale, Ire. 17/D7
Rathlin (isl.), 10/C3
Rathlin (isl.), N. Ire. 17/J1
Rathlin (sound), N. Ire. 17/J1
Rathlin O'Birne (isl.), Ire. 17/C2
Rathluirc, 10/B4
Rathluirc, Ire. 17/D7
Rathmore, Ire. 17/J5
Rathmullen, Ire. 17/F1
Rathnew-Merrymeeting, Ire. 17/J6
Rathowen, Ire. 17/F4
Rathvilly, Ire. 17/H6
Rathwell, Man. 179/D5
Ratingen, W. Ger. 22/B3
Ratio, Ark. (†72333) 203/J5
Ratlam, India 68/C4
Ratliff City, Okla. (73081) 288/M6
Ratnagiri, India 68/C5
Ratnapura, Ceylon 68/D7
Ratner, Sask. 181/G2
Ratoath, Ire. 17/J5
Raton, N. Mex., 188/F3
Raton, N. Mex. (87740) 274/E2
Rattan, Okla. (74562) 288/R6
Ratten, Austria 41/C3
Rattlesnake (creek), Kans. 232/D4
Rattlesnake (creek), Ohio 284/C7
Rattlesnake (creek), Oreg. 291/K5
Rattlesnake (hills), Wyo. 319/E3
Rattlesnake (range), Wyo. 319/E3
Rattray (head), Scot. 15/N4
Rättvik, Sweden 18/J6
Ratzeburg, W. Ger. 22/D2
Raub, Ind. (47976) 227/C3
Raub, N. Dak. (58774) 283/F4
Raub, Malaysia 72/D7
Rauch, Arg. 143/E4
Rauch, Minn. (†55740) 254/E3
Raukumara (range), N.Z. 101/F3
Raul Soares, Braz. 135/E2
Rauma, Fin. 18/M6
Rauma (riv.), Norway 18/F5
Raunds, Eng. 13/G5
Raung (mt.), Indon. 85/L2
Raurkela, India 68/F4
Rausu, Japan 81/M1
Rauville, S. Dak. (†57201) 298/P3
Ravalli (co.), Mont. 262/B4
Ravalli, Mont. (59863) 262/B3
Ravana, Ark. (†75556) 203/C7
Ravanna, Mo. (†64673) 261/E2
Ravar, Iran 59/G3
Ravar, Iran 66/K5
Ravelo, Bol. 136/C6
Raven, Va. (24639) 307/E6
Ravena, N.Y. (12143) 276/N6
Ravencliff, W. Va. (25913) 313/C7
Ravendale, Calif. (96123) 204/E3
Ravenden, Ark. (72459) 203/H1
Ravenden Springs, Ark. (72460) 203/H1
Ravenel, S.C. (29470) 296/G6
Ravenglass, Eng. 13/D3
Ravenhead, Sask. 181/D3
Raven Lake, Sask. 181/H3
Ravenna (prov.), Italy 34/D2
Ravenna, Italy 34/D2
Ravenna, Ky. (40472) 237/O5
Ravenna, Mich. (49451) 250/D5
Ravenna, Nebr. (68869) 264/F4
Ravenna, Ohio (44266) 284/H3
Ravenna, Texas (75476) 302/H4
Raven Rock, W. Va. (†26170) 313/D4
Ravensburg, W. Ger. 22/C5
Ravenscliffe, Ont. 177/E2
Ravenscrag, Sask. 181/C6
Ravensdale, Wash. (98051) 310/D3
Ravenshoe, Aust. 88/G3
Ravenshoe, Queens. 95/C3
Ravensthorpe, Aust. 88/C6
Ravensthorpe, W. Aust. 92/B6
Ravenswood, W. Va. (26164) 313/C5
Ravenwood, Mo. (64479) 261/C2
Ravi (riv.), Pak. 68/C2
Ravia, Okla. (73455) 288/N6
Ravine, Alta. 182/C3
Ravine, Pa. (17966) 294/K4
Ravinia, S. Dak. (57357) 298/N7
Rawalpindi, Pak. 59/K3
Rawalpindi, Pak. 68/C2
Rawa Mazowiecka, Poland 47/E3
Rawdon, Que. 172/D3
Rawene, N.Z. 101/D2
Rawhide (creek), Wyo. 319/G1
Rawhide (creek), Wyo. 319/H3
Rawi, Ko (isl.), Thai. 72/C6
Rawicz, Poland 47/C3
Rawlings, Md. (21557) 245/C2
Rawlings, Va. (23876) 307/N7
Rawlinna, Aust. 88/D6
Rawlinna, W. Aust. 92/D5
Rawlins (co.), Kans. 232/A2
Rawlins, Wyo., 188/E2
Rawlins, Wyo. (82301) 319/E4
Rawmarsh, Eng. 13/F4
Rawson, Arg., 120/D7
Rawson, Buenos Aires, Arg. 143/F7
Rawson, Chubut, Arg. 143/D5
Rawson, N. Dak. (58848) 283/C4
Rawson, Ohio (45881) 284/C4
Rawtenstall, 10/G2
Raxaul, India 68/E3
Ray (cape), 163/L6
Ray (mts.), Alaska 196/H1
Ray, Ill. (62679) 222/C3
Ray, Ind. (46737) 227/H1
Ray, Minn. (56669) 254/E2
Ray (co.), Mo. 261/E4
Ray, N. Dak. (58849) 283/D3
Ray (cape), Newf. 166/C4
Ray, Ohio (45672) 284/E7
Rayagada, India 68/E5
Rayak, Leb. 63/G6
Raybon, Ga. (†31553) 216/H8
Rayborn, Mo. (†65703) 261/H8
Raychikhinsk, U.S.S.R. 48/O5
Ray City, Ga. (31645) 216/F8
Rayland, Ohio (43943) 284/J5
Rayle, Ga. (30660) 216/G3
Rayleigh, Br. Col. 184/G5
Raymer (New Raymer), Colo. (80742) 208/M1
Raymond, 163/E6
Raymond, Alta. 182/D5
Raymond, Calif. (93653) 204/F6
Raymond, Idaho (†83114) 220/G7
Raymond, Ill. (62560) 222/D4
Raymond, Ind. (†45056) 227/H6
Raymond, Iowa (50667) 229/J4
Raymond, Kans. (67573) 232/D3
Raymond▵, Maine (04071) 242/B8
Raymond, Maine (04071) 242/B8
Raymond, Minn. (56282) 254/C5
Raymond, Miss. (39154) 256/D6
Raymond, Mont. (59256) 262/M2
Raymond▵, N.H. (03077) 268/E5
Raymond, Nebr. (68428) 264/H4
Raymond, Ohio (43067) 284/C5
Raymond, S. Dak. (57258) 298/O4
Raymond, Wash. (98577) 310/B4
Raymond, Wis. (†53126) 317/L2
Raymond City, W. Va. (†25159) 313/C6
Raymond Terrace, N.S.W. 97/F3
Raymondville, Mo. (65555) 261/J8
Raymondville, N.Y. (13678) 276/L1
Raymondville, Texas (78580) 302/G11
Raymore, Mo. (64083) 261/D5
Raymore, Sask. 181/G4
Rayne, La. (70578) 238/F6
Raynesford, Mont. (59469) 262/F3
Raynham▵, Mass. (02767) 249/K5
Raynham Center, Mass. (02768) 249/K5
Rayón, San Luis Potosí, Mex. 150/K6
Rayón, Sonora, Mex. 150/D2
Rayong, Thai. 72/D4
Rays (lake), Idaho 220/F6
Rays Crossing, Ind. (†46176) 227/F5
Raystown Branch, Juniata (riv.), Pa. 294/F5
Raytown, Mo. (64133) 261/P6
Rayville, La. (71269) 238/G2
Rayville, Mo. (64084) 261/E4
Raywick, Ky. (40060) 237/L5
Razgrad, Bulg. 45/H4
Razlog, Bulg. 45/F5
Ré (isl.), France 28/C4
Rea, Mo. (64480) 261/C2
Reaburn, Man. 179/E4
Reader, Ark. (71726) 203/D6
Reader, W. Va. (26167) 313/E3
Readfield▵, Maine (04355) 242/D7
Readfield, Maine (04355) 242/D7
Readfield, Wis. (54969) 317/J7
Reading, 10/F5
Reading, Eng. 13/F6
Reading, Kans. (66868) 232/F3
Reading▵, Mass. (01867) 249/C5
Reading, Mich. (49274) 250/E7
Reading, Minn. (56165) 254/C7
Reading, Ohio (45215) 284/C9
Reading, Pa., 188/L2
Reading, Pa. (*19601) 294/L5
Reading▵, Vt. (05062) 268/B5
Reading, Vt. (05062) 268/B5
Readington, N.J. (08870) 273/D2
Read Island, 163/E2
Readland, Ark. (71664) 203/H7
Readlyn, Iowa (50668) 229/J3
Readlyn, Sask. 181/F6
Readsboro▵, Vt. (05350) 268/B6
Readsboro, Vt. (05350) 268/B6
Reads Landing, Minn. (55968) 254/F6
Reads Mill, Ala. (†36279) 194/G3
Readstown, Wis. (54652) 317/E9
Readsville, Mo. (†65067) 261/J5
Readville, Mass. (02137) 249/C8
Ready, Ky. (42771) 237/J6
Readyville, Tenn. (37149) 237/J9
Reagan, Okla. (†73460) 288/N6
Reagan, Tenn. (38368) 237/E9
Reagan (co.), Texas 302/C6
Reagan, Texas (76680) 302/H6
Real, Cordillera (range), Bol. 136/A5
Real (co.), Texas 302/E8
Real del Castillo, Mex. 150/A1
Real de San Carlos, Urug. 145/A5
Realitos, Texas (78376) 302/F10
Realp, Switz. 39/F3
Ream, Cambodia 72/D5
Reamstown, Pa. (17567) 294/K5
Reao (atoll), Fr. Poly., 87/N7
Reardan, Wash. (99029) 310/H3
Reasnor, Iowa (50232) 229/G5
Reaville, N.J. (†08822) 273/D3

Saint-Charles-de-Bellechasse 429

Rushsylvania, Ohio (43347) 284/C5
Rushville, Ill. (62681) 222/C3
Rushville, Ind. (46173) 227/G5
Rushville, Mo. (64484) 261/B3
Rushville, N.Y. (14544) 276/F5
Rushville, Nebr. (69360) 264/B2
Rushville, Ohio (43150) 284/F6
Rushworth, Vic. 97/C5
Rusk, Ind. (†47581) 227/D7
Rusk (co.), Texas 302/K5
Rusk, Texas (75785) 302/J6
Rusk (co.), Wis. 317/D5
Rusk, Wis. (†54751) 317/C6
Ruskin, Br. Col. 184/L3
Ruskin, Fla. (33570) 212/C3
Ruskin, Nebr. (68974) 264/G4
Ruso, N. Dak. (58778) 283/J4
Russas, Braz. 132/G4
Russel (isl.), Aust. 88/L2
Russell (co.), Ala. 194/H6
Russell (lake), Alta. 182/C1
Russell, Ark. (72139) 203/G3
Russell, Ga. (†30680) 216/E3
Russell, Iowa (50238) 229/G7
Russell (co.), Kans. 232/D3
Russell, Kans. (67665) 232/D3
Russell (co.), Ky. 237/L7
Russell, Ky. (41169) 237/R3
Russell, Man. 179/A4
Russell▵, Mass. (01071) 249/C4
Russell, Minn. (56169) 254/C6
Russell, Miss. (39357) 256/G6
Russell, N. Dak. (†58762) 283/J2
Russell (cape), N.W.T. 187/G2
Russell (isl.), N.W.T. 187/J2
Russell (pt.), N.W.T. 187/G2
Russell, N.Y. (13684) 276/K2
Russell, N.Z. 101/E1
Russell (co.), Ont. 177/J2
Russell, Ont. 177/J2
Russell, Pa. (16345) 294/D2
Russell (co.), Va. 307/D7
Russell Cave Nat'l Mon., Ala. 194/G1
Russell Fork (riv.), Va. 307/C5
Russell Gardens‡, N.Y. (†11020) 276/R7
Russells Point, Ohio (43348) 284/C5
Russell Springs, Kans. (67755) 232/A3
Russell Springs, Ky. (42642) 237/L6
Russellton, Pa. (15076) 294/C4
Russellville, Ala. (35653) 194/C2
Russellville, Ark. (72801) 208/D3
Russellville, Ill. (†47591) 222/F5
Russellville, Ind. (46175) 227/D5
Russellville, Ky. (42276) 237/H7
Russellville, Mo. (65074) 261/H6
Russellville, Ohio (45168) 284/C8
Russellville, S.C. (29476) 296/H5
Russellville, Tenn. (37860) 237/P8
Russellville, W. Va. (26689) 313/E6
Rüsselsheim, W. Ger. 22/C4
Russia, Ohio (45363) 284/B5
Russian (riv.), Calif. 204/B4
Russian Mission, Alaska (99657) 196/F2
Russian S.F.S.R., U.S.S.R. 48/D4
Russian S.F.S.R., U.S.S.R. 52/F3
Russian S.F.S.R., U.S.S.R., 7/G3
Russian S.F.S.R., U.S.S.R., 7/J4
Russian S.F.S.R., U.S.S.R. 54/H3
Russiaville, Ind. (46975) 227/E4
Russkiy Zavorot (cape), U.S.S.R. 52/H1
Russum, Miss. (†39150) 256/B7
Rust, Austria 41/D3
Rustad, Minn. (†56560) 254/B4
Rustak, Afgh. 59/J2
Rustak, Afgh. 68/B1
Rustavi, U.S.S.R. 52/G6
Rustburg, Va. (24588) 307/K6
Rustenburg, S. Africa 118/D5
Ruston, La. (71270) 238/E1
Ruston, Wash. (†98401) 310/C3
Ruswil, Switz. 39/F2
Rusylvia, Alta. 182/E3
Rutba, Iraq 59/D3
Rutba, Iraq 66/B4
Rute, Spain 33/D4
Ruteng, Indon. 85/G7
Ruth, Mich. (48470) 250/G5
Ruth, Miss. (39662) 256/D8
Ruth, N.C. (†28139) 281/E4
Ruth, Nev. (89319) 266/F3
Rutherford, Ala. (†36860) 194/H6
Rutherford (co.), N.C. 281/E4
Rutherford, N.J. (*07070) 273/B2
Rutherford (co.), Tenn. 237/J9
Rutherford, Tenn. (38369) 237/C8
Rutherford College, N.C. (28671) 281/F3
Rutherford Fork, Obion (riv.), Tenn. 237/D8
Rutherfordton, N.C. (28139) 281/E4
Rutherglen, Ont. 177/F1
Rutherglen, 10/B1
Rutherglen, Scot. 15/C2
Ruther Glen, Va. (22546) 307/O5
Rutherglen, Vic. 97/D5
Rutheron, N. Mex. (87563) 274/C2
Rüthi, Switz. 39/J2
Ruthilda, Sask. 181/C4
Ruthin, 10/E4
Ruthin, Wales 13/D4
Ruthsburg, Md. (†21617) 245/P4
Ruthton, Minn. (56170) 254/B6
Ruthven, Ont. 177/B5
Ruthven, Iowa (51358) 229/D2
Ruthville, Va. (23147) 307/P6
Rutwell, Scot. 15/K9
Rüti, Glarus, Switz. 39/H3
Rüti, Zürich, Switz. 39/G2
Rutland, Br. Col. 184/H5
Rutland, Ill. (61358) 222/D3
Rutland, Iowa (50582) 229/E3
Rutland▵, Mass. (01543) 249/G3
Rutland, Mass. (01543) 249/G3
Rutland, N. Dak. (58067) 283/P7
Rutland (isl.), India 68/G6
Rutland, Ohio (45775) 284/F7
Rutland, S. Dak. (57057) 298/P5
Rutland, Sask. 181/B3
Rutland, Vt., 188/M2
Rutland (co.), Vt. 268/A4
Rutland▵, Vt. (05701) 268/B4
Rutland, Vt. (05701) 268/B4
Rutland Plains, Queens. 95/B2
Rutlandshire (co.), Eng. 13/G5
Rutledge, Ala. (36071) 194/F7
Rutledge, Ga. (30663) 216/E3
Rutledge, Minn. (55778) 254/F4
Rutledge, Mo. (63563) 261/H2
Rutledge, Pa. (19070) 294/M7
Rutledge, Tenn. (37861) 237/P8
Rutshuru, Dem. Rep. of the Congo 115/E4
Rutten, Neth. 27/H3
Ruurlo, Neth. 27/J4
Ruus al Jibal (dist.), Oman 59/G4
Ruvo di Puglia, Italy 34/F4
Ruvuma (riv.), 102/F6
Ruvuma (riv.), Moz. 118/F2
Ruvuma (reg.), Tanz. 115/G5
Ruvuma (riv.), Tanz. 115/G4
Ruwandiz, Iraq 66/D2
Ruwenzori (range), 102/E4
Ruwenzori (range), Dem. Rep. of the Congo. 115/E3
Ruwenzori (range), Uganda 115/E3
Ruzayevka, U.S.S.R. 52/F4
Ruzizi (riv.), Burundi 115/E4
Ruzizi (riv.), Dem. Rep. of the Congo. 115/E4
Ruzizi (riv.), Rwanda 115/E4
Ružomberok, Czech. 41/E2
Rwanda, 3/L6
RWANDA, 102/F5
RWANDA, 115/E4
Ry, Den. 21/C5
Ryan (peak), Idaho 220/D6
Ryan, Iowa (52330) 229/K4
Ryan, Okla. (73565) 288/L6
Ryan (inlet), Scot. 15/F9
Ryan Park, Wyo. (82330) 319/F4
Ryans (bay), Newf. 166/B2
Ryans Slough‡, Calif. (†95501) 204/A3
Ryazan', U.S.S.R. 48/E4
Ryazan', U.S.S.R. 52/E4
Rybachiy (pen.), U.S.S.R. 48/D2
Rybachiy (pen.), U.S.S.R. 52/D1
Rybinsk, U.S.S.R., 7/H3
Rybinsk, U.S.S.R. 48/D4
Rybinsk, U.S.S.R. 52/E3
Rybinsk (res.), U.S.S.R. 48/D4
Rybinsk (res.), U.S.S.R. 52/E3
Rybinsk (res.), U.S.S.R., 7/J3
Rybnik, Poland 47/D3
Rybnitsa, U.S.S.R. 52/C5
Rychnov nad Kněžnou, Czech. 41/D1
Rycroft, Alta. 182/A2
Ryd, Sweden 18/J8
Rydal, Ga. (30171) 216/C2
Rydal‡, Pa. (19046) 294/M5
Ryde, 10/F5
Ryde, Aust. 88/L3
Ryde, Calif. (95680) 204/B9
Ryde, Eng. 13/F7
Ryde, N.S.W. 97/J3
Ryder, N. Dak. (58779) 283/G4
Ryderwood, Wash. (98581) 310/B4
Rye, 10/G5
Rye, Ark. (†71671) 203/F6
Rye, Colo. (81069) 208/K7
Rye, Eng. 13/H7
Rye▵, N.H. (03870) 268/F5
Rye, N.H. (03870) 268/F5
Rye, N.Y. (10580) 276/P7
Rye, Texas (77369) 302/K7
Rye Beach, N.H. (†03871) 268/F6
Ryegate, Mont. (59074) 262/G4
Ryegate▵, Vt. (05042) 268/C3
Ryegate, Vt. (05042) 268/C3
Rye North Beach, N.H. (†03870) 268/F5
Rye Patch (res.), Nev. 266/C2
Ryerson, Sask. 181/K6
Rye Valley, Oreg. (†97907) 291/K3
Ryggebyen, Norway 18/D4
Ryki, Poland 47/E3
Ryland, Ala. (35767) 194/F1
Ryland, N.C. (27971) 281/R2
Ryley, Alta. 182/D3
Rylstone, N.S.W. 97/E3
Rýmařov, Czech. 41/D2
Ryotsu, Japan 81/J4
Rypin, Poland 47/D2
Rysy (mt.), Poland 47/E4
Ryugasaki, Japan 81/P2
Ryukyu (isls.), 3/R4
Ryukyu Islands, 54/R7
RYUKYU ISLANDS, 81
Rzepin, Poland 47/B2
Rzeszów (prov.), Poland 47/E4
Rzeszów, Poland 47/E3
Rzhev, U.S.S.R. 48/D4
Rzhev, U.S.S.R. 52/D3

S

Sa'ad, Israel 65/B5
Sa'ada, Yemen Arab Rep. 59/D6
Saale (riv.), E. Ger. 22/D3
Saalfeld, E. Ger. 22/D3
Saalfelden, Austria 41/B3
Saane (Sarine) (riv.), Switz. 39/D3
Saanen, Switz. 39/D4
Saanich, Br. Col. 184/K3
Saar (riv.), France 28/G3
Saar (riv.), W. Ger. 22/B4
Saarbrücken, W. Ger., 7/E4
Saarbrücken, W. Ger. 22/B4
Saarburg, W. Ger. 22/B4
Saaremaa (isl.), U.S.S.R. 48/B4
Saaremaa (isl.), U.S.S.R. 52/B3
Saaremaa (isl.), U.S.S.R. 53/B1
Saaremaa (isl.), U.S.S.R., 7/G3
Saarijärvi, Fin. 18/O5
Saarland (state), W. Ger. 22/B4
Saarlouis (Saarlautern), W. Ger. 22/B4
Saas, Switz. 39/J3
Saas-Fee, Switz. 39/E4
Saba (isl.), Neth. Ant. 156/F3
Saba (isl.), V.I.(U.S.) 161/A4
Šabac, Yugo. 45/D3
Sabadell, Spain 33/H2
Sabae, Japan 81/H5
Sabah (state), Malaysia, 3/Q5
Sabah (state), Malaysia, 54/P9
Sabah (state), Malaysia 85/F4
Sabak, Malaysia 72/D7
Sábalo, Cuba 158/A2
Sabana, Cuba 158/K4
Sabana (arch.), Cuba 158/E1
Sabana de la Mar, Dom. Rep. 156/E3
Sabana de la Mar, Dom. Rep. 158/F5
Sabana Grande, Dom. Rep. 158/E6
Sabana Grande, P. Rico 161/B2
Sabanagrande, Hond. 154/D4
Sabanalarga, Col. 126/C2
Sabana Seca, P. Rico 161/D1
Sabana Westpunt, Neth. Ant. 161/F8
Sabancuy, Mex. 150/O7
Sabaneta, Barinas, Ven. 124/D3
Sabaneta, Falcón, Ven. 124/D2
Sabang, Celebes, Indon. 85/F5
Sabang, Weh, Indon. 85/B4
Şabanözü, Turkey 63/E2
Sabará, Braz. 135/E1
Sabari, Hamun-i- (lake), Iran 66/M5
Sabattus, Maine (04280) 242/C7
Sabaudia, Italy 34/D4
Sabaya, Bol. 136/A6
Sabetha, Kans. (66534) 232/G2
Sabi (riv.), Rhod. 118/E3
Sabile, U.S.S.R. 53/B2
Sabillasville, Md. (21780) 245/J2
Sabin, Minn. (56580) 254/B4
Sabina, Ohio (45169) 284/C7
Sabinal (cay), Cuba 158/H2
Sabinal, Texas (78881) 302/E8
Sabinas, Mex. 150/J3
Sabinas (riv.), Mex. 150/J3
Sabinas Hidalgo, Mex. 150/J3
Sabine (riv.), 188/H4
Sabine (mt.), Ant. 5/B9
Sabine (par.), La. 238/C3
Sabine (lake), La. 238/C7
Sabine (passg.), La. 238/C7
Sabine (riv.), La. 238/C5
Sabine (pen.), N.W.T. 187/H2
Sabine (co.), Texas 302/L6
Sabine, Texas (†77640) 302/L8
Sabine (lake), Texas 302/L8
Sabine (riv.), Texas 302/L7
Sabine Pass, Texas (77655) 302/L8
Sabinópolis, Braz. 132/F7
Sabinoso, N. Mex. (87744) 274/E3
Sabinov, Czech. 41/F2
Sabinsville, Pa. (16943) 294/G2
Sabir, Jebel (mt.), Yemen Arab Rep. 59/D7
Sabirabad, U.S.S.R. 52/G6
Sabiya, Saudi Ar., 54/H8
Sabkha, Syria 63/H5
Sablayan, Phil. 82/C4
Sable (cape), 163/K7
Sable (isl.), 163/L7
Sable (riv.), Que. 174/D1
Sable (riv.), Ont. 177/B1
Sable (cape), Fla., 188/K5
Sable (cape), Fla. 212/E6
Sable (cape), N.S., 146/M5
Sable (isl.), N.S., 146/N5
Sable (cape), N.S. 169/C5
Sable (isl.), N.S. 169/J5
Sable River, N.S. 169/C5
Sable River West, N.S. 169/C5
Sables (lake), Que. 172/B3
Sables (lake), Que. 172/H1
Sablé-sur-Sarthe, France 28/C4
Sabougla, Miss. (†38955) 256/F3
Sabra (cape), Indon. 85/J6
Sabratha (ruins), Libya 111/B1
Sabrina Coast (reg.), Ant. 5/C6
Sabtang, Phil. 82/B2
Sabtang (isl.), Phil. 82/B2
Sabugal, Port. 33/C2
Sabula, Iowa (52070) 229/N4
Sabula, Mo. (†63620) 261/L8
Sabula, Pa. (†15801) 294/E3
Sabya, Saudi Ar. 59/D6
Sabzawar, Afgh. 59/H3
Sabzawar, Iran 59/G2
Sabzawar, Iran 66/K2
Sabzawar, Afgh. 68/A2
Sabzawaran, Iran 59/G4
Sabzawaran, Iran 66/K6
Sac (co.), Iowa 229/C4
Sac (riv.), Mo. 261/E7
Sacaba, Bol. 136/C5
Sacaca, Bol. 136/B6
Sacajawea (lake), Wash. 310/G4
Sácama, Col. 126/D4
Sacandaga (lake), N.Y. 276/L3
Sacandaga (res.), N.Y. 276/M4
Sac and Fox Ind. Res., Iowa 229/H5
Sacapulas, Guat. 154/B3
Sacaton, Ariz. (85247) 198/D5
Sacavém, Port. 33/A1
Sac City, Iowa (50583) 229/C4
Sacedón, Spain 33/E2
Săcele, Rum. 45/G3
Sac-Fox-Iowa Ind. Res., Kans. 232/G2
Sacheen (lake), Wash. 310/H2
Sachem (head), Conn. 210/E4
Sachem Head, Conn. (†06437) 210/E3
Sachigo (riv.), 163/G5
Sachigo (riv.), Ont. 175/B2
Sachojere, Bol. 136/C4
Sachse, Texas (75040) 302/H1
Sachseln, Switz. 39/F3
Sachs Harbour, 163/D1
Sachs Harbour, Canada, 4/B16
Sachs Harbour, N.W.T. 187/F2
Sackets (harb.), N.Y. 276/H3
Sackets Harbor, N.Y. (13685) 276/H3
Säckingen, W. Ger. 22/C5
Sackville, N. Br. 170/F3
Sackville, N.S. 169/E4
Saco, Ala. (†36081) 194/G7
Saco, Maine (04072) 242/C8
Saco (riv.), Maine 242/B8
Saco, Mo. (63669) 261/M8
Saco, Mont. (59261) 262/J2
Saco (riv.), N.H. 268/E3
Sacol (isl.), Phil. 82/D7
Sacramento (co.), Calif. 204/D5
Sacramento (cap.), Calif., 146/F6
Sacramento (cap.), Calif., 188/B3
Sacramento (cap.), Calif. (*95801) 204/B8
Sacramento (riv.), Calif., 188/B3
Sacramento (riv.), Calif. 204/D5
Sacramento, Braz. 132/D7
Sacramento, Braz. 135/C1
Sacramento, Ky. (42372) 237/G6
Sacramento, N. Mex. (88347) 274/D6
Sacramento (mts.), N. Mex. 274/D6
Sacramento Army Depot, Calif. 204/B8
Sacramento Wash (dry riv.), Ariz. 198/A4
Sacratif (cape), Spain 33/E4
Sacré-Coeur-de-Jésus, Que. 172/H1
Sacred Heart, Minn. (56285) 254/C6
Sacul, Texas (75788) 302/K6
Sádaba, Spain 33/F1
Sá da Bandeira, Angola 115/B6
Sadaich (riv.), Iran 66/L8
Sadani, Tanz. 115/G5
Saddell, Scot. 15/E8
Saddle, Ark. (†72554) 203/G1
Saddle (mt.), Idaho 220/D3
Saddle (mt.), Idaho 220/F6
Saddle (riv.), N.J. 273/B1
Saddle (mts.), Wash. 310/E4
Saddle Brook▵, N.J. (07662) 273/B1
Saddle Mountain, Okla. (†73023) 288/J5
Saddle River, N.J. (07458) 273/B1
Saddle Rock‡, N.Y. (†11020) 276/R7
Saddlestring, Wyo. (82840) 319/F1
Saddleworth, 10/G2
Sa Dec, S. Vietnam 72/E5
Sadhoowa, Trinidad Tobago 161/B11
Sadieville, Ky. (40370) 237/M4
Sa'diya, Iraq 66/D3
Sa'diya, Hor (lake), Iraq 66/E4
Sadiya, India 68/H3
Sadler‡, Texas (76264) 302/H4
Sadlers Village, St. Chr.-N.-A. 161/C10
Sadlersville, Tenn. (37154) 237/G7
Sado (isl.), Japan 81/J4
Sado (riv.), Port. 33/B3
Sadorus, Ill. (61872) 222/E4
Saeby, Den. 18/G8
Saeby, Den. 21/D3
Saegertown, Pa. (16433) 294/B2
Safad (Zefat), Israel 65/C2
Safaniya, Ras (cape), Saudi Ar. 59/E4
Safar, Afgh. 59/H3
Safar, Afgh. 68/A2
Šafárikovo, Czech. 41/F2
Safe, Mo. (†65559) 261/J6
Safety Bay, W. Aust. 92/A2
Safety Harbor, Fla. (33572) 212/B2
Säffle, Sweden 18/H7
Safford, Ala. (36773) 194/D6
Safford, Ariz. (85546) 198/F6
Saffordville, Kans. (66869) 232/F3
Saffron Walden, 10/G4
Saffron Walden, Eng. 13/H6
Safi, Mor. 106/C2
Safi, Jordan 65/E5
Safidar, Kuh-i- (mt.), Iran 59/F4
Safidar, Kuh-i- (mt.), Iran 66/H6
Safien Platz, Switz. 39/H3
Safir, Yemen Arab Rep. 59/E6
Safita, Syria 63/G5
Safonovo, U.S.S.R. 52/D3
Saforcada, Arg. 143/F7
Safranbolu, Turkey 63/E2
Saga (pref.), Japan 81/E7
Saga, Japan 81/E7
Sagadahoc (co.), Maine 242/D7
Sagaing (div.), Burma 72/B1
Sagaing, Burma 72/B2
Sagami (bay), Japan 81/O3
Sagami (riv.), Japan 81/O2
Sagamihara, Japan 81/O2
Sagamore, Mass. (02561) 249/M5
Sagamore, Pa. (16250) 294/D4
Sagamore Hill Nat'l Hist. Site, N.Y. 276/S6
Sagamore Hills, Ohio (†44067) 284/J10
Saganaga (lake), Ont. 175/B3
Saganaga (lake), Minn. 254/H2
Sagar, India 68/D4
Sagathun, Sask. 181/B5
Sagavanirktok (riv.), Alaska 196/J1
Sagay, Phil. 82/E6
Sage, Ark. (72573) 203/G1
Sage (mt.), V.I. (Br.) 161/D4
Sage (creek), Mont. 262/F2
Sage, Wyo. (83125) 319/B4
Sageeyah, Okla. (†74017) 288/P2
Sagemace (bay), Man. 179/B3
Sagerton, Texas (79548) 302/E4
Sageville, Iowa (†52001) 229/M3
Saggart, Ire. 17/J5
Sag Harbor, N.Y. (11963) 276/R8
Saginaw, Ala. (35137) 194/E4
Saginaw (bay), Mich., 188/K2
Saginaw, Mich., 188/K2
Saginaw (co.), Mich. 250/E5
Saginaw, Mich. (*48601) 250/F5
Saginaw (bay), Mich. 250/F5
Saginaw (riv.), Mich. 250/F5
Saginaw, Minn. (55779) 254/F4
Saginaw, Mo. (64864) 261/C8
Saginaw, Oreg. (97472) 291/E4
Saginaw, Texas (76079) 302/E1
Sagle, Idaho (83860) 220/B1
Saglek (bay), Newf. 166/B2
Saglek (fjord), Newf. 166/B2
Saglouc, 163/J3
Saglouc, Que. 174/E1
Sagñay, Phil. 82/E5
Sagola, Mich. (49881) 250/B2
Saguache (co.), Colo. 208/G6
Saguache, Colo. (81149) 208/G6
Saguache (creek), Colo. 208/F6
Sagua de Tánamo, Cuba 158/K3
Sagua la Grande, Cuba 156/B2
Sagua la Grande, Cuba 158/D1
Sagua la Grande (riv.), Cuba 158/E1
Saguaro (lake), Ariz. 198/D5
Saguaro Nat'l Mon., Ariz. 198/E6
Saguenay (riv.), Canada, 146/L5
Saguenay (co.), Que. 172/H1
Saguenay (riv.), Que. 172/G1
Saguenay (co.), Que. 174/D2
Saguenay (riv.), Que. 174/C3
Saguenay Prov. Park, Que. 174/E2
Saguia el Hamra (reg.), 102/A2
Saguia el Hamra (dry riv.), Sp. Sahara 106/B3
Saguia el Hamra (reg.), Sp. Sahara 106/B3
Sagunto, Spain 33/F3
Sahagún, Col. 126/C3
Sahagún, Spain 33/D1
Sahand, Kuh-i- (mt.), Iran 66/E2
Sahara (desert), 3/J4
Sahara (des.), 102/C2
Sahara (des.), Alg. 106/E4
Sahara (des.), Mali 106/D4
Sahara (des.), Mauritania 106/C4
Sahara (des.), Niger 106/F4
Sahara (des.), Chad 111/C3
Sahara (des.), Libya 111/C3
Sahara (des.), Sudan 111/E3
Sahara (des.), U.A.R. 111/E3
Saharan Atlas (ranges), Alg. 106/E2
Saharanpur, India 68/D3
Şahinli, Turkey 63/C6
Sahuaripa, Mex. 150/E2
Sahuarita, Ariz. (85629) 198/E7
Sahuayo de Díaz, Mex. 150/H7
Šahy, Czech. 41/E2
Saïda, Alg. 106/E2
Saida, Leb. 63/F6
Saïdia, Mor. 106/D2
Saidor, Terr. N.G. 85/B7
Saidu, Pak. 68/C2
Saignelégier, Switz. 39/D2
Saigo, Japan 81/F5
Saigon (cap.), S. Vietnam 72/E5
Saigon (cap.), S. Vietnam, 3/Q5
Saigon (cap.), S. Vietnam, 54/O8
Saihut, P.D.R. Yemen 59/F6
Saihut, P.D.R. Yemen, 54/J8
Saikai Nat'l Park, Japan 81/D7
Saiki, Japan 81/E7
Sailes, La. (†71028) 238/D2
Sailor (creek), Idaho 220/C7
Sailor Springs, Ill. (62879) 222/E5
Saimaa (lake), Fin. 18/Q6
Saimbeyli, Turkey 63/G4
Sain Alto, Mex. 150/H5
Sain Shanda, Mong. 77/H3
Saint Abb's (head), Scot. 15/M8
Saint-Adalbert, Que. 172/H3
Saint-Adelphe-de-Champlain, Que. 172/E3
Saint-Adolphe, Man. 179/E5
Saint-Adolphe-d'Howard, Que. 172/C4
Saint-Adrien, Que. 172/F4
Saint-Affrique, France 28/E6
Saint-Agapitville, Que. 172/F3
Saint Agatha▵, Maine (04772) 242/G1
Saint Agnes, Eng. 13/B7
Saint-Alban, Que. 172/E3
Saint Albans, 10/F5
Saint Albans, Eng. 13/G6
Saint Alban's (head), Eng. 13/F7
Saint Albans▵, Maine (04971) 242/E6
Saint Albans, Mo. (63073) 261/N3
Saint Alban's, Newf. 166/C4
Saint Albans▵, Vt. (05478) 268/A2
Saint Albans, Vt. (05478) 268/A2
Saint Albans, W. Va. (25177) 313/C6
Saint Albans Bay, Vt. (05481) 268/A2
Saint-Albert, Alta. 182/D3
Saint-Albert, Que. 172/E3
Saint-Albert, Ont. 177/J2
Saint-Alexandre-de-Kamouraska, Que. 172/H2
Saint-Alexandre-d'Iberville, Que. 172/D4
Saint-Alexis-de-Matapédia, Que. 172/B2
Saint-Alexis-de-Montcalm, Que. 172/D4
Saint-Alexis-des-Monts, Que. 172/D3
Saint Almo, N. Br. 170/C2
Saint-Alphonse, Que. 172/D3
Saint-Alphonse, Man. 179/C5
Saint Alphonse, N.S. 169/B4
Saint-Alphonse-de-Caplan, Que. 172/C2
Saint-Amand, N. Br. 170/C1
Saint-Amand-Mont-Rond, France 28/E4
Saint Amant, La. (70774) 238/L2
Saint-Ambroise, Man. 179/E4
Saint-Ambroise-de-Chicoutimi, Que. 172/F1
Saint-Ambroise-de-Kildare, Que. 172/D3
Saint-Anaclet, Que. 172/J1
Saint-André (cape), Malag. Rep. 118/G3
Saint-André, Réunion 118/G5
Saint-André-Avellin, Que. 172/B4
Saint-André-de-Madawaska, N. Br. 170/C1
Saint-André-de-Ristigouche, Que. 172/B2
Saint-André-du-Lac-Saint-Jean, Que. 172/E1
Saint-André-Est, Que. 172/C4
Saint Andrew (mt.), St. Vincent 161/A9
Saint Andrew (pt.), Fla. 212/D6
Saint Andrew (sound), Ga. 216/K9
Saint Andrew (lake), Man. 179/E3
Saint Andrews, 10/E2
Saint Andrews, N. Br. 170/C3
Saint Andrews, N.S. 169/F3
Saint Andrews (chan.), N.S. 169/H2
Saint Andrew's, Newf. 166/C4
Saint Andrews, S.C. (29407) 296/G6
Saint Andrews, Scot. 15/L7
Saint Andrews (bay), Scot. 15/L7
Saint Andrews, Tenn. (37372) 237/K10
Saint-Anicet, Que. 172/C4
Saint Ann, Mo. (63074) 261/O2
Saint Anne, Chan. Is. 13/E8
Saint Anne, Ill. (60964) 222/F2
Saint Ann's (bay), N.S. 169/H2
Saint Ann's Bay, Jam. 156/C3
Saint Ann's Bay, Jam. 158/J5
Saint-Anselme, Que. 172/F3
Saint-Anselme, N. Br. 170/F2
Saint Ansgar, Iowa (50472) 229/H2
Saint Anthony, Idaho (83445) 220/G6
Saint Anthony, Ind. (47575) 227/D8
Saint Anthony, Iowa (50239) 229/G4
Saint Anthony, Minn. (†56307) 254/D5
Saint Anthony, N. Dak. (58566) 283/H6
Saint Anthony, Newf. 166/C3
Saint Anthony Falls, Minn. (55414) 254/G5
Saint-Antoine, N. Br. 170/F2
Saint-Antoine-Abbé, Que. 172/D4
Saint-Antoine-des-Laurentides, Que. 172/H4
Saint-Antoine-de-Tilly, Que. 172/F3
Saint-Antoine-sur-Richelieu, Que. 172/D4
Saint-Antonin, Que. 172/H2
Saint-Antonin-Noble-Val, France 28/D5
Saint Arnaud, Aust. 88/G7
Saint Arnaud, Vic. 97/B5
Saint-Arsène, Que. 172/H2
Saint Arthur, N. Br. 170/D1
Saint Asaph, Wales 13/D4
Saint-Astier, France 28/D5
Saint-Athanase, Que. 172/H2
Saint-Aubert, Que. 172/G2
Saint Aubin, Chan. Is. 13/E8
Saint-Augustin, Que. 172/G4
Saint-Augustin, Que. 174/F2
Saint-Augustin (riv.), Que. 174/F2
Saint Augustin (riv.), Newf. 166/C3
Saint-Augustin-de-Desmaures, Que. 172/H2
Saint Augustine, Fla., 146/K7
Saint Augustine, Fla., 188/K5
Saint Augustine, Fla. (32084) 212/E2
Saint Augustine, Ill. (61474) 222/C3
Saint Augustine, Md. (†21915) 245/P3
Saint Augustine Beach, Fla. (32084) 212/E2
Saint Austell (bay), Eng. 13/C7
Saint Austell with Fowey, 10/D5
Saint Austell with Fowey, Eng. 13/C7
Saint-Barnabé-Sud, Que. 172/D4
Saint-Barthélemy (isl.), Guad. 156/F3
Saint-Barthélemy, Que. 172/D3
Saint Basile, N. Br. 170/B1
Saint-Basile-le-Grand, Que. 172/J4
Saint-Basile-Sud, Que. 172/F3
Saint Bees (head), Eng. 13/D3
Saint Benedict, Kans. (†66538) 232/F2
Saint Benedict, La. (70457) 238/K5
Saint Benedict, Oreg. (97373) 291/B3
Saint Benedict, Pa. (15773) 294/E4
Saint Benedict, Sask. 181/F3
Saint-Benjamin, Que. 172/G3
Saint-Benoît, Que. 172/C4
Saint-Benoît, Réunion 118/G5
Saint-Benoît-de-Matapédia, Que. 172/B2
Saint-Benoît-Labre, Que. 172/G3
Saint Bernard, Ala. (35138) 194/E2
Saint Bernard (par.), La. 238/L7
Saint Bernard, La. (70085) 238/L7
Saint Bernard, Ohio (45217) 284/B9
Saint-Bernard-de-Dorchester, Que. 172/F3
Saint Bernice, Ind. (47875) 227/C5
Saint Bethlehem, Tenn. (37155) 237/G7
Saint-Blaise, Switz. 39/D2
Saint-Bonaventure, Que. 172/E4
Saint Boniface, 163/G6
Saint Boniface, Man. 179/F5
Saint-Boniface-de-Shawinigan, Que. 172/D3
Saint Bonifacius, Minn. (55375) 254/F5
Saint Boswells, Sask. 181/D5
Saint Boswells, Scot. 15/L8
Saint Brandon Group (isls.), Mauritius, 54/J11
Saint Brendan's, Newf. 166/D4
Saint Brides (bay), 10/D5
Saint Bride's, Newf. 166/C2
Saint Brides (bay), Wales 13/B6
Saint-Brieuc, France 28/B3
Saint Brieux, Sask. 181/G3
Saint-Bruno, Que. 172/J4
Saint-Bruno-de-Kamouraska, Que. 172/H2
Saint-Bruno-Lac-Saint-Jean, Que. 172/F1
Saint-Calais, France 28/D4
Saint-Calixte-de-Kilkenny, Que. 172/D4
Saint-Camille, Que. 172/F4
Saint-Camille-de-Bellechasse, Que. 172/G3
Saint-Canut, Que. 172/C4
Saint-Casimir, Que. 172/E3
Saint Catharine, Mo. (64677) 261/G3
Saint Catharines, Ont. 177/E4
Saint Catherine (mt.), Grenada 161/D8
Saint Catherine, Fla. (33573) 212/D3
Saint Catherine (lake), Vt. 268/A5
Saint Catherines (isl.), Ga. 216/K7
Saint Catherines (sound), Ga. 216/K7
Saint-Céré, France 28/D5
Saint-Césaire, Que. 172/D4
Saint-Chamond, France 28/F5
Saint Charles, Ark. (72140) 203/H5
Saint-Charles, Que. 172/F1
Saint Charles, Idaho (83272) 220/G7
Saint Charles, Ill. (60174) 222/E2
Saint Charles, Iowa (50240) 229/F6
Saint Charles, Ky. (42453) 237/F6
Saint Charles (par.), La. 238/K7
Saint Charles, Mich. (48655) 250/E5
Saint Charles, Minn. (55972) 254/F7
Saint Charles (co.), Mo. 261/L5
Saint Charles, Mo. (63301) 261/O2
Saint Charles (cape), Newf. 166/C3
Saint Charles, S.C. (29134) 296/G3
Saint Charles, S. Dak. (57571) 298/L7
Saint Charles, Va. (24282) 307/B7
Saint-Charles-de-Bellechasse, Que. 172/G3

432 Salto das Sete Quedas

Salto das Sete Quedas (falls), Braz. 132/B5
Salto Grande (falls), Col. 126/D8
Salto Grande (falls), Urug. 145/A2
Saltoluokta, Sweden 18/L3
Salton Sea (lake), Calif., 188/C4
Salton Sea (lake), Calif. 204/K10
Saltpetre, W. Va. (25558) 313/A6
Salt River (bay), V.I.(U.S.) 161/F3
Salt River (range), Wyo. 319/B3
Salt River Ind. Res., Ariz. 198/D5
Salt Rock, W. Va. (25559) 313/B6
Saltrou, Haiti 158/C6
Saltsburg, Pa. (15681) 294/C4
Saltsjöbaden, Sweden 18/J1
Salt Sulphur Springs, W. Va. (†24945) 313/E7
Saltville, Va. (24370) 307/E7
Saltwater (riv.), Aust. 88/L6
Salt Wells (creek), Wyo. 319/D4
Saluda, N.C. (28773) 281/E4
Saluda (co.), S.C. 296/D3
Saluda, S.C. (29138) 296/D4
Saluda (dam), S.C. 296/E3
Saluda (riv.), S.C. 296/D3
Saluda, Va. (23149) 307/P5
Salûm, 102/E1
Salûm, U.A.R. 111/E1
Salûm (gulf), U.A.R. 111/E1
Salus, Ark. (72861) 203/D2
Salut (isls.), Fr. Gui. 131/F3
Saluzzo, Italy 34/A2
Salvador, Braz., 3/H6
Salvador, Braz., 120/G4
Salvador, Braz. 132/G6
Salvador (lake), La. 238/K7
Salvador, Sask. 181/B3
Salvage, Newf. 166/D1
Salvage (isls.), Port. 106/A2
Salvaleón de Higüey, Dom. Rep. 158/F6
Salvaterra de Magos, Port. 33/B3
Salvation (creek), Utah 304/C5
Salvisa, Ky. (40372) 237/M5
Salvo, N.C. (27972) 281/U3
Salwa, Saudi Ar. 59/F5
Salween (riv.), 54/N8
Salween (riv.), Burma 72/C3
Salween (riv.), China 77/E6
Sal'yany, U.S.S.R. 52/G7
Salybia, Dominica 161/F6
Salyer, Calif. (95563) 204/B3
Salyersville, Ky. (41465) 237/P5
Salzach (riv.), Austria 41/B2
Salzach (riv.), W. Ger. 22/E5
Salzburg, Austria, 7/F4
Salzburg (prov.), Austria 41/B3
Salzburg, Austria 41/B3
Salzgitter, W. Ger. 22/D2
Salzkammergut (reg.), Austria 41/B3
Salzwedel, E. Ger. 22/D2
Sama (riv.), Peru 128/G11
Sama, Spain 33/D1
Samagaltay, U.S.S.R. 48/K4
Samaipata, Bol. 136/D6
Samal (isl.), Phil. 82/E7
Samales Group (isls.), Phil. 82/D7
Samalkot, India 68/E5
Samalût, U.A.R. 59/B4
Samalût, U.A.R. 111/J4
Samana (cay), Bah. Is. 156/D2
Samaná, Dom. Rep. 156/E3
Samaná (bay), Dom. Rep. 156/E3
Samaná (prov.), Dom. Rep. 158/E5
Samaná, Dom. Rep. 158/F5
Samaná (bay), Dom. Rep. 158/F5
Samaná (cape), Dom. Rep. 158/F5
Samandağı, Turkey 63/F4
Samaniego, Col. 126/B7
Samantha, Ala. (35482) 194/C4
Samar, Jordan 65/D2
Samar (isl.), Phil. 82/E4
Samar (sea), Phil. 82/E4
Samar (isl.), Phil. 85/H3
Samar (isl.), Phil., 54/R8
Samara (Kuybyshev), U.S.S.R. 52/H4
Samara (riv.), U.S.S.R. 52/H4
Samara (Kuybyshev), U.S.S.R., 7/J3
Samarai, Papua 85/C8
Samarai, Papua, 87/E7
Samaria, Idaho (83252) 220/F7
Samaria, Ind. (†46181) 227/E6
Samaria (reg.), Jordan 65/C3
Samariapo, Ven. 124/E5
Samarinda, Indon., 54/P10
Samarinda, Indon. 85/F6
Samarkand, U.S.S.R. 48/G5
Samarkand, U.S.S.R., 54/K6
Samarra, Iraq 59/D3
Samarra, Iraq 66/C3
Samawa, Iraq 59/D3
Samawa (prov.), Iraq 66/D5
Samawa, Iraq 66/D5
Samba, Dem. Rep. of the Congo. 115/E4
Sambalpur, India 68/E4
Sambas, Indon. 85/D5
Sambava, Malag. Rep. 118/J2
Sambhal, India 68/D3
Sambhar (lake), India 68/C3
Sambiase, Italy 34/F5
Sambodja, Indon. 85/F6
Sambor, Cambodia 72/E4
Samborombón (bay), Arg. 143/E4
Sambre (riv.), Belg. 27/D8
Sambre (riv.), France 28/F2
Sambro, N.S. 169/E4
Samburg, Sask. 181/F2
Samburg, Tenn. (38254) 237/C8
Samch'ŏk, S. Korea 81/D5
Same, Tanz. 115/G4
Samedan, Switz. 39/J3
Samford, Aust. 88/K2
Sámi, Greece 45/E6
Samish (lake), Wash. 310/C2
Samit (pt.), Cambodia 72/D5
Samka, Burma 72/C2
Sam Lord's Castle, Barb. 161/C9
Sammamish (lake), Wash. 310/B2
Samnan, Iran 59/F2
Samnan (governorate), Iran 66/J3
Samnan, Iran 66/H3
Samnangjin, S. Korea 81/D6
Sam Neua, Laos 72/E2
Samnorwood, Texas (79077) 302/D2
Samoa, Calif. (95564) 204/A3
Samoa (isls.), Pacific, 87/J7
Samo Alto, Chile 138/A8
Samokov, Bulg. 45/F4
Samos (isl.), Greece, 7/G5
Sámos (isl.), Greece 45/H7
Samoset, Fla. (33505) 212/D4
Samothráki, Greece 45/G5
Samothráki (isl.), Greece 45/G5
Sampang, Indon. 85/K2
Samper de Calanda, Spain 33/F2
Sampit, Indon., 54/P10
Sampit, Indon. 85/E6
Sampson (co.), N.C. 281/N4
Sampwe, Dem. Rep. of the Congo. 115/E5
Sam Rayburn (res.), Texas 302/K6
Samsat, Turkey 63/H4
Samsø (isl.), Den. 21/D6
Samsø Baelt (chan.), Den. 21/D6
Samson, Ala. (36477) 194/F8
Samsula, Fla. (†32069) 212/E2
Samsun, Turkey 59/C1
Samsun (prov.), Turkey 63/F2
Samsun, Turkey 63/F2
Samsun, Turkey, 54/G5
Sams Valley, Oreg. (†97525) 291/E5
Samtown, La. (71301) 238/F4
Samu, Jordan 65/C5
Samuels, Idaho (83862) 220/B1
Samuels, Ky. (40064) 237/L5
Samui (str.), Thai. 72/D5
Samui, Ko (isl.), Thai. 72/D5
Samut Prakan, Thai. 72/D4
Samut Sakhon, Thai. 72/D4
Samut Songkhram, Thai. 72/C4
San, Mali 106/D6
San (riv.), Poland 47/F3
Saña, Peru 128/C6
San'a (cap.), Yemen Arab Rep. 59/D6
San'a (cap.), Yemen Arab Rep., 54/H8
San Acacia, N. Mex. (87831) 274/B4
San Acacio, Colo. (81150) 208/J8
Sanae Station, Ant. 5/B18
Sanaga (riv.), Cameroon 115/B3
San Agustín, Bol. 136/B7
San Agustín, Col. 126/B7
San Agustin (plains), N. Mex. 274/B5
San Agustin (cape), Phil. 82/F7
San Agustin (cape), Phil. 85/H4
San Agustín de Aguaras, Cuba 158/H3
San Agustín Loxicha, Mex. 150/L9
Sanak (isl.), Alaska 196/F4
San Ambrosio (isl.), Chile, 120/C5
Sanana, Indon. 85/H6
Sanandaj, Iran 59/E2
Sanandaj, Iran 66/E3
Sanandita, Bol. 136/D7
San Andreas, Calif. (95249) 204/E5
San Andreas (lake), Calif. 204/H2
San Andrés, Bol. 136/C4
San Andrés (isl.), Col. 126/A10
San Andrés, Antioquia, Col. 126/C4
San Andrés, San Andrés y Providencia, Col. 126/A9
San Andrés, Cuba 158/H3
San Andrés, Guat. 154/B2
San Andres (mts.), N. Mex. 274/C6
San Andrés de Giles, Arg. 143/G7
San Andrés de Machaca, Bol. 136/A5
San Andrés Tuxtla, Mex. 150/M7
San Andrés y Providencia (inten.), Col. 126/B10
San Angelo, Texas, 188/F4
San Angelo, Texas (76901) 302/D6
San Anselmo, Calif. (94960) 204/H1
San Antero, Col. 126/C3
San Antonio, Arg., 120/D5
San Antonio (cape), Arg., 120/E6
San Antonio (cape), Arg. 143/E4
San Antonio, El Beni, Bol. 136/C4
San Antonio, Santa Cruz, Bol. 136/E4
San Antonio (res.), Calif. 204/E8
San Antonio, Chile 138/F3
San Antonio, Col. 126/B6
San Antonio (cape), Cuba 156/A2
San Antonio, Cuba 158/K4
San Antonio (cape), Cuba 158/A2
San Antonio, Fla. (33576) 212/D3
San Antonio, Mex. 150/D5
San Antonio (reef), Mex. 150/L4
San Antonio, N. Mex. (87832) 274/B5
San Antonio (peak), N. Mex. 274/C2
San Antonio, Phil. 82/B3
San Antonio (bay), Phil. 82/A6
San Antonio, Central, Par. 144/A6
San Antonio, San Pedro, Par. 144/D4
San Antonio, P. Rico 161/A1
San Antonio, Texas, 146/J7
San Antonio, Texas, 188/G5
San Antonio, Texas (*78201) 302/F8
San Antonio (bay), Texas 302/H9
San Antonio (mt.), Texas 302/B10
San Antonio, Canelones, Urug. 145/B6
San Antonio, Salto, Urug. 145/B2
San Antonio, Amazonas, Ven. 124/E6
San Antonio, Monagas, Ven. 124/G2
San Antonio, Zulia, Ven. 124/C3
San Antonio Abad, Spain 33/G3
San Antonio de Areco, Arg. 143/G7
San Antonio de Caparo, Ven. 124/C4
San Antonio de Lípez, Bol. 136/B7
San Antonio de los Baños, Cuba 156/A2
San Antonio de los Baños, Cuba 158/C1
San Antonio de los Cobres, Arg. 143/C1
San Antonio del Parapetí, Bol. 136/D7
San Antonio del Táchira, Ven. 124/B4
San Antonio de Tabasca, Ven. 124/G3
San Antonio Oeste, Arg. 143/C5
San Ardo, Calif. (93450) 204/E7
Sanare, Ven. 124/D3
Sanator, S. Dak. (†57730) 298/B6
Sanatorium, Miss. (39112) 256/E7
San Augustine (co.), Texas 302/K6
San Augustine, Texas (75972) 302/K6
San Bartolomeo in Galdo, Italy 34/E4
San Bautista, Urug. 145/B6
San Benedetto del Tronto, Italy 34/E3
San Benedicto (isl.), Mex. 150/D7
San Benito (co.), Calif. 204/D7
San Benito (riv.), Calif. 204/D7
San Benito (isl.), Mex. 150/B2
San Benito, Texas (78586) 302/G12
San Bernardino, Calif., 146/G6
San Bernardino, Calif., 188/C4
San Bernardino (co.), Calif. 204/J9
San Bernardino, Calif. (*92401) 204/E10
San Bernardino (mts.), Calif. 204/J10
San Bernardino (str.), Phil. 82/E4
San Bernardino, Par. 144/B6
San Bernardino, Switz. 39/H4
San Bernardino (pass), Switz. 39/H3
San Bernardo, Chile 138/G4
San Bernardo (isls.), Col. 126/C3
San Blas (cape), Fla. 212/D7
San Blas (riv.), Mex. 150/O8
San Blas, Nayarit, Mex. 150/G6
San Blas, Sinaloa, Mex. 150/E3
San Blas (gulf), Pan. 154/H6
San Blas (pt.), Pan. 154/H6
San Blas, Cordillera de (range), Pan. 154/H6
San Borja, Bol. 136/B4
Sanborn, Iowa (51248) 229/B2
Sanborn, Minn. (56083) 254/C6
Sanborn, N. Dak. (58480) 283/O6
Sanborn, N.Y. (14132) 276/C4
Sanborn (co.), S. Dak. 298/N5
Sanborn, Wis. (†54806) 317/E3
Sanborntonᴀ, N.H. (03269) 268/D5
Sanbornton, N.H. (03269) 268/D5
Sanbornville, N.H. (03872) 268/F4
San Bruno, Calif. (94066) 204/J2
San Buenaventura, Bol. 136/A4
San Buenaventura, Mex. 150/J3
San Camillo, Arg. 143/D1
San Carlos, Corrientes, Arg. 143/E2
San Carlos, Mendoza, Arg. 143/C3
San Carlos, Santa Fe, Arg. 143/F6
San Carlos (lake), Ariz., 188/E4
San Carlos, Ariz. (85550) 198/E5
San Carlos (lake), Ariz. 198/E5
San Carlos (riv.), Ariz. 198/E5
San Carlos, Bol. 136/D5
San Carlos, Calif. (94070) 204/J3
San Carlos, Chile 138/E1
San Carlos, Coahuila, Mex. 150/J2
San Carlos, Tamaulipas, Mex. 150/K4
San Carlos, Nic. 154/E5
San Carlos, Negros Occ., Phil. 82/D5
San Carlos, Pangasinan, Phil. 82/C3
San Carlos, Eq. Guin. 115/A3
San Carlos, Pan. 154/H6
San Carlos, Central, Par. 144/B6
San Carlos, Concepción, Par. 144/D4
San Carlos, Urug. 145/E5
San Carlos, Cojedes, Ven. 124/D3
San Carlos, Zulia, Ven. 124/C2
San Carlos de Bariloche, Arg., 120/D7
San Carlos de Bariloche, Arg. 143/B5
San Carlos de la Rápita, Spain 33/G2
San Carlos del Zulia, Ven. 124/C3
San Carlos de Río Negro, Ven. 124/E7
San Carlos Ind. Res., Ariz. 198/E5
San Casimiro, Ven. 124/E3
San Cataldo, Italy 34/D6
Sancerre, France 28/E4
Sanchez (res.), Colo. 208/H8
Sánchez, Dom. Rep. 156/E3
Sánchez, Dom. Rep. 158/E5
Sánchez, Urug. 145/B3
Sánchez Ramírez (prov.), Dom. Rep. 158/E5
Sanchi, India 68/D4
San Clara, Man. 179/J4
San Clemente, Calif. (92672) 204/H10
San Clemente (isl.), Calif. 204/G11
San Clemente, Chile 138/A11
San Clemente, Spain 33/E3
Sancoins, France 28/E4
San Cosme, Par. 144/D6
San Cristóbal, Arg. 143/F5
San Cristobal (isl.), Br. Sol. Is., 87/G7
San Cristóbal, Potosí, Bol. 136/B7
San Cristóbal, Santa Cruz, Bol. 136/E3
San Cristóbal, Cuba 158/B1
San Cristóbal (prov.), Dom. Rep. 158/E6
San Cristóbal, Dom. Rep. 158/E6
San Cristóbal (isl.), Ec. 128/C9
San Cristobal, N. Mex. (87564) 274/D2
San Cristóbal, Pan. 154/G6
San Cristóbal, Ven. 124/B4
San Cristóbal de las Casas, Mex. 150/N8
Sancti-Spíritus, Cuba 156/B2
Sancti-Spíritus, Cuba 158/E2
Sanctuary, Sask. 181/D4
Sand (mt.), Ala. 194/G1
Sand, Norway 18/E7
Sand (key), Fla. 212/B3
Sand (creek), Ind. 227/F6
Sand (pt.), Mich. 250/F5
Sand (creek), Minn. 254/F5
Sand (riv.), S. Africa 118/D4
Sand (creek), S. Dak. 298/B3
Sand (creek), S. Dak. 298/C2
Sand (creek), S. Dak. 298/M5
Sand (lake), S. Dak. 298/N2
Sand (isl.), Wash. 310/A4
Sand (isl.), Wis. 317/D2
Sanda, Japan 81/H7
Sanda (isl.), Scot. 15/E9
Sandakan, Malaysia, 54/P9
Sandakan, Malaysia 85/F4
Sandalwood (Sumba) (isl.), Indon. 85/F7
Sandane, Norway 18/D6
Sandanski, Bulg. 45/F5
Sand Arroyo (dry riv.), Colo. 208/O8
Sanday (isl.), 10/E1
Sanday (sound), Scot. 15/L1
Sanday, Inverness (isl.), Scot. 15/D5
Sanday, Orkney (isl.), Scot. 15/M1
Sandbach, Eng. 13/E4
Sandbach, 10/G2
Sandborn, Ind. (47578) 227/C7
Sand Brook, N.J. (†08559) 273/D3
Sand City‡, Calif. (†93955) 204/D7
Sand Coulee, Mont. (59472) 262/E3
Sand Creek, Okla. (73769) 288/K1
Sand Creek, Wis. (54765) 317/C5
Sand Draw, Wyo. (82501) 319/D3
Sandefjord, Norway 18/C4
San de Fuca, Wash. (†98239) 310/C2
Sandel, La. (†71429) 238/D4
Sanders, Ariz. (86512) 198/F3
Sanders, Idaho (83863) 220/B2
Sanders, Ind. (†47401) 227/E6
Sanders, Ky. (41083) 237/M3
Sanders (co.), Mont. 262/A3
Sanders, Mont. (59076) 262/J4
Sanderson, Fla. (32087) 212/D1
Sanderson, Texas (79848) 302/B7
Sandersville, Ga. (31082) 216/G5
Sandersville, Miss. (39477) 256/F7
Sandford, Ind. (47877) 227/B5
Sand Fork, W. Va. (26430) 313/E5
Sandgap, Ky. (40481) 237/N6
Sandgate, Aust. 88/K2
Sandgate, Queens. 95/D2
Sandgateᴀ, Vt. (†05250) 268/A5
Sandgate, Vt. (†05250) 268/A5
Sandgirt (lake), Newf. 166/A3
Sand Hill (riv.), Minn. 254/B3
Sandhill, Miss. (39161) 256/E5
Sand Hill (riv.), Newf. 166/C3
Sand Hills-Shore Acres, Mass. (†02066) 249/M4
Sandia (peak), N. Mex. 274/C3
Sandia, Peru 128/H10
Sandia, Texas (78383) 302/F9
Sandia Base, N. Mex. 274/C3
Sandia Park, N. Mex. (87047) 274/C3
San Diego (cape), Arg., 120/D8
San Diego (cape), Arg. 143/D7
San Diego, Bol. 136/D7
San Diego, Calif., 146/G6
San Diego, Calif., 188/C4
San Diego (co.), Calif. 204/J10
San Diego, Calif. (*92101) 204/H11
San Diego (bay), Calif. 204/H11
San Diego, Texas (78384) 302/F10
San Diego de Cabrutica, Ven. 124/F3
San Diego de los Baños, Cuba 158/B1
Sandikli, Turkey 63/D3
Sandilands, Man. 179/F5
San Dimas, Calif. (91773) 204/D10
Sanding (isl.), Indon. 85/C6
Sandisfieldᴀ, Mass. (01255) 249/B4
Sand Lake‡, Alaska (†99501) 196/C1
Sand Lake, Mich. (49343) 250/D5
Sand Lake, N.Y. (12153) 276/O5
Sandnes, Norway 18/D7
Sandness, Scot. 15/M3
Sandoa, 102/E5
Sandoa, Dem. Rep. of the Congo. 115/D5
Sandomierz, Poland 47/E3
Sandon, Br. Col. 184/J5
Sandoná, Col. 126/B7
Sándorfalva, Hung. 41/F3
Sandoval, Ill. (62882) 222/D5
Sandoval (co.), N. Mex. 274/C3
Sandover (riv.), No. Terr. 93/D6
Sandoway, Burma 72/B3
Sandownᴀ, N.H. (03873) 268/E6
Sandown (bay), S. Africa 118/F7
Sandown-Shanklin, Eng. 13/F7
Sandoy (isl.), Den. 21/B3
Sand Point, Alaska (99661) 196/G3
Sandpoint, Idaho (83864) 220/B1
Sandray (isl.), Scot. 15/B6
Sandridge, Man. 179/E4
Sand Ridge‡, N.Y. (†13135) 276/H4
Sandringham, Aust. 88/M7
Sandringham, Eng. 13/H5
Sandringham, Vic. 97/J5
Sands (key), Fla. 212/F6
Sands, Mich. (†49841) 250/B2
Sand Shoal (inlet), Va. 307/S6
Sandspit, Br. Col. 184/B3
Sands Point, N.Y. (†11050) 276/N9
Sand Springs, Iowa (†52237) 229/L4
Sand Springs, Ky. (†40456) 237/N6
Sand Springs, Mont. (59077) 262/J3
Sand Springs (salt flat), Nev. 266/C3
Sand Springs, Okla. (74063) 288/O2
Sandston, Va. (23150) 307/O5
Sandstone, Aust. 88/B5
Sandstone, Minn. (55072) 254/F4
Sandstone, W. Aust. 92/B4
Sandstone, W. Va. (25985) 313/E7
Sand Tank (mt.), Ariz. 198/C6
Sandträsk, Sweden 18/M3
Sandusky, Ill. (†62988) 222/D6
Sandusky, Ind. (†47240) 227/G6
Sandusky, Mich. (48471) 250/G5
Sandusky, N.Y. (14133) 276/D6
Sandusky, Ohio, 188/K2
Sandusky (co.), Ohio 284/D3
Sandusky, Ohio (44870) 284/E3
Sandusky (bay), Ohio 284/E3
Sandusky (riv.), Ohio 284/D3
Sandvika, Norway 18/C3
Sandviken, Sweden 18/K6
Sandwich, Eng. 13/J6
Sandwich, Ill. (60548) 222/E2
Sandwichᴀ, Mass. (02563) 249/N5
Sandwich, Mass. (02563) 249/N5
Sandwichᴀ, N.H. (03270) 268/E4
Sandwich, N.H. (03270) 268/E4
Sandwich (mt.), N.H. 268/E4
Sandwich (range), N.H. 268/E4
Sandwich (bay), Newf. 166/C3
Sandwick, Scot. 15/N3
Sandwith, Sask. 181/C2
Sandy (creek), Ala. 194/H7
Sandy (lake), Alta. 182/D2
Sandy (cape), Aust. 88/J4
Sandy (lake), 163/G5
Sandy (brook), Conn. 210/C1
Sandy (pt.), V.I.(U.S.) 161/D4
Sandy (lake), Ont. 175/B2
Sandy (riv.), Maine 242/C6
Sandy (isls.), Man. 179/D2
Sandy (creek), Mont. 262/F2
Sandy (lake), Newf. 166/C4
Sandy (cape), Queens. 95/E5
Sandy, Oreg. (97055) 291/E2
Sandy, Pa. (†15801) 294/E3
Sandy (pt.), R.I. 249/H8
Sandy (pt.), S.C. 296/H6
Sandy (riv.), S.C. 296/E2
Sandy, Utah (84070) 304/O3
Sandy (creek), Wyo. 319/C3
Sandy Bay, Jam. 158/G5
Sandy Bay, Nic. 154/F3
Sandy Bay, Sask. 181/N3
Sandy Beach, Alta. 182/C3
Sandy Beach‡, N.Y. (†14072) 276/C4
Sandy Cove, N.S. 169/B4
Sandy Creek, Maine (†04009) 242/B7
Sandy Creek, N.Y. (13145) 276/H3
Sandy Hook, Conn. (06482) 210/B3
Sandy Hook, Ky. (41171) 237/P4
Sandy Hook, Man. 179/E4
Sandy Hook, Miss. (39478) 256/E8
Sandyhook, Mo. (†65046) 261/G5
Sandy Hook (spit), N.J. 273/F3
Sandy Hook, Va. (23153) 307/M5
Sandy Lake, Ont. 175/B2
Sandy Lake, Man. 179/B4
Sandy Lake, Pa. (16145) 294/B3
Sandy Lake, Sask. 181/L3
Sandy Point, St. Chr.-N.-A. 161/C10
Sandy Point, Maine (04972) 242/F7
Sandy Ridge, Ala. (†36047) 194/E6
Sandy Ridge, N.C. (27046) 281/J1
Sandy Ridge, Pa. (16677) 294/F4
Sandy Spring, Md. (20860) 245/K4
Sandy Springs, S.C. (29677) 296/B2
Sandyville, Iowa (†50001) 229/G6
Sandyville, Ohio (44671) 284/H4
Sandyville, W. Va. (25275) 313/C5
San Elizario, Texas (79849) 302/A10
San Estanislao, Par. 144/D5
San Esteban (gulf), Chile 138/D7
San Esteban, Hond. 154/D3
San Esteban de Gormaz, Spain 33/E2
San Felipe, Chile 138/G2
San Felipe, Col. 126/G7
San Felipe (cays), Cuba 156/A2
San Felipe (cays), Cuba 158/B2
San Felipe, Guat. 154/B3
San Felipe, Baja California, Mex. 150/B1
San Felipe, Guanajuato, Mex. 150/J6
San Felipe, N. Mex. (†87001) 274/C3
San Felipe, Phil. 82/B3
San Felipe‡, Texas (77473) 302/H8
San Felipe, Yaracuy, Ven. 124/D2
San Felipe, Zulia, Ven. 124/B3
San Feliu de Guixols, Spain 33/H2
San Félix (isl.), Chile, 120/B5
San Félix, Chile 138/A7
San Félix, Pan. 154/G6
San Félix, Ven. 124/C2
San Fermín, Bol. 136/A3
San Fernando, Arg. 143/G7
San Fernando (riv.), Bol. 136/F5
San Fernando, Calif. (*91340) 204/C10
San Fernando, Chile 138/G6
San Fernando, Trinidad Tobago 156/G5
San Fernando, Trinidad Tobago 161/A11
San Fernando, Chiapas, Mex. 150/N8
San Fernando, Tamaulipas, Mex. 150/L4
San Fernando, La Union, Phil. 82/C2
San Fernando, Masbate, Phil. 82/D4
San Fernando, Pampanga, Phil. 82/C3
San Fernando, Spain 33/C4
San Fernando, Ven., 120/D2
San Fernando, Ven. 124/E4
San Fernando de Atabapo, Ven. 124/E5
San Fidel, N. Mex. (87049) 274/B3
San Florencio, Par. 144/E4
Sanford, Ala. (36478) 194/F8
Sanford (mt.), Alaska 196/K2
Sanford, Colo. (81151) 208/H8
Sanford, Fla., 188/K5
Sanford, Fla. (32771) 212/E3
Sanfordᴀ, Maine (04073) 242/B9
Sanford, Maine (04073) 242/B9
Sanford, Man. 179/E5
Sanford, Mich. (48657) 250/E5
Sanford, Miss. (39479) 256/F8
Sanford, N.C. (27330) 281/L4
Sanford‡, Texas (79078) 302/C2
Sanford Nat'l Rec. Area, Texas 302/C2
San Francique, Trinidad Tobago 161/A11
San Francisco, Córdoba, Arg. 143/D3
San Francisco, San Luis, Arg. 143/C3
San Francisco (riv.), Ariz. 198/F5
San Francisco, El Beni, Bol. 136/C4
San Francisco, Santa Cruz, Bol. 136/D7
San Francisco, Calif., 146/F6
San Francisco, Calif., 188/B3
San Francisco, Calif. (*94101) 204/H2
San Francisco (bay), Calif. 204/J2
San Francisco (city county), Calif. 204/J2
San Francisco, Col. 126/B7
San Francisco (cape), Ec. 128/B2
San Francisco, Hond. 154/D3
San Francisco (riv.), N. Mex. 274/A5
San Francisco, Nic. 154/E5
San Francisco, Pan. 154/G6
San Francisco (creek), Texas 302/B8
San Francisco, U.S., 3/C4
San Francisco, Lara, Ven. 124/C2
San Francisco de la Paz, Hond. 154/D3
San Francisco del Chañar, Arg. 143/C2
San Francisco del Oro, Mex. 150/F3
San Francisco del Rincón, Mex. 150/H6
San Francisco de Macorís, Dom. Rep. 156/E3
San Francisco de Macorís, Dom. Rep. 158/E5
San Francisco de Mostazal, Chile 138/G4
San Francisco Gotera, El Salv. 154/C4
Sanga (riv.), Cameroon 115/C3
Sanga (riv.), Centr. Afr. Rep. 115/C3
Sanga (riv.), Rep. of Congo 115/C3
San Gabriel, Calif. (*91775) 204/C10
San Gabriel (res.), Calif. 204/D10
San Gabriel, Ec. 128/D2
San Gabriel Chilac, Mex. 150/K7
Sanga Cho Dzong, China 77/E6
San Gallán (isl.), Peru 128/D9
Sangamner, India 68/C5
Sangamon (co.), Ill. 222/D4
Sangamon (riv.), Ill. 222/C3
Sangar, U.S.S.R. 48/N3
Sangar, Afgh. 59/J3
Sangar, Afgh. 68/B2
Sangay (mt.), Ec. 128/C4
Sangeang (isl.), Indon. 85/F7
San Genaro, Arg. 143/F6
Sanger, Calif. (93657) 204/F7
Sanger, N. Dak. (†58547) 283/H5
Sanger, Texas (76266) 302/G4
Sangerhausen, E. Ger. 22/D3
San Germán, P. Rico 156/F1
San Germán, Cuba 158/J3
San Germán, P. Rico 161/A2
Sangervilleᴀ, Maine (04479) 242/E5
Sanggabuwana (mt.), Indon. 85/G2
Sanggau, Indon. 85/E5
Sangihe (isl.), Indon. 85/H5
Sangihe (isls.), Indon. 85/G5
San Gil, Col. 126/D4
San Giovanni in Fiore, Italy 34/F5
San Giovanni in Persiceto, Italy 34/C2
Sang-i-Sar, Iran 66/H3
San Giuliano Terme, Italy 34/C3
Sangju, S. Korea 81/D5
Sangkulirang, Indon. 85/F5
Sangli, India 68/C5
Sanglistan, Kuh-i- (mt.), Iran 66/H5
Sangmélima, Cameroon 115/B3
Sangolquí, Ec. 128/C3
Sangre de Cristo (mts.), Colo. 208/H6
Sangre de Cristo (mts.), N. Mex. 274/D3
San Gregorio, Calif. (94074) 204/J3
San Gregorio, San José, Urug. 145/C4
San Gregorio, Tacuarembó, Urug. 145/D3
Sangre Grande, Trinidad Tobago 156/G5
Sangre Grande, Trinidad Tobago 161/B10
Sangro (riv.), Italy 34/E4
Sangudo, Alta. 182/C3
Sangue (riv.), Braz. 132/B6
Sangüesa, Spain 33/F1
Sangun, Iran 66/M3
Sanho, China 77/K1
Sanibel, Fla. (33957) 212/D5
Sanibel (isl.), Fla. 212/D5
San Ignacio, Arg. 143/E2
San Ignacio, Bol., 120/D4
San Ignacio, El Beni, Bol. 136/C4
San Ignacio, Santa Cruz, Bol. 136/E5
San Ignacio, C. Rica 154/E6
San Ignacio, Chile 138/E1
San Ignacio, Baja California Sur, Mex. 150/C3
San Ignacio, Sinaloa, Mex. 150/F5
San Ignacio, Par. 144/D6
San Ignacio, Ven. 124/B2
Sanilac (co.), Mich. 250/G5
San Ildefonso, N. Mex. (†87501) 274/C3
San Ildefonso (cape), Phil. 82/D2
San Ildefonso, Spain 33/E2
San'in Kaigan Nat'l Park, Japan 81/G6
San Isabel, Colo. (†81069) 208/K7
Sanish, N. Dak. (58780) 283/E4
San Isidro, Arg. 143/C2
San Isidro, Phil. 82/E5
Saniya, Hor (lake), Iraq 66/E5
San Jacinto, Calif. (92383) 204/H10
San Jacinto, Col. 126/C3
San Jacinto, Nev. (†89825) 266/G1
San Jacinto, Phil. 82/D4
San Jacinto (co.), Texas 302/J7
San Jacinto, Urug. 145/C6
San Javier, Río Negro, Arg. 143/D5
San Javier, Santa Fe, Arg. 143/F5
San Javier, El Beni, Bol. 136/C4
San Javier, Santa Cruz, Bol. 136/D5
San Javier, Chile 138/A11
San Javier, Mex. 150/D2
San Javier, Urug. 145/A3
San Jerónimo, Cuba 158/G3
Sanjo, Japan 81/J5
San Joaquín, Bol. 136/C3
San Joaquin (riv.), Calif., 188/C3
San Joaquin (co.), Calif. 204/D6
San Joaquin, Calif. (93660) 204/E7
San Joaquin (riv.), Calif. 204/E6
San Joaquin (valley), Calif. 204/D6
San Joaquín, Par. 144/D5
San Jon, N. Mex. (88434) 274/F3
San Jorge (gulf), Arg., 120/D7
San Jorge (gulf), Arg. 143/C6
San Jorge (riv.), Col. 126/C3
San Jorge (bay), Mex. 150/C1
San Jorge, Nic. 154/E5
San Jorge (gulf), Spain 33/G2
San José, Arg. 143/G6
San José, Br. Hond. 154/C2
San José (cap.), C. Rica, 146/K9
San José (cap.), C. Rica 154/F5
San Jose, Calif., 146/F6
San Jose, Calif., 188/B3
San Jose, Calif. (*95101) 204/L3
San José, Col. 126/F6
San José (lag.), P. Rico 161/E1
San José, Guat. 154/B4
San Jose, Ill. (62682) 222/D3
San José (isl.), Mex. 150/D4
San Jose, N. Mex. (87565) 274/D3
San Jose (riv.), N. Mex. 274/B3
San Jose, Antique, Phil. 82/C5
San Jose, Bulacan, Phil. 82/C3
San Jose, Nueva Ecija, Phil. 82/C3
San Jose, Occ. Mindoro, Phil. 82/C4
San Jose, Phil. 85/G3

Senftenberg 435

Schenevus, N.Y. (12155) 276/L5
Schererville, Ind. (46375) 227/C2
Scherhorn (mt.), Switz. 39/G3
Schertz, Texas (78154) 302/F8
Schesaplana (mt.), Switz. 39/J2
Scheveningen, Neth. 27/E4
Schiedam, Neth. 27/E5
Schiermonnikoog, Neth. 27/J1
Schiermonnikoog (isl.), Neth. 27/J1
Schiers, Switz. 39/J3
Schijndel, Neth. 27/H5
Schiller Park, Ill. (60176) 222/A1
Schinznach-Dorf, Switz. 39/F2
Schio, Italy 34/C2
Schiphol, Neth. 27/B5
Schkeuditz, E. Ger. 22/E3
Schladming, Austria 41/B3
Schlarigna-Celerina, Switz. 39/J3
Schlater, Miss. (38952) 256/D3
Schlei (inlet), W. Ger. 22/C1
Schleicher (co.), Texas 302/D7
Schleitheim, Switz. 39/G1
Schleswig, Iowa (51461) 229/B4
Schleswig, W. Ger. 22/C1
Schleswig-Holstein (state), W. Ger. 22/C1
Schleusingen, E. Ger. 22/D3
Schley (co.), Ga. 216/D6
Schley, Minn. (†56633) 254/D3
Schlieren, Switz. 39/F2
Schliersee, W. Ger. 22/D5
Schlitz, W. Ger. 22/C3
Schlüchtern, W. Ger. 22/C3
Schluersburg, Mo. (†63332) 261/N3
Schmalkalden, E. Ger. 22/D3
Schmölln, E. Ger. 22/E3
Schnecksville, Pa. (18078) 294/L4
Schneeberg, E. Ger. 22/E3
Schneeberg (mt.), W. Ger. 22/D3
Schnee Eifel (plat.), Belg. 27/J8
Schneider, Ind. (46376) 227/C2
Schnellville, Ind. (47580) 227/D8
Schoelcher, Mart. 161/C6
Schoenchen, Kans. (67667) 232/C3
Schofield, Wis. (54476) 317/H6
Schofield Barracks, Hawaii (96786) 218/E2
Schoharie (co.), N.Y. 276/M5
Schoharie, N.Y. (12157) 276/M5
Schoharie (creek), N.Y. 276/M6
Schoharie (res.), N.Y. 276/M6
Scholle, N. Mex. (87054) 274/C4
Scholls, Oreg. (†97123) 291/A2
Schomberg, Ont. 177/J3
Schönberg, E. Ger. 22/D2
Schönberg, W. Ger. 22/D1
Schönebeck, E. Ger. 22/D2
Schöneberg, W. Ger. 22/E4
Schöneiche, E. Ger. 22/E2
Schönenwerd, Switz. 39/E2
Schongau, W. Ger. 22/D5
Schöningen, W. Ger. 22/D2
Schoodic (lake), Maine 242/F5
Schoolcraft (co.), Mich. 250/C2
Schoolcraft, Mich. (49087) 250/D6
Schoolcraft (riv.), Minn. 254/C3
Schooleys Mountain, N.J. (07870) 273/D2
School Hill, Wis. (†53042) 317/L8
Schoonebeek, Neth. 27/L3
Schoonhoven, Neth. 27/F5
Schoten, Belg. 27/F6
Schottegat (bay), Neth. Ant. 161/G9
Schouten (isls.), Terr. N.G. 85/B6
Schouten (isls.), Indon. 85/K6
Schouwen (isl.), Neth. 27/D5
Schramberg, W. Ger. 22/C4
Schram City, Ill. (†62049) 222/D4
Schreckhorn (mt.), Switz. 39/F3
Schreiber, Ont. 175/C3
Schreiber, Ont. 177/H5
Schrems, Austria 41/C2
Schriever, La. (70395) 238/J7
Schroeder, Minn. (55613) 254/G3
Schroon (lake), N.Y. 276/N3
Schroon (riv.), N.Y. 276/N3
Schroon Lake, N.Y. (12870) 276/N3
Schruns, Austria 41/A3
Schuermann Heights‡, Mo. (†63101) 261/P2
Schulenburg, Texas (78956) 302/H8
Schuler, Alta. 182/E4
Schull, 10/B5
Schull, Ire. 17/B8
Schulter, Okla. (74460) 288/P3
Schultz (lake), N.W.T. 187/J3
Schumacher, Ont. 175/D3
Schumacher, Ont. 177/K5
Schüpfheim, Switz. 39/F3
Schurz, Nev. (89427) 266/C4
Schussenried, W. Ger. 22/C4
Schuyler (co.), Ill. 222/C3
Schuyler (co.), Mo. 261/G2
Schuyler (co.), N.Y. 276/G6
Schuyler, Nebr. (68661) 264/G3
Schuyler, Va. (22969) 307/L5
Schuyler Lake, N.Y. (13457) 276/L5
Schuylerville, N.Y. (12871) 276/N4
Schuylkill (co.), Pa. 294/K4
Schuylkill (riv.), Pa. 294/M5
Schuylkill Haven, Pa. (17972) 294/K4
Schwaan, E. Ger. 22/E2
Schwabach, W. Ger. 22/D4
Schwäbisch Gmünd, W. Ger. 22/C4
Schwäbisch Hall, W. Ger. 22/C4
Schwanden, Switz. 39/H3
Schwandorf, W. Ger. 22/E4
Schwaner (mts.), Indon. 85/E6
Schwarzach, Austria 41/B3
Schwarzenburg, Switz. 39/D3
Schwarzhorn (mt.), Switz. 39/E4
Schwarzhorn (mt.), Switz. 39/F3
Schwarzwald (Black) (for.), W. Ger. 22/C4
Schwatka (mts.), Alaska 196/G1
Schwaz, Austria 41/A3
Schwedt, E. Ger. 22/F2
Schweinfurt, W. Ger. 22/D3
Schwelm, W. Ger. 22/B3
Schwenksville, Pa. (19473) 294/L5
Schwenningen, W. Ger. 22/C4
Schwerin (dist.), E. Ger. 22/D2
Schwerin, E. Ger. 22/D2
Schwerinersee (lake), E. Ger. 22/D2
Schwertberg, Austria 41/C2
Schwetzingen, W. Ger. 22/C4
Schwyz (canton), Switz. 39/G2
Schwyz, Switz. 39/G2
Sciacca, Italy 34/D6
Scicli, Italy 34/E6
Science Hill, Ky. (42553) 237/M6
Scilly (isls.), Eng. 13/A8
Scilly (isls.), 10/C6
Ścinawa, Poland 47/C3
Scio, N.Y. (14880) 276/E6
Scio, Ohio (43988) 284/H5
Scio, Oreg. (97374) 291/E3
Sciota, Ill. (61475) 222/C3
Sciota, Pa. (18354) 294/M4
Scioto (co.), Ohio 284/D8
Scioto (riv.), Ohio 284/D8
Sciotodale, Ohio (†45662) 284/E8
Scioto Furnace, Ohio (45677) 284/E8
Scipio, Ind. (†45053) 227/H6
Scipio, Ind. (47273) 227/F6
Scipio, Okla. (74566) 288/P4
Scipio, Utah (84656) 304/B4
Scircleville, Ind. (46066) 227/E4
Scitico, Conn. (†06036) 210/E1
Scituate∆, Mass. (02066) 249/F8
Scituate, Mass. (02066) 249/F8
Scituate (res.), R.I. 249/H5
Sclater, Man. 179/B3
Scobey, Miss. (38953) 256/E3
Scobey, Mont. (59263) 262/L2
Scofield, Oreg. (†97109) 291/D2
Scofield, Utah (84538) 304/C4
Scofield (res.), Utah 304/C4
Scollard, Alta. 182/D4
Scone, Aust. 88/J6
Scone, N.S.W. 97/F3
Scone, Scot. 15/K7
Scooba, Miss. (39358) 256/G5
Scopi (mt.), Switz. 39/G3
Scopus, Mo. (63762) 261/N8
Scoresby (sound), Greenl., 4/B10
Scoresby, Vic. 97/K5
Scoresbysund, Greenl., 4/B10
Scotch Bay, Man. 179/D4
Scotch Cap, Alaska (†99553) 196/E4
Scotch Grove, Iowa (52331) 229/L4
Scotch Plains∆, N.J. (07076) 273/E2
Scotchtown‡, N.Y. (†10940) 276/M8
Scotch Village, N.S. 169/E3
Scotfield, Alta. 182/E4
Scotia (sea), 3/G8
Scotia (sea), Ant. 5/D16
Scotia, Calif. (95565) 204/A3
Scotia, N.Y. (12302) 276/N5
Scotia, Nebr. (68875) 264/F3
Scotia, S.C. (29939) 296/E6
Scotland, U.K., 7/D3
SCOTLAND, 10/D2
SCOTLAND, 15
Scotland, Ark. (72141) 203/E2
Scotland∆, Conn. (06264) 210/G2
Scotland, Ont. 177/D4
Scotland, Ga. (31083) 216/G6
Scotland, Ind. (47457) 227/D7
Scotland, Mass. (†02324) 249/L5
Scotland, Md. (20687) 245/N8
Scotland (co.), Mo. 261/H2
Scotland (co.), N.C. 281/L5
Scotland, Pa. (17254) 294/G6
Scotland, S. Dak. (57059) 298/O7
Scotland, Texas (76379) 302/F4
Scotland Neck, N.C. (27874) 281/P2
Scotlandville, La. (70807) 238/J1
Scots (bay), N.S. 169/D3
Scots Bay, N.S. 169/D3
Scotsburn, N.S. 169/F3
Scotsguard, Sask. 181/C6
Scotstown, Que. 172/F4
Scotstown, Ire. 17/H3
Scotsville, N.S. 169/G2
Scott (cape), 163/D5
Scott (isl.), Ant., 3/A9
Scott (isl.), Ant. 5/C10
Scott (co.), Ark. 203/B4
Scott, Ark. (72142) 203/F4
Scott (cape), Br. Col. 184/C5
Scott (isls.), Br. Col. 184/C5
Scott (riv.), Calif. 204/B2
Scott, Ga. (31095) 216/G5
Scott (co.), Ill. 222/C4
Scott (co.), Ind. 227/F7
Scott, Ind. (†46746) 227/F1
Scott (co.), Iowa 229/M5
Scott (co.), Kans. 232/B3
Scott (co.), Ky. 237/M4
Scott, La. (70583) 238/F6
Scott (co.), Minn. 254/E6
Scott (co.), Miss. 256/E6
Scott, Miss. (38772) 256/B3
Scott (co.), Mo. 261/N8
Scott, Ohio (45886) 284/A4
Scott (mt.), Okla. 288/K5
Scott, Sask. 181/C3
Scott (lake), Sask. 181/M2
Scott (co.), Tenn. 237/M8
Scott (co.), Va. 307/C7
Scott A.F.B., Ill. 222/B6
Scott City, Kans. (67871) 232/B3
Scott City, Mo. (63780) 261/O8
Scottdale, Pa. (15683) 294/C5
Scott-Jonction, Que. 172/F3
Scottland, Ill. (†61924) 222/F4
Scotts (head), Dominica 161/E7
Scotts, N.C. (28699) 281/H3
Scottsbluff, Nebr., 188/F2
Scotts Bluff (co.), Nebr. 264/A3
Scottsbluff, Nebr. (69361) 264/A3
Scotts Bluff Nat'l Mon., Nebr. 264/A3
Scottsboro, Ala. (35768) 194/F1
Scottsburg, Ind. (47170) 227/F7
Scottsburg, Ky. (†42445) 237/F6
Scottsburg, Oreg. (97473) 291/D4
Scottsburg, Va. (24589) 307/L7
Scottsdale, Ariz. (*85251) 198/D5
Scottsdale, Tas. 99/D3
Scotts Hill, N.C. (†28401) 281/O6
Scotts Hill, Tenn. (38374) 237/E10
Scotts Mills, Oreg. (97375) 291/B3
Scottsmoor, Fla. (32775) 212/F3
Scotts Ridge (hills), Conn. 210/A3
Scott Station, Ant. 5/B9
Scotts Valley, Calif. (95060) 204/K4
Scottsville, Ark. (72862) 203/D3
Scottsville, Kans. (67477) 232/D2
Scottsville, Ky. (42164) 237/J7
Scottsville, N.Y. (14546) 276/E4
Scottsville, Queens. 95/C4
Scottsville‡, Texas (75688) 302/K5
Scottsville, Va. (24590) 307/L5
Scottville, Ill. (62683) 222/C4
Scottville, Mich. (49454) 250/C5
Scoudouc, N. Br. 170/F2
Scourie, Scot. 15/F3
Scout Lake, Sask. 181/F6
Scow Bay‡, Alaska (†99833) 196/M3
Scrabster, Scot. 15/J2
Scraggly (lake), Maine 242/F3
Scraggly (lake), Maine 242/H5
Scranage, Ala. (†36552) 194/C8
Scranton, Ark. (72863) 203/C3
Scranton, Iowa (51462) 229/D4
Scranton, Kans. (66537) 232/G3
Scranton, Ky. (40373) 237/O5
Scranton, N.C. (27875) 281/S4
Scranton, N. Dak. (58653) 283/D7
Scranton, N.Y. (†14075) 276/C5
Scranton, Pa., 146/L5
Scranton, Pa., 188/L2
Scranton, Pa. (*18501) 294/L3
Scranton, S.C. (29591) 296/H4
Scraper, Okla. (†74359) 288/S2
Screven (co.), Ga. 216/J5
Screven, Ga. (31560) 216/H7
Scribner, Nebr. (68057) 264/H3
Scridain (inlet), Scot. 15/D7
Scrip, Sask. 181/G3
Scugog (lake), Ont. 177/F3
Scullin, Okla. (†73086) 288/N5
Scunthorpe, Eng. 13/G4
Scunthorpe, 10/F4
Scuol-Schuls, Switz. 39/K3
Scurdie Ness (prom.), Scot. 15/M6
Scurry (co.), Texas 302/D5
Scurry, Texas (75158) 302/H5
Scutari (lake), Alb. 45/D4
Scutari (lake), Yugo. 45/D4
Scyrene, Ala. (†36436) 194/C7
Sea (isls.), Ga. 216/K9
Sea (isls.), S.C. 296/G7
Seabeck, Wash. (98380) 310/C3
Seaboard, N.C. (27876) 281/O1
Seabold, Wash. (†98110) 310/A1
Sea Breeze, N.Y. (†14617) 276/F4
Sea Bright, N.J. (07760) 273/F3
Seabrook∆, N.H. (03874) 268/F6
Seabrook, N.H. (03874) 268/F6
Seabrook, N.J. (08302) 273/C5
Seabrook, S.C. (29940) 296/F6
Seabrook (isl.), S.C. 296/G6
Seabrook, Texas (77586) 302/K2
Seabrook-Lanham, Md. (20801) 245/G4
Sea Cliff, N.Y. (11579) 276/R6
Seadrift, Texas (77983) 302/H9
Seaflower (chan.), Indon. 85/B6
Seaford, Del. (19973) 245/R6
Seaford, Eng. 13/H7
Seaford, 10/G5
Seaford‡, N.Y. (11783) 276/R7
Seaford, Va. (23428) 307/R6
Seaforth, Ont. 177/C4
Seaforth, Minn. (56287) 254/C6
Seaforth (inlet), Scot. 15/C4
Sea Girt, N.J. (08750) 273/E3
Seagoville, Texas (75159) 302/H2
Seagraves, Texas (79359) 302/B5
Seagrove, N.C. (27341) 281/K3
Seaham, Eng. 13/F3
Seaham, 10/F3
Seahorse (pt.), N.W.T. 187/L3
Seahorse (lake), Newf. 166/A3
Seahurst, Wash. (98062) 310/A2
Sea Island, Ga. (31561) 216/K8
Sea Isle City, N.J. (08243) 273/D5
Seal (riv.), 163/G4
Seal (isl.), Maine 242/F8
Seal (riv.), Man. 179/J2
Seal (isl.), N.S. 169/B5
Seal (lake), Newf. 166/B3
Seal (isl.), S. Africa 118/F7
Sea Lake, Vic. 97/B4
Seal Beach, Calif. (90740) 204/C11
Seal Cove, Maine (04674) 242/G7
Seal Cove, N. Br. 170/D4
Seal Cove, Newf. 166/C3
Seal Cove, Newf. 166/C4
Seale, Ala. (36875) 194/H6
Sealevel, N.C. (28577) 281/S5
Seal Harbor, Maine (04675) 242/G7
Seal Rock, Oreg. (97376) 291/C3
Sealston, Va. (22547) 307/O4
Sealy, Texas (77474) 302/H8
Seaman, Ohio (45679) 284/C8
Sea of Oman, Islands and Ports of the (governorate), Iran 66/H7
Sea of Oman-Persian Gulf (prov.), Iran 66/E4
Sea Pines, S.C. (†29928) 296/F7
Sea Ranch Lakes, Fla. (†33301) 212/C3
Searchlight, Nev. (89046) 266/F7
Searchmont, Ont. 177/J5
Searcy (co.), Ark. 203/E2
Searcy, Ark. (72143) 203/G3
Searight, Ala. (†36028) 194/F8
Searles, Ala. (35483) 194/D4
Searles (lake), Calif. 204/H8
Searles, Minn. (56084) 254/D6
Sears, Mich. (49679) 250/D5
Searsboro, Iowa (50242) 229/H5
Searsburg, Vt. (†05363) 268/A6
Searsmont∆, Maine (04973) 242/E7
Searsmont, Maine (04973) 242/E7
Searsport∆, Maine (04974) 242/F7
Searsport, Maine (04974) 242/F7
Seascale, Eng. 13/D3
Seaside, Calif. (93955) 204/D7
Seaside, Oreg. (97138) 291/D2
Seaside Heights, N.J. (08751) 273/E4
Seaside Park, N.J. (08752) 273/E4
Seaton, Eng. 13/D7
Seaton, Ill. (61476) 222/C2
Seatonville, Ill. (61359) 222/D2
Seat Pleasant, Md. (20027) 245/G5
Seattle, U.S., 3/C3
Seattle, Wash., 146/F5
Seattle, Wash., 188/B1
Seattle, Wash. (*98101) 310/A2
Seattle N.A.S., Wash. 310/B1
Seaview, Wash. (98644) 310/A4
Seaward Kaikouras (range), N.Z. 101/D5
Seawell, Barb. 161/B9
Seba, Indon. 85/G8
Seba Beach, Alta. 182/C3
Sebago (lake), Maine 242/B8
Sebago Lake, Maine (04075) 242/B8
Sebastian (co.), Ark. 203/B3
Sebastian, Fla. (32958) 212/F4
Sebastian (cape), Oreg. 291/C5
Sebastián Vizcaíno (bay), Mex. 150/B2
Sebasticook (lake), Maine 242/E6
Sebastopol, Calif. (95472) 204/C5
Sebastopol, Miss. (39359) 256/F5
Sebastopol, Vic. 97/B5
Sebatik (isl.), Indon. 85/F5
Sebatik (isl.), Malaysia 85/F5
Sebec∆, Maine (04481) 242/E5
Sebec, Maine (04481) 242/E5
Sebec Lake, Maine (04482) 242/E5
Sebec Station, Maine (†04426) 242/E5
Sebeka, Minn. (56477) 254/C4
Seben, Turkey 63/D2
Sebeş, Rum. 45/F3
Sebes Körös (riv.), Hung. 41/F3
Sebewaing, Mich. (48759) 250/F5
Sebha (prov.), Libya 111/B2
Sebha, Libya 111/B2
Sebha, 102/D2
Şebinkarahisar, Turkey 63/H2
Şebiş, Rum. 45/F2
Sebnitz, E. Ger. 22/F3
Seboeis∆, Maine (04484) 242/F5
Seboeis (lake), Maine 242/F5
Seboeis (riv.), Maine 242/F3
Sebollera (mt.), Spain 33/E2
Seboomook, Maine (†04478) 242/D4
Seboomook (lake), Maine 242/D4
Seboruco, Ven. 124/B3
Sebou (riv.), Mor. 106/C2
Seboyeta, N. Mex. (87055) 274/B3
Sebree, Ky. (42455) 237/F5
Sebrell, Va. (†23837) 307/O7
Sebring, Fla. (33870) 212/E4
Sebring, Ohio (44672) 284/H4
Sebringville, Ont. 177/C4
Sebuko (bay), Indon. 85/F5
Secane, Pa. (19018) 294/M7
Secas (isls.), Pan. 154/G7
Secaucus, N.J. (07094) 273/B2
Secesh (riv.), Idaho 220/C4
Sechart, Br. Col. 184/E6
Sechelt, Br. Col. 184/J2
Sechura, Peru 128/B5
Sechura (bay), Peru 128/B5
Seco, Ky. (41849) 237/R6
Second (lake), N.H. 268/E1
Second Branch, White (riv.), Vt. 268/B4
Second Cataract, Sudan 59/B5
Second Cataract (rapids), Sudan 111/F3
Secondcreek, W. Va. (24974) 313/F7
Second Mesa, Ariz. (86043) 198/E3
Secor, Ill. (61771) 222/D3
Sečovce, Czech. 41/F2
Secretan, Sask. 181/E5
Secretary, Md. (21664) 245/P6
Secretary (isl.), N.Z. 101/A6
Section, Ala. (35771) 194/G1
Secunderabad, India, 54/M8
Secunderabad, India 68/D5
Sécure (riv.), Bol. 136/C4
Security, Colo. (80911) 208/K5
Sedalia, Alta. 182/E4
Sedalia, Colo. (80135) 208/K4
Sedalia, Ind. (46067) 227/E4
Sedalia, Ky. (42079) 237/D7
Sedalia, Mo., 188/H3
Sedalia, Mo. (65301) 261/F5
Sedalia, Ohio (43151) 284/D6
Sedalia, S.C. (†29379) 296/D2
Sedan, France 28/F3
Sedan, Ind. (†46793) 227/G2
Sedan, Kans. (67361) 232/F4
Sedan, Minn. (56380) 254/C5
Sedan, N. Mex. (88436) 274/F2
Sedano, Spain 33/E1
Sedbergh, Eng. 13/E3
Sedbergh, 10/E3
Seddon, N.Z. 101/E4
Seddonville, N.Z. 101/C4
Seddülbahir, Turkey 63/B6
Sede Boqer, Israel 65/D5
Sedenak, Malaysia 72/E5
Sedgewick, Alta. 182/E3
Sedgewickville, Mo. (63781) 261/N7
Sedgwick, Ark. (72465) 203/J2
Sedgwick (co.), Colo. 208/P1
Sedgwick, Colo. (80749) 208/O1
Sedgwick (co.), Kans. 232/E4
Sedgwick, Kans. (67135) 232/E4
Sedgwick∆, Maine (04676) 242/F7
Sedhiou, Sen. 106/A6
Sedili Kechil, Tanjong (pt.), Malaysia 72/F5
Sedlčany, Czech. 41/C2
Sedley, Sask. 181/H5
Sedley, Va. (23878) 307/P7
Sedom, Israel 65/D5
Sedona, Ariz. (86336) 198/D4
Sedot Yam, Israel 65/B3
Sedro-Woolley, Wash. (98284) 310/C2
Sedrun, Switz. 39/G3
Šeduva, U.S.S.R. 53/B3
Seebe, Alta. 182/C4
Seebert, W. Va. (24975) 313/F6
Seech, Man. 179/B4
Seechelt (inlet), Br. Col. 184/J2
Seechelt (pen.), Br. Col. 184/J2
Seeheim, 102/D7
Seeheim, S.W. Afr. 118/B5
Seeis, S.W. Afr. 118/B4
Seekonk∆, Mass. (02771) 249/J5
Seeley, Calif. (92273) 204/K11
Seeley, Wis. (†54843) 317/D3
Seeley Lake, Mont. (59868) 262/C3
Seeleys Bay, Ont. 177/H3
Seely, Wyo. (†82720) 319/H1
Seelyville, Ind. (47878) 227/C6
Seelyville, Pa. (18431) 294/M2
Seesen, W. Ger. 22/D3
Seewis, Switz. 39/J3
Seez (riv.), Switz. 39/H2
Şefaatli, Turkey 63/F3
Seferihisar, Turkey 63/B3
Seffner, Fla. (33584) 212/D4
Sefid Rud (riv.), Iran 66/F2
Sefrou, Mor. 106/D2
Sefton, N.Z. 101/D5
Seg (lake), U.S.S.R. 52/D2
Segamat, Malaysia 72/D7
Segarcea, Rum. 45/F3
Segezha, U.S.S.R. 48/D3
Segezha, U.S.S.R. 52/D2
Segnes (pass), Switz. 39/H3
Segni, Italy 34/F7
Segorbe, Spain 33/F3
Ségou, 102/B3
Ségou, Mali 106/C6
Segovia, Col. 126/C4
Segovia (Coco) (riv.), Hond. 154/E3
Segovia (Coco) (riv.), Nic. 154/E3
Segovia (prov.), Spain 33/D2
Segovia, Spain 33/D2
Segré, France 28/C4
Segre (riv.), Spain 33/G2
Segreganset, Mass. (02773) 249/K5
Seguam (isl.), Alaska 196/D4
Seguam (passg.), Alaska 196/D4
Séguéla, Ivory Coast 106/C7
Seguí, Arg. 143/F6
Seguin, Kans. (†67740) 232/B2
Seguin, Texas (78155) 302/G8
Segula (isl.), Alaska 196/K4
Segundo, Colo. (81070) 208/K8
Segura, La. (†70560) 238/G6
Segura (riv.), Spain 33/F3
Sehore, India 68/D4
Sehwan, Pak. 59/J4
Sehwan, Pak. 68/B3
Sehwi Wiawso, Ghana 106/D7
Seiad Valley, Calif. (96086) 204/B2
Seibert (lake), Alta. 182/E2
Seibert, Colo. (80834) 208/O4
Seibo, Dom. Rep. 156/E3
Seiland (isl.), Norway 18/N1
Seiling, Okla. (73663) 288/J2
Sein (isl.), France 28/A3
Seinäjoki, Fin. 18/N5
Seine (riv.), Ont. 175/B3
Seine (riv.), France, 7/E4
Seine (bay), France 28/C3
Seine (riv.), France 28/D3
Seine-et-Marne (dept.), France 28/E3
Seine-Saint-Denis (dept.), France 28/C1
Seistan (reg.), Iran 66/M5
Seistan and Baluchistan (prov.), Iran 66/M6
Seixal, Port. 33/A1
Seiyun, P.D.R. Yemen 59/E6
Seize-Îles (lake), Que. 172/C4
Sejerø (isl.), Den. 21/E6
Sejny, Poland 47/F1
Sekenke, Tanz. 115/F4
Se Khong (riv.), Cambodia 72/E4
Se Khong (riv.), Laos 72/E4
Sekiu, Wash. (98381) 310/A2
Sekkane (des.), Mali 106/D4
Sekondi, Ghana 106/D8
Sekondi, Ghana 102/B4
Sekondi-Takoradi, Ghana 102/B4
Selah, Wash. (98942) 310/E4
Selama, Malaysia 72/D6
Selangor (state), Malaysia 72/D7
Selaphum, Thai. 72/E3
Selaru (isl.), Indon. 85/J7
Selatan (cape), Indon. 85/E6
Selawik, Alaska (99770) 196/G1
Selawik (lake), Alaska 196/F1
Selb, W. Ger. 22/E3
Selby, Eng. 13/F4
Selby, S. Dak. (57472) 298/J3
Selby, Vic. 97/K5
Selby-on-the-Bay‡, Md. (†21037) 245/M5
Selbyville, Del. (19975) 245/S7
Selbyville, W. Va. (26236) 313/F5
Selçuk, Turkey 63/B3
Selden, Kans. (67757) 232/B2
Selden‡, N.Y. (11784) 276/P9
Seldovia, Alaska (99663) 196/B2
Sele (riv.), Italy 34/E4
Selemiya, Syria 63/G5
Selenga (prov.), Mong. 77/G2
Selenga (riv.), Mong. 77/F2
Sélestat, France 28/G3
Selfridge, N. Dak. (58568) 283/J7
Selfridge A.F.B., Mich. 250/G6
Selfridge-Capehart‡, Mich. (†48043) 250/G6
Sélibaby, Mauritania 106/B5
Seligman, Ariz. (86337) 198/B3
Seligman, Mo. (65745) 261/D9
Selim, Turkey 63/K2
Selima (oasis), Sudan 59/A5
Selima (oasis), Sudan 111/E3
Selimiye, Turkey 63/B4
Selinsgrove, Pa. (17870) 294/J4
Selje, Norway 18/D5
Selkirk, 163/G5
Selkirk (mts.), Br. Col. 184/J4
Selkirk, Ont. 177/E5
Selkirk (mts.), Idaho 220/B1
Selkirk, Kans. (67873) 232/A3
Selkirk, 10/E3
Selkirk, Man. 179/F4
Selkirk (isl.), Man. 179/C1
Selkirk, Mich. (†48661) 250/E4
Selkirk (co.), Scot. 15/K9
Selkirk, Scot. 15/L8
Sellafield, Eng. 13/D3
Sellafield, 10/E3
Selleck, Wash. (98064) 310/D3
Sellers, Ala. (36072) 194/F6
Sellers, S.C. (29592) 296/H3
Sellersburg, Ind. (47172) 227/F8
Sellersville, Pa. (18960) 294/M5
Sells, Ariz. (85634) 198/D7
Sells, Ga. (†30548) 216/E2
Selma, Ala., 188/J4
Selma, Ala. (36701) 194/E6
Selma, Ark. (†71670) 203/G6
Selma, Calif. (93662) 204/F7
Selma, Ind. (47383) 227/G4
Selma, Iowa (52588) 229/J7
Selma, Miss. (†39120) 256/B7
Selma, N.C. (27576) 281/N3
Selma, Ohio (45364) 284/C6
Selma, Oreg. (97538) 291/D5
Selma‡, Texas (†78201) 302/F8
Selma, Va. (24474) 307/J5
Selmah, N.S. 169/E3
Selman, Okla. (73856) 288/H1
Selma Park, Br. Col. 184/K2
Selmer, Tenn. (38375) 237/D10
Selmont, Ala. (†36701) 194/E6
Selous (mt.), Yukon 187/E3
Selsey, Eng. 13/G7
Selsey Bill (pt.), Eng. 13/G7
Selukwe, Rhod. 118/E3
Selva, Arg. 143/D2
Selvas (for.), Braz., 120/D3
Selvin, Ind. (†47523) 227/C8
Selway (riv.), Idaho 220/C3
Selwyn, Aust. 88/G4
Selwyn (lake), N.W.T. 187/H4
Selwyn, Queens. 95/B4
Selwyn (range), Queens. 95/B4
Selwyn (lake), Sask. 181/M2
Selwyn, W. Va. (†25674) 313/B7
Selwyn (mts.), Yukon 187/E3
Selz, N. Dak. (58373) 283/L4
Seman, Ala. (†36092) 194/F5
Semans, Sask. 181/G4
Semara, Sp. Sahara 106/B3
Semarang, Indon., 54/O10
Semarang, Indon. 85/J2
Sematan, Malaysia 85/D5
Sembé, Rep. of Congo 115/B3
Sembrancher, Switz. 39/D4
Şemdinli, Turkey 63/L4
Semenov, U.S.S.R. 52/F3
Semeru (mt.), Indon. 85/K2
Semichi (isls.), Alaska 196/J3
Semidi (isls.), Alaska 196/G3
Semily, Czech. 41/C1
Seminary, Miss. (39479) 256/E7
Seminoe (res.), Wyo., 188/E2
Seminoe (mts.), Wyo. 319/E3
Seminoe (res.), Wyo. 319/F3
Seminoe Dam, Wyo. (82333) 319/E3
Seminole, Ala. (36574) 194/D10
Seminole (co.), Fla. 212/E3
Seminole, Fla. (33540) 212/B3
Seminole (lake), Fla. 212/B1
Seminole (co.), Ga. 216/C9
Seminole (lake), Ga. 216/B9
Seminole (co.), Okla. 288/N4
Seminole, Okla. (74868) 288/N4
Seminole, Pa. (16253) 294/D4
Seminole, Texas (79360) 302/B5
Seminole Ind. Res., Fla. 212/4F5
Semipalatinsk, U.S.S.R. 48/H4
Semipalatinsk, U.S.S.R., 54/L4
Semirara (isls.), Phil. 82/C5
Semisopochnoi (isl.), Alaska 196/K4
Semitau, Indon. 85/E5
Semmering (pass), Austria 41/C3
Semmes, Ala. (36575) 194/B9
Semois (riv.), Belg. 27/G9
Semora, N.C. (27343) 281/L2
Sempach, Switz. 39/F2
Sempach (lake), Switz. 39/F2
Semporna, Malaysia 85/F5
Semsales, Switz. 39/C3
Semur-en-Auxois, France 28/F4
Sena, Bol. 136/B2
Sena, N. Mex. (87568) 274/D3
Senado, Cuba 158/G2
Senador Pompeu, Braz. 132/G4
Senai, Malaysia 72/F5
Sena Madureira, Braz. 132/G10
Senanga, Zambia 115/D7
Senate, Sask. 181/B6
Senath, Mo. (63876) 261/M10
Senatobia, Miss. (38668) 256/E1
Sendai, Japan, 54/T6
Sendai, Honshu, Japan 81/K4
Sendai, Kyushu, Japan 81/E8
Senec, Czech. 41/D2
Seneca, Ill. (61360) 222/E2
Seneca, Kans. (66538) 232/F2
Seneca, Miss. (†39455) 256/F8
Seneca, Mo. (64865) 261/C9
Seneca, N. Mex. (88437) 274/F2
Seneca (co.), N.Y. 276/G5
Seneca (lake), N.Y. 276/G5
Seneca (riv.), N.Y. 276/G5
Seneca, Nebr. (69161) 264/D2
Seneca (co.), Ohio 284/D3
Seneca, Oreg. (97873) 291/J3
Seneca, S.C. (29678) 296/A2
Seneca (riv.), S.C. 296/B2
Seneca, S. Dak. (57473) 298/L3
Seneca, Wis. (54654) 317/E9
Seneca Army Depot, N.Y. 276/F5
Seneca Falls, N.Y. (13148) 276/G5
Seneca Gardens‡, Ky. (†40201) 237/K4
Senécal (lake), Newf. 166/B3
Senecaville, Ohio (43780) 284/H6
Senecaville (res.), Ohio 284/H6
Senegal, 3/J5
SENEGAL, 106/A5
SENEGAL, 102/A3
Senegal (riv.), 102/A3
Senegal (riv.), Mali 106/B5
Senegal (riv.), Mauritania 106/B5
Senegal (riv.), Sen. 106/B5
Senekal S Africa 118/D5
Seney, Iowa (†51031) 229/A3
Seney, Mich. (49883) 250/C2
Senftenberg, E. Ger. 22/F3

Silver 437

Shenandoah Heights‡, Pa. (†17976) 294/K4
Shenandoah Junction, W. Va. (25442) 313/L4
Shenandoah Nat'l Park, Va. 307/L3
Shenango, Pa. (16152) 294/A3
Shenango River (res.), Pa. 294/B3
Shendam, Nigeria 106/F7
Shendi, Sudan 59/B6
Shendi, Sudan 111/F4
Shëngjin, Alb. 45/D5
Shenipsit (lake), Conn. 210/F1
Shenkursk, U.S.S.R. 48/E3
Shenkursk, U.S.S.R. 52/F2
Shennington, Wis. (†54618) 317/F7
Shensi (prov.), China 77/G5
Shenstone, 10/G3
Shentsa Dzong, China 77/C5
Shenyang (Mukden), China 77/K3
Sheo, India 68/C3
Sheopur, India 68/D3
Shepard, Alta. 182/D4
Shepardsville, Ind. (47880) 227/B5
Shepaug (dam), Conn. 210/B3
Shepaug (riv.), Conn. 210/B2
Shepetovka, U.S.S.R. 52/C4
Shepetovka, U.S.S.R., 7/G3
Shepherd, Mich. (48883) 250/E5
Shepherd, Mont. (59079) 262/H5
Shepherd (bay), N.W.T. 187/J3
Shepherd, Texas (77371) 302/K7
Shepherdstown, W. Va. (25443) 313/L4
Shepherdsville, Ky. (40165) 237/K4
Shepody, N. Br. 170/F3
Shepody (bay), N. Br. 170/F3
Sheppard A.F.B., Texas 302/F3
Shepparton, Vic. 97/C5
Sheppey (isl.), Eng. 13/H6
Sheppton, Pa. (18248) 294/K4
Shepton Mallet, Eng. 13/E6
Shepton Mallet, 10/E5
Sherack, Minn. (†56722) 254/B2
Sherard, Miss. (38669) 256/C2
Sherard (cape), N.W.T. 187/L2
Sherborn△, Mass. (01770) 249/A8
Sherborne, Eng. 13/E7
Sherborne, 10/E5
Sherbro (isl.), S. Leone 106/B7
Sherbrooke, 163/J6
Sherbrooke (co.), Que. 172/E4
Sherbrooke, Que. 172/E4
Sherbrooke, N.S. 169/G3
Sherbrooke (lake), N.S. 169/D4
Sherbrooke (riv.), N.S. 169/D4
Sherburn, Minn. (56171) 254/D7
Sherburne (co.), Minn. 254/E5
Sherburne, N.Y. (13460) 276/K5
Sherburn-in-Elmet, Eng. 13/F4
Shercock, Ire. 17/G4
Shereik, Sudan 111/F4
Shergrove, Man. 179/C3
Sheridan, Ark. (72150) 203/F5
Sheridan, Calif. (95681) 204/D5
Sheridan, Colo. (†80110) 208/J3
Sheridan, Ill. (60551) 222/E2
Sheridan, Ind. (46069) 227/E4
Sheridan (co.), Kans. 232/B2
Sheridan, Maine (04775) 242/F2
Sheridan, Mich. (48884) 250/D5
Sheridan, Mo. (64486) 261/C1
Sheridan (co.), Mont. 262/M2
Sheridan, Mont. (59749) 262/D5
Sheridan (co.), N. Dak. 283/K4
Sheridan, N.Y. (14135) 276/B5
Sheridan (co.), Nebr. 264/B2
Sheridan, Oreg. (97378) 291/D2
Sheridan, W. Va. (†25506) 313/B6
Sheridan, Wis. (54477) 317/H7
Sheridan, Wyo., 146/H5
Sheridan, Wyo., 188/E2
Sheridan (co.), Wyo. 319/F1
Sheridan, Wyo. (82801) 319/F1
Sheridan Lake, Colo. (81071) 208/P6
Sheringham, Eng. 13/J5
Sheringham, 10/G4
Sherkin (isl.), Ire. 17/C9
Sherman (mt.), Colo. 208/G4
Sherman△, Conn. (06784) 210/B2
Sherman, Ill. (62684) 222/D4
Sherman (co.), Kans. 232/A2
Sherman, Kans. (†67356) 232/H4
Sherman, Ky. (†41035) 237/M3
Sherman△, Maine (†04777) 242/G4
Sherman, Maine (†04777) 242/G4
Sherman, Mich. (†49668) 250/D4
Sherman, Miss. (38869) 256/G2
Sherman, Mo. (63078) 261/O3
Sherman, N. Mex. (†88057) 274/B6
Sherman (inlet), N.W.T. 187/J3
Sherman, N.Y. (14781) 276/A6
Sherman (co.), Nebr. 264/F3
Sherman (res.), Nebr. 264/E3
Sherman (co.), Oreg. 291/G2
Sherman, S. Dak. (57060) 298/S6
Sherman, Texas, 188/G4
Sherman (co.), Texas 302/C1
Sherman, Texas (75090) 302/H4
Sherman, W. Va. (26173) 313/C5
Sherman City, Mich. (†48632) 250/D5
Sherman Mills, Maine (04776) 242/G4
Shermans Dale, Pa. (17090) 294/H5
Sherman Station, Maine (04777) 242/F4
Sherrard, Ill. (61281) 222/C2
Sherrard, W. Va. (26057) 313/E3
Sherrelwood‡, Colo. (†80030) 208/K3
Sherridon, 163/G4
Sherridon, Man. 179/H3
Sherrill, Ark. (72152) 203/F5
Sherrill, Iowa (52073) 229/M3
Sherrill, N.Y. (13461) 276/J4
Sherrington, Que. 172/D4
Sherrodsville, Ohio (44675) 284/H4
Sherry, Wis. (†54454) 317/G6
s Hertogenbosch, Neth. 27/G5
Sherwood, Ark. (72116) 203/F4
Sherwood (pt.), Conn. 210/B4
Sherwood, Mich. (49089) 250/D6
Sherwood, N. Dak. (58782) 283/G2
Sherwood, Ohio (43556) 284/A3
Sherwood, Okla. (74757) 288/S6
Sherwood, Oreg. (97140) 291/A2
Sherwood, P.E.I. 169/E2
Sherwood, Tenn. (37376) 237/K10
Sherwood, Texas (76948) 302/D6
Sherwood, Wis. (54169) 317/K7
Sherwood Park, Alta. 182/D3
Sheslay (riv.), Br. Col. 184/J2
Shetek (lake), Minn. 254/C6
Shetland (isls.), 10/G1
Shetland (isls.), Scot., 7/D2
Shetland (isls.), Scot. 15/M3
Shetucket (riv.), Conn. 210/G2
Shevchenko, U.S.S.R. 48/F5
Shevlin, Man. 179/A3
Shevlin, Minn. (56676) 254/C3
Shewa, India 68/B7
Sheyenne (riv.), N. Dak., 188/G1
Sheyenne, N. Dak. (58374) 283/M4
Sheyenne (riv.), N. Dak. 283/O6
Shiant (isls.), Scot. 15/D4
Shiawassee (co.), Mich. 250/E6
Shiawassee (riv.), Mich. 250/E5
Shibam, P.D.R. Yemen 59/E6
Shibarghan, Afgh. 59/H2
Shibarghan, Afgh. 68/B1
Shibata, Japan 81/J5
Shibetsu, Japan 81/M2
Shibin el Kom, U.A.R. 111/J3
Shibogama (lake), Ont. 175/C2
Shickley, Nebr. (68436) 264/G4
Shickshinny, Pa. (18655) 294/K3
Shickshock (mts.), Que. 172/C1
Shideler, Ind. (†47338) 227/G4
Shidler, Okla. (74652) 288/N1
Shiel (lake), 10/D2
Shiel (lake), Scot. 15/E6
Shieldaig, Scot. 15/E5
Shields, Kans. (67874) 232/B3
Shields (riv.), Mont. 262/F4
Shields, N. Dak. (58569) 283/H7
Shieldsville, Minn. (†55021) 254/E6
Shiga (pref.), Japan 81/J7
Shigatse, China 77/C6
Shigawake, Que. 172/D2
Shigma (riv.), Israel 65/B4
Shihchü, China 77/E5
Shihchüan, China 77/G5
Shihhotzu, China 77/C3
Shihkiachwang, China 77/J4
Shihr, P.D.R. Yemen 59/E7
Shihtsuishan, China 77/G4
Shijak, Alb. 45/D5
Shikarpur, Pak. 59/J4
Shikarpur, Pak. 68/B3
Shikarpur, Pak., 54/K7
Shikoku (isl.), Japan, 3/R4
Shikoku (isl.), Japan, 54/S6
Shikoku (isl.), Japan 81/F7
Shikotan (isl.), Japan 81/N2
Shikotsu (lake), Japan 81/K2
Shikotsu-Toya Nat'l Park, Japan 81/K2
Shildon, Eng. 13/F3
Shilka, U.S.S.R. 48/M4
Shilka (riv.), U.S.S.R., 54/P4
Shillelagh, 10/C4
Shillelagh, Ire. 17/J6
Shillington, Pa. (19607) 294/K5
Shillong, India 68/G3
Shilo, Man. 179/C5
Shiloh, Ala. (†36754) 194/C6
Shiloh, Ga. (31826) 216/C5
Shiloh, Ill. (†62220) 222/B6
Shiloh, N.J. (08353) 273/C5
Shiloh, Ohio (44878) 284/E4
Shiloh‡, Ohio (†45401) 284/B6
Shiloh, S.C. (†29080) 296/G4
Shiloh, Tenn. (38376) 237/E10
Shiloh, Va. (22549) 307/O4
Shiloh Nat'l Mil. Park, Tenn. 237/E10
Shimabara, Japan 81/E7
Shimane (pref.), Japan 81/F6
Shimane (pen.), Japan 81/F6
Shimanovsk, U.S.S.R. 48/N4
Shimizu, Japan 81/J6
Shimoda, Japan 81/J6
Shimoga, India 68/D6
Shimokita (pen.), Japan 81/K3
Shimonoseki, Japan 81/E6
Shin (lake), 10/D1
Shin (falls), Scot. 15/H4
Shin (lake), Scot. 15/G3
Shinano (riv.), Japan 81/J5
Shinas, Oman 59/G5
Shindand (Sabzawar), Afgh. 59/H3
Shindand (Sabzawar), Afgh. 68/A2
Shindler, S. Dak. (†57101) 298/R7
Shiner, Texas (77984) 302/G8
Shingbwiyang, Burma 72/B1
Shinglehouse, Pa. (16748) 294/F2
Shingler, Ga. (†31781) 216/E7
Shingle Springs, Calif. (95682) 204/C8
Shingleton, Mich. (49884) 250/C2
Shingu, Japan 81/H7
Shining Bank, Alta. 182/B3
Shinjo, Japan 81/K4
Shinko (riv.), Centr. Afr. Rep. 115/D2
Shinkolobwe (with Kambove), Dem. Rep. of the Congo. 115/E6
Shinnecock Ind. Res., N.Y. 276/R9
Shinnston, W. Va. (26431) 313/F4
Shin Pond, Maine (†04765) 242/F3
Shinrone, Ire. 17/F5
Shinyanga (reg.), Tanz. 115/F3
Shinyanga, Tanz. 115/F4
Shiocton, Wis. (54170) 317/K7
Shiogama, Japan 81/K4
Shiono (cape), Japan 81/H7
Ship (isl.), Miss. 256/G10
Ship Bottom, N.J. (08008) 273/E4
Ship Harbour, N.S. 169/F4
Ship Harbour, Newf. 166/D2
Shipki (pass), India 68/D2
Shipley, Eng. 13/F4
Shipman, Ill. (62685) 222/C4
Shipman, Sask. 181/F2
Shipman, Va. (22971) 307/L5
Shippan (pt.), Conn. 210/A4
Shippegan, N. Br. 170/F1
Shippegan (bay), N. Br. 170/E1
Shippegan (isl.), N. Br. 170/F1
Shippegan (gully), N. Br. 170/F1
Shippensburg, Pa. (17257) 294/H5
Shippenville, Pa. (16254) 294/D3
Shippingport‡, Pa. (15077) 294/B4
Shiprock, N. Mex. (87420) 274/A2
Ship Rock (peak), N. Mex. 274/A2
Shipshaw (riv.), Que. 172/F1
Shipshewana, Ind. (46565) 227/F1
Ship Shoal (isl.), Va. 307/S6
Shir (mt.), Iran 59/F3
Shir (mt.), Iran 66/J5
Shiragami (cape), Japan 81/J3
Shirane (mt.), Japan 81/J5
Shirane (mt.), Japan 81/H6
Shiraz, Iran, 54/J7
Shiraz, Iran 59/F4
Shiraz, Iran 66/H6
Shire (riv.), Moz. 118/E3
Shire (riv.), Malawi 115/G7
Shiremanstown‡, Pa. (17091) 294/J5
Shiretoko (cape), Japan 81/M1
Shiriya (cape), Japan 81/K3
Shirland, Ill. (61079) 222/D1
Shirley, Ark. (72153) 203/F2
Shirley, Ill. (61772) 222/E3
Shirley, Ind. (47384) 227/F5
Shirley△, Mass. (01464) 249/H2
Shirley, Mass. (01464) 249/H2
Shirley, Mo. (†63664) 261/L7
Shirley‡, N.Y. (11967) 276/P9
Shirley, W. Va. (26434) 313/E4
Shirley (basin), Wyo. 319/F3
Shirley Basin, Wyo. (82601) 319/F3
Shirley Center, Mass. (01465) 249/H2
Shirley City (Woodburn), Ind. (†46797) 227/H2
Shirley Mills△, Maine (04485) 242/D5
Shirley Mills, Maine (04485) 242/D5
Shirleysburg, Pa. (17260) 294/G5
Shiro, Texas (77876) 302/J7
Shiroishi, Japan 81/K4
Shirvan, Iran 59/G2
Shirvan, Iran 66/K2
Shirvan (riv.), Iran 66/E3
Shishaldin (vol.), Alaska 196/E4
Shishmaref, Alaska (99772) 196/E1
Shithatha, Iraq 59/D3
Shithatha, Iraq 66/C4
Shitike (creek), Oreg. 291/F3
Shiukwan, China 77/H7
Shively, Calif. (†95565) 204/B3
Shively, Ky. (40216) 237/K4
Shivers, Miss. (39164) 256/E7
Shivpuri, India 68/D3
Shivwits (plat.), Ariz. 198/B2
Shivwits Ind. Res., Utah 304/A6
Shizunai, Japan 81/L2
Shizuoka, Japan, 54/S6
Shizuoka, Japan 81/H6
Shkodër, Alb., 7/F4
Shkodër, Alb. 45/D5
Shoa (prov.), Eth. 111/G6
Shoal (riv.), Fla. 212/C6
Shoal (creek), Ill. 222/D5
Shoal (lake), Man. 179/A5
Shoal (lake), Man. 179/G5
Shoal (riv.), Man. 179/B2
Shoal (bay), N.S. 169/F4
Shoal (bay), Newf. 166/D2
Shoal (creek), Tenn. 237/F10
Shoal (creek), Utah 304/A6
Shoal Branch, Wading (riv.), N.J. 273/D4
Shoal Cove, Newf. 166/C3
Shoal Creek Drive‡, Mo. (†64801) 261/D8
Shoal Harbour, Newf. 166/C2
Shoalhaven (riv.), N.S.W. 97/E4
Shoal Lake, Man. 179/B4
Shoals, Ind. (47581) 227/D7
Shoals, N.C. (†27043) 281/J2
Shoals (isls.), N.H. 268/F6
Shoals, W. Va. (25562) 313/B6
Shoals Junction, S.C. (29680) 296/C3
Shoalwater (cape), Wash. 310/A4
Shoalwater Ind. Res., Wash. 310/B4
Shobando, China 77/E5
Shobara, Japan 81/F6
Shobonier, Ill. (62885) 222/D5
Shock, W. Va. (26638) 313/D5
Shoemakersville, Pa. (19555) 294/K4
Shoffner, Ark. (72154) 203/H2
Shohola, Pa. (18458) 294/N3
Shohsien, China 77/H4
Sholapur, India, 54/L8
Sholapur, India 68/D5
Sholes, Nebr. (†68771) 264/G2
Shona (isl.), Scot. 15/E6
Shongaloo, La. (71072) 238/D1
Shonkin, Mont. (59476) 262/F3
Shonto, Ariz. (86044) 198/E2
Shook, Mo. (63963) 261/M8
Shooting Creek, N.C. (†28904) 281/B4
Shopiere, Wis. (†53525) 317/H10
Shop Springs, Tenn. (37164) 237/J8
Shorapur, India 68/D5
Shoreacres, Br. Col. 184/J5
Shore Acres, Texas (†77571) 302/K2
Shore Acres-Sand Hills, Mass. (†02066) 249/F8
Shoreham, Mich. (†49085) 250/C6
Shoreham, Minn. (†56501) 254/C4
Shoreham, N.Y. (11786) 276/P8
Shoreham△, Vt. (05770) 268/A4
Shoreham, Vt. (05770) 268/A4
Shoreham-by-Sea, Eng. 13/G7
Shoreham-by-sea, 10/F5
Shoreview‡, Minn. (†55101) 254/G5
Shorewood‡, Ill. (60436) 222/E2
Shorewood, Minn. (†55331) 254/F5
Shorewood, Wis. (53211) 317/M1
Shorewood Hills, Mich. (†49125) 250/C7
Shorewood Hills, Wis. (†53701) 317/G9
Shorncliffe, Man. 179/E3
Short, Okla. (†72955) 288/S3
Short Beach, Conn. (†06405) 210/D3
Short Creek, Ohio (43989) 284/J5
Shortdale, Man. 179/A3
Shorter, Ala. (36075) 194/G6
Shorterville, Ala. (36373) 194/H7
Short Falls, N.H. (†03234) 268/E5
Short Hills, N.J. (07078) 273/E2
Shortleaf, Ala. (36733) 194/C6
Shortsville, N.Y. (14548) 276/F5
Shoshone, Calif. (92384) 204/J8
Shoshone (co.), Idaho 220/B2
Shoshone, Idaho (83352) 220/D7
Shoshone (falls), Idaho 220/D7
Shoshone, Nev. (†89301) 266/G4
Shoshone (mt.), Nev. 266/E6
Shoshone (lake), Wyo. 319/B1
Shoshone (riv.), Wyo. 319/D1
Shoshong, Botswana 118/D4
Shoshoni, Wyo. (82649) 319/D2
Shostka, U.S.S.R. 52/D4
Shotts, Scot. 15/E2
Shouldice, Alta. 182/D4
Shoultes, Wash. (†98270) 310/C2
Shouns, Tenn. (37689) 237/T8
Shoup, Idaho (83469) 220/D4
Shoval, Israel 65/B5
Shovel Lake, Minn. (†55785) 254/E4
Showak, Sudan 111/G5
Showell, Md. (21862) 245/T7
Show Low, Ariz. (85901) 198/F4
Shoyna, U.S.S.R. 52/F1
Shreve, Ohio (44676) 284/F4
Shreveport, La., 146/J6
Shreveport, La., 188/H4
Shreveport, La. (*71101) 238/C1
Shrewsbury, Eng. 13/E5
Shrewsbury, 10/E4
Shrewsbury△, Mass. (01545) 249/H3
Shrewsbury, Mo. (†63101) 261/P3
Shrewsbury, N.J. (07701) 273/E3
Shrewsbury, Pa. (17361) 294/J6
Shrewsbury△, Vt. (†05738) 268/B4
Shrewsbury, Vt. (†05738) 268/B4
Shropshire (Salop) (co.), Eng. 13/E5
Shrule, Ire. 17/C4
Shubenacadie, N.S. 169/E3
Shubenacadie (lake), N.S. 169/E4
Shubenacadie (riv.), N.S. 169/E3
Shubert, Nebr. (68437) 264/J4
Shubuta, Miss. (39360) 256/G7
Shue (creek), S. Dak. 298/N5
Shu'eib, Wadi (dry riv.), Jordan 65/D4
Shueyville, Iowa (†52401) 229/K5
Shu'fat, Jordan 65/C4
Shukpan (mt.), Wash. 310/D2
Shulerville, S.C. (29480) 296/H5
Shullsburg, Wis. (53586) 317/F10
Shumagin (isls.), Alaska 196/G4
Shumen (Kolarovgrad), Bulg. 45/H4
Shumerlya, U.S.S.R. 52/G3
Shumway, Ill. (62461) 222/E4
Shunat Nimrin (Nimrin), Jordan 65/D4
Shungnak, Alaska (99773) 196/G1
Shungnak Village‡, Alaska (†99773) 196/G1
Shungopavy (Shongopovi), Ariz. (†86043) 198/E3
Shunk, Pa. (17768) 294/J2
Shunock (riv.), Conn. 210/H3
Shuqaiq, Saudi Ar. 59/D6
Shuqra, P.D.R. Yemen 59/E7
Shuqualak, Miss. (39361) 256/G5
Shur (riv.), Iran 66/J7
Shuri, Ryukyu Is. 81/N6
Shush, Iran 66/F4
Shushan, N.Y. (12873) 276/O4
Shushartie Bay, Br. Col. 184/C5
Shushenskoye, U.S.S.R. 48/K4
Shushtar, Iran 66/F4
Shusp, Iran 66/L5
Shustar, Iran 59/E3
Shuswap (lake), 163/E5
Shuswap (lake), Br. Col. 184/H4
Shutesbury△, Mass. (01072) 249/E3
Shuttle Meadow (res.), Conn. 210/D2
Shuweika, Jordan 65/C3
Shuya, U.S.S.R. 52/F3
Shuyak (isl.), Alaska 196/H3
Shwangcheng, China 77/L2
Shwangliao, China 77/K3
Shwangyashan, China 77/M2
Shwebo, Burma 72/B2
Shwegyin, Burma 72/C3
Shweli (riv.), Burma 72/C2
Shwenyaung, Burma 72/C2
Shyok, India 68/D2
Siahan (range), Pak. 59/H4
Siahan (range), Pak. 68/A3
Siah Kuh (mt.), Iran 66/L3
Siaho, China 77/F4
Siak (riv.), Indon. 85/C5
Siaksriindrapura, Indon. 85/C5
Siakwan, China 77/F6
Sialkot, Pak. 59/K3
Sialkot, Pak. 68/C2
Siam (gulf), 3/Q5
Siam (gulf), 54/O9
Siam (Thailand), 54/O8
Siam (gulf), Cambodia 72/D5
Siam (gulf), Thai. 72/D5
Siam (gulf), S. Vietnam 72/D5
Sian, China, 3/Q4
Sian, China, 54/O6
Sian, China 77/G5
Siangfan, China 77/H5
Siang Kiang (riv.), China 77/H6
Siangtan, China, 54/P7
Siangtan, China 77/H6
Siangyin, China 77/H6
Siapa (riv.), Ven. 124/E7
Siapu, China 77/K6
Siargao (isl.), Phil. 82/F6
Siargao (isl.), Phil. 85/H4
Siasconset, Mass. (02564) 249/P7
Siasi, Phil. 82/C8
Siasi (isl.), Phil. 82/C8
Siátista, Greece 45/E5
Siaton, Phil. 82/D6
Siaton (pt.), Phil. 82/D6
Siau (isl.), Indon. 85/H5
Šiauliai, U.S.S.R. 48/C4
Šiauliai, U.S.S.R. 52/B3
Šiauliai, U.S.S.R. 53/B3
Šiauliai, U.S.S.R., 7/G3
Sib, Iran 66/N7
Sibalom, Phil. 82/C5
Sibanicú, Cuba 158/G3
Sibay, U.S.S.R. 52/J4
Sibay (isl.), Phil. 82/C5
Sibbald, Alta. 182/E4
Šibenik, Yugo. 45/C4
Siberia, Ind. (47582) 227/D8
Siberia (reg.), U.S.S.R. 48/M3
Siberia (reg.), U.S.S.R., 3/P2
Siberia (reg.), U.S.S.R., 4/C2
Siberia (reg.), U.S.S.R., 54/N4
Sibert, Ky. (40984) 237/O6
Siberut (isl.), Indon., 54/N10
Siberut (isl.), Indon. 85/B6
Siberut (str.), Indon. 85/B6
Sibi, Pak. 59/J4
Sibi, Pak. 68/B3
Sibi, Pak., 54/K7
Sibiti, Rep. of Congo 115/B4
Sibiu, Rum., 7/G4
Sibiu, Rum. 45/G3
Sibley, Ill. (61773) 222/E3
Sibley, Iowa (51249) 229/B2
Sibley, La. (71073) 238/D1
Sibley (co.), Minn. 254/D6
Sibley, Miss. (39165) 256/B8
Sibley, Mo. (64088) 261/S5
Sibley, N. Dak. (†58429) 283/P5
Sibley Prov. Park, Ont. 175/C3
Sibley Prov. Park, Ont. 177/H5
Sibolga, Indon., 54/N9
Sibolga, Indon. 85/B5
Siboney, Cuba 158/J4
Sibsagar, India 68/H3
Sibu, Malaysia, 54/P9
Sibu, Malaysia 85/E5
Sibube, C. Rica 154/F6
Sibuco, Phil. 82/C7
Sibuguey (bay), Phil. 82/D7
Sibundoy-Las Casas, Col. 126/B7
Sibutu (passg.), Phil. 82/B8
Sibutu, Malaysia 85/E5
Sibutu (passg.), Phil. 85/F4
Sibutu Group (isls.), Phil. 82/B8
Sibuyan (isl.), Phil. 82/D4
Sibuyan (sea), Phil. 82/D4
Sibuyan (isl.), Phil. 85/G3
Sibuyan (sea), Phil. 85/G3
Sicamous, Br. Col. 184/H5
Sicasica, Bol. 136/B5
Siccha, Bol. 136/C6
Sichang, China 77/F6
Sicilia (Sicily) (isl.), Italy, 7/F5
Sicily (reg.), Italy 34/E6
Sicily (isl.), Italy, 7/F5
Sicily (isl.), Italy 34/E6
Sicily (str.), Italy 34/D6
Sicily Island, La. (71368) 238/G3
Sicklerville, N.J. (08081) 273/D4
Sico (riv.), Hond. 154/E3
Sicuani, Peru 128/G10
Sidamo (prov.), Eth. 111/G7
Sideby, Fin. 18/M5
Side Lake, Minn. (55781) 254/E3
Sidell, Ill. (61876) 222/F4
Siderno, Italy 34/F5
Sídheros (cape), Greece 45/H8
Sidhi, India 68/E4
Sidhirókastron, Greece 45/F5
Sidhpur, India 68/C4
Sidi Barrani, U.A.R. 59/A3
Sidi Barrani, U.A.R. 111/E1
Sidi-bel-Abbès, Alg. 106/D1
Sidi-bel-Abbès, 102/C1
Sidi Ifni Mor. 102/B2
Sidi Ifni, Mor. 106/B3
Sidi-Kacem, Mor. 106/C2
Siding Springs, N.S.W. 97/E2
Sidlaw (hills), Scot. 15/K6
Sidley (mt.), Ant. 5/B12
Sidmouth, Br. Col. 184/J5
Sidmouth, Eng. 13/D7
Sidmouth, 10/E5
Sidmouth (cape), Queens. 95/C2
Sidnaw, Mich. (49961) 250/G2
Sidney, Ark. (72577) 203/G1
Sidney, Br. Col. 184/K3
Sidney, Ill. (61877) 222/E3
Sidney, Ind. (46566) 227/F2
Sidney, Iowa (51652) 229/B7
Sidney△, Maine (†04330) 242/D7
Sidney, Man. 179/C5
Sidney, Mich. (48885) 250/D5
Sidney, Mont. (59270) 262/M3
Sidney, N.Y. (13838) 276/K6
Sidney, Nebr. (69162) 264/B3
Sidney, Ohio (45365) 284/B5
Sidney, W. Va. (†25570) 313/B6
Sidney Center, N.Y. (13839) 276/K6
Sidney Lanier (lake), Ga. 216/D2
Sidoardjo, Indon. 85/K2
Sidon, Ark. (72155) 203/G3
Sidon, Miss. (38954) 256/D4
Sidon (Saida), Leb. 65/F6
Sidonia, Tenn. (†38255) 237/D8
Sidra (gulf), Libya 111/C1
Sidra (gulf), 102/D1
Siedlce, Poland 47/F2
Siegas, N. Br. 170/C1
Siegburg, W. Ger. 22/B3
Siegen, W. Ger. 22/C3
Siemianowice Śląskie, Poland 47/B4
Siemiatycze, Poland 47/F2
Siem Pang, Cambodia 72/E4
Siem Reap, Cambodia 72/D4
Siena, Italy, 7/F4
Siena (prov.), Italy 34/C3
Siena, Italy 34/C3
Sienyang, China 77/G5
Sieper, La. (71472) 238/E4
Sieradz, Poland 47/D3
Sierning, Austria 41/C2
Sierpc, Poland 47/D2
Sierra (co.), Calif. 204/E4
Sierra (co.), N. Mex. 274/B5
Sierra Ancha (mts.), Ariz. 198/D5
Sierra Apache (mts.), Ariz. 198/E5
Sierra Army Depot, Calif. 204/E3
Sierra Blanca (peak), N. Mex. 274/D5
Sierra Blanca, Texas (79851) 302/B11
Sierra City, Calif. (96125) 204/E4
Sierra Colorada, Arg. 143/C5
Sierra de Guadarrama (mts.), Spain, 7/D4
Sierra Diablo (mts.), Texas 302/C10
Sierra Gorda, Chile 138/B4
Sierra Grande, Arg. 143/C5
Sierra Leone, 3/J5
SIERRA LEONE, 106/B7
SIERRA LEONE, 102/A4
Sierra Madre, Calif. (91024) 204/D10
Sierra Madre (mts.), Phil. 82/D2
Sierra Madre (mts.), Wyo. 319/E4
Sierra Mojada, Mex. 150/H3
Sierra Morena (mts.), Spain, 7/D5
Sierra Nevada (mts.), 188/B3
Sierra Nevada (mts.), Calif. 204/E4
Sierra Nevada (mts.), Spain, 7/D5
Sierra Oscura (mts.), N. Mex. 274/C5
Sierra Vieja (mts.), Texas 302/C11
Sierraville, Calif. (96126) 204/E4
Sierra Vista, Ariz. (85635) 198/E7
Sierre, Switz. 39/D4
Siesta (key), Fla. 212/D4
Siete Cerros, Urug. 145/E5
Siete Puntas (riv.), Par. 144/D4
Sife (lake), Turkey 63/F3
Sífnos (isl.), Greece 45/G7
Sifton, Man. 179/B3
Sigean, France 28/E6
Sigel, Ill. (62462) 222/E4
Sigel, Pa. (15860) 294/D3
Siggenthal, Switz. 39/F1
Sighet, Rum. 45/F2
Sighetul-Marmației, Rum. 45/F2
Sighișoara, Rum. 45/G2
Sigiriya, Ceylon 68/E7
Sigli, Indon. 85/B4
Siglufjördhur, Ice. 21/C1
Sigmaringen, W. Ger. 22/C4
Sigmundsherberg, Austria 41/C2
Signal Hill, Calif. (90806) 204/C11
Signal Mountain, Tenn. (37377) 237/L10
Signau, Switz. 39/E3
Sigourney, Iowa (52591) 229/J6
Sigriswil, Switz. 39/E3
Sigsig, Ec. 128/C4
Sigtuna, Sweden 18/H1
Siguanea (bay), Cuba 158/B2
Siguatepeque, Hond. 154/D3
Sigüe, Ec. 128/D2
Sigüenza, Spain 33/E2
Siguiri, Guinea 106/C6
Sigulda, U.S.S.R. 53/C2
Sigurd, Utah (84657) 304/B5
Sihlsee (lake), Switz. 39/G2
Sihuas, Peru 128/D7
Siika (riv.), Fin. 18/O4
Siipyy (Sideby), Fin. 18/M5
Siirt, Turkey 59/D2
Siirt (prov.), Turkey 63/J4
Siirt, Turkey 63/J4
Sikanni Chief (riv.), Br. Col. 184/F1
Sikanni River, Br. Col. 184/F1
Sikar, India 68/D3
Sikasso, 102/B3
Sikasso, Mali 106/C6
Sikes, La. (71473) 238/F2
Sikeston, Mo. (63801) 261/N9
Sikhote-Alin' (range), U.S.S.R. 48/O5
Sikhote-Alin (range), U.S.S.R., 54/S5
Si Kiang (riv.), China, 54/O7
Si Kiang (riv.), China 77/H7
Sikkim (state), India, 54/M7
Sikkim (state), India 68/F3
Siklós, Hung. 41/E4
Siktyakh, U.S.S.R. 48/N3
Sil (riv.), Spain 33/C1
Silao, Mex. 150/J6
Silas, Ala. (36919) 194/B7
Silat Dhahr, Jordan 65/C3
Silay, Phil. 82/D5
Silchar, India 68/G4
Şile, Turkey 63/C2
Silenen, Switz. 39/G3
Siler City, N.C. (27344) 281/L3
Silerton, Tenn. (38377) 237/D10
Silesia, Mont. (59080) 262/H5
Silet, Alg. 106/E4
Siletz, Oreg. (97380) 291/D3
Silex, Mo. (63377) 261/K4
Silhouette (isl.), Seych. 118/H5
Silica, Kans. (†67526) 232/D3
Silifke, Turkey 59/B2
Silifke, Turkey 63/E4
Siliguri, India 68/F3
Silin, China 77/G7
Silinhot, China 77/J3
Silistra, Bulg. 45/H3
Silivri, Turkey 63/C2
Siljan (lake), Sweden 18/J6
Silkeborg, Den. 18/F8
Silkeborg, Den. 21/C5
Sillajguay (mt.), Bol. 136/A6
Sillajguay, Cordillera (mt.), Chile 138/B2
Silleda, Spain 33/B1
Sillery, Que. 172/J3
Sillian, Austria 41/B3
Sillikers, N. Br. 170/E2
Silloth, Eng. 13/D3
Siloam, Ga. (30665) 216/F3
Siloam, Ky. (†41175) 237/R3
Siloam, N.C. (27047) 281/H2
Siloam Springs, Ark. (72761) 203/B1
Siloam Springs, Mo. (†65775) 261/H9
Silop (riv.), Iran 66/M8
Silopi, Turkey 63/K4
Silsbee, Texas (77656) 302/K7
Sils im Domleschg, Switz. 39/H3
Silt, Colo. (81652) 208/D4
Siltcoos, Oreg. (†97441) 291/C4
Silton, Sask. 181/G5
Šilutė, U.S.S.R. 53/A3
Silva, Mo. (63964) 261/M8
Silva, N. Dak. (58375) 283/L3
Silvan, Turkey 63/J3
Silvana, Wash. (98287) 310/C2
Silvânia, Braz. 132/D7
Silvaplana, Switz. 39/J4
Silva Porto, Angola 115/C6
Silva Porto, 102/D6
Silvassa, India 68/B4
Silver (creek), Ariz. 198/E4
Silver (bank), Turks Caicos Is. 156/E2
Silver (creek), Ill. 222/D5
Silver (creek), Ind. 227/F8

438 Silver

Silver, Man. 179/E4
Silver (lake), Mass. 249/L4
Silver (lake), N.Y. 276/N1
Silver (creek), Oreg. 291/F4
Silver (creek), Oreg. 291/H4
Silver (lake), Oreg. 291/G4
Silver (lake), Oreg. 291/H4
Silver (lake), Wash. 310/C4
Silverado, Calif. (92676) 204/E11
Silver Bank (passg.), Turks Caicos Is. 156/D2
Silver Bay, Minn. (55614) 254/G3
Silver Beach, Alta. 182/D3
Silver Bell, Ariz. (85270) 198/D6
Silver Bow (co.), Mont. 262/D5
Silver Bow Park, Mont. (†59701) 262/D4
Silver City, Ga. (†30501) 216/D2
Silver City, Idaho (†83650) 220/B6
Silver City, Iowa (51571) 229/B6
Silver City, Miss. (39166) 256/C4
Silver City, N. Mex., 188/E4
Silver City, N. Mex. (88061) 274/A6
Silver City, Nev. (89428) 266/B3
Silver City, S. Dak. (57781) 298/B5
Silver Cliff, Colo. (81249) 208/J6
Silver Creek, Ga. (30173) 216/B2
Silver Creek, Minn. (55380) 254/D5
Silver Creek, Miss. (39663) 256/D7
Silver Creek‡, Mo. (†64801) 261/D9
Silver Creek, N.Y. (14136) 276/B5
Silver Creek, Nebr. (68663) 264/G3
Silver Creek, Wash. (98585) 310/C4
Silverdale, Br. Col. 184/L3
Silverdale, Kans. (67005) 232/F4
Silverdale, N.C. (†28539) 281/P5
Silverdale‡, Pa. (18962) 294/M5
Silverdale, Wash. (98383) 310/A2
Silver Grove, Ky. (41085) 237/T3
Silver Heights, Alta. 182/E3
Silverhill, Ala. (36576) 194/C9
Silverhill, Ky. (41467) 237/P5
Silver Hill, W. Va. (†26155) 313/E3
Silver Hill Suitland, Md. (20023) 245/F5
Silver Island (mts.), Utah 304/A3
Silver Lake, Ind. (46982) 227/F2
Silver Lake, Kans. (66539) 232/G2
Silver Lake, Mass. (†01887) 249/C5
Silver Lake, Mass. (†02360) 249/L5
Silver Lake, Minn. (55381) 254/D6
Silver Lake, Mo. (†63775) 261/M7
Silver Lake, N.H. (03875) 268/E4
Silver Lake, Ohio (†44221) 284/G3
Silver Lake, Oreg. (97638) 291/F4
Silverlake, Wash. (98645) 310/C4
Silver Lake, Wis. (53170) 317/K10
Silverleaf, N. Dak. (†58436) 283/O7
Silvermine (riv.), Conn. 210/B4
Silvermine (mts.), Ire. 17/E6
Silvermines, Ire. 17/E6
Silver Park, Sask. 181/G3
Silverpeak, Nev. (89047) 266/D5
Silver Peak (range), Nev. 266/D5
Silver Plains, Man. 179/E5
Silver Plume, Colo. (80476) 208/H3
Silver Point, Tenn. (38582) 237/K8
Silver Run, Ala. (†36268) 194/G3
Silver Run, Md. (†21157) 245/K2
Silvers Mills, Maine (†04930) 242/E5
Silver Spring, Md. (*20901) 245/F4
Silver Springs, Fla. (32688) 212/D2
Silver Springs, N.Y. (14550) 276/E5
Silver Star, Mont. (59751) 262/D5
Silverstreet, S.C. (29145) 296/D3
Silverthorne, Colo. (80435) 208/G3
Silverton, Aust. 88/G6
Silverton, Br. Col. 184/J5
Silverton, Colo. (81433) 208/D7
Silverton, N.S.W. 97/A2
Silverton, Ohio (†45201) 284/C9
Silverton, Oreg. (97381) 291/B3
Silverton, Texas (79257) 302/C3
Silverton, W. Va. (†26164) 313/C5
Silverton, Wash. (†98252) 310/D2
Silverton Station, Man. 179/A4
Silverville, Ind. (†47470) 227/D7
Silverwood, Alta. 182/A2
Silverwood, Ind. (†47952) 227/C5
Silverwood, Mich. (48760) 250/F5
Silves, Port. 33/B4
Silvia, Col. 126/B6
Silvies, Oreg. (†97720) 291/H3
Silvies (riv.), Oreg. 291/H4
Silvis, Ill. (61282) 222/C2
Silvretta (mts.), Switz. 39/K3
Sim (cape), Mor. 106/B2
Simanggang, Malaysia 85/E5
Simara (isl.), Phil. 82/D4
Simarańa, Ven. 124/G5
Simav, Turkey 63/C3
Simav (riv.), Turkey 63/C3
Simcoe (co.), Ont. 177/E3
Simcoe, Ont. 177/D5
Simcoe (lake), Ont. 177/E3
Simcoe, N. Dak. (†58741) 283/J3
Simen (mts.), Eth. 111/G5
Simeonovgrad (Maritsa), Bulg. 45/H4
Simeto (riv.), Italy 34/E6
Simeulue (isl.), Indon., 54/N9
Simeulue (isl.), Indon. 85/A5
Simferopol', U.S.S.R. 48/D5
Simferopol', U.S.S.R. 52/D6
Simferopol', U.S.S.R., 7/H4
Sími, Greece 45/H7
Sími (isl.), Greece 45/H7
Simikot, Nepal 68/E3
Similkameen, Br. Col. 184/G5
Similkameen (riv.), Wash. 310/F1
Simitl, Col. 126/C4
Simi Valley, Calif. (93065) 204/G9
Simla, Colo. (80835) 208/M4
Simla, India, 54/L6
Simla, India 68/D2
Şimleu Silvaniei, Rum. 45/F2
Simme (riv.), Switz. 39/D3
Simmern, W. Ger. 22/B4
Simmesport, La. (71369) 238/G5
Simmie, Sask. 181/C6
Simmons, Mo. (†65689) 261/H8
Simms, Mont. (59477) 262/E3
Simnasho, Oreg. (†97761) 291/F3
Simo (lake), Fin. 18/P3
Simo (riv.), Fin. 18/O4
Simojovel de Allende, Mex. 150/N8
Simola, Fin. 18/P6
Simon (lake), Que. 172/B4
Simonds, N. Br. 170/C2
Simonette (riv.), Alta. 182/A2
Simonstown, S. Africa 118/E7
Simonsville, Vt. (†05143) 268/B5
Simonszand (isl.), Neth. 27/J1
Simoom Sound, Br. Col. 184/D5
Simplício Mendes, Braz. 132/F4
Simplon (tunnel), Italy 34/A1
Simplon, Switz. 39/F4
Simplon (pass), Switz. 39/F4
Simplon (tunnel), Switz. 39/F4
Simpson (des.), Australia, 87/D8
Simpson (des.), Aust. 88/F5
Simpson (riv.), Chile 138/E6
Simpson, Ill. (62985) 222/E6
Simpson, Kans. (67478) 232/E2
Simpson (co.), Ky. 237/H7
Simpson, Ky. (†41301) 237/P5
Simpson, La. (71474) 238/D4
Simpson, Minn. (†55901) 254/F7
Simpson (co.), Miss. 256/E7
Simpson, Mont. (59541) 262/F2
Simpson, N.C. (27879) 281/P3
Simpson (pen.), N.W.T. 187/K3
Simpson (des.), No. Terr. 93/E8
Simpson (des.), S. Aust. 94/E1
Simpson (des.), Queens. 95/A5
Simpson, Pa. (18407) 294/L2
Simpson, Sask. 181/F4
Simpson, W. Va. (26435) 313/F4
Simpson Park (mts.), Nev. 266/E3
Simpsons, Va. (24163) 307/H6
Simpsonville, Ky. (40067) 237/L4
Simpsonville, S.C. (29681) 296/C2
Simrishamn, Sweden 18/J9
Sims, Ark. (71969) 203/C4
Sims, Ill. (62886) 222/E5
Sims, Ind. (46983) 227/F3
Sims, N.C. (27880) 281/N3
Sims (lake), Newf. 166/A3
Simsboro, Ark. (†72323) 203/K3
Simsboro, La. (71275) 238/E1
Simsbury▵, Conn. (06070) 210/D1
Simsbury, Conn. (06070) 210/D1
Sims Chapel, Ala. (36577) 194/B8
Simunul (isl.), Phil. 82/B8
Sinabang, Indon. 85/B5
Sinai (mt.), Grenada 161/D8
Sinai (pen.), 102/F2
Sinai (pen.), U.A.R. 59/B4
Sinai (mt.), U.A.R. 111/F2
Sinai (pen.), U.A.R. 111/F2
Sinai, S. Dak. (57061) 298/P5
Sinaia, Rum. 45/G3
Sinait, Phil. 82/C2
Sinaloa (state), Mex. 150/F4
Sinaloa de Leyva, Mex. 150/E4
Sinamaica, Ven. 124/B2
Sinawen, Libya 111/B1
Sincanli, Turkey 63/D3
Sincé, Col. 126/C3
Sincelejo, Col. 126/C3
Sinchu, China 77/K7
Sinclair (lake), Ga. 216/F4
Sinclair, Maine (04779) 242/G1
Sinclair, Man. 179/A5
Sinclair (head), N.Z. 101/A3
Sinclair, Wyo. (82334) 319/E4
Sinclair Mills, Br. Col. 184/G3
Sinclair's (bay), Scot. 15/K2
Sinclairville, N.Y. (14782) 276/B6
Sind (reg.), Pak. 59/J4
Sind (prov.), Pak. 68/B3
Sind (reg.), Pak. 68/B3
Sindal, Den. 21/D3
Sindañgan, Phil. 82/D6
Sindañgan (bay), Phil. 82/D6
Sindelfingen, W. Ger. 22/C4
Sindi, U.S.S.R. 53/C1
Sindirgi, Turkey 63/C3
Sindjai, Indon. 85/G7
Sines, Port. 33/B4
Sines (cape), Port. 33/B4
Sinfra, Ivory Coast 106/C7
Singa, 102/F3
Singa, Sudan 59/B7
Singac, N.J. (†07424) 273/B2
Singapore, 3/Q5
Singapore, 54/O9
Singapore (str.), Malaysia 72/F6
SINGAPORE, 72
Singapore (cap.), Sing. 72/F6
Singaradja, Indon., 54/P10
Singaradja, Indon. 85/F7
Sing Buri, Thai. 72/D4
Singen, W. Ger. 22/C5
Singer, La. (70660) 238/D5
Singers Glen, Va. (22850) 307/K3
Singhampton, Ont. 177/D3
Singida (reg.), Tanz. 115/F4
Singida, Tanz. 115/F4
Singi Obo, China 77/C5
Singkaling Hkamti, Burma 72/B1
Singkawang, Indon. 85/D5
Singkep (isl.), Indon. 85/D6
Singleton, Aust. 88/J6
Singleton, N.S.W. 97/F3
Singleton (mt.), No. Terr. 93/B6
Singora (Songkhla), Thai. 72/D6
Singsås, Norway 18/G5
Singsingsia, China 77/D3
Singtai, China 77/H4
Singu, Burma 72/C2
Singur, India 68/F1
Sinhailien (Lienyünkang), China 77/J5
Sinhsien, China 77/H4
Sinhwa, China 77/H6
Sining, China, 54/O6
Sining, China 77/F4
Siniscola, Italy 34/B4
Sinj, Yugo. 45/C4
Sinjar, Jebel (mts.), Syria 63/J4
Sinjar, Iraq 66/B2
Sinjar, Jebel (mts.), Iraq 66/B2
Sinjil, Jordan 65/C3
Sinkao Shan (mt.), China 77/K7
Sinkat, Sudan 59/C6
Sinkat, Sudan 111/G4
Sinkiang (reg.), China, 3/P3
Sinkiang (reg.), China, 54/M5
Sinkiang-Uigur (aut. reg.), China 77/B3
Sinking Spring, Ohio (45172) 284/D7
Sinking Spring, Pa. (19608) 294/K5
Sinks Grove, W. Va. (24976) 313/F7
Sinnai, Italy 34/B5
Sinnamahoning, Pa. (15861) 294/G3
Sinnamary, Fr. Gui., 120/E2
Sinnamary, Fr. Gui. 131/E3
Sinnamary (riv.), Fr. Gui. 131/E3
Sinneh (Sanandaj), Iran 66/E3
Sinnemahoning (creek), Pa. 294/F3
Sinnett, Sask. 181/G4
Sînnicolau Mare, Rum. 45/E2
Sinnûris, U.A.R. 111/J3
Sinoe (Greenville), Liberia 106/C8
Sinoia, 102/E6
Sinoia, Rhod. 118/D3
Sinop, Turkey 59/C1
Sinop (prov.), Turkey 63/F2
Sinop, Turkey 63/F2
Sinop (cape), Turkey 63/F1
Sinop, Turkey, 54/G5
Sinp'o, N. Korea 81/D4
Sins, Switz. 39/F2
Sinsiang, China, 54/P6
Sinsiang, China 77/H4
Sintaluta, Sask. 181/H5
Sint-Amandsberg, Belg. 27/D6
Sint-Andries, Belg. 27/C6
Sintang, Indon. 85/E5
Sint Anna, Neth. Ant. 161/D10
Sint Anna (bay), Neth. Ant. 161/F9
Sint Annaland, Neth. 27/E5
Sint Christoffel (mt.), Neth. Ant. 161/F8
Sint Jacobiparochie, Neth. 27/H2
Sint Jan, Neth. Ant. 161/D8
Sint Joris (bay), Neth. Ant. 161/G9
Sint Kruis, Neth. Ant. 161/F8
Sint-Lenaarts, Belg. 27/F6
Sint Martha, Neth. Ant. 161/F8
Sint Michiel, Neth. Ant. 161/F9
Sint Nicolaas, Neth. Ant. 161/E10
Sint-Niklaas, Belg. 27/E6
Sinton, Texas (78387) 302/G9
Sint-Pieters-Leeuw, Belg. 27/B9
Sintra, Port. 33/B3
Sint-Truiden, Belg. 27/G7
Sint Willebrordus, Neth. Ant. 161/F8
Sinú (riv.), Col. 126/B3
Sinuapa, Hond. 154/C3
Sinŭiju, N. Korea 81/B3
Sinyang, China 77/H5
Sió (canal), Hung. 41/E3
Siófok, Hung. 41/E3
Siokun, Phil. 82/D7
Siokun, Phil. 85/G4
Sion, Alta. 182/C3
Sion, Switz. 39/D4
Sion Mills, N. Ire. 17/G2
Sioux (co.), Iowa 229/A2
Sioux (co.), N. Dak. 283/H7
Sioux (co.), Nebr. 264/A2
Sioux Center, Iowa (51250) 229/A2
Sioux City, Iowa, 146/J5
Sioux City, Iowa, 188/G2
Sioux City, Iowa (*51101) 229/A3
Sioux Falls, S. Dak., 146/J5
Sioux Falls, S. Dak., 188/G2
Sioux Falls, S. Dak. (*57101) 298/R6
Sioux Lookout, 163/G6
Sioux Lookout, Ont. 175/B2
Sioux Lookout, Ont. 177/G4
Sioux Narrows, Ont. 177/F5
Sioux Rapids, Iowa (50585) 229/C3
Sioux Valley, Minn. (†51347) 254/C7
Sipacate, Guat. 154/B4
Sipalay, Phil. 82/D6
Sipaliwini (riv.), Sur. 131/C4
Sipapo (riv.), Ven. 124/E5
Siparia, Trinidad Tobago 156/G5
Siparia, Trinidad Tobago 161/B11
Sipí, Col. 126/B5
Sipiwesk, Man. 179/J3
Sipiwesk (lake), Man. 179/J3
Siple (mt.), Ant. 5/B12
Sipocot, Phil. 82/D4
Sipora (isl.), Indon. 85/B6
Sippola, Fin. 18/P6
Sipsey, Ala. (35584) 194/D3
Sipsey (riv.), Ala. 194/B4
Sipsey Fork (riv.), Ala. 194/D2
Sip Song Chau Thai (mts.), N. Vietnam 72/D2
Siquijor (isl.), Phil. 82/D6
Siquirres, C. Rica 154/F5
Siquisique, Ven. 124/D2
Siracuas, Par. 144/B3
Siracusa (Syracuse), Italy 34/E6
Sirajganj, Pak. 68/F4
Şiran, Turkey 63/H2
Sirdar, Br. Col. 184/J5
Sir Edward Pellew Group (isls.), Aust. 88/F3
Sir Edward Pellew Group (isls.), No. Terr. 93/E3
Siren, Wis. (54872) 317/B4
Siret (riv.), 7/G4
Siret, Rum. 45/GI
Siret (riv.), Rum. 45/H2
Sir Francis Drake (chan.), V.I. (Br.) 161/D4
Sirhan, Wadi (dry riv.), Saudi Ar. 59/C3
Şiria, Rum. 45/E2
Sirik, Iran 66/K7
Sirik (cape), Malaysia 85/E5
Siris, Jordan 65/C3
Sirius (pt.), Alaska 196/J4
Sir James MacBrien (mt.), N.W.T. 187/F3
Sirjan, Iran 59/G4
Sirjan, Iran 66/J6
Sir John's (peak), Jam. 158/K6
Sir Johns Run, W. Va. (†25411) 313/K3
Sir Joseph Banks Group (isls.), S. Aust. 94/E6
Sirnach, Switz. 39/G2
Şirnak, Turkey 63/K4
Sirohi, India 68/C4
Sironj, India 68/D4
Síros (isl.), Greece 45/G7
Sir R.A. Squires Mem. Park, Newf. 166/C4
Sirri (isl.), Iran 66/J8
Sirsa, India 68/D3
Sir Sandford (mt.), Br. Col. 184/H4
Sirsi, India 68/D6
Siruma, Phil. 82/D3
Širvintos, U.S.S.R. 53/C3
Sisak, Yugo. 45/C3
Sisaket, Thai. 72/E4
Sisi (cape), Indon. 85/F6
Sisib (lake), Man. 179/C2
Sisikon, Switz. 39/G3
Siskiwit (bay), Mich. 250/E1
Siskiyou (co.), Calif. 204/C2
Siskiyou (mts.), Calif. 204/C2
Siskiyou, Oreg. (†97520) 291/E5
Siskiyou (mts.), Oreg. 291/D6
Sisophon, Cambodia 72/D4
Sissach, Switz. 39/E2
Sisseton, S. Dak. (57262) 298/R2
Sissiboo (riv.), N.S. 169/C4
Sisson Branch, Tobique (riv.), N. Br. 170/C1
Sisson Ridge, N. Br. 170/C2
Sissonville, W. Va. (25320) 313/C5
Sister Bay, Wis. (54234) 317/M5
Sister Lakes, Mich. (49047) 250/C6
Sisteron, France 28/G5
Sisters, The (isls.), N.Z. 101/D6
Sisters, Oreg. (97759) 291/F3
Sistersville, W. Va. (26175) 313/D3
Sitapur, India 68/E3
Sites, Calif. (†95979) 204/C4
Sitges, Spain 33/G2
Sithoniá (pen.), Greece 45/F5
Sitía, Greece 45/H8
Sitio da Abadia, Braz. 132/E6
Sitionuevo, Col. 126/C2
Sitka, Alaska, 146/E4
Sitka, Alaska, 188/D6
Sitka, Alaska (99835) 196/M1
Sitka (sound), Alaska 196/M1
Sitka, Ark. (†72482) 203/H1
Sitka, Kans. (†67831) 232/C4
Sitka, U.S., 4/D16
Sitkalidak (isl.), Alaska 196/H3
Sitka Nat'l Mon., Alaska 196/M1
Sitkinak (isl.), Alaska 196/H3
Sitkinak (str.), Alaska 196/H3
Sitkum, Oreg. (†97458) 291/D4
Sittang (riv.), Burma 72/C3
Sittard, Neth. 27/H6
Sittingbourne and Milton, Eng. 13/H6
Sittwe, Burma, 54/N7
Sittwe, Burma 72/B2
Situbondo, Indon. 85/L2
Siuna, Nic. 154/E4
Siushui, China 77/J6
Siuslaw (riv.), Oreg. 291/D4
Sivand, Iran 66/H5
Sivas, Turkey 59/C1
Sivas (prov.), Turkey 63/G3
Sivas, Turkey 63/G3
Sivas, Turkey, 54/G6
Sivasli, Turkey 63/C3
Siverek, Turkey 63/H4
Sivrihisar, Turkey 63/D3
Sivry, Belg. 27/E8
Siwa, 102/E2
Siwa, U.A.R. 111/E2
Siwa (oasis), U.A.R. 111/E2
Sixes, Oreg. (97476) 291/C5
Sixes (riv.), Oreg. 291/C5
Six Lakes, Mich. (48886) 250/D5
Six Mens, Barb. 161/B8
Six Mile, S.C. (29682) 296/B2
Sixmilebridge, Ire. 17/D6
Sixmilecross, N. Ire. 17/H2
Six Mile Run, Pa. (16679) 294/F5
Six Roads, N. Br. 170/F1
Six Run (creek), N.C. 281/N4
Sixteen, Mont. (†59642) 262/F4
Sixteen Island Lake, Que. 172/C4
Sixth Cataract, Sudan 102/F3
Sixth Cataract, Sudan 59/B6
Sixth Cataract, Sudan 111/F4
Siyah Kuh (mt.), Iraq 66/D2
Siyeh (mt.), Mont. 262/C2
Sizerock, Ky. (41762) 237/P6
Sizuoka (pref.), Japan 81/H6
Sjaelland (isl.), Den. 18/H9
Sjaelland (isl.), Den. 21/E6
Sjaellands (pt.), Den. 21/E5
Skaar, N. Dak. (†59270) 283/C5
Skaarup, Den. 21/D7
Skadovsk, U.S.S.R. 52/D5
Skaelskor, Den. 21/E7
Skaerbaek, Den. 21/B7
Skagata (cape), Ice. 21/B1
Skagen, Den. 18/G8
Skagen, Den. 21/D2
Skagens Odde (cape), Den. 18/G8
Skagens Odde (pt.), Den. 21/D2
Skagerrak (str.), 7/E3
Skagerrak (str.), Den. 18/F8
Skagerrak (str.), Norway 18/F8
Skagerrak (str.), Sweden 18/F8
Skagerrak (str.), Den. 21/D2
Skagit (riv.), Br. Col. 184/G6
Skagit (co.), Wash. 310/D2
Skagit (riv.), Wash. 310/C2
Skagway, Alaska, 146/E4
Skagway, Alaska (99840) 196/M1
Skalica, Czech. 41/D2
Skals, Den. 21/C4
Skamania (co.), Wash. 310/D5
Skamania, Wash. (98646) 310/C5
Skamokawa, Wash. (98647) 310/B4
Skanderborg, Den. 18/F8
Skanderborg (co.), Den. 21/C6
Skanderborg, Den. 21/D5
Skaneateles, N.Y. (13152) 276/H5
Skaneateles (lake), N.Y. 276/H5
Skanee, Mich. (49962) 250/A2
Skåneviksjøen, Norway 18/E7
Skänninge, Sweden 18/J7
Skanör med Falsterbo, Sweden 18/H9
Skara, Sweden 18/H7
Skaraborg (co.), Sweden 18/H7
Skardu, India 68/D1
Skarżysko-Kamienna, Poland 47/E3
Skaudvilė, U.S.S.R. 53/B3
Skaw, The (Skagens Odde) (cape), Den. 18/G8
Skaw, The (Skagens Odde) (pt.), Den. 21/D2
Skedee, Okla. (74069) 288/N2
Skeena (riv.), 163/D5
Skeena (mts.), Br. Col. 184/C2
Skeena (riv.), Br. Col. 184/C3
Skeena Crossing, Br. Col. 184/D2
Skegness, Eng. 13/H4
Skegness, 10/G4
Skeir Graitich (isl.), Scot. 15/D4
Skeldon, Guyana 131/C3
Skeleton (lake), Ont. 177/E2
Skeleton Coast (reg.), S.W. Afr. 118/A3
Skellefteå, Sweden 18/M4
Skellefteälv (riv.), Sweden 18/L4
Skellytown, Texas (79080) 302/C2
Skelmerdale and Holland, Eng. 13/F2
Skelmersdale and Holland, 10/F2
Skelton, Ind. (†47570) 227/B8
Skelton and Brotton, Eng. 13/G3
Skene, Miss. (38775) 256/C3
Skerries, 10/D4
Skerries, Ire. 17/J4
Skerries (isls.), Wales 13/C4
Skerryvore (isl.), Scot. 15/B7
Ski, Norway 18/D4
Skiatook, Okla. (74070) 288/O2
Skibbereen, 10/B5
Skibbereen, Ire. 17/C8
Skibby, Den. 21/E6
Skidaway (isl.), Ga. 216/L7
Skiddaw (mt.), Eng. 13/D3
Skiddy, Kans. (†66872) 232/F3
Skidegate, Br. Col. 184/B3
Skidegate (inlet), Br. Col. 184/B3
Skidegate Mission, Br. Col. 184/A3
Skidmore, Mo. (64487) 261/B2
Skidmore, Texas (78389) 302/G9
Skien, Norway 18/F7
Skierniewice, Poland 47/D2
Skiff, Alta. 182/E5
Skiff (lake), N. Br. 170/C3
Skikda, Alg. 106/F1
Skikda, 102/C1
Skilak (lake), Alaska 196/C1
Skillet Fork (riv.), Ill. 222/E5
Skillman, N.J. (08558) 273/D3
Skinners Eddy, Pa. (†18623) 294/K2
Skipness, Scot. 15/F8
Skippack, Pa. (19474) 294/M5
Skippers, Va. (23879) 307/O7
Skipperville, Ala. (36374) 194/G7
Skipsea, Eng. 13/G4
Skipton, Eng. 13/E3
Skipton, 10/E4
Skipwith, Va. (23968) 307/L7
Skíros, Greece 45/G6
Skíros (isl.), Greece 45/G6
Skive, Den. 18/F8
Skive, Den. 21/B4
Skive (riv.), Den. 21/C5
Skjåk, Norway 18/F6
Skjálfanda (riv.), Ice. 21/C1
Skjern, Den. 21/B6
Skodborg, Den. 21/C7
Škofja Loka, Yugo. 45/A2
Skokie, Ill. (60076) 222/B1
Skokomish (mt.), Wash. 310/B3
Skokomish Ind. Res., Wash. 310/B3
Skomer (isl.), Wales 13/B6
Skookumchuck, Br. Col. 184/K5
Skootamatta (lake), Ont. 177/G3
Skópelos, Greece 45/F6
Skopin, U.S.S.R. 52/F4
Skopje, Yugo., 7/G4
Skopje, Yugo. 45/E5
Skørping, Den. 21/C4
Skövde, Sweden 18/H7
Skovorodino, U.S.S.R. 48/N4
Skovorodino, U.S.S.R., 54/R4
Skowhegan▵, Maine (04976) 242/D6
Skowhegan, Maine (04976) 242/D6
Skownan, Man. 179/C3
Skradin, Yugo. 45/C4
Skreia, Norway 18/G6
Skudeneshavn, Norway 18/D7
Skull Creek, Sask. 181/C6
Skull Valley, Ariz. (86338) 198/C4
Skull Valley Ind. Res., Utah 304/B3
Skuna (riv.), Miss. 256/F2
Skungamaug (riv.), Conn. 210/F1
Skunk (riv.), Iowa 229/K7
Skuodas, U.S.S.R. 53/A2
Skushuban, Somalia 115/J1
Skuteč, Czech. 41/D2
Skwentna, Alaska (99667) 196/B1
Skwentna (riv.), Alaska 196/A1
Skwierzyna, Poland 47/B2
Skye (isl.), 10/C2
Skye (isl.), Scot. 15/D5
Skykomish, Wash. (98288) 310/D3
Skykomish (riv.), Wash. 310/D3
Skylake, Man. 179/E4
Skyland, N.C. (28776) 281/D4
Skylight (mt.), N.Y. 276/M2
Skyline, Minn. (†56001) 254/D6
Skyline View‡, Pa. (†17101) 294/J5
Skyring (bay), Chile 138/E10
Skytop, Pa. (18357) 294/M3
Slab Fork, W. Va. (25920) 313/D7
Slabtown‡, N.Y. (14845) 276/G6
Slade, Ky. (40376) 237/O5
Slag (bay), Neth. Ant. 161/D8
Slagelse, Den. 18/G9
Slagelse, Den. 21/E7
Slagle, La. (71475) 238/D4
Slagle, W. Va. (†25654) 313/C7
Slamet (mt.), Indon. 85/J2
Slana, Alaska (†99586) 196/K2
Slana (riv.), Czech. 41/F2
Slane, Ire. 17/H4
Slanesville, W. Va. (25444) 313/K4
Slaney (riv.), Ire. 17/H7
Slangerup, Den. 21/F6
Slangkop (pt.), S. Africa 118/E7
Slănic, Rum. 45/G3
Slantsy, U.S.S.R. 52/C3
Slaný, Czech. 41/C1
Slate (mt.), Ariz. 198/D3
Slate (riv.), Colo. 208/E5
Slate (isls.), Ont. 175/C3
Slate (creek), Idaho 220/B4
Slate (riv.), Va. 307/L5
Slate, W. Va. (†26143) 313/D4
Slate (creek), Wyo. 319/C3
Slatedale, Pa. (18079) 294/L4
Slater, Colo. (81653) 208/E1
Slater, Iowa (50244) 229/F5
Slater, Mo. (65349) 261/G4
Slater, Wyo. (82230) 319/H4
Slater-Marietta, S.C. (29683) 296/C1
Slatersville, R.I. (02876) 249/H4
Slate Run, Pa. (17769) 294/H3
Slaterville Springs, N.Y. (14881) 276/H6
Slate Spring, Miss. (38955) 256/F3
Slatina, Rum. 45/G3
Slatington, Pa. (18080) 294/L4
Slaton, Texas (79364) 302/C4
Slaughter, La. (70777) 238/H5
Slaughter Beach, Del. (†19963) 245/S5
Slaughters, Ky. (42456) 237/F6
Slave (riv.), 163/E3
Slave (riv.), Alta. 182/C5
Slave (riv.), Canada, 146/G3
Slave (riv.), N.W.T. 187/G3
Slave Coast (reg.), Dahomey 106/E7
Slave Coast (reg.), Nigeria 106/E7
Slave Coast (reg.), Togo 106/E7
Slave Lake, Alta. 182/C2
Slavgorod, U.S.S.R. 48/H4
Slavgorod, U.S.S.R. 52/D4
Slavkov, Czech. 41/D2
Slavuta, U.S.S.R. 52/C4
Slavyansk, U.S.S.R. 52/E5
Slavyansk-na-Kubani, U.S.S.R. 52/E5
Sławno, Poland 47/C1
Slayden, Miss. (†38642) 256/F1
Slayden, Tenn. (37165) 237/G8
Slayton, Minn. (56172) 254/C7
Sleaford, Eng. 13/G5
Sleaford, 10/F4
Sleat (dist.), Scot. 15/E5
Sleat (pt.), Scot. 15/D5
Sleat (sound), Scot. 15/E5
Sledge, Miss. (38670) 256/D2
Sleeper, Mo. (†65536) 261/G7
Sleeping Bear Nat'l Lakeshore, Mich. 250/C4
Sleeping Deer (mt.), Idaho 220/D5
Sleepy Creek, W. Va. (25445) 313/K3
Sleepy Eye, Minn. (56085) 254/D6
Sleepy Eye (creek), Minn. 254/C6
Sleepy Hollow‡, Ill. (†60118) 222/E1
Sleetmute, Alaska (99668) 196/G2
Sleeve (lake), Man. 179/E3
Sleigh (lake), Que. 172/D2
Slemish (mt.), N. Ire. 17/J2
Slemon (lake), Man. 179/G1
Slemp, Ky. (41763) 237/P6
Slick, Okla. (74071) 288/O3
Slickford, Ky. (†42633) 237/M7
Slickville, Pa. (15684) 294/C5
Slide (mt.), N.Y. 276/L6
Slidell, La. (70458) 238/L6
Sliedrecht, Neth. 27/F5
Sliema, Malta 34/E7
Slieve Anierin (mt.), Ire. 17/F3
Slieve Aughty (mts.), Ire. 17/D5
Slieve Beagh (mt.), N. Ire. 17/G3
Slieve Bernagh (mt.), Ire. 17/D6
Slieve Bloom (mts.), Ire. 17/F5
Slieve Callan (mt.), Ire. 17/C6
Slieve Car (mt.), Ire. 17/B3
Slieve Donard (mt.), 10/D3
Slieve Donard (mt.), N. Ire. 17/K3
Slieve Elva (mt.), Ire. 17/C5
Slievefelim (mts.), Ire. 17/E6
Slieve Gamph (mts.), Ire. 17/D3
Slieve Gullion (mt.), N. Ire. 17/J3
Slieve League (mt.), Ire. 17/D2
Slieve Mishkish (mts.), Ire. 17/B8
Slievenaman (mt.), Ire. 17/F7
Sligo, 10/B3
Sligo (co.), Ire. 17/D3
Sligo, Ire. 17/E3
Sligo (bay), Ire. 17/D3
Sligo (bay), 10/B3
Sligo, La. (†71037) 238/C2
Sligo, Pa. (16255) 294/C3
Slinger, Wis. (53086) 317/K9
Slipper (isl.), N.Z. 101/F2
Slippery Rock, Pa. (16057) 294/B3
Slite, Sweden 18/L8
Sliven, Bulg., 7/G4
Sliven, Bulg. 45/H4
Sloan, Iowa (51055) 229/A4
Sloan, N.Y. (†14201) 276/C5
Sloan, Nev. (†89114) 266/F7
Sloans Valley, Ky. (42555) 237/N7
Sloat, Calif. (96127) 204/E4
Sloatsburg, N.Y. (10974) 276/M8
Slobodskoy, U.S.S.R. 48/E4
Slobodskoy, U.S.S.R. 52/H3
Slobozia, Rum. 45/H3
Slocan, Br. Col. 184/J5
Slocan (lake), Br. Col. 184/J5
Slocan Park, Br. Col. 184/J5
Slochteren, Neth. 27/K2
Slocomb, Ala. (36375) 194/G8
Slocum, R.I. (02877) 249/H6
Slocum, Texas (75839) 302/J6
Slope (co.), N. Dak. 283/C7
Sloten, Friesland, Neth. 27/H3
Sloten, North Holland, Neth. 27/B5
Sloterdijk, Neth. 27/B4
Slotermeer (lake), Neth. 27/H3
Slough, Eng. 13/G6
Sloughhouse, Calif. (95683) 204/C8
Slovak (rep.), Czech. 41/E2
Slovakia (reg.), Czech. 41/E2
Slovenia (rep.), Yugo. 45/B2
Slovenské Rudohorie (mts.), Czech. 41/E2
Słubice, Poland 47/B2
Sluis, Neth. 27/C6
Słupsk, Poland, 7/F3
Słupsk, Poland 47/C1
Slussfors, Sweden 18/K4
Slutsk, U.S.S.R. 52/C4
Slyne (head), Ire. 17/A5
Slyne (head), 10/A4
Smackover, Ark. (71762) 203/E7
Smale, Ark. (†72021) 203/H4
Small, Idaho (†83423) 220/F5
Small (cape), Maine 242/D8

440 South Barrington

South Barrington‡, Ill. (†60010) 222/E1
South Bass (isl.), Ohio 284/E2
South Bay, Fla. (33493) 212/F5
South Bay Aqueduct, Calif. 204/L3
South Baymouth, Ont. 177/B2
Southbeach, Oreg. (97366) 291/C3
South Belmar, N.J. (†07719) 273/E3
South Beloit, Ill. (61080) 222/E1
South Bend, Ind., 188/J2
South Bend, Ind. (*46601) 227/E1
South Bend, Nebr. (68058) 264/H4
South Bend, Texas (76081) 302/F5
South Bend, Wash. (98586) 310/B4
South Bennettsville, S.C. (†29512) 296/H2
South Bentinck Arm (inlet), Br. Col. 184/D4
South Berlin, Mass. (01549) 249/H3
South Berwick▵, Maine (03908) 242/B9
South Berwick, Maine (03908) 242/B9
South Bethany, Del. (†19930) 245/T6
South Bethlehem, N.Y. (12161) 276/N5
South Bethlehem, Pa. (†16242) 294/D4
South Beveland (isl.), Neth. 27/D6
South Bjerremark‡, Alaska (†99701) 196/J2
South Bloomfield, Ohio (†43103) 284/D6
South Bloomingville, Ohio (43152) 284/E7
South Boardman, Mich. (49680) 250/D4
Southborough, Eng. 13/H6
Southborough▵, Mass. (01772) 249/H3
Southborough, Mass. (01772) 249/H3
South Boston, Ind. (†47167) 227/F7
South Boston, Va. (24592) 307/L7
South Bound Brook, N.J. (08880) 273/E2
South Braintree, Mass. (†02185) 249/D8
South Branch, Mich. (48761) 250/E4
South Branch, Minn. (†56081) 254/D7
South Branch, N. Br. 170/F2
South Branch, N.J. (08881) 273/D2
South Branch, Newf. 166/C4
South Branch, Potomac (riv.), W. Va. 313/J4
Southbridge▵, Mass. (01550) 249/G4
Southbridge, Mass. (01550) 249/G4
Southbridge, N.Z. 101/D5
South Bridgewater, Mass. (†02324) 249/L5
South Bridgton, Maine (†04009) 242/B8
South Bristol▵, Maine (04568) 242/D8
South Britain, Conn. (06487) 210/B3
South Broadway, Wash. (†98901) 310/E4
South Brookfield, N.S. 169/D4
South Brooksville, Maine (†04617) 242/F7
South Brunswick▵, N.J. (†08852) 273/E3
South Bruny (isl.), Tas. 99/D5
South Burlington▵, Vt. (05401) 268/A3
South Burro (mt.), Utah 304/D3
Southbury▵, Conn. (06488) 210/C3
South Canaan, Conn. (†06031) 210/B1
South Carolina, 188/K4
SOUTH CAROLINA, 296
South Carolina (state), U.S., 146/K6
South Carrollton, Ky. (42374) 237/G6
South Carthage, Tenn. (†37030) 237/K8
South Carver, Mass. (02566) 249/M5
South Casco, Maine (04077) 242/B8
South Cave, Eng. 13/G4
South Central (sen. dist.), Alaska 196/G3
South Charleston, Ohio (45368) 284/C6
South Charleston, W. Va. (25303) 313/C6
South Chatham, Mass. (02659) 249/O6
South Chatham, N.H. (04037) 268/E3
South Cheyenne (riv.), Wyo. 319/H2
South Chicago Heights, Ill. (60411) 222/B3
South China (sea), 3/Q5
South China (sea), 54/P8
South China, Maine (04358) 242/D7
South China (sea), S. Vietnam 72/F4
South China (sea), China 77/H7
South China (sea), Phil. 82/B3
South China (sea), Indon. 85/D4
South China (sea), Malaysia 85/D4
South China (sea), Phil. 85/D4
South Cle Elum, Wash. (98943) 310/D3
South Cleveland, Tenn. (†37311) 237/M10
South Clinton, Tenn. (†37716) 237/N8
South Coatesville‡, Pa. (†19320) 294/L6
South Coffeyville, Okla. (74072) 288/P1
South Colby, Wash. (98384) 310/A2
South Colton, N.Y. (13687) 276/L1
South Congaree, S.C. (†29169) 296/E4
South Connellsville, Pa. (15425) 294/C6
South Corning, N.Y. (14830) 276/F6
South Coventry (Coventry), Conn. (†06238) 210/F1
South Cow (creek), Calif. 204/C3
South Creek, N.C. (†27806) 281/R4
South Dakota, 188/F2
SOUTH DAKOTA, 298
South Dakota (state), U.S., 146/H5
South Danbury, N.H. (†03230) 268/D5
South Danville, N.H. (03881) 268/E6
South Dartmouth, Mass. (02748) 249/L6
South Dayton, N.Y. (14138) 276/C6
South Daytona, Fla. (32021) 212/F2
South Deerfield, Mass. (01373) 249/D3
South Deerfield, N.H. (†03037) 268/E5
South Dennis, Mass. (02660) 249/O6
South Dennis, N.J. (08245) 273/D5
South Dorset, Vt. (05263) 268/A5
South Dos Palos, Calif. (93665) 204/E7
South Downs (hills), Eng. 13/G7
South Duxbury, Mass. (†02332) 249/M4
South East (cape), Australia, 87/E10
Southeast (cape), Alaska 196/E2
South East (pt.), Jam. 158/K6
South East (pt.), Vic. 97/D6
Southeastern (sen. dist.), Alaska 196/L3
South-Eastern (state), Nigeria 106/F7
Southeast Loch (inlet), Hawaii 218/B3
South Easton, Mass. (02375) 249/K4
Southeast Upsalquitch (riv.), N. Br. 170/D1
South Effingham, N.H. (03882) 268/E4
South Egremont, Mass. (01258) 249/A4
South Elgin, Ill. (60177) 222/E2
South Eliot, Maine (†03903) 242/B9
South El Monte, Calif. (91733) 204/C10
Southend, Sask. 181/N3
Southend-on-Sea, Eng. 13/H6
Southend-on-Sea, 10/G5
South English, Iowa (52335) 229/J6
Southern (dist.), Israel 65/B5
Southern Alps (range), N.Z. 101/C5
Southern Cross, Aust. 88/B6
Southern Cross, Mont. (†59711) 262/C4
Southern Cross, W. Aust. 92/B5
Southern Indian (lake), 163/G4
Southern Indian (lake), Man., 146/J4
Southern Indian (lake), Man. 179/H2
Southern Leyte (prov.), Phil. 82/E5
Southern Pines, N.C. (28387) 281/L4
Southern Shops‡, S.C. (29303) 296/D2
Southern Ute Ind. Res., Colo. 208/D8
Southern View‡, Ill. (†62701) 222/D4
South Esk (riv.), Scot. 15/K6
South Esk (riv.), Tas. 99/D3
Southesk Tablelands, W. Aust. 92/D3
South Essex, Mass. (01981) 249/L2
South Euclid, Ohio (44121) 284/H9
South Exeter, Maine (†04928) 242/E6
Southey, Sask. 181/G5
South Fallsburg, N.Y. (12779) 276/L7
South Farmingdale‡, N.Y. (11735) 276/O9
Southfield, Mass. (†01259) 249/B4
Southfield, Mich. (48075) 250/F6
Southfields, N.Y. (10975) 276/M8
South Flevoland Polder, Neth. 27/G4
South Flomaton, Fla. (†36441) 212/B5
South Floral Park‡, N.Y. (†11001) 276/R7
Southford, Conn. (†06488) 210/C3
South Fork, Kuskokwim (riv.), Alaska 196/H2
South Fork, Colo. (81154) 208/F7
South Fork, Licking (riv.), Ky. 237/N3
South Fork, Mo. (65776) 261/J9
South Fork, New (riv.), N.C. 281/G2
South Fork, Humboldt (riv.), Nev. 266/F2
South Fork, Owyhee (riv.), Nev. 266/E1
South Fork, Pa. (15956) 294/E5
South Fork, Sask. 181/C6
South Fork, Forked Deer (riv.), Tenn. 237/C9
South Fork, Obion (riv.), Tenn. 237/D8
South Fork, Powder (riv.), Wyo. 319/F2
South Fork, Shoshone (riv.), Wyo. 319/C1
South Fort George, Br. Col. 184/F3
South Foster, R.I. (†02857) 249/H5
South Fowl (lake), Minn. 254/G1
South Fox (isl.), Mich. 250/D3
South Friars (bay), St. Chr.-N.-A. 161/C10
South Fulton, Tenn. (42041) 237/D8
South Gate, Calif. (90280) 204/C11
Southgate, Ky. (41071) 237/S2
South Gate‡, Md. (†21113) 245/M4
Southgate, Mich. (48192) 250/F6
South Gate Ridge‡, Fla. (†33577) 212/D4
South Georgia (isl.), 3/H8
South Georgia (isl.), Ant. 5/D17
South Gifford, Mo. (63564) 261/G3
South Glastonbury, Conn. (06073) 210/E2
South Glens Falls, N.Y. (†12801) 276/N4
South Gobi (prov.), Mong. 77/F3
South Goldsboro‡, N.C. (†27530) 281/O4
South Grafton, Mass. (01560) 249/H4
South Greenfield, Mo. (65752) 261/E8
South Greensburg‡, Pa. (†15601) 294/C5
South Groveland, Mass. (†01830) 249/L2
South Hadley▵, Mass. (01075) 249/D4
South Hadley Falls, Mass. (01075) 249/D4
South Hampton▵, N.H. (†01913) 268/F6
South Hanover, Mass. (†02339) 249/L4
South Harbour, N.S. 169/H2
South Harpswell, Maine (04079) 242/C8
South Harwich, Mass. (02661) 249/O6
South Haven, Kans. (67140) 232/E4
South Haven, Mich. (49090) 250/C6
South Haven, Minn. (55382) 254/D5
Southhaven, Miss. (38671) 256/E1
South Haven, N.S. 169/H2
South Hazelton, Br. Col. 184/D2
South Heart, N. Dak. (58655) 283/D6
South Heights, Pa. (15081) 294/B4
South Hero▵, Vt. (05486) 268/A2
South Hero, Vt. (05486) 268/A2
South Hill, Va. (23970) 307/M7
South Hiram, Maine (04080) 242/B8
South Holbrook‡, N.Y. (†11741) 276/O9
South Holland, Ill. (60473) 222/B2
South Holland (prov.), Neth. 27/E5
South Holston (lake), Tenn. 237/T7
South Holston (lake), Va. 307/E7
South Hope, Maine (†04862) 242/E7
South Horr, Kenya 115/G3
South Houston, Texas (77587) 302/J2
South Hudson Falls‡, N.Y. (†12839) 276/N4
South Huntington‡, N.Y. (†11743) 276/O9
South Hutchinson, Kans. (†67501) 232/D3
South Indian Lake, Man. 179/H2
Southington▵, Conn. (06489) 210/D2
South International Falls, Minn. (56679) 254/E2
South Irvine, Ky. (40483) 237/N5
South Jacksonville, Ill. (62650) 222/C4
South Jordan, Utah (†84065) 304/B3
South Junction, Man. 179/G5
South Junction, Oreg. (97074) 291/F3
South Kedgwick (riv.), N. Br. 170/B1
South Kensington‡, Md. (†20795) 245/E4
South Kent, Conn. (06785) 210/B2
South Khangai (prov.), Mong. 77/F2
South Killingly, Conn. (†06239) 210/H1
South Knife (riv.), Man. 179/J2
SOUTH KOREA, 81/E5
South La Grange, Maine (†04453) 242/F5
South Laguna‡, Calif. (92677) 204/H10
Southlake, Texas (76051) 302/F1
South Lake Tahoe, Calif. (95705) 204/F5
South Lancaster, Mass. (01561) 249/H3
Southland (land dist.), N.Z. 101/A6
Southland, Texas (79368) 302/C4
South Lansing, N.Y. (14882) 276/H5
South Laurel‡, Md. (†20810) 245/L4
South Lebanon, Maine (†03901) 242/A9
South Lebanon, Ohio (45065) 284/B7
South Lee, Mass. (01260) 249/A3
South Lee, N.H. (†03042) 268/E5
South Liberty, Maine (†04949) 242/E7
South Lincoln, Maine (†04457) 242/F5
South Lincoln, Vt. (†05443) 268/B3
South Lineville, Mo. (†50147) 261/E1
South Lockport‡, N.Y. (†14094) 276/C4
South Londonderry, Vt. (05155) 268/B5
South Loup (riv.), Nebr. 264/E3
South Luconia (shoal), Asia 85/E4
South Lunenburg, Vt. (05908) 268/D3
South Lyme, Conn. (06376) 210/F3
South Lyndeboro, N.H. (03082) 268/D6
South Lynnfield, Mass. (01940) 249/D5
South Lyon, Mich. (48178) 250/F6
South Magnetic Polar Area, Ant., 3/S10
South Magnetic Polar Area, Ant. 5/C8
South Maitland, N.S. 169/E3
South Manitou, Mich. (†49654) 250/C3
South Manitou (isl.), Mich. 250/C3
South Mansfield, La. (†71052) 238/C3
South Marsh (isl.), Md. 245/O8
Southmayd‡, Texas (76268) 302/H4
South Mayo (riv.), Va. 307/H7
South Medford, Oreg. (†97501) 291/E5
South Melbourne, Vic. 97/J5
South Meriden, Conn. (†06450) 210/D2
South Merrimack, N.H. (03083) 268/D6
South Miami, Fla. (33143) 212/B5
South Miami Heights‡, Fla. (†33143) 212/B5
South Middleboro, Mass. (†02346) 249/L5
South Milford, Ind. (46786) 227/G1
South Mills, N.C. (27976) 281/S2
South Milwaukee, Wis. (53172) 317/M2
South Modesto‡, Calif. (95350) 204/D6
South Molton, Eng. 13/D6
South Molton, 10/E5
South Monmouth, Maine (†04259) 242/D7
South Monroe, Mich. (†48161) 250/F7
Southmont, N.C. (27351) 281/J3
Southmont‡, Pa. (†15901) 294/E5
South Mound, Kans. (67362) 232/G4
South Mountain, Ont. 177/J3
South Mountain, Pa. (17261) 294/H6
South Mount Vernon‡, Ohio (†43050) 284/F5
South Nahanni (riv.), N.W.T. 187/F3
South Naknek, Alaska (99670) 196/G3
South Natick, Mass. (01760) 249/A7
South Natuna (isls.), Indon. 85/D5
South Negril (pt.), Jam. 156/B3
South Negril (pt.), Jam. 158/G6
South New Berlin, N.Y. (13843) 276/K5
South Newbury, N.H. (03272) 268/D5
South Newbury, Vt. (05066) 268/C3
South New Castle‡, Pa. (16101) 294/B4
South Newfane, Vt. (05351) 268/B6
South Newport, Ga. (†31323) 216/K7
South New River (canal), Fla. 212/F5
South Norfolk, Conn. (†06058) 210/C1
South Norwalk, Conn. (†06850) 210/B4
South Nyack‡, N.Y. (†10960) 276/N8
South Ogden, Utah (†84401) 304/C2
South Ohio, N.S. 169/B5
Southold, N.Y. (11971) 276/P8
South Olive, Ohio (43724) 284/G6
South Orange, N.J. (07079) 273/A2
South Orkney (isls.), 3/G9
South Orkney (isls.), Ant. 5/C16
South Orleans, Mass. (02662) 249/O5
South Oromocto (lake), N. Br. 170/D3
South Oromocto (riv.), N. Br. 170/D3
South Oroville, Calif. (†95965) 204/D4
South Orrington, Maine (†04474) 242/F6
South Ossetian Aut. Obl., U.S.S.R. 48/E5
South Ossetian Aut. Obl., U.S.S.R. 52/F6
South Otselic, N.Y. (13155) 276/J5
South Pacific Ocean, 3/C8
South Pagai (isl.), Indon. 85/C6
South Palm Beach‡, Fla. (†33460) 212/F5
South Para (riv.), Aust. 88/E7
South Para (riv.), S. Aust. 94/C7
South Paris, Maine (04281) 242/C7
South Park Military Res., Pa. 294/B7
South Park View, Ky. (†40201) 237/K4
South Pasadena, Calif. (91030) 204/C10
South Pasadena, Fla. (33707) 212/B3
South Pass City, Wyo. (82520) 319/D3
South Patrick Shores‡, Fla. (†32935) 212/F3
South Pekin, Ill. (61564) 222/D3
South Pender, Br. Col. 184/K3
South Peninsula‡, Fla. (†32016) 212/F2
South Penobscot, Maine (04486) 242/F7
South Perry, Ohio (†43135) 284/E6
South Perth, W. Aust. 92/A1
South Philipsburg, Pa. (†16866) 294/F4
South Piney (creek), Wyo. 319/B3
South Pittsburg, Tenn. (37380) 237/K10
South Pittsfield, N.H. (†03263) 268/E5
South Plainfield, N.J. (07080) 273/E2
South Plains, Texas (79258) 302/C3
South Platte (riv.), 188/F2
South Platte (riv.), Colo. 208/N1
South Platte (riv.), Nebr. 264/C3
South Platte (riv.), U.S., 146/H5
South Point, Ohio (45680) 284/E9
South Polar (plat.), Ant. 5/A1
South Pole, 3/E10
South Pole, Ant. 5/A4
South Pomfret, Vt. (05067) 268/B4
South Porcupine, Ont. 175/D3
South Porcupine, Ont. 177/K5
Southport, Conn. (06490) 210/B4
Southport, Eng. 13/D4
Southport, Fla. (†32401) 212/C6
Southport, 10/F2
Southport, Ind. (†46201) 227/E5
Southport▵, Maine (†04569) 242/D8
Southport, Maine (04569) 242/D8
Southport, N.C. (28461) 281/N7
Southport, N.Y. (†14901) 276/G6
South Portland, Maine (04106) 242/C8
South Portsmouth, Ky. (41174) 237/P3
South Pottstown‡, Pa. (†19464) 294/L5
South Prairie, Wash. (98385) 310/D3
South Pugwash, N.S. 169/E3
South Range, Mich. (49963) 250/G1
South Range, Wis. (54874) 317/B2
South Renous (riv.), N. Br. 170/D2
South Renovo, Pa. (†17764) 294/G3
South River (peak), Colo. 208/F7
South River, Ont. 177/E2
South River, N.J. (08882) 273/E3
South Robbinston, Maine (†04671) 242/J5
South Rockwood, Mich. (48179) 250/F7
South Ronaldsay (isl.), 10/E1
South Ronaldsay (isl.), Scot. 15/L2
South Roxton, Que. 172/E4
South Royalston, Mass. (01374) 249/F2
South Royalton, Vt. (05068) 268/C4
South Russell, Ohio (†44022) 284/H3
South Ryegate, Vt. (05069) 268/C3
South Sacramento, Calif. (†95801) 204/B8
South Saint Paul, Minn. (55075) 254/G6
South Salem, Ohio (45681) 284/D7
South Salisbury‡, N.C. (†28144) 281/J3
South Salt Lake, Utah (84115) 304/C3
South Sandisfield, Mass. (†01255) 249/B4
South Sandwich (isls.), 3/H8
South Sandwich (isls.), Ant. 5/D17
South Sanford, Maine (†04073) 242/B9
South San Francisco, Calif. (94080) 204/J2
South San Gabriel‡, Calif. (91770) 204/C10
South San Jose Hills‡, Calif. (†91744) 204/D10
South San Pedro‡, Texas (†78380) 302/G10
South Santiam (riv.), Oreg. 291/E3
South Saskatchewan (riv.), Alta. 182/E4
South Saskatchewan (riv.), Sask. 181/C5
South Seabrook, N.H. (†03874) 268/F6
South Seal (riv.), Man. 179/J2
South Seaville, N.J. (08246) 273/D5
South Sevogle (riv.), N. Br. 170/D1
South Shaftsbury, Vt. (†05262) 268/A6
South Shetland (isls.), 3/F9
South Shetland (isls.), Ant. 5/C15
South Shields, Eng. 13/F3
South Shields, 10/F3
South Shore, Ky. (41175) 237/R3
South Shore, S. Dak. (57263) 298/P3
Southside, Ala. (35901) 194/F3
Southside, Tenn. (37171) 237/G8
Southside Place, Texas (†77001) 302/J2
South Sioux City, Nebr. (68776) 264/H2
South Skunk (riv.), Iowa 229/H6
South Slocan, Br. Col. 184/J5
South Solon, Ohio (43153) 284/C6
South Spectacle (lake), Conn. 210/B2
South Standard, Ill. (62686) 222/D4
South Stickney‡, Ill. (60459) 222/B2
South Stoddard, N.H. (†03464) 268/C5
South Stony Brook‡, N.Y. (†11790) 276/O9
South Strafford, Vt. (05070) 268/C4
South Streator‡, Ill. (†61364) 222/E2
South Suburban, India 68/F2
South Sudbury, Mass. (†01776) 249/J3
South Superior, Wyo. (†82945) 319/D4
South Sutton, N.H. (03273) 268/D5
South Taft, Calif. (†93268) 204/F8
South Tamworth, N.H. (03883) 268/E4
South Taranaki (bight), N.Z. 101/D3
South Thomaston▵, Maine (04858) 242/E7
South Toms River, N.J. (08753) 273/E4
South Trap (isl.), N.Z. 101/B7
South Tucson, Ariz. (85713) 198/D6
South Tunnel, Tenn. (†37066) 237/H7
South Turlock‡, Calif. (†95380) 204/E6
South Twin (mt.), N.H. 268/D3
South Tyne (riv.), Eng. 13/E3
South Uist (isl.), 10/C2
South Uist (isl.), Scot. 15/A5
South Umpqua (riv.), Oreg. 291/E4
South Uniacke, N.S. 169/E4
South Union, Ky. (42283) 237/H7
South Union, Maine (†04864) 242/E7
South Uniontown‡, Pa. (†15401) 294/C6
South Ural (mts.), U.S.S.R. 52/J4
South Valley Stream‡, N.Y. (†11580) 276/R7
South Vernon, Mass. (†01360) 249/D2
South Vienna, Ohio (45369) 284/C6
SOUTH VIETNAM, 72/F4
Southville, Mass. (†01772) 249/H3
South Wabasca (lake), Alta. 182/D2
South Wadesboro, N.C. (†28170) 281/J5
South Waldoboro, Maine (†04572) 242/E7
South Wallingford, Vt. (05771) 268/A5
South Walpole, Mass. (02071) 249/K4
South Wanatah, Ind. (†46390) 227/D2
Southwark, 10/B5
South Warren, Maine (†04864) 242/E7
South Waterford, Maine (04081) 242/B7
South Waverly, Pa. (†14892) 294/J2
South Wayne, Wis. (53587) 317/G10
South Weare, N.H. (†03281) 268/D5
South Weber‡, Utah (†84401) 304/C2
South Webster, Ohio (45682) 284/E8
South Weldon‡, N.C. (†27890) 281/O2
South Wellfleet, Mass. (02663) 249/P5
South Wellington, Br. Col. 184/J3
South West (cape), Aust. 88/G8
Southwest (cape), V.I.(U.S.) 161/E4
Southwest (passg.), La. 238/F8
Southwest (passg.), La. 238/M8
Southwest (head), N. Br. 170/D4
South West (cape), Tasmania 99/B5
South-West Africa, 3/K6
SOUTH-WEST AFRICA, 118/B3
SOUTH-WEST AFRICA, 102/D7
South West Arm (inlet), Newf. 166/D2
South West Brook (riv.), Newf. 166/C2
South Westbury‡, N.Y. (†11590) 276/R7
South West City, Mo. (64863) 261/D9
South West Gander (riv.), Newf. 166/C4
Southwest Greensburg‡, Pa. (†15601) 294/C5
Southwest Harbor▵, Maine (04679) 242/G7
South West Margaree (riv.), N.S. 169/G2
Southwest Miramichi (riv.), N. Br. 170/D2
South Westport, Mass. (02790) 249/K6
South West Port Mouton, N.S. 169/D5
South Weymouth, Mass. (†02190) 249/E8
South Whitley, Ind. (46787) 227/F2
South Whittier‡, Calif. (90605) 204/C11
Southwick, Eng. 13/G7
Southwick, Idaho (83550) 220/B3
Southwick▵, Mass. (01077) 249/C4
Southwick, Mass. (01077) 249/C4
South Williamson, Ky. (†25661) 237/S5
South Williamsport, Pa. (17701) 294/J3
South Willington, Conn. (06265) 210/F1
South Wilmington, Ill. (60474) 222/E2
South Wilton, Conn. (†06897) 210/B4
South Windham, Conn. (06266) 210/G2
South Windham, Maine (04082) 242/C8
South Windham, Vt. (†05359) 268/B5
South Windsor▵, Conn. (06074) 210/E1
Southwold, Eng. 13/J5
Southwold, 10/G4
South Wolf (isl.), Newf. 166/C3
South Wolfeboro, N.H. (†03894) 268/E4
South Woodbury, Vt. (05671) 268/C3
South Woodstock, Conn. (06267) 210/G1
South Woodstock, Vt. (05071) 268/B4
Southworth, Wash. (98386) 310/A2
South Worthington, Mass. (†01098) 249/C3
South Yadkin (riv.), N.C. 281/H3
South Yarmouth, Mass. (02664) 249/O6
South Yuba City‡, Calif. (†95991) 204/D4
South Zanesville, Ohio (43701) 284/F6
Sovereign, Sask. 181/D4
Sovereign Base Area, 63/E5
Sovetsk, U.S.S.R. 52/B4
Sovetsk, U.S.S.R. 52/G3
Sovetskaya Gavan', U.S.S.R. 48/P5
Sowerby Bridge, 10/G2
Soya (pt.), Japan 81/L1
Soyopa, Mex. 150/E2
Sozopol, Bulg. 45/H4
Spa, Belg. 27/H8
Spackenkill‡, N.Y. (†12601) 276/N7
Spades, Ind. (†47041) 227/G6
Spain, 3/J3
Spain, 7/D4
SPAIN, 33
Spalding, Eng. 13/G5
Spalding (co.), Ga. 216/D4
Spalding, 10/F4
Spalding, Mich. (49886) 250/B3
Spalding, Mo. (†63401) 261/J3
Spalding, Nebr. (68665) 264/F3
Spalding, Sask. 181/G3
Spaldings, Jam. 158/H6
Spanaway, Wash. (98387) 310/C3
Spandau, W. Ger. 22/E3
Spangle, Wash. (99031) 310/H3
Spangler, Pa. (15775) 294/E4
Spaniard's Bay, Newf. 166/D2
Spanish, Ont. 177/J5
Spanish (riv.), Ont. 177/C1
Spanish (head), I. of Man 13/C4
Spanishburg, W. Va. (25922) 313/D8
Spanish Fork, Utah (84660) 304/C3
Spanish Fork (riv.), Utah 304/C3
Spanish Fort, Ala. (36527) 194/C9
Spanish Fort, Texas (†76255) 302/G4
Spanish Lake, Mo. (†63101) 261/P2
Spanish Sahara, 3/J4
SPANISH SAHARA, 106/A4
SPANISH SAHARA, 102/A2
Spanish Ship Bay, N.S. 169/G4
Spanish Town, Jam. 156/C3
Spanish Town, Jam. 158/J6
Sparkman, Ark. (71763) 203/E6
Sparks, Ga. (31647) 216/F8
Sparks, Kans. (66082) 232/G2
Sparks, Nebr. (69220) 264/D2
Sparks, Nev., 188/C3
Sparks, Nev. (89431) 266/B3
Sparks, Okla. (74869) 288/N3
Sparks (lake), Oreg. 291/F3
Sparksville, Ky. (42778) 237/L6
Sparland, Ill. (61565) 222/D2
Sparlingville, Mich. (†48060) 250/G6
Sparr, Fla. (32690) 212/D2
Sparrow Bush, N.Y. (12780) 276/L8
Sparta, Ont. 177/C5
Sparta, Ga. (31087) 216/F4
Sparta, Greece 45/F7
Sparta, Ill. (62286) 222/D5
Sparta, Ky. (41086) 237/M3
Sparta, Mich. (49345) 250/D5
Sparta, Mo. (65753) 261/F9
Sparta, N.C. (28675) 281/G1
Sparta, N.J. (07871) 273/D1
Sparta, Ohio (43350) 284/E5
Sparta, Oreg. (†97870) 291/K3
Sparta, Tenn. (38583) 237/K9
Sparta, Va. (22552) 307/O4
Sparta, Wis. (54656) 317/E8
Spartanburg, Ind. (†47355) 227/H4
Spartanburg, S.C., 188/K4
Spartanburg (co.), S.C. 296/D2
Spartanburg, S.C. (*29301) 296/C1
Spartansburg, Pa. (16434) 294/C2
Spartivento (cape), Italy 34/B5
Spartivento (cape), Italy 34/F6
Sparwood, Br. Col. 184/K5
Spassk-Dal'niy, U.S.S.R. 48/O5
Spátha (cape), Greece 45/F8
Spaulding, Ill. (†62561) 222/D4
Spavinaw, Okla. (74366) 288/R2
Spavinaw (lake), Okla. 288/S2
Spean (riv.), Scot. 15/G6
Spean Bridge, Scot. 15/G6
Spear (cape), N. Br. 170/G2
Spear (cape), Newf. 166/D2
Spearfish, S. Dak. (57783) 298/B5
Spearhill, Man. 179/D3
Spearman, Texas (79081) 302/C1
Spearsville, Ind. (†46181) 227/E6
Spearsville, La. (71277) 238/E1
Spearville, Kans. (67876) 232/C4
Spectacle (lakes), Conn. 210/B2
Specter (range), Nev. 266/E6
Speculator, N.Y. (12164) 276/M3
Spedden, Alta. 182/E2
Spednik (lake), N. Br. 170/C3
Speed, Ind. (47172) 227/F8
Speed, Kans. (†67639) 232/C2
Speed, N.C. (27881) 281/P3
Speedway, Ind. (46224) 227/E5
Speedwell, Tenn. (37870) 237/O8
Speedwell, Va. (24374) 307/F8
Speer (mt.), Switz. 39/H2
Speers‡, Pa. (†15012) 294/C5
Speers, Sask. 181/D3
Speightstown, Barb. 156/G4
Speightstown, Barb. 161/B8
Speigner, Ala. (†36025) 194/F5
Spelterville, Ind. (†47808) 227/C5
Spenard, Alaska (99503) 196/C1
Spence Bay, N.W.T. 187/J3
Spencer (gulf), Australia, 87/D9
Spencer (cape), Alaska 196/L1
Spencer (pt.), Alaska 196/E1
Spencer (lake), Alta. 182/E2
Spencer (cape), Aust. 88/F7
Spencer (gulf), Aust. 88/F6
Spencer, Idaho (83446) 220/F5
Spencer (co.), Ind. 227/C9
Spencer, Ind. (47460) 227/D6
Spencer, Iowa (51301) 229/C2
Spencer (co.), Ky. 237/L4
Spencer, La. (71278) 238/F1
Spencer (pond), Maine 242/D4
Spencer, Maine 242/C5
Spencer▵, Mass. (01562) 249/F3

442 Stephensport

Stephensport, Ky. (40170) 237/H5
Stephentown, N.Y. (12168) 276/O5
Stephenville, 163/L6
Stephenville, Newf. 166/C4
Stephenville, Texas (76401) 302/F5
Stephenville Crossing, Newf. 166/C4
Stepney, Conn. (†06468) 210/B3
Stepnoy (Elista), U.S.S.R. 52/G5
Stepnyak, U.S.S.R. 48/H4
Stepovak (bay), Alaska 196/G3
Steprock, Ark. (72159) 203/G3
Steptoe, Wash. (99174) 310/H3
Sterling, Alaska (99672) 196/B1
Sterling, Colo., 188/F2
Sterling, Colo. (80751) 208/N1
Sterling (res.), Colo. 208/N1
Sterling△, Conn. (06377) 210/H2
Sterling, Ga. (†31520) 216/K8
Sterling, Idaho (83279) 220/F6
Sterling, Ill. (61081) 222/D2
Sterling, Kans. (67579) 232/D3
Sterling△, Mass. (01564) 249/G3
Sterling, Mich. (48659) 250/E4
Sterling, N. Dak. (58572) 283/K6
Sterling, Nebr. (68443) 264/H4
Sterling, Ohio (44276) 284/G4
Sterling, Okla. (73567) 288/K5
Sterling, Pa. (18463) 294/M3
Sterling (co.), Texas 302/C6
Sterling, Utah (84665) 304/C4
Sterling, Va. (22170) 307/O2
Sterling City, Texas (76951) 302/D6
Sterling Heights, Mich. (*48077) 250/B6
Sterling Highway, Alaska 196/B2
Sterling Run, Pa. (†15832) 294/F3
Sterlington, La. (71280) 238/F1
Sterlitamak, U.S.S.R. 48/F4
Sterlitamak, U.S.S.R. 52/J4
Sternberg, E. Ger. 22/D2
Šternberk, Czech. 41/D2
Sterrett, Ala. (35147) 194/F4
Stet, Mo. (64680) 261/E4
Stetson△, Maine (04488) 242/E6
Stetsonville, Wis. (54480) 317/F5
Stettin (bay), E. Ger. 22/F2
Stettin (Szczecin), Poland, 7/F3
Stettler, 163/E5
Stettler, Alta. 182/D3
Stettyn (mt.), S. Africa 118/G6
Steuben (co.), Ind. 227/G1
Steuben△, Maine (04680) 242/H6
Steuben, Maine (04680) 242/H6
Steuben, Mich. (†49854) 250/C2
Steuben (co.), N.Y. 276/F6
Steuben, Wis. (54657) 317/E9
Steubenville, Ohio, 188/K2
Steubenville, Ohio (43952) 284/J5
Steve, Ark. (72864) 203/D4
Stevenage, 10/F5
Stevens (isl.), Br. Col. 184/B3
Stevens (co.), Kans. 232/A4
Stevens (co.), Minn. 254/B5
Stevens (creek), S.C. 296/C4
Stevens (co.), Wash. 310/H2
Stevens (pass), Wash. 310/D3
Stevensburg, Va. (22741) 307/N4
Stevenson, Ala. (35772) 194/G1
Stevenson, Conn. (06491) 210/C3
Stevenson (lake), Man. 179/J3
Stevenson, The (riv.), S. Aust. 94/D2
Stevenson, Wash. (98648) 310/C5
Stevenson Entrance (str.), Alaska 196/H3
Stevens Point, Wis. (54481) 317/G7
Stevens Pottery, Ga. (31088) 216/F5
Stevenston, Scot. 15/G8
Stevenstown, Wis. (†54636) 317/D7
Stevens Village, Alaska (99774) 196/J1
Stevensville, Md. (21666) 245/N5
Stevensville, Mich. (49127) 250/C6
Stevensville, Mont. (59870) 262/C4
Stevns (prom.), Den. 21/F7
Steward, Ill. (60553) 222/D2
Stewardson, Ill. (62463) 222/E4
Stewart, 163/D4
Stewart, Ala. (35484) 194/C5
Stewart (cape), Aust. 88/F2
Stewart, Br. Col. 184/C2
Stewart (isl.), Chile 138/E11
Stewart, Cuba 158/F2
Stewart (co.), Ga. 216/C6
Stewart (riv.), 163/C3
Stewart, Minn. (55385) 254/D6
Stewart, Miss. (39767) 256/F4
Stewart (isl.), N.Z., 87/G10
Stewart (isl.), N.Z. 101/A7
Stewart (cape), No. Terr. 93/D1
Stewart, Ohio (45778) 284/G7
Stewart (co.), Tenn. 237/F7
Stewart, Tenn. (37175) 237/F8
Stewart (riv.), Yukon 187/E3
Stewart A.F.B., N.Y. 276/M7
Stewart Manor‡, N.Y. (†11530) 276/R7
Stewarton, Scot. 15/H8
Stewart River, 163/B3
Stewart River, Yukon 187/D3
Stewarts Point, Calif. (95480) 204/B5
Stewartstown△, N.H. (†03576) 268/E2
Stewartstown, N.H. (†03576) 268/E2
Stewartstown, N. Ire. 17/H2
Stewartstown, Pa. (17363) 294/K6
Stewartsville, Ind. (47636) 227/B8
Stewartsville, Mo. (64490) 261/C3
Stewartsville, N.J. (08886) 273/C2
Stewartsville, Ohio (43960) 284/J6
Stewart Town, Jam. 158/H6
Stewart Valley, Sask. 181/D5
Stewartville, Ala. (†35150) 194/F4
Stewartville, Minn. (55976) 254/F7
Stewiacke, N.S. 169/E3
Stewiacke (riv.), N.S. 169/E3
Steyer, Md. (†21550) 245/A3
Steyning, Eng. 13/G7
Steyr, Austria 41/C2
Stia, Italy 34/C3
Stickney, Ill. (60402) 222/B2
Stickney, N. Br. 170/C2
Stickney, S. Dak. (57375) 298/M6
Stickney, W. Va. (25188) 313/D7
Stidham, Okla. (74461) 288/P4
Stiens, Neth. 27/H2
Stigler, Okla. (74462) 288/R4
Stikine (riv.), 163/C4
Stikine (riv.), Alaska 196/N2
Stikine (str.), Alaska 196/N2
Stikine (riv.), Br. Col. 184/B1
Stikine (riv.), Canada, 146/E4
Stiles, Iowa (†52537) 229/J7
Stiles, Wis. (54172) 317/L6
Stilesboro, Ga. (†30178) 216/B2
Stilesville, Ind. (46180) 227/D5
Stilis, Greece 45/F6
Still (riv.), Conn. 210/B3
Still (riv.), Conn. 210/C1
Still (riv.), Conn. 210/G1
Stillman Valley, Ill. (61084) 222/D1
Stillmore, Ga. (30464) 216/H6
Still Pond, Md. (21667) 245/O3
Still River, Mass. (01467) 249/H3
Stillwater, Ky. (†41301) 237/O5
Stillwater, Maine (04489) 242/F6
Stillwater (riv.), Mass. 249/G3
Stillwater, Minn. (55082) 254/F5
Stillwater (co.), Mont. 262/G5
Stillwater (riv.), Mont. 262/G5
Stillwater, N.J. (07875) 273/D1
Stillwater, N.Y. (12170) 276/N5
Stillwater, Nev. (†89406) 266/C3
Stillwater (range), Nev. 266/C3
Stillwater, Ohio (44679) 284/H5
Stillwater (riv.), Ohio 284/B5
Stillwater, Okla. (74074) 288/N2
Stillwater, Pa. (17878) 294/K3
Stillwell, Ill. (†62380) 222/B3
Stillwell, Ind. (46351) 227/D1
Stilson, Ga. (30415) 216/J6
Stilwell, Kans. (66085) 232/H3
Stilwell, Okla. (74960) 288/S3
Stimson (mt.), Mont. 262/C2
Stinchar (riv.), Scot. 15/G9
Stinesville, Ind. (47464) 227/D6
Stinnett, Texas (79083) 302/C2
Stinson Beach, Calif. (94970) 204/H2
Stinson Lake, N.H. (03274) 268/D4
Štip, Yugo. 45/F5
Stiring-Wendel, France 28/G3
Stirling, Alta. 182/D5
Stirling, Ont. 177/G3
Stirling, 10/B1
Stirling, N.J. (07980) 273/E2
Stirling, No. Terr. 93/C6
Stirling (creek), No. Terr. 93/A4
Stirling (co.), Scot. 15/H7
Stirling, Scot. 15/D1
Stirling-Bridgewater, S. Aust. 94/B8
Stirling City, Calif. (95978) 204/D4
Stirling North, S. Aust. 94/E5
Stirrat, W. Va. (25645) 313/C7
Stirum, N. Dak. (58069) 283/P7
Stites, Idaho (83552) 220/C3
Stittsville, Ont. 177/J2
Stittville, N.Y. (13469) 276/K4
Stitzer, Wis. (53825) 317/E10
Stockbridge, Ga. (30281) 216/D3
Stockbridge△, Mass. (01262) 249/A3
Stockbridge, Mass. (01262) 249/A3
Stockbridge, Mich. (49285) 250/E6
Stockbridge△, Vt. (05772) 268/B4
Stockbridge, Vt. (05772) 268/B4
Stockbridge, Wis. (53088) 317/K7
Stockbridge Ind. Res., Wis. 317/J6
Stockdale, Ohio (45683) 284/E8
Stockdale‡, Pa. (15483) 294/C5
Stockdale, Texas (78160) 302/G8
Stockerau, Austria 41/D2
Stockertown, Pa. (18083) 294/M4
Stockett, Mont. (59480) 262/E3
Stockham, Nebr. (68818) 264/F4
Stockholm△, Maine (04783) 242/G1
Stockholm, N.J. (07460) 273/D1
Stockholm, S. Dak. (57264) 298/R3
Stockholm, Sask. 181/J5
Stockholm (co.), Sweden 18/L7
Stockholm (city county), Sweden 18/G1
Stockholm (cap.), Sweden 18/G1
Stockholm (cap.), Sweden, 3/K3
Stockholm (cap.), Sweden, 7/F3
Stockholm, Wis. (54769) 317/B7
Stockhorn (mt.), Switz. 39/E3
Stockland, Ill. (60967) 222/F3
Stockley, Del. (†19947) 245/S6
Stockport, Eng. 13/E4
Stockport, 10/G2
Stockport, Iowa (52651) 229/K7
Stockport, Ohio (43787) 284/G6
Stockton, Ala. (36579) 194/C9
Stockton, Calif., 186/B3
Stockton, Calif. (*95201) 204/D6
Stockton, Ga. (31649) 216/G9
Stockton, Ill. (61085) 222/C1
Stockton, Iowa (52769) 229/M5
Stockton, Kans. (67669) 232/C2
Stockton, Md. (21864) 245/S8
Stockton, Minn. (55988) 254/G6
Stockton, Mo. (65785) 261/E7
Stockton (res.), Mo. 261/E7
Stockton, N.J. (08559) 273/D3
Stockton, N.Y. (14784) 276/B6
Stockton (plat.), Texas 302/B7
Stockton, Utah (84071) 304/B3
Stockton (isl.), Wis. 317/F2
Stockton Springs△, Maine (04981) 242/F7
Stockton Springs, Maine (04981) 242/F7
Stockville, Nebr. (69042) 264/D4
Stockwell, Ind. (47983) 227/D4
Stoco, Ont. 177/G3
Stocton, Man. 179/C5
Stod, Czech. 41/B2
Stoddard (co.), Mo. 261/N9
Stoddard△, N.H. (03464) 268/C5
Stoddard, N.H. (03464) 268/C5
Stoddard, Wis. (54658) 317/D8
Stoer (pt.), Scot. 15/F3
Stoholm, Den. 21/C5
Stoke Ferry, Eng. 13/H5
Stoke-on-Trent, Eng. 13/E4
Stoke-on-Trent, 10/E4
Stokes (bay), Chile 138/D10
Stokes (co.), N.C. 281/J2
Stokes, N.C. (27884) 281/P3
Stokes Bay, Ont. 177/C2
Stokesdale, N.C. (27357) 281/K2
Stokesley, Eng. 13/F3
Stokkem, Belg. 27/H6
Stolac, Yugo. 45/D4
Stolberg, W. Ger. 22/B3
Stolbtsy, U.S.S.R., 7/G3
Ston, Yugo. 45/C4
Stone (co.), Ark. 203/F2
Stone, Eng. 13/E5
Stone, 10/E4
Stone, Idaho (83280) 220/F7
Stone, Ky. (41567) 237/S5
Stone (co.), Miss. 256/F9
Stone (co.), Mo. 261/F9
Stone (mts.), N.C. 281/F2
Stone, Sask. 181/C6
Stone (mts.), Tenn. 237/T8
Stone Bank, Wis. (†53066) 317/J1
Stonebluff, Ind. (†47987) 227/C4
Stonebluff, Okla. (†74436) 288/P3
Stoneboro, Pa. (16153) 294/B3
Stoneboro, S.C. (†29058) 296/F2
Stone City, Iowa (†52205) 229/L4
Stonecliffe, Ont. 177/F1
Stone Corral (lake), Oreg. 291/H5
Stone Creek, Ohio (43840) 284/G5
Stonefort, Ill. (62987) 222/E6
Stonega, Va. (24285) 307/C7
Stoneham, Colo. (80754) 208/M1
Stoneham, Que. 172/F2
Stoneham△, Mass. (02180) 249/C6
Stone Harbor, N.J. (08247) 273/D5
Stonehaven, 10/E2
Stonehaven, Scot. 15/M6
Stonehenge, Queens. 95/B5
Stonehenge, Sask. 181/F6
Stonehouse, Scot. 15/H8
Stone Lake, Wis. (54876) 317/C4
Stone Mountain, Ga. (30083) 216/D3
Stone Mountain Prov. Park, Br. Col. 184/L2
Stone Park, Ill. (60165) 222/A2
Stoner, Br. Col. 184/F3
Stones (riv.), Tenn. 237/H9
Stones River Nat'l Battlefield, Tenn. 237/H9
Stoneville, Miss. (38776) 256/C4
Stoneville, N.C. (27048) 281/K2
Stoneville, S. Dak. (57784) 298/D4
Stonewall, Ark. (72468) 203/J1
Stonewall, Ga. (30282) 216/C3
Stonewall, La. (71078) 238/C2
Stonewall, Man. 179/E4
Stonewall, Miss. (39363) 256/G6
Stonewall, N.C. (28583) 281/R4
Stonewall, Okla. (74871) 288/O5
Stonewall (co.), Texas 302/D4
Stonewall, Texas (78671) 302/F7
Stonewood, W. Va. (26301) 313/F4
Stoney Creek, Ont. 177/E4
Stoneykirk, Scot. 15/G10
Stoney Point, Ont. 177/B5
Stonington, Colo. (81075) 208/P8
Stonington△, Conn. (06378) 210/H3
Stonington, Conn. (06378) 210/H3
Stonington, Ill. (62567) 222/D4
Stonington△, Maine (04681) 242/F7
Stonington, Mich. (†49878) 250/C3
Stono (inlet), S.C. 296/H6
Stony (riv.), Alaska 196/G2
Stony (lake), Ont. 177/E2
Stony (lake), Ont. 177/G3
Stony (brook), N.J. 273/D3
Stony (ranges), N.S.W. 97/B2
Stony (isl.), N.Y. 276/H3
Stony (pt.), N.Y. 276/H3
Stony (isl.), Newf. 166/C3
Stony (creek), Va. 307/N6
Stony (riv.), W. Va. 313/H4
Stony Beach, Sask. 181/F5
Stony Bottom, W. Va. (24979) 313/F6
Stony Brook, N.Y. (11790) 276/O9
Stony Creek, Conn. (†06405) 210/E3
Stony Creek, N.Y. (12878) 276/M4
Stony Creek, Va. (23882) 307/N7
Stonyford, Calif. (95979) 204/C4
Stony Gorge (res.), Calif. 204/C4
Stony Island, N.S. 169/C5
Stony Lake, Mich. (49455) 250/C5
Stony Mountain, Man. 179/E4
Stony Plain, Alta. 182/C3
Stony Point‡, Mich. (†48166) 250/F7
Stony Point, N.C. (28678) 281/G3
Stony Point, N.Y. (10980) 276/M8
Stony Prairie‡, Ohio (†43420) 284/D3
Stony Rapids, Sask. 181/M2
Stony River, Alaska (99673) 196/G2
Stony Tunguska (riv.), U.S.S.R. 48/K3
Stony Wold, N.Y. (†12968) 276/M1
Storaa (riv.), Den. 21/B5
Stora Lulevatten (lake), Sweden 18/L3
Storden, Minn. (56174) 254/C6
Store Baelt (chan.), Den. 18/G9
Store Baelt (chan.), Den. 21/D6
Store-Heddinge, Den. 18/H9
Store-Heddinge, Den. 21/F7
Stor-Elvdal, Norway 18/G6
Støren, Norway 18/F5
Storey (co.), Nev. 266/B3
Storfjorden (fjord), Norway 18/D2
Storkerson (bay), N.W.T. 187/F2
Storla, S. Dak. (†57359) 298/M6
Storlien, Sweden 18/H5
Storm (bay), Aust. 88/H8
Storm (lake), Iowa 229/C3
Storm (bay), Tasmania 99/D5
Storm Lake, Iowa (50588) 229/C3
Stormont (co.), Ont. 177/K2
Stornoway, Que. 172/F4
Stornoway, 10/C1
Stornoway, Sask. 181/K4
Stornoway, Scot. 15/C3
Stornoway (harb.), Scot. 15/D3
Storøya (isl.), Norway 18/E1
Storozhevsk, U.S.S.R. 52/H2
Storr, The (mt.), Scot. 15/D4
Storrs, Conn. (06268) 210/F1
Storsjön (lake), Sweden 18/J5
Storthoaks, Sask. 182/K6
Storuman, Sweden 18/K4
Storuman (lake), Sweden 18/K4
Storvik, Sweden 18/K6
Story, Ind. (†47448) 227/E6
Story (co.), Iowa 229/G4
Story, Wyo. (82842) 319/F1
Story City, Iowa (50248) 229/F4
Stosch (isl.), Chile 138/C8
Stotesbury, Mo. (64786) 261/C7
Stotesbury, W. Va. (25929) 313/D7
Stotts City, Mo. (65756) 261/E8
Stottville, N.Y. (12172) 276/N6
Stouffville, Ont. 177/J3
Stoughton△, Mass. (02072) 249/K4
Stoughton, Sask. 181/J6
Stoughton, Wis. (53589) 317/H10
Stour (riv.), Eng. 13/H6
Stour (riv.), 10/G4
Stourbridge, Eng. 13/E5
Stourbridge, 10/G3
Stourport-on-Severn, Eng. 13/E5
Stourport-on-Severn, 10/G3
Stout (lake), Ont. 175/B2
Stout, Iowa (50673) 229/H3
Stout, Ohio (45684) 284/D8
Stoutland, Mo. (65567) 261/G7
Stoutsville, Mo. (65283) 261/J3
Stoutsville, Ohio (43154) 284/E6
Stovall, Miss. (38672) 256/C2
Stovall, N.C. (27582) 281/M2
Stover, Mo. (65078) 261/G6
Støvring, Den. 21/D4
Stow△, Maine (†04058) 242/A7
Stow△, Mass. (01775) 249/H3
Stow (creek), N.J. 273/C5
Stow, Ohio (44224) 284/H3
Stow, Scot. 15/L8
Stowe, Pa. (19464) 294/L5
Stowe△, Vt. (05672) 268/B3
Stowe, Vt. (05672) 268/B3
Stowlea, Sask. 181/G5
Stowmarket, Eng. 13/H5
Stowmarket, 10/G4
Stow-on-the-Wold, Eng. 13/F6
Stoy, Ill. (62464) 222/F5
Stoystown, Pa. (15563) 294/E5
Strabane, N. Ire. 17/G2
Strabane‡, Pa. (15363) 294/B5
Strabane, 10/C3
Strachan, Alta. 182/C3
Strachur, Scot. 15/F7
Stradbally, Laoighis, Ire. 17/G5
Stradbally, Waterford, Ire. 17/F7
Strafford, Mo. (65757) 261/F8
Strafford (co.), N.H. 268/E5
Strafford△, N.H. (03884) 268/E5
Strafford, N.H. (03884) 268/E5
Strafford△, Vt. (05072) 268/C4
Strafford, Vt. (05072) 268/C4
Straffordville, Ont. 177/D5
Strahan, Iowa (†51540) 229/B7
Strait (cliffs), Utah 304/C6
Straits, N.C. (†28579) 281/R5
Straits Pond, Mass. (†02045) 249/F7
Straitsville, Conn. (†06770) 210/C3
Strakonice, Czech. 41/B2
Stralsund, E. Ger., 7/F3
Stralsund, E. Ger. 22/E1
Strand, S. Africa 118/F7
Strandburg, S. Dak. (57265) 298/R3
Strandby, Den. 21/D3
Strandquist, Minn. (56758) 254/B2
Strang, Nebr. (68444) 264/G4
Strang, Okla. (74367) 288/R2
Strange Creek, W. Va. (26639) 313/E5
Strangford, N. Ire. 17/K3
Strangford (inlet), N. Ire. 17/K3
Strängnäs, Sweden 18/F1
Stranorlar, Ire. 17/F2
Stranraer, 10/D3
Stranraer, Sask. 181/C4
Stranraer, Scot. 15/G10
Strasbourg, France, 7/E4
Strasbourg, France 28/H3
Strasbourg, Sask. 181/G4
Strasburg, Colo. (80136) 208/L3
Strasburg, Ill. (62465) 222/E4
Strasburg, Mo. (64090) 261/D5
Strasburg, N. Dak. (58573) 283/K7
Strasburg, Ohio (44680) 284/G4
Strasburg, Pa. (17579) 294/K6
Strasburg, Va. (22657) 307/M3
Strassburg, Austria 41/C3
Strata Florida, Wales 13/D5
Stratford, Calif. (93266) 204/F7
Stratford△, Conn. (06497) 210/C4
Stratford (pt.), Conn. 210/C4
Stratford, Ont. 177/C4
Stratford, Iowa (50249) 229/F4
Stratford△, N.H. (†03590) 268/D2
Stratford, N.H. (†03590) 268/D2
Stratford, N.J. (08084) 273/B4
Stratford, N.Y. (13470) 276/L4
Stratford, N.Z. 101/E3
Stratford, Okla. (74872) 288/M5
Stratford, S. Dak. (57474) 298/N3
Stratford, Texas (79084) 302/C1
Stratford, Va. (22558) 307/P4
Stratford, Wash. (98853) 310/F3
Stratford, Wis. (54484) 317/F6
Stratford-Centre, Que. 172/F4
Stratford-upon-Avon, Eng. 13/F5
Stratford-upon-Avon, 10/F4
Strathalbyn, Aust. 88/D8
Strathalbyn, S. Aust. 94/F6
Strathallen, Sask. 181/E6
Stratham△, N.H. (03885) 268/F5
Strathaven, Scot. 15/H8
Strathbogie (dist.), Scot. 15/L5
Strathclair, Man. 179/B4
Strathcona, Minn. (56759) 254/B2
Strathcona Prov. Park, Br. Col. 184/E5
Strathdon, Scot. 15/L5
Strathfield, Aust. 88/L3
Strathfield, N.S.W. 97/J3
Strathlorne, N.S. 169/G2
Strathmere, N.J. (08248) 273/D5
Strathmoor Gardens‡, Ky. (†40201) 237/K4
Strathmoor Manor‡, Ky. (†40201) 237/K4
Strathmoor Village‡, Ky. (†40201) 237/K4
Strathmore, Alta. 182/D4
Strathmore, Calif. (93267) 204/F7
Strathmore, N.J. (†07747) 273/E3
Strathmore (dist.), Scot. 15/J7
Strathnaver, Br. Col. 184/F3
Strathpine, Aust. 88/K2
Strathroy, Ont. 177/C5
Strathy (pt.), 10/D1
Strathy (pt.), Scot. 15/H2
Strattanville, Pa. (16258) 294/D3
Stratton, Colo. (80836) 208/O4
Stratton, Ont. 175/B3
Stratton, Ont. 177/F5
Stratton, Maine (04982) 242/B5
Stratton, Nebr. (69043) 264/C4
Stratton, Ohio (43961) 284/J4
Stratton△, Vt. (†05360) 268/B5
Stratton, Vt. (†05360) 268/B5
Stratton (mt.), Vt. 268/B5
Stratton Meadows, Colo. (†80901) 208/K3
Straubing, W. Ger. 22/E4
Straubville, N. Dak. (58070) 283/O7
Straughn, Ind. (47387) 227/G5
Strausberg, E. Ger. 22/F2
Strausstown, Pa. (19559) 294/K5
Straw Mont. (†59418) 262/G4
Strawberry, Ark. (72469) 203/H2
Strawberry (lake), N. Dak. 283/J4
Strawberry (res.), Utah 304/C3
Strawberry (riv.), Utah 304/D3
Strawberry Plains, Tenn. (37871) 237/O8
Strawberry Point, Iowa (52076) 229/K3
Strawn, Ill. (61775) 222/E3
Strawn, Kans. (66839) 232/G3
Strawn, Texas (76475) 302/F5
Strayhorn, Miss. (†38665) 256/D1
Strážnice, Czech. 41/D2
Streaky (bay), Aust. 88/E6
Streaky (bay), S. Aust. 94/C5
Streaky Bay, Aust. 88/E6
Streaky Bay, S. Aust. 94/D5
Streamstown, Alta. 182/E3
Streamwood, Ill. (60103) 222/E1
Streator, Ill. (61364) 222/E2
Středočeský (reg.), Czech. 41/C2
Středoslovenský (reg.), Czech. 41/E2
Street, Eng. 13/E6
Street, 10/E5
Street, Md. (21154) 245/N2
Streeter, N. Dak. (58483) 283/M6
Streeter, Texas (†76856) 302/E7
Streetman, Texas (75859) 302/H6
Streetsboro, Ohio (44240) 284/H3
Streetsville, Ont. 177/J4
Strehaia, Rum. 45/F3
Strelka, U.S.S.R. 48/L3
Stresa, Italy 34/B2
Stretford, Eng. 13/E4
Streymoy (isl.), Den. 21/B3
Stříbro, Czech. 41/B2
Strichen, Scot. 15/M4
Strickler, Ark. (†72774) 203/B2
Strike, C.J. (res.), Idaho 220/C7
Strimón (gulf), Greece 45/G5
Stringer, Miss. (39481) 256/F7
Stringtown, Miss. (38777) 256/C3
Stringtown, Okla. (74569) 288/P6
Stripe (lake), Sask. 181/C4
Strofádhes (isls.), Greece 45/E7
Stroh, Ind. (46789) 227/G1
Strokestown, Ire. 17/E4
Stroma (isl.), Scot. 15/K2
Strömbacka, Sweden 18/K6
Strombeek-Bever, Belg. 27/C9
Stromboli (isl.), Italy 34/E5
Strome, Alta. 182/E3
Stromness, 10/E1
Stromness, Scot. 15/K2
Stromsburg, Nebr. (68666) 264/G3
Strömstad, Sweden 18/G7
Strömsund, Sweden 18/K5
Stronach, Mich. (49681) 250/C4
Stroner, Wyo. (†82722) 319/H1
Strong, Ark. (71765) 203/F7
Strong△, Maine (04983) 242/C6
Strong, Miss. (†39730) 256/G3
Strong (riv.), Miss. 256/D7
Strong City, Kans. (66869) 232/F3
Strong City, Okla. (73665) 288/G3
Strongfield, Sask. 181/E4
Stronghurst, Ill. (61480) 222/C3
Strong Pine, Sask. 181/F2
Strongs, Mich. (49790) 250/E2
Strongsville, Ohio (44136) 284/G10
Stronsay (isl.), 10/E1
Stronsay (firth), Scot. 15/L1
Stronsay (isl.), Scot. 15/M1
Strontian, Scot. 15/E6
Stropkov, Czech. 41/F2
Stroud, Ala. (†36855) 194/H4
Stroud, Ont. 177/E3
Stroud, Eng. 13/E6
Stroud, 10/E5
Stroud, N.S.W. 97/G3
Stroud, Okla. (74079) 288/N3
Stroudsburg, Pa. (18360) 294/M4
Struan, Sask. 181/D3
Struble, Iowa (51057) 229/A3
Struer, Den. 18/F8
Struer, Den. 21/B5
Struga, Yugo. 45/E5
Strum, Wis. (54770) 317/D6
Struma (riv.), Bulg. 45/F5
Strumica, Yugo. 45/F5
Strunk, Ky. (42649) 237/N7
Struthers, Ohio (44471) 284/J3
Stryker, Mont. (59933) 262/B2
Stryker, Ohio (43557) 284/B3
Strykersville, N.Y. (14145) 276/C5
Strzegom, Poland 47/C3
Strzelce Kraieńskie, Poland 47/B2
Strzelce Opolskie, Poland 47/D3
Strzelecki (creek), S. Aust. 94/G3
Strzelin, Poland 47/C3
Strzelno, Poland 47/D2
Stuart (isl.), Alaska 196/F2
Stuart (range), Aust. 88/E5
Stuart (lake), Br. Col. 184/E3
Stuart, Fla. (33494) 212/F4
Stuart, Iowa (50250) 229/E6
Stuart, Nebr. (68780) 264/E2
Stuart (range), S. Aust. 94/D3
Stuart, Okla. (74570) 288/O5
Stuart, Va. (24171) 307/H7
Stuart (mt.), Wash. 310/E3
Stuartburn, Man. 179/F5
Stuart Island, Br. Col. 184/E5
Stuarts Draft, Va. (24477) 307/L4
Stuart Town, N.S.W. 97/E3
Stubbekøbing, Den. 21/E8
Stubbenkammer (pt.), E. Ger. 22/E1
Stub Hill (mt.), N.H. 268/E1
Stubno, Alta. 182/E3
Stuckey, S.C. (29554) 296/H4
Studley, Kans. (67759) 232/B2
Studley, Va. (23162) 307/O5
Stukely-Sud, Que. 172/E4
Stump (lake), N. Dak. 283/O4
Stumptown, W. Va. (25280) 313/E5
Stumpy Point, N.C. (27978) 281/T3
Stung Sen (riv.), Cambodia 72/E4
Stung Treng, Cambodia 72/E4
Stupino, U.S.S.R. 52/E4
Stura (riv.), Italy 34/A2
Sturbridge△, Mass. (01566) 249/F4
Sturdivant, Mo. (63782) 261/M8
Sturgeon (lake), Alta. 182/B2
Sturgeon (lake), Ont. 177/G5
Sturgeon (bay), Man. 179/E3
Sturgeon (riv.), Mich. 250/C2
Sturgeon (riv.), Minn. 254/F3
Sturgeon, Mo. (65284) 261/H4
Sturgeon, P.E.I. 169/F2
Sturgeon, Pa. (15082) 294/B5
Sturgeon (riv.), Sask. 181/E2
Sturgeon Bay, Wis. (54235) 317/M6
Sturgeon Falls, 163/H6
Sturgeon Falls, Ont. 175/E3
Sturgeon Falls, Ont. 177/E1
Sturgeon Heights, Alta. 182/B2
Sturgeon Lake, Minn. (55783) 254/F4
Sturgeon Landing, Sask. 181/N4
Sturgeon River, Sask. 181/E2
Sturgeon Valley, Sask. 181/E2
Sturgis, Ky. (42459) 237/F5
Sturgis, Mich. (49091) 250/D7
Sturgis, Miss. (39769) 256/G4
Sturgis, S. Dak. (57785) 298/B5
Sturgis, Sask. 181/J4
Sturminster Newton, Eng. 13/E7
Štúrovo, Czech. 41/E3
Sturt (des.), Aust. 88/G5
Sturt (mt.), N.S.W. 97/A1
Sturt (creek), W. Aust. 92/D2
Sturt (plain), No. Terr. 93/C4
Sturt (des.), S. Aust. 94/G3
Sturt (riv.), S. Aust. 94/B8
Sturt (des.), Queens. 95/B3
Sturtevant, Wis. (53177) 317/M3
Stutsman (co.), N. Dak. 283/M5
Stutterheim, S. Africa 118/D6
Stuttgart, Ark. (72160) 203/H4
Stuttgart, Kans. (67670) 232/C2
Stuttgart, W. Ger., 7/E4
Stuttgart, W. Ger. 22/C4
Styria (prov.), Austria 41/C3
Suai, Malaysia 85/E5
Suakin, 102/F3
Suakin, Sudan 59/C6
Suakin, Sudan 111/G4
Suakin (arch.), Sudan 111/G4
Suamico, Wis. (54173) 317/K6
Suapi, Bol. 136/B4
Suapure (riv.), Ven. 124/E4
Suaqui, Mex. 150/E2
Suárez (riv.), Col. 126/D4
Subang, Indon. 85/H2
Subata, U.S.S.R. 53/D2
Subeihi, Jordan 65/D3
Subh, Jebel (mt.), Saudi Ar. 59/C5
Subiaco, Ark. (72865) 203/C3
Subiaco, Aust. 88/B2
Subiaco, W. Aust. 92/A1
Subi Besar (isl.), Indon. 85/D5
Subic (bay), Phil. 82/C3
Sublett (mts.), Idaho 220/E7
Sublett, Ky. (41470) 237/P5
Sublette, Ill. (61367) 222/D2
Sublette, Kans. (67877) 232/B4
Sublette, Mo. (†63546) 261/G2
Sublette (co.), Wyo. 319/C3
Subligna, Ga. (†30747) 216/B1
Sublimity, Oreg. (97385) 291/E3
Subotica, Yugo., 7/F4
Subotica, Yugo. 45/D2
Subtle, Ky. (42629) 237/L7
Sucarnochee, Miss. (†39352) 256/H5
Sucarnoochee (creek), Miss. 256/G5
Succasunna, N.J. (07876) 273/D2
Success, Ark. (72470) 203/J1
Success, Mo. (65570) 261/H8
Success, Sask. 181/D5
Succor (creek), Oreg. 291/K4
Suceava, Rum. 45/G2
Suchan, U.S.S.R. 48/O5
Suchedniów, Poland 47/E3
Suches, Bol. 136/A4
Suches (riv.), Bol. 136/A4
Suches, Ga. (30572) 216/E1
Suchitoto, El Salv. 154/C4
Süchow, China 77/J5
Sucia (bay), P. Rico 161/A3
Sucia (isl.), Wash. 310/C2
Sucio (riv.), Col. 126/B4
Suck (riv.), Ire. 17/E5
Sucre (cap.), Bol., 3/F6
Sucre (cap.), Bol., 120/D4
Sucre (cap.), Bol. 136/C6
Sucre, Bolívar, Col. 126/C3
Sucre, Caquetá, Col. 126/C7
Sucre (dept.), Col. 126/C3
Sucre, Ec. 128/B3
Sucre (state), Ven. 124/G2
Sucre, Ven. 124/D3
Sucúa, Ec. 128/C4
Sud (dept.), Haiti 158/A6
Suda (riv.), U.S.S.R. 52/E3
Sudak, U.S.S.R. 52/E6
Sudan, 3/L5
SUDAN, 59/B6
SUDAN, 102/E3
SUDAN, 111/E4
Sudan (reg.), 102/E3
Sudan (reg.), Chad 111/C5
Sudan (reg.), Dahomey 106/E6
Sudan (reg.), Mali 106/D6
Sudan (reg.), Niger 106/F6
Sudan (reg.), Nigeria 106/F6
Sudan (reg.), Sudan 111/E5
Sudan, Texas (79371) 302/B3
Sudan (reg.), Upp. Volta 106/D6

Tolland 447

Throckmorton, Texas (76083) 302/F4
Throne, Alta. 182/E3
Throop, Pa. (18512) 294/L3
Thrums, Br. Col. 184/J5
Thuin, Belg. 27/E8
Thule, Greenl., 3/F2
Thule, Greenl., 4/B13
Thule, Greenl., 146/M2
Thumail, Iraq 66/C4
Thun, Switz. 39/E3
Thun (lake), Switz. 39/E3
Thunder (bay), Ont. 175/C3
Thunder (bay), Mich. 250/F4
Thunder (creek), S. Dak. 298/N4
Thunder (lake), Wis. 317/H4
Thunder Bay (riv.), Mich. 250/F3
Thunder Bay, 163/H6
Thunder Bay (co.), Ont. 175/C3
Thunder Bay (co.), Ont. 177/H5
Thunder Bay, Ont., 146/K5
Thunder Bay, Ont. 175/C3
Thunder Bay, Ont. 177/H5
Thunderbird (lake), Okla. 288/M4
Thunderbolt, Ga. (31404) 216/K6
Thunder Butte (creek), S. Dak. 298/E3
Thunder Creek, Sask. 181/E5
Thunder Hawk, S. Dak. (57655) 298/F2
Thur (riv.), Switz. 39/G1
Thurgau (canton), Switz. 39/H1
Thüringer Wald (för.), E. Ger. 22/D3
Thuringia (Thüringen) (reg.), E. Ger. 22/D3
Thurles, 10/B4
Thurles, Ire. 17/F6
Thurloo Downs, N.S.W. 97/B1
Thurlow (dam), Ala. 194/G6
Thurlow, Br. Col. 184/E5
Thurlow, Mont. (†59347) 262/K4
Thurman, Iowa (51654) 229/B7
Thurman, N.Y. (†12885) 276/M3
Thurman, Ohio (45685) 284/F8
Thurmond, W. Va. (25936) 313/D7
Thurmont, Md. (21788) 245/J2
Thurrock, Eng. 13/H6
Thurrock, 10/C5
Thursday Island, Aust. 88/G2
Thursday Island, Queens. 95/B1
Thurso, Que. 172/B4
Thurso, 10/E1
Thurso, Scot. 15/K2
Thurso (riv.), Scot. 15/J3
Thurston (isl.), Ant. 5/C14
Thurston (co.), Nebr. 264/H2
Thurston, Nebr. (68062) 264/H2
Thurston, Ohio (43157) 284/E6
Thurston (co.), Wash. 310/C4
Thusis, Switz. 39/H3
Thutade (lake), Br. Col. 184/D2
Thyatira, Miss. (†33668) 256/E1
Thyborøn, Den. 21/B4
Thyregod, Den. 21/C6
Thysville, Dem. Rep. of the Congo. 115/C5
Tia, N.S.W. 97/F2
Tiahuanacu, Bol. 136/A5
Tia Juana, Ven. 124/C2
Tiaret, Alg. 106/E1
Tiatucurá, Urug. 145/C3
Tiawah, Okla. (†74017) 288/P2
Tib, Ras el (Bon) (cape), Tun. 106/G1
Tibagi, Braz. 135/A4
Tibagi (riv.), Braz. 135/A4
Tibaná, Col. 126/D5
Tibati, Cameroon 115/B2
Tibbie, Ala. (36583) 194/B8
Tibbita, N.S.W. 97/C4
Tiber (riv.), Italy, 7/F4
Tiber (riv.), Italy 34/D3
Tiber (res.), Mont. 262/E2
Tiberias, Israel 65/C2
Tiberias (lake), Israel 65/D2
Tibesti (mts.), Chad 111/C3
Tibesti, Serir (des.), Chad 111/C3
Tibesti, Serir (des.), Libya 111/C3
Tibesti (mts.), 102/D2
Tibet (reg.), China, 3/P4
Tibet (reg.), China, 54/M6
Tibet (aut. reg.), China 77/C5
Tibooburra, Aust. 88/G5
Tibooburra, N.S.W. 97/B1
Tibugá (gulf), Col. 126/B5
Tiburon, Calif. (94920) 204/J2
Tiburon (cape), Haiti 156/C3
Tiburon, Haiti 158/A6
Tiburón (isl.), Mex. 150/C2
Tiburón (cape), Pan. 154/J6
Ticaco, Peru 128/H11
Ticao (isl.), Phil. 82/D4
Tice, Fla. (33905) 212/E5
Tichigan, Wis. (†53185) 317/K2
Tichigan (lake), Wis. 317/K2
Tichitt, Mauritania 106/C5
Tichlá (well), Sp. Sahara 106/B4
Tichnor, Ark. (72166) 203/H5
Ticino (canton), Switz. 39/G4
Ticino (riv.), Switz. 39/G4
Tickfaw, La. (70466) 238/M1
Tickfaw (riv.), La. 238/M1
Tickle (bay), Newf. 166/D2
Ticonderoga, N.Y. (12883) 276/N3
Ticonic, Iowa (†51010) 229/B4
Ticul, Mex. 150/P6
Tidaholm, Sweden 18/J7
Tide Head, N. Br. 170/D1
Tidewater, Oreg. (97390) 291/D3
Tidikelt (oasis), Alg. 106/E3
Tidioute, Pa. (16351) 294/D2
Tidjikja, 102/A3
Tidjikja, Mauritania 106/B5
Tidnish, N.S. 169/E3
Tidore (isl.), Indon. 85/H5
Tidra (isl.), Mauritania 106/A5
Tiedemann (mt.), Br. Col. 184/E4
Tiefenkastel, Switz. 39/J3
Tiehling, China 77/K3
Tiekel, Alaska (†99566) 196/J2
Tiel, Neth. 27/G5
Tielt, Brabant, Belg. 27/F7
Tielt, West Flanders, Belg. 27/C7
Tien Chih (lake), China 77/F7
Tienen, Belg. 27/F7
Tien Shan (range), China, 54/L5
Tien Shan (range), China 77/B3
Tienshui, China 77/F5
Tientsin, China, 3/Q4
Tientsin, China, 54/P6
Tientsin, China 77/J4
Tien Yen, N. Vietnam 72/E2
Tie Plant, Miss. (38960) 256/E3
Tiernan, Oreg. (†97453) 291/C3
Tierp, Sweden 18/K6
Tierra Amarilla, Chile 138/A6
Tierra Amarilla, N. Mex. (87575) 274/C2
Tierra Blanca, Mex. 150/L7
Tierra Blanca (creek), N. Mex. 274/B6
Tierra Blanca (creek), Texas 302/B3
Tierra del Fuego (isl.), 3/F8
Tierra del Fuego (isl.), 120/D8
Tierra del Fuego, Antártida, e Islas del Atlántico Sur (terr.), Arg. 143/C7
Tierra del Fuego, Grande de (isl.), Arg. 143/C7
Tierra del Fuego, Grande de (isl.), Chile 138/E11
Tierralta, Col. 126/C3
Tie Siding, Wyo. (82084) 319/G4
Tietê (riv.), Braz., 120/E5
Tietê (riv.), Braz. 132/D8
Tietê, Braz. 135/C3
Tietê (riv.), Braz. 135/B2
Tieton, Wash. (98947) 310/E4
Tieton (riv.), Wash. 310/D4
Tieyon, S. Aust. 94/C2
Tiff, Mo. (63674) 261/L6
Tiffany, Colo. (†81137) 208/D8
Tiffany (mt.), Wash. 310/F2
Tiff City, Mo. (64868) 261/C9
Tiffin, Iowa (52340) 229/K5
Tiffin, Mo. (†64744) 261/E7
Tiffin, Ohio (44883) 284/D3
Tiffin (riv.), Ohio 284/B3
Tiflis (Tbilisi), U.S.S.R. 52/F6
Tift (co.), Ga. 216/E7
Tifton, Ga. (31794) 216/F8
Tiftona, Tenn. (†37401) 237/L11
Tigalda (isl.), Alaska 196/F4
Tigard, Oreg. (97223) 291/A2
Tiger, Ga. (30576) 216/F1
Tiger (falls), Guyana 131/C4
Tiger (Matjan) (isls.), Indon. 85/G7
Tiger (falls), Sur. 131/C4
Tiger, Wash. (99177) 310/H2
Tiger Hills, Sask. 181/F3
Tiger Lily, Alta. 182/C2
Tigerton, Wis. (54486) 317/H6
Tigerville, S.C. (29688) 296/C1
Tighina (Bendery), U.S.S.R. 52/C5
Tigil', U.S.S.R. 48/Q4
Tigil', U.S.S.R., 54/U4
Tignall, Ga. (30668) 216/G3
Tignamar, Chile 138/B1
Tignish, P.E.I. 169/D2
Tigre, Arg. 143/G7
Tigre (isl.), N. Vietnam 72/E3
Tigre (prov.), Eth. 111/H5
Tigre (riv.), Peru, 120/C3
Tigre (riv.), Peru 128/E4
Tigre (isl.), Urug. 145/A7
Tigre (riv.), Ven. 124/G3
Tigrett, Tenn. (38070) 237/C9
Tigris (riv.), 54/H6
Tigris (riv.), Iran 59/E3
Tigris (riv.), Iraq 59/E3
Tigris (riv.), Syria 59/E3
Tigris (riv.), Turkey 59/E3
Tigris (riv.), Syria 63/K4
Tigris (Dicle) (riv.), Turkey 63/J4
Tigris (riv.), Iraq 66/E4
Tiguabos, Cuba 158/J4
Tiguentourine, Alg. 106/F3
Tihama (reg.), Saudi Ar. 59/C5
Tihama (reg.), Yemen Arab Rep. 59/C5
Tihany, Hung. 41/D3
Tihuatlán, Mex. 150/L6
Tihwa (Urumchi), China, 54/M5
Tijamuchi (riv.), Bol. 136/C4
Tijeglo, Somalia 115/H3
Tijeras, N. Mex. (87059) 274/C3
Tijuana, Mex. 150/A1
Tijucas, Braz. 132/D9
Tikchik (lakes), Alaska 196/G2
Tikhoretsk, U.S.S.R. 52/F5
Tikhvin, U.S.S.R. 52/D3
Tiko, Cameroon 115/A3
Tikopia (isl.), Br. Sol. Is., 87/G7
Tikrit, Iraq 59/D3
Tikrit, Iraq 66/C3
Tiksi, U.S.S.R. 48/N2
Tiksi, U.S.S.R., 4/B3
Tilburg, Neth. 27/G5
Tilbury, Ont. 177/B5
Tilcara, Arg. 143/C1
Tilcha, S. Aust. 94/G3
Tilden, Ill. (62292) 222/D5
Tilden, Ky. (†42409) 237/F5
Tilden, Miss. (†38843) 256/H2
Tilden, Nebr. (68781) 264/G2
Tilden, Texas (78072) 302/F9
Tilemsi (valley), Mali 106/E5
Tilford, S. Dak. (†57769) 298/C5
Tilghman, Md. (21671) 245/N6
Tilin, Burma 72/B2
Tiline, Ky. (42083) 237/E6
Till (riv.), Eng. 13/F2
Tillabéry, Niger 106/E6
Tillamook (co.), Oreg. 291/D2
Tillamook, Oreg. (97141) 291/D2
Tillamook (head), Oreg. 291/C2
Tillanchong (isl.), India 68/G7
Tillar, Ark. (71670) 203/H6
Tillatoba, Miss. (38961) 256/E3
Tillberga, Sweden 18/K7
Tilleda, Wis. (54978) 317/J6
Tiller, Oreg. (97484) 291/E5
Tillery, N.C. (27887) 281/O2
Tillery (lake), N.C. 281/J4
Tilley, Alta. 182/E4
Tilley, N. Br. 170/C2
Tilley Road, N. Br. 170/E1
Tillicoultry, 10/B1
Tillicoultry, Scot. 15/J7
Tillicum, Wash. (98492) 310/C3
Tillman, Miss. (†39150) 256/C7
Tillman (co.), Okla. 288/J6
Tillman, S.C. (29943) 296/E7
Tillson, N.Y. (12486) 276/M7
Tillsonburg, Ont. 177/D5
Tilney, Sask. 181/F5
Tilomonte, Chile 138/B4
Tílos (isl.), Greece 45/H7
Tilpa, N.S.W. 97/C2
Tilston, Man. 179/A5
Tilt (riv.), Scot. 15/J6
Tiltagara, N.S.W. 97/C2
Tiltil, Chile 138/G2
Tilting, Newf. 166/D4
Tilton, Ark. (72380) 203/J3
Tilton, Ga. (†30720) 216/B1
Tilton, Ill. (†61832) 222/F3
Tilton△, N.H. (03276) 268/D5
Tilton-Northfield, N.H. (03276) 268/D5
Tiltonsville, Ohio (43963) 284/J5
Timagami (lake), Ont. 175/D3
Timagami, Ont. 177/K5
Timagami (lake), Ont. 177/K5
Timan (ridge), U.S.S.R. 52/G1
Timaná, Col. 126/C7
Timane (riv.), Par. 144/C3
Timaru, N.Z. 101/C6
Timashevsk, U.S.S.R. 52/E5
Timbákion, Greece 45/G8
Timbalier (bay), La. 238/K8
Timbalier (isl.), La. 238/K8
Timbarra (riv.), N.S.W. 97/G1
Timbédra, Mauritania 106/C5
Timber (mt.), Nev. 266/F4
Timber (mt.), Nev. 266/E5
Timber, Oreg. (97144) 291/D2
Timberlake, N.C. (27583) 281/M2
Timberlake, Ohio (†44094) 284/J8
Timber Lake, S. Dak. (57656) 298/H3
Timberlea, N.S. 169/E4
Timberville, Va. (22853) 307/L3
Timbío, Col. 126/B6
Timbiquí, Col. 126/B6
Timblin, Pa. (15778) 294/D4
Timbo, Ark. (72680) 203/F2
Timboulaga (well), Niger 106/F5
Timbuktu, 102/B3
Timbuktu, Mali 106/D5
Time, Ill. (†62363) 222/C4
Times Beach, Mo. (†63025) 261/O3
Timeu, Alta. 182/C2
Timewell, Ill. (62375) 222/C3
Timgad (ruins), Alg. 106/F1
Timimoun, Alg. 106/E3
Timiris (cape), Mauritania 106/A5
Timiș (riv.), Rum. 45/E3
Timiskaming (lake), 163/J6
Timiskaming (co.), Ont. 175/D3
Timiskaming (lake), Ont. 175/E3
Timiskaming (co.), Ont. 177/K5
Timișoara, Rum., 7/G4
Timișoara, Rum. 45/E3
Timken, Kans. (67582) 232/C3
Timmendorferstrand, W. Ger. 22/D1
Timmins, 163/H6
Timmins, Ont. 175/D3
Timmins, Ont. 177/J5
Timmins, Ont., 146/K5
Timmissao (well), Alg. 106/E4
Timmonsville, S.C. (29161) 296/H3
Timms Hill (mt.), Wis. 317/F5
Timnath, Colo. (80547) 208/J2
Timok (riv.), Bulg. 45/F3
Timok (riv.), Yugo. 45/F3
Timoleague, Ire. 17/D8
Timonium-Lutherville, Md. (21093) 245/M3
Timor (isl.), 3/R6
Timor (sea), Aust. 88/D2
Timor (isl.), Indon., 54/R10
Timor (reg.), Indon. 85/H7
Timor (sea), Indon. 85/H7
Timor (sea), W. Aust. 92/D1
Timor (sea), No. Terr. 93/A2
Timote, Urug. 145/D4
Timotes, Ven. 124/C3
Timothy, Tenn. (†38568) 237/L8
Timpahute (range), Nev. 266/F5
Timpanogos Cave Nat'l Mon., Utah 304/C3
Timpas, Colo. (81079) 208/M7
Timpas (creek), Colo. 208/M7
Timpson, Texas (75975) 302/K6
Timrå, Sweden 18/K5
Tims Ford (lake), Tenn. 237/J10
Tina (mt.), Dom. Rep. 158/D6
Tina, Mo. (64682) 261/F3
Tinabely, Ire. 17/H6
Tinaca (pt.), Phil. 82/E8
Tinaca (pt.), Phil. 85/H4
Tinaco, Ven. 124/D3
Tinaquillo, Ven. 124/D3
Tinca, Rum. 45/F2
Tin City, Alaska (†99778) 196/E1
Tincup, Colo. (†81210) 208/F5
Tindall, Mo. (†64683) 261/E2
Tindouf, Alg. 106/C3
Tindouf, Sebkra de (salt lake), Alg. 106/C3
Tindouf, 102/B2
Tinela, Ala. (†36452) 194/D7
Tineo, Spain 33/C1
Tinggi, Pulau (isl.), Malaysia 72/E7
Tingha, N.S.W. 97/F1
Tinghai, China 77/K5
Tingiarmiut, Greenl., 4/C12
Tinglev, Den. 21/C8
Tingley, Iowa (50863) 229/E7
Tingmerkpuk (mt.), Alaska 196/F1
Tingo María, Peru 128/D7
Tingri Dzong, China 77/C6
Tingsi, China 77/G5
Tingsin, China 77/E3
Tinguiririca, Chile 138/G6
Tinguiririca (riv.), Chile 138/F5
Tingwick, Que. 172/F4
Tinharé (isl.), Braz. ...
Tinjoub, Mor. 106/C3
Tinker A.F.B., Okla. 288/M4
Tinkers (creek), Md. 245/F6
Tinley Park, Ill. (60477) 222/B2
Tinmouth△, Vt. (†05773) 268/A5
Tinmouth, Vt. (†05773) 268/A5
Tinnie, N. Mex. (88351) 274/D5
Tinogasta, Arg., 120/D5
Tinogasta, Arg. 143/C2
Tínos, Greece 45/G7
Tínos (isl.), Greece 45/G7
Tinquipaya, Bol. 136/C6
Tinrhert Hamada (des.), Alg. 106/F3
Tinrhert Hamada (des.), Libya 111/B2
Tinsley, Ky. (40993) 237/O7
Tinsman, Ark. (71767) 203/F6
Tinsukia, India 68/H3
Tintagel, Br. Col. 184/E3
Tintah, Minn. (56583) 254/B5
Tintina, Arg. 143/D2
Tinto (riv.), Spain 33/C4
Tinui, N.Z. 101/F4
Tiny, Sask. 181/J4
Tin-Zaouatene, Mali 106/E5
Tioga, Ill. (62351) 222/B3
Tioga, La. (71477) 238/F4
Tioga, N. Dak. (58852) 283/E3
Tioga (co.), N.Y. 276/H6
Tioga (co.), Pa. 294/H2
Tioga, Pa. (16946) 294/H2
Tioga (riv.), Pa. 294/H1
Tioga, Texas (76271) 302/H4
Tioga, W. Va. (26691) 313/E6
Tioman, Pulau (isl.), Malaysia 72/E7
Tiona, Pa. (16352) 294/D2
Tionesta, Pa. (16353) 294/C2
Tionesta Creek (res.), Pa. 294/D3
Tiosa, Ind. (†46975) 227/E2
Tioughnioga (riv.), N.Y. 276/H6
Tipitapa, Nic. 154/E4
Tipler, Wis. (†49935) 317/J4
Tiplersville, Miss. (38674) 256/G1
Tippah (co.), Miss. 256/G1
Tipp City, Ohio (45371) 284/B6
Tippecanoe (co.), Ind. 227/D4
Tippecanoe, Ind. (46570) 227/E2
Tippecanoe (riv.), Ind. 227/E2
Tippecanoe, Ohio (44699) 284/H5
Tipperary, 10/B4
Tipperary (co.), Ire. 17/F6
Tipperary, Ire. 17/E7
Tippettville, Ga. (†31092) 216/E6
Tippo, Miss. (38962) 256/D3
Tipton, Calif. (93272) 204/F7
Tipton (co.), Ind. 227/E4
Tipton, Ind. (46072) 227/E4
Tipton, Iowa (52772) 229/L5
Tipton, Kans. (67485) 232/D2
Tipton, Mo. (65081) 261/G5
Tipton, Okla. (73570) 288/H6
Tipton, Pa. (16684) 294/F4
Tipton (co.), Tenn. 237/B9
Tipton, Tenn. (38071) 237/B10
Tiptonville, Tenn. (38079) 237/B8
Tip Top (mt.), Ont. 175/C3
Tip Top (mt.), Ont. 177/H5
Tiptop, Ky. (†41409) 237/P5
Tiptop, Va. (24655) 307/F6
Tipuani, Bol. 136/B4
Tiran, Kans. (67582) 232/C3
Tiran (str.), U.A.R. 59/C4
Tiran (isl.), Saudi Ar. 59/C4
Tiran (str.), Saudi Ar. 59/C4
Tiran (str.), U.A.R. 111/F2
Tiranë (cap.), Alb., 7/F4
Tiranë (Tirana) (cap.), Alb. 45/E5
Tirano, Italy 34/C1
Tiraque, Bol. 136/C5
Tiraspol', U.S.S.R. 52/D5
Tiraspol', U.S.S.R., 7/G4
Tirat Hakarmel, Israel 65/B2
Tirat Zevi, Israel 65/D3
Tire, Turkey 59/A2
Tire, Turkey 63/B3
Tirebolu, Turkey 63/H2
Tiree (isl.), 10/C2
Tiree (isl.), Scot. 15/C6
Tîrgoviște, Rum. 45/G3
Tîrgu Frumos, Rum. 45/H2
Tîrgu Jiu, Rum. 45/F3
Tîrgu Mureș, Rum. 45/G2
Tîrgu Neamț, Rum. 45/G2
Tîrgu Ocna, Rum. 45/H2
Tîrgu Secuiesc, Rum. 45/H2
Tirich Mir (mt.), Pak. 59/K2
Tirich Mir (mt.), Pak. 68/C1
Tirlemont (Tienen), Belg. 27/F7
Tîrnava Mare (riv.), Rum. 45/G2
Tîrnăveni, Rum. 45/F2
Tírnavos, Greece 45/F6
Tiro, Ohio (44887) 284/E4
Tirol (prov.), Austria 41/B3
Tirol (reg.), Austria 41/A3
Tirry (riv.), Scot. 15/H3
Tirschenreuth, W. Ger. 22/E4
Tirso (riv.), Italy 34/B4
Tiruchchirappalli, India, 54/M8
Tiruchchirappalli, India 68/D6
Tiruchendur, India 68/D7
Tirunelveli, India 68/D7
Tiruntán, Peru 128/E6
Tirupati, India 68/D6
Tiruppattur, India 68/D6
Tiruvannamalai, India 68/D6
Tirzah, S.C. (†29745) 296/E2
Tisbury, Eng. 13/F6
Tisch Mills, Wis. (54240) 317/L7
Tisdale, 163/F5
Tisdale, Sask. 181/H3
Tishomingo (co.), Miss. 256/H1
Tishomingo, Miss. (38873) 256/H1
Tishomingo, Okla. (73460) 288/N6
Tiskilwa, Ill. (61368) 222/D2
Tišnov, Czech. 41/D2
Tisovec, Czech. 41/E2
Tistrup, Den. 21/B6
Tisvildeleje, Den. 21/E5
Tisza (riv.), Hung. 41/F3
Tisza (riv.), Yugo. 45/E3
Tiszacsege, Hung. 41/F3
Tiszaföldvár, Hung. 41/F3
Tiszafüred, Hung. 41/F3
Tiszakécske, Hung. 41/E3
Tiszalök, Hung. 41/F2
Tiszavasvári, Hung. 41/F3
Titagarh, India 68/F1
Tit-Ary, U.S.S.R. 48/N2
Titicaca (lake), 3/F6
Titicaca (lake), 120/D4
Titicaca (lake), Bol. 136/A4
Titicaca (lake), Peru 128/H10
Titicus, Conn. (†06877) 210/A3
Titicus (mt.), Conn. 210/A3
Titicus (riv.), Conn. 210/A3
Titihira (head), N.Z. 101/B5
Titirangi, N.Z. 101/B1
Titlagarh, India 68/E4
Titlis (mt.), Switz. 39/F3
Titograd, Yugo. 45/D4
Titonka, Iowa (50480) 229/E2
Titovo Užice, Yugo. 45/D4
Titov Veles, Yugo. 45/E5
Tittabawassee (riv.), Mich. 250/E5
Titule, 102/E4
Titule, Dem. Rep. of the Congo. 115/E3
Titus, Ala. (36080) 194/F5
Titus (mt.), Conn. 210/B1
Titus, Ga. (†30546) 216/E1
Titus (lake), N.Y. 276/M1
Titus (co.), Texas 302/K4
Titusville, Fla. (32780) 212/F3
Titusville, N.J. (08560) 273/D3
Titusville, Pa. (16354) 294/C2
Tiumpan (head), Scot. 15/D3
Tivaouane, Sen. 106/A5
Tiverton, Ont. 177/C3
Tiverton, Eng. 13/D7
Tiverton, 10/E5
Tiverton, N.S. 169/B4
Tiverton△, R.I. (02878) 249/K6
Tiverton, R.I. (02878) 249/K6
Tiverton Four Corners, R.I. (†02878) 249/K6
Tivoli, Italy 34/F6
Tivoli, N.Y. (12583) 276/N6
Tivoli, Texas (77990) 302/G9
Tiv'on, Israel 65/C2
Tiwi, Phil. 82/D4
Tixmucuy, Mex. 150/O7
Tixtla de Guerrero, Mex. 150/K8
Tizard (bank), Asia 85/E3
Tizayuca, Mex. 150/L1
Tizimín, Mex. 150/Q6
Tizi-Ouzou, Alg. 106/E1
Tiznit, Mor. 106/B3
Tjalang, Indon. 85/B5
Tjareme (mt.), Indon. 85/H2
Tjeukemeer (lake), Neth. 27/H3
Tjiamis, Indon. 85/H2
Tjiandjur, Indon. 85/H2
Tjidulang, Indon. 85/H2
Tjilatjap, Indon. 85/H2
Tjimahi, Indon. 85/H2
Tjirebon, Indon. 85/H2
Tjurup, Indon. 85/C6
Tjuv (fjord), Norway 18/D2
Tlachichuca, Mex. 150/O1
Tlacolula de Matamoros, Mex. 150/L8
Tlacotalpan, Mex. 150/M7
Tlacotepec de Mejiá, Mex. 150/P1
Tlahualilo de Zaragoza, Mex. 150/H3
Tlalixcoyan, Mex. 150/Q2
Tlalmanalco de Velásquez, Mex. 150/L1
Tlalnepantla de Comonfort, Mex. 150/L1
Tlalpan, Mex. 150/L1
Tlaltenango, Mex. 150/H6
Tlaltizapan, Mex. 150/L2
Tlapacoyan, Mex. 150/P1
Tlapa de Comonfort, Mex. 150/K8
Tlaquiltenango, Mex. 150/L2
Tlaxcala (state), Mex. 150/N1
Tlaxcala de Xicotencatl, Mex. 150/M1
Tlaxco de Morelos, Mex. 150/N1
Tlaxiaco, Mex. 150/L8
Tlayacapan, Mex. 150/L1
Tlell, Br. Col. 184/B3
Tlemcen, Alg. 106/D2
Tlemcen, 102/C1
Tmessa, Libya 111/C2
Tni Haïa (well), Alg. 106/D4
Toa, Cuchillas de (mts.), Cuba 158/K4
Toa Alta, P. Rico 161/D1
Toa Baja, P. Rico 161/D1
Toad (riv.), Br. Col. 184/L2
Toadlena, N. Mex. (87324) 274/A2
Toana (range), Nev. 266/G2
Toano, Va. (23168) 307/P6
Toast, N.C. (27049) 281/H2
Toay, Arg. 143/D4
Toba, Arg. 143/F4
Toba (inlet), Br. Col. 184/E5
Toba, Japan 81/H6
Toba (lake), Indon. 85/B5
Tobago (isl.), Trinidad Tobago 156/G5
Tobarra, Spain 33/F3
Tobasco, Ohio (†45245) 284/C10
Tobatí, Par. 144/B6
Tobeatic (lake), N.S. 169/C4
Tobelo, Indon. 85/H5
Tobermory, Ont. 177/C2
Tobermory, 10/C2
Tobermory, Scot. 15/D6
Tobetsu, Japan 81/K2
Tobi (isl.), Japan 81/J4
Tobi (isl.), Pac. Is., 87/D5
Tobias, Nebr. (68453) 264/G4
Tobin (lake), Sask. 181/H2
Tobinsport, Ind. (47587) 227/D9
Tobique, N. Br. 170/E1
Tobique (riv.), N. Br. 170/C2
Tobique Narrows, N. Br. 170/C2
Tobol (riv.), U.S.S.R. 48/G4
Tobol (riv.), U.S.S.R., 54/K4
Tobol'sk, U.S.S.R. 48/G4
Tobol'sk, U.S.S.R., 54/L4
Tobolski, Jam. 158/J6
Tobruk, Libya 111/D1
Tobruk, 102/E1
Tobseda, U.S.S.R. 52/H1
Toby (mt.), Mass. 249/E3
Tobyhanna, Pa. (18466) 294/M3
Tocache, Peru 128/D7
Tocantínia, Braz. 132/D5
Tocantinópolis, Braz., 120/F3
Tocantinópolis, Braz. 132/D4
Tocantins (riv.), Braz., 3/G6
Tocantins (riv.), Braz., 120/F4
Tocantins (riv.), Braz. 132/D4
Toccoa, Ga. (30577) 216/F1
Toccopola, Miss. (38874) 256/F2
Tochcha (lake), Br. Col. 184/E3
Tochigi (pref.), Japan 81/K5
Toco, Chile 138/B3
Toco, Trinidad Tobago 161/B10
Tocoa, Hond. 154/E3
Tocomechi, Bol. 136/D5
Toconao, Chile 138/C4
Tocópero, Ven. 124/D2
Tocopilla, Chile, 120/C5
Tocopilla, Chile 138/A3
Tocorpuri, Cerros de (mt.), Bol. 136/A8
Tocorpuri, Cerro de (mt.), Chile 138/B3
Tocsin, Ind. (46790) 227/G3
Tocuco (riv.), Ven. 124/B3
Tocumen, Pan. 154/H6
Tocumwal, N.S.W. 97/C4
Tocuyo (riv.), Ven. 124/D2
Tocuyo de la Costa, Ven. 124/D2
Todd, Alaska (†99820) 196/M1
Todd (co.), Ky. 237/G7
Todd (co.), Minn. 254/D4
Todd (mt.), N. Br. 170/D2
Todd, N.C. (28684) 281/F2
Todd (riv.), No. Terr. 93/D8
Todd (co.), S. Dak. 298/H7
Toddville, Iowa (52341) 229/K4
Toddville, Md. (21672) 245/O7
Toddville, S.C. (†29526) 296/J4
Todenyang, Kenya 115/G3
Todi, Italy 34/D3
Tödi (mt.), Switz. 39/G3
Todmorden, 10/G2
Todos Santos, Cochabamba, Bol. 136/C5
Todos Santos, La Paz, Bol. 136/B3
Todos Santos, Oruro, Bol. 136/A6
Todos Santos, Mex. 150/D5
Toe (head), Ire. 17/C9
Toe (head), Scot. 15/B4
Toekomstig (res.), Sur. 131/C3
Toeterville, Iowa (50481) 229/H2
Tofield, Alta. 182/D3
Tofino, Br. Col. 184/E5
Tofte, Minn. (55615) 254/H3
Toftlund, Den. 21/C7
Togane, Japan 81/K6
Toggenburg (dist.), Switz. 39/H2
Togiak, Alaska (99678) 196/F3
Togiak (bay), Alaska 196/F3
Togian (isls.), Indon. 85/G6
Togliatti, U.S.S.R. 52/G4
Togo, 3/J5
TOGO, 106/E7
TOGO, 102/C4
Togo, Minn. (55788) 254/E3
Togo, Sask. 181/K4
Tohamiyam, Sudan 59/C6
Tohatchi, N. Mex. (87325) 274/A3
Tohma (riv.), Turkey 63/G3
Tohopekaliga (lake), Fla. 212/E3
Toibalawe, India 68/G6
Toijala, Fin. 18/N6
Toimi, Minn. (†55602) 254/G3
Toivola, Minn. (55789) 254/F3
Toiyabe (range), Nev. 266/D3
Tojo, Japan 81/F6
Tok, Alaska (99780) 196/K2
Tokaanu, N.Z. 101/E3
Tokachi (mt.), Japan 81/L2
Tokachi (riv.), Japan 81/L2
Tokaj, Hung. 41/F2
Tokanui, N.Z. 101/B7
Tokar, Sudan 59/C6
Tokar, Sudan 111/G4
Tokara (isls.), Japan 81/O5
Tokat, Turkey 59/C1
Tokat (prov.), Turkey 63/G2
Tokat, Turkey 63/G2
Tokeen, Alaska (†99901) 196/M2
Tokeland, Wash. (98590) 310/A4
Tokelau (isls.), 87/J6
Tokewamna (peak), Utah 304/D3
Tokio, N. Dak. (58379) 283/N4
Tokio, Texas (79376) 302/B4
Tokke (riv.), Norway 18/F7
Tokmak, U.S.S.R. 48/H5
Tokmak, U.S.S.R. 52/E5
Toko, N.Z. 101/E3
Tokomaru Bay, N.Z. 101/G3
Tokoroa, N.Z. 101/F3
Tokoto, China 77/H3
Tokra, Libya 111/D1
Toksook Bay, Alaska (99637) 196/E2
Tokuno (isl.), Japan 81/O5
Tokushima (pref.), Japan 81/G7
Tokushima, Japan 81/G7
Tokuyama, Japan 81/F6
Tokyo (cap.), Japan, 3/R4
Tokyo (cap.), Japan, 54/T6
Tokyo (pref.), Japan 81/O2
Tokyo (cap.), Japan 81/O2
Tokyo (bay), Japan 81/O2
Tolaga Bay, N.Z. 101/G3
Tolar, Texas (76476) 302/G5
Tolbukhin, Bulg. 45/H4
Tolchester Beach, Md. (†21620) 245/N4
Tolé, Pan. 154/G6
Toledo, Bol. 136/B6
Toledo, Col. 126/D4
Toledo, Ont. 177/H3
Toledo, Ill. (62468) 222/E4
Toledo, Iowa (52342) 229/H4
Toledo, Ohio, 146/K5
Toledo, Ohio, 188/K2
Toledo, Ohio (*43601) 284/D2
Toledo, Oreg. (97391) 291/D3
Toledo, Spain, 7/D5
Toledo (prov.), Spain 33/D3
Toledo, Spain 33/D3
Toledo (mts.), Spain 33/E3
Toledo, Urug. 145/B6
Toledo, Wash. (98591) 310/C4
Toledo Bend (dam), La. 238/C4
Toledo Bend (res.), La. 238/C4
Toledo Bend (dam), Texas 302/L6
Toledo Bend (res.), Texas 302/L6
Tolentino, Italy 34/D3
Tolima (mt.), Col., 120/C2
Tolima, Col. 126/D8
Tolima (dept.), Col. 126/C5
Tolima, Nevada del (mt.), Col. 126/C5
Tolimán, Mex. 150/K6
Töling, China 77/B5
Tolitoli, Indon. 85/G5
Tolland, Alta. 182/E3
Tolland (co.), Conn. 210/F1
Tolland△, Conn. (06084) 210/F1

448 Tolland

Tolland∆, Mass. (†01034) 249/B4
Tollensee (lake), E. Ger. 22/E2
Tollesboro, Ky. (41189) 237/O3
Tolleson, Ariz. (85353) 198/C5
Tollette, Ark. (†71851) 203/C6
Tolley, N. Dak. (58787) 283/G2
Toll Gate, W. Va. (26442) 313/E4
Tølløse, Den. 21/E6
Tollville, Ark. (†72041) 203/G4
Tollygunge, India 68/F2
Tolly's Nullah (riv.), India 68/F2
Tolna (co.), Hung. 41/E3
Tolna, Hung. 41/E3
Tolna, N. Dak. (58380) 283/O4
Tolo (gulf), Indon. 85/G6
Tolo, Dem. Rep. of the Congo. 115/C4
Tolona, Mo. (†63450) 261/J2
Tolong (bay), Phil. 82/D6
Tolono, Ill. (61880) 222/E3
Tolosa, Spain 33/F1
Tolovana Park, Oreg. (97145) 291/C2
Tolsta (head), Scot. 15/D3
Tolstoi, Man. 179/F5
Tolstoy, S. Dak. (57475) 298/K3
Toltén, Chile 138/D2
Toltén (riv.), Chile 138/D2
Tolt River (res.), Wash. 310/D3
Tolú, Col. 126/C3
Tolu, Ky. (42084) 237/E6
Toluca, Ill. (61369) 222/D2
Toluca, Mex., 146/H8
Toluca de Lerdo, Mex. 150/K7
Tolun, China 77/J3
Tom (mt.), Conn. 210/B1
Tom (mt.), Mass. 249/D4
Tom (mt.), N.H. 268/E3
Tom, Okla. (74762) 288/S7
Tomah, Wis. (54660) 317/F8
Tomahawk, Alta. 182/C3
Tomahawk, N.C. (28465) 281/N5
Tomahawk, Wis. (54487) 317/G5
Tomakomai, Japan 81/K2
Tomales, Calif. (94971) 204/C5
Tomales (pt.), Calif. 204/B5
Tomanao, Phil. 82/E8
Tomar, Port. 33/B3
Tomarza, Turkey 63/F3
Tomasaki (mt.), Utah 304/E5
Tomás Barrón, Bol. 136/B5
Tomás Gomensoro, Urug. 145/B1
Tomaszów Lubelski, Poland 47/F3
Tomaszów Mazowiecki, Poland 47/E3
Tomatlán, Mex. 150/G6
Tomave, Bol. 136/B7
Tomayapo, Bol. 136/C7
Tombador (range), Braz. 132/B6
Tomball, Texas (77375) 302/J7
Tombe, Sudan 111/F6
Tom Bean‡, Texas (75489) 302/H4
Tombigbee (riv.), 188/J4
Tombigbee (riv.), Ala. 194/B7
Tombigbee (riv.), Miss. 256/H4
Tombstone, Ariz. (85638) 198/F7
Tomé, Chile 138/D1
Tome, N. Mex. (87060) 274/C4
Tomelilla, Sweden 18/J9
Tomelloso, Spain 33/E3
Tom Green (co.), Texas 302/D6
Tomhannock (res.), N.Y. 276/O5
Tomichi (creek), Colo. 208/F5
Tomifobia, Que. 172/E4
Tomina, Bol. 136/C6
Tomingley, N.S.W. 97/E3
Tomini (gulf), Indon., 54/R10
Tomini (gulf), Indon. 85/G6
Tomintoul, Scot. 15/K5
Tomiyama, Japan 81/O3
Tomkinson (ranges), W. Aust. 92/E4
Tommerup, Den. 21/D7
Tommot, U.S.S.R. 48/N4
Tommot, U.S.S.R., 54/R4
Tomnolen, Miss. (39770) 256/F4
Tomo (riv.), Col. 126/F5
To Mo, Thai. 72/D6
Tomor (mt.), Alb. 45/E5
Tompkins (co.), N.Y. 276/H6
Tompkins, Sask. 181/C5
Tompkinsville, Ky. (42167) 237/K7
Tompkinsville, Md. (†20664) 245/L7
Tom Price (mt.), W. Aust. 92/B3
Toms (riv.), N.J. 273/E3
Toms Brook, Va. (22660) 307/L3
Toms Creek, Va. (†24230) 307/D7
Tomsk, U.S.S.R. 48/J4
Tomsk, U.S.S.R., 54/M4
Toms River, N.J. (08753) 273/E4
Tömük, Turkey 63/F4
Tonalá, Mex. 150/N8
Tonalea, Ariz. (86044) 198/E2
Tonasket, Wash. (98855) 310/F2
Tonate, Fr. Gui. 131/E3
Tonawanda, N.Y. (14150) 276/B4
Tonawanda Ind. Res., N.Y. 276/D4
Tonbridge, Eng. 13/H6
Tonbridge, 10/G5
Tonckens (falls), Sur. 131/C3
Tondabayashi, Japan 81/J8
Tondano, Indon. 85/H5
Tønder, Den. 18/F9
Tønder (co.), Den. 21/B8
Tønder, Den. 21/C8
Tondo, Dem. Rep. of the Congo. 115/C4
Tone (riv.), Japan 81/K6
Tonegrama, Peru 128/D4
Toney, Ala. (35773) 194/E1
Tonga, 3/A6
Tonga, 87/J8
Tonga, Sudan 111/F6
Tongala, Vic. 97/C5
Tonganoxie, Kans. (66086) 232/G2
Tongareva (atoll), Cook Is., 87/L6
Tongatapu (isls.), Tonga, 87/J8
T'ongch'ŏn, N. Korea 81/D4
Tongeren, Belg. 27/G7
Tongo, N.S.W. 97/B2
Tongo (lake), N.S.W. 97/B2
Tongoy, Chile 138/A8
Tongoy (bay), Chile 138/A8
Tongquil (isl.), Phil. 82/D8
Tongres (Tongeren), Belg. 27/G7
Tongs, Ky. (†41175) 237/R3
Tongsa Dzong, India 68/G3
Tongue (riv.), Mont. 262/K5
Tongue (riv.), N. Dak. 283/P2
Tongue (pt.), N.Z. 101/A3
Tongue, Scot. 15/H3
Tongue, Kyle of (inlet), Scot. 15/G2
Tongue (riv.), Wyo. 319/E1
Tongue of the Ocean (chan.), Bah. Is. 156/C1
Tongue River (res.), Mont. 262/K5
Tongue River Ind. Res., Mont. 262/K5
Tonica, Ill. (61370) 222/E2
Tonj, Sudan 111/E6
Tonk, India 68/D3
Tonka Bay, Minn. (†55331) 254/F5
Tonkawa, Okla. (74653) 288/M1
Tonkhil, Mong. 77/D2
Tonkin (gulf), 54/O8
Tonkin (gulf), N. Vietnam 72/E3
Tonkin (gulf), China 77/G8
Tonkin, Sask. 181/J4
Tonle Sap (lake), Cambodia 72/D4
Ton Mhor (pt.), Scot. 15/C8
Tonneins, France 28/D5
Tonnerre, France 28/E4
Tönning, W. Ger. 22/C1
Tonopah, Ariz. (85354) 198/B5
Tonopah, Nev., 188/C3
Tonopah, Nev. (89049) 266/D4
Tonosí, Pan. 154/G7
Tonota, Botswana 118/D4
Tønsberg, Norway 18/D4
Tonsina, Alaska (†99686) 196/J2
Tontitown, Ark. (72770) 203/B1
Tonto (basin), Ariz. 198/D4
Tonto (creek), Ariz. 198/D4
Tonto Basin, Ariz. (85553) 198/D5
Tontogany, Ohio (43565) 284/C3
Tonto Nat'l Mon., Ariz. 198/D5
Tony, Wis. (54563) 317/E5
Tonya, Turkey 63/H2
Toodyay, Aust. 88/B2
Toodyay, W. Aust. 92/B1
Tooele, Utah, 188/D2
Tooele (co.), Utah 304/A3
Tooele, Utah (84074) 304/B3
Tooele Army Depot, Utah 304/B3
Toole (co.), Mont. 262/E2
Toombs (co.), Ga. 216/H6
Toomevara, Ire. 17/E6
Toomsboro, Ga. (31090) 216/F5
Toomsuba, Miss. (39364) 256/G6
Toone, Tenn. (38381) 237/D10
Tooraweenah, N.S.W. 97/E2
Toowoomba, Australia, 87/F8
Toowoomba, Aust. 88/J5
Toowoomba, Queens. 95/D5
Top (lake), U.S.S.R. 52/D1
Topador, Urug. 145/C1
Topanga, Calif. (90290) 204/B10
Topanga Beach, Calif. (†90290) 204/B10
Topará, Peru 128/D9
Topawa, Ariz. (85639) 198/D7
Topaz (lake), Nev. 266/B4
Topeka, Ill. (61567) 222/D3
Topeka, Ind. (46571) 227/F1
Topeka (cap.), Kans., 146/J6
Topeka (cap.), Kans., 188/G3
Topeka (cap.), Kans. (*66601) 232/G2
Topia, Mex. 150/F4
Topinabee, Mich. (49791) 250/E3
Topl'a (riv.), Czech. 41/F2
Topland, Alta. 182/C2
Topley, Br. Col. 184/D3
Toplița, Rum. 45/G2
Topocalma (pt.), Chile 138/A10
Topock, Ariz. (86436) 198/A4
Topol'čany, Czech. 41/D2
Topolobampo, Mex. 150/E4
Topolovgrad, Bulg. 45/H4
Toponas, Colo. (80479) 208/F2
Toppenish, Wash. (98948) 310/E4
Toppenish (creek), Wash. 310/E4
Topsail, Newf. 166/D2
Topsfield, Maine (04490) 242/H5
Topsfield∆, Mass. (01983) 249/L2
Topsham, Eng. 13/D7
Topsham∆, Maine (04086) 242/D8
Topsham, Maine (04086) 242/D8
Topsham∆, Vt. (05076) 268/C3
Topsham, Vt. (05076) 268/C3
Top Springs, No. Terr. 93/C4
Topton, N.C. (28781) 281/B4
Topton, Pa. (19562) 294/L5
Toqsun, China 77/C3
Toquepala, Peru 128/G11
Toquerville, Utah (84774) 304/A6
Toquima (range), Nev. 266/E4
Tor (bay), Eng. 13/D7
Tor (bay), N.S. 169/G3
Tora, Dem. Rep. of the Congo. 115/E3
Torata, Peru 128/G11
Torawitan (cape), Indon. 85/G5
Torbali, Turkey 63/B3
Torbay, Eng. 13/D7
Torbay, Newf. 166/D2
Torbay (pt.), Newf. 166/D2
Torbeck, Haiti 158/A6
Torch (key), Fla. 212/E7
Torch (lake), Mich. 250/D3
Torch, Ohio (45781) 284/G7
Torch (riv.), Sask. 181/H2
Torch River, Sask. 181/G2
Tordesillas, Spain 33/D2
Torgau, E. Ger. 22/E3
Torgelow, E. Ger. 22/F2
Torhout, Belg. 27/C6
Tori, Eth. 111/F6
Torino (Turin), Italy, 7/E4
Torino (Turin), Italy 34/A2
Torit, Sudan 111/F7
Törmänen, Fin. 18/Q2
Torne (riv.), 7/G2
Torneälv (riv.), Sweden 18/M3
Tor Ness (prom.), Scot. 15/K2
Torneträsk (lake), Sweden 18/L2
Torngat (mts.), Newf. 166/B2
Tornillo, Texas (79853) 302/A10
Tornio, Fin. 18/O4
Tornio (riv.), Fin. 18/O3
Tornio, Fin., 7/G2
Tornquist, Arg. 143/D4
Toro, Cerro del (mt.), Arg. 143/B2
Toro (lake), Chile 138/D9
Toro (pt.), Chile 138/A10
Toro, Cerro del (mt.), Chile 138/B7
Toro, El (mt.), P. Rico 161/F2
Toro, La. (†71429) 238/C4
Toro, Spain 33/D2
Törökszentmiklós, Hung. 41/F3
Toronaic (gulf), Greece 45/F5
Toronto, Iowa (52343) 229/M5
Toronto, Kans. (66777) 232/G4
Toronto (res.), Kans. 232/F4
Toronto, N.S.W. 97/F3
Toronto (res.), N.Y. 276/L7
Toronto, Ohio (43964) 284/J5
Toronto, Canada, 3/F3
Toronto (cap.), Ont., 146/K5
Toronto (cap.), Ont. 163/H7
Toronto (cap.), Ont. 177/K4
Toronto, S. Dak. (57268) 298/R4
Toropalca, Bol. 136/B7
Toropets, U.S.S.R. 52/D3
Tororo, Uganda 115/F3
Torote (riv.), Spain 33/G4
Torotoro, Bol. 136/C6
Torpedo, Pa. (†16340) 294/D2
Torpoint, Eng. 13/C7
Torquay, 10/E5
Torquay, Sask. 181/H6
Torquemada, Spain 33/D1
Torr (head), N. Ire. 17/K1
Torrance, Calif. (*90501) 204/C11
Torrance, Ont. 177/E3
Torrance (co.), N. Mex. 274/D4
Torrance, Pa. (15779) 294/D5
Torre, Cerro de la (mt.), Chile 138/E4
Torre Annunziata, Italy 34/E4
Torreblanca, Spain 33/G2
Torrecilla (lag.), P. Rico 161/E1
Torre del Greco, Italy 34/E4
Tôrre de Moncorvo, Port. 33/C2
Torredonjimeno, Spain 33/D4
Torre Gaia, Italy 34/F6
Torrejoncillo, Spain 33/C3
Torrejón de Ardoz, Spain 33/G4
Torrelaguna, Spain 33/E2
Torrelavega, Spain 33/D1
Torremaggiore, Italy 34/E4
Torremolinos, Spain 33/D4
Torrens (lake), Australia, 87/D9
Torrens (lake), Aust. 88/F6
Torrens (riv.), Aust. 88/E7
Torrens (lake), S. Aust. 94/E4
Torrens (riv.), S. Aust. 94/C7
Torrente, Spain 33/F3
Torreón, Mex., 146/H7
Torreón, Mex. 150/H4
Torreon, N. Mex. (87061) 274/C4
Torre-Pacheco, Spain 33/F4
Torres (str.), Aust. 88/G2
Torres (isls.), New Hebr., 87/G7
Torres (strait), 87/E7
Torres (str.), Terr. N.G. 85/A7
Torres (str.), Queens. 95/B1
Torres Martinez Ind. Res., Calif. 204/J10
Tôrres Novas, Port. 33/B3
Tôrres Vedras, Port. 33/B3
Torrevieja, Spain 33/F4
Torrey, Utah (84775) 304/C5
Torridon, Scot. 15/F5
Torridon (inlet), Scot. 15/E4
Torriente, Cuba 158/D1
Torrijos, Phil. 82/D4
Torrijos, Spain 33/D2
Tørring, Den. 21/C6
Torringford, Conn. (†06790) 210/C1
Torrington, Alta. 182/D4
Torrington, Conn. (06790) 210/C1
Torrington, Eng. 13/C7
Torrington, Wyo. (82240) 319/H3
Torroella de Montgrí, Spain 33/H1
Torrowangee, N.S.W. 97/A2
Torrox, Spain 33/E4
Torsby, Sweden 18/H6
Tors Cove, Newf. 166/D2
Torshälla, Sweden 18/K7
Tórshavn, Den., 7/D2
Tórshavn (cap.), Faerøe Is., Den. 21/A3
Tortilla Flat, Ariz. (85290) 198/D5
Tortola (isl.), V.I. (Br.) 156/H1
Tortola (isl.), V.I. (Br.) 161/D3
Tórtolas, Cerro de las (mt.), Chile 138/B8
Tortona, Italy 34/B2
Tortorici, Italy 34/E6
Tortosa, Spain 33/G2
Tortosa (cape), Spain 33/G2
Tortue (Tortuga) (isl.), Haiti 156/D2
Tortue (chan.), Haiti 158/C5
Tortue (Tortuga) (isl.), Haiti 158/C4
Tortuga (isl.), Haiti 156/D2
Tortuga (isl.), Haiti 158/C4
Tortugas (gulf), Col. 126/B6
Tortuguero (lag.), P. Rico 161/D1
Tortuguilla (pt.), Cuba 158/K4
Tortum, Turkey 63/J2
Torul, Turkey 63/H2
Toruń, Poland 47/D2
Torunos, Ven. 124/C3
Törva, U.S.S.R. 53/C1
Tory (isl.), Ire. 17/E1
Tory (sound), Ire. 17/E1
Tory (isl.), 10/B3
Torysa (riv.), Czech. 41/F2
Torzhok, U.S.S.R. 52/D3
Tosa, Japan 81/F7
Tosa (bay), Japan 81/F7
Tosashimizu, Japan 81/F7
Töss (riv.), Switz. 39/G1
Tostado, Arg. 143/D2
Toston, Mont. (59643) 262/E4
Tosu, Japan 81/E7
Tosya, Turkey 63/F2
Tota (lag.), Col. 126/D5
Totana, Spain 33/F4
Tótkomlós, Hung. 41/F3
Tot'ma, U.S.S.R. 48/E4
Tot'ma, U.S.S.R. 52/F3
Totnes, Eng. 13/D7
Totnes, 10/E5
Totnes, Sask. 181/C4
Totness, Sur. 131/C3
Toto, Ind. (†46534) 227/D2
Totoket, Conn. (†06405) 210/D3
Totonicapán, Guat. 154/B3
Totora, Cochabamba, Bol. 136/C5
Totora, Oruro, Bol. 136/A5
Totoral, Chile 138/A6
Totoral, Quebrada (riv.), Chile 138/A6
Totoral, Urug. 145/C3
Totowa, N.J. (07511) 273/B1
Tottenham, Aust. 88/H6
Tottenham, Ont. 177/E3
Tottenham, N.S.W. 97/D3
Tottori (pref.), Japan 81/G6
Tottori, Japan 81/G6
Touat (oasis), Alg. 106/E3
Touba, Ivory Coast 106/C7
Touba, Sen. 106/A6
Toubkal, Jebel (mt.), Mor. 106/C2
Touchet, Wash. (99360) 310/G4
Touchet (riv.), Wash. 310/G4
Touchwood (lake), Alta. 182/E2
Touchwood (hills), Sask. 181/G4
Toufourine (well), Mali 106/C4
Tougaloo, Miss. (39174) 256/D6
Tougan, Upp. Volta 106/D6
Touggourt, Alg. 106/F2
Touggourt, 102/C1
Toughkenamon, Pa. (19374) 294/L6
Tougué, Guinea 106/B6
Touila (well), Alg. 106/C3
Touila (well), Mauritania 106/C3
Toul, France 28/F3
Touladi (lake), Que. 172/J1
Toulnustouc (riv.), Que. 174/D2
Toulon, France, 7/E4
Toulon, France 28/F6
Toulon, Ill. (61483) 222/D2
Toulouse, France, 7/E4
Toulouse, France 28/D6
Toumodi, Ivory Coast 106/D7
Toungo, Nigeria 106/G7
Toungoo, Burma 72/C3
Tourakom, Laos 72/D3
Tourane (Da Nang), S. Vietnam 72/E3
Tourane (cape), S. Vietnam 72/F3
Tourbis (lake), Que. 172/C2
Tourcoing, France 28/E2
Tour d'Aï (mt.), Switz. 39/C4
Tournai, Belg. 27/C7
Tournavista, Peru 128/E7
Tournon, France 28/F5
Tournus, France 28/F4
Touros, Braz. 132/H4
Touro Synagogue Nat'l Hist. Site, R.I. 249/J7
Tours, France, 7/E4
Tours, France 28/D4
Tourville, Que. 172/H2
Toutes Aides, Man. 179/C3
Toutle, Wash. (98649) 310/C4
Toutle, North Fork (riv.), Wash. 310/C4
Toutle, South Fork (riv.), Wash. 310/C4
Toužim, Czech. 41/B1
Tovar, Ven. 124/C3
Tovey, Ill. (62570) 222/D4
Towaco, N.J. (07082) 273/E2
Towada, Japan 81/K3
Towada (lake), Japan 81/K3
Towada-Hachimantai Nat'l Park, Japan 81/K3
Towakaima, Guyana 131/B2
Towanda, Ill. (61776) 222/E3
Towanda, Kans. (67144) 232/E4
Towanda, Pa. (18848) 294/J2
Towanda (creek), Pa. 294/J2
Towaoc, Colo. (81334) 208/B8
Towcester, Eng. 13/F5
Tower, Mich. (49792) 250/E3
Tower, Minn. (55790) 254/F3
Tower, Wyo. (†82190) 319/B1
Tower City, N. Dak. (58071) 283/P6
Tower City, Pa. (17980) 294/J4
Tower Hamlets‡, 10/B5
Tower Hill, Ill. (62571) 222/E4
Tower Lake‡, Ill. (†60010) 222/E1
Towers of Silence, India 68/B7
Tow Law, Eng. 13/F3
Town (creek), Ala. 194/C1
Town (creek), Md. 245/E2
Town and Country‡, Mo. (†63101) 261/O3
Town and Country‡, Wash. (†99218) 310/H3
Town Creek, Ala. (35672) 194/D1
Towner, Colo. (81080) 208/P6
Towner (co.), N. Dak. 283/M2
Towner, N. Dak. (58788) 283/K3
Townley, Ala. (35587) 194/D3
Town Line‡, N.Y. (14165) 276/C5
Town of Pines, Ind. (†46360) 227/D1
Town Point, Md. (†21915) 245/P3
Towns (co.), Ga. 216/E1
Towns, Ga. (†31055) 216/G7
Townsend, Del. (19734) 245/R3
Townsend, Ga. (31331) 216/J7
Townsend∆, Mass. (01469) 249/H2
Townsend, Mass. (01469) 249/H2
Townsend, Mont. (59644) 262/E4
Townsend (inlet), N.J. 273/D5
Townsend, Tenn. (37882) 237/O9
Townsend, Va. (23443) 307/R6
Townsend, Wis. (54175) 317/K5
Townsend Harbor, Mass. (†01469) 249/G2
Townshend∆, Vt. (05353) 268/B5
Townshend, Vt. (05353) 268/B5
Townsville, Australia, 87/E7
Townsville, Aust. 88/H3
Townsville, Australia, 3/S6
Townsville, N.C. (27584) 281/N1
Townsville, Queens. 95/C3
Townville, Pa. (16360) 294/C2
Townville, S.C. (29689) 296/B2
Towot, Sudan 111/F6
Towson, Md. (21204) 245/M3
Towuti (lake), Indon. 85/G6
Towy (riv.), 10/E5
Towy (riv.), Wales 13/D6
Toxey, Ala. (36921) 194/B7
Toya (lake), Japan 81/K2
Toyah, Texas (79785) 302/D11
Toyah (creek), Texas 302/D11
Toyah (lake), Texas 302/A6
Toyahvale, Texas (79786) 302/D11
Toyama (pref.), Japan 81/H5
Toyama, Japan 81/H5
Toyama (bay), Japan 81/H5
Toyohashi, Japan, 54/S6
Toyohashi, Japan 81/H6
Toyonaka, Japan 81/J7
Toyooka, Japan 81/G6
Toyota, Japan 81/H6
Tozeur, 102/C1
Tozeur, Tun. 106/F2
Trabzon, Turkey 59/C1
Trabzon (prov.), Turkey 63/H2
Trabzon, Turkey 63/H2
Trabzon, Turkey, 54/G5
Tracadie, N. Br. 170/F1
Tracadie, N.S. 169/G3
Tracadie (bay), P.E.I. 169/F2
Trachselwald, Switz. 39/E2
Tracy, Calif. (95376) 204/D6
Tracy, Conn. (†06492) 210/D2
Tracy, Que. 172/D3
Tracy, Iowa (50256) 229/H6
Tracy, Ky. (†42123) 237/K7
Tracy, Minn. (56175) 254/C6
Tracy, Mo. (64091) 261/C4
Tracy, N. Br. 170/D3
Tracy Arm (inlet), Alaska 196/N1
Tracy City, Tenn. (37387) 237/K10
Tracyton, Wash. (98393) 310/A2
Trade, Tenn. (37691) 237/T8
Trade Lake, Wis. (†54837) 317/A4
Tradesville, S.C. (†29720) 296/F2
Tradewater (riv.), Ky. 237/F6
Trading (bay), Alaska 196/B1
Trading Post, Kans. (†66075) 232/H3
Tradom, China 77/B6
Traer, Iowa (50675) 229/J4
Traer, Kans. (67760) 232/B2
Trafalgar, Ind. (46181) 227/E6
Trafalgar (cape), Spain 33/C4
Trafaria, Port. 33/A1
Trafford, Ala. (35172) 194/E3
Trafford, Pa. (15085) 294/C5
Traghen, Libya 111/B2
Traiguén, Chile 138/D2
Traiguén (isl.), Chile 138/D6
Trail, 163/E6
Trail, Br. Col. 184/J6
Trail, Minn. (56684) 254/C3
Trail, Oreg. (97541) 291/E5
Trail City, S. Dak. (57657) 298/H3
Trail Creek, Ind. (†46360) 227/D1
Trailcreek, Mont. (†59928) 262/B2
Trailer Estates‡, Fla. (33505) 212/D4
Traill (isl.), Greenl., 4/B10
Traill (co.), N. Dak. 283/R5
Trainer, Pa. (†19013) 294/L7
Traiskirchen, Austria 41/D2
Trakai, U.S.S.R. 53/C3
Tralake, Miss. (38757) 256/C4
Tralee, 10/B4
Tralee, Ire. 17/B7
Tralee (bay), Ire. 17/B7
Tramán-tepuí (mt.), Ven. 124/G5
Tramelan, Switz. 39/D2
Trammel, Va. (24289) 307/D6
Tramore, 10/C4
Tramore, Ire. 17/G7
Tramore (bay), Ire. 17/G7
Trampas, N. Mex. (87576) 274/D2
Tramperos (creek), N. Mex. 274/F2
Tramping (lake), Sask. 181/C3
Tramping Lake, Sask. 181/B3
Tranås, Sweden 18/J7
Trancoso, Port. 33/C2
Tranebjerg, Den. 21/D6
Tranebjerg (mt.), Den. 21/C6
Tranent, Scot. 15/L8
Trang, Thai. 72/C6
Trangan (isl.), Indon. 85/J7
Trangie, N.S.W. 97/D3
Trani, Italy 34/F4
Tran Ninh (plat.), Laos 72/D3
Tranquebar, India 68/E6
Tranqueras, Urug. 145/D2
Tranqui (isl.), Chile 138/D4
Tranquility, N.J. (07879) 273/D2
Tranquille, Br. Col. 184/G5
Tranquillity, Calif. (93668) 204/E7
Transantarctic (mts.), Ant. 5/A11
Trans-Carpathian Oblast, U.S.S.R. 52/B5
Transcona, Man. 179/F5
Transfer, Pa. (16154) 294/A3
Trans-Himalayas (range), China, 54/M6
Trans-Himalayas (range), China 77/E5
Transkei (prov.), 102/E8
Transkei (prov.), S. Africa 118/D6
Transquaking (riv.), Md. 245/P7
Transvaal (prov.), 102/E7
Transvaal (prov.), S. Africa 118/D4
Transylvania, La. (71286) 238/H1
Transylvania (co.), N.C. 281/D4
Transylvanian Alps (mts.), Rum. 45/G3
Trapani (prov.), Italy 34/D5
Trapani, Italy 34/D5
Trap Falls (res.), Conn. 210/C3
Traphill, N.C. (28685) 281/H2
Trappe, Md. (21673) 245/O6
Trappe‡, Pa. (†19426) 294/M5
Trappers (lake), Colo. 208/E3
Traquair, Scot. 15/K8
Traralgon, Vic. 97/D6
Trarza (reg.), Mauritania 106/A5
Trasimeno (lake), Italy 34/D3
Traskwood, Ark. (72167) 203/E5
Trás-os-Montes e Alto Douro (prov.), Port. 33/C2
Trat, Thai. 72/D4
Traun, Austria 41/C2
Traun (riv.), Austria 41/C2
Traun See (lake), Austria 41/B3
Traunstein, W. Ger. 22/E5
Travancore (reg.), India 68/D7
Travelers Rest, S.C. (29690) 296/C2
Travellers (lake), N.S.W. 97/B3
Travellers Rest, Ky. (41314) 237/O6
Travemünde, W. Ger. 22/D2
Travers, Alta. 182/D4
Traverse (isl.), Mich. 250/A1
Traverse (pt.), Mich. 250/A1
Traverse (co.), Minn. 254/B5
Traverse, Minn. (†56082) 254/D6
Traverse (lake), Minn. 254/B5
Traverse (lake), S. Dak. 298/R2
Traverse Beach, Man. 179/F4
Traverse City, Mich., 188/K2
Traverse City, Mich. (49684) 250/D4
Tra Vinh, S. Vietnam 72/E5
Travis (co.), Texas 302/G7
Travis (lake), Texas 302/G7
Travis A.F.B., Calif. 204/L1
Travnik, Yugo. 45/C3
Trawbreaga (bay), Ire. 17/F1
Traynor, Sask. 181/C3
Traytown, Newf. 166/D1
Trbovlje, Yugo. 45/B2
Treadway, Tenn. (37883) 237/P8
Treasure (isl.), Fla. 212/B3
Treasure (co.), Mont. 262/J4
Treasure Beach, Jam. 158/H6
Treasure Island, Fla. (33740) 212/B3
Treaty, Ind. (†46992) 227/F3
Trebbia (riv.), Italy 34/B2
Třebíč, Czech. 41/C2
Trebinje, Yugo. 45/D4
Trebišov, Czech. 41/F2
Trebizond (Trabzon), Turkey 63/H2
Trebloc, Miss. (38875) 256/G3
Třeboň, Czech. 41/C2
Treece, Kans. (66778) 232/H4
Treelon, Sask. 181/C6
Trees, La. (71081) 238/B1
Treesbank, Man. 179/C5
Tregaron, 10/E4
Tregaron, Wales 13/D5
Tregarva, Sask. 181/G5
Trego (co.), Kans. 232/C3
Trego, Mont. (59934) 262/B2
Trego, Wis. (54888) 317/C4
Treherne, Man. 179/D5
Treig (lake), Scot. 15/G6
Treinta y Tres (dept.), Urug. 145/E4
Treinta y Tres, Urug. 145/E4
Trelew, Arg. 143/C5
Trelleborg, Sweden 18/H9
Tremadoc (bay), 10/D4
Tremadoc (bay), Wales 13/C5
Tremblant (lake), Que. 172/C3
Trembleur (lake), Br. Col. 184/E3
Trementina, N. Mex. (88439) 274/E3
Tremiti (isls.), Italy 34/E3
Tremont, Ill. (61568) 222/D3
Tremont∆, Maine (†04653) 242/G7
Tremont, Maine (†04653) 242/G7
Tremont, Miss. (38876) 256/H2
Tremont, Pa. (17981) 294/K4
Tremont City, Ohio (45372) 284/C5
Tremonton, Utah (84337) 304/B2
Tremp, Spain 33/G1
Trempealeau (co.), Wis. 317/D7
Trempealeau, Wis. (54661) 317/C8
Trempealeau (riv.), Wis. 317/C7
Trenary, Mich. (49891) 250/C2
Trenčín, Czech. 41/E2
Trenel, Arg. 143/D4
Trenggalek, Indon. 85/K2
Trenque Lauquen, Arg. 143/D4
Trent (riv.), Eng. 13/G4
Trent (riv.), N.C. 281/P4
Trent, Oreg. (†97431) 291/E4
Trent (riv.), 10/F4
Trent, S. Dak. (57065) 298/R6
Trent, Texas (79561) 302/D5
Trente-et-un-Milles (lake), Que. 172/B3
Trentham, Man. 179/F5
Trentham Cliffs, N.S.W. 97/B4
Trentino-Alto Adige (reg.), Italy 34/C1
Trento, Italy, 7/F4
Trento (prov.), Italy 34/C1
Trento, Italy 34/C1
Trenton, Ala. (35774) 194/F1
Trenton, Ark. (†72374) 203/J5
Trenton, Ont. 177/G3
Trenton, Fla. (32693) 212/D2
Trenton, Ga. (30752) 216/A1
Trenton, Ill. (62293) 222/D5
Trenton, Iowa (†52641) 229/K6
Trenton, Ky. (42286) 237/G7
Trenton∆, Maine (†04605) 242/G7
Trenton, Maine (†04605) 242/G7
Trenton, Md. (†21155) 245/L2
Trenton, Mich. (48183) 250/B7
Trenton, Miss. (†39153) 256/E6
Trenton, Mo. (64683) 261/E2
Trenton, N.C. (28585) 281/P4
Trenton, N. Dak. (58853) 283/C3
Trenton (cap.), N.J., 146/L5
Trenton (cap.), N.J., 188/M2
Trenton (cap.), N.J. (*08601) 273/D3
Trenton, N.S. 169/F3
Trenton (Barneveld), N.Y. (13304) 276/K4
Trenton, Nebr. (69044) 264/D4
Trenton, Ohio (45067) 284/B7
Trenton, S.C. (29847) 296/D4
Trenton, Tenn. (38382) 237/D9
Trenton, Texas (75490) 302/H4
Trenton, Utah (84338) 304/B2
Trent Woods, N.C. (†28560) 281/P4
Trepassey, Newf. 166/D2
Trepassey (bay), Newf. 166/D2
Treptow, E. Ger. 22/F4
Tres Árboles, Urug. 145/C3
Tres Arroyos, Arg. 143/D4
Tres Bocas, Urug. 145/B2
Tresckow, Pa. (18254) 294/K4
Tresco (isl.), Eng. 13/A7
Três Corações, Braz. 132/E8
Três Corações, Braz. 135/D2
Trescott, Maine (†04652) 242/J6
Tres Cruces, Nevada (mt.), Chile 138/B6
Tres Esquinas, Col. 126/C7
Treshnish (isls.), Scot. 15/C7
Tres Islas, Urug. 145/E3
Três Lagoas, Braz. 132/C8
Tres Lomas, Arg. 143/D4
Tres Marías (isls.), Mex. 150/F6
Tres Montes (cape), Chile, 120/C7
Tres Montes (cape), Chile 138/C7
Tres Montes (gulf), Chile 138/D6
Tres Montes (pen.), Chile 138/C6
Tres Palmas, Col. 126/B3
Tres Picos, Cerro (mt.), Arg. 143/B5
Tres Piedras, N. Mex. (87577) 274/D2
Tres Pinos, Calif. (95075) 204/D7

Turgeon 449

Três Pontas, Braz. 135/D2
Tres Puntas (cape), Arg., 120/D7
Tres Puntas (cape), Arg. 143/D6
Tres Puntas (cape), Guat. 154/C3
Três Rios, Braz. 132/F8
Três Rios, Braz. 135/E3
Tres Ritos, N. Mex. (†87579) 274/D2
Třešť, Czech. 41/C2
Treuchtlingen, W. Ger. 22/D4
Treungen, Norway 18/F7
Treutlen (co.), Ga. 216/G6
Trevelín, Arg. 143/B5
Trevett, Maine (04571) 242/D8
Treviglio, Italy 34/B2
Trevino, Condado de, Spain 33/E1
Treviso (prov.), Italy 34/D2
Treviso, Italy 34/D2
Trevlac, Ind. (†47448) 227/E6
Trevor, Wales 13/C5
Trevorton, Pa. (17881) 294/J4
Trevose (head), Eng. 13/B7
Trévoux, France 28/F5
Trewdale, Sask. 181/E5
Treynor, Iowa (51575) 229/B6
Treysa, W. Ger. 22/C3
Treyvaux, Switz. 39/D3
Trezevant, Tenn. (38258) 237/D8
Trhové Sviny, Czech. 41/C2
Triadelphia (lake), Md. 245/L4
Triadelphia, W. Va. (26059) 313/E2
Triana, Ala. (†35758) 194/E1
Triangle, Alta. 182/B2
Triangle, Va. (22172) 307/O3
Triángulo Este (isl.), Mex. 150/N6
Triángulo Oeste (isl.), Mex. 150/N6
Tribbett, Miss. (38779) 256/C4
Tribbey, Okla. (†74852) 288/M4
Tribble, W. Va. (†25095) 313/C5
Triberg, W. Ger. 22/C4
Tribes Hill‡, N.Y. (12177) 276/M5
Tribune, Kans. (67879) 232/A3
Tribune, Sask. 181/H6
Tricao Malal, Arg. 143/C4
Tricase, Italy 34/G5
Trichur, India 68/D6
Trida, N.S.W. 97/C3
Tridell, Utah (84076) 304/E3
Trident, Mont. (59753) 262/E5
Trident (peak), Nev. 266/C1
Trieben, Austria 41/C3
Trier, W. Ger. 22/B4
Triesen, Liecht. 39/H2
Trieste, Italy, 7/F4
Trieste (prov.), Italy 34/E2
Trieste, Italy 34/E2
Trieste (gulf), Italy 34/D2
Trigal, Bol. 136/C6
Trigg (co.), Ky. 237/F7
Triglav (mt.), Yugo. 45/A2
Trigueros, Spain 33/C4
Tríkkala, Greece, 7/G5
Tríkkala, Greece 45/E6
Tri Lakes, Ind. (†46725) 227/G2
Trilby, Fla. (33593) 212/D3
Trilla, Ill. (62469) 222/E4
Trillick, N. Ire. 17/G3
Trim, 10/C4
Trim, Ire. 17/H4
Trimble, Ill. (†62454) 222/F4
Trimble (co.), Ky. 237/L3
Trimble, Ky. (42559) 237/M6
Trimble, Mo. (64492) 261/D4
Trimble, Ohio (45782) 284/F7
Trimble, Tenn. (38259) 237/C8
Trim Cane (creek), Miss. 256/G4
Trimmis, Switz. 39/J3
Trimont, Minn. (56176) 254/D7
Trin, Switz. 39/H3
Trinchera, Colo. (81081) 208/M8
Trinchera (peak), Colo. 208/J8
Trinchera (riv.), Colo. 208/H8
Trincomalee, Ceylon, 54/M9
Trincomalee, Ceylon 68/E7
Třinec, Czech. 41/E2
Tring, 10/F5
Tring-Jonction, Que. 172/F3
Trinidad (isl.), Arg. 143/D4
Trinidad, Bol., 120/D5
Trinidad, El Beni, Bol. 136/C4
Trinidad, Pando, Bol. 136/B2
Trinidad, Calif. (95570) 204/A2
Trinidad (head), Calif. 204/A2
Trinidad (gulf), Chile 138/D8
Trinidad, Col. 126/E5
Trinidad, Colo., 146/H6
Trinidad, Colo., 188/F3
Trinidad, Colo. (81082) 208/L8
Trinidad, Cuba 156/B2
Trinidad (isl.), Trinidad Tobago 156/G5
Trinidad, Cuba 158/E2
Trinidad (isl.), Trinidad Tobago 161/A9
Trinidad, Hond. 154/C3
Trinidad, Par. 144/E6
Trinidad, Texas (75163) 302/J5
Trinidad, Urug. 145/B4
Trinidad, Wash. (†98848) 310/F3
Trinidad and Tobago, 3/G5
TRINIDAD and TOBAGO, 156/G5
TRINIDAD and TOBAGO, 161
Trinité, Mart. 161/D6
Trinity, Ala. (35673) 194/D1
Trinity (isls.), Alaska 196/H3
Trinity (bay), Aust. 88/H3
Trinity (co.), Calif. 204/B3
Trinity (riv.), Calif. 204/B3
Trinity (mt.), Idaho 220/C6
Trinity, Ky. (41190) 237/O3
Trinity (range), Nev. 266/C2
Trinity, Newf. 166/D2
Trinity, Newf. 166/D4
Trinity (bay), Newf. 166/D2
Trinity (bay), Queens. 95/C3
Trinity (riv.), Texas, 188/G4
Trinity (co.), Texas 302/J6
Trinity, Texas (75862) 302/J7
Trinity (bay), Texas 302/L2
Trinity (riv.), Texas 302/H5
Trinity Center, Calif. (96091) 204/C2
Trinity Springs, Ind. (†47581) 227/D7
Trinityville, Jam. 158/K6
Trinkitat, 102/F3
Trinkitat, Sudan 59/C6
Trinkitat, Sudan 111/G4
Trino, Italy 34/B2
Trinway, Ohio (43842) 284/F5
Trio, S.C. (29595) 296/H5
Trion, Ga. (30753) 216/B1
Tri Par Estates‡, Fla. (†33577) 212/D4
Triplet, Va. (23886) 307/N7
Triplett, Mo. (65286) 261/F4
Tripoli, Iowa (50676) 229/J3
Tripoli (Tarabulus), Leb. 59/C3
Tripoli (Tarabulus), Leb. 63/F5
Tripoli (prov.), Libya 111/B1
Tripoli (cap.), Libya, 3/K4
Tripoli (cap.), Libya 111/B1
Tripoli (cap.), Libya 102/D1
Tripoli, Wis. (54564) 317/G4
Tripolis, Greece 45/F7
Tripolitania (reg.), Libya 111/B1
Tripolitania (reg.), 102/D1
Tripp (co.), S. Dak. 298/K7
Tripp, S. Dak. (57376) 298/N7
Tripura (terr.), India 68/G4
Trischen (isl.), W. Ger. 22/C1
Tristan da Cunha (isl.), St. Helena, 3/J7
Triste (gulf), Ven. 124/D2
Triton, Que. 172/E2
Triton (isl.), China 85/E2
Triumph, Ill. (61371) 222/E2
Triumph-Buras, La. (†70041) 238/L8
Triune, Tenn. (†37014) 237/H9
Trivandrum, India, 54/L9
Trivandrum, India 68/D7
Trivoli, Ill. (61569) 222/D3
Trnava, Czech. 41/D2
Trobriand (isls.), Papua 85/C7
Trobriand (isls.), Papua, 87/F6
Trochu, Alta. 182/D4
Trodday (isl.), Scot. 15/D4
Troense, Den. 21/D7
Trofaiach, Austria 41/C3
Trogen, Switz. 39/H2
Trogir, Yugo. 45/C4
Trois-Îlets, Mart. 161/D7
Trois-Pistoles, Que. 172/H1
Trois Pitons, Morne (mt.), Dominica 161/E6
Trois-Rivières, 163/J6
Trois-Rivières (riv.), Haiti 158/B5
Trois-Rivières, Guad. 161/A7
Trois-Rivières, Que. 172/E3
Trois-Rivières, Que., 146/L5
Trois-Saumons, Que. 172/G2
Troisvierges, Lux. 27/J9
Troitsa (lake), Br. Col. 184/D3
Troitsk, U.S.S.R. 48/G4
Troitsk, U.S.S.R., 54/K4
Troitsko-Pechorsk, U.S.S.R. 52/J2
Trojan, S. Dak. (†57754) 298/B5
Trollhättan, Sweden 18/H7
Trombay, India 68/B7
Trombetas (riv.), Braz. 132/B3
Trommald, Minn. (†56455) 254/D4
Troms (co.), Norway 18/L2
Tromsø, Norway 18/L2
Tromsø, Norway, 4/B9
Tromsø, Norway, 7/G2
Trona, Calif. (93562) 204/H8
Tronador (mt.), Arg. 143/B5
Tronador, Cerro (mt.), Chile 138/E3
Tronchiennes (Drongen), Belg. 27/D6
Trondheim, Norway 18/F5
Trondheim, Norway, 7/F2
Trondheimsfjorden (fjord), Norway 18/G5
Trondheimsfjorden (fjord), Norway, 7/E2
Troodos (mt.), Cyprus 63/E5
Troon, 10/D3
Troon, Scot. 15/G8
Tropic, Utah (84776) 304/B6
Trosa, Sweden 18/K7
Trosky, Minn. (56177) 254/B7
Trossachs, Sask. 181/G6
Trossachs, The (valley), Scot. 15/H7
Trostan (mt.), N. Ire. 17/J1
Trotternish (dist.), Scot. 15/D4
Trotters, N. Dak. (58657) 283/C5
Trotwood‡, Ohio (45426) 284/B6
Trou-du-Nord, Haiti 158/C5
Troup (co.), Ga. 216/B4
Troup (head), Scot. 15/M4
Troup, Texas (75789) 302/J5
Troupsburg, N.Y. (14885) 276/F6
Trousdale, Kans. (67145) 232/C4
Trousdale, Okla. (†74878) 288/M4
Trousdale (co.), Tenn. 237/J8
Trousers (lake), N. Br. 170/C1
Trout (lake), 163/D3
Trout (mt.), Alta. 182/C1
Trout (riv.), Alta. 182/C1
Trout (creek), Ariz. 198/B3
Trout (creek), Colo. 208/E2
Trout (lake), Ont. 175/B2
Trout (lake), Ont. 177/E1
Trout (lake), Ont. 177/F1
Trout (creek), Idaho 220/B1
Trout, La. (71371) 238/F3
Trout (lake), Minn. 254/F2
Trout (lake), N.W.T. 187/F3
Trout (creek), Oreg. 291/J5
Trout (creek), Oreg. 291/F3
Trout (riv.), Sask. 181/L2
Trout (riv.), Vt. 268/B2
Trout, W. Va. (24982) 313/F6
Trout (lake), Wis. 317/G3
Trout Brook, N. Br. 170/E1
Trout Brook, N.S. 169/H3
Trout Creek, Ont. 177/E2
Trout Creek, Mich. (49967) 250/G2
Trout Creek, Mont. (59874) 262/A3
Trout Creek, Utah (84077) 304/A4
Troutdale, Maine (†04985) 242/D5
Troutdale, Oreg. (97060) 291/E2
Trout Dale, Va. (24378) 307/F7
Trout Hall, Jam. 158/J6
Trout Lake, Br. Col. 184/J5
Trout Lake, Ont. 175/C2
Trout Lake, Mich. (49793) 250/E2
Trout Lake, N.W.T. 187/F3
Trout Lake, Wash. (98650) 310/D5
Troutman, Ga. (†31721) 216/C7
Troutman, N.C. (28166) 281/H3
Trout River, Newf. 166/C4
Trout Run, Pa. (17771) 294/H3
Troutville, Pa. (15866) 294/E3
Troutville, Va. (24175) 307/J6
Trowbridge, Eng. 13/E6
Trowbridge, 10/E5
Troxelville, Pa. (17882) 294/H4
Troy, Ala. (36081) 194/G7
Troy, Idaho (83871) 220/B3
Troy, Ill. (62294) 222/B6
Troy, Ind. (47588) 227/D9
Troy, Iowa (52537) 229/J7
Troy, Kans. (66087) 232/G2
Troy▵, Maine (04987) 242/E6
Troy, Mich. (48084) 250/B6
Troy, Miss. (†38863) 256/G2
Troy, Mo. (63379) 261/L5
Troy, Mont. (59935) 262/A2
Troy, N.C. (27371) 281/K4
Troy▵, N.H. (03465) 268/C6
Troy, N.S. 169/G3
Troy, N.Y., 188/M2
Troy, N.Y. (*12180) 276/N5
Troy (Ilium) (ruins), Turkey 63/B6
Troy, Ohio (45373) 284/B5
Troy, Okla. (†74856) 288/N6
Troy, Oreg. (†97885) 291/K2
Troy, Pa. (16947) 294/J2
Troy, S.C. (29848) 296/C4
Troy, S. Dak. (†57265) 298/R3
Troy, Tenn. (38260) 237/C8
Troy‡, Texas (76579) 302/G6
Troy, Va. (22974) 307/M5
Troy▵, Vt. (05868) 268/C2
Troy, Vt. (05868) 268/C2
Troy, W. Va. (26443) 313/E4
Troyan, Bulg. 45/G4
Troy Center, Wis. (53180) 317/J2
Troyes, France 28/F3
Troy Grove, Ill. (61372) 222/E2
Troy Mills, Iowa (52344) 229/K4
Trstená, Czech. 41/E2
Truandó (riv.), Col. 126/B4
Truax, Sask. 181/G6
Trub, Switz. 39/E3
Truba, Saudi Ar. 59/D4
Trubchevsk, U.S.S.R. 52/D4
Truc Giang, S. Vietnam 72/E5
Truchas, N. Mex. (87578) 274/D2
Trucial States, 54/J7
TRUCIAL STATES, 59/F5
Truckee, Calif. (95734) 204/E4
Truckee (riv.), Calif. 204/F4
Truckee (riv.), Nev. 266/B3
Truckton, Colo. (†80864) 208/L5
Truesdail, Mo. (63380) 261/K5
Truesdale, Iowa (50592) 229/C3
Truesdell, Wis. (†53140) 317/L3
Trufant, Mich. (49347) 250/D5
Truganina, Vic. 97/H5
Trujillo, Hond. 154/E3
Trujillo, N. Mex. (87748) 274/E3
Trujillo, Peru, 120/C3
Trujillo, Peru 128/C7
Trujillo, Spain 33/D3
Trujillo (creek), Texas 302/A2
Trujillo, Ven., 120/D2
Trujillo (state), Ven. 124/C3
Trujillo, Ven. 124/C3
Trujillo Alto, P. Rico 161/E1
Truk (isls.), Pac. Is., 87/F5
Truman, Minn. (56088) 254/D7
Trumann, Ark. (72472) 203/J2
Trumansburg, N.Y. (14886) 276/G5
Trumbauersville, Pa. (18970) 294/M5
Trumbull (mt.), Ariz. 198/B2
Trumbull▵, Conn. (06611) 210/C4
Trumbull, Conn. (06611) 210/C4
Trumbull (lake), Iowa 229/C2
Trumbull, Nebr. (68980) 264/F4
Trumbull (co.), Ohio 284/J3
Trŭn, Bulg. 45/F4
Trun, Switz. 39/G3
Trundle, N.S.W. 97/D3
Trung Khanh Phu, N. Vietnam 72/E2
Truro, 163/K6
Truro, Eng. 13/C7
Truro, 10/D5
Truro, Iowa (50257) 229/F6
Truro▵, Mass. (02666) 249/O5
Truro, N.S. 169/E3
Truscott, Texas (79260) 302/E4
Truskmore (mt.), Ire. 17/E3
Trussville, Ala. (35173) 194/E3
Trustrup, Den. 21/D5
Truth or Consequences, N. Mex. (87901) 274/B5
Trutnov, Czech. 41/D1
Truxno, La. (†71260) 238/F1
Truxton, Mo. (63381) 261/K4
Truxton, N.Y. (13158) 276/H5
Tryon, N.C. (28782) 281/E4
Tryon, Nebr. (69167) 264/C3
Tryon, Okla. (74875) 288/N3
Tryonville, Pa. (†16404) 294/C2
Trysil, Norway 18/H6
Trysil (riv.), Norway 18/H6
Trzcianka, Poland 47/C2
Trzebiatów, Poland 47/E1
Trzebnica, Poland 47/C3
Tržič, Yugo. 45/B2
Tsagan Gol, Mong. 77/F2
Tsagan Ula, Mong. 77/E2
Tsagan Usu, China 77/E4
Tsaidam (swamp), China, 54/N6
Tsaidam (swamp), China 77/E4
Tsala Apopka (lake), Fla. 212/D3
Tsamkong, China, 54/P7
Tsangchow, China 77/J4
Tsangpo (riv.), China, 54/M7
Tsangpo (riv.), China 77/C6
Tsaochwang, China 77/J4
Tsau, Botswana 118/C4
Tsavo, Kenya 115/G4
Tsawwassen, Br. Col. 184/K3
Tschida (lake), N. Dak. 283/G6
Tschlin, Switz. 39/K3
Tseelim, Wadi (dry riv.), Israel 65/C5
Tselinograd, U.S.S.R. 48/H4
Tselinograd, U.S.S.R., 54/L4
Tselo (Chira), China 77/B4
Tses, S.W. Afr. 118/B5
Tsetserlig, Mong. 77/F2
Tshabong, Botswana 118/C5
Tshane, Botswana 118/C4
Tshela, Dem. Rep. of the Congo. 115/B4
Tshikapa, Dem. Rep. of the Congo. 115/D5
Tshofa, Dem. Rep. of the Congo. 115/D5
Tshuapa (riv.), Dem. Rep. of the Congo. 115/D4
Tsiafajavona (mt.), 102/G6
Tsiafajavona (mt.), Malag. Rep. 118/H3
Tsiaotso, China 77/H4
Tsihombe, Malag. Rep. 118/H5
Tsimlyansk (res.), U.S.S.R. 48/E5
Tsimlyansk (res.), U.S.S.R. 52/F5
Tsimlyansk (res.), U.S.S.R., 7/J4
Tsinan, China, 54/P6
Tsinan, China 77/J4
Tsinghai (prov.), China 77/E4
Tsing Hai (Koko Nor) (lake), China 77/E4
Tsingkiang, Kiangsi, China 77/J6
Tsingkiang, Kiangsu, China 77/J5
Tsingshih, China 77/H6
Tsingtao, China, 54/R6
Tsingtao, China 77/K4
Tsining, Inner Mong., China 77/H3
Tsining, Shantung, China 77/J4
Tsinling Shan (range), China 77/G5
Tsiribihina (riv.), Malag. Rep. 118/G3
Tsiroanomandidy, Malag. Rep. 118/H3
Tsitsihar, China, 54/R5
Tsitsihar, China 77/K2
Tsivory, Malag. Rep. 118/H4
Tskhinvali, U.S.S.R. 48/E5
Tskhinvali, U.S.S.R. 52/F6
Tsodilo Hill (mt.), Botswana 118/C3
Tsu, Japan 81/H6
Tsubame, Japan 81/J5
Tsuchiura, Japan 81/J5
Tsugaru (str.), Japan 81/K3
Tsumeb, 102/D6
Tsumeb, S.W. Afr. 118/B3
Tsunyi, China 77/G6
Tsuruga, Japan 81/G6
Tsurugi (mt.), Japan 81/G7
Tsuruoka, Japan 81/J4
Tsushima (isls.), Japan 81/D6
Tsushima (str.), Japan 81/D7
Tsuyama, Japan 81/F6
Tsuyung, China 77/F6
Tszaq, Mong. 77/E2
Tuadook (lake), N. Br. 170/D2
Tuakau, N.Z. 101/E2
Tual, Indon. 85/J7
Tualatin, Oreg. (97062) 291/A2
Tualatin (riv.), Oreg. 291/A2
Tuam, 10/B4
Tuam, Ire. 17/D4
Tuamotu (arch.), Fr. Poly., 87/M7
Tuamotu (arch.), Fr. Poly., 3/C6
Tuapse, U.S.S.R. 52/E6
Tuapse, U.S.S.R., 7/H4
Tuatapere, N.Z. 101/A7
Tuath (inlet), Scot. 15/D7
Tubac, Ariz. (85640) 198/E7
Tuba City, Ariz. (86045) 198/D2
Tubal, Wadi al (dry riv.), Iraq 66/B4
Tuban, Indon. 85/K2
Tubarão, Braz. 132/D10
Tubas, Jordan 65/C3
Tubbataha (reefs), Phil. 82/B6
Tubbataha (reefs), Phil. 85/G4
Tubbercurry, Ire. 17/D3
Tubeke (Tubize), Belg. 27/E7
Tuberose, Sask. 181/C5
Tubigon, Phil. 82/D6
Tübingen, W. Ger. 22/C4
Tubize, Belg. 27/E7
Tubod, Phil. 82/D6
Tubuai (isl.), Fr. Poly., 87/M8
Tubuai (Austral) (isls.), Fr. Poly., 87/M8
Tuburan, Phil. 82/D5
Tucacas, Ven. 124/D2
Tucannon (riv.), Wash. 310/G4
Tucano, Braz. 132/G5
Tucavaca, Bol. 136/F6
Tucavaca (riv.), Bol. 136/F6
Tuchola, Poland 47/C2
Tuckahoe (creek), Md. 245/P5
Tuckahoe, N.J. (08250) 273/D5
Tuckahoe (riv.), N.J. 273/D5
Tuckahoe, N.Y. (10707) 276/O7
Tucker, Ark. (72168) 203/G5
Tucker (co.), W. Va. 313/G4
Tuckerman, Ark. (72473) 203/H2
Tuckernuck (isl.), Mass. 249/N7
Tuckerton, N.J. (08087) 273/E4
Tucson, Ariz., 146/G6
Tucson, Ariz., 188/D4
Tucson, Ariz. (*85701) 198/D6
Tucumán, Arg., 120/D5
Tucumán (prov.), Arg. 143/C2
Tucumán, Arg. 143/D2
Tucumcari, N. Mex., 188/F3
Tucumcari, N. Mex. (88401) 274/F3
Tucupido, Ven. 124/F3
Tucupita, Ven. 124/H3
Tudela, Spain 33/F1
Tudela de Duero, Spain 33/D2
Tudor, Alta. 182/D4
Tuena, N.S.W. 97/E3
Tuensang, India 68/G3
Tuffnell, Sask. 181/H4
Tufi, Papua 85/C7
Tuftonboro▵, N.H. (†03816) 268/E4
Tuftonboro, N.H. (†03816) 268/E4
Tugaloo (riv.), Ga. 216/F1
Tugaloo (riv.), S.C. 296/A2
Tugaske, Sask. 181/E5
Tug Fork (riv.), Ky. 237/S5
Tug Fork (riv.), Va. 307/D5
Tug Fork (riv.), W. Va. 313/B7
Tuggerah (lake), N.S.W. 97/F3
Tugidak (isl.), Alaska 196/G3
Tugnug (pt.), Phil. 82/E5
Tuguegarao, Phil. 82/C2
Tuguegarao, Phil. 85/G2
Tugur, U.S.S.R. 48/O4
Tuhshan, China 77/G6
Tuichi (riv.), Bol. 136/A4
Tuiserkan, Iran 66/F3
Tujunga, Calif. (91042) 204/C10
Tukangbesi (isls.), Indon. 85/G7
Tuktoyaktuk, 163/C2
Tuktoyaktuk, Canada, 4/C16
Tuktoyaktuk, N.W.T. 187/E3
Tukuhnikivatz (mt.), Utah 304/E5
Tukums, U.S.S.R. 52/B3
Tukums, U.S.S.R. 53/B2
Tukuran, Phil. 82/D7
Tukuyu, Tanz. 115/F5
Tukwila, Wash. (98188) 310/B2
Tula, U.S.S.R. 48/D4
Tula, U.S.S.R. 52/E4
Tula, Mex. 150/K5
Tula (riv.), Mex. 150/L1
Tula, Miss. (38675) 256/F2
Tula, U.S.S.R., 7/H3
Tulak, Afgh. 59/H3
Tulak, Afgh. 68/A2
Tulalip, Wash. (†98270) 310/C2
Tulalip Ind. Res., Wash. 310/C2
Tulameen, Br. Col. 184/G5
Tulan, China 77/E4
Tulancingo, Mex. 150/K7
Tulare (lake), Calif., 188/B3
Tulare (co.), Calif. 204/G7
Tulare, Calif. (93274) 204/F7
Tulare (lake), Calif. 204/F7
Tulare, S. Dak. (57476) 298/N4
Tularosa, N. Mex. (88352) 274/C5
Tularosa (valley), N. Mex. 274/C6
Tulcán, Ec. 128/D2
Tulcea, Rum. 45/J3
Tul'chin, U.S.S.R. 52/C5
Tulcingo de Valle, Mex. 150/M2
Tule (lake), Calif. 204/D2
Tule (des.), Nev. 266/G5
Tuléar, 102/G7
Tuléar (prov.), Malag. Rep. 118/G4
Tuléar, Malag. Rep. 118/G4
Tulelake, Calif. (96134) 204/D2
Tule River Ind. Res., Calif. 204/G7
Tuli, Rhod. 118/D4
Tulia, Texas (79088) 302/C3
Tulip, Ark. (†71725) 203/E5
Tulip, Ind. (†47424) 227/D6
Tulkarm, Jordan 65/C3
Tull, Ark. (72015) 203/E5
Tulla, Ire. 17/D6
Tullahassee, Okla. (74466) 288/P3
Tullahoma, Tenn. (37388) 237/J10
Tullamore, 10/C4
Tullamore, Ire. 17/G5
Tullamore, N.S.W. 97/D3
Tullaroan, Ire. 17/G6
Tulle, France 28/D5
Tullibigeal, N.S.W. 97/D3
Tulliby Lake, Alta. 182/E3
Tullis, Sask. 181/D4
Tulln, Austria 41/D2
Tullos, La. (71479) 238/F3
Tullow, 10/C4
Tullow, Ire. 17/H6
Tully, Aust. 88/H3
Tully, Mass. (†01364) 249/E2
Tully, N.Y. (13159) 276/H5
Tully, Queens. 95/C3
Tully (falls), Queens. 95/C3
Tullytown, Pa. (19007) 294/N5
Tuloma (riv.), U.S.S.R. 52/D1
Tulot, Ark. (72483) 203/K2
Tulsa, Okla., 146/J6
Tulsa, Okla., 188/G3
Tulsa (co.), Okla. 288/P2
Tulsa, Okla. (*74101) 288/O2
Tulsequah, Br. Col. 184/J2
Tulsi (lake), India 68/B6
Tultepec, Mex. 150/L1
Tuluá, Col. 126/B5
Tuluksak, Alaska (99679) 196/F2
Tulun, U.S.S.R. 48/L4
Tulun, U.S.S.R., 54/O4
Tulungagung, Indon. 85/K2
Tuma (riv.), Nic. 154/E4
Tumacacori, Ariz. (85640) 198/D7
Tumacacori Nat'l Mon., Ariz. 198/E7
Tumaco, Col., 120/C2
Tumaco, Col. 126/A7
Tumaco, Rada de (bay), Col. 126/A6
Tumalo, Oreg. (†97701) 291/F3
Tumalo (creek), Oreg. 291/F3
Tumatumari, Guyana 131/B3
Tumba (lake), Dem. Rep. of the Congo. 115/C4
Tumbarumba, Aust. 88/H7
Tumbarumba, N.S.W. 97/D4
Tumbes (penn.), Chile 138/D1
Tumbes (riv.), Ec. 128/B4
Tumbes (dept.), Peru 128/B4
Tumbes, Peru 128/B4
Tumbes (riv.), Peru 128/B4
Tumblong, N.S.W. 97/D4
Tumby Bay, S. Aust. 94/E6
Tumegl-Tomils, Switz. 39/H3
Tumeka (lake), Br. Col. 184/C1
Tumen, China, 54/R5
Tumen, China 77/M3
Tumen (riv.), China 77/L3
Tumen (riv.), N. Korea 81/D2
Tumeremo, Ven. 124/H4
Tumereng, Guyana 131/B2
Tumindao (isl.), Phil. 82/B8
Tumkur, India 68/D6
Tummel, Man. 179/A3
Tummel (lake), Scot. 15/J6
Tummel (riv.), Scot. 15/J6
Tummo (El War) (well), Niger 106/G4
Tump, Pak. 59/H4
Tump, Pak. 68/A3
Tumpat, Malaysia 72/D6
Tumtum (lake), Oreg. 291/J5
Tumtum, Wash. (99034) 310/H3
Tumu, Ghana 106/D6
Tumucumaque (range), Braz. 132/C2
Tumucumaque, Serra de (range), Fr. Gui. 131/D5
Tumucumaque, Serra de (range), Sur. 131/D5
Tumupasa, Bol. 136/B4
Tumusla, Bol. 136/C7
Tumut, Aust. 88/H7
Tumut, N.S.W. 97/E4
Tumut (res.), N.S.W. 97/E4
Tumwater, Wash. (98501) 310/B3
Tun (Firdaus), Iran 59/G3
Tun (Firdaus), Iran 66/K3
Tuna (pt.), P. Rico 161/E3
Tunahí, Sierra (mts.), Col. 126/E7
Tunapuna, Trinidad Tobago 161/B10
Tunas, Mo. (65764) 261/F7
Tunas de Zaza, Cuba 156/B2
Tunas de Zaza, Cuba 158/E2
Tunbridge, N. Dak. (†58368) 283/K3
Tunbridge▵, Vt. (05077) 268/C4
Tunbridge, Vt. (05077) 268/C4
Tunbridge Wells (Royal Tunbridge Wells), Eng. 13/H6
Tunbridge Wells (Royal Tunbridge Wells), 10/G5
Tunceli (prov.), Turkey 63/H3
Tunceli (Kalan), Turkey 63/H3
Tuncurry, N.S.W. 97/G3
Tunduru, Tanz. 115/G6
Tundzha (riv.), Bulg. 45/G4
Tungabhadra (riv.), India 68/D5
Tungchwan, Shensi, China 77/G4
Tungchwan, Yünnan, China 77/F6
Tungfang, China 77/G8
Tungho, China 77/L2
Tunghwa, China 77/L3
Tungjen, Kweichow, China 77/G6
Tungjen, Tsinghai, China 77/F4
Tungkiang, China 77/M2
Tungkwan, China 77/H5
Tungliao, China 77/K3
Tungsha (Pratas) (isl.), China 77/J7
Tungsten, N.W.T. 187/F3
Tungsten, Nev. (†89418) 266/C2
Tungting (lake), China, 54/P7
Tungting (lake), China 77/H6
Tungü, China 77/K2
Tungurahua (prov.), Ec. 128/C3
Tunhwa, China 77/L3
Tunhwang, China 77/D3
Tuni, India 68/E5
Tunica, La. (70782) 238/G5
Tunica (co.), Miss. 256/D1
Tunica, Miss. (38676) 256/D1
Tunis, N.C. (†27986) 281/R2
Tunis (cap.), Tun., 3/K4
Tunis (cap.), Tun. 102/D1
Tunis (cap.), Tun. 106/G1
Tunis (gulf), Tun. 106/G1
Tunisia, 3/K4
TUNISIA, 106/F1
TUNISIA, 102/C1
Tunis Mills, Md. (†21601) 245/O5
Tunja, Col., 120/C2
Tunja, Col. 126/D5
Tunker, Ind. (†46787) 227/F2
Tunkhannock, Pa. (18657) 294/L2
Tunki, Nic. 154/E4
Tunki, China 77/J6
Tunn (lake), Norway 18/H4
Tunnel, Alaska (†99587) 196/C1
Tunnel City, Wis. (54662) 317/E7
Tunnel Hill, Ga. (30755) 216/C1
Tunnelhill‡, Pa. (†16641) 294/E5
Tunnel Springs, Ala. (36479) 194/D7
Tunnelton, Ind. (47467) 227/E7
Tunnelton, W. Va. (26444) 313/G4
Tunstall, Va. (23172) 307/O5
Tuntutuliak, Alaska (99680) 196/F2
Tununak, Alaska (99681) 196/E2
Tunungayualok (isl.), Newf. 166/B2
Tunuyán, Arg. 143/C3
Tunuyán (riv.), Arg. 143/C3
Tuolumne (co.), Calif. 204/F5
Tuolumne, Calif. (95379) 204/E6
Tupã, Braz. 132/D8
Tupã, Braz. 135/A2
Tupambaé, Urug. 145/E3
Tupanciretã, Braz. 132/C10
Tupelo, Ark. (72169) 203/H3
Tupelo, Miss. (38801) 256/G2
Tupelo, Okla. (74572) 288/O5
Tupelo Nat'l Battlefield, Miss. 256/G2
Tupi, Ven. 124/D2
Tupiza, Bol., 120/D5
Tupiza, Bol. 136/C7
Tupman, Calif. (93276) 204/F8
Tupper, Br. Col. 184/G2
Tupper (lake), N.S. 169/D4
Tupper (lake), N.Y. 276/M2
Tupper Lake, N.Y. (12986) 276/M2
Tuppers Plains, Ohio (45783) 284/G7
Tupungato, Cerro (mt.), Arg. 143/B3
Tupungato, Cerro (mt.), Chile 138/B9
Túquerres, Col. 126/B7
Tur, Jordan 65/C4
Tura, Hung. 41/E3
Tura, India 68/G3
Tura, U.S.S.R. 48/L3
Tura, U.S.S.R., 54/N3
Turaba, Saudi Ar. 59/D5
Turagua, Serranía (mts.), Ven. 124/F4
Turakina, N.Z. 101/E4
Turakirae (head), N.Z. 101/B3
Turan, U.S.S.R. 48/K4
Tur'an, Israel 65/C2
Turbaco, Col. 126/C2
Turbat, Pak. 59/H4
Turbat, Pak. 68/A3
Turbat-i-Haidari, Iran 59/G2
Turbat-i-Haidari, Iran 66/L3
Turbat-i-Shaikh Jam, Iran 59/H2
Turbat-i-Shaikh Jam, Iran 66/M3
Turbenthal, Switz. 39/G2
Turbeville, S.C. (29162) 296/G4
Turbeville, Va. (24596) 307/K7
Turbo, Col., 120/C2
Turbo, Col. 126/B3
Turbotville, Pa. (17772) 294/J3
Turčianske Teplice, Czech. 41/E2
Turco, Bol. 136/A6
Turda, Rum. 45/G2
Tureia (atoll), Fr. Poly., 87/N8
Turek, Poland 47/D2
Turema, St. Vincent 161/A8
Turen, Indon. 85/K2
Turén, Ven. 124/D3
Turfan, China, 54/N5
Turfan, China 77/C3
Turfan (depr.), China 77/C3
Turgay, U.S.S.R. 48/G5
Turgeon, N. Br. 170/E1

450 Turgi

Turgi, Switz. 39/F1
Tŭrgovishte, Bulg. 45/H4
Turgutlu, Turkey 63/B3
Turhal, Turkey 63/F2
Türi, U.S.S.R. 53/C1
Turia (riv.), Spain 33/F3
Turiaçu, Braz. 132/E3
Turiaçu (riv.), Braz. 132/E3
Turiamo, Ven. 124/E2
Turin, Alta. 182/D5
Turin, Ga. (30289) 216/C4
Turin, Iowa (51059) 229/B4
Turin, Italy, 7/E4
Turin (prov.), Italy 34/A2
Turin, Italy 34/A2
Turin, N.Y. (13473) 276/K3
Türkeli, Turkey 63/F2
Turkestan, U.S.S.R. 48/G5
Túrkeve, Hung. 41/F3
Turkey, 3/L4
Turkey, 7/H5
Turkey, 54/G6
TURKEY, 59/B2
TURKEY, 63/D3
Turkey (riv.), Iowa 229/K2
Turkey, Ky. (41382) 237/P6
Turkey, N.C. (28393) 281/N4
Turkey (creek), Okla. 288/L2
Turkey (creek), S.C. 296/E2
Turkey, Texas (79261) 302/D3
Turkey Creek, Aust. 88/D3
Turkey Creek, La. (70585) 238/F5
Turkey Creek, W. Aust. 92/E2
Turkey Point, Ont. 177/D5
Türkmen Daği (mt.), Turkey 63/D3
Turkmen S.S.R., U.S.S.R. 48/F6
Turkmen S.S.R., U.S.S.R., 54/J6
Türkoğlu, Turkey 63/G4
Turks (isls.), Turks Caicos Is. 156/D2
Turks and Caicos (isls.), 146/L7
TURKS and CAICOS ISLANDS, 156/D2
Turks Island (passg.), Turks Caicos Is. 156/D2
Turku, Fin. 18/N6
Turku-Pori (prov.), Fin. 18/N6
Turlock, Calif. (95380) 204/E6
Turmero, Ven. 124/E2
Turnagain (riv.), Br. Col. 184/K2
Turnagain (cape), N.Z. 101/F4
Turnagain Arm (inlet), Alaska 196/B1
Turnavik (isls.), Newf. 166/C2
Turnberry (pt.), Scot. 15/G9
Turneffe (isls.), Br. Hond. 154/D2
Turnen (mt.), Switz. 39/D3
Turner, Ark. (72383) 203/H5
Turner (co.), Ga. 216/E7
Turner▵, Maine (04282) 242/C7
Turner, Maine (04282) 242/C7
Turner, Mich. (48765) 250/F4
Turner, Mont. (59542) 262/H2
Turner, Oreg. (97392) 291/E3
Turner (co.), S. Dak. 298/P7
Turner, Wash. (†99328) 310/H4
Turner Center, Maine (04283) 242/C7
Turnercrest, Wyo. (†82716) 319/G2
Turner Hole (bay), V.I.(U.S.) 161/G4
Turners, Mo. (65765) 261/F8
Turnersburg, N.C. (28688) 281/H3
Turners Falls, Mass. (01376) 249/D2
Turners Station, Ky. (40075) 237/L3
Turnersville, Texas (76580) 302/G6
Turner Valley, Alta. 182/C4
Turnerville, Wyo. (†83112) 319/A3
Turney, Mo. (64493) 261/D3
Turnhout, Belg. 27/F6
Turnov, Czech. 41/C1
Turnu Măgurele, Rum. 45/G4
Turnu Severin, Rum. 45/F3
Turon, Kans. (67583) 232/D4
Turpin, Okla. (73950) 288/E1
Turquino (peak), Cuba 158/H4
Turrell, Ark. (72384) 203/K3
Turrialba, C. Rica 154/F6
Turriff, 10/E2
Turriff, Scot. 15/M4
Turtkul', U.S.S.R. 48/G5
Turtle (mt.), Man. 179/B5
Turtle (riv.), Man. 179/C3
Turtle (lake), Mich. 250/F4
Turtle (lake), N. Dak. 283/H4
Turtle (mts.), N. Dak. 283/K2
Turtle (isls.), Phil. 82/B7
Turtle (Penju) (isls.), Indon. 85/H7
Turtle (creek), S. Dak. 298/M4
Turtle (lake), Sask. 181/C2
Turtle Beach, Sask. 181/C2
Turtle Creek, N. Br. 170/F3
Turtle Creek, Pa. (15145) 294/C7
Turtle Creek, W. Va. (25203) 313/C6
Turtleford, Sask. 181/B2
Turtle Lake, N. Dak. (58575) 283/J4
Turtle Lake, Wis. (54889) 317/B5
Turtle Mountain Ind. Res., N. Dak. 283/L2
Turtle Mountain Prov. Park, Man. 179/B5
Turtlepoint, Pa. (16750) 294/F2
Turtle River, Minn. (†56601) 254/D3
Turtletown, Tenn. (37391) 237/N10
Turtola, Fin. 18/O3
Turton, S. Dak. (57477) 298/N3
Turtu, Mong. 77/F1
Turukhansk, U.S.S.R. 48/J3
Turukhansk, U.S.S.R., 54/N3
Turun, Iran 59/G2
Turun, Iran 66/K3
Turut, Iran 59/F2
Turut, Iran 66/J3
Turvo (riv.), Braz. 135/B2
Turzovka, Czech. 41/E2
Tuscaloosa, Ala., 188/J4
Tuscaloosa (co.), Ala. 194/C4
Tuscaloosa, Ala. (35401) 194/C4
Tuscan (arch.), Italy 34/B3
Tuscany (reg.), Italy 34/C3
Tuscarawas (co.), Ohio 284/H5
Tuscarawas, Ohio (44682) 284/H5
Tuscarawas (riv.), Ohio 284/H5
Tuscarora, Nev. (89834) 266/E1
Tuscarora (mts.), Nev. 266/E1
Tuscarora (mt.), Pa. 294/G5
Tuscarora Ind. Res., N.Y. 276/B4
Tuscola, Ill. (61953) 222/E4
Tuscola (co.), Mich. 250/F5
Tuscola, Mich. (48769) 250/F5
Tuscola, Texas (79562) 302/E5
Tuscor, Mont. (†59874) 262/A3
Tusculum, Ga. (†31329) 216/K6
Tusculum, Tenn. (37743) 237/R8
Tuscumbia, Ala. (35674) 194/C1
Tuscumbia, Mo. (65082) 261/H6
Tushantze, China 77/B3
Tushka, Okla. (74573) 288/O6
Tuskahoma, Okla. (74574) 288/R5
Tuskegee, Ala. (36083) 194/G6
Tuskegee Institute, Ala. (36088) 194/G6
Tusket, N.S. 169/C5
Tusket (isl.), N.S. 169/B5
Tusket (riv.), N.S. 169/C4
Tussy, Okla. (73088) 288/L6
Tustin, Calif. (92680) 204/D11
Tustin, Mich. (49688) 250/D4
Tustin, Wis. (†54940) 317/J7
Tustumena (lake), Alaska 196/C1
Tutak, Turkey 63/K3
Tutamoe (range), N.Z. 101/D1
Tutayev, U.S.S.R. 52/E3
Tuthill, S. Dak. (57574) 298/G7
Tuticorin, India 68/D7
Tutóia, Braz. 132/F3
Tutrakan, Bulg. 45/H4
Tuttle, Idaho (83354) 220/D7
Tuttle (lake), Iowa 229/D2
Tuttle, N. Dak. (58488) 283/L5
Tuttle, Okla. (73089) 288/L4
Tuttle Creek (res.), Kans. 232/F2
Tuttlingen, W. Ger. 22/C5
Tutuila (isl.), Amer. Samoa, 87/J7
Tutwiler, Miss. (38963) 256/D2
Tuun (mt.), N. Korea 81/C3
Tuvinian A.S.S.R., U.S.S.R. 48/K4
Tuwaiq, Jebel (range), Saudi Ar. 59/E5
Tuweep, Ariz. (†84770) 198/B2
Tuxedo, Man. 179/E5
Tuxedo, Md. (20781) 245/G5
Tuxedo Park, N.Y. (10987) 276/M8
Tuxford, Sask. 181/F5
Tuxpan, Jalisco, Mex. 150/H7
Tuxpan, Nayarit, Mex. 150/G6
Tuxpan de Rodríguez Caño, Mex. 150/L6
Tuxtepec, Mex. 150/L7
Tuxtla Gutiérrez, Mex. 150/N8
Túy, Spain 33/B1
Tuy (riv.), Ven. 124/E2
Tuya (riv.), Br. Col. 184/K2
Tuyen Quang, N. Vietnam 72/E2
Tuy Hoa, S. Vietnam 72/F4
Tuymazy, U.S.S.R. 52/H4
Tuyün, China 77/G6
Tuz (lake), Turkey 59/B2
Tuz (lake), Turkey 63/E3
Tuzigoot Nat'l Mon., Ariz. 198/D4
Tuz Khurmatu, Iraq 66/D3
Tuzla, Yugo. 45/D3
Tuzluca, Turkey 63/K3
Tuzlukçu, Turkey 63/D3
Tvedestrand, Norway 18/F7
Tver (Kalinin), U.S.S.R., 7/H3
Tversted, Den. 21/D2
Twain, Calif. (95984) 204/D4
Twain Harte, Calif. (95383) 204/E6
Tway, Sask. 181/F3
Tweed, Ont. 177/G3
Tweed (riv.), Eng. 13/E2
Tweed (riv.), 10/E3
Tweed (riv.), Scot. 15/M8
Tweed Heads, N.S.W. 97/G1
Tweedsmuir, Scot. 15/J9
Tweedsmuir Prov. Park, Br. Col. 184/D3
Twello, Neth. 27/J4
Twelve Mile, Ind. (46988) 227/E3
Twelvemile (lake), Sask. 181/E6
Twelve Mile (creek), Utah 304/C2
Twelve Pins (mt.), Ire. 17/B4
Twelvepole (creek), W. Va. 313/A6
Twentynine Palms, Calif. (92277) 204/K9
Twentynine Palms Marine Base, Calif. 204/J9
Twig, Minn. (55791) 254/F4
Twiggs (co.), Ga. 216/F5
Twila, Ky. (†40873) 237/P7
Twilight‡, Pa. (†15022) 294/C5
Twillingate, Newf. 166/C4
Twin (lakes), Conn. 210/B1
Twin (falls), Idaho 220/D7
Twin (lakes), Maine 242/F4
Twin (lakes), Wash. 310/G2
Twin Bridges, Mo. (†65775) 261/H9
Twin Bridges, Mont. (59754) 262/D5
Twin Brooks, S. Dak. (57269) 298/R3
Twin Butte, Alta. 182/C5
Twin City, Ga. (30471) 216/H5
Twin Falls, Idaho, 188/C2
Twin Falls (co.), Idaho 220/D7
Twin Falls, Idaho (83301) 220/D7
Twin Falls, Newf. 166/B3
Twin Hills‡, Alaska (†99576) 196/G3
Twining, Mich. (48766) 250/F4
Twin Lake, Mich. (49457) 250/C5
Twin Lakes, Calif. (†95060) 204/K4
Twin Lakes, Colo. (81251) 208/G4
Twin Lakes (res.), Colo. 208/G4
Twin Lakes, Minn. (56089) 254/E7
Twin Lakes, Wis. (53181) 317/K11
Twin Mountain, N.H. (03595) 268/D3
Twin Oaks‡, Mo. (†63088) 261/O3
Twin Peaks, Calif. (92391) 204/H9
Twin Peaks (mt.), Idaho 220/D5
Twin River, Alta. 182/D5
Twin Rocks, Oreg. (†97136) 291/C2
Twin Rocks, Pa. (15960) 294/E4
Twinsburg, Ohio (44087) 284/J10
Twin Sisters (mt.), Wash. 310/D2
Twin Valley, Minn. (56584) 254/B3
Twin Valley, Sask. 181/E6
Twisp, Wash. (98856) 310/E2
Twisp (pass), Wash. 310/E2
Twisp (riv.), Wash. 310/E2
Twitchell (res.), Calif. 204/E9
Two Arm (bay), Alaska 196/C2
Two Buttes, Colo. (81084) 208/P7
Two Buttes (creek), Colo. 208/N7
Two Buttes (res.), Colo. 208/O7
Two Creeks, Man. 179/B4
Twodot, Mont. (59085) 262/F4
Twofold (bay), N.S.W. 97/F5
Two Harbors, Minn. (55616) 254/G3
Two Hearted (riv.), Mich. 250/D2
Two Hills, Alta. 182/E3
Two Rivers (riv.), Minn. 254/A1
Two Rivers, Wis. (54241) 317/M7
Two Water (creek), Utah 304/E4
Tyachev, U.S.S.R. 52/B5
Tyaskin, Md. (21865) 245/P7
Tybee Roads (chan.), S.C. 296/F7
Tychy, Poland 47/B4
Tye, Texas (79563) 302/E5
Tyende (creek), Ariz. 198/E2
Tye River, Va. (22975) 307/L5
Tygart (lake), W. Va. 313/G4
Tygart Valley (riv.), W. Va. 313/F5
Tyger (riv.), S.C. 296/D2
Tygh Valley, Oreg. (97063) 291/F2
Tyler, Ala. (36785) 194/E6
Tyler (lake), Conn. 210/B1
Tyler, Minn. (56178) 254/B6
Tyler, Mo. (†63877) 261/N10
Tyler, N. Dak. (†58075) 283/S7
Tyler, Pa. (†15849) 294/F3
Tyler, Texas, 188/H4
Tyler (co.), Texas 302/K7
Tyler, Texas (75701) 302/J5
Tyler (co.), W. Va. 313/E4
Tyler, Wash. (99035) 310/H3
Tylersburg, Pa. (16361) 294/D3
Tylersville, Pa. (17773) 294/G4
Tylertown, Miss. (39667) 256/D8
Tylerville, Conn. (†06438) 210/F3
Tym (riv.), U.S.S.R. 48/J3
Týn, Czech. 41/C2
Tynagh, Ire. 17/E5
Tynan, N. Ire. 17/H3
Tynan, Texas (78391) 302/G9
Tyndall, Man. 179/F4
Tyndall, S. Dak. (57066) 298/O8
Tyndall A.F.B., Fla. 212/C6
Tyndinskiy, U.S.S.R. 48/N4
Tyne (riv.), Eng. 13/F3
Tyne (riv.), 10/F3
Tyne (riv.), Scot. 15/M7
Tynemouth, Eng. 13/F2
Tynemouth, 10/F3
Tyner, Ind. (46572) 227/E2
Tyner, Ky. (40486) 237/O6
Tyner, N.C. (27980) 281/R2
Tyner, Sask. 181/C4
Tyne Valley, P.E.I. 169/E2
Tyngsboro▵, Mass. (01879) 249/J2
Tynset, Norway 18/G5
Tyntynder Central, Vic. 97/B4
Tyonek, Alaska (99682) 196/B1
Tyra (cays), Nic. 154/F4
Tyre (Sur), Leb. 63/F6
Tyri (fjord), Norway 18/C3
Tyringham▵, Mass. (01264) 249/A4
Tyrnyauz, U.S.S.R. 52/F6
Tyro, Kans. (67364) 232/G4
Tyro, Miss. (†38668) 256/E1
Tyro, Va. (22976) 307/K5
Tyrone, Colo. (†81059) 208/L8
Tyrone, Ont. 177/F3
Tyrone, Ga. (30290) 216/C4
Tyrone, Ky. (†40342) 237/M4
Tyrone, Mo. (†65564) 261/J8
Tyrone (co.), N. Ire. 17/G2
Tyrone, N. Mex. (88065) 274/A6
Tyrone, Okla. (73951) 288/D1
Tyrone, Pa. (16686) 294/F4
Tyronza, Ark. (72386) 203/K3
Tyronza (riv.), Ark. 203/K2
Tyrrell (co.), N.C. 281/S3
Tyrrell (lake), Vic. 97/B4
Tyrrellspass, Ire. 17/G5
Tyrrhenian (sea), 7/F5
Tyrrhenian (sea), Italy 34/C4
Tysnes, Norway 18/D6
Tyson, Vt. (†05149) 268/B5
Tyson Wash (dry riv.), Ariz. 198/A5
Ty Ty, Ga. (31795) 216/E8
Tyubelyakh, U.S.S.R. 48/O3
Tyumen', U.S.S.R. 48/G4
Tyumen', U.S.S.R., 54/K4
Tyung (riv.), U.S.S.R. 48/M3
Tyvan, Sask. 181/H5
Tywyn, 10/D4
Tywyn, Wales 13/C5
Tzaneen, S. Africa 118/E4
Tzekung, China 77/G6
Tzekwei, China 77/H5
Tzepo, China 77/J4

U

Uahuka, Fr. Poly., 87/N6
Uanda, Queens. 95/C4
Uanle Uen, Somalia 115/H3
Uapou (isl.), Fr. Poly., 87/M6
Uatumã (riv.), Braz. 132/B3
Uaupés, Braz. 132/G9
Uaupés (riv.), Braz. 132/G9
Ubá, Braz. 132/F8
Ubá, Braz. 135/E2
Ubaíra, Braz. 132/G6
Ubaitaba, Braz. 132/G6
Ubaiyidh, Wadi (dry riv.), Iraq 66/B5
Ubangi (riv.), 102/E4
Ubangi (riv.), Centr. Afr. Rep. 115/C3
Ubangi (riv.), Rep. of Congo 115/C3
Ubangi (riv.), Dem. Rep. of the Congo. 115/C3
Ubari (prov.), Libya 111/B2
Ubari, Libya 111/B2
Ubaté, Col. 126/D5
Ubatuba, Braz. 135/D3
Ubay, Phil. 82/E5
Ube, Japan 81/E6
Úbeda, Spain 33/E3
Uberaba (mts.), Bol. 136/F5
Uberaba, Braz., 120/F4
Uberaba, Braz. 132/D7
Uberaba, Braz. 135/C1
Uberlândia, Braz. 132/E7
Überlingen, W. Ger. 22/C5
Ubina, Bol. 136/B7
Ubinas, Peru 128/G11
Ubly, Mich. (48475) 250/G5
Ubombo, S. Africa 118/E5
Ubon, Thai. 72/E4
Ubon, Thai., 54/O8
Ubrique, Spain 33/D4
Ubsa Nor (prov.), Mong. 77/D2
Ubsa Nor (lake), Mong. 77/D1
Ucayali (riv.), Peru, 3/F6
Ucayali (riv.), Peru, 120/C3
Ucayali (riv.), Peru 128/F5
Uccle, Belg. 27/B9
Uch, Pak. 68/B3
Uchaly, U.S.S.R. 52/J4
Ucharonidge, No. Terr. 93/D4
Uchee, Ala. (†36858) 194/H6
Uchinoura, Japan 81/E8
Uchiura (bay), Japan 81/K2
Uchiza, Peru 128/D7
Uch Turfan, China 77/A3
Uckange, France 28/G3
Ücker (riv.), E. Ger. 22/E2
Uckfield, Eng. 13/H7
Uckfield, 10/G5
Ucluelet, Br. Col. 184/E6
Ucon, Idaho (83454) 220/F6
Ucross, Wyo. (†82835) 319/F1
Ucumasi, Bol. 136/B6
Udall, Kans. (67146) 232/E4
Udaypur, India 68/C4
Udby, Den. 21/D4
Uddevalla, Sweden 18/G7
Uddjaur (lake), Sweden 18/L4
Udell, Iowa (52593) 229/H7
Uden, Neth. 27/H5
Udhampur, India 68/D2
Udine (prov.), Italy 34/D1
Udine, Italy 34/D2
Udipi, India 68/C6
Udmurt A.S.S.R., U.S.S.R. 48/F4
Udmurt A.S.S.R., U.S.S.R. 52/H3
Udon Thani, Thai. 72/D3
Ueberstorf, Switz. 39/D3
Ueckermünde, E. Ger. 22/F2
Ueda, Japan 81/J5
Uehling, Nebr. (68063) 264/H3
Uele (riv.), Dem. Rep. of the Congo. 115/E3
Uelen, U.S.S.R. 48/T3
Uelen, U.S.S.R., 4/C18
Uel'kal, U.S.S.R. 48/S3
Uelzen, W. Ger. 22/D2
Uetendorf, Switz. 39/E3
Uetersen, W. Ger. 22/C2
Ufa, U.S.S.R. 48/F4
Ufa, U.S.S.R. 52/J4
Ufa (riv.), U.S.S.R. 52/J3
Ufa, U.S.S.R., 3/M3
Ufa, U.S.S.R., 7/K3
Uffington, W. Va. (†26505) 313/G3
Ugab (riv.), S.W. Afr. 118/A4
Uganda, 3/L5
UGANDA, 102/F4
UGANDA, 115/F3
Ugashik, Alaska (99683) 196/G3
Ugashik (lakes), Alaska 196/G3
Ugie (riv.), Scot. 15/N4
Ugljar, Spain 33/E4
Ugjoktok (bay), Newf. 166/B2
Uglich, U.S.S.R. 52/E3
Ugo, Japan 81/K4
Uh (riv.), Czech. 41/G2
Uherské Hradiště, Czech. 41/D2
Uherský Brod, Czech. 41/D2
Úhlava (riv.), Czech. 41/B2
Uhlířské Janovice, Czech. 41/C2
Uhrichsville, Ohio (44683) 284/H5
Uichin, S. Korea 81/D5
Uig, 10/C2
Uig, Inverness, Scot. 15/D4
Uig, Ross and Cromarty, Scot. 15/B3
Uige (dist.), Angola 115/C5
Uiju, N. Korea 81/B3
Uinkaret (plat.), Ariz. 198/C2
Uinta (mts.), Utah 304/D3
Uinta (riv.), Utah 304/D3
Uinta (co.), Wyo. 319/B4
Uintah (co.), Utah 304/E3
Uintah, Utah (†84401) 304/C2
Uintah and Ouray Ind. Res., Utah 304/D3
Uisŏng, S. Korea 81/D5
Uitenhage, 102/E8
Uitenhage, S. Africa 118/C6
Uitgeest, Neth. 27/F3
Uithoorn, Neth. 27/F4
Uithuizen, Neth. 27/K2
Uivak (cape), Newf. 166/B2
Ujelang (atoll), Pac. Is., 87/F5
Újfehértó, Hung. 41/F3
Újhartyán, Hung. 41/E3
Uji, Hond. 154/F3
Uji, Japan 81/J7
Ujjain, India 68/D4
Újpest, Hung. 41/E3
Uka, U.S.S.R. 48/R4
Ukasiksalik (isl.), Newf. 166/B2
Ukhta, U.S.S.R. 48/F3
Ukiah, Calif. (95482) 204/B4
Ukiah, Oreg. (97880) 291/J2
Ukkel (Uccle), Belg. 27/B9
Ukmergė, U.S.S.R. 52/C3
Ukmergė, U.S.S.R. 53/C3
Ukraina, Man. 179/B3
Ukrainian S.S.R., U.S.S.R. 48/C5
Ukrainian S.S.R., U.S.S.R. 52/D5
Ukrainian S.S.R., U.S.S.R., 7/H4
Ula, Turkey 63/C4
Ulah, N.C. (†27203) 281/K3
Ulak (isl.), Alaska 196/K4
Ulan Bator (cap.), Mong., 3/Q3
Ulan Bator (cap.), Mong., 54/O5
Ulan Bator (cap.), Mong. 77/G2
Ulangom, Mong., 54/N5
Ulangom, Mong. 77/D2
Ulanhot, China 77/K2
Ulan-Ude, U.S.S.R. 48/L4
Ulan-Ude, U.S.S.R., 3/Q3
Ulan-Ude, U.S.S.R., 54/O5
Ulapes, Arg. 143/C3
Ulaş, Turkey 63/G3
Ulcinj, Yugo. 45/D5
Uldum, Den. 21/C6
Ulee Lheue, Indon. 85/A4
Ulen, Ind. (†46052) 227/E4
Ulen, Minn. (56585) 254/B3
Ulen Muren (riv.), China 77/D5
Uler, W. Va. (25282) 313/D5
Ulfborg, Den. 21/B5
Ulhasnagar, India 68/C5
Uliassutai, Mong., 54/N5
Uliassutai, Mong. 77/E2
Ulindi (riv.), Dem. Rep. of the Congo. 115/E4
Uling (mt.), Phil. 82/D5
Ulithi (atoll), Pac. Is., 87/D4
Ulla (riv.), Spain 33/B1
Ulladulla, N.S.W. 97/F4
Ullapool, 10/D2
Ullapool, Scot. 15/F4
Ullared, Sweden 18/H8
Ulla Ulla, Bol. 136/A4
Ulldecona, Spain 33/G2
Ullensvang, Norway 18/E6
Ullin, Ill. (62992) 222/D6
Ulloma, Bol. 136/A5
Ullŭng (isl.), S. Korea 81/E5
Ulm, Ark. (72170) 203/H4
Ulm, Mont. (59485) 262/E3
Ulm, W. Ger. 22/C4
Ulm, Wyo. (82835) 319/F1
Ulman, Mo. (65083) 261/H6
Ulmarra, N.S.W. 97/G1
Ulmer, Iowa (51464) 229/D4
Ulmer, S.C. (29849) 296/E5
Ulricehamn, Sweden 18/H8
Ulriksfors, Sweden 18/K5
Ulrum, Neth. 27/J2
Ulsan, S. Korea 81/D6
Ulster (part) (prov.), Ire. 17/G2
Ulster (part) (prov.), N. Ire. 17/G2
Ulster (co.), N.Y. 276/M7
Ulster, Pa. (18850) 294/J2
Ulster Spring, Jam. 158/H6
Última Esperanza (sound), Chile 138/E9
Ulúa (riv.), Hond. 154/D3
Ulubey, Turkey 63/C3
Uluborlu, Turkey 63/D3
Uludağ (mt.), Turkey 63/C3
Uludere, Turkey 63/K4
Ulugan (bay), Phil. 82/B5
Ulughchat, China 77/A4
Ulugh Muztagh (mt.), China 77/C4
Ulukişla, Turkey 63/F4
Ulumalu, Hawaii (†96708) 218/K2
Ulupalakua, Hawaii (†96790) 218/J2
Ulu Tiram, Malaysia 72/F5
Ulva (isl.), Scot. 15/D7
Ulverston, Eng. 13/D3
Ulverston, 10/E3
Ulverstone, Aust. 88/H8
Ulverstone, Tasmania 99/C3
Ulvik, Norway 18/E6
Ulvila, Fin. 18/N6
Ul'yanovsk, U.S.S.R. 48/E4
Ul'yanovsk, U.S.S.R. 52/G4
Ul'yanovsk, U.S.S.R., 7/J3
Ulysses, Kans. (67880) 232/A4
Ulysses, Ky. (41264) 237/R5
Ulysses, Nebr. (68669) 264/G3
Ulysses, Pa. (16948) 294/G2
Ulyungur Nor (lake), China 77/C2
Umala, Bol. 136/B5
Uman', U.S.S.R. 52/D5
Umán, Mex. 150/P6
Umanun (pt.), Phil. 82/F6
Umapine, Oreg. (97881) 291/J2
Umarkot, Pak. 59/J4
Umarkot, Pak. 68/B3
Umatilla, Fla. (32784) 212/E3
Umatilla (co.), Oreg. 291/J2
Umatilla, Oreg. (97882) 291/H2
Umatilla (lake), Oreg. 291/G2
Umatilla (riv.), Oreg. 291/H2
Umatilla (lake), Wash. 310/E5
Umatilla Army Depot, Oreg. 291/H2
Umatilla Ind. Res., Oreg. 291/J2
Umbagog (lake), Maine 242/A6
Umbagog (lake), N.H. 268/E2
Umbarger, Texas (79091) 302/B3
Umbeara, No. Terr. 93/C8
Umbertide, Italy 34/D3
Umbrail (mt.), Switz. 39/K3
Umbría, Col. 126/B7
Umbria (reg.), Italy 34/D3
Umcalcus (lake), Maine 242/G3
Umeå, Sweden 18/M5
Umeå, Sweden, 7/F2
Umeälv (riv.), Sweden 18/L4
Umfors, Sweden 18/J4
Umiakovik (lake), Newf. 166/B2
Umiat, Alaska (†99701) 196/H1
Umikoa, Hawaii (†96776) 218/H4
Um Jauza, Jordan 65/D3
Umm al Qaiwain (cap.), Trucial States 59/G4
Umm el Abid, Libya 111/C2
Umm el Fahm, Israel 65/C2
Umm Hajar, Eth. 111/G5
Umm Keddada, Sudan 111/E5
Umm Lajj, Saudi Ar. 59/C4
Umm Qasr, Iraq 66/E5
Umm Ruwaba, Sudan 59/B7
Umm Ruwaba, Sudan 111/F5
Umm Sa'id, Qatar 59/F5
Umnak (isl.), Alaska 196/E4
Umnak (passg.), Alaska 196/E4
Umnak (isl.), U.S., 4/D18
Umpire, Ark. (71971) 203/B5
Umpqua, Oreg. (97486) 291/D4
Umpqua (riv.), Oreg. 291/D4
Umrer, India 68/D4
Umsaskis (lake), Maine 242/E2
Umtali, 102/F6
Umtali, Rhod. 118/E3
Umtata, 102/E8
Umtata, S. Africa 118/D6
Umurbey, Turkey 63/C6
Umvukwe (range), Rhod. 118/E3
Umvuma, Rhod. 118/D3
Umzinto, S. Africa 118/E6
Una (mt.), N.Z. 101/D5
Una (riv.), Yugo. 45/C3
Unadilla, Ga. (31091) 216/E6
Unadilla, N.Y. (13849) 276/K6
Unadilla (riv.), N.Y. 276/K5
Unadilla, Nebr. (68454) 264/H4
Unaí, Braz. 132/E7
Unaka, N.C. (28908) 281/A4
Unaka (mts.), N.C. 281/E2
Unaka (mts.), Tenn. 237/S8
Unalakleet, Alaska, 188/C5
Unalakleet, Alaska (99684) 196/G2
Unalaska, Alaska, 188/C6
Unalaska, Alaska (99685) 196/E4
Unalaska (isl.), Alaska 196/E4
Unalaska (isl.), U.S., 4/D18
Unango, Moz. 118/F2
Unare (riv.), Ven. 124/F3
Uncas, Alta. 182/D3
Uncas, Okla. (74601) 288/M1
Uncastillo, Spain 33/F1
Uncasville, Conn. (06382) 210/G3
Uncertain, Texas (†75661) 302/K5
Uncía, Bol. 136/B6
Uncompahgre (peak), Colo. 208/E6
Uncompahgre (plat.), Colo. 208/B5
Uncompahgre (riv.), Colo. 208/D5
Underbool, Vic. 97/A4
Underhill, Man. 179/B5
Underhill▵, Vt. (05489) 268/B2
Underhill, Vt. (05489) 268/B2
Underhill, Wis. (54176) 317/K6
Underhill Center, Vt. (05490) 268/B2
Underwood, Ont. 177/C3
Underwood, Ind. (47177) 227/F7
Underwood, Iowa (51576) 229/B6
Underwood, Minn. (56586) 254/C4
Underwood, N. Dak. (58576) 283/H5
Underwood, Wash. (98651) 310/D5
Undur Khan, Mong. 77/H2
Undzha (riv.), U.S.S.R. 52/F3
Uneeda, W. Va. (25205) 313/C6
Unga (isl.), Alaska 196/F3
Ungalik, Alaska (†99684) 196/F2
Ungarie, N.S.W. 97/D3
Ungava (bay), Canada, 146/M4
Ungava (Nouveau-Québec) (dist.), Que. 174/E1
Ungava (bay), Que. 174/F1
Ungava (pen.), Que. 174/E1
Ungava (bay), 163/K4
Ungava (pen.), 163/J3
Ungava (bay), N.W.T. 187/M4
Unger, W. Va. (25447) 313/K4
Unggi, N. Korea 81/E2
União, Braz. 132/F4
União da Vitória, Braz. 132/D9
União dos Palmares, Braz. 132/H5
Unicoi (mts.), N.C. 281/A4
Unicoi (co.), Tenn. 237/S8
Unicoi, Tenn. (37692) 237/S8
Unicoi (mts.), Tenn. 237/N10
Uničov, Czech. 41/D2
Uniform, Ala. (†36583) 194/B8
Uniket, China 77/J2
Unimak (isl.), Alaska, 188/C6
Unimak (bight), Alaska 196/F4
Unimak (isl.), Alaska 196/E4
Unimak (passg.), Alaska 196/F4
Unimak (isl.), U.S., 4/D18
Unini, Peru 128/F8
Union, Ala. (†35462) 194/C5
Unión, Arg. 143/C3
Union (mt.), Ariz. 198/C4
Union (co.), Ark. 203/E7
Union, Ark. (72582) 203/G1
Union▵, Conn. (†06076) 210/G1
Union (isl.), St. Vincent 156/G4
Union, Grenada 161/D8
Union (co.), Fla. 212/D1
Union (co.), Ga. 216/E1
Union (co.), Ill. 222/D6
Union, Ill. (60180) 222/E1
Union (co.), Ind. 227/H5
Union, Ind. (†47540) 227/C8
Union (co.), Iowa 229/E7
Union, Iowa (50258) 229/G4
Union (co.), Ky. 237/F5
Union, Ky. (41091) 237/M3
Union (par.), La. 238/F1
Union, La. (70723) 238/L3
Union▵, Maine (04862) 242/E7
Union, Maine (04862) 242/E7
Union, West Branch (riv.), Maine 242/G6
Union (co.), Miss. 256/F2
Union, Miss. (39365) 256/F5
Union, Mo. (63084) 261/L6
Union (co.), N.C. 281/H4
Union, N. Dak. (58279) 283/O2
Union, N.H. (03887) 268/E5
Union (co.), N.J. 273/E2
Union▵, N.J. (07083) 273/A2
Union (lake), N.J. 273/C5
Union (co.), N. Mex. 274/F2
Union, Nebr. (68455) 264/J4
Union (co.), Ohio 284/D5
Union, Ohio (45322) 284/B6
Union, Okla. (73090) 288/L4
Union (co.), Oreg. 291/J2
Union, Oreg. (97883) 291/K2
Union (co.), Pa. 294/H4
Unión, Par. 144/D5
Union (co.), S.C. 296/D2
Union, S.C. (29379) 296/D2
Union (co.), S. Dak. 298/R8
Union (co.), Tenn. 237/O8
Unión, Urug. 145/B7
Union, W. Va. (24983) 313/E7
Union, Wash. (98592) 310/B3
Union (lake), Wash. 310/B2
Union Bay, Br. Col. 184/H2
Union Beach, N.J. (07735) 273/E3
Union Bridge, Md. (21791) 245/K2
Union Center, S. Dak. (57787) 298/D4
Union Center, Wis. (53962) 317/F8
Union Church, Miss. (39668) 256/C7
Union City, Calif. (94587) 204/K2
Union City, Conn. (†06770) 210/C2
Union City, Ga. (30291) 216/D3
Union City, Ind. (47390) 227/H4
Union City, Mich. (49094) 250/D6
Union City, N.J. (07087) 273/C2
Union City, Ohio (†47390) 284/A5
Union City, Pa. (16438) 294/C2

Valley Brook 451

Union City, Tenn. (38261) 237/C8
Union Creek, Oreg. (†97536) 291/E5
Uniondale, Ind. (46791) 227/G3
Uniondale‡, N.Y. (11553) 276/R7
Union Dale, Pa. (18470) 294/M2
Unión de Reyes, Cuba 158/C1
Union Furnace, Ohio (43158) 284/F7
Union Gap, Wash. (98903) 310/E4
Union Grove, Ala. (35175) 194/E2
Union Grove, N.C. (28689) 281/H2
Union Grove, Wis. (53182) 317/L3
Union Hall, Va. (24176) 307/J6
Unión Hidalgo, Mex. 150/M8
Union Hill, Ill. (60969) 222/E2
Union Hill, N.Y. (14563) 276/F4
Union Level, Va. (23973) 307/M7
Union Mills, Ind. (46382) 227/D2
Union Mills, Md. (†21157) 245/K2
Union Mills, N.C. (28167) 281/F3
Union of Soviet Socialist Republics, 3/L2
Union of Soviet Socialist Republics, 4/C2
Union of Soviet Socialist Republics, 7/H3
Union of Soviet Socialist Republics, 54/M3
UNION of SOVIET SOCIALIST REPUBLICS, 48
UNION of SOVIET SOCIALIST REPUBLICS, 52
Union Park‡, Fla. (†32801) 212/E3
Union Pier, Mich. (49129) 250/C7
Union Point, Ga. (30669) 216/F3
Union Point, Man. 179/E5
Unionport, Ind. (†47340) 227/G4
Unionport, Ohio (43966) 284/J5
Union Springs, Ala. (36089) 194/G6
Union Springs, N.Y. (13160) 276/G5
Union Star, Ky. (40171) 237/H5
Union Star, Mo. (64494) 261/C2
Uniontown, Ala. (36786) 194/D6
Uniontown, Ark. (72955) 203/B2
Uniontown, Ind. (47589) 227/D8
Uniontown, Kans. (66779) 232/G4
Uniontown, Ky. (42461) 237/F5
Uniontown, Md. (21157) 245/K2
Uniontown, Mo. (63783) 261/N7
Uniontown, Ohio (44685) 284/H4
Uniontown (Fultonham), Ohio (†43738) 284/F6
Uniontown, Pa. (15401) 294/C6
Uniontown, Wash. (99179) 310/H4
Union Village, Vt. (05078) 268/C4
Unionville, Conn. (06085) 210/D1
Unionville, Ont. 177/K4
Unionville, Ga. (†31794) 216/F8
Unionville, Ill. (†61270) 222/E6
Unionville, Ind. (47468) 227/E6
Unionville, Iowa (52594) 229/H7
Unionville, Maine (†04622) 242/H6
Unionville, Md. (21792) 245/K3
Unionville, Mich. (48767) 250/F5
Unionville, Mo. (63565) 261/G2
Unionville, N.C. (†28110) 281/J4
Unionville, N.Y. (10988) 276/L8
Unionville, Nev. (†89418) 266/C2
Unionville, Ohio (44088) 284/J2
Unionville (Fleming), Pa. (19375) 294/G4
Unionville, Tenn. (37180) 237/H9
Unionville, Va. (22567) 307/N4
Unionville Center, Ohio (43077) 284/D5
Uniopolis, Ohio (45888) 284/B4
United, Pa. (15689) 294/D5
United Arab Republic, 3/L4
UNITED ARAB REPUBLIC, 59/A4
UNITED ARAB REPUBLIC (EGYPT), 102/E2
UNITED ARAB REPUBLIC (EGYPT), 111/E2
United Kingdom, 3/J3
United Kingdom, 7/E3
UNITED KINGDOM, 10
United States, 3/D4
United States, 4/C17
United States, 146/H6
UNITED STATES, 188
United States (range), 163/N3
Unity▵, Maine (04988) 242/E6
Unity, Md. (†20729) 245/K4
Unity, Mo. (64063) 261/R6
Unity▵, N.H. (†03743) 268/C5
Unity, Ohio (†44413) 284/J4
Unity, Oreg. (97884) 291/J3
Unity, Sask. 181/B3
Unity, Wis. (54488) 317/F6
Unityville, Pa. (17774) 294/K3
Unityville, S. Dak. (†57058) 298/P6
Universal, Ind. (47884) 227/C5
Universal, Pa. (15235) 294/C7
Universal City‡, Texas (78148) 302/F8
University‡, Fla. (33606) 212/D3
University, N.C. (†27701) 281/L2
University City, Mo., 188/H3
University City, Mo. (63130) 261/P3
University Heights, Iowa (†52240) 229/K5
University Heights, Ohio (44118) 284/H9
University Park, Calif. (90007) 204/D11
University Park‡, Fla. (†33432) 212/F5
University Park, Iowa (52595) 229/H6
University Park, Md. (†20740) 245/F4
University Park, N. Mex. (88001) 274/C6
University Park, Texas (78228) 302/H2
University Place‡, Wash. (†98401) 310/C3
Unley, Aust. 88/D8
Unley, S. Aust. 94/B8
Unnao, India 68/E3
Uno, Man. 179/B4
Unsan, N. Korea 81/C4
Unst (isl.), 10/H1
Unst (isl.), Scot. 15/N2
Unstrut (riv.), E. Ger. 22/D3
Unterägeri, Switz. 39/G2
Unterkulm, Switz. 39/F2
Untersee (lake), Switz. 39/H1
Unterseen, Switz. 39/E3
Untervaz, Switz. 39/H3
Unterwalden (canton), Switz. 39/F3
Unuk (riv.), Alaska 196/N2
Unuk (riv.), Br. Col. 184/B2
Unwin, Sask. 181/B3
ünye, Turkey 59/C1
ünye, Turkey 63/G2
Unzen (mt.), Japan 81/D7
Unzen-Amakusa Nat'l Park, Japan 81/D7
Uozu, Japan 81/H5
Upalco, Utah (†84007) 304/D3
Upata, Ven. 124/G3
Upatoi, Ga. (31829) 216/C5
Upemba (lake), Dem. Rep. of the Congo. 115/E5
Upemba Nat'l Park, Dem. Rep. of the Congo. 115/E5
Upernavik, Greenl., 4/B12
Upham, N. Br. 170/E3
Upham, N. Dak. (58789) 283/J2
Upía (riv.), Col. 126/D5
úpice, Czech. 41/C1
Upington, S. Africa 118/C5
Upland, Calif. (91786) 204/E10
Upland, Ind. (46989) 227/F4
Upland, Kans. (†67431) 232/E2
Upland, Nebr. (68981) 264/F4
Upland, Pa. (†19013) 294/L7
Uplands Park‡, Mo. (†63101) 261/P3
Upolu (pt.), Hawaii 218/G3
Upolu (isl.), W. Samoa, 87/J7
Upper Alkali (lake), Calif. 204/E2
Upper Ammonoosuc (riv.), N.H. 268/E2
Upper Arlington, Ohio (43221) 284/D6
Upper Arrow (lake), Br. Col. 184/H5
Upper Austria (prov.), Austria 41/B2
Upper Black Eddy, Pa. (18972) 294/N4
Upper Blackville, N. Br. 170/E2
Upper Brookville‡, N.Y. (†11545) 276/R7
Upper Charlo, N. Br. 170/D1
Upper Chateaugay (lake), N.Y. 276/M1
Upperchurch, Ire. 17/E6
Upper Clyde River, N.S. 169/C5
Upperco, Md. (21155) 245/L2
Upper Dam, Maine (†04293) 242/B6
Upper Darby▵, Pa. (*19082) 294/M6
Upper Des Lacs (lake), N. Dak. 283/F2
Upper Engadine (valley), Switz. 39/J4
Upper Fairmount, Md. (21867) 245/P8
Upper Falls, Md. (21156) 245/N3
Upper Fraser, Br. Col. 184/G3
Upper Frenchville, Maine (04784) 242/G1
Upper Gagetown, N. Br. 170/D3
Upper Gaspereau, N. Br. 170/E2
Upperglade, W. Va. (26266) 313/F6
Upper Greenwood Lake, N.J. (†07421) 273/E1
Upper Hainesville, N. Br. 170/C2
Upper Horton, N.S.W. 97/F2
Upper Hutt, N.Z. 101/B2
Upper Iowa (riv.), Iowa 229/K2
Upper Island Cove, Newf. 166/D2
Upper Jay, N.Y. (12987) 276/N2
Upper Juba (prov.), Somalia 115/H3
Upper Kennetcook, N.S. 169/E3
Upper Kent, N. Br. 170/C2
Upper Klamath (lake), Oreg., 188/B2
Upper Klamath (lake), Oreg. 291/E5
Upper Lake, Calif. (95485) 204/C4
Upper Lough Erne (lake), 10/C3
Upper Lough Erne (lake), N. Ire. 17/F3
Upper Macopin, N.J. (†07435) 273/E1
Upper Manzanilla, Trinidad Tobago 161/B10
Upper Marlboro, Md. (20870) 245/M5
Upper Matecumbe (key), Fla. 212/F7
Upper Mills, N. Br. 170/C3
Upper Musquodoboit, N.S. 169/F3
Upper Nappan, N.S. 169/D3
Upper New York (bay), N.J. 273/B2
Upper Nile (prov.), Sudan 111/F6
Upper Nyack‡, N.Y. (†10960) 276/N9
Upper Rawdon, N.S. 169/E3
Upper Red (lake), Minn. 254/D2
Upper Red Rock (lake), Mont. 262/E6
Upper Rockport, N. Br. 170/F3
Upper Sackville, N. Br. 170/F3
Upper Saddle River, N.J. (†07458) 273/B1
Upper Sandusky, Ohio (43351) 284/D4
Upper Sandy Point, N.S. 169/C5
Upper Saranac (lake), N.Y. 276/M2
Upper Sheikh, Somalia 115/J2
Upper Sheila, N. Br. 170/E1
Upper South River, N.S. 169/G3
Upper Spavinaw (lake), Okla. 288/S2
Upper Stepney, Conn. (†06468) 210/B3
Upper Stewiacke, N.S. 169/F3
Upper Strasburg, Pa. (17265) 294/G5
Upper Tract, W. Va. (26866) 313/H5
Upper Tunguska (riv.), U.S.S.R. 48/K4
Upper Tygart, Ky. (41178) 237/P4
Upper Vaughan, N.S. 169/D4
Upperville, Va. (22176) 307/N2
Upper Volta, 3/J5
UPPER VOLTA, 106/D6
UPPER VOLTA, 102/B3
Upper Woodstock, N. Br. 170/C2
Uppingham, Eng. 13/G5
Uppsala (co.), Sweden 18/K6
Uppsala, Sweden 18/L7
Uppsala, Sweden, 7/F3
Upright (cape), Alaska 196/D2
Upsala, Ont. 175/B3
Upsala, Ont. 177/G5
Upsala, Minn. (56384) 254/D5
Upsalquitch, N. Br. 170/D1
Upsalquitch (riv.), N. Br. 170/D1
Upshur (co.), Texas 302/K5
Upshur (co.), W. Va. 313/F5
Upson (co.), Ga. 216/D5
Upson, Wis. (54565) 317/F3
Upton, Que. 172/E4
Upton, Ky. (42784) 237/K6
Upton▵, Maine (04261) 242/B6
Upton▵, Mass. (01568) 249/H4
Upton, Mo. (65579) 261/H8
Upton (co.), Texas 302/B6
Upton, Wyo. (82730) 319/H1
Upton-on-Severn, Eng. 13/E5
Upton-West Upton, Mass. (01568) 249/H4
Ur (ruins), Iraq 66/E5
Urabá (gulf), Col. 126/B3
Urachiche, Ven. 124/D2
Uracoa, Ven. 124/G3
Uraidla, S. Aust. 94/B8
Urakawa, Japan 81/L2
Ural (mts.), U.S.S.R. 48/F4
Ural (riv.), U.S.S.R. 48/F5
Ural (mts.), U.S.S.R. 52/J2
Ural (riv.), U.S.S.R. 52/J4
Ural (mts.), U.S.S.R., 4/C6
Ural (mts.), U.S.S.R., 7/L2
Ural (mts.), U.S.S.R., 54/J4
Ural (riv.), U.S.S.R., 54/J5
Uralla, N.S.W. 97/F2
Ural'sk, U.S.S.R. 48/F4
Urambo, Tanz. 115/F4
Uran, India 68/B7
Urana, N.S.W. 97/D4
Urana (lake), N.S.W. 97/D4
Urania, La. (71480) 238/F3
Uranium City, 163/F4
Uranium City, Sask. 181/L2
Urapunga, Aust. 88/E2
Urapunga, No. Terr. 93/D3
Uraricuera (riv.), Braz. 132/H8
Uravan, Colo. (81436) 208/B6
Urawa, Japan 81/O2
Urbain‡, Ill. (†62822) 222/D6
Urban, Ky. (40765) 237/O6
Urban, Pa. (†17830) 294/J4
Urban, Wash. (98296) 310/C2
Urbana, Ark. (71768) 203/E7
Urbana, Ill. (61801) 222/E3
Urbana, Ind. (46990) 227/F3
Urbana, Iowa (52345) 229/K4
Urbana, Md. (†21701) 245/J3
Urbana, Mo. (65767) 261/F7
Urbana, Ohio (43078) 284/C5
Urbancrest, Ohio (†43123) 284/D6
Urbandale, Iowa (50322) 229/F5
Urbanette, Ark. (72681) 203/D1
Urbank, Minn. (†56361) 254/C4
Urbanna, Va. (23175) 307/P5
Urbenville, N.S.W. 97/G1
Urbino, Italy 34/D3
Urcos, Peru 128/G9
Urda, Spain 33/E3
Urdinarrain, Arg. 143/G6
Ure (riv.), Eng. 13/F3
Uren, Sask. 181/E5
Urenui, N.Z. 101/E3
Ures, Mex. 150/D2
Urfa, Turkey 59/C2
Urfa (prov.), Turkey 63/H4
Urfa, Turkey 63/H4
Urfa, Turkey, 54/G6
Urgel (plain), Spain 33/G2
Urgench, U.S.S.R. 48/F5
ürgüp, Turkey 63/F3
Uri (canton), Switz. 39/G3
Uriah, Ala. (36480) 194/D8
Uribe, Col. 126/C6
Uribia, Col. 126/D2
Urica, Ven. 124/F3
Urich, Mo. (64788) 261/E6
Urim, Israel 65/B5
Urimán, Ven. 124/G5
Uriondo, Bol. 136/C7
Urique (riv.), Mex. 150/F3
Urirotstock (mt.), Switz. 39/G3
Urituyacu (riv.), Peru 128/D5
Urk, Neth. 27/H3
Urla, Turkey 63/B3
Urlaţa, Rum. 45/H3
Urlingford, Ire. 17/F6
Urmia (lake), Iran, 54/H6
Urmia (Reza'iyeh), Iran 59/D2
Urmia (Reza'iyeh), Iran 66/D2
Urmia (lake), Iran 59/E2
Urmia (lake), Iran 66/D2
Urmiri, Bol. 136/B6
Urnäsch, Switz. 39/H2
Uromi, Nigeria 106/F7
Urrao, Col. 126/B4
Ursa, Ill. (62376) 222/B3
Ursina, Pa. (15485) 294/D6
Ursine, Nev. (†89043) 266/G5
úrsulo Galván, Mex. 150/Q1
Uruáchic, Mex. 150/E3
Uruaçu, Braz. 132/D6
Uruapan del Progreso, Mex. 150/H7
Urubamba (riv.), Peru, 120/C4
Urubamba, Peru 128/F9
Urubamba (riv.), Peru 128/F8
Urubichá, Bol. 136/D4
Urubu (riv.), Braz. 132/A3
Urucará, Braz. 132/B3
Uruçuí, Braz. 132/E4
Urucún (mt.), Braz. 132/B7
Urucurituba, Braz. 132/B3
Uruguai (riv.), Braz. 132/C9
Uruguaiana, Braz., 120/E5
Uruguaiana, Braz. 132/B10
Uruguay, 3/G7
Uruguay, 120/E6
URUGUAY, 145
Uruguay (riv.), 120/E5
Uruguay (riv.), Arg. 143/E3
Uruguay (riv.), Urug. 145/A3
Urumaco, Ven. 124/C2
Urumchi, China, 3/P3
Urumchi, China, 54/M5
Urumchi, China 77/C3
Urunga, N.S.W. 97/G2
Urungu (riv.), China 77/C2
Urup (isl.), U.S.S.R., 54/U5
Uruyén, Ven. 124/G5
Uryupinsk, U.S.S.R. 52/F4
Urzhum, U.S.S.R. 52/G3
Urziceni, Rum. 45/H3
Usa (riv.), U.S.S.R. 52/K1
Usa (riv.), U.S.S.R., 7/K2
Uşak, Turkey 59/A2
Uşak (prov.), Turkey 63/C3
Uşak, Turkey 63/C3
Usakos, S.W. Afr. 118/B4
Usedom (isl.), E. Ger. 22/F1
Ushakov (isl.), U.S.S.R., 4/B5
Ushant (isl.), France, 7/D4
Ushant (Ouessant) (isl.), France 28/A3
Usherville, Sask. 181/J3
Ushibuka, Japan 81/D7
Ushnuiyeh, Iran 66/D2
Ushtaran, Kuh-i- (mt.), Iran 66/F4
Ushuaia, Arg., 120/D8
Ushuaia, Arg. 143/C7
Usibelli‡, Alaska (99787) 196/J2
Usibelli Mines‡, Alaska (†99787) 196/J2
Usk, Br. Col. 184/C3
Usk (riv.), 10/E5
Usk (riv.), Wales 13/D6
Usk, Wash. (99180) 310/H2
üsküdar, Turkey 63/D6
Uslar, W. Ger. 22/C3
Usman', U.S.S.R. 52/E4
U.S. Nav. Air Sta., V.I.(U.S.) 161/A4
U.S. Naval Base, Trinidad Tobago 161/A10
Usona, Alta. 182/D3
Usquepaug, R.I. (†02892) 249/H6
Ussel, France 28/E5
Ussuri (riv.), 54/S5
Ussuri (riv.), U.S.S.R. 48/O5
Ussuri (riv.), China 77/M2
Ussuriysk, U.S.S.R. 48/O5
Ust'-Bol'sheretsk, U.S.S.R., 54/T4
Ust'-Chaun, U.S.S.R. 48/S3
Ust'-Chaun, U.S.S.R., 4/C1
úštěk, Czech. 41/C1
Uster, Switz. 39/G2
Ustica (isl.), Italy 34/D5
Ust'-Ilimsk, U.S.S.R. 48/L4
ústí nad Labem, Czech. 41/C1
ústí nad Orlicí, Czech. 41/D2
Ustka, Poland 47/C1
Ust'-Kamchatsk, U.S.S.R. 48/R4
Ust'-Kamchatsk, U.S.S.R., 54/V4
Ust'-Kamenogorsk, U.S.S.R. 48/J5
Ust'-Kara, U.S.S.R. 48/G3
Ust'-Kara, U.S.S.R. 52/L1
Ust'-Kulom, U.S.S.R. 52/H2
Ust'-Kut, U.S.S.R. 48/L4
Ust'-Maya, U.S.S.R. 48/O3
Ust'-Maya, U.S.S.R., 54/S3
Ust'-Nera, U.S.S.R. 48/P3
Ust'-Ordynskiy, U.S.S.R. 48/L4
Ust'-Ordynskiy Nat'l Okr., U.S.S.R. 48/L4
Ust'-Pinega, U.S.S.R. 52/F2
Ust'-Port, U.S.S.R. 48/J2
Ust'-Shchugor, U.S.S.R. 52/J2
Ust'-Srednikan, U.S.S.R. 48/Q3
Ust'-Tsil'ma, U.S.S.R. 52/H1
Ust'-Tsil'ma, U.S.S.R., 7/J2
Ust'-Urt (plat.), U.S.S.R. 48/F5
Ust'-Usa, U.S.S.R. 52/J1
Ustyuzhna, U.S.S.R. 52/E3
Usuki, Japan 81/F7
Usulután, El Salv. 154/C4
Usumacinta (riv.), Guat. 154/B2
Usumacinta (riv.), Mex. 150/O8
Utah, 188/D3
UTAH, 304
Utah (beach), France 28/C3
Utah (state), U.S., 146/G6
Utah (lake), Utah, 188/D2
Utah (co.), Utah 304/C3
Utah (lake), Utah 304/C3
Utajärvi, Fin. 18/P4
Ute, Iowa (51060) 229/B4
Ute (creek), N. Mex. 274/F3
Ute (peak), N. Mex. 274/D2
Ute (res.), N. Mex. 274/F3
Ute Mountain Ind. Res., Colo. 208/B8
Ute Mountain Ind. Res., N. Mex. 274/A1
Utena, U.S.S.R. 52/C3
Utena, U.S.S.R. 53/C3
Ute Park, N. Mex. (87749) 274/D2
Utete, 102/F5
Utete, Tanz. 115/G5
Uthai Thani, Thai. 72/C4
Uthal, Pak. 59/J4
Uthal, Pak. 68/B3
Utica, Ill. (61373) 222/E2
Utica, Ind. (†47130) 227/F8
Utica, Kans. (67584) 232/B3
Utica, Ky. (42376) 237/G5
Utica, Mich. (48087) 250/F6
Utica, Minn. (55979) 254/G7
Utica, Miss. (39175) 256/C6
Utica, Mo. (64686) 261/E3
Utica, Mont. (59452) 262/F4
Utica, N.Y., 188/M2
Utica, N.Y. (*13501) 276/K4
Utica, Nebr. (68456) 264/G4
Utica, Ohio (43080) 284/F5
Utica, Okla. (74763) 288/O7
Utica, Pa. (16362) 294/C3
Utica, S.C. (†29678) 296/B2
Utica, S. Dak. (57067) 298/P8
Utica, Wis. (†53589) 317/H10
Utica Junior College, Miss. (39175) 256/C6
Utiel, Spain 33/F3
Utikuma (lake), Alta. 182/C2
Utikuma (riv.), Alta. 182/C1
Utikumasis (lake), Alta. 182/C2
Utila, Hond. 154/D2
Utila (isl.), Hond. 154/D2
Utleyville, Colo. (81086) 208/O8
Utopia, Alaska (†99745) 196/H1
Utopia (lake), N. Br. 170/D3
Utopia, No. Terr. 93/D7
Utopia, Texas (78884) 302/E8
Utrecht, Neth., 7/E3
Utrecht (prov.), Neth. 27/G4
Utrecht, Neth. 27/G4
Utrera, Spain 33/D4
Utsjoki, Fin. 18/P2
Utsunomiya, Japan 81/K5
Uttaradit, Thai. 72/D3
Uttarpara, India 68/F1
Uttar Pradesh (state), India 68/D3
Utterson, Ont. 177/E2
Uttoxeter, Eng. 13/F5
Uttoxeter, 10/F4
Utuado, P. Rico 156/F1
Utuado, P. Rico 161/B2
Utukok (riv.), Alaska 196/F1
Uturoa, Fr. Poly., 87/L7
Utzenstorf, Switz. 39/E2
Uusikaarlepyy (Nykarleby), Fin. 18/N5
Uusikaupunki, Fin. 18/M6
Uusimaa (prov.), Fin. 18/O6
Uva (riv.), Col. 126/E5
Uva (lag.), Col. 126/E6
Uvalda, Ga. (30473) 216/H6
Uvalde (co.), Texas 302/E8
Uvalde, Texas (78801) 302/E8
Uvat, U.S.S.R. 48/G4
Uvéa (isl.), New Cal., 87/G7
Uvera, 102/E5
Uverito, Ven. 124/F3
Uvero Quemado, Cuba 158/A2
Uvinza, Tanz. 115/F5
Uvira, Dem. Rep. of the Congo. 115/E4
Uwajima, Japan 81/F7
Uwchland, Pa. (19480) 294/L5
'Uweinat, Jebel (mt.), 102/E2
'Uweinat, Jebel (mt.), Libya 111/E3
'Uweinat, Jebel (mt.), Sudan 111/E3
'Uweinat, Jebel (mt.), U.A.R. 111/E3
Uxbridge, Ont. 177/E3
Uxbridge▵, Mass. (01569) 249/H4
Uxbridge, Mass. (01569) 249/H4
Uxmal (ruins), Mex. 150/P6
Uyak, Alaska (†99624) 196/H3
Uyuni, Bol., 120/D5
Uyuni, Bol. 136/B7
Uyuni (salt dep.), Bol. 136/B7
Uzbek S.S.R., U.S.S.R. 48/G5
Uzbek S.S.R., U.S.S.R., 54/J5
Uzès, France 28/F5
Uzhgorod, U.S.S.R. 52/B5
Uzlovaya, U.S.S.R. 52/E4
Uznach, Switz. 39/H2
Uznam (Usedom) (isl.), Poland 47/B1
üzümlü, Turkey 63/D4
Uzunköprü, Turkey 63/B2
Uzwil, Switz. 39/H2
Uzza, Israel 65/B4

V

Vaal (riv.), 102/E7
Vaal (riv.), S. Africa 118/D5
Vaala, Fin. 18/P4
Vaals, Neth. 27/H7
Vaalserberg (mt.), Belg. 27/J7
Vaalserberg (mt.), Neth. 27/J7
Vaasa (prov.), Fin. 18/N5
Vaasa, Fin. 18/M5
Vaasa, Fin., 7/G2
Vác, Hung. 41/E3
Vaca (key), Fla. 212/E7
Vacaville, Calif. (95688) 204/D5
Vaccarès (lag.), France 28/F6
Vache (isl.), Haiti 156/D3
Vache (isl.), Haiti 158/B6
Vacherie, La. (70090) 238/L3
Vacía Talega (pt.), P. Rico 161/E1
Vada, Ky. (41383) 237/O5
Vaden, Ark. (†71923) 203/E6
Vader, Wash. (98593) 310/B4
Vadis, W. Va. (26445) 313/E4
Vadito, N. Mex. (87579) 274/D2
Vadnais Heights, Minn. (†55101) 254/G5
Vado, N. Mex. (88072) 274/C6
Vadret (mt.), Switz. 39/J3
Vadsø, Norway 18/Q1
Vadsø, Norway, 7/H1
Vadstena, Sweden 18/J7
Vaduz (cap.), Liecht. 39/H2
Vaerøy (isl.), Norway 18/H3
Vagå (lake), Norway 18/F6
Vaga (riv.), U.S.S.R. 52/F2
Vaggeryd, Sweden 18/J8
Vagos, Port. 33/B2
Vagthus (pt.), V.I.(U.S.) 161/F4
Váh (riv.), Czech. 41/D2
Vahitahi (atoll), Fr. Poly., 87/N7
Vaiden, Miss. (39176) 256/E4
Vail, Ariz. (85641) 198/E6
Vail, Colo. (81657) 208/G3
Vail, Iowa (51465) 229/C4
Vail Homes, N.J. (†07724) 273/E3
Vails, N.J. (†07832) 273/D2
Vaitupu (atoll), Gilb. and Ell., 87/H6
Vajinanu (mt.), Iran 66/J2
Vakfikebir, Turkey 63/H2
Vakh (riv.), U.S.S.R. 48/J3
Vál, Hung. 41/E3
Vålådalen, Sweden 18/H5
Valais (canton), Switz. 39/E4
Val-Alain, Que. 172/F3
Valašské Klobouky, Czech. 41/D2
Valašské Meziříčí, Czech. 41/D2
Valatie, N.Y. (12184) 276/N6
Val-Barrette, Que. 172/B3
Valbrand, Sask. 181/E2
Val-Brillant, Que. 172/B1
Valcartier Village, Que. 172/F3
Valcheta, Arg. 143/C5
Val-Comeau, N. Br. 170/F1
Valcour (isl.), N.Y. 276/N1
Valcourt, Que. 172/E4
Valdagno, Italy 34/C2
Val d'Amour, N. Br. 170/D1
Val-David, Que. 172/C3
Valday, U.S.S.R. 52/D3
Valday (hills), U.S.S.R. 52/D3
Val-de-Marne (dept.), France 28/C1
Valdemarsvik, Sweden 18/K7
Valdemoro, Spain 33/F4
Valdepeñas, Spain 33/E3
Valderas, Spain 33/D1
Valderrobres, Spain 33/F2
Valders, Wis. (54245) 317/L7
Valdés (pen.), Arg., 120/D7
Valdés (pen.), Arg. 143/D5
Valdes (isl.), Br. Col. 184/K3
Val-des-Bois, Que. 172/B4
Valdese, N.C. (28690) 281/F3
Val-d'Espoir, Que. 172/D1
Valdeverdeja, Spain 33/D3
Valdez, Alaska (99686) 196/D1
Valdez, Colo. (†81082) 208/K8
Valdez, Ec. 128/C2
Valdez, N. Mex. (87580) 274/D2
Valdivia, Chile, 3/F7
Valdivia, Chile, 120/C6
Valdivia (prov.), Chile 138/D3
Valdivia, Chile 138/D3
Valdivia, Col. 126/C4
Val-d'Oise (dept.), France 28/E3
Val-d'Or, 163/J6
Val-d'Or, Que. 174/B3
Valdosta, Ga., 188/K4
Valdosta, Ga. (31601) 216/F9
Val Doucet, N. Br. 170/E1
Vale, N.C. (28168) 281/G3
Vale, Oreg. (97918) 291/K4
Vale, S. Dak. (57788) 298/C4
Vale, Tenn. (38386) 237/E8
Valeda, Kans. (†67337) 232/G4
Valeene, Ind. (†47125) 227/E8
Valemount, Br. Col. 184/H4
Valença, Braz. 132/G6
Valença, Port. 33/B2
Valença do Piauí, Braz. 132/F4
Valence, France 28/F5
Valencia, Calif. (91355) 204/G9
Valencia, Trinidad Tobago 161/B10
Valencia (Valentia) (isl.), Ire. 17/A8
Valencia (Valentia) (isl.), 10/A5
Valencia (co.), N. Mex. 274/A4
Valencia, N. Mex. (†87031) 274/C4
Valencia, Phil. 82/C7
Valencia, Pa. (16059) 294/C4
Valencia (reg.), Spain 33/F3
Valencia (prov.), Spain 33/F3
Valencia, Spain, 7/D5
Valencia, Spain 33/F3
Valencia (gulf), Spain 33/G3
Valencia (lag.), Spain 33/G3
Valencia, Ven., 120/D2
Valencia, Ven. 124/E2
Valencia (lake), Ven. 124/E2
Valencia de Alcántara, Spain 33/C3
Valencia de Don Juan, Spain 33/D1
Valenciennes, France 28/E2
Valendas, Switz. 39/H3
Valentia (isl.), Ire. 17/A8
Valentia (isl.), 10/A5
Valentine, Ariz. (86437) 198/B3
Valentine, Ind. (†46761) 227/G1
Valentine, Nebr. (69201) 264/D2
Valentine, Texas (79854) 302/C11
Valentines, Urug. 145/E4
Valentines, Va. (23887) 307/N7
Valenza, Italy 34/B2
Valenzuela, Par. 144/B6
Valeport, Sask. 181/G5
Valera, Texas (76884) 302/E6
Valera, Ven., 120/C2
Valera, Ven. 124/C3
Valeria, Iowa (50260) 229/G5
Vale Summit, Md. (†21532) 245/C2
Valga, U.S.S.R. 52/C3
Valga, U.S.S.R. 53/D2
Valhalla, Alta. 182/A2
Valhalla, N.Y. (10595) 276/P6
Valhalla Centre, Alta. 182/A2
Valhermoso Springs, Ala. (35775) 194/E2
Valiente (pen.), Pan. 154/G6
Valier, Ill. (62891) 222/D5
Valier, Mont. (59486) 262/D2
Valier, Pa. (15780) 294/D4
Valinda‡, Calif. (91744) 204/D10
Val-Jalbert, Que. 172/E1
Valjean, Sask. 181/E5
Valjevo, Yugo. 45/D3
Valka, U.S.S.R. 53/C2
Valkeakoski, Fin. 18/N6
Valkenswaard, Neth. 27/H6
Valladolid, Mex., 146/K7
Valladolid, Mex. 150/P6
Valladolid, Spain, 7/E4
Valladolid (prov.), Spain 33/D2
Valladolid, Spain 33/D2
Vallay (isl.), Scot. 15/A4
Vall de Uxó, Spain 33/F3
Valle, Norway 18/E7
Valle Alegre, Chile 138/F2
Vallecas, Spain 33/G4
Vallecito (res.), Colo. 208/D8
Vallecitos, N. Mex. (87581) 274/C2
Valle d'Aosta (reg.), Italy 34/A2
Valle d'Aosta (prov.), Italy 34/A2
Valle de Bravo, Mex. 150/J7
Valle de Guanape, Ven. 124/F3
Valle de la Pascua, Ven. 124/F3
Valle del Cauca (dept.), Col. 126/B6
Valle de Santiago, Mex. 150/J6
Valledupar, Col. 126/D2
Vallée-Jonction, Que. 172/G3
Valle Fértil, Arg. 143/C3
Vallegrande, Bol. 136/C6
Valle Hermoso, Mex. 150/L4
Vallehermoso, Spain 33/A5
Vallejo, Calif., 188/B3
Vallejo, Calif. (94590) 204/J1
Vallenar, Chile, 120/C5
Vallenar, Chile 138/A7
Valles Mines, Mo. (63087) 261/L6
Valletta (cap.), Malta, 7/F5
Valletta (cap.), Malta 34/E7
Valley (co.), Idaho 220/C5
Valley (riv.), Man. 179/B4
Valley (co.), Mont. 262/K2
Valley, N.S. 169/E3
Valley (co.), Nebr. 264/E3
Valley, Nebr. (68064) 264/H3
Valley, Wash. (99181) 310/H2
Valley, Wis. (†54639) 317/F8
Valley, Wyo. (82414) 319/C1
Valley Bend, W. Va. (26293) 313/F5
Valley Brook, Okla. (†73101) 288/M4

452 Valley Center

Valley Center, Kans. (67147) 232/E4
Valley Centre, Sask. 181/D4
Valley City, Ill. (†62340) 222/C4
Valley City, N. Dak. (58072) 283/P6
Valley City, Ohio (44280) 284/G3
Valley Cottage‡, N.Y. (10989) 276/M8
Valley Falls, Kans. (66088) 232/G2
Valley Falls, N.Y. (12185) 276/N5
Valley Falls, Oreg. (†97630) 291/G5
Valley Falls, R.I. (†02864) 249/J5
Valley Farms, Ariz. (85291) 198/D6
Valleyfield, Que. 172/C4
Valleyford, Wash. (99036) 310/H3
Valley Forge, Pa. (19481) 294/L5
Valley Grove, W. Va. (26060) 313/E2
Valley Head, Ala. (35989) 194/G1
Valley Head, W. Va. (26294) 313/G5
Valley Hi, Ohio (†43360) 284/C5
Valley Lee, Md. (20692) 245/M8
Valley Mills, Texas (76689) 302/G6
Valley Park, Miss. (39177) 256/C5
Valley Park, Mo. (63088) 261/O3
Valley Point, W. Va. (†26519) 313/G3
Valley River, Man. 179/B3
Valley Spring, Texas (76885) 302/F7
Valley Springs, Ark. (72682) 203/D1
Valley Springs, Calif. (95252) 204/C9
Valley Springs, S. Dak. (57068) 298/S6
Valley Station, Ky. (40272) 237/K4
Valley Stream, N.Y. (*11580) 276/N9
Valleyview, Alta. 182/B2
Valley View‡, Ill. (†60120) 222/E2
Valley View, Ky. (†40475) 237/N5
Valley View, Ohio (†43201) 284/D6
Valley View, Ohio (†44101) 284/H9
Valley View, Pa. (17983) 294/J4
Valley View, Texas (76272) 302/H4
Vallgrund (isl.), Fin. 18/M5
Valliant, Okla. (74764) 288/R6
Vallière, Haiti 158/C5
Vallimanca (riv.), Arg. 143/F7
Vallonia, Ind. (47281) 227/E7
Vallon-Pont-d'Arc, France 28/F5
Vallorbe, Switz. 39/B3
Valls, Spain 33/G2
Val Marie, Sask. 181/D6
Valmeyer, Ill. (62295) 222/C5
Valmiera, U.S.S.R. 52/C3
Valmiera, U.S.S.R. 53/C2
Valmont, Que. 172/E3
Valmont, Que. 172/H2
Valmontone, Italy 34/F7
Valmora, N. Mex. (87750) 274/D3
Val-Morin, Que. 172/C3
Valmy, Nev. (89438) 266/D2
Valmy, Wis. (†54235) 317/M6
Valognes, France 28/C3
Valona, Ga. (31332) 216/K8
Valpaços, Port. 33/C2
Valparaiso, Braz. 132/D8
Valparaíso (prov.), Chile 138/A9
Valparaíso, Chile, 3/F7
Valparaíso, Chile, 120/C6
Valparaíso, Chile 138/E2
Valparaiso, Fla. (32580) 212/C6
Valparaiso, Ind. (46383) 227/C2
Valparaiso, Nebr. (68065) 264/H3
Valparaiso, Sask. 181/G3
Val-Racine, Que. 172/G4
Vals (cape), Indon. 85/K7
Vals, Switz. 39/H3
Val-Saint-Michel, Que. 172/H3
Valsequillo (res.), Mex. 150/N2
Valserrhein (riv.), Switz. 39/H3
Valsetz, Oreg. (97393) 291/D3
Value, Miss. (39178) 256/D6
Valuyki, U.S.S.R. 52/E4
Valverda, La. (†70757) 238/G5
Valverde (prov.), Dom. Rep. 158/D5
Valverde, Dom. Rep. 158/D5
Val Verde (co.), Texas 302/C8
Valverde del Camino, Spain 33/C4
Vamdrup, Den. 21/C7
Vammala, Fin. 18/N6
Vámos, Greece 45/F8
Van, Ky. (41857) 237/R6
Van (lake), N. Dak. 283/L5
Van, Oreg. (†97904) 291/J4
Van, Pa. (16363) 294/C3
Van, Texas (75790) 302/J5
Van (prov.), Turkey 63/K3
Van, Turkey 59/D2
Van, Turkey 63/K3
Van (lake), Turkey, 54/H6
Van (lake), Turkey 59/D2
Van (lake), Turkey 63/K3
Van, W. Va. (25206) 313/C7
Vanadium, N. Mex. (88073) 274/A6
Van Alstyne, Texas (75095) 302/H4
Vananda, Br. Col. 184/E5
Vananda, Mont. (†59237) 262/K4
Vanatta, Ohio (†43055) 284/E5
Vanavara, U.S.S.R. 48/L3
Van Blommestein (lake), Sur. 131/D3
Van-Bruyssel, Que. 172/E2
Van Buren (co.), Ark. 203/E2
Van Buren, Ark. (72956) 203/B3
Van Buren, Ind. (46991) 227/F3
Van Buren (co.), Iowa 229/K7
Vanburen, Ky. (†40046) 237/L5
Van Buren▵, Maine (04785) 242/G1
Van Buren, Maine (04785) 242/G1
Van Buren (co.), Mich. 250/C6
Van Buren, Mo. (63965) 261/L8
Van Buren, Ohio (45889) 284/C3
Van Buren (co.), Tenn. 237/L9
Vance, Ala. (35490) 194/D4
Vance, Miss. (38964) 256/D2
Vance (co.), N.C. 281/N2
Vance, S.C. (29163) 296/G5
Vance, Sask. 181/C3
Vance A.F.B., Okla. 288/K2
Vanceboro▵, Maine (04491) 242/J4
Vanceboro, N.C. (28586) 281/P4
Vanceburg, Ky. (41179) 237/P3
Vancleave, Miss. (†39564) 256/G9
Van Cleve, Iowa (†50162) 229/G5
Vancourt, Texas (76955) 302/D6
Vancouver, 163/D6
Vancouver (isl.), 163/D6
Vancouver (mt.), Alaska 196/L2
Vancouver, Br. Col., 146/F5
Vancouver (isl.), Br. Col., 146/F5
Vancouver, Br. Col. 184/K3
Vancouver (isl.), Br. Col. 184/D5
Vancouver, Canada, 3/C3
Vancouver (isl.), Canada, 3/C3
Vancouver, Wash., 188/B1
Vancouver, Wash. (*98660) 310/C5
Vancouver (lake), Wash. 310/C5
Vandalia, Ill. (62471) 222/D5
Vandalia, Mich. (49095) 250/D7
Vandalia, Mo. (63382) 261/J4
Vandalia, Mont. (59273) 262/J2
Vandalia, Ohio (45377) 284/B6
Vandalia, W. Va. (†26423) 313/F5
Vandemere, N.C. (28587) 281/R4
Vandenberg A.F.B., Calif. 204/E9
Vanderbilt, Mich. (49795) 250/E3
Vanderbilt, Pa. (15486) 294/C5
Vanderbilt, Texas (77991) 302/H9
Vanderburgh (co.), Ind. 227/B8
Vandergrift, Pa. (15690) 294/D4
Vanderhoof, 163/D5
Vanderhoof, Br. Col. 184/E3
Vanderlin (isl.), Aust. 88/F3
Vanderlin (isl.), No. Terr. 93/E3
Vanderpool, Texas (78885) 302/E8
Vanderpool, Va. (24481) 307/J4
Vandervoort, Ark. (71972) 203/B5
Van Diemen (cape), Aust. 88/D2
Van Diemen (gulf), Aust. 88/E2
Van Diemen (cape), No. Terr. 93/A1
Van Diemen (gulf), No. Terr. 93/B1
Vandiola, Bol. 136/C5
Vandiver, Ala. (35176) 194/F4
Vandiver‡, Mo. (†65265) 261/J4
Vandling, Pa. (18421) 294/M2
Vändra, U.S.S.R. 53/C1
Vandura, Sask. 181/K5
Vanduser, Mo. (63784) 261/N9
Vanegas, Mex. 150/J5
Vänern (lake), Sweden 18/H7
Vänern (lake), Sweden, 7/F3
Vänersborg, Sweden 18/G7
Van Etten, N.Y. (14889) 276/G6
Van Ewijcksluis, Neth. 27/F3
Vanga, Dem. Rep. of the Congo, 115/C4
Vanga, Kenya 115/G4
Vangaindrano, Malag. Rep. 118/H4
Van Gia, S. Vietnam 72/F4
Vanguard, Sask. 181/D6
Vang Vieng, Laos 72/D3
Van Hoa, N. Vietnam 72/E2
Van Horn, Texas (79855) 302/C11
Van Horne, Iowa (52346) 229/J4
Van Hornesville, N.Y. (13475) 276/L5
Vanier, Ont. 177/J2
Vanikoro (isl.), Br. Sol. Is., 87/G7
Vanil Noir (mt.), Switz. 39/D3
Vanimo, Terr. N.G. 85/B6
Vanino, U.S.S.R. 48/P5
Vaniyambadi, India 68/D6
Vankarem, U.S.S.R., 4/C1
Van Keurens‡, N.Y. (†12601) 276/N7
Vankleek Hill, Ont. 177/K2
Van Lear, Ky. (41265) 237/R5
Vanleer, Tenn. (37181) 237/G8
Vanlue, Ohio (45890) 284/C4
Van Meter, Iowa (50261) 229/E5
Vanna, Ga. (30672) 216/F2
Vännäs, Sweden 18/L5
Vanndale, Ark. (72387) 203/J3
Vannes, France 28/B4
Vannøy (isl.), Norway 18/L1
Van Nuys, Calif. (*91401) 204/B10
Van Orin, Ill. (61374) 222/D2
Vanoss, Okla. (74876) 288/N5
Vanrhynsdorp, S. Africa 118/B6
Vanrook, Queens. 95/B3
Vansant, Va. (24656) 307/D6
Vansbro, Sweden 18/H6
Vanscoy, Sask. 181/D4
Vansittart (isl.), N.W.T. 187/K3
Vantage, Sask. 181/F6
Vantage, Wash. (98950) 310/E4
Van Tassell, Wyo. (82242) 319/H3
Vanua Levu (isl.), Fiji, 87/H7
Van Vleck‡, Texas (77482) 302/J9
Van Vleet, Miss. (†38851) 256/G3
Vanvoorhis, W. Va. (†26505) 313/G3
Van Wert, Iowa (50262) 229/F7
Van Wert (co.), Ohio 284/A4
Van Wert, Ohio (45891) 284/A4
Van Wyck, S.C. (29744) 296/F2
Van Yen, N. Vietnam 72/E2
Vanylven, Norway 18/E5
Van Zandt (co.), Texas 302/J5
Van Zandt, Wash. (98244) 310/C2
Vanzant, Mo. (65768) 261/H9
Var (dept.), France 28/G6
Vara, Sweden 18/H7
Vara de María, Ven. 124/C4
Varadero, Cuba 158/D1
Varaklāni, U.S.S.R. 53/D2
Varallo, Italy 34/B2
Varanasi, India, 54/M7
Varanasi, India 68/E3
Varangerfjord (fjord), Norway 18/Q2
Varanger Halvøy (pen.), Norway 18/Q1
Varano (lake), Italy 34/F3
Varaždin, Yugo. 45/B2
Varazze, Italy 34/B2
Varberg, Sweden 18/G8
Vardaman, Miss. (38878) 256/F3
Vardar (riv.), Greece 45/E5
Vardar (riv.), Yugo. 45/E5
Varde, Den. 18/F9
Varde, Den. 21/B6
Varde (riv.), Den. 21/B6
Vardø, Norway 18/R1
Varel, W. Ger. 22/C2
Varella (cape), S. Vietnam 72/F4
Varėna, U.S.S.R. 53/C3
Varennes, Que. 172/J4
Vareš, Yugo. 45/D3
Varese (prov.), Italy 34/B2
Varese, Italy 34/B2
Varginha, Braz. 132/E8
Varginha, Braz. 135/D2
Varina, Iowa (50593) 229/D3
Varkaus, Fin. 18/Q5
Värmland (co.), Sweden 18/H7
Varna, Bulg., 7/G4
Varna, Bulg. 45/J4
Varna, Ill. (61375) 222/D2
Varnado, La. (70467) 238/L5
Värnamo, Sweden 18/J8
Varnek, U.S.S.R. 52/J1
Varnell, Ga. (30756) 216/C1
Varner, Kans. (67148) 232/D4
Varney, Ont. 177/D3
Varney, W. Va. (25696) 313/B7
Varnsdorf, Czech. 41/C1
Varnville, S.C. (29944) 296/E6
Várpalota, Hung. 41/E3
Vars, Ont. 177/J2
Vartholomión, Greece 45/E7
Varto, Turkey 63/J3
Varysburg, N.Y. (14167) 276/D5
Vas (co.), Hung. 41/D3
Vasa (Vaasa), Fin. 18/M5
Vasa, Minn. (†55089) 254/F6
Vasa Barris (riv.), Braz. 132/G5
Vascongadas (reg.), Spain 33/E1
Vashi, India 68/B7
Vashon, Wash. (98070) 310/A2
Vasile Roaită, Rum. 45/J3
Vasil'kov, U.S.S.R. 52/D4
Vaslui, Rum. 45/H2
Vass, N.C. (28394) 281/L4
Vassalboro▵, Maine (04989) 242/D7
Vassalboro, Maine (04989) 242/D7
Vassar, Kans. (66543) 232/G3
Vassar, Man. 179/G5
Vassar, Mich. (48768) 250/F5
Vastenjaure (lake), Sweden 18/K3
Västerås, Sweden 18/J7
Västerås, Sweden, 7/F3
Västerbotten (co.), Sweden 18/K4
Västerdalälven (riv.), Sweden 18/H6
Västerhaninge, Sweden 18/H1
Västernorrland (co.), Sweden 18/K5
Västervik, Sweden 18/K8
Västmanland (co.), Sweden 18/K7
Vasto, Italy 34/E3
Vasvár, Hung. 41/D3
Vaternish (dist.), Scot. 15/C4
Vaternish (pt.), Scot. 15/C4
Vatersay (isl.), Scot. 15/A6
Vathí, Greece 45/H7
Vatican City, 7/F4
VATICAN CITY, 34/B6, D4
Vaticano (cape), Italy 34/E5
Vatna (glac.), Ice. 21/C1
Vatomandry, Malag. Rep. 118/H3
Vatra Dornei, Rum. 45/G2
Vättern (lake), Sweden 18/J7
Vättern (lake), Sweden, 7/F3
Vauclin, Mart. 161/D6
Vauclin (mt.), Mart. 161/D6
Vaucluse (dept.), France 28/F6
Vaucluse, S.C. (29850) 296/D7
Vaud (canton), Switz. 39/C3
Vauderens, Switz. 39/C3
Vaudreuil (co.), Que. 172/C4
Vaudreuil, Que. 172/C4
Vaughan, Miss. (39179) 256/D5
Vaughan, N.C. (27586) 281/N2
Vaughan, W. Va. (†26656) 313/D6
Vaughn, Mont. (59487) 262/E3
Vaughn, N. Mex. (88353) 274/D4
Vaughn, Wash. (98394) 310/C3
Vaughnsville, Ohio (45893) 284/B4
Vaulruz, Switz. 39/C3
Vaupés (riv.), Col., 120/C2
Vaupés (riv.), Col. 126/E7
Vaupés (comm.), Col. 126/E7
Vauxhall, Alta. 182/D4
Vauxhall, N.J. (07088) 273/A2
Vava'u Group (isls.), Tonga, 87/J7
Vavenby, Br. Col. 184/H4
Vavuniya, Ceylon 68/E7
Vawn, Sask. 181/C2
Vaxholm, Sweden 18/J1
Växjö, Sweden 18/J8
Vaygach (isl.), U.S.S.R. 52/K1
Vaygach (isl.), U.S.S.R., 4/C6
Vayland, S. Dak. (57377) 298/M5
Važec, Czech. 41/E2
Vazhgort, U.S.S.R. 52/G2
Vaz-Obervaz, Switz. 39/J3
Veagh (lake), Ire. 17/F1
Vealmoor, Texas (79720) 302/C5
Veazie▵, Maine (04401) 242/F6
Veazie, Maine (04401) 242/F6
Veblen, S. Dak. (57270) 298/P2
Vechigen, Switz. 39/E3
Vecht (riv.), Neth. 27/J4
Vechta, W. Ger. 22/C2
Vechte (riv.), Neth. 27/J3
Vechte (riv.), W. Ger. 22/B2
Vecsés, Hung. 41/E3
Vedder Crossing, Br. Col. 184/M3
Vedia, Arg. 143/F7
Veedersburg, Ind. (47987) 227/C4
Veendam, Neth. 27/K2
Veenendaal, Neth. 27/G4
Veenhuizen, Neth. 27/J2
Veere, Neth. 27/D5
Veeregat (chan.), Neth. 27/D5
Vega (pt.), Alaska 196/J4
Vega, Alta. 182/C2
Vega (fjord), Norway 18/G4
Vega (isl.), Norway 18/G4
Vega, Texas (79092) 302/B2
Vega Alta, P. Rico 161/D1
Vega Baja, P. Rico 161/D1
Vegas Creek‡, Nev. (†89101) 266/F6
Veghel, Neth. 27/H5
Vègreville, 163/E5
Vègreville, Alta. 182/E3
Veguita, N. Mex. (87062) 274/C4
Veguitas, Cuba 158/H4
Vehar (lake), India 68/B7
Veillardville, Sask. 181/J3
25 de Agosto, Urug. 145/A6
Veinticinco de Mayo, Arg. 143/F7
25 de Mayo, Urug. 145/C5
27 de Noviembre (Fortín Gabino Mendoza), Par. 144/B3
Vejen, Den. 21/C7
Vejer de la Frontera, Spain 33/C4
Vejle, Den. 18/F9
Vejle (co.), Den. 21/C6
Vejle, Den. 21/C6
Vejle (fiord), Den. 21/C6
Vejprty, Czech. 41/B1
Vela, La (cape), Col. 126/D1
Vela, Roca que (cay), Col. 126/B8
Vélan (mt.), Switz. 39/D5
Velarde, N. Mex. (87582) 274/C2
Velas (cape), C. Rica 154/D5
Velasco, Cuba 158/H3
Velázquez, Urug. 145/E5
Velda‡, Mo. (†63101) 261/P3
Velda Village Hills‡, Mo. (†63101) 261/P3
Velden, Austria 41/C3
Veldrif, S. Africa 118/B6
Vélez, Col. 126/D4
Vélez Blanco, Spain 33/E4
Vélez-Málaga, Spain 33/E4
Vélez Rubio, Spain 33/E4
Velhas (riv.), Braz. 132/E7
Velikaya (riv.), U.S.S.R. 52/C3
Veliki Bečkerek (Zrenjanin), Yugo. 45/E3
Velikiye Luki, U.S.S.R., 7/H3
Velikiye Luki, U.S.S.R. 48/D4
Velikiye Luki, U.S.S.R. 52/D3
Velikiy Ustyug, U.S.S.R. 48/E3
Velikiy Ustyug, U.S.S.R. 52/F2
Velikiy Ustyug, U.S.S.R., 7/J2
Veliko Tŭrnovo, Bulg. 45/G4
Velikovisochnoye, U.S.S.R. 52/H1
Velizh, U.S.S.R. 52/D3
Velká Bíteš, Czech. 41/D2
Velká Bystřice, Czech. 41/D2
Veľké Kapušany, Czech. 41/G2
Velké Meziříčí, Czech. 41/D2
Veľké Rovné, Czech. 41/E2
Velletri, Italy 34/F7
Velling, Den. 21/B5
Vellore, India 68/D6
Velluda, Sierra (mt.), Chile 138/E1
Velma, Okla. (73091) 288/L6
Velp, Neth. 27/J5
Velpen, Ind. (47590) 227/C8
Velsen, Neth. 27/F4
Vel'sk, U.S.S.R. 48/E3
Vel'sk, U.S.S.R. 52/F2
Velten, E. Ger. 22/E2
Veluwe (reg.), Neth. 27/H4
Velva, N. Dak. (58790) 283/J3
Velvendós, Greece 45/F5
Vemb, Den. 21/B5
Venadillo, Col. 126/C5
Venado, Mex. 150/J5
Venado Tuerto, Arg. 143/D3
Venafro, Italy 34/E4
Venamo (mt.), Guyana 131/A3
Venamo (riv.), Ven. 124/H4
Venamo, Cerro (mt.), Ven. 124/H4
Venango, Nebr. (69168) 264/C4
Venango (co.), Pa. 294/C3
Venango, Pa. (16440) 294/B2
Vena Park, Queens. 95/B3
Vence, France 28/G6
Vendas Novas, Port. 33/B3
Vendée (dept.), France 28/C4
Vendôme, France 28/D4
Vendrell, Spain 33/G2
Venedocia, Ohio (45894) 284/B4
Venedy, Ill. (62296) 222/D5
Veneta, Oreg. (97487) 291/D3
Venetia (reg.), Italy 34/C2
Venetian Village‡, Ill. (†60046) 222/E1
Venetie, Alaska (99781) 196/J1
Venezia (Venice), Italy, 7/F4
Venezia (Venice), Italy 34/D2
Venezuela, 3/F5
Venezuela, 120/D2
VENEZUELA, 124
VENEZUELA, 156
Venezuela (gulf), Ven., 120/C1
Venezuela (gulf), Ven. 124/C2
Vengurla, India 68/C5
Veniaminof (crater), Alaska 196/F3
Venice, Alta. 182/E2
Venice, Calif. (90291) 204/B11
Venice, Fla. (33595) 212/D4
Venice, Ill. (62090) 222/A6
Venice, Italy, 7/F4
Venice (prov.), Italy 34/D2
Venice, Italy 34/D2
Venice (gulf), Italy 34/D2
Venice, La. (70091) 238/M8
Venice, Ohio (44870) 284/B9
Venice, Utah (84777) 304/C5
Vénissieux, France 28/F5
Venkatagiri, India 68/D6
Venlaw, Man. 179/B3
Venlo, Neth. 27/J6
Venn, Sask. 181/F4
Venosa, Italy 34/E4
Venosta, Que. 172/A4
Venraij, Neth. 27/H6
Venta (riv.), U.S.S.R. 53/B2
Ventimiglia, Italy 34/A3
Ventnor, Eng. 13/F7
Ventnor, 10/F5
Ventnor City, N.J. (08406) 273/E5
Ventotene (isl.), Italy 34/D4
Ventry, Ire. 17/A7
Ventspils, U.S.S.R. 48/B4
Ventspils, U.S.S.R. 52/B3
Ventspils, U.S.S.R. 53/A2
Ventspils, U.S.S.R., 7/G3
Ventuari (riv.), Ven. 124/E5
Ventura (co.), Calif. 204/F9
Ventura, Calif. (*93001) 204/F9
Ventura, Iowa (50482) 229/F2
Venturia, N. Dak. (58489) 283/L7
Venus, Fla. (33960) 212/E4
Venus, Pa. (16364) 294/C3
Venus‡, Texas (76084) 302/G5
Venus (bay), Vic. 97/C6
Venustiano Carranza, Mex. 150/N8
Venustiano Carranza (res.), Mex. 150/J3
Vera, Ill. (†62080) 222/D4
Vera, Okla. (74082) 288/P2
Verá (lag.), Par. 144/B7
Vera, Sask. 181/B3
Vera, Spain 33/F4
Vera, Texas (76383) 302/E4
Vera, Va. (†24522) 307/L6
Vera Cruz, Braz. 135/B3
Vera Cruz, Ind. (†46714) 227/G3
Veracruz (state), Mex. 150/L7
Veracruz Llave, Mex., 3/E5
Veracruz Llave, Mex., 146/J8
Veracruz Llave, Mex. 150/Q1
Veradale, Wash. (99037) 310/H3
Veragua Abajo, Dom. Rep. 158/E5
Veramin, Iran 66/G3
Veras, Urug. 145/C2
Veraval, India 68/C4
Verbania, Italy 34/B2
Verbena, Ala. (36091) 194/E5
Verboort, Oreg. (†97116) 291/A2
Vercelli (prov.), Italy 34/B2
Vercelli, Italy 34/B2
Verchères (co.), Que. 172/J4
Verchères, Que. 172/J4
Verçinin Tepesi (mt.), Turkey 63/J2
Verda, Ky. (40872) 237/P7
Verda, La. (71481) 238/E3
Verde (riv.), Ariz., 188/D4
Verde (riv.), Ariz. 198/D5
Verde (riv.), Braz. 132/C7
Verde (cay), Bah. Is. 156/C2
Verde (cape), 102/A3
Verde (riv.), Mex. 150/F3
Verde (riv.), Mex. 150/L8
Verde (riv.), Par. 144/C4
Verde (cape), Sen. 106/A6
Verde Island (passg.), Phil. 82/C4
Verdel, Nebr. (68762) 264/F2
Verden, Okla. (73092) 288/K4
Verden, W. Ger. 22/C2
Verdery, S.C. (†29819) 296/C3
Verdi, Minn. (56179) 254/B6
Verdi, Nev. (89439) 266/B3
Verdigre, Nebr. (68783) 264/F2
Verdigris (riv.), Kans. 232/G5
Verdigris, Okla. (†74017) 288/P2
Verdigris (riv.), Okla. 288/P2
Verdinho (riv.), Braz. 132/D7
Verdon, Nebr. (68457) 264/J4
Verdon, S. Dak. (57478) 298/N3
Verdun, Que. 172/H4
Verdún, Urug. 145/D5
Verdun-sur-Meuse, France 28/F3
Verdunville, W. Va. (25649) 313/B7
Vereeniging, S. Africa 118/D5
Veregin, Sask. 181/K4
Verendrye, N. Dak. (†58717) 283/J3
Vereshchagino, U.S.S.R. 48/J3
Verga (cape), Guinea 106/B6
Vergara, Arg. 143/H7
Vergara, Spain 33/E1
Vergara, Urug. 145/E3
Vergas, Minn. (56587) 254/C4
Vergeletto, Switz. 39/G4
Vergennes, Ill. (62994) 222/D6
Vergennes, Vt. (05491) 268/A3
Veribest, Texas (76886) 302/D6
Verín, Spain 33/C2
Verkhne-Vilyuysk, U.S.S.R. 48/N3
Verkhniy Ufaley, U.S.S.R. 48/F4
Verkhnyaya Toyma, U.S.S.R. 52/G2
Verkhoyansk, U.S.S.R. 48/N3
Verkhoyansk (range), U.S.S.R. 48/N3
Verkhoyansk, U.S.S.R., 3/R2
Verkhoyansk (range), U.S.S.R., 4/C3
Verkhoyansk, U.S.S.R., 4/C3
Verkhoyansk, U.S.S.R., 54/R3
Verlo, Sask. 181/C5
Vermejo (riv.), N. Mex. 274/E2
Vermejo Park, N. Mex. (†81091) 274/D2
Vermilion, Alta. 182/E3
Vermilion (riv.), Alta. 182/E3
Vermilion (cliffs), Ariz. 198/D2
Vermilion (riv.), Que. 172/D2
Vermilion (co.), Ill. 222/F3
Vermilion, Ill. (61955) 222/F4
Vermilion (riv.), Ind. 227/B4
Vermilion (par.), La. 238/F7
Vermilion (bay), La. 238/F7
Vermilion (lake), Minn., 188/H1
Vermilion (lake), Minn. 254/F3
Vermilion (range), Minn. 254/F3
Vermilion (riv.), Minn. 254/F2
Vermilion, Ohio (44089) 284/F3
Vermilion (riv.), Ohio 284/F3
Vermilion Bay, Ont. 175/B3
Vermilion Bay, Ont. 177/G4
Vermilion Grove, Ill. (†61870) 222/F4
Vermillion (co.), Ind. 227/C5
Vermillion, Kans. (66544) 232/F2
Vermillion, Minn. (55085) 254/F6
Vermillion, S. Dak. (57069) 298/R8
Vermillion (riv.), S. Dak. 298/P6
Vermont, 188/M2
VERMONT, 268
Vermont, Ill. (61484) 222/C3
Vermont (state), U.S., 146/L5
Vermontville, Mich. (49096) 250/E6
Vernal, Utah (84078) 304/E3
Vernayaz, Switz. 39/D4
Verndale, Minn. (56481) 254/C4
Verndon, Minn. (†55752) 254/E4
Verner, Ont. 177/D1
Verneuil-sur-Avre, France 28/D3
Vernon, 163/E5
Vernon, Ala. (35592) 194/B3
Vernon, Ariz. (85940) 198/F4
Vernon, Br. Col. 184/H5
Vernon‡, Calif. (90058) 204/C10
Vernon, Colo. (80755) 208/P3
Vernon▵, Conn. (06086) 210/F1
Vernon, Ont. 177/J2
Vernon (lake), Ont. 177/E2
Vernon, Fla. (32462) 212/C6
Vernon, France 28/D3
Vernon, Ill. (62892) 222/D5
Vernon, Ind. (47282) 227/F7
Vernon, Ky. (†42151) 237/L7
Vernon (par.), La. 238/D4
Vernon, La. (†71228) 238/E2
Vernon (lake), La. 238/D4
Vernon, Mich. (48476) 250/F6
Vernon (co.), Mo. 261/D7
Vernon, N.J. (07462) 273/E1
Vernon‡, N.Y. (13476) 276/J4
Vernon, Okla. (74877) 288/P4
Vernon, P.E.I. 169/E2
Vernon, Texas (76384) 302/E3
Vernon, Utah (84080) 304/B3
Vernon▵, Vt. (05354) 268/B6
Vernon, Vt. (05354) 268/B6
Vernon (co.), Wis. 317/E8
Vernonburg, Ga. (†31401) 216/K7
Vernon Center, Conn. (†06086) 210/F1
Vernon Center, Minn. (56090) 254/D7
Vernon Fork (creek), Ind. 227/F7
Vernon Hill, Va. (24597) 307/K7
Vernon Hills‡, Ill. (†60060) 222/F1
Vernonia, Oreg. (97064) 291/D2
Vernon Valley‡, N.Y. (†11768) 276/O9
Vero Beach, Fla. (32960) 212/F4
Veroli, Italy 34/D4
Verona, Ont. 177/H3
Verona, Ill. (60479) 222/E2
Verona, Italy, 7/F4
Verona (prov.), Italy 34/C2
Verona, Italy 34/C2
Verona, Ky. (41092) 237/M3
Verona, Miss. (38879) 256/G2
Verona, Mo. (65769) 261/E9
Verona, N.C. (28540) 281/O5
Verona, N. Dak. (58490) 283/O7
Verona, N.J. (07044) 273/B2
Verona, Ohio (45378) 284/A6
Verona, Pa. (15147) 294/C6
Verona, Va. (24482) 307/K4
Verona, Wis. (53593) 317/G9
Verona Park‡, Mich. (†49014) 250/D6
Verónica, Arg. 143/H7
Verret (lake), La. 238/K4
Verret, N. Br. 170/B1
Verrettes, Haiti 158/C5
Vérroia, Greece 45/F5
Versailles, Conn. (06383) 210/G2
Versailles, France, 7/E4
Versailles, France 28/A2
Versailles, Ill. (62378) 222/C4
Versailles, Ind. (47042) 227/G6
Versailles, Ky. (40383) 237/M4
Versailles, Mo. (65084) 261/G6
Versailles, N.Y. (14168) 276/B6
Versailles, Ohio (45380) 284/A5
Versailles, Pa. (15132) 294/C7
Versalles, Bol. 136/D3
Vershire▵, Vt. (05079) 268/C4
Vershire, Vt. (05079) 268/C4
Versoix, Switz. 39/B4
Verte (isl.), Que. 172/H1
Verte (bay), N. Br. 170/G2
Verte (bay), N.S. 169/D2
Vertientes, Cuba 158/G3
Vert-Pré, Mart. 161/D6
Vertus, France 28/E3
Verviers, Belg. 27/H7
Verwood, Sask. 181/F6
Vesava, India 68/B7
Vesdre (riv.), Belg. 27/H7
Veseleyville, N. Dak. (†58237) 283/R3
Veseli, Minn. (55086) 254/E6
Veselí nad Lužnicí, Czech. 41/C2
Veselí nad Moravou, Czech. 41/D2
Vesoul, France 28/F4
Vesper, Kans. (†67455) 232/D2
Vesper, Sask. 181/D5
Vesper, Wis. (54489) 317/F7
Vesta, C. Rica 154/F6
Vesta, Minn. (56292) 254/C6
Vesta, Va. (24177) 307/H7
Vestaburg, Mich. (48891) 250/E5
Vest-Agder (co.), Norway 18/E7
Vestal, N.Y. (13850) 276/H6
Vestavia Hills, Ala. (35216) 194/E4
Vesterålen (isls.), Norway 18/J2
Vesterålen (isls.), Norway, 7/F2
Vester Skerninge, Den. 21/D7
Vester Vedsted, Den. 21/B7
Vestfjord (fjord), Norway 18/H3
Vestfjord (fjord), Norway, 7/F2
Vestfold (co.), Norway 18/D4
Vestmannaeyjar, Ice. 21/B2
Vestvågoy (isl.), Norway 18/H3
Vesuvius (vol.), Italy, 7/F4
Vesuvius (vol.), Italy 34/E4
Vesuvius, Va. (24483) 307/K5
Ves'yegonsk, U.S.S.R. 52/E3
Veszprém (co.), Hung. 41/D3
Veszprém, Hung. 41/D3
Vésztő, Hung. 41/F3
Vetal, S. Dak. (57575) 298/G7
Veteran, Alta. 182/E3
Veteran, Wyo. (82243) 319/H4
Vetlanda, Sweden 18/J8
Vetluga, U.S.S.R. 52/G3
Vetluga (riv.), U.S.S.R. 52/G3
Veurne, Belg. 27/B6
Vevay, Ind. (47043) 227/G7
Vevey, Switz. 39/C4
Veyo, Utah (†84722) 304/A6
Veyrier, Switz. 39/B4
Vezirköprü, Turkey 63/F2
Viacha, Bol. 136/A5
Viadana, Italy 34/C2
Viale, Arg. 143/F5
Vian, Okla. (74962) 288/S4
Viana, Braz. 132/E3
Viana, Port. 33/B2
Viana del Bollo, Spain 33/C1
Viana do Alentejo, Port. 33/C3
Vianden, Lux. 27/J9
Vianen, Neth. 27/G5
Viareggio, Italy 34/C3
Vibank, Sask. 181/H5
Vibbard, Mo. (†64062) 261/D4
Viborg, Den. 18/F8
Viborg (co.), Den. 21/C4
Viborg, Den. 21/C5
Viborg, S. Dak. (57070) 298/P7
Vibo Valentia, Italy 34/F5
Viburnum, Mo. (65566) 261/K7
Viby, Den. 21/E6
Vicálvaro, Spain 33/G4
Vicars, W. Va. (25284) 313/D5
Vicco, Ky. (41773) 237/P6
Vicente Guerrero, Durango, Mex. 150/G5
Vicente Guerrero, Tlaxcala, Mex. 150/M1
Vicente López, Arg. 143/G7
Vicenza (prov.), Italy 34/C2
Vicenza, Italy 34/C2
Viceroy, Sask. 181/F6
Vich, Spain 33/H2
Vichacla, Bol. 136/C7
Vichada (riv.), Col., 120/D2

454 Vólos

Vólos, Greece, 7/G5
Vólos, Greece 45/F6
Vol'sk, U.S.S.R. 48/E4
Vol'sk, U.S.S.R. 52/G4
Volta (lake), Ghana 106/D7
Volta (riv.), Ghana 106/E7
Volta (lake), 102/B4
Volta (riv.), 102/C4
Voltaire, N. Dak. (58792) 283/J3
Volta Redonda, Braz. 132/E8
Volta Redonda, Braz. 135/D3
Volterra, Italy 34/C3
Volturno (riv.), Italy 34/E4
Voluntown▵, Conn. (06384) 210/H2
Volusia (co.), Fla. 212/E2
Vólvi (lake), Greece 45/F5
Volyně, Czech. 41/B2
Volyn Oblast, U.S.S.R. 52/C4
Volzhsk, U.S.S.R. 52/G3
Volzhskiy, U.S.S.R. 52/G5
Vom, Nigeria 106/F7
Vona, Colo. (80861) 208/O4
Vonda, Sask. 181/F3
Vónitsa, Greece 45/E6
Vonore, Tenn. (37885) 237/N9
Voorburg, Neth. 27/E4
Voorheesville, N.Y. (12186) 276/M5
Voorhies, Iowa (†50643) 229/J4
Voorne (isl.), Neth. 27/D5
Voorst, Neth. 27/J4
Vopnafjörd (fjord), Ice. 21/D1
Vorab (mt.), Switz. 39/H3
Vorarlberg (prov.), Austria 41/A3
Vorbasse, Den. 21/B6
Vorden, Neth. 27/J4
Vordernberg, Austria 41/C3
Vorderrhein (riv.), Switz. 39/G3
Vordingborg, Den. 18/G9
Vordingborg, Den. 21/E7
Vorgod (riv.), Den. 21/B6
Vorkuta, U.S.S.R. 48/G3
Vorkuta, U.S.S.R. 52/K1
Vorkuta, U.S.S.R., 4/C6
Vorkuta, U.S.S.R., 7/L2
Vormsi (isl.), U.S.S.R. 53/B1
Vorona (riv.), U.S.S.R. 52/F4
Voronezh, U.S.S.R. 48/E4
Voronezh, U.S.S.R. 52/E4
Voronezh, U.S.S.R., 7/J3
Voroshilovgrad, U.S.S.R. 48/E5
Voroshilovgrad, U.S.S.R. 52/E5
Voroshilovgrad, U.S.S.R., 7/H4
Vorsaa, Den. 21/D3
Vorskla (riv.), U.S.S.R. 52/E4
Vorst (Forest), Belg. 27/B9
Võrtsjärv (lake), U.S.S.R. 53/D1
Võru, U.S.S.R. 53/D2
Vosges (dept.), France 28/G3
Vosges (mts.), France 28/G3
Voss, Norway 18/E6
Voss, N. Dak. (58280) 283/R3
Vossburg, Miss. (39366) 256/F7
Vostok (isl.), 3/B6
Vostok (isl.), Pacific, 87/L7
Votamo (riv.), Ven. 124/F6
Votice, Czech. 41/C2
Votkinsk, U.S.S.R. 48/F4
Votkinsk, U.S.S.R. 52/H3
Votuporanga, Braz. 135/B2
Vouvry, Switz. 39/C4
Voúxa (cape), Greece 45/F8
Vouziers, France 28/F3
Voxna, Sweden 18/J6
Voyvodina (aut. prov.), Yugo. 45/D3
Voy-Vozh, U.S.S.R. 48/F3
Voy-Vozh, U.S.S.R. 52/H2
Vozhe (lake), U.S.S.R. 52/F2
Vozhega, U.S.S.R. 52/F2
Voznesensk, U.S.S.R. 52/D5
Vraa, Den. 21/C3
Vrâble, Czech. 41/E2
Vracov, Czech. 41/D2
Vranje, Yugo. 45/F4
Vranov, Czech. 41/F2
Vratsa, Bulg. 45/F4
Vrbas, Yugo. 45/D3
Vrbas (riv.), Yugo. 45/C3
Vrbno, Czech. 41/D1
Vrbovce, Czech. 41/D2
Vrbové, Czech. 41/D2
Vrchlabí, Czech. 41/C1
Vrede, S. Africa 118/D5
Vredenburgh, Ala. (36481) 194/D7
Vreed-en-Hoop, Guyana 131/B2
Vreeswijk, Neth. 27/G4
Vrieseveen, Neth. 27/K4
Vrondádhes, Greece 45/G6
Vršac, Yugo. 45/E3
Vrútky, Czech. 41/E2
Vryburg, S. Africa 118/C5
Vryheid, S. Africa 118/E5
Vsetín, Czech. 41/D2
Vsevidof (mt.), Alaska 196/E4
Vught, Neth. 27/G5
Vukovar, Yugo. 45/D3
Vulcan, Alta. 182/D4
Vulcan, Mich. (49892) 250/B3
Vulcan, Mo. (63675) 261/L8
Vulcan, W. Va. (25697) 313/B7
Vulcano (isl.), Italy 34/E5
Vu Liet, N. Vietnam 72/E3
Vung Tau, S. Vietnam 72/E5
Vuolvojaure (lake), Sweden 18/L3
Vuotso, Fin. 18/P2
Vya, Nev. (†96104) 266/B1
Vyatka (riv.), U.S.S.R. 52/H3
Vyatka (Kirov), U.S.S.R., 7/J3
Vyatskiye Polyany, U.S.S.R. 52/H3
Vyaz'ma, U.S.S.R. 52/D3
Vyborg, U.S.S.R. 48/C3
Vyborg, U.S.S.R. 52/C2
Vyborg, U.S.S.R., 7/G2
Vychegda (riv.), U.S.S.R. 52/G2
Východočeský (reg.), Czech. 41/C1
Východoslovenský (reg.), Czech. 41/F2
Vyg (lake), U.S.S.R. 52/E2
Vyksa, U.S.S.R. 52/F3
Vym' (riv.), U.S.S.R. 52/H2
Vyshniy Volochek, U.S.S.R. 48/D4
Vyshniy Volochek, U.S.S.R. 52/D3
Vyškov, Czech. 41/D2
Vysoké Mýto, Czech. 41/D2
Vysoké Tatry, Czech. 41/F2
Vyšší Brod, Czech. 41/C2
Vytegra, U.S.S.R. 52/E2

W

Wa, Ghana 106/D6
Waal (riv.), Neth. 27/G5
Waalwijk, Neth. 27/F5
Waarschoot, Belg. 27/D6
Waas (mt.), Utah 304/E5
Waasis, N. Br. 170/D3
Waasten (Warneton), Belg. 27/B7
Wabamun, Alta. 182/C3
Waban, Mass. (†02168) 249/B7
Wabana, Newf. 166/D2
Wabaningo, Mich. (49463) 250/C5
Wabasca (riv.), 163/E4
Wabasca, Alta. 182/D2
Wabasca (riv.), Alta. 182/C1
Wabash (riv.), 188/J3
Wabash, Ark. (72389) 203/J5
Wabash (co.), Ill. 222/F5
Wabash (riv.), Ill. 222/F5
Wabash (co.), Ind. 227/F3
Wabash, Ind. (46992) 227/F3
Wabash (riv.), Ind. 227/B7
Wabash, Ohio (†45822) 284/A4
Wabash (riv.), Ohio 284/A5
Wabasha (co.), Minn. 254/F6
Wabasha, Minn. (55981) 254/G6
Wabasso, Fla. (32970) 212/F4
Wabasso, Minn. (56293) 254/C6
Wabatawangang (lake), Minn. 254/D3
Wabaunsee (co.), Kans. 232/F3
Wabaunsee, Kans. (†66547) 232/F2
Wabbaseka, Ark. (72175) 203/G5
Wabeno, Wis. (54566) 317/J5
Wabi (riv.), Eth. 111/H6
Wabigoon, Ont. 175/B3
Wabigoon, Ont. 177/G5
Wabi Shebelle (riv.), Eth. 111/H6
Wabi Shebelle (riv.), Somalia 115/H3
Wabowden, Man. 179/J3
Wąbrzeźno, Poland 47/D2
Wabuk (pt.), Ont. 175/D1
Wabush, Newf. 166/A3
Wabush (lake), Newf. 166/A3
Wabush Lake, 163/K5
Wabuska, Nev. (†89447) 266/B3
Waccamaw (lake), N.C. 281/N6
Waccamaw (riv.), N.C. 281/M7
Waccamaw (riv.), S.C. 296/J5
Waccasassa (bay), Fla. 212/D2
Waccasassa (riv.), Fla. 212/D2
Wachapreague, Va. (23480) 307/S5
Wachapreague (inlet), Va. 307/T6
Wachee, Sask. 181/J3
Wachusett (mt.), Mass. 249/G3
Wachusett (res.), Mass. 249/G3
Wacissa, Fla. (32361) 212/B1
Waco, Ga. (30182) 216/B3
Waco, Ky. (40385) 237/N5
Waco, Mo. (63869) 261/C8
Waco, N.C. (28169) 281/G4
Waco, Nebr. (68460) 264/G4
Waco, Texas, 146/J6
Waco, Texas, 188/G4
Waco, Texas (*76701) 302/G6
Waconia, Minn. (55387) 254/E6
Wadai (reg.), Chad 111/D5
Waddan, Libya 111/C2
Waddell, Ariz. (85355) 198/C5
Waddenzee (sound), Neth. 27/G2
Waddington (mt.), 163/D5
Waddington (mt.), Br. Col. 184/E4
Waddington, N.Y. (13694) 276/K1
Waddy, Ky. (40076) 237/L4
Wade, Miss. (39575) 256/G9
Wade, N.C. (28395) 281/M4
Wade (lake), Newf. 166/A3
Wade, Okla. (74765) 288/O7
Wadebridge, Eng. 13/B7
Wade-Hampton, S.C. (29607) 296/C2
Wadena, Ind. (†47944) 227/C3
Wadena, Iowa (52169) 229/K3
Wadena (co.), Minn. 254/D4
Wadena, Minn. (56482) 254/C4
Wadena, Sask. 181/H4
Wädenswil, Switz. 39/G2
Wadesboro, La. (†70454) 238/M2
Wadesboro, N.C. (28170) 281/J5
Wadestown, W. Va. (26589) 313/F3
Wadesville, Ind. (47638) 227/B8
Wadeville, N.C. (†27306) 281/J4
Wadhams, Br. Col. 184/D4
Wadhams, N.Y. (12990) 276/N2
Wadi, India 68/D5
Wadi es Sir, Jordan 65/D4
Wadi Musa, Jordan 65/E5
Wading (riv.), N.J. 273/D4
Wading River, N.Y. (11792) 276/P9
Wadley, Ala. (36276) 194/G4
Wadley, Ga. (30477) 216/H5
Wadmalaw (isl.), S.C. 296/G6
Wad Medani, 102/F3
Wad Medani, Sudan 59/B7
Wad Medani, Sudan 111/F5
Wadowice, Poland 47/D4
Wadsworth, Ala. (†36022) 194/E5
Wadsworth, Ill. (60083) 222/F1
Wadsworth, Nev. (89442) 266/B3
Wadsworth, Ohio (44281) 284/G3
Wadsworth, Texas (77483) 302/J9
Waelder, Texas (78959) 302/G8
Wafania, Dem. Rep. of the Congo. 115/D4
Wagarville, Ala. (36585) 194/B8
Wagener, S.C. (29164) 296/E4
Wageningen, Neth. 27/H5
Wageningen, Sur. 131/C3
Wager (bay), 163/G3
Wager (bay), N.W.T., 146/K3
Wager (bay), N.W.T. 187/K3
Wagga Wagga, Australia, 87/E9
Wagga Wagga, Aust. 88/H7
Wagga Wagga, N.S.W. 97/D4
Waggoner, Ill. (62572) 222/D4
Waggrakine, W. Aust. 92/A5
Wagin, Aust. 88/B6
Wagin, W. Aust. 92/B2
Wagner, Mont. (59543) 262/H2
Wagner, S. Dak. (57380) 298/N7
Wagoner (co.), Okla. 288/P3
Wagoner, Okla. (74467) 288/R3
Wagon Mound, N. Mex. (87752) 274/E2
Wagontire, Oreg. (†97720) 291/H4
Wagon Wheel Gap, Colo. (†81130) 208/F7
Wagram, N.C. (28396) 281/L5
Wągrowiec, Poland 47/C2
Waha, Belg. 27/G8
Wahai, Indon. 85/H6
Wahalak, Miss. (†39358) 256/G5
Wahiawa, Hawaii, 188/F5
Wahiawa, Hawaii (96766) 218/E2
Wahkiacus, Wash. (98670) 310/D5
Wahkiakum (co.), Wash. 310/B4
Wahkon, Minn. (56386) 254/E4
Wahlern, Switz. 39/D3
Wahnapitae, Ont. 177/D1
Wahneta‡, Fla. (33880) 212/E4
Wahoo, Nebr. (68066) 264/H3
Wahpeton, Iowa (†51360) 229/C2
Wahpeton, N. Dak., 188/G1
Wahpeton, N. Dak. (58075) 283/S7
Wahsatch, Utah (†82930) 304/C2
Wah Wah (mts.), Utah 304/A5
Wahwashkesh (lake), Ont. 177/D2
Wahweap (creek), Utah 304/C6
Waiakoa, Hawaii (†96788) 218/J2
Waialeale (mt.), Hawaii 218/C1
Waialee, Hawaii (†96731) 218/E1
Waialua, Hawaii, 188/F5
Waialua, Molokai, Hawaii (†96748) 218/H1
Waialua, Oahu, Hawaii (96791) 218/E1
Waianae, Hawaii (96792) 218/D2
Waiau, N.Z. 101/D5
Waiau (riv.), N.Z. 101/A6
Waidhofen an der Thaya, Austria 41/C2
Waidhofen an der Ybbs, Austria 41/C3
Waidsboro, Va. (24181) 307/J7
Waigama, Indon. 85/H6
Waigeo (isl.), Indon. 85/J5
Waihee, Hawaii (†96793) 218/J2
Waiheke (isl.), N.Z. 101/E2
Waihi, N.Z. 101/E2
Waikabubak, Indon. 85/F7
Waikanae, N.Z. 101/E4
Waikane, Hawaii (†96744) 218/F2
Waikapu, Hawaii (†96793) 218/J2
Waikaremoana (lake), N.Z. 101/F3
Waikari, N.Z. 101/D5
Waikato (riv.), N.Z. 101/E2
Waikawa, N.Z. 101/B7
Waikerie, Aust. 88/G6
Waikerie, S. Aust. 94/F6
Waikii, Hawaii (†96743) 218/H4
Waikiki, Hawaii (96815) 218/C4
Waikiki (beach), Hawaii 218/C4
Waikiwi, N.Z. 101/B7
Waikouaiti, N.Z. 101/C6
Wailau, Hawaii (†96748) 218/H1
Wailea, Hawaii (†96710) 218/J4
Wailua, Hawaii (†96746) 218/D2
Wailuku, Hawaii, 188/F5
Wailuku, Hawaii (96793) 218/J2
Wailuku (riv.), Hawaii 218/J5
Waimakariri (riv.), N.Z. 101/D5
Waimalu, Hawaii (†96701) 218/B3
Waimanalo, Hawaii (96795) 218/F2
Waimanalo Beach, Hawaii (†96795) 218/F2
Waimate, N.Z. 101/C6
Waimea (bay), Hawaii 218/B2
Waimea (riv.), Hawaii 218/C2
Waimea (Kamuela), Hawaii, Hawaii (†96743) 218/G3
Waimea, Kauai, Hawaii (96796) 218/B2
Waimea, Oahu, Hawaii (†96712) 218/E1
Waimes, Belg. 27/J8
Wainfleet, Ont. 177/E4
Wainfleet, Eng. 13/H4
Waingapu, Indon. 85/G7
Waini (riv.), Guyana 131/B2
Wainiha, Hawaii (†96714) 218/C1
Wainiha (riv.), Hawaii 218/C1
Wainuiomata, N.Z. 101/B3
Wainui-o-mata (riv.), N.Z. 101/B3
Wainwright, Alaska (99782) 196/F1
Wainwright, Alta. 182/E3
Wainwright, Ohio (44686) 284/G5
Wainwright, Okla. (74468) 288/R3
Wainwright, U.S., 4/B18
Waiohinu, Hawaii (†96772) 218/G7
Waipa (riv.), N.Z. 101/E2
Waipahu, Hawaii, 188/F5
Waipahu, Hawaii (96797) 218/A3
Waipara, N.Z. 101/D5
Waipawa, N.Z. 101/F3
Waipio, Hawaii (†96758) 218/H3
Waipio (bay), Hawaii 218/H3
Waipio (pen.), Hawaii 218/A3
Waipio (pt.), Hawaii 218/A4
Waipio Acres, Hawaii (†96786) 218/E2
Waipiro Bay, N.Z. 101/G3
Waipukurau, N.Z. 101/F4
Wairau (riv.), N.Z. 101/D4
Wairoa, N.Z. 101/F3
Wairoa (riv.), N.Z. 101/E1
Wais, Iran 66/F5
Waitakere, N.Z. 101/B1
Waitakere (range), N.Z. 101/A1
Waitaki (riv.), N.Z. 101/C6
Waitangi, N.Z. 101/D7
Waitara, N.Z. 101/E3
Waite▵, Maine (04492) 242/H5
Waite Hill, Ohio (†44094) 284/H2
Waitemata (harb.), N.Z. 101/B1
Waite Park, Minn. (56387) 254/D5
Waiteville, W. Va. (24984) 313/F8
Waitotara, N.Z. 101/E3
Waits (riv.), Vt. 268/C3
Waitsburg, Wash. (99361) 310/G4
Waitsfield▵, Vt. (05673) 268/B3
Waitsfield, Vt. (05673) 268/B3
Waits River, Vt. (†05076) 268/C3
Waiuku, N.Z. 101/E2
Wajabula, Indon. 85/H5
Wajima, Japan 81/H5
Wajir, Kenya 115/H3
Waka, Eth. 111/G6
Waka, Dem. Rep. of the Congo. 115/D3
Waka, Texas (79093) 302/D1
Wakarusa, Ind. (46573) 227/F1
Wakarusa, Kans. (66546) 232/G3
Wakasa, Japan 81/G6
Wakasa (bay), Japan 81/G6
Wakatipu (lake), N.Z. 101/B6
Wakaw, Sask. 181/F3
Wakayama, Japan, 54/S6
Wakayama (pref.), Japan 81/G6
Wakayama, Japan 81/G6
Wakde (isl.), Indon. 85/K6
Wake (co.), N.C. 281/M3
Wake (isl.), Pacific, 87/G4
WaKeeney, Kans. (67672) 232/C2
Wakefield, Que. 172/B4
Wakefield, Eng. 13/F4
Wakefield, 10/F4
Wakefield, Kans. (67487) 232/E2
Wakefield, La. (70784) 238/H5
Wakefield▵, Mass. (01880) 249/C5
Wakefield, Mich. (49968) 250/F2
Wakefield▵, N.H. (03888) 268/F4
Wakefield, N.H. (03888) 268/F4
Wakefield, Nebr. (68784) 264/H2
Wakefield, Ohio (45687) 284/E8
Wakefield, Va. (23888) 307/O7
Wakefield-Peace Dale, R.I. (02879) 249/J7
Wake Forest, N.C. (27587) 281/M3
Wakeham (Maricourt), 163/J3
Wakeham (Maricourt), Que. 174/F1
Wakema, Burma 72/B3
Wakeman, Ohio (44889) 284/F3
Wakenaam (isl.), Guyana 131/B2
Wakenda, Mo. (64687) 261/F4
Wake Village, Texas (75501) 302/K4
Wakita, Okla. (73771) 288/L1
Wakkanai, Japan 81/K1
Wakonda, S. Dak. (57073) 298/P7
Wakool, N.S.W. 97/C4
Wakopa, Man. 179/C5
Wakpala, S. Dak. (57658) 298/H2
Wakulla (co.), Fla. 212/B1
Wakulla, Fla. (†32327) 212/B1
Wakwekobi (lake), Ont. 177/A1
Wala, Kuh-i- (mt.), Afgh. 59/H3
Walbridge, Ohio (43465) 284/C2
Wałbrzych, Poland 47/B3
Walbundrie, N.S.W. 97/D4
Walcha, Aust. 88/J6
Walcha, N.S.W. 97/F2
Walchensee (lake), W. Ger. 22/D5
Walcheren (isl.), Neth. 27/C5
Walcott, Ark. (72474) 203/J1
Walcott, Iowa (52773) 229/M5
Walcott, N. Dak. (58077) 283/R6
Walcott, Wyo. (82335) 319/F4
Walcourt, Belg. 27/F8
Wałcz, Poland 47/C2
Wald, Switz. 39/G2
Waldeck, Sask. 181/D5
Walden, Colo. (80480) 208/G1
Walden, Ga. (†31201) 216/E5
Walden, Ky. (40768) 237/N7
Walden (pond), Mass. 249/A6
Walden, N.Y. (12586) 276/M7
Walden▵, Vt. (†05873) 268/C3
Walden, Vt. (†05873) 268/C3
Waldenburg, Ark. (72475) 203/J2
Waldenburg, Mich. (†48043) 250/G6
Waldenburg, Switz. 39/E2
Walden Heights, Vt. (†05873) 268/C3
Waldersee, Man. 179/D4
Waldheim, E. Ger. 22/E3
Waldheim, La. (†70433) 238/L5
Waldheim, Sask. 181/E3
Waldia, Eth. 111/G5
Waldkirch, Switz. 39/H2
Waldkirch, W. Ger. 22/B4
Waldkraiburg, W. Ger. 22/E4
Waldo, Ark. (71770) 203/D7
Waldo, Br. Col. 184/K5
Waldo, Fla. (32694) 212/D2
Waldo, Kans. (67673) 232/D2
Waldo (co.), Maine 242/E6
Waldo▵, Maine (†04915) 242/E7
Waldo, Ohio (43356) 284/D5
Waldo (lake), Oreg. 291/E4
Waldo, Wis. (53093) 317/L8
Waldoboro▵, Maine (04572) 242/E7
Waldoboro, Maine (04572) 242/E7
Waldorf, Md. (20601) 245/L6
Waldorf, Minn. (56091) 254/E7
Waldport, Oreg. (97394) 291/C3
Waldron, Ark. (72958) 203/B4
Waldron, Ind. (46182) 227/F6
Waldron, Kans. (67150) 232/D4
Waldron, Mich. (49288) 250/E7
Waldron, Mo. (64092) 261/O5
Waldron, Sask. 181/J5
Waldron, Wash. (98297) 310/B2
Waldrup, Miss. (†39422) 256/F7
Waldsassen, W. Ger. 22/E3
Waldshut, W. Ger. 22/C5
Waldwick, N.J. (07463) 273/B1
Waldwick, Wis. (†53565) 317/G10
Wales, U.K., 7/D3
WALES, 10/E4
WALES, 13
Wales, Alaska, 188/C5
Wales, Alaska (99783) 196/E1
Wales▵, Mass. (01081) 249/F4
Wales, Minn. (†55616) 254/G3
Wales, N. Dak. (58281) 283/N2
Wales (isl.), N.W.T. 187/K3
Wales, Tenn. (38484) 237/G10
Wales, Utah (84667) 304/C4
Wales, Wis. (53183) 317/J1
Walesboro, Ind. (†47201) 227/F6
Waleska, Ga. (30183) 216/D2
Walford, Ont. 177/B1
Walford, Iowa (52351) 229/K5
Walgett, Aust. 88/H6
Walgett, N.S.W. 97/E2
Walgreen Coast (reg.), Ant. 5/B13
Walhachin, Br. Col. 184/G5
Walhalla, Mich. (49458) 250/C5
Walhalla, N. Dak. (58282) 283/P2
Walhalla, S.C. (29691) 296/A2
Walhonding, Ohio (43843) 284/F5
Walikale, Dem. Rep. of the Congo. 115/E4
Walker (co.), Ala. 194/D3
Walker (creek), Ariz. 198/F2
Walker (mt.), Ark. 203/E2
Walker (co.), Ga. 216/B1
Walker, Iowa (52352) 229/K4
Walker, Kans. (67674) 232/C3
Walker, Ky. (40997) 237/O7
Walker, La. (70785) 238/L1
Walker, Mich. (49504) 250/D6
Walker, Minn. (56484) 254/D3
Walker, Mo. (64790) 261/D7
Walker (bay), N.W.T. 187/G2
Walker, N.Y. (14566) 276/E4
Walker (lake), Nev., 188/C3
Walker (lake), Nev. 266/C4
Walker (riv.), Nev. 266/C3
Walker, Oreg. (†97426) 291/D4
Walker, S. Dak. (57659) 298/G2
Walker (co.), Texas 302/J7
Walker (creek), Va. 307/F6
Walker, W. Va. (26180) 313/D4
Walker Mill‡, Md. (†20023) 245/G5
Walker River Ind. Res., Nev. 266/C3
Walker Springs, Ala. (36586) 194/C7
Walkersville, Md. (21793) 245/J3
Walkersville, W. Va. (26447) 313/F5
Walkerton, Ont. 177/C3
Walkerton, Ind. (46574) 227/E2
Walkerton, Va. (23177) 307/O5
Walkertown, N.C. (27051) 281/J2
Walkerville, Mich. (49459) 250/C5
Walkerville, Mont. (59701) 262/D4
Wall▵, N.J. (07719) 273/E3
Wall, Pa. (†15148) 294/C5
Wall, S. Dak. (57790) 298/E6
Wall, Texas (76957) 302/D6
Wallace, Ala. (†36426) 194/D8
Wallace (mt.), Alta. 182/C2
Wallace, Calif. (95254) 204/C9
Wallace, Idaho (83873) 220/C2
Wallace, Ind. (47988) 227/C5
Wallace (co.), Kans. 232/A3
Wallace, Kans. (67761) 232/A3
Wallace, La. (70049) 238/M3
Wallace (lake), La. 238/C2
Wallace (lake), Man. 179/G3
Wallace, Mich. (49893) 250/B3
Wallace, N.C. (28466) 281/N5
Wallace, N.S. 169/E3
Wallace (harb.), N.S. 169/E3
Wallace, N.Y. (14890) 276/E6
Wallace, Nebr. (69169) 264/C4
Wallace, S.C. (29596) 296/H2
Wallace, S. Dak. (57272) 298/P3
Wallace, W. Va. (26448) 313/E4
Wallaceburg, Ont. 177/B5
Wallaceton, Pa. (16876) 294/F4
Wallacetown, Ont. 177/C5
Wallaga (prov.), Eth. 111/G6
Wallal Downs, W. Aust. 92/C2
Walland, Tenn. (37886) 237/O9
Wallard, Sask. 181/D6
Wallaroo, Aust. 88/F6
Wallaroo, S. Aust. 94/E5
Wallasey, Eng. 13/D4
Wallasey, 10/F2
Walla Walla, N.S.W. 97/D4
Walla Walla (riv.), Oreg. 291/J1
Walla Walla, Wash., 188/C1
Walla Walla (co.), Wash. 310/G4
Walla Walla, Wash. (99362) 310/G4
Walla Walla (riv.), Wash. 310/G4
Wallback, W. Va. (25285) 313/D5
Wallburg, N.C. (27373) 281/J3
Walldürn, W. Ger. 22/C4
Walled Lake, Mich. (48088) 250/F6
Wallen, Ind. (†46802) 227/G2
Wallendbeen, N.S.W. 97/E4
Wallenpaupack (lake), Pa. 294/M3
Wallenstadt, Switz. 39/H2
Wallenstadt (lake), Switz. 39/H2
Waller (co.), Texas 302/J8
Waller‡, Texas (77484) 302/J7
Wallerawang, N.S.W. 97/F3
Wallerville, Miss. (†38652) 256/G2
Wallhamn, Sweden 18/G7
Wallibu, St. Vincent 161/A8
Walling, Tenn. (38587) 237/K9
Wallingford▵, Conn. (06492) 210/D3
Wallingford, Eng. 13/F6
Wallingford, Iowa (51365) 229/D2
Wallingford, Ky. (41093) 237/O4
Wallingford, Pa. (19086) 294/L7
Wallingford▵, Vt. (05773) 268/B5
Wallingford, Vt. (05773) 268/B5
Wallington, N.J. (07055) 273/B2
Wallins Creek, Ky. (40873) 237/O7
Wallis (lake), N.S.W. 97/G3
Wallis, Texas (77485) 302/H8
Wallis (isls.), Wallis and Futuna, 87/J7
Wallis and Futuna, 87/J7
Wallisville, Texas (77597) 302/L1
Wallkill (riv.), N.J. 273/D1
Wallkill, N.Y. (12589) 276/M7
Wallkill (riv.), N.Y. 276/L8
Wall Lake, Iowa (51466) 229/C4
Wallo (prov.), Eth. 111/H5
Wallonia, Ky. (†42405) 237/F7
Walloon (lake), Mich. 250/E3
Walloon Lake, Mich. (49796) 250/E3
Wallops (isl.), Va. 307/T5
Wallowa (co.), Oreg. 291/K2
Wallowa, Oreg. (97885) 291/K2
Wallowa (mts.), Oreg. 291/K2
Wallowa (riv.), Oreg. 291/K2
Wallpack Center, N.J. (07881) 273/D1
Walls, Miss. (38680) 256/D1
Walls, Scot. 15/M3
Wallsburg, Utah (84082) 304/C3
Wallsend, Eng. 13/F2
Wallula (lake), Oreg. 291/H1
Wallula, Wash. (99363) 310/G4
Wallula (lake), Wash. 310/F4
Walney (isl.), Eng. 13/D3
Walney (isl.), 10/E3
Walnut, Calif. (91789) 204/D10
Walnut (creek), Calif. 204/K1
Walnut, Ill. (61376) 222/D2
Walnut, Iowa (51577) 229/C6
Walnut, Kans. (66780) 232/G4
Walnut (creek), Kans. 232/B3
Walnut (riv.), Kans. 232/E4
Walnut, Miss. (38683) 256/G1
Walnut, N.C. (28753) 281/D3
Walnut, Pa. (†17082) 294/G4
Walnut (creek), Texas 302/F2
Walnut Bottom, Pa. (17266) 294/H5
Walnut Canyon Nat'l Mon., Ariz. 198/D3
Walnut Cove, N.C. (27052) 281/J2
Walnut Creek, Calif. (*94595) 204/K2
Walnut Creek, Ohio (44687) 284/G4
Walnut Grove, Ala. (35990) 194/E2
Walnut Grove, Calif. (95690) 204/B9
Walnut Grove, Ga. (†30209) 216/E3
Walnut Grove, Ill. (61487) 222/C3
Walnut Grove, Ky. (42563) 237/M6
Walnut Grove, Minn. (56180) 254/C6
Walnut Grove, Miss. (39189) 256/F5
Walnut Grove, Mo. (65770) 261/F8
Walnut Hill, Ark. (†71826) 203/C7
Walnut Hill, Fla. (32568) 212/B5
Walnut Hill, Ill. (62893) 222/E5
Walnut Hill, Maine (†04021) 242/C8
Walnut Park‡, Calif. (†90255) 204/C11
Walnutport, Pa. (18088) 294/L4
Walnut Ridge, Ark. (72476) 203/J1
Walnut Springs, Texas (76690) 302/G5
Walpole (isl.), Ont. 177/B5
Walpole▵, Mass. (02081) 249/B8
Walpole▵, N.H. (03608) 268/C5
Walpole, N.H. (03608) 268/C5
Walpole, Sask. 181/K6
Walrus (isl.), Alaska 196/E3
Walrus (isls.), Alaska 196/F3
Walsall, Eng. 13/F5
Walsall, 10/G3
Walsenburg, Colo. (81089) 208/K7
Walsh, Alta. 182/E5
Walsh, Aust. 88/G3
Walsh, Colo. (81090) 208/P8
Walsh (co.), N. Dak. 283/P3
Walsh, Queens. 95/B3
Walshville, Ill. (62091) 222/D4
Walsingham (cape), 163/L2
Walsingham, Eng. 13/J5
Walsingham (cape), N.W.T. 187/M3
Walsoken, Eng. 13/H5
Walsoken, 10/G4
Walsrode, W. Ger. 22/C2
Walston, Pa. (15781) 294/D4
Walstonburg, N.C. (27888) 281/O3
Waltair, India 68/E5
Walterboro, S.C. (29488) 296/F6
Walter F. George (dam), Ala. 194/H7
Walter F. George (dam), Ga. 216/B7
Walterhill, Tenn. (†37130) 237/J9
Walter Reed Army Med. Ctr., D.C. 245/E4
Walter Reed Army Med. Ctr. Annex, Md. 245/E4
Walters, La. (71374) 238/G3
Walters, Minn. (56092) 254/E7
Walters, Okla. (73572) 288/K6
Walters Falls, Ont. 177/D3
Waltershausen, E. Ger. 22/D3
Waltersville, Ky. (†40312) 237/N5
Waltersville, Miss. (†39180) 256/C6
Walterville, Oreg. (97489) 291/E3
Walthall (co.), Miss. 256/D8
Walthall, Miss. (39771) 256/F3
Waltham▵, Maine (†04605) 242/G6
Waltham, Mass. (02154) 249/B6
Waltham, Minn. (55982) 254/F7
Waltham▵, Vt. (†05491) 268/A3
Waltham, Vt. (†05491) 268/A3
Waltham Forest, 10/B5
Waltham Holy Cross, 10/B5
Walthill, Nebr. (68067) 264/H2
Walthourville, Ga. (31333) 216/J7
Waltman, Wyo. (†82648) 319/E2
Walton, Ont. 177/C4
Walton (co.), Fla. 212/C6
Walton, Fla. (†33457) 212/F4
Walton (co.), Ga. 216/E3
Walton, Ind. (46994) 227/E3
Walton, Kans. (67151) 232/E3
Walton, Ky. (41094) 237/M3
Walton, N.S. 169/E3
Walton, N.Y. (13856) 276/K6
Walton, Nebr. (68461) 264/H4
Walton, Oreg. (97490) 291/D3
Walton, W. Va. (25286) 313/D5
Walton and Weybridge, 10/B6
Walton Hills, Ohio (†44146) 284/J10
Waltonville, Ill. (62894) 222/D5
Waltreak, Ark. (72866) 203/C4
Waltz, Mich. (†48164) 250/F6
Walum, N. Dak. (58491) 283/O5
Walupt (lake), Wash. 310/D4
Walvis (bay), S. Africa 118/A4
Walvis Bay, 102/D7
Walvis Bay, S. Africa 118/A4
Walvis Bay, S. Afr., 3/K7
Walworth, N.Y. (14568) 276/F4
Walworth (co.), S. Dak. 298/J3
Walworth (co.), Wis. 317/J10
Walworth, Wis. (53184) 317/J10
Walzenhausen, Switz. 39/J2
Wamac, Ill. (†62801) 222/D5
Wamba, Nigeria 106/F7
Wamba, Dem. Rep. of the Congo. 115/E3
Wamego, Kans. (66547) 232/F2
Wamel, Neth. 27/H5
Wamena, Indon. 85/K6
Wamgumbaug (lake), Conn. 210/F1
Wami (riv.), Tanz. 115/G5
Wamic, Oreg. (97063) 291/F2

456 Waverly

Waverly, Ill. (62692) 222/D4
Waverly, Ind. (†46151) 227/E5
Waverly, Iowa (50677) 229/J3
Waverly, Kans. (66871) 232/G3
Waverly, Ky. (42462) 237/F5
Waverly, La. (71290) 238/H2
Waverly, Minn. (55390) 254/E5
Waverly, Mo. (64096) 261/E4
Waverly, N.S. 169/E4
Waverly, Nebr. (68462) 264/H4
Waverly, Ohio (45690) 284/D7
Waverly, S. Dak. (57202) 298/R3
Waverly, Tenn. (37185) 237/F8
Waverly, Va. (23890) 307/O6
Waverly, W. Va. (26184) 313/D4
Waverly, Wash. (99039) 310/H3
Waverly Hall, Ga. (31831) 216/C5
Waves, N.C. (27982) 281/U3
Wavre, Belg. 27/F7
Wawa, Ont. 175/C3
Wawa, Ont. 177/J5
Wawa (riv.), Nic. 154/F3
Wawaka, Ind. (46794) 227/F2
Wawanesa, Man. 179/C5
Wawasee (lake), Ind. 227/F2
Wawayanda (lake), N.J. 273/E1
Waweig, N. Br. 170/C3
Wawina, Minn. (55794) 254/E3
Wawota, Sask. 181/J6
Wawpecong, Ind. (†46901) 227/F3
Wax, Ky. (42787) 237/J6
Waxahachie, Texas (75165) 302/H5
Waxhaw, N.C. (28173) 281/H5
Way, Miss. (†39046) 256/E5
Way, Poulo (isls.), S. Vietnam 72/D5
Way (lake), W. Aust. 92/C4
Wayagamak (lake), Que. 172/E2
Wayan, Idaho (83285) 220/G7
Wayatinah, Tas. 99/C4
Waycross, Ga., 188/K4
Waycross, Ga. (31501) 216/H8
Wayerton, N. Br. 170/E1
Wayland, Iowa (52654) 229/K6
Wayland, Ky. (41666) 237/R6
Wayland△, Mass. (01778) 249/A7
Wayland, Mass. (01778) 249/A7
Wayland, Mich. (49348) 250/D6
Wayland, Mo. (63472) 261/J2
Wayland, N.Y. (14572) 276/E5
Wayland, Ohio (44285) 284/H3
Waymansville, Ind. (†47201) 227/E6
Waymart, Pa. (18472) 294/M2
Wayne, Ala. (†36763) 194/C6
Wayne, Alta. 182/D4
Wayne (co.), Ga. 216/J7
Wayne (co.), Ill. 222/E5
Wayne‡, Ill. (60184) 222/E2
Wayne (co.), Ind. 227/G5
Wayne (co.), Iowa 229/G7
Wayne, Kans. (66969) 232/E2
Wayne (co.), Ky. 237/M7
Wayne△, Maine (04284) 242/D7
Wayne, Maine (04284) 242/D7
Wayne (co.), Mich. 250/F6
Wayne, Mich. (48184) 250/F6
Wayne (co.), Miss. 256/G7
Wayne (co.), Mo. 261/L8
Wayne (co.), N.C. 281/N4
Wayne△, N.J. (07470) 273/A1
Wayne (co.), N.Y. 276/F4
Wayne, N.Y. (14893) 276/F6
Wayne (co.), Nebr. 264/G2
Wayne, Nebr. (68787) 264/G2
Wayne (co.), Ohio 284/G4
Wayne, Ohio (43466) 284/C3
Wayne, Okla. (73095) 288/M5
Wayne (co.), Pa. 294/M2
Wayne, Pa. (19087) 294/M6
Wayne (co.), Tenn. 237/F10
Wayne (co.), Utah 304/C5
Wayne (co.), W. Va. 313/B6
Wayne, W. Va. (25570) 313/B6
Wayne City, Ill. (62895) 222/E5
Wayne Heights‡, Pa. (†17268) 294/G6
Waynesboro, Ga. (30830) 216/J4
Waynesboro, Miss. (39367) 256/G7
Waynesboro, Pa. (17268) 294/G6
Waynesboro, Tenn. (38485) 237/F10
Waynesboro, Va. (22980) 307/K4
Waynesburg, Ky. (40489) 237/M6
Waynesburg, Ohio (44688) 284/H4
Waynesburg, Pa. (15370) 294/B6
Waynesfield, Ohio (45896) 284/C4
Waynesville, Ga. (31566) 216/J8
Waynesville, Ill. (61778) 222/D3
Waynesville, Ind. (†47201) 227/F6
Waynesville, Mo. (65583) 261/H7
Waynesville, N.C. (28786) 281/D4
Waynesville, Ohio (45068) 284/B6
Waynetown, Ind. (47990) 227/C4
Waynoka, Okla. (73860) 288/J1
Wayside, Ga. (†31032) 216/E4
Wayside, Kans. (67366) 232/G4
Wayside, Miss. (38780) 256/C4
Wayside, Texas (79094) 302/C3
Wayside, Wis. (†54126) 317/L7
Wayzata, Minn. (55391) 254/G5
Wazirabad, Pak. 59/K3
Weakley (co.), Tenn. 237/D8
Wear (riv.), Eng. 13/F3
Wear (riv.), 10/F3
Weare△, N.H. (03281) 268/D5
Weare P.O. (North Weare), N.H. (03281) 268/D5
Weasel Creek, Alta. 182/D2
Weatherby, Mo. (64497) 261/D3
Weatherby Lake, Mo. (†64152) 261/O5
Weatherford, Okla. (73096) 288/J4
Weatherford, Texas (76086) 302/G5
Weatherly, Pa. (18255) 294/L4
Weathers, Okla. (†74560) 288/P5
Weathersby, Miss. (†39114) 256/E7
Weatogue, Conn. (06089) 210/D1
Weaubleau, Mo. (65774) 261/F7
Weaver, Ala. (36277) 194/G3
Weaver (lake), Man. 179/F2
Weaver, Minn. (55984) 254/G6
Weaver, N. Dak. (†58352) 283/N2
Weaverville, Calif. (96093) 204/B3
Weaverville, N.C. (28787) 281/D3
Webb, Ala. (36376) 194/H8
Webb, Iowa (51366) 229/D3
Webb (lake), Maine 242/C6
Webb, Miss. (38966) 256/D3
Webb (bay), Newf. 166/B2
Webb, Sask. 181/C5
Webb (co.), Texas 302/E10
Webb, Texas (†76010) 302/F2
Webb A.F.B., Texas 302/C5
Webb City, Ark. (†72949) 203/C3
Webb City, Mo. (64870) 261/D8
Webb City, Okla. (74654) 288/N1
Webber, Kans. (66970) 232/D2
Webbers Falls, Okla. (74470) 288/R3
Webbers Falls (res.), Okla. 288/R3
Webberville, Mich. (48892) 250/E6
Webb Lake, Wis. (54892) 317/B3
Webbs Cross Roads, Ky. (42652) 237/L6
Webbville, Ky. (41180) 237/R4
Webbwood, Ont. 177/C1
Weber (co.), Utah 304/B2
Weber (riv.), Utah 304/C3
Weber City, Va. (24251) 307/C7
Webster, Alta. 182/A2
Webster, Fla. (33597) 212/D3
Webster (co.), Ga. 216/C6
Webster, Ind. (47392) 227/H5
Webster (co.), Iowa 229/E4
Webster, Iowa (52355) 229/J6
Webster (res.), Kans. 232/C2
Webster (co.), Ky. 237/F5
Webster, Ky. (40176) 237/J5
Webster (par.), La. 238/D1
Webster△, Maine (†04250) 242/C7
Webster (brook), Maine 242/E3
Webster△, Mass. (01570) 249/G4
Webster, Mass. (01570) 249/G4
Webster (lake), Mass. 249/G4
Webster, Minn. (55088) 254/E6
Webster (co.), Miss. 256/F3
Webster (co.), Mo. 261/G8
Webster, Mont. (†59313) 262/M4
Webster, N.C. (28788) 281/C4
Webster, N. Dak. (58382) 283/N3
Webster△, N.H. (†03301) 268/D5
Webster, N.Y. (14580) 276/F4
Webster (co.), Nebr. 264/F4
Webster, Pa. (15087) 294/C5
Webster, S. Dak. (57274) 298/P3
Webster, Texas (77598) 302/K2
Webster (co.), W. Va. 313/F6
Webster, Wis. (54893) 317/B4
Webster City, Iowa (50595) 229/F4
Webster Groves, Mo. (63119) 261/P3
Webster Mills, Pa. (†17233) 294/F6
Webster Springs, W. Va. (26288) 313/F6
Websterville, Vt. (05678) 268/B3
Wecota, S. Dak. (57480) 298/L3
Weda, Indon. 85/H5
Wedau, Papua 85/C7
Weddell (sea), Ant., 3/H10
Weddell (sea), Ant. 5/C16
Wedderburn, Oreg. (97491) 291/C5
Wedderburn, Vic. 97/B5
Wedel, W. Ger. 22/C2
Wedgefield, S.C. (29168) 296/F4
Wedgeport, N.S. 169/C5
Wedgeworth, Ala. (†36776) 194/C5
Wedington, Ark. (†72701) 203/B1
Wedowee, Ala. (36278) 194/H4
Weed, Calif. (96094) 204/C2
Weed, N. Mex. (88354) 274/D6
Weed (hills), Sask. 181/J5
Weed Heights, Nev. (89443) 266/B4
Weedon, Eng. 13/F5
Weedon-Centre, Que. 172/F4
Weedsport, N.Y. (13166) 276/G4
Weedville, Pa. (15868) 294/F3
Weehawken△, N.J. (07087) 273/C2
Week (isls.), Chile 138/D10
Weekapaug, R.I. (02891) 249/G7
Weekes, Sask. 181/J3
Weeki Wachee, Fla. (33512) 212/D3
Weeks, La. (†70569) 238/G7
Weeks (isl.), N.Z. 101/B1
Weeks, Nev. (†89447) 266/B3
Weeksbury, Ky. (41667) 237/R6
Weeks Mills, Maine (04361) 242/E7
Weeksville, N.C. (27909) 281/S2
Weems, Va. (22576) 307/P5
Weeping Water, Nebr. (68463) 264/J4
Weert, Neth. 27/H6
Weesatche, Texas (77993) 302/G9
Weesen, Switz. 39/H2
Weesp, Neth. 27/G4
Wee Waa, N.S.W. 97/E2
Wegdahl, Minn. (†56265) 254/C6
Weggis, Switz. 39/F2
Węgorzewo, Poland 47/E1
Wegra-Flat Creek, Ala. (†35129) 194/D3
Węgrów, Poland 47/E2
Weh (isl.), Indon. 85/B4
Weida, E. Ger. 22/D3
Weiden, W. Ger. 22/D4
Weidman, Mich. (48893) 250/D5
Weifang, China 77/J4
Weihai, China 77/K4
Wei Ho (riv.), China 77/G5
Weilburg, W. Ger. 22/C3
Weilheim, W. Ger. 22/D5
Weimar, E. Ger. 22/D3
Weimar, Texas (78962) 302/H8
Weiner, Ark. (72479) 203/J2
Weinert, Texas (76388) 302/E4
Weinfelden, Switz. 39/H1
Weingarten, W. Ger. 22/C5
Weinheim, W. Ger. 22/C4
Weining, China 77/F6
Weinsberg, W. Ger. 22/C4
Weipa, Aust. 88/G1
Weipa, Queens. 95/B2
Weippe, Idaho (83553) 220/C3
Weir (lake), Fla. 212/E2
Weir, Kans. (66781) 232/H4
Weir, Miss. (39772) 256/F4
Weirdale, Sask. 181/F2
Weirgor, Wis. (†54835) 317/D4
Weirsdale, Fla. (32695) 212/D3
Weirton, W. Va. (26062) 313/E2
Weirwood, Va. (23484) 307/S6
Weisburg, Ind. (47044) 227/H6
Weiser, Idaho (83672) 220/B5
Weiser (riv.), Idaho 220/B5
Weisi, China 77/E6
Weismes (Waimes), Belg. 27/J8
Weiss (res.), Ala. 194/G2
Weiss (res.), Ga. 216/B2
Weissenburg, W. Ger. 22/D4
Weissenfels, E. Ger. 22/D3
Weissensee, E. Ger. 22/F3
Weissenstein (mts.), Switz. 39/D2
Weisserstein (mt.), Belg. 27/J8
Weissert, Nebr. (68880) 264/E3
Weisshorn (mt.), Switz. 39/E4
Weisshorn (mt.), Switz. 39/J3
Weissmies (mt.), Switz. 39/F4
Weissport‡, Pa. (18235) 294/L4
Weisswasser, E. Ger. 22/F3
Weitchpec, Calif. (†95546) 204/B2
Weitensfeld, Austria 41/B3
Weitra, Austria 41/C2
Weiz, Austria 41/C3
Wejh, Saudi Ar. 59/C4
Wejherowo, Poland 47/D1
Wekusko, Man. 179/H3
Welaka, Fla. (32093) 212/E2
Welby‡, Colo. (†80022) 208/K3
Welby, Sask. 181/K5
Welch, Okla. (74369) 288/R1
Welch, Texas (79377) 302/B5
Welch, W. Va. (24801) 313/C8
Welches, Oreg. (†97067) 291/E2
Welchman Hall, Barb. 161/B8
Welchville, Maine (†04270) 242/C7
Welcome, La. (70093) 238/L3
Welcome, Md. (20693) 245/K7
Welcome, Minn. (56181) 254/D7
Welcome, N.C. (27374) 281/J3
Weld (co.), Colo. 208/L1
Weld△, Maine (04285) 242/C6
Weld (range), W. Aust. 92/B4
Welda, Kans. (66091) 232/G3
Weldon, Ark. (72177) 203/H3
Weldon, Calif. (93283) 204/G8
Weldon, Ill. (61882) 222/E3
Weldon, Iowa (50264) 229/F7
Weldon, N.C. (27890) 281/O2
Weldon, Sask. 181/F2
Weldon, Texas (75863) 302/J6
Weldona, Colo. (80653) 208/M2
Weldon Spring, Mo. (†63301) 261/O2
Weleetka, Okla. (74880) 288/O4
Welford, Aust. 88/G5
Welford, Queens. 95/C5
Welkom, S. Africa 118/D5
Welland (co.), Ont. 177/E4
Welland, Ont. 177/E5
Welland (riv.), 10/F4
Welland Junction, Ont. 177/E4
Wellandport, Ont. 177/E4
Wellborn, Fla. (32094) 212/D1
Wellersburg, Pa. (15564) 294/E6
Wellesley (isls.), Australia, 87/D7
Wellesley (isls.), Aust. 88/G3
Wellesley, Ont. 177/D4
Wellesley△, Mass. (02181) 249/B7
Wellesley (isls.), Queens. 95/A3
Wellesley Hills, Mass. (02181) 249/B7
Wellfleet△, Mass. (02667) 249/O5
Wellfleet (harb.), Mass. 249/O5
Wellfleet, Nebr. (69170) 264/D4
Wellford, S.C. (29385) 296/C2
Welling, Alta. 182/D5
Welling, Okla. (74471) 288/S3
Wellingborough, 10/F4
Wellingborough, Eng. 13/G5
Wellington (chan.), 163/G1
Wellington, Ala. (36279) 194/G3
Wellington, Aust. 88/H6
Wellington, Br. Col. 184/J3
Wellington (isl.), Chile, 120/C7
Wellington (isl.), Chile 138/D8
Wellington, Colo. (80549) 208/K1
Wellington (co.), Ont. 177/D4
Wellington, Ont. 177/G4
Wellington, Shropshire, Eng. 13/E5
Wellington, Somerset, Eng. 13/D7
Wellington, Ill. (60973) 222/F3
Wellington, Kans. (67152) 232/E4
Wellington‡, Ky. (†40201) 237/K4
Wellington, Ky. (40387) 237/O5
Wellington△, Maine (04990) 242/D5
Wellington, Mo. (64097) 261/E4
Wellington, N.S. 169/E4
Wellington, N.S.W. 97/E3
Wellington (bay), N.W.T. 187/H3
Wellington (chan.), N.W.T. 187/J2
Wellington (prov. dist.), N.Z. 101/E4
Wellington (cap.), N.Z., 3/T8
Wellington (cap.), N.Z., 87/H10
Wellington (cap.), N.Z. 101/A3
Wellington, Nev. (89444) 266/B4
Wellington, Ohio (44090) 284/F3
Wellington, P.E.I. 169/D2
Wellington, Shropshire, 10/E4
Wellington, Somerset, 10/E5
Wellington, S. Africa 118/B6
Wellington, Texas (79095) 302/D3
Wellington, Utah (84542) 304/D4
Wellington (lake), Vic. 97/D6
Wellman, Iowa (52356) 229/K6
Wellman (lake), Man. 179/B3
Wellman, Texas (79378) 302/B5
Wellpinit, Wash. (99040) 310/G3
Wells (lake), Aust. 88/C5
Wells, Br. Col. 184/G3
Wells, Norfolk, Eng. 13/H5
Wells, Somerset, Eng. 13/E6
Wells (co.), Ind. 227/G3
Wells, Kans. (67488) 232/E2
Wells△, Maine (04090) 242/B9
Wells, Maine (04090) 242/B9
Wells, Mich. (49894) 250/B3
Wells, Minn. (56097) 254/E7
Wells, Norfolk, 10/G4
Wells (co.), N. Dak. 283/L4
Wells, N.Y. (12190) 276/M4
Wells, Nev. (89835) 266/G1
Wells (lake), W. Aust. 92/C4
Wells, Somerset, 10/E5
Wells, Texas (75976) 302/J6
Wells△, Vt. (05774) 268/A5
Wells, Vt. (05774) 268/A5
Wells (riv.), Vt. 268/C3
Wells (dam), Wash. 310/F3
Wells Beach, Maine (04090) 242/B9
Wellsboro, Ind. (†46382) 227/D1
Wellsboro, Pa. (16901) 294/H2
Wells Bridge, N.Y. (13859) 276/K6
Wellsburg, Iowa (50680) 229/H4
Wellsburg, N. Dak. (†58341) 283/L4
Wellsburg, N.Y. (14894) 276/G6
Wellsburg, W. Va. (26070) 313/E2
Wellsford, Kans. (†67059) 232/C4
Wellsford, N.Z. 101/E2
Wells Gray Prov. Park, Br. Col. 184/H4
Wells River, Vt. (05081) 268/C3
Wellston, Mich. (49689) 250/D4
Wellston, Mo. (63112) 261/P3
Wellston, Ohio (45692) 284/F7
Wellston, Okla. (74881) 288/M3
Wellsville, Kans. (66092) 232/G3
Wellsville, Mo. (63384) 261/K4
Wellsville, N.Y. (14895) 276/E6
Wellsville, Ohio (43968) 284/J4
Wellsville, Pa. (17365) 294/J5
Wellsville, Utah (84339) 304/C2
Wellton, Ariz. (85356) 198/A6
Wellwood, Man. 179/C4
Wels, Austria 41/C2
Welsford, N. Br. 170/D3
Welsh, La. (70591) 238/E6
Welshfield, Ohio (†44021) 284/H3
Welshpool, 10/E4
Welshpool, N. Br. 170/D4
Welshpool, Wales 13/D5
Welton, Iowa (52774) 229/M5
Welty, Okla. (74882) 288/O3
Welwyn (Welwyn Garden City), Eng. 13/G6
Welwyn (Welwyn Garden City), 10/F5
Welwyn, Sask. 181/K5
Wem, Eng. 13/E5
Wembere (riv.), Tanz. 115/F4
Wembley, Alta. 182/A2
Wemme, Oreg. (97067) 291/E2
Wemmel, Belg. 27/B9
Wenamu (riv.), Guyana 131/A2
Wenas (creek), Wash. 310/E4
Wenasoga, Miss. (38886) 256/G1
Wenatchee, Wash., 188/B1
Wenatchee, Wash. (98801) 310/E3
Wenatchee (lake), Wash. 310/E3
Wenatchee (mts.), Wash. 310/E3
Wenatchee (riv.), Wash. 310/E3
Wenchi, Ghana 106/D7
Wenchow, China, 54/H5
Wenchow, China 77/J6
Wendel, Calif. (96136) 204/E3
Wendel, W. Va. (26450) 313/F4
Wendell, Idaho (83355) 220/D7
Wendell△, Mass. (01379) 249/E2
Wendell, Minn. (56590) 254/B4
Wendell, N.C. (27591) 281/N3
Wendell, N.H. (03783) 268/C5
Wendell Depot, Mass. (01380) 249/E2
Wenden, Ariz. (85357) 198/B5
Wendover, Ont. 177/J2
Wendover, Utah (84083) 304/A3
Wendover, Wyo. (†82214) 319/H3
Wendte, S. Dak. (†57532) 298/H5
Wenduine, Belg. 27/C6
Wenham△, Mass. (01984) 249/L2
Wenhsien, China 77/F5
Wenlock, Eng. 13/E5
Wenlock, 10/E4
Wenman (isl.), Ec. 128/B8
Wenona, Ga. (†31015) 216/E7
Wenona, Ill. (61377) 222/E2
Wenona, Md. (21870) 245/P8
Wenona, N.C. (†27860) 281/R3
Wenonah, Ill. (†62075) 222/D4
Wenonah, N.J. (08090) 273/C4
Wenshan, China 77/F7
Wentworth, Aust. 88/G6
Wentworth (co.), Ont. 177/D4
Wentworth, Mo. (64873) 261/D8
Wentworth, N.C. (27375) 281/K2
Wentworth△, N.H. (03282) 268/D4
Wentworth, N.H. (03282) 268/D4
Wentworth (lake), N.H. 268/E4
Wentworth, N.S. 169/E3
Wentworth, N.S.W. 97/B4
Wentworth, S. Dak. (57075) 298/R6
Wentworth, Wis. (54894) 317/C2
Wentworth Centre, N.S. 169/E3
Wentworths Location△, N.H. (†03579) 268/E2
Wentworths Location, N.H. (†03579) 268/E2
Wentzville, Mo. (63385) 261/M2
Weobley, Eng. 13/E5
Weogufka, Ala. (35183) 194/F4
Weohyakapka (lake), Fla. 212/E4
Weott, Calif. (95571) 204/A3
Wepawaug (riv.), Conn. 210/C3
Wequetequock, Conn. (†02891) 210/H3
Werdau, E. Ger. 22/E3
Werder, E. Ger. 22/E2
Werner, N. Dak. (†58636) 283/F5
Wernersville, Pa. (19565) 294/K5
Wernigerode, E. Ger. 22/D3
Werra (riv.), E. Ger. 22/D3
Werra (riv.), W. Ger. 22/D3
Werribee, Aust. 88/L7
Werribee (riv.), Aust. 88/L7
Werribee, Vic. 97/C5
Werribee South, Vic. 97/C5
Werrimull, Vic. 97/A4
Werris Creek, N.S.W. 97/F2
Wertheim, W. Ger. 22/C4
Wervik, Belg. 27/B7
Wesco, Mo. (65586) 261/K7
Wesel, W. Ger. 22/B3
Weser (riv.), Ger., 7/E3
Weser (riv.), W. Ger. 22/C2
Weskan, Kans. (67762) 232/A3
Weslaco, Texas (78596) 302/G11
Weslemkoon, Ont. 177/G3
Weslemkoon (lake), Ont. 177/G2
Wesley, Ark. (72773) 203/C1
Wesley, Dominica 161/F5
Wesley, Ga. (†30401) 216/H6
Wesley, Iowa (50483) 229/E2
Wesley△, Maine (04686) 242/H6
Wesley, Maine (04686) 242/H6
Wesleyville, Newf. 166/D4
Wesleyville, Pa. (16510) 294/C1
Wes-Rand, S. Africa 118/G6
Wessel (isls.), Australia, 87/D7
Wessel (cape), Aust. 88/F2
Wessel (isls.), Aust. 88/F2
Wessel (cape), No. Terr. 93/E1
Wessel (isls.), No. Terr. 93/E1
Wessington, S. Dak. (57381) 298/M5
Wessington Springs, S. Dak. (57382) 298/M5
Wesson, Ark. (71771) 203/E7
Wesson, Miss. (39191) 256/D7
West (riv.), Conn. 210/E3
West (riv.), Conn. 210/D3
West (pt.), Que. 174/E3
West, Iowa (52357) 229/J5
West (bay), La. 238/M8
West (isl.), Mass. 249/L6
West (riv.), Mass. 249/H4
West, Miss. (39192) 256/E4
West (isls.), N. Br. 170/D4
West (bay), N.S. 169/G3
West (pt.), N.S. 169/H5
West (riv.), N.S. 169/F3
West (cape), N.Z. 101/A6
West (pt.), P.E.I. 169/D2
West, Texas (76691) 302/G6
West (bay), Texas 302/K8
West (riv.), Vt. 268/B5
West Acton, Mass. (01720) 249/H3
West Alexander, Pa. (15376) 294/B5
West Alexandria, Ohio (45381) 284/A6
West Allis, Wis. (53214) 317/L1
Westalton, Mo. (63386) 261/R2
West Alton, N.H. (†03246) 268/E4
West Amboy, N.Y. (†13493) 276/J4
West Amityville‡, N.Y. (†11701) 276/O9
West Arichat, N.S. 169/G3
West Ashford, Conn. (†06251) 210/G1
West Aspetuck (riv.), Conn. 210/B2
West Athens‡, Calif. (†90301) 204/C11
West Athens, Maine (†04912) 242/D6
West Auburndale‡, Fla. (†33823) 212/E3
West Augusta, Va. (24485) 307/K4
West Avon, Conn. (†06001) 210/D1
West Babylon‡, N.Y. (11704) 276/O9
West Baden Springs, Ind. (47469) 227/D7
West Baines (riv.), No. Terr. 93/A4
West Baldwin, Maine (04091) 242/B8
Westbank, Br. Col. 184/H5
West Baraboo, Wis. (†53913) 317/G9
West Barnet, Vt. (05870) 268/C3
West Barnstable, Mass. (02668) 249/N6
West Barrington, R.I. (02890) 249/J5
West Bath△, Maine (†04530) 242/D8
West Baton Rouge (par.), La. 238/H6
Westbay, Fla. (32401) 212/C6
West Bay, N.S. 169/G3
West Bay, Newf. 166/C3
West Bay Road, N.S. 169/G3
West Bend, Iowa (50597) 229/D3
Westbend, Ky. (40388) 237/N5
West Bend, Sask. 181/H4
West Bend, Wis. (53095) 317/K9
West Bengal (state), India 68/F4
West Berbice (dist.), Guyana 131/C2
West Berkshire, Vt. (05493) 268/B2
West Berlin, Mass. (†01503) 249/H3
West Bethel, Maine (04286) 242/B7
West Blocton, Ala. (35184) 194/D4
West Bloomfield, Wis. (†54983) 317/J7
Westboro△, Mass. (01581) 249/H3
Westboro, Mass. (01581) 249/H3
Westboro, Mo. (64498) 261/B1
Westboro, Ohio (45175) 284/C7
Westboro, Wis. (54490) 317/F5
West Bountiful, Utah (†84087) 304/B3
Westbourne, Man. 179/D4
Westbourne, Tenn. (†37766) 237/O7
West Boxford, Mass. (01885) 249/K2
West Boylston△, Mass. (01583) 249/G3
West Bradenton‡, Fla. (†33505) 212/D4
West Braintree (Braintree P.O.), Vt. (†05646) 268/B4
West Branch (res.), Conn. 210/C1
West Branch, Lièvre (riv.), Que. 172/B2
West Branch, Iowa (52358) 229/L5
West Branch, Farmington (riv.), Mass. 249/B4
West Branch, Mich. (48661) 250/E4
West Branch, Rocky (riv.), Ohio 284/G10
West Branch, Susquehanna (riv.), Pa. 294/G3
West Brattleboro, Vt. (05301) 268/B6
West Brentwood, N.H. (†03848) 268/E6
West Brewster, Mass. (†02631) 249/O5
Westbridge, Br. Col. 184/H5
West Bridgewater△, Mass. (02379) 249/K4
West Bridgewater, Mass. (02379) 249/K4
West Bridgewater, Vt. (†05034) 268/B4
West Bromwich, Eng. 13/F5
West Bromwich, 10/G3
Westbrook△, Conn. (06498) 210/F3
Westbrook, Conn. (06498) 210/F3
Westbrook, Maine (04092) 242/C8
Westbrook, Minn. (56183) 254/C6
Westbrook, N.S. 169/D3
Westbrook, Texas (79565) 302/C5
West Brookfield△, Mass. (01585) 249/F4
West Brookfield, Mass. (01585) 249/F4
West Brooklyn, Ill. (61378) 222/D2
West Brooksville, Maine (†04617) 242/F7
West Brownsville, Pa. (15417) 294/C5
West Buechel‡, Ky. (†40218) 237/K4
West Burke, Vt. (05871) 268/C2
West Burlington, Iowa (52655) 229/L7
West Burlington‡, N.C. (†27215) 281/L2
West Burra (isl.), Scot. 15/M3
West Bury, Eng. 13/E6
Westbury, N.Y. (11590) 276/R7
Westbury, 10/E5
Westbury, Tas. 99/C3
West Buxton, Maine (04093) 242/B8
Westby, Mont. (59275) 262/M2
Westby, Wis. (54667) 317/E8
West Calder, Scot. 15/K8
West Caldwell, N.J. (07006) 273/A2
West Campton, N.H. (03228) 268/D4
West Canaan, N.H. (03741) 268/C4
West Cape May, N.J. (†08204) 273/D6
West Carroll (par.), La. 238/H1
West Carrollton, Ohio (45449) 284/B6
West Carson‡, Calif. (†90744) 204/C11
West Carthage, N.Y. (†13619) 276/J3
West Charleston, Vt. (05872) 268/C2
West Chatham, Mass. (02669) 249/O6
West Chazy, N.Y. (12992) 276/N1
West Chelmsford, Mass. (†01824) 249/J2
West Cheshire, Conn. (†06410) 210/D3
Westchester, Conn. (†06474) 210/F2
Westchester, Ill. (60153) 222/A2
West Chester, Iowa (52359) 229/K6
Westchester (co.), N.Y. 276/N8
West Chester, Ohio (45069) 284/C9
West Chester, Pa. (19380) 294/L6
West Chesterfield, Mass. (01084) 249/C3
Westchester Station (North Westchester), Conn. (†06474) 210/F2
Westchester Station, N.S. 169/E3
West Chicago, Ill. (60185) 222/E2
West Chop (pt.), Mass. 249/M7
West City, Ill. (†62812) 222/E5
West Clarkston-Highland‡, Wash. (†99403) 310/H4
Westcliffe, Colo. (81252) 208/H6
West College Corner, Ind. (†47353) 227/H5
West Columbia, S.C. (29169) 296/E4
West Columbia, Texas (77486) 302/J8
West Columbia, W. Va. (25287) 313/B5
West Compton‡, Calif. (†90220) 204/C11
West Concord, Mass. (01781) 249/A6
West Concord, Minn. (55985) 254/F6
West Concord‡, N.C. (28025) 281/H4
West Conshohocken‡, Pa. (19428) 294/M5
West Corinth, Vt. (†05039) 268/C3
West Cornwall, Conn. (06796) 210/B1
West Cornwall, Vt. (†05753) 268/A4
West Cote Blanche (bay), La. 238/G7
Westcott, Alta. 182/C4
Westcott Cove (bay), Conn. 210/A4
West Covina, Calif. (*91790) 204/D10
Westcreek, Colo. (†80135) 208/J4
West Creek, N.J. (08092) 273/E4
West Crossett, Ark. (†71635) 203/F7
West Cummington, Mass. (01265) 249/B3
West Danville, Vt. (05873) 268/C3
West Demerara (dist.), Guyana 131/B3
West Dennis, Mass. (02670) 249/O6
West Derry (Derry), N.H. (†03038) 268/E6
West Derry‡, Pa. (†15627) 294/D3
West Des Moines, Iowa (50265) 229/F5
West Dover, N.S. 169/E4
West Dover, Vt. (05356) 268/B6
West Dublin, N.S. 169/D4
West Dudley, Mass. (†01550) 249/F4
West Dummerston, Vt. (05357) 268/B6
West Dundee (Dundee), Ill. (†60118) 222/E1
West Easton‡, Pa. (†18042) 294/M4
West Eau Gallie‡, Fla. (32935) 212/F3
West Elizabeth, Pa. (15088) 294/C5
West Elkton, Ohio (45070) 284/A6
West Elmira, N.Y. (†14901) 276/G6
West Eminence, Mo. (†65466) 261/J8
Westend, Calif. (93564) 204/H8
West End, V.I. (Br.) 161/C4
West End‡, Fla. (32446) 212/D2
West End‡, Ill. (†61101) 222/D1
West End, N.C. (27376) 281/K4
West End‡, N.Y. (†13820) 276/K6
West End-Cobb Town, Ala. (†36201) 194/G3
Westende, Belg. 27/B6
Westend Saltpond (lag.), V.I.(U.S.) 161/E4
West Enfield, Maine (04493) 242/F5
West Epping, N.H. (†03042) 268/E5
Wester Eems (chan.), Neth. 27/K1
Westerland, W. Ger. 22/C1
Westerlo, Belg. 27/F6
Westerlo, N.Y. (12193) 276/M6
Westerly△, R.I. (02891) 249/G7
Westerly, R.I. (02891) 249/G7
Western (head), N.S. 169/D5
Western, Nebr. (68464) 264/G4
Western (state), Nigeria 106/E7
Western (prov.), Kenya 115/G3
Western Australia (state), Australia, 87/C8
WESTERN AUSTRALIA, 88/C5
WESTERN AUSTRALIA, 92
Western Bay, Newf. 166/D2
Western Dvina (riv.), U.S.S.R. 48/C4
Western Dvina (riv.), U.S.S.R. 52/C3
Western Dvina (riv.), U.S.S.R. 53/C2
Western Ghats (mts.), India 68/C5
Western Grove, Ark. (72685) 203/D1
Westernport, Md. (21562) 245/B3
Western Port (inlet), Vic. 97/C6
Western Samoa, 3/A6
Western Samoa, 87/J7
Western Scheldt (De Honte) (bay), Neth. 27/D6
Western Shore, N.S. 169/D4
Western Shoshone Ind. Res., Idaho 220/B7
Western Shoshone Ind. Res., Nev. 266/E1
Western Springs, Ill. (60558) 222/A2
Western State Hospital, Tenn. (38074) 237/C10

White 457

Westernville, N.Y. (13486) 276/K4
Westerose, Alta. 182/C3
Westerstede, W. Ger. 22/B2
Westervelt, Ill. (62574) 222/E4
Westerville, Nebr. (68881) 264/E3
Westerville, Ohio (43081) 284/D5
Westerville, S. Dak. (†57069) 298/P8
Westerwald (for.), W. Ger. 22/B3
West Fairlee∆, Vt. (05083) 268/C4
West Fairlee, Vt. (05083) 268/C4
West Fairview‡, Pa. (17025) 294/J5
West Falkland (isl.), Falk Is., 120/D8
Westfall, Kans. (67489) 232/D3
Westfall, Oreg. (97920) 291/K3
West Falmouth, Mass. (02574) 249/M6
West Fargo, N. Dak. (58078) 283/S6
West Fargo Industrial Park, N. Dak. (†58078) 283/S6
West Farmington, Maine (04992) 242/C6
West Farmington, Ohio (44491) 284/J3
West Feliciana (par.), La. 238/H5
Westfield, Conn. (†06457) 210/E2
Westfield, Ill. (62474) 222/F4
Westfield, Ind. (46074) 227/E4
Westfield, Iowa (51062) 229/A3
Westfield∆, Maine (04787) 242/G2
Westfield, Mass. (01085) 249/D4
Westfield (riv.), Mass. 249/C3
Westfield, N.C. (27053) 281/H2
Westfield, N. Dak. (†58542) 283/K7
Westfield, N.J. (*07090) 273/E2
Westfield, N.S. 169/C4
Westfield, N.Y. (14787) 276/A6
Westfield, Pa. (16950) 294/H2
Westfield∆, Vt. (05874) 268/C2
Westfield, Vt. (05874) 268/C2
Westfield, Wis. (53964) 317/H8
Westfield Centre, N. Br. 170/D3
West Finley, Pa. (15377) 294/B5
Westfir, Oreg. (97492) 291/E4
West Flanders (prov.), Belg. 27/B7
Westford, Conn. (†06076) 210/G1
Westford∆, Mass. (01886) 249/J2
Westford, Pa. (16134) 294/A2
Westford∆, Vt. (05494) 268/A2
Westford, Vt. (05494) 268/A2
West Fork, Ark. (72774) 203/B2
West Fork, Ind. (47178) 227/D8
West Fork, White (riv.), Ind. 227/C7
West Fork, Bruneau (riv.), Nev. 266/F1
West Fork, Trinity (riv.), Texas 302/F2
West Fork (riv.), W. Va. 313/E5
West Forks, Maine (04985) 242/D5
West Frankfort, Ill. (62896) 222/E6
West Franklin, Ind. (†47620) 227/B9
West Franklin, Maine (†04634) 242/G6
West Frisian (isls.), Neth. 27/F2
West Gardiner∆, Maine (†04345) 242/D7
West Garland, Maine (†04930) 242/E5
Westgat (chan.), Neth. 27/F3
Westgate, Iowa (50681) 229/K3
Westgate, Man. 179/A2
West Germany, 7/E3
WEST GERMANY, 22
West Glacier, Mont. (59936) 262/C2
West Glen Park‡, Ind. (†46401) 227/C1
West Glens Falls, N.Y. (†12801) 276/N4
West Glocester, R.I. (†02814) 249/G5
West Glover, Vt. (05875) 268/C2
West Gorham, Maine (†04038) 242/C8
West Goshen, Conn. (†06797) 210/B1
West Gouldsboro, Maine (†04607) 242/G7
West Granby, Conn. (06090) 210/D1
West Grand (lake), Maine 242/H5
West Granville, Mass. (†01034) 249/C4
West Green, Ga. (31567) 216/G7
West Greene, Ala. (35491) 194/B5
West Green Harbour, N.S. 169/C5
West Groton, Mass. (01472) 249/H2
West Grove, Iowa (52538) 229/J7
West Grove, Pa. (19390) 294/L6
West Gulfport, Miss. (†39501) 256/F10
West Halifax, Vt. (05358) 268/B6
West Hamlin, W. Va. (25571) 313/B6
West Hampden, Maine (†04445) 242/E6
West Hampstead, N.H. (03889) 268/E6
Westhampton∆, Mass. (†01027) 249/C3
Westhampton, N.Y. (11977) 276/P9
Westhampton Beach, N.Y. (11978) 276/P9
West Hanover, Mass. (02339) 249/L4
West Harrison, Ind. (†45030) 227/H6
West Hartford∆, Conn. (06107) 210/D1
West Hartford, Vt. (05084) 268/C4
West Hartland, Conn. (06091) 210/D1
West Harwich, Mass. (02671) 249/O6
West Haven, Conn. (06516) 210/D3
Westhaven, Ill. (†60462) 222/A2
West Haven∆, Vt. (†05743) 268/A4
West Haven, Vt. (†05743) 268/A4
West Haverstraw‡, N.Y. (10993) 276/M8
West Hawk (lake), Man. 179/G5
Westhawk Lake, Man. 179/G5
West Hawley, Mass. (†01339) 249/C2
Westhazel, Sask. 181/B2
West Hazleton, Pa. (18201) 294/K4
West Helena, Ark. (72390) 203/J4
West Hempstead‡, N.Y. (11552) 276/R7
West Henniker, N.H. (†03242) 268/D5
West Hickory, Pa. (16370) 294/C2
West Hill (pond), Conn. 210/C1
West Hillsborough‡, N.C. (†27278) 281/L2
Westhoff, Texas (77994) 302/G8
West Hollywood, Calif. (†90025) 204/B10
Westholme, Br. Col. 184/J3
West Homestead‡, Pa. (†15120) 294/B7
Westhope, N. Dak. (58793) 283/H2
West Hopkinton, N.H. (03283) 268/D5
West Hurley, N.Y. (12491) 276/M6
West Ice Shelf, Ant. 5/C5
West Indies (isls.), 3/G5
WEST INDIES, 156
West Irian (reg.), Indon., 3/R6
West Irian (reg.), Indon. 85/J6
West Irvine, Ky. (40491) 237/N5
West Islip‡, N.Y. (11795) 276/O9
West Jefferson, Ala. (†35005) 194/D4
West Jefferson, N.C. (28694) 281/F2
West Jefferson, Ohio (43162) 284/D6
West Jersey, Ill. (†61483) 222/D2
West Jonesport Maine (04649) 242/H6
West Jordan, Utah (84084) 304/B3
Westkapelle, Neth. 27/C5
West Kennebunk, Maine (04094) 242/B9
West Kilbride, Scot. 15/G8
West Kildonan, Man. 179/E5
West Kingston, R.I. (02892) 249/H7
West Kittanning, Pa. (†16201) 294/C4
West Korea (bay), China 77/K4
West Korea (bay), N. Korea 81/B4
West La Crosse, Wis. (†54601) 317/D8
West Lafayette, Ind. (47906) 227/D4
West Lafayette, Ohio (43845) 284/G5
Westlake, La. (70669) 238/D6
West Lake (reg.), Tanz. 115/F3
Westlake, Ohio (44145) 284/G9
Westlake, Oreg. (97493) 291/C4
Westlake, Texas (†76101) 302/F1
Westlake, Wash. (†98837) 310/F3
West Lake Hills‡, Texas (†78701) 302/G7
Westland, Mich. (48185) 250/F6
Westland (prov. dist.), N.Z. 101/C5
Westland, Pa. (15378) 294/B5
West Lanham Hills, Md. (†20784) 245/G4
West Laurel‡, Md. (†20810) 245/L4
West Lawn, Pa. (19609) 294/K5
West Lawrencetown, N.S. 169/E4
West Lebanon, Ind. (47991) 227/C4
West Lebanon, Maine (04027) 242/B9
West Lebanon, N.H. (03784) 268/C4
West Ledge (flats), Berm. 156/G3
West Leechburg, Pa. (†15656) 294/C4
West Leipsic, Ohio (†45856) 284/B3
West Leyden, N.Y. (13489) 276/J4
West Liberty, Ill. (62475) 222/E5
West Liberty, Iowa (52776) 229/L5
West Liberty, Ky. (41472) 237/P5
West Liberty, Ohio (43357) 284/C5
West Liberty, Pa. (†16057) 294/B4
West Liberty, W. Va. (26074) 313/E2
West Lima, Wis. (54668) 317/E8
West Line, Mo. (64791) 261/C5
Westline, Pa. (16751) 294/E2
West Linn, Oreg. (97068) 291/B2
West Linton, 10/C1
West Linton, Scot. 15/K8
West Liscomb (riv.), N.S. 169/F3
West Loch (inlet), Hawaii 218/A3
West Loch Tarbert (inlet), Scot. 15/B4
Westlock, Alta. 182/C2
West Logan, W. Va. (25601) 313/C7
West Long (lake), N. Br. 170/D3
West Long Branch, N.J. (07764) 273/F3
West Lorne, Ont. 177/C5
West Los Angeles, Calif. (90025) 204/B10
West Lothian (co.), Scot. 15/J8
West Louisville, Ky. (42377) 237/G5
West Lubec, Maine (†04652) 242/J6
West Manchester, Ohio (45382) 284/A6
West Mansfield, Mass. (02083) 249/K5
West Mansfield, Ohio (43358) 284/C5
West Marion‡, N.C. (†28752) 281/E3
West Mayfield‡, Pa. (†15010) 294/B4
Westmeath, Ont. 177/H2
Westmeath (co.), Ire. 17/G5
West Medway, Mass. (†02053) 249/J4
West Melbourne, Fla. (†32901) 212/F3
West Memphis, Ark. (72301) 203/K3
Westmere‡, N.Y. (†12201) 276/N5
West Mersea, 10/G5
West Miami, Fla. (†33101) 212/B5
West Middlesex, Pa. (16159) 294/B3
West Middleton, Ind. (46995) 227/E4
West Middletown, Pa. (15379) 294/A5
West Mifflin, Pa. (15122) 294/C7
West Milan, N.H. (†03588) 268/E2
West Milford, N.J. (07480) 273/E1
West Milford, W. Va. (26451) 313/F4
West Millbury, Mass. (01586) 249/G4
West Millgrove, Ohio (43467) 284/C3
West Mills, Maine (†04938) 242/C6
West Milton, Ohio (45383) 284/B6
West Milton, Pa. (17886) 294/J3
West Milwaukee, Wis. (†53201) 317/L1
West Mineral, Kans. (66782) 232/H4
West Minot, Maine (04288) 242/C7
Westminster, Calif. (92683) 204/D11
Westminster, Colo. (80030) 208/J3
Westminster, Conn. (†06331) 210/G2
Westminster∆, Mass. (01473) 249/G2
Westminster, Mass. (01473) 249/G2
Westminster, Md. (21157) 245/L2
Westminster, 10/B5
Westminster, S.C. (29693) 296/A2
Westminster‡, Texas (75096) 302/H4
Westminster∆, Vt. (05158) 268/C5
Westminster, Vt. (05158) 268/C5
Westminster Station, Vt. (05159) 268/B5
Westminster West, Vt. (†05158) 268/B5
West Modesto‡, Calif. (†95350) 204/D6
West Monroe, La. (71291) 238/F1
Westmont‡, Calif. (†90301) 204/C11
Westmont, Ill. (60559) 222/A2
Westmont, Pa. (†15901) 294/D5
West Monterey, Pa. (16060) 294/C3
Westmore∆, Vt. (†05860) 268/C2
Westmore, Vt. (†05860) 268/C2
Westmoreland, Kans. (66549) 232/F2
Westmoreland∆, N.H. (03467) 268/C6
Westmoreland, N.H. (03467) 268/C6
Westmoreland, Queens. 95/A3
Westmoreland (co.), Pa. 294/D5
Westmoreland, Tenn. (37186) 237/J7
Westmoreland (co.), Va. 307/P4
Westmorland, Calif. (92281) 204/K10
Westmorland (co.), Eng. 13/E3
Westmorland (co.), N. Br. 170/F2
Westmount, Que. 172/H4
Westmount, N.S. 169/H2
West Mountain‡, Texas (†75647) 302/K5
West Musquash (lake), Maine 242/H5
West Mystic, Conn. (06388) 210/H3
West Newbury∆, Mass. (01985) 249/L1
West Newbury, Vt. (05085) 268/C3
West Newfield, Maine (04095) 242/B8
West Newton, Mass. (†02165) 249/B7
West Newton, Pa. (15089) 294/C5
West New York, N.J. (07093) 273/C2
West Nicholson, Rhod. 118/D4
West Nishnabotna (riv.), Iowa 229/C6
West Norwalk, Conn. (†06856) 210/B4
West Nottingham, N.H. (03291) 268/E5
West Nyack‡, N.Y. (10994) 276/N8
West Okoboji, Iowa (†51351) 229/C2
West Olive, Mich. (49460) 250/C6
Weston, Ala. (†35570) 194/B2
Weston, Colo. (81091) 208/K8
Weston∆, Conn. (06880) 210/B4
Weston, Conn. (06880) 210/B4
Weston, Ont. 177/J4
Weston, Ga. (31832) 216/C7
Weston, Idaho (83286) 220/F7
Weston, Ill. (†61726) 222/E3
Weston, Iowa (†51576) 229/B6
Weston∆, Maine (04494) 242/H4
Weston∆, Mass. (02193) 249/B6
Weston, Mich. (49289) 250/E7
Weston, Mo. (64098) 261/C4
Weston, N.S. 169/D3
Weston, Nebr. (68070) 264/H3
Weston, Malaysia 85/F4
Weston, Ohio (43569) 284/C3
Weston, Oreg. (97886) 291/J2
Weston, Pa. (18256) 294/K4
Weston∆, Vt. (05161) 268/B5
Weston, Vt. (05161) 268/B5
Weston, W. Va. (26452) 313/F4
Weston, Wis. (†54751) 317/C6
Weston, Wis. (†54476) 317/G6
Weston (co.), Wyo. 319/H2
Weston, Wyo. (82731) 319/G1
Westonaria, S. Africa 118/H7
Westons Mills, N.Y. (14788) 276/D6
Weston-super-Mare, Eng. 13/E6
Weston-super-Mare, 10/E5
West Orange, N.J. (07052) 273/A2
West Orange, Texas (77630) 302/L7
West Ossipee, N.H. (03890) 268/E4
Westover, Ala. (35185) 194/E4
Westover, Md. (21871) 245/R8
Westover, Pa. (16692) 294/E4
Westover, S. Dak. (†57559) 298/H6
Westover, W. Va. (26505) 313/G3
Westover A.F.B., Mass. 249/D4
Westover Hills, Texas (†76101) 302/E2
West Paducah, Ky. (42086) 237/D6
West Palm Beach, Fla., 146/K7
West Palm Beach, Fla., 188/K5
West Palm Beach, Fla. (*33401) 212/F5
West Palm Beach (canal), Fla. 212/F5
West Panama City Beach, Fla. (32401) 212/C6
West Paris∆, Maine (04289) 242/B7
West Paterson, N.J. (07424) 273/B2
West Pawlet, Vt. (05775) 268/A5
West Pelzer, S.C. (29669) 296/B2
West Pembroke, Maine (†04666) 242/J6
West Pensacola, Fla. (32505) 212/B6
West Peoria‡, Ill. (†61601) 222/D3
West Peru, Maine (04290) 242/C7
West Peterborough, N.H. (03468) 268/C6
West Petersburg, Alaska (†99833) 196/M1
Westphalia, Ind. (47596) 227/C7
Westphalia, Iowa (51578) 229/C5
Westphalia, Kans. (66093) 232/G3
Westphalia, Mich. (48894) 250/E6
Westphalia, Mo. (65085) 261/J6
West Pittsburg, Calif. (94565) 204/K1
West Pittsburg, Pa. (16160) 294/B4
West Pittston‡, Pa. (18643) 294/L3
West Plains (Plains), Kans. (67869) 232/B4
West Plains, Mo. (65775) 261/J9
West Plains, Sask. 181/B6
West Point (res.), Ala. 194/J4
West Point (mt.), Alaska 196/K2
West Point, Ark. (72178) 203/G3
West Point, Calif. (95255) 204/E5
West Point, Ga. (31833) 216/B5
West Point (res.), Ga. 216/B4
West Point, Ill. (62380) 222/B3
Westpoint, Ind. (47992) 227/C4
West Point, Iowa (52656) 229/K7
West Point, Ky. (40177) 237/J4
West Point, Miss. (39773) 256/G3
West Point, N.Y. (10996) 276/M8
West Point, Nebr. (68788) 264/H3
West Point, Ohio (44492) 284/J4
Westpoint, Tenn. (38486) 237/G10
West Point‡, Utah (†84015) 304/B2
West Point, Va. (23181) 307/P6
West Pointe a la Hache, La. (†70082) 238/L7
West Poland, Maine (04291) 242/C7
Westport, Calif. (95488) 204/B4
Westport∆, Conn. (06880) 210/B4
Westport, Ont. 177/H3
Westport, 10/B4
Westport, Ind. (47283) 227/F6
Westport, Ire. 17/C4
Westport, Ky. (40077) 237/K4
Westport∆, Mass. (02790) 249/K6
Westport, Minn. (56388) 254/C5
Westport, N.H. (†03470) 268/C6
Westport, N.S. 169/B4
Westport, N.Y. (12993) 276/N2
Westport, N.Z. 101/C4
Westport, Oreg. (97016) 291/D1
Westport, Pa. (17778) 294/G3
Westport, S. Dak. (57481) 298/M2
Westport, Tenn. (38387) 237/E9
Westport, Wash. (98595) 310/A4
West Portal, N.J. (†08802) 273/D2
Westport P.O. (North Westport), Mass. (02790) 249/K6
Westport Point, Mass. (02791) 249/K6
West Portsmouth, Ohio (†45662) 284/D8
West Pubnico, N.S. 169/C5
Westpunt, Neth. Ant. 161/D10
West Quaco, N. Br. 170/E3
West Quoddy (head), Maine 242/K6
Westray (isl.), 10/E1
Westray (firth), Scot. 15/K1
Westray (isl.), Scot. 15/K1
West Reading‡, Pa. (19602) 294/L5
West Redding, Conn. (06896) 210/B3
Westree, Ont. 177/J5
West Richland, Wash. (99352) 310/F4
West Ridge, Ark. (72391) 203/K2
West Rindge, N.H. (†03461) 268/C6
West River, Md. (20881) 245/M5
West River Station, N.S. 169/F3
West Road (riv.), Br. Col. 184/E3
West Rockport, Maine (04865) 242/E7
West Rock Ridge (hills), Conn. 210/D3
West Rumney, N.H. (†03266) 268/D4
West Rupert, Vt. (05776) 268/A5
West Rushville, Ohio (43163) 284/E6
West Rutland∆, Vt. (05777) 268/A4
West Rutland, Vt. (05777) 268/A4
West Rye, N.H. (†03870) 268/F6
West Sacramento, Calif. (95691) 204/B8
West Saint Mary's (riv.), N.S. 169/F3
West Saint-Modeste, Newf. 166/C3
West Saint Paul, Minn. (55118) 254/G5
West Salem, Ill. (62476) 222/F5
West Salem, Ohio (44287) 284/F4
West Salem, Wis. (54669) 317/D8
West Salisbury, Pa. (15565) 294/D6
West Salisbury, Vt. (†05769) 268/A4
West Sand Lake‡, N.Y. (12196) 276/N5
West Sayville, N.Y. (11796) 276/O9
West Scarborough, Maine (04074) 242/C8
West Sebois, Maine (†04484) 242/F4
West Seneca∆, N.Y. (14224) 276/C5
West Shoal (lake), Man. 179/E4
Westside, Iowa (51467) 229/C4
West Side, Oreg. (†97630) 291/G5
West Siloam Springs, Okla. (†72761) 288/S2
West Simsbury, Conn. (06092) 210/D1
West Sister (isl.), Ohio 284/D2
West Somerset, Ky. (42564) 237/M6
West Springfield∆, Mass. (01089) 249/D4
West Springfield, N.H. (03284) 268/C5
West Springfield, Pa. (16443) 294/B2
West Springfield‡, Va. (22152) 307/O3
West Springs, S.C. (†29374) 296/D2
West Stafford, Conn. (†06076) 210/F1
West Statesville‡, N.C. (28677) 281/H3
West Stewartstown, N.H. (03597) 268/E2
West Stockbridge∆, Mass. (01266) 249/A3
West Stockholm, N.Y. (13696) 276/K1
West Suffield, Conn. (06093) 210/E1
West Sumner, Maine (04292) 242/B7
West Sunbury, Pa. (16061) 294/C3
West Swan (riv.), Minn. 254/F3
West Swanzey, N.H. (03469) 268/C6
West Tapinac, Phil. 82/C3
West Tawakoni‡, Texas (†75474) 302/J4
West Terre Haute, Ind. (47885) 227/B6
West-Terschelling, Neth. 27/G2
West Thompson, Conn. (†06255) 210/H1
West Thornton, N.H. (03285) 268/D4
West Thumb-Grant Village, Wyo. (†82190) 319/B1
West Tisbury∆, Mass. (02575) 249/M7
West Torrens, Aust. 88/D7
West Torrens, S. Aust. 94/A8
West Torrington, Conn. (†06790) 210/C1
West Townsend, Mass. (01474) 249/H2
West Townshend, Vt. (05359) 268/B5
West Tremont, Maine (04690) 242/G7
West Trenton, N.J. (08628) 273/D3
West Union, Ill. (62477) 222/F4
West Union, Iowa (52175) 229/K3
West Union, Minn. (56389) 254/C5
West Union, Ohio (45693) 284/C8
West Union, S.C. (29696) 296/B2
West Union, W. Va. (26456) 313/E4
West Unity, Ohio (43570) 284/B2
West University Place, Texas (†77001) 302/J2
West Upton-Upton, Mass. (01587) 249/H4
Westvale‡, N.Y. (†13201) 276/H4
West Valley, N.Y. (14171) 276/C6
West Vancouver, Br. Col. 184/K3
West Van Lear, Ky. (41268) 237/R5
Westview, Ohio (†44138) 284/G10
West View, Pa. (15229) 294/B6
Westview‡, S.C. (†29301) 296/D2
Westville, Fla. (32464) 212/C6
Westville, Ill. (61883) 222/F3
Westville, Ind. (46391) 227/D1
Westville, N.H. (03892) 268/E6
Westville, N.J. (08093) 273/B3
Westville, N.S. 169/F3
Westville, Okla. (74965) 288/S2
Westville, Pa. (15869) 294/E3
Westville, S.C. (29175) 296/F3
West Virginia, 188/K3
WEST VIRGINIA, 313
West Virginia (state), U.S., 146/K6
Westward Ho, Alta. 182/C4
West Wardsboro, Vt. (05360) 268/B5
West Wareham, Mass. (02576) 249/L5
West Warren, Mass. (01092) 249/F4
West Warwick, R.I. (02893) 249/H6
West Weber, Utah (†84401) 304/B2
Westwego, La. (70094) 238/O4
West Wenatchee, Wash. (†98801) 310/E3
West Whittier-Los Nietos‡, Calif. (90606) 204/C11
West Wildwood, N.J. (†08260) 273/D6
West Willington, Conn. (06279) 210/F1
West Windham, N.H. (†03087) 268/E6
West Winfield, N.Y. (13491) 276/K5
West Winfield, Pa. (16062) 294/C4
West Wingham, Alta. 182/E4
West Winter Haven‡, Fla. (†33880) 212/E3
West Winterport, Maine (†04496) 242/E6
Westwold, Br. Col. 184/G5
Westwood, Calif. (96137) 204/D3
Westwood, Calif. (96137) 204/B10
Westwood‡, Kans. (†66101) 232/H2
Westwood, Ky. (41101) 237/R4
Westwood‡, Ky. (†40201) 237/K4
Westwood∆, Mass. (02090) 249/B8
Westwood‡, Mich. (†49001) 250/D6
Westwood‡, Mo. (†63101) 261/P3
West Woodburn, Oreg. (†97071) 291/A3
Westwood Hills‡, Kans. (†66101) 232/H2
Westwood Lakes, Fla. (†33101) 212/B5
West Woodstock, Conn. (†06260) 210/G1
West Woodstock, Vt. (†05091) 268/B4
Westworth, Texas (†76101) 302/E2
West Wyalong, N.S.W. 97/D3
West Wyoming‡, Pa. (18644) 294/L3
West Yarmouth, Mass. (02673) 249/N6
West Yellowstone, Mont. (59758) 262/E6
West York, Ill. (62478) 222/F4
West York, Pa. (†17401) 294/J6
West Yuma, Ariz. (†85364) 198/A6
Westzaan, Neth. 27/A4
Wetar (isl.), Indon., 54/R1
Wetar (isl.), Indon. 85/H7
Wetaskiwin, 163/E5
Wetaskiwin, Alta. 182/D3
Wete, Tanz. 115/G4
Wetheral, Eng. 13/E3
Wethersfield, Conn. (06109) 210/E2
Wetipquin, Md. (†21856) 245/P7
Wetmore, Colo. (81253) 208/J6
Wetmore, Kans. (66550) 232/G2
Wetmore, Mich. (49895) 250/C2
Wetmore, Tenn. (†37325) 237/N10
Wetonka, S. Dak. (57482) 298/M2
Wetteren, Belg. 27/D7
Wetterhorn (peak), Colo. 208/D6
Wetterhorn (mt.), Switz. 39/F3
Wettingen, Switz. 39/F2
Wetumka, Okla. (74883) 288/O4
Wetumpka, Ala. (36092) 194/F5
Wetuppa, N.S.W. 97/B4
Wetzel (co.), W. Va. 313/E3
Wetzikon, Switz. 39/G2
Wetzlar, W. Ger. 22/C3
Wever, Iowa (52658) 229/L7
Weverton, Md. (†21758) 245/H3
Wewahitchka, Fla. (32465) 212/D6
Wewak, Terr. N.G. 85/B6
Wewak, Terr. N.G., 87/E6
Weweantic (riv.), Mass. 249/L5
Wewela, S. Dak. (57578) 298/K7
Wewoka, Okla. (74884) 288/O4
Wexford, 10/C4
Wexford (co.), Ire. 17/H7
Wexford, Ire. 17/H7
Wexford (bay), Ire. 17/J7
Wexford (harb.), Ire. 17/J7
Wexford (harb.), 10/C4
Wexford (co.), Mich. 250/D4
Weyanoke, La. (70787) 238/H5
Weyauwega, Wis. (54983) 317/H7
Weybridge∆, Vt. (†05753) 268/A3
Weybridge, Vt. (†05753) 268/A3
Weyburn, 163/F6
Weyburn, Sask. 181/H6
Weyer, Austria 41/C3
Weyerhauser, Wis. (54895) 317/D5
Weyers Cave, Va. (24486) 307/L4
Weymouth (bay), Eng. 13/E7
Weymouth, Mass. (†02188) 249/D8
Weymouth, N.S. 169/C4
Weymouth and Melcombe Regis, Eng. 13/E7
Weymouth and Melcombe Regis, 10/E5
Wezembeek-Oppem, Belg. 27/D9
Wezet (Visé), Belg. 27/H7
Whakatane, N.Z. 101/F2
Whalan, Minn. (55986) 254/G7
Whalan (creek), N.S.W. 97/E1
Whale (bay), Alaska 196/M1
Whaleback (mt.), W. Aust. 92/B3
Whale Cove, N.W.T. 187/J3
Whaletown, Br. Col. 184/E5
Whaley Bridge, 10/G2
Whaleysville, Md. (21872) 245/S7
Whaleyville, Va. (23485) 307/P7
Whallonsburg, N.Y. (12994) 276/O2
Whalsay (isl.), 10/H1
Whalsay (isl.), Scot. 15/N3
Whangamata, N.Z. 101/F2
Whangarei, N.Z. 101/E1
Wharfe (riv.), Eng. 13/F4
Wharfe (riv.), 10/F3
Wharncliffe, W. Va. (25651) 313/C7
Wharton (pen.), Chile 138/D8
Wharton, N.J. (07885) 273/D2
Wharton (lake), N.W.T. 187/H3
Wharton, Ohio (43359) 284/D4
Wharton, Pa. (†16720) 294/G2
Wharton (co.), Texas 302/H8
Wharton, Texas (77488) 302/J8
Wharton, W. Va. (25208) 313/C7
Whataroa, N.Z. 101/C5
Whatatutu, N.Z. 101/F3
What Cheer, Iowa (50268) 229/J6
Whatcom (co.), Wash. 310/D2
Whatcom (lake), Wash. 310/C2
Whately∆, Mass. (01093) 249/D3
Whatley, Ala. (36482) 194/C7
Wheatcroft, Ky. (42463) 237/F5
Wheatfield, Ind. (46392) 227/C2
Wheatland, Calif. (95692) 204/D4
Wheatland, Ind. (47597) 227/C7
Wheatland, Iowa (52777) 229/M5
Wheatland, Man. 179/B4
Wheatland, Mo. (65779) 261/F7
Wheatland (co.), Mont. 262/G4
Wheatland, N. Dak. (58079) 283/R6
Wheatland, N. Mex. (†88120) 274/F4
Wheatland, Pa. (16161) 294/B3
Wheatland, Wyo. (82201) 319/H3
Wheatland (res.), Wyo. 319/G4
Wheatley, Ark. (72392) 203/H4
Wheatley, Ont. 177/B5
Wheatley, Ky. (40389) 237/M3
Wheaton, Ill. (60187) 222/E2
Wheaton, Kans. (66551) 232/F2
Wheaton, Md. (20902) 245/E3
Wheaton, Minn. (56296) 254/B5
Wheaton, Mo. (64874) 261/E9
Wheat Ridge, Colo. (80033) 208/J3
Wheeler (lake), Ala., 188/J4
Wheeler, Ala. (†35618) 194/D1
Wheeler (dam), Ala. 194/D1
Wheeler (lake), Ala. 194/D1
Wheeler (peak), Calif. 204/F5
Wheeler (riv.), Que. 174/D1
Wheeler (co.), Ga. 216/G6
Wheeler, Ill. (62479) 222/E4
Wheeler, Ind. (46393) 227/C1
Wheeler, Kans. (67763) 232/A2
Wheeler, Ky. (†40906) 237/O7
Wheeler, Mich. (48662) 250/E5
Wheeler, Miss. (38880) 256/G1
Wheeler (peak), N. Mex., 188/F3
Wheeler (peak), N. Mex. 274/D2
Wheeler (co.), Nebr. 264/F3
Wheeler (peak), Nev. 266/G4
Wheeler (co.), Oreg. 291/G3
Wheeler, Oreg. (97147) 291/D2
Wheeler (co.), Texas 302/D2
Wheeler, Texas (79096) 302/D2
Wheeler, Wash. (†98837) 310/F3
Wheeler, Wis. (54772) 317/C5
Wheeler A.F.B., Hawaii 218/E1
Wheeler Ridge, Calif. (93284) 204/G8
Wheelersburg, Ohio (45694) 284/E8
Wheeless, Okla. (73952) 288/A1
Wheeling, Ill. (60090) 222/F1
Wheeling, Ind. (†47342) 227/G4
Wheeling, Ind. (†47534) 227/C8
Wheeling, Mo. (64688) 261/F3
Wheeling, W. Va., 188/K2
Wheeling, W. Va. (26003) 313/E2
Wheelock, N. Dak. (58855) 283/D3
Wheelock∆, Vt. (†05851) 268/C2
Wheelock, Vt. (†05851) 268/C2
Wheelwright, Ky. (41669) 237/R6
Wheelwright, Mass. (01094) 249/F3
Whelan, Sask. 181/B2
Whelen Springs, Ark. (71772) 203/D6
Whetstone (buttes), N. Dak. 283/E7
Whetstone (creek), S. Dak. 298/R3
Whick, Ky. (41390) 237/P6
Whidbey (isls.), S. Aust. 94/D6
Whidbey (isl.), Wash. 310/C2
Whidbey I. N.A.S., Wash. 310/C2
Whigham, Ga. (31797) 216/D9
Whigville, Conn. (†06010) 210/D2
Whipholt, Minn. (56485) 254/D3
Whippany, N.J. (07981) 273/E2
Whipple (mts.), Calif. 204/L9
Whipple, Ohio (45788) 284/H6
Whiskeytown-Shasta-Trinity Nat'l Rec. Area, Calif. 204/C3
Whisky Gap, Alta. 182/D5
Whispering Pines, N.C. (28327) 281/L4
Whitaker, Ind. (†46166) 227/D6
Whitaker, Pa. (15120) 294/C7
Whitakers, N.C. (27891) 281/O2
Whitbourne, Newf. 166/D2
Whitburn, 10/C1
Whitburn, Scot. 15/E2
Whitby, Ont. 177/F4
Whitby, Eng. 13/G3
Whitby, 10/F3
Whitchurch, Eng. 13/E5
Whitcomb, Ind. (†47012) 227/H6
Whitcombe (mt.), N.Z. 101/C5
White (bay), 163/L5
White (mts.), Alaska 196/J1
White (pass), Alaska 196/N1
White (riv.), Alaska 196/K2
White (riv.), Ariz. 198/E5
White (riv.), Ark., 188/H3
White (co.), Ark. 203/G3
White, Ark. (†71635) 203/G7
White (riv.), Ark. 203/H5
White (riv.), Colo. 208/B2
White (lake), Ont. 177/F2
White (lake), Ont. 177/H2
White (co.), Ga. 216/E1
White, Ga. (30184) 216/C2
White (co.), Ill. 222/E5
White (co.), Ind. 227/D3
White (riv.), Ind. 227/B8
White (lake), La. 238/E7
White (riv.), Mich. 250/C5
White (riv.), Mo. 261/G10
White (butte), N. Dak. 283/D7
White (isl.), N.H. 268/F6
White (mts.), N.H. 268/E3
White (isl.), N.W.T. 187/K3
White (isl.), N.Z. 101/F2
White (riv.), Nebr. 264/A2
White (bay), Newf. 166/C3
White (lake), No. Terr. 93/A6
White (riv.), Oreg. 291/F2
White, S. Dak. (57276) 298/R5
White (lake), S. Dak. 298/M6
White (riv.), S. Dak. 298/D7
White (co.), Tenn. 237/L9
White (riv.), Texas 302/C4
White (sea), U.S.S.R., 4/C8
White (sea), U.S.S.R. 48/D3
White (sea), U.S.S.R. 52/E1

Z

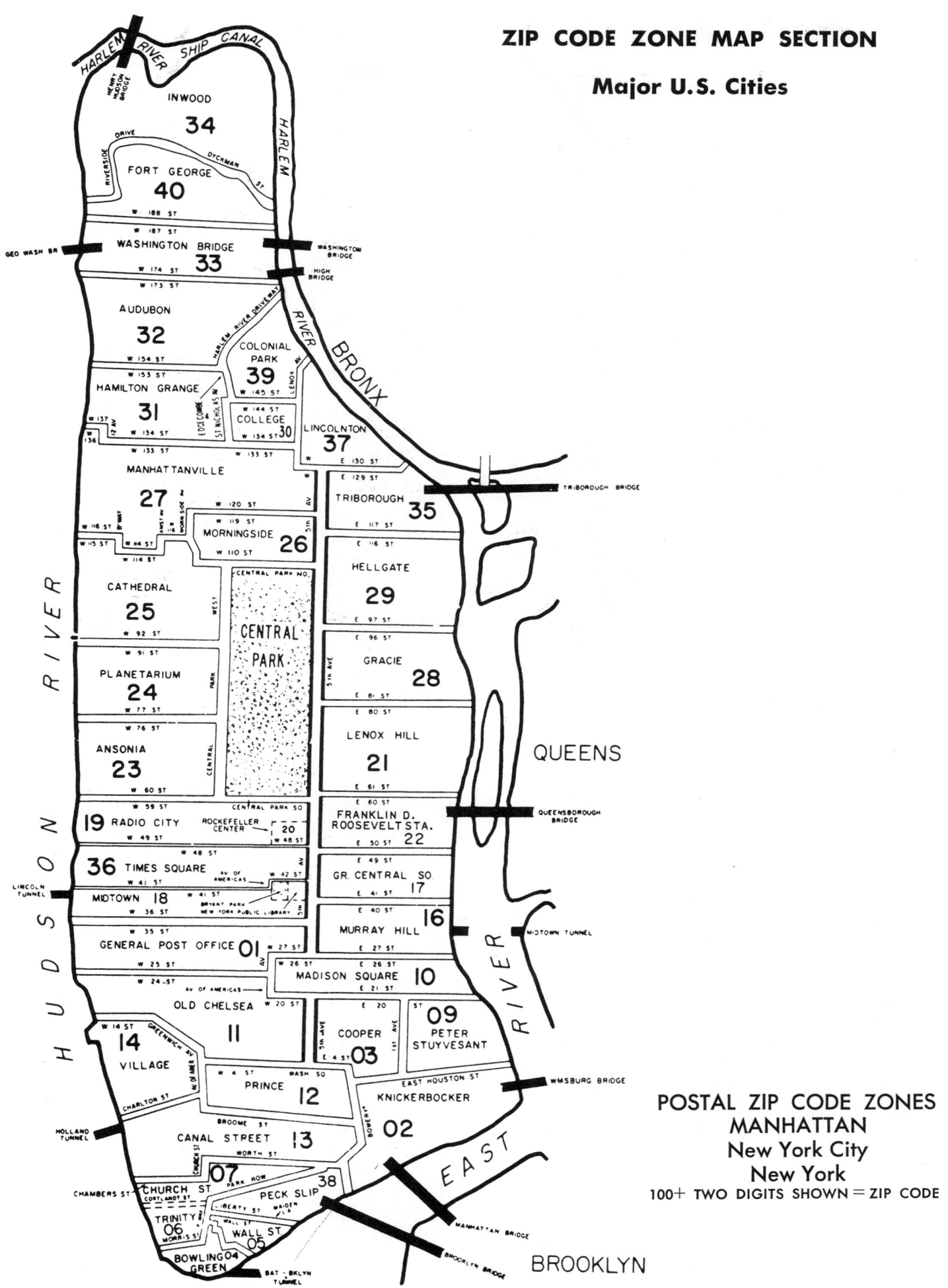

ZIP CODE ZONE MAP SECTION

Major U.S. Cities

INWOOD 34

FORT GEORGE 40

WASHINGTON BRIDGE 33

AUDUBON 32

COLONIAL PARK 39

HAMILTON GRANGE 31

COLLEGE 30

LINCOLNTON 37

MANHATTANVILLE 27

MORNINGSIDE 26

TRIBOROUGH 35

HELLGATE 29

CATHEDRAL 25

CENTRAL PARK

GRACIE 28

PLANETARIUM 24

LENOX HILL 21

ANSONIA 23

RADIO CITY 19

ROCKEFELLER CENTER 20

FRANKLIN D. ROOSEVELT STA. 22

TIMES SQUARE 36

GR. CENTRAL SO. 17

MIDTOWN 18

NEW YORK PUBLIC LIBRARY

MURRAY HILL 16

GENERAL POST OFFICE 01

MADISON SQUARE 10

OLD CHELSEA 11

COOPER 03

PETER STUYVESANT 09

VILLAGE 14

PRINCE 12

KNICKERBOCKER

02

CANAL STREET 13

CHURCH ST 07

PECK SLIP 38

TRINITY 06

WALL ST 05

BOWLING GREEN 04

QUEENS

BRONX

HUDSON RIVER

EAST RIVER

BROOKLYN

POSTAL ZIP CODE ZONES MANHATTAN
New York City
New York
100+ TWO DIGITS SHOWN = ZIP CODE

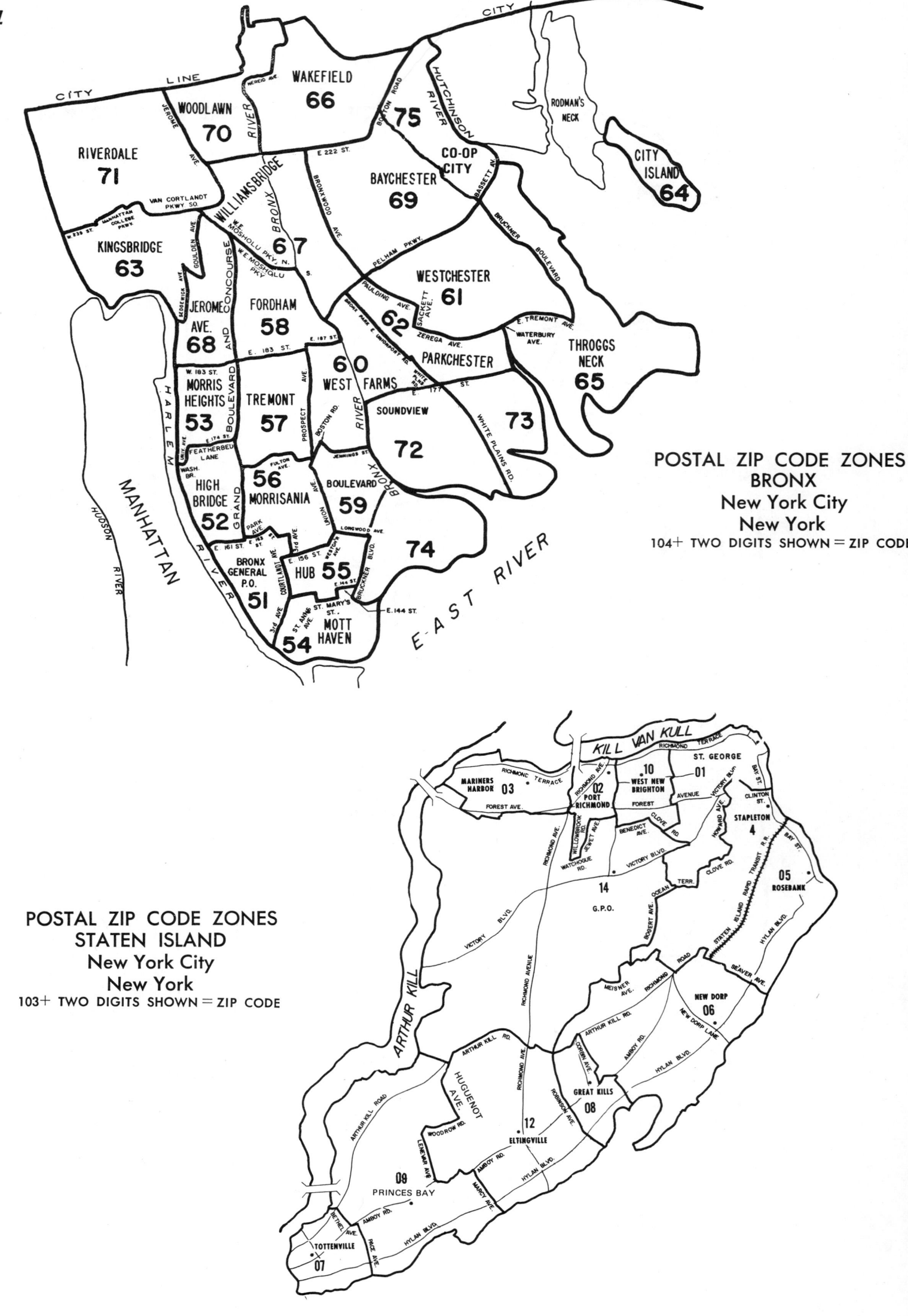

**POSTAL ZIP CODE ZONES
BRONX
New York City
New York
104+ TWO DIGITS SHOWN = ZIP CODE**

**POSTAL ZIP CODE ZONES
STATEN ISLAND
New York City
New York
103+ TWO DIGITS SHOWN = ZIP CODE**

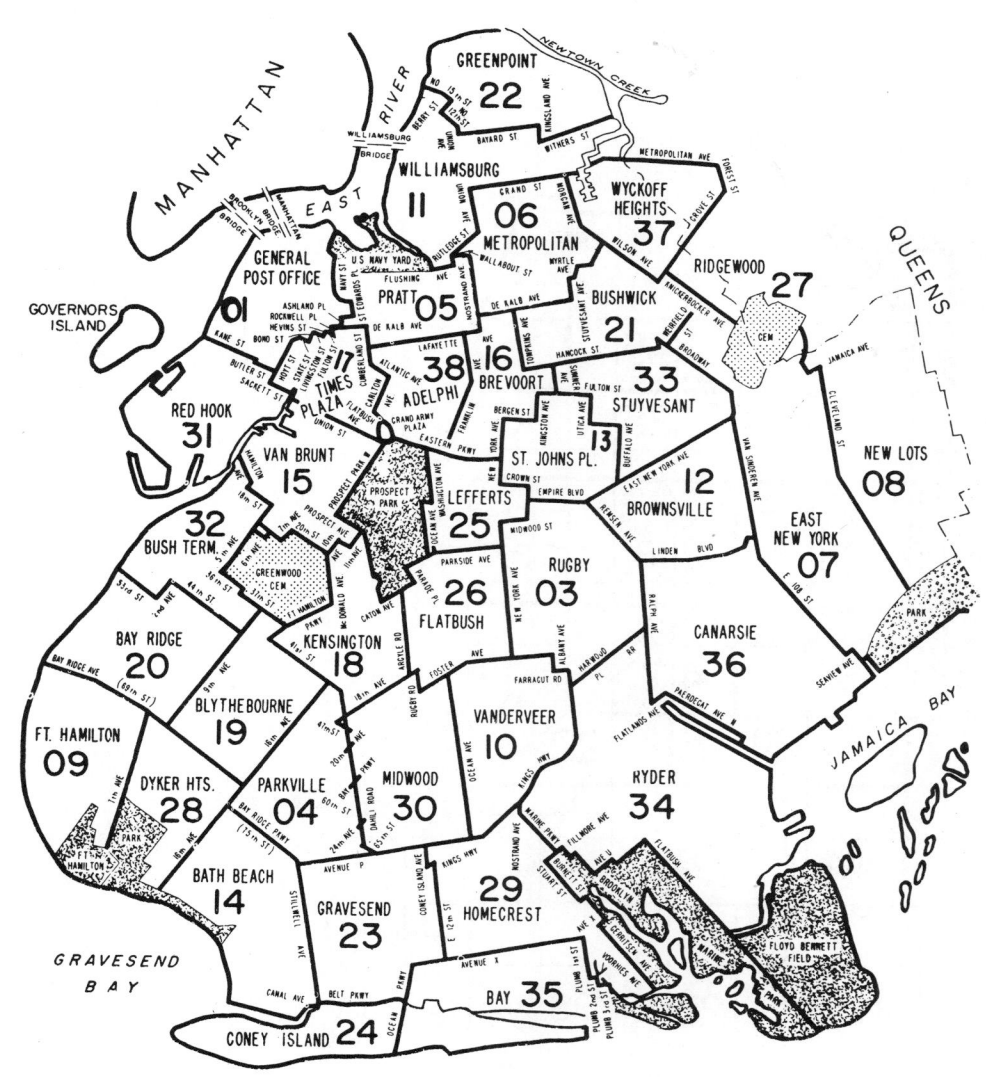

POSTAL ZIP CODE ZONES
BROOKLYN
New York City
New York
112+ TWO DIGITS SHOWN = ZIP CODE

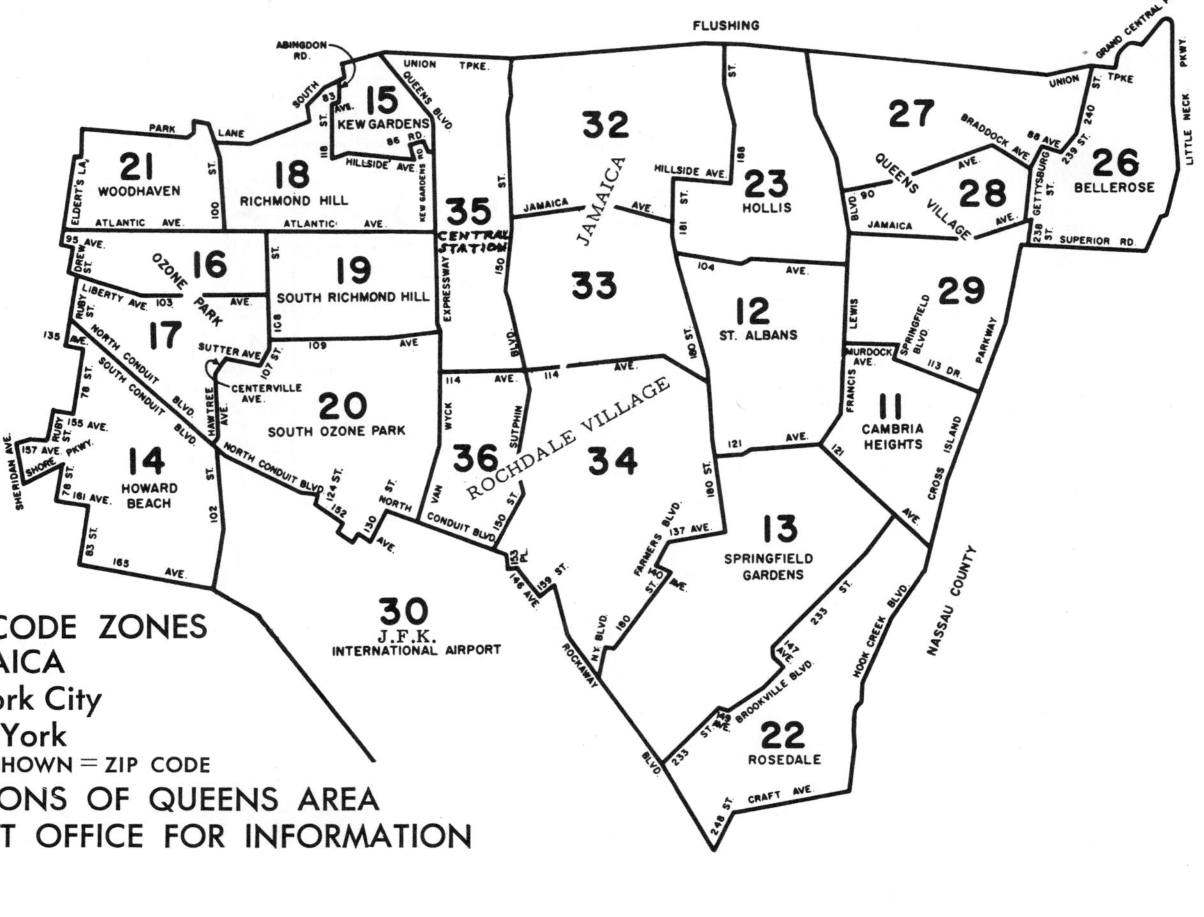

POSTAL ZIP CODE ZONES
JAMAICA
New York City
New York
114+ TWO DIGITS SHOWN = ZIP CODE
FOR REMAINING PORTIONS OF QUEENS AREA
CONTACT YOUR LOCAL POST OFFICE FOR INFORMATION

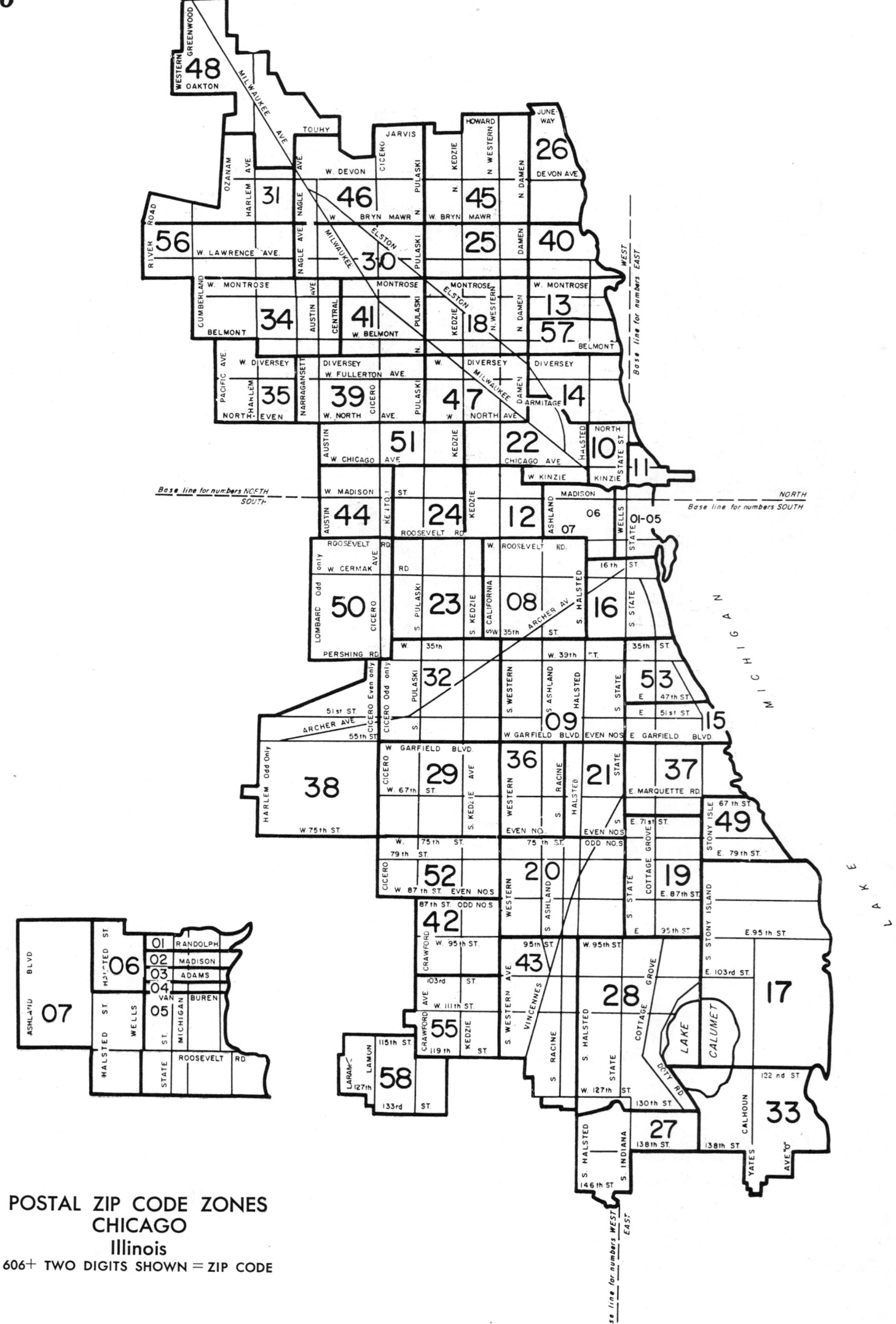

POSTAL ZIP CODE ZONES
CHICAGO
Illinois
606+ TWO DIGITS SHOWN = ZIP CODE

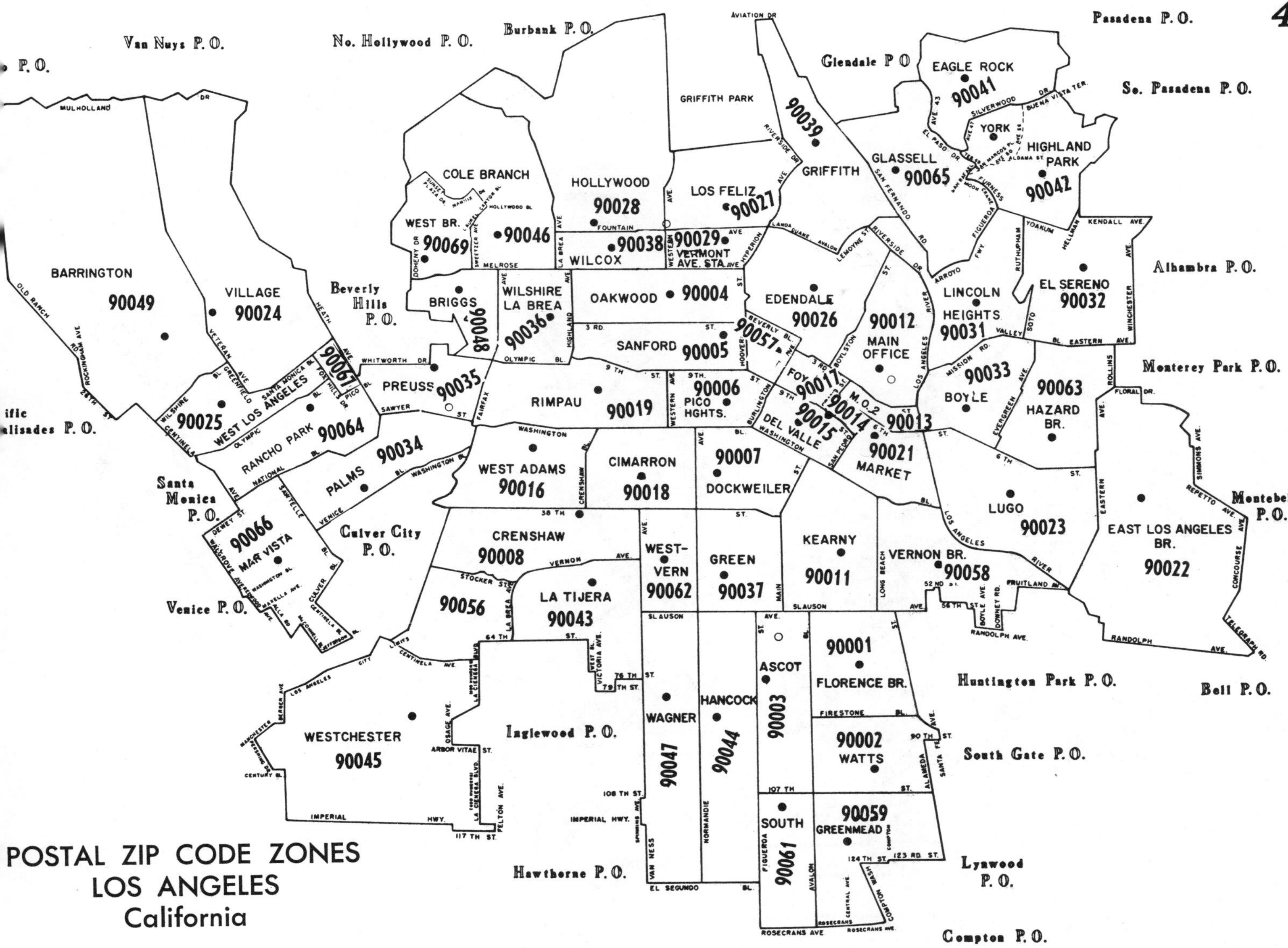

467

POSTAL ZIP CODE ZONES
LOS ANGELES
California

Van Nuys P.O. — No. Hollywood P.O. — Burbank P.O. — Aviation Dr — Pasadena P.O.

Glendale P O — EAGLE ROCK 90041 — So. Pasadena P.O.

GRIFFITH PARK

90039 — YORK — HIGHLAND PARK

GLASSELL 90065 — 90042 — Alhambra P.O.

GRIFFITH

COLE BRANCH — HOLLYWOOD 90028 — LOS FELIZ 90027

WEST BR. 90069 — 90046 — 90038 — 90029 VERMONT AVE. STA. — EL SERENO 90032 — Monterey Park P.O.

WILCOX — LINCOLN HEIGHTS 90031

BARRINGTON 90049 — VILLAGE 90024 — Beverly Hills P.O. — BRIGGS 90048 — WILSHIRE LA BREA 90036 — OAKWOOD 90004 — EDENDALE 90026 — 90012 MAIN OFFICE

90057 — 90033 — 90063 HAZARD BR.

SANFORD 90005 — BOYLE

PREUSS 90035 — RIMPAU 90019 — 90006 PICO HGHTS. — 90017 — 90014 M.O.2 — 90013

90061 — WEST LOS ANGELES 90025 — RANCHO PARK 90064 — 90034 — PALMS — DEL VALLE 90015 — 90021 MARKET

Santa Monica P.O. — 90066 MAR VISTA — Culver City P.O. — WEST ADAMS 90016 — CIMARRON 90018 — 90007 DOCKWEILER — LUGO 90023 — EAST LOS ANGELES BR. 90022 — Montebello P.O.

CRENSHAW 90008 — WEST-VERN 90062 — GREEN 90037 — KEARNY 90011 — VERNON BR. 90058

Venice P.O. — 90056 — LA TIJERA 90043 —

WESTCHESTER 90045 — Inglewood P.O. — WAGNER 90047 — HANCOCK 90044 — 90003 ASCOT — 90001 FLORENCE BR. — Huntington Park P.O. — Bell P.O.

90002 WATTS — South Gate P.O.

SOUTH 90061 — 90059 GREENMEAD — Lynwood P.O.

Hawthorne P.O. — Compton P.O.

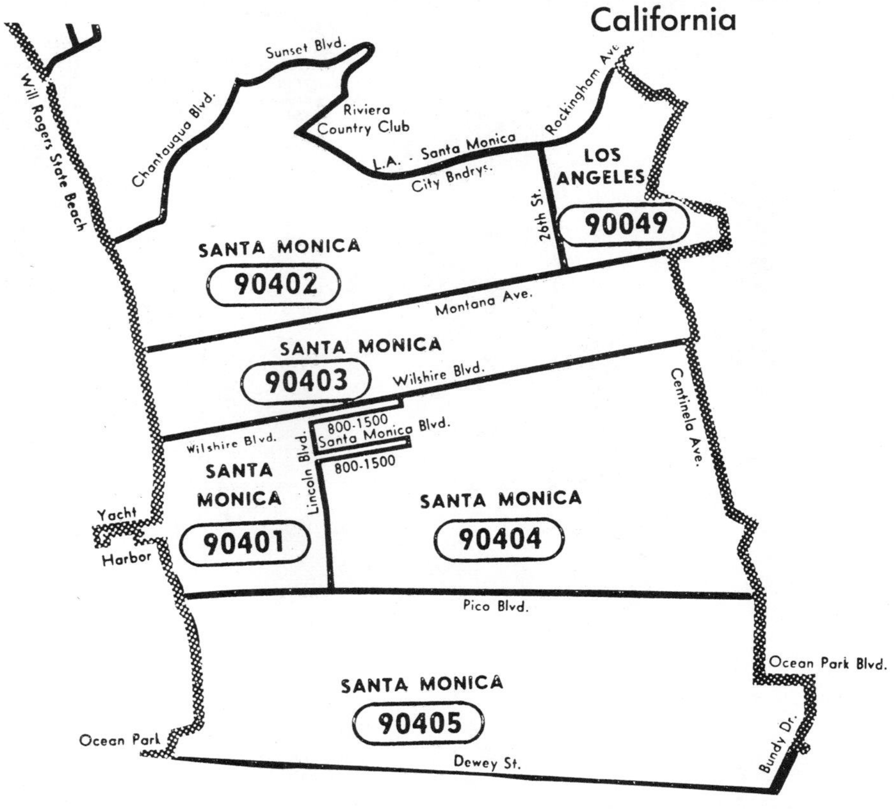

FOR REMAINING PORTIONS OF LOS ANGELES AREA CONTACT YOUR LOCAL POST OFFICE FOR INFORMATION

POSTAL ZIP CODE ZONES
NO. HOLLYWOOD
California

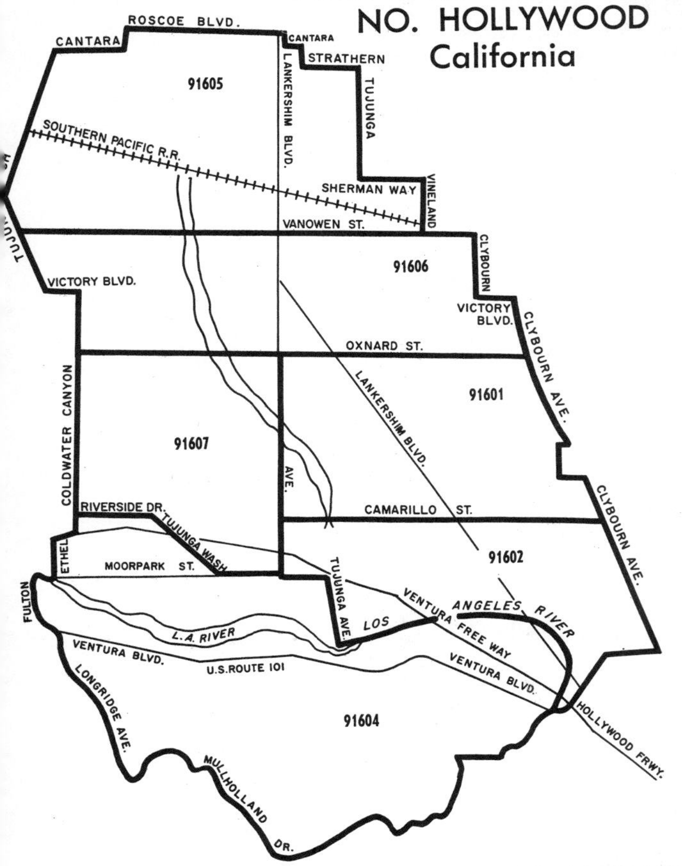

91605 — 91606 — 91601 — 91607 — 91602 — 91604

POSTAL ZIP CODE ZONES
SANTA MONICA
California

LOS ANGELES 90049

SANTA MONICA 90402

SANTA MONICA 90403

SANTA MONICA 90401

SANTA MONICA 90404

SANTA MONICA 90405

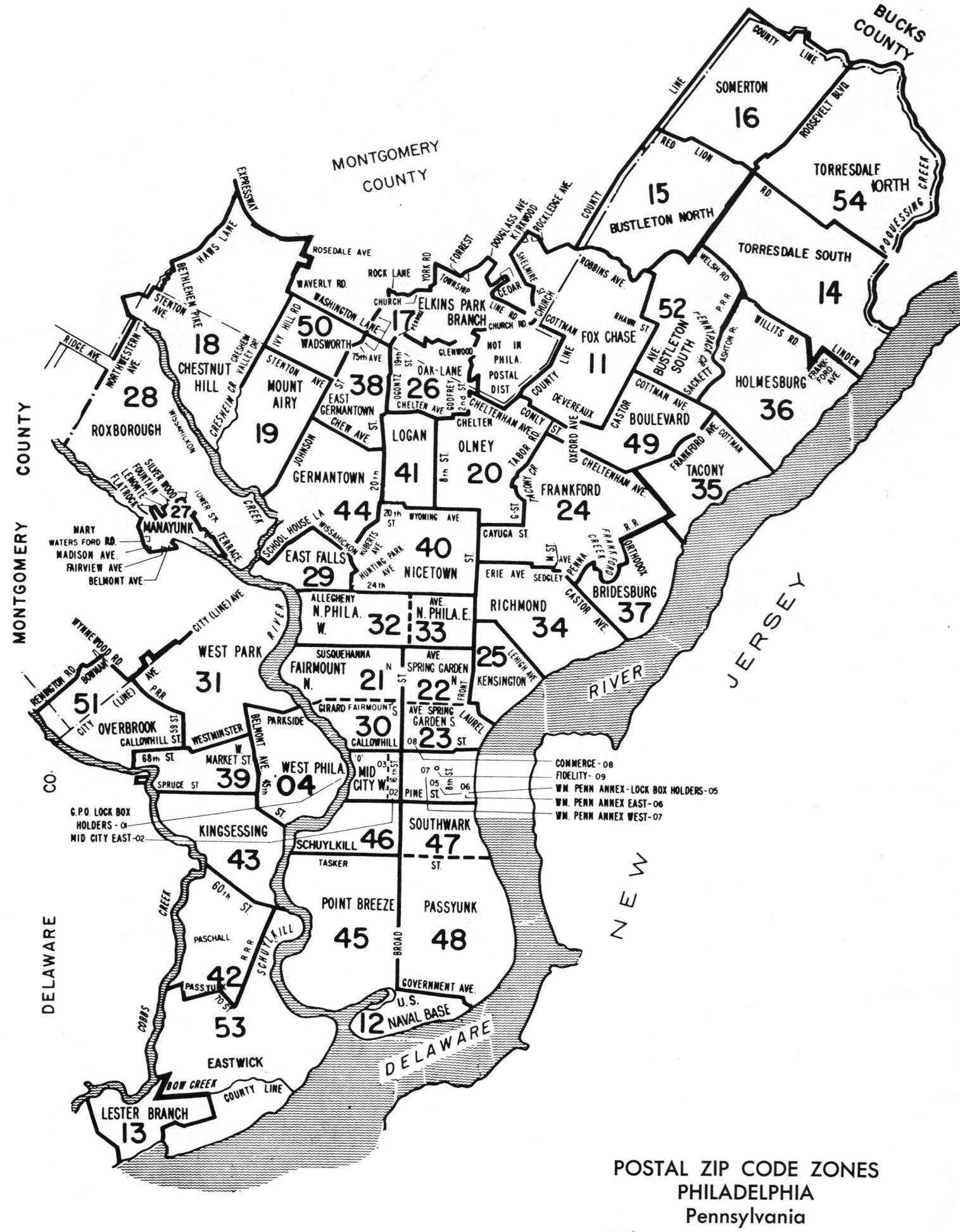

POSTAL ZIP CODE ZONES
PHILADELPHIA
Pennsylvania
191+ TWO DIGITS SHOWN = ZIP CODE

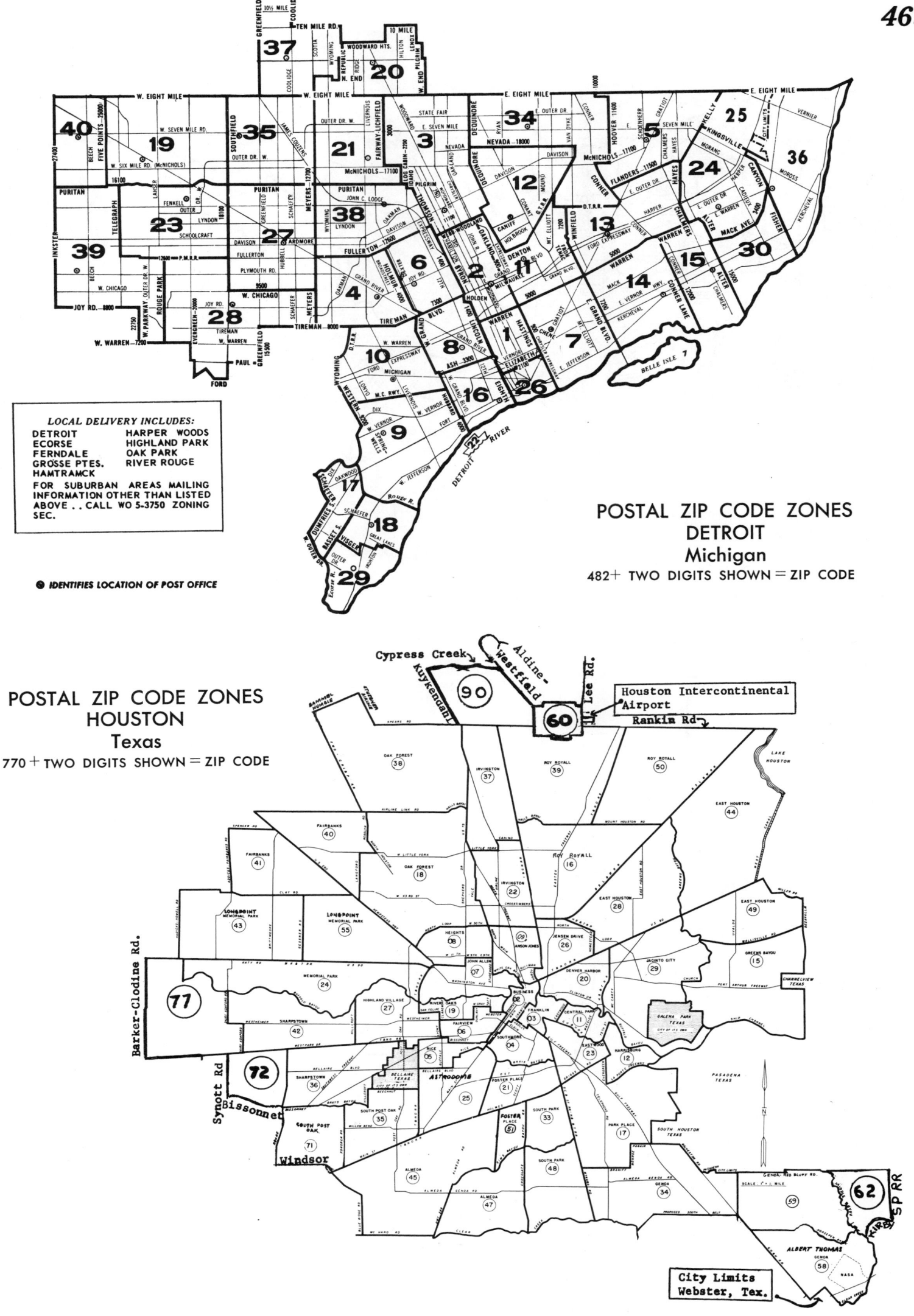

POSTAL ZIP CODE ZONES
DETROIT
Michigan
482+ TWO DIGITS SHOWN = ZIP CODE

LOCAL DELIVERY INCLUDES:
DETROIT .... HARPER WOODS
ECORSE .... HIGHLAND PARK
FERNDALE ...... OAK PARK
GROSSE PTES. .. RIVER ROUGE
HAMTRAMCK
FOR SUBURBAN AREAS MAILING
INFORMATION OTHER THAN LISTED
ABOVE .. CALL WO 5-3750 ZONING
SEC.

● IDENTIFIES LOCATION OF POST OFFICE

POSTAL ZIP CODE ZONES
HOUSTON
Texas
770+ TWO DIGITS SHOWN = ZIP CODE

City Limits
Webster, Tex.

POSTAL ZIP CODE ZONES
BALTIMORE
Maryland

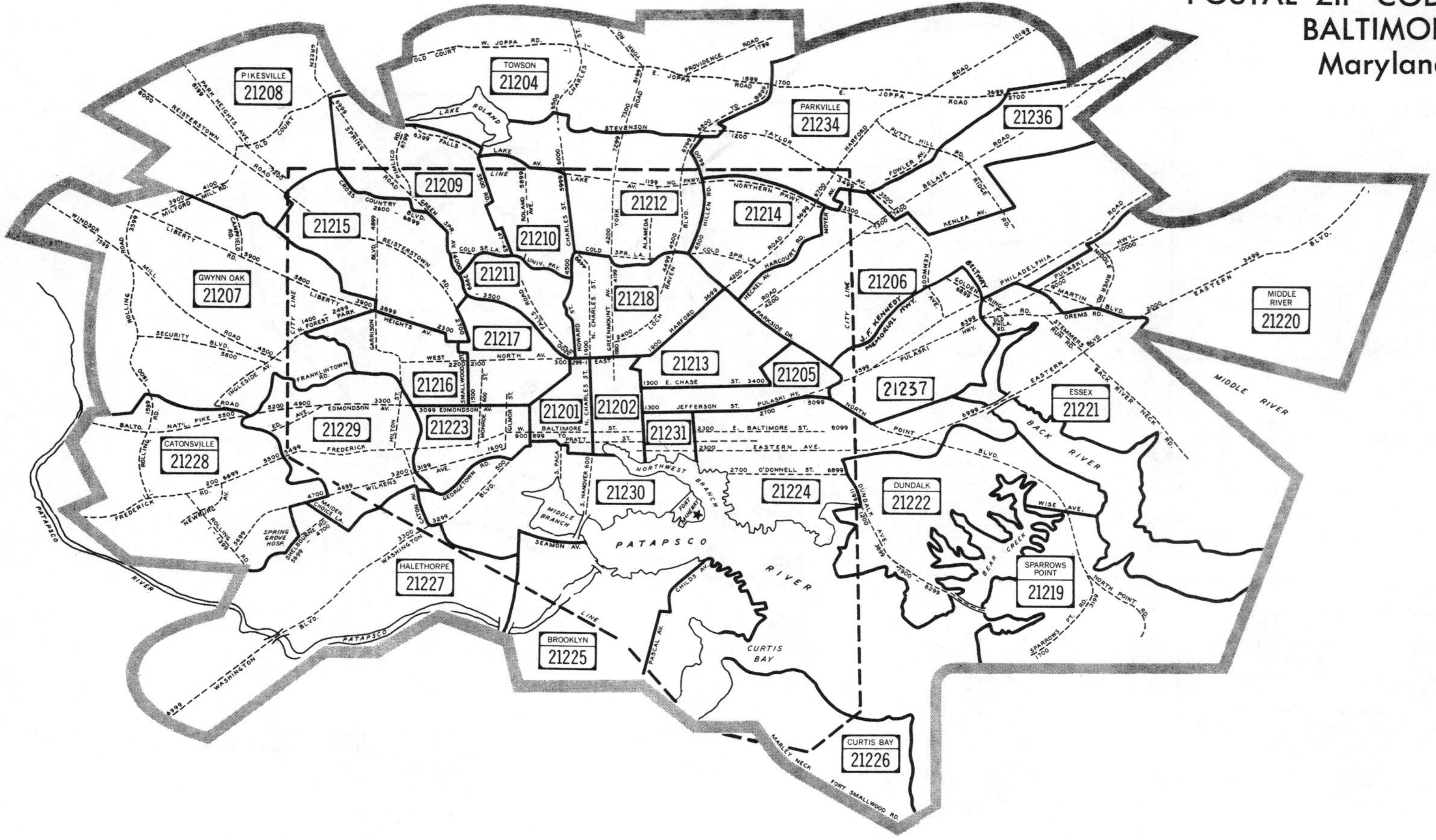

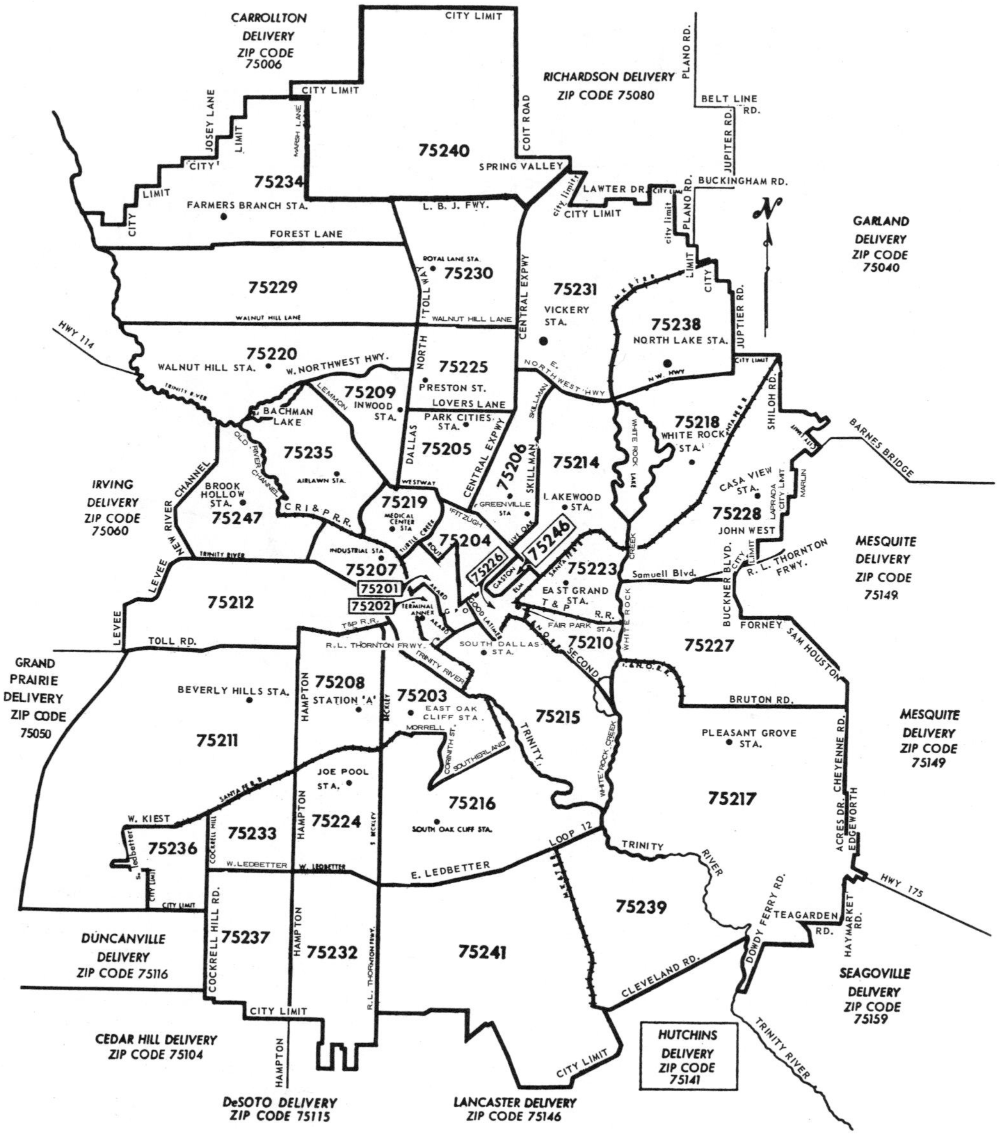

PIKESVILLE 21208
TOWSON 21204
PARKVILLE 21234
21236
21209
21215
21212
21214
GWYNN OAK 21207
21210
21211
21218
21206
MIDDLE RIVER 21220
21217
21216
21213
21205
21237
ESSEX 21221
21201
21202
21229
21223
21231
CATONSVILLE 21228
21230
21224
DUNDALK 21222
SPARROWS POINT 21219
HALETHORPE 21227
BROOKLYN 21225
CURTIS BAY
PATAPSCO RIVER
MIDDLE RIVER
BACK RIVER
CURTIS BAY 21226

POSTAL ZIP CODE ZONES
DALLAS
Texas

CARROLLTON DELIVERY ZIP CODE 75006
CITY LIMIT
RICHARDSON DELIVERY ZIP CODE 75080
PLANO RD.
BELT LINE RD.
75240
SPRING VALLEY
75234
FARMERS BRANCH STA.
L. B. J. FWY.
FOREST LANE
GARLAND DELIVERY ZIP CODE 75040
75230
ROYAL LANE STA.
75231
VICKERY STA.
75238
NORTH LAKE STA.
75229
WALNUT HILL LANE
75220
WALNUT HILL STA.
75225
PRESTON ST.
75209
INWOOD STA.
LOVERS LANE
PARK CITIES STA.
75218
WHITE ROCK STA.
BACHMAN LAKE
75235
AIRLAWN STA.
75205
75206
75214
CASA VIEW STA.
75228
IRVING DELIVERY ZIP CODE 75060
BROOK HOLLOW STA.
75247
75219
MEDICAL CENTER STA.
GREENVILLE STA.
LAKEWOOD STA.
JOHN WEST
MESQUITE DELIVERY ZIP CODE 75149
INDUSTRIAL STA.
75204
75226
75246
75223
EAST GRAND STA.
SAMUELL BLVD.
75212
75207
75201
75202
TERMINAL ANNEX
EAST GRAND T & P R.R.
FAIR PARK STA.
75210
75227
SOUTH DALLAS STA.
GRAND PRAIRIE DELIVERY ZIP CODE 75050
BEVERLY HILLS STA.
75208
STATION "A"
75203
EAST OAK CLIFF STA.
75215
PLEASANT GROVE STA.
MESQUITE DELIVERY ZIP CODE 75149
75211
JOE POOL STA.
75216
SOUTH OAK CLIFF STA.
75217
W. KIEST
75233
75224
75236
E. LEDBETTER
75239
DUNCANVILLE DELIVERY ZIP CODE 75116
75237
75232
75241
SEAGOVILLE DELIVERY ZIP CODE 75159
CEDAR HILL DELIVERY ZIP CODE 75104
HUTCHINS DELIVERY ZIP CODE 75141
DeSOTO DELIVERY ZIP CODE 75115
LANCASTER DELIVERY ZIP CODE 75146
TRINITY RIVER

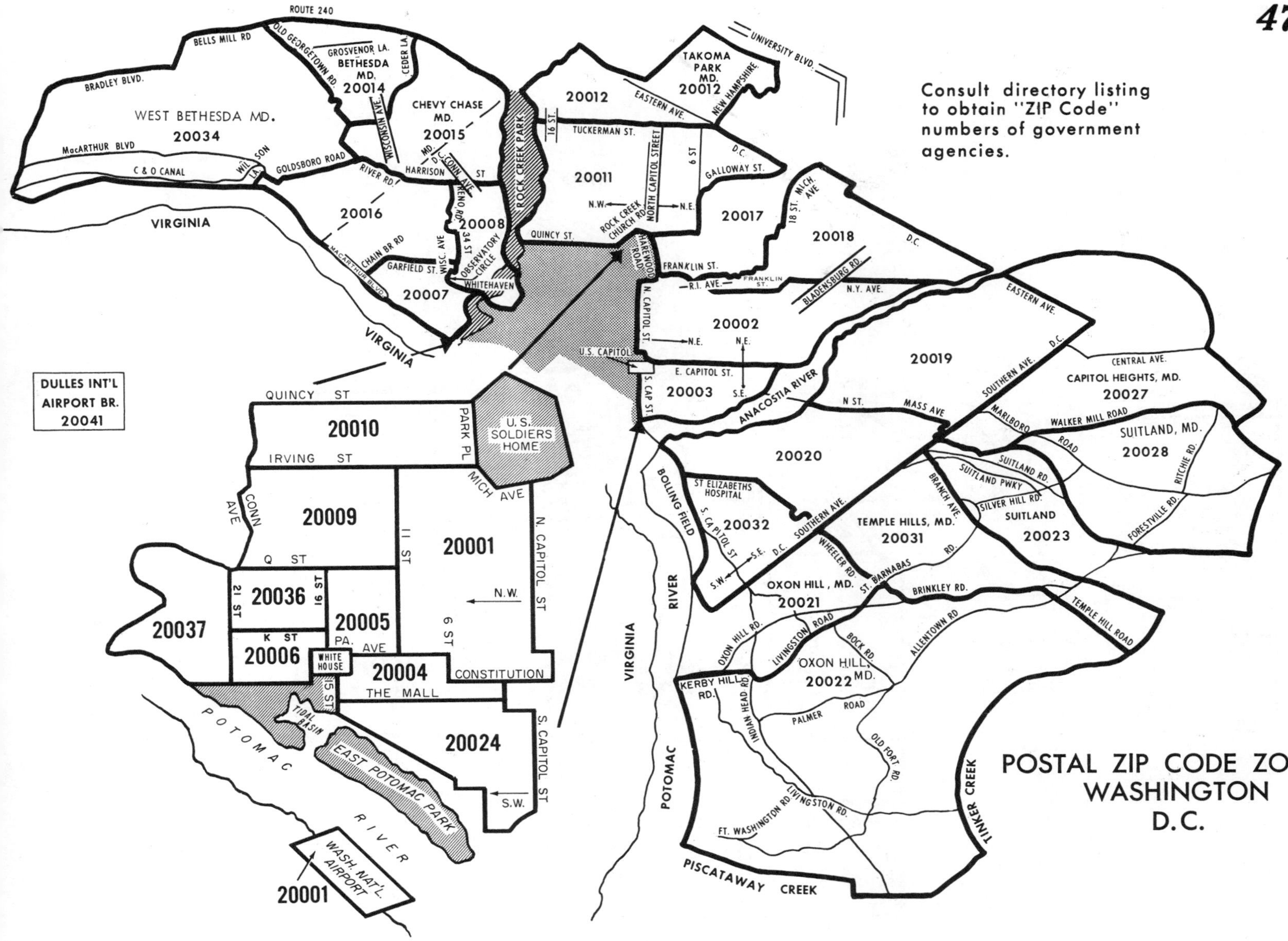

POSTAL ZIP CODE ZONES WASHINGTON D.C.

Consult directory listing to obtain "ZIP Code" numbers of government agencies.

WEST BETHESDA MD. 20034

ROUTE 240

BELLS MILL RD

BRADLEY BLVD.

BETHESDA MD. 20014

GROSVENOR LA.

OLD GEORGETOWN RD

CEDER LA.

MacARTHUR BLVD.

C & O CANAL

WILSON LA.

GOLDSBORO ROAD

RIVER RD.

CHEVY CHASE MD. 20015

WISCONSIN AVE.

HARRISON ST.

JOHN AVE.

34 ST.

ROCK CREEK PARK

16 ST

TUCKERMAN ST.

TAKOMA PARK MD. 20012

EASTERN AVE.

NEW HAMPSHIRE

UNIVERSITY BLVD.

20012

20011

6 ST.

GALLOWAY ST.

D.C.

18 ST. MICH. AVE.

VIRGINIA

20016

RENO RD.

20008

QUINCY ST.

N.W.

N.E.

ROCK CREEK CHURCH NORTH CAPITOL STREET

20017

20018

BLADENSBURG RD.

D.C.

CHAIN BR RD.

GARFIELD ST.

WISC. AVE.

OBSERVATORY CIRCLE

WHITEHAVEN

20007

FRANKLIN ST.

FRANKLIN ST.

R.I. AVE.

N.Y. AVE.

EASTERN AVE.

D.C.

VIRGINIA

U.S. CAPITOL

20002

N CAPITOL ST.

N.E.

N.E.

S CAP ST

20003

E. CAPITOL ST.

S.E.

ANACOSTIA RIVER

20019

N ST.

MASS AVE

SOUTHERN AVE.

D.C.

MARLBORO

SUITLAND RD.

WALKER MILL ROAD

CENTRAL AVE.

CAPITOL HEIGHTS, MD. 20027

SUITLAND, MD. 20028

RITCHIE RD.

DULLES INT'L AIRPORT BR. 20041

QUINCY ST

20010

IRVING ST

U.S. SOLDIERS HOME

PARK PL

MICH. AVE.

BOLLING FIELD

ST. ELIZABETHS HOSPITAL

S. CAPITOL ST.

S.E.

20020

20032

SUITLAND PWKY

BRANCH AVE.

SILVER HILL RD.

SUITLAND 20023

FORESTVILLE RD.

CONN AVE.

20009

Q ST

21 ST

20036

16 ST

20001

II ST

N CAPITOL ST.

N.W.

6 ST

TEMPLE HILLS, MD. 20031

WHEELER RD.

ST. BARNABAS RD.

BRINKLEY RD.

ALLENTOWN RD.

TEMPLE HILL ROAD

20037

20005

K ST

20006

PA. AVE.

15 ST

WHITE HOUSE

20004

CONSTITUTION

THE MALL

OXON HILL, MD. 20021

OXON HILL RD.

LIVINGSTON ROAD

ROCK RD.

OXON HILLS MD. 20022

POTOMAC

TIDAL BASIN

EAST POTOMAC PARK

20024

S. CAPITOL ST.

S.W.

VIRGINIA

POTOMAC RIVER

KERBY HILL RD.

INDIAN HEAD RD.

PALMER ROAD

OLD FORT RD.

TINKER CREEK

RIVER

WASH NAT'L AIRPORT

20001

LIVINGSTON ROAD

FT. WASHINGTON RD

PISCATAWAY CREEK

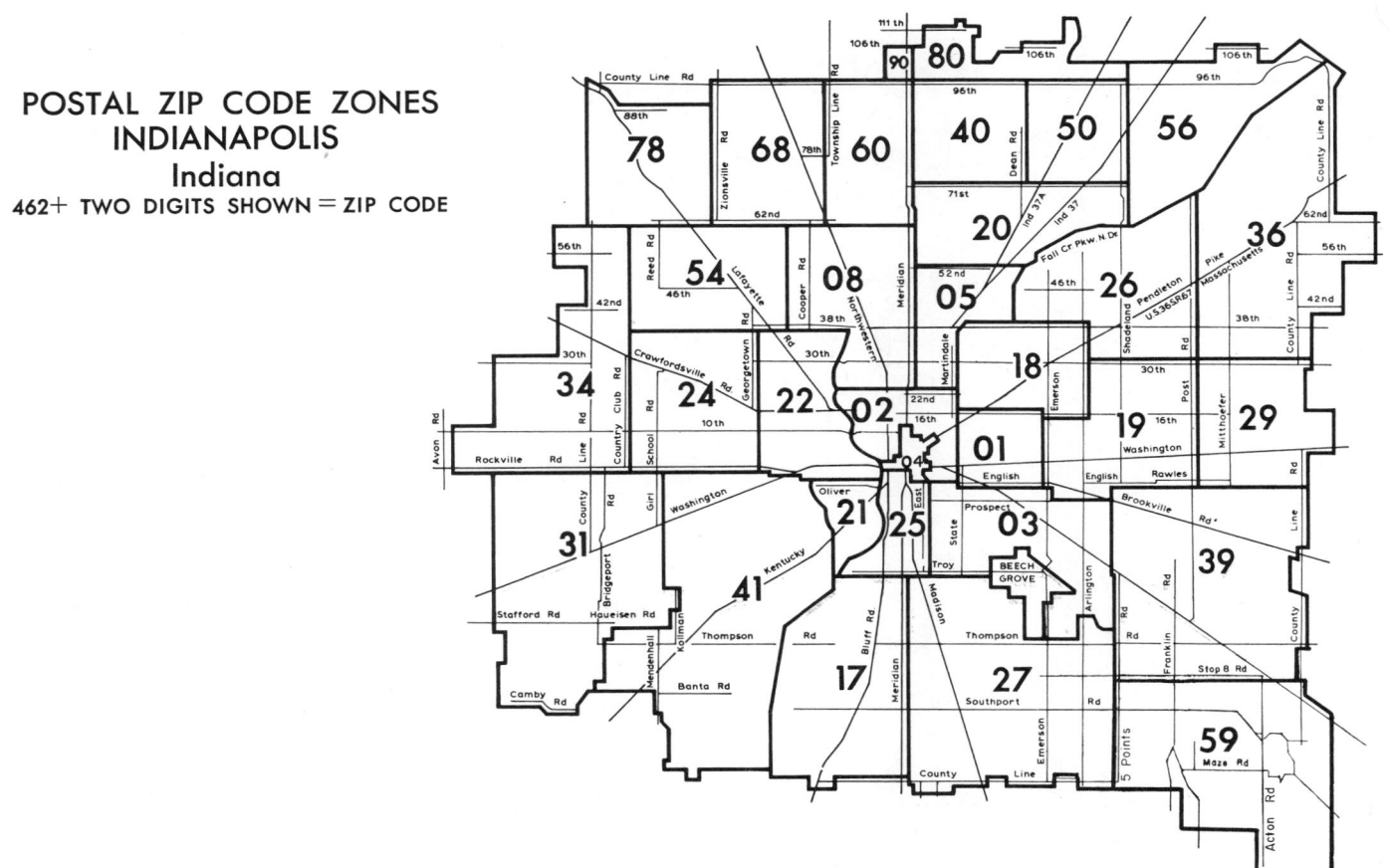

POSTAL ZIP CODE ZONES INDIANAPOLIS
Indiana
462+ TWO DIGITS SHOWN = ZIP CODE

111 th

106 th

County Line Rd

90

80

106th

106th

96th

96th

88th

78

Zionsville Rd

68

Township Line Rd

78th

62nd

60

40

Dean Rd

50

56

56th

Reed Rd

54

Lafayette Rd

Cooper Rd

08

Meridian

71st

Ind 37A

Ind 37

Fall Cr Pkw N Dr

20

52nd

46th

05

26

Shadeland

U.S.36&RE7

Pendleton

Pike

Massachusetts

36

62nd

County Line Rd

56th

42nd

30th

42nd

34

Crawfordsville Rd

24

Georgetown Rd

30th

22

38th

Northwestern

02

22nd

16th

18

Martindale

Emerson

30th

Post Rd

19

Mitthoefer Rd

29

38th

16th

Washington

Avon Rd

Rockville Rd

Country Club Rd

Line Rd

School Rd

Girl School Rd

Washington

10th

01

04

English

English

Rawles

25

East St

03

Prospect

BEECH GROVE

Arlington

Brookville Rd

39

County Line Rd

31

County Line Rd

Bridgeport Rd

Oliver

21

State

Troy

Madison

Thompson Rd

Franklin Rd

Stop 8 Rd

Stafford Rd

Haueisen Rd

41

Kentucky

Kalliman Rd

Thompson Rd

Camby Rd

Mendenhall Rd

Banta Rd

17

Meridian

Bluff Rd

27

Southport Rd

Emerson

5 Points

Thompson Rd

County Line

59

Maze Rd

Acton Rd

POSTAL ZIP CODE ZONES
CLEVELAND
Ohio
441+ TWO DIGITS SHOWN = ZIP CODE

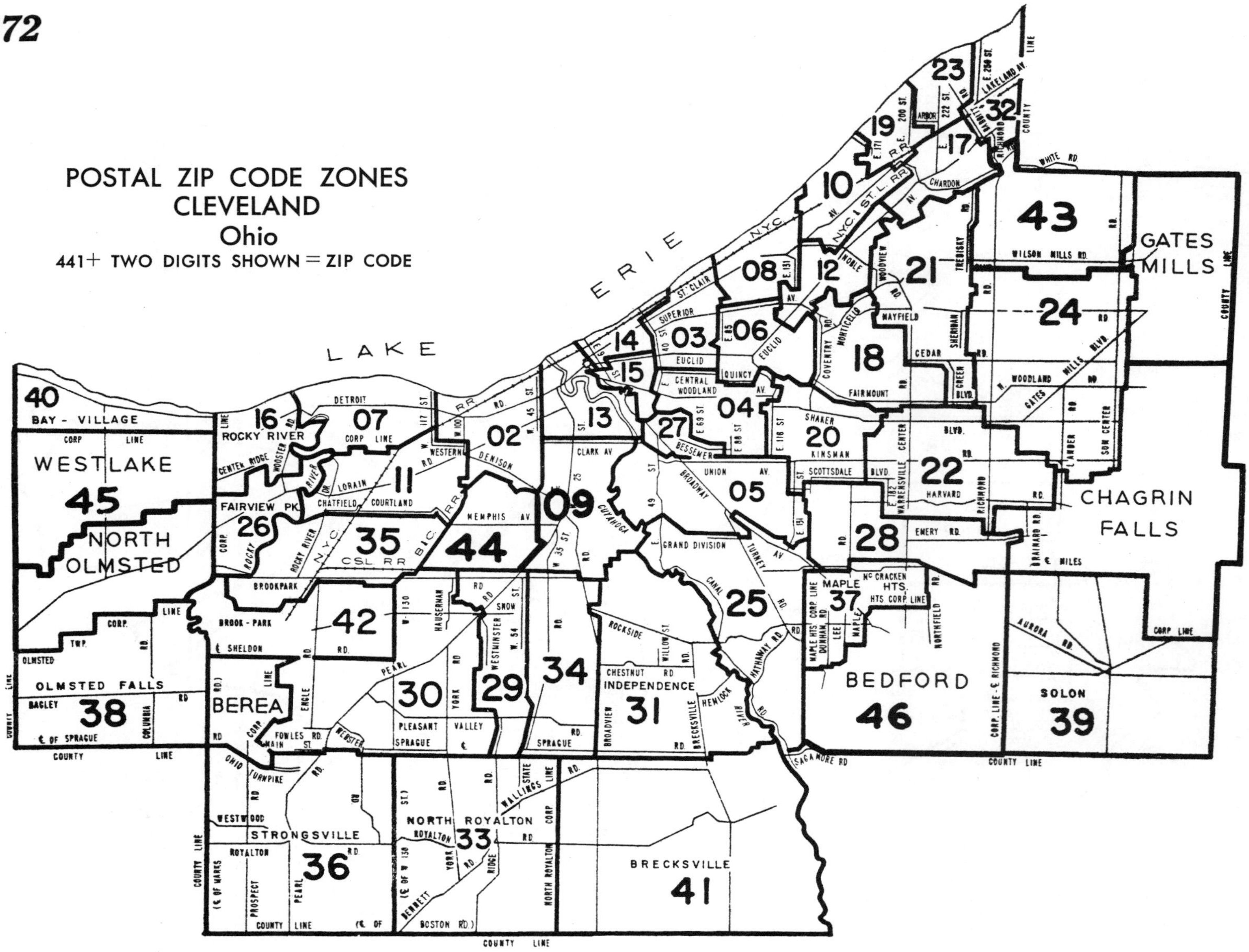

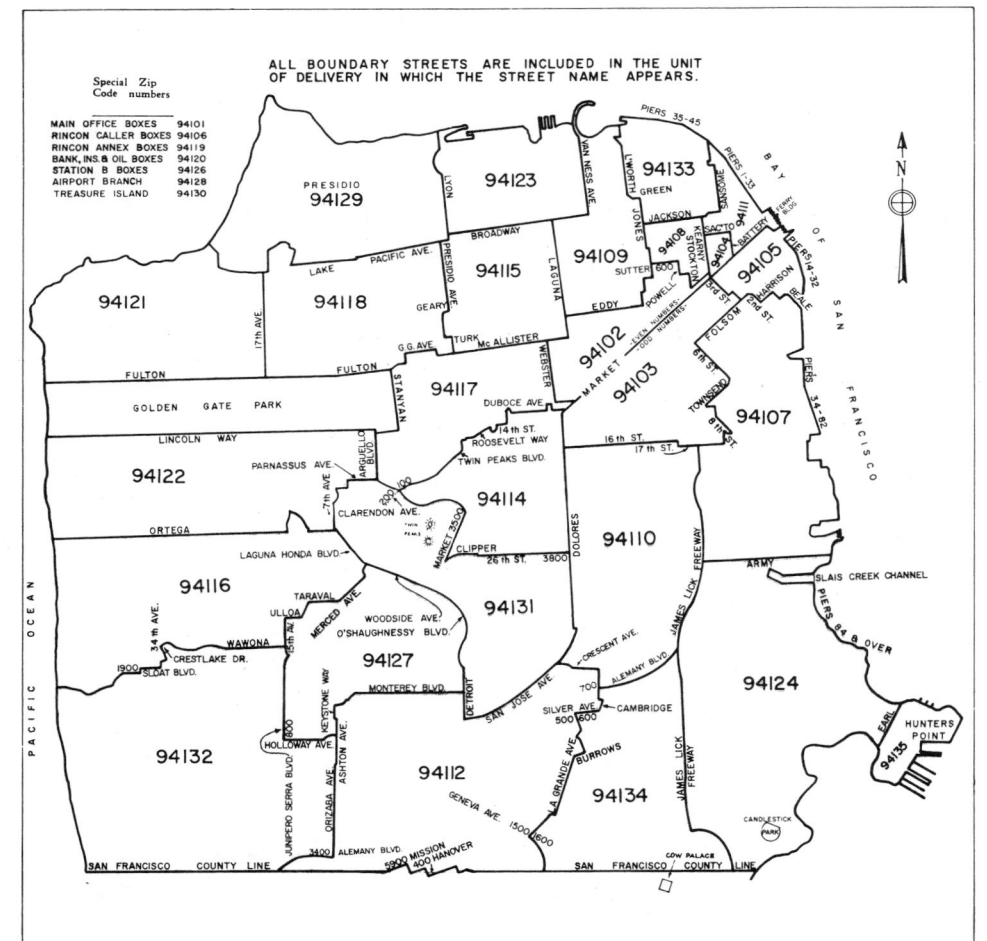

POSTAL ZIP CODE ZONES
SAN FRANCISCO
California

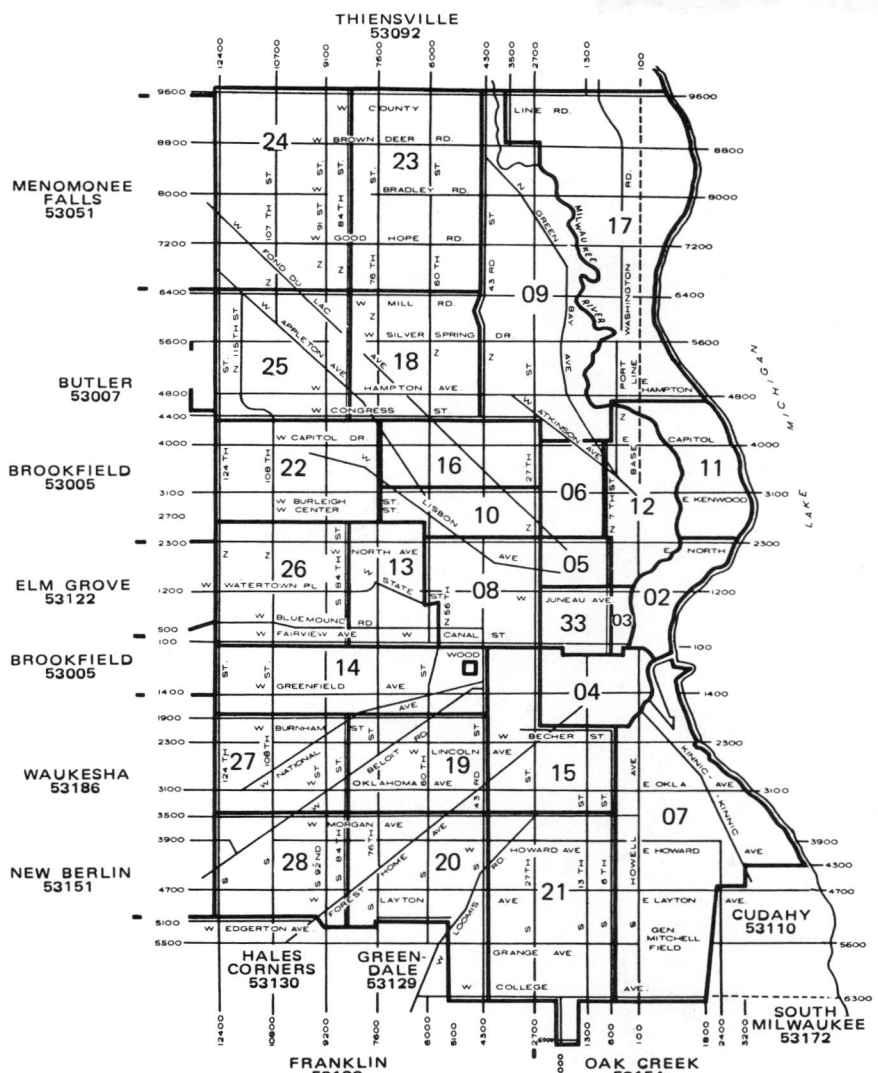

POSTAL ZIP CODE ZONES
MILWAUKEE
Wisconsin
532+ TWO DIGITS SHOWN = ZIP CODE

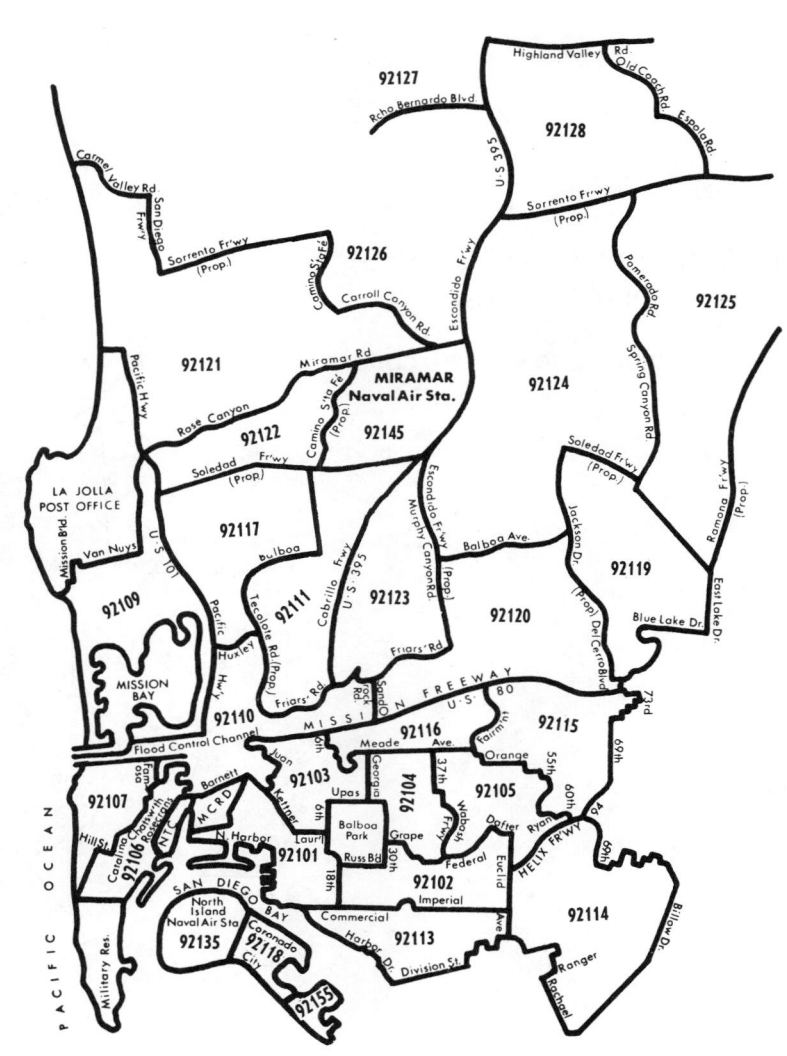

POSTAL ZIP CODE ZONES
SAN DIEGO
California

474

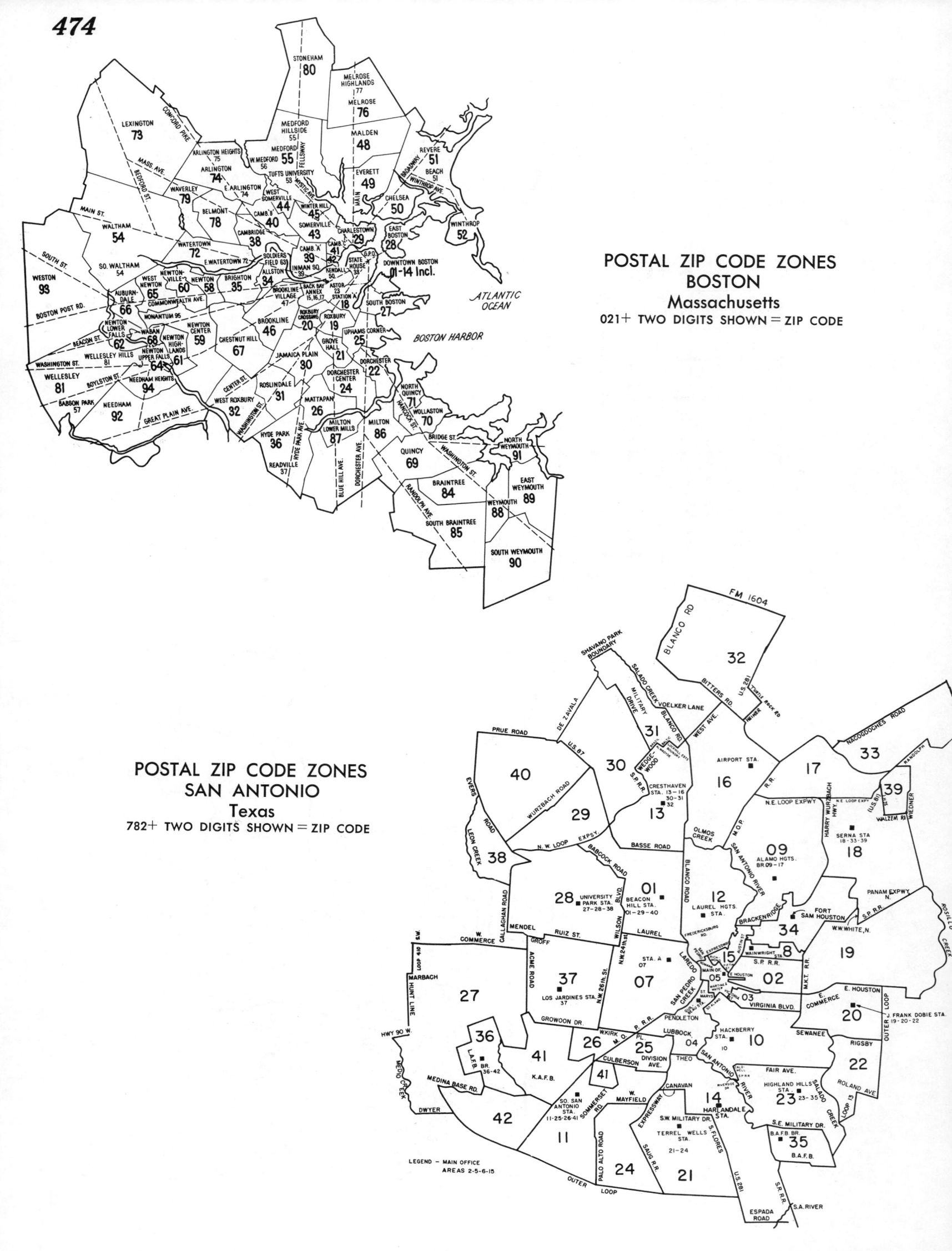

POSTAL ZIP CODE ZONES
BOSTON
Massachusetts
021+ TWO DIGITS SHOWN = ZIP CODE

POSTAL ZIP CODE ZONES
SAN ANTONIO
Texas
782+ TWO DIGITS SHOWN = ZIP CODE

MAP PROJECTIONS

by Erwin Raisz

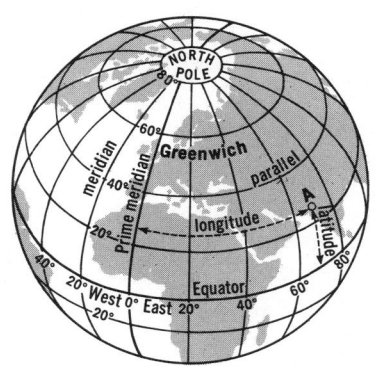

Our earth is rotating around its *axis* once a day. The two end points of its axis are the *poles;* the line circling the earth midway between the poles is the *equator.* The arc from either of the poles to the equator is divided into 90 *degrees.* The distance, expressed in degrees, from the equator to any point is its *latitude* and circles of equal latitude are the *parallels.* On maps it is customary to show parallels of evenly-spaced degrees such as every fifth or every tenth.

The equator is divided into 360 degrees. Lines circling from pole to pole through the degree points on the equator are called *meridians.* They are all equal in length but by international agreement the meridian passing through the Greenwich Observatory in London has been chosen as *prime meridian.* The distance, expressed in degrees, from the prime meridian to any point is its *longitude.* While meridians are all equal in length, parallels become shorter and shorter as they approach the poles. Whereas one degree of latitude represents everywhere approximately 69 miles, one degree of longitude varies from 69 miles at the equator to nothing at the poles.

Each degree is divided into 60 minutes and each minute into 60 seconds. One minute of latitude equals a nautical mile.

The map is flat but the earth is nearly spherical. Neither a rubber ball nor any part of a rubber ball may be flattened without stretching or tearing unless the part is very small. To present the curved surface of the earth on a flat map is not difficult as long as the areas under consideration are small, but the mapping of countries, continents, or the whole earth requires some kind of *projection.* Any regular set of parallels and meridians upon which a map can be drawn makes a map projection. Many systems are used.

In any projection only the parallels or the meridians or some other set of lines can be *true* (the same length as on the globe of corresponding scale); all other lines are too long or too short. Only on a globe is it possible to have both the parallels and the meridians true. The scale given on a flat map cannot be true everywhere. The construction of the various projections begins usually with laying out the parallels or meridians which have true lengths.

Rectangular Projection

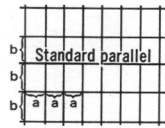

RECTANGULAR PROJECTION — This is a set of evenly-placed meridians and horizontal parallels. The central or *standard parallel* and all meridians are true. All other parallels are either too long or too short. The projection is used for simple maps of small areas, as city plans, etc.

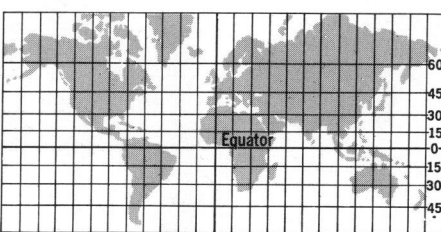

Mercator Projection

MERCATOR PROJECTION — In this projection the meridians are evenly-spaced vertical lines. The parallels are horizontal, spaced so that their length has the same relation to the meridians as on a globe. As the meridians converge at higher latitudes on the globe, while on the map they do not, the parallels have to be drawn also farther and farther apart to maintain the correct relationship. When every very small area has the same shape as on a globe we call the projection *conformal.* The most interesting quality of this projection is that all *compass directions* appear as straight lines. For this reason it is generally used for marine charts. It is also frequently used for world maps in spite of the fact that the high latitudes are very much exaggerated in size. Only the equator is true to scale; all other parallels and meridians are too long. The Mercator projection did *not* derive from projecting a globe upon a cylinder.

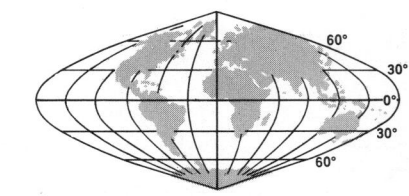

Sinusoidal Projection

SINUSOIDAL PROJECTION — The parallels are truly-spaced horizontal lines. They are divided truly and the connecting curves make the meridians. It does not make a good world map because the outer regions are distorted, but the central portion is good and this part is often used for maps of Africa and South America. Every part of the map has the same area as the corresponding area on the globe. It is an *equal-area* projection.

MOLLWEIDE PROJECTION — The meridians are equally-spaced ellipses; the parallels are horizontal lines spaced so that every belt of latitude should have the same area as on a globe. This projection is popular for world maps, especially in European atlases.

GOODE'S INTERRUPTED PROJECTIONS—Only the good central part of the Mollweide or sinusoidal (or both) projection is used and the oceans are cut. This makes an equal-area map with little distortion of shape. It is commonly used for world maps.

ECKERT PROJECTIONS — These are similar to the sinusoidal or the Mollweide projections, but the poles are shown as lines half the length of the equator. There are several variants; the meridians are either sine curves or ellipses; the parallels are horizontal and spaced either evenly or so as to make the projection equal area. Their use for world maps is increasing. The figure shows the elliptical equal-area variant.

CONIC PROJECTION — The original idea of the conic projection is that of capping the globe by a cone upon which both the parallels and meridians are projected from the center of the globe. The cone is then cut open and laid flat. A cone can be made tangent to any chosen *standard parallel.*

The actually-used conic projection is a modification of this idea. The radius of the standard parallel is obtained as above. The meridians are straight radiating lines spaced truly on the standard parallel. The parallels are concentric circles spaced at true distances. All parallels except the standard are too long. The projection is used for maps of countries in middle latitudes, as it presents good shapes with small scale error.

There are several variants: The use of *two standard parallels,* one near the top, the other near the bottom of the map, reduces the scale error. In the *Albers projection* the parallels are spaced unevenly, to make the projection equal-area. This is a good projection for the United States. In the *Lambert conformal conic projection* the parallels are spaced so that any small quadrangle of the grid should have the same shape as on the globe. This is the best projection for air-navigation charts as it has relatively straight azimuths.

An *azimuth* is a great-circle direction reckoned clockwise from north. A *great-circle direction* points to a place along the shortest line on the earth's surface. This is not the same as compass direction. The center of a great circle is the center of the globe.

BONNE PROJECTION — The parallels are laid out exactly as in the conic projection. All parallels are divided truly and the connecting curves make the meridians. It is an equal-area projection. It is used for maps of the northern continents, as Asia, Europe, and North America.

POLYCONIC PROJECTION — The central meridian is divided truly. The parallels are non-concentric circles, the radii of which are obtained by drawing tangents to the globe as though the globe were covered by several cones rather than by only one. Each parallel is divided truly and the connecting curves make the meridians. All meridians except the central one are too long. This projection is used for large-scale topographic sheets — less often for countries or continents.

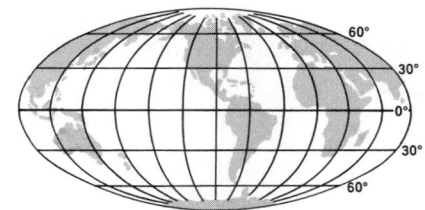

Mollweide Projection

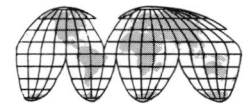

Goode's Interrupted Projection

Eckert Projection

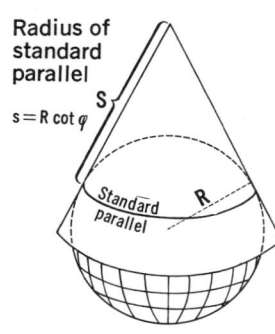

Radius of standard parallel

$s = R \cot \varphi$

Conic Projection

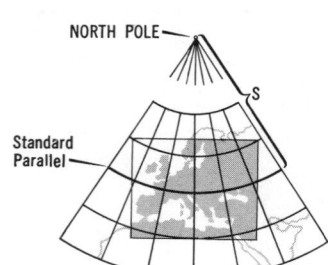

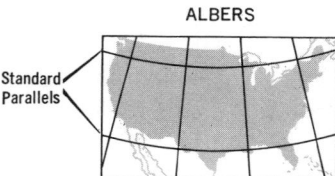

ALBERS

Albers Projection

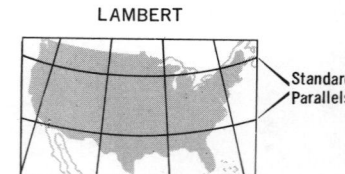

LAMBERT

Lambert Conformal Conic Projection

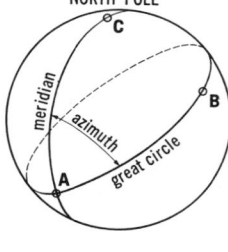

Bonne Projection

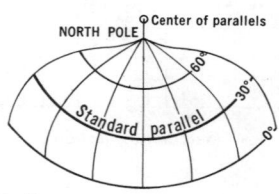

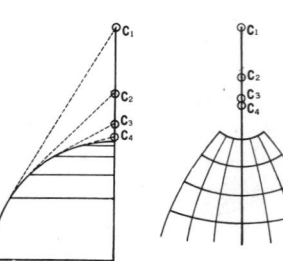

Polyconic Projection

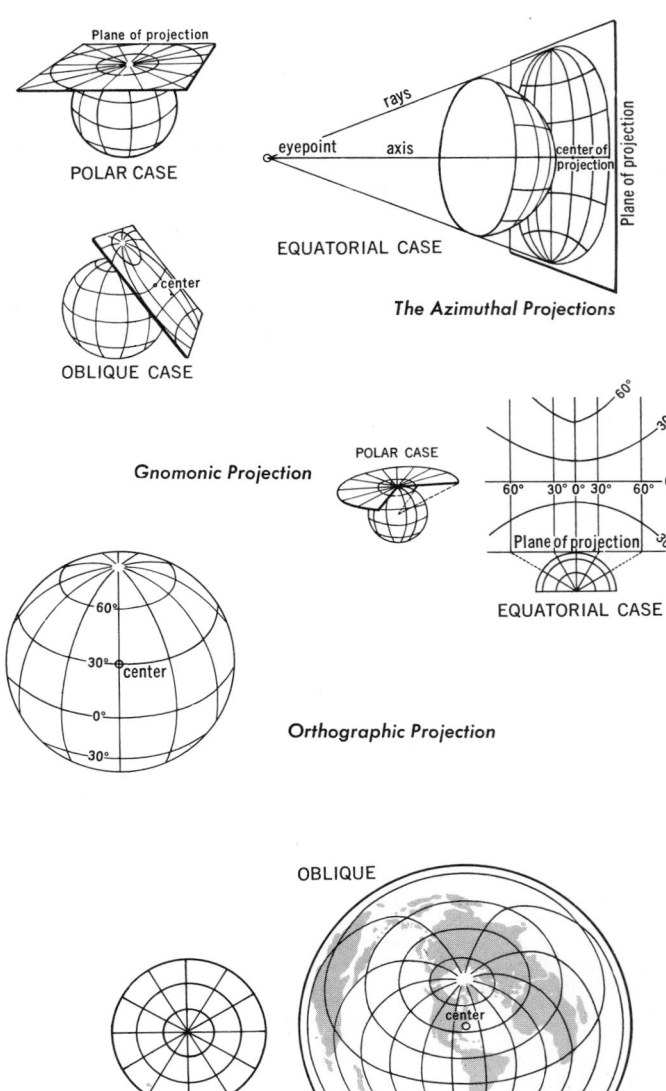

The Azimuthal Projections

Gnomonic Projection

Orthographic Projection

Azimuthal Equidistant Projection

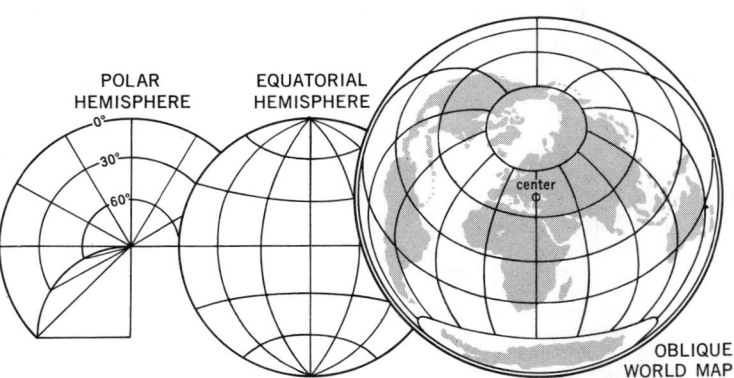

Lambert Azimuthal Equal-Area Projection

THE AZIMUTHAL PROJECTIONS — In this group a part of the globe is projected from an eyepoint onto a plane. The eyepoint can be at different distances, making different projections. The plane of projection can be tangent at the equator, at a pole, or at any other point on which we want to focus attention. The most important quality of all azimuthal projections is that they show every point at its true direction (azimuth) from the center point, and all points equally distant from the center point will be equally distant on the map also.

GNOMONIC PROJECTION — This projection has the eyepoint at the center of the globe Only the central part is good; the outer regions are badly distorted. Yet the projection has one important quality, all great circles being shown as straight lines. For this reason it is used for laying out the routes for long range flying or trans-oceanic navigation.

ORTHOGRAPHIC PROJECTION — This projection has the eyepoint at infinite distance and the projecting rays are parallel. The polar or equatorial varieties are rare but the oblique case became very popular on account of its visual quality. It looks like a picture of a globe. Although the distortion on the peripheries is extreme, we see it correctly because the eye perceives it not as a map but as a picture of a three-dimensional globe. Obviously only a hemisphere (half globe) can be shown.

Some azimuthal projections do not derive from the actual process of projecting from an eyepoint, but are arrived at by other means:

AZIMUTHAL EQUIDISTANT PROJECTION — This is the only projection in which every point is shown both at true great-circle direction and at true distance from the center point, but all other directions and distances are distorted. The principle of the projection can best be understood from the polar case. Most polar maps are in this projection. The oblique case is used for radio direction finding, for earthquake research, and in long-distance flying. A separate map has to be constructed for each central point selected.

LAMBERT AZIMUTHAL EQUAL-AREA PROJECTION—The construction of this projection can best be understood from the polar case. All three cases are widely used. It makes a good polar map and it is often extended to include the southern continents. It is the most common projection used for maps of the Eastern and Western Hemispheres, and it is a good projection for continents as it shows correct areas with relatively little distortion of shape. Most of the continent maps in this atlas are in this projection.

IN THIS ATLAS, on almost all maps, parallels and meridians have been marked because they are useful for the following:

(a) They show the north-south and east-west directions which appear on many maps at oblique angles especially near the margins.

(b) With the help of parallels and meridians every place can be exactly located; for instance, New York City is at 41° N and 74° W on any map.

(c) They help to measure distances even in the distorted parts of the map. The scale given on each map is true only along certain lines which are specified in the foregoing discussion for each projection. One degree of latitude equals nearly 69 statute miles or 60 nautical miles. The length of one degree of longitude varies (1° long. = 1° lat. × cos lat.).

WORLD STATISTICAL TABLES

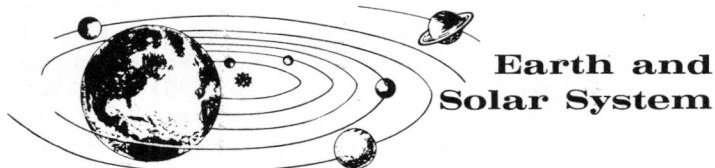

Earth and Solar System

Elements of the Solar System

	Mean Distance From Sun in Miles	Period of Revolution Around Sun	Period of Rotation on Axis	Equatorial Diameter in Miles	Surface Gravity (Earth=1)	Mean Density (Water=1)	Number of Satellites
SUN	....	....	25.4 days	864,000	27.95	1.4	....
MERCURY	36,001,000	87.97 days	59 days (?)	3,100	0.38	5.3	0
VENUS	67,272,000	224.70 days	247 days (?)	7,700	0.88	4.9	0
EARTH	93,003,000	365.26 days	23h 56m	7,927	1.00	5.5	1
MARS	141,708,000	687 days	24h 37m	4,200	0.39	4.0	2
JUPITER	483,880,000	11.86 years	9h 50m	88,698	2.65	1.3	12
SATURN	887,141,000	29.46 years	10h 14m	75,060	1.17	0.7	10
URANUS	1,782,000,000	84.02 years	10h 45m	29,200	1.05	1.3	5
NEPTUNE	2,792,000,000	164.79 years	15h 48m	27,700	1.23	1.6	2
PLUTO	3,664,000,000	247.7 years	6.4 days (?)	8,700 (?)	0.7 (?)	?	0

Dimensions of the Earth

Superficial area	197,272,000	sq. miles
Land surface	57,491,000	" "
North America	9,363,000	" "
South America	6,875,000	" "
Europe	4,063,000	" "
Asia	17,032,000	" "
Africa	11,682,000	" "
Australia	2,967,741	" "
Water surface	139,781,000	" "
Atlantic Ocean	31,862,000	" "
Pacific Ocean	64,186,000	" "
Indian Ocean	28,350,000	" "
Arctic Ocean	3,662,000	" "
Equatorial circumference	24,902	miles
Meridional circumference	24,860	"
Equatorial diameter	7,926.677	"
Polar diameter	7,899.988	"
Equatorial radius	3,963.34	"
Polar radius	3,949.99	"
Volume of the Earth	260,000,000,000 cubic miles	
Mass, or weight	6,592,000,000,000,000,000,000 tons	
Mean distance from the Sun	93,003,000 miles	

The Moon is the Earth's natural satellite. The mean distance which separates the Earth from the Moon is 238,857 miles. The Moon's true period of revolution (sidereal month) is 27⅓ days. The Moon rotates on its own axis once during this time. The phase period or time between new moons (synodic month) is 29½ days. The Moon's diameter is 2,160 miles, its density is 3.3 and its surface gravity is 0.2.

Principal Lakes and Inland Seas

	AREA IN SQ. MILES
Caspian Sea	143,200
Lake Superior	32,483
Lake Victoria	26,828
Aral Sea	24,630
Lake Huron	23,860
Lake Michigan	22,178
Lake Tanganyika	12,700
Great Bear Lake	12,275
Lake Baykal	12,162
Lake Nyasa	11,500
Great Slave Lake	10,980
Lake Erie	9,889
Lake Winnipeg	9,465
Lake Ontario	7,313
Lake Ladoga	7,100
Lake Balkhash	6,700
Lake Chad	6,500
Lake Onega	3,765
Lake Titicaca	3,200
Lake Athabasca	3,120
Lake Nicaragua	3,100
Lake Rudolf	2,473
Reindeer Lake	2,467
Issyk-Kul'	2,276
Vänern	2,149
Lake Winnipegosis	2,103
Kariba Lake	2,050
Lake Urmia	1,795
Lake Albert	1,640
Lake Peipus	1,400
Lake Tana	1,219
Great Salt Lake	1,100
Lake Bangweulu	Approx. 1,000
Vättern	733
Dead Sea	405
Lake Balaton	266
Lake Geneva	225
Lake of Constance	208
Lake Garda	143
Lake of Neuchâtel	83
Lake Maggiore	82
Lake Como	56
Lake of Lucerne	44.5
Lake of Zurich	34

Oceans and Seas of the World

	AREA IN SQ. MILES	GREATEST DEPTH IN FEET	VOLUME IN CUBIC MILES
Pacific Ocean	64,186,000	36,198	167,025,000
Atlantic Ocean	31,862,000	28,374	77,580,000
Indian Ocean	28,350,000	25,344	68,213,000
Arctic Ocean	3,662,000	17,880	3,026,000
Mediterranean Sea	960,000	16,896	1,019,400
Bering Sea	875,000	13,422	788,500
Caribbean Sea	970,000	24,720	2,298,400
Sea of Okhotsk	590,000	11,070	454,700
East China Sea	482,000	10,500	52,700
Hudson Bay	476,000	1,500	37,590
Japan Sea	389,000	13,242	383,200
North Sea	222,000	2,654	12,890
Red Sea	169,000	7,254	53,700
Black Sea	185,000	7,200	....
Baltic Sea	163,000	1,506	5,360

Great Ship Canals

	LENGTH IN MILES	DEPTH IN FEET
Baltic-White Sea, U.S.S.R.	141	....
Suez, U.A.R.	100.76	34
Albert, Belgium	81	16.5
Moscow-Volga, U.S.S.R.	80	18
Kiel, West Germany	61	37
Göta, Sweden	54	10
Panama, Canal Zone	50.72	41
Houston Ship, U.S.A.	50	36
Amsterdam-Rhine, Netherlands	45	41
Beaumont-Port Arthur, U.S.A.	40	32
Manchester Ship, England	35.5	28
Chicago Sanitary and Ship, U.S.A.	30	22
Welland, Canada	27.6	30
Juliana, Netherlands	21	11.8
Chesapeake and Delaware, U.S.A.	19	27
Cape Cod, U.S.A.	13	25
Lake Washington, U.S.A.	8	30
Corinth, Greece	4	26.25
Sault Ste. Marie, U.S.A.	1.6	24.5
Sault Ste. Marie, Canada	1.4	18.25

Principal Islands of the World

	AREA IN SQ. MILES		AREA IN SQ. MILES		AREA IN SQ. MILES		AREA IN SQ. MILES
Greenland	840,000	Tierra del Fuego	18,500	Wrangel	2,819	Orkney Islands	376
New Guinea	320,000	Melville	16,369	Canary Islands	2,808	Madeira Islands	308
Borneo	287,000	Kyushu	16,200	Kerguélen	2,700	Dominica	290
Madagascar	226,467	Southampton	15,700	Prince Edward	2,184	Tonga	270
Baffin	183,810	Solomon Islands	15,580	Trindad and Tobago	1,980	Caroline Islands	267
Sumatra	164,148	New Britain	14,098	Balearic Islands	1,936	Molokai	261
Philippines	115,707	Taiwan (Formosa)	13,948	Madura	1,752	St. Lucia	238
New Zealand	103,736	Hainan	13,000	South Georgia	1,600	Corfu	229
Honshu	88,923	Prince of Wales	12,830	Cape Verde Islands	1,557	Bornholm	227
England-Scotland-Wales	88,755	Vancouver	12,408	Long I., New York	1,401	Isle of Man	227
Ellesmere	82,119	Timor	11,527	Socotra	1,400	Singapore	226
Victoria	81,930	Sicily	9,926	Gotland	1,225	Guam	212
Celebes	72,986	Somerset	9,370	Isle of Pines	1,180	Isle Royale	210
Java	48,842	Sardinia	9,301	Samoa	1,173	Virgin Islands	192
Cuba	44,206	Shikoku	7,244	Réunion	969	Curaçao	182
Newfoundland	43,359	New Caledonia	7,335	Azores	893	Barbados	166
Luzon	40,420	Fiji Islands	7,015	Ryukyu Islands	848	St. Vincent	150
Iceland	39,768	New Hebrides	5,700	Fernando Po	786	Isle of Wight	147
Mindanao	36,537	Kuril Islands	5,700	Tenerife	785	Lanai	141
Ireland	32,059	Falkland Islands	4,618	Maui	728	Grenada	133
Novaya Zemlya	31,900	Jamaica	4,411	Mauritius	709	Maltese Islands	122
Hokkaido	30,305	Bahama Islands	4,404	Zanzibar	640	Tobago	116
Molucca Islands	30,168	Hawaii	4,036	Oahu	604	Seychelles	109
Hispaniola	29,398	Cape Breton	3,970	Guadeloupe	583	Martha's Vinyard	109
Sakhalin	28,215	New Ireland	3,800	Ahvenanmaa (Aland Is.)	564	Channel Islands	75
Tasmania	26,215	Cyprus	3,473	Kauai	551	Nantucket	57
Ceylon	25,332	Puedto Rico	3,435	Shetland Islands	551	St. Helena	47
Svalbard	23,958	Corsica	3,368	Rhodes	542	Ascension	34
Banks	23,230	Crete	3,218	Martinique	425	Hong Kong	29
Devon	20,861	Galápagos Islands	3,042	Tahiti	402	Manhattan, New York	22
Bismarck Arch.	18,770	Hebrides	3,000	Pemba	380	Bermudas	21

Principal Mountains of the World

	FEET		FEET
Everest, Nepal-China	29,028	Dykh-Tau, U.S.S.R.	17,054
Godwin Austen (K2), India	28,250	Ararat, Turkey	16,946
Kanchenjunga, Nepal-India	28,208	Vinson Massif, Antarctica	16,864
Dhaulagiri, Nepal	26,810	Margherita (Ruwenzori), Africa	16,795
Nanga Parbat, India	26,660	Kazbek, U.S.S.R.	16,558
Annapurna, Nepal	26,504	Djaja, Indonesia	16,503
Nanda Devi, India	25,645	Blanc, France	15,771
Kamet, India	25,447	Klyuchevskaya Sopka, U.S.S.R.	15,584
Gurla Mandhata, China	25,355	Rosa (Dufourspitze), Italy-Switzerland	15,203
Tirich Mir, Pakistan	25,230	Ras Dashan, Ethiopia	15,157
Minya Konka, China	24,902	Matterhorn, Switzerland	14,688
Muztagh Ata, China	24,757	Whitney, California	14,494
Communism, U.S.S.R.	24,590	Elbert, Colorado	14,433
Pobeda Peak, U.S.S.R.	24,406	Rainer, Washington	14,410
Chomo Lhari, India-China	23,997	Markham, Antarctica	14,272
Muztagh, China	23,891	Shasta, California	14,162
Aconcagua, Argentina	22,831	Pikes Peak, Colorado	14,110
Ojos del Salado, Chile-Arg.	22,572	Finsteraarhorn, Switzerland	14,022
Tupungato, Chile-Argentina	22,310	Tajumulco, Guatemala	13,845
Mercedario, Argentina	22,211	Mauna Kea, Hawaii	13,796
Huascarán, Peru	22,205	Mauna Loa, Hawaii	13,680
Llullaillaco Volcano, Chile-Arg.	22,057	Toubkal, Morocco	13,665
Ancohuma, Bolivia	21,489	Jungfrau, Switzerland	13,642
Illampu, Bolivia	21,276	Cameroon, Cameroon	13,350
Chimborazo, Ecuador	20,561	Gran Paradiso, Italy	13,323
McKinley, Alaska	20,320	Robson, British Columbia	12,972
Logan, Yukon	19,850	Grossglockner, Austria	12,461
Cotopaxi, Ecuador	19,347	Fuji, Japan	12,389
Kilimanjaro, Tanzania	19,340	Cook, New Zealand	12,349
El Misti, Peru	19,199	Pico de Teide, Canary Is.	12,172
Citlaltépetl (Orizaba), Mexico	18,855	Semeru, Java, Indonesia	12,060
El'brus, U.S.S.R.	18,481	Mulhacén, Spain	11,411
Demavend, Iran	18,376	Etna, Italy	11,053
St. Elias, Alaska-Yukon	18,008	Lassen Peak, California	10,457
Vilcanota, Peru	17,999	Kosciusko, Australia	7,316
Popocatépetl, Mexico	17,887	Mitchell, North Carolina	6,684
Kenya, Kenya	17,058		

Longest Rivers of the World

	LENGTH IN MILES		LENGTH IN MILES
Nile, Africa	4,145	Japurá, S.A.	1,500
Amazon, S.A.	3,900	Arkansas, U.S.A.	1,450
Mississippi-Missouri, U.S.A.	3,741	Colorado, U.S.A.-Mexico	1,450
Ob-Irtysh, U.S.S.R.	3,460	Dnieper, U.S.S.R.	1,418
Yangtze, China	3,400	Negro, S.A.	1,400
Hwang (Yellow), China	2,900	Orange, Africa	1,350
Congo, Africa	2,718	Kolyma, U.S.S.R.	1,335
Amur, Asia	2,700	Irrawaddy, Burma	1,325
Lena, U.S.S.R.	2,680	Ohio, U.S.A.	1,306
Mackenzie, Canada	2,635	Kama, U.S.S.R.	1,262
Mekong, Asia	2,600	Red, U.S.A.	1,222
Niger, Africa	2,600	Don, U.S.S.R.	1,222
Yenisey, U.S.S.R.	2,543	Columbia, U.S.A.-Canada	1,214
Paraná, S.A.	2,450	Saskatchewan, Canada	1,205
Murray-Darling, Australia	2,310	Peace, Canada	1,195
Volga, U.S.S.R.	2,194	Darling, Australia	1,160
Madeira, S.A.	2,000	Angara, U.S.S.R.	1,151
St. Lawrence, Canada-U.S.A.	1,900	Tigris, Asia	1,150
Rio Grande, U.S.A.-Mexico	1,885	Sungari, Asia	1,130
Yukon, Alaska-Canada	1,875	Pechora, U.S.S.R.	1,111
Purus, S.A.	1,850	Snake, U.S.A.	1,000
São Francisco, Brazil	1,800	Churchill, Canada	1,000
Salween, Asia	1,750	Pilcomayo, S.A.	1,000
Danube, Europe	1,725	Uruguay, S.A.	1,000
Euphrates, Asia	1,700	Magdalena, Colombia	1,000
Indus, Asia	1,700	Platte-N. Platte, U.S.A.	990
Tocantins, Brazil	1,700	Oka, U.S.S.R.	918
Brahmaputra, Asia	1,680	Canadian, U.S.A.	906
Syr-Dar'ya, U.S.S.R.	1,680	Colorado, Texas, U.S.A.	894
Si, China	1,650	Brazos, U.S.A.	870
Ganges, Asia	1,650	Tennessee, U.S.A.	869
Orinoco, S.A.	1,600	South Saskatchewan, Canada	865
Nelson, Canada	1,600	Dniester, U.S.S.R.	852
Zambezi, Africa	1,600	Fraser, Canada	850
Ural, U.S.S.R.	1,574	Northern Dvina, U.S.S.R.	803
Amu-Dar'ya, Asia	1,550	Tisza, Europe	800
Olenek, U.S.S.R.	1,500	North Canadian, U.S.A.	784
Paraguay, S.A.	1,500	Athabasca, Canada	765

GEOGRAPHICAL TERMS

A. = Arabic Camb. = Cambodian Ch. = Chinese Czech. = Czechoslovakian Dan. = Danish Du. = Dutch Finn. = Finnish Fr. = French Ger. = German Ice. = Icelandic
It. = Italian Jap. = Japanese Mong. = Mongol Nor. = Norwegian Per. = Persian Port. = Portuguese Russ. = Russian Sp. = Spanish Sw. = Swedish Turk. = Turkish

Å	Nor., Sw.	Stream
Aas	Dan., Nor.	Hills
Abajo	Sp	Lower
Ada, Adasi	Turk	Island
Altipiano	It	Plateau
Altiplano	Sp	Plateau
Alv, Alf, Elf	Sw	River
Arrecife	Sp	Reef
Asa	Nor., Sw.	Hill
Asaga	Turk	Lower
Austral	Sp	Southern
Baai	Du	Bay
Bab	Arabic	Gate or Strait
Bahia	Sp	Bay
Bahr	Arabic	Marsh, Lake, Sea, River
Baia	Port	Bay
Baie	Fr	Bay, Gulf
Baizo	Port	Low
Bakke	Dan	Hill
Bana	Jap	Cape
Bañados	Sp	Marshes
Band	Per	Mt. Range
Barra	Sp	Reef
Bel	Turk	Pass
Belt	Ger	Strait
Ben	Gaelic	Mountain
Bera	Du	Mountain
Berg	Ger., Du.	Mountain
Bir	Arabic	Well
Birket	Arabic	Pond
Boca	Sp	Gulf, Inlet
Boğhaz	Turk	Strait
Bolshoi, Bolshaya	Russ	Big
Bolson	Sp	Depression
Bong	Korean	Mountain
Boreal	Sp	Northern
Breen	Nor	Glacier
Bro	Dan., Nor., Sw.	Bridge
Bucht	Ger	Bay
Bugt	Dan	Bay
Bukhta	Russ	Bay
Bukit	Malay	Hill, Mountain
Bukt	Nor., Sw.	Bay, Gulf
Burnu, Burun	Turk	Cape, Point
By	Dan., Nor., Sw.	Town
Cabo	Port., Sp.	Cape
Campos	Port	Plains
Canal	Port., Sp.	Channel
Cap, Capo	Fr., It	Cape
Cataratas	Sp	Falls
Catena	It	Mt. Range
Catingas	Port	Open Woodlands
Central, Centrale	Fr., It	Middle
Cerrito, Cerro	Sp	Hill
Cerros	Sp	Hills, Mountains
Chai	Turk	River
Chow	Ch	Town of the second rank
Ciénaga	Sp	Swamp
Ciudad	Sp	City
Col	Fr	Pass
Cordillera	Sp	Mt. Range, Mts.
Côte	Fr	Coast
Csatoria	Magyar	Canal
Cuchilla	Sp	Mt. Range
Curiche	Sp	Swamp
Dag, Dagh	Turk	Mountain
Dağlari	Turk	Mt. Range
Dal	Nor., Sw.	Valley
Dar	Arabic	Land
Darya	Per	Salt Lake
Dasht	Per	Desert, Plain
Deniz, Denizi	Turk	Sea, Lake
Desierto	Sp	Desert
Détroit	Fr	Strait
Djeziret	Arabic, Turk	Island
Do	Korean	Island
Doi	Thai	Mountain
Eiland	Du	Island
Elv	Dan., Nor	River
Embalse	Sp	Reservoir
Emi	Berber	Mountain
Erg	Arabic	Dune, Desert
Eski	Turk	Old
Est, Este	Fr., Port., Sp.	East
Estero	Sp	Estuary, Creek
Estrecho, Estreito	Sp., Port	Strait
Etang	Fr	Pond, Lagoon, Lake
Fedja, Feij	Arabic	Pass
Fiume	It	River
Fjäll	Sw	Mountain
Fjeld, Fjell	Nor	Hills, Mountain
Fjord	Dan., Nor., Sw.	Fiord
Fleuve	Fr	River
Fljót	Icelandic	Stream
Fluss	Ger	River
Fokani, Fukani	Arabic	Upper
Fors	Sw	Waterfall
Fos, Foss	Dan., Nor	Waterfall
Fu	Ch	Town of importance
Gamla	Nor	Old
Gamle	Dan	Old
Gata	Jap	Lake
Gawa	Jap	River
Gebel	Arabic	Mountain
Gebergte	Du	Mt. Range
Gebirge	Ger	Mt. Range
Ghubbet	Arabic	Bay
Gobi	Mongol	Desert
Goe	Jap	Pass
Gol	Mongol, Turk	Lake, Stream
Golf	Ger., Du.	Gulf
Golfe	Fr	Gulf
Golfo	Sp., It., Port	Gulf
Gölü	Turk	Lake
Gora	Russ	Mountain
Grand, Grande	Fr., Sp	Big
Groot	Du	Big
Gross	Ger	Big
Grosso	It., Port	Big
Guba	Russ	Bay, Gulf
Gunto	Jap	Archipelago
Gunung	Malay	Mountain
Hai	Ch	Sea
Halbinsel	Ger	Peninsula
Hamáda, Hammada	Arabic	Rocky Plateau
Hamn	Sw	Harbor
Hamún	Per	Marsh
Hanto	Jap	Peninsula
Has, Hassi	Arabic	Well
Hav	Dan., Nor., Sw.	Sea, Ocean
Havet	Nor	Bay
Havn	Dan., Nor	Harbor
Havre	Fr	Harbor
Higashi, Higasi	Jap	East
Ho	Ch	River
Hochebene	Ger	Plateau
Hoek	Du	Cape
Hoku	Jap	North
Holm	Dan., Nor., Sw.	Island
Hory	Czech	Mountains
Hoved	Dan., Nor	Cape, Promontory
Hsien	Ch	Town of the third class
Hu	Ch	Lake
Huk	Dan., Nor., Sw.	Point
Hus, Huus	Dan., Nor., Sw.	House
Hwang	Ch	Yellow
Ile	Fr	Island
Ilet	Fr	Islet
Ilot	Fr	Islet
Indre	Dan., Nor	Inner
Inferieur, Inferiore	Fr., It	Lower
Inner, Inre	Sw	Inner
Insel	Ger	Island
Irmak	Turk	River
Isla	Sp	Island
Isola	It	Island
Jabal, Jebel	Arabic	Mountains
Järvi	Finn	Lake
Jaure	Sw	Lake
Jezira	Arabic	Island
Jima	Jap	Island
Joki	Finn	River
Kaap	Du	Cape
Kabir, Kebir	Arabic	Big
Kai	Jap	Sea
Kaikyo	Jap	Strait
Kami	Turk	Upper
Kanaal	Du	Canal
Kanal	Russ., Ger	Canal, Channel
Kao	Thai	Mountain
Kap, Kapp	Nor., Sw., Ice	Cape
Kaupunki	Finn	Town
Kawa	Jap	River
Khao	Thai	Mountain
Khrebet	Russ	Mt. Range
Kiang	Ch	River
Kiao	Ch	Point
Kita	Jap	North
Klein	Du., Ger	Small
Klint	Dan	Promontory
Kô	Jap	Lake
Ko	Thai	Island
Koh	Camb., Khmer	Island
Kong	Ch	River
Kop	Du	Peak, Head
Köping	Sw	Market, Borough
Körfez, Körfezi	Turk	Gulf
Kosa	Russ	Spit
Kosui	Jap	Lake
Kraal	Du	Native Village
Kuchuk	Turk	Small
Kuh	Per	Mountain
Kul	Sinkiang Turki	Lake
Kum	Turk	Desert
Kuro	Jap	Black
Laag	Du	Low
Lac	Fr	Lake
Lago	Port., Sp., It	Lake
Lagoa	Port	Lagoon
Laguna	Sp	Lagoon
Lagune	Fr	Lagoon
Lahti	Finn	Bay, Bight
Län	Sw	County
Lilla	Sw	Small
Lille	Dan., Nor	Small
Ling	Ch	Mountain
Llanos	Sp	Plains
Mae Nam	Thai	River
Mali, Malaya	Russ	Small
Man	Korean	Bay
Mar	Sp., Port	Sea
Mare	It	Sea
Medio	Sp	Middle
Meer	Du	Lake
Meer	Ger	Sea
Mer	Fr	Sea
Meridionale	It	Southern
Meseta	Sp	Plateau
Middelst, Midden	Du	Middle
Minami	Jap	Southern
Mir	Per	Mountain
Mis	Russ	Cape
Misaki	Jap	Cape
Mittel	Ger	Middle
Mont	Fr	Mountain
Montagne	Fr	Mountain
Montaña	Sp	Mountains
Monte	Sp., It., Port	Mountain
More	Russ	Sea
Morro	Port., Sp	Mountain, Promontory
Morue	Fr	Hill
Moyen	Fr	Middle
Muong	Siamese	Town
Mys	Russ	Cape
Nada	Jap	Sea
Naka	Jap	Middle
Nam	Burm., Lao	River
Nan	Ch., Jap	South
Nes	Nor	Cape, Point
Nevado	Sp	Snow covered peak
Nieder	Ger	Lower
Nishi, Nisi	Jap	West
Nizhni, Nizhnyaya	Russ	Lower
Njarga	Finn	Peninsula, Promontory
Nong	Thai	Lake
Noord	Du	North
Nor	Mong	Lake
Nord	Fr., Ger	North
Norte	Sp., It., Port	North
Nos	Russ	Cape
Novi, Novaya	Russ	New
Nusa	Malay	Island
Ny, Nya	Nor., Sw.	New
O	Jap	Big
Ö	Nor., Sw.	Island
Ober	Ger	Upper
Occidental, Occidentale	Sp., It	Western
Odde	Dan	Point
Oeste	Port	West
Ola	Mong	Mountains
Ooster	Du	Eastern
Opper, Over	Du	Upper
Oriental	Sp., Fr	Eastern
Orientale	It	Eastern
Orta	Turk	Middle
Ost	Ger	East
Ostrov	Russ	Island
Ouest	Fr	West
öy	Nor	Island
Ozero	Russ	Lake
Pampa	Sp	Plain
Pas	Fr	Channel, Strait
Paso	Sp	Pass
Passo	It., Port	Pass
Peh, Pei	Ch	North
Peña	Sp	Rock, Mountain
Penisola	It	Peninsula
Pequeño	Sp	Small
Pereval	Russ	Pass
Peski	Russ	Desert
Petit	Fr	Small
Phu	Lao, Annamese	Mtn.
Pic	Fr	Mountain
Piccolo	It	Small
Pico	Port., Sp	Mountain, Peak
Pik	Russ	Mountain, Peak
Piton	Fr	Mountain, Peak
Planalto	Port	Plateau
Plato	Russ	Plateau
Pointe	Fr	Point
Poluostrov	Russ	Peninsula
Ponta	Port	Point
Presa	Sp	Reservoir
Presqu'île	Fr	Peninsula
Proliv	Russ	Strait
Pulou, Pulo	Malay	Island
Punt	Du	Point
Punta	Sp., It., Port	Point
Qum	Turk	Desert
Rada	Sp	Inlet
Rade	Fr	Bay, Inlet
Ras	Arabic	Cape
Reka	Russ	River
Retto	Jap	Archipelago
Ria	Sp	Estuary
Río	Sp	River
Rivier, Rivière	Du., Fr	River
Rud	Per	River
Saghir	Arabic	Small
Sai	Jap	West
Saki	Jap	Cape
Salar, Salina	Sp	Salt Deposit
Salto	Sp., Port	Falls
San	Ch., Jap., Korean	Hill
Sanmaek	Korean	Mt. Range
Schiereiland	Du	Peninsula
Se	Camb., Khmer	River
See	Ger	Sea, Lake
Selvas	Sp., Port	Woods, Forest
Seno	Sp	Bay, Gulf
Serra	Port	Mts.
Serranía	Sp	Mts.
Seto	Jap	Strait
Settentrionale	It	Northern
Severni, Severnaya	Russ	North
Shan	Ch., Jap	Hill, Mts.
Shang	Ch	Upper
Shatt	Arabic	River
Shima	Jap	Island
Shimo	Jap	Lower
Shin	Jap	Land
Shiro	Jap	White
Shoto	Jap	Islands
Si	Ch	West
Siao	Ch	Small
Sierra	Sp	Mt. Range, Mts.
Sjö	Nor., Sw	Lake, Sea
Sok, Suk, Souk	Arabic, Ar. Fr	Market
Song	Annamese	River
Sopka	Russ	Volcano
Spitze	Ger	Mt. Peak
Sredni, Srednyaya	Russ	Middle
Stad	Dan., Nor., Sw	City
Stari, Staraya	Russ	Old
Step	Russ	Treeless Plain
Straat	Du	Strait
Strasse	Ger	Strait
Stretto	It	Strait
Ström	Dan., Nor., Sw	Sound
Stung	Camb., Khmer	River
Su	Turk	River
Sud, Süd	Sp., Fr., Ger	South
Suido	Jap	Strait, Channel
Sul	Port	South
Sund	Dan., Nor., Sw	Sound
Sungei	Malay	River
Supérieur	Fr	Upper
Superior, Superiore	Sp., It	Upper
Sur	Sp	South
Suyu	Turk	River
Ta	Ch	Big
Tafelland	Du	Plateau
Tagh	Turk	Mt. Range
Take	Jap	Peak, Ridge
Takht	Arabic	Lower
Tal	Ger	Valley
Tandjong, Tanjung	Malay	Cape, Point
Tao	Ch	Island
Tell	Arabic	Hill
Thale	Thai	Sea, Lake
Tind	Nor	Peak
Tö	Jap	East
To	Jap	Island
Toge	Jap	Pass
Trask	Finn	Lake
Tso	Tibetan	Lake
Tugh	Somali	Dry River
Tung	Ch	Eastern
Udjung	Malay	Point
Umi	Jap	Bay
Unter	Ger	Lower
Ura	Jap	Inlet
Val	Fr	Valley
Vatn	Nor	Lake
Vecchio	It	Old
Veld	Du	Plain, Field
Velho	Port	Old
Verkhni	Russ	Upper
Vesi	Finn	Lake
Vieho	Sp	Old
Vik	Nor., Sw	Bay
Vishni, Vishnyaya	Russ	High
Vodokhranilishche	Russ	Reservoir
Volcán	Sp	Volcano
Vostochni, Vostochnaya	Russ	East, Eastern
Wadi	Arabic	Dry River
Wald	Ger	Forest
Wan	Jap	Bay
Westersch	Du	Western
Wüste	Ger	Desert
Yama	Jap	Mountain
Yarim Ada	Turk	Peninsula
Yokara	Turk	Upper
Yug, Yuzhni, Yuzhnaya	Russ	South, Southern
Zaki	Jap	Cape
Zaliv	Russ	Bay, Gulf
Zapadni, Zapadnaya	Russ	Western
Zee	Du	Sea
Zemlya	Russ	Land
Zuid	Du	South

Atlas of the Bible Lands

Edited by HARRY THOMAS FRANK

Professor of Religion
Oberlin College

HAMMOND INCORPORATED   MAPLEWOOD, NEW JERSEY

Title page illustration:
Aerial view of Jerusalem from the east.
Buildings in foreground are on the Mount
of Olives. Beyond is the Dome of the Rock.

Wall painting from tomb at Beni-hasan
depicts Asian people, probably Amorites,
entering Egypt about 1900 B.C.

ATLAS OF THE BIBLE LANDS, New Edition
Entire contents © Copyright MCMLXXVII
by HAMMOND INCORPORATED
*All rights reserved. No part of this book may
be reproduced or utilized in any form or by any
means, electronic or mechanical including photo-
copying, recording or by any information storage
and retrieval system, without permission in writing
from the publisher.*

*The maps "Routes in Palestine" and "Economy of
Palestine" on pages 5 and 7 were prepared especially for
Abingdon Press and published in* The Interpreter's
Dictionary of the Bible, Supplementary Volume. *They are
reproduced here with Abingdon's permission.*

Library of Congress Cataloging in Publication Data

Hammond Incorporated.
    Atlas of the Bible Lands.

    Includes index.
    1. Bible—Geography—Maps.   I. Frank, Harry Thomas.
II. Title.
G2230.H3   1977   912'.33   77-6292

Printed in the United States of America

Contents

Preface

THE BIBLE is a universal book, restricted neither by time nor place. Over the centuries on all continents its words have carried a message of hope, solace and salvation for the believer, and on the authority of the Holy Word, societies have been shaped and great events set afoot. Moreover, for the individual person of faith, now as in the past, the Bible is both an indispensable guide and a fundamental point of reference.

Yet the events spoken of in the Bible took place at certain times and in definite places. It is, in fact, basic to a Biblical understanding of revelation that its timeless message was given in historical events, through real persons and at places which can be visited by you and by me. The Bible is thus neither a speculative nor a philosophical book. Rather, it is concrete. It offers no essays on the goodness or the near presence of God, but speaks, for instance, of his being with Abraham as he leaves Ur to journey with many adventures and at God's beckoning to Haran, Shechem and Egypt before returning to settle in Beer-sheba (Genesis 11:28-22:19). It was through Moses in "the Wilderness of Sinai" that Israel received the Ten Commandments (Exodus 19-20). God, says the Bible, was present in the struggles of Deborah and her followers ". . . at Taanach, by the waters of Megiddo" (Judges 5:19). And he was revealing himself in the actions of Joseph, who "went up from Galilee, from the city of Nazareth, to Judea, to the city of David, which is called Bethlehem, because he was of the house and lineage of David, to be enrolled with Mary, his betrothed, who was with child" (Luke 2:4-5).

Where are Ur, Haran, Shechem, Egypt, Beer-sheba, the Wilderness of Sinai, Taanach, Megiddo, Galilee, Nazareth, Judea and Bethlehem? Even the casual reader of the Bible will be struck by the frequency and importance of places in the narrative, and no serious student of the Bible can long afford to be without detailed and accurate knowledge of the lands of the Bible. Indeed, from Haran in the north of Syria to Beer-sheba in the south of Israel, Biblical memories haunt almost every ancient site, and once you pass below the towering Lebanon Mountains and the majestic heights of Hermon there is virtually no town or city, no valley, mountain pass or plain which was not the location of some Biblical event.

Consider Paul as he walked northward from Jerusalem, making his way slowly toward Damascus and his startling conversion to Christianity. What places did he pass, and what memories did they hold? We do not know his exact route, but whatever way he went from the Holy City, Biblical memories lay all about him and whispered to him from the soil of the great deeds of God. If Paul went straight north along the mountain ridge, he passed Gibeah within the hour — Gibeah, the home of Saul, first king of Israel — and shortly passed Ramah and Mizpah, both hallowed by Samuel. The next day Paul would ascend slowly as he neared the desolate site of Bethel, which once echoed to Amos' ringing denunciations. Thus along the road through Samaria, following the course of the great Biblical cities that trace that route: Shiloh, Shechem, Samaria, Dothan — and then into and across the Great Plain where Deborah won an astounding victory with the aid of ". . . the onrushing torrent, the torrent Kishon." As the road winds up into the Galilee hills Nazareth lies nestled to the west, and to the east there are the brooding heights of Gilboa on which Saul and Jonathan ". . . swifter than eagles, stronger than lions . . ." had fallen before the Philistines. And so eventually past the Sea of Galilee with all of its associations with Jesus, and up to the Syrian Heights (The Golan) and into Damascus.

Obviously geography alone cannot convey the Biblical message. But geography, history and religion are inseparably bound together in the Bible. Full understanding and a more complete appreciation of the Bible's unique historical revelation depend upon a certain level of knowledge of its physical setting.

With the aid of this completely new edition of *Hammond's Atlas of the Bible Lands,* sites mentioned in the text of both the Old and New Testaments can quickly be located. Journeys — from that of Abraham to those of the early Christian missionaries — can be easily traced, understood and learned. Fresh, up-to-date maps have been combined with evocative photographs and graphic city plans to serve as a readily usable and convenient companion to the study of the Scriptures. Not only does the user of this Atlas gain a sense of the land itself, but because of the large number of concise, uncluttered, historically-oriented maps each Biblical period comes alive. This historical orientation of the maps is aided by the Time Charts which show parallel events at a glance. These charts help the student of the Bible place Biblical events in their larger historical context.

> ". . . the land which you are going over to possess is a land
> of hills and valleys, which drinks water by the rain from
> heaven, a land which the Lord your God cares for; the eyes
> of the Lord your God are always upon it, from the beginning
> of the year to the end of the year."
> — Deuteronomy 11:11-12

HARRY THOMAS FRANK

Oberlin, Ohio
February 23, 1977

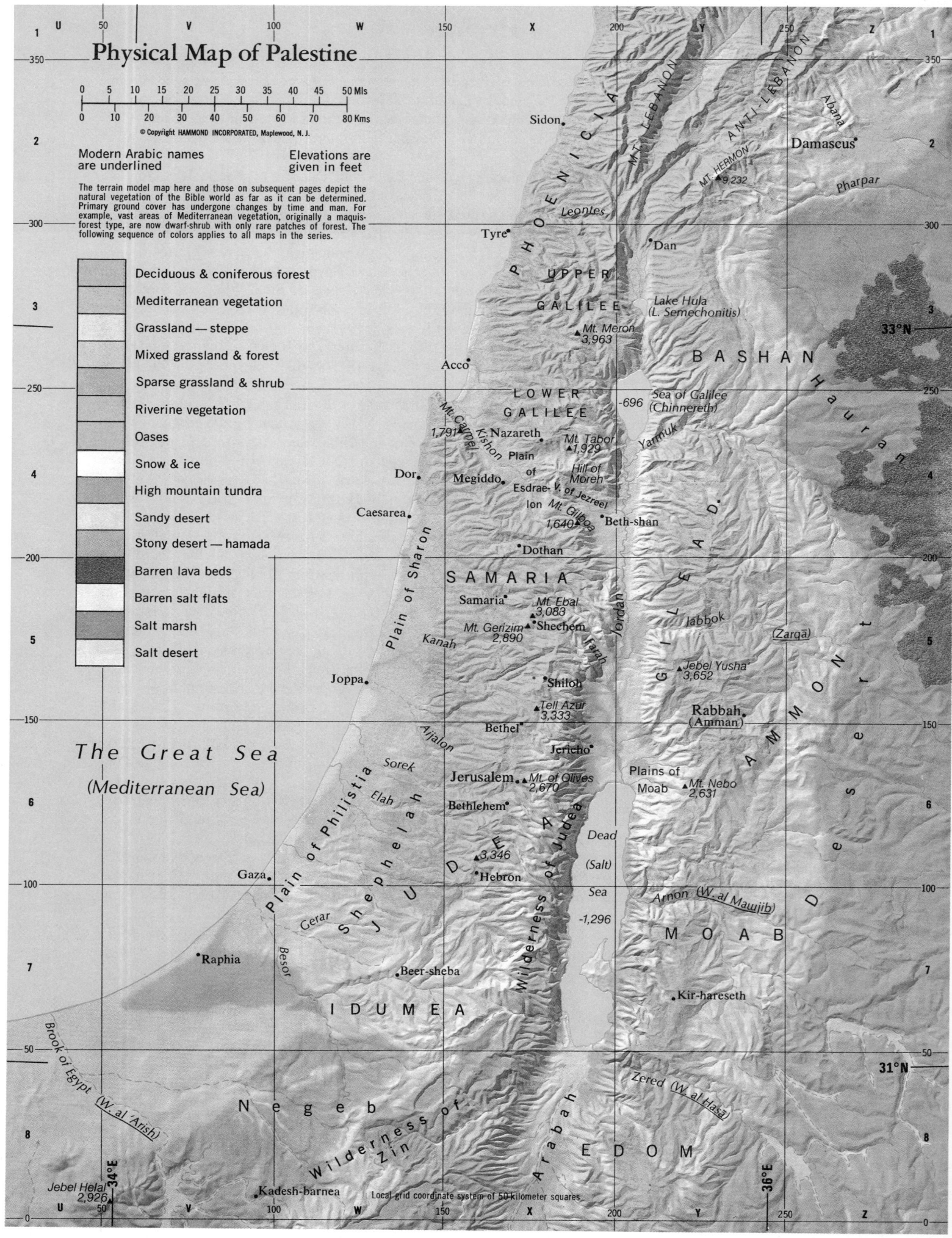

Physical Map of Palestine

| 0 | 5 | 10 | 15 | 20 | 25 | 30 | 35 | 40 | 45 | 50 Mls |

| 0 | 10 | 20 | 30 | 40 | 50 | 60 | 70 | 80 Kms |

© Copyright HAMMOND INCORPORATED, Maplewood, N.J.

Modern Arabic names are underlined

Elevations are given in feet

The terrain model map here and those on subsequent pages depict the natural vegetation of the Bible world as far as it can be determined. Primary ground cover has undergone changes by time and man. For example, vast areas of Mediterranean vegetation, originally a maquis-forest type, are now dwarf-shrub with only rare patches of forest. The following sequence of colors applies to all maps in the series.

Deciduous & coniferous forest

Mediterranean vegetation

Grassland — steppe

Mixed grassland & forest

Sparse grassland & shrub

Riverine vegetation

Oases

Snow & ice

High mountain tundra

Sandy desert

Stony desert — hamada

Barren lava beds

Barren salt flats

Salt marsh

Salt desert

The Great Sea
(Mediterranean Sea)

Local grid coordinate system of 50 kilometer squares

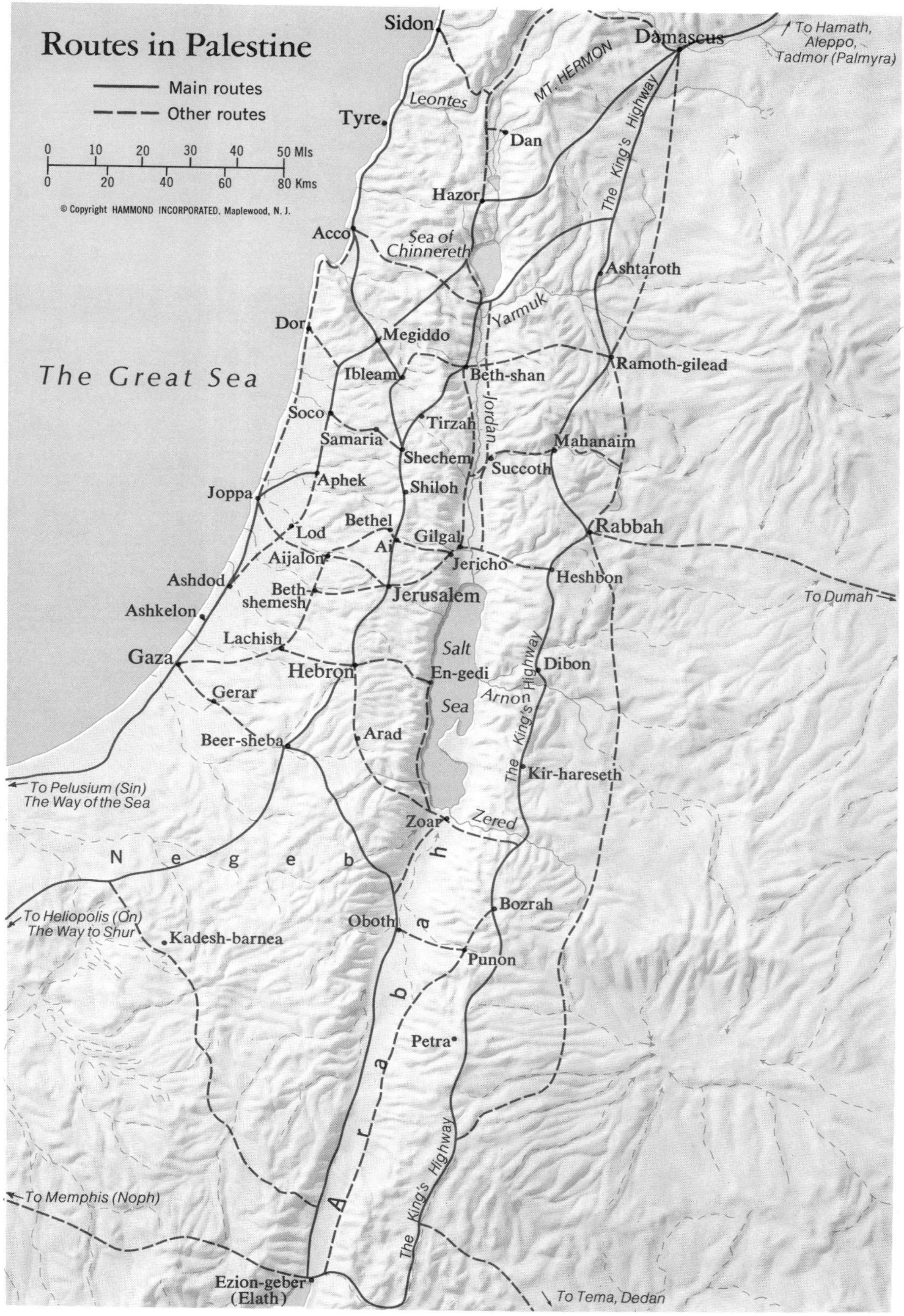

Routes in Palestine

— Main routes
- - - Other routes

0 10 20 30 40 50 Mls
0 20 40 60 80 Kms

© Copyright HAMMOND INCORPORATED, Maplewood, N.J.

The Great Sea

Sidon
To Hamath, Aleppo, Tadmor (Palmyra)
Damascus
MT. HERMON
Leontes
Tyre
The King's Highway
Dan
Hazor
Acco
Sea of Chinnereth
Ashtaroth
Dor
Yarmuk
Megiddo
Ibleam
Beth-shan
Ramoth-gilead
Soco
Tirzah
Jordan
Samaria
Shechem
Succoth
Mahanaim
Aphek
Shiloh
Joppa
Bethel
Lod
Ai
Gilgal
Rabbah
Aijalon
Jericho
Ashdod
Beth-shemesh
Jerusalem
Heshbon
Ashkelon
Salt
En-gedi
Dibon
To Dumah
Lachish
Gaza
Hebron
Sea
Arnon
The King's Highway
Gerar
Kir-hareseth
Beer-sheba
Arad
Zered
To Pelusium (Sin) The Way of the Sea
Zoar
N e g e b
A r a b a h
To Heliopolis (On) The Way to Shur
Oboth
Bozrah
Kadesh-barnea
Punon
To Memphis (Noph)
Petra
The King's Highway
Ezion-geber (Elath)
To Tema, Dedan

The Plain of Esdraelon looking north toward Mount Tabor.

Goats graze in the forbidding central Samaria hills, where the invading Hebrews found a home for their flocks in Biblical times.

Today children frolic in the cool waters beneath the waterfalls of En-gedi, celebrated in the Song of Songs.

The placid Dead Sea looking eastward toward the hills of Transjordan. Wind erosion at this lowest spot on earth produces an eerie, lunar landscape along the western shore.

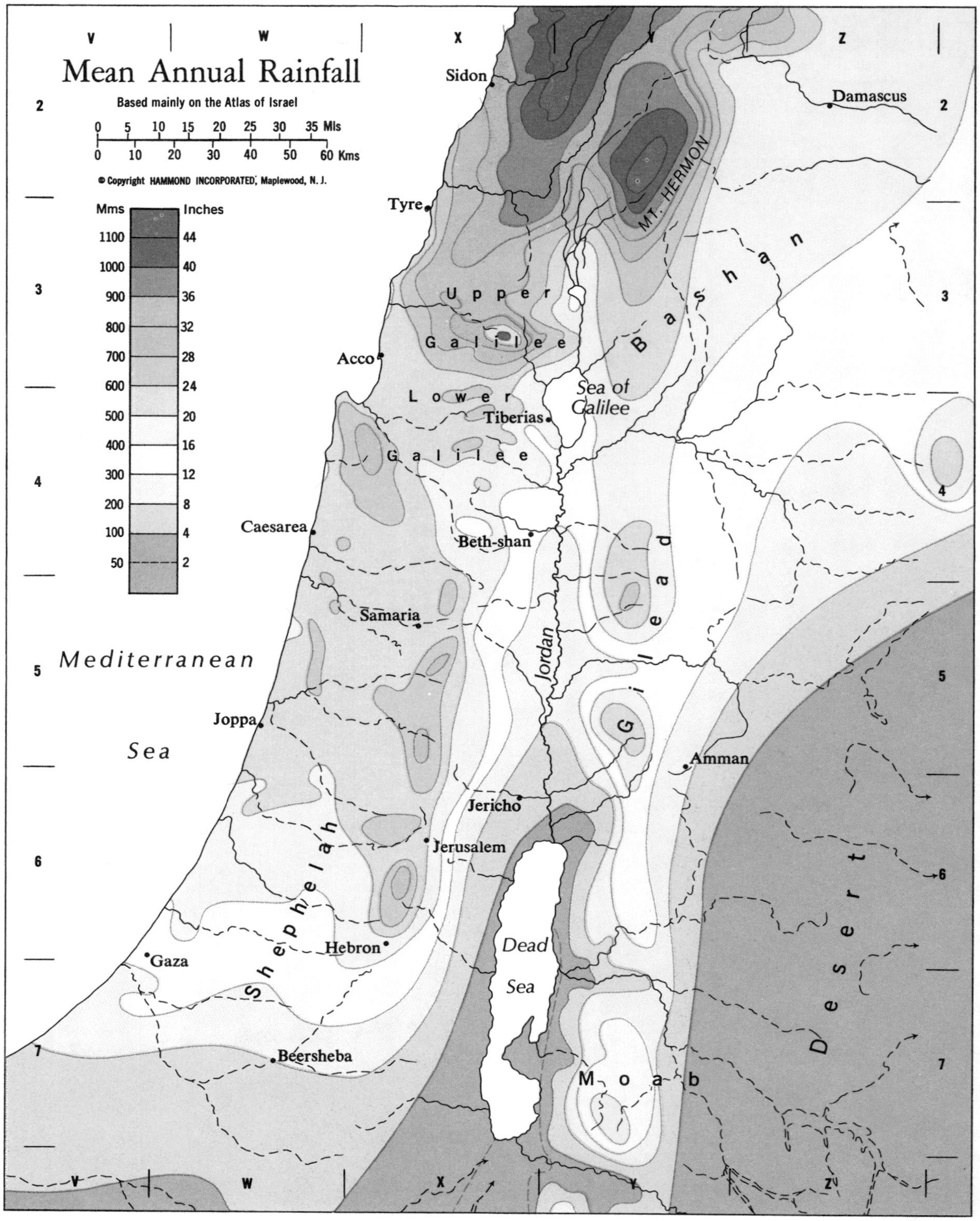

Mean Annual Rainfall

Based mainly on the Atlas of Israel

0 5 10 15 20 25 30 35 Mls
0   10   20   30   40   50   60 Kms

© Copyright HAMMOND INCORPORATED, Maplewood, N.J.

Mms		Inches
1100		44
1000		40
900		36
800		32
700		28
600		24
500		20
400		16
300		12
200		8
100		4
50		2

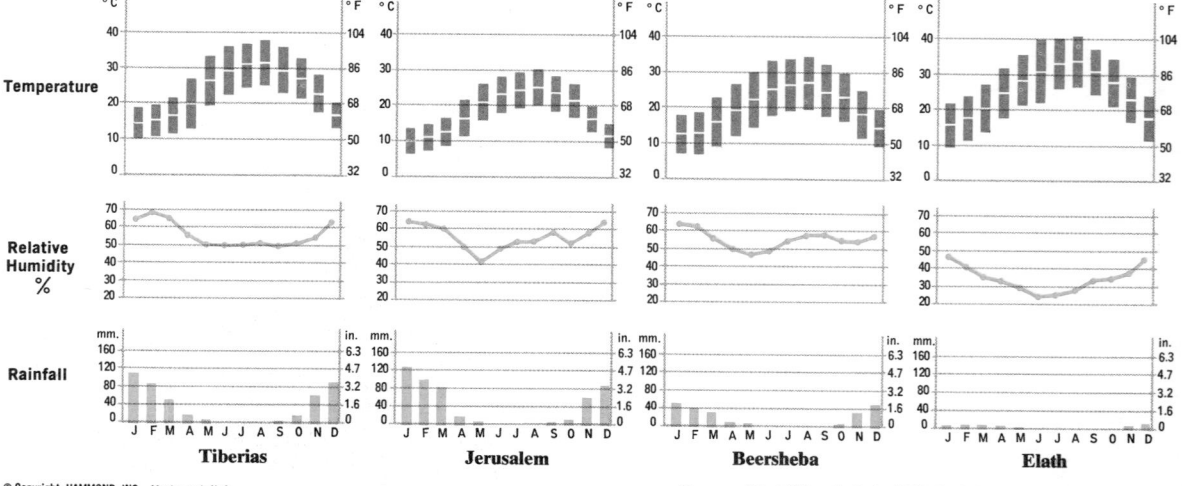

Temperature, rainfall, and relative humidity for selected stations

Tiberias   Jerusalem   Beersheba   Elath

© Copyright HAMMOND INC., Maplewood, N.J.

Sources: World Climatic Data, 1972; Statistical Abstract of Israel, 1969

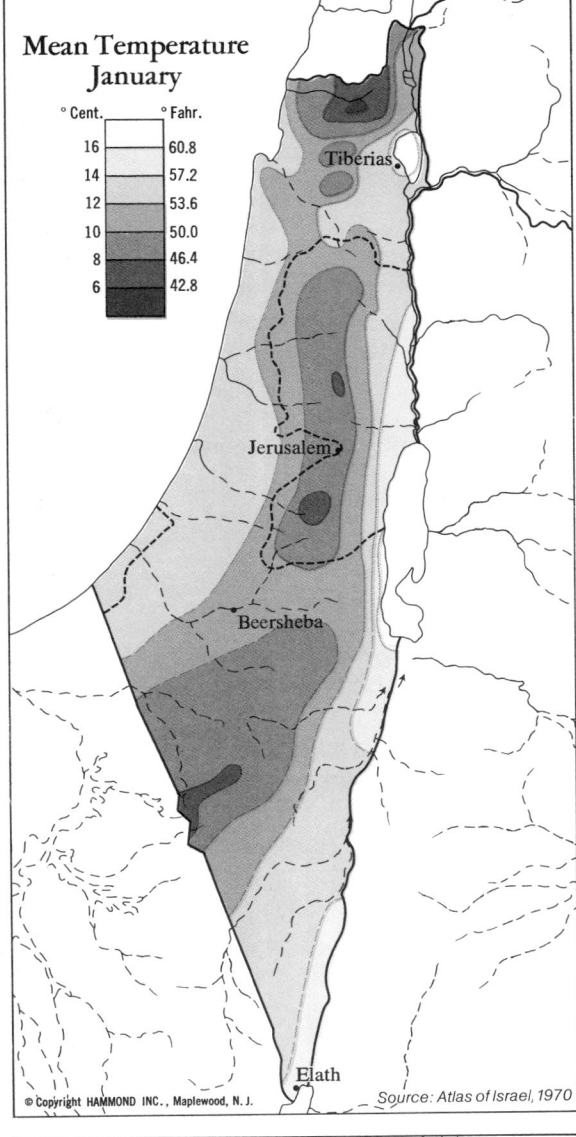

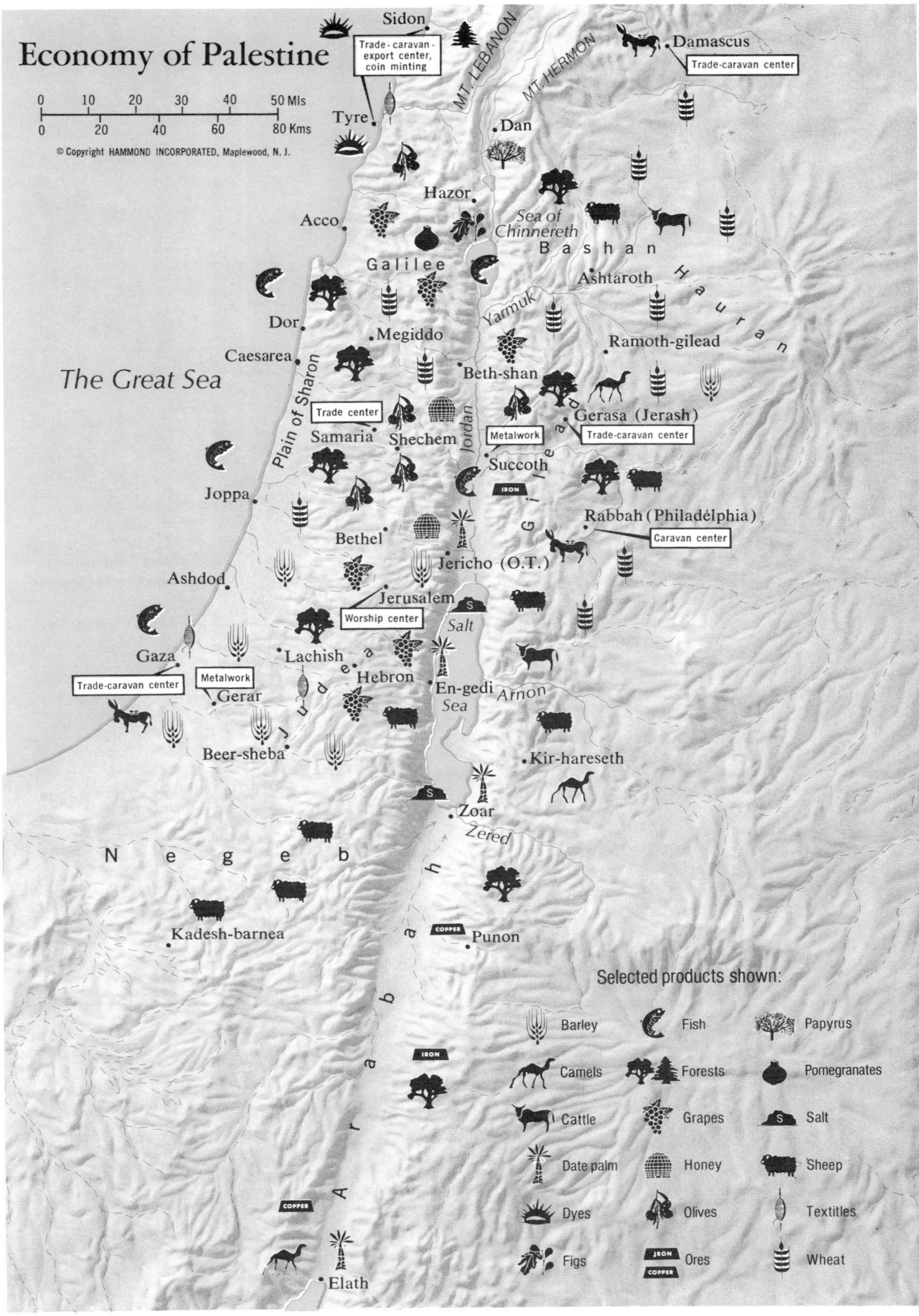

Mean Temperature January

°Cent.	°Fahr.
16	60.8
14	57.2
12	53.6
10	50.0
8	46.4
6	42.8

Tiberias

Jerusalem

Beersheba

Elath

© Copyright HAMMOND INC., Maplewood, N.J.   *Source: Atlas of Israel, 1970*

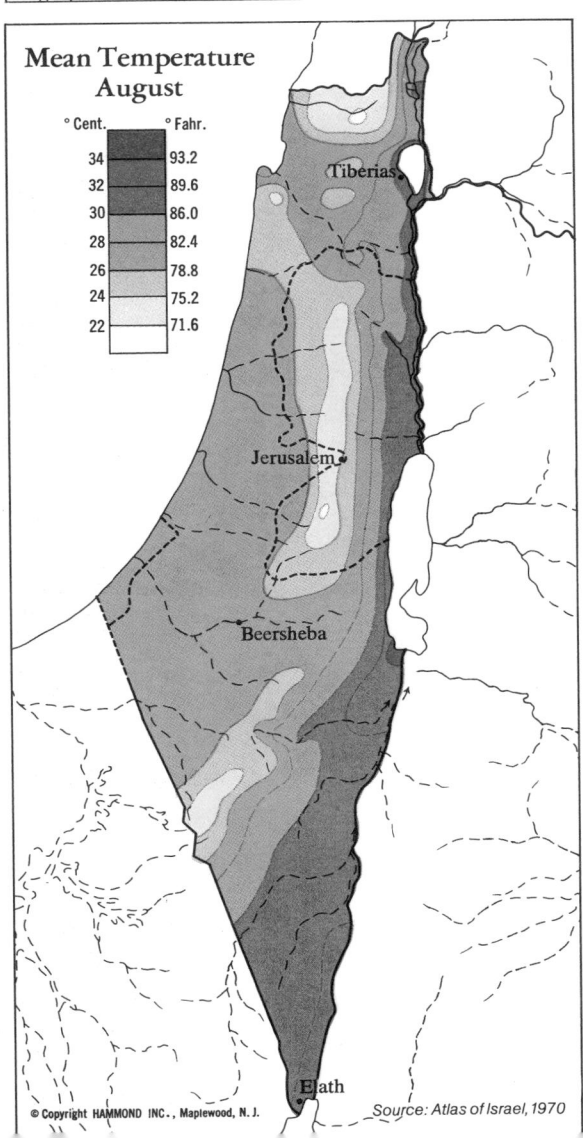

Mean Temperature August

°Cent.	°Fahr.
34	93.2
32	89.6
30	86.0
28	82.4
26	78.8
24	75.2
22	71.6

Tiberias

Jerusalem

Beersheba

Elath

© Copyright HAMMOND INC., Maplewood, N.J.   *Source: Atlas of Israel, 1970*

Economy of Palestine

| 0 | 10 | 20 | 30 | 40 | 50 Mls |
| 0 | 20 | 40 | 60 | 80 Kms |

© Copyright HAMMOND INCORPORATED, Maplewood, N.J.

Sidon

Trade-caravan-export center, coin minting

MT. LEBANON

MT. HERMON

Damascus

Trade-caravan center

Tyre

Dan

Hazor

Acco

Sea of Chinnereth

Bashan

Galilee

Ashtaroth

Hauran

Dor

Megiddo

Yarmuk

Ramoth-gilead

Caesarea

Beth-shan

The Great Sea

Trade center

Gerasa (Jerash)

Samaria

Shechem

Metalwork

Trade-caravan center

Jordan

Joppa

Succoth

IRON

Gilead

Rabbah (Philadelphia)

Bethel

Caravan center

Jericho (O.T.)

Ashdod

Jerusalem

Worship center

Salt

Gaza

Lachish

En-gedi

Arnon

Trade-caravan center

Metalwork

Hebron

Sea

Gerar

Beer-sheba

Kir-hareseth

Judea

S

Zoar

Zered

N e g e b

Kadesh-barnea

COPPER

Punon

Arabah

IRON

COPPER

Elath

Selected products shown:

Barley	Fish	Papyrus
Camels	Forests	Pomegranates
Cattle	Grapes	Salt
Date palm	Honey	Sheep
Dyes	Olives	Textitles
Figs	Ores	Wheat

Grapes being weighed in a manner reminiscent of a period when both kings and prophets in Israel were concerned with honest measure.

A cluster of dates suggests the richness and plenty of well-watered date palm plantations such as those at Jericho.

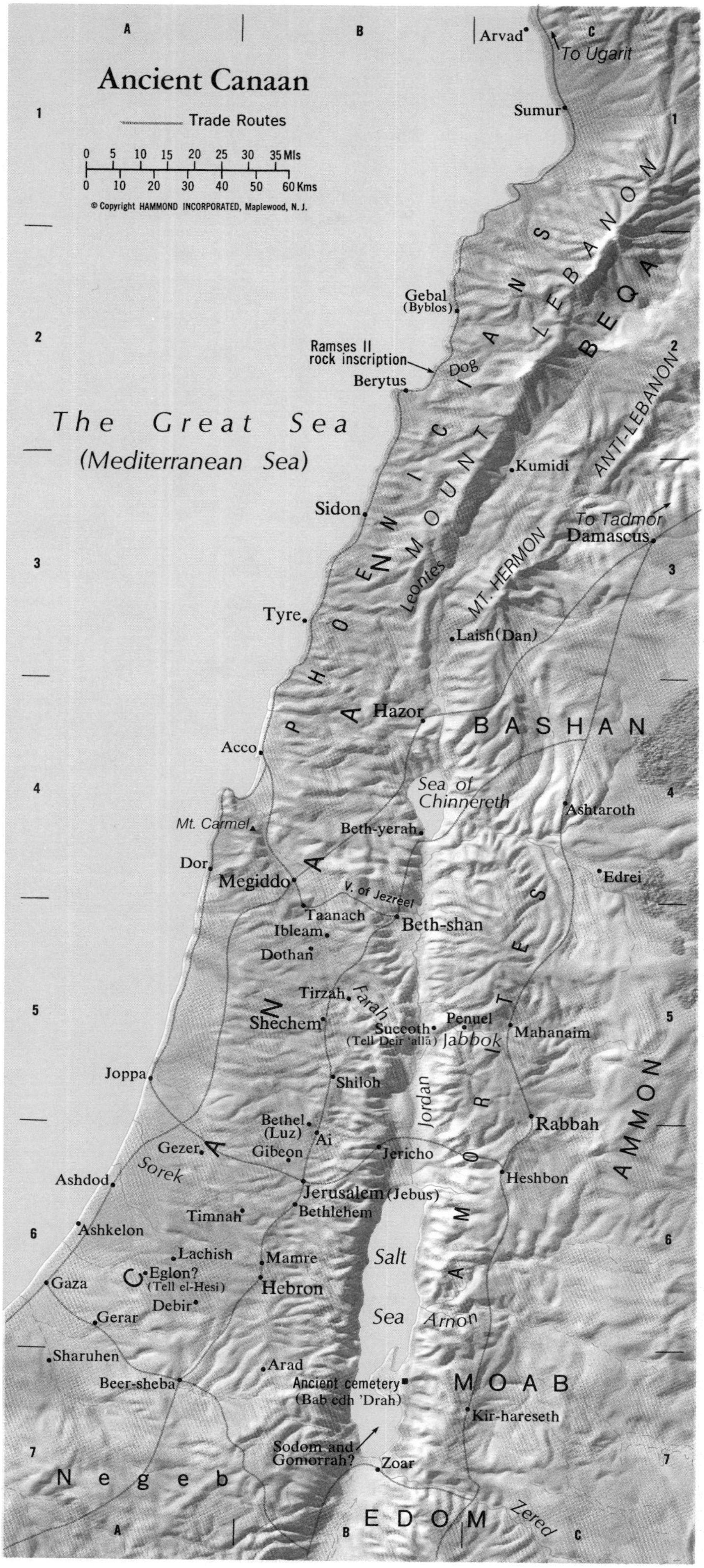

Ancient Canaan

—— Trade Routes

0 5 10 15 20 25 30 35 Mls
0   10   20   30   40   50   60 Kms

© Copyright HAMMOND INCORPORATED, Maplewood, N.J.

The Great Sea
(Mediterranean Sea)

Arvad
To Ugarit
Sumur

PHOENICIAN MOUNTAINS LEBANON
BEQA
ANTI-LEBANON

Gebal (Byblos)
Ramses II rock inscription
Berytus
Dog
Kumidi

Sidon
To Tadmor
Damascus
MT. HERMON
Leontes

Tyre
Laish (Dan)

BASHAN
Hazor
Acco
Sea of Chinnereth
Ashtaroth

Mt. Carmel
Beth-yerah
Dor
Edrei
Megiddo
V. of Jezreel
Taanach
Beth-shan
Ibleam
Dothan
Tirzah
Farah
Shechem
Succoth (Tell Deir 'alla)
Penuel
Mahanaim
Jabbok
Joppa
Shiloh
Jordan
Bethel (Luz)
Ai
Gezer
Gibeon
Rabbah
Jericho
Ashdod
Sorek
Heshbon
Timnah
Jerusalem (Jebus)
Bethlehem
Ashkelon
Lachish
Mamre
Salt
Gaza
Eglon? (Tell el-Hesi)
Hebron
Sea
Arnon
Debir
Gerar
Sharuhen
Arad
Beer-sheba
Ancient cemetery (Bab edh 'Drah)
MOAB
Kir-hareseth
Negeb
Sodom and Gomorrah?
Zoar
EDOM
Zered

AMORITES
AMMON

Bla
Troy
ASSUWA
Hermes
Karabel
Maeander
Beyces
ARZAWA
LUKKA
MINOAN-MYCENAEAN DOMAIN
Rhodes
Cnossus
CAPHTOR (Crete)

Mediterranean S
(Great or Upper Sea)

Lower Egypt
Memphis (Noph)
Heracleopolis
Akhetaton (Tell el-Amarna)
Herm
Abyo
Up
E

Libyan Desert

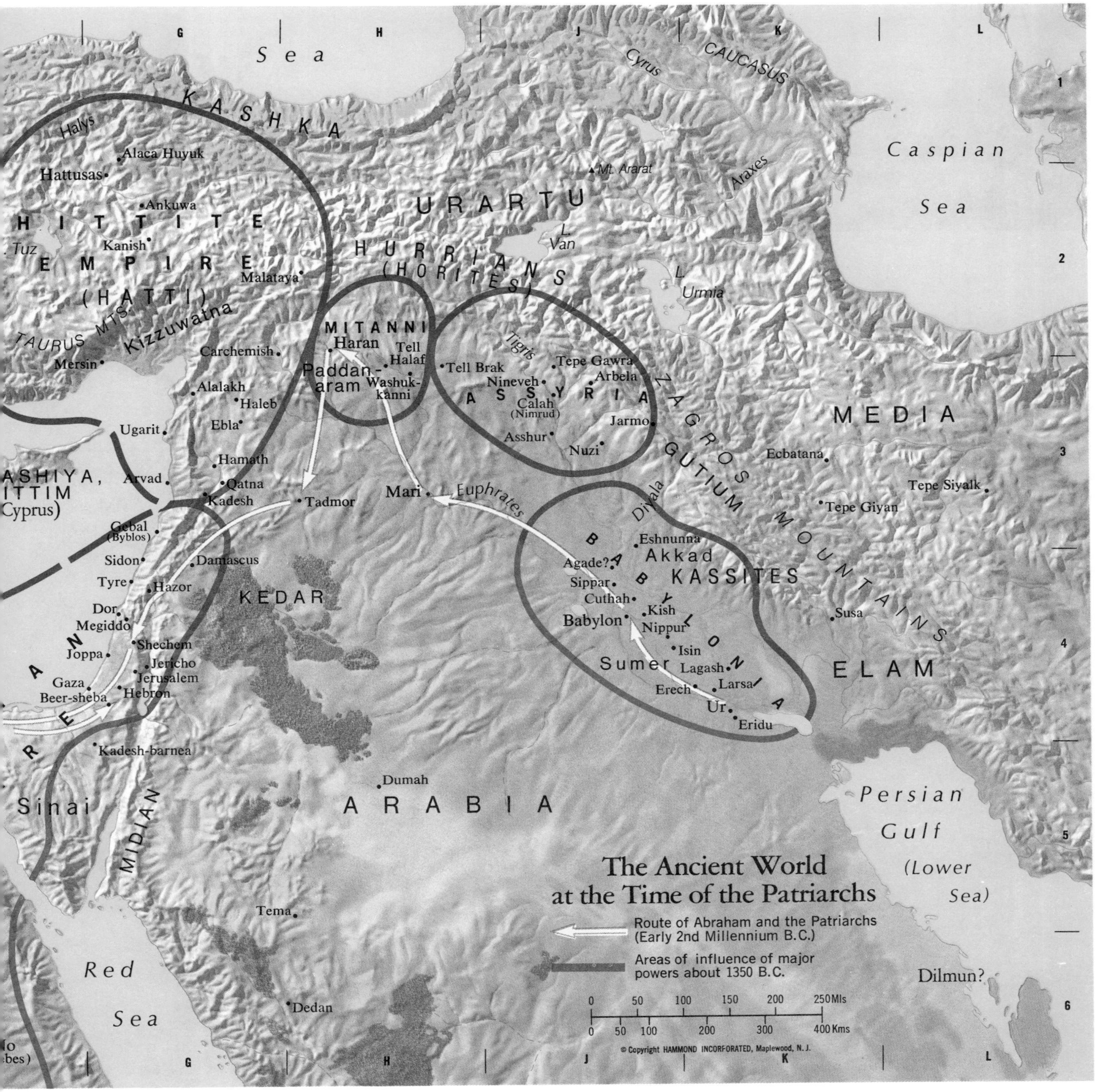

Sea

KASHKA

CAUCASUS

Cyrus

Halys

Alaca Huyuk

Hattusas

Ankuwa

HITTITE

Kanish

Tuz

EMPIRE

Malataya

URARTU

Mt. Ararat

Araxes

Caspian
Sea

HURRIANS

(HORITES)

L. Van

MITANNI

(HATTI)

TAURUS MTS.

Kizzuwatna

Carchemish

Haran

Tell
Halaf

Paddan-
aram

Washuk-
kanni

Tell Brak

Tigris

Tepe Gawra

L. Urmia

Mersin

Alalakh

Nineveh

Arbela

MEDIA

ASHIYA,

Haleb

Ebla

A S S Y R I A

Calah
(Nimrud)

Jarmo

ZAGROS

Ecbatana

ITTIM

Ugarit

Hamath

Asshur

Nuzi

Tepe Siyalk

Cyprus)

Arvad

Qatna

Kadesh

Tadmor

Mari

Euphrates

GUTIUM

Tepe Giyan

Gebal
(Byblos)

Sidon

Damascus

KEDAR

Diyala

Eshnunna

Agade?

Akkad

KASSITES

MOUNTAINS

Susa

Tyre

Hazor

Sippar

B

Dor

Megiddo

Cuthah

Kish

Babylon

Nippur

ELAM

Joppa

Shechem

Jericho

Isin

Jerusalem

Sumer

Lagash

Gaza

Beer-sheba

Hebron

Erech

Larsa

Ur

Kadesh-barnea

Eridu

Persian

Dumah

Gulf

Sinai

A R A B I A

(Lower

MIDIAN

Tema

Sea)

Dilmun?

The Ancient World
at the Time of the Patriarchs

Route of Abraham and the Patriarchs
(Early 2nd Millennium B.C.)

Areas of influence of major
powers about 1350 B.C.

Red

Sea

Dedan

0   50   100   150   200   250 Mls

0   50   100   200   300   400 Kms

© Copyright HAMMOND INCORPORATED, Maplewood, N.J.

Discoveries in the royal tombs at Ur
have made it possible to reconstruct
this magnificent sounding box of a lyre
The bull's head is of gold, silver and
lapis lazuli. Below the head are panels
of shell inlay.

The Canaanite altar for burnt
offerings at Megiddo. This
splendid "high place" was
built in the Early Bronze Age
and continued in use as late as
the 19th century B.C., the time
of the Hebrew Patriarchs.

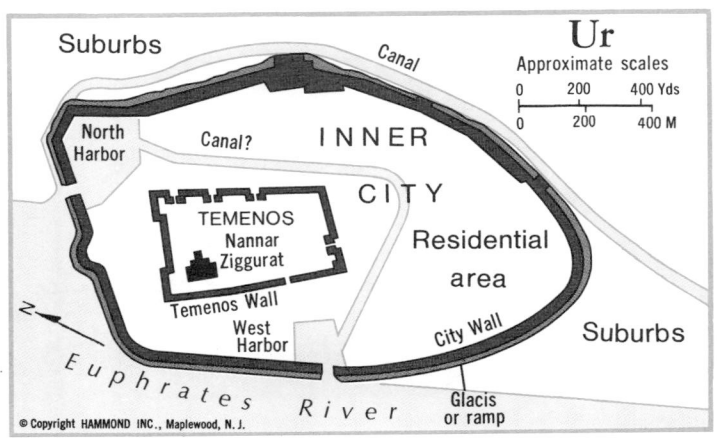

Ur
Approximate scales

0   200   400 Yds

0   200   400 M

Suburbs

Canal

North
Harbor

Canal?

INNER

CITY

TEMENOS

Nannar
Ziggurat

Residential
area

Temenos Wall

West Harbor

City Wall

Suburbs

Euphrates River

Glacis
or ramp

© Copyright HAMMOND INC., Maplewood, N.J.

In a timeless scene the pyramids dominate the sandy Egyptian horizon beyond the fertile fields of the Nile River plain.

A wall painting from the reign of Thutmoses III (15th century B.C.) shows the various stages of brickmaking.

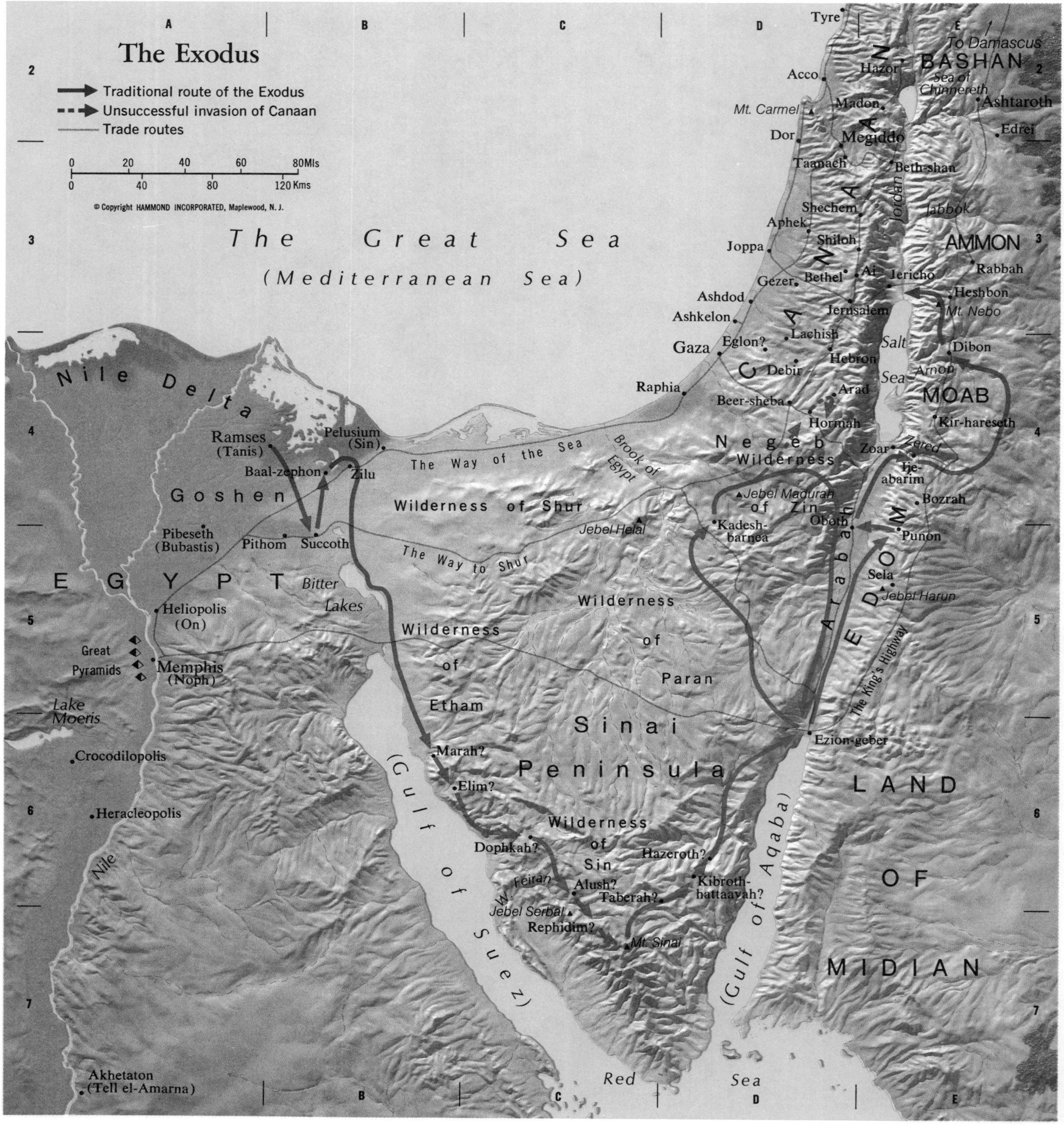

The Exodus

→ Traditional route of the Exodus
⇢ Unsuccessful invasion of Canaan
— Trade routes

0   20   40   60   80Mls
0   40   80   120 Kms

© Copyright HAMMOND INCORPORATED, Maplewood, N.J.

The Great Sea
(Mediterranean Sea)

Nile Delta

Tyre
Acco
Hazor
BASHAN
Sea of Chinnereth
Ashtaroth
Mt. Carmel
Madon
Edrei
Dor
Megiddo
Taanach
Beth-shan
Shechem
Jordan
Jabbok
Aphek
Shiloh
AMMON
Joppa
Bethel
Ai
Jericho
Rabbah
Gezer
Heshbon
Ashdod
Jerusalem
Mt. Nebo
Ashkelon
Lachish
Gaza
Eglon?
Salt
Dibon
Raphia
Debir
Hebron
Sea
Arnon
Beer-sheba
Arad
MOAB
Hormah
Kir-hareseth
Negeb
Zoar
Zered
Wilderness
Ije-abarim
Jebel Maqurah
Bozrah
Jebel Helal
Kadesh-barnea
Oboth
Punon
Wilderness of Shur
Brook of Egypt
Sela
The Way of the Sea
Jebel Harun
The Way to Shur
EDOM

Ramses (Tanis)
Pelusium (Sin)
Baal-zephon
Zilu
Goshen
Pibeseth (Bubastis)
Pithom
Succoth
EGYPT
Bitter Lakes
Heliopolis (On)
Wilderness of Paran
Great Pyramids
Memphis (Noph)
Wilderness of
Lake Moeris
Etham
Wilderness of Sin
Crocodilopolis
Marah?
Sinai
Ezion-geber
Elim?
Peninsula
LAND
Heracleopolis
Wilderness of Sin
Nile
Dophkah?
Hazeroth?
OF
Feiran
Alush?
Kibroth-hattaavah?
Jebel Serbal
Taberah?
Rephidim?
Mt. Sinai
MIDIAN
(Gulf of Suez)
(Gulf of Aqaba)
The King's Highway
Arabah

Akhetaton (Tell el-Amarna)
Red   Sea

Mount Tabor, where the forces of Deborah gathered to give battle to the army of Sisera (Judges 4:6f.). A torrent turned the Esdraelon Plain (in the foreground) into a quagmire, rendering Sisera's Canaanite chariots ineffective.

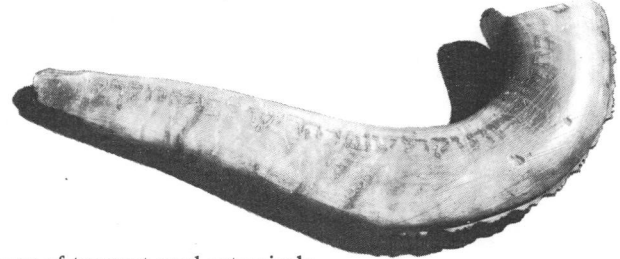

A *shofar,* a type of trumpet used extensively in ancient Israel for special religious purposes in both war and peace.

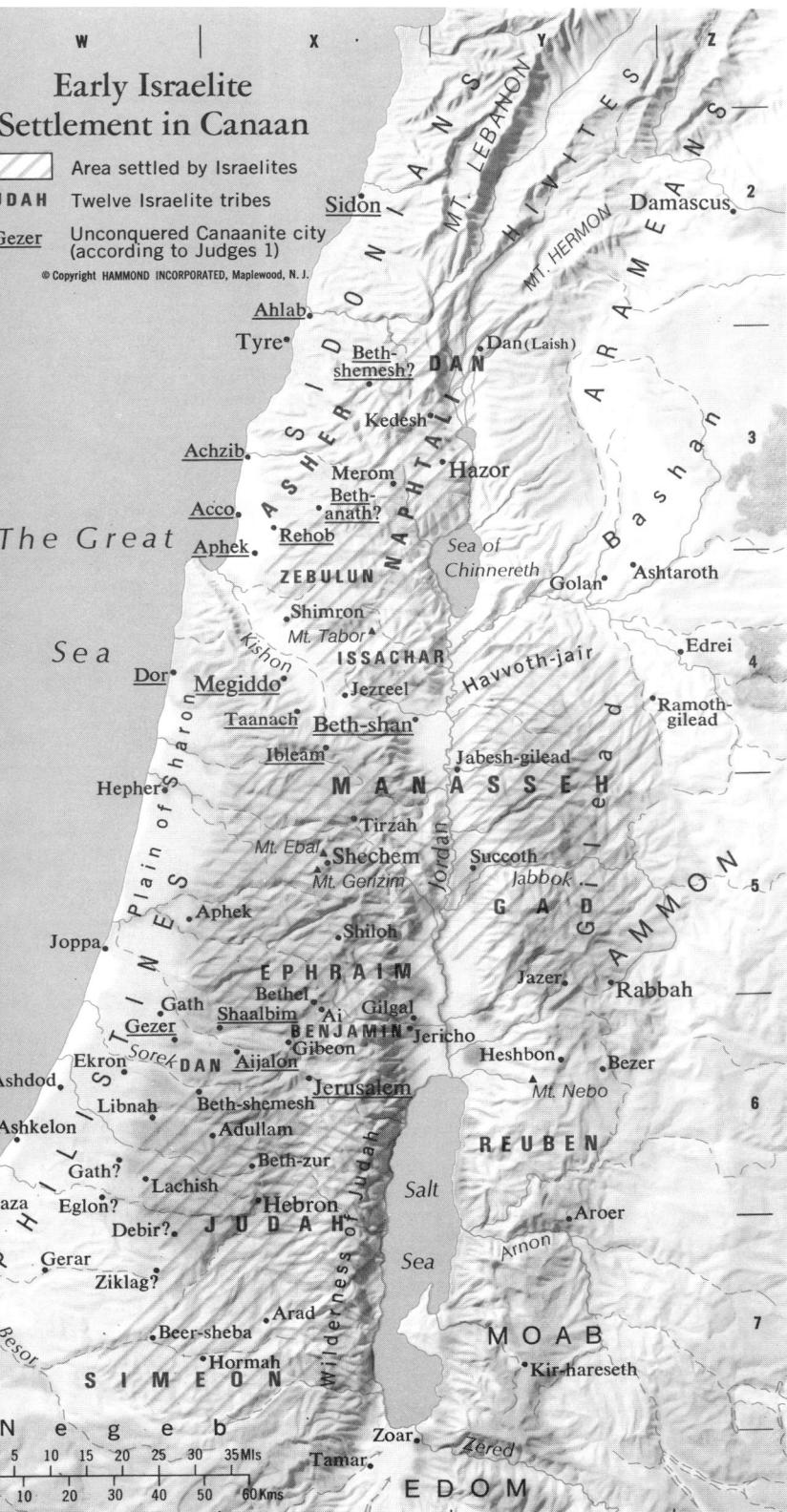

Early Israelite Settlement in Canaan

Area settled by Israelites

DAH Twelve Israelite tribes

Gezer Unconquered Canaanite city (according to Judges 1)

© Copyright HAMMOND INCORPORATED, Maplewood, N. J.

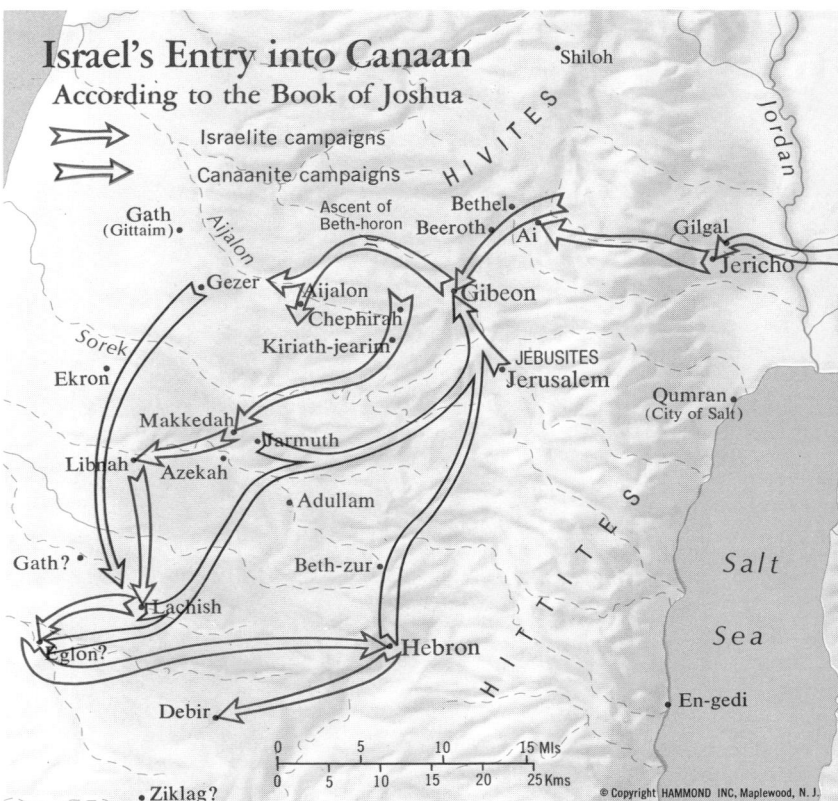

Israel's Entry into Canaan
According to the Book of Joshua

Israelite campaigns

Canaanite campaigns

© Copyright HAMMOND INC, Maplewood, N. J.

The fortress-temple of Baal-berith, probably the scene of Joshua's covenant (Joshua 24:1-28), was built at Shechem around 1650 B.C. and with modifications continued in use throughout the Period of the Judges.

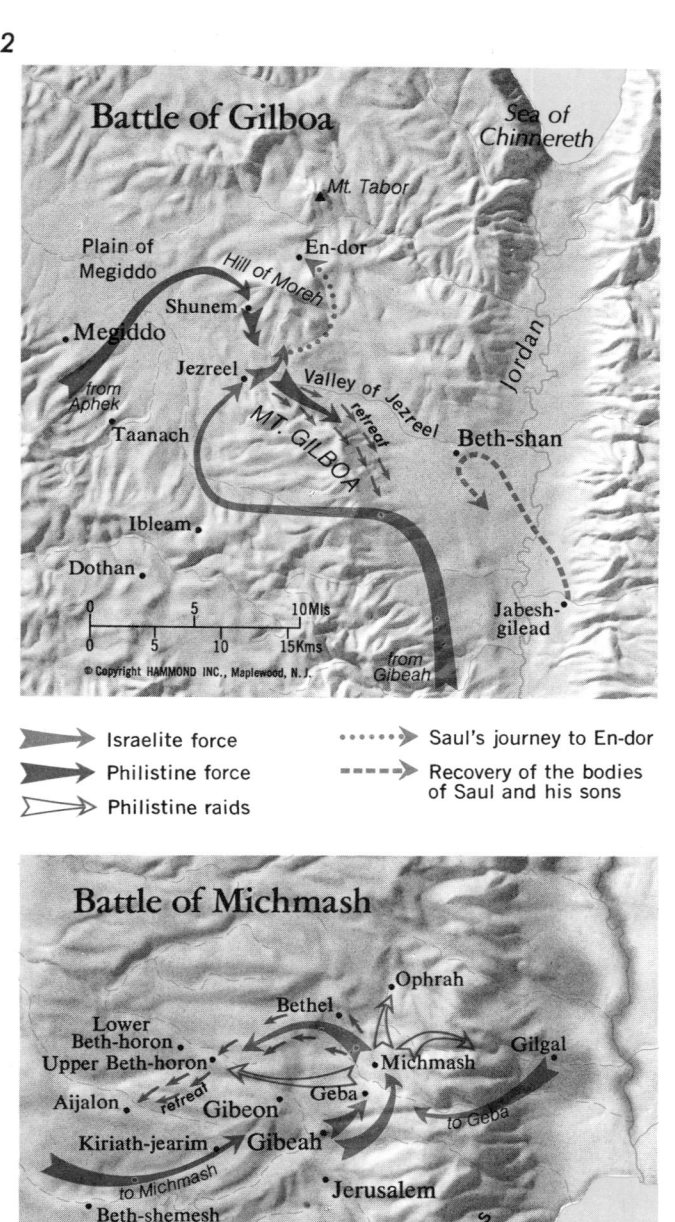

Battle of Gilboa

Sea of Chinnereth

Plain of Megiddo · En-dor · Mt. Tabor
Shunem · Hill of Moreh
Megiddo
Jezreel · Valley of Jezreel · *retreat*
from Aphek · MT. GILBOA · Beth-shan
Taanach
Ibleam · Jordan
Dothan · Jabesh-gilead
from Gibeah

0 5 10Mls
0 5 10 15Kms
© Copyright HAMMOND INC., Maplewood, N.J.

→ Israelite force
→ Philistine force
⊳ Philistine raids
···› Saul's journey to En-dor
--→ Recovery of the bodies of Saul and his sons

Battle of Michmash

Ophrah
Bethel
Lower Beth-horon
Upper Beth-horon · Michmash · Gilgal
Aijalon · *retreat* · Geba
Gibeon · to Geba
Kiriath-jearim · Gibeah
to Michmash
Beth-shemesh · Jerusalem
Bethlehem
Wilderness of Judah
Salt Sea

0 5 10 15Mls
0 5 10 15 20 25Kms
© Copyright HAMMOND INC., Maplewood, N.J.

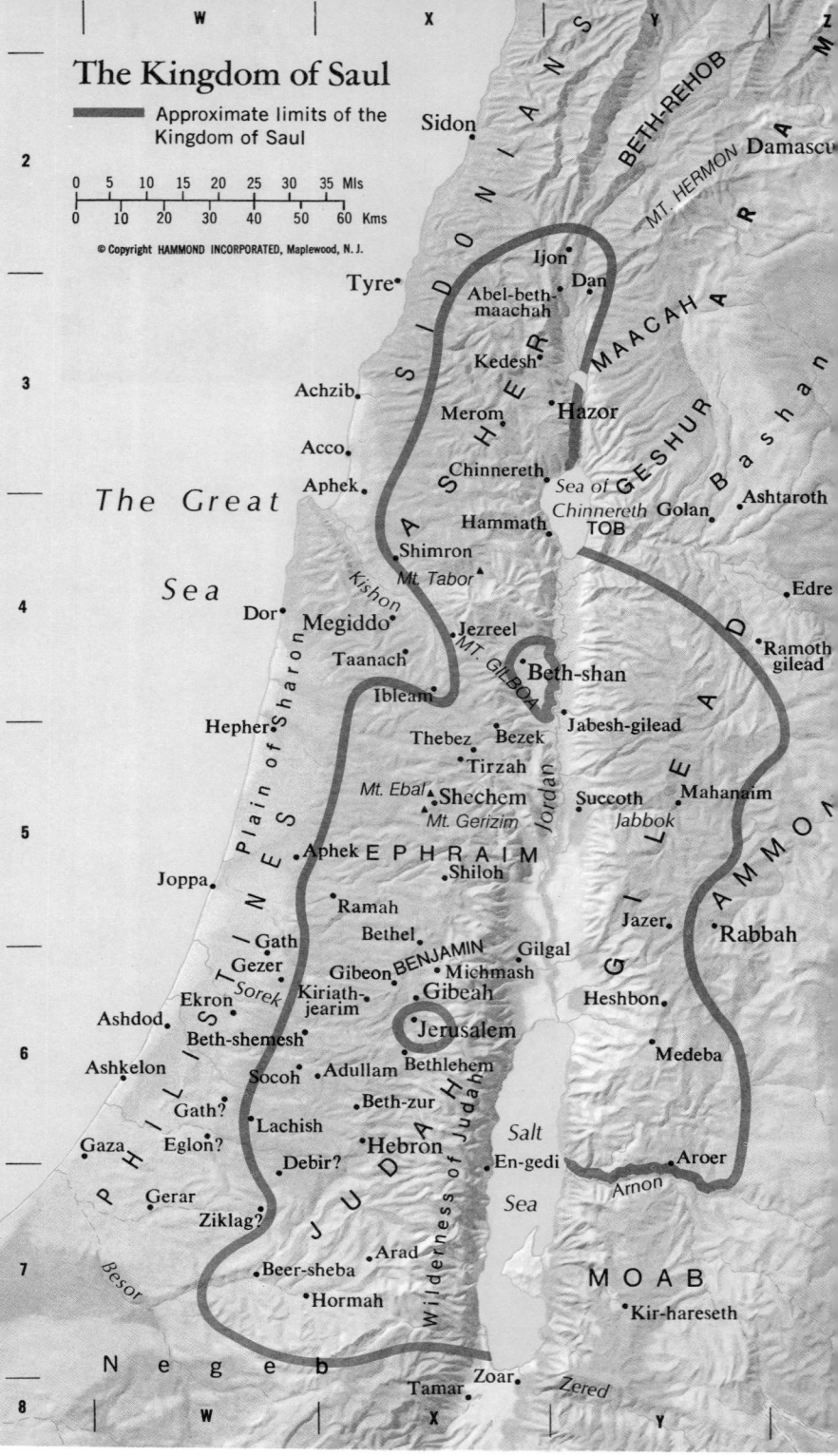

The Kingdom of Saul

━━ Approximate limits of the Kingdom of Saul

0 5 10 15 20 25 30 35 Mls
0 10 20 30 40 50 60 Kms
© Copyright HAMMOND INCORPORATED, Maplewood, N.J.

W · X · Y · Z

SIDONIANS · BETH-REHOB
Sidon · MT. HERMON · Damascu
Tyre · Ijon · Dan
Abel-beth-maachah · MAACAH
Achzib · Kedesh · GESHUR · Bashan
Acco · Merom · Hazor
Aphek · Chinnereth · Sea of Chinnereth · Golan · Ashtaroth
Hammath · TOB
The Great · Shimron · Mt. Tabor · Edre
Dor · Kishon · Jezreel · Ramoth gilead
Megiddo · MT. GILBOA · Beth-shan
Sea · Taanach · Ibleam · Jabesh-gilead
Hepher · Thebez · Bezek
Plain of Sharon · Tirzah · Succoth · Mahanaim
Mt. Ebal · Shechem · Jabbok
Mt. Gerizim
Aphek · EPHRAIM · AMMON
Joppa · Shiloh
Ramah
Gath · Bethel · Jazer · Rabbah
Gezer · Gibeon · BENJAMIN · Gilgal
Ekron · Sorek · Kiriath-jearim · Michmash · Heshbon
Ashdod · Beth-shemesh · Gibeah
Jerusalem
Ashkelon · Socoh · Adullam · Bethlehem · Medeba
Gath? · Beth-zur
Gaza · Eglon? · Lachish · Hebron · Salt · Aroer
Debir? · En-gedi · Sea · Arnon
Gerar · JUDAH
Ziklag · Arad · MOAB
Besor · Beer-sheba · Kir-hareseth
Hormah
Negeb · Tamar · Zoar · Zered

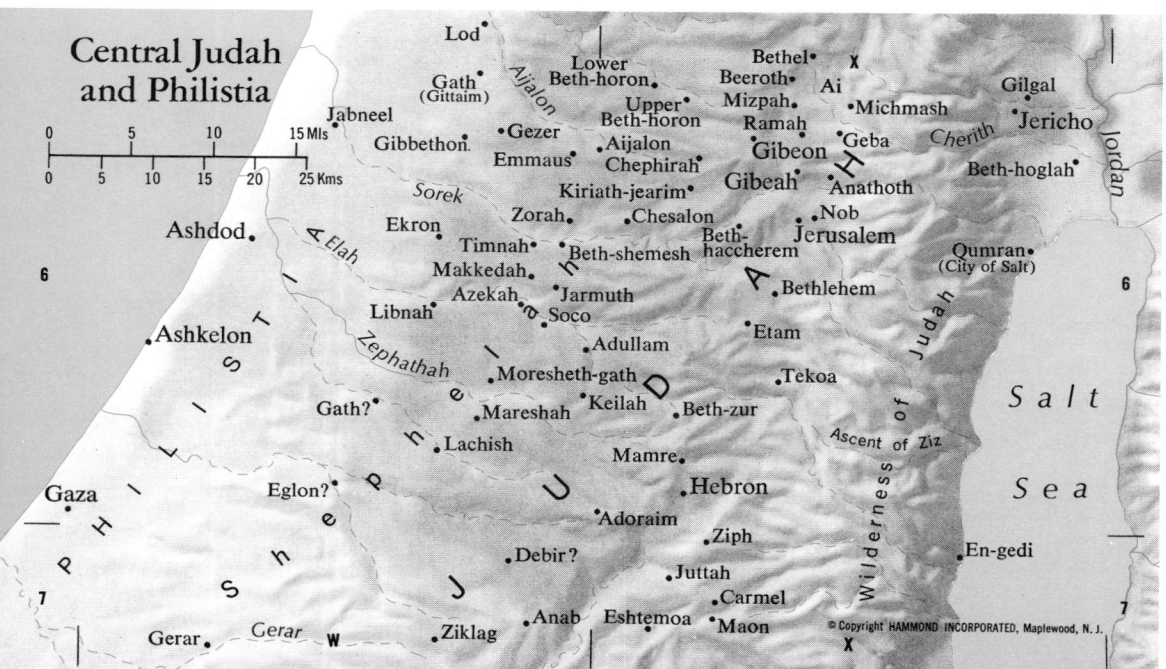

Central Judah and Philistia

0 5 10 15Mls
0 5 10 15 20 25Kms

Lod
Gath (Gittaim) · Lower Beth-horon · Bethel · Ai · Gilgal
Jabneel · Upper Beth-horon · Beeroth · Michmash · Jericho
Gibbethon · Gezer · Emmaus · Aijalon · Mizpah · Geba · Cherith
Chephirah · Ramah · Gibeon · Beth-hoglah
Sorek · Kiriath-jearim · Anathoth · Jordan
Ekron · Zorah · Chesalon · Nob
Ashdod · Timnah · Beth-shemesh · Beth-haccherem · Jerusalem
Makkedah · Bethlehem · Qumran (City of Salt)
Azekah · Jarmuth · Etam
Libnah · Soco · Tekoa
Ashkelon · Zephathah · Adullam
Moresheth-gath · Salt
Gath? · Mareshah · Keilah · Beth-zur · Ascent of Ziz · Sea
Lachish · Mamre
Eglon? · Hebron · Wilderness of Judah
Adoraim
Gaza · Gerar · Ziph
Debir? · En-gedi
Juttah
Gerar · Anab · Eshtemoa · Carmel
Ziklag · Maon

© Copyright HAMMOND INCORPORATED, Maplewood, N.J.

At Gibeah the remains of Saul's fortress-palace (background) are surrounded by later construction (foregound). The rude simplicity of Saul's capital contrasted sharply with Solomon's magnificent buildings constructed four miles away in Jerusalem only a few years later.

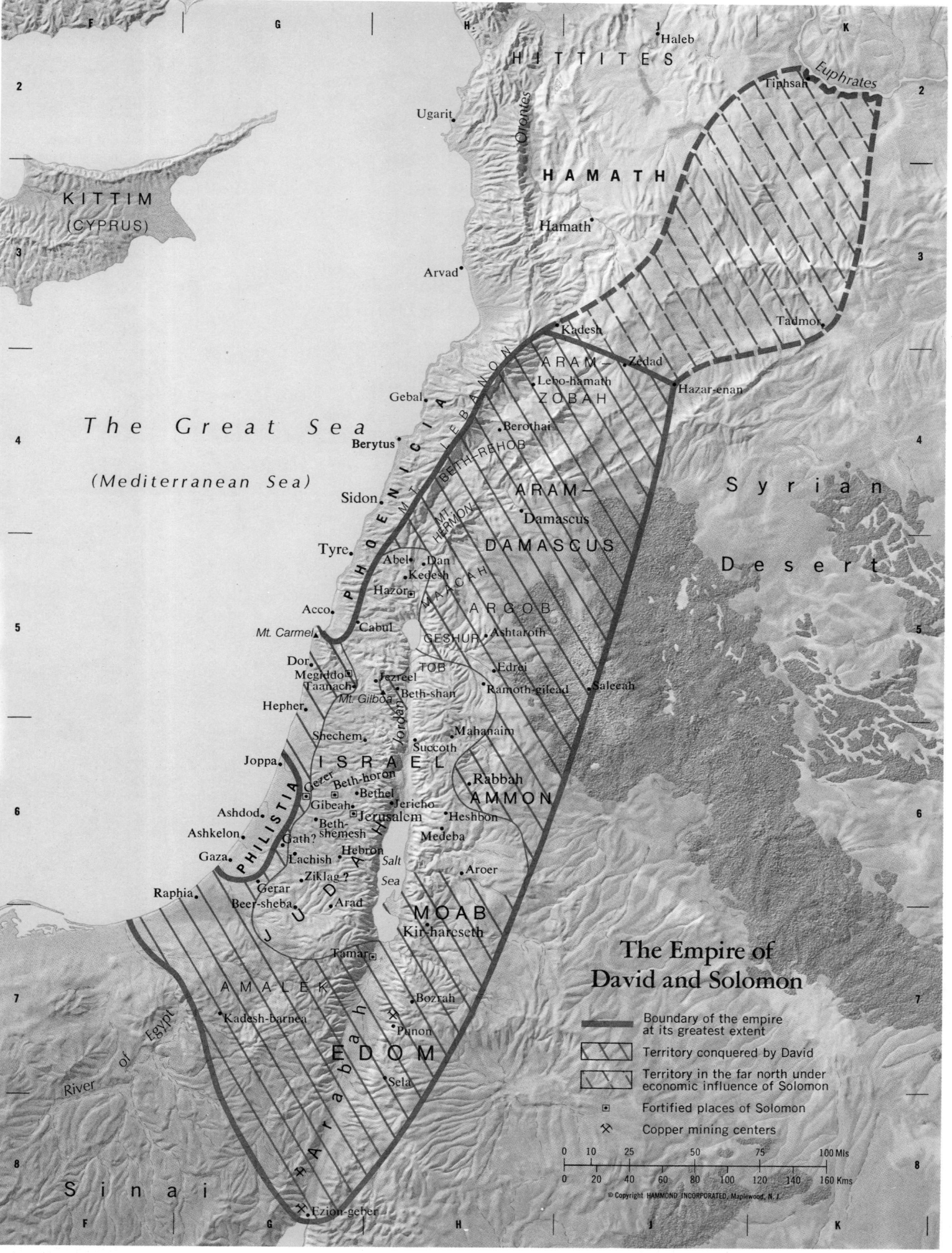

The Empire of David and Solomon

Boundary of the empire at its greatest extent

Territory conquered by David

Territory in the far north under economic influence of Solomon

⊡ Fortified places of Solomon

✕ Copper mining centers

| 0 | 10 | 25 | | 50 | | 75 | 100 Mls |

| 0 | 20 | 40 | 60 | 80 | 100 | 120 | 140 | 160 Kms |

© Copyright HAMMOND INCORPORATED, Maplewood, N.J.

The Israelite gate at Gezer is one of the finest Solomonic structures yet found. Its design of two outer towers and six flanking guardrooms is virtually identical to Solomon's fortification gates at Megiddo and Hazor.

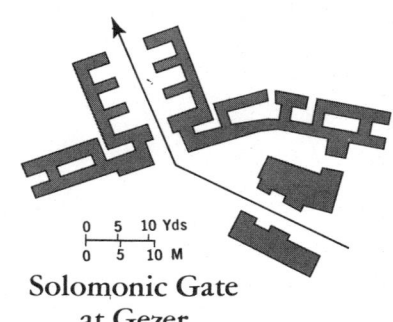

0 5 10 Yds
0 5 10 M

Solomonic Gate at Gezer

A proto-Ionic capital of the type that graced the gates of the royal cities and palaces of Israel and Judah: Samaria, Megiddo, Hazor, Ramat Rahel and most likely Jerusalem and Gezer.

Jerusalem of David & Solomon

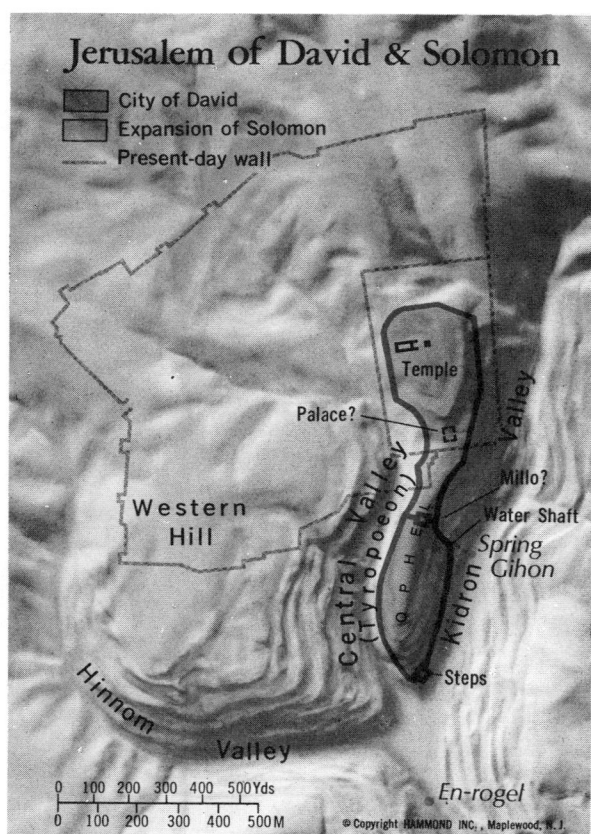

City of David
Expansion of Solomon
Present-day wall

Western Hill

Temple
Palace?
Millo?
Water Shaft
Spring Gihon
Steps

Central Valley (Tyropoeon)
OPHEL
Kidron Valley

Hinnom Valley

En-rogel

0 100 200 300 400 500Yds
0 100 200 300 400 500M

© Copyright HAMMOND INC., Maplewood, N.J.

Temple of Solomon

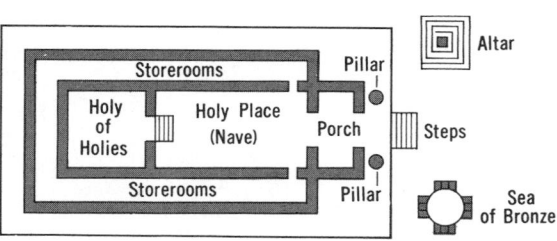

Storerooms
Holy of Holies
Holy Place (Nave)
Porch
Pillar
Pillar
Storerooms

Altar
Steps
Sea of Bronze

0 10 20 30 Cubits
0 5 10 15 M

Solomon's Twelve Districts

Boundary of tax districts
Gezer Royal City of Solomon
⊡ Places fortified by Solomon

0 5 10 15 20 25 30 35 Mls
0 10 20 30 40 50 60 Kms

© Copyright HAMMOND INCORPORATED, Maplewood, N.J.

MT. LEBANON
BETH-REHOB
Sidon
MT. HERMON
ARAM
Tyre
Abel
Dan
Kedesh
MAACAH
The Great
Hazor ⊡
ARGOB
GESHUR
Acco
Cabul
Sea of Chinnereth
TOB
Ashtaroth
Sea
Mt. Carmel
Shimron
Kishon
Mt. Tabor
Havvoth-jair
Edrei
Dor
IV
Jezreel
MT. GILBOA
Ramoth-gilead
Megiddo ⊡
Taanach
V
Beth-shean (Beth-shan)
Ibleam
Hepher
Soco
Plain of Sharon
Mt. Ebal
Shechem
Succoth
Mahanaim
III
Kanah
Mt. Gerizim
Jabbok
Aphek
VII
Joppa
AMMON
II
Lower Beth-horon
Bethel
Rabbah
Shaalbim
Gibeon
Jericho
Baalath?
Gezer ⊡
Gibeah
Heshbon
Ashdod
Ekron
Beth-shemesh
Jerusalem
Medeba
Ashkelon
Libnah
Bethlehem
Gath?
XII
Lachish
Hebron
Salt
Dibon
Gaza
JUDAH
Sea
Aroer
Arnon
Gerar
Preferential tax area
Ziklag?
Arad
Ar?
Beer-sheba
MOAB
Besor
Kir-hareseth
Negeb
Zered
AMALEK
Tamar ⊡

PHOENICIA
Bashan
G
PHILISTIA

The Kingdoms of Israel and Judah

- - - - Approximate frontiers
ISRAEL Hebrew kingdoms
AMMON Foreign kingdoms

0 5 10 15 20 25 30 35 40 45 50 Mls
0 10 20 30 40 50 60 70 80 Kms

© Copyright HAMMOND INCORPORATED, Maplewood, N.J.

SYRIA (ARAM)

Damascus

Sidon

PHOENICIA

MT. HERMON

Tyre

Leontes

Ijon

Abel-beth-maachah

Dan

Kedesh

Hazor

Bashan

Merom

Galilee

Acco

Chinnereth

Cabul

Sea of Chinnereth

Karnaim

Ashtaroth

Rumah

Hammath

Gath-hepher

Aphek

Mt. Tabor

Plain of

Yarmuk

Edrei

Dor

Shunem

Esdraelon

Havvoth-jair

Kishon

Megiddo

Jezreel

Mt. Gilboa

Ramoth-gilead

Taanach

Beth-shan

Beth-haggan

Ibleam

Abel-meholah

Dothan

Jabesh-gilead

Tishbe

The Great Sea

(Mediterranean Sea)

Socoh

ISRAEL

Tirzah

Samaria

Mt. Ebal

Shechem

Penuel

Mahanaim

Mt. Gerizim

Succoth

Jabbok

Gilead

Kanah

Aphek

Shiloh

AMMON

Plain of Sharon

Zeredah

Joppa

Rabbah

Lod

Bethel

Zemaraim

Gath

Mizpah

Gilgal

Jabneel

Geba

Jericho

Shittim?

Gezer

Heshbon

Gibbethon

Aijalon

Gibeon

Ramah

Ekron

Zorah

Jerusalem

Mt. Nebo

Ashdod

Beth-shemesh

Bethlehem

Medeba

Jahaz

Ashkelon

Socoh

Adullam

Etam

Mareshah

Tekoa

Beth-zur

Ataroth

Salt

Lachish

JUDAH

Hebron

En-gedi

Sea

Gaza

Adoraim

Dibon

Debir?

Ziph

Aroer

Wilderness of Judah

Arnon

Ziklag?

Raphia

Ar

Sharuhen

Arad

MOAB

Besor

Beer-sheba

Kir-hareseth

Zoar

Zered

Tamar

Ziph

Arabah

Ascent of Akrabbim

N e g e b

EDOM

Bozrah

PHILISTIA

Jordan

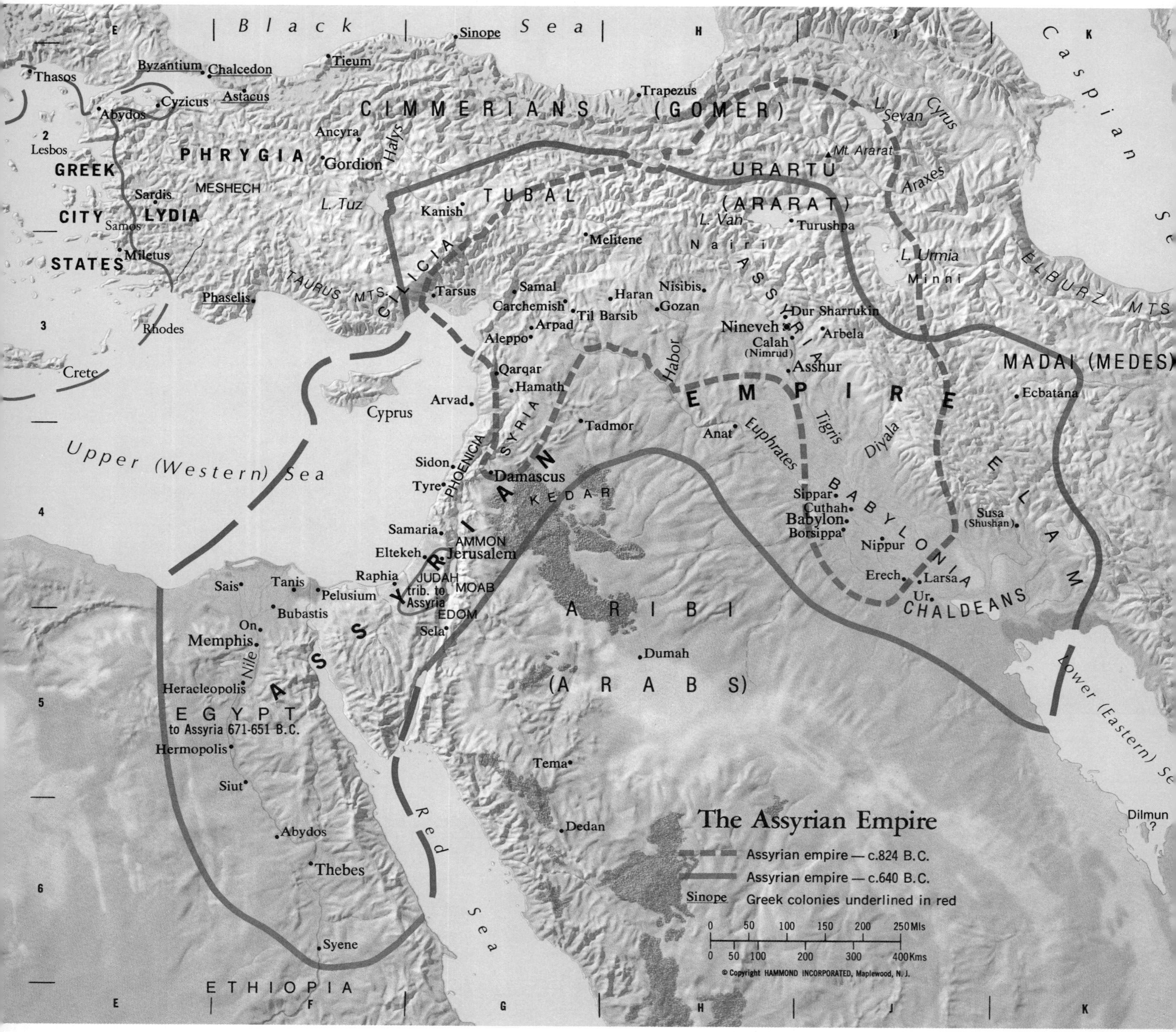

Black Sea

Sinope

GREEK

CITY

STATES

Thasos
Lesbos
Samos
Miletus
Rhodes
Crete

Byzantium Chalcedon
Abydos Cyzicus Astacus
Tieum

PHRYGIA

Sardis
MESHECH

LYDIA

Phaselis

Ancyra
Gordion

L. Tuz

Kanish

TAURUS MTS.

CILICIA

Tarsus

CIMMERIANS (GOMER)

Trapezus

TUBAL

Melitene

Samal
Carchemish
Aleppo
Arpad

URARTU

(ARARAT)

Mt. Ararat

L. Van

Nairi

Haran
Til Barsib
Gozan

Nisibis

L. Sevan
Cyrus
Araxes

Turushpa

L. Urmia
Minni

Dur Sharrukin
Nineveh
Calah
(Nimrud)
Asshur

Arbela

Caspian

ELBURZ MTS

MADAI (MEDES)

Ecbatana

Upper (Western) Sea

Cyprus

Arvad

Sidon
Tyre

Qarqar
Hamath

PHOENICIA

SYRIA

Damascus

Tadmor

KEDAR

Anat

Euphrates

Habor

EMPIRE

Tigris

Diyala

ASSYRIA

BABYLONIA

Sippar
Cuthah
Babylon
Borsippa

Nippur

Erech

Larsa

Ur

CHALDEANS

ELAM

Susa
(Shushan)

Samaria
Eltekeh
Raphia

ASSYRIAN

Jerusalem

AMMON

JUDAH
trib. to
Assyria

MOAB

EDOM

Sela

ARIBI

(ARABS)

Dumah

Lower (Eastern) Se

Sais
Memphis

Tanis
Bubastis
On

Pelusium

Heracleopolis

EGYPT
to Assyria 671-651 B.C.

Hermopolis

Siut

Abydos

Thebes

Red Sea

Tema

Dedan

ETHIOPIA

Syene

Dilmun
?

The Assyrian Empire

- - - Assyrian empire — c.824 B.C.
—— Assyrian empire — c.640 B.C.

<u>Sinope</u> Greek colonies underlined in red

0   50   100   150   200   250 Mls

0 50 100   200   300   400 Kms

© Copyright HAMMOND INCORPORATED, Maplewood, N.J.

Tiglath-pileser III extended the
Assyrian Empire in the 8th
century B.C. and caused political
chaos in Israel.

The only contemporary picture of a Hebrew
monarch occurs on the Black Obelisk, an
Assyrian monument from Nimrud. It shows
Jehu on his knees before Shalmaneser III.

Assyrian wall relief from the throne room of
Sennacherib shows Hebrews fleeing the doomed
city of Lachish in southwest Judah when it was
under Assyrian siege in 701 B.C.

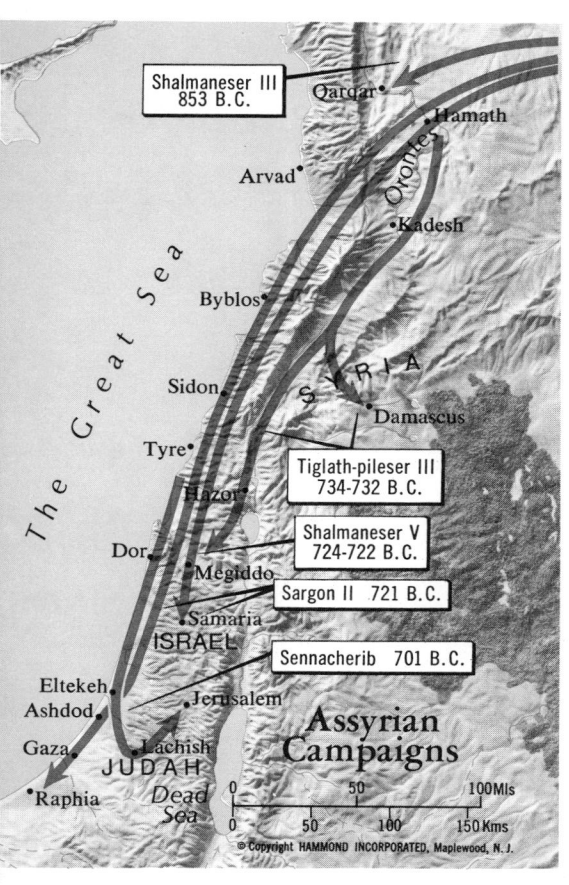

Assyrian Campaigns

Shalmaneser III
853 B.C.

Qatqar

Hamath

Arvad

Kadesh

Byblos

SYRIA

Sidon

Damascus

Tyre

Tiglath-pileser III
734-732 B.C.

Hazor

Shalmaneser V
724-722 B.C.

Dor

Megiddo

Sargon II 721 B.C.

Samaria

ISRAEL

Sennacherib 701 B.C.

Eltekeh

Jerusalem

Ashdod

Gaza

Lachish

JUDAH

Raphia

Dead Sea

The Great Sea

Orontes

© Copyright HAMMOND INCORPORATED, Maplewood, N.J.

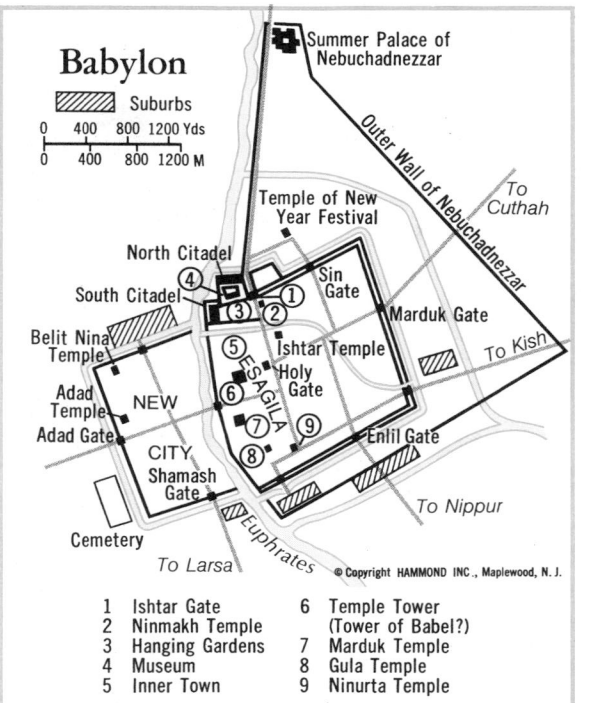

Babylon

Suburbs

Summer Palace of Nebuchadnezzar

Outer Wall of Nebuchadnezzar

To Cuthah

Temple of New Year Festival

North Citadel

South Citadel

Sin Gate

Marduk Gate

To Kish

Belit Nina Temple

Ishtar Temple

ESAGILA

Ishtar Holy Gate

Adad Temple

NEW

Adad Gate

CITY

Shamash Gate

Enlil Gate

To Nippur

Cemetery

To Larsa

Euphrates

© Copyright HAMMOND INC., Maplewood, N.J.

1 Ishtar Gate
2 Ninmakh Temple
3 Hanging Gardens
4 Museum
5 Inner Town
6 Temple Tower (Tower of Babel?)
7 Marduk Temple
8 Gula Temple
9 Ninurta Temple

A reconstruction of the Ishtar Gate at Babylon, with the famous "hanging gardens" in the right background. The king entering the gate is Nebuchadnezzar II (605-562 B.C.), who destroyed Jerusalem.

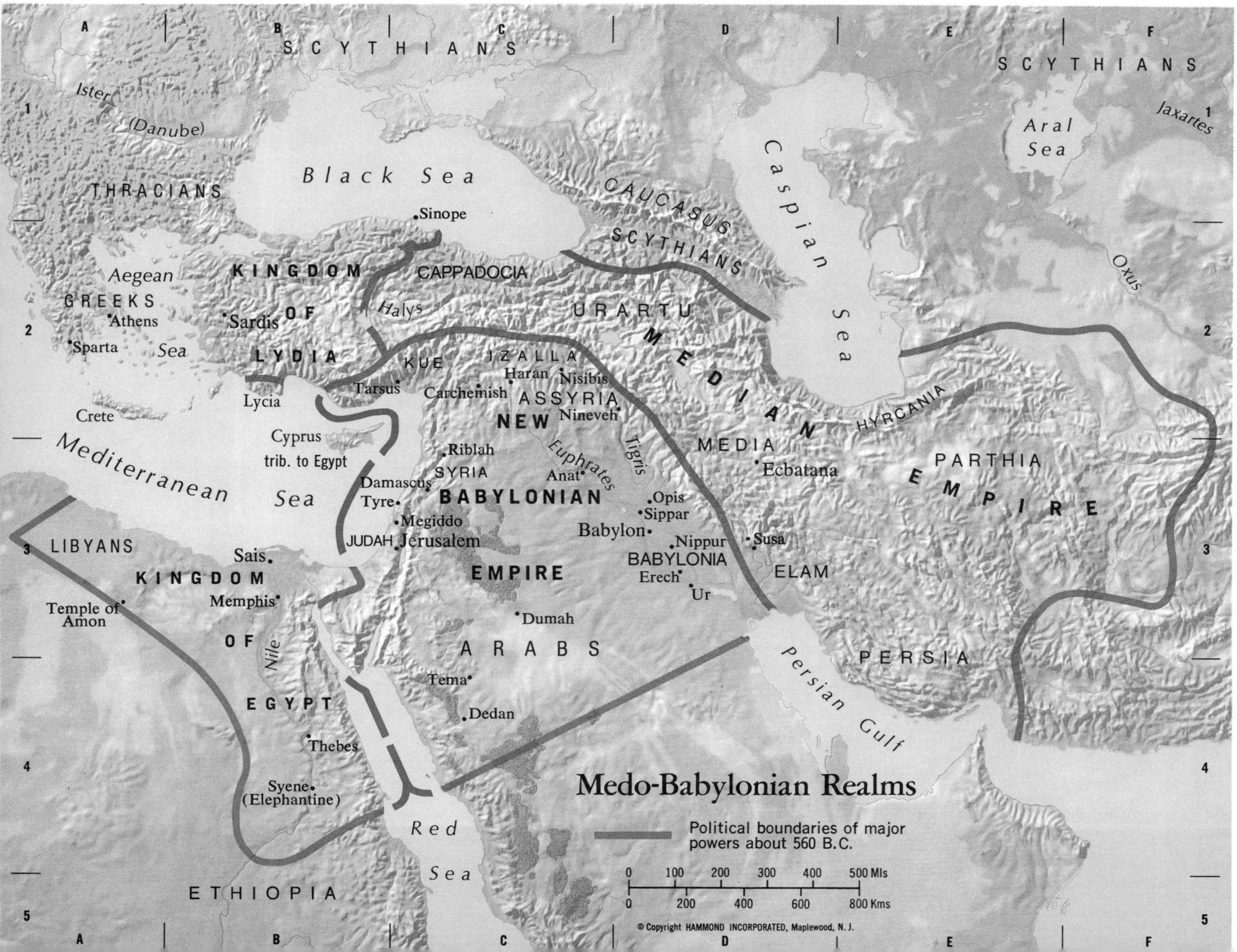

Medo-Babylonian Realms

Political boundaries of major powers about 560 B.C.

SCYTHIANS

Ister (Danube)

Jaxartes

Aral Sea

THRACIANS

Black Sea

Sinope

SCYTHIANS

CAUCASUS

Caspian Sea

Oxus

Aegean Sea

KINGDOM OF LYDIA

CAPPADOCIA

URARTU

MEDIAN

GREEKS

Athens

Sardis

Halys

Sparta

KUE

IZALLA

Haran Nisibis

HYRCANIA

Lycia

Tarsus

Carchemish

ASSYRIA

PARTHIA

Crete

Cyprus trib. to Egypt

NEW

Nineveh

MEDIA

EMPIRE

Mediterranean Sea

Riblah

Euphrates

Tigris

Ecbatana

Damascus

SYRIA

Anat

Tyre

BABYLONIAN

Opis

Megiddo

Sippar

JUDAH Jerusalem

Babylon

Nippur

Susa

LIBYANS

EMPIRE

BABYLONIA

ELAM

KINGDOM

Sais

Erech

Ur

PERSIA

Temple of Amon

Memphis

OF

Dumah

ARABS

Persian Gulf

EGYPT

Tema

Dedan

Nile

Thebes

Syene (Elephantine)

Red Sea

ETHIOPIA

© Copyright HAMMOND INCORPORATED, Maplewood, N.J.

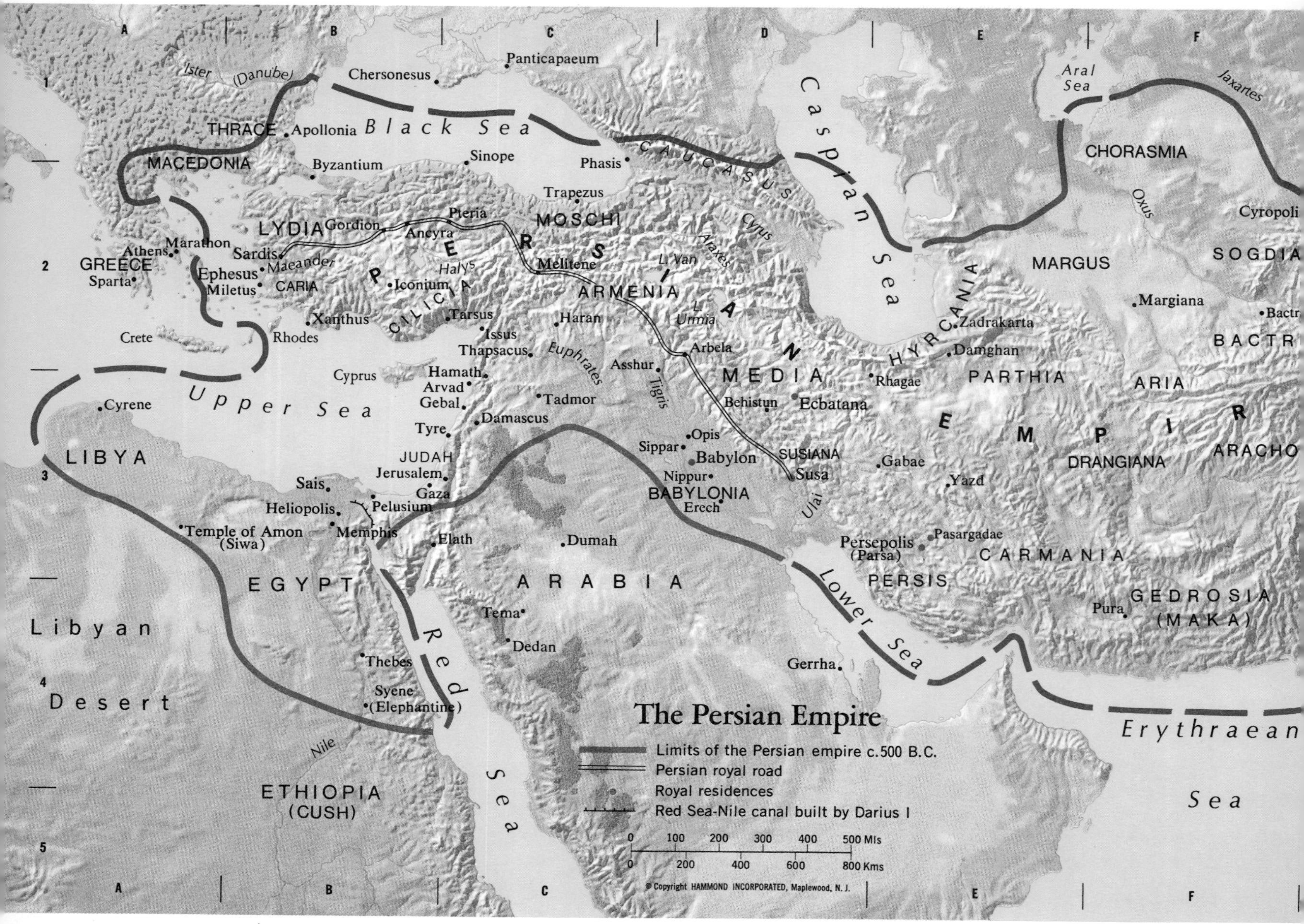

The Persian Empire

Map labels (selected):

Ister (Danube), Chersonesus, Panticapaeum, Black Sea, Aral Sea, Jaxartes, THRACE, Apollonia, CHORASMIA, MACEDONIA, Byzantium, Sinope, Phasis, CAUCASUS, Oxus, Cyropoli, Trapezus, Cyrus, LYDIA, Gordion, Pieria, MOSCHI, Araxes, SOGDIA, Aneyra, Melitene, MARGUS, Athens, Marathon, Sardis, L. Van, Bactr, GREECE, Maeander, Halys, ARMENIA, Urmia, Margiana, Sparta, Ephesus, Miletus, CARIA, Iconium, CILICIA, HYRCANIA, Zadrakarta, BACTR, Xanthus, Tarsus, Haran, Damghan, Rhodes, Issus, Arbela, MEDIA, PARTHIA, Crete, Thapsacus, Euphrates, Asshur, Rhagae, Ecbatana, ARIA, Cyprus, Hamath, Tigris, Behistun, EMPIR, Upper Sea, Arvad, Gebal, Tadmor, Opis, Gabae, DRANGIANA, ARACHO, Cyrene, Tyre, Damascus, Sippar, Babylon, Yazd, LIBYA, JUDAH, Nippur, BABYLONIA, SUSIANA, Jerusalem, Gaza, Erech, Susa, Persepolis (Parsa), Pasargadae, CARMANIA, Sais, Heliopolis, Pelusium, Ulai, PERSIS, Temple of Amon (Siwa), Memphis, Elath, Dumah, GEDROSIA (MAKA), EGYPT, ARABIA, Pura, Libyan, Tema, Lower Sea, Dedan, Thebes, Gerrha, Erythraean, Syene (Elephantine), Red Sea, Nile, ETHIOPIA (CUSH), Sea, Desert

Limits of the Persian empire c. 500 B.C.
Persian royal road
Royal residences
Red Sea-Nile canal built by Darius I

0 100 200 300 400 500 Mls
0 200 400 600 800 Kms

© Copyright HAMMOND INCORPORATED, Maplewood, N.J.

On this clay cylinder of 538 B.C., Cyrus provides royal authorization for the rebuilding of temples "beyond the Euphrates."

Tomb of Cyrus the Great at Pasargadae, Iran. When he conquered Babylon, Cyrus allowed the Jews to return to Jerusalem and rebuild their temple.

The earliest coin used in the Holy Land is this 4th-century silver Persian piece. The obverse has a falcon with the inscription "Yahud." The reverse has a lily with no inscription.

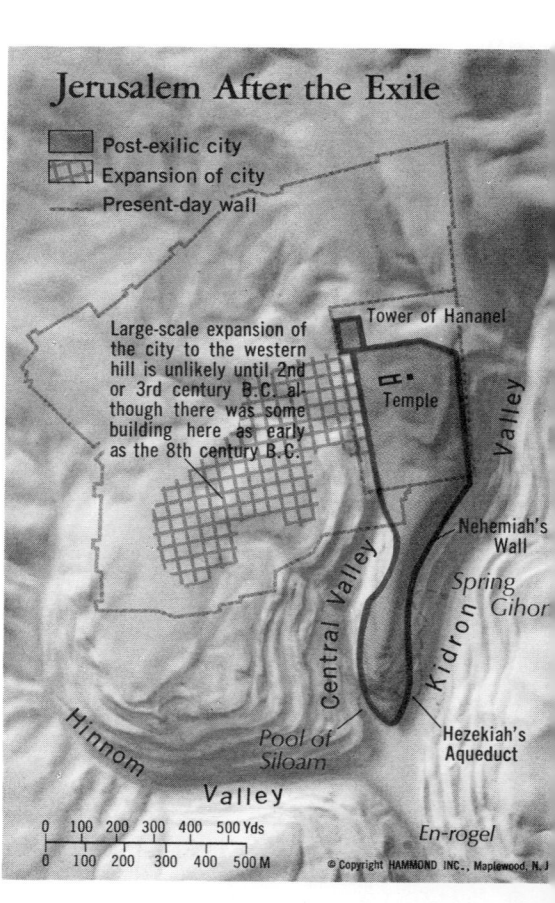

Jerusalem After the Exile

Post-exilic city
Expansion of city
Present-day wall

Large-scale expansion of the city to the western hill is unlikely until 2nd or 3rd century B.C. although there was some building here as early as the 8th century B.C.

Tower of Hananel
Temple
Valley
Nehemiah's Wall
Spring Gihor
Central Valley
Kidron
Hinnom
Pool of Siloam
Hezekiah's Aqueduct
Valley
En-rogel

0 100 200 300 400 500 Yds
0 100 200 300 400 500 M

© Copyright HAMMOND INC., Maplewood, N.J.

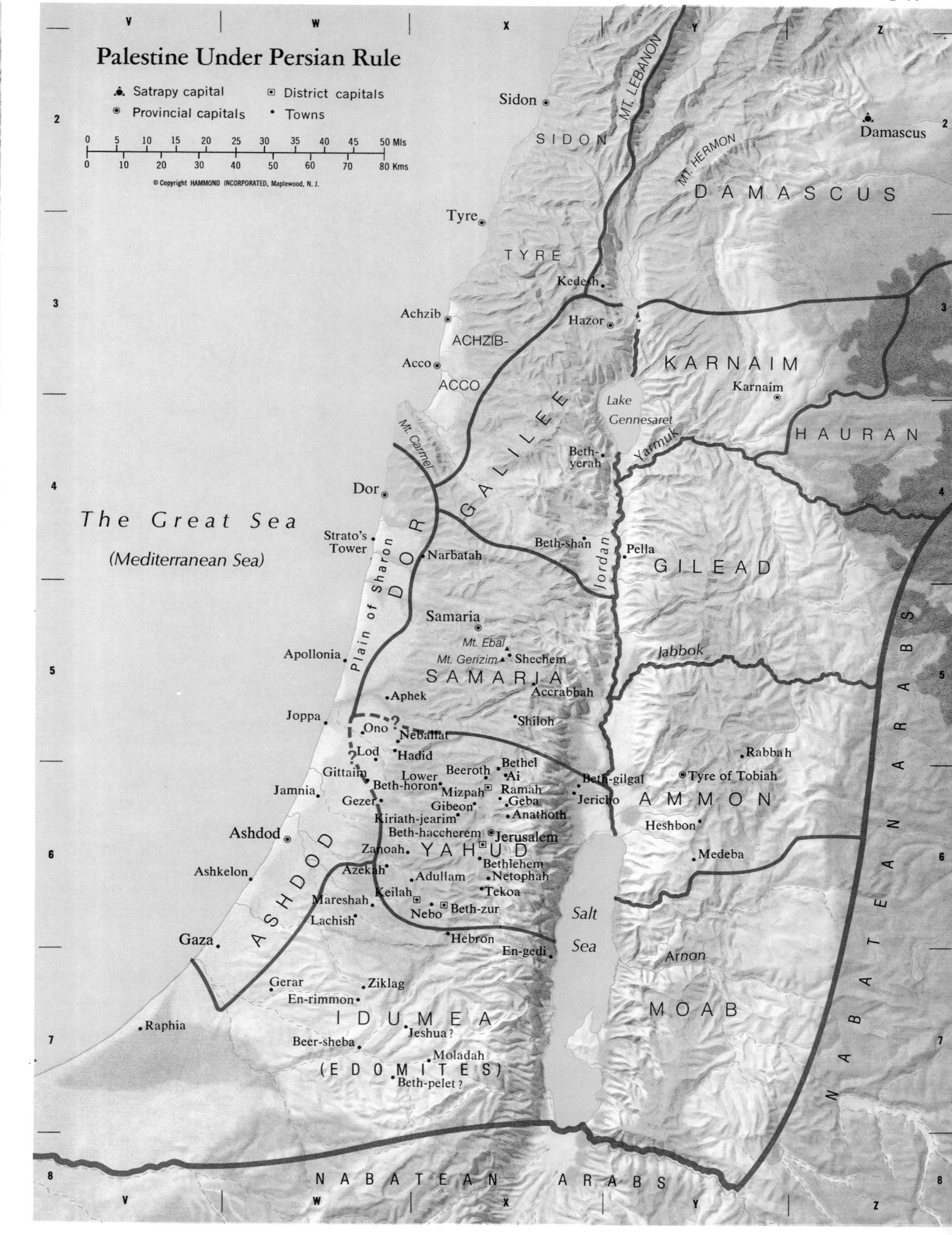

Palestine Under Persian Rule

- ⚭ Satrapy capital
- ◉ Provincial capitals
- ⊡ District capitals
- • Towns

0 5 10 15 20 25 30 35 40 45 50 Mls
0 10 20 30 40 50 60 70 80 Kms

© Copyright HAMMOND INCORPORATED, Maplewood, N.J.

Sidon

Damascus

SIDON

DAMASCUS

MT. LEBANON

MT. HERMON

Tyre

TYRE

Kedesh

Achzib

ACHZIB-

Hazor

KARNAIM

Karnaim

Acco

ACCO

GALILEE

Lake
Gennesaret

HAURAN

Yarmuk

Beth-
yerah

Mt. Carmel

Dor

DOR

Beth-shan

Pella

GILEAD

The Great Sea

Strato's
Tower

Narbatah

Jordan

(Mediterranean Sea)

Plain of Sharon

Samaria

Jabbok

Apollonia

Mt. Ebal
Mt. Gerizim ▲ Shechem

SAMARIA

Accrabbah

Aphek

Shiloh

Joppa

Ono

Neballat

Rabbah

Lod

Hadid

Bethel

Gittaim

Lower
Beth-horon

Beeroth

Ai

Beth-gilgal

Tyre of Tobiah

Jamnia

Mizpah

Ramah

Jericho

AMMON

Gezer

Gibeon

Geba

Kiriath-jearim

Anathoth

Heshbon

Beth-haccherem

Jerusalem

Ashdod

ASHDOD

Zanoah

YAHUD

Bethlehem

Medeba

Ashkelon

Azekah

Adullam

Netophah

Keilah

Tekoa

Mareshah

Nebo

Beth-zur

Salt

Lachish

Sea

Gaza

Hebron

En-gedi

Arnon

Gerar

Ziklag

En-rimmon

MOAB

Raphia

IDUMEA

Beer-sheba

Jeshua ?

Moladah

(EDOMITES)

Beth-pelet ?

NABATEAN ARABS

NABATEAN ARABS

THIANS
(SAKA)

G

KUSH

ophen
abul)

ANDARA

Taxila

INDUSH
(INDIA)

tala

Probable
ancient
coastline

G

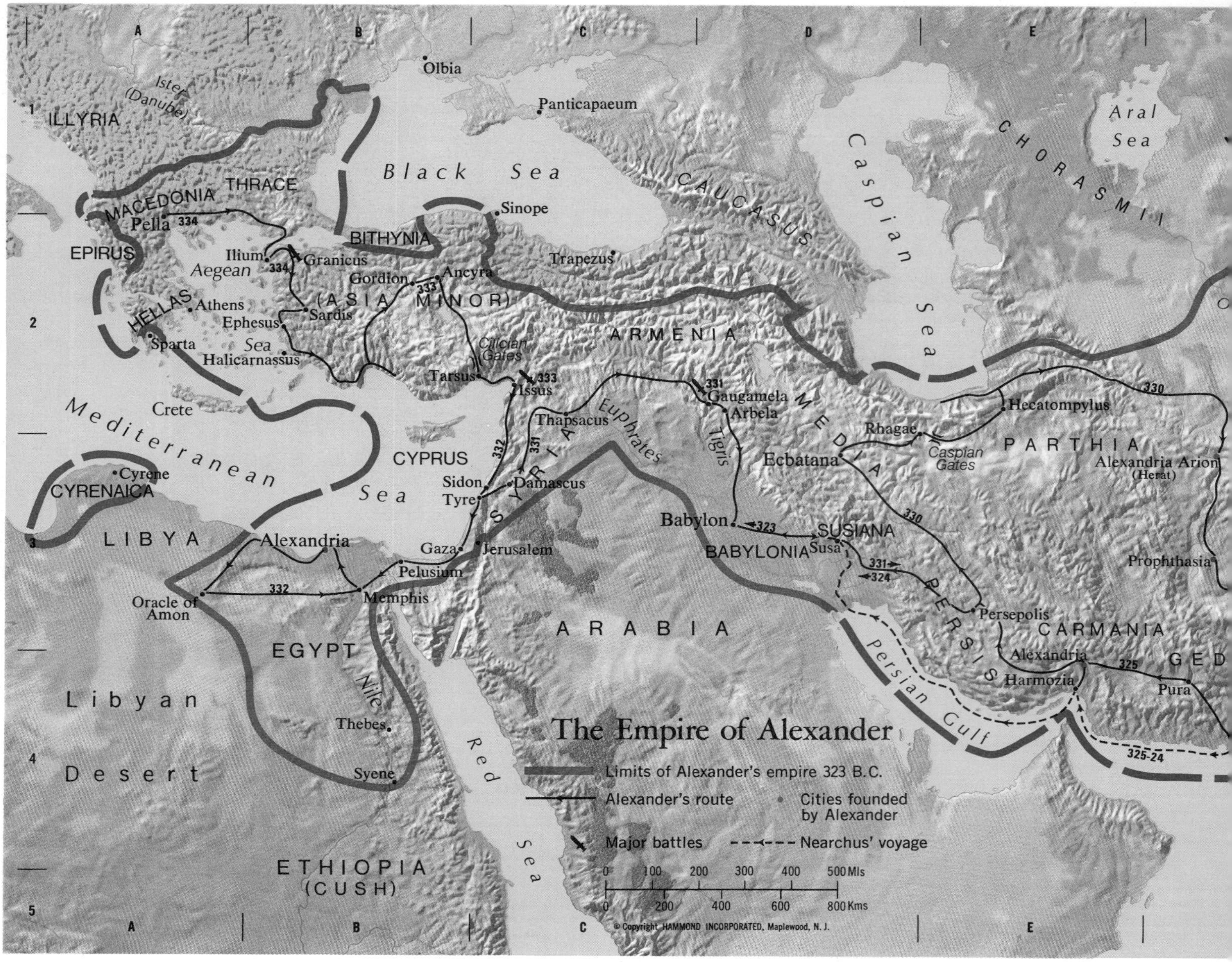

The Empire of Alexander

ILLYRIA
Ister (Danube)
Olbia
Panticapaeum
Black Sea
Aral Sea
CHORASMIA
MACEDONIA
THRACE
Pella 334
EPIRUS
BITHYNIA
Sinope
CAUCASUS
Caspian Sea
Ilium
Granicus 334
Aegean
Gordion
Ancyra
Trapezus
(ASIA MINOR)
333
ARMENIA
HELLAS
Athens
Sardis
Ephesus
Sea
Sparta
Halicarnassus
Clician Gates
Tarsus
333
Issus
Gaugamela 331
Arbela
MEDIA
Hecatompylus
330
Rhagae
Caspian Gates
PARTHIA
Crete
Mediterranean
Thapsacus
Euphrates
Tigris
Ecbatana
Alexandria Arion (Herat)
Sea
332
Sidon
Damascus
Babylon 323
SUSIANA
330
Tyre
BABYLONIA
Susa
331
PERSIS
Prophthasia
CYRENAICA
Cyrene
Gaza
Jerusalem
ARABIA
324
Persepolis
CARMANIA
LIBYA
Alexandria
Pelusium
Alexandria
325
GED
Oracle of Amon
332
Memphis
Persian Gulf
Harmozia
Pura
EGYPT
Libyan
Nile
325-24
Thebes
Desert
Syene
Red Sea

The Empire of Alexander

— Limits of Alexander's empire 323 B.C.
— Alexander's route   • Cities founded by Alexander
↗ Major battles   - - -◄- - - Nearchus' voyage

0   100   200   300   400   500 Mls
0   200   400   600   800 Kms

© Copyright HAMMOND INCORPORATED, Maplewood, N.J.

ETHIOPIA (CUSH)

Alexander the Great at the Battle of Issus, where he defeated the Persians. This Roman mosaic from Pompeii shows the determination of this brilliant soldier who established an empire at age thirty.

Silver tetradrachm of Ptolemy I struck in Egypt shows Alexander wearing an elephant head-dress. Reverse: the goddess Athena.

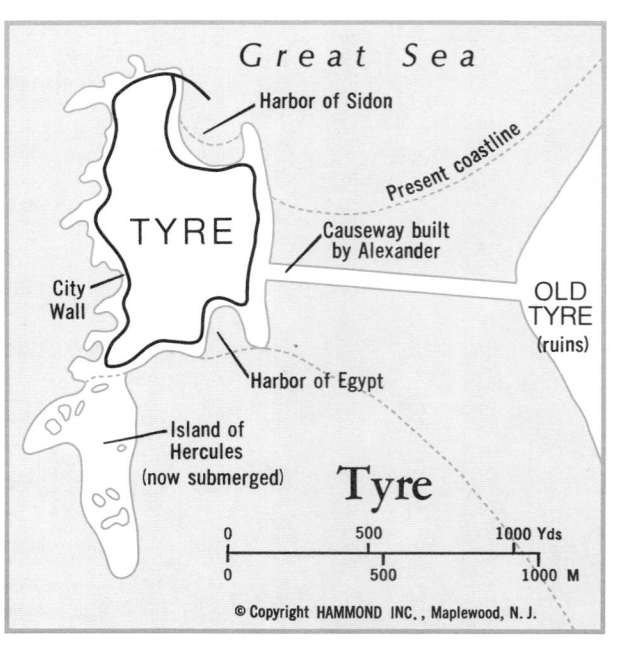

Great Sea

Harbor of Sidon

Present coastline

TYRE

Causeway built by Alexander

City Wall

OLD TYRE (ruins)

Harbor of Egypt

Island of Hercules (now submerged)

Tyre

0   500   1000 Yds
0   500   1000 M

© Copyright HAMMOND INC., Maplewood, N.J.

Massive round towers such as this one were set into Israelite walls at Samaria by Alexander's military engineers. Samaria, once capital of Israel, became one of the most Hellenized cities of Palestine.

Seleucus I, "Nicator," continued Alexander's Hellenizing policies.

Ptolemy I, "Soter," turned Egypt into his personal domain.

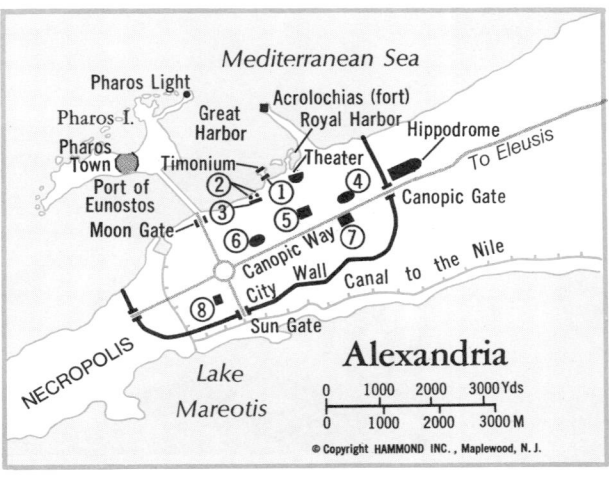

Alexandria

1 Poseidium
2 Obelisks (later Cleopatra's Needles)
3 Caesarium
4 Stadium
5 Library and Museum
6 Amphitheater
7 Sports Grounds
8 Serapeion

Terracotta statuette of a war elephant with driver and tower.

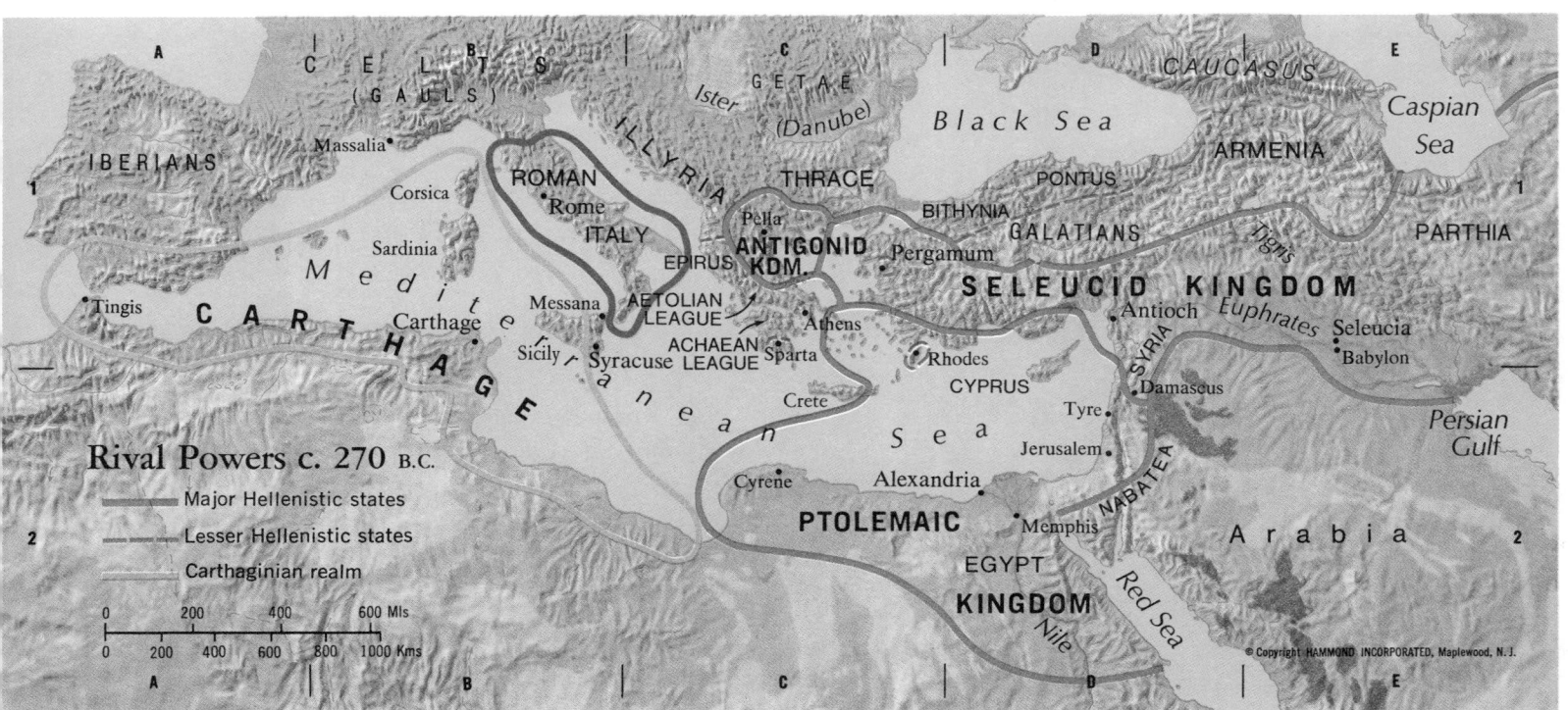

Rival Powers c. 270 B.C.

Major Hellenistic states
Lesser Hellenistic states
Carthaginian realm

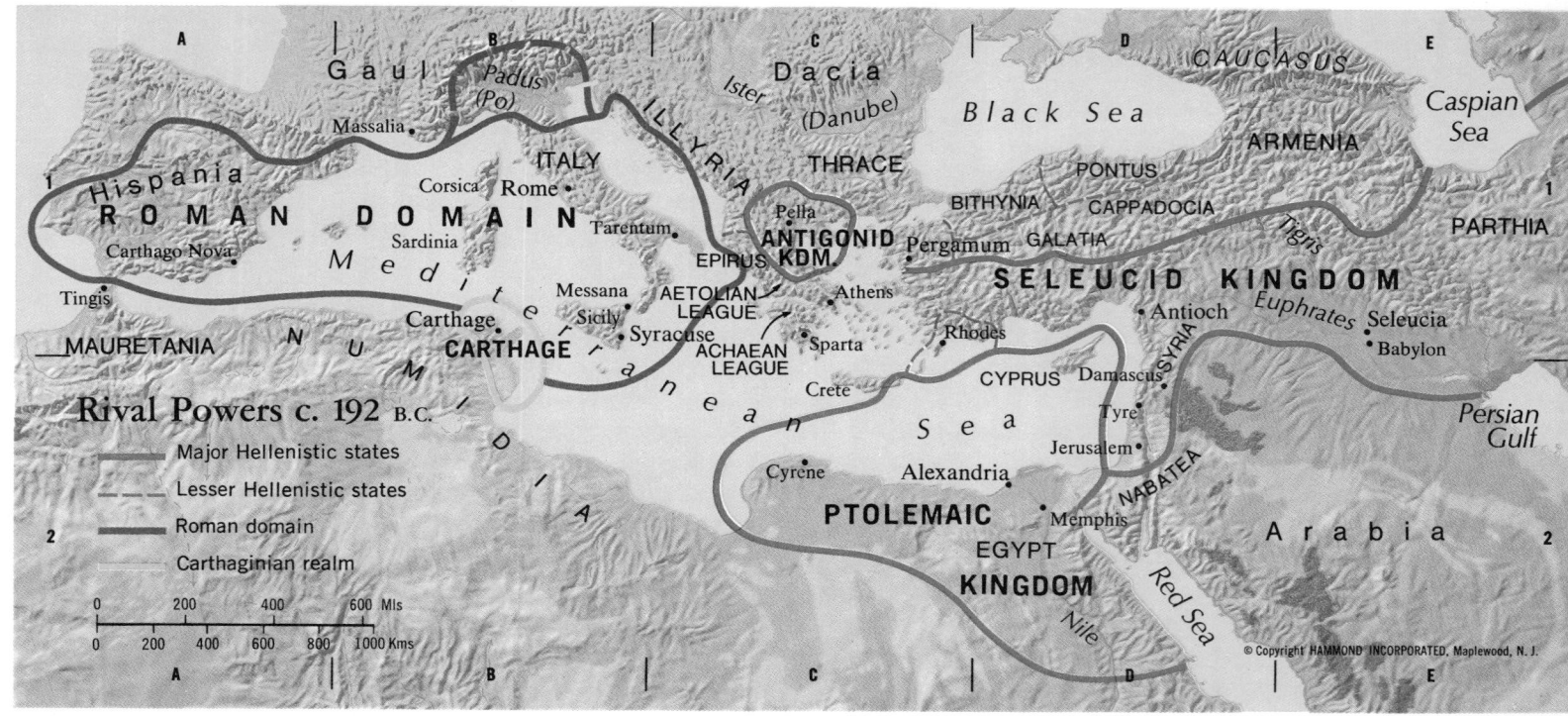

Rival Powers c. 192 B.C.

- Major Hellenistic states
- Lesser Hellenistic states
- Roman domain
- Carthaginian realm

Antiochus III, "The Great," who took Palestine from the Ptolemies at the Battle of Panias in 197 B.C.

Naked Greek youths participating in athletic contests are pictured on this 6th-century B.C. Greek vase. Such practices introduced into Jerusalem were a cause of the Maccabean Revolt.

Jerusalem of the Maccabees

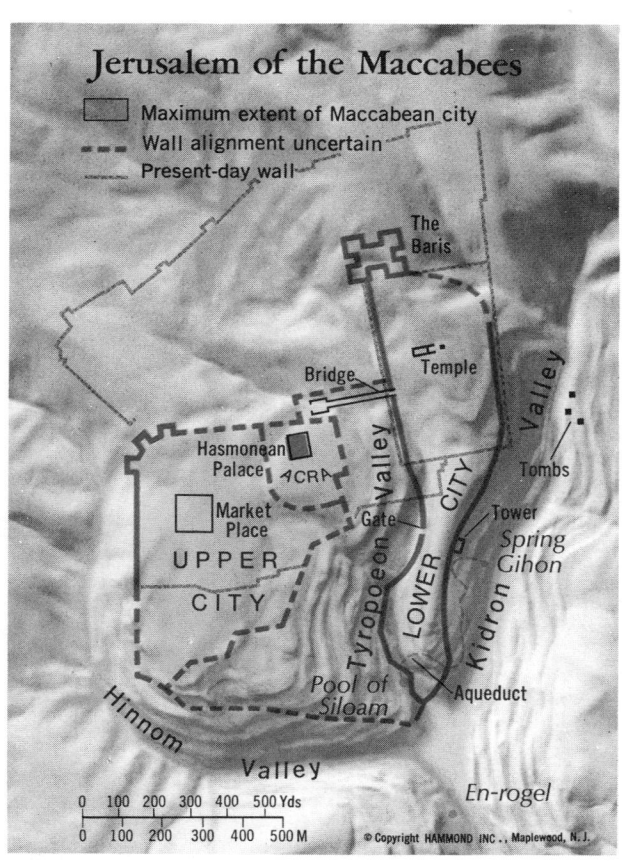

- Maximum extent of Maccabean city
- Wall alignment uncertain
- Present-day wall

Antiochus IV, "Epiphanes," tried to Hellenize the Jews, which led to the Maccabean War in 166 B.C.

A lepton of Alexander Jannaeus (103-76 B.C.), who expanded the Jewish Hasmonean Kingdom to its greatest limits. This coin is popularly known as the "widow's mite" of the New Testament. (Mark 12:42, Luke 21:2).

A Jewish "slipper lamp" from the time of the Hasmonean Kingdom.

Antigonus II (40-37 B.C.), the last of the Hasmonean rulers, issued debased coinage, but did show the Menorah on some coins such as this perutah. He lost his throne to Herod the Great.

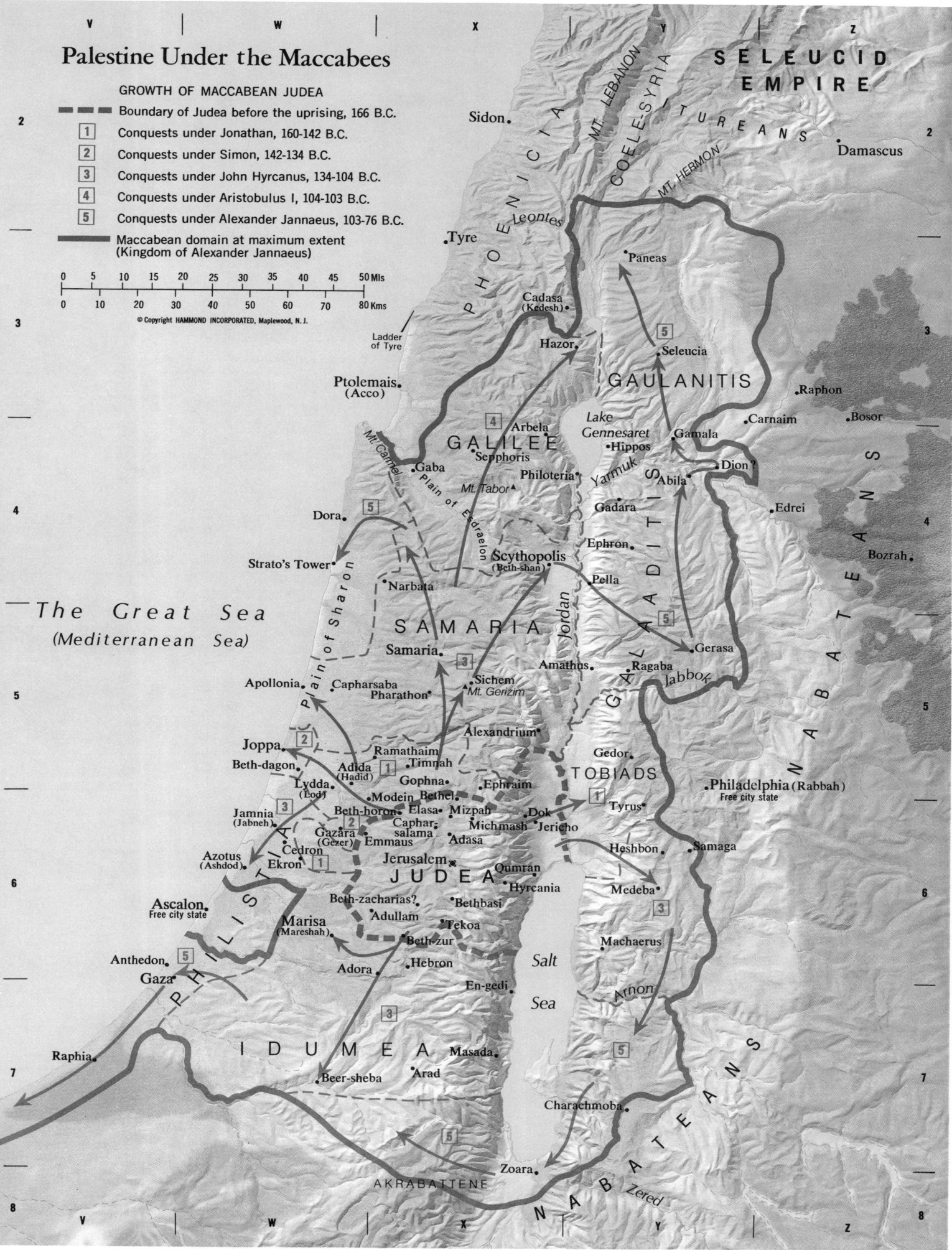

Palestine Under the Maccabees

GROWTH OF MACCABEAN JUDEA

- – – – Boundary of Judea before the uprising, 166 B.C.
- 1 Conquests under Jonathan, 160-142 B.C.
- 2 Conquests under Simon, 142-134 B.C.
- 3 Conquests under John Hyrcanus, 134-104 B.C.
- 4 Conquests under Aristobulus I, 104-103 B.C.
- 5 Conquests under Alexander Jannaeus, 103-76 B.C.
- —— Maccabean domain at maximum extent (Kingdom of Alexander Jannaeus)

0 5 10 15 20 25 30 35 40 45 50 Mls
0 10 20 30 40 50 60 70 80 Kms

© Copyright HAMMOND INCORPORATED, Maplewood, N.J.

SELEUCID EMPIRE

PHOENICIA

COELE-SYRIA

ITUREANS

Sidon

Damascus

Mt. Lebanon

Mt. Hermon

Tyre

Leontes

Paneas

Cadasa (Kedesh)

Ladder of Tyre

Hazor

Seleucia

GAULANITIS

Ptolemais (Acco)

Arbela

Lake Gennesaret

Raphon

Carnaim

Bosor

GALILEE

Gaba

Sepphoris

Hippos

Gamala

Dion

Mt. Carmel

Plain of Esdraelon

Mt. Tabor

Philoteria

Yarmuk

Abila

Edrei

Dora

Gadara

Bozrah

Strato's Tower

Scythopolis (Beth-shan)

Ephron

Pella

GALAADITIS

Narbata

Jordan

Samaria

Amathus

Ragaba

Gerasa

NABATEANS

The Great Sea
(Mediterranean Sea)

Plain of Sharon

SAMARIA

Jabbok

Apollonia

Capharsaba

Pharathon

Sichem

Mt. Gerizim

Alexandrium

Gedor

TOBIADS

Joppa

Ramathaim

Timnah

Ephraim

Philadelphia (Rabbah)
Free city state

Beth-dagon

Adida (Hadid)

Gophna

Tyrus

Lydda (Lod)

Modein

Bethel

Dok

Jericho

Jamnia (Jabneh)

Beth-horon

Elasa

Mizpah

Michmash

Heshbon

Samaga

Gazara (Gezer)

Caphar-salama

Adasa

Azotus (Ashdod)

Cedron

Emmaus

Jerusalem

Qumran

Medeba

Ekron

JUDEA

Hyrcania

PHILISTIA

Ascalon
Free city state

Beth-zacharias?

Bethbasi

Machaerus

Gaza

Anthedon

Marisa (Mareshah)

Adullam

Tekoa

Beth-zur

Salt Sea

Adora

Hebron

En-gedi

Arnon

Raphia

IDUMEA

Masada

Beer-sheba

Arad

Charachmoba

Zoara

AKRABATTENE

NABATEANS

Zered

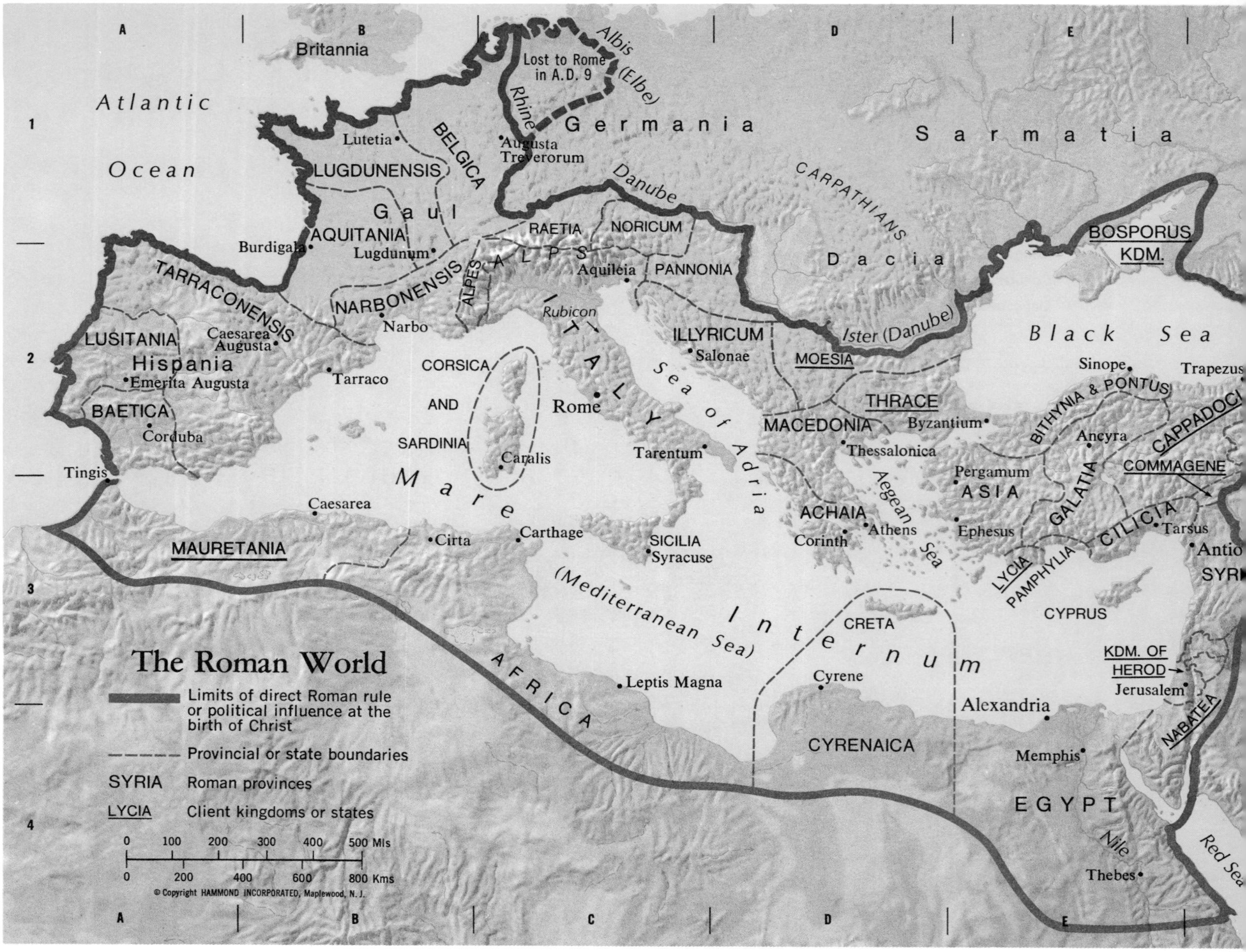

The Roman World

Limits of direct Roman rule or political influence at the birth of Christ

------- Provincial or state boundaries

SYRIA Roman provinces

<u>LYCIA</u> Client kingdoms or states

```
0    100   200   300   400   500 Mls
0    200   400   600   800 Kms
```

© Copyright HAMMOND INCORPORATED, Maplewood, N.J.

Map labels: Britannia · Atlantic Ocean · Lutetia · Lost to Rome in A.D. 9 · Albis (Elbe) · Germania · Sarmatia · Rhine · BELGICA · Augusta Treverorum · Danube · CARPATHIANS · LUGDUNENSIS · Gaul · RAETIA · NORICUM · Dacia · BOSPORUS KDM. · AQUITANIA · Burdigala · Lugdunum · ALPES · ALPS · Aquileia · PANNONIA · Black Sea · TARRACONENSIS · NARBONENSIS · ITALY · Rubicon · ILLYRICUM · Ister (Danube) · Sinope · Trapezus · Narbo · Salonae · MOESIA · BITHYNIA & PONTUS · LUSITANIA · Caesarea Augusta · Hispania · CORSICA · Rome · Sea of Adria · THRACE · Byzantium · Ancyra · CAPPADOCIA · Emerita Augusta · Tarraco · AND · MACEDONIA · Thessalonica · Pergamum · ASIA · GALATIA · COMMAGENE · BAETICA · SARDINIA · Caralis · Tarentum · Aegean Sea · ACHAIA · Ephesus · CILICIA · Tarsus · Corduba · Mare · Corinth · Athens · LYCIA · PAMPHYLIA · Antioch · Tingis · Caesarea · SICILIA · Syracuse · CYPRUS · SYRIA · Cirta · Carthage · Internum · CRETA · KDM. OF HEROD · Jerusalem · MAURETANIA · (Mediterranean Sea) · Cyrene · Alexandria · NABATEA · AFRICA · Leptis Magna · CYRENAICA · Memphis · EGYPT · Nile · Red Sea · Thebes

Senate House in the Imperial Forum.

Octavian (Caesar Augustus).

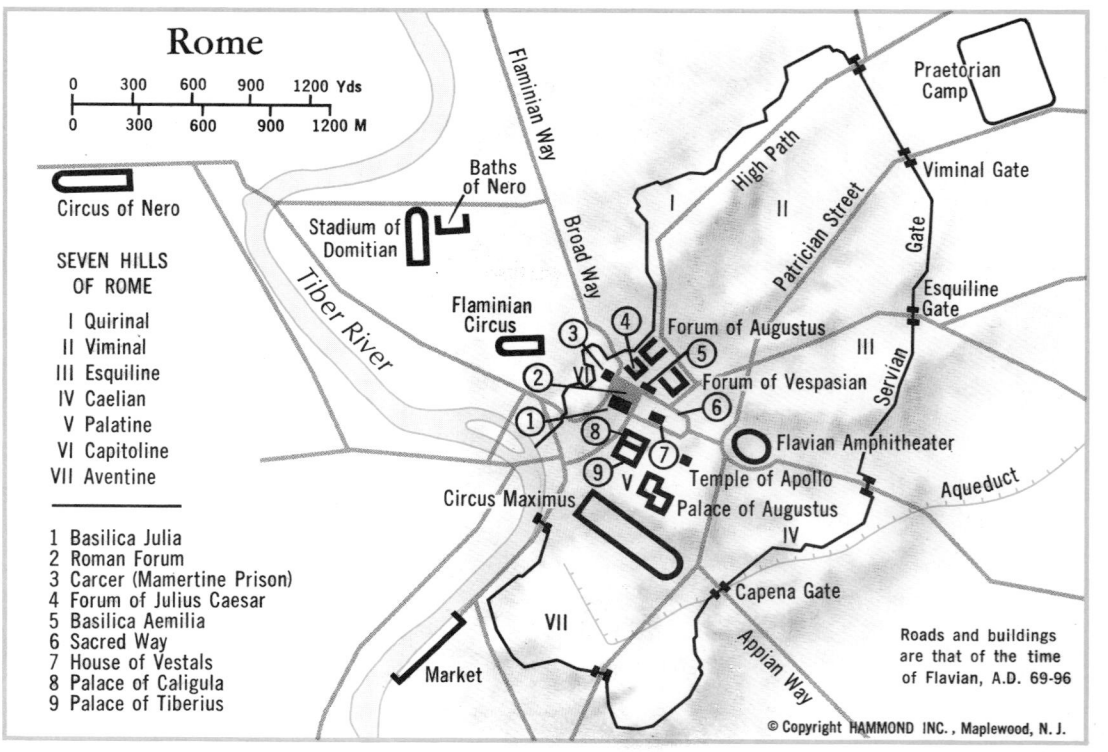

Rome

```
0    300   600   900   1200 Yds
0    300   600   900   1200 M
```

Circus of Nero

SEVEN HILLS OF ROME

I Quirinal
II Viminal
III Esquiline
IV Caelian
V Palatine
VI Capitoline
VII Aventine

1 Basilica Julia
2 Roman Forum
3 Carcer (Mamertine Prison)
4 Forum of Julius Caesar
5 Basilica Aemilia
6 Sacred Way
7 House of Vestals
8 Palace of Caligula
9 Palace of Tiberius

Map labels: Flaminian Way · Praetorian Camp · Baths of Nero · High Path · Stadium of Domitian · Viminal Gate · Broad Way · Patrician Street · Tiber River · Flaminian Circus · Forum of Augustus · Esquiline Gate · Forum of Vespasian · Servian · Gate · Flavian Amphitheater · Circus Maximus · Temple of Apollo · Aqueduct · Palace of Augustus · Capena Gate · Market · Appian Way

Roads and buildings are that of the time of Flavian, A.D. 69-96

© Copyright HAMMOND INC., Maplewood, N.J.

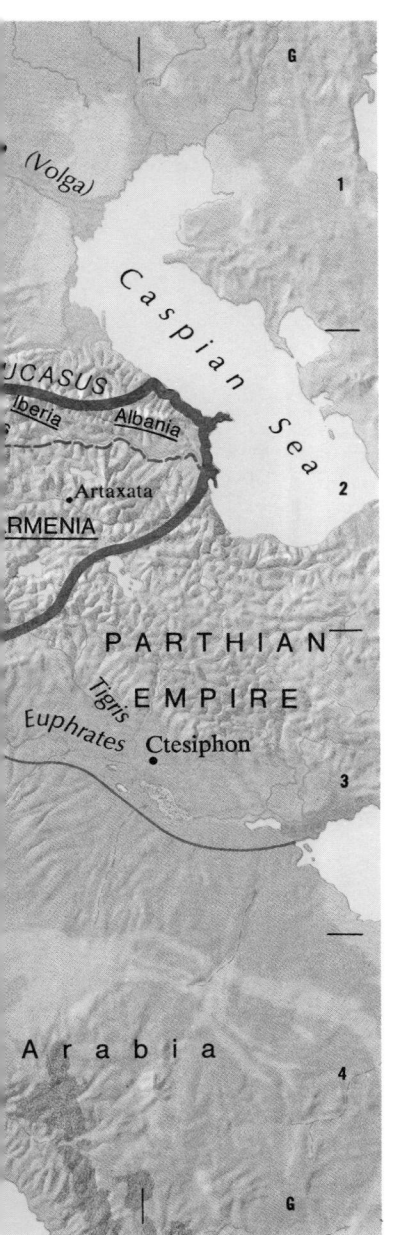

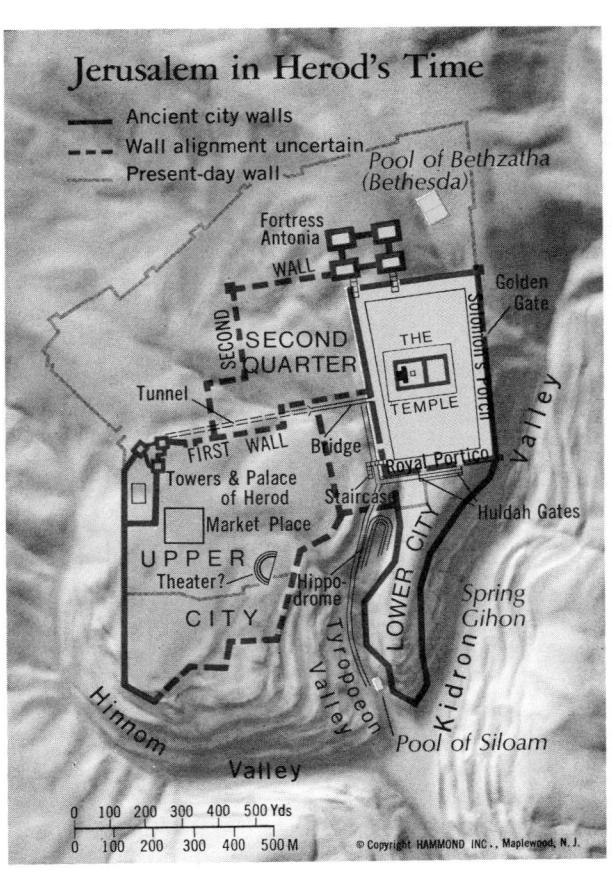

The Kingdom of Herod the Great

Boundary of Herod's kingdom
Other boundaries
⊡ Cities of the Decapolis
⨝ Fortresses

| 0 5 10 15 20 25 30 35 40 45 50 Mls |
| 0 10 20 30 40 50 60 70 80 Kms |

© Copyright HAMMOND INCORPORATED, Maplewood, N. J.

(Volga)

Caspian Sea

CAUCASUS
Iberia Albania
ARMENIA
• Artaxata

PARTHIAN EMPIRE
Tigris Euphrates
• Ctesiphon

Arabia

Mediterranean Sea

Chalcis
ABILENE
• Abila
Sidon
SYRIA
MT. LEBANON
Iturea • Damascus ⊡
Tyre
Leontes
Paneas
• Paneas
Ulatha
Cadasa
Gischala
Gaulanitis
Trachonitis
Batanea
• Raphana
Ptolemais
GALILEE
• Bethsaida
Taricheae (Magadan)
Sea of Galilee
⊡ Hippos
Auranitis
Gabae
• Sepphoris
• Dion ?
Mt. Carmel ▲
Nazareth
⊡ Gadara
• Abila
Dora
Scythopolis ⊡
⊡ Pella
DECAPOLIS
Caesarea (Strato's Tower)
Narbata
• Bostra
Plain of Sharon
SAMARIA
Jordan
⨝ Amathus
• Gerasa
Sebaste (Samaria)
Jabbok
Apollonia
Mt. Gerizim ▲
Antipatris
Gadara
Joppa
Alexandrium ⨝
PEREA
• Philadelphia
Phasaelis
Lydda
Gophna
Jamnia
Emmaus
Jericho
Betharamphtha
Jerusalem • Bethany
Cyprus ⨝
Esbus
Azotus
Bethlehem
Qumran
Medeba
Ascalon (free city)
JUDEA
Hyrcania ⨝
Herodium ⨝
Callirrhoe ⨝
Agrippias (Anthedon)
• Hebron
Lake Asphaltitis (Dead Sea)
Machaerus ⨝
Gaza
Adora
Engaddi
Arnon
IDUMEA
Bersabe
Masada ⨝
NABATEA
Malatha ⨝
Elusa
Nessana
• Khirbet Tannur
Nabatean sanctuary

Jerusalem in Herod's Time

Ancient city walls
Wall alignment uncertain
Present-day wall

Pool of Bethzatha (Bethesda)
Fortress Antonia
WALL
Golden Gate
SECOND QUARTER
Solomon's Porch
THE TEMPLE
Tunnel
FIRST WALL Bridge
Royal Portico
Towers & Palace of Herod
Staircase
Huldah Gates
Market Place
UPPER Theater?
Hippodrome
CITY
Spring Gihon
Tyropoeon Valley
LOWER CITY
Kidron Valley
Hinnom Valley
Pool of Siloam

| 0 100 200 300 400 500 Yds |
| 0 100 200 300 400 500 M |

© Copyright HAMMOND INC., Maplewood, N.J.

Temple of Herod

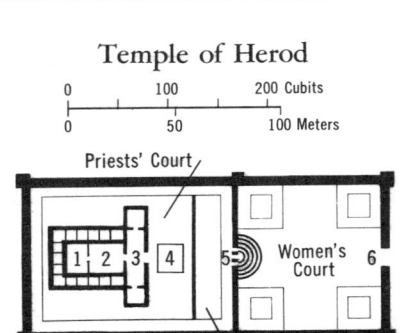

| 0 100 200 Cubits |
| 0 50 100 Meters |

Priests' Court
1 2 3 4 5 6
Women's Court
Court of Israel

1 Holy of Holies
2 Holy Place (Nave)
3 Porch
4 Altar
5 Nicanor Gate
6 Beautiful Gate?

Model of Herod's Temple, with surrounding courts and Royal Portico in the background.

Palestine in New Testament Times

▬▬▬	Political boundaries A.D. 6-44
───	Major roads
----	Other roads
⊡	Cities of the Decapolis
⋈	Fortresses

0 — 10 — 20 — 30 — 40 Mls
0 — 20 — 40 — 60 Kms

© Copyright HAMMOND INCORPORATED, Maplewood, N.J.

Mediterranean

Sea

ABILENE

Abila

Sidon

Sarepta

SYRIA

Iturea

Damascus

MT. LEBANON

Paneas

Tyre

Leontes

MT. HERMON

Caesarea Philippi
(Paneas)

Ulatha

Ladder
of Tyre

Ecdippa

Cadasa

Gischala

Gaulanitis

Trachonitis

Batanea

Ptolemais

Chorazin

Bethsaida-Julias

GALILEE

Capernaum

Raphana

Cana

Magadan

Bosor

Asochis

Tiberias

Sea
of
Galilee

Hippos

Dion?

Auranitis

Sepphoris

Nazareth

Philoteria

Yarmuk

Abila

Gabae

Plain

Mt. Tabor

Nain

Gadara

Capitolias

Dora

of

Agrippina

Bostra

Crocodilon

Esdraelon

Arbela

Caesarea

Scythopolis

Narbata

Ginae

Pella

DECAPOLIS

Salim
Aenon

Jordan

SAMARIA

Sebaste
(Samaria)

Mt. Ebal

Gerasa

Apollonia

Neapolis

Sychar

Amathus

Mt. Gerizim

Jabbok

Antipatris

Alexandrium

Joppa

Phasaelis

Gadara

Arimathea?

PEREA

Gophna

Ephraim

Philadelphia

Lydda

Archelais

Jamnia

Jericho

Betharamphtha
(Livias, Julias)

Emmaus
(Nicopolis)

Emmaus?

Cyprus

Jerusalem

Bethany

Esbus

Azotus

Bethlehem

Qumran
Essene community

Medeba

Ascalon

Marisa

Hyrcania

JUDEA

Herodium

Callirrhoe

Bethsura

Lake

Machaerus

Agrippias

Hebron

Asphaltitis

Gaza

(Dead Sea)

Arnon

Raphia

Engaddi

IDUMEA

Masada

Areopolis

Bersabe

Malatha

NABATEA

Charachmoba

Elusa

Plain of Sharon

Mt. Carmel

Phoenicia

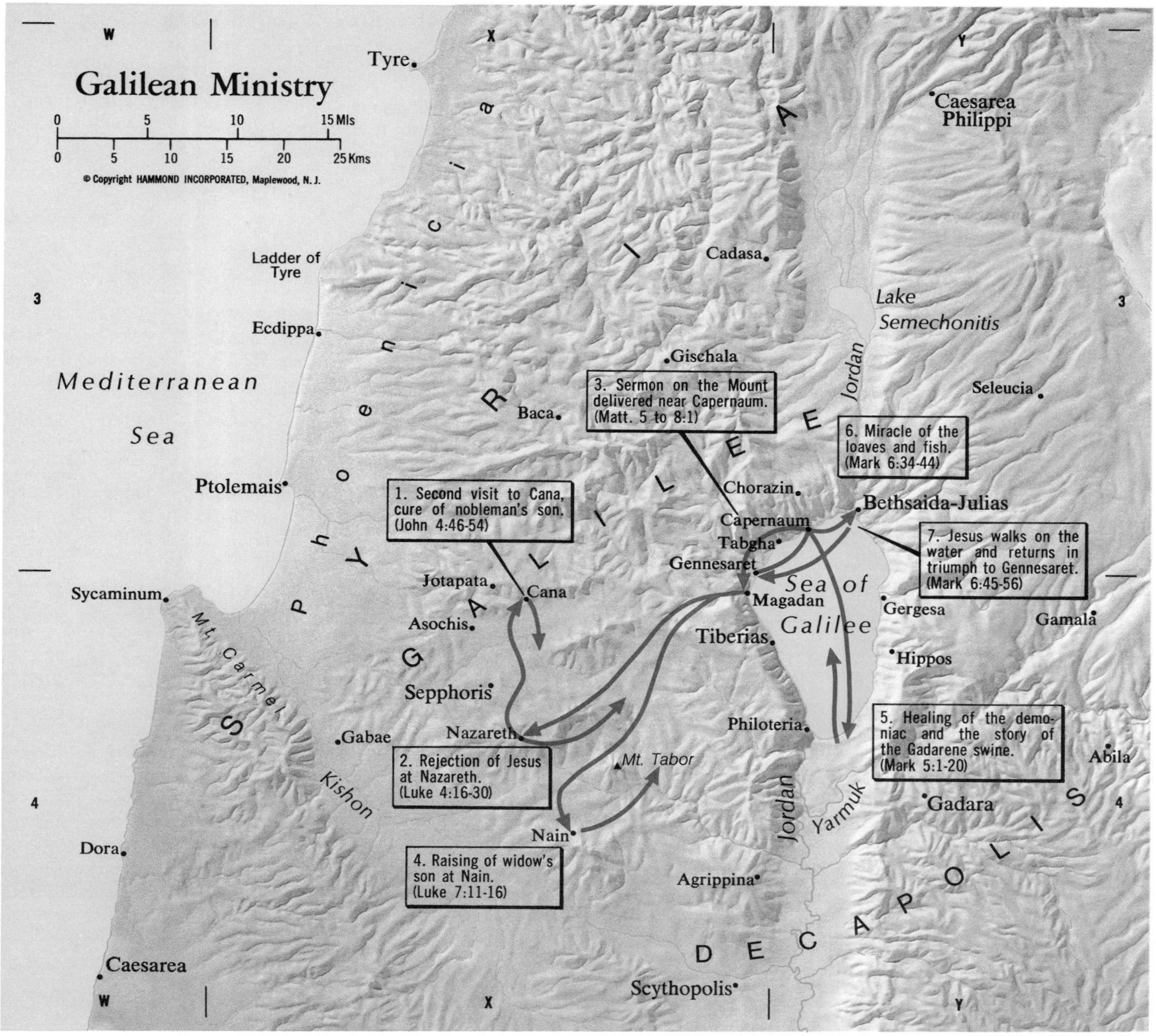

Galilean Ministry

0 5 10 15 Mls
0 5 10 15 20 25 Kms
© Copyright HAMMOND INCORPORATED, Maplewood, N.J.

Mediterranean

Sea

Tyre.

Ladder of
Tyre

Ecdippa.

Cadasa.

Lake
Semechonitis

Caesarea
Philippi

Seleucia

.Gischala

**3. Sermon on the Mount
delivered near Capernaum.
(Matt. 5 to 8:1)**

Baca.

**6. Miracle of the
loaves and fish.
(Mark 6:34-44)**

Ptolemais•

**1. Second visit to Cana,
cure of nobleman's son.
(John 4:46-54)**

Chorazin.

Capernaum.

Bethsaida-Julias

**7. Jesus walks on the
water and returns in
triumph to Gennesaret.
(Mark 6:45-56)**

Sycaminum.

Jotapata.

Cana

Tabgha•

Gennesaret

Sea of
Galilee

•Magadan

Gergesa

Gamala

Asochis.

Tiberias.

•Hippos

Sepphoris•

•Gabae

Nazareth

Philoteria.

**5. Healing of the demo-
niac and the story of
the Gadarene swine.
(Mark 5:1-20)**

Abila

**2. Rejection of Jesus
at Nazareth.
(Luke 4:16-30)**

•Mt. Tabor

•Gadara

Dora.

Nain

**4. Raising of widow's
son at Nain.
(Luke 7:11-16)**

Agrippina•

Caesarea

Scythopolis•

D E C A P O L I S

Above the waters of the Sea of
Galilee the Church of the Beatitudes
dominates the hill where tradition
says Jesus preached the Sermon on
the Mount.

The excavated synagogue at
Capernaum (right) is later than
the time of Jesus, but recalls
that the Galilean Ministry was
based in Capernaum, where
Jesus spent much time teaching
and healing in the synagogue.

The traditional site of Jesus' baptism
is here at the Jordan River.

Machaerus, where John the Baptist was put to
death on orders of Herod Antipas.

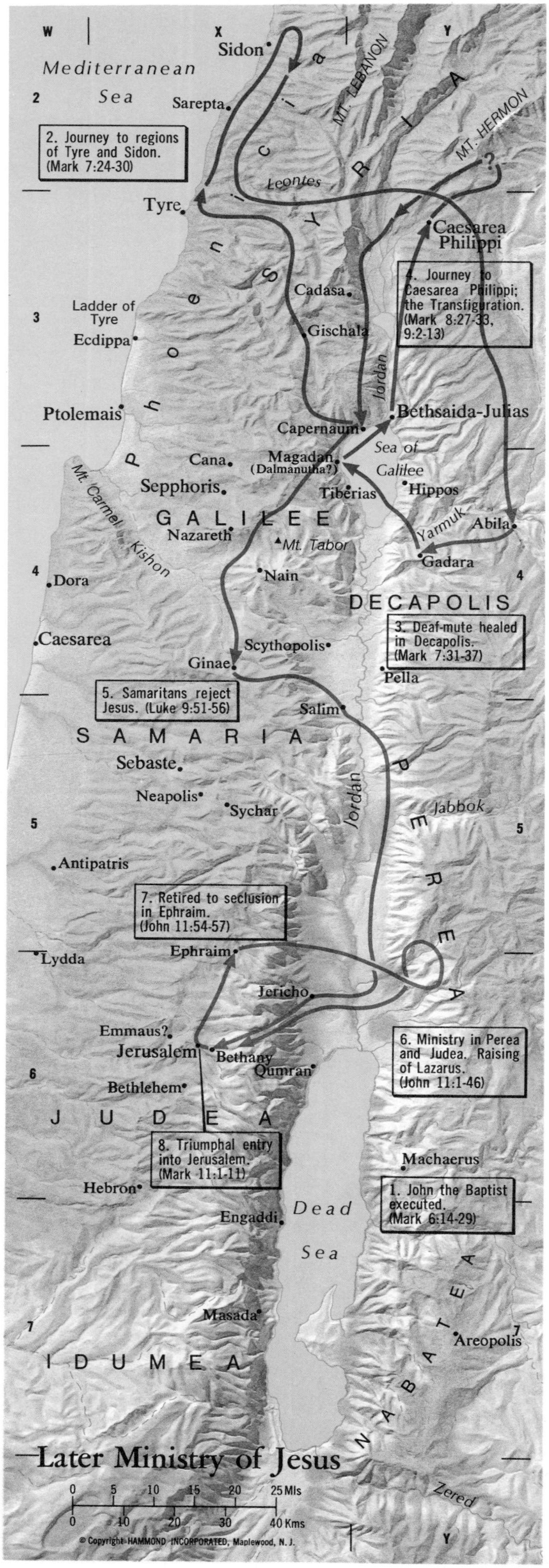

Map: Later Ministry of Jesus

W X Y

Mediterranean
Sea
Sidon
Sarepta

2. Journey to regions of Tyre and Sidon. (Mark 7:24-30).

Leontes
Tyre

MT. LEBANON
MT. HERMON

?

Caesarea Philippi

Cadasa
Gischala

4. Journey to Caesarea Philippi; the Transfiguration. (Mark 8:27-33, 9:2-13).

Ladder of Tyre
Ecdippa

Ptolemais

Capernaum
Bethsaida-Julias

Jordan

Sea of Galilee

Cana
Magadan (Dalmanutha?)
Sepphoris
Tiberias
Hippos

GALILEE
Nazareth
Mt. Tabor
Yarmuk
Abila

Nain
Gadara

Dora

DECAPOLIS

Caesarea
Scythopolis

3. Deaf-mute healed in Decapolis. (Mark 7:31-37).

Ginae
Pella

5. Samaritans reject Jesus. (Luke 9:51-56).

Salim

SAMARIA
Sebaste

Jordan

Neapolis
Sychar

Jabbok

Antipatris

P E R E A

7. Retired to seclusion in Ephraim. (John 11:54-57).

Lydda
Ephraim

Jericho

Emmaus?
Jerusalem
Bethany
Qumran

6. Ministry in Perea and Judea. Raising of Lazarus. (John 11:1-46).

Bethlehem

J U D E A

8. Triumphal entry into Jerusalem. (Mark 11:1-11).

Hebron

Machaerus

1. John the Baptist executed. (Mark 6:14-29).

Dead Sea

Engaddi

I D U M E A

Masada
Areopolis

N A B A T E A

Later Ministry of Jesus

0 5 10 15 20 25 Mis
0 10 20 30 40 Kms

© Copyright HAMMOND INCORPORATED, Maplewood, N.J.

Zered

The Events of Passion Week
(According to the Synoptic Gospels)

	MATT.	MARK	LUKE
SUNDAY (Palm Sunday)			
Triumphal entry into Jerusalem	21:1-9	11:1-10	19:28-44
Visit to Temple and return to Bethany	21:10-17	11:11	19:45-46
MONDAY			
On the way to Jerusalem Jesus curses an unfruitful fig tree	21:18-19	11:12-14	
The Temple court cleansed		11:15-19	19:45-48
TUESDAY			
Returning to Jerusalem, Jesus explains the withering of the fig tree	21:20-22	11:20-26	
Jesus' authority is questioned	21:23-27	11:27-33	20:1-8
Teachings in the Temple	21:28-46; 22	12:1-37a	20:9-44
Condemnation of scribes and Pharisees	23:1-36	12:37b-40	20:45-47
Jesus in Temple treasury calls attention to widow's gift		12:41-44	21:1-4
Prediction of destruction of the Temple and the end of the World	24:1-44	13:1-37	21:5-38
WEDNESDAY			
Conspiracy against Jesus	26:1-5	14:1-2	22:1-2
Anointing at Bethany	26:6-13	14:1-9	
Judas agrees to betray Jesus	26:14-16	14:10-11	22:3-6
THURSDAY (Maundy Thursday)			
Jesus prepares to celebrate Passover	26:17-19	14:12-16	22:7-13
The Last Supper	26:20-29	14:17-25	22:14-38
Withdrawal to Gethsemane	26:30-46	14:26-42	22:39-46
Betrayal and arrest of Jesus	26:47-56	14:43-52	22:47-53
Jesus before Caiaphas and members of the Sanhedrin; Peter's denial	26:57-75	14:53-72	22:54-71
FRIDAY (Good Friday)			
Trial before Pilate; Judas' suicide	27:1-2	15:1-5	23:1-5
Jesus sent to Herod			23:6-16
Pilate imposes sentence of death	27:15-26	15:6-15	23:17-25
Jesus scourged and led to Golgotha	27:27-32	15:15-21	
Jesus' crucifixion and death	27:33-56	15:22-41	23:33-49
Jesus is buried	27:57-61	15:42-47	23:50-56
SATURDAY			
The guarded tomb	27:62-66		
SUNDAY (Easter)			
The empty tomb and the risen Christ	28:1-10	16:1-8	24:1-12

A modern church at ancient Bethany marks the traditional place where Jesus raised Lazarus from the dead (John 11:1-44).

Silver denarius of Tiberius, "tribute money" of Luke 20:21-26.

At Caesarea, residence of the Roman governors, archaeologists found this dedication stone with the only known inscriptional reference to Pontius Pilate.

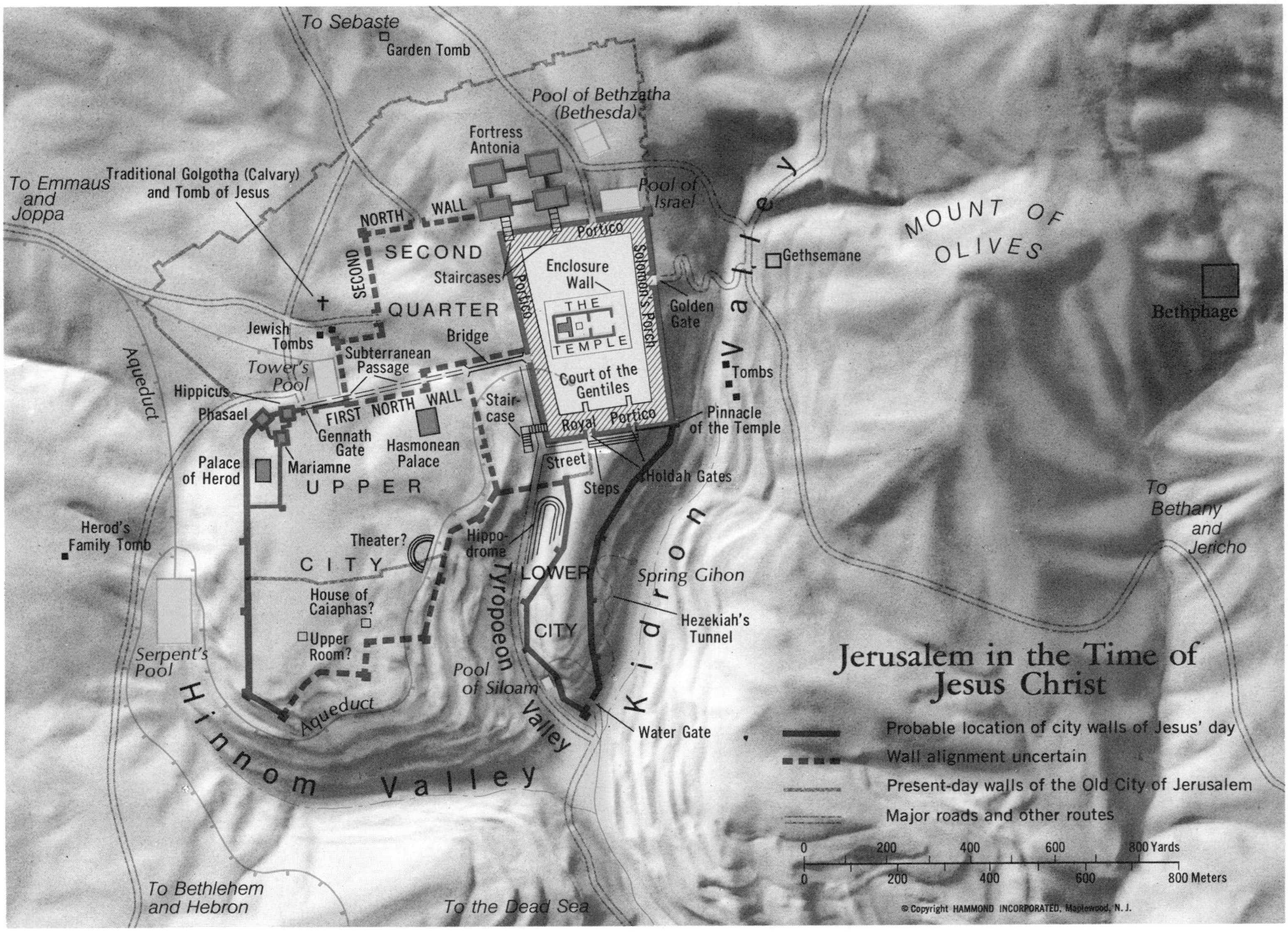

Jerusalem in the Time of Jesus Christ

Probable location of city walls of Jesus' day
Wall alignment uncertain
Present-day walls of the Old City of Jerusalem
Major roads and other routes

0   200   400   600   800 Yards
0   200   400   600   800 Meters

© Copyright HAMMOND INCORPORATED, Maplewood, N.J.

Map labels:
To Sebaste
Garden Tomb
Pool of Bethzatha (Bethesda)
Fortress Antonia
Traditional Golgotha (Calvary) and Tomb of Jesus
To Emmaus and Joppa
NORTH WALL
SECOND
Pool of Israel
Portico
MOUNT OF OLIVES
Staircases
Enclosure Wall
QUARTER
THE TEMPLE
Solomon's Porch
Gethsemane
Jewish Tombs
Bridge
Court of the Gentiles
Golden Gate
Bethphage
Tower's Pool
Subterranean Passage
Hippicus
FIRST NORTH WALL
Staircase
Pinnacle of the Temple
Phasael
Gennath Gate
Hasmonean Palace
Royal Portico
Tombs
Palace of Herod
Mariamne
Street
Holdah Gates
UPPER
Steps
Herod's Family Tomb
Theater?
Hippodrome
CITY
To Bethany and Jericho
House of Caiaphas?
LOWER
Spring Gihon
Serpent's Pool
Upper Room?
CITY
Hezekiah's Tunnel
Pool of Siloam
Aqueduct
Water Gate
Tyropoeon Valley
Kidron Valley
Hinnom Valley
To Bethlehem and Hebron
To the Dead Sea

Today a mosque, the magnificent Dome of the Rock, occupies the platform where Herod's Temple stood in Jesus' day.

Judas' 30 pieces of silver may have been Tyrian shekels of this type.

A model of Jerusalem shows the Temple platform and four towers of Fortress Antonia. The Pool of Bethzatha where Jesus healed the crippled man is the square-shaped building with reddish roof in the foreground.

The Garden Tomb, a rock-cut tomb of the type in which Jesus was buried. North of Jerusalem, this quiet spot just outside the present north wall is a rival to the traditional site of the crucifixion and burial.

"The Pavement" (courtyard) of the Fortress Antonia was possibly the place where Jesus was tried by Pilate. Today it is the crypt of a church and convent.

Theodotus synagogue inscription found on Mount Zion in Jerusalem. Some think this dedicatory inscription refers to the "Synagogue of the Freedmen" mentioned in Acts 6:9.

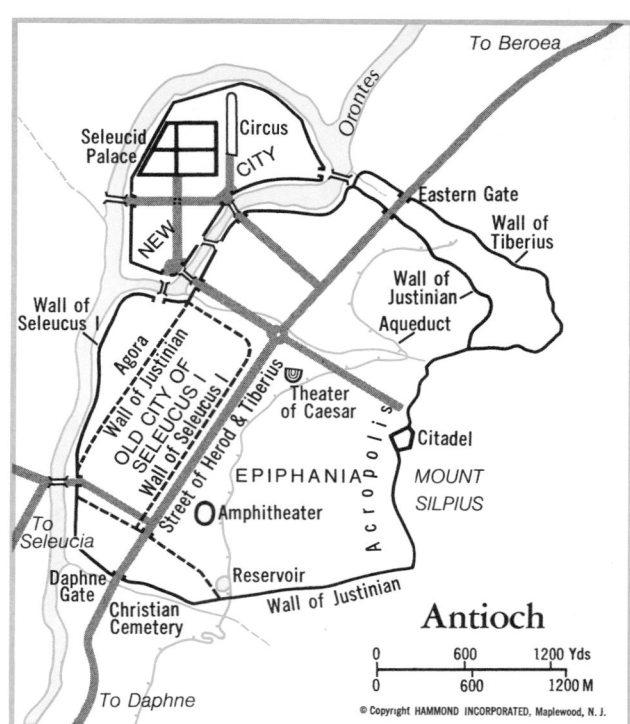

Antioch

The Lion Gate in Jerusalem's east wall. Medieval Christian tradition locates the martyrdom of Stephen (Acts 7:58-60) nearby. Therefore Christians call this "St. Stephen's Gate."

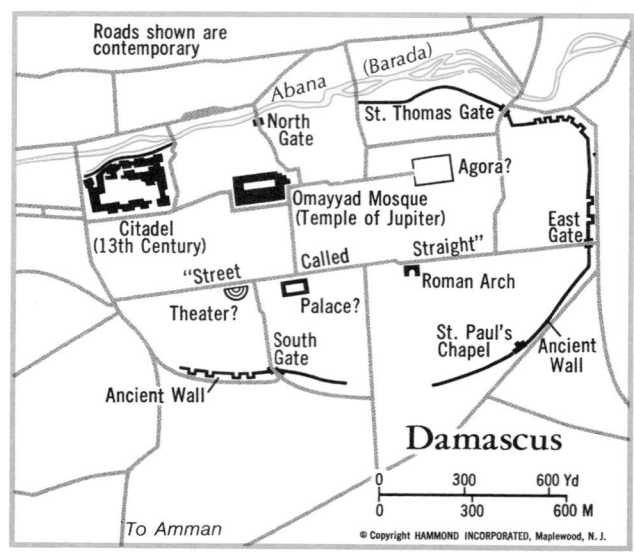

Damascus

St. Paul's Chapel, Damascus. This is the traditional location of Paul's escape over the city wall (Acts 9:25).

The theater by the sea at Caesarea where in 10 B.C. Herod dedicated his splendid new city. Now restored, it is used for concerts.

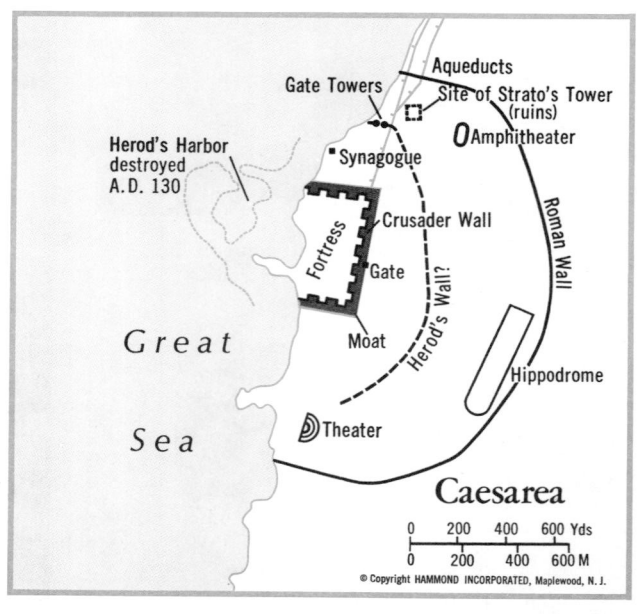

Caesarea

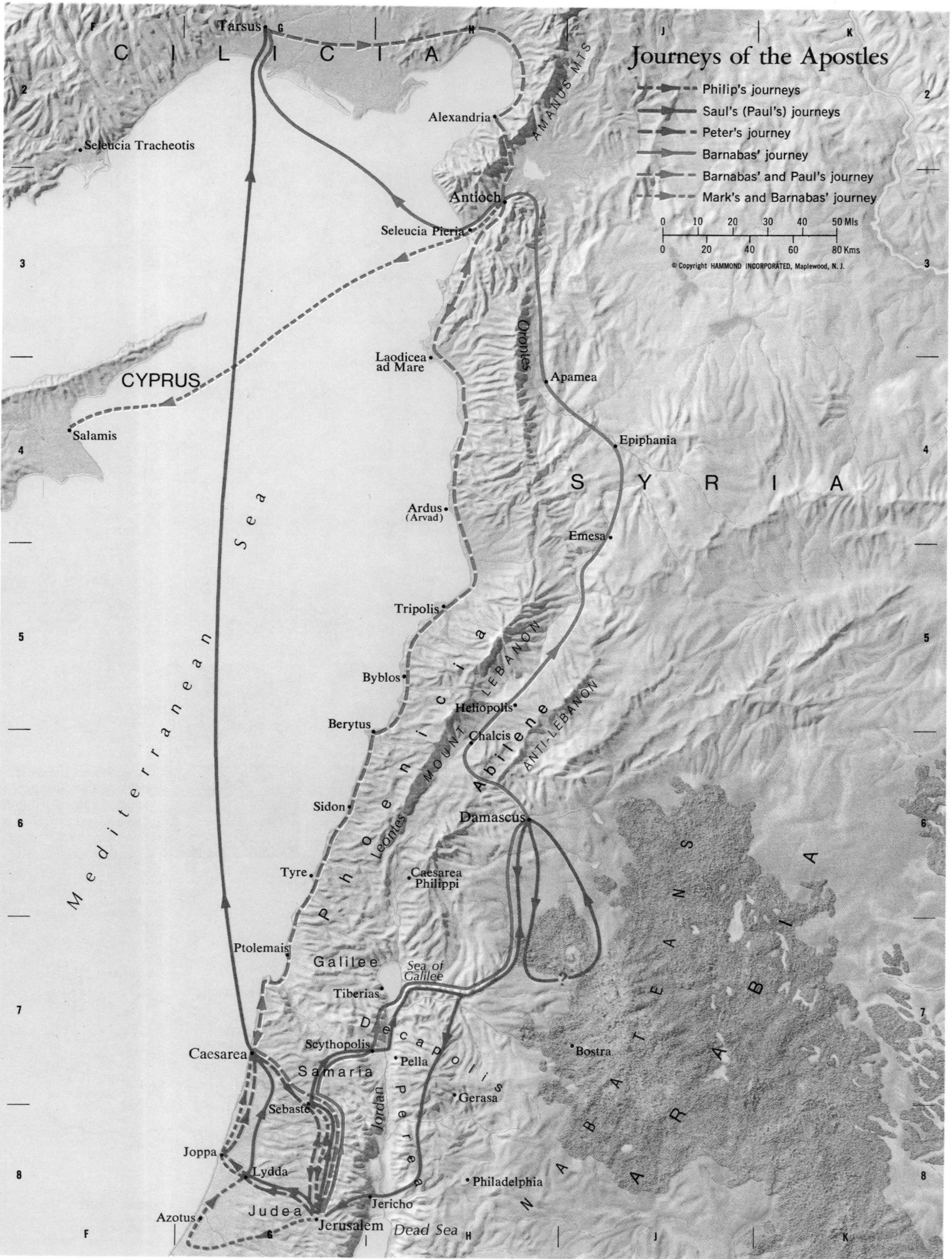

Journeys of the Apostles

- – – – → Philip's journeys
- ───→ Saul's (Paul's) journeys
- ━━━→ Peter's journey
- ────→ Barnabas' journey
- – – – → Barnabas' and Paul's journey
- – – – → Mark's and Barnabas' journey

0 10 20 30 40 50 Mls
0 20 40 60 80 Kms

© Copyright HAMMOND INCORPORATED, Maplewood, N. J.

CILICIA

Tarsus

Seleucia Tracheotis

Alexandria

Antioch

Seleucia Pieria

CYPRUS

Salamis

Laodicea ad Mare

Apamea

Orontes

Epiphania

S Y R I A

Ardus (Arvad)

Emesa

Tripolis

Byblos

Berytus

Heliopolis

Chalcis

Abilene

ANTI-LEBANON

MOUNT LEBANON

Sidon

Damascus

Tyre

Caesarea Philippi

Mediterranean Sea

Phoenicia

Leontes

Ptolemais

Galilee

Sea of Galilee

Tiberias

N A B A T E A N S

A R A B I A

Caesarea

Scythopolis

Samaria

Pella

Bostra

Sebaste

Decapolis

Gerasa

Joppa

Jordan

Perea

Philadelphia

Lydda

Judea

Jericho

Azotus

Jerusalem

Dead Sea

AMANUS MTS.

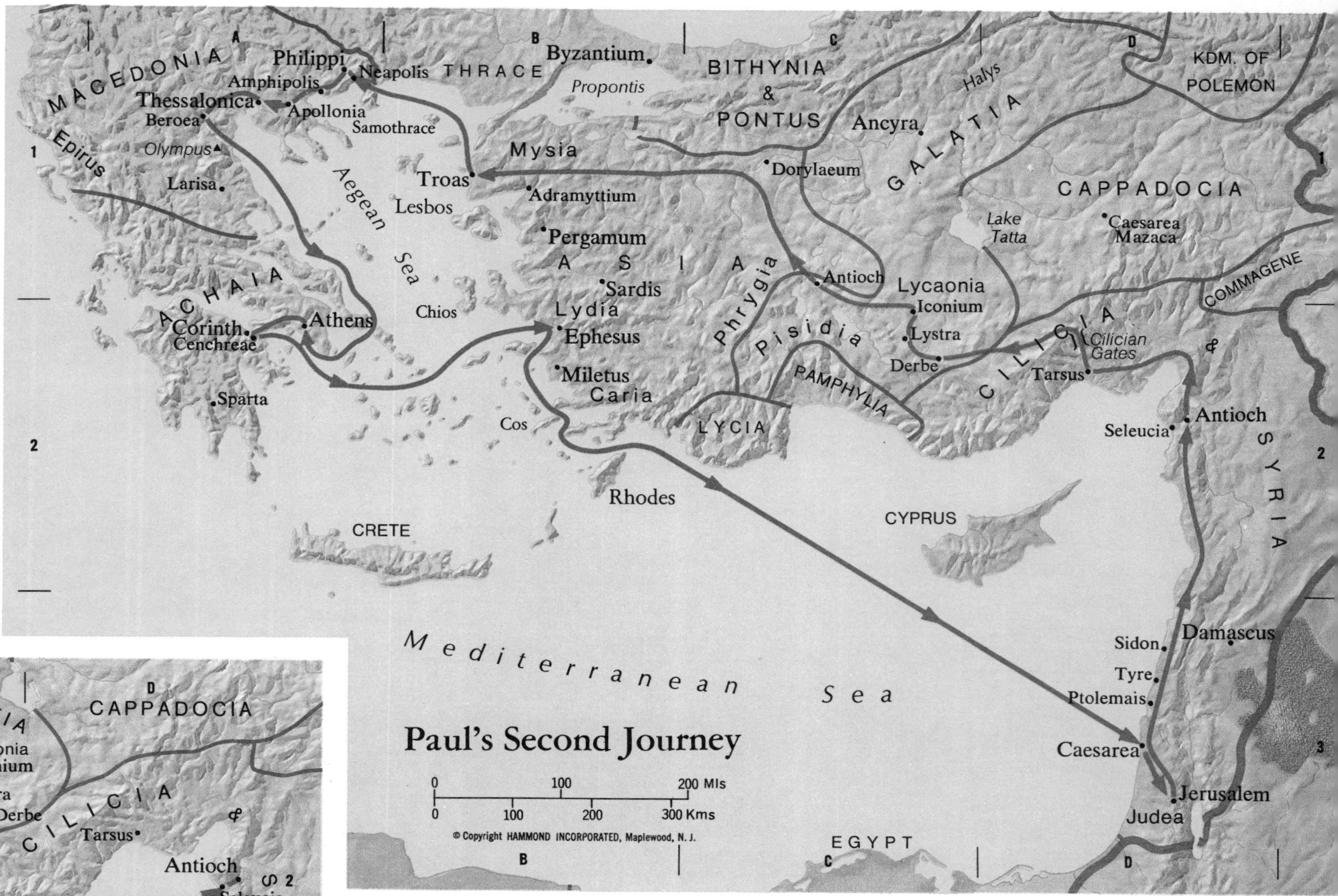

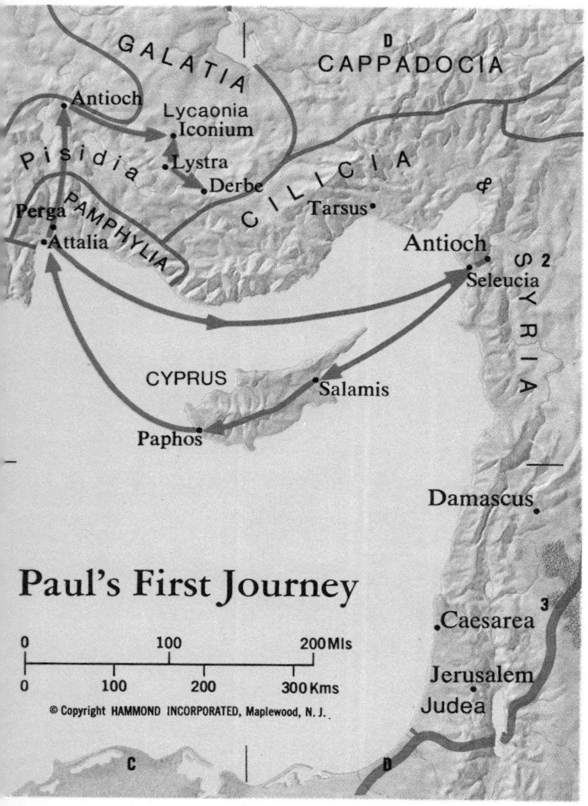

Paul's Second Journey

MACEDONIA
Philippi
Amphipolis • Neapolis THRACE Byzantium BITHYNIA & PONTUS KDM. OF POLEMON
Thessalonica • Apollonia
Beroea • Samothrace
Epirus Olympus▲ Mysia Adramyttium Dorylaeum Ancyra GALATIA CAPPADOCIA Halys
Larisa • Troas
Aegean Lesbos ASIA Antioch Lycaonia Caesarea Mazaca
Sea Pergamum Phrygia Iconium COMMAGENE
ACHAIA Chios Sardis Pisidia Lystra
Corinth • Athens Lydia Derbe CILICIA
Cenchreae • Ephesus Pamphylia Tarsus Cilician Gates
Sparta • Miletus Caria LYCIA
Cos Seleucia • Antioch SYRIA
Rhodes CYPRUS

Mediterranean Sea
Sidon • Damascus
Tyre •
Ptolemais •

Paul's Second Journey

```
0           100         200 MIs
0     100   200   300 Kms
© Copyright HAMMOND INCORPORATED, Maplewood, N.J.
```

Caesarea •
Jerusalem
Judea
EGYPT

Paul's First Journey

GALATIA CAPPADOCIA
Antioch
Pisidia Lycaonia
Iconium
Perga Lystra
Attalia Pamphylia Derbe CILICIA
Tarsus
Antioch
Seleucia
CYPRUS SYRIA
Salamis
Paphos

Damascus •

Paul's First Journey

```
0           100         200 MIs
0     100   200   300 Kms
© Copyright HAMMOND INCORPORATED, Maplewood, N.J.
```

Caesarea •
Jerusalem
Judea

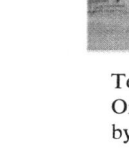

Temple of Apollo, Corinth.
Only 7 of the 38 columns seen
by Paul are now standing.

The Acropolis rises behind the Areopagus
(foreground) where Paul was mocked by the
Athenian elders (Acts 17:32).

Artemis was the chief
deity of Ephesus. Paul's
attack on the worship of
this goddess provoked a
riot (Acts 19:23f.).

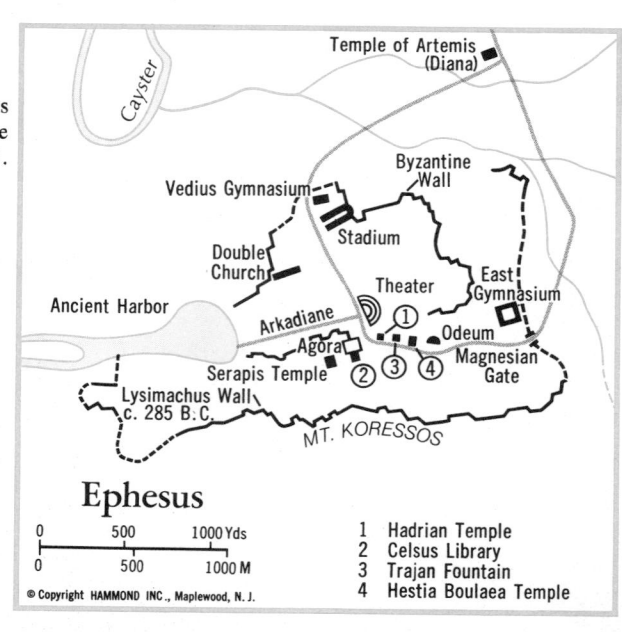

Cayster
Temple of Artemis (Diana)
Vedius Gymnasium
Byzantine Wall
Stadium
Double Church
Theater
East Gymnasium
Ancient Harbor
Arkadiane
① Odeum
Agora ② ③ ④ Magnesian Gate
Serapis Temple
Lysimachus Wall c. 285 B.C.
MT. KORESSOS

Ephesus

```
0        500      1000 Yds
0        500      1000 M
© Copyright HAMMOND INC., Maplewood, N.J.
```

1 Hadrian Temple
2 Celsus Library
3 Trajan Fountain
4 Hestia Boulaea Temple

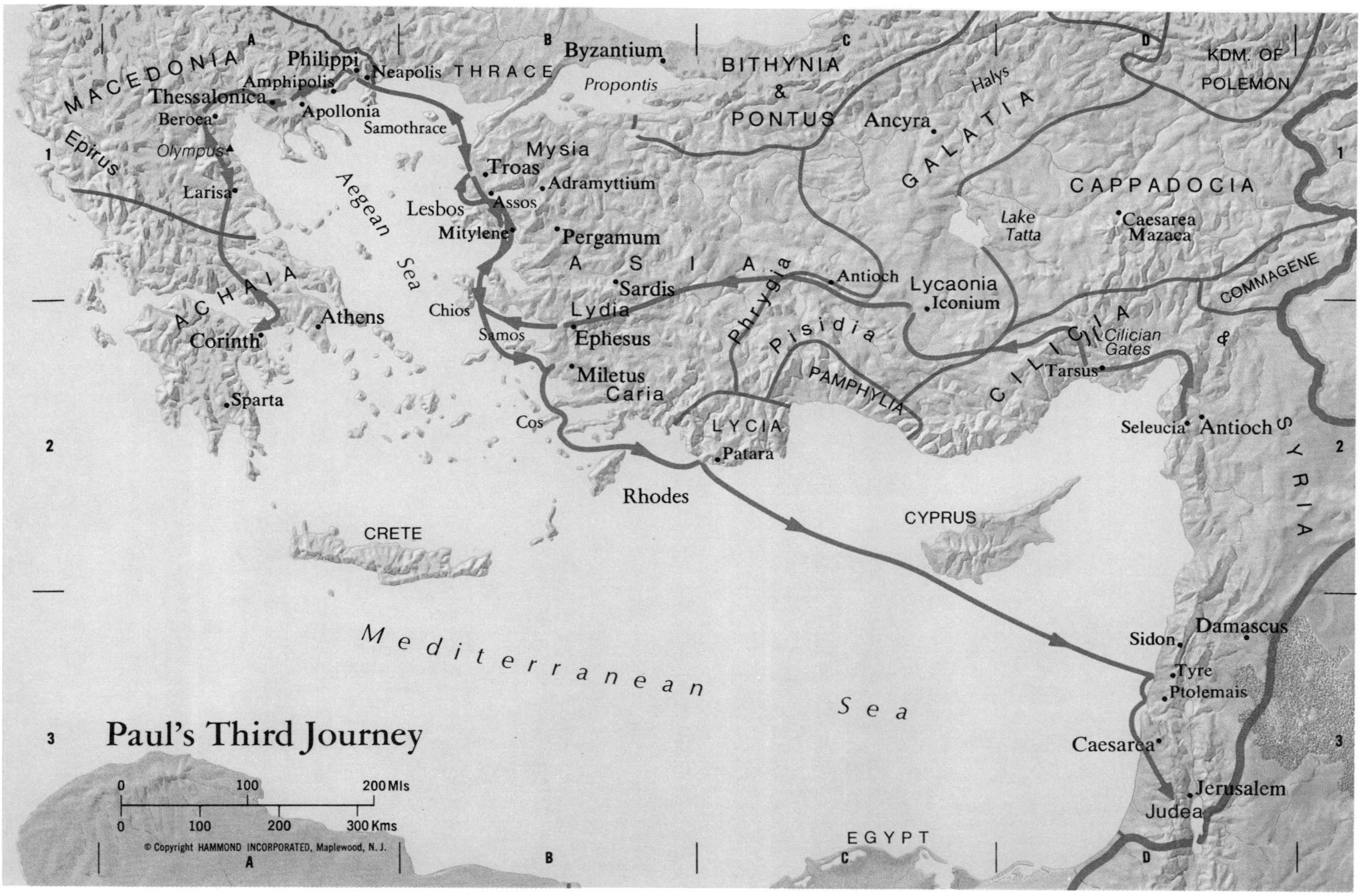

Paul's Third Journey

MACEDONIA
Philippi
Amphipolis • Neapolis THRACE
Thessalonica •
Beroea • • Apollonia
Epirus Samothrace
Olympus ▲ Larisa
Aegean Sea
Byzantium
Propontis
BITHYNIA & PONTUS
KDM. OF POLEMON
Ancyra Halys
GALATIA
CAPPADOCIA
Lake Tatta
Caesarea Mazaca

Mysia
Troas • Adramyttium
Assos
Lesbos
Mitylene
Pergamum •
ASIA
Sardis •
Chios Lydia
Ephesus •
Samos
Miletus •
Caria
Cos

Phrygia
Antioch
Lycaonia
Iconium
Pisidia
PAMPHYLIA
LYCIA
Patara •
CILICIA
Cilician Gates
Tarsus •
COMMAGENE &

Athens •
Corinth •
ACHAIA
Sparta •

Rhodes

CYPRUS

Seleucia • Antioch
SYRIA

Sidon • Damascus •
Tyre •
Ptolemais •

Caesarea •

Jerusalem •
Judea

Mediterranean Sea

EGYPT

Scale:
0 — 100 — 200 Mls
0 — 100 — 200 — 300 Kms
© Copyright HAMMOND INCORPORATED, Maplewood, N.J.

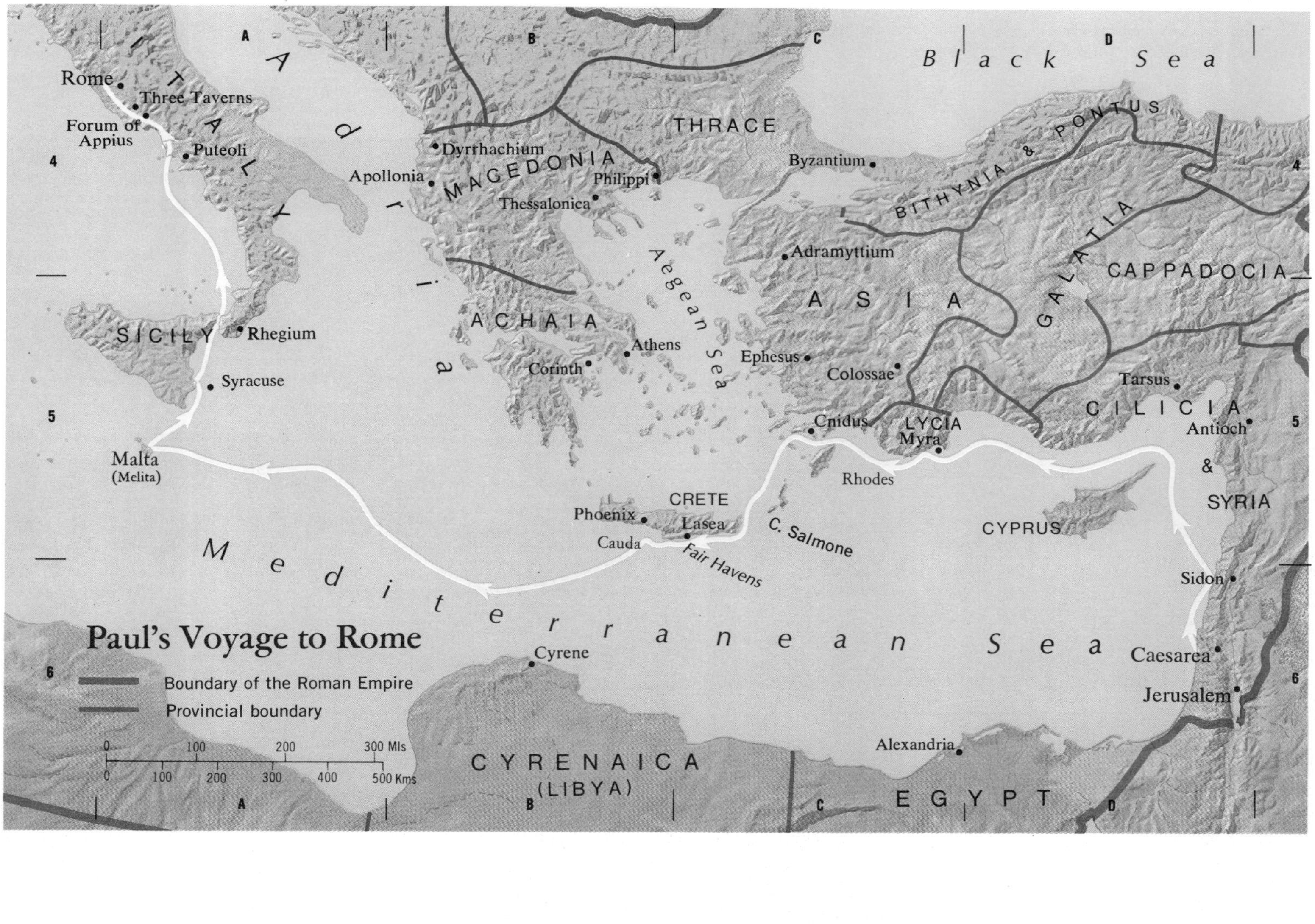

Paul's Voyage to Rome

Rome •
Three Taverns
Forum of Appius
Puteoli •
ITALY
Adriatic
Dyrrhachium •
Apollonia • MAGEDONIA
Thessalonica •
Philippi •
THRACE
Byzantium •
BITHYNIA & PONTUS
Black Sea
Adramyttium •
GALATIA
CAPPADOCIA

SICILY
Rhegium •
Syracuse •
ACHAIA
Athens •
Corinth •
Aegean Sea
ASIA
Ephesus •
Colossae •
Tarsus •
CILICIA
Antioch •
&

Malta (Melita)
Phoenix • CRETE
Cauda Lasea
Fair Havens
Cnidus •
LYCIA
Myra
C. Salmone
Rhodes
CYPRUS
SYRIA
Sidon •

Mediterranean Sea
Caesarea •
Jerusalem •

Cyrene •
CYRENAICA (LIBYA)
Alexandria •
EGYPT

— Boundary of the Roman Empire
— Provincial boundary

Scale:
0 — 100 — 200 — 300 Mls
0 — 100 — 200 — 300 — 400 — 500 Kms

A Roman eagle
on an altar
in Jerusalem.

Masada from the north showing the archaeologically
recovered fortress of Herod. Behind the imperial apartments
is a bathhouse surrounded by storerooms.

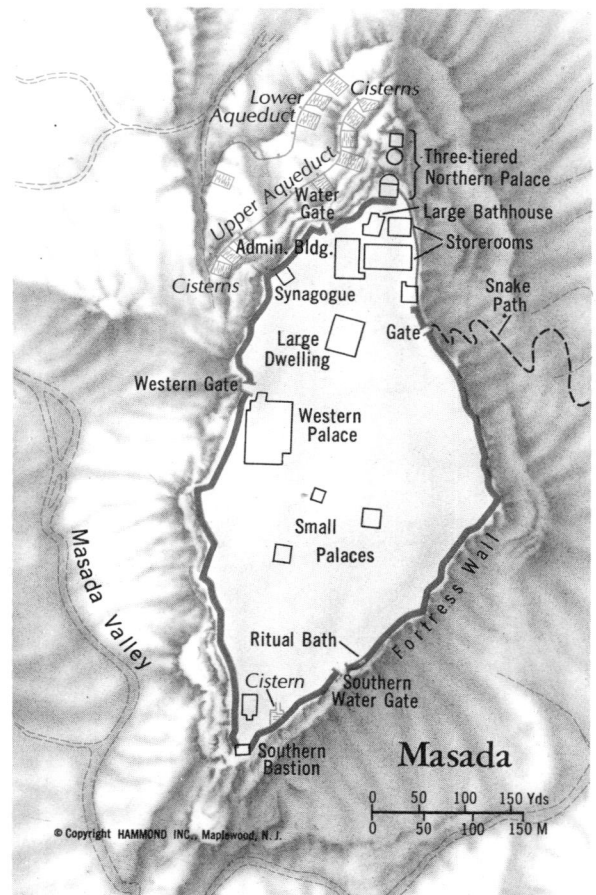

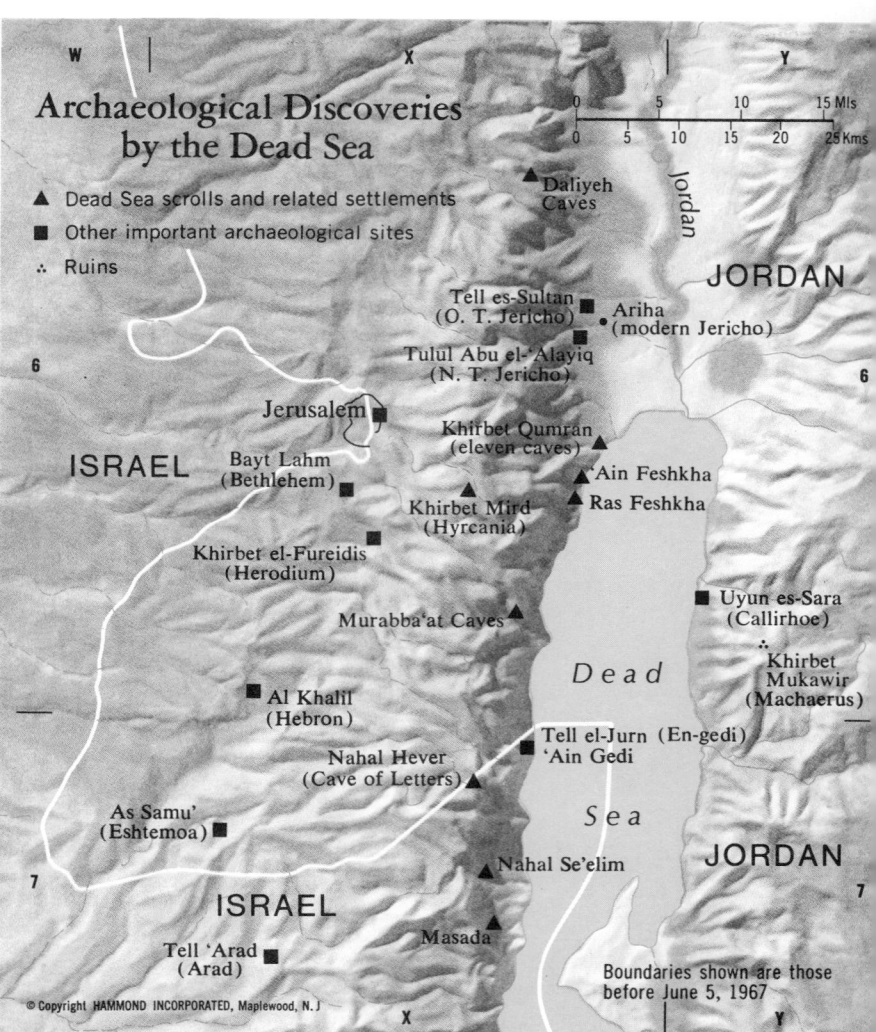

Archaeological Discoveries by the Dead Sea

▲ Dead Sea scrolls and related settlements
■ Other important archaeological sites
∴ Ruins

Daliyeh Caves

JORDAN

Tell es-Sultan
(O. T. Jericho)
Ariha
(modern Jericho)

Tulul Abu el-'Alayiq
(N. T. Jericho)

Jerusalem

ISRAEL

Bayt Lahm
(Bethlehem)

Khirbet Qumran
(eleven caves)

'Ain Feshkha
Ras Feshkha

Khirbet Mird
(Hyrcania)

Khirbet el-Fureidis
(Herodium)

Murabba'at Caves

Uyun es-Sara
(Callirhoe)

Dead

Al Khalil
(Hebron)

Khirbet
Mukawir
(Machaerus)

Nahal Hever
(Cave of Letters)

Tell el-Jurn (En-gedi)
'Ain Gedi

As Samu'
(Eshtemoa)

Sea

JORDAN

Nahal Se'elim

ISRAEL

Tell 'Arad
(Arad)

Masada

Boundaries shown are those
before June 5, 1967

© Copyright HAMMOND INCORPORATED, Maplewood, N.J.

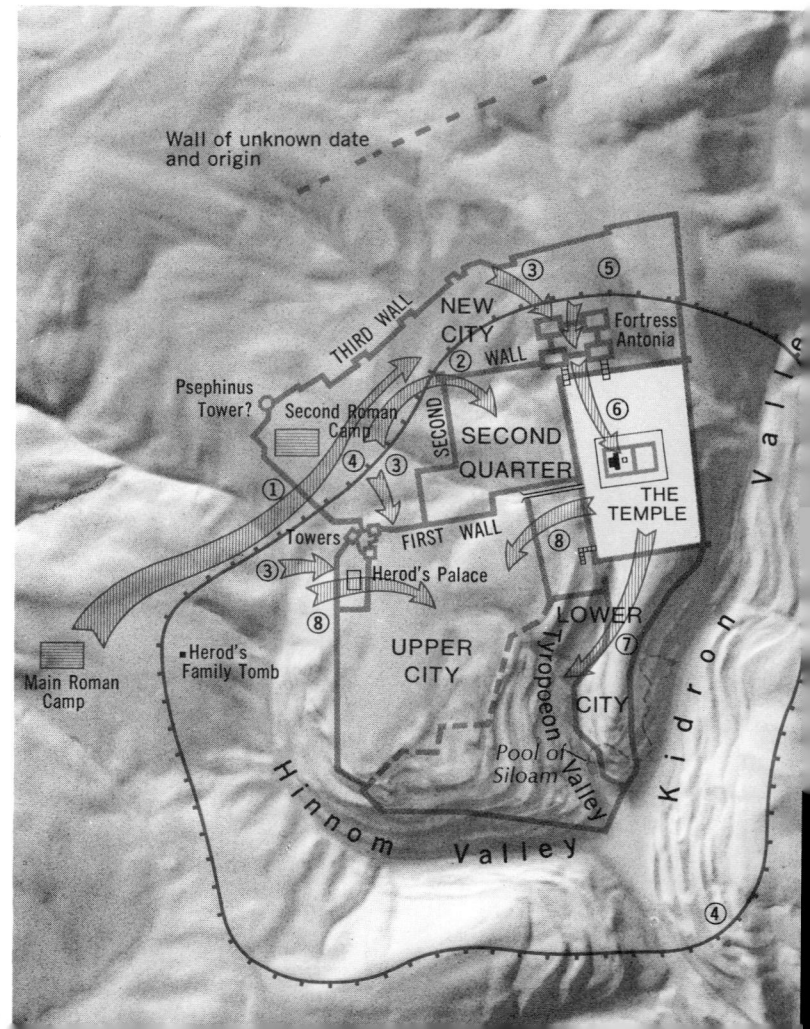

Masada:
Lower Aqueduct, Cisterns, Upper Aqueduct, Water Gate, Three-tiered Northern Palace, Large Bathhouse, Storerooms, Admin. Bldg., Synagogue, Cisterns, Large Dwelling, Gate, Snake Path, Western Gate, Western Palace, Small Palaces, Fortress Wall, Masada Valley, Ritual Bath, Cistern, Southern Water Gate, Southern Bastion, **Masada**

© Copyright HAMMOND INC., Maplewood, N.J.

Wall of unknown date and origin

THIRD WALL, NEW CITY, Fortress Antonia, Psephinus Tower?, Second Roman Camp, SECOND WALL, SECOND QUARTER, THE TEMPLE, Towers, FIRST WALL, Herod's Palace, Main Roman Camp, Herod's Family Tomb, UPPER CITY, LOWER CITY, Tyropoeon Valley, Pool of Siloam, Kidron Valley, Hinnom Valley

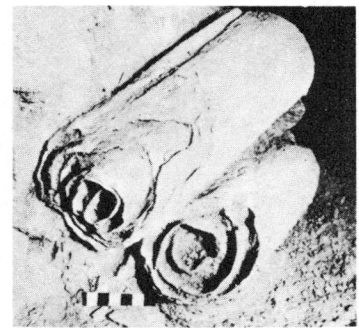

Copper Scrolls found at Qumran.

Cave Four at Qumran (center) in which a wealth of precious scrolls were found.

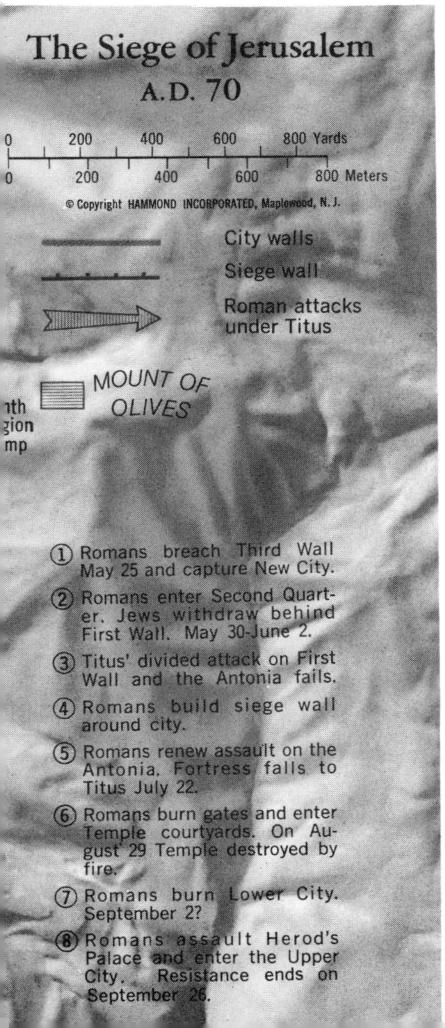

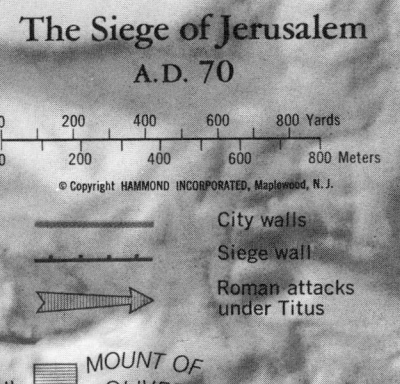

The Siege of Jerusalem
A.D. 70

0 200 400 600 800 Yards

0 200 400 600 800 Meters

© Copyright HAMMOND INCORPORATED, Maplewood, N.J.

━━━━━ City walls

━·━·━ Siege wall

⟹ Roman attacks under Titus

▤ MOUNT OF OLIVES

nth
gion
mp

① Romans breach Third Wall May 25 and capture New City.

② Romans enter Second Quarter. Jews withdraw behind First Wall. May 30-June 2.

③ Titus' divided attack on First Wall and the Antonia fails.

④ Romans build siege wall around city.

⑤ Romans renew assault on the Antonia. Fortress falls to Titus July 22.

⑥ Romans burn gates and enter Temple courtyards. On August 29 Temple destroyed by fire.

⑦ Romans burn Lower City. September 2?

⑧ Romans assault Herod's Palace and enter the Upper City. Resistance ends on September 26.

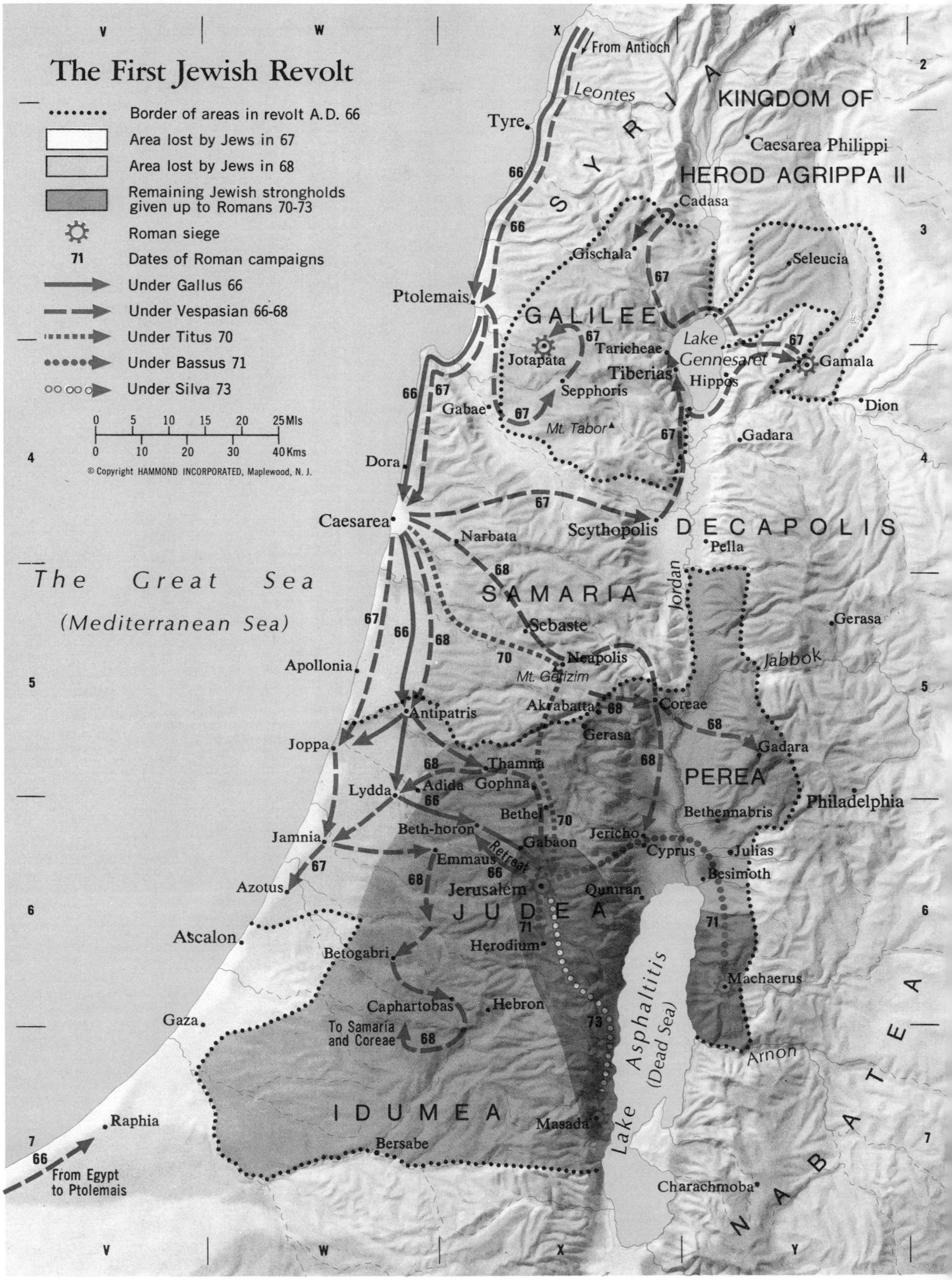

The First Jewish Revolt

∙∙∙∙∙∙ Border of areas in revolt A.D. 66

☐ Area lost by Jews in 67

▨ Area lost by Jews in 68

▨ Remaining Jewish strongholds given up to Romans 70-73

⚙ Roman siege

71 Dates of Roman campaigns

→ Under Gallus 66

⇢ Under Vespasian 66-68

⋯→ Under Titus 70

••••→ Under Bassus 71

∘∘∘∘→ Under Silva 73

0 5 10 15 20 25 Mls

0 10 20 30 40 Kms

© Copyright HAMMOND INCORPORATED, Maplewood, N.J.

The Great Sea

(Mediterranean Sea)

From Antioch

KINGDOM OF

Caesarea Philippi

HEROD AGRIPPA II

Tyre

Leontes

Cadasa

Seleucia

Gischala

GALILEE

Lake Gennesaret

Gamala

Ptolemais

Taricheae

Jotapata

Tiberias

Hippos

Dion

Sepphoris

Gabae

Mt. Tabor

Gadara

Dora

Scythopolis DECAPOLIS

Caesarea

Narbata

Pella

Gerasa

SAMARIA

Jordan

Sebaste

Jabbok

Apollonia

Neapolis

Mt. Gerizim

Akrabatta

Coreae

Antipatris

Gerasa

Gadara

Joppa

Thamna

PEREA

Lydda

Adida Gophna

Philadelphia

Bethel

Bethennabris

Jamnia

Beth-horon

Gabaon

Jericho

Julias

Emmaus

Cyprus

Besimoth

Azotus

Jerusalem

Qumran

Ascalon

JUDEA

Betogabri

Herodium

Lake Asphaltitis (Dead Sea)

Machaerus

Gaza

Caphartobas

Hebron

To Samaria and Coreae

NABATEA

IDUMEA

Masada

Arnon

Raphia

Bersabe

From Egypt to Ptolemais

Charachmoba

Silver shekel from the "year three," the third year of the Revolt (A.D. 68).

Roman "Judaea Capta" coins. Above are Vespasian and Titus. Sestertius, right, shows a captive Jewess.

GERMANIA

Rhine

Cologne

Trier

GAUL

Danube

Lugdunum
(Lyons)
Vienne

ILLYRICUM

DA

Astorga
Leon

Salona

Saragossa

T

SPAIN

MACEDONIA

Ph

Merida

Beroea
Thessal

Rome

Larissa

Hispalis
Corduba

Ostia
Antium

Nicopolis

ACHAIA

Puteoli

Mediterranean

Sicily

Patrae

Corinth
At

MAURETANIA

Sitifi
Cirta
Thuburba
Carthage

Syracuse

Sparta

Lambesis
Madaurus
Uthina
Hadrumetum

Numidia
Thysdrus

AFRICA

The Spread of Christianity

Gor

⋮ The Seven Churches of Asia (Rev. 1-3)

•   City with Christian church recorded in second century

▨ Regions known to contain Christians by A.D. 185
    (the time of Irenaeus)

—   Boundary of the Roman empire
    for most of second century

--- Temporarily controlled by Rome

Cyrene

CYRENAIC

| 0 | 100 | 200 | 300 | 400 | 500Mls |
| 0 | 200 | 400 | 600 | 800Kms |

© Copyright HAMMOND INCORPORATED, Maplewood, N.J.

St. Paul's-Outside-the-Walls, Rome,
traditional site of the tomb of Paul.

The Flavian Amphitheater (Colosseum) in
Rome, where many Christians were martyred.

Constantine made Christianity
a "legal religion" in A.D. 311.

Limestone statuette of Coptic Christian woman with cross, from 4th-century A.D. Egypt.

Map labels: Caspian Sea, Black Sea, Anchialus, Debeltum, Ionopolis, Amastris, Sinope, PONTUS, Amisus, ARMENIA, yzantium, BITHYNIA, Nicomedia, Mysia, Ancyra, GALATIA, Caesarea, Melitene, PARTHIA, Phrygia, CAPPADOCIA, oas, Pergamum, Samosata, Nisibis, Beit Zabde, atira, Sardis, Antioch, Edessa, na, Philadelphia, Iconium, Tarsus, MESOPOTAMIA, sus, Laodicea, Lystra, Derbe, CILICIA, Tigris, Miletus, Colossae, Perga, Rhossus, Antioch, Euphrates, Seleucia, SYRIA, Dura-Europos, Myra, Laodicea, Apamea, Cyprus, Salamis, Paphos, Tripolis, Sidon, Damascus, Paphos, Sidon, Tyre, ARABIA, Caesarea, Pella, Joppa, Jerusalem, Alexandria, Naucratis, Memphis, Nile, EGYPT

Chalice of Antioch shows Christ and apostles. It dates from 4th or 5th century A.D.

Patmos, where The Revelation to St. John the Divine, the last book in the New Testament, was written.

Papyrus fragment of the Gospel of Matthew from Oxyrhynchus, Egypt.

Lid of Philistine anthropoid coffin from Beth-shan.

The Moabite Stone, found in 1868 at Mesha's capital. Carved about 840-820 B.C., it tells of the events of 2 Kings 3:4-27 and their aftermath from a Moabite point of view.

The mound of Tell el-Hesi. One of the first sites to be excavated in Palestine, it is thought to be Biblical Eglon, a Canaanite royal city taken by Joshua (Joshua 10).

Archaeological Sites in Israel and Jordan

⬤ Prehistoric cave sites
■ Major excavated sites
▪ Other important excavations

```
0    5   10   15   20  25 Mls
0   10   20   30    40 Kms
```

© Copyright HAMMOND INCORPORATED, Maplewood, N.J.

Tyre
Dan
LEB.
SYRIA
Kafr Bir'im
Nahariyah
HAZOR
Meiron
Acco—
Ptolemais
Capernaum
Tabgha
Irbid
Sea of
Galilee
Sepphoris
Tiberias
Beth-yerah
Wadi el-Mughara
Beth Shearim
Dor
MEGIDDO
Beth-Alfa
Taanach
BETH-SHAN—SCYTHOPOLIS
Caesarea

Mediterranean

Dothan

Sea

TIRZAH
Jordan
Tell es-Saidiyeh
(Zarethan?)
Jerash
SAMARIA—SEBASTE
SHECHEM
Tell Deir 'alla
(Succoth)
Qasile
Aphek—Antipatris
Shiloh
JORDAN
Joppa
Amman
Yavne Yam
BETHEL
Ai
Kh. el-Mefjir
(Gilgal?)
Araq el-Emir
Tell en-Nasbeh
(Mizpah?)
GEZER
JERICHO
Gibeon
Gibeah
Heshbon
'Ain Karim
JERUSALEM
Teleilat el-Ghassul
Ashdod
BETH-SHEMESH
Ramat
Qumran
Bethlehem
Rahel
'Ain Feshkha
Tell es-Safi
Azekah
Herodium
Hyrcania
Madaba
Ascalon
Tell el-Judeideh
Beth-zur
Murabba'at Caves
LACHISH
Mareshah
Dead
Tell el-Hesi
(Eglon?)
Hebron
'Ain Gedi
Dibon
TELL AJJUL
TELL BEIT MIRSIM
(Debir?)
Sea
Khirbet 'Ar'ir
Tell Jemmeh
Tell el-Far'a
Tell 'Arad
Masada
Tell Abu Matar
Tell es-Seba
Bab edh 'Drah
Khirbet el-Kerak
Khalasa
Karnub
Khirbet et-Tannur
Auja el-Hafir
Isbeita
EGYPT
Avdat
Kadesh-barnea

This four-spouted lamp is from Patriarchal times.

A footed lamp from the period of the Hebrew kings.

Jesus knew this type of Herodian lamp.

Lands of the Bible in Modern Times

International boundary
Armistice line, 1949
Israeli-occupied area
UN buffer zone

National capital
Ancient site
Port facility
Oil pipeline
Canal

0	20	40	60	80	100Mls
0	40	80	120	160Kms	

© Copyright HAMMOND INCORPORATED, Maplewood, N.J.

Mediterranean Sea

LEBANON
Tripoli (Tarābulus)
Al Harmal
Cedars of Lebanon
Byblos
Baalbek
Beirut
Zahlah
Sidon
Damascus (Dimashq)
Az Zahrāni
Mt. Hermon
Tyre
Baniyās
Al Qunayţirah
Golan Heights
'Akko
Zefat
Lake Tiberias
Haifa
Ḥaqrayot
Tiberias
Nazareth
Dar'ā
Afula
Yarmuk
Irbid
Caesarea
Jenin
Bet She'an
Ajlūn
Al Mafraq
Hadera
Ţulkarm
Zarqā'
Netanya
Nābulus
ISRAEL
Ramat Gan
West Bank
As Salt
Az Zarqā'
Tel Aviv-Yafo
Ram Allah
Amman
Holon
Jericho
Ramla
Ma'daba
Ashdod
Jerusalem
Qiryat Gat
Bethlehem
Ashqelon
Hebron
Dead Sea
Dhībān
GAZA STRIP
Gaza
Masada
Mawjib
Rafaḥ
Arad
Al Qaţrānah
Beersheba
Al Karak
Dimona
Yeroham
Sedom
Nizzana
Oron
Tannur
Sede Boqer
Negeb
En Yahav
Wādī al 'Arabah
Kadesh-barnea
Petra
Ma'ān
Al Qusaymah
Har Ramon
Wādī Mūsā
Yotvata
Al Kuntillah
Ra's an Naqb
Mikhrot Timna'
Elat
Al 'Aqabah
Al Mudawwarah
Haql
Ḥallat 'Ammar
JORDAN

SYRIA

Sinai Peninsula
Al 'Arīsh
Wādī al 'Arīsh
Bi'r Jifjālah
An Nakhl
Nuweiba
St. Catherine's Monastery
Jaba Mūsā (Mt. Sinai)
Dhahab
Magna
Aţ Ţūr
Sharm ash Shaykh
Str. of Tiran
Şanāfir
Al Khuraybah

SAUDI ARABIA

Gulf of Aqaba

EGYPT
Baltīm
Damietta
Port Said
Nile Delta
Al Maḥallah al Kubrá
Al Manşūrah
Tanis
Pelusium
Mişfaq
Tanţā
Daphne
Suez
Al Qanţarah
Al Firdān
Canal
Shibīn al Kawm
Az Zaqāzīq
Ismailia
Banhā
Succoth
Bitter Lakes
Imbābah
Heliopolis (On)
Giza
Cairo (Al Qāhirah)
Sphinx and Pyramids
Memphis
Ḥulwān
Birkat Qārūn
Mitla Pass
Suez
Port Tawfiq
Al Fayyūm
Ra's as Sidr
Nile
'Ayn Sukhnah
Banī Suwayf
Za'farānah
Abū Zanīmah
Umm Bugma
Abū Rudays
Maghāghah
Wādī aţ Ţarfā'
Ra's Ghārib
Al Minyā
Aţ Ţūr
Ra's Shukheir
Tell el Amarna

Eastern Desert

Gulf of Suez

Red Sea

Time Chart of Bible History

DATE	PALESTINE	EGYPT	MESOPOTAMIA & PERSIA	ANATOLIA & SYRIA	GREECE & ROME
4000 BC	Neolithic culture (Jericho)	— First use of metal: copper and bronze —			
	Ghassulian culture c. 3500	Hieroglyphic writing developed	Halaf culture Cuneiform writing developed		
	The Canaanites, a Semitic people, were ancestral to the Phoenicians	**Archaic Period** Menes unifies Egypt	Sumerian city states c. 2800-2360	Early Bronze cities Byblos, Troy, Ugarit	
	Early Bronze urban culture c. 3300	**Old Kingdom** The Great Pyramids at Gizeh c. 2550	**Akkadian Empire** Sargon I 2360-2305	Syria under Akkadian Empire	Beginning of Minoan civilization on Crete
	Amorite invasions c. 2500-2300	Old Kingdom falls	Gutian kings Ur dominance	Hittites enter Anatolia	Greeks invade Balkan peninsula
2000 BC			Ur falls c. 1950	Amorite invasions	
	Egypt controls Canaan	**Middle Kingdom**	**Isin-Larsa Period** **Old Babylonian Empire**	Hittites intro. Iron	**Minoan Sea Empire**
	Abraham — oral tradition	Hyksos invaders from Asia c. 1720-1550	Hammurabi 1728-1686	Labarnas I c. 1600	
	Israelite sojourn in Egypt	**New Kingdom**	**Kassite Period**	**Old Hittite Kingdom**	Mycenae shaft graves
	Battle of Megiddo 1468 Amarna letters c. 1370-1353	Akhenaton 1370-1353 Tutankhamen 1353-1344	Hittites sack Babylon 1531 Mitanni Kdm.	Mursilis I c. 1540	Cretan palaces destroyed c. 1400
	The Exodus c. 1290 Israelite invasion	Ramses II 1290-1224 Ramses III defeats Sea Peoples c. 1170	**Rise of Assyria** Shalmaneser I	Suppilullumas **Hittite Empire**	Dorians invade Greece
	Philistine penetration Kdm. of Saul c. 1020-1000	**Late Dynastic Period**	Tiglath-pileser I 1115-1078	Battle of Kedesh 1296 Sack of Troy 1192	Trojan War c. 1200
1000 BC	**United Kingdom**			Arameans flood into Syria	Decline of Aegean Bronze Age civilization
	David c. 1000-961 Solomon c. 961-922	Period of decline		Hiram of Tyre 969-936	
	First Temple completed c. 950	Shishak c. 935-914	**Assyrian Empire**	Damascus city state	Latins settle in central Italy
	Divided Kingdom Rehoboam & Jeroboam I	Libyan dynasties 950-710	Asshurnasirpal II 883-859	Ben-hadad II	
	Omri dynasty 876-842 Samaria founded c. 875		Shalmaneser III 859-824	Battle of Qarqar 853	
	Jehu dynasty 842-745		Adad-nirari III 807-782	Phoenicians found Carthage 814	
800 BC	Israel resurgence under Jeroboam II 786-746 Amos, Hosea				First Olympics 776 Legendary founding of Rome 753
	Fall of Samaria and exile of Israel 722/721	Nubian dynasties 715-663	Tiglath-pileser III 745-727 Sargon II 722-705	Phrygian Kdm. Midas c. 715	Etruscan period Homer
	Hezekiah of Judah 715-687/6	Egypt under Assyrian rule 671-652	Sennacherib 705-681 Asshurbanapal 669-633	Lydian Kdm.	
	Isaiah Micah Judah resurgence under Josiah 640-609	Thebes sacked 663	Rise of Babylon under Nabopolassar	Gyges of Lydia 680-652	Draco codifies Athenian law 621
600 BC	Jeremiah	Neco II 609-593	Fall of Nineveh to Medes and Babylonians 612		

Kings of Judah and Israel

JUDAH	ISRAEL		JUDAH	ISRAEL
Rehoboam 922-915 ●	● 922-901 Jeroboam I		Jotham 750-735 ●	● 746-745 Zechariah
Abijah 915-913 ●	● 901-900 Nadab			● 745 Shallum
Asa 913-873 ●	● 900-877 Baasha			● 745-738 Menahem
	● 877-876 Elah			● 738-737 Pekahiah
	● 876 Zimri		Ahaz 735-715 ●	● 737-732 Pekah
Jehoshaphat 873-849 ●	● 876-869 Omri			● 732-724 Hoshea
	● 869-850 Ahab		Hezekiah 715-687/6 ●	
	● 850-849 Ahaziah		Manasseh 687/6-642 ●	
Jehoram 849-842 ●	● 849-842 Jehoram		Amon 642-640 ●	
Ahaziah 842 ●	● 842-815 Jehu		Josiah 640-609 ●	
Athaliah 842-837 ●			Jehoahaz 609 ●	
Joash 837-800 ●	● 815-801 Jehoahaz		Jehoiakim 609-598 ●	
Amaziah 800-783 ●	● 801-786 Jehoash		Jehoiachin 598-597 ●	
Uzziah 783-742 ●	● 786-746 Jeroboam II		Zedekiah 597-587 ●	

DATE	PALESTINE	EGYPT	MESOPOTAMIA & PERSIA	ANATOLIA & SYRIA	GREECE & ROME
600 BC	Destruction of Jerusalem and exile of Judah 587 Ezekiel **Babylonian Captivity** Edict of Cyrus allows return of Jews 538 Zerubbabel Temple rebuilt 520-515 **Persian Period** Ezra's mission 458?? Nehemiah comes to Judah 445 (440?)	Egypt under Persian rule 525-401 Unsuccessful revolt Return to native rule	**New Babylonian Empire** Nebuchadnezzar II 605-562 **Persian Empire** Cyrus 550-530 Babylon falls 539 Cambyses 530-522 Darius I 522-486 Xerxes I 486-465 Artaxerxes I Darius II 433-404	Syria and Anatolia under Persian rule Phoenicians provide fleet for Persian attacks on Greece	Solon's judicial reforms c.590 Rome ruled by Etruscan kings Roman Republic established 509 Persian Wars 499-479 Thermopylae-Salamis 480 Pericles 461-429 Herodotus
400 BC	Ezra's mission 398? Palestine passes under Alexander's rule and Hellenization begins 332 Ptolemaic Egyptian rule 312	Persian rule 342-332 Alexander conquers Egypt 332 Ptolemy I 323-284 **Ptolemaic Kingdom** Alexandrian Jews translate Pentateuch into Greek Ptolemy V 203-181	Artaxerxes III 358-338 Alexander invades Persia 331 Seleucid rule Parthians and Bactrians gain independence c.250	Alexander takes Tyre 332 Seleucid rule Seleucus I 312-280 **Seleucid Empire** Antiochus I 280-261 Seleucus II 246-226 Antiochus III (The Great) 223-187	Socrates' death Sack of Rome by Gauls Philip II of Macedon Alexander the Great 336-323 **Alexander's Empire** Wars of the Diodochi 1st and 2nd Punic Wars Hannibal in Italy 218
200 BC	Palestine comes under Seleucid Syrian control 198 **Maccabean Period** Judas Maccabeus leads revolt of Jews 166-160 Temple rededicated 164 Jonathan 160-142 Simon 142-134 John Hyrcanus I 134-104 Aristobulus I 104-103	Ptolemy VI 181-146 Antiochus IV campaigns in Egypt Ptolemy VII 146-116	**Parthian Empire** Mithridates I 171-138 Mithridates II 124-88	Battle of Magnesia 190 Antiochus IV (Epiphanes) 175-163 Antiochus V 163-162 Demetrius I 162-150 Demetrius II 145-139 Tyre independent	Spain annexed by Rome **Empire of the Roman Republic** 3rd Punic War Romans destroy Carthage and Corinth 146 Reforms of the Gracchi
100 BC 50 BC	Alexander Jannaeus 103-76 Alexandra 76-67 Aristobulus II 67-63 Pompey takes Jerusalem for Rome 63 Hyrcanus II, high priest 63-40 Antipater governor 55	Ptolemy VIII 116-81 Ptolemy XI 80-81 Cleopatra VII 51-30	Tigranes of Armenia Phrates III 70-57 Orodes I 57-38 War with Rome 55-38 Crassus defeated	Mithridatic Wars Antiochus XIII 68-67 Anatolia and Syria under Roman control	Sulla dictator 82-79 1st Triumvirate Pompey's campaigns in Asia 66-63 Caesar's Gallic Wars 58-51

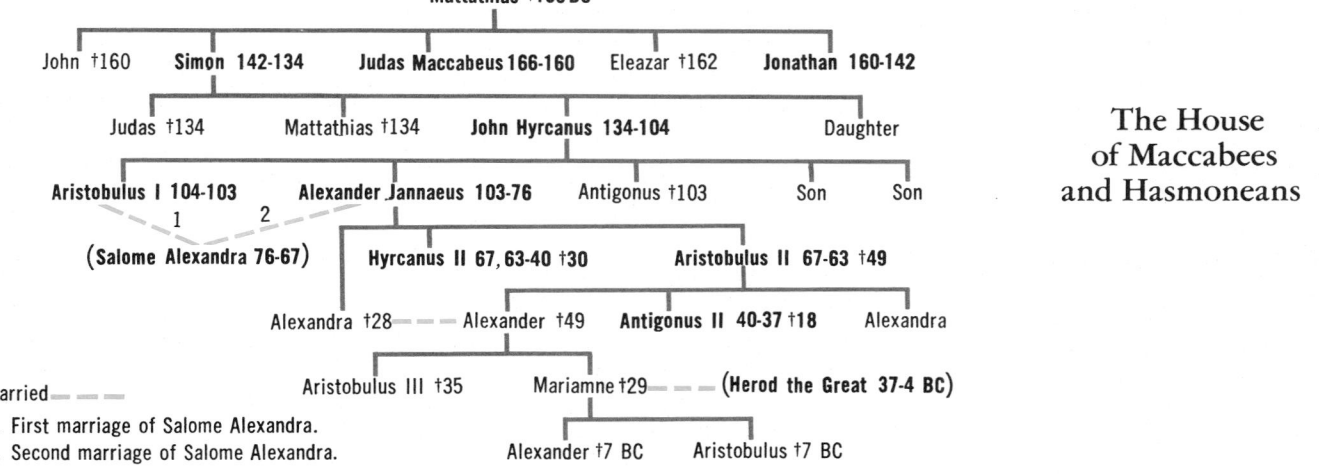

Married - - - -
1. First marriage of Salome Alexandra.
2. Second marriage of Salome Alexandra.

The House
of Maccabees
and Hasmoneans

Time Chart of Bible History, Continued

DATE	PALESTINE	THE WEST	THE EAST
50 BC	**Roman Rule** Caesar in Judea 47 Parthian invasion 40 Antigonus 40-37 Herod the Great 37-4 BC Herod's Temple begun 18 Birth of Christ c.4 BC Archelaus 4 BC-AD 6	Death of Pompey 48 Death of Caesar 44 2nd Triumvirate Battle of Philippi 42 Battle of Actium 31 Augustus — First emperor 27 BC-AD 14 **Roman Empire**	**Parthian Empire** Phraates 37-32 Parthians defeat Antony 36
0	Roman governors 6-41 Pontius Pilate 27-37 Death of Christ c.29 Herod Agrippa I 41-44 Paul's 1st journey, Council at Jerusalem 46/47	Varus defeated in Germany 9 Tiberius 14-37 Gaius (Caligula) 37-41 Claudius 41-54 Conquest of Britain begun 43	Artabanus II 10-40
50 AD	Antonius Felix 52-60 Imprisonment of Paul 58 Porcius Festus 60-62 Paul sent to Rome 60 Gessius Florus 64-66 First Jewish Revolt 66-73 Destruction of Jerusalem 70 Fall of Masada 73 Jewish center at Jamnia	Nero 54-68 1st Persecution of Christians 64 Galba, Otho, Vitellius 68/69 Vespasian 69-79 Titus 79-81 Domitian 81-96 Nerva 96-98 Trajan 98-117	Vologases I 51-80 Parthian War with Rome 53-63 Osroes (Chosroes) 89-128
100 AD **135 AD**	Jewish uprisings in Palestine, Egypt, Mesopotamia 116-117 Bar-Kochba Revolt 132-135 Jerusalem razed, Aelia Capitolina built on site	Campaigns in Dacia 101-107 Hadrian 117-138	Conquest of Nabateans by Romans Trajan invades Parthia 114 Territory lost to Romans regained 118

Herod and His Descendants

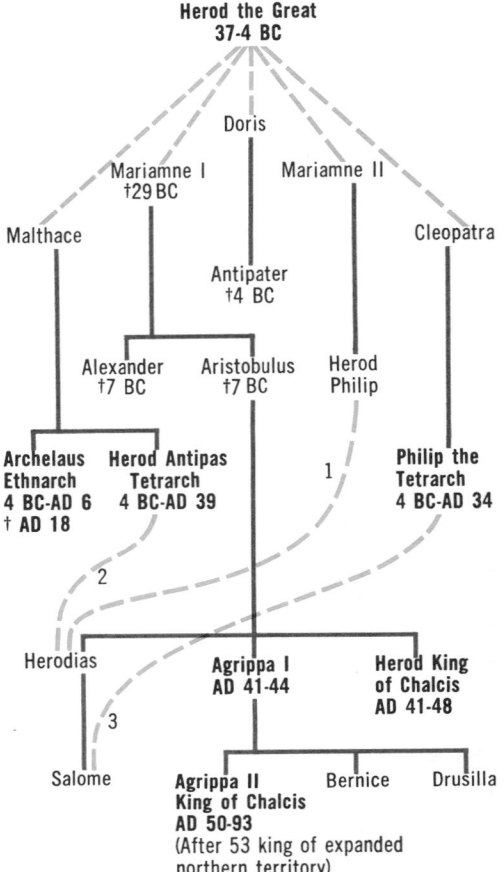

Married – – – – –
1. First marriage of Herodias.
2. Second marriage of Herodias.
3. Salome, daughter of Herodias and Herod (sometimes referred to as Philip), danced before Herod Antipas for John the Baptist's head. She married her great-uncle Philip the Tetrarch.

Roman catapult. A type of artillery used
effectively by both Romans and Jews in
the battle for Jerusalem, A.D. 69-70.

Gazetteer-Index

This Gazetteer-Index is an alphabetical listing of all geographical names found on the maps of this volume. The spelling of Biblical names used on maps and index is that found in the Revised Standard Version (RSV). Alternative Biblical or other ancient names are given in parentheses. Wherever possible, the modern equivalent (Arabic, Hebrew, Turkish, etc.) of an ancient name is given in italic type. A question mark after the identification of a site indicates that the location is possible or probable but not yet certain. The page numbers of the maps on which the name appears are listed in sequence. The key or grid reference (a letter-figure combination) following the page number(s) refers to the letters and figures at the margins of the maps. For example, Azotus (Ashdod in Old Testament times) [Arabic *Isdud*, Hebrew *Tel Ashdod*] can be found on the maps on pages 23, 25, 26 and 35 at key reference W6 and on page 31 at G8. Entries for locations within or near Jerusalem give the page numbers only for the appropriate Jerusalem maps.

ABBREVIATIONS

T. = Tell, Tel (mound)
Kh. = Khirbet (ruin)
H. = Horvat (ruin)
J. = Jebel (hill or mount)
W. = Wadi (seasonal stream)

A

Abana, *Nahr Barada,* river. 4:Z2
Abel, (Abel-beth-maachah), *T. Abil.* 12, 14, 15:Y3; 13:H5
Abel-meholah, *Kh. el-Maqlub.* 15:Y4
Abila, *T. Abil,* in Decapolis. 23, 25, 26, 27, 28:Y4
Abila, *T. Abila,* in Abilene. 25, 26:Z2
Abilene, region. 25, 26:X2; 31:H6
Abū Rudays. 39:C6
Abū Zanimah. 39:C6
Abydos, *Arabet el-Madfuneh,* in Egypt. 9, 16:F6
Abydos, *Canakkale,* in Asia Minor. 16:E2
Accaron, *see* Ekron
Acco, (Ptolemais, Acre), *'Akko, T. el-Fukhkhar.* 4, 11, 12, 14, 15, 19, 23, 38:X3; 8:B4; 10:D2; 13:G5
Accrabbah, (Akrabatta), *'Aqraba.* 19:X5
Achaean League. 21, 22:C1
Achaia, Roman province. 32, 33:A1; 36:F3
Achmetha, *see* Ecbatana
Achzib, (Ecdippa), *es-Zib.* 11, 12, 19:X3
Achzib-Acco, region. 19:X3
Acra, in Jerusalem. 22
Adasa, *Kh. 'Addasa.* 23:X6
Adida, (Hadid), *el-Haditheh.* 23, 35:W5
Adora, (Adoraim), *Dura.* 23, 25:W6
Adoraim, (Adora), *Dura.* 12, 15:W6
Adramyttium, *Edremit.* 32, 33:B1; 33:C4
Adria, (Adriatic Sea). 33:A4
Adullam, *T. esh-Sheikh Madhkur.* 11, 12, 15, 19, 23:X6
Aegean Sea. 17, 20, 32, 33:A1
Aenon, spring north of *Kh. Umm el-'Umdan* (?). 26:X5
Aetolian League. 21, 22:C1
Africa, Roman province. 36:C4
'Afula. 39:D3
Agade, *Abu Ghubar* (?). 9:J4
Agrippias, (Anthedon), *el-Blahiyeh.* 25,26:V6
Agrippina, *Kaukab el-Hawa.* 26, 27:X4
Ahlab, *Kh. el-Mahalib.* 11:X2
Ai, *et-Tell.* 8:B6; 10:E3; 11, 12, 19, 38:X6
Aijalon, *Yalo.* 11, 12, 15:X6
Aijalon, Valley of, *W. Selman.* 4, 11, 12:W6
'Ain Feshkha, spring. 34, 38:X6

'Ain Gedi, (En-gedi). 34, 38:X7
'Ain Karim, (Beth-haccherem). 38:X6
'Ajlūn. 39:E3
Akhetaton, *Tell el-Amarna.* 8:E5; 10:A7
Akkad, region. 9:J4
'Akko, (Acco, Ptolemais). 39:D2
Akrabatta, (Accrabbah), *'Aqraba.* 35:X5
Akrabattene, region. 23:X8
Akrabbim, Ascent of, *Naqb es-Safa.* 15:X8
Alaca Huyuk. 9:G1
Alalakh. 9:G3
Al 'Aqabah. 39:D5
Al 'Arīsh. 39:C4
Alashiya, (Cyprus). 9:F3
Aleppo, (Haleb), *Halab.* 16:G3
Alexandria, *Alexandretta,* in Syria. 31:H2
Alexandria, *Gulashkird,* in Carmania. 20:E4
Alexandria, *Iskandariyeh,* in Egypt. 20:B3; 21, 22:D2; 33:66; 37:G5; *see also city plan p. 21*
Alexandria Arachosiorum, *Ghazni.* 20:F3
Alexandria Arion, *Herat.* 20:F3
Alexandria Eschata, *Khodzent.* 21:G2
Alexandrium, *Qarn Sartabeh.* 23, 25, 26:X5
Al Fayyūm. 39:A6
Al Firdān. 39:B4
Al Harmal. 39:E1
Al Karak. 39:E4
Al Khalil, (Hebron). 34:X6
Al Khuraybah. 39:D7
Al Kuntillah. 39:D5
Al Mafraq. 39:E3
Al Mahallah al Kubra. 39:A4
Al Manṣurāh. 39:A4
Al Minyā. 39:A7
Al Mudawwarah. 39:E6
Al Qāhirah, (Cairo). 39:A5
Al Qantarah. 39:B4
Al Qatrānah. 39:E4
Al Qunayţirah. 39:E2
Al Qusaymah. 39:D4
Alush, *Wadi el-Esh* (?). 10:C6
Amalek, Amalekites, people. 12:X6; 13:G7; 14:W8
Amanus Mts. 31:H2
Amarna, Tell el-, (Akhetaton). 10, 39:A7
Amastris. 37:G3
Amathus, *T. 'Ammata.* 23, 25, 26:Y5
Amisus. 37:H3
Amman, (Rabba, Philadelphia). 38:Y5; 39:E3
Ammon, region. 4, 11, 12, 14, 15, 19:Z5; 8:C5; 10:E3; 13:H6; 16:G4

Amon, Temple of, *Siwa.* 18, 20:A3
Amorites, people. 8:B6
Amphipolis, *Neochori.* 32, 33:A1
Anab, *Kh. 'Anab es-Saghireh.* 12:W6
Anat, *'Anah.* 16:H4; 17:C3
Anathoth, *Ras el-Kharrubeh.* 12, 19:X6
Anchialus. 37:G3
Ancyra, *Ankara.* 16:F2; 18, 20:B2; 32, 33:C1; 37:G3
Ankuwa, *Alisar Huyuk* (?). 9:G2
An Nakhl. 39:C5
Anthedon, (Agrippias), *el-Blahiyeh.* 23, 25:V6
Antigonid Kingdom. 21, 22:C1
Anti-Lebanon, mts. 4:Y2; 8:C2; 31:J5
Antioch, *Antakya,* in Syria. 22:D1; 31:H3; 32, 33:D2; 37:H4; *see also city plan p. 30*
Antioch, *Yalvac,* in Pisidia. 32:C1; 32:C2; 37:G3
Antipatris, (Aphek), *Ras el-'Ain.* 25, 26, 28, 35, 38:W5
Antium, *Anzio.* 36:D3
Antonia Fortress, in Jerusalem. 25, 29, 34
Apamea, *Qal'at el-Mudiq.* 31, 37:H4
Aphek, (Antipatris), *Ras el-'Ain.* 10:D3; 11, 12, 14, 15, 38:X5
Aphek, *Fiq,* in Transjordan. 15:Y4
Aphek, *T. Kurdaneh,* in Asher. 11, 12:X3
Apollonia, *Arsuf,* in Palestine. 19, 23, 25, 26, 35:W5
Apollonia, *Pollinia,* in Macedonia. 32, 33:A1
Apollonia, *Sozopol,* on Black Sea. 18:B1
Appius, Forum of, (Appi Forum). 33:A4
Aqaba, Gulf of. 10, 39:D6
Ar, *el-Misna'.* 14, 15:Y7
Arabah, *el- Ghor, Wadi al 'Arabah.* 4, 15:X8; 10:D5; 13:H8; 39:E4
Arabia, region. 9:H5; 18, 20:C3; 21, 22:E2; 37:J5
Arabian Sea. 21:F4
Arabs, people. 16:H5; 17:C3
Arachosia, region. 18, 20:F3
Arad, *T. 'Arad.* 8:B7; 10:D4; 11, 12, 14, 15, 23, 34:X7; 13:G6
'Arad. 39:D3
Aral Sea. 17, 18, 20:E1
Aram, (Syria), region. 14, 15:Y2
Aram-Damascus, region. 13:H4
Arameans, people. 11:Y2
Aram-zobah, region. 13:J4
Araq, el-Emir, (Tyrus). 38:Y6

Ararat, (Urartu), region. 16:H2
Ararat, Mt., *Buyuk Agri Dagi.* 9, 16:J2
Araxes, river. 9:K2; 16:J2; 18:D1
Arbela, *Erbil,* in Assyria. 9, 16:J3; 18, 20:D2
Arbela, *Irbid,* in Decapolis. 26:Y4
Arbela, *Kh. Irbid,* in Galilee. 23:X4
Archelais, *Kh. 'Auja et-Tahta.* 26:X5
Ardus, (Arvad), *Erwad, Ruwad.* 31:H4
Areopolis, (Rabbath-moab), *Kh. er-Rabba.* 26, 28:Y7
Argob, region. 13:H5; 14:Y3
Aria, region. 18, 21:F3
Aribi, (Arabs), people. 16:H4
Ariha, (Jericho). 34:X6
Arimathea, (Ramathaim), *Rentis.* 26:X5
'Arish, Wadi al-, (River of Egypt). 4:V8; 39:C5
Armenia, region. 18, 20:C2; 21, 22:E1; 37:J3
Arnon, *W. al-Mawjib,* river. 4, 11, 12, 14, 15, 19, 23, 25, 26, 35:Y7; 8:B6; 10:E4
Aroer, *'Ara'ir,* in Moab. 11, 12:Y6; 13:H6
Arpad, *T. Erfad.* 16:G3
Arvad, (Ardus), *Erwad, Ruwad.* 9, 16:G3; 13:H3; 18:C3; 31:H4
Arzawa, region. 8:E2
Ascalon, (Ashkelon), *'Ashqelon.* 23, 25, 26, 35, 38:W6
Ashdod, (Azotus), *Isdud, T. Ashdod.* 8:A6; 11, 12, 14, 15, 19, 23, 38:W6; 10, 39:D3
Ashdod, region. 19:W6
Asher, tribe. 11, 12:X3
Ashkelon, (Ascalon), *'Ashqelon.* 8:A6; 10:D3; 11, 12, 14, 15, 19, 23:W6; 13:G6
'Ashqelon. 39:D3
Ashtaroth, *T. 'Ashtarah.* 8:C4; 10:E2; 11, 12, 14, 15:Y4; 13:H5
Asia, Roman province. 32, 33:B1; 33:C5; 37:G3
Asia Minor, region. 20:B2
Asochis, *Kh. el-Lon.* 26, 27:X4
Asphaltitis, Lake, (Dead Sea). 25, 26, 35:X6
As Salţ. 39:E3
As Samu', (Eshtemoa). 34:X7
Asshur, *Qal'at Sherqat.* 9:J3; 16:J3; 18:C2
Assuwa, region. 8:E1
Assyria, region. 9:J3; 16:H3; 17:C2
Assyrian Empire. 16:G4
Astacus. 16:F2
Astorga. 36:A2
Ataroth, *Kh. Attarus.* 15:Y6

E

Eastern Sea, (Persian Gulf). 16:K5
Ebal, Mt., *Jebel Eslamiyeh.* 4, 11, 12, 14, 15, 19, 26:X5
Ebla. 9:E3
Ecbatana, near *Hamadan.* 9, 16:K3; 17, 18, 20:D3
Ecdippa, (Achzib), *es-Zib.* 26, 27, 28:X3
Edessa, *Urfa.* 37:H3
Edom, region. 4, 11, 12, 15:Y8; 8:B7; 10:E5; 13:H7; 16:G5
Edomites, people. 19:X7
Edrei, *Der'a.* 8:C4; 10:E2; 11, 12, 14, 15, 23:Z4; 13:H5
Eglon, *Tell el-Hesi*(?). 8:A6; 10:D4; 11, 38:W6
Egypt, nation. 39:A5
Egypt, region. 10:A5; 16:F5; 17, 18, 20:C4; 21, 22:D2; 32, 33:C3; 37:G5
Egypt, Brook of, *Wadi al 'Arish.* 4:U8; 10:C4; 13:F7
Egypt, Lower, region. 8:E4
Egypt, Upper, region. 8:F5
Egyptian Empire. 8:E5
Ekron, (Accaron), *Kh. el-Muqanna'* (?). 11, 12, 14, 15, 23:W6
Elah, *W. es-Sant,* valley. 4, 12:W6
Elam, region. 9, 16:K4; 17:D3
Elasa, *Kh. Ilasa.* 23:X5
Elat, (Elath). 39:D6
Elath, *T. el-Kheleifeh.* 18:C3
Elburz Mts. 16:K3
Elephantine, (Syene), *Aswan.* 17, 18:B4
Elim, *Wadi Gharandel* (?). 10:C6
Eltekeh, *Kh. el-Muqanna'* (?). 16:F4
Elusa, *el-Khalasa.* 25, 26:W7
Emesa, *Homs.* 31:J4
Emmaus, (Nicopolis), *'Imwas.* 12, 23, 25, 26, 35:W6
Emmaus, *Qaloniyeh* (?). 26, 28:X6
En-dor, near *'Indur.* 12
Engaddi, (En-gedi), *'Ain Gedi, Tell el-Jurn.* 26, 28:X7; *see illust. p. 5*
En-gedi, (Engaddi), *'Ain Gedi, Tell el-Jurn.* 11, 12, 15, 19, 23, 34:X7
En-rimmon, *Kh. Ummer-Ramamin.* 19:W7
En-rogel, spring in Jerusalem. 14, 18, 22
'En Yahav. 39:D5
Ephesus. 18, 20, 32, 33:B2; 35:C5; 37:F4; *see also city plan p. 32*
Ephraim, (Ophrah, Aphairema), *et-Taiyibeh* (?). 23, 26, 28:X5
Ephraim, tribe. 11, 12:X5
Ephron, *et-Taiyibeh.* 23:Y4
Epirus, region. 18:A2; 21, 22:C1; 32, 33:A1
Erech, (Uruk), *Warka.* 9, 16:J4; 17, 18:D3
Eridu, *Abu Shahrein.* 9:K4
Erythraean Sea, (Arabian Sea). 18:F4
Esbus, (Heshbon), *Hesban.* 25, 26:Y6
Esdraelon, Plain of, (Plain of Megiddo). 4, 15, 23, 26:X4; *see illust. p. 5*
Eshnunna, *T. Asmar.* 9:J3
Eshtemoa, *es-Samu',* 12, 34:X7
Etam, *Kh. el-Khokh.* 12, 15:X6
Etham, Wilderness of. 10:B5
Ethiopia, (Cush), region. 16:F6; 17, 18, 20:B5
Euphrates, river. 9:H3; 16:H4; 17, 18, 20:C3; 21, 22:E1; 37:J4

F

Ezion-geber, *T. el-Khaleifeh.* 10:D6; 13:G8

Fair Havens, *Limenes Kali,* harbor. 33:C5
Farah, wadi. 4:X5; 8:B5
Feiran, wadi. 10:C6

G

Gaba, (Gabae), *Sheikh Abreiq.* 23:X4
Gabae, (Gaba), *Sheikh Abreiq.* 25, 26, 27, 35:X4
Gabae, *Isfahan.* 18:E3
Gabaon, (Gibeon), *el-Jib.* 35:X6
Gad, tribe. 11:Y5
Gadara, *T. Jadur,* in Perea. 25, 26, 35:Y5
Gadara, *Umm Qeis,* in Decapolis. 23, 25, 26,27, 28, 35:Y4
Galaaditis, region. 23:Y4
Galatia, region. 22:D1; 32, 33:C1; 37:G3
Galatians, people. 21:D1
Galilee, region. 15, 19, 23, 25, 26, 27, 28, 35:X4; 31:G7
Galilee, Lower. 4:X4
Galilee, Sea of, (Sea of Chinnereth). 4, 25, 26, 27, 38:Y4; 31:H7
Galilee, Upper. 4:X3
Gamala, *Ras el Hal.* 23, 27, 35:Y4
Gandara, region. 19:G3
Garden Tomb, in Jerusalem. 29; *see illust. p. 29*
Gath, (Gittaim), *T. Ras Abu Hamad.* 12, 15:W6
Gath, *T. es Safi* (?). 11, 12, 14:W6; 13:G6
Gaugamela, battle site. 20:D2
Gaul, region. 22:B1; 36:C2
Gaulanitis, region. 23, 25, 26:X4
Gaza, *el-Ghazzeh.* 4, 11, 12, 14, 15, 19, 23, 25, 26, 35, 38:Y6; 8:A6; 9:F4; 10, 39:D4; 13:G6; 18, 20:B3
Gazara, (Gezer), *T. Jezer.* 23:W6
Geba, *Jeba'.* 12, 15, 19:X6
Gebal, (Byblos), *Jebeil.* 8:B2; 9:G3; 13:H4; 18:C3
Gedor, (Gadara), *T. Jadur.* 23:Y5
Gedrosia, (Maka), region. 18, 20:F4
Gennath Gate, in Jerusalem. 29
Gennesaret, *T. el-'Ureimeh.* 27:X3
Gennesaret, Lake, (Sea of Galilee). 19, 23, 35:Y4
Gerar, *T. Abu Hureirah.* 8:A6; 11, 12, 14, 19:W7; 13:G6
Gerar, wadi. 4, 12:W7
Gerasa, *Jerash.* 23, 25, 26, 35:Y5; 31:H7
Gergasa, *el-Kursi.* 27:Y4
Gerizim, Mt., *Jebel et-Tur.* 4, 11, 12, 14, 15, 19, 23, 25, 26, 35:X5
Gerrha, *Ugair* (?). 18:D4
Geshur, region. 12, 14:Y3; 13:H5
Getae, people. 21:C1
Gethsemane, in Jerusalem. 29
Gezer, (Gazara), *T. Jezer.* 8:A6; 10:D3; 12, 14, 15, 19, 23, 38:W6; 13:G6; *see illust. p. 14*
Gibbethon, *T. el-Melat.* 12, 15:W6
Gibeah, *T. el-Ful.* 12, 14, 38:X6; 13:G6; *see illust. p. 12*
Gibeon, *el-Jib.* 8:B6; 11, 12, 14, 15, 19, 38:X6
Gihon, Spring, in Jerusalem. 14, 18, 22, 25, 29
Gilboa, Mt., *Jebel Fuqu'ah.* 4, 12, 14, 15:X4; 13:H5
Gilead, region. 4, 11, 15, 19:Y5

Gilgal, *Kh. el-Mefjir* (?). 11, 12, 15:X6
Ginae, (En-gannim), *Jenin.* 26, 28:X4
Ginnesar, *see* Gennesaret
Gischala, *el-Jish.* 25, 26, 27, 28, 35:X3
Gittaim, (Gath), *T. Ras Abu Hamad.* 12, 19:W6
Giza. 39:A5
Golan, *Sahm el-Jaulan.* 11, 12:Y4
Golan Heights. 39:E1
Golden Gate, in Jerusalem. 25, 29
Golgotha, in Jerusalem. 29
Gomer, people. 16:H2
Gomorrah, southern end of Dead Sea (?). 8:B7
Gophna, *Jiphna.* 23, 25, 26, 35:X5
Gordion, (Gordium), near *Polatli.* 16:F2; 18, 20:B2
Gortyna. 36:F4
Goshen, region. 10:A4
Gozan, *T. Halaf.* 16:H3
Granicus, battle site. 20:B2
Great Sea, (Mediterranean Sea). 8:E4
Greece. 18:A2
Greek City States. 16:E2
Gutium, region. 9:K3

H

Habor, river. 16:H3
Hadera. 39:D3
Hadid, (Adida), *el-Haditheh.* 23:W5
Hadrumetum. 36:D4
Haifa. 39:D2
Haleb, (Aleppo), *Halab.* 9:G3; 13:J2
Halicarnassus, *Bodrum.* 20:B2
Hallat 'Ammār. 39:E6
Halys, *Kizil Irmak,* river. 9:F1; 16:F2; 17, 18, 32, 33:C1
Hamath, *Hama.* 9, 16:G3; 13:J3; 18:C2
Hamath, *Hammam Tabariyeh,* in Naphtali. 12, 15:X4
Hamath, region. 13:J3
Hananel, Tower of, in Jerusalem. 18
Haql. 39:D6
Haqrāyot. 39:D2
Haran, *Harran.* 9:H2; 16:H3; 17, 18:C2
Harmozia, *Minab.* 20:E4
Har Ramon, mt. 39:D5
Harun, Jebel. 10:E5
Hasmonean Palace, in Jerusalem. 22, 29
Hatti, (Hittites), people. 9:G2
Hattusas, *Bogazkoy.* 9:F1
Hauran, region. 4, 19:Y3
Havvoth-jair, region. 11, 14, 15:Y4
Hazar-enan, *Qaryatein* (?). 13:J4
Hazeroth, *'Ain Hudra* (?). 10:D6
Hazor, *T. el-Qedah,* (or *Waqqas*). 8:B4; 9:G4; 10:E2; 11, 12:Y3; 13:H5; 14, 15, 19, 23, 38:X3
Hebron, *Al Khalil, el-Khalil.* 4, 11, 12, 14, 15, 19, 23, 25, 26, 28, 34, 35, 38:X6; 9:B6, G4; 10:D4; 13:G6
Hecatompylus, *Damghan.* 20:E2
Helal, Jebel. 4:U8; 10:C5
Heliopolis, *Baalbek.* 31:H5
Heliopolis, *T. Husn,* in Egypt. 10, 39:A5; 18:B3
Hellas, (Greece). 20:A2
Hepher, *T. Ifshar* (?). 11, 12, 14:W5; 13:G5
Heracleopolis, *Ahnas el-Medineh.* 9, 16:E5; 10:A6
Herat, (Alexandria Arion). 20:F3
Hermes, river. 8:E2

Hermon, Mount, *Jebel esh-Sheikh.* 4, 11, 12, 14, 15, 19,23, 26, 28:Y2; 9:C3; 13:H4; 39:F2
Hermopolis, *el-Ashmunein.* 9, 16:F5
Herodium, *Kh. el-Fureidis.* 25, 26, 34, 35, 38:X6
Herod's Palace, in Jerusalem. 25, 29, 34
Heshbon, *Hesban.* 8:C4; 10:E3; 11, 12, 14, 15, 19, 23, 38:Y6; 13:H6
Hezekiah's Tunnel, in Jerusalem. 18, 29
Hindu Kush, mts. 19, 21:G2
Hindush, (India), region. 19:G4
Hinnon Valley, in Jerusalem. 14, 18, 22, 25, 29, 34
Hippicus Tower, in Jerusalem. 29
Hippos, *Qal'at el-Husn.* 23, 25, 26, 27, 28, 35:Y4
Hispalis. 36:A3
Hittite Empire. 9:G2
Hittites, people. 11:Y2; 13:J2
Holon. 39:D3
Horites, people. 9:H2
Hormah, *Kh. el-Mishash.* 10:D4; 11, 12:X7
Hula, Lake, (L. Semechonitis). 4:Y3
Hulwān. 39:A5
Hurrians, people. 9:H2
Hydaspes, river. 21:G3
Hyphasis, *Beas,* river. 21:G3
Hyrcania, *Kh. Mird.* 23, 25, 26, 34, 38:X6
Hyrcania, region. 17, 18:E2

I

Iberians, people. 21:A1
Ibleam, *T. Bel'ameh.* 8:B5; 11, 12, 14, 15:X4
Iconium, *Qoniyah.* 18:B2; 32, 33:C2; 37:G3
Iconopolis. 37:G3
Idumea, region. 4, 19, 23, 25, 26, 28, 35:W7
Ije-abarim, near Brook Zered. 10:E4
Ijon, *T. ed-Dibbin.* 12, 15:Y2
Ilium, (Troy), *Hisarlik.* 20:B2
Illyria, region. 20:A1; 21, 22:C1
Illyricum, region. 36:E2
Imbabāh. 39:A5
India, region. 19:G4; 21:G3
Indus, river. 19, 21:G3
Irbid. 39:E3
Isbeita. 38:W8
Isin, *Bahriyat.* 9:K4
Ismailia. 39:B5
Israel, nation. 39:D3
Israel, region. 13:H6; 15:X5
Israel, Kingdom of. 15:X5
Israel, Pool of, in Jerusalem. 29
Issachar, tribe. 11:X4
Issus, battle site. 18, 20:C2
Ister, (Danube), river. 17, 18, 20:A1; 21, 22:C1
Italy, region. 21, 22:B1; 33:A4; 36:D3
Iturea, region. 25, 26:Y2
Itureans, people. 23:Y2
Izalla, region. 17:C2

J

Jabbok, *Nahr es-Zarqā,* river. 4, 11, 12, 14, 15, 19, 23, 25, 26, 28, 35:Y5; 8:B5; 10:E3
Jabesh-gilead, *T. Abu Kharaz.* 11, 12, 15:Y4
Jabneel, (Jabneh, Jamnia), *Yebna.* 12, 15:W6
Jabneh, (Jabneel, Jamnia), *Yebna.* 23:W6

Picture Credits

The editor and publisher wish to express their thanks and appreciation to the following for supplying illustrations:

The American Numismatic Society, New York: pages 20 (bottom), 21 (top right), 22 (center left), 28 (bottom right), 29 (bottom left), 35 (bottom). Henry Angelo-Castrillon: page 32 (top right), 36 (right). The Bettmann Archive, New York: page 42. The Trustees of the British Museum: pages 16 (all three photos), 18 (top). The Brooklyn Museum, Charles Edwin Wilbour Fund: page 37 (top right). Ernest J. Dupuy: pages 32 (top left), 36 (center), 37 (center). GAF Pana-Vue Slides: pages 24 (top), 28 (top). Hebrew University, Jerusalem, Department of Archaeology: page 22 (bottom right). Iran National Tourist Office, New York: page 18 (left). Israel Government Tourist Office, New York: title page, pages 5 (bottom left), 11 (two photos at top), 27 (left), 29 (top left), 30 (second from top), 34 (center left), 35 (center left). The Israel Museum, Jerusalem: pages 14 (top right), 18 (bottom right), 28 (bottom left). Istanbul Museum: page 30 (top). Italian Government Travel Office: page 36 (left). Nancy L. Lapp: page 12. From Lepsius, *Denkmaeler:* page 10 (right). Herbert G. May: page 27 (bottom right). The Metropolitan Museum of Art: pages 2, 22 (top left and top right), 37 (bottom right). Museo Nazionale, Naples: pages 20 (top), 21 (center right). Museum of Fine Arts, Boston: page 24 (bottom). Notre Dame de Sion, Jerusalem: page 29 (center bottom). The Oriental Institute, University of Chicago: pages 17, 38 (center). William L. Reed, courtesy American Schools of Oriental Research: page 35 (top). The University Museum, University of Pennsylvania: pages 9, 37 (left). Wide World Photos: page 30 (third from top).

Photographs from collection of Professor Harry Thomas Frank: pages 5 (three photos at right), 7 (both), 8, 10 (left), 11 (bottom), 14 (top left), 21 (top left), 22 (center right and bottom left), 25, 27 (center and top right), 29 (center top and right), 30 (bottom), 32 (bottom), 34 (top), 38 (top and four bottom photos). Copyright © 1977 by Harry Thomas Frank

WORLD HISTORY ATLAS

A collection of maps illustrating geographically the most significant periods and events in the history of civilization.

EUROPE
PHYSICAL

RELIEF

METERS	FEET
3,658	12,000
1,829	6,000
914	3,000
305	1,000
Sea	Level
Depression	Depression

183 METERS ------ 100 FATHOMS

Copyright by C. S. HAMMOND & Co., N.Y.

TABLE OF CONTENTS

Published by

HAMMOND
INCORPORATED

MAPLEWOOD, NEW JERSEY

Printed in U. S. A.

Maps updated 1980
© Copyright by Hammond Incorporated, MCMLXXIX

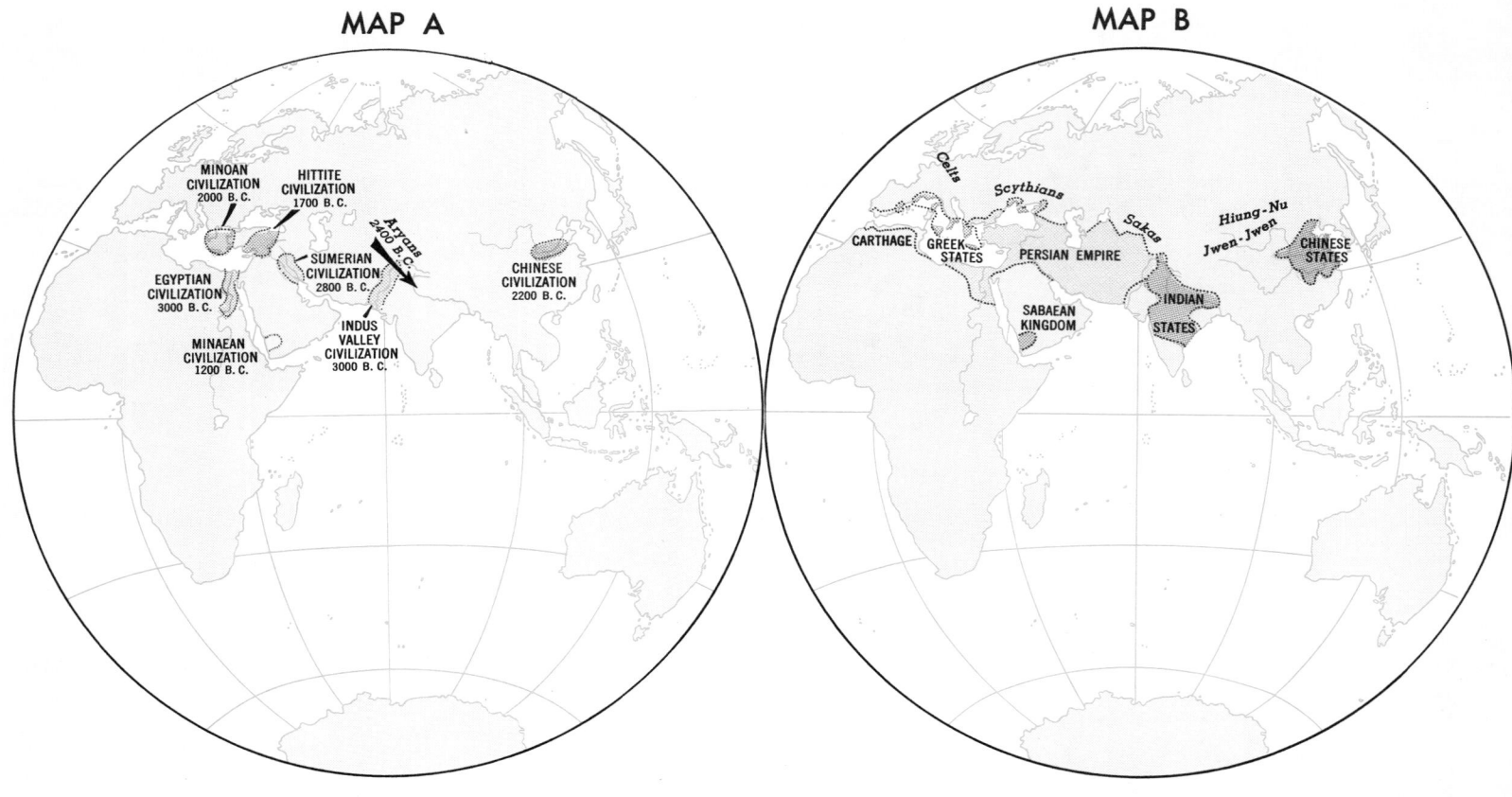

MAP A

MINOAN CIVILIZATION 2000 B.C.

HITTITE CIVILIZATION 1700 B.C.

Aryans 2000 B.C.

EGYPTIAN CIVILIZATION 3000 B.C.

SUMERIAN CIVILIZATION 2800 B.C.

CHINESE CIVILIZATION 2200 B.C.

MINAEAN CIVILIZATION 1200 B.C.

INDUS VALLEY CIVILIZATION 3000 B.C.

*The Cradles of Civilization
3000-1000 B.C.*

MAP B

Celts

Scythians

Hiung-Nu

CARTHAGE

GREEK STATES

PERSIAN EMPIRE

Sakas

Jwen-Jwen

CHINESE STATES

SABAEAN KINGDOM

INDIAN STATES

*Major States and Empires
in 500 B.C.*

MAP C

MAYAN STATES

Huns

KOKURYO

WEI EMPIRE

JAPANESE EMPIRE

Germans

Slavs

White Huns

SUNG EMPIRE

WESTERN ROMAN

Berbers

Kanggü

EASTERN EMPIRE

KUSHAN STATES

PYU

FUNAN

K. OF MULAVARMAN

KINGDOM OF GHANA

SASSANID EMPIRE

GUPTA EMPIRE

Hindus

LANGKASUKA

Hindus

Nubians

HIMYARITIC KINGDOM

PALLAVA CONFEDERACY

SINHALA

YAVADVIPA

TARUMA

AXUMITE KINGDOM

*Major States and Empires
in 400 A.D.*

MAP D

Spaniards

JAPAN

KOREA

TIDORE

TERNATE

MING DYNASTY OF CHINA

BRUNEI

MACASSAR

Russians

AZTEC EMPIRE (1519)

MAYAN STATES (1527)

French

English

RUSSIAN EMPIRE

BUKHARA

ANNAM

BURMA

SIAM

MATARAM

Spaniards

Moslems

Spaniards

MOROCCO

MOGUL EMPIRE

PERSIA

ATJEH

Portuguese

Dutch

INCA EMPIRE (1533)

OTTOMAN EMPIRE

BORNU

SONGHOY EMPIRE

HAUSA

DARFUR

ETHIOPIA

BAGUIRMI

Portuguese

Portuguese

Dutch

*The Expansion
of Western Civilization
1600 A.D.*

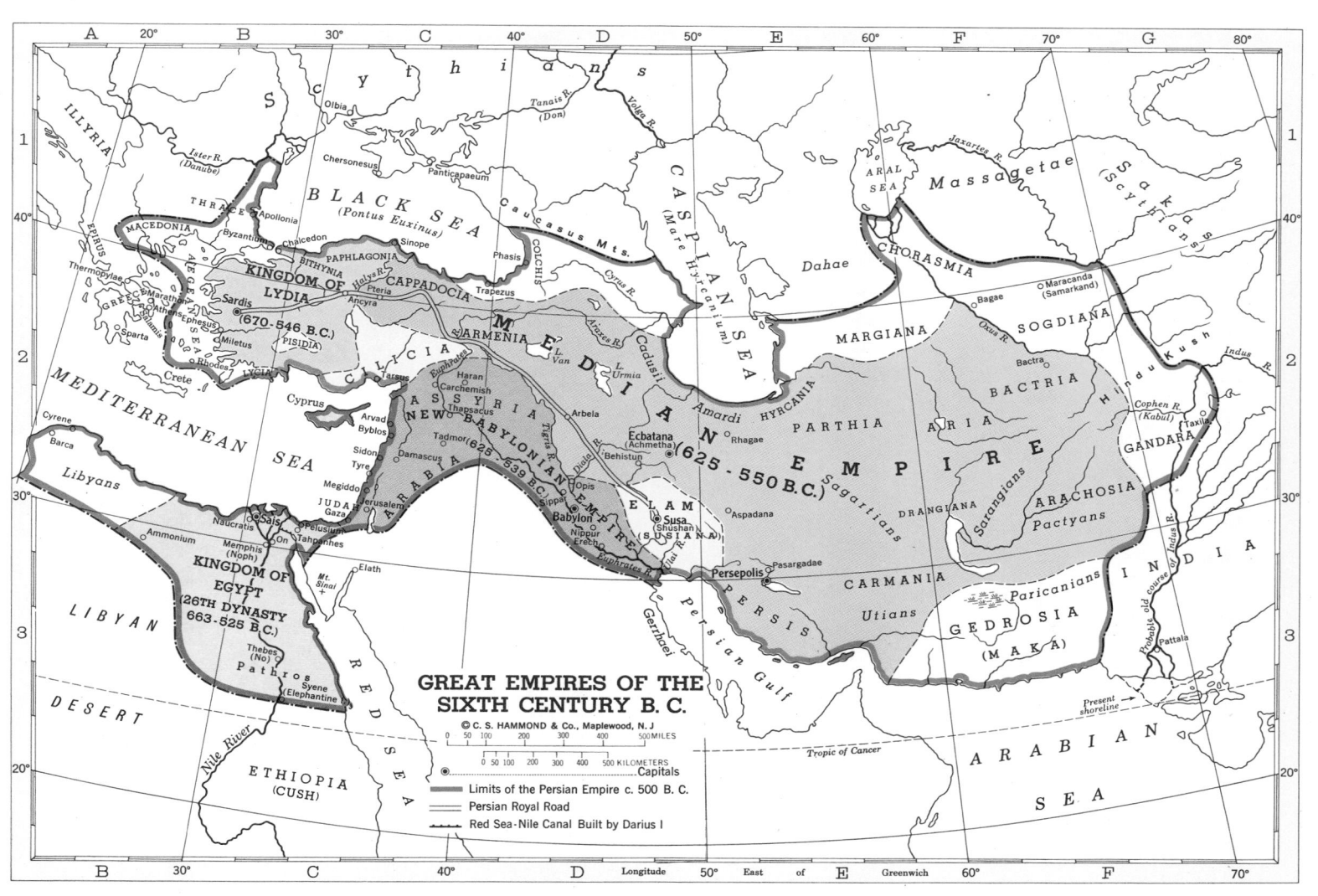

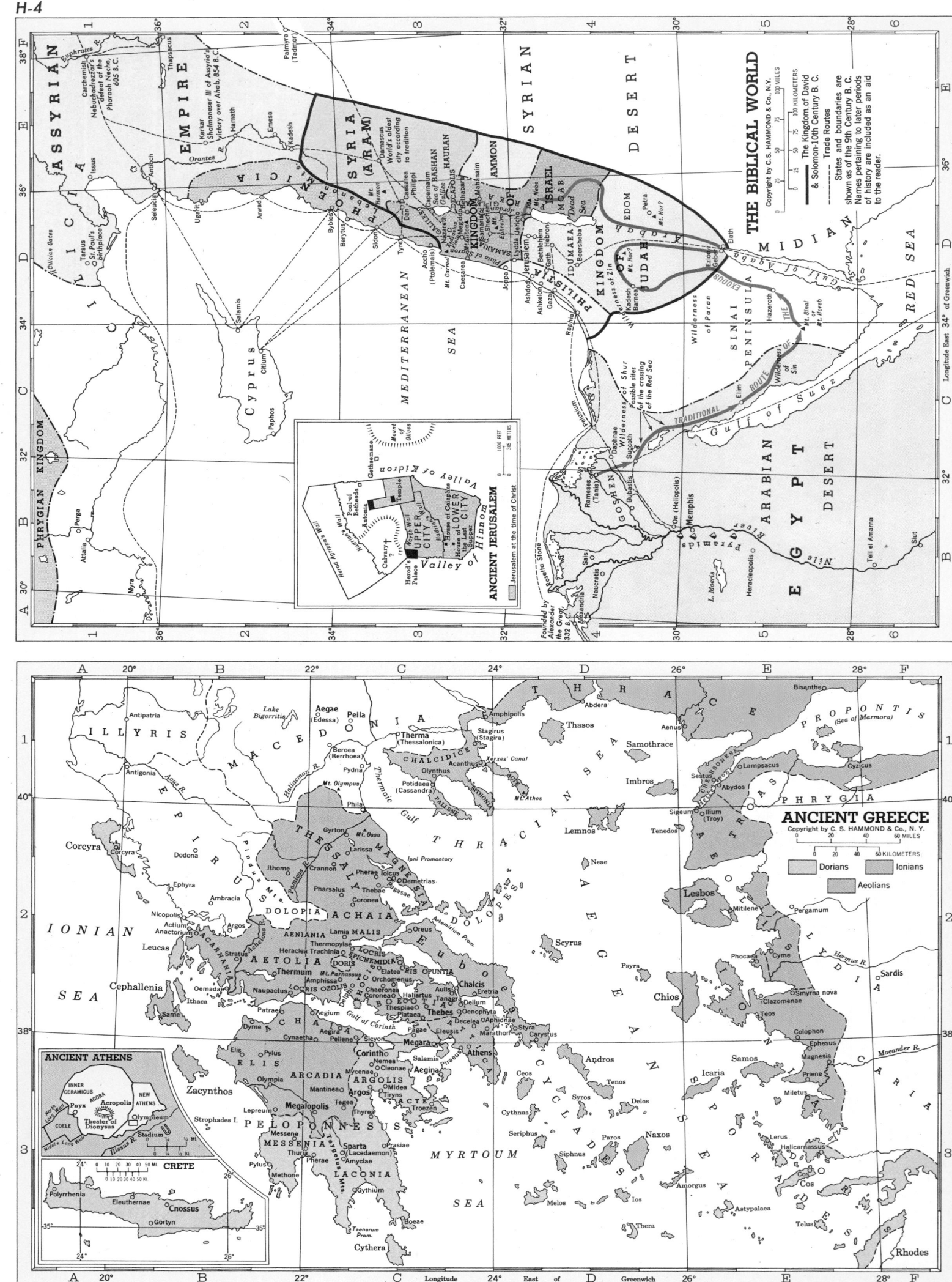

THE BIBLICAL WORLD

Copyright by C. S. HAMMOND & Co., N.Y.

The Kingdom of David
& Solomon-10th Century B. C.

Trade Routes

States and boundaries are
shown as of the 9th Century B. C.
Names pertaining to later periods
of history are included as an aid
to the reader.

0 25 50 75 100 KILOMETERS
0 25 50 75 100 MILES

ANCIENT JERUSALEM

Jerusalem at the time of Christ

ANCIENT GREECE

Copyright by C. S. HAMMOND & Co., N.Y.

0 20 40 60 MILES
0 20 40 60 KILOMETERS

Dorians

Ionians

Aeolians

ANCIENT ATHENS

CRETE

THE PERSIAN EMPIRE
ABOUT 500 B. C.
AND THE EMPIRE OF
ALEXANDER THE GREAT
323 B. C.

Limits of the Persian Empire: ▬▬▬▬
Dominions of Alexander:

Alexander's Route
shown thus: ·······

Directions indicated
by arrows: →

0 100 200 300 400 500 MILES
0 100 200 300 400 500 KILOMETERS

Copyright by C. S. HAMMOND & CO., N.Y.

THE
ROMAN EMPIRE
AT ITS GREATEST EXTENT
ABOUT 117 A. D.

Copyright by C. S. HAMMOND & CO., N.Y.

0 50 100 200 300 400 500 600 MILES
0 50 100 200 300 400 500 600 KILOMETERS

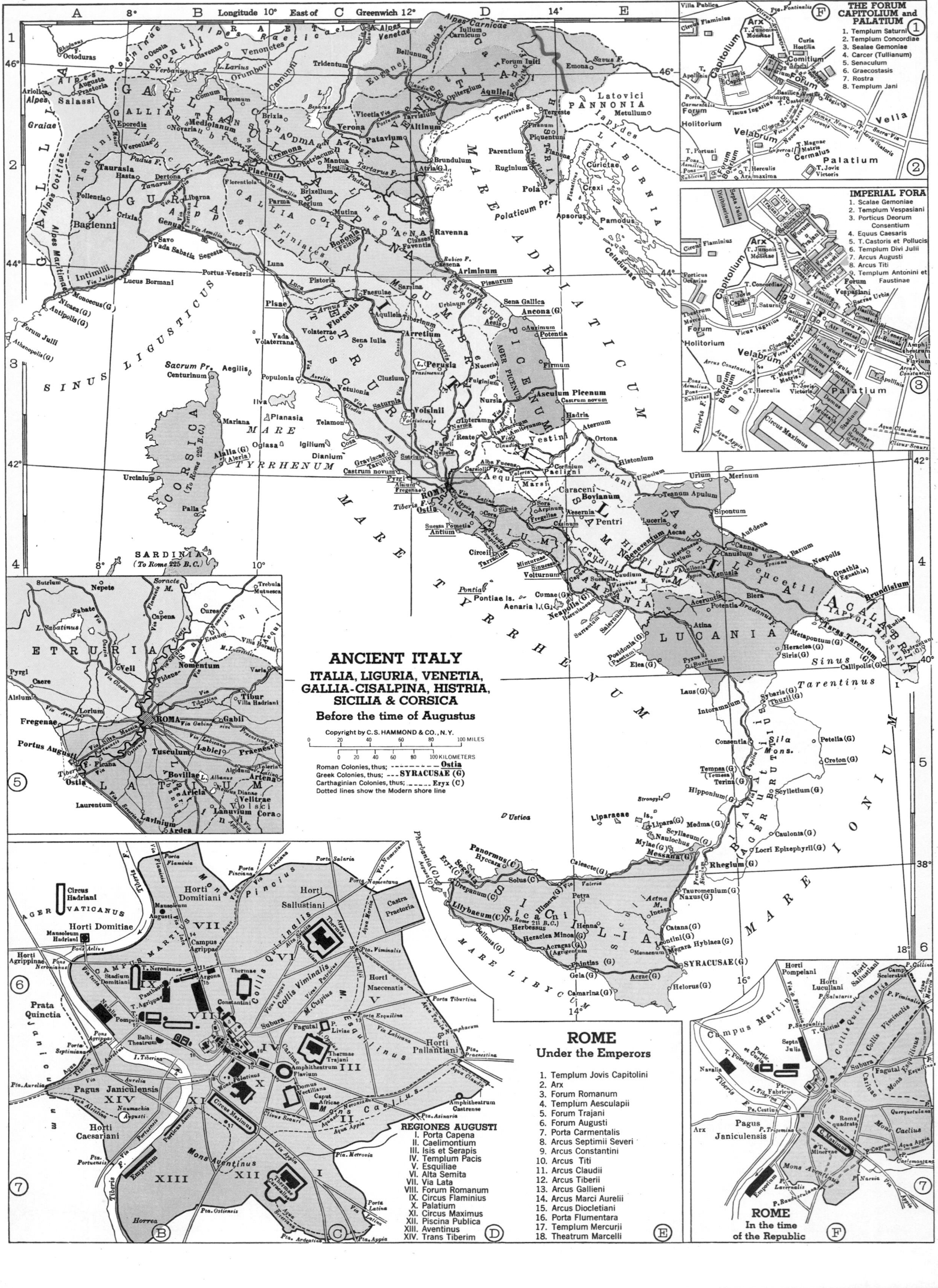

ANCIENT ITALY
ITALIA, LIGURIA, VENETIA, GALLIA-CISALPINA, HISTRIA, SICILIA & CORSICA
Before the time of Augustus
Copyright by C.S. HAMMOND & CO., N.Y.
0 20 40 60 80 100 MILES
0 20 40 60 80 100 KILOMETERS
Roman Colonies, thus; Ostia
Greek Colonies, thus; SYRACUSAE (G)
Carthaginian Colonies, thus; Eryx (C)
Dotted lines show the Modern shore line
Longitude 10° East of Greenwich 12°
MARE ADRIATICUM
MARE TYRRHENUM
SINUS LIGUSTICUS
MARE IONIUM
MARE LIBYCUM
THE FORUM CAPITOLIUM and PALATIUM
1. Templum Saturni
2. Templum Concordiae
3. Sealae Gemoniae
4. Carcer (Tullianum)
5. Senaculum
6. Graecostasis
7. Rostra
8. Templum Jani
IMPERIAL FORA
1. Scalae Gemoniae
2. Templum Vespasiani
3. Porticus Deorum Consentium
4. Equus Caesaris
5. T.Castoris et Pollucis
6. Templum Divi Julii
7. Arcus Augusti
8. Arcus Titi
9. Templum Antonini et Faustinae
ROME
Under the Emperors
1. Templum Jovis Capitolini
2. Arx
3. Forum Romanum
4. Templum Aesculapii
5. Forum Trajani
6. Forum Augusti
7. Porta Carmentalis
8. Arcus Septimii Severi
9. Arcus Constantini
10. Arcus Titi
11. Arcus Claudii
12. Arcus Tiberii
13. Arcus Gallieni
14. Arcus Marci Aurelii
15. Arcus Diocletiani
16. Porta Flumentara
17. Templum Mercurii
18. Theatrum Marcelli
REGIONES AUGUSTI
I. Porta Capena
II. Caelimontium
III. Isis et Serapis
IV. Templum Pacis
V. Esquiliae
VI. Alta Semita
VII. Via Lata
VIII. Forum Romanum
IX. Circus Flaminius
X. Palatium
XI. Circus Maximus
XII. Piscina Publica
XIII. Aventinus
XIV. Trans Tiberim
ROME
In the time of the Republic

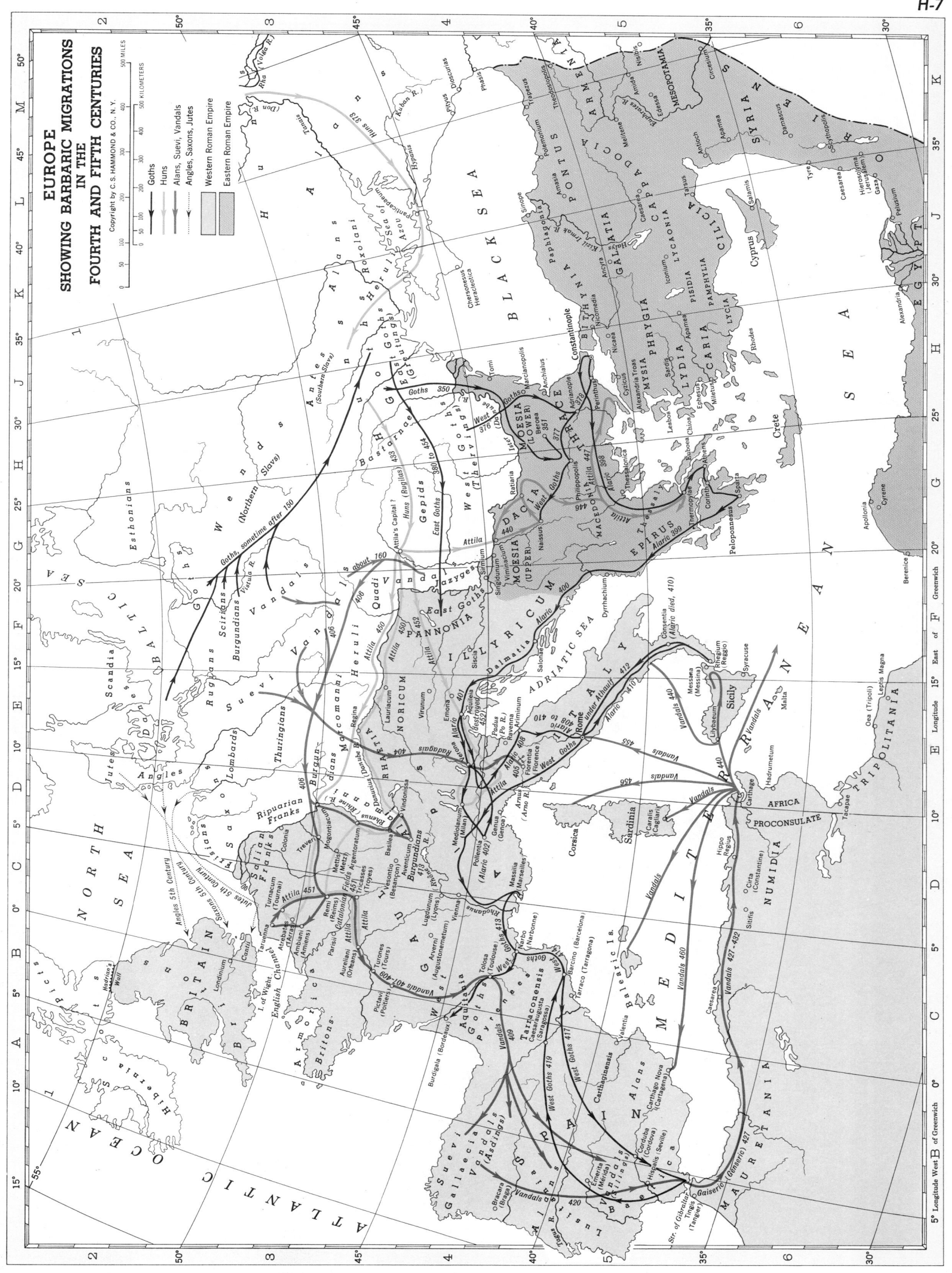

EUROPE
SHOWING BARBARIC MIGRATIONS IN THE FOURTH AND FIFTH CENTURIES

Copyright by C. S. HAMMOND & CO., N.Y.

Goths
Huns
Alans, Suevi, Vandals
Angles, Saxons, Jutes
Western Roman Empire
Eastern Roman Empire

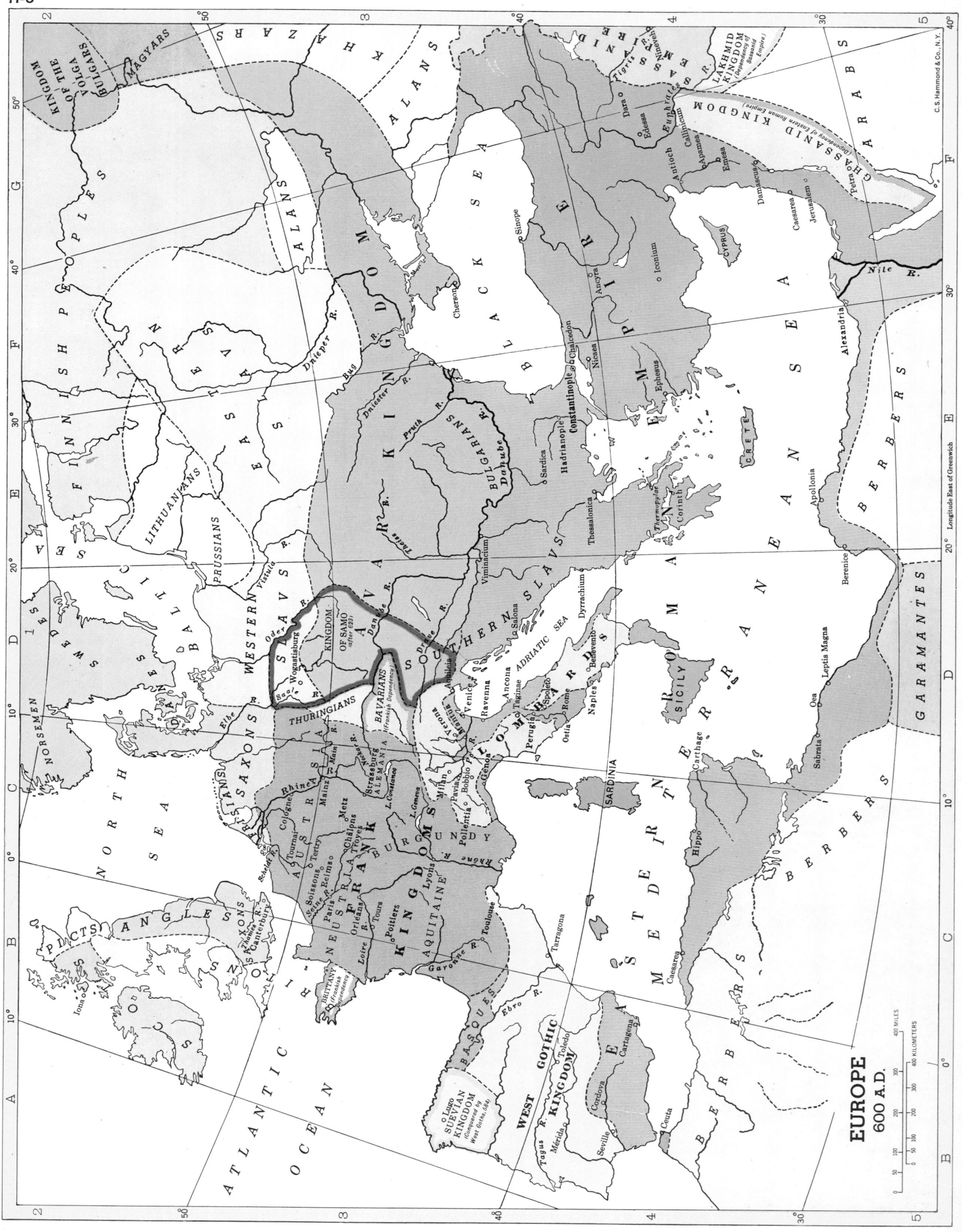

EUROPE
600 A.D.

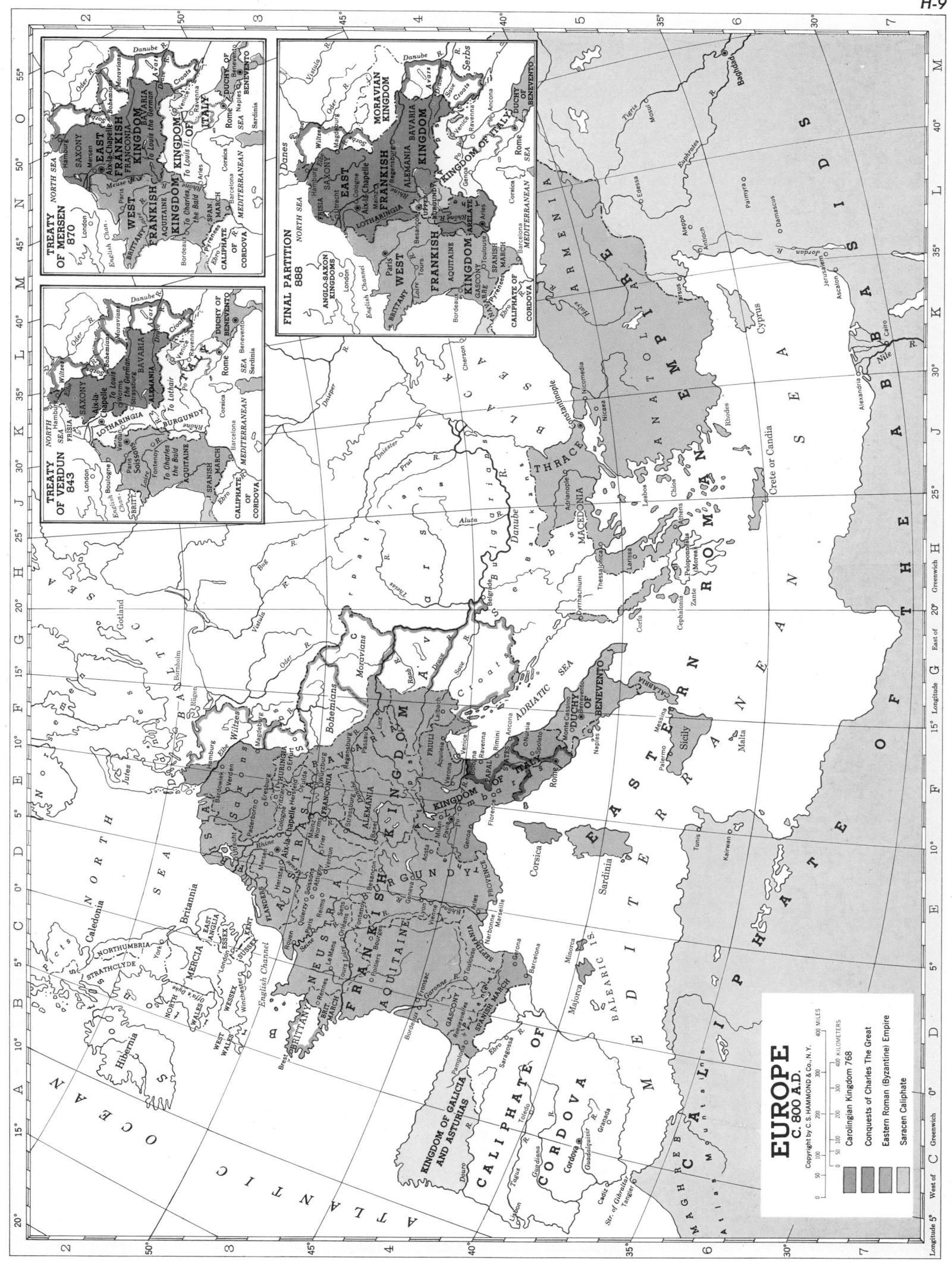

EUROPE
C. 800 A.D.

Copyright by C. S. HAMMOND & Co., N.Y.

- Carolingian Kingdom 768
- Conquests of Charles The Great
- Eastern Roman (Byzantine) Empire
- Saracen Caliphate

TREATY OF VERDUN 843

TREATY OF MERSEN 870

FINAL PARTITION 888

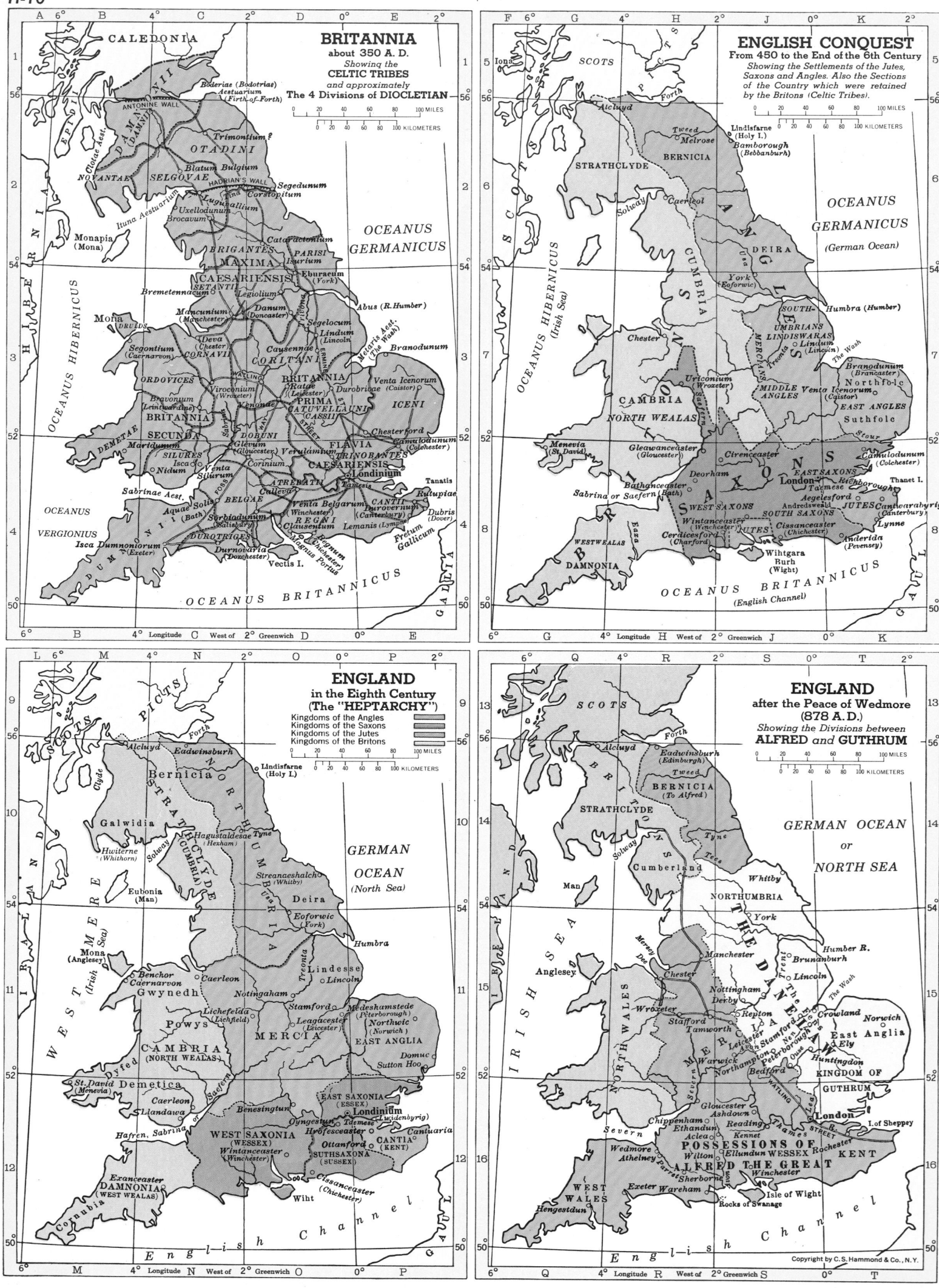

BRITANNIA
about 350 A.D.
Showing the
CELTIC TRIBES
and approximately
The 4 Divisions of DIOCLETIAN

ENGLISH CONQUEST
From 450 to the End of the 6th Century
Showing the Settlements of the Jutes, Saxons and Angles. Also the Sections of the Country which were retained by the Britons (Celtic Tribes).

ENGLAND
in the Eighth Century
(The "HEPTARCHY")
Kingdoms of the Angles
Kingdoms of the Saxons
Kingdoms of the Jutes
Kingdoms of the Britons

ENGLAND
after the Peace of Wedmore
(878 A.D.)
Showing the Divisions between
ALFRED *and* **GUTHRUM**

Copyright by C. S. Hammond & Co., N.Y.

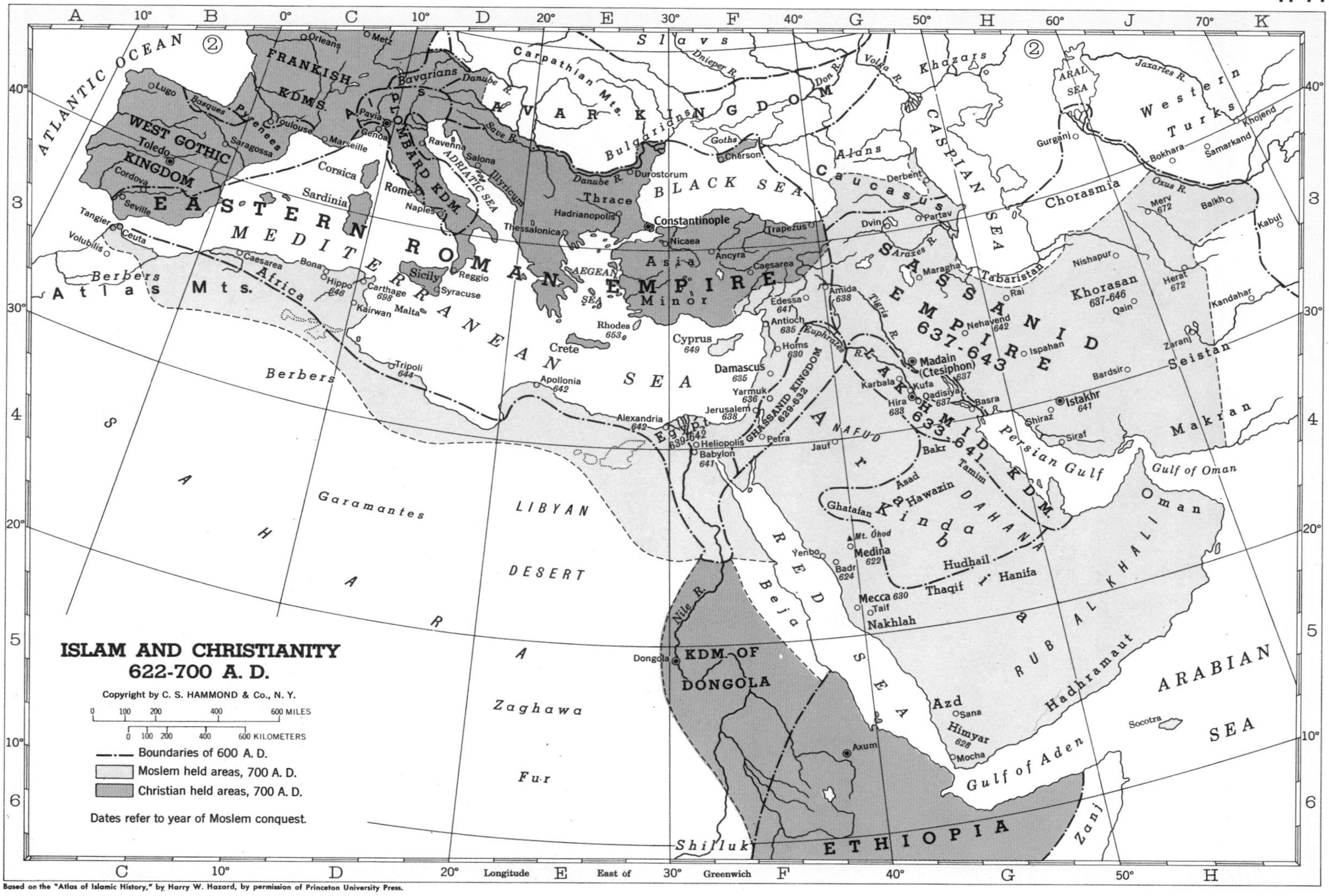

Map 1 (top)

A 10° B 0° C 10° D 20° E 30° F 40° G 50° H 60° J 70° K

②

ATLANTIC OCEAN

Orleans · Metz
FRANKISH KDMS.
Bavarians
Carpathian Mts.
Danube
Slavs
Dnieper R.
Khazars
Volga R.
Western Turks
ARAL SEA
Jaxartes R.

WEST GOTHIC KINGDOM
Lugo · Boxques · Pyrenees
Toledo · Toulouse · Marseille · Genoa
Saragossa
Cordova
Pavia · **LOMBARD KDM.** · Ravenna
Rome
AVAR KINGDOM
Goths
Alans
Gurgani
Chorasmia
Bokhara · Samarkand
Khojand

EASTERN ROMAN
Corsica
Sardinia
Salona
ILLYRICUM
Durostorum
Bulgarians
Thrace
BLACK SEA
Caucasus
Derbent
Merv 672
Balkh
Kabul

Tangier · Ceuta
Volubilis
Berbers
Atlas Mts.
Africa
Carthage 698
Hippo
Bona
Hadrumetum
Sicily
Reggio · Syracuse
Malta
MEDITERRANEAN
Naples
Rome
Adriatic Sea
Aegean Sea
Thessalonica
Hadrianopolis
Constantinople
Nicaea
Ancyra
Caesarea
Trapezus
Dvin
Partav
Araxes R.
Rai
Maragha
SASSANID
Tabaristan
Nishapur
Herat 672
Kandahar

Berbers
Tripoli 644
Apollonia 642
Crete
Rhodes 653?
Cyprus 649
Antioch 635
Amida 638
Edessa 641
Nehavend 642
Kufa
Ispahan
EMPIRE 637-643
Khorasan 637-646
Qain

SAHARA
LIBYAN DESERT
Garamantes
Alexandria 642
Heliopolis 640
Babylon 641
Damascus 635
Homs 636
Yarmuk 636
Jerusalem 638
Petra
Jauf
Madain (Ctesiphon)
Karbala · Kufa · Qadisiya 637
Hira 633
Basra
Shiraz · Istakhr 641
Siraf
Bardsir
Seistan
Makran

Zaghawa
Fur
Dongola · **KDM. OF DONGOLA**
Nile R.
RED SEA
Beja
Yenbo
Medina 622
Badr 624
Mecca 630
Taif
Nakhlah
Thaqif · Hanifa
Hudhail
DAHANA
Azd
Himyar 628
Sana · Mocha
Axum
ETHIOPIA
Shilluk
RUB AL KHALI
Hadramaut
Oman
Gulf of Oman
ARABIAN SEA
Socotra
Gulf of Aden
Zanj

ISLAM AND CHRISTIANITY
622-700 A.D.

Copyright by C. S. Hammond & Co., N. Y.

0 100 200 400 600 MILES
0 100 200 400 600 KILOMETERS

— · — Boundaries of 600 A.D.
☐ Moslem held areas, 700 A.D.
▨ Christian held areas, 700 A.D.

Dates refer to year of Moslem conquest.

C 10° D 20° Longitude E East of 30° Greenwich F 40° G 50° H

Based on the "Atlas of Islamic History," by Harry W. Hazard, by permission of Princeton University Press.

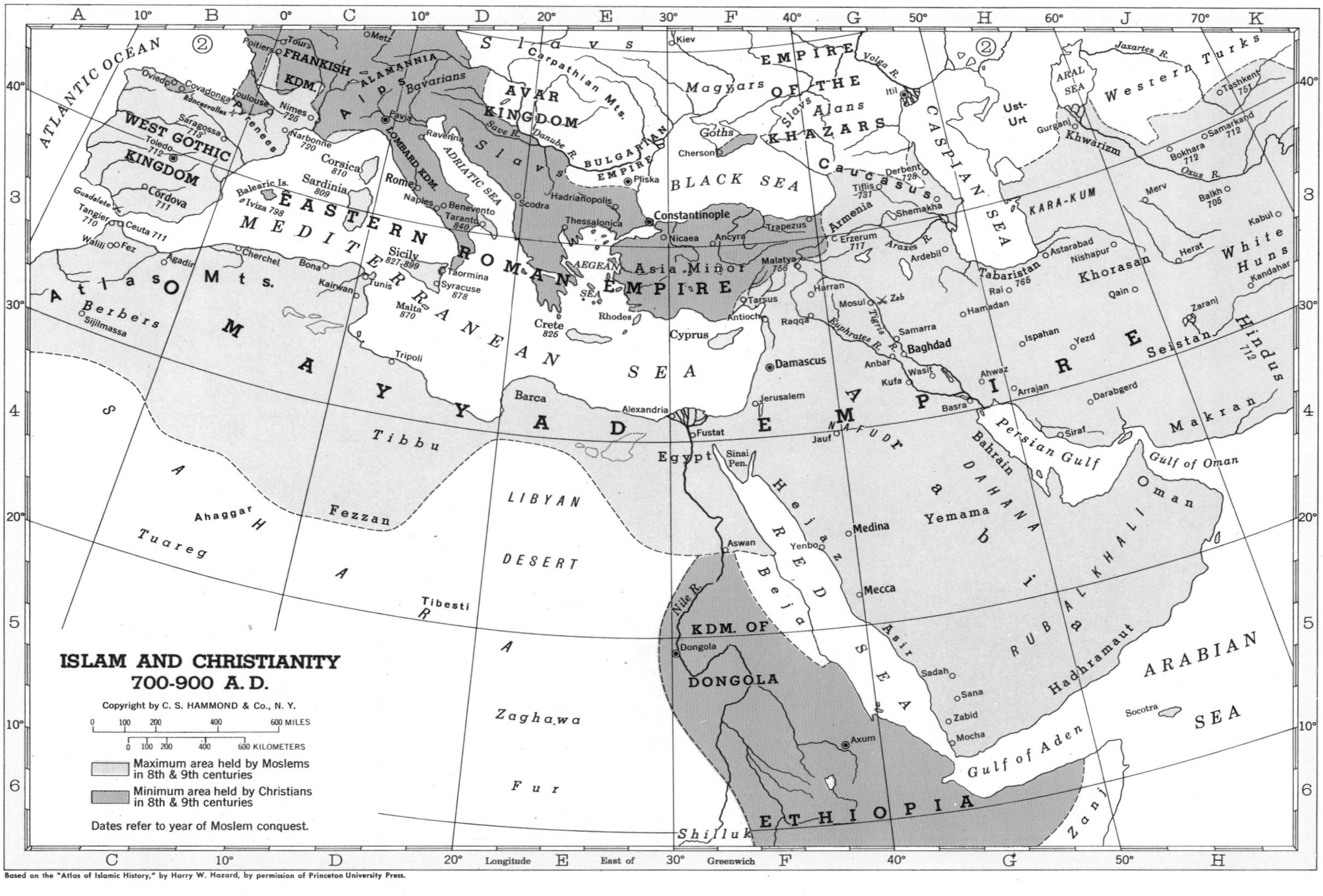

Map 2 (bottom)

A 10° B 0° C 10° D 20° E 30° F 40° G 50° H 60° J 70° K

②

ATLANTIC OCEAN

Tours · Metz
Poitiers · 732
FRANKISH KDM.
ALAMANNIA · Bavarians
Slavs
Kiev
Carpathian Mts.
EMPIRE OF THE
Volga R.
Western Turks
ARAL SEA
Jaxartes R.
Tashkent 751

WEST GOTHIC KINGDOM
Oviedo · Covadonga 718
Roncesvalles 778
Toledo 712 · Toulouse 721
Saragossa 712
Cordova 711
Nîmes 725
Narbonne 720
Pavia · **LOMBARD KDM.** · Ravenna
Rome
AVAR KINGDOM
Slavs
Goths
Magyars
KHAZARS
Alans
Itil
Ust-Urt
Gurgani
Khwarizm
Bokhara
Samarkand 712
Balkh 705
Kabul

Guadalete 711 · Corsica 810
Balearic Is. 809
Iviza 798
Sardinia
Benevento
Taranto 840
BULGARIAN EMPIRE
Pliska
Scodra
Hadrianopolis
Thessalonica
Constantinople
Nicaea · Ancyra
Trapezus
BLACK SEA
Cherson
Armenia
Erzerum 717
Derbent 728
Caucasus
Tiflis 731
KARA-KUM
Merv
Balkh
White Huns
Kandahar
Hindus

Tangier 709 · Ceuta 711
Walili 770 · Fez
Agadir
Cherchel
Bona
Kairwan
Tunis
Sicily 827-899
Taormina
Syracuse 878
Malta 870
MEDITERRANEAN
Naples
EASTERN ROMAN
Crete 825
Rhodes
Cyprus
Asia Minor EMPIRE
Tarsus
Antioch
Malatya 756
Harran
Mosul
Z'ab
Samarra
Baghdad
Anbar · Wasit
Kufa · Basra
Ahwaz
Arrajan
Hamadan
Rai 765
Tabaristan
Astarabad
Nishapur
Khorasan
Qain
Herat
Zaranj
Seistan
Makran

Berbers
Sijilmassa
Atlas Mts.
OMAYYAD
Tripoli
Barca
Alexandria
Fustat
Sinai Pen.
Jerusalem
Damascus
Jauf
EMPIRE
Bahrain
Persian Gulf
Siraf
Darabgerd
Gulf of Oman
Oman

S A H A R A
Ahaggar · Tibbu · Fezzan
Tuareg
Tibesti
LIBYAN DESERT
Egypt
Aswan
RED SEA
Beja
Yenbo
Medina
Mecca
Taif
Hejaz
Yemama
DAHANA
Asir
Sadah
Sana · Zabid · Mocha
Axum
Shilluk
ETHIOPIA
RUB AL KHALI
Hadramaut
ARABIAN SEA
Socotra
Gulf of Aden
Zanj

Zaghawa
Fur
Dongola · **KDM. OF DONGOLA**
Nile R.

ISLAM AND CHRISTIANITY
700-900 A.D.

Copyright by C. S. Hammond & Co., N. Y.

0 100 200 400 600 MILES
0 100 200 400 600 KILOMETERS

☐ Maximum area held by Moslems in 8th & 9th centuries
▨ Minimum area held by Christians in 8th & 9th centuries

Dates refer to year of Moslem conquest.

C 10° D 20° Longitude E East of 30° Greenwich F 40° G 50° H

Based on the "Atlas of Islamic History," by Harry W. Hazard, by permission of Princeton University Press.

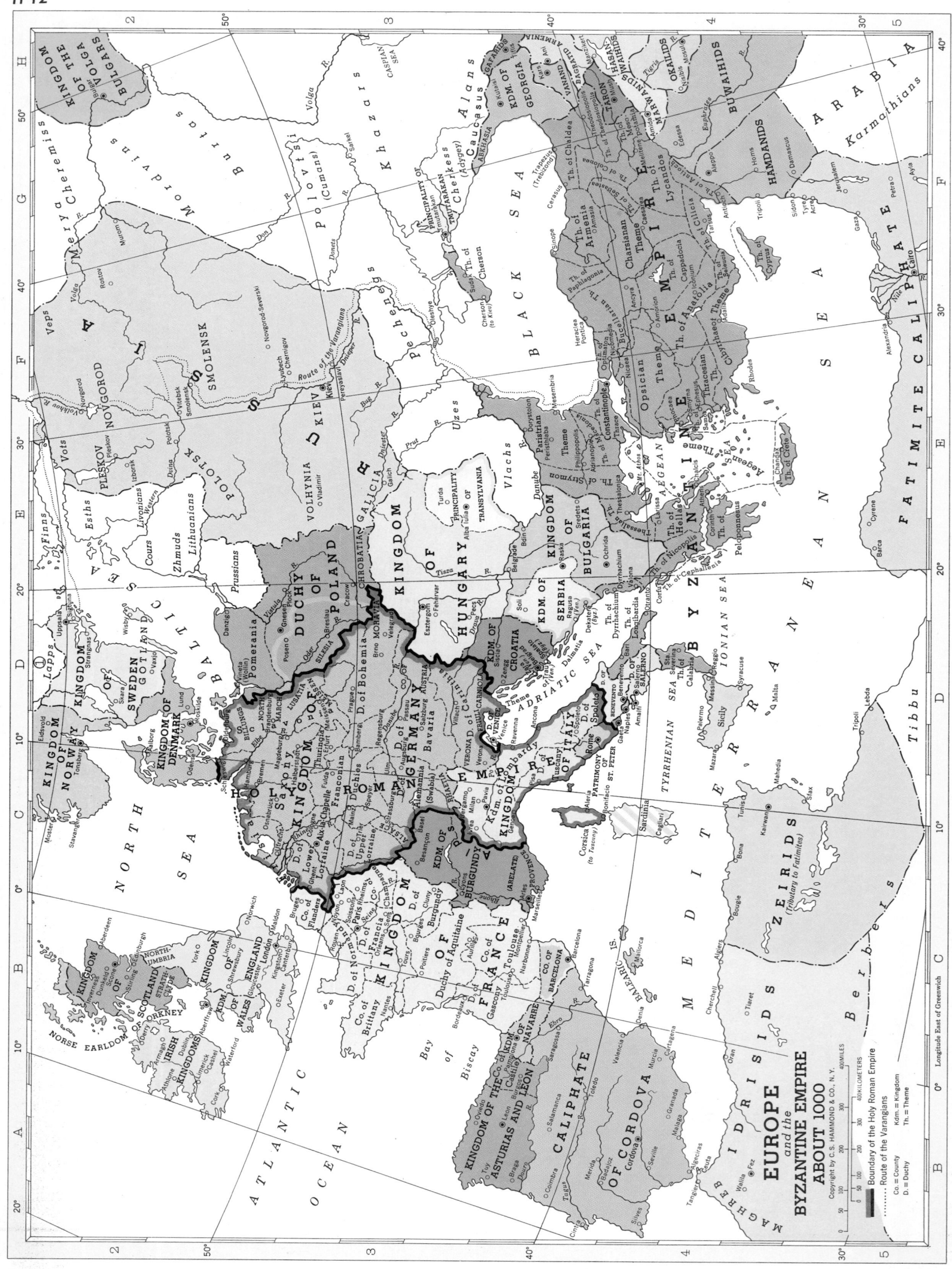

EUROPE
and the
BYZANTINE EMPIRE
ABOUT 1000

Copyright by C. S. Hammond & Co. N.Y.

Boundary of the Holy Roman Empire
...... Route of the Varangians

Co. = County
Kdm. = Kingdom
D. = Duchy
Th. = Theme

KINGDOM OF THE VOLGA BULGARS

Merya Cheremiss

Mordvins

Poloutsi (Cumans)

Khazars

CASPIAN SEA

ALANIA

KDM. OF GEORGIA

ARMENIA

CAPARIDS

HASAN
JWAIHIDS

OKAILIDS

BUWAIHIDS

ARABIA

Karmathians

BLACK SEA

BYZANTINE EMPIRE

HAMDANIDS

FATIMITE CALIPHATE

FINLAND

SMOLENSK

NOVGOROD

PLESKOV

POLOTSK

KIEV

VOLHYNIA

GALICIA

CHROBATIA

KINGDOM OF POLAND

DUCHY OF POLAND

Pomerania

KINGDOM OF HUNGARY

PRINCIPALITY OF TRANSYLVANIA

Vlachs

KINGDOM OF BULGARIA

KDM. OF SERBIA

KDM. OF CROATIA

ADRIATIC SEA

AEGEAN SEA

KINGDOM OF SWEDEN

GOTLAND

KINGDOM OF DENMARK

KINGDOM OF NORWAY

BALTIC SEA

Prussians

Lithuanians

Esths

Livonians

Cours

Zhmuds

Finns

Lapps

NORTH SEA

HOLY ROMAN EMPIRE

KINGDOM OF GERMANY

D. of Bohemia

MORAVIA

Bavaria

AUSTRIA

CARINTHIA

CARNIOLA

D. OF VENICE

KINGDOM OF ITALY

Lombardy

Tuscany

PATRIMONY OF ST. PETER

D. of Spoleto

KDM. OF BURGUNDY

PROVENCE

KINGDOM OF FRANCE

Duchy of Aquitaine

Co. of Flanders

D. of Normandy

D. of Brittany

Co. of Toulouse

Co. of Barcelona

KDM. OF NAVARRE

CALIPHATE OF CORDOVA

KINGDOM OF THE ASTURIAS AND LEON

KINGDOM OF ENGLAND

KINGDOM OF SCOTLAND

WALES

IRISH KINGDOMS

NORSE EARLDOM OF ORKNEY

ATLANTIC OCEAN

Bay of Biscay

MEDITERRANEAN SEA

TYRRHENIAN SEA

IONIAN SEA

Sicily

Sardinia

Corsica

ZEIRIDS (Tributary to Fatimites)

IDRISIDS

MAGHREB

Berbers

Tibbu

MEDITERRANEAN LANDS IN 1097

Copyright by C.S. HAMMOND & Co., N.Y.

First Crusade, 1096-99
Second Crusade, 1147-49
Third Crusade, 1189-91

THE CALIFATE IN 750

Copyright by C. S. HAMMOND & Co., N.Y.

Dominions of Mohammed (632)
Conquests of the first three Califs (632-659)
Conquests of the Omayyads (661-750)

MEDITERRANEAN LANDS AFTER 1204

Copyright by C.S. HAMMOND & Co., N.Y.

Fourth Crusade, 1202-04
Crusade of Friedrich II, 1228-29
Crusades of Louis IX, 1248-54 and in 1270
Venetian possessions
Genoese acquisitions after 1261 underlined: Pera

LATIN STATES IN SYRIA
After the 1st Crusade

Dates are those of conquests by the Crusaders; years of losses in italics.

Kingdom of Jerusalem 1099 (1187) 1229 (1244)

Copyright by C.S. HAMMOND & Co., N.Y.

Area held by Crusaders after the Treaty of 1229.

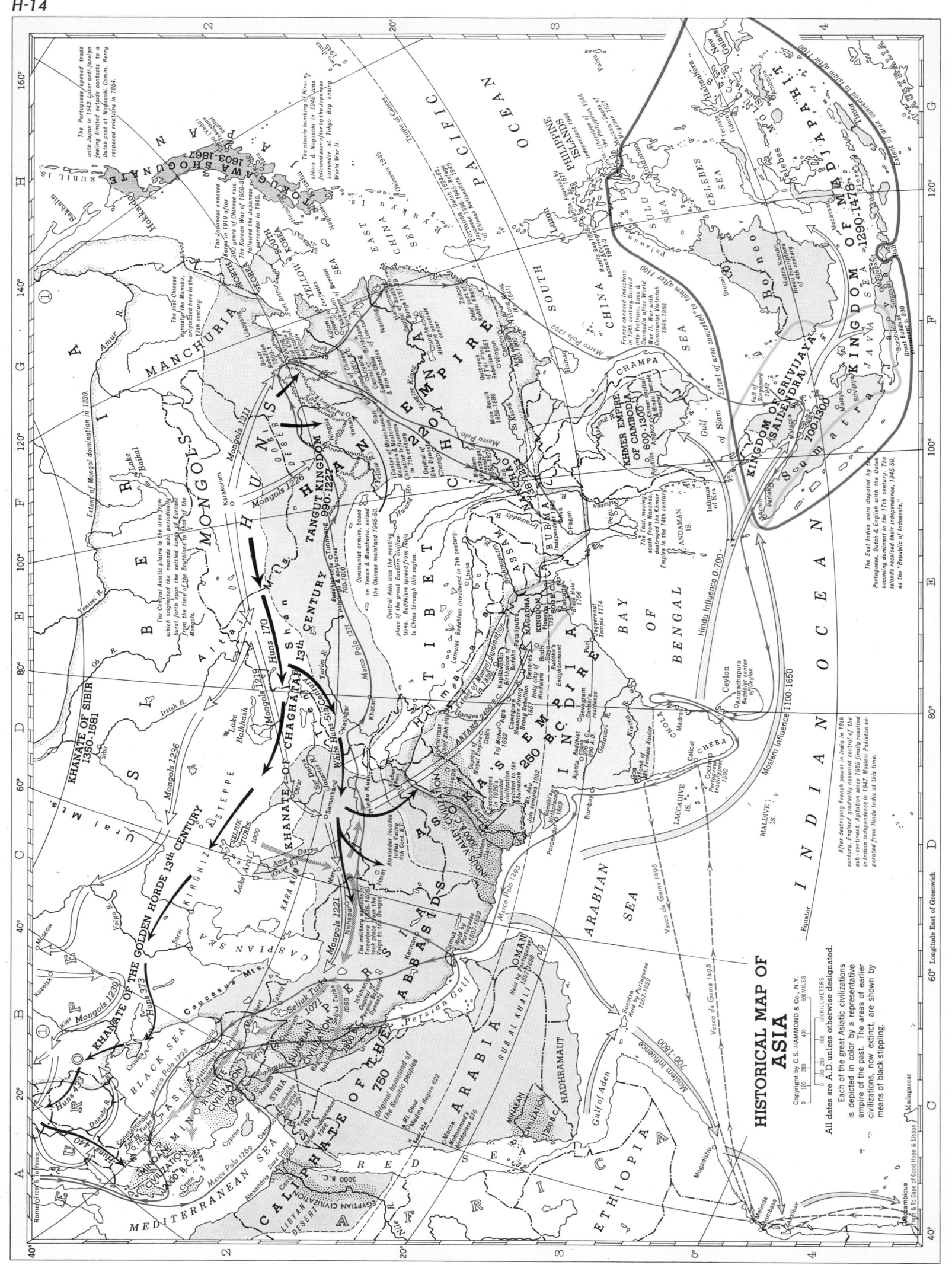

HISTORICAL MAP OF ASIA

Copyright by C.S. HAMMOND & Co., N.Y.

All dates are A.D. unless otherwise designated.

Each of the great Asiatic civilizations is depicted in color by a representative empire of the past. The areas of earlier civilizations, now extinct, are shown by means of black stippling.

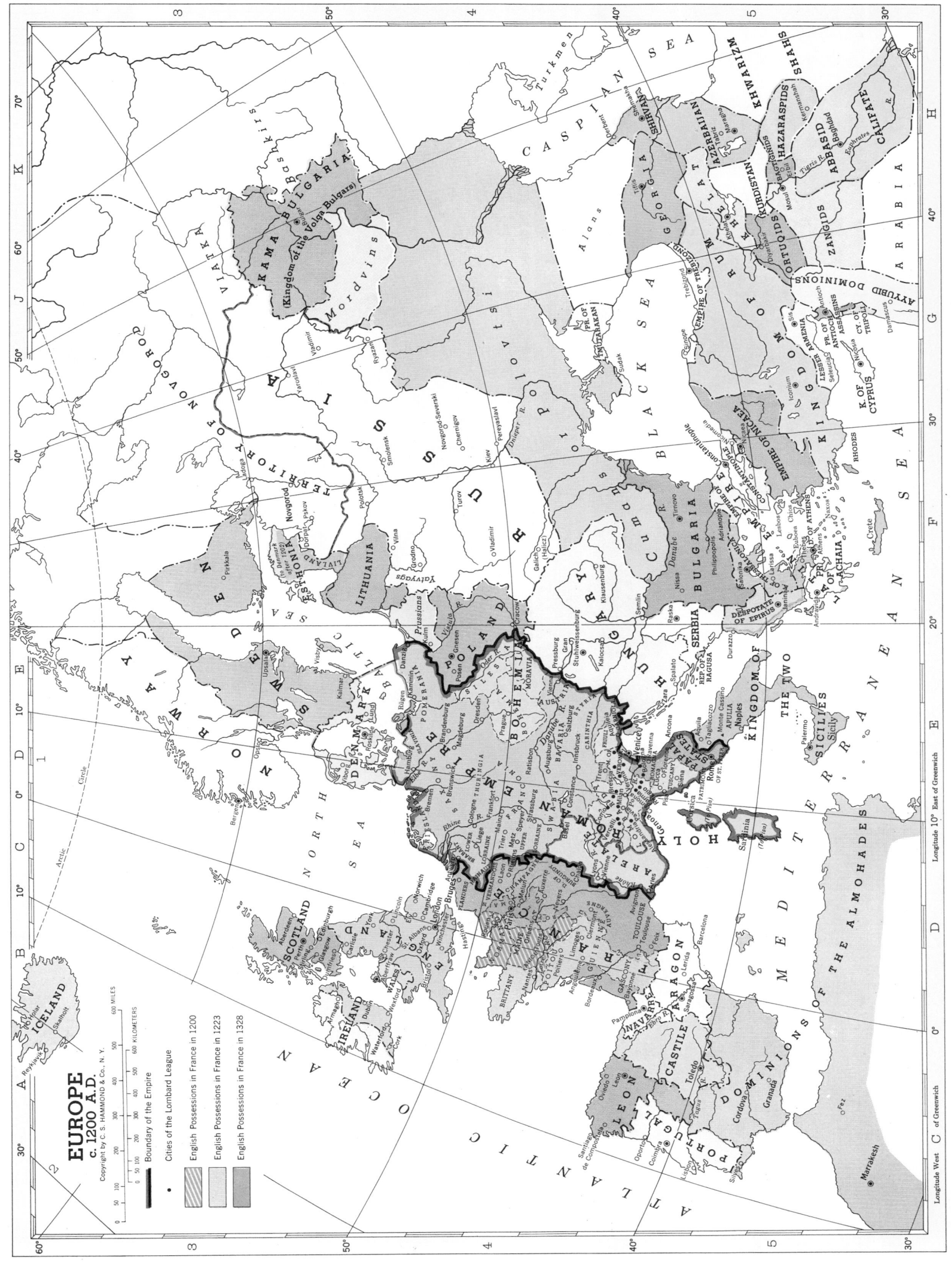

EUROPE
c. 1200 A.D.

Copyright by C. S. HAMMOND & Co., N.Y.

Boundary of the Empire

• Cities of the Lombard League

English Possessions in France in 1200

English Possessions in France in 1223

English Possessions in France in 1328

GREENLAND

Gardar

(To Trondjem)

Same scale as main map

ECCLESIASTICAL MAP OF
EUROPE
c. 1300 A.D.

Archbishoprics
Bishoprics
Monasteries
Universities
The Archepiscopal provinces are colored

C.S. HAMMOND & CO., N.Y.

Longitude West 0° East of Greenwich

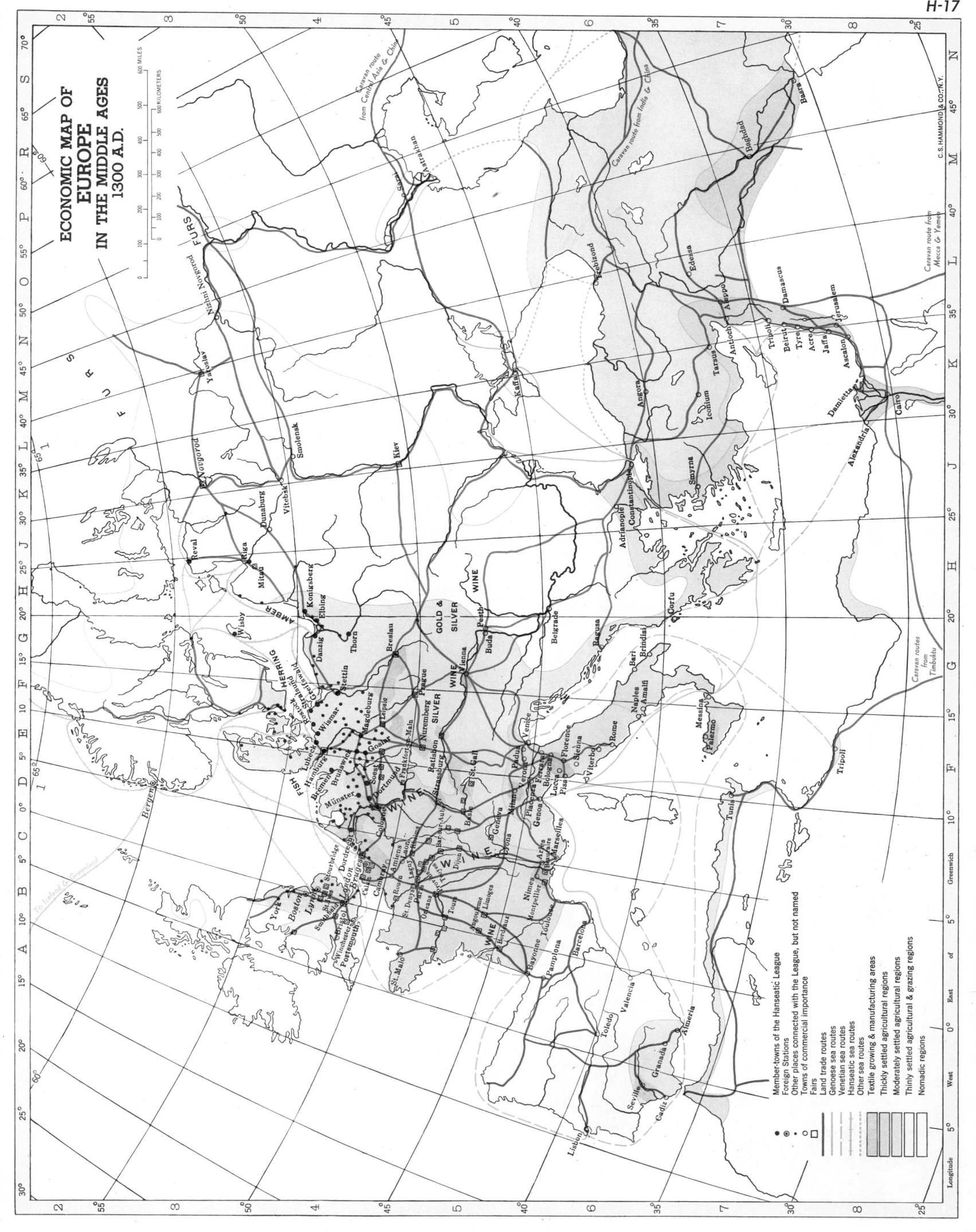

ECONOMIC MAP OF
EUROPE
IN THE MIDDLE AGES
1300 A.D.

600 MILES
600 KILOMETERS

C.S. HAMMOND & CO., N.Y.

Member-towns of the Hanseatic League
Foreign Stations
Other places connected with the League, but not named
Towns of commercial importance
Fairs
Land trade routes
Genoese sea routes
Venetian sea routes
Hanseatic sea routes
Other sea routes
Textile growing & manufacturing areas
Thickly settled agricultural regions
Moderately settled agricultural regions
Thinly settled agricultural & grazing regions
Nomadic regions

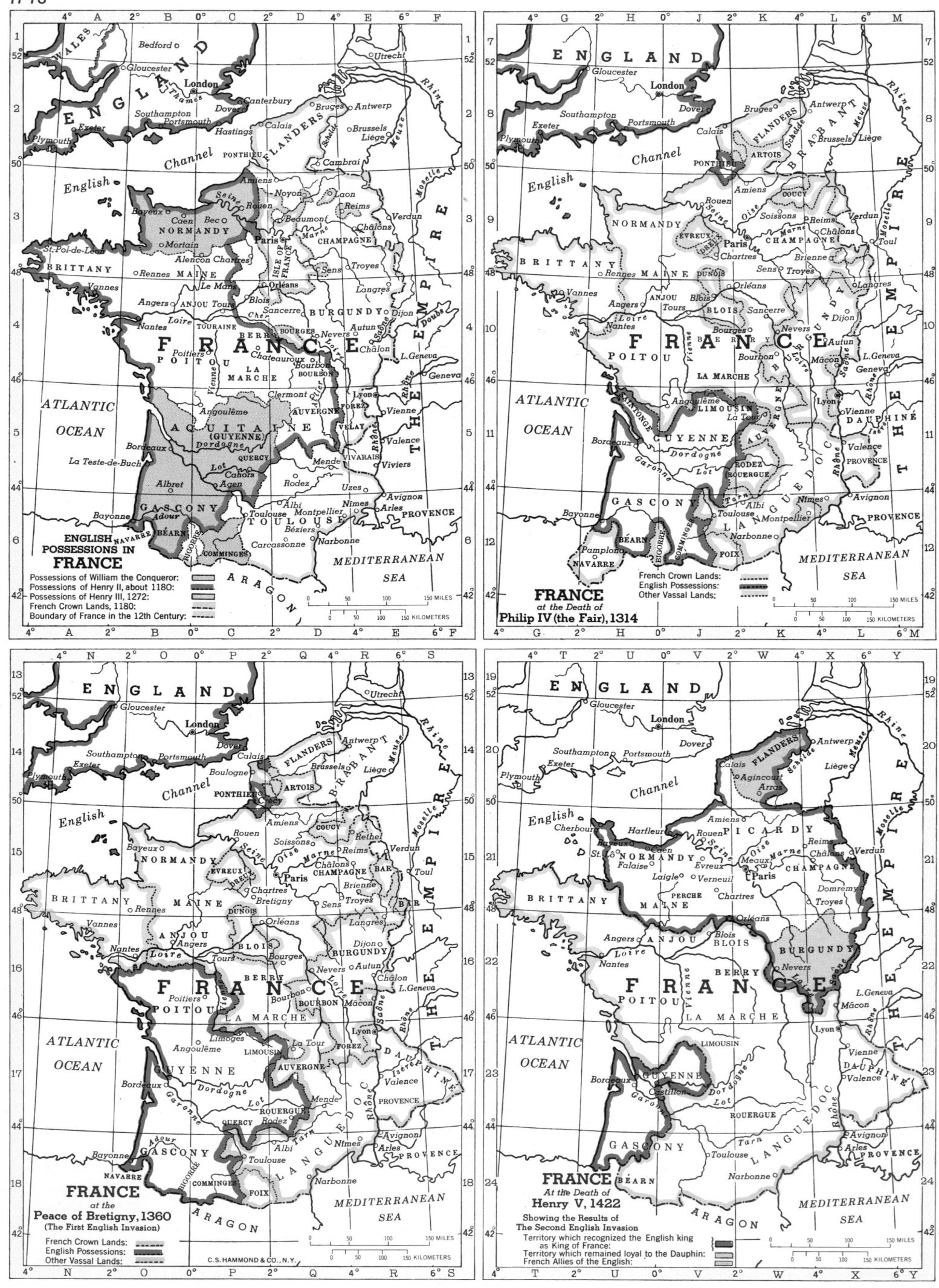

ENGLISH POSSESSIONS IN FRANCE

Possessions of William the Conqueror:
Possessions of Henry II, about 1180:
Possessions of Henry III, 1272:
French Crown Lands, 1180:
Boundary of France in the 12th Century:

FRANCE
at the Death of
Philip IV (the Fair), 1314

French Crown Lands:
English Possessions:
Other Vassal Lands:

FRANCE
at the
Peace of Bretigny, 1360
(The First English Invasion)

French Crown Lands:
English Possessions:
Other Vassal Lands:

C. S. HAMMOND & CO., N.Y.

FRANCE
At the Death of
Henry V, 1422

Showing the Results of
The Second English Invasion
Territory which recognized the English king
as King of France:
Territory which remained loyal to the Dauphin:
French Allies of the English:

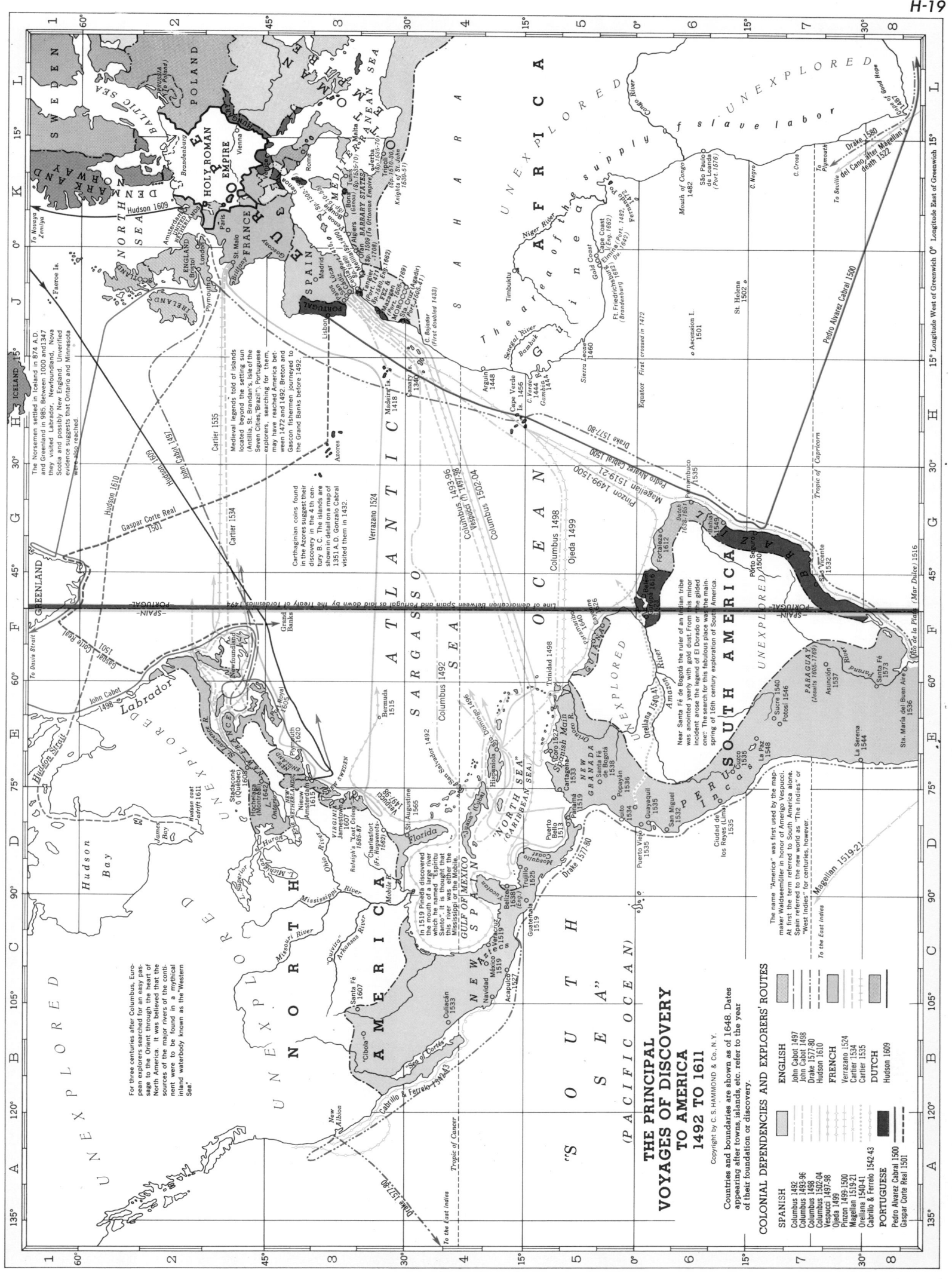

THE PRINCIPAL VOYAGES OF DISCOVERY TO AMERICA 1492 TO 1611

Copyright by C. S. HAMMOND & Co., N.Y.

Countries and boundaries are shown as of 1648. Dates appearing after towns, islands, etc. refer to the year of their foundation or discovery.

COLONIAL DEPENDENCIES AND EXPLORERS' ROUTES

SPANISH
Columbus 1492
Columbus 1493-96
Columbus 1498
Vespucci 1497-98
Ojeda 1499
Pinzón 1499-1500
Magellan 1519-21
Orellana 1540-41
Cabrillo & Ferrelo 1542-43

ENGLISH
John Cabot 1497
John Cabot 1498
Drake 1577-80
Hudson 1610

FRENCH
Verrazano 1524
Cartier 1534
Cartier 1535

DUTCH
Hudson 1609

PORTUGESE
Pedro Alvarez Cabral 1500
Gaspar Corte Real 1501

For three centuries after Columbus, European explorers searched for an easy passage to the Orient through the heart of North America. It was believed that the sources of the major rivers of the continent were to be found in a mythical inland waterbody known as the "Western Sea."

Medieval legends told of islands located beyond the setting sun (Antilia, St. Brandan's, Isle of the Seven Cities, "Brazil"). Portuguese explorers, searching for them, may have reached America between 1472 and 1492. Breton and Gascon fishermen journeyed to the Grand Banks before 1492.

Carthaginian coins found in the Azores suggest their discovery in the 4th century B.C. The islands are shown in detail on a map of 1351 A.D. Gonzalo Cabral visited them in 1432.

The Norsemen settled in Iceland in 874 A.D. and Greenland in 985. Between 1000 and 1347 they visited Labrador, Newfoundland, Nova Scotia and possibly New England. Unverified evidence suggests that Ontario and Minnesota were also reached.

In 1519 Pineda discovered the mouth of a large river which he named "Espíritu Santo". It is thought that this river was either the Mississippi or the Mobile.

Near Santa Fé de Bogotá the ruler of an Indian tribe was anointed yearly with gold dust. From this minor incident arose the legend of El Dorado or the gilded one". The search for this fabulous place was the mainspring of 16th century exploration of South America.

The name "America" was first used by the mapmaker Waldseemüller in honor of Amerigo Vespucci. At first the term referred to South America alone. Spain referred to the new world as "The Indies" or "West Indies" for centuries, however.

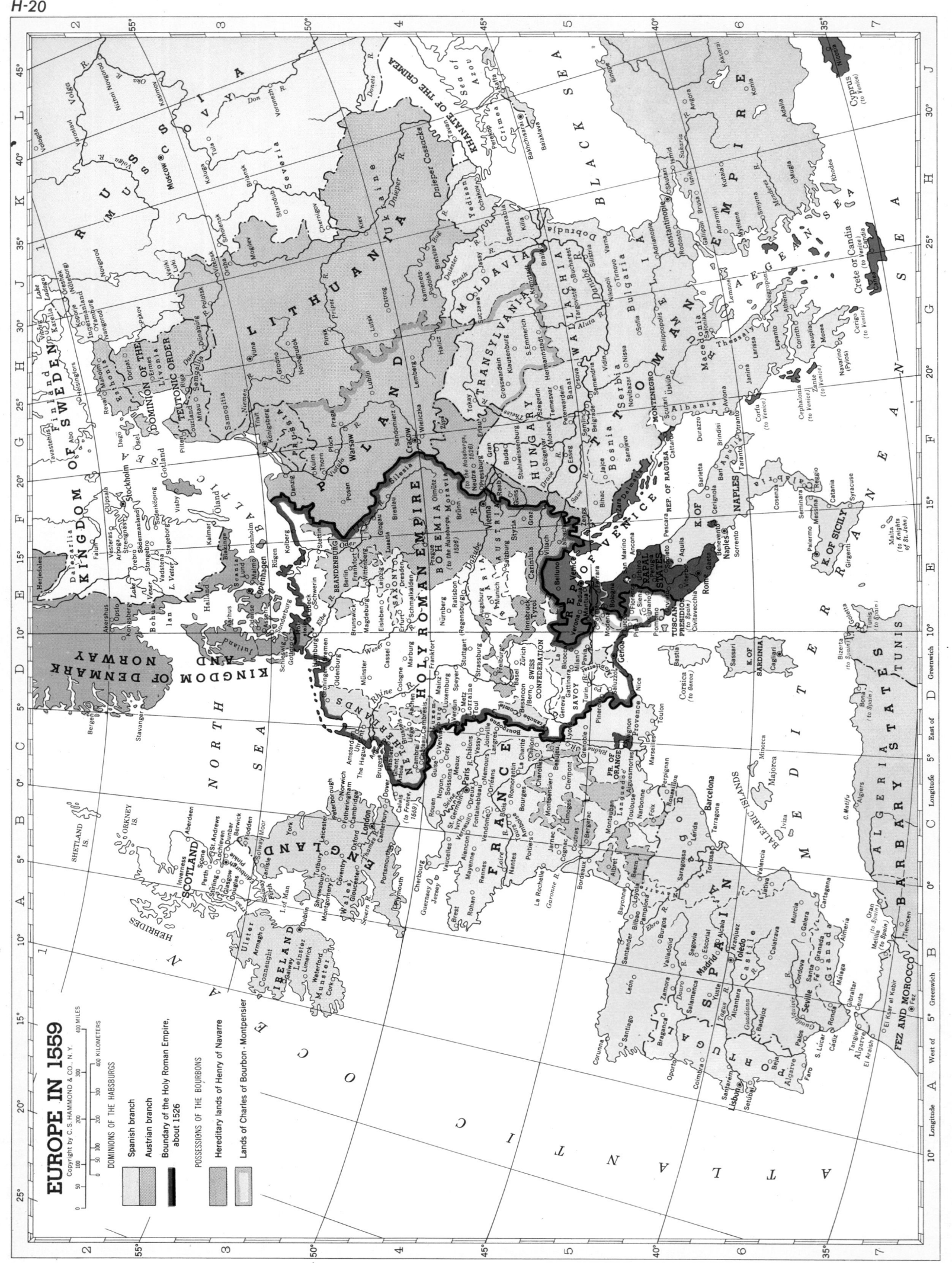

EUROPE IN 1559

Copyright by C.S. HAMMOND & CO., N.Y.

DOMINIONS OF THE HABSBURGS
- Spanish branch
- Austrian branch
- Boundary of the Holy Roman Empire, about 1526

POSSESSIONS OF THE BOURBONS
- Hereditary lands of Henry of Navarre
- Lands of Charles of Bourbon-Montpensier

EUROPE IN 1648
AT THE PEACE OF WESTPHALIA

Copyright by C. S. HAMMOND & CO., N.Y.

Boundary of the Empire

Church Lands

Transylvania, independent of
Hungarian Kingdom with Turkish
Backing.

DOMINIONS OF THE HABSBURGS

Spanish Branch

Austrian Branch

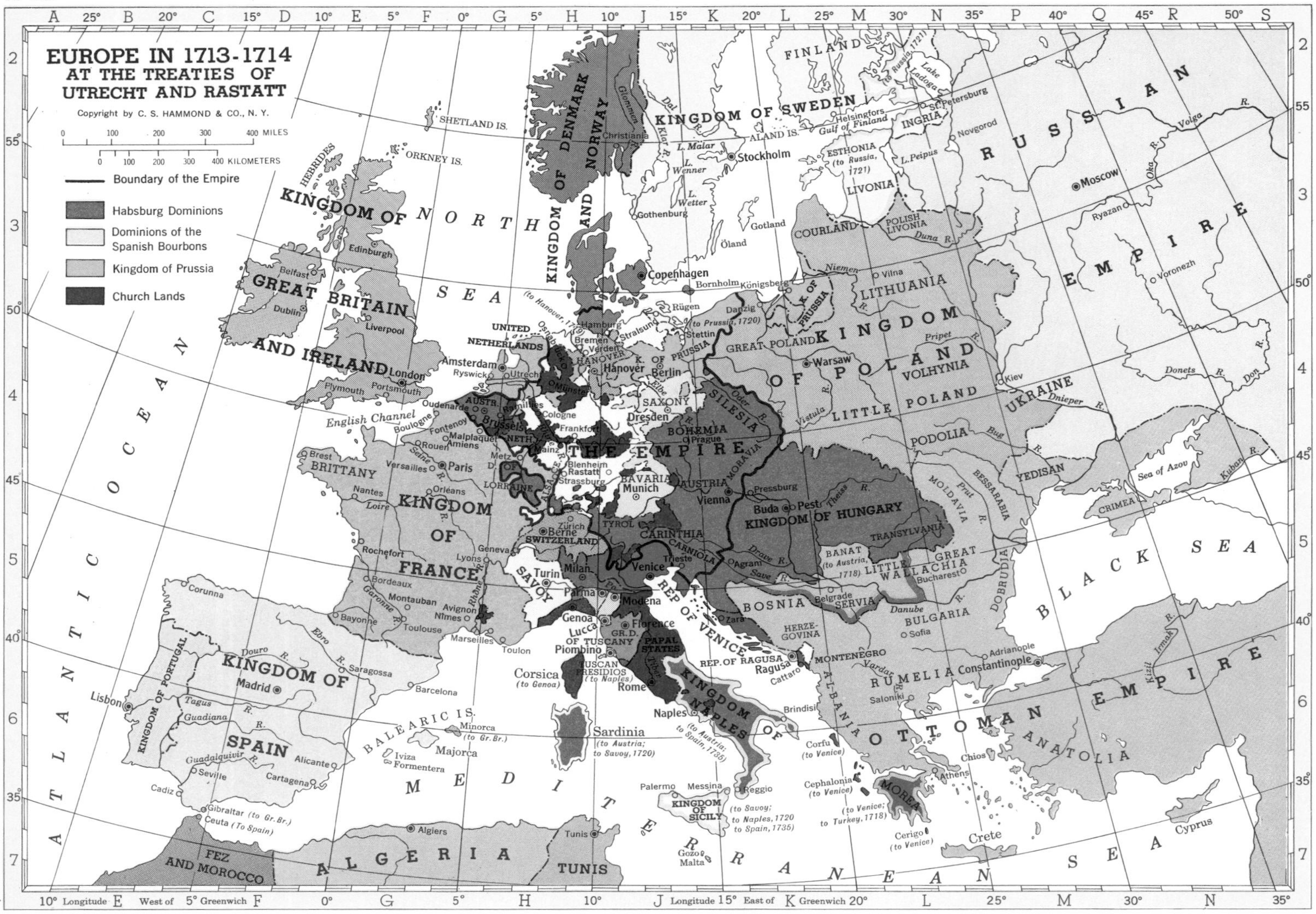

EUROPE IN 1713-1714
AT THE TREATIES OF
UTRECHT AND RASTATT
Copyright by C. S. HAMMOND & CO., N. Y.
MILES
KILOMETERS
Boundary of the Empire
Habsburg Dominions
Dominions of the Spanish Bourbons
Kingdom of Prussia
Church Lands
KINGDOM OF GREAT BRITAIN AND IRELAND
NORTH SEA
ATLANTIC OCEAN
KINGDOM OF DENMARK AND NORWAY
KINGDOM OF SWEDEN
RUSSIAN EMPIRE
KINGDOM OF POLAND
LITHUANIA
THE EMPIRE
KINGDOM OF FRANCE
KINGDOM OF SPAIN
KINGDOM OF PORTUGAL
KINGDOM OF HUNGARY
KINGDOM OF NAPLES
KINGDOM OF SICILY
OTTOMAN EMPIRE
BLACK SEA
MEDITERRANEAN SEA
ALGERIA
TUNIS
FEZ AND MOROCCO
UNITED NETHERLANDS
SWITZERLAND
SAVOY
REP. OF VENICE
PAPAL STATES
Sardinia (to Austria; to Savoy, 1720)
Corsica (to Genoa)
Gibraltar (to Gr. Br.)
Minorca (to Gr. Br.)
Longitude West of Greenwich
Longitude East of Greenwich

1682
1713
1763
1783
Copyright by C. S. HAMMOND & Co., N. Y.
CHANGING OWNERSHIP OF THE CONTINENT
ENGLISH
FRENCH
SPANISH
INDEPENDENT
2561

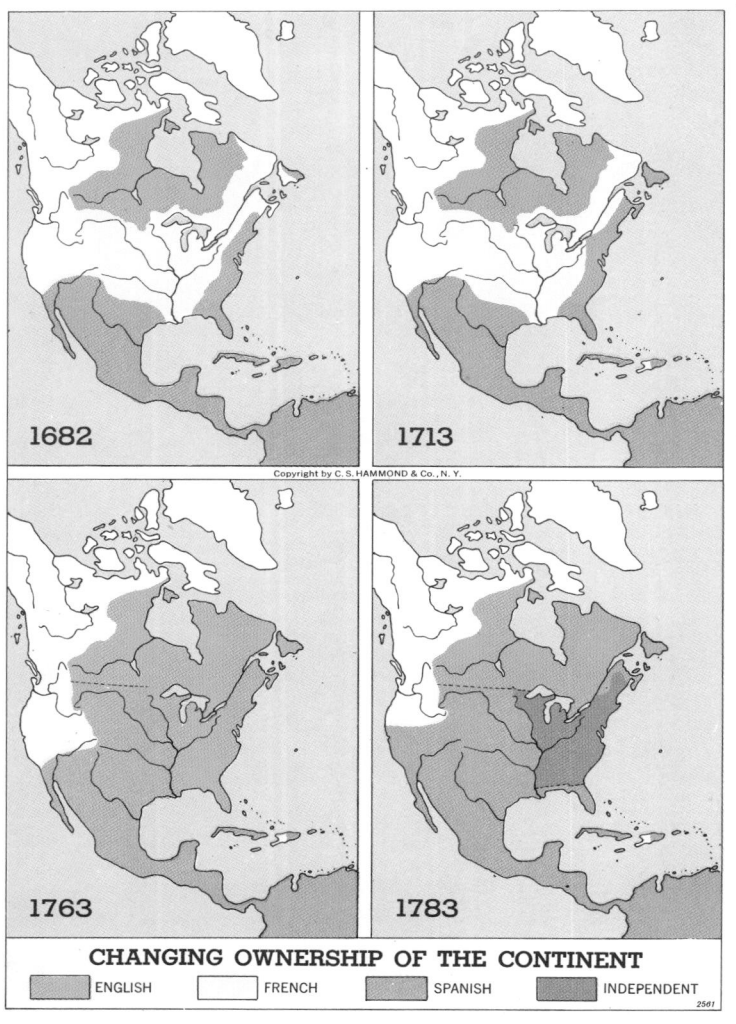

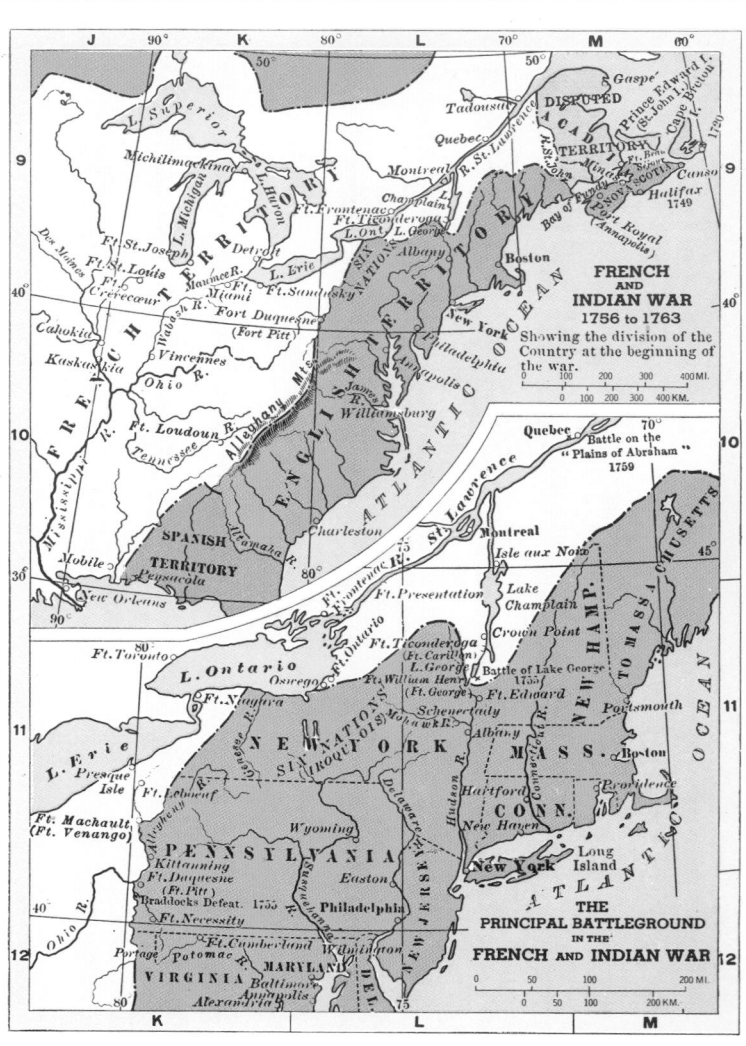

FRENCH AND INDIAN WAR
1756 to 1763
Showing the division of the Country at the beginning of the war.
FRENCH TERRITORY
ENGLISH TERRITORY
SPANISH TERRITORY
DISPUTED ACADIAN TERRITORY
ATLANTIC OCEAN
Battle on the "Plains of Abraham" 1759
THE PRINCIPAL BATTLEGROUND IN THE FRENCH AND INDIAN WAR
NEW YORK
PENNSYLVANIA
MASS.
CONN.
NEW HAMP.
NEW JERSEY
MARYLAND
VIRGINIA
SIX NATIONS (IROQUOIS)
Battle of Lake George 1755
Braddocks Defeat. 1755
L. Ontario
L. Erie

EUROPE IN 1763

Copyright by C. S. HAMMOND & CO., N.Y.

Boundary of the Holy Roman Empire

Habsburg Dominions

Kingdom of Prussia

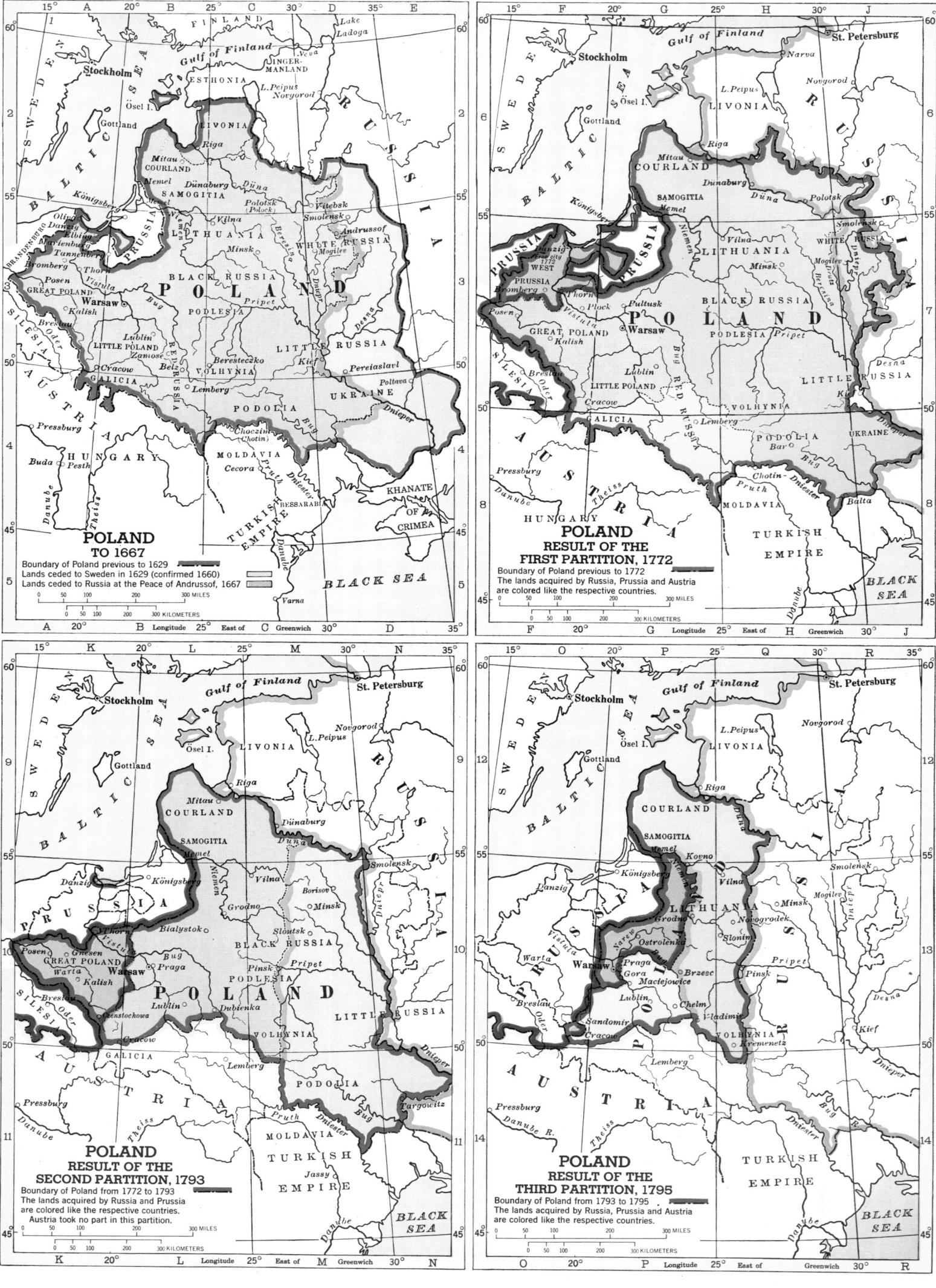

POLAND
TO 1667

Boundary of Poland previous to 1629
Lands ceded to Sweden in 1629 (confirmed 1660)
Lands ceded to Russia at the Peace of Andrussof, 1667

0   50 100   200   300 MILES
0   50 100   200   300 KILOMETERS

POLAND
RESULT OF THE
FIRST PARTITION, 1772

Boundary of Poland previous to 1772
The lands acquired by Russia, Prussia and Austria
are colored like the respective countries.

0   50 100   200   300 MILES
0   50 100   200   300 KILOMETERS

POLAND
RESULT OF THE
SECOND PARTITION, 1793

Boundary of Poland from 1772 to 1793
The lands acquired by Russia and Prussia
are colored like the respective countries.
Austria took no part in this partition.

0   50 100   200   300 MILES
0   50 100   200   300 KILOMETERS

POLAND
RESULT OF THE
THIRD PARTITION, 1795

Boundary of Poland from 1793 to 1795
The lands acquired by Russia, Prussia and Austria
are colored like the respective countries.

0   50 100   200   300 MILES
0   50 100   200   300 KILOMETERS

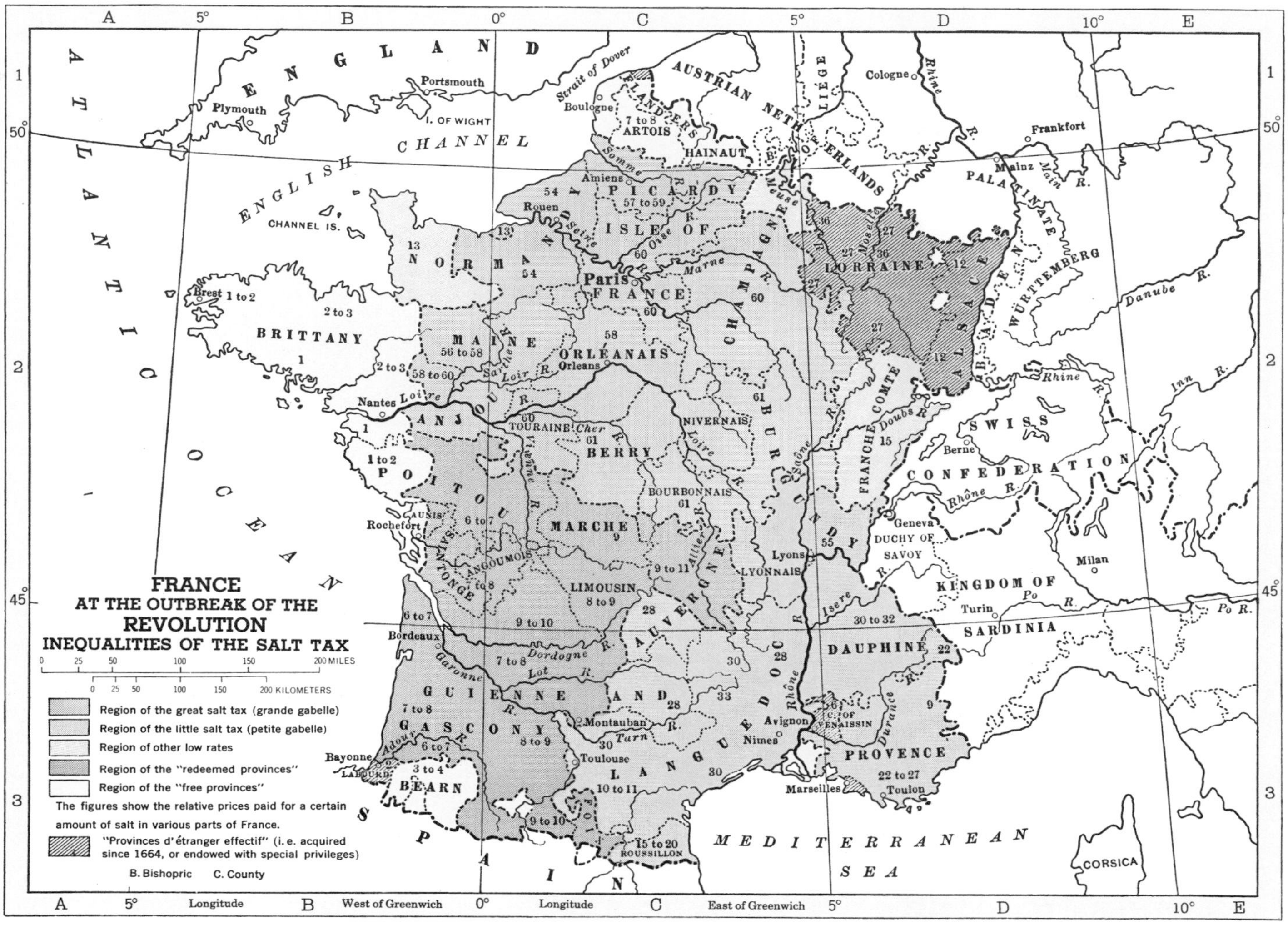

FRANCE
AT THE OUTBREAK OF THE REVOLUTION
INEQUALITIES OF THE SALT TAX

ATLANTIC OCEAN

ENGLAND
Portsmouth
Plymouth
I. OF WIGHT
ENGLISH CHANNEL
CHANNEL IS.
Strait of Dover
Boulogne
AUSTRIAN NETHERLANDS
FLANDERS
ARTOIS 7 to 8
HAINAUT
Liège
Cologne
Rhine R.
Frankfort
Mainz
Amiens
Rouen
PICARDY 57 to 59
54
ISLE OF FRANCE
Somme R.
Oise R.
PALATINATE
Main R.
NORMANDY 13
54
Seine R.
Paris
Marne R.
CHAMPAGNE
LORRAINE 36
ALSACE 12
27
WÜRTTEMBERG
Danube R.
Brest 1 to 2
2 to 3
BRITTANY 1
MAINE 56 to 58
Loir R.
ORLEANAIS 58
Orleans
60
FRANCHE COMTÉ 15
Rhine
SWISS CONFEDERATION
Berne
Nantes
Loire R.
2 to 3
58 to 60
ANJOU 61
TOURAINE
Cher R.
Vienne R.
BERRY
NIVERNAIS
Loire R.
BURGUNDY
Doubs R.
55
Milan
POITOU 1 to 2
MARCHE 9
BOURBONNAIS 61
AUVERGNE
9 to 11
Saône R.
Rhône R.
Lyons
LYONNAIS
55
Geneva
DUCHY OF SAVOY
KINGDOM OF SARDINIA
Turin
Po R.
AUNIS 6 to 7
Rochefort
LIMOUSIN 8 to 9
28
Isère R.
30 to 32
Bordeaux
9 to 10
Dordogne R.
Lot R.
30
28
33
28
LANGUEDOC 33
DAUPHINE 22
Rhône R.
Durance R.
ANGOUMOIS 6 to 8
SAINTONGE 7 to 8
GUIENNE AND GASCONY 7 to 8
8 to 9
Garonne R.
Montauban
Tarn R.
30
Toulouse 10 to 11
Avignon
C. OF VENAISSIN
Nîmes
PROVENCE 22 to 27
Marseilles
Toulon
Bayonne
LABOURD 6 to 7
BÉARN 3 to 4
9 to 10
SPAIN
15 to 20 ROUSSILLON
MEDITERRANEAN SEA
CORSICA

Legend
- Region of the great salt tax (grande gabelle)
- Region of the little salt tax (petite gabelle)
- Region of other low rates
- Region of the "redeemed provinces"
- Region of the "free provinces"

The figures show the relative prices paid for a certain amount of salt in various parts of France.

"Provinces d'étranger effectif" (i. e. acquired since 1664, or endowed with special privileges)

B. Bishopric   C. County

SCALE
0 25 50 100 150 200 MILES
0 25 50 100 150 200 KILOMETERS

Longitude West of Greenwich 0° Longitude East of Greenwich

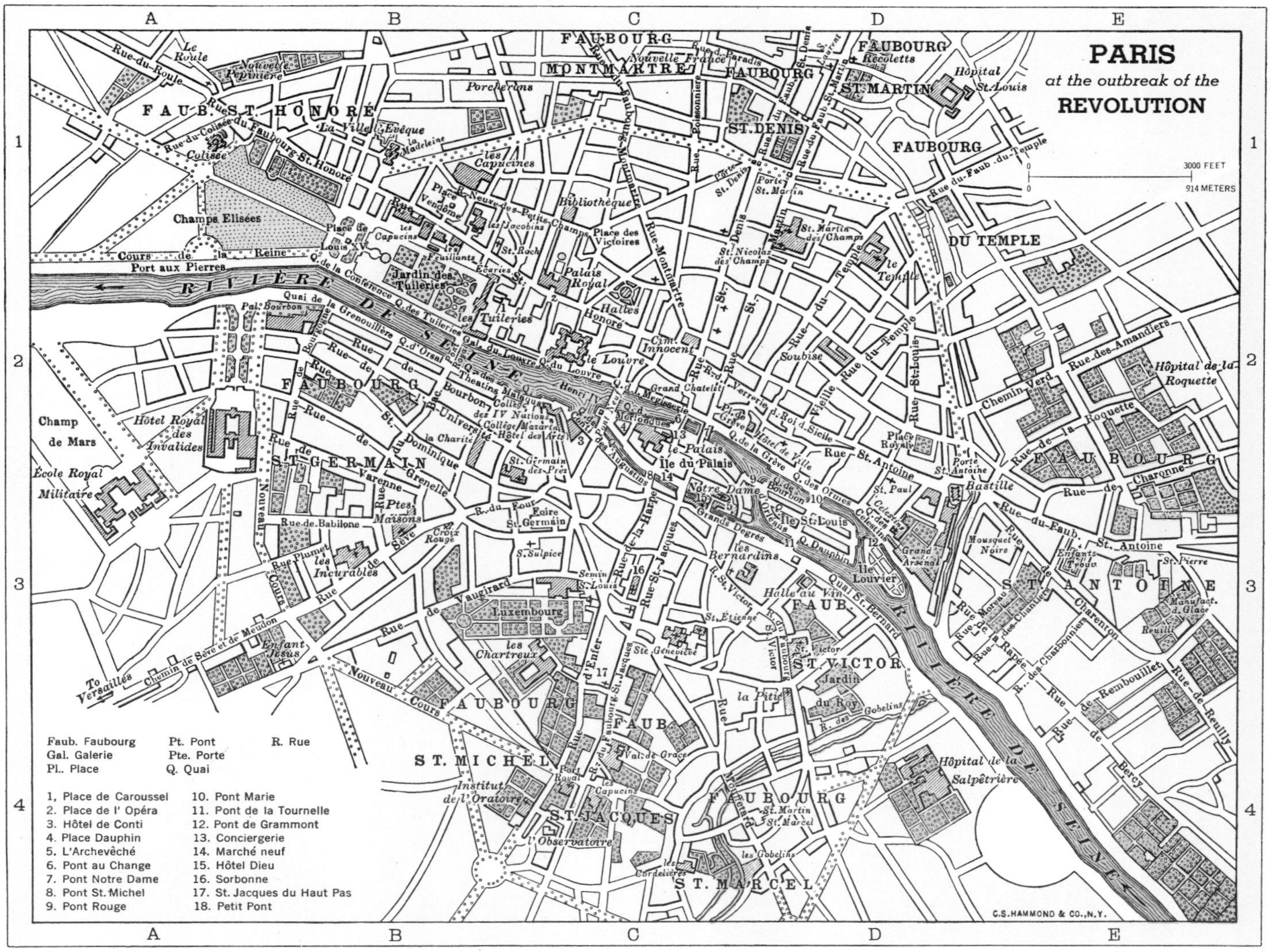

PARIS
at the outbreak of the REVOLUTION

SCALE
0 3000 FEET
0 914 METERS

RIVIÈRE DE SEINE

FAUB. ST. HONORÉ
Le Roule
Rue du Roule
Nouvelle Pépinière
FAUBOURG MONTMARTRE
FAUBOURG ST. DENIS
FAUBOURG ST. MARTIN
Hôpital St. Louis
FAUBOURG DU TEMPLE
Champs Elisées
Cours de la Reine
Port aux Pierres
Jardin des Tuileries
les Tuileries
Palais Royal
Bibliothèque
les Capucines
Place des Victoires
Porte St. Denis
Porte St. Martin
le Temple
Rue des Amandiers
Champ de Mars
Hôtel Royal des Invalides
École Royal Militaire
FAUBOURG ST. GERMAIN
Collège des IV Nations
le Louvre
Halles
Grand Châtelet
Île du Palais
Place de Grève
St. Antoine
Porte St. Antoine
Bastille
FAUBOURG ST. ANTOINE
Hôpital de la Roquette
Notre Dame
l'Arsenal
Luxembourg
les Chartreux
Sorbonne
FAUBOURG ST. VICTOR
Jardin du Roy
les Gobelins
FAUBOURG ST. MICHEL
FAUBOURG ST. JACQUES
Institut de l'Oratoire
Observatoire
FAUBOURG ST. MARCEL
Hôpital de la Salpêtrière

Abbreviations
Faub. Faubourg   Pt. Pont   R. Rue
Gal. Galerie   Pte. Porte
Pl. Place   Q. Quai

1. Place de Caroussel
2. Place de l' Opéra
3. Hôtel de Conti
4. Place Dauphin
5. L'Archevêché
6. Pont au Change
7. Pont Notre Dame
8. Pont St. Michel
9. Pont Rouge
10. Pont Marie
11. Pont de la Tournelle
12. Pont de Grammont
13. Conciergerie
14. Marché neuf
15. Hôtel Dieu
16. Sorbonne
17. St. Jacques du Haut Pas
18. Petit Pont

To Versailles

C.S. HAMMOND & CO., N.Y.

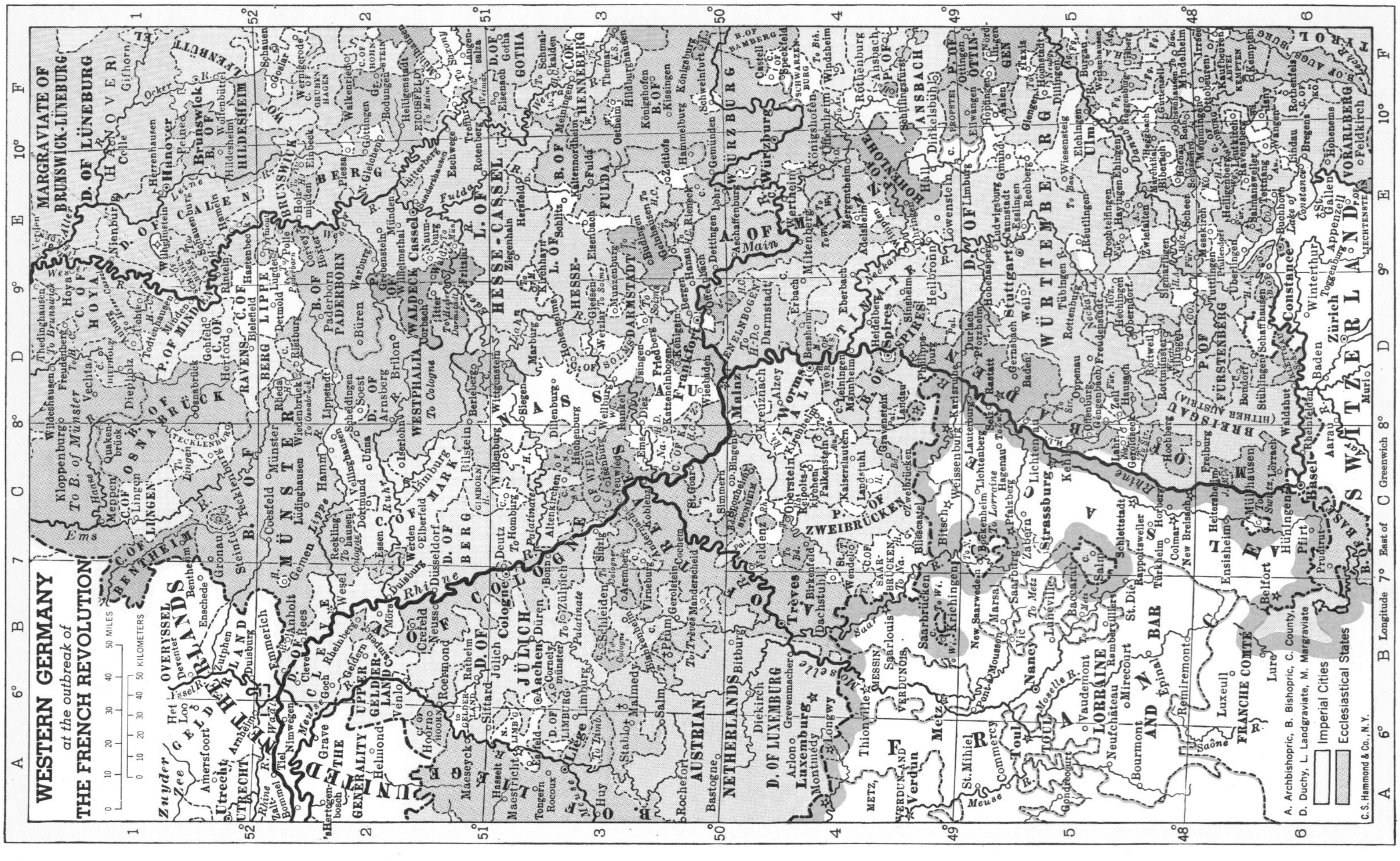

WESTERN GERMANY
at the outbreak of
THE FRENCH REVOLUTION

C.S. Hammond & Co., N.Y.

A. Archbishopric, B. Bishopric, C. County,
D. Duchy, L. Landgraviate, M. Margraviate

Imperial Cities

Ecclesiastical States

MARGRAVIATE OF BRUNSWICK-LÜNEBURG

D. OF LÜNEBURG (HANOVER)

THE NETHERLANDS

UNITED

GENERALITY

HESSE-CASSEL

HESSE-DARMSTADT

WÜRTTEMBERG

SWITZERLAND

AUSTRIAN NETHERLANDS

D. OF LUXEMBURG

LORRAINE

FRANCHE COMTÉ

BAR AND

METZ, VERDUN AND Verdun

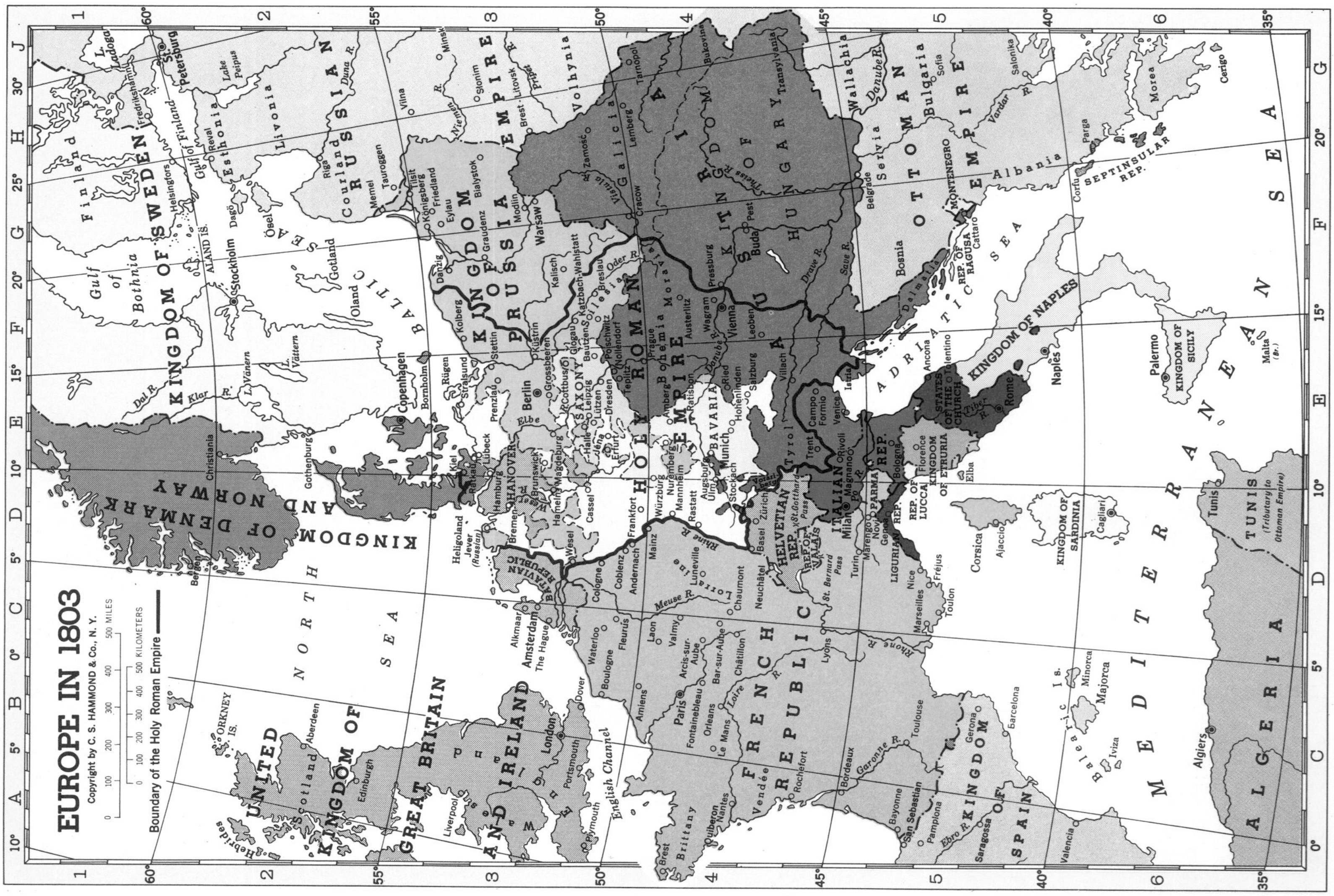

EUROPE IN 1803

Copyright by C. S. Hammond & Co., N.Y.

Boundary of the Holy Roman Empire

UNITED KINGDOM OF GREAT BRITAIN AND IRELAND

KINGDOM OF SWEDEN

KINGDOM OF DENMARK AND NORWAY

RUSSIAN EMPIRE

KINGDOM OF PRUSSIA

HOLY ROMAN EMPIRE

HANOVER

SAXONY

BAVARIA

AUSTRIA

HUNGARY

OTTOMAN EMPIRE

FRENCH REPUBLIC

HELVETIAN REP.

BATAVIAN REPUBLIC

ITALIAN REP.

LIGURIAN REP.

PARMA

REP. OF LUCCA

KINGDOM OF ETRURIA

STATES OF THE CHURCH

KINGDOM OF NAPLES

KINGDOM OF SICILY

KINGDOM OF SARDINIA

KINGDOM OF SPAIN

REP. OF RAGUSA

SEPTINSULAR REP.

MONTENEGRO

TUNIS (Tributary to Ottoman Empire)

ALGERIA

NORTH SEA

BALTIC SEA

MEDITERRANEAN SEA

ADRIATIC SEA

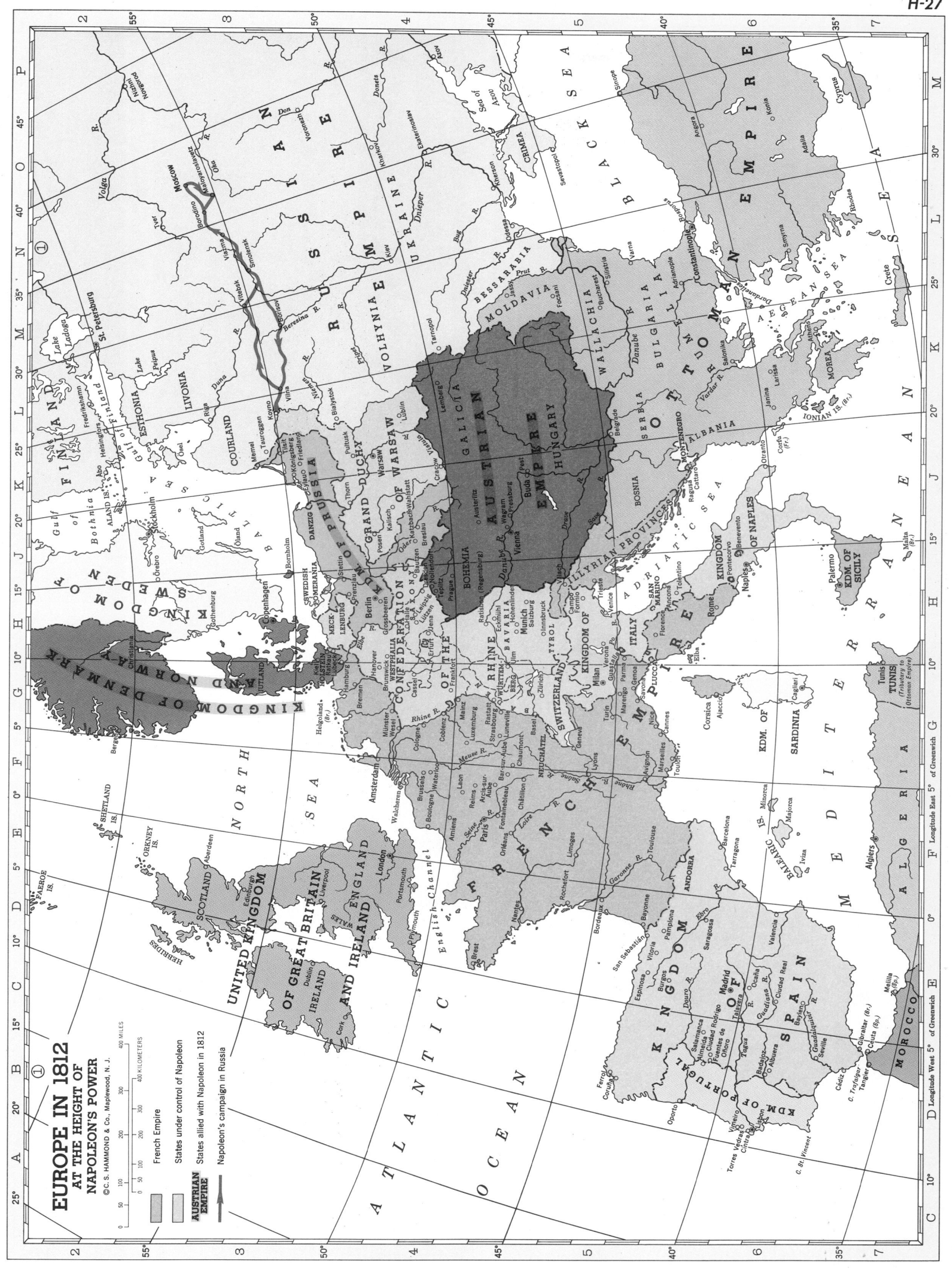

EUROPE IN 1812
AT THE HEIGHT OF
NAPOLEON'S POWER

© C. S. HAMMOND & Co., Maplewood, N. J.

French Empire

States under control of Napoleon

States allied with Napoleon in 1812

Napoleon's campaign in Russia

AUSTRIAN EMPIRE

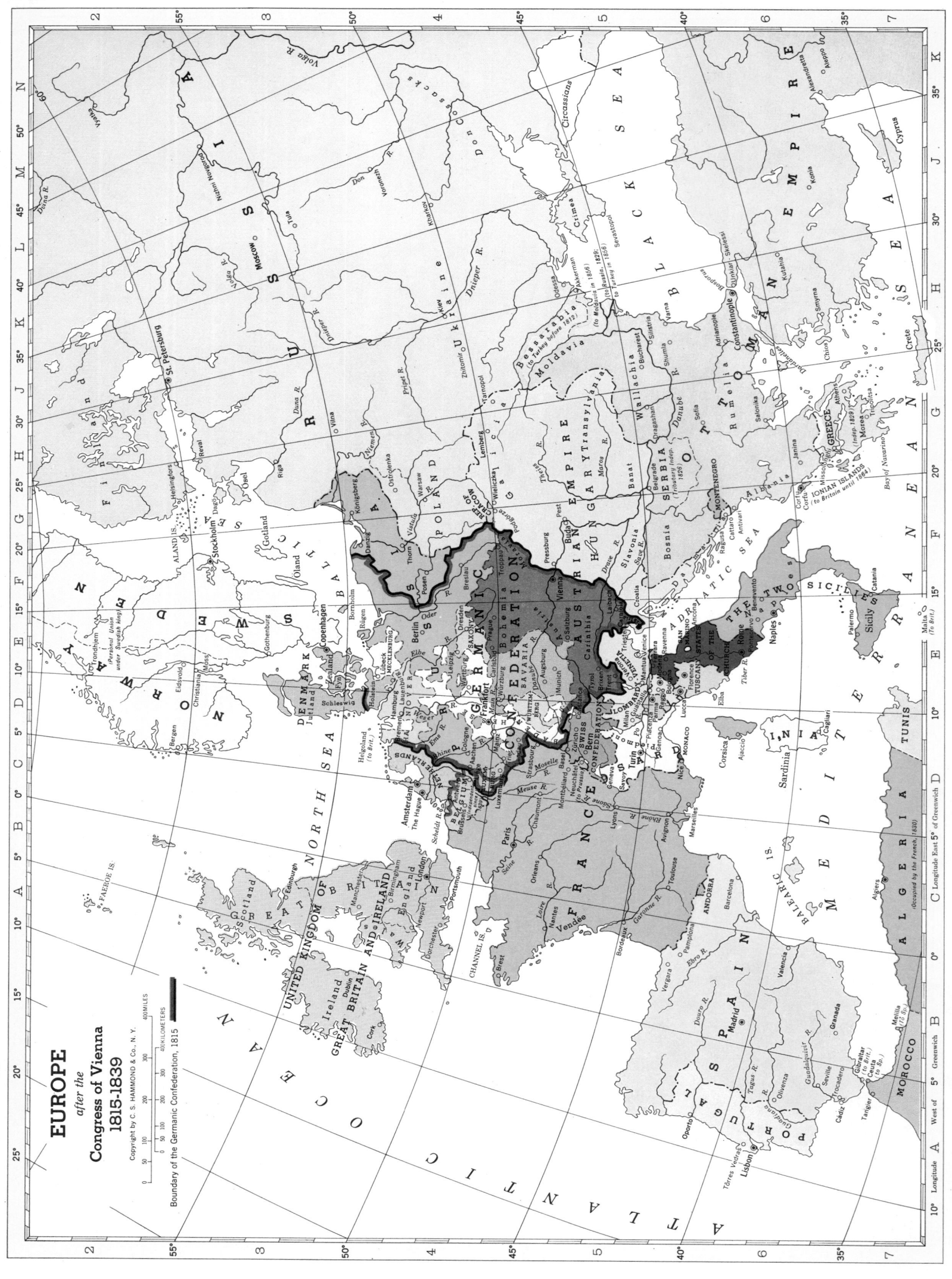

EUROPE
after the
Congress of Vienna
1815-1839

Copyright by C. S. HAMMOND & Co., N. Y.

Boundary of the Germanic Confederation, 1815

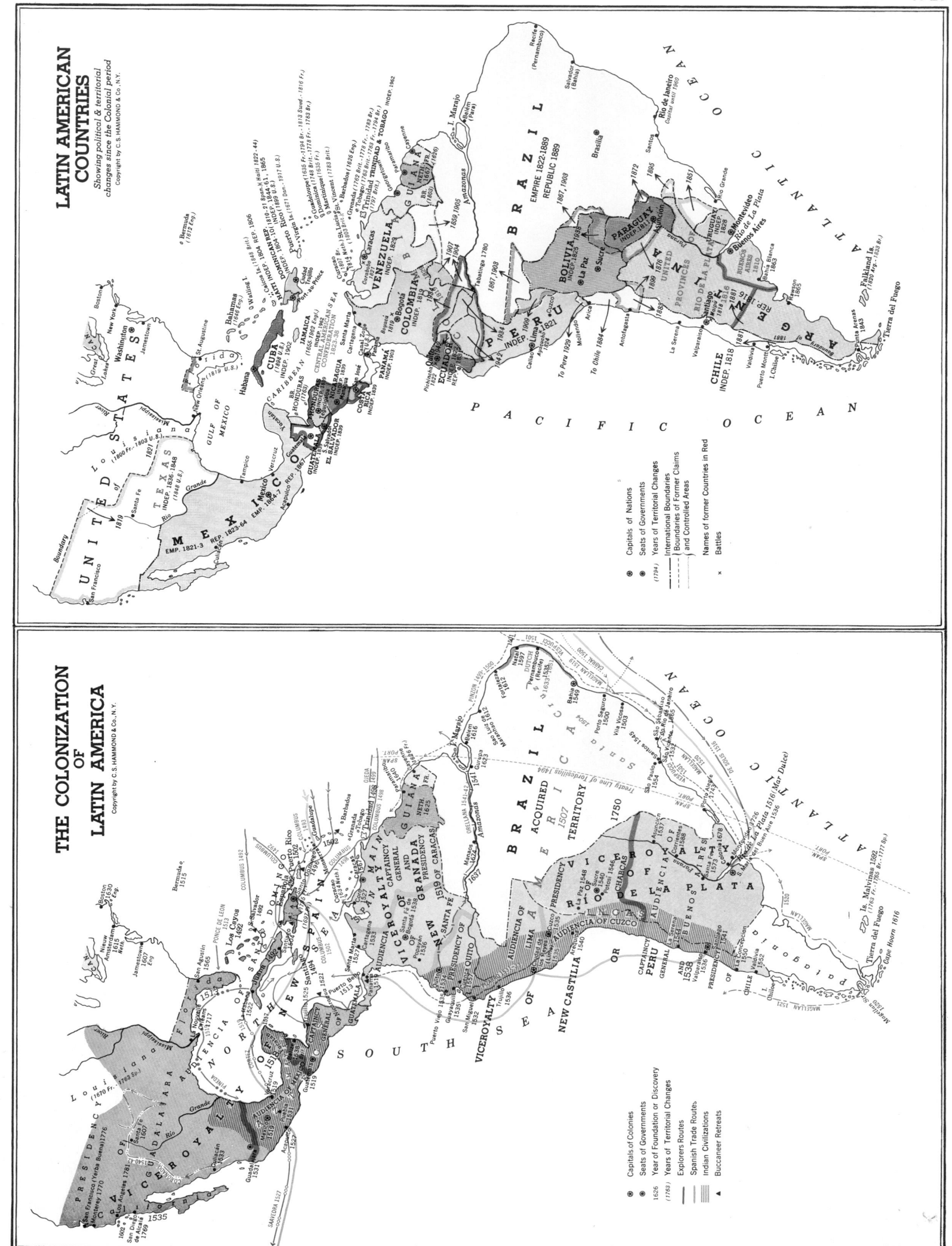

LATIN AMERICAN COUNTRIES

Showing political & territorial changes since the Colonial period

Copyright by C. S. HAMMOND & Co., N.Y.

Legend:
- ⊛ Capitals of Nations
- ⊛ Seats of Governments
- (1794) Years of Territorial Changes
- —·— International Boundaries
- — — — Boundaries of Former Claims
- ·········· and Controlled Areas
- Names of former Countries in Red
- × Battles

THE COLONIZATION OF LATIN AMERICA

Copyright by C. S. HAMMOND & Co., N.Y.

Legend:
- ⊛ Capitals of Colonies
- ⊛ Seats of Governments
- 1626 Year of Foundation or Discovery
- (1763) Years of Territorial Changes
- Explorers Routes
- Spanish Trade Routes
- |||||| Indian Civilizations
- ▲ Buccaneer Retreats

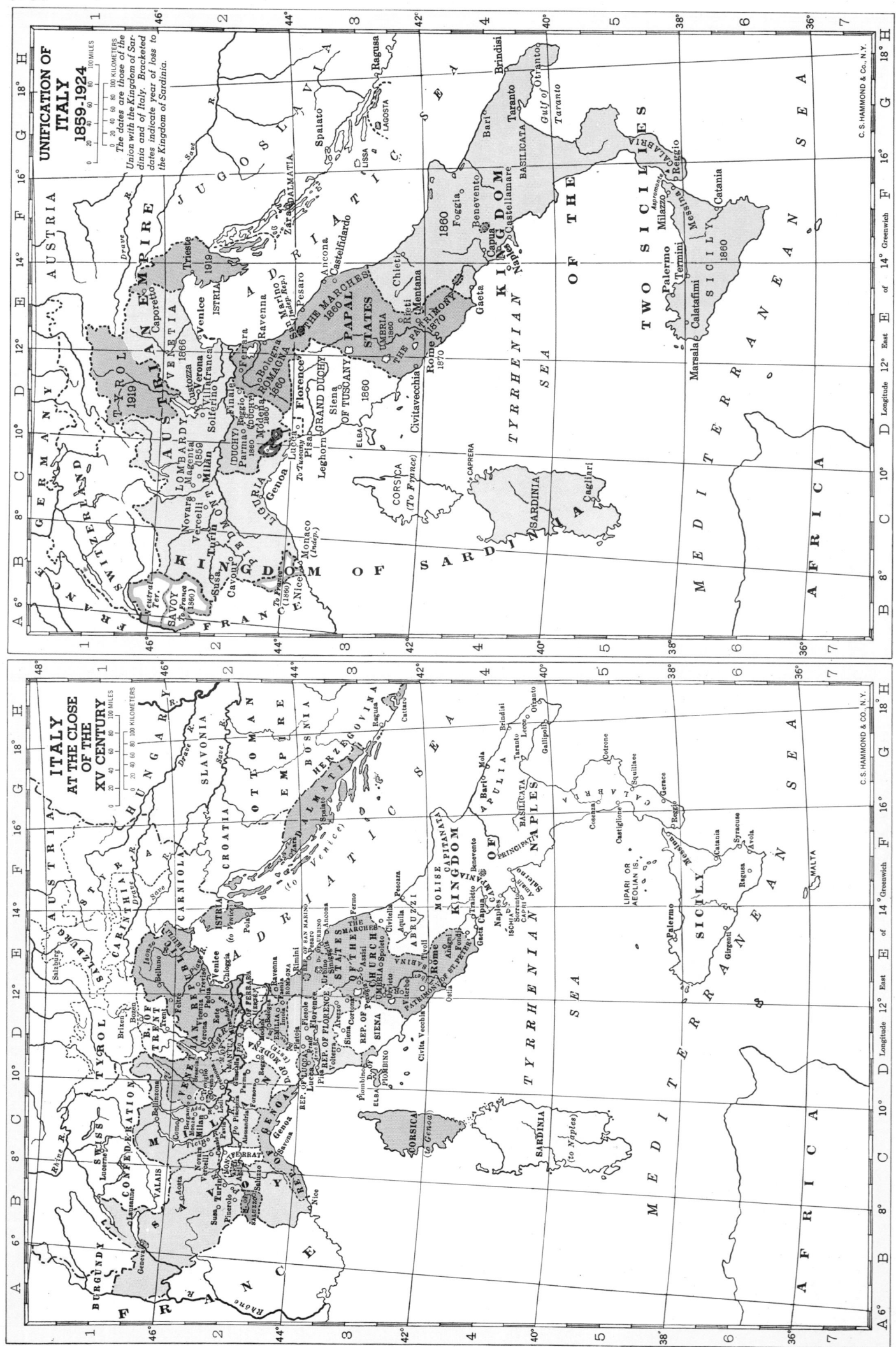

UNIFICATION OF ITALY
1859-1924

The dates are those of the Union with the Kingdom of Sardinia and of Italy. Bracketed dates indicate year of loss to the Kingdom of Sardinia.

C. S. HAMMOND & Co., N.Y.

ITALY AT THE CLOSE OF THE XV CENTURY

C. S. HAMMOND & CO., N.Y.

CENTRAL EUROPE
1815-1871

- ——— Boundary of German Confederation 1815-1866
- •••••• Boundary of North German Confederation 1860-1871
- – – – Boundary of German Empire in 1871

0 25 50 100 150 200 MILES

0 25 50 100 150 200 KILOMETERS

Longitude 12° East of Greenwich

© The Century Co., 1932

LANGUAGE MAP OF
EUROPE
1910

Copyright by C.S. HAMMOND & Co., N.Y.

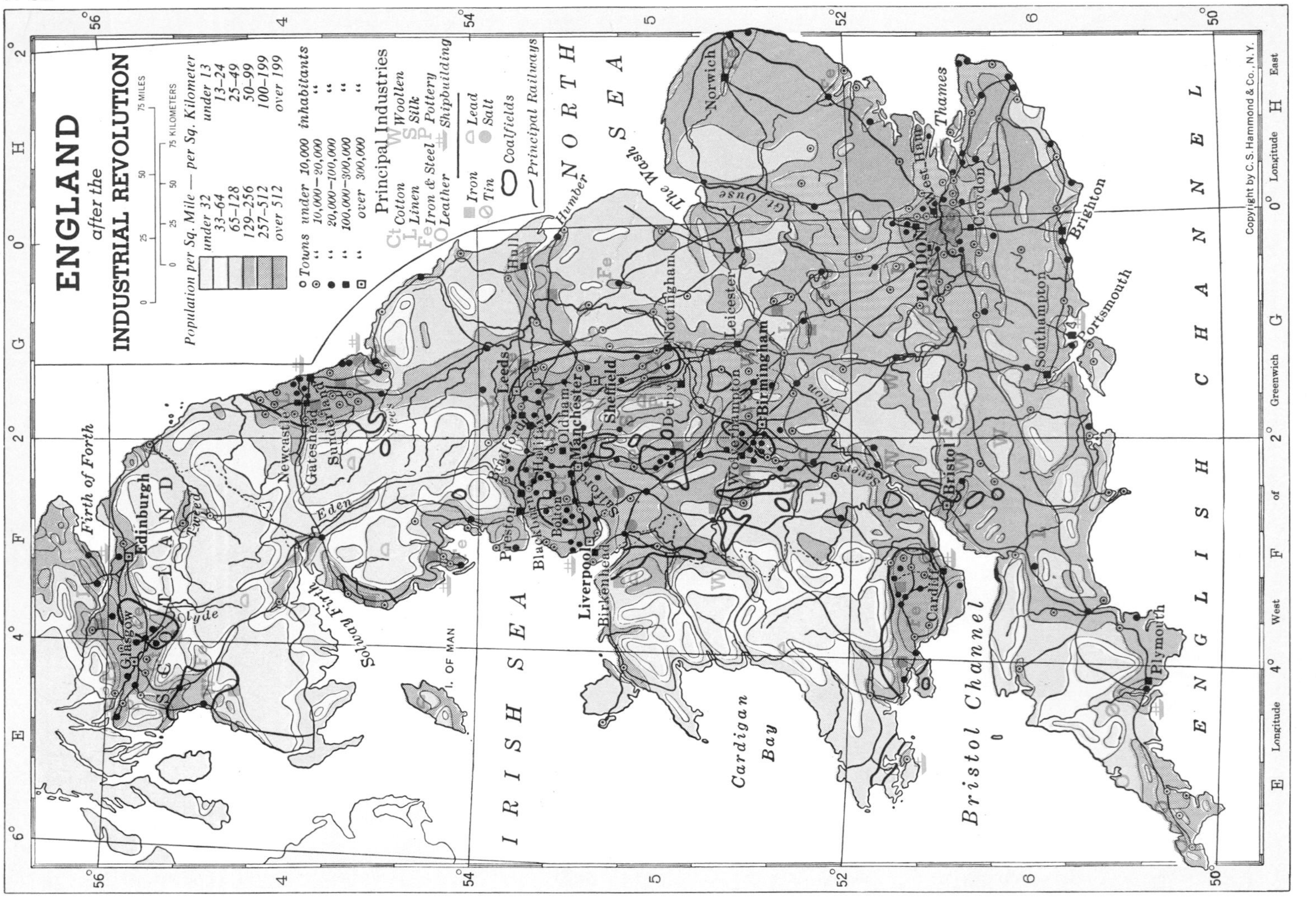
ENGLAND
after the
INDUSTRIAL REVOLUTION
Population per Sq. Mile — per Sq. Kilometer
under 32 — under 13
33–64 — 13–24
65–128 — 25–49
129–256 — 50–99
257–512 — 100–199
over 512 — over 199
Towns under 10,000 inhabitants
10,000–20,000
20,000–100,000
100,000–300,000
over 300,000
Principal Industries
Ct Cotton
L Linen
Fe Iron & Steel
O Leather
W Woollen
S Silk
P Pottery
Shipbuilding
Iron
Tin
Lead
Salt
Coalfields
Principal Railways
IRISH SEA
NORTH SEA
ENGLISH CHANNEL
Bristol Channel
Cardigan Bay
LONDON
Copyright by C.S. Hammond & Co., N.Y.

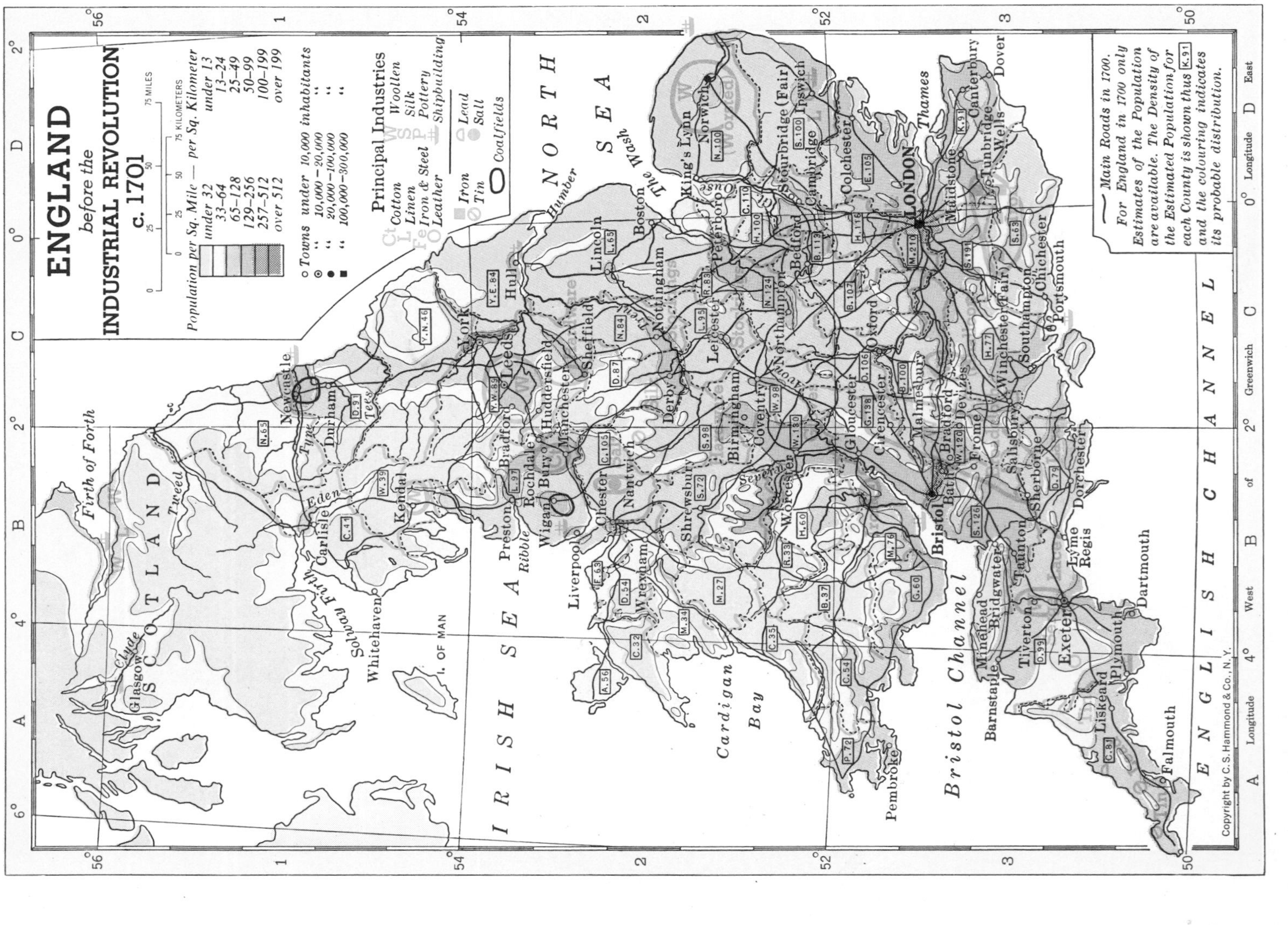
ENGLAND
before the
INDUSTRIAL REVOLUTION
c. 1701
Population per Sq. Mile — per Sq. Kilometer
under 32 — under 13
33–64 — 13–24
65–128 — 25–49
129–256 — 50–99
257–512 — 100–199
over 512 — over 199
Towns under 10,000 inhabitants
10,000–20,000
20,000–100,000
100,000–300,000
Principal Industries
Ct Cotton
L Linen
Fe Iron & Steel
O Leather
W Woollen
S Silk
P Pottery
Shipbuilding
Iron
Tin
Lead
Salt
Coalfields
Main Roads in 1700.
For England in 1700 only Estimates of the Population are available. The Density of the Estimated Population for each County is shown thus K.91 and the colouring indicates its probable distribution.
IRISH SEA
NORTH SEA
ENGLISH CHANNEL
Bristol Channel
Cardigan Bay
LONDON
Copyright by C.S. Hammond & Co., N.Y.

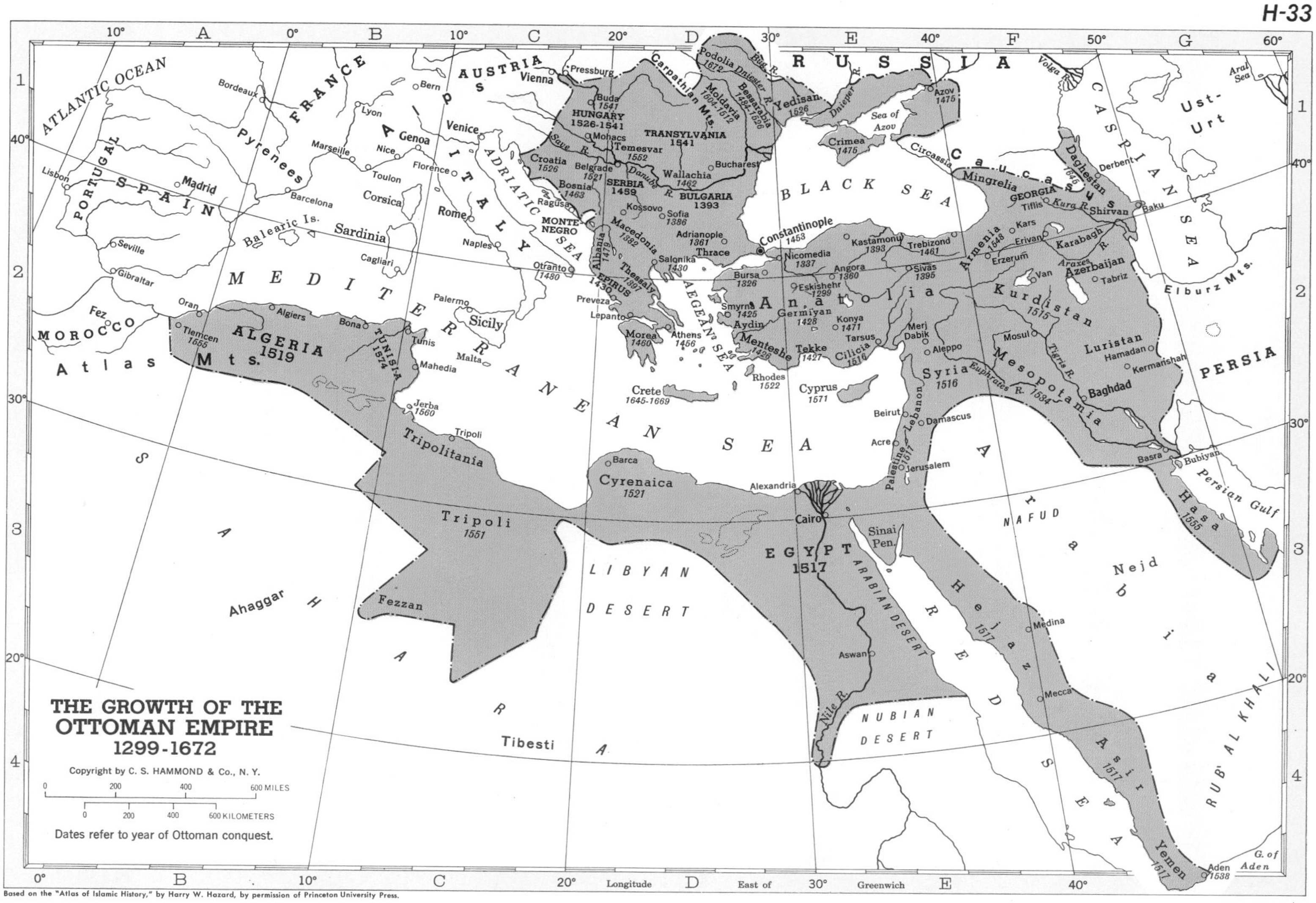

THE GROWTH OF THE OTTOMAN EMPIRE 1299-1672

Copyright by C. S. HAMMOND & Co., N.Y.

0 200 400 600 MILES

0 200 400 600 KILOMETERS

Dates refer to year of Ottoman conquest.

Based on the "Atlas of Islamic History," by Harry W. Hazard, by permission of Princeton University Press.

Map labels (Growth map): ATLANTIC OCEAN, FRANCE, AUSTRIA, Vienna, Pressburg, RUSSIA, Podolia 1672, Moldavia 1504–1513, Bessarabia 1484, Yedisan 1526, PORTUGAL, SPAIN, Madrid, Lisbon, Bordeaux, Lyon, Bern, Genoa, Venice, Marseille, Nice, Toulon, Florence, Rome, Naples, Corsica, Sardinia, Balearic Is., Seville, Gibraltar, Barcelona, Fez, MOROCCO, Oran, Tlemcen 1555, ALGERIA 1519, Tunis, Tunisia 1574, Bona, Algiers, Mahedia, Jerba 1560, Tripoli, Tripolitania, Tripoli 1551, Fezzan, SAHARA, Ahaggar, Tibesti, MEDITERRANEAN SEA, ITALY, ADRIATIC SEA, Palermo, Sicily, Malta, Cagliari, HUNGARY 1526–1541, Buda 1541, TRANSYLVANIA 1541, Temesvar 1552, Croatia 1526, Belgrade 1521, Bosnia 1463, SERBIA 1459, BULGARIA 1393, Wallachia 1462, Bucharest, Sofia 1386, Kossovo 1386, Macedonia 1382, MONTE NEGRO, Ragusa, Adrianople 1361, Thrace, Constantinople 1453, Salonika 1430, Thessaly, EPIRUS, Preveza, Otranto 1480, Athens 1456, Morea 1460, Lepanto, Smyrna 1425, Aydin, Crete 1645–1669, Rhodes 1522, Cyprus 1571, AEGEAN SEA, Anatolia, Bursa 1326, Eskishehr 1299, Angora 1360, Germiyan 1428, Konya 1471, Menteshe, Tekke 1427, Cilicia 1516, Tarsus, BLACK SEA, Crimea 1475, Azov 1475, Sea of Azov, Circassia, Caucasus, Mingrelia, GEORGIA, Tiflis, Armenia, Trebizond 1461, Erzerum, Kars, Erivan, Van, Kurdistan 1515, Azerbaijan, Araxes R., Shirvan, Karabagh, Baku, CASPIAN SEA, Ust-Urt, Aral Sea, Volga, PERSIA, Elburz Mts., Luristan, Hamadan, Kermanshah, Mosul, Tigris R., Mesopotamia, Baghdad, Euphrates R. 1534, Sivas 1395, Merj Dabik, Aleppo, Syria 1516, Lebanon, Damascus, Beirut, Acre, Palestine 1517, Jerusalem, Arabia, NAFUD, Nejd, Hasa 1555, Persian Gulf, Bubiyan, Basra, EGYPT 1517, Cairo, Alexandria, Barca, Cyrenaica 1521, LIBYAN DESERT, Sinai Pen., RED SEA, ARABIAN DESERT, Nile R., Aswan, Hejaz 1517, Medina, Mecca, NUBIAN DESERT, Asir 1517, RUB' AL KHALI, Yemen 1517, Aden 1538, G. of Aden

---

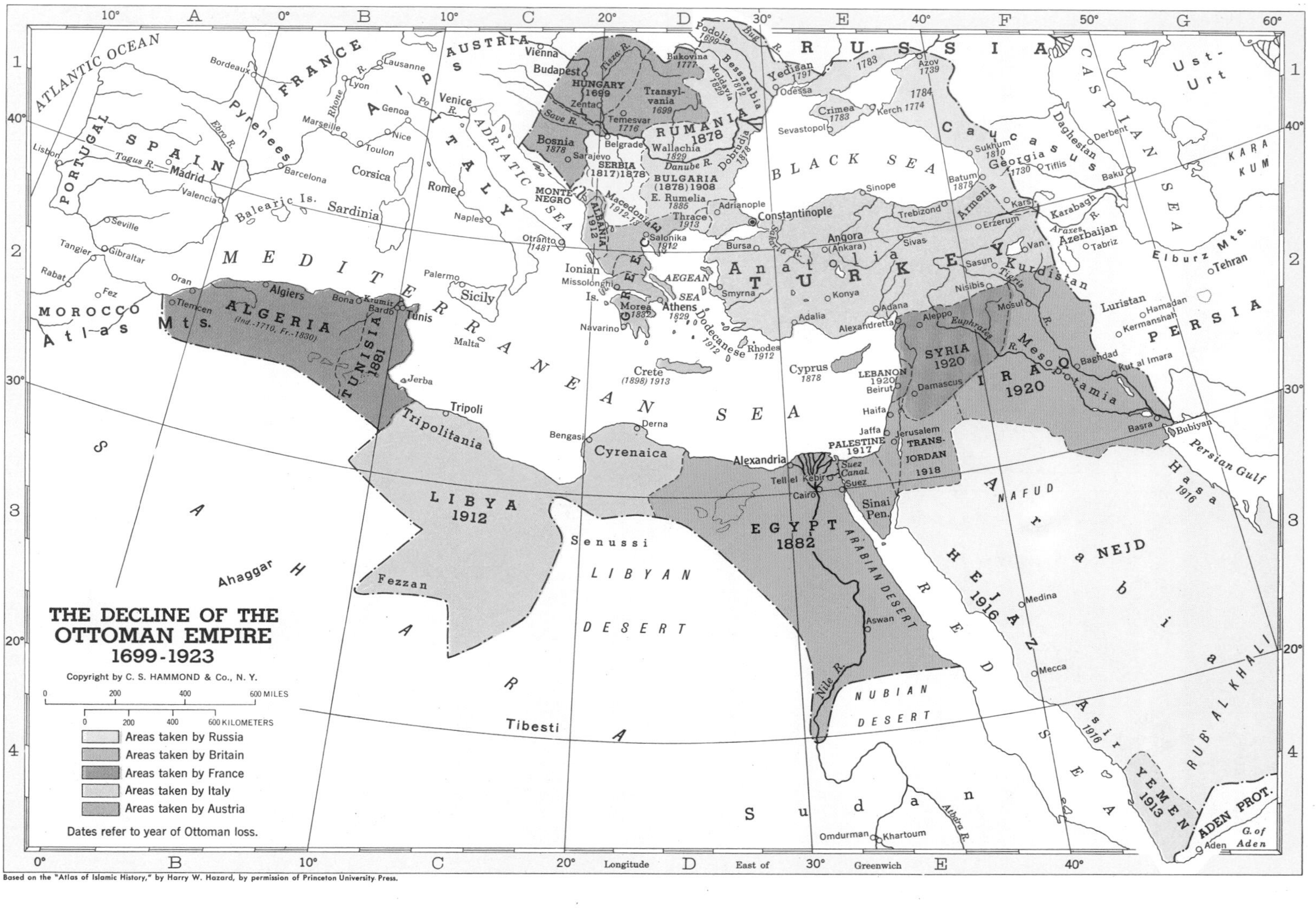

THE DECLINE OF THE OTTOMAN EMPIRE 1699-1923

Copyright by C. S. HAMMOND & Co., N.Y.

0 200 400 600 MILES

0 200 400 600 KILOMETERS

Legend:
- Areas taken by Russia
- Areas taken by Britain
- Areas taken by France
- Areas taken by Italy
- Areas taken by Austria

Dates refer to year of Ottoman loss.

Based on the "Atlas of Islamic History," by Harry W. Hazard, by permission of Princeton University Press.

Map labels (Decline map): ATLANTIC OCEAN, FRANCE, AUSTRIA, Vienna, Budapest, RUSSIA, PORTUGAL, SPAIN, Madrid, Lisbon, Bordeaux, Lausanne, Lyon, Geneva, Rhone R., Nice, Toulon, Genoa, Venice, Po R., Rome, Naples, Corsica, Sardinia, Balearic Is., Valencia, Seville, Tangier, Gibraltar, Rabat, Fez, MOROCCO, Oran, Tlemcen, Algiers, ALGERIA (Ind.-1710, Fr.-1830), Tunis, TUNISIA 1881, Bona, Kamini, Bardo, Jerba, Tripolitania, LIBYA 1912, Fezzan, SAHARA, Ahaggar, Tibesti, MEDITERRANEAN SEA, ITALY, ADRIATIC SEA, Palermo, Sicily, Malta, HUNGARY 1699, Zentac, Transylvania 1699, Temesvar 1716, Belgrade, BOSNIA 1878, Sarajevo, SERBIA (1817) 1878, Save R., Tisza R., Danube R., Wallachia 1829, RUMANIA 1878, Dobrudja, Bukovina 1775, Moldavia 1792, Bessarabia 1812, Yedisan 1791, Odessa, BULGARIA (1876) 1908, E. Rumelia 1885, Macedonia 1912, Thrace 1913, MONTE NEGRO, ALBANIA 1912–3, Salonika 1912, Adrianople, Constantinople, Otranto 1481, Ionian Is., Missolonghi, Morea 1829, Athens 1829, AEGEAN SEA, Navarino, Crete (1898) 1913, Rhodes 1912, Dodecanese 1912, Cyprus 1878, Smyrna, Anatolia, TURKEY, Bursa, Angora (Ankara), Konya, Adana, Adalia, Alexandretta, BLACK SEA, Sinope, Sevastopol, Crimea 1783, Kerch 1774, Sea of Azov, Azov 1739, Caucasus, Georgia 1801, Tiflis, Batum 1878, Trebizond, Erzerum, Kars 1878, Sasun, Armenia, Nisibis, Kurdistan, Azerbaijan, Tabriz, Araxes R., Karabagh, Baku, Daghestan, Derbent, Sukhum 1810, CASPIAN SEA, KARA KUM, Ust-Urt, PERSIA, Elburz Mts., Tehran, Luristan, Hamadan, Kermanshah, Mosul, Tigris R., Mesopotamia, IRAK 1920, Baghdad, Rut el Imara, Euphrates R., SYRIA 1920, Aleppo, LEBANON 1920, Beirut, Damascus, Haifa, Jaffa, PALESTINE 1917, Jerusalem, TRANS-JORDAN 1918, Tell el Kebir, Suez Canal, Suez, Sinai Pen., Arabia, NAFUD, NEJD, Hasa 1916, Persian Gulf, Bubiyan, Basra, EGYPT 1882, Cairo, Alexandria, Bengasi, Derna, Cyrenaica, Senussi, LIBYAN DESERT, RED SEA, ARABIAN DESERT, Nile R., Aswan, HEJAZ 1916, Medina, Mecca, NUBIAN DESERT, Atbara R., Omdurman, Khartoum, Sudan, Asir 1916, YEMEN 1913, RUB' AL KHALI, ADEN PROT., Aden, G. of Aden

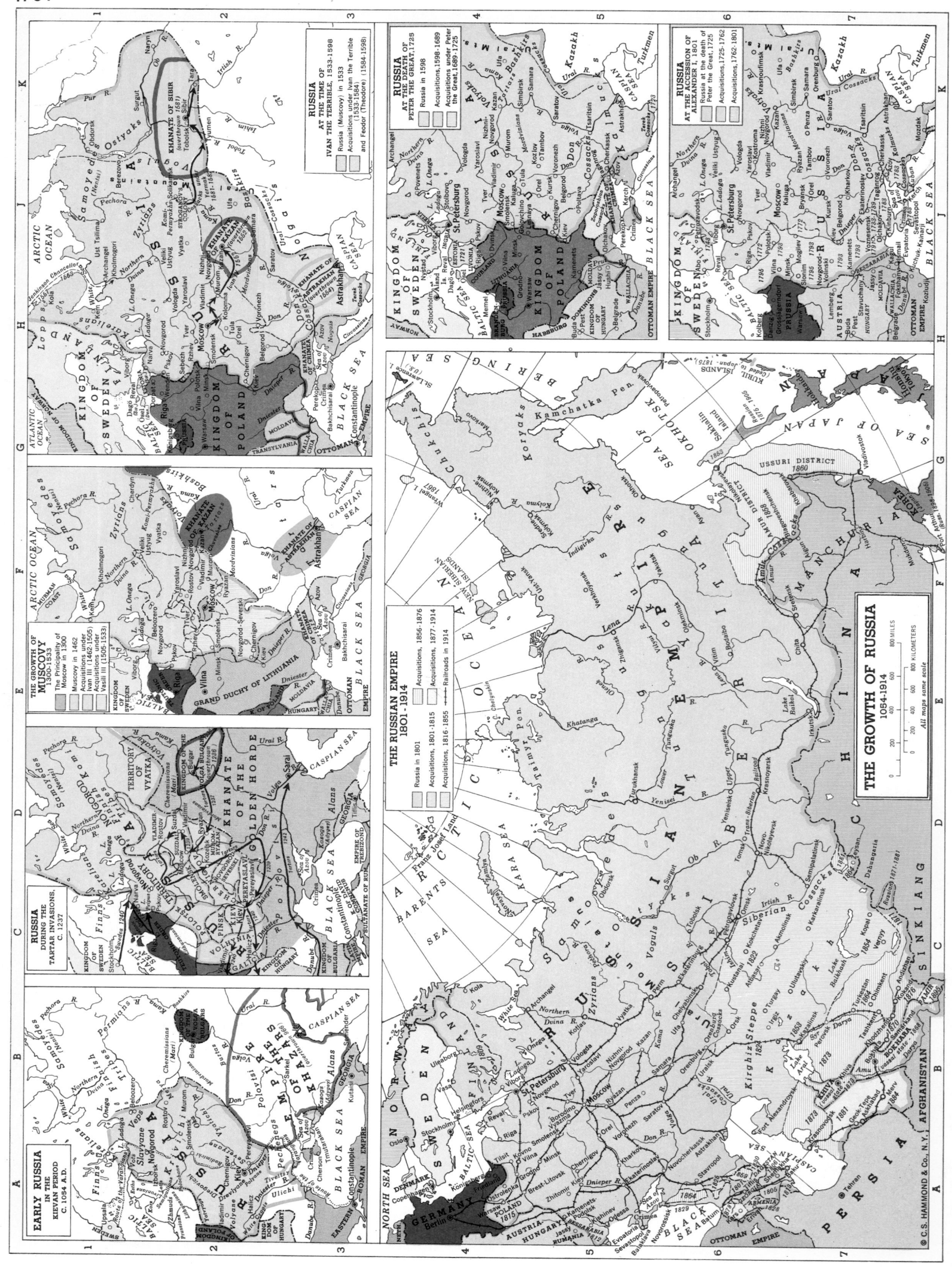

EARLY RUSSIA IN THE KIEVAN PERIOD C. 1054 A.D.

RUSSIA DURING THE TARTAR INVASIONS, C. 1237

THE GROWTH OF MUSCOVY 1300-1533

	The Principality of Moscow in 1300
	Muscovy in 1462
	Acquisitions under Ivan III (1462-1505)
	Acquisitions under Vasili III (1505-1533)

RUSSIA AT THE TIME OF IVAN THE TERRIBLE, 1533-1598

| | Russia (Muscovy) in 1533 |
| | Acquisitions under Ivan the Terrible (1533-1584) and Feodor (Theodore) (1584-1598) |

RUSSIA AT THE DEATH OF PETER THE GREAT, 1725

	Russia in 1598
	Acquisitions, 1598-1689
	Acquisitions under Peter the Great, 1689-1725

RUSSIA AT THE ACCESSION OF ALEXANDER I, 1801

	Russia at the death of Peter the Great, 1725
	Acquisitions, 1725-1762
	Acquisitions, 1762-1801

THE RUSSIAN EMPIRE 1801-1914

	Russia in 1801
	Acquisitions, 1801-1815
	Acquisitions, 1816-1855
	Acquisitions, 1856-1876
	Acquisitions, 1877-1914
+++	Railroads in 1914

THE GROWTH OF RUSSIA 1054-1914

MILES
0 200 400 600 800
KILOMETERS
0 200 400 600 800
All maps same scale

© C.S. HAMMOND & Co., N.Y.

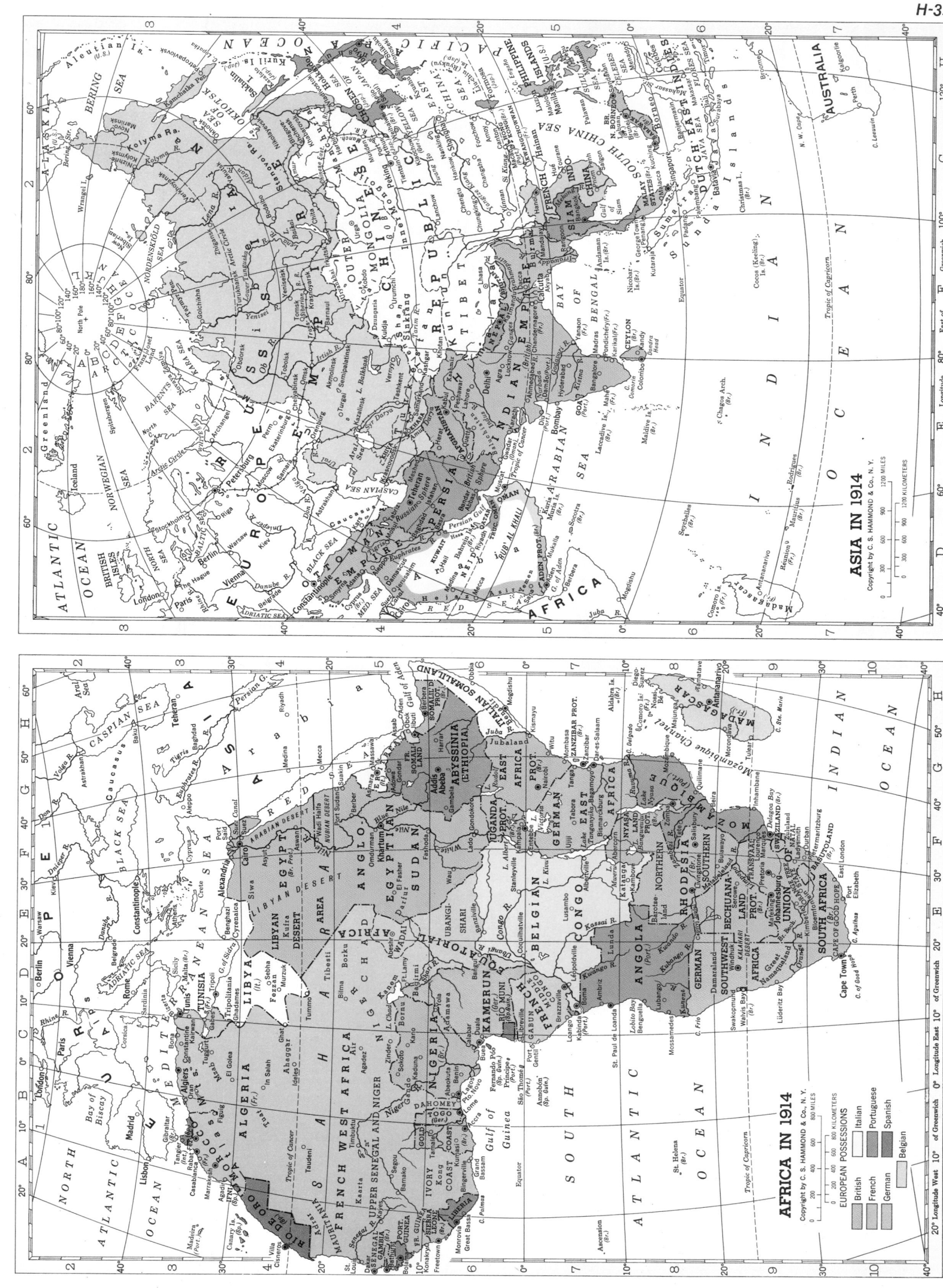

ASIA IN 1914

AFRICA IN 1914

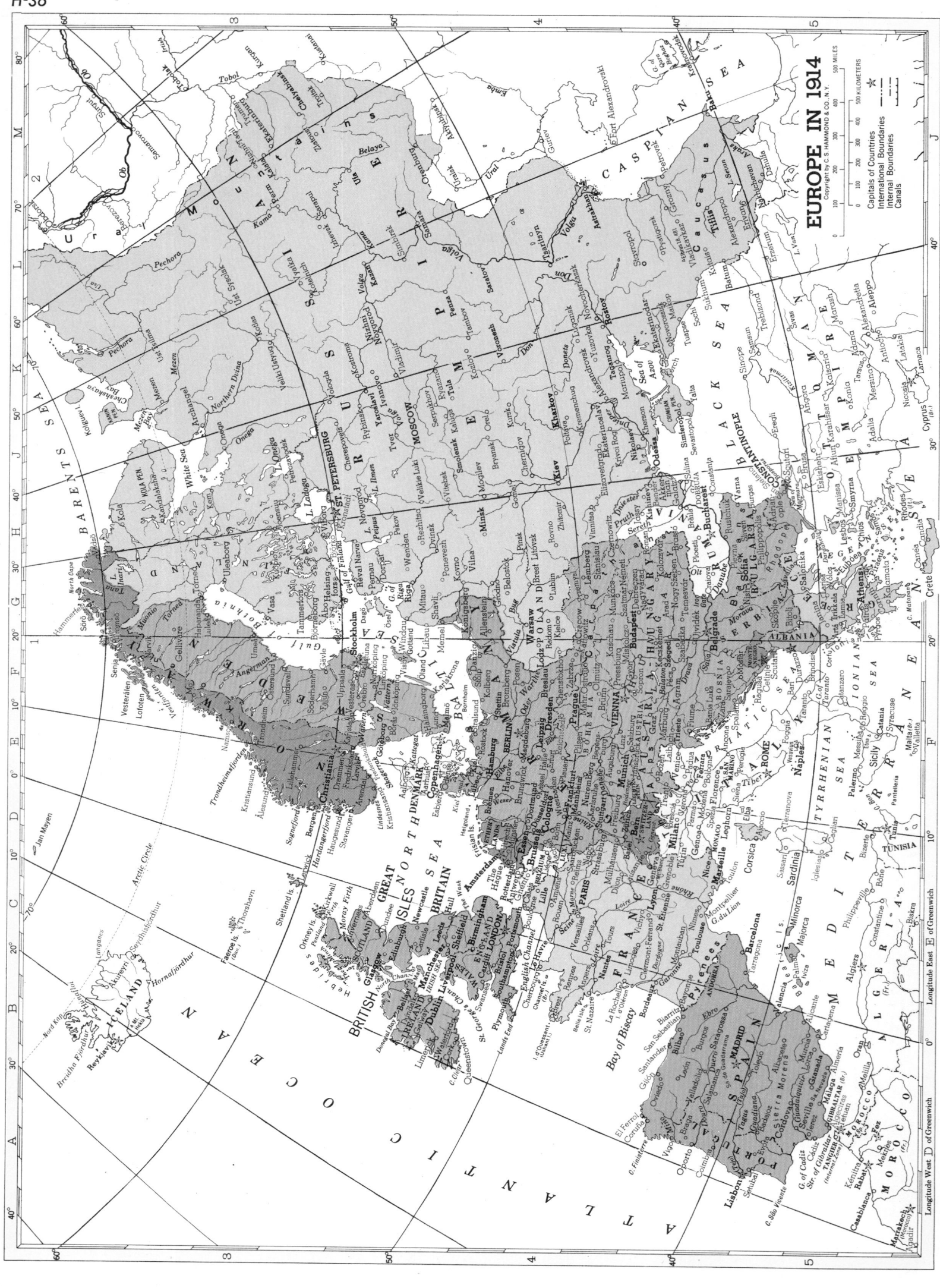

EUROPE IN 1914

Copyright by C. S. HAMMOND & CO., N.Y.

EUROPE AND THE
NEAR EAST

100   200   300   400   500 MILES
100   200   300   400   500 KILOMETERS

- - - Stabilized Line on the
Western Front, 1914-1917

- - - Eastern Front on the Eve of the
Russian Revolution, Oct. 1917

· · · · Limit of Allied Advances
in the East

Area Occupied by the Central
Powers after Brest Litovsk
Treaty, 1918

THE FIRST WORLD WAR
1914-1918

© C. S. HAMMOND & Co., Maplewood, N.J.

The Allies

The Central Powers

Neutral States

Areas Occupied by
the Central Powers

Advances of the Allies

Advances of the Central Powers

THE WESTERN FRONT

0   20   40   60   80 MILES
0   20   40   60   80 KILOMETERS

——— Limit of German Advance, 1914

——— Limit of Trench Warfare, 1914-1917

– – – Hindenburg Line, 1917

– – – Limit of Final German Advance, 1918

· · · · Armistice Line, November 11, 1918

——— Limit of Allied Occupation Zone

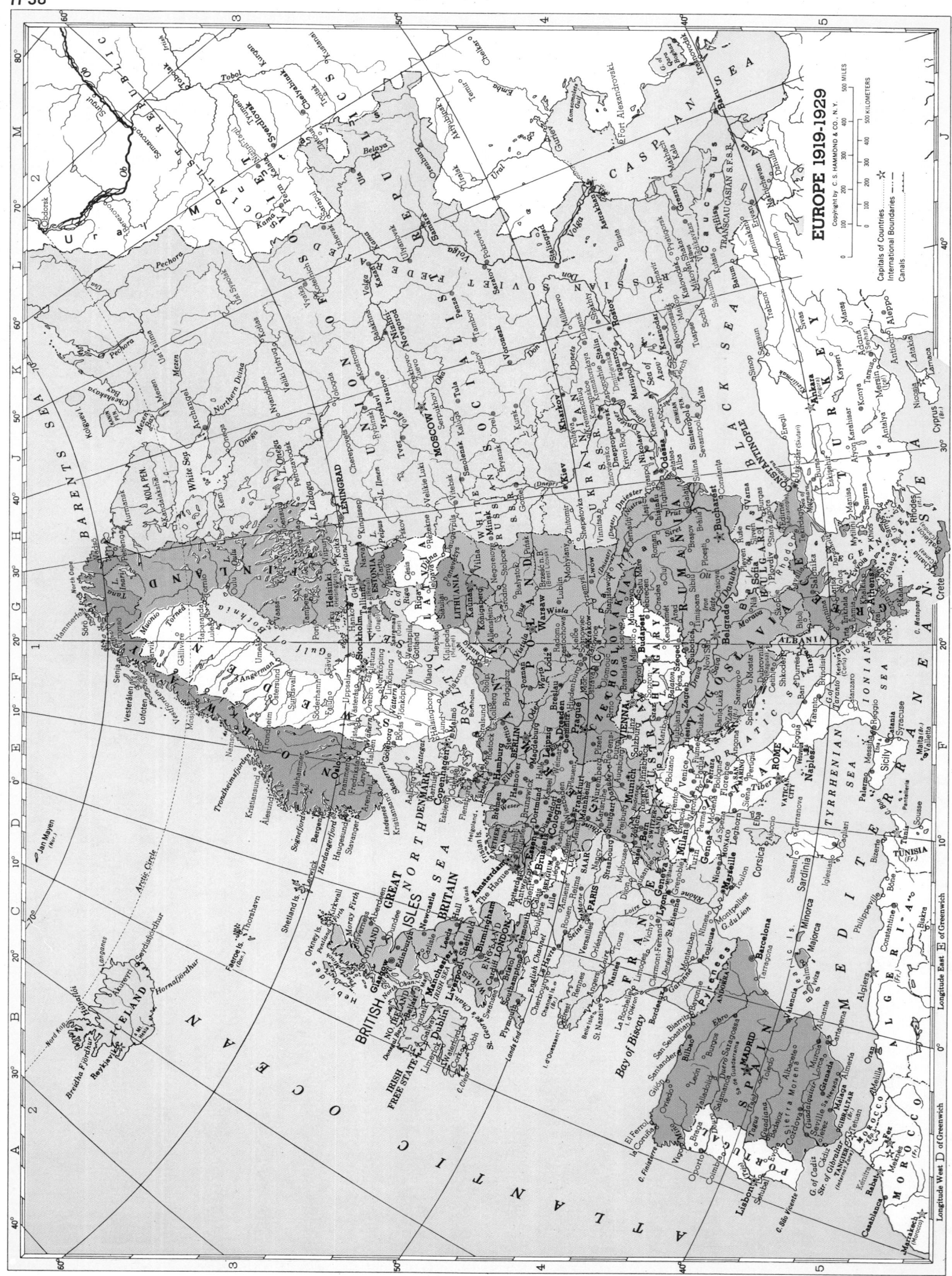

EUROPE 1919-1929

Copyright by C. S. Hammond & Co., N.Y.

Capitals of Countries .... ★
International Boundaries ....
Canals ....

0 100 200 300 400 500 MILES
0 100 200 300 400 500 KILOMETERS

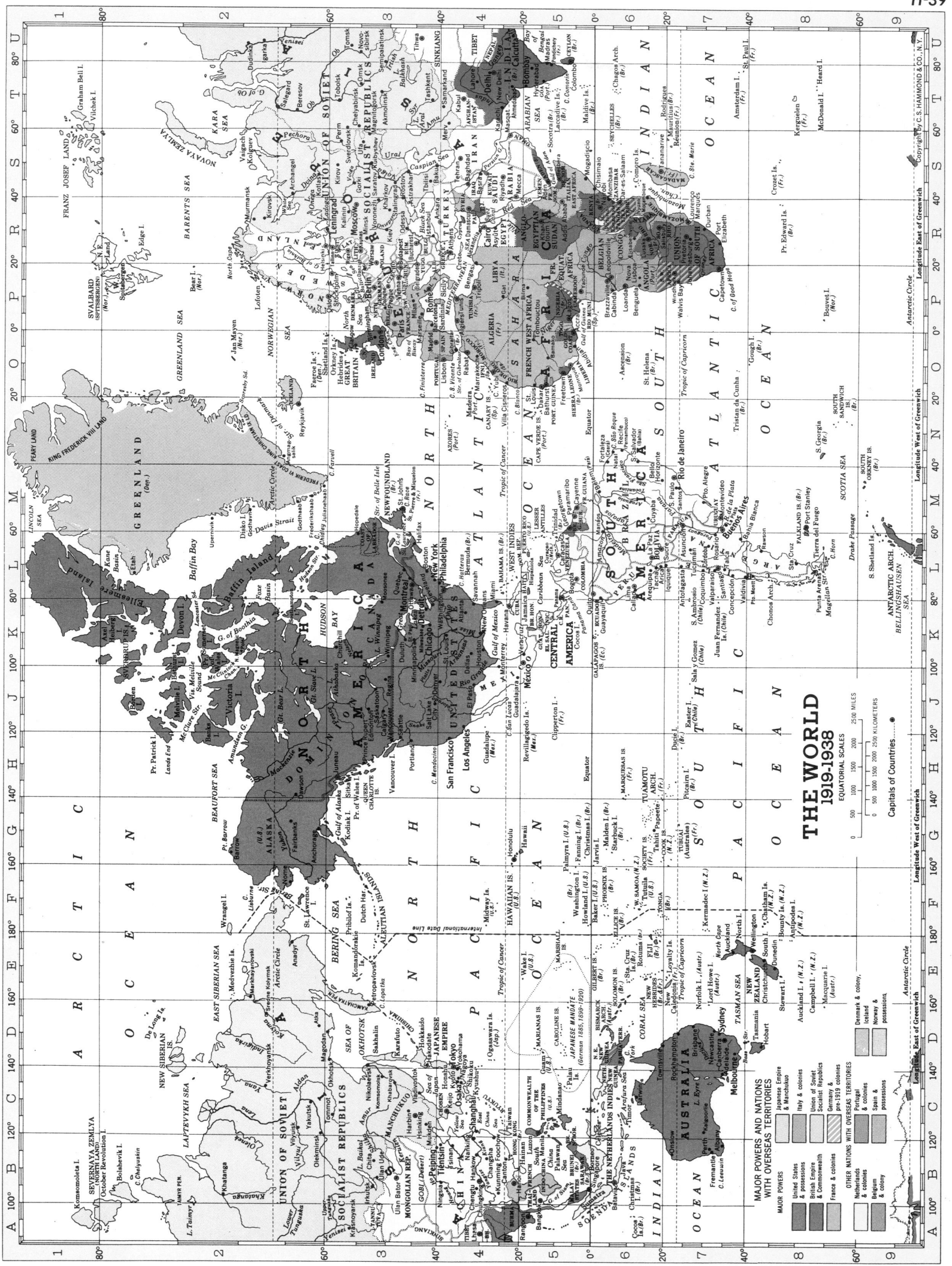

THE WORLD
1919-1938

EQUATORIAL SCALES

0   500   1000   1500   2000   2500 MILES

0   500 1000 1500 2000 2500 KILOMETERS

Capitals of Countries........●

MAJOR POWERS AND NATIONS
WITH OVERSEAS TERRITORIES

MAJOR POWERS

United States
& possessions

Italy & colonies

British Empire
& Commonwealth

France & colonies

OTHER NATIONS WITH OVERSEAS TERRITORIES

Netherlands
& colonies

Belgium
& colony

Japanese Empire
& Manchukuo

Union of Soviet
Socialist Republics

Germany
pre-1919 colonies

Portugal
& colonies

Spain & possessions

Denmark &
Iceland

Norway &
possessions

Copyright by C. S. HAMMOND & CO., N.Y.

Longitude East of Greenwich

Longitude West of Greenwich

Longitude East of Greenwich

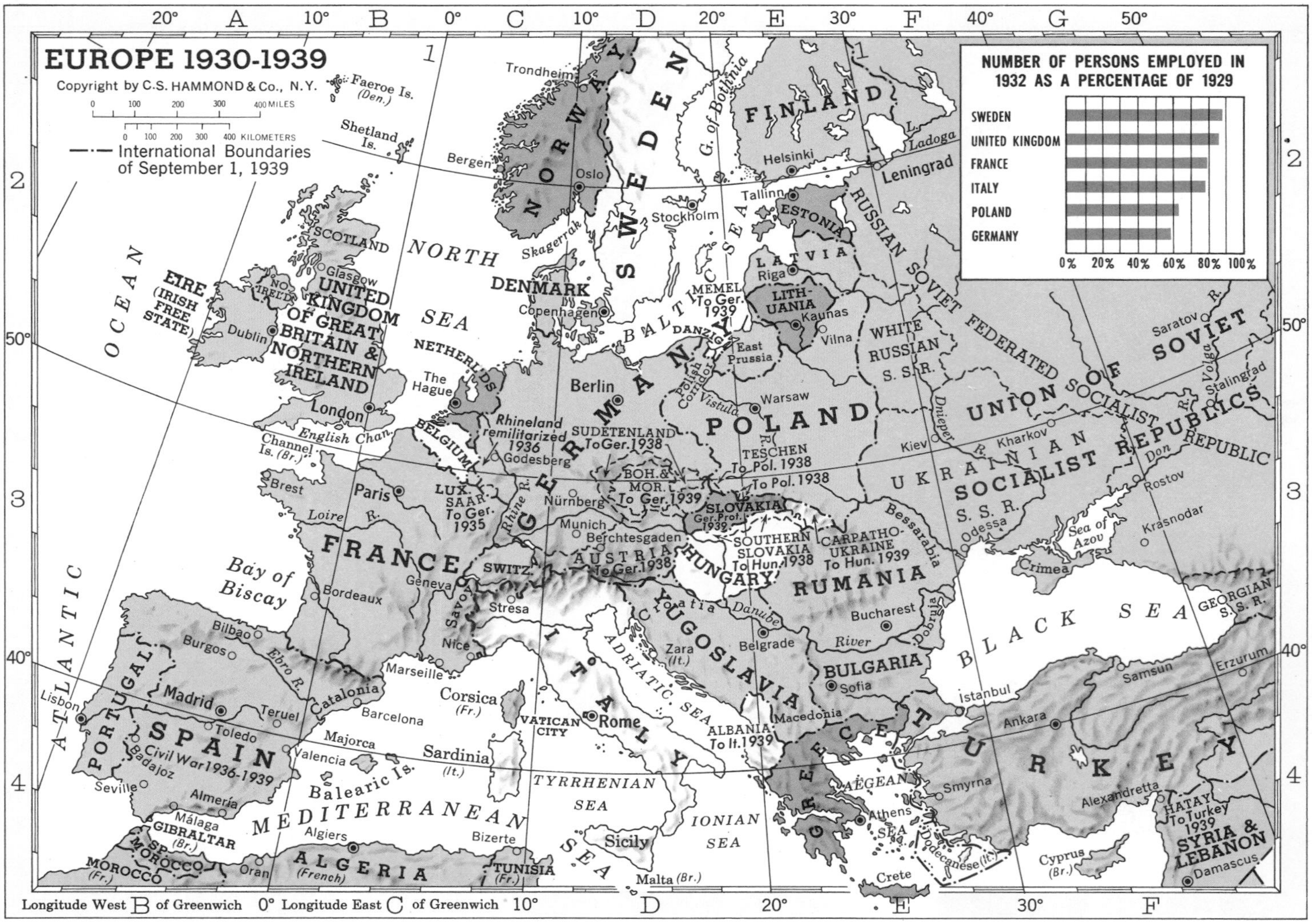

EUROPE 1930-1939

Copyright by C.S. HAMMOND & Co., N.Y.

0 100 200 300 400 MILES
0 100 200 300 400 KILOMETERS

—·—·— International Boundaries of September 1, 1939

NUMBER OF PERSONS EMPLOYED IN 1932 AS A PERCENTAGE OF 1929

SWEDEN
UNITED KINGDOM
FRANCE
ITALY
POLAND
GERMANY

0% 20% 40% 60% 80% 100%

Longitude West **B** of Greenwich   0° Longitude East **C** of Greenwich   10°

ATLANTIC OCEAN
Faeroe Is. (Den.)
Shetland Is.
Trondheim
Bergen
Oslo
NORWAY
SWEDEN
Stockholm
Skagerrak
NORTH SEA
DENMARK
Copenhagen
Helsinki
FINLAND
G. of Bothnia
L. Ladoga
Leningrad
Tallinn
ESTONIA
Riga
LATVIA
Memel To Ger. 1939
LITHUANIA
Kaunas
Vilna
BALTIC SEA
RUSSIAN SOVIET FEDERATED SOCIALIST REPUBLIC
WHITE RUSSIAN S.S.R.
SCOTLAND
Glasgow
N. IRELAND
EIRE (IRISH FREE STATE)
Dublin
UNITED KINGDOM OF GREAT BRITAIN & NORTHERN IRELAND
London
English Chan.
Channel Is. (Br.)
NETHERLDS
The Hague
BELGIUM
Berlin
DANZIG
East Prussia
POLAND
Warsaw
Vistula
Bug
Kiev
UKRAINIAN SOCIALIST REPUBLICS S.S.R.
Kharkov
Saratov R.
SOVIET UNION OF SOCIALIST REPUBLICS
Stalingrad
Volga
Brest
Paris
Loire R.
FRANCE
LUX.
SAAR To Ger. 1935
Rhineland remilitarized 1936
Godesberg
Nürnberg
GERMANY
SUDETENLAND To Ger. 1938
BOH. & MOR. To Ger. 1939
TESCHEN To Pol. 1938
SLOVAKIA Ger. Prot. 1939
SOUTHERN SLOVAKIA To Hun. 1938
CARPATHO-UKRAINE To Hun. 1939
Dnieper
Odessa
Bessarabia
Don
Rostov
Sea of Azov
Krasnodar
Bordeaux
Geneva
SWITZ.
Munich
Berchtesgaden
AUSTRIA To Ger. 1938
HUNGARY
Danube
RUMANIA
Bucharest
Belgrade
YUGOSLAVIA
Croatia
Stresa
Nice
Marseille
Corsica (Fr.)
ITALY
Rome
Zara (It.)
ADRIATIC SEA
BULGARIA
Sofia
Macedonia
ALBANIA To It. 1939
GREECE
BLACK SEA
GEORGIAN S.S.R.
Erzurum
Istanbul
Ankara
TURKEY
Samsun
Portugal
Lisbon
Madrid
Toledo
Teruel
SPAIN
Civil War 1936-1939
Catalonia
Barcelona
Burgos
Bilbao
Ebro R.
Badajoz
Seville
Málaga
Almería
GIBRALTAR (Br.)
SP. MOROCCO
MOROCCO (Fr.)
Oran
Algiers
ALGERIA (French)
Majorca
Valencia
Balearic Is.
Sardinia (It.)
TYRRHENIAN SEA
Sicily
Bizerte
TUNISIA (Fr.)
Malta (Br.)
MEDITERRANEAN SEA
IONIAN SEA
Athens
AEGEAN SEA
Smyrna
Dodecanese (It.)
Crete
Cyprus (Br.)
Alexandretta
HATAY To Turkey 1939
SYRIA & LEBANON
Damascus
Bay of Biscay

Longitude West **B** of Greenwich   0° Longitude East **C** of Greenwich   10°
20°   30°

THE FAR EAST 1930-1941

Copyright by C.S. HAMMOND & CO., N.Y.

0 100 200 300 400 500 MILES
0 100 200 300 400 500 KILOMETERS

—·—·— International Boundaries of December 7, 1941
+—+—+ Major Railroads

[shaded] The Japanese Empire in 1930
[shaded] Japanese dominated or occupied areas on December 7, 1941
[shaded] Unoccupied China

◄— Soviet, Mongolian and Chinese Communist military movements
◄═ Japanese and Manchukuoan military movements against Soviet and Mongolian forces

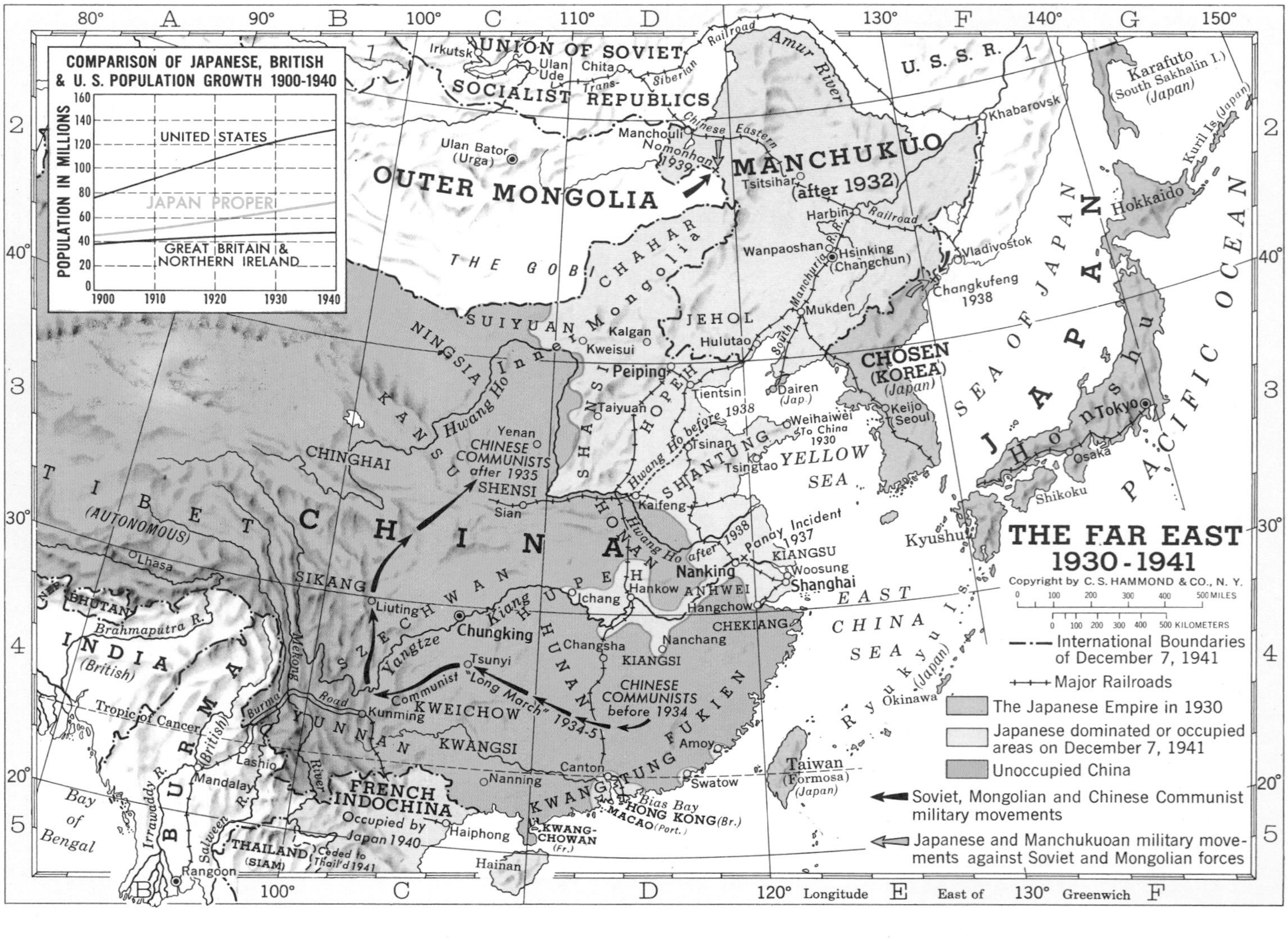

COMPARISON OF JAPANESE, BRITISH & U.S. POPULATION GROWTH 1900-1940

POPULATION IN MILLIONS
160
140
120
100
80
60
40
20

UNITED STATES
JAPAN PROPER
GREAT BRITAIN & NORTHERN IRELAND

1900 1910 1920 1930 1940

Irkutsk
UNION OF SOVIET SOCIALIST REPUBLICS
Ulan Ude
Chita
Trans-Siberian Railroad
Amur River
U.S.S.R.
Khabarovsk
Karafuto (South Sakhalin I.) (Japan)
Chinese Eastern Railroad
Manchouli
Nomonhan 1939
MANCHUKUO (after 1932)
Tsitsihar
OUTER MONGOLIA
Ulan Bator (Urga)
THE GOBI
CHAHAR
Inner Mongolia
Harbin
Railroad
Vladivostok
Changkufeng 1938
Hokkaido
Mukden
Hsinking (Changchun)
Wanpaoshan
SUIYUAN
NINGSIA
Kalgan
Kweisui
JEHOL
South Manchuria
CHOSEN (KOREA) (Japan)
Keijo Seoul
SEA OF JAPAN
JAPAN
Honshu
Tokyo
PACIFIC OCEAN
KANSU
Hwang Ho
SHANSI
HOPEH
Peiping
Tientsin
Dairen (Jap.)
Weihaiwei To China 1930
Tsinan
SHANTUNG
Tsingtao
YELLOW SEA
Osaka
Shikoku
Kyushu
TIBET (AUTONOMOUS)
Lhasa
CHINGHAI
Yenan
CHINESE COMMUNISTS after 1935
SHENSI
Sian
Hwang Ho before 1938
Taiyuan
HONAN
Kaifeng
Hwang Ho after 1938
Panay Incident 1937
KIANGSU
Woosung
Shanghai
EAST CHINA SEA
SIKANG
Liuting
SZECHWAN
Chungking
HUPEH
Hankow
Ichang
ANHWEI
Nanking
Hangchow
CHEKIANG
Ryukyu Is. (Japan)
Okinawa
Yangtze Kiang
Tsunyi
KWEICHOW
HUNAN
Changsha
Nanchang
KIANGSI
FUKIEN
Amoy
Taiwan (Formosa) (Japan)
INDIA (British)
Brahmaputra R.
BHUTAN
BURMA (British)
Mandalay
Lashio
Irrawaddy R.
Salween R.
Mekong R.
Burma Road
"Long March" Communist Road 1934-5
Kunming
YUNNAN
CHINESE COMMUNISTS before 1934
KWANGSI
Nanning
KWANGTUNG
Canton
HONG KONG (Br.)
MACAO (Port.)
Bias Bay
Swatow
KWANG-CHOWAN (Fr.)
Hainan
FRENCH INDOCHINA
Occupied by Japan 1940
Haiphong
THAILAND (SIAM)
Ceded to Thai'd 1941
Bay of Bengal
Rangoon
Tropic of Cancer

80° 90° 100° 110° 120° Longitude East of 130° Greenwich 140° 150°

THE WORLD AT WAR 1939-1945

The following states, neutral throughout the greater part of the war, joined the conflict against the Axis after 1944 -

ARGENTINA	LEBANON	SYRIA
CHILE	PARAGUAY	TURKEY
ECUADOR	PERU	URUGUAY
EGYPT	SAUDI ARABIA	VENEZUELA

Legend:

- Sphere of German U-boat Operations
- Neutral States
- Allied Advances
- Naval & air bases obtained by U.S. from Great Britain are underlined.

- Areas Occupied by the Allies
- The Axis Powers (including Thailand and Japanese-occupied areas on Dec. 7, 1941)
- Areas Occupied by the Axis Powers
- Vichy-controlled Areas (later to Allies)

- – – – International Boundaries of September 1, 1939 (December 7, 1941 in Far East)
- – – – Allied Maritime Supply Routes
- ———— U. S. Military Airways
- The Allies

ECKERT PROJECTION
SCALE OF MILES ALONG EQUATOR

0 500 1000 1500 2000 2500 MILES
0 500 1000 1500 2000 2500 KILOMETERS

Copyright by C. S. HAMMOND & Co., N.Y.

ARCTIC OCEAN

NORTH AMERICA

SOUTH AMERICA

ATLANTIC OCEAN

PACIFIC OCEAN

INDIAN OCEAN

EUROPE

AFRICA

ASIA

AUSTRALIA

ANTARCTICA

UNION OF SOVIET SOCIALIST REPUBLICS

UNITED STATES

BRAZIL

CANADA

MEXICO

AUSTRALIA

NEW ZEALAND

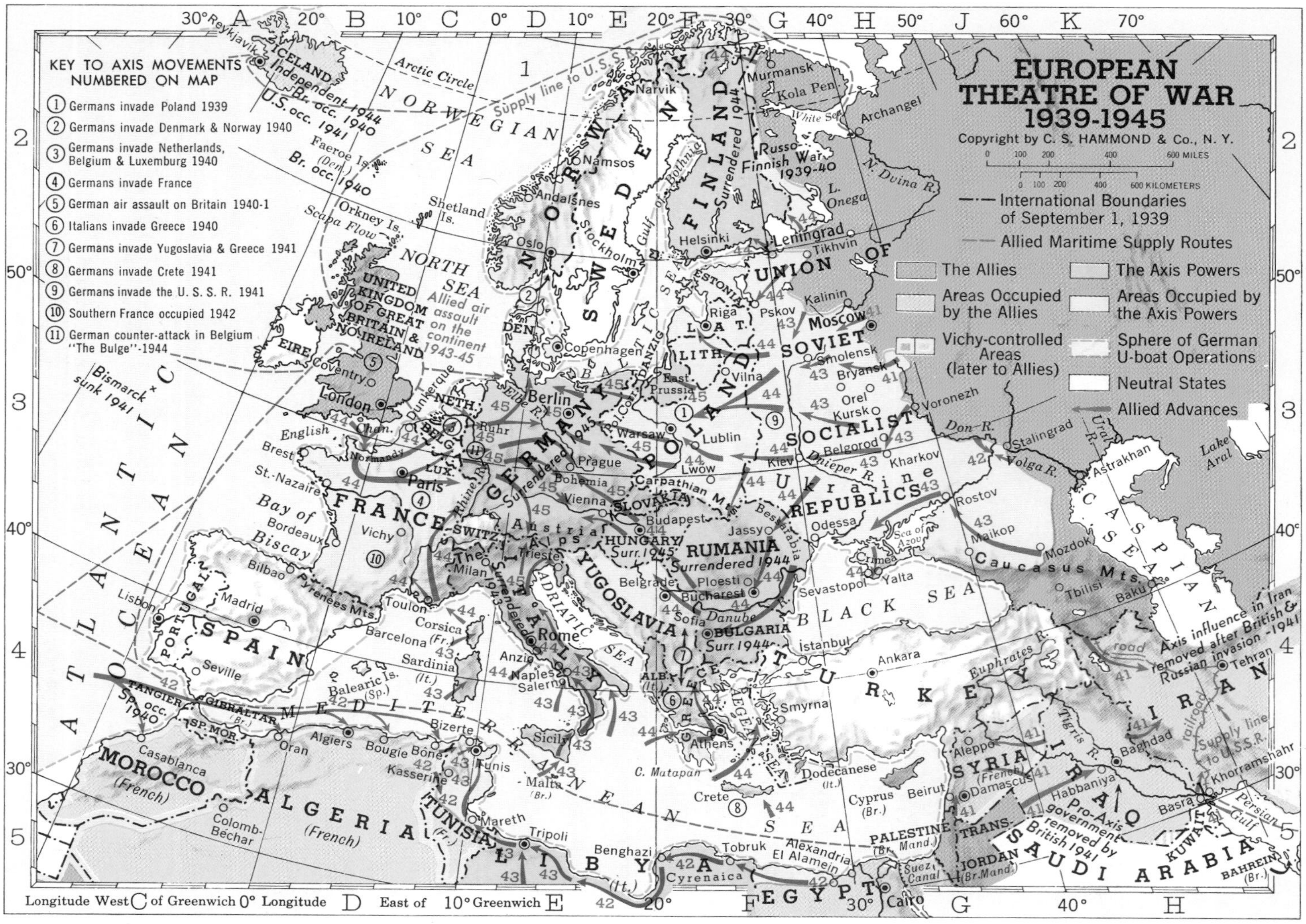
EUROPEAN THEATRE OF WAR 1939-1945
Copyright by C. S. HAMMOND & Co., N. Y.
KEY TO AXIS MOVEMENTS NUMBERED ON MAP
1 Germans invade Poland 1939
2 Germans invade Denmark & Norway 1940
3 Germans invade Netherlands, Belgium & Luxemburg 1940
4 Germans invade France
5 German air assault on Britain 1940-1
6 Italians invade Greece 1940
7 Germans invade Yugoslavia & Greece 1941
8 Germans invade Crete 1941
9 Germans invade the U. S. S. R. 1941
10 Southern France occupied 1942
11 German counter-attack in Belgium "The Bulge"-1944
International Boundaries of September 1, 1939
Allied Maritime Supply Routes
The Allies
The Axis Powers
Areas Occupied by the Allies
Areas Occupied by the Axis Powers
Vichy-controlled Areas (later to Allies)
Sphere of German U-boat Operations
Neutral States
Allied Advances
Longitude West of Greenwich 0° Longitude East of 10° Greenwich

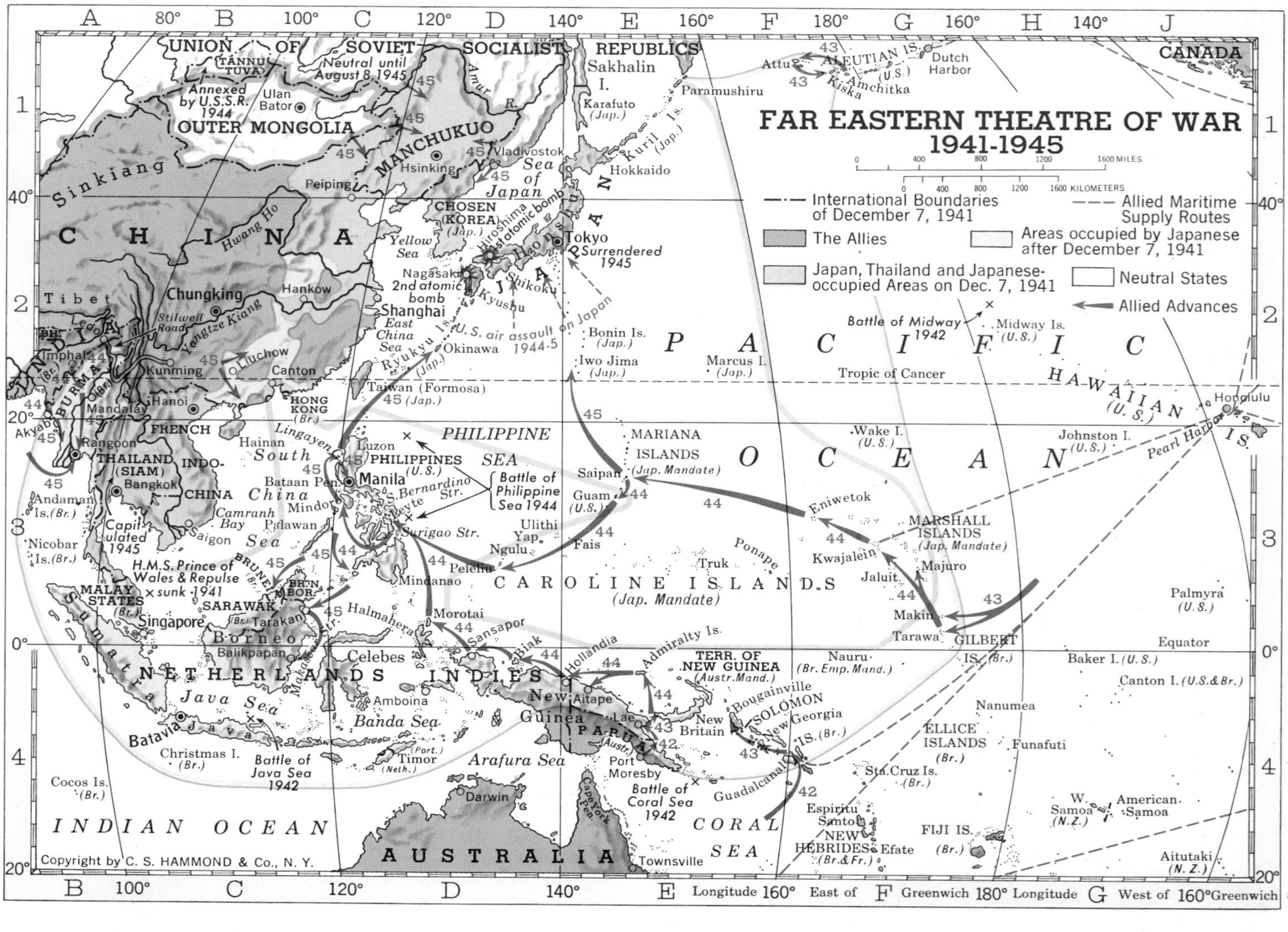
FAR EASTERN THEATRE OF WAR 1941-1945
International Boundaries of December 7, 1941
Allied Maritime Supply Routes
The Allies
Areas occupied by Japanese after December 7, 1941
Japan, Thailand and Japanese-occupied Areas on Dec. 7, 1941
Neutral States
Allied Advances
Copyright by C. S. HAMMOND & Co., N. Y.
Longitude 160° East of Greenwich 180° Longitude West of 160° Greenwich

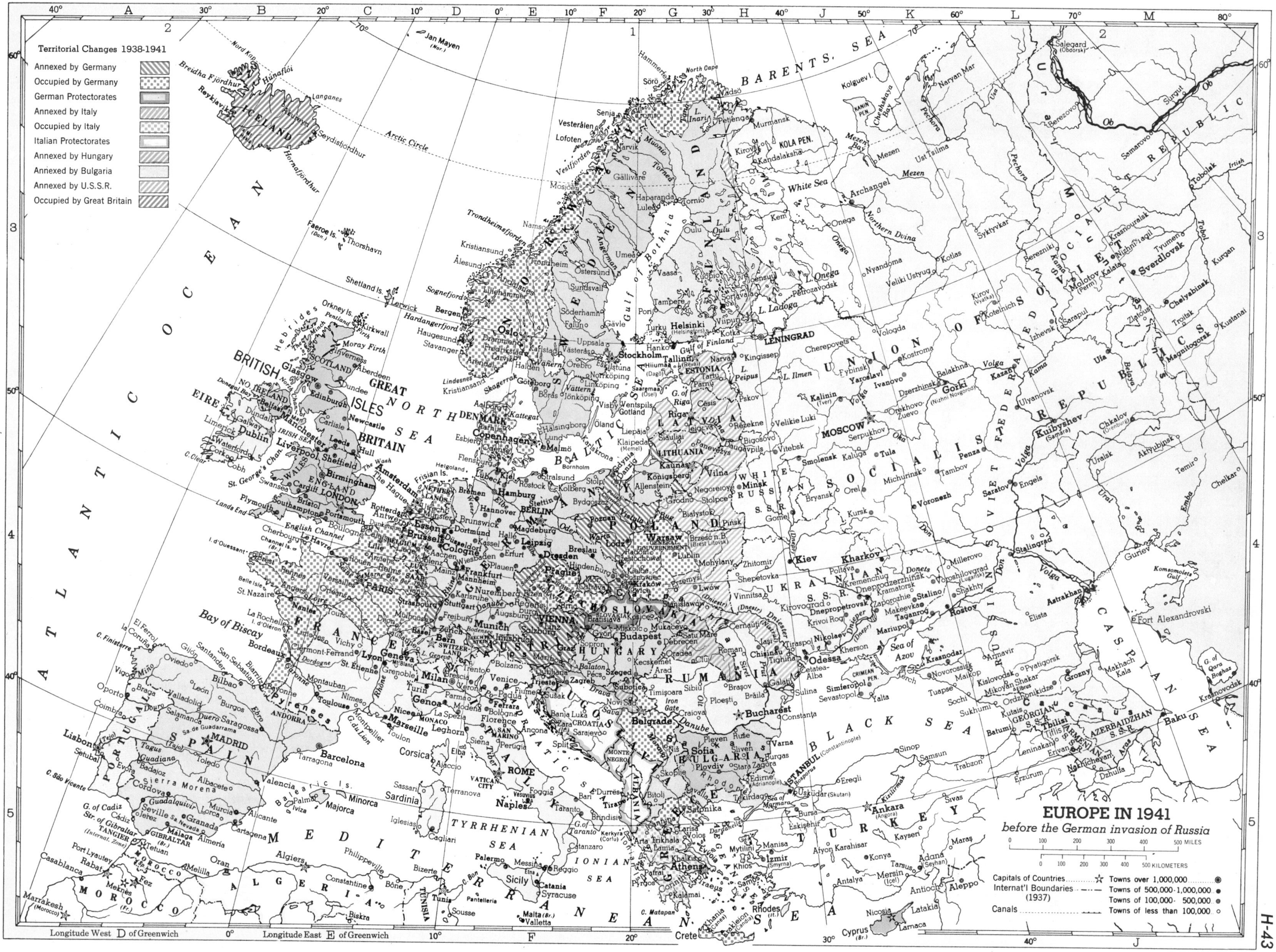

EUROPE IN 1941
before the German invasion of Russia
Territorial Changes 1938-1941
Annexed by Germany
Occupied by Germany
German Protectorates
Annexed by Italy
Occupied by Italy
Italian Protectorates
Annexed by Hungary
Annexed by Bulgaria
Annexed by U.S.S.R.
Occupied by Great Britain
Capitals of Countries
Internat'l Boundaries (1937)
Canals
Towns over 1,000,000
Towns of 500,000-1,000,000
Towns of 100,000-500,000
Towns of less than 100,000
0 100 200 300 400 500 MILES
0 100 200 300 400 500 KILOMETERS
ATLANTIC OCEAN
BARENTS SEA
NORTH SEA
BALTIC SEA
BLACK SEA
CASPIAN SEA
MEDITERRANEAN SEA
TYRRHENIAN SEA
IONIAN SEA
Bay of Biscay
UNION OF SOVIET SOCIALIST REPUBLICS
Longitude West D of Greenwich
Longitude East E of Greenwich

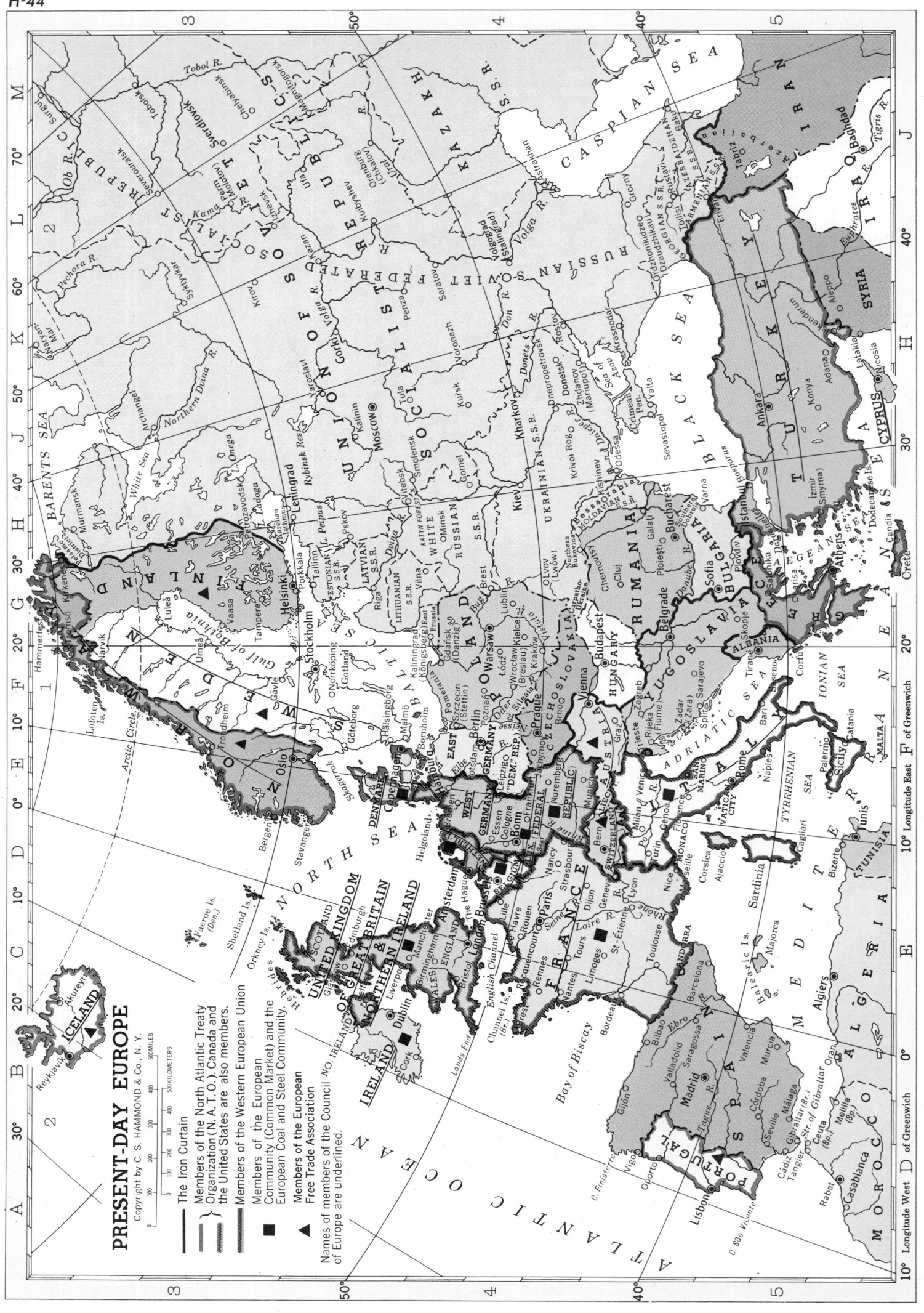

PRESENT-DAY EUROPE

Copyright by C. S. HAMMOND & Co., N.Y.

The Iron Curtain

Members of the North Atlantic Treaty Organization (N.A.T.O.). Canada and the United States are also members.

Members of the Western European Union

Members of the European Community (Common Market) and the European Coal and Steel Community.

Members of the European Free Trade Association

Names of members of the Council of Europe are underlined.

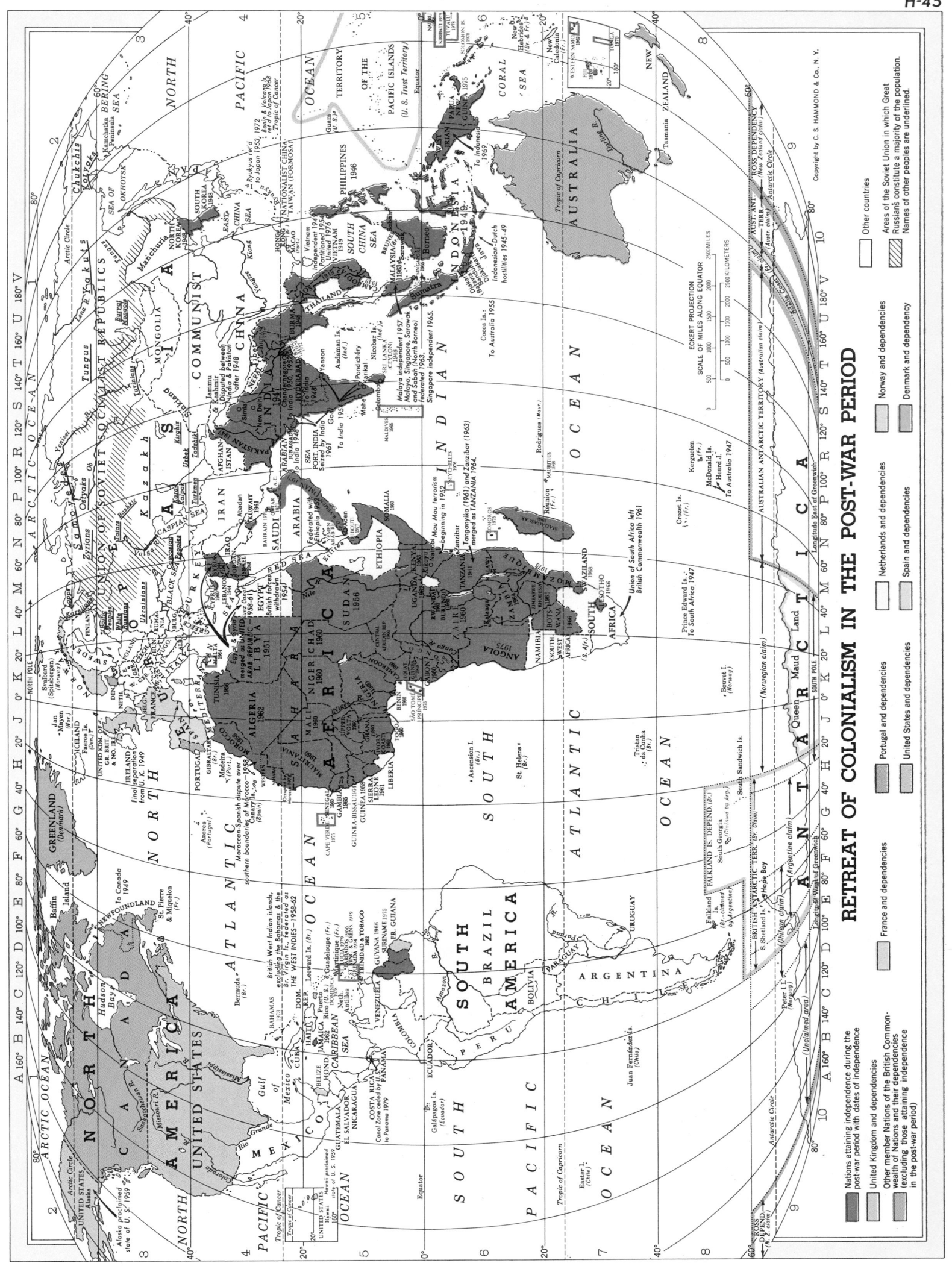

RETREAT OF COLONIALISM IN THE POST-WAR PERIOD

Legend (lower left):

- Nations attaining independence during the post-war period with dates of independence
- United Kingdom and dependencies
- Other member Nations of the British Commonwealth of Nations and their dependencies (excluding those attaining independence in the post-war period)

Legend (lower center/right):

- France and dependencies
- Portugal and dependencies
- Netherlands and dependencies
- United States and dependencies
- Norway and dependencies
- Spain and dependencies
- Denmark and dependency
- Other countries
- Areas of the Soviet Union in which Great Russians constitute a majority of the population.
- Names of other peoples are underlined.

ECKERT PROJECTION
SCALE OF MILES ALONG EQUATOR

Copyright by C. S. HAMMOND & Co., N.Y.

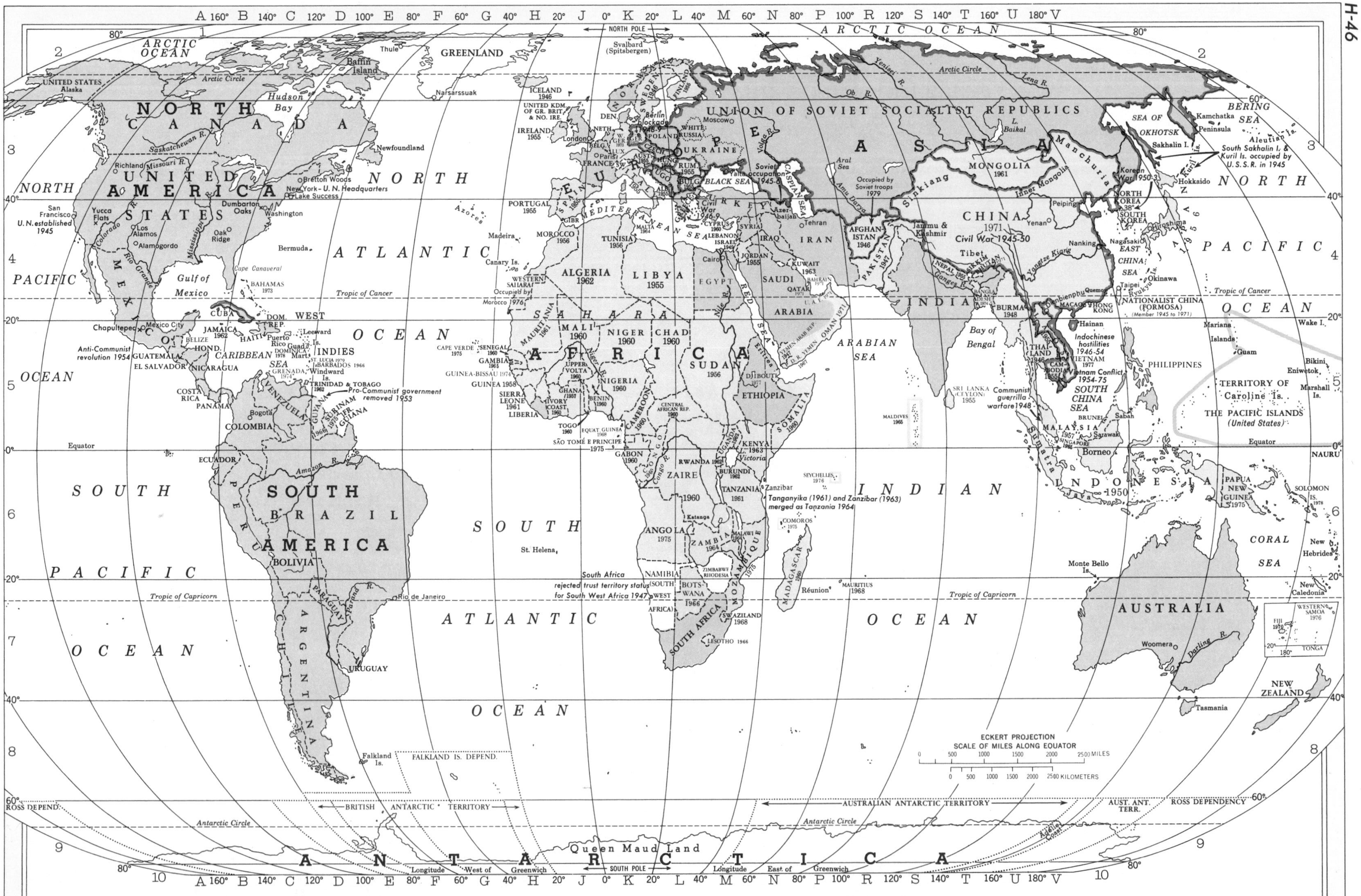

THE WORLD OF THE UNITED NATIONS AND THE COLD WAR

Legend:
- Original members of the United Nations ·1945
- Entrants after 1945 with dates of entry
- Non-members
- Trust Territories
- Communist States

ECKERT PROJECTION
SCALE OF MILES ALONG EQUATOR
0 500 1000 1500 2000 2500 MILES
0 500 1000 1500 2000 2500 KILOMETERS

EUROPE
PHYSICAL

Copyright by C. S. HAMMOND & CO., N.Y.

Mountain Altitudes in Feet

500 MILES
500 KILOMETERS

Feet
9840
6560
3280
1640
656
328
Sea Level
Depression
109
1640
3000
Fathoms

Metres
3000
2000
1000
500
200
100
Sea
Depression
200
3000
Metres

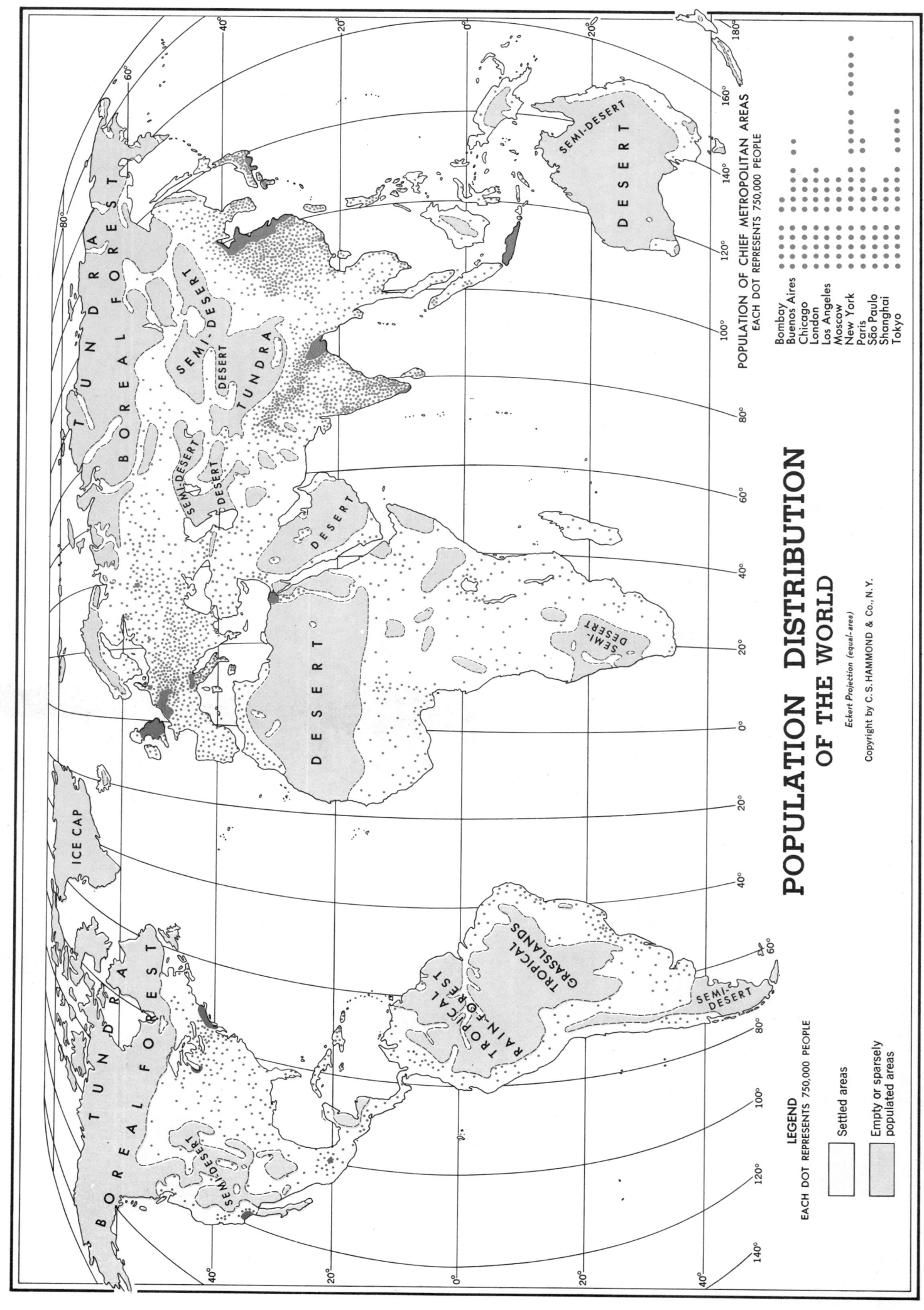

POPULATION DISTRIBUTION
OF THE WORLD

Eckert Projection (equal-area)

Copyright by C. S. HAMMOND & Co., N.Y.

POPULATION OF CHIEF METROPOLITAN AREAS
EACH DOT REPRESENTS 750,000 PEOPLE

Bombay
Buenos Aires
Chicago
London
Los Angeles
Moscow
New York
Paris
São Paulo
Shanghai
Tokyo

LEGEND
EACH DOT REPRESENTS 750,000 PEOPLE

Settled areas

Empty or sparsely
populated areas

United States History Atlas

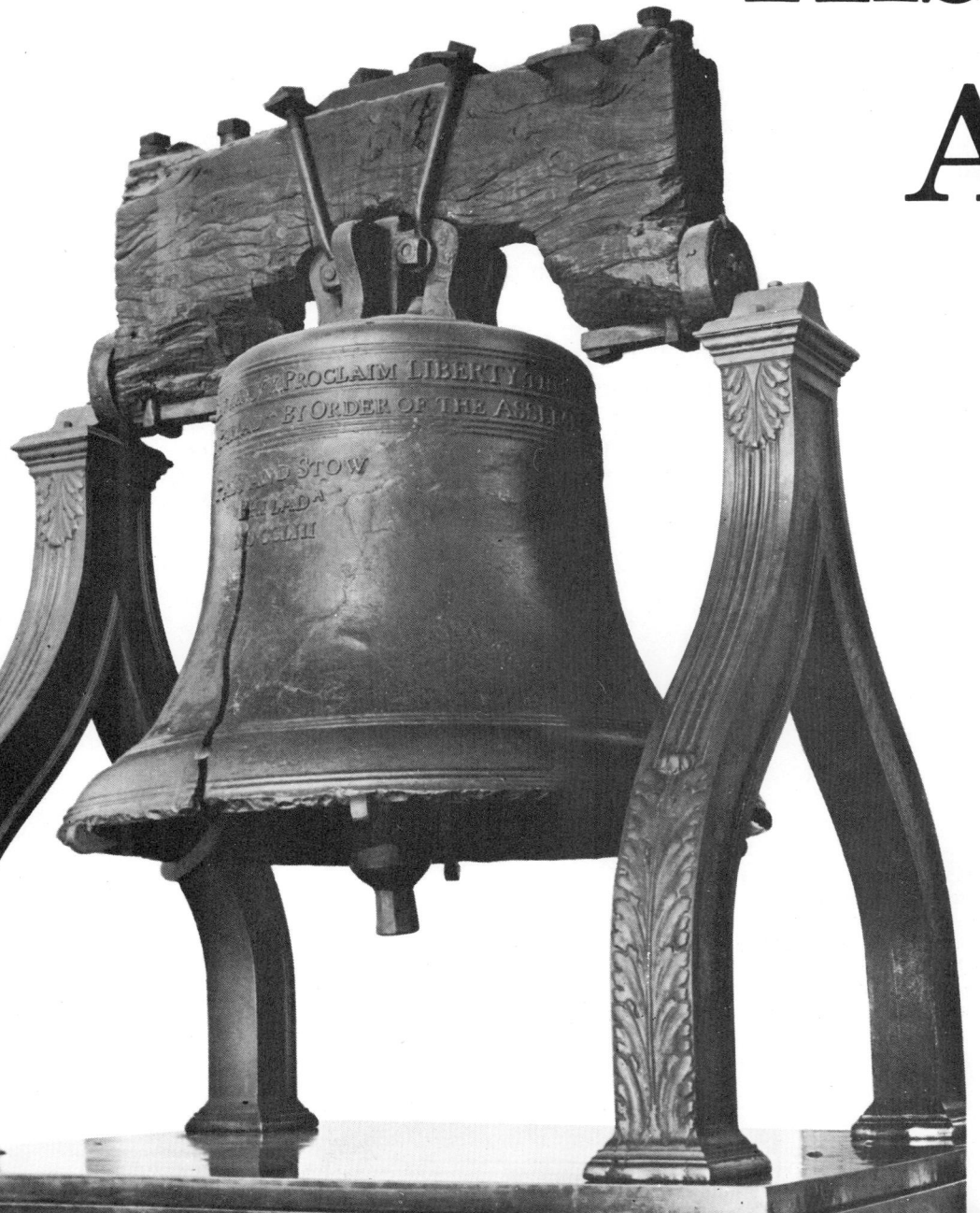

HAMMOND®
INCORPORATED
MAPLEWOOD, NEW JERSEY   07040

Introduction

The *United States History Atlas* was developed to help the student discover the geographic patterns underlying much of our nation's history. Using the maps and diagrams of this atlas, the student will develop a feeling of involvement in the great territorial, geopolitical and economic questions that constitute the American story. Such involvement should motivate the student to inquire on his own, into the geographic factors that underlie 400 years of political, economic and social life on this continent.

It will be noted that the contents of this atlas consist of far more than simple political maps merely showing political boundaries and towns at various dates. Instead, the maps and diagrams bring out the economic, social, demographic and ecological factors that have molded American history. For example, the maps of *Colonial America in 1770* on pages 12 and 13 present not only the boundaries of the thirteen colonies but, also, cartographic representation of colonial settlement patterns at three different dates, distribution maps showing the colonial economy, and an ethnic map illustrating the cultural diversity of the Atlantic seaboard area in the eighteenth century. Many other maps and graphs in the atlas bring out the socio-geographic elements of various periods in our history.

The sequence of maps in the atlas is broadly chronological, beginning with maps portraying the major Indian tribes and families and ending with maps and diagrams depicting current urban problems, economic data and election results. However, many topical maps, covering long periods of time, appear throughout the work. Thus the map of *Expansion of the United States* on page 16 shows the territorial growth of our nation from 1783 to 1898 — a single topic through 116 years of time. The maps entitled *Growth of Industry and Cities* on pages 34 and 35 cover modern industrial and urban development from its beginning at the time of the Civil War to the present decade. At the end of the atlas is a useful index locating specific place names important in American history.

The publishers of this wholly new teaching tool have succeeded in producing maps and graphs that are notable for their conciseness, legibility and scholarship. The type faces used for place names on the maps are distinguished for their clarity and large size. Colors have been selected to delineate clearly one geographic area from another. Confusing detail and overcrowding have been avoided by creating several maps for each topic and period of American history. Many of the maps indicate terrain by a shaded relief technique, so that the student will be made aware of the influence of topography on the events and movements of history. The result is a historical atlas that is both eye-pleasing and authoritative.

Contents

A

CREE

MONTAGNAIS

SALISHAN TRIBES

KUTENAI

BLACKFEET (SIKSIKA)

NOOTKA

ATSINA

ASSINIBOIN

CHIPPEWA (OJIBWA)

OTTAWA

ALGONKIN

MICMAC

MALECITE

ABNAKI

YAKIMA PALOUSE

FLATHEAD (SALISH)

NEZ PERCÉ

CHINOOK

YAQUINA

CAYUSE

HIDATSA MANDAN 22

DAKOTA (SIOUX)

HURON

IROQUOIS 20

MASSACHUSET

SIUSLAW

KLAMATH MODOC

BANNOCK

CROW

MENOMINEE

SAUK

WINNEBAGO 22

POTAWATOMI

NEUTRAL

ERIE

SUSQUEHANNA

2 PEQUOT

YUROK SHASTA

SHOSHONI

2 SUTAIO

21 ARIKARA

FOX

MIAMI

DELAWARE

MAIDU

PAIUTE 11

CHEYENNE 2

PONCA OMAHA

IOWA

ILLINOIS 2

NANTICOKE

WASHO 8

UTE

OTO

SHAWNEE

MANAHOAC TUTELO

POWHATAN

POMO

MIWOK YOKUTS

SHOSHONI

ARAPAHO

PAWNEE 21

MISSOURI 22

22 CATAWBA

TUSCARORA 20

COSTANOAN

SALINAN

CHUMASH 16

PAIUTE

NAVAHO

MOHAVE

HOPI 11

ZUÑI 19 12

KIOWA 12

KANSA

OSAGE

CHEROKEE 20

YUCHI

CUSABO

CAHUILLA

YUMA

PUEBLOS 1

APACHE

COMANCHE 11

WICHITA 21

QUAPAW

CHICKASAW

CREEK 23

CADDO

13 CHOCTAW

NATCHEZ

YAMASEE

DIEGUEÑO

PAPAGO

PIMA

WACO

TONKAWA

13 ATAKAPA

13

22 BILOXI

SEMINOLE

UTINA 24

CONCHO

KARANKAWA

11

COAHUILTECAN TRIBES 17

CALUSA 23

LAGUNERO

TAMAULIPEC TRIBES

1	ATHAPASCAN		
2	ALGONKIAN		
3	RITWAN	14	HOKAN
4	KUTENAI	15	YUMAN
5	WAKASHAN	16	SALINAN–SERIAN
6	CHIMAKUAN	17	COAHUILTECAN
7	SALISHAN	18	YUKIAN
8	PENUTIAN	19	KERESAN
9	CHINOOKAN	20	IROQUOIAN
10	SAHAPTIAN	21	CADDOAN
11	UTO–AZTECAN	22	SIOUAN–YUCHI
12	TANO–ZUÑIAN	23	MUSKHOGEAN
13	TUNICAN	24	TIMUCUAN

© Copyright HAMMOND INCORPORATED, Maplewood, N.J.
Printed in U.S.A.

AMERICAN INDIANS
•
LINGUISTIC FAMILIES
•
MAJOR TRIBES

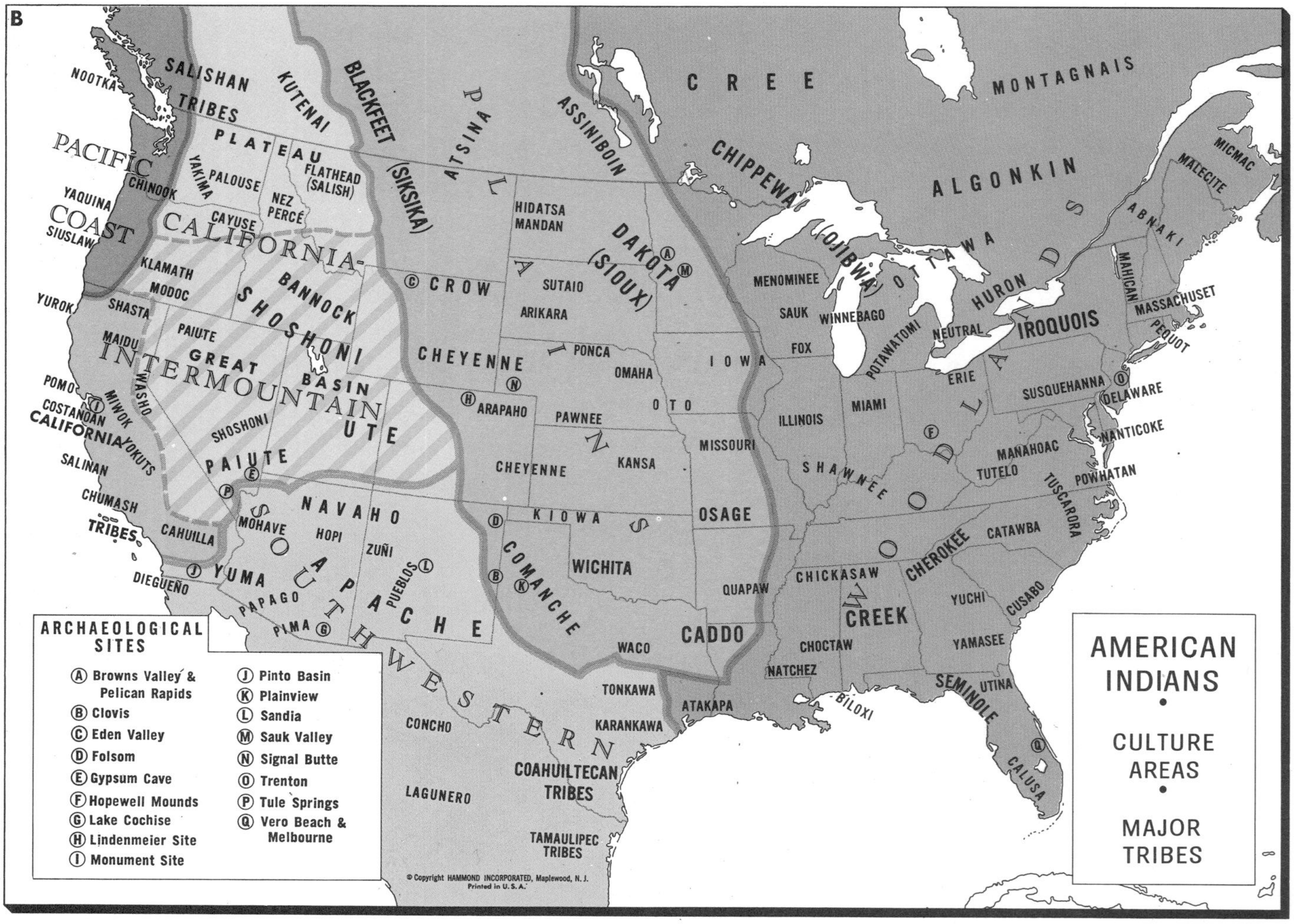

B

CREE

MONTAGNAIS

SALISHAN TRIBES

KUTENAI

BLACKFEET (SIKSIKA)

NOOTKA

PACIFIC

PLATEAU

ATSINA

ASSINIBOIN

CHIPPEWA (OJIBWA)

OTTAWA

ALGONKIN

MICMAC

MALECITE

YAKIMA PALOUSE

FLATHEAD (SALISH)

NEZ PERCÉ

COAST

CALIFORNIA-

CHINOOK

YAQUINA

CAYUSE

HIDATSA MANDAN

DAKOTA (SIOUX)

HURON

IROQUOIS

ABNAKI

SIUSLAW

KLAMATH MODOC

BANNOCK

Ⓒ CROW

MENOMINEE

SAUK

WINNEBAGO

POTAWATOMI

NEUTRAL ERIE

MASSACHUSET

PEQUOT

YUROK SHASTA

SHOSHONI

PAIUTE

SUTAIO

ARIKARA

FOX

MIAMI

SUSQUEHANNA

DELAWARE

MAIDU

GREAT BASIN

CHEYENNE

PONCA OMAHA

IOWA

ILLINOIS

NANTICOKE

POMO

WASHO

INTERMOUNTAIN

UTE

Ⓗ ARAPAHO

Ⓝ

PAWNEE

OTO

MISSOURI

SHAWNEE

MANAHOAC TUTELO

POWHATAN

COSTANOAN

MIWOK YOKUTS

SHOSHONI

KANSA

OSAGE

CHEROKEE

CATAWBA

TUSCARORA

CALIFORNIA

SALINAN

PAIUTE

Ⓔ

NAVAHO

KIOWA

WICHITA

QUAPAW

CHICKASAW

YUCHI

CUSABO

CHUMASH

TRIBES

CAHUILLA

MOHAVE

HOPI

ZUÑI

Ⓛ

Ⓓ

Ⓑ COMANCHE

CREEK

YAMASEE

DIEGUEÑO

YUMA Ⓙ

PUEBLOS

Ⓚ

CADDO

CHOCTAW

SEMINOLE

UTINA

PAPAGO

PIMA Ⓖ

APACHE

SOUTHWESTERN

WOODLANDS

NATCHEZ

WACO

TONKAWA

ATAKAPA

BILOXI

CONCHO

KARANKAWA

CALUSA

LAGUNERO

COAHUILTECAN TRIBES

TAMAULIPEC TRIBES

ARCHAEOLOGICAL SITES

Ⓐ Browns Valley & Pelican Rapids	Ⓙ Pinto Basin
Ⓑ Clovis	Ⓚ Plainview
Ⓒ Eden Valley	Ⓛ Sandia
Ⓓ Folsom	Ⓜ Sauk Valley
Ⓔ Gypsum Cave	Ⓝ Signal Butte
Ⓕ Hopewell Mounds	Ⓞ Trenton
Ⓖ Lake Cochise	Ⓟ Tule Springs
Ⓗ Lindenmeier Site	Ⓠ Vero Beach & Melbourne
Ⓘ Monument Site	

© Copyright HAMMOND INCORPORATED, Maplewood, N.J.
Printed in U.S.A.

AMERICAN INDIANS
•
CULTURE AREAS
•
MAJOR TRIBES

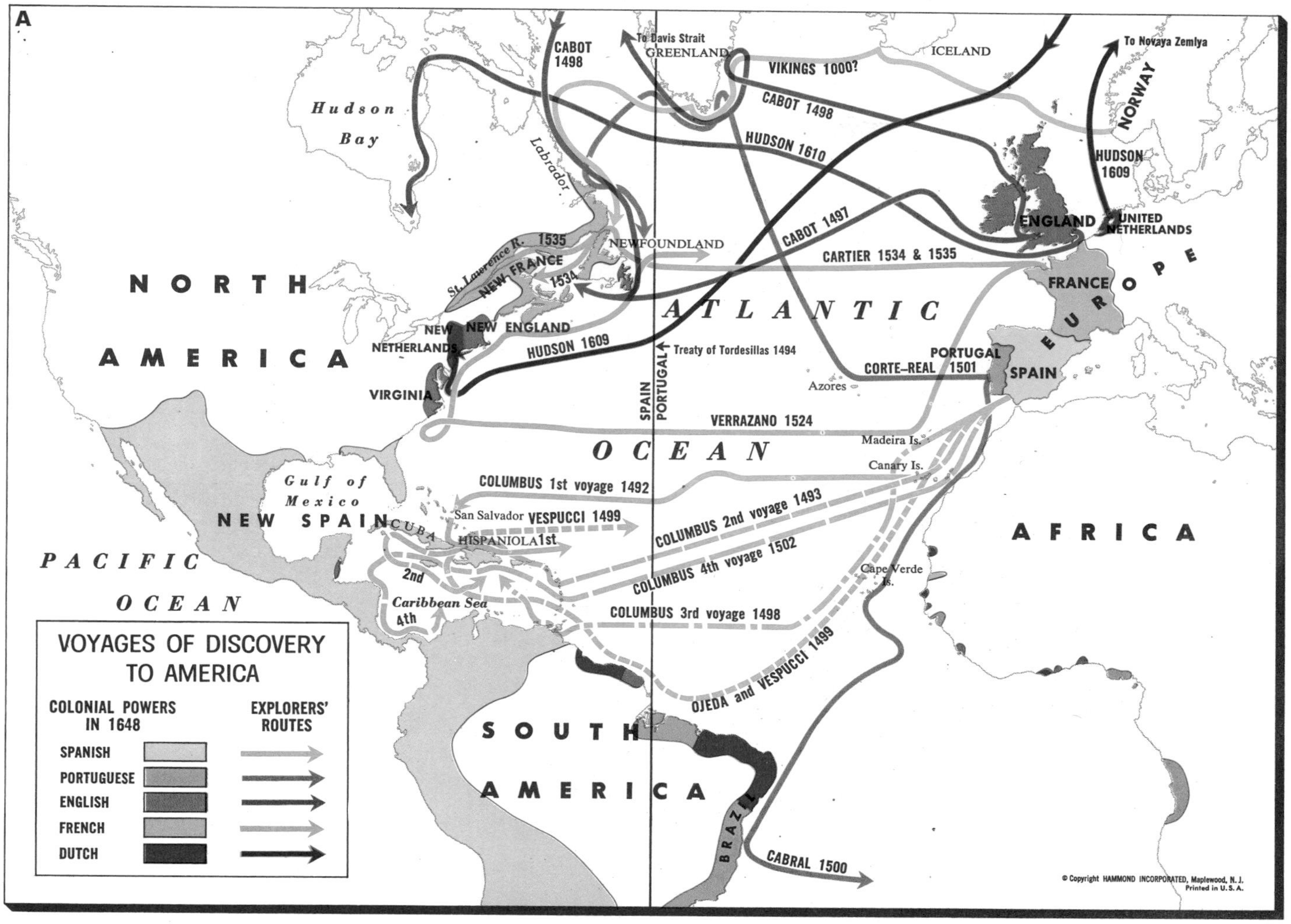
A
VOYAGES OF DISCOVERY TO AMERICA
COLONIAL POWERS IN 1648
EXPLORERS' ROUTES
SPANISH
PORTUGUESE
ENGLISH
FRENCH
DUTCH
NORTH AMERICA
SOUTH AMERICA
AFRICA
EUROPE
ATLANTIC OCEAN
PACIFIC OCEAN
Hudson Bay
Gulf of Mexico
Caribbean Sea
Labrador
GREENLAND
ICELAND
NORWAY
NEWFOUNDLAND
NEW FRANCE
St. Lawrence R.
NEW ENGLAND
NEW NETHERLANDS
VIRGINIA
NEW SPAIN
CUBA
HISPANIOLA
San Salvador
BRAZIL
ENGLAND
UNITED NETHERLANDS
FRANCE
SPAIN
PORTUGAL
Azores
Madeira Is.
Canary Is.
Cape Verde Is.
Treaty of Tordesillas 1494
SPAIN
PORTUGAL
To Davis Strait
To Novaya Zemlya
CABOT 1498
VIKINGS 1000?
CABOT 1498
HUDSON 1610
HUDSON 1609
CABOT 1497
CARTIER 1534 & 1535
1535
1534
HUDSON 1609
CORTE-REAL 1501
VERRAZANO 1524
COLUMBUS 1st voyage 1492
VESPUCCI 1499
COLUMBUS 2nd voyage 1493
COLUMBUS 4th voyage 1502
COLUMBUS 3rd voyage 1498
1st
2nd
4th
OJEDA and VESPUCCI 1499
CABRAL 1500

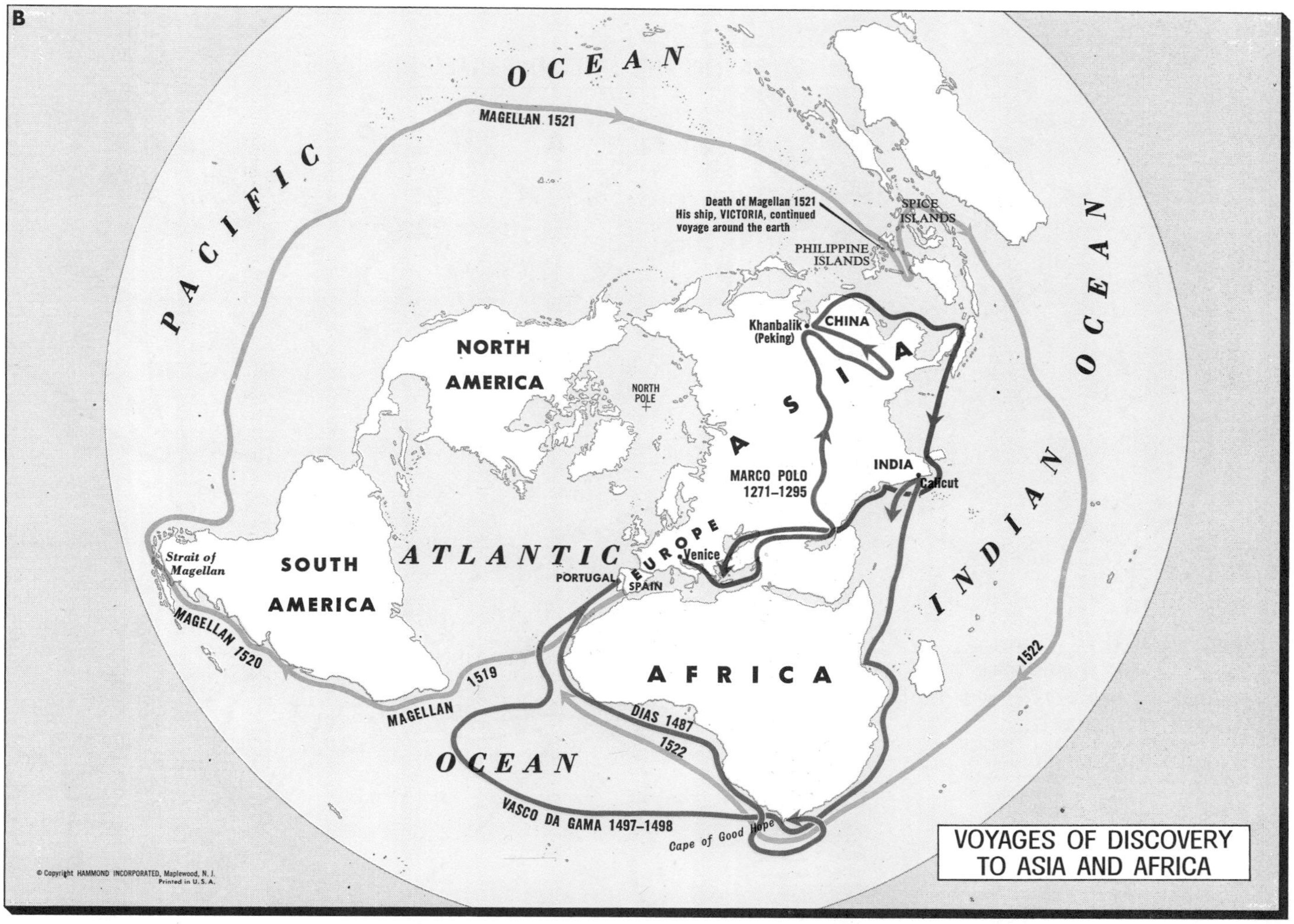
B
VOYAGES OF DISCOVERY TO ASIA AND AFRICA
PACIFIC OCEAN
ATLANTIC OCEAN
INDIAN OCEAN
NORTH AMERICA
SOUTH AMERICA
AFRICA
EUROPE
ASIA
NORTH POLE
CHINA
INDIA
Khanbalik (Peking)
Calicut
Venice
PORTUGAL
SPAIN
SPICE ISLANDS
PHILIPPINE ISLANDS
Strait of Magellan
Cape of Good Hope
Death of Magellan 1521
His ship, VICTORIA, continued voyage around the earth
MAGELLAN 1521
MAGELLAN 1520
MAGELLAN
1519
1522
MARCO POLO 1271–1295
DIAS 1487
1522
VASCO DA GAMA 1497–1498

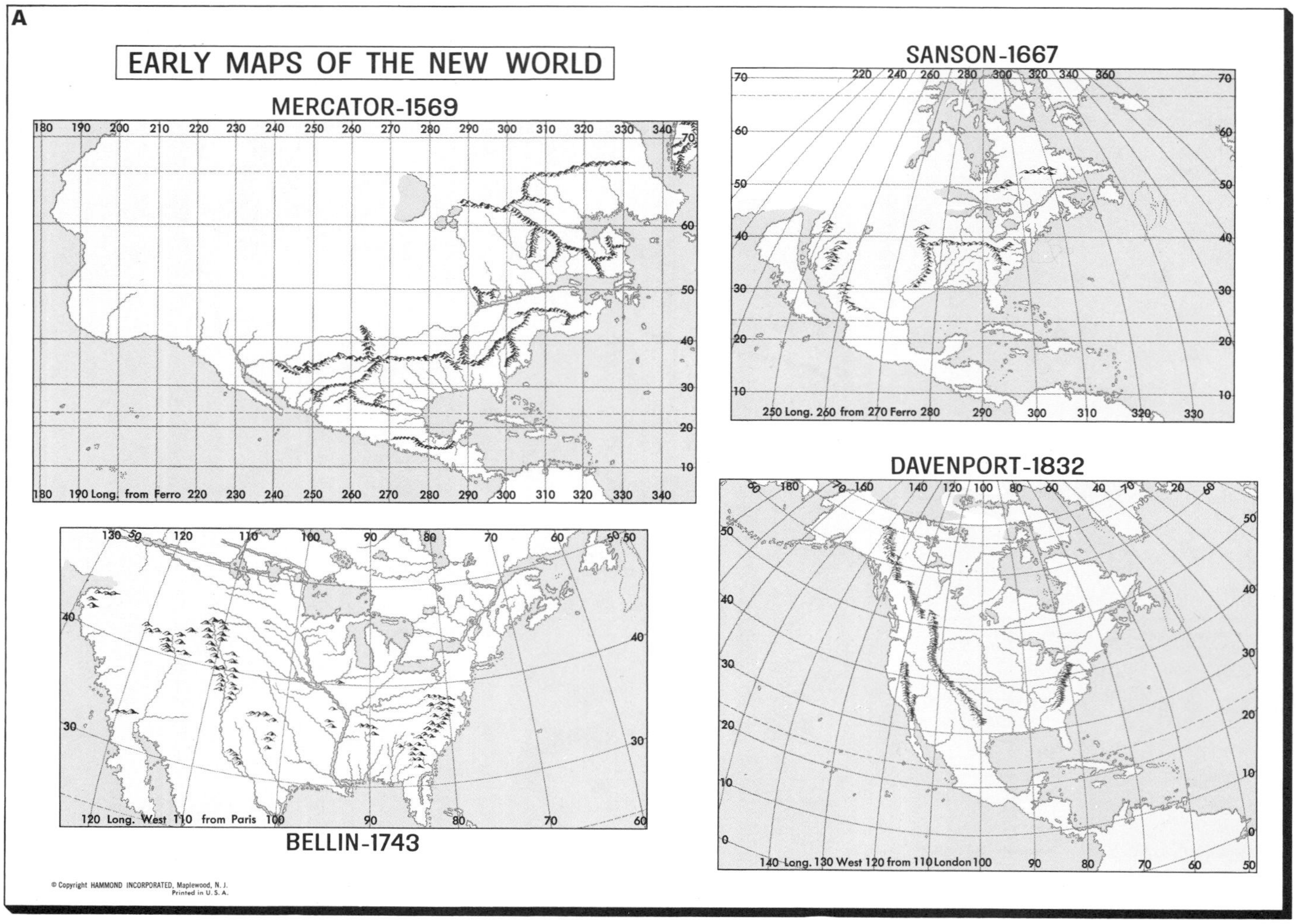

A

EARLY MAPS OF THE NEW WORLD

MERCATOR-1569

SANSON-1667

DAVENPORT-1832

BELLIN-1743

© Copyright HAMMOND INCORPORATED, Maplewood, N.J.
Printed in U.S.A.

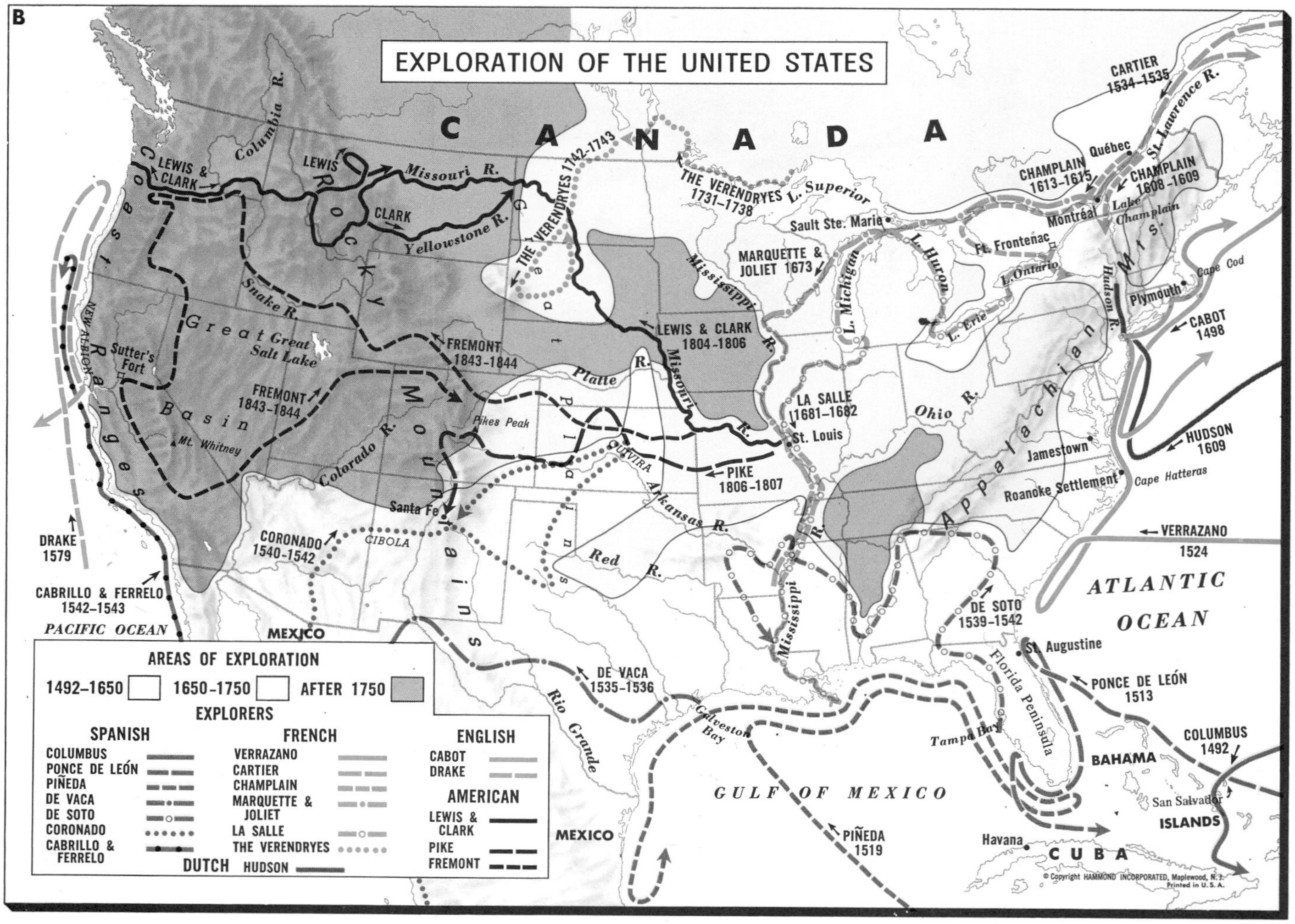

B

EXPLORATION OF THE UNITED STATES

CANADA

CARTIER 1534-1535

LEWIS & CLARK

Columbia R.

LEWIS

Missouri R.

CLARK

Yellowstone R.

THE VERENDRYES 1742-1743

THE VERENDRYES 1731-1738

L. Superior

Sault Ste. Marie

MARQUETTE & JOLIET 1673

CHAMPLAIN 1613-1615

Québec

St. Lawrence R.

CHAMPLAIN 1608-1609

Montréal

Lake Champlain

Ft. Frontenac

L. Huron

L. Michigan

L. Ontario

L. Erie

Hudson R.

Plymouth

Cape Cod

CABOT 1498

Snake R.

Great Salt Lake

Great Basin

Mt. Whitney

FREMONT 1843-1844

FREMONT 1843-1844

Pikes Peak

Platte R.

LEWIS & CLARK 1804-1806

Missouri R.

LA SALLE 1681-1682

St. Louis

Ohio R.

Jamestown

HUDSON 1609

Roanoke Settlement

Cape Hatteras

Colorado R.

Santa Fe

PIKE 1806-1807

CIBOLA

Arkansas R.

VERRAZANO 1524

DRAKE 1579

CORONADO 1540-1542

Red R.

ATLANTIC OCEAN

CABRILLO & FERRELO 1542-1543

PACIFIC OCEAN

MEXICO

DE SOTO 1539-1542

St. Augustine

DE VACA 1535-1536

DE VACA

Mississippi R.

Rio Grande

Galveston Bay

Florida Peninsula

PONCE DE LEÓN 1513

MEXICO

GULF OF MEXICO

Tampa Bay

COLUMBUS 1492

BAHAMA

PIÑEDA 1519

Havana

CUBA

San Salvador

ISLANDS

AREAS OF EXPLORATION

1492–1650   1650–1750   AFTER 1750

EXPLORERS

SPANISH
COLUMBUS
PONCE DE LEÓN
PIÑEDA
DE VACA
DE SOTO
CORONADO
CABRILLO & FERRELO

FRENCH
VERRAZANO
CARTIER
CHAMPLAIN
MARQUETTE & JOLIET
LA SALLE
THE VERENDRYES

DUTCH HUDSON

ENGLISH
CABOT
DRAKE

AMERICAN
LEWIS & CLARK
PIKE
FREMONT

© Copyright HAMMOND INCORPORATED, Maplewood, N.J.
Printed in U.S.A.

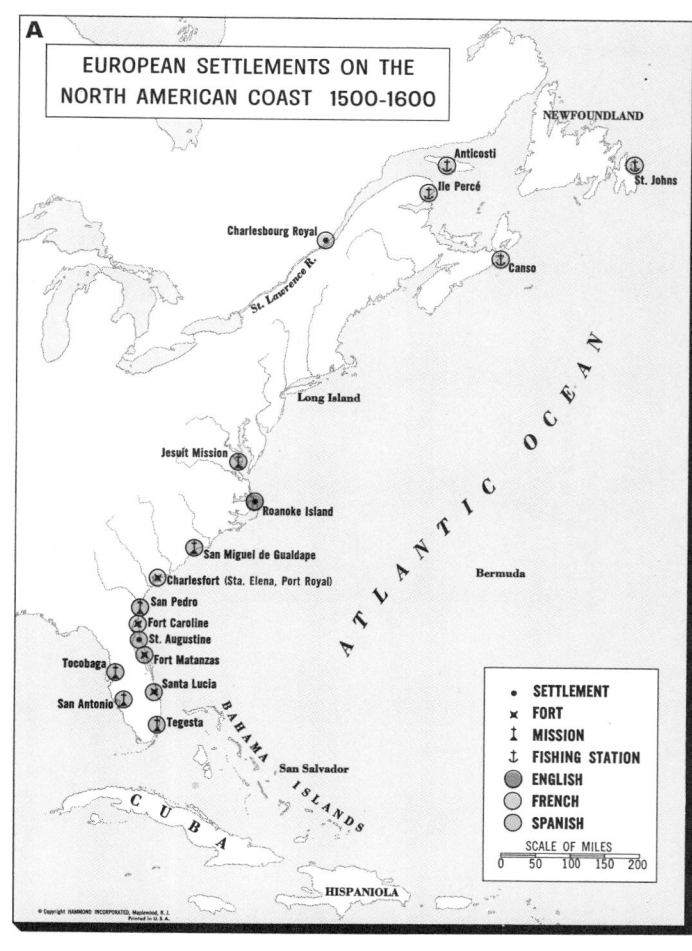

A

EUROPEAN SETTLEMENTS ON THE NORTH AMERICAN COAST 1500-1600

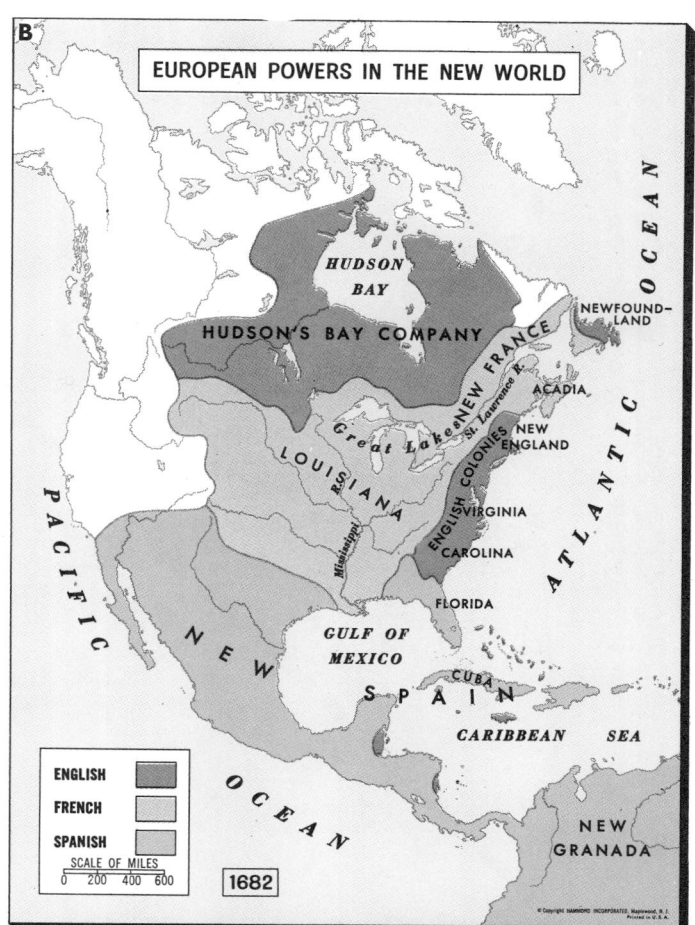

B

EUROPEAN POWERS IN THE NEW WORLD

1682

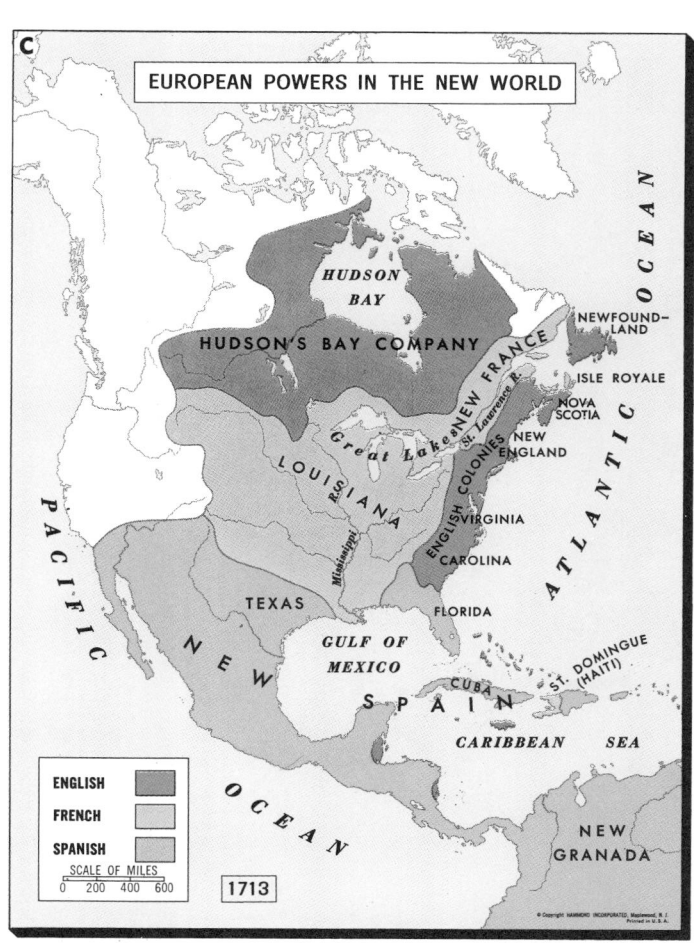

C

EUROPEAN POWERS IN THE NEW WORLD

1713

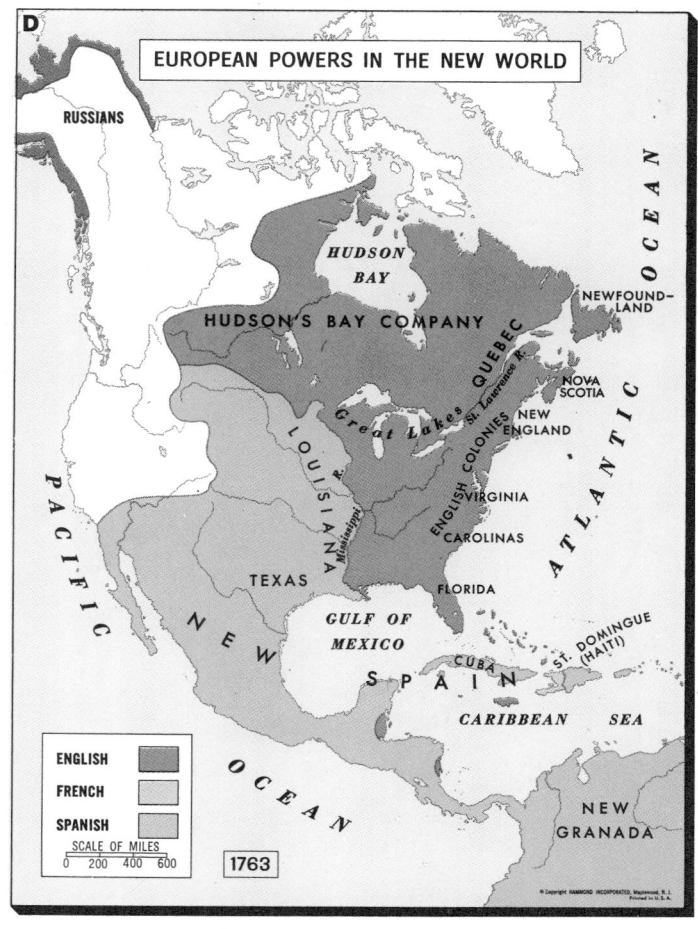

D

EUROPEAN POWERS IN THE NEW WORLD

1763

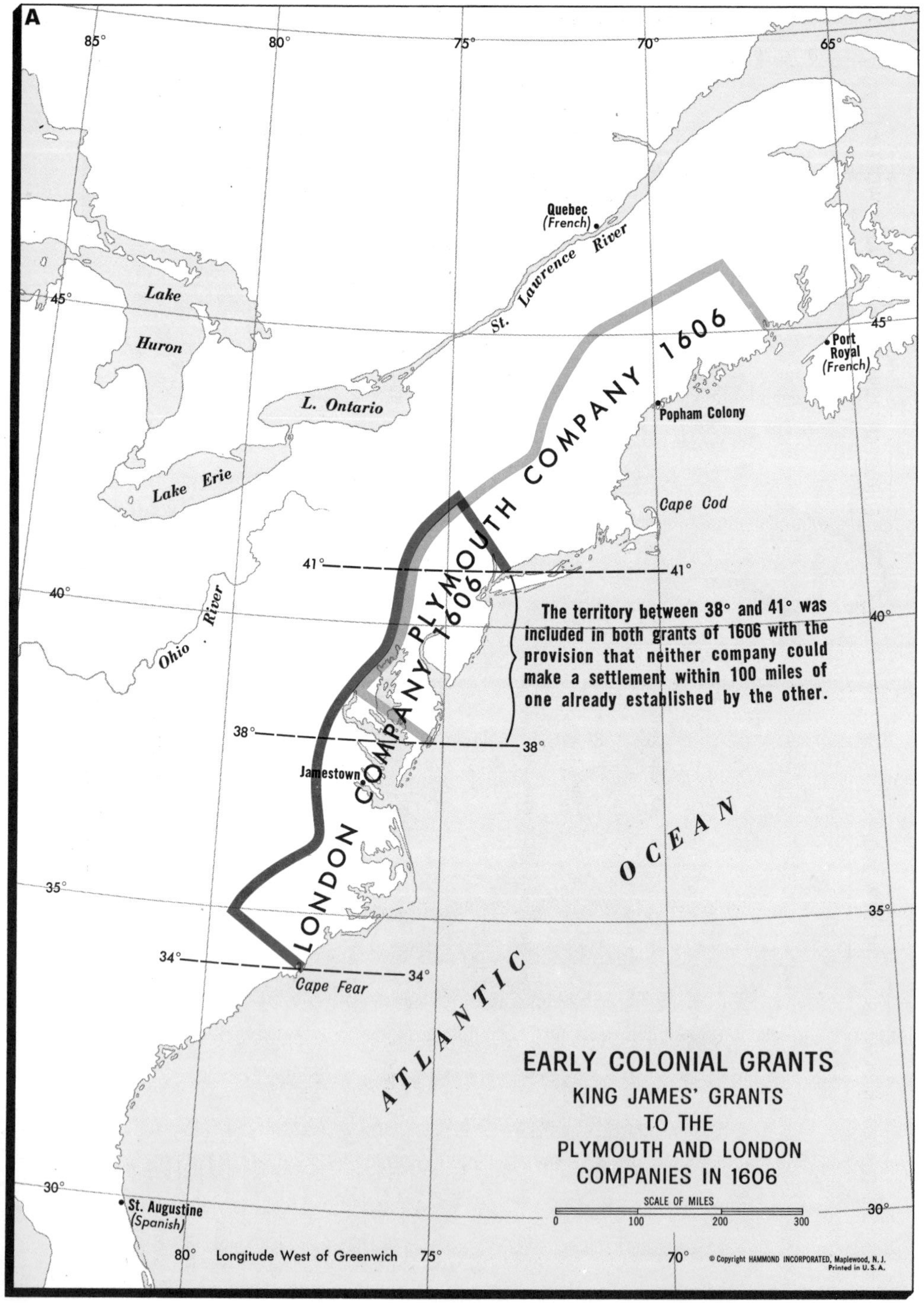

Map B — EARLY COLONIAL GRANTS
GRANTS TO THE VIRGINIA COMPANY OF LONDON 1609 AND THE PLYMOUTH COUNCIL FOR NEW ENGLAND 1620

PLYMOUTH COUNCIL FOR NEW ENGLAND 1620

VIRGINIA COMPANY OF LONDON 1609

"from sea to sea"

ATLANTIC OCEAN

Port Royal (French)
Quebec (French)
St. Lawrence River
Cape Cod
Plymouth
L. Ontario
Lake Erie
Lake Huron
Ohio River
Jamestown
Point Comfort
Cape Fear
St. Augustine (Spanish)

Longitude West of Greenwich

SCALE OF MILES

© Copyright HAMMOND INCORPORATED, Maplewood, N.J. Printed in U.S.A.

Map A — EARLY COLONIAL GRANTS
KING JAMES' GRANTS TO THE PLYMOUTH AND LONDON COMPANIES IN 1606

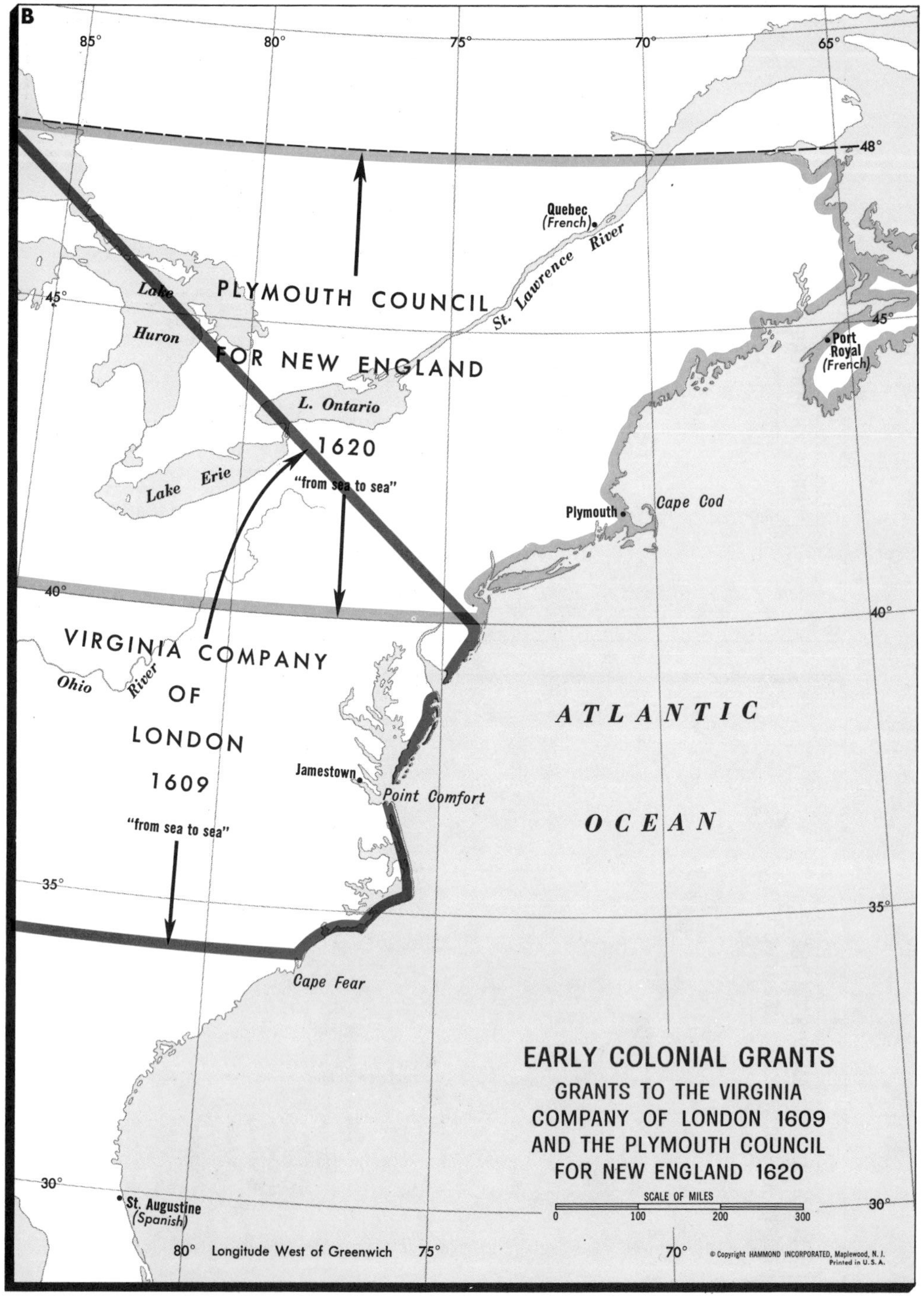

PLYMOUTH COMPANY 1606

LONDON COMPANY 1606

The territory between 38° and 41° was included in both grants of 1606 with the provision that neither company could make a settlement within 100 miles of one already established by the other.

ATLANTIC OCEAN

Port Royal (French)
Quebec (French)
St. Lawrence River
Popham Colony
Cape Cod
L. Ontario
Lake Erie
Lake Huron
Ohio River
Jamestown
Cape Fear
St. Augustine (Spanish)

Longitude West of Greenwich

SCALE OF MILES

© Copyright HAMMOND INCORPORATED, Maplewood, N.J. Printed in U.S.A.

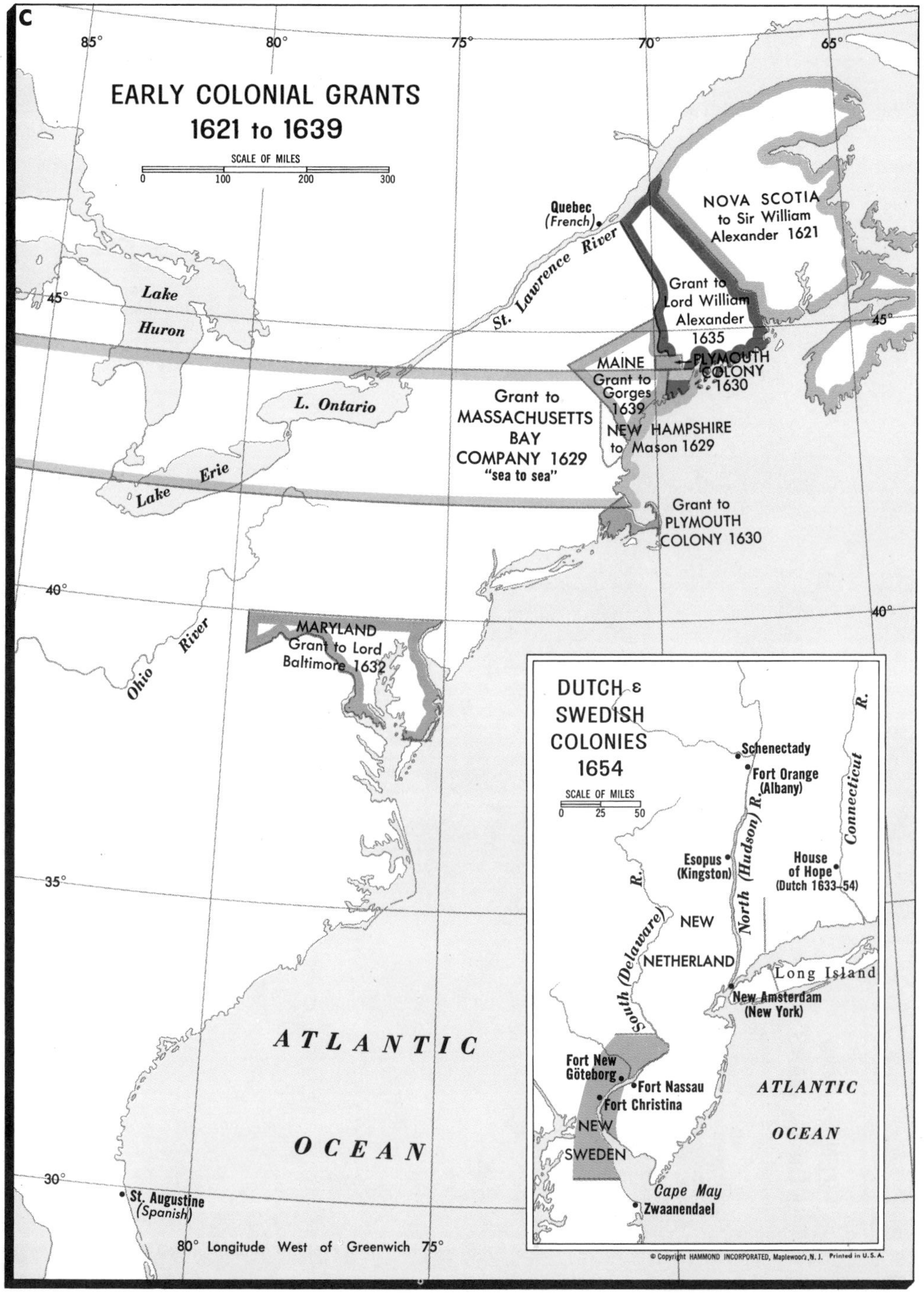

EARLY COLONIAL GRANTS 1662 to 1732

SCALE OF MILES
0 100 200 300

Quebec (French)

St. Lawrence River

Lake Huron
Lake Ontario
Lake Erie
Ohio River

L. Ontario

Grant to Duke of York 1664

Grant to RHODE ISLAND & PROVIDENCE PLANTATIONS 1663

NEW YORK Grant to Duke of York 1664

Grant to CONNECTICUT COL. CO. 1662 "sea to sea"

PENNSYLVANIA Grant to William Penn 1681

NEW JERSEY Grant by Duke of York to Lord Berkeley & Sir George Carteret 1664

DELAWARE Grant by Duke of York to William Penn 1682

CAROLINA Grant to Earl of Clarendon "sea to sea" & others 1665

GEORGIA Grant to James Oglethorpe & others 1732 "sea to sea"

ATLANTIC OCEAN

St. Augustine (Spanish)

80° Longitude West of Greenwich

CONNECTICUT AND NEW HAVEN COLONIES 1635-1664 AND THE DIVISION OF NEW JERSEY 1676-1702

SCALE OF MILES
0 25 50

■ NEW HAVEN COLONY TOWNS
● CONNECTICUT COLONY TOWNS

Boundary of 1703
Boundary of 1662 (modified)
Hartford
CONNECTICUT COLONY
New Haven
NEW HAVEN COLONY
Long Island
New York
Hudson R.
Boundary of 1683 (New York's title confirmed 1664)
Boundary of 1664
Boundary of 1773
NEW YORK
EAST JERSEY
Perth Amboy
WEST JERSEY
Burlington
PENNSYLVANIA
Philadelphia
Delaware R.
Delaware Bay
Cape May

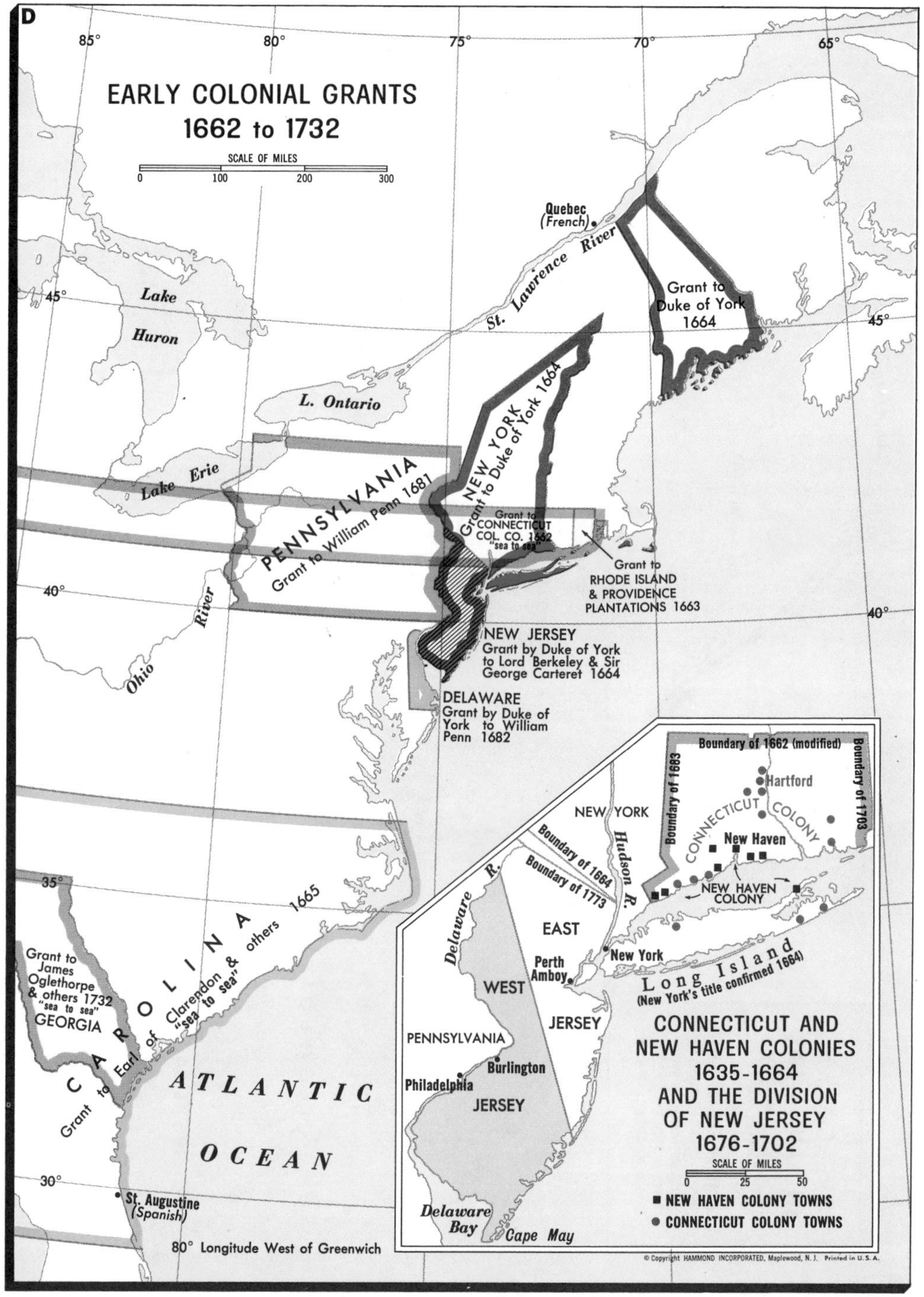

© Copyright HAMMOND INCORPORATED, Maplewood, N.J. Printed in U.S.A.

EARLY COLONIAL GRANTS 1621 to 1639

SCALE OF MILES
0 100 200 300

Quebec (French)

St. Lawrence River

Lake Huron
Lake Ontario
Lake Erie
Ohio River

L. Ontario

NOVA SCOTIA to Sir William Alexander 1621

Grant to Lord William Alexander 1635

PLYMOUTH COLONY 1630

MAINE Grant to Gorges 1639

NEW HAMPSHIRE Grant to Mason 1629

Grant to MASSACHUSETTS BAY COMPANY 1629 "sea to sea"

Grant to PLYMOUTH COLONY 1630

MARYLAND Grant to Lord Baltimore 1632

ATLANTIC OCEAN

St. Augustine (Spanish)

75° Longitude West of Greenwich

DUTCH & SWEDISH COLONIES 1654

SCALE OF MILES
0 25 50

Connecticut R.
House of Hope (Dutch 1633-54)
Schenectady
Fort Orange (Albany)
Esopus (Kingston)
North (Hudson) R.
NEW NETHERLAND
New Amsterdam (New York)
Long Island
ATLANTIC OCEAN
South (Delaware) R.
Fort Nassau
Fort Christina
Fort New Göteborg
NEW SWEDEN
Cape May
Zwaanendael

© Copyright HAMMOND INCORPORATED, Maplewood, N.J. Printed in U.S.A.

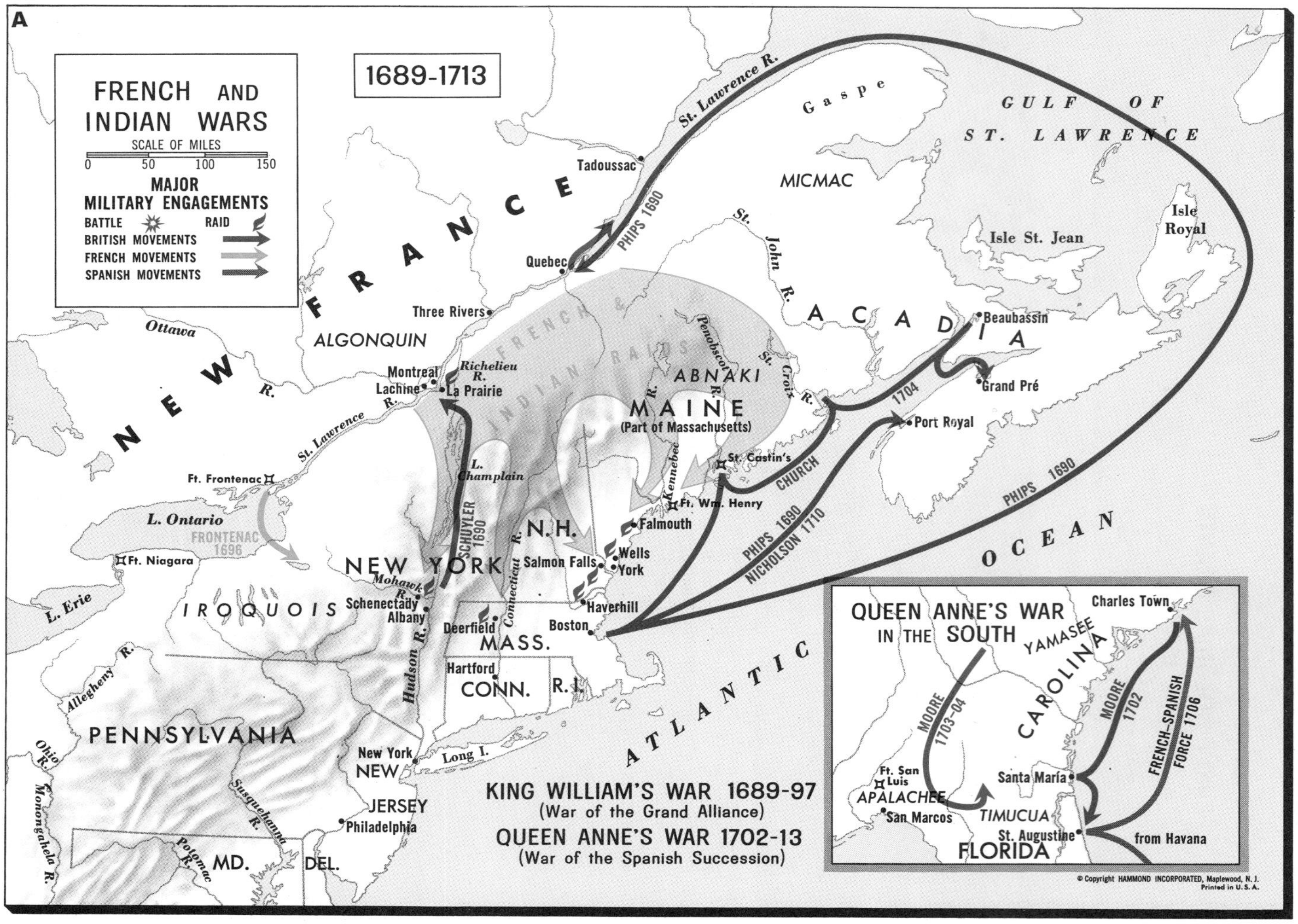

A

1689-1713

FRENCH AND INDIAN WARS
SCALE OF MILES
0 50 100 150
MAJOR MILITARY ENGAGEMENTS
BATTLE   RAID
BRITISH MOVEMENTS
FRENCH MOVEMENTS
SPANISH MOVEMENTS

NEW FRANCE

GULF OF ST. LAWRENCE

St. Lawrence R.

Gaspe

MICMAC

Tadoussac

PHIPS 1690

Quebec

Isle St. Jean

Isle Royal

Three Rivers

ALGONQUIN

Ottawa R.

Montreal
Lachine
La Prairie
Richelieu R.
St. Lawrence R.

St. John R.

St. Croix R.

Penobscot R.

ACADIA

Beaubassin

Grand Pré

ABNAKI

MAINE
(Part of Massachusetts)

1704

Port Royal

Ft. Frontenac

L. Champlain

SCHUYLER 1690

St. Castin's

CHURCH

PHIPS 1690
NICHOLSON 1710

L. Ontario
FRONTENAC 1696

Ft. Niagara

L. Erie

IROQUOIS

Mohawk R.
Schenectady
Albany

NEW YORK

Ft. Wm. Henry
Falmouth
Salmon Falls
Wells
York

Kennebec R.

N.H.

Connecticut R.

Deerfield
Haverhill
Boston

MASS.
Hartford
CONN.
R.I.

PHIPS 1690

ATLANTIC OCEAN

PENNSYLVANIA

Allegheny R.

Ohio R.

Monongahela R.

Susquehanna R.

Hudson R.

New York
NEW JERSEY

Long I.

Philadelphia

Potomac R.

MD.   DEL.

KING WILLIAM'S WAR 1689-97
(War of the Grand Alliance)
QUEEN ANNE'S WAR 1702-13
(War of the Spanish Succession)

QUEEN ANNE'S WAR IN THE SOUTH

Charles Town

YAMASEE

CAROLINA

MOORE 1703-04

MOORE 1702

FRENCH-SPANISH FORCE 1706

Ft. San Luis
APALACHEE
San Marcos

Santa María

TIMUCUA

St. Augustine

from Havana

FLORIDA

© Copyright HAMMOND INCORPORATED, Maplewood, N.J.
Printed in U.S.A.

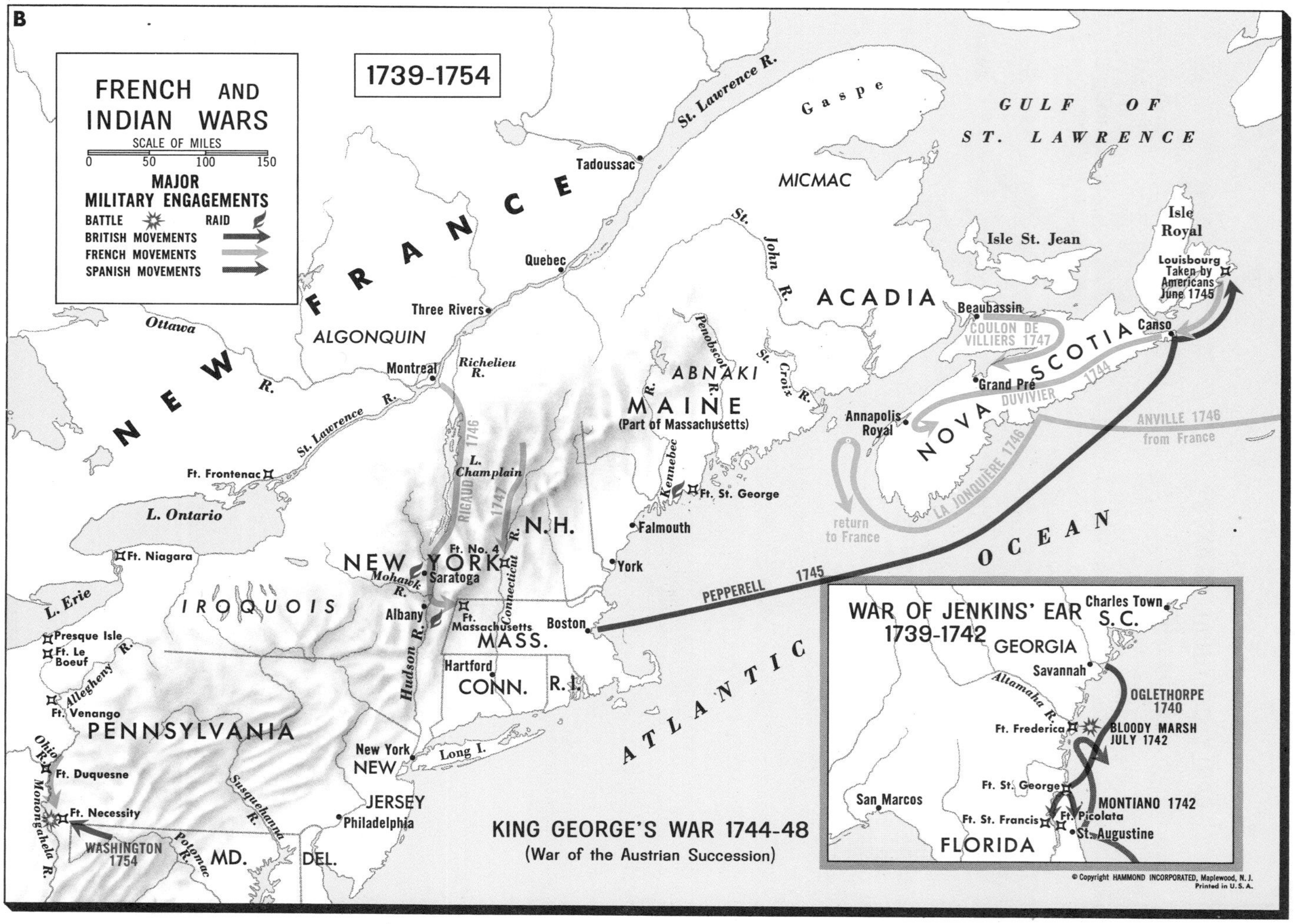

B

1739-1754

FRENCH AND INDIAN WARS
SCALE OF MILES
0 50 100 150
MAJOR MILITARY ENGAGEMENTS
BATTLE   RAID
BRITISH MOVEMENTS
FRENCH MOVEMENTS
SPANISH MOVEMENTS

NEW FRANCE

GULF OF ST. LAWRENCE

St. Lawrence R.

Gaspe

MICMAC

Tadoussac

Quebec

Isle St. Jean

Isle Royal
Louisbourg Taken by Americans June 1745

Three Rivers

ALGONQUIN

Ottawa R.

Montreal
Richelieu R.
St. Lawrence R.

St. John R.

St. Croix R.

Penobscot R.

ACADIA

Beaubassin

COULON DE VILLIERS 1747

NOVA SCOTIA

Grand Pré
Annapolis Royal

Canso

DUVIVIER 1744

LA JONQUIÈRE 1746

ANVILLE 1746
from France

ABNAKI

MAINE
(Part of Massachusetts)

Ft. St. George

Kennebec R.

return to France

Ft. Frontenac

L. Champlain

RIGAUD 1746

Ft. Niagara

L. Ontario

L. Erie

Presque Isle
Ft. Le Boeuf
Allegheny R.
Ft. Venango

IROQUOIS

Mohawk R.
Ft. No. 4
Saratoga
Albany
Ft. Massachusetts

NEW YORK

N.H.

Connecticut R.

Falmouth
York

Hudson R.

Boston

PEPPERELL 1745

MASS.
Hartford
CONN.
R.I.

ATLANTIC OCEAN

PENNSYLVANIA

Ft. Duquesne
Ft. Necessity
WASHINGTON 1754
Monongahela R.

Ohio R.

Susquehanna R.

Potomac R.

New York
NEW JERSEY

Long I.

Philadelphia

MD.   DEL.

KING GEORGE'S WAR 1744-48
(War of the Austrian Succession)

WAR OF JENKINS' EAR 1739-1742

Charles Town S.C.

GEORGIA

Savannah

Altamaha R.

OGLETHORPE 1740

Ft. Frederica

BLOODY MARSH JULY 1742

San Marcos

Ft. St. George

Ft. St. Francis

MONTIANO 1742

Ft. Picolata
St. Augustine

FLORIDA

© Copyright HAMMOND INCORPORATED, Maplewood, N.J.
Printed in U.S.A.

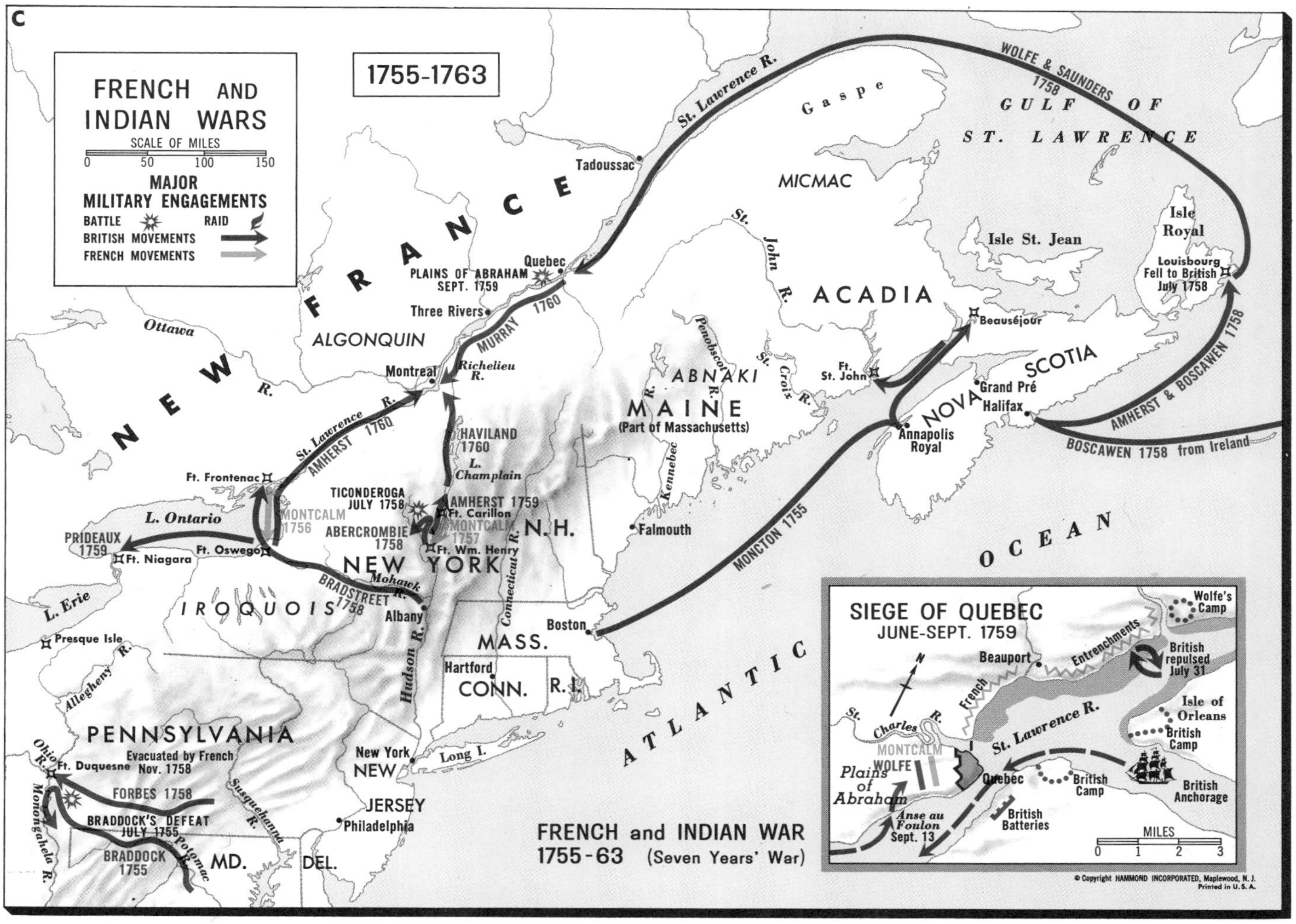

C

FRENCH AND INDIAN WARS

1755-1763

SCALE OF MILES
0   50   100   150

MAJOR MILITARY ENGAGEMENTS

BATTLE ✳   RAID
BRITISH MOVEMENTS →
FRENCH MOVEMENTS →

N E W   F R A N C E

Ottawa R.

ALGONQUIN

St. Lawrence R.

Gaspe

WOLFE & SAUNDERS 1758

GULF OF ST. LAWRENCE

Tadoussac

MICMAC

Isle St. Jean

Isle Royal

Louisbourg Fell to British July 1758

PLAINS OF ABRAHAM SEPT. 1759   Quebec

Three Rivers   MURRAY 1760

Montreal   Richelieu R.

St. John R.

ACADIA

St. Croix R.

Beauséjour

AMHERST & BOSCAWEN 1758

St. Lawrence R.   AMHERST 1760

Ft. Frontenac

L. Champlain   HAVILAND 1760

Penobscot R.

ABNAKI

MAINE (Part of Massachusetts)

Ft. St. John

Kennebec R.

NOVA SCOTIA

Grand Pré   Halifax

Annapolis Royal

BOSCAWEN 1758 from Ireland

L. Ontario   MONTCALM 1756

PRIDEAUX 1759   Ft. Niagara   Ft. Oswego

TICONDEROGA JULY 1758   AMHERST 1759

ABERCROMBIE 1758   Ft. Carillon MONTCALM 1757

Ft. Wm. Henry   N.H.

Falmouth

MONCTON 1755

L. Erie   BRADSTREET 1758

Mohawk R.

Albany

IROQUOIS

NEW YORK

Connecticut R.

MASS.

Boston

Hartford   CONN.   R.I.

Presque Isle

Allegheny R.

Hudson R.

Long I.

New York

NEW JERSEY

Philadelphia

A T L A N T I C   O C E A N

PENNSYLVANIA

Ohio R.   Ft. Duquesne   Evacuated by French Nov. 1758

FORBES 1758

BRADDOCK'S DEFEAT JULY 1755

Susquehanna R.

BRADDOCK 1755   MD.   DEL.

Monongahela R.   Potomac R.

FRENCH and INDIAN WAR
1755-63 (Seven Years' War)

SIEGE OF QUEBEC
JUNE-SEPT. 1759

Wolfe's Camp

Beauport   Entrenchments

British repulsed July 31

St. Charles R.

MONTCALM   WOLFE

Plains of Abraham

St. Lawrence R.

Isle of Orleans

British Camp

Quebec   British Camp

British Anchorage

Anse au Foulon Sept. 13

British Batteries

MILES
0   1   2   3

© Copyright HAMMOND INCORPORATED, Maplewood, N. J.
Printed in U.S.A.

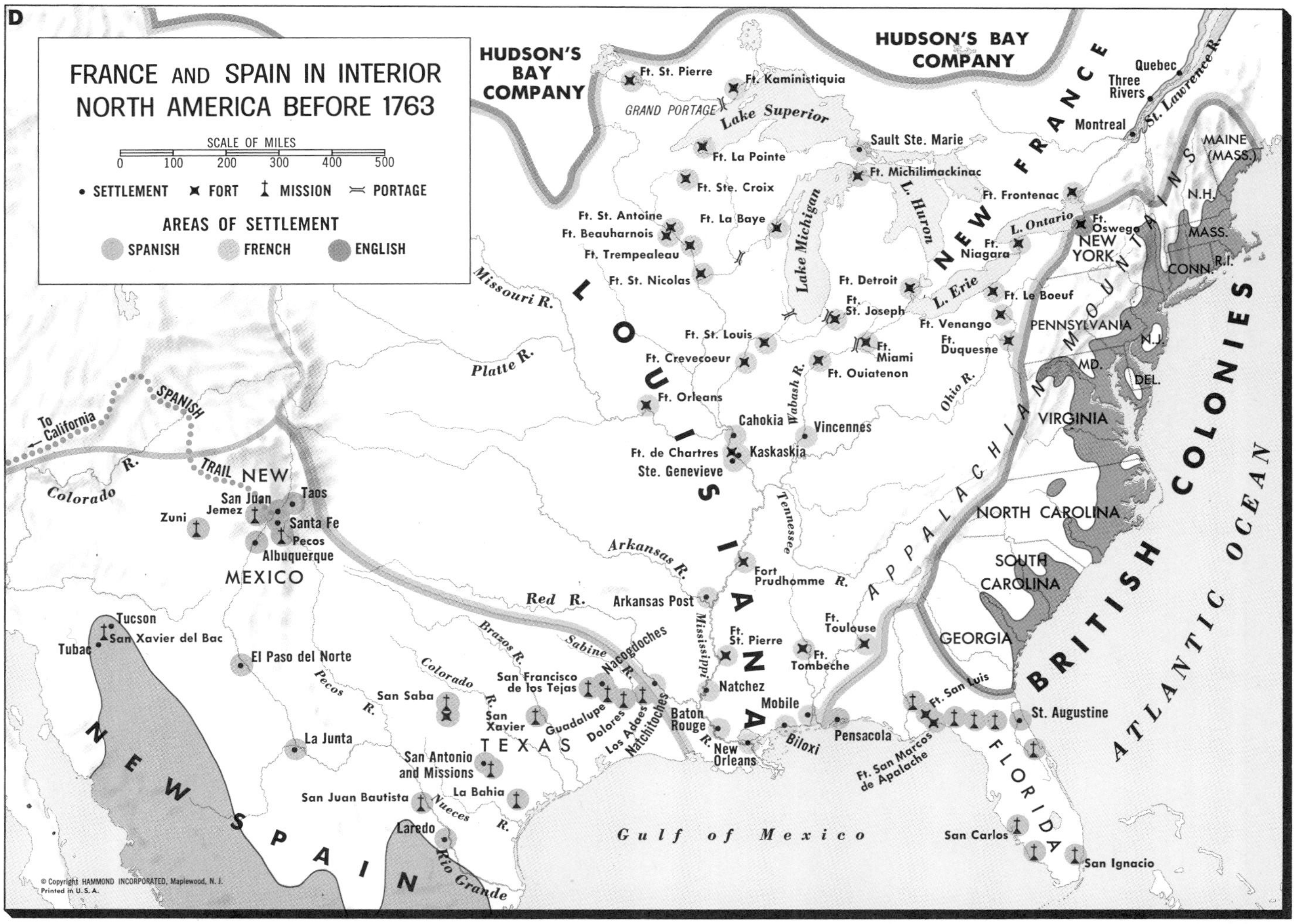

D

FRANCE AND SPAIN IN INTERIOR NORTH AMERICA BEFORE 1763

SCALE OF MILES
0   100   200   300   400   500

● SETTLEMENT   ✕ FORT   ⊺ MISSION   ⋈ PORTAGE

AREAS OF SETTLEMENT
⬤ SPANISH   ⬤ FRENCH   ⬤ ENGLISH

HUDSON'S BAY COMPANY

HUDSON'S BAY COMPANY

Quebec

Three Rivers

NEW FRANCE

Montreal   St. Lawrence R.

Ft. St. Pierre   Ft. Kaministiquia

GRAND PORTAGE   Lake Superior

Sault Ste. Marie

MAINE (MASS.)

N.H.

Ft. La Pointe

Ft. Michilimackinac

Ft. Ste. Croix

Ft. Frontenac

Ft. St. Antoine   Ft. La Baye

L. Huron

L. Ontario   Ft. Oswego

MASS.

Ft. Beauharnois

Lake Michigan

Ft. Niagara

NEW YORK   CONN.   R.I.

Ft. Trempealeau

Ft. St. Nicolas

Ft. Detroit

L. Erie   Ft. Le Boeuf

Missouri R.

Ft. St. Joseph

Ft. Venango   PENNSYLVANIA

Ft. St. Louis

Ft. Miami   Ft. Duquesne

N.J.   MD.   DEL.

L O U I S I A N A

Ft. Crevecoeur   Wabash R.

Ft. Ouiatenon

Ohio R.

Platte R.

Ft. Orleans

Cahokia   Vincennes

VIRGINIA

Ft. de Chartres   Kaskaskia

Ste. Genevieve

SPANISH   TRAIL

To California

Colorado R.

NEW   Taos

San Juan   Jemez

Zuni   Santa Fe

Pecos

Albuquerque

MEXICO

Arkansas R.

Tennessee R.

Fort Prudhomme

NORTH CAROLINA

APPALACHIAN MOUNTAINS

B R I T I S H   C O L O N I E S

Tucson   San Xavier del Bac

Tubac

El Paso del Norte

Pecos R.

San Saba

La Junta

Colorado R.

Brazos R.

Sabine R.

Red R.

Arkansas Post

Ft. St. Pierre

Ft. Toulouse

SOUTH CAROLINA

Ft. Tombeche

GEORGIA

San Francisco de los Tejas

Nacogdoches

Natchez

Mobile

Ft. San Luis

St. Augustine

San Xavier

Guadalupe   Dolores   Los Adaes

Natchitoches

Baton Rouge

Pensacola

FLORIDA

San Antonio and Missions

La Bahia

TEXAS

New Orleans

Biloxi

Ft. San Marcos de Apalache

San Juan Bautista

Nueces R.

Laredo

Rio Grande

N E W   S P A I N

Gulf of Mexico

San Carlos

San Ignacio

A T L A N T I C   O C E A N

© Copyright HAMMOND INCORPORATED, Maplewood, N. J.
Printed in U.S.A.

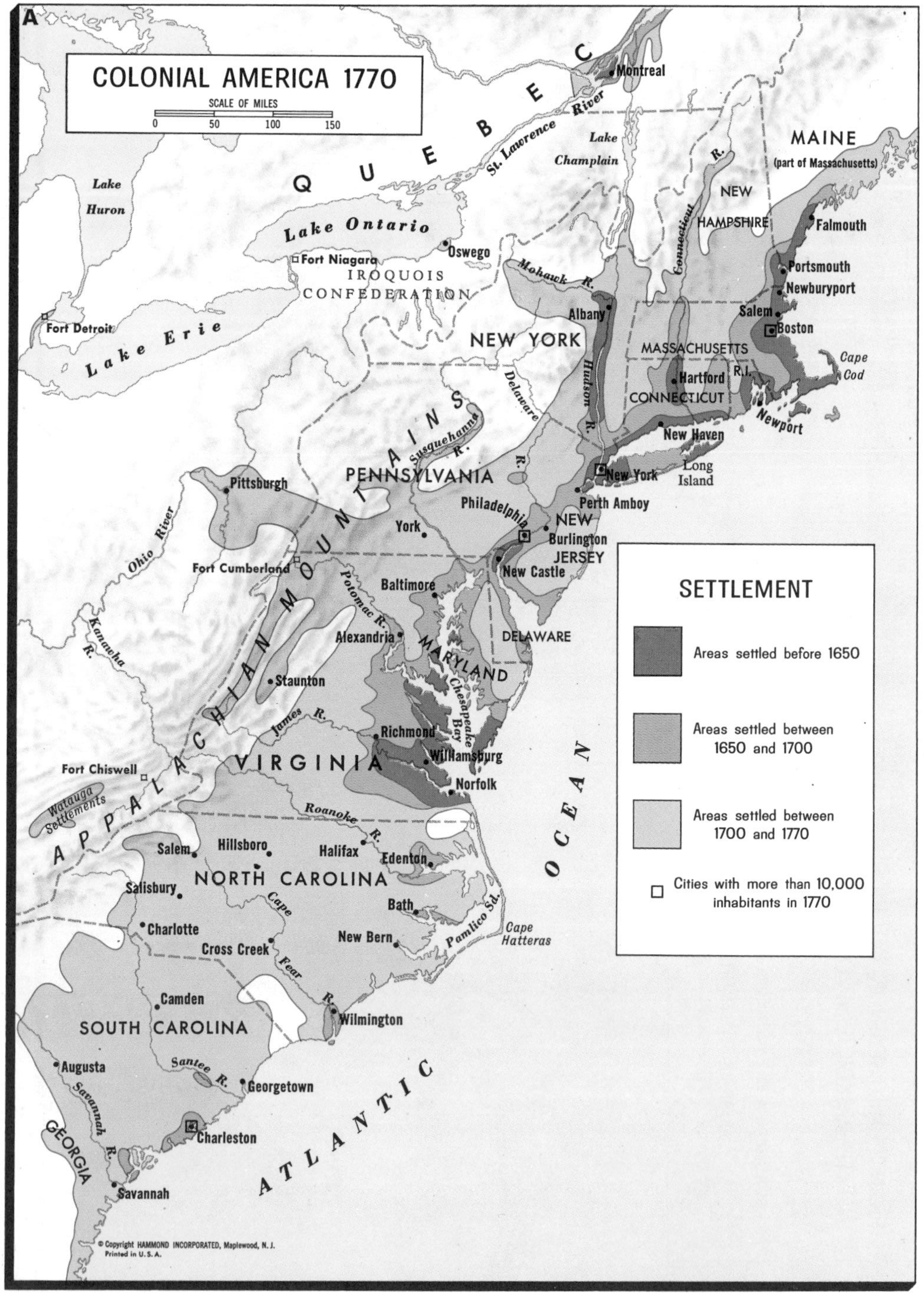

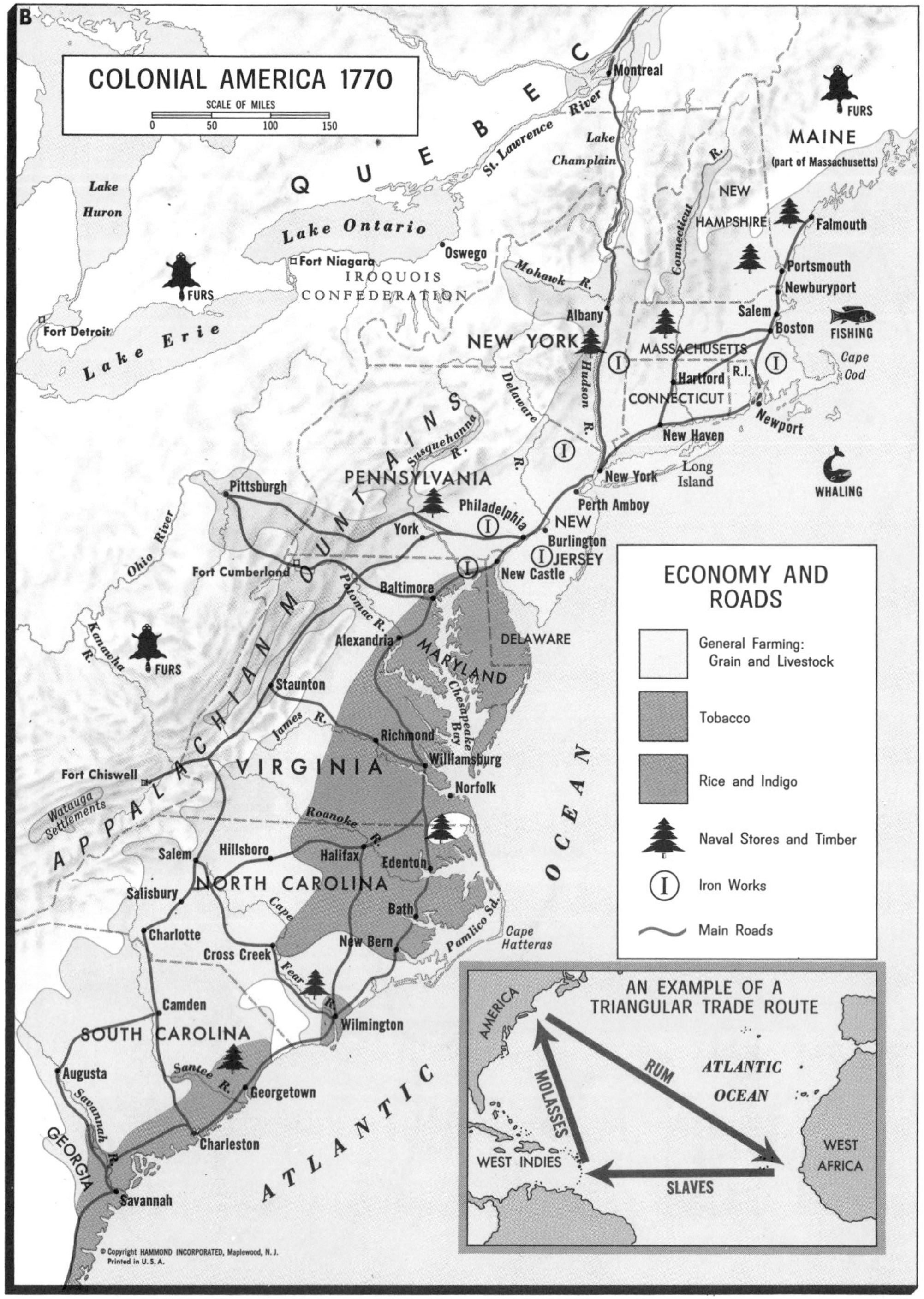

B

COLONIAL AMERICA 1770

SCALE OF MILES
0 50 100 150

ECONOMY AND ROADS

General Farming:
Grain and Livestock
Tobacco
Rice and Indigo
Naval Stores and Timber
Iron Works
Main Roads

AN EXAMPLE OF A TRIANGULAR TRADE ROUTE

ATLANTIC OCEAN
WEST AFRICA
SLAVES
RUM
MOLASSES
AMERICA
WEST INDIES

MAINE (part of Massachusetts)
FURS
Falmouth
Portsmouth
Newburyport
FISHING
Cape Cod
NEW HAMPSHIRE
Salem
Boston
Newport
WHALING
Hartford
R.I.
MASSACHUSETTS
CONNECTICUT
New Haven
New York
Long Island
Perth Amboy
NEW JERSEY
Burlington
Montreal
Lake Champlain
St. Lawrence River
Lake Ontario
Fort Niagara
IROQUOIS CONFEDERATION
Oswego
Albany
Hudson R.
Mohawk R.
Delaware R.
QUEBEC
Lake Erie
FURS
Lake Huron
Fort Detroit
Fort Chiswell
New Castle
Philadelphia
PENNSYLVANIA
Susquehanna R.
York
Baltimore
DELAWARE
MARYLAND
Chesapeake Bay
OCEAN
Potomac R.
Alexandria
Richmond
Williamsburg
Norfolk
VIRGINIA
Pamlico Sd.
Cape Hatteras
Staunton
James R.
Roanoke R.
Edenton
Bath
New Bern
Halifax
APPALACHIAN MOUNTAINS
Pittsburgh
Fort Cumberland
Hillsboro
NORTH CAROLINA
Cape Fear
Cross Creek
Wilmington
Ohio River
FURS
Kanawha R.
Salem
Salisbury
Charlotte
Camden
Georgetown
Santee R.
SOUTH CAROLINA
Charleston
ATLANTIC
Augusta
Savannah R.
Savannah
GEORGIA
Watauga Settlements

© Copyright HAMMOND INCORPORATED, Maplewood, N.J.
Printed in U.S.A.

A

COLONIAL AMERICA 1770

SCALE OF MILES
0 50 100 150

SETTLEMENT

Areas settled before 1650
Areas settled between 1650 and 1700
Areas settled between 1700 and 1770
Cities with more than 10,000 inhabitants in 1770

MAINE (part of Massachusetts)
Falmouth
Portsmouth
Newburyport
Cape Cod
NEW HAMPSHIRE
Salem
Boston
Newport
Hartford
R.I.
MASSACHUSETTS
CONNECTICUT
New Haven
New York
Long Island
Perth Amboy
NEW JERSEY
Burlington
Montreal
Lake Champlain
St. Lawrence River
Lake Ontario
Fort Niagara
IROQUOIS CONFEDERATION
Oswego
Albany
Hudson R.
Mohawk R.
Delaware R.
QUEBEC
Lake Erie
Lake Huron
Fort Detroit
Fort Chiswell
New Castle
Philadelphia
PENNSYLVANIA
Susquehanna R.
York
Baltimore
DELAWARE
MARYLAND
Chesapeake Bay
OCEAN
Potomac R.
Alexandria
Richmond
Williamsburg
Norfolk
VIRGINIA
Pamlico Sd.
Cape Hatteras
Staunton
James R.
Roanoke R.
Edenton
Bath
New Bern
Halifax
APPALACHIAN MOUNTAINS
Pittsburgh
Fort Cumberland
Hillsboro
NORTH CAROLINA
Cape Fear
Cross Creek
Wilmington
Ohio River
Kanawha R.
Salem
Salisbury
Charlotte
Camden
Georgetown
Santee R.
SOUTH CAROLINA
Charleston
ATLANTIC
Augusta
Savannah R.
Savannah
GEORGIA
Watauga Settlements

© Copyright HAMMOND INCORPORATED, Maplewood, N.J.
Printed in U.S.A.

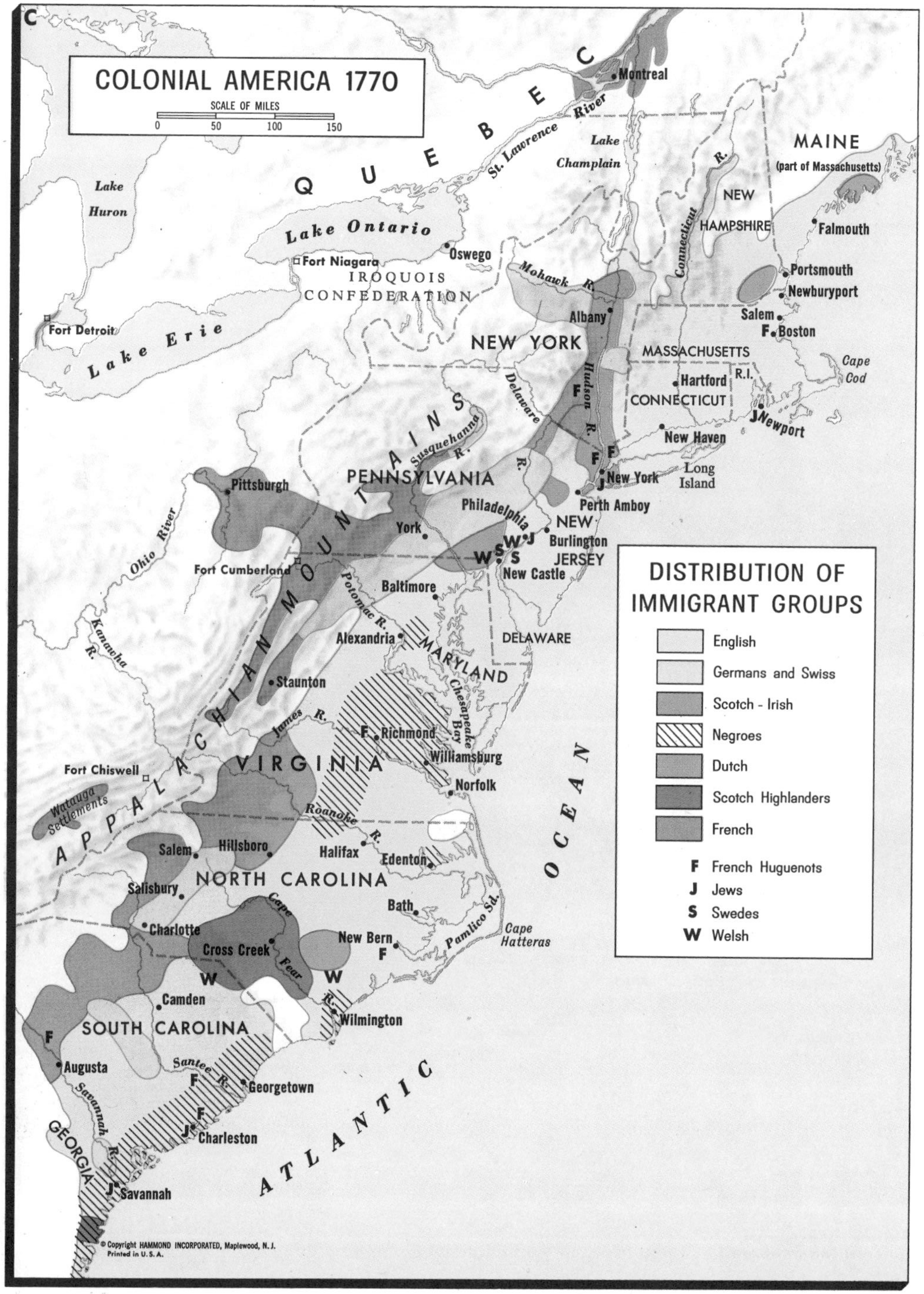

COLONIAL CALIFORNIA

SCALE OF MILES
0 25 50 75 100

SIERRA NEVADA

COAST RANGES

Sacramento R.

San Joaquin R.

Mojave Desert

SPANISH TRAIL

Cajon Pass

EL CAMINO REAL

San Francisco Solano 1823

Fort Ross (Russian)

San Rafael 1817

San Francisco de Asis 1776

San Francisco

Santa Clara 1777

San José 1797

San José

Santa Cruz 1791

Santa Cruz

Monterey

San Carlos Borromeo 1770

San Juan Bautista 1797

Soledad 1791

Salinas R.

San Antonio de Padua 1771

San Miguel Arcangel 1797

San Luis Obispo 1772

La Purísima 1787

Santa Inés 1804

Santa Barbara 1786

San Buenaventura 1782

Santa Barbara

San Fernando 1797

San Gabriel 1771

Los Angeles

San Juan Capistrano 1776

San Luis Rey 1798

San Diego

San Diego de Alcalá 1769

SANTA BARBARA ISLANDS

PACIFIC OCEAN

Settlement (Civic Pueblo) •
Mission ✝
Presidio or Fort ▲
Areas settled by 1823 □

© Copyright HAMMOND INCORPORATED, Maplewood, N.J.
Printed in U.S.A.

D

COLONIAL AMERICA 1770

SCALE OF MILES
0 50 100 150

DISTRIBUTION OF IMMIGRANT GROUPS

English
Germans and Swiss
Scotch - Irish
Negroes
Dutch
Scotch Highlanders
French
French Huguenots   F
Jews   J
Swedes   S
Welsh   W

QUEBEC

Lake Huron

Lake Erie

Lake Ontario

Lake Champlain

St. Lawrence River

Montreal

Fort Detroit

Fort Niagara

Oswego

IROQUOIS CONFEDERATION

NEW YORK

Mohawk R.

Albany

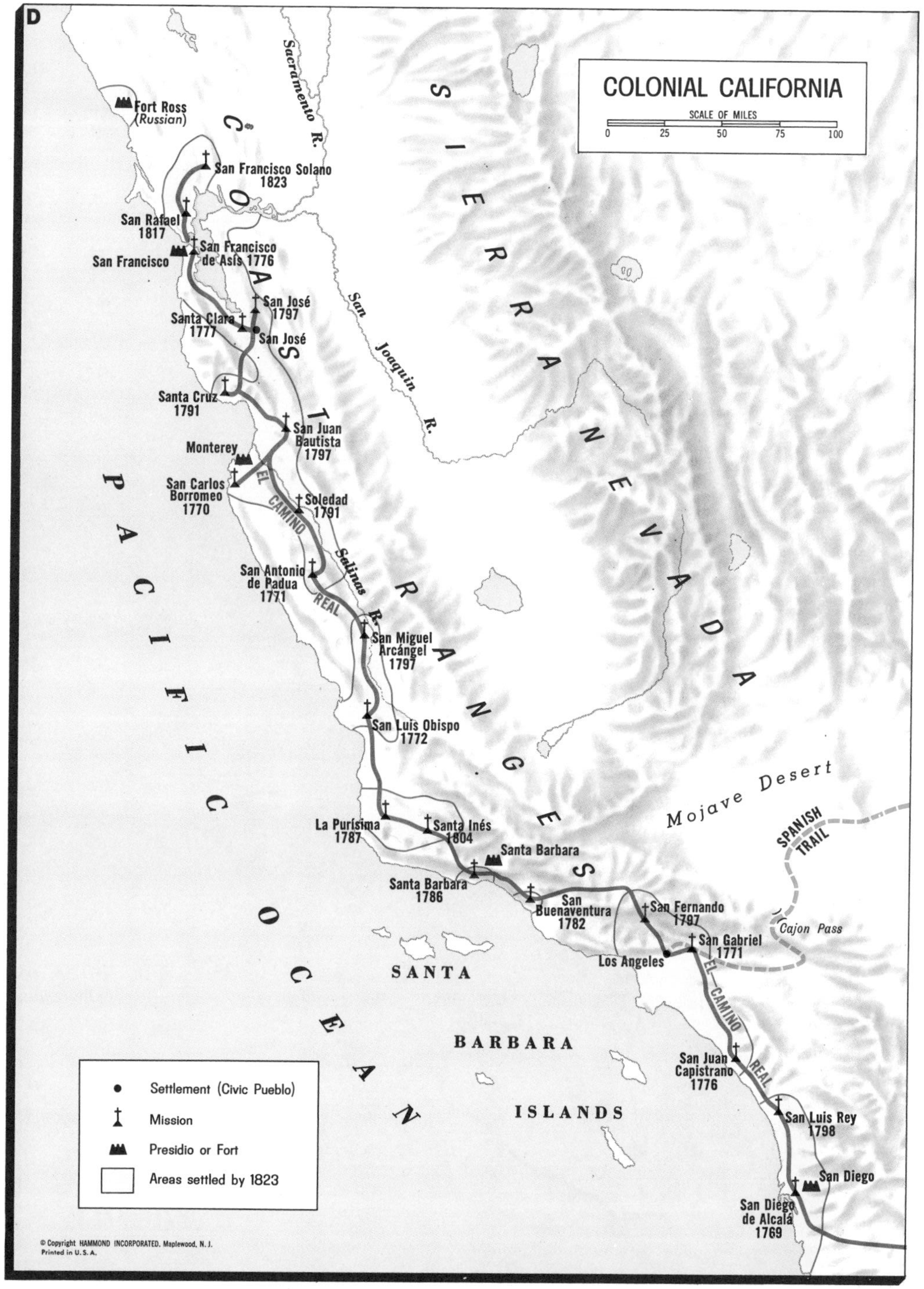

Hudson R.

Ohio River

Kanawha R.

Fort Cumberland

Pittsburgh

PENNSYLVANIA

Susquehanna R.

York

Fort Chiswell

APPALACHIAN MOUNTAINS

MAINE (part of Massachusetts)

Falmouth

Portsmouth

Newburyport

NEW HAMPSHIRE

Salem

Boston

Connecticut R.

MASSACHUSETTS

Hartford

R.I.

Newport

CONNECTICUT

New Haven

Long Island

New York

Perth Amboy

NEW JERSEY

Burlington

Philadelphia

New Castle

DELAWARE

Delaware R.

Baltimore

MARYLAND

Chesapeake Bay

Potomac R.

Alexandria

Staunton

VIRGINIA

Richmond

Williamsburg

Norfolk

ATLANTIC OCEAN

Cape Cod

Cape Hatteras

Pamlico Sd.

Edenton

Bath

New Bern

Halifax

Hillsboro

Roanoke R.

NORTH CAROLINA

Salem

Salisbury

Charlotte

Cross Creek

Cape Fear R.

Wilmington

SOUTH CAROLINA

Camden

Charleston

Georgetown

Santee R.

GEORGIA

Augusta

Savannah

Savannah R.

© Copyright HAMMOND INCORPORATED, Maplewood, N.J.
Printed in U.S.A.

C

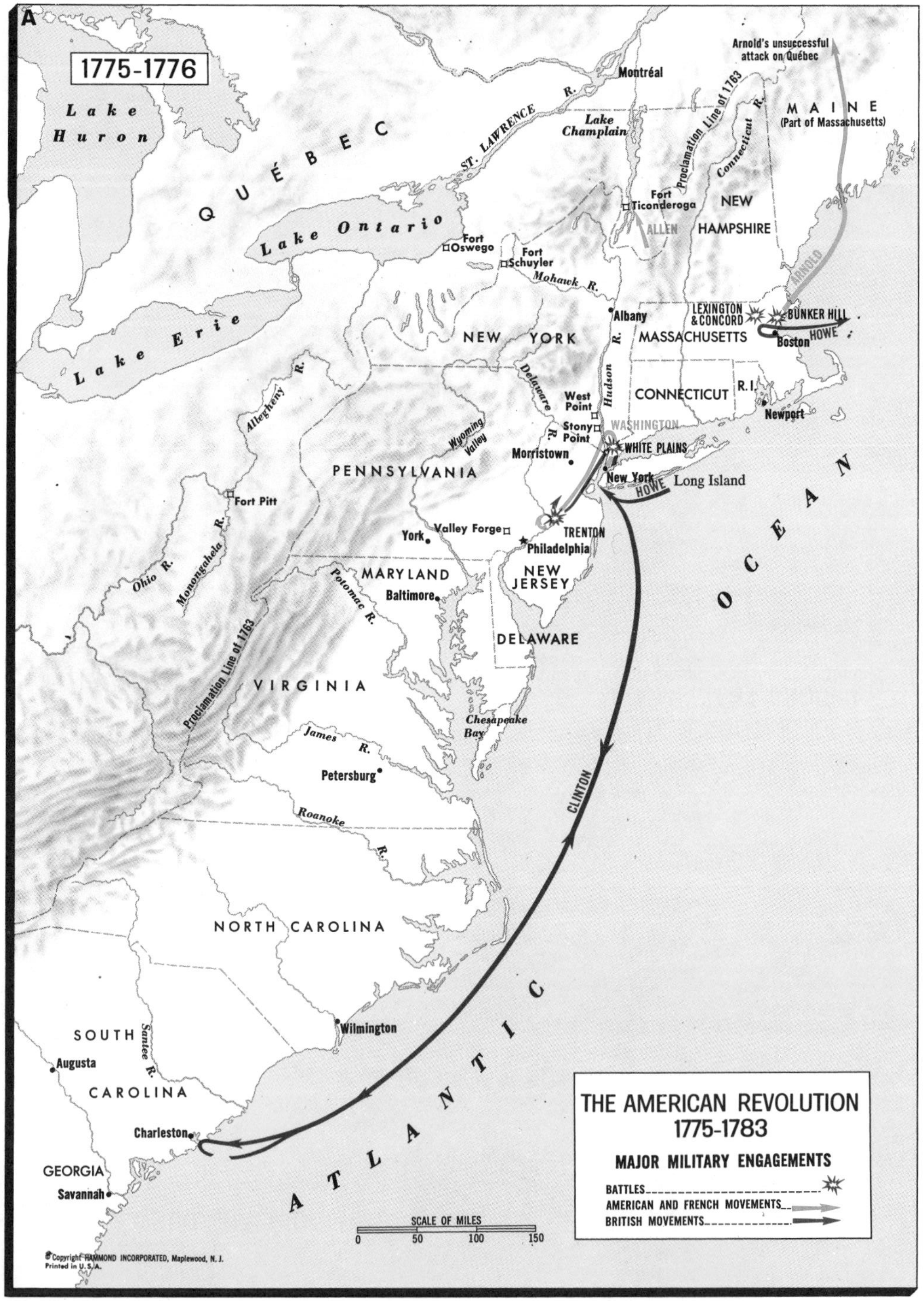
A
1775-1776
THE AMERICAN REVOLUTION
1775-1783
MAJOR MILITARY ENGAGEMENTS
BATTLES
AMERICAN AND FRENCH MOVEMENTS
BRITISH MOVEMENTS
SCALE OF MILES
0 50 100 150
Arnold's unsuccessful attack on Québec
Lake Huron
Lake Erie
Lake Ontario
QUÉBEC
Montréal
ST. LAWRENCE R.
Lake Champlain
Proclamation Line of 1763
Connecticut R.
MAINE
(Part of Massachusetts)
ARNOLD
Fort Ticonderoga
ALLEN
NEW HAMPSHIRE
Fort Oswego
Fort Schuyler
Mohawk R.
Albany
LEXINGTON & CONCORD
BUNKER HILL
Boston
HOWE
NEW YORK
MASSACHUSETTS
CONNECTICUT
R.I.
Newport
Hudson R.
Delaware R.
West Point
Stony Point
WASHINGTON
WHITE PLAINS
Morristown
New York
Long Island
PENNSYLVANIA
Allegheny R.
Fort Pitt
Monongahela R.
Ohio R.
York
Valley Forge
TRENTON
Philadelphia
MARYLAND
Baltimore
NEW JERSEY
DELAWARE
Potomac R.
Proclamation Line of 1763
VIRGINIA
Chesapeake Bay
James R.
Petersburg
Roanoke R.
CLINTON
OCEAN
NORTH CAROLINA
Wilmington
SOUTH CAROLINA
Santee R.
Augusta
Charleston
GEORGIA
Savannah
ATLANTIC
© Copyright HAMMOND INCORPORATED, Maplewood, N.J.
Printed in U.S.A.

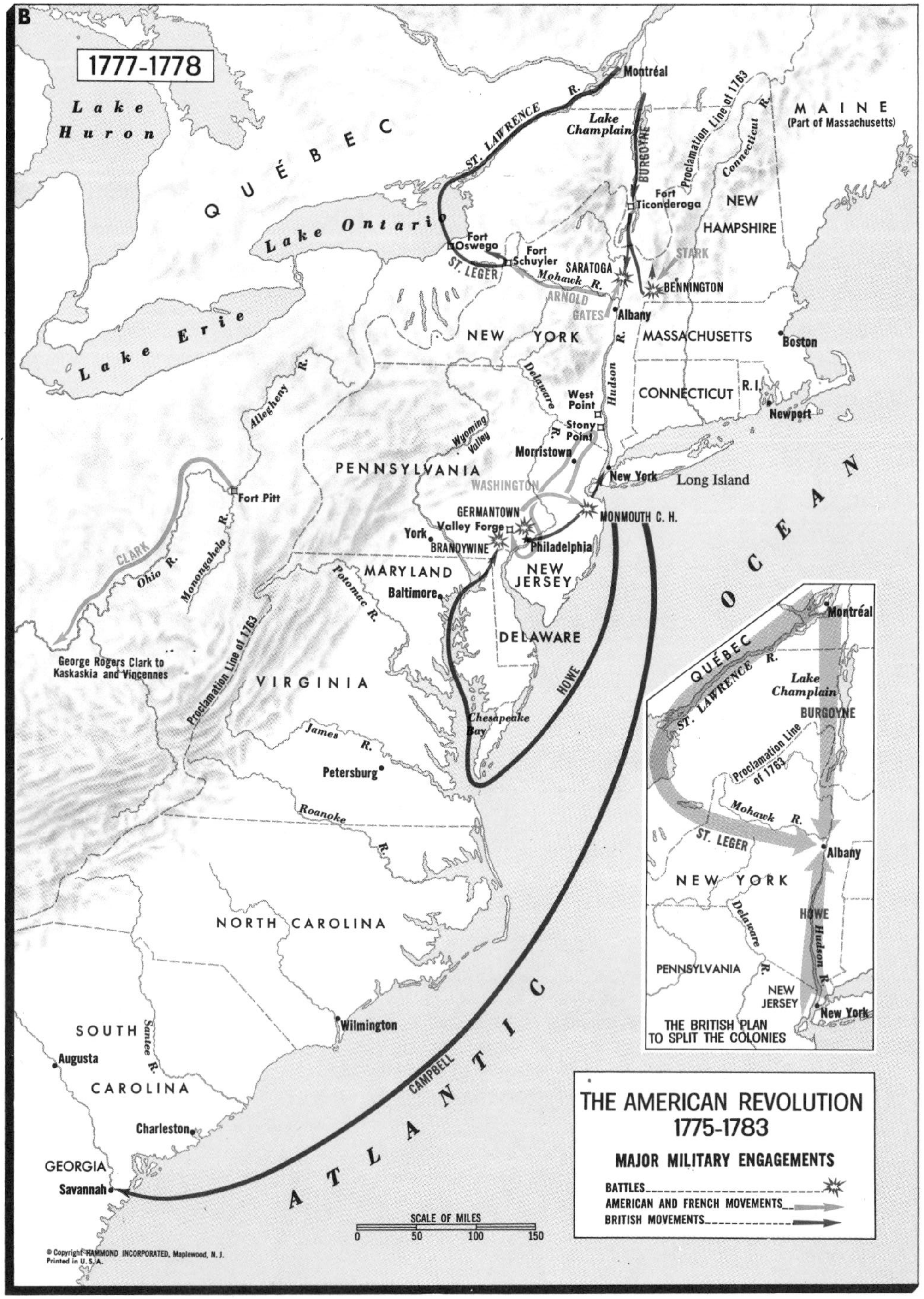
B
1777-1778
THE AMERICAN REVOLUTION
1775-1783
MAJOR MILITARY ENGAGEMENTS
BATTLES
AMERICAN AND FRENCH MOVEMENTS
BRITISH MOVEMENTS
SCALE OF MILES
0 50 100 150
Lake Huron
Lake Erie
Lake Ontario
QUÉBEC
Montréal
ST. LAWRENCE R.
Lake Champlain
BURGOYNE
Proclamation Line of 1763
Connecticut R.
MAINE
(Part of Massachusetts)
Fort Ticonderoga
STARK
BENNINGTON
NEW HAMPSHIRE
Fort Oswego
ST. LEGER
Fort Schuyler
Mohawk R.
SARATOGA
ARNOLD
GATES
Albany
NEW YORK
MASSACHUSETTS
Boston
CONNECTICUT
R.I.
Newport
Hudson R.
Delaware R.
West Point
Stony Point
Morristown
WASHINGTON
New York
Long Island
MONMOUTH C. H.
GERMANTOWN
Valley Forge
BRANDYWINE
Philadelphia
PENNSYLVANIA
Wyoming Valley
Allegheny R.
Fort Pitt
CLARK
Ohio R.
Monongahela R.
George Rogers Clark to Kaskaskia and Vincennes
Proclamation Line of 1763
York
MARYLAND
Baltimore
NEW JERSEY
DELAWARE
Potomac R.
HOWE
VIRGINIA
Chesapeake Bay
James R.
Petersburg
Roanoke R.
OCEAN
NORTH CAROLINA
Wilmington
CAMPBELL
SOUTH CAROLINA
Santee R.
Augusta
Charleston
GEORGIA
Savannah
ATLANTIC
QUÉBEC
ST. LAWRENCE R.
Lake Champlain
BURGOYNE
Proclamation Line of 1763
Mohawk R.
ST. LEGER
Albany
NEW YORK
HOWE
Hudson R.
Delaware R.
PENNSYLVANIA
NEW JERSEY
New York
THE BRITISH PLAN TO SPLIT THE COLONIES
© Copyright HAMMOND INCORPORATED, Maplewood, N.J.
Printed in U.S.A.

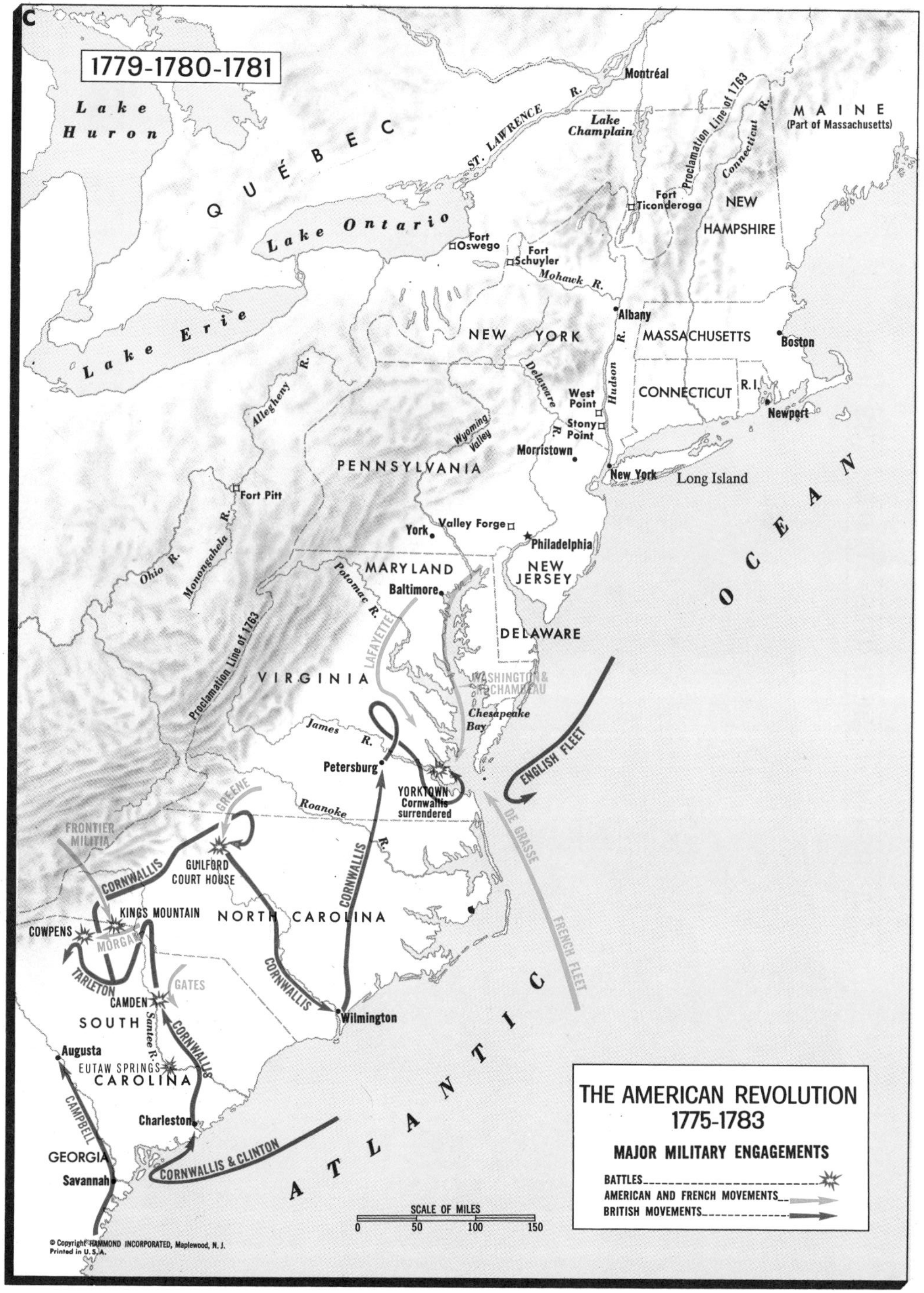

ENGAGEMENTS NEAR BOSTON
1775-1776

SCALE OF MILES
0 1 2 3 4

AMERICAN LINES
PAUL REVERE'S RIDE
DAWES' ROUTE
PRESCOTT'S ROUTE

© Copyright HAMMOND INCORPORATED, Maplewood, N.J. Printed in U.S.A.

Smith and Percy retreat to Boston

BUNKER HILL
Breeds Hill
GAGE
Charlestown
North Church
HOWE
to Halifax
Boston Harbor
Boston
Dorchester Heights

Roxbury

Medford
Mystic R.
SMITH
Charles R.

Cambridge

Brookline

Arlington (Menotomy)
Dawes joins Revere

Watertown

Charles R.

Waltham

Weston

Percy to Lexington to support British retreat toward Boston

MINUTEMEN
Lexington
LEXINGTON
Prescott joins Revere and Dawes

Revere captured, Dawes turns back
X
PRESCOTT

Lincoln

MINUTEMEN

MASSACHUSETTS

North Bridge
CONCORD
Concord
British retreat toward Boston
MINUTEMEN

Sudbury R.

D

THE WESTERN CAMPAIGNS
1778-1781

SCALE OF MILES
0 50 100 150

Lake Erie

Ft. Pitt
Redstone Old Fort
Proclamation Line of 1763

Ft. Henry
Ohio R.
CLARK

Detroit

Maumee R.

HAMILTON

Lake Michigan

Ft. St. Joseph

X Blue Licks (Indian Battle)
Boonesboro

Wabash R.
Kaskaskia R.
Kaskaskia R.

Vincennes
CLARK
VINCENNES

Falls of the Ohio
Harrodstown

Cumberland R.

POURE (Spanish)

CLARK

Illinois R.

Ohio R.

Tennessee R.

Missouri R.
St. Louis • Cahokia
Kaskaskia

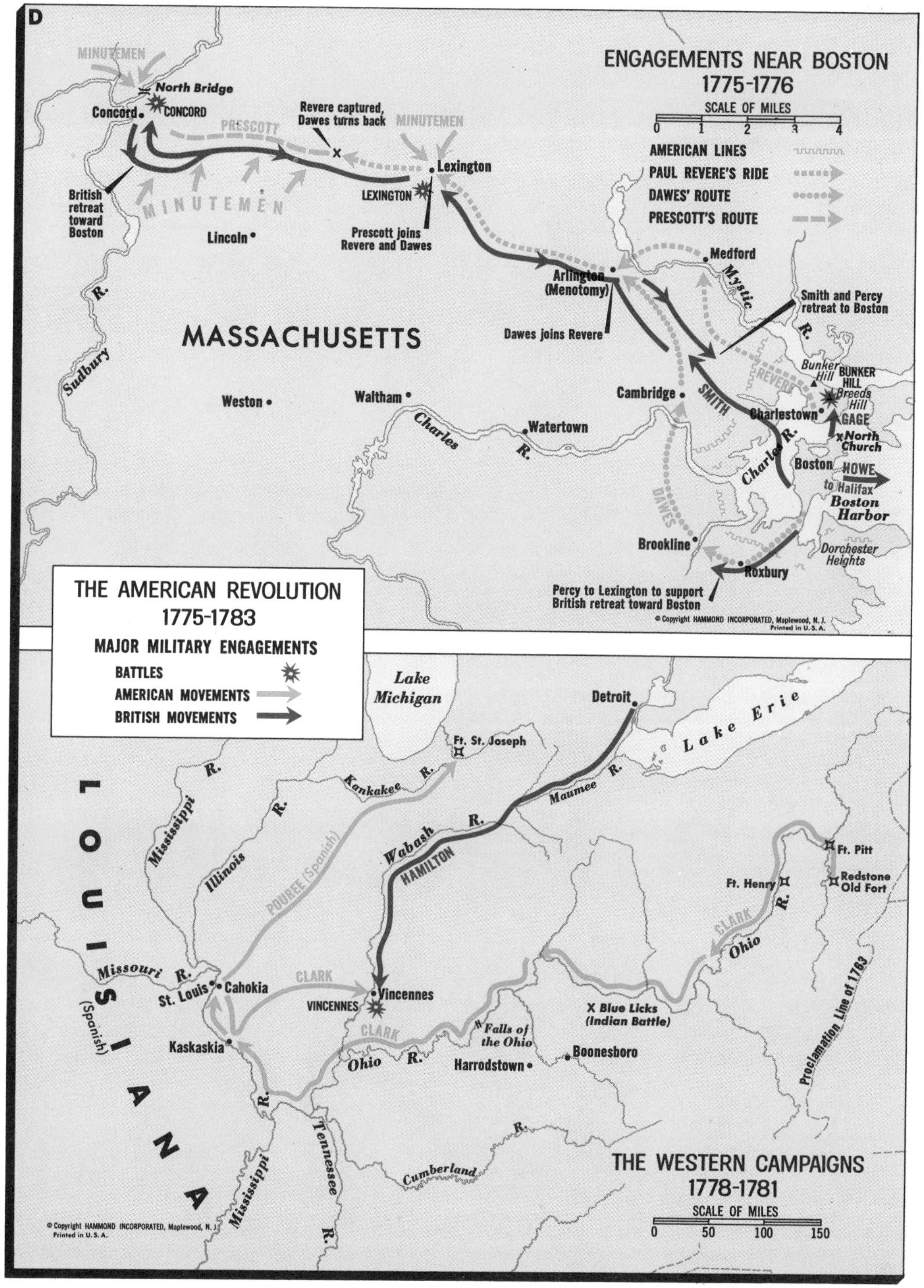

Mississippi R.

Mississippi R.

L O U I S I A N A
(Spanish)

© Copyright HAMMOND INCORPORATED, Maplewood, N.J. Printed in U.S.A.

THE AMERICAN REVOLUTION
1775-1783
MAJOR MILITARY ENGAGEMENTS

BATTLES
AMERICAN MOVEMENTS
BRITISH MOVEMENTS

C

1779-1780-1781

Lake Huron

Lake Erie

Lake Ontario

Q U É B E C

Montréal

Fort Ticonderoga
Lake Champlain

Fort Schuyler
Fort Oswego
Mohawk R.

MAINE (Part of Massachusetts)

NEW HAMPSHIRE

Connecticut R.
Proclamation Line of 1763

Boston

Newport
R.I.

MASSACHUSETTS
CONNECTICUT

Albany
Hudson R.
West Point
Stony Point
New York
Long Island

NEW YORK

Allegheny R.

Fort Pitt

Monongahela R.

PENNSYLVANIA
York

Valley Forge

Morristown
NEW JERSEY
Delaware R.
Philadelphia

DELAWARE

MARYLAND
Baltimore

Potomac R.

LAFAYETTE

VIRGINIA
James R.
Petersburg

Roanoke R.

YORKTOWN
Cornwallis surrendered

ENGLISH FLEET
DE GRASSE
FRENCH FLEET

WASHINGTON
Chesapeake Bay

Proclamation Line of 1763

CORNWALLIS
Wilmington

NORTH CAROLINA

GREENE

GUILFORD COURT HOUSE

FRONTIER MILITIA
KINGS MOUNTAIN
MORGAN
COWPENS
GATES
Camden
CORNWALLIS
Santee R.
EUTAW SPRINGS
TARLETON
Charleston

SOUTH CAROLINA
CORNWALLIS & CLINTON

Augusta
CAMPBELL
GEORGIA
Savannah

A T L A N T I C   O C E A N

SCALE OF MILES
0 50 100 150

THE AMERICAN REVOLUTION
1775-1783
MAJOR MILITARY ENGAGEMENTS

BATTLES
AMERICAN AND FRENCH MOVEMENTS
BRITISH MOVEMENTS

© Copyright HAMMOND INCORPORATED, Maplewood, N.J. Printed in U.S.A.

A

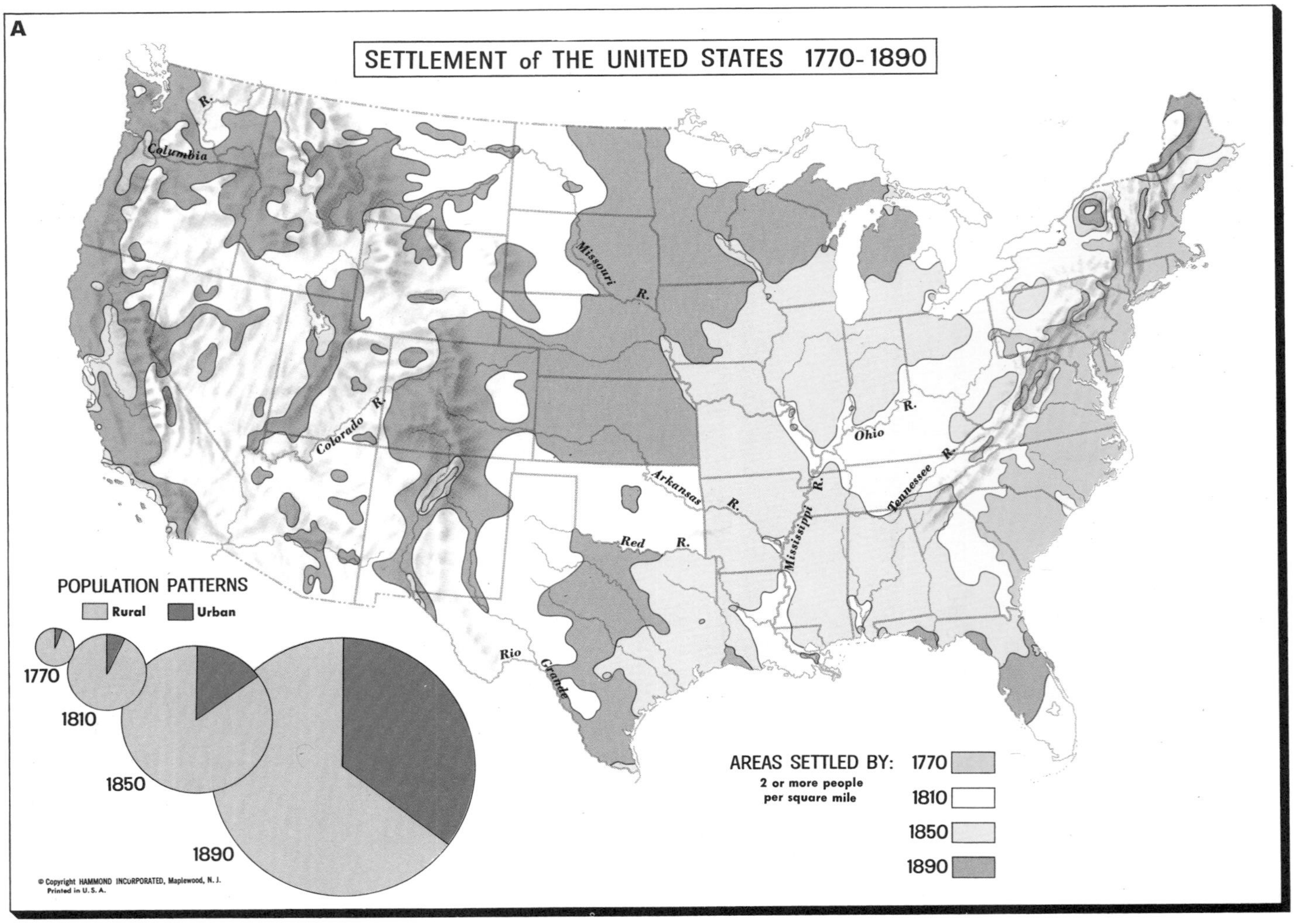
SETTLEMENT of THE UNITED STATES 1770-1890
Columbia
R.
Missouri
R.
Colorado R.
Arkansas R.
Red R.
Rio Grande
Ohio R.
Mississippi R.
Tennessee R.
POPULATION PATTERNS
Rural
Urban
1770
1810
1850
1890
AREAS SETTLED BY:
2 or more people per square mile
1770
1810
1850
1890
© Copyright HAMMOND INCORPORATED, Maplewood, N. J.
Printed in U. S. A.

B

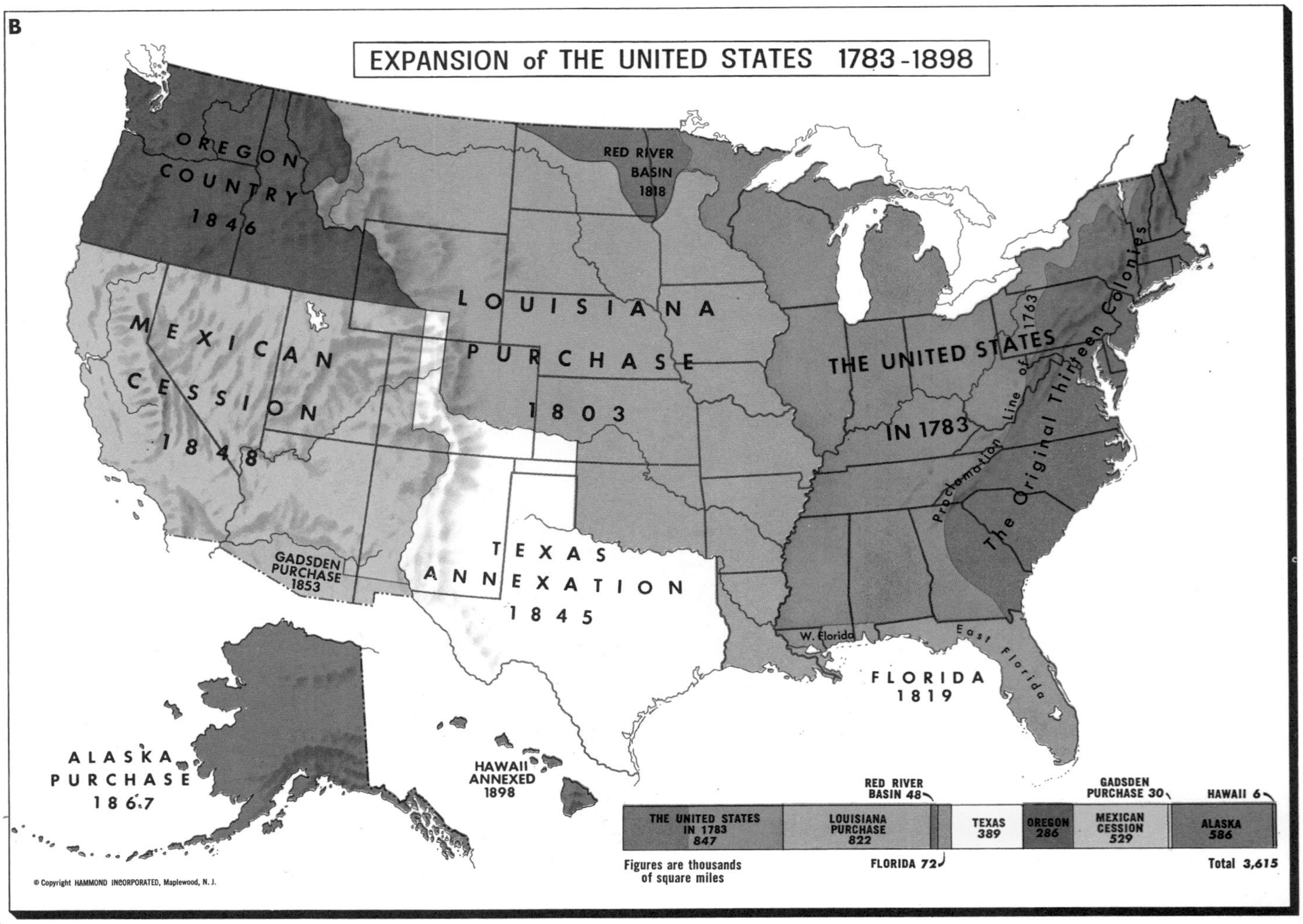
EXPANSION of THE UNITED STATES 1783-1898
OREGON COUNTRY 1846
RED RIVER BASIN 1818
LOUISIANA PURCHASE 1803
MEXICAN CESSION 1848
THE UNITED STATES IN 1783
Proclamation Line of 1763
The Original Thirteen Colonies
GADSDEN PURCHASE 1853
TEXAS ANNEXATION 1845
W. Florida
East Florida
FLORIDA 1819
ALASKA PURCHASE 1867
HAWAII ANNEXED 1898
RED RIVER BASIN 48
GADSDEN PURCHASE 30
HAWAII 6
THE UNITED STATES IN 1783 847
LOUISIANA PURCHASE 822
TEXAS 389
OREGON 286
MEXICAN CESSION 529
ALASKA 586
Figures are thousands of square miles
FLORIDA 72
Total 3,615
© Copyright HAMMOND INCORPORATED, Maplewood, N. J.

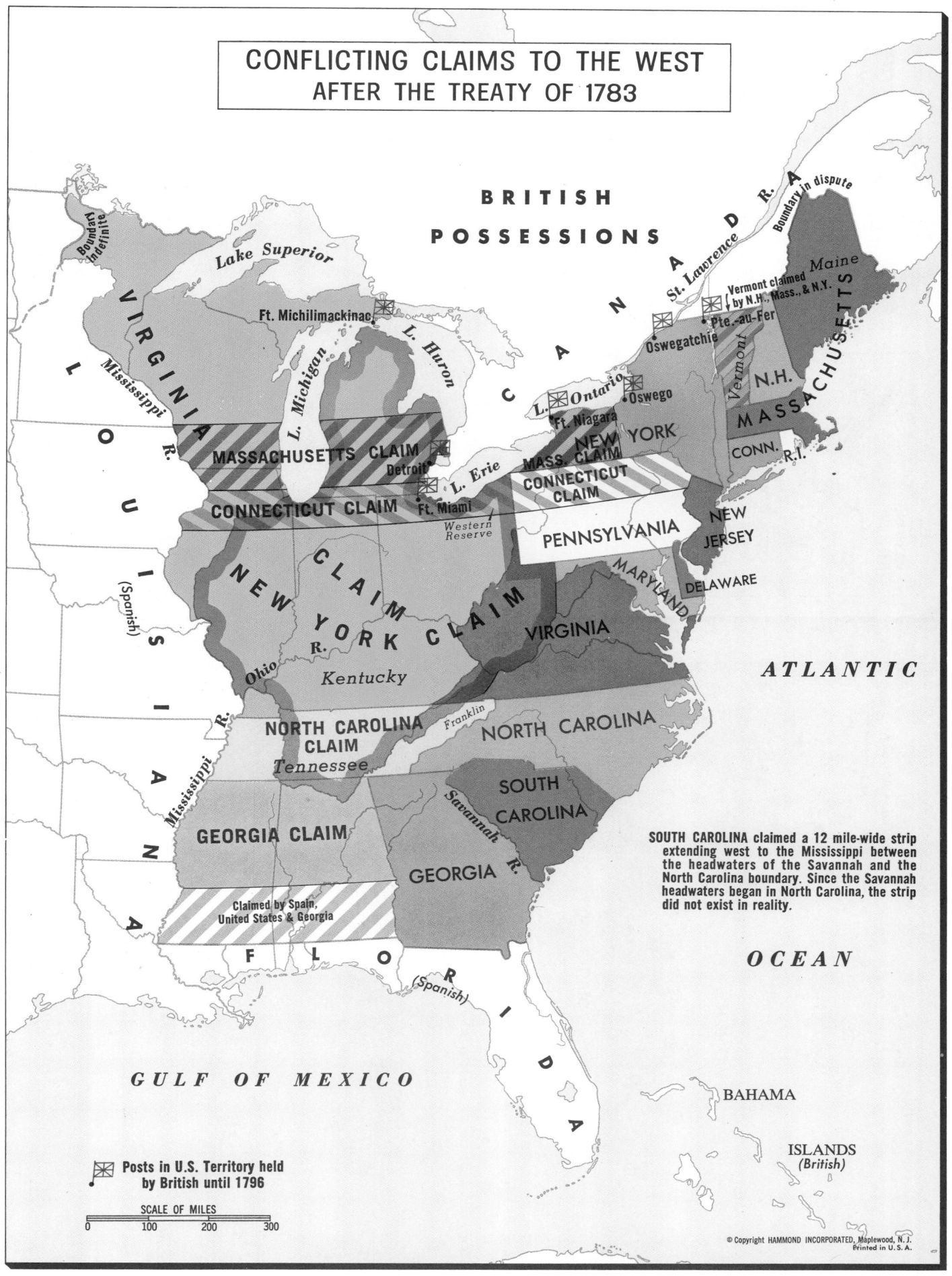

CONFLICTING CLAIMS TO THE WEST
AFTER THE TREATY OF 1783

BRITISH

POSSESSIONS

C A N A D A

Boundary in dispute

Boundary Indefinite

Lake Superior

St. Lawrence R.

Maine

Ft. Michilimackinac

L. Michigan

L. Huron

Vermont claimed by N.H., Mass. & N.Y.

Pte.-au-Fer

Oswegatchie

MASSACHUSETTS

L O U I S I A N A

Mississippi R.

V I R G I N I A

L. Ontario

Oswego

Ft. Niagara

Vermont

N.H.

(Spanish)

MASSACHUSETTS CLAIM

Detroit

L. Erie

NEW YORK

MASS. CLAIM

CONN.

R.I.

CONNECTICUT CLAIM

Ft. Miami

Western Reserve

CONNECTICUT CLAIM

PENNSYLVANIA

NEW JERSEY

C L A I M

MARYLAND

DELAWARE

N E W   Y O R K   C L A I M

R.

VIRGINIA

ATLANTIC

Ohio R.

Kentucky

NORTH CAROLINA CLAIM

Franklin

NORTH CAROLINA

Tennessee

SOUTH CAROLINA

Mississippi R.

GEORGIA CLAIM

Savannah R.

GEORGIA

SOUTH CAROLINA claimed a 12 mile-wide strip extending west to the Mississippi between the headwaters of the Savannah and the North Carolina boundary. Since the Savannah headwaters began in North Carolina, the strip did not exist in reality.

Claimed by Spain, United States & Georgia

OCEAN

F L O R I D A

(Spanish)

GULF OF MEXICO

BAHAMA

ISLANDS
(British)

⊠ Posts in U.S. Territory held
by British until 1796

SCALE OF MILES

0   100   200   300

© Copyright HAMMOND INCORPORATED, Maplewood, N.J.
Printed in U.S.A.

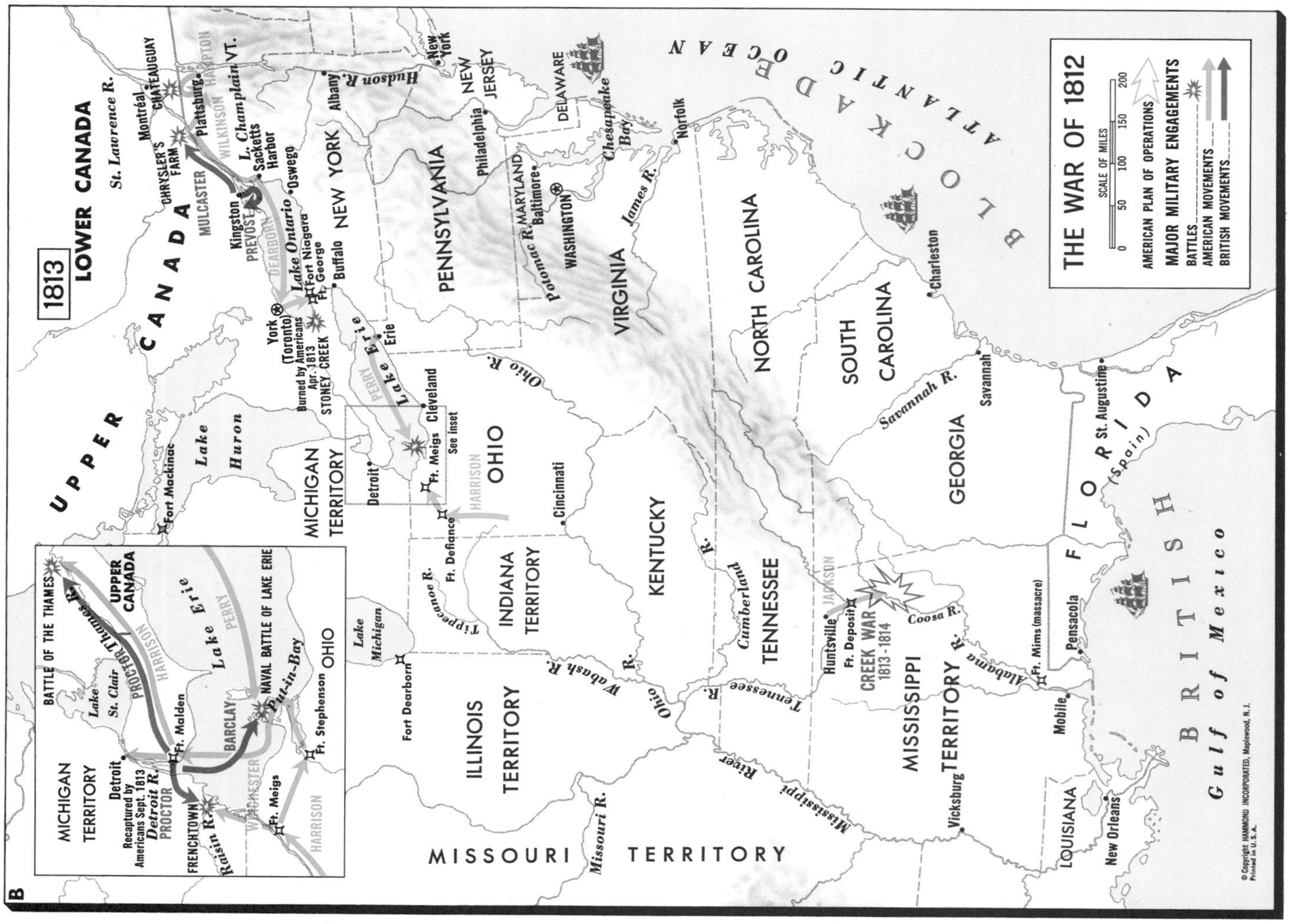

Map B — 1813

THE WAR OF 1812

SCALE OF MILES
0 50 100 150 200

AMERICAN PLAN OF OPERATIONS
MAJOR MILITARY ENGAGEMENTS
BATTLES
AMERICAN MOVEMENTS
BRITISH MOVEMENTS

1813

LOWER CANADA
UPPER CANADA
ATLANTIC OCEAN
BLOCKADE

St. Lawrence R.
CHATEAUGUAY
Montréal
HAMPTON
L. Champlain, VT.
Plattsburg
WILKINSON
CHRYSLER'S FARM
MULCASTER
Sacketts Harbor
Kingston
PREVOST
Oswego
DEARBORN
Lake Ontario
Ft. George
Fort Niagara
Buffalo
York (Toronto)
Burned by Americans Apr. 1813
STONEY CREEK
Lake Erie
Erie
PERRY
Cleveland
Ft. Meigs — See inset
HARRISON
Detroit
Ft. Defiance
Fort Mackinac
Lake Huron
Lake Michigan
Fort Dearborn

NEW YORK
Hudson R.
New York
Albany
NEW JERSEY
PENNSYLVANIA
Philadelphia
DELAWARE
Chesapeake Bay
MARYLAND
Baltimore
WASHINGTON
Potomac R.
VIRGINIA
James R.
Norfolk
NORTH CAROLINA
Charleston
SOUTH CAROLINA
GEORGIA
Savannah R.
Savannah
FLORIDA (Spain)
St. Augustine
BRITISH

MICHIGAN TERRITORY
OHIO
Cincinnati
Tippecanoe R.
INDIANA TERRITORY
KENTUCKY
Wabash R.
Ohio R.
TENNESSEE
Cumberland R.
Huntsville
JACKSON
Ft. Deposit
CREEK WAR 1813–1814
Coosa R.
Ft. Mims (massacre)
Alabama R.
Pensacola
Mobile
MISSISSIPPI TERRITORY
Vicksburg
LOUISIANA
New Orleans
ILLINOIS TERRITORY
MISSOURI TERRITORY
Missouri R.
Mississippi River
Tennessee R.
Gulf of Mexico

© Copyright HAMMOND INCORPORATED, Maplewood, N.J.
Printed in U.S.A.

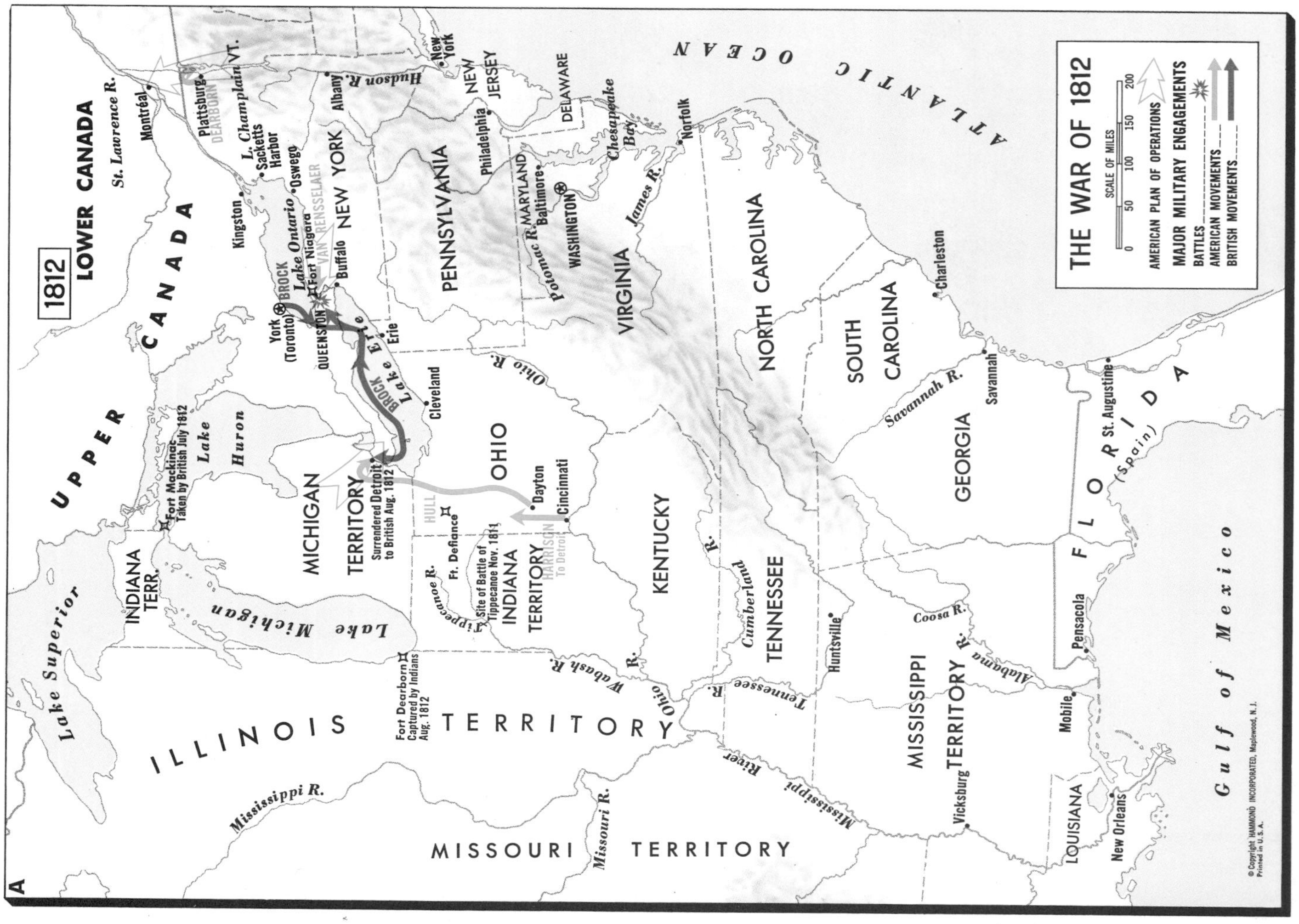

Inset (Map B):
MICHIGAN TERRITORY
UPPER CANADA
BATTLE OF THE THAMES
Lake St. Clair
PROCTOR
Thames R.
Ft. Malden
Detroit — Recaptured by Americans Sept. 1813
Detroit R.
PROCTOR
FRENCHTOWN
Raisin R.
WINCHESTER
HARRISON
Ft. Meigs
Ft. Stephenson
NAVAL BATTLE OF LAKE ERIE
BARCLAY
PERRY
Put-in-Bay
Lake Erie
OHIO

Map A — 1812

THE WAR OF 1812

SCALE OF MILES
0 50 100 150 200

AMERICAN PLAN OF OPERATIONS
MAJOR MILITARY ENGAGEMENTS
BATTLES
AMERICAN MOVEMENTS
BRITISH MOVEMENTS

1812

LOWER CANADA
UPPER CANADA
ATLANTIC OCEAN

St. Lawrence R.
Montréal
Plattsburg
L. Champlain, VT.
DEARBORN
Sacketts Harbor
Kingston
Oswego
Lake Ontario
Fort Niagara
York (Toronto)
BROCK
QUEENSTON
VAN RENSSELAER
Buffalo
Lake Erie
Erie
BROCK
Cleveland
Ohio R.
HULL
Surrendered Detroit to British Aug. 1812
Fort Mackinac Taken by British July 1812
Lake Huron
Lake Superior
Lake Michigan
MICHIGAN TERRITORY
Detroit
Ft. Defiance
HARRISON To Detroit
INDIANA TERR.
Site of Battle of Tippecanoe Nov. 1811
Tippecanoe R.
Dayton
Cincinnati
OHIO
Fort Dearborn Captured by Indians Aug. 1812

NEW YORK
Hudson R.
New York
Albany
NEW JERSEY
PENNSYLVANIA
Philadelphia
DELAWARE
Chesapeake Bay
MARYLAND
Baltimore
WASHINGTON
Potomac R.
VIRGINIA
James R.
Norfolk
NORTH CAROLINA
Charleston
SOUTH CAROLINA
GEORGIA
Savannah R.
Savannah
FLORIDA (Spain)
St. Augustine

ILLINOIS TERRITORY
MISSOURI TERRITORY
Missouri R.
Mississippi R.
Wabash R.
Ohio R.
KENTUCKY
TENNESSEE
Cumberland R.
Tennessee R.
Huntsville
Coosa R.
Alabama R.
MISSISSIPPI TERRITORY
Vicksburg
Mobile
Pensacola
LOUISIANA
New Orleans
Gulf of Mexico

© Copyright HAMMOND INCORPORATED, Maplewood, N.J.
Printed in U.S.A.

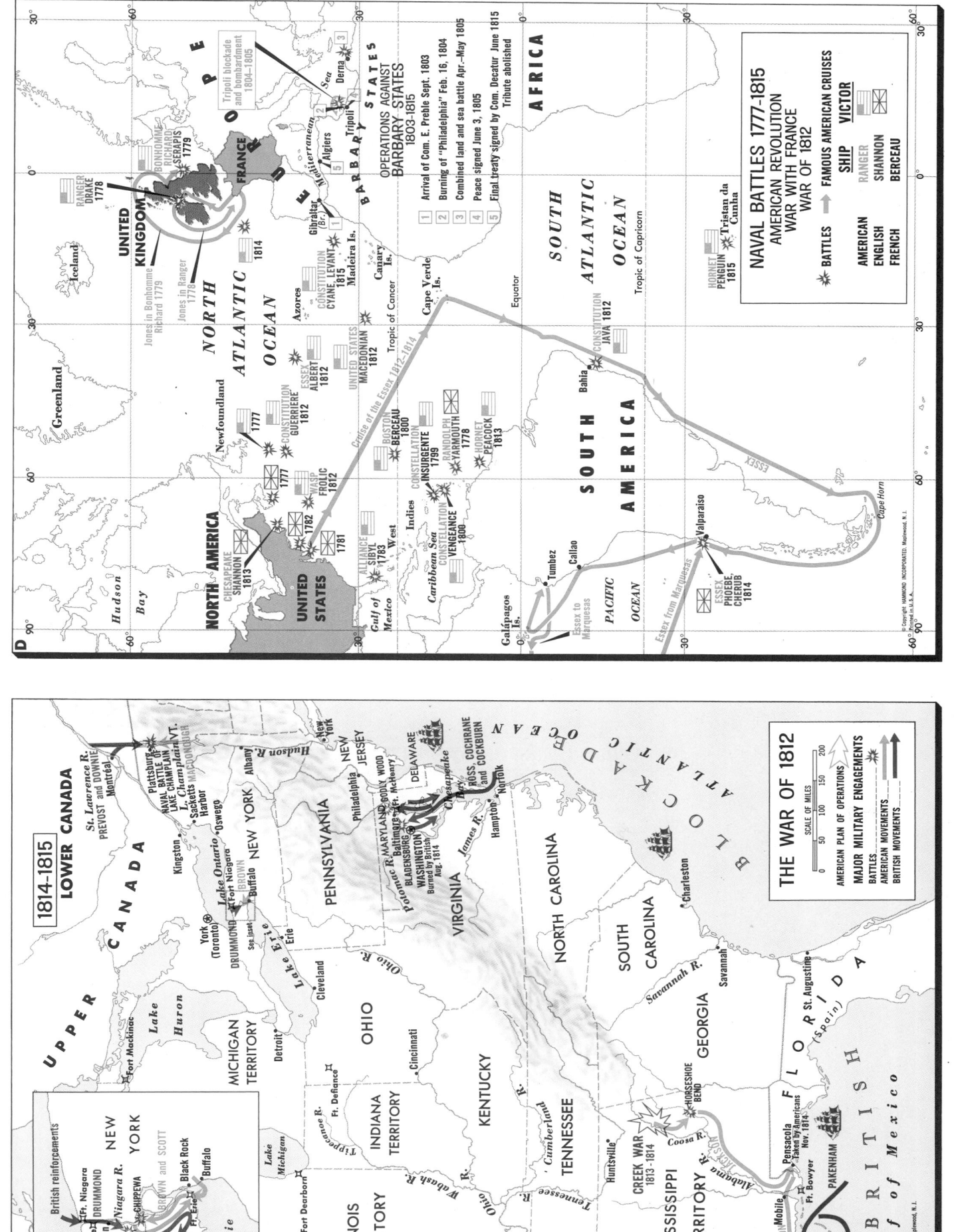

NAVAL BATTLES 1777-1815
AMERICAN REVOLUTION
WAR WITH FRANCE
WAR OF 1812

	SHIP	VICTOR
BATTLES — FAMOUS AMERICAN CRUISES	RANGER	SHANNON
	SHANNON	
	BERCEAU	

AMERICAN
ENGLISH
FRENCH

★ BATTLES → FAMOUS AMERICAN CRUISES

OPERATIONS AGAINST
BARBARY STATES
1803-1815

1 Arrival of Com. E. Preble Sept. 1803
2 Burning of "Philadelphia" Feb. 16, 1804
3 Combined land and sea battle Apr.-May 1805
4 Peace signed June 3, 1805
5 Final treaty signed by Com. Decatur June 1815 Tribute abolished

THE WAR OF 1812

SCALE OF MILES
0   50   100   150   200

⇨ AMERICAN PLAN OF OPERATIONS
★ BATTLES
➡ AMERICAN MOVEMENTS
➡ BRITISH MOVEMENTS

MAJOR MILITARY ENGAGEMENTS

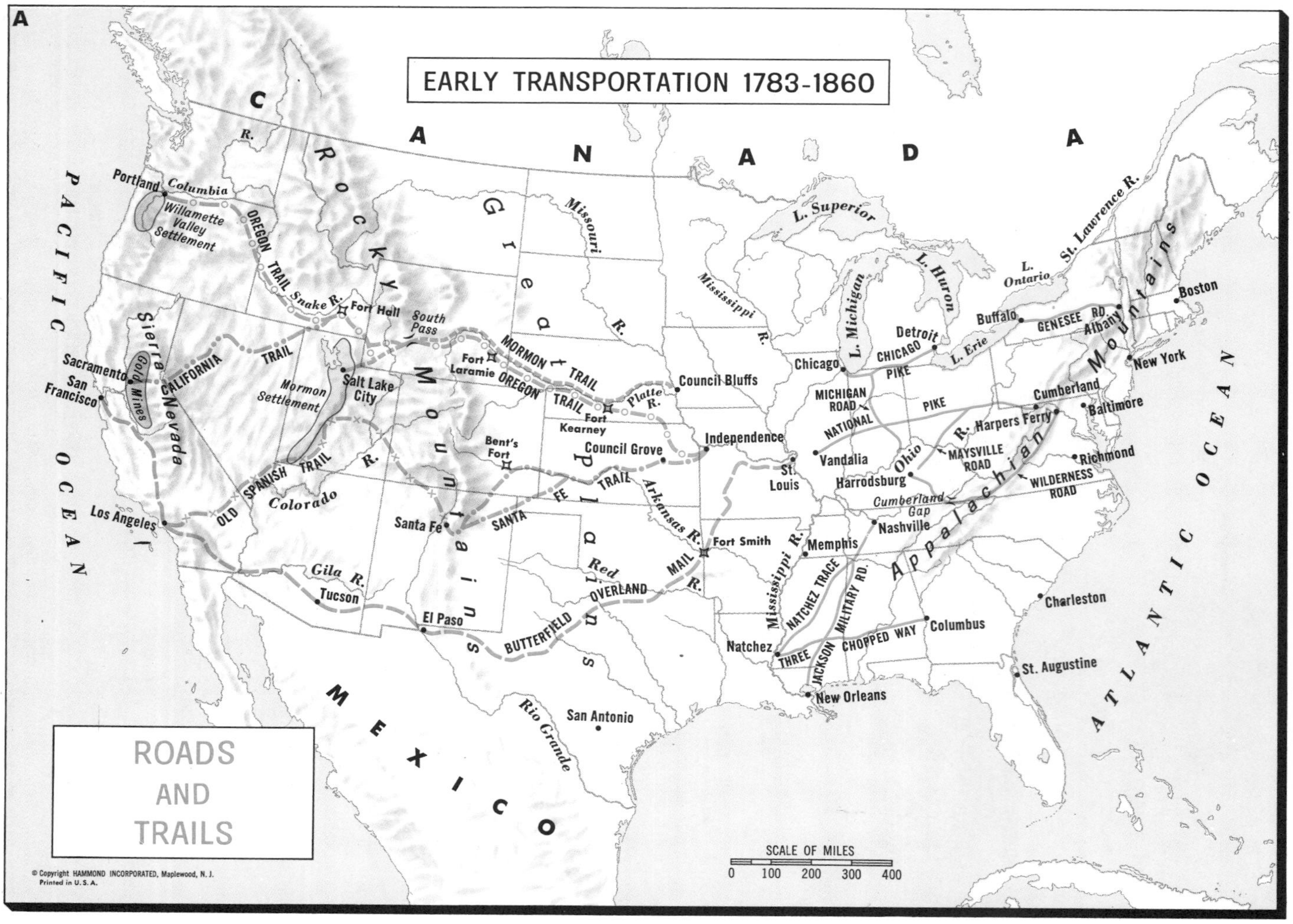

A

EARLY TRANSPORTATION 1783-1860

C A N A D A

PACIFIC OCEAN

ATLANTIC OCEAN

MEXICO

ROCKY Mountains

Great Plains

Sierra Nevada

Appalachian Mountains

L. Superior
L. Michigan
L. Huron
L. Ontario
L. Erie

St. Lawrence R.
Missouri R.
Mississippi R.
Columbia R.
Snake R.
Platte R.
Colorado R.
Gila R.
Arkansas R.
Red R.
Rio Grande
Ohio R.

Portland
Columbia
Willamette Valley Settlement
OREGON TRAIL
Fort Hall
South Pass
MORMON TRAIL
Fort Laramie
OREGON TRAIL
Fort Kearney
Council Bluffs
Chicago
Detroit
Buffalo
Albany
Boston
New York
GENESEE RD.
CHICAGO PIKE
Sacramento
San Francisco
CALIFORNIA TRAIL
Salt Lake City
Mormon Settlement
Independence
MICHIGAN ROAD
NATIONAL PIKE
Cumberland
Baltimore
Harpers Ferry
St. Louis
Vandalia
Harrodsburg
MAYSVILLE ROAD
Richmond
Los Angeles
OLD SPANISH TRAIL
Bent's Fort
Council Grove
SANTA FE TRAIL
Santa Fe
Cumberland Gap
WILDERNESS ROAD
Tucson
Memphis
Nashville
Charleston
El Paso
BUTTERFIELD OVERLAND MAIL
Fort Smith
MAIL RD.
NATCHEZ TRACE
NATCHEZ MILITARY RD.
Columbus
St. Augustine
San Antonio
Natchez
THREE CHOPPED WAY
JACKSON CHOPPED WAY
New Orleans

ROADS AND TRAILS

© Copyright HAMMOND INCORPORATED, Maplewood, N.J.
Printed in U.S.A.

SCALE OF MILES
0 100 200 300 400

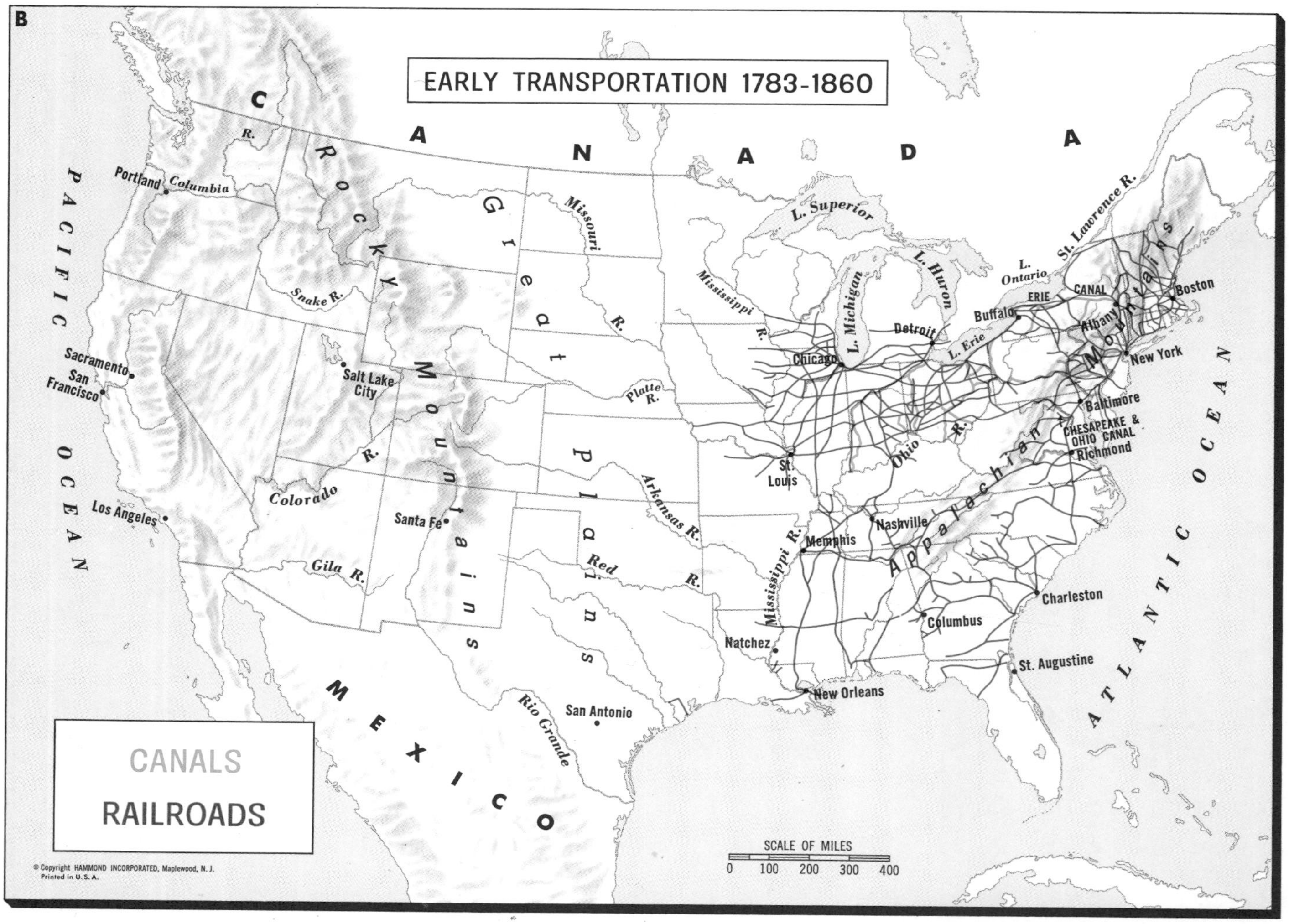

B

EARLY TRANSPORTATION 1783-1860

C A N A D A

PACIFIC OCEAN

ATLANTIC OCEAN

MEXICO

ROCKY Mountains

Great Plains

Sierra Nevada

Appalachian Mountains

L. Superior
L. Michigan
L. Huron
L. Ontario
L. Erie

St. Lawrence R.
Missouri R.
Mississippi R.
Columbia R.
Snake R.
Platte R.
Colorado R.
Gila R.
Arkansas R.
Red R.
Rio Grande
Ohio R.

Portland
Columbia
Sacramento
San Francisco
Salt Lake City
Los Angeles
Santa Fe
Chicago
Detroit
Buffalo
ERIE CANAL
Albany
Boston
New York
Baltimore
CHESAPEAKE & OHIO CANAL
Richmond
St. Louis
Memphis
Nashville
Charleston
Columbus
Natchez
St. Augustine
San Antonio
New Orleans

CANALS
RAILROADS

© Copyright HAMMOND INCORPORATED, Maplewood, N.J.
Printed in U.S.A.

SCALE OF MILES
0 100 200 300 400

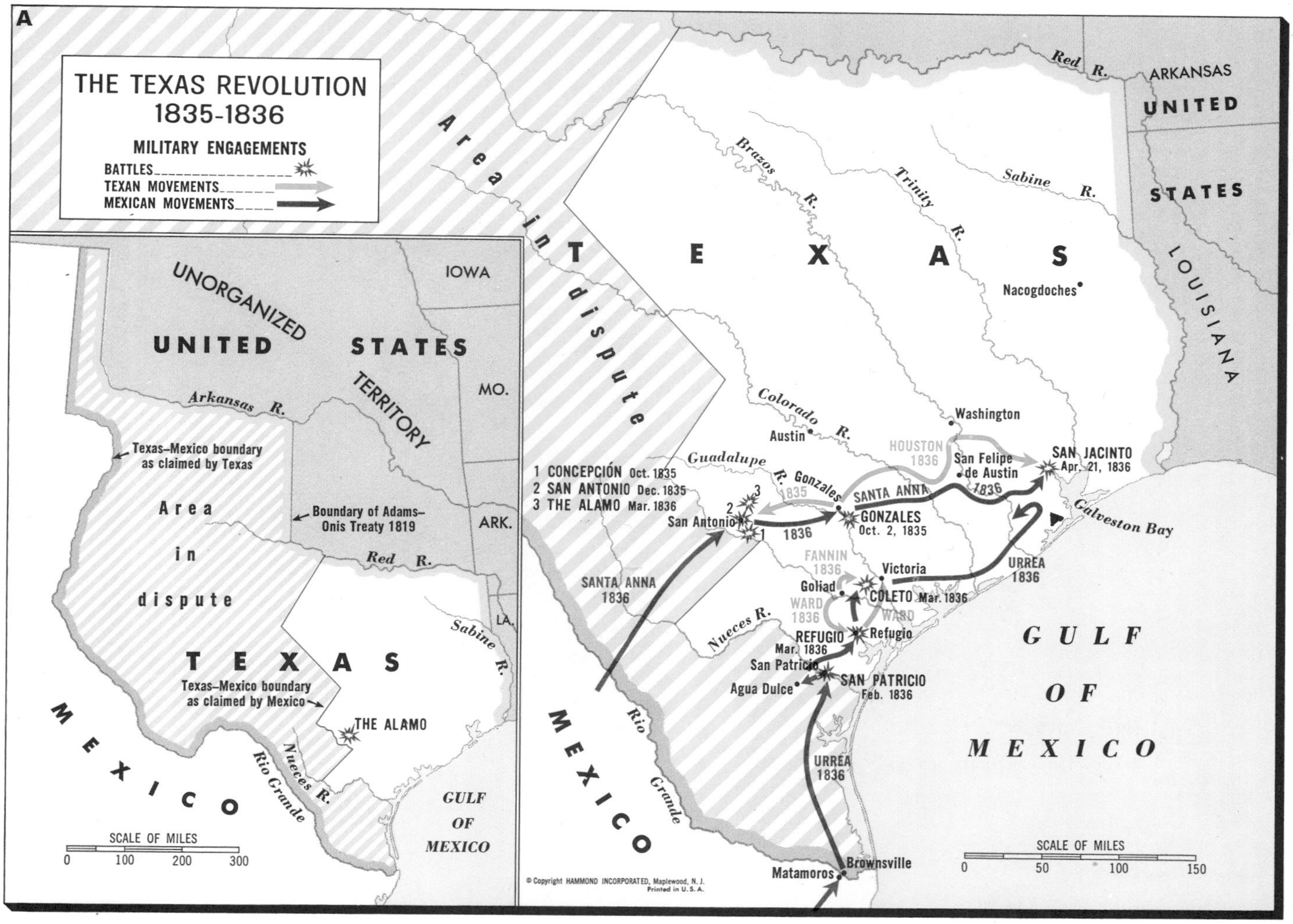

A

THE TEXAS REVOLUTION 1835-1836

MILITARY ENGAGEMENTS

BATTLES
TEXAN MOVEMENTS
MEXICAN MOVEMENTS

Red R.

ARKANSAS

UNITED

STATES

Area in dispute

Brazos R.

Trinity R.

Sabine R.

LOUISIANA

T E X A S

Nacogdoches

Inset map:

UNORGANIZED

IOWA

UNITED STATES TERRITORY

MO.

Arkansas R.

Texas–Mexico boundary as claimed by Texas

Boundary of Adams–Onis Treaty 1819

ARK.

A r e a

Red R.

LA.

i n

Sabine R.

d i s p u t e

T E X A S

Texas–Mexico boundary as claimed by Mexico →

THE ALAMO

M E X I C O

Rio Grande

Nueces R.

GULF OF MEXICO

SCALE OF MILES
0   100   200   300

Main map:

Colorado R.

Washington

Austin

Guadalupe R.

Gonzales 1835

HOUSTON 1836

San Felipe de Austin 1836

SAN JACINTO Apr. 21, 1836

1 CONCEPCIÓN Oct. 1835
2 SAN ANTONIO Dec. 1835
3 THE ALAMO Mar. 1836

SANTA ANNA

GONZALES Oct. 2, 1835

Galveston Bay

San Antonio

1836

SANTA ANNA 1836

FANNIN 1836

Victoria

URREA 1836

WARD 1836

Goliad

COLETO Mar. 1836

Nueces R.

WARD

REFUGIO Mar. 1836

Refugio

GULF

San Patricio

OF

Agua Dulce

SAN PATRICIO Feb. 1836

MEXICO

Rio Grande

M E X I C O

URREA 1836

Matamoros

Brownsville

© Copyright HAMMOND INCORPORATED, Maplewood, N.J.
Printed in U.S.A.

SCALE OF MILES
0   50   100   150

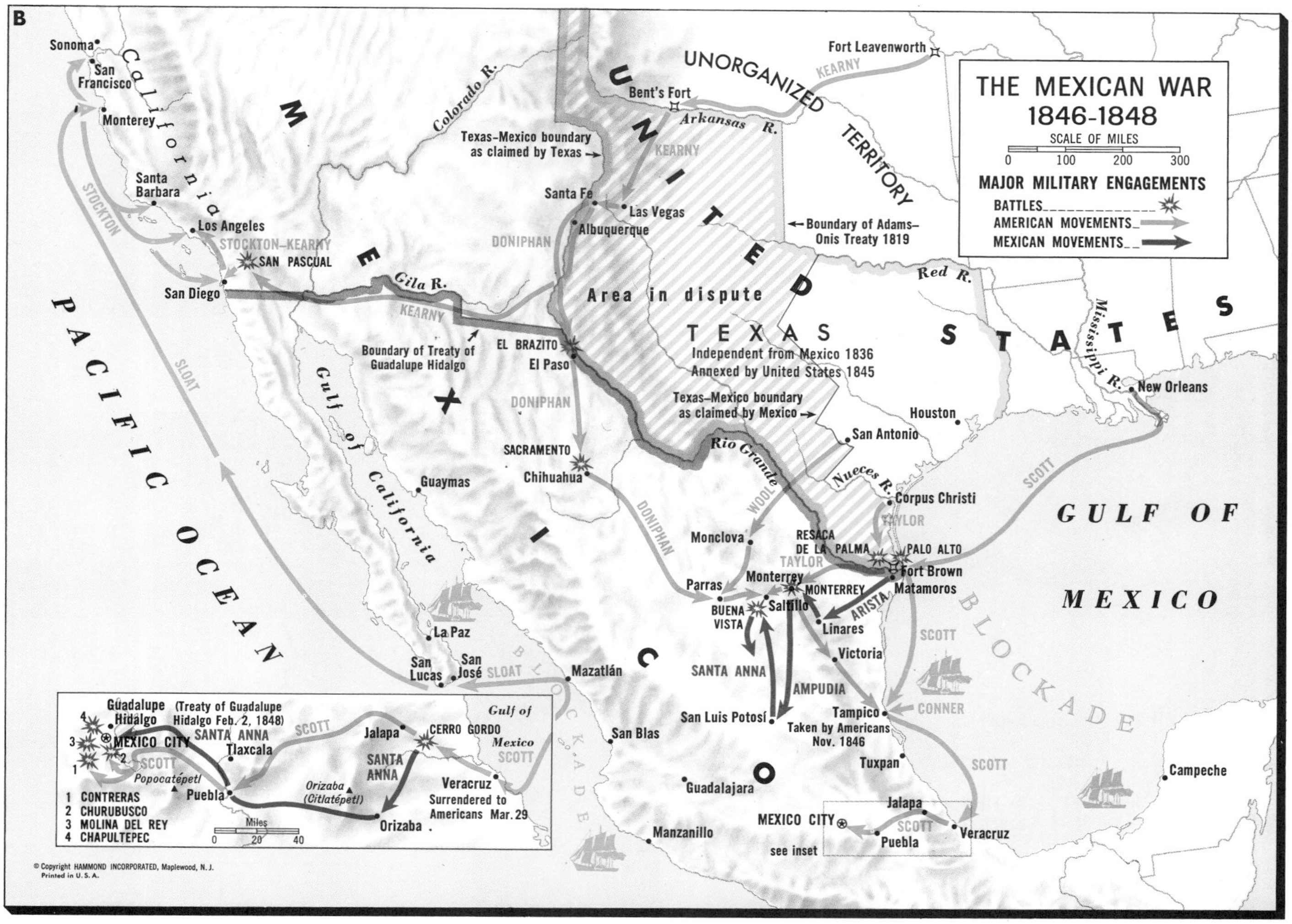

B

THE MEXICAN WAR 1846-1848

SCALE OF MILES
0   100   200   300

MAJOR MILITARY ENGAGEMENTS

BATTLES
AMERICAN MOVEMENTS
MEXICAN MOVEMENTS

Sonoma

San Francisco

California

Monterey

STOCKTON

Santa Barbara

Los Angeles

STOCKTON–KEARNY

San Diego

SAN PASCUAL

SLOAT

Colorado R.

Texas–Mexico boundary as claimed by Texas →

UNORGANIZED

Fort Leavenworth

KEARNY

Bent's Fort

Arkansas R.

TERRITORY

Santa Fe

KEARNY

Las Vegas

DONIPHAN

Albuquerque

Boundary of Adams–Onis Treaty 1819

Gila R.

KEARNY

Boundary of Treaty of Guadalupe Hidalgo

EL BRAZITO

El Paso

DONIPHAN

Area in dispute

T E X A S

Independent from Mexico 1836
Annexed by United States 1845

Texas–Mexico boundary as claimed by Mexico →

Red R.

UNITED

STATES

Mississippi R.

New Orleans

M E X I C O

Gulf of California

SACRAMENTO

Chihuahua

DONIPHAN

Rio Grande

Houston

San Antonio

Nueces R.

Corpus Christi

TAYLOR

GULF OF

Guaymas

Monclova

WOOL

BLOCKADE

Parras

Monterrey

RESACA DE LA PALMA

PALO ALTO

Fort Brown

Matamoros

SCOTT

MEXICO

La Paz

San Lucas

San José

SLOAT

Mazatlán

BUENA VISTA

Saltillo

ARISTA

Linares

SANTA ANNA

Victoria

SCOTT

AMPUDIA

San Luis Potosí

Tampico Taken by Americans Nov. 1846

CONNER

San Blas

Tuxpan

SCOTT

Guadalajara

Jalapa

Campeche

PACIFIC OCEAN

Inset map (lower left):

Guadalupe (Treaty of Guadalupe Hidalgo Feb. 2, 1848)

4
3
SANTA ANNA

MEXICO CITY

Tlaxcala

2

SCOTT

1

Popocatépetl

Puebla

1 CONTRERAS
2 CHURUBUSCO
3 MOLINA DEL REY
4 CHAPULTEPEC

Jalapa

Orizaba (Citlatépetl)

SANTA ANNA

CERRO GORDO

Gulf of Mexico

SCOTT

Veracruz Surrendered to Americans Mar. 29

Orizaba

Miles
0   20   40

Inset map (lower right):

MEXICO CITY
see inset

SCOTT

Puebla

Jalapa

Veracruz

Manzanillo

© Copyright HAMMOND INCORPORATED, Maplewood, N.J.
Printed in U.S.A.

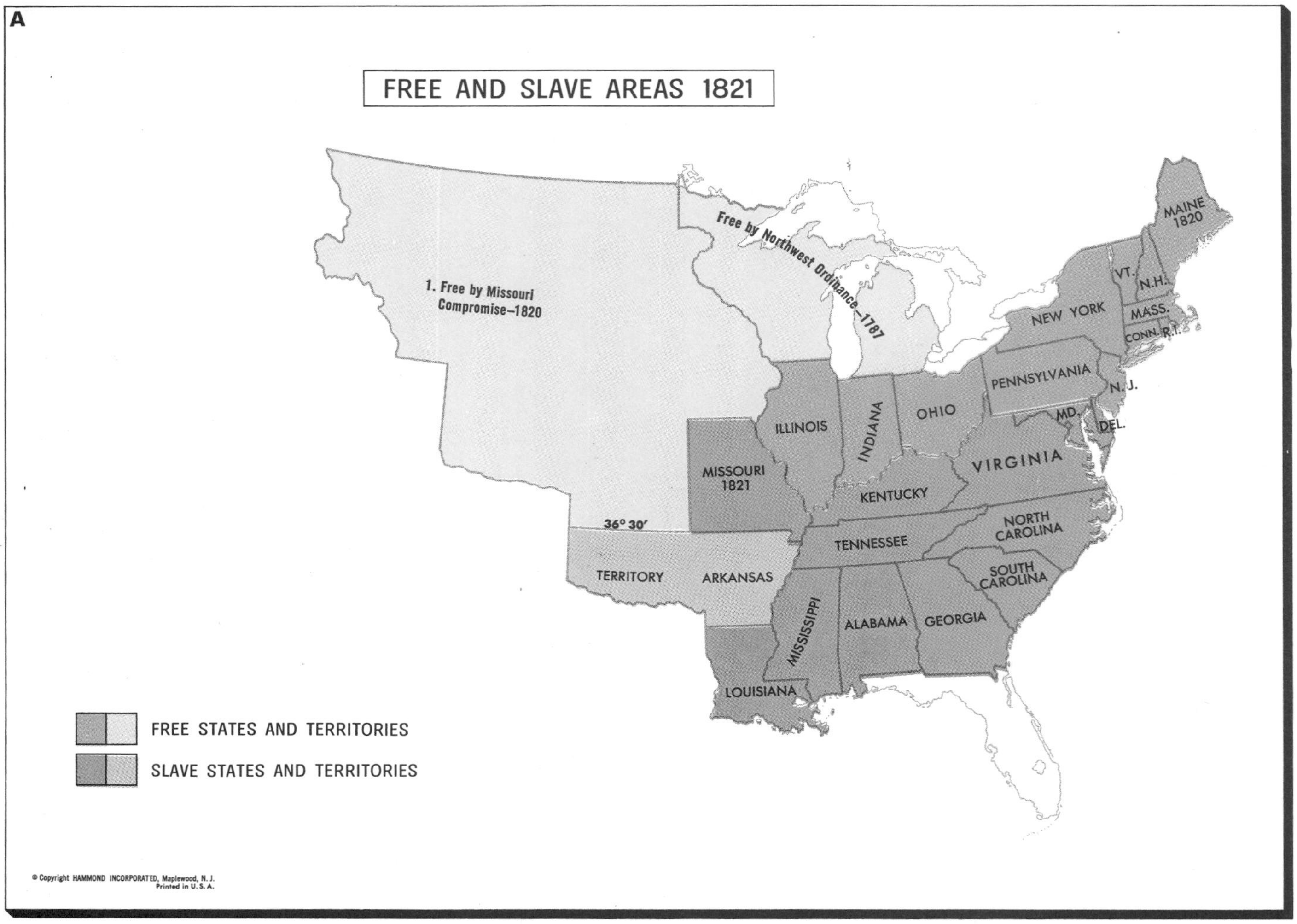

FREE AND SLAVE AREAS 1821

FREE STATES AND TERRITORIES

SLAVE STATES AND TERRITORIES

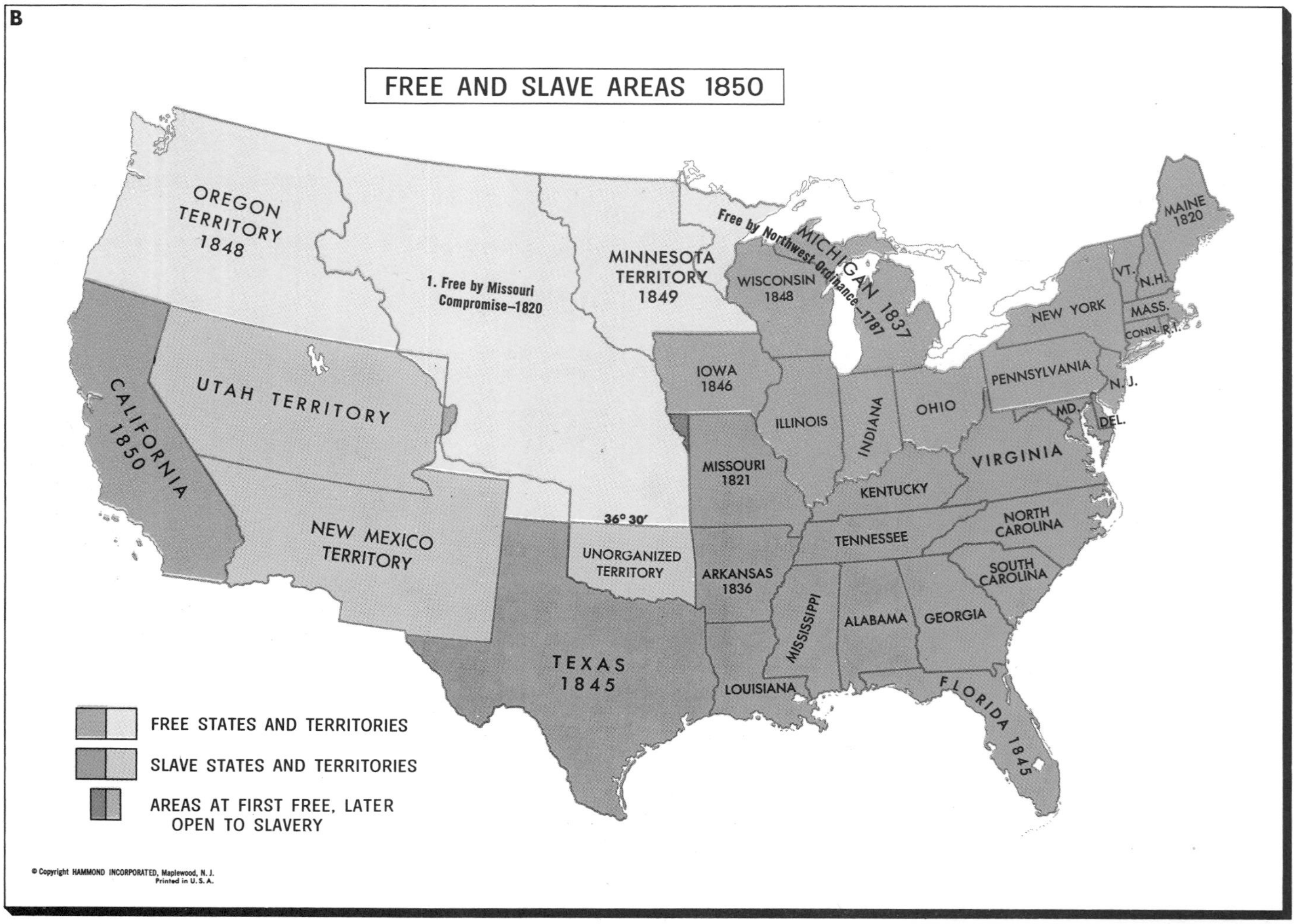

FREE AND SLAVE AREAS 1850

FREE STATES AND TERRITORIES

SLAVE STATES AND TERRITORIES

AREAS AT FIRST FREE, LATER OPEN TO SLAVERY

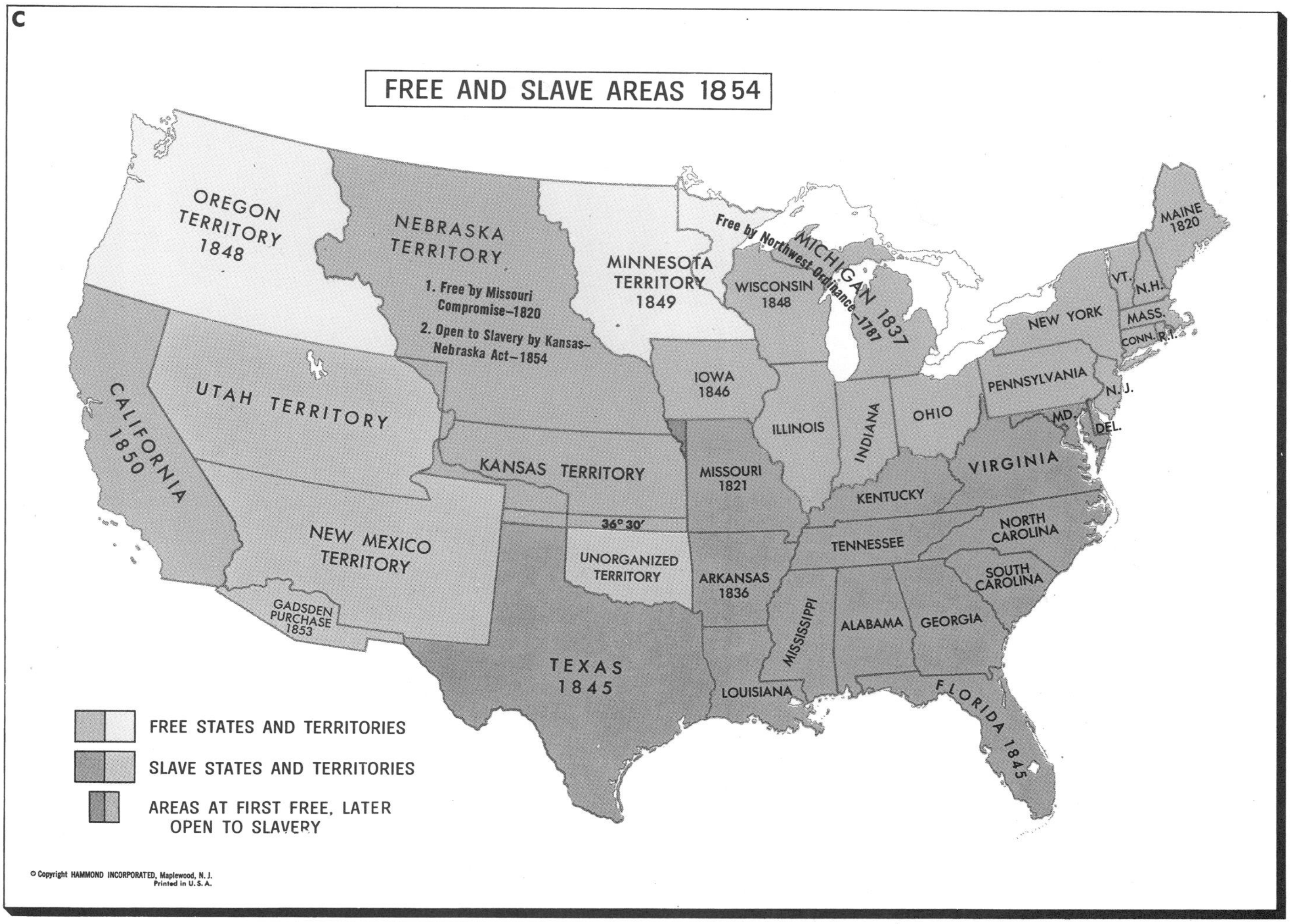

C

FREE AND SLAVE AREAS 1854

OREGON TERRITORY 1848

NEBRASKA TERRITORY.
1. Free by Missouri Compromise—1820
2. Open to Slavery by Kansas—Nebraska Act—1854

MINNESOTA TERRITORY 1849

Free by Northwest Ordinance—1787

MICHIGAN 1837

WISCONSIN 1848

MAINE 1820

VT.
N.H.

NEW YORK

MASS.
CONN. R.I.

UTAH TERRITORY

CALIFORNIA 1850

IOWA 1846

PENNSYLVANIA

N.J.

ILLINOIS

INDIANA

OHIO

MD.

DEL.

KANSAS TERRITORY

MISSOURI 1821

KENTUCKY

VIRGINIA

36° 30'

NEW MEXICO TERRITORY

UNORGANIZED TERRITORY

TENNESSEE

NORTH CAROLINA

GADSDEN PURCHASE 1853

ARKANSAS 1836

SOUTH CAROLINA

MISSISSIPPI

ALABAMA

GEORGIA

TEXAS 1845

LOUISIANA

FLORIDA 1845

FREE STATES AND TERRITORIES

SLAVE STATES AND TERRITORIES

AREAS AT FIRST FREE, LATER OPEN TO SLAVERY

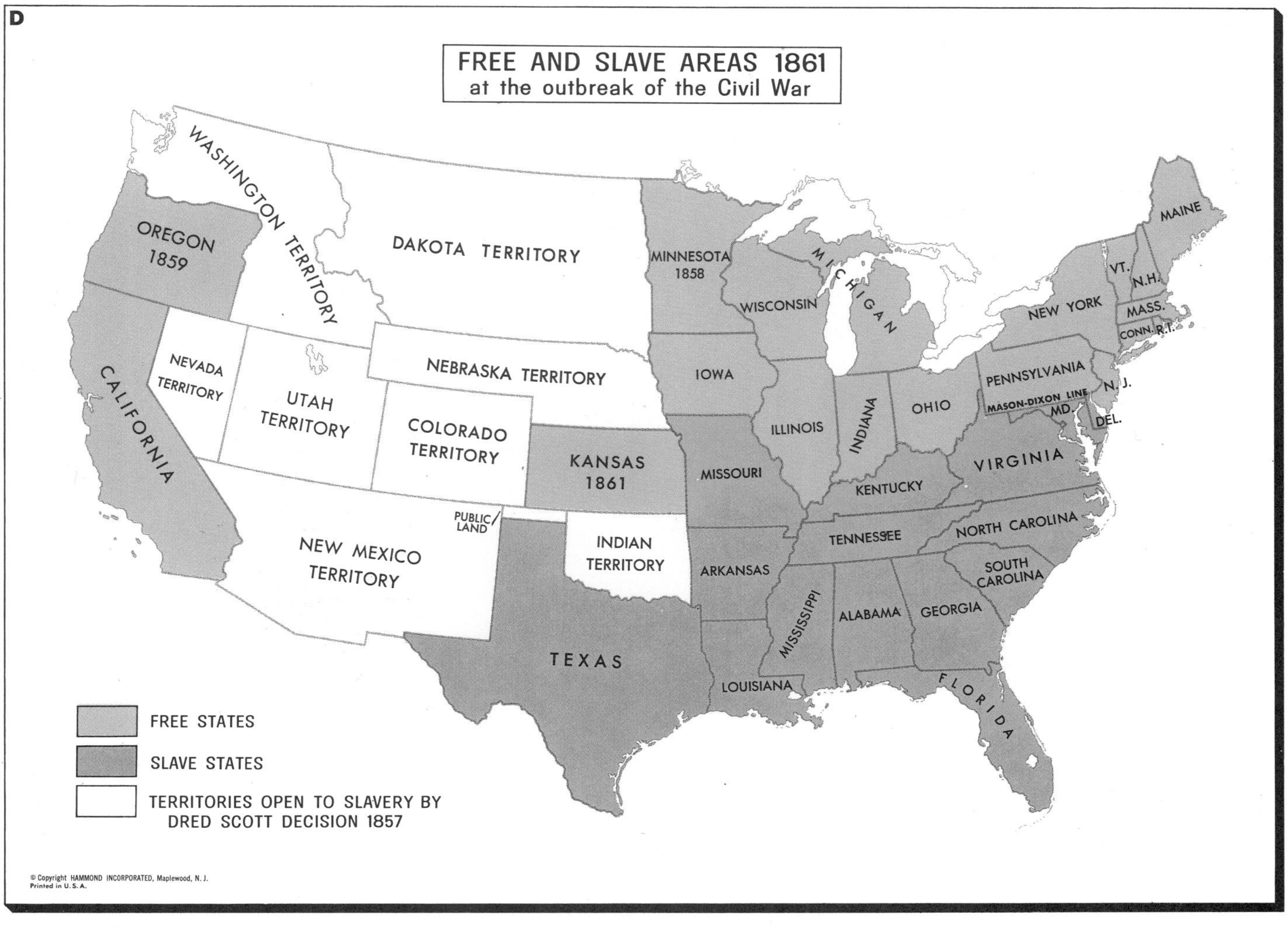

D

FREE AND SLAVE AREAS 1861
at the outbreak of the Civil War

WASHINGTON TERRITORY

OREGON 1859

DAKOTA TERRITORY

MINNESOTA 1858

MICHIGAN

MAINE

NEVADA TERRITORY

UTAH TERRITORY

NEBRASKA TERRITORY

WISCONSIN

VT.
N.H.

NEW YORK

MASS.
CONN. R.I.

CALIFORNIA

COLORADO TERRITORY

IOWA

PENNSYLVANIA

N.J.

KANSAS 1861

ILLINOIS

INDIANA

OHIO

MASON-DIXON LINE

MD.

DEL.

MISSOURI

KENTUCKY

VIRGINIA

PUBLIC LAND

NEW MEXICO TERRITORY

INDIAN TERRITORY

ARKANSAS

TENNESSEE

NORTH CAROLINA

SOUTH CAROLINA

MISSISSIPPI

ALABAMA

GEORGIA

TEXAS

LOUISIANA

FLORIDA

FREE STATES

SLAVE STATES

TERRITORIES OPEN TO SLAVERY BY DRED SCOTT DECISION 1857

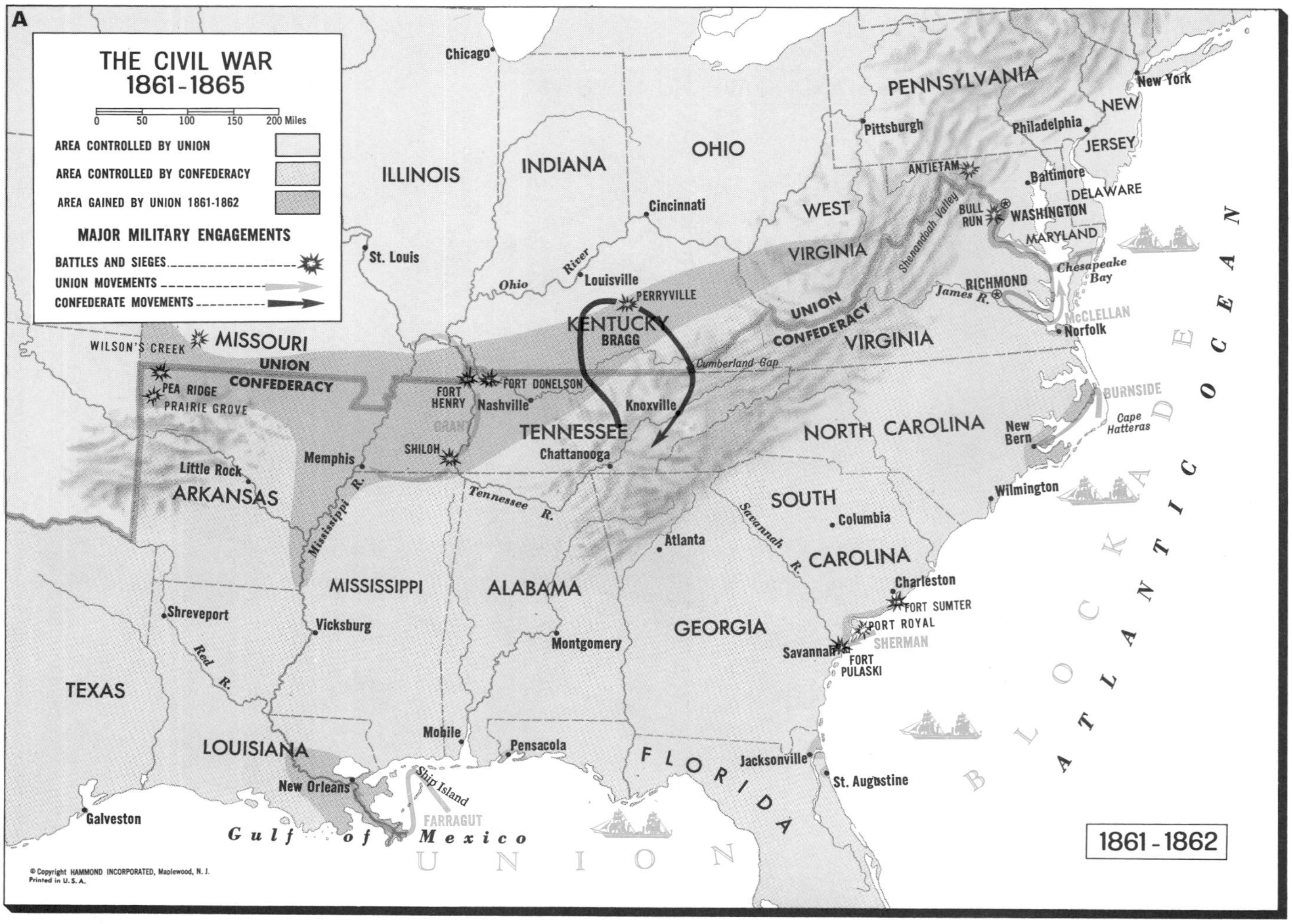
A
THE CIVIL WAR
1861-1865
0 50 100 150 200 Miles
AREA CONTROLLED BY UNION
AREA CONTROLLED BY CONFEDERACY
AREA GAINED BY UNION 1861-1862
MAJOR MILITARY ENGAGEMENTS
BATTLES AND SIEGES
UNION MOVEMENTS
CONFEDERATE MOVEMENTS
Chicago
ILLINOIS
INDIANA
OHIO
PENNSYLVANIA
Pittsburgh
Philadelphia
New York
NEW JERSEY
ANTIETAM
Baltimore
DELAWARE
BULL RUN
WASHINGTON
MARYLAND
WEST VIRGINIA
Cincinnati
St. Louis
Ohio River
Louisville
PERRYVILLE
KENTUCKY
BRAGG
Shenandoah Valley
RICHMOND
James R.
Chesapeake Bay
McCLELLAN
Norfolk
UNION
CONFEDERACY
VIRGINIA
WILSON'S CREEK
MISSOURI
UNION
CONFEDERACY
PEA RIDGE
PRAIRIE GROVE
FORT HENRY
FORT DONELSON
Nashville
Cumberland Gap
Knoxville
BURNSIDE
Cape Hatteras
New Bern
NORTH CAROLINA
TENNESSEE
GRANT
SHILOH
Memphis
Chattanooga
Little Rock
ARKANSAS
Mississippi R.
Tennessee R.
Wilmington
SOUTH CAROLINA
Columbia
Savannah R.
Atlanta
MISSISSIPPI
ALABAMA
Charleston
FORT SUMTER
PORT ROYAL
SHERMAN
Shreveport
Vicksburg
Montgomery
GEORGIA
Savannah
FORT PULASKI
Red R.
TEXAS
Mobile
Pensacola
LOUISIANA
FLORIDA
Jacksonville
St. Augustine
New Orleans
Ship Island
FARRAGUT
Galveston
Gulf of Mexico
UNION
BLOCKADE
ATLANTIC OCEAN
1861-1862
© Copyright HAMMOND INCORPORATED, Maplewood, N. J.
Printed in U. S. A.

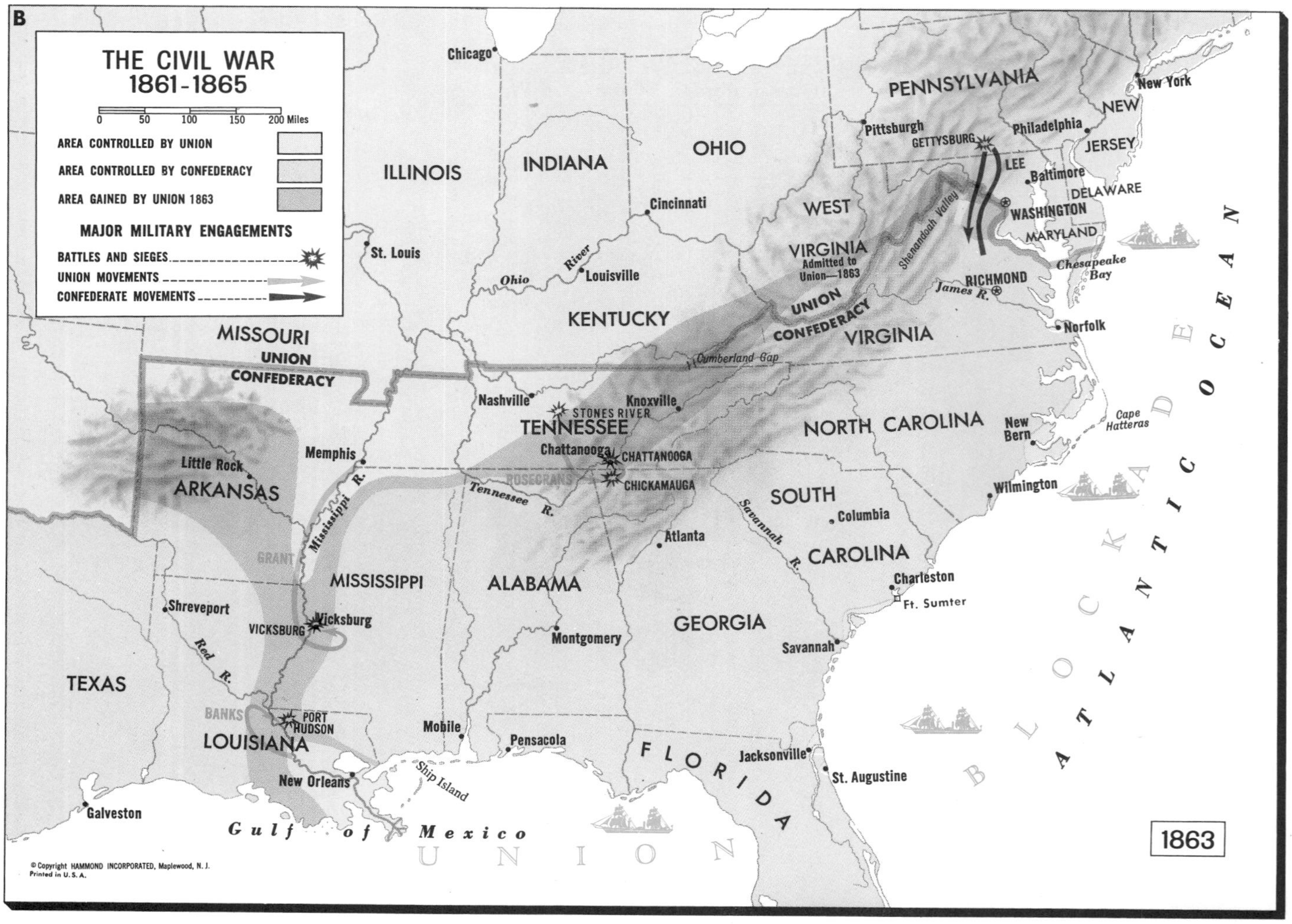
B
THE CIVIL WAR
1861-1865
0 50 100 150 200 Miles
AREA CONTROLLED BY UNION
AREA CONTROLLED BY CONFEDERACY
AREA GAINED BY UNION 1863
MAJOR MILITARY ENGAGEMENTS
BATTLES AND SIEGES
UNION MOVEMENTS
CONFEDERATE MOVEMENTS
Chicago
ILLINOIS
INDIANA
OHIO
PENNSYLVANIA
Pittsburgh
GETTYSBURG
Philadelphia
New York
NEW JERSEY
LEE
Baltimore
DELAWARE
WASHINGTON
MARYLAND
Cincinnati
St. Louis
Ohio River
Louisville
WEST VIRGINIA
Admitted to Union—1863
Shenandoah Valley
RICHMOND
James R.
Chesapeake Bay
KENTUCKY
UNION
CONFEDERACY
VIRGINIA
Norfolk
MISSOURI
UNION
CONFEDERACY
Cumberland Gap
Nashville
STONES RIVER
Knoxville
TENNESSEE
NORTH CAROLINA
New Bern
Cape Hatteras
Memphis
Chattanooga
CHATTANOOGA
ROSECRANS
CHICKAMAUGA
Little Rock
ARKANSAS
Mississippi R.
Tennessee R.
SOUTH CAROLINA
Columbia
Wilmington
Savannah R.
Atlanta
GRANT
MISSISSIPPI
ALABAMA
Charleston
Ft. Sumter
Shreveport
VICKSBURG
Vicksburg
Montgomery
GEORGIA
Savannah
Red R.
TEXAS
BANKS
PORT HUDSON
LOUISIANA
Mobile
Pensacola
FLORIDA
Jacksonville
St. Augustine
New Orleans
Ship Island
Galveston
Gulf of Mexico
UNION
BLOCKADE
ATLANTIC OCEAN
1863
© Copyright HAMMOND INCORPORATED, Maplewood, N. J.
Printed in U. S. A.

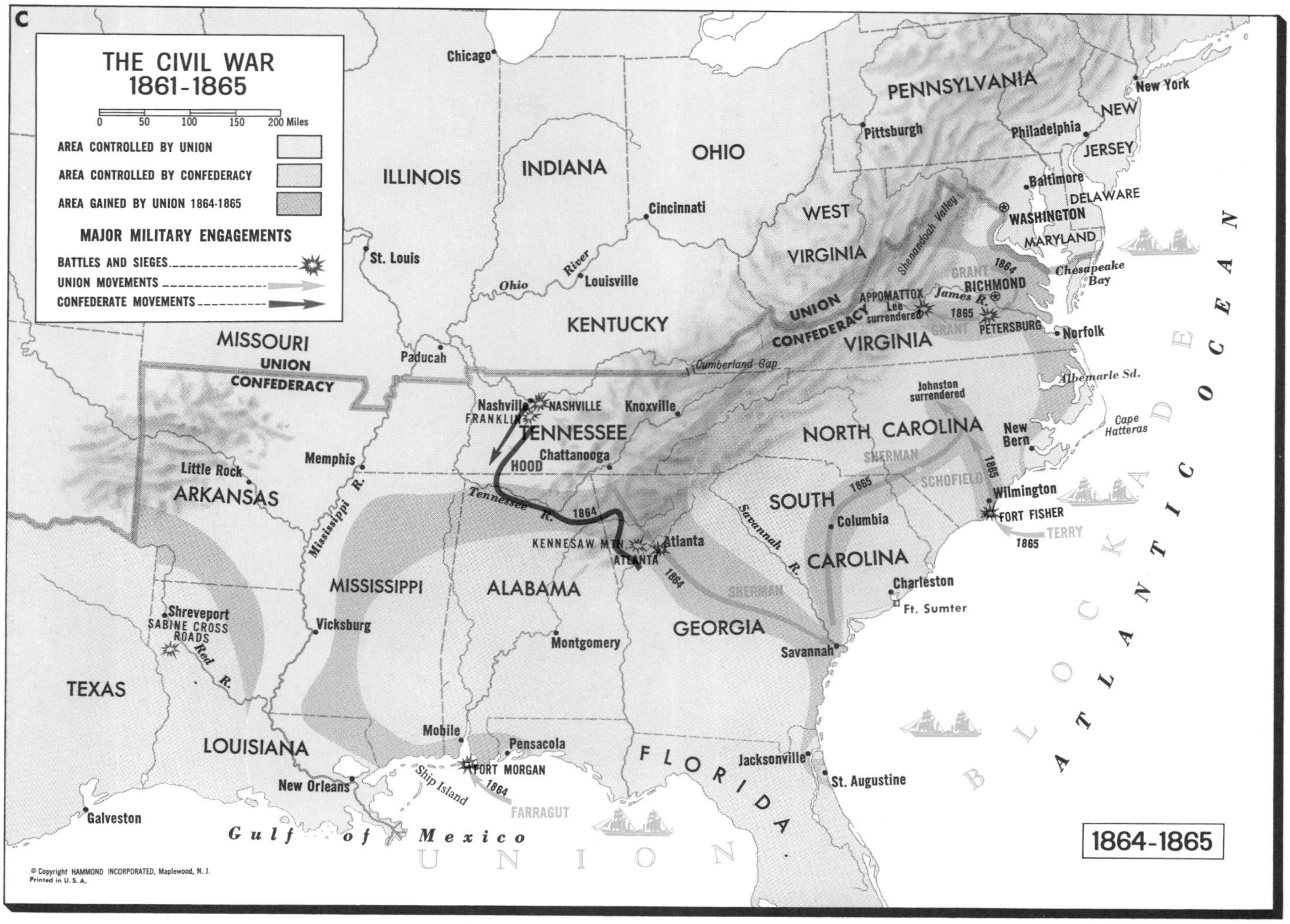

C

THE CIVIL WAR
1861-1865

0 50 100 150 200 Miles

AREA CONTROLLED BY UNION

AREA CONTROLLED BY CONFEDERACY

AREA GAINED BY UNION 1864-1865

MAJOR MILITARY ENGAGEMENTS

BATTLES AND SIEGES

UNION MOVEMENTS

CONFEDERATE MOVEMENTS

Chicago

PENNSYLVANIA

New York

NEW

JERSEY

ILLINOIS

INDIANA

OHIO

Pittsburgh

Philadelphia

Baltimore

DELAWARE

WEST

VIRGINIA

WASHINGTON

MARYLAND

Cincinnati

St. Louis

Ohio

River

Louisville

GRANT 1864

RICHMOND

Chesapeake

Bay

MISSOURI

UNION

CONFEDERACY

KENTUCKY

UNION

CONFEDERATE

APPOMATTOX

Lee

surrendered

James

R.

1865

GRANT

PETERSBURG

Norfolk

ATLANTIC OCEAN

Paducah

VIRGINIA

Cumberland Gap

Albemarle Sd.

Johnston

surrendered

Little Rock

Memphis

Mississippi R.

Nashville

FRANKLIN

NASHVILLE

Knoxville

NORTH CAROLINA

SHERMAN

New

Bern

Cape

Hatteras

ARKANSAS

TENNESSEE

Chattanooga

HOOD

Tennessee R.

1864

SOUTH

SCHOFIELD

1865

Columbia

1865

Wilmington

FORT FISHER

TERRY

1865

Shreveport

SABINE CROSS

ROADS

Red R.

Vicksburg

MISSISSIPPI

ALABAMA

KENNESAW MTN

ATLANTA

Atlanta

1864

CAROLINA

Charleston

Ft. Sumter

SHERMAN

BLOCKADE

TEXAS

Montgomery

GEORGIA

Savannah R.

Savannah

LOUISIANA

Mobile

Pensacola

Jacksonville

New Orleans

Ship Island

FORT MORGAN

1864

FARRAGUT

FLORIDA

St. Augustine

Galveston

Gulf of Mexico

UNION

1864-1865

© Copyright HAMMOND INCORPORATED, Maplewood, N. J.
Printed in U.S.A.

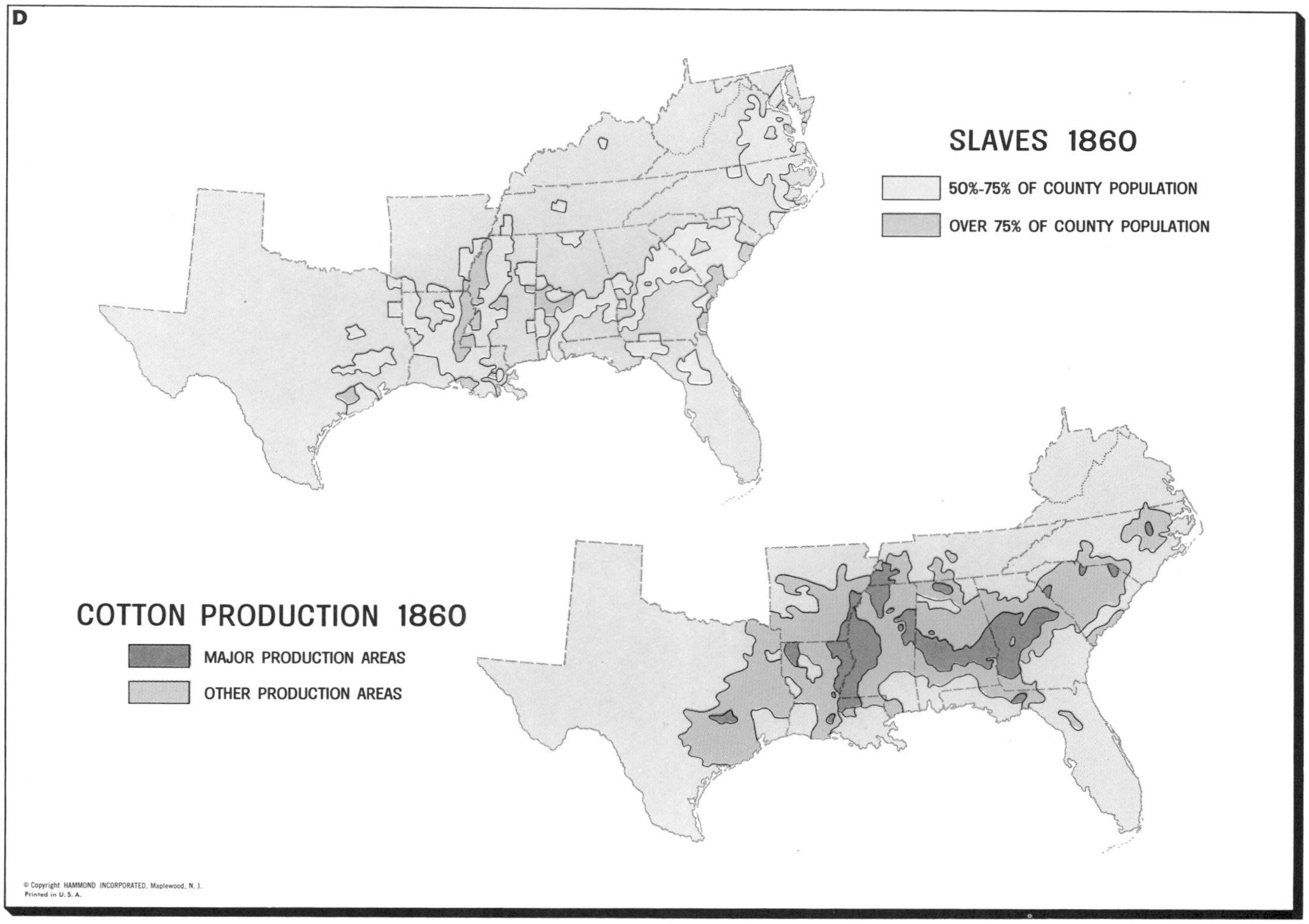

D

SLAVES 1860

50%-75% OF COUNTY POPULATION

OVER 75% OF COUNTY POPULATION

COTTON PRODUCTION 1860

MAJOR PRODUCTION AREAS

OTHER PRODUCTION AREAS

© Copyright HAMMOND INCORPORATED, Maplewood, N. J.
Printed in U.S.A.

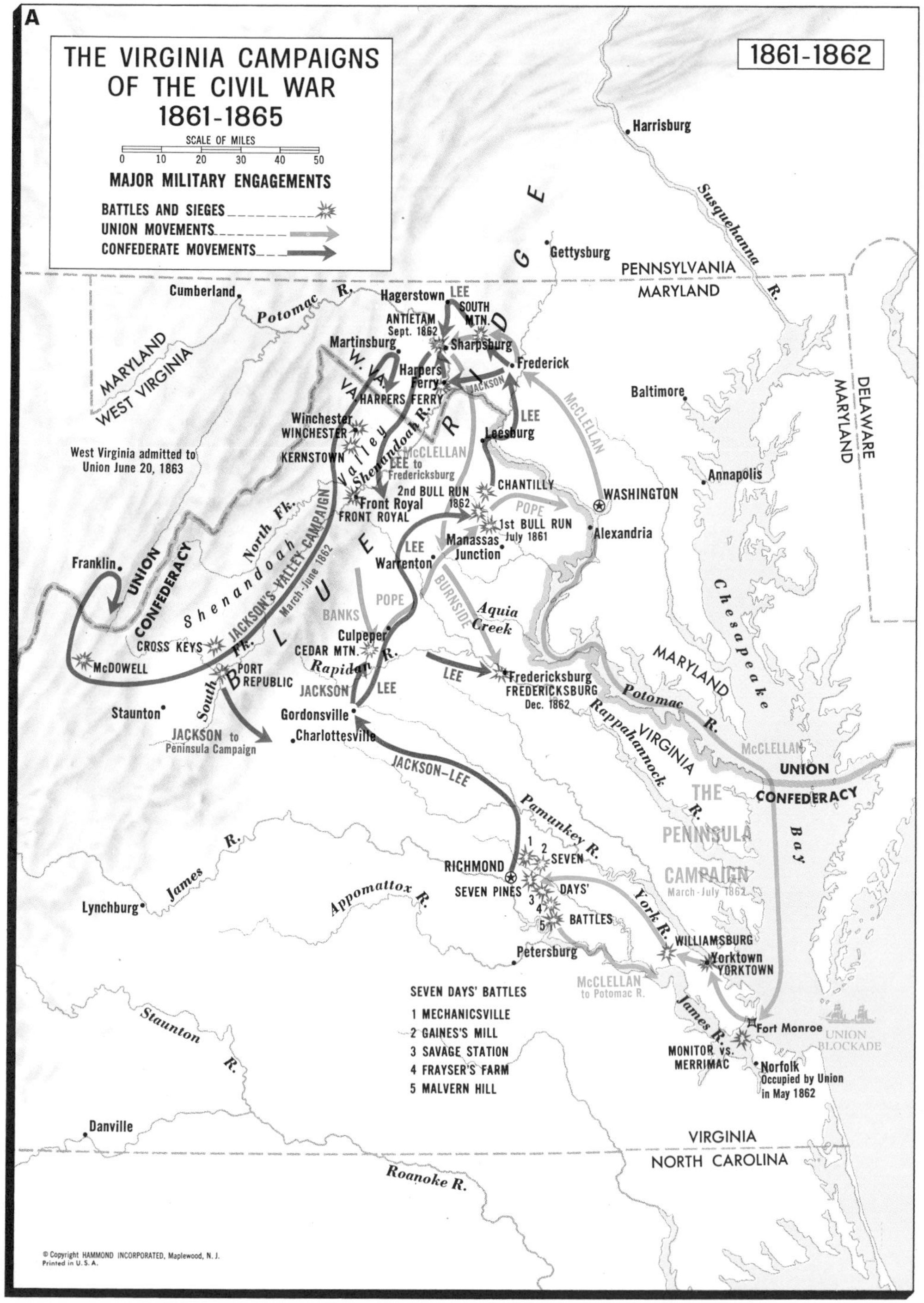

B | **1863**

THE VIRGINIA CAMPAIGNS OF THE CIVIL WAR 1861-1865

SCALE OF MILES
0 10 20 30 40 50

MAJOR MILITARY ENGAGEMENTS

BATTLES AND SIEGES
UNION MOVEMENTS
CONFEDERATE MOVEMENTS

West Virginia admitted to Union June 20, 1863

DELAWARE
MARYLAND
PENNSYLVANIA
MARYLAND
VIRGINIA
NORTH CAROLINA
WEST VIRGINIA
W. VA.
VA.
UNION
CONFEDERACY

Chesapeake Bay

Harrisburg
Wrightsville
Susquehanna R.
York
Carlisle
Gettysburg July 1863
Gettysburg
Chambersburg
Hagerstown
Sharpsburg
Hagers Ferry
Martinsburg
Winchester
Front Royal
Frederick
Leesburg
Baltimore
Annapolis
WASHINGTON
Alexandria
Manassas Junction
Warrenton
Aquia Creek
Fredericksburg
Culpeper
Brandy Station
Rapidan R.
CHANCELLORSVILLE May 1863
Charlottesville
RICHMOND
Petersburg
Fort Monroe
Norfolk
Yorktown
UNION BLOCKADE

EARLY
EWELL
LEE
MEADE
HOOKER
STUART to Gettysburg
STUART
R. LEE

Potomac R.
Shenandoah R.
North Fk.
South Fk. Shenandoah
Rappahannock R.
Pamunkey R.
York R.
James R.
Appomattox R.
Roanoke R.
Staunton
Cumberland
Franklin
Lynchburg
Danville

© Copyright HAMMOND INCORPORATED, Maplewood, N.J.
Printed in U.S.A.

A | **1861-1862**

THE VIRGINIA CAMPAIGNS OF THE CIVIL WAR 1861-1865

SCALE OF MILES
0 10 20 30 40 50

MAJOR MILITARY ENGAGEMENTS

BATTLES AND SIEGES
UNION MOVEMENTS
CONFEDERATE MOVEMENTS

West Virginia admitted to Union June 20, 1863

SEVEN DAYS' BATTLES
1 MECHANICSVILLE
2 GAINES'S MILL
3 SAVAGE STATION
4 FRAYSER'S FARM
5 MALVERN HILL

DELAWARE
MARYLAND
PENNSYLVANIA
MARYLAND
VIRGINIA
NORTH CAROLINA
WEST VIRGINIA
W. VA.
VA.
UNION
CONFEDERACY
THE CONFEDERACY

Chesapeake Bay

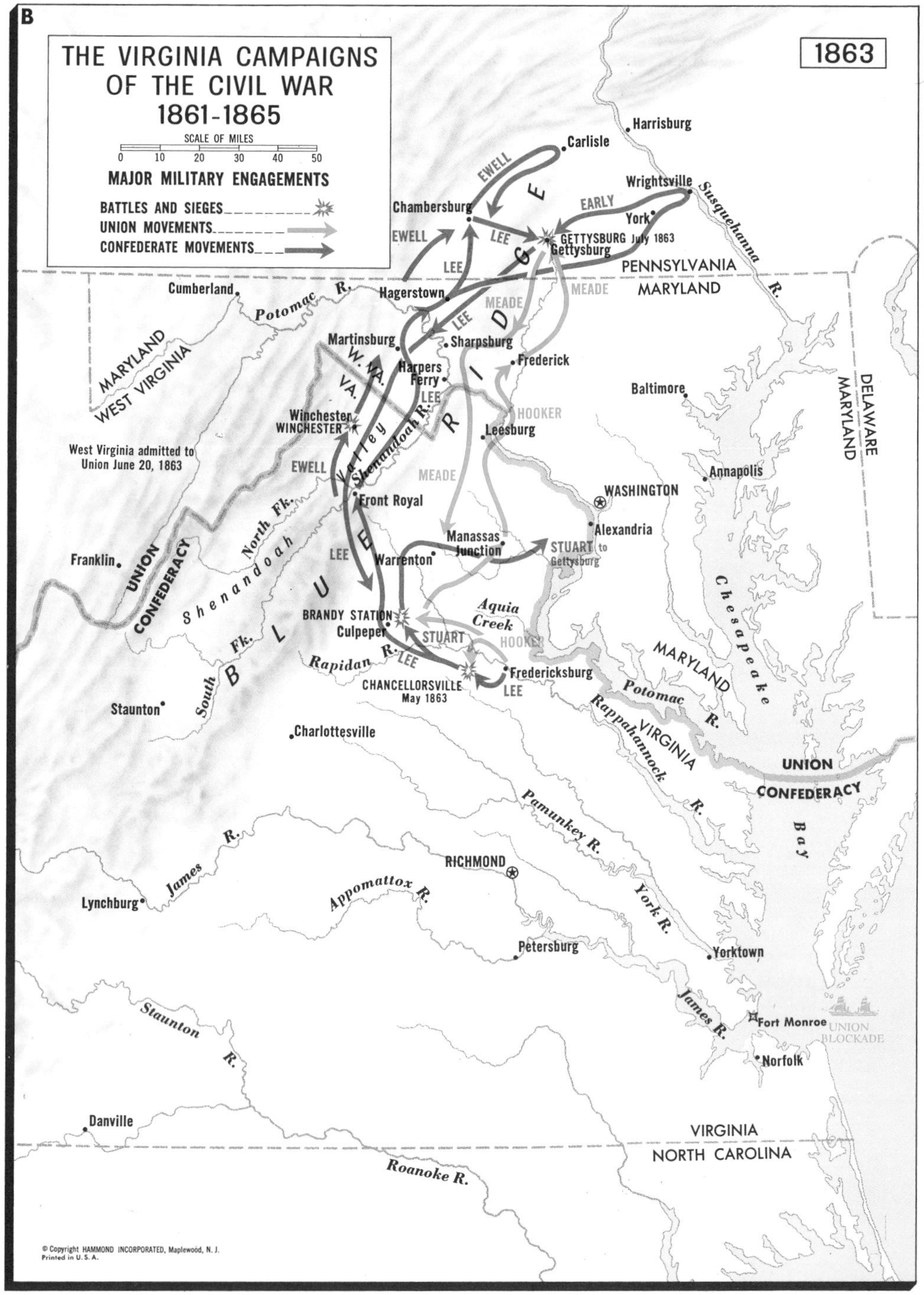

Harrisburg
Susquehanna R.
Gettysburg
Cumberland
Hagerstown
ANTIETAM Sept. 1862
SOUTH MTN.
Sharpsburg
Hagers Ferry
HARPERS FERRY
Martinsburg
Winchester
KERNSTOWN
FRONT ROYAL
Front Royal
CROSS KEYS
PORT REPUBLIC
McDOWELL
Franklin
Staunton
CEDAR MTN.
Gordonsville
Charlottesville
Culpeper
Rapidan
Warrenton
CHANTILLY
1st BULL RUN July 1861
2nd BULL RUN 1862
Manassas Junction
Frederick
Leesburg
Baltimore
Annapolis
WASHINGTON
Alexandria
Aquia Creek
FREDERICKSBURG Dec. 1862
Fredericksburg
SEVEN PINES
RICHMOND
SEVEN DAYS' BATTLES
Petersburg
WILLIAMSBURG
YORKTOWN
Yorktown
Fort Monroe
Norfolk Occupied by Union in May 1862
MONITOR vs. MERRIMAC
UNION BLOCKADE

JACKSON'S VALLEY CAMPAIGN March–June 1862
JACKSON to Peninsula Campaign
JACKSON–LEE
THE PENINSULA CAMPAIGN March–July 1862
McCLELLAN
McCLELLAN to Potomac R.
McCLELLAN to Fredericksburg
LEE to Fredericksburg
POPE
BANKS
BURNSIDE
LEE

Potomac R.
Shenandoah R.
North Fk.
South Fk.
Rappahannock R.
Pamunkey R.
York R.
James R.
Appomattox R.
Roanoke R.
Lynchburg
Danville

© Copyright HAMMOND INCORPORATED, Maplewood, N.J.
Printed in U.S.A.

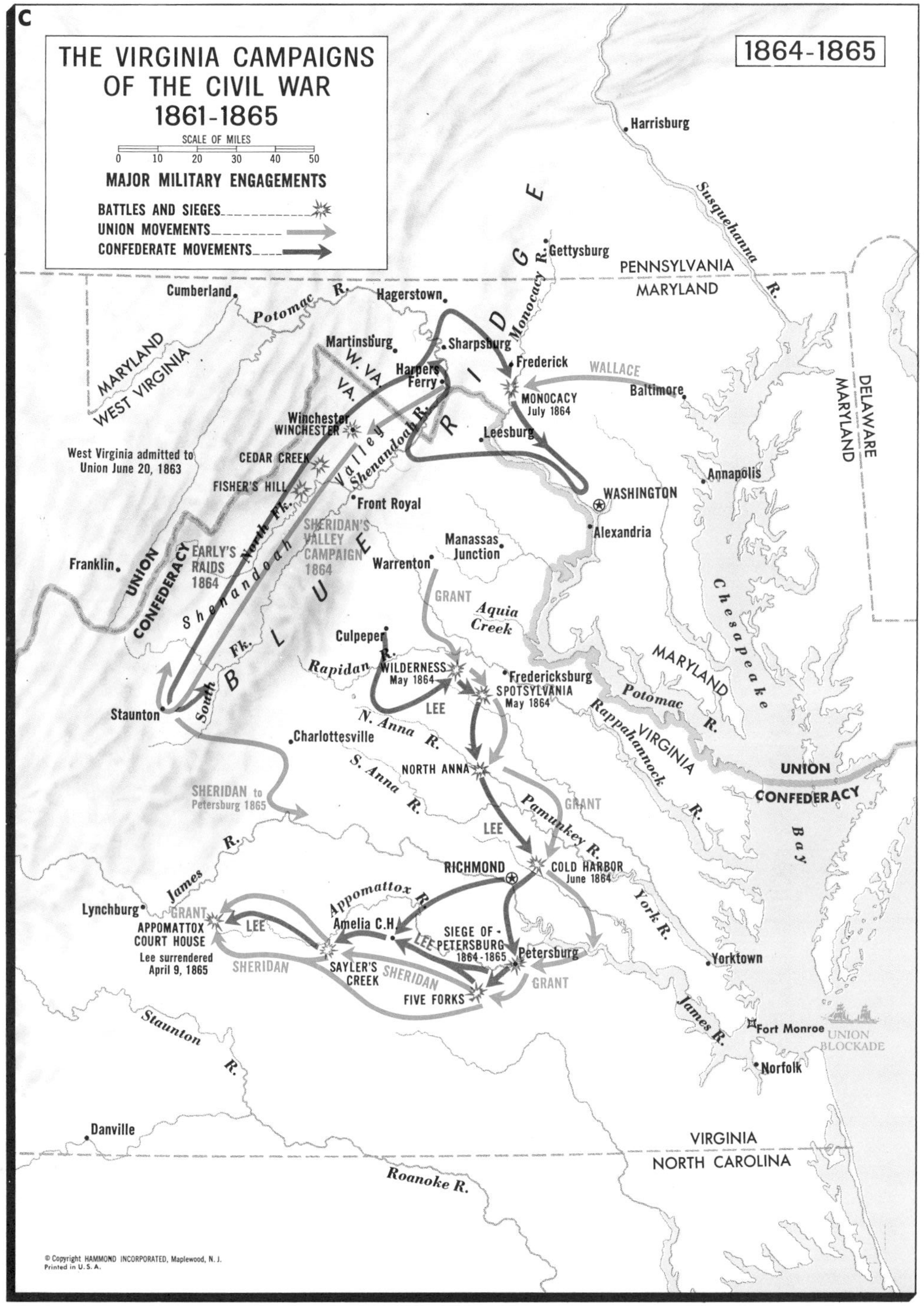

THE BATTLE OF GETTYSBURG
JULY 1-3, 1863

SCALE OF MILES

UNION MOVEMENTS
UNION BATTLE LINES
CONFEDERATE MOVEMENTS
CONFEDERATE BATTLE LINES

Initial Engagement

To Harrisburg

Confederate Troops advance toward Gettysburg July 1

Rock Cr.

July 1

Early

EWELL

Oak Hill

Buford

Union Line

July 1

Heth

A.P. HILL

Confederate Troops advance toward Gettysburg July 1

To Cashtown

Union Troops retreat to Cemetery Hill July 1

Confederate Attack July 2

Cavalry Battlefield

SLOCUM SEDGWICK July 2

To Baltimore

MEADE

Rock Cr.

July 2

Culp's Hill

Cemetery Hill

Gettysburg

Union Line July 2-3

HANCOCK

Cemetery Ridge

July 3

Seminary Ridge

Peach Orchard

Wheat Field

Devil's Den

Little Round Top

Round Top

HANCOCK July 1

To Taneytown

Plum Run

Pickett's Charge July 3

LONGSTREET

July 2

Confederate Attack July 2

Willoughby Run

Union Troops withdraw to Cemetery Ridge July 2

REYNOLDS (DOUBLEDAY) HOWARD SICKLES July 1

To Emmitsburg

Marsh Cr.

LEE

© Copyright HAMMOND INCORPORATED, Maplewood, N.J. Printed in U.S.A.

THE VIRGINIA CAMPAIGNS
OF THE CIVIL WAR
1861-1865

1864-1865

SCALE OF MILES

MAJOR MILITARY ENGAGEMENTS

BATTLES AND SIEGES
UNION MOVEMENTS
CONFEDERATE MOVEMENTS

West Virginia admitted to Union June 20, 1863

DELAWARE
MARYLAND

CONFEDERACY

UNION BLOCKADE

Chesapeake Bay

Susquehanna R.

Harrisburg

PENNSYLVANIA
MARYLAND

Gettysburg

Monocacy R.

Frederick

WALLACE

Baltimore

MONOCACY July 1864

Sharpsburg

Leesburg

WASHINGTON

Alexandria

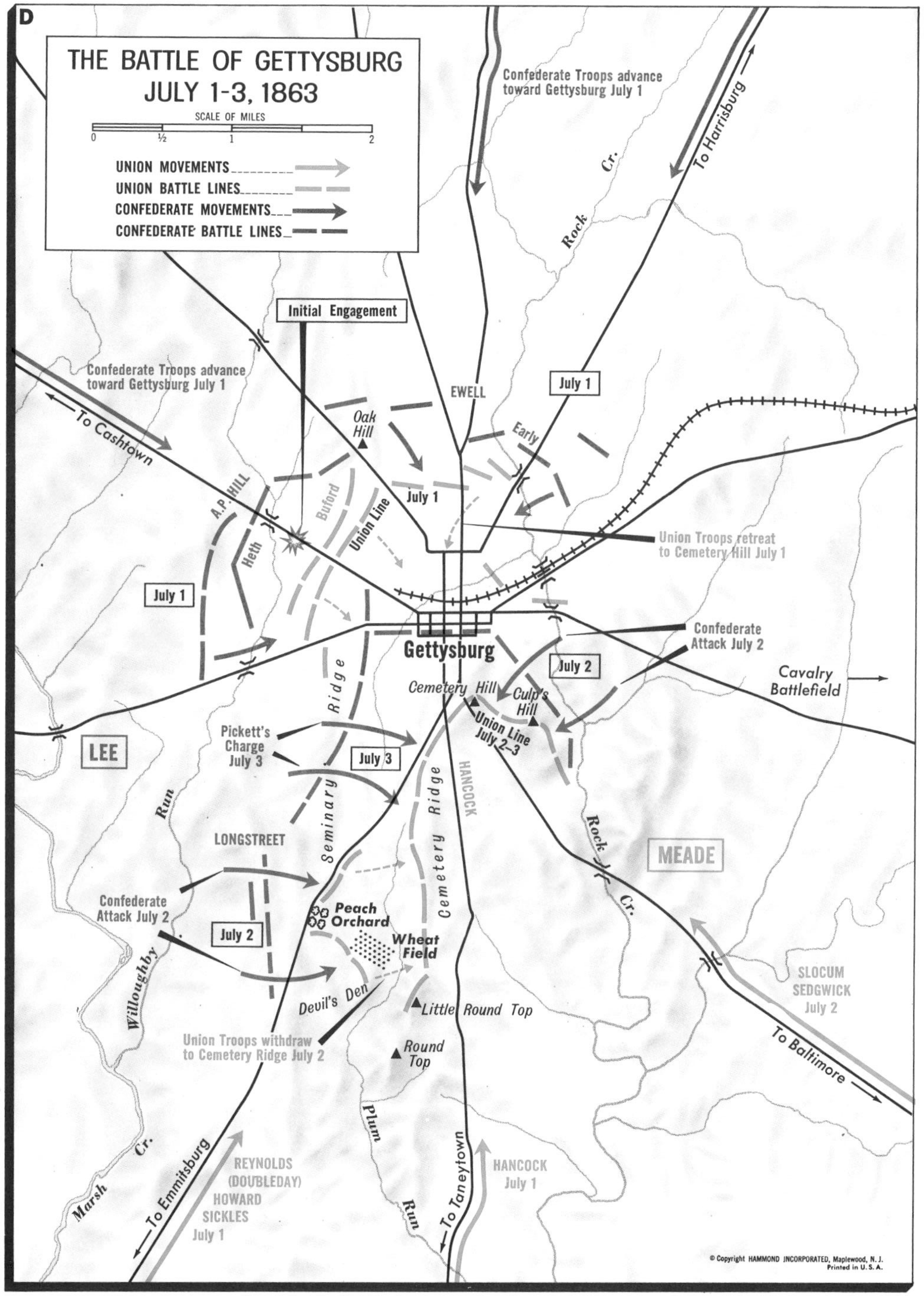

Annapolis

MARYLAND

Potomac R.

Potomac R.

VIRGINIA

York R.

Yorktown

James R.

Fort Monroe

Norfolk

VIRGINIA
NORTH CAROLINA

Cumberland

Hagerstown

Martinsburg

W. VA.
VA.

Harpers Ferry

Winchester

WINCHESTER

CEDAR CREEK

FISHER'S HILL

SHERIDAN'S VALLEY CAMPAIGN 1864

EARLY'S RAIDS 1864

Shenandoah R.

North Fk. Shenandoah R.

South Fk. Shenandoah R.

Front Royal

Manassas Junction

Warrenton

Aquia Creek

Culpeper

Rapidan R.

Fredericksburg

WILDERNESS May 1864

SPOTSYLVANIA May 1864

LEE

GRANT

N. Anna R.

NORTH ANNA

S. Anna R.

Charlottesville

Pamunkey R.

COLD HARBOR June 1864

GRANT

LEE

RICHMOND

Petersburg

SIEGE OF LEE-PETERSBURG 1864-1865

GRANT

FIVE FORKS

SHERIDAN

Appomattox R.

Amelia C.H.

SAYLER'S CREEK

SHERIDAN

SHERIDAN to Petersburg 1865

James R.

Staunton

Staunton R.

Roanoke R.

Lynchburg

APPOMATTOX COURT HOUSE
Lee surrendered April 9, 1865

GRANT

LEE

Danville

WEST VIRGINIA
MARYLAND

UNION
CONFEDERACY

Franklin

© Copyright HAMMOND INCORPORATED, Maplewood, N.J. Printed in U.S.A.

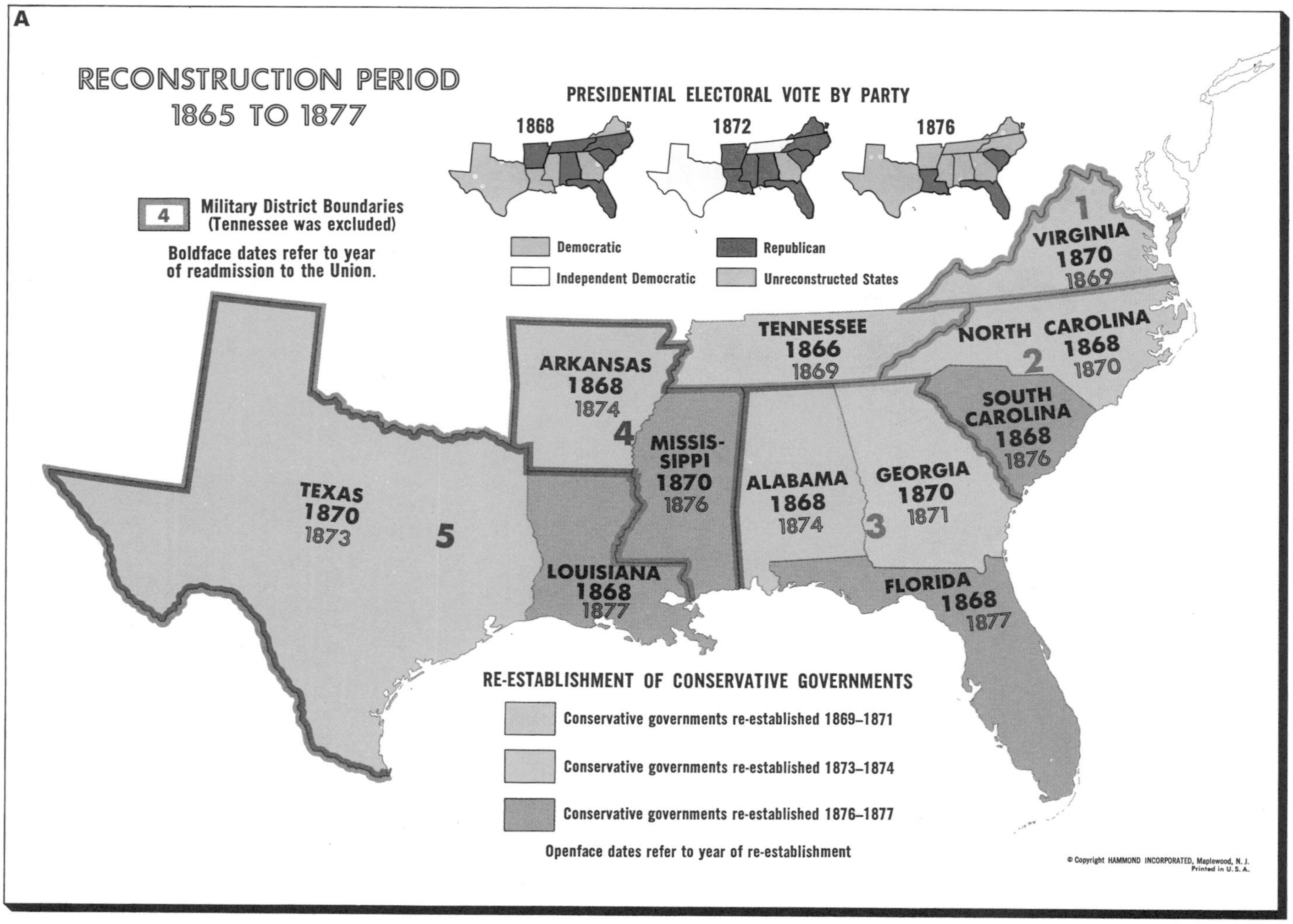

A

RECONSTRUCTION PERIOD
1865 TO 1877

PRESIDENTIAL ELECTORAL VOTE BY PARTY

1868   1872   1876

4 Military District Boundaries
(Tennessee was excluded)

Boldface dates refer to year
of readmission to the Union.

Democratic — Republican

Independent Democratic — Unreconstructed States

VIRGINIA
1870
1869

1

TENNESSEE
1866
1869

NORTH CAROLINA 1868
1870

2

ARKANSAS
1868
1874

4

SOUTH CAROLINA 1868
1876

MISSIS-SIPPI
1870
1876

ALABAMA
1868
1874

GEORGIA
1870
1871

3

TEXAS
1870
1873

5

LOUISIANA
1868
1877

FLORIDA
1868
1877

RE-ESTABLISHMENT OF CONSERVATIVE GOVERNMENTS

Conservative governments re-established 1869–1871

Conservative governments re-established 1873–1874

Conservative governments re-established 1876–1877

Openface dates refer to year of re-establishment

© Copyright HAMMOND INCORPORATED, Maplewood, N.J.
Printed in U.S.A.

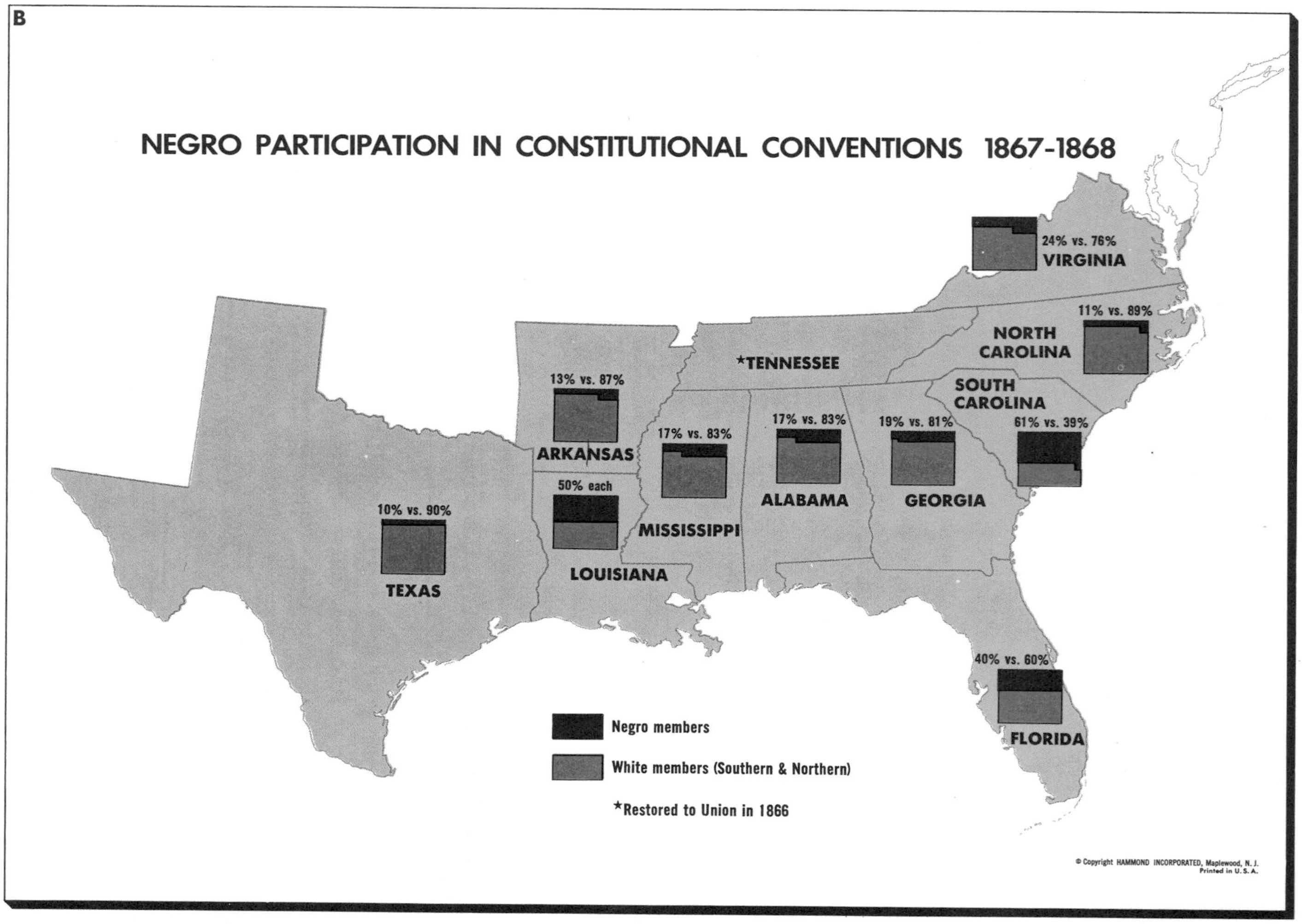

B

NEGRO PARTICIPATION IN CONSTITUTIONAL CONVENTIONS 1867-1868

24% vs. 76% **VIRGINIA**

11% vs. 89% **NORTH CAROLINA**

***TENNESSEE**

SOUTH CAROLINA

61% vs. 39%

13% vs. 87% **ARKANSAS**

17% vs. 83% **MISSISSIPPI**

17% vs. 83% **ALABAMA**

19% vs. 81% **GEORGIA**

50% each

10% vs. 90% **TEXAS**

LOUISIANA

40% vs. 60% **FLORIDA**

Negro members

White members (Southern & Northern)

*Restored to Union in 1866

© Copyright HAMMOND INCORPORATED, Maplewood, N.J.
Printed in U.S.A.

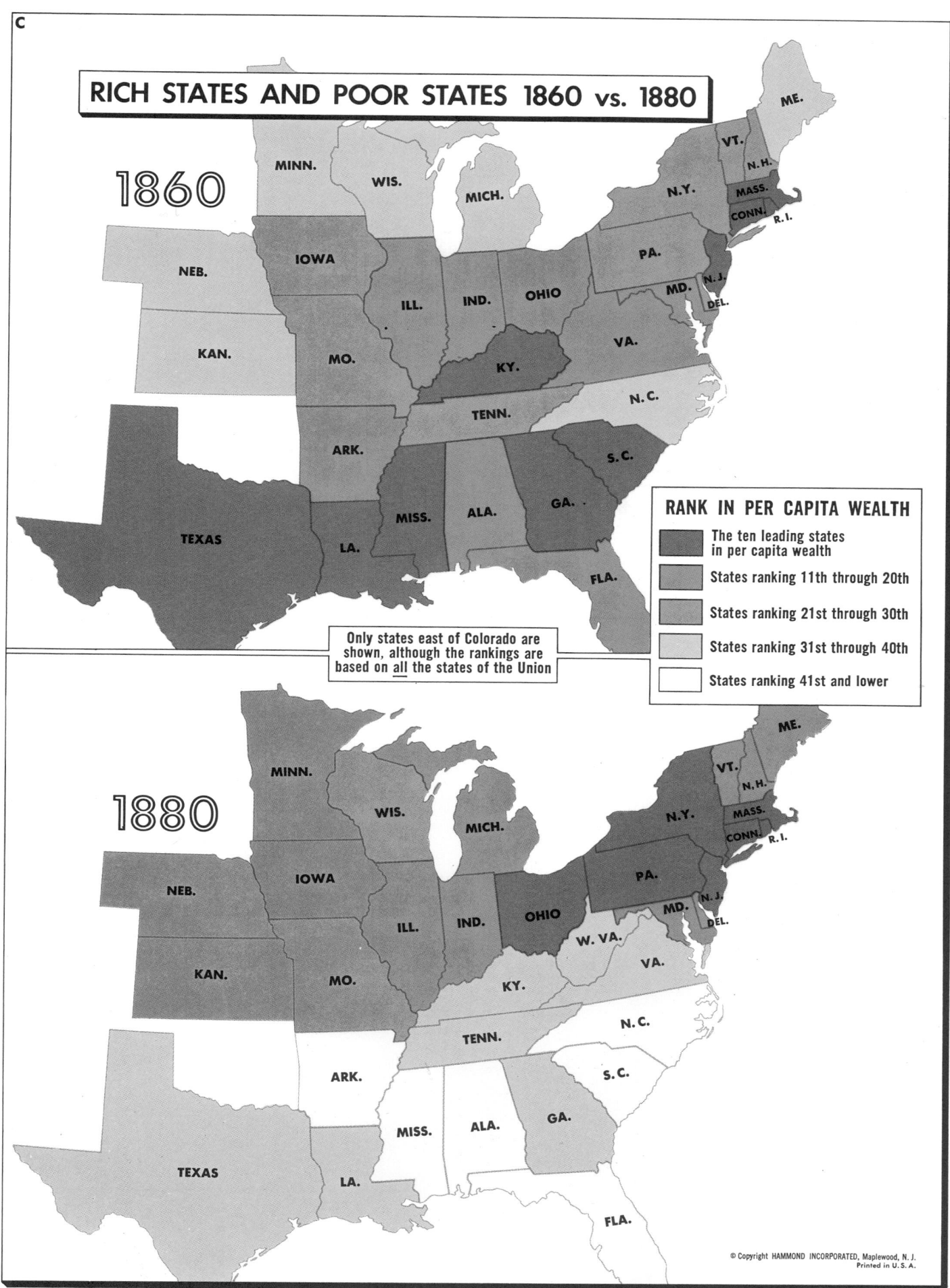

RICH STATES AND POOR STATES 1860 vs. 1880

1860

MINN. WIS. MICH. ME. VT. N.H. N.Y. MASS. CONN. R.I. NEB. IOWA PA. N.J. ILL. IND. OHIO MD. DEL. KAN. MO. VA. KY. N.C. TENN. ARK. S.C. MISS. ALA. GA. TEXAS LA. FLA.

RANK IN PER CAPITA WEALTH

The ten leading states in per capita wealth

States ranking 11th through 20th

States ranking 21st through 30th

States ranking 31st through 40th

States ranking 41st and lower

Only states east of Colorado are shown, although the rankings are based on all the states of the Union

1880

MINN. WIS. MICH. ME. VT. N.H. N.Y. MASS. CONN. R.I. NEB. IOWA PA. N.J. ILL. IND. OHIO MD. DEL. W. VA. KAN. MO. VA. KY. TENN. N.C. ARK. S.C. MISS. ALA. GA. TEXAS LA. FLA.

© Copyright HAMMOND INCORPORATED, Maplewood, N.J.
Printed in U.S.A.

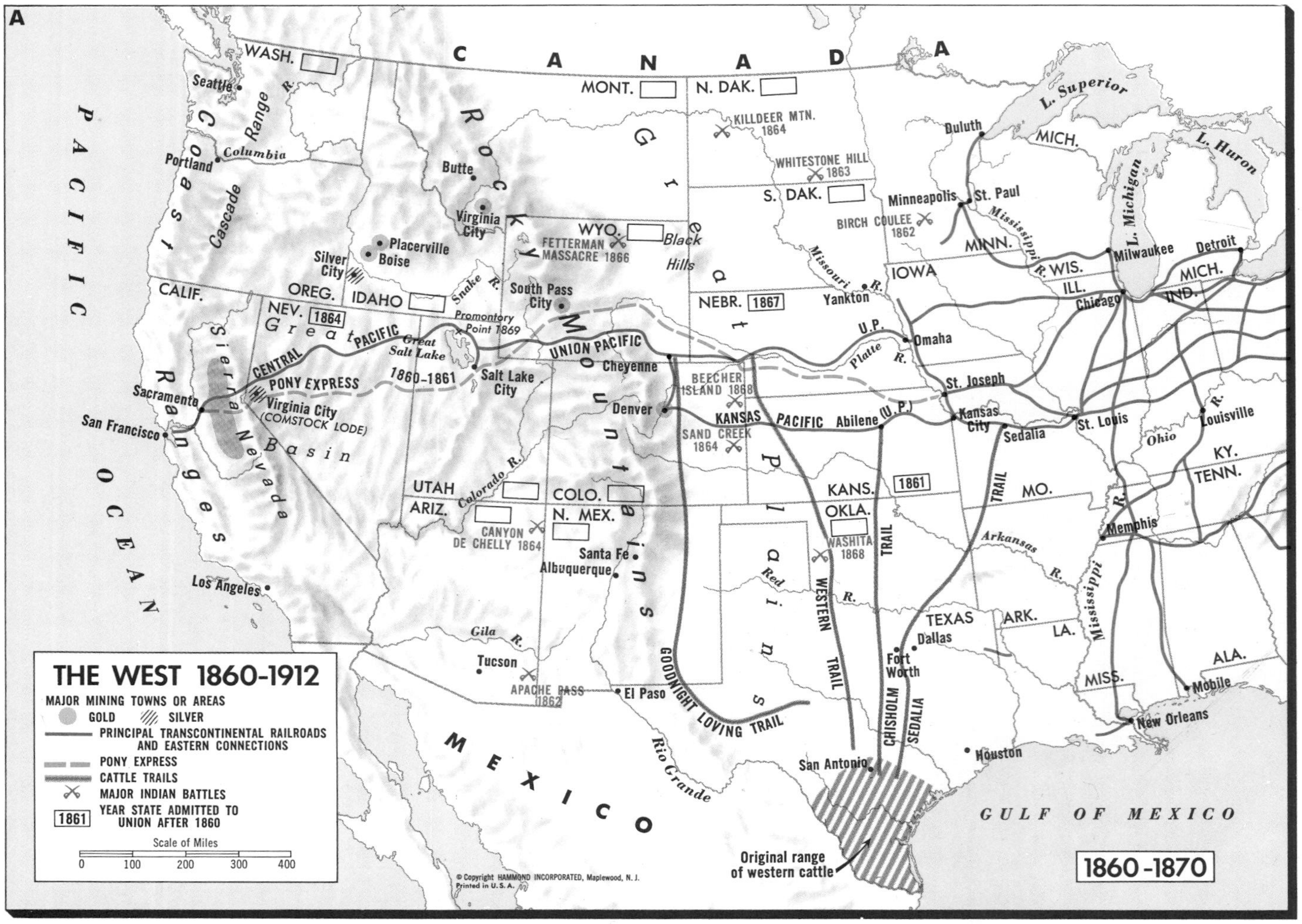

A

THE WEST 1860-1912

MAJOR MINING TOWNS OR AREAS
- ● GOLD
- ▨ SILVER
- —— PRINCIPAL TRANSCONTINENTAL RAILROADS AND EASTERN CONNECTIONS
- – – – PONY EXPRESS
- ▦ CATTLE TRAILS
- ✕ MAJOR INDIAN BATTLES
- 1861 YEAR STATE ADMITTED TO UNION AFTER 1860

Scale of Miles
0 100 200 300 400

© Copyright HAMMOND INCORPORATED, Maplewood, N.J.
Printed in U.S.A.

1860-1870

CANADA

WASH.
Seattle
Portland
Columbia R.
Coast Range
Cascade
PACIFIC OCEAN
OREG.
CALIF.
Sacramento
San Francisco
Sierra Nevada Ranges
CENTRAL PACIFIC
PONY EXPRESS
Virginia City (COMSTOCK LODE)
Los Angeles
Silver City
Placerville
Boise
Virginia City
IDAHO
Snake R.
Great Salt Lake
Great Basin
UTAH
ARIZ.
Gila R.
Tucson
APACHE PASS 1862
NEV. 1864
South Pass City
Promontory Point 1869
Salt Lake City
UNION PACIFIC 1860-1861
Colorado R.
CANYON DE CHELLY 1864
N. MEX.
Santa Fe
Albuquerque
El Paso
Rio Grande
MEXICO
MONT.
N. DAK.
KILLDEER MTN. 1864
WHITESTONE HILL 1863
S. DAK.
BIRCH COULEE 1862
WYO.
FETTERMAN MASSACRE 1866
Black Hills
Rocky Mountains
Great Plains
Platte R.
Cheyenne
Denver
SAND CREEK 1864
BEECHER ISLAND 1868
KANSAS PACIFIC
Abilene (U.P.)
COLO.
KANS. 1861
OKLA.
WASHITA 1868
Red R.
WESTERN TRAIL
TEXAS
Dallas
Fort Worth
SEDALIA
CHISHOLM
GOODNIGHT LOVING TRAIL
San Antonio
Original range of western cattle
NEBR. 1867
Yankton
U.P.
Omaha
St. Joseph
Kansas City
Sedalia
St. Louis
IOWA
Missouri R.
MINN.
Duluth
Minneapolis
St. Paul
L. Superior
MICH.
WIS.
ILL.
Chicago
Milwaukee
Detroit
IND.
L. Michigan
L. Huron
MO.
Arkansas R.
Mississippi R.
Ohio R.
Louisville
KY.
TENN.
Memphis
ARK.
LA.
MISS.
ALA.
Mobile
New Orleans
Houston
GULF OF MEXICO

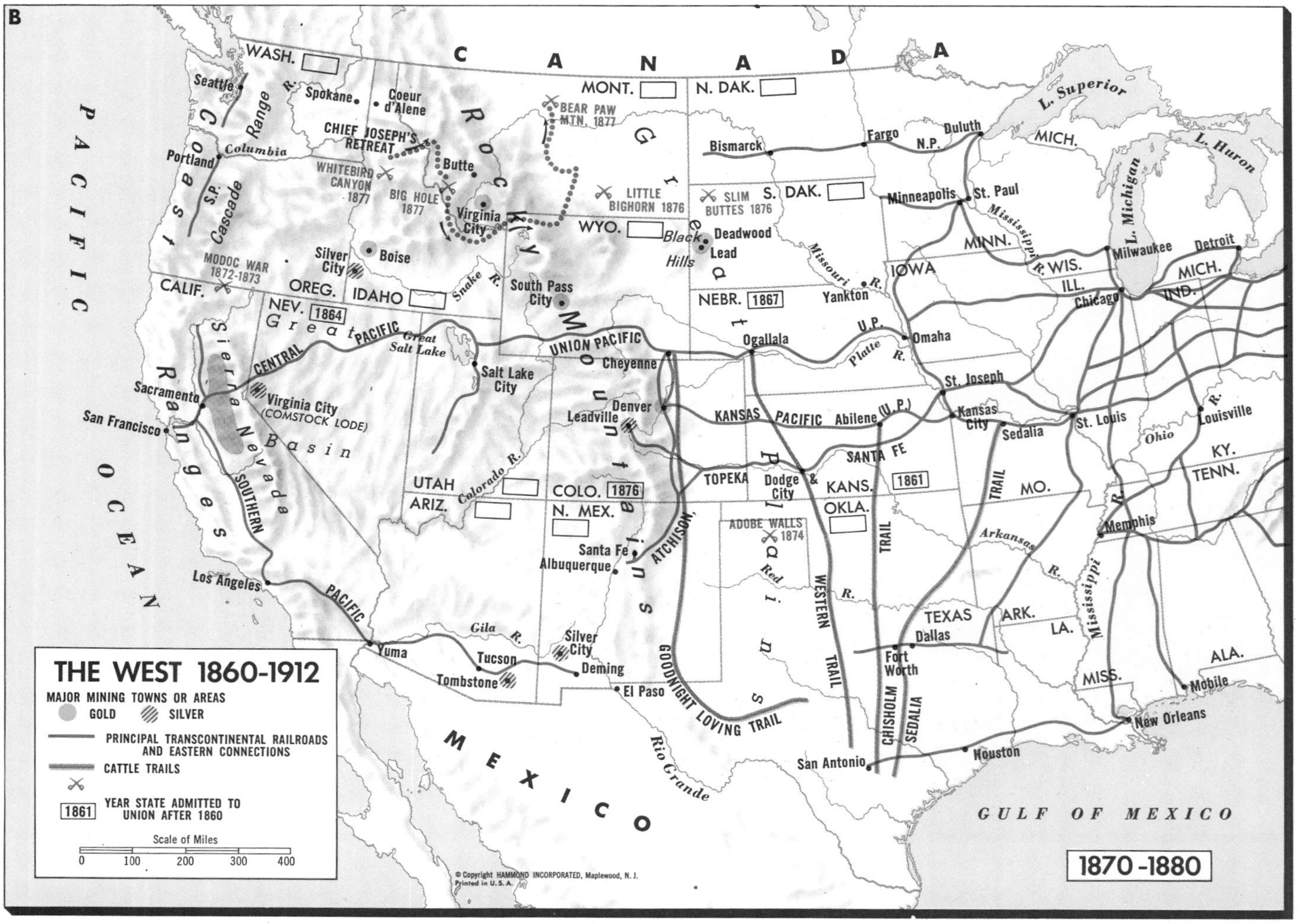

B

THE WEST 1860-1912

MAJOR MINING TOWNS OR AREAS
- ● GOLD
- ▨ SILVER
- —— PRINCIPAL TRANSCONTINENTAL RAILROADS AND EASTERN CONNECTIONS
- ✕ CATTLE TRAILS
- 1861 YEAR STATE ADMITTED TO UNION AFTER 1860

Scale of Miles
0 100 200 300 400

© Copyright HAMMOND INCORPORATED, Maplewood, N.J.
Printed in U.S.A.

1870-1880

CANADA

WASH.
Seattle
Spokane
Coeur d'Alene
Portland
Columbia R.
Coast Range
Cascade
S.P.
PACIFIC OCEAN
OREG.
CALIF.
Sacramento
San Francisco
Sierra Nevada Ranges
SOUTHERN PACIFIC
CENTRAL PACIFIC
Virginia City (COMSTOCK LODE)
Los Angeles
MODOC WAR 1872-1873
Silver City
Boise
Virginia City
WHITEBIRD CANYON 1877
BIG HOLE 1877
CHIEF JOSEPH'S RETREAT
Butte
IDAHO
Snake R.
Great Salt Lake
Great Basin
NEV. 1864
South Pass City
Salt Lake City
UNION PACIFIC
UTAH
ARIZ.
Colorado R.
Gila R.
Yuma
Tucson
Tombstone
Deming
Silver City
N. MEX.
Santa Fe
Albuquerque
El Paso
Rio Grande
MEXICO
MONT.
BEAR PAW MTN. 1877
N. DAK.
Bismarck
Fargo
N.P.
LITTLE BIGHORN 1876
SLIM BUTTES 1876
S. DAK.
Deadwood
Lead
Black Hills
WYO.
Rocky Mountains
Great Plains
Cheyenne
Denver
Leadville
Ogallala
Platte R.
KANSAS PACIFIC
Abilene (U.P.)
SANTA FE
TOPEKA
Dodge City
COLO. 1876
KANS. 1861
OKLA.
ADOBE WALLS 1874
Red R.
ATCHISON
WESTERN TRAIL
TEXAS
Dallas
Fort Worth
CHISHOLM
SEDALIA
GOODNIGHT LOVING TRAIL
San Antonio
Houston
NEBR. 1867
Yankton
U.P.
Omaha
St. Joseph
Kansas City
Sedalia
St. Louis
IOWA
Missouri R.
MINN.
Duluth
Minneapolis
St. Paul
L. Superior
MICH.
WIS.
ILL.
Chicago
Milwaukee
Detroit
IND.
L. Michigan
L. Huron
MO.
Arkansas R.
Mississippi R.
Ohio R.
Louisville
KY.
TENN.
Memphis
ARK.
LA.
MISS.
ALA.
Mobile
New Orleans
GULF OF MEXICO

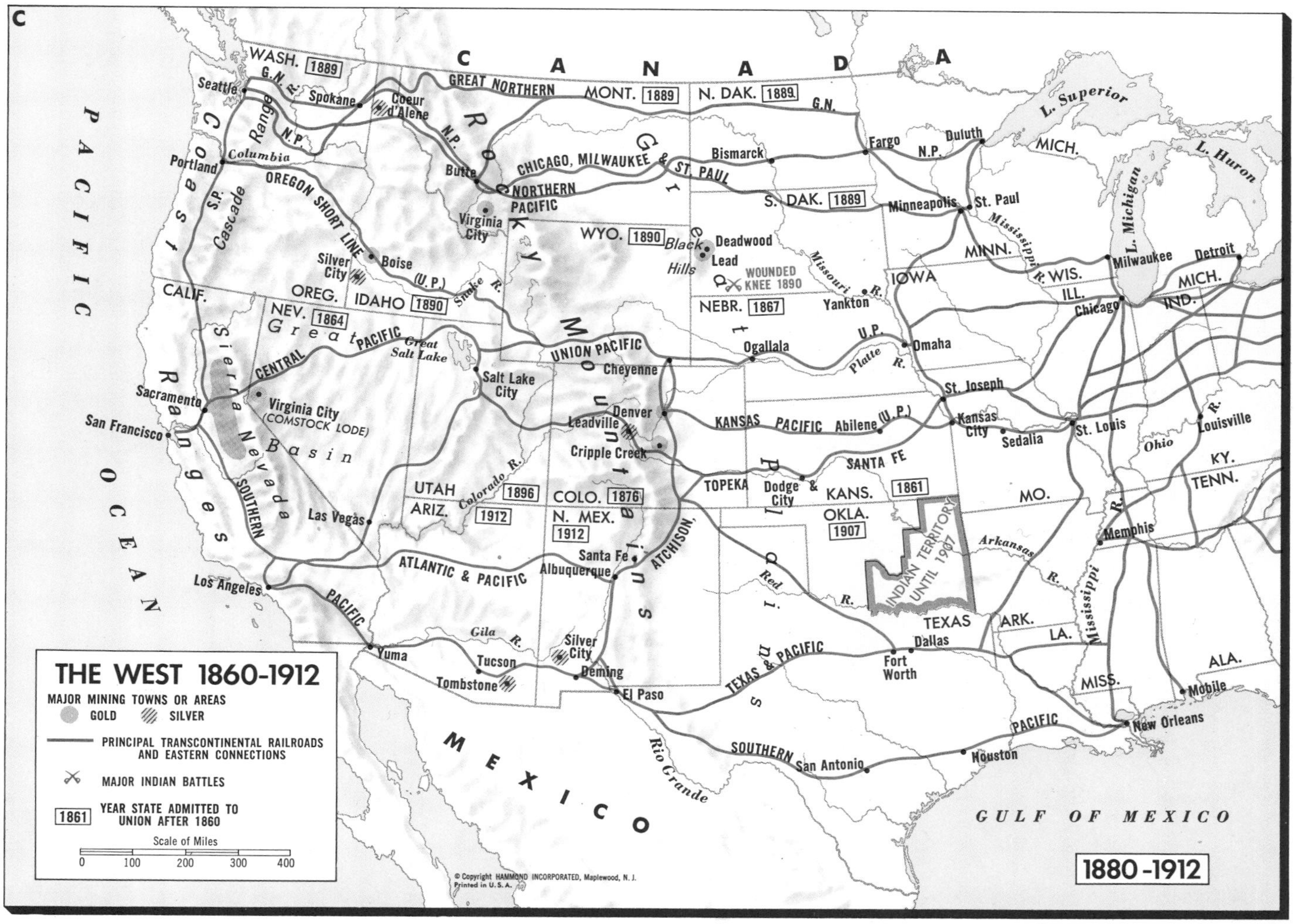

Map C — THE WEST 1860-1912

THE WEST 1860-1912

MAJOR MINING TOWNS OR AREAS
- GOLD
- SILVER

PRINCIPAL TRANSCONTINENTAL RAILROADS AND EASTERN CONNECTIONS

MAJOR INDIAN BATTLES

1861 YEAR STATE ADMITTED TO UNION AFTER 1860

Scale of Miles
0 100 200 300 400

© Copyright HAMMOND INCORPORATED, Maplewood, N.J. Printed in U.S.A.

1880-1912

CANADA

PACIFIC OCEAN

WASH. 1889 — Seattle, Spokane, Coeur d'Alene
GREAT NORTHERN — MONT. 1889 — N. DAK. 1889 — G.N.
Columbia — Portland — OREGON SHORT LINE
CHICAGO, MILWAUKEE & ST. PAUL — Bismarck — Fargo — N.P. — Duluth — MICH. — L. Superior — L. Huron
NORTHERN PACIFIC — Butte — Virginia City
Coast Range — Cascade — Sierra Nevada — SOUTHERN RANGES
Silver City — Boise (U.P.) — IDAHO 1890 — Snake R.
S. DAK. 1889 — Minneapolis — St. Paul — MINN. — WIS. — ILL. — Milwaukee — Detroit
Deadwood — Lead — Black Hills — WOUNDED KNEE 1890
WYO. 1890
NEV. 1864 — Great Basin — PACIFIC
CENTRAL — Great Salt Lake — Salt Lake City — UNION PACIFIC — Cheyenne
Sacramento — Virginia City (COMSTOCK LODE) — Denver — Leadville
San Francisco — Las Vegas — Cripple Creek — KANSAS PACIFIC — Abilene (U.P.) — Kansas City
UTAH 1896 — COLO. 1876 — TOPEKA — KANS. 1861 — St. Joseph — St. Louis — Louisville — KY. — TENN.
ARIZ. 1912 — N. MEX. 1912 — Dodge City — SANTA FE — OKLA. 1907 — MO. — Ohio R. — Memphis
Los Angeles — ATLANTIC & PACIFIC — Santa Fe — Albuquerque — INDIAN TERRITORY UNTIL 1907 — Arkansas R. — Red R.
Yuma — Gila R. — Silver City — Deming — ATCHISON — TEXAS — Dallas — ARK. — LA. — ALA. — Mobile
Tucson — Tombstone — El Paso — TEXAS & PACIFIC — Fort Worth — MISS.
Rio Grande — SOUTHERN PACIFIC — San Antonio — Houston — New Orleans — PACIFIC
MEXICO — GULF OF MEXICO
Rocky Mountains — Great Plains — Platte R. — Ogallala — Omaha — Yankton — NEBR. 1867 — IOWA — Missouri R.

Map D — INDIAN RESERVATIONS AND ARMY POSTS IN THE WEST

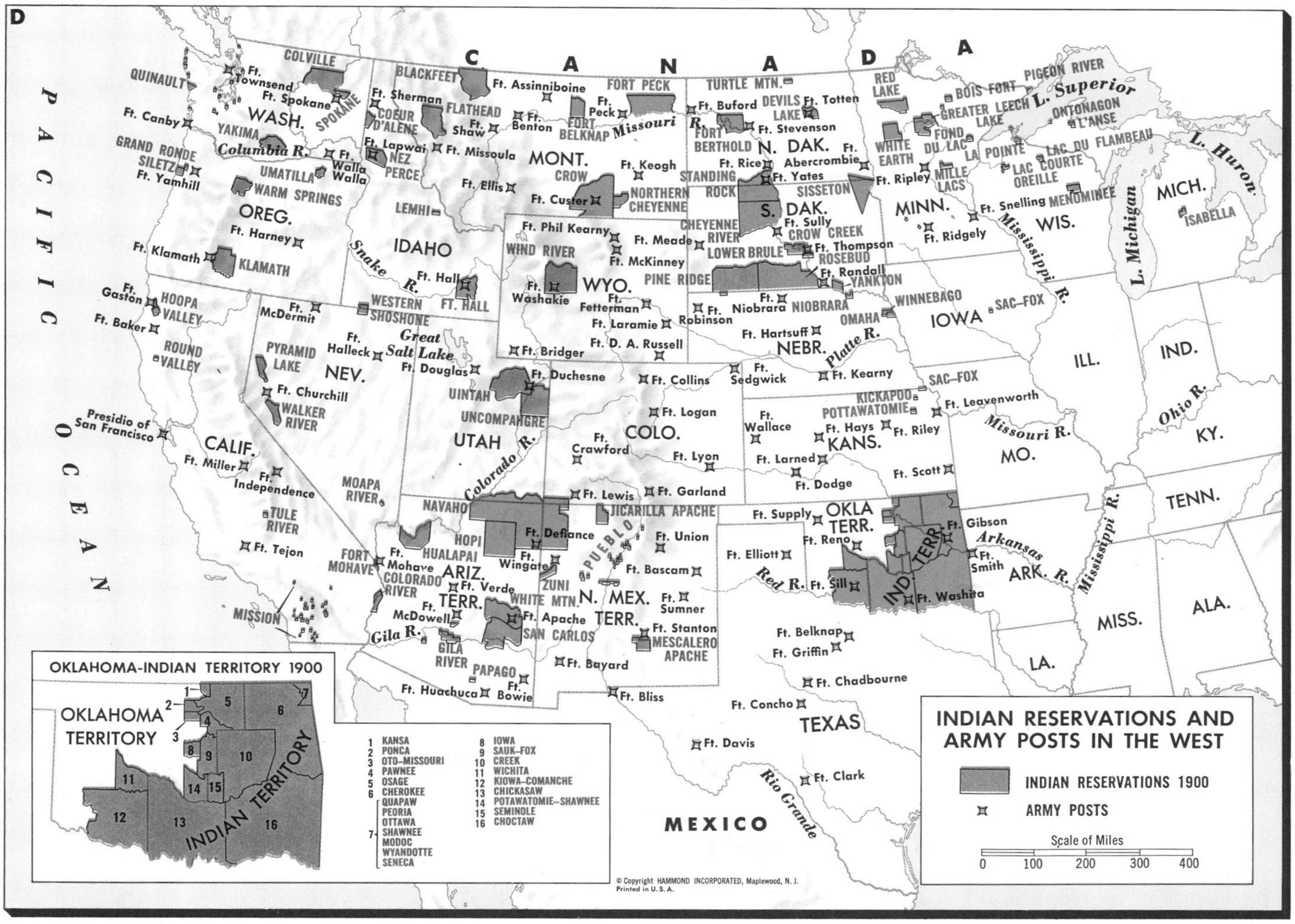

INDIAN RESERVATIONS AND ARMY POSTS IN THE WEST

INDIAN RESERVATIONS 1900

ARMY POSTS

Scale of Miles
0 100 200 300 400

© Copyright HAMMOND INCORPORATED, Maplewood, N.J. Printed in U.S.A.

CANADA

PACIFIC OCEAN

QUINAULT — COLVILLE — Ft. Townsend — Ft. Spokane — BLACKFEET — Ft. Assinniboine — FORT PECK — TURTLE MTN. — RED LAKE — BOIS FORT — PIGEON RIVER — GREATER LEECH LAKE — ONTONAGON — L'ANSE — L. Superior
Ft. Canby — Ft. Sherman — FLATHEAD — Ft. Shaw — Ft. Benton — FORT BELKNAP — Ft. Peck — Ft. Buford — DEVILS LAKE — Ft. Totten — Ft. Stevenson — WHITE EARTH — FOND DU LAC — LA POINTE — LAC DU FLAMBEAU — MICH.
WASH. — YAKIMA — SPOKANE — COEUR D'ALENE — Ft. Lapwai — NEZ PERCE — Ft. Missoula — MONT. — Ft. Keogh — FORT BERTHOLD — N. DAK. — Ft. Rice — Ft. Yates — Ft. Ripley — MILLE LACS — LAC COURTE OREILLE — ISABELLA — L. Huron
GRAND RONDE — SILETZ — Ft. Yamhill — Columbia R. — Walla Walla — Ft. Ellis — CROW — STANDING ROCK — Ft. Snelling — MENOMINEE — L. Michigan
UMATILLA — WARM SPRINGS — Ft. Harney — OREG. — Ft. Phil Kearny — NORTHERN CHEYENNE — S. DAK. — Ft. Sully — CROW CREEK — Ft. Ridgely — MINN. — WIS.
KLAMATH — Ft. Klamath — LEMHI — IDAHO — WIND RIVER — Ft. Custer — CHEYENNE RIVER — SISSETON — Ft. Thompson — ROSEBUD — YANKTON — IOWA — Ft. Ridgely
Ft. Gaston — HOOPA VALLEY — Ft. McDermit — Ft. Hall — WYO. — Ft. Washakie — LOWER BRULE — Ft. Randall — NIOBRARA — WINNEBAGO — SAC-FOX
Ft. Baker — ROUND VALLEY — Ft. Halleck — WESTERN SHOSHONE — Great Salt Lake — FT. HALL — Ft. Fetterman — PINE RIDGE — Ft. Robinson — Ft. Niobrara — NIOBRARA — OMAHA — Ft. Hartsuff — ILL. — IND.
PYRAMID LAKE — Ft. Bridger — Ft. Laramie — Ft. D. A. Russell — NEBR. — Platte R. — Ft. Kearny — SAC-FOX — Ohio R. — KY.
Ft. Churchill — NEV. — Ft. Douglas — UINTAH — Ft. Duchesne — Ft. Collins — Ft. Sedgwick — KICKAPOO — POTTAWATOMIE — Ft. Leavenworth
WALKER RIVER — UNCOMPAHGRE — UTAH — Ft. Logan — COLO. — Ft. Wallace — Ft. Hays — Ft. Riley — Missouri R. — MO.
Presidio of San Francisco — CALIF. — Colorado R. — Ft. Crawford — KANS. — Ft. Larned — Ft. Scott
Ft. Miller — Ft. Independence — MOAPA RIVER — Ft. Lyon — Ft. Dodge — TENN.
TULE RIVER — NAVAHO — Ft. Lewis — Ft. Garland — JICARILLA APACHE — OKLA TERR. — Ft. Supply — Ft. Gibson — Arkansas R.
Ft. Tejon — HOPI — Ft. Defiance — PUEBLO — Ft. Union — IND. TERR. — Ft. Reno — Ft. Smith — ARK. — MISS. — ALA.
HUALAPAI — Wingate — ZUNI — Ft. Bascam — Ft. Elliott — Ft. Sill — Ft. Washita — Red R.
MISSION — FORT MOHAVE — COLORADO RIVER — ARIZ. TERR. — Ft. Verde — WHITE MTN. — N. MEX. TERR. — Ft. Sumner — Ft. Belknap
Gila R. — McDowell — Apache — SAN CARLOS — Ft. Stanton — MESCALERO APACHE — Ft. Griffin — LA.
GILA RIVER — PAPAGO — Ft. Bayard — Ft. Concho
Ft. Huachuca — Ft. Bowie — Ft. Bliss — TEXAS — Ft. Chadbourne
Ft. Davis — Ft. Clark — Rio Grande — MEXICO

Inset — OKLAHOMA-INDIAN TERRITORY 1900

OKLAHOMA TERRITORY

INDIAN TERRITORY

1 KANSA	8 IOWA
2 PONCA	9 SAUK–FOX
3 OTO–MISSOURI	10 CREEK
4 PAWNEE	11 WICHITA
5 OSAGE	12 KIOWA–COMANCHE
6 CHEROKEE	13 CHICKASAW
7 QUAPAW	14 POTAWATOMIE–SHAWNEE
PEORIA	15 SEMINOLE
OTTAWA	16 CHOCTAW
SHAWNEE	
MODOC	
WYANDOTTE	
SENECA	

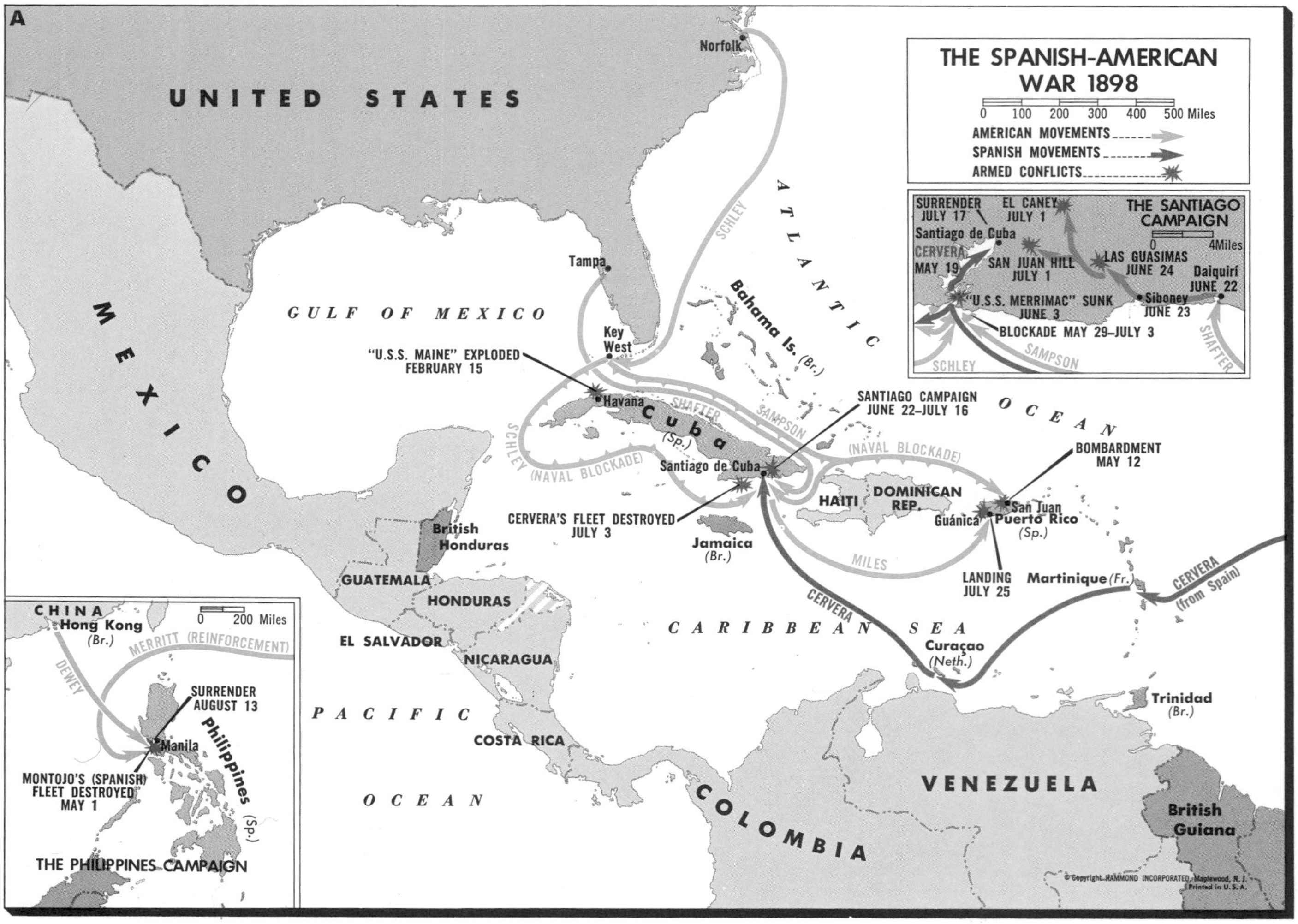

A

THE SPANISH-AMERICAN WAR 1898

0   100   200   300   400   500 Miles

AMERICAN MOVEMENTS
SPANISH MOVEMENTS
ARMED CONFLICTS

THE SANTIAGO CAMPAIGN

SURRENDER JULY 17
EL CANEY JULY 1
Santiago de Cuba
CERVERA MAY 19
SAN JUAN HILL JULY 1
LAS GUASIMAS JUNE 24
Daiquirí JUNE 22
"U.S.S. MERRIMAC" SUNK JUNE 3
Siboney JUNE 23
BLOCKADE MAY 29–JULY 3

0   4 Miles

UNITED STATES

Norfolk

ATLANTIC OCEAN

Tampa

Bahama Is. (Br.)

GULF OF MEXICO

Key West

"U.S.S. MAINE" EXPLODED FEBRUARY 15

Havana
Cuba (Sp.)

SANTIAGO CAMPAIGN JUNE 22–JULY 16

SCHLEY (NAVAL BLOCKADE)
SHAFTER
SAMPSON
(NAVAL BLOCKADE)

BOMBARDMENT MAY 12

Santiago de Cuba
CERVERA'S FLEET DESTROYED JULY 3

HAITI
DOMINICAN REP.

San Juan
Guánica   Puerto Rico (Sp.)

Jamaica (Br.)

MILES

LANDING JULY 25

Martinique (Fr.)

CERVERA (from Spain)

CERVERA

MEXICO

British Honduras

GUATEMALA
HONDURAS

EL SALVADOR
NICARAGUA

CARIBBEAN   SEA

Curaçao (Neth.)

Trinidad (Br.)

COSTA RICA

PACIFIC   OCEAN

VENEZUELA

COLOMBIA

CHINA
Hong Kong (Br.)

0   200 Miles

MERRITT (REINFORCEMENT)
DEWEY

SURRENDER AUGUST 13

Manila
Philippines (Sp.)

MONTOJO'S (SPANISH) FLEET DESTROYED MAY 1

THE PHILIPPINES CAMPAIGN

British Guiana

© Copyright. HAMMOND INCORPORATED, Maplewood, N.J.
Printed in U.S.A.

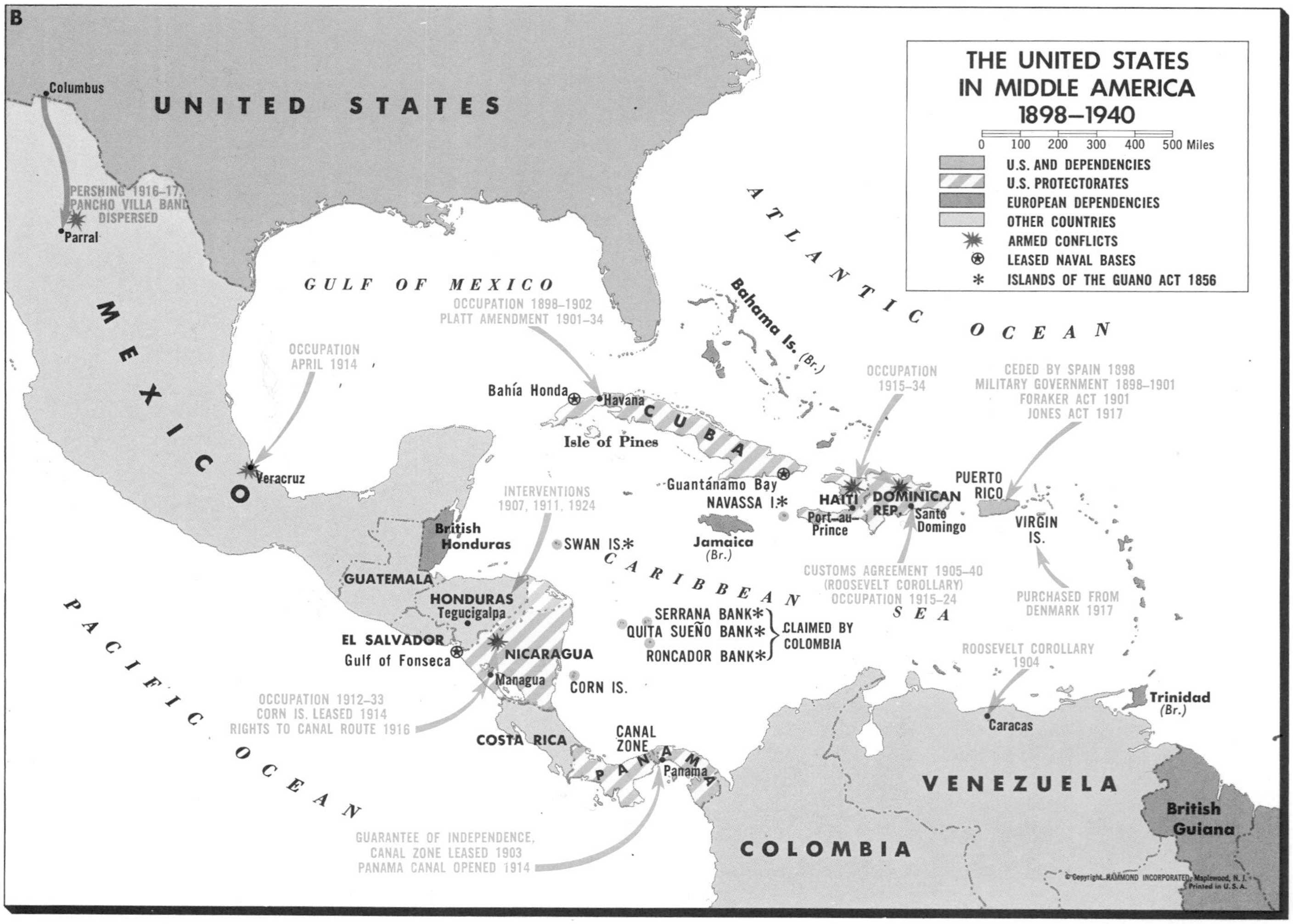

B

THE UNITED STATES IN MIDDLE AMERICA 1898–1940

0   100   200   300   400   500 Miles

U.S. AND DEPENDENCIES
U.S. PROTECTORATES
EUROPEAN DEPENDENCIES
OTHER COUNTRIES
ARMED CONFLICTS
LEASED NAVAL BASES
ISLANDS OF THE GUANO ACT 1856

Columbus

UNITED STATES

PERSHING 1916–17, PANCHO VILLA BAND DISPERSED

Parral

MEXICO

GULF OF MEXICO

OCCUPATION 1898–1902 PLATT AMENDMENT 1901–34

OCCUPATION APRIL 1914

ATLANTIC OCEAN

Bahama Is. (Br.)

OCCUPATION 1915–34

CEDED BY SPAIN 1898
MILITARY GOVERNMENT 1898–1901
FORAKER ACT 1901
JONES ACT 1917

Bahía Honda
Havana

Veracruz

CUBA

Isle of Pines

INTERVENTIONS 1907, 1911, 1924

Guantánamo Bay
NAVASSA I.✳

HAITI ✳ DOMINICAN REP.
Port-au-Prince   Santo Domingo

PUERTO RICO

VIRGIN IS.

PURCHASED FROM DENMARK 1917

British Honduras

GUATEMALA

SWAN IS.✳

Jamaica (Br.)

CARIBBEAN   SEA

CUSTOMS AGREEMENT 1905–40 (ROOSEVELT COROLLARY)
OCCUPATION 1915–24

HONDURAS
Tegucigalpa

SERRANA BANK✳
QUITA SUEÑO BANK✳
RONCADOR BANK✳
CLAIMED BY COLOMBIA

ROOSEVELT COROLLARY 1904

EL SALVADOR
Gulf of Fonseca

NICARAGUA
Managua

CORN IS.

OCCUPATION 1912–33
CORN IS. LEASED 1914
RIGHTS TO CANAL ROUTE 1916

COSTA RICA

CANAL ZONE

PANAMA
Panama

Caracas

Trinidad (Br.)

VENEZUELA

PACIFIC OCEAN

GUARANTEE OF INDEPENDENCE,
CANAL ZONE LEASED 1903
PANAMA CANAL OPENED 1914

COLOMBIA

British Guiana

© Copyright. HAMMOND INCORPORATED, Maplewood, N.J.
Printed in U.S.A.

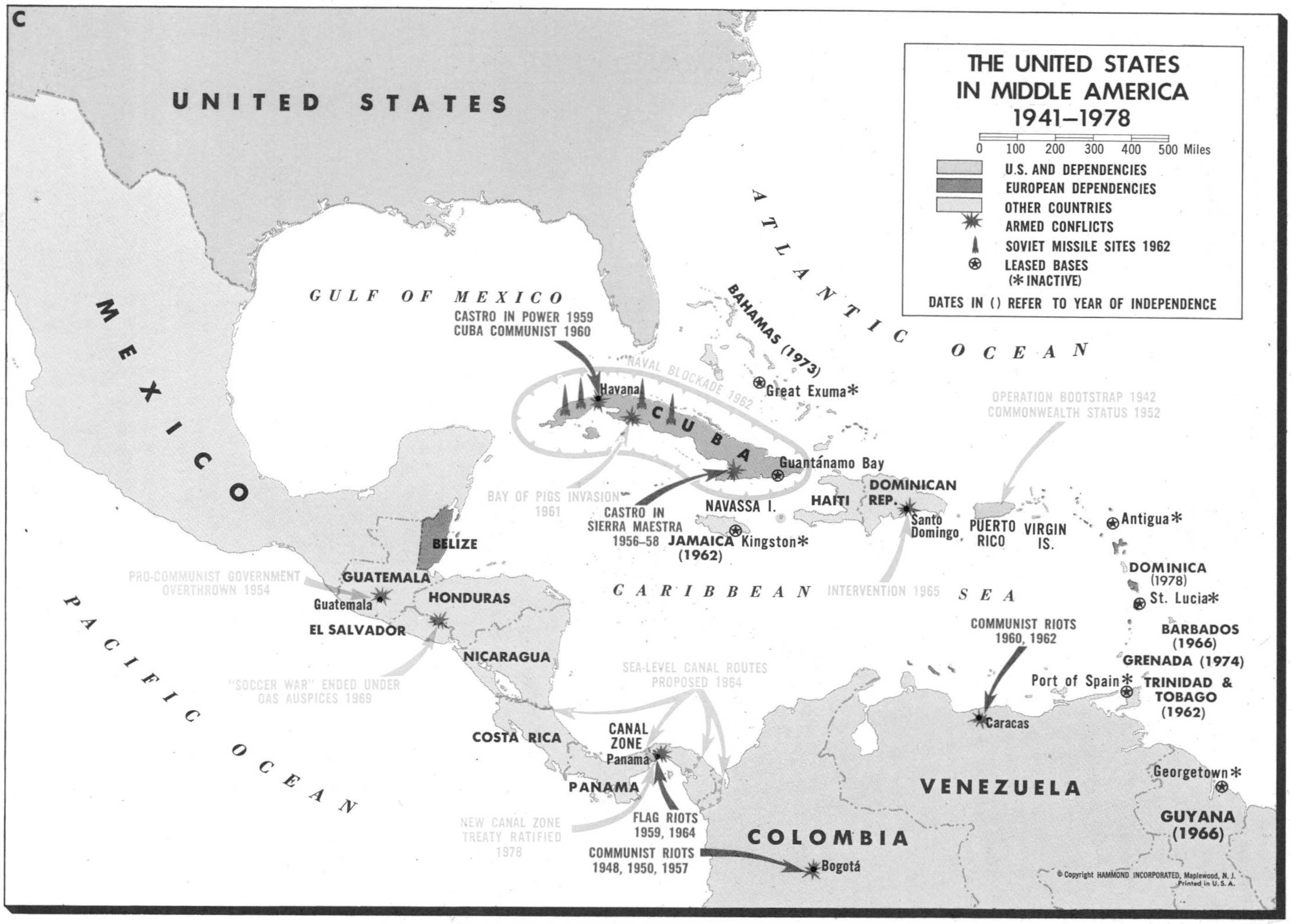

THE UNITED STATES IN MIDDLE AMERICA 1941–1978

0 100 200 300 400 500 Miles

- U.S. AND DEPENDENCIES
- EUROPEAN DEPENDENCIES
- OTHER COUNTRIES
- ARMED CONFLICTS
- SOVIET MISSILE SITES 1962
- LEASED BASES (* INACTIVE)

DATES IN ( ) REFER TO YEAR OF INDEPENDENCE

UNITED STATES

GULF OF MEXICO

MEXICO

PACIFIC OCEAN

ATLANTIC OCEAN

BAHAMAS (1973)

CASTRO IN POWER 1959
CUBA COMMUNIST 1960

NAVAL BLOCKADE 1962

Havana

Great Exuma *

OPERATION BOOTSTRAP 1942
COMMONWEALTH STATUS 1952

CUBA

Guantánamo Bay

BAY OF PIGS INVASION 1961

CASTRO IN SIERRA MAESTRA 1956–58

NAVASSA I.

HAITI

DOMINICAN REP.

JAMAICA (1962)

Kingston *

Santo Domingo

PUERTO RICO

VIRGIN IS.

Antigua *

DOMINICA (1978)

St. Lucia *

BELIZE

GUATEMALA

Guatemala

HONDURAS

EL SALVADOR

NICARAGUA

PRO-COMMUNIST GOVERNMENT OVERTHROWN 1954

"SOCCER WAR" ENDED UNDER OAS AUSPICES 1969

CARIBBEAN SEA

INTERVENTION 1965

COMMUNIST RIOTS 1960, 1962

BARBADOS (1966)

GRENADA (1974)

Port of Spain *

TRINIDAD & TOBAGO (1962)

SEA-LEVEL CANAL ROUTES PROPOSED 1964

COSTA RICA

CANAL ZONE

Panama

PANAMA

Caracas

VENEZUELA

Georgetown *

NEW CANAL ZONE TREATY RATIFIED 1978

FLAG RIOTS 1959, 1964

COMMUNIST RIOTS 1948, 1950, 1957

COLOMBIA

Bogotá

GUYANA (1966)

© Copyright HAMMOND INCORPORATED, Maplewood, N.J.
Printed in U.S.A.

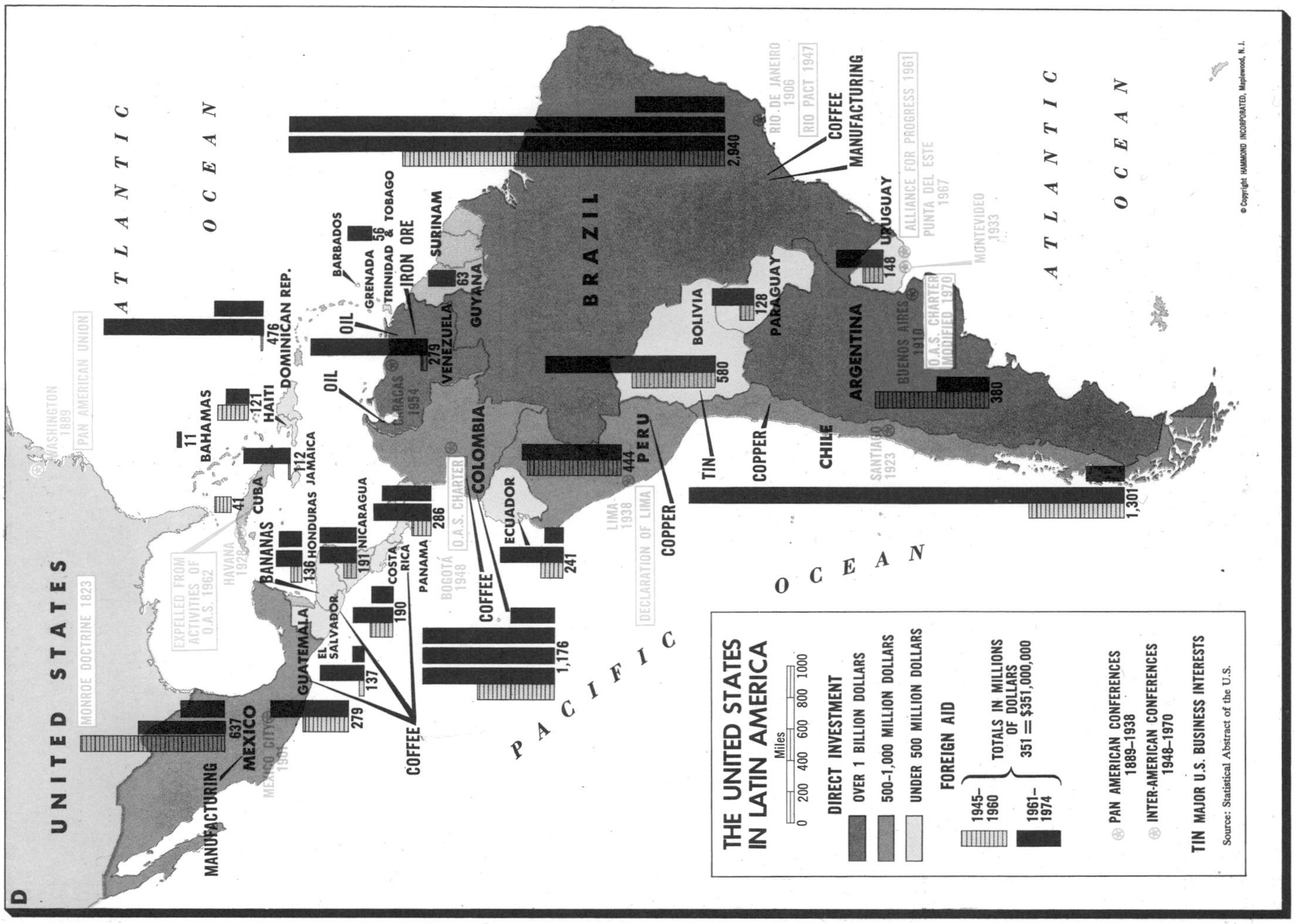

THE UNITED STATES IN LATIN AMERICA

ATLANTIC OCEAN

PACIFIC OCEAN

UNITED STATES

MONROE DOCTRINE 1823

WASHINGTON 1889 PAN AMERICAN UNION

EXPELLED FROM ACTIVITIES OF O.A.S. 1962

HAVANA 1928

MEXICO CITY 1945

MEXICO 637

MANUFACTURING

BAHAMAS 11

CUBA 41

HAITI 121

DOMINICAN REP. 476

JAMAICA 112

BANANAS

HONDURAS 136

NICARAGUA 191

COSTA RICA 190

PANAMA 1,176

GUATEMALA 279

EL SALVADOR 137

COFFEE

BARBADOS

GRENADA

TRINIDAD & TOBAGO 56

IRON ORE

SURINAM 63

GUYANA

VENEZUELA 279

CARACAS 1954

OIL

O.A.S. CHARTER

COLOMBIA 286

BOGOTÁ 1948

DECLARATION OF LIMA

ECUADOR 241

COFFEE

PERU 444

LIMA 1938

TIN

COPPER

BOLIVIA 128

PARAGUAY

BRAZIL 2,940

RIO DE JANEIRO 1906

RIO PACT 1947

COFFEE

MANUFACTURING

ALLIANCE FOR PROGRESS 1961

PUNTA DEL ESTE 1967

URUGUAY 148

MONTEVIDEO 1933

O.A.S. CHARTER MODIFIED 1970

ARGENTINA 580

BUENOS AIRES 1910

CHILE 1,301

COPPER

SANTIAGO 1923

380

ATLANTIC OCEAN

THE UNITED STATES IN LATIN AMERICA

Miles
0 200 400 600 800 1000

DIRECT INVESTMENT
- OVER 1 BILLION DOLLARS
- 500–1,000 MILLION DOLLARS
- UNDER 500 MILLION DOLLARS

FOREIGN AID
- 1945–1960
- 1961–1974

TOTALS IN MILLIONS OF DOLLARS
351 = $351,000,000

⊛ PAN AMERICAN CONFERENCES 1889–1938
⊛ INTER-AMERICAN CONFERENCES 1948–1970

TIN MAJOR U.S. BUSINESS INTERESTS

Source: Statistical Abstract of the U.S.

© Copyright HAMMOND INCORPORATED, Maplewood, N.J.

A

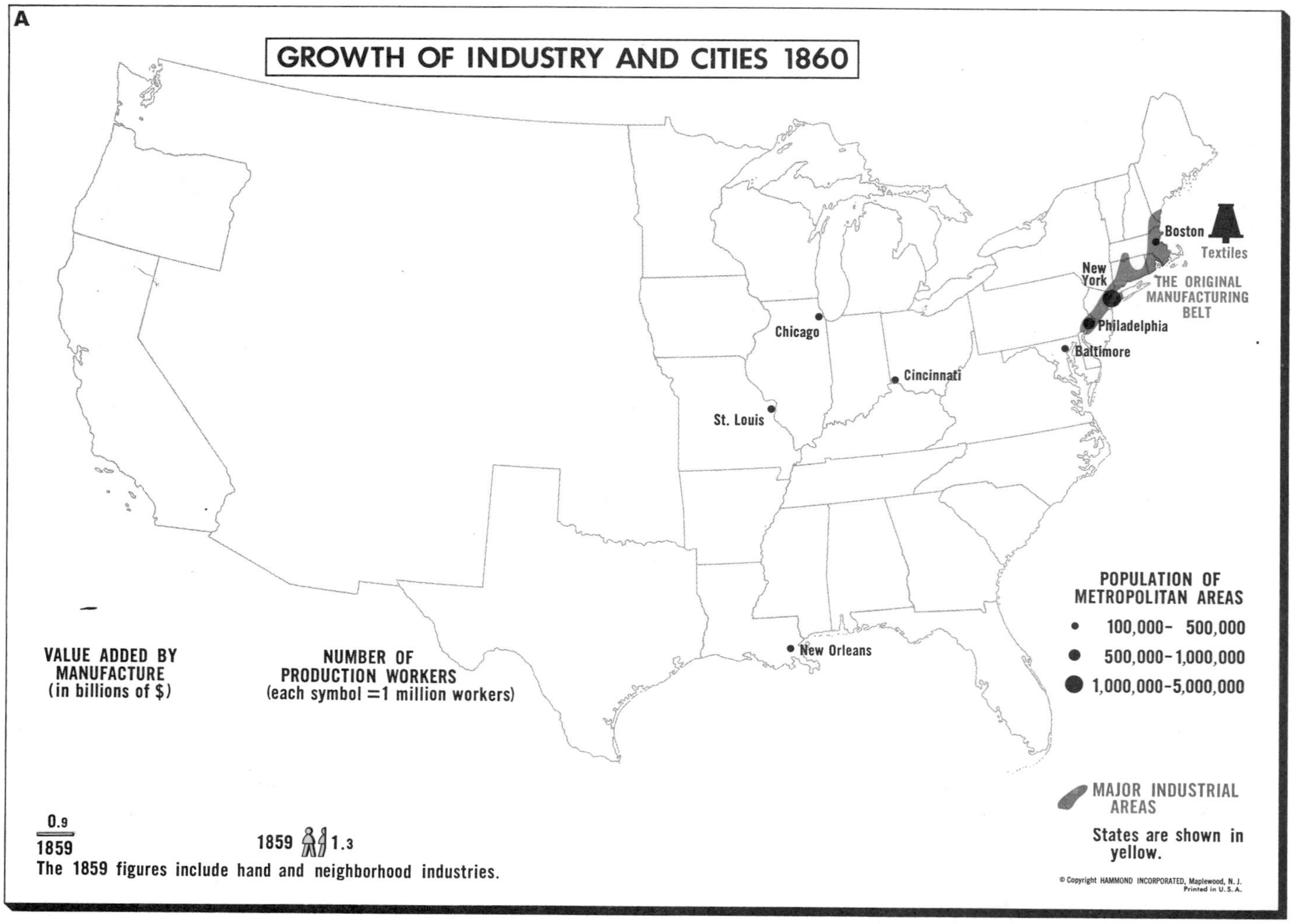

GROWTH OF INDUSTRY AND CITIES 1860

Boston
Textiles

New York

THE ORIGINAL MANUFACTURING BELT

Chicago

Philadelphia

Baltimore

Cincinnati

St. Louis

New Orleans

VALUE ADDED BY MANUFACTURE
(in billions of $)

NUMBER OF PRODUCTION WORKERS
(each symbol =1 million workers)

POPULATION OF METROPOLITAN AREAS

· 100,000- 500,000
● 500,000-1,000,000
⬤ 1,000,000-5,000,000

MAJOR INDUSTRIAL AREAS

States are shown in yellow.

0.9
——
1859

1859 1.3

The 1859 figures include hand and neighborhood industries.

B

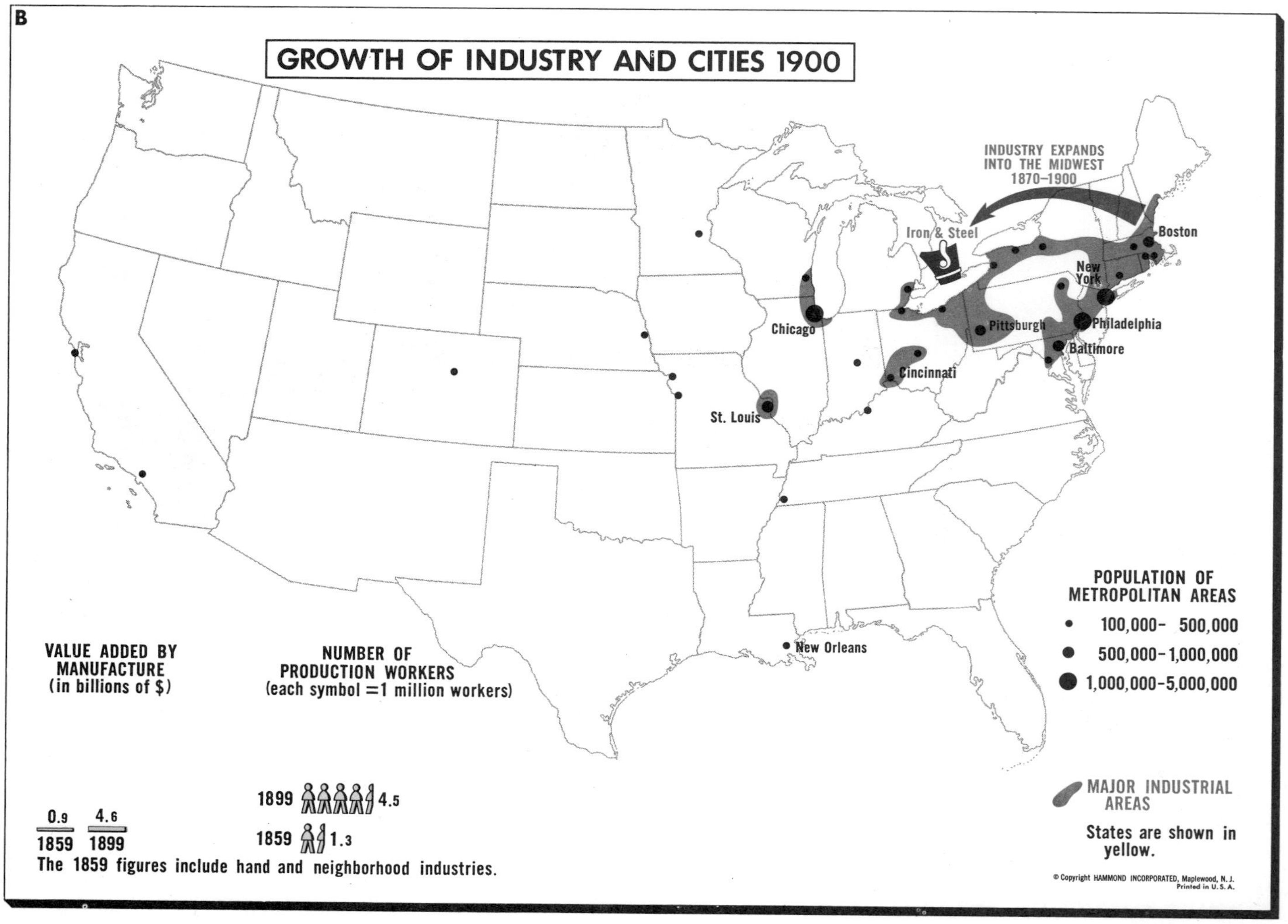

GROWTH OF INDUSTRY AND CITIES 1900

INDUSTRY EXPANDS INTO THE MIDWEST 1870–1900

Iron & Steel

Boston

New York

Chicago

Pittsburgh

Philadelphia

Baltimore

Cincinnati

St. Louis

New Orleans

VALUE ADDED BY MANUFACTURE
(in billions of $)

NUMBER OF PRODUCTION WORKERS
(each symbol =1 million workers)

POPULATION OF METROPOLITAN AREAS

· 100,000- 500,000
● 500,000-1,000,000
⬤ 1,000,000-5,000,000

MAJOR INDUSTRIAL AREAS

States are shown in yellow.

0.9   4.6
——   ——
1859   1899

1899 4.5

1859 1.3

The 1859 figures include hand and neighborhood industries.

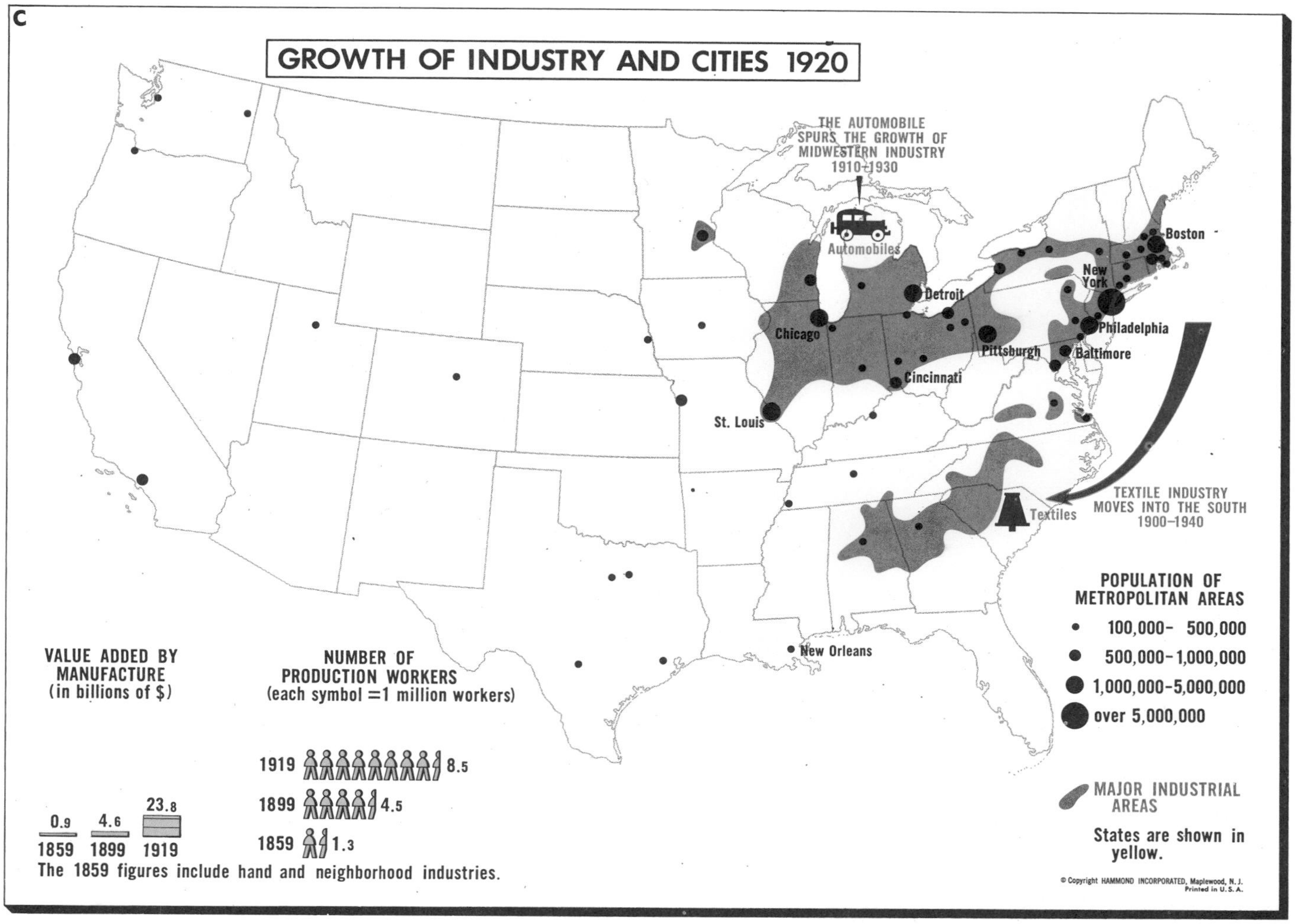

C

GROWTH OF INDUSTRY AND CITIES 1920

THE AUTOMOBILE
SPURS THE GROWTH OF
MIDWESTERN INDUSTRY
1910–1930

Automobiles

Boston
New York
Detroit
Philadelphia
Chicago
Pittsburgh
Baltimore
Cincinnati
St. Louis

Textiles

TEXTILE INDUSTRY
MOVES INTO THE SOUTH
1900–1940

New Orleans

POPULATION OF METROPOLITAN AREAS

· 100,000– 500,000
• 500,000–1,000,000
● 1,000,000–5,000,000
⬤ over 5,000,000

VALUE ADDED BY MANUFACTURE
(in billions of $)

NUMBER OF PRODUCTION WORKERS
(each symbol =1 million workers)

1919   8.5
1899   4.5
1859   1.3

0.9   4.6   23.8
1859   1899   1919

The 1859 figures include hand and neighborhood industries.

MAJOR INDUSTRIAL AREAS

States are shown in yellow.

© Copyright HAMMOND INCORPORATED, Maplewood, N.J.
Printed in U.S.A.

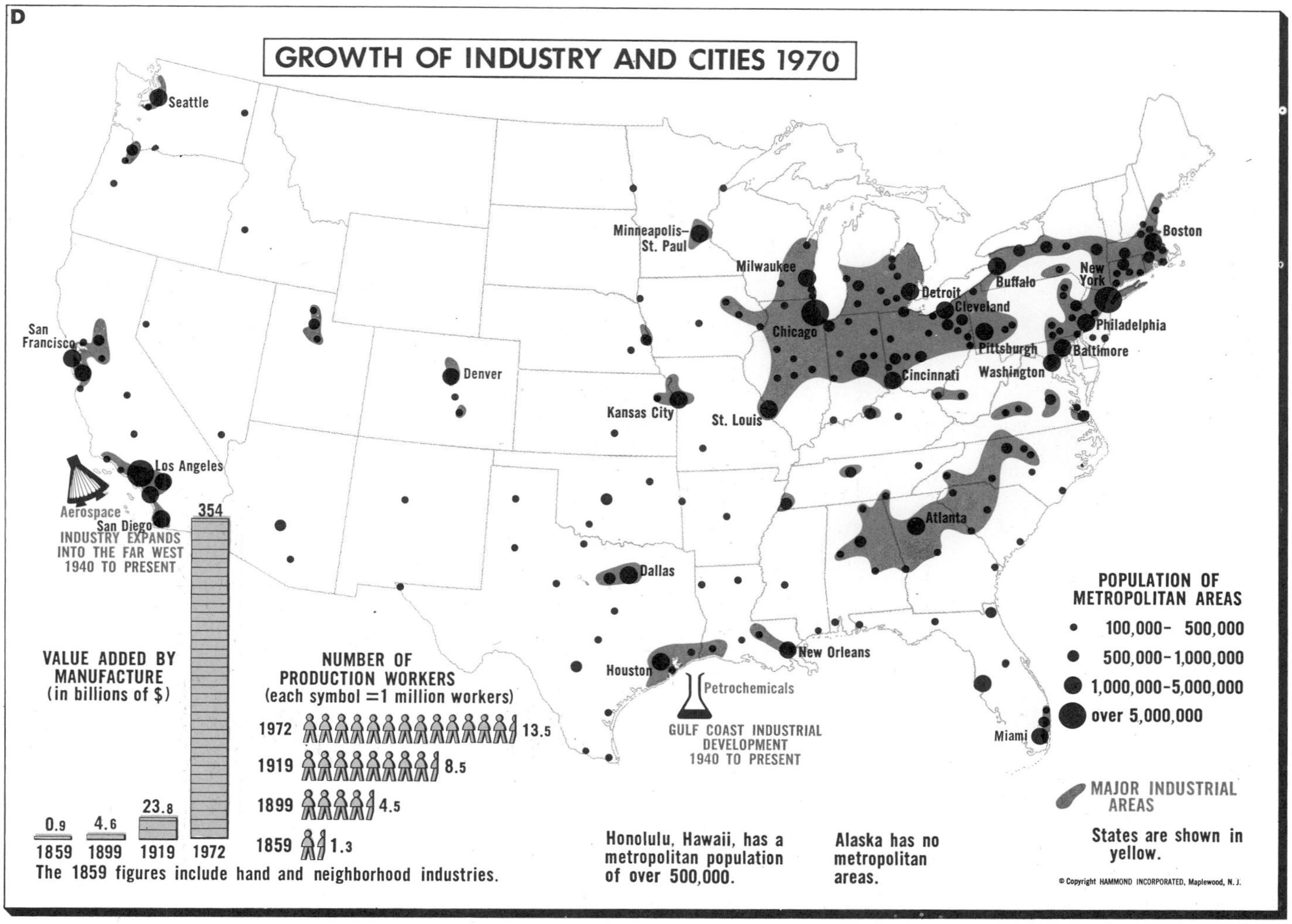

D

GROWTH OF INDUSTRY AND CITIES 1970

Seattle

Minneapolis–St. Paul
Milwaukee
Buffalo
Boston
Detroit
New York
Cleveland
Chicago
Pittsburgh
Philadelphia
Cincinnati
Washington
Baltimore

San Francisco

Denver

Kansas City
St. Louis

Los Angeles

Aerospace
San Diego

INDUSTRY EXPANDS
INTO THE FAR WEST
1940 TO PRESENT

Atlanta

Dallas

Houston
New Orleans
Petrochemicals

GULF COAST INDUSTRIAL
DEVELOPMENT
1940 TO PRESENT

Miami

354

VALUE ADDED BY MANUFACTURE
(in billions of $)

NUMBER OF PRODUCTION WORKERS
(each symbol =1 million workers)

1972   13.5
1919   8.5
1899   4.5
1859   1.3

0.9   4.6   23.8   354
1859   1899   1919   1972

The 1859 figures include hand and neighborhood industries.

Honolulu, Hawaii, has a metropolitan population of over 500,000.

Alaska has no metropolitan areas.

POPULATION OF METROPOLITAN AREAS

· 100,000– 500,000
• 500,000–1,000,000
● 1,000,000–5,000,000
⬤ over 5,000,000

MAJOR INDUSTRIAL AREAS

States are shown in yellow.

© Copyright HAMMOND INCORPORATED, Maplewood, N.J.

A

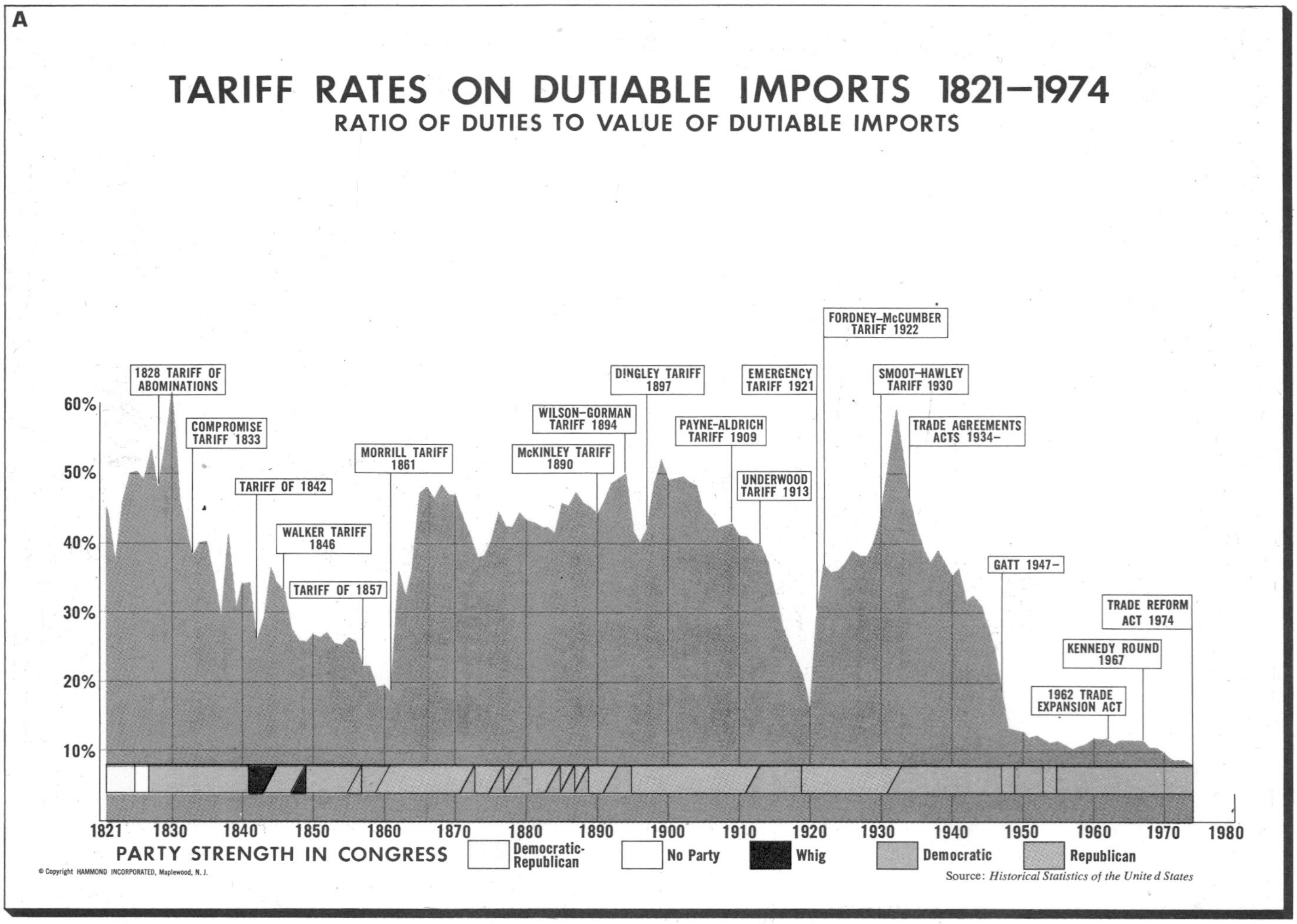

TARIFF RATES ON DUTIABLE IMPORTS 1821–1974
RATIO OF DUTIES TO VALUE OF DUTIABLE IMPORTS

1828 TARIFF OF ABOMINATIONS

COMPROMISE TARIFF 1833

TARIFF OF 1842

WALKER TARIFF 1846

TARIFF OF 1857

MORRILL TARIFF 1861

McKINLEY TARIFF 1890

WILSON–GORMAN TARIFF 1894

DINGLEY TARIFF 1897

PAYNE-ALDRICH TARIFF 1909

UNDERWOOD TARIFF 1913

EMERGENCY TARIFF 1921

FORDNEY–McCUMBER TARIFF 1922

SMOOT–HAWLEY TARIFF 1930

TRADE AGREEMENTS ACTS 1934–

GATT 1947–

TRADE REFORM ACT 1974

KENNEDY ROUND 1967

1962 TRADE EXPANSION ACT

PARTY STRENGTH IN CONGRESS   Democratic-Republican   No Party   Whig   Democratic   Republican

© Copyright HAMMOND INCORPORATED, Maplewood, N.J.

Source: *Historical Statistics of the United States*

B

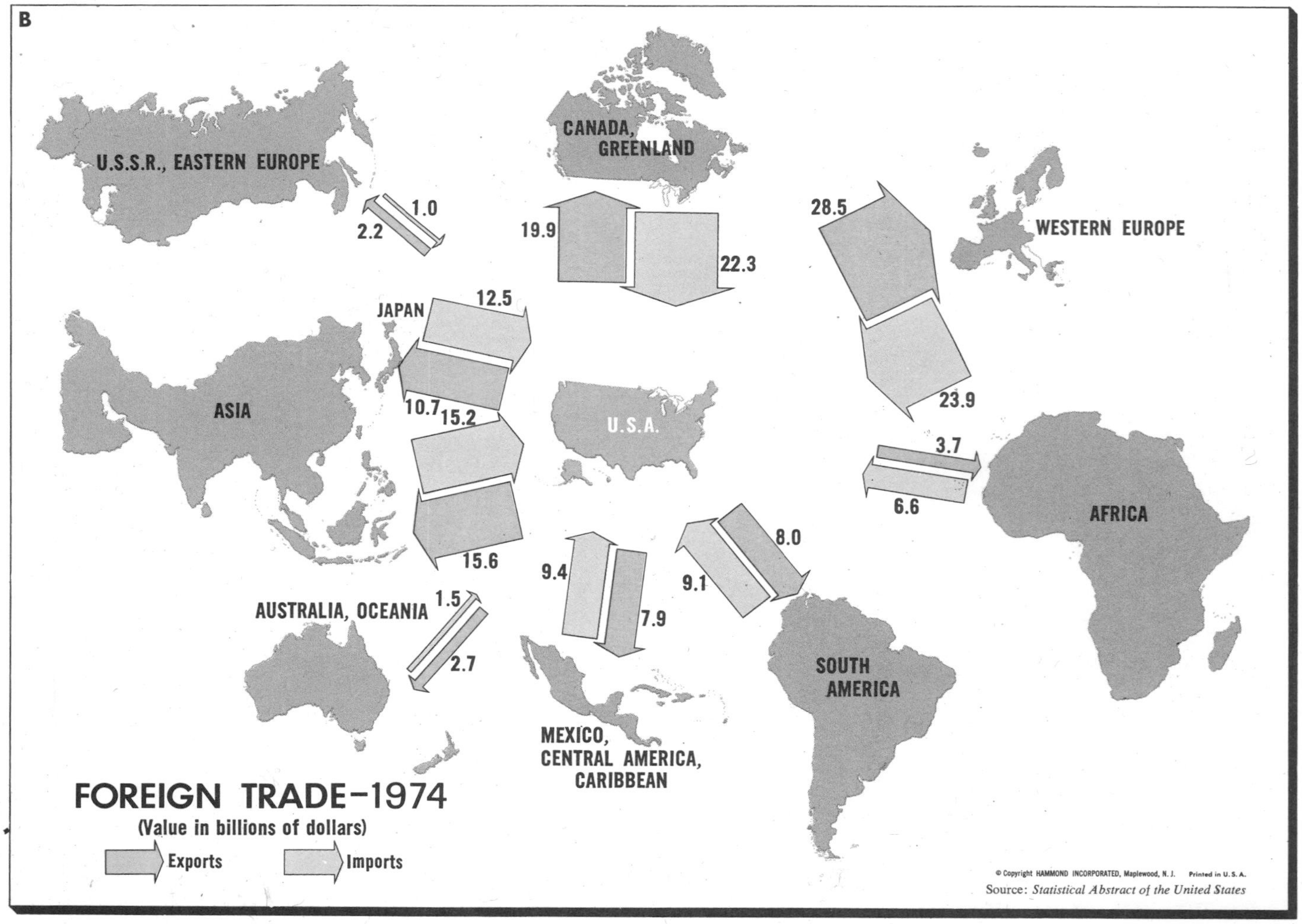

U.S.S.R., EASTERN EUROPE   1.0 / 2.2

CANADA, GREENLAND   19.9 / 22.3

WESTERN EUROPE   28.5 / 23.9

JAPAN   12.5 / 10.7 / 15.2

ASIA   15.6

U.S.A.

AFRICA   3.7 / 6.6

AUSTRALIA, OCEANIA   1.5 / 2.7

MEXICO, CENTRAL AMERICA, CARIBBEAN   9.4 / 7.9

SOUTH AMERICA   8.0 / 9.1

FOREIGN TRADE–1974
(Value in billions of dollars)

Exports   Imports

© Copyright HAMMOND INCORPORATED, Maplewood, N.J.   Printed in U.S.A.

Source: *Statistical Abstract of the United States*

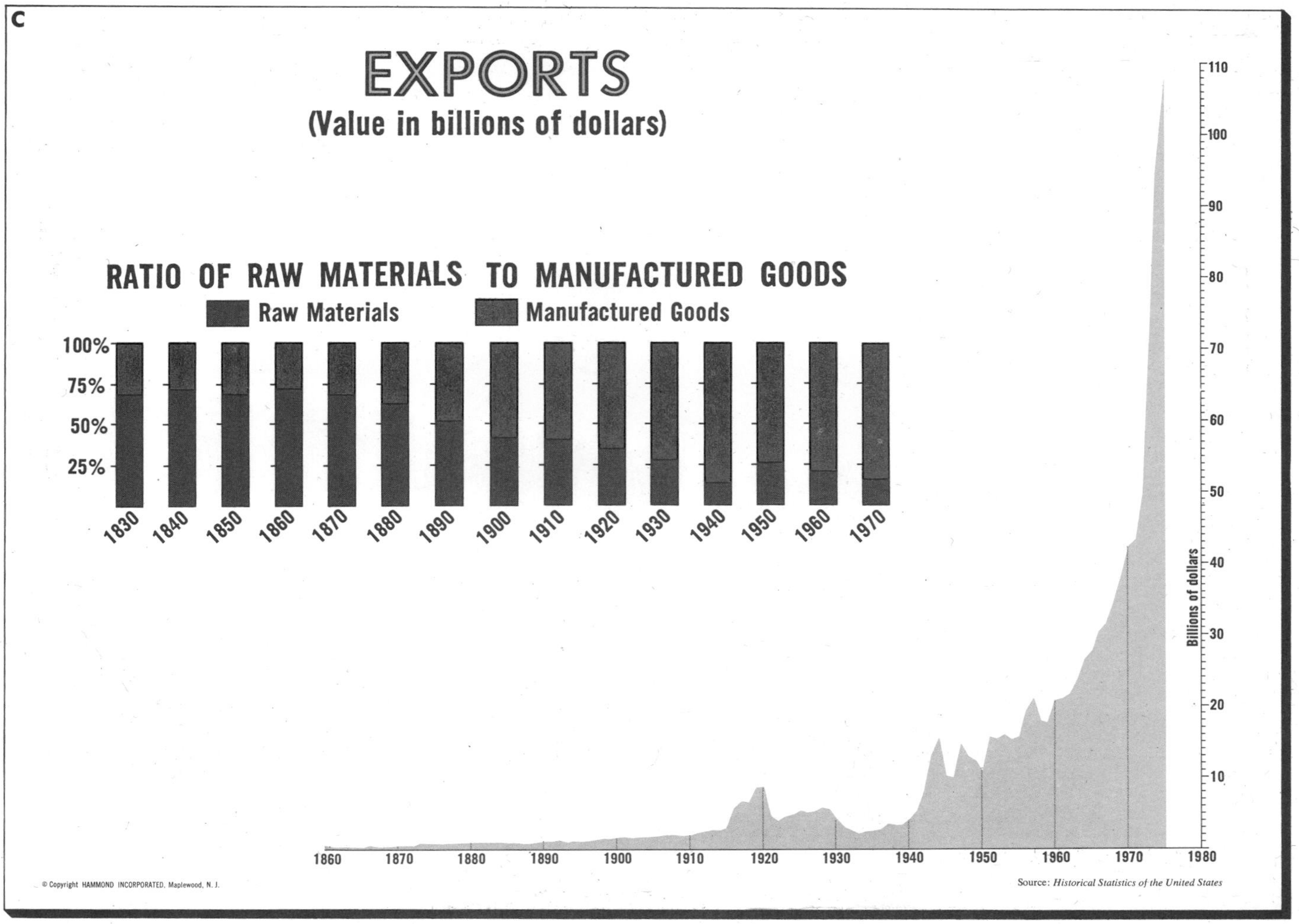

C

EXPORTS
(Value in billions of dollars)

RATIO OF RAW MATERIALS TO MANUFACTURED GOODS

■ Raw Materials ▩ Manufactured Goods

Billions of dollars

© Copyright HAMMOND INCORPORATED, Maplewood, N. J.

Source: *Historical Statistics of the United States*

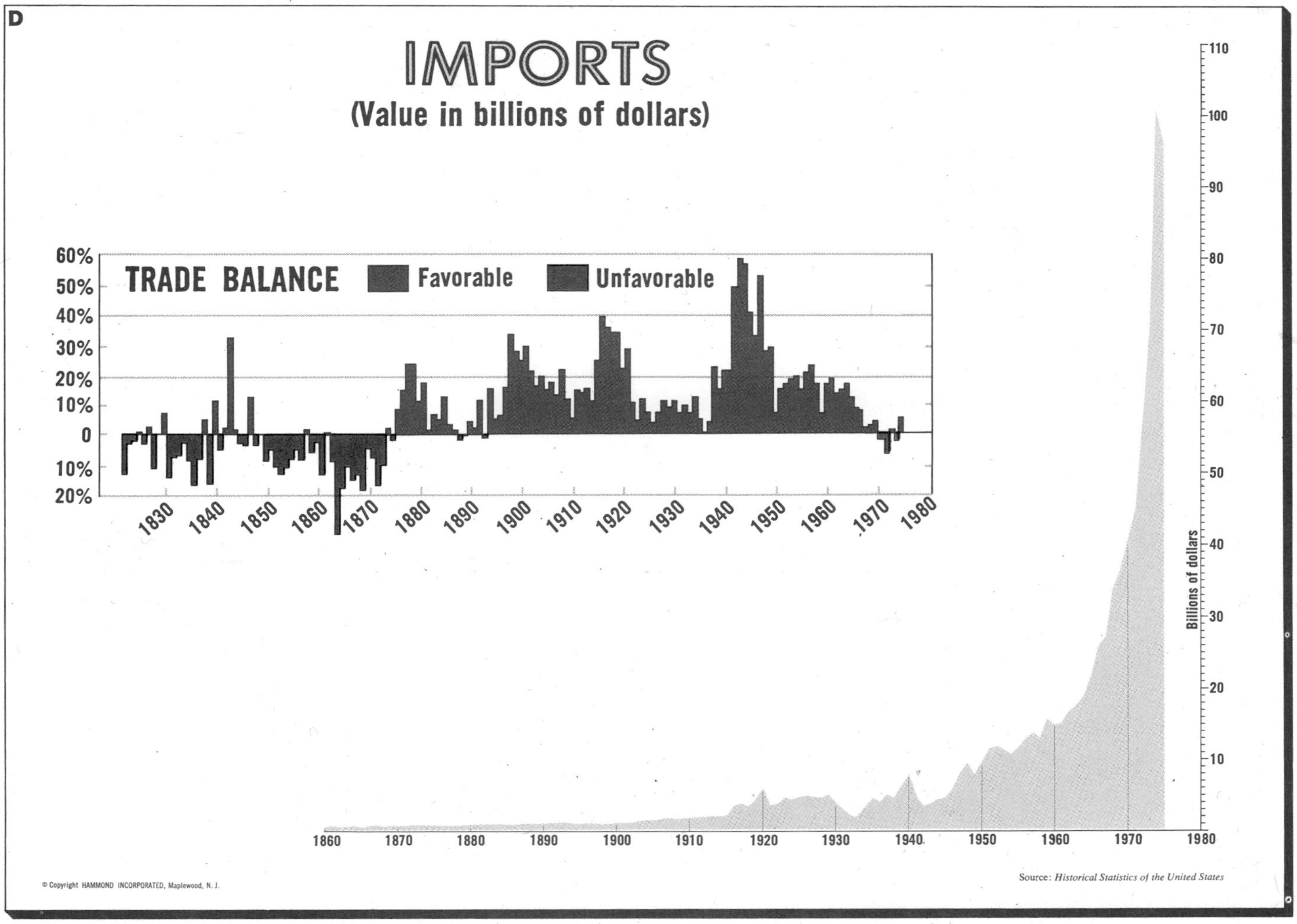

D

IMPORTS
(Value in billions of dollars)

TRADE BALANCE ■ Favorable ■ Unfavorable

Billions of dollars

© Copyright HAMMOND INCORPORATED, Maplewood, N. J.

Source: *Historical Statistics of the United States*

A

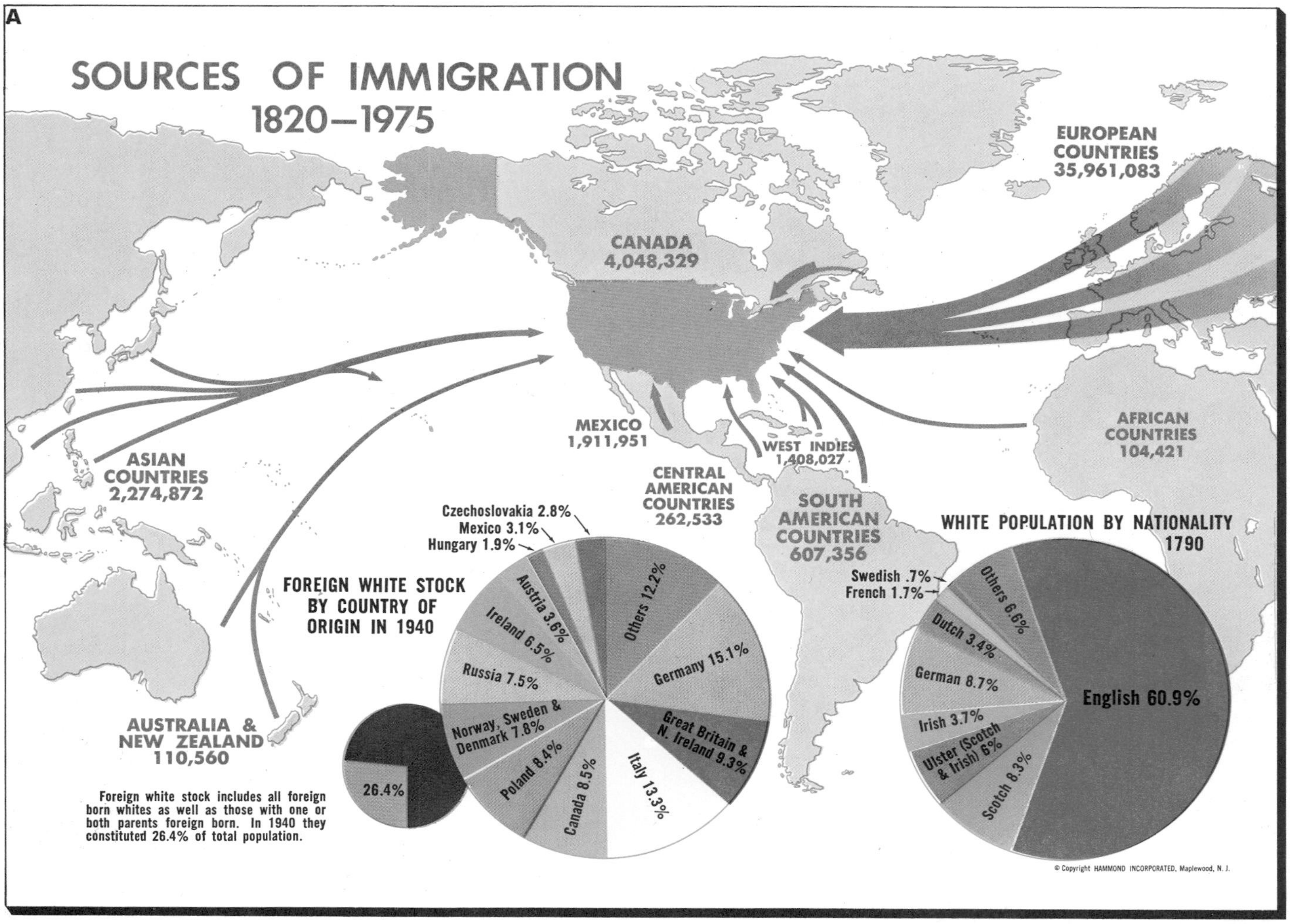

SOURCES OF IMMIGRATION
1820–1975

EUROPEAN COUNTRIES
35,961,083

CANADA
4,048,329

ASIAN COUNTRIES
2,274,872

MEXICO
1,911,951

WEST INDIES
1,408,027

CENTRAL AMERICAN COUNTRIES
262,533

SOUTH AMERICAN COUNTRIES
607,356

AFRICAN COUNTRIES
104,421

AUSTRALIA & NEW ZEALAND
110,560

Foreign white stock includes all foreign born whites as well as those with one or both parents foreign born. In 1940 they constituted 26.4% of total population.

FOREIGN WHITE STOCK BY COUNTRY OF ORIGIN IN 1940

Czechoslovakia 2.8%
Mexico 3.1%
Hungary 1.9%
Austria 3.6%
Ireland 6.5%
Russia 7.5%
Norway, Sweden & Denmark 7.8%
Poland 8.4%
Canada 8.5%
Italy 13.3%
Great Britain & N. Ireland 9.3%
Germany 15.1%
Others 12.2%

26.4%

WHITE POPULATION BY NATIONALITY 1790

Swedish .7%
French 1.7%
Others 6.6%
Dutch 3.4%
German 8.7%
Irish 3.7%
Ulster (Scotch & Irish) 6%
Scotch 8.3%
English 60.9%

© Copyright HAMMOND INCORPORATED, Maplewood, N. J.

B

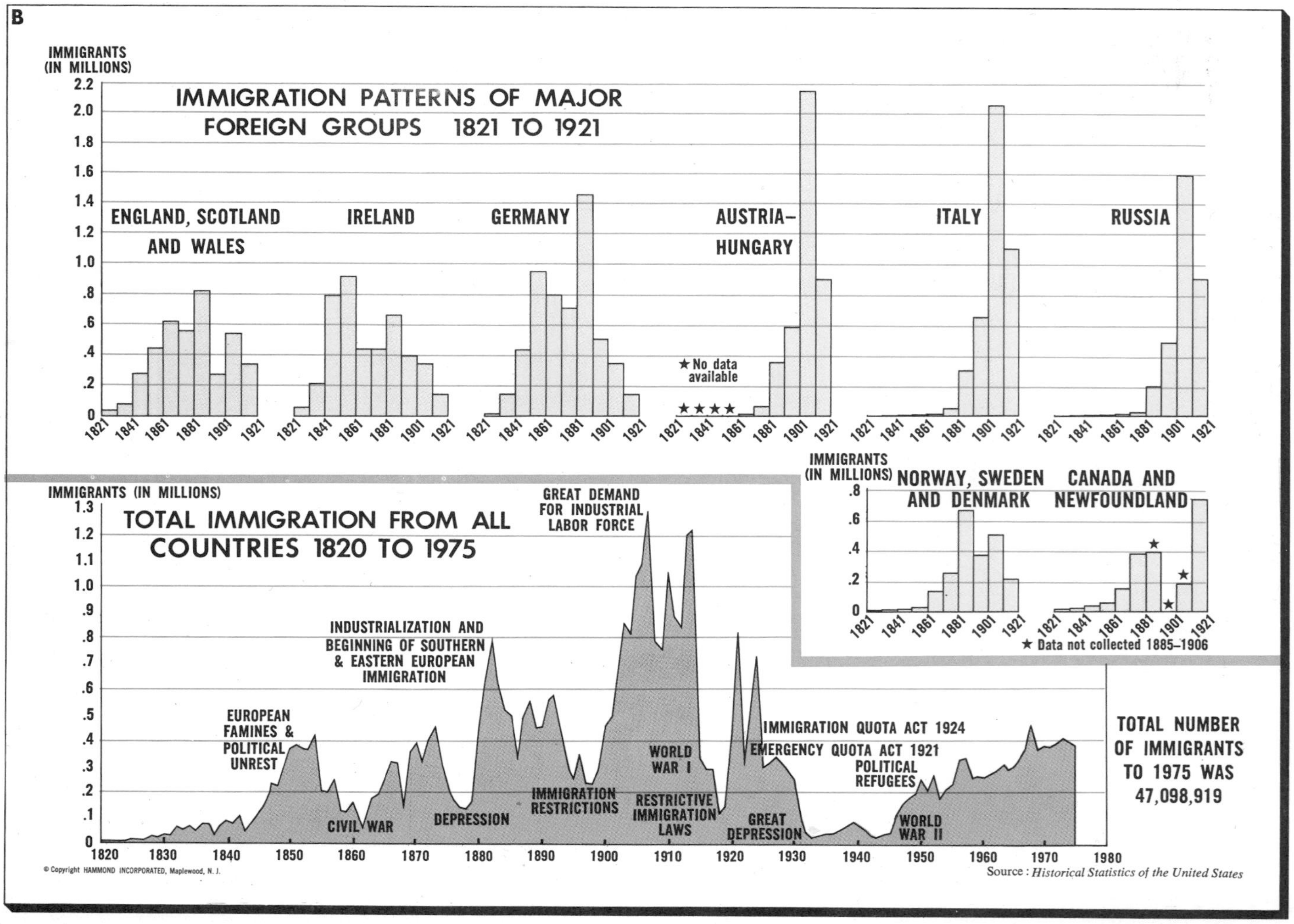

IMMIGRANTS (IN MILLIONS)

IMMIGRATION PATTERNS OF MAJOR FOREIGN GROUPS   1821 TO 1921

ENGLAND, SCOTLAND AND WALES

IRELAND

GERMANY

AUSTRIA–HUNGARY

★ No data available
★ ★ ★ ★

ITALY

RUSSIA

1821 1841 1861 1881 1901 1921

IMMIGRANTS (IN MILLIONS)

TOTAL IMMIGRATION FROM ALL COUNTRIES 1820 TO 1975

GREAT DEMAND FOR INDUSTRIAL LABOR FORCE

INDUSTRIALIZATION AND BEGINNING OF SOUTHERN & EASTERN EUROPEAN IMMIGRATION

EUROPEAN FAMINES & POLITICAL UNREST

CIVIL WAR

DEPRESSION

IMMIGRATION RESTRICTIONS

RESTRICTIVE IMMIGRATION LAWS

WORLD WAR I

IMMIGRATION QUOTA ACT 1924
EMERGENCY QUOTA ACT 1921
POLITICAL REFUGEES

GREAT DEPRESSION

WORLD WAR II

1820 1830 1840 1850 1860 1870 1880 1890 1900 1910 1920 1930 1940 1950 1960 1970 1980

TOTAL NUMBER OF IMMIGRANTS TO 1975 WAS 47,098,919

IMMIGRANTS (IN MILLIONS)

NORWAY, SWEDEN AND DENMARK

CANADA AND NEWFOUNDLAND

★ Data not collected 1885–1906

1821 1841 1861 1881 1901 1921

© Copyright HAMMOND INCORPORATED, Maplewood, N. J.

Source : *Historical Statistics of the United States*

DISTRIBUTION OF FOREIGN BORN IN UNITED STATES
1910

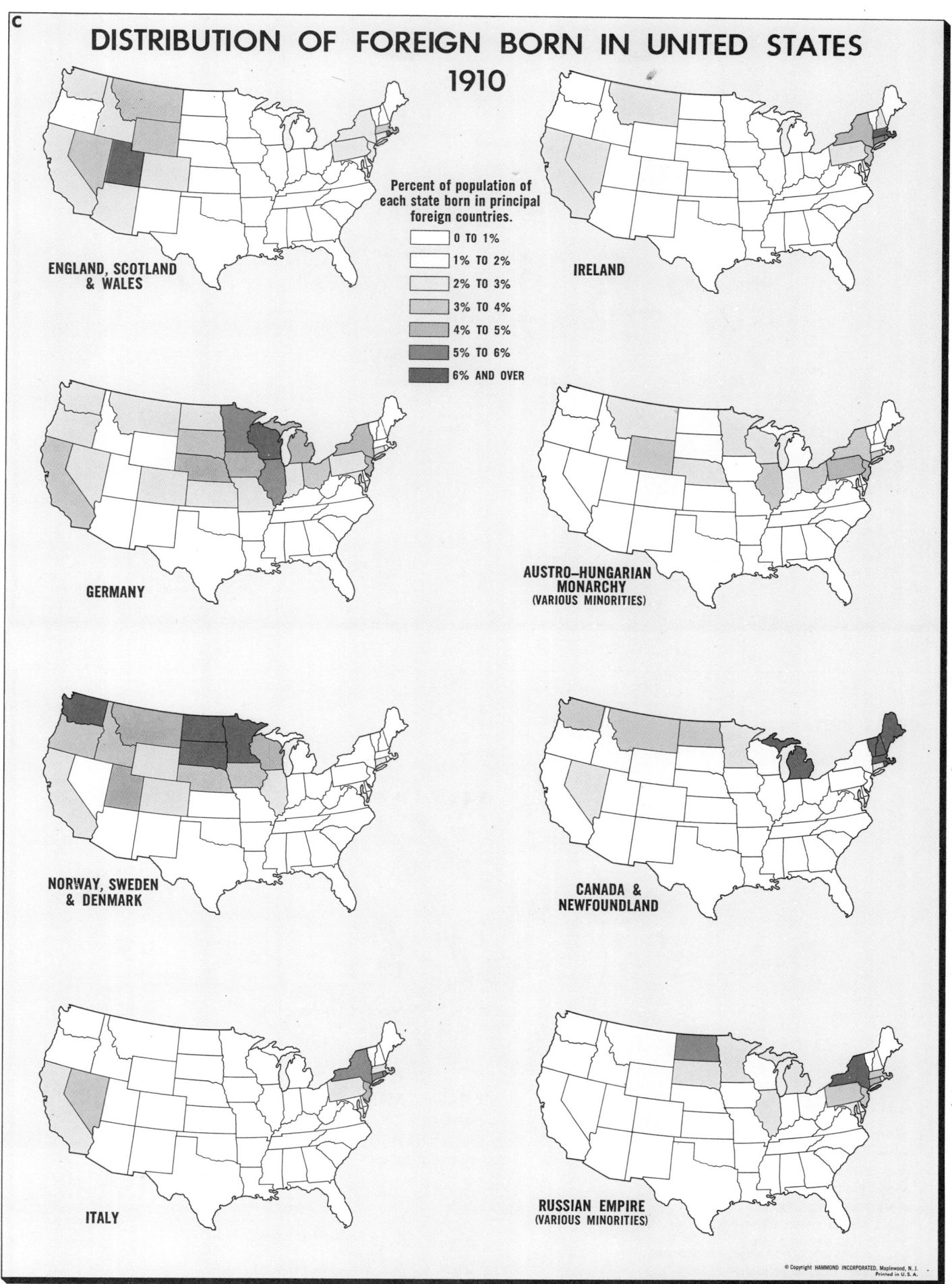

Percent of population of each state born in principal foreign countries.

- 0 TO 1%
- 1% TO 2%
- 2% TO 3%
- 3% TO 4%
- 4% TO 5%
- 5% TO 6%
- 6% AND OVER

ENGLAND, SCOTLAND & WALES

IRELAND

GERMANY

AUSTRO–HUNGARIAN MONARCHY (VARIOUS MINORITIES)

NORWAY, SWEDEN & DENMARK

CANADA & NEWFOUNDLAND

ITALY

RUSSIAN EMPIRE (VARIOUS MINORITIES)

C

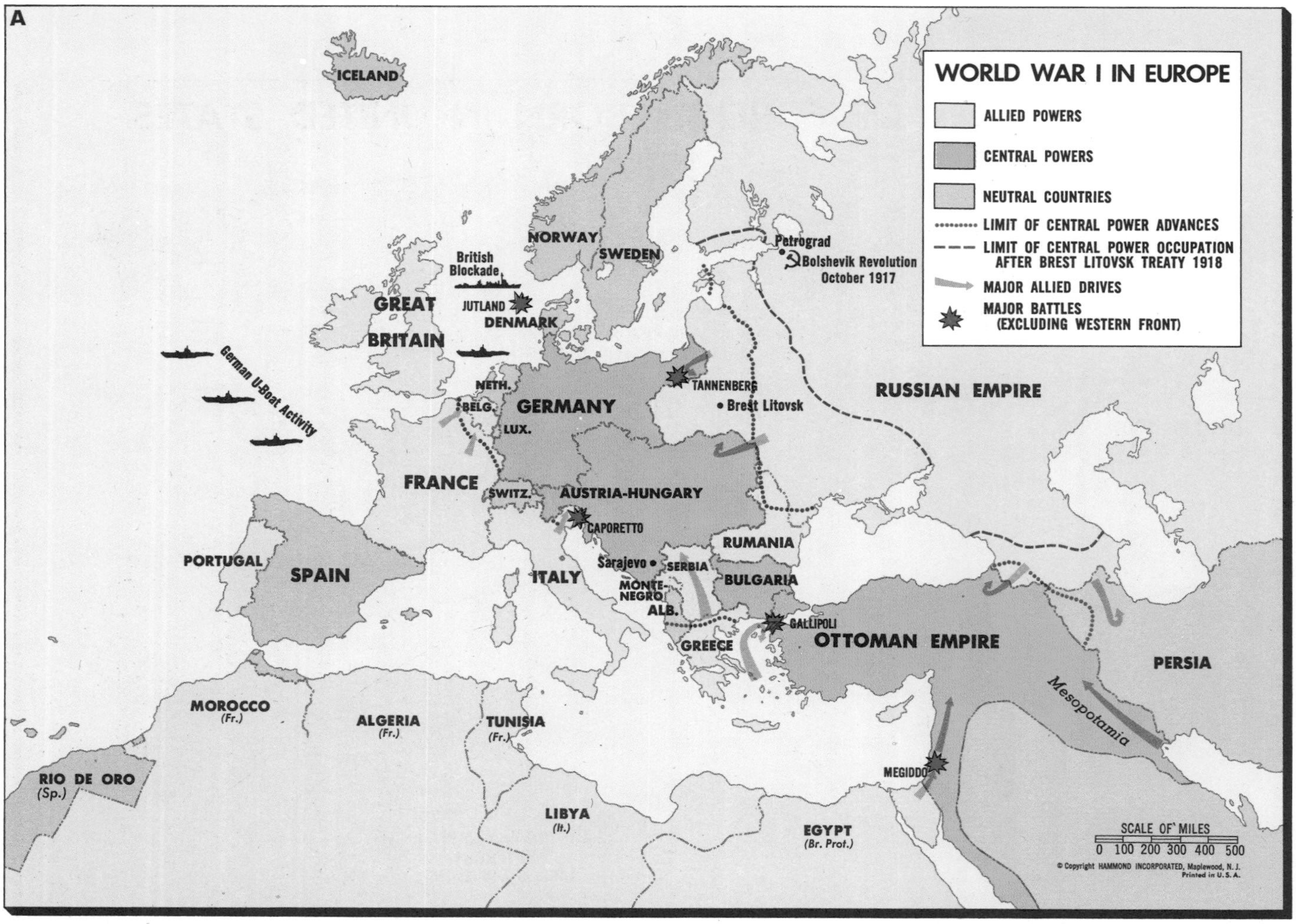

A

ICELAND

WORLD WAR I IN EUROPE

	ALLIED POWERS
	CENTRAL POWERS
	NEUTRAL COUNTRIES
....	LIMIT OF CENTRAL POWER ADVANCES
‒ ‒ ‒	LIMIT OF CENTRAL POWER OCCUPATION AFTER BREST LITOVSK TREATY 1918
➙	MAJOR ALLIED DRIVES
✹	MAJOR BATTLES (EXCLUDING WESTERN FRONT)

NORWAY
SWEDEN
Petrograd
Bolshevik Revolution October 1917

British Blockade

GREAT BRITAIN
JUTLAND
DENMARK

German U-Boat Activity

TANNENBERG
• Brest Litovsk

RUSSIAN EMPIRE

NETH.
BELG.
GERMANY
LUX.

FRANCE
SWITZ.
AUSTRIA-HUNGARY

CAPORETTO

PORTUGAL
SPAIN
ITALY
Sarajevo • SERBIA
MONTE-NEGRO
ALB.

RUMANIA
BULGARIA

GREECE
GALLIPOLI
OTTOMAN EMPIRE
PERSIA

Mesopotamia

MOROCCO (Fr.)
ALGERIA (Fr.)
TUNISIA (Fr.)
RIO DE ORO (Sp.)
LIBYA (It.)
EGYPT (Br. Prot.)

MEGIDDO

SCALE OF MILES
0 100 200 300 400 500

© Copyright HAMMOND INCORPORATED, Maplewood, N.J.
Printed in U.S.A.

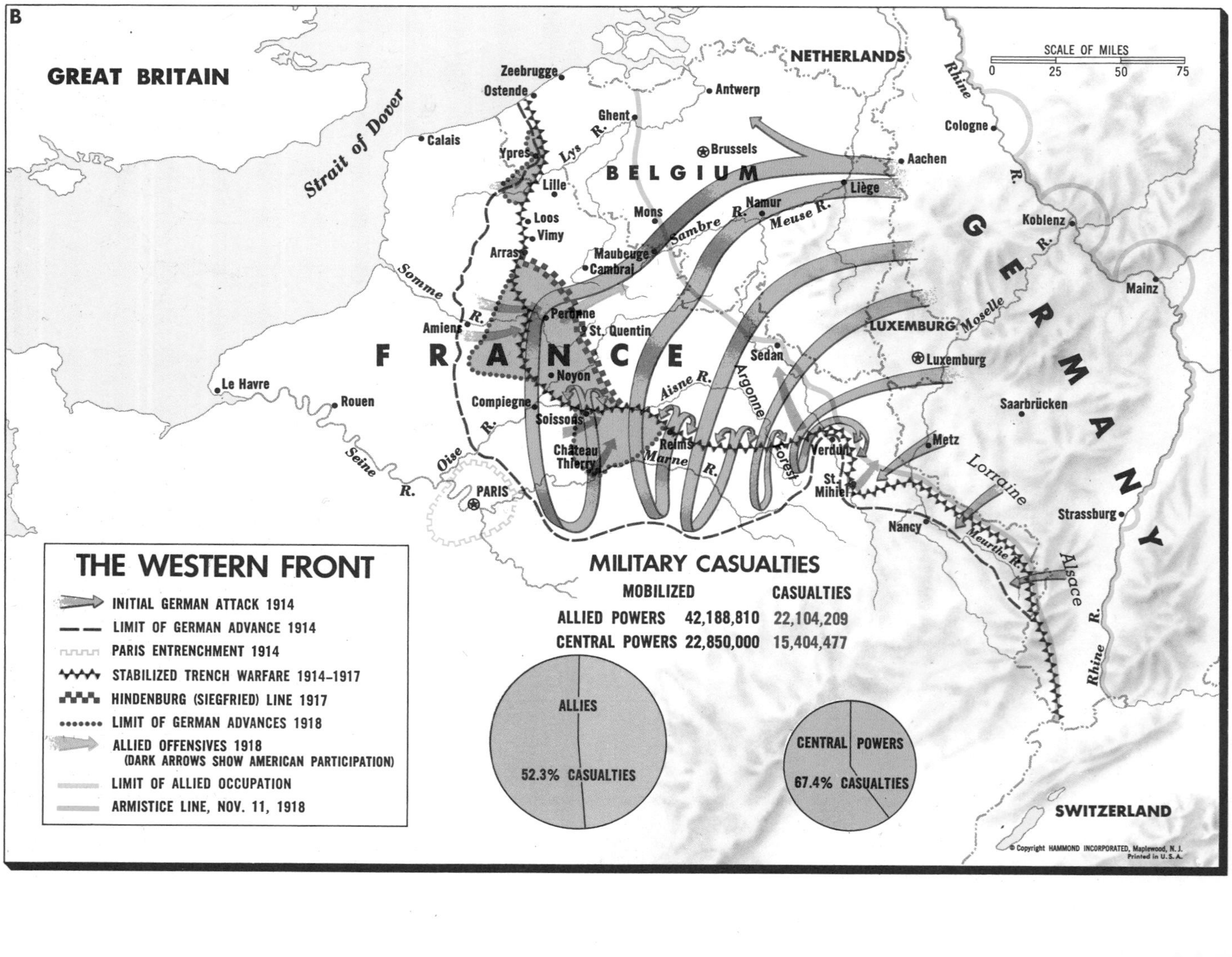

B

GREAT BRITAIN
NETHERLANDS

SCALE OF MILES
0 25 50 75

Zeebrugge
Ostende
Strait of Dover
Calais
Ypres
Lille
Loos
Vimy
Arras

Lys R.
Ghent
• Antwerp
BELGIUM
⊕ Brussels
Mons
Namur
Sambre R.
Meuse R.
Maubeuge
Cambrai

Rhine R.
Cologne
Aachen
Liège
Koblenz

GERMANY

Mainz

Somme R.
Amiens
Perronne
St. Quentin
FRANCE
Noyon
Compiegne
Soissons
Château Thierry
Reims
Marne R.
Argonne Forest
Verdun
St. Mihiel

Sedan
LUXEMBURG
⊕ Luxemburg
Moselle R.
Metz

Saarbrücken

Le Havre
Rouen
Seine R.
Oise R.
Aisne R.

PARIS ⊕

Nancy
Lorraine
Meurthe R.
Strassburg
Alsace
Rhine R.

SWITZERLAND

THE WESTERN FRONT

➙	INITIAL GERMAN ATTACK 1914
‒ ‒ ‒	LIMIT OF GERMAN ADVANCE 1914
∿∿∿	PARIS ENTRENCHMENT 1914
⋀⋀⋀	STABILIZED TRENCH WARFARE 1914–1917
▰▰▰	HINDENBURG (SIEGFRIED) LINE 1917
••••••	LIMIT OF GERMAN ADVANCES 1918
➙	ALLIED OFFENSIVES 1918 (DARK ARROWS SHOW AMERICAN PARTICIPATION)
	LIMIT OF ALLIED OCCUPATION
	ARMISTICE LINE, NOV. 11, 1918

MILITARY CASUALTIES

	MOBILIZED	CASUALTIES
ALLIED POWERS	42,188,810	22,104,209
CENTRAL POWERS	22,850,000	15,404,477

ALLIES
52.3% CASUALTIES

CENTRAL POWERS
67.4% CASUALTIES

© Copyright HAMMOND INCORPORATED, Maplewood, N.J.
Printed in U.S.A.

C

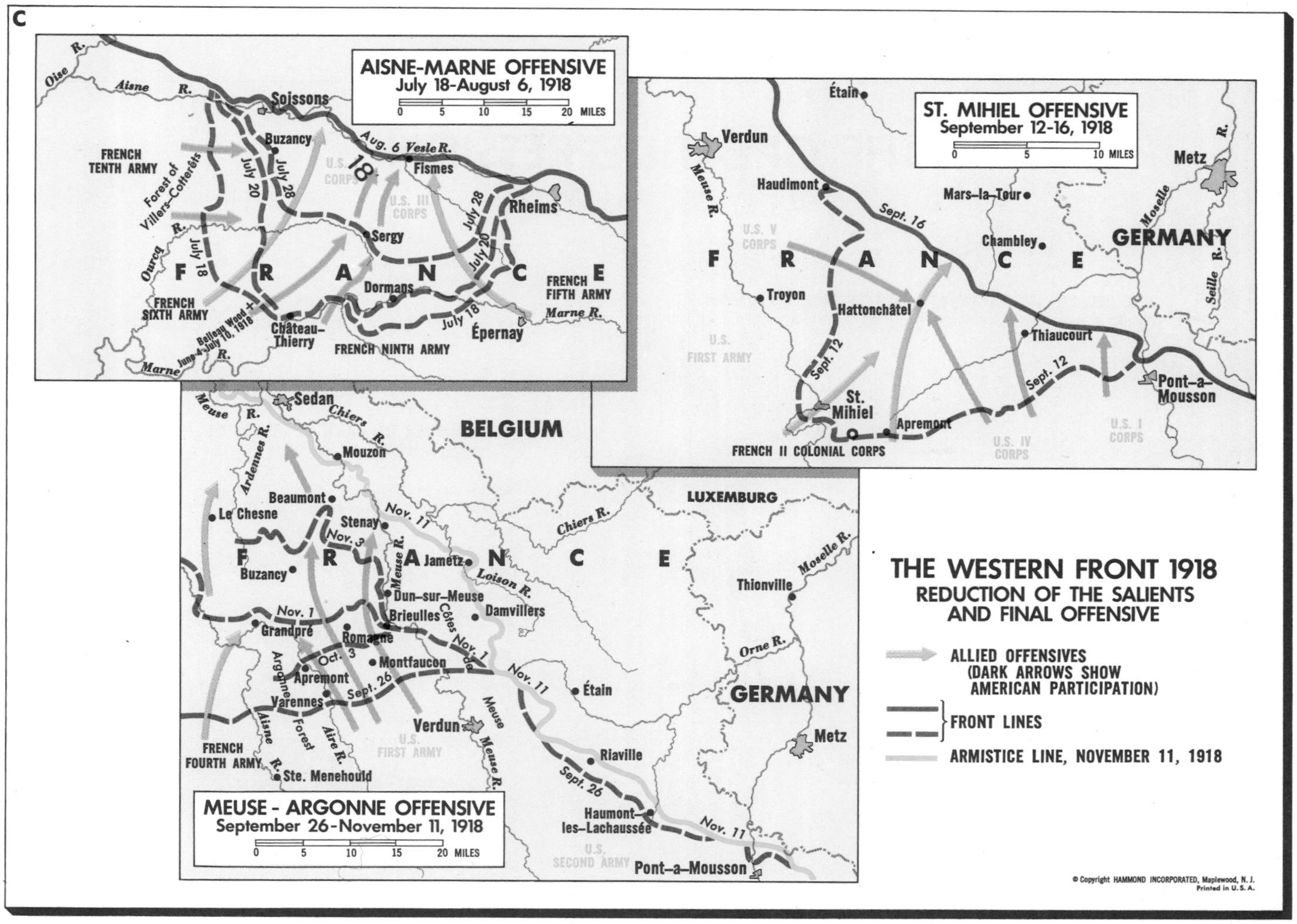

AISNE-MARNE OFFENSIVE
July 18-August 6, 1918
0   5   10   15   20 MILES

Oise R.
Aisne R.
Soissons
Buzancy
FRENCH TENTH ARMY
Aug. 6 Vesle R.
July 26
July 20
Fismes
U.S. CORPS 18
U.S. III CORPS
Rheims
Forest of Villers-Cotterêts
Ourcq R.
July 18
July 28
July 20
Sergy
F R A N C E
FRENCH FIFTH ARMY
FRENCH SIXTH ARMY
Dormans
July 18
Belleau Wood June 4-July 10, 1918
Château-Thierry
Épernay
Marne R.
Marne R.
FRENCH NINTH ARMY

ST. MIHIEL OFFENSIVE
September 12-16, 1918
0   5   10 MILES

Étain
Verdun
Metz
Meuse R.
Haudimont
Sept. 16
Mars-la-Tour
Chambley
GERMANY
Moselle R.
U.S. V CORPS
F R A N C E
Seille R.
Troyon
Hattonchâtel
Thiaucourt
U.S. FIRST ARMY
Sept. 12
Sept. 16
Sept. 12
St. Mihiel
Apremont
Pont-a-Mousson
FRENCH II COLONIAL CORPS
U.S. IV CORPS
U.S. I CORPS

Meuse R.
Sedan
Chiers R.
BELGIUM
LUXEMBURG
Mouzon
Chiers R.
Le Chesne
Beaumont
Nov. 11
Stenay
Nov. 3
F R A N C E
Jametz
Loison R.
Thionville
Moselle R.
Buzancy
Meuse R.
Dun-sur-Meuse
Damvillers
GERMANY
Nov. 1
Grandpré
Brieulles
Nov. 1
Orne R.
Romagne
Côtes
Étain
Argonne Forest
Oct. 3
Montfaucon
Metz
Apremont
Sept. 26
Varennes
Nov. 11
Aire R.
Aisne R.
Verdun
Riaville
FRENCH FOURTH ARMY
U.S. FIRST ARMY
Meuse R.
Ste. Menehould
Sept. 26

MEUSE - ARGONNE OFFENSIVE
September 26-November 11, 1918
0   5   10   15   20 MILES

Haumont les-Lachaussée
Nov. 11
U.S. SECOND ARMY
Pont-a-Mousson

THE WESTERN FRONT 1918
REDUCTION OF THE SALIENTS AND FINAL OFFENSIVE

→ ALLIED OFFENSIVES (DARK ARROWS SHOW AMERICAN PARTICIPATION)

━━ FRONT LINES

- - - ARMISTICE LINE, NOVEMBER 11, 1918

© Copyright HAMMOND INCORPORATED, Maplewood, N.J.
Printed in U.S.A.

D

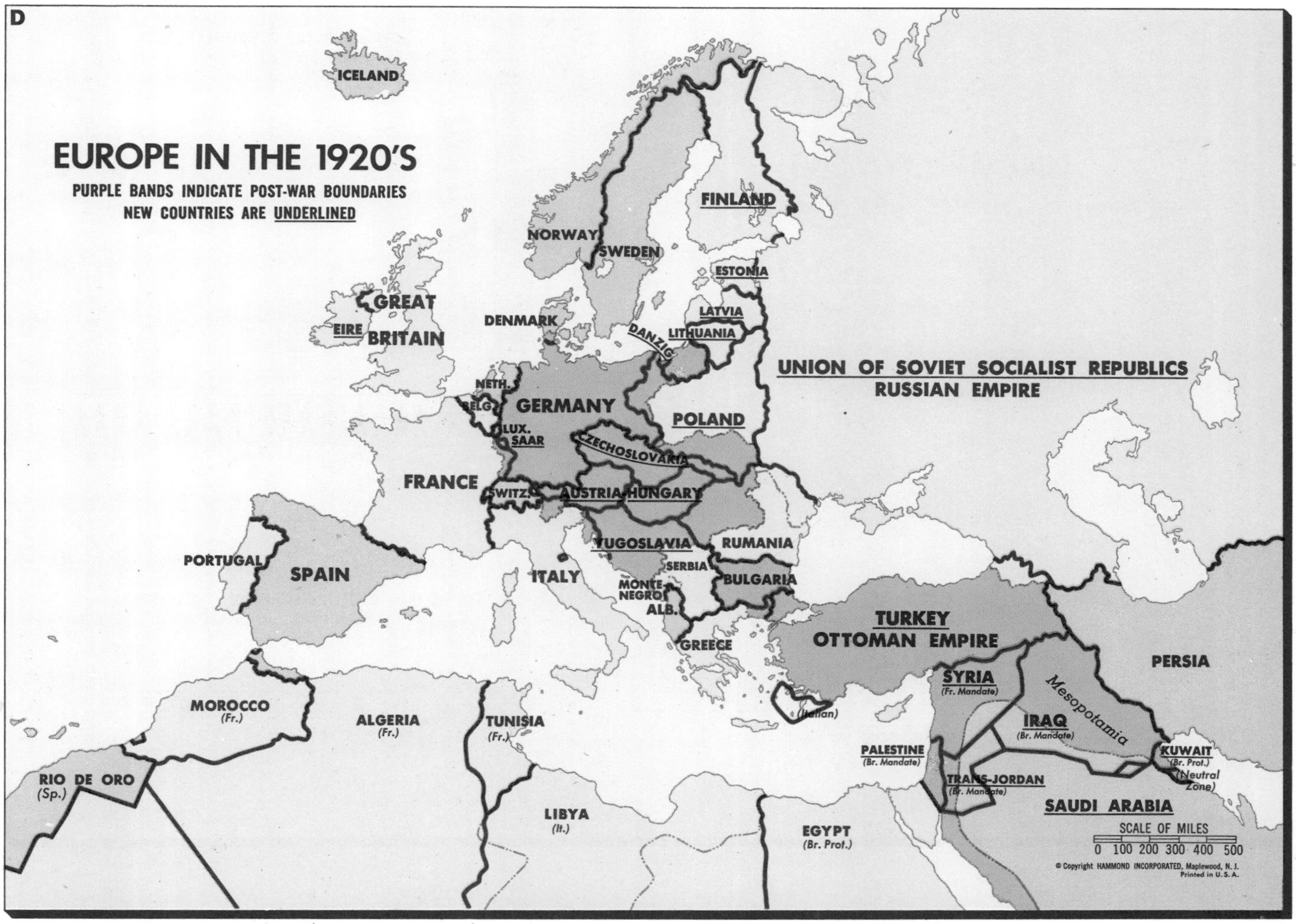

EUROPE IN THE 1920'S

PURPLE BANDS INDICATE POST-WAR BOUNDARIES
NEW COUNTRIES ARE UNDERLINED

ICELAND

FINLAND
NORWAY
SWEDEN
ESTONIA
GREAT BRITAIN
EIRE
DENMARK
LATVIA
LITHUANIA
DANZIG

UNION OF SOVIET SOCIALIST REPUBLICS
RUSSIAN EMPIRE

NETH.
BELG.
GERMANY
POLAND
LUX.
SAAR
CZECHOSLOVAKIA
FRANCE
SWITZ.
AUSTRIA-HUNGARY
YUGOSLAVIA
RUMANIA
SERBIA
PORTUGAL
ITALY
MONTE-NEGRO
ALB.
BULGARIA
SPAIN
GREECE
TURKEY
OTTOMAN EMPIRE
PERSIA
SYRIA (Fr. Mandate)
Mesopotamia
MOROCCO (Fr.)
ALGERIA (Fr.)
TUNISIA (Fr.)
IRAQ (Br. Mandate)
KUWAIT (Br. Prot.) (Neutral Zone)
PALESTINE (Br. Mandate)
RIO DE ORO (Sp.)
LIBYA (It.)
EGYPT (Br. Prot.)
TRANS-JORDAN (Br. Mandate)
SAUDI ARABIA

SCALE OF MILES
0 100 200 300 400 500

© Copyright HAMMOND INCORPORATED, Maplewood, N.J.
Printed in U.S.A.

A

THE GREAT DEPRESSION

THE DECLINE AND RECOVERY OF THE NATIONAL ECONOMY

IN BILLIONS OF DOLLARS

TOTAL GROSS NATIONAL PRODUCT

PERSONAL INCOME

THE GREAT DEPRESSION

NUMBER OF BANK SUSPENSIONS 1919–1933

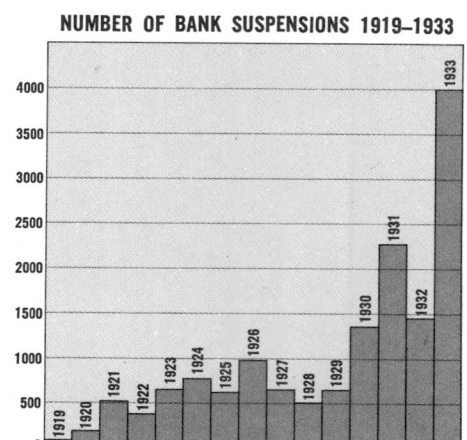

UNEMPLOYMENT

THE UNEMPLOYED AS A PERCENT OF THE CIVILIAN LABOR FORCE

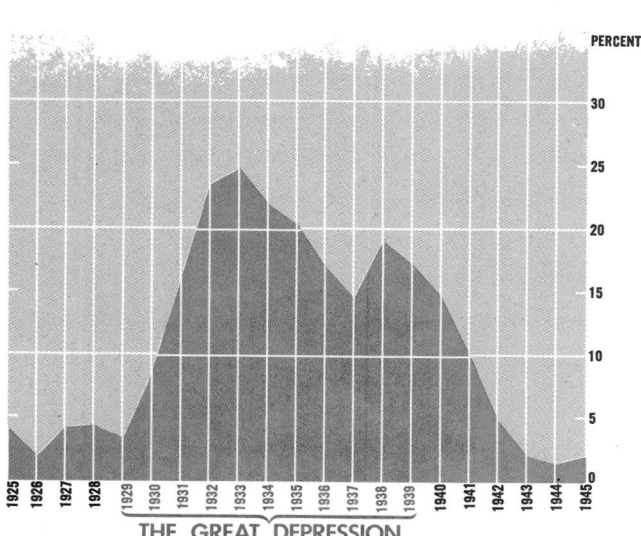

PERCENT

THE GREAT DEPRESSION

HOW U.S. TOTAL PERSONAL INCOME WAS DIVIDED IN 1929

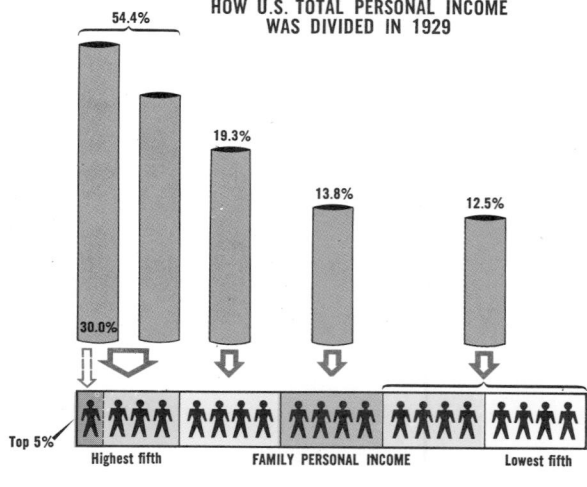

54.4%

30.0%

19.3%

13.8%

12.5%

Top 5%

Highest fifth

FAMILY PERSONAL INCOME

Lowest fifth

HOURS WORKED IN MANUFACTURING (1925–1945)
(WEEKLY AVERAGE)

HOURS

Source: *Historical Statistics of the United States*

THE GREAT DEPRESSION
SPECULATION IN THE STOCK MARKET

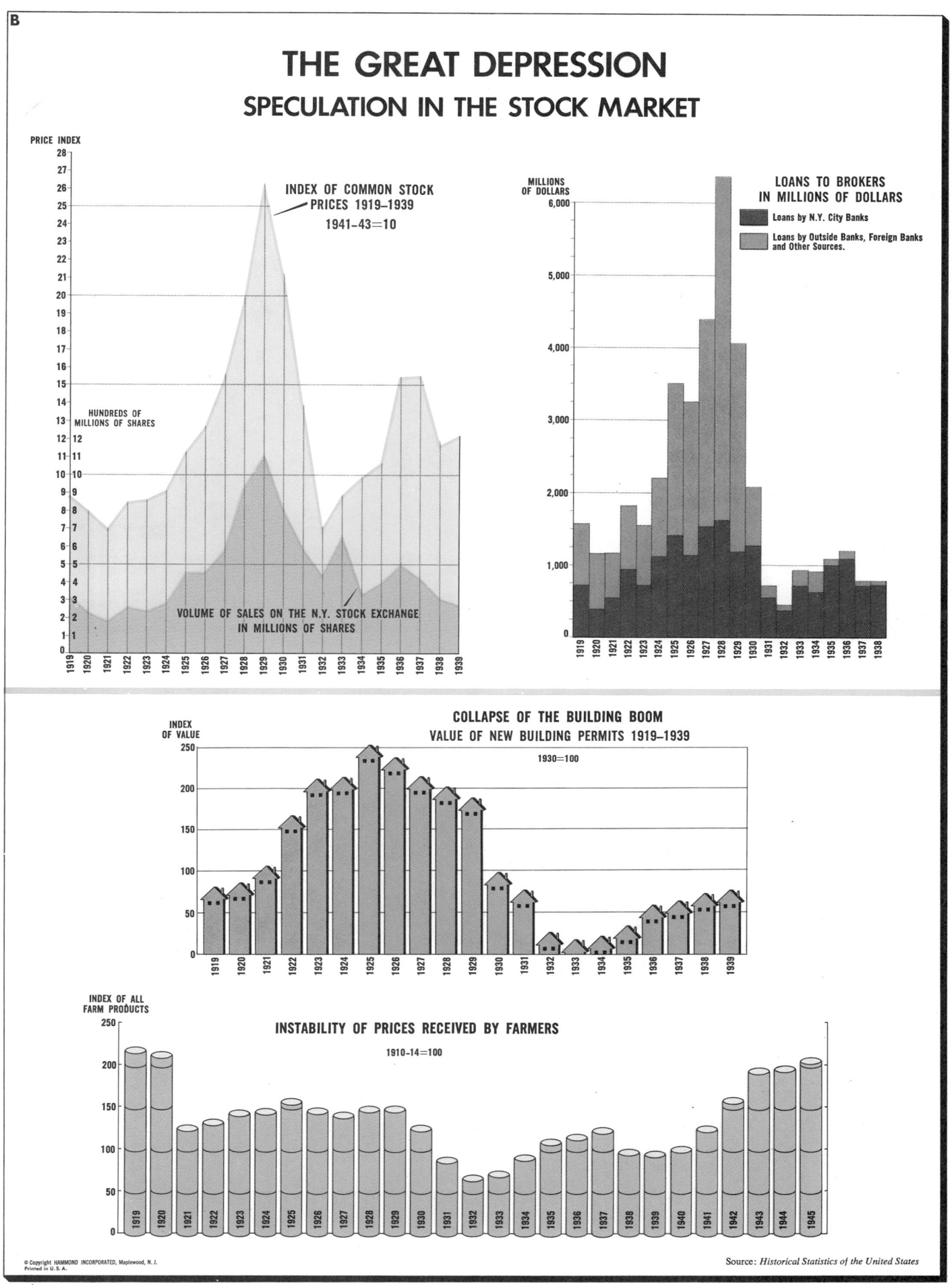

INDEX OF COMMON STOCK PRICES 1919–1939
1941–43=10

VOLUME OF SALES ON THE N.Y. STOCK EXCHANGE IN MILLIONS OF SHARES

LOANS TO BROKERS IN MILLIONS OF DOLLARS
- Loans by N.Y. City Banks
- Loans by Outside Banks, Foreign Banks and Other Sources.

COLLAPSE OF THE BUILDING BOOM
VALUE OF NEW BUILDING PERMITS 1919–1939
1930=100

INSTABILITY OF PRICES RECEIVED BY FARMERS
1910–14=100

Source: *Historical Statistics of the United States*

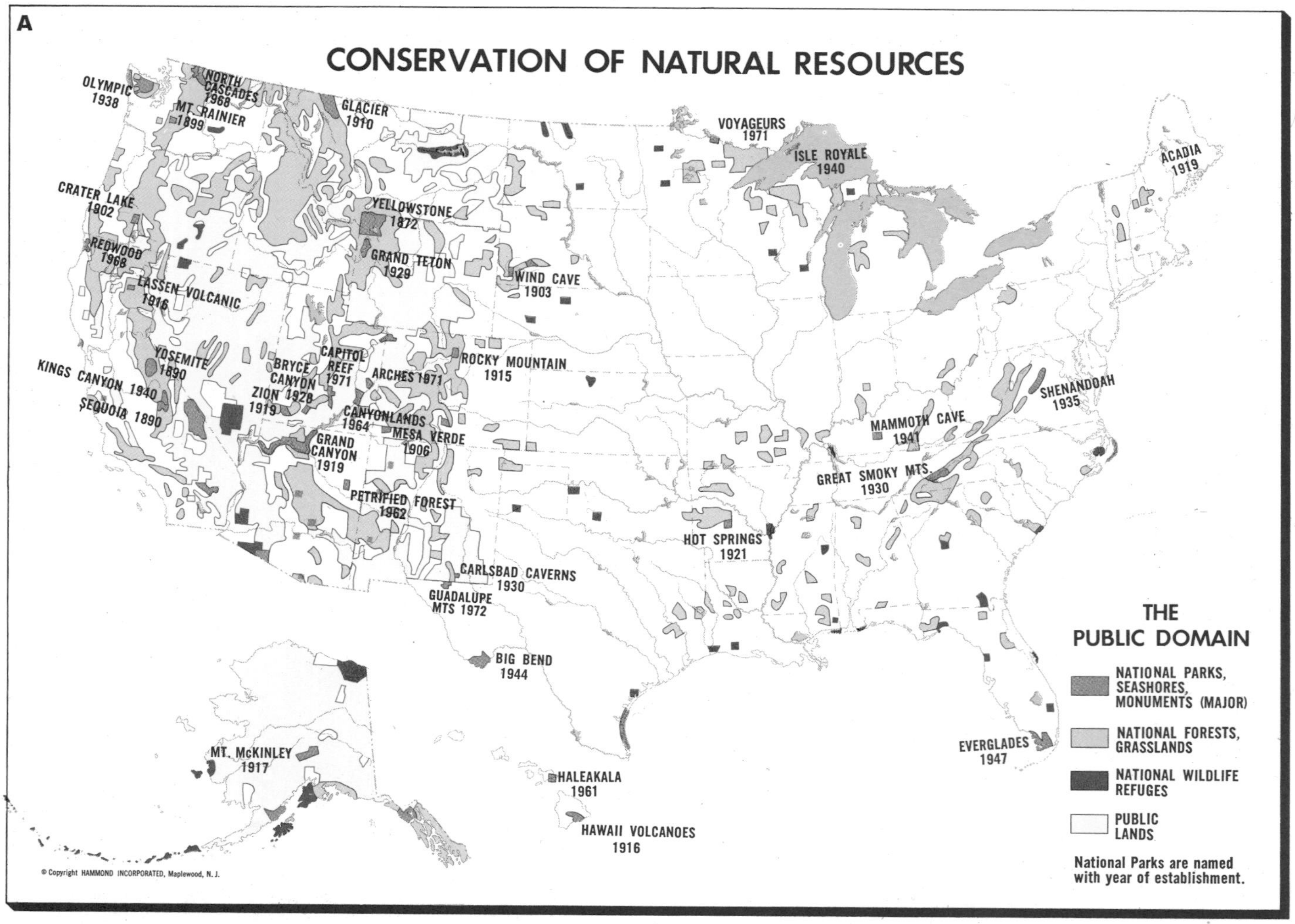

A

CONSERVATION OF NATURAL RESOURCES

OLYMPIC 1938
NORTH CASCADES 1968
MT. RAINIER 1899
GLACIER 1910
VOYAGEURS 1971
ISLE ROYALE 1940
ACADIA 1919
CRATER LAKE 1902
YELLOWSTONE 1872
REDWOOD 1968
GRAND TETON 1929
WIND CAVE 1903
LASSEN VOLCANIC 1916
SHENANDOAH 1935
YOSEMITE 1890
BRYCE CANYON 1971
CAPITOL REEF 1971
ARCHES 1971
ROCKY MOUNTAIN 1915
KINGS CANYON 1940
ZION 1928 1919
CANYONLANDS 1964
MESA VERDE 1906
MAMMOTH CAVE 1941
SEQUOIA 1890
GRAND CANYON 1919
GREAT SMOKY MTS. 1930
PETRIFIED FOREST 1962
HOT SPRINGS 1921
CARLSBAD CAVERNS 1930
GUADALUPE MTS 1972
BIG BEND 1944
MT. McKINLEY 1917
HALEAKALA 1961
EVERGLADES 1947
HAWAII VOLCANOES 1916

© Copyright HAMMOND INCORPORATED, Maplewood, N. J.

THE PUBLIC DOMAIN

- NATIONAL PARKS, SEASHORES, MONUMENTS (MAJOR)
- NATIONAL FORESTS, GRASSLANDS
- NATIONAL WILDLIFE REFUGES
- PUBLIC LANDS

National Parks are named with year of establishment.

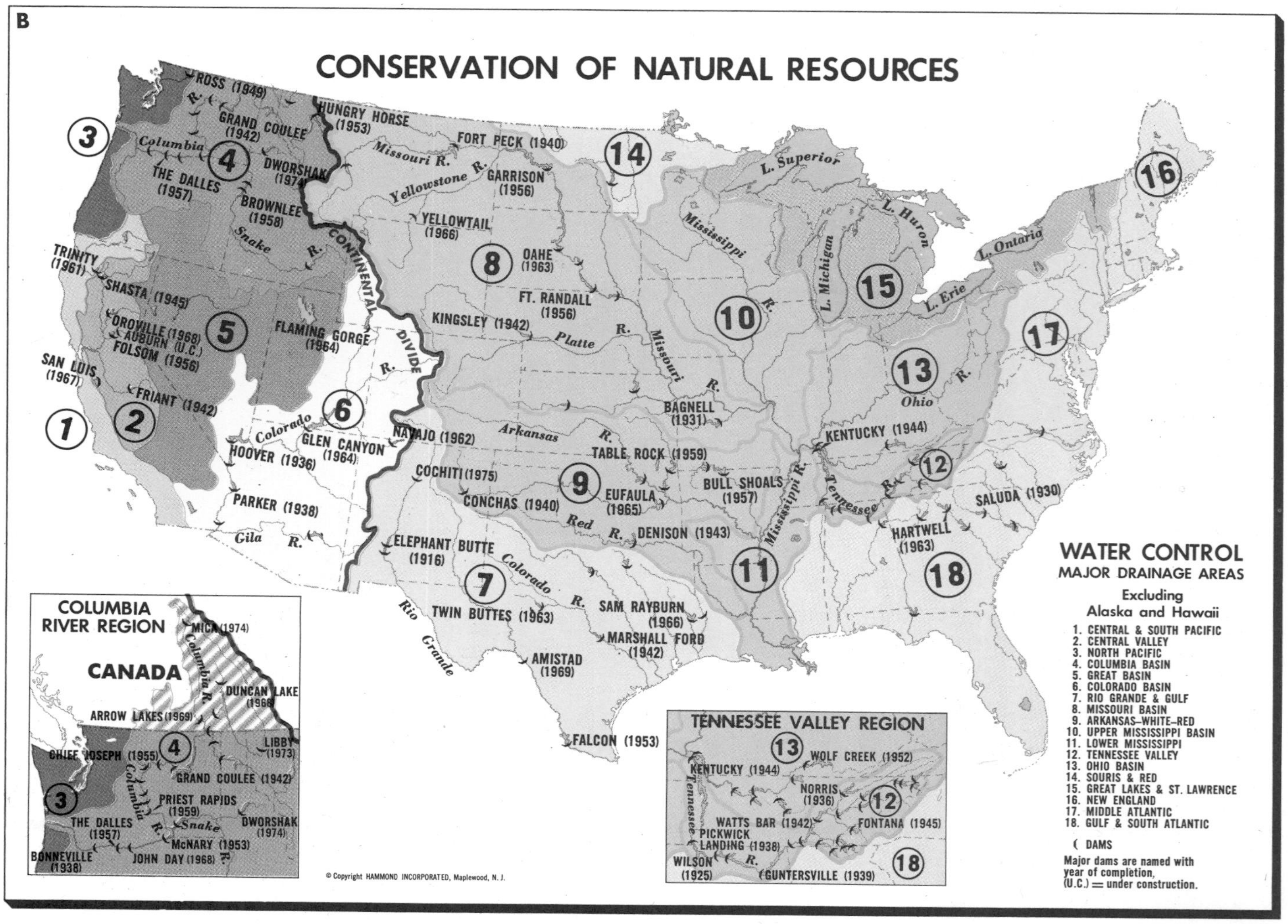

B

CONSERVATION OF NATURAL RESOURCES

ROSS (1949)
GRAND COULEE (1942)
HUNGRY HORSE (1953)
FORT PECK (1940)
③
④
THE DALLES (1957)
DWORSHAK (1974)
Columbia
Missouri R.
Yellowstone R.
GARRISON (1956)
⑭
L. Superior
⑯
BROWNLEE (1958)
YELLOWTAIL (1966)
Mississippi
L. Huron
TRINITY (1961)
Snake R.
CONTINENTAL
OAHE (1963)
⑧
L. Ontario
SHASTA (1945)
L. Michigan
⑮
L. Erie
OROVILLE (1968)
AUBURN (U.C.)
FOLSOM (1956)
FLAMING GORGE (1964)
⑤
FT. RANDALL (1956)
KINGSLEY (1942)
R.
⑩
⑰
SAN LUIS (1967)
DIVIDE
Platte
R.
Missouri
⑬
FRIANT (1942)
R.
BAGNELL (1931)
Ohio
⑥
NAVAJO (1962)
Arkansas
R.
KENTUCKY (1944)
①
②
Colorado
GLEN CANYON (1964)
TABLE ROCK (1959)
⑫
HOOVER (1936)
COCHITI (1975)
EUFAULA (1965)
BULL SHOALS (1957)
Tennessee R.
SALUDA (1930)
PARKER (1938)
CONCHAS (1940)
⑨
DENISON (1943)
Mississippi R.
Gila R.
Red R.
HARTWELL (1963)
ELEPHANT BUTTE (1916)
Colorado R.
⑪
⑱
⑦
SAM RAYBURN (1966)
TWIN BUTTES (1963)
MARSHALL FORD (1942)
Rio Grande
AMISTAD (1969)
FALCON (1953)

COLUMBIA RIVER REGION

MICA (1974)
CANADA
Columbia R.
DUNCAN LAKE (1968)
ARROW LAKES (1969)
LIBBY (1973)
CHIEF JOSEPH (1955)
④
GRAND COULEE (1942)
③
PRIEST RAPIDS (1959)
DWORSHAK (1974)
THE DALLES (1957)
Snake R.
Columbia R.
McNARY (1953)
BONNEVILLE (1938)
JOHN DAY (1968)

TENNESSEE VALLEY REGION

⑬
WOLF CREEK (1952)
KENTUCKY (1944)
NORRIS (1936)
⑫
Tennessee
WATTS BAR (1942)
FONTANA (1945)
PICKWICK LANDING (1938)
WILSON (1925)
R.
GUNTERSVILLE (1939)
⑱

© Copyright HAMMOND INCORPORATED, Maplewood, N. J.

WATER CONTROL
MAJOR DRAINAGE AREAS
Excluding Alaska and Hawaii

1. CENTRAL & SOUTH PACIFIC
2. CENTRAL VALLEY
3. NORTH PACIFIC
4. COLUMBIA BASIN
5. GREAT BASIN
6. COLORADO BASIN
7. RIO GRANDE & GULF
8. MISSOURI BASIN
9. ARKANSAS–WHITE–RED
10. UPPER MISSISSIPPI BASIN
11. LOWER MISSISSIPPI
12. TENNESSEE VALLEY
13. OHIO BASIN
14. SOURIS & RED
15. GREAT LAKES & ST. LAWRENCE
16. NEW ENGLAND
17. MIDDLE ATLANTIC
18. GULF & SOUTH ATLANTIC

(DAMS

Major dams are named with year of completion.
(U.C.) = under construction.

CONSERVATION OF NATURAL RESOURCES

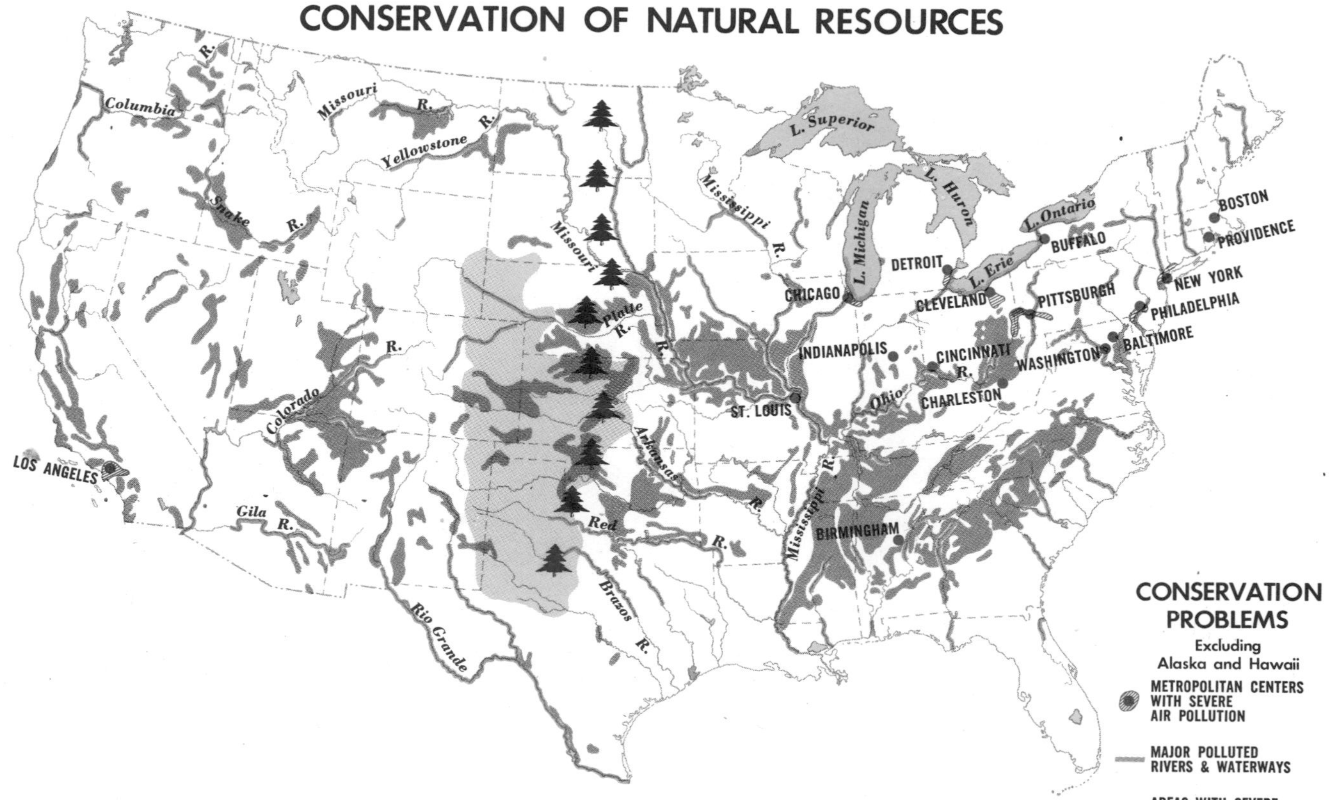

CONSERVATION PROBLEMS

Excluding Alaska and Hawaii

METROPOLITAN CENTERS WITH SEVERE AIR POLLUTION

MAJOR POLLUTED RIVERS & WATERWAYS

AREAS WITH SEVERE SOIL EROSION

"DUST BOWL" OF THE GREAT PLAINS (1931–38)

SHELTERBELT ZONE

FORESTS–1620

VIRGIN FOREST

FORESTS–TODAY

VIRGIN FOREST

FOREST AND CUT-OVER LAND

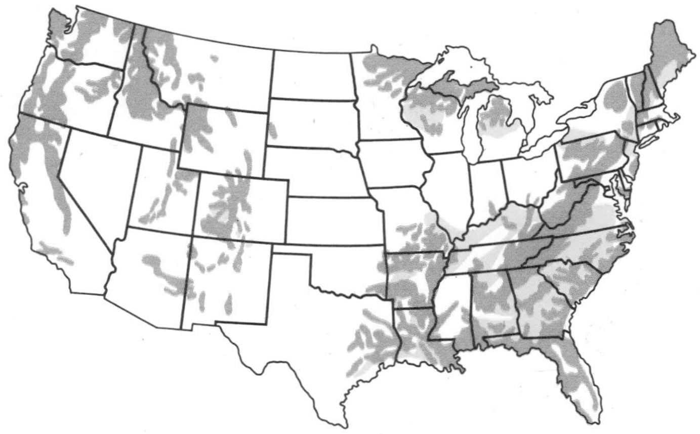

A

GERMAN EXPANSION 1935-1939*

SCALE OF MILES
0 100 200 300 400

- Germany 1933
- Area gained by Plebiscite 1935
- Areas annexed 1938
- Area annexed 1939
- German Protectorates

*To Invasion of Poland Sept. 1, 1939

UNION OF SOVIET SOCIALIST REPUBLICS

FINLAND

NORWAY

SWEDEN

ESTONIA

LATVIA

LITHUANIA

UNITED KINGDOM

GREAT BRITAIN

NORTH SEA

DENMARK

NO. IRELAND

IRELAND

BALTIC SEA

MEMEL To Germany 1939

DANZIG

East Prussia

Polish Corridor

NETHERLANDS

BELGIUM

LUX.

Rhineland

Saar

Rhineland remilitarized 1936

Berlin

GERMANY

POLAND

BOHEMIA & MORAVIA German Protectorate and occupation 1939

SAAR To Germany 1935

SUDETENLAND To Germany 1938

Sudetenland BOHEMIA & MORAVIA CZECHOSLOVAKIA

SLOVAKIA

To Hung. 1939

FRANCE

Munich

AUSTRIA

HUNGARY

SLOVAKIA German Protectorate 1939

SWITZ.

AUSTRIA To Germany 1938

RUMANIA

ATLANTIC OCEAN

PORTUGAL

SPAIN

Civil War 1936-1939

ITALY

ADRIATIC SEA

YUGOSLAVIA

Danube R.

BLACK SEA

BULGARIA

MEDITERRANEAN SEA

ALBANIA (To Italy 1939)

GREECE

TURKEY

© Copyright HAMMOND INCORPORATED, Maplewood, N.J.
Printed in U.S.A.

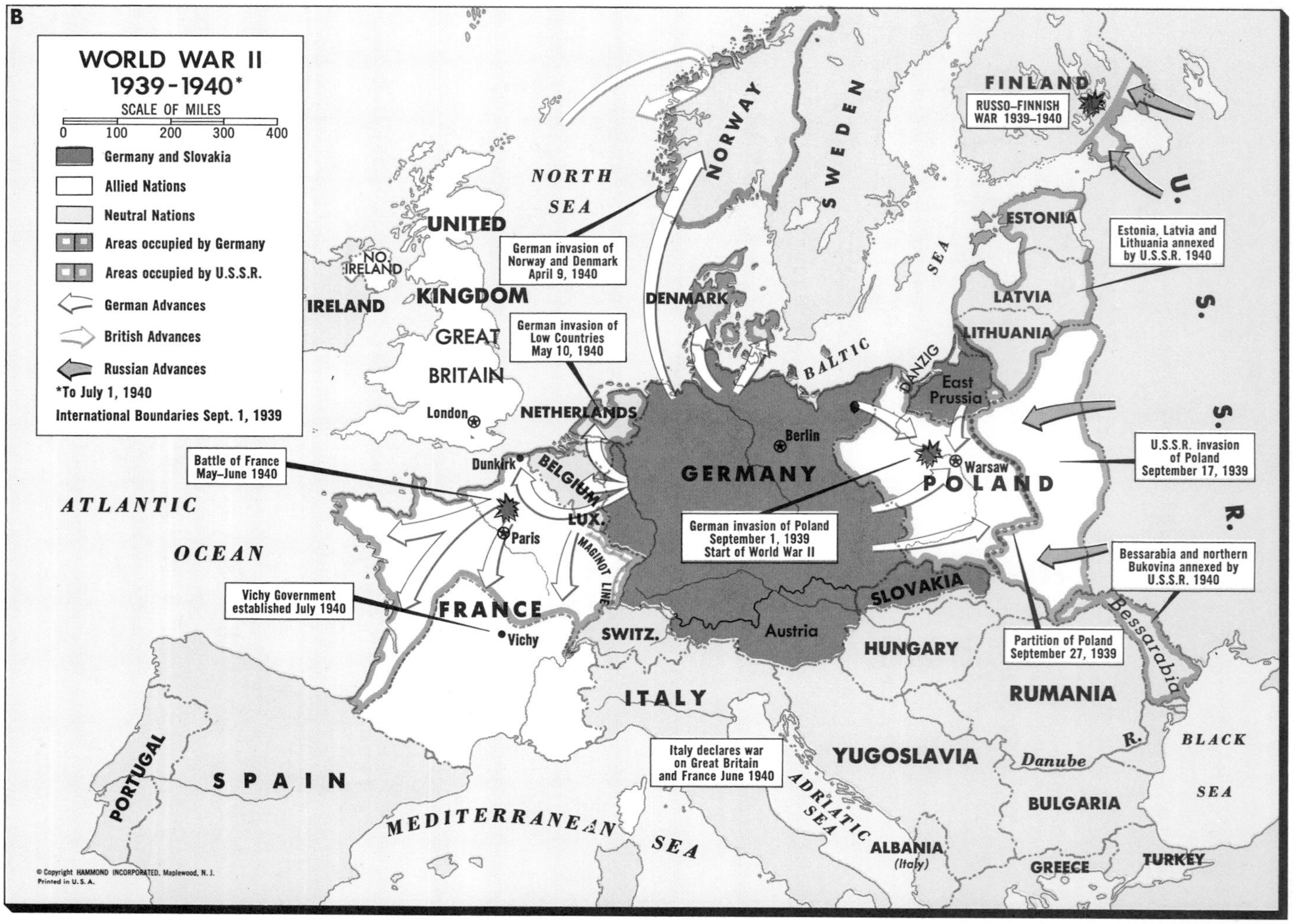

B

WORLD WAR II 1939-1940*

SCALE OF MILES
0 100 200 300 400

- Germany and Slovakia
- Allied Nations
- Neutral Nations
- Areas occupied by Germany
- Areas occupied by U.S.S.R.
- German Advances
- British Advances
- Russian Advances

*To July 1, 1940
International Boundaries Sept. 1, 1939

FINLAND

RUSSO–FINNISH WAR 1939–1940

U.

NORTH SEA

NORWAY

SWEDEN

ESTONIA

Estonia, Latvia and Lithuania annexed by U.S.S.R. 1940

S.

UNITED KINGDOM

NO. IRELAND

IRELAND

GREAT BRITAIN

German invasion of Norway and Denmark April 9, 1940

DENMARK

BALTIC SEA

LATVIA

LITHUANIA

DANZIG

East Prussia

S.

German invasion of Low Countries May 10, 1940

London

NETHERLANDS

BELGIUM

LUX.

Berlin

GERMANY

Warsaw

POLAND

U.S.S.R. invasion of Poland September 17, 1939

R.

Battle of France May–June 1940

Dunkirk

MAGINOT LINE

Paris

German invasion of Poland September 1, 1939 Start of World War II

Bessarabia

ATLANTIC OCEAN

Vichy Government established July 1940

SLOVAKIA

Bessarabia and northern Bukovina annexed by U.S.S.R. 1940

FRANCE

Vichy

SWITZ.

Austria

HUNGARY

Partition of Poland September 27, 1939

ITALY

RUMANIA

SPAIN

PORTUGAL

Italy declares war on Great Britain and France June 1940

YUGOSLAVIA

Danube R.

BLACK SEA

MEDITERRANEAN SEA

ADRIATIC SEA

BULGARIA

ALBANIA (Italy)

GREECE

TURKEY

© Copyright HAMMOND INCORPORATED, Maplewood, N.J.
Printed in U.S.A.

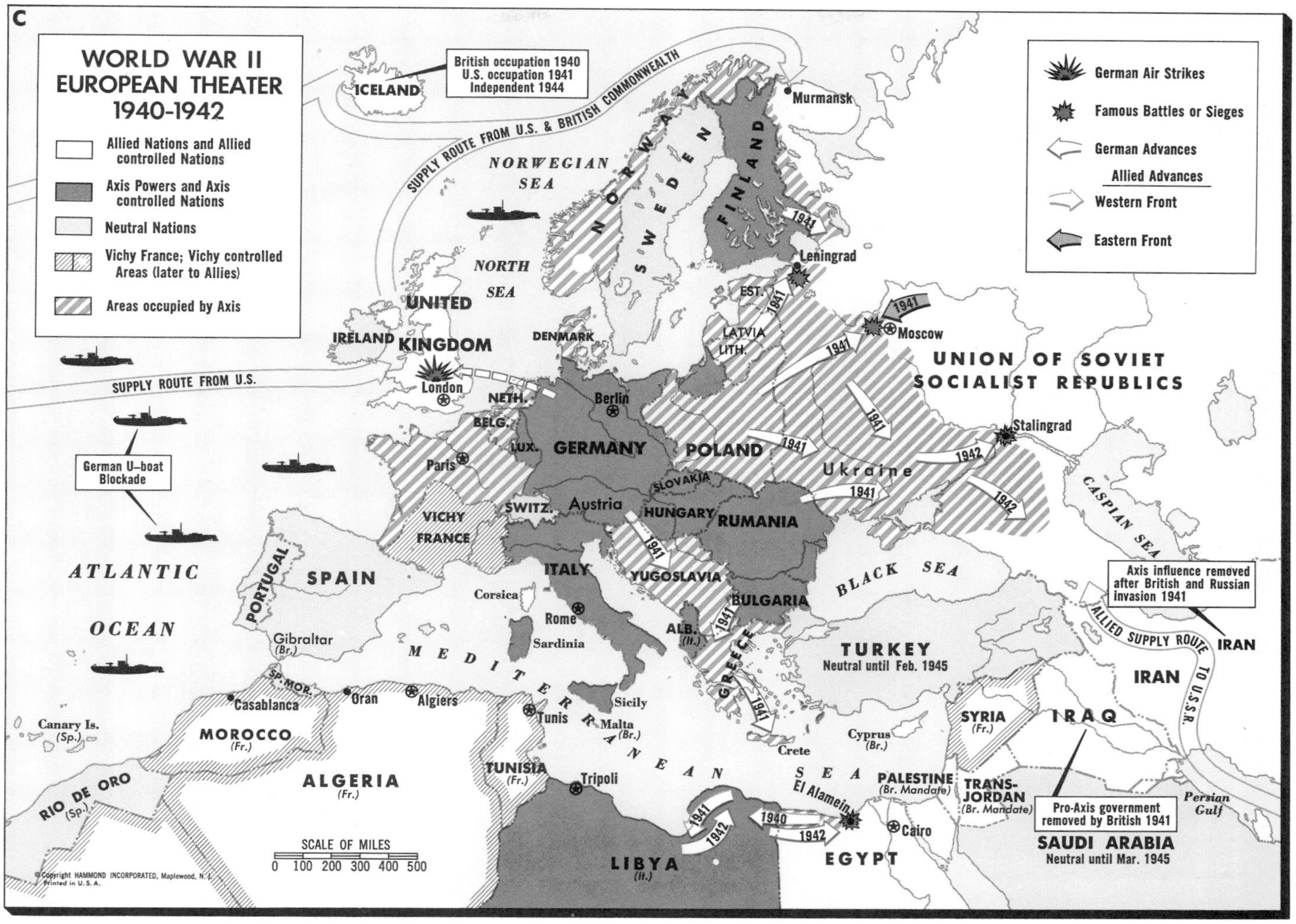

C

WORLD WAR II EUROPEAN THEATER 1940-1942

Allied Nations and Allied controlled Nations

Axis Powers and Axis controlled Nations

Neutral Nations

Vichy France; Vichy controlled Areas (later to Allies)

Areas occupied by Axis

German Air Strikes

Famous Battles or Sieges

German Advances

Allied Advances

Western Front

Eastern Front

British occupation 1940 U.S. occupation 1941 Independent 1944

ICELAND

SUPPLY ROUTE FROM U.S. & BRITISH COMMONWEALTH

Murmansk

NORWEGIAN SEA

NORWAY SWEDEN FINLAND

1941

Leningrad

NORTH SEA

UNITED KINGDOM

IRELAND

DENMARK

EST.

LATVIA LITH.

1941

Moscow

UNION OF SOVIET SOCIALIST REPUBLICS

SUPPLY ROUTE FROM U.S.

London

NETH.

BELG.

Lux.

Berlin

GERMANY

POLAND

1941

1941

Stalingrad

German U-boat Blockade

Paris

SWITZ. Austria

SLOVAKIA

HUNGARY

RUMANIA

Ukraine

1942

1941

1942

CASPIAN SEA

ATLANTIC OCEAN

PORTUGAL SPAIN

VICHY FRANCE

ITALY

YUGOSLAVIA

BULGARIA

BLACK SEA

Axis influence removed after British and Russian invasion 1941

IRAN

Corsica

Rome

Sardinia

ALB. (It.)

GREECE

TURKEY Neutral until Feb. 1945

IRAN

Gibraltar (Br.)

MEDITERRANEAN

Sicily

1941

ALLIED SUPPLY ROUTE TO U.S.S.R.

SP. MOR.

Casablanca

Oran

Algiers

Tunis

Malta (Br.)

Crete

Cyprus (Br.)

SYRIA (Fr.)

IRAQ

Canary Is. (Sp.)

MOROCCO (Fr.)

ALGERIA (Fr.)

TUNISIA (Fr.)

Tripoli

SEA

El Alamein

PALESTINE (Br. Mandate)

TRANS-JORDAN (Br. Mandate)

Persian Gulf

RIO DE ORO (Sp.)

SCALE OF MILES
0 100 200 300 400 500

LIBYA (It.)

Cairo

EGYPT

Pro-Axis government removed by British 1941

SAUDI ARABIA Neutral until Mar. 1945

Copyright HAMMOND INCORPORATED, Maplewood, N.J. Printed in U.S.A.

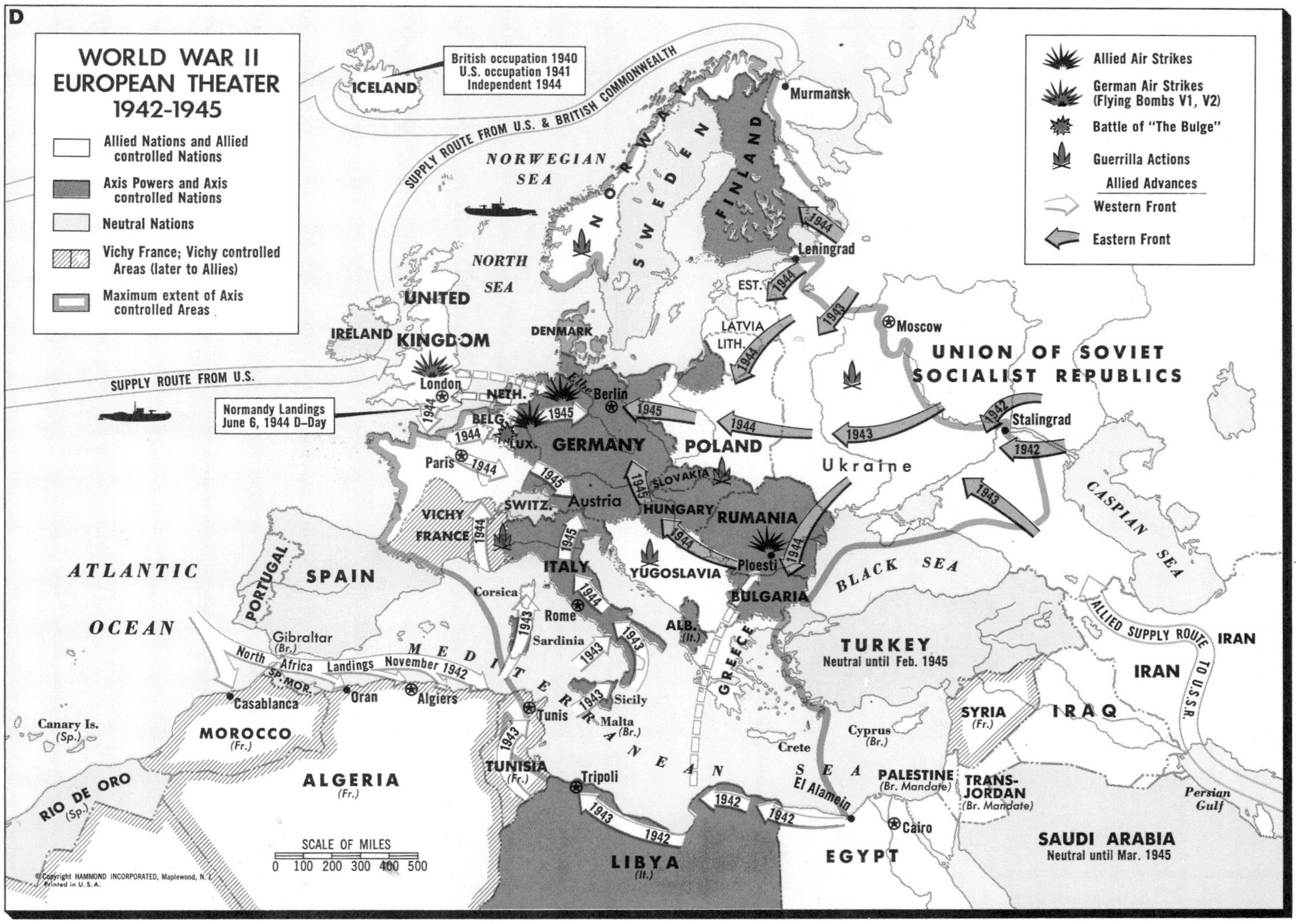

D

WORLD WAR II EUROPEAN THEATER 1942-1945

Allied Nations and Allied controlled Nations

Axis Powers and Axis controlled Nations

Neutral Nations

Vichy France; Vichy controlled Areas (later to Allies)

Maximum extent of Axis controlled Areas

Allied Air Strikes

German Air Strikes (Flying Bombs V1, V2)

Battle of "The Bulge"

Guerrilla Actions

Allied Advances

Western Front

Eastern Front

British occupation 1940 U.S. occupation 1941 Independent 1944

ICELAND

SUPPLY ROUTE FROM U.S. & BRITISH COMMONWEALTH

Murmansk

NORWEGIAN SEA

NORWAY SWEDEN FINLAND

1944

Leningrad

NORTH SEA

UNITED KINGDOM

IRELAND

DENMARK

EST. 1944

LATVIA LITH.

1944

1943

Moscow

UNION OF SOVIET SOCIALIST REPUBLICS

SUPPLY ROUTE FROM U.S.

London

NETH.

BELG.

Lux.

Berlin

1945

1945

GERMANY

POLAND

1945

1944

1943

Stalingrad

Normandy Landings June 6, 1944 D-Day

Paris

1944

1945

SWITZ.

Austria

SLOVAKIA

HUNGARY

RUMANIA

Ukraine

1943

1942

1944

Ploesti

1943

CASPIAN SEA

ATLANTIC OCEAN

PORTUGAL SPAIN

VICHY FRANCE

1944

ITALY

1944

YUGOSLAVIA

BULGARIA

BLACK SEA

IRAN

Corsica

Rome

1943

Sardinia

1943

ALB. (It.)

GREECE

TURKEY Neutral until Feb. 1945

IRAN

Gibraltar (Br.)

North Africa Landings November 1942

MEDITERRANEAN

Sicily

1943

Malta (Br.)

Crete

Cyprus (Br.)

SYRIA (Fr.)

IRAQ

ALLIED SUPPLY ROUTE TO U.S.S.R.

SP. MOR.

Casablanca

Oran

Algiers

Tunis

1943

Canary Is. (Sp.)

MOROCCO (Fr.)

ALGERIA (Fr.)

TUNISIA (Fr.)

Tripoli

1943

SEA

El Alamein

1942

PALESTINE (Br. Mandate)

TRANS-JORDAN (Br. Mandate)

Persian Gulf

RIO DE ORO (Sp.)

SCALE OF MILES
0 100 200 300 400 500

LIBYA (It.)

1942

1942

Cairo

EGYPT

SAUDI ARABIA Neutral until Mar. 1945

Copyright HAMMOND INCORPORATED, Maplewood, N.J. Printed in U.S.A.

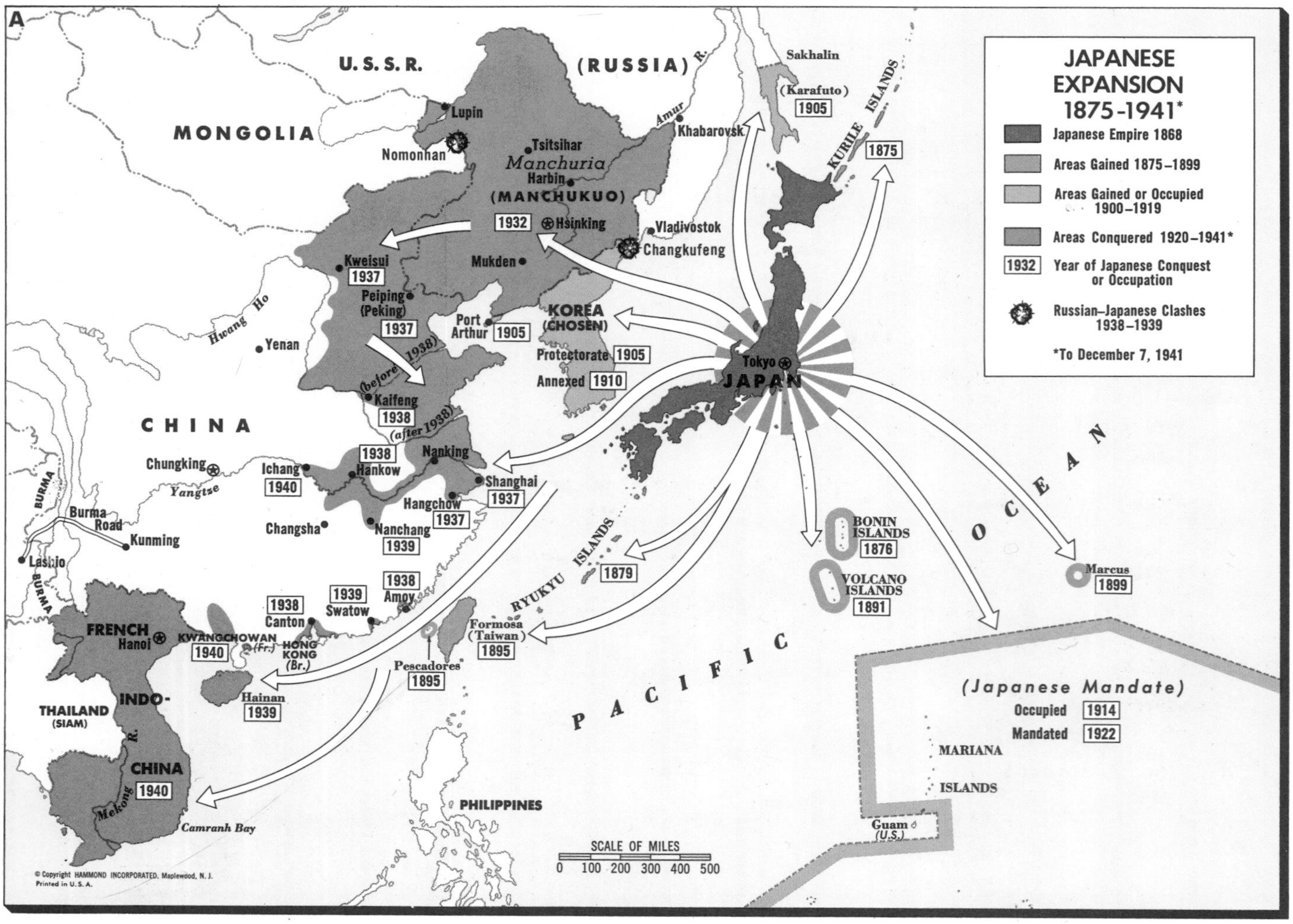

A

JAPANESE EXPANSION 1875-1941*

- Japanese Empire 1868
- Areas Gained 1875–1899
- Areas Gained or Occupied 1900–1919
- Areas Conquered 1920–1941*
- 1932 Year of Japanese Conquest or Occupation
- Russian–Japanese Clashes 1938–1939

*To December 7, 1941

U.S.S.R. (RUSSIA)

MONGOLIA

Lupin
Nomonhan
Tsitsihar
Manchuria
Harbin
(MANCHUKUO)
1932 Hsinking
Mukden
Kweisui 1937
Peiping (Peking) 1937
1938 (before 1938)
Port Arthur 1905
KOREA (CHOSEN)
Protectorate 1905
Annexed 1910
Vladivostok
Changkufeng
Khabarovsk
Amur R.
Sakhalin (Karafuto) 1905
KURILE ISLANDS 1875
Tokyo
JAPAN
Hwang Ho
Yenan
CHINA
Kaifeng 1938 (after 1938)
Nanking 1937
Chungking
Ichang 1940
Yangtze
Hankow 1938
Shanghai 1937
Hangchow 1937
Changsha
Nanchang 1939
RYUKYU ISLANDS 1879
Amoy 1938
1939 1938
Swatow
Canton 1938
Formosa (Taiwan) 1895
Pescadores 1895
BONIN ISLANDS 1876
VOLCANO ISLANDS 1891
Marcus 1899
Burma Road
Lashio
Kunming
BURMA
FRENCH Hanoi
KWANGCHOWAN (Fr.) 1940
HONG KONG (Br.)
Hainan 1939
THAILAND (SIAM)
INDO-CHINA 1940
Mekong R.
Camranh Bay
PHILIPPINES

PACIFIC OCEAN

(Japanese Mandate)
Occupied 1914
Mandated 1922
MARIANA ISLANDS
Guam (U.S.)

SCALE OF MILES
0 100 200 300 400 500

© Copyright HAMMOND INCORPORATED, Maplewood, N.J.
Printed in U.S.A.

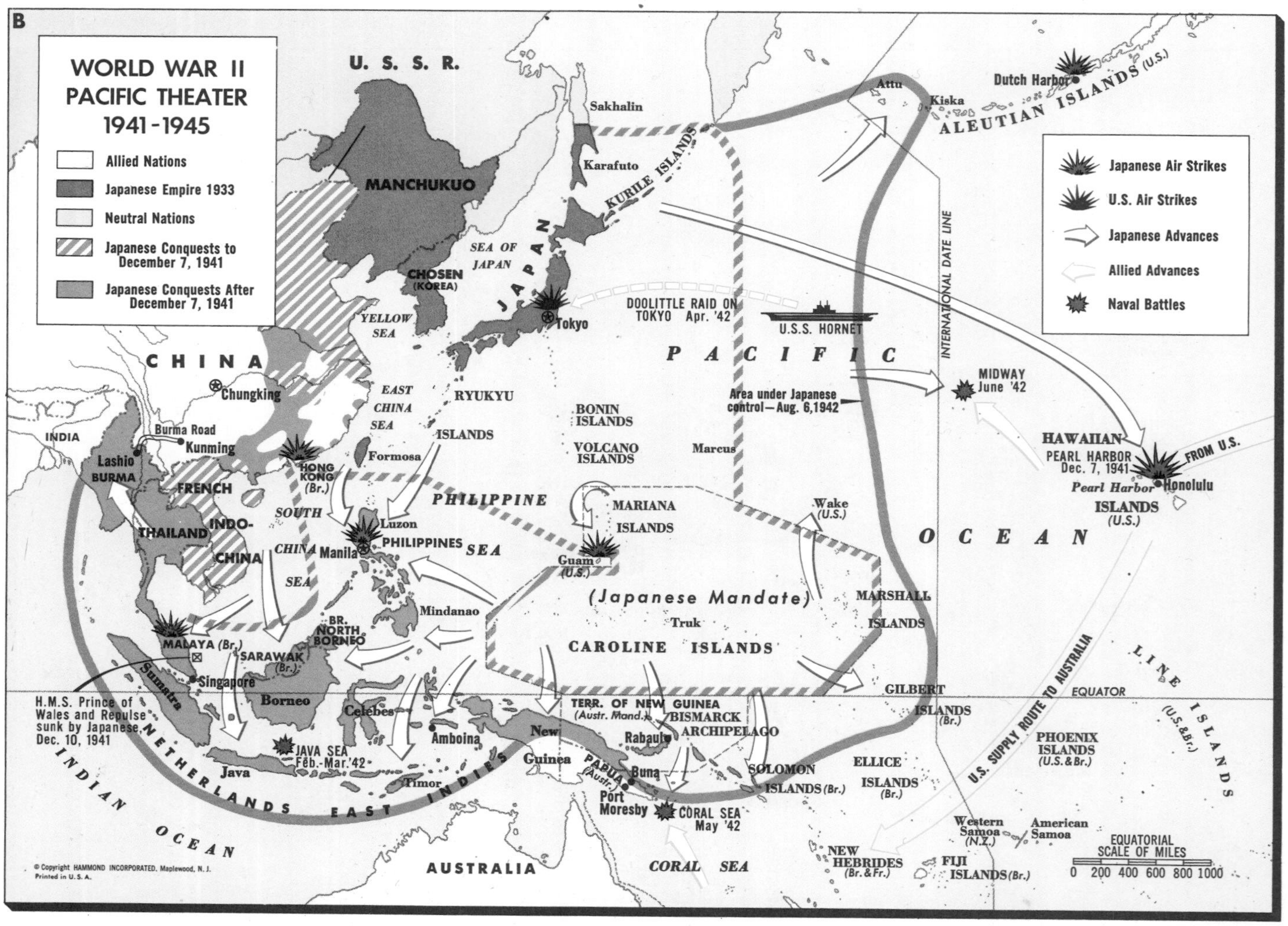

B

WORLD WAR II PACIFIC THEATER 1941-1945

- Allied Nations
- Japanese Empire 1933
- Neutral Nations
- Japanese Conquests to December 7, 1941
- Japanese Conquests After December 7, 1941

- Japanese Air Strikes
- U.S. Air Strikes
- Japanese Advances
- Allied Advances
- Naval Battles

U.S.S.R.
Sakhalin
Karafuto
MANCHUKUO
CHOSEN (KOREA)
SEA OF JAPAN
JAPAN
KURILE ISLANDS
Attu
Kiska
Dutch Harbor (U.S.)
ALEUTIAN ISLANDS
INTERNATIONAL DATE LINE
DOOLITTLE RAID ON TOKYO Apr. '42
Tokyo
U.S.S. HORNET
PACIFIC OCEAN
MIDWAY June '42
YELLOW SEA
CHINA
Chungking
RYUKYU ISLANDS
EAST CHINA SEA
Formosa
BONIN ISLANDS
VOLCANO ISLANDS
Marcus
Area under Japanese control—Aug. 6, 1942
HAWAIIAN PEARL HARBOR Dec. 7, 1941 FROM U.S.
Pearl Harbor Honolulu
ISLANDS (U.S.)
INDIA
Burma Road
Kunming
Lashio
BURMA
HONG KONG (Br.)
SOUTH CHINA SEA
Luzon
Manila
PHILIPPINES
PHILIPPINE SEA
MARIANA ISLANDS
Guam (U.S.)
Wake (U.S.)
FRENCH INDO-CHINA
THAILAND
Mindanao
(Japanese Mandate)
MARSHALL ISLANDS
Truk
CAROLINE ISLANDS
H.M.S. Prince of Wales and Repulse sunk by Japanese Dec. 10, 1941
MALAYA (Br.)
SARAWAK (Br.)
BR. NORTH BORNEO
Singapore
Sumatra
Borneo
Celebes
NETHERLANDS EAST INDIES
JAVA SEA Feb.-Mar. '42
Java
Amboina
Timor
New Guinea
PAPUA (Austr.)
Port Moresby
TERR. OF NEW GUINEA (Austr. Mand.)
Buna
BISMARCK ARCHIPELAGO
Rabaul
SOLOMON ISLANDS (Br.)
CORAL SEA May '42
GILBERT ISLANDS (Br.)
ELLICE ISLANDS (Br.)
EQUATOR
U.S. SUPPLY ROUTE TO AUSTRALIA
PHOENIX ISLANDS (U.S. & Br.)
LINE ISLANDS (U.S. & Br.)
NEW HEBRIDES (Br. & Fr.)
FIJI ISLANDS (Br.)
Western Samoa (N.Z.)
American Samoa (U.S.)
INDIAN OCEAN
AUSTRALIA
CORAL SEA

EQUATORIAL SCALE OF MILES
0 200 400 600 800 1000

© Copyright HAMMOND INCORPORATED, Maplewood, N.J.
Printed in U.S.A.

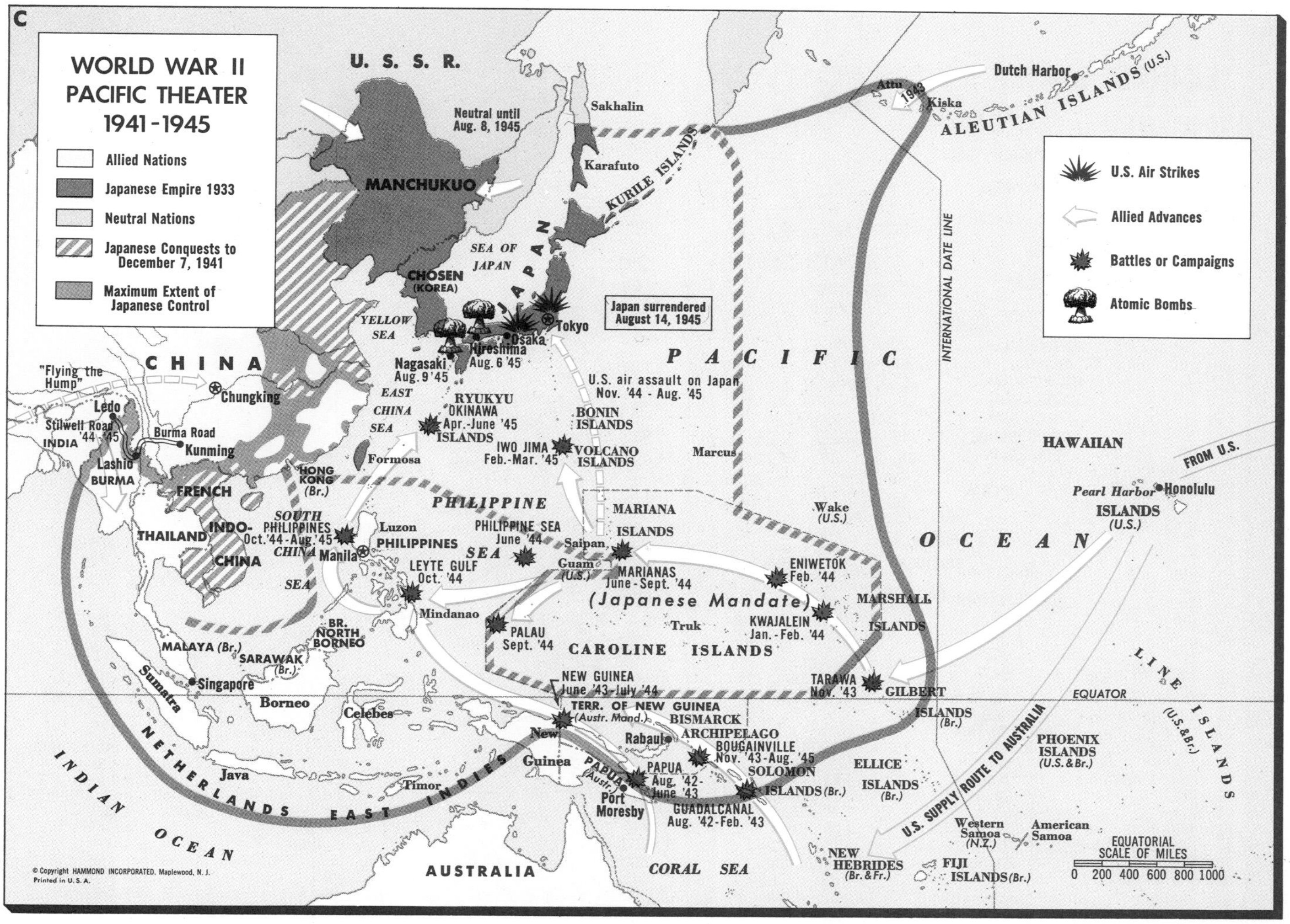

C

WORLD WAR II PACIFIC THEATER 1941-1945

- ☐ Allied Nations
- ■ Japanese Empire 1933
- ☐ Neutral Nations
- ▨ Japanese Conquests to December 7, 1941
- ▤ Maximum Extent of Japanese Control

U.S.S.R.

Neutral until Aug. 8, 1945

Sakhalin

Karafuto

MANCHUKUO

KURILE ISLANDS

SEA OF JAPAN

JAPAN

CHOSEN (KOREA)

CHINA

YELLOW SEA

Japan surrendered August 14, 1945

Tokyo

Osaka

Hiroshima Aug. 6 '45

Nagasaki Aug. 9 '45

EAST CHINA SEA

U.S. air assault on Japan Nov. '44 - Aug. '45

P A C I F I C

"Flying the Hump"

Ledo
Stilwell Road INDIA '44-'45
Lashio
Kunming
BURMA
Burma Road

Chungking

RYUKYU OKINAWA Apr.-June '45 ISLANDS

BONIN ISLANDS

IWO JIMA Feb.-Mar. '45

VOLCANO ISLANDS

Marcus

HAWAIIAN

FROM U.S.

FRENCH INDO- CHINA

THAILAND

HONG KONG (Br.)

Formosa

PHILIPPINE SEA

MARIANA ISLANDS

Wake (U.S.)

Pearl Harbor Honolulu

O C E A N

ISLANDS (U.S.)

SOUTH CHINA SEA

Luzon

PHILIPPINES

Manila

LEYTE GULF Oct. '44

Saipan

Guam (U.S.)

MARIANAS June-Sept. '44

ENIWETOK Feb. '44

Mindanao

Truk

KWAJALEIN Jan.- Feb. '44

MARSHALL ISLANDS

SOUTH PHILIPPINES Oct.'44-Aug.'45

MALAYA (Br.)

BR. NORTH BORNEO

SARAWAK (Br.)

PALAU Sept. '44

CAROLINE ISLANDS

(Japanese Mandate)

EQUATOR

LINE ISLANDS (U.S.&Br.)

Sumatra

Singapore

Borneo

Celebes

NEW GUINEA June '43-July '44

TERR. OF NEW GUINEA (Austr. Mand.)

BISMARCK ARCHIPELAGO

TARAWA Nov. '43

GILBERT ISLANDS (Br.)

NETHERLANDS EAST INDIES

Java

Timor

New Guinea

PAPUA (Austr.)

Port Moresby

Rabaul

BOUGAINVILLE Nov. '43-Aug. '45

SOLOMON ISLANDS (Br.)

ELLICE ISLANDS (Br.)

PHOENIX ISLANDS (U.S. & Br.)

PAPUA Aug. '42- June '43

GUADALCANAL Aug. '42-Feb. '43

U.S. SUPPLY ROUTE TO AUSTRALIA

Western Samoa (N.Z.)

American Samoa

INDIAN OCEAN

AUSTRALIA

CORAL SEA

NEW HEBRIDES (Br. & Fr.)

FIJI ISLANDS (Br.)

Legend (right)

- ✴ U.S. Air Strikes
- ◁ Allied Advances
- ✸ Battles or Campaigns
- ☁ Atomic Bombs.

INTERNATIONAL DATE LINE

EQUATORIAL SCALE OF MILES
0 200 400 600 800 1000

© Copyright HAMMOND INCORPORATED. Maplewood, N.J.
Printed in U.S.A.

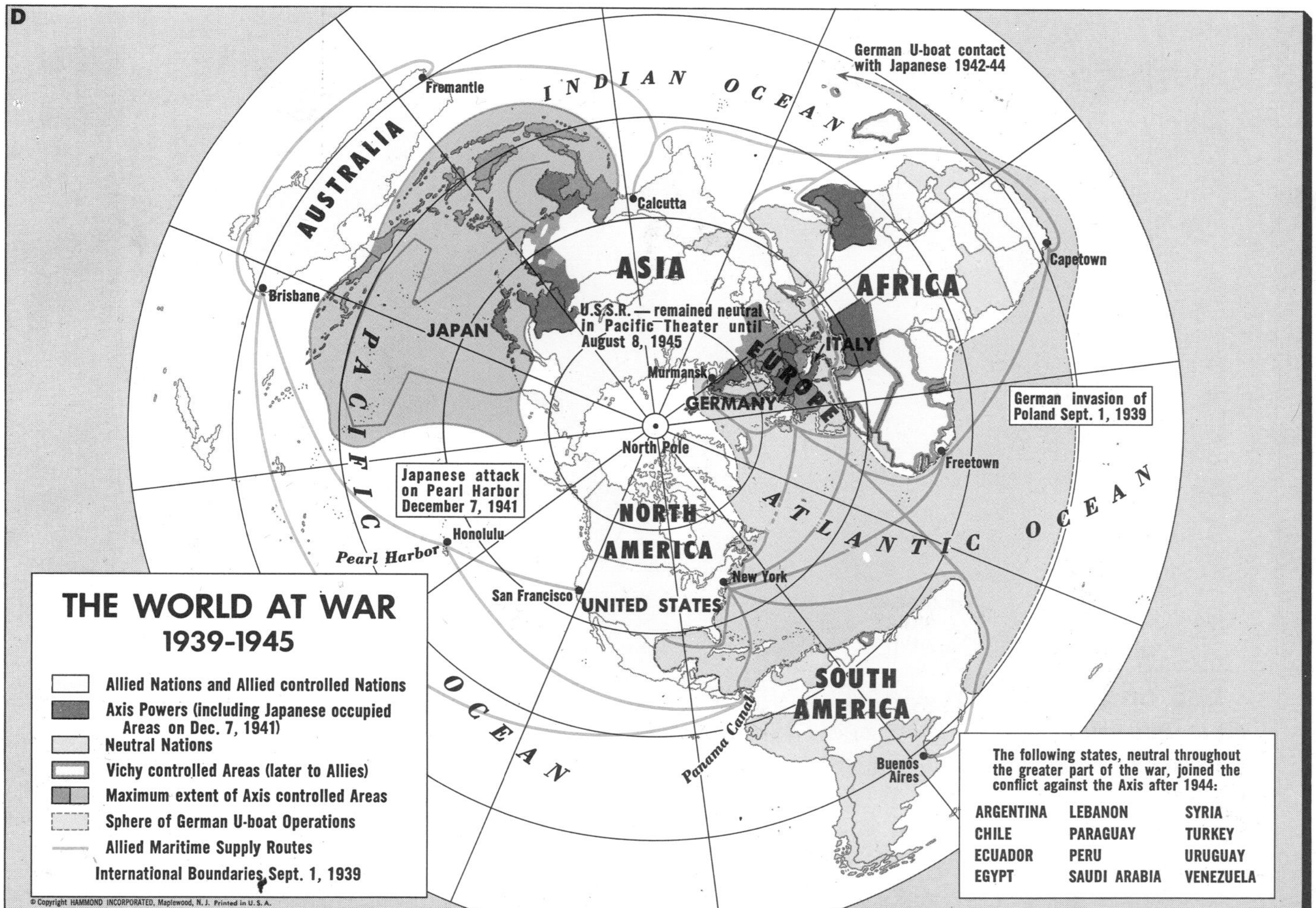

D

German U-boat contact with Japanese 1942-44

INDIAN OCEAN

Fremantle

Calcutta

Capetown

AUSTRALIA

Brisbane

ASIA

U.S.S.R. — remained neutral in Pacific Theater until August 8, 1945

AFRICA

PACIFIC

JAPAN

Murmansk

EUROPE

ITALY

GERMANY

German invasion of Poland Sept. 1, 1939

North Pole

Japanese attack on Pearl Harbor December 7, 1941

Freetown

ATLANTIC OCEAN

NORTH AMERICA

Honolulu

Pearl Harbor

San Francisco

UNITED STATES

New York

OCEAN

SOUTH AMERICA

Panama Canal

Buenos Aires

THE WORLD AT WAR 1939-1945

- ☐ Allied Nations and Allied controlled Nations
- ■ Axis Powers (including Japanese occupied Areas on Dec. 7, 1941)
- ☐ Neutral Nations
- ▨ Vichy controlled Areas (later to Allies)
- ▤ Maximum extent of Axis controlled Areas
- ⊡ Sphere of German U-boat Operations
- ～ Allied Maritime Supply Routes
- International Boundaries Sept. 1, 1939

© Copyright HAMMOND INCORPORATED, Maplewood, N.J. Printed in U.S.A.

The following states, neutral throughout the greater part of the war, joined the conflict against the Axis after 1944:

ARGENTINA	LEBANON	SYRIA
CHILE	PARAGUAY	TURKEY
ECUADOR	PERU	URUGUAY
EGYPT	SAUDI ARABIA	VENEZUELA

A

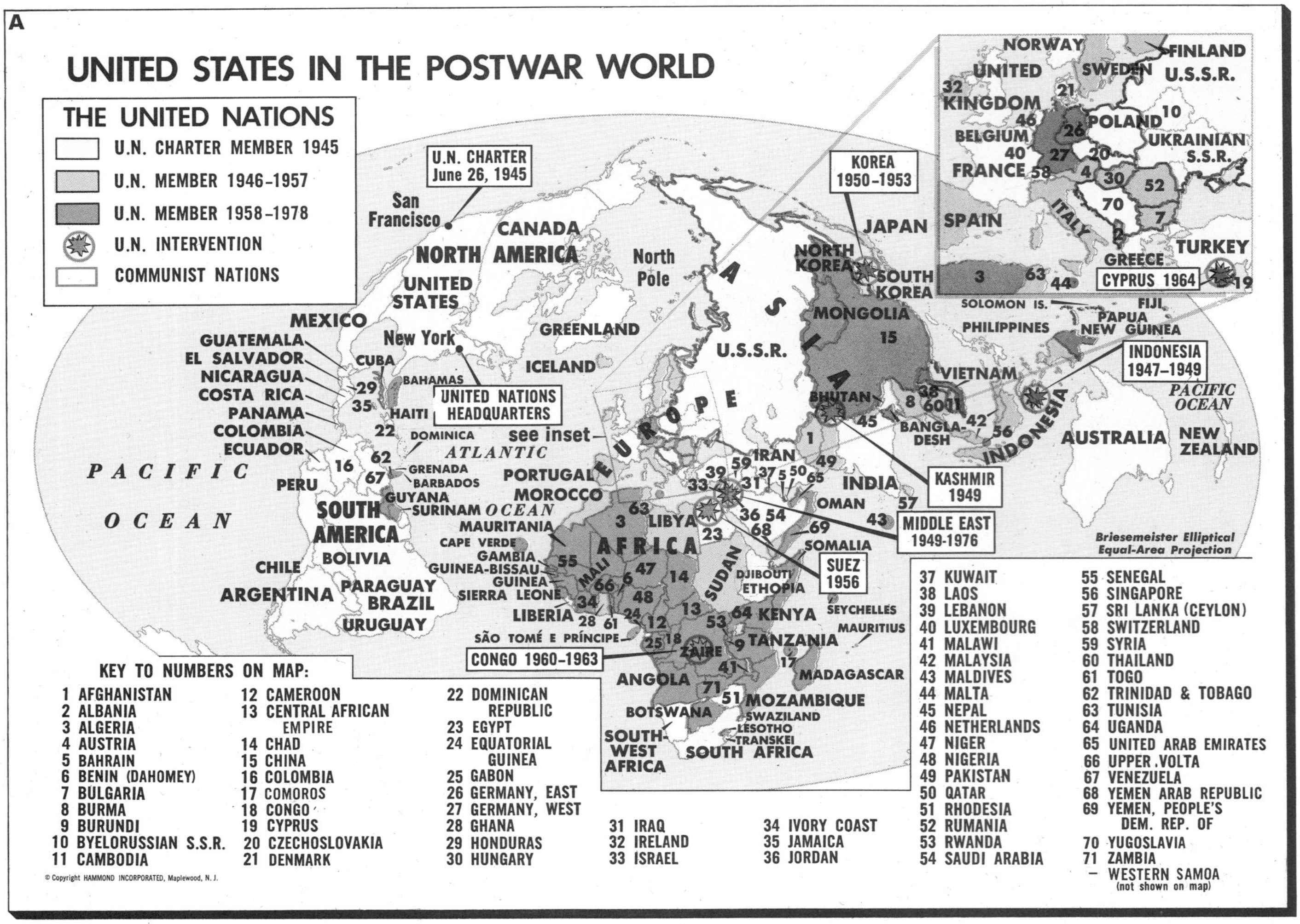

UNITED STATES IN THE POSTWAR WORLD

THE UNITED NATIONS

☐	U.N. CHARTER MEMBER 1945
▨	U.N. MEMBER 1946–1957
▨	U.N. MEMBER 1958–1978
✳	U.N. INTERVENTION
☐	COMMUNIST NATIONS

U.N. CHARTER June 26, 1945

KOREA 1950–1953

San Francisco

CANADA

NORTH AMERICA

North Pole

UNITED STATES

NORTH KOREA

SOUTH KOREA

JAPAN

New York

GREENLAND

MEXICO

GUATEMALA
EL SALVADOR
NICARAGUA
COSTA RICA
PANAMA
COLOMBIA
ECUADOR

CUBA

ICELAND

U.S.S.R.

MONGOLIA

ASIA

15

BAHAMAS

HAITI

UNITED NATIONS HEADQUARTERS

BHUTAN

VIETNAM

38
60 01

29
35
22

DOMINICA

see inset—

EUROPE

1

45

8

BANGLA-DESH

42
56

INDONESIA 1947–1949

PACIFIC OCEAN

AUSTRALIA

NEW ZEALAND

DATLANTIC

16

62
67

GRENADA
BARBADOS

PORTUGAL

MOROCCO

39
33

59
31

IRAN
37
5

49
50
65

KASHMIR 1949

INDIA

57

PERU

GUYANA
SURINAM

GUINEA

OMAN

OCEAN

SOUTH AMERICA

MAURITANIA

3

LIBYA

63

36 54
68

69

43

MIDDLE EAST 1949–1976

Briesemeister Elliptical Equal-Area Projection

CAPE VERDE
GAMBIA
GUINEA-BISSAU

AFRICA

23

SOMALIA

CHILE

BOLIVIA

55

MALI

47

14

SUDAN

DJIBOUTI
ETHIOPIA

SUEZ 1956

ARGENTINA

PARAGUAY

GUINEA
SIERRA LEONE

66

48

13

SEYCHELLES

64

KENYA

BRAZIL

LIBERIA

34

24

MAURITIUS

URUGUAY

28

61

12

53

9

TANZANIA

SÃO TOMÉ E PRÍNCIPE

25
18

ZAIRE

41

17

MADAGASCAR

CONGO 1960–1963

ANGOLA

71

51

MOZAMBIQUE

BOTSWANA

SWAZILAND
LESOTHO
TRANSKEI

SOUTH-WEST AFRICA

SOUTH AFRICA

KEY TO NUMBERS ON MAP:

1 AFGHANISTAN	12 CAMEROON	22 DOMINICAN REPUBLIC	
2 ALBANIA	13 CENTRAL AFRICAN EMPIRE	23 EGYPT	
3 ALGERIA	14 CHAD	24 EQUATORIAL GUINEA	
4 AUSTRIA	15 CHINA	25 GABON	
5 BAHRAIN	16 COLOMBIA	26 GERMANY, EAST	
6 BENIN (DAHOMEY)	17 COMOROS	27 GERMANY, WEST	
7 BULGARIA	18 CONGO	28 GHANA	
8 BURMA	19 CYPRUS	29 HONDURAS	
9 BURUNDI	20 CZECHOSLOVAKIA	30 HUNGARY	
10 BYELORUSSIAN S.S.R.	21 DENMARK		
11 CAMBODIA			

31 IRAQ	34 IVORY COAST	37 KUWAIT	55 SENEGAL
32 IRELAND	35 JAMAICA	38 LAOS	56 SINGAPORE
33 ISRAEL	36 JORDAN	39 LEBANON	57 SRI LANKA (CEYLON)
		40 LUXEMBOURG	58 SWITZERLAND
		41 MALAWI	59 SYRIA
		42 MALAYSIA	60 THAILAND
		43 MALDIVES	61 TOGO
		44 MALTA	62 TRINIDAD & TOBAGO
		45 NEPAL	63 TUNISIA
		46 NETHERLANDS	64 UGANDA
		47 NIGER	65 UNITED ARAB EMIRATES
		48 NIGERIA	66 UPPER VOLTA
		49 PAKISTAN	67 VENEZUELA
		50 QATAR	68 YEMEN ARAB REPUBLIC
		51 RHODESIA	69 YEMEN, PEOPLE'S DEM. REP. OF
		52 RUMANIA	70 YUGOSLAVIA
		53 RWANDA	71 ZAMBIA
		54 SAUDI ARABIA	— WESTERN SAMOA (not shown on map)

Inset (Europe):
NORWAY
UNITED KINGDOM
SWEDEN
FINLAND
U.S.S.R.
32
21
46
26
POLAND
10
BELGIUM
40
FRANCE
58
27
4
30
52
UKRAINIAN S.S.R.
70
7
SPAIN
ITALY
3
63
44
GREECE
TURKEY
CYPRUS 1964
19
SOLOMON IS.
FIJI
PAPUA NEW GUINEA
PHILIPPINES

© Copyright HAMMOND INCORPORATED, Maplewood, N.J.

B

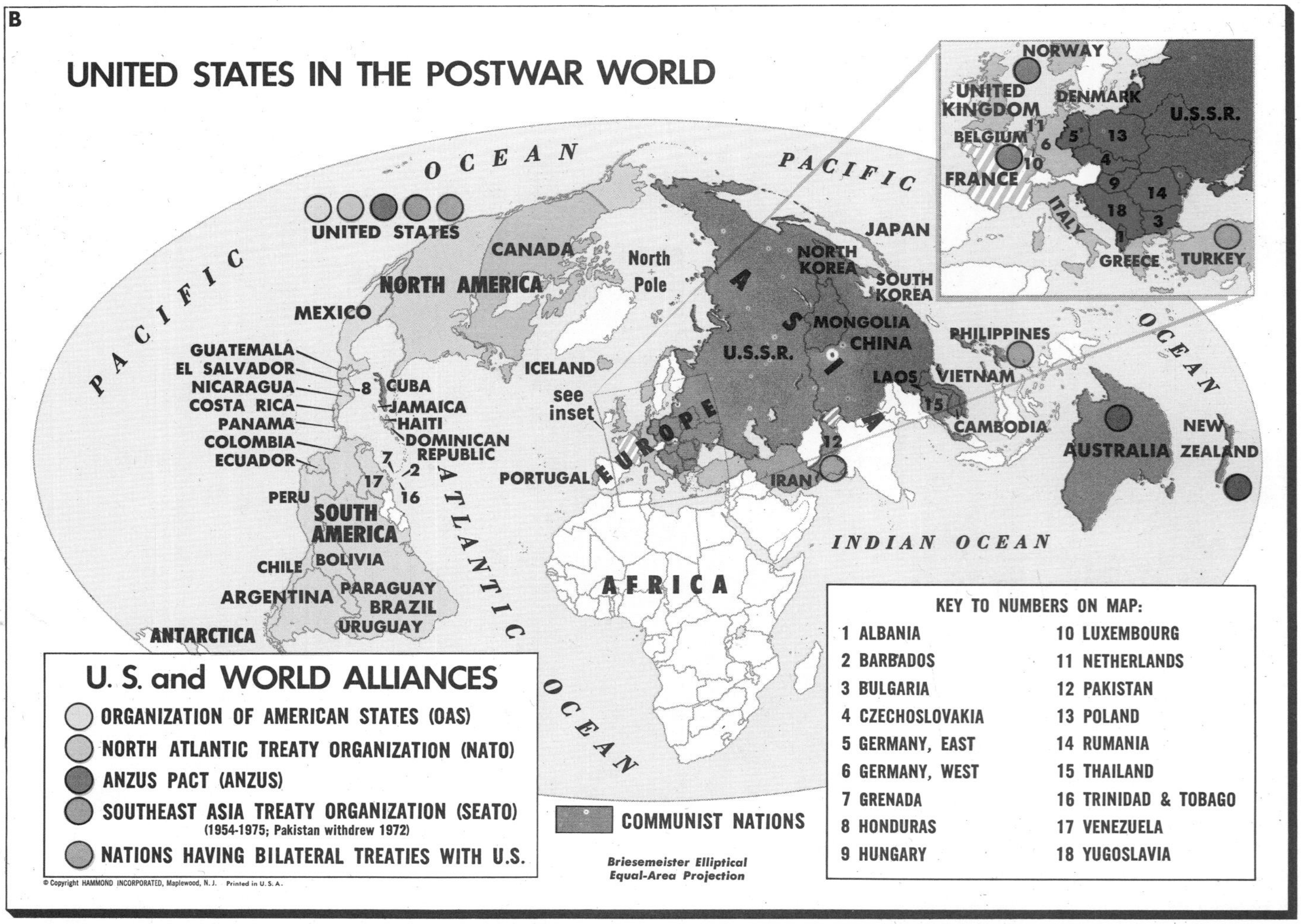

UNITED STATES IN THE POSTWAR WORLD

OCEAN

PACIFIC

⊙ ⊙ ⊙ ⊙ ⊙
UNITED STATES

CANADA

NORTH AMERICA

North Pole

JAPAN

NORTH KOREA

SOUTH KOREA

PACIFIC

MEXICO

ICELAND

ASIA

MONGOLIA

CHINA

U.S.S.R.

PHILIPPINES

GUATEMALA
EL SALVADOR
NICARAGUA
COSTA RICA
PANAMA
COLOMBIA
ECUADOR

8

CUBA

JAMAICA

HAITI

DOMINICAN REPUBLIC

see inset

EUROPE

LAOS

VIETNAM

15

OCEAN

CAMBODIA

NEW ZEALAND

7

2

PERU

17

2

16

PORTUGAL

12

IRAN

AUSTRALIA

SOUTH AMERICA

DATLANTIC

INDIAN OCEAN

CHILE

BOLIVIA

AFRICA

ARGENTINA

PARAGUAY

BRAZIL

URUGUAY

ANTARCTICA

OCEAN

U.S. and WORLD ALLIANCES

⊙	ORGANIZATION OF AMERICAN STATES (OAS)
⊙	NORTH ATLANTIC TREATY ORGANIZATION (NATO)
⊙	ANZUS PACT (ANZUS)
⊙	SOUTHEAST ASIA TREATY ORGANIZATION (SEATO) (1954–1975; Pakistan withdrew 1972)
⊙	NATIONS HAVING BILATERAL TREATIES WITH U.S.

▨ COMMUNIST NATIONS

Briesemeister Elliptical Equal-Area Projection

KEY TO NUMBERS ON MAP:

1 ALBANIA	10 LUXEMBOURG
2 BARBADOS	11 NETHERLANDS
3 BULGARIA	12 PAKISTAN
4 CZECHOSLOVAKIA	13 POLAND
5 GERMANY, EAST	14 RUMANIA
6 GERMANY, WEST	15 THAILAND
7 GRENADA	16 TRINIDAD & TOBAGO
8 HONDURAS	17 VENEZUELA
9 HUNGARY	18 YUGOSLAVIA

Inset (Europe):
NORWAY
UNITED KINGDOM
DENMARK
U.S.S.R.
BELGIUM
11
6
5
13
FRANCE
10
4
ITALY
9
14
8
3
GREECE
TURKEY

© Copyright HAMMOND INCORPORATED, Maplewood, N.J.   Printed in U.S.A.

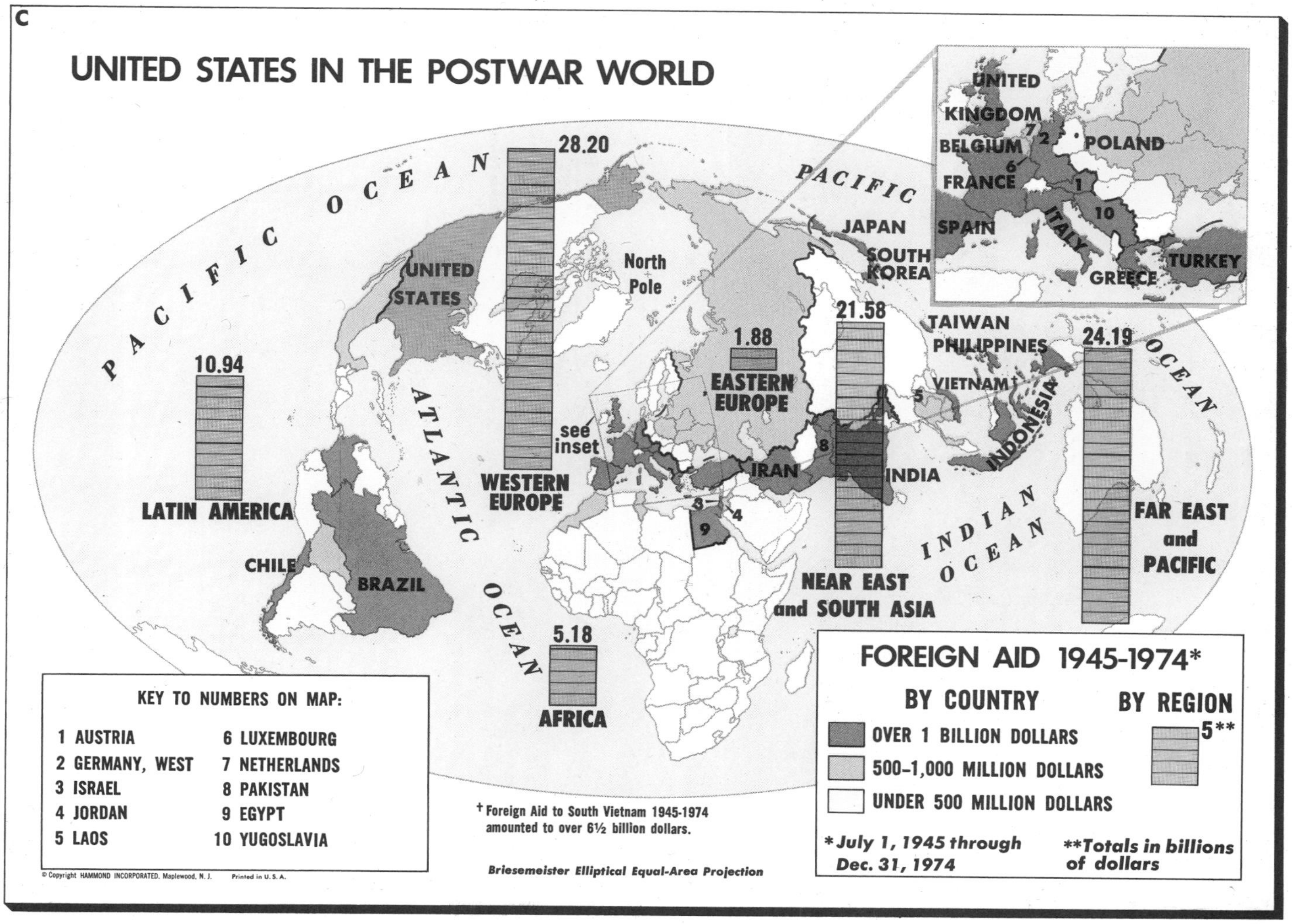

C

UNITED STATES IN THE POSTWAR WORLD

PACIFIC OCEAN

ATLANTIC OCEAN

PACIFIC OCEAN

INDIAN OCEAN

North Pole

UNITED STATES

JAPAN
SOUTH KOREA

TAIWAN
PHILIPPINES

VIETNAM†

INDONESIA

28.20

10.94

LATIN AMERICA

CHILE

BRAZIL

see inset

1.88
EASTERN EUROPE

WESTERN EUROPE

21.58

IRAN

3
9
4

INDIA

8

24.19

FAR EAST and PACIFIC

NEAR EAST and SOUTH ASIA

5.18

AFRICA

5

Inset:
UNITED KINGDOM
BELGIUM
FRANCE
SPAIN
POLAND
ITALY
GREECE
TURKEY
7 2
6
1
10

KEY TO NUMBERS ON MAP:

1 AUSTRIA	6 LUXEMBOURG
2 GERMANY, WEST	7 NETHERLANDS
3 ISRAEL	8 PAKISTAN
4 JORDAN	9 EGYPT
5 LAOS	10 YUGOSLAVIA

© Copyright HAMMOND INCORPORATED, Maplewood, N. J.   Printed in U.S.A.

† Foreign Aid to South Vietnam 1945-1974 amounted to over 6½ billion dollars.

Briesemeister Elliptical Equal-Area Projection

FOREIGN AID 1945-1974*

BY COUNTRY
- OVER 1 BILLION DOLLARS
- 500–1,000 MILLION DOLLARS
- UNDER 500 MILLION DOLLARS

BY REGION
5**

*July 1, 1945 through Dec. 31, 1974   **Totals in billions of dollars

---

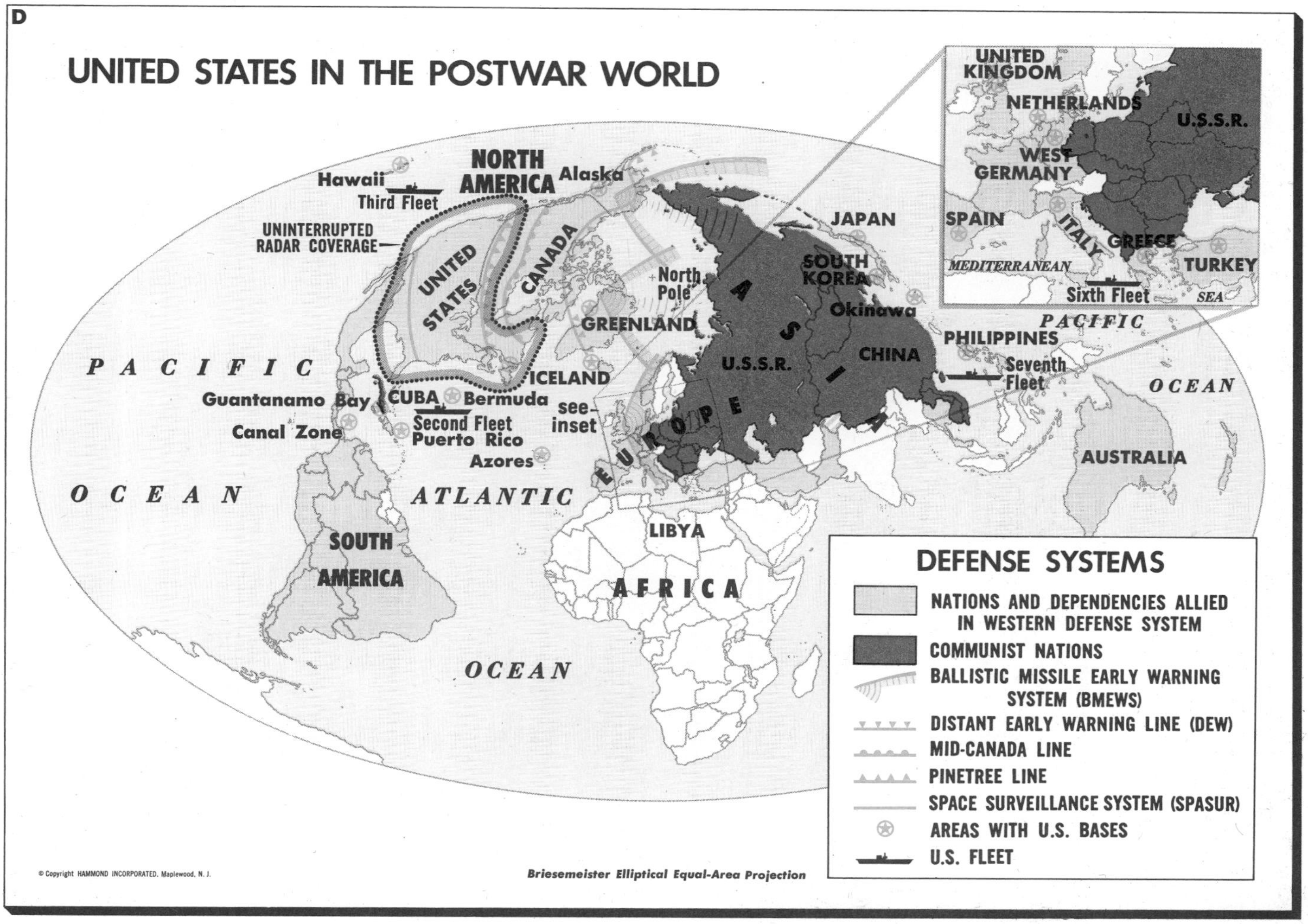

D

UNITED STATES IN THE POSTWAR WORLD

PACIFIC OCEAN

ATLANTIC OCEAN

PACIFIC OCEAN

Hawaii
Third Fleet

NORTH AMERICA   Alaska

UNINTERRUPTED RADAR COVERAGE

UNITED STATES

CANADA

North Pole

GREENLAND

ICELAND

Guantanamo Bay
Canal Zone
CUBA Bermuda
Second Fleet
Puerto Rico
Azores

see inset

JAPAN

SOUTH KOREA

Okinawa

ASIA

U.S.S.R.

CHINA

EUROPE

PHILIPPINES
Seventh Fleet

AUSTRALIA

LIBYA

SOUTH AMERICA

AFRICA

OCEAN

Inset:
UNITED KINGDOM
NETHERLANDS
WEST GERMANY
SPAIN
U.S.S.R.
ITALY GREECE
TURKEY
MEDITERRANEAN
Sixth Fleet
SEA

DEFENSE SYSTEMS

- NATIONS AND DEPENDENCIES ALLIED IN WESTERN DEFENSE SYSTEM
- COMMUNIST NATIONS
- BALLISTIC MISSILE EARLY WARNING SYSTEM (BMEWS)
- DISTANT EARLY WARNING LINE (DEW)
- MID-CANADA LINE
- PINETREE LINE
- SPACE SURVEILLANCE SYSTEM (SPASUR)
- AREAS WITH U.S. BASES
- U.S. FLEET

© Copyright HAMMOND INCORPORATED, Maplewood, N. J.

Briesemeister Elliptical Equal-Area Projection

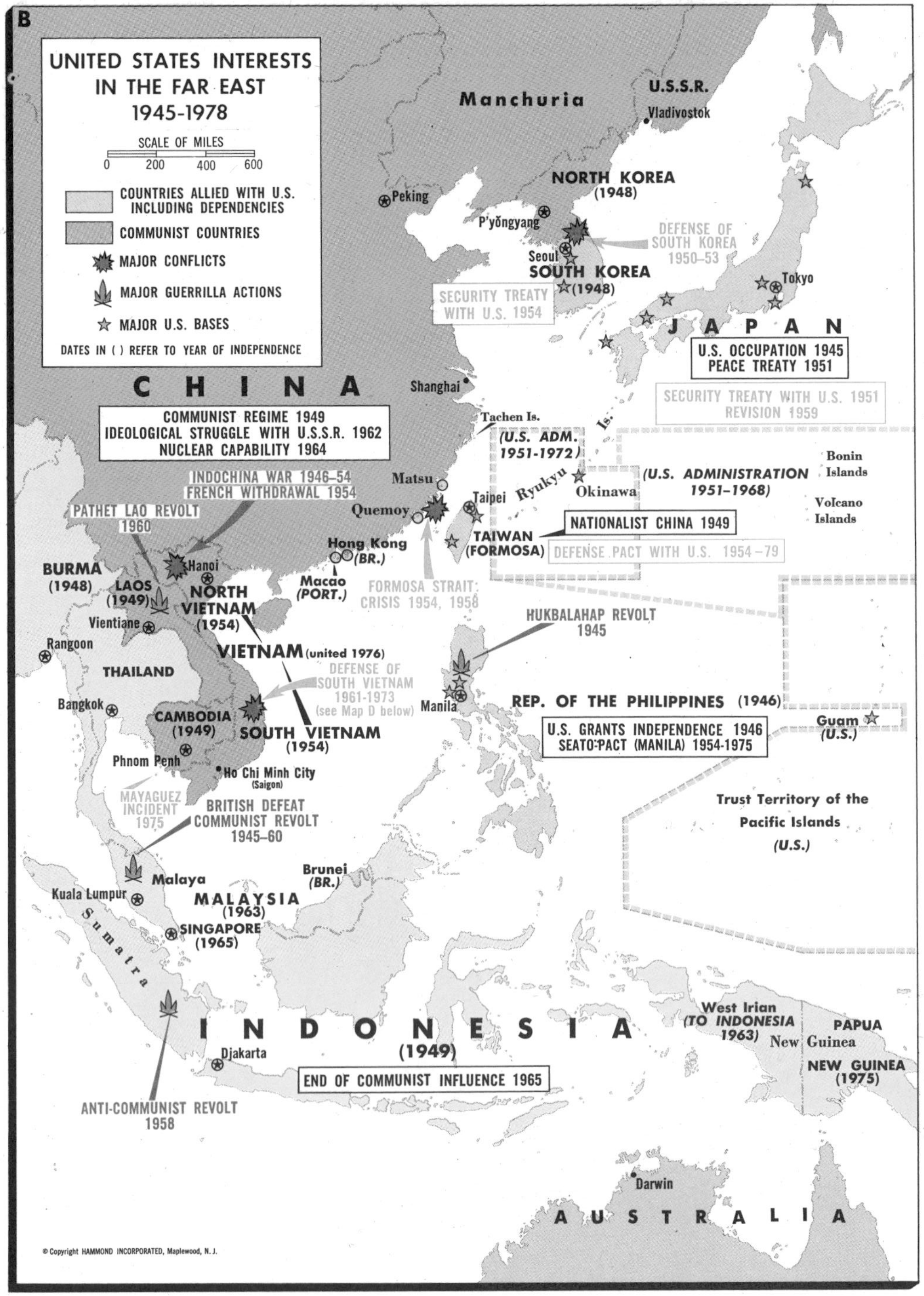

B

UNITED STATES INTERESTS IN THE FAR EAST 1945-1978

SCALE OF MILES
0 200 400 600

COUNTRIES ALLIED WITH U.S. INCLUDING DEPENDENCIES

COMMUNIST COUNTRIES

✳ MAJOR CONFLICTS

⚔ MAJOR GUERRILLA ACTIONS

★ MAJOR U.S. BASES

DATES IN ( ) REFER TO YEAR OF INDEPENDENCE

U.S.S.R.
Vladivostok

Manchuria

Peking ⊕

NORTH KOREA (1948)
P'yŏngyang ⊕

DEFENSE OF SOUTH KOREA 1950-53

SOUTH KOREA (1948)
Seoul ⊕

SECURITY TREATY WITH U.S. 1954

J A P A N
Tokyo ★

U.S. OCCUPATION 1945 PEACE TREATY 1951

SECURITY TREATY WITH U.S. 1951 REVISION 1959

Bonin Islands
Volcano Islands

U.S. ADMINISTRATION 1951-1968

Okinawa

Guam (U.S.) ★

Trust Territory of the Pacific Islands (U.S.)

Shanghai ⊙

C H I N A

COMMUNIST REGIME 1949
IDEOLOGICAL STRUGGLE WITH U.S.S.R. 1962
NUCLEAR CAPABILITY 1964

INDOCHINA WAR 1946-54
FRENCH WITHDRAWAL 1954

Matsu
Quemoy
FORMOSA STRAIT CRISIS 1954, 1958

U.S. ADM. 1951-1972
Tachen Is.

Taipei ★
TAIWAN (FORMOSA)
NATIONALIST CHINA 1949

Hong Kong (BR.)
Macao (PORT.)

HUKBALAHAP REVOLT 1945

REP. OF THE PHILIPPINES (1946)

DEFENSE PACT WITH U.S. 1954-79

Manila ★
U.S. GRANTS INDEPENDENCE 1946
SEATO PACT (MANILA) 1954-1975

PATHET LAO REVOLT 1960

Hanoi ✳
NORTH VIETNAM (1954)
BURMA (1948)
LAOS (1949)
Vientiane ⊕
THAILAND
Rangoon
Bangkok ⊕

VIETNAM (united 1976)
DEFENSE OF SOUTH VIETNAM 1961-1973 (see Map D below)

CAMBODIA (1949)
Phnom Penh ⊕

SOUTH VIETNAM (1954)
Ho Chi Minh City (Saigon)

MAYAGUEZ INCIDENT 1975

BRITISH DEFEAT COMMUNIST REVOLT 1945-60

Brunei (BR.)

MALAYSIA (1963)
Malaya (BR.)
SINGAPORE (1965)
Kuala Lumpur ⊕

I N D O N E S I A (1949)

Djakarta ⊙

END OF COMMUNIST INFLUENCE 1965

ANTI-COMMUNIST REVOLT 1958

Sumatra

A U S T R A L I A
Darwin •

West Irian (TO INDONESIA 1963) New Guinea

PAPUA NEW GUINEA (1975)

© Copyright HAMMOND INCORPORATED, Maplewood, N.J.

A

UNITED STATES INTERESTS IN THE FAR EAST 1854-1937

SCALE OF MILES
0 200 400 600

U.S. DEPENDENCIES

OTHER DEPENDENCIES

■ MAJOR TREATY PORTS

✳ CONFLICTS INVOLVING U.S. FORCES

RUSSIA (U.S.S.R.)
Vladivostok ✳

INTERVENTION IN RUSSIAN CIVIL WAR 1918-20

J A P A N
Hakodate •
Tokyo ⊕
Shimoda

TREATY PORT AGREEMENT (PERRY)

PRESIDENT T. ROOSEVELT MEDIATES IN RUSSIAN-JAPANESE WAR 1905

TREATY PORT AGREEMENT 1854-99

Osaka •
Nagasaki •

Manchuria (Manchukuo) (JAP.)
Mukden •

Korea (Chosen) (JAP.)

Dairen (JAP.)
Weihaiwei (BR. UNTIL 1930)
Kiaochow (GER. UNTIL 1914)

BOXER REBELLION 1900

Peking ⊕
Tientsin ■

C H I N A

Nanking ■

JAPAN EXTENDS OCCUPATION OF CHINA 1937

OPEN DOOR POLICY 1899
STIMSON DOCTRINE 1932

Shanghai ■
Ningpo ■
Foochow ■
Amoy ■

PANAY INCIDENT 1937

Ryukyu Islands (JAP.)

Formosa (JAP.)

PACIFIC OCEAN

Mariana Is. (JAP. MANDATE)
Guam (U.S.)

CEDED BY SPAIN 1898

Caroline Islands (JAP. MANDATE)

CEDED BY SPAIN 1898
MILITARY GOVERNMENT 1898-1901
JONES ACT 1916
COMMONWEALTH STATUS 1935

PHILIPPINE INSURRECTION 1899-1902

Mindanao
Luzon
Manila ✳
Philippine Islands

SPANISH-AMERICAN WAR, PHILIPPINES CAMPAIGN 1898

Chungking ■

Hankow ■
Nanning ■
Hanoi •
Canton ■
Kwangchowan (FR.)
Hong Kong (BR.)
Macao (PORT.)

French Indochina

S I A M
Bangkok ⊕

Burma (BR.)
Rangoon •

Malay States (BR.)
Singapore (BR.) ⊙

Netherlands East Indies

Br. North Borneo (BR.)
Brunei (BR.)
Sarawak (BR.)

Saigon •

Batavia •
Surabaya •

Timor (PORT.)

Terr. of New Guinea
New Guinea
Papua

A U S T R A L I A

COMMONWEALTH STATUS 1901

INDIAN OCEAN

© Copyright HAMMOND INCORPORATED, Maplewood, N.J.
Printed in U.S.A.

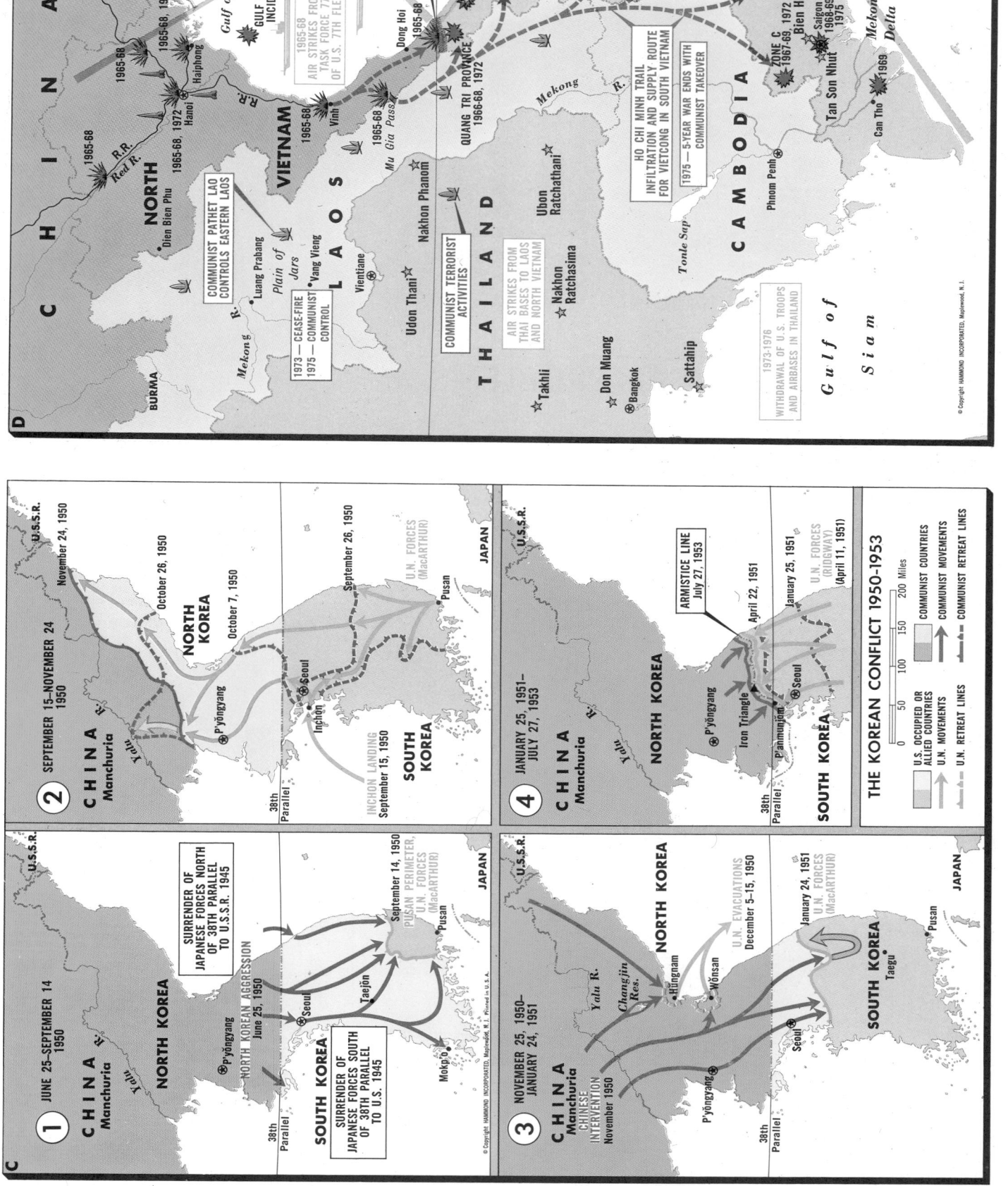

THE VIETNAM CONFLICT
1961-1975
SCALE OF MILES
0   50   100   150

- COUNTRIES ALLIED WITH U.S.
- COMMUNIST COUNTRIES
- MAJOR CONFLICTS
- GUERRILLA ACTIONS
- AIR STRIKE TARGETS
- SOVIET MISSILE SITES
- MAJOR U.S. BASES
- U.S. MARINE AND ARMY LANDINGS

C H I N A

R.R.

Gulf of Tonkin

GULF OF TONKIN INCIDENT 1964

1965-68

1965-68, 1972

Hanoi
Haiphong
1965-68, 1972

1965-68

Red R.
R.R.

NORTH
VIETNAM

Dien Bien Phu

COMMUNIST PATHET LAO CONTROLS EASTERN LAOS

Plain of Jars

Luang Prabang
Vang Vieng

1973— CEASE-FIRE
1975— COMMUNIST CONTROL

Vientiane

L A O S

BURMA

Mekong R.

Vinh
1965-68

1965-68

Mu Gia Pass

1965-68 AIR STRIKES FROM TASK FORCE 77 OF U.S. 7TH FLEET

Dong Hoi
1965-68

PARTITION LINE 1954 DEMILITARIZED ZONE (DMZ)

17th Parallel

QUANG TRI PROVINCE 1966-68, 1972

Hue
1968-69

Nakhon Phanom

COMMUNIST TERRORIST ACTIVITIES

Udon Thani

T H A I L A N D

Nakhon Ratchasima

Ubon Ratchathani

AIR STRIKES FROM THAI BASES TO LAOS AND NORTH VIETNAM

Don Muang
Bangkok

Takhli

Sattahip

1973-1976 WITHDRAWAL OF U.S. TROOPS AND AIRBASES IN THAILAND

Gulf of Siam

South China Sea

Hainan (CHINA)

Danang
1968-69, 1975

Chu Lai 1965, 1968

Dak To 1966-68

Kontum 1972, 1975

Pleiku 1965, 1972

An Khe

Plei Me

IA DRANG VALLEY 1965

Qui Nhon

Ban Me Thuot 1975

Nha Trang

Da Lat

Cam Ranh Bay

Phan Rang

1965-68 AIR STRIKES OF B-52 BOMBERS FROM GUAM

SOUTH VIETNAM

ZONE C 1967-69, 1972

Bien Hoa 1975

Saigon 1968-69, 1975

Tan Son Nhut 1969

Can Tho

Mekong Delta

C A M B O D I A

Phnom Penh

Mekong R.

Tonle Sap

HO CHI MINH TRAIL INFILTRATION AND SUPPLY ROUTE FOR VIETCONG IN SOUTH VIETNAM

1975— 5-YEAR WAR ENDS WITH COMMUNIST TAKEOVER

1970— U.S. AND SOUTH VIETNAMESE TROOPS ENTER CAMBODIA TO STAMP OUT ENEMY SANCTUARIES

1973— CEASE-FIRE, U.S. TROOPS LEAVE VIETNAM, U.S. ENDS ALL BOMBING IN INDOCHINA

1975— COMMUNISTS STEP UP MILITARY OFFENSIVE IN THE SOUTH, SOUTH VIETNAM SURRENDERS TO THE VIET CONG

© Copyright HAMMOND INCORPORATED, Maplewood, N.J.

---

1 JUNE 25–SEPTEMBER 14 1950

C H I N A
Manchuria

U.S.S.R.

Yalu

NORTH KOREA

P'yŏngyang

38th Parallel

NORTH KOREAN AGGRESSION June 25, 1950

Seoul

SURRENDER OF JAPANESE FORCES SOUTH OF 38TH PARALLEL TO U.S. 1945

SURRENDER OF JAPANESE FORCES NORTH OF 38TH PARALLEL TO U.S.S.R. 1945

September 14, 1950

PUSAN PERIMETER, U.N. FORCES (MacARTHUR)

Taejŏn

SOUTH KOREA

Pusan

Mokp'o

JAPAN

© Copyright HAMMOND INCORPORATED, Maplewood, N.J. Printed in U.S.A.

---

2 SEPTEMBER 15–NOVEMBER 24 1950

C H I N A
Manchuria

U.S.S.R.

November 24, 1950

October 26, 1950

Yalu

October 7, 1950

NORTH KOREA

P'yŏngyang

September 26, 1950

38th Parallel

Seoul

Inchon

INCHON LANDING September 15, 1950

U.N. FORCES (MacARTHUR)

SOUTH KOREA

Pusan

JAPAN

---

3 NOVEMBER 25, 1950– JANUARY 24, 1951

C H I N A
Manchuria

U.S.S.R.

CHINESE INTERVENTION November 1950

Yalu R.

Changjin Res.

NORTH KOREA

Hŭngnam

Wŏnsan

U.N. EVACUATIONS December 5–15, 1950

P'yŏngyang

Seoul

January 24, 1951 U.N. FORCES (MacARTHUR)

SOUTH KOREA

Taegu

Pusan

JAPAN

---

4 JANUARY 25, 1951– JULY 27, 1953

C H I N A
Manchuria

U.S.S.R.

ARMISTICE LINE July 27, 1953

January 25, 1951

April 22, 1951

U.N. FORCES (RIDGWAY) (April 11, 1951)

Yalu

NORTH KOREA

P'yŏngyang

Iron Triangle

P'anmunjŏm

38th Parallel

Seoul

SOUTH KOREA

THE KOREAN CONFLICT 1950-1953

0   50   100   150   200 Miles

- U.S. OCCUPIED OR ALLIED COUNTRIES
- COMMUNIST COUNTRIES
- U.N. MOVEMENTS
- COMMUNIST MOVEMENTS
- U.N. RETREAT LINES
- COMMUNIST RETREAT LINES

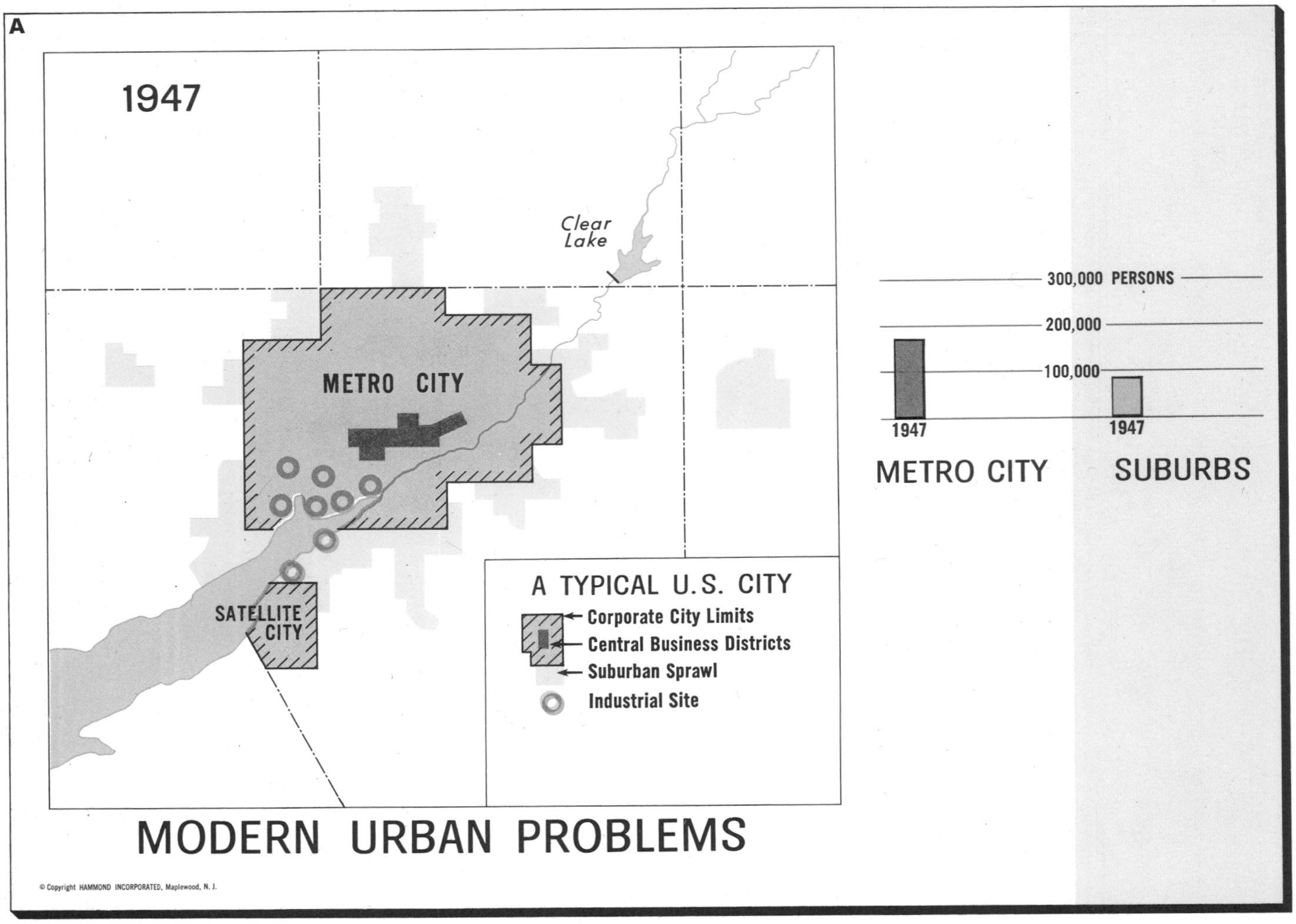

A

1947

Clear
Lake

METRO CITY

SATELLITE
CITY

300,000 PERSONS

200,000

100,000

1947 | 1947

METRO CITY | SUBURBS

A TYPICAL U.S. CITY

Corporate City Limits
Central Business Districts
Suburban Sprawl
⊚ Industrial Site

MODERN URBAN PROBLEMS

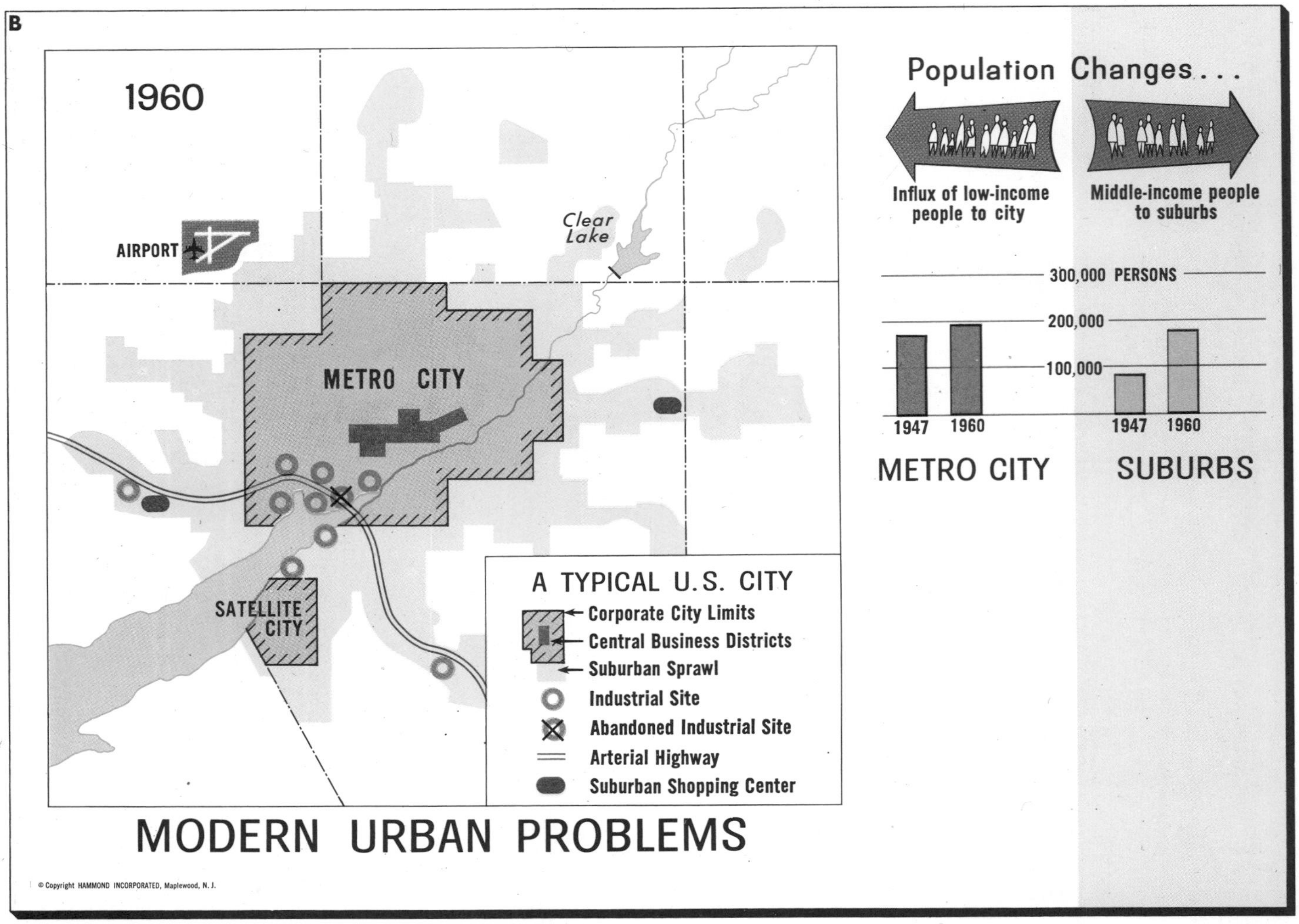

B

1960

AIRPORT

Clear
Lake

METRO CITY

SATELLITE
CITY

Population Changes...

Influx of low-income
people to city

Middle-income people
to suburbs

300,000 PERSONS

200,000

100,000

1947 1960 | 1947 1960

METRO CITY | SUBURBS

A TYPICAL U.S. CITY

Corporate City Limits
Central Business Districts
Suburban Sprawl
⊚ Industrial Site
⊗ Abandoned Industrial Site
═ Arterial Highway
⬤ Suburban Shopping Center

MODERN URBAN PROBLEMS

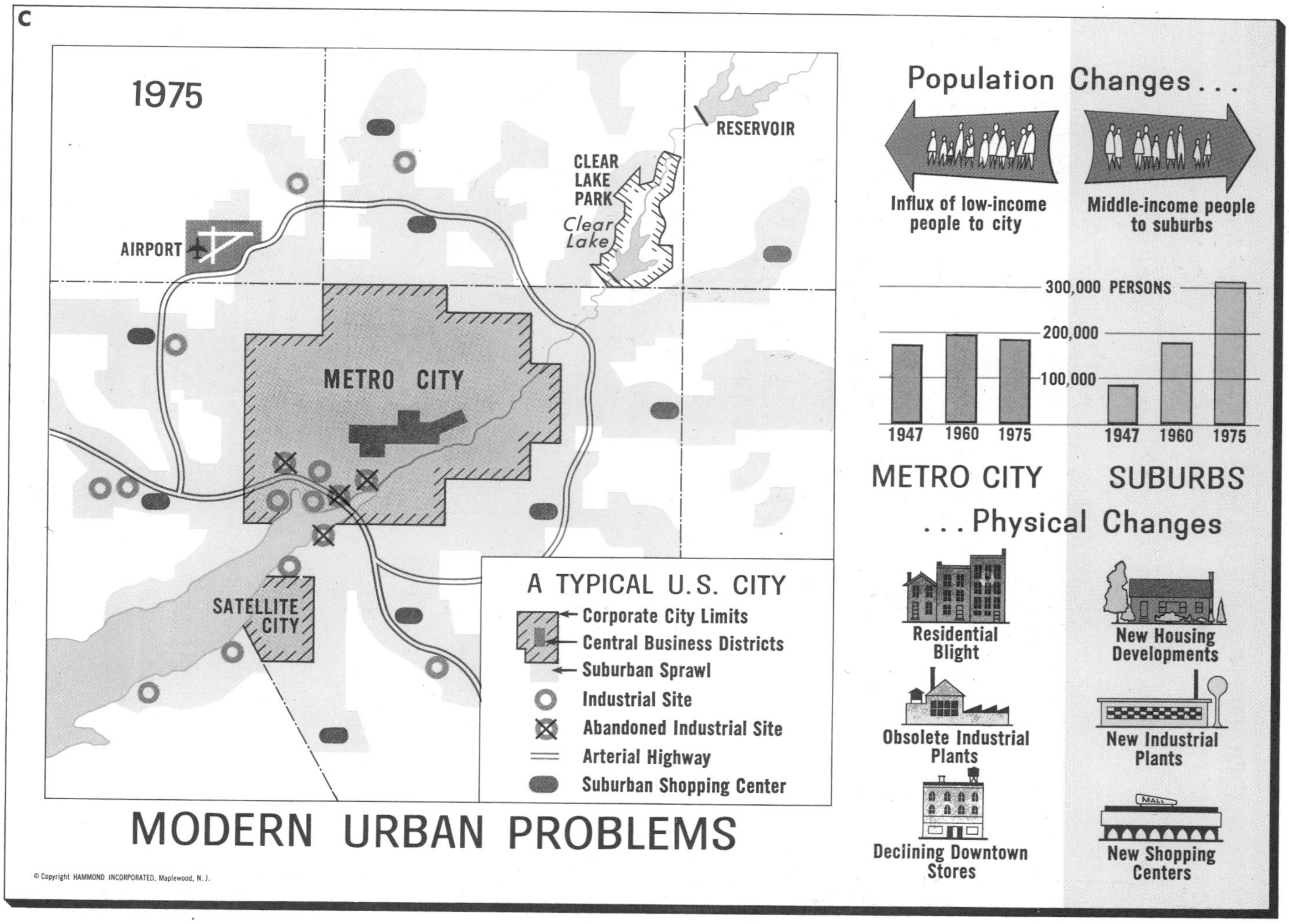

C

1975

RESERVOIR

CLEAR
LAKE
PARK

*Clear
Lake*

AIRPORT

METRO CITY

SATELLITE
CITY

A TYPICAL U.S. CITY

← Corporate City Limits
← Central Business Districts
← Suburban Sprawl
○ Industrial Site
⊗ Abandoned Industrial Site
═ Arterial Highway
⬤ Suburban Shopping Center

MODERN URBAN PROBLEMS

Population Changes...

Influx of low-income
people to city

Middle-income people
to suburbs

300,000 PERSONS

200,000

100,000

1947 1960 1975   1947 1960 1975

METRO CITY   SUBURBS

...Physical Changes

Residential
Blight

New Housing
Developments

Obsolete Industrial
Plants

New Industrial
Plants

Declining Downtown
Stores

New Shopping
Centers

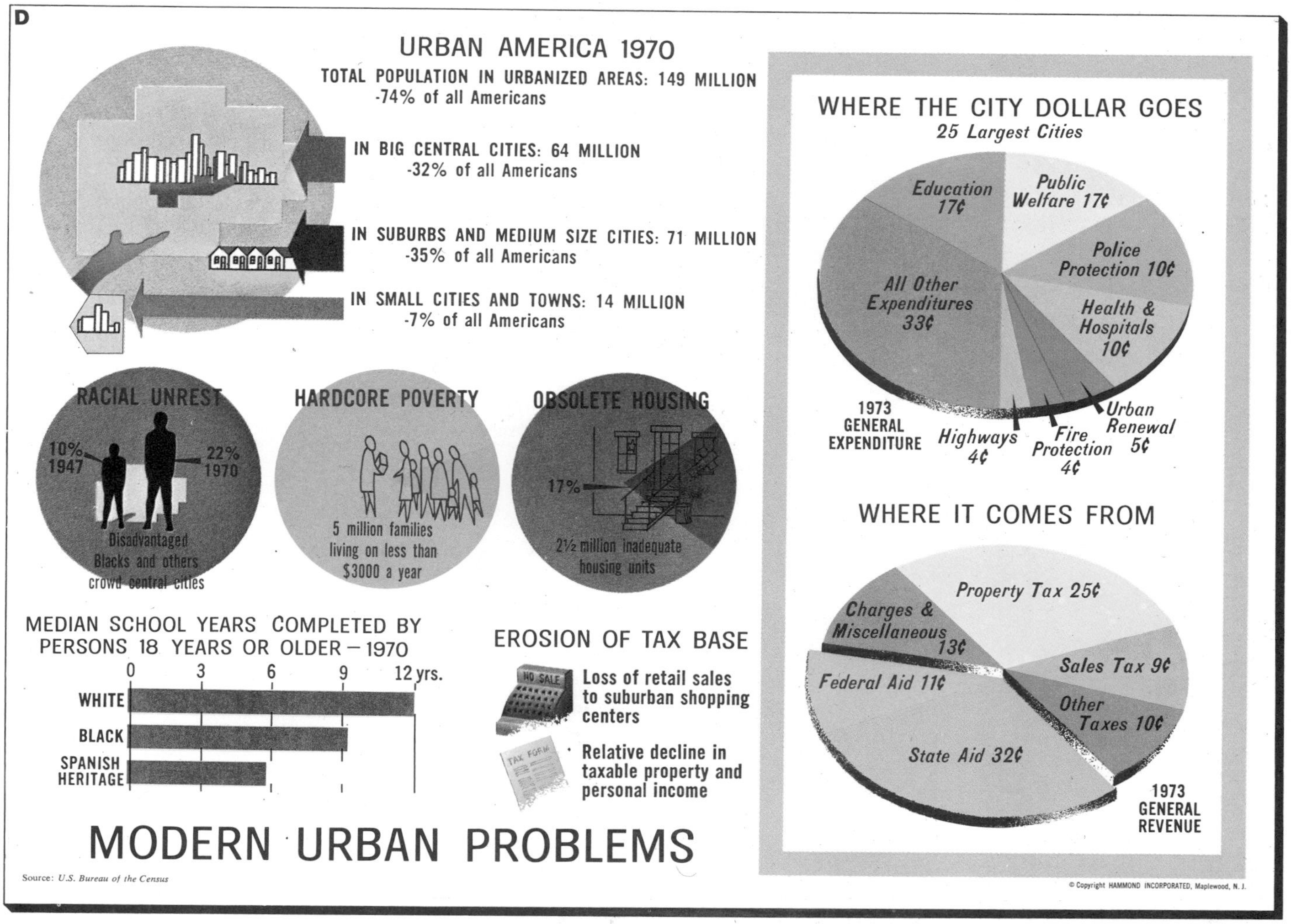

D

URBAN AMERICA 1970

TOTAL POPULATION IN URBANIZED AREAS: 149 MILLION
-74% of all Americans

IN BIG CENTRAL CITIES: 64 MILLION
-32% of all Americans

IN SUBURBS AND MEDIUM SIZE CITIES: 71 MILLION
-35% of all Americans

IN SMALL CITIES AND TOWNS: 14 MILLION
-7% of all Americans

RACIAL UNREST

10%
1947

22%
1970

Disadvantaged
Blacks and others
crowd central cities

HARDCORE POVERTY

5 million families
living on less than
$3000 a year

OBSOLETE HOUSING

17%

2½ million inadequate
housing units

MEDIAN SCHOOL YEARS COMPLETED BY
PERSONS 18 YEARS OR OLDER – 1970

0   3   6   9   12 yrs.

WHITE

BLACK

SPANISH
HERITAGE

EROSION OF TAX BASE

NO SALE
• Loss of retail sales
to suburban shopping
centers

TAX FORM
• Relative decline in
taxable property and
personal income

MODERN URBAN PROBLEMS

Source: U.S. Bureau of the Census

WHERE THE CITY DOLLAR GOES
25 Largest Cities

Education
17¢

Public
Welfare 17¢

Police
Protection 10¢

All Other
Expenditures
33¢

Health &
Hospitals
10¢

1973
GENERAL
EXPENDITURE

Highways
4¢

Fire
Protection
4¢

Urban
Renewal
5¢

WHERE IT COMES FROM

Property Tax 25¢

Charges &
Miscellaneous
13¢

Sales Tax 9¢

Federal Aid 11¢

Other
Taxes 10¢

State Aid 32¢

1973
GENERAL
REVENUE

B

GROWTH OF UNITED STATES ECONOMY
AGRICULTURE

PERCENTAGES OF FARM WORKERS TO TOTAL GAINFUL LABOR FORCE

1820 — 72%
1840 — 69%
1870 — 53%
1900 — 37%
1930 — 21%
1970 — 2%

GAINFUL FARM WORKERS

Millions
12 10 8 6 4 2 0
1820 1840 1870 1900 1930 1960 1970

Experienced Farm Workers

PRODUCTION INCREASE PER FARM WORKER

In 1970 one experienced farm worker fed 80 people.

In 1840 one farm worker fed 4½ people.
1840
1970

VALUE OF FARM MACHINERY AND EQUIPMENT

=1 Billion Dollars

$0.8 — 1900
$1.3 — 1910
$3.6 — 1920
$3.3 — 1930
$3.1 — 1940
$12.2 — 1950
$22.3 — 1960
$31.8 — 1970
$53.2 — 1975

NUMBER OF FARMS

1850
1870
1900
1935
1975

Each symbol represents one million farms.

MAJOR EVENTS IN THE GROWTH OF AGRICULTURE

PUBLIC LAND ACT 1820
McCORMICK REAPER 1831
DEPT. OF AGRICULTURE ESTABLISHED; MORRILL ACT; HOMESTEAD ACT 1862
NATIONAL GRANGE ORGANIZED 1867
TRACTOR 1876
BARBED WIRE PATENTED 1874
HATCH ACT 1887
PURE FOOD AND DRUGS ACT 1906
FARM BUREAU ORGANIZED 1920
1933 AGRICULTURAL ADJUSTMENT ACT
AGRICULTURAL RESEARCH ADMINISTRATION 1942
AGRICULTURAL STABILIZATION AND CONSERVATION SERVICE EST. 1961
SOIL BANK SET UP 1956

1820 1840 1860 1880 1900 1920 1940 1960 1970

© Copyright HAMMOND INCORPORATED, Maplewood, N. J.

Sources: Historical Statistics of the United States
Statistical Abstract of the United States

A

GROWTH OF UNITED STATES ECONOMY
POPULATION AND LABOR FORCE

POPULATION GROWTH 1820-1975

MILLIONS
200 175 150 125 100 75 50 25 0
1820 1840 1860 1880 1900 1920 1940 1960 1975

TOTAL LABOR FORCE

U.S. Percentage of World Total 1975

5½%

POPULATION PYRAMID 1970

AGE GROUP
85+
75–79
65–69
55–59
45–49
35–39
25–29
15–19
5–9
UNDER 5

12 10 8 6 4 2 0 2 4 6 8 10 12

UNION MEMBERSHIP AS PERCENT OF TOTAL LABOR FORCE

1910 — 6%
1920 — 12%
1930 — 7%
1940 — 16%
1950 — 22%
1960 — 26%
1970 — 25%

SHIFTS IN MAJOR OCCUPATIONS 1920-1940-1970

MILLIONS OF WORKERS
30 25 20 15 10 5 0

FARMING
MANUFACTURING
TRADE & SERVICES
GOVERNMENT

SHIFTS IN RESIDENCY

1860
1900
1940
1970

RURAL
URBAN

EACH SYMBOL REPRESENTS 10% OF THE TOTAL POPULATION FOR EACH GIVEN YEAR.

MAJOR EVENTS IN THE LABOR MOVEMENT

WORKINGMEN'S PARTY 1828
NATIONAL TRADES' UNION FOUNDED 1834
NATIONAL LABOR UNION ORGANIZED 1866
KNIGHTS OF LABOR FOUNDED 1869
BUR. OF LABOR CREATED 1884
AFL FOUNDED 1886
DEPT. OF LABOR ORGANIZED 1913
1932 NORRIS-LA GUARDIA ACT
WAGNER ACT 1935
WAGES AND HOURS ACT, CIO FORMED 1938
TAFT-HARTLEY ACT 1947
AFL-CIO MERGER 1955
LANDRUM-GRIFFIN ACT 1959
RAILROAD ARBITRATION ACT 1963

1820 1840 1860 1880 1900 1920 1940 1960 1970

© Copyright HAMMOND INCORPORATED, Maplewood, N. J.

Sources: Historical Statistics of the United States
Statistical Abstract of the United States

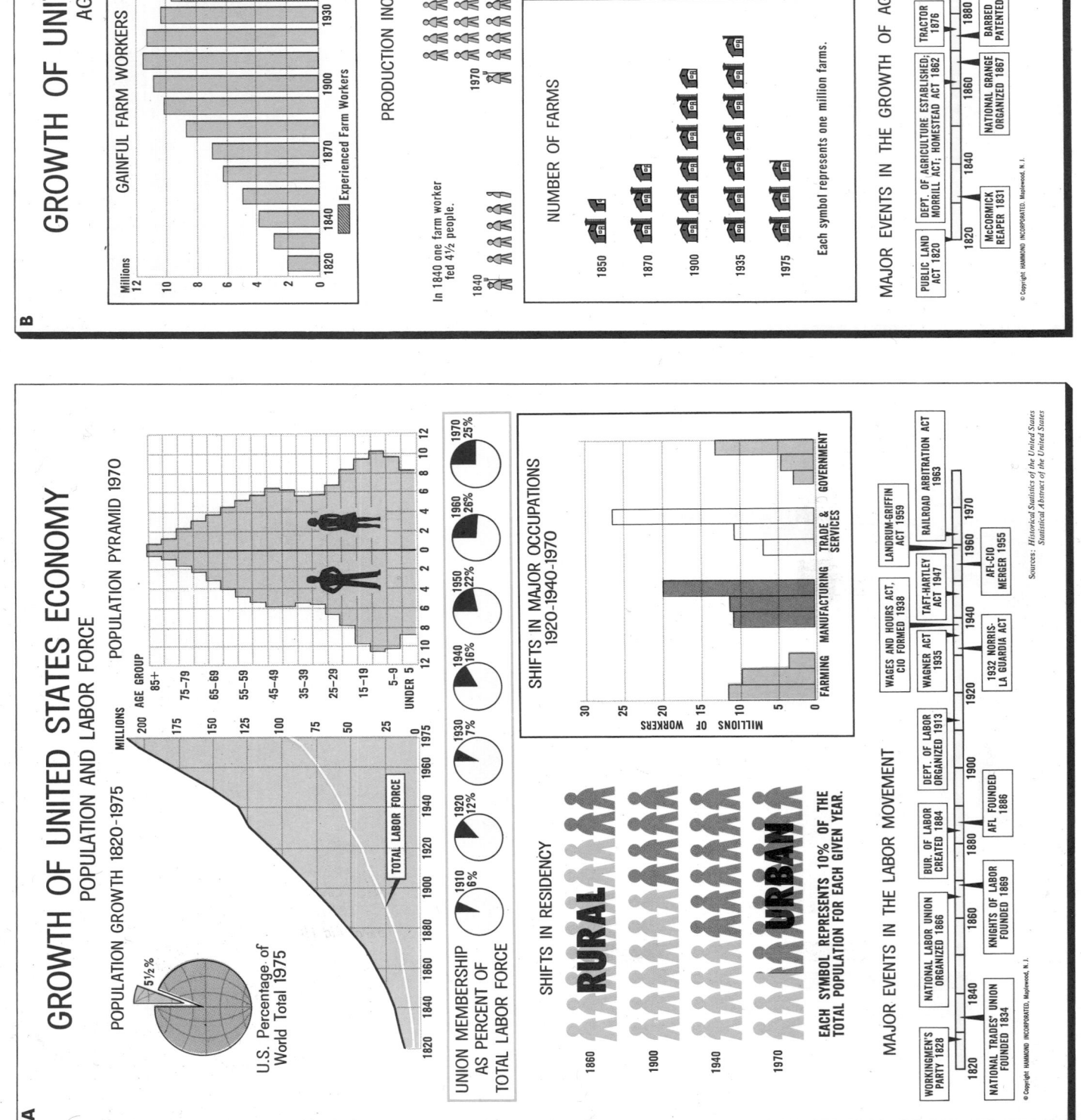

GROWTH OF UNITED STATES ECONOMY
NATIONAL PRODUCT AND INCOME

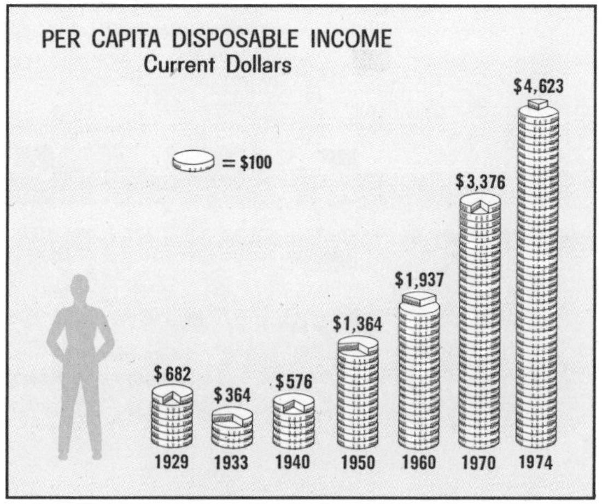

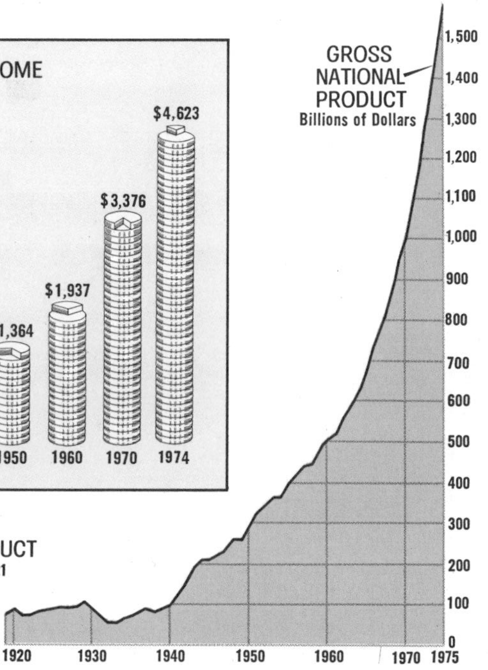

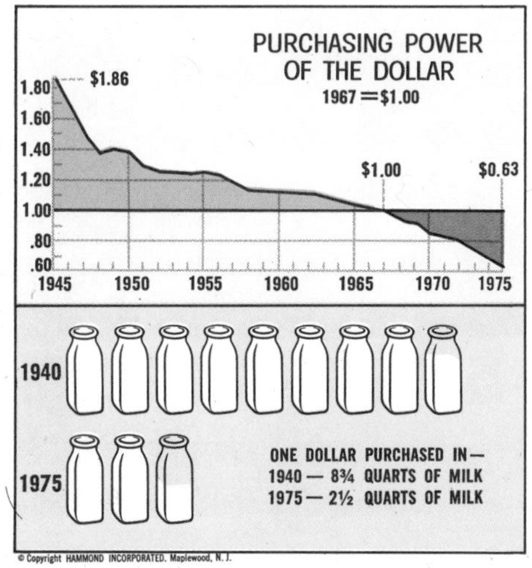

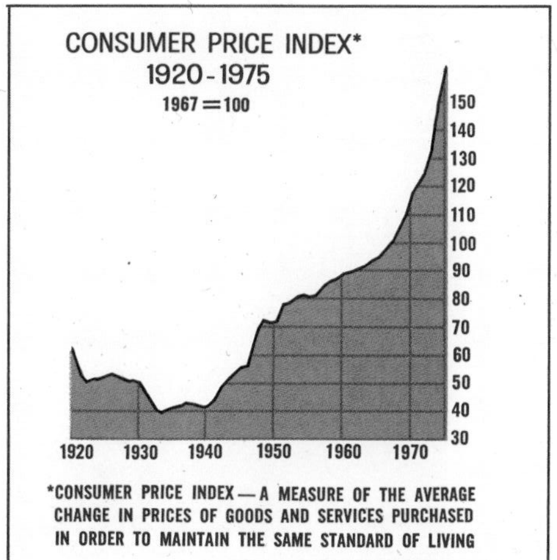

D

GROSS NATIONAL PRODUCT
Billions of Dollars

1,500
1,400
1,300
1,200
1,100
1,000
900
800
700
600
500
400
300
200
100
0

1975 1970 1960 1950 1940 1930 1920 1910 1900 1892

GROSS NATIONAL PRODUCT
FIVE YEAR AVERAGES 1892-1921

PER CAPITA DISPOSABLE INCOME
Current Dollars

= $100

$682 — 1929
$364 — 1933
$576 — 1940
$1,364 — 1950
$1,937 — 1960
$3,376 — 1970
$4,623 — 1974

CONSUMER PRICE INDEX*
1920 - 1975
1967 = 100

150
140
130
120
110
100
90
80
70
60
50
40
30

1920 1930 1940 1950 1960 1970

*CONSUMER PRICE INDEX — A MEASURE OF THE AVERAGE CHANGE IN PRICES OF GOODS AND SERVICES PURCHASED IN ORDER TO MAINTAIN THE SAME STANDARD OF LIVING

PURCHASING POWER OF THE DOLLAR
1967 = $1.00

1.80
1.60
1.40
1.20
1.00
.80
.60

$1.86
$1.00
$0.63

1945 1950 1955 1960 1965 1970 1975

ONE DOLLAR PURCHASED IN—
1940 — 8¾ QUARTS OF MILK
1975 — 2½ QUARTS OF MILK

1940
1975

Sources: Historical Statistics of the United States
Statistical Abstract of the United States

GROWTH OF UNITED STATES ECONOMY
TRANSPORTATION

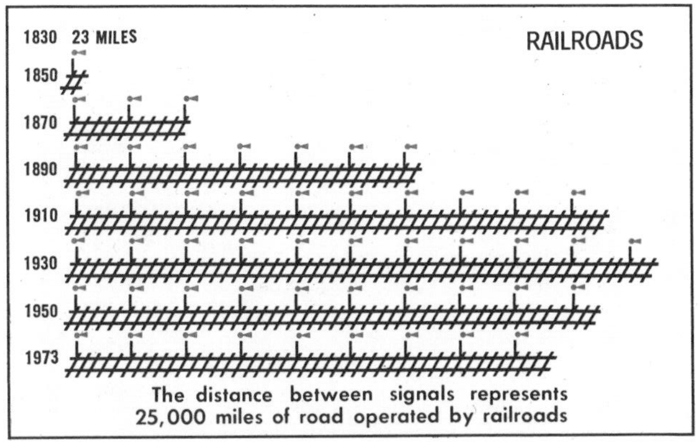

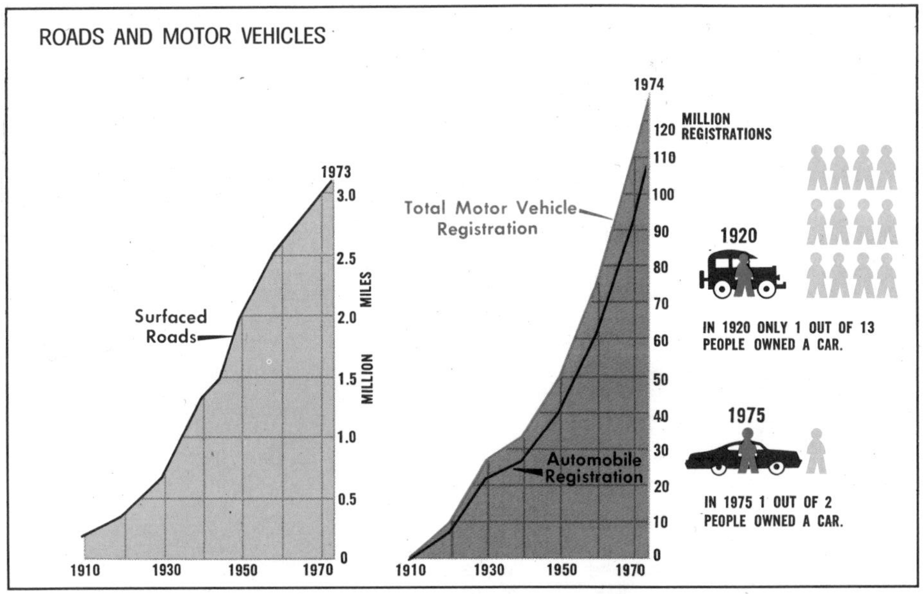

C

AIRLINES
Domestic Passenger-Miles Flown

BILLIONS OF MILES

120
100
80
60
40
20
0

1974 1970 1960 1950 1940 1930

RAILROADS

MILES

1830 23 MILES
1850
1870
1890
1910
1930
1950
1973

The distance between signals represents 25,000 miles of road operated by railroads

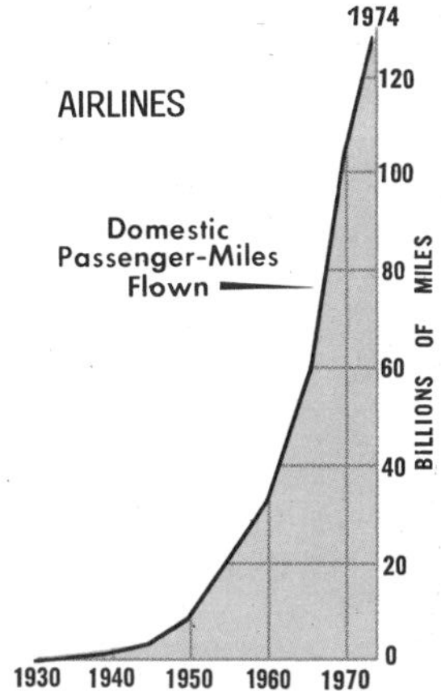

ROADS AND MOTOR VEHICLES

MILLION REGISTRATIONS

120
110
100
90
80
70
60
50
40
30
20
10
0

1974 1970 1950 1930 1910

Automobile Registration

Total Motor Vehicle Registration

1920 ONLY 1 OUT OF 13 PEOPLE OWNED A CAR.
1975 1 OUT OF 2 PEOPLE OWNED A CAR.

1920
1975

MILLION MILES

3.0
2.5
2.0
1.5
1.0
0.5
0

1973 1970 1950 1930 1910

Surfaced Roads

MAJOR EVENTS IN THE GROWTH OF TRANSPORTATION

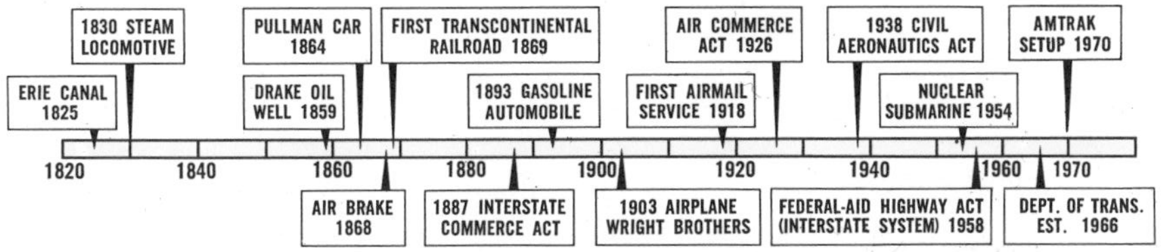

ERIE CANAL 1825
1820
1830 STEAM LOCOMOTIVE
1840
AIR BRAKE 1868
1860
DRAKE OIL WELL 1859
PULLMAN CAR 1864
FIRST TRANSCONTINENTAL RAILROAD 1869
1880
1887 INTERSTATE COMMERCE ACT
1893 GASOLINE AUTOMOBILE
1900
1903 AIRPLANE WRIGHT BROTHERS
FIRST AIRMAIL SERVICE 1918
AIR COMMERCE ACT 1926
1920
1938 CIVIL AERONAUTICS ACT
FEDERAL-AID HIGHWAY ACT (INTERSTATE SYSTEM) 1958
NUCLEAR SUBMARINE 1954
1940
DEPT. OF TRANS. EST. 1966
AMTRAK SETUP 1970
1960
1970

Sources: Historical Statistics of the United States
Statistical Abstract of the United States

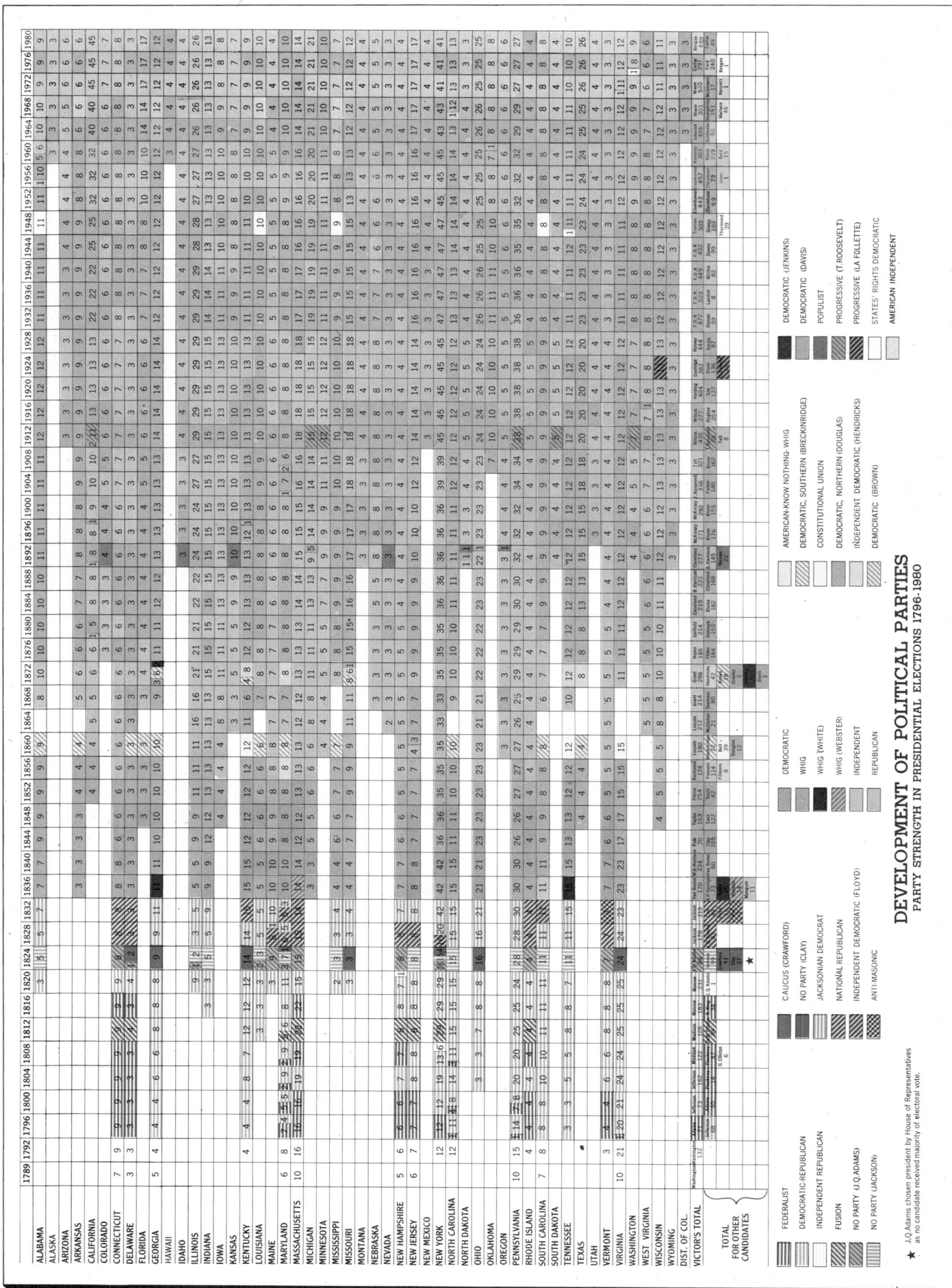

DEVELOPMENT OF POLITICAL PARTIES

PARTY STRENGTH IN PRESIDENTIAL ELECTIONS 1796-1980

★ J.Q.Adams chosen president by House of Representatives as no candidate received majority of electoral vote.

POLITICAL SECTIONALISM 1796-1868
PRESIDENTIAL ELECTORAL VOTE BY STATES AND PARTIES

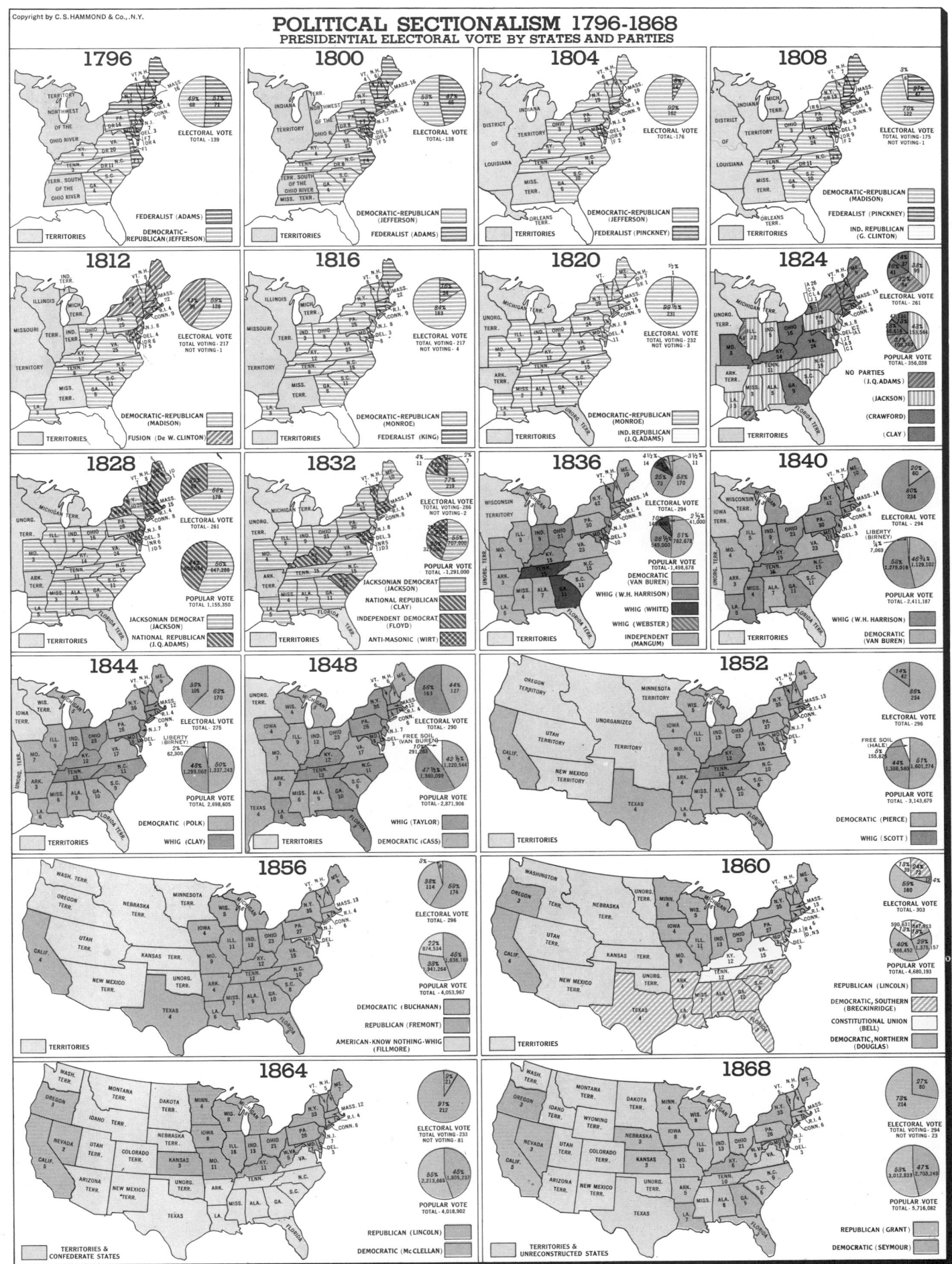

POLITICAL SECTIONALISM 1872-1916
PRESIDENTIAL ELECTORAL VOTE BY STATES AND PARTIES

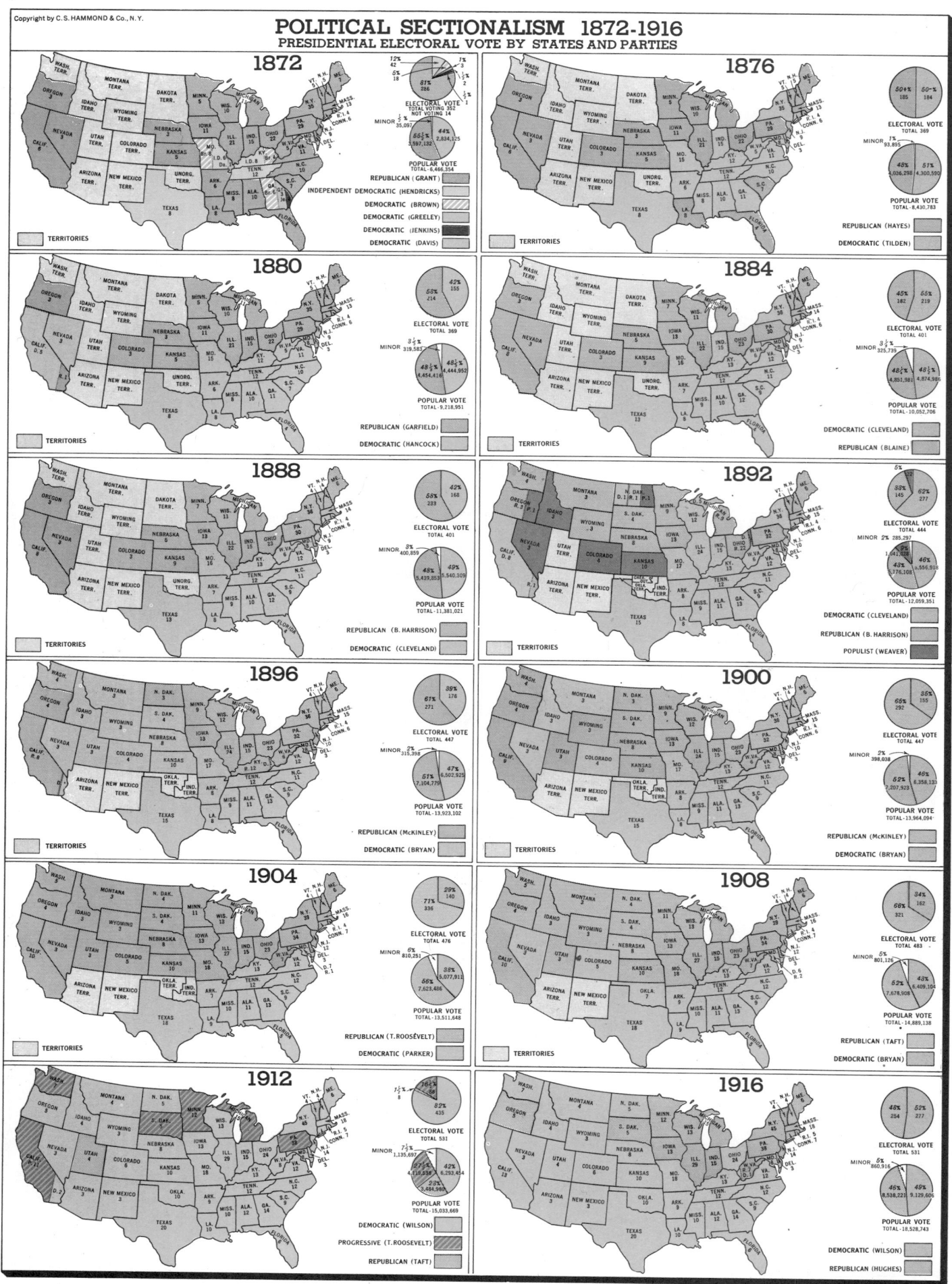

POLITICAL SECTIONALISM 1920-1964
PRESIDENTIAL ELECTORAL VOTE BY STATES AND PARTIES

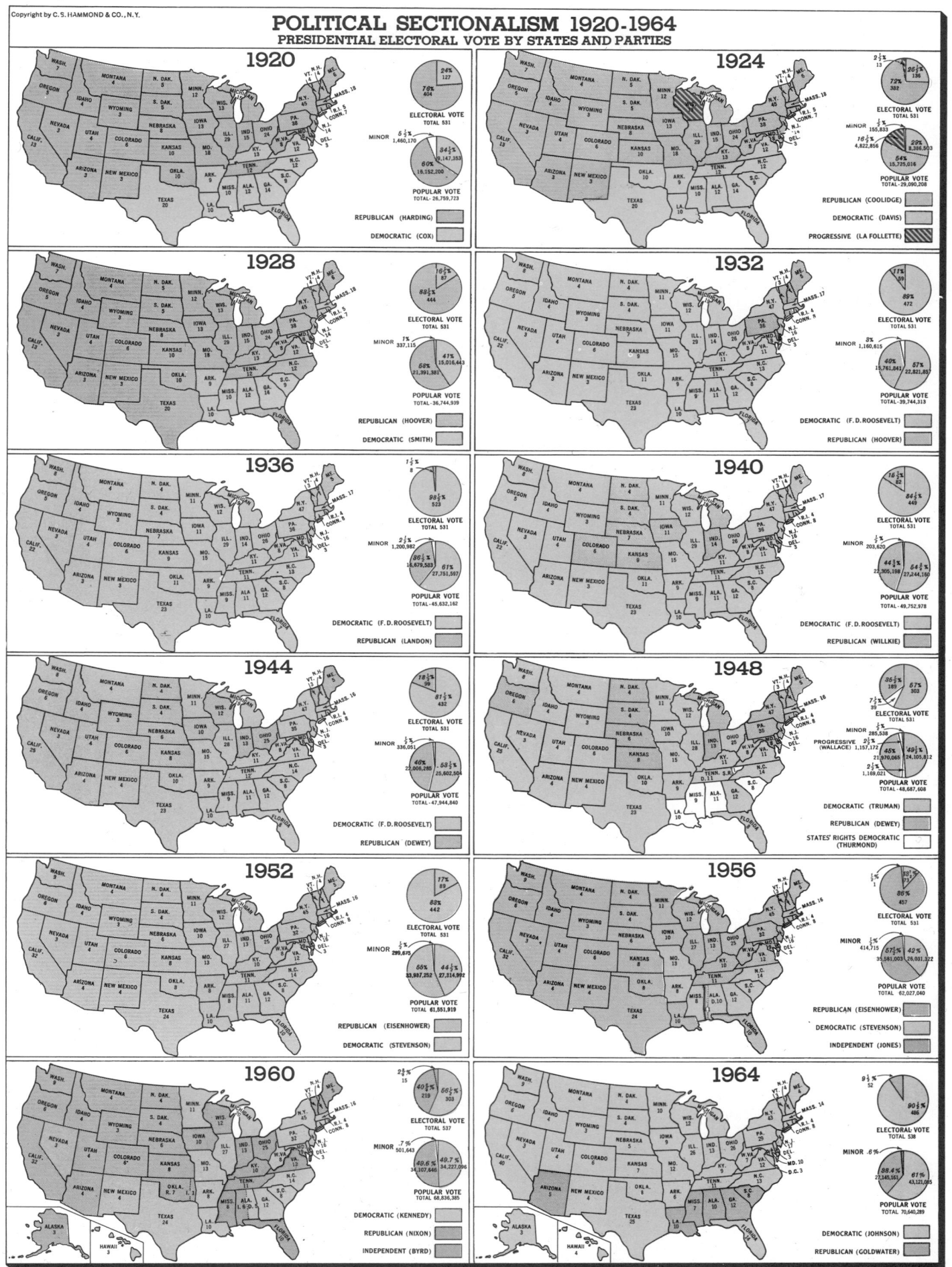

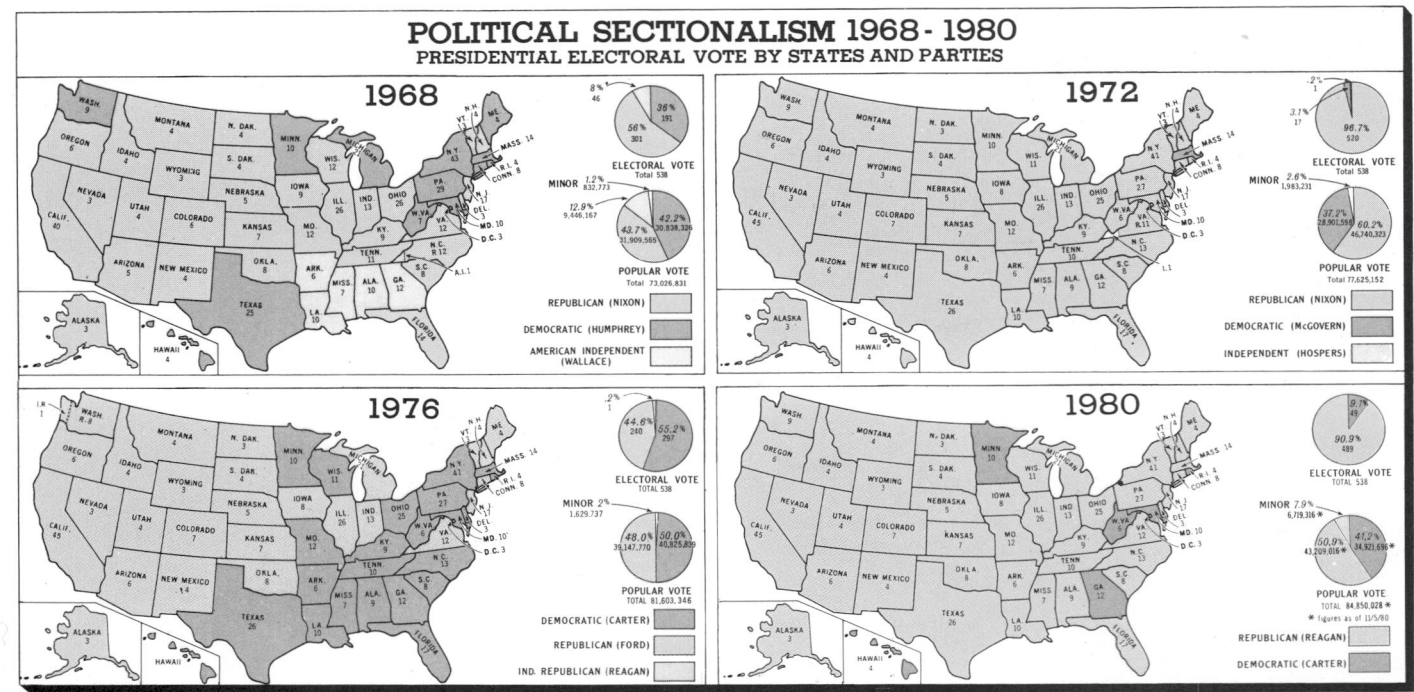

POLITICAL SECTIONALISM 1968-1980
PRESIDENTIAL ELECTORAL VOTE BY STATES AND PARTIES

PRESIDENTS OF THE UNITED STATES

No.	Name	Politics	Native State	Age at Inauguration	Age at Death
1	George Washington	Federalist	Va.	57	67
2	John Adams	Federalist	Mass.	61	90
3	Thomas Jefferson	Rep.-Dem.	Va.	57	83
4	James Madison	Rep.-Dem.	Va.	57	85
5	James Monroe	Rep.-Dem.	Va.	58	73
6	John Quincy Adams	Rep.-Dem.	Mass.	57	80
7	Andrew Jackson	Democrat	S.C.	61	78
8	Martin Van Buren	Democrat	N.Y.	54	79
9	William Henry Harrison	Whig	Va.	68	68
10	John Tyler	Whig	Va.	51	71
11	James Knox Polk	Democrat	N.C.	49	53
12	Zachary Taylor	Whig	Va.	64	65
13	Millard Fillmore	Whig	N.Y.	50	74
14	Franklin Pierce	Democrat	N.H.	48	64
15	James Buchanan	Democrat	Pa.	65	77
16	Abraham Lincoln	Republican	Ky.	52	56
17	Andrew Johnson	Democrat	N.C.	56	66
18	Ulysses Simpson Grant	Republican	Ohio	46	63
19	Rutherford B. Hayes	Republican	Ohio	54	70
20	James Abram Garfield	Republican	Ohio	49	49
21	Chester Alan Arthur	Republican	Vt.	50	56
22	Grover Cleveland	Democrat	N.J.	47	71
23	Benjamin Harrison	Republican	Ohio	55	67
24	Grover Cleveland	Democrat	N.J.	55	71
25	William McKinley	Republican	Ohio	54	58
26	Theodore Roosevelt	Republican	N.Y.	42	60
27	William Howard Taft	Republican	Ohio	51	72
28	Woodrow Wilson	Democrat	Va.	56	67
29	Warren G. Harding	Republican	Ohio	55	57
30	Calvin Coolidge	Republican	Vt.	51	60
31	Herbert Clark Hoover	Republican	Iowa	54	90
32	Franklin D. Roosevelt	Democrat	N.Y.	51	63
33	Harry S. Truman	Democrat	Mo.	60	88
34	Dwight D. Eisenhower	Republican	Texas	62	78
35	John F. Kennedy	Democrat	Mass.	43	46
36	Lyndon B. Johnson	Democrat	Texas	55	64
37	Richard M. Nixon	Republican	Calif.	56	....
38	Gerald R. Ford	Republican	Mich.	61	....
39	James E. Carter, Jr.	Democrat	Ga.	52	....
40	Ronald W. Reagan	Republican	Ill.	69	....

Index

This index lists historically important places, areas, events and geographical features appearing on the maps of the United States History Atlas. Each entry is followed by the page number on which the name appears. The letters following the page number designate a particular map on pages containing more than one map. Names that appear on more than one map are indexed to the map or maps portraying the place at its most historically significant period.